MYUNG MOON

Webster's
ENGLISH-ENGLISH-KOREAN DICTIONARY

웹스터
英英韓辭典

監修
鄭 炳 祖 〈前서울大敎授〉

編者
吳 昌 根 〈前慶熙大講師〉

明文堂

머 리 말

영어를 배우는 데 있어서, English through English를 중시하는 현대 영어 교육의 방침 아래, 「英英」사전이 차지하는 중요성은 이미 상식화되어 있는 일이므로 새삼스레 논할 필요조차 없다 할 것이다.

그런데 우리의 현실은 어떠한가. 과연 어느 정도의 사람이 실지로 「英英」사전을 이용하여 영어를 배웠으며, 또 몇 퍼센트나 되는 사람이 현재 실지로 「英英」사전으로 영어를 익히고 있는가——매우 의심스러운 바 있다 할 것이다. 대부분의 사람들이 「英英」의 중요성과 필요성을 충분히 알고 있으면서도, 실지로는 「英韓」사전을 이용하고 있는 사실은 누구나 알고 있는 현실이다.

이런 현실에 눈을 감고서, 아무리 「英英」사전의 중요성만을 역설해도, 실질적인 효과를 거두기는 어려울 뿐 아니라, 오히려 영어를 배우려는 사람들로 하여금 영어에서 점점 더 멀어져 가게 할 우려마저 있다 할 것이다. 이러한 관점에 입각하여, 우리는 오랜 연구 검토 끝에 새로운 아이디어로, 여태까지 없었던 특수한 스타일의 「**英英韓**」사전을 기획·편찬하기에 이르렀다. 즉 「英英」에 곁들여 활용하기 편리한 체제의 한국어 난을 마련하면, 영어학습에 있어서의 현실과 이상이 합치되는 획기적인 사전이 될 수 있다는 결론을 얻은 것이다.

이리하여 탄생한 것이 바로 이 English-English-Korean Dictionary이다.

이 사전이 지니고 있는 근본적인 특장과 이점은 다음과 같다.

① 「英英」만을 바로 대하기에는 확고한 자신이 없어서 불안감이 따를 때, 「英英韓」은 그 불안감을 깨끗이 해소시켜 준다.

② 「英英」의 말뜻풀이로 이해한 내용을 역어(譯語) 난으로 곧바로 재확인할 수 있으므로, 흔히 일어날 수 있는 오해와 착각을 미연에 방지할 수 있다.

③ 「英英」의 말뜻풀이만으로는 아무래도 명확한 개념 파악이 어려워서, 다시 다른 「英韓」을 찾아보고 싶을 때, 그 불필요한 수고를 덜어 준다.

④ 초보자는 「英韓」사전으로 활용하기도 편리할 뿐만 아니라, 보통의 「英韓」에서는 볼 수 없는 풍부한 예문과 영문의 말뜻풀이를 대할 수 있어, 부지불식간에 영어 실력이 향상된다.

따라서 이 「英英韓」은 「英英+英韓」의 단순한 합성본이 아니라, 서로의 특장과 이점이 상승작용을 하여, 일석삼조(一石三鳥)의 효과를 발휘하는 획기적인 사전이다.

이 밖에 이 사전 편집상의 특장을 열거하면 다음과 같다.

1. 학습 및 일반원서 해독에 필요·충분한 52,000단어를 수록하였다.

특수한 고유명사, 전문용어, 영속성이 의심스러운 신어 등 영어학습에 불필요한 것은 제외하고, 영어의 근간(根幹)을 이루는 기본어 및 일반적인 단어를 최대한으로 수록하였다. 표제어 가운데 특히 중요도가 높은 단어는, 각종 통계자료를 바탕으로 하여, 3단계의 별표를 붙여 표시하였다.

2. 단어의 활용면을 중시하고, 계수(計數)·불계수(不計數)·목적어 등을 상세히 표시하였다.

명사는 각 단어마다 ⓒⓤ의 기호로 계수·불계수의 구별을 표시하고, 타동사의 말뜻풀이 속에 그 단어가 취하는 목적어를 명시하였다. 이 밖에 흔히 결합하여 쓰이는 전치사 등의 어귀나 절(clause) 등도 명시함으로써, 문형(文型)과 활용상에 도움이 되게 하였다.

3. 문법상의 참고 난(Usage, N.B.)을 충실히 다루었다.

우리나라 사람으로서 영어를 배우는 데 있어 특히 주의를 환기시킬 필요가 있는 문법상의 포인트에 대하여는 한국어 난에 Usage 항목을 마련하여 설명하였다. 또 표제어에 따라 함께 이해해 두면 편리한 배경이나 부가적(附加的)인 사항에 대하여는 N.B. 항목을 한국어 난에 마련하여, 빠짐없이 설명하였다.

4. 발음은 미국 발음을 우선 표기하고, 영국 발음도 아울러 표기하였다. 그 밖의 방면에서도 미식 영어를 기준으로 삼았다.

시대의 추세나, 장래의 방향을 고려하여, 미·영의 발음이 서로 다를 경우, 먼저 미국 발음을 적고 뒤이어 영국 발음을 표기하였다. 말뜻풀이에 있어서도 주로 미국계의 사전을 기준으로 하였다. 그러나 영국 특유의 말뜻이 있을 경우, 그 뜻도 빠뜨림없이 수록하였다.

이상과 같은 특장을 지닌 이 사전이, 올바르고 효과적인 영어 학습의 촉매작용을 하고 영어를 더욱 가까이 익히려는 분들에게 좋은 반려가 되기를 빌어 마지않는다.

英英韓辭典編纂委員會

代表委員　吳　昌　根　識

英英辭典 이용을 위한 가이드

 대부분의 한국사람에게 있어서 영어보다 한국말이 더 이해하기 쉽다는 것은 말할 필요가 없다. 그렇다면 한국말로 풀이된 「英韓辭典」이 있는 터에, 굳이 「英英辭典」을 써야 할 필요는 없지 않은가──이런 의문을 품을 사람도 없지 않을 것이다. 사전이 단순히 「모르는 단어의 뜻을 찾아보기 위한 도구」라고 한다면 그렇게도 말할 수 있을 것이다. 그러나 사전이란 결코 그것만으로 끝나는 것이 아니다. 「도구」인 동시에 그 사용법을 익혀 가는 과정에서 영어의 실력이 몸에 붙게 되는, 다시 말해서 이 도구를 사용하는 그 자체가 바로 「학습」이 되게 마련인 것이다.

 특히 英英辭典을 이용한다는 것은, 그 자체가 영어로 생각하며 영어로 표현하는 훈련에 직결되고, 영어의 발상법(發想法)을 몸에 익히는 데 있어서 이상적인 학습방법이라 할 수 있다. 英英辭典을 이용하는 최대의 목적도 바로 이 점에 있다고 해도 과언이 아니다.

 그러면 英英辭典을 효율적으로 사용하기 위해서는 어떻게 해야 할까. 이에 대한 해답을 얻기 위해서는 먼저 英英辭典의 특질을 충분히 이해해 둘 필요가 있다. 이 책, English-English-Korean Dictionary의 내용을 보기로 하여 살펴보기로 한다.

1. 말뜻풀이[語釋]의 구조를 분해할 것

 말뜻풀이는 보통 중심이 되는 말[核]과, 그것의 상태·성질 등을 설명하고 있는 한정·수식어귀[條件]와의 결합으로 성립되어 있다. 핵(核)은 그 사물 자체를 나타내며, 조건(條件)은 다른 사물과 구별하기 위한, 그 사물의 가장 현저한 특징을 나타내고 있다.

 보기 : **dog**→a common domestic animal, kept as a pet, for hunting, etc.

  cat→a small fur-covered animal often kept as a pet, to catch mice, etc.

 양쪽 다같이 말뜻풀이의 핵은 animal이다. 곧, dog나 cat나 「사물 그 자체」로서는 「동물」이다. 이 핵을 찾아내는 것으로써 dog, cat에 대한 제1단계의 정의(동물이라는 것)는 파악한 셈이다.

 물론 핵을 찾아낸 것만으로 dog, cat를 이해하였다고는 할 수 없다. 이것만으로는

  dog = animal   cat = animal   ∴ dog = cat

라는 이론이 성립되고 만다.

 그래서 문제되는 것이 조건의 부분이다. 동물은 동물이라도, 서로 어떤 특징을 지닌 동물인가──하는 점을 규정짓는 것이 이 부분이다.

	조 건 A	핵	조 건 B
dog	a common domestic	animal	kept as a pet, for hunting, etc.
cat	a small fur-covered	animal	often kept as a pet, to catch mice, etc.

dog, cat 양쪽 다 앞뒤에 조건을 수반하고 있다. 「조건 A」의 부분에서는

 dog→흔히 볼 수 있는, 집안에서 기르는

 cat→조그마하고 모피(毛皮)로 덮인

이라고 규정되어 있다. 각각 dog, cat의 일면을 표현하고 있지만, 결정적 조건이라고는 할 수 없다. 경우에 따라서는 서로 맞바꾸어 놓을 수도 있는 조건이다. 따라서 「조건 A」의 단계에서는 아직 dog, cat를 충분히 설명하고 있다고는 할 수 없다. 다음에 「조건 B」를 살펴보자

　　dog→애완용으로, 또는 수렵용 등으로 기르는
　　cat→애완용으로, 또는 쥐를 잡게 하려고 기르는

이 부분, 곧 「수렵용」「쥐를 잡게 하려고」에 와서 비로소 dog와 cat가 명확하게 구별된 셈이다.

이 밖에 다른 몇 가지 실례를 들어 말뜻풀이의 구성을 살펴보자. 밑줄친 부분이 「핵」이다.

　보기 :
　　wait→<u>stay or remain</u> until someone comes or something happens
　　increase→<u>become greater</u> in number, size, value, etc.
　　rocket→a <u>machine</u> propelled by means of self-contained gases
　　sack←a <u>bag</u> made of coarse cloth used for holding corn, coal, etc.

2. 英英辭典 특유의 표현에 익숙해질 것

국어사전에서도 마찬가지이지만, 사전의 말뜻풀이는 간결하여야만 한다. 한정된 스페이스에 될수록 많은 내용을 담기 위해서이기도 하지만, 그보다는 오히려 군더더기가 없는 간결한 표현으로써 말의 본질을 강조하고, 인상을 강화한다는 적극적인 효과를 노린다고 볼 수 있다. 英英辭典에서 쓰이고 있는 간결한 표현의 바탕을 살펴보자

1) 분사(分詞)에 의한 표현

앞에 나온 dog의 보기 a common domestic animal, kept as a pet, for hunting, etc.에서는 kept의 앞에 wich is 가 생략되어 있다. 관계대명사는 사전적 표현에 있어서 가장 흔히 생략의 대상이 된다. 바꾸어 말하면, 英英辭典의 말뜻풀이에는 분사에 의한 표현이 많다는 것이 된다.

분사에 의한 표현에는 「과거분사」에 의한 것과 「현재분사」에 의한 것의 두 가지가 있다.

a) 과거분사에 의한 표현 : 피동적 의미를 나타낸다. 분사 앞에 which is 등을 보완해 보면 이해하기 쉽다.

　보기 : **tide**→the regular rise and fall of the ocean <u>caused</u> by the waves
　　　　beach→a smooth shore of sand or pebbles, esp. <u>washed</u> over by the waves at high tide
　　　　nail→a metal pin <u>pointed</u> at one end, <u>used</u> to hold separate pieces of wood, etc, together.

b) 현재분사에 의한 표현 : 능동적 의미를 나타낸다. 그 동사를 사용하여 which ~ 로 바꿔 놓고 보면 이해하기 쉽다.

　보기 : **rain**→the water <u>falling</u> to earth in small drops
　　　　oyster→an edible shellfish living in shallow sea water and which has a rough shell

numeral→a word, letter, or figure expressing a number

분사에 의한 표현은 명사의 말뜻풀이에서뿐만이 아니라, 형용사의 말뜻풀이로서도 가끔 쓰인다.

 보기 : **healthy**→having good health; showing good health
    own→belonging to oneself
    rigid→not bending
    overdue→unpaid at the time expected for payment

이상과 같이 분사에 의한 표현은 英英辭典에서 아주 빈번히 쓰이고 있으므로, 잘 익혀 둘 필요가 있다.

2) 동명사(動名詞)에 의한 표현 : 분사에 의한 표현과 더불어 익혀 두어야 할 것으로 「전치사+동명사」를 쓴 표현이다. 동사를 명사화하여 씀으로써 단순한 구문으로 표현할 수가 있다.

 보기 : **tablecloth**→a cloth for covering a table
    bread→a kind of food made by baking a mixture of flour and water
    poach→cook(an egg) by breaking it into boiling water
    twist→join(two or more threads, etc.) by winding one around another

만일, 동명사를 쓰지 않고 위의 보기를 표현하려고 하면,

    poach→break(an egg) into boiling water and cook it
    twist→wind(two or more threads, etc.) one around another and join them

등과 같이 표현하게 될 것이다. 이렇게 되면 말뜻풀이의 「핵」은 형식상으로 cook, join으로부터 각각 break, wind로 옮아가 버리고, 말뜻풀이의 엄밀성이 손상되고 만다. 이것을 break, wind라는 부수적인 동사를 동명사화함으로써 cook, join이라는 말뜻풀이의 핵을 앞쪽에 내세움과 동시에, 말뜻풀이 전체를 단문(simple sentence)의 형태로 할 수 있게 되는 셈이다.

3. 「…함」「…음」을 영어로 나타내면

국어사전에서 추상적인 의미의 명사를 찾아보면 「…함」「…음」 등과 같이 표현하고 있는 경우가 많다.(다음의 보기는 이희승편 「국어대사전」에서 인용한 것임)

 보기 : **정확**(正確)→바르고 확실함.
   무력(無力)→힘이 없음. 세력이 없음.

한국어에서는 동작·상태 등을 「…함」「…음」으로 나타낼 수 있으나, 영어에서는 이와 같은 편리한 말이 없고, 경우에 따라 각각 다음과 같은 여러 가지 말을 선택 사용하지 않으면 안된다.

「…함」 { 동작…act / 경과…process / 기술…art } 「…음」 { 상태…state, condition / 성질…quality / 능력…ability, power }

추상명사의 경우, 이러한 말에 「of+동명사」가 붙어서 표현되는 일이 아주 많다.

 보기 :
  (동작) **division**→the act of dividing
     breach→the act of breaking a law, promise, etc.

英英辭典 이용을 위한 가이드

haste→the act of hurrying
(동작·능력) **imagination**→the act or power of forming pictures of what is not actually present
(기술) **poetry**→the art of writing poems
(상태) **politeness**→the state of being polite
health→the state of being well
(성질) **absurdity**→the quality of being absurd
(상태·성질) **manhood**→the state or quality of being a man
hastiness→the quality or state of being hasty

4. 알고 있는 단어를 찾아본다

다음 표는 중학 정도에서 배우는 아주 쉬운 단어 4개를 들어, 보통의 영한사전에 나타나는 표준적인 역어(譯語)와, 이 사전에 나타난 말뜻풀이를 대비시켜 본 것이다.

farm	농 장	a piece of land used to raise crops or animals, usu. plus a house and the other necessary buildings belonging to it
beach	바닷가	a smooth shore of sand or pebbles, esp. washed over by the waves at high tide
branch	가 지	a part of tree growing out from the trunk
dive	잠수하다	go down headfirst into water

위 표의 영문 말뜻 풀이에서 밑줄친 부분에 주목해 주기 바란다. 그저 무심코 「farm=농장」으로만 받아들이고 있는 그 내용 속에, 과연 「가옥 및 그 밖의 필요한 건조물이 있는」이라는 이미지까지 내포되어 있는가 어떤가―나머지 3개의 보기에 있어서도 밑줄친 부분까지 포함하여 이해하고 있다면, 여러분의 영어 실력은 상당한 수준이라고 할 만하다. 이러한 지식은 보통의 영한사전에서는 좀처럼 얻을 수 없는 경우가 많다.

이와 같이 英英辭典이 아니고서는 알 수 없는, 말뜻의 미묘한 뉘앙스를 알아내는 것도, 英英辭典을 이용하는 커다란 목적이며 동시에 이점(利點)이기도 하다.

다음에, 외국어가 우리말화하여 쓰이고 있는 경우, 원어가 나타내는 뜻 가운데 일부분만이 채택되어 사용되는 수가 많다.

boat	노를 저어 움직이는 작은 배	a small open ship; a ship
yacht	돛배, 요트	a boat for pleasure or racing
garage	자동차의 차고	a building or place where automobiles and airplanes are kept or repaired
boss	폭력배 등의 두목	a person who gives orders to workmen; a headman of any business

boat, yacht에 대하여 먼저 깨닫게 되는 것은, 동력원에 대하여는 전혀 언급하지 않고 있는 점이다. 언급이 전혀 없다는 것은, 동력원의 종류는 무엇이었든 상관이 없다는 것을 의미하고 있다. 즉, 돛으로 움직이든 엔진으로 움직이든 혹은 노를 저어 움직이든, 그것은 boat, yacht를 정의하는 결정적 조건이 아니라는 점을 알게 된다. 엔진으로 움직이는 yacht도 있는가 하면, 돛으로 달려가는 boat도 있다.

garage도 「자동차의 차고」만이 아니라, 「비행기의 격납고」도 가리키며, 또 반드시 지붕이 있는 건조물에 한정되지 않고, 그러한 목적에 사용되는 장소까지도 가리키고 있다.

boss는 일을 지시하는 웃사람 전반을 가리키는 단어로서, 우리가 쓰는 「보스」보다는 훨씬 넓은 사용 범위를 지니고 있다.

이러한 것들은 영한사전으로써도 주의깊게 찾아보면 어느 정도 알 수 있기는 하지만, 실제로 英英辭典의 말뜻풀이를 대함으로써 더욱 확실한 「산 지식」으로 몸에 붙게 되는 것이다.

영한사전이 주로 「모르는 단어의 뜻을 알기」 위하여 사용되는 데 대하여, 英英辭典은 「알고 있는 단어」(좀더 정확히 말하면 「안다고 생각하고 있는 단어」)를 재확인하고, 나아가서는 의미의 정확성을 기하여 활용하는 것이 바람직한 일이다.

5. 입체적인 학습의 필요성

다시 beach를 보기로 들어

    beach→a smooth shore of sand or pebbles, esp. washed over by the waves at high tide

이 말뜻풀이의 「핵」인 shore를 다시 이 사전에서 찾아보면

    shore→the land on the edge of a sea, a lake, etc.

로 나와 있다. beach가 「모래나 자갈로 된 평탄한 shore」인 데 대하여, shore는 지형·지질에는 관계없이 물가의 땅 전반을 가리키는 말임을 알 수 있다. 즉 낭떠러지인 shore도 있고, 땅으로 된 shore도 있지만, beach는 이런 여러 가지 형태의 shore 가운데, 어느 한 가지의 특별한 형태를 가진 경우만을 가리키는 말인 것이다.

이와 같이 어떤 단어를 찾았을 때, 그 말뜻풀이 가운데 있는 단어를 다시 찾아보는 습관을 몸에 붙이는 것이 바람직하다. 찾아보고 싶은 단어를 찾고는 바로 그대로 사전을 덮어 버리는 평면적인 이용법에서 탈피하여, 관련된 다른 말을 차례차례로 찾아보는 방법——즉 사전의 입체적 이용법에 의하여 이해도 깊어질 뿐 아니라, 비슷한 말끼리의 미묘한 의미의 상이점도 알게 되어, 어휘 실력의 향상이 두드러지게 나타날 수 있다.

보기 :
    barricade→a barrier roughly made for defense
    barrier→a fence, wall, etc. which stands in the way to prevent passage
    appear→come into sight
    sight→the range or field that one can see
    heave→raise (something) with effort
    raise→cause (someone or something) to rise
    tool→an instrument used with the hands in doing work
    instrument→a tool used for delicate or scientific work

英英辞典 이용을 위한 가이드

6. 말뜻풀이로 표제어를 생각한다

먼저 알고자 하는 표제어를 찾아내어 그 말뜻풀이를 보는 것이 정통적인 사전의 사용법이다. 알지 못하는 단어의 뜻을 조사하려고 할 경우, 이 순서를 밟는 길 외에는 도리가 없을 것이다. 그러나 앞서 말한 바와 같이, 특히 英英辭典에서는 「알고 있는 단어를 찾아본다」는 것도 중요한 이용법의 하나이다. 사전을 이와 같이 이용할 경우, 「표제어에서 말뜻풀이로」라는 정통적인 사용법에 굳이 구애받을 필요는 없을 것이다. 이와 정반대로 「말뜻 풀이에서 표제어로」라는 사용법도, 英英辭典을 효율적으로 이용하는 데 극히 유효한 방법이다. 즉, 표제어를 가려 놓고, 말뜻풀이만을 읽고서 그것이 어떤 표제어의 말뜻풀이인가를 생각해 내는 것이다. 이렇게 하면 퀴즈를 즐기는 기분으로, 부지불식간에 영어 실력이 부쩍 향상될 것이다.

다음에 보인 것들은 모두 이 사전에 나오는 말뜻풀이다. 우선 연습삼아 이들을 읽고, 각각 해당하는 표제어를 생각해 보면 재미있을 것이다. (해답은 맨 아래쪽)

1. a group of musicians who play together on their instruments, esp. stringed instruments
2. a muscular organ that pumps the blood throughout the body
3. express ideas by spoken words
4. an instrument with lenses which makes distant object appear nearer and larger
5. a book containing the words of a language, usu. arranged alphabetically, with explanations of their meaning
6. come to the end of life
7. an image or a thought passing through a sleeping person's mind
8. a painful feeling caused by need of something to drink
9. one side of a leaf of paper in a book
10. change (food) into a state in which the body can absorb it
11. the part of the body of a person or monkey between the shoulder and the hand
12. an office for receiving, lending, exchanging, and issuing money
13. bend the head or body in greeting, respect, worship, or obedience
14. having lived or existed for a long time
15. the regular rise and fall of the ocean caused by the pull of the moon and the sun
16. come or go near or nearer to (a place)
17. greater in amount or degree
18. change the position of (something)
19. tie (something) with a cord, wire, etc.
20. what one thinks about a subject

[answer] 1. orchestra 2. heart 3. talk 4. telescope 5. dictionary
6. die 7. dream 8. thirst 9. page 10. digest
11. arm 12. bank 13. bow 14. old 15. tide
16. approach 17. more 18. move 19. bind 20. opinion

일러두기

[1] 표제어

(1) 철자는 미국식 철자를 우선적으로 게재하고, 그뒤에 *Brit.*로 표시하여 영국식 철자를 아울러 적었다.

　　보기: **la·bor**, *Brit.* **-bour** [léibər] *n.* ...

(2) 미국식·영국식의 구별 이외에, 한 단어로 2가지의 철자가 있는 것 가운데 발음이 같은 것은 아울러 적었다. 또 발음이 다르더라도, 표제어 배열상 가까이 인접하는 것도 아울러 적었다.

　　보기: **ax, axe** [æks] *n.* ...
　　　　 e·go·is·tic [ì:gouístik / ègou-], **-ti·cal** [-tik(ə)l] *adj....*

(3) 철자는 같아도 어원이 다른 것은 원칙적으로 별개 표제어로 잡고, 우측 상단에 작은 숫자를 붙여 구별하였다.

　　보기: **rear**[1] [ri(:)ər] *n.* ⓒ **1.** the back part of something. ...
　　　　 rear[2] [ri(:)ər] *vt.* **1.** make (someone or something) grow; ...

(4) 음절과 음절 사이는 가운뎃점 「·」으로 표시하였다. 또 2단어 이상으로 된 표제어로서 각 단어가 독립된 표제어로 게재되어 있을 경우는 음절 표시를 생략하였다.

　　보기: **Ham·mond organ** [hǽməndɔ́:rgən]

(5) 배열은 모두 알파벳순으로 하고, 철자가 같은 경우에는, 보통말·고유명사·접두어·접미어·약어(소문자·대문자·피어리어드, 하이픈이 없는 것·있는 것)의 순서로 하였다

(6) 중요 단어에는 별표를 붙였으며, 그 중요도에 따라 다음 3단계로 나누었다.
　　　　✹ 가장 중요한 단어(973 단어)
　　　　✦ 2차적 중요 단어(1914 단어)
　　　　✱ 3차적 중요 단어(2722 단어)

[2] 발음

(1) 표제어 바로 뒤 [ ] 속에 국제음성기호(International Phonetic Alphabet)를 써서 표시하였다. 미국 발음은 Kenyon & Knott의 *A Pronouncing Dictionary of American English* 및 *Webster's Seventh New Collegiate Dictionary*; 영국 발음은 D. Jones의 *English Pronouncing Dictionary*(13판); *The Concise Oxford Dictionary*(5판)와 그밖의 각종 최신 사전을 참고로 하여 최근의 영·미 발음을 병기하였다(p.16의 「발음기호표」 참조).

(2) 악센트 표시는 직상식(直上式)으로 하였으며, 제1 악센트는 「´」, 제2 악센트는 「`」로 나타내었다.

(3) 영·미 발음의 상이점은 [미국 발음/영국 발음]으로 나타내었으며, 흔히 쓰이는 발음이 두 가지 이상 있을 경우에는, 각각 다른 부분을 음절 단위로 아울러 표기하였다. 또 악센트의 위치만이 바뀔 경우는, 음절 수만큼의 하이픈 「-」을 배열하고 악센트가 있는 음절을 「´」「`」 등으로 나타내었다.

　　보기: **dic·tate** *v.* [díkteit, -´ / -´] *vt.* ...

일러두기

(4) 한 표제어가, 미·영, 품사, 말뜻 따위에 따라 발음이 다를 경우에는, 각각 다음과 같이 나타내었다.

　　보기 : **re·cast** vt. [rí:kǽst → n. / -kά:st] ... ――n. [U.S. rí:kǽst] ⓒ ...
　　　　　(미국에서는 n.의 경우 [rí:kǽst]로 된다. 영국에서는 v.와 마찬가지로 [rí:kά:st])
　　　　　in·car·nate adj. [inkά:rnit / -neit → v.] ... ――vt. [inkά:rneit] ...
　　　　　(v.에서는 미·영 다같이 [inkά:rneit]로 발음한다)
　　　　　re·tail [rí:teil → v.] n. ⓤ ...
　　　　　――v. [rí:teil → 2. / ri(:)téil] vt. **1.** ... **2.** [U.S. ritéil] ...
　　　　　(영국에서는 v.의 경우 [ri(:)téil]이 된다. 또 v.의 2.의 경우 미국에서는 [ritéil]로 된다).
　　　　　es·say n. [ései, ési → v.] ⓒ ... ――vi., vt. [eséi] ...
　　　　　cig·a·rette [sìgərét, +U.S. ∠-∸] n. ...
　　　　　(미국에서는 [sígərèt]라고도 발음한다)
　　　　　e·lite, é·lite [eilí:t, +U.S. i-, +Brit. e-] n. ...

(5) 2단어 이상으로 된 표제어에서는 연어(連語)로서의 악센트를 표시하였다. 이 경우 각 단어가 독립 표제어로 게재되어 있으면 하이픈 「-」을 써서 악센트의 위치만을 나타내었으며, 한 단어라도 독립 표제어로 게재되지 않은 것이 있으면, 전체적인 발음기호를 표시하였다.

　　보기 : **Labor Day** [∠-∸] n. ...
　　　　　Ham·mond organ [hǽməndɔ́:rgən]

(6) 표제어를 병기할 경우, 발음이 같으면 뒤에 일괄하여 표시하였다.
　　보기 : **cat·a·log, -logue** [kǽtəlɔ̀(:)g, +U.S. -làg] n. ...

(7) 생략할 수 있는 발음은 ( )로 묶었다.
　　보기 : **re·ac·tion** [ri(:)ǽkʃ(ə)n] n. ...

[3] 품 사

(1) 품사명은 원칙적으로 발음기호의 바로 다음에 n., adj., adv.등과 같이 약자를 써서 표시하였다. 한 표제어가 두 가지 이상의 품사로 나누어져 있을 경우에는 각각 그 바로 앞에 「――」를 붙여 나타내었다.

(2) 2단어 이상으로 된 연어(連語)에도 품사기호를 나타내었다.

(3) 고유명사에도 n.으로 하여 품사를 표시하였다.

(4) 동사는 원칙적으로 자동사·타동사를 각각 vi, vt.로 구별 표시하였으나, 양쪽에 두루 통하는 명칭으로서 v.를 사용한 경우도 있다.

　　보기 : **weep** [wi:p] v. (**wept**) vi. **1.** express grief ... by shedding tears; ...
　　　　　――vt. **1.** weep for (someone or something); ...

(5) 관계대명사, 의문부사 등 문법상 설명이 필요한 것은 말뜻 번호 다음에 (interrogative pronoun) ... 등으로 표시하였다.

　　보기 : **who** [hu:] pron. **1.** (*interrogative pronoun*) what or which person[s] ... **2.** (*relative pronoun*) ...

일러두기

[4] 어형 변화

(1) 다음 종류의 단어는 그 변화형을 품사 바로 뒤에 ( )로 묶어, 굵은 활자로 표시하였다.

　　명사 : 1. 불규칙 복수형
　　　　 2. 어미가 「자음+y」로 끝나는 것의 복수형
　　　　 3. 어미가 「f, o」로 끝나는 것의 복수형
　　　　 4. 변화형이 두 가지 있는 것의 복수형

　　보기 : **wom·an** [wúmən] *n.* ⓒ (pl. **wom·en**) …
　　　　　leaf [li:f] *n.* ⓒ (pl. **leaves**) …
　　　　　chief [tʃi:f] *n.* ⓒ (pl. **chiefs**) …
　　　　　hero [híərou] *n.* ⓒ (pl. **-roes**) …
　　　　　cod [kɑd / kɔd] *n.* ⓒ (pl. **cods** or *collectively* **cod**) …
　　　　　sheep [ʃi:p] *n.* ⓒ (pl. **sheep**) …

　　동사 : 1. 불규칙 변화형
　　　　 2. 어미의 자음 글자를 포개는 변화형
　　　　 3. 어미가 「자음+y」로 끝나는 것의 변화형
　　　　 4. 미국과 영국에서 서로 다른 변화를 하는 것의 변화형
　　　　 5. 두 가지 변화가 있는 것의 변화형

　　보기 : **go** [gou] *vi.* (**went, gone**) …
　　　　　put [put] *v.* (**put, put·ting**) …
　　　　　stop [stɑp / stɔp] *v.* (**stopped, stop·ping**) …
　　　　　bur·y [béri] *vt.* (**bur·ied**) …
　　　　　lie [lai] *vi.* (**lay, lain, ly·ing**) …
　　　　　die [dai] *vi.* (ppr. **dy·ing**) …
　　　　　trav·el [trǽvl] *v.* (**-eled, -el·ing** or *Brit.* **-elled, -el·ling**) …

　　형용사 : 1. 불규칙 비교변화를 하는 것의 변화형(형용사・부사)
　　부　사　 2. 2음절 이상으로 -er, -est의 형태로 변화하는 것의 변화형(형용사)
　　　　　 3. 변화형은 사용되는 빈도에 따라 usu., often, sometimes의 단서를 변화형 바로 앞에 표시하였다.

　　보기 : **pret·ty** [príti] *adj.* (**-ti·er, -ti·est**) …
　　　　　fat [fæt] *adj.* (**fat·ter, fat·test**) …
　　　　　far [fɑːr] *adv.* (**far·ther** or **fur·ther, far·thest** or **fur·thest**) … ─ *adj.* …
　　　　　well [wel] *adv.* (**bet·ter, best**) …
　　　　　com·plete [kəmplíːt] *adj.* (often **-plet·er, -plet·est**) …

(2) 원칙적으로 변화하지 않는 음절을 하이픈「-」으로 생략하였다.

　　보기 : **o·ver·run** [òuvərʌ́n] *vt.* (**-ran, -run**) …

(3) 변화형에는 모두 분절(分節) 표시를 하였으며, 독립 표제어로 게재되지 않은 변화형 및 특수한 발음을 하는 것에는 발음을 표기하였다.

　　보기 : **gen·tle·wom·an** [dʒéntlwùmən] *n.* ⓒ (pl. **-wom·en** [-wìmin]) …
　　　　　mouth *n.* [mauθ → *v.*] ⓒ (pl. **mouths** [mauðz]) …

일러두기

[5] 말뜻·역어

(1) 말뜻의 구분은 품사마다 **1. 2. 3.** …, 다시 세분할 때는 ⓐⓑⓒ를 썼다.
(2) 말뜻풀이를 연이어 적을 경우는 「세미콜론(;)」을 사용하였다.
(3) 말뜻의 배열 순서는 원칙적으로, 일반적인 것에서 차차 특수한 것으로 가게 하였다.
(4) 표제어의 특수 용법은 《 》로 묶어 다음과 같이 나타내었다.

　보기 : 《usu. *pl.*》……복수형을 취할 경우
　　　　《usu. *H·*》……첫글자가 대문자로 되는 경우
　　　　《often *the S·*》……정관사를 앞에 붙이고 첫글자를 대문자로 하는 경우
　　이밖에 《in *passive*》, 《*collectively*》, 《*sing.* only》, 《as *predicative*》
　　등으로 표시하였다.

(5) 미국에서 쓰는 것은 (*U.S.*), 영국에서 쓰는 것은 (*Brit.*)으로 표시하였다.
(6) 타동사에 말뜻풀이에는 ( ) 속에 someone, something 등의 목적어를 표시하였다. 보기 : **cov·er** [kʌ́vər] *vt.* **1.** put over the top or surface
　　　　of (something); hide (something) from view.

(7) 특정한 목적어를 취하는 것은 구체적인 명사를 들어 나타내었다.

　보기 : **ar·gue** [áːrgjuː] *vt.* **1.** discuss (a problem, etc.);
　　　　maintain (an opinion, etc.) …

(8) 표제어와 밀접하게 결합되는 중요한 전치사·부사 등은 말뜻풀이 뒤에 《 》로 묶어 이탤릭체로 표시하였다.

　보기 : **de·pend·ent** [dipéndənt] *adj.* **1.** getting help or
　　　　support from another. 《~ *on* or *upon*》 …

(9) 「자동사+전치사」의 경우는, someone, something, 또는 구체적인 명사로 그 전치사의 목적어를 나타내었으며, 부정사(infinitive), 동명사, 절(clause) 등을 목적어로 취하는 것은 그것을 명시함으로써 문형적(文型的) 이해를 도모하였다.

　보기 : **re·joice** [ridʒɔ́is] *vi.* feel joy; be glad. 《~ *at* (or
　　　　in, over) something; ~ *to do*; ~ *that* …》 …
　　　　state [steit] *n.* …
　　　　──*vt.* **1.** express (a fact, an opinion, etc.) in
　　　　words; say. 《~ *that* …; ~ *what* …; ~ someone *to do*》

[6] 용　례

(1) 용례는 품사·말뜻마다 ¶표 다음에 게재하였다.
(2) 용례와 용례 사이는 「/」로 구분하였다.
(3) 같은 뜻의 용례는 ; 표로 연이어 적었다.
(4) 표제어가 변화없이 그대로 쓰일 경우는 ~로 나타내었다.
(5) 용례·숙어 가운데에서, 바꿔 쓸 수 있는 어귀는 그 바로 뒤에 ( )로 묶어 나타내었다.

　보기 : *a large*(*small*) *amount of money*
　다른 영어로 바꾸어 말해도 뜻이 변하지 않는 경우는 다음과 같이 나타내었다.
　보기 : *keep up* (or *save*) *appearances* …

(6) 생략해도 괜찮은 어귀는 [ ]로 묶어 표시하였다.

(7) 행(行) 끝에서 단어가 끊길 경우는 -를 붙여 표시하였다.

(8) 영문만으로는 알기 어려운 용례에는, 우측 상단에 ①②③의 번호를 붙이고 한국어 난에서 번역을 게재했다. ⇨[10] 한국어난(2) 참조

보기 : **no·ta·ble** [nóutəbl] *adj*. worthy of notice ; remarkable.
¶*a ~ increase of population*① / *His deed was very ~.*②

—[형] 주목할 만한 ¶①인구의 뚜렷한 증가/②그의 공적은 주목할 만하다

[7] 숙 어

(1) 숙어는 이탤릭 고딕체로, 각 품사의 맨 뒤에 일괄하여 게재하였다.

(2) 배열은 단어 단위에 의한 알파벳순으로 하였고(단 앞의 관사는 무시), 모두 별행으로 실었다.

(3) 전치사를 가진 동사구 등에서는 목적어의 관계를 나타내기 위해, 다음과 같은 방식으로 표시하였다.

보기 : ***keep step*** *(=move at the same pace)* ***with*** *someone.*

[8] 계수명사 · 불계수명사

셀 수 있는 명사(countable noun), 셀 수 없는 명사(uncountable noun)에는 각각 [C][U]를 붙여 계수 · 불계수의 구별을 명시하였다.

(1) 말뜻 · 역어에 따라 [C][U]가 다른 것은 각각 그 말뜻 번호의 직후, 또는 역어의 직전에 표시하였다. 한 표제어의 말뜻의 대다수가 [C] 또는 [U]의 어느 쪽일 때는 품사의 바로 뒤에 대표적으로 표시하고, 예외적으로 다른 것이 섞여 들 때에 해당하는 말뜻 번호의 직후 또는 역어의 직전에 그 예외적인 경우의 기호를 표시하였다.

(2) 계수 · 불계수의 양쪽으로 다 쓰일 경우는 [C][U] 또는 [U][C]로 나란히 적어 표시하였다. 일반적으로는 앞에 나온 기호 쪽이 많이 쓰이는 것을 뜻하기도 하지만, 때로는 동등한 것도 있다.

[9] [usage] [N.B.]

본문 중에서 [usage] [N.B.] 등의 특수 활자를 써서 표시하고, 문법상의 문제점, 참고사항 등을 한국어난에서 해설하였다. ⇨[10]한국어난 (4) 참조

[10] 한국어난

각 페이지의 오른쪽에, 영문과 행의 위치를 맞추어 우리말 역어 및 해설 기사 등을 실었다.

(1) 표제어의 역어는 말뜻마다 모두 게재하였다.

(2) 「英英」난의 용례중 알기 어려운 것의 번역문을 ①②③…의 번호로 대응시켜 실었다.

(3) [熟]으로 표시하여, 숙어 · 성구의 역어를 1) 2) 3)…의 번호로 대응시켜 게재하였다.

(4) 문법상의 문제점은 [usage] 난에서, 주의사항이나 참고사항은 [N.B.] 난에서 해설하고, 「英英」난에서는 ⇨[usage], [N.B.]로 표시하여, 한국어난을 참조케 하였다.

[註] N.B.는 라틴어의 nota bene(=note well 주목하라)의 약자

(5) 변화형의 표제어, 약어 등은 원칙적으로 우리말 역어를 생략하였다.

発音記号表

母 音 (VOWELS)					子 音 (CONSONANTS)			
	記号	綴字	發音 (美) (英)			記号	綴字	發音
単母音 (SIMPLE VOWELS)	iː	each	iːtʃ		破裂音	p	pencil	pénsl
	i	ink	iŋk			b	book	buk
	e	end	end			t	table	téibl
	æ	apple	æpl			d	deep	diːp
	ɑː	palm	pɑːm			k	cook	kuk
	ɑːr	cart	kɑːrt / kɑːt			g	good	gud
	ɔ	stop	── / stɔp		鼻音	m	money	mʌ́ni
	ɑ	stop	stɑp / ──			n	nose	nouz
	ɔː	ought	ɔːt			ŋ	angle	æŋgl
	ɔːr	oar	ɔːr / ɔː		側音	l	live	liv
	u	could	kud		摩擦音	f	foot	fut
	uː	two	tuː			v	voice	vɔis
	ʌ	up	ʌp			θ	truth	truːθ
	əːr	birth	bəːrθ / bəːθ			ð	then	ðen
	ə	about	əbáut			s	swim	swim
	ər	runner	rʌ́nər / rʌ́nə			z	zone	zoun
二重母音 (DIPHTHONGS)	ei	eight	eit			ʃ	sheep	ʃiːp
	ou	coat	kout			ʒ	vision	víʒ(ə)n
	ai	like	laik			h	handle	hændl
	au	loud	laud			r	roof	ruːf
	ɔi	toy	tɔi			j	you	juː
	iər	ear	iər / iə			w	with	wið
	ɛər	heir	ɛər / ɛə		破擦音	tʃ	choose	tʃuːz
	uər	poor	puər / puə			dʒ	bridge	bridʒ
					特殊外國音	ç	Reich	raiç
						x	Bach	baːx
						~	restaurant	rést(ə)rɔ̃ː(ŋ)

ENGLISH-ENGLISH-KOREAN DICTIONARY

A

A, a [ei] *n.* [C] (pl. **A's, As, a's, as** [eiz]) **1.** the first letter of the English alphabet. **2.** the first in a series or group. **3.** (*U.S.*) the highest grade at school. ¶*straight A's.*① **4.** (*Mathematics*) the first of known numbers or qualities. **5.** the sixth note or tone of the musical scale of C major. ¶*a sonata in A major.*② **6.** anything shaped like the letter A.
1) ***do not know A from B,*** know nothing.
2) ***from A to Z,*** from beginning to end; thoroughly.
—*adj.* **1.** first in a series, group, rank, etc. **2.** having the shape of the letter A. ¶*an A tent.*③

—[名] **1.** 영어 알파벳의 첫째 글자 **2.** [연속하는 것 중의] 첫번째 것 **3.** 《美》 [학업 성적에서의] 수(秀) ¶①전과목 수(秀) **4.** 《數》 제1의 기지수(량) **5.** 《樂》 「가」음(조) ¶②「가」장조 소나타 **6.** A자형의 것
[熟] 1)낫 놓고 기역자도 모르다 2)처음부터 끝까지; 모조리
—[形] **1.** 첫째의; 일류의 **2.** A자형의 ¶③A자형 천막

‡a [ə, ei], **an** [ən, æn] *indef. art.* 《*a* before consonants, *an* before vowels and silent *h*-》 **1.** one. ¶~ *book* / *an apple* / *an hour.* **2.** a certain. ¶*It is true in ~ sense.*① **3.** any; every. ¶*A dog is a faithful animal.* **4.** per; each. ¶*He came home twice ~ month.*② **5.** one and the same. ¶*Birds of ~ feather flock together.*③

—[冠] **1.** 하나의 **2.** 어떤 ¶①그것은 어떤 의미에서는 진실이다 **3.** …이라는 것은 어느 것이나 **4.** …에 대하여 ¶②그는 한 달에 두 번 집에 왔다 **5.** 동일한 ¶③깃털이 같은 새(동류)는 한 떼 모인다; 유유상종

A 1 [éiwʌ́n] *n.* (*colloq.*) the first-class; superior. ⇨[N.B.] ¶~ *tea*① / *an ~ musician.*

—[名] 《口》 일류, 최고 [N.B.] A one으로도 씀 ¶①최고급의 차(茶)

ab·a·ci [ǽbəsài] *n.* pl. of **abacus.**

a·back [əbǽk] *adv.* to the back; backward.
be taken aback, be surprised. ¶*I was taken ~ by the news.*

—[副]뒤로, 뒤쪽으로
[熟] 깜짝 놀라다

ab·a·cus [ǽbəkəs] *n.* [C] (pl. **-cus·es** [-kəsiz] or **-ci**) a frame with rows of sliding beads which are put back and forth in doing calculation.

—[名] 주판

a·baft [əbǽft / əbɑ́:ft] (*Nautical*) *adv.* toward the rear end of a ship. **—*prep.*** behind. ¶~ *the mast*① / *the wind from ~.*②

—[副] 《海》[배의] 후반부(고물)로 —[前] …의 뒤에 ¶①돛대 뒤에/②[배의] 뒤에서 불어오는 바람

‡a·ban·don [əbǽndən] *vt.* **1.** give up (something) entirely. ¶~ *the attempt.*① **2.** leave (a place) for ever. ¶~ *one's home*② / *The crew abandoned the wrecked ship.* **3.** 《*reflexively*》 yield (oneself) completely. 《~ oneself *to*》 ¶*She abandoned herself to despair.*③

—[他] **1.** …을 버리다, 단념하다 ¶①계획을 포기하다 **2.** [장소]를 버리고 떠나다 ¶②집을 버리고 떠나다 **3.** [몸]을 맡기다 ¶③그녀는 자포자기가 되었다

a·ban·doned [əbǽndənd] *adj.* **1.** given up; forsaken. ¶*an ~ child.*① **2.** desperate; wicked.

—[形] **1.** 버림받은 ¶①기아(棄兒) **2.** 자포자기의; 사악한

a·ban·don·ment [əbǽndənmənt] *n.* [U] **1.** the act of abandoning; the state of being abandoned. ¶*the ~ of a right.*① **2.** lack of self-control.

—[名] **1.** 포기 ¶①권리 포기 **2.** 자포자기

a·base [əbéis] *vt.* make (someone) lower in rank, position, character, etc. ¶~ *oneself.*①

—[他] …의 지위·품격 따위를 떨어뜨리다 ¶①스스로 품격을 떨어뜨리다

a·base·ment [əbéismənt] *n.* [U] **1.** the state of being abased. **2.** loss of dignity and respect; humility.

—[名] **1.** 면목을 잃음 **2.** 영락(零落), 몰락; 스스로 낮추기

a·bash [əbǽʃ] *vt.* 《usu. in *passive*》 make (someone) feel confused and ashamed; embarrass. ¶*be* (or *feel*) ~① / *The girl was abashed when she saw the young man.*

—[他] …의 얼굴을 붉히게 하다; 무안하게 하다 ¶①부끄러워하다, 얼굴을 붉히다

a·bate [əbéit] *vt.* **1.** make (something) less in amount or intensity; lessen; decrease. ¶*The pain is abated.*① **2.** cut down the cost or price of (something). **—*vi.*** become less in amount or intensity. ¶*The storm abated.*②

—[他] **1.** …을 경감하다, 덜하게 하다 ¶①고통이 줄었다. **2.** …의 값(가치)을 내리다 —[自] 줄다, 약해지다; 가라앉다 ¶②폭풍이 잤다.

a·bate·ment [əbéitmənt] *n.* [U] the act of abating; the state of being abated. ¶*make an ~ of the price.*①

—[名] 감소, 감가(減價), 완화 ¶①값을 깎다

ab·bess [ǽbis] *n.* [C] the chief nun of an abbey. ↔abbot

—[名] 수녀원 원장

ab·bey [ǽbi] *n.* **1.** ⓒ a building where men or women lead a religious life. **2.** ⓒ a large church that is used or was once used as an abbey. ¶*Westminster Abbey.*① **3.** (*collectively*) all the men and women in an abbey.
—⑬ 1. 대수도원, 수녀원 2. 대사원 ¶①웨스트민스터 대사원 3. [수도원 전체의] 수도사, 수녀

ab·bot [ǽbət] *n.* ⓒ the head man of an abbey. ↔abbess
—⑬ 대수도원 원장

ab·bre·vi·ate [əbríːvièit] *vt.* make (a word, phrase, or story) shorter; shorten. ¶*We can ~ "foot" to "ft."*
—⑬ [말·이야기 따위]를 짧게 줄이다, 생략(단축)하다

ab·bre·vi·a·tion [əbrìːviéiʃ(ə)n] *n.* **1.** Ⓤ the act of abbreviating. **2.** ⓒ a shortened form of a word or phrase.
—⑬ 1. 단축, 생략 2. 생략형, 약자, 약어

ABC [éibìːsíː] *n.* (*pl.* **ABC's**) **1.** (*usu. pl.*) the English alphabet. **2.** (*often the ~*) something to be learned first; a basic element. ¶*The ABC's of economics.*①
—⑬ 1. 알파벳 2. 초보 ¶①경제학 입문

ab·di·cate [ǽbdikèit] *vt., vi.* abandon (one's position, right, etc.); resign. ¶*~ [from] the throne.*① ▷**ab·di·ca·tor** [-ər] *n.* [resignation.
—⑬ⓥ [지위·권리 따위를] 포기하다 ¶①퇴위하다

ab·di·ca·tion [æ̀bdikéiʃ(ə)n] *n.* Ⓤ the act of abdicating;
—⑬ 퇴위, 사직, 기권

ab·do·men [ǽbdəmən, æbdóu- / ǽbdəmèn] *n.* ⓒ the part of the body below the chest.
—⑬ [사람의] 배, 복부

ab·dom·i·nal [æbdámin(ə)l / -dɔ́m-] *adj.* of the abdomen. ¶*an ~ belt*① / *~ breathing*② / *an ~ operation.*③
—⑬ 복부의 ¶①배 띠/②복식(腹式) 호흡/③개복 수술

ab·duct [æbdʌ́kt] *vt.* carry off (someone, esp. a child) by force, often for money; kidnap.
—⑬ [특히 유아]를 유괴하다

ab·duc·tion [æbdʌ́kʃ(ə)n] *n.* Ⓤⓒ the act of abducting.
—⑬ 유괴

ab·duc·tor [æbdʌ́ktər] *n.* ⓒ a person who abducts.
—⑬ 유괴범

Abe [eib] *n.* nickname of Abraham.
—⑬ Abraham의 애칭

a·beam [əbíːm] *adv.* (*Nautical*) at a right angle to a ship's side. ¶*have the wind ~.*
—⑬ [배의] 정우현(正右舷, 또는 正左舷)으로

A·bel [éib(ə)l] *n.* **1.** a man's name. **2.** (in the Bible) the second son of Adam and Eve; he was killed by Cain, his elder brother.
—⑬ 1. 남자 이름 2. 아벨(아담의 둘째 아들. 형 Cain에게 죽음)

ab·er·rant [æbérənt] *adj.* straying from normal courses.
—⑬ 정도에서 벗어난, 탈선한

ab·er·ra·tion [æ̀bəréiʃ(ə)n] *n.* Ⓤ the state of being abnormal; an abnormal act. ¶*mental ~.*①
—⑬ 상궤(常軌)를 벗어남; 탈선 ¶①정신이상

a·bet [əbét] *vt.* (**a·bet·ted, a·bet·ting**) help (someone) in a wrong way, esp. in a crime. ¶*~ a crime*① / *~ someone in a crime.*② ▷**a·bet·tor, a·bet·ter** [-ər] *n.*
—⑬ 부추기다, 선동(교사)하다 ¶①범죄를 부추기다/②남을 부추겨 범죄를 저지르게 하다

a·bey·ance [əbéiəns] *n.* Ⓤ the state in which something is not in use or is delayed for a short time. ¶*fall into ~*① / *hold a question in ~.*②
—⑬ 중지, 정지 ¶①[법령·관습 따위가] 일시 정지되다 / ②문제를 일시 미정인 채로 두다

ab·hor [əbhɔ́ːr] *vt.* (**-horred, -hor·ring**) hate (something) very much. ¶*We ~ cruelty.*①
—⑬ …을 몸서리치도록 싫어하다 ¶①우리는 잔인성을 증오한다

ab·hor·rence [əbhɔ́ːrəns / -hɔ́r-] *n.* **1.** Ⓤ the act of abhorring; great hatred. **2.** ⓒ a cause of great hatred.
—⑬ 1. 증오 2. 질색인 것

ab·hor·rent [əbhɔ́ːrənt / -hɔ́r-] *adj.* causing (someone) to feel great hatred; hateful; detestable.
—⑬ 아주 싫은, 질색인

* **a·bide** [əbáid] *vt.* (**a·bode** or **a·bid·ed**) *vt.* **1.** wait for (something). ¶*~ one's time.*① **2.** (usu. in *negative* or *interrogative*) put up with (something); endure. ¶*I can't ~ such a rude fellow.*② / *She can't ~ his rudeness.*③ —*vi.* remain.
abide by (=remain true or faithful to) something. ¶*A man must ~ by his word.*③   [¶*~ faith.*
—⑬ 1. …을 기다리다 ¶①때를 기다리다 2. 참다 ¶②그런 건방진 녀석은 용서할 수 없다 —ⓥ [어떤 상태에] 머무르다, 지속하다

🔲 …을 지키다 ¶③사람은 약속을 지켜야 한다

a·bid·ing [əbáidiŋ] *adj.* permanent; lasting; unchanging.
—⑬ 영구적인, 불변의

‡ a·bil·i·ty [əbíliti] *n.* (*pl.* **-ties**) **1.** Ⓤ power to do something; skill. ¶*the ~ to speak* / *a man of ~.*① **2.** (usu. *pl.*) talents. ¶*manifold abilities*② / *She showed ~ in music.* ¶*well as one can.*
to the best of one's ability; to one's best ability, as
—⑬ 1. 능력; 수완, 솜씨 ¶①수완가 2. 재능 ¶②다방면의 재능

🔲 힘껏, 될 수 있는 한

ab·ject [ǽbdʒekt, +U.S. æbdʒékt] *adj.* **1.** miserable. ¶*~ poverty.*① **2.** mean; contemptible. ¶*an ~ time-server.*② ▷**ab·ject·ly** [-li] *adv.*
—⑬ 1. 비참한, 불쌍한 ¶①지독한 가난 2. 비열한, 천한 ¶②비열한 기회주의자

ab·jec·tion [æbdʒékʃ(ə)n] *n.* Ⓤ the state of being abject.
—⑬ 비천, 비열, 비굴

ab·ju·ra·tion [æ̀bdʒu(ə)réiʃ(ə)n] *n.* Ⓤ the act of abjuring; the state of being abjured.
—⑬ [신앙·국적 따위의] 포기

ab·jure [əbdʒúər] *vt.* declare to give up (one's right, faith, demand, nationality, etc.).
—[他] [의견·신앙·국적 따위]를 버리기로 맹세하다

a·blaze [əbléiz] *adj.* 《only in *predicative*》 **1.** on fire. **2.** shining in bright color; excited. ¶*His face was ~ with anger.*①
—[形] 1. 불타는 2. 반짝이는;흥분한 ¶①그는 몹시 성이 나 있었다

‡ **a·ble** [éibl] *adj.* (**a·bler, a·blest**) **1.** having power to do something. ↔unable **2.** skillful; clever. ¶*an ~ man*① / *an ~ speech.*②
—[形] 1. …할 수 있는 2. 유능한, 솜씨 있는, 뛰어난 ¶①수완가/②훌륭한 연설

be able to do, can do. ⇒[N.B.] ¶*He is ~ to speak French. / I shall be ~ to visit you tomorrow. / He has not been ~ to attend school for a week.*
[熟] 할 수 있다 [N.B.] 조동사 can은 미래형·완료형이 없으므로 be able to로 씀

-a·ble [-əbl] *suf.* **1.** able to: *durable* (=able to last). **2.** fit to; suitable for: *drinkable* (=fit to drink). **3.** tending to; likely to: *changeable* (=likely to change). **4.** having qualities of: *comfortable* (=having qualities of comfort). **5.** worthy of: *lovable* (=worthy of loving).
—《接尾》 1.「…할 수 있는」 2.「…에 알맞은」 3.「…하기 쉬운」 4.「…질(質)의」「… 같은」 5.「…할 가치가 있는」

a·ble-bod·ied [éiblbádid / -bɔ́d-] *adj.* strong in health.
—[形] 강건한

a·bloom [əblúːm] *adv., adj.* 《only in *predicative*》 in bloom. ¶*The garden is ~ with tulips.*
—[副][形] 꽃이 피어, 개화하여

ab·lu·tion [əblúːʃ(ə)n] *n.* [U][C] the act of washing one's body or a part of it, esp. as a religious ceremony.
—[名] [특히 종교의식으로서의] 목욕

a·bly [éibli] *adv.* in an able manner; skillfully.
—[副] 훌륭히, 잘

ab·ne·ga·tion [æ̀bnigéiʃ(ə)n] *n.* [U] **1.** refusal. **2.** (of one's rights, etc.) abandonment.
—[名] 1. 거절, 거부 2. [권리 따위의] 포기

ab·nor·mal [æbnɔ́ːrm(ə)l] *adj.* not normal; unusual; uncommon. ¶*~ psychology.*① ▷**ab·nor·mal·ness** [-nis] *n.*
—[形] 변태의, 변칙의, 정상이 아닌 ¶①변태 심리학

ab·nor·mal·i·ty [æ̀bnɔːrmǽliti] *n.* (pl. **-ties**) **1.** [U] the state of being abnormal. **2.** [C] an abnormal thing.
—[名] 1. 비정상, 변태 2. 예사가 아닌 것, 기형, 불구

ab·nor·mal·ly [æbnɔ́ːrməli] *adv.* in an abnormal manner; to an abnormal extent.
—[副] 예사가 아니게, 병적으로

* **a·board** [əbɔ́ːrd] *adv., prep.* on or in a ship; (*U.S.*) on or in a bus, train, airplane, etc. ¶*step ~ / go* (or *come*) *~ a ship*① / *All ~.*②
—[副][前] 배로, 배에;《美》 기차·버스·비행기 따위에[타고] ¶①승선하다/②승선(승차)해 주시오.

fall aboard [*of another ship*], strike against the side of another ship.
[熟] 다른 배에 부딪치다

* **a·bode**[1] [əbóud] *n.* [C] a place where a person lives. ¶*make* (or *take up*) *one's ~.*①
—[名] 거처, 주소 ¶①거처를 정하다

a·bode[2] [əbóud] *v.* pt. and pp. of **abide**.

* **a·bol·ish** [əbáliʃ / -bɔ́l-] *vt.* put an end to (laws, customs, etc.). ¶*~ slavery.*① ▷**a·bol·ish·ment** [-mənt] *n.*
—[他] [법률·관습 따위]를 폐지하다, 철폐하다 ¶①노예제도를 폐지하다

ab·o·li·tion [æ̀bəlíʃ(ə)n] *n.* [U] **1.** the act of abolishing. **2.** (*U.S.*) the act of abolishing slavery. ▷**ab·o·li·tion·ist** [-ʃ(ə)nist] *n.*
—[名] 1. 폐지 2. 노예제도 폐지

* **A-bomb** [éibàm / -bɔ̀m] *n.* [C] an atomic bomb.
—[名] 원자폭탄

a·bom·i·na·ble [əbáminəbl / əbɔ́m-] *adj.* **1.** hateful; horrible. **2.** (*colloq.*) very unpleasant. ¶*~ weather.*①
—[形] 1. 밉살맞은; 지긋지긋한 2.《口》 지독한, 불쾌한 ¶①지독한 날씨

a·bom·i·nate [əbáminèit / əbɔ́m-] *vt.* hate strongly; abhor. ▷**a·bom·i·na·tor** [-ər] *n.*
—[他] …을 몹시 싫어하다

a·bom·i·na·tion [əbàminéiʃ(ə)n / əbɔ̀m-] *n.* **1.** [U] hatred. **2.** [C] anything which causes hatred.
—[名] 1. 혐오, 몹시 싫어함 2. 몹시 싫은 것

ab·o·rig·i·nal [æ̀bərídʒin(ə)l] *adj.* **1.** existing from the earliest days; primitive. **2.** originally found in a certain country or region; native. ¶*an ~ animal.* **—*n.*** [C] (pl. **-i·nes**) an original inhabitant, animal, or plant of a country or region.
—[形] 1. 원시의, 원생(原生)의 2. 토착민의
—[名] 원주민, 토착 동식물

ab·o·rig·i·nes [æ̀bərídʒiniːz] *n. pl.* 《*collectively*》 aboriginal inhabitants; natives.
—[名] 토착민, 원주민

a·bor·tion [əbɔ́ːrʃ(ə)n] *n.* [U][C] **1.** the birth of a baby before it has not yet grown enough to live. ¶*criminal ~.*① **2.** a failure [of a plan or an idea].
—[名] 1. 유산(流產), 낙태 ¶①낙태죄 2. [계획 따위의] 실패

a·bor·tive [əbɔ́ːrtiv] *adj.* **1.** born before grown enough to live. ¶*~ birth.*① **2.** not successful; fruitless.
—[形] 1. 유산(流產)의, 낙태의 ¶①유산 2. 실패의, 열매를 맺지 않는

* **a·bound** [əbáund] *vi.* exist in plenty. 《*~ in* or *with* something》 ¶*Fish ~ in this river.; This river abounds in* (or *with*) *fish.*①
—[自] 많이 있다, 풍부하다 ¶①이 강에는 물고기가 많다

A

⁝ **a·bout** [əbáut] *prep.* **1.** concerning; of. ¶*What are you speaking ~?* **2.** on; by; with. ¶*There is something elegant ~ her.*① | *I had lost all I had ~ me.* **3.** near. ¶*~ three o'clock.* **4.** somewhere near; not far from. ¶*You will find my son somewhere ~ the house.* **5.** here and there; to and fro; [all] around. ¶*walk ~ the streets* | *There is a fence ~ the garden.*② **6.** engaged in; attending to. ¶*What are you ~ here?*③ | *He is busy ~ his packing.*

—[前] 1. …에 대하여, …에 관한 2. 신변에; …의 몸에 지니고; …의 수중에 ¶①그녀에게는 어딘가 우아한 데가 있다 3. …쯤에.; 약… 4. …의 근처에 5. …의 여기저가에;의 둘레에 ¶②정원 둘레에는 울타리가 있다 6. …에 종사하여 ¶③여기서 무엇을 하고 있는가

be about to *do,* be going to do; be on the point of doing. ¶*She was ~ to start.*

[熟] 방금 …하려 하고 있다

—*adv.* **1.** around; in every direction. ¶*She looked ~.* **2.** nearly; almost. ¶*The buckets are ~ full.* | *It is ~ time to start.* **3.** somewhere around; nearby; somewhere near. ¶*scatter the toys ~* | *There was nobody ~.* **4.** in the opposite direction. ¶*turn ~.* **5.** alternately; in succession; by turns. **6.** going on; in action. ¶*Rumors are ~.* | *He is already up ana ~.*④

—[副] 1. 둘레에;주위에(를) 2. 대략, 거의 3. 근처[어딘가]에, 여기 저기에 4. 반대의 위치로; 빙 돌아서 5. 번갈아, 차례로 6. 움직여서, 일하여; 진행중 ¶④그는 이미 일어나서 움직이고 있다

⁝ **a·bove** [əbʌ́v] *prep.* **1.** higher than, over; on the top of. ↔below ¶*~ the horizon* | *the clouds ~ the mountains* | *3,000 meters ~ sea level* | *The sun is blazing ~ our heads.* | *Her voice was heard ~ the noise.* **2.** earlier in history than; upstream from. ¶*the period ~ the 6th century*① | *There is a waterfall ~ the bridge.*② **3.** superior to; more than; better than. ¶*~ a thousand* | *~ the average*③ | *Health is ~ wealth.* | *He is ~ all the other boys in his class.* **4.** surpassing; beyond, ashamed of. ¶*He is ~ criticism.*④ | *This book is ~ my understanding.* | *You must not be ~ asking questions.*⑤

—[前] 1. …보다 높이; …의 위에 2. …을 거슬러 올라가서; …보다 상류에 ¶①6세기 이전의 시대/②다리 상류에 폭포가 있다 3. …보다 뛰어나게; …이상으로 ¶③평균 이상 4. …을 초월하여 ;…이 따를 수 없는; …을 부끄러워하는 ¶④그는 비평할 여지가 없을 만큼 훌륭하다/⑤질문하기를 부끄러워해서는 안 된다.

—*adv.* **1.** in or at a higher place; overhead. ¶*clear sky ~.* **2.** upstairs. ¶*an iron stair leading ~.* **3.** in heaven. ¶*God ~* **4.** higher in rank or power. ¶*the courts ~.*⑥ **5.** upstream. ¶*There is good fishing ~.*⑦ **6.** (esp. in a book) before; earlier ¶*as [is] mentioned ~.*⑧ **7.** over; in addition. ¶*Children of six and ~ should attend school.*

—[副] 1. 보다 높이; 위쪽에 2. 층계 위에 3. 하늘 위에 4. 상급에, 윗자리에 ¶⑥상급 법원 5. 강의 상류로(에) ¶⑦상류에서는 낚시가 잘 된다 6. 책의 페이지 위쪽에;전문(前文)에 ¶⑧위에서 말한 바와 같이 7. …이상, 그 이상으로

—*adj.* written above; foregoing. ¶*the ~ explanations* | *judging by* (*or* from) *the ~ facts.*

—[形] 위에서 말한, 상기한

a·bove·board [əbʌ́vbɔ̀ːrd] *adv.* without dishonesty; openly. ¶*He treated us ~.* —*adj.* honest, open. ¶*His dealings are all ~.*①

—[副] 공명정대하게, 솔직하게 —[形] 공정한, 솔직한 ¶①그의 거래는 공명정대하다

a·bove-men·tion·ed [əbʌ́vménʃ(ə)nd] *adj.* mentioned before.

—[形] 앞서 말한, 상술(上述)한

a·brade [əbréid] *vt.* rub off (the surface, the skin, etc.). ¶*A glacier abrades rocks.*①

—[他] …을 닳려 없애다; 깎다 ¶①빙하가 바위를 깎는다

A·bra·ham [éibrəhæm, -həm] *n.* **1.** a man's name. **2.** (in the Bible) the first head of the Hebrews.

—[名] 1. 남자 이름 2. 아브라함(유대인의 시조)

a·bra·sion [əbréiʒ(ə)n] *n.* **1.** [U] the state of being abraded. ¶*~ of a coin.*① **2.** [C] an abraded place or spot.

—[名] 1. 벗겨짐, 마손, 마멸 ¶①주화(鑄貨)의 마멸 2. 벗겨진 곳, 찰과상

a·breast [əbrést] *adv.* side by side.

—[副] …과 병행하여, 나란히

keep abreast of (=*keep up with*) *something.* ¶*Keep ~ of the times.*①

[熟] …에 뒤지지 않도록 하다 ¶①시대에 뒤지지 않도록 해라

a·bridge [əbrídʒ] *vt.* make (a story, a book, etc.) shorter without changing the chief contents; shorten. ↔lengthen ¶*~ a long story for school.*①

—[他] [이야기·책 따위]를 단축하다, 요약하다 ¶①긴 이야기를 교재용으로 요약하다

a·bridg·ment, -bridge- [əbrídʒmənt] *n.* **1.** [U] the act of abridging. **2.** [C] an abridged story, book, etc.

—[名] 1. 요약, 단축 2. 요약한 이야기나 책

⁝ **a·broad** [əbrɔ́ːd] *adv.* **1.** out of one's own country; to or in a foreign land. ¶*go ~.* **2.** far and wide; broadly. ¶*The news of his coming spread ~*

—[副] 1. 해외로; 외국으로 2. 널리; [소문 따위가] 퍼져서

ab·ro·gate [ǽbrougèit] *vt.* abolish (laws, customs, etc.); repeal.

—[他] [법률·습관 따위]를 폐지하다

ab·ro·ga·tion [æ̀brougéiʃ(ə)n] *n.* [U] the act of abrogating; the state of being abrogated.

—[名] 폐지

* **ab·rupt** [əbrʌ́pt] *adj.* ↔gentle **1.** sudden; unexpected. ¶*an ~ death*① | *an ~ change in the weather.* **2.** rough;

—[形] 1. 갑작스러운, 뜻밖의 ¶①급사 2. 무뚝뚝한 ¶②무뚝뚝한 대답/③무뚝

abruptly [21] **abstain**

impolite ; rude. ¶*an ~ reply*① / *answer in an ~ manner.*② **3.** very steep. ¶*an ~ slope.*　「ly ; rudely.」

• **ab·rupt·ly** [əbrʌ́ptli] *adv.* in an abrupt manner ; sudden-」

ab·rupt·ness [əbrʌ́ptnis] *n.* Ⓤ the state of being abrupt ; rudeness. ¶*with ~.*①

ab·scess [ǽbsis] *n.* Ⓒ a painful part of the body, swollen with pus often resulting from an infection.

ab·scond [əbskánd / -skɔ́nd] *vi.* go away suddenly and hide.

: ab·sence [ǽbs(ə)ns] *n.* **1.** Ⓤ the state of being away or not present. ↔presence ¶*~ from school.*① **2.** Ⓒ a time when a person is away. ¶*after a long ~*② / *during one's ~.*③ **3.** the state of being without something ; lack. ¶*~ of mind*④ / *~ of order.*⑤

: ab·sent *adj.* [ǽbs(ə)nt→*v.*] **1.** not here ; away in another place. ↔present ¶*He is ~ from class today.* / *~ friends.* **2.** not existing ; lacking. ¶*Snow is ~ in some countries.* **3.** not paying attention. ↔attentive ¶*an ~ air.*① ——*vt.* [æbsént] (*reflexively*) stay (oneself) away ; keep (oneself) away. (*~ oneself from*) ¶*~ oneself from class.*

ab·sen·tee [æ̀bs(ə)ntíː] *n.* Ⓒ a person who is absent from school, work, home, etc.　「lessly. 」

ab·sent·ly [ǽbs(ə)ntli] *adv.* in an absent manner ; care-」

ab·sent-mind·ed [ǽbs(ə)ntmáindid] *adj.* paying no attention to what is happening around one ; careless. ▷**ab·sent-mind·ed·ly** [-li] *adv.* ——**ab·sent-mind·ed·ness** [-nis] *n.*

: ab·so·lute [ǽbsəluːt, -ljùːt] *adj.* **1.** complete ; perfect. ¶*~ ignorance.* **2.** not mixed with anything else ; pure. ¶*~ alcohol.*① **3.** not limited ; uncontrolled ; free. ¶*an ~ ruler*② / *the Absolute* (=God). **4.** certain ; real ; definite. ¶*an ~ proof* / *an ~ fact.*

: ab·so·lute·ly [ǽbsəlùːtli, -ljùːt-] *adv.* **1.** completely ; thoroughly. ¶*That's ~ ridiculous.* **2.** (*colloq.*) (used in *conversation*) quite so ; yes. ⇒N.B. ¶"*Are you fine?*" "*Absolutely.*"

ab·so·lu·tion [æ̀bsəlúːʃ(ə)n, -ljúː-] *n.* Ⓤ the act of absolving ; [a formal declaration of] freedom from guilt or punishment.

ab·solve [æbsálv, -zálv / əbzɔ́lv] *vt.* **1.** declare (someone) free from guilt or punishment ; forgive. (*~ someone of a sin*) ¶*The priest absolved him of all his sins.*① **2.** set (someone) free from a duty or promise. (*~ someone from*)

• **ab·sorb** [əbsɔ́ːrb] *vt.* **1.** take in (moisture, heat, light, etc.) wholly. ¶*Blotting paper absorbs ink.*① / *Black absorbs light.*② **2.** cause (someone) to have a deep interest ; attract (someone's attention or interest) fully. ¶*His lecture absorbs me* (or *my interest*).

be absorbed (=be deeply interested) **in something.** ¶*He is absorbed in reading.*

ab·sorb·ent [əbsɔ́ːrbənt] *adj.* having the quality of absorbing. ¶*~ cotton*① / *~ powder.*② ——*n.* Ⓒ anything that absorbs.

ab·sorb·ing [əbsɔ́ːrbiŋ] *adj.* occupying someone's attention wholly ; very interesting. ¶*an ~ book.*

ab·sorp·tion [əbsɔ́ːrpʃ(ə)n] *n.* Ⓤ **1.** the act of absorbing **2.** great interest. ¶*His ~ in sports prevents his progress in his studies.*①

ab·sorp·tive [əbsɔ́ːrptiv] *adj.* having the quality of absorbing ; absorbent. ▷**ab·sorp·tive·ness** [-nis] *n.*

ab·stain [æbstéin] *vi.* hold (oneself) back ; refrain. (*~ from something, ~ from doing*) ¶*~ from smoking.*①

둑하게 대답하다 **3.** 가파른

——働 갑자기 ; 무뚝뚝하게

——働 갑작스러움, 무뚝뚝함 ¶①갑작스럽게 ; 무뚝뚝하게

——働 종기, 농양(膿瘍)

——働 도망하다, 자취를 감추다

——働 **1.** 부재, 출타 ; 결석 ¶①결석 **2.** 부재 기간 ¶②오래간만에/③부재중에 **3.** 결여, 결핍 ¶④방심/⑤무질서

——働 **1.** 결석의 ; 부재의 **2.** …이 없는 ; 결여된 **3.** 멍하니 있는 ¶①멍하고 있는 모습
——働 …을 결석시키다, 결근시키다

——働 결석자, 결근자, 부재자

——働 멍하니
——働 멍하고 있는, 얼빠진

——働 **1.** 완전한 ; 순전한 **2.** 순수한 ¶①무수(無水) 알코올 **3.** 무제한의, 억제(제약)받지 않은 ¶②전제 군주 **4.** 확실한 ; 실제의 ; 확고부동의

——働 **1.** 절대적으로, 완전히 **2.** (口)정말로 [그렇습니다] N.B. 특히 강조할 때는 [æ̀bsəlúːtli]로 발음

——働 무죄 언도 ; 죄상 소멸[의 선언]

——働 **1.** …을 무죄로 하다, …에게 무죄 언도를 하다 ¶①목사는 그의 죄장(罪障) 소멸을 선언했다 **2.** [남]의 [의무·책임]을 면제하다

——働 **1.** …을 흡수하다, 동화하다 ¶①압지는 잉크를 빨아들인다/②검정색은 광선을 흡수한다 **2.** [남]을 열중(열광)시키다, [남의 주목·관심]을 끌다

熟 …에 정신이 팔려 있다

——働 흡수성의 ¶①탈지면/②땀며약
——働 흡수제

——働 열중(열광)시키는 ; 아주 재미있는

——働 **1.** 흡수 **2.** 열중, 골몰, 전심 ¶①그는 운동에 너무 열중해서 학과가 진보하지 않는다
——働 흡수성의

——働 [의지력으로 …을] 삼가다, 억제하다 ¶①금연하다

ab·stain·er [əbstéinər] *n.* [C] a person who abstains, esp. from taking alcoholic drinks. ¶*a total ~.*①

—[명] 절제하는 사람, [특히] 금주가 ¶①절대 금주가

ab·ste·mi·ous [æbstí:miəs] *adj.* not eating and drinking too much; moderate. ¶*~ life.*① ¶*~ from wine.*①

—[형] 폭음(폭식)하지 않는; 절제 있는 ¶①절제 생활

ab·sten·tion [æbsténʃ(ə)n] *n.* [U] the act of abstaining.

—[명] 절제; 회피 ¶①금주

ab·sti·nence [ǽbstinəns] *n.* [U] the act of abstaining, esp. from eating and drinking. ¶*total ~*① | *~ from wine.*②

—[명] 절제, 금욕, 금주 ¶①절대 금주 ②금주

ab·sti·nent [ǽbstinənt] *adj.* moderate in eating and drinking.

—[형] [음식 따위] 절제 있는, 금욕의

***ab·stract** *adj.* [ǽbstrækt → *v.*] **1.** considered apart from any real things; only in idea; not concrete. ↔concrete ¶*an ~ conception*① | *an ~ noun*② | *~ art.*③ **2.** hard to understand; difficult. ¶*~ theories about the nature of the soul.*④

—[형] 1. 추상적인 ¶①추상적 개념/②추상 명사/③추상 예술 2. 난해한, 심원한 ¶④영혼의 본질에 관한 난해한 이론

—*n.* [C] a shortened form of the main ideas of a book or argument; a summary.

—[명] 적요(摘要), 발췌

1) ***in the abstract,*** in an abstract way. ¶*He has no idea of poverty except in the ~.*⑤
2) ***make an abstract*** (=*sum up the main points*) ***of*** *a book, argument, etc.*

[熟] 1)추상적으로 ¶⑤그는 가난을 추상적으로밖에 모른다 2)[책·의론 따위의] 요점을 발췌하다

—*vt.* [æbstrǽkt] **1.** make an abstract of (a book, argument, etc.); summarize. ¶*~ a passage from a book.* **2.** take away. ¶*~ others' attention from one's fault.*①

—[타] 1. [책 따위]를 발췌하다, 요약하다 2. …을 떼어내다 ¶①자기의 과실에서 남의 주의를 돌리게 하다

ab·stract·ed [æbstrǽktid] *adj.* absent-minded; lost in thought. ¶*with an ~ air.*① ▷**ab·stract·ed·ly** [-li] *adv.*

—[형] 멍하고 있는 ¶①멍하니

ab·strac·tion [æbstrǽkʃ(ə)n] *n.* **1.** [U] the act of abstracting; the state of being abstracted. **2.** [C] an abstract idea. **3.** [U] absent-mindedness. ¶*with an air of ~.*①

—[명] 1. 추상화 2. 추상 개념 3. 방심 상태 ¶①멍하니, 넋을 잃고

ab·struse [æbstrú:s] *adj.* difficult to understand; deep in meaning. ¶*~ questions.* ▷**ab·struse·ly** [-li] *adv.* —**ab·struse·ness** [-nis] *n.*

—[형] 난해한; 심원한

***ab·surd** [əbsə́:rd, +*U.S.* -zə́:rd] *adj.* very foolish; ridiculous; unreasonable. ¶*an ~ opinion* | *Don't be ~!*①

—[형] 어리석은; 불합리한 ¶①어이없는 짓을 말아라

ab·surd·i·ty [əbsə́:rditi, +*U.S.* -zə́:rd-] *n.* (pl. **-ties**) **1.** [U] the quality of being absurd; unreasonableness. **2.** [C] an absurd idea, act, thing, etc. ¶*He said a number of absurdities.*

—[명] 1. 불합리 2. 어리석은 일(짓·말)

ab·surd·ly [əbsə́:rdli, +*U.S.* -zə́:rd-] *adv.* in an absurd manner; foolishly.

—[부] 불합리하게, 어리석게

***a·bun·dance** [əbʌ́ndəns] *n.* [U] 《sometimes *an ~*》 an amount or quantity that is more than enough. ¶*an ~ of food* | *An ~ of rice is produced every year.*①

—[명] 풍부, 다량 ¶①해마다 쌀이 풍부하게 산출된다

1) ***in abundance,*** in plenty.
2) ***live in abundance,*** have many things to make life pleasant and comfortable. ¶*They live in ~.*②

[熟] 1)풍부하게, 유복하게 2)유복하게 살다 ¶②그들은 유복하게 살고 있다

***a·bun·dant** [əbʌ́ndənt] *adj.* plentiful; very rich in something. ¶*an ~ harvest*① | *an ~ crop of rice.*②
be abundant (=*be rich*) ***in*** *something.* ¶*This country is ~ in natural resources.*③

—[형] 많은, 풍부한 ¶①풍작/②쌀의 풍작
[熟] 1)…이 풍부하다 ¶③이 나라는 천연 자원이 풍부하다

a·bun·dant·ly [əbʌ́ndəntli] *adv.* in a great number or amount.

—[부] 풍부하게

***a·buse** *vt.* [əbjú:z → *n.*] **1.** use (a position, privilege, etc.) for a wrong purpose; make a wrong use of (words, etc.). ¶*~ one's authority.* **2.** treat (someone) cruelly. **3.** use bad or violent language to (someone).

—[타] 1. [권력 따위]를 남용(악용)하다; [말 따위]를 잘못 쓰다 2. …을 학대하다 3. …을 욕지거리하다

—*n.* [əbjú:s] **1.** [U][C] bad or wrong use. ¶*the ~ of power* | *~ of words.*① **2.** [U] bad language that hurts others. ¶*a term of ~.*② **3.** [U] severe and cruel treatment of persons. **4.** [C] 《often *pl.*》 a bad or unjust custom or practice. ¶*the abuses of modern times*③ | *the abuses of government.*④ ▷**a·bus·er** [-zər] *n.*

—[명] 1. 남용, 오용 ¶①말의 오용 2. 욕지거리 ¶②폭언 3. 학대 4. 악습, 폐해, 악폐 ¶③현대의 악폐/④정치의 폐해

a·bu·sive [əbjú:siv] *adj.* **1.** using wrong and insulting language. ¶*become ~*① | *use ~ language.* **2.** used in a wrong way. ¶*an ~ exercise of power.*②

—[형] 1. 입버릇 나쁜 ¶①입버릇이 사나와지다 2. 남용하는 ¶②권력의 남용

a·but [əbʌ́t] *v.* (**a·but·ted, a·but·ting**) *vi.* be in contact at an end or edge. 《*~ on* (or *upon, against*) something》

—[자] [토지 따위가 다른 것과] 경계를 접하다 ¶①그의 정원은 도로에 인접

¶*His garden abuts on the road.*① | *The street abuts against the railroad.* —*vt.* border upon (something).

해 있다 —[他] …과 접경(接境)하다

a·but·ment [əbʌ́tmənt] *n.* **1.** [U] the state of being abutted. **2.** [C] (*Architecture*) that which supports an arch or a bridge.

—[名] 1. 인접, 접촉 2.《建》 홍예(虹霓) 받이, 교대(橋臺)

a·bys·mal [əbízməl] *adj.* very deep; bottomless. ¶~ *ignorance.*

—[形] 끝없이 깊은, 심원한

a·byss [əbís] *n.* [C] **1.** bottomless depth. **2.** anything bottomless or unlimited. ¶*an ~ of time*① **3.** hell.

—[名] 1. 심연(深淵) 2. 끝이 없는 것 ¶①영원 3. 지옥

a·ca·cia [əkéiʃə] *n.* [C] a tree with very small leaves and yellow or white flowers that grows in warm regions.

—[名] 아카시아

ac·a·dem·ic [æ̀kədémik] *adj.* **1.** of a school, esp. a college or university; scholarly. ¶*the ~ curriculum*① | *an ~ degree*② | *~ freedom.*③ **2.** (*U.S.*) of general education rather than technical or professional education. **3.** of a learned society. ¶*~ circles.*④ **4.** having no practical effect; theoretical. ¶*an ~ question.*⑤

—[形] 1. 대학의; 학구적인 ¶①대학의 교과 과정/②학위/③학문의 자유 2. 일반 교양의 3. 학계 ¶④학계 4. 이론상의, 비실제적인 ¶⑤탁상공론

ac·a·dem·i·cal [æ̀kədémik(ə)l] *adj.* =academic. —*n.* 《*pl.*》 traditional formal clothes worn in some colleges or universities. ⇒[N.B.], fig. ▷**ac·a·dem·i·cal·ly** [-kəli] *adv.*

—[名] 대학의 의식복(儀式服) [N.B.] cap and gown 이라고도 함

〔academicals〕

a·cad·e·mi·cian [əkæ̀dəmíʃ(ə)n] *n.* [C] **1.** a learned man who belongs to a society or institution for the advancement of literature, science, or art. **2.** 《*A-*》 a member of the Royal Academy, the French Academy, or the American Academy of Arts and Letters.

—[名] 1. [학사원 · 예술원 따위의] 회원 2. 영국 왕립 예술원 · 프랑스 학사원 · 미국 예술원의 회원

⁎**a·cad·e·my** [əkǽdəmi] *n.* [C] (pl. **-mies**) **1.** a place for higher learning. **2.** (*U.S.*) a private secondary or high school. **3.** a school for special study and instruction. ¶*an ~ of music*① | *a naval ~*② | *a military ~.*③ **4.** a society of learned men for the advancement of literature, science, or art.

—[名] 1. 학교, 학원, 고등학교 정도의 각종 학교 2. 사립 중 · 고등학교 3. 전문학교 ¶①음악 전문학교 / ②해군 사관학교/③육군 사관학교 4. 학사원, 예술원, 학회

ac·cede [æksí:d, +*Brit.* ək-] *vi.* **1.** agree. 《~ *to* something》 ¶*~ to a proposal*① | *~ to a request.*② **2.** take up a position; succeed. ¶*~ to the throne* | *~ to the estate.*③ **3.** become a member of an organization.

—[自] 1. 동의하다 ¶①제안에 동의하다 /②요구에 응하다 2. 취임하다; 상속하다 ¶③재산을 이어받다 3. 가입하다

⁎**ac·cel·er·ate** [æksélərèit / ək-] *vt.* **1.** make (something) move faster; speed up. **2.** make (something) happen or come sooner. ¶*~ someone's recovery*① | *Death was accelerated by grief.* —*vi.* increase in speed.

—[他] 1. …의 속력을 빨리하다 2. …을 촉진하다 ¶①회복을 촉진하다 —[自] 빨라지다

ac·cel·er·a·tion [æksèləréiʃ(ə)n / ək-] *n.* [U] **1.** the act of accelerating; the state of being accelerated. **2.** (*Physics*) a change in the rate of speed of a body in motion. ¶*~ of gravity*① | *positive* (*negative*) *~.*②

—[名] 1. 가속; 촉진 2. 가속도 ¶①중력에 의한 가속도/②가(감)속도

ac·cel·er·a·tor [æksélərèitər / əksélərèitə] *n.* [C] **1.** a person or thing that causes an increase in the speed of something. **2.** a device for increasing the speed of a motor engine.

—[名] 1. 가속자(加速者) 2. [자동차의] 가속 장치, 악셀

⁑**ac·cent** *n.* [ǽksent / -s(ə)nt ‖ → *v.*] [C] **1.** a special force given by the voice to one part of a word; a mark to show such a part. ¶*In "letter", the ~ is on the first syllable.* **2.** [C] [U] a special way of pronouncing. ¶*the Irish ~* | *the Southern ~.* **3.** 《*pl.*》 tone of voice. ¶*She spoke in tender accents.*① —*vt.* [æksént] **1.** pronounce (a word) with an accent. **2.** place special value on (something); stress.

—[名] 1. 악센트[부호]; 강세, 강조 2. 발음의 양식; 사투리 3. 어조, 말투 —[他] 1. …을 악센트를 붙여 발음하다 2. …을 강조하다

ac·cen·tu·ate [ækséntʃuèit / -tju-] *vt.* **1.** pronounce (a word, syllable, phrase, etc.) with an accent or a stress on it. **2.** put an emphasis upon (something); distinguish (something) from others. ¶*Her black hair accentuated the whiteness of her skin.*①

—[他] 1. [음절 따위에] 악센트를 붙여 발음하다 2. …을 강조하다; 두드러지게 하다 ¶①검은 머리 때문에 그녀의 흰 살갗이 두드러져 보였다

ac·cen·tu·a·tion [æksèntʃuéiʃ(ə)n / -tju-] *n.* [U] **1.** the act of accentuating. **2.** emphasis.

⁑ ac·cept [æksépt] *vt.* **1.** receive gladly. ¶*~ a favor.*① **2.** agree to (something). ¶*~ a proposal*② | *~ an appointment.*③ **3.** take (something) as true. ¶*~ the excuse* | *His theory was widely accepted.*

ac·cept·a·bil·i·ty [æksèptəbíliti] *n.* [U] the quality of being acceptable.

· ac·cept·a·ble [ækséptəbl] *adj.* **1.** worth accepting. **2.** agreeable; welcome. ¶*an ~ gift to a sick person.*

· ac·cept·ance [æksépt(ə)ns / ək-, æk-] *n.* [U] **1.** the act of accepting; the state of being accepted. ↔refusal **2.** approval; assent. ↔disapproval ¶*The invention found widespread ~.*① **3.** (*Commerce*) a promise to pay.

ac·cep·ta·tion [æ̀kseptéiʃ(ə)n] *n.* [C] the recognized meaning of a word or expression.

ac·cept·ed [ækséptid / əksépt-] *adj.* approved in general by people. ¶*a generally ~ theory*① | *Once it was an ~ belief that the world was flat.*

· ac·cess [ǽkses] *n.* **1.** [U] the act of coming near. ¶*Access to the top of the mountain is difficult.*① **2.** [C] a way, chance, or right of approaching. ¶*the only ~ to the castle.*② **3.** [C] a fit or attack of illness. ¶*an ~ of fever*③ | *in an ~ of fury.*④

1) ***be easy (difficult) of access,*** be easy (difficult) to approach.
2) ***gain*** (or ***obtain***) ***access to,*** ⓐ approach to (someone). ⓑ enter (a building).
3) ***have access to,*** ⓐ approach to (someone or something). ⓑ can make use of (something).

ac·ces·sa·ry [æksésəri / əks-] *adj., n.* (pl. **-ries**) =accessory.

ac·ces·si·bil·i·ty [æksèsibíliti / ək-] *n.* [U] the state of being easy to approach or enter.

ac·ces·si·ble [æksésibl / əks-] *adj.* **1.** easy to approach, enter, or obtain. ↔inaccessible ¶*The place is not ~ by land.*① **2.** that can be easily influenced by something. ¶*Women are more ~ to pity than men.*

ac·ces·sion [ækséʃ(ə)n] *n.* [U] **1.** the act of attaining to a certain condition. 《*~ to*》 ¶*~ to manhood*① | *~ to the throne.*② **2.** the act of joining; consent. ¶*~ to the party*③ | *~ to demand.*④

ac·ces·so·ry [æksésəri / əks-] *adj.* **1.** additional. **2.** (*Law*) helping in a crime. ¶*be made ~.*①
—*n.* [C] (pl. **-ries**) **1.** an extra article attached to something. ¶*the accessories of a motorcar*② | *toilet accessories.*③ **2.** 《usu. *pl.*》 an article that is worn besides the basic clothing, such as gloves, earrings, etc. **3.** (*Law*) a person who helps in a crime. ¶*an ~ to a crime.*④

⁑ ac·ci·dent [ǽksid(ə)nt] *n.* [C] **1.** something that happens unexpectedly. **2.** a harmful or unfortunate happening; a disaster. ¶*an automobile ~*① | *an inevitable ~* | *meet with an ~*② | *He was killed in a traffic ~.*
by accident, by chance. ↔on purpose, by design

ac·ci·den·tal [æ̀ksidéntl] *adj.* happening by chance or unexpectedly. ¶*an ~ death.*①

ac·ci·den·tal·ly [æ̀ksidéntəli] *adv.* in an accidental manner; by accident.

ac·claim [əkléim] *vt.* welcome (someone) with praise, joy, and applause along with loud shouts. ¶*~ the victor* | *The people acclaimed him king.*①

ac·cla·ma·tion [æ̀kləméiʃ(ə)n] *n.* [U] [C] the act of acclaiming; a shout of welcome or approval. ¶*hail someone with acclamation[s].*①

ac·cli·mate [əkláimit, ǽklimèit] *vt.* accustom (someone or something) to a new environment, climate, etc.

—[名] 1. 악센트를 붙이기 2. 역설, 강조

—[他] 1. …을 받아들이다 ¶①호의를 받아들이다 2. …을 승낙하다 ¶②제안에 응하다/③임명을 수락하다 3. …을 믿어 주다, 용인하다

—[名] [기분좋게] 받아들일 수 있음, 승낙, 만족

—[形] 1. 수락할 수 있는 2. 마음에 드는, 만족스러운

—[名] 1. 받아들임, 수령 2. 승낙, 용인 ¶①그 발명은 세상에서 널리 인정받았다 3. [어음 따위의] 인수

—[名] [말의] 널리 인정되는 의미

—[形] 일반적으로 인정된, 공인된 ¶①일반적으로 인정된 이론

—[名] 1. 접근 ¶①그 산꼭대기에 이르기는 힘들다 2. 접근하는 방법(기회·권리) ¶②그 성으로 가는 유일한 길 3. [병 따위의] 발작 ¶③발열/④화가 나서

[熟] 1)접근하기 쉽다(힘들다) 2)ⓐ[남]에게 접근하다 ⓑ[건물]에 들어가다 3)ⓐ…에 접근하다 ⓑ…을 이용할 수 있다

—[名] 접근할 수 있음, 가까이 하기 쉬움

—[形] 1. 접근(출입·입수)하기 쉬운 ¶①그 곳은 육로로 갈 수 없다 2. 영향받기 쉬운, [마음이] 잘 움직여지는

—[名] 1. [어떤 사태로의] 도달; 즉위, 취임 ¶①성년이 됨/②즉위 2. 가입; 동의 ¶③정당 가입/④요구 수락

—[形] 1. 부속의, 보조적인 2. 《法》 종범(從犯)의 ¶①종범자로 몰리다
—[名] 1. 부속품 ¶②자동차의 부속품/③화장 용품류 2. 액세서리, 장신구 3. 《法》 종범자 ¶④공범자

—[名] 1. 우발적인 일; 우연 2. 불행한 사고, 재난 ¶①자동차 사고/②횡액을 만나다

[熟] 우연히
—[形] 우연의, 예기치 않은 ¶①횡사(橫死)
—[副] 우연히, 뜻하지 않게
—[他] …에게 갈채하다, 환호하다 ¶①국민은 환호하여 그를 국왕으로 맞이했다
—[名] 갈채, 환호[의 소리] ¶①[남을] 환호성을 올려 맞이하다

—[他] …을 새로운 환경·기후 따위에 적응시키다

ac·cli·ma·tize [əkláimətàiz] *vi., vt.* (chiefly *Brit.*) =acclimate.
ac·cliv·i·ty [əklíviti] *n.* ⓒ (pl. **-ties**) a slope which goes upwards. ↔declivity
ac·co·lade [ækəléid, ⸺ / ǽkouleid, -là:d] *n.* ⓒ a light tap on a man's shoulder with the flat of a sword in making him a knight.
* **ac·com·mo·date** [əkámədèit / -kɔ́m-] *vt.* **1.** make (someone or something) fit; adjust; adapt. 《~ something or someone *to*》 ¶ ~ *oneself to circumstances*① / ~ *facts to a theory*.② **2.** kindly give (someone) what he wants. 《~ someone *with*》 ¶ *He will ~ me with the use of his car*. **3.** have rooms for (persons). ¶ *The hospital can ~ 300 patients.* / *The hotel is admirably accommodated.*③ **4.** reconcile (disputes). ¶ ~ *a quarrel*.
ac·com·mo·dat·ing [əkámədèitiŋ / əkɔ́m-] *adj.* kind and willing to help. ¶ *an ~ man*.
ac·com·mo·da·tion [əkàmədéiʃ(ə)n / əkɔ̀mə-] *n.* **1.** Ⓤ the act of making fit. ¶ ~ *to a new environment.*① **2.** ⓒ settlement of differences. ¶ *come to an ~*.② **3.** (*pl.*) (*U. S.*) food and/or lodging. ¶ *We have no sleeping accommodations.* **4.** ⓒ anything that helps or is convenient. ¶ *for the ~ of someone*③ / *This hotel has good accommodations.*④ **5.** ⓒ a loan.
ac·com·pa·ni·ment [əkʌ́mp(ə)nimənt] *n.* ⓒ **1.** something that naturally goes along with another thing. **2.** music played to support the main music. ¶ *play one's ~*① / *sing to the ~ of a piano*.
ac·com·pa·nist [əkʌ́mp(ə)nist] *n.* ⓒ a person who plays a musical accompaniment.
:**ac·com·pa·ny** [əkʌ́mp(ə)ni] *vt.* (**-nied**) **1.** go along with (someone). ¶ ~ *a friend on a walk*. **2.** happen or exist together with (something); attend. ¶ *Light is accompanied by heat.*① **3.** cause (something) to be together with other things. ¶ ~ *a present with a letter.*② **4.** play music in order to help (other music). ¶ ~ *the violin on* (or *at*) *the piano*.③
ac·com·plice [əkámplis / əkɔ́m-] *n.* ⓒ a person who helps another in a wrong act. ¶ *an ~ in murder*.①
:**ac·com·plish** [əkámpliʃ / əkɔ́m-] *vt.* complete successfully. ¶ ~ *a journey*① / ~ *one's object*.
* **ac·com·plished** [əkámpliʃt / əkɔ́m-] *adj.* **1.** completed; done. ¶ *an ~ task* / *an ~ fact*.① **2.** skillful in social arts; well-trained. ¶ *an ~ gentleman*② / *an ~ lady*.
* **ac·com·plish·ment** [əkámpliʃmənt / əkɔ́m-] *n.* **1.** Ⓤ achievement; completion. **2.** ⓒ a thing that has been achieved. **3.** ⓒ (often *pl.*) an excellent skill or ability acquired by training. ¶ *a man of many accomplishments*① / *Sewing is not among her accomplishments*.② / *He had every ~ except that of making money.*③
* **ac·cord** [əkɔ́:rd] *vt.* give; grant. ¶ ~ *praise to someone; ~ someone praise* / *They accorded a hearty welcome to me*.① ─*vi.* agree. 《~ *with* something》 ¶ *That does not ~ with what you said before.*
  ─*n.* **1.** Ⓤ the state of being in harmony or agreement. **2.** ⓒ reconciliation. **3.** ⓒ the combination of musical sounds in harmony. ↔discord
  1) *be in accord* (=*harmonize*) *with* something.
  2) *be of one accord,* be in agreement.
  3) *be out of accord* (=*do not harmony*) *with* something.
  4) *of one's own accord,* without being asked; willingly.
  5) *with one accord,* unanimously.
* **ac·cord·ance** [əkɔ́:rd(ə)ns] *n.* Ⓤ agreement; harmony. *in accordance with*, according to. ¶ *Everything has been done in ~ with the rules.*①

─ⓝ 치받이[경사]
─ⓝ 나이트 작위 수여[식]

─ⓥ **1.** …을 적응시키다 ¶①환경에 적응하다/②사실을 이론에 적합시키다 **2.** [남]에게 …을 빌려주다, 편의를 도모하다 **3.** [손님]을 숙박시키다, …을 수용하다 ¶③그 호텔은 시설이 아주 좋다 **4.** [분쟁]을 화해시키다, 조절하다

─ⓐ 친절한, 융통성 있는

─ⓝ **1.** 적응 ¶①새로운 환경에의 적응 **2.** 화해 ¶②타협이 되다 **3.** (美) 숙박 **4.** 편의, [숙박]시설, 설비 ¶③[남]의 편의를 도모하기 위해/④이 호텔은 숙박 설비가 좋다 **5.** 대부[금]

─ⓝ **1.** 부속물, 딸리는 것 **2.** 반주 ¶①반주하다

─ⓝ 반주자

─ⓥ **1.** …와 동반하다; …을 데리고 가다 **2.** …와 함께 일어나다(존재하다) ¶①광선에는 열이 따른다 **3.** …에 덧붙이다, 첨부하다 ¶②선물에 편지를 함께 보내다 **4.** …에 반주하다 ¶③바이올린에 피아노 반주를 하다

─ⓝ 공범자, 공모자 ¶①살인 공범자

─ⓥ [일・계획 따위]를 완수(성취)하다, 다하다 ¶①여정을 끝내다
─ⓐ **1.** 성취(완성)한 ¶①기정 사실 **2.** 능숙한, 교양 있는, 세련된 ¶②세련된 신사
─ⓝ **1.** 성취; 수행, 실천 **2.** 업적 **3.** 예능; 재주, 교양 ¶①재주 많은 사람/②그녀는 재봉의 재주가 없다/③그는 돈벌이 말고는 없는 재주가 없다

─ⓥ …을 주다 ¶①그들은 나를 진정으로 환영해 주었다 ─ⓥ 일치하다, 조화하다

─ⓝ **1.** 일치, 조화 **2.** 화해 **3.** 화음

圖 1) …와 조화되다 2) 일치되어 있다 3) …와 조화되지 않다 4) 자발적으로, 기꺼이 5) 일제히

─ⓝ 일치, 조화
圖 …에 따라서 ¶①모든 것은 규칙에 따라 행해졌다

ac·cor·dant [əkɔ́:rd(ə)nt] *adj.* in harmony; agreeing or in agreement. 《~ *with, to*》 ¶~ *to reason.*①
—[形] 일치되는, 조화하는 ¶①도리에 맞는

⁝ **ac·cord·ing** [əkɔ́:rdiŋ] *adv.* in harmony.
—[副] …에 따라서

. 1) ***according as,*** in proportion as. ¶*We have different views of a thing ~ as we are rich or poor.*
2) ***according to,*** ⓐ in agreement with; in accordance with. ¶*living ~ to one's income*① / *~ to his promise.* ⓑ following what is said by; on the authority of. ¶*~ to the Bible, God made the world in six days.*②
[熟] 1)…에 준하여, 에 따라서 2)ⓐ…에 따라, 일치되게 ¶①수입에 맞추어 살다 ⓑ[…이 말하는 바]에 의하면 ¶②성경에 따르면 하나님은 엿새 동안에 세상을 만들었다

· **ac·cord·ing·ly** [əkɔ́:rdiŋli] *adv.* **1.** in agreement with what has been said. ¶*The students were given new instructions and told to act ~.* **2.** for this reason.
—[副] 1. [사정에 따라] 적당히, 그에 따라서 2. 그러므로

ac·cor·di·on [əkɔ́:rdiən] *n.* [C] a portable musical instrument with a bellows and a keyboard.
—[名] 아코오디언

accordion pleats [-´-- ´] *n. pl.* (in clothing) folds like the bellows of an accordion.
—[名] [주름 치마의] 좁다란 주름

ac·cost [əkɔ́:st / əkɔ́st] *vt.* come up and speak to (someone). ¶*I was accosted by a beggar.*
—[他] …에게 다가가서 말을 걸다

⁝ **ac·count** [əkáunt] *n.* **1.** [C] a report; a story; description. ¶*newspaper accounts.*① **2.** [C] a record of money spent and received. **3.** [U] value; importance. ¶*a matter of great ~.*② **4.** [U] profit; advantage; benefit. ¶*I find no ~ in it.*③
—[名] 1. 보고[서]; 설명[기사] ¶①신문의 보도 2. 회계[기록] 3. 가치; 중요성 ¶②중요한 일 4. 이익, 편의 ¶③그것으로는 이익이 되지 않는다

1) ***call to account,*** ⓐ demand an explanation. ⓑ scold.
2) ***on account,*** as part-payment.
3) ***on account of,*** because of.
4) ***on no account,*** under no circumstances; never.
5) ***on one's own account,*** for oneself; for one's own sake.
6) ***take account of,*** make allowance for (something); consider.
7) ***take something into account,*** consider; give attention to something.
8) ***turn to account,*** make (something) useful or helpful; get advantage or profit from (something).
[熟] 1)ⓐ해명을 요구하다 ⓑ꾸짖다 2)계약금으로서 3)…때문에; …한 까닭으로 4)결코 …하지 않다 5)혼자의 힘으로; 자기의 이익을 위해서 6)7)…을 고려에 넣다 8)…을 이용하다

—*vt.* consider; estimate; judge. ¶*I ~ myself* [*to be*] *happy.*
—[他] …을 […이라고] 생각하다; 평가하다

account for, ⓐ explain; make (something) plain. ¶*I want you to ~ for every penny you spent.* / *How do you ~ for your absence yesterday?* ⓑ be the reason for (something). ¶*Poor health accounts for his failure.*④
[熟] ⓐ…을 설명하다; …의 이유를 분명히 하다 ⓑ …때문이다, …의 원인이다 ¶④나쁜 건강이 그의 실패의 원인이다

ac·count·a·bil·i·ty [əkàuntəbíliti] *n.* [U] the quality or state of being accountable.
—[名] 책임[이 있음]

ac·count·a·ble [əkáuntəbl] *adj.* **1.** responsible. 《~ *to*》 ¶*I am ~ to him for the loss.* **2.** that can be explained.
—[形] 1. 책임이 있는 2. 설명(변명)할 수 있는

ac·count·ant [əkáuntənt] *n.* [C] a person whose business is to inspect and manage business accounts.
—[名] 회계원; 계리사

ac·cou·ter, *Brit.* **-tre** [əkú:tər] *vt.* 《usu. in *passive*》 provide (someone) with special equipment and clothes, esp. for military service.
—[他] …에게 어떤 복장을 하게 하다; [특히] 군장(軍裝)을 갖추게 하다

ac·cou·ter·ments, *Brit.* **-tre-** [əkú:tərmənts] *n. pl.* **1.** a soldier's military equipment, such as a belt, blanket, knapsack, etc. in addition to his actual clothes and weapons. **2.** one's own clothes.
—[名] 1. [군복·무기를 제외한] 군장 2. 복장

ac·cred·it [əkrédit] *vt.* **1.** send (an ambassador) with letters of his own government. 《~ someone *to*》 **2.** credit; attribute. 《~ something *to*》 ¶*He is accredited with these words.; They accredited these words to him.*① **3.** believe in (someone).
—[他] 1. [대사 등]에게 신임장을 주어 파견하다 2. [말 따위]를 …에게 돌리다 ¶①그들은 이런 말을 그가 한 말로 돌렸다 3. …을 믿다

ac·cre·tion [ækrí:ʃ(ə)n] *n.* [U] increase in size by growth or adding bits on; [C] a matter so added.
—[名] 증대; 부가[물]

ac·crue [əkrú:] *vi.* **1.** come as a natural result. **2.** come as a natural increase (esp. of money). ¶*interest accruing from principal.*①
—[自] 1. [자연 증가의 결과로] 생기다 2. [이자 따위가] 붙다, 생기다 ¶①원금에서 생기는 이자

* **ac·cu·mu·late** [əkjú:mjulèit] *vt.* collect; gather. ¶~ *wealth.* —*vi.* increase in amount; (of misfortune) fall. ¶*Dust accumulated on the floor.* | *Disaster accumulated round his path.*①
—[他] …을 쌓다(축적하다), 모으다 —[自] 모이다; [불행 따위가] 겹쳐지다 ¶①그의 앞길에는 불행이 겹쳐 있었다

ac·cu·mu·la·tion [əkjù:mjuléiʃ(ə)n] *n.* **1.** [U] the act of accumulating. ¶~ *of wealth.*① **2.** [C] things accumulated. ¶*an* ~ *of freight*② | *an* ~ *of odds and ends in the attic.*③
—[名] 1. 축적 ¶①부(富)의 축적 2. 축적물 ¶②체화(滯貨)/③고미다락에 쌓인 잡동사니

ac·cu·mu·la·tive [əkjú:mjulèitiv / -lə-] *adj.* tending to accumulate.
—[形] 축적의, 축재의

ac·cu·mu·la·tor [əkjú:mjulèitər] *n.* [C] **1.** a person or thing that accumulates. **2.** (*Machine*) an apparatus to collect and store energy. **3.** (*Brit.*) a storage battery.
—[名] 1. 축적(재)자 2. 《機》 축열기, 축압기, 어큐뮬레이터 3. 《英》 축전지

* **ac·cu·ra·cy** [ǽkjurəsi] *n.* [U] the state or quality of being accurate. ¶*with* ~.①
—[名] 정확, 엄밀, 정밀 ¶①정확히

* **ac·cu·rate** [ǽkjurit] *adj.* **1.** careful not to make errors. **2.** free from errors or mistakes. ¶~ *statements.*① **3.** working with accuracy. ¶~ *machines.*
—[形] 1. [사람이] 조심성 있는 2. [이야기 따위가] 정확한 ¶①틀림없는 진술 3. [기계·장치가] 정확한

* **ac·cu·rate·ly** [ǽkjuritli] *adv.* in an accurate manner.
—[副] 정확히, 정밀하게

ac·curs·ed [əkə́:rsid, +*U.S.* əkə́:rst], **-curst** [əkə́:rst] *adj.* **1.** under a curse. **2.** filled with hatred. ¶*an* ~ *deed.*① **3.** (*colloq.*) troublesome.
—[形] 1. 저주받은 2. 몹시 싫은 ¶①가증스러운 짓 3. 《口》 골치아프기 짝이 없는

ac·cu·sa·tion [æ̀kju(:)zéiʃ(ə)n] *n.* [U] [C] the act of accusing or charging. ¶*bring an* ~ *against someone.*①
—[名] 비난, 트집, 고소 ¶①남을 고발하다

* **ac·cuse** [əkjú:z] *vt.* **1.** find fault with (someone); blame. ¶*He accused me because of my mistake.*① **2.** charge (someone) with having broken the law. ¶~ *someone of a crime* | *be accused of stealing money.*
—[他] 1. …을 나무라다, 비난하다 ¶①그는 내 잘못을 나무랐다 2. …을 고발하다

ac·cused [əkjú:zd] *n.* 《*the* ~》 the person who is charged with guilt in a court of law. ↔accuser
—[名] 피고

ac·cus·er [əkjú:zər] *n.* [C] **1.** a person who brings a charge against others. ↔the accused **2.** a person who blames others.
—[名] 1. 고발인, 원고 2. 비난자

* **ac·cus·tom** [əkʌ́stəm] *vt.* get (a person or an animal) used to or familiar with. 《~ someone *to*》 ¶~ *a dog to racing* | *She will soon* ~ *herself to the school.*① | *She is* ~ *to rising early* (or *to rise early*).②
—[他] …을 습관들이다, 익히다 ¶①그녀는 곧 학교에 익숙해질 것이다/②그녀는 일찍 일어나는 일에 익었다

ac·cus·tomed [əkʌ́stəmd] *adj.* usual; habitual. ¶*one's* ~ *way.*①
—[形] 평소의, 늘 하는; 익숙한 ¶①늘 쓰는 방법

ace [eis] *n.* [C] **1.** a single spot on a card, domino, or side of a die. **2.** a person with great skill. ¶*a football* ~
—[名] 1. [카아드·주사위의] 1 2. 최고의 사람, 우수 선수

1) ***an ace in the hole,*** (*colloq.*) a man or thing helpful in an emergency.
2) ***within an ace of,*** escaping from something by a hair's breadth. ¶*He came within an* ~ *of death.*
[熟] 1)《口》만일의 경우에 쓰일 사람(물건) 2)아슬아슬하게 …을 피하여

—*adj.* (*colloq.*) first-class; expert. ¶*an* ~ *athlete.*
—[形] 《口》 일류의

a·cer·bi·ty [əsə́:rbiti] *n.* [U] **1.** a sharp taste. **2.** a severe and bitter quality of words, manner, or temper.
—[名] 1. 신(떫은) 맛 2. [언동의] 신랄함, 가혹성

ac·e·tate [ǽsitit, -teit] *n.* [U] a salt of acetic acid.
—[名] 초산염

a·ce·tic [əsí:tik, əsétik] *adj.* having the taste of acid; of acid.
—[形] 신, 초의

a·cet·y·lene [əsétilì:n] *n.* [U] a colorless gas with a strong odor that burns brightly with a very hot flame.
—[名] 아세틸렌[가스]

* **ache** [eik] *vi.* **1.** have a continuous pain. ¶*I am aching all over.* **2.** feel sympathy, pity, etc. ¶*My heart aches.* **3.** (*colloq.*) wish very much. 《~ *for* something or someone; ~ *to do*》 ¶*She ached to be near him.* —*n.* [C] [U] a continuous pain. ¶*have a headache.*
—[自] 1. 아프다, 쑤시다 2. [동정심이나 불쌍해서] 마음이 쓰리다 3. 《口》…하고 싶어 못 견디다 —[名] 아픔

⁑ **a·chieve** [ətʃí:v] *vt.* **1.** do successfully; accomplish. ↔fail ¶*We have achieved all that we expected.*① **2.** gain (something) by effort. ¶~ *success.*
—[他] 1. …을 성취하다 ¶①우리는 기대하던 바 전부를 이룩했다 2. …을 얻다

* **a·chieve·ment** [ətʃí:vmənt] *n.* **1.** [U] the act of achieving. **2.** [C] something achieved. ¶*an* ~ *test.*
—[名] 1. 달성, 성취 2. 달성한 것; 위업, 업적; 성적

A·chil·les['] tendon [əkíli:zténdən] *n.* the tendon which joins the calf muscles to the heelbone.
—[名] 아킬레스 건(腱)

A

ach·ro·mat·ic [ækroumǽtik] *adj.* colorless.
—[形] 무색의

*__ac·id__ [ǽsid] *n.* **1.** [U] [C] a chemical substance with a sour taste which turns blue litmus paper red. **2.** [C] a substance with a sour taste. —*adj.* **1.** having the qualities of acid. **2.** having a sour and bitter taste.
—[名] 1. 산(酸) 2. 신 것 —[形] 1. 산의 산성의 2. 신

a·cid·i·fy [əsídifài] *vt.* (**-fied**) **1.** make (something) sour. **2.** change (something) into an acid. —*vi.* turn sour.
—[他] 1. …을 시게 하다 2. …을 산성화하다 —[自] 시어지다

a·cid·i·ty [əsíditi] *n.* [U] the acid quality or condition.
—[名] 신 맛, 산성(酸性)

*__ac·knowl·edge__ [əknálidʒ / -nɔ́l-] *vt.* **1.** admit (something) to be true. 《~ *that* …; ~ *doing*; ~ something *as*》 ↔deny ¶~ *one's fault*① / *be acknowledged to be true*② / ~ *the news as false* / *He did not* ~ *that he stole my watch.*; *He did not* ~ *having stolen my watch.*③ **2.** say that one has received (something). ¶*I beg to* ~ *your letter.*④ **3.** express thanks for (something). ¶~ *a letter* / ~ *gifts.*
—[他] 1. …을 인정하다 ¶①자기의 과실을 인정하다/②사실임을 인정받다/③그는 내 시계를 훔친 일을 인정하지 않았다 2. [도착·접수 따위]를 알리다 ¶④편지는 확실히 받았읍니다 3. …에 대해 감사하다

ac·knowl·edg·ment, *Brit.* **-edge·ment** [əknálidʒmənt / -nɔ́l-] *n.* **1.** [U] the act of acknowledging. **2.** [C] an official document of acknowledging; a receipt. **3.** [U] [C] an expression of thanks.
—[名] 1. 승인 2. 접수증; 영수증 3. 감사

ac·me [ǽkmi] *n.* 《*the* ~》 the top or highest point.
—[名] 절정, 극치

ac·o·lyte [ǽkəlàit] *n.* [C] **1.** a person who attends in public worship and helps a priest. **2.** an assistant.
—[名] 1. [가톨릭에서 미사 때의] 시제(侍祭) 2. 조수

ac·o·nite [ǽkənàit] *n.* **1.** [C] a poisonous plant. **2.** [U] a drug obtained from this plant.
—[名] 1. 바곳(독초) 2. 아코닛[바곳에서 채취한 진통제]

a·corn [éikɔːrn, +*U.S.* -kərn] *n.* [C] the fruit or nut of an oak tree.
—[名] 도토리

a·cous·tic [əkúːstik], **-ti·cal** [-tik(ə)l] *adj.* **1.** of sound or the sense of hearing. ¶~ *nerves*① / ~ *education*② / *Earphones are* ~ *aids for deaf people.* **2.** of the science of sound.
—[形] 1. 청각의 ¶①청신경/②음감(音感) 교육 2. 음향학의

a·cous·tics [əkúːstiks] *n. pl.* **1.** 《used as *sing.*》 the science of sound. **2.** the qualities of a room, hall, etc., that determine how clearly sound can be heard in it.
—[名] 1. 음향학 2. [극장 따위의] 음향 효과

*__ac·quaint__ [əkwéint] *vt.* **1.** tell. 《~ someone *with* or *of*》 ¶*Did you* ~ *him with the fact?*① **2.** make (someone) known; introduce. 《~ someone *with*》
—[他] 1. …에게 알리다 ¶①그에게 사실을 알렸느냐? 2. …에게 자세히 알게 하다

be (or ***get, become***) ***acquainted with,*** ⓐ have personal knowledge of (someone). ⓑ be familiar with (something). ¶*He is well acquainted with history.*②
[熟] ⓐ…와 아는 사이(가 되다)이다 ⓑ…을 알고 있다, 에 밝다 ¶②그는 역사에 밝다

*__ac·quaint·ance__ [əkwéint(ə)ns] *n.* **1.** [U] knowledge through experience. ¶*gain* ~ *with something*① / *I have a slight* (*no*) ~ *with him.*② **2.** [C] a person whom one knows to some extent; 《*collectively*》 such persons. ¶*a nodding* ~③ / *renew one's* ~.④
—[名] 1. 알고 있음, 면식, 교제; 지식 ¶①…을 알게 되다/②나는 그를 좀 알고 있다(전혀 모른다) 2. 친지, 아는 사람 ¶③만나면 고개를 끄떡할 정도로 아는 사람/④옛정을 새로이하다

1) ***make the acquaintance of*** *someone;* ***make*** *someone's* ***acquaintance,*** become friends with someone.
2) ***strike up an acquaintance*** (=*become friendly*) ***with*** *someone.*
[熟] 1)…와 알게 되다 2)…와 친한 사이가 되다

ac·qui·esce [ækwiés] *vi.* give consent silently; agree. 《~ *in* a conclusion, plan, etc.》
—[自] 묵인하다; [제안·제의 따위에] 묵묵히 따르다

ac·qui·es·cence [ækwiésns] *n.* [U] the act of consenting or agreeing quietly.
—[名] 묵인, 묵종, [어쩔 수 없는] 동의

ac·qui·es·cent [ækwiésnt] *adj.* agreeing quietly.
—[形] 묵묵히 따르는, 묵인의

__ac·quire__ [əkwáiər] *vt.* **1. get (something) by effort. ¶~ *a knowledge of English*① / *He acquired a name for honesty.* **2.** obtain (something) as one's own. ¶~ *land by purchase.*②
—[他] 1. [노력하여] …을 얻다 ¶①영어를 배우다 2. [권리 따위]를 획득하다 ¶②토지를 구입하다

ac·quire·ment [əkwáiərmənt] *n.* **1.** [U] the act of acquiring. **2.** [C] 《often *pl.*》 something acquired by learning or practice. ¶*I am proud of my son's acquirements.*① / *Her musical acquirements surprised every one.*②
—[名] 1. [학문·학술 따위의] 습득 2. [습득한] 예능, 학식 ¶①아들의 학식이 자랑스럽다/②그녀의 음악 솜씨에 모두 놀랐다

ac·qui·si·tion [ækwizíʃ(ə)n] *n.* **1.** [U] the act of gaining as one's own. **2.** [C] something gained or acquired. ¶*recent acquisitions to the library.*①
—[名] 1. [재산·학문 따위의] 획득, 취득 2. 취득물 ¶①도서관의 새 구입 도서

ac·quis·i·tive [əkwízitiv] *adj.* eager to get and keep as one's own. ¶*an ~ person.*① ▷**ac·quis·i·tive·ly** [-li] *adv.* —**ac·quis·i·tive·ness** [-nis] *n.*
—[形] [지식·재산 따위를] 욕심내는, 탐내는 ¶①욕심 많은 사람

ac·quit [əkwít] *vt.* (**-quit·ted, -quit·ting**) **1.** set (someone) free from a charge of crime or from duty. 《~ someone *of*》 ¶*They acquitted him of the charge.*① **2.** 《*reflexively*》 behave; conduct; do one's part. ¶~ *oneself well in the game.*②
—[他] 1. …을 무죄 방면하다; [책임 따위를 남에게] 면제해 주다 ¶①그들은 그를 방면했다 2. 처신하다; 수행하다 ¶②경기에서 활약하다

ac·quit·tal [əkwítl] *n.* [U] [C] **1.** the performance of a duty, etc. **2.** (*Law*) a decision freeing a person from a charge of crime.
—[名] 1. [의무 따위의] 수행 2. 방면, 석방

ac·quit·tance [əkwít(ə)ns] *n.* **1.** [U] freedom from a debt or duty. **2.** [C] a record showing that a debt has been paid.
—[名] 1. [채무·의무 따위의] 면제, 반제(返濟) 2. 채무 반제 증서, 영수증

***a·cre** [éikər] *n.* [C] **1.** a unit of measure of land equal to 43,560 square feet. **2.** 《*pl.*》 lands. ¶*broad acres.*
—[名] 1. 에이커[4,046.8 평방 미터] 2. 지면; 논밭, 토지

a·cre·age [éikəridʒ] *n.* [U] the number of acres; the area of land measured in acres. ¶*the ~ under cultivation*① / *the ~ of the park.*
—[名] 에이커 수(數); 면적 ¶①경작 면적

ac·rid [ǽkrid] *adj.* **1.** bitter and stinging to the mouth or nose. ¶*the ~ smoke of gasoline.* **2.** bitter or sharp in manner, temper, or speech. ¶~ *remarks.*
—[形] 1. [맛·냄새 따위가] 쓴, 매운 2. [말·성질 따위가] 신랄한, 엄한

ac·ro·bat [ǽkrəbæ̀t] *n.* [C] a person who can do skillful and bold exercises, such as walking on a tight rope.
—[名] 곡예사, 광대

ac·ro·bat·ic [æ̀krəbǽtik] *adj.* of an acrobat or like his tricks. ¶*an ~ dance*① / ~ *feats.*②
—[形] 곡예[사]의 ¶①곡예 댄스/②곡예

ac·ro·bat·ics [æ̀krəbǽtiks] *n. pl.* the tricks or performances of an acrobat. ¶*aerial ~.*①
—[名] 곡예 ¶①공중 곡예

***a·cross** [əkrɔ́:s / əkrɔ́s] *adv.* **1.** from one side to the other; to or on the other side. ¶*What is the distance ~? / The lake is 5 miles ~.* **2.** so as to cross; in the form of a cross. ¶*with arms ~.*①
—[副] 1. 이쪽에서 저쪽까지; 직경으로, 가로질러서 2. 십자로 교차하여 ¶①팔짱을 끼고

—*prep.* **1.** to the other side of; from one side to the other of. ¶*walk ~ a street.* **2.** on the other side of; beyond. ¶*He lives ~ the river.*②
—[前] 1. …을 가로질러서; …의 맞은편으로 2. …의 맞은편에[서] ¶②그는 강 건너에 살고 있다

come across (=*happen to meet* or *find*) *someone* or *something.* ¶*He came ~ an old friend.*
[熟] …을 우연히 만나다; …을 우연히 발견하다

***act** [ækt] *n.* [C] **1.** a thing done; a deed. ¶*an ~ of kindness.* **2.** 《*the ~*》 the process of doing something. **3.** a section of a play or drama. ¶*a comedy in three acts*① / *Act II, scene iii.*② **4.** a law passed by a law-making body. ¶*an Act of Congress.*③ **5.** each part in a television program, variety show, etc.
—[名] 1. 행위, 소행 2. 현행(現行) 3. [극·오페라의] 막 ¶①3막짜리의 희극/②제2막 3장 4. 법령, 조례 ¶③법령 5. [방송국 따위의] 한 프로

1) ***an act*** (or ***Act***) ***of God,*** (*Law*) an accident due to natural forces which could not be controlled.
2) ***the Acts*** [***of the Apostles***], the fifth book of the New Testament.
3) ***in the*** [***very***] ***act of*** *doing,* while one is doing. ¶*The thief was caught in the* [*very*] *~ of taking the money.*④
[熟] 1)《法》 불가항력 2)[신약 성서의] 사도행전 3)…의 현행 중에, …하고 있을 때에 ¶④도둑은 돈을 훔치는 현장에서 붙잡혔다

—*vt.* **1.** play the part of (something); perform. ¶~ *the Queen in "Hamlet".* **2.** behave like (something). ¶*Don't ~ the child.*
—[他] 1. [극]을 상연하다; …의 배역을 맡아하다 2. …인 체하다

—*vi.* **1.** conduct oneself; behave. ¶~ *quickly in an emergency* / ~ *like a lady.* **2.** produce effects. ⇨***act on*** ⓑ **3.** operate; function. ¶*The brakes failed to ~.* **4.** pretend; perform as an actor. **5.** serve.
—[自] 1. 행동(실행)하다, 처신하다 2. 작용하다 3. […하게] 처신하다; 배우 노릇을 하다 4. 근무하다

1) ***act as*** (=*do the work of*) *someone* or *something.* ¶~ *as go-between.*⑤ ⇨[usage]
2) ***act for,*** ⓐ take someone's place. ¶*He acted for his absent brother.* ⓑ do (someone) a service.
3) ***act on,*** ⓐ obey; follow. ¶*I will ~ on your suggestion.* ⓑ have an effect on (something). ¶*Acids ~ on metal.*
[熟] 1)…노릇을 하다 ¶⑤중매장이 노릇을 하다 [usage] as 다음에 오는 단수 보통명사에는 관사를 붙이지 않음 2)ⓐ…의 대리 역할을 하다 ⓑ…을 위해서 하다 3)ⓐ…에 입각하여 행동하다 ⓑ…에 영향을 미치다

***act·ing** [ǽktiŋ] *adj.* **1.** doing duties in place of someone else. ¶*an ~ manager*① / *an ~ principal.*② **2.** used for
—[形] 1. 대리의 ¶①지배인 대리/②교장 대리 2. 연출용의 ¶③대본 —[名]

A

the performance of a play. ¶*an ~ copy.*① —*n.* ⓤ the act or art of performing in plays or films. ¶*a play suitable for ~ | good ~.*④

ac·tion [ǽkʃ(ə)n] *n.* **1.** ⓤ the process or fact of acting. **2.** ⓤ activity. ¶*men of ~.*① **3.** ⓒ an act or a thing done; conduct; behavior. ¶*a dishonest ~.*② **4.** ⓤ effect; influence. ¶*the ~ of acid on iron.* **5.** ⓒ the way or manner of moving or working. **6.** ⓤ function; mechanism. ¶*the ~ of a typewriter.* **7.** ⓒⓤ a small battle; fight between bodies of troops. **8.** ⓤ series of events in a story or play. **9.** ⓒ a legal process.
1) *in action,* active; working; taking part. ¶*put a machine in ~.*②
2) *take action,* ⓐ begin to act. ⓑ start a lawsuit.

ac·tion·a·ble [ǽkʃ(ə)nəbl] *adj.* (*Law*) giving cause for an action at law.

ac·ti·vate [ǽktivèit] *vt.* **1.** make (something) active, esp. by chemical reaction. **2.** (*Physics*) make (something) radioactive.

ac·tive [ǽktiv] *adj.* **1.** lively in action; working or moving. ¶*an ~ volcano*① */ a soldier on ~ service.*② **2.** energetic; busy. ¶*an ~ life | be ~ on doing good to others.* **3.** real; effective. ¶*I want ~ help.* **4.** (*Grammar*) showing the subject of a verb as acting. ↔passive

ac·tive·ly [ǽktivli] *adv.* in an active manner.

ac·tiv·ism [ǽktiviz(ə)m] *n.* ⓤ the doctorine or practice that emphasizes energetic action.

ac·tiv·i·ty [æktíviti] *n.* (pl. *-ties*) **1.** ⓤ the state of being active. ¶*mental ~.*① **2.** (*usu. pl.*) things to do. ¶*homeroom activities.*② *The police started activities.*③ ⓤ liveliness. ¶*the ~ of the market.*③

ac·tor [ǽktər] *n.* ⓒ a person who plays a part in a [drama. ↔actress

ac·tress [ǽktris] *n.* ⓒ a woman actor. ↔actor

ac·tu·al [ǽktʃu(ə)l] *adj.* **1.** really existing. ↔imaginative ¶*Davy Crockett was an ~ person.* **2.** present. ¶*the ~ condition.*①

ac·tu·al·i·ty [æktʃuǽliti] *n.* (pl. *-ties*) **1.** ⓤ the state of being actual. **2.** (*usu. pl.*) real conditions. ¶*in ~.*①

ac·tu·al·ly [ǽktʃuəli] *adv.* **1.** at the present moment. **2.** in fact; really. ¶*Actually, it was only a rumor.*

ac·tu·ate [ǽktʃuèit / -tju-] *vt.* **1.** put (something) into motion or action. **2.** force (someone) to act. (*~ someone to do*) ¶*What actuated him to kill his friend?*

a·cu·men [əkjúːmən, ǽkjəmən / əkjúːmen, ǽkjumen] *n.* ⓤ keenness of mind; quickness of insight.

a·cute [əkjúːt] *adj.* **1.** pointed; sharp at the end. ¶*an ~ angle.*① **2.** (of illness) very painful; sudden and severe. ↔chronic ¶*~ pain*② */ an ~ disease.*③ **3.** keen; sharp. ¶*an ~ sense / an ~ observation.*④

a·cute·ly [əkjúːtli] *adv.* keenly; sharply. ⌈acute.

a·cute·ness [əkjúːtnis] *n.* ⓤ the state or quality of being⌋

ad [ǽd] *n.* ⓒ (*U.S. colloq.*) an advertisement.

A.D. [éidíː, ǽnoudámināi / -dóːmi-] (*Latin*) *Anno Domini* (=in the year of our Lord). ↔B.C.

A·da [éidə] *n.* a woman's name.

ad·age [ǽdidʒ] *n.* ⓒ an old and well-known saying; a [proverb.

a·da·gi·o [ədáːdʒiòu, +*U.S.* -dʒou] (*Music*) *adv.* slowly. —*adj.* slow. —*n.* ⓒ (pl. *-gi·os*) a slow part in music.

Ad·am [ǽdəm] *n.* (in the Bible) the first man God made in the Garden of Eden. ↔Eve
1) *Adam's apple,* a part that projects in the front of
2) *as old as Adam,* very old. ⌊the human throat.
3) *do not know someone from Adam,* (*colloq.*) do not know someone at all.

ad·a·mant [ǽdəmənt, -mæ̀nt] *n.* [U] a thing too hard to be cut or broken. ¶*as hard as ~.*① —*adj.* very hard.
—[名] 견고한 것 ¶①더할나위 없이 굳은 —[形] 견고무비한

ad·a·man·tine [æ̀dəmǽnti(:)n, -tain / -tain] *adj.* very hard; firm. ¶*~ courage.*
—[形] 견고한, 굳센

* **a·dapt** [ədǽpt] *vt.* **1.** make (someone) suitable. 《~ someone *for* or *to*》 ¶*She is not adapted for such work. / He adapted himself to a new job.*① **2.** change (sɔmething) for another purpose. 《~ something *for*》 ¶*The book is adapted for beginners.*②
—[他] 1. …을 적응시키다, 순응하게 하다 ¶①새로운 일을 할 수 있는 태세를 취했다 2. [작품]을 개작(번안·각색)하다 ¶②이 책은 초심자용으로 개작되었다

a·dapt·a·bil·i·ty [ədæ̀ptəbíliti] *n.* [U] the quality of being adaptable.
—[名] 적응성

a·dapt·a·ble [ədǽptəbl] *adj.* able to change or to be changed easily to fit different conditions.
—[形] [사람이] …에 적응할 수 있는, [사물이] 고쳐 쓸 수 있는

ad·ap·ta·tion [æ̀dəptéiʃ(ə)n / æ̀dæp-] *n.* **1.** [U] the act or process of adapting; the condition of being adapted. **2.** [C] something made by a process of adapting. ¶*an ~ from an English novel.*①
—[名] 1. [장소 따위에 대한] 적응, 순응 2. 각색, 개작 ¶①영국 소설로부터의 번안

a·dapt·ed [ədǽptid] *adj.* suitable. 《~ *for*》 ¶*a book ~ for children.*①
—[形] 적합한 ¶①아동용의 책

‡ **add** [æd] *vt.* **1.** join; unite. 《~ one thing *to* another》 **2.** combine (two or more numbers) so as to get a sum total. ↔subtract ¶*Add 8 and 4 and you get twelve.* **3.** say or write further. ¶*"And come tomorrow, please," he added.* —*vi.* **1.** increase. 《~ *to* something》 **2.** find a sum; do addition in arithmetic. ¶*The little boy is learning to ~ and subtract.*①
—[他] 1. …을 더하다, 가산하다 2. …을 합계하다 3. 말을 덧붙이다, 써 넣다 —[自] 1. 늘다 2. 덧셈하다 ¶①그 어린 소년은 덧셈과 뺄셈을 배우고 있다.

1) ***add to,*** ⓐ increase. ¶*~ to one's cares.* ⓑ put. ¶*~ sugar to coffee.*
2) ***add up,*** find the sum of. ¶*Add up these figures.*
3) ***add up to,*** ⓐ amount to. ⓑ mean. ¶*What do her remarks ~ up to?*
[熟] 1)ⓐ…을 늘리다 ⓑ…을 보태다 2) …을 합계하다 3)ⓐ합계 …이 되다 ⓑ…을 의미하다

ad·den·da [ədéndə] *n.* pl. of **addendum**.

ad·den·dum [ədéndəm] *n.* [C] (pl. **-da**) a thing added to something, esp. an added note.
—[名] 부록, 부가물

ad·der¹ [ǽdər] *n.* [C] a small poisonous snake of Europe; one of several harmless snakes of North America.
—[名] 뱀의 일종(유럽산은 유독, 북미산은 무독)

ad·der² [ǽdər] *n.* [C] an adding machine.
—[名] 계산기

ad·dict [ədíkt →*n.*] *vt.* 《*reflexively*》 devote (oneself) to a bad habit. ¶*He addicted himself to drinking.*① —*n.* [ǽdikt] [C] a person who devotes himself to some bad habit.
—[他] …을 나쁜 버릇에 빠지게 하다 ¶①그는 술에 빠졌다 —[名] […에] 빠진 사람, 마약(알코올) 중독자

ad·dic·tion [ədíkʃ(ə)n] *n.* [U] the state of being addicted.
—[名] 탐닉, 열중

‡ **ad·di·tion** [ədíʃ(ə)n] *n.* **1.** [U] the act of adding a thing. **2.** [C] something added. **3.** [U] the process of getting a sum total by combining two or more numbers.
—[名] 1. 부가 2. 부가물 3. 덧셈, 가산법

in addition to, besides; as well as. ¶*In ~ to automobiles, Henry Ford built many other things.*
[熟] …에 더하여; 그 밖에 [또]

* **ad·di·tion·al** [ədíʃ(ə)n(ə)l] *adj.* added. ¶*an ~ tax.*① ▷**ad·di·tion·al·ly** [-ʃ(ə)nəli] *adv.*
—[形] 추가의 ¶①부가세

ad·dle [ǽdl] *vt.* make (something) rotten or confused. —*vi.* (of eggs) go bad; become confused. —*adj.* (of eggs) rotten; confused.
—[他] …을 썩이다, 혼란시키다 —[自] [달걀이] 썩다; 혼란하다 —[形] [달걀이] 썩은, 상한; 혼란된

ad·dle-brained [ǽdlbrèind] *adj.* having confused ideas; stupid.
—[形] 머리가 둔한

‡ **ad·dress** *n.* [ədrés →*n.* 2.] **1.** [C] a written or spoken speech. ¶*an opening (a closing) ~*① */ an ~ of thanks.*② **2.** [+*U.S.* ǽdres] [C] a place where mail is received; a written direction on an envelope, parcel, etc., that shows where it is to be sent. ¶*one's name and ~.*③
—[名] 1. 연설, 인사말 ¶①개회(폐회)사 /②감사의 말 2. 주소; [편지의] 겉봉 ¶③주소 성명

—*vt.* **1.** make a speech to (persons); speak or write to (someone). ¶*~ the nation over the radio.*④ **2.** speak or write to (someone) by using titles. ¶*How do you ~ a mayor?* **3.** write on (a letter, parcel, etc.) where it is to be sent; direct. ¶*~ a letter to someone.*
—[他] 1. [사람들]에게 연설하다; 말을 걸다 ¶④라디오를 통해 국민에게 연설하다 2. […할 칭호로] …에게 말을 걸다 3. …에 겉봉(주소 성명)을 쓰다

address oneself to, ⓐ speak to (someone). ¶*~ oneself to the chairman.*⑤ ⓑ devote one's energies to (a task).
[熟] ⓐ…에게 말을 걸다 ¶⑤의장에게 발언하다 ⓑ…에 착수(전념)하다

ad·dress·ee [æ̀dresí:] *n.* [C] a person to whom a piece of mail is addressed. ↔addresser
—[名] 수신인

ad·duce [əd(j)ú:s / ədjú:s] *vt.* offer (something) as evidence or as an example.
—[타] [증거·예로서] …을 제시하다

ad·e·noids [ǽdinɔ̀idz] *n. pl.* a spongy growth between the upper part of the throat and the back of the nose, often diseased.
—[명] 아데노이드(편도선 증식 비대증)

ad·ept [ədépt, +*Brit.* ǽdept → *n.*] *adj.* highly skilled. ¶*be ~ in* (or *at*) *diving.* —*n.* [C] [ǽdept, ədépt] a person with great skill; an expert.
—[형] 숙달한, 정통한 —[명] 명인, 명수

ad·e·qua·cy [ǽdikwəsi] *n.* [U] the state of being adequate.
—[명] 적당, 충분

• **ad·e·quate** [ǽdikwit] *adj.* sufficient; suitable. ¶*~ intelligence*① / *the means ~ for the purpose.*
—[형] [어떤 목적에] 충분한; 적당한 ¶①상당한 지능

ad·e·quate·ly [ǽdikwitli] *adv.* in an adequate manner.
—[부] 적당히, 충분히

ad·here [ədhíər] *vi.* **1.** stick. 《~ *to* something》 ¶*Wax adheres to the finger.*① **2.** be attached fast; support firmly. 《~ *to* a principle, etc.》 ¶*He adhered to the party.*② ▷**ad·her·er** [-ər] *n.*
—[자] 1. [물건에] 달라붙다 ¶①밀랍은 손가락에 달라붙는다 2. …을 고수하다; …에 충실하다 ¶②그는 당에 충실했다

ad·her·ence [ədhíərəns] *n.* [U] the act of adhering. 《~ *to*》 ¶*~ to one's resolution.*①
—[명] 부착; 고수 ¶①주의(主義)의 고수

ad·her·ent [ədhíərənt] *adj.* attached. —*n.* [C] a follower; a supporter.
—[형] 부착(고수)하는 —[명] 같은 편, 지지자

ad·he·sion [ədhí:ʒ(ə)n, æd-] *n.* [U] **1.** the act of adhering; the state of being adhered. **2.** the act of supporting or following something; faithfulness.
—[명] 1. 부착, 달라붙음 2. 고수

ad·he·sive [ədhí:siv, æd-] *adj.* **1.** sticking. **2.** sticky. ¶*~ plaster.* —*n.* [U] a sticky substance.
—[형] 1. [사람이] 붙어서 떨어지지 않는 2. 접착성의 —[명] 접착성 물질

a·dieu [əd(j)ú: / ədjú:] *interj.* Goodbye; Farewell. —*n.* (pl. **a·dieus** or **a·dieux**) a farewell.
—[감] 안녕, 잘 있거라 —[명] 고별, 작별

a·dieux [əd(j)ú:z / -djú:z] *n.* pl. of **adieu.**

ad·i·pose [ǽdipous] *adj.* of fat. —*n.* [U] animal fat.
—[형] 지방질의 —[명] [동물성] 지방

adj. **1.** adjective. **2.** adjunct. **3.** adjustment.

ad·ja·cent [ədʒéis(ə)nt] *adj.* lying near or next to. 《~ *to*》 ¶*an ~ angle*① / *a house ~ to the church.*②
—[형] 인접한 ¶①인접각/②교회의 옆집

ad·jec·ti·val [æ̀dʒiktáiv(ə)l, / -dʒek-] *adj.* of an adjective.
—[형] 형용사의

: **ad·jec·tive** [ǽdʒiktiv] *n.* [C] (*Grammar*) a word used to limit or describe a noun or pronoun. —*adj.* of an adjective.
—[명] 형용사 —[형] 형용사의

• **ad·join** [ədʒɔ́in] *vt.* be next to (something). ¶*Canada adjoins the United States.*① —*vi.* be in contact. 《~ *to* or *on* something》 ¶*The two houses ~.*
—[타] …에 인접하다 ¶①캐나다는 미국에 인접해 있다 —[자] 서로 접해 있다

ad·join·ing [ədʒɔ́iniŋ] *adj.* in contact; bordering; next. ¶*the ~ rooms.*①
—[형] 이웃의, 부근의 ¶①이웃 방

• **ad·journ** [ədʒə́:rn] *vt.* put off or stop (a meeting, etc.) until a later time. —*vi.* **1.** come to a close. ¶*~ without day.*① **2.** (*colloq.*) go to another place. 《~ *to* another place》
—[타] [모임 따위]를 연기하다, 휴회하다 —[자] 1. 휴회하다 ¶①무기 연기하다 2. 《口》 자리를 옮기다

ad·journ·ment [ədʒə́:rnmənt] *n.* **1.** [U] the act of adjourning; the state of being adjourned. **2.** [C] the time during which a meeting is adjourned.
—[명] 1. 연기, 휴회 2. 휴회 기간

ad·judge [ədʒʌ́dʒ] *vt.* **1.** decide or judge by law. 《~ someone *to*, ~ *that* …》 ¶*~ him to death.*① **2.** give (something) according to the decision, often by law. 《~ something *to*》 ¶*~ a prize to him.*
—[타] 1. 판결(선고)하다 ¶①그에게 사형을 언도하다 2. 심사하여 [상 따위]를 주다

ad·ju·di·cate [ədʒú:dikèit] *vt., vi.* give a judgment. 《~ someone *to be*; ~ *on* or *upon* something》
—[타][자] 판결을 내리다

ad·ju·di·ca·tion [ədʒù:dikéiʃ(ə)n] *n.* **1.** [U] the act of adjudicating. **2.** [C] a decision of bankruptcy.
—[명] 1. 판결 2. 파산 선고

ad·junct [ǽdʒʌŋ(k)t] *n.* [C] **1.** something added to another thing, but not essential. ¶*a mere ~.*① **2.** (*Grammar*) words or phrases that modify other words or phrases, such as adjectives and adverbs.
—[명] 1. 부속물 ¶①단순한 부속물 2. 《文法》 수식어구

ad·jure [ədʒúər] *vt.* **1.** give orders to (someone) solemnly under oath. **2.** appeal to (someone) earnestly. 《~ someone *to do*》 ¶*I ~ you to do it.*①
—[타] 1. …에게 엄명하다 2. …에 간청하다 ¶①제발 그것을 해 주시오

• **ad·just** [ədʒʌ́st] *vt.* **1.** make (someone or something) fit. 《~ something *to*》 ¶*~ oneself to new circumstances.*①
—[타] 1. …을 적응시키다 ¶①새로운 환경에 적응하다 2. [기계 따위]를 조

2. put (something) in a right order or position. ¶~ *the length of a coat* | ~ *a radio dial.* **3.** settle rightly. ¶~ *a difference of opinion.*

정하다; [몸차림 따위]를 단정히 하다 **3.** 조정(조화)시키다

ad·just·a·ble [ədʒʌ́stəbl] *adj.* that can be adjusted.

—[形] 조정할 수 있는

***ad·just·ment** [ədʒʌ́stmənt] *n.* [U] [C] the act of adjusting.

—[名] 정리, 조정

ad·ju·tant [ǽdʒut(ə)nt] *n.* [C] **1.** an assistant. **2.** an army officer who does office work for the commanding officer. **3.** a large bird found in India and Africa.

—[名] **1.** 조수 **2.** 부관 **3.** [동인도산] 학의 일종

ad·lib [ædlíb] *vt., vi.* (**-libbed, -lib·bing**) (*U.S. colloq.*) act, speak, etc. without any preparation.

—[他][自] 《美口》 …을 즉석에서 하다, 즉흥적으로 말하다

***ad·min·is·ter** [ədmínistər] *vt.* **1.** manage the affairs of (a country, business, etc.); direct; conduct. **2.** give; supply. ¶~ *justice*① | *A doctor administers medicine to sick people.* | *I administered him a box on the ear.*② **3.** put (something) into effect. ¶~ *the laws.* —*vi.* **1.** act as manager or administrator. **2.** be helpful. 《~ *to* something》 ¶~ *to someone's comfort.*③

—[他] **1.** …을 처리(관리·지배)하다 **2.** …을 주다, 공급하다 ¶①재판을 하다/②그의 따귀를 한 대 후려갈겼다. **3.** [법]을 집행하다 —[自] **1.** 관리하다 **2.** 공헌하다, 도움이 되다 ¶③남의 위안에 도움이 되다

⁑**ad·min·is·tra·tion** [ədmìnistréiʃ(ə)n] *n.* [U] **1.** the act of managing a business, office, etc. **2.** the management of a government. ¶*metropolitan* ~.① **3.** (*U.S.*) 《*the A-*》 the President, the members of his cabinet, and the executive departments of the government. **4.** the application of law or medicine. ¶*the* ~ *of justice.*

—[名] **1.** 관리, 통제 **2.** 정치, 행정 ¶①수도 행정 **3.** 《美》 행정부; 내각 **4.** [법의] 집행; 투약(投藥)

ad·min·is·tra·tive [ədmínistrèitiv / -trətiv] *adj.* relating to administration. ▷**ad·min·is·tra·tive·ly** [-li] *adv.*

—[形] 관리(행정)의

ad·min·is·tra·tor [ədmínistrèitər] *n.* [C] **1.** a person who manages and directs public affairs. **2.** a person who legally manages another's property.

—[名] **1.** 행정관, 위정자; 장관 **2.** 재산관리인

***ad·mi·ra·ble** [ǽdm(ə)rəbl] *adj.* **1.** worthy of praise. **2.** very good.

—[形] **1.** 칭찬할 만한 **2.** 훌륭한

ad·mi·ra·bly [ǽdm(ə)rəbli] *adv.* in a wonderful and excellent manner.

—[副] 훌륭하게, 뛰어나게

***ad·mi·ral** [ǽdm(ə)r(ə)l] *n.* [C] **1.** an officer of the navy who commands a fleet. **2.** an officer of the highest rank of the navy. ⇨[N.B.] ¶(*U.S.*) *Fleet Admiral;* (*Brit.*) *Admiral of the Fleet*① | *Vice Admiral.*②

—[名] **1.** 해군 대장 **2.** 해군 장성, 제독 [N.B.] adm.으로 줄여 씀 ¶①해군 원수 ②해군 중장

ad·mi·ral·ty [ǽdm(ə)r(ə)lti] *n.* (pl. **-ties**) **1.** [U] the rank or authority of an admiral. **2.** 《*the A-*》 (*Brit.*) the governmental department managing naval affairs.

—[名] **1.** 해군 대장의 직권 **2.** 《英》 해군성

***ad·mi·ra·tion** [æ̀dməréiʃ(ə)n] *n.* [U] **1.** a feeling of wonder, approval, and pleasure. ¶*I was struck with* ~ *for their courage.*① **2.** any object of this feeling. ¶*She is the* ~ *of all.*

—[名] **1.** 감탄, 칭찬 ¶①나는 그들의 용기에 완전히 탄복했다 **2.** 칭찬의 대상

1) ***in admiration of,*** with admiration for.
2) ***to admiration,*** in an admirable manner.

[熟] 1)…을 찬미하여 2)훌륭히

⁑**ad·mire** [ədmáiər] *vt.* **1.** regard (something) with wonder, approval, and pleasure. 《~ someone *for*》 ¶*I admired him for his honesty.*① **2.** think highly of (someone or something); respect. **3.** (*U.S. colloq.*) wish; like. 《~ *to do*》

—[他] **1.** …에 감탄하다, …을 칭찬하다 ¶①나는 그의 정직에 감탄했다 **2.** …을 존경(숭배)하다 **3.** …하고 싶어하다; …을 좋아하다

ad·mir·er [ədmáiərər] *n.* [C] **1.** a person who admires. ¶*a great* ~ *of Soseki.*① **2.** a man who admires or loves a woman.

—[名] **1.** 찬미자 ¶①밀톤의 애독자 **2.** 여성 숭배자, 구혼자

ad·mir·ing [ədmáiəriŋ] *adj.* filled with admiration. ¶*an* ~ *glance.*

—[形] 찬미의, 감탄하는

ad·mir·ing·ly [ədmáiəriŋli] *adv.* with admiration.

—[副] 감탄하여

ad·mis·si·ble [ədmísibl] *adj.* **1.** that can be admitted. **2.** worthy of being admitted. ▷**ad·mis·si·bly** [-i] *adv.*

—[形] **1.** 허락할 수 있는 **2.** [지위 따위에] 취임할 자격이 있는

***ad·mis·sion** [ədmíʃ(ə)n] *n.* **1.** [U] the right or permission to enter. ¶*grant someone* ~① | *Admission to the school is by examination only.* **2.** [C] (*colloq.*) the money which must be paid to enter. ¶*Admission Free.*② | *an* ~ *ticket.* **3.** [C] a statement that something is true. ¶*He made an* ~ *of his guilt at last.*

—[名] **1.** [입학·입장 따위의] 허가 ¶①[남]에게 입장을 허가하다 **2.** 입장료 ¶②입장 무료 **3.** 승인, 자백

⁑**ad·mit** [ədmít] *v.* (**-mit·ted, -mit·ting**) *vt.* **1.** allow (someone or something) to enter; let (someone or something)

—[他] **1.** …의 입장을 허락하다; …을 들이다 ¶①이 표로 두 사람이 입장할 수

A

in. ¶~ *a girl into* (or *to*) *a school* | ~ *air into a room* | *This ticket admits two persons.*① | *He admitted me to his secret.*② **2.** accept (something) as true or sure; acknowledge; confess. 《~ something *to be*; ~ *doing*; ~ *that* ...》 ¶*He admitted his guilt.* | *He admits that it is true; He admits it to be true.* | *She admits having done it herself.* **3.** have room or space for (someone or something). ¶*This room admits five persons.* **—*vi.*** permit to enter. ¶*This key admits to the garden.*③

있다/②그는 내게 비밀을 털어놓았다 2. …을 인정하다 3. …을 수용할 수 있다 —[自] 들어갈 수 있다 ¶③이 열쇠로 정원에 들어갈 수 있다

admit of (=*leave room for*) *something.* ¶*Circumstances do not ~ of this.*④

[熟] …의 여지가 있다 ¶④여러가지 사정으로 이것은 무리다

ad·mit·tance [ədmít(ə)ns] *n.* [U] the act of admitting; the right or permission to enter. ¶*No ~* [*except on business*].① | *Admittance only to adults.*②

—[名] 입장;입장 허가 ¶①[무용자] 출입 금지/②미성년자 입장 사절

ad·mit·ted·ly [ədmítidli] *adv.* by general agreement.

—[副] 의심할 여지 없이, 명백히

ad·mix [ədmíks] *vt.* mix (things) together. 《~ something *with*》 **—*vi.*** become mixed.

—[他] …을 섞다, 혼합하다 —[自] 섞이다

ad·mix·ture [ədmíkstʃər] *n.* **1.** [U] the act of mixing. **2.** [C] something added by mixing.

—[名] 1. 혼합 2. 혼합물

ad·mon·ish [ədmániʃ / -mɔ́n-] *vt.* **1.** give advice to (someone). 《~ someone *to do*》 ¶ *The policeman admonished him to drive carefully.* **2.** blame or scold gently. ¶*The teacher admonished the student for his careless mistake.*①

—[他] 1. [남]에게 …하도록 권하다 2. [남]을 부드럽게 꾸짖다, 타이르다 ¶①선생이 그 학생의 조심성 없는 과실을 타일렀다

ad·mo·ni·tion [ædmənίʃ(ə)n] *n.* [U] the act of warning.

—[名] 훈계, 경고

ad·mon·i·to·ry [ədmánətɔ̀:ri / -mɔ́nitəri] *adj.* warning.

—[形] 타이르는, 경고(권고)하는

a·do [ədú:] *n.* [U] trouble; fuss; excitement. ¶*make much ~*① | *much ~ about nothing*② | *with much ~.*

—[名] 수고; 소동 ¶①큰 소동을 벌이다/②헛소동

ad·o·les·cence [ædoulésns], **-cen·cy** [-snsi] *n.* [U] a period between childhood and manhood or womanhood.

—[名] 청년기, 청춘기

ad·o·les·cent [ædoulésnt] *adj.* growing from childhood to manhood or womanhood. **—*n.*** [C] a young person in adolescence.

—[形] 청년의, 청춘기의 —[名] 청년, 젊은이

:a·dopt [ədápt / ədɔ́pt] *vt.* **1.** choose and use (something) as one's own. ¶~ *a new method* | *words adopted from a foreign language.*① **2.** take another's child legally into one's family and bring up as one's own child. ¶*an adopted child*② | ~ *a child into a family.*③ **3.** vote to accept (a plan).

—[他] 1. [방법·생각 따위]를 채택하다 ¶①외래어 2. …을 양자로 삼다 ¶②양자/③아이를 가족의 한 사람으로 삼다 3. …을 가결하다

·a·dop·tion [ədápʃ(ə)n / ədɔ́p-] *n.* [U][C] the act of adopting.

—[名] 채택; 양자 결연

a·dop·tive [ədáptiv / ədɔ́p-] *adj.* taken by adoption. ¶~ *parents.*①

—[形] 양자 관계의 ¶①양부모

a·dor·a·ble [ədɔ́:rəbl] *adj.* **1.** worthy of being respected. **2.** (*colloq.*) very charming. ▷**a·dor·a·bly** [-i] *adv.*

—[形] 1. 숭배할 만한 2. 《口》 귀여운, 반할 만한

ad·o·ra·tion [ædəréiʃ(ə)n / ædɔ:réi-] *n.* [U] **1.** the act of worshiping. **2.** deep, great love and devotion.

—[名] 1. 숭배 2. 동경

·a·dore [ədɔ́:r] *vt.* **1.** love greatly. ¶~ *a woman.* **2.** worship. **3.** (*colloq.*) like very much.

—[他] 1. …을 사랑하다 2. 승상(숭배)하다 3. 《口》 아주 좋아하다

a·dor·er [ədɔ́:rər] *n.* [C] a person who adores; an admirer.

—[名] 동경하는 사람; 숭배자

·a·dorn [ədɔ́:rn] *vt.* **1.** make (something) beautiful. 《~ something or someone *with*》 ¶~ *oneself with jewels.* **2.** add splendor to (something). ¶~ *one's character*① | ~ *the stage.*②

—[他] 1. …을 꾸미다, 장식하다 2. …을 돋보이게 하다 ¶①인격을 닦다/②무대를 돋보이게 하다

a·dorn·ment [ədɔ́:rnmənt] *n.* **1.** [U] the act of adorning; the state of being adorned. **2.** [C] something that adorns.

—[名] 1. 장식하기 2. 장식품

a·drift [ədríft] *adv., adj.* 《as *predicative*》 **1.** floating; drifting. ¶*be ~ upon the world.*① **2.** without being guided.

—[副][形] 1. 표류하여 ¶①세계를 떠돌고 있다 2. [사람이] 어찌할 바를 몰라서

go adrift, ⓐ float at random. ⓑ wander from the main subject.

[熟] ⓐ표류하다 ⓑ[이야기가] 탈선하다

a·droit [ədrɔ́it] *adj.* having the ability to do something well; skillful. ¶*an ~ workman.* ▷**a·droit·ness** [-nis] *n.*

—[形] 솜씨있는, 교묘한

a·droit·ly [ədrɔ́itli] *adv.* with skill and cleverness.

—[副] 솜씨있게

adulate [ˈædʒuleɪt / ˈædju-] vt. speak too highly of (someone); praise (someone) too much. ▷**ad·u·la·tor** [-tər] n.
— 他 …에게 알랑거리다

ad·u·la·tion [ˌædʒuˈleɪʃ(ə)n / ˌædju-] n. ⓤ the act of adulating; excessive praise. ▷**ad·u·la·to·ry** [ˈædʒulətɔːri / ˈædjuleɪtəri] adj.
— 名 아첨, 아양

* **a·dult** [əˈdʌlt / ˈædʌlt] adj. full-grown; mature. ¶ ~ education.① — n. ⓒ a full-grown person or animal. ¶ Adults' Day. ▷**a·dult·ness** [-nis] n.
— 形 성장한, 어른의 ¶①성인 교육 — 名 성인, 어른; 성장한 동물(식물)

a·dul·ter·ate [əˈdʌltəreɪt] vt. make (something) poorer in quality by adding something improper. 《~ something with》 ¶ ~ milk with water.
— 他 [조악품을 섞어] …의 품질을 떨어뜨리다

a·dul·ter·a·tion [əˌdʌltəˈreɪʃ(ə)n] n. 1. ⓤ the act of adulterating. 2. ⓒ something adulterated.
— 名 1. [조악품의] 혼합 2. 조악품

a·dul·ter·ous [əˈdʌlt(ə)rəs] adj. guilty of adultery.
— 形 간통의

a·dul·ter·y [əˈdʌltəri] n. ⓤ ⓒ (pl. -ter·ies) unfaithfulness of a husband or wife.
— 名 간통

adv. 1. adverb; adverbial. 2. advertisement.

‡ **ad·vance** [ədˈvæns / -ˈvɑːns] vi. 1. go forward. ¶ The troops advanced. / We advanced three miles a day. 2. progress; develop. ¶ He advanced in mathematics.① 3. rise in rank, price, etc. ¶ ~ in life (or in the world) / ~ in years② / Prices have advanced 8 per cent during the year. — vt. 1. put (someone or something) forward. ¶ The troops were advanced. 2. promote; hasten. ¶ ~ one's work. 3. raise (someone) to a higher rank. ¶ ~ someone from clerk to manager.③ 4. raise (prices). 5. pay (money) before the appointed time; lend (money). — n. 1. ⓤ the act of moving forward; progress; improvement. ¶ the ~ of science / the ~ of evening (old age)④ / the ~ of the enemy. 2. ⓒ a rise in price, rank, etc. ¶ an ~ of 7 per cent in the cost of living.
1) **in advance,** beforehand.
2) **in advance of,** before; ahead of.
— 自 1. 전진하다 2. 진보하다; 발달하다 ¶①그는 수학이 늘었다 3. 출세하다; [물가 따위가] 상승(앙등)하다 ¶②다 늙다 — 他 1. …을 전진시키다 2. …을 촉진(진보)시키다 3. …을 출세시키다 ¶③ 점원에서 지배인으로 승격시키다 4. [값]을 올리다 5. 기일 전에 [돈]을 치르다; [돈]을 빌려주다
— 名 1. 전진; 진보, 발전 ¶④밤이 깊어 감(나이를 먹음) 2. [가격 따위의] 상승; 승격
熟 1) 미리, 전부터 2) …에 앞서서

* **ad·vanced** [ədˈvænst / -ˈvɑːnst] adj. far ahead of others in age, ideas, progress, action, etc. ¶ an ~ age① / an ~ course② / an ~ philosopher③ / be ~ in years.④
— 形 전진한, 진보한; [시간이] 오래된 ¶①고령(高齡)의 / ②고등과 / ③진보적인 철학자 / ④나이가 많다

ad·vance·ment [ədˈvænsmənt / -ˈvɑːns-] n. ⓤ the act of advancing; the state of being advanced. ¶ the ~ of learning① / ~ in fortune② / ~ in life.③
— 名 전진, 진보, 승진 ¶①학문의 진보 / ②재산의 증가 / ③출세

‡ **ad·van·tage** [ədˈvæntɪdʒ / -ˈvɑːn-] n. 1. ⓤ benefit; gain. ¶ There is no ~ in doing such a thing.① 2. ⓒ anything that helps someone to lead over others; superiority; better position. ¶ the ~ of ground.②
1) **take advantage of,** ⓐ make use of (something). ¶ He took full ~ of his position.③ ⓑ deceive (someone). 　　　　　　　　　　　　　　　　　[to ~.⑤]
2) **to advantage,** to good effect. ¶ appear to ~④ / sell
— 名 1. 이익; 편의 ¶①그런 일을 해도 아무 이익이 없다 2. 이점, 강점; 우월 ¶②지리(地利)
熟 1) ⓐ …을 이용하다 ¶③그는 자기의 지위를 십분 이용했다 ⓑ…을 속이다 2) ⓓ효과적으로 ¶④돋보이다 / ⑤비싸게 팔다

ad·van·ta·geous [ˌædvənˈteɪdʒəs] adj. giving a benefit or help; favorable. ▷**ad·van·ta·geous·ly** [-li] adv.
— 形 유리한, 기회가 좋은

ad·vent [ˈædvent / -vənt] n. ⓤ 1. (usu. the ~) a coming; arrival. ¶ the ~ of spring.① 2. (A-) the birth of Christ.; the season including the four Sundays before Christmas.
— 名 1. 내도(來到), 출현 ¶①봄이 옴 2. 그리스도의 탄생; 그리스도 강림절

ad·ven·ti·tious [ˌædvenˈtɪʃəs / -vent-] adj. 1. happening by chance; accidental. 2. coming from outside.
— 形 1. 우연의 2. 외래(外來)의

‡ **ad·ven·ture** [ədˈventʃər] n. 1. ⓒ ⓤ a bold undertaking filled with excitement and danger. ¶ the adventures of Arctic exploration. 2. ⓒ an exciting or unusual experience. ¶ a strange ~① / quite an ~② / the Adventures of Robinson Crusoe"③ / seek adventures.④ 3. ⓤ a liking for excitement and risk. ¶ His life was full of ~.
— vi. do a bold thing. — vt. take a chance on (something). ¶ ~ one's life on the undertaking.
— 名 1. 모험, 희한한 경험; 모험담 ¶①기묘한 일 / ②정말로 진기한 경험 / ③로빈슨 크루소우의 모험담 / ④신기한 일을 찾아다니다 3. 모험심
— 自 모험하다 — 他 흥망(생사)을 걸고 해보다

ad·ven·tur·er [ədˈventʃərər] n. ⓒ 1. a person who has or likes to have adventures. 2. a person who tries to
— 名 1. 모험가 2. 투기자(投機者)

get money by questionable means.

ad·ven·tur·ous [ədvéntʃ(ə)rəs] *adj.* fond of adventure; bold. **2.** filled with danger. ¶*an ~ journey.*
—[형] 1. 모험을 좋아하는, 대담한 2. 위험한

: ad·verb [ǽdvə:rb] *n.* [C] a word which modifies a verb, adjective, or another adverb, by telling time, place, degree, etc.
—[명] 부사(副詞)

ad·ver·bi·al [ædvə́:rbiəl / ədvə́:bjəl] *adj.* of or used as an adverb.
—[형] 부사의

ad·ver·sar·y [ǽdvərsèri / -vəs(ə)ri] *n.* [C] (pl. **-ries**) a person or group that opposes another; an enemy.
—[명] 적, 상대, 적대자

ad·verse [ædvə́:rs,/ ǽdvə:s] *adj.* **1.** contrary in direction. ¶*an ~ current.*① **2.** unfavorable and opposing. ¶*~ fortune*② / *under ~ circumstances*③ / *The situation was ~ to us.*④ ▷**ad·verse·ly** [-li] *adv.*
—[형] 1. 거꾸로의 ¶①역류 2. 불리한, 반대의 ¶②불운/③역경 속에서/④형세는 우리에게 불리했다

ad·ver·si·ty [ædvə́:rsiti / ədvə́:s-] *n.* [U][C] (pl. **-ties**) misfortune; great trouble.
—[명] 역경, 불리

ad·vert [ædvə́:rt / ədvə́:t] *vi.* **1.** turn attention. ⟪~ *to* something⟫ **2.** refer. ⟪~ *to* something⟫
—[자] 1. 주의를 돌리다 2. 언급하다

• ad·ver·tise, -tize [ǽdvərtàiz, +*U.S.* æ̀dvərtáiz] *vt.* **1.** make (something) generally known by means of printed matter, radio, or the like. ¶*~ a house for sale*① / *~ one's wares.*② **2.** inform. ⟪~ someone *of*⟫ **—*vi.*** put a notice in a newspaper, etc. ¶*~ for a job.*③
—[타] 1. …을 광고하다, 공고하다 ¶①집을 판다고 광고하다/②상품 광고를 하다 2. …을 통고하다 —[자] 광고하다 ¶③구직 광고를 하다

• ad·ver·tise·ment, -tize- [æ̀dvərtáizmənt / ədvə́:tizmənt, -tis-] *n.* **1.** [U] the act of advertising. ⇒[N.B.] ¶*~ column.*① **2.** [C] a public notice.
—[명] 1. 광고 [N.B.] ad., adv., advt. 로 줄여 씀 ¶①광고란 2. 공고; 선전

ad·ver·tis·er, -tiz- [ǽdvərtàizər] *n.* [C] a person who advertises.
—[명] 광고하는 사람

• ad·ver·tis·ing, -tiz- [ǽdvərtàiziŋ] *n.* [U] **1.** the business of advertising. **2.** advertisement. ¶*newspaper ~.*① **—*adj.*** of advertisement. ¶*~ agency.*②
—[명] 1. 광고업 2. 광고 ¶①신문 광고 —[형] 광고의 ¶②광고 대리점

: ad·vice [ədváis] *n.* **1.** [U] an opinion about what to do; counsel. ¶*take (follow) someone's ~ / give someone a piece of ~ / take the doctor's ~* **2.** ⟪usu. *pl.*⟫ news; information. ¶*advices from New York / diplomatic advices.*①
—[명] 1. 충고, 조언, 권고 2. 통지, 보고 ¶①외교상의 보고

ad·vis·a·bil·i·ty [ədvàizəbíliti] *n.* [U] the quality of being advisable.
—[명] 권할 만함, 상책

ad·vis·a·ble [ədváizəbl] *adj.* advised; wise. ¶*It would be ~ to do so.*① ▷**ad·vis·a·bly** [-i] *adv.*
—[형] 권할 만한; 현명한 ¶①그렇게 하는 것이 좋을 것이다

: ad·vise [ədváiz] *vt.* **1.** give advice to (someone); give an opinion of the best thing to do. ⟪~ someone *to do*⟫ **2.** give notice to (someone); make (someone) know; teach. ⟪~ someone *of*⟫ ¶*He advised me of his arrival. / We were advised of the danger.*①
—[타] 1. …에게 충고하다, 조언해 주다 2. …에 통지하다; 알리다 ¶①우리들은 위험하다는 통지를 받았다

ad·vised [ədváizd] *adj.* considered.
—[형] 곰곰이 생각한

ad·vis·ed·ly [ədváizidli] *adv.* after careful thought; on purpose.
—[부] 심사숙고한 끝에; 고의로

ad·vise·ment [ədváizmənt] *n.* [U] careful consideration.
—[명] 숙고

• ad·vis·er, (*U.S.*) **-vi·sor** [ədváizər] *n.* [C] **1.** a person who gives advice. **2.** (*U.S.*) a teacher who advises students.
—[명] 1. 충고자, 조언자 2. [美] 지도교사

ad·vi·so·ry [ədváizəri] *adj.* having authority to give advice. ¶*an ~ committee.*①
—[형] 조언의, 자문의 ¶①자문 위원회

ad·vo·ca·cy [ǽdvəkəsi] *n.* [U] the act of speaking in favor.
—[명] 변호, 옹호, 지지

• ad·vo·cate *vt.* [ǽdvəkèit → *n.*] speak in favor of (something); defend. ⟪~ *doing*⟫ ⇒[usage] **—*n.*** [ǽdvəkit, -kèit] [C] **1.** a person who advocates. **2.** a person who defends others in a court of law. ▷**ad·vo·ca·tion** [æ̀dvəkéiʃ(ə)n] *n.*
—[타] …을 옹호하다, 주창하다 [usage] 뒤에 that-clause 가 오지 않음 —[명] 1. 옹호자 2. 변호사

adz, adze [ædz] *n.* [C] a curved tool like an axe, used for shaping wood. ⇒ fig.
—[명] 큰 자귀

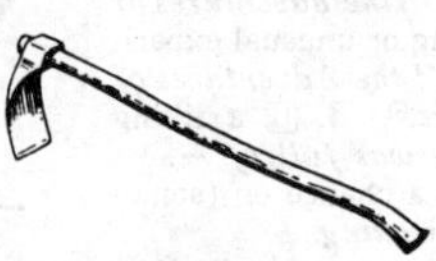

[adz]

Ae·ge·an [i(:)dʒí:ən] *adj.* of the Aegean. **—*n.*** ⟪the ~⟫ the sea between Greece and Turkey. ¶*the ~ [Sea]*① / *the ~ Islands.*②
—[형] 에게해의 —[명] 에게해 ¶①에게해, 다도해 ②에게해 제도

ae·gis [í:dʒis] *n.* **1.** [C] a shield used by Zeus or Athena. **2.** [U] protection. ¶*appear under the ~ of a person.*①
—[名] 1. 방패 2. 보호 ¶①남의 보호(후원)를 받고 나타나다

ae·on, e·on [í:ən] *n.* [C] a very long period of time that can not be measused.
—[名] 영구, 영겁(永劫)

aer·ate [éiərèit, +*Brit.* éər-] *vt.* **1.** expose (something) to the action of the air. **2.** fill (liquid) with air or gas. ¶*aerated water.*①
—[他] 1. …을 공기에 쐬다 2. [액체]에 탄산가스[따위]를 함유시키다 ¶①탄산수

aer·i·al [éəriəl] *adj.* **1.** of, like, or in the air. ¶*an ~ current*① | *an ~ telegraph*② | *an ~ wire*③ | *an ~ performance.*④ **2.** not real. **3.** of aircraft or flight. ¶*an ~ chart*⑤ | *an ~ photograph.* **—*n.*** [C] wires or rods for sending out or receiving electric waves; an antenna.
—[形] 1. 공기의, 공중의 ¶①기류/②무선전신/③공중선/④공중 곡예 2. 가공(架空)의 3. 항공[기]에 관한 ¶⑤항공도(航空圖) —[名] 공중선, 안테나

aer·ie, aer·y [éəri, íəri] *n.* [C] **1.** a high nest of an eagle, etc. **2.** a house or castle built on a high rock or hill.
—[名] 1. [독수리·매 따위의] 높은 둥지 2. 높은 곳의 집 또는 성채

aer·o·bat·ics [èərəbǽtiks] *n. pl.* **1.** the acrobatic flight of an airplane. **2.** 《used as *sing.*》 the art of doing such flights.
—[名] 1. 곡예 비행 2. 고등 비행술

aer·o·drome [éərədròum] *n.* (*Brit.*) =airdrome.

aer·o·gram, -gramme [éərougræ̀m] *n.* [C] **1.** a message sent by radio. **2.** a letter, parcel, or the like sent by air mail.
—[名] 1. 무선 전보(전신) 2. 항공 봉함엽서, 항공 소포

aer·o·nau·tics [èərənɔ́:tiks] *n. pl.* 《used as *sing.*》 the science of building and operating aircraft. ▷**aer·o·nau·tic** [-tik] *adj.* —**aer·o·nau·ti·cal** [-k(ə)l] *adj.*
—[名] 비행술, 항공학

⁑ **aer·o·plane** [éərəplèin] *n.* [C] (*Brit.*) =airplane.

Ae·sop [í:sɑp, -səp / -sɔp] *n.* (620?–560 B.C.) a Greek fable writer. ¶*Aesop's Fables.*①
—[名] 이솝(그리이스의 우화 작가) ¶①이솝 우화

aes·thete [ésθi:t / í:s-] *n.* [C] **1.** a person who has a keen sensibility to beauty and art. **2.** a person who pays too much attention to art and beauty, neglecting practical matters.
—[名] 1. 심미가 2. 유미(唯美)주의자

aes·thet·ic [esθétik / i:sθétik] *adj.* **1.** the philosophy of beauty. ¶*an ~ point of view.*① **2.** having a sense of beauty in art or nature. **3.** artistic.
—[形] 1. 미학적인 ¶①미학적 견지 2. 심미적인 3. 미적(美的)인

ae·ther [í:θər] *n.* =ether.

a·far [əfɑ́:r] *adv.* (*poetic*) **1.** from a distance. **2.** far off.
—[副] (詩) 1. 멀리서부터 2. 멀리에

af·fa·bil·i·ty [æ̀fəbíliti] *n.* [U] the quality of being friendly and polite in speech and manner.
—[名] 붙임성이 있음, 상냥함, 공손함

af·fa·ble [ǽfəbl] *adj.* **1.** easy to talk to. **2.** friendly and polite.
—[形] 1. 붙임성 있는, 2. 상냥한, 예의바른

⁑ **af·fair** [əféər] *n.* [C] **1.** an event; a happening. ¶*a strange ~* | *a private (public) ~.*① **2.** 《*pl.*》 business. ¶*a man of affairs* | *a talent for affairs* | *He has many affairs to look after.*② **3.** any matter; a thing. ¶*The journey was a very pleasant ~.*③
—[名] 1. 사건; 일 ¶①개인의 일(공무) 2. 직책, 사무, 업무 ¶②그는 보살펴야 할 일이 많다 3. [막연한] 일; 것, 물건 ¶③그 여행은 즐거웠다

⁑ **af·fect** [əfékt] *vt.* **1.** have an influence on (something or someone). ¶*Cares ~ the health.*① **2.** move the feelings of (someone). ¶*He was deeply affected by sorrow.* **3.** be fond of (something). ¶*~ a foreign style of dress.* **4.** pretend. ¶*~ ignorance* | *~ illness* | *He affects carelessness in dress.*
—[他] 1. …에 영향을 미치다, [병이] …을 침범하다 ¶①근심 걱정은 건강에 나쁘다 2. …을 감동시키다 3. …을 좋아하다 4. …을 가장하다, …인 체하다

af·fec·ta·tion [æ̀fektéiʃ(ə)n] *n.* [U] [C] the act of pretending; a false show of manners, etc.; unnatural behavior. ¶*an ~ of kindness*① | *with an ~ of wit*② | *without ~.*③
—[名] 젠체하기, 가식; 뽐냄 ¶①친절한 체하기/②지혜 있는 체하고/③솔직히

af·fect·ed [əféktid] *adj.* **1.** influenced seriously. ¶*an ~ part*① | *the ~ district.*② **2.** moved in emotion. ¶*well-affected.*③ **3.** pretended; not natural. ¶*an ~ girl.*
—[形] 1. 영향을 받은; 침범당한 ¶①아픈 곳/②피해지 2. 감동한 ¶③호의를 가진 3. 젠체하는

af·fect·ing [əféktiŋ] *adj.* having the power to move the emotions. ¶*an ~ sight.*① ▷**af·fect·ing·ly** [-li] *adv.*
—[形] 감동시키는; 가슴 아픈 ¶①애처로운 광경

⁑ **af·fec·tion** [əfékʃ(ə)n] *n.* [U] love; good-will. ↔dislike ¶*motherly ~*① | *the object of ~*② | *have an ~ for a girl.*
—[名] 애정; 호의 ¶①모성애/②연모의 대상

* **af·fec·tion·ate** [əfékʃ(ə)nit] *adj.* full of love and tenderness. ¶*an ~ mother.*①
—[形] 애정에 가득찬, 자애로운 ¶①자모(慈母)

af·fec·tion·ate·ly [əfékʃ(ə)nitli] *adv.* with love; in an affectionate manner. ¶*Yours ~.; Affectionately yours.*①
—[副] 자애스럽게 ¶①친구·근친간의 편지에서 끝맺는 말

af·fi·ance [əfáiəns] *n.* **1.** [U] firm trust. **2.** [C] a promise of marriage. **—*vt.*** ⟪usu. in *passive*⟫ promise (someone) to marry. ¶*He is affianced to my sister.*①
—[名] 1. 신용 2. 약혼 —[他] …와 약혼하다 ¶①그는 내 누이와 약혼했다

af·fi·da·vit [æ̀fidéivit] *n.* [C] a written statement made with an oath, usu. in a court of law.
—[名] 선서 구술서(口述書)

af·fil·i·ate [əfílièit] *vt.* **1.** bring (someone or something) into close association; have (someone or something) as a member. ⟪~ someone *with* or *to*⟫ ¶*~ oneself with* (or *to*) *the club*① | *Our school is affiliated to* (or *with*) *the University.*② **2.** adopt (a child) as one's own.
—[他] 1. …을 깊은 관계를 맺게 하다; …을 회원으로 넣다 ¶①클럽에 가입하다/②우리 학교는 그 대학교의 부속 학교이다 2. …을 양자로 삼다

af·fil·i·a·tion [əfìliéiʃ(ə)n] *n.* [U] [C] **1.** the act of joining; union. **2.** (*U.S.*) a friendly relationship.
—[名] 1. 가입, 합동 2. 우호관계

af·fin·i·ty [əfíniti] *n.* [C] [U] (pl. **-ties**) **1.** a close relationship. ¶*an ~ between the two races.* **2.** likeness.
—[名] 1. 밀접한 관계 2. 유사성(점)

• **af·firm** [əfə́:rm] *vt.* **1.** declare the truth of (something). ¶*~ one's loyalty.*① **2.** confirm. **—*vi.*** testify in a court without an oath.
—[他] 1. …을 단언하다 ¶①충성을 맹세하다 2. 확인하다 —[自] 증언하다

af·fir·ma·tion [æ̀fərméiʃ(ə)n] *n.* [U] [C] **1.** the act of affirming. ↔denial, negation **2.** (*Law*) a statement in court which gives evidence about something.
—[名] 1. 긍정; 단언하기 2. 증언

af·firm·a·tive [əfə́:rmətiv] *adj.* answering "yes" to a question; positive. ↔negative **—*n.*** ⟪*the* ~⟫ a statement of "yes"; the "yes" side in an argument.
—[形] 긍정의; 시인하는 —[名] 긍정어구; 찬성자측

answer in the affirmative, answer "yes." ¶*He answered in the ~.*
[熟] 그렇다고 대답하다, 긍정하다

▷**af·firm·a·tive·ly** [-li] *adv.*

af·fix *vt.* [əfíks → *n.*] fix (one thing) to or on another; write down (one's signature) on a document; stick (a stamp) on a letter. **—*n.*** [ǽfiks] [C] (*Grammar*) a prefix, suffix, or infix.
—[他] …을 첨부하다; [서명 따위]를 써넣다; [우표 따위]를 붙이다 —[名] ⟪文法⟫ 접사(接辭)(접두사·접미사)

af·flict [əflíkt] *vt.* cause pain or grief to (someone's body or mind); make (someone) miserable; trouble greatly.
—[他] [심신]을 괴롭히다; 슬퍼하게 하다

af·flic·tion [əflíkʃ(ə)n] *n.* **1.** [U] pain; distress; great trouble. ¶*people in ~.*① **2.** [C] a cause of pain, distress, or trouble; a misfortune. ¶*live in ~.*
—[名] 1. 고뇌; 고생 ¶①고통받는 사람들 2. 고뇌의 원인; 불행

af·flu·ence [ǽfluəns] *n.* [U] rich supply; great wealth.
—[名] 풍요; 부유

af·flu·ent [ǽfluənt] *adj.* abundant; wealthy. **—*n.*** [C] a river or stream flowing into a larger one.
—[形] 풍부한; 부유한 —[名] 지류(支流)

⁝ **af·ford** [əfɔ́:rd] *vt.* **1.** ⟪usu. with *can, be able to,* or *could*⟫ have enough money, time, etc. for (something). ¶*We can ~ a new car now.* | *I can't ~ a holiday.*① | *Can you ~ the time?* **2.** (of things) give; supply. ¶*Music affords me great pleasure.* | *The trees ~ pleasant shade.* | *The sea affords fish.*
—[他] 1. …할 시간·금전 따위의 여유가 있다; …할 수 있다 ¶①나는 휴가를 갈 여유가 없다 2. 주다, 공급하다; [천연 자원 따위]를 산출하다

af·for·est [əfɔ́:rist, əfɑ́r- / əfɔ́r-] *vt.* change (bare or cultivated land) into a forest.
—[他] …에 숲을 만들다, 조림하다

af·fray [əfréi] *n.* [C] **1.** a noisy quarrel. **2.** (*Law*) a fight in a public place.
—[名] 1. 싸움, 난투 2. ⟪法⟫ 소요(騷擾)

af·front [əfrʌ́nt] *vt.* **1.** insult (someone) openly and on purpose. **2.** meet (death) face to face. **—*n.*** [C] an open insult. ¶*put an ~ upon someone.*①
—[他] 1. [고의로] …을 모욕하다 2. [죽음 따위]에 과감하게 맞서다 —[名] 모욕 ¶①[남]을 모욕하다

Af·ghan [ǽfgæn, +*U.S.* -gən] *n.* [C] a person of Afghanistan; [U] the language spoken there. **—*adj.*** of Afghanistan or its people.
—[名] 아프가니스탄 사람; 아프가니스탄 말 —[形] 아프가니스탄[사람]의

Af·ghan·i·stan [æfgǽnistæ̀n] *n.* a country in south-western Asia.
—[名] 아프가니스탄

a·field [əfí:ld] *adv.* **1.** to, on, or in the field. **2.** to or at a distance; [far] away.
—[副] 1. 들로; 전쟁터로 2. 멀리 떨어져서

a·fire [əfáiər] *adv., adj.* on fire. ¶*The woods were ~.*
—[副][形] 불타올라

a·flame [əfléim] *adv., adj.* in flames; as if on fire.
—[副][形] 불타올라; [감정이] 격하여

a·float [əflóut] *adv., adj.* **1.** at sea; on board a ship. **2.** floating in the water or air. **3.** covered with water; flooded. ¶*The kitchen was ~.* **4.** going around, as a rumor. **5.** out of debt.
—[副][形] 1. 바다 위에 2. [물 위·하늘에] 떠서 3. 물을 뒤집어 써서 4. [소문 따위가]떠돌아 5. 빚지지 않고

a·foot [əfút] *adv., adj.* **1.** on foot. **2.** about to happen; going on. ¶*There is trouble ~.*
—[副][形] 1. 도보로 2. 진행중; 발생하여

a·fore·men·tioned [əfɔ́ːrmènʃ(ə)nd] *adj.* talked about above or before.
—[形] 앞서 말한; 앞에 적은

a·fore·said [əfɔ́ːrsèd] *adj.* said above or before.
—[形] 앞서 말한

a·fore·time [əfɔ́ːrtàim] *adv.* previously; formerly.
—[副] 앞서서, 미리; 이전에

a·foul [əfául] *adv., adj.* in collision.
—[副][形] 충돌하여

⁑ **a·fraid** [əfréid] *adj.* ⟪as *predicative*⟫ **1.** frightened; filled with fear. ⟪~ *of*; ~ *that* ...; ~ *to do*⟫ ¶*I am ~ of dogs. / He was ~ of dying. / Don't be ~ of being late. / The girl was ~ to go through the wood. / I am ~ [that] I shall die.* **2.** (*colloq.*) sorry; feeling regret, unhappiness, etc.
—[形] **1.** 무서워하는, 두려워하는; 염려(걱정)하는 **2.** ⟪口⟫ …을 유감스럽게 생각하는

I'm afraid [that], (*colloq.*) I'm sorry; I have to admit with regret. ↔I hope [that] ... ¶*I am ~ I cannot help you. / "Will it rain?" "I'm ~ so."*
[熟] ⟪口⟫ …이 아닐지 염려하다; [유감스럽지만] …이라고 생각하다

a·fresh [əfréʃ] *adv.* anew; again.
—[副] 다시, 새로이

⁑ **Af·ri·ca** [ǽfrikə] *n.* the second largest continent, south of Europe.
—[名] 아프리카

Af·ri·can [ǽfrikən] *adj.* of Africa or its people. —*n.* [C] a person of Africa.
—[形] 아프리카의; 아프리카 사람의 —[名] 아프리카 사람

aft [æft / ɑːft] *adv.* (*Nautical*) at or toward the back part of a ship.
—[副] ⟪海⟫ 고물(선미)에

⁑ **af·ter** [ǽftər / ɑ́ːftə] *prep.* **1.** behind in place, time, or order; next to; later than; (*U.S.*) (of time) past. ¶*~ school*① */ ~ eight o'clock / five minutes ~ six / ~ a while / the day ~ tomorrow*② */ the great dramatists ~ Shakespeare / Shut the door ~ you.*③ **2.** in spite of. ¶*After all my objections, why did you do it?* **3.** because of. ¶*Nobody trusts her ~ that lie.*④ **4.** in search of. ¶*The policeman ran ~ the thief / seek ~ happiness / What is he ~?*⑤ **5.** about; concerning. ¶*ask (inquire) ~ someone*⑥ */ look ~ the children.*⑦ **6.** according to; in imitation of; in agreement with. ¶*act ~ one's ideas*⑧ */ She was named Elizabeth ~ her grandmother. / take ~ one's mother*⑨ */ copy ~ a model / a novel ~ Hemingway's style.*
—[前] **1.** [장소·시간·위치가] …의 뒤(나중)에, …에 이어서; ⟪美⟫ [몇 시] 지나서 ¶①방과후/②모래/③문 닫고 들어오시오 **2.** [···함]에도 불구하고 **3.** …했기 때문에, …에 비추어 ¶④그런 거짓말을 해서 아무도 그녀를 안 믿는다 **4.** …을 찾아 ¶⑤그는 무엇을 찾고 있는가 **5.** …에 관하여 ¶⑥남의 안부를 묻다/⑦아이들을 돌보다 **6.** …에 좇아서; …을 본떠서 / ¶⑧자기의 생각에 따라 행동하다 ⑨어머니를 닮다

1) ***after all,*** in spite of all that has been said or done.
2) ***one after another,*** one by one; in succession.
3) ***one after the other,*** by turns; alternately.
[熟] 1)결국; …에도 불구하고 2)연달아, 줄이어 3)번갈아, 교대로

—*adv.* behind; later; afterward. ¶*six days ~ / soon ~ / look before and ~ / follow ~.*
—[副] 뒤에, 나중에

—*conj.* later than the time at which [something happens]. ¶*We shall start ~ he comes. / ~ all is said and done.*⑩
—[接] …한 후에 ¶⑩결국, 역시

—*adj.* later in time. ¶*In ~ years I never heard from her.*⑪
—[形] 후의 ¶⑪후년에 그녀의 소식을 못 들었다

af·ter-din·ner [ǽftərdínər / ɑ́ːftədínə] *adj.* following dinner. ¶*an ~ speech.*①
—[形] 정찬(만찬) 후의 ¶①탁상 연설

af·ter·ef·fect [ǽftərifèkt / ɑ́ːftə-] *n.* [C] a result or effect that follows later.
—[名] 여파, 여세; [약을 먹은 뒤의] 작용

af·ter·glow [ǽftərglòu / ɑ́ːftə-] *n.* [C] the glow in the sky after the sun has set.
—[名] 저녁놀

af·ter·math [ǽftərmæ̀θ / ɑ́ːftə-] *n.* [C] an undesirable result; that which follows from a disaster, such as a flood, or fire. ¶*the ~ of the storm.*
—[名] [재해 따위에 따르는 불쾌한] 여파, 후유증

af·ter·most [ǽftərmòust / ɑ́ːftəməst] *adj.* **1.** last. **2.** (*Nautical*) nearest the back part of a ship.
—[形] **1.** 최후의 **2.** ⟪海⟫ [배의] 가장 뒤쪽의

⁑ **af·ter·noon** [æ̀ftərnúːn / ɑ̀ːftə-] *n.* [C] the time between noon and evening. ¶*in the ~ / in the ~ next Monday.*
—[名] 오후

af·ter·thought [ǽftərθɔ̀ːt / ɑ́ːftə-] *n.* [U][C] a later thought about an action or decision; a second thought.
—[名] 때늦은 생각, 뒤늦게 떠오른 묘안

⁑ **af·ter·ward** [ǽftərwərd / ɑ́ːftə-], *Brit.* **-wards** [ǽftərwərdz / ɑ́ːftə-] *adv.* subsequently; at a later time.
—[副] 뒤에, 나중에; 그 후

⁑ **a·gain** [əgén, +*Brit.* əgéin] *adv.* **1.** once more. ¶*try ~ / come ~.* **2.** moreover; furthermore. ¶*Again, I must say.*① **3.** back (into a former position). ¶*come home ~ / return ~.* **4.** in return or reply. ¶*answer ~.* **5.** on the other hand. ¶*It might happen, and ~ it might not.*
—[副] **1.** 다시, 또 **2.** 그만큼 더, 그 위에 ¶①그 위에 더 한마디 해둔다 **3.** 본래의 자리(상태)로 **4.** 응하여, 대답하여 **5.** 또 한편

A

1) ***again and again,*** very often.
2) ***as many*** (or ***much***) ***again,*** twice as much; twice as many; double.
3) ***now and again,*** occasionally.

[熟] 1)몇번이고 2)…의 두 배의 분량(수) 3)때때로

: **a·gainst** [əgénst, +*Brit.* əgéinst] *prep.* **1.** in opposition to; in an opposite direction to; toward; contrary to. ↔ for ¶*push ~ the door*① / *ride ~ the wind* / *~ reason*② / *vote ~ him.* **2.** in contact with; facing; next to. ¶ *lean ~ the wall* / *put the desk ~ the wall.* **3.** in contrast to; having as background. ¶*~ the evening sky* / *forty votes ~ twelve.* **4.** in preparation for. ¶*Save ~ a rainy day.*③

—[前] 1.…에 향하여, 대하여, 거슬러서, 반대하여 ¶①몸으로 밀어 문을 열다/②이치에 안맞는 2.…에 기대어, 의지하여; …의 이웃에 3.대조하여; …을 배경으로 하여 4.…에 대비하여 ¶③만일에 대비하여 저축하다

1) ***as against,*** [as] compared with. ¶*twenty airplanes of theirs as ~ our three.*④
2) ***over against,*** just in front of; right opposite.

[熟] 1)…에 비교하여 ¶④아군기 3대에 대해 적기 20대 2)…의 정면에

a·gape [əgéip] *adv.* with the mouth wide open in a state of wonder or surprise.

—[副] [놀라서] 입을 헤벌리고, 멍하니

a·gar-a·gar [éigɑ:réigɑ:r] *n.* [U] a jellylike substance produced from certain seaweeds, used to grow bacteria.

—[名] 우뭇가사리류, 한천[세균 배양기]

ag·ate [ǽgət, ǽgit] *n.* [C] **1.** a kind of precious stone. **2.** (*U.S.*) a child's playing marble.

—[名] 1.마노(瑪瑙) 2.(美) [마노 비슷한 어린이의] 공기돌

Ag·a·tha [ǽgəθə] *n.* a woman's name.

—[名] 여자 이름

: **age** [eidʒ] *n.* **1.** [U][C] the time of life already passed. ¶*at the ~ of forty* / *middle ~* / *a girl of your ~* / *He is just my ~.* / *He looks young for his ~.*① **2.** [C] the entire time of life. ¶(*proverb*) *Threescore and ten is the ~ of man.*② **3.** [C] a generation; a period of time in history. ¶*from ~ to ~*③ / *the Golden Age.* **4.** [U] old age; the latter part of life; advanced years. ↔youth ¶*the wisdom of ~* / *His eyes were dim with ~.* **5.** [U] the time of life when a person receives full legal rights. ⇒[N.B.] ¶*under ~*④ / *over ~.*⑤ **6.** [C] (*colloq.*) a long time. ¶*ages ago* / *for an ~* (or *ages*).

—[名] 1.나이, 연령 ¶①나이에 비해 젊어 보인다 2.수명 ¶②70세는 사람의 수명 3.세대; 시대 ¶③대대로 4.노령(老齡) 5.성년 [N.B.] 영·미에서는 만 21세 ¶④미성년의/⑤성년 이상 6.(口) 오랜 동안

1) ***of age,*** 21 years old or over. ¶*be* (or *come*) *~.*⑥
2) ***with*** (or ***from***) ***age,*** because of old age.

[熟] 1)성년의 ¶⑥성년에 이르다(이다) 2)나이 탓으로

—vi. grow old. ¶*His mother aged rapidly.* ***—vt.*** make (someone) old; make (wine, cheese, etc.) mature. ¶*Worry and illness ~ a man.*⑦ / *~ wine.*⑧

—[自] 나이를 먹다, 늙다; 해가 가다, 낡아지다 —[他] …을 낡게 하다; [술 따위]를 묵히다; …에게 나이먹게 하다 ¶⑦걱정과 질병은 사람을 늙게 만든다/⑧포도주를 묵히다

* **a·ged** *adj.* **1.** [éidʒid →2.] old; advanced in years. ¶*an ~ man* / *the ~.*① **2.** [eidʒd] of the age of. ¶*a girl ~ seven* [*years*].

—[形] 1.늙은; 오래 묵은 ¶①노인들 2. …살(세)의

age·less [éidʒlis] *adj.* never growing old; timeless.

—[形] 늙지 않은, 영원히 젊은

age·long [éidʒlɔ̀(:)ŋ / -lɔ̀ŋ] *adj.* lasting for a long time.

—[形] 다년간의; 영속하는

: **a·gen·cy** [éidʒ(ə)nsi] *n.* (pl. **-cies**) **1.** [U][C] action; operation; power; a means. **2.** [C] the business of a person or firm that acts for another; an office of such a person or firm. ¶*a sole* (*general*) *~*① / *hold an ~ for ...*②

—[名] 1.발동력; 작용; 힘; 수단 2.대리[권]; 대리점 ¶①독점 판매점(총대리점)/②…의 대리점을 하다

through (or ***by***) ***the agency of ...,*** by the good offices of.

[熟] …의 매개로, …을 거쳐서

a·gen·da [ədʒéndə] *n. pl.* (*sing.* **-dum**) ((usu. used as *sing.*)) [a program of] things or a list of things to be done.

—[名] 의사 일정, 협의 사항, 의제

a·gen·dum [ədʒéndəm] *n.* sing. of **agenda**.

: **a·gent** [éidʒ(ə)nt] *n.* [C] **1.** a person or firm that acts for another; a representative; (*colloq.*) a [traveling] salesman. **2.** a power or cause that has a certain effect.

—[名] 1.대리인(점); 외무 판매원 2.작인(作因), 동인(動因)

ag·glom·er·ate *vi., vt.* [əglámərèit / -glɔ́m- // → *n., adj.*] gather or collect into a mass or heap.

—[自他] 덩어리로 되다, 응집하다

—n. [əglámərit / -glɔ́m-] [U] a mass or collection of things.
—adj. [əglámərit / -glɔ́m-] gathered together into a mass.

—[名] 덩어리, 집괴(集塊) —[形] 덩어리진, 응집한

ag·glom·er·a·tion [əglàməréiʃ(ə)n / -glɔ̀m-] *n.* [U][C] the act of gathering into a mass; a mass; a heap.

—[名] 덩어리로 하기(되기); 응집한 것; 집적(集積)

ag·glu·ti·nate [əglú:tinèit →*adj.*] *vt.* join together (something) as with a sticky substance. ***—vi.*** become a sticky substance; combine. ***—adj.*** [əglú:tənit] joined together.

—[他] …교착(점착)시키다; 접합하다 —[自] 아교처럼 되다; 점착(粘着)하다 —[形] 교착한

ag·glu·ti·na·tion [əglùːtinéiʃ(ə)n] *n.* [U] the act or process of agglutinating; such a condition.
—[名] 접합(교착)하기; 접합된 상태

ag·gran·dize [əgrǽndaiz, ǽgrəndàiz] *vt.* make (someone or a nation) greater in power, wealth, rank, etc.; make (one's opinion) appear greater; exaggerate. ▷**ag·gran·dize·ment** [-mənt] *n.*
—[他] [권력·재산·지위 따위]를 증대하다; [의견 따위]를 과장하다

ag·gra·vate [ǽgrəvèit] *vt.* **1.** make (an existing trouble) worse or more severe. **2.** (*colloq.*) anger.
—[他] 1. …을 더욱 악화시키다 2. …을 화나게 하다

ag·gra·vat·ing [ǽgrəvèitiŋ] *adj.* making worse or more severe; (*colloq.*) troublesome; provoking; irritating.
—[形] 더욱 악화하는; 화나는, 괘씸한

ag·gra·va·tion [æ̀grəvéiʃ(ə)n] *n.* [U] [C] **1.** the act of aggrating; a thing that makes worse or more severe. **2.** the state of being irritated.
—[名] 1. 더욱 악화시키기(시키는 것) 2. 약오르는 것(일)

ag·gre·gate *vt., vi.* [ǽgrigèit → *adj., n.*] **1.** collect. **2.** (*colloq.*) amount to. ¶*The money collected has aggregated one million won.*① —*adj.* [ǽgrigit] total; formed into a mass. —*n.* [ǽgrigit] ⦅usu. *the* ~⦆ the total; a mass formed of separate things.
—[他][自] 1. 모으다 2. 합계 …이 되다 ¶①모은 돈은 모두 100만원이 되었다
—[形] 총계의, 총합의 —[名] 총계; 집합체

in the aggregate, as a whole; totally.
[熟] 전체로서; 총계하여

ag·gre·ga·tion [æ̀grigéiʃ(ə)n] *n.* [U] [C] the act of aggregating; separate things collected into one whole.
—[名] 집합, 집성(集成); 집합체

ag·gres·sion [əgréʃ(ə)n] *n.* [U] [C] an attack without just cause; the act of starting a fight by entering the territory of another country; an assult. ¶*a war of* ~.①
—[名] [까닭없는, 불법적인] 공격, 침략; 침해 ¶①침략 전쟁

ag·gres·sive [əgrésiv] *adj.* **1.** quick to attack; offensive; quarrelsome. **2.** (*U.S.*) energetic; enterprising. ¶*an* ~ *salesman.*
—[形] 1. 침략적인; 공격의; 툭하면 다투는 2. 활동적인, 적극적인

assume (or ***take***) ***the aggressive,*** start a fight; take the offensive; become active before others.
[熟] 공격으로 나오다; 공세를 취하다

▷**ag·gres·sive·ly** [-li] *adv.* —**ag·gres·sive·ness** [-nis] *n.*

ag·gres·sor [əgrésər] *n.* [C] a person or country that makes the first move in a quarrel or war.
—[名] 침략자(국); 공격자(국)

ag·grieve [əgríːv] *vt.* ⦅usu. in *passive*⦆ trouble or injure (someone) by unjust treatment. ¶*be* (or *feel*) *aggrieved.*①
—[他] …을 괴롭히다, 못살게 굴다 ¶①불만을 품다, 분개하다

a·ghast [əgǽst / əgɑ́ːst] *adj.* ⦅in *predicative*⦆ struck with sudden surprise, terror, etc. ⦅~ *at*⦆ ¶*stand* ~ *at the sight* (*the news*).
—[形] 어안이벙벙해진

ag·ile [ǽdʒəl, ǽʒil / ǽdʒail] *adj.* able to move quickly and easily.
—[形] 민첩한, 재빠른; 경쾌한

a·gil·i·ty [ədʒíliti] *n.* [U] the quickness or readiness of movement.
—[名] 재빠름, 민첩함; 경쾌성

ag·i·tate [ǽdʒitèit] *vt.* **1.** move or shake violently. **2.** disturb; excite. ¶*be agitated by* (or *with*) …① —*vi.* stir up the public by means of slogans, demonstrations, etc. ⦅~ *for* something⦆ ¶~ *for reform.*
—[他] 1. …을 뒤흔들다 2. [마음]을 어지럽히다; 선동하다 ¶① …으로 [마음이] 어지럽다 —[自] [데모 따위로] 여론을 불러일으키다

***ag·i·ta·tion** [æ̀dʒitéiʃ(ə)n] *n.* **1.** [U] [C] a disturbed or troubled state of the mind; excitement. **2.** [U] discussion to arouse public interest.
—[名] 1. [인심의] 동요; 흥분 2. [사회적·정치적인] 선동

ag·i·ta·tor [ǽdʒitèitər] *n.* [C] a person who tries to make a political or industrial disturbance by making people dissatisfied with the present state of affairs.
—[名] 선동가

a·glow [əglóu] *adj.* ⦅as *predicative*⦆ glowing; flushed. ¶*be* ~ *with delight.* —*adv.* in a glow.
—[形] [얼굴 따위가] 붉어져서, 홍조를 띠어 —[副] 불타올라

Ag·nes [ǽgnis] *n.* a woman's name.
—[名] 여자 이름

ag·nos·tic [ægnɑ́stik / -nɔ́s-] *n.* [C] a person who believes that a man cannot know the final nature of things, or who does not say either that God is or that God is not. —*adj.* of such a belief.
—[名] 불가지론자(不可知論者)
—[形] 불가지론(不可知論)의

‡**a·go** [əgóu] *adj.* ⦅always placed after the *noun*⦆ past; back; gone by. ¶*a few years* ~. —*adv.* ⦅used after the adverb *long*⦆ in past time. ¶*It happened long* ~.
—[形] 이전의; [지금으로부터] … 전[의] —[副] 이전에

a·gog [əgɑ́g / -gɔ́g] *adj.* ⦅as *predicative*⦆ excited by eagerness, expectation, etc. —*adv.* in a state of eagerly desiring. ¶*be all* ~ *for* …① / *all* ~ *to know.*②
—[形][副] 흥분하여, 야단법석이 나서 ¶① …을 갈망하다/②…을 알기를 열망하여

ag·o·nize [ǽgənàiz] *vi.* **1.** suffer greatly. **2.** make a great effort. **—***vt.* make (someone) suffer extremely. ¶*~ oneself.*①
—[自] 1. 고민하다 2. 죽을 힘을 다하다 —[他] …을 괴롭히다 ¶①고민하다

ag·o·niz·ing [ǽgənàiziŋ] *adj.* being in agony; suffering greatly.
—[形] 괴로움을 주는, 고민하는

• **ag·o·ny** [ǽgəni] *n.* [U] [C] (pl. **-nies**) **1.** great pain of body or mind; great excitement. ¶*in an ~ of joy.*① **2.** death struggle.
—[名] 1. 고민; 격정, [슬픔·기쁨의] 절정 2. 단말마의 고통

a·grar·i·an [əgrέəriən] *adj.* of land, its use, or its ownership.
—[形] 토지의, 경작지의

⁑ **a·gree** [əgríː] *vi.* **1.** consent; say 'yes'. 《*~ to* something; *to do*》 ¶*~ to a plan* / *She agreed to go.* **2.** have the same opinion. 《*~ with* someone》 ¶*I ~ with you.* **3.** be in harmony; correspond. 《*~ with* something》 ¶*Her story agreed with his.* **4.** meet the taste; suit. 《*~ with* someone》 ¶*So much candy does not ~ with me.* **5.** get on well together; decide together. 《*~ on* a price, terms, etc.》 ¶*~ on a price.* **—***vt.* admit. 《*~ that* or *how* …》 ⇒[N.B.] ¶*I ~ that it is too late.*
—[自] 1. 동의하다, 찬성하다, 승낙하다 2. 같은 의견이다 3. [사물이] 일치하다, 부합하다 4. [음식·기후가] 성미에 맞다 5. 마음이 맞다; 사이가 좋다 —[他] 동의(승인)하다 [N.B.] agree to it that …의 to it가 탈락되어 생겼다고 생각됨

• **a·gree·a·ble** [əgríəbl] *adj.* **1.** pleasant. ¶*~ manners* / *~ to the ears.*① **2.** suitable. ¶*an act ~ to the law.*
agreeable to, according to (a promise, etc.).
—[形] 1. 기분 좋은, 유쾌한 ¶①듣기 좋은 2. 알맞는
[熟] …에 따라서

a·gree·a·bly [əgríəbli] *adv.* pleasantly.
—[副] 기분 좋게, 유쾌하게

⁑ **a·gree·ment** [əgríːmənt] *n.* **1.** [U] [C] mutual understanding; harmony of opinions or feelings. ¶*a conditional ~.*① **2.** [C] a contract. ¶*bring about an ~.*② **3.** [U] (*Grammar*) correspondence of one word with another in gender, number, etc.
1) ***arrive at*** (or ***come to***) ***an agreement,*** come to an understanding or make an arrangement.
2) ***in agreement with,*** in accord with; according to.
—[名] 1. 동의; [감정·의견 따위의] 일치 ¶①조건부 동의 2. 협정, 계약 ¶②협정을 맺다 3. 《文法》 [성·수·격 따위의] 일치
[熟] 1)합의되다, 협정이 성립되다 2)…와 일치하여, …에 좇아서

• **ag·ri·cul·tur·al** [æ̀grikʌ́ltʃ(ə)r(ə)l] *adj.* of agriculture.
▷**ag·ri·cul·tur·al·ly** [-rəli] *adv.*
—[形] 농업의, 농학의

⁑ **ag·ri·cul·ture** [ǽgrikʌ̀ltʃər] *n.* [U] the science and art of raising crops and animals on a farm.
—[名] 농업, 농예, 농학

a·ground [əgráund] *adv.* (of a ship) on or onto the ground. ¶*The ship goes* (or *runs*) *~.*①
—[副] 좌초하여 ¶①배가 좌초한다

a·gue [éigjuː] *n.* [U] a malarial fever; a fit of fever; a fit of shivering.
—[名] 학질; 오한

⁑ **ah** [ɑː] *interj.* a natural exclamation of sudden emotion, such as sorrow, joy, or contempt.
—[感] 아아(슬픔·기쁨·경멸 따위의 감정을 나타냄)

a·ha [ɑ(ː)háː, əháː] *interj.* an exclamation of triumph, surprise, or contempt.
—[感] 아하, 흐흥

⁑ **a·head** [əhéd] *adv.* in or to the front; toward the front; forward; onward; into the future. ¶*There is a crossing ~.*
1) ***ahead of,*** before; in advance of. ¶*Run ~ of us.* / *The ship left ~ of time*① / *She is ~ of her class in French.*②
2) ***be ahead,*** be in front.
3) ***get ahead,*** succeed, as in business.
4) ***get ahead of,*** exceed; surpass. ¶*He will get ~ of others in English.*
5) ***go ahead,*** ⓐ move onward. ¶*Go ~.*③ ⓑ improve; make progress. ⓒ continue. ¶*Go ~ with the cake.*④
—[副] 앞에, 전방에; 앞서서; 앞장서서; 전도에; [시간적으로] 먼저
[熟] 1)…의 앞에; …보다 먼저 ¶①배는 정각보다 먼저 떠났다/②그녀는 프랑스어에 있어서 학급에서 앞서 있다 2)앞에 있다 3)출세하다 4)…을 앞서다; 능가하다 5)ⓐ앞으로 나아가다 ¶③[이야기를] 계속해라!; 전진!; 자, 시작!; [상대에게] 먼저 하시오 ⓑ진보하다 ⓒ계속하다 ¶④케이크를 계속 드시오

a·hem [əhém, hm, mm'm] *interj.* a slight cough to attract attention, express doubt, gain time, etc.
—[感] 에헴, 흐흥(기침소리 또는 주의를 환기시키는 소리)

a·hoy [əhɔ́i] *interj.* (*Nautical*) a call used by sailors for calling a ship. ¶*Ship ~!*
—[感] 《海》 어어이! [다른 배를 부를 때의 소리]

⁑ **aid** [eid] *n.* **1.** [U] help; support; assistance. ¶*go to someone's ~*① / *give* (or *render*) *~ to someone.*② **2.** [C] something that helps; a helper; an assistant. ¶*an ~ in solving the problem*③ / *an ~ to health.*
—*vt.* help; assist. ¶*~ someone in an enterprise* / *He aided his wife in dressing.* **—***vi.* give help or assistance.
—[名] 1. 도와줌, 조력; 원조 ¶① 남을 도우러 가다/② …을 돕다 2. 도움이 되는 것; 조력자, 조수 ¶③문제 해결의 실마리
—[他] …을 돕다, 거들다 —[自] 돕다, 도와주다

aide [eid] *n.* [C] **1.** =an aide-de-camp. **2.** a helper; an assistant.
—[名] 1. 부관 2. 조수; 조력자

aide-de-camp [éiddəkǽmp / -kɑ́:(ŋ)] *n.* [C] (pl. **aides-de-camp** [éidzdəkǽmp]) (*Military*) an army or navy assistant officer.
—[名] 부관

ail [eil] *vt.* give or cause pain or discomfort to (someone); trouble. —*vi.* be ill; feel sick. ⇒[N.B.]
—[他] …을 괴롭히다, 번민하게 하다 —[自] 앓다 [N.B.] 가벼운 병을 말할 때 씀

ai·ler·on [éilərɑ̀n / -rɔ̀n] *n.* [C] the movable section of an airplane wing.
—[名] [비행기의] 보조익

ail·ment [éilmənt] *n.* [C] a slight disease or disorder of the body or mind; illness; sickness.
—[名] 병; 편찮음

⁑ **aim** [eim] *vt.* **1.** point (a missile, weapon, blow, etc.) at a particular object; direct (words, acts, etc.). ⟪~ a gun at⟫ ¶*The remark was aimed at me.*① **2.** try to do (something); intend. ¶*He aims to lead the class in English.*② —*vi.* **1.** direct a missile, remark, etc.; point a weapon at an object. **2.** direct efforts toward a particular object; intend; try. ⟪~ *at* something⟫ ¶~ *high* (*low*)③ / *We ~ at success.*
—[他] 1. [총 따위]를 돌리다, 겨냥하다; 빗대어 말하다 ¶①그 말은 내게 빗대어 한 말이다 2. 뜻하다, 목표삼다 ¶②그는 영어에서는 학급에서 1등이 되려 하고 있다 —[自] 1. 겨냥하다 2. 뜻하다; 목표삼다 ¶③큰(작은) 뜻을 품다

—*n.* **1.** [U] the act of pointing a weapon, etc. ¶*take good ~ at the target.*④ **2.** [C] something aimed at; an object; a purpose; an intention. ¶*miss one's ~*⑤ / *What is your ~ in life? / He studied English with the ~ of going abroad.*⑥
—[名] 1. 겨냥, 조준 ¶④과녁을 잘 겨냥하다 2. 과녁; 목적[물]; 목적 ¶⑤과녁을 못 맞히다/⑥그는 해외에 갈 목적으로 영어를 공부했다

aim·less [éimlis] *adj.* without aim or purpose. ▷**aim·less·ly** [-li] *adv.* —**aim·less·ness** [-nis] *n.*
—[形] 목적이 없는; 시시한

* **ain't** [eint] (*colloq.*)=am not; (*slang*)=is (are, have, has) not.

Ai·nu [áinu:] *n.* [C] (pl. **Ainus** or *collectively* **Ainu**) a member of a primitive race in north Japan, now beocming extinct; [U] their language.
—[名] 아이누 사람; 아이누 말

⁑ **air** [ɛər] *n.* **1.** [U] the mixture of gases surrounding the earth; the atmosphere. ¶*breathe fresh* (*foul*) ~ / *a breath of ~.*① **2.** [U] space above the earth; the sky. ¶*leap into the ~*② / *fly in the ~.* **3.** [U] circulation. ¶*Queer rumors are in the ~.*③ **4.** (*Music*) [C] a melody; a tune. ¶*a sweet ~.*④ **5.** [C] an outward appearance; a look; a bearing; a style; a manner. ¶*with a sad* (*cheerful*) ~.⑤ **6.** ⟪*pl.*⟫ affected manner. ¶*assume* (or *put on*) *airs.*⑥
—[名] 1. 공기; 대기 ¶①산들바람 2. 공중, 공간, 하늘 ¶②공중으로 도약하다 3. 퍼짐, 유포 ¶③이상한 소문이 퍼지고 있다 4. ⟪樂⟫ 선율, 가락 ¶④아름다운 선율 5. 외양, 모양; 태도 ¶⑤슬픈(기쁜) 모습으로 6. 젠체하는 태도 ¶⑥젠체하는 태도

1) ***beat the air,*** make vain efforts.
2) ***by air,*** by airplane.
3) [*a*] ***change of air,*** a change of (or in) climate. ¶*a change of ~ for the health.*⑦
4) ***in the air,*** ⓐ in circulation. ⓑ =[up] in the air.
5) ***live on air,*** live without food.
6) ***off the air,*** (*Radio*) not being broadcast.
7) ***on the air,*** (*Radio*) being broadcast.
8) ***take the air,*** ⓐ go outdoors. ⓑ (*Radio*) start broadcasting. ⓒ (*slang*) leave hurriedly ⓓ (of an airplane) take off.
9) ***take to the air,*** become an aviator.
10) [*up*] ***in the air,*** not yet decided; vague.
11) ***walk*** (or ***tread***) ***on air,*** feel very happy.

[熟] 1)헛수고하다 2)비행기로 3)전지(轉地) ¶⑦전지 요법 4)ⓐ[풍문 따위가] 퍼져서 ⓑ막연하여 5)아무것도 먹지 않고 있다 6)방송되지 않는 7)방송 중인 8)ⓐ외출하다, 산책하다 ⓑ방송을 개시하다 ⓒ⟪俗⟫ 급히 가버리다 ⓓ이륙하다 9)비행가가 되다 10)미결정으로 남겨두고, 막연하여 11)기뻐 날뛰다

—*vt.* **1.** expose (something) to the air; dry or purify. ¶*You must ~ the room.* **2.** make (something) public; display. ¶*Don't ~ your troubles too often.*
—[他] 1. …을 바람에 쐬다; 누기를 없애다 2. …을 공표하다; 자랑삼아 보이다

air balloon [∸ ─∸] *n.* a toy balloon.
—[名] [장난감] 고무 풍선

air·borne [ɛ́ərbɔ:rn] *adj.* carried by air. ¶~ *troops.*
—[形] 공수(空輸)된

air brake [∸ ∸] *n.* a brake operated by compressed air.
—[名] 공기 제동기

air-con·di·tion [ɛ́ərkəndìʃ(ə)n] *vt.* **1.** furnish (a room, building, etc.) with an air-conditioning apparatus. **2.** treat (air) with such an apparatus.
—[他] 1. [방·건물]에 공기 조절 장치를 시설하다 2. …을 공기 조절하다

air-con·di·tioned [ɛ́ərkəndìʃ(ə)nd] *adj.* having an air conditioning system.
—[形] 공기 조절 장치가 있는; 냉(난)방장치가 있는

air conditioning [ɛ́ərkəndìʃ(ə)niŋ] *n.* a system to control the temperature, humidity, etc. in a building or house, esp. to cool.
—[名] [온도·습도 따위의] 공기 조절 장치법

air·craft [ɛ́ərkræft / ɛ́əkrɑ̀:ft] *n.* ⓒ (pl. **-craft**) any machine for flight in the air, such as an airplane, an airship, a balloon, etc. ⇒USAGE
—图 항공기 USAGE 단수의 뜻으로 쓰이는 일은 비교적 드뭄

aircraft carrier [⌐ ⌐⌐] *n.* a warship designed to carry airplanes and to serve as a landing field. 「field.」
—图 항공모함

air·drome [ɛ́ərdròum] *n.* ⓒ (*U.S.*) an airport; an air-
—图 (美) 비행장; 공항

air·field [ɛ́ərfì:ld] *n.* ⓒ a field from which airplanes take off and on which they land.
—图 비행장

air force [⌐ ⌐] *n.* a unit of military or naval forces that uses airplanes. ¶*The Royal Air Force*.① ⇒N.B. / *the United States* (or *U.S.*) *Air Force*.②
—图 공군 ¶①영국 공군 N.B. the R.A.F.로 줄여 씀/②미국 공군

air gun [⌐ ⌐] *n.* a gun operated by compressed air.
—图 공기총

air hostess [⌐ ⌐⌐] *n.* an air stewardess.
—图 [여객기의] 여자 안내원

air·i·ly [ɛ́ərili] *adv.* in an airy manner; lightly.
—图 경쾌하게; 쾌활하게

air·ing [ɛ́əriŋ] *n.* ⓒ **1.** the act of exposing to the air for drying, freshening, etc. ¶*give something an* ~.① **2.** a walk, drive, etc., in the open air.
—图 1. 공기에 쐬기 ¶①…을 공기에 쐬다 2. 외출

air·less [ɛ́ərlis] *adj.* without a breeze or fresh air; stuffy.
—图 바람 없는; 통풍이 잘 안 되는

air letter [⌐ ⌐⌐] *n.* **1.** an airmail letter; an aerogram. **2.** a very light letter-sheet for air mail.
—图 1. 항공우편 2. 항공우편 용지

air·lift [ɛ́ərlìft] *n.* ⓒ a system for carrying persons or cargo by aircraft, esp. in an emergency; something carried by such a system. —*vt.* carry (something) by airlift.
——图 공수; 공수물자 —働 …을 공수하다

air·line [ɛ́ərlàin] *n.* ⓒ **1.** a system for carrying persons and cargo regularly by aircraft. **2.** (*pl.* used as *sing.*) a company that operates such a system. ¶*Korean Air Lines* **3.** a direct line. 「airlines.」
—图 1. 항공로, 정기 항공 2. 항공회사 3. 일직선

air·lin·er [ɛ́ərlàinər] *n.* ⓒ a passenger aircraft of an
—图 [대형] 정기 여객기

air mail [⌐ ⌐] *n.* the system of sending mail by aircraft; mail carried by aircraft.
—图 항공우편[물]

air·mail, air-mail [ɛ́ərmèil] *adj.* of air mail. ¶*an ~ letter.* —*vt.* send (a letter) by air [mail]. ¶*I airmailed your letter.*
—图 항공우편의 —働 [편지]를 항공우편으로 부치다

air·man [ɛ́ərmən] *n.* ⓒ (pl. **-men** [-mən]) the pilot of an airplane; (*U.S. Air Force*) a member of a [military] aircrew. ⇒N.B.
—图 비행사; (美空軍) 항공병 N.B. 항공병의 경우 남녀에 모두 쓰이며 air-woman은 여류 비행사의 뜻

air·mind·ed [ɛ́ərmàindid] *adj.* interested in flying aircraft; fond of flying aircraft or of air travel.
—图 항공에 흥미를 가진; 항공(비행)열(熱)의

:air·plane [ɛ́ərplèin] *n.* ⓒ (*U.S.*) a winged machine for flight. ⇒N.B.
—图 비행기 N.B. 영국에서는 aeroplane으로 씀

air pocket [⌐ ⌐ ⌐] *n.* an upright current in the air that causes an airplane to make a sudden drop.
—图 에어포켓(수직 기류에 의해 비행기가 급강하하는 곳)

:air·port [ɛ́ərpɔ̀:rt] *n.* ⓒ a place where airplanes land and take off; an airdrome. ¶*Haneda Airport*.
—图 공항

air pump [⌐ ⌐] *n.* a machine for exhausting, compressing, or drawing in air.
—图 공기 펌프, 배기(排氣) 펌프

air-raid [ɛ́ərèid] *adj.* for or against a raid by aircraft. ¶*an* ~ *shelter*① / *an* ~ *warning* (or *alarm*).②
—图 공습의 ¶①방공호/②공습 경보

air raid [⌐ ⌐] *n.* an attack by aircraft, esp. to bomb a certain area.
—图 공습

air·ship [ɛ́ərʃìp] *n.* ⓒ a balloon that is driven by engines in the air. ⇒N.B., fig.
—图 비행선 N.B. 현재는 일반적으로 dirigible이라 함

[airship]

air·sick [ɛ́ərsìk] *adj.* sick as a result of air travel.
—图 항공병(航空病)에 걸린, 비행기 멀미를 하는

air·sick·ness [ɛ́ərsìknis] *n.* Ⓤ the state of being airsick.
—图 비행기 멀미

air·strip [ɛ́ərstrìp] *n.* ⓒ a long runway on which planes land and from which they take off.
—图 [가설] 활주로

air·tight [ɛ́ərtàit] *adj.* **1.** so closed that no air can enter. **2.** having no weak points [open to an enemy's attack, open to criticism, etc.].
—图 1. 밀폐한 2. 공격할 틈이 없는

air·way [έərwèi] *n.* [C] **1.** a main route for aircraft. **2.** a passage used for changing the air in a room, etc.; an air course.
—[名] 1. 항공로 2. 통풍구

air·y [έəri] *adj.* (**air·i·er, air·i·est**) **1.** in or of the air; open to the air; high up. **2.** like air; imaginary. ¶~ *dreams.* **3.** light in manner; lively; gay. ¶~ *songs.*
—[形] 1. 공기의; 공중의; 통풍이 잘 되는 2. 공기 같은; 꿈 같은 3. 경쾌한; 쾌활한

* **aisle** [ail] *n.* [C] **1.** a passage between rows of seats in a church, theater, hall, etc. **2.** part of a church separated from the main interior area by a row of pillars. **3.** any long or narrow passageway.
—[名] 1. [교회·극장·집회장 따위의] 통로 2. [교회의] 측면 복도 3. 좁다란 통로

a·jar[1] [ədʒά:r] *adj., adv.* (of a gate or door) slightly opened. ¶*leave the door* ~.①
—[形][副] [문 따위가] 조금 열려 ¶①문을 조금 열어 두다

a·jar[2] [ədʒά:r] *adj., adv.* out of harmony. ¶~ *with the world.*
—[形][副] 조화되지 않고

a·kim·bo [əkímbou] *adv., adj.* with the hands on the hips and the elbows turned outward. ¶*with hands* ~.
—[副][形] 두 손을 허리에 대고 팔꿈치를 펴고

a·kin [əkín] *adj.* 《as *predicative*》 **1.** of the same kin; related. ¶*She is* ~ *to me.*① **2.** similar. ¶*Most girls are* ~ *in their love of dolls.*
—[形] 1. 동족의 ¶①그녀는 나의 친족이다 2. 유사한

Al·a·bam·a [æ̀ləbǽmə] *n.* a southern State of the United States. ⇒[N.B.]
—[名] 앨러배머 주 [N.B.] Ala.로 줄여 씀 수도는 Montgomery

al·a·bas·ter [ǽləbæ̀stər / -bὰ:stə] *n.* [U] a white, glass-like mineral.
—[名] 설화석고(雪花石膏)

à la carte [ὰ:lɑ:kά:rt] *adv., adj.* by the menu. ↔table d'hôte ¶*an* ~ *dinner.*①
—[副][形] 메뉴에 따라서(따른) ¶①일품요리

a·lac·ri·ty [əlǽkriti] *n.* [U] cheerful readiness or willingness; liveliness.
—[名] 민활, 민첩

A·lad·din [əlǽd(i)n] *n.* a youth with a magic lamp in "*The Arabian Nights.*"
—[名] 알라딘(마법의 남포로 무슨 소망이든 이룬 「천일야화」 속의 인물)

à la mode [ὰ:ləmóud] *adj.* **1.** according to the fashion; fashionable. **2.** (of dessert, pie, etc.) served with a portion of ice cream; (of beef) stewed with vegetables.
—[形] 1. 유행의 2. 아이스크리임을 얹은; 야채와 함께 삶은

Al·an [ǽlən] *n.* a man's name.
—[名] 남자 이름

⁑ **a·larm** [əlά:rm] *n.* **1.** [C] a sound telling of danger; any device that gives such a warning. ¶*a fire* ~.① **2.** [U] sudden fright. ¶*in* ~② / *without* ~③ / *take* [*the*] ~ *at something.*④ —*vt.* strike (something) with sudden fear. ¶*be alarmed at the sound.*⑤
—[名] 1. 경보[기] ¶①화재 경보 2. 놀람 ¶②놀라서/③침착하게/④…에 깜짝 놀라다 —[他] …을 깜짝 놀라게 하다 ¶⑤그 소리에 깜짝 놀라다

alarm clock [-ˊ ˋ] *n.* a clock with a bell.
—[名] 자명종

a·larm·ist [əlά:rmist] *n.* [C] a person who is always warning of danger without sufficient reason.
—[名] 부질없이 세상을 놀래는 사람; 군걱정을 하는 사람

⁑ **a·las** [əlǽs / əlά:s] *interj.* exclamation of unhappiness, pity, or grief.
—[感] 아아, 슬프도다

A·las·ka [əlǽskə] *n.* a State of the United States in northwest North America. ⇒[N.B.]
—[名] 알래스카 주 [N.B.] Alas.로 줄여 씀, 수도 Juneau

Al·ba·ni·a [ælbéiniə] *n.* a country in southeastern Europe. ⇒[N.B.]
—[名] 알바니아 [N.B.] Alb.로 줄여 씀, 수도 Jirona

Al·ba·ni·an [ælbéiniən] *adj.* of Albania, its people, or their language. —*n.* [C] a person of Albania; [U] the language of Albania.
—[形] 알바니아[사람·말]의 —[名] 알바니아 사람; 알바니아 말

al·ba·tross [ǽlbətrɔ̀s] *n.* [C] any of several large white sea birds that can fly long distance and which chiefly appears over the Pacific and southern oceans.
—[名] 신천옹(信天翁)(남태평양에서 사는 바다새)

Al·bert [ǽlbərt] *n.* a man's name. ⇒[N.B.]
—[名] 남자 이름 [N.B.] 애칭은 Bert.

al·bi·no [ælbáinou / -bí:-] *n.* [C] (pl. **-nos**) a person or other animal that is pale and has not the usual coloring from birth.
—[名] 피부 색소 결핍증에 걸린 사람(동물)

Al·bi·on [ǽlbiən,] *n.* (*poetic*) England.
—[名] 《詩》 영국

⁑ **al·bum** [ǽlbəm] *n.* [C] a blank book for storing autographs, photographs, stamps, or the like.
—[名] 앨범, 사진(서화·우표)첩

al·bu·men [ælbjú:min, ǽlbjumin] *n.* [U] **1.** the white of an egg. **2.** (*Botany*) a nourishing substance in a seed.
—[名] 1. 알의 흰자위 2. 《植》 배유(胚乳)

al·che·mist [ǽlkimist] *n.* [C] a person who studied alchemy in the Middle Ages.
—[名] 연금술사(鍊金術師)

al·che·my [ǽlkimi] *n.* [U] the chemistry of the Middle Ages, the aim of which was to change the cheaper metals into gold.
—[名] 연금술

* **al·co·hol** [ǽlkəhɔ̀:l, -hὰl / -hɔ̀l] *n.* [U] a colorless liquid
—[名] 알코홀

in wine, whisky, etc.; drinks which contain alcohol.
al·co·hol·ic [ælkəhɔ́lik, -hɔ́:l- / -hɔ́l-] *adj.* of or containing alcohol. —*n.* ⓒ a person who drinks too much wine. ―❷ 알코올의 ; 알코올을 함유한 ―❷ 술고래
al·co·hol·ism [ǽlkəhɔ̀:liz(ə)m, -hɑ̀l- / -hɔ̀l-] *n.* Ⓤ a diseased condition resulting from drinking too much liquor. ―❷ 알코올 중독
al·cove [ǽlkouv] *n.* ⓒ **1.** a space in a room for a bed, bookcases, etc. ⇒fig. **2.** a small house in the garden. ―❷ 1.[큰 방에 딸린] 작은 방, 후미진 곳 2.[정원의] 정자

[alcove 1.]

al·der [ɔ́:ldər] *n.* ⓒ a tree usu. growing in wet places. ―❷ 오리나무
al·der·man [ɔ́:ldərmən] *n.* ⓒ (pl. -men [-mən]) **1.** (*Brit.*) an officer next in rank to the mayor. **2.** (*U.S.*) a member of a law-making body in a city. ―❷ 1.(英) 부시장, 시참사회원 2.(美) 시의원
*** ale** [eil] *n.* Ⓤ a drink, more bitter than beer, made from hops and malt. [other drinks are sold.] ―❷ 맥주의 일종
ale·house [éilhàus] *n.* ⓒ a house or place where ale and ―❷ 맥주 호울, 술집
***a·lert** [ələ́:rt] *adj.* watchful; brisk. —*n.* Ⓤ (*the ~*) watchfulness. ―❷ 방심 않는, 빈틈없는 ―❷ 경계
be on the alert, be wide-awake; be watchful. 國 빈틈없이 감시하다
a·lert·ly [ələ́:rtli] *adv.* in an alert manner; watchfully. ―❶ 빈틈없이
a·lert·ness [ələ́:rtnis] *n.* Ⓤ the state of being alert. ―❷ 경계 ; 기민, 민첩
Al·ex·an·der [æ̀ligzǽndər / -zɑ́:ndə] *n.* a man's name. ―❷ 남자 이름
*** Alexander the Great** [―́―́―́ ―́] *n.* (356-323 B.C.) a king of Macedonia (336-323 B.C.) ―❷ 알렉산더 대왕(기원전 4세기의 마케도니아의 왕)
Al·ex·an·dri·a [æ̀ligzǽndriə / -zɑ́:n-] *n.* a seaport in the Nile delta in Egypt, founded by Alexander the Great in 323 B.C. ―❷ 알렉산드리아(알렉산더대왕이 창건한 이집트의 항구 도시)
al·fal·fa [ælfǽlfə] *n.* Ⓤ (*U.S.*) a clover-like plant of the pea family, used as food for horses and cattle. ⇒fig. ―❷ 자주개자리(가축 사료용의 식물)
Al·fred [ǽlfrid] *n.* a man's name. ―❷ 남자 이름
al·ga [ǽlgə] *n.* sing. of **algae**.
al·gae [ǽldʒi:] *n. pl.* (sing. **al·ga**) a kind of water plant. ―❷ 말무리, 해초
*** al·ge·bra** [ǽldʒibrə] *n.* Ⓤ a branch of mathematics. ―❷ 대수학
al·ge·bra·ic [æ̀ldʒibréiik], **-i·cal** [-ik(ə)l] *adj.* of algebra. ▷**al·ge·bra·i·cal·ly** [-ikəli] *adv.* ―❷ 대수학[상]의
Al·ger·i·a [ældʒíəriə] *n.* a country in northwest Africa. ⇒**N.B.** [alfalfa] ―❷ 알제리아 **N.B.** 아프리카 북부의 공화국, 수도 Algiers
a·li·as [éiliæs] *adv.* otherwise called. ¶*William ~ Big Bill.* —*n.* ⓒ other name. ¶*go by the ~ of George.* ―❶ 일명…, 별명은 … ―❷ 별명, 가명
al·i·bi [ǽlibài] *n.* ⓒ **1.** (*Law*) the fact of having been somewhere else when a crime was committed. **2.** (*U.S. colloq.*) an excuse. ―❷ 1. 현장 부재 증명, 알리바이 2.(美口) 구실, 핑계
Al·ice [ǽlis] *n.* a woman's name. ―❷ 여자 이름
*** al·ien** [éiliən] *adj.* **1.** foreign. ¶*~ friends.*① **2.** different in nature [from others]. ¶*a style ~ from genuine English.*② **3.** in opposition. ¶*~ to his thoughts.* —*n.* ⓒ a foreigner. ―❷ 1. 외국의 ¶①[국내에 있는] 외국인 2. 성질을 달리하는 ¶②참된 영어와는 다른 문체 3. 서로 용납되지 않는 ―❷ 거류 외인
al·ien·ate [éiliənèit] *vt.* **1.** turn away; make (someone) unfriendly. ¶*~ A from B*③ / *I'm alienated from her.*④ **2.** (*Law*) give the ownership of (something) to another. ―❶ 1. …을 멀리하다, 따돌리다 ¶③A와 B를 이간하다/④나는 그녀와 사이가 틀렸다 2.[재산]을 양도하다
al·ien·a·tion [èiliənéiʃ(ə)n] *n.* Ⓤ **1.** the act of alienating; the state of being alienated. **2.** (*Law*) change in the ownership of property. ―❷ 1. 따돌림, 소원(疎遠) 2. 양도
*** a·light**¹ [əláit] *vi.* **1.** get off or down. 《*~ from* something》 ¶*~ from a train* (*horse, carriage, plane*). **2.** (of birds, airplanes, etc.) come down and settle. 《*~ on* some place》 ¶*The plane alighted on the ground.*/ *Some birds alighted on the tree.* ―❶ 1. …에서 내리다 2.[새가] 내려앉다 ; [비행기가] 착륙하다

a·light[2] [əláit] *adj.* ((as *predicative*)) lighted; on fire. ¶*set a candle alight*① | *Her face was alight with joy.*
—[形] 불 붙인; 불타는 ¶①양초에 불을 켜다

a·lign [əláin] *vt., vi.* bring (something) into a straight line; form in a line. ¶*The students aligned themselves.*
—[他][自] 일직선으로 하다(되다)

a·lign·ment [əláinmənt] *n.* [U] the act of aligning; the state of being aligned; adjustment to a straight line.
—[名] 일직선으로 하기, 정렬; 직선, 일렬

‡ **a·like** [əláik] *adj.* ((as *predicative*)) resembling each other; similar. ¶*They are very much* ~.① —*adv.* in the same way; equally. ¶*treat all people* ~.
—[形] 서로 비슷한; 한결같은 ¶①그들은 아주 닮았다 —[副] 한결같이; 똑같이

al·i·ment [ǽlimənt] *n.* [U] food; nutriment.
—[名] 영양물, 음식물

al·i·men·ta·ry [æliméntəri] *adj.* of food or nutrition.
—[形] 영양의, 음식의

a·line [əláin] *v.* =align.

a·line·ment [əláinmənt] *n.* =alignment.

‡ **a·live** [əláiv] *adj.* ((as *predicative*)) **1.** living. ↔dead ¶*He was buried* ~.① | *He is the greatest man* ~. **2.** lively; active. ¶*keep the fire* ~② | *He is* ~ *and well.*③
1) ***alive to*** (=*aware of*) *something.* ¶~ *to dangers* | ~ *to one's interests.*④
2) ***alive with*** (=*full of*) *something.* ¶*a lake* ~ *with* ⌈*boats* (or *fish*).⌋
3) ***Look alive!***, Hurry up!; Be quick!
—[形] 1. 살아 있는 ¶①그는 생매장됐다 2. 활동적인, 활발한 ¶②불을 끄지 않고 두다/③죽지 않고 살아 있다
[熟] 1)알아채다 ¶④이해관계에 빠른 2)떼지어 있는; 가득 찬 3)서둘러라

al·ka·li [ǽlkəlài] *n.* [C] (pl. **-lis** or **-lies**) a chemical substance that turns red litmus blue.
—[名] 알칼리

al·ka·line [ǽlkəlàin] *adj.* of or containing an alkali.
—[形] 알칼리[성]의

al·ka·loid [ǽlkəlɔ̀id] *n.* [C][U] any basic, organic substance containing nitrogen.
—[名] 알칼로이드(식물의 염기성 유해물질)

‡ **all** [ɔ:l] *adj.* **1.** ((with *sing. noun*)) ⓐ the whole of. ¶~ *day* (*night*) | ~ *yesterday* | ~ *the year* | ~ *one's life* | ~ *this time.* ⓑ only. ¶*All work and no play makes Jack a dull boy.*① ⓒ the greatest possible; as much as possible. ¶*with* ~ *haste* | *in* ~ *kindness.* **2.** ((with *pl. noun*)) ⓐ every one of. ¶~ *men* | ~ *the students* | ~ *his friends* | *These are* ~ *the books I have.*② ⓑ only. ¶~ *words and no thought.*③ ⓒ full of. ¶*He was* ~ *smiles* (*ears*).④
—[形] 1. ⓐ 전체의, 전부의; 모든 … ⓑ 단지 …만 ¶①공부만 하고 쉬지 않으면 아무 소용이 없다 ⓒ최대한의, 있는 대로의 2. ⓐ모든, 온갖 ¶②이것이 내가 갖고 있는 책의 전부이다 ⓑ…만 ¶③말뿐이고 사상이 없는 ⓒ…으로 가득찬 ¶④그는 만면에 미소를 짓고 있었다(열심히 귀를 기울이고 있었다)

—*adv.* **1.** entirely; completely; altogether; quite. ¶~ *over the world* | ~*covered with mud* | ~ *alone* | ~ *too soon.* **2.** each. ¶*The score was one* ~.
—[副] 1. 전혀; 아주; 통틀어 2. 각각

all at once, ⓐ suddenly. ⓑ at the same time.
[熟] ⓐ갑자기 ⓑ일제히

—*n.* [U] everything one has. ¶*He lost his* ~. | *It was my little* ~.⑤
—[名] 전부; 소유물(재산) 전부 ¶⑤그것은 적지만 내 재산의 전부이다

—*pron.* **1.** ((used as *sing.*)) everything; the whole of anything. ¶*All is over.* | *All is not gold that glitters.*⑥ | *All that he said was true.* **2.** ((used as *pl.*)) everyone. ¶*All are happy.* | *All of us* (or *We* ~ [*of us*]) *are going there.* | *They are* ~ *happy.*
—[代] 1. 전부; 모두; 전체 ¶⑥반짝인다고 전부 금은 아니다 2. 모든 사람들

1) ***above all,*** before everything else; especially.
2) ***after all,*** after considering everything; finally; nevertheless.
3) ***all but,*** almost; nearly. ¶*He is* ~ *but dead.*⑦
4) ***all in all,*** ⓐ in general; on the whole. ⓑ completely; everything. ¶*Tell me* ~ *in* ~.
5) ***at all,*** in any way; to any extent. ¶*I wasn't surprised at* ~.
6) ***for all*** [***that*** ...], in spite of; notwithstanding.
7) ***in all,*** altogether; all included.
8) ***when all is said*** [***and done***], after all; finally.
[熟] 1)무엇보다도 먼저, 특히 2)결국, 역시 3)거의, …이나 다름없이 ¶⑦그는 죽은 것이나 다름없다 4)ⓐ전체로서, 대개 ⓑ모두, 전부 5)전혀; 조금도 [… 않다] 6)…에도 불구하고 7)모두 [합쳐서] 8) 결국; 최후로

Al·lah [ǽlə, ɑ́:lə / ǽlə, ǽlɑ:] *n.* the name of the Supreme Being or God of Islam.
—[名] [회교의] 신, 알라

Al·lan [ǽlən] *n.* a man's name.
—[名] 남자 이름

al·lay [əléi] *vt.* **1.** put (fear, anger, etc.) at rest; quiet; calm. **2.** lessen (pain, etc.). ¶*His headache was allayed by the medicine.*
—[他] 1. [공포·분노 따위]를 가라앉히다, 누이다 2. [고통]을 경감하다

al·le·ga·tion [æligéiʃ(ə)n] *n.* [U] [C] the act of alleging; affirmation or assertion without proof.
—[名] [증거가 없는데도 사실·이유로서] 단언하기, 주장

allege [48] **allowance**

*al·lege [əlédʒ] vt. 1. speak clearly about (something) without proof. (~ that ...) ¶She alleges that her watch has been stolen. 2. say (something) as an excuse. ¶~ illness.①
　—㉻ 1. [증거 없이] …을 강력히 주장하다 2. [구실로서] …이라고 주장하다, …의 탓이라고 말하다 ¶①병 때문이라고 말하다

al·le·giance [əlí:dʒ(ə)ns] n. Ⓤ loyalty; faithfulness. ¶owe ~ to someone / pledge ~ to someone.①
　—㉻ [군주·국가에 대한] 충성, 신의 ¶① …에 충성을 서약하다

al·le·gor·i·cal [æligɔ́:rik(ə)l, -gár- / -gɔ́r-] adj. of an alle-⎫
al·le·go·ry [æligɔ̀:ri / -gəri] n. Ⓒ (pl. -ries) a story in⎬ gory.⎭ which a teaching is given symbolically.
　—㉻ 우의적(寓意的)인, 풍유(諷喩)의
　—㉻ 우화, 비유담

al·le·gro [əléigrou] adv. (Music) in fast tempo; lively.
　—㉿ (樂) 빠르게

al·ler·gy [ǽlərdʒi] n. Ⓤ Ⓒ 1. (Medicine) the state of being exceptionally sensitive to certain substances, such as food, pollen, and animals. 2. (colloq.) a strong dislike.
　—㉻ 1. (醫) 알레르기 2. 반감

al·le·vi·ate [əlí:vièit] vt. lighten (suffering); make (pain, agony, etc.) easier to endure.
　—㉻ [심신의 고통]을 경감하다

al·le·vi·a·tion [əlì:viéiʃ(ə)n] n. Ⓤ the act of alleviating; Ⓒ something that alleviates.
　—㉻ [심신의 고통의] 경감, 완화; 경감시키는 것

*al·ley [ǽli] n. Ⓒ 1. a path or a walk bordered with a hedge or trees in a park or garden; a narrow back street in a city. ¶a blind ~.① 2. a long, narrow lane for bowling.
　—㉻ 1. 오솔길; [빈민가의] 좁은 길, 골목길 ¶①막다른 골목 2. [보울링의] 경기대, 레인

All Fools' Day [ɔ́:lfú:lzdèi] n. April Fools' Day (April⎫
All·hal·lows [ɔ̀:lhǽlouz / ɔ́:l-] n. All Saints' Day (Nov. 1).⎭ 1).
　—㉻ 만우절(4월 1일)
　—㉻ 만성절(11월 1일)

*al·li·ance [əláiəns] n. 1. Ⓒ a union between nations, parties, or families. ¶an ~ between A and B① / make an ~ against ...② 2. Ⓤ relationship by marriage.
　—㉻ 1. [국가·당파 사이의] 동맹 ¶① A와 B와의 동맹 / ② …에 대하여 동맹하다 2. 결연(結緣)

*al·lied [əláid, ǽlaid] adj. 1. joined by agreement. 2. related by marriage. 3. similar.
　—㉿ 1. 동맹을 맺은 2. 혼인으로 인연을 맺은 3. 유사한

al·li·ga·tor [ǽligèitər] n. Ⓒ a large cold-blooded animal like the crocodile, living in rivers of the southern part of America or China.
　—㉻ [미국·중국산의] 악어 (이집트·아프리카산의 악어는 crocodile)

all-im·por·tant [ɔ́:limpɔ́:rt(ə)nt] adj. very important.
　—㉿ 아주 중요한

al·lit·er·a·tion [əlìtəréiʃ(ə)n] n. Ⓤ the use of the same initial sound in a group of words or line, as in "secret snow, silent snow."
　—㉻ 두운법(頭韻法)

al·lit·er·a·tive [əlítərèitiv / -ətiv] adj. of alliteration.
　—㉿ 두운의, 두운을 사용하는

al·lo·cate [ǽləkèit] vt. 1. divide (a sum of money, a share, work, etc.) for a particular purpose. ¶~ funds to new plans. 2. fix the place of (something).
　—㉿ 1. …을 할당하다, 배분하다 2. …의 위치를 정하다

al·lo·ca·tion [ǽləkéiʃ(ə)n] n. Ⓤ Ⓒ the act of allocating; the state of being allocated; the share alloted.
　—㉻ 할당, 배치; 할당된 상태; 배당액

al·lot [əlát / əlɔ́t] vt. (-lot·ted, -lot·ting) give a part of (something) to each. ¶~ some work to each; ~ each some work.①
　—㉿ …을 할당하다; 분배하다 ¶①자에게 일을 할당하다

al·lot·ment [əlátmənt / əlɔ́t-] n. 1. Ⓤ the act of allotting; Ⓒ a part given to each; a portion. 2. Ⓤ (chiefly Brit.) public land allotted for a family garden. 3. Ⓤ destiny.
　—㉻ 1. 할당, 분배; 배당, 몫 2. 배분된 땅 3. 운명

‡**al·low** [əláu] vt. 1. permit; let. ((~ someone or something to do)) ¶Smoking is not allowed here. / Allow a door to stand open. / She allowed her imagination full play.① / Allow me to introduce Mr. Smith to you. 2. give; grant. ¶~ him 30,000 yen a month. 3. admit. ((~ that..., ~ someone to be)) ¶Allow his claim. / He allowed that he was in the wrong.; He allowed himself to be in the wrong. / We must ~ her to be a beauty. 4. take off; deduct. ¶~ two cents in the dollar.
　1) allow for, take into consideration; provide for. ¶~ an hour for dinner / She purposely made the dress larger to ~ for shrinking when it was washed.②
　2) allow of, permit (something) to happen or exist. ¶~ of no excuse③ / The situation allows of no delay. ⇒ⓊⓈⒶⒼⒺ
　—㉿ 1. …을 그대로 시켜 두다; 허락하다 ¶①그녀는 마음껏 상상에 잠겼다 2. …을 주다 3. [제의 따위]를 인정하다; …이라고 생각하다 4. …을 빼다, 할인하다
　圀 1)고려하다; [사정을] 참작하다; …에 대비하다 ¶②그녀는 빨면 줄 것이라는 것을 참작하여 드레스를 좀 큼직하게 만들었다 2)…의 여지가 있다 ¶③핑계를 댈 여지가 없다 ⓊⓈⒶⒼⒺ allow of는 사람을 주어로 하는 구문에 쓸 수 없음

al·low·a·ble [əláuəbl] adj. permissible; lawful; accept-⎫able.⎭
　—㉿ 허용(승인)할 수 있는; 정당한

*al·low·ance [əláuəns] n. Ⓒ 1. a sum of money given
　—㉻ 1. 수당, 급여[금] ¶①가족수당/

weekly or monthly. ¶*a family* ~① / *retirement* ~② / *She has an* ~ *of 5,000 yen a month.* **2.** the amount taken off from the value of goods.
②퇴직금 2. 공제, 할인

make allowance[s] for, take (something) into consideration.
[熟] …을 참작하다

al·loy *vt.* [əlɔ́i →*n.*] **1.** mix (metals); mix (a metal) with other cheaper metal. ¶~ *gold with copper.* **2.** make (something) worse or less valuable.
—[他] 1. …을 합금하다; 합금하여 질을 떨어뜨리다 2. …의 품질을 저하시키다

—*n.* [ǽlɔi, əlɔ́i] **1.** [C] [U] a metal made by mixing two or more metals; a less valuable metal mixed with other metal. ¶*without* ~① / *an* ~ *of gold and* (or *with*) *copper.* **2.** [U] standard or quality of gold, silver, etc.
—[名] 1. 합금; 혼합용의 금속 ¶①순수한, 혼합물이 없는 2. [금·은의] 품위

all-round [ɔ́:lráund] *adj.* able to do many things well. ¶*an* ~ *athlete.*①
—[形] 다방면에 걸친 ¶①만능 선수

All Saints' Day [ɔ́:lséintsdèi] *n.* November 1, celebrated in honor of all the saints.
—[名] 만성절(萬聖節) (11월 1일)

all·spice [ɔ́:lspàis] *n.* **1.** [C] a kind of berry of the West Indies. **2.** [U] spice made from it.
—[名] 1. [서인도제도산의] 딸기의 일종 2. [그 열매로 만든] 양념

al·lude [əlú:d, +*Brit.* əljú:d] *vi.* speak of something indirectly. 《~ *to* something or someone》 ¶*Who[m] do you* ~ *to?*①
—[自] [넌지시] 언급하다 ¶①누구의 말을 하고 있는가?

al·lure [əlúər / əl(j)úə] *vt.* tempt (someone) to do something by promising to give something good; fascinate. 《~ someone *into* or *from,* ~ someone *to do*》
—[他] …을 유혹하다; 매혹하다

al·lure·ment [əlúərmənt / əl(j)úə-] *n.* [U] [C] the act of alluring; temptation; fascination.
—[名] 부추김, 유혹

al·lur·ing [əlúəriŋ / əl(j)úər-] *adj.* attracting; fascinating; charming.
—[形] 마음을 끄는; 매혹적인; 황홀하게 하는

al·lu·sion [əlú:ʒ(ə)n / əl(j)ú:-] *n.* [U] [C] indirect speech about something.
—[名] 암시

in allusion to, mentioning indirectly; hinting at.
[熟] 넌지시 …을 가리켜

al·lu·sive [əlú:siv / əl(j)ú:-] *adj.* suggestive; figurative.
—[形] 암시적인, 비유적인

al·lu·vi·al [əlú:viəl / əl(j)ú:vjəl] *adj.* consisting of or made of clay or mud left by running water. ¶~ *epoch.*①
—[形] 충적(沖積)의 ¶①충적기

* **al·ly** *vt.* [əlái →*n.*] (**-lied**) **1.** 《*reflexively* or in *passive*》 unite (two countries, companies, persons, etc.) by treaty, marriage, etc. 《~ *to* or *with* something》 ¶~ *itself* (*be allied*) *with other country.* **2.** 《usu. in *passive*》 make (something) related; belong to some kind. 《~ *to* something》 ¶*Dogs are allied to wolves.*①
—[他] 1. …을 동맹시키다; 결연시키다 2. …을 관련시키다 ¶①개와 늑대는 동류이다

—*n.* [ǽlai, əlái] [C] (pl. **-lies**) a person or nation united with another by treaty, friendship, etc.; a helper. ↔ enemy, foe
—[名] 동맹자(국); 협력자, 조력자

al·ma ma·ter, Al·ma Ma·ter [ǽlməméitər / -má:tə] *n.* the college or university in which one has been educated. ⇨[N.B.]
—[名] 모교, 출신교 [N.B.] 라틴어로 fostering mother 의 뜻

al·ma·nac [ɔ́:lmənæ̀k] *n.* [C] a calendar.
—[名] 달력

* **al·might·y** [ɔ:lmáiti] *adj.* **1.** having all power. **2.** (*U.S. colloq.*) very great; huge. —*n.* 《the *A-*》 God. —*adv.* extremely.
—[形] 1. 전능의 2. 《美口》 엄청난 —[名] 전능의 신 —[副] 대단히

al·mond [á:mənd, +*U.S.* ǽm-] *n.* [C] the nut or seed of a peach-like fruit. ⇨**fig.**; the tree itself.
—[名] 편도(扁桃); 그 편도나무

[almond]

al·mond-eyed [á:məndàid, +*U.S.* ǽm-] *adj.* having long, narrow, oval-shaped eyes, as the Chinese.
—[形] 편도 모양의 눈을 가진

‡ **al·most** [ɔ́:lmoust, +*U.S.* ɔ:lmóust] *adv.* nearly; all but. ¶*She* ~ *fell.*① / *It is* ~ *finished.*
—[副] 거의, 대부분 ¶①그녀는 거의 넘어질 뻔했다

alms [a:mz] *n.* [C] (pl. **alms**) money or gifts given to the poor. ¶*A beggar lives by* ~.
—[名] [거지에게 동냥으로 주는] 물건(돈); [빈민 구제를 위한] 의연금

alms·giv·ing [á:mzgìviŋ] *n.* [U] the act of giving alms; charity.
—[名] 자선, 희사[행위]

alms·house [á:mzhàus] *n.* [C] (*Brit.*) a private poorhouse; (*U.S.*) a public poorhouse.
—[名] 《英》 사립 구빈원(救貧院) (양로원); 《美》 공립 구빈원

aloe — already

al·oe [ǽlou] *n.* **1.** Ⓤ a plant of the lily family. ⇒fig. **2.** (*pl.* used as *sing.*) a drug made from aloes.

a·loft [əlɔ́:ft, əláft / əlɔ́ft] *adv.* **1.** high up; far above the earth. **2.** (*Nautical*) to the top of the mast.

a·lo·ha [ɑ:lóuə, ɑ:lóuhɑ:] *interj.* (*Hawaiian*) Hello!; Good-bye!

‡ **a·lone** [əlóun] *adj.* (as *predicative*) **1.** quite by oneself; apart from others; solitary; single. ¶*She lives ~ in this house.* / *She likes to be ~.* **2.** (following the *noun* or *pronoun*) without anyone or anything else. ¶*He ~ remained.* / *Man shall not live by bread ~.*①

[aloe 1.]

1) *let alone,* not to mention. ¶*It takes up too much time, let ~ the money.*
2) *let* (or *leave*) *someone* or *something alone,* do not trouble or interfere; ignore; do not touch or move. ¶*leave her ~* / *Let him ~ to do that.*②
—*adv.* by oneself; without aid or help; solely. ¶*I can do it ~.*

‡ **a·long** [əlɔ́:ŋ / əlɔ́ŋ] *prep.* from one end to the other end of; on or by the whole length of. ¶*walk ~ a lake.*
—*adv.* **1.** forward; onward. ¶*run ~* / *Let us walk ~.*① **2.** by the side; near. (*~ by*) ¶*~ by the hedge.* **3.** in company; with me (or you, him, etc.). ¶*I took my wife ~.*
1) *all along,* all the time.
2) *along with,* together with. ¶*Come ~ with me.*

• **a·long·side** [əlɔ́:ŋsáid / əlɔ́ŋ-] *adv., prep.* at or by the side [of]; side by side [with].
alongside of, by the side of; beside.

a·loof [əlú:f] *adv., adj.* (as *predicative*) apart; cold in manner; not interested. ¶*stand* (or *keep*) *~ from something.*①

‡ **a·loud** [əláud] *adv.* so as to be heard; loudly.
think aloud, talk to oneself.

alp [ælp] *n.* Ⓒ a high mountain.

al·pac·a [ælpǽkə] *n.* Ⓒ a South American animal like a sheep. ⇒ fig.; Ⓤ its wool; the cloth made from its wool.

al·pen·stock [ǽlpinstɑ̀k / -stɔ̀k] *n.* Ⓒ a strong stick with an iron point, used by mountain climbers.

al·pha [ǽlfə] *n.* Ⓒ **1.** the first letter of the Greek alphabet, *A, α* **2.** (*the ~*) the first.
[alpaca]

the Alpha and Omega, the beginning and the end.

• **al·pha·bet** [ǽlfəbit, -bèt] *n.* Ⓤ Ⓒ **1.** the letters of a language arranged in order. ⇒NB **2.** the basic elements to be learned first. ¶*the ~ of English conversation.*

al·pha·bet·i·cal [æ̀lfəbétik(ə)l] *adj.* of the alphabet; arranged in the order of the letters of a language.

al·pha·bet·i·cal·ly [æ̀lfəbétikəli] *adv.* in the order of the letters of the alphabet.

Al·pine [ǽlpain] *adj.* **1.** of the Alps. **2.** (*A-, a-*) of or growing on a high mountain. ¶*alpine plants* (or *flora*)①

Al·pin·ist [ǽlpinist] *n.* Ⓒ a person who climbs the Alps; (*a-*) a mountain climber.

Alps [ælps], *the n. pl.* a mountain range in south Europe.

‡ **al·read·y** [ɔ:lrédi] *adv.* before or by this time. ¶*I have ~ done it.* / *It's ~ finished.* / *Is she back ~?*①

‡ **al·so** [ɔ́:lsou] *adv.* in addition; as well; too; besides. ¶*He ~ agreed with me.*① —[副] [···도] 또한; 마찬가지로 ¶①그도 나에게 동의했다

al·so-ran [ɔ́:lsouræ̀n] *n.* [C] (*colloq.*) a horse which fails to come in among the first three in a race; a person defeated in a competition. —[名] [경마에서] 등수에 들지 못한 말; [경주·선거에서] 패배한 선수, 낙선자

* **al·tar** [ɔ́:ltər] *n.* [C] a raised place on which sacrifices are offered to a god; a table or stand in a church, used in the communion service. —[名] 제단;성찬대

* **al·ter** [ɔ́:ltər] *vt.* make (something) different; change; modify. ¶~ *clothes*① / ~ *a house.*② **—*vi.*** become different. —[他] ···을 바꾸다; 고치다 ¶①옷을 고치다/②집을 개조하다 —[自] 바뀌다

al·ter·a·tion [ɔ̀:ltəréiʃ(ə)n] *n.* [U][C] the act of altering; a change; a modification. ¶*make an ~ on something.*① —[名] 변경, 개조 ¶① ···을 변경(개조)하다

al·ter·ca·tion [ɔ̀:ltərkéiʃ(ə)n] *n.* [U][C] an angry dispute; a quarrel. —[名] 말다툼, 언쟁, 싸움

* **al·ter·nate** *v.* [ɔ́:ltərnèit →*adj., n.*] *vi.* take place or happen by turns; change. ¶*Night and day ~ with each other.*① **—*vt.*** cause (things) to happen by turns. ¶~ *work with pleasure.*② **—*adj.*** [ɔ́:ltə:rnit] taking place or happening by turns; every other. ¶*on ~ days.*③ **—*n.*** [ɔ́:ltərnit] [C] (*U.S.*) a person officially named to take the place of another. —[自] 번갈아 일어나다, 교대하다 ¶①밤과 낮은 번갈아 온다 —[他] ···을 교대하다 ¶②일과 즐거움을 교대로 하다 —[形] 교대의;하나 걸러의 ¶③격일로 —[名] 《美》 대리인

al·ter·nate·ly [ɔ́:ltərnitli / ɔ:ltə́:-] *adv.* in an alternate manner; one after another; every other. —[副] 교대로, 번갈아; 하나 건너서

al·ter·nat·ing [ɔ́:ltərnèitiŋ] *adj.* first one and then the other. —[形] 교대의

alternating current [⌐−−− ⌐−] *n.* an electric current that changes its direction at regular intervals. —[名] 교류

al·ter·na·tion [ɔ̀:ltərnéiʃ(ə)n] *n.* [U][C] the act of alternating; the state of being alternated; a change. —[名] 교호(交互); 교대

* **al·ter·na·tive** [ɔ:ltə́:rnətiv] *adj.* that can be chosen between two, or sometimes more, things. ¶*We have no ~ course.*① **—*n.*** [C] a choice between two things; one of two things which must be chosen. ¶*The alternatives are death or submission.* —[形] [둘, 때로는 둘 이상 가운데에서] 하나를 고르는 ¶①달리 길이 없다 —[名] 양자 택일; 선택하여야 할 둘(두 개)

al·ter·na·tive·ly [ɔ:ltə́:rnətivli] *adv.* so as to choose between two; as an alternative. —[副] 양자 택일로

‡ **al·though** [ɔ:lðóu] *conj.* though; even if. ¶*Although he was poor, he was always honest.* / *Although it rained hard, I went shopping.* —[接] ···이기는 하나, 비록 ···일지라도

al·tim·e·ter [ǽltimì:tər, æltímitər] *n.* [C] an instrument for finding distance above sea level. —[名] 고도계(高度計)

* **al·ti·tude** [ǽltit(j)ù:d / -tjù:d] *n.* [U][C] **1.** the height above the earth's surface or sea level. **2.** 《usu. *pl.*》 a high point or place. —[名] 1. [산·천체·비행기 따위의] 높이, 고도, 표고(標高) 2. 높은 곳

al·to [ǽltou] *n.* (pl. **-tos**) (*Music*) [U] the voice between soprano and tenor; [C] a singer having such a voice. —[名] 알토; 알토 가수

‡ **al·to·geth·er** [ɔ̀:ltəgéðər] *adv.* **1.** entirely; wholly; without exception. ¶*His story is not ~ false.*① ⇒[Usage] **2.** on the whole. **3.** all included. ¶*How much ~?* —[副] 1. 전혀, 예외 없이 ¶①그의 이야기가 전혀 거짓말은 아니다 [Usage] 부분 부정 2. 대체로 3. 통틀어

taken altogether, with everything considered. ¶*Taken ~, there's no hope yet.* [熟] 대체로 보아

al·tru·ism [ǽltruiz(ə)m] *n.* [U][C] the principle of considering others' interests and happiness first; unselfishness. ↔egoism —[名] 이타심; 이타(애타)주의

al·tru·is·tic [æ̀ltruístik] *adj.* unselfish; disinterested. —[形] 이타적인; 사심이 없는

al·um [ǽləm] *n.* [C] a mineral salt used in medicine or in dyeing. —[名] 명반(明礬)

al·u·min·i·um [æ̀ljumíniəm] *n.* (esp. *Brit.*)=aluminum.

a·lu·mi·num [əlú:minəm] *n.* [U] (*U.S.*) a light, silver-white metal. —[名] 알루미늄

a·lum·na [əlʌ́mnə] *n.* [C] (pl. **-nae**) (*U.S.*) a woman graduate of a school, college, etc. —[名] 여자 졸업생, 여자 동창생

a·lum·nae [əlʌ́mni:] *n.* pl. of **alumna.**

a·lum·ni [əlʌ́mnai] *n.* pl. of **alumnus.**

A

a·lum·nus [əlʌ́mnəs] *n.* [C] (pl. **-ni**) (*U.S.*) a male graduate of a school, college, etc. —[名] 남자 졸업생, 남자 동창생

‡ **al·ways** [ɔ́:lwəz, -weiz] *adv.* at all times; on all occasions. ⇒[usage] ¶*He is ~ disappointed.* —[副] 언제나, 늘 [usage] 조동사와 be 동사 이외에는 동사 앞에 둠

‡ **am** [æm, əm] *vi.* the first person singular present indicative of **be**. —[自] be 동사의 제1인칭·단수·현재형

‡ **A.M., a.m.** [éiém] before noon. ¶*at 8 a.m.* / *the 10:30 a.m. train.* ⇒[usage] —《略》 오전 [usage] 표제·시각표. 이외에서는 보통 소문자

a·main [əméin] *adv.* (*poetic*) with full force; at full speed; in haste. —[副] 《詩》 힘껏; 쏜살같이; 매우 급히

a·mal·gam [əmǽlgəm] *n.* [U] any metallic mixture of mercury with some other metal[s]. —[名] 아말감(주성분은 수은)

a·mal·gam·ate [əmǽlgəmèit] *vt.* **1.** unite (a metal) with mercury. **2.** join together; combine. ¶*~ three companies into one* / *be amalgamated with something.*① **—*vi.*** (of companies, etc.) unite; join together. —[他] **1.** …을 수은과 혼합하다 **2.** [회사 따위]를 합병(병합)하다 ¶①…과 결합하다 —[自] [회사 따위가] 합병하다

a·mal·gam·a·tion [əmæ̀lgəméiʃ(ə)n] *n.* [U][C] the act of amalgamating; mixture; union. —[名] 아말감을 만들기; 융합; 합병

am·a·ryl·lis [æ̀mərílis] *n.* [C] a plant like a lily. —[名] 아마릴리스

a·mass [əmǽs] *vt.* collect a large quantity of (something); pile up; accumulate (a fortune). —[他] …을 쌓다, 모으다; [재산]을 축적하다

* **am·a·teur** [ǽmətʃuər / ǽmətə(:)] *n.* [C] a person who studies an art or plays a game for pleasure, not for money. **—*adj.*** of or by amateurs; made or done by an amateur. —[名] …아마튜어, 소인(素人); 애호가 —[形] 아마튜어의

am·a·teur·ish [æ̀mətə́:riʃ, -tʃúər- / -tə́:r-, -tjúər-] *adj.* made or done as an amateur might do it; crude; clumsy. —[形] 아마튜어다운, 미숙한

am·a·teur·ism [ǽmətʃuərìz(ə)m / æ̀mətə́:riz(ə)m] *n.* [U] amateurish practice or quality. —[名] 아마튜어 연예; 도락; 비직업적인 방법

am·a·to·ry [ǽmətɔ̀:ri / -təri] *adj.* of love. —[形] 연애의, 애인의

* **a·maze** [əméiz] *vt.* surprise or astonish greatly; fill (someone) with wonder. ¶*She was amazed at the news.* / *We were amazed that she should want to marry such a man.* —[他] …을 깜짝 놀라게 하다

a·mazed [əméizd] *adj.* filled with wonder; lost in astonishment. —[形] 깜짝 놀란

a·maz·ed·ly [əméiz(i)dli] *adv.* in wonder or astonishment. —[副] 깜짝 놀라

* **a·maze·ment** [əméizmənt] *n.* [U] the state of being amazed; astonishment; great surprise. ¶*She looked at me in ~.*① —[名] 경악, 크게 놀람 ¶①그녀는 놀라서 나를 보았다

to one's amazement, to one's astonishment. ¶*To my ~, he called on me at midnight.* [熟] 놀라운 일은

* **a·maz·ing** [əméiziŋ] *adj.* causing great astonishment. —[形] 놀랄 만한

Am·a·zon [ǽməzɑn / -z(ə)n] *n.* **1.** 《*the ~*》 a river in northwest South America. **2.** (in Greek mythology) one of a race of warlike women. ⇒[N.B.] **3.** 《*a-*》 [C] a big, powerful, manly woman. —[名] **1.** 아마존강 **2.** 아마존 [N.B.] 흑해 연안에 살았다고 하는 용맹한 여걸 **3.** 여걸

* **am·bas·sa·dor** [æmbǽsədər] *n.* [C] **1.** a government officer sent to another country to act for his own country. ¶*an ~ extraordinary* [*and plenipotentiary*].① ⇒[N.B.] **2.** an official messenger. ¶*an ~ of peace.*② —[名] **1.** 대사 ¶①특명[전권]대사 [N.B.] 호칭은 Your Excellency **2.** [외교]사절 ¶②평화의 사절

am·bas·sa·dress [æmbǽsədris] *n.* [C] **1.** the wife of an ambassador. **2.** a woman ambassador. —[名] **1.** 대사 부인 **2.** 여자 대사(사절)

am·ber [ǽmbər] *n.* [U] **1.** a pale yellow substance used for jewerry. **2.** the color of amber; yellow or yellowish-brown. ⇒[N.B.] **—*adj.*** yellowish in color; [made] of amber. —[名] **1.** 호박(琥珀) **2.** 호박색 [N.B.] 미국에서는 교통신호의 황색을 흔히 amber라 함 —[形] 호박색의; 호박으로 만든

am·ber·gris [ǽmbərgrì(:)s] *n.* [U] a grey fat produced from whales, used in making perfumes. —[名] 용연향(龍涎香)

am·bi·gu·i·ty [æ̀mbigjú(:)iti] *n.* (pl. **-ties**) **1.** [U] doubtfulness of meaning. **2.** [C] a word or expression with more than one meaning. —[名] **1.** [의미의] 애매함 **2.** 애매한 어구(표현)

am·big·u·ous [æmbígjuəs] *adj.* obscure (in meaning); doubtful; uncertain. —[形] 애매한, 불명료한; 이도 저도 아닌

‡ **am·bi·tion** [æmbíʃ(ə)n] *n.* [U][C] the state of being ambitious; an eager desire for fame, wealth, success, position, etc.; the object of the desire itself. ⇒[usage] —[名] 야심; 대망; 야망의 대상 [usage] 좋은 뜻으로나 나쁜 뜻으로나 다 쓰임

• **am·bi·tious** [æmbíʃəs] *adj.* **1.** full of ambition; showing great ambition. ¶*an ~ plan.* **2.** ((as *predicative*)) strongly desiring. ¶*Boys, be ~! | He is ~ to succeed* (or *of success*).①
—[形] 1. 대망·패기에 찬 2. 열망하는 ¶①그는 성공을 열망하고 있다

am·biv·a·lent [æmbív(ə)lənt / æ̀mbivei-] *adj.* having opposite and conflicting feelings, esp. love and hate, toward the same object. ▷**am·biv·a·lence** [-ləns] *n.*
—[形] [감정 따위가] 서로 용납하지 않는

am·ble [ǽmbl] *vi.* (of a person) walk at a slow pace; (of a horse) move at an easy pace by lifting both legs on the same side at once. ((~ *about* or *along* a street)) —*n.* [C] such an easy pace of a horse; an easy walk of a person; a stroll.
—[自] [사람이] 천천히 걷다; [말이]같은 편의 두 발을 동시에 올리며 걷다 —[名] [말의] 측대보(側對步); 느린 걸음

am·bro·sia [æmbróuʒə / -ziə, -zjə] *n.* [U] **1.** (in Greek and Roman mythology) the food of the gods. **2.** anything delicious to taste or smell.
—[名] 1. [그리이스·로마 신화의] 신의 음식 2. 맛 좋고 향기로운 음식

am·bro·sial [æmbróuzəl / -ziəl] *adj.* very delicious.
—[形] 아주 맛있는

am·bu·lance [ǽmbjuləns] *n.* [C] **1.** a field hospital. **2.** a vehicle for carrying sick or wounded persons.
—[名] 1. 야전 병원 2. 부상병 운반차(선·비행기), 구급차

am·bus·cade [æ̀mbʌskéid] *n., vt.* =ambush.

am·bush [ǽmbuʃ] *n.* [U] the act of lying in wait to attack an enemy; [C] ((*collectively*)) soldiers so hidden; a place where they are hidden. —*vi., vt.* lie in wait; hide soldiers for a surprise attack.
—[名] 매복, 기습; 복병; 매복 장소 —[自][他] 매복하다; 복병을 두다

a·mel·io·rate [əmíːliərèit] *vt.* make (something) better; improve. —*vi.* become or grow better ↔deteriorate
—[他] …을 개선하다, 개량하다 —[自] 좋아지다; 개선되다

a·mel·io·ra·tion [əmìːliəréiʃ(ə)n] *n.* [U][C] improvement.
—[名] 향상; 개선, 개량

a·men [áːmén, éimén / ɑːmén] *n.* [C] a word, meaning "So be it," used at the end of a prayer.
—[名] 아멘(「그렇게 되기를 바라나이다」의 뜻)

say amen (=*agree*) *to something.*
[熟] …에 동의하다

a·me·na·ble [əmíːnəbl] *adj.* **1.** answerable; responsive. ¶*~ to law.* **2.** willing or ready to obey. ¶*He is ~ to reason.*①
—[形] 1. 복종해야 할, [법의] 제재를 받는 2. 기꺼이 따르는, 순종하는 ¶①그는 도리에 따른다

• **a·mend** [əménd] *vt.* **1.** change or revise (a law, bill, etc.). ¶*~ a bill.* **2.** make (one's behavior, etc.) better; improve. ¶*~ one's life* (or *ways*). —*vi.* become better in conduct, etc.
—[他] 1. [의안 따위]를 개정(수정)하다, 정정하다 2. [행실 따위]를 고치다 —[自] 개심하다

• **a·mend·ment** [əméndmənt] *n.* **1.** [U][C] a change for the better; a correction. **2.** [C] a change in a law or bill. ¶*propose an ~ to a law.*①
—[名] 1. [행실·마음 따위를]고치기, 정정; 개정, 개량 2. 수정 ¶①법률의 수정안을 내다

a·mends [əméndz] *n. pl.* ((used as *sing.*)) something to pay for harm done.
—[名] 보상

make amends (=*do something to pay*) *for a loss or injury.*
[熟] [손실·손상]에 대해 보상하다

a·men·i·ty [əméniti, əmíːn-] *n.* **1.** [U] the quality of being pleasant. **2.** ((*the -ties*)) agreeable manners or ways.
—[名] 1. [태도·기후 따위의] 쾌적함; 온화 2. 예의

⁑ **A·mer·i·ca** [əmérikə] *n.* **1.** the United States of America. **2.** North America. **3.** South America. **4.** ((often *the ~s*)) ((*collectively*)) North and South America.
—[名] 1. 아메리카 합중국 2. 북아메리카 3. 남아메리카 4. 남북 아메리카, 미주

⁑ **A·mer·i·can** [əmérikən] *adj.* of or belonging to America, esp. the United States. —*n.* **1.** [C] a person of America, esp. a citizen of the United States. **2.** [U] American English.
—[形] 아메리카의, 합중국의 —[名] 1. 미국인 2. [영어에 대해서] 미어(美語)

A·mer·i·can·ism [əmérikənìz(ə)m] *n.* **1.** [U][C] an American word or phrase. **2.** an American custom. **3.** [U] loyalty to the United States and its customs and manners; American spirit.
—[名] 1. 미국식 말투, 미어 2. 미국식 3. 친미주의, 미국인 기질, 미국 정신

A·mer·i·can·i·za·tion [əmèrikənizéiʃ(ə)n / -kənai-] *n.* [U] the act of Americanizing.
—[名] 미국화

A·mer·i·can·ize [əmérikənàiz] *vt.* make (someone or something) American in character, habits, or nationality.
—[他] …을 미국화하다; 미국에 귀화시키다

ame·thyst [ǽmiθist] *n.* [U] a precious stone, clear purple or violet in color.
—[名] 자석영(紫石英), 자수정

a·mi·a·bil·i·ty [èimiəbíləti] *n.* [U] the quality of being amiable.
—[名] 온순; 상냥함, 애교

a·mi·a·ble [éimiəbl] *adj.* good-natured; friendly; kindhearted.
—[形] 귀염성 있는, 상냥한, 온순한

a·mi·a·bly [éimiəbli] *adv.* good-naturedly; agreeably.
—[副] 우호적으로; 상냥하게

am·i·ca·ble [ǽmikəbl] *adj.* friendly; peaceful. ↔hostile
am·i·ca·bly [ǽmikəbli] *adv.* in a friendly manner; peacefully.
* **a·mid** [əmíd] *prep.* in the middle of; among. ¶ ~ *tears.*①
a·mid·ships [əmídʃips] *adv.* in or near the middle of a ship.
a·midst [əmídst] *prep.* amid; in the middle of.
a·miss [əmís] *adv.* out of order; badly; wrongly. ¶*She*
1) *go amiss*, go wrong.   [*thinks* ~.]
2) *take something amiss*, be offended at something.
—*adj.* ((as *predicative*)) wrong; out of order. ((~ *with*))
¶*Is there anything* ~ *with your watch?*
am·i·ty [ǽmiti] *n.* ⓤ friendly relations, esp. between nations; friendship. ¶*live in* ~ *with someone.*①
am·me·ter [ǽmmɪ:tər / ǽmitə] *n.* ⓒ an instrument for measuring an electric current in amperes.
am·mo·ni·a [əmóuniə] *n.* ⓤ 1. a colorless gas with a very sharp smell, used in making ice and in medicine. 2. a liquid containing this gas.
am·mo·nite [ǽmənàit] *n.* ⓒ a coiled, chambered shellfish which lived long ago. ⇒fig.
am·mu·ni·tion [æ̀mjuníʃ(ə)n] *n.* ⓤ powder, bullets, or shells to be used in war.
am·ne·sia [æmní:ʒə / -zjə] *n.* ⓤ total or partial loss of memory caused by brain injury, shock, etc.

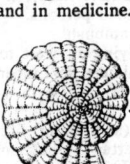
[ammonite]

am·nes·ty [ǽmnèsti / ni-] *n.* (pl. **-ties**) ⓒⓤ a general pardon, given esp. to political offenders. —*vt.* (**-tied**) give an amnesty to (someone).
a·moe·ba [əmí:bə] *n.* ⓒ (pl. **-bas** or **-bae**) a tiny water animal that has only one cell and that constantly changes in shape as it moves. ▷**a·moe·ba·like** [-làik] *adj.*
a·moe·bae [əmí:bi:] *n.* pl. of **amoeba**.
‡ **a·mong** [əmʌ́ŋ] *prep.* 1. in the middle of; surrounded by. ¶*She sat* ~ *her friends.* 2. in shares with; within. ¶*Divide the books* ~ *the students.* / *Decide* ~ *yourselves.* 3. in the class or group of. ¶*This is the best* ~ *the pictures of this year.* 4. by or with the whole of. ¶*This song is popular* ~ *young people.* 5. each with the other; mutually. ¶*They quarrelled* ~ *themselves.* ⇒USAGE
* **a·mongst** [əmʌ́ŋst] *prep.* =among.
am·o·rous [ǽmərəs] *adj.* 1. inclined to [esp. sexual] love. 2. showing love. 3. of [esp. sexual] love.
a·mor·phous [əmɔ́:rfəs] *adj.* 1. formless; shapeless. 2. unorganized. ▷**a·mor·phous·ly** [-li] *adv.*
‡ **a·mount** [əmáunt] *vi.* add up; be equal.
amount to, ⓐ add up to; come up to (a sum, quantity, etc.). ¶*The bill amounts to 300 dollars.* / *It amounts to much.*① / ~ *to nothing* (or *little*).② ⓑ be equal to. ¶*His words* ~ *almost to a threat.*
—*n.* 1. ⓤ ((*the* ~)) sum; total. ¶*What is the full* ~ *I owe you?* / *the* ~ *of today's sales.* 2. ((*the* ~)) total meaning. ¶*This is the* ~ *of what she said.*① 3. ⓒ a quantity. ¶*a large* (*small*) ~ *of money* | *a great* ~ *of*
1) *in amount*, in all; in substance.   [*intelligence.*]
2) *to the amount of*, as much as.
a·mour [əmúər] *n.* ⓒ a [secret] love affair.
am·pere, -père [ǽmpiər, æmpíər / ǽmpɛə] *n.* ⓤ a unit for measuring the strength of an electrical current. ⇒N.B.
am·phib·i·an [æmfíbiən] *n.* ⓒ 1. an animal or plant that can live both on land and in water. 2. an air-

plane that can take off from and land on both land and water. **3.** a tank or other vehicle, that can be used both on land and water. —*adj.* able to live or to operate both on land and in water; amphibious.
수륙 양용(양서)의

am·phib·i·ous [æmfíbiəs] *adj.* **1.** able to live or to operate both on land and in water. ¶ *~ plants / an ~ tank.* **2.** of military operations by land, water, and air forces. ¶ *an ~ attack.*
—[形] 1. 수륙 양용(양서)의 2. 육·해·공 공동 작전의

am·phi·the·a·ter, *Brit.* **-tre** [ǽmfiθìətər] *n.* [C] **1.** a circular building with rows of seats around an open area. ⇒fig. **2.** anything resembling an amphitheater' in shape.
—[名] 1. 원형극장; 투기장(주위에 계단식 관람석이 있음) 2. 원형극장 비슷한 장소

〔amphitheater 1.〕

* **am·ple** [ǽmpl] *adj.* **1.** of a large size or amount; extensive. **2.** enough; sufficient. **3.** abundant. ↔scanty
—[形] 1. 광대한; 넓은 2. 충분한 3. 풍부한

am·pli·fi·ca·tion [æ̀mplifikéiʃ(ə)n] *n.* [U] **1.** the act of amplifying; the state of being amplified; expansion; enlargement. **2.** an increase in the strength of an electric current, voltage, or power.
—[名] 1. 확대, 확장 2. 증폭(增幅)

am·pli·fi·er [ǽmplifàiər] *n.* [C] **1.** a person or thing that amplifies. **2.** a device to increase the strength of an electric current.
—[名] 1. 확대하는 사람(것) 2. 증폭기

am·pli·fy [ǽmplifài] *vt.* **(-fied) 1.** make (something) larger or louder; enlarge; expand. **2.** explain (something) more fully. **3.** increase the strength of (an electric current, voltage, or power). —*vi.* write or talk in great detail. ⟪*~ on* or *upon* a story, etc.⟫ ¶ *~ upon a matter.*①
—[他] 1. …을 확대하다 2. …을 상세히 설명하다 3. [전압·전력]을 증폭하다 —[自] 상세히 말하다 ¶①일을 상술하다

am·pli·tude [ǽmplit(j)ù:d / -tjù:d] *n.* [U] the state or quality of being ample.
—[名] 넓이; 충분; 증폭

am·ply [ǽmpli] *adv.* **1.** sufficiently. **2.** in detail.
—[副] 1. 충분히 2. 상세히

am·pu·tate [ǽmpjutèit] *vt.* cut off (an arm, a leg, etc.), esp. by surgery.
—[他] [손발 따위]를 절단하다

am·pu·ta·tion [æ̀mpjutéiʃ(ə)n] *n.* [U][C] the act of amputating.
—[名] 절단[수술]

* **Am·ster·dam** [ǽmstərdæ̀m / ⌐⌐⌐] *n.* an important seaport and the nominal capital of the Netherlands. ⇒[N.B.]
—[名] 암스테르담 [N.B.] 행정상의 수도는 The Hague

a·muck [əmʌ́k] *adv.* madly; wildly.
—[副] 미쳐 날뛰어

run amuck, rush about madly, attacking everybody whom one meets.
[熟] 미쳐 날뛰다, 닥치는 대로 때려부수다

am·u·let [ǽmjulit] *n.* [C] a small object worn as a charm against evil or harm.
—[名] 부적; 액막이

* **a·muse** [əmjú:z] *vt.* **1.** cause (someone) to feel happy; entertain. **2.** cause (someone) to laugh or smile. ⟪~ someone *by* or *with* a story, etc.⟫ ▷**a·mus·er** [-ər] *n.*
—[他] 1. …을 재미나게 하다 2. …을 즐겁게 하다

* **a·muse·ment** [əmjú:zmənt] *n.* **1.** [U] the state of being amused. **2.** [C] an entertainment; a pleasure.
—[名] 1. 즐거움, 즐기기 2. 오락, 여흥

* **a·mus·ing** [əmjú:ziŋ] *adj.* **1.** pleasant; entertaining. **2.** causing laughter. ¶ *an ~ motion picture.* ▷**a·mus·ing·ly** [-li] *adv.*
—[形] 1. 재미있는 2. 우스운

A·my [éimi] *n.* a woman's name.
—[名] 여자 이름

‡ **an** [ən, æn] *indef. art.* ⟪used before words beginning with a *vowel* sound⟫. =a.

a·nach·ro·nism [ənǽkrənìz(ə)m] *n.* [U][C] the state of being out of date; a person or thing out of date.
—[名] 시대 착오; 시대에 뒤진 사람(것)

a·nach·ro·nis·tic [ənæ̀krənístik] *adj.* out of date.
—[形] 시대 착오의

an·a·con·da [æ̀nəkɑ́ndə / -kɔ́n-] *n.* [C] a very large snake of South America that coils around and crushes its prey.
—[名] [남미산의] 구렁이의 일종

a·nae·mi·a [əní:miə] *n.* =anemia.

a·nae·mic [əní:mik] *adj.* =anemic.

an·aes·thet·ic [æ̀nisθétik] *adj., n.* =anesthetic.

an·a·gram [ǽnəgræ̀m] *n.* [C] **1.** a word or phrase obtained by changing the order of the letters of another word or phrase. ⇒[N.B.] **2.** ⟪*pl.* used as *sing.*⟫ a game in which the players make words by changing and
—[名] 1. 글자수수께끼 [N.B.] live를 evil, time을 emit로 하는 따위 2. 철자 바꾸기 놀이

adding letters.

a·nal·o·gous [ənǽləgəs] *adj.* having analogy; similar. —[형] 유사한, 비슷한

a·nal·o·gy [ənǽlədʒi] *n.* [C][U] (pl. **-gies**) likeness; similarity. ¶*bear* (or *have*) *some ~ with* (or *to*) *something*① / *by ~ with something; on the ~ of something.*② —[명] 유사, 상사 ¶①…과 유사하다/②…에서 유추(類推)하여

an·a·lyse [ǽnəlàiz] *vt.* (chiefty *Brit.*) =analyze.

a·nal·y·ses [ənǽlisi:z] *n.* pl. of **analysis.**

• **a·nal·y·sis** [ənǽlisis] *n.* [U][C] (pl. **-ses**) **1.** the act of separating something into its parts or elements to find out what it is made of. ↔synthesis **2.** (*Chemistry*) the separation of materials into their elements to find their kind or nature. **3.** a critical examination of an idea, a book, an event, etc. —[명] 1. 분해; 분석 2. [화학적인] 분석 3. 검토

in the last analysis, after all. [熟] 결국은

an·a·lyst [ǽnəlist] *n.* [C] **1.** a person who analyzes; an analyzer. **2.** a psychoanalyst. —[명] 1. 분석(분해)하는 사람 2. 정신분석학자

an·a·lyt·ic [æ̀nəlítik], **-i·cal** [-ik(ə)l] *adj.* separating a thing into its parts or elements for the purpose of study. ↔synthetic ▷**an·a·lyt·i·cal·ly** [-kəli] *adv.* —[형] 분석(분해)적인

• **an·a·lyze** [ǽnəlàiz] *vt.* **1.** separate (something) into its parts or elements. ↔synthesize ¶*~ a sentence.*① **2.** examine (something) critically. ▷**an·a·lyz·er** [-ər] *n.* —[타] 1. …을 분석(분해)하다 ¶①문장을 분해하다 2. …을 검토하다

an·ar·chism [ǽnərkìz(ə)m] *n.* [U] the doctrine that all existing governmental systems are wrong and undesirable. —[명] 무정부주의

an·ar·chist [ǽnərkist] *n.* [C] a person who believes in anarchism. —[명] 무정부주의자

an·ar·chy [ǽnərki] *n.* [U] **1.** the absence of government and law. **2.** the absence of political order; lawlessness; confusion; disorder. —[명] 1. 무정부 2. 무질서

a·nath·e·ma [ənǽθimə] *n.* [C] (pl. **-mas** or **-ma·ta**) **1.** a solemn curse that excludes someone from membership in the church. **2.** a thing or person greatly disliked. —[명] 1. 파문(破門) 2. 저주받은 사람

a·nath·e·ma·ta [ənǽθimətə] *n.* pl. of **anathema.**

an·a·tom·i·cal [æ̀nətámik(ə)l / -tɔ́m-] *adj.* **1.** of anatomy. **2.** structural. ▷**an·a·tom·i·cal·ly** [-kəli] *adv.* —[형] 1. 해부[학상]의 2. 구조의

a·nat·o·mist [ənǽtəmist] *n.* [C] a specialist in anatomy. —[명] 해부학자

a·nat·o·mize [ənǽtəmàiz] *vt.* **1.** cut (an animal, a plant, etc.) into parts to study its structure; dissect. **2.** analyze minutely. —[타] 1. [동식물체]를 해부하다 2. …을 세밀하게 분해하다

a·nat·o·my [ənǽtəmi] *n.* [U] **1.** the study of the structure of animals and plants. **2.** the act of cutting up animals or plants to study their structures. **3.** [C] the structure of an animal or plant. —[명] 1. 해부학 2. 해부 3. 해부적 조직

• **an·ces·tor** [ǽnsestər / -sis-] *n.* [C] a person from whom another person is descended; a forefather. ↔descendant —[명] 선조, 조상

an·ces·tral [ænséstrəl] *adj.* **1.** of ancestors; belonging to ancestors. **2.** inherited from ancestors. ¶*~ estate.* —[형] 1. 선조의 2. 조상 전래의

an·ces·try [ǽnsestri / -sis-] *n.* [U] ⟪*collectively*⟫ **1.** all of one's ancestors. **2.** the line of family descent. ¶*She was born of good ~.*① / *He is an American of Korean ~.*② —[명] 1. 선조, 조상 2. 가계(家系); 가문 ¶①그녀는 명문 출신이다/②그는 한국계 미국인이다

• **an·chor** [ǽŋkər] *n.* [C] **1.** a heavy iron or steel instrument used to keep a ship from moving. **2.** anything that makes someone feel safe and secure; a support. **3.** a person who runs the last part of the way in a relay race. —[명] 1. 닻 2. 믿고 의지하는 것 3. [계주·역전 마라톤의] 최종 주자

1) ***be*** (or ***lie, ride***) ***at anchor,*** (of a ship) be kept from moving by an anchor.
2) ***cast*** (or ***drop, slip***) ***anchor,*** let the anchor down.
3) ***weigh anchor,*** take up the anchor; depart.

[熟] 1)정박해 있다 2)닻을 내리다 3)닻을 올리다

—*vt.* **1.** keep (a ship) from moving by an anchor. **2.** fix firmly; make (something) secure. ¶*She anchored her hopes in her son's talent for music.*① —*vi.* **1.** cast an anchor. **2.** be firmly fixed. —[타] 1. [배]를 정박시키다 2. …을 고정시키다 ¶①그녀는 아들의 음악적 재능에 기대를 걸었다 —[자] 1. 닻을 내리다; 정박하다 2. 고정하다

an·chor·age [ǽŋkəridʒ] *n.* **1.** Ⓤ the act of anchoring; the state of being anchored. **2.** Ⓒ a place where ships are anchored. **3.** Ⓒ money that must be paid for anchoring a ship.
an·cho·ret [ǽŋkərèt, -rit] *n.* =anchorite.
an·cho·rite [ǽŋkəràit] *n.* Ⓒ a person who has retired to a solitary place for religious meditation.
an·cho·vy [ǽntʃouvi / -tʃə-] *n.* Ⓒ (pl. **-vies** or *collectively* **-vy**) a very small fish of the herring family, found chiefly in the Mediterranean Sea. ⇒N.B.
ːan·cient [éinʃ(ə)nt] *adj.* **1.** of or in times long past. ¶ ~ *history.* **2.** very old. ↔new ¶*an ~ tree.* **3.** old-fashioned. ↔modern —*n.* Ⓒ **1.** a person who lived in ancient times. **2.** 《*the* ~s》 the civilized peoples who lived long time ago, as the Greeks or Romans. ▷**an·cient·ly** [-li] *adv.*
ːand [ænd, ənd, ən, n] *conj.* **1.** with; in addition to; joined together; plus. ¶*You ~ she ~ I are friends.* / *three ~ forty*① / *Four ~ five is (or are) nine.* / *man ~ wife* / *pen ~ ink* / *bread ~ butter* [brédnbʌ́tər]② / *a watch ~ chain*③ / *He is a scholar ~ writer.* ⇒usage **2.** as a result. ¶*The teacher told her ~ she wept.* / *Work hard ~ you will succeed in the examination.* **3.** then again; then once more. ¶*for hours ~ hours* / *again ~ again* / *He walked miles ~ miles.* **4.** 《expressing *different examples* of the same kind》 ¶*There are books ~ books.*④ **5.** on the other hand; but. ¶*She is so rich, ~ lives like a beggar.* **6.** also; what is more important. ¶*give ~ take* / *He did it, ~ did it well.*⑤ **7.** (*colloq.*) in order to. ⇒usage ¶*go ~ see him* / *try ~ help him.* **8.** 《placed between *two adjectives*》 (*colloq.*). ⇒usage ¶*nice ~ warm* / *good ~ tired.*⑥
1) *and how!*, of course.
2) *and so*, therefore; so.
3) *and so on* (or *forth*), and the like; et cetera.
an·dan·te [ændǽnti] *adj., adv.* (*Music*) moderately slow. —*n.* Ⓒ a moderately slow movement of music.
An·des [ǽndi:z], **the** *n. pl.* a mountain range in west South America. ⇒N.B.
and·i·ron [ǽndàiərn] *n.* Ⓒ one of a pair of metal supports for holding firewood in a fireplace. ⇒fig.
and/or [ǽndɔːr] *conj.* both or either. ⇒N.B. ¶*fish ~ meat.*
An·drew [ǽndruː] *n.* a man's name. ⇒N.B.
[andiron]
an·ec·dote [ǽnikdòut] *n.* Ⓒ a brief story, usu. amusing or instructive, told about some person or incident. ¶*Many anecdotes are told about him.*
a·ne·mi·a [əníːmiə] *n.* Ⓤ lack of blood; an illness because of lack of blood. ⌜anemia.⌝
a·ne·mic [əníːmik] *adj.* lacking in blood; suffering from
an·e·mom·e·ter [ænimάmitər / -mɔ́mitə] *n.* Ⓒ an instrument for measuring the speed or pressure of the wind.
a·nem·o·ne [ənéməni] *n.* Ⓒ **1.** a plant with a slender stem and white, red, or purple flowers. **2.** a sea animal with a tube-like body and many feelers or tentacles; a sea anemone.
an·es·thet·ic [ænisθétik] *n.* Ⓒ a drug or **gas**, such as chloroform or ether, which causes loss of sensation for a time. —*adj.* causing loss of sensation for a time.
a·new [ən(j)úː / ənjúː] *adv.* **1.** over again; once more.

—명 1. 투묘(投錨), 정박 2. 투묘 장소, 정박 장소 3. 정박세

—명 [특히 종교 때문에 속세를 등진] 은사(隱士), 은자
—명 [지중해산] 멸치 비슷한 물고기 N.B. anchovy sauce를 만듦

—형 1. 고대의 2. [사물이] 낡은, 오래된 3. 구식의 —명 1. 고대인 2. 고대 문명 민족[고대 그리이스·로마인 등]

—접 1. 그리고, 또, 및; 게다가, 더하여 ¶①43/②버터 바른 빵/③사슬 달린 시계 usage 이와같이 한 개의 관념를 나타내는 경우의 동사는 단수형 2. (결과를 나타내어) 하면;만일 …하면 3. (반복·연속을 나타내어) 다시 [도] 4. 여러가지의 ¶④책에는 좋은 책도 나쁜 책도 여러가지가 있다 5. 그런데도 6. (강조) 더구나, 그것도 ¶⑤그는 그것을 했다, 그리고 훌륭하게 7. (口) …하러, …하려고 usage 동사의 원형 다음에 써서 부정사의 to의 대용 8. 《두 개의 형용사를 연결하여 앞의 형용사를 부사적으로 만듦》¶⑥몹시 지친

圖 1)물론 2)그러니까, 그래서 3)따위, 등등
—형·부 느린(느리게) —명 안단테 조[의 곡]
—명 안데스 산맥 N.B. 최고봉은 Aconcagua
—명 [벽난로의] 장작 받침쇠

—접 양쪽 모두 또는 한쪽 N.B. 상용문·공문 따위에서 씀
—명 남자 이름 N.B. 애칭은 Andy

—명 일화

—명 빈혈[증]

—명 빈혈[증]의
—명 풍속계, 풍력계

—명 1. 아네모네 2. 말미잘

—명 마취제 —형 마취의

—부 1. 다시 2. 새로, 신규로

2. in a new form or manner; afresh.

‡ an·gel [éindʒ(ə)l] *n.* [C] **1.** a messenger of God, usu. pictured with wings. **2.** a good, innocent, or lovely person. ¶*an ~ of a child*① | *Be an ~ and do it.*② **3.** a guardian spirit.
—[名] 1. 천사 2. 천사 같은 사람 ¶①천사 같은 아이/②착한 아이니까 그것을 해 다오 3. 수호신

an·gel·ic [ændʒélik], **-i·cal** [-ik(ə)l] *adj.* of or like an angel.
—[形] 천사의(같은)

An·ge·lus [ǽndʒiləs] *n.* [C] **1.** a Roman Catholic prayer said three times a day. **2.** the bell that announces the time for this prayer; an Angelus bell.
—[名] 1. 아침 6시, 정오, 저녁 6시에 세 번 울리는 도고(禱告) 기도 2. 안젤루스의 종

‡ an·ger [ǽŋgər] *n.* [U] strong, hostile emotion aroused by a wrong act or remark of another person. **—***vt.* make (someone) angry; offend. ¶*His dishonesty angered his friends.* **—***vi.* become angry.
—[名] 노여움 —[他] …을 성나게 하다 —[自] 성내다

‡ an·gle[1] [ǽŋgl] *n.* [C] **1.** (*Geometry*) the space between two lines that meet at a point. ¶*an acute ~*① | *an obtuse ~*② | *a right ~.*③ **2.** a corner. **3.** a point of view. **—***vt.* move or bend (something) in an angle. **—***vi.* move or go at an angle.
—[名] 1. 각도 ¶①예각/②둔각/③직각 2. 모퉁이, 모서리 3. 견지, 관점 —[他] …을 어떤 각도로 움직이다(구부리다) —[自] 어떤 각도로 되다(구부러지다)

an·gle[2] [ǽŋgl] *vi.* **1.** catch fish with a hook and line. 《~ *for* fish》 **2.** try to get by using tricks. 《~ *for* something》 ¶~ *for praise.*
—[自] 1. 낚시질하다 2. 꾀어내다

An·gli·can [ǽŋglikən] *adj.* **1.** of the Church of England. **2.** (cheifly *U.S.*) English. **—***n.* [C] a member of the Church of England.
—[形] 1. 영국 국교회[파]의 2. 영국[민]의 —[名] 영국 국교회파의 사람

An·gli·cise, *Brit.* **-cize** [ǽŋglisàiz] *vt.* make (something) English in customs, character, words, pronunciation, etc.
—[他] [습관·성질 따위]를 영국식으로 하다; [외국어]를 영어화하다

an·gling [ǽŋgliŋ] *n.* [U] the act or art of fishing with a hook and line.
—[名] 낚시질

An·glo- [ǽŋglou-] a word element meaning *English.*
—「영국」이라는 뜻의 연결형

An·glo-A·mer·i·can [ǽŋglouəmérikən] *adj.* **1.** English and American. **2.** of Anglo-Americans. **—***n.* [C] an American of English origin or birth.
—[形] 1. 영미의 2. 영국계 미국인의 —[名] 영국계 미국인

An·glo-Sax·on [ǽŋglousǽks(ə)n] *n.* **1.** [C] a person of the English-speaking world. **2.** [C] a person who lived in England before the Norman Conquest. **3.** [C] a person of English descent. **4.** [U] the language used in Britain before the Norman Conquest; Old English. **—***adj.* **1.** of the Anglo-Saxons or their language. **2.** of the English people.
—[名] 1. 영어를 국어로 쓰는 사람 2. 앵글로색슨 사람 3. 영국계의 사람; 영국인 4. 앵글로색슨 말; 고대 영어 —[形] 1. 앵글로색슨 민족(어)의 2. 영국인의

An·go·ra [æŋgɔ́:rə] *n.* **1.** [C] a cat or goat with very long, soft hair. **2.** 《*a*-》 [U] cloth made from the wool of an Angora goat; mohair.
—[名] 1. 앙고라 고양이; 앙고라 염소 2. 앙고라 직물

an·gri·ly [ǽŋgrili] *adv.* in anger.
—[副] 성나서

‡ an·gry [ǽŋgri] *adj.* (**-gri·er, -gri·est**) feeling or showing anger or rage. 《~ *at, with,* or *about*》
—[形] 성난

an·guish [ǽŋgwiʃ] *n.* [U] great pain, grief, or suffering.
—[名] 고통; 고뇌

an·guished [ǽŋgwiʃt] *adj.* full of anguish.
—[形] 고뇌에 찬

an·gu·lar [ǽŋgjulər] *adj.* **1.** having angles; having sharp corners. **2.** lean; bony.
—[形] 1. 모가 있는, 모난 2. 말라빠진

an·gu·lar·i·ty [æ̀ŋgjulǽriti] *n.* [U] the quality of having sharp corners.
—[名] 모남, 모짐

an·i·line [ǽnilin / -lì:n], **-lin** [-lin] *n.* [U] a poisonous, colorless, oily liquid, usu. obtained from nitrobenzene, used in making dyes, drugs, etc. **—***adj.* made from aniline.
—[名] 아닐린 —[形] 아닐린의

an·i·mad·ver·sion [æ̀nimædvə́:rʒ(ə)n / -və́:ʃ(ə)n] *n.* [U] [C] criticism; blame.
—[名] 비평; 비난

an·i·mad·vert [æ̀nimædvə́:rt] *vt.* comment critically; blame.
—[他] …을 비평하다; 비난하다

‡ an·i·mal [ǽnim(ə)l] *n.* [C] **1.** any living thing that can feel and move about by itself, such as a man, dog, bird, fish, insect, etc. **2.** any animal other than man. **3.** a four-legged animal. **4.** a person like a brute or beast. **—***adj.* of animals; like an animal.
—[名] 1. [식물·광물에 대하여] 동물 2. [인간과 구별하여] 짐승, 동물 3. 네 발 짐승 4. 짐승 같은 사람 —[形] 동물의; 짐승 같은

an·i·mate *vt.* [ǽnimèit → *adj.*] **1.** give life to (someone). **2.** make (someone or something) lively, gay, or energetic.
—[他] 1. …을 살리다 2. …을 활기 띠게 하다 3. …을 격려하다 4. …을 행동시

animated [59] **annoyance**

¶*Joy animates his face.* **3.** give courage to (someone); inspire; encourage. **4.** move (someone) to action.
——*adj.* [ǽnimit] **1.** living; alive. **2.** lively; gay. ↔ inanimate ——웽 1. 살아 있는 2. 활기 띤

an·i·mat·ed [ǽnimèitid] *adj.* full of life or spirit; lively. ——웽 생기 있는, 활발한

an·i·ma·tion [æniméiʃ(ə)n] *n.* Ⓤ **1.** liveliness; spirit; life. **2.** the process of preparing an animated cartoon. ——웽 1. 활기; 생기 2. 만화 영화 제작

an·i·mos·i·ty [ænimɔ́siti / -mɔ́s-] *n.* (pl. **-ties**) **1.** Ⓤ hatred; dislike; hostility. 《~ *against, toward* or *between*》 **2.** Ⓒ conduct of this nature. ——웽 1. 원한; 증오, 악의 2. 원한(악의)에 찬 행동

an·ise [ǽnis] *n.* **1.** Ⓒ a plant with sweet-smelling seeds. **2.** Ⓤ the seed of this plant. ⇒fig. ——웽 1. 아니스 2. 아니스 열매

an·i·seed [ǽnisìːd] *n.* Ⓤ the seed of anise, used both in medicine and in flavoring. ——웽 아니스의 열매

* **an·kle** [ǽŋkl] *n.* Ⓒ **1.** the joint which connects the foot with the leg. **2.** the slender part of the leg between this joint and the calf. ——웽 1. 복사뼈, 거골(距骨) 2. 발목

an·klet [ǽŋklit] *n.* Ⓒ **1.** a sock that reaches just above the ankle. **2.** an decorative ring or chain worn around the ankle. ——웽 1. [여자·아동용] 짧은 양말 2. 발목 장식; 차꼬

[anise 2.]

Ann [æn], **An·na** [ǽnə] *n.* women's names. ——웽 여자 이름

an·nal·ist [ǽnəlist] *n.* Ⓒ a writer of annals. ——웽 연대기 편자

an·nals [ǽnlz] *n. pl.* **1.** a list of events recorded year by year. **2.** historical records. **3.** yearly reports published by an organization. ——웽 1. 연대기 2. [역사의] 기록 3. 연보(年報)

an·nex *vt.* [ənéks → *n.*] **1.** add or join (something) to a larger thing. **2.** attach. 《~ something *to*》 ——*n.* [ǽneks] Ⓒ **1.** something added. **2.** an addition to a building. ——퉁 1. …을 병합하다 2. …을 부가하다 ——웽 1. 부가물 2. [호텔 따위의] 별관; 분교(分校)

an·nex·a·tion [æneksséiʃ(ə)n] *n.* **1.** Ⓤ the act of joining or adding something to a large thing. **2.** Ⓒ something added. ——웽 1. 병합/부가 2. 합병한 영토; 부가물

an·nexe [ǽneks] *n. Brit.*=annex.

an·ni·hi·late [ənáiəlèit] *vt.* **1.** destroy completely. **2.** put an end to (something). ——퉁 1. …을 전멸시키다 2. [법령 따위]를 폐기하다

an·ni·hi·la·tion [ənàiəléiʃ(ə)n] *n.* Ⓤ complete destruction. ——웽 전멸, 멸종

* **an·ni·ver·sa·ry** [æ̀nivə́ːrs(ə)ri] *n.* (pl. **-ries**) **1.** the yearly return of the date on which an event happened. **2.** the celebration of the yearly return of such a date. ——*adj.* **1.** returning each year; annual. **2.** of such a date. ——웽 1. 기념일 2. 기념 축전 ——퉁 1. 예년의 2. 기념일의

An·no Dom·i·ni [ǽnoudɔ́minai / -dɔ́m-] *adv.* since Christ was born; in the year of our Lord. ⇒N.B. ——튱 서력 기원 N.B. A.D.로 줄여 씀. 「기원전」은 B.C.

an·no·tate [ǽnoutèit] *vt.* add explaining notes or comments to (a book, etc.). ——*vi.* make notes or comments on a book, etc. 《~ *on* or *upon* something》 ——퉁 1. …에 주석을 달다 ——튱 주석을 달다

an·no·ta·tion [æ̀noutéiʃ(ə)n] *n.* **1.** Ⓤ the act of annotating. **2.** Ⓒ a note added to a text. ——웽 1. 주석[을 달기] 2. [텍스트 따위의] 주(註)

‡**an·nounce** [ənáuns] *vt.* **1.** make (something) known publicly; tell. ¶~ *a dinner.* **2.** make known the presence or coming of (someone); say the name of (a guest). ¶~ *a visitor.* ——퉁 1. …을 발표하다; 알리다 2. [손님]의 내방을 알리다

* **an·nounce·ment** [ənáunsmənt] *n.* **1.** Ⓒ a public notice; something made known. **2.** Ⓤ the act of announcing. ——웽 1. 공표; 발표 2. 고지(告知)

* **an·nounc·er** [ənáunsər] *n.* Ⓒ **1.** a person who makes announcements over the radio or television. **2.** a person who announces. ——웽 1. [방송] 아나운서 2. 통보자

* **an·noy** [ənɔ́i] *vt.* **1.** trouble; irritate. ¶*He was much annoyed with her.* **2.** harm. ——퉁 1. …을 괴롭히다; 애타게 하다 2. …을 해치다

an·noy·ance [ənɔ́iəns] *n.* **1.** Ⓤ the act of annoying. **2.** Ⓤ the feeling of being annoyed. **3.** Ⓒ a thing or person that annoys. ——웽 1. 괴롭힘, 시달림 2. 귀찮음 3. 골 칫거리

an·noy·ing [ənɔ́iiŋ] *adj.* troublesome.
—[形] 귀찮은, 골치아픈

⁑ **an·nu·al** [ǽnjuəl] *adj.* **1.** in a year; for a year; during a year. **2.** coming or occuring once a year; yearly. **3.** (of plants) living only one year or season. **4.** taking a year to complete. **—*n.*** [C] **1.** a plant living for one year or season. **2.** a book, magazine, etc. that is published once a year.
—[形] 1. 1년간의 2. 한해 한번의 3. [식물이] 1년생의 4. 1년 걸리는 —[名] 1. 1년생 식물 2. 연보, 연감

an·nu·al·ly [ǽnjuəli] *adv.* yearly; each year.
—[副] 한해 한번; 매년

an·nu·i·ty [ən(j)ú:iti / ənjú(:)i-] *n.* (pl. **-ties**) **1.** [C] a sum of money paid or given each year regularly. ¶*a life ~.*① **2.** [U] the right to receive or the duty to pay such money.
—[名] 1. 연금 ¶①종신 연금 2. 연금을 받는 권리; 지불 의무

an·nul [ənʌ́l] *vt.* (**-nulled, -nul·ling**) destroy the effect of (a law, etc.); do away with (something); cancel.
—[他] [법률 따위]를 폐지하다; …을 소멸시키다; 취소하다

an·nul·ment [ənʌ́lmənt] *n.* [U] [C] the act of annulling or canceling.
—[名] 폐지; 취소

An·nun·ci·a·tion [ənʌ̀nsiéiʃ(ə)n], **the** *n.* **1.** the announcement by the angle Gabriel to the Virgin Mary that she was to be the mother of Christ. **2.** the festival in memory of this, Lady Day [March 25].
—[名] 1. 수태 고지(그리스도의 수태를 성모 마리아께 알린 일) 2. 수태 고지의 축제

an·ode [ǽnoud] *n.* [C] the positive pole of a battery. ↔ cathode
—[名] 양극(陽極)

an·o·dyne [ǽnoudàin] *n.* [C] a medicine that relieves pain. **—*adj.*** relieving pain.
—[名] 진통제 —[形] 진통의

a·noint [ənɔ́int] *vt.* **1.** put oil or ointment on (something or someone). **2.** pour oil on the head of (someone) in a religious ceremony. ▷**a·noint·ment** [-mənt] *n.*
—[他] 1. …에 기름(연고)을 바르다 2. …에 성유(聖油)를 부어 깨끗이 하다

a·nom·a·lous [ənɑ́mələs / -nɔ́m-] *adj.* away from the common rule or type; irregular; abnormal.
—[形] 불규칙의; 변칙의

a·nom·a·ly [ənɑ́məli / -nɔ́m-] *n.* [C] [U] (pl. **-lies**) the state of being away from the common rule or type; irregularity; a person or thing that is abnormal.
—[名] 변칙; 이례적인 사람(것)

∗ **a·non** [ənɑ́n / ənɔ́n] *adv.* (*archaic*) **1.** soon. **2.** at once; immediately.
—[副] 《古》 1. 곧 2. 즉각

ever and anon, every now and then; occasionally.
[熟] 때때로, 가끔

anon. anonymous.

a·non·y·mous [ənɑ́niməs / ənɔ́n-] *adj.* **1.** without the author's name listed. **2.** not known by name; nameless. ▷**a·non·y·mous·ly** [-li] *adv.*
—[形] 1. 작자 불명의 2. 무명의; 익명의

⁑ **an·oth·er** [ənʌ́ðər] *adj.* **1.** one more. ¶*in ~ nine months*① / *Have ~ cup of coffee.* **2.** different; of a different kind. ¶*I don't like this necktie. Show me ~ one.* / *One man's meat is ~ man's poison.*② **3.** second; similar. ¶*He will be ~ Newton some day.*③ **—*pron.*** **1.** one more thing or person. ¶*Try ~.* **2.** a different one; something different. ¶*I don't like this one. Show me ~.* **3.** one just like; one like the first. ¶*He is a fool, and his brother is ~.*
—[形] 1. 또 하나의 ¶①9개월만 더 있으면 2. 별개의, 다른 ¶②A에겐 약이 되어도 B에겐 독이 될 수 있다 3. 제2의; 동류의 ¶③그는 언제고 제2의 뉴우턴이 될 것이다
—[代] 1. 또 하나의 것(사람) 2. 다른 사람(것) 3. …도 또한 같은 것

ans. answer; answered.

⁑ **an·swer** [ǽnsər / ɑ́:nsə] *vt.* **1.** reply 《~ *that* ...》; respond to (a question). ¶*~ my question* / *~ a letter* / *She answered that she knew something about it.* / *She didn't ~ a word to us.* / *Answer me this question.* / *~ blows with blows.*① **2.** defend oneself against (something); prove (something) not to be true. ¶*~ the charge.*② **3.** be enough for (something); serve; fulfill; satisfy. ¶*The knife answers my purpose.*③ / *My prayer was answered.*④ / *The boy will ~ your desires.* **—*vi.*** **1.** reply. ¶*They called again and again, but no one answered.* / *To the question he answered decidedly.*⑤ **2.** serve the purpose; succeed. ¶*Such an excuse will not ~.*⑥ / *Our plan has answered.*⑦
—[他] 1. …이라고 대답하다, …에게 응수하다 ¶①주먹에는 주먹으로 응수하다 2. [비난]에 응수하다; 자기 변호하다 ¶②고소에 응수하다 3. [목적·요건]에 충족되다; 합치하다; 쓸모가 있다 ¶③이 나이프로 된다/④내 기도는 효험이 있었다 —[自] 1. 대답을 하다 ¶⑤그 질문에 그는 단호히 대답했다 2. 소용이 되다; 효험을 보다; 성공하다 ¶⑥그런 핑계는 통하지 않는다/⑦우리 계획은 성공했다

1) ***answer back,*** (*colloq.*) answer in a rude manner.
2) ***answer for,*** ⓐ promise; be responsible for (some-
[熟] 1)거만하게 대답하다 2)ⓐ…을 약속하다; …의 책임을 지다 ⓑ… 때문에

thing). ¶*I can't ~ for his honesty.* ⓑ be punished for (something). ¶*You must ~ for your telling a lie.*⑧
처벌되다 ¶⑧너는 거짓말을 한 벌을 받아야 한다

—*n.* [C] **1.** a reply. ¶*give an ~*. **2.** a solution. ¶*an ~ to a riddle.*
—[名] 1. 대답, 회답 2. 해답

an·swer·a·ble [ǽns(ə)rəbl / ɑ́:n-] *adj.* **1.** responsible. 《~ *to, for*》 ¶*You are ~ to me for your conduct.* **2.** that can be answered.
—[形] 1. 책임이 있는 2. 대답할 수 있는

⁑ **ant** [ænt] *n.* [C] a small insect that lives in crowds in tunnels under the ground or in wood.
—[名] 개미

an·tag·o·nism [æntǽgənìz(ə)m] *n.* [U] dislike or opposition between two persons or groups of people; hostility; hatred.
—[名] 반대; 적대; 적의

an·tag·o·nist [æntǽgənist] *n.* [C] a person who fights or struggles with another; a rival; an opponent.
—[名] 적대; 경쟁 상대

an·tag·o·nis·tic [æntæ̀gənístik], **-ti·cal** [-k(ə)l] *adj.* opposing; hostile. 《~ *to*》 ▷**an·tag·o·nis·ti·cal·ly** [-kəli] *adv.*
—[形] 반대의; 적대하는

an·tag·o·nize [æntǽgənàiz] *vt.* **1.** make (someone) an enemy. **2.** oppose.
—[他] 1. …을 적으로 돌리다 2. …에 적대하다

* **ant·arc·tic** [æntɑ́:rktik] *adj.* near the South Pole; of the south polar region. ↔arctic —*n.* 《*the A-*》 the South Pole; the region around the South Pole.
—[形] 남극의 —[名] 남극[지방]

Ant·arc·ti·ca [æntɑ́:rktikə] *n.* the continent around the South Pole.
—[名] 남극 대륙

an·te-[ǽnti-] *pref.* before: *anteroom* (=waiting room).
—《接頭》 전…

ant·eat·er [ǽntì:tər] *n.* [C] an animal with a long, slender tongue that feeds chiefly on ants.
—[名] [남미산] 개미핥기

an·te·ced·ent [æ̀ntisí:d(ə)nt] *adj.* going before. 《~ *to*》
—[形] 선행의

—*n.* [C] **1.** a person or thing that goes before. **2.** 《*pl.*》 an ancestor; one's past life. **3.** (*Grammar*) a noun, pronoun, etc., that is followed by a relative pronoun or relative adverb.
—[名] 1. 선행하는 것 2. 선조; 신원(身元), 경력 3. 《文法》 선행사

an·te·cham·ber [ǽntitʃèimbər] *n.* [C] a room leading into a larger room; a waiting room.
—[名] [큰 방으로 통하는] 대기실; 대합실

an·te·di·lu·vi·an [æ̀ntidilú:viən] *adj.* **1.** of the time before the Flood. **2.** very old; oldfashioned. —*n.* [C] a person who lived before the Flood.
—[形] 1. 노아의 홍수 이전의 2. 태고의; 아주 오래된 —[名] 노아의 홍수 이전 사람

an·te·lope [ǽntilòup] *n.* [C] (pl. **-lopes** or *collectively* **-lope**) an animal like a deer which can move very quickly.
—[名] 영양(羚羊)

an·te me·rid·i·em [ǽntimərídiəm] *adj.* before noon. ↔post meridiem ⇒[N.B.]
—[形] 오전[의] [N.B.] a.m., A.M.으로 줄임

an·ten·na [ænténə] *n.* [C] **1.** (pl. **-nas** → 2.) wires or rods used in radio and television for receiving or sending out electric waves. **2.** (pl. **-nae**) a feeler on the heads of insects, lobsters, etc.
—[名] 1. 공중선, 안테나 2. 촉각

an·ten·nae [ænténi:] *n.* pl. of **antenna**.

an·te·ri·or [æntíəriər] *adj.* **1.** fore; toward the front. **2.** coming before; earlier. 《~ *to*》 ↔posterior
—[形] 1. 전방의 2. [장소·시간이] 앞의, 먼저의

an·te·room [ǽntirù(:)m] *n.* [C] a room leading into a large room; a waiting room.
—[名] 대기실

an·them [ǽnθəm] *n.* [C] **1.** a song of praise. ¶*a national ~*.① **2.** a sacred song, usu. with words taken from the Bible; a hymn.
—[名] 1. 축가, 송가 ¶①국가 2. 찬미가

an·ther [ǽnθər] *n.* [C] the top part of the stamen of a flower.
—[名] 《植》 약(葯)

ant hill [∸ ∸] *n.* a pile of earth heaped up by ants in digging their tunnels to their nest.
—[名] 개미둑

an·thol·o·gy [ænθɑ́lədʒi / -θɔ́l-] *n.* [C] (pl. **-gies**) a collection of poems or prose passages by various authors.
—[名] 명시 선집; 문집

An·tho·ny [ǽntəni, -θə-] *n.* a man's name. ⇒[N.B.]
—[名] 남자 이름 [N.B.] 애칭은 Tony

an·thra·cite [ǽnθrəsàit] *n.* [U] hard coal that gives out great heat and little smoke or flame.
—[名] 무연탄

an·thrax [ǽnθræks] *n.* [U] a disease of cattle, sheep, etc. that can spread and that usu. causes death.
—[名] 탄저열(炭疽熱)

an·thro·poid [ǽnθrəpɔ̀id] *adj.* man-like; resembling man. —*n.* [C] a man-like ape, such as a chimpanzee or gorilla.
—[形] 인간 비슷한 —[名] 유인원

an·thro·po·log·ic [ӕnθrəpəládʒik / -lɔ́dʒ-], **-i·cal** [-k(ə)l] *adj.* of anthropology. —[形] 인류학의

an·thro·po·lo·gist [ӕnθrəpáləd3ist / -pɔ́l-] *n.* [C] a person who specializes in anthropology. —[名] 인류학자

an·thro·pol·o·gy [ӕnθrəpálədʒi / -pɔ́l-] *n.* [U] the science of the origin and development of mankind. —[名] 인류학

an·ti-[ǽntai-, -ti- / ǽnti-] *pref.* **1.** against; opposed to: *anti-aircraft* (=against enemy aircraft); *anti-Japanese* (=opposed to Japan). **2.** not: *antisocial* (=not social). **3.** preventing an effect: *antitoxin* (=preventing poisoning). ⇒[N.B.] —《接頭》 1. 반(反)… 2. 비(非)… 3. 항(抗)… [N.B.] 모음으로 시작되는 낱말이나 고유명사·형용사에 붙는 경우는 보통 하이픈을 붙임

an·ti·air·craft [ӕntiέərkrӕft / -έəkrὰ:ft] *adj.* used in defense against enemy aircraft. ¶*an ~ gun.*① —[形] 방공용의 ¶①고사포

an·ti·bi·ot·ic [ӕntibaiátik / -ɔ́t-] *n.* [C] a chemical product that kills or weakens germs, such as penicillin and streptomycin. —*adj.* able to kill or weaken germs. —[名] 항생물질 —[形] 항생의

an·ti·bod·y [ǽntibὰdi / -bɔ̀di] *n.* [C] (pl. **-bod·ies**) a substance in a person's blood that kills or weakens germs and other poisons. —[名] 항독소, 항체(抗體)

an·ti·christ [ǽntikrὰist] *n.* [C] 《often *A-*》 an enemy of Christ; an opponent of Christ. —[名] 그리스도의 적; 그리스도의 반대자

an·ti·chris·tian [ӕntikrístʃən / -tjən] *adj.* 《often *A-*》 of an Antichrist; opposed to Christianity. —*n.* [C] an opponent of Christianity. —[形] 그리스도 반대의; 그리스도교 반대의 —[名] 그리스도교 반대자

an·tic·i·pate [ӕntísipèit] *vt.* **1.** guess (something) correctly before it happens. ¶*~ one's wish.*① **2.** go ahead of (another) in doing something. ¶*~ the enemy's move.* —[他] 1. …을 예기하다 ¶①남의 소원을 미리 알고 해주다 2. [상대방]에 앞서다

an·tic·i·pa·tion [ӕntìsipéiʃ(ə)n] *n.* [U] the act of anticipating.
1) ***in anticipation,*** previously.
2) ***in anticipation of,*** looking forward to.
—[名] 예기(豫期)
[熟] 1)미리 2)…을 예기하여

an·tics [ǽntiks] *n. pl.* comical actions; grotesque gesture. —[名] 익살[스런 몸짓]; 광대짓

an·ti·cy·clone [ӕntisáikloun] *n.* [C] a circulation of winds moving outward from a center of high pressure; the area of high pressure. —[名] 역선풍; 고기압권

an·ti·dote [ǽntidòut] *n.* [C] a medicine which works against a poison. 《*~ to, for,* or *against*》 —[名] 해독제

An·til·les [ӕntíli:z], **the** *n. pl.* a chain of islands in the West Indies, including Cuba, Haiti, Jamaica and Puerto Rico. —[名] 앤틸리이즈 열도

an·ti·mo·ny [ǽntimòuni / -mə-] *n.* [U] a silvery-white metal that is often combined with tin and lead. —[名] 안티몬

an·tip·a·thy [ӕntípəθi] *n.* [U] [C] (pl. **-thies**) a strong dislike; a feeling against someone or something. 《*~ to, against*》 ↔sympathy —[名] [뿌리 깊고 본능적인] 혐오; 반감

an·tip·o·des [ӕntípədì:z] *n. pl.* places on exactly opposite sides of the earth. —[名] 대척지(對蹠地)(지구상의 정반대쪽에 있는 두 지점)

an·ti·quar·i·an [ӕntikwέ(ə)riən] *adj.* of the study of ancient things. —*n.* [C] a person who studies or collects ancient things. —[形] 골동품 연구의 —[名] 골동품 연구(수집)가

an·ti·quar·y [ǽntikwèri / -kwəri] *n.* [C] (pl. **-quar·ies**) a person who studies, collects, or sells ancient things. —[名] 골동품 연구(수집)가; 골동품상

an·ti·quat·ed [ǽntikwèitid] *adj.* **1.** old-fashioned; out-of-date. **2.** old; aged. —[形] 1. 시대에 뒤진 2. 낡아빠진, 헌; 노후한

an·tique [ӕntí:k] *adj.* **1.** belonging to an age long past; ancient. **2.** old-fashioned. ↔modern —*n.* [C] **1.** something made long ago. **2.** 《*the ~*》 the antique style, usu. Greek or Roman, esp. in art. —[形] 1. 고대의 2. 구식의 —[名] 1. 골동품 2. [특히 고대 그리이스·로마의] 미술 양식

an·tiq·ui·ty [ӕntíkwiti] *n.* (pl. **-ties**) **1.** [U] ancientness. **2.** [U] ancient times, esp. before the Middle Ages. **3.** 《usu. *pl.*》 the things of ancient times. —[名] 1. 낡음 2. 먼 옛날 [특히 중세 이전] 3. 고대의 유물

an·ti·sep·tic [ӕntiséptik] *adj.* having the power of killing harmful germs. —*n.* [C] a thing that kills germs. —[形] 살균(방부)성의 —[名] 살균(방부)제

an·ti·slav·er·y [ӕntisléivəri / ǽnti-] *n.* [U] opposition to slavery. —*adj.* opposed to slavery. —[名] 노예제도 반대 —[形] 노예제도 반대의

an·ti·so·cial [æ̀ntisóuʃ(ə)l / ǽnti-] *adj.* **1.** opposed to companionship with other people. **2.** opposed to social order.
—[形] 1. 비사교적인 2. 반사화적인

an·tith·e·ses [æntíθisìːz] *n.* pl. of **antithesis.**

an·tith·e·sis [æntíθisis] *n.* (pl. **-tith·e·ses**) **1.** [U] opposition; contrast. ⟪~ *of, between*⟫ **2.** [U] the direct opposite. ⟪~ *of, to*⟫ **3.** [C] a contrast of idea, such as "Give me liberty, or give me death."
—[名] 1. 대조 2. 정반대 3. 대조법, 대구(對句)

an·ti·tox·in [æ̀ntitáksin / ǽntitɔ́ks-] *n.* [C] a substance formed in the body to resist a poison or the effects of germs.
—[名] 항독소

ant·ler [ǽntlər] *n.* [C] **1.** the horn of a deer. **2.** a branch of the horn of deer.
—[名] 1. 사슴 뿔 2. 가지진 뿔

ant·li·on [ǽntlàiən] *n.* [C] an insect which, early in its life, digs a pit in which it lies in wait for ants or other insects.
—[名] 개미귀신(명주잠자리의 유충)

an·to·nym [ǽntənim] *n.* [C] a word that has the opposite meaning to another word. ↔synonym
—[名] 반의어, 반대말

a·nus [éinəs] *n.* [C] the opening at the lower end of the body through which waste substance goes out.
—[名] 항문

an·vil [ǽnvil] *n.* [C] a block of iron or steel on which a blacksmith hammers metal into shape. ⇨fig.
—[名] [대장간의] 모루

[anvil]

·anx·i·e·ty [æŋzáiəti] *n.* [U] **1.** fear of what may happen. **2.** strong desire. ⟪~ *for, to do*⟫
—[名] 1. 근심, 걱정 2. 갈망, 열망

:anx·ious [ǽŋ(k)ʃəs] *adj.* **1.** afraid of what may happen; deeply troubled or worried. **2.** desiring very strongly. ⟪~ *for, to do*⟫ ▷**anx·ious·ness** [-nis] *n.*
—[形] 1. 근심스러운 2. 갈망하는

anx·ious·ly [ǽŋ(k)ʃəsli] *adv.* with anxiety.
—[副] 근심하여

:an·y [éni] *adj.* **1.** no matter which. ¶*Any book will do.*① **2.** ⟪in *interrogative* or *subjunctive*⟫ some. ¶*Have you ~ money with you? | If you have ~ interesting book, please lend it to me.* **3.** every. ¶*Any pupil knows it.* **4.** ⟪in *negative*⟫ even one; even a little. ¶*I haven't ~ money.*
—[形] 1. 어떤, 어떠한 [···이라도] ¶①어느 책이라도 좋다 2. 얼마간의; 다소의 3. 각각의; 모든 4. 조금의

—*pron.* ⟪in *negative*⟫ any person or thing; any part. ¶*Were ~ of you absent yesterday? | Take ~ you like.*② *| She hasn't got ~.*
—[代] 어느 것이라도; 누구라도; 어느 ¶②어느 것이든 좋은 것을 가져라

—*adv.* **1.** somewhat. ¶*Is she ~ better today?* **2.** ⟪usu. in *interrogative* or *subjunctive*⟫ in some degree; at all ¶*If she is ~ better, let me know. | He couldn't go ~ further. | Could you sleep ~ last night?*③
—[副] 1. 조금은, 얼마간은 2. 조금이라도 ¶③어젯밤은 조금은 잤느냐

:an·y·bod·y [énibàdi, -bʌ̀di / -bɔ̀di] *pron.* any person; anyone. ¶*~ else's book*① *| Anybody can do that. | I didn't know ~. | I haven't seen ~. | Does ~ know?*
—[代] 누구라도, 누군가 ¶①누군가 다른 사람의 책

—*n.* [C] **1.** an important person. ¶*Everybody who was ~ was there.*② **2.** ⟪often *pl.*⟫ not important persons. ¶*Two or three anybodies.*
—[名] 1. 중요한 사람; 제 구실을 하는 사람 ¶②다소 이름 있는 사람이면 다 왔었다 2. 이름 없는 사람들

·an·y·how [énihàu] *adv.* **1.** in any way. **2.** by any means; in any case. **3.** carelessly.
—[副] 1. 어떻게 해서라도 2. 어떻게든 3. 아무렇게나

all anyhow, carelessly.
[熟] 아무렇게나

:an·y·one [éniwʌ̀n] *pron.* any person; anybody.
—[代] 누군가; 누구라도

:an·y·thing [éniθìŋ] *pron.* any thing; everything. **—*adv.*** in any degree.
—[代] 무엇이든지; 무엇인가; 아무것도
—[副] 조금은

:an·y·way [éniwèi] *adv.* **1.** in any manner. **2.** by any means; in any case. **3.** carelessly.
—[副] 1. 어떻게 해서라도 2. 어떻게든 3. 아무렇게나

:an·y·where [éni(h)wɛ̀ər] *adv.* to, in, or at any place.
—[副] 어디엔가, 어디든지

an·y·wise [éniwàiz] *adv.* in any way.
—[副] 어떻게 해서든지

a·pace [əpéis] *adv.* quickly; speedily.
—[副] 빨리; 급히

:a·part [əpάːrt] *adv.* **1.** in or into pieces. **2.** separated from someone or something; independently.
—[副] 1. 따로 [떨어져서] 2. 떼어서

1) ***apart from,*** except for; not considering.
2) ***take something apart,*** break up.
[熟] 1)···은 별문제로 하고 2)[기계 따위]를 분해하다

:a·part·ment [əpάːrtmənt] *n.* [C] a room or a few rooms to live in.
—[名] 방, [부엌 달린] 셋방

ap·a·thet·ic [æpəθétik] *adj.* lacking in feeling or interest; unemotional; indifferent.
—[形] 무감각한, 감정이 없는; 냉담한

ap·a·thy [ǽpəθi] *n.* [U] lack of feeling or interest; indifference.
—[名] 무감각; 무관심; 냉담

ape [eip] *n.* [C] **1.** a large monkey without a tail, such as a chimpanzee or a gorilla. **2.** any monkey. **3.** a person who imitates. —*vt.* imitate.
—[名] 1. 유인원 2. 원숭이 3. 흉내내는 사람 —[他] …을 흉내내다

a·pe·ri·ent [əpíəriənt] *adj.* emptying the bowels. —*n.* [C] a medicine used to empty the bowels.
—[形] 변통(便通)게 효력이 있는 —[名] 하제(下劑)

ap·er·ture [ǽpərtʃər / -tjuə] *n.* [C] a small opening; a hole; a gap.
—[名] 구멍; 틈

a·pex [éipeks] *n.* [C] (pl. **-es** or **a·pi·ces**) **1.** the top; the peak; the summit. **2.** a climax.
—[名] 1. 꼭대기, 정상 2. 절정

a·phid [èifid, ǽf-] *n.* [C] a small insect that sucks the juice of plants; a plant louse.
—[名] 진디

aph·i·des [ǽfidì:z] *n.* pl. of **aphis**.

a·phis [éifis, ǽf-] *n.* [C] (pl. **aph·i·des**) =aphid.

aph·o·rism [ǽfərìz(ə)m] *n.* [C] a concise sentence expressing a general truth; a proverb.
—[名] 격언, 금언

Aph·ro·di·te [æfrədáiti] *n.* (in Greek mythology) the goddess of love and beauty. ⇒[N.B.]
—[名] 아프로디테 [N.B.] 로마신화의 비너스에 해당

a·pi·ar·y [éipièri / -piəri] *n.* [C] (pl. **-ar·ies**) a place in which bees are kept; a beehouse.
—[名] 양봉장(통)

a·pi·ces [ǽpisi:z, éi-] *n.* pl. of **apex**.

a·pi·cul·ture [éipikʌ̀ltʃər] *n.* [U] the care and management of bees for the sale of honey.
—[名] 양봉

a·piece [əpí:s] *adv.* to or for each one. ¶*He gave us one thousand won* ~.①
—[副] 각각, 하나하나 ¶①그는 우리에게 각각 천원씩 주었다

a·poc·a·lypse [əpákəlips / əpɔ́k-] *n.* **1.** (*the A-*) the last book in the New Testament. **2.** [C] a prediction of the future, esp. in early Christian history.
—[名] 1. 묵시록 2. 묵시

a·poc·a·lyp·tic [əpàkəlíptik / əpɔ́k-] *adj.* of the Apocalypse.
—[形] 묵시적인, 묵시록의

:A·pol·lo [əpálou / əpɔ́l-] *n.* (pl. **-los**) **1.** (in Greek and Roman mythology) the god of the sun, poetry, music, prophecy, and youthful manly beauty. **2.** [C] a handsome young man.
—[名] 1. 아폴로 2. 미남자

a·pol·o·get·ic [əpàlədʒétik / əpɔ̀l-], **-i·cal** [-k(ə)l] *adj.* expressing an apology or regret; excusing a fault or an error.
—[形] 변명의, 사과하는

a·pol·o·get·i·cal·ly [əpàlədʒétikəli / əpɔ̀l-] *adv.* in an apologetic manner; as an apology.
—[副] 변명으로

***a·pol·o·gize** [əpálədʒàiz / əpɔ́l-] *vi.* express regret; make an excuse. (~ *for* a failure, mistake, etc.) ▷**a·pol·o·giz·er** [-ər] *n.*
—[自] 사과하다; 변명하다

***a·pol·o·gy** [əpálədʒi / -pɔ́l-] *n.* [C] (pl. **-gies**) **1.** an expression of regret. ¶*make an* ~ *for something.*① **2.** a formal excuse or defense in speech or writing. ¶*a letter of* ~; *a written* ~.②
—[名] 1. 사과, 사죄 ¶①사과하다 2. 정식 변명 ¶②사과장

ap·o·plec·tic [æpəpléktik] *adj.* **1.** of apoplexy. **2.** having or likely to have apoplexy. ¶*an* ~ *fit.*① —*n.* [C] a person who has apoplexy.
—[形] 1. 졸도의 2. 졸도에 걸리기 쉬운 ¶①졸도 —[名] 졸도성이 있는 사람

ap·o·plex·y [ǽpəplèksi] *n.* [U] the sudden loss of the power to feel or move. ¶*be seized with* ~.①
—[名] 졸도 ¶①졸도를 일으키다

a·pos·ta·sy [əpástəsi / əpɔ́s-] *n.* [U][C] (pl. **-sies**) the act of giving up one's religion, principles, political party, etc.
—[名] 배교(背教); 변절; 탈당

a·pos·tate [əpástit, -teit / əpɔ́s-] *n.* [C] a person who gives up his religion, principles, political party, etc. —*adj.* of apostasy.
—[名] 배교자; 배신자; 탈당자 —[形] 배교의; 탈당한

a·pos·tle [əpásl / -pɔ́sl] *n.* **1.** (*A-*) one of the twelve men chosen by Jesus Christ to teach the Gospel to the world. **2.** [C] the first Christian missionary in any region.
—[名] 1. 그리스도의 12사도 중 한 사람 2. [어떤 지방에 있어서의] 최초의 전도자

·a·pos·tro·phe [əpástrəfi / əpɔ́s-] *n.* [C] the sign (') used in writing to show: ⓐ the omission of one or more letters, as in *I'll* (=I will); *can't* (=cannot), *'68* (=
—[名] 어포스트러피(') ⓐ생략을 나타냄 ⓑ소유격을 만듦 ⓒ글자·숫자의 복수를 나타냄 ⓓ회화에서 발음되지 않

1968); ⓑ the possessive case of nouns or indefinite pronouns, as a *dog's* tail, *everybody's* duty; ⓒ the plural of letters and figures, as three *A's*, *5's*; ⓓ that the sound represented in the usual spelling has not been spoken, as Good *mornin'* (=morning).

a·poth·e·car·y [əpάθəkèri / əpɔ́θikəri] *n.* ⓒ (pl. **-car·ies**) a person who is licensed to prescribe medicine.

—명 약제사

ap·pall, -pal [əpɔ́:l] *vt.* fill (someone) with horror; frighten; shock. ¶ *I was appalled at the sight.*

—타 …에 공포심을 품게 하다; …을 오싹하게 하다

ap·pall·ing [əpɔ́:liŋ] *adj.* causing horror; dreadful; shocking. ▷**ap·pall·ing·ly** [-li] *adv.*

—형 간담이 서늘해지는, 오싹해지는

• **ap·pa·ra·tus** [æ̀pəréitəs, +U.S. æ̀pərǽtəs] *n.* ⓒ (pl. **-tus** or **-tus·es** [-təsiz]) 1. an equipment, instrument, etc. necessary for a special purpose. ¶ *an electric ~.*① 2. bodily organs. ¶ *the digestive ~.*②

—명 1. 기구 ¶①전기 기구 2. 기관(器官) ¶②소화 기관

ap·par·el [əpǽr(ə)l] *n.* Ⓤ 1. clothing; garments. 2. (*Nautical*) things used to equip a ship, such as sails and an anchor. ——*vt.* (**-eled, -el·ing** or *Brit.* **-elled, -el·ling**) clothe; dress.

—명 1. 의복 2. [배의] 장구(裝具)
—타 …을 입히다; 차려입다

• **ap·par·ent** [əpǽr(ə)nt, əpέər-] *adj.* 1. easily seen or to be seen. 2. easily understood; evident; plain. 3. seeming to be, but not really true. ¶ *Her reluctance was only ~.*①

—형 1. 눈에 보이는 2. 명백한 3. 외견 상의 ¶①그녀가 싫어한 것은 외관뿐 이었다

: **ap·par·ent·ly** [əpǽr(ə)ntli, əpέər-] *adv.* 1. seemingly. ¶ *He is ~ a gentleman.* 2. clearly; obviously.

—부 1. 보기에는 2. 명백히

ap·pa·ri·tion [æ̀pəríʃ(ə)n] *n.* 1. ⓒ a ghost; a specter. 2. ⓒ anything strange or unexpected that comes into sight; a phantom.

—명 1. 유령, 도깨비 2. 갑자기 나타나는 이상한 것; 환영(幻影)

: **ap·peal** [əpí:l] *vi.* 1. ask or request earnestly. (*~ for* or *to* something; *~ to* someone *to do*; *~ to* someone *for mercy, aid, etc.*) ¶ *~ for funds* / *The lost child appealed to the policeman for help.* 2. use something as a means; resort. (*~ to* something) ¶ *~ to arms.* 3. take a law case to a higher court. ¶ *~ the judgment to the Supreme Court.* 4. move the feelings; be interesting or attractive. (*~ to* someone) ¶ *These pictures do not ~ to the young.* 〔and hold a general election.〕 **appeal to the country,** (*Brit.*) break up Parliament 〕 ——*n.* 1. ⓒ an earnest request; a prayer. ¶ *an ~ to someone for help* / *make an ~ to reason* / *make an ~ for support.* 2. Ⓤⓒ a request to have a law case heard again before a higher court or judge; the right to have a law case heard again. ¶ *a court of ~*① / *direct ~.*② 3. Ⓤ attraction; interest. ¶ *sex ~* / *This sort of music has much ~ for* (or *to*) *them.*

—자 1. 애원(간청)하다 2. [무력 따위에] 호소하다 3. 상고(공소)하다 4. [사물이 사람의] 마음에 들다, 흥미를 끌다, 매력이 있다

圞 《英》[의회를 해산하고] 여론에 묻다
—명 1. 애원, 애소, 간청; [무력·여론에의] 호소 2. 상고, 공소; 공소권 ¶① 공소심 재판소/②직접 소송 3. 매력, 마음에 호소하는 힘

ap·peal·ing [əpí:liŋ] *adj.* attractive; interesting; touching.

—형 애원하는[듯한]; 심금을 울리는

: **ap·pear** [əpíər] *vi.* 1. come into sight; become clear or plain. ↔disappear ¶ *The moon appeared in the sky.* / *One by one the stars appeared.* 2. seem or look. (*~ [to be] ill, happy, etc.*) ¶ *She appears [to be] rich.*① / *She appears to have been rich.* 3. be published. ¶ *~ in the Times* / *The book will ~ next month.*② 4. act or perform publicly. ¶ *~ as Hamlet*③ / *He appears on television.* 5. present oneself. ¶ *~ in court* / *~ before a committee.*
    It appears [to me] that ..., It seems [to me] that ..., I think that .... ¶ *It appears to me that he is dishonest.*

—자 1. 나타나다 2. …인 듯하다 ¶① 그녀는 부자 같다 3. 발행되다 ¶② 이 책은 내달에 나온다 4. [극에] 출연하다 ¶③햄릿역으로 출연하다 5. 출두하다

圞 [나에게는] …이라고 생각되다

: **ap·pear·ance** [əpíərəns] *n.* 1. ⓒ the act of appearing (before the public, in a law court, etc.); the publication of a book. ¶ *The first ~ of this book.* 2. Ⓤⓒ outward look; outward show. ¶ *one's personal ~* / *a man of noble ~* / *judge by appearances* / *outward ~* / *put on the ~ of innocence.*① 3. (*pl.*) outward impressions;

—명 1. 출현, 출두, 출정; 출판, 발간 2. 모습; 외관, 풍채, 겉치레 ¶①순진한 체하다 3. 형세, 상황, 정세 ¶②보기에는 그는 재미를 보고 있었다

appease [66] **application**

circumstances. ¶*By all appearances, he enjoyed himself.*② / *Appearances are against us.*

1) *keep up* (or *save*) *appearances,* keep an outward show of prosperity. 「pear publicly; attend.」
2) *make* (or *put in*) *an* (or *one's*) *appearance,* ap-
3) *to all appearance*[*s*], as far as one can see or judge.

ap·pease [əpíːz] *vt.* **1.** quiet (an angry person, etc.). **2.** satisfy (an appetite, etc.). **3.** yield to the demands of (someone). 「the state of being appeased.」

ap·pease·ment [əpíːzmənt] *n.* Ⓤ the act of appeasing;

ap·pel·lant [əpélənt] *n.* Ⓒ a person who appeals to a higher court. —*adj.* of appeals.

ap·pel·la·tion [æpəléiʃ(ə)n] *n.* Ⓒ a name or title by which a person or thing is known.

ap·pend [əpénd] *vt.* **1.** attach; add. (《~ a supplement *to* a book, etc.》 **2.** hang.

ap·pend·age [əpéndidʒ] *n.* Ⓒ **1.** anything attached to a greater thing; an addition. **2.** any subordinate part of a body, such as an arm, a leg, or a tail.

ap·pen·di·ces [əpéndisìːz] *n.* pl. of **appendix**.

ap·pen·di·ci·tis [əpèndisáitis] *n.* Ⓤ a diseased condition of the human appendix.

ap·pen·dix [əpéndiks] *n.* Ⓒ (pl. **-dix·es** or **-di·ces** [-disìːz]) **1.** anything appended; an additional part of a book to give further information. **2.** (*Anatomy*) a worm-like tube attached to the large intestine.

ap·per·tain [æpərtéin] *vi.* belong; be related or fit. (《~ *to* something》 ¶*a piece of furniture appertaining to a living room.*

* **ap·pe·tite** [æpitàit] *n.* Ⓒ Ⓤ **1.** a desire for food or drink; hunger. ¶(*proverb*) *A good ~ is a good sauce.*② **2.** a strong and active desire. ¶*an ~ for reading.*②

ap·pe·tiz·er [æpitàizər] *n.* Ⓒ a kind of food or 「k to arouse the appetite. 「meal.」

ap·pe·tiz·ing [æpitàiziŋ] *adj.* arousing the appetite. ¶~」

* **ap·plaud** [əplɔ́ːd] *vi.* show approval by clapping hands or cheering. —*vt.* **1.** show approval of (something), esp. by clapping hands. **2.** admire; commend.

* **ap·plause** [əplɔ́ːz] *n.* Ⓤ **1.** approval, esp. shown by clapping hands. **2.** admiration; praise.

‡ **ap·ple** [æpl] *n.* Ⓒ a round, usu. red, yellow, or green fruit; the tree that bears this fruit.

1) *the apple of contention* (or *discord*), the cause of discord. ⇒N.B.
2) *an apple of love; a love apple,* a tomato.
3) *the apple of the eye,* ⓐ the pupil of the eye. ⓑ something very important. ¶*love a child as the ~ of the eye.*① 「under a crust.」

apple pie [≤ ≤] *n.* a pie baked with apples and sugar

ap·ple-pie order [æplpaiɔ́ːrdər] *n.* (*colloq.*) perfect or excellent order.

in apple-pie order, in perfect order.

ap·ple·sauce [æplsɔ̀ːs] *n.* Ⓤ **1.** apples stewed until soft. **2.** (*U.S. colloq.*) nonsense.

ap·pli·ance [əpláiəns] *n.* **1.** Ⓤ the act of applying. **2.** Ⓒ an article for some special purpose; an apparatus. ¶*a medical ~.*① 「applicable.」

ap·pli·ca·bil·i·ty [æplikəbíliti] *n.* Ⓤ the quality of being

ap·pli·ca·ble [æplikəbl] *adj.* that can be applied; suitable.

ap·pli·cant [æplikənt] *n.* Ⓒ a person who asks for something or some position; a candidate. ¶*an ~ for a position*① / *an ~ for entrance.*②

‡ **ap·pli·ca·tion** [æplikéiʃ(ə)n] *n.* **1.** Ⓤ the act of applying; the state of being applied. ¶*the ~ of a theory*

圈 1)체면을 차리다 2)나타나다, 얼굴을 내밀다, 출두하다 3)보기에는

—⑩ 1. …을 달래다 2. …을 만족시키다 3. …에게 양보하다

—③ 위로, 진정; 유화(宥和)
—③ 공소인 —⑬ 공소의

—③ 명칭, 칭호

—⑩ 1. …을 붙이다, 부가하다 2. …을 매달다
—③ 1. 부가물 2. [손·발 따위] 부속기관

—③ 충수염, 맹장염

—③ 1. 부가물; 부록 2. 《解》 충양돌기

—⑥ 속하다; 관련하다; 적합하다

—⑩ 1. 식욕 ¶①시장이 반찬이다 2. 욕구 ¶②독서욕

—③ 식욕을 돋구는 것

—⑬ 식욕을 돋구는
—⑥ 박수갈채하다 —⑩ 1. …을 박수갈채하다 2. …을 칭찬하다

—③ 1. 박수갈채 2. 칭찬

—③ 사과; 사과나무

圈 1)불화의 사과; 불화의 원인 N.B. Troy 전쟁의 원인이 된 황금의 사과 2) 토마토의 별명 3)ⓐ눈동자 ⓑ소중한 것 ¶①아이를 지독히 사랑하다

—③ 사과파이
—③ 질서정연

圈 질서 정연하게
—③ 1. 사과 소오스 2. 《美口》 헛소리; 아첨
—③ 1. 적용; 응용 2. 기구; 장치 ¶① 의료기구

—③ 적응성
—⑬ 적용할 수 있는; 적절한
—③ 지원자; 후보자 ¶①취직 지망자 /②입학 지원자

—③ 1. 적용, 응용 ¶①이론의 실지 응용 2. 신청; 출원; 원서 ¶②신청 용

*to practice.*① **2.** [C] a spoken or written request for a position, membership, etc. ¶*an ~ form* (or *blank*)② / *make an ~ for employment.*③ **3.** [U] attention; diligence; effort. ¶*a man of close ~.*④

지/③취직을 신청하다 3. 전심, 전력; 근면 ¶④아주 부지런한 사람

ap·plied [əpláid] *adj.* put to or used in practical purposes. ¶*~ chemistry.*①

—[形] [실제로] 응용된 ¶①응용화학

ap·pli·qué [æplikéi / æplí:kei] *adj.* ornamented by a different material sewn on. —*n.* [U] an ornament made of a different material sewn on.

—[形] [의복 따위에] 다른 재료를 꿰매 붙인 —[名] 아플리케

‡ ap·ply [əplái] *v.* (**-plied**) *vt.* **1.** put on; place (something) in contact. ⦅~ something *to*⦆ ¶*~ a match to a candle* / *~ a plaster to a wound.* **2.** use practically; put (something) into practice. ⦅~ something *to*; ~ a word or expression *to*⦆ ¶*~ a theory to a case* / *~ force.* **3.** use (something) for a special purpose. ¶*~ the money for the benefit of the poor.* —*vi.* **1.** ask; make a request. ⦅~ *for* something; ~ *to* someone *for*⦆ ¶*~ for a job* / *~ to a friend for aid* / *You can ~ by letter.* **2.** fit; be suitable; have a connection. ⦅~ *to* someone or something⦆ ¶*This does not ~ to women.*
apply oneself (or *one's* ***mind***) ***to*** (=*concentrate on*) *something.*

—[他] 1. …을 대다, 덧붙이다, 바르다 2. …을 적용하다; 응용(사용)하다 3. [어떤 목적]에 충당하다, 쓰다 —[自] 1. 지원하다, 신청하다; 조회(문의)하다 2. 적용되다, 적합하다

[熟] …에 전력(전심)하다

‡ ap·point [əpɔ́int] *vt.* **1.** name or choose (someone) for a position; designate. ⦅~ someone *to* a post⦆ **2.** decide on (the time, date, place, etc.); fix; set. ¶*~ the time for the meeting.* ▷**ap·point·or** [-ər] *n.*

—[他] 1. …을 임명하다 2. [시일·장소 따위]를 정하다.

*** ap·point·ment** [əpɔ́intmənt] *n.* [C][U] **1.** the act of appointing. **2.** office; position. **3.** a mutual agreement to meet; an engagement. ¶*make an ~*① / *I have an ~ with my dentist at two.*②

—[名] 1. 지정; 선정; 임명 2. 임무; 관직 3. [모임 따위의] 약속 ¶①약속하다/②두 시에 치과 의사에게 간다는 약속이 있다

ap·por·tion [əpɔ́:rʃ(ə)n] *vt.* give a part of (something) to each; divide; distribute; allot.

—[他] …을 배분하다

ap·por·tion·ment [əpɔ́:rʃ(ə)nmənt] *n.* [U][C] the act of apportioning; the state of being apportioned; distribution.

—[名] 배분; 할당

ap·po·site [ǽpəzit] *adj.* proper; apt; suitable.

—[形] 적절한

ap·po·si·tion [æpəzíʃ(ə)n] *n.* [U] **1.** the act of placing side by side. **2.** (*Grammar*) the addition of one noun as a supplement to another. ⇒[N.B.]

—[名] 1. 병치(並置) 2. ⦅文法⦆ 동격 [N.B.] "Mary, my sister, is sick." 중에서 Mary와 sister는 동격

ap·prais·al [əpréiz(ə)l] *n.* [U][C] the act of appraising; the state of being appraised; valuation.

—[名] 평가; 값을 매기기; 감정(鑑定)

ap·praise [əpréiz] *vt.* judge the quality, value, importance, etc. of (something); estimate.

—[他] …을 평가하다, 값을 매기다

ap·pre·ci·a·ble [əprí:ʃ(i)əbl] *adj.* that can be felt or estimated. ¶*an ~ difference between two ideas.*

—[形] 감지할 수 있는; 평가할 수 있는

ap·pre·ci·a·bly [əprí:ʃ(i)əbli] *adv.* to an appreciable degree; somewhat.

—[副] 다소

‡ ap·pre·ci·ate [əprí:ʃièit] *vt.* **1.** feel and understand the value of (something or someone); like; enjoy. ¶*~ French poetry* / *~ good food* / *~ one's friends.* **2.** understand; judge rightly. ¶*~ someone's situation* / *~ small differences in sounds.* **3.** be grateful for (something). ¶*I greatly ~ your kindness.* / *We appreciated a rest after our hard work.*

—[他] 1. [사물·사람]의 진가(眞價)를 인정하다; 맛있게 맛보다; 감상하다 2. …을 올바르게 평가하다, 알아차리다 3. …을 고맙게 여기다

*** ap·pre·ci·a·tion** [əprì:ʃiéiʃ(ə)n] *n.* [U] **1.** the act of appreciating. ¶*in ~ of something.*① **2.** the act or ability of understanding the value. ¶*~ of painting.* **3.** gratitude; thankfulness.

—[名] 1. 진가를 인정하기; 감상 ¶①…을 충분히 알고, 칭찬하여 2. 이해 3. 감사

ap·pre·ci·a·tive [əprí:ʃiətiv, -ʃièitiv] *adj.* able to appreciate; feeling gratitude. ▷**ap·pre·ci·a·tive·ly** [-li] *adv.*
be appreciative of (=*be thankful for*) *something* ¶*I am always ~ of his kindness.*①

—[形] 감식력이 있는; 감사한

[熟] …을 감사하고 있다 ¶①그의 친절을 언제나 감사하고 있다

ap·pre·hend [æprihénd] *vt.* **1.** arrest; seize. ¶*The thief was apprehended by a policeman.* **2.** grasp the meaning of (something); understand thoroughly. **3.** expect

—[他] 1. …을 체포하다 2. [의미]를 이해하다 3. …을 염려하다, 걱정하다 ¶①…할 염려가 있다 —[自] 이해하다;

(something) with fear; dread. ¶*It is apprehended that* ...① —*vi.* understand; be fearful.

불안하게 생각하다

ap·pre·hen·si·ble [æprihénsibl] *adj.* that can be understood.

—[形] 이해할 수 있는, 납득이 가는

ap·pre·hen·sion [æprihénʃ(ə)n] *n.* [U] **1.** 《often *pl.*》 fear of what might happen. ¶*entertain apprehensions.*① **2.** 《sometimes *an* ~》 the ability to understand; conception. ¶*be above one's* ~.② **3.** the act of arresting.

—[名] 1. [장래에 대한] 불안 ¶①불안을 품다 2. 이해; 이해력 ¶②이해가 되지 않다 3. 체포

ap·pre·hen·sive [æprihénsiv] *adj.* **1.** fearful about something that might happen; anxious; uneasy. ¶*be ~ for someone's safety*① / *be ~ of failure.*② **2.** quick to understand; intelligent. **3.** perceptive. ▷**ap·pre·hen·sive·ly** [-li] *adv.* —**ap·pre·hen·sive·ness** [-nis] *n.*

—[形] 1. 염려(걱정)하는 ¶①남의 안전을 염려하다 2. 이해가 빠른 3. 지각적(知覺的)인

* **ap·pren·tice** [əpréntis] *n.* [C] **1.** a person who works under a skilled worker to learn a trade. **2.** a beginner; a learner. —*vt.* put (someone) under a master to learn a trade. ¶*He was apprenticed to a tailor.*

—[名] 1. 도제(徒弟) 2. 초심자 —[他] …을 도제로 보내다

ap·pren·tice·ship [əpréntisʃip] *n.* [U] **1.** the state of being an apprentice. **2.** the period of time for which a person works as an apprentice.

—[名] 1. 도제[의 신분] 2. 도제의 연한

‡ **ap·proach** [əpróutʃ] *vt.* **1.** come or go near or nearer to (a place). **2.** bring (something) near. 《~ something *to*》 ¶~ *a magnet to a piece of iron.* **3.** come near to (something or someone) in quality, character, time, or condition; come to resemble. ¶~ *completion* / *As a poet he hardly approaches Shakespeare.* **4.** try to have personal relations with; speak to (someone). ¶~ *someone with a proposal* (*on a matter*). **5.** begin to study (something). ¶~ *a problem.* —*vi.* go near or nearer; come close or closer. 《~ *to* something》 ¶*Winter is approaching.* / *Her reply approached to a denial.*

—[他] 1. [장소]에 다가가다, 접근하다 2. …에 가까와지게 하다 3. [시간·상태 따위]에 가까와지다 4. …에 접근하다, 접촉을 시작하다 5. …을 연구하다 —[自] 접근하다; …에 가깝다, 근사하다

—*n.* **1.** [U] the act of coming near or nearer, or of going near or nearer. ¶*the ~ of summer* / *easy* (*difficult*) *of* ~① / *He waited for her* ~. **2.** [C] a way of reaching a place or beginning something; access. ¶*an ~ to literature*② / *the ~ to the cave.* **3.** 《*pl.*》 attempts to open personal relations; advances. ¶*make approaches to someone*③ / *make one's approaches to someone.*④

—[名] 1. 접근, 가까이하기 ¶①가까이하기 쉬운(어려운) 2. 접근하는 길, 입구, 길목, 어귀; 연구법, 길잡이, 개론 ¶②문학의 길잡이 3. 교섭, 친근책; 치근거림; 제의 ¶③…에게 접근하다/④…에게 알랑거리다

ap·proach·a·ble [əpróutʃəbl] *adj.* **1.** that can be approached. **2.** easy to talk with; friendly.

—[形] 1. 가까이하기 쉬운 2. 사귀기 쉬운

ap·pro·ba·tion [æprəbéiʃ(ə)n] *n.* [U] approval.

—[名] 시인(是認); 칭찬

* **ap·pro·pri·ate** *adj.* [əpróupriit → *v.*] suitable; proper. ¶~ *to the occasion*① / *goods ~ for Christmas gifts.*

—[形] 알맞은, 적당한 ¶①그 경우에 어울리는

—*vt.* [əpróuprièit] **1.** use (something) for a special purpose. 《~ something *to* or *for* a plan, etc.》 ¶~ *the money for one's new house.* **2.** take and use (something) for oneself; steal. ¶~ *public money to oneself.* ▷**ap·pro·pri·ate·ly** [-itli] *adv.* —**ap·pro·pri·ate·ness** [-nis] *n.* —**ap·pro·pri·a·tor** [-èit(ə)r] *n.*

—[他] 1. [특수 목적에] …을 유용하다 2. …을 사용(私用)으로 쓰다; 횡령(착복)하다

ap·pro·pri·a·tion [əpròupriéiʃ(ə)n] *n.* **1.** [U] the act of appropriating; the state of being appropriated. **2.** [C] money kept or used for some special purpose.

—[名] 1. 전유(專有); 유용(流用) 2. 지출금

* **ap·prov·al** [əprú:v(ə)l] *n.* [U] **1.** the act of approving. **2.** formal permission.

—[名] 1. 시인(是認) 2. 인가

goods on approval, goods that can be sent back if not satisfactory.

[熟] 써 보고 마음에 들면 사는 물건

‡ **ap·prove** [əprú:v] *vt.* **1.** speak or think well of (someone or something). ¶~ *a plan.* **2.** permit formally. —*vi.* speak or think favorably. 《~ *of* something》 ¶*Mother did not ~ of my idea.*①

—[他] 1. …을 좋다고 인정하다 2. …을 인가하다 —[自] 좋게 말(생각)하다 ¶①어머니는 내 생각을 좋게 생각하지 않았다

ap·prov·ing [əprú:viŋ] *adj.* satisfactory.

—[形] 만족스러운

ap·prov·ing·ly [əprú:viŋli] *adv.* in an approving manner; with satisfaction.

—[副] 만족하여

ap·prox·i·mate *adj.* [əprɑ́ksimit / -prɔ́ksi- // → *v.*] fairly exact; very near; very similar. ¶~ *estimate.*①

—[形] 비슷한, 정확에 가까운 ¶①개산(概算)

—*vt.* [əprάksəmèit / -rɔ́ksi-] come close to (something); approach. ¶ ~ *perfection.*② —*vi.* be nearly equal. ⟪~ *to* something⟫ ¶ *Her description approximates to reality.*③

—[他] …에 다가가다 ¶②완성에 가까와지다 —[自] [분량·성질 따위] …에 가깝다 ¶③그녀의 묘사는 진실에 가깝다

* **ap·prox·i·mate·ly** [əprάksimitli / -prɔ́ksi-] *adv.* in an approximate manner; very nearly; about.

—[副] 대략, 거의

ap·prox·i·ma·tion [əprὰksiméiʃ(ə)n / -rɔ̀ksi-] *n.* **1.** [C] a fairly exact estimate. **2.** [U] [C] the state of being more or less exact; a close approach. ¶*an ~ to perfection.*①

—[名] 1. 개산(概算) 2. 근사; 접근 ¶①완전에 가까운 것

ap·pur·te·nance [əpə́:rtinəns] *n.* ⟪usu. *pl.*⟫ an accessory.

—[名] 부속물

Apr. April.

a·pri·cot [éiprikὰt / -kɔ̀t] *n.* **1.** [C] a small, soft, round, orange-colored fruit, somewhat like a peach; [C] the tree that bears this fruit. **2.** [U] pale orange-yellow; pinkish yellow.

—[名] 1. 살구; 살구나무 2. 살구빛

‡ **A·pril** [éipr(ə)l, -pril] *n.* the fourth month of the year. ⇒[N.B.]

—[名] 4월 [N.B.] Apr.로 줄임

a pri·o·ri [èipraiɔ́:rai, ὰ:priɔ́:ri: / ⌐-⌐-] *adv., adj.* from cause to effect; from a general rule to each instance.

—[副][形] 원인에서 결과로[의]; 연역적(演繹的)으로(인)

* **a·pron** [éipr(ə)n] *n.* [C] **1.** a covering made of cloth, rubber, leather, etc., worn to protect clothes. **2.** anything like an apron in shape or use. ¶*an ~ stage.*①

—[名] 1. 앞치마, 에이프런 2. 에이프런 모양의 것 ¶①[극장의] 막 앞의 돌출무대

tied to one's mother's (wife's) apron strings, completely depending on one's mother (wife).

[熟] 어머니(아내)에게 쥐어 살다

ap·ro·pos [æ̀prəpóu / ǽprəpòu] *adv.* to the point; suitably.

—[副] 적절히

1) ***apropos of,*** with reference to.

2) ***apropos of nothing,*** without any previous notice; suddenly; unconnected with the subject being talked about.

[熟] 1)…에 관하여 2)불쑥, 갑자기

—*adj.* fitting; suitable. ¶ ~ *words.*

—[形] 적절한, 계제 좋은

apse [æps] *n.* [C] a half-round place at the east end of a church.

—[名] 후진(後陣)(교회당 동쪽 끝의 반원형의 부분)

* **apt** [æpt] *adj.* **1.** inclined; likely. ¶*We are ~ to make mistakes.* **2.** quick to learn; intelligent. ¶*She is ~ at music.*① **3.** suitable; appropriate. ¶*an ~ remark / He is ~ for this kind of job.*

—[形] 1. …하는 경향이 있는; …할 듯한 2. 영리한, 이해가 빠른 ¶①그녀는 음악에 재능이 있다 3. 적당한; 적절한

ap·ti·tude [ǽptit(j)ù:d / -tjù:d] *n.* [C] [U] fitness; ability or quickness to learn; talent; intelligence; inclination. ¶*an ~ test*① */ have an ~ for languages.*②

—[名] 적응성; 소질; 재능; 이해력; 경향 ¶①적성 검사/②어학의 재능이 있다

apt·ly [ǽptli] *adv.* in an apt manner; suitably.

—[副] 적절히

apt·ness [ǽptnis] *n.* [U] the quality of being apt; aptitude.

—[名] 적응성

aq·ua·lung [ǽkwəlʌ̀ŋ] *n.* [C] a cylinder of oxygen fastened to a person's back for underwater swimming. ⇒fig.

—[名] 수중폐(水中肺)(압축공기를 넣은 잠수용 수중 호흡기)

(aqualung)

a·quar·i·a [əkwέəriə] *n.* pl. of **aquarium.**

a·quar·i·um [əkwέəriəm] *n.* [C] (pl. **-ums** or **a·quar·i·a**) **1.** a tank, pond, or bowl for keeping water animals and water plants. **2.** a building used for showing collections of water animals and water plants.

—[名] 1. 양어(養魚)통; 양어 연못 2. 수족관(水族館)

a·quat·ic [əkwǽtik, +*U.S.* əkwάt-, +*Brit.* əkwɔ́t-] *adj.* **1.** living in the water. **2.** in or on water. ¶ ~ *sports.* —*n.* [C] an animal or plant living in the water.

—[形] 1. 수생(水生)의 2. 수중의, 물 위의 —[名] 수생 동물; 수초

aq·ue·duct [ǽkwidʌ̀kt] *n.* [C] **1.** a pipe or a man-made channel through which water is led from a distance. **2.** a tube or passage in the body.

—[名] 1. 수도, 수로(水路) 2. 맥관(脈管)

a·que·ous [éikwiəs, ǽk-] *adj.* **1.** of water. **2.** produced by water.

—[形] 1. 물의 2. 수성(水成)의

aq·ui·line [ǽkwilàin, +*U.S.* -lin] *adj.* **1.** of or like an eagle. ¶ ~ *features.* **2.** hooked like an eagle's beak.

—[形] 1. 독수리 같은 2. 갈고리 모양으로 굽은

Ar·ab [ǽrəb] *n.* [C] **1.** a person of the Arabian Peninsula or north Africa. **2.** an Arab horse. —*adj.* of the Arabs; of Arabia.

—[名] 1. 아라비아 사람 2. 아라비아 말(馬) —[形] 아라비아[사람]의

ar·a·besque [ærəbésk] *n.* ⓒ a kind of fanciful Arabian design of flowers, leaves, geometrical figures, etc. ⇒fig.

A·ra·bi·a [əréibiə] *n.* a peninsula in the southwestern part of Asia.

A·ra·bi·an [əréibiən] *adj.* of Arabia; of the Arabs. ——*n.* ⓒ an Arab.

Ar·a·bic [ǽrəbik] *adj.* **1.** of the language of the Arabs. **2.** of the Arabs. **3.** of Arabia. ¶~ *architecture.* ——*n.* Ⓤ the language of the Arabs.

[arabesque]

Arabic numerals [⌐⌐⌐] *n. pl.* the figures 0, 1, 2, 3, 4, 5, 6, 7, 8, 9.

ar·a·ble [ǽrəbl] *adj.* fit to be plowed or to produce crops.

ar·bi·ter [á:rbitər] *n.* ⓒ a person chosen to settle a quarrel; a judge whose decision is final.

ar·bit·ra·ment [a:rbítrəmənt] *n.* Ⓤ the act of deciding; ⓒ decision by an arbiter.

ar·bi·trar·i·ly [á:rbitrèrili / á:rbitrər-] *adv.* in an arbitrary manner; without sufficient reason.

ar·bi·trar·y [á:rbitrèri / á:rbitrəri] *adj.* **1.** decided or done according to one's own wishes. **2.** ruled by one's own will or absolute authority. ¶~ *rule.*①

ar·bi·trate [á:rbitrèit] *vt.* settle (something) by arbitration. ——*vi.* act as an arbiter; decide.

ar·bi·tra·tion [à:rbitréiʃ(ə)n] *n.* Ⓤⓒ settlement of a difference of opinion by the decision of a judge or an umpire. *submit something to arbitration,* decide by arbitration.

ar·bi·tra·tor [á:rbitrèitər] *n.* ⓒ a person who is chosen to settle a dispute. ↔arbitrate

ar·bor [á:rbər] *n.* ⓒ a place in a garden or park made shady by trees or climbing plants. [trees.]

ar·bo·re·al [a:rbɔ́:riəl] *adj.* **1.** of trees. **2.** living among

ar·bour [á:rbər] *n. Brit.* =arbor. [*lamp*].①

• **arc** [a:rk] *n.* ⓒ a part of a circle. ¶*an* ~ *light* (or

ar·cade [a:rkéid] *n.* ⓒ **1.** a series of arches supported by columns. ⇒fig. **2.** a covered street, usu. having an arched roof and shops along the sides.

:arch¹ [a:rtʃ] *n.* ⓒ **1.** a curved structure supporting the weight of what is above it, as in gateways, bridges, etc. **2.** anything like an arch. ¶*a triumphal* ~① / *the* ~ *of the heavens.*②
[arcade 1.]
——*vt.* curve (something) like an arch; form (something) in the shape of an arch. ¶*A cat arches its back.*③ ——*vi.* become like an arch.

arch² [a:rtʃ] *adj.* **1.** chief. ⇒N.B. ¶*an archbishop.* **2.** pleasantly mischievous; cunning. [archaeology.]

ar·chae·o·log·i·cal [à:rkiələdʒik(ə)l / à:kiəlɔ́dʒ-] *adj.* of

ar·chae·ol·o·gist [à:rkiálədʒist / à:kiɔ́l-] *n.* ⓒ an expert in archaeology. [ancient things.]

ar·chae·ol·o·gy [à:rkiálədʒi / à:kiɔ́l-] *n.* Ⓤ the study of

ar·cha·ic [a:rkéiik] *adj.* gone out of use or date; ancient; of ancient times. ¶*an* ~ *word.*①

ar·cha·ism [á:rkiiz(ə)m, -keiiz(ə)m] *n.* **1.** ⓒ a word or expression no longer used. **2.** Ⓤ use of what is archaic, as in art, etc. [order.]

arch·an·gel [á:rkèindʒ(ə)l] *n.* ⓒ an angel of the highest

• **arch·bish·op** [á:rtʃbíʃəp] *n.* ⓒ the highest of a group of bishops.

arch·duke [á:rtʃd(j)ú:k / á:tʃdjú:k] *n.* ⓒ a son of an Emperor of Austria. [arch.]

arched [a:rtʃt] *adj.* shaped like an arch; having an

——ⓝ 아라비아 무늬, 당초(唐草) 무늬

——ⓝ 아라비아

——ⓐ 아라비아[사람]의
——ⓝ 아라비아 사람
——ⓐ 1. 아라비아어의 2. 아라비아 사람의 3. 아라비아 식의 ——ⓝ 아라비아어

——ⓝ 아라비아 숫자

——ⓐ 경작에 알맞는
——ⓝ 중재인, 전권 결재자

——ⓝ 재결(裁決), 심판

——ⓐⓓ 제멋대로, 독단적으로

——ⓐ 1. 제멋대로의, 독단적인 2. 전제(專制)의 ¶①전제 정치

——ⓥⓣ …을 중재에 의해 결정하다, 중재에 붙이다 ——ⓥⓘ 중재하다
——ⓝ 중재[재판]

熟 [분쟁]을 중재에 붙이다
——ⓝ 중재인(자)

——ⓝ 녹음이 우거진 장소

——ⓐ 1. 나무의 2. 나무 사이에서 사는
——ⓝ 호(弧) ¶①아아크등
——ⓝ 1. 아아치[기둥]의 열(列) 2. [양쪽에 점포가 늘어선] 지붕 있는 도로, 아아케이드

——ⓝ 1. 아아치[형의 문], 홍예문 2. 활 모양의 것 ¶①개선문/②창공

——ⓥⓣ 아아치형으로 구부리다 ¶③고양이는 등을 활처럼 구부린다 ——ⓥⓘ 아아치형이 되다
——ⓐ 1. 주요한 N.B. 주로 합성어에 씀 2. 장난꾸러기의; 교활한
——ⓐ 고고학[상]의, 고고학적인
——ⓝ 고고학자

——ⓝ 고고학
——ⓐ 고대의, 시대에 뒤진, 낡은 ¶①고어(古語)
——ⓝ 1. 고어 2. 고체(古體), 의고(擬古)주의, 고풍

——ⓝ 대천사(大天使)
——ⓝ 대감독, 대사교, 대승정

——ⓝ 대공(大公)

——ⓐ 아아치형의, 아아치가 있는

arch·er [á:rtʃər] *n.* **1.** [C] a person who shoots arrows with a bow. **2.** ⦅*the A-*⦆ the group of stars named Sagittarius.
—[名] 1. 사수(射手), 궁술가 2. ⦅天⦆사수좌

arch·er·y [á:rtʃəri] *n.* [U] the art of shooting with bows and arrows.
—[名] 궁술

ar·che·type [á:rkitàip] *n.* [C] an original model or pattern.
—[名] 원형

Ar·chi·bald [á:rtʃibəld, -bɔ̀:ld] *n.* a man's name.
—[名] 남자 이름

Ar·chi·me·des [à:rkimí:di:z] *n.* (287?–212 B.C.) a Greek mathematician and scientist.
—[名] 아르키메데스 (옛 그리이스의 수학자·과학자)

ar·chi·pel·a·go [à:rkipéligou, -pélə-] *n.* [C] (pl. **-goes** or **-gos**) **1.** a group of many islands in a sea. **2.** a sea having such a group of islands.
—[名] 1. 제도(諸島) 2. 다도해

* **ar·chi·tect** [á:rkitèkt] *n.* [C] a person who plans buildings or, sometimes, ships. ¶*a naval ~.*①
—[名] 건축가, 설계자 ¶①조선 기사

ar·chi·tec·tur·al [à:rkitéktʃ(ə)r(ə)l] *adj.* of architecture.
—[形] 건축[술]의, 건축상의

* **ar·chi·tec·ture** [á:rkitèktʃər] *n.* [U] **1.** the science or art of building. **2.** a style or system of building. **3.** ⦅*collectively*⦆ buildings; structures.
—[名] 1. 건축술, 건축학 2. 건축 양식 3. 건축물

ar·chives [á:rkaivz] *n. pl.* **1.** a place where public documents or records are kept. **2.** public or historical records.
—[名] 1. 기록(공문서) 보관소 2. 고문서(古文書), 기록류, 공문서

arch·ly [á:rtʃli] *adv.* cleverly; mischievously.
—[副] 교활하게, 장난꾸러기처럼

arch·way [á:rtʃwèi] *n.* [C] an entrance or passage covered with an arch.
—[名] 아아치 밑의 통로

arc lamp [ˊ ˊ] *n.* an arc light.
—[名] 아아크 등

arc light [ˊ ˊ] *n.* a lamp giving light by means of an electric arc.
—[名] 아아크 등

* **arc·tic** [á:rktik] *adj.* **1.** of or near the North Pole. ↔ antarctic **2.** very cold; frigid. **—*n.*** ⦅*the A-*⦆ the north polar district.
—[形] 1. 북극의 2. 극한(極寒)의 —[名] 북극[지방]

Arctic Circle [ˊ– ˊ–], **the** *n.* a line parallel to the equator at the latitude of 66°73′ North.
—[名] 북극권

Arctic Ocean [ˊ– ˊ–], **the** *n.* the ocean to the north of North America, Asia and the Arctic Circle.
—[名] 북극해

Arctic Pole [ˊ– ˊ], **the** *n.* the North Pole.
—[名] 북극

ar·dent [á:rd(ə)nt] *adj.* **1.** eager; with strong feelings. ¶*an ~ lover of music.* **2.** burning; hot. ¶*~ spirit.*①
—[形] 1. 열심인, 열렬한 2. 불타는 [듯한] ¶①독한 술

ar·dent·ly [á:rd(ə)ntli] *adv.* with eagerness; eagerly.
—[副] 열심히, 열렬하게

ar·dor, *Brit.* **-dour** [á:rdər] *n.* [U] warm, strong feeling; strong love. ¶*with ~.*①
—[名] 열심, 열정 ¶①열심히

ar·du·ous [á:rdʒuəs / á:dju-] *adj.* **1.** very difficult; requiring much hard work. **2.** using much energy; energetic. ¶*an ~ effort*① / *an ~ worker.* **3.** steep; hard to climb.
—[形] 1. 힘이 드는, 곤란한 2. 끈기있는 ¶①끊임없는 노력 3. 가파른, 험준한

‡ **are**[1] [ɑ:r, ər] *v., auxil. v.* (**were, been**) present plural and second person singular of **be**.
—[自] be의 2인칭 단수, 1·2·3인칭의 복수 현재

are[2] [ɛər, ɑ:r / ɑ:] *n.* [C] a unit of land-measure equal to 100 square meters.
—[名] 아아르(100평방 미터)

‡ **ar·e·a** [ɛ́əriə] *n.* **1.** [U][C] the size of any surface such as land, water, or a floor. **2.** [C] a part of a country or district. ¶*an industrial ~.*① **3.** [C] a field. ¶*a wide ~ of scientific investigation.*②
—[名] 1. 면적 2. 지역, 지방 ¶①공업지대 3. [활동 따위의] 영역, 분야 ¶②과학연구의 넓은 분야

a·re·na [ərí:nə] *n.* [C] **1.** the central place of an ancient Roman amphitheater where games or fights took place. **2.** any place of public action. ¶*the political ~.*①
—[名] 1. 투기장(鬪技場) 2. 활동 무대, …계(界) ¶①정계

‡ **aren't** [ɑ:rnt] are not.

ar·gent [á:rdʒ(ə)nt] *n.* [U] (*archaic, poetic*) silver. **—*adj.*** like silver; silver-colored.
—[名] 은(銀) —[形] 은의(같은), 은빛의

Ar·gen·ti·na [à:rdʒ(ə)ntí:nə] *n.* a country in South America. ⇒[N.B.]
—[名] 아르헨티나 [N.B.] 수도 Buenos Aires

Ar·gen·tine [á:rdʒ(ə)ntàin, -tì:n] *adj.* of Argentina or its people. **—*n.*** [C] a person of Argentina.
—[形] 아르헨티나[사람]의 —[名] 아르헨티나 사람

ar·go·sy [á:rgəsi] *n.* [C] (pl. **-sies**) a large merchant ship.
—[名] 큰 상선

‡ **ar·gue** [á:rgju:] *vt.* **1.** discuss (a problem, etc.); maintain (an opinion, etc.). ⦅*~ that …*⦆ ¶*They argued a very difficult matter.* / *He argued that the plan was impracticable.* **2.** make (someone) consent or understand by giving reasons. ⦅~ someone *into* or *out of*⦆ ¶*He*
—[他] 1. …을 논하다, 논의하다; 주장하다 2. [사람]을 설득하다, 설득하여 …시키다 3. …을 나타내다, 입증하다 —[自] 토론하다, 논쟁하다

A

argument

argued her into going with him. **3.** indicate; prove; show. 《~ *someone to be*; ~ *that* ...》 ¶*Her clothes ~ poverty.* / *His attitude argues him [to be] a gentleman.* / *Her rich clothes ~ that she is wealthy.* ——*vi.* discuss; dispute. 《~ *for* or *against* a proposal, etc.; ~ *with someone about*》 ¶*He argued for justice.* / *They argued against the passage of the bill.* / *He argued with his father about the matter.*

:ar·gu·ment [á:rgjumənt] *n.* **1.** ⓤⓒ a discussion; a reason for or against something. **2.** ⓒ a short statement of what is in a story, book, etc.; a summary.
—명 1. 의론;논증 2. [이야기·서적 따위의] 요지(要旨),개요,줄거리

ar·gu·men·ta·tion [à:rgjuməntéiʃ(ə)n] *n.* ⓤⓒ **1.** the act of arguing; a discussion. **2.** a process of reasoning.
—명 1. 논쟁 2. 논증, 증명

ar·gu·men·ta·tive [à:rgjuméntətiv] *adj.* **1.** fond of arguing; disputative. **2.** full of arguments.
—형 1. 논쟁을 좋아하는, 이유를 따지는 2. 왈가왈부하는, 논쟁적인

Ar·gus [á:rgəs] *n.* (in Greek mythology) a giant having a hundred eyes who was killed by Hermes.
—명 아르고스(그리이스 신화에서 100개의 눈을 가진 거인)

a·ri·a [á:riə] *n.* ⓒ a melody sung, usu. by one voice, in an opera.
—명 아리아; 독창곡

ar·id [ǽrid] *adj.* **1.** (of soil, land) dry; not rich; barren. ↔humid **2.** dull; uninteresting. ▷**ar·id·ly** [-li] *adv.*
—형 1. 건조한; 불모의 2. 무미건조한

a·rid·i·ty [əríditi] *n.* ⓤ the state of being arid; dryness; barrenness; dullness.
—명 건조,불모; 무미건조

a·right [əráit] *adv.* rightly; correctly. ¶*if I remember ~.*
—부 바르게 ¶①내 기억이 틀림없다면

:a·rise [əráiz] *vi.* (**a·rose**, **a·ris·en**) come about; appear. 《~ *from* or *out of* something》 ¶*Difficulties arose out of the affair.*
—자 일어나다; 나타나다, 발생하다 ¶①여러가지 곤란이 그 사건에서 발생했다

:a·ris·en [ərízn] *v.* pp. of *arise*.

ar·is·toc·ra·cy [ǽristákrəsi / -tɔ́k-] *n.* **1.** ⓤ a government ruled by persons of the highest social class. ↔democracy **2.** ⓒ 《*collectively*》 the nobles; the social class to which the nobles belong. **3.** ⓒ a group distinguished more than most people, as because of wealth or intelligence. ¶*the ~ of intellect.*
—명 1. 귀족 정치 2. 귀족; 귀족 사회 3. [재산·학식 따위가] 일류인 사람들 ¶①일류의 지식인

ar·is·to·crat [ərístəkræt / ǽristə-] *n.* ⓒ a person who belongs to the class of nobles, esp. by birth; a nobleman; a person who is attached to or who favors aristocracy.
—명 귀족[의 일원]; 귀족정치 주의자

a·ris·to·crat·ic [ərìstəkrǽtik / ǽristə-] *adj.* **1.** of or like an aristocrat. **2.** attached to aristocracy. **3.** grand. ▷**a·ris·to·crat·i·cal·ly** [-kəli] *adv.*
—형 1. 귀족의, 귀족적인 2. 귀족정치[주의]의 3. 당당한

Ar·is·tot·le [ǽristàtl / -tɔ̀tl] *n.* (384-322 B.C.) a Greek philosopher.
—명 아리스토텔레스(엣 그리이스의 철학자)

:a·rith·me·tic [əríθmətik] *n.* ⓤ the science of using numbers, as by adding, subtracting, multiplying, or dividing. ¶*mental ~.*
—명 산수, 셈 ¶①암산

ar·ith·met·i·cal [ærlθmétik(ə)l] *adj.* of arithmetic.
—형 산수의(에 관한)

arithmetical progression [-´-`---´-] *n.* a series of numbers that shows increase or decrease by a constant quantity, such as 1, 3, 5, 7, etc., or 7, 5, 3, etc.
—명 등차 수열(等差數列)

a·rith·me·ti·cian [ərìθmətíʃ(ə)n] *n.* ⓒ a person who is skilled in arithmetic.
—명 산수가(算數家)

Ariz. Arizona.

Ar·i·zo·na [ǽrizóunə] *n.* a southwestern State of the United States. ⇒ⓃⒷ.
—명 아리조나주 ⓃⒷ Ariz.로 줄임. 수도 Phoenix.

ark [a:rk] *n.* **1.** (*Bible*) the ship of Noah; a ship like Noah's. ⇒ⓃⒷ. **2.** ⓒ (*poetic, dialect*) a box; a chest.
—명 1. 노아의 방주(方舟) ⓃⒷ 노아와 그의 일족이 태고의 대홍수 때에 탔던 배 2. 궤, 갑(匣)

Ark. Arkansas.

Ar·kan·sas [á:rkənsɔ̀:] *n.* a south central State of the United States. ⇒ⓃⒷ.
—명 아아칸소우주 ⓃⒷ Ark.로 줄임. 수도 Little Rock

:arm¹ [a:rm] *n.* ⓒ **1.** the part of the body of a person or monkey between the shoulder and the hand. **2.** anything like an arm in shape or use. ¶*the arms of a chair* / *an ~ of the sea* / *the arms of the coat.* **3.** power; authority. ¶*the ~ of the law.*
—명 1. 팔 2. 팔 모양의 것 ¶①의자의 팔걸이/②작은 만(灣) 3. 힘, 권력 ¶③법의 힘

1) ***arm in arm,*** (of two persons) with arms linked. ¶*walk ~ in ~.*
2) ***a child in arms,*** a child too young to walk.
3) ***keep someone at arm's length,*** treat someone coldly.
4) ***with one's arms folded,*** with folded arms.
5) ***with open arms,*** in a warm, friendly way. ¶*receive someone with open arms.*

[熟] 1)[두 사람이] 팔짱을 끼고 2)아직 걷지 못하는 아이 3)[남]을 가까이하지 않다, 쌀쌀하게 대하다 4)팔짱을 끼고 5)두 팔을 벌리고, 진심으로

‡arm² [ɑ:rm] *n.* **1.** ⟪usu. *pl.*⟫ weapons. ¶*small arms*① / *a man of arms.*② **2.** ⟪*pl.*⟫ deeds of war; fighting. ¶*appeal to arms.*③ **3.** [C] a branch or division of a country's military services. ¶*the infantry* ~④ / *the air* ~. **4.** ⟪*pl.*⟫ mark on a shield or flag as a sign of noble families.

—[名] 1. 병기, 무기 ¶①소화기[권총·소총 따위]/②전사(戰士) 2. 전투 ¶③무력에 호소하다 3. 병과; 병종(兵種) ¶④보병과 4. 문장(紋章)

1) ***be up in arms,*** be protesting strongly; be in rebellion.
2) ***bear arms,*** serve as a soldier.
3) ***coat of arms,*** a mark on a shield, etc. as a sign of one's family or rank.
4) ***in arms,*** armed; ready to fight.
5) ***lay down arms,*** stop fighting.
6) ***take up arms,*** rise up in arms; get ready to fight.
7) ***To arms!,*** a call to take up arms
8) ***under arms,*** having weapons; equipped for fighting.

[熟] 1)무기를 들고 일어서다; 반기를 들다 2)병역에 복무하다 3)문장 4)무장하고, 전투태세를 갖추고 5)무기를 버리다, 항복하다 6)무기를 들다, 전단(戰端)을 열다 7)전투 준비 8)전투 태세를 갖추고

—*vt.* provide (someone or something) with weapons; protect or defend; provide (someone) with what is needed. ¶~ *a castle* / ~ *oneself against danger.*⑤ / *be armed with patience.*⑥ —*vi.* prepare for war; take weapons. ¶*The soldiers armed themselves for battle.*

—[他] …을 무장시키다; 무기를 잡다; [필수품]을 몸에 지니다, 공급하다 ¶⑤위험에 대비해서 무장하다/⑥인내심을 갖추고 있다 —[自] 무장하다

ar·ma·da [ɑ:rmá:də, +*U.S.* -méidə] *n.* [C] a fleet of warships. ¶*the Invincible* (or *Spanish*) *Armada.*①

—[名] 함대 ¶①스페인 무적함대

ar·ma·dil·lo [ɑ̀:rmədílou] *n.* [C] (pl. **-los**) a small animal with a hard, armor-like covering, living chiefly in South America. ⇒fig.

—[名] [남미산] 아르마딜로

〔armadillo〕

ar·ma·ment [á:rməmənt] *n.* [U] **1.** ⟪often *pl.*⟫ military forces of a nation. ¶*limitation* (*reduction*) *of armaments.*① **2.** ⟪*collectively*⟫ all the things used for fighting. ¶*anti-torpedo* ~.②

—[名] 1. [한 나라의] 군비 ¶①군비 제한(축소) 2. 병기 ¶②어뢰 방어포(防禦砲)

ar·ma·ture [á:rmətʃər / á:mətjuə] *n.* [C] **1.** a defensive covering worn by a person for fighting; armor. **2.** a defensive, armor-like covering of an animal or a plant. **3.** ⟪*electricity*⟫ a piece of soft iron joining the poles of a magnet; the essential part of a dynamo.

—[名] 1. 갑옷, 투구 2. [동식물의] 방호기관(防護器官) 3. [자철(磁鐵)의] 접극자(接極子); 전기자(電機子)

arm·chair [á:rmtʃὲər / ˊ-ˋ] *n.* [C] a chair with side-rests for the arms.

—[名] 팔걸이 의자

arm·ful [á:rmfùl] *n.* [C] as much as can be held in one arm or both arms. ¶*an* ~ *of hay.*①

—[名] 한팔 가득, 한 아름 ¶①한 아름의 건초

arm·hole [á:rmhòul] *n.* [C] an opening for the arm in clothes.

—[名] [옷의] 진동, 소맷부리

ar·mi·stice [á:rmistis] *n.* [C] an agreement to stop fighting for a while. ¶*a separate* ~.①

—[名] 휴전 ¶①단독 휴전

arm·let [á:rmlit] *n.* [C] **1.** a band worn round the upper part of the arm. **2.** a small inlet of the sea.

—[名] 1. 팔찌, 팔장식 2. 작은 만(灣)

‡ar·mor, *Brit.* **-mour** [á:rmər] *n.* [U] **1.** a covering, usu. of metal, to protect the body from attack or in fighting. ¶*be* [*clad*] *in* ~.① **2.** defensive metal covering or plates for tanks, warships, or motor vehicles. **3.** any protective covering of animals or plants. —*vt., vi.* put armor on (someone or something).

—[名] 1. 갑옷 ¶①갑옷을 입고 있다 2. [군함의] 장갑(裝甲) 3. [동식물의] 갑옷 같은 방호기관 —[他][自] 갑옷을 입히다; 장갑(裝甲)하다

ar·mored, *Brit.* **-moured** [á:rmərd] *adj.* covered with armor.

—[形] 갑옷을 입은, 장갑(裝甲)을 한

ar·mor·er, *Brit.* **-mour-** [á:rmərər] *n.* [C] a person who makes, repairs, or takes care of arms or armor.

—[名] 갑옷(병기) 제조자; 병기계(兵器係)

ar·mo·ri·al [ɑ:rmɔ́:riəl] *adj.* of a coat of arms.

—[形] 문장(紋章)의

armor plate [ˊ- ˋ] *n.* an iron or steel plate with which warships, tanks, etc. are covered.

—[名] 장갑판(裝甲板), 장갑 철판

ar·mor·y, *Brit.* **-mour-** [ɑ́ːrməri] *n.* [C] (pl. **-mor·ies**) **1.** a place where arms are kept. **2.** (*U.S.*) a place where arms are manufactured.
—[名] 1. 병기고 2. 병기 공장

arm·pit [ɑ́ːrmpìt] *n.* [C] the hollow place under the arm at the shoulder.
—[名] 겨드랑 밑

: ar·my [ɑ́ːrmi] *n.* [C] (pl. **-mies**) **1.** a large number of soldiers organized and trained to fight on land. ¶*a standing* (or *reserve*) *~*① / *enter* (or *join, go into*) *the ~*② / *leave* (or *retire from*) *the ~*③ / *serve in the ~.*④ **2.** a body of men organized for a purpose. ¶*the Blue Ribbon Army*⑤ / *the Salvation Army.*⑥ **3.** a very large number of anything. ¶*a great ~ of locusts.*⑦
—[名] 1. 육군, 군대 ¶①상비(예비)군/②입대하다/③제대하다/④병역에 복무하다 2. 단체, …군(軍) ¶⑤푸른 리본단(금주 단체 이름)/⑥구세군 3. 큰 떼, 대군 ¶⑦메뚜기의 대군

Ar·nold [ɑ́ːrn(ə)ld] *n.* **1.** a man's name. **2.** a family names.
—[名] 1. 남자 이름 2. 성(姓)의 하나

a·ro·ma [əróumə] *n.* [U] [C] a sweet smell.
—[名] 향기, 방향(芳香)

ar·o·mat·ic [æ̀roumǽtik] *adj.* sweet-smelling.
—[形] 향기로운, 방향(芳香)의

*** a·rose** [əróuz] *v.* pt. of **arise.**

: a·round [əráund] *adv.* **1.** on every side; all round. ¶*He looked ~ in wonder.* / *The garden is fenced all ~.* **2.** forming a circle. ¶*gather ~.*① / *fly ~ and ~.* **3.** here and there. ¶*travel ~.* **4.** with a rotating movement. ¶*the wheels turned ~.* **5.** by all the distance of the outside edge; in circumference. ¶*The pond is 2 miles ~.* **6.** with a return to the starting point. ¶*The season came ~.*② **7.** not by the shortest route. ¶*He goes a long way ~.*③ **8.** from one to another. ¶*pass the candy ~ to the boys.* **9.** from beginning to end; throughout. ¶*the year ~.* **10.** to a certain place. ¶*He came ~ to see me.* **11.** (*U.S. colloq.*) somewhere near. ¶*I waited ~ for her.*④
—[副] 1. 사면에, 빙 둘러 2. 둥글게, 원을 이루어 ¶①둥글게 모이다 3. 여기저기; 사방에 4. 회전하여 5. 둘레가 6. 일주하여, 한 바퀴 돌아 ¶②계절이 한 바퀴 돌아왔다 7. 멀리 돌아서 ¶③ 그는 멀리 돌아갔다 8. 차례차례 9. 시종, 쭉 10. 어떤 장소에 11. 어딘가 그 근처에서 ¶④그녀는 근처에서 기다렸다

have been around, (*U.S. colloq.*) have had much worldly experience.
[熟] 《美口》 경험이 많다; 지각이 있다

—*prep.* **1.** surrounding; in a circle about. ¶*We sat ~ the fire.* / *She looked happy with her grandchildren ~ her.* **2.** in all directions from. ¶*She looked ~ her.* **3.** rotating about the center of. ¶*the motion of wheels ~ their axis.* **4.** along the outer side of. ¶*go ~ the lake.* **5.** (*U.S. colloq.*) here and there in. ¶*travel ~ the country.* **6.** near. ¶*They were playing ~ the house.* **7.** (*U.S. colloq.*) about. ¶*~ here* / *It's ~ six o'clock.* / *~ ten dollars.* **8.** (*U.S. colloq.*) reached by making a turn. ¶*the church ~ the corner.*
—[前] 1. …을 둘러싸고 2. …의 주위에 3. …을 중심으로 돌아서 4. …에 따라서 5. …을 사방으로; …의 여기저기 6. …의 근처 7. 대략 8. …을 돌아서

: a·rouse [əráuz] *vt.* **1.** awaken. **2.** stir (someone) to action; excite; stir up. ¶*~ fear* / *A red rag arouses the anger of a bull.*
—[他] 1. …의 눈을 뜨게 하다 2. …을 자극하다, 환기하다, 분기시키다

ar·raign [əréin] *vt.* **1.** call a prisoner before a court of law in order to examine him. **2.** find fault with (someone or something); accuse; charge.
—[他] 1. [피고]를 법정에 소환하여 소인(訴因)의 인부(認否)를 묻다 2. …을 비난하다

ar·raign·ment [əréinmənt] *n.* [U] [C] **1.** the act of arraigning. **2.** unfavorable criticism; blame.
—[名] 1. 고소, 소환, 죄상 인부(罪狀認否) 2. 비난

: ar·range [əréindʒ] *vt.* **1.** put (things) in order; adjust. ¶*~ flowers*① / *~ books on the shelf* / *~ one's hair.* **2.** bring (something) to an end; settle; decide. ¶*~ a dispute.*② **3.** prepare; plan. ¶*~ a meeting* / *~ a marriage for someone* / *The party was arranged for Sunday evening.* / *It is arranged that ...*③ **4.** change (something) so as to make it suitable for a new purpose; fit; adapt. 《~ something *for*》 ¶*~ a novel for the stage.* **—*vi.*** **1.** make plans; prepare. 《~ *for* something; ~ *to do*》 ¶*We'll ~ to do as you wish.*④ / *Let's ~ for the trip.* / *Can you ~ to start early tomorrow morning?* **2.** come to an agreement. 《~ *with* someone; ~ *about* something》 ¶*We are going to ~ with him about it.* / *I have arranged for him to see her home.*
—[他] 1. …을 정리정돈하다; 가지런히 하다 ¶①꽃꽂이하다 2. …을 끝내다, 마무리하다 ¶②분쟁을 조정하다 3. …하도록 짜 놓다, 준비하다 ¶③…할 예정으로 되어 있다 4. …을[…용으로] 개작하다, 편곡하다, 각색하다 —[自] 1. 준비하다, …하도록 정해 놓다 ¶④네가 바라는 대로 하도록 해 놓겠다 2. 결정하다; 협정하다

: ar·range·ment [əréindʒmənt] *n.* **1.** [U] the act of setting or the state of being set in order. ¶*flower ~.*① **2.** [C]
—[名] 1. 정돈; 배열 ¶①꽃꽂이 2. 협정; 결정 3. 준비 ¶②등산에 필요한

the act of setting or deciding. **3.** ⦅usu. *pl.*⦆ preparations. ¶*make necessary arrangements for mountaineering.*② **4.** [U] the act of changing a piece of music (or novel, etc.) to make it suitable for a new purpose. **5.** [C] something arranged in a particular way; adaptation.
1) ***come to*** (or ***arrive at***) ***an arrangement*** (=*reach an understanding*) ***with*** *someone.*
2) ***make an arrangement*** (=*arrange*) ***with*** *someone.*

준비를 해 놓다 **4.** 편곡, 각색 **5.** [편곡·각색된] 작품
[熟] 1)[남]과 타협이 되다 2)[남]과 협정을 맺다

ar·rant [ǽrənt] *adj.* well-known for bad deeds.
—[形] 소문난, 극악(極惡)의

ar·ras [ǽrəs] *n.* **1.** [U] a kind of cloth with pictures on it. **2.** [C] a cloth hung on a wall as interior decoration.
—[名] **1.** 애러스 천 **2.** 애러스 천 벽걸이

* **ar·ray** [əréi] *vt.* **1.** put or arrange (something) in order. **2.** dress (someone) up. —*n.* **1.** [U] order. ¶*be in battle ~.*① **2.** [C] a large group of persons or things; display. ¶*an ~ of actors | make an ~.*② **3.** [C] a military force; soldiers. **4.** [U] dress; clothes. ¶*be in fine ~.*
—[他] **1.** …을 배열시키다 **2.** …을 성장(盛裝)하다 —[名] **1.** 배열; 대열 ¶①전투대형을 취하고 있다 **2.** 죽 늘어서기 ¶②죽 늘어서다 **3.** 군대; 병사 **4.** 옷

ar·rear [əríər] *n.* ⦅usu. *pl.*⦆ **1.** money that is due, but not paid; debts. **2.** work that is undone.
1) ***in arrear***[***s***], behind in payments, work, etc.
2) ***in arrear***[***s***] ***of,*** later than. ↔in advance of
—[名] **1.** 미불금; 빚 **2.** [일 따위의] 지체
[熟] 1)[지불·일 따위가] 지체되어 2) …보다 늦게

⁑ **ar·rest** [ərést] *vt.* **1.** stop; check. ¶*~ development.*① **2.** seize; capture (someone) by means of the law. ¶*~ someone for a crime.* **3.** attract. ¶*~ someone's attention.* —*n.* [U] [C] the act of arresting; imprisonment.
under arrest, held by the police.
—[他] **1.** …을 막다; …을 방해하다 ¶①발전을 저해하다 **2.** …을 체포하다; 구인(拘引)하다 **3.** [주의 따위]를 끌다
—[名] 체포; 감금
[熟] 구금(수감)되어

⁑ **ar·riv·al** [əráiv(ə)l] *n.* **1.** [U] the act of arriving. ↔departure ¶*the ~ of spring | an ~ platform.*① **2.** [C] a person or thing that arrives. ¶*a new ~*② *| He was the first ~ here.*
on arrival, as soon as someone arrives.
—[名] **1.** 도착, 도달 ¶①[열차] 도착 플랫포옴 **2.** 도착자; 도착물 ¶②새로 온 사람; 새로 들어온 상품(책)
[熟] 도착하는 대로

⁑ **ar·rive** [əráiv] *vi.* **1.** get or come to (some place); reach. ↔depart ⦅*~ at* or *in* a place⦆ ¶*~ at the station | ~ home | He arrived in London before seven.* ⇒[usage] **2.** come to a certain stage in a process. ¶*~ at full age*① *| ~ at a conclusion* (*decision*). **3.** (of time or opportunity) come; occur. ¶*The time has arrived for you to work.*
—[自] **1.** 닿다; 도착하다 [usage] 도착하는 것이 어떤 지점이면 at, 어떤 지역이면 in을 씀 **2.** [어떤 나이·결론·확신에] 도달하다 ¶①성년에 달하다 **3.** [시간·기회 따위가] 이르다, 오다

ar·ro·gance [ǽrəgəns] *n.* [U] the state or manner of having too great pride in oneself.
—[名] 거만함, 교만

ar·ro·gant [ǽrəgənt] *adj.* very proud of oneself.
—[形] 거만한, 건방진

ar·ro·gate [ǽrəgèit] *vt.* take (something) to oneself without right.
—[他] …을 가로채다, 탈취하다

⁑ **ar·row** [ǽrou] *n.* **1.** [C] a stick pointed at one end and used for shooting from a bow. ¶*Time flies like an ~.* **2.** the sign "→".
—[名] **1.** 화살 ¶①시간은 화살 같다 **2.** 화살표

ar·row·head [ǽrouhèd] *n.* [C] **1.** the head of an arrow. ⇒fig. **2.** a plant that has a leaf shaped like arrowheads. ⇒fig.
—[名] **1.** 화살촉 **2.** 쇠귀나물

〔arrowhead 1., 2.〕

ar·row·root [ǽrourù:t] *n.* [U] a tropical plant in America.
—[名] 칡의 일종

ar·se·nal [á:rsn(ə)l] *n.* [C] a place where weapons are made or stored.
—[名] 병기창, 군수공장; 병기고

ar·se·nic [á:rsnik] *n.* [U] a grayish-white chemical element.
—[名] 비소(砒素)

ar·son [á:rsn] *n.* [U] the act or crime of setting fire to buildings or goods illegally.
—[名] 방화; 방화죄

⁑ **art**¹ [a:rt] *n.* **1.** [U] the expression or creation of what is beautiful or impressive, esp. by painting a picture. ⇒[N.B.] ¶*a work of art*① *| an ~ critic*② *| Art is long, life is short.*③ **2.** [C] ⦅usu. *pl.*⦆ literature, languages, and history studied in college or university. ¶*a Bachelor*
—[名] **1.** 예술; 미술 [N.B.] 그림·조각 따위의 하나하나를 가리킬 때는 복수로 되는 일도 있음 ¶①미술 작품/②미술 평론가/③예술은 길고 인생은 짧다 **2.** 문예, 인문과학 ¶④문학사/⑤문

*of Arts*④ | *a college of arts and sciences.*⑤ **3.** [U] [C] skill; some special kind of skill. ¶*the healing* ~⑥ | *industrial* ~⑦ | *the useful arts.*⑧ **4.** 《often *pl.*》 trick; intentional way of acting. ¶*In spite of all her arts, I was not attracted to her.*⑨

리학부 **3.** 기술, 기교 ¶⑥의술/⑦공예/⑧수예 **4.** 책략, 술책 ¶⑨그녀의 여러가지 술책에도 불구하고 나는 그녀에게 마음이 끌리지 않았다

art² [ɑːrt] *vi.* (*archaic, poetic*) =are.

Ar·te·mis [ɑ́ːrtimis] *n.* (in Greek mythology) the goddess of the hunt and the moon. ⇒[N.B.]
—[名] 아르테미스 [N.B.] 로마 신화의 Diana에 해당

ar·te·ri·al [ɑːrtíəriəl] *adj.* **1.** of an artery. **2.** like an artery. ¶*an ~ road* (*highway*).①
—[形] **1.** 동맥의 **2.** 동맥 모양을 한 ¶①간선도로

ar·ter·y [ɑ́ːrtəri] *n.* [C] **1.** a tube through which blood runs from the heart to other parts of the body. ↔vein **2.** a main road.
—[名] **1.** 동맥 **2.** 주요(간선)도로

ar·te·sian well [ɑːrtíːʒənwél / ɑːtíːzjənwél, -ziən-] *n.* a deep and narrow well filled with water.
—[名] [지하수 압력을 이용한] 깊은 우물

art·ful [ɑ́ːrtf(u)l] *adj.* **1.** cunning; deceitful. **2.** skillful. ▷**art·ful·ly** [-fuli] *adv.*
—[形] **1.** 교활한 **2.** 능수능란한

Ar·thur [ɑ́ːrθər] *n.* a man's name.
—[名] 남자 이름

ar·ti·choke [ɑ́ːrtitʃòuk] *n.* [C] a plant with thick leaves whose flowering head is eaten as a vegetable. ⇒fig.
—[名] 양엉겅퀴

[artichoke]

‡**ar·ti·cle** [ɑ́ːrtikl] *n.* [C] **1.** a piece of writing in a newspaper or magazine. ¶(*Brit.*) *a leading ~*; (*U.S.*) *an editorial ~*① | *an ~ on housekeeping.* **2.** one thing written in a list. ¶*the ninth ~ of the Constitution.*② **3.** thing [for sale]. ¶*An armchair is an ~ of furniture.* | *What is the next ~, madam?*③ **4.** (*Grammar*) one of the words *a, an,* or *the.* ¶*a definite ~*④ | *an indefinite ~.*⑤
—[名] **1.** [신문·잡지의] 기사; 논설 ¶①사설 **2.** [계약·법령 따위의] 조항 ¶②헌법 제9조 **3.** 물품; 상품 ¶③부인, 또 무엇을 드릴까요? **4.** 관사 ¶④정관사/⑤부정관사

ar·tic·u·late [ɑːrtíkjulit →*v.*] *adj.* **1.** having distinct parts; jointed. **2.** (of words) spoken in distinct syllables. ¶*~ speech.*① —*vt., vi.* [ɑːrtíkjulèit] **1.** unite (something) by joints; become jointed. **2.** speak or pronounce (a word) distinctly.
—[形] **1.** 관절이 있는 **2.** 발음이 똑똑한 ¶①명료한 말 —[他][自] **1.** …을 관절로 잇다; 결합하다 **2.** 명료하게 말하다; [단어·음절]을 똑똑히 발음하다

ar·tic·u·la·tion [ɑːrtìkjuléiʃ(ə)n] *n.* **1.** [C] (*Anatomy*) a joint. **2.** [U] the act of connecting joints. **3.** [C] the method of speaking clearly or distinctly. ⇒[N.B.] ¶*His ~ is poor.*
—[名] **1.** 《解》 관절 **2.** [관절의] 접합 **3.** [낱말의] 똑똑한 발음 [N.B.] 문자(A,B C,…) 하나하나의 발음은 pronunciation 이라고 함

ar·ti·fice [ɑ́ːrtifis] *n.* **1.** [U] device; skill. **2.** [C] a trick; craft. ¶*by ~.*①
—[名] **1.** 기술, 교묘한 고안 **2.** 술책 ¶①책략을 써서

ar·tif·i·cer [ɑːrtífisər]′ *n.* [C] a craftsman; a workman, esp. a skilled one.
—[名] [우수한] 세공인, 숙련공; 기술자

•**ar·ti·fi·cial** [ɑ̀ːrtifíʃ(ə)l] *adj.* **1.** made by human skill or art; made in imitation of a natural product. ↔natural ¶*~ flowers*① | *an ~ foot*② | *~ silk.*③ **2.** pretended; unnatural; not real. ¶*an ~ smile*④ | *~ manners.*⑤
—[形] **1.** 인공의, 가짜의 ¶①조화/②의족(義足)/③인조견 **2.** 거짓의, 부자연스러운 ¶④억지 웃음/⑤허례(虛禮)

ar·ti·fi·ci·al·i·ty [ɑ̀ːrtifìʃiǽliti] *n.* (pl. **-ties**) **1.** [U] the state or quality of being artificial. **2.** [C] something unnatural or made by human skill.
—[名] **1.** 부자연함, 인위적임 **2.** 부자연한 것; 인공물

ar·ti·fi·cial·ly [ɑ̀ːrtifíʃəli] *adv.* in an artificial manner; with artifice; unnaturally.
—[副] 인공적으로; 인위적으로

•**ar·til·ler·y** [ɑːrtíləri] *n.* [U] **1.** 《*collectively*》 large guns; cannon. **2.** 《*collectively*》 the part of an army in charge of the cannon. ¶*heavy* (*light*) ~.① **3.** the skill or science of firing large guns.
—[名] **1.** 대포 **2.** 포병 ¶①중(경) 포병 **3.** 포술

ar·til·ler·y·man [ɑːrtílərimən] *n.* [C] (pl. **-men** [-mən]) a soldier in the artillery; a gunner.
—[名] 포병

ar·ti·san [ɑ́ːrtiz(ə)n / ɑ̀ːtizǽn] *n.* [C] a workman, esp. a skilled one.
—[名] 직공, [특히] 숙련공

‡**art·ist** [ɑ́ːrtist] *n.* [C] a person who practices any creative art, esp. a person who is skilled in painting.
—[名] 예술가, [특히] 화가

ar·tiste [ɑːrtíːst] *n.* [C] a skillful performer, esp. a singer, dancer, barber, cook, etc.
—[名] 예능인, [특히] 가수·댄서·이발사·요리사

* **ar·tis·tic** [ɑːrtístik] *adj.* **1.** of art or artists. **2.** (of the fine arts) done beautifully or skillfully. **3.** having the ability to appreciate arts; loving fine arts.
—[形] 1. 예술[가]의 2. 예술적인, 운치 있는 3. 예술을 이해하는, 예술 애호의

ar·tis·ti·cal·ly [ɑːrtístikəli] *adv.* in an artistic manner; from an artistic standpoint.
—[副] 예술적으로; 미술적으로, 예술적으로 보아

art·ist·ry [áːrtistri] *n.* [U] **1.** artistic workmanship or skill. **2.** artistic effect.
—[名] 1. 예술가의 일(수완) 2. 예술적 효과

art·less [áːrtlis] *adj.* **1.** simple and natural. **2.** lacking skill; clumsy; unskillful.
—[形] 1. 꾸미지 않은; 순진한 2. 서투른

Ar·y·an [έəriən, áːr-] *adj.* of the Indo-European languages, such as Sanskrit, Persian and most European languages. —*n.* [U] the Indo-European languages; [C] the people speaking any of these languages.
—[形] 아리아(인도·유럽)[어]계의 —[名] 아리아어; 아리아 사람

⁑ **as** [æz, əz] *adv.* ⟪often used in *as ... as ...*⟫ to the same degree or extent; equally. ⇒[N.B.] ¶*Her mother is ~ tall as she* [*is*]. / *Take ~ many as you want.* / *Her face looked* [*~*] *white as snow.* / *She has ~ many* [*as I have*]. / *I can do it ~ well* [*as you can*].① ⇒[usage] / *I did it in three hours, but it took her ~ many days.*②
—[副] …과 같은 정도, …만큼; …과 마찬가지로 [N.B.] as … as ~에서는 앞의 as는 부사, 뒤의 as는 접속사 ¶①나도 너만큼 그것을 잘 할 수 있다 [usage] 뒤의 as 이하는 때때로 생략됨/②나는 세 시간에 했는데 그녀는 사흘이나 걸렸다

—*conj.* **1.** ⟪often used in *as ... as ~, so ... as ~*⟫ to the same degree or extent that. ¶*He is as tall ~ I* (or *me*). / *This is not so easy ~ you think.* / *He was so kind ~ to come to see me off.*③ **2.** in the same way or state that. ¶*Do ~ you like.* / *Parks are to the city ~ lungs are to the body.*④ **3.** during the time that; while; when. ¶*He entered the room ~ I was studying.* / *I trembled ~ I spoke.* / *As a child he lived in Seoul.* / *He will improve ~ he grows older.*⑤ **4.** since; because. ¶*As she is honest, she is trusted by everyone.* / *Young ~ he was, it is natural that he should have acted so foolishly.*⑥ **5.** though. ¶*Rich ~ he is, he is not happy.*
—[接] 1. …만큼, …과 동등하게 ¶③친절하게도 그는 나를 전송해 주었다 2. …과 같은, …처럼 ¶④공원과 도시의 관계는 폐와 몸의 관계와 같다 3. …의 사이; …하는 대로 ¶⑤성장함에 따라 그는 향상할 것이다 4. …이므로, 까닭에 ¶⑥그는 젊기 때문에 그런 바보 같은 짓을 했대도 무리는 아니다 5. …이지만, …이면서도

1) ***as for,*** about; concerning; in regard to; speaking of.
2) ***as from,*** on and after.
3) ***as it were,*** so to speak.
4) ***as to,*** ⓐ about; concerning. ⓑ in order to.
[熟] 1)…에 관한 한, …은 어떤가 하면 2)…부터 3)말하자면 4)ⓐ…에 관하여 [말하자면] ⓑ…하기 위해서

—⟪*relative pronoun*⟫ **1.** that; which. ⇒[usage] ¶*as much money ~ I have* / *such books ~ you read* / *Such men ~ saw him admired him.* / *This is the same watch ~ I lost.* **2.** a fact that ... ⇒[N.B.] ¶*He is very clever, ~ I know from his work.* / *He failed, ~ was expected.* / *As might have been expected, they were spoiled.* / *As is often the case with girls of her age, she is very bashful.*⑦
—⟪關代⟫ 1. …인 바의; …같은 [usage] 선행사로서 such, the same, as many, as much 따위를 씀 2. …이라는 사실 [N.B.] 문장 전체를 받음 ¶⑦그만한 나이의 소녀들에게 흔히 있는 일인데 그녀는 굉장히 수줍어한다

—*prep.* **1.** in the capacity or character of. ¶*He is famous ~ a scholar.* / *He is a scientist, and ought to be treated ~ such.* / *Who will act ~ go-between?*⑧ **2.** like. ¶*Her lips were ~ lilies.*
—[前] 1. …으로서 ¶⑧누가 조정자 노릇을 할 것인가? 2. …과 같은

as·bes·tos, as·bes·tus [æsbéstəs, æz- / æzbéstɔs, -təs] *n.* [U] a soft, white, mineral material which cannot be burnt, used as fireproofing.
—[名] 석면(石綿)

⁑ **as·cend** [əsénd] *vi.* go up; rise. ↔descend ¶*watch an airplane ~.* —*vt.* climb. ¶*~ a mountain* / *~ the throne.*①
ascend to heaven, die.
—[自] 오르다; 올라가다 —[他] …을 올라가다 ¶①왕위에 오르다
[熟] 죽다

as·cend·an·cy, -en·cy [əséndənsi] *n.* [U] the quality of being ascendant; power; domination.
—[名] 우세, 지배

as·cend·ant, -ent [əséndənt] *adj.* **1.** ascending. **2.** superior. —*n.* [U] ⟪*the ~*⟫ **1.** the fortune decided by the positions of stars at the time of birth. **2.** controlling power.
—[形] 1. 상승적인 2. 우세한 —[名] 1. [태어날 때의] 운수 2. 지배력

as·cen·sion [əsénʃ(ə)n] *n.* [U] **1.** the act of ascending. **2.** ⟪*the A-*⟫ the bodily ascent of Jesus Christ to Heaven.
—[名] 1. 상승 2. 그리스도의 승천

as·cent [əsént] *n.* [C] **1.** the act of ascending or going up. ¶*the ~ of Mt. Halla*① **2.** advancement in one's position, rank, etc. **3.** a place or way which slopes up. ¶*a gentle* (*rapid*) *~.*②
—[名] 1. 올라감 ¶①한라산 등산 2. [지위 따위의] 승진 3. 오르막길, 치받이 ¶②완만한(급한) 오르막길

as·cer·tain [æ̀sərtéin] *vt.* find out (a fact, etc.); make sure.
—[他] [사실 따위]를 확인하다

as·cet·ic [əsétik] *adj.* giving up pleasure and comforts; self-denying. ¶*an ~ life.*①
—[形] 금욕주의의, 고행(苦行)의 ¶①금욕생활

as·cet·i·cism [əsétisiz(ə)m] *n.* [C] the belief that it is better not to enjoy the pleasures of this world.
—[名] 금욕주의, 고행

as·crib·a·ble [əskráibəbl] *adj.* that can be ascribed.
—[形] …의 탓으로 돌릴 수 있는

as·cribe [əskráib] *vt.* give the cause, etc. of (something); believe (something or someone) to belong; attribute. ⟪~ something *to*⟫ ¶*He ascribes his failure to fate.*①
—[他] [원인 따위]를 …으로 돌리다 ¶①그는 자기의 실패의 원인을 운명의 탓으로 돌린다

as·crip·tion [əskrípʃ(ə)n] *n.* **1.** [U] the act of ascribing; the state of being ascribed. **2.** [C] a statement, esp. the words of praise for God at the end of a sermon.
—[名] 1. [원인 따위를] …에 돌리기, 귀속 2. 설교를 끝마치면서 신을 찬미하는 말

a·sep·tic [əséptik / æsép-] *adj.* free from bacteria causing disease. —*n.* [C] a drug which keeps off bacteria causing disease.
—[形] 무균(無菌)의 —[名] 방부제

⁑ **ash**¹ [æʃ] *n.* [U] ⟪often *pl.*⟫ the fine grayish dust left after something has been burnt. ¶*be burnt* (or *reduced*) *to ashes*① | *Peace to his ashes!*②
—[名] 재 ¶①몽땅 타 버리다/②그의 영혼에 평안이 깃들기를!

ash² [æʃ] *n.* [C] a tree whose wood is used for making furniture.
—[名] 서양물푸레나무

⁑ **a·shamed** [əʃéimd] *adj.* ⟪usu. as *predicative*⟫ **1.** feeling shame because one has done something wrong or silly. ⟪~ *of*⟫ ¶*I am ~ of having done so.*① | *He was ~ of his shabby clothes.* **2.** not willing to do because of shame. ⟪~ *to do*⟫ ¶*He was ~ to tell us that he had failed.*
—[形] 1. …을 부끄러워하는 ¶①그런 짓을 해서 부끄럽다 2. …하는 것이 부끄러운

ash·en [ǽʃn] *adj.* of the color of ashes; grayish; pale. ¶*John turned ~ when he heard the report.*
—[形] 잿빛의; 창백한

* **a·shore** [əʃɔ́ːr] *adv.* to or on the shore. ¶*go* (or *come*) *~*① | *run ~.*②
—[副] 해변(으로) ¶①[배에서] 상륙하다/②좌초하다

ash·y [ǽʃi] *adj.* (**ash·i·er, ash·i·est**) **1.** of or like ashes; covered with ashes. **2.** pale.
—[形] 1. 재의; 재투성이의 2. 창백한

⁑ **A·sia** [éiʒə, éiʃə / éiʃə] *n.* the largest continent in the world.
—[名] 아시아 대륙

A·si·at·ic [èiʒiǽtik, èiʃi- / èiʃiǽtik] *adj.* of Asia or its people. —*n.* [C] the people of Asia.
—[形] 아시아[사람]의 —[名] 아시아 사람

⁑ **a·side** [əsáid] *adv.* **1.** on one side. **2.** to one side. ¶*move the chair ~* | *take* (or *draw*) *someone ~.* **3.** apart from. ¶*Joking ~, I mean to do it.*① | *That is ~ from the question.*
—[副] 1. 곁에서; 옆에서 2. 곁으로; 옆으로 3. 떨어져서, 따로 ¶①농담은 젖혀놓고 난 정말로 그걸 할 작정이다

1) ***aside from,*** except. ¶*Others, ~ from the captain, had noticed it.*
2) ***lay*** (or ***put, set***) ***aside,*** ⓐ discard. ⓑ store.
[熟] 1)…은 별문제로 하고 2)ⓐ포기하다 ⓑ따로 간수해 두다

as·i·nine [ǽsinàin] *adj.* **1.** of or like an ass. **2.** silly; stupid.
—[形] 1. 당나귀의(같은) 2. 어리석은

⁑ **ask** [æsk / ɑːsk] *vt.* **1.** put a question to (someone); try to get an answer to (something) by putting a question. ⇒[usage] ⟪~ someone *a question*; ~ a question *of* someone; ~ someone *what* (or *how, where, if*) ...⟫ ¶*~ the way to the post-office* | *May I ~ you a question?; May I ~ a question of you?* | *Ask him what he wants.* | *Ask him if* (or *whether*) *he knows it.*① | *I asked him where he had been.* | *I asked* [*him*] *how to do it.* | *A few questions were asked* [*of*] *us.* **2.** request; beg. ⇒[usage] ⟪~ someone *a favor*; ~ a favor *of* someone; ~ someone *for*; ~ someone *to do*; *~ to do; ~ that* ...⟫ ¶*It is too much to ~ of me.*② | *The boy asked his father for some money.*③ | *Ask him to return the book.* | *I asked to read the book.; I asked that I might be allowed to read the book.* | *My mother asked for the curtains to be drawn.*④ **3.** demand; claim; require. ⟪~ something *for*⟫ ¶*How much do you ~ for this hat?* | *He asks 2,000 yen for the book.* | *The job asks much time.*⑤ **4.** invite. ⟪~ someone *to*⟫ ¶*We asked her to the party.* | *I was asked out to dinner.* —*vi.* inquire; beg. ¶*Ask, and it shall be given you.*⑥
—[他] 1. …에게 묻다; …에게 질문하다 [usage] 이 의미의 뒤에는 that-clause가 올 수 없음 ¶①그가 그 일을 아는지 물어보아라 2. 부탁하다, 요구하다 [usage] 이 의미의 뒤에는 부정사 또는 that-clause가 올 수 있음 ¶②그것은 나로서는 무리한 부탁이다/ ¶③그 소년은 부친에게 돈을 달라고 말했다/④어머니는 커어튼을 치라고 말했다 3. [사물이] …을 필요로 하다 ¶⑤이 일에는 많은 시간이 필요하다 4. …을 초대하다 —[自] 요구하다, 구하다 ¶⑥구하라, 그러면 주실 것이요

1) ***ask after*** (=*put a question about the health of*) *someone.*
2) ***ask for,*** ⓐ request to be given or to be told. ¶*~ for a pound of butter* | *be asked for one's name.* ⓑ
[熟] 1)[…의 건강·안부]를 묻다 2)ⓐ…을 달라고 [가르쳐 달라고] 말하다 ⓑ…을 만나려고 하다 ⓒ⟪口⟫일부러

try or want to see (someone). ¶*Here is a lady asking for you.* [c] (*colloq.*) run the risk of (something). 3) ***ask out,*** invite (someone) out.
위험을 무릅쓰다 3)…을 초대하다

a·skance [əskǽns] *adv.* **1.** sideways; to one side. **2.** with suspicion or disapproval. ¶*look ~ at something.*①
—[副] 1. 비스듬히, 곁눈으로 2. 수상쩍게 ¶①…을 수상쩍게 노려보다

a·skew [əskjú:] *adv., adj.* not straight; out of order. ¶*look ~ at something*① / *hang a picture ~.*
—[副][形] 비스듬히, 삐뚜러져 ¶①…을 곁눈으로 보다

a·slant [əslǽnt / əslɑ́:nt] *adv.* not straight up and down; obliquely.
—[副] 경사하여

⁝ **a·sleep** [əslí:p] *adj.* ⦅as *predicative*⦆ **1.** in a state of sleep; sleeping. ↔awake ¶*fall ~*① / *The dog is ~.* **2.** (of the spirit) dull; inactive; (of the limbs) numb. ¶*My left hand is ~.*
be fast asleep, be sleeping soundly.
—[形] 1. 잠든 ¶①잠들다 2. [정신이] 잠든, 죽은 듯한; [손발이] 저린, 마비한
[熟] 푹 잠들어 있다

asp [æsp] *n.* (*poetic*)=aspen.

as·par·a·gus [əspǽrəgəs] *n.* [U] a vegetable whose green tender shoots are eaten for food.
—[名] 아스파라거스

* **as·pect** [ǽspekt] *n.* [C] **1.** a look; an appearance. ¶*a gentle ~.*① **2.** the direction in which a house, window, etc. faces. ¶*His house has a southern ~.* **3.** a way of thinking about or looking at a problem, etc. ¶*Let's consider the question from every ~.* **4.** the side or part of a subject. ¶*the aspects of things.*②
take on (or ***assume***) ***a new aspect,*** become entirely new. ¶*The situation of war has taken on a new ~.*③
—[名] 1. 생김새, 용모 ¶①점잖은 용모 2. [집 따위의] 방향, 쪽 3. [문제 따위의] 보는 법, 견지 4. [어떤 일의] 양상, 국면, 형세, 정세 ¶②정세
[熟] 새로운 국면을 띠다, 면목을 일신하다 ¶③전쟁의 양상이 달라졌다

as·pen [ǽspən] *n.* [C] a kind of poplar tree whose leaves tremble easily, even in still air. **—*adj.*** **1.** of or like an aspen. **2.** trembling; quivering.
—[名] 포플라 —[形] 1. 포플라의(같은) 2. 잘 떠는

as·per·i·ty [æspériti] *n.* (pl. **-ties**) [U][C] (of character, voice, surroundings, etc.) roughness, severity or harshness.
—[名] [기질·목소리 따위의] 거칠음, 매서움; 고생스러움

as·perse [əspə́:rs] *vt.* **1.** sprinkle (water). **2.** say cruel or false things about (someone); speak ill of (someone).
—[他] 1. [물]을 뿌리다 2. [남]을 중상(비난)하다

as·per·sion [əspə́:rʒ(ə)n, -ʃ(ə)n / -ʃ(ə)n] *n.* [U][C] the act of aspersing or speaking ill of someone.
—[名] [물을] 뿌리기; [세례 때의] 관수(灌水); 중상, 욕설

as·phalt [ǽsfɔ:lt, -fælt / ǽsfælt] *n.* [U] hard, black material used in making roads. ¶*an ~ pavement.*① **—*vt.*** pave (a road) with asphalt.
—[名] 아스팔트 ¶①아스팔트 포장도로 —[他] [도로]를 아스팔트로 포장하다

as·pir·ant [əspáiərənt, ǽspirənt] *n.* [C] a person who aspires after a high position, honors, etc.; an ambitious person.
—[名] 큰 뜻을 품은 사람, 야심가

as·pi·ra·tion [æ̀spəréiʃ(ə)n] *n.* [U][C] the act of aspiring; a strong desire. ¶*have an ~ for* (or *after*) *fame.*① / *His ~ to do the work has been realized.*②
—[名] 대망, 포부; 열망 ¶①명성을 열망하다/②그 일을 하고 싶다는 그의 소망은 이루어졌다

as·pire [əspáiər] *vi.* desire eagerly or strongly. ⦅*~ after* or *to* something; *~ to do*⦆ ¶*He aspires to high literary honors.*① / *The whole nation aspired after independence.*
—[自] 열망하다 ¶①그는 문학계의 높은 명성을 얻기를 바라고 있다

as·pi·rin [ǽsp(ə)rin, -pirin] *n.* [U] [C] a medicine used to drive away pain.
—[名] 아스피린(해열 진통제)

* **ass** [æs, +*Brit.* ɑ:s] *n.* [C] **1.** an animal with long ears related to the horse; a donkey. ⇒[N.B.] **2.** a stupid person. ¶*You ~!*①
—[名] 1. 나귀 [N.B.] 보통 donkey를 더 많이 씀 2. 바보 ¶①이 바보녀석아!

* **as·sail** [əséil] *vt.* attack violently. ¶*~ someone with questions.*
—[他] …을 공격하다

as·sail·ant [əséilənt] *n.* [C] a person who attacks; an attacker.
—[名] 공격자

as·sas·sin [əsǽsin] *n.* [C] a person who murders, esp. for political purposes.
—[名] 암살자

as·sas·si·nate [əsǽsinèit] *vt.* murder (someone) by a secret or sudden attack.
—[他] …을 암살하다

as·sas·si·na·tion [əsæ̀sinéiʃ(ə)n] *n.* [U] [C] the act of assassinating; the state of being assassinated.
—[名] 암살

* **as·sault** [əsɔ́:lt] *n.* [C] a sudden attack. ¶*make an ~ on* (or *upon*) *someone*① / *take a castle by ~.*② **—*vt.*** make an attack on (someone or something).
—[名] 습격, 강습(强襲) ¶①남을 습격하다/②성을 강습하여 점령하다 —[他] …을 강습하다

as·say [əséi, ǽsei] *vt.* analyse (an ore) to find out the quantities of gold, silver, or other metals in it. **—*n.*** [U] analysis of an ore.
—[他] [광석]의 분석 시험을 하다; 시험하다 —[名] [광석의] 분석 시험

as·sem·blage [əsémblidʒ] *n.* **1.** Ⓒ a group of people who have come together for some purpose. **2.** Ⓤ the act of putting the parts of a machine, etc. together.
—[名] 1. [사람의] 모임, 군중 2. [기계의] 짜맞춤, 조립

: as·sem·ble [əsémbl] *vi.* come together in a group. ¶~ *in a playground.* —*vt.* **1.** bring (persons) together in a meeting. **2.** put (the parts of a machine) together.
—[自] 집합하다 —[他] 1. [사람]을 모으다, 집합시키다 2. [기계]를 짜맞추다

: as·sem·bly [əsémbli] *n.* Ⓒ (pl. **-blies**) **1.** a group of people gathered together for some purpose. ¶*the city* (or *municipal*) ~.① **2.** the act of putting or fitting the parts of a machine, etc. together.
—[名] 1. 집회, 집합 ¶①시의회 2. [기계의] 조립

assembly line [–ˊ– ˊ] *n.* a process of mass production by which the parts of a thing are assembled as on a conveyor belt.
—[名] [공장의] 일관 작업(一貫作業)

as·sem·bly·man [əsémblimən] *n.* Ⓒ (pl. **-men** [mən]) **1.** a member of a law-making body. **2.** 《*A-*》 (*U.S.*) a member of the lower house of a state law-making body.
—[名] 1. [일반적으로] 의원 2. 《美》[주의회의] 하원 의원

assembly room [–ˊ– ˊ] *n.* **1.** a room for a meeting. **2.** a factory where the parts of a machine, etc. are put together.
—[名] 1. 회의실; 강당 2. [기계 따위의] 조립공장

*** as·sent** [əsént] *vi.* agree to (something). 《~ *to* a statement, etc.》 ↔dissent —*n.* Ⓤ agreement. ¶*by common* ~① / *give one's* ~ *to someone* or *something.*②
—[自] 동의하다 —[名] 동의 ¶①모두 일치하여/②…에 동의하다

with one assent, unanimously.
[熟] 만장일치의 동의로

: as·sert [əsə́:rt] *vt.* declare or insist on (something) solemnly and with certainty. ¶~ *oneself*① / *Virtue will* ~ *itself.*②
—[他] …을 단언하다; 주장하다 ¶①자기권리를 주장하다; 주제넘게 나서다; 밖에 드러내다/덕이란 스스로 나타나는 법이다

as·ser·tion [əsə́:rʃ(ə)n] *n.* Ⓤ Ⓒ the act of asserting; positive statement; declaration.
—[名] 단언, 주장

as·ser·tive [əsə́:rtiv] *adj.* too confident in one's statements; positive. ¶(*Grammar*) *an* ~ *sentence.*①
—[形] 단정적인; 자신이 강한 ¶①서술문

as·sess [əsés] *vt.* **1.** determine or fix the value of (property, income, etc.). **2.** fix the amount of (a tax, fine, damages, etc.). ¶~ *a tax on* (or *upon*) *someone.*
—[他] 1. [재산·수입 따위]를 사정하다 2. [세금·벌금·손해 따위]를 할당[부과]하다

as·sess·ment [əsésmənt] *n.* Ⓤ the act of assessing; valuation; Ⓒ an amount assessed.
—[名] 사정, 세액 [평가]

as·ses·sor [əsésər] *n.* Ⓒ **1.** a person who gives advice to a judge or magistrate on technical matters. **2.** a person who determines the value of property, incomes, etc. for taxation.
—[名] 1. 보좌역, 고문; 《法》 배석판사 2. 세액 사정자

as·set [ǽset] *n.* Ⓒ something that has value; a desirable thing to have. ¶*Good health is a great* ~.①
—[名] 재산, 이익, 가치 있는 것 ¶①건강은 큰 재산이다

as·sets [ǽsets] *n. pl.* valuable things; property, esp. that which may be used to pay one's debts.
—[名] 자산; 자산 목록

as·sev·er·ate [əsévərèit] *vt.* declare solemnly; say strongly.
—[他] …을 증언하다; 단언하다

as·sev·er·a·tion [əsèvəréiʃ(ə)n] *n.* Ⓤ the act of asseverating; an oath.
—[名] 맹세의 말, 증언

as·si·du·i·ty [æ̀sid(j)ú:iti / æ̀sidjú(:)-] *n.* (pl. **-ties**) **1.** Ⓤ the state of being assiduous; diligence. ¶*with* ~.① **2.** 《*pl.*》 careful and eager attention.
—[名] 1. 근면, 부지런함 ¶①부지런하게 2. 배려, 노파심

as·sid·u·ous [əsídʒuəs / əsídju-] *adj.* working steadily; eagerly attentive; diligent. ↔lazy ▷**as·sid·u·ous·ly** [-li] *adv.*
—[形] 근면한

*** as·sign** [əsáin] *vt.* **1.** give a part of (something) to each; allot. 《~ work, etc. *to*》 ¶*A large room has been assigned to us.*① **2.** fix. 《~ a day *for*》 ¶~ *a day for a meeting.*② **3.** appoint. 《~ someone *for* or *to*》 **4.** give a cause of (something or someone); ascribe. 《~ *to* something》 ¶~ *the failure to the lack of study.*③
—[他] 1. …을 할당하다 ¶①넓은 방이 우리에게 할당되었다 2. …을 지정하다 ¶②회합 날짜를 지정하다 3. …을 선임하다 4. [원인 따위를] …에 돌리다 ¶③실패를 연구 부족의 탓으로 돌리다

as·sign·ment [əsáinmənt] *n.* **1.** Ⓤ the act of assigning; the state of being assigned; Ⓒ something assigned, esp. given as a piece of work to be done. **2.** Ⓒ a lesson; homework. **3.** Ⓤ Ⓒ appointment; designation. ¶*his* ~ *to America.*
—[名] 1. [할당된] 일 2. 과제; 숙제 3. 임명; 지정

as·sim·i·late [əsímilèit] *vt.* **1.** cause (someone) to be like others (in customs, etc.). 《~ someone *to* or *with*》
—[他] 1. …을 동화시키다 2. …과 비교하다; …에 견주다 ¶①자신의 인생을

2. compare with (something); liken. 《~ something *to* or *with*》 ¶~ *one's life to a voyage.*① **3.** take (something) in and make it a part of oneself; digest; absorb. **4.** master (knowledge); understand fully. —*vi.* absorb oneself; become like others.
항해에 비유하다 **3.** …을 동화하다, 소화・흡수하다 **4.** …을 습득하다; 충분히 이해하다 —[自] 동화하다, 흡수하다; 똑같이 되다

as·sim·i·la·tion [əsìmiléiʃ(ə)n] *n.* Ⓤ the act of assimilating; the state of being assimilated; digestion; absorption. ↔dissimilation
—[名] 동화[작용], 소화, 흡수

⁑ as·sist [əsíst] *vt.* help. 《~ someone *in*》 ¶*John assisted me in my work.*
—[他] …을 돕다

*** as·sist·ance** [əsíst(ə)ns] *n.* Ⓤ the act of assisting; help. ¶*come* (or *go*) *to someone's* ~① / *My sister gave* ~ *to me in my homework.*②
—[名] 조력, 원조 ¶①남을 도우러 가다 /②누이가 내 숙제를 거들어 주었다

*** as·sist·ant** [əsíst(ə)nt] *n.* Ⓒ a person who assists; a helper; a co-worker. —*adj.* assisting; helping; helpful. ¶*an* ~ *professor*① / *an* ~ *manager.*②
—[名] 조수; 점원 —[形] 보좌의; 보조의 ¶①조교수/②부지배인

as·siz·es [əsáiziz] *n. pl.* sessions of a special court of law held periodically in each county of England.
—[名] [영국의] 순회 재판

⁑ as·so·ci·ate [əsóuʃièit → *n., adj.*] *vi.* **1.** keep company. 《~ *with* someone》 ¶*You must not* ~ *with dishonest people.*① **2.** cooperate; work together. 《~ *with* someone》 —*vt.* **1.** 《often *reflexively*》 bring (oneself or someone) with others, usu. for a special purpose. ¶~ *oneself with an enterprise.*② / *We associated him with us in the attempt.*③ **2.** connect (things) in the mind. 《~ something *with*》 ¶*We* ~ *the name of Einstein with the theory of relativity.*④
—[自] **1.** …과 교제하다 ¶①부정직한 사람과 사귀어서는 안 된다 **2.** …과 제휴하다 —[他] **1.** …을 연합시키다 ¶②사업에 한몫 들다/③우리들은 그 계획에 그를 참가시켰다 **2.** 연상하다 ¶④우리들은 아인시타인의 이름을 보면 상대성 원리를 연상한다

—*n.* [əsóuʃiit] Ⓒ a person joined with others; a member of a group; a companion; a partner. ¶*He has been my* ~ *for a long time.*⑤
—[名] 친구, 동료; 준회원 ¶⑤그는 오래 전부터 나의 동료이다

—*adj.* [əsóuʃiit] united or joined for a common purpose. ¶*an* ~ *judge.*⑥
—[形] 연합한; 같은 동료의 ¶⑥배석판사

as·so·ci·at·ed [əsóuʃièitid] *adj.* being in association; united; joint. ¶*the Associated Press.*① ⇒[N.B.]
—[形] 연합한; 조합의 ¶①[미국의] 연합통신사 [N.B.] A.P.로 줄임

⁑ as·so·ci·a·tion [əsòusiéiʃ(ə)n] *n.* **1.** Ⓤ the act of associating; the state of being associated; companionship; partnership. **2.** Ⓒ a group of persons acting together for some special purpose; a society. ¶*a cooperative* ~① / *the Young Men's* (*Women's*) *Christian Association* ~.② ⇒[N.B.] **3.** Ⓤ the act of connecting ideas in the mind; Ⓒ ideas connected in the mind. ¶~ *of ideas.*③
—[名] **1.** 교제; 제휴 **2.** 협회; 조합 ¶①협동조합 / ②그리스도교 청년(여자청년)회 [N.B.] Y.M.(W.)C.A.로 줄임 **3.** [관념의] 연합, 연상 ¶③관념 연합

in association with, in cooperation with; in connection with.
[熟] …과 협동하여; …에 관련하여

association football [-ˊ-ˋ-- ˊ-] *n.* (*Brit.*) soccer.
—[名] 아식 축구

as·sort [əsɔ́ːrt] *vt.* divide (things) into separate classes; classify. —*vi.* match; suit. 《~ *with* something》 ¶*The hat assorts well with his suit.*
—[他] …을 분류하다 —[自] 어울리다, 조화되다

as·sort·ed [əsɔ́ːrtid] *adj.* divided into groups.
—[形] 분류한; 골고루 갖춘

as·sort·ment [əsɔ́ːrtmənt] *n.* ⓊⒸ the act of assorting; the state of being assorted; a set of various kinds of things. ¶*We have a complete* ~ *of traveling requisites.*①
—[名] 유별; 여러가지를 갖춘 것(상품) ¶①우리 상점에 여행용품이 전부 갖추어져 있다

as·suage [əswéidʒ] *vt.* lessen (pain, anger, sorrow, etc.); soften; calm.
—[他] [고통・노여움・슬픔 따위]를 완화시키다

as·sum·a·ble [əsúːməbl / -s(j)úːm-] *adj.* that can be assumed.
—[形] 가정할 수 있는

⁑ as·sume [əsúːm / -s(j)úːm] *vt.* **1.** suppose or accept (something) to be a fact; suppose or believe (someone) to be something. 《~ *that* …; ~ someone *to do*》 ¶*We assumed that the news was true.* / *They assumed him to be an American.* / *Assuming that this is true, what should I do?*① **2.** take (something) upon oneself; undertake; adopt. ¶~ *new duties* / ~ *the chair*② / ~ *a responsibility.* **3.** pretend. 《~ *to do*》 ¶~ *an air of innocence* / *He assumes to have knowledge of this fact.* **4.** take (something) as one's own.
—[他] **1.** …을 가정하다, 간주하다, 추정하다, 당연한 것으로 여기다 ¶①이것이 정말이라고 한다면 나는 어찌하면 좋을까? **2.** [책임・임무]를 떠맡다, [태도]를 취하다 ¶②의장직을 맡다 **3.** …인 체하다, 가장하다, [외관]을 나타내다 **4.** [남의 것]을 횡령하다, 자기 것이라 하다

as·sum·ing [əsúːmiŋ / -s(j)úːm-] *adj.* too bold or self-confident; arrogant.
—[形] 주제넘은

* **as·sump·tion** [əsʌ́mpʃ(ə)n] *n.* [U] [C] **1.** the act of assuming; the state of being assumed; something assumed; [a] supposition. ¶*a mere ~.*① **2.** the act of taking a position, power, etc. ¶*His ~ of power was welcomed by everyone.*② **3.** the act of taking (something) without right. **4.** pretense; disguise.
—[名] 1. 가정 ¶①전혀 근거 없는 억설 2. 취임; 떠맡기; [권력의] 장악, 찬탈 ¶②그의 권력 장악은 누구에게나 환영받았다 3. 횡령 4. 가장, …인 체하기; 위장

on the assumption (=*supposing*) *that ...*
[熟] …이라는 가정하에

* **as·sur·ance** [əʃúərəns] *n.* **1.** [C] th act of assuring; the state of being assured; guarantee. ¶*give an ~ that...*① **2.** [U] certainty; sureness; confidence; self-confidence. ¶*with ~*② **3.** [U] (chiefly *Brit.*) life insurance.
—[名] 1. 보증 ¶①…이라는 보증을 주다 2. 확신; 자신 ¶②확신을 가지고 3. [생명]보험

⁑ **as·sure** [əʃúər] *vt.* **1.** bring (a certain result) without fail. ¶*Does hard work always ~ success?*① **2.** convince (someone) of something; say as a sure act (fact) to (someone); try to make (someone) believe. 《~ someone *of* his safety, etc.; ~ someone *that* ...》 ¶*I ~ you of his honesty.*② / *I ~ you that there is no danger.*
—[他] 1. …을 약속하다, …의 결과를 보증하다 ¶①열심히 일하면 성공은 보증되는가? 2. …을(…이라고) 확신하다; 보증하다; …에게 확신시키다; 납득시키다 ¶②그가 정직하다는 것을 보증하겠다

as·sured [əʃúərd] *adj.* **1.** certain; sure. ¶*Our victory is quite ~.*① **2.** feeling certain that ...; confident. 《~ *of*; ~ *that* ...》 ¶*I am ~ that he will succeed.*
—[形] 1. 확실한 ¶①우리의 승리는 틀림이 없다 2. …이라고 확신하는

as·sur·ed·ly [əʃúəridli] *adv.* in an assured manner; without doubt; surely; confidently.
—[副] 확실히; 단호하게

as·ter [ǽstər] *n.* [C] a plant with blue, pink, or white star-like flowers.
—[名] 해국(海菊), 갯알

as·ter·isk [ǽst(ə)rìsk] *n.* [C] a starlike mark (*) used in printing or writing to call attention.
—[名] 별표(*)

a·stern [əstə́:rn] *adv.* (*Nautical*) at or toward the back end of a ship. ¶*fall* [*drop*] *~*① / *Go ~!*②
—[副] 《海》고물에; 후방으로 ¶①다른 배에 뒤떨어지다/②후진하라

as·ter·oid [ǽstərɔ̀id] *n.* [C] **1.** (*Astronomy*) a small star or planet. **2.** a starfish. —*adj.* starlike in shape.
—[名] 1. 《天》 소유성(小遊星); 소혹성 2. 불가사리 —[形] 별 모양의

asth·ma [ǽzmə, ǽs- / ǽs-] *n.* [U] a disease that makes breathing noisy and difficult.
—[名] 천식(喘息)

asth·mat·ic [æzmǽtik, æs- / æs-] *adj.* **1.** of asthma. **2.** suffering from asthma. —*n.* [C] a person suffering from asthma.
—[形] 1. 천식의 2. 천식을 앓는 —[名] 천식 환자

a·stig·ma·tism [æstígmətìz(ə)m] *n.* [U] a diseased state of the eyes that causes a person to see certain parts of a thing less clearly than the rest.
—[名] 난시(亂視)

a·stir [əstə́:r] *adv., adj.* 《always as *predicative*》 **1.** in [a state of] motion; moving; excited. ¶*The town was ~ with the news.*① **2.** out of bed. ¶*be early ~.*
—[副][形] 1. 움직여, 떠들썩하여 ¶①거리는 그 소식으로 떠들썩했다 2. 일어나서

* **as·ton·ish** [əstániʃ / -tɔ́n-] *vt.* 《often in the *passive*》 surprise (someone) greatly. ¶*I was astonished at the news.*① / *I was astonished that she married such a man.*
—[他] …을 깜짝 놀라게 하다 ¶①그 소식을 듣고 깜짝 놀랐다

as·ton·ish·ing [əstániʃiŋ / -tɔ́n-] *adj.* very surprising. ¶*an ~ man*① ⇒[N.B.] / *The news was ~ to every country in the world.* ▷**as·ton·ish·ing·ly** [-li] *adv.*
—[形] 놀랄 만한 ¶①놀라운 인물 [N.B.] an *astonished man*은 놀라는 사람의 뜻

* **as·ton·ish·ment** [əstániʃmənt / -tɔ́n-] *n.* **1.** [U] the state of being astonished; great surprise. **2.** [C] something astonishing.
—[名] 1. 놀람 2. 놀라운 사물

1) ***in*** (or ***with***) ***astonishment,*** in surprise or amazement.
2) ***to one's astonishment,*** to one's surprise.
[熟] 1)놀라서, 놀란 나머지 2)놀랍게도

as·tound [əstáund] *vt.* astonish (someone) greatly; overwhelm (someone) with surprise.
—[他] …을 깜짝 놀라게 하다; 간담을 서늘하게 하다

as·tound·ing [əstáundiŋ] *adj.* very astonishing.
—[形] 깜짝 놀랄 만한

as·tra·khan, -chan [ǽstrəkæ̀n / æ̀strəkǽn] *n.* [U] a young lamb's skin with curled wool. ⇒[N.B.]
—[名] 아스트라칸 양피 [N.B.] 소련의 Astrakhan 지방에서 남

a·stray [əstréi] *adj.* 《as *predicative*》 *adv.* wandering out of the right way.
—[形][副] 길을 잃고

1) ***go astray,*** ⓐ go out of the right way; lose one's way. ⓑ go wrong.
2) ***lead someone astray,*** lead someone out of the right way.
[熟] 1)ⓐ길을 잃다 ⓑ타락하다 2)나쁜 길로 끌어들이다, 타락시키다

a·stride [əstráid] *adv.* with the legs apart, as in horseback riding. ¶*ride a horse ~.*①
—[副] 걸터앉아 ¶①말을 타다

as·trin·gen·cy [əstríndʒ(ə)nsi] *n.* [U] the state of being astringent.
—[名] 수렴성(收斂性); 엄함

as·trin·gent [əstríndʒ(ə)nt] *adj.* **1.** (*Medicine*) causing the skin to contract or shrink; tightening. ¶*an ~ liquid for the skin.*① **2.** stern; severe; harsh. —*n.* [C] a substance that makes the skin contracted or shrinken.
—[形] 1.《醫》 수렴성(收斂性)의 ¶①피부의 수렴제 2. 엄한 —[名]수렴제

as·trol·o·ger [əstrálədʒər / -trɔ́l-] *n.* [C] a person who studies the stars in order to predict the future.
—[名] 점성가(占星家)

as·tro·log·i·cal [æ̀strəládʒik(ə)l / -lɔ́dʒ-] *adj.* of astrology.
—[形] 점성술의

as·trol·o·gy [əstrálədʒi / -trɔ́l-] *n.* [U] the study of the stars in order to know what will happen in the future.
—[名] 점성술

as·tro·naut [ǽstrənɔ̀:t] *n.* [C] a traveler through space.
—[名] 우주 비행사

as·tron·o·mer [əstránəmər / -trɔ́nəmə] *n.* [C] a person who studies the science of the sun, stars, and planets.
—[名] 천문학자

as·tro·nom·i·cal [æ̀strənámik(ə)l / -nɔ́m-] *adj.* **1.** of astronomy. ¶*an ~ observatory.*① **2.** (of a number or amount) enormous. ¶*~ figures.*
—[形] 1. 천문학의 ¶①천문대 2. [숫자·수량 따위가] 천문학적인, 거대한

as·tron·o·my [əstránəmi / -trɔ́n-] *n.* [U] the scientific study of the stars, planets, and other heavenly bodies.
—[名] 천문학

as·tute [əst(j)ú:t / əstjú:t] *adj.* very clever; shrewd; cunning.
—[形] 기민한; 빈틈없는

as·tute·ness [əst(j)ú:tnis / -tjú:t-] *n.* [U] keenness; shrewdness.
—[名] 기민, 교활

a·sun·der [əsʌ́ndər] *adv.* 《as *predicative*》 into pieces; separately. ¶*tear paper ~.*
—[副] 따로따로 떨어져서, 산산이

a·sy·lum [əsáiləm] *n.* [C] a place where madmen, orphans or old people are taken care of. ¶*an ~ for the aged / a lunatic ~.*
—[名] [고아·광인 따위의] 보호소, 양육원

⁑ **at** [æt, ət] *prep.* **1.** (of a place or space) in; on; near; by. ¶*stand ~ the front door / ~ a distance*① */ arrive ~ the destination / Knock ~ the door. / He was present ~ the meeting.* **2.** (of a place) through; by way of; from. ¶*enter ~ the front door*② */ go out of the house ~ the back door. / look out ~ the window.* **3.** (of time) on or upon the point of; during the time of. ¶*~ noon / ~ present / ~ eight [o'clock] / ~ the age of 80 / ~ the end of the month / for days ~ a time.*③ **4.** engaged in; doing. ¶*~ school / ~ work / ~ supper / ~ play / ~ table / What are you ~ now?* **5.** as to the ability in. ¶*poor ~ music / slow ~ understanding.* **6.** in the state or condition of. ¶*~ ease / ~ peace / ~ war / ~ anchor*④ */ The storm was ~ its worst about noon.* **7.** to; toward; in the direction of. ¶*aim ~ a mark / throw a stone ~ a dog / laugh ~ someone / catch ~ a butterfly*⑤ */ run ~ the enemy.*⑥ **8.** because of; by reason of. ¶*He was happy ~ the news. / ~ his command.*⑦ **9.** in the amount, degree, number, price, or rate of. ¶*~ 8 dollars apiece / ~ a high speed / ~ the rate of 45 miles an hour / I bought the book ~ 3 dollars.* **10.** according to; dependent on. ¶*~ will / ~ one's mercy*⑧ */ Come ~ your convenience.*
—[前] 1. …에, …에서 ¶①멀리서 2. …을 통하여, …으로 ¶②정면 현관으로 들어가다 3. …할 때부터, …때에 ¶③한 번에 며칠씩이나 4. …에 종사중인, …하여 5. …의 능력에 대하여 6. …중, …하여 ¶④정박중 7. [방향·목표·목적을 정하고] …으로 향하여 ¶⑤나비를 잡으려고 하다/⑥적을 향하여 달려들다 8. …의 원인(이유)으로 ¶⑦그의 명령으로 9. [분량·정도·숫자·가격 따위가] …으로, …인 10. [방법을 제시하고] …에, …으로; …대로 ¶⑧남이 하는 대로

at that, moreover; nevertheless.
[熟] 그 위에; 게다가; 말할 것도 없이

⁑ **ate** [eit / et] *vt., vi.* pt. of **eat**.

at·el·ier [ǽtəljèi / ǽtəlièi, -ljèi] *n.* [C] a room where a painter or craftsman works; a workshop; a studio.
—[名] 아틀리에, 제작실, 화실

a·the·ism [éiθiìz(ə)m] *n.* [U] the belief that there is no God. ↔theism.
—[名] 무신론

a·the·ist [éiθiist] *n.* [C] a person who believes that there is no God. ↔theist
—[名] 무신론자

a·the·is·tic [èiθiístik] *adj.* of atheism. ↔theistic
—[形] 무신론[자]의, 무신론적인

A·the·na [əθí:nə] *n.* (in Greek mythology) the goddess of wisdom and the arts. ⇒[N.B.]
—[名] 아테나 신 [N.B.] 로마 신화에서는 Minerva

A·the·ne [əθí:ni(:)] *n.* =Athena.

A·the·ni·an [əθí:niən] *adj.* of Athens. —*n.* [C] a person born or living in Athens.
—[形] 아테네[사람]의 —[名] 아테네 사람

Ath·ens [ǽθinz] *n.* the capital of Greece.
—[名] 아테네

a·thirst [əθə́:rst] *adj.* 《as *predicative*》 thirsty; wanting to drink. ¶*be ~ for information.*①
—[形] 갈망하는 ¶①지식을 갈망하다

athlete [8 4] attache

ath·lete [ǽθliːt] *n.* ⓒ a person who is trained for games or sports.
—ⓝ 운동가, 운동 경기자

* **ath·let·ic** [æθlétik] *adj.* of athletics; like an athlete. ¶ *an ~ meet* (or *meeting*).
—ⓐ 운동경기의; 운동가다운

ath·let·ics [æθlétiks] *n. pl.* **1.** exercises of physical power, speed, and skill; active games and sports. **2.** ((used as *sing.*)) the principles of athletic training.
—ⓝ 1. 운동경기 2. 체육 실기 [과목]

at-home, at home [əthóum] *n.* ⓒ informal reception at an appointed time. ¶*an at-home day.*①
—ⓝ [가정적인] 초대회 ¶①면회일

a·thwart [əθwɔ́ːrt] *adv.* across from one side to another. —*prep.* across; against.
—ⓐ [비스듬히] 가로질러 —ⓟ …을 가로질러; 거슬러서

‡ **At·lan·tic** [ətlǽntik, ət- / ət-], **the** *n.* the ocean on the east of North and South America. —*adj.* of the Atlantic Ocean. ¶(*U. S.*) *the ~ states.*①
—ⓝ 대서양 —ⓐ 대서양의 ¶①[미국의] 대서양 연안 제주(諸州)

at·las [ǽtləs] *n.* **1.** ⓒ a book of maps. ⇒NB. **2.** ((*A-*)) (in Greek mythology) a giant who supported the heavens on his shoulders. ⇒fig.
—ⓝ 지도책 NB atlas는 map(한 장의 지도)를 모아 책으로 만든 것 2. 아틀라스(그리이스 신화에 나오는 거인)

‡ **at·mos·phere** [ǽtməsfīər] *n.* **1.** Ⓤ the air surrounding the earth; the air in some place. **2.** ⓒ a general feeling ¶*the political ~ of the country.*①
—ⓝ 1. 대기; [특정 장소의] 공기 2. 주위의 상황·분위기 ¶①그 나라의 정치 상황

at·mos·pher·ic [ætməsférik] *adj.* of atmosphere. ¶*high* (*low*) *atmospheric pressure.*①
—ⓐ 대기의; 대기 속의 ¶①고(저)기압

at·oll [ǽtɔːl, ətál / ǽtɔl, ətɔ́l] *n.* ⓒ a coral island which is in the shape of a ring. ⇒fig.
—ⓝ 환초(環礁)

[Atlas]

* **at·om** [ǽtəm] *n.* **1.** ⓒ (*Physics*) the smallest element of matter. **2.** a very small amount.
—ⓝ 1. 원자 2. 극소의 것

* **a·tom·ic** [ətámik / ətɔ́m-] *adj.* **1.** of atoms. ¶*an ~ bomb*① / *an ~ power plant.*② **2.** very small; minute.
—ⓐ 1. 원자의 ¶① 원자폭탄/②원자력 발전소 2. 아주 작은, 극히 미세한

[atoll]

at·om·ize [ǽtəmàiz] *vt.* **1.** separate (a matter) into atoms. **2.** change (a liquid, etc.) into a minute spray.
—ⓥ 1. …을 원자로 만들다 2. [액체를] 분무로 뿜다; [원자탄으로] 분쇄하다

at·om·iz·er [ǽtəmàizər] *n.* ⓒ an instrument used to blow a liquid in the form of a very fine spray.
—ⓝ 분무기; 분무식 향수 뿌리개

a·tone [ətóun] *vi.* make repayment for a wrong or fault.
—ⓥ 보상하다, 갚다

a·tone·ment [ətóunmənt] *n.* Ⓤ **1.** the act of atoning. **2.** ((*the A-*)) the sufferings and death of Christ to atone for the sins of mankind.
—ⓝ 1. 보상 2. 그리스도의 속죄

a·top [ətáp / -tɔ́p] *adv.* on or at the top. —*prep.* on or at the top of.
—ⓐ 꼭대기에 —ⓟ …의 꼭대기에

a·tro·cious [ətróuʃəs] *adj.* very cruel; very wicked. ▷ **a·tro·cious·ly** [-li] *adv.*
—ⓐ 잔인한, 흉악한

a·troc·i·ty [ətrásiti / -rɔ́s-] *n.* Ⓤ cruelty; brutality; ⓒ a very cruel act.
—ⓝ 극악, 포학; 잔학한 행위

at·ro·phy [ǽtrəfi] *n.* Ⓤ (*Medicine*) the state in which a part of the body wastes away.
—ⓝ [영양 불량 따위에서 오는] 위축[증]

‡ **at·tach** [ətǽtʃ] *vt.* **1.** join; fasten. ((~ *something to*)) ¶ ~ *a rope to a dog* / *Tom attached a label to the baggage.*① **2.** make (someone or something) belong; include. ((~ *someone or something to*)) ¶*a high school attached to a university*② / *She attached herself to the party.*③ **3.** attribute. ¶*The police attached the blame to the driver.*④ —*vi.* go with; belong to. ¶*No honor attaches to this position.*
be attached to (=*be fond of; love*) someone. ¶*She is very attached to her aunt.*
—ⓥ 1. …을 매다, 붙이다 ¶①톰은 수하물에 꼬리표를 붙이다 2. …을 소속시키다, 부속시키다 ¶②대학 부속 고등학교/③그녀는 그 모임에 가입했다 3. [책임 따위]를 돌리다 ¶④경찰은 그 책임이 운전수에게 있다고 했다
—ⓥ 붙다, 부속하다

熟 애착을 갖다

at·tach·a·ble [ətǽtʃəbl] *adj.* that can attached.
—ⓐ 붙일 수 있는; 차압할 수 있는

at·ta·ché [ætəʃéi / ətǽʃei] *n.* ⓒ a person who goes with an ambassador to a foreign country.
—ⓝ 대(공)사관원, 대(공)사 수행원

attaché case [-´-´] *n.* a small, flat case for documents shaped like a suitcase.

at·tach·ment [ətǽtʃmənt] *n.* **1.** Ⓤ the act of attaching; the state of being attached; Ⓒ something that is fixed. **2.** Ⓤ affection. ¶ ~ *to one's mother.*①

— Ⓝ 서류용 손가방

— Ⓝ 1. 붙이기, 부착; 부속물 2. 애착
¶①어머니에 대한 사랑

‡ at·tack [ətǽk] *vt.* **1.** fight against (someone or something). ¶ ~ *the enemy.* **2.** (of a disease, medicines, etc.) act harmfully on (a person or thing). ¶ *Influenza attacked the whole town.*① / *She was attacked by pneumonia.* **3.** begin to work energetically on (something). ¶ *He attacked a very difficult calculation.*②
— *n.* **1.** Ⓤ Ⓒ the act of attacking. ¶ *Attack is the best form of defense.* / *make an ~ on the enemy.*③ **2.** Ⓒ a sudden occurrence of illness; a fit. ¶ *have an ~ of a disease* / *He is suffering from an ~ of gout.*④

— Ⓥ 1. …을 공격하다 2. [병이] …을 엄습하다, [약품 따위가] …에 나쁘게 작용하다 ¶①인플루엔자가 온 읍내를 휩쓸었다 3. …에 착수하다 ¶②그는 아주 힘든 계산을 하려고 들었다

— Ⓝ 1. 공격 ¶③적을 공격하다 2. 발병, 병에 걸리기 ¶④그는 통풍(痛風)의 발작으로 고생하고 있다

at·tack·er [ətǽkər] *n.* Ⓒ a person who attacks.

— Ⓝ 공격자

‡ at·tain [ətéin] *vt.* **1.** arrive at (some place); reach. ¶ *He attained the opposite bank of the river.* **2.** perform. ¶ *It is now impossible to ~ your ambition.* — *vi.* come to reach. ¶ *Wisdom is a hard thing to ~ to.*①

— Ⓥ 1. …에 도달하다 2. [애써서] 성취하다, 달성하다 — Ⓥ [자연히] …되다; [노력하여] 도달하다 ¶①지혜란 도달하기 힘든 것이다

at·tain·a·ble [ətéinəbl] *adj.* that can be attained.

— Ⓐ 도달할 수 있는

at·tain·ment [ətéinmənt] *n.* Ⓤ **1.** the act of attaining; achievement. **2.** (*pl.*) skill or knowledge gained by training or study; accomplishments. ¶ *a man of great (or high) attainments.*①

— Ⓝ 1. 달성 2. 학식, 예능 ¶①박식한 사람

at·tar [ǽtər] *n.* Ⓤ a sweet-smelling liquid made from 「flowers petal.」

— Ⓝ 꽃의 엑스, 장미 기름

‡ at·tempt [ətém(p)t] *vt.* **1.** try; endeavor. (*~ to do*) ¶ ~ *a discussion*① / ~ [*to climb*] *an unconquered peak.*② **2.** attack; destroy.
1) ***attempt someone's life,*** try to kill someone.
2) ***attempt one's own life,*** try to kill oneself; try to commit suicide.
— *n.* Ⓒ **1.** an effort; an endeavor; a trial. ¶ *a murderous ~.*③ **2.** an attack. ¶ *an ~ on the enemy camp.*④
1) ***make an attempt at*** (*=try*) *something.* ¶ *She made an ~ at suicide.*
2) ***make an attempt on,*** try to kill (someone); attack.
3) ***make an attempt*** (*=try*) ***to do.***

— Ⓥ 1. …을 시도하다, 기도하다 ¶토론을 시도하다/②미정복의 봉우리의 등반을 시도하다 2. …을 습격하다
熟 1)…의 목숨을 노리다 2)자살을 꾀하다

— Ⓝ 1. 시도; 기도 ¶③살해 기도 2. 공격, 습격 ¶④적진 습격

熟 1)…을 시도하다 2)[남]의 목숨을 노리다; …을 공격하다 3)…하려고 꾀하다

‡ at·tend [əténd] *vt.* **1.** be present at (a meeting, etc.). ¶ ~ *school*① / ~ *a lecture.*② **2.** look after or take care of (someone). ¶ ~ *a patient*③ / *He is always attended by a nurse.* **3.** accompany; follow. ¶ *Great difficulties attended our plan.*④ — *vi.* **1.** pay attention. (*~ to something*) ¶ *You must ~ to your duty as a student.* **2.** wait on someone; serve. (*~ on someone*) **3.** be engaged in something.

— Ⓥ 1. [모임 따위]에 참석(출석)하다 ¶①학교에 출석하다/②강의에 출석하다 2. …을 보살피다; …의 시중을 들다 ¶③환자의 시중들다 3. …에 동행하다; 동반하다 ¶④우리 계획에는 큰 곤란이 따랐다 1.주의하다 2.시중들다 3.종사하다

· at·tend·ance [əténdəns] *n.* Ⓤ **1.** the act of being present. ¶ *Our English class has very good ~ today.*① **2.** Ⓤ Ⓒ (*collectively*) those who are present. ¶ *There was a large (a small) ~ at the ceremony.*② **3.** the act of serving or waiting on someone; service; care.
be in attendance (*=wait*) ***on someone.***

— Ⓝ 1. 출석 ¶①오늘 영어 수업에는 출석 상황이 좋다 2. 출석자 ¶②식에는 출석자가 많았다(적었다) 3.시중들기, 봉사; 보살피기

熟 …에 시중들다

· at·tend·ant [əténdənt] *adj.* **1.** accompanying; following. ¶ *war and its ~ inflation*① / *Diseases are ~ on famine.*② **2.** present. — *n.* Ⓒ **1.** a person who waits on others; a servant; a nurse; a follower. ¶ *The president called all his attendants together.* **2.** a person who is present.

— Ⓐ 1. 따라다니는; 부수하는 ¶①전쟁과 이에 따르는 인플레/②기근에는 질병이 따른다 2. 출석한 — Ⓝ 1.시중드는 사람, 수행원; 심부름꾼; 간호원 2. 출석자

‡ at·ten·tion [ətén∫(ə)n] *n.* Ⓤ **1.** the act of giving one's mind; careful observation. ¶ *attract* (or *draw, arrest*) ~ ① / *give ~ to something* / *call someone's attention to a fact*② / *She was all ~.*③ / *Attention !*④ **2.** care; treatment. **3.** (often *pl.*) kindness; consideration; courtesy, esp. for women.

— Ⓝ 1. 주의, 유의 ¶①주의를 끌다/②남의 주의를 환기시키다/③그녀는 열심히 듣고 있었다/④차려!(구령) 2. 시중, 돌봄 3. 친절; 공손, 정중; 구혼(求婚)

1) ***come to attention,*** take an erect, motionless position. 2) ***devote*** *one's* ***attention*** (=*apply oneself*) ***to*** *something.* 3) ***stand at attention,*** stand erect and motionless.

[熟] 1)차려의 자세로 서다 2)…에 전렴하다 3)부동자세를 취하다

* **at·ten·tive** [əténtiv] *adj.* **1.** paying attention; careful; observant. ¶*Be more ~ to your studies.*① **2.** considerate; polite; courteous. ⟪~ *to*⟫ ¶*He is very ~ to his little sister.*②

—[形] 1. 주의 깊은 ¶①공부에 더욱 열의를 쏟아라 2. 정중한; 다정한 ¶②그는 어린 누이에게 다정했다

at·ten·tive·ly [əténtivli] *adv.* with attention; carefully.

—[副] 주의 깊게

at·ten·u·ate [əténjuèit] *vi.* become thin or slender; lessen. —*vt.* make (something) thin or slender; weaken.

—[自] 가늘게 되다; 줄다 —[他] …을 가늘게 하다; 약하게 하다

at·test [ətést] *vi., vt.* **1.** declare the truth of (one's words); testify; certify. **2.** give proof of (something); prove. ¶*His ability is attested by his rapid promotion.*

—[自][他] 1. …의 진실임을 맹세하다 2. 입증하다; 증거가 되다

attest to (=*be proof of*) *something.* ¶*This attests to his innocence.*①

[熟] …의 증거가 되다 ¶①이것이 그의 무죄를 증명한다

at·tes·ta·tion [æ̀testéiʃ(ə)n] *n.* [U] [C] the act of attesting; testimony; proof.

—[名] 증명; 증거; 증언

* **at·tic** [ǽtik] *n.* [C] a room just under the roof of a house.

—[名] 고미다락방

* **at·tire** [ətáiər] *vt.* ⟪chiefly in the *passive* or *reflexively*⟫ dress up; put clothes on (someone). ¶~*oneself in black.*①

—[他] 차려입다 ¶①검정 옷을 입다

* **at·ti·tude** [ǽtit(j)ù:d / -tjù:d] *n.* [C] **1.** the way of thinking, feeling, or acting; manner. ¶*a serious ~*① / *What is your ~ toward this question?*② **2.** a position of the body.

—[名] 1. 태도 ¶①진지한 태도/②이 문제에 대한 너의 태도는 어떤가? 2. 자세

strike an attitude, put on airs; pretend.

[熟] 젠체하다, 허세부리다

* **at·tor·ney** [ətə́:rni] *n.* [C] **1.** a person who acts legally for another; an agent. **2.** a lawyer.

—[名] 1. 대리인 2. 변호사

1) ***by attorney,*** by an agent who has a letter of attorney. ↔in person 2) ***a letter*** (or ***warrant***) ***of attorney,*** a letter indicating that a person is appointed as an agent.

[熟] 1)[위임장을 가진] 대리인에 의하여 2)위임장

at·tor·ney-at-law [ətə́:rniətlɔ́:] *n.* [C] a lawyer.

—[名] 변호사

attorney general [-ˊ- ˊ--] *n.* (pl. **attorneys ~** or **~ generals**) **1.** the chief law officer of a country. **2.** ⟪*A- G-*⟫ (*U.S.*) the head of the Department of Justice, who helps his President as his chief legal advisor.

—[名] 1. 검찰 총장 2.⟪美⟫ 법무장관

‡ **at·tract** [ətrǽkt] *vt.* **1.** draw (someone or something) toward oneself. ¶*The art exhibition attracted a crowd of visitors.*① / *A magnet attracts iron.*② **2.** make (someone) interested; charm. ¶*The actress attracted the town's people.*

—[他] 1. …을 끌다, 끌어당기다 ¶①미술 전람회는 많은 관중을 끌었다/②자석은 쇠를 끌어당긴다 2. [주의·흥미 따위]를 끌다; …을 매혹하다

* **at·trac·tion** [ətrǽkʃ(ə)n] *n.* **1.** [U] the act of attracting; (*Physics*) the power that attracts. **2.** [C] a person or thing that attracts or charms people. ¶*Susie has many attractions.*① / *The lions were the chief ~ at the circus.*

—[名] 1. 끌기, 당기기; 인력 2. [이목을] 끄는 것 ¶①수우지한테는 사람을 끌어당기는 점이 많이 있다

‡ **at·trac·tive** [ətrǽktiv] *adj.* pleasing; charming; arousing interest.

—[形] 끄는, 끌어당기는; 매력이 있는

at·trac·tive·ly [ətrǽktivli] *adv.* in an attractive manner; charmingly.

—[副] 매력적으로, 눈에 띄게

at·trib·ut·a·ble [ətríbjutəbl] *adj.* that can be attributed.

—[形] [원인 따위가] 돌릴 수 있는

* **at·trib·ute** [ətríbju(:)t →*n.*] *vt.* consider (one thing) as belonging to or caused by another. ⟪~ something *to*⟫ ¶*They attributed his success to good luck.* / *We ~ wisdom to him.* / *The painting is attributed to Van Gogh.*

—[他] [결과 따위]를 …에 돌리다, [원인]을 …의 탓으로 하다; [성질]을 …에 속하게 하다, …을 …의 작품이라 하다

—*n.* [ǽtribju:t] [C] **1.** a quality or an object that belongs to a special person or thing; a characteristic; a symbol. ¶*Reason is an ~ of man.* / *Winged feet are the ~ of Mercury.* **2.** (*Grammar*) an attributive adjective.

—[名] 1. 특성, 속성; 부수물, 딸린 것; 상징 2.⟪文法⟫ 한정 형용사

at·tri·bu·tion [æ̀tribjú:ʃ(ə)n] *n.* **1.** [U] the act of attributing. **2.** [C] a thing attributed.

—[名] 1. [원인 따위의] 돌리기; 귀속 2. [부속된] 권한; 직권

at·trib·u·tive [ətríbjutiv] *adj.* **1.** expressing a quality of belonging to something. **2.** (*Grammar*) (of an adjective) used before or, sometimes, after a noun; restrictive. ↔predicative —*n.* [C] (*Grammar*) an attributive adjective; a restrictive word.

—[形] 1. 속성(屬性)을 나타내는 2. 한정적인, 직접 수식하는 —[名] 한정 형용사, 한정사

at·tri·tion [ətríʃ(ə)n] *n.* ⓤ the act of wearing out; the state of being gradually worn out. ¶*Pebbles become smooth by* ~.①

at·tune [ət(j)úːn / ətjúːn] *vt.* **1.** make (the sounds of one musical instrument) agree with those of another. **2.** cause (one's feelings) to agree with those of another.

au·burn [ɔ́ːbə(ː)rn] *n., adj.* (of hair, etc.) red-brown.

auc·tion [ɔ́ːkʃ(ə)n] *n.* ⓤⓒ a public sale in which goods are sold to the buyer who offers the highest price.

auc·tion·eer [ɔ̀ːkʃəníər] *n.* ⓒ a person who sells goods at auction, usu. as a business. —*vt.* sell (goods) at auction. ⌈*was auctioned off.*⌉
auction off, sell (goods) at auction. ¶*The bookcase*

au·da·cious [ɔːdéiʃəs] *adj.* very daring; impudent; shameless. ▷**au·da·cious·ly** [-li] *adv.*

au·dac·i·ty [ɔːdǽsiti] *n.* ⓤ the state of being audacious; boldness; impudence. ¶*He had the* ~ *to break his promise.*

au·di·bil·i·ty [ɔ̀ːdibíliti] *n.* ⓤ the state of being audible.

au·di·ble [ɔ́ːdibl] *adj.* loud enough to be heard.

‡au·di·ence [ɔ́ːdiəns] *n.* **1.** ⓒ (*collectively*) persons gathered in a place to hear a singer, a speaker, etc. or to see a play, movie, etc. ¶*The* ~ *was composed of ladies.*① / *Most of the* ~ *at the movie were* (or *was*) *young men.*② ⇒ⓤⓢⓐⓖⓔ **2.** ⓒⓤ a formal interview with a person of high rank.
1) *be received in audience,* be admitted into a formal interview with a person of high rank.
2) *give audience to; grant an audience to,* admit (someone) to speak to someone else. ⌈*someone.*⌉
3) *have audience of* (=*have the chance to speak to*)
4) *in open* (or *general*) *audience,* in public.
5) *in the audience* (=*in the presence*) *of someone.*

au·di·o [ɔ́ːdiou] *adj.* (*Radio*) **1.** of a frequency which can be heard. **2.** of sound.

au·di·o-vis·u·al aids [ɔ́ːdiouvíʒu(ə)léidz] *n. pl.* educational apparatuses designed for hearing and seeing.

au·dit [ɔ́ːdit] *n.* ⓤ an official examination of business accounts. —*vt.* **1.** examine (business accounts) officially. **2.** (*U.S.*) attend (a college class) as a special student.

au·di·tion [ɔːdíʃ(ə)n] *n.* ⓤ the act or power of hearing; ⓒ an examination to test a singer, an actor, etc. before he is hired.

au·di·tor [ɔ́ːditər] *n.* ⓒ **1.** a hearer; a listener. **2.** a person whose job is to audit business accounts.

au·di·to·ri·a [ɔ̀ːditɔ́ːriə] *n.* pl. of **auditorium.**

au·di·to·ri·um [ɔ̀ːditɔ́ːriəm] *n.* ⓒ (pl. **-ums** or **-ri·a**) a large hall or room in which meetings are held or lectures, concerts, etc. are given.

au·di·to·ry [ɔ́ːditɔ̀ːri / -t(ə)ri] *adj.* of [the sense of] hearing. ¶~ *nerves*① / ~ *education.*②

Au·drey [ɔ́ːdri] *n.* a woman's name.

Aug. August.

au·ger [ɔ́ːgər] *n.* ⓒ an instrument for making holes in wood. ⇒ N.B. ⇒fig.

aught [ɔːt] *pron.* (*archaic, poetic*) anything.
1) *for aught I care,* I don't care. ¶*You may get sick for aught I care.*①
2) *for aught I know,* perhaps. ¶*He may be a millionaire for aught I know.*
—*adv.* (*archaic*) at all, in any way.

aug·ment [ɔːgmént] *vt., vi.* increase; enlarge.

aug·men·ta·tion [ɔ̀ːgmentéiʃ(ə)n] *n.* **1.** ⓤ

[auger]

—⒨ 마찰;마멸 ¶①자갈은 마찰로 매끈매끈하다

—⒨ 1.〔악기의〕음조를 다른 것에 맞추다 2.〔마음을〕남의 기분에 조화시키다

—⒨⒨ 〔머리털 따위가〕적갈색〔의〕
—⒨ 경매, 공매

—⒨ 경매인 —⒨ …을 경매하다

⒩ 〔물건〕을 경매로 팔다.
—⒨ 대담한, 뻔뻔스러운

—⒨ 대담함; 뻔뻔스러움

—⒨ 들을 수 있음, 가청
—⒨ 〔똑똑히〕들을 수 있는
—⒨ 1.청중, 관객 ¶①청중들은 여자들이다/②영화 관객의 대개는 청년들이다
ⓤⓢⓐⓖⓔ 개개의 청중을 가리키는 경우는 복수 취급 2.공식 접견, 알현, 접견

⒩ 1)알현을 허락받다 2)…을 접견하다; …에 알현을 허락하다 3)…에 배알하다 4)공개 석상에서 5)…의 면전에서

—⒨ 1. 가청주파(可聽周波)의 2. 음의

—⒨ 시청각 교재

—⒨ 회계 검사; 〔회사 따위의〕감사; 결산 —⒨ 1.(美)〔회계〕를 검사하다 2.〔대학의 강좌를 청강생으로서〕청강하다

—⒨ 청취(력); 〔가수 등과 계약할 때의〕심사 시험; 〔레코드 따위의〕시청(試聽)

—⒨ 1.듣는 사람; 〔라디오 따위의〕청취자 2.회계 검사관, 감사역

—⒨ 강당;〔강당·교회·극장 따위의〕청중석; 공회당

—⒨ 귀의, 청각의 ¶①청각 신경/②음감 교육
—⒨ 여자 이름

—⒨ 큰 송곳 ⒩.⒝. 작은 것은 gimlet

—⒞ (古·詩)어떤 일(것), 무엇인가
⒩ 1)…해도 내가 알 바가 아니다 ¶①네가 병이 걸려도 내 알 바 아니다 2)잘은 모르지만, 뭐라 할 수 없으나 아마
—⒨ 조금도, 아무래도
—⒨⒨ …을 늘리다, 증가하다
—⒨ 1.증가, 부가 2. 증가물, 부가물

increase; addition. **2.** [C] something increased.

au·gur [ɔ́:gər] *n.* [C] **1.** an official in ancient Rome that told the fortune from the appearance of birds. **2.** a fortune teller. —*vt.* foretell. —*vi.* be a sign of the future. ¶~ *well* (*bad*) *for.*①

—[名] 1. 복점관(卜占官) 2. 점장이 —[他] …을 점치다 —[自] …의 전조가 되다 ¶①…의 길조(흉조)가 되다

au·gu·ry [ɔ́:gjuri] *n.* (pl. **-ries**) **1.** [U] an art of fortune-telling. **2.** [C] a prophecy; an omen.

—[名] 1. 점 2. 예언; 전조

⁑**Au·gust** [ɔ́:gəst] *n.* the eighth month of the year. ⇒[N.B.]

—[名] 8월 [N.B.] Aug.로 줄임

au·gust [ɔ:gʌ́st] *adj.* majestic; causing a feeling of fear and respect.

—[形] 위엄이 있는; 존엄한

⁑**Au·gus·tan** [ɔ:gʌ́st(ə)n] *adj.* of Augustus, a Roman Emperor; of the period of his reign.

—[形] [로마 황제] 아우구스투스의, 아우구스투스 시대의

auld lang syne [ɔ́:ldlæŋsáin] *n.* (*Scot.*) the good old times.

—[名] 《스코》 그리운 옛날

⁑**aunt** [ænt / ɑ:nt] *n.* [C] a father's or mother's sister; the wife of one's uncle.

—[名] 숙모, 아주머니

aunt·ie, aunt·y [ǽnti / ɑ́:n-] *n.* [C] (*child's word*) aunt.

—[名] 《小兒》 아줌마

au·ra [ɔ́:rə] *n.* [C] (pl. **-ras** or **-rae**) a faint smell or atmosphere lying around a thing or person like the smell round flowers.

—[名] [물체에서 발산되는] 기(氣); 분위기

au·rae [ɔ́:ri:] *n.* pl. of **aura**.

au·ral [ɔ́:r(ə)l] *adj.* of the ear or hearing. ↔oral

—[形] 귀의; 청각의

au·re·ole [ɔ́:riòul], **au·re·o·la** [ɔ:ríələ] *n.* [C] a circle of bright light round the head or figure of a holy person as shown in a picture.

—[名] [성상(聖像)의] 후광(後光); 광륜(光輪)

au·ri·cle [ɔ́:rikl] *n.* [C] the outer part of the ear.

—[名] 외이(外耳), 귓바퀴

au·ric·u·lar [ɔ:ríkjulər] *adj.* **1.** of the ear. **2.** shaped like an ear. **3.** of an auricle of the heart.

—[形] 1. 귀의 2. 귀 모양의 3. 심이(心耳)의

au·ro·ra [ɔ:rɔ́:rə] *n.* **1.** 《*A-*》 (in Roman mythology) the goddess of the dawn. ⇒[N.B.] **2.** 《*the* ~》 the colored bands of light in the sky around the North Pole.

—[名] 1. 여명의 여신 [N.B.] 그리이스 신화의 Eos에 해당 2. 극광(極光)

au·ro·ra aus·tra·lis [ɔ:rɔ́:rəɔ:stréilis] *n.* the bands of light in the southern area corresponding to the aurora.

—[名] 남극광

aus·pice [ɔ́:spis] *n.* **1.** 《usu. *pl.*》 patronage; sponsorship. **2.** [C] a sign of good fortune.

—[名] 1. 후원; 주최 2. 좋은 전조

under the auspices of, sponsored by.

[熟] …의 후원으로, 주최로

aus·pi·cious [ɔ:spíʃəs] *adj.* promising good fortune; fortunate. ↔inauspicious

—[形] 길조(吉兆)의; 행운의

aus·tere [ɔ:stíər] *adj.* **1.** very plain and simple in appearance or living. **2.** strict in character or manner.

—[形] 1. [생활 · 양식 따위가] 간소한 2. [성격 · 태도가] 엄격한, 엄한

aus·ter·i·ty [ɔ:stériti] *n.* **1.** [U] strictness; severity. **2.** 《*pl.*》 severe practices; a hard life.

—[名] 1. 엄격 2. 내핍생활

***Aus·tral·ia** [ɔ:stréiljə] *n.* **1.** the continent to the southeast of Asia. **2.** the Commonwealth of Australia. ⇒[N.B.]

—[名] 1. 오스트레일리아 대륙 2. 오스트레일리아 [연방] [N.B.] 수도 Canberra

Aus·tral·ian [ɔ:stréiljən] *adj.* of Australia or its people. —*n.* [C] a person of Australia.

—[形] 오스트레일리아[사람]의 —[名] 오스트레일리아 사람

***Aus·tri·a** [ɔ́:striə] *n.* a country in central Europe.

—[名] 오스트리아

Aus·tri·an [ɔ́:striən] *adj.* of Austria or its people. —*n.* [C] a person of Austria.

—[形] 오스트리아[사람]의 —[名] 오스트리아 사람

au·tar·ky [ɔ́:tɑ:rki] *n.* [U] economical self-sufficiency; the state of needing no help from others.

—[名] [경제의] 자급자족

au·then·tic [ɔ:θéntik] *adj.* trustworthy; true; genuine.

—[形] 신뢰할 만한; 진정한, 진짜의

au·then·ti·cate [ɔ:θéntikèit] *vt.* show or make (something or someone) to be true, reliable, or genuine.

—[他] [사물의 진정함 따위]를 증명하다

au·then·ti·ca·tion [ɔ:θèntikéiʃ(ə)n] *n.* [U] the act of authenticating; the state of being authenticated.

—[名] 확증; 증명

au·then·tic·i·ty [ɔ:θentísiti] *n.* [U] reliability; genuineness.

—[名] 확실성; 진정(眞正)

***au·thor** [ɔ́:θər] *n.* [C] **1.** the writer of a book, novel, play, etc. ¶*I like modern authors.* **2.** a writer's publication. ¶*He has many authors on his shelves.*① **3.** the first beginner of a new thing; a creator.

—[名] 1. 작가; 저자 2. 저작물 ¶①그의 서가에는 많은 작가의 작품이 있다 3. 창시자; 장본인

the Author of our being (or ***the universe***), God.

[熟] 조물주; 신

au·thor·ess [ɔ́:θəris] *n.* [C] a woman author.

—[名] 여류 작가

au·thor·i·tar·i·an [əθɔ̀:ritέəriən / ɔ:θɔ̀:r-] *adj.* giving more importance to authority than to individual liberty.

—[形] 관권주의의; 독재주의의

authoritative [89] **automobile**

—*n.* ⓒ a person who has such a principle.
au·thor·i·ta·tive [əθɔ́:ritèitiv / ɔ:θɔ́ritə-] *adj.* **1.** having authority; commanding. ¶*an ~ manner / in ~ tones.*① **2.** that can be trusted; reliable. 「mandingly; reliably.」
au·thor·i·ta·tive·ly [əθɔ́:ritèitivli / ɔ:θɔ́ritə-] *adv.* com-
: **au·thor·i·ty** [əθɔ́:riti, əθɑ́r- / ɔ:θɔ́ri-] *n.* (pl. **-ties**) **1.** Ⓤ the right and power to command. ¶*A king used to have greater ~ over* (or *with*) *people.* **2.** Ⓤ permission. ¶*Who gave you ~ to come into this room?* **3.** (usu. *pl.*) the group of persons who have the right and power to govern. ¶*the school authorities.*① **4.** ⓒ a person or book that can be relied on reading some subject. ¶*He is a great ~ on children's diseases.*② */ The book is the best ~ on the history of English literature.*③
au·thor·i·za·tion [ɔ̀:θəraizéiʃ(ə)n / -rai-] *n.* Ⓤ the act of authorizing.
* **au·thor·ize** [ɔ́:θəràiz] *vt.* **1.** give (someone) the right and power to act. ¶*He has authorized me to act for him during his absence.* **2.** permit; make legal. ¶*a parade authorized by the police.*① **3.** justify.
* **au·thor·ized** [ɔ́:θəràizd] *adj.* supported by authority; given authority. ¶*an ~ textbook / an ~ agent.*①
Authorized Version [`--- --`] **the,** *n.* the English translation of the Bible published in 1611. ⇒N.B.
au·thor·ship [ɔ́:θərʃip] *n.* Ⓤ the occupation of an author; the source or origin [of a book].
au·to [ɔ́:tou] *n.* ⓒ (pl. **au·tos**)・(*colloq.*) an automobile.
au·to- [ɔ́:tou-] a word element meaning *self*: *autobiography* (=a life-history written by oneself) / *autograph* (=a person's own handwriting).
au·to·bi·o·graph·i·cal [ɔ̀:təbàiəgræfik(ə)l]**, -graph·ic** [-græfik] *adj.* of an autobiography.
au·to·bi·og·ra·phy [ɔ̀:təbaiɔ́grəfi / -ɔ́grə-] *n.* ⓒ a story of a person's life written by himself.
au·toc·ra·cy [ɔ:tákrəsi / -tɔ́k-] *n.* (pl. **-ra·cies**) **1.** Ⓤ government by a ruler who has absolute power; dictatorship. **2.** ⓒ a government that has unlimited power.
au·to·crat [ɔ́:təkræt] *n.* ⓒ a ruler or person who has absolute power over a group of persons.
au·to·crat·ic [ɔ̀:təkrǽtik] *adj.* of or like an autocrat.
au·to·gi·ro, -gy·ro [ɔ̀:tədʒáiərou / ɔ́:t-] *n.* ⓒ (pl. **-ros**) an airplane that can rise straight up from the ground.
au·to·graph [ɔ́:təgræf / -grà:f] *n.* ⓒ **1.** a person's own handwriting. **2.** a person's name written by himself.
—*vt.* **1.** write one's signature in or on (something). **2.** write (letters, etc.) with one's own hand.
au·to·mat [ɔ́:təmæt] *n.* ⓒ (*U.S.*) a restaurant in which food and drink are sold by machines.
au·tom·a·ta [ɔ:támətə / -tɔ́m-] *n.* pl. of **automaton.**
* **au·to·mat·ic** [ɔ̀:təmǽtik] *adj.* **1.** self-moving; acting by itself. ¶*an ~ door / an ~ elevator.* **2.** done without thought or attention; unconscious. ¶*Swallowing food is usually ~.* —*n.* ⓒ a machine which works by itself; a gun which works by itself.
* **au·to·mat·i·cal·ly** [ɔ̀:təmǽtikəli] *adv.* in an automatic manner; by itself.
au·to·ma·tion [ɔ̀:təméiʃ(ə)n] *n.* Ⓤ the technique, or system of doing mechanical processes by automatic means.
au·tom·a·ton [ɔ:támət(ə)n / -tɔ́m-] *n.* ⓒ (pl. **-tons** or **-ta** [-tə]) **1.** a machine that imitates the actions of living people; a robot. **2.** a person who acts like a machine, without thought of his own.
: **au·to·mo·bile** [ɔ́:təməbì:l, ɔ̀:təmóubi:l, ɔ̀:təməbí:l] *n.* ⓒ (chiefly *U.S.*) a motorcar.

—图 관권(독재)주의자
—圈 1.권력이 있는; 명령적인 ¶①명령적인 말투로 2.권위 있는; 믿을 만한
—團 권력적으로; 명령투로
—图 1.권위; 권력 2.권한; 허가 3.당국,관청 ¶①학교 당국 4.[믿을 만한] 전거; 대가(大家); 권위자 ¶②그는 소아과의 권위다/③그 책은 영문학사에 관한 최고의 전거이다

—图 권한을 줌; 인가

—働 1.…에 권한을 주다 2.[행동을] 인가하다 ¶①경찰에서 인가한 퍼레이드 3. …을 정당하다고 인정하다

—囮 인가받은, 권한이 부여된 ¶①지정 대리인
—图 흠정역(欽定譯)성서 N.B. 별칭 the King James Version
—图 저작자임, 저술; [소문 따위의] 출처, 근원
—图 자동차
—「자신의; 독자적인; 자기의」따위의 뜻을 나타내는 연결형

—囮 자서전의

—图 자서전

—图 1.독재정치 2.독재 정부

—图 독재자; 독재 군주

—囮 독재적인
—图 오오토자이로우

—图 1.자필 2.자서(自署) —働 1.…에 자필 서명하다 2.[편지 따위] 자필로 쓰다

—图 자동 판매 식당

—囮 1.자동의 2.기계적인; 무의식의
—图 자동 기계; 자동 소총

—團 자동적으로; 기계적으로

—图 자동 조작; 오오토메이션

—图・1.자동 기계; 자동 인형 2.기계적으로 움직이는 사람

—图 자동차

A

au·ton·o·mous [ɔːtɑ́nəməs / -tɔ́n-] *adj.* self-governing; ruled by its own laws only. ▷**au·ton·o·mous·ly** [-li] *adv.*
—[形] 자치의; 자율적인

au·ton·o·my [ɔːtɑ́nəmi / -tɔ́n-] *n.* (pl. **-mies**) **1.** [U] [the right of] self-government. **2.** [C] a self-governing community.
—[名] 1. 자치[권] 2. 자치 단체

au·top·sy [ɔ́ːtɑpsi / -təp-] *n.* [C] (pl. **-sies**) an examination of a body after death to find the cause of death.
—[名] 검시(檢屍)

⁑ **au·tumn** [ɔ́ːtəm] *n.* [U][C] the third season of the year; the season between summer and winter. (cf. *U.S.* fall) **—*adj.*** of autumn.
—[名] 가을 —[形] 가을의

au·tum·nal [ɔːtʌ́mn(ə)l] *adj.* of autumn.
—[形] 가을의

aux·il·ia·ry [ɔːgzíljəri, +*U.S.* -lièri] *adj.* **1.** additional. **2.** helpful. **—*n.*** [C] (pl. **-ries**) **1.** a person or thing that gives aid. **2.** (*Grammar*) a word helping the function of verbs, such as *have, be, may, shall, and will.*
—[形] 1. 추가의 2. 보조의 —[名] 1. 보조자(물) 2. 조동사

* **a·vail** [əvéil] *vi.* be of use; help. ¶*Such arguments will not* ~.① **—*vt.*** profit. ¶*Our wealth avails us nothing.*② *avail oneself* (=*take advantage or make use*) ***of** something.*
—*n.* [U] ⟪chiefly in *negative*⟫ use; benefit.
—[自] 쓸모있다, 소용되다 ¶①그런 의론은 아무 소용없다 —[他] …에 이익되다 ¶②재산이 우리에게 아무 이익되는 바가 없다 [熟] …을 이용하다
—[名] 이익

a·vail·a·bil·i·ty [əvèiləbíliti] *n.* (pl. **-ties**) **1.** [U] the state of being available. **2.** [C] a person or thing that is available.
—[名] 1. 유용[성] 2. 쓸모있는 사람(것)

⁑ **a·vail·a·ble** [əvéiləbl] *adj.* **1.** of use; ready for use. **2.** that can be obtained.
—[形] 1. 쓸모있는 2. 입수할 수 있는

av·a·lanche [ǽvəlæntʃ / -lɑːnʃ] *n.* [C] **1.** a great mass of snow, ice, etc. suddenly sliding down a mountainside. **2.** anything like an avalanche. **—*vi.*** come down like an avalanche.
—[名] 1. 눈사태 2. [눈사태 같은] 쇄도 —[自] [눈사태처럼] 밀려오다

av·a·rice [ǽvəris] *n.* [U] too strong desire for riches. ↔generosity
—[名] 탐욕

av·a·ri·cious [æ̀vəríʃəs] *adj.* anxious for riches; greedy. ↔generous
—[形] 탐욕스러운

AVE, Ave., ave. Avenue.

A·ve Ma·ri·a [ɑ́ːveiməríːə / ɑ́ːvimərίə] *n.* **1.** the first words of the Latin version of a prayer in the Roman Catholic Church in praise of Mary, mother of Christ. **2.** a recitation of this prayer.
—[名] 1. 아베마리아 2. 성모 마리아에게 바치는 기도

a·venge [əvéndʒ] *vt.* punish (someone) in return for his wrong act or injury. ¶~ *one's father* / ~ *a murder* / ~ *oneself* (or *be avenged*) *on someone.*①
—[他] …의 복수를 하다, 원수 갚다 ¶①…에게 원수(원한)를 갚다

a·ven·ger [əvéndʒər] *n.* [C] a person who avenges.
—[名] 복수하는 사람

⁑ **av·e·nue** [ǽvinjuː] *n.* [C] **1.** a wide or main street. **2.** a way to approach or leave. **3.** a wide road with trees on each side.
—[名] 1. 가로, 큰 거리 2. 접근 수단 3. 가로수길

a·ver [əvə́ːr] *vt.* assert; affirm; declare as true. ⟪~ *that…*⟫
—[他] …을 단언하다, 주장하다

⁑ **av·er·age** [ǽv(ə)ridʒ] *n.* [C] **1.** the ordinary amount, quality, type, etc.; a common standard. **2.** the middle value or quantity of a set of numbers.
on an (or ***the***) ***average,*** approximately.
—*adj.* **1.** of an average. **2.** ordinary; usual.
—*vt.* **1.** find the average of (something); have (some quantity) as an average. ¶~ *15 miles* / ~ *eight hours a day.*① **2.** divide evenly. **—*vi.*** be of an average.
—[名] 1. 보통[의 분량·질]; 표준 2. 평균 [熟] 평균하여
—[形] 1. 평균의 2. 보통의; 통상의 —[他] 1. …의 평균을 내다; 평균하여 …이 되다 ¶①하루 평균 8시간 2. …을 평균하다; 균분하다 —[自] 평균되다, 균등하게 되다

a·verse [əvə́ːrs] *adj.* unwilling; opposed.
—[形] 싫어하는; 반대의

a·ver·sion [əvə́ːrʒ(ə)n / -ʃ(ə)n] *n.* **1.** [U] a strong feeling of dislike. ⟪~ *to*⟫ **2.** [C] a person or thing disliked.
—[名] 1. 염오, 싫음 2. 싫어하는 사람(것)

a·vert [əvə́ːrt] *vt.* **1.** turn away. ⟪~ *one's eyes* or *face from*⟫ ¶*He averted his eyes from the horrible sight.*① **2.** prevent; avoid.
—[他] 1. …을 돌리다 ¶①그는 소름끼치는 광경에서 눈을 돌렸다 2. …을 피하다, 막다

a·vi·ar·y [éivièri / -vjəri] *n.* [C] (pl. **-ar·ies**) a large cage in which many birds are kept.
—[名] [대형의] 새장; 조류 사육장

a·vi·a·tion [èiviéiʃ(ə)n] *n.* [U] the act or art of flying in airplanes.
—[名] 비행; 항공술

a·vi·a·tor [éivièitər] *n.* [C] a person who flies an airplane; a pilot of an airplane.
—[名] 비행가(사)

a·vi·a·tress, -trice [éivièitris] *n.* [C] a woman who flies an airplane.
—[名] 여류 비행가

av·id [ǽvid] *adj.* eager; very keen; greedy. ⟪~ *of, for*⟫
—[形] 갈망하는; 열심인; 탐욕스러운

a·vid·i·ty [əvíditi] *n.* [U] eagerness; greediness.
—[名] 갈망; 탐욕

av·o·ca·tion [æ̀voukéiʃ(ə)n] *n.* [C] an occupation besides one's regular work; a hobby.
—[名] 부업; 취미삼아 하는 일

⁑a·void [əvɔ́id] *vt.* keep away from (something); refrain from (something). 《~ *doing*》 ¶ ~ *making any promise.*
—[他] …을 피하다

a·void·a·ble [əvɔ́idəbl] *adj.* that can be avoided.
—[形] 피할 수 있는

a·void·ance [əvɔ́id(ə)ns] *n.* [U] the act of avoiding.
—[名] 피하기, 회피

av·oir·du·pois [æ̀vərdəpɔ́iz] *n.* [U] **1.** a system of weights used in the United States and Great Britain, based on 16 ounces to the pound. **2.** (*colloq.*) one's weight; weight.
—[名] 1. 상형(常衡)(영미에서는 귀금속·보석·약품 이외의 것에 대해서는 16온스를 1파운드로 정하는 형량) 2. 체중; 무게

a·vouch [əváutʃ] *vt.* **1.** affirm or declare positively. **2.** acknowledge; confess frankly.
—[他] 1. …을[정말이라고] 주장하다 2. …을 인정하다; 고백하다

a·vow [əváu] *vt.* declare openly; acknowledge; confess; admit frankly.
—[他] …을 공언하다; 인정하다; 고백하다; 솔직히 인정하다

a·vow·al [əváuəl] *n.* [U][C] an open declaration; acknowledgment; confession.
—[名] 공언; 자인(自認)

a·vowed [əváud] *adj.* acknowledged; declared openly.
—[形] 스스로 인정한; 공언한

a·vow·ed·ly [əváuidli] *adv.* openly.
—[副] 공공연히

⁑a·wait [əwéit] *vt.* **1.** wait for (someone or something); expect. ¶*I ~ your reply.* **2.** be prepared for (someone or something). ¶*A hearty welcome awaits you.*
—[他] 1. …을 기다리다; 예기하다 2. [사물]이 …을 기다리고 있다; 준비되어 있다

⁑a·wake [əwéik] *v.* (**a·woke, a·waked** or **a·woke**) *vt.* **1.** rouse (someone) from sleep; arouse; awaken. ¶*The noise awoke me from my sleep.* **2.** stir up; excite. ¶ ~ *a desire* / ~ *old memories* / *The affair awoke her to a sense of sin.* —*vi.* **1.** stop sleeping. ¶*One morning he awoke to find himself famous.*① **2.** become aware; realize. 《~ *to* something》 ¶*I awoke to my danger.*② —*adj.* 《as *predicative*》 **1.** not sleeping. ↔asleep ¶*He was wide ~ all night.* **2.** watchful; alert.
be awake to (=*be aware of*) *something.* ¶*He was ~ to the danger.*
—[他] 1. [잠에서] …을 깨우다, 각성시키다 2. [죄 따위]를 자각시키다; [기억 따위]를 불러일으키다 —[自] 1. 눈이 띄다, 일어나다 ¶①어느 날 아침 눈을 뜨니까 유명해져 있었다 2. 깨닫다, 알아차리다 ¶②내게 다가온 위험을 알아챘다 —[形] 1. 잠들지 않은, 깨어 있는 2. 빈틈없는; 알아차린
[熟] …을 알고 있다; …을 눈치채고 있다

⁑a·wak·en [əwéik(ə)n] *vt.* **1.** wake up (someone). **2.** make (someone) aware. —*vi.* awake; become aware.
—[他] 1. …의 눈을 뜨게 하다, 깨우다 2. …에 알아차리게 하다 —[自] 깨다; 알아차리다

a·wak·en·ing [əwéikniŋ] *adj.* arousing. —*n.* [U][C] the act of waking up; sudden awareness.
—[形] 깨어 있는 —[名] 깨기

***a·ward** [əwɔ́ːrd] *vt.* give (something) as the result of judging or consideration. ¶ ~ *someone a prize* (*reward*); ~ *a prize* (*reward*) *to someone.* —*n.* [C] a thing given as the result of judging or consideration; a prize.
—[他] [심사한 뒤에 상품 따위를] …에게 수여하다 —[名] 상

⁑a·ware [əwέər] *adj.* knowing; conscious. 《~ *of*》 ▷**a·ware·ness** [-nis] *n.*
—[形] 알고 있는; 깨달은

a·wash [əwɑ́ʃ / əwɔ́ʃ] *adj., adv.* 《as *predicate*》 (*Nautical*) scarcely above the surface of the water; just covered with water.
—[形][副] [바위·침몰선 따위가] 거의 수면과 같은 높이로; 파도로 덮일 정도로

⁑a·way [əwéi] *adv.* **1.** off; from this or that place; not at home; absent; at or to a distance; remote. ¶*far* ~ / *miles* ~ / ~ [*to the*] *west* / *He was ~ from home.* / *He is ~ in the country.* / *She talks ~ from the subject.* **2.** aside; in another direction. ¶*go* ~ / *come* ~ / *turn your eyes ~.* **3.** out of existence or notice; out of one's possession. ¶*wash* ~ / *fade* ~ / *die* ~ / *boil* ~ / *burn* ~ / *give free catalogs ~.* **4.** continuously; without stopping; on and on; without hesitation. ¶*work* ~ / *Sing ~.*① **5.** (*U.S. colloq.*) far. ¶*He is ~ behind the others in class.*②
—[副] 1. 떨어져서, 멀리에; 부재(不在)로; 떠나서 2. [동사와 함께] 저쪽에, 다른 쪽에(으로) 3. [동사와 함께] 사라져, 없어져, 꺼져 4. 계속, 끊임없이; 망설이지 않고 ¶①망설이지 말고 노래해라! 5. 《美口》 훨씬, 저 멀리 ¶②그는 반에서 남들을 훨씬 앞서 있다

1) ***away back,*** (*U.S. colloq.*) as (*or* so) far back as; long ago.
2) ***Away with you!,*** Go away!
3) ***far and away,*** beyond all doubt; very much; by far. ¶*This is far and ~ the best.*
4) ***from away,*** from a distance.
5) ***make*** (or ***do***) ***away with,*** ⓐ get rid of (something). ⓑ kill.
6) ***out and away,*** by far.
7) ***right away,*** at once.

[熟] 1)《美口》 훨씬 전에 2)나가라! 꺼져라! 3)비길데 없이 4)멀리에서 5)ⓐ…을 처분하다 ⓑ…을 죽이다 6)멀리에 7)곧, 당장

awe

- **awe** [ɔː] *n.* Ⓤ a feeling of combined fear, respect, and wonder. —*vt.* **1.** cause (someone) to feel awe; fill (someone) with awe. **2.** influence or overcome (someone) by awe.
  awe·in·spir·ing [ɔ́ːinspáiəriŋ] *adj.* arousing awe.
  awe·some [ɔ́ːsəm] *adj.* causing awe; inspiring awe.
  awe·strick·en [ɔ́ːstrìk(ə)n] *adj.* =awe-struck.
  awe·struck [ɔ́ːstrʌk] *adj.* filled with awe.
: **aw·ful** [ɔ́ːf(u)l] *adj.* **1.** dreadful; terrible. **2.** (*colloq.*) extremely bad; very ugly. —*adv.* (*colloq.*) very; extremely. ▷**aw·ful·ness** [-nis] *n.*
: **aw·ful·ly** *adv.* **1.** [ɔ́ːfuli→] dreadfully; terribly. **2.** [ɔ́ːfli] (*colloq.*) very; extremely.
- **a·while** [ə(h)wáil] *adv.* for a short time.
- **awk·ward** [ɔ́ːkwərd] *adj.* **1.** not skillful or graceful in movement or shape; clumsy. ↔skillful **2.** not convenient or comfortable; dangerous or difficult to deal with. ↔handy ▷**awk·ward·ly** [-li] *adv.* —**awk·ward·ness** [-nis] *n.*

awl [ɔːl] *n.* Ⓒ a pointed instrument for making small holes in leather or wood, used esp. by shoemakers. ⇒fig.

awn·ing [ɔ́ːniŋ] *n.* Ⓒ a canvas roof over or in front of a door, window, etc. [awl]

- **a·woke** [əwóuk] *v.* pt. and pp. of **awake**.
  a·wry [ərái] *adv., adj.* **1.** with a turn or twist to one side. **2.** away from the expected direction; wrong. *go awry*, go wrong.
: **ax, axe** [æks] *n.* Ⓒ (pl. **ax·es**) an instrument with a bladed head on a handle, used for cutting down trees. *have an ax to grind,* (*colloq.*) have a selfish motive or a special purpose for acting.
  ax·es [ǽksiːz] *n.* **1.** pl. of **ax** or **axe**. **2.** pl. of **axis**.
  ax·i·om [ǽksiəm] *n.* Ⓒ **1.** a truth which everybody accepts as true without proof. **2.** an established principle; a maxim; a proverb. 「evident.」
  ax·i·o·mat·ic [æksiəmǽtik], **-i·cal** [-ik(ə)l] *adj.* self-
  ax·is [ǽksis] *n.* Ⓒ (pl. **ax·es** [-siːz]) **1.** a straight line around which a body, such as the earth, turns. **2.** a central line dividing a regular body or form symmetrically. **3.** an agreement of two or more nations.
  ax·le [ǽksl] *n.* Ⓒ a pin or bar on or with which a wheel turns; a rod that joins two wheels. 「~.①」
- **ay, aye**¹ [ai] *adv.* (*archaic*) always; ever. ¶*forever and*
- **ay, aye**² [ai] *adv.* yes. —*n.* an affirmative vote or voter.
  a·zal·ea [əzéiliə] *n.* Ⓒ **1.** a bush with many handsome flowers of various colors. **2.** the flower of this plant.
  az·ure [ǽʒər, éiʒər] *adj.* sky-blue. —*n.* Ⓤ **1.** sky-blue color. **2.** the clear, cloudless sky.

B

B¹, **b** [biː] *n.* Ⓒ (pl. **B's, Bs, b's, bs** [biːz]) **1.** the second letter of the English alphabet. **2.** (*Music*) the seventh note in the scale of C major. —*adj.* second.
B² **1.** black. ⇒N.B. **2.** (*Chemistry*) boron. **3.** (*Chess*) bishop.
B. A. Bachelor of Arts. ⇒N.B.

baa [bæː / bɑː] *n.* [C] a trembling cry, as of a sheep or lamb. **—***vi.* (of a sheep) make this sound.
—[名] 양의 울음 소리 —[自] [양이] 울다

bab·ble [bǽbl] *vi.* **1.** make meaningless sounds like a baby; talk childishly or foolishly. **2.** (of a brook, etc.) murmur. **—***vt.* tell thoughtlessly; make (something) known foolishly. 《~ *out* a secret, etc.》 **—***n.* [U] **1.** indistinct talk. **2.** idle talk. **3.** a continuous murmuring sound.
—[自] 1. 서투른 말로 지껄이다; 재잘재잘 지껄이다 2. [물이] 졸졸 소리를 내다 —[他] …을 재잘재잘 지껄이다; [비밀 따위]를 입밖에 내다 —[名] 1. [어린애의] 서투른 말 2. 수다 3. [시냇물의] 졸졸 소리

* **babe** [beib] *n.* [C] (*poetic*) a baby.
—[名] 《詩》 갓난아이

Ba·bel [béib(ə)l] *n.* **1.** (in the Bible) the tower described the Genesis 11. ⇒[N.B.] **2.** 《usu. *a b-*》 the confused state in which many languages are spoken at a time; great disorder.
—[名] 1. 《聖》 바벨의 탑 [N.B.] 하늘까지 쌓아 올리려다가 신의 노여움을 사서 실패로 끝난 탑 2. 언어의 혼란; 떠들썩한 소리

ba·boon [bæbúːn / bə-] *n.* [C] a large, fierce monkey of Arabia and Africa with a dog-like face.
—[名] 비비(狒狒)

⁑ **ba·by** [béibi] *n.* (pl. **-bies**) [C] **1.** a very young child; an infant. **2.** a childish person.
—[名] 1. 갓난아이 2. 어린애 같은 사람

hold (*or* ***carry***) ***the baby,*** be given a troublesome task.
[熟] 성가신 일을 떠맡다

—*adj.* **1.** young; childish. **2.** small in size.
—[形] 1. 젊은, 어린 2. 소형의

ba·by·hood [béibihùd] *n.* [U] **1.** the time or condition of being a baby. **2.** 《*collectively*》 babies.
—[名] 1. 유년시대; 유치함 2. 젖먹이

ba·by·ish [béibiiʃ] *adj.* childish; silly.
—[形] 어린애 같은; 어리석은

Bab·y·lon [bǽbilən] *n.* **1.** the capital of Babylonia. **2.** [C] any great, rich, but vicious city.
—[名] 1. 바빌론 2. 악덕의 도시, 화려하고 타락한 대도시

Bab·y·lo·ni·a [bæ̀b(i)lóuniə] *n.* the ancient empire in southwest Asia. ⇒[N.B.]
—[名] 바빌로니아 [N.B.] 고대(2800–1000 B.C.)에 번영한 왕국

Bab·y·lo·ni·an [bæ̀b(i)lóuniən] *adj.* **1.** of or like Babylon or Babylonia. **2.** sinful.
—[形] 1. 바빌론(바빌로니아)의 2. 사악한, 거대한

ba·by-sat [béibisæ̀t] *v. pt.* or *pp.* of baby-sit.

ba·by-sit [béibisìt] *vi.* (**-sat, -sit·ting**) take care of a child while the parents are away. 《~ ***with*** a child》
—[自] [부모 외출시에] 아이를 보아주다

ba·by-sit·ter [béibisìtər] *n.* [C] a person who babysits.
—[名] 집 지키며 애봐주는 사람, 안저지

Bac·cha·nal [bǽkənl, + *U.S.* -nɑːl] *adj.* of Bacchus.
—[形] 바커스의

Bac·chus [bǽkəs] *n.* (in Roman mythology) the god of wine. ⇒[N.B.]
—[名] 주신(酒神) 바커스 [N.B.] 그리이스 신화에서는 Dionysus

Bach [bɑːk, bɑːx], **Johann Sebastian** *n.* (1685–1750) a German composer of music and organist.
—[名] 세바스티안 바하(독일의 작곡가·오르가니스트)

* **bach·e·lor** [bǽtʃ(ə)lər] *n.* [C] **1.** a man who has not married yet. ↔spinster **2.** a person who has taken the first degree at a college or university. ⇒[N.B.]
—[名] 1. 독신 남자 2. 학사 [N.B.] Bachelor of Arts=B.A. (문학사)라 말함

ba·cil·li [bəsílai] *n.* pl. of **bacillus**.

ba·cil·lus [bəsíləs] *n.* (pl. **-cil·li**) [C] a bacterium, esp. a rod-shaped one.
—[名] 바칠루스, 간상균(桿狀菌)

⁑ **back** [bæk] *n.* [C] **1.** the hinder surface of the human body; the upper surface of an animal's body. ¶*sit on the horse's ~ / She has a baby on her ~.* **2.** the opposite side from the front; the farthest part from a spectator. ¶*the ~ of a house*① / *the ~ of a room*② / *the ~ of a hand*③. **3.** the rear part of a thing. ¶*the ~ of a chair*④. **4.** (of football or other games) a player placed behind. ↔forward ⇒[N.B.]
—[名] 1. [사람·동물의]등 2. 뒤쪽; 안쪽 ¶①집 뒤/②방 안쪽/③손등 3. 등부분 ¶④의자의 등받이 4. [축구 따위의] 후위, 수비[진] [N.B.] 경기에 따라서 fullback, halfback 따위로 나뉨

1) ***at the back of,*** behind, esp. in support or pursuit of.
2) ***the back of beyond,*** (*colloq.*) a very distant place.
3) ***back to back,*** directing one's back toward another's back.
4) ***back to front,*** (*colloq.*) having the back where the front should be.
5) ***be on one's back,*** be ill in bed; be helpless.
6) ***be on someone's back,*** find fault with someone.
7) ***behind someone's back,*** when someone is absent; without someone's knowledge or consent.
8) ***break someone's back,*** ⓐ cause someone to fail; cause someone to become bankrupt. ⓑ be too hard for someone to do.
9) ***break the back of,*** ⓐ finish the major or most difficult part of (a project, job, etc.). ⓑ defeat the

[熟] 1)…의 뒤에, …을 후원하여 2)《口》 머나먼 곳 3)등을 맞대고 4)《口》 뒤집혀서 5)앓아 누워 있다; 어찌할 바를 모르게 되다 6)…을 비난하다, 헐뜯다 7)남몰래, 뒤에서; 무단히 8)ⓐ실패시키다; 파산시키다 ⓑ…에게 짐이 너무 무겁다, 힘에 부치다 9)ⓐ…의 고비를 넘기다 ⓑ…을 무력하게 만들다, …에게 짐이 너무 무겁다 10)성내다 11)ⓐ[남]을 성나게 하다 ⓑ…에게 거역하다 12)《美口》 궁지에 몰려 있다 13)…의 뒤에 14)ⓐ…의 뒤에 ⓑ…에 뒤이어 [usage] 사건, 특히 불운한 사건 따위에 대해서만 씀 15)…에 전력을

B

strength.
10) ***get*** (or ***put***) *one's* ***back up,*** get angry.
11) ***get*** (or ***put***) *someone's* ***back up,*** ⓐ make someone angry. ⓑ do not obey someone.
12) ***have*** *one's* ***back to the wall,*** be in a difficult or hopeless situation.
13) ***in back of,*** (*U.S. colloq.*) behind.
14) ***on the back of,*** ⓐ on the reverse side of. ⓑ immediately following. ⇒[usage]
15) ***put*** *one's* ***back into,*** do (something) with all one's energy.
16) ***turn*** *one's* ***back on,*** forsake; neglect.

다하다 16)…을 저버리다; 무시하다

—*adj.* (superl. **back·most**) **1.** situated behind; opposite to the front. ¶*a ~ door.* **2.** far from the main area; remote. ¶*a ~ country.* **3.** moving backward. ¶*~ current*⑤ **4.** belonging to the past. ¶*the ~ numbers of a magazine.*⑥

—[形] 1. 배후의, 뒤쪽의 2. 외딴, 먼 3. 뒷걸음의, 거꾸로의 ¶⑤역류 4. 기왕의, 과거의 ¶⑥묵은 잡지

—*adv.* **1.** to the rear. **2.** into or in an earlier, normal, or true position. **3.** in return. **4.** to or in a retired or remote position. **5.** to an earlier time.

—[副] 1. 후방으로 2. 원래 장소로; 제자리에(돌아와서) 3. 답례로서 4. 안쪽에, 먼 곳에 5. 거슬러 올라가서, 이전에

back and forth, to and fro.

[熟] 앞뒤로

—*vt.* **1.** cause (someone or something) to move backward. **2.** support. 《~ someone *in* something》 —*vi.* go backward.

—[他] 1. …을 후퇴시키다 2. …을 후원하다 —[自] 후퇴하다

1) ***back and fill,*** (*U.S. colloq.*) change one's opinion or position from time to time.
2) ***back down,*** give up an argument, a claim, etc.
3) ***back on to,*** have the back (usu. of a house) close against (something).
4) ***back out,*** withdraw or fail to keep one's promise.
5) ***back up,*** ⓐ support. ⓑ move backward.

[熟] 1)《美口》 [생각 따위가] 자꾸 바뀌다, 동요하다 2)…에서 손을 떼다 3) [건물 따위가] …에 인접하다 4)약속을 취소하다(깨뜨리다) 5)ⓐ…을 지원하다 ⓑ후퇴하다

back·bit [bǽkbìt] *v.* pt. of **backbite.**

back·bite [bǽkbàit] *vt., vi.* (**-bit, -bit·ten**) speak ill of someone who is not present. ▷**back·bit·er** [-ər] *n.*

—[他][自] 험담을 하다

back·bit·ten [bǽkbìtn] *v.* pp. of **backbite.**

back·bone [bǽkbòun] *n.* **1.** [C] the main bone along the center of the back in man or other animals; the spine. **2.** [C] the most important part. **3.** [U] the strength of character; moral courage.

—[名] 1. 등뼈 2. 중심 세력, 중견; 중추 3. 기골(氣骨); 정신력

back·door [bǽkdɔ̀ːr] *adj.* secret.

—[形] 비밀의

back·er [bǽkər] *n.* [C] a person who helps another.

—[名] 후원자

back·fire [bǽkfàiər] *n.* [U][C] **1.** (in a gasoline engine) an explosion of gas before the right time. **2.** a fire which is set to stop the advance of a forest or field fire. —*vi.* **1.** (of gas) burst before the right time. **2.** start a backfire.

—[名] 1. [내연기관의] 역화(逆火) 2. [번지는 산불을 막는] 맞불 —[自] 1. 역화가 일어나다 2. 맞불을 놓다

back·gam·mon [bǽkgæ̀mən / ˊ-ˋ-] *n.* [U] a game played by two persons with a board and a dice.

—[名] 서양 주사위놀이

***back·ground** [bǽkgràund] *n.* [U] **1.** the distant part of a scene; the part of a picture on which the distant scene is represented. **2.** the surface on or to which things are placed, attached, or drawn.

—[名] 1. 원경(遠景) 2. 배경

in the background, out of sight or notice.

[熟] 뒤에 숨어서, 표면에 나서지 않고

back·hand [bǽkhæ̀nd] *n.* [U][C] **1.** (in tennis, etc.) a stroke made from the side of the body opposite to that of the hand holding the racket. **2.** handwriting which slopes to the left.

—[名] 1.《테니스》 역타(逆打) 2. [문자의] 좌사체(左斜體)

back·hand·ed [bǽkhæ̀ndid] *adj.* of backhand

—[形] [필적이] 왼쪽으로 기운; 역타의

back·ing [bǽkiŋ] *n.* [U][C] **1.** something placed behind anything to support or strengthen it. **2.** help; support. **3.** 《*collectively*》 supporters.

—[名] 1. [책의] 등붙이기; [건축의] 속널 2. 후원; 지지 3. 후원자들

back·slid [bǽkslìd] *v.* pt. and pp. of **backslide.**

back·slid·den [bǽkslìdn] *v.* pp. of **backslide.**

back·slide [bǽkslàid] *vi.* (**-slid, -slid** or **-slid·den**) return from the good ways to the bad former ways; turn away from a religion once believed in. ▷**back·slid·er** [-ər] *n.*

—[自] 뒷걸음치다; 신앙을 버리다; 타락하다

back·stage [bǽkstéidʒ] *adv.* in the dressing room in a theater; at or to the rear of a stage.
—⚃ 무대 뒤에서

back·stroke [bǽkstròuk] *n.* Ⓒ **1.** a return blow. **2.** (in tennis, etc.) a backhand stroke. **3.** a stroke made by a swimmer lying on his back.
—⚂ 1. 되치기 2. 《베니스》 역타(逆打) 3. 배영(背泳)

* **back·ward** [bǽkwərd] *adj.* **1.** directed to the back. ¶~ *motion.* **2.** done in a way opposite to the usual or right way. **3.** unwilling; shy. **4.** behind the times; not developed. ¶~ *nations.*①
—⚃ 1. 뒤쪽[으로]의 2. 거꾸로의 3. 마음내키지 않는, 수줍어하는 4. 철늦은, 시기가 늦은; [학문·정보 따위가] 늦은 ¶①후진국
—*adv.* **1.** toward the back; toward the starting point. **2.** with the back first. **3.** in a way opposite to the usual or right way. **4.** toward the past. ¶*look ~ to one's youth.* **5.** from better to worse.
—⚃ 1. 뒤쪽으로; 원래대로 2. 뒤를 향해 3. 거꾸로 4. 과거로 5. 퇴보하여
backward and forward, thoroughly.
▨ 완전히, 철저히
▷**back·ward·ness** [-nis] *n.*

* **back·wards** [bǽkwərdz] *adv.* (*Brit.*)=backward.
back·wa·ter [bǽkwɔ̀:tər, +*U.S.* -wɑ̀t-] *n.* **1.** Ⓒ⒰ water held back by a dam, etc.; calm water lying to one side of a river. **2.** Ⓒ an inactive state or condition.
—⚂ 1. 둑에 부딪쳐 나가는 물; 역류 2. 침체

back·woods [bǽkwùdz] *n. pl.* forests or wild regions far away from towns; back country.
—⚂ [특히 미국·캐나다의] 미개간지; 외딴 신개척지

back·woods·man [bǽkwùdzmən] *n.* Ⓒ (pl. **-men** [-mən]) a man who lives in the backwoods.
—⚂ 벽지 사람, 시골뜨기

back·yard [bǽkjɑ:rd] *n.* Ⓒ (*U. S.*) the yard at the back of a house or other building.
—⚂ 《美》 뒤뜰

* **ba·con** [béik(ə)n] *n.* ⒰ salted and smoked pork.
—⚂ 베이컨

* **Ba·con** [béikən], *n.* **1.** Francis (1561-1626) an English essayist, philosopher and statesman. **2.** Roger (1214 ? -1294) an English philosopher and scientist.
—⚂ 1. 영국의 수필가·철학가·정치가 2. 영국의 철학가·과학자

bac·te·ri·a [bæktíəriə] *n. pl.* (sing. **bac·te·ri·um**) tiny plants of one cell. ⌜bacteria.⌝
—⚂ 세균, 박테리아

bac·te·ri·al [bæktíəriəl] *adj.* of bacteria; caused by⌟
—⚃ 박테리아의; 세균에 의한

bac·te·ri·o·log·i·cal [bæktìəriəlɑ́dʒik(ə)l / -lɔ́dʒi-] *adj.* of bacteriology.
—⚃ 세균학[상]의

bac·te·ri·ol·o·gist [bæktìəriɑ́lədʒist / -ɔ́lə-] *n.* Ⓒ an expert in bacteriology.
—⚂ 세균학자

bac·te·ri·ol·o·gy [bæktìəriɑ́lədʒi / -ɔ́lə-] *n.* ⒰ the science that deals with bacteria.
—⚂ 세균학

bac·te·ri·um [bæktíəriəm] *n.* sing. of **bacteria.**

‡**bad**¹ [bæd] *adj.* (**worse, worst**) ↔ **good 1.** not good; not right. **2.** of poor quality; worthless. **3.** incorrect; full of mistakes. ¶*a ~ guess* / *a ~ composition.* **4.** not morally right; wicked; evil. ¶*It is ~ to tell a lie.* **5.** rotten; spoiled. ¶*a ~ apple.* **6.** harmful; injurious. ¶*Heavy smoking is ~ for the health.* **7.** disagreeable; unpleasant. ¶*a ~ smell.* **8.** severe; serious. ¶*a ~ cold* / *a ~ accident.* **9.** ill; sick; in pain. ¶*I feel ~ today.* **10.** unlucky; unfortunate. ¶*He came at ~ time.* **11.** (*the ~*) persons of wicked character.
—⚃ 1. 나쁜, 부정한, 불량한 2. 품질이 나쁜, 가치없는 3. 부정확한, 틀린 데가 많은 4. 부도덕한, 사악한, 5. 썩은, 상한, 곯은 6. 해로운, 유해의 7. 불쾌한 8. 심한, 지독한 9. 병에 걸린, 편찮은 10. 불운한, 재수 나쁜 11. 악인

1) *feel bad for (or about),* regret; be sorry for (one's⌝
2) *go bad,* rot; spoil.   ⌊mistakes).⌟
3) *not bad,* (*colloq.*) rather good.
4) *That's too bad,* I'm very sorry.
▨ 1)후회하다 2)썩다, 상하다 3)(口)상당히 좋은 4)참 안됐읍니다

—*n.* **1.** ⒰ (*the ~*) what is bad; bad quality or state.
—⚂ 나쁜 일, 나쁜 상태
1) *go from bad to worse,* grow worse.
2) *go to the bad,* become wicked; ruin morally.
3) *in bad,* ⓐ in trouble. ⓑ in disfavor.
▨ 1)더욱 더 악화되다 2)타락하다 3) ⓐ골치아프게 된 ⓑ미움을 산

bad² [bæd] *v.* pt. of **bid.**

* **bade** [bæd, +*Brit* beid] *v.* pt. of **bid.**

badge [bædʒ] *n.* Ⓒ a special mark or token worn as a sign of membership, authority, etc.; a symbol.
—⚂ 배지, 기장(記章)

* **badg·er** [bǽdʒər] *n.* Ⓒ a hairy animal of Europe and America which lives in holes and is active at night.
—⚂ 오소리
—*vt.* tease; annoy; worry.
—⚄ …을 못살게 굴다; 괴롭히다

* **bad·ly** [bǽdli] *adv.* (**worse, worst**) **1.** in a bad manner. **2.** (*colloq.*) very much; to a great degree.
—[副] 1. 나쁘게; 서투르게; 잘못 2. 크게, 몹시

bad·min·ton [bǽdmintən] *n.* [U] a game like tennis played with a feathered cork and rackets. ⇒[N.B.]
—[名] 배드민턴 [N.B.] Duke of Beaufort의 영지의 이름에서

bad·ness [bǽdnis] *n.* [U] the state of being bad.
—[名] 악; 부정; 불량; 유해

baf·fle [bǽfl] *vt.* **1.** bring (the efforts of someone) to nothing; perplex; puzzle. **2.** prevent (plans, etc.) from being carried out. **—*vi.*** struggle without success. 《~ *with* something》
—[他] 1. [남의 노력 따위]를 좌절시키다, 꺾다; 괴롭히다 2. [계획 따위]를 방해하다 —[自] 헛되이 애쓰다

be baffled (=*fail*) ***in one's attempt.***
[熟] 헛수고로 끝나다

—*n.* [C] a wall or screen for checking the flow of air, water, etc.
—[名] [기류·수류 따위의] 조절 장치

⁑ **bag** [bæg] *n.* [C] **1.** a sack or case made of paper, cloth, leather, etc. **2.** a purse; a handbag. **3.** a suitcase; a traveling bag. **4.** the amount a bag holds. **5.** (*colloq.*) what is contained in a bag. **6.** all birds or animals shot by a hunter in a day. **7.** (in baseball) a base.
—[名] 1. 가방, 자루 2. 지갑, 손가방 3. 여행용 가방 4. 가방 가득[한 분량] 5. 가방 [자루] 속에 든 것 6. [하루에 잡은] 불치(새·짐승 따위) 7. [야구의] 누(壘), 베이스

1) ***bag and baggage,*** [with] all one's belongings.
2) ***a bag of bones,*** a very thin person.
3) ***in the bag,*** (*colloq.*) captured; gained.
4) ***let the cat out of the bag,*** (*colloq.*) give away a secret.
5) ***the whole bag of tricks,*** everything needed for some purpose.

[熟] 1)소지품(가재도구) 일체; 이것저것 죄다 2)말라빠진 사람 3)《口》 수중에 든, [성공이] 확실한 4)《口》 비밀을 누설하다 5)온갖 수단(술책)

—*v.* (**bagged; bag·ging**) *vt.* **1.** put (something) in a bag. **2.** kill or catch (animals) in hunting. **3.** (*colloq.*) take possession of (something); steal. **4.** swell (something) outward. **—*vi.* 1.** swell outward. **2.** hang loosely.
—[他] 1. …을 자루(가방)에 넣다 2. [사냥감을] 잡다 3. …을 손에 넣다; 훔치다 4. …을 부풀리다 —[自] 1. 부풀다 2. [빈 자루처럼] 처지다

Bag·dad, Bagh·dad [bǽgdæd / ‐ˊ] *n.* the capital of Iraq.
—[名] 바그다드

* **bag·gage** [bǽgidʒ] *n.* [U] (*U.S.*) the trunks, bags, suitcases, etc. used for a traveler to carry with. (cf. *Brit.* luggage); (*Military*) the portable things of an army, such as tents, sleeping bags, etc.
—[名] 《美》 수하물; 《軍》 군용 행낭

bag·gy [bǽgi] *adj.* (**-gi·er; -gi·est**) baglike; hanging loose.
—[形] 자루 같은; 헐렁헐렁한

bag·pipe [bǽgpàip] *n.* [C] 《often *pl.*》 a Scottish musical instrument made of a windbag and pipes. ⇒fig.
—[名] [가죽 부대로 만든] 풍적(風笛)

〔bagpipe〕

bag·pi·per [bǽgpàipər] *n.* [C] a person who plays the bagpipe.
—[名] 풍적을 부는 사람

bah [bɑː, +*U.S.* bæː] *interj.* an exclamation to show the feeling of contempt or disgust.
—[感] 흥(경멸·염오감 따위를 나타내는 소리)

bail[1] [beil] *n.* (pl. **bail**) (*Law*) **1.** [U] freedom given to a prisoner for a certain time; money paid for getting such freedom. **2.** [C] a person or persons who pay such money for a prisoner. **—*vt.*** make (a prisoner) free by paying bail. 《~ someone *out*》
—[名] 1. 보석(保釋); 보석금 2. 보석 보증인 —[他] …을 보석시키다

bail[2] [beil] *n.* [C] a handle of a pail, kettle, etc.
—[名] [물통 따위의] 손잡이, 자루

bail[3] [beil] *n.* [C] a pail or scoop used in dipping water out of a boat. **—*vi., vt.*** dip out water with a bail.
—[名] 배에 괸 물을 퍼내는 기구 —[自][他] 괸 물을 퍼내다

bail out, jump from an airplane by parachute.
[熟] 낙하산으로 탈출하다

bail·iff [béilif] *n.* [C] **1.** an assistant to a sheriff. **2.** an officer of a court who guards prisoners and jurymen. **3.** (*Brit. History*) a governer in certain towns.
—[名] 1. 집행인(sheriff의 부하) 2. 법정의 수위, 정리(廷吏) 3. 시장(市長)

* **bait** [beit] *n.* [C][U] **1.** anything used to attract fish or other animals in order to catch them. **2.** temptation.
—[名] 1. [낚시·사냥 따위의] 미끼 2. 유혹

—*vt.* 1. put a bait on (something). 《~ a fishhook, trap, etc. *with*》 **2.** tempt; attract. **3.** make dogs attack (an animal, such as a chained bear) for sport. **4.** give trouble to (someone) by unkind or unpleasant words. **—*vi.*** (*Brit.*) take a rest during a journey.
—[他] 1. …에 미끼를 달다 2. …을 유혹하다 3. [매어 놓은 곰 따위에] 개를 부추겨 집적이게 하다 4. …을 불쾌한 말로 괴롭히다 —[自] 《英》 [여행 중에] 식사를 위해 쉬다

baize [beiz] *n.* [U] a thick and rough woolen cloth, used for curtains, table covers, etc.
—[名] 초록빛의 거친 나사(羅紗)

:bake [beik] *vt.* **1.** cook (bread, cake, etc.) in an oven. **2.** dry and harden (bricks, china, etc.) by heat. ***—vi.*** **1.** become baked. **2.** become brown with sunburn.

—[他] 1. [빵 따위]를 굽다 2. [벽돌 따위를] 구워 굳히다 —[自] 1. 구워지다 2. [햇볕에 살갗이] 타다

ba·ke·lite [béik(ə)làit] *n.* [U] (*Trademark*) an artificial material used in place of bone, ivory, etc. ⇒[N.B.]

—[名] 베이클라이트 [N.B.] 발명자의 이름에서

•bak·er [béikər] *n.* [C] **1.** a person who makes and sells bread, cakes, etc. **2.** (*U.S.*) a portable oven.

a baker's dozen, thirteen.

—[名] 1. 빵집 2. 《美》 [휴대용] 빵 굽는 화덕

[熟] 13개

bak·er·y [béikəri] *n.* [C] (pl. **-er·ies**) a place where bread, cakes, etc. are made or sold; a baker's shop.

—[名] 빵집, 제빵소

bak·ing [béikiŋ] *n.* [U] the act or process of cooking in a dry heat; [C] the quantity baked at one time.

—[名] 빵굽기; 한번 구워내는 분량

baking powder [ˊ-- ˋ-] *n.* white powder used to make cake or biscuit larger in baking.

—[名] 베이킹파우더

:bal·ance [bǽləns] *n.* **1.** [C] an instrument for measuring weight. **2.** [C] a gear of a clock which causes it to go regularly. **3.** [U] the state of having the same amount on both sides. **4.** [U][C] a steady condition or position. ¶*lose one's* ~. **5.** 《*the* ~》 sum of money not yet spent. ¶*the* ~ *in hand.*① **6.** [U] (*colloq.*) the rest; the remainder.

1) ***hold the balance,*** have the power to decide.

2) ***in the balance,*** not yet settled or decided. ¶*hang in the* ~② / *hold something in the* ~.③

3) ***off one's balance,*** in a position where one loses one's balance.

—vt. **1.** measure the weight of (something). **2.** bring (something) into or keep (something) in the state of balance. **3.** make (two things) equal in weight or importance. 《~ something *with* (or *by, against*)》

—vi. be equal; come into the state of balance. 《~ *with* something》

—[名] 1. 천칭, 저울 2. [시계의] 평형바퀴 3. 균형잡힌 상태; 균형 4. 침착, 안정 상태 5. 잔고 ¶①수지 잔고 6. 《口》 나머지

[熟] 1)결정권을 가지다 2)미결 상태로; 불안정하여 ¶②불안 상태에 있다/③미결된 채로 내버려 두다 3) 쓰러져; 당황(낭패)하여

—[他] 1. …의 무게를 재다 2. …의 균형을 잡다 3. [무게·가치 따위]의 균형을 맞추다, 일치시키다 —[自] [계산·장부가] 맞다; 균형이 맞다

balance sheet [ˊ-- ˋ] *n.* a written paper to show the sum of money spent and earned by a business.

—[名] 대차 대조표, 손익 계산서

•bal·co·ny [bǽlkəni] *n.* [C] (pl. **-nies**) a platform built out from an upper floor of a building.

—[名] 발코니

bald [bɔːld] *adj.* **1.** without hair on the head, wholly or partly. **2.** without natural covering, as of feathers, leaves, etc. ¶*a* ~ *mountain.*① **3.** not hiding; open; plain.

—[形] 1. 벗어진, 대머리진 2. 깃털·잎사귀 [따위]가 없는 ¶①민둥산 3. 노골적인, 솔직한

bald·head·ed [bɔ́ːldhèdid] *adj.* having a bald head.

—[形] 대머리의

bald·ly [bɔ́ːldli] *adv.* frankly; openly; without reserve.

—[副] 노골적으로, 솔직히

bald·ness [bɔ́ːldnis] *n.* [U] **1.** the state of being bald. **2.** the state or quality of being frank. **3.** dullness.

—[名] 1. 벗어짐 2. 노골적임 3. 단조로움, 무미건조

bale [beil] *n.* **1.** [C] a large package or bundle of goods tightly bound or wrapped for storing or shipping. **2.** 《*pl.*》 goods. ***—vt.*** make or form (something) into bales; pack.

—[名] 1. [상품의] 짐짝, 가마니 2. 화물 —[他] …을 가마니에 넣다, 포장하다

bale·ful [béilf(u)l] *adj.* **1.** harmful. **2.** with evil intent.

—[形] 1. 해로운 2. 악의를 품은

balk, baulk [bɔːk] *n.* [C] **1.** an obstacle; a hindrance. **2.** a mistake. **3.** (in baseball) an unfair motion by a pitcher. ***—vt.*** prevent (someone) from doing what he wishes to do; hinder. 《~ someone *in* (or *of*)》 ***—vi.*** stop and refuse to go; shrink.

—[名] 1. 장해 2. 실패, 실수 3. 《野球》 보오크 —[他] …을 방해하다; 꺾다; 실망시키다 —[自] [말 따위가] 갑자기 서서 나아가지 않다; 뒷걸음질치다

:ball[1] [bɔːl] *n.* [C] **1.** a round body. ¶*the earthly* ~.① **2.** a game played with a ball. **3.** [U] baseball. **4.** a bullet or cannon ball. **5.** a ball the batter ought not strike at.

1) ***carry the ball,*** bear the responsibility; act an important part. ¶*carry the* ~ *for the victory.*

2) ***have the ball at one's feet,*** see one's way to success.

3) ***keep the ball rolling,*** cause a conversation, project, etc. to continue smoothly.

4) ***play ball,*** ⓐ begin playing a ball game. ⓑ start or continue any action. ⓒ work together; cooperate.

—vt. make (something) into a ball. ***—vi.*** form into a ball.

—[名] 1. 공, 구(球) ¶①지구 2. 구기(球技) 3. 야구 4. 탄환, 포탄 5. 《野球》 보올

[熟] 1)책임을 지다; 중요한 역할을 하다 2)성공할 전망이 보이다 3)대화(계획 따위)가 끊기지 않도록 하다 4)ⓐ경기를 시작하다 ⓑ동작을 시작(계속)하다 ⓒ협동하여 일하다

—[他] …을 공 모양으로 만들다 —[自] 공 모양이 되다

ball

ball² [bɔ:l] *n.* ⓒ a large, formal social party for dancing. —ⓝ 무도회

bal·lad [bǽləd] *n.* ⓒ 1. a simple song with several verses sung to the same melody. 2. a poem that tells a story. —ⓝ 1. 민요, 짧은 노래 2. 발라드(민요시)

bal·last [bǽləst] *n.* ⓤ 1. (*Nautical*) heavy material carried in a ship to make it balanced. 2. bags of sand carried below a balloon. 3. small stones used for the bed of a road or railroad track. —*vt.* 1. place ballast in (ships, balloons, etc.). 2. put ballast on (a railroad bed). —ⓝ 1. [배를 안정시키기 위해 싣는] 바닥짐 2. [기구(氣球)의] 모래주머니 3. [철도·도로에 까는] 자갈 —ⓥ 1. …에 바닥짐(모래주머니)를 싣다 2. [선로·도로]에 자갈을 깔다

ball bear·ing [⌐ ⌐] *n.* a bearing in which a number of metal balls are set. —ⓝ 볼베어링

bal·le·ri·na [bæ̀ləríːnə] *n.* ⓒ (pl. **-nas** or **-ne**) a woman
bal·le·ri·ne [bæ̀lərí:ne] *n.* pl. of **ballerina**. —ⓝ 발레리이나, 발레 댄서

bal·let [bǽléi, ⌐ ⌐] *n.* ⓒⓤ 1. an artistic dance with a story performed to music. 2. ((*collectively*)) ballet dancers. —ⓝ 1. 무용극, 발레 2. 무용단, 발레단

bal·lis·tic [bəlístik] *adj.* (of missiles) intended to be shot or thrown. —ⓐ 탄도(彈道)의

• **bal·loon** [bəlúːn] *n.* ⓒ a round bag filled with some gas that is lighter than air to make it rise and float in the air. —*vi.* 1. go up in a balloon. 2. swell out like a balloon. —ⓝ [경]기구(氣球); 풍선 —ⓥ 1. 기구로 상승하다 2. 풍선처럼 부풀다

• **bal·lot** [bǽlət] *n.* 1. ⓒ a paper used in voting. 2. the whole number of votes cast in an election. 3. ⓤ secret voting. —*vi.* 1. vote or decide by ballot. ((~ *for* or *against* something)) 2. draw lots. —ⓝ 1. 투표용지 2. 투표 총수 3. 무기명(비밀)투표 —ⓥ 1. [비밀] 투표하다 (로 정하다) 2. 제비를 뽑다

ballot box [⌐ ⌐] *n.* a box into which ballots are put. —ⓝ 투표함

ball-point pen [bɔ́:lpɔ̀intpén] *n.* a fountain pen whose point is a small ball bearing. —ⓝ 볼펜

ball·room [bɔ́:lrùː(ː)m] *n.* ⓒ a large room used for dancing. —ⓝ 무도실(장)

balm [bɑːm] *n.* 1. ⓤ a sweet-smelling oil or oily paste obtained from certain trees, used esp. as medicine for a wound. 2. ⓤ anything used for relieving pain. 3. ⓒ a sweet-smelling plant. —ⓝ 1. 향유(香油) 2. 진통제 3. 박하

balm·y [bɑ́:mi] *adj.* (**balm·i·er, balm·i·est**) 1. sweet-smelling; fragrant. 2. mild; gentle. —ⓐ 1. 향기로운 2. 기분좋은, 온화한

bal·sam [bɔ́:lsəm] *n.* 1. ⓤ balm. 2. ⓒ a plant from which balm is taken. 3. ⓒ any of flowering plant of the touch-me-not family. —ⓝ 1. 향유 2. 향유의 원료가 되는 나무 3. 봉숭아

Bal·tic Sea [bɔ́:ltiksíː], **the** *n.* a sea northeast of Germany. —ⓝ 발트해

bal·us·ter [bǽləstər] *n.* ⓒ 1. an erect pillar or support for a railing. ⇒fig. 2. ((*pl.*)) a balustrade. —ⓝ 1. [손잡이·난간의] 기둥 2. 난간

bal·us·trade [bæ̀ləstréid, ⌐ ⌐ ⌐] *n.* ⓒ a row of balusters. ⇒fig. —ⓝ [계단] 손잡이, 난간

[balustrade]

• **bam·boo** [bæmbúː] *n.* ⓤⓒ (pl. **-boos**) a tall, tree-like grass with hard, hollow, jointed stems. —ⓝ 대나무

ban [bæn] *n.* ⓒ an order that something must not be done or said. —*vi., vt.* (**banned, ban·ning**) forbid; prohibit. —ⓝ 금지령 —ⓥⓐ …을 금하다

ba·nal [bənǽl, bənɑ́:l, bǽn(ə)l, béinl] *adj.* (of ideas, opinions, etc.) not new; not original. —ⓐ 평범한; 케케묵은

‡ **ba·nan·a** [bənǽnə / -nɑ́:nə] *n.* ⓒ a tropical tree-like plant; its fruit. —ⓝ 바나나

‡ **band** [bænd] *n.* ⓒ 1. a group of persons doing something together. 2. a group of persons playing music together. 3. a thin flat material for binding, fastening, etc. 4. a stripe. —*vt.* 1. tie (something) with a band; put a band on or around (something). 2. mark with stripes on (something). 3. cause (something or someone) to unite in a group. ((~ something *together*)) —*vi.* unite or join in a group. ((~ *together*; ~ *with* something)) —ⓝ 1. [공통의 목적으로 행동하는]그루우프, 한 떼 2. 악단 3. [물건을 묶는] 띠, 끈, 테; 허리머 4. 줄무늬 —ⓥ 1. …을 끈[띠]으로 묶다 2. …에 줄무늬를 달다 3. 단결시키다 —ⓥ 단결하다

• **band·age** [bǽndidʒ] *n.* ⓒ a strip of cloth or other material used for binding wounds. ¶*apply a ~ to* —ⓝ 붕대 ¶①상처에 붕대를 하다

band·box [bǽn(d)bɑ̀ks / -bɔ̀ks] *n.* ⓒ a light box of thick and stiff paper for holding hats, collars, etc.
ban·dit [bǽndit] *n.* ⓒ (pl. **-dits** or **-dit·ti**) a highwayman;
ban·dit·ti [bændíti(:)] *n.* pl. of **bandit**. a robber.
band·mas·ter [bǽn(d)mæ̀stər / -mɑ̀:stə] *n.* ⓒ the leader of a musical band. ber of a musical band.
bands·man [bǽn(d)zmən] *n.* ⓒ (pl. **-men** [-mən]) a mem-
band·stand [bǽn(d)stæ̀nd] *n.* ⓒ a platform, usu. with a roof, for outdoor band concerts.
ban·dy [bǽndi] *vt.* (**-died**) **1.** throw, toss, or knock (a ball) to and fro. **2.** give and receive (words). —*adj.* bent or curved outward. ¶ ~ *legs.* bandy legs.
ban·dy-leg·ged [bǽndilègid, -légd / -lègd] *adj.* having
bane [bein] *n.* Ⓤ **1.** poison. **2.** cause of destruction, ruin, death, or any other trouble.
bane·ful [béinf(u)l] *adj.* harmful; troublesome.
• **bang**¹ [bæŋ] *vt.* **1.** strike noisily. **2.** shut (a door) noisily. —*vi.* **1.** strike noisily. **2.** make a sudden and bursting sound. ¶ *The doors banged back.*
—*n.* ⓒ **1.** a sudden or bursting sound. **2.** a sharp blow.
—*adv.* **1.** with a bang. **2.** suddenly.
bang² [bæŋ] *n.* ⓒ (often *pl.*) hair cut straight over the forehead. —*vt.* cut (hair) straight across.
• **ban·ish** [bǽniʃ] *vt.* **1.** order (someone) to go away from a place or country; exile. **2.** force (someone or something) to go or to be put away.
ban·ish·ment [bǽniʃmənt] *n.* ⓤⓒ the act of banishing; the state of being banished.
ban·is·ter [bǽnistər] *n.* **1.** ⓒ a baluster. **2.** (*pl.*) a balustrade of a staircase.
ban·jo [bǽndʒou] *n.* ⓒ (pl. **-jos** or **-joes**) a stringed musical instrument played like a guitar.
‡ **bank**¹ [bæŋk] *n.* ⓒ **1.** a long mound or heap of earth along a river, lake, road, railway, etc. **2.** a slope. **3.** a shallow place in the sea or at the mouth of a river. **4.** anything moundlike, as of clouds or snow.
—*vt.* **1.** make a bank of (earth, snow, etc.); pile; heap. **2.** make (something) safe with a bank. (~ *up*) **3.** cover (a fire) with ashes to prevent rapid burning.
—*vi.* form into a bank.
‡ **bank**² [bæŋk] *n.* ⓒ **1.** an office for receiving, lending, exchanging, and issuing money. **2.** any place for keeping things safe. ¶ *a blood* ~.①
—*vt.* put (money) in a bank. —*vi.* **1.** keep money in a bank. **2.** keep or manage a bank.
bank·a·ble [bǽŋkəbl] *adj.* that can be accepted at a bank.
bank·book [bǽŋkbùk] *n.* ⓒ a book in which a bank records a person's account.
• **bank·er** [bǽŋkər] *n.* ⓒ a person who owns or manages a bank. ⇒N.B. closed by law.
bank holiday [´ ⌐ ¬] *n.* a weekday on which banks are
bank·ing [bǽŋkiŋ] *n.* Ⓤ the business of a bank or banker.
bank·note [bǽŋknòut] *n.* ⓒ a note or bill issued by a bank, used as money.
bank·rupt [bǽŋkrʌpt, -rəpt] *n.* ⓒ (*Law*) a person who is legally declared unable to pay the money he has borrowed from others and whose property is divided among them. —*adj.* unable to pay the money one has borrowed. —*vt.* make (someone) bankrupt.
bank·rupt·cy [bǽŋkrʌptsi, -rəp(t)si] *n.* ⓤⓒ (pl. **-cies**) the state of being bankrupt.
• **ban·ner** [bǽnər] *n.* ⓒ a flag, usu. with some design or letters on it. —*adj.* (*U.S.*) leading; foremost.

* **ban·quet** [bǽŋkwit] ***n.*** [C] a feast. **—*vi., vt.*** give a banquet to (someone); enjoy a banquet.
—[名] 연회 —[自][他] 연회를 열어 …을 대접하다; 연회를 즐기다

ban·tam [bǽntəm] ***n.*** [C] a small domestic fowl.
—[名] 밴텀닭, 당닭

ban·ter [bǽntər] ***n.*** [C] a good-natured, teasing talk. **—*vt.*** make fun of (someone) good-humoredly. **—*vi.*** talk jokingly.
—[名] [악의 없는] 농담 —[他] …을 놀리다 —[自] 농담을 하다

bap·tism [bǽptiz(ə)m] ***n.*** [U] [C] the act or ceremony of baptizing.
—[名] [그리스도교의] 세례[식]

bap·tis·mal [bæptízm(ə)l] ***adj.*** of baptism.
—[形] 세례의

Bap·tist [bǽptist] ***n.*** **1.** ⟪*the* ~⟫ John the Baptist. **2.** [C] ⟪*b-*⟫ a person who baptizes. **3.** [C] a member of a Christian church who holds the opinion that baptism should be given only to an adult believer and by dipping his whole body under water.
—[名] 1. 세례 요한 2. 세례를 베푸는 사람 3. 침례교회 신도

bap·tize [bæptáiz, ´--] ***vt.*** **1.** dip (someone) into water, or put water on (someone), as a sign to wash away his sin and to admit him into the Christian church. **2.** give a first name to (someone). **3.** purify; cleanse.
—[他] 1. …에게 세례를 베풀다; …을 그리스도 교도로 만들다 2. …에게 명명(命名)하다 3. …을 깨끗하게 하다

⁑ **bar** [bɑːr] ***n.*** [C] **1.** a long, evenly shaped piece of hard material. ¶ ~ *of chocolate.* **2.** a fence or pole used to prevent people from passing; a barrier. **3.** a law court; the place in a law court where a prisoner stands. **4.** an obstacle; a moral obstacle. ¶*Poor health is a ~ to success.* | *a ~ of conscience*① | *the ~ of public opinion.*② **5.** a place or counter at which alcoholic drinks or food are served. **6.** ⟪*collectively*⟫, ⟪*the* ~ or *the B-*⟫ the profession of law; the group of lawyers. **7.** a sand bar.
—[名] 1. 막대기[모양의 것] 2. 방책(防柵); 문살; 빗장, 가로장 3. 법정; 피고석 4. 장애[물] ¶①양심의 가책 ②여론의 반대 5. 술집·식당의 술 파는 대 6. 변호사직(단) 7. 모래톱

1) ***be at the Bar,*** work as a lawyer.
2) ***behind the bars,*** in prison.
3) ***cross the bar,*** die.
4) ***go to the Bar,*** become a lawyer.
[熟] 1)변호사로서 일하다 2)옥중에[서] 3)죽다 4)변호사가 되다

—*vt.* (**barred, bar·ring**) **1.** fasten (something) with bars. **2.** shut off (a road, gate, etc.) from passage. ¶ ~ *a road.* **3.** do not allow; prohibit. ¶ ~ *the use of atomic weapons.*③ **4.** keep or shut (something or someone) out; prevent (someone) from getting in. ⟪~ someone *from* a club, etc.⟫ ¶ ~ *someone from the committee.*④
—[他] 1. …에 빗장을 지르다 2. …의 통행을 차단하다 3. …을 금지하다 ¶③핵무기의 사용을 금지하다 4. …을 들어오지 못하게 하다 ¶④사람을 위원회에 들어오지 못하게 하다

—*prep.* except; save.
—[前] …을 제외하고

barb [bɑːrb] ***n.*** [C] a sharp point projecting backward from the main point, as on an arrow, a fishhook, etc. **—*vt.*** furnish (something) with barbs.
—[名] [화살촉·낚시 따위의] 미늘; [철조망의] 가시 —[他] …에 미늘을 달다

Bar·ba·ra [bɑ́ːrb(ə)rə] ***n.*** a woman's name.
—[名] 여자 이름

bar·bar·i·an [bɑːrbέəriən] ***n.*** [C] **1.** an uncivilized person. **2.** (*History*) a person who was not a Greek; a person outside of the Roman Empire; a person who was not a Christian. **—*adj.*** not civilized; rude.
—[名] 1. 야만인 2. ⟪史⟫ 그리이스인 이외의 사람; 로마 제국 외의 이민족; [그리스도 교도 쪽에서 본] 이교도 —[形] 미개한; 야만의

bar·bar·ic [bɑːrbǽrik] ***adj.*** of or like barbarians; rough and rude.
—[形] 미개인의(같은); 거친, 야만의

bar·ba·rism [bɑ́ːrbərìz(ə)m] ***n.*** [U] uncivilized condition.
—[名] 야만, 미개

bar·bar·i·ty [bɑːrbǽriti] ***n.*** [U] [C] (pl. **-ties**) **1.** a brutal or cruel act; cruelty. **2.** a barbaric taste, manner, etc.
—[名] 1. 만행; 잔인[한 행위] 2. 야비, 조야(粗野)

bar·ba·rous [bɑ́ːrb(ə)rəs] ***adj.*** **1.** savage; uncivilized; harsh and cruel. **2.** unrefined; crude.
—[形] 1. 야만의; 미개한; 거칠고 잔인한 2. 야비한; 상스러운

bar·be·cue [bɑ́ːrbikjùː] ***n.*** **1.** [C] an animal roasted whole; [U] meat roasted over an open fire. **2.** [C] (*U.S.*) an out-of-door party at which animals (or meat) are roasted over an open fire. **—*vt.*** roast (an animal) whole.
—[名] 1. [돼지·소 따위의] 통째로 구운 것 2. ⟪美⟫ 야외 연회 —[他] …을 통째로 굽다

barbed [bɑːrbd] ***adj.*** having a barb.
—[形] 미늘이 있는

* **bar·ber** [bɑ́ːrbər] ***n.*** [C] a person whose business is haircutting, hairdressing, and shaving.
—[名] 이발사

bard [bɑːrd] ***n.*** [C] **1.** an ancient poet and singer. **2.** a poet.
—[名] 1. 음영(吟詠)시인 2. 시인

⁑ **bare** [bεər] ***adj.*** **1.** unclothed; uncovered; naked. **2.** exposed; not hidden. ¶*The guilt laid ~ to the world.*① **3.** without decoration; unfurnished. ¶*a ~ room* | ~
—[形] 1. 벌거벗은, 나체의 2. 노출된, 발각된 ¶①범죄가 세상에 폭로되었다 3. 장식이 없는; 설비가 없는 4. 근소한,

walls. **4.** small in amount; scanty. **5.** mere. ¶*a ~ hundred pounds.* **6.** empty. ¶*be ~ in purse.*
얼마 안되는 5. 겨우 …한 6. 텅 빈

—*vt.* make (something) bare; expose; uncover; reveal. ¶*~ a tree of its leaves.*
—[他] …을 벗기다, 드러내다

bare·back [bέərbæ̀k] *adj., adv.* on a horse without a saddle.
—[形][副] 안장 없는; 안장 없이

bare·faced [bέərféist] *adj.* without concealment; shameless.
—[形] 얼굴을 가리지 않은; 뻔뻔스러운

bare·foot [bέərfùt] *adj., adv.* with bare feet.
—[形][副] 맨발의

bare·foot·ed [bέərfùtid] *adj.* barefoot.
—[形] 맨발의

bare·head·ed [bέərhédid] *adj., adv.* with the head uncovered.
—[形][副] 모자를 쓰지 않은(않고)

* **bare·ly** [bέərli] *adv.* hardly; scarcely.
—[副] 겨우, 간신히; 거의 …이 아닌

bare·ness [bέərnis] *n.* [U] the state of being bare; lack of covering.
—[名] 나체; 노출

‡ **bar·gain** [bɑ́:rgin] *n.* [C] **1.** an agreement in trade or business; a contract. **2.** something offered or bought at a low price. **3.** the result of shopping. ¶*a good (bad) ~.*①
1) ***into the bargain,*** moreover; also.
2) ***strike a bargain,*** reach an agreement. ¶*strike a ~ with him.*
—[名] 1. 매매 계약 2. 값이 싼 물건, 싸게 산 것 3. 거래, 흥정 ¶①싸게(비싸게) 산 것
熟 1)게다가, 그 위에 2)매매 계약을 맺다

—*vi.* make an agreement; discuss the price. 《*~ with* someone》
1) ***bargain for,*** be ready for (something); expect.
2) ***bargain on,*** count or rely on (something).
—[自] 매매 거래를 하다, 흥정하다
熟 1)…을 예기하다; 기대하다 2)…을 기대로 삼다

* **barge** [bɑ:rdʒ] *n.* [C] **1.** a flat-bottomed boat for carrying goods. **2.** a pleasure boat. **3.** (*U.S.*) a coach.
—[名] 1. 거룻배; 밑이 평평한 짐배 2. 유람선 3. 《美》 마차
—*vt.* carry (something) by barge.
—[他] 거룻배로 나르다

barge·man [bɑ́:rdʒmən] *n.* [C] (pl. **-men** [-mən]) a person who works on a barge.
—[名] 거룻배(유람선)사공

bar·i·tone, *Brit.* **bar·y·tone** [bǽritòun] *n.* (*Music*) **1.** [U] a male voice between tenor and bass. **2.** [C] a singer having such a voice. **3.** [C] a musical instrument having such a sound.
—[名] 《樂》 1. 바리톤 2. 바리톤 가수 3. 바리톤 악기

bar·i·um [bέəriəm] *n.* [U] a soft, silver-white, metallic element.
—[名] 바륨

‡ **bark¹** [bɑ:rk] *n.* [U] the outer covering of trees or plants. —*vt.* take the bark off (a tree).
—[名] 나무껍질 —[他] …의 나무껍질을 벗기다

‡ **bark²** [bɑ:rk] *n.* [C] **1.** a cry made by a dog. **2.** a cry or sound like this. —*vi.* cry, as a dog does. ¶(*proverb*) *A barking dog seldom bites.*
—[名] 1. [개 따위의] 짖는 소리 2. 짖는 듯한 소리 —[自] 짖다; 고함치다

bark³ [bɑ:rk] *n.* [C] **1.** a small three-masted ship. **2.** (*poetic*) a ship.
—[名] 1. 세 돛대의 돛배 2. 《詩》 배

bar·keep·er [bɑ́:rkì:pər] *n.* [C] **1.** a person who runs a bar. **2.** a barman.
—[名] 1. 술집 주인 2. 바아텐더

bark·er [bʌ́:rkər] *n.* [C] a person who stands before a theater, etc., calling out to the crowd to enter.
—[名] [상점·흥행장 따위의] 손님 끄는 사람

* **bar·ley** [bɑ́:rli] *n.* [U] a sort of grain used as a food.
—[名] 보리

bar·ley·corn [bɑ́:rlikɔ̀:rn] *n.* [C] a grain of barley.
—[名] 보리쌀

bar·maid [bɑ́:rmèid] *n.* [C] (*Brit.*) a girl who serves food and alcoholic drinks in a bar.
—[名] 바아의 여급, 술집 여자

bar·man [bɑ́:rmən] *n.* [C] (pl. **-men** [-mən]) a man who serves drinks in a bar; a bartender.
—[名] 바아텐더

‡ **barn** [bɑ:rn] *n.* [C] a farm building for storing hay, grain, etc., or for keeping cows, horses, etc.
—[名] [농가의] 헛간, 창고; 가축 우리

bar·na·cle [bɑ́:rnəkl] *n.* [C] a sea animal with a shell that attaches itself to rocks, logs, etc.
—[名] 조개삿갓

barn·yard [bɑ́:rnjɑ̀:rd] *n.* [U] a yard around or before a barn.
—[名] 헛간의 앞뜰, 농가의 안뜰

ba·rom·e·ter [bərɑ́mitər / -rɔ́mitə] *n.* [C] **1.** an instrument for measuring the pressure of air. **2.** anything that shows changes.
—[名] 1. 기압계, 청우계 2. [변화를 아는] 실마리; [여론의] 지표

* **bar·on** [bǽr(ə)n] *n.* [C] **1.** a nobleman of the lowest rank in Britain. ⇒[N.B.] **2.** (*History*) a nobleman who held his land under a direct grant from the king. **3.** (*U.S.*) a powerful man in business.
—[名] 1. 남작 [N.B.] 호칭은 영국인의 경우는 Lord …, 외국인의 경우만 Baron …이라 함 2. [봉토를 받은] 귀족 3. 대실업가, 거상(巨商)

bar·on·ess [bǽrənes] *n.* [C] the wife of a baron; a woman baron. ⇒[N.B.]
—[名] 남작 부인; 여자 남작 [N.B.] 호칭은 Lady …, Baroness …

bar·on·et [bǽrənèt] *n.* [C] a person holding the degree of honor between baron and knight. ⇒[N.B.]
—[名] 준남작 [N.B.] 귀족은 아님 Sir …, Bart.

ba·roque [bəróuk] *adj.* **1.** of or like a style of art and
—[形] 1. 바로크 식의 2. 환상적인; 괴기

architecture in Europe about 1550 to the late 18th century. **2.** fantastic; grotesque. **—*n.*** [U] ⟪*the* ~⟫ the baroque period; the baroque style.
한 —[名] 바로크 시대; 바로크 양식

bar·que [bɑːrk] *n.* =bark³

bar·rack [bǽrək] *n.* [C] ⟪usu. *pl.*⟫ a building or a row of buildings for lodging soldiers or people.
—[名] 병사(兵舍); 바라크 [식 건물]

bar·rage [bərɑ́ːʒ / bǽrɑːʒ] *n.* [C] (*Military*) a curtain of machine-gun fire to protect advancing troops or to conceal their movements.
—[名] ⟪軍⟫ 탄막

:bar·rel [bǽr(ə)l] *n.* [C] **1.** a cask or container with a round, flat head and end and slightly curved sides. **2.** the quantity that a barrel can contain. **3.** the metal tube of a gun. **—*vt.*** (**-reled, -rel·ing,** or *Brit.* **-relled, -rel·ling**) put or pack (something) in a barrel.
—[名] 1. [중배가 불룩한] 통 2. 한 통[의 분량] 3. 총신 —[他] …을 통에 넣다

barrel organ [⌐– ⌐–] *n.* a portable pipe organ.
—[名] 휴대용 파이프 오르간

·bar·ren [bǽr(ə)n] *adj.* **1.** not producing anything; not fertile. ¶~ *land.* **2.** (of a plant) not able to bear fruit or seed; (of an animal) unable to bear young. **3.** unprofitable. **4.** dull in mind; not attractive.
—[形] 1. 불모의, 메마른 2. 열매를 맺지 않는; 새끼를 낳지 않는 3. 이익이 없는 4. 둔한; 매력이 없는

—*n.* [U] ⟪usu. *pl.*⟫ a stretch of land with sandy soil and few trees. ▷**bar·ren·ness** [-nis] *n.*
—[名] 불모지, 황무지

bar·ri·cade [bæ̀rikéid, +*U.S.* ⌐–⌐] *n.* a barrier roughly made for defense; any obstruction. **—*vt.*** obstruct or stop up (the street, etc.) with a barricade.
—[名] [급히 쌓은] 방책(防柵); 바리케이드; 장해 —[他] 바리케이드로 [도로 따위]를 막다

·bar·ri·er [bǽriər] *n.* [C] **1.** a fence, wall, etc. which stands in the way to prevent passage. **2.** anything that prevents progress. ¶*a* ~ *to success.*
—[名] 1. 울타리, 장벽; 관문; 장해물 2. 방해, 장해

bar·ris·ter [bǽristər] *n.* [C] (*Brit.*) a lawyer who practices in the courts; (*U.S. colloq.*) a lawyer.
—[名] 법정 변호사; 변호사

bar·room [bɑ́ːrrù(ː)m] *n.* [C] a room in a ship, hotel, etc. where alcoholic drinks are served over a counter.
—[名] [호텔 따위의] 바아

bar·row¹ [bǽrou] *n.* [C] a flat frame with handles at each end, used for carrying things; a handcart.
—[名] 운반대; 두 바퀴 손수레

bar·row² [bǽrou] *n.* [C] an ancient mound over a grave.
—[名] 분묘, 고총(古塚)

bar·tend·er [bɑ́ːrtèndər] *n.* [C] (*U.S.*) a person who serves alcoholic drinks in a bar.
—[名] ⟪美⟫ 바아텐더

bar·ter [bɑ́ːrtər] *vi.* trade by exchanging one kind of goods for other goods without money payment. ⟪~*with* someone *for*⟫ **—*vt.*** exchange. ⟪~ something *for*⟫ **—*n.*** [C] trade by bartering.
—[自] 물물교환하다 —[他] …을 교환하다 —[名] 물물교환

bar·y·tone [bǽritòun] *n. adj.* (*Brit.*)=baritone

bas·al [béisl] *adj.* forming a basis; basic; fundamental.
—[形] 기초의; 기본적인

ba·salt [bəsɔ́ːlt, bǽsɔːlt] *n.* [U] a dark, heavy rock of volcanic origin.
—[名] 현무암

bas·cule [bǽskjuːl] *n.* [C] anything working like a seesaw. ¶*a* ~ *bridge.*①
—[名] 뒤개장치 ¶①도개교(跳開橋)

base¹ [beis] *adj.* **1.** morally low; mean; ignoble. ¶*a* ~ *action.* **2.** not pure; of inferior value. ¶~*coin.* **3.** (of language) not classical. ¶ ~ *Latin.* **4.** (*Music*) bass.
—[形] 1. 비열한; 치사한 2. 질이 나쁜; 불순한 3. [언어가] 불순화된 4. ⟪樂⟫ 베이스(저음)의

:base² [beis] *n.* [C] **1.** what a thing rests on; a bottom. **2.** a principle. ¶*act on the* ~ *of*.... **3.** a starting point. **4.** a military center; headquarters. **5.** alkali. **6.** the main element of a mixture.
—[名] 1. 기부(基部), 바닥 2. 주의(主義) 3. 출발점 4. 군사 기지; 사령부 5. 염기(鹽基), 알칼리 6. 혼합물의 주성분

—*vt.* found; rest; establish. ⟪~ a theory, etc. *on*⟫
—[他] …의 기초를 두다

:base·ball [béisbɔ̀ːl] *n.* [U] a game played with a bat and a ball by two teams.
—[名] 야구

base·less [béislis] *adj.* without a base; groundless.
—[形] 근거 없는

base·man [béismən] *n.* [C] (pl. **-men** [-mən]) a baseball player guarding the first, second, or third base.
—[名] 1(2. 3)루수

base·ment [béismənt] *n.* [C] the lowest story of a building, partly or wholly underground; a cellar.
—[名] [건물의] 최하부, 지하실

base·ness [béisnis] *n.* [U] moral meanness; inferiority in conduct or character.
—[名] 천함, 비열

ba·ses [béisiːz] *n.* pl. of **basis.**

bash·ful [bǽʃf(u)l] *adj.* shy. ▷**bash·ful·ly** [-i] *adv.*
—[形] 수줍어하는

* **bas·ic** [béisik] *adj.* fundamental; essential. —[形] 기초적인; 근본적인

bas·i·cal·ly [béisik(ə)li] *adv.* fundamentally; essentially. —[副] 근본적으로; 기본적으로

ba·sil·i·ca [bəsílikə, +*Brit.* -zíl-] *n.* [C] **1.** an oblong hall, used as a court or an assembly in ancient Rome. **2.** a Christian church built in this form in the earliest or medieval period. —[名] 1. 바실리카 공회당 2. 바실리카 풍의 교회당

bas·i·lisk [bǽsilìsk, bǽzi-] *n.* [C] (in Greek and Roman legend) a fearful animal like a serpent. ⇒[N.B.] —[名] 뱀 비슷한 괴물 [N.B.] 눈길과 숨길로 사람을 죽였다고 함

* **ba·sin** [béisn] *n.* [C] **1.** a round, shallow bowl. **2.** a hollow place containing water; a reservoir. **3.** an area surrounded by higher lands. **4.** all the land along a river. —[名] 1. 대야, 세면기 2. 물웅덩이; 못 3. 분지(盆地) 4. [강의] 유역

‡ **ba·sis** [béisis] *n.* [C] (pl. **ba·ses**) **1.** a base or foundation. **2.** the chief element of a mixture. —[名] 1. 기초; 근거[지] 2. 주성분

bask [bǽsk/bɑːsk] *vi.* lie in pleasant warmth; enjoy a cheerful situation. —[自] 몸을 녹이다; 햇볕을 쬐다; [애정·은혜 따위]를 입다

‡ **bas·ket** [bǽskit / bɑ́ːs-] *n.* [C] **1.** a container made of rushes, twigs, etc. woven together. **2.** the amount that a basket holds. **3.** anything like a basket. **4.** (in basketball) a score or goal. —[名] 1. 광주리, 바구니 2. 바구니 가득[한 분량] 3. 바구니 모양의 것 4. [농구] 고울, 득점

‡ **bas·ket·ball** [bǽskitbɔ̀ːl / bɑ́ːs-] *n.* **1.** [U] a game played with a large ball by two teams of five persons. **2.** [C] a ball used in this game. —[名] 1. 농구 2. [농구용] 보올, 공

bas·ket·ful [bǽskitfùl / bɑ́ːs-] *n.* [C] the quantity to fill a basket. —[名] 바구니 가득[한 분량]

bas-re·lief [bɑ̀ːrilíːf / bǽsrilìːf] *n.* [U] [C] (*Art*) sculpture in which the figures stand out slightly from the background. —[名] 얕은 돋을새김

bass[1] [beis] (*Music*) *adj.* of the lowest pitch or range. —*n.* **1.** [U] the lowest male voice or part. **2.** [C] a bass singer or instrument. —[形] 베이스의, 저음의 —[名] 1. 남성 최저 음부 2. 저음 가수; 저음 악기

bass[2] [bæs] *n.* [C] (pl. **bass·es** [bǽsiz] or *collectively* **bass**) a fish found in both fresh and salt water in North America. —[名] [북미산] 농어류

bas·si·net [bæ̀sinét, ⌐‒⌐] *n.* [C] a baby's basketlike cradle. ⇒fig. —[名] 포장 달린 요람; 유모차

〔bassinet〕

bas·soon [bæsúːn, bəs-, +*Brit.* bəzúːn] *n.* [C] (*Music*) a deep-toned wind instrument. —[名] 저음 목관 악기의 하나, 파곳

bast [bæst] *n.* [U] the inner layer of the bark. ⇒[N.B.] —[名] 나무껍질의 속 껍질 [N.B.] 돗자리·밧줄 따위를 만듦

bas·tard [bǽstərd] *n.* [C] **1.** a child whose parents are not legally married. **2.** anything inferior or not genuine. —*adj.* **1.** born of unmarried parents. **2.** not genuine; false. **3.** inferior. **4.** not standard. —[名] 1. 사생아, 서자(庶子) 2. [동물의] 잡종; 가짜; 열등품 —[形] 1. 서자의, 사생아의 2. 불순한; 가짜의 3. 열등한 4. 표준에서 벗어난, 기형의

bas·tion [bǽstʃən, -tiən / -tiən] *n.* [C] a projecting part of a wall of a castle. —[名] 능보(稜堡), 요새

* **bat**[1] [bæt] *n.* **1.** [C] a heavy stick or club used to hit the ball in baseball, cricket, etc. **2.** [C] a batsman. —[名] 1. [야구 따위의] 배트, 타구봉 2. 타자(打者)

at bat, (in baseball) taking one's turn to bat. [熟] 1)타석에 서서

—*v.* (**bat·ted, bat·ting**) *vt.* hit (a ball) with a bat. —[他] …을 배트로 치다

—*vi.* use a bat. —[自] 배트를 사용하다

‡ **bat**[2] [bæt] *n.* [C] a flying animal with a mouse-like body and wings. —[名] 박쥐

blind as a bat, completely blind. [熟] 장님이나 다름 없는

batch [bætʃ] *n.* **1.** [C] the quantity of bread baked at one time; the quantity of anything made at one time. **2.** a group of persons or things taken together. —[名] 1. [빵·도자기 따위의] 한 가마(솥), 1회분 2. 한 묶음, 한 무리, 한 다발; 한 떼

bate [beit] *vt.* make (strength, etc.) less; make (a price) low. —[他] [힘 따위]를 약하게 하다; [값 따위]를 깎다

with bated breath, holding one's breath in great fear, interest, etc. [熟] 숨을 죽이다

‡ **bath** [bæθ / bɑːθ] *n.* (pl. **baths** [bæðz / bɑːðz]) **1.** [C] the act of washing or cleaning the body with water, steam, etc. ¶*take a* ~. **2.** [U] water for bathing. **3.** [C] a tub or room for bathing. —[名] 1. 목욕, 목간 2. [목욕용의] 물, 데운 물 3. 목욕실(탕)

B

B

‡**bathe** [beið] *vt.* **1.** give a bath to (someone); wash (a baby, wound, hand, etc.) with water or other liquid. **2.** dip (something) into any liquid; make (something) wet with any liquid. 《~ something *in* water》 ¶*be bathed in tears*①. **3.** 《in *passive*》 cover (something) as water does. ¶*The garden was bathed in moonlight.*②
—*vi.* **1.** have or take a bath. **2.** swim; go swimming. ¶*~ in the river.*
—*n.* [C] (*Brit.*) the act of swimming in a river or the sea. ¶*take a ~.*

—[他] 1. …을 목욕통에 넣다; 씻다 2. …을 담그다; 적시다 ¶①눈물젖다 3. …을 온통 덮다; …에 가득 차다 ¶②정원은 달빛으로 가득 차 있었다 —[自] 1. 목욕하다 2. 수영하다, 헤엄치다
—[名] 《英》 [강·바다에서의] 수영; 목욕

bath·er [béiðər] *n.* [C] a person who takes a bathe or a bath.
—[名] 수영자; [온천의] 요양객

bath·robe [bǽθròub / bɑ́:θ-] *n.* [C] (*U.S.*) a long, loose garment worn before and after a bath. (cf. *Brit.* dressing gown)
—[名] 《美》 [목욕 전후에 입는] 욕의(浴衣)

bath·room [bǽθrù:m / bɑ́:θ-] *n.* [C] **1.** a room for taking a bath. **2.** a toilet.
—[名] 1. 욕실, 목욕탕 2. 화장실, 변소

bath·tub [bǽθtʌ̀b / bɑ́:θ-] *n.* [C] a tub to bathe in.
—[名] 목욕통, 욕조(浴槽)

ba·ton [bətɑ́n, bǽt(ɑ)n / bǽt(ə)n] *n.* [C] **1.** a stick used by the leader of an orchestra or a band for beating time. **2.** a stick which is passed from one to the next runner in a relay race.
—[名] 1. 지휘봉 2. [릴레이용의] 바톤

bats·man [bǽtsmən] *n.* [C] (pl. **-men** [-mən]) (*Brit.*) a player at bat in baseball, cricket, etc.
—[名] 《英》 [야구·크리켓 따위의] 타자(打者)

bat·tal·ion [bətǽljən] *n.* [C] **1.** (*Military*) two or more companies of soldiers. **2.** 《*pl.*》 armies; military forces. **3.** an organized group.
—[名] 1. 보병 대대 2. 대부대, 군대 3. 집단

bat·ten [bǽtn] *n.* [C] **1.** a narrow strip of wood used in fastening two boards. **2.** a board used for flooring.
—*vt.* fasten (two boards) with battens; strengthen.
—[名] 1. 작은 널빤지(각목) 2. 마루 판자 —[他] …을 작은 널빤지로 잇다(받치다)

bat·ter[1] [bǽtər] *vt.* **1.** beat or strike (something) with repeated heavy blows; beat (something) out of shape; crush; pound. **2.** damage (something) by hard use.
—[他] 1. …을 연달아 치다; 때려부수다; 파괴하다 2. …을 거칠게 다루어 못쓰게 만들다

bat·ter[2] [bǽtər] *n.* [U] a mixture of flour, milk, and eggs, beaten together.
—[名] [밀가루·우유·달걀의] 반죽

***bat·ter**[3] [bǽtər] *n.* [C] =batsman.

bat·ter·ing ram [bǽt(ə)riŋræ̀m] *n.* an ancient military machine to break the walls or gates of a castle or city. ⇒fig.
—[名] 파성추(破城槌)

[battering ram]

***bat·ter·y** [bǽtəri] *n.* (pl. **-ter·ies**) [C] **1.** a set of cells, or a single cell, producing electric current. **2.** [C] a set of similar articles, machines, etc. ¶*a cooking ~*① / *a ~ of cameras.*② **3.** (*Military*) a set of big guns. **4.** (*Baseball*) the pitcher and the catcher together.
—[名] 1. 전지 2. 한 벌의 기구·장치 ¶①요리 도구 한 벌/②카메라 한 세트 3. 《軍》 포대; 포열(砲列) 4. [야구의] 배터리(투수와 포수)

‡**bat·tle** [bǽtl] *n.* [C] **1.** a fight between two forces (in a war); a combat. ¶*the ~ of Waterloo.* **2.** [U] any hard struggle. ¶*the ~ of life.*①
1) ***fall in battle,*** die in battle.
2) ***gain a battle,*** gain victory in a battle.
3) ***join battle,*** accept the enemy's challenge.
4) ***lose a battle,*** be defeated in a battle.
—*vi.* fight; struggle; make a great effort. ¶*~ with* (or *against*) *ones' enemy* / *~ for peace.*
—[名] 1. 전투 2. 투쟁 ¶①생존 투쟁
[熟] 1)전장에서 죽다 2)싸움에 이기다 3)응전하다 4)싸움에 지다
—[自] 싸우다; 분투하다

bat·tle-ax, -axe [bǽtlæ̀ks] *n.* [C] an ax used as a weapon.
—[名] [옛날 싸움에 쓰던] 큰 도끼

bat·tle·dore [bǽtldɔ̀:r] *n.* [C] a racket used in badminton.
—[名] 배드민턴의 라켓

bat·tle·field [bǽtlfì:ld] *n.* [C] a place on which a battle is fought.
—[名] 전장, 싸움터

bat·tle·ground [bǽtlgràund] *n.* [C] a battlefield.
—[名] 전장

bat·tle·ment [bǽtlmənt] *n.* 《usu. *pl.*》 a castle wall with open spaces for shooting.
—[名] 총안이 있는 흉벽(胸壁)

bat·tle·plane [bǽtlplèin] *n.* [C] an airplane made for combat.
—[名] 전투기

bat·tle·ship [bǽtlʃìp] *n.* [C] the largest and most powerful warship.
—[名] 전[투]함

bau·ble [bɔ́:bl] *n.* [C] a thing which is good in appearance but valueless; a child's plaything.
—[名] 번드르르한 싸구려 물건; 장난감

baulk [bɔ:k] *n., v.* =balk.

baux·ite [bɔ́:ksait] *n.* [U] a claylike material from which aluminum is obtained.
—[名] 보오크사이트

bawl [bɔ:l] *vi., vt.* shout; cry out loudly.
—[自][他] 외치다, 고함지르다

—*n.* [C] loud crying; noisy shouts.
—[名] 고함, 외침소리

⁑ **bay**¹ [bei] *n.* [C] a part of a sea or lake extending into the shore.
—[名] 만(灣); 후미

bay² [bei] *n.* [C] **1.** a part of a wall between pillars. **2.** a separate part in an airplane, esp. for carrying bombs. **3.** a place for storing hay in a barn.
—[名] **1.** 기둥과 기둥 사이의 우묵한 벽 **2.** [비행기의] 격실(隔室) **3.** [헛간의] 건초 두는 곳

bay³ [bei] *n.* [U] **1.** the long, low cry of a dog. **2.** a state or situation from which escape is impossible. ¶*be* (or *stand*) *at* ~① / *bring* (or *drive*) *someone to* ~②.
—[名] **1.** 짖는 소리, 으르렁 소리 **2.** 쫓겨서 몰린 상태, 궁지 ¶①궁지에 빠지다 /②남을 궁지에 몰아넣다

—*vi.* cry with a deep sound; bark. —*vt.* bark at (someone or something).
—[自] 짖다 —[他] …에 짖어대다

bay⁴ [bei] *n.* [C] **1.** a small evergreen tree; laurel tree. **2.** ⦅*pl.*⦆ a laurel ring or crown given to successful poets or victors. **3.** ⦅*pl.*⦆ honor; fame.
—[名] **1.** 월계수 **2.** 월계관 **3.** 영예

bay⁵ [bei] *n.* **1.** [U] color of reddish brown. **2.** [C] a reddish brown horse. —*adj.* reddish brown in color.
—[名] **1.** 적갈색 **2.** 적갈색의 말
—[形] 적갈색의

bay·o·net [bé(i)ənit] *n.* [C] a dagger attached to a gun.
—[名] 총검

bay rum [´ ´] *n.* a sweet-smelling toilet liquid.
—[名] 베이럼(머릿기름)

bay window [´ ´–] *n.* a window projecting from the outside wall of a building. ⇒fig.
—[名] 퇴창, 밖으로 내민 창

(bay window)

ba·zaar, ba·zar [bəzɑ́:r] *n.* [C] **1.** a market place in Oriental countries. **2.** a place for the sale of various kinds of goods. **3.** a sale of various kinds of articles for charity or other such purpose.
—[名] **1.** [동양의] 상점가 **2.** 시장 **3.** 자선시(慈善市)

ba·zoo·ka [bəzú:kə] *n.* [C] a portable rocket gun, esp. used against tanks.
—[名] 바주우카 포

* **B. C.** Before Christ.

⁑ **be** [bi:, bi] *vi.*(pres. **am, are, is,** pt. **was, were,** pp. **been**) **1.** ⓐ be equal in meaning; regard or recognize as the same. ¶*January is the first month.* / *Let x ~ 10.*① / *The first person I met was my brother.* ⓑ have as a quality or character. ¶*The leaves are green.* ⓒ belong to the class of. ¶*The fish is a salmon.* **2.** ⓐ exist; occupy a place or position. ¶*I think, therefore I am.*② / *Once upon a time there was a knight.* / *The book is on the table.* / *Let it be.*③ ⓑ occur; take place. ¶*There was a fire last night.* ⓒ amount to; cost. ¶*Twice 2 is 4.* / *It is nothing to me.*④
—[自] **1.** ⓐ…이다, 같다 ¶①*x*의 값을 10으로 하라 ⓑ…의 성질을 지니다 ⓒ…에 속하다 **2.** ⓐ존재하다, 있다; 위치를 차지하다 ¶②나는 생각한다, 고로 존재한다/③그대로 놔두어라/ⓑ일어나다 ⓒ이르다; 걸리다 ④그것은 내게 아무 것도 아니다

1) ***be off,*** (*colloq.*) go; depart; leave somewhere. ¶*We must be off early tomorrow morning.*
2) ***Be off*** [***with you***]*!* Leave here!; Get away!
[熟] ⦅口⦆ 1)떠나다, 출발하다 2)꺼져라!, 없어져라!

—*auxil. v.* **1.** ⦅with *pp.* of *vt.*, forming *passive*⦆ ¶*He was killed.* / *He has been killed.* / *The house is being built.* **2.** ⦅with *pp.* of some *vi.*, forming *perfect*⦆ ¶*The sun is set.* / *How he is grown!* **3.** ⦅with *pres. part.*, expressing *incomplete action*⦆ ¶*He is building a house.* **4.** ⦅with *to-infinitive*, expressing *duty, intention, possibility,* or *hypothesis*⦆ ¶*I am to inform you.* / *He is to be there.* / *Nothing was to be seen.* / *If I were to die....*
—[助] **1.** ⦅타동사의 과거분사와 함께 수동태를 만듦⦆ **2.** ⦅어떤 자동사와 함께 완료를 나타냄⦆ **3.** ⦅현재분사와 함께 진행형을 만듦⦆ **4.** ⦅부정사와 함께 의무·예정·당연 따위의 뜻을 나타냄⦆

⁑ **beach** [bi:tʃ] *n.* [C] **1.** a smooth shore of sand or pebbles, esp. washed over by the waves at high tide. **2.** ⦅*collectively*⦆ the sand of the shore of a sea or a lake.
—[名] **1.** 물가, 해안 **2.** 해변의 모래

beachhead [bíːtʃhèd] *n.* ⓒ (*Military*) the first position taken by a military force landing on an enemy shore.
— ⓝ 상륙 거점(據點), 교두보

bea·con [bíːk(ə)n] *n.* ⓒ **1.** a signal fire used to guide or warn. **2.** a radio signal used for guiding airplanes or ships. **3.** a lighthouse **4.** a warning. —*vt.* give light to (something) as a signal; furnish (something) with guiding lights. —*vi.* shine brightly.
— ⓝ 1. 봉화, 횃불 2. 무선 표지(標識) 3. 등대 4. 경고 — ⓣ …에 대해 봉화를 올리다; …에 지표를 설치하다 — ⓘ 빛나다

* **bead** [biːd] *n.* ⓒ **1.** a small ball or piece of glass, metal, etc. with a hole through it, used in a necklace. **2.** (*pl.*) a necklace of such balls; a rosary. **3.** a drop of a liquid. ¶ *beads of sweat.*① 「a rosary. *count* (or *say, tell*) *one's beads,* say one's prayers with」 —*vi., vt.* decorate (something) with beads; form beads.
— ⓝ 1. 구슬, 염주알, 유리알 2. 목걸이, 염주 3. 방울 ¶①땀방울
📖 [염주알을 세며] 기도문을 외다
— ⓘⓣ 구슬로 장식하다; 구슬처럼 되다

* **beak** [biːk] *n.* ⓒ **1.** the bill of a bird, esp. as of an eagle, a hawk, etc. **2.** anything which looks like a bill; a hooked nose of a man.
— ⓝ 1. 부리 2. 부리 모양의 것(주전자의 주둥이·피리코 따위); [사람의] 매부리코

beaked [biːkt] *adj.* having a beak; shaped like a beak.
— ⓣ 부리가 있는; 부리 모양의

beak·er [bíːkər] *n.* ⓒ **1.** a large drinking glass with a wide mouth. **2.** a thin glass cup with a pouring lip, used in chemical experiments.
— ⓝ 1. 아가리가 넓은 유리컵 2. [화학 실험용의] 비이커

: beam [biːm] *n.* ⓒ **1.** a long piece of wood or metal used in building. **2.** a supporting bar of wood or metal. ¶ *the ~ of a balance.*① **3.** a ray of light. ¶ *a ~ of light.*② **4.** a bright look or smile. **5.** a set of radio signals used to guide airplanes or ships. —*vi.* **1.** shine. ¶ *The sun beams.* **2.** smile happily. ¶ *~ with joy.* —*vt.* send forth (rays or radio waves). *beam upon,* smile happily at (something).
— ⓝ 1. 들보, 도리 2. 들보 모양의 재목 (장대) ¶①저울대 3. 광선 ¶②한줄기 빛 4. [표정의] 밝음, 환함 5. 신호 전파
— ⓘ 1. 빛나다 2. 미소하다 — ⓣ …을 발사(放射)하다
— …을 보고 미소하다

: bean [biːn] *n.* ⓒ **1.** a seed used as a vegetable. **2.** any seed shaped like a bean. ¶ *Coffee-beans.*① ▷ **bean·like** [-laik] *adj.*
— ⓝ 1. 콩 2. [콩 비슷한] 열매 ¶① 코오피 열매

bean·stalk [bíːnstɔ̀ːk] *n.* ⓒ the stem of a bean plant.
— ⓝ 콩줄기

: bear¹ [bɛər] *v.* (**bore, borne,** →6.) *vt.* **1.** carry. ¶ *~ a heavy load.* **2.** support; sustain. **3.** put up with (something); endure. (*~ to do*) ¶ *I cannot ~ the sight of him* (or *~ to see him*).① ⇒ USAGE **4.** be fit for or worthy of (something). (*~ doing*) ¶ *This cloth will ~ washing.*② / *Your opinion will ~ repeating.*③ **5.** experience; undergo. **6.** (pp. **born** except after *have* or before *by*) give birth to (someone).; produce; yield. ¶ *She has borne him five children.*④ / *He was born in 1926 in Seoul* / *This tree bears much fruit.* **7.** have; hold. ¶ *~ something in mind.*⑤ / *This letter bears his signature.* —*vi.* **1.** be able to support. **2.** be fruitful; take effect. **3.** have relation. (*~ on* someone or something) **4.** lean; press. (*~ on* something)
1) *bear a hand in,* help someone in doing something.
2) *bear down,* ⓐ press down. ⓑ defeat; overcome.
3) *bear down on* (or *upon*), ⓐ approach. ⓑ put pressure on (someone).
4) *bear fruit,* have results, usu. good.
5) *bear hard on* (=*deal severely with*) *someone.*
6) *bear in mind,* do not forget; remember.
7) *bear on* (or *upon*), ⓐ force upon. ⓑ have relation
8) *bear oneself,* behave; conduct. ⌊to (something).⌋
9) *bear out,* prove (a statement, etc.) to be true.
10) *bear up,* keep one's courage; do not despair.

— ⓣ 1. …을 나르다 2. …을 버티다, 지탱하다 3. …에 견디다, 참다 ¶①그녀석은 보기도 싫다 USAGE can, could 와 함께 부정문·의문문에 쓰이다 4. …에 알맞다; …의 가치가 있다 ¶②이 천은 세탁은 잘된다 / ③내 의견은 되풀이 들을 가치가 있다 5. …을 경험하다; …을 겪다 6. …을 낳다; 산출하다 ¶ ④그녀는 그의 아이를 다섯이나 낳았다 7. …을 지니다; 마음에 품다 ¶⑤기억해 두다 — ⓘ 1. 지탱하다, 배겨나다 2. 열매를 맺다, 성과가 있다 3. 관계가 있다 4. 기대다; 누르다

🔲 1)거들다 2)ⓐ…을 압도하다 ⓑ…에 이기다, 극복하다 3)ⓐ…에 접근하다 ⓑ…을 압박하다 4)성과를 거두다 5)…을 학대하다 6)기억하다 7)ⓐ…을 압박하다 ⓑ…과 관계를 맺다 8)처신(행동)하다 9)…을 증명하다, 뒷받침하다 10)용기를 잃지 않다

: bear² [bɛər] *n.* ⓒ **1.** a large animal with long, hard hair and a short tail. **2.** a rough or rude person. **3.** (*the B-*) either of two groups of stars. ¶ *Great Bear*① / *Little Bear.*②
— ⓝ 1. 곰 2. 난폭자 3. 웅좌(熊座) ¶ ①대웅좌 / ②소웅좌

bear·a·ble [bɛ́ərəbl] *adj.* endurable.
— ⓣ 참을 수 있는, 견딜 만한

: beard [biərd] *n.* ⓒ **1.** the hair growing on the chin of an adult man. ⇒ N.B. **2.** the hairs on the heads of
— ⓝ 1. 턱수염 N.B. 때로 moustache [məstɑ́ːʃ](코밑수염)의 뜻을 포함

bearded

plants, like oats or wheat.
beard·ed [bíərdid] *adj.* having a beard.
beard·less [bíərdlis] *adj.* **1.** having no beard. **2.** young.
bear·er [béərər] *n.* ⓒ **1.** a person or thing that carries. **2.** a person who holds a check, or who requests the payment for a check. **3.** a tree or plant which produces fruit or flowers. ¶*That cherry tree is a good ~.*①
∗**bear·ing** [béəriŋ] *n.* Ⓤ **1.** manner; behavior. **2.** ⓊⒸ relation. ¶*That has no ~ on this accident.*① **3.** (usu. *pl.*) direction; relative position. ¶*lose one's bearings.*② **4.** ⓒ (usu. *pl.*) a part of a machine that supports a turning shaft.
bear·ish [béəriʃ] *adj.* like a bear; rough.
bear·skin [béərskin] *n.* Ⓤ the skin or fur of a bear. ⓒ a coat made of such skin or fur.
‡**beast** [bi:st] *n.* **1.** ⓒ any four-footed animal, esp. a large and fierce one. **2.** (*collectively*) cattle. **3.** ⓒ a coarse, brutal person. ▷**beast·like** [-laik] *adj.*
beast·ly [bí:stli] *adj.* (**-li·er, -li·est**) **1.** like a beast; brutal; dirty. **2.** (*Brit. colloq.*) unpleasant; nasty.
‡**beat** [bi:t] *v.* (**beat, beat·en** or **beat**) *vt.* **1.** strike (something) again and again. **2.** punish (someone) by hitting. **3.** win a victory over (someone); defeat; overcome. ·(*~ someone at* or *in* battle, a contest, etc.) ¶*~ the enemy* / *~ him at chess.* **4.** puzzle; perplex. **5.** make (something) flat; change the shape of (metal) with a hammer. **6.** show (rhythm or time) in music by hand or stick. **7.** stir (eggs, cream, etc.) vigorously. **8.** move (wings) up and down. —*vi.* **1.** strike again and again; throb. ¶*The heart beats.* **2.** make a sound by being beaten.
  1) ***beat about,*** search around. ((*~* about *for* something))
  2) ***beat back,*** make (an enemy, a dog, etc.) retreat; defeat. 「one) accept a lower price.」
  3) ***beat down,*** ⓐ defeat; overcome. ⓑ make (some-
  4) ***beat out,*** ⓐ make (metal) flat by beating. ⓑ win a victory over (someone). ⓒ make (someone) tired.
  5) ***beat up,*** ⓐ sail against the wind. ⓑ attack (an enemy) suddenly. ⓒ mix (eggs, cream, etc.) by stirring. ⓓ gather (persons) together.
—*n.* ⓒ **1.** a stroke or blow made again and again as of the heart or a drum. ¶*The ~ of the drum.* **2.** a unit of rhythm in music. **3.** a regular or assigned course of a policeman or a watchman. ¶*The watchman is on his ~.*①
be off one's beat, be different from one's usual work.
‡**beat·en** [bí:tn] *v.* pp. of **beat**.
—*adj.* **1.** whipped. **2.** defeated; overcome. **3.** shaped by beating. **4.** hardened by footsteps; much used. ¶*the ~ path.* **5.** exhausted; worn out.
beat·er [bí:tər] *n.* ⓒ **1.** a person or thing that beats. **2.** a person who makes animals or birds come out from their hiding place in hunting. 「ness. **2.** blissful; happy.」
be·a·tif·ic [bì:ətífik] *adj.* **1.** giving blessings or happi-
be·at·i·fy [biǽtifài] *vt.* (**-fied**) **1.** make (someone) happy. **2.** (*Catholic*) declare (a dead person) to be among the blessed in heaven. ▷**be·at·i·fi·ca·tion** [biæ̀tifikéiʃ(ə)n] *n.*
beat·ing [bí:tiŋ] *n.* ⓊⒸ **1.** whipping, esp. as punishment. **2.** a severe defeat. **3.** the act of throbbing.
be·at·i·tude [biǽtit(j)ù:d / bi(:)ǽtitju:d] *n.* Ⓤ supreme and perfect happiness; blessing.
beat·nik [bí:tnik] *n.* ⓒ (*colloq.*) a member of persons who reject conventional things and social inhibitions.
Be·a·trice [bí:ətris / bíə-] *n.* a woman's name.

Beatrice

(植) 꺼끄러기
—圏 턱수염을 기른
—圏 1. 수염이 없는 2. 젊은; 애숭이의
—名 1. 나르는 사람(것) 2. [수표 따위의] 지참인 3. 열매 맺는(꽃 피는) 초목 ¶①저 벚나무는 열매를 잘 맺는다.
—名 1. 태도, 처신 2. [남에 대한] 관계 ¶①그것은 이 사건에 관계가 없다 3. 방향; 위치 ¶②방향을 모르게 되다 4. [기계의] 축받이, 베어링

—圏 곰 같은; 난폭한
—名 곰가죽; 곰가죽 옷

—名 1. 네발 짐승, 짐승; 맹수 2. 가축 3. 짐승같은 사람

—圏 1. 짐승 같은; 흉악한; 불결한 2. 《英口》불쾌한, 싫은
—働 1. …을 연달아 치다 2. [벌로서]…을 때리다 3. …에게 이기다, …을 타도하다 4. …을 괴롭히다 5. …을 두들겨 펴다, (壓延)하다 6. [박자]를 맞춰 치다 7. …을 휘젓다 8. [깃 따위]를 아래위로 움직이다 —働 1. 연달아 치다; 고동하다 2. [두들겨 맞아] 소리내다, 울리다

團 1)[구실·해결책]을 찾다 2)…을 격퇴하다 3)ⓐ을 격파하다 ⓑ[값]을 깎다 4)ⓐ두들겨서 …을 펴다 ⓑ…에 이기다 ⓒ…을 지치게 하다 5)ⓐ바람을 안고 항해하다 ⓑ…을 기습하다 ⓒ…을 휘젓다 ⓓ…을 한데 모으다, 소집하다

—名 1. 치기, 때리기; 심장의 고동, 되풀이 치는 소리 2. 박자 3. 순찰(담당) 구역 ¶①그 경비원은 순찰 중이다

熟 자기의 전문 밖이다
—圏 1. 얻어 맞은 2. 패배당한; 정복된 3. 두들겨 편 4. 밟아 다져진; 많이 사용된 5. 지쳐빠진

—名 1. 치는 사람(것) 2. [사냥의] 몰이꾼

—圏 1. 축복을 주는 2. 행복에 겨운
—働 1. …을 행복하게 하다 2. 《가톨릭》…을 시복(諡福)하다

—名 1. 치기, 두들김; 매질 2. 패배 3. [심장의] 고동, 동계(動悸)
—名 무상의 행복; 지복(至福)

—名 비이트족의 사람

—名 여자 이름

beau [bou] *n.* ⓒ (pl. **beaus** or **beaux**) **1.** a man who pays much attention to the fashion of his clothes; a dandy. **2.** a male companion or escort for a girl or woman; a lover; a suitor.
—㉠ 1. 멋쟁이 [남자] 2. 여자의 상대역(호위역)이 되는 사람; 애인; 정부

beau·te·ous [bjú:tiəs] *adj.* (*poetic*) beautiful.
—㉠ 아름다운

beau·ti·ful [bjú:tif(u)l] *adj.* pleasant to the eye, ear, or mind; lovely; excellent.
—㉠ 아름다운; 사랑스러운; 훌륭한

beau·ti·ful·ly [bjú:tifuli] *adv.* excellently.
—㉠ 훌륭하게

beau·ti·fy [bjú:tifài] *vt.* (**-fied**) make (something) beautiful; adorn. —*vi.* become beautiful.
—㉠ …을 아름답게 하다; 꾸미다
—㉠ 아름다와지다

beau·ty [bjú:ti] *n.* (pl. **-ties**) **1.** ⓤ a quality which pleases the mind and senses. **2.** ⓒ something beautiful. **3.** ⓒ a beautiful girl or woman; (*the* ~) (*collectively*) beautiful girls or women.
—㉠ 1. 미(美); 아름다움 2. 아름다운 것 3. 미인; 미인들

beaux [bouz] *n.* pl. of **beau**.

bea·ver [bí:vər] *n.* **1.** ⓒ a four-legged animal with soft fur and a flat tail living both in water and on land. ⇒fig. **2.** ⓤ its soft and brown fur. **3.** ⓒ a high silk hat. **4.** ⓤ a heavy woolen cloth.
[beaver 1.]
—㉠ 1. 해리(海狸), 비이버 2. 그 모피 3. 실크햇(이전에는 비이버 모피로 만들었음) 4. 두꺼운 나사(羅紗) 천

be·calm [biká:m] *vt.* **1.** make (something) calm; tranquilize. **2.** make (a ship) unable to move because of lack of wind.
—㉠ 1. …을 가라앉히다 2. 바람이 자서 [돛배]를 나아갈 수 없게 하다

be·came [bikéim] *v.* pt. of **become**.

be·cause [bikɔ́:z, +U.S. -kʌ́z] *conj.* for the reason that; since; for. ¶*He plays baseball* ~ *he likes it.*
because of, on account of.
—㉠ …이라는 이유로; …이니까, …때문에
㉰ …때문에

beck [bek] *n.* ⓒ a nod or other gesture, as of a call or command. ⌈complete control.
be at someone's beck [*and call*], be under someone's⌋
—㉠ 고갯짓; 손짓
㉰ [남]이 시키는 대로 하다

beck·on [bék(ə)n] *vi., vt.* make a signal by a motion of the head or hand. (~ *to someone*; ~ *someone to do*)
—㉠㉰ 손짓[고갯짓]으로 부르다, 신호하다

be·cloud [bikláud] *vt.* darken; obscure.
—㉰ …을 어둡게 하다; 애매하게 하다

be·come [bikʌ́m] *v.* (**-came, -come**) *vi.* come or grow to be. ¶~ *king* (*rich, noted*). —*vt.* be suitable to; look well on (something or someone). ¶*This hat becomes you.* ⌈*has* ~ *of him?*⌋
become of (=*happen to*) *someone or something.* ¶*What*
—㉰ …이 되다 —㉰ …에 어울리다, 알맞다
㉰ [사람·물건이 어떻게] 되다 ¶① 그는 어찌 됐을까?

be·com·ing [bikʌ́miŋ] *adj.* suitable; proper. ¶*Her new hat is very* ~ *to* (or *on*) *her.* | *It is not* ~ *in a man to*
—㉠ 어울리는, 알맞는

be·com·ing·ly [bikʌ́miŋli] *adv.* suitably. ⌊*tell a lie.*⌋
—㉰ 어울리게

bed [bed] *n.* ⓒ **1.** a piece of furniture for sleeping on. **2.** a piece of ground for growing plants. ¶*a flower* ~. **3.** a bottom or base on which a thing rests. **4.** the bottom of a river. **5.** a layer of rock or earth.
1) *be brought to bed,* give birth to a child.
2) *die in one's bed,* die of natural causes.
3) *keep one's bed,* be in bed from illness.
4) *lie in the bed one has made,* accept the results of one's acts.
5) *take to one's bed,* go to bed because one is ill.
—*vt.* (**bed·ded, bed·ding**) **1.** prepare a bed for (someone). **2.** plant (grass, etc.) in a bed. **3.** lay (things) flat or in order.
—㉠ 1. 침대, 잠자리 2. 묘판, 화단, 밭 3. 토대, 기초 4. 강바닥 5. 지층; 암층
㉰ 1) 해산(解産)하다 2) 제 명에 죽다 3) 병으로 누워 있다 4) 자기가 한 일에 보답을 받다 5) 앓아 눕다
—㉰ 1. …을 위해 잠자리를 마련하다 2. …을 화단에 심다 3. …을 평평하게 놓다, 쌓아 올리다

be·dab·ble [bidǽbl] *vt.* sprinkle.
—㉰ [물 따위]를 튀기다

be·daub [bidɔ́:b] *vt.* smear (something) with dirty or oily material; decorate (something) in a showy way.
—㉰ …을 더덕더덕 칠하다; 야하게 꾸미다

bed·bug [bédbʌ̀g] *n.* ⓒ (*U.S.*) a small bloodsucking insect. ⌈ing room.
—㉠ (美) 빈대

bed·cham·ber [bédtʃèimbər] *n.* ⓒ a bedroom; a sleep-⌋
—㉠ 침실

bed·clothes [bédklòuz, -klòuðz] *n. pl.* the sheets, blankets, quilts, etc. used on a bed.
—㉠ 침구(matress 제외)

bed·ding [bédiŋ] *n.* [U] **1.** the materials for a bed. **2.** a foundation of any kind.
—[名] 1. 침구 2. 토대; 기초

be·deck [bidék] *vt.* decorate; ornament.
—[他] …을 장식하다

be·dew [bid(j)ú: / -djú:] *vt.* make (something) wet with dew or something like dew.
—[他] …을 이슬(눈물)로 적시다

bed·fel·low [bédfèlou] *n.* [C] **1.** a wife. **2.** a companion.
—[名] 1. 아내 2. 동료

be·dim [bidím] *vt.* (**-dimmed, -dim·ming**) make (something) dark or dim.
—[他] [눈·마음 따위]를 흐리게 하다

be·di·zen [bidáizn, -dízn] *vt.* dress or decorate (something) in a showy way. 《~ oneself *with*》
—[他] …을 야하게 꾸며대다(치장하다)

bed·lam [bédləm] *n.* [C] **1.** a scene of great confusion or disorder. **2.** a hospital for mad persons; a madhouse.
—[名] 1. 시끄러움; 혼란 2. 정신병원

Bed·ou·in [béduin] *n.* [C] a wandering Arab of the desert in Arabia, Syria, or northern Africa.
—[名] 아라비아·시리아·북 아프리카 사막의 아랍 유목민

bed·post [bédpòust] *n.* [C] a supporting post of a bed.
—[名] [네 귀의] 침대 기둥

be·drag·gle [bidrǽgl] *vt.* make (a dress, etc.) weak and dirty by dragging.
—[他] [옷자락 따위]를 질질 끌어 더럽히다

bed·rid·den [bédrìdn] *adj.* in bed for a long time because of age or sickness.
—[形] [오랫동안] 누워만 있는

bed·rock [bédràk / -rɔ̀k] *n.* [U][C] **1.** the solid rock beneath the soil. **2.** a firm foundation.
—[名] 1. 반암(盤岩) 2. 튼튼한 토대; 기반

⁑**bed·room** [bédrù(:)m] *n.* [C] a room used for sleeping.
—[名] 침실

bed·side [bédsàid] *n.* [C] 《*one's* ~》 the side of a bed. ¶*sit by a sick person's* ~.①
—[名] 침대 곁 ¶①환자의 머리맡에서 시중들다

bed·sore [bédsɔ̀:r] *n.* [C] (of a sick person) a sore caused by lying too long in bed.
—[名] [환자의] 욕창(褥瘡)

bed·spread [bédsprèd] *n.* [C] a cover for a bed.
—[名] 침대 덮개

bed·stead [bédstèd] *n.* [C] the framework of a bed.
—[名] 침대의 뼈대

bed·time [bédtàim] *n.* [U] the time to go to bed.
—[名] 취침 시간

⁑**bee** [bi:] *n.* [C] an insect with four wings and a sting that gathers honey from flowers. ¶*as busy as a* ~① / *a queen* ~② / *a working* ~.③
—[名] 꿀벌 ¶①몹시 바쁜/②여왕벌/③일벌

have a bee in one's bonnet, ⓐ think of one thing only. ⓑ have eccentric ideas.
[熟] ⓐ한 가지를 골똘히 생각하다 ⓑ머리가 좀 돈 듯하다

beech [bi:tʃ] *n.* **1.** [C] a tree having a smooth gray bark and bearing nuts that can be eaten. **2.** [U] its wood.
—[名] 1. 너도밤나무 2. 그 재목

beech·en [bí:tʃ(ə)n] *adj.* made of beechwood.
—[形] 너도밤나무 재목으로 만든

⁑**beef** [bi:f] *n.* (pl. **beeves**) **1.** [U] meat from a cow or bull. ¶~ *cattle*.① **2.** [C] 《*pl.*》 adult cows or bulls raised for their meat.
—[名] 1. 쇠고기 ¶①육우(肉牛) 2. 식용우(食用牛)

beef·eat·er [bí:fì:tər] *n.* [C] **1.** a person who eats beef. **2.** a guardsman of English royalty. **3.** a guard of the Tower of London. ⇒fig.
—[名] 1. 쇠고기를 먹는 사람 2. 영국 왕의 호위병 3. 런던탑의 수위

〔beefeater 3.〕

beef·steak [bí:fstèik / ⌐ ⌐] *n.* [U][C] a slice of beef, broiled or fried, or suitable for broiling or frying.
—[名] 두꺼운 쇠고기점; 비이프 스테이크

beef tea [⌐ ⌐] *n.* a strong beef soup.
—[名] 진한 쇠고기 수우프, 곰국

beef·y [bí:fi] *adj.* (**beef·i·er, beef·i·est**) **1.** like beef. **2.** strong; solid. ▷**beef·i·ness** [-nis] *n.*
—[形] 1. 쇠고기 같은 2. 건장한

bee·hive [bí:hàiv] *n.* [C] a box made for bees in which they live.
—[名] 꿀벌통

bee·keep·er [bí:kì:pər] *n.* [C] a person who keeps bees.
—[名] 양봉가

bee·line [bí:làin] *n.* [C] a direct line. ¶*in a* ~.①
—[名] 일직선 ¶①일직선으로

⁑**been** [bin / bi:n] *v.* pp. of **be**.

***beer** [biər] *n.* [U] an alcoholic drink made from dried grain flavored with hops; [C] a drink or a glass of beer. ¶*draft* ~① / *ginger* ~② / *be in* ~.③
—[名] 맥주; 한 잔의 맥주 ¶①생맥주 ②생강이 든 청량음료/③맥주에 취하여

bees·wax [bí:zwæ̀ks] *n.* [U] wax produced by bees.
—[名] 밀랍(蜜蠟)

beet [bi:t] *n.* [C] **1.** a plant having a fleshy red or white root that is eaten. ¶*a sugar* ~.① **2.** the root of such a plant. ▷**beet·like** [-làik] *adj.*
—[名] 1. 사탕무우, 근대 ¶①사탕무우 2. 그 뿌리

***Bee·tho·ven** [béit(h)ouv(ə)n], **Ludwig van** [lú:tviçfan] *n.* (1770–1827) a German musical composer.
—[名] 독일의 작곡가

bee·tle¹ [bí:tl] *n.* ⓒ an insect having hard wing-cases.
bee·tle² [bí:tl] *vi.* project ; overhang.
beet root [´ ´] *n.* the root of a beet plant.
beet sugar [´ ´] *n.* sugar made from white beets.
beeves [bi:vz] *n.* pl. of beef.
be·fall [bifɔ́:l] *vt., vi.* (-fell, -fall·en) (of a bad matter) happen to (someone). ¶*What befell him? / Evil befell the old man.*
be·fall·en [bifɔ́:ln] *v.* pp. of befall.
be·fell [bifél] *v.* pt. of befall.
be·fit [bifít] *vt.* (-fit·ted, -fit·ting) be suited to (something) ; become. ¶*Her clothes did not ~ the occasion.*
be·fit·ting [bifítiŋ] *adj.* suitable ; becoming.
be·fit·ting·ly [bifítiŋli] *adv.* suitably ; properly.
be·fog [bifɔ́g, -fɔ́:g / -fɔ́g] *vt.* (-fogged, -fog·ging) hide (something) in fog ; obscure ; confuse.
be·fool [bifú:l] *vt.* make a fool of (someone) ; deceive.
‡**be·fore** [bifɔ́:r] *adv.* 1. (of place) ahead ; in front. ¶*He ran on ~.*① 2. (of time) earlier ; already. ¶*I have heard this ~.*
　—*prep.* 1. in front of ; ahead of. ↔behind ¶*She stood ~ the door.* 2. in the presence of. ¶*He appeared ~ the judge.* 3. earlier than. ¶*They arrived ~ me.* 4. (*colloq.*) rather than. ¶*I would do anything ~ that.* 5. superior to. ¶*Work should come ~ pleasure.*②
　1) *before long,* soon.
　2) *before one's time,* ahead of one's time.
　—*conj.* 1. earlier than. ¶*We got home ~ it got dark.* 2. rather than. ¶*I would die ~ I told him.*
be·fore·hand [bifɔ́:rhæ̀nd] *adv.* ahead of time ; in advance. ↔behindhand ¶*You are rather ~ in your suspicions.*①
be·foul [bifául] *vt.* make (something) dirty.
be·friend [bifrénd] *vt.* act as a friend to (someone) ; aid.
‡**beg** [beg] *v.* (begged, beg·ging) *vt.* 1. ask for (money, food, etc.) as a kindness. (*~ something of* ; *~ someone for*) ¶*I begged something to eat of him. / May I ~ you for some money?*① 2. ask earnestly ; entreat ; request. (*~ someone to do* ; *~ that …* ; *~ to do*) ¶*~ one's life*② */ I begged him to forgive me.*③ */ I ~ you to tell the truth.*④ 　—*vi.* 1. live as a beggar. (*~ on the street.* 2. ask earnestly. (*~ for something*)
　I beg your pardon, ⓐ I ask you to forgive me. ⓑ Say it once more, please.
‡**be·gan** [bigǽn] *v.* pt. of begin.
be·get [bigét] *vt.* (be·got, be·got·ten or be·got, be·get·ting) 1. become the father of (a son). ⇒NB ¶*He begot a son.* 2. be the cause of (something). ¶*Power begets power.* ▷**be·get·ter** [-ər] *n.*
‡**beg·gar** [bégər] *n.* ⓒ 1. a person who lives by begging. ¶*die a ~.*① 2. a very poor person. 　—*vt.* make (someone) poor. ¶*His thoughtless spending will ~ his father.*
beg·gar·ly [bégərli] *adj.* like a beggar ; very poor.
beg·gar·y [bégəri] *n.* Ⓤ extreme poverty.
‡**be·gin** [bigín] *vi.* (be·gan, be·gun) *vi.* 1. start. ¶*School begins at eight.* 2. come into existence ; arise. ¶*The river begins in the mountains.*① 　—*vt.* 1. start the activity of (something). (*~ to do* ; *~ doing*) ¶*~ one's breakfast / ~ to read* (or *reading*) *a new book.*② 2. found ; invent.
　1) *begin at,* start from.
　2) *begin on* (or *upon*), set to work at.
　3) *begin with,* take (something) first.
　4) *to begin with,* in the first place.
be·gin·ner [bigínər] *n.* ⓒ 1. a person who is doing some-

―ⓝ 무구풍뎅이
―ⓥ [벼랑 따위가] 쑥 튀어나오다
―ⓝ 사탕무우의 뿌리
―ⓝ 사탕무우로 만든 설탕

―ⓥ [나쁜 일이] 일어나다 ; …의 몸에 닥치다

―ⓥ …에 적합하다, 어울리다

―ⓐ 적당한, 어울리는
―ⓐ 적당히, 어울리게
―ⓥ …을 짙은 안개로 덮다 ; 낯처네 만들다 ; [설명 따위를] 흐리멍덩하게
―ⓥ …을 놀리다 ; 속이다　[하다
―ⓐ 1. 앞쪽에(을), 전면에 ¶①그는 앞으로 달렸다 2. 앞서서, 미리, 이미

―ⓟ 1. [장소]의 앞에 2. …의 면전에 3. …보다 먼저(빨리) ; 이전에 4. (口) …보다 오히려 5. …보다 우위의, 상위의 ¶②일이 즐거움에 앞서야 한다
圈 1)곧, 오래지 않아 2)태어나기 전에 ; 시대에 앞서서
―ⓒ 1. …보다 앞서(빨리) ; …이 되기 전에 2. …보다 오히려
―ⓐ 미리, 앞서서 ¶①너는 의심이 너무 지나치다

―ⓥ …을 더럽히다
―ⓥ …의 편이 되다, …을 돕다
―ⓥ 1. …을 구걸하다 ¶①돈을 좀 주지 않겠소? 2. …을 빌다, 간청하다 ¶②살려 달라고 빌다/③그에게 용서해 달라고 빌었다/④제발 진실을 말해 주시오　—ⓥ 1. 걸식하다 2. 부탁하다, 간청하다

圈 ⓐ용서하십시오 ⓑ다시 한번 말해 주시오

―ⓥ 1. [아버지가] 자식을 보다 NB 모친의 경우는 bear 2. …을 초래하다, …의 원인이 되다

―ⓝ 1. 거지 ¶①객사하다 2. 가난뱅이
―ⓥ …을 가난하게 만들다

―ⓐ 거지 같은, 아주 가난한
―ⓝ 거지 신세, 빈곤
―ⓥ 1. 시작되다 2. 일어나다, 발생하다 ¶①그 강은 저 산맥에서 시작된다　—ⓥ 1. …에 착수하다, …을 시작하다 ¶②새 책을 읽기 시작하다 2. …을 설립하다 ; 발명하다

圈 1)…부터 시작하다 2)…에 착수하다 3)…부터 시작하다 4)우선 제일 먼저

―ⓝ 1. 초심자 2. 창시자

thing for the first time. **2.** a person who begins anything.

⁑ **be·gin·ning** [bigíniŋ] *n.* [C] ↔end **1.** the start. ¶*at* (or *in*) *the ~ of the year.*① **2.** the time or place at which anything begins; the origin; the source. **3.** the first part.
—[名] 1. 시초 ¶①연초에 2. 발단, 기원 3. 초기, 당초

be·gone [bigɔ́:n / -gɔ́n] *interj., vi.* go away. ¶*Begone!* / *She bade him ~.*
—[感] 물러가라! —[自] 가 버리다

be·got [bigɑ́t / -gɔ́t] *v.* pt. and pp. of **beget.**

be·got·ten [bigɑ́tn / -gɔ́tn] *v.* pp. of **beget.**

be·grime [bigráim] *vt.* make (something) dirty.
—[他] …을 더럽히다

be·grudge [bigrʌ́dʒ] *vt.* **1.** envy. ¶*~ someone his good luck.* **2.** be unwilling to give. ¶*He begrudges his wife money.*① ▷**be·grudg·ing·ly** [-iŋli] *adv.*
—[他] 1. …을 시기하다 2. …을 내기 싫어하다 ¶①그는 아내에게 돈 주기를 아까와한다

be·guile [bigáil] *vt.* **1.** deceive; mislead. 《~ someone *into doing*; ~ someone *of* (or *out of*)》 **2.** entertain; amuse. 《~ someone *with*》
—[他] 1. …을 속이다 2. …을 즐겁게 하다; 재미있게 하다

⁑ **be·gun** [bigʌ́n] *v.* pp. of **begin.**

* **be·half** [bihǽf / -hɑ́:f] *n.* [U] interest; favor. ⇒[usage]
1) ***in behalf of*** (=*in the interest of; for*) ***someone.***
2) ***on behalf of someone; on someone's behalf,*** ⓐ as a representative of someone. ¶*I attended the meeting on his ~.*① ⓑ in behalf of someone.
—[名] 이익 [usage] 다음 숙어에만 씀
[熟] 1)…을 위해서 2)ⓐ…을 대표하여; …에 대신하여 ¶①그를 대신하여 내가 모임에 나갔다 ⓑ…을 위해서

* **be·have** [bihéiv] *vt.* 《*reflexibly*》 conduct. ¶*Behave yourself!*① / *~ oneself like a man.* **—*vi.*** **1.** conduct. **2.** act well. ¶*Did the child ~?*
—[他] 처신하다 ¶①얌전하게 굴어라
—[自] 1. 처신하다 2. 얌전하게 굴다

* **be·hav·ior** [bihéivjər] *n.* [U] **1.** acts. **2.** manners. ¶*good ~.*
—[名] 1. 행위 2. 태도, 행실, 품행

be·head [bihéd] *vt.* cut off the head of (someone).
—[他] …의 목을 자르다

* **be·held** [bihéld] *v.* pt. and pp. of **behold.**

be·hest [bihést] *n.* [C] (*poetic*) a command; an order.
—[名] 명령

⁑ **be·hind** [biháind] *adv.* **1.** in a former place; at an earlier time. ¶*leave someone ~.*① **2.** in or to the back. ¶*Look ~.* **3.** not so good as. **4.** late; slow. ¶*The watch runs ~.*② **5.** at one's back; at the back.
—[副] 1. 먼저 장소에, 일찌기 ¶①남을 뒤에 남겨 놓다 2. 뒤에, 뒤로 3. …보다 나쁘게 4. 늦어서, 뒤져서 ¶②이 시계는 늦는다 5. 배후에, 이면에[서]

—*prep.* **1.** at the back of; hidden from view by. ¶*The sun has sunk ~ the hill.* **2.** later than. ¶*The train is five minutes ~ time.* **3.** alone after someone has gone away. ¶*He left his wife ~ him.*③ **4.** inferior to; less advanced. ¶*Tom is ~ other boys in his class.*
1) ***behind one's back,*** secretly.
2) ***behind the times,*** out of date.
—[前] 1. …의 뒤에 2. …보다 늦어서 3. [사람이] 사라진 후 ¶③그는 아내를 남기고 죽었다 4. …보다 못하여, 뒤떨어져서
[熟] 1)몰래 2)시대에 뒤진

be·hind·hand [biháindhæ̀nd] *adv., adj.* late; behind in progress. ↔beforehand ⇒[usage]
—[副][形] 늦어서, 늦은 [usage] 형용사로서는 서술용법에만 씀

⁑ **be·hold** [bihóuld] *vt.* (**be·held**) watch; look at.
—[他] …을 보다

be·hold·en [bihóuld(ə)n] *adj.* under an obligation; indebted. ¶*I am greatly ~ to you for your kindness.*①
—[形] 은혜를 입은, 신세를 진 ¶①정말로 신세졌읍니다

be·hoof [bihú:f] *n.* [U] use; advantage. ⇒[usage]
in (or ***for, to, on***) ***someone's behoof,*** for someone's own use or advantage. ¶*spend money for his children's ~.*
—[名] [usage] 다음 숙어에만 씀
[熟] …을 위하여

be·hoove [bihú:v] *vt.* be necessary for (some one). 《~ someone *to do*》 ¶*It behooves him to do so.*① ⇒[usage]
—[他] …의 의무이다 ¶①그는 그렇게 하는 것이 마땅하다 [usage] 항상 it를 주어로 함

be·hove [bihóuv] *vt.* (chiefly *Brit.*)=behoove.

beige [beiʒ] *n.* [U] **1.** soft material of natural wool. **2.** a very light brown color; the color of natural wool.
—[名] 1. 원모 그대로의 모직물 2. 회갈색; 베이지색

⁑ **be·ing** [bí:iŋ] *n.* **1.** [U] existence; life. ¶*the aim of our ~* / *~ in itself.*① **2.** [C] a living creature; a human creature. ¶*a human ~* / *human beings.*② **3.** [U] essential nature.
1) ***come into being,*** begin to exist; be made.
2) ***the Supreme Being,*** God.
—[名] 1. 존재; 인생 ¶①실재(實在) 그 자체 2. 살아 있는 것, 인간 ¶②인류 3. 본질; 천성
[熟] 1)태어나다, 생기다 2)신

be·jew·el [bidʒú(:)əl] *vt.* (**-eled, -el·ing** or *Brit.* **-elled, -el·ling**) adorn (something) with jewels.
—[他] …을 보석으로 꾸미다

be·lat·ed [biléitid] *adj.* **1.** too late; delayed. ¶*a ~ letter.* **2.** overtaken by darkness. ▷**be·lat·ed·ly** [-li] *adv.*
—[形] 1. 늦어진 2. [나그네가] 길이 저문

belch [beltʃ] *vi., vt.* **1.** throw out gas from the stomach through the mouth. **2.** throw out (flame, smoke, etc.) with force. **—*n.*** [U] the act of belching.
—[自][他] 1. 트림하다 2. [불길·연기 따위]를 뿜어내다, 분출하다 —[名] 트림; 분출

bel·fry [bélfri] *n.* ⓒ (pl. **-fries**) a bell tower. ⇒fig. —ⓝ 종루(鐘樓)

Bel·gian [béldʒ(ə)n, +U.S. -dʒiən] *adj.* of Belgium or its people. —*n.* ⓒ a person of Belgium. —ⓐ 벨기에[사람]의 —ⓝ 벨기에 사람

* **Bel·gium** [béldʒəm, +U.S. -dʒiəm] *n.* a country in western Europe. ⇒N.B. —ⓝ 벨기에 N.B. 수도 Brussels

be·lie [bilái] *vt.* (**-lied, -ly·ing**) **1.** give a false impression of (something). ¶*Her cheerful speaking belied her feelings.*① **2.** disappoint. ¶*The result has belied our expectations.*② —ⓥ 1. …을 속이다 ¶①그녀의 쾌활한 이야기는 그녀의 감정을 속이고 있다 2. …어기다, 배반하다 ¶②결과는 우리 기대에 어긋났다

‡ **be·lief** [bilíːf] *n.* (pl. **-liefs**) ⓤ **1.** something believed; a convinced opinion. **2.** acceptance as true or existing. (~ *in*) ¶~ *in ghosts.*① **3.** trust. **4.** ⓤⓒ a religious faith. ¶*the Buddhist ~ / I have no ~ in God.*
 1) *beyond belief,* that cannot be believed.
 2) *to the best of one's belief,* as far as one knows.
[belfry] —ⓝ 1. 신념; 소신 2. 정말이라고 믿음 ¶①유령의 존재를 믿음 3. 신용 4. 신앙

圏 1) 믿을 수 없는 2) …이 믿는(아는) 바로는

be·liev·a·ble [bilíːvəbl] *adj.* that can be believed. —ⓐ 믿을 수 있는

‡ **be·lieve** [bilíːv] *vt.* **1.** accept (something or someone) as true or honest. ¶*I ~ you. / I ~ what he says. / I ~ him to be honest.* **2.** hold (something) as an opinion; think; suppose. —*vi.* **1.** have firm religious faith. **2.** have a firm conviction. **3.** think; suppose.
 believe in, have faith in the existence, truth, possibility, etc. of (something). ⌈*in Buddhism.*①⌉ —ⓥ 1. …을 믿다 2. …이라고 생각하고 있다 —ⓥ 1. 신앙하다 2. 믿다, 확신하다 3. 생각하고 있다

圏 …의 존재(효력·현명함)를 믿다

be·liev·er [bilíːvər] *n.* ⓒ a person who believes. —ⓝ 믿는 사람 ¶①불교 신자

be·lit·tle [bilítl] *vt.* **1.** regard (something) as less important than it is; speak of (something) as unimportant. ¶~ *someone's merit.* **2.** make (something) small. —ⓥ 1. …을 얕보다, 경시하다; 헐뜯다 2. …을 작아지게 하다

‡ **bell** [bel] *n.* ⓒ **1.** a hollow metal cup that makes a sound when struck by a hammer. **2.** the sound of a bell. **3.** a thing shaped like a bell. —*vt.* put a bell on (something). *bell the cat,* attempt something dangerous. ⌊thing.⌋ —ⓝ 1. 종; 방울, 벨 2. 종 모양의 것 —ⓥ …에 종(방울)을 달다

圏 위험한 일을 시도하다

Bell [bel], **Alexander Graham** (1847-1922), *n.* an American scientist and the inventor of the telephone. —ⓝ 미국의 과학자·전화기 발명가

bell·boy [bélbɔ̀i] *n.* ⓒ (U.S.) a man whose work is carrying baggage and doing errands at a hotel or club. —ⓝ (美) [호텔·클럽의] 급사, 보이

bell buoy [˂ ˂] *n.* a buoy with a bell rung by waves' motion. —ⓝ 타종부표(打鐘浮標)

* **belle** [bel] *n.* ⓒ a beautiful woman or girl, esp. the most beautiful one in a group. ¶*She was the~of the party.* —ⓝ 미녀; 제일가는 미녀

belles-let·tres [bellétr(ə), -létər / -létr] *n. pl.* ((used as *sing.*)) the finer forms of literature; writings of the purely literary kind. ⌈like bells.⌉ —ⓝ 순문학

bell·flow·er [bélflàuər] *n.* ⓒ a plant with flowers shaped —ⓝ 초롱꽃

bel·li·cose [bélikòus] *adj.* fond of war; inclined to fight. ▷ **bel·li·cos·i·ty** [bèlikásiti / -kɔ́s-] *n.* ⌈belligerent.⌉ —ⓐ 싸움을 좋아하는; 호전적인

bel·lig·er·en·cy [bilídʒərənsi] *n.* ⓤ the state of being —ⓝ 교전상태

bel·lig·er·ent [bilídʒərənt] *adj.* **1.** fond of war. **2.** being at war. ¶~ *powers.*① **3.** of nations at war. —*n.* ⓒ a nation at war. ▷ **bel·lig·er·ent·ly** [-li] *adv.* —ⓐ 1. 호전적인 2. 교전중인 ¶①교전국 3. 교전국의 —ⓝ 교전국

* **bel·low** [bélou] *vi., vt.* **1.** make a loud and deep cry, as of a bull. **2.** cry loudly and deeply. ¶*a man bellowing with anger.* —*n.* ⓒ the sound of bellowing. —ⓥ 1. [소 따위가] 큰 소리로 울다 2. 울부짖다, 으르렁거리다 —ⓝ [소 따위의] 울음소리, 짖는 소리, 고함

bel·lows [bélouz] *n.* ⓒ (pl. **-lows**) **1.** an instrument for producing a strong blast of air. ⇒fig. **2.** the folding part of a camera, etc. —ⓝ 1. 풀무 2. [사진기 따위의] 주름통

bell tent [˂ ˂] *n.* a tent shaped like a bell. —ⓝ 종 모양의 텐트

bell tower [˂ ˂–] *n.* a tower that supports or shelters a bell or bells. —ⓝ 종루(鐘樓)

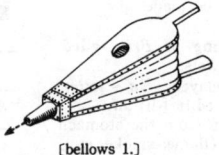
[bellows 1.]

bell·weth·er [bélwèðər] *n.* ⓒ **1.** a male sheep with a bell on his neck, usu. the leader of the group. **2.** a leader.
—ⓝ **1.** 방울을 달고 양떼를 인도해 가는 수양 **2.** 지도자

* **bel·ly** [béli] *n.* ⓒ (pl. **-lies**) **1.** the lower front of the human body; the under part of an animal's body; the abdomen; the stomach. →ᴜꜱᴀɢᴇ **2.** the swelling part of anything. —*vi., vt.* (**-lied**) swell out. ¶*Sails ~ out.*
—ⓝ **1.** [사람·짐승의] 배, 복부; 위 ᴜꜱᴀɢᴇ 여성의 경우는 보통 stomach 를 씀 **2.** 부푼 부분 —ⓥ 부풀다, 부풀리다

bel·ly·ful [bélifùl] *n.* ⓒ as much as one can eat.
—ⓝ 배 가득, 만복

‡ **be·long** [bilɔ́:ŋ / -lɔ́ŋ] *vi.* **1.** have a proper place. **2.** be the property of (someone); be a member of (something). 《~ *to* someone or something》 ¶*This book belongs to my brother.* / *He belongs in this club.* →ᴜꜱᴀɢᴇ
—ⓥ **1.** [있어야 할 곳에] 있다 **2.** […의] 소유물이다; […의] 일원이다; 속하다 ᴜꜱᴀɢᴇ 미국에서는 to 이외의 전치사도 씀

be·long·ings [bilɔ́:ŋiŋz / -lɔ́ŋ-] *n. pl.* a person's property; possessions.
—ⓝ 재산, 소유물

* **be·lov·ed** [bilʌ́vd, -lʌ́vid] *adj.* dearly loved. —*n.* 《one's ~》 a person who is loved ¶*my ~.*①
—ⓐ 귀여운 —ⓝ 사랑하는 사람 ¶①여보, 당신

‡ **be·low** [bilóu] *adv.* ↔above **1.** in or to a lower place; downstairs. **2.** on earth. **3.** in or to hell. **4.** in or to a lower rank or number.
—*prep.* ↔above **1.** in or to a lower place than. ¶*~ one's eyes*① / *The sun has sunk ~ the horizon.* **2.** (as in rank) inferior to; less than. ¶*She is ~ me in the class.* **3.** not worthy of; beneath. ¶*This job is ~ his ability.*
—ⓐ **1.** 밑에, 밑으로; 아래층에 **2.** 저상에[서]; 이 세상에서 **3.** 지옥에서 **4.** 아래 계급에[서], 아래 숫자에
—ⓟ **1.** …보다 밑(아래)에 ¶①눈아래에 **2.** [계급 따위] …보다 낮은(못한); …보다 적은 **3.** …의 가치가 없는

‡ **belt** [belt] *n.* ⓒ **1.** a strip of leather, cloth, etc. put around the waist; a band. ¶*undo one's ~.*① **2.** a district having distinctive characteristics. 《*a forest ~* / *a ~ of cotton plantations.*② **3.** an endless band that moves by wheels. ¶*a ~ conveyer.*③
below the belt, unfair; unfairly.
tighten one's belt, be more economical.
—*vt.* **1.** put a belt around (something). **2.** fasten (something) with a belt. ¶*~ on a sword.*④
—ⓝ **1.** 허리띠, 혁대 ¶①허리띠를 늦추다 **2.** 지대 ¶②목화 재배지대 **3.** 벨트, 피대 ¶③벨트 콘베이어

🔲 1)부정(不正)한, 부정하게 2)내핍생활을 하다; 긴축재정을 쓰다
—ⓥ **1.** …에 띠를 감다 **2.** …을 띠로 비끄러매다 ¶④칼을 차다

be·ly·ing [biláiiŋ] *v.* ppr. of belie.
be·moan [bimóun] *vt.* moan over (something); lament for (something).
—ⓥ …을 슬퍼하다

Ben [ben] *n.* a nickname of Benjamin.
—ⓝ Benjamin의 애칭

‡ **bench** [bentʃ] *n.* ⓒ **1.** a long seat. **2.** a judge's seat. **3.** 《*collectively*》 ⓤ judges. ¶*~ and bar.*① **4.** a law court.
on the bench, ⓐ serving as a judge in a law court. ⓑ (*in sports*) sitting as a substitute player.
—ⓝ **1.** 벤치 **2.** 판사석 **3.** 재판관 ¶①판사와 변호사 **4.** 법정

🔲 ⓐ판사석에 앉아 있는 ⓑ[야구선수가] 보결선수로서 벤치에 앉아 있는

‡ **bend** [bend] *v.* (**bent**) *vt.* **1.** force (a straight line) into a curve or an angle. **2.** force (someone) to submit. 《~ someone *to*》 **3.** turn (efforts, eyes, etc.) in a certain direction. —*vi.* **1.** become curved; turn. **2.** stoop; crouch; bow. **3.** submit; yield. 《~ *to* someone's will》
be bent (=*be determined*) *on something.*
—*n.* **1.** ⓤ the act of bending. **2.** ⓒ a curved part.
—ⓥ **1.** …을 구부리다 **2.** …을 굴복시키다 **3.** …을 [어떤 방향]으로 돌리다 —ⓥ **1.** 구부러지다 **2.** 구부리다; 절하다 **3.** 굴복하다

🔲 …에 마음이 기울어져 있다
—ⓝ **1.** 구부리기 **2.** 굽은 부분

‡ **be·neath** [binf:θ] *adv.* below; underneath. —*prep.* **1.** below; under; lower in place than. ¶*A lieutenant is ~ a captain.* **2.** unworthy of. ¶*A~ contempt.*
—ⓐ 아래에 —ⓟ **1.** …의 아래에; [신분·지위가] 보다 낮은 **2.** …의 가치가 없는

Ben·e·dic·tine [bènidíkti:n→] *adj.*) *n.* **1.** ⓒ a monk or nun following the teachings of Saint Benedict. **2.** ⓤ 《*b-*》 a kind of liqueur. —*adj.* bènidíktin, +U.S. -ti:n] of Saint Benedict or the Benedictines.
—ⓝ **1.** 베네딕트파의 수도사(수녀) **2.** 베네딕틴 술 —ⓐ 성(聖) 베네딕트[파]의

ben·e·dic·tion [bènidíkʃ(ə)n] *n.* ⓤⓒ **1.** the act of asking a blessing at the end of a church service. **2.** a blessing.
—ⓝ **1.** 예배 전후의 기도 **2.** 축복

ben·e·fac·tion [bènifækʃ(ə)n] *n.* **1.** ⓤ the act of doing good. **2.** ⓒ a benefit given; a gift for charity.
—ⓝ **1.** 선행(善行) **2.** 희사(喜捨)

ben·e·fac·tor [bénifæktər, ⸌⸌⸌⸌] *n.* ⓒ a person who has given money to a school, hospital, etc.; a person who kindly helps.
—ⓝ 은인; 후원자

ben·e·fac·tress [bénifæktris, ⸌⸌⸌⸌] *n.* ⓒ a woman benefactor.
—ⓝ benefactor의 여성형

be·nef·i·cence [binéfis(ə)ns] *n.* **1.** ⓤ kindness; the act of doing good. **2.** ⓒ a kind act. **3.** ⓒ a gift.
—ⓝ **1.** 친절; 선행 **2.** 친절한 행위 **3.** 기증하는 물건

be·nef·i·cent [binéfis(ə)nt] *adj.* kind; doing good.
—[形] 친절한; 선행의

ben·e·fi·cial [bèniffʃ(ə)l] *adj.* helpful; producing good results.
—[形] 유익한

ben·e·fi·ci·ar·y [benifíʃəri] *n.* [C] (pl. **-ar·ies**) **1.** a person who receives benefits or profits. **2.** a person who receives money or other property under an insurance policy or a will.
—[名] 1. 은혜를 입는 사람 2. [보험의] 수익자(受益者); 유산 상속인

‡ ben·e·fit [bénifit] *n.* [C] **1.** [U] anything that is helpful; an advantage. **2.** a kind act; a favor. **3.** money paid to a sick or an old person. **4.** a bazaar, dance, show, etc. held for charity.
—[名] 1. 이익 2. 친절한 행위; 친절 3. [환자·노인에 대한] 급여금 4. 자선 흥행

—*vt.* do good to (someone or something); help. ¶*The fresh air benefits you.* —*vi.* get good; receive help.
—[他] …의 이익이 되다; …을 돕다 —[自] 이익(도움)을 받다

be·nev·o·lence [binévələns] *n.* **1.** [U] good will; mercy. ↔malevolence **2.** [C] a kind act.
—[名] 1. 자비심, 박애 2. 선행, 자선

be·nev·o·lent [binévələnt] *adj.* ↔malevolent **1.** kind. ¶*a ~ rich man.* **2.** generous.
—[形] 1. 자애로운; 자선적인 2. 인정 많은

be·nev·o·lent·ly [binévələntli] *adv.* in a benevolent manner.
—[副] 자애롭게; 인정 많게

be·night·ed [bináitid] *adj.* **1.** overtaken by night; being in darkness. ¶*a ~ traveler.*① **2.** not knowing right and wrong; not educated.
—[形] 1. 밤이 된, 갈 길이 저문 ¶①길이 저문 나그네 2. 어리석은; 무식한

be·nign [bináin] *adj.* **1.** kind; gentle. ¶*a ~ old master.* **2.** favorable; mild. ¶*a ~ climate.* **3.** (of diseases) not very serious. ↔malignant
—[形] 1. 친절한, 상냥한 2. 좋은, 온화한 3. [병이] 악성이 아닌

be·nig·nant [binígnənt] *adj.* **1.** kind; gentle. **2.** useful.
—[形] 1. 자비심 깊은, 인정있는 2. 유익한

be·nig·nant·ly [binígnəntli] *adv.* **1.** with kindness. **2.** in a useful manner.
—[副] 1. 인자하게, 상냥하게, 자애롭게 2. 유익하게

be·nig·ni·ty [binígniti] *n.* (pl. **-ties**) **1.** [U] the state of being kind. **2.** [C] a kind act; a favor.
—[名] 1. 인자함, 자애로움 2. 자비로운 행위; 은혜

be·nign·ly [bináinli] *adv.* gently; with kindness.
—[副] 다정하게, 친절하게

Ben·ja·min [béndʒəmin] *n.* a man's name.
—[名] 남자 이름

‡ bent [bent] *v.* pt. and pp. of **bend.** —*adj.* **1.** not straight. **2.** strongly inclined; determined. ¶*He is ~ on becoming an artist.*① —*n.* 《*a ~; one's ~*》 a natural interest or ability. ¶*a ~ for poetry.*②
—[形] 1. 똑바르지 않은, 굽은 2. 열중한; 결심한 ¶①그는 화가가 되기로 결심하고 있다 —[名] 경향, 성벽 ¶②시재(詩才)

be·numb [binʌ́m] *vt.* 《usu. in *passive*》 **1.** make (one's fingers, etc.) have no feeling or powerless. ¶*My fingers were benumbed with cold.*① **2.** make (the mind, will, feelings, etc.) senseless.
—[他] 1. [추위 따위가] …을 무감각하게 하다 ¶①내 손가락은 추위로 마비되었다 2. [마음·의지·가정 따위]를 마비시키다

ben·zene [bénzi:n, -ˊ] *n.* [U] a colorless liquid which is got from coal-tar and which burns easily.
—[名] 벤젠

ben·zine [bénzi:n, -ˊ] *n.* [U] a colorless, light liquid obtained from oil.
—[名] 벤진, 휘발유

be·queath [bikwí:ð, -kwí:θ] *vt.* **1.** give or leave (a property, etc.) by a will. ¶*The father bequeathed the old house to his son.*① **2.** hand down or pass on (something) to those who come after. ¶*The old story has been bequeathed by word of mouth.*②
—[他] 1. [재산]을 유언으로 양도하다 ¶①부친은 오래된 집을 유언으로 아들에게 넘겨 주었다 2. …을 후세에 남기다; 전하다 ¶②그 옛이야기는 입으로 전하여져 왔다

be·quest [bikwést] *n.* **1.** [C] money, property, etc. left to someone by a will. **2.** [U] the act of bequeathing.
—[名] 1. 유증물(遺贈物), 유산, 유물 2. 유증

be·reave [birí:v] *vt.* (**-reaved** or **-reft**) take away; rob. 《~ someone *of*》 ¶*His death bereft her of all her hope.*① / *Death bereaved him of his wife.*②
—[他] …에서 빼앗다 ¶①그의 죽음으로 그녀는 모든 희망을 빼앗겼다/②그는 상처를 했다

be·reaved [birí:vd] *adj.* having lost one's husband, wife, etc. ¶*a war-bereaved widow*① / *be ~ of one's wife.*②
—[形] [가족 따위를] 잃은 ¶①전쟁 미망인/②상처하다

be·reave·ment [birí:vmənt] *n.* [U][C] loss of a relative or friend by death. ¶*We sympathize with you in your ~.*①
—[名] 상실, 사별(死別) ¶①당하신 불행에 동정을 드립니다

be·reft [biréft] *v.* pt. and pp. of **bereave.**
—*adj.* having lost someone; left sad and lonely by death.
—[形] 잃은; 빼앗긴; 사별한

be·ret [bəréi, bérei] *n.* [C] a soft, flat and round woolen cap.
—[名] 베레모자

berg [bə:rg] *n.* [C] a large mass of ice in the sea.
—[名] 빙산

ber·i·ber·i [béribéri] *n.* [U] a disease caused by a lack of vitamin B.
—[名] 각기병

Ber·ing Sea [bériŋsí:, +*U.S.* bíər-], **the** *n.* the sea in the north Pacific between Alaska and Siberia.
—[名] 베링해(시베리아와 알래스카 사이)

Bering Strait [bériŋstréit, +*U.S.* bíər-], **the** *n.* the narrow channel between the Bering Sea and the Arctic Ocean.
—[名] 베링 해협

Berk·shire [bə́:rkʃ(i)ər / bɑ́:k-] *n.* **1.** a county in south England. **2.** [C] a kind of black-and-white pig.
—[名] 1. 영국 남부의 주 2. 검은 돼지의 일종

* **Ber·lin** [bə:rlín] *n.* the capital of East Germany.
—[名] 베를린(동독의 수도)

Ber·mu·da [bərmjú:də] *n.* a group of British islands in the west Atlantic.
—[名] 대서양 서부의 영령 제도

Bern, Berne [bə:rn] *n.* the capital of Switzerland.
—[名] 베른(스위스의 수도)

Ber·nard [bə́:rnərd] *n.* a man's name.
—[名] 남자 이름

‡ **ber·ry** [béri] *n.* [C] (pl. **-ries**) **1.** a small, juicy fruit with many seeds, such as strawberries. **2.** a dry seed of various plants, as of the coffee plant. —*vi.* gather or pick berries. ¶*go berrying.*①
—[名] 1. 장과(漿果) 2. [밀·코오피 따위의] 열매, 알갱이 —[自] 열매를 따다 ¶①딸기를 따러 가다

berth [bə:rθ] *n.* [C] **1.** a sleeping place on a ship, train, etc. **2.** a place for a ship to anchor. **3.** a place to live in for a time.
—[名] 1. [배·기차 따위의] 침대 2. [배의] 정박 위치, 정박 장소 3. 숙박소
give a wide berth to, keep a safe distance from (someone or something); avoid.
[熟] …을 경원하다, 멀리하다
—*vt.* put (a ship) in a berth; provide (someone) with a berth. —*vi.* have or occupy a berth.
—[他] [배]를 정박시키다; …에게 침대(방)를 주다 —[自] 숙박하다

Ber·tha [bə́:rθə] *n.* a woman's name. ⇒[N.B.]
—[名] 여자 이름 [N.B.] 애칭은 Bertie

ber·yl [béril] *n.* [U] a very hard jewel stone, green or blue.
—[名] 녹주석(綠柱石)

* **be·seech** [bisí:tʃ] *vt.* (**be·sought**) ask earnestly; beg. 《~ someone *to do*; ~ someone *for*》 ¶*I ~ you to tell me the truth.*①
—[他] …을 간청하다, 탄원하다 ¶①제발 사실을 말해 주시오

be·seech·ing·ly [bisí:tʃiŋli] *adv.* in a begging manner.
—[副] 간청(애원)하듯이

be·set [bisét] *vt.* (**-set, -set·ting**) **1.** attack (someone or something) on all sides; attack; worry. ¶*be beset by many doubts.*① **2.** surround. ¶*Dangers ~ her path. / The story is beset with contradictions.*② **3.** 《usu. in *passive*》 set. ¶*a bracelet beset with jewels.*
—[他] 1. …을 사방에서 공격하다; 괴롭히다 ¶①여러가지 의심에 사로잡히다 2. …을 둘러싸다 ¶②그 이야기는 모순 투성이다 3. …을 끼워(박아) 넣다

be·set·ting [bisétiŋ] *adj.* 《usu. as *attributive*》 constantly attacking. ¶*~ sins*① / *a ~ temptation.*
—[形] 늘 붙어다니는 ¶①사람이 늘 빠지기 쉬운 죄

‡ **be·side** [bisáid] *prep.* **1.** by the side of; near. ¶*Come and sit ~ me. / I want to live ~ the sea.* **2.** compared with. ¶*You are quite tall ~ your sister.*① **3.** away from.
1) ***beside oneself,*** out of one's mind; mad.
2) ***beside the point*** (or ***mark***)***,*** having nothing to do with the subject being discussed.
—[前] 1. …의 곁(옆)에[서], …의 가까이에 2. …와 비교하여 ¶①누이에 비하면 너는 키가 퍽 크다 3. …을 떠나서
[熟] 1)정신이 나가서; 미쳐서 2)엉뚱한

‡ **be·sides** [bisáidz] *adv.* **1.** also; moreover; further. ¶*I'm tired; ~ I'm sleepy.* **2.** otherwise; else. —*prep.* **1.** in addition to. ¶*There were six people ~ Tom.* **2.** except; other than. ⇒[usage] ¶*He has nothing ~ his salary.*
—[副] 1. 그 위에, 게다가 2. 따로 —[前] 1. …에 더하여 2. …외에는, …을 제외하고 [usage] 이 의미는 부정문·의문문의 경우에만 쓰임

be·siege [bisí:dʒ] *vt.* **1.** surround or attack (a place) with armed forces. ¶*~ a city.* **2.** crowd. ¶*The famous pianist was besieged by many admirers.*① **3.** trouble (someone) with requests, questions, etc. 《~ someone *with*》 ¶*The teacher was besieged with questions.*
—[他] 1. …을 포위하다; 습격하다 2. …에 떼지어 모이다, 쇄도하다 ¶①그 유명한 피아니스트는 많은 팬에게 둘러싸였다 3. [탄원·질문 따위로] …을 괴롭히다

be·sieg·er [bisí:dʒər] *n.* [C] a member of a besieging army; 《*pl.*》 a besieging army. ⇒[N.B.]
—[名] 포위자; 포위군 [N.B.] 「포위당한 사람」은 the besieged

be·smear [bismíər] *vt.* cover (something) with oil, etc.
—[他] …에 기름 따위를 처바르다

be·smirch [bismə́:rtʃ] *vt.* make (something) dirty; bring shame upon (someone's honor, fame, etc.).
—[他] …을 더럽히다; [명예·명성 따위]를 더럽히다

be·som [bí:zəm] *n.* [C] a long brush for sweeping, made of thin branches.
—[名] 싸리비, 대비

be·sot·ted [bisɑ́tid / -sɔ́t-] *adj.* **1.** foolish; stupid; senseless. **2.** drunk.
—[形] 1. 어리석은, 의식이 없는 2. 술취한

be·sought [bisɔ́:t] *v.* pt. and pp. of **beseech.**

be·span·gle [bispǽŋgl] *vt.* make (something) beautiful with small pieces of bright metal.
—[他] …을 반짝이는 것으로 장식하다

be·spat·ter [bispǽtər] *vt.* **1.** splash. 《~ someone or something *with*》 **2.** speak ill of (someone).
—[他] 1. …을 뿌리다, 튀기다 2. …에게 욕지거리하다, 욕설을 퍼붓다

be·speak [bispí:k] *vt.* (**-spoke, -spok·en** or **-spoke**) **1.** order; reserve. ¶ ~ *tickets for the opera.* **2.** give evidence of (something); show. ¶ *This bespeaks his generous nature.*① —[他] 1. …을 예약하다; 주문하다 2. …을 나타내다 ¶①이것으로 그가 인자한 성격임을 알 수 있다

be·spoke [bispóuk] *v.* pt. and pp. of **bespeak.**

be·spok·en [bispóuk(ə)n] *v.* pp. of **bespeak.**

Bess [bes] *n.* a nickname for Elizabeth. —[名] Elizabeth의 애칭

Bes·sie, Bes·sy [bési] *n.* =Bess.

:best [best] *adj.* (superl. of **good**) excelling all others; having the highest degree of quality. —[形] 제일 좋은, 최상의

1) ***get the best of,*** win in a contest; outdo.
2) ***make the best of,*** utilize (something) as well as one can.
3) ***to the best of one's ability,*** as well as one can.
4) ***You had best do,*** It is your best course to do.

[熟] 1)이기다 2)…을 가장 잘 이용하다 3)힘 자라는 대로, 최선을 다하여 4)…하는 것이 제일 좋다

bes·tial [béstʃəl, ·tiəl / ·tiəl] *adj.* like a beast; cruel; very bad. ▷**bes·tial·ly** [-i] *adv.* —[形] 짐승 같은, 흉포한, 천한

·be·stow [bistóu] *vt.* present (something) as a gift; give. (~ something *on*) ¶*He bestowed all his books on me.* —[他] …을 수여(증여)하다

be·stow·al [bistóuəl] *n.* [U] [C] the act of giving. —[名] 증여, 수여

be·strew [bistrú:] *vt.* (**-strewed, -strewed** or **-strewn**) **1.** throw (things) here and there. **2.** scatter things over (a place). (~ a place *with*) ¶~ *the room with flowers* / *the streets bestrewn with dead leaves.*① —[他] 1. …을 흩뿌리다 2. …에 뿌리다 ¶①낙엽이 쌓인 가로

be·strewn [bistrú:n] *v.* pp. of **bestrew.**

be·strid [bistríd] *v.* pt. and pp. of **bestride.**

be·strid·den [bistrídn] *v.* pp. of **bestride.**

be·stride [bistráid] *vt.* (**-strode** or **-strid, -strid·den** or **-strid**) **1.** get on or sit on (something) with legs apart. ¶~ *a horse.* **2.** step over. ¶~ *a fence.* ⇒[N.B.] —[他] 1. …에 걸터앉다 2. …을 건너뛰다 [N.B.] 무지개 따위가 하늘에 걸칠 때에도 쓰임

be·strode [bistróud] *v.* pt. of **bestride.**

best seller [´ ´-] *n.* **1.** a book, record, etc. that has the largest sale in a given period. **2.** an author of a book with a very large sale. —[名] 1. 베스트셀러 2. 베스트셀러의 작가

·bet [bet] *v.* (**bet** or **bet·ted, bet·ting**) *vt.* agree to give (money, etc.) to another if he guesses right. ¶*I ~ you a dollar on his success.*① —*vi.* make a bet. (~ *on* or *against* one's success, etc.) —[他] [돈 따위]를 걸다 ¶①그가 성공하느냐에 너와 1달러 걸겠다 —[自] 내기를 하다

I bet you; You bet!, Certainly.; without fail. ¶*I ~ you he will fail.*② [熟] 꼭, 반드시 ¶②그는 꼭 실패할 게다

—*n.* [C] **1.** a promise to give money, etc. to another if he guesses right. ¶*an even ~*③ / *lose* (*win*) *a ~.* **2.** the money or thing bet. —[名] 1. 내기 ¶③반반의 내기 2. 건 돈

be·ta [béitə, bí:tə / bí:tə] *n.* [C] the second letter of the Greek alphabet (B, β). —[名] 베타(그리이스 자모의 둘째 자)

be·take [bitéik] *vt.* (**-took, -tak·en**) (usu. *reflexively*) **1.** cause (someone) to go. ¶*He betook himself to the river.*① **2.** apply oneself to (something). —[他] 1. 가다 ¶①그는 강으로 갔다 2. …에 전렴하다

be·tak·en [bitéik(ə)n] *v.* pp. of **betake.**

Beth [beθ] *n.* a nickname for Elizabeth. —[名] …에 전렴하다

be·think [biθíŋk] *vt.* (**-thought**) (usu. *reflexively*) consider; remember. ¶~ *oneself how …*① / ~ *oneself of …*② / ~ *oneself that.* —[他] 생각하다, 숙고하다; 기억해 내다 ¶①…은 어떤지 잘 생각하다 / ②…을 생각해 내다

Beth·le·hem [béθlihèm, ·liəm] *n.* a town in Palestine; the birthplace of Jesus. —[名] 베들레헴; 그리스도의 출생지

be·thought [biθɔ́:t] *v.* pt. and pp. of **bethink.**

be·tide [bitáid] *vt., vi.* happen [to]. ¶*Woe ~ the man!* —[他][自] 일어나다, 생기다

be·times [bitáimz] *adv.* **1.** early. ¶*rise ~.* **2.** in good time; before it is too late. —[副] 1. 일찍 2. 때마침 좋은 때에; 늦기 전에

be·to·ken [bitóuk(ə)n] *vt.* be a sign of (something); show. ¶*Clouds ~ rain.*① —[他] …의 전조이다, …을 나타내다 ¶①검은 구름은 비가 올 전조이다

be·took [bitúk] *v.* pt. of **betake.**

:be·tray [bitréi] *vt.* **1.** sell (a country, etc.) to the enemy. **2.** make (a secret) known; show. ¶~*a secret* / *His words betrayed him.* / *The gate betrays its age.*① **3.** deceive. ¶*He was betrayed into buying an old car.* —[他] 1. …을 적에게 팔다; 배신하다 2. …을 누설하다; [무심코] 드러내다 ¶①그 문은 오래되었음을 나타내고 있다 3. …을 속이다

be·tray·al [bitréi(i)əl] *n.* [C] [U] the act of betraying. —[名] 배신; 밀고; 매국 행위

be·tray·er [bitréi(i)ər] *n.* [C] a person who sells his country, etc. to the enemy. —[名] 배신자; 매국노

be·troth [bitróuð, -tróuθ] *vt.* ⟪usu. in *passive*⟫ arrange (someone) to marry. ¶*His daughter was betrothed to a banker.*①
—[他] …을 약혼시키다 ¶①그의 딸은 은행가와 약혼했다

be·troth·al [bitróuð(ə)l, +*U.S.* -trɔ́:θ-] *n.* [C] a promise to marry.
—[名] 약혼

be·trothed [bitróuðd, +*U.S.* -trɔ́:θt] *n.* ⟪*the* ~; *one's* ~⟫ a person engaged to be married. ¶*my* ~ / *the* ~.①
—[名] 약혼자 ¶①[한 쌍의] 약혼자

‡ **bet·ter**¹ [bétər] *adj.* (compar. of **good**) excelling another; having a higher degree in quality.
—[形] 보다 좋은, 보다 뛰어난

1) ***get the better of*** (=*win a victory over; defeat*) *someone.*
2) ***You had better do,*** It is better for you to do.
3) ***no better than,*** mere. ¶*He is no ~ than a fool.*①
4) ***the better part,*** the majority.

[熟] 1)…에 이기다 2)…하는 편이 낫다 3)단지; …에 불과한 ¶①그는 바보에 지나지 않는다

—*n.* **1.** ⟪*the* ~; *one's* ~⟫ something better. **2.** [C] ⟪usu. *pl.*⟫ a person of higher rank, ability, etc. ¶*his betters.*①
—[名] **1.** 보다 좋은 것 **2.** 손위 사람, 상사, 뛰어난 사람 ¶①그의 손위 사람들

—*adv.* (compar. of **well**) in a more excellent manner.
—[副] 보다 좋게

1) ***better off,*** richer.
2) ***know better,*** be not such a fool. ¶*I know ~ than to do such a thing.*

[熟] 1)한층 더 유복한 2)그런 바보가 아니다

—*vi., vt.* improve; improve upon ¶~ *oneself.*
—[自][他] 좋아지다, 개선하다

bet·ter², **-tor** [bétər] *n.* [C] a person who bets or makes an agreement about paying money if a certain thing happens.
—[名] 내기를 하는 사람

bet·ter·ment [bétərmənt] *n.* [U][C] **1.** improvement. **2.** ⟪usu. *pl.*⟫ an improvement to the value of real property.
—[名] **1.** 개량 **2.** [부동산의] 가격 앙등

bet·ting [bétiŋ] *n.* [U] the act of making bets.
—[名] 내기

Bet·ty [béti] *n.* a nickname for Elizabeth.
—[名] Elizabeth의 애칭

‡ **be·tween** [bitwí:n] *prep.* **1.** in the time, space, or interval that separates. ¶~ *eight and nine.*① **2.** in common to. ¶*a treaty ~ two powers.*② **3.** in comparison of. ¶*There is not much to choose ~ the two.* **4.** from one to the other or another of. ¶*It is about thirty miles ~ this city and that.*
—[前] **1.** [시간·공간]의 사이에서[의] ¶① 8시부터 9시까지의 사이에 **2.** [공통하여] …의 사이에 ¶②양국간의 조약 **3.** [정도 따위] …의 중간에서; 비교하여 **4.** …에서 …까지

—*adv.* between two or more points; between extremes in quantity, character, etc.
—[副] 사이에(로); 이도저도 아니게; 사이를 두고

1) ***between times,*** in the interval between.
2) ***between you and me; between ourselves,*** speaking in confidence.
3) ***in between,*** between. ¶*There were flowers in ~ the trees.*

[熟] 1)이따금 2)비밀이지만 3)…의 사이에

* **be·twixt** [bitwíkst] *prep., adv.* (*archaic*)=between.

bev·el [bév(ə)l] *n.* [C] **1.** a sloping edge. **2.** an instrument for measuring or drawing angles. —*vt.* (**-eled, -el·ing** or esp. *Brit.* **-elled, -el·ling**) give a sloping edge to (something).
—[名] **1.** 사각(斜角), 경사 **2.** 각도자(尺)
—[他] …을 비스듬히 자르다, 사각을 만들다

bev·er·age [bév(ə)ridʒ] *n.* [C] something to drink, such as tea, beer, wine, etc. ¶*intoxicating beverages.*①
—[名] 음료 ¶①알코홀성 음료

bev·y [bévi] *n.* (pl. **bev·ies**) a small group, esp. of women or girls; a flock of birds, esp. of larks or quail.
—[名] [여자의] 떼, 무리; [메추리·종달새 따위의] 떼

be·wail [biwéil] *vt., vi.* mourn; weep; regret deeply.
—[他][自] 슬퍼하다, 울다

* **be·ware** [biwέər] *vi., vt.* guard against (something); be careful. ⟪~ *of* something⟫ ¶*Beware of pickpockets!*① / *Tell him to ~ of the dog.* ⇒[usage]
—[自][他] 조심하다 ¶①소매치기에 조심하시오 [usage] 언제나 원형으로만 쓰임

* **be·wil·der** [biwíldər] *vt.* ⟪chiefly in *passive*⟫ confuse completely. ¶*Tom was bewildered by the examination questions.*①
—[他] …을 당황하게 하다, 갈피를 못잡게 하다 ¶①톰은 시험문제에 당황했다

be·wil·der·ing [biwíldəriŋ] *adj.* causing puzzlement; confusing.
—[形] 당황하게 하는, 갈피를 못잡게 하는

be·wil·der·ing·ly [biwíldəriŋli] *adv.* in a puzzle.
—[副] 당황하여, 어찌할 바를 몰라

be·wil·der·ment [biwíldərmənt] *n.* [U] the state of being confused; complete confusion.
—[名] 당황, 난처함

be·witch [biwítʃ] *vt.* use a magic effect on (someone); charm; delight.
—[他] …에 마법을 걸다; …을 매혹하다

be·witch·ing [biwítʃiŋ] *adj.* delightful; charming.
—[形] 넋을 잃게 하는, 매력있는

be·witch·ing·ly [biwítʃiŋli] *adv.* in a charming manner.
—[副] 매력적으로

‡ **be·yond** [bijánd / -jɔ́nd] *prep.* **1.** at or to the farther side of. **2.** outside the range of; out of sight or hearing of. **3.** more than. **4.** ⟪usu. in *negative* or *interrogative*⟫ except; other than. ¶*Beyond this I know nothing.*①
—[前] **1.** …의 저쪽에 **2.** …의 범위를 넘어서 **3.** …이상의(으로) **4.** …이외에는 ¶①이 이상은 아무것도 모른다

1) *beyond measure,* exceedingly; too much.
2) *It is beyond me,* I cannot understand it.
—*adv.* 1. at or to the farther side; further on; outside. 2. besides.
bi- [bai] *pref.* twice; two; double.: *bicycle* (=a two-wheeled vehicle): *bimonthly* (=every two months).
bi·an·nu·al [baiǽnjuəl] *adj.* coming twice a year.
bi·as [báiəs] *n.* 1. ⓒ a slanting line. ¶*cut a cloth on the ~.*① 2. ⓒⓤ an opinion formed before examining the facts; a prejudice. ¶*She is free from ~.*② 3. ⓒ the weight or force that makes something lean; particular fondness. ⌈one side.⌉
1) *have* (or *be under*) *a bias toward,* have a liking for
2) *without bias and without favor,* fairly.
—*adj.* slanting; sloping.
—*adv.* from corner to corner. ⌈usu.not fairly.⌉
—*vt.* (**-ased, -as·ing** or *Brit.* **-assed, -as·sing**) influence,
bib [bib] *n.* ⓒ 1. a cloth worn under the chin by a baby to keep his other clothing clean. 2. the top part of an apron.
* **Bi·ble** [báibl] *n.* 1. ⓒ (usu. *the ~*) the sacred book of the Christian religion; the Old and New Testaments. ¶*kiss the ~.*① / *on the ~.*② 2. ⓒ (*b-*) any book accepted as an authority. ⌈*quotation.*①⌉
Bib·li·cal, bib- [bíblik(ə)l] *adj.* of the Bible. ¶*~*
bib·li·og·ra·pher [bìbliɔ́grəfər / -ɔ́grəfə] *n.* ⓒ a person who studies the histories of books or who describes and lists them. ⌈raphy.⌉
bib·li·o·graph·i·cal [bìbliəgrǽfik(ə)l] *adj.* of bibliog-
bib·li·og·ra·phy [bìbliɔ́grəfi / -ɔ́g-] *n.* (pl. **-phies**) 1. ⓒ a list of books about a subject or person. ¶*a Shakespeare ~.*① 2. ⓤ the study of the writers, editions, dates, etc., of books. ⌈collects books.⌉
bib·li·o·phile [bíblioufàil] *n.* ⓒ a person who loves or
bi·cam·er·al [baikǽm(ə)rəl] *adj.* having two law-making assemblies, as the Congress of the United States.
bi·car·bo·nate [baiká:rbənit] *n.* ⓤⓒ a salt of carbonic acid, used in cooking or for medicine. ¶*sodium ~.*①
bi·cen·te·nar·y [baiséntinèri / bàisentínəri, -tén-] *adj.* of 200 years; happening every 200 years. —*n.* ⓒ (pl. **-nar·ies**) 1. a period of 200 years. 2. the celebration of the 200th anniversary of an event.
bi·cen·ten·ni·al [bàisenténiəl] *adj., n.* =bicentenary.
bick·er [bíkər] *vi.* 1. quarrel over or about small matters. 2. flow noisily. 3. (of light, flame) flash.
: **bi·cy·cle** [báisikl] *n.* ⓒ a machine with two wheels moved by turning pedals with one's feet. ⇒N.B. —*vi.* ride a bicycle.
bi·cy·clist [báisiklist] *n.* ⓒ a bicycle rider.
: **bid** [bid] *v.* (**bade** or *Brit.* **bad, bid·den** → 3, 4, 5, **bid·ding**) *vt.* 1. give an order to (someone); command. (*~* someone [*to*] *do*) ¶*~ him go; ~ him to go.* 2. say (goodby, good morning, etc.). ¶*~ him good-by; ~ good-by to him.* 3. (pt., pp. **bid**) offer a price for (something). ¶*~ five dollars for.* 4. (pt., pp. **bid**) make (something) known to the public. 5. (pt., pp. **bid**) invite.
bid fair to do, seem likely to.
—*n.* ⓒ 1. an offer of money; the amount offered for something. 2. an attempt to get.
make a bid for (=*try to get*) *something.*
* **bid·den** [bídn] *v.* pp. of **bid.** ⌈auction sale.⌉
bid·der [bídər] *n.* ⓒ a person who bids, esp. at an
bid·ding [bídiŋ] *n.* ⓤⓒ 1. a command. 2. an invitation. 3. an offering of money for something.

—閑 1)굉장히, 몹시 2)이해할 수 없다

—劚 1. 저쪽에, 저 멀리에 2. 그 밖에

—《接頭》 둘…, 쌍…, 복(複)…, 중(重)…

—劚 1년에 두 번의

—劚 1. 사선(斜線) ¶①천을 비스듬히 자르다 2. 편견, 선입관 ¶②그녀에게는 편견이 없다 3. 편중, 치우침

閑 1)…에 치우치다, …의 경향이 있다 2) 공평하게
—劚 엇갈리는, 비스듬한
—劚 비스듬히, 엇갈리게
—劚 …을 한쪽으로 치우치게 하다; 편견을 갖게 하다

—劚 1. 턱받이 2. [앞치마 따위의] 가슴 부분

—劚 1. 성서 ¶①[성서에 입을 맞추고] 선서하다/②성서에 맹세하여 2. 권위 있는 책

—劚 성서의 ¶①성서에서의 인용
—劚 서적 해제편자(解題編者); 서지(書誌)학자

—劚 서지의, 서지 해제의; 서지학적인
—劚 1. [어떤 문제·사람에 관한] 서적목록 ¶①셰익스피어 문헌 2. 서지학

—劚 서적 애호가, 애서가
—劚 상하 양원이 있는, 양원제의

—劚 중(重)탄산염 ¶①중탄산 소오다

—劚 200년[째]의 —劚 1. 200년 2. 200년[기념]제

—劚 1. 말다툼하다 2. [시냇물이] 졸졸 흐르다 3. 반짝이다
—劚 자전거 N.B. 회화에서는 bike를 씀 —劚 자전거를 타다

—劚 자전거 타는 사람
—劚 1. …에게 명령하다 2. …에게 인사말을 하다 3. …의 값을 부르다 4. …을 공표하다 5. …을 초대하다

閑 …할 가망이 있다
—劚 1. 매기는 값, 입찰가격 2. [얻으려는] 노력, 시도
閑 …을 얻으려고 하다

—劚 명령자; 값을 매기는 사람, 입찰자
—劚 1. 명령 2. 초대 3. 입찰, 값을 매기기

1) ***at the bidding of*** (=*obedient to*) *someone.*
2) ***do the bidding*** (=*carry out the orders*) ***of*** *someone.*

[熟] 1)…의 분부대로 2)…의 명령대로 하다

bi·en·ni·al [baiéniəl] *adj.* **1.** (of plants) lasting two years. **2.** happening every two years. **—*n.*** [C] **1.** a plant that lives two years. **2.** an event that happens every two years.

—[形] 1. 2년생의 2. 2년에 한번의 —[名] 1. 2년생 식물 2. 2년마다 일어나는 일

bi·en·ni·al·ly [baiéniəli] *adv.* once in two years.

—[副] 2년마다

bier [biər] *n.* [C] a base for carrying a box containing a dead body; a frame of wood.

—[名] 관(棺) [놓는 대]

bi·fo·cal [bàifóuk(ə)l] *adj.* (of a lens) having two focuses. **—*n.*** **1.** 《usu. *pl.*》 a pair of glasses having bifocal lenses. **2.** [C] a bifocal lens.

—[形] 두 초점이 있는 —[名] 1. 두 초점 렌즈의 안경 2. 두 초점의 렌즈

‡**big** [big] *adj.* **(big·ger, big·gest) 1.** large. **2.** grown-up. **3.** (*colloq.*) important. ¶*the ~ event.* **4.** boastful. ¶*~ words.*①
big with (=*full of*) *something.* ¶*eyes ~ with tears.*

—[形] 1. 큰 2. 성장한 3. 《口》 중요한 4. 뽐내는, 자랑하는 ¶①호언장담
[熟] …에 가득차서; …을 임신하여

big·a·my [bígəmi] *n.* [U] the crime of having two wives or husbands at the same time.

—[名] 중혼(重婚)[죄], 이중 결혼

bight [bait] *n.* [C] **1.** a curve in a coastline. **2.** a bay. **3.** a loop made in a rope.

—[名] 1. 해안(강)의 만곡부 2. 만(灣), 후미 3. 밧줄의 고리

big·ness [bígnis] *n.* [U] the state of being big; greatness; importance.

—[名] 큼; 위대함; 중대함

big·ot [bígət] *n.* [C] a person who sticks blindly to his own opinion; a prejudiced person.

—[名] 완고한 미신가, 고집통이

big·ot·ed [bígətid] *adj.* sticking to one's opinion, belief, etc., without reason.

—[形] 완고한, 고집불통의

big·ot·ry [bígətri] *n.* (pl. **-ries**) [U][C] the state of being bigoted; prejudice.

—[名] 완고, 고집

bike [baik] *n., v.* (*colloq.*) =bicycle.

bi·lat·er·al [bailǽt(ə)rəl] *adj.* with two sides; of two sides.

—[形] 두 면이 있는; 양면의

bile [bail] *n.* [U] **1.** bitter, yellow, or greenish liquid produced by the liver to aid the digestion of food. **2.** bad temper; anger.

—[名] 1. 담즙(膽汁) 2. 분통, 화, 역정

bi·lin·gual [bailíŋgwəl] *adj.* **1.** able to speak two languages. **2.** written in two languages.

—[形] 1. 2개 국어를 말하는 2. 두 나라 말로 쓰인

bil·ious [bíliəs] *adj.* **1.** suffering from or caused by some trouble with the liver. ¶*a ~ patient.* **2.** bad-tempered.

—[形] 1. 간장(肝臟) 질환의 2. 성미 까다로운

‡**bill**¹ [bil] *n.* [C] **1.** a list of things for which money should be paid. ¶*a ~ for …*① / *collect bills*② / *settle a ~.*③ **2.** a piece of paper money. ¶*a ten-dollar ~.*④ **3.** a printed or written advertisement; a poster. **4.** a plan of a law presented for discussion by a parliament. ¶*pass a ~.*⑤ **5.** a written or printed public notice. ¶*a ~ of debt*⑥ / *a ~ of exchange*⑦ / *a ~ of sale*⑧ / *a ~ of lading.*⑨
1) ***a bill of fare,*** a menu.
2) ***a bill of health,*** a list of people on a ship showing whether they are ill or well. ¶*give someone a clean ~ of health.*⑩
3) ***foot the bill,*** (*colloq.*) pay the cost; settle the bill.
—*vt.* **1.** send a bill to (someone). **2.** enter (charges) on a bill. **3.** announce (something) publicly. ¶*~ a new shop.* **4.** post bills in or on (a wall, etc.).

—[名] 1. 청구서, 명세서 ¶①…의 청구서/②수금하다/③셈을 치르다 2. 지폐 ¶④10달러 지폐 3. 삐라, 포스터 4. 의안, 법안 ¶⑤의안을 통과시키다 5. 증서, 어음 ¶⑥약속어음/⑦환어음/⑧매도증서/⑨선하(船荷)증권
[熟] 1)식단표 2)[선객·선원의] 건강증명서 ¶⑩…에게 완전히 건강하다는 증명을 해주다 3)셈을 치르다; 비용을 부담하다
—[他] 1. …에게 계산서를 보내다 2. 계산서에 …을 적다 3. …을 광고(발표)하다 4. …에 삐라(포스터)를 붙이다

‡**bill**² [bil] *n.* [C] **1.** a hard part of a bird's mouth; a beak. **2.** anything like a bird's bill. **—*vi.*** **1.** join beaks; touch bills together. **2.** show affection.
bill and coo, kiss and talk as lovers do.

—[名] 1. 부리 2. 부리 모양의 것 —[自] 1. 부리를 가볍게 쪼아대다 2. 애무하다
[熟] 입을 맞추며 서로 속삭여대다

Bill [bil] *n.* a nickname for William.

—[名] William의 애칭

bill·board [bílbɔ̀ːrd] *n.* [C] a signboard for advertisements, notices and announcements.

—[名] 게시판, 광고판

bil·let [bílit] *n.* [C] a place where a soldier is lodged.

—[名] 병사(兵舍)

bill·fold [bílfòuld] *n.* [C] a folding, pocket size leather case for carrying money, paper, etc.; a wallet.

—[名] 지갑

bil·liards [bíljədz] *n. pl.* 《used as *pl.* and *sing.*》 a game played with a long stick and balls on a table. ¶*play* [at] *~.*①

—[名] 당구 ¶①당구를 치다

billiard table [⌐– ⌐] *n.* an oblong table for playing the game of billiards.

—[名] 당구대

* **bil·lion** [bíljən] *n.*, [C] **1.** (*U.S.*) one thousand million; 1,000,000,000. **2.** (*Brit.*) one million million; 1,000,000,000,000.
—[名] 1.《美》10억 2.《英》1조

bil·low [bílou] *n.* [C] a great wave of the sea. **—*vi.*** rise, fall or roll like big waves.
—[名] 큰 물결, 파도; 바다 —[自] 크게 물결치다

bil·low·y [bíloui] *adj.* rising or rolling like big waves.
—[形] 큰 파도가 치는, 큰 물결의

bil·ly [bíli] *n.* (pl. **-lies**) [C] (*colloq.*) a policeman's club.
—[名]《口》[경찰의] 곤봉

billy goat [ˊ-ˋ] *n.* (*colloq.*) a male goat.
—[名]《口》수양

bi·month·ly [bàimʌ́nθli] *adj.* **1.** happening once every two months. **2.** happening twice a month; semimonthly. ⇒[N.B.] **—*n.*** [C] (pl. **-lies**) a magazine published bimonthly. **—*adv.*** **1.** once every two months. **2.** twice a month; semimonthly.
—[形] 1. 두 달에 한 번의, 한 달 걸러의 2. 한 달에 두 번의 [N.B.] 이 뜻으로는 semimonthly를 씀 —[名] 격월간(隔月刊) 잡지 —[副] 1. 한 달 걸러 2. 한 달에 두 번

bin [bin] *n.* [C] a box or enclosed place, usu. with a cover, for storing grain, coal, etc.
—[名] [곡물·석탄 따위의] 저장통, 큰 상자

⁑ **bind** [baind] *v.* (**bound**) *vt.* **1.** tie (something) with a cord, wire, etc.; hold (things) together; fasten. **2.** deprive (someone) of his liberty; restrain. **3.** wind. 《~ a cord, etc. *around*》 **—*vi.*** **1.** hold together. **2.** stick together.
1) ***be bound*** (=*be compelled; be obliged*) ***to something.***
2) ***bind up,*** tie up (something) with a bandage.
—[他] 1. …을 묶다; 매다; 다발짓다 2. …을 속박하다 3. …을 둘러감다 —[自] 1. 다발로 되다 2. 들러붙다
[熟] 1)…할 의무가 있다 2)…에 붕대를 감다

bind·er [báindər] *n.* [C] **1.** a person who binds; a bookbinder. **2.** anything that ties or holds together. **3.** a cover for holding loose sheets of paper together. **4.** a machine for cutting and binding grain.
—[名] 1. 묶는 사람; 제본업자 2. [끈·밧줄 따위] 묶는 재료 3. 띠처럼 두르는 표지 4. [곡식 베는 기계의] 단 묶는 기구

bind·ing [báindiŋ] *n.* [C] a covering of a book. **—*adj.*** **1.** binding, fastening, or connecting something. **2.** having power to hold to some agreement. ¶*a ~ engagement*① / *be ~ on someone.*②
—[名] 제본; 장정(裝幀) —[形] 1. 묶는, 잇는 2. 구속력이 있는 ¶①의무적인 약속/②…에 의무를 지우다

bi·noc·u·lar [bainákjulər, bi- / -nɔ́kjulə] *adj.* using both eyes; for both eyes. ¶*a ~ telescope.*① **—*n.*** 《usu. *pl.*, used as *sing.*》 a field glass or opera glass for both eyes.
—[形] 두 눈의 ¶①쌍안경
—[名] 쌍안경

bi·o·chem·is·try [bàioukémistri] *n.* [U] the chemistry of living animals and plants.
—[名] 생화학

bi·og·ra·pher [baiágrəfər / -ɔ́grəfə] *n.* [C] a person who writes a biography.
—[名] 전기(傳記)작가

bi·o·graph·i·cal [bàiougrǽfik(ə)l] *adj.* of or about some-one's life. ¶*a ~ sketch*① / *a ~ dictionary.*② ▷**bi·o·graph·i·cal·ly** [-ikəli] *adv.*
—[形] 전기의 ¶①약전(略傳)/② 인명사전

* **bi·og·ra·phy** [baiágrəfi / -ɔ́g-] *n.* (pl. **-phies**) **1.** [C] the story of someone's life written by another. **2.** [U] the part of literature that consists of biographies.
—[名] 1. 전기(傳記) 2. 전기 문학

bi·o·log·ic [baiəládʒik / -lɔ́dʒ-], **-log·i·cal** [-k(ə)l] *adj.* of plant and animal life; of biology.
—[形] 생물의, 생물학의

bi·ol·o·gist [baiálədʒist / -ɔ́lə-] *n.* [C] an expert in biology.
—[名] 생물학자

* **bi·ol·o·gy** [baiálədʒi / -ɔ́lə-] *n.* [U] the science of life or living things.
—[名] 생물학

bi·ped [báiped] *n.* [C] an animal having two feet, as a man or bird. **—*adj.*** having two feet.
—[名] [사람·새와 같은] 두발동물
—[形] 발이 두 개 있는

bi·plane [báiplèin] *n.* [C] an airplane having two pairs of wings, one above the other.
—[名] 복엽(複葉)비행기

* **birch** [bəːrtʃ] *n.* **1.** [C] a tree with smooth bark and slender branches. **2.** [U] its wood. **3.** [C] a birch stick, or a bundle of birch twigs, used for whipping; a birch rod.
—[名] 1. 자작나무 2. 자작나무 재목 3. [자작나무] 회초리

birch·en [bə́ːrtʃ(ə)n] *adj.* **1.** of a birch tree. **2.** made of birchwood.
—[形] 1. 자작나무의 2. 자작나무로 만든

⁑ **bird** [bəːrd] *n.* [C] a two-legged animal that has wings and feathers, and lays eggs.
1) ***a bird in the bush,*** what is uncertain.
2) ***a bird in the hand,*** what is certain.
3) ***a bird of passage,*** a bird which comes and goes with the seasons.
4) ***birds of a feather,*** people of like character.
—[名] 새
[熟] 1)불확실한 것 2)확실한 것 3)철새; 떠돌이 4)동류, 같은 부류의 사람들

bird·cage [bə́ːrdkèidʒ] *n.* [C] a cage for birds.
—[名] 새장

bird fancier [ˊ ˋ—] *n.* a person who knows, collects, breeds, or sells birds; a person having an interest in birds.
—[名] 새장수; 조류 애호가

bird·ie [bə́:rdi] *n.* [C] a little bird.
—[名] 새 새끼, 작은 새

bird·lime [bə́:rdlàim] *n.* [U] a sticky material put on branches to catch small birds.
—[名] [새잡는] 끈끈이

bird's-eye [bə́:rdzài] *adj.* seen from above or from a distance; general. ¶*a ~ view of the city.*①
—[形] 위에서 내려다본; 개관(概觀)의 ¶①시의 조감도

Bir·ming·ham [bə́:rmiŋhæ̀m / bə́:miŋəm] *n.* **1.** a city in England. **2.** a city in central Alabama.
—[名] 1. 영국의 도시 2. 미국 Alabama 주의 도시

⁑ **birth** [bə:rθ] *n.* [U] [C] **1.** the act of coming into life. ¶*the ~ of a son / the ~ of Christ.* **2.** the beginning; the origin. ¶*the ~ of a new country.* **3.** descent; family. ¶*by ~*① */ from ~*② */ a woman of noble ~.* **4.** a noble family or descent. ¶*a man of ~ and breeding*③ */ Birth is much, but breeding is more.*④ **5.** something produced.
—[名] 1. 탄생, 출생 2. 기원(起源) 3. 태생, 가문 ¶①태생은, 고향은/②태어날 때부터 4. 명문, 문벌 ¶③가문도 좋고 교육도 받은 사람/④가문도 중하지만 교육이 더 중요하다 5. 출산, 분만

give birth to, bear; bring forth (a child, an idea, etc.); originate. ¶*She gave ~ to a daughter.*
[熟] …을 낳다; 생기다; …의 근원이 되다

⁑ **birth·day** [bə́:rθdèi] *n.* [C] the yearly return of the day on which someone was born. ¶*celebrate one's 20th ~.*①
—[名] 생일 ¶①20세의 생일을 축하하다

birth·mark [bə́:rθmɑ̀:rk] *n.* [C] a mark on a person's skin at birth.
—[名] 멍

birth·place [bə́:rθplèis] *n.* [C] the place or house where someone was born.
—[名] 출생지, 태어난 집

birth rate [ˊ ˋ] *n.* the proportion of the number of births in a place during a certain period of time to the total population.
—[名] 출생률

birth·right [bə́:rθràit] *n.* [C] the rights belonging to a person because he was born in a certain country or family; the rights belonging to the eldest son.
—[名] 생득권(生得權); [장자] 상속권

* **bis·cuit** [bískit] *n.* (pl. **-cuits** or **-cuit**) [C] **1.** (*U. S.*) a kind of bread baked in small, soft cakes. **2.** (*esp. Brit.*) a flat, dry cake. (cf. *U.S.* cracker)
—[名] 1.《美》과자 비슷한 빵 2.《英》비스킷

bi·sect [baisékt] *vt.* cut or divide (something) into two [equal] parts.
—[他] …을 등분하다, 양분하다

bi·sec·tion [baisékʃ(ə)n] *n.* [U] the act of bisecting.
—[名] 양단(兩斷); 2등분

⁑ **bish·op** [bíʃəp] *n.* [C] **1.** a clergyman of high rank who administers the affairs of a church district. ⇒fig. **2.** one of the pieces in the game of chess. **3.** a kind of wine.
—[名] 1. [그리스도 신교의] 감독; [정교회의] 주교; [가톨릭의] 사교(司敎) 2. [서양장기의] 비숍 3. 일종의 포도주

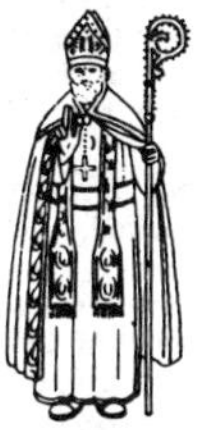
[bishop 1.]

bish·op·ric [bíʃəprik] *n.* [U] [C] **1.** the office or rank of a bishop. **2.** a church district under the charge of a bishop.
—[名] 1. 비숍의 직위 2. 비숍의 관할구

bis·muth [bízməθ] *n.* [U] a hard, red-white metal used in medicine.
—[名] 창연(蒼鉛)

bi·son [báisn, +*U.S.* -zn] *n.* [C] (pl. **-son**) an American buffalo; a wild ox-like animal. ⇒fig.
—[名] 들소

bit[1] [bit] *n.* [C] **1.** the part of a bridle that goes in a horse's mouth, used for controlling the horse. **2.** anything that restrains. **3.** the cutting part of a tool. **4.** a tool for boring or drilling.
—[名] 1. [굴레의] 재갈 2. 구속하는 것 3. [대패 따위의] 날 4. [송곳 따위의] 끝

—*vt.* (**bit·ted, bit·ting**) **1.** put a bit in the mouth of (a horse). **2.** restrain.
—[他] 1. [말]에 재갈을 물리다 2. …을 구속하다

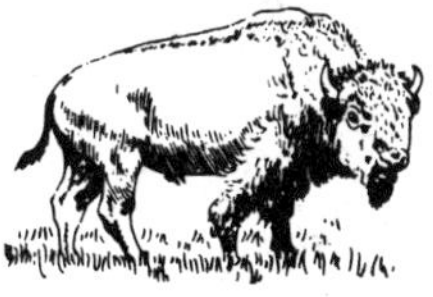
[bison]

⁑ **bit**[2] [bit] *n.* [C] **1.** a small piece; a small amount. **2.** (*colloq.*) a short time. **3.** (*U.S. colloq.*) 12½ cents.
—[名] 1. 조금, 소량, 한 입, 작은 조각 2. 잠깐, 잠시 3.《美口》12센트 반

1) ***bit by bit,*** little by little; gradually.
2) ***a bit of,*** rather. ¶*He is a ~ of a poet.*①
3) ***come*** (*or* ***go***) ***to bits,*** get (*or* be) broken.
4) ***do one's bit,*** do one's share (of the duty).
5) ***every bit,*** ⓐ all. ⓑ in every way; perfectly. ¶*She is every ~ a lady.*②

[熟] 1)조금씩, 차차 2)다소, 조금은 ¶①그는 조금은 시를 쓴다 3)부서지다 4)자기의 할 바를 다하다 5)ⓐ모든 ⓑ어느 점에서 보아도 ¶②그녀는 어느 모로나 숙녀다 6) 잠깐[사이] 7) 솔직히 말하다; 꾸짖다 8) ⓐ천만에

bit [122] **blackberry**

6) *for a bit,* for a little time.
7) *give someone a bit of one's mind,* speak frankly; scold.
8) *not a bit,* ⓐ not at all. ⓑ not in the least.

: **bit³** [bit] *v.* pt. and pp. of **bite**.
bitch [bitʃ] *n.* ⓒ a female dog, wolf, or fox. —ⓐ [개·여우 따위의] 암컷
: **bite** [bait] *v.* (**bit, bit** or **bit·ten**) *vi.* 1. snap with the teeth. (~ *at* something) 2. accept bait. —*vt.* 1. cut into (something) with the teeth; cut (something) off with the teeth. 2. rot or destroy (esp. metals) by chemicals, etc. swering back or laughing.
1) *bite one's lips,* keep oneself with difficulty from an-
2) *bite off more than one can chew,* attempt too great a task.
—*n.* ⓒ 1. the act of biting. 2. wound made by biting. 3. (of a fish) the act of taking bait 4. a piece cut off with the teeth.
bite and sup, hurried meal.
bit·er [báitər] *n.* ⓒ 1. a person or an animal that bites; a dog 2. a cheater. ¶*The ~ is bitten.*
bit·ing [báitiŋ] *adj.* 1. sharp; cutting. ¶*a ~ wind* / ~ *cold.* 2. sneering. ¶*a ~ remark.*
bit·ing·ly [báitiŋli] *adv.* sharply; cuttingly.
: **bit·ten** [bítn] *v.* pp. of **bite**.
: **bit·ter** [bítər] *adj.* (usu. ~**er,** ~**est**) 1. tasting like black coffee. ↔sweet 2. unpleasant to the mind. 3. biting; harsh; severe.
to the bitter end, to the last extremity.
• **bit·ter·ly** [bítərli] *adv.* with bitterness; with cruelty.
bit·tern [bítərn] *n.* ⓒ a small kind of bird that lives in marshes and is known for its loud cry.
• **bit·ter·ness** [bítərnis] *n.* Ⓤ the state of being bitter; something that causes bitter feeling.
bit·ter·sweet [bítərswì:t] *adj.* both bitter and sweet; both painful and pleasant.
bi·tu·men [bait(j)ú:mən / bítjumin] *n.* Ⓤ asphalt. men.
bi·tu·mi·nous [bit(j)ú:minəs / -tjú:-] *adj.* containing bitu-
bi·valve [báivælv] *n.* ⓒ a water-animal with a shell, as oysters or clams. —*adj.* having two parts hinged together.
biv·ou·ac [bívuæk, -vwǽk] *n.* ⓒ a rest for the night outside, often without tents. —*vi.* (**-acked, -ack·ing**) pass the night without tents.
biv·ou·acked [bívuækt, -vwǽkt] *v.* pt. of **bivouac**.
biv·ou·ack·ing [bívuækiŋ, -vwǽk-] *v.* ppr. of **bivouac**.
bi·week·ly [bàiwí:kli] *adj.* 1. happening once every two weeks. 2. happening twice a week; semiweekly. —*n.* ⓒ a newspaper or magazine issued biweekly. —*adv.* 1. once every two weeks. 2. twice a week; semiweekly.
bi·zarre [bizá:r] *adj.* queer; grotesque; strange.
blab [blæb] *vt., vi.* (**blabbed, blab·bing**) tell (a secret); talk too much.
blab·ber [blǽbər] *n.* ⓒ a person who blabs.
: **black** [blæk] *adj.* 1. opposite to white. 2. quite dark; without any light. ¶*a ~ night.* 3. dark-skinned. 4. dim; gloomy. 5. wicked; evil. ¶*a ~ heart.*
—*n.* 1. Ⓤ black color; black paint. 2. Ⓤⓒ a black speck. 3. Ⓤ black clothes. 4. ⓒ a Negro.
—*vt.* make (something) black; polish (something) with blacking. skinned person.
black·a·moor [blǽkəmùər] *n.* ⓒ 1. a Negro. 2. a dark-
black art [ˊ ˋ] *n.* evil magic.
black·ball [blǽkbɔ̀:l] *vt.* vote against (a candidate); shut out (someone) from a club, etc. by vote. —*n.* ⓒ a vote against (someone or something).
black·ber·ry [blǽkbèri, -b(ə)ri] *n.* ⓒ (pl. **-ries**) a small,

ⓑ 조금도 …않다

—ⓐ [개·여우 따위의] 암컷
—ⓑ 1. 물다 2. 미끼를 물다 —ⓐ 1. …을 물다, 깨물다; …을 물어뜯다 2. …을 부식(腐蝕)하다

🅱 1)[웃음 따위를] 참다 2)분에 넘치는 일을 하려고 하다
—ⓐ 1. 물기, 깨물기 2. 물린 상처 3. 물고기가 미끼를 물기 4. 물어뜯은 조각
🅱 간단한 식사
—ⓐ 1. 깨무는 사람(것); 먹는 짐승(개) 2. 사기꾼
—ⓐ 1. 살을 에는 듯한, 날카로운 2. 신랄한, 통렬한
—ⓑ 신랄하게, 찌르는 듯이

—ⓐ 1. 쓴 2. 불쾌한, 지독한 3. 신랄한, 격렬한

🅱 최후까지, 죽을 때까지
—ⓑ 쓰게; 몹시, 비통하게, 잔인하게
—ⓐ 알락해오라기(철새)

—ⓐ 피로움, 신랄함, 비통

—ⓑ 쓰고도 단; 피로우면서도 즐거운

—ⓐ 아스팔트
—ⓑ 아스팔트를 함유한
—ⓐ 쌍각류의 조개(굴·대합 따위) —ⓑ 쌍각류의; [식물이] 양판(兩瓣)의

—ⓐ 노영(露營), 노영지 —ⓑ 노영하다

—ⓑ 1. 격주(隔週)의 2. 1주 2회의 —ⓐ 격주 간행물 —ⓑ 1. 격주로 2. 1주에 2회

—ⓑ 기괴한, 별난, 피이한
—ⓑⓐ [비밀을] 입싸게 지껄이다

—ⓐ 수다장이
—ⓑ 1. 검은 2. 암흑의, 어둠의 3. 피부가 검은 4. 음산한, 우울한 5. 사악한

—ⓐ 1. 검정; 흑색 도료(안료) 2. 검정 얼룩, 오점 3. 검은 옷 4. 흑인
—ⓑ …을 검게 하다; …에 검정 약칠을 하다
—ⓐ 1. 흑인 2. 빛깔이 검은 사람
—ⓐ 마술, 마법
—ⓑ [후보자]에게 반대 투표하다; …을 배척하다 —ⓐ [검은 공을 투표함에 넣는] 반대 투표
—ⓐ 나무딸기[열매]

black or dark-purple eatable fruit; a plant bearing this fruit.

black·bird [blǽkbə̀:rd] *n.* [C] any of various birds the male of which is mostly black.
—[名] 검은 새[지빠귀류]

⁑ **black·board** [blǽkbɔ̀:rd] *n.* [C] a board for writing on with chalk or crayon.
—[名] 흑판

black coffee [ˊ ˊ-] *n.* coffee without milk or sugar.
—[名] 설탕·밀크를 넣지 않은 코오피

black·en [blǽk(ə)n] *vt.* **1.** make (something) black. **2.** speak evil of (someone); injure. —*vi.* become black.
—[他] 1. …을 검게 하다 2. …을 헐뜯다 —[自] 검게 되다

black·guard [blǽgɑ:rd, -gərd / -gɑ:d] *n.* [C] a person who has no sense of honor; a rascal. —*vt.* abuse (someone) with very bad language. —*vi.* behave like a rascal.
—[名] 악한, 불량배 —[他] …에게 욕설을 퍼붓다 —[自] 악한처럼 굴다

black·guard·ly [blǽgɑ:rd-, -gərd- / -gɑ:d-] *adj.* of or like a blackguard. —*adv.* in the manner of a rascal.
—[形] 악한의(같은) —[副] 악한처럼

black·ing [blǽkiŋ] *n.* [U] anything for making (shoes, boots, etc.) black and polished.
—[名] 검게 하는 것; 구두약; 검정 물감

black·ish [blǽkiʃ] *adj.* black.
—[形] 거무스름한, 검은

black lead [ˊ ˊ] *n.* soft grey-black carbon, used in pencils.
—[名] 흑연(黑鉛), 석묵(石墨)

black·leg [blǽklèg] *n.* [C] **1.** (*colloq.*) a person who cheats; a swindler. **2.** (*Brit.*) a worker who works when the regular workers are on strike.
—[名] 1. 《口》 사기꾼 2. 《英》 파업 방해자

black list [ˊ ˋ] *n.* a list of persons who are believed to be dangerous or who are to be punished.
—[名] 요시찰인 명부, 블랙리스트

black·mail [blǽkmèil] *n.* [U] any money gained from someone by threatening to tell something bad or dishonorable about him. —*vt.* get or try to get blackmail from (someone.)
—[名] 갈취, 공갈하여 빼앗기 —[他] 돈을 갈취하다

black·mail·er [blǽkmèilər] *n.* [C] a person who blackmails.
—[名] 갈취자, 공갈자

black market [ˊ ˊ-] *n.* a place where things are sold and bought at illegal prices or by illegal routes.
—[名] 암시장

black·ness [blǽknis] *n.* [U] **1.** the state of being black; a black color. **2.** wickedness.
—[名] 1. 검정; 흑색 2. 음험

black·out [blǽkàut] *n.* [C] **1.** the act of turning out or covering all the lights to protect a city, etc. against an air attack. **2.** temporary loss of consciousness or memory.
—[名] 1. [공습 때의] 등화 관제 2. [비행중의 급강하 따위로 일어나는] 일시적 의식 상실

black sheep [ˊ ˊ] *n.* an unusual or bad member of a family or group.
—[名] 말썽꾼, 골칫거리

* **black·smith** [blǽksmìθ] *n.* [C] a man who works with iron to make tools, horseshoes, etc.
—[名] 대장장이

black·thorn [blǽkθɔ̀:rn] *n.* [C] **1.** a thorny European bush that has white flowers and dark-purple fruit. **2.** a walking stick made from this shrub.
—[名] 1. 인목(橉木) 2. 인목 지팡이

blad·der [blǽdər] *n.* [C] 《*the* ~》 a soft, thin bag of skin in a human and animal body that stores waste liquid before it is passed out.
—[名] 방광(膀胱)

⁑ **blade** [bleid] *n.* [C] **1.** the cutting part of a knife, tool, etc; 《*the* ~》 a sword. **2.** a leaf of grass. ¶*in the* ~.① **3.** a flat, wide part of anything, such as an oar, a paddle, etc. ¶*the shoulder* ~.② ▷**blade·like** [-làik] *adj.*
—[名] 1. 칼날; 칼몸, 검 2. 풀잎 ¶①(이삭이 아직 나오기 전) 잎이 나와 3. 평평한 부분 ¶②견갑골(肩甲骨)

blam·a·ble [bléiməbl] *adj.* fit to be blamed; having a fault.
—[形] 비난할 만한

⁑ **blame** [bleim] *vt.* **1.** find fault with (someone or something). 《~ someone *for*》 ¶*He is blamed for neglect of duty.*① / *I don't ~ you for doing that.* **2.** say that a person or a thing is the cause of a certain trouble. 《~ something *on*》 ¶*We blamed the accident on him.*
—[他] 1. 책망하다, 비난하다 ¶①그는 직무 태만으로 책망 받고 있다 2. …의 탓으로 하다; [과실 따위]의 책임을 …에게 지게 하다

be to blame, be held responsible. ¶*I am to ~ for it.*② / *Who is to ~?*
[熟] 책임이 있다 ¶②그것은 내가 나쁘다

—*n.* [U] **1.** the act of finding fault. **2.** the responsibility for something wrong or bad. ¶*bear the ~ for ...*③ / *lay the ~ at the door of another*④ / *lay* (or *put*) *the ~ on someone for ....*⑤
—[名] 1. 비난, 책망 2. 책임 ¶③…의 책임을 지다/④죄를 남에게 뒤집어씌우다/⑤남에게 …의 책임을 지게 하다

blame·less [bléimlis] *adj.* free from blame; doing nothing wrong; pure.
—[形] 나무랄 데 없는, 결백한

blame·wor·thy [bléimwə̀:rði] *adj.* to be blamed.
—[形] 책망 받을 만한

B

blanch [blæntʃ / blɑːntʃ] *vt.* make (something) white. **—*vi.*** turn white or pale. ¶ *He blanched with fear.*
blanch over, make (someone) believe what is not true.
—[他] …을 표백하다 —[自] 희어지다; [안색이] 창백해지다
[熟] …을 속이다

bland [blænd] *adj.* **1.** smooth; gentle; mild. ¶ ~ *food* / *a* ~ *medicine.* **2.** agreeable; polite. ▷**bland·ness** [-nis] *n.*
—[形] 1. 입에 맞는, 순한; 온화한 2. 기분 좋은; 예의 바른

blan·dish [blǽndiʃ] *vt.* flatter.
—[他] 알랑거리다

blan·dish·ment [blǽndiʃmənt] *n.* ⟪often *pl.*⟫ a soft and gentle word or action that flatters.
—[名] 아첨의 말, 감언; 아첨

bland·ly [blǽndli] *adv.* in a polite manner; gently.
—[副] 온화하게, 부드럽게

:blank [blæŋk] *adj.* **1.** not written or printed on. **2.** (of a face) without expression. ¶ *a* ~ *look.* **3.** without effect or interest. **4.** without any clear idea; having nothing in mind. ¶ *My memory is* ~ *on the subject.*① **5.** complete; thorough. ¶ ~ *despair.*
—*n.* [C] a blank space in a document; an empty or vacant space; an empty surface. ¶ *Leave a* ~ *after each word.*②
—[形] 1. 기입하지 않은 2. 무표정한 3. 효과 없는; 흥미가 없는 4. 얼빠진, 멍청한; 기억 없는 ¶①그 문제에 대해서는 아무 기억도 없다 5. 순전한, 정말의
—[名] 빈칸, 공백, 여백; 빈터 ¶②각 단어 뒤에 빈칸을 남겨라

:blan·ket [blǽŋkit] *n.* [C] **1.** a large, soft piece of woolen cloth. **2.** anything like a blanket. ¶ *a* ~ *of snow.*
—*vt.* **1.** cover (something) with a blanket. **2.** cover. ¶ *The snow blanketed the ground.*
—[名] 1. 담요 2. 전면에 덮인 것 —[他] 1. …을 담요로 덮다 2. …을 싸다, 온통 덮어 가리다

blank·ly [blǽŋkli] *adv.* in a blank manner; vacantly. ¶ *She looked at me* ~.
—[副] 헛되게, 멍청하게

blank·ness [blǽŋknis] *n.* [U] the state of being blank or empty.
—[名] 공백, 공허; 단조로움

blare [blɛər] *vt., vi.* **1.** make a loud sound like a trumpet. ¶ *The radio blared.* **2.** cry. **—*n.*** [C][U] **1.** a loud sound. **2.** brightness of color.
—[他][自] 1. 큰소리로 울리다 2. 큰 소리로 외치다 —[名] 1. 외침 2. 화려한 색채

blar·ney [blɑ́ːrni] *n.* [U] flattering talk; too much praise. **—*vi., vt.*** flatter.
—[名] 아첨의 말 —[自][他] 아첨하다

blas·pheme [blæsfíːm] *vi., vt.* speak ill of (something sacred). ¶ ~ *against God.*
—[自][他] …을 모독하다; 욕지거리하다

blas·phem·er [blæsfíːmər] *n.* [C] a person who speaks ill of God, holy things, etc.
—[名] 신성 모독자; 욕설하는 사람

blas·phe·mous [blǽsfiməs] *adj.* speaking ill of God or holy things.
—[形] 신을 모독하는, 불경한

blas·phe·my [blǽsfimi] *n.* (pl. **-mies**) [U] contempt for God or holy things; [C] a talk showing no respect for God.
—[名] 불경, 모독; 신을 모독하는 말

:blast [blæst / blɑːst] *n.* [C] **1.** a strong rush of wind. **2.** a sound of a musical wind-instrument. **—*vt.*** **1.** blow up (something) with gunpowder. **2.** make (a plant) dry up and die; make (someone's hope, happiness, etc.) come to nothing; ruin; wither.
Blast it (or ***him, you, etc.***)!, Damn it!
—[名] 1. 한 바탕 일어나는 강풍 2. 관악기의 소리 —[他] 1. …을 폭발시키다 2. …을 마르게 하다; 망치다
[熟] 빌어먹을!

blast furnace [⌐ ⌐-] *n.* a furnace for melting iron by blowing hot air into it.
—[名] 용광로, 고로(高爐)

bla·tant [bléit(ə)nt] *adj.* **1.** noisy. **2.** bright and gay, but in bad taste.
—[形] 1. 시끄러운 2. 야한

:blaze[1] [bleiz] *n.* [C] **1.** a bright flame or fire. **2.** a sudden and violent outburst of passion. **3.** a bright display; a strong, direct light.
—*vi.* **1.** burn with a bright flame. **2.** explode; burst. **3.** glow or shine like a flame. **4.** burst out with strong feeling. ⟪~ *with* anger, etc.⟫
1) ***blaze away*** (= *fire a gun continuously*) ***at the enemy, etc.***
2) ***blaze up,*** burst into flames.
—[名] 1. 불꽃, 화염 2. 감정의 불타오름, 격발(激發) 3. 반짝임, 섬광
—[自] 1. 활활 타다 2. 폭발하다 3. 반짝이다 4. 감정을 폭발시키다
[熟] 1)…을 향해 총을 마구 쏘다 2)확 타오르다

blaze[2] [bleiz] *vt.* make (news, etc.) known; announce.
blaze about (or ***abroad***), spread.
—[他] …을 선언하다, 공언하다
[熟] …의 소문을 퍼뜨리다

blaz·er [bléizər] *n.* [C] a bright-colored sports jacket.
—[名] 블레이저 코우트

blaz·ing [bléiziŋ] *adj.* **1.** burning. ¶ *a* ~ *sun.*① **2.** unusual; clear.
—[形] 1. 불타는 [듯한] ¶①염천(炎天) 2. 심한; 뚜렷한

bla·zon [bléizn] *vt.* decorate (something) with the special mark of a family.
—[他] …을 문장(紋章)으로 장식하다

bldg. (pl. **bldgs.**) building.

bleach [bliːtʃ] *vt.* make (something) white. **—*vi.*** become white or pale. **—*n.*** [C] **1.** a chemical product used in bleaching. **2.** the act of bleaching.
—[他] …을 표백하다, 희게 하다 —[自] 희어지다 —[名] 1. 표백제 2. 표백

bleach·er [blíːtʃər] *n.* **1.** [C] a person or thing that makes something white. **2.** ⟪*pl.*⟫ seats at a baseball game or
—[名] 1. 표백업자; 표백기; 표백제 2. 지붕 없는 관람석

bleaching powder [`-´-`] *n.* any powder used in making something white. —총 표백제, 표백분

bleak [bli:k] *adj.* **1.** laid open to wind and cold. ¶ ~ *hills.* **2.** cold. ¶*a ~ wind.* **3.** without cheer; dull. ¶*a ~ prospect.*① ▷**bleak·ly** [-li] *adv.* —형 1. 바람받이의, 황량한 2. 몹시 추운 3. 음울한, 슬픈 ¶①어두운 전망

blear [bliər] *adj.* dim. —*vt.* make (an eye, a surface, etc.) dim. —형 눈이 흐린 —타 …을 흐리게 하다, 희미하게 하다

blear-eyed [blíəràid] *adj.* having dim eyes. —형 눈이 흐린

bleat [bli:t] *n.* ⓒⓊ the cry made by a sheep. —*vi.* (of a sheep) cry. —총 양의 울음소리 —자 [양이] 울다

bled [bled] *v.* pt. and pp. of **bleed**.

* **bleed** [bli:d] *v.* (**bled**) *vi.* **1.** lose blood. ¶ ~ *at the nose*① / *His knee is bleeding.* | ~ *to death.*② **2.** (of a tree) lose sap (or liquid). **3.** feel pity or sorrow. 《~ *for* someone》 ¶*My heart bleeds for you.* —*vt.* take blood from (someone). ¶ ~ *sick people.*③ —자 1. 출혈하다 ¶①코피를 흘리다/②출혈 과다로 죽다 2. [식물이] 진을 내다 3. 동정하다, 마음아파하다 —타 …을 출혈시키다 ¶③환자의 피를 뽑다

bleed·ing [blí:diŋ] *n.* Ⓤ loss of blood; a flow of blood. —*adj.* losing blood. —총 출혈 —형 피를 흘리는

blem·ish [blémiʃ] *n.* ⓒ a spot; a fault. ¶*a ~ on the skin.* —*vt.* **1.** make (something) dirty. **2.** spoil the beauty or fame of (someone or something); injure. —총 오점, 흠, 결점 —타 1. …을 더럽히다, …에 얼룩을 만들다 2. [명성 따위]를 해치다

blench [blentʃ] *vi.* jump back; draw back. —자 뒷걸음치다; 움츠리다

* **blend** [blend] *vt.* mix (things) together; make (something) by mixing together. 《~ something *with*》 ¶ ~ *paints*① / ~ *coffee* / ~ *amusement with instruction.*② —*vi.* mix; become mixed. 《~ *with* something》 ¶*Oil will not ~ with water.* —*n.* ⓒ something made by mixing. ¶*a ~ of coffee.* —타 …을 혼합하다; …을 섞어서 새 종류를 만들다 ¶①그림물감을 섞다/②재미와 교훈을 뒤섞다 —자 뒤섞이다, 혼합하다 —총 혼합[물]

: **bless** [bles] *vt.* (**blessed** [blest] or **blest**) **1.** make (something) holy. ¶*God blessed the seventh day.* **2.** ask God's favor for (someone or something). **3.** feel grateful to (God); praise ¶*God be blessed.*① / *We ~ the Lord.*② **4.** (of God) make (someone) happy or successful. 《~ someone *with*》 ¶*God has blessed me with riches.* / *God ~ you!*③ / *She is blessed with children.*④ **5.** guard; protect. ¶*Bless me from all evils!*
  1) *Bless me!*; *Bless my soul!*; *Well, I'm blest!*, What a surprise!; Oh, never!
  2) *bless one's stars*, be grateful for one's good fortune.
  3) *I am blessed* (or *blest*) *if*, I am completely ignorant. ¶*I am blessed if I know.*⑤
—타 1. …을 신성하게 하다, 정하게 하다 2. …을 위해 신의 가호를 빌다 3. …을 신에게 감사하다; 신을 숭상하다 ¶①신을 찬미하다/②신에게 감사하다 4. [신이] …에게 은혜를 베풀다, 축복하다 ¶③신의 축복이 있으시기를/④그녀에게는 자식 복이 있다 5. 수호하다
감 1)아아!; 아차!, 저런! 2)하늘의 은혜를 감사하다 3)결코 …하지 않는다 ¶⑤그런 것을 내가 알 게 뭐야

bless·ed [blésid] *adj.* **1.** holy. **2.** happy; successful. ¶ ~ *ignorance*① / *the Blessed Virgin*② / *Blessed are the pure in heart.* **3.** (*colloq.*) giving trouble. —형 1. 신성한 2. 축복받은, 행복한 ¶①모르는 게 약/②성모 마리아 3.(口) 골치아픈, 성가신

bless·ed·ness [blésidnis] *n.* Ⓤ happiness. ¶*single ~.*① —총 행복, 행운 ¶①행복한 독신

: **bless·ing** [blésiŋ] *n.* ⓒ **1.** a prayer asking God to show His favor; the favor of God; thanks to God before or after a meal. ¶*ask a ~*① / *He sent us his ~.*② **2.** anything that makes happy. ¶*Health is a great ~.* —총 1. 신의 축복, 식전(식후)의 기도 ¶①식전의 기도를 드리다/②그는 우리에게 행운이 있기를 빌어 왔다 2. 하늘의 은혜; 행복

* **blest** [blest] *v.* pt. and pp. of **bless**. —*adj.* =blessed.

* **blew** [blu:] *v.* pt. of **blow**².

blight [blait] *n.* **1.** Ⓤ any disease that makes plants dry and lifeless. **2.** ⓒ an insect that causes such a disease. **3.** ⓒ anything that causes ruin. —*vt.* **1.** make (a plant) dry and lifeless. **2.** destroy. —총 1. [식물의] 말라죽는 병 2. 그 병을 일으키는 해충 3. 파괴 [파멸]의 원인 —타 1. …을 시들게 하다, 해치다 2. 파괴하다

: **blind** [blaind] *adj.* **1.** without sight; unable to see. **2.** without mental or moral ability to distinguish between right and wrong. ¶*He is ~ to his own defects.* **3.** careless about results; reckless; without aim. **4.** hidden. ¶*a ~ ditch.*① —*vt.* **1.** deprive (someone) of his sight. **2.** make (someone) mentally blind. **3.** hide; conceal. —*n.* ⓒ a screen for a window. —형 1. 보이지 않는 2. 선악의 판단을 내리지 못하는 3. 맹목적인 4. 숨겨진 ¶①암거(暗渠) —타 1. …을 눈멀게 하다 2. …의 이성을 빼앗다 3. …을 숨기다 —총 차양, 발, 덧문

B

blind·fold [bláin(d)fòuld] *vt.* cover (someone's eyes) with a cloth, etc. **—*adj.*** **1.** with the eyes covered. ¶*a ~ test.* **2.** not caring about danger. ¶*~ rage*① / *do something ~.*② **—*adv.*** **1.** with the eyes covered. **2.** in a blind manner. **—*n.*** [C] a cloth or bandage put before the eyes to prevent seeing.
—[他] …의 눈을 가리다 —[形] 1. 눈을 가린 2. 맹목적인 ¶①맹목적인 분노/②무턱대고 …을 하다 —[副] 1. 눈을 가리고 2. 맹목적으로 —[名] 눈가리개

blind·ly [bláindli] *adv.* recklessly; without judgment.
—[副] 맹목적으로, 분별없이

blind·man's buff [bláindmænzbʌ́f] *n.* a game played by children in which one child, with his eyes covered, tries to catch the other players.
—[名] 장님놀이

blind·ness [bláindnis] *n.* [U] the state of being blind; lack of judgment; lack of knowledge.
—[名] 맹목; 무분별; 무식

blink** [bliŋk] *vi., vt.* **1.** open and close the eyes quickly; wink. **2.** glance. 《~ *at* something》 **3.** shine with an unsteady light; turn (light) on and off quickly. **4.** refuse to know a fact; ignore. 《~ *at* something》 ¶*~ at someone's mistake* / *~ the fact that ….*① **—*n. [C] a glance; a moment. ¶*in a ~.*②
—[自][他] 1. 깜짝거리다 2. 흘깃 보다 3. 깜박이다, 명멸하다(시키다) 4. …을 무시하다, 못 본 체하다 ¶①…이라는 사실을 모르는 체하다 —[名] 흘깃 보기; 순간 ¶②순식간에

blink·ers [blíŋkərz] *n. pl.* **1.** colored glasses. **2.** pieces of leather fixed at the sides of a horse's eyes.
—[名] 1. 색안경 2. [말의] 눈가리개 가죽

***bliss** [blis] *n.* [U] happiness; joy. ¶*Ignorance is ~.*①
—[名] 행복; 기쁨 ¶①모르는 게 약

bliss·ful [blísf(u)l] *adj.* very happy. ▷**bliss·ful·ly** [-fuli] *adv.* —**bliss·ful·ness** [-nis] *n.*
—[形] 더할 나위 없이 행복한, 기쁨에 넘친

blis·ter [blístər] *n.* [C] a little, raised spot on the skin with liquid under it, caused by burns or rubbing. **—*vt., vi.*** cause a blister on (the skin); become covered with blisters.
—[名] 물집, 수포(水疱) —[他][自] …에 물집이 생기게 하다; 물집이 되다

blithe [blaið] *adj.* gay; joyful; cheerful. ▷**blithe·ly** [-li] *adv.*
—[形] 즐거운, 명랑한

blithe·some [bláiðsəm] *adj.* gay; cheerful.
—[形] 즐거운

blitz [blits] *n.* [C] a sudden, violent attack by airplanes and tanks. **—*vt.*** attack (a place, an enemy, etc.) in this way.
—[名] 전격 직전(기습) —[他] …을 전격 기습하다

bliz·zard [blízərd] *n.* [C] a storm with a strong, cold wind and much snow.
—[名] 눈보라, 폭풍설

bloat [blout] *vt.* cause (something) to swell. **—*vi.*** swell.
—[他] …을 부풀리다 —[自] 부풀다

bloat·ed [blóutid] *adj.* **1.** fat and large in an unhealthy way. **2.** with too much pride.
—[形] 1. 부푼 2. 자만심을 품은, 거만한

bloat·er [blóutər] *n.* [C] a salted and smoked herring.
—[名] 훈제(燻製)한 청어

bloc [blɑk / blɔk] *n.* [C] a group of persons combined for a common purpose. ¶*the Communist ~*① / *the dollar ~.*②
—[名] [정치·경제 상의] 블록, 권(圈) ¶①공산권/②달러권

‡**block** [blɑk / blɔk] *n.* [C] **1.** a thick and solid piece of stone, wood, etc. **2.** a large piece of wood for cutting meat, fish, wood, etc. ¶*send someone to the ~.*① **3.** a wheel or set of wheels used for lifting heavy things. **4.** a square part of a city bounded by four streets. **—*vt.*** **1.** make (a way) unable to be passed through. **2.** oppose. **3.** (*Cricket*) stop (a ball) with a bat.
1) ***block in*** (*or* ***out***), sketch roughly; plan.
2) ***block up,*** keep (something) shut in; obstruct.
—[名] 1. 덩어리, 돌덩어리, 블록 2. 받침판; 도마 ¶①남을 단두대에 보내다 3. 도르레, 활차 4. [도시의] 한 구획 —[他] 1. [길]을 막다 2. …에 반대하다 3. 《크리켓》 배트로 [보올]을 막다
[熟] 1)대충 계획을 세우다 2)봉쇄(방해)하다; 가로막다

block·ade [blɑkéid / blɔk-] *n.* [C] the act of shutting off a place by soldiers or ships to prevent passage. ¶*run* (or *break*) *the ~.*① **—*vt.*** put (a place, etc.) under blockade.
—[名] 봉쇄; 교통 차단 ¶①…의 봉쇄선을 뚫다 —[他] …을 봉쇄하다; 막다

block·head [blɑ́khèd / blɔ́k-] *n.* [C] a fool; a stupid person.
—[名] 바보, 얼간이

block·house [blɑ́khàus/blɔ́k-] *n.* [C] a strong military building of wood with holes for firing through. ⇒fig.
—[名] [총안(銃眼)이 있는] 요새, 방책(防柵)

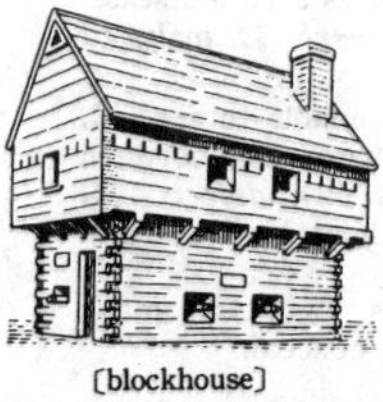

〔blockhouse〕

block letter [⌐ ⌐⌐] *n.* a printing type cut from wood; a style of printing type or a letter with tight curves.
—[名] 목판 문자; 블록 글자체

***blond, blonde** [blɑnd / blɔnd] *adj.* having light-colored hair, blue or gray eyes, and light
—[形] 피부는 희고 금발에 푸른 눈을 한 —[名] 그러한 사람 [usage] blond는 남성, blonde는 여성에 씀

skin. ↔brunette —*n.* [C] a person with such hair, eyes, and skin. ⇒[usage]

:blood [blʌd] *n.* [U] **1.** red liquid in bodies of the higher animals. **2.** passion; temperament. ¶ *His ~ is up.*① **3.** relationship by birth.
1) ***bad blood,*** ill feeling; dislike; hatred.
2) ***blue blood,*** high birth.
3) ***flesh and blood,*** the human body; the animal nature.
4) ***in cold blood,*** on purpose; cruelly.

—[名] 1. 피, 혈액 2. 격정; 기질 ¶①그는 몹시 화가 났다 3. 혈연
[熟] 1)악감정; 불화; 증오 2)고귀한 태생 3)육체; 수성(獸性) 4)고의로; 잔인하게

blood·cur·dling [blʌ́dkə:rdliŋ] *adj.* horrible; causing terror.
—[形] 오싹하게 하는; 소름끼치는

blood·hound [blʌ́dhàund] *n.* [C] a large, powerful dog with a keen sense of smell, used for looking for a person, etc.
—[名] 경찰견

blood·i·ly [blʌ́dili] *adv.* **1.** covered with blood. **2.** in a cruel manner.
—[副] 1. 피투성이가 되어 2. 무참하게

blood·i·ness [blʌ́dinis] *n.* **1.** [U] the quality of being cruel. **2.** the state of being covered with blood.
—[名] 1. 피투성이 2. 잔인

blood·less [blʌ́dlis] *adj.* **1.** without blood; pale. ¶ *~ lips.* **2.** without losing blood. ¶ *~ revolution.*① **3.** without energy; without spirit. **4.** cold-hearted; cruel.
—[形] 1. 핏기 없는, 창백한 2. 피를 흘리지 않는 ¶①무혈 혁명 3. 힘이 없는; 영혼이 없는 4. 냉담한, 무정한

blood·let·ting [blʌ́dlètiŋ] *n.* [U] (*Medicine*) the act of opening a vein to take out blood.
—[名] 《醫》 방혈(放血)

blood poisoning [ˊ ˋ--] *n.* (*Medicine*) a diseased condition of blood, esp. through a wound, etc.
—[名] 《醫》 패혈증(敗血症)

blood·shed [blʌ́dʃèd] *n.* [U] the flowing of blood; the killing of people.
—[名] 유혈; 살해

blood·shot [blʌ́dʃɑt / -ʃɔt] *adj.* (of the eyes) red and sore; colored slightly with blood.
—[形] [눈이] 충혈한, 핏발선

blood·stained [blʌ́dstèind] *adj.* **1.** stained with blood. **2.** guilty of murder.
—[形] 1. 핏자국이 있는 2. 살인범의

blood stream [ˊ ˋ] *n.* the circulating stream of blood in a body.
—[名] [인체 내의] 혈류(血流)

blood·suck·er [blʌ́dsʌ̀kər] *n.* [C] **1.** an animal that sucks blood. **2.** a person who gets money from others by power.
—[名] 1. 거머리, 흡혈동물 2. 착취자; 욕심꾸러기

blood test [ˊ ˋ] *n.* an examination of a person's blood.
—[名] 혈액 검사

blood·thirst·y [blʌ́dθə̀:rsti] *adj.* eager to kill others; cruel.
—[形] 피에 굶주린, 잔인한

blood transfusion [ˊ -ˋ-] *n.* an injection of blood from one person or animal into another.
—[名] 수혈[법]

blood type [ˊ ˋ] *n.* any one of four groups of human blood.
—[名] 혈액형

blood vessel [ˊ ˋ-] *n.* a tube in the body through which the blood flows.
—[名] 혈관

·blood·y [blʌ́di] *adj.* (**blood·i·er, blood·i·est**) **1.** bleeding. **2.** stained with blood. **3.** cruel. ¶ *a ~ battle / a ~ murderer.* —*vt.* make (something) dirty with blood.
—[形] 1. 피흘리는 2. 피투성이의 3. 잔인한; 피비린내 나는
—[他] …을 피로 더럽히다

:bloom [blu:m] *n.* **1.** [C] a flower; a blossom; 《*collectively*》 flowers. **2.** [U] the time of flowering. ¶ *be in* [*full*] *~*① / *come into ~.*② **3.** 《usu. *the ~*》 a time of greatest health or beauty. ¶ *She is in the ~ of youth.*③ **4.** [C] a bright, warm color of health and beauty. ¶ *take the ~ off ….*④ —*vi.* **1.** have flowers; blossom. ¶ *This flower blooms all the year round.* **2.** be in the time of greatest health or beauty.
—[名] 1. 꽃 2. 개화[기] ¶①꽃이 피어(만발하여) 있다/②꽃이 피다 3. 전성기 ¶③그녀는 한창 젊을 때다 4. 건강색; 신선미 ¶④…의 젊음을 빼앗다
—[自] 1. [꽃이] 피다 2. 한창 때(전성기)에 있다

bloom·ers [blú:mərz] *n. pl.* loose trousers worn by girls for physical training. ⇒[N.B.]
—[名] 블루우머 [N.B.] 창시자는 Bloomer

bloom·ing [blú:miŋ] *adj.* **1.** blossoming. **2.** youthful; young.
—[形] 1. 한창 때의 2. 청춘의

:blos·som [blɑ́səm / blɔ́s-] *n.* [C] **1.** a flower, esp. of a fruit tree. **2.** [U] the time of flowering. ¶ *come into blossom*① / *be in full ~.*② **3.** [C] a youth. —*vi.* **1.** (of a tree) have blossoms. **2.** (of a person) become, usu. something good. ¶ *He has blossomed into a great novelist.*③
—[名] 1. [과수의] 꽃 2. 개화기 ¶①꽃 피다/②만발해 있다 3. 청춘 —[自] 1. 꽃이 피다 2. 발달하여 …이 되다 ¶③그는 훌륭한 소설가가 되었다

·blot [blɑt / blɔt] *v.* (**blot·ted, blot·ting**) *vt.* **1.** spot (something) with ink, etc. **2.** dry (ink) with soft paper. **3.** bring shame or dishonor upon (someone). —*vi.* become blotted.
—[他] 1. …을 더럽히다 2. [압지로] 빨아들이다 3. …의 인격·명성 따위를 해치다 —[自] 번지다

blot out, ⓐ cover up. ¶*The fog blotted out the view.* ⓑ wipe out. ¶*~ out a memory.*
—*n.* [C] a spot of ink; a fault; an ugly object. ¶*a ~ on one's character.*

[熟] ⓐ…을 보이지 않게 하다 ⓑ[문자 따위]를 지우다
—[名] 잉크 얼룩; 더럼; 결점; 눈에 거슬리는 것

blotch [blɑtʃ/blɔtʃ] *n.* [C] **1.** a large, irregular spot. **2.** a red spot on the skin. —*vt.* cover (something) with blotches.

—[名] 1. 얼룩, 오점 2. 부스럼, 종기
—[他] …을 더럽히다

blot·ter [blɑ́tər/blɔ́tə] *n.* [C] **1.** a piece of paper for drying ink. **2.** a book for writing down things that happen.

—[名] 1. 압지 2. [원대장에 올리기 전의] 임시 장부, 치부책

blotting paper [blɑ́tiŋpèipər/blɔ́tiŋpèipə] *n.* a special kind of paper for drying ink.

—[名] 압지

blouse [blaus, +*U.S.* blauz] *n.* [C] a kind of shirt worn by women and children on the upper part of the body.

—[名] 블라우스

:blow¹ [blou] *n.* [C] **1.** a hard hit; a knock. ¶*be at blows*① / *exchange blows.*② / *He gave me a heavy ~ on the face.* **2.** a sudden misfortune; a shock. ¶*It was a great ~ to me.*
1) ***at one*** (or ***a***) ***blow,*** by a single act or effort.
2) ***come*** (or ***fall***) ***to blows,*** begin fighting.
3) ***deal*** (or ***give, strike***) ***a blow to,*** beat.
4) ***without striking a blow,*** without any effort; quite easily.

—[名] 1. 타격, 강타 ¶①서로 치고받다/ ②싸움을 하다 2. 불의의 충격, 재난
[熟] 1)한대에; 단숨에 2)주먹다짐을 시작하다 3)…을 때리다 4)쉽게, 힘들이지 않고

:blow² [blou] *v.* (**blew, blown**) *vi.* **1.** move as the wind does. ⇒[usage] **2.** send strong wind from the mouth. **3.** be moved or carried by the wind. ¶*The curtain blew in the wind.* **4.** breathe fast; puff; pant. **5.** burst with a loud noise; explode. **6.** boast. —*vt.* **1.** send strong wind to (something). **2.** make (a wind instrument or whistle) sound. ¶*~ a trumpet.* **3.** ((usu. in *passive*)) exhaust of breath (esp. of a horse).
1) ***blow hot and cold,*** constantly change one's mood.
2) ***blow in,*** (*U. S. slang*) go in; enter; call to see someone.
3) ***blow off*** (=*send out*) *water, steam, etc.*
4) ***blow out,*** ⓐ extinguish by blowing. ⓑ fill (something) with air or gas by blowing.
5) ***blow over,*** (*colloq.*) (of trouble, a quarrel, etc.) pass away.
6) ***blow one's own trumpet,*** boast of oneself.
7) ***blow up,*** ⓐ fill (something) with air or gas. ⓑ explode; burst. ⓒ destroy (something) by an explosive. ⓓ (*slang*) scold. ⓔ (of a storm, etc.) arise.
—*n.* [C] **1.** a strong wind; a gale; a blast. **2.** (*slang*) a person who speaks proudly of himself. **3.** the act of speaking proudly of oneself.

—[自] 1. 불다 [usage] wind 또는 it 어느 것을 주어로 해도 좋음 2. 입김을 불다 3. 바람에 날리다, 흔들리다 4. 헐떡이다 5. 폭발하다 6. 허풍떨다 —[他] 1. …을 강하게 불다, 휘몰아치다 2. [취주악기]를 취주하다 3. [말(馬)]을 헐떡이게 하다
[熟] 1)항상 기분을 바꾸다, 변덕스럽다 2)((美俗))들어가다; 뜻밖에 찾아가다 3)…을 불어 날리다 4)ⓐ…을 불어서 끄다 ⓑ…을 가스로 채우다 5)((口)) [싸움 따위가] 가라앉다 6)허풍떨다, 자랑하다 7)ⓐ…을 가스로 채우다 ⓑ폭발하다 ⓒ…을 폭파하다 ⓓ((俗))꾸짖다 ⓔ[폭풍우 따위가] 발생하다
—[名] 1. 불기; 강풍 2. 허풍선이 3. 허풍떨기

blow·er [blóuər] *n.* [C] **1.** a person who blows. ¶*a glass ~.*① **2.** a machine to send air into a building, furnace, etc.

—[名] 1. 부는 사람 ¶①유리 부는 직공 2. 송풍기

:blown [bloun] *v.* pp. of **blow²**.
—*adj.* **1.** out of breath; breathless. **2.** tainted by flies; dirty.

—[形] 1. 숨가쁜, 지쳐빠진 / 2. 파리가 쉬를 슨; 더러운

blow·out [blóuàut] *n.* [C] **1.** a burst in an automobile tire; a puncture. **2.** a sudden escape of air, steam, etc.

—[名] 1. [타이어의] 빵꾸 2. [공기·증기 따위의] 분출

blow·pipe [blóupàip] *n.* [C] a tube for sending air or gas into a flame to make it hotter.

—[名] 불어서 불을 세게 하는 대롱

blow·torch [blóutɔ̀:rtʃ] *n.* [C] a lamp that shoots out a hot flame for melting metal. ⇒fig.

—[名] 토오치램프

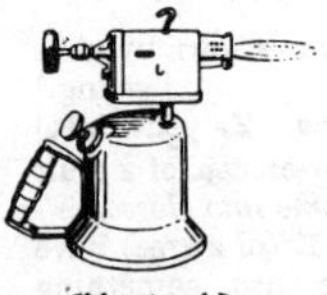
[blowtorch]

blub·ber [blʌ́bər] *n.* [U] the fat of whales and some other sea animals from which oil is obtained.

—[名] 고래 기름

bludg·eon [blʌ́dʒ(ə)n] *n.* [C] a short, thick stick with a heavy end. —*vt.* strike (someone or something) with a bludgeon; strike; hit.

—[名] 곤봉 —[他] 곤봉으로 때리다

:blue [blu:] *adj.* **1.** colored like the clear sky or the deep sea. **2.** low-spirited; depressed; hopeless. **3.** (of women) learned.

—[形] 1. 푸른 2. 기운없는; 희망없는 3. [여자가] 학식이 있는

bluebell *once in a blue moon,* very rarely.
—*n.* ⓤ **1.** blue color. **2.** blue paint or dye. **3.** ((*the* ~)) the sky; the sea. **4.** ⓒ a woman scholar. **5.** ((*pl.* often used as *sing.*)) low spirits.
—*vt.* make (something) blue. 「shaped flowers.」
blue·bell [blú:bèl] *n.* ⓒ a wild plant with blue, bell-
blue·bird [blú:bə̀:rd] *n.* ⓒ a small North American songbird with a bright blue back.
blue-black [blú:blǽk] *adj.* very dark blue.
blue blood [⌣ ⌣] *n.* blood of a noble family.
blue book [⌣ ⌣] *n.* **1.** (*U.S.*) a list of famous people. **2.** a British official report with a blue cover.
blue·jack·et [blú:dʒækit] *n.* ⓒ a sailor in the navy.
blue-pen·cil [blú:pénsl] *vt.* (**-ciled, -cil·ing** or esp. *Brit.* **-cilled, -cil·ling**) correct or cross out (a manuscript) with a blue pencil; edit.
blue·print [blú:prìnt] *n.* ⓒ **1.** a photograph made in white lines on blue paper, for building plans, etc. **2.** a detailed plan; a scheme. —*vt.* make a blueprint of (something); plan.
blue ribbon [⌣ ⌣⌣] *n.* the highest honor, given to the first-place winner in a contest; the ribbon of the Order of the Garter.
blue·stock·ing [blú:stàkiŋ/-stɔ̀k-] *n.* ⓒ a learned woman; a woman who pretends to be learned.
* **bluff**¹ [blʌf] *n.* ⓒ a high, steep place; a cliff. —*adj.* **1.** (of a cliff) having a wide, steep front. **2.** frank and rough in manner.
blu·ish [blú(:)iʃ] *adj.* somewhat blue; slightly blue.
blun·der [blʌ́ndər] *n.* ⓒ a foolish and careless mistake. ¶*commit a* ~.① —*vi., vt.* **1.** make a foolish mistake. **2.** stumble. **3.** say (something) thoughtlessly.
1) *blunder away,* miss (a chance, etc.) carelessly.
2) *blunder on,* find (someone or something) by chance.
blun·der·buss [blʌ́ndərbʌ̀s] *n.* ⓒ **1.** an old short gun with a wide mouth. **2.** a foolish person.
blun·der·er [blʌ́ndərər] *n.* ⓒ a careless person.
* **blunt** [blʌnt] *adj.* **1.** not having a sharp edge or point. ↔ sharp **2.** frank or plain in speech or manner. ¶ ~ *of speech.* **3.** slow in understanding. —*vt.* make (something) blunt. —*vi.* become blunt.
blunt·ly [blʌ́ntli] *adv.* in a blunt manner; plainly.
blunt·ness [blʌ́ntnis] *n.* ⓤ the state of being blunt.
blur [blə:r] *vt., vi.* (**blurred, blur·ring**) **1.** make (something) not clear in shape or appearance. ¶*Tears blurred my sight.*① **2.** become dim. ¶*Mists blurred the view.*② **3.** make (something) dirty; become dirty; stain. ¶*She blurred her new dress with red ink.*
—*n.* ⓒ **1.** the state of being not clear. **2.** a thing not seen clearly. **3.** a stain; a blot. ¶*a* ~ *on the mirror.*③
blurt [blə:rt] *vt.* tell suddenly or thoughtlessly. ((~ *out* something)) ¶ ~ *out a secret.*
* **blush** [blʌʃ] *n.* ⓒ **1.** the red color of the cheek or face caused by embarrassment or excitement. ¶*put someone to the* ~.① **2.** a rosy color.
at first blush, on first glance.
—*vi.* become rosy because of embarrassment or excitement; feel shame; be ashamed or embarrassed. ((~ *at* something; ~ *for* something or someone; ~ *to do*)) ¶ ~ *up to the root of one's hair*② | ~ *for shame*③ | *I blushed to hear the story.*④
blus·ter [blʌ́stər] *vi., vt.* **1.** blow noisily and violently; be windy. **2.** talk noisily and violently. **3.** boast.
—*n.* ⓒⓤ **1.** stormy noise. **2.** noisy and violent talk.

圈 아주 드물게
—영 1. 파랑, 남 2. 파랑 그림감(염료) 3. 바다; 창공 4. 여류 학자 5. 침울, 우울
—타 …을 푸르게 하다; …의 기운을
—영 종 모양의 남빛 꽃이 피는 야생초 「없애다」
—영 파랑새

—영 암청색의
—영 귀족의 혈통
—영 1. (美) 명사 인명록 2. 청서(青書) (영국 의회의 보고서)
—영 수병
—영 [원고 따위]를 푸른 연필로 수정하다; 편집하다

—영 1. 청사진 2. 상세한 설계도, 계획
—타 …을 청사진으로 찍다; 계획하다

—영 최고의 영예; 가아터 훈장의 푸른 리본

—영 여류 학자; 학식 있는 체하는 여자
—영 벼랑, 절벽 —영 1. 절벽의 2. 무뚝뚝한; 솔직한; 촌스러운

—영 푸르스름한
—영 큰 실수 ¶큰 실수를 하다 —자타 1. 큰 실수를 하다 2. 넘어지다 3. 무심코 말하다
圈 1) [기회 따위]를 실수로 놓치다 2) 우연히 만나다
—영 1. [18세기 경의] 총구가 넓고 짧은 총 2. 바보, 얼간이
—영 실수 잘하는 사람
—영 1. 날이 무딘, 둔한 2. 솔직한; 무뚝뚝한 3. 둔감한; 어리석은 —타 …을 무디게 하다 —자 둔감해지다, 무디어지다
—영 무뚝뚝하게, 버릇없이
—영 무딤, 무뚝뚝함
—타자 1. …을 희미하게 하다 ¶①눈물로 희미해지다 2. 흐려지다 ¶②안개로 똑똑히 보이지 않게 되었다 3. 더러워지다; 더럽히다
—영 1. 몽롱함, 흐림, 희미함 2. 희미한 것 3. 더럼, 얼룩 ¶③거울의 얼룩
—타 …을 불쑥 말하다; 부지중에 말하다
—영 1. 얼굴을 붉히기 ¶①남을 얼굴을 붉히게 하다 2. 장미빛

圈 얼핏 보기에, 일견
—자 얼굴을 붉히다; 붉어지다 ¶②새빨갛게 되다/③부끄러워서 붉어지다/④그 이야기를 듣고 얼굴이 붉어졌다

—자타 1. 바람이 휘몰아치다 2. 고함치다 3. 으쓱거리다 —영 1. 거칠게 몰아침 2. 호령, 고함

blus·ter·ous [blʌ́st(ə)rəs] *adj.* **1.** blowing noisily and violently; blowing like a storm. **2.** talking noisily.
—[形] 1. 휘몰아치는 2. 고함지르는, 뽐내는

bo·a [bóuə] *n.* [C] **1.** a large, long tropical American snake that is not poisonous. **2.** a long scarf of fur or feathers worn by a woman.
—[名] 1. 구렁이 2. 목도리

boa constrictor [⌐- -⌐-] *n.*=boa.

* **boar** [bɔːr] *n.* [C] **1.** a male pig. **2.** a wild pig.
—[名] 1. 수퇘지 2. 산돼지

‡ **board** [bɔːrd] *n.* [C] **1.** a long, wide, thin piece of wood. **2.** a large, thick, flat piece. **3.** a thick, stiff paper. **4.** ⟪*pl.*⟫ the stage. ¶*go on the boards.*① **5.** [U] food served; daily meals. **6.** a council; a committee.
—[名] 1. 널빤지 2. 널따란 판 3. 판지(板紙) 4. 무대 ¶①배우가 되다 5. 식사 6. 회의, 이사회

1) ***go by the board,*** ⓐ (of a mast) fall into the sea out of a ship. ⓑ fail completely; come to nothing.
2) ***on board,*** on or into a train or a ship.
[熟] 1)ⓐ[돛대가] 쓰러져서 바다에 떨어지다 ⓑ완전히 실패하다 2)승차(승선)하여

—*vt.* **1.** cover (something) with boards. **2.** provide (someone) with daily meals at a fixed price. **3.** go on or get in (a ship, train, plane, etc.). —*vi.* get one's daily meals at a fixed price.
—[他] 1. …을 판자로 덮다 2. …에게 식사를 주다 3. …에 타다 —[自] 하숙하다, 기숙하다

board·er [bɔ́ːrdər] *n.* [C] a person who pays for meals or for room and meals at other's house, a school, etc. ¶*a ~ at the school.*① ⇒[N.B.]
—[名] 하숙인; 기숙인 ¶①기숙생 [N.B.] 통학생은 dayboy, daygirl

boarding house [⌐- ⌐] *n.* a house where persons are given meals, or room and meals, at a fixed price.
—[名] 하숙집; 기숙사

boarding school [⌐- ⌐] *n.* a school where pupils are given room and meals as well as lessons. ⇒[N.B.]
—[名] 기숙학교 [N.B.] 자택에서 통학하는 학교는 day school

board·walk [bɔ́ːrdwɔ̀ːk] *n.* [C] a sidewalk made of thick boards, esp. along a beach.
—[名] [해변 따위의] 판자를 깐 산책로

‡ **boast** [boust] *vi., vt.* speak too well about oneself; be proud; be proud of having (something). ⟪~ *of* or *about* something; ~ *that* ...⟫ ¶*Our city boasts a fine park.*① / *He boasts of his wealth.*②
—[自][他] 자랑하다, 자랑으로 여기다 ¶① 우리 시는 훌륭한 공원이 자랑이다 /②그는 자기의 재산을 자랑한다

—*n.* [C] **1.** the act of praising oneself. **2.** a thing to be proud of.
—[名] 1. 자랑 2. 자랑거리

make a boast (=*be proud*) ***of something.***
[熟] …을 자랑하다

boast·er [bóustər] *n.* [C] a person who boasts.
—[名] 자랑하는 사람, 허풍선이

boast·ful [bóustf(u)l] *adj.* **1.** boasting. **2.** fond of boasting. ▷**boast·ful·ly** [-fuli] *adv.* —**boast·ful·ness** [-nis] *n.*
—[形] 1. 자랑하는 2. 자랑하기 좋아하는

‡ **boat** [bout] *n.* [C] **1.** a small open ship; a ship. ¶*cross a river in a ~ / row a ~ / go by ~.* **2.** a dish shaped like a boat.
—[名] 1. 보우트; [일반적으로] 배 2. 배 모양의 그릇(접시)

be in the same boat (=*be in the same condition*) ***with someone.***
[熟] …과 같은 처지에 있다

—*vi., vt.* **1.** go in a boat; row a boat. ¶*go boating.* **2.** carry (something) in a boat.
—[自][他] 1. 배로 가다; 배를 젓다 2. …을 배로 나르다

boat·house [bóuthàus] *n.* [C] a house for keeping boats safely.
—[名] 정고(艇庫), 배를 넣는 창고

boat·ing [bóutiŋ] *n.* [U] the act of rowing a boat, esp. for pleasure.
—[名] 보우트놀이

boat·man [bóutmən] *n.* [C] (pl. **-men** [-mən]) **1.** a man who rents boats. **2.** a man who rows boats for pay.
—[名] 1. 보우트 세놓는 사람 2. 보우트 젓는 사람, 뱃사공

boat·race [bóutrèis] *n.* [C] a race among rowing boats.
—[名] 보우트 경조

boat·swain [bóusn, bóutswèin] *n.* [C] the chief of common seamen on a ship. ⇒[N.B.]
—[名] 갑판장, 수부장 [N.B.] bosun이라고도 씀

boat train [⌐ ⌐] *n.* a train that carries passengers to or from a steamer.
—[名] 임항(臨港) 열차

bob[1] [bɑb/bɔb] *vt., vi.* (**bobbed, bob·bing**) move (something) up and down with short, quick motions; move about with short, quick motions.
—[他][自] 급히 아래위로 움직이다, 흔들리다, 깐닥하고 움직이다

bob up, appear suddenly. ¶*~ up like a cork.*①
[熟] 갑자기 나타나다 ¶①힘차게 다시 일어나다

—*n.* [C] a short, quick up-and-down motion; a sudden movement.
—[名] 깐닥하고 움직이기

bob[2] [bɑb/bɔb] *n.* [C] **1.** a short haircut for a woman or girl. **2.** a weight on the end of a line. **3.** a float for a fishing line. —*vt.* (**bobbed, bob·bing**) cut (hair) short and straight.
—[名] 1. 단발 2. [진자(振子)의] 추, 저울추 3. 낚시찌 —[他] [머리]를 짧게 자르다

Bob [bɑb / bɔb] *n.* a nickname of Robert.
—[名] Robert의 애칭

* **bob·by** [bɑ́bi/bɔ́bi] *n.* [C] (pl. **-bies**) (*Brit. slang*) a policeman.
—[名] ⟪英俗⟫ 순경

bob·sled [bɑ́bslèd/bɔ́b-] *n.* [C] (*U.S.*) two short sleds
—[名] ⟪美⟫ [두 대를 앞뒤로 이은] 연결

fastened together by a thick board, used for sliding down a snowy slope. ⇒fig.
썰매

bob·sleigh [bábslèi / bɔ́b-] *n.* =bobsled.

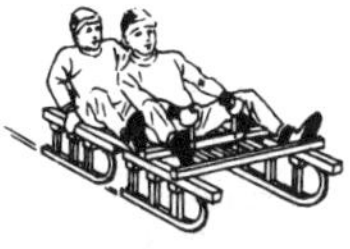
〔bobsled〕

bob·tail [bábtèil / bɔ́b-] *n.* [C] **1.** a short tail; a tail cut short. **2.** a horse or dog with a bobtail. **—*adj.*** having a bobtail.
—[名] 1. 짧은 꼬리; 자른 꼬리 2. 꼬리를 자른 말(개 따위) —[形] 꼬리를 자른; 꼬리가 짧은

bode [boud] *vt., vi.* be a sign of (something).
—[他][自] …의 전조가 되다

bode ill (well), be a bad (good) sign of (something).
[熟] …의 흉조(길조)이다

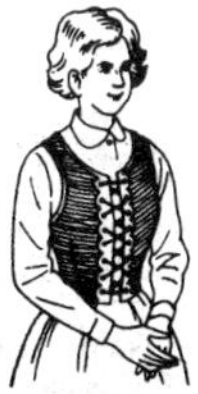
〔bodice〕

bod·ice [bádis / bɔ́d-] *n.* [C] the close-fitting waist of a dress for women. ⇒fig.
—[名] 코르셋 위에 입는 여자용 웃옷

bod·i·less [bádilis / bɔ́d-] *adj.* without a body.
—[形] 몸(동체)이 없는

* **bod·i·ly** [bádili / bɔ́d-] *adj.* having to do with the body. ↔mental ¶～ *pain.*① **—*adv.*** **1.** in person. **2.** all together; entirely.
—[形] 신체(육체)의 ¶①육체적 고통 —[副] 1. 자신이, 몸소 2. 송두리째, 통틀어서

bod·kin [bádkin / bɔ́d-] *n.* [C] a large, thick needle with a large eye.
—[名] 돗바늘

⁑ **bod·y** [bádi / bɔ́di] *n.* (pl. **bod·ies**) [C] **1.** the physical structure of a man or an animal, dead or alive. **2.** the central part of a man or an animal without the head or limbs. **3.** the main part of something. **4.** a person. ¶*anybody / somebody.* **5.** a group of persons or things as a unit. ¶*in a ～.*① **6.** a piece of matter. ¶*a heavenly ～.*② **7.** [U] solidity; substance; thickness. ¶*wine of good ～.*③ **—*vt.*** (**bod·ied**) give a real shape to (something); put (an idea, etc.) into some shape which can be seen or heard. 《～ *forth* something》
—[名] 1. 몸, 신체, 육체 2. 동체 3. 주요부 4. 사람 5. 무리, 다수 ¶①떼지어 6. 물체 ¶②천체 7. 실질(實質); [술 따위의] 농도, 밀도 ¶③진국 포도주 —[他] …을 구체화하다; …에 형체를 주다

bod·y·guard [bádigà:rd / bɔ́digá:d] *n.* [C] a man or group of men who guard an important person.
—[名] 호위[병], 경호원

bog [bag, bɔ:g / bɔg] *n.* [C] soft, wet, spongy ground; marsh. **—*vt.*** (**bogged, bog·ging**) sink (something) in a bog. **—*vi.*** fall into a bog. ¶～ *down.*①
—[名] 늪, 수렁, 소택지 —[他] …을 수렁에 빠뜨리다 —[自] 수렁에 빠지다 ¶①[궁지에 빠져] 꼼짝 못하다

bo·gey [bóugi] *n.* [C] an evil spirit; a person or a thing that causes fear.
—[名] 도깨비, 유령; 무시무시한 사람(것)

bog·gle [bágl / bɔ́g-] *vi.* hesitate.
—[自] 망설이다

bog·gy [bági, bɔ́:gi / bɔ́g-] *adj.* (**-gi·er, -gi·est**) soft, wet, and spongy like a bog.
—[形] 수렁 같은

bo·gie [bóugi] *n.* =bogey.

bo·gle [bóugl] *n.* =bogey.

bo·gus [bóugəs] *adj.* (*U.S*) false; untrue.
—[形] 《美》 가짜의, 위조의

bo·gy [bóugi] *n.* (pl. **-gies**) =bogey.

Bo·he·mi·a [bouhí:miə] *n.* a region of Czechoslovakia; a former country in central Europe.
—[名] 보헤미아 지방

Bo·he·mi·an [bouhí:miən] *adj.* **1.** of Bohemia, its people, or their language. **2.** free and easy. **—*n.*** [C] **1.** a person of Bohemia. **2.** [U] the language of Bohemia. **3.** 《often *b-*》 an artist, a writer, etc. who leads a free and easy way of life. **4.** a gypsy.
—[形] 1. 보헤미아의; 보헤미아 사람(말)의 2. 방랑의, 방종하는 —[名] 1. 보헤미아 사람 2. 보헤미아 말 3. 제멋대로 사는 사람(예술가) 4. 방랑자

⁑ **boil** [bɔil] *vt., vi.* **1.** heat (liquid) to the point of becoming gas; (of liquid) grow hot; cook (something) in water. ¶*boiling point.*① **2.** be very angry or excited.
—[他][自] 1. 끓이다, 끓다; 익히다, 익다; 삶다 ¶①비등점(沸騰點) 2. 핏대를 올리다, 격분하다

1) ***boil down,*** make (something) smaller in quantity.
2) ***boil over,*** ⓐ overflow the side of a vessel while boiling. ⓑ become very excited.
3) ***make** someone's **blood boil,*** make someone very angry.
[熟] 1)바짝 졸이다; 요약하다 2)ⓐ끓어 넘치다 ⓑ노발대발하다 3)[남]을 핏대올리게 하다

—*n.* [C] 《often *the* ～》 the act of boiling; the state of being boiled.
—[名] 끓음, 비등

boil·er [bɔ́ilər] *n.* [C] a large metal vessel for producing steam, keeping hot water, or boiling something.
—[名] 끓이는 기구; 증기 솥; 보일러

B

bois·ter·ous [bɔ́ist(ə)rəs] *adj.* violent; noisy; stormy; rough. —[形] 맹렬한, 시끄러운, 거친, 사나운

bois·ter·ous·ly [bɔ́ist(ə)rəsli] *adv.* in a boisterous manner. —[副] 시끄럽게, 사납게

‡ **bold** [bould] *adj.* **1.** fearless; brave; courageous. ↔cowardly ¶*a ~ idea.*① **2.** without feelings of shame; impudent. ¶*as ~ as brass.*② **3.** clear; striking; well-marked. —[形] 1. 대담한, 용감한 ¶①대담한 생각 2. 뻔뻔스러운, 창피한 줄 모르는 ¶②철면피의 3. 뚜렷한; 굵은

be (*or* ***make***) ***bold to,*** dare to do (something); have the courage to do (something). [熟] 대담하게 …하다

bold·faced [bóuldfèist] *adj.* **1.** impudent; impolite. **2.** having thick, heavy lines. ¶ *~ type.*① —[形] 1. 뻔뻔스러운, 버릇없는 2. [활자 따위] 고딕체의 ¶①고딕체 활자

B

* **bold·ly** [bóuldli] *adv.* **1.** in a bold manner. **2.** clearly. —[副] 1. 대담하게 2. 두드러지게

bold·ness [bóuldnis] *n.* [U] the state of being bold. —[名] 대담함, 배짱좋음; 두드러짐

bole [boul] *n.* [C] the trunk of a tree. —[名] 나무의 줄기

bo·le·ro [bouléərou] *n.* [C] (pl. **-ros**) **1.** a lively Spanish dance; the music for it. **2.** a short, loose jacket for women. —[名] 1. 볼레로 춤; 볼레로 춤곡 2. [여자용의] 짧은 웃옷

boll [boul] *n.* [C] a round seed case of cotton or flax. —[名] [목화·아마 따위의] 둥근 꼬투리

bo·lo·gna [bəlóunə / -njə] *n.* [U] a large sausage made of beef, pork, etc. —[名] 볼로냐 소시지

Bol·she·vik [bálʃivik / bɔ́l-] *n.* [C] (pl. **-viks** or **-viki**) **1.** a member of the Communist party of Russia. **2.** an extreme radical. ▷**Bol·she·vism** [-vizəm] *n.* —[名] 1. 볼셰비키(러시아 사회 민주 노동당의 다수파) 2. 과격파

Bol·she·vi·ki [bàlʃəví:ki / bɔ̀l-] *n.* pl. of **Bolshevik.**

bol·ster [bóulstər] *n.* [C] **1.** a long pillow for a bed. **2.** a cushion. —*vt.* support. —[名] 1. 긴 베개 2. [서까래 따위의] 받침 —[他] …을 지지하다

bolster up, support; keep (something) from falling. [熟] …을 지지하다; 받치다

* **bolt** [boult] *n.* [C] **1.** a metal pin used with a nut in fastening and holding things together. **2.** a sliding bar for locking a door or gate. **3.** a short heavy arrow of a crossbow. **4.** a flash of lightning; a thunderbolt. **5.** the act of bolting (*v.* 1) —[名] 1. 볼트, 죔못 2. 빗장 3. [crossbow의] 굵은 화살 4. 번개 5. 탈주, 도망

do a bolt; make a bolt for it, run away quickly. [熟] 뺑소니치다

—*vi., vt.* **1.** escape, depart, or run away suddenly from (a place). **2.** swallow (food) unchewed. **3.** fasten (a door) with a bolt. —[自][他] 1. 갑자기 도망치다 2. [음식을] 통째로 삼키다 3. [문에] 빗장을 걸다

bolt in (***out***), shut (someone) in (out). [熟] …을 가두어 넣다(안에 들이지 않다)

—*adv.* in an erect position. ¶ *~ upright.*① —[副] 곧추 서서 ¶①꼿꼿이

* **bomb** [bam / bɔm] *n.* [C] a metal ball or shell filled with bursting material for causing destruction, usu. dropped from an aircraft. ¶*an atomic ~*① / *a hydrogen ~.*② —[名] 폭탄 ¶①원자폭탄/②수소폭탄

—*vt., vi.* drop bombs on (a place, etc.). ¶*be bombed out.*③ —[他][自] 폭탄을 투하하다 ¶③공습으로 집이 타서 쫓겨나다

bom·bard [bambá:rd / bɔmbá:d] *vt.* **1.** attack (a place, etc.) with shells from big guns. **2.** attack (someone) with questions, arguments, etc. 《~ someone *with*》 —[他] 1. …을 포격하다 2. …에 질문을 퍼붓다

bom·bard·ment [bambá:rdmənt / bɔmbá:d-] *n.* [C][U] an attack with shells or with bombs. —[名] 포격

bom·bast [bámbæst / bɔ́m-] *n.* [U] big words or big talk with little meaning. —[名] 호언장담

bom·bas·tic [bambǽstik / bɔm-] *adj.* using many fine words with little thought. —[形] 과장된, 허풍의

Bom·bay [bambéi / bɔm-] *n.* a seaport in western India. —[名] 봄베이(인도 서부의 항구)

bomb·er [bámər / bɔ́mə] *n.* [C] **1.** an airplane used for dropping bombs on the enemy. **2.** a person who drops bombs. —[名] 1. 폭격기 2. 폭격수

bomb·proof [bámprù:f / bɔ́m-] *adj.* safe from bombs and shells. —[形] 방탄(防彈)의

bomb·shell [bámʃèl / bɔ́m-] *n.* [C] **1.** a bomb. **2.** something sudden and surprising. —[名] 1. 폭탄 2. 돌발 사건, 놀랄 만한 일

bo·na fi·de [bóunəfáidi] *adv.* sincerely; truely. —[副] 성실하게, 참말로

bo·nan·za [bounǽnzə] *n.* [C] (*U.S.*) **1.** a rich mass of metal in a mine. **2.** (*colloq.*) anything that brings good fortune and prosperity. ¶*in ~.*① —[名] 1. 《美》 노다지 2. 《口》대통한 운수, ¶①행운재수 좋게, 운수 대통으로

bon·bon [bánbàn / bɔ́nbɔ̀n] *n.* [C] a small piece of candy. —[名] 봉봉[과자]

‡ **bond** [band / bɔnd] *n.* [C] **1.** anything that joins or unites; 《*pl.*》 anything that controls someone's liberty. ¶*a ~* —[名] 1. 기반(羈絆), 맺는 것; 구속, 속박 ¶①우정의 기반/②속박되어/③인습의

bondage [133] **bookcase**

*of friendship*① / *in bonds*② / *break the bonds of convention.*③ **2.** a printed paper sold by a government or company promising to pay back money. ¶*a public ~* / *a treasury ~*. **3.** (*Law*) a written agreement. 속박을 타파하다 **2.** 차용증서, 공채증서, 사채(社債) **3.** 약정

bond·age [bándidʒ / bɔ́nd-] *n.* Ⓤ **1.** the condition of not being free; slavery. **2.** the condition of being under some power or influence. —명 **1.** 노예의 신분 **2.** 속박

bond·man [bándmən / bɔ́nd-] *n.* Ⓒ (*pl.* **-men** [-mən]) a slave. —명 노예

bonds·man [bándzmən / bɔ́ndz-] *n.* (*pl.* **-men** [-mən]) =bondman.

‡**bone** [boun] *n.* Ⓒ **1.** a single part of a skeleton; Ⓤ the material of which bones consist. **2.** (*pl.*) a skeleton; a body, dead or alive. **3.** a bone-like substance. **4.** a thing made of bone or ivory. —명 **1.** 뼈; 골질(骨質) **2.** 골격체 **3.** 뼈 모양의 물질 **4.** 뼈·상아 제품

 1) *a bone of contention,* a cause of a quarrel.
 2) *feel in one's bones,* ⓐ feel sure. ⓑ feel without reasoning.
 3) *make no bones of* (*or about*), not mind doing (something); do not care about (something).
 4) *spare bones,* do not try one's best.
 5) *to the bone,* completely.

숙 1) 불화의 씨 2) ⓐ 확신하다 ⓑ 직감하다 3) …을 개의치 않다, …을 예사로 하다 4) 꾀를 부리다 5) 철저히, 철두철미하게

—*vt.* rid (a body) of bones. —타 …의 뼈를 없애다

bone-dry [bóundrái] *adj.* (*colloq.*) very dry or thirsty. —형 《口》 바싹 마른

bone-set·ter [bóunsètər] *n.* Ⓒ a person who sets broken bones. —명 정골사(整骨師)

bon·fire [bánfàiər / bɔ́nfàiə] *n.* Ⓒ a large fire made out of doors for burning dead leaves, rubbish etc., or in celebration of some public event. —명 화톳불; 모닥불

bo·ni·to [bouní:tou] *n.* Ⓒ (*pl.* **-tos** or **-toes**, *collectively* **-to**) a large salt-water food fish. —명 가다랭이

Bonn [ban / bɔn] *n.* the capital of West Germany. —명 본(서독의 수도)

∗**bon·net** [bánit / bɔ́n-] *n.* Ⓒ **1.** a woman's or baby's hat, usu. tied under the chin with strings or ribbons. **2.** a cap without edge worn by men and boys in Scotland. **3.** (*Brit.*) the part of an automobile covering the engine, etc. —명 **1.** 보닛(부인·소아용의 챙 없는 모자) **2.** [스코틀랜드의] 남자 모자 **3.** 《英》 [자동차의] 보닛

bon·ny, bon·nie [báni / bɔ́ni] *adj.* (**-ni·er, -ni·est**) **1.** pretty; handsome. **2.** fine; merry; gay. **3.** healthy-looking. ▷ **bon·ni·ness** [-nis] *n.* —형 **1.** 예쁜, 귀여운 **2.** 좋은; 쾌활한, 즐거운 **3.** 토실토실한, 건강해 보이는

bo·nus [bóunəs] *n.* Ⓒ a special money given to workers or stockholders etc., besides their usual income. —명 보우너스, 상여금; 특별 배당금

bon·y [bóuni] *adj.* (**bon·i·er, bon·i·est**) **1.** of or like bone. **2.** full of bones. **3.** thin. ¶*a ~ man*. —형 **1.** 뼈의(같은) **2.** 뼈가 많은 **3.** 앙상한, 마른

boo·by [bú:bi] *n.* Ⓒ (*pl.* **-bies**) a foolish, slow person; a fool. —명 바보, 얼간이

booby prize [‿ ‿] *n.* a prize given to a person who is last in a race or game —명 꼴찌상, 최하위상

‡**book** [buk] *n.* Ⓒ **1.** a bundle of printed sheets of paper fastened together as a thing to be read. **2.** Ⓤ literary work. **3.** a main division of such a volume. **4.** (*the B-*) Bible. **5.** anything fastened like a book. **6.** a set of tickets, checks, etc. bound together. —명 **1.** 책, 서적 **2.** 저술, 저작 **3.** [책의] 권, 장(章) **4.** 성서 **5.** 장부, 책자 **6.** 어음철, 우표첩

 1) *bring someone to book,* force someone to explain.
 2) *by the book,* according to the usual way.
 3) *in someone's bad* (*or black*) *books,* out of favor with someone.
 4) *in someone's good books,* in someone's favor.
 5) *know something like a book,* know something very well.
 6) *on the books,* ⓐ recorded. ⓑ listed.

숙 1) 해명을 요구하다 2) 일반적으로는, 규칙에 따라서 3) …에게 미움받아 4) …의 호감을 사서 5) …을 잘 알고 있다 6) ⓐ 기록된 ⓑ 등록된

—*vt.* **1.** record (names, data, etc.) in a book or a list. **2.** reserve. ¶*~ a seat*. —*vi.* issue a ticket. —타 **1.** …을 기장하다 **2.** …을 예약하다

book down (*or in*), write down (something) in a book. 숙 …을 기록하다

book·case [búkkèis] *n.* Ⓒ a cabinet or set of shelves to hold books in. —명 책장, 서가(書架)

book end [´-`] *n.* ((usu. *pl.*)) a support placed at the end of a row of books to hold them upright. —⊛ [책이 쓰러지지 않게 받치는] 책꽂이

book·ing clerk [búkiŋklə̀:rk] *n.* **1.** a person who sells tickets. **2.** a person who makes seating reservations. —⊛ 1. 출찰계원, 매표원 2. [호텔 따위의] 예약계

booking office [´- `-] *n.* (*Brit.*) a place where tickets are sold. (cf. *U.S.* ticket office) —⊛ (英) 매표소

book·ish [búkiʃ] *adj.* **1.** fond of books. ¶ *a* ~ *girl.* **2.** knowing from books better than from real life. **3.** of books. **4.** formal; pedantic. ¶ ~ *English* ① / *a* ~ *speech.* ▷ **book·ish ness** [-nis] *n.* —⊛ 1. 책을 좋아하는 2. 서적상의, 실제에 어두운 3. 서적의 4. 딱딱한, 학자인 체하는 ¶①딱딱한 영어

book·keep·er [búkkì:pər] *n.* ⓒ a person who records business accounts. —⊛ 장부 계원, 기장자

book·keep·ing [búkkì:piŋ] *n.* Ⓤ the work of recording business accounts. —⊛ 부기

book·let [búklit] *n.* ⓒ a small book; a pamphlet. —⊛ 소책자, 팜플렛

book·mak·er [búkmèikər] *n.* ⓒ **1.** a maker of books. **2.** a person who makes a business of accepting bets on horse races. —⊛ 1. [돈벌이 목적의] 저작자, 편집자 2. [경마의] 마권(馬券)업자

book·mark [búkmà:rk] *n.* ⓒ anything put between the pages of a book to mark a certain place. —⊛ 서표(書標)

book·sell·er [búksèlər] *n.* ⓒ a person whose business is selling books. —⊛ 서적상, 책 장수

book·shelf [búkʃèlf] *n.* ⓒ (pl. **-shelves**) a shelf, usu. part of a bookcase, for holding books. —⊛ 책장, 서가

book·shelves [búkʃèlvz] *n.* pl. of **bookshelf.**

book·shop [búkʃàp / -ʃɔ̀p] *n.* (*Brit.*) =bookstore.

book·stall [búkstɔ̀:l] *n.* ⓒ **1.** a stall at which books, usu. secondhand ones, are sold. **2.** (*Brit.*) a stand at which newspapers are sold; a newsstand. —⊛ 1. 책방, 서점, 고본(古本)의 노점 2. (英) 신문 매점

book·store [búkstɔ̀:r] *n.* ⓒ (*U.S.*) a store where books are sold. —⊛ (美) 서점, 책방

book·worm [búkwə̀:rm] *n.* ⓒ **1.** a person who is always reading books. **2.** a small worm that makes holes in books. —⊛ 1. 독서광, 책벌레 2. 좀, 책좀

boom¹ [bu:m] *n.* ⓒ **1.** a deep sound, as of waves or a big gun. **2.** a sudden rapid increase of activity; a rise in popularity. ¶ *a* ~ *town*① / *a war* ~.② —*vi.* **1.** make a deep sound. **2.** increase suddenly in activity; grow rapidly. ¶*Business is booming.*③ —*vt.* speak (something) with a booming sound. ((~ *out* something)) ¶ *The clocks* ~ *out the hour.*④ [boom² 1.]
—⊛ 1. 쾅 울리는 소리 2. 벼락 경기(景氣), 붐; [인기 따위의] 급상승 ¶①신흥도시 /②전시 경기(戰時景氣)
—ⓥⓘ 1. 쿵(쾅)하고 울리다 2. 갑자기 경기가 좋아지다 ¶③장사가 갑자기 잘된다 —ⓥⓣ …을 쿵(쾅)하고 울리다 ¶④시계가 땡땡하고 시간을 알린다

boom² [bu:m] *n.* ⓒ **1.** a long pole by which a sail is stretched; the lifting arm of a derrick. ⇒fig. **2.** a chain, cable, etc. that keeps logs from floating away. —⊛ 1. 돛의 아래 활죽; 데릭 기중기의 물건 올리는 부분 2. [강·항구 따위의] 방재(防材)

boom·er·ang [bú:məræŋ] *n.* ⓒ a curved piece of wood used by Australian natives as a weapon which comes back when thrown. ⇒fig. —⊛ 부우머랭(던지면 되돌아오는 오스트레일리아 토인의 무기)

boon¹ [bu:n] *n.* ⓒ a blessing; a great favor. —⊛ 은혜, 은전

boon² [bu:n] *adj.* jolly; gay; merry; close. ¶*a* ~ *companion.*① ⇒ usage [boomerang]
—ⓐ 유쾌한, 재미있는 ¶①다정한 친구 usage 이 숙어에만 쓰임

boor [buər] *n.* ⓒ **1.** a rude person with bad manners. **2.** a peasant, esp. a Dutch or German peasant. —⊛ 1. 시골뜨기, 무식한 촌사람 2. [네덜란드 또는 등지의] 농민, 농군

boor·ish [búəriʃ] *adj.* rude; ill-mannered; clumsy. —⊛ 야비한, 버릇없는

boost [bu:st] *vt.* **1.** lift or push (something) from below or behind. **2.** support very earnestly. ¶*She always boosts her home town.* **3.** raise or increase. ¶ ~ *prices.* —*n.* ⓒ the act of boosting.
—ⓥ 1. …을 뒤에서 밀다, 밀어 올리다 2. …을 후원하다 3. [세세 따위를] 올리다 4. 뒤를 밀기; 가격 인상, 등귀(騰貴)

boost·er [búːstər] *n.* ⓒ (*U.S. colloq.*) a person or a thing that boosts; an earnest supporter. —명 《美口》후원자, 조력자

boot [buːt] *n.* ⓒ **1.** (usu. *pl.*) (*U.S.*) a covering made of leather or rubber for the foot and leg; (*Brit.*) a shoe or outer foot covering reaching above the ankle. ¶*a pair of boots.* **2.** any protecting cover. —명 1. 《美》 장화; 《英》목이 긴 구두 2. 덮개
1) *bet your boots,* (*U.S.*) be certain; be quite sure.
2) *The boot is on the other leg* (or *foot*). The situation is changed.
3) *get the boot,* ⓐ be kicked. ⓑ lose one's employment; be fired.
4) *give someone the boot,* ⓐ kick. ⓑ force away.
5) *have one's heart in one's boots,* be afraid; be in low spirits with fear.
6) *lick the boots of* (=*flatter*) *someone.*
—*vt.* **1.** put boots on (someone). **2.** kick.
熟 1)《美》틀림없다 2)당치도 않은 소리다; 책임(진상)은 딴 데 있다 3)ⓐ걸어차이다 4)ⓐ걸어차다 ⓑ…를 해고하다 5)겁을 먹고 있다 6)…에게 아첨하다
—타 1. [남]에게 구두를 신기다 2. …을 차다

boot·black [búːtblæ̀k] *n.* ⓒ a person whose work is shining shoes and boots on the street. —명 [거리의] 구두닦기

boot·ed [búːtid] *adj.* having boots on. —형 구두를 신은

boot·ee [buːtíː / búːtiː, buːtíː] *n.* (usu. *pl.*) **1.** a baby's soft shoe of knitted wool. **2.** a woman's short boot. —명 1. 털실로 짠 어린이 구두 2. 가벼운 부인용 구두

booth [buːθ, buːð / buːð] *n.* ⓒ (pl. **booths** [buːðz]) **1.** a covered stall or stand at a fair or a market. **2.** a small, enclosed place for a special purpose. ¶*a telephone ~* / *a voting ~*. **3.** a partly enclosed place in a café or the like, for use by a few persons. —명 1. [거리·시장 따위의] 매점 2. 간막이 방 3. [다방 따위의] 간막이 좌석

boot·lace [búːtlèis] *n.* (chiefly *Brit.*)=shoelace.

boot·leg [búːtlèg] *vt., vi.* (*U.S. slang*) make, carry or sell (wine or other things) unlawfully. —타재 《美俗》 [술 따위를] 밀조하다, 밀매하다

boot·leg·ger [búːtlègər] *n.* ⓒ a person who bootlegs. —명 [주류] 밀조자, 밀매자, 밀수입자

boot·less [búːtlis] *adj.* useless. —형 쓸데없는, 무익한

boot·mak·er [búːtmèikər] *n.* ⓒ a person who makes shoes. —명 구두 직공

boo·ty [búːti] *n.* ⓤ **1.** things taken from the enemy in time of war; goods stolen by thieves. **2.** gain; profits. —명 1. 전리품, 노획품, 약탈품 2. 벌이, 이득

booze [buːz] *n.* ⓤ (*colloq.*) any alcoholic liquor or strong drink. —*vi.* drink very much. —명 술 —자 술을 고래로 마시다

bo·peep [boupíːp] *n.* ⓤ a cry meaning "I see you" in a game played with a very young child. —명 아웅, 때꾹(어린애를 놀릴 때 내는 소리)

bo·rac·ic [bourǽsik] *adj.* =boric.

bo·rax [bɔ́ːræks] *n.* ⓤ a white salt-like powder used for cleaning and in glass-making. —명 붕사(硼砂)

Bor·deaux [bɔːrdóu] *n.* ⓤ a red or white wine made in the Bordeaux region. —명 보르도 포도주

bor·der [bɔ́ːrdər] *n.* ⓒ **1.** an edge. ¶*a hotel on the ~ of the lake.* **2.** a narrow strip along or around something. **3.** a line of division between two countries or states; a frontier. **4.** a decorative edge. ¶*a ~ of lace.* —*vt.* put a border on (something). —*vi.* touch; approach closely in character. (*~ on* or *upon* something) ¶*~ on the lake*① / *His actions ~ on madness.*② —명 1. 가장자리, 가, 변두리 2. 가장자리의 좁다란 부분 3. 경계, 변경, 국경 4. 가장자리 장식 —타 …과 경계를 접하다; …의 가장자리를 대다 —자 ①접하다; 비슷하다 ¶①호수에 접하다/②그의 행동은 미친 짓에 가깝다

bor·der·er [bɔ́ːrdərər] *n.* ⓒ a person who lives on the border of a country. —명 국경 지방에 사는 사람

bor·der·land [bɔ́ːrdərlæ̀nd] *n.* (*the ~*) **1.** the land on or near a frontier between two countries. **2.** an uncertain district or space. —명 1. 국경 지방, 경계지 2. 어중간한 지역

bor·der·line [bɔ́ːrdərlàin] *n.* ⓒ a boundary line; a dividing line. —*adj.* **1.** on a border or boundary. **2.** uncertain; doubtful; between. ¶*a ~ case*① —명 국경선, 경계선 —형 1. 국경선상의 2. 어중간한, 불명확한 ¶①한계를 짓기 어려운 사건

bore¹ [bɔːr] *vt., vi.* **1.** make a hole with a drill, etc. **2.** make (a hole, passage, tunnel, etc.) by pushing through or digging out. **3.** push forward; advance step by step. ¶*~ one's way through the crowd.*① —*n.* ⓒ **1.** a hole made by boring. **2.** empty space inside a pipe, tube, etc. **3.** distance across the inside of a hole or a tube. —타자 1. 구멍을 뚫다 2. 뚫다 3. 밀어젖히고 나아가다 ¶①군중 사이를 뚫고 나아가다
—명 1. [송곳 따위로 뚫은] 구멍 2. 파이프 구멍 3. 구경(口徑)

bore

bore² [bɔːr] *vt.* make (someone) weary by being dull or tiresome. (~ someone *with*) —*n.* ⓒ a dull, tiresome person or thing.
—ⓤ …을 지루하게 하다, 싫증나게 하다 —ⓒ 지루한 사람(것)

* **bore³** [bɔːr] *v.* pt. of **bear¹**.

bore⁴ [bɔːr] *n.* ⓒ a very high sea-wave at the mouth of a river or narrow channel.
—ⓒ 해일(海溢), 높은 파도

bo·re·al [bɔ́ːriəl] *adj.* northern.
—ⓐ 북쪽의

bore·dom [bɔ́ːrdəm] *n.* **1.** ⓤ the state of being tired and not interested. **2.** ⓒ an instance of being bored.
—ⓒ 1. 지루함, 권태 2. 지루한 일

bor·er [bɔ́ːrər] *n.* ⓒ **1.** a person who drills holes; a tool for drilling holes. **2.** an insect or a worm that bores into wood, fruit, etc.
—ⓒ 1. 구멍을 뚫는 사람; 송곳, 천공기(穿孔機) 2. 나무 좀

bo·ric acid [bɔ́ːrikǽsid] *n.* a white, crystalline substance.
—ⓒ 붕산(硼酸)

bor·ing¹ [bɔ́ːriŋ] *n.* ⓤ the act of making or enlarging a hole.
—ⓒ 구멍을 뚫기, 천공

bor·ing² [bɔ́ːriŋ] *adj.* tiresome; dull.
—ⓐ 지루한, 싫증나는

* **born** [bɔːrn] *v.* pp. of **bear¹**.
—*adj.* **1.** brought into life; brought forth. **2.** by birth; by natural qualities. ¶*a ~ poet.*
—ⓐ 1. 태어난 2. 타고난, 천성의

* **borne** [bɔːrn] *v.* pp. of **bear¹**.

Bor·ne·o [bɔ́ːrniòu] *n.* an island in the East Indies.
—ⓒ 보르네오 섬

bo·ron [bɔ́ːran / -rɔn] *n.* ⓤ a chemical element found in borax.
—ⓒ 붕소(硼素)

bor·ough [bɔ́ːrou / bʌ́rə] *n.* ⓒ **1.** (*U.S.*) a combined town smaller than a city. **2.** (*U.S.*) one of the five political divisions of New York City. **3.** (*Brit.*) a town with powers of self-government.
—ⓒ 1 (美) 자치읍 2.(美) 뉴우요오크시의 구(區) 3.(英) 자치 도시

bor·row [bárou, bɔ́ː- / bɔ́r-] *vt.* **1.** get (something) from another person on a promise of return. (~ something *from*) ↔**lend 2.** copy or adopt (another's thoughts, words, ideas, etc.) as one's own. —*vi.* borrow money. (~ *from* someone) borrows.
—ⓤ 1. …을 빌리다, 차용하다 2. …을 모방하다, 표절하다 —ⓥ 돈을 빌리다

bor·row·er [bárouər, bɔ́ːr- / bɔ́rouə] *n.* ⓒ a person who borrows.
—ⓒ 차용인; 표절자

bosh [baʃ / bɔʃ] *n.* ⓤ (*colloq.*) nonsense; foolish talk or ideas. ¶*Bosh!*
—ⓒ 허튼 소리, 터무니없는 생각 ¶① 바보 같은 소리!

* **bos·om** [búzəm] *n.* ⓒ **1.** the upper, front part of the human body; the human breast, esp. of a woman. **2.** the part of a garment covering the breast. **3.** the center or inmost part of (something). ¶*on the ~ of the Pacific Ocean / in the ~ of the mountains.* **4.** the place where one feels deeply. ¶*speak one's ~.*① **5.** the surface of a sea, lake, etc. —*adj.* close; trusted; very familiar. ¶*a ~ friend.*
—ⓒ 1. 가슴 2. [의류의] 가슴 부분 3. 한가운데, 내부, 속 4. 마음, 흉중 ¶① 가슴속을 이야기하다 5. [바다·호수 따위의] 표면 —ⓐ 친한

* **boss¹** [bɔːs, bas / bɔs] *n.* ⓒ (*colloq.*) **1.** a person who gives orders to workmen; a headman of any business; a foreman; a manager; a master. **2.** a politician who controls his party organization, usu. in a certain place. —*vt., vi.* be the boss of (a party); give orders to (someone); control.
—ⓒ 1. 우두머리, 두목, 수령, 감독 2. [어떤 지역의] 정당 영수 —ⓤⓥ 두목(보스·수령)이 되다; …을 지배하다

boss² [bɔːs, bas / bɔs] *n.* ⓒ a round part or ornament which stands up on a flat surface.
—ⓒ 양각 돋기(陽刻突起), 양각 장식

boss·y [bɔ́ːsi, bási / bɔ́si] *adj.* (*U.S. colloq.*) (**boss·i·er, boss·i·est**) with a character to be a boss; fond of ordering others.
—ⓐ 두목 행세를 하는, 뻐기는

* **Bos·ton** [bɔ́ːst(ə)n / bɔ́s-] *n.* a seaport and capital of Massachusetts, U.S.A.
—ⓒ 보스턴(미국의 도시)

Bos·to·ni·an [bɔːstóuniən / bɔs-] *adj.* of Boston. —*n.* ⓒ a person of Boston.
—ⓐ 보스턴의 —ⓒ 보스턴 시민

bo·tan·ic [bətǽnik] *adj.*=botanical.

bo·tan·i·cal [bətǽnik(ə)l] *adj.* of plants or botany.
—ⓐ 식물의; 식물학[상]의

bot·a·nist [bátənist / bɔ́t-] *n.* ⓒ a person who studies botany; a specialist in botany.
—ⓒ 식물학자

bot·a·nize [bátənàiz / bɔ́t-] *vi.* **1.** collect plants for study. **2.** study plants. ▷**bot·a·niz·er** [-ər] *n.*
—ⓤ 1. 식물을 채집하다 2. 식물을 연구하다

* **bot·a·ny** [bátəni / bɔ́t-] *n.* ⓤ the scientific study of plants; the study of plants and plant life.
—ⓒ 식물학

botch [batʃ / bɔtʃ] *vt.* **1.** spoil (something) by poor work;
—ⓤ 1. …을 망쳐 놓다 2. 보기 흉하게

do (work) badly. **2.** mend roughly. —*n.* ⓒ **1.** a poor piece of work ; a bad job. **2.** a badly mended part.

‡both [bouθ] *adj.* the two ; the pair of. ¶*~brothers | the brothers.* ⇒USAGE
—*pron.* the two ; the one and the other. ¶*~ of them | Both are dead. | They ~ went. | They are ~ true.* ⇒USAGE
—*conj.* 《in form of *both ... and*》together with ; at once ; not only ... but also. ↔neither ... nor ¶*Both he and she are dead. | She is ~ dead and buried.*

‡both·er [báðər / bɔ́ðə] *vt.* trouble ; worry. 《*~ someone with*》 ¶*Don't ~ me with foolish questions. | That does not ~ me. | Don't ~ yourself* (or *your head*) *about it.*
—*vi.* trouble oneself. 《*~ about* something》 ¶*Don't ~ about it. | Don't ~ about my dinner.*①
—*n.* **1.** ⓒ a cause or condition of worry or anxiety ; Ⓤ trouble. ¶*This broken zipper is a ~.*② *| I find the work a great ~.* **2.** ⓒ a person or thing that causes worry or trouble.

both·er·some [báðərsəm / bɔ́ðə-] *adj.* causing trouble ; troublesome ; troubling.

‡bot·tle [bátl / bɔ́tl] *n.* ⓒ **1.** a narrow-necked container, usu. of glass, for holding liquids. ¶*the neck of a ~.* **2.** the contents of such a container ; amount that a bottle holds. **3.** 《*the ~*》 the act or habit of drinking wine, etc. ; alcoholic liquor.
—*vt.* put (liquid, fruits, vegetables, etc.) into bottles.
bottle up, ⓐ keep (something) in a bottle ; hold in ; shut in. ⓑ control ; hide. ¶*~ one's anger.*①

bot·tle·neck [bátlnèk / bɔ́tl-] *n.* ⓒ **1.** the neck of a bottle. **2.** a narrow part of a passage or street that cannot be passed through. **3.** anything that hinders progress ; a check. **4.** a condition in which progress is stopped.

‡bot·tom [bátəm / bɔ́t-] *n.* ⓒ **1.** the base ; the lowest part. **2.** the ground under the water. ¶*the ~ of the sea.* **3.** real nature or essential facts that exist below the surface. **4.** the lowest person or thing in a class, etc. **5.** a ship ; the outer part of a ship below the water. **6.** (*pl.*) low lying land along the river. **7.** Ⓤ staying power ; stamina.
1) *be at the bottom of* (=*be the real reason for*) something.
2) *from* (or *to*) *the bottom of one's heart,* sincerely.
3) *get to the bottom of* (=*find out the real reason for*) something.
4) *go to the bottom,* sink.
5) *send to the bottom,* make (a ship) sink.
6) *stand on one's own bottom,* be independent.
7) *touch bottom,* ⓐ (of a ship) run on a rock. ⓑ be at the lowest point.

bot·tom·less [bátəmlis / bɔ́t-] *adj.* without a bottom ; very deep.

bou·doir [búːdwɑːr] *n.* ⓒ a lady's private sitting room 「for dressing room.」

• **bough** [bau] *n.* ⓒ one of the main branches of a tree.

‡bought [bɔːt] *v.* pt. and pp. of **buy.** 「beef.」

bouil·lon [búːljən / búːjɔːŋ] *n.* Ⓤ a clear soup, usu. of

boul·der [bóuldər] *n.* ⓒ a large piece of rock rounded or worn by water and weather.

boul·e·vard [búl(ː)ləvɑːrd / búːlvɑːd, -vɑːd] *n.* ⓒ a broad main street, usu. having trees on each side.

bounce [bauns] *vi.* **1.** bound like a ball. ¶*The ball bounces well.* **2.** move in a sudden or noisy rush. 《*~ about* (or *out of, into*) *a room*》 ¶*~ out of one's bed*① *| He bounced out of the room.* —*vt.* **1.** cause (something) to bounce. ¶*~ a ball | ~ a child up and down.* **2.** make (someone) do by force. 《*~ someone into* or

깁다 —名 **1.** 서투른 일(작품) **2.** 보기 흉하게 기운 곳

—形 양쪽의. 쌍방의 USAGE 정관사의 앞에 놓임

—代 양쪽, 둘 모두 USAGE 동사가 불완전 동사의 경우 both 는 그 뒤에 놓임

—接 어느 쪽이나, 함께

—他 …을 귀찮게 굴다, 걱정을 끼치다
—自 마음쓰다, 걱정하다 ¶①내 식사에는 마음을 쓰지 마시오

—名 **1.** 성가신 일, 골칫거리 ; 성가심, 귀찮음 ; 분규 ¶②이 망가진 지퍼가 골칫거리다 **2.** 귀찮은 사람(일·것)

—形 귀찮은, 성가신

—名 **1.** 병 **2.** 한 병의 분량 **3.** 음주 ; 술

—他 …을 병에 넣다
熟 ⓐ …을 병에 넣다 ⓑ …을 억누르다 ; 감추다 ¶①분노를 누르다

—名 **1.** 병 모가지 **2.** 좁은 통로 **3.** 애로, 장애 **4.** 사물의 발전을 저해하는 상

—名 **1.** 밑바닥 [부분], 기부(基部) **2.** 강바닥, 물밑 **3.** 마음속, 내심 ; [일의] 진상 **4.** 최하층 계급의 사람, 말석 **5.** 배 ; [물 밑에 들어가는] 선복(船腹) **6.** 강가의 낮은 지대 **7.** 지구력, 뚝심, 끈기

熟 1)…의 원인이다 2)충심으로 3)…의 진상을 밝히다 4)가라앉다 5)[배]를 가라앉히다 6)독립하다 7)ⓐ좌초하다 ⓑ최저가 되다

—形 밑바닥이 없는 ; 한 없이 깊은

—名 부인의 내실
—名 큰 가지

—名 맑은 쇠고기·닭고기 수우프
—名 [비바람에 모가 없어진] 둥근 돌

—名 가로수길, 한길, 대로

—自 **1.** 뛰다 **2.** 거칠게 움직이다 ¶①침대에서 뛰어 일어나다 —他 **1.** …을 뛰게 하다 **2.** …을 위협하여 억지로 시키다 ¶②남을 억지로 떠나게 하다

out of doing》 ¶ *~ someone into starting.*② **—*n.* 1.** Ⓒ a bound; a spring. **2.** Ⓤ a boast; a lie.
—[名] 1. 튀기, 되튐 2. 허풍, 거짓말

bounc·ing [báunsiŋ] *adj.* **1.** big; strong. **2.** lively; healthy. ¶ *a ~ baby.*
—[形] 1. 거대한, 힘센 2. 건강한, 원기 있는

⁑ **bound**[1] [baund] *v.* pt. and pp. of **bind**.
—*adj.* 1. having a cover or binding. ¶ *a ~ book.* **2.** obliged; forced; compelled. **3.** certain; sure. ¶ *He is ~ to fail in his examination.* **4.** determined; resolved.
1) ***be bound up in*** (=*be much devoted to*) *something.*
2) ***be bound up in*** (*or* ***with***) (=*be closely connected with*) *something.*
—[形] 1. 장정(裝幀)한 2. …할 의무가 있는; 속박된 3. 확실한 4. …하려고 결심한
[熟] 1)…에 열중해 있다 2)…와 밀접한 관계가 있다

⁑ **bound**[2] [baund] *vi.* **1.** jump; leap. **2.** leap or spring upward or onward. **3.** spring back; bounce. **—*n.*** Ⓒ **1.** a leap or spring upward or onward. **2.** a bounce.
—[自] 1. 뛰다, 도약하다 2. …뛰어오르다 3. 튀다, 되튀다 —[名] 1. 뛰어오르기, 도약 2. 튐, 되튐

⁑ **bound**[3] [baund] *n.* 《usu. *pl.*》 **1.** a limit; a boundary; a limiting line. ¶ *within the bounds of reason.* **2.** the land on or near a boundary; the area within boundaries. **—*vt.*** form the boundary of (a place); limit.
—[名] 1. 한계; 경계[선] 2. 경계 안의 영토
—[他] …에 경계를 짓다; …을 제한하다

* **bound**[4] [baund] *adj.* going; on the way. 《*~ for*》 ¶ *a ship ~ for New York.*
—[形] …으로 가고 있는, 가는 중인; …행의

⁑ **bound·a·ry** [báund(ə)ri] *n.* Ⓒ (pl. **-ries**) a limiting line; a limit; a border.
—[名] 경계선; 한계, 범위

bound·en [báundən] *adj.* required; that one must do.
—[形] 하여야 하는

bound·less [báundlis] *adj.* not limited; infinite; vast.
—[形] 한이 없는, 가없는

boun·te·ous [báuntiəs] *adj.* **1.** generous; given freely. **2.** plentiful; abundant.
—[形] 1. 아낌없는, 관대한 2. 풍부한

boun·ti·ful [báuntif(u)l] *adj.* =bounteous.

boun·ty [báunti] *n.* Ⓒ **1.** Ⓤ generosity. **2.** a generous gift. **3.** money, offered by a government, usu. as a reward.
—[名] 1. 관대, 박애 2. 은혜 3. [정부]보조금, 장려금

bou·quet *n.* **1.** [boukéi / bu(:)kéi ∥ →2.] Ⓒ a bunch of flowers. **2.** [bu:kéi, bou- / bu(:)kéi, bú:kei] Ⓤ sweet smell; pleasant odor.
—[名] 1. 꽃다발 2. 향기, 방향

bour·geois [búərʒwɑ:, buərʒwɑ́:] *n.* Ⓒ (pl. **bour·geois**) a person of the middle class. **—*adj.*** of the middle class.
—[名] 부르조아, 중산계급의 사람
—[形] 유산(중산)계급의 사람

bour·geoi·sie [bùərʒwɑ:zí:] *n.* Ⓤ 《*the ~*》 the middle class.
—[名] 중산(유산)계급

bourn, bourne [buərn, bɔərn] *n.* Ⓒ a small stream; a brook.
—[名] 실개천, 시내

bout [baut] *n.* Ⓒ **1.** a test of strength or ability; a contest. ¶ *a boxing ~.* **2.** a period of time; a spell. **3.** a fit. ¶ *a ~ of illness.*①
—[名] 1. 한 판의 시합(승부) 2. 기간, 한바탕 …하는 동안 3. 발작 ¶①병의 발작

'bout *adv., prep.* =about.

bo·vine [bóuvain] *adj.* **1.** of or like an ox or a cow. **2.** slow; stupid. **—*n.*** Ⓒ an ox; a cow.
—[形] 1. 소의, 소 같은 2. 느린, 굼벵이의
—[名] 소과(科)의 동물

⁑ **bow**[1] [bau] *vi.* **1.** bend the head or body in greeting, respect, worship, or obedience. **2.** submit; yield. 《*~ to someone or something*》 ¶ *~ to the inevitable.*① **—*vt.* 1.** express (one's feelings) by a bow. ¶ *~ one's thanks.* **2.** cause (someone) to submit; obey. **3.** cause (something) to bend down. ¶ *Age had bowed his head.*
—*n.* Ⓒ the act of bending of the head or body in greeting, respect, worship, etc.
—[自] 1. 절하다 2. 굴복하다 ¶①피할 수 없는 운명에 굴복하다 —[他] 1. 절하여 …을 나타내다 2. …을 굴복시키다 3. …을 구부리다
—[名] 절, 인사

⁑ **bow**[2] [bou] *n.* Ⓒ **1.** a weapon for shooting arrows; anything shaped like this. **2.** a slender stick with horsehairs for playing a violin, etc. **3.** a looped knot. **4.** a curve; a bend. **—*vt., vi.* 1.** bend (something) into the form of a bow (*n.* 1.). **2.** play (a violin, etc.) with a bow (*n.* 2.).
—[名] 1. 활; 활 모양의 것 2. 악기의 활 3. 나비 매듭 4. 굽음, 만곡(彎曲) —[他][自] 1. …을 활 모양으로 구부리다 2. …을 활로 켜다

bow[3] [bau] *n.* Ⓒ 《usu. *pl.*》 the front part of a ship, boat, or airship.
—[名] 뱃머리, 이물

* **bow·el** [báu(ə)l] *n.* Ⓒ 《usu. *pl.*》 **1.** a tube in the body through which food passes from the stomach; the intestines. **2.** the inner part. ¶ *the bowels of the earth.*
—[名] 1. 창자, 장(腸) 2. 내부

* **bow·er** [báuər] *n.* Ⓒ **1.** a shelter of tree branches or vines with leaves. **2.** a summer house; an arbor.
—[名] 1. 나뭇그늘[의 휴식처] 2. 정자

bow·er·y [báuəri] *adj.* like a bower; leafy; shady.
—[形] 정자 모양의; 나뭇그늘의

bow·ie knife [bóuinàif] *n.* a long hunting knife. ⇒fig.

‡ **bowl¹** [boul] *n.* ⓒ **1.** a hollow, rounded dish. **2.** the amount that such a dish can hold. **3.** a hollow, rounded part. **4.** a large drinking cup. **5.** any bowl-shaped thing.

[bowie knife]

bowl² [boul] *n.* ⓒ a wooden ball used in games. ─*vi.* **1.** play the game of bowling. **2.** roll or move rapidly and smoothly.

bow·leg·ged [bóulèg(i)d] *adj.* having the legs curved outward.

bowl·er [bóulər] *n.* ⓒ **1.** a person who bowls. **2.** (*Brit.*) a derby hat.

bowl·ing [bóuliŋ] *n.* Ⓤ the game of bowls in which one tries to hit 10 pins down.

bow·man [bóumən] *n.* ⓒ (pl. **-men** [-mən]) a soldier who shoots with a bow and arrows; an archer.

bow·shot [bóuʃàt/-ʃɔ̀t] *n.* Ⓤ the distance that a bow will shoot an arrow.

bow·sprit [bóusprìt, +*U.S.* báu-] *n.* ⓒ a long pole projecting forward from the front part of a ship. ⇒fig.

bow·string [bóustrìŋ] *n.* ⓒ a string of a bow² (*n.* 2.).

bow·tie [bóutài] *n.* ⓒ a small necktie tied in a bow at the collar.

bow window [´ ´] *n.* a curved bay window.

bow·wow [báuwáu → *n.* 2.] *n.* ⓒ **1.** the bark of a dog; an imitation of this. **2.** [´ ´] (chiefly *baby talk*) a dog.

[bowsprit]

‡ **box¹** [baks / bɔks] *n.* ⓒ **1.** a case or container of rigid material, usu. with a lid. **2.** the contents of a box; the quality that a box can hold. ¶*a ~ of coins.* **3.** any enclosed space; a compartment.
─*vt.* **1.** put (something) in a box. **2.** keep (something or someone) within limits; confine.
1) ***box in*** (*or* ***up***), shut up (something) in a box.
2) ***box the compass,*** (in discussion) make a complete change and return to the starting point.

• **box²** [baks / bɔks] *n.* ⓒ a blow with the open hand or the fist, esp. on the ear or the side of the head. ¶*give a ~ on the ear.*① ─*vi., vt.* **1.** strike (someone) with such a blow. **2.** fight with the fists as a sport.

box³ [baks / bɔks] *n.* **1.** ⓒ a small evergreen tree or shrub. **2.** Ⓤ its hard wood.

box·er [báksər / bɔ́ksə] *n.* ⓒ **1.** a person who fights with his fists in gloves as a sport. **2.** a short-haired brown dog.

box·ing [báksiŋ / bɔ́ks-] *n.* Ⓤ the sport of fighting with the fists.

Boxing Day [´ ´] *n.* (*Brit.*) the first weekday after Christmas Day. ⇒N.B.

box office [´ ´] *n.* the place where tickets are sold in a theater, hall, etc.

box·wood [bákswùd / bɔ́ks-] *n.* **1.** Ⓤ the hard, fine-grained wood of the box³. **2.** ⓒ the tree itself.

‡ **boy** [bɔi] *n.* ⓒ **1.** a male child from birth to about eighteen. **2.** a young servant; a page.

boy·cott [bɔ́ikàt / -kɔ̀t] *vt.* **1.** make a promise with others to have nothing to do with (someone, a business, a nation, etc.). **2.** refuse to buy or use (goods, etc.). ─*n.* ⓒ the act of boycotting.

• **boy·hood** [bɔ́ihùd] *n.* Ⓤ **1.** the time or condition of being a boy. **2.** (*collectively*) boys.

boy·ish [bɔ́iiʃ] *adj.* **1.** of a boy. **2.** like a boy.

Boy Scouts [´ ´] *n.* a world-wide boy's organization.

─명 사냥칼

─명 1. 사발, 주발, 공기 2. 사발(주발) 가득 3. [숟가락 따위의] 오목한 부분 4. 큰 술잔 5. 사발 모양의 것

─명 [게임용의] 나무 공 ─자 1. 공굴리기를 하다 2. 미끄러지듯이 나아가다

─형 안짱다리의
─명 1. 공굴리기(보울링)를 하는 사람 2.《英》중산모자
─명 보울링

─명 궁술가, 활량

─명 화살이 닿는 거리, 사정(射程)

─명 뱃머리에 있는 사장(斜檣)

─명 활시위

─명 나비 넥타이

─명 밖으로 불룩 나온 창(窓)

─명 1. 개짖는 소리 2.《小兒》멍멍, 개

─명 1. 상자, 통 2. 한 상자 가득 3. 간막이한 곳

─타 1. …을 상자에 넣다 2. …을 간막이하다, 가두어 넣다
짧 1) …을 상자에 넣어 포장하다 2) [의론 따위가] 결국 원점으로 되돌아오다

─명 [손바닥·주먹의] 일격, 때리기 ¶① 따귀를 때리다 ─자타 1. 손바닥(주먹)으로 때리다 2. 권투하다

─명 1. 회양목 2. 회양목 재목

─명 1. 권투가 2. 복서종의 개

─명 권투
─명《英》크리스마스 다음날 N.B. 하인 등에게 선물을 줌
─명 [극장 따위의] 매표소
─명 1. 회양목 2. 회양목 재목

─명 1. 소년, 사내 아이 2. 급사, 사동

─타 1. …을 보이콧하다 2. 불매동맹을 맺어 …을 배척하다
─명 불매동맹, 보이콧

─명 1. 소년기, 소년시대 2. 소년들

─형 1. 소년의 2. 어린이다운
─명 보이스카우트

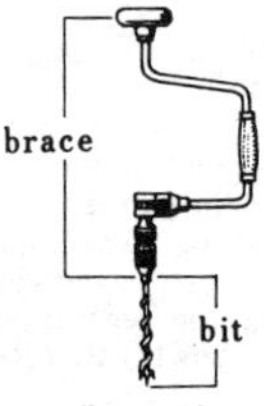

[brace 4.]

* **brace** [breis] *n.* [C] **1.** anything which supports, strengthens, or holds parts together. **2.** a piece of wood, metal, etc., for supporting another piece of framework. **3.** (pl. **brace**) pair; couple. ¶*two ~ of ducks.*① **4.** a handle of a drill used for holding and rotating it. ⇒fig. **5.** either of these signs { }, used to enclose words, figures, etc. **6.** (*Brit.*) (*pl.*) suspenders. **—*vt.*** **1.** fasten tightly. **2.** give strength to (someone or something). ¶*~ oneself.*②
—[명] 1. 버팀대 2. 지주(支柱) 3. 한쌍 ¶①오리 두 쌍 4. [송곳의] 굽은 손잡이 5. 대괄호 6. (英) 바지 멜빵 —[타] 1. …을 꽉 죄다 2. …을 기운내게 하다 ¶②기운내다

brace·let [bréislit] *n.* [C] **1.** an ornamental band for the wrist or arm. **2.** (*colloq.*) a handcuff.
—[명] 1. 팔찌 2. 수갑

brack·en [brǽk(ə)n] *n.* [U][C] a large fern.
—[명] 양치(羊齒), 고사리

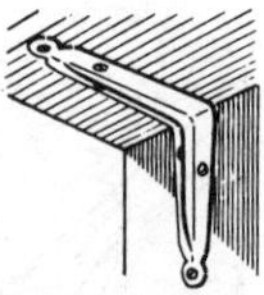
[bracket 1.]

brack·et [brǽkit] *n.* [C] **1.** an L-shaped support for a shelf. ⇒fig. **2.** (*pl.*) either of these signs ( ) [ ], used to enclose words or figures. ⇒[N.B.]
—*vt.* **1.** support (a shelf) with brackets (*n.* 1). **2.** enclose (a word) within brackets (*n.* 2).
—[명] 1. [선반 따위를 받치는] 까치발, 선반받이 2. 괄호 [N.B.] ( )는 round brackets, [ ]는 square brackets라 함 —[타] 1. …에 까치발을 달다 2. …을 괄호로 묶다

brack·ish [brǽkiʃ] *adj.* **1.** a little salty. **2.** distasteful; unpleasant.
▷**brack·ish·ness** [-nis] *n.*
—[형] 1. 소금기가 있는 2. 맛없는, 불쾌한

brag [bræg] *n.* [U] boasting talk **—*vt., vi.*** (**bragged, brag·ging**) boast.
—[명] 허풍 —[타][자] 자랑하다

brag·gart [brǽgərt] *n.* [C] a person who boasts.
—[명] 허풍선이

Brah·man [brɑ́:mən] *n.* [C] (pl. **-mans**) a member of the highest caste in the Hindu social system.
—[명] 바라문(婆羅門) (인도의 4성 중의 최고위인 승려 계급)

Brah·man·ism [brɑ́:mənìz(ə)m] *n.* [U] a Hindu religious and social system.
—[명] 바라문교

Brah·min [brɑ́:min] *n.* =Brahman.

Brahms [brɑ:mz], **Johannes** *n.* (1833-97) a German composer of music.
—[명] 독일의 작곡가

braid [breid] *n.* **1.** [U] a band of woven material used esp. for the decoration of clothing. **2.** [C] a plait of hair.
—*vt.* **1.** weave together stripes or strands of (hair, a ribbon, etc.); plait. **2.** form (something) by such weaving. **3.** trim or bind (clothing) with braid.
—[명] 1. 끈 끈, 짠 끈, 합사 2. 땋아 늘인 머리
—[타] 1. …을 짜다, 꼬다 2. …을 끈으로 꼬다 3. …을 끈 끈으로 장식하다

Braille, braille [breil] *n.* [U] **1.** the system of writing and printing for blind people by using raised dots. **2.** the letters themselves. ⇒[N.B.]
—[명] 1. [장님용] 점자법 2. 점자 [N.B.] 고안자는 프랑스의 Louis Braille(1809-52)

⁑ **brain** [brein] *n.* [C] **1.** the central nervous system within the skull. **2.** (*often pl.*) mind; intelligence.
beat one's brains, try hard to think.
—[명] 1. 뇌 2. 두뇌, 지력(知力)
[숙] 골똘히 궁리하다, 머리를 짜다

brain·less [bréinlis] *adj.* **1.** without a brain. **2.** stupid; foolish.
—[형] 1. 지능이 모자라는 2. 어리석은

brain trust [ˊˋ] *n.* a group of advisers to a political leader, etc.
—[명] 자문 위원회

brain·wash·ing [bréinwɑ̀ʃiŋ / -wɔ̀ʃiŋ] *n.* [U] a method for changing someone's thoughts or beliefs.
—[명] 세뇌(洗腦), 사상 개조 교육

* **brake**[1] [breik] *n.* [C] anything used for slowing or stopping the motion of a wheel or vehicle. **—*vt.*** slow up or stop (a car) by a brake.
—[명] 제동기, 브레이크 —[타] …에 브레이크를 걸다

brake[2] [breik] *n.* [C] a place covered with a thick growth of bushes; a thicket.
—[명] 덤불

brake[3] [breik] *n.* [C] a large fern.
—[명] 고사리류

brake·man [bréikmən] *n.* [C] (pl. **-men** [-mən]) a man who works brakes or helps the conductor of a railroad train.
—[명] 제동수(制動手)

bram·ble [brǽmbl] *n.* [C] **1.** a blackberry-bush; a wild blackberry. **2.** any rough, prickly shrub.
—[명] 1. 나무 딸기, 검정 딸기 2. 찔레, 들장미

bram·bly [brǽmbli] *adj.* **1.** full of brambles. **2.** like brambles; prickly.
—[형] 1. 검정 딸기가 많은 2. 가시덤불이 우거진

bran [bræn] *n.* [U] the outside coat of the grains of wheat, rye, etc.
—[명] 겨, 밀기울

branch [bræntʃ / brɑ:ntʃ] *n.* [C] **1.** a part of a tree growing out from the trunk. ⇒fig. **2.** any division like a branch of a tree. ¶*a ~ of a river.*① **3.** a division; a part. ¶*a ~ of study*② **4.** a local office. ¶*a ~ office.*
—[名] 1. 가지 2. 가지 모양의 것; 분파; 지류, 지맥(支脈) ¶①강의 지류 3. 부문, 학과, 과(科) ¶②학과 4. 지부, 지점, 출장소

—*vi.* **1.** put out branches. **2.** separate into branches.
—[自] 1. 가지를 벋다 2. 갈라지다

1) ***branch off,*** divide (something) into branches.
2) ***branch out,*** ⓐ put out branches. ⓑ extend (business, activities, etc.).
[熟] 1)…을 나누다 2)ⓐ가지가 퍼지다 ⓑ사업을 확장하다

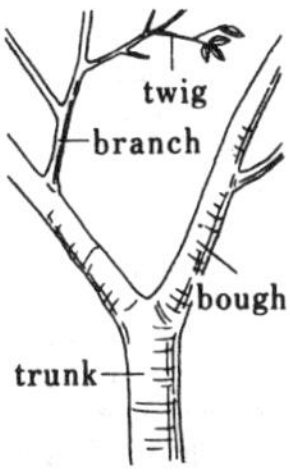

(branch 1.)

brand [brænd] *n.* [C] **1.** a certain kind, grade, or make of goods. ¶*the best ~ of tea.*① **2.** a trademark. **3.** a mark made by burning the skin with a hot iron. **4.** a mark of disgrace. —*vt.* **1.** mark (cattle) by burning the skin with a hot iron. **2.** put a mark of disgrace on (someone). ⟪~ someone *as*⟫ ¶*~ him as a liar.*②
—[名] 1. 품종 ¶①최고급의 차 2. 상표 3. 낙인, 소인(燒印) 4. 오점, 불명예 —[他] 1. …에 낙인을 찍다 2. …에 오명을 씌우다 ¶②그에게 거짓말장이라는 낙인을 찍다

bran·dish [brǽndiʃ] *vt.* wave or shake (a sword, etc.) as a threat.
—[他] [칼 따위]를 휘둘러 위협하다

brand-new [brǽn(d)n(j)ú: / brǽn(d)njú:] *adj.* very new; quite new.
—[形] 아주 새로운, 신품인

bran·dy [brǽndi] *n.* [U] a strong alcoholic liquor made from wine. ¶*a ~.*①
—[名] 브랜디 ¶①브랜디 한 잔

brass [bræs / brɑ:s] *n.* [U] **1.** a yellow metal made by melting copper and zinc together. **2.** ⟪usu. *pl.*⟫ things made of brass, such as ornaments, dishes, etc. **3.** ⟪usu. *the ~*⟫ the trumpets, horns, etc. in an orchestra. **4.** (*colloq.*) money. **5.** (*colloq.*) shamelessness; impudence.
—[名] 1. 놋쇠, 황동 2. 놋쇠 그릇 3. 취주악기 4. ⟪口⟫ 돈 5. ⟪口⟫ 뻔뻔스러움

—*adj.* made of brass.
—[形] 놋쇠로 만든

brass band [ˊ ˊ] *n.* a group of musicians playing brass wind instruments.
—[名] 취주악단

bras·siere [brəzíər / brǽsiə] *n.* [C] a bust support worn by women.
—[名] 브래지어, 젖가리개

brass·y [brǽsi / brɑ́:si] *adj.* (**brass·i·er, brass·i·est**) **1.** of brass. **2.** like brass. **3.** loud and harsh.
—[形] 1. 놋쇠의 2. 놋쇠 같은 3. 시끄러운

brat [bræt] *n.* [C] a child.
—[名] 아이, 애새끼

bra·va·do [brəvɑ́:dou] *n.* [U][C] (pl. **-dos** or **-does**) a great show of boldness, often without much real courage.
—[名] 허세, 허장성세

brave [breiv] *adj.* **1.** without fear; having courage. **2.** making a fine appearance; showy. —*n.* [C] a brave person. —*vt.* **1.** face or meet (someone or something) with courage. **2.** dare. ▷**brave·ness** [-nis] *n.*
—[形] 1. 용감한, 대담한 2. [복장이] 화려한 —[名] 용사 —[他] 1. …에 용감하게 맞서다 2. 감히 …하다

brave·ly [bréivli] *adv.* without fear; finely.
—[副] 용감하게

brav·er·y [bréiv(ə)ri] *n.* [U] **1.** courage; fearlessness. **2.** fine appearance; showy dress.
—[名] 1. 용감, 용기 2. 옷치장, 화려한 옷

bra·vo[1] [brɑ́:vou] *interj.* Well done!; Fine!; Excellent! —*n.* [C] (pl. **-vos** or **-voes**) a cry of "bravo!"
—[感] 브라보! 잘한다! —[名] 갈채의 소리

bra·vo[2] [brɑ́:vóu, +*U.S.* bréi-] *n.* [C] (pl. **-vos** or **-voes**) a hired fighter or murderer.
—[名] 자객, 흉한

brawl [brɔ:l] *n.* [C] a noisy quarrel or fight. —*vi.* quarrel noisily.
—[名] 말다툼, 싸움 —[自] 말다툼하다, 싸우다

brawn [brɔ:n] *n.* [U] **1.** firm, strong muscles. **2.** muscular strength.
—[名] 1. 근육 2. 완력, 근력

brawn·y [brɔ́:ni] *adj.* (**brawn·i·er, brawn·i·est**) strong; muscular. ▷**brawn·i·ness** [-nis] *n.*
—[形] 힘센; 근육이 탄탄한

bray [brei] *n.* [C] the loud, rough sound made by a donkey; noise like it. —*vi.* **1.** make a loud, rough sound. **2.** speak something in a loud, rough voice.
—[名] [나귀의] 울음소리; 떠들썩한 소리 —[自] 1. [나귀 따위가] 울다 2. 큰 소리로 말하다

bra·zen [bréizn] *adj.* **1.** made of brass. **2.** like brass in color or strength. **3.** loud and rough. **4.** shameless; impudent. ¶*a ~ lie.*
—[形] 1. 놋쇠로 만든 2. 놋쇠 같은 3. 귀에 거슬리는, 시끄러운 4. 뻔뻔스러운

—*vt.* do shamelessly or impudently.
—[他] …을 뻔뻔스럽게 해치우다

brazen it out; brazen through, behave shamelessly to get rid of a bad situation.
[熟] 뻔뻔스럽게 밀고 나아가다

bra·zen-faced [bréiznfèist] *adj.* openly shameless; impudent.
—[形] 뻔뻔스러운, 철면피의

bra·zier[1] [bréiʒər, +*Brit.* -zjə] *n.* [C] a metal container to hold burning charcoal or coal.
—[名] 화로

bra·zier[2] [bréiʒər +*Brit.* -zjə] *n.* [C] a person who works with brass.
—[名] 놋쇠 세공사

Bra·zil [brəzíl] *n.* the largest country in South America. ⇒[N.B.]
—[名] 브라질 [N.B.] 수도 Brasilia

Bra·zil·ian [brəzíliən] *adj.* of Brazil or its people. —*n.* [C] a person of Brazil.
—[形] 브라질[사람]의 —[名] 브라질 사람

breach [bri:tʃ] *n.* [C] **1.** an opening made by breaking through; gap. **2.** the act of breaking a law, promise, duty, etc.; neglect. **3.** an act of breaking friendly relations; a quarrel. —*vt.* make a breach in (something); break.
—[名] 1. 갈라진 틈, 돌파구 2. 위반, 불이행 3. 불화, 절교 —[他] …위반하다

⁑**bread** [bred] *n.* [U] **1.** a kind of food made by baking a mixture of flour and water. **2.** food; livelihood. ¶*earn one's ~ | Man shall not live by ~ alone.*①
1) ***break bread,*** eat; share a meal with (someone).
2) ***know which side one's bread is buttered on,*** know what is to one's advantage.
—*vt.* cover (something) with bread crumbs before cooking.
—[名] 1. 빵 2. 먹을 것, 양식; 생계 ¶① 사람은 빵으로만 사는 것이 아니다
[熟] 1)먹다; [남]과 식사를 같이 하다 2)이해관계에 빈틈이 없다
—[他] …에 빵가루를 묻히다

bread·fruit [brédfrù:t] *n.* [C] **1.** a large, round, starchy, tropical fruit of the Pacific islands which tastes like bread when baked. **2.** the tree bearing this fruit.
—[名] 1. 빵나무의 열매 2. 빵나무

***breadth** [bredθ, bretθ] *n.* [U] **1.** the distance from side to side; width. **2.** (of mind, thought, etc.) largeness; broadness. ¶*He has ~ of mind.*
—[名] 1. 폭, 넓이 2. [생각 따위의] 폭, 관용

bread·win·ner [brédwìnər] *n.* [C] a person who earns a living for his family.
—[名] 한 집안의 생계를 꾸리는 사람

⁂**break** [breik] *v.* (**broke, bro·ken**) *vt.* **1.** cause (something) to come to pieces by a blow or strain; destroy; crack; smash. ¶*~ a cup.* **2.** hurt; injure. ¶*~ the skin.* **3.** put (something) out of order. ¶*~ a watch | ~ a line.*① **4.** act against (a law, rule, etc.); disobey. ¶*~ the rules | ~ one's promise.*② **5.** escape from (a place); make one's way; open (something) or enter (a place) by force. ¶*~ prison.*③ **6.** lessen the force of (something); weaken. **7.** stop; put an end to (something); interrupt. ¶*~ one's journey | ~ a person's sleep.* **8.** change (a state), usu. suddenly. ¶*~ silence | ~ one's bad habit.* **9.** make (a bank, company, etc.) bankrupt. ¶*~ a bank.* **10.** make (something) known. 《~ something *to*》 **11.** tame (a wild animal).
—[他] 1. …을 부수다, 쪼개다, 깨다, 찢다, 꺾다, 갈다 2. …을 다치다 3. …을 흩뜨리다, 고장내다 ¶①줄을 흩뜨리다 4. [법률 따위]를 어기다, 범하다 ¶② 약속을 깨뜨리다 5. …을 탈주하다; 부수고 열다, 부수고 들어가다 ¶③탈옥하다 6. …을 약하게 하다 7. …을 중단시키다, 끊기게 하다 8. [침묵 따위]를 깨뜨리다 9. …을 파산시키다 10. …을 알리다, 전하다 11. [동물 따위]를 길들이다

—*vi.* **1.** come into pieces by a blow or strain. ¶*Glass breaks easily.* **2.** fall into confusion; get out of order. **3.** come suddenly; burst into activity. ¶*The storm broke.* **4.** change suddenly. ¶*His voice broke when he told the story.*④ **5.** dawn. ¶*The day is breaking.* **6.** become weak; lose vigor. **7.** go bankrupt.
1) ***break away,*** ⓐ go away suddenly; escape. ⓑ give up (habits, thoughts, etc.).
2) ***break down,*** ⓐ destroy. ⓑ fail. ⓒ stop working rightly; get out of order.
3) ***break free,*** get free by force; escape.
4) ***break in,*** ⓐ get ready for work or use. ¶*A new car has to be broken in.*⑤ ⓑ enter (a place) by force.
5) ***break into,*** ⓐ enter suddenly; begin suddenly. ⓑ enter (a place) by force.
6) ***break loose,*** =break free.
7) ***break someone of,*** force someone to give up (something).
8) ***break off,*** come or bring to an end.
9) ***break open,*** open (a place) by breaking.
10) ***break out,*** ⓐ escape from prison. ⓑ shout suddenly. ⓒ (of a fire, disease, war, etc.) start suddenly. ¶*A*
—[自] 1. 부서지다, 깨지다, 쪼개지다, 꺾이다 2. 혼란을 일으키다 3. 갑자기 일어나다 4. 급변하다 ¶④그 이야기를 할 때 그의 목소리는 갑자기 바뀌었다 5. 동이 트다 6. 약해지다, 쇠퇴하다 7. 파산하다
[熟] 1)ⓐ갑자기 가 버리다, 도망치다 ⓑ[습관 따위]를 갑자기 중단하다 2)ⓐ…을 파괴하다 ⓑ실패하다 ⓒ 고장을 일으키다 3)도망치다 4)ⓐ…을 길들이다, 훈련하다 ¶⑤새 차는 길이 들어야 한다 ⓑ…에 억지로 들어가다 5)ⓐ…에 불쑥 들어가다, …을 갑자기 시작하다 ⓑ…에 침입하다 7)[남]에게 단념시키다 8)…을 중지하다 9)부수고 열다 10)ⓐ탈옥하다 ⓑ별안간 외치다 ⓒ갑자기 일어나다 11)…을 돌파하다 12)ⓐ[모임 따위]를 끝내다; [학교 따위가] 방학이 되다 ⓑ산산이 부서지다(흩어지다) 13)…와 관계를 끊다

fire broke out last night.
11) ***break through,*** force a way through (a place).
12) ***break up,*** ⓐ put an end to (something); end; stop. ⓑ separate into parts. ¶*The crowd broke up.*
13) ***break with,*** stop relations with (someone).
—*n.* [C] **1.** a gap; a broken place; an opening. ¶*a ~ in the wall.* **2.** a short rest; a pause in work, etc. ¶*work without a ~ / a coffee ~.*⑥ **3.** the beginning. ¶*at· ~ of day.* **4.** a sudden change. **5.** (in boxing) the act of separating after a clinch **6.** a fault. **7.** failure. **8.** (*colloq.*) a good chance; a piece of good luck.
—[名] **1.** 갈라진 틈, 째진 곳 **2.** 잠깐의 휴식 ¶⑥코오피를 마시는 휴식 시간 **3.** 새벽, 여명 **4.** 급변 **5.** [권투의] 브레이크[의 선언] **6.** 결점, 실수 **7.** 실패 **8.** 〔口〕 좋은 기회, 행운

break·a·ble [bréikəbl] *adj.* easily broken.
—[形] 깨지기(부서지기) 쉬운

break·age [bréikidʒ] *n.* [U] **1.** the act of breaking; a break. **2.** things broken; damage or loss caused by breaking.
—[名] **1.** 파손 **2.** 파손물

break·down [bréikdàun] *n.* [C] **1.** (of a train or machine) trouble; a failure to work. **2.** loss of health; weakness. ¶*a nervous ~.*① **3.** a failure in business, etc. **4.** analysis.
—[名] **1.** 파손, 고장 **2.** 건강 장해; 쇠약 ¶①신경쇠약 **3.** 붕괴, 몰락; 실패 **4.** 분석

break·er [bréikər] *n.* [C] **1.** a person or thing that breaks. **2.** a wave that breaks into foam on the shore or rocks.
—[名] **1.** 부수는 사람(것) **2.** 부서지는 파도, 흰 파도

⁑ break·fast [brékfəst] *n.* [U][C] the first meal of the day. ¶*at ~ / have a good ~.* —*vi.* eat breakfast. ¶*~ on bread.*① —*vt.* supply (someone) with breakfast.
—[名] 조반 —[自] 조반을 먹다 ¶①빵으로 조반을 먹다 —[他] …에게 조반을 주다

break·neck [bréiknèk] *adj.* very dangerous, esp. because it is too fast. ¶*at ~ speed.*①
—[形] 위험하기 짝이 없는 ¶①살인적인 스피이드로

break·through [bréikθrùː / ⌐⌐] *n.* [C] (*Military*) a movement or advance through and beyond an enemy's line.
—[名] [적의 방어선] 돌파

break·wa·ter [bréikwɔ̀ːtər, +*U.S.* -wɑ̀t-] *n.* [C] a wall to protect a harbor against waves.
—[名] 방파제

bream [briːm] *n.* [C] (pl. **breams** or *collectively* **bream**) a fresh-water fish of the carp family.
—[名] 잉어의 일종

⁑ breast [brest] *n.* [C] **1.** the upper, front part of the human and animal body; the chest. ¶*a pain in the ~.* **2.** the upper, front part of a coat, dress, etc. **3.** the gland that gives milk. ¶*give the ~ to a baby.* **4.** heart; feelings. ¶*have a troubled ~.*①
—[名] **1.** 가슴, 흉부 **2.** [의류·갑옷 따위의] 가슴 부분 **3.** 유방 **4.** 가슴속, 마음 ¶①고민이 있다

make a clean breast of, confess (something) completely.
[熟] …의 흉중을 죄다 털어놓다

—*vt.* advance against (something); face (something) with resolution.
—[他] …을 향해 나아가다; …에 결연히 맞서다

breast·bone [bréstbòun] *n.* [C] the thin, flat bone in the front of the chest to which the ribs are attached.
—[名] 가슴뼈, 흉골

breast-high [brésthái] *adj.* reaching to the height of the breast.
—[形] 가슴까지 높이의

breast·plate [bréstplèit] *n.* [C] **1.** a piece of armor for the breast, used in the Middle Ages. **2.** a garment ornamented with jewels, worn by a Jewish high priest.
—[名] **1.** [갑옷의] 가슴받이 **2.** [유대인 성직자가 보석을 박아 가슴에 늘어뜨리는] 가슴받이

breast·stroke [bréststròuk] *n.* (*the ~*) a kind of swimming style in which a swimmer moves both his hands from the head to the sides, at the same time moving the legs in a frog kick.
—[名] 개구리헤엄, 평영(平泳)

breast·work [bréstwə̀ːrk] *n.* [C] a low, quickly-built wall for defense.
—[名] 흉벽(胸壁)

⁑ breath [breθ] *n.* **1.** [U] air drawn into and let out of the lungs. **2.** [C] a single act of breathing. ¶*take* (or *draw*) *a deep breath.*① **3.** [C] a light, gentle wind; a slight movement in the air. **4.** [U] spirit; life.
—[名] **1.** 숨, 호흡 **2.** 한번에 들이(내)쉬는 숨 ¶①심호흡하다 **3.** 살랑거림, 속삭임 **4.** 생명, 목숨

1) ***below*** (or ***under***) ***one's breath,*** in a whisper; not to be heard.
2) ***catch*** (or ***hold***) ***one's breath,*** stop breathing for a moment.
3) ***in the same breath,*** at the same time.
4) ***out of breath,*** breathless, as from too much exercise.
5) ***spend*** (or ***waste***) ***one's breath,*** talk vainly.
6) ***take breath,*** pause; rest.
[熟] 1)작은 목소리로 2)숨을 죽이다 3)동시에 4)헐떡이면서 5)쓸데없이 지껄이다 6)쉬다

⁑ breathe [briːð] *vi., vt.* **1.** draw air into and let it out of
—[自][他] **1.** 호흡하다 **2.** 휴식하다 **3.** 조

B

breather [144] **bricklayer**

lungs; respire. **2.** pause to breathe; stop to rest. **3.** speak softly; whisper. **4.** be alive; live.
1) *breathe a word*, say the slightest thing. 「safe.」
2) *breathe again* (*or freely*), recover calmness; feel
breath·er [bríːðər] *n.* ⓒ **1.** a short interval for rest. **2.** a vigorous exercise that causes heavy breathing.
breath·ing [bríːðiŋ] *n.* ⓊⒸ **1.** the act of one that breathes. **2.** ⓒ the time needed for a single breath; a moment. **3.** ⓒ a gentle breeze.
* **breath·less** [bréθlis] *adj.* **1.** out of breath. **2.** unable to breathe because of fear, interest, or excitement. ¶*with ~ interest.*Ⓓ **3.** dead; lifeless. **4.** without a breeze. ¶*a ~ summer evening.*
* **breath·less·ly** [bréθlisli] *adv.* in a breathless manner.
breath-tak·ing [bréθtèikiŋ] *adj.* causing a thrill; exciting. ¶*~ horse-riding.*
* **bred** [bred] *v.* pt. and pp. of **breed**.
—*adj.* brought up in a certain way. ¶*ill-bred.*Ⓓ
breech·es [brítʃiz] *n. pl.* **1.** short trousers reaching to the knees. **2.** (*colloq.*) trousers.
* **breed** [briːd] *vt., vi.* (**bred**) **1.** produce young; bear offspring. **2.** cause (plants or animals) to grow; raise. **3.** educate; bring up; train. **4.** be the cause of (something); bring about; result in. ¶*Poverty breeds crime.*Ⓓ
—*n.* ⓒ a race or a family with the same qualities.
breed·er [bríːdər] *n.* ⓒ **1.** a person who raises animals. **2.** an animal that produces young.
breed·ing [bríːdiŋ] *n.* Ⓤ **1.** the act of producing young. ¶*the ~ season.* **2.** training; good manners and behavior. ¶*a man of ~.*
: **breeze** [briːz] *n.* ⓒ **1.** a gentle wind. ¶*spring breezes.* **2.** (*Brit. colloq.*) a slight quarrel. **3.** idle talk. ¶*shoot the ~.*Ⓓ —*vi.* (*colloq.*) blow calmly.
breez·y [bríːzi] *adj.* (**breez·i·er, breez·i·est**) **1.** having a breeze; with light winds blowing. **2.** lively; fresh.
* **breth·ren** [bréðrin] *n. pl.* (sing. **broth·er**) the members of a church or society.
brev·i·ty [bréviti] *n.* Ⓤ **1.** shortness of time. ¶*~ of human life.* **2.** briefness; conciseness. ¶*Brevity is the soul of wit.*Ⓓ
brew [bruː] *vt., vi.* **1.** make (beer, wine, etc.) through chemical change caused by bacteria. **2.** (make a drink) by boiling or mixing. ¶*~ tea.* **3.** plan; plot. **4.** begin to form. —*n.* ⓒ a drink that is brewed.
brew·er [brúː(ː)ər] *n.* ⓒ a person who makes beer, ale, etc.
brew·er·y [brúː(ː)əri] *n.* ⓒ (pl. **-er·ies**) a place where beer,
bri·ar [bráiər] *n.* =brier¹; brier². ⌊ale, etc., are made.⌋
* **bribe** [braib] *n.* ⓒ money or other gift given to someone to get his help, favor, etc., dishonestly. —*vt.* influence (someone) by giving a bribe. ▷**brib·a·ble** [bráibəbl] *adj.* —**brib·er** [-ər] *n.*
brib·er·y [bráibəri] *n.* Ⓤ **1.** the act of giving or offering as a bribe. **2.** the act of taking a bribe.
bric-a-brac [bríkəbræ̀k] *n.* Ⓤ small things of former times having artistic value.
: **brick** [brik] *n.* ⓊⒸ (pl. **bricks** or *collectively* **brick**) **1.** a block of clay baked by sun or fire, used in building a house or paving a street. ¶*build a house of red ~.* **2.** ⓒ anything shaped like a brick. **3.** ⓒ (*colloq.*) a good fellow. ¶*He is a regular ~.*Ⓓ
—*adj.* made of bricks. —*vt.* build or pave (something) with bricks. ▷**brick·like** [-làik] *adj.*
brick·lay·er [bríklèi(ə)r] *n.* ⓒ a person whose work is building with bricks.

—용히 이야기하다, 속삭이다 **4.** 살아 있다
熟 1)한마디 하다 2)평정을 되찾다
—图 **1.** 휴식 **2.** 과격한 운동

—图 **1.** 호흡 **2.** 잠깐; 짧은 휴식 **3.** 미풍

—颐 **1.** 숨이 가쁜 **2.** 숨을 죽인 ¶① 숨을 죽이고 **3.** 죽은, 생명 없는 **4.** 바람 한점 없는

—團 헐떡이면서, 숨을 죽이고
—颐 아슬아슬한, 손에 땀을 쥐게 하는

—颐 …하게 자란 ¶①버릇없이 자란

—图 **1.** [승마용] 반바지 **2.** 《口》바지, 즈봉
—颐酌 **1.** 낳다, 번식하다(시키다) **2.** 사육하다 **3.** 양육하다, 가꾸다 **4.** 일으키다, 야기하다 ¶①빈곤은 범죄를 일으킨다
—图 [동식물의] 품종, 종류
—图 **1.** 사육자 **2.** 종축(種畜)

—图 **1.** 번식; 부화(孵化) **2.** 사육; 양육; 훈육

—图 **1.** 미풍, 산들바람 **2.** 《英口》싸움, 소동 **3.** 잡담, 한담 ¶①호언장담하다
—勯 《口》산들산들 불다
—颐 **1.** 산들바람이 부는, 바람이 잘 통하는 **2.** 쌕쌕한, 발랄한
—图 교우(敎友)

—图 **1.** [시간 따위의] 짧음, 덧없음 **2.** 간결 ¶①간결은 기지(機知)의 생명이다
—颐酌 **1.** 양조하다 **2.** [차 따위를] 끓이다 **3.** …을 꾀하다 **4.** …을 일으키다, 야기하다 —图 양조물

—图 《맥주》양조자
—图 《맥주 따위의》양조장

—图 뇌물 —颐 …을 매수하다, …에게 뇌물을 주다

—图 **1.** 증회(贈賄) **2.** 수회

—图 고물, 골동품

—图 **1.** 벽돌 **2.** 벽돌 모양의 것 **3.** 《口》 호남아, 좋은 친구 ¶①그는 정말 좋은 녀석이다

—颐 벽돌로 만든 —颐 …을 벽돌로 짓다, …에 벽돌을 깔다
—图 벽돌 직공

brick·work [bríkwə̀:rk] *n.* [U] a thing made of bricks. —[名] 벽돌로 만든 것

brick·yard [bríkjɑ̀:rd] *n.* [C] a place where bricks are made or sold. —[名] 벽돌 공장

brid·al [bráidl] *adj.* of a bride or a wedding. —*n.* [C] a wedding. —[形] 신부의; 결혼의 —[名] 결혼식

⁑ **bride** [braid] *n.* [C] a woman just married or about to be married. —[名] 신부, 새색시

bride·cake [bráidkèik] *n.* [C] [U] a wedding-cake. —[名] 결혼 케이크

* **bride·groom** [bráidgrù(:)m] *n.* [C] a man just married or about to be married. —[名] 신랑

brides·maid [bráidzmèid] *n.* [C] a young, usu. unmarried woman attending on the bride at a wedding. —[名] 신부 들러리[처녀]

⁑ **bridge**[1] [bridʒ] *n.* [C] **1.** a structure built over a river, road, etc., that can be crossed. **2.** a platform above the deck of a ship. **3.** the upper, bony part of the nose. **4.** a metal clip for keeping false teeth in place. **5.** a movable piece over which the strings of a violin, etc., are stretched. —[名] **1.** 다리, 교량 **2.** 선교(船橋), 함교 **3.** 콧마루 **4.** [의치를 받치는] 치교(齒橋) **5.** [현악기의] 기러기발, 브리지

burn one's bridges, cut off all chances to return; make a decision which cannot be changed. [熟] 배수의 진을 치다

—*vt.* **1.** build a bridge over (something). ¶ *~ the river.* **2.** extend over; make a passage over (something). **3.** overcome. —[他] **1.** …에 다리를 놓다 **2.** …에 다리처럼 걸치다 **3.** [곤란 따위]를 극복(타개)하다

bridge[2] [bridʒ] *n.* [U] a kind of card game. —[名] 브리지

bridge·head [brídʒhèd] *n.* [C] a defense covering or protecting the end of a bridge; a protected place on the enemy's side of a river. —[名] 교두보

* **bri·dle** [bráidl] *n.* [C] **1.** the head part of a horse's leather bands, by which the rider can control a horse. ⇒fig. **2.** anything that holds back or controls. —*vt.* **1.** put a bridle on (a horse) **2.** bring (something) under control. —*vi.* draw up the head in anger. —[名] **1.** 말굴레(말머리에 다는 재갈·고삐 따위의 총칭), [특히] 고삐 **2.** 구속[물] —[他] **1.** …에 말굴레를 씌우다 **2.** …을 제어(억제)하다 —[自] 머리를 쳐들고 으쓱대다

▷**bri·dler** [-dlər] *n.*

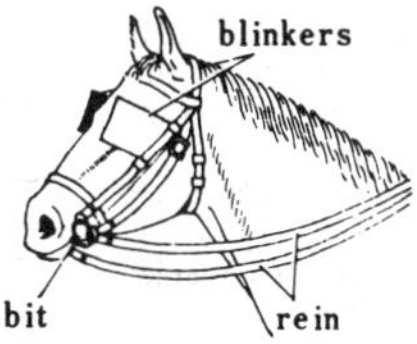
blinkers
bit
rein
〔bridle 1.〕

⁑ **brief** [bri:f] *adj.* **1.** (of time) short. ¶ *a ~ meeting.* **2.** using few words; concise. ¶ *a ~ letter.* —[形] **1.** 짧은, 단시간의 **2.** 간단한, 간결한

—*n.* [C] (pl. **briefs**) **1.** a short statement; a summary. **2.** an outline of a law case spoken by lawyers in court. **3.** 《*pl.*》 close-fitting, legless underpants. —[名] **1.** 요점, 요약, 줄거리 **2.** 소송사건 적요서(摘要書) **3.** 짧은 팬츠

1) ***hold a brief*** (=*defend; support*) ***for someone.*** ¶ *He holds a ~ for me.*
2) ***in brief,*** in a few words; in short.
[熟] **1.** …을 변호하다 **2.** 간단히 말하면, 요는

—*vt.* give a brief instruction to (someone). —[他] …에 간단한 지시를 주다

brief case [´ ˏ] *n.* a flat case, usu. made of leather, for carrying loose papers, books, drawings, etc. —[名] 서류 가방

* **brief·ly** [brí:fli] *adv.* in brief; shortly. —[副] 간단히, 짧게

bri·er[1] [bráiər] *n.* [C] a thorny plant or bush of the rose family; a wild rose. —[名] 들장미, 찔레

bri·er[2] [bráiər] *n.* **1.** [C] [U] a white heath tree found in southern Europe, the root of which is used in making tobacco pipes. **2.** [C] a tobacco pipe made of this root. —[名] **1.** 브라이어(유럽산 석남과의 관목) **2.** [그 뿌리로 만든] 브라이어의 파이프

brig [brig] *n.* [C] a ship with two masts and square sails. —[名] 쌍돛대의 범선

bri·gade [brigéid] *n.* [C] **1.** a military unit smaller than a division. **2.** a group of people organized for some purpose. ¶ *a fire ~.*① —[名] **1.** 여단 **2.** 대(隊), 단(團) ¶①소방대

brig·a·dier [brìgədíər] *n.* [C] an officer who commands a brigade; a brigadier general. —[名] 여단장

brigadier general [ˏ-ˋ ˊ--] *n.* (*U. S.*) an army officer ranking between colonel and major general. —[名] 《美》 육군 준장

brig·and [brígənd] *n.* [C] a man who lives in the forests or mountains and who robs travelers on the road; a robber. —[名] 산적, 강도

brig·and·age [brígəndidʒ] *n.* [U] the act of robbing by force.
—[名] 강탈

⁑**bright** [brait] *adj.* **1.** giving much light. ¶~ *sunlight.* **2.** very light or clear. ↔dark ¶*a* ~ *day.* **3.** clever ↔dull ¶*a* ~ *boy.* **4.** glowing; vivid. ¶~ *fire.* **5.** lively; cheerful. ¶*a* ~ *smile.* **6.** favorable. ¶~ *prospects for the future.* —*adv.* in a bright manner.
—[形] **1.** 밝은, 빛나는 **2.** 개인, 환한 **3.** 영리한, 총명한 **4.** [빛깔 따위] 선명한 **5.** 쾌활한, 즐거운 **6.** 유망한 —[副] 빛나서, 밝게

***bright·en** [bráitn] *vt.* make (something) bright; make (someone) happy or cheerful. —*vi.* become bright; become happy or cheerful.
—[他] …을 빛나게 하다, 밝게 하다; 명랑하게 하다 —[自] 빛나다, 즐거워지다, 명랑해지다

***bright·ly** [bráitli] *adv.* in a bright manner.
—[副] 밝게; 슬기롭게

***bright·ness** [bráitnis] *n.* [U] the quality of being bright.
—[名] 빛남; 선명; 쾌활; 현명

bril·liance [bríljəns], **bril·lian·cy** [-si] *n.* [U] **1.** great brightness; glitter. **2.** splendor; magnificence. **3.** great ability; keen intelligence. ¶*a man of* ~.①
—[名] **1.** 광휘, 광명 **2.** 훌륭함 **3.** 슬기, 총명

⁑**bril·liant** [bríljənt] *adj.* **1.** shining brightly; very bright. ¶~ *sunshine.* **2.** splendid; magnificent. ¶*a* ~ *discovery.* **3.** having great ability; very clever. ¶*a* ~ *idea* / *a* ~ *scientist.* —*n.* [C] a diamond or other gem cut so as to sparkle greatly.
—[形] **1.** 빛나는, 반짝반짝하는 **2.** 훌륭한 **3.** 총명한 —[名] 브릴리언트 형의 다이아몬드

bril·liant·ly [bríljəntli] *adv.* in a brilliant manner.
—[副] 반짝반짝, 선명하게

***brim** [brim] *n.* [C] ⟪usu. *the* ~⟫ **1.** the edge of a cup, bowl, etc.; a rim. ¶*I have filled my glass to the* ~. **2.** the projecting edge of a hat. **3.** the edge bordering water. —*v.* (**brimmed, brim·ming**) *vi.* be full to the brim. —*vt.* fill (a glass, etc.) to the brim. ▷**brim·less** [-lis] *adj.*
—[名] **1.** 가장자리 **2.** [모자의] 차양 **3.** 샘가, 강가, 물가
—[自] 가득하다 —[他] …을 가득 붓다

brim·ful, -full [brímfúl] *adj.* full to the brim.
—[形] 넘칠 듯한

brim·stone [brímstòun / -stən] *n.* [U] a pale-yellow substance that burns with a blue flame and strong smell.
—[名] 유황

brin·dled [bríndld] *adj.* (esp. of cows, dogs, etc.) gray, tan, or brown with darker streaks and spots.
—[形] 얼룩진, 얼룩무늬가 있는

brine [brain] *n.* [U] **1.** very salty water. **2.** ⟪*the* ~⟫ a salt lake; the sea; the ocean.
—[名] **1.** 소금물 **2.** 함수호(鹹水湖); 바다

⁑**bring** [briŋ] *vt.* (**brought**) **1.** come with; be accompanied by (something or someone); carry. ¶~ *someone a book;* ~ *a book to someone.* **2.** make (someone) come. ¶*What has brought you here?*① **3.** persuade; lead. ⟪~ someone *to do*⟫
—[他] **1.** …을 데리고 오다, 가져오다, 날라 오다 **2.** …을 오게 하다 ¶①무슨 일로 여기 왔느냐? **3.** [남]을 …으로 이끌다, …할 생각이 들게 하다

1) ***bring about,*** cause (something) to happen.
2) ***bring around (or round),*** ⓐ make (someone) recover consciousness. ⓑ persuade. ⟪~ someone around *to* one's opinion⟫
3) ***bring back,*** ⓐ come back with (something). ⓑ remember.
4) ***bring down,*** ⓐ cause (something) to come down. ⓑ cause (something) to lessen; make (prices) low.
5) ***bring forth,*** ⓐ produce; give birth to (something). ⓑ make (something) clear to the public; show.
6) ***bring forward,*** show; introduce.
7) ***bring in,*** ⓐ introduce. ⓑ yield or produce (profits, etc.). ⓒ declare (guilty or not guilty).
8) ***bring off,*** (*colloq.*) accomplish.
9) ***bring on,*** cause (something) to happen.
10) ***bring out,*** ⓐ show; exhibit clearly; publish (a book, etc). ⓑ introduce (someone) to society.
11) ***bring over,*** persuade; cause (someone) to change an opinion.
12) ***bring through,*** save (a sick person, etc.).
13) ***bring to,*** ⓐ make (someone) recover consciousness. ⓑ cause (a ship) to stop.
14) ***bring up,*** ⓐ take care of (someone) in his childhood; rear; educate. ⓑ begin to speak of (something).

[熟] 1)…을 일으키다 2)ⓐ…의 의식을 회복시키다 ⓑ…을 설득하다 3)ⓐ…을 다시 데려오다 ⓑ…을 상기시키다 4)ⓐ…을 내리다, 떨어뜨리다 ⓑ…을 적게 하다, [값]을 내리다 5)ⓐ…을 낳다, 만들어 내다 ⓑ…을 널리 알리다, 공표하다 6)…을 나타내다; 소개하다 7)ⓐ…을 들여 오다 ⓑ[이익·수입 따위가] 생기다 ⓒ…[죄의 유무를] 언도(선고)하다 8)⟪口⟫…을 성취하다 9)…을 일으키다, 가져오다 10)ⓐ…을 명시하다; 출판하다 ⓑ…을 사교계에 넣다 11)…을 자기 편에 끌어넣다 12)…을 구하다 13)ⓐ…을 정신들게 하다 ⓑ…[배]를 멈추다 14)ⓐ…을 보살피다, 기르다 ⓑ…에 언급하다

brink [briŋk] *n.* [C] **1.** ⟪usu. *the* ~⟫ the edge of a steep place or of land bordering water. **2.** a serious or dangerous situation.
—[名] **1.** [벼랑 따위의] 가장자리, 가; 물가 **2.** 위험, 위기

briny [147] **broad-minded**

on the brink of, very near; on the point of (something). ¶*They were on the ~ of war.*① 「salty.」
brin·y [bráini] *adj.* (**brin·i·er, brin·i·est**) of or like brinc;
—㉰ 소금물의, 짠
* **brisk** [brisk] *adj.* **1.** quick and active; lively. ¶*a ~ walk.* **2.** sharp. ¶*cold and ~ wind.* **3.** (of liquors) giving off bubbles of gas. ¶*~ cider.* ▷**brisk·ness** [-nis]
—㉰ **1.** 활발한, 팔팔한 **2.** 상쾌한, 마음이 후련한 **3.** 거품이 잘 이는
bris·ket [brískit] *n.* ⓤ **1.** the meat cut from the breast of an·animal. **2.** the breast of an animal.
—㉭ **1.** [짐승고기의] 양지머리 **2.** [짐승의] 가슴 부분
brisk·ly [brískli] *adv.* in a brisk manner.
—㉯ 활발하게
* **bris·tle** [brísl] *n.* ⓒ one of the short, hard, rough hairs of certain animals, esp. hogs, used to make brushes.
—㉭ 거센 털, 강모(剛毛)
—*vi.* **1.** raise bristles in anger or fear. ¶*The cat bristled.* **2.** be full. 《*~ with* something》 ¶*The project bristled with difficulties.* —*vt.* erect (something) like bristles.
—㉠ **1.** 털이 곤두서다 **2.** [장해·곤란 따위로] 가득 차 있다 —㉣ [털]을 곤두세우다
bris·tly [brísli] *adj.* **1.** rough with bristles; having bristles. ¶*a ~ chin.* **2.** like bristles; short and stiff.
—㉰ **1.** 거센 털의(이 있는) **2.** 강모 같은; 짧고 빳빳한
: **Brit·ain** [brít(ə)n] *n.* England, Scotland, and Wales; Great Britain.
—㉭ 영국; 대영제국
Bri·tan·ni·a [britániə] *n.* **1.** Britain; Great Britain. **2.** the British Empire. **3.** a woman figure symbolizing Britain or the British Empire used in coin, etc.
—㉭ **1.** 영국 **2.** 영제국 **3.** 브리타니아상(像)
Bri·tan·nic [británik] *adj.* of Britain; British.
—㉰ 영국의
: **Brit·ish** [brítiʃ] *adj.* of Great Britain; of the British Empire, or its people. —*n.* 《*the ~*》 people of Great Britain or the British Empire.
—㉰ 영국의; 영국인의 —㉭ 영국인
Brit·ish·er [brítiʃər] *n.* ⓒ a person of Britain.
—㉭ 영국인
Brit·on [brít(ə)n] *n.* ⓒ **1.** a person of Great Britain or the British Empire. **2.** one of the Celtic people who lived in south Britain at the time of the Roman invasion.
—㉭ **1.** 영국인 **2.** [옛]브리튼 사람
brit·tle [brítl] *adj.* very easily broken.
—㉰ 잘 부서지는, 깨지기 쉬운
broach [broutʃ] *n.* ⓒ a sharp-pointed, slender rod or bar to roast meat with.
—㉭ [고기 굽는] 꽂이, 꼬챙이
—*vt.* **1.** open (a cask or barrel of beer, etc.) by making a hole. **2.** begin to talk about (something); speak of (something) for the first time. ▷**broach·er** [-ər] *n.*
—㉣ **1.** [술통 따위]에 구멍을 내다 **2.** …에 관한 말을 하기 시작하다; …에 관한 [이야기]를 처음 꺼내다
: **broad** [brɔːd] *adj.* ↔narrow **1.** wide from side to side. ¶*a ~ road.* **2.** vast; spacious. ¶*a ~ ocean.* **3.** not limited; liberal. ¶*a ~ mind.* **4.** much; large in amount. ¶*~ knowledge.* **5.** plain; clear. ¶*a ~ fact.* **6.** general. ¶*in a ~ sense.*① **7.** not delicate; rough.
—㉰ **1.** 넓은 **2.** 널따란, 광대한 **3.** [마음이] 넓은 **4.** [지식 따위가] 광범위한, 깊은 **5.** 명백한 **6.** 일반적인 ¶① 넓은 뜻으로는 **7.** 천한, 거친
broad bean [ˊ ˊ] *n.* a large eatable flat bean.
—㉭ 잠두(蠶豆)
broad·brim [brɔ́ːdbrìm] *n.* ⓒ a hat with a very wide brim, esp. worn by Quakers.
—㉭ [퀘이커 교도가 쓰는] 챙 넓은 모자
* **broad·cast** [brɔ́ːdkæst / -kɑ̀ːst] *vt., vi.* (**-cast** or **-cast·ed**) **1.** send out (news, etc.) by radio or television. **2.** scatter widely. —*n.* ⓤⓒ **1.** the act of broadcasting. **2.** a thing or things broadcast; a radio program. —*adj.* **1.** sent out by radio or television. **2.** scattered widely. —*adv.* over a wide surface.
—㉣㉠ **1.** 방송하다 **2.** 흩뿌리다 —㉭ **1.** 방송, 흩뿌리기 **2.** 방송되는 것; 방송 프로 —㉰ **1.** 방송의 **2.** 널리 퍼진
—㉯ 널리
broad·cast·er [brɔ́ːdkæ̀stər / -kɑ̀ːstə] *n.* ⓒ a person who broadcasts; an announcer.
—㉭ 방송자, 어나운서
broad·cast·ing [brɔ́ːdkæ̀stiŋ / -kɑ̀ːst-] *n.* ⓤ **1.** the act of sending out speech, music, news, etc. by radio or television. **2.** radio or television as a business.
—㉭ **1.** 방송 **2.** 방송 사업
broad·cloth [brɔ́ːdklɔ̀ːθ / -klɔ̀(ː)θ] *n.* ⓤ cloth of double width used in making shirts and dresses.
—㉭ [드레스·샤쓰용의] 폭 넓은 고급 천
broad·en [brɔ́ːdn] *vt., vi.* make or become broad or broader. ¶*The river broadens at this point.*
—㉣㉠ 넓게 하다, 넓어지다
broad jump [ˊ ˊ] *n.* a jump as long as possible. ↔high jump 「openly.」
—㉭ 넓이뛰기
broad·ly [brɔ́ːdli] *adv.* widely; general y; about; nearly;
—㉯ 넓게; 개괄적으로; 대략; 솔직히
broad-mind·ed [brɔ́ːdmáindid] *adj.* liberal; generous; without prejudice. ▷**broad·mind·ed·ness** [-nis] *n.*
—㉰ 마음이 넓은; 편견이 없는

broad·ness [brɔ́:dnis] *n.* [U] the quality of being broad. —[名] 넓음, 관대

broad·sheet [brɔ́:dʃì:t] *n.* [C] a large sheet of paper printed on one side only. —[名] 한쪽만 인쇄된 큰 종이

broad·side [brɔ́:dsàid] *n.* [C] **1.** the whole side of a ship above the water line. **2.** all the guns that can be fired from one side of a ship. **3.** the firing of all the guns on one side of a warship at the same time. **4.** (*colloq.*) a violent attack in words, esp. in a newspaper. —*adv.* with the side turned. —[名] 1. 뱃전 2. 한쪽 뱃전에 있는 포 전부 3. [그 포에 의한] 일제 사격 4. 《口》 욕설·비난을 일제히 퍼붓기 —[副] 뱃전을 돌리고

broad·sword [brɔ́:dsɔ̀:rd] *n.* [C] a sword with a broad, flat blade. —[名] 날 폭이 넓은 칼

Broad·way [brɔ́:dwèi] *n.* a street in New York City. —[名] 브로오드웨이(New York의 극장가)

bro·cade [broukéid] *n.* [U] a rich silk cloth with raised designs in gold and silver on it. —[名] 금란(金襴), 능라(綾羅)(무늬를 두드러지게 짠 비단)

bro·cad·ed [broukéidid] *adj.* woven into a rich cloth with a raised design. —[形] 무늬를 두드러지게 짠

broc·co·li [brákəli / brɔ́k-] *n.* [C] a kind of vegetable with flower heads. —[名] 모란채(cauliflower의 일종)

bro·chure [brouʃúər / bróuʃjuə] *n.* [C] a small book; a pamphlet. —[名] 소책자, 팜플렛

brogue [broug] *n.* [C] a heavy, strong country shoe formerly used by Irishmen. —[名] 생가죽 구두

broil[1] [brɔil] *vt.* **1.** cook (meat, etc.) by direct heat. **2.** make (something) very hot. —*vi.* be very hot. ¶*a broiling day.*① —*n.* [C][U] **1.** the act or state of broiling. **2.** something broiled; broiled meat. —[他] 1. …을 굽다 2. …을 뜨겁게(덥게) 하다 —[自] 찌는 듯이 덥다 ¶①찌는 듯이 더운 날 —[名] 1. 굽기 2. 구워진 것, 불고기

broil[2] [brɔil] *n.* [C] an angry quarrel or struggle. —[名] 싸움, 말다툼

broil·er [brɔ́ilər] *n.* [C] **1.** any device for roasting. **2.** a young chicken for roasting. —[名] 1. 고기 굽는 기구 2. 불고기용 영계

‡ **broke** [brouk] *v.* pt. of **break**.
—*adj.* (*colloq.*) having no money; unable to pay one's debts. —[形] 빈털털이의, 파산한

‡ **bro·ken** [bróuk(ə)n] *v.* pp. of **break**.
—*adj.* **1.** separated into parts by a blow or by strain; crushed. ¶*a ~ cup.* **2.** weakened in spirit, strength, etc. **3.** tamed. ¶*a ~ elephant.* **4.** uneven; rough. ¶*~ ground.* **5.** not kept; violated. ¶*a ~ promise.* **6.** imperfectly spoken. ¶*~ English.* **7.** interrupted. ¶*~ sleep.* **8.** shocked by grief. ¶*a ~ heart.* —[形] 1. 부서진, 쪼개진, 부러진, 꺾인, 깨진 2. 약해진, 풀죽은 3. 길든 4. 울퉁불퉁한 5. [약속 따위가] 지켜지지 않은, 어겨진 6. [말이] 변칙의, 엉터리의 7. 중단된 8. 슬픔에 잠긴

bro·ken-down [bróuk(ə)ndáun] *adj.* **1.** broken in health; ruined. **2.** unfit for use; out of order. —[形] 1. 쇠약해진 2. [기계가] 파손된, 고장난

bro·ken-heart·ed [bróuk(ə)nhá:rtid] *adj.* shocked by sorrow or grief; very sad; disappointed in love. —[形] 슬픔에 잠긴, 절망에 빠진, 실연(失戀)한

bro·ken-wind·ed [bróuk(ə)nwíndid] *adj.* (of a horse) breathing with difficulty. —[形] [말(馬)이] 헐떡이는

bro·ker [bróukər] *n.* [C] a person who buys and sells for other people. —[名] 주식 중매인(仲買人), 중개인

bro·ker·age [bróukəridʒ] *n.* [U] **1.** the business of a broker. **2.** the money paid to a broker for his services. —[名] 1. 중매업 2. 중매 수수료

bro·mide [bróumaid, +*U.S.* -mid] *n.* [C] **1.** [U][C] a compound material of bromine. ¶*~ paper.*① **2.** a calming medicine. **3.** a commonplace and boring person. —[名] 1. 취화물(臭化物) ¶①[사진의] 인화지 2. 진정제 3. 평범한 사람

bro·mine [bróumi(:)n] *n.* [U] a chemical element which is a dark red liquid with a strong smell. —[名] 취소(臭素)

bron·chi [bráŋkai / brɔ́ŋ-] *n. pl.* (sing. **bron·chus**) the two main branches of the windpipe. —[名] 기관지(氣管支)

bron·chi·al [bráŋkiəl / brɔ́ŋ-] *adj.* of the bronchi or bronchus. —[形] 기관지(氣管支)의

bron·chi·tis [braŋkáitis, bran- / brɔŋkáitis, brɔn-] *n.* [U] a disease of the bronchi. —[名] 기관지염

bron·cho [bráŋkou / brɔ́ŋ-] *n.* (pl. **-chos**) =bronco.

bron·chus [bráŋkəs / brɔ́ŋ-] *n.* sing. of **bronchi.**

bron·co [bráŋkou / brɔ́ŋ-] *n.* [C] (pl. **-cos**) a wild-natured pony of the western United States. —[名] [미국 서부산] 야생(반야생)의 말

* **bronze** [branz / brɔnz] *n.* **1.** [U] a brown mixture of copper and tin. **2.** [C] a statue, medal, etc., made of bronze.
—*adj.* **1.** made of bronze. ¶*a ~ statue.*① **2.** metallic brown. —[名] 1. 청동 2. 청동제품 —[形] 1. 청동제의 ¶①동상 2. 청동빛의

Bronze Age [∠ ∠], **the** *n.* a period when bronze tools, weapons, etc., were used. —[名] 청동기 시대

brooch [broutʃ, +U.S. bruːtʃ] n. ⓒ an ornamental or jeweled pin worn on the clothes at the neck or breast. —ⓝ 브로우치, 장식핀

• **brood** [bruːd] n. ⓒ 1. a group of young birds hatched at one time. 2. a group; a kind. —ⓝ 1. 한 배의 병아리(새 새끼) 2. 한 떼; 종류
sit on brood, think about something for a long time. 꽁꽁이 생각하다
—vi. 1. sit on eggs in order to hatch them. 2. think deeply. 《~ *on* or *over* something》 ¶*She was brooding over her past.* 3. hang low. ¶*Dusk was brooding* —ⓥ 1. 알을 품다 2. 심사숙고하다 3. [구름·어둠 따위가] 내려 덮이다

‡ **brook**¹ [bruk] n. ⓒ a small stream. *over the town.* —ⓝ 시내, 개울

brook² [bruk] vt. 《in *negative* or *interrogative*》 suffer; bear. ¶*I cannot ~ your interference.*① —ⓥ …을 참다, …에 견디다 ¶①네 간섭은 참을 수 없다

brook·let [brúklit] n. ⓒ a little brook. —ⓝ 시내, 실개천

Brook·lyn [brúklin] n. a division of New York City. —ⓝ 뉴우요오크의 한 구

• **broom** [bru(ː)m] n. ⓒ 1. a brush with a long handle used for sweeping. ¶(*proverb*) *A new ~ sweeps clean.*① 2. a kind of plant with yellow flowers. —ⓝ 1. 비 ¶①신임자는 일을 잘한다 2. 금작화

broom·stick [brú(ː)mstik] n. ⓒ the long handle of a broom. —ⓝ 빗자루

bros., Bros. brothers.

broth [brɔːθ / brɔ(ː)θ] n. ⓤ ⓒ water in which meat has been boiled; thin meat soup. —ⓝ 육즙(肉汁); 묽은 고기 수우프

broth·el [brɑ́θəl, -ðəl / brɔ́θəl] n. ⓒ a house of ill fame. —ⓝ 매음굴, 유곽

‡ **broth·er** [brʌ́ðər] n. ⓒ 1. one of the sons of the same parents; one of the sons of only the same mother or father. ↔sister ¶*an elder* (or *older*) *~* / *a half ~*① / *a whole ~*② / *a younger ~*. 2. a close friend; a companion. ¶*a ~ in arms.*③ 3. (pl. **breth·ren**) a member of a church, union, etc. ¶*professional brethren.*④ —ⓝ 1. 형제, 형, 아우 ¶①배다른 형제 /②부모가 같은 형(동생) 2. 동료, 동기생 ¶③전우 3. 교우(敎友); 동업자 ¶④[의사·변호사 등의] 동업자

• **broth·er·hood** [brʌ́ðərhùd] n. 1. ⓤ the condition or quality of being a brother or brothers. 2. ⓒ a group of persons with common interests. —ⓝ 1. 형제임, 형제의 인연 2. 조합, 단체, 협회

broth·er-in-law [brʌ́ðə(r)inlɔ̀ː] n. ⓒ (pl. **broth·ers-**) a brother of one's husband or wife; a sister's husband. —ⓝ 남편 또는 아내의 형제, 자매의 남편

broth·er·ly [brʌ́ðərli] adj. of or like a brother; kind; gentle and loving. ¶*in an ~ manner.* —ⓝ 형제의, 형제다운; 친절한, 우애깊은

brough·am [brúː(ə)m / brú(ː)əm] n. ⓒ a closed carriage with four wheels, drawn by one horse. —ⓝ 한 마리가 끄는 4륜마차

‡ **brought** [brɔːt] v. pt. and pp. of **bring**.

‡ **brow** [brau] n. (usu. *pl.*) 1. the arch of hair over each eye. ¶*knit* (or *bend*) *one's brows.*① 2. the front of the head above the eyes. 3. the steep slope of a hill. —ⓝ 1. 눈썹 ¶①눈썹을 찌푸리다; 상을 찡그리다 2. 이마 3. 벼랑; 낭떠러지

brow·beat [bráubiːt] vt. (**-beat, -bea·ten**) make (someone) afraid by using rough words; frighten. 《~ someone *into doing*》 —ⓥ …을 위협하다, 위압하다

brow·bea·ten [bráubiːtn] v. pp. of **browbeat**.

‡ **brown** [braun] n. ⓤ 1. a dark color like that of toast, coffee, etc. 2. a paint having this color. —adj. of this color. —vt., vi. make (something) brown; become brown. ▷ **brown·ness** [-nis] n. —ⓝ 1. 갈색, 밤색 2. 갈색 그림물감 —ⓐ 갈색의, 밤빛의 —ⓥⓝ 갈색으로 하다(되다)

brown·ie [bráuni] n. ⓒ 1. a good-natured fairy who helps secretly in household work. 2. (*U.S.*) a flat, sweet chocolate bar containing nuts. 3. 《*B-*》 a junior member of the Girl Scouts. —ⓝ 1. 밤에 농가에 와서 집안 일을 도와 준다는 요정(妖精) 2.(美) 초콜렛 케이크 3. [8~11세의] 소녀단 단원

Brown·ing [bráuniŋ], **Robert** n. (1812-89) an English poet. —ⓝ 영국의 시인

brown·ish [bráuniʃ] adj. somewhat brown. —ⓐ 갈색을 띤

browse [brauz] vi., vt. 1. eat grass and young leaves; feed. 《~ *on* leaves》 2. read here and there in books. —n. ⓤ ⓒ soft leaves of trees. —ⓥⓝ 1. [동물이] 새싹(순)을 먹다; [마음대로] 먹게 하다 2. [책 따위] 마음내키는 대로 읽다 —ⓝ 새싹, 순

bru·in, Bru·in [brú(ː)in] n. ⓒ (usu. in fairy tales) a bear. —ⓝ 곰서방, 곰아저씨

bruise [bruːz] n. ⓒ a colored place on the skin caused by a blow. —vt. 1. cause a bruise. 2. injure; hurt. ¶*His words bruised her feelings.* —vi. become bruised. —ⓝ 타박상, 멍 —ⓥ 1. …에 타박상을 입히다 2. [감정 따위]를 해치다 —ⓥ 상처가 나다

bru·net, bru·nette [bruːnét, +Brit. brunét] adj. 1. (of skin, eyes, or hair) dark; brown. 2. (of a person) having dark or brown hair, eyes, or skin. —n. ⓒ a —ⓐ 1. [피부·눈·머리칼이] 거무스름한 2. [사람이] 머리·눈·피부가 거무스름한 —ⓝ 빛깔이 거무스름한

brunt [150] **buckle**

person, esp. a woman, with dark hair, eyes, and skin. ↔blonde ⇒ N.B.
—여자 N.B. brunet 은 남자, brunette 은 여자

brunt [brʌnt] *n.* Ⓒ the main force or violence of an attack ; the hardest part. ¶*bear the ~ of a criticism.*①
—웝 충격 ; 난국 ¶①비난을 정면으로 맞받다

‡brush¹ [brʌʃ] *n.* Ⓒ **1.** a tool made of stiff hairs or wires fastened to a handle, used in cleaning, rubbing, painting, etc. **2.** an act of brushing. **3.** a light touch in passing. **4.** a short, quick fight or quarrel. **5.** a fox's tail.
—웝 1. 솔, 브러시, 붓 2. 브러시질, 솔질 3. 스쳐 지나가기 4. 작은 충돌(전투) 5. 여우 꼬리

—*vt.* **1.** clean, rub, or paint (something) with a brush. **2.** sweep or remove (the dirt) away with a brush. (*~ the dirt away, off*) **3.** wipe (something) away. **4.** touch (something) lightly in passing. —*vi.* move lightly and quickly. 「passing.」
—匜 1. …에 솔질을 하다, 붓으로 …을 그리다 2. [먼지 따위]를 솔로 털어 없애다 3. …을 닦아(훔쳐)내다 4. …에 가볍게 스치다 —匜 가볍게 움직이다

1) *brush against,* touch lightly against (something) in
2) *brush aside* (or *away*), ⓐ put (something) aside. ⓑ pay little or no attention to (something or someone).
3) *brush over,* paint lightly.
4) *brush up,* refresh (one's knowledge, etc.).
熟 1)…을 가볍게 스치다 2)ⓐ…을 치우다 ⓑ…을 무시하다 3)가볍게 칠하다 4)[지식 따위]를 새로이하다, …을 복습하다

brush² [brʌʃ] *n.* Ⓤ a thick growth of small trees, etc.
—웝 덤불

brush·wood [brʌ́ʃwùd] *n.* Ⓤ small trees growing thickly together.
—웝 작은 나뭇가지, 결가지

brusque [brʌsk / brusk] *adj.* quick and rough in manner.
—퀭 무뚝뚝한

brusque·ly [brʌ́skli / brúsk-] *adv.* in a quick and rough manner.
—뷘 무뚝뚝하게

Brus·sels [brʌ́slz] *n.* the capital of Belgium.
—웝 벨기에의 수도

Brussels sprouts [⌞-⌞] *n.* a kind of cabbage having small heads along the central stick.
—웝 양배추의 일종

bru·tal [brúːtl] *adj.* cruel ; like a beast.
—퀭 잔인한 ; 야만적인, 상스러운

bru·tal·i·ty [bruːtǽliti] *n.* (*pl.* **-ties**) **1.** Ⓤ the state of being cruel. **2.** Ⓒ a very cruel act.
—웝 1. 잔인 2. 만행

bru·tal·ize [brúːt(ə)làiz] *vi.* become cruel. —*vt.* make (someone) cruel or animal-like.
—匜 잔인하게 되다 —匜 …을 잔인하게(짐승처럼) 만들다

bru·tal·ly [brúːt(ə)li] *adv.* in a brutal manner.
—뷘 무정하게, 짐승처럼

*****brute** [bruːt] *n.* Ⓒ **1.** an animal without power to think ; a beast. **2.** a cruel person. ¶*the ~.*① —*adj.* **1.** of or like an animal ; not human. **2.** cruel ; without feeling. ¶*~ force.*②
—웝 1. 짐승 ; 축생 2. 짐승 같은 사람 ¶①수성(獸性) ; 수욕(獸慾) ; [인간의] 색욕 —퀭 1. 짐승같은 2. 잔인한, 무감각한 ¶②폭력

brut·ish [brúːtiʃ] *adj.* like a beast ; cruel ; rude.
—퀭 짐승 같은, 잔인한, 야만적인

B. S. Bachelor of Science ; Bachelor of Surgery.

‡bub·ble [bʌ́bl] *n.* Ⓒ **1.** a thin ball of liquid containing air or gas ; an air space in a liquid. ¶*blow bubbles.*① **2.** a plan or an idea that produces no actual results.
—웝 1. 거품, 기포(氣泡) ¶①비눗방울을 불다 2. 허무한 계획(야심)

—*vi., vt.* **1.** form or produce bubbles ; make sounds like water boiling. **2.** rise in bubbles ; spring.
—匜匜 1. 거품 일다 ; 거품 일게 하다, 부글부글 끓다 2. [샘 따위가] 솟다

buc·ca·neer [bʌ̀kəníər] *n.* Ⓒ a sea robber.
—웝 해적

*****buck**¹ [bʌk] *n.* Ⓒ **1.** a male deer, rabbit, etc. **2.** a man who is too careful of his dress.
—웝 1. 수사슴, [토끼] 수컷 2. 멋쟁이

buck² [bʌk] *vt., vi.* **1.** (of a horse) jump up with all four feet off the ground. **2.** hit (something) with the head ; push against (someone or something).
—匜匜 1. [말이] 뛰어오르다 2. …을 머리로 받다, …에 돌진하다

1) *buck off,* (of a horse) throw off (a rider).
2) *buck up,* make (someone) more cheerful ; become more cheerful.
熟 1)[말이 사람]을 내동댕이치다 2)…을 기운내게 하다 ; 기운을 내다

‡buck·et [bʌ́kit] *n.* Ⓒ a pail made of metal or wood. ¶*a fire ~.*① / *a ~ of water* / *a drop in the ~.*②
kick the bucket, die.
—웝 바께쓰, 물통 ¶①소화용 바께쓰/②큰 바다의 물 한 방울
熟 죽다

buck·et·ful [bʌ́kitfùl] *n.* Ⓒ the amount that a bucket can hold. ¶*a ~ of water.*
—웝 바께쓰 하나 가득

Buck·ing·ham [bʌ́kiŋəm, +*U.S.* -hæm] *n.* a county in southern England ; Buckinghamshire.
—웝 영국 남부의 주

buck·le [bʌ́kl] *n.* Ⓒ **1.** a thing that fastens together the ends of a belt, etc. **2.** a metal ornament for a shoe. —*vt., vi.* **1.** fasten (things) with a buckle. **2.** bend. **3.** work hard.
—웝 1. 물림쇠, 혁대 장식 2. [구두의] 장식용 쵬쇠 —匜匜 1. …을 쵬쇠로 죄다 2. 구부리다, 구부러지다 3. 열심히 일하다

buckler [151] **buffoon**

buckle [down] to (or *buckle oneself to*) *a job,* work very hard. 「that protects.」 — 熟 [일]에 온힘을 기울이다
buck·ler [bʌ́klər] *n.* ⓒ a small, round shield; a thing — 名 (작은) 둥근 방패; 방어물
buck·ram [bʌ́krəm] *n.* ⓤ a rough cloth made stiff with paste. — 名 아교·풀을 빳빳하게 먹인 아마포의 일종
buck·saw [bʌ́ksɔ̀ː] *n.* ⓒ (*U. S.*) a saw set in a frame. — 名 (美) 큰 톱
buck·skin [bʌ́kskìn] *n.* **1.** ⓤ the skin of a deer. **2.** (*pl.*) short trousers made of buckskin. — 名 1. 사슴 가죽, 녹비 2. 녹비 반바지
buck·wheat [bʌ́k(h)wìːt] *n.* ⓤ a plant producing small black grain; flour made from this grain. — 名 메밀; 메밀가루
bu·col·ic [bju(ː)kálik / -kɔ́l-] *adj.* of country life; of shepherds. —*n.* ⓒ **1.** (*usu.pl.*) a poetry about shepherds; poets who write such poems. **2.** a country person. — 形 시골풍의; 양치기의, 목가적인 — 名 1. 목가; 전원시인 2. 시골사람
: bud [bʌd] *n.* ⓒ **1.** a small, early stage of a flower, leaf, or branch. ¶ *a flower ~ | put forth buds.*① **2.** any person or thing that is not fully grown.
  1) *in bud,* having buds. ¶ *The tree is in ~.*②
  2) *in the bud,* at an early stage; at the very beginning. ¶ *a poet in the ~*③ */nip in the ~.*④
  —*v.* (**bud·ded; bud·ding**) *vi.* **1.** put forth buds. **2.** begin to grow and develop. —*vt.* put a young bud into another tree to get a new shoot, branch, etc.
— 名 1. 꽃봉오리, 싹 ¶①싹트다 2. 덜 된 것, 소녀, 소년
熟 1)싹터서, 꽃봉오리져서 ¶②그 나무는 싹이 텄다 2)초기에, 시초에 ¶③시인 초년생/④봉오리졌을 때 따다
— 自 1. 꽃봉오리지다, 싹트다 2. 자라기 시작하다 — 他 …을 눈접하다
Bu·da·pest [b(j)úːdəpèst, ⸌‐⸍] *n.* the capital of Hungary. — 名 헝가리의 수도
* **Bud·dha** [búdə] *n.* (563?-483? B. C.) a great religious leader of Asia, the founder of Buddhism. — 名 부처, 석가여래
* **Bud·dhism** [búdiz(ə)m] *n.* ⓤ a religion started in India by Buddha in the sixth century B.C. — 名 불교
* **Bud·dhist** [búdist] *adj.* of Buddha or Buddhism. ¶ *a ~ temple.*① —*n.* ⓒ a person who believes in Buddhism. — 形 부처의, 불교의 ¶①절, 사원 — 名 불교도
bud·ding [bʌ́diŋ] *adj.* **1.** putting forth buds. **2.** just beginning to show signs of future success. ¶ *a ~ author.* — 形 1. 싹트기 시작하는 2. 신진의
bud·dy [bʌ́di] *n.* ⓒ (pl. **-dies**) (*U. S. colloq.*) a good friend. — 名 (美口) 동료, 친구, 짝패
budge [bʌdʒ] *vi., vt.* (usu. in *negative*) move slightly; cause (something) to move. ¶ *He won't ~ an inch.* — 自他 [조금] 움직이다; …을 움직이게 하다
* **budg·et** [bʌ́dʒit] *n.* ⓒ **1.** a plan how to use money for a certain period in the future. ¶ *open the ~.*① **2.** a collection; a bundle. ¶ *a ~ of letters.*② —*vi.* make a plan for using money. —*vt.* divide (something) by a plan. ¶ *~ one's time.*
— 名 1. 예산안 ¶①[의회에] 예산안을 제출하다 2. 무더기, 다발 ¶②한 다발의 편지 — 自 예산을 세우다 — 他 [자금·시간·따위의] 배분을 정하다
budg·et·ar·y [bʌ́dʒitèri / -təri] *adj.* of a budget. — 形 예산상의
Bue·nos Ai·res [bwéinəsáiəriz, bóunəsɛ́əri:z / bwénəs ái(ə)riz] *n.* the capital of Argentina. — 名 아르헨티나의 수도
buff [bʌf] *n.* ⓤ **1.** a soft, dull-yellow leather made from the skin of an ox, etc. **2.** a dull yellow. —*vt.* polish (something) with a buff. — 名 1. [물소·소 따위의] 무두질한 가죽 2. 황갈색 — 他 …을 무두질한 가죽으로 닦다
* **buf·fa·lo** [bʌ́fəlòu] *n.* ⓒ (pl. **-loes, -los** or *collectively* -**lo**) any of various wild oxen, as the water buffalo of India. 「Lake Erie.」 — 名 들소, 물소
Buf·fa·lo [bʌ́fəlou] *n.* a city in west New York State, on — 名 미국 New York 주의 도시
buff·er [bʌ́fər] *n.* ⓒ anything that lessens the shock of a blow. ⇒fig. — 名 완충기, 완충 장치
* **buf·fet**¹ [bʌ́fit] *n.* ⓒ **1.** a blow of the hand; a knock. **2.** misfortune. —*vt.* give a blow to (someone). —*vi.* struggle with or against something.

[buffer]
— 名 1. 타격, 때리기 2. 불운, 불행 — 他 …을 때려눕히다 — 自 [물결·역경 따위]와 싸우다
buf·fet² *n.* ⓒ **1.** [bʌféi, bə-, bu-/ bʌ́fi // → 2] a piece of furniture for holding dishes, silver, and table linen. **2.** [búféi, +*U.S.* buféi] a counter for lunch or drinks, esp. in a station or on a train. ¶ *a ~ car.*① 「acting in a foolish way.」
— 名 1. 찬장, 식기 선반 2. 간이식당 ¶①식당차
buf·foon [bəfúːn] *n.* ⓒ a person who amuses people by — 名 광대

buf·foon·er·y [bʌfúːnəri] *n.* Ⓤ Ⓒ (pl. **-er·ies**) tricks or jokes of a buffoon; foolish actions. — ⑤ 광대짓, 익살

bug [bʌg] *n.* Ⓒ **1.** any insect. ¶*a lighting ~.*① **2.** (*Brit.*) a small, biting insect without wings; (*U.S.*) an insect with hard front wings; a beetle. **3.** (*colloq.*) a germ. **4.** (*U.S. colloq.*) a fan. **5.** (*U.S.*) a defect.
a big bug, an important man.
— ⑤ **1.** 곤충 ¶①개똥벌레 **2.**《英》빈대;《美》투구풍뎅이 **3.**《口》미생물, 병원균 **4.**《美口》열광자, 팬 **5.**《美》[기계의] 고장, 결함
圈 거물, 높은 양반

bug·a·boo [bʌ́gəbùː] *n.* Ⓒ (pl. **-boos**) an imaginary thing causing unnecessary fear.
— ⑤ 도깨비, 유령

bug·bear [bʌ́gbɛ̀ər] *n.* =bugaboo.

bug·gy [bʌ́gi] *n.* Ⓒ (pl. **-gies**) a small carriage with one horse and one seat. ⇒ⓃⒷ
— ⑤ 한 필이 끄는 작은 마차 ⓃⒷ 영국에서는 2륜, 미국에서는 4륜

· **bu·gle** [bjúːgl] *n.* Ⓒ a musical instrument like a small trumpet. ¶*blow a ~ / a ~ call.*① —*vi.* sound a bugle. —*vt.* call (persons) with a bugle.
— ⑤ 〖군용〗나팔 ¶①소집 나팔 — ⓔ 나팔을 불다
— ⓣ …을 나팔로 소집하다

bu·gler [bjúːglər] *n.* Ⓒ a person who plays the bugle.
— ⑤ 나팔수

‡ **build** [bild] *v.* (**built**) *vt.* **1.** make (a house, building, machine, etc.) by putting materials or parts together; construct. ¶*~ a church (a bridge, a ship, a radio).* **2.** make a basis for (something); form; establish. ¶*~ one's theory on facts.* **3.** form gradually; develop. ¶*~ a fortune.*① —*vi.* **1.** have a house built. **2.** be built. ¶*The house is building.*②
build up, ⓐ make (something) step by step; form (something) by degrees. ⓑ make (something) strong; make (someone) healthy. ⓒ erect buildings in (a place).
—*n.* Ⓤ the shape or structure of the human body.
— ⓔ **1.** …을 세우다, 짓다, 건축하다 **2.** …의 기초를 마련하다 **3.** …을 차츰 쌓아 올리다; 증진하다 ¶①재산을 만들다 ②집을 짓다 **2.**건설되다 ¶②그 집은 건축중이다

圈 ⓐ…을 쌓아 올리다, 증진하다 ⓑ …을 강화하다; 건강하게 하다 ⓒ…을 건물로 막다(메우다)

— ⑤ 체격

· **build·er** [bíldər] *n.* Ⓒ a person who builds; a person whose business is building. ¶*a master ~.*①
— ⑤ 건설자, 건조자; 건축업자 ¶①건축 청부업자

‡ **build·ing** [bíldiŋ] *n.* **1.** Ⓒ anything built, such as a house, factory, barn, store, etc. ¶*the Empire State Building / a public ~.*① **2.** Ⓤ the art or work of making houses, etc.
— ⑤ **1.**건물 ¶①공공 건축물 **2.**건축

‡ **built** [bilt] *v.* pt. and pp. of **build**. 「*~ bookcase.*」
built-in [bíltín] *adj.* built as a part of the building. ¶*a*」
— ⓔ 〖옷장 따위〗건물의 일부로 짜넣은

· **bulb** [bʌlb] *n.* **1.** Ⓒ a round part of such plants as the onion, tulip, and lily, usu. under the ground. **2.** anything shaped like a bulb; an electric lamp.
— ⑤ **1.**구근(球根), 구경(球莖) **2.**공 모양의 것; 전구

bulb·ous [bʌ́lbəs] *adj.* **1.** of the round root of certain plants. **2.** shaped like a bulb. ¶*a ~ plant.*①
— ⓔ **1.**구경(球莖)의 **2.**구경 모양의 ¶①구근식물

Bul·gar·i·a [bʌlgɛ́əriə, +*U.S.* bul-] *n.* a country in southeast Europe.
— ⑤ 불가리아

Bul·gar·i·an [bʌlgɛ́əriən, +*U.S.* bul-] *adj.* of Bulgaria, its people, or their language. —*n.* **1.** Ⓒ a person of Bulgaria. **2.** Ⓤ the language of Bulgaria.
— ⓔ 불가리아의; 불가리아 사람(말)의 — ⑤ **1.**불가리아 사람 **2.**불가리아 말

bulge [bʌldʒ] *n.* Ⓒ **1.** a rounded part which stands out; swelling. **2.** 〘*the ~*〙 (*U.S. colloq.*) advantage.
get (or *have*) *the bulge on* (=*be in a better position than; defeat*) *someone.*
—*vi.* swell. (*~ with* something) ¶*His pockets were bulging with apples.* —*vt.* cause (something) to swell.
— ⑤ **1.**부품 **2.**우세
圈 …을 능가하다, …보다 우세하다
— ⓔ 부풀다 — ⓣ …을 부풀게 하다

· **bulk** [bʌlk] *n.* Ⓤ **1.** large size. **2.** 〘*the ~*〙 the main part. **3.** goods or cargo not in packages, boxes, etc.
in bulk, ⓐ loose; not in packages. ⓑ in large quantities.
—*vi.* **1.** give the appearance of great size or importance. ¶*The matter bulks large.*① **2.** grow large.
— ⑤ **1.**크기 **2.**대부분 **3.**비포장 화물
圈 ⓐ포장되지 않은 ⓑ대량으로
— ⓔ **1.**[크게 또는 중대하게] 생각되다 ¶①그 문제는 중요해 보인다 **2.**[부피가] 붇다

bulk·head [bʌ́lkhèd] *n.* Ⓒ a wall inside a ship for forming watertight compartments. 「of space.」
— ⑤ 〖배 내부의〗칸막이 벽

bulk·y [bʌ́lki] *adj.* (**bulk·i·er, bulk·i·est**) taking up a lot」
— ⓔ 부피가 큰, 거대한

· **bull**¹ [bul] *n.* Ⓒ **1.** the male of cattle. ⇒ⓃⒷ **2.** the male of other large animals, such as the elephant, whale, etc. **3.** a person who buys stocks and tries to raise their market price. ↔bear **4.** (*U.S. slang*) a policeman.
— ⑤ **1.**수소 ⓃⒷ 암소는 cow, 거세한 수소는 ox **2.**[코끼리 따위의] 수컷 **3.**[시세를 올리려고 증권을] 사 두는 사람 **4.**《美俗》순경

take the bull by the horns, attack a problem fearlessly. — [熟] 용감하게 난국에 처하다

bull² [bul] *n.* [C] a formal writing or an official order from the Pope. — [名] [로마 교황의] 교시

bull·dog [búldɔ̀:g / -dɔ̀g] *n.* [C] one of an English breed of short-haired dogs. — [名] 불독

bull·doz·er [búldòuzər] *n.* [C] a powerful tractor for leveling rough ground and removing obstacles. — [名] 불도우저, 토목공사용 트랙터

* **bul·let** [búlit] *n.* [C] a small piece of lead, steel, etc. to be shot from a gun. — [名] 탄환, 소총탄

* **bul·le·tin** [búlitin] *n.* [C] **1.** a short public announcement. **2.** a magazine, newspaper, or any publication appearing regularly. **—***vt.* make (something) known by a bulletin. — [名] **1.** 고시, 게시 **2.** 공보, 회보 —[他] …을 고시하다, 게시하다

bulletin board [∠-- ∸] *n.* a board on which notices are put up. — [名] 게시판

bul·let·proof [búlitprù:f] *adj.* that a bullet cannot go through. — [形] 방탄의

bull·fight [búlfàit] *n.* [C] a traditional Spanish and Latin American spectacle in which men and a bull fight in an enclosed place. — [名] 투우

bull·fight·er [búlfàitər] *n.* [C] a man who fights a bull. — [名] 투우사

bull·finch [búlfìntʃ] *n.* [C] a European song bird with beautifully colored feathers and a short, rounded bill. — [名] 피리새의 일종

bull·frog [búlfràg, -frɔ̀:g / -frɔ̀g] *n.* [C] a large frog of North America that makes a deep, loud sound. — [名] [북미산] 식용개구리

bull·head·ed [búlhédid] *adj.* stupidly stubborn: obstinate. ▷**bull·head·ed·ness** [-nis] *n.* — [形] 완고한, 고집센

bul·lion [búljən] *n.* [U] gold or silver in mass. — [名] 금괴, 은괴

bull·ock [búlək] *n.* [C] **1.** a young bull. **2.** a bull from which the male sex organ has been removed. — [名] **1.** 수 송아지 **2.** 거세한 소

bull ring [∠ ∸] *n.* an enclosed place for bullfights. — [名] 투우장

bull's-eye [búlzài] *n.* [C] **1.** the center of a target, or a shot hitting it. **2.** a small, round window. — [名] **1.** 과녁의 중심점 **2.** 둥근 창

bull terrier [∠ ∠--] *n.* a breed of dog between bulldog and terrier. — [名] 불독과 테리어의 잡종 개

bul·ly [búli] *n.* [C] (pl. **bul·lies**) a person who frightens, hurts or makes fun of smaller or weaker persons. **—***vi., vt.* (**bul·lied**) be a bully. — [名] 약자를 괴롭히는 사람 —[自][他] 약한 자를 괴롭히다

bully** someone **into** (**out of**) **doing, force someone to do (not to do) something by frightening. — [熟] [남]을 위협하여 …시키다(그만두게 하다)

—*adj.* (*Brit. colloq.*) fine; excellent. — [形] 《英口》 멋들어진

—*interj.* (*Brit. colloq.*) good!; well done! — [感] 잘했다!, 멋지다!

bul·rush [búlrʌʃ] *n.* [C] **1.** a tall, thin plant that grows in water and on wet land. **2.** (in the Bible) the papyrus — [名] **1.** 큰고랭이속의 식물 **2.** [성경에서] 갈대

bul·wark [búlwərk] *n.* [C] **1.** a wall of earth or other material built for defense. **2.** a defense; a protection. **3.** a breakwater. **4.** 《usu. *pl.*》 a ship's side above the deck. ⇒fig. **—***vt.* provide (a place, etc.) with a bulwark or bulwarks. — [名] **1.** 성채, 보루(堡壘) **2.** 방어물, 옹호자 **3.** 방파제 **4.** 현장(舷牆) —[他] …을 성채로 견고히 하다, 방어하다

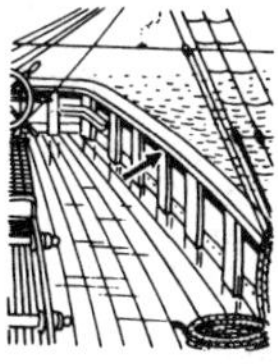
[bulwarks 4.]

bum [bʌm] *n.* [C] (*U.S. slang*) **1.** a good-for-nothing fellow. **2.** a lazy person. **—***v.* (**bummed, bum·ming**) *vi.* lead an idle life. **—***vt.* borrow (something) without intention of returning. — [名] **1.** 《美俗》 건달, 룸펜 **2.** 게으름뱅이 —[自] 빈둥빈둥 지내다 —[他] 공짜로 얻다, 갚을 수도 없이 꾸다

bum·ble·bee [bʌ́mblbì:] *n.* [C] a large hairy bee with a loud buzz. — [名] 땅벌

* **bump** [bʌmp] *vt.* **1.** strike (something) heavily. ¶ *My car bumped a truck.* **2.** dismiss (someone) from a job. **—***vi.* **1.** hit or strike against something or someone. 《~*against* or *into* something or someone》 ¶ *He bumped into me.* **2.** move with a jerk. ¶ *Our car bumped down the road.* — [他] **1.** …을 쾅하고 부딪치다 **2.** [남]을 지위에서 몰아내다 —[自] **1.** 충돌하다 **2.** [차가] 덜커덕거리며 나아가다

—*n.* [C] **1.** a heavy blow or knock. **2.** a swelling caused by a blow. **3.** unevenness on a road surface. — [名] **1.** 충돌 **2.** 타박상, 혹 **3.** 울퉁불퉁함

bump·er [bʌ́mpər] *n.* [C] **1.** a metal guard for protecting the front or rear of an automobile, a truck, etc. **2.** a — [名] **1.** [자동차의] 완충기 **2.** 가득 채운 잔 **3.** 《口》 풍작, 풍어(豊漁); 대만원

B

cup or glass filled to the brim. **3.** (*colloq.*) something unusually abundant —*adj.* unusually abundant ¶*a ~ harvest.*① —[形] 아주 풍부한, 풍족한 ¶①대풍작

bump·kin [bʌ́mpkin] *n.* [C] an ungraceful person from the country. —[名] 시골뜨기, 촌사람

bump·y [bʌ́mpi] *adj.* (**bump·i·er, bump·i·est**) causing bumps; uneven; rough. ¶*a ~ road.* ▷**bump·i·ness** [-nis] *n.* —[形] 덜컹거리는, 울퉁불퉁한

bun [bʌn] *n.* [C] a small, round, sweet roll. —[名] 단 빵

:bunch [bʌntʃ] *n.* [C] **1.** a connected group; a cluster. ¶*a ~ of flowers / Bananas grow in bunches.* **2.** a group of things. ¶*a ~ of papers.* **3.** (*colloq.*) a group of people. ¶*a ~ of students.* —*vt.* make a bunch of (something). —*vi.* gather together; collect into a group. —[名] 1. 송이 2. 다발 3. ((口)) [사람의] 한 떼, 한 무리 —[他] …을 다발짓다 —[自] 한데 모이다, 떼짓다

bund [bʌnd] *n.* [C] (in India, China, Korea, etc.) a bank along a river, etc.; an embankment. —[名] [동양에서 흔히 볼 수 있는] 제방

***bun·dle** [bʌ́ndl] *n.* [C] **1.** a number of things tied or wrapped together. **2.** a package. **3.** a group. —[名] 1. 다발 2. 꾸러미 3. 무리, 일단

—*vt.* **1.** tie or wrap (things) together. **2.** put (something) away without order. **3.** send (persons or animals) in a hurry. —*vi.* leave hurriedly. —[他] 1. …을 뭉치(다발)로 만들다 2. 뒤섞어 던져 넣다 3. [사람·짐승]을 급히 몰아대다 —[自] 급히 가 버리다

bundle up, dress warmly. [熟] 따뜻하게 몸을 감싸다

bung [bʌŋ] *n.* [C] a stopper for the opening of a cask, etc. —*vt.* close (something) with a stopper. —[名] [통 따위의] 마개, 꼭지 —[他] …에 마개를 하다

bun·ga·low [bʌ́ŋgəlou] *n.* [C] a cottage, usu. one-storied. —[名] 방갈로[식 주택]

bun·gle [bʌ́ŋgl] *vt., vi.* do or make (something) badly. —*n.* [C] a clumsy, unskillful performance. —[他][自] 서투르게 만들다, 실수하다 —[名] 실수, 실책

bun·gler [bʌ́ŋglər] *n.* [C] a person who does work badly. —[名] 실수하는 사람, 솜씨 없는 사람

bunk [bʌŋk] *n.* [C] **1.** a bed built against a wall like a shelf, esp. in a ship, etc. **2.** (*colloq.*) any bed. —*vi.* (*colloq.*) sleep in a bunk. —[名] 1. [배·기차 따위의] 침대 2. ((口)) [보통의] 침대 —[自] 침대에서 자다; ((口))뒹굴어 자다

bunk·er [bʌ́ŋkər] *n.* [C] **1.** a place for fuel on a ship. **2.** a sandy hollow or other obstruction on a golf course. —[名] 1. [배 안의] 연료 창고 2. [골프장의] 모랫구멍, 장애

***bun·ny** [bʌ́ni] *n.* [C] (pl. **-nies**) (*colloq.*) **1.** (*child's word*) a rabbit. **2.** (*U. S.*) a squirrel. —[名] ((口)) 1. 토끼 2. ((美)) 다람쥐

Bun·sen burner [bʌ́nsnbə́:rnər] *n.* a gas burner that produces a hot, blue flame. —[名] 분젠 등(燈)

bunt [bʌnt] *vt.* **1.** strike (something) with the horns, etc., as a goat does. **2.** (*Baseball*) hit (a pitched ball) very gently so that the ball rolls only a short distance on the ground. —*n.* [C] **1.** a push. **2.** (*Baseball*) the act of bunting; a bunted ball. —[他] 1. …을 뿔[따위]로 받다 2. ((야구)) 연타(번트)하다 —[名] 1. 받기, 찌르기 2. ((野球)) 번트, 연타(軟打)

bun·ting [bʌ́ntiŋ] *n.* [U] **1.** a thin cloth used for flags. **2.** ((*collectively*)) flags. —[名] 1. 기·휘장 만드는 천 2. [장식을 위한] 기; 휘장

Bun·yan [bʌ́njən], **John** *n.* (1628-88) an English preacher and religious writer. —[名] 영국의 종교 작가

buoy [bɔi, +*U.S.* bu:i] *n.* [C] **1.** a floating thing fastened to the bottom of the water with a chain to show the presence of dangerous rocks, the safe part of the channel, etc. **2.** a floating ring used to save a person from drowning. —[名] 1. 부표(浮標) 2. 구명대

—*vt.* **1.** keeps (something) from sinking. **2.** sustain. —[他] 1. …을 띄우다 2. 지지하다

buoy up, ⓐ keep (something) from sinking. ⓑ cause (someone) to rise. ¶*~ oneself up with hope.* [熟] ⓐ…을 띄우다 ⓑ…의 기운을 북돋우다

buoy·an·cy [bɔ́iənsi, +*U.S.* bú:jən-] *n.* [U] **1.** the ability to float. **2.** the power to keep things afloat. **3.** cheerfulness; high spirits. —[名] 1. 부력, 뜨는 힘 2. 뜨는 성질 3. 경쾌, 쾌활

buoy·ant [bɔ́iənt, +*U.S.* bú:jənt] *adj.* **1.** able to float; very light. **2.** able to keep things afloat. ¶*~ force.*① **3.** gay; cheerful. ▷**buoy·ant·ly** [-li] *adv.* —[形] 1. [물건이] 잘 뜨는 2. [물이] 띄우는 힘이 있는 ¶①부력 3. 쾌활한

bur [bə:r] *n.* [C] **1.** the rough, prickly case around the seeds of certain plants. **2.** any plant with burs. —[名] 1. [밤 따위의] 가시 2. 가시 있는 열매를 맺는 식물

Bur·ber·ry [bə́:rbèri, -bəri / -bəri] *n.* **1.** [C] a light rain coat made of a waterproof cotton cloth. **2.** [U] such cloth. —[名] 1. 바아바리 비옷 2. 방수포(防水布)

:bur·den[1] [bə́:rdn] *n.* [C][U] **1.** anything that is carried; a —[名] 1. 짐; 무거운 짐 ¶①짐 나르는

load. ¶*a beast of ~.*① **2.** something hard to bear. ¶*the ~ of taxation / be a ~ to* (or *on*) *society*② */ bear the ~.*③ **3.** the weight of a ship's cargo; the carrying capacity of a ship. ¶*a ship of 150 tons ~.* **—*vt.*** put a burden on (someone). 《~ someone *with*》

짐승 **2.** 부담, 의무 ¶②사회의 부담이 되다/③어려운 일에 견디다 **3.** 적재량 —[他] …에 무거운 짐(부담)을 지우다

bur·den² [bə́:rdn] *n.* [C] **1.** 《usu. *the ~*》 the most important idea or message. **2.** the part of a song repeated often; the refrain.

—[名] **1.** 요지(要旨), 취지 **2.** 노래의 후렴

bur·den·some [bə́:rdnsəm] *adj.* hard to bear; troublesome; oppressive.

—[形] 짐이 되는; 골치아픈, 성가신

bur·dock [bə́:rdàk / -dɔ̀k] *n.* [C] a plant with prickly burs, large leaves, and a strong smell.

—[名] 우엉

⁑bu·reau [bjúərou] *n.* [C] (pl. **bu·reaus** or **bu·reaux**) **1.** a government office. **2.** (*Brit.*) a large writing table with drawers. **3.** (*U.S.*) a chest of drawers for clothing, etc.

—[名] **1.** 국(局), 부; 관청 **2.**《英》 서랍 달린 큰 책상 **3.**《美》 [거울 달린] 침실용 장롱

bu·reauc·ra·cy [bju(ə)rákrəsi / -rɔ́k-] *n.* [U][C] (pl. **-cies**) **1.** government by bureaus and group of officials. **2.** 《*collectively*》 officials managing the government. **3.** concentration of authority in administrative bureaus.

—[名] **1.** 관료주의 **2.** 관리, 관료 **3.** 관료주의

bu·reau·crat [bjúərəkræ̀t] *n.* [C] **1.** an official of a bureaucracy. **2.** a formal government official who tries to center power in himself.

—[名] **1.** 관리 **2.** 관료주의자

bu·reau·crat·ic [bjùəroukrǽtik] *adj.* of a bureaucracy or a bureaucrat.

—[形] 관료 정치의, 관료적인

bu·reaux [bjúərouz] *n.* pl. of **bureau.**

burgh [bə:rg / bʌ́rə] *n.* [C] a town having powers of self-goverment in Scotland.

—[名] [스코틀랜드의] 자치도시

burgh·er [bə́:rgər] *n.* [C] a citizen of a town; a citizen.

—[名] 시민, 공민

bur·glar [bə́:rglər] *n.* [C] a thief who breaks into a building, etc. to steal.

—[名] 밤도둑, 강도

bur·gla·ry [bə́:rgləri] *n.* [U][C] (pl. **-gla·ries**) the act of breaking into a house to steal, esp. after dark.

—[名] 밤도둑질(죄)

bur·go·mas·ter [bə́:rgoumæ̀stər / bə́:goumà:stə] *n.* [C] the mayor of a town in the Netherlands, Germany, etc.

—[名] [네덜란드·독일 등지의] 시장(市長)

bur·i·al** [bériəl] *n.* [U][C] the act of burying a dead body. ¶*~ at sea.*① **—*adj. of burying

—[名] 매장, 장례 ¶①수장(水葬) —[形] 장례식의

burial ground [´-- ˌ] *n.* a graveyard; a cemetery.

—[名] 묘지, 매장지

burial service [´-- ´-] *n.* the ceremony of burying.

—[名] 매장식

bur·ied [bérid] *adj.* laid in a grave.

—[形] 매장된

bur·lap [bə́:rlæp] *n.* [U] very rough cloth made from jute or hemp used for making sacks.

—[名] [자루용의] 누른 삼베

bur·lesque [bərlésk] *n.* [C][U] **1.** foolish imitation of a serious literary or dramatic work. **2.** (*U.S.*) a cheap, vulgar kind of light musical comedy. **—*vt.*** make (something) nonsensial and laughable by imitating foolishly. **—*adj.*** comical; making people laugh.

—[名] **1.** [문학작품 따위의] 익살스런 모작(模作), 희극 번안 **2.**《美》 저속한 희가극 —[他] …을 익살스럽게 만들다 —[形] 익살맞은, 우스운

bur·ly [bə́:rli] *adj.* (**-li·er, -li·est**) stout; strong; big.

—[形] 건장한, 힘센

Bur·ma [bə́:rmə] *n.* a country in the southeast Asia. ⇨ [N.B.]

—[名] 버어마 [N.B.] 수도는 Rangoon

Bur·mese [bə:rmí:z] *n.* (pl. **-mese**) **1.** [C] a person of Burma. **2.** [U] the language of Burma. **—*adj.*** of Burma, its people, or their language.

—[名] **1.** 버어마 사람 **2.** 버어마 말 —[形] 버어마의

⁑burn [bə:rn] *v.* (**burnt** or **burned**) *vi.* **1.** be on fire; blaze. ¶*Paper burns well.* **2.** give light; glow. ¶*The light burned in the room.* **3.** be destroyed or damaged by fire, heat, or acid. ¶*Her skin burns easily in the sun.*① **4.** feel hot. **5.** feel strong emotion. 《~ *with* anger, shame, love, etc.》 **6.** go brown with heat or light. **—*vt.*** **1.** cause (something) to be on fire; destroy or damage (something) by fire, heat, or acid. **2.** use (something) as fuel. ¶*~ wood (coal).* **3.** produce (something) by the action of fire or heat. ¶*~ bricks / ~ wood into charcoal.*② **4.** exhaust. **5.** (*slang*) irritate.

—[自] **1.** 불타다 **2.** 빛나다 **3.** 타다, 데다 ¶①그녀의 피부는 볕에 잘 탄다 **4.** 뜨겁게 느끼다 **5.** 발끈하다, 흥분하다; 열중하다 **6.** 눋다 —[他] **1.** …을 태우다, 불사르다 **2.** …을 때다, 연료로 하다 **3.** …을 태워서 만들다 ¶②나무를 태워 숯을 굽다 **4.** …을 다 써 없애다 **5.**《俗》 성나게 하다

1) ***burn away,*** ⓐ destroy or ruin by burning. ⓑ go on

[熟] 1)ⓐ…을 태워 버리다 ⓑ 계속 불

burning. ⓒ be exhausted through burning.
2) ***burn daylight,*** waste time or energy.
3) ***burn down,*** burn (a house, etc.) to the ground.
4) ***burn*** oneself ***out,*** use up all one's energy through overwork.
5) ***burn up,*** burn completely.
6) ***have*** something ***to burn,*** have very much of something to spend.
—*n.* [C] an injury or a damage caused by burning.

타다 ⓒ타 없어지다 2)시간(정력·돈)을 낭비하다 3)…을 몽땅 태워 버리다 4)[과로로] 정력을 몽땅 소모하다 5)몽땅 타다 6)…을 남아돌 정도로 갖고 있다
—[名] 불에 뎀, 화상

burn·er [bə́:rnər] *n.* [C] **1.** the part of a lamp, furnace, etc., where the flame is produced. ¶*a gas-burner.*① **2.** anything that burns. **3.** a person whose work is burning something. ¶*a charcoal ~.*②
—[名] 1. 화구(火口) ¶①가스 화구 2. 연소기 3. 태우는 사람 ¶②숯굽는 사람

burn·ing [bə́:rniŋ] *adj.* very hot; exciting; urgent or very important. ▷**burn·ing·ly** [-li] *adv.*
—[形] 타는 듯한; 흥분시키는; 긴급의

bur·nish [bə́:rniʃ] *vt.* polish (the surface of metal, etc.) by rubbing. ▷**bur·nish·er** [-ər] *n.*
—[他] [금속 표면 따위]를 닦다, 갈다

⁑ **burnt** [bə:rnt] *v.* pt. and pp. of **burn**[1].

burr [bə:r] *n.* =bur.

* **bur·row** [bə́:rou / bʌ́rou] *n.* [C] **1.** a hole in the ground made by a rabbit, fox, etc. for living in. **2.** a similar place of retreat. —*vi., vt.* **1.** make a hole or passage in the ground. **2.** research; investigate. 《~ *into* reference books, etc.》 **3.** hide.
—[名] 1. [토끼·여우 따위의] 굴 2. 숨는 곳 —[自][他] 1. 굴을 파다 2. 철저히 조사하다 3. [구멍에 몸]을 숨기다

⁑ **burst** [bə:rst] *v.* (**burst**) *vi.* **1.** break open or into pieces violently and suddenly; explode; split. **2.** be filled to the breaking point. —*vt.* cause (something) to break violently and suddenly.
1) ***be bursting*** (=*be eager*) ***to do.***
2) ***be bursting with*** (=*be full of*) ***something.***
3) ***burst in,*** ⓐ open violently inward. ⓑ interrupt. 《~ in *upon* a conversation》 ⓒ appear or come in suddenly. 《~ in *upon* someone》
4) ***burst into,*** ⓐ come into suddenly. ⓑ begin to do something suddenly. ¶~ *into flames*① / ~ *into tears*② / ~ *into laughter.*③
5) ***burst open,*** open violently or suddenly.
6) ***burst out,*** ⓐ exclaim; begin to speak loudly. 《~ out *into* something》 ⓑ start suddenly. 《~ out *of* a room》 ⓒ begin to do suddenly. 《~ out *doing*》
7) ***burst up,*** explode.
8) ***burst upon*** (or ***on***), ⓐ come suddenly in sight of (someone). ⓑ attack suddenly.
—*n.* [C] **1.** the act of bursting; a split; an explosion. **2.** an outbreak. ¶*a ~ of laughter.*④ **3.** a sudden activity or spurt.

—[自] 1. 폭발하다; 파열하다; 찢어지다 2. [터질 듯이] 가득 차다 —[他] …을 파열시키다
[熟] 1)…하고 싶어하다 2)…으로 가득 차 있다 3)ⓐ[문 따위] 안쪽으로 세차게 열리다 ⓑ[이야기 따위]를 방해하다 ⓒ갑자기 나타나다, 난입(亂入)하다 4)ⓐ난입하다 ⓑ갑자기 시작하다 ¶①확 타오르다/②갑자기 울음을 터뜨리다/③갑자기 웃음을 터뜨리다 5)활짝 피다 6)ⓐ외치다; 큰 소리로 말하기 시작하다 ⓑ갑자기 떠나다 ⓒ갑자기 시작하다 7)폭발하다 8)ⓐ갑자기 시야에 들어오다 ⓑ급습하다
—[名] 1. 폭발; 파열 2. 돌발 ¶①갑자기 일어나는 웃음소리 3. 분발, 단숨

⁑ **bur·y** [béri] *vt.* (**bur·ied**) **1.** put (a dead body) in the earth. **2.** hide (something) from view; cover up. ¶*She buried her face in her hands.*① **3.** plunge; sink. ¶*He buried himself in his work.*②
—[他] 1. …을 묻다, 매장하다 2. …을 덮어 가리다 ¶①그녀는 두 손으로 얼굴을 가렸다 3. …에 몰두시키다 ¶②그는 일에 몰두했다

⁑ **bus** [bʌs] *n.* [C] a large automobile having seats or benches for passengers; an omnibus.
—[名] 버스, 합승 자동차

bus·by [bʌ́zbi] *n.* [C] (pl. **-bies**) a tall fur hat worn for parades by soldiers of certain British armies. ⇒fig.
—[名] 모자(영국의 기병·공병 등이 쓰는 모피제 정모)

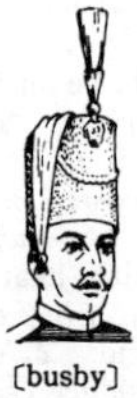
(busby)

⁑ **bush** [buʃ] *n.* **1.** [C] a low-growing plant with several branches growing from the root. **2.** 《*the* ~》 wild land.
beat around the bush, approach a matter in a long, slow way.
—[名] 1. 관목 2. 미개간지, 덤불, 총림지대
[熟] 둘러대어(넌지시) 말하다

* **bush·el** [búʃ(ə)l] *n.* [C] measure for grain, fruit, vegetables, etc., equal to eight gallons.
—[名] 부셸

bush·y [búʃi] *adj.* (**bush·i·er, bush·i·est**) **1.** spreading out like a bush. **2.** covered with thick hair.
—[形] 1. 덤불이 우거진(무성한) 2. 털이 많은

* **bus·i·ly** [bízili] *adv.* in a busy manner.
—[副] 바쁘게, 열심히

⁑busi·ness [bíznis] *n.* [U] **1.** one's work; occupation. ¶*What's his ~?* **2.** the selling and buying of goods; trade. ¶*He is in the cotton ~.*① **3.** a commercial or industrial enterprise. **4.** the activities of selling and buying. ¶*Business is dull.*② **5.** [C] an affair; a matter. ¶*a strange ~.* **6.** duty; mission. ¶*go to Paris on urgent ~.*③ **7.** ⟪usu. in *negative*⟫ what has to do with someone; right to concern. ¶*It's none of your ~.*④

—[名] **1.** 일, 사무, 업무; 직업 **2.** 장사; 매매 ¶①목화 장사를 하고 있다 **3.** 기업 **4.** 상황(商況) ¶②장사는 불황이다 **5.** 사건, 일 **6.** 의무; 사명, 볼일 ¶③급한 볼일로 파리에 가다 **7.** 관계할 권리(필요) ¶④그것은 네가 알 바가 아니다

1) ***Business is business.***, Business comes before personal circumstances.
2) ***come*** (or ***get***) ***to business,*** start the work that is to be done.
3) ***do business,*** carry on one's work or trade.
4) ***do one's business for someone,*** defeat or kill someone.
5) ***do business*** (=*be connected in business*) ***with someone.***
6) ***enter business,*** begin one's work.
7) ***Go about your business!,*** Get away!
8) ***go into business,*** become a man of business.
9) ***make it one's business to do,*** decide to do; do often as one's business.
10) ***out of business,*** going bankrupt.
11) ***send someone about his business,*** dismiss.

[熟] 1)장사는 장사(관용·감정은 금물) 2)할일에 착수하다 3)장사(일)를 하다 4)죽이다, 해치우다 5)…와 거래하다 6)일을 시작하다 7)네 일이나봐!, 저리 가! 8)실업가가 되다 9)반드시 …하다; …하기를 떠맡다 10)파산하여 11)…을 해고하다

busi·ness·like [bíznislàik] *adj.* having system and method; practical.

—[形] 조직적인, 사무적인, 실제적인

busi·ness·man [bíznismæ̀n] *n.* [C] (pl. **-men** [-mèn]) a man engaged in business; a man who runs a business.

—[名] 실업가, 상인

∗bust[1] [bʌst] *n.* [C] **1.** a sculpture of a person's head, shoulders, and chest. **2.** the upper, front part of the body. **3.** a woman's bosom.

—[名] **1.** 반신상 **2.** 가슴 부분 **3.** [여자의] 앞가슴

bus·tle [bʌ́sl] *vi.* move or act noisily and in a hurry. ⟪~ *about* something⟫ —*vt.* make (others) hurry or work hard. —*n.* [U] ⟪sometimes *a* ~⟫ activity with great show of energy. ¶*in a ~.*① ▷**bus·tler** [-lər] *n.*

—[自] 부산떨다, 떠들어대다 —[他] …을 서두르게 하다 —[名] 법석, 소동 ¶① 떠들며, 혼잡하여

⁑bus·y [bízi] *adj.* (**bus·i·er, bus·i·est**) **1.** working; active; not free. ¶*I'm ~ now.* **2.** full of work or activity; crowded. ¶*a ~ day* / *a ~ street.* **3.** (*U.S.*) (of a telephone line) in use.

—[形] **1.** 일하고 있는, 여가가 없는 **2.** 바쁜, 볼일이 많은; 떠들썩한, 혼잡한 **3.** ⟪美⟫ [전화가] 통화중인

—*vt.* (**bus·ied**) make or keep (oneself, one's hands, etc.) busy. ⟪~ oneself *with* or *about*; ~ oneself [*in*] *doing*⟫

—[他] …을 바쁘게 하다(움직이다)

bus·y·bod·y [bízibɑ̀di / -bɔ̀di] *n.* [C] (pl. **-bod·ies**) a person who wants to do the affairs of others.

—[名] 잘하는 사람

⁑but [bʌt, bət] *conj.* **1.** on the other hand; yet; however; still. ¶*I was not there, ~ my sister was.* / *It's not difficult, ~ easy.* **2.** unless; if ... not. ¶*She would have fallen ~* [that] *I caught her.*① **3.** other than. ¶*I cannot choose ~ laugh.*② **4.** (*old*) that ... not. ¶*He is not such a fool ~* [that] *he can tell that.*③ **5.** that. ¶*I have no doubt ~* [*that* or *what*] *he will succeed.*④

—[接] 그러나, 허나; 그 한편 **2.** …하지 않으면 ¶①내가 붙들지 않았더면 그녀는 넘어졌을 게다 **3.** …을 제외하고 ¶②웃지 않을 수 없었다 **4.** …하지 않는 것 같은 ¶③그는 그걸 모를 정도의 바보는 아니다 **5.** …이라는 것은 ¶④그가 성공할 것은 틀림없다

1) ***all but,*** nearly; almost.
2) ***anything but,*** far from.
3) ***but for,*** if it were not for; if it had not been for.
4) ***But me no buts.***, Don't object to me.
5) ***but then,*** but on the other hand.
6) ***cannot but do,*** cannot help doing; must do.
7) ***not but what that*** (or ***what***) ..., though at the same time it is true that....
8) ***not only A but also B,*** B as well as A.
9) ***nothing but,*** only. ¶*War brings nothing ~ misery.*

[熟] 1)거의 2)…이기는커녕 3)…이 없다면 4)「그러나, 그러나」하고 자꾸 변명하지 말게 5)그러나 그 반면에 6)…하지 않을 수 없다 7) 아니라는 것은 아니지만 8)A뿐 아니라 B도 또한 9)단지 …만

—*prep.* except; save ¶*the last ~ one*⑤ / *They are all wrong ~ him.*⑥ —*pron.* ⟪*relative pronoun*⟫ who...not; that...not. ¶*There is no one ~ knows it.*⑦ / *There is no rule ~ has exceptions.*⑧ —*adv.* only. ¶*She is ~ a child.*

—[前] …을 제외하고, …외에 ¶⑤마지막에서 두번째 / ⑥그를 제외하고는 모두 틀린다 —[代] …이 아닌 [것] ¶⑦그것을 모르는 사람은 없다 / ⑧예외 없는 규칙은 없다 —[副] 단지

∗butch·er [bútʃər] *n.* [C] **1.** a person whose business is to

—[名] **1.** 도살자 **2.** 푸줏간 **3.** ⟪美⟫ [특히

kill animals for food. **2.** a person who sells meat. **3.** (*U.S.*) a seller. **—*vt.* 1.** kill (animals) for food. **2.** kill brutally. **3.** spoil (something) by poor work.
열차내의] 판매원 —[他] 1. …을 도살하다 2. …을 학살하다 3. …을 망쳐 놓다

butch·er·y [bútʃəri] *n.* (pl. **-er·ies**) **1.** [U] brutal killing. **2.** [C] a house for killing animals; a butcher's work.
—[名] 1. 도살, 학살 2. 도살장

* **but·ler** [bʌ́tlər] *n.* [C] the chief manservant of a household who has charge of the plates and wine.
—[名] 집사, 하인의 우두머리

butt[1] [bʌt] *n.* [C] the thicker end of a tool, weapon, fishing-rod, etc.
—[名] [연장·무기·낚싯대 따위의] 굵은 끝, 밑동

butt[2] [bʌt] *n.* [C] **1.** a target for shooting. **2.** a person who is laughed at or blamed by others.
—[名] 1. 과녁, 표적 2. [조소·비평 따위의] 대상, …거리

butt[3] [bʌt] *vt.* strike or push (something) with the head or horns. **—*n.*** [C] a push or blow with the head or horns.
—[他] [머리·뿔 따위로] …을 받다 —[名] 머리로 받기

⁑ **but·ter** [bʌ́tər] *n.* [U] **1.** the solid yellowish fat made from cream. **2.** something like butter. ¶*peanut ~.*
—*vt.* 1. put butter on (bread, etc.). **2.** (*colloq.*) flatter. 《*~ up* someone》
—[名] 1. 버터 2. 버터 비슷한 것
—[他] 1. …에 버터를 바르다 2. …에 아첨하다

but·ter·cup [bʌ́tərkʌ̀p] *n.* [C] a wild plant with bright yellow cup-shaped flowers.
—[名] 애기미나리아재비

* **but·ter·fly** [bʌ́tərflài] *n.* [C] (pl. **-flies**) an insect with feelers and four wings.
—[名] 나비

but·ter·milk [bʌ́tərmìlk] *n.* [U] liquid remaining after butter has been separated from milk.
—[名] 버터 밀크(버터를 빼고 남는 신 우유)

but·ter·scotch [bʌ́tərskɑ̀tʃ / -skɔ̀tʃ, -skɔ́tʃ] *n.* [U] candy made from brown sugar and butter. **—*adj.*** flavored with brown sugar and butter.
—[名] 버터들이 사탕과자 —[形] 흑설탕과 버터로 맛을 낸

but·ter·y [bʌ́təri] *adj.* **1.** like butter. **2.** containing butter.
—[形] 1. 버터 같은 2. 버터가 들어 있는

but·tocks [bʌ́təks] *n. pl.* the part of the body on which a person sits; a rump.
—[名] 궁둥이, 둔부

⁑ **but·ton** [bʌ́tn] *n.* [C] **1.** a small object fastened to. **2.** any knob or button-shaped object to push. **3.** 《*pl.*》 (*Brit. colloq.*) a boy who serves in a hotel, club, etc. in uniform. **—*vt.*** fasten with buttons. ¶*This dress buttons down the back.*① ▷**but·ton·less** [-lis] *adj.*
—[名] 1. [의복의] 단추 2. [초인종의] 누름단추 3. 급사 —[他] …을 단추로 채우다 ¶①이 드레스는 등에서 단추로 채운다

but·ton·hole [bʌ́tnhòul] *n.* [C] a hole through which a button is passed. **—*vt.*** make buttonholes in (cloth, etc.).
—[名] 단추 구멍 —[他] …에 단추 구멍을 내다

but·tress [bʌ́tris] *n.* [C] **1.** a structure built against a wall as a support. ⇒fig. **2.** a support. **—*vt.* 1.** make (something) strong with a buttress. **2.** support.
—[名] 1. 버팀벽 2. 버티는 물건 —[他] 1. 을 버팀벽으로 버티다 2. …을 버티다

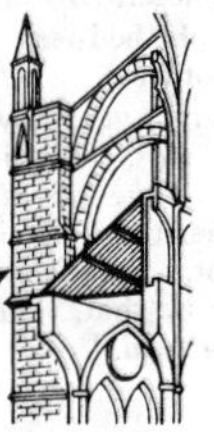
〔buttress 1.〕

bux·om [bʌ́ksəm] *adj.* (of women) rounded and good to look at, healthy and cheerful.
—[形] [여자가] 토실토실하고 예쁜, 건강하고 쾌활한

⁑ **buy** [bai] *vt.* (**bought**) **1.** get (something) in exchange for money; purchase. **2.** get (something) by means of some sacrifice. ¶*~ fame with health.*① **3.** (of money, etc.) serve to get (something). ¶*Money cannot ~ happiness.* **4.** bribe.
—[他] 1. …을 사다 2. 희생을 치르고 …을 얻다 ¶①건강의 댓가로 명성을 얻다 3. [돈 따위가] …을 사는 데에 쓸모 있다 4. …을 매수하다

1) ***buy in,*** buy stock (in a company, etc.).
2) ***buy off,*** get rid of (something) by payment; bribe.
3) ***buy out,*** get all rights of business by paying money.
4) ***buy over,*** bribe.
5) ***buy up,*** buy as much of (something) as one can.

[熟] 1)…을 사들이다 2)돈을 주고 …을 모면하다; …에게 뇌물을 주다 3)[회사 따위]를 매수하다 4)…에게 뇌물을 주다 5)…을 가능한 한 매점하다

buy·a·ble [báiəbl] *adj.* that can be bought.
—[形] 살 수 있는

* **buy·er** [báiər] *n.* [C] a person who buys.
—[名] 사는 사람, 사는 쪽

* **buzz** [bʌz] *n.* [C] **1.** the humming sound of a bee, etc. **2.** the confused sound of many people talking quietly. **—*vi., vt.* 1.** make a buzz; cause (something) to make a low, humming sound. **2.** speak with a low, humming voice. **3.** spread (a rumor, gossip, etc.) secretly.
—[名] 1. [벌 따위의] 윙윙 소리 2. 웅성거림 —[自][他] 1. 윙윙 소리내다; 윙윙 소리내게 하다 2. 웅성거리다, 떠들다 3. [소문 따위]를 몰래 퍼뜨리다

1) ***buzz about*** (or ***around***), move about noisily.
2) ***buzz off,*** (*Brit. colloq.*) ring off on the telephone; (*colloq.*) go away.

[熟] 1)바쁘게 여기저기 돌아다니다 2)《英口》 전화를 끊다; 《口》 가 버리다

buz·zard [bʌ́zərd] *n.* [C] a bird of the falcon family.
—[名] 말똥가리

buzz·er [bʌ́zər] *n.* [C] an electrical instrument that makes a buzzing sound as a signal or warning.
—[名] 버저(전기 자석 신호 장치)

‡ **by** [bai] *prep.* **1.** near to; beside. ¶*a house ~ the lake* | *A cat is ~ the gate.* **2.** along; at the side of. ¶*a path ~ the river* | *He went ~ me.* **3.** through; across; over; via. ¶*go ~ sea (land, air)*① | *travel ~ Siberia.*② **4.** through the act or means of. ¶*travel ~ airplane.*③ | *America was discovered ~ Columbus.* **5.** to the extent of. ¶*short ~ an inch*④ | *too many ~ one.*⑤ **6.** according to a unit of; in the measure of. ¶*sell ~ the pound*⑥ | *He was employed ~ the month.*⑦ **7.** according to. ¶*judge someone ~ his appearance*⑧ | *What time is it ~ your watch?* **8.** concerning; in relation to; in respect of. ¶*He is a German ~ birth.*⑨ | *She did well ~ her daughter.*⑩ **9.** with a succession of. ¶*~ degrees* | *~ hundreds* | *little ~ little* | *step ~ step.* **10.** during. ¶*He works ~ day and studies ~ night.* **11.** not later than. ¶*I will come back ~ five.* **12.** toward. ¶*North ~ East.*

—[前] **1.** …의 옆(곁)에[서의] **2.** …을 따라, …의 옆을 **3.** …을 지나서; 건너서 ¶①해로(육로·공로)로/②시베리아 경유로 여행하다 **4.** …을 써서, …에 의하여 ¶③비행기로 여행하다 **5.** …만큼 ¶④1인치 짧은/⑤하나가 많은 **6.** …단위로, …당 ¶⑥파운드 단위로 팔다/⑦그는 월급제로 고용되었다 **7.** …에 따라, …으로 ¶⑧사람을 용모로 판단하다 **8.** …에 관하여, …의 점에서 ¶⑨그는 태생이 독일인이다/⑩그는 딸에 관한 점에서는 잘 해주었다 **9.** …씩 **10.** …의 사이 **11.** …까지에 **12.** …에 대하여, …으로 치우친

—*adv.* **1.** near at hand. **2.** past. ¶*pass ~* | *go ~* | *days gone ~.* **3.** aside; away. ¶*lay something ~.* **4.** in reserve. ¶*lay ~ money.*

—[副] **1.** 가까이에 **2.** [시간이] 지나서, 흘러서 **3.** 옆에, 곁에 **4.** 예비로, 따로 두어

1) ***by and by,*** before long; soon.
2) ***by and large,*** on the whole; in general.
3) ***by the by,*** in passing; by the way.

[熟] 1)멀지 않아 2)대체로 3)그런데, 말이 났으니 말이지

by-and-by [báiən(d)bái, bái(ə)mbái] *n.* 《*the* ~》 future.
—[名] [그다지 멀지 않은] 미래

bye-bye [báibài] *interj.* (*colloq.*) good-by.
—[感] 《口》 안녕 !

by-e·lec·tion [báiilèkʃ(ə)n] *n.* [C] (*Brit.*) a special election to fill a vacancy.
—[名] 《英》 보궐선거

by·gone [báigɔ̀:n / -gɔ̀n] *adj.* past. —*n.* [C] 《*pl.*》 something in the past.
—[形] 과거의 —[名] 지나간 일, 과거

by·law [báilɔ̀:] *n.* [C] **1.** a law made by a local government. **2.** a secondary law or rule.
—[名] **1.** 지방법 **2.** 내규(內規), 세칙

by-line [báilàin] *n.* [C] (*U. S.*) a line at the beginning of a newspaper or magazine article giving the name of the writer.
—[名] 《美》 [신문·잡지에서] 필자 이름이 씌어 있는 행

by·name [báinèim] *n.* [C] a nickname.
—[名] 별명

by-pass [báipæ̀s / -pɑ̀:s] *n.* [C] a side road parallel to the main road, built for fast traffic to pass by, and not through, a town. —*vt.* avoid (a city, etc.) by following a by-pass; go around.
—[名] 우회로(迂回路), 옆길 —[他] …을 피하여 지나가다; 우회하다

by-path [báipæ̀θ / -pɑ̀:θ] *n.* [C] a side path.
—[名] 옆길, 샛길

by-play [báiplèi] *n.* [U] an action or speech on the stage apart from that of the main situation.
—[名] [연극의] 곁줄거리

by-prod·uct [báiprɑ̀dəkt / -prɔ̀d-] *n.* [C] something produced while some other thing is made.
—[名] 부산물

by-road [báiròud] *n.* [C] a side road.
—[名] 옆길

By·ron [báiər(ə)n], **George Gordon** *n.* (1788-1824) an English poet.
—[名] 영국의 시인

By·ron·ic [bairɑ́nik / -rɔ́n-] *adj.* of Byron or his poetry.
—[形] 바이런풍의

by·stand·er [báistæ̀ndər] *n.* [C] a person who stands near or looks on but does not take part in an event and activity.
—[名] 구경군, 방관자, 국외자(局外者)

by·street [báistrì:t] *n.* [C] a side street.
—[名] 뒷길, 뒷골목

by·way [báiwèi] *n.* [C] a side path or road.
—[名] 옆길, 샛길

by·word [báiwə̀:rd] *n.* [C] **1.** a proverb. **2.** an object of contempt.
—[名] **1.** 속담 **2.** 웃음거리

Byz·an·tine [bíz(ə)ntì:n, -tàin, bizǽntin / bizǽntain] *adj.* of Byzantium esp. the style of architecture developed there. —*n.* [C] a person of Byzantium.
—[形] 비잔티움의, 비잔티움식의 —[名] 비잔티움 사람

By·zan·ti·um [bizǽntiəm, +*U.S.* -ʃi-] *n.* the capital of the Eastern Roman Empire. ⇨[N.B.]
—[名] 비잔티움 [N.B.] 오늘날의 Istanbul

C

C, c [siː] *n.* [C] (pl. **C's, Cs, c's, cs** [siːz]) **1.** the third letter of the English alphabet. **2.** the first note of the musical scale of C major.
—[名] 1. 영어 자모의 세째 글자 2.《樂》「다」음,「다」조

C 1. (*Chemistry*) carbon. **2.** the Roman number 100.

C. 1. Centigrade. **2.** Cape. **3.** Catholic.

c. 1. cent; cents. **2.** chapter. **3.** circa. **4.** cubic.

***cab** [kæb] *n.* [C] **1.** an automobile for hire; a taxi. **2.** the covered part of a locomotive or truck where the engineer or driver sits. **3.** a carriage for hire, pulled by one horse.
—[名] 1. 택시 2. [기관차의] 기관사석, [트럭의] 운전대 3. 한 필이 끄는 합승 마차

ca·bal [kəbǽl] *n.* [C] **1.** a small group of persons who work for a secret plan. **2.** a secret plan of such a group, esp. in politics.
—[名] 1. 음모단, 비밀 결사 2. [특히 정치상의] 음모

cab·a·ret [kæbəréi / kǽbərèi] *n.* [C] **1.** a restaurant where entertainment of singing and dancing is given during meals. **2.** an entertainment or show given at a restaurant.
—[名] 1. 카바레(음악·춤 따위 여흥이 있는 술집) 2. 카바레 쇼우

***cab·bage** [kǽbidʒ] *n.* [C] a kind of vegetable whose leaves are folded into a round head; [U] these leaves cooked as a vegetable. ⇒[N.B.]
—[名] 양배추; 요리한 양배추 잎 [N.B.] 중심부는 head 또는 heart

cab·by [kǽbi] *n.* [C] (pl. **-bies**) (*colloq.*) the driver of a cab.
—[名] 택시 운전수; 마차 마부

‡**cab·in** [kǽbin] *n.* [C] **1.** a small, roughly-built house, usu. of wood; a hut. **2.** a small room, esp. in a ship or an airplane, for officers or passengers.
—[名] 1. [통나무] 오두막 2. 선실(船室)

cabin boy [ˊ-ˋ] *n.* a boy who waits on the officers and passengers on a ship.
—[名] 선실(선장실) 급사

cabin class [ˊ-ˋ] *n.* the class between the first and second class on a passenger ship.
—[名] 캐빈급, 특2등(여객선의 1등과 2등의 중간급)

***cab·i·net** [kǽbinit] *n.* [C] **1.** a piece of furniture with shelves or drawers used to hold things, such as dishes or jewels. **2.** 《usu. *the C-*》 a group of persons chosen by the head of a nation to advise him in government administration.
—[名] 1. [보석·접시 따위를 넣어 두는] 서랍 달린 장롱, 식기장 2. 내각

cab·i·net·mak·er [kǽbinetmèikər] *n.* [C] a person who makes furniture and other things of wood.
—[名] 가구사(家具師)

***ca·ble** [kéibl] *n.* [C] **1.** a strong, thick rope, usu. made of twisted wires. **2.** a protected bundle of wires under the ocean used for sending messages by electric telegraph. **3.** a message sent by ocean cable. ¶*send a* ~.①
—[名] 1. 닻줄, 굵은 밧줄 2. 해저전선 3. 해저전신 ¶①해외로 전보를 치다

—*vt., vi.* send (a message) by ocean cable.
—[他][自] 해저전신으로 통신하다

cable car [ˊ-ˋ] *n.* a car pulled by a moving cable.
—[名] 케이블 카아

ca·ble·gram [kéiblgræ̀m] *n.* [C] a message sent by ocean cable.
—[名] 해저전보

cab·man [kǽbmən] *n.* [C] (pl. **-men** [-mən]) a man who drives a cab.
—[名] 택시 운전수, [마차의] 마부

ca·boose [kəbúːs] *n.* [C] **1.** (*U.S.*) the last, small car on a freight train, used chiefly by the trainmen **2.** a kitchen on the deck of a ship.
—[名] 1.《美》[화물열차 뒤의] 승무원차, 차장차 2. 상선의 상갑판의 부엌

ca·ca·o [kəkéiou / -kɑ́ː-] *n.* [C] (pl. **-ca·os**) seeds of a tropical tree from which cocoa and chocolate are made; the tree itself.
—[名] 카카오 열매(나무)

cache [kæʃ] *n.* [C] **1.** a hiding place for food or anything useful. **2.** a hidden store of food or anything useful.
—[名] 1. [식량 따위의] 저장소, 은닉처 2. 저장물, 은닉 물자

—*vt.* put (something) in a cache; hide.
—[他] …을 감추다

cach·in·nate [kǽkinèit] *vi.* laugh loudly.
—[自] [주착없이] 껄껄 웃다

cack·le [kǽkl] *vi.* **1.** (of a hen) make a shrill, broken noise after laying an egg. **2.** laugh or talk noisily.
—[自] 1. [암탉이 알을 낳고] 꼬꼬꼬꼬 울다 2. 낄낄(껄껄) 웃다

—*n.* **1.** [U][C] the noise made by a hen when it has laid an egg. **2.** [C] laughter. **3.** [U] noisy chatter; idle talk.
—[名] 1. 꼬꼬꼬꼬 우는 소리 2. 째지는 듯한 웃음소리 3. 수다, 장담

cac·ti [kǽktai] *n.* pl. of **cactus.**

cac·tus [kǽktəs] *n.* [C] (pl. **-tus·es** or **-ti**) a tropical plant without leaves, whose thick stems are covered with prickles.
—[名] 선인장

cad [kæd] *n.* [C] a fellow whose behavior is bad, esp. toward women.
—[名] 비열한 사내

ca·dav·er·ous [kədǽv(ə)rəs] *adj.* **1.** like a dead body. **2.** deadly pale.
—[形] 1. 시체 같은 2. 창백한

cad·die [kǽdi] *n.* [C] a person who attends a golf player, carrying golf clubs, finding lost balls, etc.
—[名] 캐디(골프장에서 공을 줍거나 짐을 나르는 사람)

cad·dish [kǽdiʃ] *adj.* like a cad; ill-mannered.
—[形] [태도·말이] 상스러운

cad·dy[1] [kǽdi] *n.* [C] (pl. **-dies**) a small box or a can, often used to hold tea.
—[名] [작은] 차통(茶筒)

cad·dy[2] [kǽdi] *n.* (pl. **-dies**) =caddie.

ca·dence [kéid(ə)ns] *n.* [U] [C] **1.** rhythm. **2.** the rise and fall of the voice. **3.** (*Music*) a series of chords that shows the end of a melody.
—[名] 1. 운율 2. 억양 3. [악장의] 마침, 종지(終止)

ca·det [kədét] *n.* [C] a student in training for service as an officer in a naval or military college. ¶ ~ *corps.*①
—[名] [육해군] 사관학교 생도, 사관 후보생 ¶①학생 군사훈련단

cadge [kædʒ] *vi., vt.* (*colloq.*) beg. ¶ *He is always cadging.*
▷**cadg·er** [-ər] *n.*
—[自][他] 《口》 빌어먹다; 조르다

cad·mi·um [kǽdmiəm] *n.* [U] a soft, silverwhite metal like tin.
—[名] 카드뮴

ca·du·ce·i [kəd(j)ú:siài / -djú:-] *n.* pl. of **caduceus.**

ca·du·ce·us [kəd(j)ú:siəs / -djú:-] *n.* [C] (pl. **-ce·i**) a stick with two snakes twined around it and a pair of wings on top, often used as a symbol of the medical profession. ⇒fig.
—[名] Mercury의 지팡이(두 마리의 뱀이 감겨 있고 꼭대기에 두 개의 날개가 있음; 의술·평화의 상징)

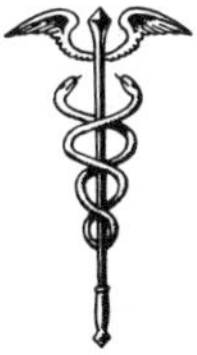

〔caduceus〕

***Cae·sar** [sí:zər] *n.* **1.** , **Gaius Julius** (100?–44 B.C.) a Roman general and statesman. **2.** the title of the Roman emperors from Augustus to Hadrian. **3.** [C] an emperor. **4.** [C] a dictator; a tyrant.
—[名] 1. 시이저(로마의 장군·정치가) 2. 로마 황제(칭호) 3. 황제 4. 전제군주, 폭군

ca·fé [kəféi, kæf- / kǽfei] *n.* **1.** [C] a restaurant; a teashop; a coffeehouse. **2.** [U] coffee.
—[名] 1. 요리점; 다방; 경식당 2. 코오피

caf·e·te·ri·a [kæ̀fitíəriə] *n.* [C] a lunch room or a restaurant where people serve themselves.
—[名] 간이식당(손님이 스스로 날라다 먹음)

caf·feine, -fein [kæfí:n, ⌐⌐ / kǽfi:n] *n.* [U] a bitter compound found in coffee beans and tea leaves, used as a stimulating drug.
—[名] 카페인(흥분제)

‡**cage** [keidʒ] *n.* [C] **1.** a boxlike structure or enclosure with wires or bars for keeping birds and wild animals. **2.** a thing shaped like a cage. **3.** a prison.
—*vt.* put or keep (something) in a cage. ¶ *a caged bird.*①
—[名] 1. 새장, 우리 2. 새장 모양의 것, [특히 탄갱 내의] 승강대 3. 감옥
—[他] …을 새장(우리)에 넣다 ¶①새장 안에 갇힌 새

Cain [kein] *n.* **1.** (in the Bible) the eldest son of Adam and Eve, who killed his brother Abel. **2.** [C] a murderer.
—[名] 1. 카인 2. 살인자

cairn [kɛərn] *n.* [C] a heap of stones used as a memorial, tomb, or landmark.
—[名] 도정표(道程標)

Cai·ro [káiərou] *n.* the capital of the United Arab Republic.
—[名] 카이로

cais·son [kéis(ə)n, -sɑn / kəsú:n, kéis(ə)n] *n.* [C] **1.** a box or chest for explosives, such as shells and bombs. **2.** a wagon to carry shells, bombs, etc. **3.** (*Engineering*) an iron box in which men can work under water.
—[名] 1. 탄약 상자 2. 탄약차 3. 잠함(潛函)(수중 공사용의 토목 기구)

ca·jole [kədʒóul] *vt.* persuade (someone) to do something with pleasant words. ¶ ~ *someone into going*① / ~ *someone out of money;* ~ *money out of someone.*②
—[他] …을 감언으로 속이다 ¶① …을 추어올려 가게 하다/②…을 구슬려서 돈을 빼앗다

‡**cake** [keik] *n.* **1.** [U] [C] a sweet baked food made with flour, sugar, eggs, etc. ¶ *a sponge* ~① / (*proverb*) *You cannot eat your* ~ *and have it, too.*② **2.** [C] a pancake; a griddlecake. **3.** [C] a small and flat mass shaped and pressed. ¶ *a* ~ *of soap* / *a* ~ *of ice.*
cakes and ale, merry-making.
—*vt., vi.* cause (something) to harden; become hard.
—[名] 1. 케이크 ¶①카스텔라/②《俚》 과자란 먹으면 없어지는 법; 이쪽 저쪽 다 좋을 수 없다 2. 납작한 빵 3. 일정한 모양의 덩어리
[熟] 즐거운 것, 인생의 즐거움
—[他][自] …을 굳히다; 굳어지다

C

Cal. California.
ca·lam·i·tous [kəlǽmitəs] *adj.* disastrous.
* **ca·lam·i·ty** [kəlǽmiti] *n.* ⓤⓒ (pl. **-ties**) a great misfortune; sudden disaster; misery. ¶*the ~ of war.*①
cal·ci·fy [kǽlsifài] *v.* (**-fied**) *vi.* become hard by the deposit of lime. —*vt.* change (something) into lime.
cal·ci·mine [kǽlsimàin] *n.* ⓤ a white or colored liquid used on ceilings and walls. ⌈element.⌉
cal·ci·um [kǽlsiəm] *n.* ⓤ a soft, silvery-white chemical⌋
cal·cu·la·ble [kǽlkjuləbl] *adj.* **1.** that can be measured. **2.** reliable; dependable.
* **cal·cu·late** [kǽlkjulèit] *vi., vt.* **1.** add, divide, multiply, etc. by working with numbers. ¶*~ the cost*① / *the lunar eclipse*② / *be calculated at one million dollars.*③ **2.** rely; depend; count. ⟪*~ on* or *upon* someone or something⟫ **3.** (usu. in *passive*) plan; intend; count. ⟪*~ to do*⟫ ¶*This room is calculated to hold a hundred people.*④ **4.** (*U.S. colloq.*) think; suppose; believe. ¶*I ~ we're going to have thunder.*⑤
  be calculated for, be fitted to (something); be suitable for (something). ¶*This law is not calculated for modern Korea*⑥
cal·cu·lat·ed [kǽlkjulèitid] *adj.* **1.** arranged beforehand; designed. ¶*a ~ crime.*① **2.** likely; suitable.
cal·cu·lat·ing [kǽlkjulèitiŋ] *adj.* shrewd; careful. ¶*a ~ politician.*①
calculating machine [╌╌╌ ╌-] *n.* a machine that calculates mechanically.
* **cal·cu·la·tion** [kæ̀lkjuléiʃən] *n.* **1.** ⓤ the act of calculating. **2.** ⓤ careful thinking. **3.** ⓒ a result found by calculating.
cal·cu·la·tive [kǽlkjulèitiv / -lə-] *adj.* **1.** of calculation. **2.** tending to be calculating; shrewd. ⌈that calculates.⌉
cal·cu·la·tor [kǽlkjulèitər] *n.* ⓒ a person or machine⌋
cal·cu·li [kǽlkjulài] *n.* pl. of **calculus**.
cal·cu·lus [kǽlkjuləs] *n.* (pl. **-li** or **-lus·es**) **1.** ⓤ a way of calculation in higher mathematics. ¶*differential (integral) ~.*① **2.** ⓒ (*Medicine*) a stony mass that has formed in the body.
Cal·cut·ta [kælkʌ́tə] *n.* a seaport in East India.
cal·dron, caul- [kɔ́:ldrən] *n.* ⓒ a large kettle or boiler.
Cal·e·do·ni·a [kæ̀lidóuniə] *n.* (*poetic*) Scotland.
Cal·e·do·ni·an [kæ̀lidóuniən] *n.* ⓒ (*poetic*) a person of ancient Scotland.
: **cal·en·dar** [kǽləndər] *n.* ⓒ **1.** a list of the months, weeks and the days printed year by year. **2.** a method by which the beginning, length, and divisions of the year are fixed. ¶*the lunar (solar) ~.*① **3.** a list; a record; a catalog.
cal·en·der [kǽləndər] *n.* ⓒ a roller-machine in which cloth, paper, etc. is pressed and smoothed.
—*vt.* put (something) through a calender.
* **calf**¹ [kæf / ka:f] *n.* (pl. **calves**) **1.** ⓒ the young of a cow or of some other animals. **2.** ⓤ leather with a smooth finish made from the skin of a calf.
  kill the fatted calf, make a feast to celebrate (something) or welcome (someone). ⇒N.B.
calf² [kæf / ka:f] *n.* (pl. **calves**) the thick part of the back of the leg between the knee and the foot.
calf·skin [kǽfskìn / ká:f-] *n.* ⓤ **1.** the skin of a calf. **2.** leather with a smooth finish, made from the skin of a calf.
cal·i·ber, *Brit.* **-bre**[kǽləbər] *n.* **1.** ⓒ the inside diameter of a tube, bore of a gun, etc. **2.** ⓤ ability or character.

cal·i·co [kǽlikou] *n.* ⓤⓒ (*pl.* **-coes** or **-cos**) **1.** (*U. S.*) a cotton cloth usu. printed on one side. **2.** (*Brit.*) a plain white cloth, used for bed sheets.
- **Cal·i·for·nia** [kæ̀lifɔ́:rnjə] *n.* a western state of the United States, on the Pacific coast. ⇒[N.B.]
Cal·i·for·ni·an [kæ̀lifɔ́:rniən] *adj.* of California.
— *n.* ⓒ a person of California.
cal·i·pers, cal·li- [kǽlipərz] *n.* ⓒ *pl.* a tool with two legs resembling a draftsman's compass, used to obtain inside and outside measurements.
ca·liph [kǽlif, kéi-] *n.* ⓒ the head of an Islamic state; the title, given to him. ⇒[N.B.]
cal·is·then·ics, cal·lis- [kæ̀lisθéniks] *n. pl.* **1.** (used as *sing.*) the practice or art of developing a strong and graceful body. **2.** (used as *pl.*) exercises of this.
calk [kɔ:k] *vt.* fill or close a seam, joint, etc. as in a boat; make (a ship) watertight.
‡**call** [kɔ:l] *vt.* **1.** cry out (something) in a loud voice. ¶*He called her name to see if she was home.*① **2.** read over (something) in a loud voice. ¶*The teacher called the roll of the class.* **3.** cry out to (someone) in order to make him come; ask (someone) to come or to pay attention by sending a message or signal or by telephoning. ¶*~ a doctor* / *Call a taxi for me.*② **4.** command; request. ¶*~ a halt.*③ **5.** gather persons to hold (a meeting); summon. ¶*~ a meeting.* **6.** rouse (someone) from sleep. ¶*Call me at seven o'clock.* **7.** name; consider; regard (someone or something a being.something. (*~ someone Tom*; *~ something a success*) ¶*Do you ~ English an easy language?*④ / *All called the party a success.* **8.** (*U.S.*) telephone to (someone). ¶*Call me when you arrive.* —*vi.* **1.** speak loudly, as to attract attention; cry. (*~ to someone*) ¶*She called to the children.* **2.** go to someone's house, office, etc. for a short visit or on business. ¶*I am sorry I was out when you called.* **3.** telephone. ¶*She promised to ~ at noon.*
 1) ***call at,*** visit (some place) for a short time. ¶*She called at the store for the package.*
 2) ***call away,*** cause (someone) to leave or go; summon.
 3) ***call back,*** ⓐ bring back; recall. ⓑ take back (something one has said). ⓒ telephone to someone who has called earlier.
 4) ***call down,*** ⓐ pray for. ⓑ (*colloq.*) scold.
 5) ***call for,*** ⓐ need; require. ⓑ go or come to get (something); fetch.
 6) ***call forth,*** bring out and use (something); summon (someone) into action.
 7) ***call in,*** ⓐ order the return of (something). ⓑ ask (someone) to come. ⌈draw.⌉
 8) ***call off,*** ⓐ take away. ⓑ (*colloq.*) cancel; with-
 9) ***call on,*** visit (someone) for a short time.
 10) ***call out,*** ⓐ speak in a loud voice. (*~ out to someone for help*) ⓑ summon (persons) into service or action. ⓒ bring out.
 11) ***call over,*** read out a list of names.
 12) ***call up,*** ⓐ cause to remember (something). ⓑ telephone to (someone). ⓒ summon.
—*n.* ⓒ **1.** a loud shout; a cry. **2.** a signal given by sound. **3.** attraction; charm. ¶*the ~ of the sea.* **4.** a short visit or stop at some place. ¶*make a ~ on someone.* **5.** (usu. in *negative* or *interrogative*) necessity. ¶*There is no ~ for you to worry.*⑤ **6.** ⓒⓤ demand; need; occasion. ¶*a ~ of nature.*⑥ **7.** demand for payment.

—㊇ 1.《美》사라사(한쪽에 날염한 무명) 2.《英》흰 무명의 일종

—㊇ 미국 태평양 연안의 주 [N.B.] Calif.로 줄임, 수도 Sacramento
—㊋ 캘리포오니아의 —㊇ 캘리포오니아주의 사람
—㊇ 캘리퍼스, 측경기(測徑器)

—㊇ 칼리프(회교국의 왕) [N.B.] calif, khalif 로도 씀
—㊇ 1.미용 체조법 2.미용 체조

—㊌ [배의 널판 틈을] 뱃밥·타르 따위로 메우다
—㊌ 1. …을 부르다 ¶①그는 그녀가 집에 있는지를 알려고 이름을 불렀다 2. …을 큰소리로 읽다 3. …을 오라고 부르다; …의 주의를 촉구하다 ¶②택시를 불러 주시오 4. …을 명하다, 요구하다 ¶③정지를 명하다 5. …을 소집하다 6. …을 불러 깨우다 7. …을 (이라고) 이름짓다, 칭하다; 간주하다, 여기다 ¶④영어는 쉬운 언어라 생각하느냐? 8.《美》…에게 전화걸다 —㊉ 1. 부르다; 외치다 2. 방문하다 3. 전화를 걸다

圖 1)[장소에] 들르다 2)[남을 불러서 가게 하다 3)ⓐ소환하다 ⓑ[앞서의 말을] 취소하다 ⓒ[전화를 해온 상대에게] 나중에 다시 걸다 4)ⓐ…을 기도하다 ⓑ《口》꾸짖다 5)ⓐ…을 필요로 하다 ⓑ…을 가지러(데리러) 가다(오다) 6)…을 불러 일으키다; 분기(환기)시키다 7)ⓐ…을 회수하다 ⓑ…을 부르다(청하다) 8)ⓐ…을 가져(데려)가다 ⓑ…을 중지(취소)하다 9)…을 방문하다 10)ⓐ외치다 ⓑ…을 불러 내다; 소집하다 ⓒ…을 끌어내다 11)[이름]을 큰 소리로 부르다, 출석을 부르다 12)ⓐ…을 생각나게 하다 ⓑ전화를 걸다 ⓒ…을 소집하다

—㊇ 1. 외침소리 2.신호 3.매력 4.들르기; [잠깐의] 방문 5.필요 ¶⑤내가 걱정할 필요는 없다 6.요구; 필요; 이유 ¶⑥편의(便宜) 7.청구

call bell [164] **Calvinism**

1) *at* (or *on*) *call,* (of money) that should be paid any time requested; (of a doctor, etc.) available for serve at any time.
2) *close call,* narrow escape.
3) *make* (or *pay*) *a call,* stop at a place; visit.
4) *within call,* not far away; close at hand.

— 熟 1)[돈이] 청구하는 대로 지불되는; 언제나 이용할 수 있는 2)위기일발 3)방문하다; 들르다 4)가까이에, 소리가 들리는 곳에

call bell [⌐⌐] *n.* a bell used to call others. —ⓝ 초인종
call box [⌐⌐] *n.* (*Brit.*) a booth with a public telephone. —ⓝ 공중전화실
call boy [⌐⌐] *n.* Ⓒ **1.** a bellboy in a hotel, on a ship, etc. **2.** a boy who calls actors when it is time for them to go on the stage. —ⓝ 1.[호텔·배 따위의] 보이 2.[극장의] 호출계
call·er [kɔ́:lər] *n.* Ⓒ **1.** a person who makes a short visit; a visitor. **2.** a person who calls. —ⓝ 1.방문객, 내방자 2.부르는 사람
cal·lig·ra·phy [kəlígrəfi] *n.* Ⓤ **1.** handwriting; penmanship. **2.** beautiful handwriting. —ⓝ 1.필적 2.달필
call·ing [kɔ́:liŋ] *n.* Ⓒ **1.** an occupation; a business; a profession; a trade. **2.** an invitation; summons. —ⓝ 1.직업 2.부름; 초대, 소집
calling card [⌐⌐] *n.* a small card with a person's name, occupation, address, etc. on it, used in business and on visits; a visiting card. —ⓝ 명함
cal·li·pers [kǽlipərz] *n. pl.* =calipers.
cal·lis·then·ics [kæˌlisθéniks] *n. pl.* =calisthenics.
call loan [⌐⌐] *n.* a loan that must be paid back when demanded. —ⓝ [은행 사이의] 요구불 당좌대금 (貸金)
call money [⌐⌐] *n.* money borrowed that must be paid back when requested. —ⓝ 요구불 단기 차입금
call number [⌐⌐] *n.* a number used for books in a library. —ⓝ [도서관의] 청구 번호
cal·los·i·ty [kəlɔ́siti, kæl-/kælɔ́siti] *n.* (pl. **-ties**) **1.** Ⓒ a thick, hardened part of the skin; callus. **2.** Ⓤ lack of feeling; hardness of heart. —ⓝ 1.[피부 따위의] 못, 경결(硬結) 2.무정, 무감각
cal·lous [kǽləs] *adj.* **1.** (of the skin) hard; hardened. **2.** (of the mind) unfeeling; not sensitive. ↔sensitive —ⓐ 1.[피부가] 굳어진 2.무정한, 무감각한
cal·low [kǽlou] *adj.* **1.** young and without experience. ¶*a ~ youth.*① **2.** (of birds) without feathers for flying. —ⓐ 1.풋내기의 ¶①풋내기 2.[새가] 깃털이 나지 않은
cal·lus [kǽləs] *n.* Ⓒ (pl. **-lus·es**) **1.** a hard, thickened part of the skin. **2.** (of plants) a substance growing over a wounded or cut surface of a stem. —ⓝ 1.[피부의] 못 2.[식물의] 유합(癒合) 조직, 가피(假皮)
:calm [kɑ:m] *adj.* **1.** not stormy or windy; quiet. ¶*a ~ sea.*① **2.** peaceful; (of a person) not excited. ¶*a ~ voice.* —*n.* **1.** Ⓤ (usu. *a ~*) absence of motion or wind; quietness; stillness. ¶*a ~ before the storm.*② **2.** Ⓤ absence of excitement; peacefulness. —*vi.* become calm. (*~ down*) —*vt.* make (something) calm. ¶*~ oneself.* —ⓐ 1.온화한, 고요한 ¶①고요한 바다 2.평온한, 침착한 —ⓝ 1.무풍상태, 평온 ¶②폭풍 전의 고요 2.침착, 태평 —ⓥ 조용해지다 —ⓥ …을 가라앉히다
·**calm·ly** [kɑ́:mli] *adv.* in a calm manner; quietly; coolly. —ⓐⓓ 조용히, 침착하게
calm·ness [kɑ́:mnis] *n.* Ⓤ the state of being calm. —ⓝ 평온, 냉정, 침착
cal·o·mel [kǽləm(ə)l, -mèl/-mèl] *n.* Ⓤ a white, tasteless, crystalline powder, used in medicine. —ⓝ 감홍(甘汞)
ca·lor·ic [kəlɔ́:rik, -lɑ́r-/-lɔ́r-] *n.* Ⓤ heat. —*adj.* of heat or calorie. —ⓝ 열 —ⓐ 열의, 칼로리의
cal·o·rie, -ry [kǽləri] *n.* Ⓒ (pl. **-ries**) **1.** (*Physics*) a unit of heat. **2.** a unit of the energy supplied by food. —ⓝ 1.칼로리(열량의 단위) 2.식품의 열량 단위
cal·o·rim·e·ter [kæ̀lərímitər] *n.* Ⓒ an instrument for measuring quantities of heat or calories. —ⓝ 열량계(熱量計)
ca·lum·ni·ate [kəlʌ́mnièit] *vt.* say untrue things about (someone); slander. ▷**ca·lum·ni·a·tor** [-ər] *n.* —ⓥ …을 중상하다, 헐뜯다
cal·um·ny [kǽləmni] *n.* Ⓤ Ⓒ (pl. **-nies**) a false statement made to hurt someone's reputation; slander. —ⓝ 중상, 비방
Cal·va·ry [kǽlvəri] *n.* the place near Jerusalem where Jesus died on the cross. —ⓝ 그리스도가 못박힌 곳
calves [kævz/kɑ:vz] *n. pl.* of **calf.**
Cal·vin [kǽlvin], **John** *n.* (1509-64) a French leader of the Protestant Reformation in Switzerland. —ⓝ 스위스에서 활동한 프랑스의 종교 개혁가
Cal·vin·ism [kǽlvinìz(ə)m] *n.* Ⓤ the religious teachings of John Calvin. —ⓝ 칼빈주의

cam [kæm] *n.* [C] (*Machinery*) a projecting part of a wheel or shaft that changes a circular motion into an up-and-down or back-and-forth motion. ⇒fig.
—[名] 《機》 캠(임의 형태를 하고 일정한 축의 둘레를 회전함으로써 여러가지 운동을 주는 장치)

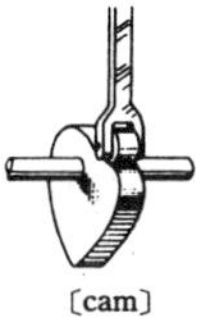
[cam]

cam·ber [kǽmbər] *n.* [C] [U] **1.** a slight arch, as of a road or piece of timber. **2.** the slight arch of the wing of an airplane. —*vi.* have a camber. —*vt.* give (something) a camber.
—[名] 1.[도로·갑판 따위의] 휘어 오른 부분 2.[비행기 날개의] 만곡(彎曲)[도(度)] —[自] 위로 휘다 —[他] …을 위로 휘게 하다

Cam·bo·di·a [kæmbóudiə] *n.* a country in southeast Asia. ⇒[N.B.]
—[名] 캄보디아 [N.B.] 수도 Pnompenh

Cam·bria [kǽmbriə] *n.* (*poetic*) the old name of Wales.
—[名] 《詩》 웨일즈

cam·bric [kéimbrik] *n.* [U] fine, thin, white linen or cotton cloth.
—[名] 흰 삼베의 일종

∗ **Cam·bridge** [kéimbridʒ] *n.* **1.** a city in eastern England. **2.** the university located there. **3.** a city in Massachusetts. ⇒[N.B.]
—[名] 1.영국 동부의 도시 2.케임브리지 대학 3.미국의 도시 [N.B.] Harvard 대학 소재지

⁑ **came** [keim] *v.* pt. of **come**.

∗ **cam·el** [kǽm(ə)l] *n.* [C] a long-necked animal with one or two humps on its back, used for riding and for carrying goods in the desert.
—[名] 낙타

ca·mel·li·a [kəméliə, -míː-, -ljə / -míːljə, -mél-] *n.* [C] a shrub with shiny evergreen leaves and white or red roselike flowers; the flower of this shrub.
—[名] 동백나무

cam·e·o [kǽmiòu] *n.* [C] (pl. **-os**) a precious stone or shell having two layers and with a figure carved in one layer.
—[名] [조가비 따위에 돋을새김을 한] 보석, 카메오

⁑ **cam·er·a** [kǽm(ə)rə] *n.* [C] **1.** a machine for taking photographs or motion pictures. **2.** a machine that changes images into electrical impulses for television broadcasting.
—[名] 1.사진기, 카메라 2.텔레비전 카메라

cam·er·a·man [kǽm(ə)rəmæ̀n] *n.* [C] (pl. **-men** [-mèn]) a person who operates a camera.
—[名] 사진사, 사진기자, 카메라맨

cam·ou·flage [kǽmuflɑ̀ːʒ] *n.* [U] [C] **1.** the art of giving things a false appearance to deceive others. **2.** disguise; concealment. —*vt.* disguise; deceive.
—[名] 1.위장(僞裝), 카무플라즈 2.기만, 속임 —[他] …을 위장하다; 속이다

⁑ **camp** [kæmp] *n.* [C] **1.** a group of tents, huts, etc. where people live for a short time. **2.** a place where a camp is put up. **3.** 《*collectively*》 a group of people living in a camp. **4.** 《*collectively*》 a group of people who agree on a subject or work together. —*vt., vi.* **1.** make a camp. **2.** live or stay in a camp.
—[名] 1.야영(野營) 캠프 2.야영지 3.야영하는 사람들 4.동지 —[他][自] 1.캠프를 설치하다 2.야영하다

⁑ **cam·paign** [kæmpéin] *n.* [C] **1.** military operations with a particular purpose. **2.** organized action for a particular purpose. ¶*a political ~.*① —*vi.* take part in or go on a campaign.
—[名] 1.작전, 전투 2.운동 ¶①정치운동 —[自] 작전(운동)에 참가하다

cam·paign·er [kæmpéinər] *n.* [C] a person who takes part in a campaign.
—[名] 종군자

camp·er [kǽmpər] *n.* [C] a person who camps.
—[名] 야영자

camp·fire [kǽmpfàiər] *n.* [C] **1.** a fire in a camp used for warmth or cooking. **2.** a social gathering around such a fire.
—[名] 1.야영의 모닥불 2.모닥불을 둘러싼 사교 모임

cam·phor [kǽmfər] *n.* [C] a white substance with a strong odor obtained from the camphor tree and used in medicine, mothballs, etc. ¶*a ~ tree.*①
—[名] 장뇌(樟腦) ¶①녹나무

cam·pus [kǽmpəs] *n.* [C] (*U.S.*) the grounds of a school, college, or university.
—[名] 《美》 [특히 대학의] 교정(校庭), 구내

⁑ **can**[1] [kæn; kən, kn] *auxil. v.* (pt. **could**) **1.** be able to; know how to. ¶ *He ~ read rapidly.* / *He ~ run that machine.* **2.** have the right to. ¶*You can't attend the meeting.* **3.** 《usu. in *interrogative*》 be possible. ¶*Can it be true?* **4.** 《usu. in *negative*》 have no probability. ↔must ¶*The report cannot be true.* / *I cannot have said so.* **5.** may; be allowed to. ⇒[N.B.] ¶*You ~ go at four o'clock.* / *Can I have a little talk with you?* **6.** want to; feel inclined to. ¶*You may leave whenever you ~.*
—[助] 1.…할 수 있다 2.…할 권리가 있다 3.…일까 4.있을 수 없다 5.…해도 좋다 [N.B.] 미국 구어에서는 May I…? 대신에 Can I…?를 쓰는 일이 많음 6.…하고 싶다

can [166] **cane**

can² [kæn] *n.* ⓒ **1.** a metal container. ¶ *a milk ~ / an oil ~.* **2.** contents of a can. ── *vt.* (**canned, can·ning**) put (food) into a can to preserve it.
─명 1. 생철통, 통조림통 2. 통 안에 든 것 ─타 …을 통조림으로 만들다

Ca·naan [kéinən] *n.* (in the Bible) the region that God promised to the Israelites. ⇒N.B.
─명 (聖) 가나안의 땅 N.B. 현재의 Palestine 서부 지방

• **Can·a·da** [kǽnədə] *n.* a country in North America. ⇒N.B.
─명 캐나다 N.B. 수도 Ottawa

Ca·na·di·an [kənéidiən] *adj.* of Canada or its people. ──*n.* ⓒ a person of Canada.
─형 캐나다의, 캐나다 사람의 ─명 캐나다 사람

: ca·nal [kənǽl] *n.* ⓒ **1.** a man-made waterway for ships or for irrigation. **2.** a tube-like passage in an animal body or a plant for carrying food, liquid, air, etc.
─명 1. 운하 2. [체내의] 도관(導管)

ca·nard [kəná:rd] *n.* ⓒ a false rumor.
─명 유언비어, 헛소문

: ca·nar·y [kənέəri] *n.* (pl. **-nar·ies**) **1.** ⓒ a small yellow songbird. **2.** Ⓤ light yellow.
─명 1. 카나리아 2. 담황색

can·cel [kǽns(ə)l] *vt.* (**-celed, -cel·ing** or *Brit.* **-celled, -cel·ling**) **1.** cross out; mark (something) so as to make it void. ¶ *~ a stamp.* **2.** take back; withdraw. ¶ *He canceled his order for the books.*
──*n.* ⓒ the act of canceling.
─타 1. …을 말소하다, …에 소인(消印)을 찍다 2. …을 취소하다
─명 말소, 취소, 해약

can·cel·la·tion [kænsəléiʃ(ə)n] *n.* Ⓤⓒ **1.** the act of canceling; the state of being canceled. **2.** ⓒ the mark showing that something has been canceled.
─명 1. 취소, 해약 2. 소인

can·cer [kǽnsər] *n.* **1.** Ⓤⓒ a growth in the body of a person or an animal that is very harmful to life. **2.** ⓒ anything bad or harmful that destroys by growing.
─명 1. 암(癌) 2. 해악, 폐해

can·cer·ous [kǽns(ə)rəs] *adj.* of, like, or having cancer.
─형 암의, 암 같은, 암에 걸린

can·de·la·bra [kændilá:brə] *n. pl.* of **candelabrum.**

can·de·la·brum [kændilá:brəm] *n.* (pl. **-bra** or **-brums**) a candlestick with ornamental branches. ⇒fig.
─명 가지 모양의 장식 촛대

can·did [kǽndid] *adj.* frank; sincere; outspoken. ¶ *a ~ opinion.*
─형 솔직한, 정직한, 거리낌없는

can·di·da·cy [kǽndidəsi] *n.* Ⓤ (*U. S.*) the fact or state of being a candidate.
─명 (美) 입후보

• **can·di·date** [kǽndidèit, -didit / -didit] *n.* ⓒ a person who seeks or takes part in a contest for a prize or position. ¶ *a ~ for President.*
─명 후보자 ¶ ①대통령 후보자

can·di·da·ture [kǽndiditʃər] *n.* (*Brit.*) =candidacy.

[candelabrum]

can·did·ly [kǽndidli] *adv.* in a candid manner; frankly.
─부 솔직히

: can·dle [kǽndl] *n.* ⓒ **1.** a stick of tallow or wax with a wick through its center that is burned to give light. **2.** a unit of luminous intensity.
 1) ***burn the candle at both ends,*** work or play too much, so that one's energy or money is quickly wasted.
 2) ***not worth the candle,*** not worth doing.
─명 1. 양초 2. 촉광(燭光)
熟 1)[정력·금전 따위]를 다 써 없애다 2)할 가치가 없는

can·dle·light [kǽndllàit] *n.* Ⓤ **1.** the light of a candle. **2.** dusk; twilight.
─명 1. 촛불 2. 등불 켤 무렵, 저녁 때

candle power [⸺⸺] *n.* a unit of luminous intensity.
─명 촉광

can·dle·stick [kǽndlstìk] *n.* ⓒ a holder for a candle.
─명 촛대

can·dle·wick [kǽndlwìk] *n.* ⓒ the wick of a candle.
─명 [초의] 심지

: can·dy [kǽndi] *n.* Ⓤⓒ (pl. **-dies**) **1.** (*U. S.*) something to eat made chiefly of sugar combined with fruits, nuts, etc. (cf. *Brit.* sweets) **2.** Ⓤ (*Brit.*) sugar candy. **3.** ⓒ one piece of such a sweet.
──*vt.* (**-died**) cook (food) in sugar syrup; coat or preserve (food) with sugar. ──*vi.* turn into sugar.
─명 1. (美) 캔디, 사탕과자 2. (英) 얼음 사탕 3. 캔디 한 개
─타 …을 설탕에 재다, 설탕을 치다
─자 설탕이 되다

• **cane** [kein] *n.* ⓒ **1.** the slender, long, and flexible stem of certain plants, such as bamboo, rattan, and blackberry. **2.** a walking stick. **3.** a stick used for beating.
──*vt.* **1.** beat (someone or something) with a cane. **2.** make or furnish (chairs, etc.) with cane.
─명 1. [대나무·등나무 따위의] 줄기 2. 지팡이 3. 채찍, 회초리
─타 1. …을 지팡이로 치다 2. …을 등나무로 만들다

cane sugar [ˊ ˋ-] *n.* sugar obtained from sugar cane. — 名 자당(蔗糖)

ca·nine [kéinain] *adj.* **1.** of or like a dog. **2.** of the dog family. —*n.* ⓒ a canine tooth. — 形 1. 개의(같은) 2. 개과(科)의 — 名 송곳니

canine tooth [ˊ- ˋ] *n.* one of the four sharp-pointed teeth of a man or an animal. — 名 송곳니

can·is·ter [kǽnistər] *n.* ⓒ a box or can for tea, coffee, tobacco, etc. — 名 [차 따위를 넣는] 깡통

can·ker [kǽŋkər] *n.* ⓒ **1.** a sore, esp. in the mouth. **2.** a disease of plants that causes them to decay slowly. **3.** ⓤ anything causing decay or rot. —*vt., vi.* **1.** infect or be infected with canker. **2.** decay; rot. — 名 1. [입안의] 궤양 2. [나무의] 암종병(癌腫病) 3. 해독 — 他⃝自 1. 궤양을 옮기다(에 걸리다) 2. 썩게 하다, 썩다

can·ker·worm [kǽŋkərwəːrm] *n.* ⓒ a caterpillar that feeds on the leaves of plants. — 名 자벌레

can·na [kǽnə] *n.* ⓒ a tropical plant with large, pointed leaves and large red, pink, or yellow flowers; the flower of this plant. — 名 칸나

* **canned** [kænd] *adj.* put or preserved in a can. — 形 통조림한

can·ner·y [kǽnəri] *n.* ⓒ (*pl.* **-ner·ies**) a factory where foods are canned. — 名 통조림 공장

can·ni·bal [kǽnib(ə)l] *n.* ⓒ **1.** a person who eats human flesh. **2.** any animal that eats its own kind. —*adj.* of or like cannibals. — 名 1. 식인종의 사람 2. 같은 동족을 잡아먹는 짐승 — 形 식인종의, 동류를 잡아먹는

can·ni·bal·ism [kǽnibəlìz(ə)m] *n.* ⓤ the act or habit of eating one's own kind. — 名 식인의 풍습, 동류를 잡아먹음

can·ni·kin [kǽnikin] *n.* ⓒ a small can; a small cup. — 名 작은 깡통; 작은 물컵

* **can·non** [kǽnən] *n.* ⓒ (*pl.* **-nons** or *collectively* **-non**) a large, heavy gun. — 名 대포

can·non·ade [kæ̀nənéid] *n.* ⓒ a continuous firing of cannons; an attack with cannons. — 名 포격

can·non·ball [kǽnənbɔ̀ːl] *n.* ⓒ a heavy, large ball of iron or other metal, formerly fired from cannons. — 名 [옛날의] 둥근 포탄

* **can·not** [kǽnat, -ˊ, kǽnət / kǽnɔt, -nət] =can not.

can·ny [kǽni] *adj.* (**-ni·er, -ni·est**) shrewd; cautious. — 形 교활한, 빈틈없는

‡ **ca·noe** [kənúː] *n.* ⓒ a light, narrow boat moved with paddles. —*vi.* go in a canoe. — 名 통나무배, 카누우 — 自 카누우로 가다

* **can·on** [kǽnən] *n.* ⓒ **1.** a law or rule of a church. **2.** a principle or rule by which things are judged. **3.** the list of books of the Bible accepted by the church. — 名 1. 교회 법규, 계율 2. 판단의 규준, 규범 3. 정전(正典)

ca·non [kǽnjən] *n.* =canyon.

ca·non·i·cal [kənɑ́nik(ə)l / -nɔ́ni-] *adj.* **1.** according to the church law. **2.** belonging to the canon of the Bible. **3.** authorized; accepted. —*n.* (*pl.*) the clothes that a clergyman must wear at a church service. — 形 1. 교회법에 의거한 2. 정전(正典)으로 인정된 3. 규범적인 — 名 법복(法服)

can·on·ize [kǽnənàiz] *vt.* **1.** declare (a dead person) to be a saint; add (a dead person's name) to the list of saints. **2.** recognize (some book) as canonical. **3.** glorify. — 他 1. [죽은 사람]을 성자로 모시다 2. …을 정전(正典)으로 인정하다 3. …을 칭찬하다

can·o·py [kǽnəpi] *n.* ⓒ (*pl.* **-pies**) **1.** a cloth covering fixed above a bed, throne, entrance, etc. ⇒fig. **2.** any overhanging covering. ¶*a ~ of leaves.*① **3.** the sky. —*vt.* (**-pied**) cover (something or someone) with a canopy. — 名 1. 천개(天蓋) 2. 천개처럼 가리는 것 ¶①지붕처럼 덮인 나뭇잎 3. 창공 — 他 …을 천개로 덮다

[canopy 1.]

* **canst** [kænst] *auxil. v.* (*archaic*) =can. ⇒N.B. — 助 N.B. 주어가 thou 의 경우에 씀

cant¹ [kænt] *n.* ⓤ **1.** an insincere statement expressive of goodness or piety. **2.** the peculiar language of a special group. —*vi.* talk in cant. — 名 1. 위선적인 말, 형식적인 신앙 2. 변말, 은어 — 自 은어로 말하다

cant² [kænt] *n.* **1.** a sloping or slanting surface; a slope; a slant. **2.** a corner. —*vt., vi.* slant; slope. — 名 1. 경사면 2. 모퉁이, 구석 — 他⃝自 기울이다; 기울다

‡ **can't** [kænt / kɑːnt] =cannot.

can·ta·bi·le [kɑːntɑ́ːbilèi / kæntɑ́ːbili] (*Music*) *adj., adv.* songlike; in an easy and flowing manner. — 形⃝副 《樂》 노래하는 듯한(듯이), 우아한, 우아하게

can·ta·loup, -loupe [kǽntəlòup / -lùːp] *n.* [C] a sort of melon with sweet and juicy flesh.
—[名] 참외의 일종

can·tan·ker·ous [kæntǽŋk(ə)rəs] *adj.* ill-natured; quarrelsome.
—[形] 심술궂은, 곧잘 싸우는

can·ta·ta [kæntάːtə] *n.* [C] a musical composition telling a story.
—[名] 교성곡(交聲曲), 칸타타

can·teen [kæntíːn] *n.* [C] **1.** a small container used for carrying water or other drinks. **2.** a small store in a factory, office, or camp where food, drinks, tobacco, etc. are sold.
—[名] 1. 수통 2. 구내 매점, 주보

can·ter [kǽntər] *n.* [C] a slow gallop. ¶*The horse had an easy ~.* —*vi.* go at a canter. —*vt.* make (a horse) go at a canter.
—[名] [말의] 느린 구보 —[自] 구보로 가다 —[他] [말]을 구보시키다

Can·ter·bur·y [kǽntərbèri / -b(ə)ri] *n.* a city in southeast England. ⇒[N.B.]
—[名] 캔터베리 [N.B.] 영국 국교의 총본산이 있음

can·ti·cle [kǽntikl] *n.* [C] a song whose words are taken from the Bible, used in church services.
—[名] [성경 문구에 곡을 붙인] 성가, 영창

can·to [kǽntou] *n.* [C] (pl. **-tos**) one of the main divisions of a long poem.
—[名] [장시(長詩)의] 편(篇)

can·ton [kǽntən, -tɑn / -tɔn] *n.* [C] a small political division of a country, esp. of Switzerland.
—[名] [스위스 등지의] 주(州)

can·ton·ment [kæntάnmənt / -tóun-, -túːn-] *n.* 《usu. *pl.*》 a place where soldiers live for a short time.
—[名] [군대의] 숙영지

***can·vas** [kǽnvəs] *n.* **1.** [U] rough, thick, and strong cloth made of cotton, hemp, etc. used for tents, sails, tennis shoes, etc. **2.** [C][U] a material on which to paint in oil; [C] an oil painting. **3.** [C] something made of canvas, as a tent or sail.
—[名] 1. 돛베, 즈크 2. [유화용의] 화포(畫布), 캔버스; 유화 3. 즈크 제품

can·vass [kǽnvəs] *vt.* **1.** examine or look over (something) thoroughly; discuss (something) in detail. **2.** go through (places) or among (people) asking for votes, opinions, orders, etc. 《~ places or persons *for* votes, etc.》 —*n.* [C] the act of canvassing.
—[他] 1. …을 정밀 검사하다, 세밀하게 논의하다 2. [지구(地區)·사람들]에 선거운동을 하다, 주문을 받으러 다니다 —[名] 정밀 검사, 조사; 권유; 선거운동

can·yon [kǽnjən] *n.* [C] a deep, long valley between high cliffs, usu. along a stream; a gorge.
—[名] 계곡, 협곡

‡**cap** [kæp] *n.* [C] **1.** a covering for the head, usu. without a brim. **2.** anything like a cap in use or shape. ¶*the ~ of a mushroom.*① **3.** the highest part; the top.
—[名] 1. [챙 없는] 모자 2. 모자 모양의 것 ¶①버섯의 갓 3. 절정, 꼭대기

1) ***cap in hand,*** humbly.
2) ***set one's cap for,*** attempt to catch (a man) as one's husband or lover.
[熟] 1) 공손히 2) [여자가 남자의] 마음을 끌려고 하다

—*v.* (**capped, cap·ping**) *vt.* **1.** put a cap on (someone); cover the top of (something). **2.** complete. **3.** do or say something better than (what somebody else has done or said). ¶*~ a story or joke.* —*vi.* raise one's cap to someone.
—[他] 1. …에 모자를 씌우다; …의 꼭대기를 덮다 2. …을 끝내다 3. …보다 이상의 일(말)을 하다 —[自] 탈모하다

cap the climax, go beyond expectation or belief; go to the extreme limit.
[熟] 의표(意表)로 달리다; 극단으로 달리다

ca·pa·bil·i·ty [kèipəbíliti] *n.* [U] ability; the power of doing something.
—[名] 재능; 능력

‡**ca·pa·ble** [kéipəbl] *adj.* skillful; able; having ability.
—[形] 숙련된; 능력이 있는

capable of (=*having the necessary ability or qualities for*) [*doing*] *something.* ¶*a man ~ of hard work / a man ~ of murder*① */ This room is ~ of holding five persons.*
[熟] …의 능력이 있는, …할 수 있는; …도 서슴지 않을 ¶①살인도 서슴지 않을 사내

ca·pa·bly [kéipəbli] *adv.* with ability; in a capable manner.
—[副] 잘, 훌륭하게

ca·pa·cious [kəpéiʃəs] *adj.* that can hold much; spacious. ¶*a ~ room.*①
—[形] 용적이 큰, 너른 ¶①너른 방

ca·pac·i·tate [kəpǽsitèit] *vt.* enable; make (someone) capable. 《~ someone *to do*》
—[他] …에게 […을] 할 수 있게 하다, […할] 능력을 주다

‡**ca·pac·i·ty** [kəpǽsiti] *n.* (pl. **-ties**) **1.** [U] 《often *a ~*》 the power or ability of receiving and holding. ¶*be filled to ~*① */ The hall has a ~ of 500.*② **2.** [U] 《sometimes *a ~*》 ability; power. ¶*a man of great ~.*③ **3.** [C] a position; a relation; a character. ¶*in one's ~ as a judge*④ */ He went in a private ~.*
—[名] 1. 수용력, 용량 ¶①만원이다/②이 호올에는 500명 들어갈 수 있다 2. 능력, 역량 ¶③아주 능력이 있는 사람 3. 자격, 지위 ¶④재판관의 자격으로

cap-a-pie [kæ̀pəpíː] *adv.* from head to foot; completely.
—[副] 온몸에, 빈틈없이

ca·par·i·son [kəpǽrisn] *n.* [C] ⟪often *pl.*⟫ **1.** an ornamental cloth for a horse. ⇒fig. **2.** gay or rich dress. **—***vt.* put a caparison on (a horse); dress (someone) richly.
—[名] 1. 마의(馬衣) 2. 성장(盛裝) —[他] …에 마의를 입히다; …에 성장시키다

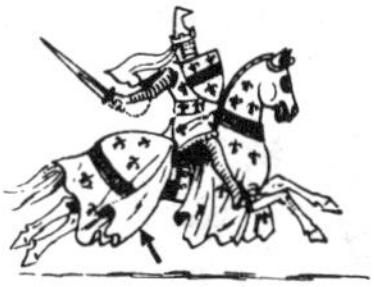
〔caparison 1.〕

cape¹ [keip] *n.* [C] an outer sleeveless garment worn loosely over the shoulders.
—[名] 케이프, 어깨 망토

* **cape²** [keip] *n.* **1.** [C] a point of land going out into the sea. **2.** ⟪*the C-*⟫ the Cape of Good Hope.
—[名] 1. 갑(岬), 곶 2. [남아프리카 남단의] 희망봉

Cape Ken·ne·dy [kèipkénədi] *n.* the base camp for experiments on rockets in Florida, U. S. A.
—[名] 케이프 케네디(미국의 우주 로켓 발사 기지)

ca·per [kéipər] *vi.* jump about playfully. **—***n.* [C] a playful jump.
cut a caper (or *capers*), jump about playfully.
—[自] 뛰어 돌아다니다 —[名] 뛰어 돌아다님
[熟] 뛰어 돌아다니다

cap·il·lar·i·ty [kæ̀pilǽriti] *n.* [U] the state of being capillary; the power of exerting capillary attraction or repulsion.
—[名] 털 모양; 모세관 현상

cap·il·lar·y [kǽpilèri / kəpíləri] *n.* [C] (pl. **-lar·ies**) a hair-like tube with a very slender opening. **—***adj.* **1.** like hair, very thin. **2.** of or in capillary tubes.
—[名] 모세관 —[形] 1. 털 모양의 2. 모세관의

* **cap·i·tal¹** [kǽpitl] *n.* [C] **1.** a city or a town where the government of a country or State is placed. ¶*Seoul is the ~ of Korea*① **2.** a large letter of the alphabet like A, B, C and D. **3.** [U] ⟪often *a ~*⟫ the amount of money or wealth that is used in carrying on a business. ¶*The company has a ~ of 30,000,000 won*②
make capital (=*take advantage*) *of something.*
—*adj.* **1.** of capital. **2.** very important; main; chief; principal. **3.** very good; excellent. **4.** punishable by death. ¶*a ~ crime.*③
—[名] 1. 서울, 수도 ¶①서울은 한국의 수도이다 2. 대문자 3. 자본[금] ¶②그 회사의 자본금은 3,000만 원이다
[熟] …을 이용하다, …을 틈타다
—[形] 1. 수도의 2. 주요한 3. 우수한; 멋진 4. 죽어 마땅한 ¶③사형을 받을 만한 죄

cap·i·tal² [kǽpitl] *n.* [C] the top part of a column.
—[名] 기둥머리

cap·i·tal·ism [kǽpitəlìz(ə)m] *n.* [U] an economic system based on the owners of capital.
—[名] 자본주의

cap·i·tal·ist [kǽpitəlist] *n.* [C] **1.** a person who owns much wealth used in business. **2.** a person who believes in capitalism.
—[名] 1. 자본주, 자본가 2. 자본주의자

cap·i·tal·is·tic [kæ̀pitəlístik] *adj.* of capitalism or capitalists.
—[形] 자본가의; 자본주의의

cap·i·tal·i·za·tion [kæ̀pitəlizéiʃ(ə)n / -təlai-] *n.* [U] **1.** the act of capitalizing. **2.** the sum resulting from a process of capitalizing. **3.** the capital stock of a business.
—[名] 1. 자본화 2. 자본 총액 3. 주식 자본

cap·i·tal·ize [kǽpitəlàiz / kəpítəlaiz] *vt.* **1.** write or print (words) with a capital letter. **2.** turn (money) into capital; use (money) as capital. **3.** calculate the present value of (an income). **4.** (*U. S.*) take advantage of (something). ¶*~ on a rival's mistake.*
—[他] 1. …을 대문자로 쓰다(인쇄하다) 2. …을 자본화하다 3. [수입 따위]의 현가(現價)를 계산하다 4. …을 이용하다

capital stock [ˊ-- ˊ] *n.* the total stock issued by a corporation, used in carrying on a business.
—[名] 주식 자본

cap·i·ta·tion [kæ̀pitéiʃ(ə)n] *n.* [C] a tax or fee of the same amount for every person.
—[名] 인두세(人頭稅)

* **Cap·i·tol** [kǽpitl] *n.* **1.** ⟪*the ~*⟫ the building in which the U. S. Congress meets, located in Washington, D. C. **2.** [C] ⟪often *c-*⟫ the building in which a state's law-making body meets. **3.** the ancient temple of Jupiter in Rome.
—[名] 1. [미국의] 국회 의사당 2. 주의회 의사당 3. [옛 로마의] 주피터 신전

ca·pit·u·late [kəpítʃulèit / -tju-] *vi.* surrender on certain conditions.
—[自] [조건을 붙여] 항복하다

ca·pit·u·la·tion [kəpìtʃuléiʃ(ə)n / -tju-] *n.* **1.** [U][C] the act of capitulaltng. **2.** ⟪*pl.*⟫ agreement; condition.
—[名] 1. [조건부] 항복 2. [항복의] 문서; 조건

ca·price [kəpríːs] *n.* [U][C] a sudden change of mind or behavior without reason; whim.
—[名] 변덕, 일시적 기분

ca·pri·cious [kəpríʃəs] *adj.* guided by caprice; change-
—[形] 변덕스러운

able.

cap·size [kǽpsaiz, -ˊ / -ˊ] *vi., vt.* turn upside down; upset. —[自][他] 전복하다(시키다)

cap·stan [kǽpstən] *n.* [C] a machine used for lifting or pulling, around which men walk pushing levers. ⇒fig. —[名] 닻을 감아 올리는 장치

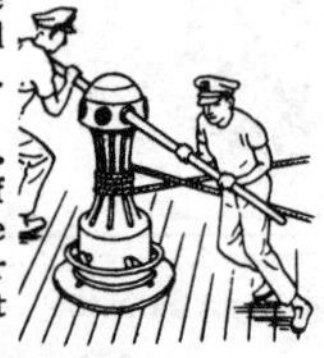
(capstan)

cap·sule [kǽps(ə)l / -sju:l] *n.* [C] **1.** a small soluble case for a dose of medicine. **2.** (*Botany*) a small case containing dry seeds. **3.** a cap for a bottle. **4.** the part of a rocket holding instruments or persons. —[名] 1. [약을 싸는] 캡슈울 2. [씨의] 꼬투리, 삭과(蒴果) 3. [유리병의] 병마개 4. [로켓의] 캡슈울

Capt. Captain.

⁑ **cap·tain** [kǽpt(ə)n / -tin] *n.* [C] **1.** a leader; a chief. **2.** an army officer ranking below a major and above a lieutenant. **3.** a navy officer ranking below an admiral and above a commander. **—*vt.*** lead (a team) as the captain; command. ¶*He captained the team.*① —[名] 1. 우두머리, 수령 2. 육군 대위 3. 해군 대령; 선장 —[他] …을 지휘하다, 통솔하다 ¶①그는 티임을 통솔했다

cap·tain·ship [kǽpt(ə)nʃìp / -tin-] *n.* [U] **1.** the position of a captain. **2.** leadership. —[名] 1. 주장(主將)의 지위 2. 통솔력

cap·tion [kǽpʃ(ə)n] *n.* [C] a title or heading used to explane a picture, photograph, etc. **—*vt.*** put a caption on (something). —[名] [그림·영화·사진 따위의] 표제, 설명, 자막 —[他] …에 표제를 달다

cap·tious [kǽpʃəs] *adj.* ready to find fault. —[形] 헐뜯는, 흠잡기 좋아하는

cap·ti·vate [kǽptivèit] *vt.* take hold of (something) by beauty or interest; charm; fascinate; enchant. ¶*He was captivated by the poem.*① ▷**cap·ti·va·tor** [-ər] *n.* —[他] …을 매혹하다, 사로잡다 ¶①그는 그 시에 매혹되었다

cap·ti·vat·ing [kǽptivèitiŋ] *adj.* charming; fascinating. —[形] 매력있는, 매혹적인

cap·ti·va·tion [kæ̀ptivéiʃ(ə)n] *n.* [U] the act of captivating; the state of being captivated; charm. —[名] 매혹, 뇌살(腦殺)

• **cap·tive** [kǽptiv] *n.* [C] a prisoner; a person who is captivated. ¶*He was taken ~.*① —[名] 포로, 넋을 빼앗긴 사람 ¶①그는 포로가 되었다

—*adj.* taken or kept as a prisoner. —[形] 사로잡힌, 포로가 된

captive balloon [ˊ-- ˊ] *n.* [C] a balloon which is fixed by a rope from the ground. —[名] 계류(繫留) 기구

cap·tiv·i·ty [kæptíviti] *n.* [U] the condition of being held as a prisoner; the state of being in prison. ¶*in ~*① —[名] 사로잡힘, 감금 ¶①사로잡혀

cap·tor [kǽptər] *n.* [C] a person who holds a prisoner. —[名] 잡는 사람, 체포자

⁑ **cap·ture** [kǽptʃər] *vt.* take (someone) as a prisoner; seize or catch. ¶*The policeman captured the thief.*① / *The boy will ~ the prize.* **—*n.*** **1.** [C] a captured person or thing. **2.** [U] the act of capturing or seizing. —[他] …을 사로잡다, 붙잡다, 손에 넣다 ¶①경관은 도둑을 잡았다 —[名] 1. 포로; 노획품 2. 노획, 점령

⁑ **car** [kɑ:r] *n.* [C] **1.** a vehicle or carriage that moves on wheels. **2.** an automobile; a motorcar. ⇒[N.B.] **3.** a railroad vehicle that carries things or passengers. **4.** a vehicle that runs on rails; a streetcar; a carriage. **5.** a part of an elevator, a balloon, etc. for things or passengers. **6.** (*poetic*) a chariot. —[名] 1. 차, 수레 2. 자동차 [N.B.] 미국에서는 승용차는 automobile, auto, auto-car 보다 car를 보통 씀. 3. 객차, 화차 4. 열차, 전차(電車) 5. [승강기의] 통, [기구(氣球) 따위의] 조롱(吊籠) 6. 전차(戰車)

ca·rafe [kərǽf / -rɑ́:f] *n.* [C] a glass water bottle to be used at the table. —[名] 물주전자, 물병

car·a·mel [kǽrəmèl] *n.* **1.** [U] burnt sugar used for coloring or flavoring food. **2.** [C] a small piece of candy made of burnt sugar. —[名] 1. 캐러멜(흑맥주·과자의 착색제) 2. 캐러멜(과자)

car·at [kǽrət] *n.* [C] **1.** a unit of weight for jewels, equal to $^1/_5$ gram. **2.** a unit to measure the amount of pure gold. —[名] 1. 캐럿(보석의 중량 단위) 2. 금의 순도

car·a·van [kǽrəvæ̀n / ˊ-ˊ, ˊ--] *n.* [C] **1.** a group of persons traveling together across a desert or a dangerous land. **2.** a large, covered wagon used by people in traveling ⇒fig.; a house on wheels; a trailer; a van. —[名] 1. [사막 따위의] 대상(隊商) 2. [서어커스·집시 대위의] 포장마차; 이동주택

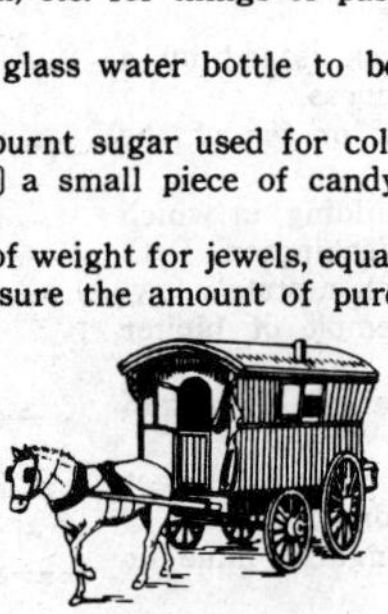
(caravan 2.)

car·a·van·sa·ry [kǽrəvǽnsəri] *n.* ⓒ (*pl.* **-ries**) **1.** a kind of inn, usu. with a large courtyard, where caravans rest in. **2.** a large inn.
— 圀 1. 대상의 여관(보통 넓은 안뜰이 있음) 2. 큰 여관

car·a·van·se·rai [kǽrəvǽnsərài, -sərèi] *n.* =caravansary.

car·bide [káːrbaid] *n.* Ⓤ a compound of carbon.
— 圀 카아바이드, 탄화물

car·bine [káːrbain, +*U.S.* -biːn] *n.* ⓒ a short rifle or musket, used esp. by horsemen.
— 圀 기총(騎銃), 기병총

car·bo·hy·drate [kàːrbouháidreit] *n.* Ⓤⓒ a substance made of carbon, hydrogen, and oxygen.
— 圀 탄수화물, 함수(含水)탄소

car·bo·lize [káːrbəlaiz] *vt.* treat (something) with carbolic acid.
— 働 …을 석탄산으로 처리하다

∗**car·bon** [káːrbən] *n.* **1.** Ⓤ a very common nonmetallic element. **2.** ⓒ a carbon rod used in arc lamps, etc. **3.** Ⓤⓒ a piece of carbon paper; ⓒ a copy made with carbon paper.
— 圀 1. 탄소 2. [아아크등의] 탄소봉 3. 카아본지(紙), 묵지; 사본

car·bon·ate [káːrbənit →*v.*] *n.* Ⓤⓒ salt of carbonic acid. —*vt.* [káːrbənèit] **1.** change (something) into carbonate. **2.** charge water, etc. with carbon dioxide.
— 圀 탄산염 — 働 1. …을 탄산염으로 만들다 2. …을 탄산가스로 채우다

carbon di·ox·ide [káːrbəndaiɔ́ksaid / káːbəndaiɔ́ks-] *n.* a heavy, colorless gas with no smell.
— 圀 탄산가스, 이산화탄소

car·bon·ic [kɑːrbɑ́nik / -bɔ́nik] *adj.* made from carbon.
— 働 탄소의

carbonic acid [-́-́ -́] *n.* a weak acid which is made when carbon dioxide is dissolved in water.
— 圀 탄산

carbonic acid gas [-́-́ -́- -́] *n.* a gas which is made when carbonic acid is dissolved.
— 圀 탄산가스

carbon mon·ox·ide [káːrbənmɑnɑ́ksaid / káːbənmɔnɔ́k-] *n.* a very poisonous gas with no color and smell, formed when carbon burns without enough air.
— 圀 일산화탄소

car·bun·cle [káːrbʌŋkl] *n.* Ⓒ **1.** a painful swelling under the skin. **2.** Ⓤⓒ a smooth, deep-red jewel.
— 圀 1. 옹(癰) 2. 홍옥, 석류석

car·bu·ret [káːrb(j)urèt] *vt.* (**-ret·ed, -ret·ing** or esp. *Brit.* **-ret·ted, -ret·ting**) combine (something) with carbon.
— 働 …을 탄소와 화합시키다, …에 탄소를 혼입하다

car·case [káːrkəs] *n.* =carcass.

car·cass [káːrkəs] *n.* ⓒ the dead body of an animal.
— 圀 [짐승의] 시체

‡**card**¹ [kɑːrd] *n.* ⓒ **1.** a rectangular piece of stiff paper. ¶*a postal ~ | a calling ~*. **2.** one of a pack of cards used in playing games. **3.** (*pl.*) a game or games played with cards.
 1) **have one's** (or **a**) **card up one's sleeve,** have a secret plan in reserve.
 2) **in** (*or* **on**) **the cards,** likely to happen; probable.
 3) **put one's cards on the table,** conceal nothing; make one's plans, intentions, etc. known; be absolutely frank about one's plans.
 4) **speak by the card,** speak accurately or precisely.
— 圀 1. 카아드 2. 트럼프의 카아드; 화투 3. 카아드놀이

熟 1)숨겨둔 계획(수단)이 있다 2)있을 수 있는 3)계획을 공개하다; 비밀을 터놓다 4)명확하게 말하다

card² [kɑːrd] *n.* ⓒ a wire brush. —*vt.* clean or comb (wool) with a card.
— 圀 [양털을 빗는] 얼레빗 — 働 [털 따위]를 빗다, …에 보풀을 세우다

card·board [káːrdbɔ́ːrd] *n.* Ⓤ a thick, stiff paper used in making cards or boxes.
— 圀 두꺼운 종이, 마분지

car·di·ac [káːrdiæk] *adj.* **1.** of the heart. **2.** of the upper part of the stomach. —*n.* ⓒ medicine to stimulate the heart or the stomach.
— 働 1. 심장의 2. [위(胃)의] 분문(噴門)의 — 圀 강심제, 건위제(健胃劑)

car·di·gan [káːrdigən] *n.* ⓒ a knitted woolen sweater.
— 圀 카아디건(스웨터)

car·di·nal [káːrdin(ə)l] *adj.* **1.** chief; fundamental; of first importance. **2.** bright-red. —*n.* **1.** Ⓤ a bright red color. **2.** ⓒ a high member of the Roman Catholic Church, appointed by the Pope. **3.** ⓒ an American song bird with a bright-red color. ⇒N.B. **4.** (usu. *pl.*) =cardinal numbers. [↔ordinal numbers]
 cardinal numbers, the numbers one, two, three, etc.
— 働 1. 주요한, 기본적인 2. 진홍빛의 — 圀 1. 진홍빛 2. 추기경(로마 교황의 최고의 고문 성직자) 3. 홍관조(紅冠鳥) N.B. 별명 cardinal bird 4. 기수(基數)

熟 기수(基數)

‡**care** [kɛər] *n.* **1.** Ⓤⓒ troubled state of mind caused by doubt or fear; anxiety. ¶*Care had aged him.*① **2.** (often *pl.*) cause of sorrow and anxiety. ¶*He was rich*
— 圀 1. 근심 ¶①근심으로 그는 늙었다 2. 근심거리 ¶②그는 부자이고 아무런 근심거리도 없었다 3. 감독, 보호,

*and free from cares of every kind.*② **3.** [U] watchful keeping; charge; protection. ¶*The child was left in her sister's ~.* **4.** [U] serious attention. ¶*Take ~ not to break the glass.*③ **5.** [U] pains.

보살핌 4. 주의, 조심 ¶③이 유리잔을 깨지 않도록 주의하시오 5. 수고

1) ***have a care; take care,*** be careful.
2) ***take care of,*** ⓐ look after; watch over (a baby, a patient, etc.). ⓑ be careful about (something). ⓒ (*colloq.*) deal with; attend to (something).

[熟] 1)…에 주의하다 2)ⓐ…을 돌보다 ⓑ…에 조심하다 ⓒ…을 처분하다; …에 종사하다

—*vi.* **1.** feel anxiety, sorrow, or interest. 《*~ that* …; *~ what* (or *how*, etc.) … ; *~ for* or *about* something》 ¶*He doesn't ~ what I say.* **2.** 《usu. in *negative* or *interrogative*》 wish; be willing. 《*~ to do*》 ¶*I don't ~ to answer.*④

—[自] 1. 근심하다, 관심을 갖다 2. 좋아하다; …하고 싶어하다 ¶④대답하고 싶지 않다

1) ***care about,*** ⓐ 《usu. in *negative* or *interrogative*》 feel anxiety; be worried about (something). ¶*I don't ~ about the matter.* ⓑ be interested in (something). ¶*He cares about music.*
2) ***care for,*** ⓐ look after; watch over (a baby, a patient, etc.); protect. ⓑ 《in *negative* or *interrogative*》 want; like; love. ¶*Would you ~ for a walk? / She does not ~ for him.*

[熟] 1)ⓐ…을 근심하다 ⓑ…에 관심을 갖다 2)ⓐ…을 보살피다 ⓑ…을 좋아하다, …하고 싶어하다

ca·reen [kəríːn] *vi.* lean to one side; tilt. **—*vt.*** cause (a ship) to lean to one side for repair or cleaning.

—[自] 기울다 —[他] [수리·청소를 위해 배]를 기울이다

* **ca·reer** [kəríər] *n.* [C] **1.** a general course of action or development through life. ¶*Young people should read much of the careers of great men.*① **2.** a way of living; a profession. ¶*He is going to take up education for his ~.*② **3.** one's progress through life; development. **4.** [U] speed; full speed.

—[名] 1. 생애, 경력 ¶①젊은이는 위인전을 많이 읽어야 한다 2. 직업 ¶②그는 교육을 직업으로 삼으려고 한다 3. 출세; 발전 4. 속력, 전속력

1) ***in full career,*** at full speed. ¶*His car was in full ~.*③
2) ***make a career,*** rise in the world; be successful.

[熟] 1)전속력으로 ¶③그의 차는 전속력으로 달렸다 2)출세하다

—*vi.* run along wildly; dash.

—[自] 질주하다

—*adj.* (*U. S.*) professional. ¶*a ~ woman.*④

—[形] 직업적인 ¶④직업 여성

care·free [kέərfrìː] *adj.* without worry; gay.

—[形] 근심걱정이 없는, 태평한

⁑ **care·ful** [kέərf(u)l] *adj.* **1.** thinking much about what one says or does; watchful; cautious. 《*~ about*》 ¶*Be ~ not to go too far.*① / *Be ~ what you eat.* **2.** done with enough thought or care; exact; thorough. ¶*a ~ study / The doctor gave us a ~ examination.*②

—[形] 1. 주의깊은 ¶①멀리 가지 않도록 주의해라 2. 용의주도한, 공들인 ¶②이 의사는 면밀히 진찰했다

be careful (=*take good care*) ***of something.*** ¶*be ~ of money / be ~ of another's feelings.*

[熟] 소중히 하다; 주의하다

⁑ **care·ful·ly** [kέərf(u)li] *adv.* with care.

—[副] 주의깊게

care·ful·ness [kέərf(u)lnis] *n.* [U] the state of being careful.

—[名] 주의깊음, 용의주도, 세심함

* **care·less** [kέərlis] *adj.* **1.** not thinking much about what one says or does; not careful or cautious. ¶*How ~ you are to say such a thing to him!*① **2.** done without enough thought or care; thoughtless. ¶*a ~ mistake*② / *He is a ~ reader.*③ **3.** not troubling; meeting without complaining. **4.** without worry; happy; light-hearted.

—[形] 1. 부주의한 ¶①그에게 그런 말을 하다니 너는 부주의했다 2. 경솔한, 아무렇게나 한 ¶②경솔한 잘못/③그는 아무렇게나 독서를 한다 3. 무관심한, 4. 근심없는; 태평한, 마음편한

1) ***be careless about*** (=*be indifferent to*) ***something.***
2) ***be careless*** (=*be regardless*) ***of something.*** ¶*Those people were ~ of discomfort.*④

[熟] 1)…에 개의하지 않다 2)…에 무관심하다 ¶④그들은 불편한 점에 개의치 않는다

care·less·ly [kέərlisli] *adv.* without care; in a careless manner.

—[副] 부주의하게 아무렇게나

care·less·ness [kέərlisnis] *n.* [U] the state of being careless.

—[名] 부주의, 경솔

* **ca·ress** [kərés] *n.* [C] a touch or stroke showing love; an embrace; a kiss. **—*vt.*** touch or stroke (someone) with love; embrace; kiss.

—[名] 애무, 포옹, 키스 —[他] …을 애무하다, 포옹하다, 입맞추다

ca·ress·ing [kərésiŋ] *adj.* showing love.

—[形] 애무하는, 귀여워하는

ca·ress·ing·ly [kərésiŋli] *adv.* in a caressing manner.

—[副] 애무하여

car·et [kǽrət, kéi- / kǽrət] *n.* [C] a mark (∧) in writing or printing to show where something should be put in.

—[名] 탈자(脫字) 부호(∧)

care·tak·er [kέərtèikər] *n.* [C] a person who takes care of someone or something.

—[名] 관리인, 돌보는(집지키는) 사람

care·worn [kέərwɔ̀:rn] *adj.* tired; weary. —[形] 근심에 시달린(야윈)

car·fare [ká:rfὲər] *n.* [C] money paid for riding on a bus, train, etc. —[名] 찻삯, 차비

* **car·go** [ká:rgou] *n.* [U] [C] (pl. **-goes** or **-gos**) goods carried on a ship. —[名] 뱃짐, 적하(積荷)

car·go-boat [ká:rgoubòut] *n.* [C] a ship to carry cargo. —[名] 화물선

Car·ib·be·an [kæ̀ribí(:)ən] *n.* the sea bounded by Central America, the West Indies, and South America. —*adj.* **1.** of this sea. **2.** of the Caribs, a tribe of Indians living in the southern West Indies or in northeastern South America. —[名] 1. 카리브해 —[形] 카리브해의 2. 카리브 사람의

Caribbean Sea [⊥-⊥- ⊥], **the** *n.* =the Caribbean.

car·i·ca·ture [kǽrikətʃùər / kæ̀rikətjúə] *n.* **1.** [C] a funny picture drawn or description made in an exaggerated way. **2.** [U] the art of making such pictures or descriptions. —*vt.* make a caricature of (something). —[名] 1. 풍자화, 만화 2. 만화화(漫畫化), 희작(戲作) —[他] …을 만화로 그리다, 풍자하다

car·i·ca·tur·ist [kǽrikətʃùərist / kæ̀rikətjúər-] *n.* [C] a person who makes caricatures by profession. —[名] 풍자 화가, 만화가

car·ies [kέər(i)ì:z / kέərii:z] *n.* [U] decay of teeth or bones. —[名] 카리에스

car·il·lon [kǽrəlàn / kəríljən] *n.* [C] **1.** a set of bells for playing melodies. **2.** a melody played on such bells. —[名] 1. 한 벌의 종 2. 종악(鐘樂)

car·load [ká:rlòud] *n.* [U] goods carried by a car; the minimum weight of goods that a car can hold or carry. —[名] 화차 적재 화물; [대절에 필요한] 화차의 최저 적재량

Car·lyle [ka:rláil], **Thomas** *n.* (1795–1881) an English philosopher, historian, and essayist. —[名] 영국의 철학가·역사가·수필가

car·man [ká:rmən] *n.* [C] (pl. **-men** [-mən]) **1.** a person who drives a cart. **2.** a motorman; a conductor of a streetcar. —[名] 1. 짐마차 마부 2. 전차 승무원

car·mine [ká:rmin, -main / ká:main] *n.* [U] a deep red color. —*adj.* deep red; purplish-red. —[名] 카아민, 양홍색(洋紅色) —[形] 양홍색의

car·nage [ká:rnidʒ] *n.* [U] the act of killing a great many people; slaughter. —[名] 살륙, 대학살

car·nal [ká:rn(ə)l] *adj.* of the body; sensual. —[形] 육체의, 육욕의

car·na·tion [ka:rnéiʃ(ə)n] *n.* **1.** [C] a flower of a red, white, or pink color and with a sweet smell. **2.** [U] a rosy pink or deep red color. —*adj.* rosy-pink; deep-red. —[名] 1. 카아네이션 2. 분홍색; 살빛 —[形] 분홍색의; 살빛의

car·ni·val [ká:rniv(ə)l] *n.* [C] **1.** ⦅often without *an article*⦆ [U] a time of feasting and merrymaking during the week before Lent. **2.** a traveling show with merry-go-round etc. **3.** feasting and merrymaking. —[名] 1. 사육제(가톨릭의 사순절 직전 1주 동안의 축제) 2. 순회 흥행 3. 북새통, 진탕만탕 놀기

car·ni·vore [ká:rnivɔ̀:r] *n.* [C] an animal that eats flesh. —[名] 식육 동물

car·niv·o·rous [ka:rnív(ə)rəs] *adj.* flesh-eating. —[形] 고기를 먹는, 식육의

car·ol [kǽr(ə)l] *n.* [C] a song of joy; a joyful religious song; a hymn. ¶*Christmas carols.*① —*vt.* (**-oled, -ol·ing** or *Brit.* **-olled, -ol·ling**) sing joyously. —[名] 기쁨의 노래, 축가 ¶①크리스마스 축가 —[他] …을 즐겁게 노래 부르다, 지저귀다

Car·o·li·na [kæ̀rəláinə] *n.* either North Carolina or South Carolina, States in the south of the United States. —[名] 북(남) 캐롤라이너주(미국 동남부의 주)

Car·o·line [kǽrəlàin, -lin] *n.* a woman's name. —[名] 여자 이름

ca·rous·al [kəráuz(ə)l] *n.* [C] a noisy drinking party. —[名] 흥겨운 큰 잔치, 큰 주연

ca·rouse [kəráuz] *n.* [C] a noisy drinking party or feast. —*vi.* drink heavily; drink merrily at a feast. —[名] 술잔치, 주연 —[自] 술을 진탕 마시다; 술마시며 떠들다

car·ou·sel [kæ̀ruzél, +*U.S.* kæ̀r-] *n.* =carrousel.

carp[1] [ka:rp] *vi.* find fault; complain about a trifle. ⦅~ *at* someone or something⦆ ¶*He is always carping at my faults.*① ▷**carp·er** [-ər] *n.* —[自] 허물을 들추다, 트집잡다 ¶①그는 언제나 내 결점만을 들추고 있다

carp[2] [ka:rp] *n.* [C] (pl. **carps** or esp. *collectively* **carp**) a fresh-water fish living in a lake or pond. —[名] 잉어

* **car·pen·ter** [ká:rpintər] *n.* [C] a man whose work is to make a thing or building of wood. —*vt., vi.* do such work. —[名] 목수 —[他][自] 목수 일을 하다

car·pen·try [ká:rpintri] *n.* [U] **1.** the work of a carpenter. **2.** a thing or building made by a carpenter. —[名] 1. 목수 일 2. 목공품

* **car·pet** [ká:rpit] *n.* [C] a thick cloth used for covering floors and stairs; something like this. ¶*a ~ of flowers.*① —[名] 융단, 양탄자 ¶①만발한 꽃밭
on the carpet, under discussion or consideration. [熟] 토의중, 심의중

—*vt.* cover (something) with a carpet. ¶*In the autumn, the ground is carpeted with fallen leaves.*

—[他] …에 융단을 깔다

car·pet·bag [ká:rpitbæ̀g] *n.* [C] a traveling bag made of carpet.

—[名] [융단으로 만든] 여행 가방

carp·ing [ká:rpiŋ] *adj.* fault-finding; captious.

—[形] 트집잡는, 흠잡는

car·port [ká:rpɔ̀:rt] *n.* [C] (*U.S.*) a roof projecting from the side of building and serving to make a garage.

—[名] 《美》 [다른 건물에 부수한] 간이 자동차 차고

˸car·riage [kæ̀ridʒ] *n.* **1.** [C] a vehicle with wheels, usu. pulled by horses and used to carry people. ¶*a ~ and pair.*① **2.** [C] (*Brit.*) a part of a train in which passengers sit; a railway coach. (cf. *U.S.* car) ¶*a first(second)-class ~.* **3.** [U] the act or cost of carrying. **4.** 《usu. *a ~*》 bearing; manner. ¶*She has a graceful ~.*② **5.** [U] management; handling.

—[名] 1. 마차 ¶①네 필이 끄는 4륜마차 2.《英》 [철도의] 객차 3. [여객·화물의] 수송, 운반; 운임 4. 태도, 몸가짐 5. [사업 따위의] 처리

carriage drive [ˊ-- ˋ] *n.* a road from a gate to a main, large building.

—[名] [현관으로 통하는] 차도

***car·ri·er** [kæ̀riər] *n.* [C] **1.** a person or thing that carries something. **2.** (*U.S.*) a person who carries or delivers mail. (cf. chiefly *Brit.* postman) **3.** (*Medicine*) a person or thing that gives a disease to others.

—[名] 1. 운송하는 사람(것) 2.《美》 우편 배달부 3.《醫》 보균자(물)

carrier pigeon [ˊ--- ˋ-] *n.* a pigeon used to carry messages; a homing pigeon.

—[名] 전서구(傳書鳩)

car·ri·on [kæ̀riən] *n.* [U] dead or decaying flesh. —*adj.* **1.** of or like carrion. **2.** feeding on carrion.

—[名] 썩은 고기, 죽은 짐승고기 —[形] 1. 썩은 고기의 2. 썩은 고기를 먹는

carrion crow [ˊ-- ˋ] *n.* a common European crow.

—[名] [유럽산] 까마귀의 일종

car·rot [kæ̀rət] *n.* [C] a vegetable whose long orange-red root is eaten.

—[名] 당근

car·rot·y [kæ̀rəti] *adj.* **1.** like a carrot in color. **2.** having red hair.

—[形] 1. 당근 빛깔의 2. 붉은 머리털의

car·rou·sel [kæ̀rəsél, -zél / kæ̀ruzél] *n.* [C] a merry-go-round.

—[名] 회전목마

˸car·ry [kæ̀ri] *v.* (**-ried**) *vt.* **1.** take or move (something) from one place to another place. ¶*He was carrying a box on his shoulder.* / *Railroads ~ coals from the mines to your town.* **2.** possess; wear. ¶*Mr. A carries great authority.*① / *Do you always ~ an umbrella?* **3.** bear the weight of (something); support; hold up. ¶*Those columns ~ the roof.* **4.** hold (one's body and head) in a certain way. ¶*~ one's head on one side.*② **5.** 《*reflexively*》 behave. ¶*He carries himself like a soldier.* / *She carries herself gracefully.*③ **6.** have (something) as a result of belonging; involve. ¶*Power carries responsibility with it.*④ / *His opinion carries great weight.* **7.** make (something) longer; extend; continue. ¶*carry a fence around a field.* **8.** overcome; win. ¶*Our troops carried the enemy's fort.*⑤ **9.** influence greatly. —*vi.* **1.** act as bearer. **2.** have the power to reach; cover the distance. ¶*His voice will ~ to the back of the room.*⑥

—[他] 1. …을 나르다 2. …을 가지고 있다 ¶①A씨는 큰 세력을 갖고 있다 3. […의 무게 따위]를 지탱하다 4. [몸·머리]를 어떤 자세로 하다 ¶②머리를 한쪽으로 기울이다 5. 처신하다 ¶③그녀는 우아하게 처신한다 6. [필연적으로] …을 가져오다; 포함하다 ¶④권력에는 책임이 따른다 7. …을 연장하다 8. 이기다, 함락시키다 ¶⑤우리 부대는 적의 요새를 뺏았다 9. …에 영향을 주다
—[自] 1. 물건을 나르다 2. [소리·탄환 따위가] 미치다, 도달하다 ¶⑥그의 목소리는 방 뒤까지 들릴 것이다

1) ***carry away,*** ⓐ 《usu. in *passive*》 cause (someone) to lose self-control. ⓑ take (something) to another place.
2) ***carry someone back,*** cause someone to recollect.
3) ***carry forward,*** ⓐ make progress with (something). ⓑ take (figures) to the top of the next page.
4) ***carry off,*** ⓐ win (a prize, honor, etc.). ⓑ deal with (something) successfully. ⓒ cause the death of (someone).
5) ***carry on,*** ⓐ continue (something) without stopping. ⓑ manage.
6) ***carry out,*** put (something) into operation; execute.
7) ***carry something over,*** hold something until a later time.
8) ***carry through,*** ⓐ complete; accomplish. ⓑ support (something) through a difficult situation.
9) ***carry something too far,*** make something go beyond the limits of good tastes, sense, etc.

[熟] 1)ⓐ…을 넋을 잃게 하다 ⓑ…을 가져가다 2)…에게 회상시키다 3)ⓐ[사업 따위를] 진행시키다 ⓑ[부기에서] 이월하다 4)ⓐ[상·명예]를 획득하다 ⓑ…을 잘 처리하다 ⓒ…의 죽음의 원인이 되다 5)ⓐ…을 계속하다 ⓑ…을 경영하다 6)…을 실행하다 7)…을 미루다, 이월하다 8)ⓐ…을 완성하다 ⓑ…을 지지하다, 지원하다 9)극단에 흐르다

—*n.* [C] the distance that something goes; range.

—[名] 물건이 도달하는 거리; 사정(射程)

car·ry·ing [kǽriiŋ] *adj.* taking a person or thing from one place to another. —[形] 운송의

car·sick [kɑ́:rsìk] *adj.* sick because of a car's motion. —[形] 차멀미의

‡ **cart** [kɑ:rt] *n.* [C] **1.** a vehicle with two wheels pulled by a horse and used for carrying heavy goods. **2.** a light wagon for delivery. **3.** a small vehicle on wheels, moved by hand. —[名] 1. [2륜의] 짐마차 2. 경장(輕裝) 마차 3. 손수레
put the cart before the horse, do or place things in the wrong order. [熟] 본말을 전도하다
—*vt.* carry (something) in a cart. —*vi.* drive a cart. —[他] …을 짐마차로 나르다 —[自] 짐마차를 몰다

cart·age [kɑ́:rtidʒ] *n.* [U] [the cost of] carrying in a cart. —[名] 짐수레 운반(운임)

carte blanche [kɑ́:rtblɑ́:nʃ] *n.* **1.** a blank sheet given to a person on which to write his own opinion. ⇒[N.B.] **2.** freedom to use one's own judgment. —[名] 1. 백지 위임장 [N.B.] 원래 프랑스어로서 문자 그대로의 뜻은 백지 2. [행동·선택 따위의] 자유

car·tel [kɑ:rtél, kɑ́:rtl] *n.* [C] **1.** a large group of business companies formed to control prices, etc. **2.** a written agreement relating to exchange of prisoners. **3.** a letter of challenge. —[名] 1. 카르텔, 기업 연합 2. 포로 교환 조약서 3. 결투장

car·ter [kɑ́:rtər] *n.* [C] a person whose work is driving a cart. —[名] 짐마차꾼

cart horse [ˊ ˋ] *n.* a big, strong horse fit for drawing heavy loads. —[名] 짐마차 말

car·ti·lage [kɑ́:rtilidʒ] *n.* [C] a firm, elastic substance at the ends of bones. —[名] 연골(軟骨)

car·ti·lag·i·nous [kɑ̀:rtilǽdʒinəs] *adj.* of or like cartilage. —[形] 연골[질]의

cart·load [kɑ́:rtlòud] *n.* [C] **1.** the amount that a cart can carry. **2.** (*colloq.*) an indefinitely large amount. —[名] 1. 한 수레의 적재량 2. 《口》 대량

car·ton [kɑ́:rtn] *n.* [C] a box made of strong cardboard. —[名] 마분지 상자

car·toon [kɑ:rtú:n] *n.* [C] a comic sketch or drawing for the purpose of making a person laugh or think (esp. about political events). —*vt.* draw a cartoon of (something). —*vi.* draw a cartoon. —[名] [정치 따위의] 풍자화 —[他] …을 만화화하다 —[自] 만화를 그리다

car·toon·ist [kɑ:rtú:nist] *n.* [C] a person who draws cartoons. —[名] 만화가

car·tridge [kɑ́:rtridʒ] *n.* [C] **1.** a small, round case for holding gunpowder. **2.** a roll of camera film. —[名] 1. 탄약통 2. [필름을 감아 넣는] 파트로네

cart·wheel [kɑ́:rt(h)wì:l] *n.* [C] **1.** a wheel of a cart. **2.** a sideways somersault. —[名] 1. [짐수레의] 차바퀴 2. 옆으로 재주넘기

cart·wright [kɑ́:rtràit] *n.* [C] a person who makes carts. —[名] 수레목수

* **carve** [kɑ:rv] *vt.* **1.** cut (stone or wood). **2.** make (figures) by cutting. ¶~ *a statue out of stone.* **3.** cut (something) into pieces or slices. ¶~ *the meat at the table.* —*vi.* **1.** carve figures. **2.** cut meat. —[他] 1. [돌·나무]를 새기다 2. …을 조각하다 3. [식탁에서 고기 따위]를 잘라서 나누다 —[自] 1. 새기다, 조각하다 2. 고기를 잘라 나누다

carved [kɑ:rvd] *adj.* decorated by cutting. —[形] 조각이 되어 있는

carv·er [kɑ́:rvər] *n.* [C] **1.** a person who carves. **2.** a knife used for cutting up meat. —[名] 1. 조각가 2. 고기 써는 나이프

carv·ing [kɑ́:rviŋ] *n.* **1.** [C] a work produced by cutting. ¶*a wood* ~.① **2.** [U] the act or art of one that carves. —[名] 1. 조각물 ¶①목각(木刻) 2. 조각[술]

cas·cade [kæskéid] *n.* [C] a small waterfall. —*vi.* fall in the form of a small waterfall. —[名] 작은 폭포 —[自] 폭포를 이루어 떨어지다

‡ **case**[1] [keis] *n.* [C] **1.** something that has happened; an instance; an occurence. ¶*a* ~ *of poor judgment.* **2.** a situation; a condition. ¶*It is a different* ~.① **3.** 《*the* ~》 the actual state of things. ¶*That is not the* ~.② **4.** a question or problem of moral conduct. ¶*a* ~ *of conscience* / *a* ~ *of murder.* **5.** a question to be decided in a law court; a suit. ¶*The* ~ *will be tried in the law court next week.* **6.** a person who has a disease or an injury. ⇒[N.B.] —[名] 1. 사례(事例) 2. 사정; 경우 ¶① 그것은 별문제다 3. 사실, 진상 ¶②그것은 사실이 아니다 4. 문제; 사건 5. 소송[사건] 6. 환자 [N.B.] case는 병에 중점을 두고, patient는 환자 자체를 가리킴

1) ***in any case,*** whatever happens or may have happened.
2) ***in case,*** if it should happen that …
3) ***in case of,*** in the event of.
4) ***in no case,*** never; under no condition.
5) ***in the case of,*** as regards.
6) ***in this (that) case,*** if this (that) happens; if this (that) is true; in these (those) circumstances.
7) ***make out someone's case,*** prove that someone is right.

[熟] 1)어쨌든, 하여튼 2)만일 …이면 3)…의 경우에는 4)어떤 경우라도 …않다 5)…에 대해서는 6)이러한(그러한) 경우에는 7)…의 옳음을 입증하다

case² [keis] *n.* ⓒ **1.** a box ; a bag. **2.** a sheath ; an outer covering. ¶ *a watch* ~.① **3.** a glass box for exhibiting goods ; a showcase. **4.** a framework ; a surrounding frame. ¶ *a window* ~.② **5.** the amount that a case can hold. —*vt.* put (something) in a case ; enclose.
—㉿ **1.** 상자 ; 자루 **2.** 케이스, [칼]집, 덮개 ¶①시계 뚜껑 **3.** 진열 케이스 **4.** 틀, 테 ¶②창틀 **5.** 한 상자의 분량
—㉰ …을 상자에 넣다 ; …을 싸다

case·hard·ened [kéishà:ァdnd] *adj.* **1.** made hard by heat treatment. **2.** insensible ; impudent.
—㉲ **1.** [쇠를]담금질하다 **2.** 철면피의, 뻔뻔스러운

ca·se·in [kéisiin / kéisi(:)in] *n.* Ⓤ the solid part of milk, of which cheese is made. 「wards or inwards.」
—㉿ 카세인, 건락소(乾酪素)

case·ment [kéismənt] *n.* ⓒ a window which opens out-
—㉿ 젖혀서 여는 창

• **cash** [kæʃ] *n.* Ⓤ **1.** money, esp. money on hand ; coins and bills. **2.** money, or an equivalent, such as a check. —*vt.* turn (something) into cash. ¶ ~ *a check*.
1) *cash in*, turn (something) into cash.
2) *cash in on*, ⓐ make a profit from (something). ⓑ turn (something) to one's advantage.
—㉿ **1.** 현금, 소지금 **2.** [지불을 위한] 돈, 수표 —㉰ [어음 따위]를 현금으로 바꾸다
圖 1)…을 현금으로 바꾸다 2)ⓐ…으로 이익을 보다 ⓑ…을 이용하다

cash·book [kǽʃbùk] *n.* ⓒ a book to record the sum of money received and paid out.
—㉿ 현금 출납부

cash·ew [kǽʃu:, kəʃú: / kæʃú:, kə-] *n.* ⓒ a tropical American tree and its nut.
—㉿ [열대산] 옻나무과의 식물, 그 열매

cash·ier [kæʃíər] *n.* ⓒ a person in a bank or restaurant who receives and pays out money.
—㉿ 현금 출납계

cash·mere [kǽʃmiəァ / kǽʃmíə] *n.* Ⓤ fine, soft wool from Kashmir and Tibet goats. ¶ *a* ~ *shawl*.①
—㉿ 캐시미어직(織) ¶①캐시미어 쇼올

cash register [-´-´-] *n.* a cash box to indicate the amount of a sale.
—㉿ 자동 금전 출납 계산기

cas·ing [kéisiŋ] *n.* **1.** ⓒ a case or covering ; Ⓤ enclosing material. **2.** ⓒ a frame.
—㉿ **1.** 상자에 넣기 ; 포장 ; 포장 재료 **2.** 틀, 테

ca·si·no [kəsí:nou] *n.* (pl. **-nos**) **1.** ⓒ a public building or room for shows, dancing, gambling, etc. **2.** Ⓤ a game played for money.
—㉿ **1.** 카지노, [댄스·도박 따위의] 오락장 **2.** 카아드 놀이의 일종

cask [kæsk / kɑ:sk] *n.* ⓒ **1.** a barrel to hold liquids. ¶ *a* ~ *of beer*. **2.** the amount that a cask can hold.
—㉿ **1.** 통 **2.** 한 통의 분량

cas·ket [kǽskit / kɑ́:s-] *n.* ⓒ **1.** a small box to hold jewels, letters, etc. **2.** (*U.S.*) a coffin.
—㉿ **1.** [귀중품 따위의] 작은 상자 **2.** 《美》관(棺)

cas·sock [kǽsək] *n.* ⓒ a long garment, usu. black, worn by a clergyman. ⇒fig.
—㉿ 법의(法衣)

cas·so·war·y [kǽsəwèəri] *n.* ⓒ a large, running bird like the ostrich, found in Australia and New Guinea.
—㉿ 화식조(火食鳥)

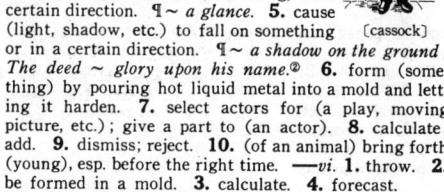
[cassock]

‡ **cast** [kæst / kɑ:st] *v.* (**cast**) *vt.* **1.** throw ; throw up or down ; throw off or away. ¶ ~ *a stone at a dog*. **2.** put off ; shed. ¶ *The snake* ~ *its skin*. **3.** let (something) fall or drop ; throw out. ¶ ~ *anchor*.① **4.** direct ; turn (something) in a certain direction. ¶ ~ *a glance*. **5.** cause (light, shadow, etc.) to fall on something or in a certain direction. ¶ ~ *a shadow on the ground* / *The deed* ~ *glory upon his name*.② **6.** form (something) by pouring hot liquid metal into a mold and letting it harden. **7.** select actors for (a play, moving picture, etc.); give a part to (an actor). **8.** calculate ; add. **9.** dismiss ; reject. **10.** (of an animal) bring forth (young), esp. before the right time. —*vi.* **1.** throw. **2.** be formed in a mold. **3.** calculate. **4.** forecast.
1) *cast about for*, look around for (something) ; try to find (something).
2) *cast away*, ⓐ throw away ; abandon. ⓑ shipwreck. ⓒ spend (money) foolishly.
3) *cast back*, recollect ; recall. 「discouraged.」
4) *cast down*, ⓐ turn downward. ⓑ make (someone)
5) *cast off*, ⓐ put off (clothes, etc.) ; let go or let loose, as a boat. ⓑ abandon.

—㉰ **1.** …을 던지다 ; 버리다 **2.** [껍질 따위]를 벗겨 던지다, [털·과실 따위]를 떨어뜨리다 **3.** …을 내리다, 가라앉히다 ; 내던지다 ¶①닻을 내리다 **4.** …을 돌리다 **5.** [빛·그림자 따위]를 던지다, 비추다 ¶②그 행위가 그의 명성을 높여 주었다 **6.** …을 주조하다 **7.** [극]에 배우를 배정하다 ; [배우]에게 배역을 주다 **8.** …을 계산하다 **9.** …을 해고하다, 폐기하다 **10.** [동물이 새끼]를 조산하다 —㉯ **1.** 던지다 **2.** 주조되다 **3.** 계산하다 **4.** 예상하다

圖 1)…을 찾아 돌아다니다 2)ⓐ[불필요한 것·습관 따위]를 버리다 ⓑ…을 난파시키다 ⓒ…을 낭비하다 3)…을 회상하다 4)ⓐ…을 넘어뜨리다 ⓑ…을 낙담시키다 5)ⓐ[옷]을 벗다 ; [매 놓은 배]를 풀어놓다 ⓑ체념하다 ⓒ물아내다, 쫓아내다

6) ***cast out,*** drive away; force out; expel.

—*n.* [C] **1.** the act of casting. **2.** fortune. **3.** a thing formed by molding or pressing. **4.** a mold into which metal is poured or soft material pressed. **5.** appearance; style; inclination. ¶*a ~ of mind.*③ **6.** calculation. **7.** (of the eyes) a slight squint. **8.** a slight tinge of some color. **9.** the set of actors in a play.
—[名] **1.** 던지기 **2.** 운수 **3.** 주조물; 주형(鑄型)으로 만든 물건 **4.** 주형 **5.** 용모; 특색, 기질 ¶③기질 **6.** 계산 **7.** 사팔뜨기 **8.** [빛깔의] 흔적 **9.** 배역

cas·ta·nets [kæ̀stənéts] *n. pl.* a pair of instruments of hard wood or ivory used to beat time to music.
—[名] 캐스터네츠(나무 또는 상아로 만든 타악기)

cast·a·way [kǽstəwèi / kɑ́:st-] *adj.* **1.** thrown away; of no value. **2.** shipwrecked. —*n.* [C] **1.** a person or thing thrown away. **2.** a shipwrecked person.
—[形] **1.** 버림받은; 가치없는 **2.** 난파한
—[名] **1.** 버림받은 사람(것) **2.** 표류자

caste [kæst / kɑ:st] *n.* **1.** [C] a Hindu social class. **2.** [C] an exclusive social group. **3.** [U] social position.
—[名] **1.** 카아스트, 사성(四姓) **2.** 배타적 계급 **3.** 사회적 지위

lose caste, lose social position or rank.
[熟] 사회적 지위를 잃다

cast·er [kǽstər / kɑ́:stə] *n.* [C] **1.** a person or thing that casts. **2.** a small wheel for supporting and moving furniture. **3.** a bottle on the table for serving salt, vinegar, or other seasoning. **4.** a stand for such bottles. ⇒[N.B.]
—[名] **1.** 던지는 사람 **2.** [가구의] 다리 바퀴 **3.** [식탁용] 양념 그릇 **4.** 양념 그릇을 올려놓는 받침 [N.B.] 2, 3, 4의 의미일 때는 castor라고도 씀

cas·ti·gate [kǽstigèit] *vt.* **1.** punish. **2.** criticize severely.
—[他] **1.** 벌주다 **2.** …을 혹평하다

cas·ti·ga·tion [kæ̀stigéiʃ(ə)n] *n.* [U][C] **1.** punishment. **2.** severe criticism.
—[名] **1.** 엄벌, 견책 **2.** 혹평

cast·ing [kǽstiŋ / kɑ́:st-] *n.* [U] **1.** throwing. **2.** [C] a thing formed by pouring a liquid into a mold to harden. **3.** [C] a part; a role.
—[名] **1.** 던지기 **2.** 주조품 **3.** 배역

casting vote [´- ´] *n.* the deciding vote of the chairman when the votes are equally divided.
—[名] 결정 투표(찬부 동수일 때에 의장이 던지는 한 표)

cast iron [´ ´-] *n.* a soft and strong mixture of iron, carbon, and other elements.
—[名] 주철(鑄鐵)

cast-iron [kǽstáiərn / kɑ́:stáiən] *adj.* **1.** made of cast iron. **2.** inflexible; stern.
—[形] **1.** 주철로 만든 **2.** 불굴의; 엄격한

⁑**cas·tle** [kǽsl / kɑ́:sl] *n.* [C] **1.** a large house of old times strengthened against attack. **2.** a large and stately mansion. **3.** a piece in chess, shaped like a castle tower.
—[名] **1.** 성(城) **2.** 대저택 **3.** [서양 장기의] 성장(城將)

cast·off [kǽstɔ̀:f / kɑ́:stɔ̀(:)f] *adj.* thrown away.
—[形] 버림받은

cas·tor[1] [kǽstər / kɑ́:stə] *n.* =caster (2., 3., 4.).

cas·tor[2] [kǽstər / kɑ́:stə] *n.* [C] **1.** a beaver. **2.** a hat made of beaver fur. **3.** [U] an oily substance with a strong smell produced by beavers.
—[名] **1.** 비이버, 바다삵 **2.** 비이버 모자 **3.** 해리향(海狸香)

cas·trate [kǽstreit / -´, ´-] *vt.* **1.** remove the male sexual glands from (an animal). **2.** omit; deprive (something) of its most important part. ▷**cas·tra·tion** [kæstréiʃ(ə)n] *n.*
—[他] **1.** …을 거세하다 **2.** …의 중요부분을 없애다

***cas·u·al** [kǽʒu(ə)l, kǽʒuəl] *adj.* **1.** happening by chance. ¶*a ~ meeting.* **2.** without serious intention. ¶*a ~ remark.*① **3.** irregular; occasional. ¶*~ expenses / ~ labor.*② **4.** (of clothes) designed for wearing at home; informal. ¶*We dressed in ~ clothes for the picnic.*
—[形] **1.** 우연한 **2.** 부주의한, 되는 대로의 ¶①문득 생각난 말 **3.** 임시의 ¶②뜨내기 일 **4.** 평상복의, 집에서 입는

cas·u·al·ly [kǽʒu(ə)li / kǽʒuəli] *adv.* accidentally; occasionally; carelessly.
—[副] 우연히; 이따금; 아무 생각없이

cas·u·al·ty [kǽʒu(ə)lti / kǽʒuəl-] *n.* [C] **1.** an accident; an unfortunate accident. **2.** 《*pl.*》 (*Military*) soldiers wounded or killed in a battle. **3.** a person hurt or killed in an accident.
—[名] **1.** 재해; 재난 **2.** 《軍》 사상자[수] **3.** 조난자, 부상자, 사망자

cas·u·ist [kǽʒuist / kǽzju-] *n.* **1.** [C] a person who studies and solves cases of conscience or conduct. **2.** a sophist.
—[名] **1.** 결의론자(決疑論者) **2.** 궤변가

⁑**cat** [kæt] *n.* [C] **1.** a small, fur-covered animal often kept as a pet, to catch mice, etc.; any animal of the cat family, such as a lion or a tiger. **2.** an ill-natured woman; a malicious woman.
—[名] **1.** 고양이; 고양이과의 동물 **2.** 심술궂은 여자

1) ***bell the cat,*** attempt something dangerous.
2) ***lead a cat and dog life; live like cat-and-dog,*** be always quarreling.
3) ***let the cat out of the bag,*** tell a secret.

[熟] 1)스스로 어려운 일을 떠맡다 2)늘 아옹다옹하며 살다 3)비밀을 누설하다 4)억수같이 퍼붓다 5)형세를 관망하다

4) ***rain cats and dogs,*** rain very heavily.
5) ***see how the cat jumps; see which way the cat will jump; wait for the cat to jump,*** refuse to make plans until other people act.

cat·a·clysm [kǽtəklìz(ə)m] *n.* [C] **1.** a great flood of water. **2.** an earthquake, or any sudden and violent physical change in the earth. **3.** a sudden overturning of society, or the political system.
—[名] 1. 대홍수 2. 지진, 지각(地殼)의 격변 3. [사회 · 정치의] 대변혁

cat·a·comb [kǽtəkòum] *n.* ((usu. *pl.*)) an underground place for graves or tombs.
—[名] 지하 납골당(納骨堂)

* **cat·a·log** [kǽtəlɔ(:)g, +*U.S.* -làg] *n., vt.* =catalogue.

* **cat·a·logue** [kǽtəlɔ̀(:)g, +*U.S.* -làg] *n.* [C] **1.** a list of things to be shown or for sale. **2.** (*U.S.*) a book or pamphlet of a college or university listing rules, courses to be given, etc. (cf. *Brit.* calendar)
—[名] 1. 목록, 카탈로그 2. ((美)) [대학의] 요람

—*vt.* to make a catalogue of (something), enter (something) in a catalogue.
—[他] …의 목록을 만들다, …을 목록에 싣다

cat·a·pult [kǽtəpʌlt] *n.* [C] **1.** an ancient military engine for throwing stones, spears, etc. **2.** a device for launching an airplane from the deck of a ship. **3.** (*Brit.*) a slingshot. —*vt.* shoot (a stone, an airplane, etc.) from a catapult.
—[名] 1. 쇠뇌, 석궁(石弓) 2. [배에 싣는] 비행기 사출기(射出機) 3. [장난감] 새총 —[他] …을 쇠뇌(새총)로 쏘다

cat·a·ract [kǽtərӕkt] *n.* [C] **1.** a great waterfall. **2.** a rush of water; a deluge. **3.** (*Medicine*) a disease of the eye.
—[名] 1. 폭포 2. 분류(奔流), 홍수 3. ((醫)) 백내장(白內障)

ca·tarrh [kətɑ́:*r*] *n.* [U] **1.** a diseased condition of the throat or back of nose, as in a cold. **2.** (*Brit. colloq.*) a cold.
—[名] 1. 카타르(점막(粘膜)의 염증) 2. [기침] 감기

ca·tas·tro·phe [kətǽstrəfi] *n.* [C] **1.** a sudden and widespread disaster. **2.** an unhappy ending. **3.** a sudden violent change in nature.
—[名] 1. [갑작스러운] 큰 재난 2. [비극 따위의] 대단원 3. 대변동

cat·a·stroph·ic [kӕtəstrɑ́fik / -strɔ́f-] *adj.* disastrous; calamitous.
—[形] 비참한, 재난의

cat·call [kǽtkɔ̀:l] *n.* [C] a cry like that of a cat, used to express disapproval at a theater, a meeting, etc.
—[名] 고양이 울음소리를 흉내낸 야유

‡ **catch** [kætʃ] *v.* (**caught**) *vt.* **1.** take and hold; capture. ↔lose ¶~ *a rat in a trap* / ~ *a thief.* **2.** stop the motion of (something) and seize it. ¶~ *a ball.* **3.** hear clearly; understand. ¶*I cannot* ~ *what you say.* **4.** be in time for; be in time to get aboard (a train, boat, etc.). ¶~ *the 9:00 limited express.* **5.** become infected with (a disease); form (habits). ¶~[*a*] *cold* / ~ *the measles*① / ~ *his manner.*② **6.** take; get; bring (something) on oneself. ¶*Paper catches fire easily.*③ **7.** attract (the attention). ¶*She caught his fancy.* / *His speech caught our attention.* **8.** come on (someone) suddenly. ((~ someone *doing* something wrong)) ¶*I caught him stealing apples in my garden.* / *She was caught* [*in the act of*] *stealing.*④ **9.** hit; strike. ¶*He caught her on the cheek.*⑤ / *He caught a stone on the forehead.*⑥ **10.** make (something) entangled or hooked. ¶*I caught my coat on a nail.*⑦
—[他] 1. …을 잡다, 붙들다 2. 받아 내다, 잡다 3. [말]을 알아듣다, 이해하다 4. [기차 · 배 따위]가 제시간에 대다 5. [병]에 걸리다; [습관]에 동화되다 ¶①홍역에 걸리다/②그의 태도를 흉내내게 되다 6. …을 가지고 오다, 끌어 넣다; 생기게 하다 ¶③종이는 금방 불이 붙는다 7. [눈길 · 주의]를 끌다 8. […하고 있는 현장]을 발견하다, 붙잡다 ¶④그녀는 도둑질 현장에서 붙들렸다 9. …에 맞다; …을 치다 ¶⑤그는 그녀의 뺨을 때렸다/⑥그는 이마에 돌을 얻어맞았다 10. …을 걸다, 얽히게 하다 ¶⑦나는 웃옷을 못에 걸었다

—*vi.* **1.** try to seize suddenly or rudely. ((~ *at* something)) **2.** become entangled or hooked. ¶*The kite caught in a tree.* **3.** take fire. **4.** be communicated, as a disease or enthusiasm. **5.** (*Baseball*) play as a catcher.
—[自] 1. 붙잡으려고 하다 2. 얽히다, 걸리다 3. 불이 붙다 4. [병이] 유행하다, [정열]이 옮다 5. ((野球)) 포수노릇을 하다

1) ***catch a glimpse of,*** see (something) for a short time.
2) ***catch as catch can,*** act without any plan or order.
3) ***catch at,*** try to catch (something) eagerly. ¶(*proverb*) *A drowning man will* ~ *at a straw.*⑧
4) ***catch it,*** be scolded or punished.
5) ***catch on,*** ⓐ (*colloq.*) become popular. ⓑ understand; grasp the point of (something).
6) ***catch up,*** lift suddenly.

[熟] 1)…을 흘깃 보다 2)닥치는 대로 붙들다 3)[물건]을 붙잡으려고 하다, …에 달려들다 ¶⑧물에 빠진 사람은 지푸라기라도 붙든다 4)꾸지람 듣다, 벌받다 5)ⓐ유행하다 ⓑ…을 이해하다 6)갑자기 쳐들다 7)…을 따라 잡다

7) ***catch up with,*** overtake.
—*n.* [C] **1.** the act of catching. **2.** what is caught, as a quantity of fish. ¶*The fisherman brought home a large ~.* **3.** a person or thing that is worth getting. ¶*Most of the girls think Tommy is quite a ~.*⑨ **4.** something intended to trick; a cunning question. ¶*This question has a ~ in it.*⑩ **5.** (*Music*) a song for a number of voices starting one after another. **6.** a game of throwing and catching a ball. ¶*play ~.*
—[名] 1. 붙잡기, 붙들기 2. 어획고 3. 소망하는 물건(사람) ¶⑨대개의 여자들은 토미를 멋진 결혼 상대로 알고 있다 4. [남을 속여 넘기려는] 함정 ¶⑩이 문제에는 함정이 있다 5. ⦅樂⦆ 윤창 6. 공던지기

catch·er [kǽtʃər] *n.* [C] **1.** a person or thing that catches. **2.** a baseball player behind the batter and home base to catch the pitched ball.
—[名] 1. 잡는 사람(물건) 2. 포수, 캐처

catch·ing [kǽtʃiŋ] *adj.* **1.** liable to spread from one to another. **2.** attractive.
—[形] 1. 전염하기 쉬운 2. 매혹적인

catch·up [kǽtʃəp, +*U.S.* kétʃ-] *n.* =ketchup, catsup.

catch·word [kǽtʃwə:*rd*] *n.* [C] **1.** a slogan. **2.** a word printed at the top of a page in a dictionary.
—[名] 1. 표어, 슬로우건 2. [사전 따위의] 난외(欄外) 표제어

catch·y [kǽtʃi] *adj.* (**catch·i·er, catch·i·est**) **1.** easily remembered. **2.** tricky.
—[形] 1. 외기 쉬운 2. 걸려들기 쉬운

cat·e·chism [kǽtikìz(ə)m] *n.* [C] **1.** an elementary book used for teaching Christian doctrine. **2.** a set of questions and answers about a subject, esp. religion.
—[名] 1. [기독교] 교리 문답서 2. [일반적으로] 종교 문답집

cat·e·chize [kǽtikàiz] *vt.* **1.** instruct by questions and answers. **2.** question searchingly or excessively.
—[他] 1. [교리]를 문답으로 가르치다 2. …을 신문하다

cat·e·gor·i·cal [kæ̀tigɔ́(:)rik(ə)l, +*U.S.* -gɑ́r-] *adj.* **1.** of or in a category. **2.** absolute; positive and definite. ▷**cat·e·gor·i·cal·ly** [-i] *adv.*
—[形] 1. 범주에 속하는 2. 절대적인; 명백한

cat·e·go·ry [kǽtigɔ̀:ri / -gə] *n.* [C] (pl. **-ries**) **1.** (*Logic*) any of the basic concepts into which all knowledge can be classified. **2.** a class; a division.
—[名] 1. ⦅論⦆ 범주 2. 종류, 부류

ca·ter [kéitə*r*] *vi.* **1.** provide food, supplies, etc. ⦅~ *for* something⦆ **2.** provide means of pleasure; satisfy a need or taste. ⦅~ *for* something; ~ *to* someone⦆
—[自] 1. 음식(보급)을 공급하다 2. 기쁘게 하다; 요구·기호 따위를 만족시키다

ca·ter·er [kéitərə*r*] *n.* [C] a person who caters.
—[名] 음식 조달자(공급자)

•**cat·er·pil·lar** [kǽtə*r*pìlə*r*] *n.* [C] a worm with many legs which later changes into a butterfly or moth.
—[名] 나비·나방의 유충

cat·er·waul [kǽtə*r*wɔ̀:l] *vi.* cry like a cat in mating season. **—*n.*** [C] such a cry.
—[自] [고양이가] 야옹야옹 울다 —[名] 야옹야옹 우는 소리

cat·fish [kǽtfìʃ] *n.* [C] (pl. **-fish**) a scaleless fish having some fancied resemblance to a cat.
—[名] 메기

cat·gut [kǽtgʌ̀t] *n.* [U] a strong string, used for musical instruments, etc.
—[名] [현악기의] 장선(腸線)

ca·thar·tic [kəθɑ́:*r*tik] *n.* [C] a strong medicine used for emptying out the bowels. **—*adj.*** emptying out the bowels; purgative.
—[名] 하제(下劑) —[形] 하제의

Ca·thay [kæθéi] *n.* (*poetic* or *archaic*) China.
—[名] ⦅古·詩⦆ 중국

⁑**ca·the·dral** [kəθí:drəl] *n.* [C] a large or important church presided over by a bishop.
—[名] [bishop이 있는] 대성당

Cath·e·rine [kǽθ(ə)rin] *n.* a woman's name.
—[名] 여자 이름

⁑**cath·o·lic** [kǽθəlik] *adj.* universal; general; having a broad mind.
—[形] 보편적인; 마음이 넓은

⁑**Cath·o·lic** [kǽθəlik] *adj.* **1.** of the Christian church led by the Pope; Roman Catholic. **2.** of the orthodox Christian churches, different from Reformed or Protestant churches. **—*n.*** [C] a member of a Catholic church.
—[形] 1. [교황이 통치하는] 그리스도 교회의, 로마 가톨릭 교회의 2. 구교의 —[名] [로마] 가톨릭 교도; 구교도

Ca·thol·i·cism [kəθɑ́lisìz(ə)m / -θɔ́l-] *n.* [U] the faith, doctrine, and system of the Roman Catholic Church.
—[名] [로마] 카톨릭교의 신앙·교리 조직

cath·o·lic·i·ty [kæ̀θəlísiti] *n.* [U] the quality of being universal; the quality of having a wide mind.
—[名] 보편성; 너그러움, 포용성

Cath·y [kǽθi] *n.* a nickname for Catherine.
—[名] Catherine의 애칭

cat·like [kǽtlàik] *adj.* like a cat; secret.
—[形] 고양이 같은; 발소리를 죽인

cat·kin [kǽtkin] *n.* [C] a kind of hanging flower, as of the willow.
—[名] [버들 따위의] 개지

cat-o'-nine-tails [kæ̀tənáintèilz / kǽt-] *n.* [C] (pl. **-tails**) a whip with nine tied cords fastened to a handle.
—[名] 아홉 개의 끈을 자루에 맨 채찍

cat's-meat [kǽtsmìːt] *n.* [U] meat for a cat; poor meat. —[名] 고양이 먹이; 맛없는 고기

cat's-paw, cats·paw [kǽtspɔ̀ː] *n.* [C] a person used as a tool by another. —[名] 앞잡이, 끄나불(원숭이에게 속은 고양이의 옛이야기에서)

make a cat's-paw of, use (someone) as a tool. [熟] …을 앞잡이로 부리다

cat·sup [kǽtsəp, kétʃəp] *n.* [U] catchup; ketchup. —[名] 케첩

⁑**cat·tle** [kǽtl] *n.* 《*collectively*, used as *pl.*》 **1.** cows; bulls; oxen. **2.** domestic animals. **3.** worthless people. —[名] 1. 축우(畜牛) 2. 가축 3. [사람을 경멸하여] 짐승들

cat·ty [kǽti] *adj.* (**-ti·er, -ti·est**) **1.** sly; cunning. **2.** like a cat. —[形] 1. 교활한; 음험한 2. 고양이 같은

Cau·ca·sian [kɔːkéiʒən, -ʃən / -zjən, -ziən] *adj.* **1.** of the Caucasus or its inhabitants. **2.** of the white race. —[形] 1. 코오카서스 지방(사람)의 2. 백인의

—*n.* [C] **1.** a native of the Caucasus. **2.** a white person. —[名] 1. 코오카서스인 2. 백인

cau·cus [kɔ́ːkəs] *n.* [C] (*U.S.*) a meeting of leaders of a political party. —[名] 《美》 [정당의] 비공식 간부회 —*vi.* hold a caucus. —[自] 간부회를 열다

cau·dal [kɔ́ːdl] *adj.* of or near the tail; like a tail. —[形] 꼬리의; 꼬리 비슷한

C

⁑**caught** [kɔ́ːt] *vt.* pt. and pp. of **catch**.

caul·dron [kɔ́ːldr(ə)n] *n.* =caldron.

cau·li·flow·er [kɔ́ːliflàuər / kɔ́liflàuə] *n.* [C][U] a kind of cabbage having a head with large white flowers, used as a vegetable. —[名] 꽃양배추

caulk [kɔːk] *vt.* =calk.

caus·al [kɔ́ːz(ə)l] *adj.* **1.** of a cause. **2.** expressing a cause or reason. ▷**caus·al·ly** [-i] *adv.* —[形] 1. 원인의 2. 원인을 나타내는

cau·sal·i·ty [kɔːzǽliti] *n.* [U] the relation of cause and effect. —[名] 인과관계

cau·sa·tion [kɔːzéiʃ(ə)n] *n.* [U] **1.** the relation of cause and effect. **2.** a cause. —[名] 1. 인과관계 2. 원인

caus·a·tive [kɔ́ːzətiv] *adj.* acting as a cause 《~ *of*》; productive. —[形] 원인이 되는

⁑**cause** [kɔːz] *n.* **1.** [U][C] anything that produces an effect or a result. ↔effect ¶*the ~ of the fire* / *~ and effect.*① **2.** [U] reason; motive. ¶*There is no ~ for anxiety.* **3.** [C] a great enterprise, movement, principle, or aim. ¶*the Socialist ~.* **4.** [C] (*Law*) a case to be decided by the court; a suit. —[名] 1. 원인 ¶①원인과 결과 2. 이유; 동기 3. 주의(主義); 목적; 운동 4. 《法》 소송[사건]

in the cause of, in order to; for the purpose of. [熟] …때문에

—*vt.* be the cause of (something); make (something) happen. 《~ someone or something *to do*》 ¶*The fire caused much damage.*② / *The rain caused the river to overflow.*③ —[他] …의 원인이 되다; …에게 …시키다 ¶②화재가 큰 손해를 가져왔다/③비 때문에 강이 넘쳤다

cause·less [kɔ́ːzlis] *adj.* **1.** having no apparent cause. **2.** without proper reason. ¶*~ anger.* **3.** happening by chance. —[形] 1. 뚜렷한 이유가 없는 2. 까닭없는 3. 우연의

cause·way [kɔ́ːzwèi] *n.* [C] **1.** a raised road or path across low or wet ground. **2.** a paved road. —[名] 1. 방죽길, 둑길 2. 포장도로

caus·tic [kɔ́ːstik / kɔ́(ː)s-] *adj.* **1.** having the power of burning or destroying flesh by chemical action. **2.** sharp; bitter. ¶*a ~ tongue.*① —*n.* [C] a caustic substance. —[形] 1. 부식성(腐蝕性)의 2. [풍자·비평이] 신랄한 ¶①독설 —[名] 부식제

cau·ter·ize [kɔ́ːtəràiz] *vt.* burn (a wound, etc.) with a hot iron or needle, or with a caustic substance. —[他] [가열한 바늘·부식제 따위로 상처]를 지지다

***cau·tion** [kɔ́ːʃ(ə)n] *n.* [U] **1.** carefulness. **2.** [C] a warning or advice. —[名] 1. 조심 2. 경고

1) ***by way of caution,*** as a warning.
2) ***with caution,*** carefully.

[熟] 1)경고로서 2)조심하여, 신중하게

—*vt.* give a caution to (someone); warn; advise. 《~ someone *against*; ~ someone *not to do*》 ¶*He cautioned me not to be late again.* —[他] …에게 조심시키다; 경고하다

cau·tion·ar·y [kɔ́ːʃ(ə)nèri / -əri] *adj.* warning; urging caution. —[形] 경계의; 경고하는

***cau·tious** [kɔ́ːʃəs] *adj.* very careful. ↔careless ¶*Be ~ not to do such a thing again.* ▷**cau·tious·ness** [-nis] *n.* —[形] 신중한; 조심성 깊은

***cau·tious·ly** [kɔ́ːʃəsli] *adv.* very carefully. —[副] 조심스럽게, 신중하게

cav·al·cade [kæ̀v(ə)lkéid, +*U.S.* ⌐–⌐] *n.* [C] **1.** a long line of moving people riding on horses or in carriages. **2.** a line of people or things. —[名] 1. 기마(마차) 행렬 2. 행렬

cav·a·lier [kæ̀vəlíər] *n.* [C] **1.** a knight; a soldier on a horse. **2.** a brave and polite gentleman; an escort for a lady. —*adj.* **1.** very proud. **2.** free and easy. —[名] 1. 기사(騎士) 2. 예의바른 신사; 부인을 호위하는 사람 —[形] 1. 기사연하는, 우쭐해하는 2. 태평한

cav·al·ry [kǽv(ə)lri] *n.* ⓒ (*pl.* **-ries**) **1.** ((*collectively*, usu. used as *pl.*)) soldiers on horses. **2.** a branch of the armed forces equipped with horses or, now, armed motor vehicles.
—ⓝ **1.** 기병대 **2.** 기갑부대

cav·al·ry·man [kǽvəlrimən, -mæ̀n] *n.* ⓒ (*pl.* **-men** [-mən, -mèn]) a member of a force of soldiers on horses.
—ⓝ 기병

: cave [keiv] *n.* ⓒ a large hole under the ground or in a cliff. —*vi.* fall down; collapse.
cave in, fall in; collapse.
—ⓝ 동굴 —ⓥ 빠지다, 함몰하다

圖 함몰하다(시키다)

cave dweller [⌣⌣] *n.* a cave man.
—ⓝ 혈거인(穴居人)

cave man [⌣⌣] *n.* **1.** a human being who lived in a cave before history began. **2.** (*colloq.*) a rude man.
—ⓝ **1.** [유사(有史) 이전의] 혈거인 **2.** 난폭한 사람

* **cav·ern** [kǽvərn] *n.* ⓒ a large cave.
—ⓝ 동료

cav·ern·ous [kǽvərnəs] *adj.* like a large cave.
—ⓐ 동료 같은

cav·i·ar, -are [kǽviɑ̀ːr, ⌣⌣⌣ / ⌣⌣⌣, ⌣⌣⌣] *n.* Ⓤ the salted eggs of large fish.
—ⓝ 캐비아[철갑상어의 알젓]

cav·il [kǽvil] *vi.* (**-iled, -il·ing** or *Brit.* **-illed, -il·ling**) find fault; blame. ((~ *at* or *about* something)) —*n.* ⓒ a small objection.
—ⓥ 트집잡다, 흠잡다 —ⓝ 트집, 헐뜯기

cav·i·ty [kǽviti] *n.* ⓒ (*pl.* **-ties**) a hole. ¶ *a ~ in a tooth.*① / *the mouth ~.*②
—ⓝ 공동(空洞), 움푹한 곳 ¶ ①충치 구멍 / ②구강(口腔)

ca·vort [kəvɔ́ːrt] *vi.* (*U. S. colloq.*) (usu. of a horse) jump around.
—ⓥ (美口) [말이] 날뛰다

caw [kɔː] *n.* ⓒ the cry of a crow. —*vi.* make this cry or similar sound.
—ⓝ 까마귀 울음소리 —ⓥ 까악까악 울다

cay·enne [keién] *n.* Ⓤ a kind of pepper.
—ⓝ 고추

* **cease** [siːs] *vi., vt.* come to an end; stop. ((~ [*from*] *doing*; ~ *to do*))
—ⓥⓥ 그치다, 그만두다; 끝나다; 중지하다

cease-fire [síːsfàiər] *n.* ⓒ a stop of fighting for a time.
—ⓝ 휴전

: cease·less [síːslis] *adj.* never ending; going on without a stop.
—ⓐ 끊임없는

cease·less·ly [síːslisli] *adv.* without stopping; constantly.
—ⓐⓓ 끊임없이

Cec·il [sés(i)l / sésl, sís(i)l] *n.* a man's name.
—ⓝ 남자 이름

* **ce·dar** [síːdər] *n.* ⓒ a tree with green leaves all the year.
—ⓝ 히말라야 삼목(杉木)

cede [siːd] *vt.* **1.** give up. ((~ *to* another)) ↔keep **2.** give way to force; surrender.
—ⓥ **1.** [권리·영토 따위]를 양도하다 **2.** …에게 양보하다

ce·dil·la [sidílə] *n.* ⓒ a mark [,] placed under *c* as a sign that it is sounded as [s].
—ⓝ ç처럼 C자 밑에 붙여 [s]음을 나타내는 기호

: ceil·ing [síːliŋ] *n.* ⓒ **1.** the inside top roof of a room, opposite to the floor. **2.** (*U.S.*) a top limit set for prices, wages, etc. **3.** the highest place to which an airplane or airship can rise under certain conditions.
—ⓝ **1.** 천장(반자) **2.** [가격·임금 따위]의 최고한도 **3.** 상승한도

cel·an·dine [sélədàin] *n.* ⓒ a kind of yellow spring field flower.
—ⓝ 애기똥풀

: cel·e·brate [sélibrèit] *vt., vi.* **1.** perform a ceremony for (a person or event). ¶ ~ *Christmas.* **2.** praise; honor. ¶ ~ *a brave soldier in a song.* ⌜*for*⌝
—ⓥⓥ **1.** […을 위해] 의식·축전을 거행하다, [식을 올려] …을 축하하다 **2.** 칭찬하다

* **cel·e·brat·ed** [sélibrèitid] *adj.* famous; well-known. ((~
—ⓐ 유명한; 세상에 알려진

* **cel·e·bra·tion** [sèlibréiʃ(ə)n] *n.* ⓒⓤ the act of showing that an event or time is important. ¶ *hold a ~.*
in celebration of, in honor of (an event).
—ⓝ 축하; 축전, 의식

圖 …을 축하하여, 기념하여

ce·leb·ri·ty [silébriti] *n.* (*pl.* **-ties**) **1.** Ⓤ fame. **2.** ⓒ a famous person.
—ⓝ **1.** 명성 **2.** 명사(名士)

ce·ler·i·ty [silériti] *n.* Ⓤ the quality of being quick; speed.
—ⓝ 민첩, 날램

cel·er·y [séləri] *n.* Ⓤ a vegetable, used raw for salads.
—ⓝ 셀러리(미나리과에 속하는 야채)

ce·les·tial [siléstʃəl / -tjəl] *adj.* **1.** of the heavens; of the sky. ¶ ~ *body.*① **2.** of or coming from heaven; very beautiful. ¶ *a ~ music.* **ce·les·tial·ly** [-i] *adv.*
—ⓐ **1.** 천국의, 하늘의 ¶ ①천체 **2.** 거룩한, 거룩할 정도로 아름다운

cel·i·ba·cy [sélibəsi] *n.* Ⓤ the unmarried state.
—ⓝ 독신[생활]

: cell [sel] *n.* ⓒ **1.** a small room in a large building, such as a prison, etc.; a small hut. **2.** a very small hollow, as of a nest of a bee. **3.** (*Electricity*) a box containing materials for producing electricity. **4.** (*Biology*) a very small unit of living things. **5.** a small political group.
—ⓝ **1.** [수도원의] 암자; [교도소의] 독방; 작은 방 **2.** [벌집의] 구멍 **3.** (電) 전지 **4.** (生) 세포 **5.** [정치 단체의] 세포

‡**cel·lar** [sélər] *n.* [C] **1.** a room under the ground of a building. **2.** a stock of wines. ¶*keep a good ~.*
—[名] 1. 지하 저장실, 지하실 2. 저장된 포도주

cel·list, 'cel·list [tʃélist] *n.* [C] a person who plays the cello.
—[名] 첼로 연주가

cel·lo, 'cel·lo [tʃélou] *n.* [C] (pl. **-los**) a musical instrument like a violin, but larger and deeper in tone. ⇒[N.B.]
—[名] 첼로 [N.B.] violoncello의 준말

cel·lo·phane [séləfèin] *n.* [U] a clear, paper-like material, used to wrap food, tobacco, etc. ¶*wrapped in ~.*①
—[名] 셀로판 ¶①가까이하기 어려운

cel·lu·lar [séljulər] *adj.* of or like a cell.
—[形] 세포[모양]의

cel·lule [sélju:l] *n.* [C] a very small cell.
—[名] 작은 세포

cel·lu·loid [séluləid / sélju-] *n.* [U] a material which looks like glass, but that can be bent and that burns easily.
—[名] 셀룰로이드

cel·lu·lose [séljulòus] *n.* [U] the substance forming the chief part of all plants and trees.
—[名] 셀룰로오즈, 섬유소

ce·ment** [simént] *n.* [U] **1.** a gray powder used for joining bricks, making concrete, etc. **2.** anything used to bind or unite things together. **3.** something which holds firm. **—*vt., vi. **1.** join with cement. **2.** unite; make solid. ¶*~ a friendship.*
—[名] 1. 시멘트 2. 접착제 3. [친구간의] 유대, 기반(羈絆) —[他][自] 1. 시멘트로 굳히다(를 바르다) 2. 결합되다; [우정 따위를] 굳히다

***cem·e·ter·y** [sémitèri / -tri] *n.* [C] (pl. **-ter·ies**) a place for burying the dead that is not next to a church.
—[名] [교회에 부속되지 않은] 묘지, 공동묘지

cen·o·taph [sénətæf / -tà:f] *n.* [C] a monument built in memory of a dead person whose body is buried somewhere else.
—[名] 기념비

cen·ser [sénsər] *n.* [C] a hanging pot in which sweet-smelling powder is burned.
—[名] 향로(香爐)

cen·sor [sénsər] *n.* [C] **1.** a person who examines books, news reports, movies, etc. to remove or prohibit anything considered unsuitable. ¶*a film ~.*① **2.** a Roman officer who controlled the manners or morals of citizens. **3.** a person who tells others how they ought to behave. **4.** a person who finds fault.
—[名] 1. [출판물·영화 따위의] 검열관 ¶①영화 검열관 2. 고대 로마의 감찰관 3. 풍기 단속반원; [대학의] 학생감 4. 남의 허물만 찾는 사람, 잔소리꾼

—*vt.* examine (letters, books, etc.).
—[他] …을 검열하다

cen·so·ri·ous [sensɔ́:riəs] *adj.* severely critical; fond of finding fault.
—[形] 비평적인; 잔소리 심한, 비평을 잘하는

cen·sor·ship [sénsərʃìp] *n.* [U] **1.** the act or system of censoring. **2.** the work or position of a censor.
—[名] 1. 검열[제도] 2. 검열관의 직무(지위)

cen·sure [sénʃər] *n.* [U][C] blame; severe judgment. ¶*a vote of ~.*① **—*vt.*** blame; find fault with. 《~ someone *for*》
—[名] 비난; 혹평 ¶①불신임 결의 —[他] …을 나무라다; …의 허물을 찾다, …을 혹평하다

cen·sus [sénsəs] *n.* [C] an official count of the population of a country, etc. ¶*take a ~ of unemployment.*①
—[名] 국세 조사, 인구 조사 ¶①실업자 조사를 하다

‡**cent** [sent] *n.* **1.** [C] the hundredth part of the U.S. dollar; a copper coin with that value. **2.** [U] a hundred.
—[名] 1. 센트; 1센트 주화 2. [단위로서] 100

cen·taur [séntɔ:r] *n.* [C] (in Greek mythology) an animal having the head, breast, and arms of a man, and the body and legs of a horse. ⇒fig.
—[名] 켄타우루스(상반신은 사람, 하반신은 말의 몸을 가진 괴물)

[centaur]

cen·te·nar·i·an [sèntinέəriən] *n.* [C] a person who is at least 100 years old. **—*adj.*** of 100 years.
—[名] 백세[이상]된 사람 —[形] 백세[이상]의

cen·te·nar·y [séntənèri, senténəri / sentí:nəri] *n.* [C] (pl. **-nar·ies**) **1.** a period of 100 years; a century. **2.** a 100th return of a certain date. **—*adj.*** of a centenary.
—[名] 1. 백년[간]; 1세기 2. 백년제 —[形] 백년[째]의; 백년제의

cen·ten·ni·al [senténiəl] *adj.* **1.** of 100 years. **2.** of the 100th return of a certain date. **—*n.*** [C] a 100th return of a certain date.
—[形] 1. 백년의 2. 백년제(째)의 —[名] 백년제

‡**cen·ter,** *Brit.* **-tre** [séntər] *n.* [C] **1.** 《usu. *the ~*》 the middle part or point. ¶*the ~ of a circle / the ~ of the town.* **2.** the point, object, or place about which things gather or to which they come. ¶*a ~ of trade*① / *an*
—[名] 1. 중앙, 중심 2. 중심지 ¶①무역의 중심/②오락가 3. [축구·농구 따위의] 센터

centerpiece

amusement ~ ② / *a shopping ~*. **3.** a person who takes the middle position of the forward line in many athletic games, such as football and basketball.
— *vt.* **1.** place (something) in or on a center. ¶*She centered the clock on the desk.* **2.** collect (things) to or around a center. — *vi.* be in or at the center; gather or come, as toward a center. 《~ *on* (or *around*, *in*) something》 ¶*Our thoughts ~ upon one idea.*②

—⑮ 1. …을 중심에 두다 2. …을 중심에 모으다 —⑯ 중심에 있다, 집중하다 ¶③우리의 생각은 하나의 사상으로 집중된다

cen·ter·piece [séntərpìːs] *n.* ⓒ a beautiful piece of silver, glass, lace, etc. put in the center of a table.

—⑯ [테이블의] 중앙 장식

cen·ti- [sénti-] a word element meaning *100* or a *100th part*.

—「100」「1/100」을 나타내는 연결형

cen·ti·are [séntièər / -àː] *n.* ⓒ one square meter.

—⑯ 1평방미터

cen·ti·grade [séntigrèid] *adj.* **1.** divided into 100 degrees. **2.** of a centigrade thermometer. ⇒N.B.

—⑯ 1. 백분도(百分度)의 2. 섭씨의 N.B. C.,c.,cent.로 줄임

cen·ti·gram, *Brit.* **-gramme** [séntigræm] *n.* ⓒ a 100th part of a gram. ⇒N.B.

—⑯ 센티그람, 1/100그람 N.B. cg.으로 줄임

cen·ti·me·ter, *Brit.* **-tre** [séntimìːtər] *n.* ⓒ a 100th part of a meter.

—⑯ 센티미터 N.B. cm,cm.로 줄임

cen·ti·pede [séntipìːd] *n.* ⓒ a small animal like a worm, with many pairs of legs.

—⑯ 지네

‡**cen·tral** [séntr(ə)l] *adj.* **1.** of the center. ¶*the ~ Government.*① **2.** principal; chief. ¶*the ~ figure in a drama.*② —*n.* ⓒ 《often C-》 《*U.S.*》 a telephone exchange. ¶*get ~.*③

—⑯ 1. 중심의,중앙의 ¶①중앙 정부 2. 주요한 ¶②극의 중심 인물 —⑯ 《美》전화 교환국 ¶③교환국을 불러내다

Central America [≤−≤−−] *n.* the part of North America between Mexico and South America.

—⑯ 중앙 아메리카, 중미

central heating [≤− ≤−] *n.* a system used for heating all parts of a building by carrying hot steam, water, or air from a central place.

—⑯ 중앙 난방

cen·tral·ism [séntrəlìz(ə)m] *n.* Ⓤ a system of bringing power or authority under the central government.

—⑯ 중앙 집권제(주의)

cen·tral·i·za·tion [sèntrəlizéiʃ(ə)n / -lai-] *n.* Ⓤ **1.** the act of bringing things to a center. **2.** the act of bringing power or authority to the central government.

—⑯ 1. 집중 2. 중앙 집권화

cen·tral·ize [séntrəlàiz] *vt.* **1.** bring (things) to a center; gather together. **2.** bring (things) under one control.

—⑯ 1. …을 집중시키다 2. …을 중앙 집권화로 하다

cen·tral·ized [séntrəlàizd] *adj.* brought to a center or under one control.

—⑯ 집중(중앙 집권)의

cen·tral·ly [séntrəli] *adv.* at or near the center.

—⑯ 중심으로; 중앙에

‡**cen·tre** [séntər] *n., v.* 《*Brit.*》=center.
‡**cen·tre·piece** [séntərpìːs] *n.* 《*Brit.*》=centerpiece.
cen·tric [séntrik], **-tri·cal** [-trik(ə)l] *adj.* central.

—⑯ 중앙의

cen·trif·u·gal [sentrífjug(ə)l] *adj.* **1.** having a tendency away from the center. ¶*~ force.*① **2.** making use of this force. ↔centripetal ▷**cen·trif·u·gal·ly** [-gəli] *adv.*

—⑯ 1. 중심을 떠나려고 하는; 원심성(遠心性)의 ¶①원심력 2. 원심력을 이용한

cen·trip·e·tal [sentrípitl] *adj.* **1.** having a tendency to the center. **2.** making use of this force. ↔centrifugal

—⑯ 1. 중심으로 향하는, 구심성(求心性)의 2. 구심력을 이용한

‡**cen·tu·ry** [séntʃuri] *n.* ⓒ (pl. **-ries**) **1.** 100 years. **2.** one of the units of 100 years before or after the birth of Christ. ¶*the 20th ~.*

—⑯ 1. 백년 2. 1세기

ce·phal·ic [seffælik / ke-] *adj.* of the head.

—⑯ 머리의,두부의

ce·ram·ic [sirǽmik] *adj.* of products made from clay, like pottery; of the art of making such products. ⇒N.B. ¶*the ~ industry.*①

—⑯ 질그릇의,제도술(製陶術)의 N.B. Keramic으로도 씀 ¶①요업(窯業)

ce·ram·ics [sirǽmiks] *n. pl.* **1.** 《used as *sing.*》 the art of making pottery, etc. **2.** articles made of clay, pottery, etc.

—⑯ 1. 제도술, 요업 2. 질그릇, 도기

• **ce·re·al** [síəriəl] *n.* 《usu. *pl.*》 **1.** a grain used for food, such as rice and corn. **2.** any plant that produces a grain used for human food. **3.** Ⓤ 《*U.S.*》 food made from grain, esp. a breakfast food.

—⑯ 1. [쌀·옥수수 따위의] 곡류, 곡물 2. 곡류 식물 3. [oatmeal, cornflakes 따위] 곡류로 된 조반

cer·e·bel·la [sèribélə] *n. pl.* of **cerebellum**.
cer·e·bel·lum [sèribéləm] *n.* ⓒ (pl. **-lums** or **-la**) 《*Anatomy*》 the small back part of the brain.

—⑯ 소뇌(小腦)

cer·e·bra [séribrə] *n. pl.* of **cerebrum**.

cerebral

cer·e·bral [séribr(ə)l] *adj.* (*Anatomy*) of the brain. —형 대뇌(大腦)의, 뇌의
cer·e·brum [séribrəm] *n.* ⓒ (*pl.* **-brums** or **-bra**) (*Anatomy*) the upper, front, and largest part of the brain. —명 대뇌
cer·e·mo·ni·al [sèrimóuniəl] *adj.* **1.** of ceremony. **2.** formal; used in a ceremony. ¶ *~ costumes.* —*n.* ⓒ **1.** a system or rules of ceremony. **2.** a formality, esp. of etiquette; the observance of ceremony. 「manner.
—형 1.의식(儀式)의 2.정식의 —명 1.의식 2.정식,예식
cer·e·mo·ni·al·ly [sèrimóuniəli] *adv.* in a ceremonial
cer·e·mo·ni·ous [sèrimóuniəs] *adj.* full of ceremony; formally polite; stiff. 「ous manner.
—형 의례적으로, 예의상
—형 의식적인, 엄숙한; 딱딱할 정도로 예의바른, 격식을 차리는
cer·e·mo·ni·ous·ly [sèrimóuniəsli] *adv.* in a ceremoni-
—문 예의바르게, 격식을 차려
* **cer·e·mo·ny** [sérimòuni / -mə-] *n.* (*pl.* **-nies**) **1.** ⓒ (often *pl.*) the solemn show that goes with a religious or important public event. ¶ *a wedding ~ | perform a ~.*① **2.** Ⓤ very polite conduct; manners. ¶ *He opened the show with great ~.* **3.** Ⓤ an empty formality.
—명 1.의식 ¶①식을 거행하다 2.예의, 예식 3.격식

 1) *a master of ceremonies,* a person who sees that a program is carried through in an orderly way. ⇒Ⓝ.Ⓑ.
 2) *stand on* (or *upon*) *ceremony,* be very formal; be too polite. 「ture.
圖 1)사회자 Ⓝ.Ⓑ. 이런 의미로 쓰일 때는 M.C. [émsí:]로 줄임 2)격식(형식)을 차리다

Cer·es [síəri:z] *n.* the ancient Roman goddess of agricul-
—명 곡물의 여신
ce·rise [sərí:z, -rí:s] *adj.* of a cherry-red color. —*n.* Ⓤ cherry-red; a light, clear red.
—형 버찌 빛깔의 —명 담홍색

: **cer·tain** [sə́:rt(i)n] *adj.* **1.** beyond doubt or question; (of the future) true. ¶ *a ~ fact | There is no ~ cure for this disease.* **2.** (as *predicative*) not doubtful; sure. ¶ *Are you ~ that your answer is right? | He is ~ to come.*① **3.** sure to come or to happen; inevitable. ¶ *Death is ~.* **4.** (as *attributive*) definite but not named or described. ⇒ⓊⓈⒶⒼⒺ ¶ *a ~ person | a ~ John Miles*② *| at a ~ place.* **5.** (as *attributive*) some; not much. ¶ *to a ~ extent.*③ *| There is a ~ charm about him.*
—형 1.확실한 2.확신하고 있는 ¶①그는 꼭 올 겁니다 3.[장래] 피할 수 없는 4.일정한, 어떤, 어느 Ⓤ.Ⓢ.Ⓐ.Ⓖ.Ⓔ. 말하는 사람이 알고는 있으나 입밖에 내기를 꺼릴 때 씀 ¶②존 마일스인가 하는 사람 5.상당한, 다소의 ¶③어느 정도

 1) *for certain,* without doubt; surely. 「sure.
 2) *make certain of* (or *that*), find out and become
圖 1)확실히 2)…을 확인하다
: **cer·tain·ly** [sə́:rt(i)nli] *adv.* **1.** surely; without fail; without doubt. ¶ *He will ~ come.* **2.** (in answer to questions) yes, of course. ¶ *" May I take it? " " Certainly."*
—문 1.확실히; 반드시; 꼭; 의심할 여지없이 2.[대답으로서] 그렇고말고, 알았읍니다
* **cer·tain·ty** [sə́:rt(i)nti] *n.* (*pl.* **-ties**) **1.** Ⓤ the state of being sure. **2.** ⓒ something that is sure to occur. ¶ *Death and taxes are certainties.*
—명 1.확실[성] 2.확실한 것(일)

 1) *for* (or *to*) *a certainty,* surely; without doubt.
 2) *with certainty,* certainly. ¶ *I cannot say with ~ whether he is still alive.*①
圖 1)확실히, 꼭 2)확실히, 분명히 ¶①그가 아직 살아 있는지도 분명히 알 수 없다
* **cer·tif·i·cate** *n.* [sərtífikit] ⓒ a written or printed statement that declares something to be a fact. ¶ *a birth ~ | a health ~ | a teacher's ~.*
—명 증명서, 면허장

cer·ti·fi·ca·tion [sə̀:rtifikéiʃ(ə)n] *n.* Ⓤ **1.** the act of declaring the truth of something by a written statement. **2.** the state of being confirmed; assurance. **3.** a formal notice.
—명 1.증명서 교부 2.보증, 확인 3.증명[서], 검정(檢定)

cer·ti·fy [sə́:rtifài] *vt.* declare (something) true or correct, usu. in writing; approve the quality or value of (something). ((~ someone or something *as* or *for*; ~ *that...*)) ¶ *~ a check*① *| ~ it as true | The doctor certified that Mary had been vaccinated.* —*vi.* give assurance. ((~ *to* or *for* something)) ¶ *She certified to the character of her friend.*
—타 …을 증명하다, 인증(認證)하다 ¶①[은행이] 수표의 지불을 보증하다
—자 보증하다, 증인이 되다

cer·ti·tude [sə́:rtit(j)ù:d / -titjù:d] *n.* Ⓤ the state of being sure; confidence. 「sky-blue.
—명 확실[성]; 확신
ce·ru·le·an [sirú:liən, -ljən] *adj.* of a deep clear blue;
—형 하늘빛의
Cer·van·tes [sərvǽnti:z / sə:vǽntiz], **Miguel de** *n.* (1547-1616) the Spanish author who wrote *Don Quixote.*
—명 스페인의 소설가(돈키호테의 작가)
ces·sa·tion [seséiʃ(ə)n] *n.* Ⓤⓒ a stop; a pause. ¶ *~ of arms*① *| without ~.*②
—명 중지, 휴지(休止) ¶①휴전/②끊임없이

ces·sion [séʃ(ə)n] *n.* [U] [C] the act of giving up land, rights, etc. to another.
—[名] [영토의] 할양(割讓), [권리·재산의] 양도

cess·pool [séspù:l] *n.* [C] a pool or hollow for holding the dirty water which flows out of a house.
—[名] 구정물 웅덩이

Cey·lon [silán / -lɔ́n] *n.* an island country in the Indian Ocean, south of India. ⇒[N.B.]
—[名] 실론 [N.B.] 수도는 Colombo

cf. [sí:éf, kənfə́:r, +*Brit.* kəmpὲə] compare; confer.

ch., Ch. **1.** chapter. **2.** chief. **3.** church.

chafe [tʃeif] *vt., vi.* **1.** rub (the skin, etc.) to make it warm. ¶~ *cold hands.* **2.** wear or be worn away by rubbing. **3.** make or become painful by rubbing. ¶*The stiff collar chafed his neck.* **4.** make (someone) angry; irritate. ¶*A noisy baby chafes her parents.* **5.** become angry; be irritated. 《~ *at* or *under* something》 ¶~ *at the slightest delay.* **6.** (of a beast, a river, etc.) rub itself. 《~ *against* something》
—*n.* **1.** [C] a chafed place on the skin. **2.** [U] irritation.
in a chafe, in the state of nervous irritation.
—[他][自] **1.** [피부 따위를] 비벼 따뜻하게 하다 **2.** [마찰하여 …을] 닳려 없애다(없어지다), **3.** …을 쓸려 벗어지(게 하)다 **4.** …을 짜증나게 하다, 성나게 하다 **5.** 성내다, 짜증내다 **6.** [짐승이] 몸을 비벼대다; [강물이 기슭에] 부딪치다
—[名] **1.** 찰상(擦傷) **2.** 안달, 초조
[熟] 안달이 나서, 초조하여

chaff[1] [tʃæf / tʃɑ:f] *n.* [U] **1.** the outer coverings of grains, usu. separated from the seed. **2.** hay or straw cut fine for cattle. **3.** worthless matter; rubbish. ¶~ *and dust.*①
—[名] **1.** 왕겨 **2.** [마소의] 여물, 꼴 **3.** 쓸모없는 것; 쓰레기 ¶①쓰레기

chaff[2] [tʃæf / tʃɑ:f] *vt.* make fun of (someone) in a good-humored way. 《~ someone *about*》 —*n.* [U] good-natured joking or teasing; banter. ¶*be caught with* ~.①
—[他] [악의 없이] …을 희롱하다, 놀리다 —[名] 희롱, 놀림 ¶①쉽게 속아 넘어가다

chaf·fer [tʃǽfər] *vi.* bargain; argue about a price. ¶~ *away.* —*vt.* trade or deal in. —*n.* [C] bargain.
—[自] 값을 깍다, 흥정하다 —[他] …을 거래하다 —[名] 값을 깍기

chaf·finch [tʃǽfintʃ] *n.* [C] a European songbird.
—[名] 되새, 방울새

cha·grin [ʃəgrín / ʃǽgrin, ʃəgrí:n] *n.* [U] a feeling of disappointment; regret. ¶*to one's* ~.① —*vt.* 《usu. in *passive*》 cause (someone) to feel chagrin. ¶*be* (or *feel*) *chagrined at* (or *by*) *something.*②
—[名] 분함, 원통함 ¶①원통하게도 —[他] …을 분하게 하다, 원통하게 하다 ¶① …을 분해하다

‡chain [tʃein] *n.* [C] **1.** a series of links or rings joined together. **2.** 《usu. *pl.*》 bonds; imprisonment. **3.** a series of connected things or events. ¶*a* ~ *of events*① / *a* ~ *of ideas* / *a* ~ *of mountains.* **4.** a measuring instrument like a chain.
be in chains, be bound; be not free.
—*vt.* fasten (something) with a chain; restrain. ¶~ *a dog to a post.*
—[名] **1.** 사슬 **2.** 속박; 감금 **3.** 연속[한 것] ¶①잇따른 사건 **4.** 측쇄(測鎖)
[熟] 감옥에 갇혀 있다, 구속되어 있다
—[他] …을 사슬로 매다; 속박하다

chain mail [ˊ ˋ] *n.* a kind of armor made of metal rings linked together.
—[名] 쇠사슬 갑옷

chain reaction [ˊ -ˋ-] *n.* a chemical change resulting in products which themselves cause more changes, and then these changes are similarly repeated again and again.
—[名] 연쇄반응

chain smoker [ˊ ˋ-] *n.* a person who smokes continually.
—[名] 연거푸 담배를 피우는 사람

chain stitch [ˊ ˋ] *n.* a kind of ornamental sewing.
—[名] 쇠사슬 모양으로 뜨기(짜기)

chain store [ˊ ˋ] *n.* (*U.S.*) one of a group of stores owned and managed by the same company.
—[名] 《美》 연쇄점, 체인 스토어

‡chair [tʃεər] *n.* [C] **1.** a seat with four legs and a back, usu. for one person. ¶*take a* ~.① **2.** 《*the* ~》 a seat from which a professor delivers his lectures; an official office or position, esp. of a professor. **3.** [the seat of] a chairman. ¶*appeal to the* ~② / *leave the* ~③ / *take the* ~.④
—*vt.* **1.** put (someone) into a chair; seat. **2.** put (someone) in a position of authority.
—[名] **1.** 의자 ¶①착석하다 **2.** 대학의 강좌; [특히 대학 교수의] 지위 **3.** 의장, 의장석 ¶②의장의 재결을 호소하다/③토의를 끝내다, 의장석을 떠나다/④토의를 개시하다, 의장석에 앉다
—[他] **1.** …을 의자에 앉히다 **2.** …을 [권위있는] 지위에 앉히다

‡chair·man [tʃέərmən] *n.* [C] (pl. **-men** [-mən]) a person who controls a meeting; a master of ceremonies; a person at the head of a committee.
—[名] 의장; 사회자; 위원장

chair·man·ship [tʃέərmənʃìp] *n.* [U] the office or position of a chairman.
—[名] chairman의 직위(신분, 지위, 자격)

chaise [ʃeiz] *n.* [C] a light open carriage, usu. with a hood.
—[名] [4륜 또는 2륜의 여행용] 경마차

C

chal·et [ʃæléi, ʃǽli / ʃǽlei] n. ⓒ **1.** a Swiss summer hut. **2.** a cottage or house built in this style. ⇒fig.

chal·ice [tʃǽlis] n. ⓒ **1.** (*poetic*) a drinking-cup. **2.** a cup used in church services. **3.** a flower shaped like a cup.

[chalet 2.]

‡**chalk** [tʃɔːk] n. **1.** ⓤ a soft, white, natural stone. **2.** ⓒ a stick of this or of a like substance used for writing or drawing. ¶*a piece of* ~.
 1) *as like as chalk and cheese,* unlike in essentials.
 2) *by a long chalk; by [long] chalks,* (*colloq.*) by far, by much.
 —*vt.* mark, draw, or write (something) with chalk; rub or whiten (something) with chalk. ¶*They chalked*
 1) *chalk out,* plan; mark out.　　　　*the sidewalk.*
 2) *chalk up,* record; score.

chalk·y [tʃɔ́ːki] *adj.* (**chalk·i·er, chalk·i·est**) **1.** of chalk. **2.** like chalk; white as chalk.

***chal·lenge** [tʃǽlindʒ] n. ⓒ **1.** a call to fight, play a game, etc. to see which is better in strength, skill, etc. **2.** a demand to answer and explain. **3.** a guard's cry, 'Who goes there?' **4.** (*Law*) a formal objection made to a person's serving on a jury.
 —*vt.* **1.** offer to fight or contest with (someone). 《~ someone *to* a duel, game, fight; ~ someone *to do*》 **2.** call on (someone, etc.) to answer and explain; question; doubt.　《~ someone's right *to do*》¶*The sentry challenged him. / He challenged the statement.* **3.** demand (attention, etc.); claim (something) as due. ¶ ~ *attention.* **4.** (*Law*) object to (a jury, vote).

chal·leng·er [tʃǽlindʒər] n. ⓒ a person who challenges.

‡**cham·ber** [tʃéimbər] n. ⓒ **1.** a room; a bedroom. **2.** a meeting hall where a governing body meets; a government body itself; a committee with a special purpose. ¶*the Chamber of Commerce.*① **3.** (*pl.*) the [private] office of a judge or lawyer; (*Brit.*) a set of rooms used as a dwelling or as business offices. **4.** a walled or enclosed space in the body of an animal or plant; the back end of a gun or pistol.

cham·ber·lain [tʃéimbərlin] n. ⓒ **1.** a palace official; the manager of a great nobleman's house, lands, etc. **2.** a treasurer.

cham·ber·maid [tʃéimbərmèid] n. ⓒ a maid who takes care of bedrooms in a hotel or an inn.

chamber music [⌃ ⌃⌣] n. music played in a room or a small concert hall, usu. for a trio, quartet, etc.

chamber pot [⌃ ⌣] n. a pot for urine used in a bedroom.

cha·me·le·on [kəmíːliən, -ljən] n. ⓒ **1.** a small animal that changes the color of its skin according to its background. **2.** a person of changeable character or habits.

cham·ois [ʃǽmi / ʃǽmwɑː] n. **1.** ⓒ (pl. **-ois**) a small goatlike animal. **2.** ⓤ soft leather made from the skin of chamois, sheep, deer, etc.

champ [tʃæmp] *vi., vt.* **1.** (of horses) bite (food) noisily or impatiently. **2.** grind one's teeth with impatience.

cham·pagne [ʃæmpéin] n. ⓤ a high-priced white wine, first made in Champagne, France.

cham·paign [ʃæmpéin / tʃǽmpein] n. ⓒ a level, open country; a plain.

‡**cham·pi·on** [tʃǽmpiən, -pjən] n. ⓒ **1.** a person who

chalet

[186]

champion

—ⓝ **1.** 샬레이(스위스 산속의 목동의 집) **2.** 샬레이식의 집(별장)

—ⓝ **1.** 술잔 **2.** 성찬배(聖餐杯)(성찬 때 포도주를 따라 마심) **3.** 술잔 모양의 꽃

—ⓝ **1.** 백악(白堊), 호분(胡粉) **2.** 백묵, 분필

圞 1)외양은 같으나 실제는 딴판인 2) 《口》 훨씬, 월등히

—ⓥ …을 분필로 쓰다; …에 초크칠을 하다
圞 1)…을 설계하다, 계획하다 2)[득점 따위]를 기록하다
—ⓐ 백악질의; 백악같이 흰

—ⓝ **1.** 도전, 결투장 **2.** 설명의 요구 **3.** [보초의] 수하(誰何) **4.** 《法》[배심원에 대한] 기피, 거부

—ⓥ **1.** …에 도전하다, 결투를 신청하다 **2.** 누구냐고 소리쳐 묻다; …에게 설명을 요구하다; …을 의심하다 **3.** [주의 따위]를 요구하다; 당연한 것으로서 요구하다 **4.** [배심원]을 기피하다

—ⓝ 도전자; 누구냐고 묻는 사람
—ⓝ **1.** 방, 침실 **2.** 회의장, 의회; 회의소 ¶①상업 회의소 **3.** [법원의] 판사실, 변호사실; 《英》잇따라 있는 거실 (사무실) **4.** [동식물 체내의] 강(腔), 구멍; [총의] 약실(藥室)

—ⓝ **1.** 시종(侍從), 의전관, 청지기 **2.** 출납계

—ⓝ 호텔의 하녀, 여관 하녀

—ⓝ 실내악

—ⓝ 〔침실용〕 변기, 요강

—ⓝ **1.** 카멜레온(도마뱀) **2.** 변덕장이, 절조 없는 사람

—ⓝ **1.** [남 유럽·서남 아시아 산의] 알프스영양(羚羊) **2.** 새미 가죽(영양의 무두질 가죽)
—ⓥⓘ **1.** 소리내며 씹다 **2.** 이를 갈며 분해하다
—ⓝ 샴페인(고급 백포도주)

—ⓝ 평원, 평야

—ⓝ **1.** [남이나 주의·주장 따위를

defends or fights for another or for some good cause; a supporter. ¶*a ~ of the poor.* **2.** a person, animal, or thing that takes the first place in a sport or contest. **—*adj.*** **1.** having won the first place in a sport or contest. **2.** first-class; very good. **—*vt.*** fight for; defend; support.

해 싸우는] 투사, 전사; 옹호자 **2.** [경기의] 우승자, 선수권자; 최고상을 받은 사람(것)
—[形] **1.** 우승한 **2.** 일류의, 뛰어난 —[他] …을 위해서 싸우다; …을 옹호하다

cham·pi·on·ship [tʃǽmpiənʃìp, -pjən-] *n.* [C] **1.** the state of being a champion. **2.** the defense of a person or cause.

—[名] **1.** 선수권 **2.** 옹호

‡**chance** [tʃæns / tʃɑːns] *n.* **1.** [U] the cause of events for no known reason; fortune; luck; fate. ¶*Chance governs all.* **2.** [C] opportunity. ¶*a ~ to make some money.*① **3.** [U][C] possibility; probability. ¶*a good ~ of success.*② **4.** [C] a risk; a gamble.
1) ***by chance,*** by accident; not on purpose.
2) ***on the chance of*** (or ***that ...***), hoping for the possibility of (or that)...
3) ***on the off chance,*** in the very slight hope.
4) ***stand a good chance*** (=*be hopeful*) ***of** something.*
—*vi.* **1.** happen by chance. 《~ *to do*》 ¶*I chanced to meet him.* **2.** 《after *it*》 come about by accident. 《~ *that...*》 ¶*It chanced that our arrivals coincided.*③
—*vt.* take a risk of; venture to do (something). ¶*Let's ~ it.*④
chance on (or ***upon***), meet or find (someone or something) by chance; come across.

—[名] **1.** 우연[한 사건]; 운수 **2.** 좋은 기회 ¶①돈을 벌 좋은 기회 **3.** 가능성 ¶②성공할 충분한 가망 **4.** 내기, 모험
[熟] 1)우연히 2)…을 은근히 기대하여 3)가망이 극히 없는 4)가망이 충분히 있다
—[自] **1.** 우연히 …하다 **2.** 우연히 발생하다 ¶③우연히 우리의 도착은 일치했다 —[他] [모험적으로] …을 해보다 ¶④운을 하늘에 맡기고 해보다
[熟] 우연히 만나다(발견하다)

chan·cel [tʃǽns(ə)l / tʃɑ́ːn-] *n.* [C] the space about the altar of a church for the clergy and the choir.

—[名] [교회당의] 내진(內陣)(성단(聖壇)주위의 성직자·합창단을 위한 장소)

chan·cel·lor [tʃǽnsələr / tʃɑ́ːnsələ] *n.* [C] **1.** (*Brit.*) a title given to a chief minister of state. ¶*Chancellor of the Exchequer*① / *Lord Chancellor.*② **2.** (*U.S.*) a chief judge of a court of chancery. **3.** (*Brit.*) the head of a university. (cf. *U.S.* president) ⇒[N.B.] **4.** the prime minister in West Germany.

—[名] **1.** 《英》 [각 성(省)의] 대신, 장관; 고관의 칭호 ¶①재무상/②대법관 **2.** 《美》 형평법 재판소장 **3.** 《英》 대학총장 [N.B.] Chancellor는 사실상 명예직이며 실무는 Vice-Chancellor가 봄 **4.** [서독의] 수상

chan·cer·y [tʃǽns(ə)ri / tʃɑ́ːn-] *n.* [C] (pl. **-cer·ies**) **1.** (*Brit.*) a high court of law. **2.** (*U.S.*) a court of equity. **3.** an office where public records are kept.

—[名] **1.** 《英》 대법원(지금은 고등법원의 일부) **2.** 《美》 형평법 재판소 **3.** 공공기록

chan·de·lier [ʃæ̀ndilíər] *n.* [C] a branched support for lights suspended from a ceiling.

—[名] 샹들리에

chan·dler [tʃǽndlər / tʃɑ́ːndlə] *n.* [C] **1.** a maker or seller of candles. **2.** a merchant selling candles, soap, oil, etc. ¶*a ship's ~*① / *a corn ~.*②

—[名] **1.** 양초 제조(판매)업자 **2.** 잡화상, 상인 ¶①선구상(船具商)/②잡곡상

‡**change** [tʃeindʒ] *vt.* **1.** make (something) different; alter. ¶*~ one's opinion.* **2.** exchange. ¶*Shall we ~ seats?*① / *I changed seats with him.* **3.** give or get smaller money of a sum equal to (larger money); give or get another money of equal value to (one money). ¶*~ dollars into francs.*② **4.** put on (other clothes).
—*vi.* **1.** become different. 《~ *to* (or *with, into*) something》 ¶*Colors ~ if they are exposed to the sun.*③ / *Summer changed to autumn.* **2.** make an exchange. **3.** get off one train, bus, etc. and get on another. ¶*~ at Kobe* / *~ for Osaka.* **4.** put on other clothes.
1) ***change hands,*** pass from one owner to another.
2) ***change one's mind,*** change one's opinion; decide on a new plan.
—*n.* **1.** [C] the act or fact of changing. ¶*a ~ of heart.* **2.** [C] anything or any person taking the place of another; substitution. **3.** [C] a fresh set of clothing. **4.** [U] the money returned to a buyer as the difference between the price and the amount he has paid; smaller units of money. ¶*I have no ~ about me.*④
ring the changes, repeat the same thing in different ways.

—[他] **1.** …을 바꾸다 **2.** …을 교환하다 ¶①좌석을 교환할까요? **3.** …을 환전(換錢)하다 ¶②달러를 프랑으로 바꾸다 **4.** [옷]을 갈아 입다 —[自] **1.** 바뀌다, 변화하다 ¶③빛깔은 햇볕을 쬐면 변한다 **2.** 교환하다 **3.** 바꿔 타다 **4.** 갈아 입다
[熟] 1)소유주가 바뀌다 2)생각을 바꾸다
—[名] **1.** 변화, 변경, 변혁 **2.** 대용[품]; 교대 **3.** 갈아입기 **4.** 바꿀 돈, 거스름돈, 잔돈 ¶④잔돈을 가진 것이 없다
[熟] 여러가지 방법으로 해 보다

change·a·bil·i·ty [tʃèindʒəbíliti] *n.* [U] the state of being changeable.

—[名] 변하기 쉬운 성질, 불안정

⁎ **change·a·ble** [tʃéindʒəbl] *adj.* **1.** that can be changed. **2.** likely to change or vary; fickle.
—[形] 1. 변하기 쉬운 2. 가변성의

change·ful [tʃéindʒf(u)l] *adj.* variable; full of change. ▷**change·ful·ly** [-fuli] *adv.*
—[形] 변화가 풍부한; 변하기 쉬운; 바꿀 수 있는

change·less [tʃéindʒlis] *adj.* **1.** not changing; not likely to change; constant. **2.** monotonous.
—[形] 1. 변화가 없는; 일정한 2. 단조로운

⁑ **chan·nel** [tʃǽn(ə)l] *n.* [C] **1.** a passage for water; the bed of a river; a narrow stretch of sea. ¶*the English Channel.* **2.** a means or route through which anything passes and is carried. **3.** a range of wave frequencies used by a radio or television station. **4.** a hollow line cut into something. —*vt.* (**-neled, -nel·ing** or *Brit.* **-nelled, -nel·ling**) form a channel in; cut out as a channel; carry or direct through a channel.
—[名] 1. 수로(水路); 강바닥, 하상(河床); 해협 2. 경로; 수단 3. [라디오·텔레비전의] 주파수대(周波數帶), 채널 4. [문지방 따위의] 홈 —[他] …에 수로를 열다; …에 홈을 파다; …을 수로로 나르다

C

⁎ **chant** [tʃænt / tʃɑːnt] *n.* [C] **1.** a slow song, esp. used in a church service; prayer. **2.** a dull way of talking. —*vi., vt.* sing; sing as to a chant; praise in song; say or tell over and over again.
—[名] 1. 찬미가, 노래; 성가; 영창 2. 단조로운 말투
—[自][他] 노래하다; 찬미하다; [단조로운 말투로] 말하다, 되풀이하다

cha·os [kéiɑs / -ɔs] *n.* [U] **1.** the state of being infinite or formless before the world began. **2.** the state of being completely confused or in disorder.
—[名] 1. [천지 창조 이전 세계의] 혼돈 2. 무질서; 혼란[상태]

cha·ot·ic [keiɑ́tik / -ɔ́t-] *adj.* in a state of chaos; completely disordered; very confused.
—[形] 혼돈된, 무질서한

⁎ **chap**[1] [tʃæp] *n.* [C] (*colloq.*) a fellow; a man or boy.
—[名] 《口》 놈, 녀석

⁎ **chap**[2] [tʃæp] *n.* 《usu. *pl.*》 a crack in the skin caused by frost, etc. —*vi., vt.* (of the skin) crack; make or become rough.
—[名] [갈라진] 금; [살갗의] 튼 데
—[自][他] 살갗이 트(게 하)다, 금이 가(게 하)다

chap. chapter.

⁎ **chapel** [tʃǽp(ə)l] *n.* [C] **1.** a small place of worship in a cathedral. **2.** a place of worship in a school, palace, prison, etc. **3.** a service held in a chapel. **4.** (*Brit.*) a church not belonging to the Church of England or the Roman Catholic Church.
—[名] 1. [교회에 딸린] 작은 예배당 2. [학교·왕실·교도소 따위의] 예배당 3. [대학 따위의] 예배[식] 4. 《英》 [비(非) 국교도의] 교회당

chap·er·on, -one [ʃǽpəròun] *n.* [C] a married or older woman who watches over a young unmarried woman on public occasions. —*vt.* act as a chaperon to (a girl).
—[名] [미혼 여자가 사교계에 처음 나갈 때] 시중드는 부인 —[他] [젊은 여자]의 시중을 들다

chap·fall·en [tʃǽpfɔ̀ːl(ə)n] *adj.* in low spirits; sad and hopeless.
—[形] 기운없는, 풀이 죽은

chap·lain [tʃǽplin] *n.* [C] a clergyman or priest who performs religious services in the army or navy, a school, a private house, etc.
—[名] [궁정·학교·군대 따위의] 목사, 종군 목사; [교도소의] 교회사(敎誨師)

chap·let [tʃǽplit] *n.* [C] a circle of flowers, gold, etc. for the head; a string of beads.
—[名] 화관(花冠); 염주

chap·man [tʃǽpmən] *n.* [C] (pl. **-men** [-mən]) (*Brit.*) a person who buys or sells at the door.
—[名] 《英》 행상인

⁑ **chap·ter** [tʃǽptər] *n.* [C] **1.** a main division of a book. ⇨[N.B.] **2.** an important part or section of anything. **3.** a branch of a society or organization. **4.** a meeting of clergymen.
1) ***chapter and verse,*** exact authority for a statement.
2) ***a chapter of accidents,*** accident after accident.
3) ***to*** (or ***till***) ***the end of the chapter,*** for ever, throughout.
—[名] 1. [서적의] 장(章) [N.B.] chap. ch. 또는 c.로 줄임 2. [역사·인생 따위의] 한 시기, 한토막 3. [조합·정당 따위의] 지부, 분회(分會) 4. 성직자 집회
[熟] 1)정확한 출처(전거) 2)잇따른 재난(사고) 3)영구히, 최후까지

char[1] [tʃɑːr] *vt., vi.* (**charred, char·ring**) change (wood) into charcoal; burn slightly or partly.
—[他][自] 숯을 굽다, 새까맣게 타다(태우다)

char[2] [tʃɑːr] *n., v.* (*Brit.*) =chare.

⁑ **char·ac·ter** [kǽriktər] *n.* [C] **1.** [U][C] qualities that make any person or thing different from others; any distinctive mark; moral and mental nature. ¶*a man of* ~.① / *the national* ~.② **2.** [U] position; status. **3.** a person in a play or novel. ¶*the characters in the novels of Charles Dickens.* **4.** (*colloq.*) a person, esp. who does something unusual. ¶*a bad* ~ / *a historical* ~. **5.** reputation. ¶*get a good* ~. **6.** a letter given by a former employer to an employee to aid in obtaining a job; a recommendation. **7.** a figure; a sign; a letter.
—[名] 1. 특징, 품성 ¶①인격자/②국민성 2. 자격 3. [극·소설의] 인물 4. 《口》 사람; 괴짜 5. 명성, 평판 6. [전고용주가 사용인에게 주는] 인물 증명서, 추천장 7. 기호; 문자

1) ***in character,*** as expected; right; suitable.
2) ***out of character,*** not as expected; not right; not suitable.

[熟] 1)역에 말맞은,어울리는 2)역에 맞지 않는,어울리지 않는

⁑ char·ac·ter·is·tic [kæ̀riktərístik] *adj.* different from others; special. ¶*It's ~ of him.*① —*n.* [C] a special mark or quality. ¶*An elephant's trunk is its most noticeable ~.*

—[形] 특유의,독특한 ¶①그것은 그에게 특유한 것이다 —[名] 특징,특성,특질

char·ac·ter·is·ti·cal·ly [kæ̀riktərístikəli] *adv.* in a characteristic way; specially.

—[副] 특질(특성)로서,특질상

char·ac·ter·i·za·tion [kæ̀rikt(ə)rizéiʃ(ə)n / -tərai-] *n.* [U] **1.** the act of characterizing. **2.** the description of characteristics.

—[名] 1.특성 표시 2.성격 묘사

*** char·ac·ter·ize** [kǽriktəràiz] *vt.* show or describe the special qualities or features of (someone or something).

—[他] …의 특색을 나타내다;특성을 묘사하다

char·coal [tʃɑ́:rkòul] *n.* [U] wood burnt black, used as fuel.

—[名] 숯,목탄

charcoal burner [⌐- ⌐-] *n.* **1.** a person who makes charcoal. **2.** a kind of stove in which charcoal is burned.

—[名] 1.숯 굽는 사람 2.숯풍로

chard [tʃɑ:rd] *n.* [C] a variety of beet.

—[名] 《植》 근대

chare [tʃɛər] *n.* (*Brit.*) **1.** [C] a woman hired to do housework or cleaning. **2.** 《usu. *pl.*》 a part-time job, esp. of housework or cleaning. —*vi.* work at cleaning house by the day or hour. —*vt.* do (a part-time jobs, housework, etc.).

—[名] 《英》 1.[가정의] 잡역부, 빨래하는 여자 2.잡일,허드렛일 —[名] 세탁소에서 일하다 —[他] [허드렛일]을 하다

⁑ charge [tʃɑ:rdʒ] *vt.* **1.** ask (a sum of money) as a price. 《~ [someone] one dollar *for*》 ¶*That store charges $10 for gloves.* / *He charged me five dollars for mending a pair of shoes.* **2.** 《usu. in *passive*》 give (someone) a task as a duty. ¶*He was charged with an important mission.*① **3.** blame; accuse (someone) formally. 《~ someone *with*》 ¶*They charged him with reckless driving.* **4.** put into; put upon; fill. ¶*~ a storage battery*② / *~ a gun with bullets.*③ **5.** load; burden. ¶*His mind was charged with weighty matters.* **6.** command; instruct. 《~ someone *to do*》 ¶*He charged me not to forget what he said.* **7.** attack. —*vi.* **1.** demand a price. ¶*He charges too high.* **2.** attack. 《~ *on* or *at* someone or something》

—[他] 1.[대금]을 청구하다 2.[일·임무]를 지우다 ¶①그는 중요한 일을 맡았다 3.…을 비난(고발)하다 4.[물건]을 …에 채우다,…을 가득 넣다 ¶②축전지에 충전하다/③총에 탄알을 재다 5.…에 짐을 싣다, 무거운 짐을 지게 하다 6.…에 명령하다 7.…을 공격하다 —[自] 1.청구하다 2.습격하다

1) ***charge off,*** take away (some amount of money) as a loss.
2) ***charge off to,*** regard as the result of (something).
3) ***charge oneself with*** (=*hold oneself responsible for*) *something.*
4) ***charge someone with,*** accuse someone in, esp. a court of law.

[熟] 1)결손으로서 빼다 2)…의 탓으로 하다 3)…의 책임을 떠맡다 4) …을 고소하다

—*n.* **1.** [C] 《often *pl.*》 expense; fee; tax. ¶*No ~ for admission.*④ **2.** [U] load; burden. **3.** [C] a work as a duty; [U] responsibility. ¶*lay the mistake to his ~.*⑤ **4.** [U] care; management; trust. ¶*The baby is in Susie's ~.* **5.** [C] accusation. **6.** [U] command; order.

—[名] 1.비용; 세금 ¶④입장 무료 2.짐,부담 3.[의무로서의] 일; 책임 ¶⑤잘못을 그의 탓으로 하다 4.보호; 위탁 5.비난,고발 6.명령

1) ***give someone in charge,*** ⓐ entrust. ⓑ give someone up to the police.
2) ***in charge of,*** having the responsibility of.
3) ***take charge of*** (=*be responsible for*) *something.*

[熟] 1)ⓐ…을 맡기다 ⓑ[경찰에] 인도하다 2)…을 맡아보는, …담당의 3)…을 맡다,담당하다

charge·a·ble [tʃɑ́:rdʒəbl] *adj.* that may or should be charged. ¶*The expense is ~ on him.*

—[形] [죄·세금·부담·비용 따위] 져야 할,맡아야 할

charg·er [tʃɑ́:rdʒər] *n.* [C] an army officer's horse.

—[名] 군마(軍馬)

*** char·i·ot** [tʃǽriət] *n.* [C] a cart with two wheels, drawn by horses and used in war in ancient times. ⇒fig.

—[名] [고대 그리이스·로마의] 두 바퀴 전차(戰車)

(chariot)

char·i·ot·eer [tʃæ̀riətíər] *n.* [C] a person who drives a chariot.

—[名] chariot 을 모는 사람

char·i·ta·ble [tʃǽritəbl] *adj.* merciful; generous; kindly. ▷**char·i·ta·bly** [-i] *adv.*

—[形] 자비로운; 관대한

char·i·ty [tʃǽriti] *n.* **1.** Ⓤ mercy; Christian love; kindness in judging people's faults. **2.** Ⓤ a gift to the poor; the help given to the sick and the poor. **3.** (usu. *pl.*) a society for helping the sick and the poor.
—명 1.자비심; 박애; 그리스도교적인 사랑; 관용 2.자선[행위],보시(布施) 3.자선 시설(사업)

char·la·tan [ʃáːrlət(ə)n] *n.* Ⓒ a person who pretends to have more knowledge or more wonderful cures than he really has.
—명 허풍선이; 야바위꾼; 아는 체하는 사람; 돌팔이 의사

Charles [tʃɑːrlz] *n.* a man's name.
—명 남자 이름

Char·lotte [ʃáːrlət] *n.* a woman's name.
—명 여자 이름

charm [tʃɑːrm] *n.* **1.** ⓊⒸ power to attract or please; magic power. ¶*be under a* ~. **2.** (usu. *pl.*) appeal; beauty. ¶*He fell a victim to her charms.* **3.** Ⓒ a word or words having magical power. **4.** Ⓒ anything supposed to have magic power or to bring good luck.
—명 1.매력; 마력 2.애교; 아름다운 용모 3.주문(呪文) 4.부적, 호부(護符)

—*vt.* **1.** attract. **2.** give pleasure to (someone). ¶*I am charmed to meet you.* **3.** influence (something) as by magic power; protect (something) as by a spell; use magic on (something). —*vi.* be attractive.
—타 1.…을 매혹하다 2.…에 기쁨을 주다 ¶①만나서 기쁩니다 3.…에 마법을 걸다; …을 마술의 힘으로 보호하다
—자 매력이 있다

charm·er [tʃáːrmər] *n.* Ⓒ **1.** a person who charms. ¶*a snake* ~. **2.** a beautiful woman.
—명 1.마술사 ¶①뱀을 부리는 사람 2. 미녀

charm·ing [tʃáːrmin] *adj.* full of charm; attractive; delightful. ▷**charm·ing·ly** [-li] *adv.*
—형 매력이 있는; 아름다운; 즐거운

char·nel house [tʃáːrn(ə)lhàus] *n.* a place where the bodies or the bones of the dead are laid.
—명 납골당(納骨堂)(소); 묘지

* **chart** [tʃɑːrt] *n.* Ⓒ **1.** a sailor's map of the sea. **2.** a sheet giving information by means of curves, lines, etc.; a rough map; a list; a table. ¶*a weather* ~.
—*vt.* draw a chart of (something); show (something) on a chart. ▷**chart·less** [-lis] *adj.*
—명 1.해도(海圖) 2.백지도, 도표 ¶①기상도 —타 …의 해도(도표)를 만들다; …을 도표로 나타내다

* **char·ter** [tʃáːrtər] *n.* Ⓒ **1.** a formal paper of rights, permission to do something, etc. given by a ruler or government. **2.** a formal paper defining the right to organize a new organization, chapter, branch, etc. ¶*the Charter of the United Nations.* —*vt.* **1.** give a charter to (someone). **2.** hire (a ship, airplane, etc.). ¶~ *a bus.* 「chart (or charter). **2.** hired.」
—명 1.[나라의 지배자·정부가 주는] 특허장,면허장 2.헌장; [목적·강령의] 선언[서] —타 1.…에게 특허를 주다, …을 면허하다 2.…을 용선(傭船)하다; …을 대절하다

char·tered [tʃáːrtərd] *adj.* **1.** given or allowed by a
—형 1.특허를 받은,공인의 2.대절한

char·wom·an [tʃáːrwùmən] *n.* Ⓒ (pl. -wom·en [-wìmin]) a woman hired by the day for doing odd jobs in a house or public building.
—명 날품팔이 여자, 잡역부(雜役婦)

char·y [tʃέəri] *adj.* (**char·i·er, char·i·est**) **1.** careful; cautious. ¶*A burnt child is* ~ *of fire.* **2.** shy. ¶*be* ~ *of strangers.* **3.** stingy. ¶*He is* ~ *of his praise.*
—형 1.조심성 있는 2.부끄러워하는 3.인색한, 구두쇠의 ¶①그는 여간해서 칭찬을 않는다

chase¹ [tʃeis] *vt.* **1.** run after (someone or something) to catch or kill; pursue. ¶~ *a prisoner.* **2.** drive away. ¶~ *cats out of the garden* | ~ *fear from the mind.* —*vi.* follow in pursuit.
—*n.* Ⓒ **1.** an earnest pursuit. ¶*a* ~ *after a murderer.* | *in* ~ *of an animal, etc.* **2.** (usu. *the* ~) hunting as a sport; (*collectively*) hunters; a hunted animal.
give chase to, run after (someone); chase. ¶*give chase to the enemy.*
—타 1.…을 쫓다, 추적(추격)하다 ¶①죄수를 추적하다 2.…을 사냥하다; 몰아내다 ¶②공포심을 털어 없애다
—자 쫓다, 추적하다
—명 1. 추적, 추격 ¶③살인자의 추격 /④동물 따위를 쫓아서 사냥, 수렵; 사냥꾼들· 사냥할 짐승, 엽수(獵獸) ¶…을 쫓다 ¶⑤적을 쫓다

chase² [tʃeis] *vt.* ornament (metal or other hard material) by engraving or embossing.
—타 [쇠붙이]에 돋을새김을 하다; [무늬를] 양각(陽刻)하다

chas·er [tʃéisər] *n.* Ⓒ **1.** a person or thing that chases; a hunter; a pursuer. **2.** (*Military*) a small, fast airplan or ship used to pursue the enemy. **3.** a gun on a ship, used during pursuit or by another ship.
—명 1.쫓는 사람(것), 사냥군,추격자 2.추격기,추격함 3.[함선의] 추격포

chasm [kǽz(ə)m] *n.* Ⓒ **1.** a deep opening in the earth; gap. **2.** a wide difference of feelings or opinions, etc. between people or groups.
—명 1.[지면 따위의] 깊이 갈라진 틈, 간극 2.[감정·의견 따위] 차이, 격차

chas·sis [ʃǽsi(ː)] *n.* Ⓒ (pl. **chas·sis** [-si(ː)z]) **1.** the frame, wheels or machinery that supports the body of an automobile, airplane, etc. **2.** the framework in which
—명 1.[자동차의] 차대(車臺), [비행기의] 기대(機臺), 각부(脚部) 2.[라디오·빌레비전의] 샤시

chaste [tʃeist] *adj.* **1.** pure; virtuous. ↔immoral **2.** modest. **3.** simple in taste, style, etc.
chas·ten [tʃéisn] *vt.* **1.** punish (someone) in order to correct; train (someone) by pain or trials. **2.** bring (something) under control; subdue. ¶ ~ *one's passions.*① **3.** refine; purify. ▷**chas·ten·er** [-*ə*r] *n.*
chas·tise [tʃæstáiz] *vt.* **1.** correct (a child, etc.) with a rod. **2.** punish. ⌈punishment; beating.⌉
chas·tise·ment [tʃǽstizmənt, +*U. S.* tʃæstáiz-] *n.* Ⓤ Ⓒ
chas·ti·ty [tʃǽstiti] *n.* Ⓤ **1.** purity; virtue; virginity. **2.** simplicity of taste, style, etc.
* **chat** [tʃæt] *n.* Ⓒ an easy and familiar conversation; gossip. ¶*have a ~ with a friend.*① ——*vi.* (**chat·ted, chat·ting**) talk in an easy and friendly way. ¶*I chatted with a friend about the matter.*
châ·teau [ʃætóu / ʃá:tou] *n.* Ⓒ (pl. **-teaux**) a French castle or country mansion.
châ·teaux [ʃætóuz / ʃá:tou] *n.* pl. of **château**.
chat·tel [tʃǽtl] *n.* Ⓒ (usu. *pl.*) a movable possession; a piece of personal property besides houses or land. ¶*goods and chattels.*①
* **chat·ter** [tʃǽtər] *vi.* **1.** (of a person) talk fast, constantly and foolishly. **2.** (of birds, monkeys, etc.) make short, quick sounds. **3.** (of teeth, parts of a machine, etc.) make a noise by hitting each other. ¶*His teeth chattered from the cold.* ——*n.* ⒸⓊ **1.** idle, rapid talk. **2.** quick, short sounds. ⌈chatters a great deal.⌉
chat·ter·box [tʃǽtərbɑ̀ks / -tɔ̀bks] *n.* Ⓒ a person who
chat·ter·er [tʃǽtərər] *n.* Ⓒ a person who chatters.
chat·ty [tʃǽti] *adj.* (**-ti·er, -ti·est**) fond of chatting; talk·ative. ⌈poet.⌉
Chau·cer [tʃɔ́:sər], **Geoffrey** *n.* (1340?-1400) an English
chauf·feur [ʃóufə:r, ʃoufə́:r] *n.* Ⓒ a person whose work is to drive another's automobile.
chau·vin·ism [ʃóuvinìz(ə)m] *n.* Ⓤ unreasoning devotion to one's country; warlike patriotism.
chau·vin·ist [ʃóuvinist] *n.* Ⓒ an unreasoning patriot; a warlike person. ——*adj.* =chauvinistic. ⌈vinists.⌉
chau·vin·is·tic [ʃòuvinístik] *adj.* of chauvinism or chau-
Ch. E. Chemical Engineer.
: cheap [tʃi:p] *adj.* **1.** low in price; not expensive. ↔expensive; dear. ¶~ *and nasty*① / *a ~ edition.*② **2.** of poor quality; worthless; easily obtained; common. ¶*a ~ novel*③ / *make oneself* [*too*] ~④ / *Cheap clothes are useless.*
1) **dirt cheap** (or **cheap as dirt**), extremely cheap.
2) **feel cheap**, ⓐ feel ill. ⓑ feel inferior and ashamed.
3) **hold** *someone* or *something* **cheap**, put little value on someone or something; despise.
——*adv.* at a low price; cheaply. ¶*get* (or *buy*) *something* ~⑤ ⌈become cheap.⌉
cheap·en [tʃí:p(ə)n] *vt.* make (something) cheap. ——*vi.*
cheap·ly [tʃí:pli] *adv.* at a low price; in a cheap manner.
cheap·ness [tʃí:pnis] *n.* Ⓤ the state of being cheap.
* **cheat** [tʃi:t] *vt.* **1.** deceive; deprive (someone) of something by trickery. 《~ *someone* [*out*] *of something*; ~ *something out of someone*; ~ *someone into something* or *into* doing》 ¶~ *someone into the belief that* ...① / *He cheated his customers in business.* / *He cheated her out of her money.*② **2.** escape. ¶~ *the gallows.*③ ——*vi.* act dishonestly. ¶~ *on* (or *in*) *a test.*④
——*n.* Ⓒ a person who deceives another; a cheater; a dishonest trick.

——形 1. 순결한, 정숙한 2. 조심성 있는 3. [취미・문체가] 간결한
——他 1. [잘 되게 하기 위해서] …을 응징하다; …을 단련시키다 2. …을 억제하다 ¶①격정을 억제하다 3. …을 세련되게 하다, 고상하게 하다
——他 1. [아이]를 징벌하다, 때려 주다 2. …을 처벌하다
——名 징벌, 응징
——名 1. 순결, 동정(童貞), 처녀성 2. [문체・취미 따위의] 간결, 고상함
——名 잡담, 한담 ¶①친구와 잡담하다
——自 잡담하다, [한가롭게] 담소하다

——名 [프랑스의] 성, 대저택

——名 동산(動産), 가재도구 ¶①가재도구

——自 1. [사람이] 재잘재잘 지껄이다 2. [원숭이・새 따위가] 짹짹거리다, 지저귀다 3. [이・기계 따위] 달각달각 소리내다 ——名 1. 지껄임, 수다 2. 짹짹소리, 졸졸소리; 달각달각 소리
——名 수다쟁이
——名 수다 떠는 사람
——形 수다스러운, 잘 지껄이는

——名 영국의 시인
——名 자가용 운전수

——名 맹목적 애국주의, 호전적 애국주의

——名 맹목적 애국주의자, 호전적 애국주의자
——形 맹목적 애국주의[자]의
——(略) 화학 공업 기사
——形 1. 값싼, 염가의, 돈이 들지 않는 ¶①싸게 나쁘건간에/②염가판 2. 싸구려의, 보잘것 없는; 쉽게 입수되는; 값싸게 여겨지는 ¶③싸구려 소설/④자신을 얕보다, 경솔히 행동하다
(熟) 1)터무니없이 싼 2)ⓐ기분이 나쁘다 ⓑ기가 죽다, 창피하게 여기다 3) …을 얕보다

——副 싸게 ¶⑤물건을 싸게 입수하다 (사다)
——他 …을 싸게 하다, 얕보다 ——自 싸지다
——副 싸게, 쉽사리 [게 되다]
——名 염가, 값쌈
——他 1. …을 속이다, 속여 빼앗다 ¶①남을 속여 …이라고 믿게 하다/②그는 그녀에게서 돈을 속여 빼앗다 3. …을 운 좋게 면하다; [지루함 따위]를 이럭저럭 넘기다 ¶③운 좋게 교수형을 면하다 ——自 속임수를 쓰다 ¶④시험에서 부정행위를 하다

——名 사기꾼, 협잡, 사기

C

:check [tʃek] *n.* [C] **1.** a sudden stop. ¶*meet with a ~.*① **2.** any person or thing that controls or restrains. **3.** an examination to prove that something is true or correct; (*U.S.*) a mark to show that something has been examined or compared. **4.** (*U.S.*) a written order for money, drawn upon a bank. (cf. *Brit.* cheque) **5.** a checkered pattern.
—*vt.* **1.** stop or control (something) by force or suddenly. **2.** examine (something) to prove it true or correct, as by comparison. **3.** (*U.S.*) put or leave (something) in a safe place for a short time. **4.** (*U.S.*) get a ticket, a piece of wood, metal, etc. that shows one's right to receive (something). **—*vi.*** **1.** make a stop. **2.** (*U.S.*) change a check for cash.
1) ***check in,*** register one's name as a guest at a hotel.
2) ***check something off,*** mark something as having been examined or done.
3) ***check out,*** pay one's bill and leave, as from a hotel.
4) ***check up*** (or ***upon***)***,*** test; compare to prove (something) correct.

—[名] 1. 저지, 방해 ¶①방해를 만나다 2. 억제하는 사람(것·수단) 3. 검사, 대조; 대조표 4.《美》 수표 5. 격자무늬
—[他] 1. …을 저지(방해)하다 2. [대조 따위에 의해] …을 확인하다 3.《美》 물표를 받고 맡기다 4.《美》 물표(영수증)를 받고 넘겨주다
[熟] 1)소정 절차를 밟고 [호텔]에 들다 2)기입(대조)필의 표를 하다 3)[호텔에서] 셈을 치르고 나오다 4)…을 조사하다, 대조하다

check·book [tʃékbùk] *n.* [C] (*U.S.*) a book containing blank checks on a bank. (cf. *Brit.* chequebook)
—[名] 《美》 수표장

checked [tʃekt] *adj.* with a checker pattern.
—[形] 바둑판 무늬의

check·er [tʃékər] *vt.* mark (something) with small squares of different colors; mark (something) with light and shade. ¶*be checkered with sunlight and shade.*①
—*n.* [C] **1.** a pattern with squares of different colors. **2.** one of the flat, round pieces used in the game of checkers. **3.** (*U.S.*) 《*pl.* used as *sing.*》 a game played on a checkerboard. (cf. *Brit.* draughts) ⇒[N.B.]
—[他] …을 바둑판 무늬로 하다, 변화를 주다; 명암을 번갈아 배열하다 ¶①햇볕과 그늘이 격자무늬를 이루다 —[名] 1. 격자(바둑판)무늬 2. [서양 장기의] 말 3.《美》 체커 [N.B.] 12개의 말을 써서 노는 서양 장기

check·er·board [tʃékərbɔ̀:rd] *n.* [C] a board divided into 32 red squares and 32 black squares, on which the games of checkers and chess are played. ⇒[N.B.]
—[名] 체커판 [N.B.] 검정·빨강의 64개의 눈이 있으며 체커·체스 놀이에 쓰임

check·ered [tʃékərd] *adj.* **1.** of a checker pattern; checked. **2.** various; with many ups and downs. ¶*a ~ career.*
—[形] 1. 바둑판 무늬의, 알락달락한 2. 변화가 풍부한

check·list [tʃéklìst] *n.* [C] a list of things to be checked off.
—[名] 대조표

check·mate [tʃékmèit] *vt.* **1.** (in chess) put (an opponent's king) in a position from which escape is impossible. **2.** defeat completely. **—*n.*** [C] **1.** (in chess) the act of putting the opponent's king in check, thus ending the game. **2.** a complete defeat.
—[他] 1. [체스에서] 외통수로 몰다 2. 완전히 패배시키다 —[名] 1. [장기의] 외통수 2. 궁지, 대실패

check·room [tʃékrù(:)m] *n.* [C] a room where coats, hats, etc. may be left until called for later.
—[名] 휴대품 보관소

check-up [tʃékʌ̀p] *n.* (*U.S.*) [C] a careful examination; a physical examination.
—[名] 대조, 검사, 건강진단

:cheek [tʃi:k] *n.* **1.** [C] 《usu. *pl.*》 either side of the face below the eye. ¶*rosy cheeks.*① ⇒[usage] **2.** 《*pl.*》 something suggesting the human cheek in shape or position. **3.** [U] (*colloq.*) rudeness. ¶*What ~ !*② / *give someone ~.*③ / *None of your cheek !*④
1) ***cheek by jowl*** (=*close together; intimate*) ***with*** *someone.*
2) ***have the cheek to do,*** have the rudeness to do; dare to do.
3) ***tongue in cheek,*** insincerely.
—[名] 1. 뺨, 볼 ¶①장미빛의 뺨 [usage] eyes, ears처럼 보통 복수로 씀 2. [기계·도구 따위의] 볼 비슷한 부분, 측면 3.《口》 건방짐, 뻔뻔스러움 ¶②뻔뻔스럽기도 하구나! /③남에게 건방지게 대하다/④건방진 소리 마라
[熟] 1)…와 밀접하게, 다정하게 2)뻔뻔스럽게도 …하다 3)불성실한

cheek·bone [tʃí:kbòun] *n.* [C] either of the bones just below the eye.
—[名] 광대뼈

cheek·y [tʃí:ki] *adj.* (**cheek·i·er, cheek·i·est**) (*colloq.*) rude. ▷**cheek·i·ly** [-li] *adv.* —**cheek·i·ness** [-nis] *n.*
—[形] 《口》 건방진

cheep [tʃi:p] *vi.* make a short, weak, shrill sound like a young bird, etc.; chirp; peep. **—*n.*** [C] a short, weak, shrill sound like that of a young bird, etc.; chirp; peep.
—[自] [병아리 따위가] 삐약삐약 울다 —[名] 삐약삐약 [소리]

:cheer [tʃiər] *n.* **1.** [U] joy; gladness. **2.** [C] encouragement; something that promotes cheerfulness. ¶*words*
—[名] 1. 기분 좋음 2. 격려 ¶①격려의 말 3. 박수갈채; 환호 4. 기분, 심기 ¶

of ~.① **3.** ((chiefly *pl.*)) a shout of joy, applause, or encouragement. **4.** the state of mind. ¶*He is of good* ~.② **5.** good food or drink. ¶*make good* ~.③
②그는 기분이 좋다 **5.** 좋은 음식, 진수성찬 ¶③진수성찬을 먹다

1) ***give three cheers,*** cry or shout 'Hurrah!' three times. ⇒[N.B.]
2) ***with good cheer,*** cheerfully; willingly.
[熟] 1)만세삼창을 하다 [N.B.] Hip, hip, hurrah를 세 번 되풀이함 2)기꺼이

—*vt.* **1.** comfort. **2.** applaud; shout for joy; give approval or encouragement. ¶*The boys cheered their football team to victory.*
—[他] **1.** …을 기운나게 하다 **2.** …에게 박수갈채하다

cheer up, become or make (someone) more cheerful. ¶*Your visit cheered up the sick man.*
[熟] 기운나다(내다)

⁑**cheer·ful** [tʃíərf(u)l] *adj.* **1.** in good spirits; joyful; glad. ¶*a* ~ *old man.* **2.** filled with cheer; bright and pleasant. ¶*a* ~ *room.* **3.** willing; eager.
—[形] **1.** 기운찬, 기뻐하는, 기분 좋은 **2.** 즐거운, 유쾌한 **3.** 기꺼이 …하는

***cheer·ful·ly** [tʃíərf(u)li] *adv.* in a cheerful manner.
—[副] 기운차게, 기분 좋게

cheer·ful·ness [tʃíərf(u)lnis] *n.* [U] the state of being cheerful.
—[名] 기분 좋음, 쾌활

cheer·i·ly [tʃíərili] *adv.* in a cheery manner.
—[副] 원기 있게, 명랑하게

cheer·io [tʃíərióu] *interj.* (chiefly *Brit. colloq.*) goodby! good luck!
—[感] 잘 있거라, 안녕히

cheer·less [tʃíərlis] *adj.* without cheer; gloomy; dreary.
—[形] 즐거움 없는, 쓸쓸한, 침울한

cheer·y [tʃíəri] *adj.* (**cheer·i·er, cheer·i·est**) merry; pleasant; gay; lively.
—[形] 쾌활한, 즐거운, 활발한

⁑**cheese** [tʃiːz] *n.* **1.** [U] a kind of solid food made from milk. ¶*green* ~① / *Say* ~!② **2.** [C] a mass of this cheese pressed into a shape. ▷**cheese·like** [-làik] *adj.*
—[名] **1.** 치이즈 ¶①생(生) 치이즈/②웃으시오 **2.** [일정한 모양으로 굳힌] 치이즈

chee·tah [tʃíːtə] *n.* [C] a flesh-eating animal like a leopard.
—[名] ((動)) 치이타아

chef [ʃef] *n.* [C] a head cook in a hotel, etc.
—[名] 요리사(쿡)의 우두머리

***chem·i·cal** [kémik(ə)l] *adj.* of chemistry; produced by or used in chemistry. ¶a ~ *combination*① / ~ *engineering*② / *a* ~ *formula.*③
—[形] 화학의, 화학작용에 의한 ¶①화합/②화학 공업/③화학식

—*n.* ((usu. *pl.*)) a substance produced by or used in a chemical process.
—[名] 화학 약품(제품)

chem·i·cal·ly [kémik(ə)li] *adv.* according to chemistry; by chemical means.
—[副] 화학적으로

che·mise [ʃimíːz] *n.* [C] a woman's loose, shirtlike undergarment.
—[名] [여자용] 속옷, 시미이즈

***chem·ist** [kémist] *n.* [C] **1.** a expert or student in chemistry. **2.** (*Brit.*) a druggist.
—[名] **1.** 화학자 **2.** 약제사

***chem·is·try** [kémistri] *n.* [U] [C] (pl. **-tries**) the science that deals with or examines the nature of elements or simple substances. ¶*applied* (or *practical*) ~① / *organic* (*inorganic*) ~.②
—[名] 화학 ¶①응용화학/②유기(무기) 화학

⁑**cheque** [tʃek] *n.* (*Brit.*) =check.

cheque·book [tʃékbùk] *n.* (*Brit.*) =checkbook.

cheq·uer [tʃékər] *vt., n.* (*Brit.*) =checker.

cheq·uered [tʃékərd] *a.* (*Brit.*) =checkered.

***cher·ish** [tʃériʃ] *vt.* **1.** love; treat (someone) with affection; care for (someone) tenderly or kindly. **2.** keep (something) in mind; entertain; cling to. ¶~ *the memory of a happy life*① / ~ *a grudge against someone.*
—[他] **1.** …을 귀여워하다, 소중히 하다 **2.** …을 마음속에 품다, 가슴에 간직하다, …에 집착하다 ¶①행복했던 생활을 그리워하다

⁑**cher·ry** [tʃéri] *n.* (pl. **-ries**) **1.** [C] a small, round, bright red fruit with a stone in the center; the tree that it grows on. **2.** [U] the wood of this tree. **3.** [U] a bright red. —*adj.* **1.** made of cherry wood. **2.** bright-red.
—[名] **1.** 버찌, 벚나무 **2.** 벚나무 재목 **3.** 버찌 빛깔, 진분홍 —[形] **1.** 벚나무 재목으로 만든 **2.** 버찌 빛깔의, 진분홍의

cherry stone [⌐–⌐] *n.* [C] **1.** the stone of a cherry. **2.** a kind of shellfish; a clam.
—[名] **1.** 버찌의 씨 **2.** 무명조개

cher·ub [tʃérəb] *n.* [C] (pl. **cher·u·bim** →3.) **1.** an angel of the second class. ⇒[N.B.] **2.** a picture or statue of a child with wings or the head of such a child. ⇒fig. **3.** (pl. **cher·ubs**) a sweet, innocent, good child; a child with a round, innocent face.
—[名] **1.** 케루빔, 지천사(智天使) [N.B.] 아홉 천사 중 둘째 천사로서 신의 지혜와 정의를 상징 **2.** cherub의 그림(상(像)) **3.** 천사 같은 아이; 토실토실 살찐 귀여운 아이

[cherub 2.]

cher·u·bim [tʃérəbìm] *n.* pl. of **cherub.**

chess [tʃes] *n.* [U] a game played by two persons on a chessboard. ⇒[N.B.]
—[名] 체스, 서양장기 [N.B.] 두 사람이 32개의 말을 써서 둠

chess·board [tʃésbɔ̀:rd] *n.* [C] a board divided into 32 red squares and 32 black squares, used in playing chess.
—[名] 체스판

chess·man [tʃésmæ̀n] *n.* (pl. **-men** [-mèn]) [C] one of the pieces used in the game of chess.
—[名] [체스의] 말

⁑chest [tʃest] *n.* [C] **1.** the upper front part of the body between the neck and the stomach. ¶*a cold in the* ~.① / *have a weak* ~.② **2.** a large box with a lid. ¶*a carpenter's* ~③ / *a medicine* ~.④ **3.** a sealed container for gas, steam, etc. **4.** the place where money is kept; treasury; a [public] fund. ¶*the community* ~.⑤
—[名] 1. 가슴, 폐 ¶①기침 감기/②가슴이 나쁘다, 폐병이다 2. 큰 상자 ¶③목수의 도구 상자/④약상자 3. [가스·액체 따위를 넣는] 밀폐 용기(容器) 4. 금고, 자금 ¶⑤공동 모금

1) ***a chest of drawers,*** a case fitted with sliding drawers. (cf. *U. S.* bureau)
2) ***get*** *(something)* ***off one's chest,*** *(colloq.)* relieve oneself of (some annoyance, trouble, etc.) by talking about it.
[熟] 1)장롱 [N.B.] 침실·화장실에 둠 2)《口》[털어놓고 이야기하여] 마음의 짐을 덜다

·chest·nut [tʃésnət / -nʌt] *n.* **1.** [C] a kind of eatable nut; the tree it grows on. **2.** [U] the wood of this tree; the color of a chestnut; a reddishbrown color. **3.** [C] a reddish brown horse.
—[名] 1. 밤; 밤나무 2. 밤나무 재목, 밤빛, 적갈색 3. 밤색 털의 말

pull someone's chestnuts out of the fire, be pressed into rescuing someone from difficulty, etc.
[熟] 남을 위해 불 속의 밤을 줍다; 남의 앞잡이 노릇을 하다

—*adj.* reddish-brown.
—[形] 밤색의, 밤색 털의

chev·ron [ʃévrən] *n.* [C] **1.** a V-shaped design worn on the sleeves of a police or military uniform, etc. ⇒[N.B.], fig. **2.** a V-shaped design used in coats of arms, architecture, etc.
—[名] 1. 수장(袖章) [N.B.] ∧모양으로서 하사관복·경관복의 소매에 닮. 영국에서는 근무 연한, 미국에서는 계급을 나타냄 2. ∧자형 장식

〔chevron 1.〕

·chew [tʃu:] *vt.* crush or grind (something) with the teeth. **—*vi.*** **1.** think very much; consider. ¶~ *on* (or *over, upon*) *it.*① **2.** bite repeatedly with the teeth.
—[他] …을 씹다, 깨물어 부수다 —[自] 1. 곰곰이 생각하다 ¶①그것을 심사숙고하다 2. 씹다

bite off more than one can chew, undertake something which is beyond one's capacity or power.
[熟] 능력 이상의 일을 하려고 하다

—*n.* [C] the act of chewing; a piece [of food, etc.] to be chewed.
—[名] 씹기, 저작(咀嚼); 씹는 것

chew·ing gum [tʃú:iŋgʌ̀m] *n.* a gum for chewing.
—[名] 추우잉검, 껌

chic [ʃi(:)k] *n.* [U] a smart, elegance of style and manner. **—*adj.*** (**chicqu·er, chiqu·est**) stylish.
—[名] 멋, 우아함, 독특한 스타일 —[形] 멋진, 우아한

·Chi·ca·go [ʃikɑ́:gou, -kɔ́:-] *n.* a large city of the United States, in the state of Illinois. ⇒[N.B.]
—[名] 시카고 [N.B.] Michigan 호수에 면한 미국 제2의 대도시

chi·can·er·y [ʃikéinəri] *n.* [U][C] (pl. **-er·ies**) trickery; unfair practice; false arguments. ¶*use* ~.①
—[名] 교활, 속임수, 책략; 궤변 ¶①속임수를 쓰다

chick [tʃik] *n.* [C] **1.** a baby chicken; a young bird. **2.** a child; a young girl.
—[名] 1. 병아리; 새 새끼 2. 어린애, 계집애

⁑chick·en [tʃíkin] *n.* [C] **1.** a young hen or rooster; (*U. S.*) a hen or rooster of any age. ¶(*proverb*) *Don't count your chickens before they are hatched.*① **2.** any young bird. **3.** [U] the flesh of a chicken. **4.** (*U. S. colloq.*) a young person or girl. **—*adj.*** young; small; of or like a chicken; cowardly.
—[名] 1. 병아리; 《美》 [일반적으로] 닭 ¶①까지도 않은 병아리 수부터 세지 마라 2. [일반적으로] 새 새끼 3. 닭고기 4. 《美口》 풋나기, 애숭이; 어린이; 젊은 여자 —[形] 어린애의; 병아리의; 소심한

chick·en-heart·ed [tʃíkinhɑ́:rtid] *adj.* lacking courage; timid.
—[形] 소심한, 겁 많은

chick·weed [tʃíkwì:d] *n.* [C] a common, white-flowering weed.
—[名] 별꽃

chic·o·ry [tʃíkəri] *n.* [U] a plant whose leaves are used for salad.
—[名] 꽃상치류(잎은 샐러드용)

chid [tʃid] *v.* pt. and pp. of **chide.**

chid·den [tʃídn] *v.* pp. of **chide.**

chide [tʃaid] *vi., vt.* (**chid** or **chid·ed, chid·den** or **chid** or **chid·ed**) blame; scold; find fault. 《~ someone *for*》 ¶*Our teacher chided a boy for coming late.*①
—[自][他] […을] 꾸짖다, 나무라다, 잔소리하다 ¶①우리 선생님은 지각했다고 학생을 꾸짖었다

⁑chief [tʃi:f] *n.* [C] (pl. **chiefs**) a leader; a commander; the head of a tribe, etc. ¶*a* ~ *judge* (or *justice*)① / (*U. S.*) *a* ~ *of police.*② (cf. *Brit.* chief constable) / *the* ~ *of staff.*③
—[名] 우두머리, 수령, 장관, 추장, 족장 ¶①재판장/ ②《美》 경찰서장/ ③참모장

in chief, ⓐ chiefly. ⓑ at the head. ¶*a commander-in-chief.*④
[熟] ⓐ주로 ⓑ우두머리의, 장관의 ¶④총사령관

—*adj.* **1.** highest in rank; at the head. **2.** most important; main. ¶*the ~ object.*⑤ / *the ~ point.*⑥ ▷**chief·less** [tʃíːflis] *adj.*
—[形] 1. 우두머리의, 제1의, 최고의 2. 주요한 ¶⑤주안(主眼)/⑥주요점

⁑chief·ly [tʃíːfli] *adv.* **1.** mainly; mostly. **2.** most of all; first of all.
—[副] 1. 주로, 대개 2. 우선 첫째로, 맨 먼저

chief·tain [tʃíːftən] *n.* [C] the leader of a tribe, etc.; a leader; the head of a group.
—[名] 수령, 추장, 대장, 단장

chief·tain·cy [tʃíːftənsi] *n.* [U][C] (pl. **-cies**) the position or rank of a chieftain.
—[名] 대장(추장)의 지위(임무)

chif·fon [ʃifɑ́n, ⌐⌐ / ʃífɔn] *n.* **1.** [U] a very soft, thin silk or rayon cloth. **2.** ⟪usu. *pl.*⟫ laces, ribbons, etc.
—[名] 1. 비단 메린스 2. 드레스의 장식 레이스(리본)

chif·fo·nier [ʃìfəníər] *n.* [C] a high, narrow bureau or chest of drawers, sometimes with a mirror.
—[名] [거울 달린] 서양 양복장

chil·blain [tʃílblèin] *n.* ⟪usu. *pl.*⟫ a red swelling on the hands or feet caused by cold.
—[名] 동상(凍傷)

⁑child [tʃaild] *n.* (pl. **chil·dren**) [C] **1.** a boy or girl; a baby; an infant; a son or daughter. ¶*as a ~*① / *from a ~* / *Don't be a ~.*② / (*proverb*) *The ~ is father of* (or *to*) *the man.*③ **2.** a descendant. ¶*a ~ of Abraham.*④ **3.** a person regarded as the product of a particular place, time, etc. ¶*a ~ of the age*⑤ / *a ~ of the Renaissance* / *a ~ of nature.* **4.** a childish person. **5.** product; result.
—[名] 1. 어린이, 갓난애, 유아, 아들, 딸, ¶①어린 시절에/②어린애 같은 짓 마라/③세 살 적 버릇이 여든까지 2. 자손 ¶④아브라함의 자손, 유대인 3. [특정의 장소·시대에 자란] 사람 ¶⑤시대의 총아 4. 어린애 같은 사람 5. 소산, 결과

with child, having a baby in the body.
[熟] 임신한

child·bed [tʃáildbèd] *n.* [U][C] the state of a woman giving birth to a child.
—[名] 분만

child·birth [tʃáildbə̀ːrθ] *n.* [U] the act of giving birth to a child; the birth rate.
—[名] 출산, 출생률

⁑child·hood [tʃáildhùd] *n.* [U] the state or time of being a child. ¶*in someone's ~*① / *in someone's second ~.*②
—[名] 어린 시절, 유년시대 ¶①어린 시절에/②늘그막에

·child·ish [tʃáildiʃ] *adj.* **1.** of or like a child. **2.** not grown-up; weak; silly; foolish.
—[形] 1. 어린이의, 어린애다운 2. 유치한, 철없는; 노망한

child·ish·ly [tʃáildiʃli] *adv.* in the state of being a child or acting like a child; sillily.
—[副] 어린이답게; 어린애 같게, 유치하게

child·ish·ness [tʃáildiʃnis] *n.* [U] the state of being childish.
—[名] 어린이다움; 유치함

child·less [tʃáildlis] *adj.* having no child.
—[形] 어린애가 없는

child·like [tʃáildlàik] *adj.* like a child; fit for a child; innocent; frank; simple. ▷**child·like·ness** [-nis] *n.*
—[形] 어린애 같은, 어린이다운, 순진한, 솔직한, 단순한

⁑chil·dren [tʃíldr(ə)n] *n.* pl. of **child.**

child's play [⌐⌐] *n.* something very easy to do; play which a child does.
—[名] 어린애 장난, 아주 쉬운 일

Chil·e [tʃíli] *n.* a country in southwestern South America. ⇒[N.B.]
—[名] 칠레 [N.B.] 수도 Santiago

chil·i [tʃíli] *n.* (pl. **chil·ies**) **1.** [C] a hot-tasting red pepper; the tropical American plant that bears this pepper. **2.** [U] a dish made of beans and this pepper.
—[名] 1. [열대 아메리카산] 고추의 일종 2. 콩과 그 고추로 만든 요리

⁑chill [tʃil] *n.* [C] **1.** coldness. ¶*a ~ in the air.* **2.** a sudden bodily coldness with shivering. ¶*catch* (or *take*) *a ~*① / *A ~ came over me.* **3.** unfriendliness; coolness in manner. **4.** a sudden fear; discouragement.
—[名] 1. 차가움, 냉기 2. 오한, 으스스함 ¶①으스스 떨려 오다 3. 냉담, 쌀쌀함 4. 풀죽음, 낙심, 싫증

—*adj.* **1.** cold. **2.** unfriendly; cold in manner. **3.** in low spirits; discouraging.
—[形] 1. 차가운, 냉랭한 2. 냉담한, [태도가] 쌀쌀한 3. 풀이 죽은, 실망한

—*vt.* **1.** make (something) cool; cause (someone) to become cool. **2.** discourage; dispirit. ¶*~ the enthusiasm.* —*vi.* become cool; feel cool. ▷**chill·ness** [-nis] *n.*
—[他] 1. …을 식히다, 냉동하다, 오싹해지게 하다 2. [열의 따위]를 꺾다, [흥]을 깨다 —[自] 식다, 오한이 나다

·chill·y [tʃíli] *adj.* (**chill·i·er, chill·i·est**) **1.** uncomfortably cool; rather cold. **2.** cold in manner; unfriendly.
—[形] 1. 쌀쌀한, 으스스한 2. 냉담한, 차가운

·chime [tʃaim] *n.* **1.** [C] a set of bells in tune. **2.** ⟪often *pl.*⟫ the musical sound of these bells. ¶*listen to the chimes.* **3.** [U] harmony; agreement. ¶*keep ~ with someone.*①
—[名] 1. 조율한 한 벌의 종, 차임 2. 그 종소리 3. 조화, 일치 ¶①…와 조화를 이루게 하다

1) ***fall into chime with,*** be harmonious with (something or someone).
2) ***in chime,*** in harmony.
[熟] 1)…와 조화하다 2)조화하여

—*vt.* **1.** ring or strike a bell or a set of bells. **2.** tell the hour by chimes. ¶*The clock chimed five.* —*vi.* **1.** ring out musically. **2.** harmonize; agree. ⟪*~with* something⟫. ¶*~ with one's mood.*②
—[他] 1. 종을 울리다 2. [시간]을 종으로 알리다 —[自] 1. 종이 울리다 2. 조화하다, 일치하다 ¶②기분과 일치하다

chime in, ⓐ break into or join in a conversation. ⓑ harmonize; agree. 《*~ in with* something》
[熟] ⓐ맞장구치다, 대화에 끼다 ⓑ조화하다, 일치하다

chi·me·ra, -mae- [kaimíərə] *n.* [C] **1.** (in Greek mythology) a fire-breathing monster. ⇒[N.B.] **2.** a terrible imaginary creature; a wild dream.
—[名] 1. 키메라 [N.B.] 사자의 머리, 양의 몸, 용의 꼬리를 가졌고 불을 뿜는 괴물 2. 괴물, 망상

chi·mer·i·cal [kaimérik(ə)l] *adj.* imaginary; nonsensical; wildly fanciful.
—[形] 공상의, 터무니없는, 환상적인

:chim·ney [tʃímni] *n.* [C] **1.** an upright structure for carrying smoke from a fireplace, a furnace, etc. **2.** a glass tube around a lamp flame. **3.** a crack or opening in a rock, mountain, etc. ⇒[N.B.]
—[名] 1. 굴뚝 2. [남포의] 등피 3. 침니 [N.B.] 바위 벽에 세로로 갈라진 틈. 등산가가 이용함

chimney corner [´-- ˋ-] *n.* the corner or side of a fireplace.
—[名] 벽로 앞의 따뜻한 자리

chimney piece [´-- ˋ] *n.* a mantelshelf; a mantelpiece.
—[名] 벽로 선반, 벽로 장식

chimney pot [´-- ˋ] *n.* a pipe of earthenware or metal fitted to the top of a chimney. ⇒[N.B.]
—[名] 굴뚝 꼭대기의 통풍관 [N.B.] 통풍이 잘 되도록 닮

chimney stack [´-- ˋ] *n.* a number of pipes embodied in one chimney; the part of a chimney rising above a roof. ⇒fig.
—[名] 여러 개를 한데 맞붙인 굴뚝 [N.B.] 그 하나하나를 chimney pot라 함

〔chimney stack〕

chimney sweep [´-- ˋ] *n.* a person whose work is to clean out chimneys.
—[名] 굴뚝 소제부

chim·pan·zee [tʃìmpænzí: / -pən-] *n.* [C] an dark brown manlike African monkey.
—[名] 침팬지이, 검정성성(猩猩)이

·chin [tʃin] *n.* [C] the part of the face below the mouth.
—[名] 턱

—*v.* **(chinned, chin·ning)** *vt.* pull (oneself) up by the hands until one's chin is on a level with a horizontal bar. —*vi.* talk too much; chatter.
—[他] [철봉에서] 턱걸이하다 —[自] 수다떨다

chi·na [tʃáinə] *n.* [U] 《*collectively*》 **1.** a fine, white object made of clay baked by a special process. **2.** dishes, vases, etc. made of china. ¶*a piece of ~.*
—[名] 1. 자기(磁器) 2. [일반적으로] 도자기

:Chi·na [tʃáinə] *n.* a large country in East Asia. ¶***the People's Republic of ~***① | ***the Republic of ~.***②
—[名] 중국 ¶①중공/②중화민국

Chi·na·man [tʃáinəmən] *n.* [C] (pl. **-men** [-mən]) a person of China; a Chinese. ⇒[usage]
—[名] 중국인 [usage] Chinese에 비하여 다소 경멸적 용법

chi·na·ware [tʃáinəwɛ̀ər] *n.* [U] dishes, vases, etc. made of china.
—[名] 사기그릇, 도자기

chin·chil·la [tʃintʃílə] *n.* **1.** [C] a South American animal like a squirrel. **2.** [U] its fur. ⇒[N.B.]
—[名] 1. 친칠라(남미산의 다람쥐 비슷한 동물) 2. 그 고급 모피

chine [tʃain] *n.* [C] **1.** the backbone; spine; (of meat) a cut of an animal's backbone with the meat still on it. **2.** a ridge.
—[名] 1. 등뼈, 등뼈 고기 2. 산등성이, 산마루

:Chi·nese [tʃáiní:z] *n.* (pl. **-nese**) **1.** [C] a person of China. **2.** [U] the language of China. —*adj.* of China, its people, or their language. ¶*~ characters*① | *~ ink.*②
—[名] 1. 중국인 2. 중국어 —[形] 중국[인·어]의 ¶①한자/②먹

chink¹ [tʃiŋk] *n.* [C] a narrow opening; a crack. —*vt.* fill up the chinks in (something). 《*~up* something》
—[名] 갈라진 틈, 째진 금 —[他] …의 금(틈)을 메우다

chink² [tʃiŋk] *n.* [C] a sharp, ringing sound as of coins or glasses struck lightly. —*vt.* cause (something) to jingle. —*vi.* jingle.
—[名] 쟁그랑, 짤랑(쇠붙이·유리의 부딪치는 소리) —[他] …을 쨍그랑 울리다 —[自] 쟁그랑하고 울리다

chintz [tʃints] *n.* [U] a cotton cloth printed in various colored patterns.
—[名] 사라사 천의 일종

·chip [tʃip] *n.* [C] **1.** a small piece that is cut or cut off. **2.** a gap left when a small piece is cut or broken off from something. **3.** 《usu *pl.*》 a small, thin piece of food or candy. ¶*potato chips.*① **4.** 《*pl.*》 wood or straw, etc. in thin strips for weaving into hats or baskets.
—[名] 1. 잘린 토막 2. 잘라낸 자국 3. [먹을것·과자의] 작은 조각 ¶①잘게 썬 감자 튀김 4. [모자·상자 따위를 만드는] 얄팍한 대팻밥

a chip off the old block, a child that is very much like either of its parents.
[熟] 부모를 고대로 닮은 아이

—*v.* **(chipped, chip·ping)** *vt.* **1.** cut or break off a small part of (something). **2.** chop or cut (as with an ax); shape (something) by cutting. —*vi.* become small pieces.
—[他] 1. …을 잘라 내다, 깎아 내다 2. [도끼 따위로] …을 쪼개다, 자르다; …의 모양을 파다 —[自] [사기그릇이] 이가 빠지다

chip at, find fault with (someone or something) severely.
[熟] …을 혹평하다

chip·munk [tʃípmʌŋk] *n.* [C] a small, striped squirrel living in North America.
—[名] [북미산의] 줄무늬다람쥐

* **chirp** [tʃəːrp] *vi.* make a short, sharp sound such as certain birds or insects do. —*vt.* utter (something) in a short, sharp tone. —*n.* [C] a short, sharp sound.
—[自] 짹짹 울다 —[他] 째지는 듯한 소리로 말하다 —[名] [참새 따위의] 짹짹소리

chir·rup [tʃírəp, +*U.S.* tʃə́ːrəp] *vi.* **1.** chirp repeatedly. **2.** make such sounds. —*n.* [C] the sound or the act of chirruping.
—[自] 1. 지저귀다 2. 지저귀는 듯한 소리를 내다 —[名] 지저귐

chis·el [tʃízl] *n.* [C] a tool with a sharp edge for cutting or shaping wood, stone, or metal. —*vt.* (**-eled, -el·ing** or *Brit.* **-elled, -el·ling**) **1.** cut or sharpen (something) with such a tool. ¶*chiseled features.*① **2.** (*colloq.*) cheat; get (something) by cheating. 《~ someone *out of*》
—[名] 끌, 정
—[他] 1. …을 끌로 파다(새기다) ¶① 잘 생긴 얼굴 2.《口》…을 속이다; 속여 빼앗다

chit [tʃit] *n.* [C] a child; a young, small, slender girl. ⇒[usage]
—[名] 아이, 계집애 [usage] 경멸적으로 쓰이는 일이 많음

chit-chat [tʃíttʃæ̀t] *n.* [U] light, friendly, informal talk.
—[名] 잡담, 한담

chiv·al·ric [ʃív(ə)lrik] *adj.* related to a knight; like a knight; chivalrous.
—[形] 기사도의, 기사 같은, 용맹한

chiv·al·rous [ʃív(ə)ləs] *adj.* having to do with chivalry; having the qualities of an ideal knight; brave; polite; honorable.
—[形] 기사[도]의, 용맹한, 의협적인

chiv·al·rous·ly [ʃív(ə)lrəsli] *adv.* in the qualities of being chivalrous.
—[副] 기사답게, 의협적으로

chiv·al·ry [ʃív(ə)lri] *n.* [U] **1.** the ideal quality of a knight. **2.** the systems of knighthood in the Middle Ages. **3.** 《*collectively*》 a group of knights.
—[名] 1. 기사도[정신] 2. [중세의] 기사제도 3. 기사들

chlo·ride [klɔ́ːraid] *n.* [U][C] (*Chemistry*) a compound of chlorine. ¶*~ of lime.*①
—[名] 《化》 염화물 ¶①표백분

chlo·rine [klɔ́ːriːn] *n.* [U] a greenish-yellow, poisonous, gaseous chemical element with an unpleasant smell.
—[名] 염소(鹽素)

chlo·ro·form [klɔ́ːrəfɔ̀ːrm / klɔ́(ː)rəfɔ́ːm] *n.* [U] a colorless liquid with a rather sweet smell. ⇒[N.B.] —*vt.* make (someone) unconscious or dead with chloroform.
—[名] 클로로포름 [N.B.] 마취약 —[他] …을 클로로포름으로 마취시키다(죽이다)

chlo·ro·phyll, chlo·ro·phyl [klɔ́(ː)rəfìl] *n.* [U] the green coloring matter of plants.
—[名] 엽록소 (葉綠素)

* **choc·o·late** [tʃɑ́kəlit, tʃɔ́ːkə- / tʃɔ́k(ə)-] *n.* [U] **1.** a piece of candy made of chocolate; a drink made of chocolate. ¶*a bar of ~.*① **2.** a dark-brown color. —*adj.* made of chocolate; dark-brown.
—[名] 1. 초콜렛; 초콜렛 음료 ¶①초콜렛 한 개 2. 초콜렛 빛 —[形] 초콜렛[빛깔]의

‡ **choice** [tʃɔis] *n.* **1.** [C] selection; the act of choosing. ¶*the book of one's ~*① / *You may take your ~.*② **2.** [U] power or right to choose. ¶*I have a ~ between you and he for my secretary.*③ **3.** [C] a thing or person that is chosen. ¶*This book is my ~.*
—[名] 1. 선택 ¶①스스로 고른 책/②마음에 드는 것을 골라라 2. 선택권(력) ¶③나는 당신이나 그 사람 중에서 내 비서를 고를 수 있다 3. 선택된 것

1) ***at*** [*one's* ***own***] ***choice,*** as one likes.
2) ***by*** (or ***for***) ***choice,*** ⓐ of one's free will; willingly. ⓑ if one must choose.
3) ***have no choice to do,*** cannot help doing; must do.
4) ***make choice of*** (=*choose*) *something.*

[熟] 1)마음대로 [골라서] 2)ⓐ좋아하여, 자유 의사로 ⓑ만일 고른다면 3)…할 밖에 없다 4)…을 고르다

—*adj.* **1.** excellent. **2.** carefully selected.
—[形] 1. 뛰어난 2. 가려뽑은, 정선한

* **choir** [kwáiər] *n.* [C] **1.** a group of singers, usu. in a church. **2.** the part of a church in which the choir sings. —*vi., vt.* (*poetic*) sing in chorus.
—[名] 1. [교회의] 성가대, 합창단 2. 성가대석 —[自][他] 《詩》 [새·천사 등이] 합창하다

* **choke** [tʃouk] *vt.* **1.** stop the breathing of (someone). **2.** fill completely; prevent or stop up the passage through (something) by filling. ¶*The chimney was choked with soot.* **3.** stop the growth of (a plant); put out (a fire). **4.** control; hold; prevent. ¶*Sobs choked her utterance.*① —*vi.* **1.** be unable to breathe. **2.** be filled up.
—[他] 1. …을 질식시키다 2. …을 막히게 하다, 막다 3. [식물]의 발육을 멈추게 하다; [불]을 끄다 4. …을 억누르다 ¶①그녀는 울음으로 말도 못했다 —[自] 1. 질식하다 2. 막히다

1) ***choke back*** (or ***down***), hold back (feelings, sobs, etc.).
2) ***choke off,*** ⓐ kill (someone) by choking. ⓑ persuade (someone) not to do. ⓒ get rid of (something); put away.

[熟] 1)[감정 따위]를 억누르다 2)ⓐ…을 목졸라 죽이다 ⓑ…을 그만두게 하다 ⓒ…을 없애다, 치우다 3)…을 막다, 메우다

C

3) ***choke up,*** fill up; block up.

choke·damp [tʃóukdæ̀mp] *n.* [U] a heavy gas which causes difficulty in breathing. ⇒[N.B.]
—[명] 질식 가스 [N.B.] 탄갱·깊은 우물 따위에서 생기는 탄산가스

chol·er [kálər / kɔ́lə] *n.* [U] great anger.
—[명] 격분, 분노

chol·er·a [kálərə / kɔ́l-] *n.* [U] an infectious and deadly Asiatic disease. ¶*Asiatic* (or *malignant*) ~① / *European* (or *summer*) ~.②
—[명] 콜레라 ¶①진성 콜레라/②비(非) 전염성 콜레라

chol·er·ic [kálərik / kɔ́l-] *adj.* easily angry.
—[형] 화를 잘 내는, 성마른

cho·les·ter·ol [kəléstəròul / kɔléstərɔl] *n.* [U] white waxy substance found in human tissues.
—[명] 콜레스테롤(지방 조직에 함유되어 있는 성분)

:choose [tʃu:z] *v.* (**chose, cho·sen**) *vt.* **1.** select (something) as most desirable. ¶*You may ~ the largest apple in the dish.* **2.** elect. **3.** decide; please or think proper. 《~ *to do*》 ¶*He chose to run for president.*① —*vi.* **1.** make a choice. ¶*There is nothing to ~ between the two.*② **2.** make a decision. ¶*You may stay here if you ~.*
—[타] 1. …을 고르다 2. …을 선출하다 3. …을 바라다, 결정하다 ¶①그는 대통령에 입후보하기로 결정했다 —[자] 1. 선택하다 ¶②그 두 개는 대단한 차이가 없다 2 결정하다

cannot choose but, must; have to.
[숙] …하지 않을 수 없다

:chop¹ [tʃɑp / tʃɔp] *v.* (**chopped, chop·ping**) *vt.* **1.** cut or make (something) by strokes with an axe. ¶*~ twigs with an axe.*① **2.** cut (something) into small pieces. ¶*~ up an onion.* —*vi.* make cutting strokes as with an axe.
—[타] 1. [도끼 따위로] …을 자르다 ¶①도끼로 가지를 치다 2. …을 잘게 썰다 —[자] 자르다; 잘게 썰다

1) ***chop about*** (or ***round***), (of the wind) change direction suddenly.
2) ***chop and change,*** always change one's opinions, plans, etc.
3) ***chop logic*** (or ***words***), exchange opinions by talking or discussing with someone.
4) ***chop through,*** make (one's way) by cutting trees down. ¶*~ a path through a forest.*
5) ***chop up,*** cut (something) into small pieces.
[숙] 1)[바람의 방향이] 갑자기 바뀌다 2)[의견·계획이] 쉴새 없이 바뀌다 3)논쟁하다 4)베어 젖히며 나아가다 5)…을 잘게 썰다

—*n.* **1.** [C] a short, cutting blow; the act of chopping. **2.** [C] a slice of meat (as of lamb, pork, etc.). **3.** [U] a sudden motion of waves.
—[명] 1. 일격, 자르기, 절단 2. 두껍게 썬 고깃점 3. 불규칙한 잔물결

chop² [tʃɑp / tʃɔp] *n.* [C] 《usu. *pl.*》 the jaws; the chin.
—[명] 턱

chop·house [tʃáphàus / tʃɔ́p-] *n.* [C] a restaurant dealing chiefly with slices of meat, etc.
—[명] 대중식당, 고기 요릿집

chop·per [tʃápər / tʃɔ́pə] *n.* [C] **1.** a person who chops. **2.** a tool or machine for chopping.
—[명] 1. 자르는 사람 2. 자르는 것, 도끼

chop·py¹ [tʃápi / tʃɔ́pi] *adj.* (**-pi·er, -pi·est**) **1.** with sharp, sudden movements. **2.** (of a lake etc.) moving in short, rough waves. **3.** full of cracks.
—[형] 1. 덜컹덜컹 움직이는 2. [호수 따위] 거칠게 물결이 이는 3. 갈라진 틈이 많은

chop·py² [tʃápi / tʃɔ́pi] *adj.* (**-pi·er, -pi·est**) (of the wind, etc.) changing suddenly.
—[형] [바람이] 끊임없이 바뀌는

chop·stick [tʃápstìk / tʃɔ́p-] *n.* [C] 《usu. *pl.*》 a small stick used in pairs by the Koreans and Chinese to carry food to the mouth.
—[명] 젓가락

chop su·ey [tʃápsú:i / tʃɔ́ps(j)ú(:)i] *n.* a Chinese-American dish. ⇒[N.B.]
—[명] 잡채 [N.B.] 스튜우 비슷한 미국식 중국 요리

cho·ral [kɔ́:rəl →*n.*] *adj.* of a choir or chorus; sung by a choir or chorus. —*n.* [*U.S.* kərǽl] [C] a hymn tune.
—[형] 합창[대]의
—[명] 성가, 찬미가

chord¹ [kɔ:rd] *n.* [C] (*Music*) a combination of several musical notes sounded together in harmony.
—[명] 화음

chord² [kɔ:rd] *n.* [C] **1.** (*Mathematics*) a straight line joining any two points on a circle. **2.** (*Anatomy*) a chordlike structure in an animal body. ¶*the vocal chord*[*s*].① **3.** a string of a musical instrument. **4.** [U] feeling; emotion.
—[명] 1.《數》현(弦) 2.《解》건(腱) ¶①성대 3. [악기의] 현(絃) 4. 감정, 느낌, 심금(心琴)

strike (or ***touch***) ***the right chord,*** appeal deeply to emotion.
[숙] 심금을 울리다

chore [tʃɔ:r] *n.* [C] **1.** a small or odd job. **2.** a hard or disagreeable task.
—[명] 1. 허드렛일, 자질구레한 일 2. 힘드는(싫은) 일

chor·is·ter [kárìstər, kɔ́:r- / kɔ́r-] *n.* [C] **1.** a singer in a choir. **2.** a leader of a choir.
—[명] 1. [교회의] 합창자 2. 합창대 지휘자

chor·tle [tʃɔ́:rtl] *vi.* laugh loudly and joyously. —*n.* [C] a joyous laugh.
—[자] 소리 높이 웃다 —[명] 기쁜 웃음

·cho·rus [kɔ́:rəs] *n.* [C] **1.** a group of singers who sing
—[명] 1. 합창대, 합창[곡] ¶①혼성합창

chose [199] **chronological**

together; a piece of song or musical composition sung by many singers together. ¶*mixed ~.*① / *join in a ~.*② **2.** the repeated part of a song. **3.** something said or called out by many at the same time. ¶*in ~.*③ —*vt., vi.* sing or speak all together.
/②합창에 끼어들다 2. 노래의 후렴 3. 많은 사람 소리를 합쳐 일제히 말하기 ¶③합창으로, 이구동성으로 —⑩@ 합창하다, 이구동성으로 말하다

- **chose** [tʃouz] *v.* pt. of **choose**.
- **cho·sen** [tʃóuzn] *v.* pp. of **choose**.
  —*adj.* selected ¶*the ~ people.*①
  —⑧ 선택된 ¶①신의 선민(選民)(유 「대인」

chow·der [tʃáudər] *n.* Ⓤ a thick soup-like food which usu. contains fish, shellfish, and various vegetables.
—⑧ 잡탕(생선·조개·야채 따위의 모듬 남비 요리)

:**Christ** [kraist] *n.* a title given to Jesus, the founder of the Christian religion; the Savior.
—⑧ 그리스도, 구세주

chris·ten [krísn] *vt.* **1.** take (someone) into a Christian church by baptism; baptize. **2.** give a first name to (a baby) at baptism. ¶*He was christened John after his grandfather.* 「and countries.」
—⑩ 1. …에 세례를 베풀다, …을 그리스도 교도로 하다 2. …에게 세례를 베풀어 명명하다

Chris·ten·dom [krísndəm] *n.* Ⓤ Ⓒ all Christians people
—⑧ 전(全) 그리스도 교도(교국)

chris·ten·ing [krísniŋ] *n.* Ⓒ Ⓤ the act or ceremony at which a baby is christened; baptism.
—⑧ 세례, 세례식, 명명식

:**Chris·tian** [krístʃən] *adj.* **1.** of Christ; believing in Christ. ¶*a ~ name*① / *the ~ Era.*② **2.** showing the good qualities taught by Christ. ⇒N.B. **3.** of Christianity or Christians. —*n.* Ⓒ **1.** a believer in Christ; a member of the religion founded by Jesus Christ. **2.** (*colloq.*) a good and honorable person.
—⑩ 1. 그리스도의, 그리스도교를 믿는 ¶①세례명/②서력 기원 2. 그리스도교적인 N.B. 사랑·겸손·친절을 나타냄 3. 그리스도교도[의] —⑧ 1. 그리스도 교도 2. (口) 훌륭한 사람

Chris·ti·an·i·ty [krìstʃiǽniti] *n.* Ⓤ the religion taught by Christ; the Christian religion; Christian beliefs, faith, spirit, etc.
—⑧ 그리스도교; 그리스도교 신앙, 그리스도교적인 정신

Chris·tian·ize [krístʃənàiz / -tjən-] *vt.* make (someone) Christian or like a Christian; convert (someone) to Christianity.
—⑩ …을 그리스도 교도로 만들다, 그리스도교화하다

:**Christ·mas** [krísməs] *n.* the celebration held on December 25th in honor of the birth of Christ.
—⑧ 크리스마스, 성탄절

Christmas box [´-´] *n.* (*Brit.*) a present given at Christmas to the postman, delivery boys, etc. in return for their services.
—⑧ (英) [우체부·배달부 등에게 주는] 크리스마스 선물

Christmas card [´-´] *n.* a card for mailing at Christmas to express good wishes. ⇒usage
—⑧ 크리스마스 카아드 usage send a Christmas card 라고 함

Christmas carol [´-´´] *n.* a Christmas song. 「Day.」
—⑧ 크리스마스 축가

Christmas Eve [´-´] *n.* the evening before Christmas 」
—⑧ 크리스마스 전야

Christmas tree [´-´] *n.* an evergreen tree decorated with candles or small electric lights at Christmas time.
—⑧ 크리스마스 트리

Chris·to·pher [krístəfər] *n.* a man's name.
—⑧ 남자 이름

chro·mat·ic [kroumǽtik / krə-] *adj.* **1.** of color or colors. ¶*~ printing.*① **2.** (*Music*) progressing by half tones.
—⑩ 1. 빛깔의, 색채의 ¶①색채 인쇄 [물] 2.(樂) 반음계의, 반음의

chrome [kroum] *n.* Ⓤ **1.** chromium. **2.** chrome yellow.
—⑧ 1. 크로움 2. 황연(黃鉛)

chrome steel [´ ´] *n.* a very strong, hard, steel that contains chromium.
—⑧ 크로움강(鋼)

chro·mi·um [króumiəm] *n.* Ⓤ a shiny, hard, rust-resisting metallic element.
—⑧ 크로움, 크로뮴

chron·ic [kránik / krɔ́n-] *adj.* **1.** (of a disease) lasting for a long time; long-continued. ↔acute ¶*a ~ case.*① **2.** constant; habitual. ¶*a ~ smoker.*②
—⑩ 1. 만성의, 오래 끄는 ¶①만성병 환자 2. 장기에 걸친, 습관적인 ¶② 골초

chron·i·cal·ly [kránik(ə)li / krɔ́n-] *adv.* in a manner of being chronic.
—⑩ 만성적으로, 질질 끌어

- **chron·i·cle** [kránikl / krɔ́n-] *n.* Ⓒ a record of events in the order in which they happened. ¶*the Chronicles.*①
  —*vt.* record (something) in a chronicle; write or tell the history or story of (something).
  —⑧ 연대기, 편년사(編年史), 기록, 이야기 ¶①역대지략(歷代志略) —⑩ …을 연대기에 싣다, 기록에 올리다

chron·i·cler [krániklər / krɔ́nikla-] *n.* Ⓒ a writer of a chronicle; a recorder of events; a historian.
—⑧ 연대기 작자, 기록자, 역사가

chron·o·log·i·cal [krànəládʒik(ə)l / krɔ̀nəlɔ́dʒ-] *adj.* arranged in the order of occurrence. ¶*in ~ order.*①
▷**chron·o·log·i·cal·ly** [-i] *adv.*
—⑩ 연대순의 ¶①연대순으로

chro·nol·o·gy [krənálədʒi / -nɔ́l-] *n.* (pl. **-gies**) **1.** Ⓤ the science dealing with events and arranging their dates in proper order. **2.** Ⓒ a table or list of events arranged in their proper order of occurrence; the arrangement of events in their proper order of occurrence.
— ⓝ 1. 연대학(年代學) 2. 연표, 연대표, 연대기

chro·nom·e·ter [krənámitər / -nɔ́m-] *n.* Ⓒ an instrument like a clock or watch for measuring time very exactly.
— ⓝ 크로노미터[경도(經度) 측정용의 정밀 시계]

chrys·al·i·des [krisǽlidìːz] *n.* pl. of **chrysalis**.

chrys·a·lis [krísəlis] *n.* Ⓒ (pl. **chrys·a·lis·es** or **chrys·al·i·des**) **1.** the inactive form of an insect when it is in a case; a pupa. **2.** anything in such a stage; an undeveloped stage.
— ⓝ 1. [특히 나비류의] 번데기 2. 준비기간, 과도기; 미발달의 상태

chry·san·the·mum [krisǽnθ(ə)məm] *n.* Ⓒ a plant of the aster family which blooms late in the autumn. ⇒N.B.
— ⓝ 국화 N.B. 미국 구어에서는 mum 이라 함

chub·by [tʃʎbi] *adj.* (**-bi·er, -bi·est**) round and plump; rather fat. ▷**chub·bi·ness** [-nis] *n.*
— ⓐ 토실토실 살찐, 똥똥한

chuck¹ [tʃʌk] *vt.* **1.** pat or tap lovingly, esp. under the chin. ¶ ~ *someone under the chin.* **2.** throw; toss. ¶ ~ *a ball* | ~ *the letter into the wastebasket* | ~ *me the suitcase.* **3.** (*colloq.*) throw away; dismiss. ¶ ~ *one's friend.*①
1) *chuck away,* ⓐ throw away. ⓑ waste (time, money, etc.).
2) *chuck up,* give up; abandon (one's job, etc.) in disgust. — *n.* Ⓒ **1.** a light pat or tap [under the chin]. **2.** a toss; a throw.
— ⓥ 1. …을 가볍게 치다(두드리다) 2. …을 내던지다 3. (口) 포기하다, 사직하다 ¶①친구를 버리다
熟 1)ⓐ …을 던져 버리다 ⓑ …을 낭비하다 2)…을 [싫증나서] 팽개치다; 포기하다 — ⓝ 1. [턱 밑을] 가볍게 때리기 2. 내던지기; 포기

chuck² [tʃʌk] *n.* **1.** Ⓒ a device for holding a tool or a piece of wood or metal in a lathe or drill. **2.** Ⓤ the part or cut of beef between the neck and the shoulder.
— ⓝ 1. 척(선반(旋盤) 따위에 고정시키는 일종의 회전 바이스) 2. 소의 목덜미 고기

• **chuck·le** [tʃʎkl] *vi.* laugh quietly to oneself. ¶*He chuckled to himself over the funny cartoon.* — *n.* Ⓒ a soft, quiet laugh. ▷**chuck·ler** [-lər] *n.*
— ⓥ 껄껄 웃다 — ⓝ 껄껄 웃음, 킬킬거림

chug [tʃʌg] *n.* Ⓒ a short, loud, explosive sound. — *vi.* (**chugged, chug·ging**) make short, loud, explosive sounds; move while making such sounds.
— ⓝ [발동기 따위의] 풍풍 소리 — ⓥ 풍풍 소리내다(내며 나아가다)

chum [tʃʌm] *n.* Ⓒ **1.** an intimate, dear friend. **2.** a roommate. — *vi.* (**chummed, chum·ming**) **1.** be intimate friends with someone. ¶ ~ *up* (or *in*) *with someone.*① **2.** room together. (~ *with* someone)
— ⓝ 1. 친구 2. 한방 친구 — ⓥ 1. 친하게 지내다 ¶①…와 사이좋게 지내다 2. …와 한방에 거처하다

chum·my [tʃʎmi] *adj.* (**-mi·er, -mi·est**) (*colloq.*) very friendly; intimate. ▷**chum·mi·ly** [-li] *adv.*
— ⓐ 친한, 친밀한

chump [tʃʌmp] *n.* Ⓒ **1.** (*colloq.*) a foolish or silly person. **2.** a short, thick piece of wood. **3.** (*slang*) the head.
— ⓝ 1. (口) 바보 2. 통나무 토막 3. (俗) 머리

chunk [tʃʌŋk] *n.* Ⓒ **1.** a short, thick piece or lump, as of wood, meat, or cheese. **2.** (*U.S.*) a stocky person or animal. ¶*a fine ~ of man.*①
— ⓝ 1. 큰 조각 2. (美) 땅딸막한 사람 (짐승) ¶①체격이 훌륭한 사내

‡ **church** [tʃəːrtʃ] *n.* **1.** Ⓒ a building for public Christian worship.
— ⓝ 1. 교회 N.B. 보통 그리스도교의 교회만을 이르나 영국에서는 국교의 교회당만을 가리키는 경우도 있음 2. [교회에서] 예배 N.B. 이 의미에서는 관사를 붙이지 않음 ¶①예배보러 가다/②그들은 예배 중이다 N.B. They are in the church.는 「그들은 교회당에 있다」는 뜻 3. [모든] 그리스도 교도

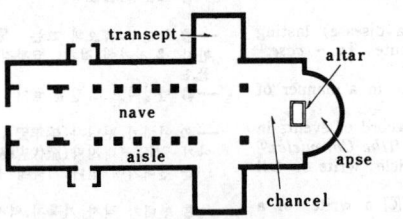
[church 1.]

⇒N.B., fig. **2.** Ⓤ (without *an article*) public worship; religious service in a church. ⇒N.B. ¶*go to* (or *attend*) ~① | *They are at* (or *in*) ~.② ⇒N.B. **3.** ((*the*

churchgoer [201] **cinecamera**

C-, *collectively*) all Christians. **4.** ⓒ a group of people with the same religious beliefs. ¶*the Church of England*③ / *the Church of Rome.*④ **5.** Ⓤ (*the C-*) the clergy as a profession.

1) *as poor as a church mouse*, very poor.
2) *enter* (or *go into*) *the Church*, become a priest.
—*vt.* bring or conduct (someone) to church, esp. for special services; perform a church service of thanksgiving for (a woman after childbirth). ¶*The mother was churched.*⑤ 「church regularly.」

church·go·er [tʃə́ːrtʃgòuər] *n.* ⓒ a person who goes to
church·go·ing [tʃə́ːrtʃgòu(u)iŋ] *n.* Ⓤ church attendance esp. when habitual. —*adj.* attending church regularly.
church·man [tʃə́ːrtʃmən] *n.* ⓒ (pl. **-men** [-mən]) **1.** a clergyman; a priest. **2.** (*Brit.*) (sometimes *C-*) a member of the Church of England.
church·ward·en [tʃə́ːrtʃwɔ̀ːrdn] *n.* ⓒ **1.** a church officer, not a priest, whose duties are chiefly concerned with the management of church business, property, finances, etc. ⇒[N.B.] **2.** (*Brit. colloq.*) a long clay tobacco pipe.
church·yard [tʃə́ːrtʃjàːrd] *n.* ⓒ a yard or graveyard very near a church; a cemetery.
churl·ish [tʃə́ːrliʃ] *adj.* rude; ill-bred; mean.
churn [tʃəːrn] *n.* **1.** ⓒ a wooden tub or machine in which milk or cream is made into butter. ⇒fig. **2.** ⓒ (*Brit.*) a large milk can. **3.** Ⓤ the act of stirring violently. —*vt.* **1.** stir or shake (cream or milk) in a churn. **2.** make (butter) in a churn. **3.** shake (water, etc.) violently. —*vi.* **1.** work a churn. **2.** move as if churned. ¶*The water churns around* (or *among*) *the rocks.*④ [churn 1.]

chute [ʃuːt] *n.* ⓒ **1.** an inclined passage, tube, etc. for conveying things from a higher to a lower level. ¶*a letter ~.*④ **2.** rapids in a river; waterfall. **3.** a long, narrow ledge; a steep slope. **4.** (*colloq.*) a parachute.
ci·ca·da [sikéidə, -káːdə] *n.* ⓒ (pl. **-das** or **-dae**) a large insect with four transparent wings. ⇒[N.B.]
ci·ca·dae [sikéidiː / -kaː-] *n.* pl. of **cicada**.
cic·e·ro·ne [sìsəróuni / tʃìtʃə-] *n.* ⓒ (pl. **-nes** or **-ni**) a guide for sightseers who explains the history or interesting places, etc.
cic·e·ro·ni [sìsəróuniː / tʃìtʃə-] *n.* pl. of **cicerone**.
ci·der [sáidər] *n.* Ⓤ **1.** apple juice. **2.** (*Brit.*) a light wine.
cider press [⌣–⌣] *n.* a machine that presses the juice out of apples. 「smoking.」
* **ci·gar** [sigáːr] *n.* ⓒ a small roll of tobacco leaves for
* **cig·a·rette** [sìgərét, +*U.S.* ⌣–⌣] *n.* ⓒ a thin roll of finely cut tobacco wrapped in a thin sheet of paper for smoking. ¶*a carton of cigarettes.*④
cin·cho·na [siŋkóunə] *n.* **1.** ⓒ a tropical tree of South America, the East Indies, India, and Java, valuable for its bark. ⇒[N.B.] **2.** Ⓤ its bitter bark. ⇒[N.B.]
cinc·ture [síŋktʃər] *n.* **1.** ⓒ a belt or girdle. **2.** Ⓤ enclosure.
cin·der [síndər] *n.* **1.** Ⓤ (often *pl.*) a small piece of coal, etc. partly burned and no longer flaming. ¶*be burnt to cinders.*④ **2.** (*pl.*) ashes.
Cin·der·el·la [sìndərélə] *n.* **1.** a pretty girl in a fairy tale. ⇒[N.B.] **2.** ⓒ a beautiful girl who is oppressed in poor surroundings. 「motion pictures.」
cin·e·cam·e·ra [sìnikǽm(ə)rə] *n.* ⓒ a camera for making

4. [조직체로서의] 교회, 교파, ¶③영국 국교회/④로마 가톨릭 교회 5. 성직

圀 1) 아주 가난한 2) 성직에 취임하다, 목사가 되다
—㉮ [안산(安産)·감사 따위의 특별 예배에] …을 교회에 안내하다; …을 위해 [안산의] 감사 예배를 드리다 ¶⑤어머니는 감사 예배를 받았다

—㉯ 교회에 다니는 사람
—㉯ 교회에 다니기 —㉮ 교회에 다니는
—㉯ 1. 목사 2. 영국 국교도

—㉯ 1. [성직자가 아닌] 교구 위원 [N.B.] 영국 교회나 미국 성공회에서는 parish(교구)를 대표하여 교회 일을 돌보는 사람 2. (英口) 긴 사기 담뱃대
—㉯ 교회의 구내; [교회에 부속된] 묘지
—㉮ 야비한, 천한; 인색한
—㉯ 1. 교유기(攪乳器) 2. 대형 우유통 3. 세게 휘젓기 —㉮ 1. …을 [교유기로] 휘젓다 2. [휘저어서] …을 만들다 3. …을 세게 휘젓다 —㉳ 1. 교유기를 쓰다 2. 심하게 동요하다 ¶①물이 바위 사이에서 세게 소용돌이치고 있다

—㉯ 1. 비탈진 도랑(홈통) ¶①우편 투하 장치 2. 급류, 폭포 3. 활주사면(滑走斜面); 급사면 4. (口) 낙하산

—㉯ 매미 [N.B.] 미국에서는 locust 라고도 함

—㉯ [명소·고적의] 안내인

—㉯ 1. 사과즙 2. 사과술

—㉯ 사과 압착기

—㉯ 엽궐련, 시가아
—㉯ 궐련 ¶①(열 갑 들이) 담배 한 상자

—㉯ 1. 기나수(幾那樹) [N.B.] 원산지는 남미 2. 기나피(皮) [N.B.] 키니네를 채취함
—㉯ 1. 끈, 띠 2. 울타리, 담

—㉯ 1. 탄 나무, 뜬숯(완전히 재가 되지 않은 것) ¶①새까맣게 타다 2. 재

—㉯ 1. 신데렐라 [N.B.] 계모와 자매에게 혹사당하다가 나중에 왕비가 되었음 2. 숨은 미인
—㉯ 영화 촬영기

‡ **cin·e·ma** [sínimə] *n.* [C] (chiefly *Brit.*) **1.** a motion picture; a motion-picture theater. ¶*go to the* (or *a*) ~.① **2.** 《*the* ~, *collectively*》 motion pictures; the business or art of motion pictures.
—[名] 《英》 1. [한 편의] 영화; 영화관 ¶ ①영화를 보러 가다 2. 영화; 영화 사업(예술)

cin·e·mat·o·graph [sìnimǽtəgræ̀f / -grὰ:f] *n.* [C] **1.** (*Brit.*) a motion-picture projector. **2.** a camera for taking motion pictures. ⇨[N.B.]
—[名] 1. 《英》 영사기 2. 영화 촬영기 [N.B.] kinematograph 라고도 함

cin·na·mon [sínəmən] *n.* **1.** [C] an East Indian tree; [U] the bark of this tree. **2.** [U] the yellowish-brown spice made from the inner bark of this tree. ⇨[N.B.] **3.** [U] a light, rather red brown.
—[名] 1. 육계수(肉桂樹); 육계피 2. 육계 [N.B.] 육계수 껍질의 가루로서 향미료 3. 육계빛

ci·pher [sáifər] *n.* [C] **1.** zero; 0. **2.** a person or thing of no importance. **3.** a code; a method of secret writing. ¶*in* ~.① **4.** [U] a key explaining secret writing or a code. ¶*a* ~ *code* (*telegram*).② **5.** interlaced initials; a monogram. —*vt.* **1.** solve (problems) with figures. **2.** express (something) in secret writing. ↔decipher —*vi.* **1.** solve arithmetical problems. **2.** use a secret code.
—[名] 1. 영(零), 0 2. 보잘것 없는 사람(것). 3. 암호, 암호로 쓰는 법 ¶①암호로 쓴 4. 암호 해독법 ¶②암호 전신부(전보) 5. [이름의 머리글자의] 짜맞춘 문자 —[他] 1. …을 계산하다 2. …을 암호로 쓰다 —[自] 1. 계산을 하다 2. 암호문을 쓰다

cir·ca [sə́:rkə] *prep., adv.* about. ⇨[N.B.] ¶*He was born c. 1500.*
—[前][副] 약(約) [N.B.] c. circ.로 줄임

Cir·ce [sə́:rsi] *n.* **1.** (in Greek mythology) a female magician. ⇨[N.B.] **2.** [C] a very charming woman.
—[名] 1. 키르케 [N.B.] 남자를 돼지로 변하게 한 마녀 2. 요부(妖婦)

‡ **cir·cle** [sə́:rkl] *n.* [C] **1.** a plane figure of perfectly round. **2.** something round like a circle; a ring. ¶*stand in a* ~.① **3.** [U] a series ending at the starting point. ¶*the* ~ *of the seasons.*② **4.** a section of seats in a theater. **5.** a society of persons having the same interests. ¶*business circles.*③ **6.** (*Astronomy*) the path in which a heavenly body moves about another.
—[名] 1. [평면적인] 원 2. 원 모양의 물건; 고리 ¶①원을 이루어 서다 3. 순환 ¶②사철의 순환 4. [극장의] 원형 관람석 5. 한패; 동호회; 사회 ¶③실업계 6. [천체의] 궤도

—*vt.* **1.** enclose (something) with a circle; surround. **2.** move in a circle around (a place). —*vi.* move in a circle.
—[他] 1. …을 둘러싸다 2. …의 둘레를 회전하다; 선회하다 —[自] 회전하다

cir·clet [sə́:rklit] *n.* [C] **1.** a small circle. **2.** a round ornament for the head, neck, arm, or finger.
—[名] 1. 작은 원 2. [금·보석 따위의] 장식고리, 목걸이, 반지, 팔찌

* **cir·cuit** [sə́:rkit] *n.* [C] **1.** [U] the boundary line around an area; the area so bounded. ¶*the* ~ *of the earth.*① **2.** the act of going around; a round trip; a detour. ¶*make a* ~ *of*....② **3.** a way or district over which a person or group regularly travels at certain times for the purpose of holding court or performing certain duties. ¶*on the* ~③ / *ride the* ~④ / *make a* ~. **4.** the path of an electric current. ¶*a leak in an electric* ~.⑤
—[名] 1. 주위, 범위 ¶①지구의 주위 2. 순회[여행], 우회[로]; 멀리 돌기 ¶②…을 일주하다 3. [목사·재판관 따위의] 순회, 순회 교구, 순회 재판[구], 순회 변호사회 ¶③순회중/④말을 타고 순시하다 4. [전류의] 회로(回路), 회선 ¶⑤누전

circuit court [⌐– ⌐] *n.* a Federal court whose judges hold court regularly at certain places in a district. ⇨[N.B.]
—[名] 순회 재판소 [N.B.] 1911년 폐지

cir·cu·i·tous [sə(:)rkjú(:)itəs] *adj.* roundabout; indirect.
—[形] 돌아가는, 우회하는; 넌지시 하는

* **cir·cu·lar** [sə́:rkjulər] *adj.* **1.** round. **2.** going around a circle; revolving. **3.** sent to each of many persons. ¶*a* ~ *letter.*① **4.** roundabout; indirect. ¶*a* ~ *ticket.*② —*n.* [C] a letter, notice, or advertisement sent to each of many persons. ▷**cir·cu·lar·ly** [-li] *adv.*
—[形] 1. 둥근 2. 빙글빙글 도는, 순환성의 3. 회람의, 여러 사람에게 돌리는 ¶①회람 4. 순회의 ¶②순회 차표 —[名] 회람판, 안내장

cir·cu·late [sə́:rkjulèit] *vi.* **1.** go around; pass from one person or place to another. ¶*Blood circulates in the body.*① **2.** be handed from person to person. **3.** go from one person or place to another. ¶*Money circulates.* / *The rumor circulated.* / *The story circulated through the village.*② —*vt.* cause (something) to move around from one person or place to another; place (something) in circulation.
—[自] 1. 빙글빙글 돌다, 순회하다 ¶①혈액은 체내를 순환한다 2. [신문 따위가] 배포되다 3. 유포되다, 전해지다 ¶②그 이야기는 온 마을에 퍼졌다 —[他] …을 돌리다, 퍼뜨리다, 배부하다, 회람하다, 유통시키다

* **cir·cu·la·tion** [sə̀:rkjuléiʃ(ə)n] *n.* [U] **1.** the act of circulating; the movement of the blood. ¶~ *of the air*① / ~ *of the blood.* **2.** the distribution of newspapers, etc. **3.** [U][C] the number of copies of a newspaper, etc. that are sent out or sold in a given time. ¶*have a large* ~② / *have a wide* ~ / *The paper has a* ~ *of 100,000.*③
—[名] 1. [공기·물 따위의] 유통, 혈액의 순환 ¶①공기의 유통 2. 배포, 배부 3. 발행부수, 매상고 ¶②발행부수가 많다 /③그 신문은 10만의 발행부수를 갖고 있다 4. [화폐의] 유통; [뉴우스의] 유포 ¶④[화폐가] 유통하고 있다; [소문

4. the passage of something, such as money or news, from one person or place to another. ¶*be in* ~④ / *put … in* ~.⑤

이] 나돌고 있다/⑤…을 유통시키다, 유포시키다

cir·cu·la·to·ry [sə́:rkjulətɔ̀:ri / sə̀:kjuléit(ə)ri] *adj.* of circulation.

—[形] [혈액·물 따위의] 순환의

cir·cum·fer·ence [sərkʌ́mf(ə)r(ə)ns] *n.* [U] the line that bounds a cirle; the distance around. ¶*the* ~ *of one's chest.*①

—[名] 원주, 주변, 주위; 경계선 ¶①가슴둘레

cir·cum·fer·en·tial [sərkʌ̀mfərénʃəl] *adj.* of, at, or near the circumference.

—[形] 원주의, 주위의

cir·cum·lo·cu·tion [sə̀:rkəmləkjú:ʃ(ə)n] *n.* [U] [C] a roundabout or indirect expression.

—[名] 넌지시 돌려 말하기; 완곡한 표현

cir·cum·loc·u·to·ry [sə̀:rkəmlákjutɔ̀:ri / -lɔ́kjut(ə)ri] *adj.* characterized by circumlocution.

—[形] 넌지시 돌려 말하는

cir·cum·nav·i·gate [sə̀:rkəmnǽvigèit] *vt.* sail completely around (the earth, etc.). ▷**cir·cum·nav·i·ga·tor** [-ər] *n.*

—[他] …을 두루 항해하다, 배로 일주하다

cir·cum·nav·i·ga·tion [sə̀:rkəmnæ̀vigéiʃ(ə)n] *n.* [U] the act of sailing around the earth, etc.

—[名] [세계] 주항(周航)

cir·cum·scribe [sə̀:rkəmskráib, ⌐—⌐] *vt.* **1.** draw a line around (something); encircle; encompass. **2.** limit; keep (something) within bounds; show clearly; restrict.

—[他] 1. …의 주위에 선을 긋다; 주위를 둘러싸다 2. …을 제한하다; 한정하다; 속박하다

cir·cum·spect [sə́:rkəmspèkt] *adj.* careful; cautious; prudent.

—[形] 조심성 있는, 신중한

cir·cum·spec·tion [sə̀:rkəmspékʃ(ə)n] *n.* [U] care; caution; prudence.

—[名] 주의, 조심, 신중

⁑cir·cum·stance [sə́:rkəmstæ̀ns / sə́:kəmstəns] *n.* **1.** ⦅usu. *pl.*⦆ all the conditions of an act or event; environment. ¶*without considering all the circumstances*① / *as far as circumstances permit.*② **2.** ⦅*pl.*⦆ the facts or events which surround and influence something; financial condition. ¶*in bad (easy) circumstances.*③ **3.** [C] an event; a happening; a fact. ¶*His arrival was a fortunate* ~.④ **4.** [U] full detail. ¶*He told of his adventure with great* ~.

—[名] 1. 사정 ¶①모든 사정을 고려하지 않고/②사정이 허락하는 한 2. 환경, 경우, 경제 사정 ¶③곤궁하여(안락하게) 3. 일, 사건, 사실 ¶④그의 도착은 운 좋은 일이었다 4. 자초지종, 상세

1) ***under no circumstances,*** never; by no means.
2) ***under the circumstances,*** since such is the case; because of the conditions.

[熟] 1)결코 …않다 2)이러한 사정(조건)하에

—*vt.* ⦅in *passive*⦆ place (someone) in certain circumstances.

—[他] …을 특수한 사정하에 두다

cir·cum·stan·tial [sə́:rk(ə)mstǽnʃ(ə)l] *adj.* **1.** depending on circumstances. ¶~ *evidence.*① ↔direct evidence **2.** happening; not important. **3.** full of details; detailed. ¶*a* ~ *story.*② ▷**cir·cum·stan·tial·ly** [-ʃəli] *adv.*

—[形] 1. [증거 따위가] 상황에 따르는 ¶①정황(情況) 증거 2. 우연한, 중요하지 않은 3. 상세한, 자세한 ¶②자세한 이야기

cir·cum·vent [sə̀:rkəmvént] *vt.* **1.** go around (something). **2.** catch (someone) in a trap; defeat or block (someone's plan, etc.) by better trickery; outwit.

—[他] 1. …을 일주하다 2. …을 함정에 빠뜨리다; 덫에 걸다; 능가하다; 속이다, …보다 한수 더 뜨다

cir·cum·ven·tion [sə̀:rkəmvénʃ(ə)n] *n.* [U] the act of circumventing; the state of being circumvented.

—[名] 속여 넘기기; 계략에 빠뜨리기; 우회

•cir·cus [sə́:rkəs] *n.* [C] **1.** a traveling show of acrobats, clowns, horses, wild animals, etc.; a building or large tent for such a performance. **2.** in ancient Rome, a round or level space with rows of seats around it, used for chariot races, games, etc. **3.** (*Brit.*) a circular open place where many streets meet. ⇒[N.B.] ¶*Piccadilly Circus.*①

—[名] 1. 곡예, 곡마단, 서어커스; [계단식] 원형 흥행장 2. [고대 로마의] 경기장 3. ⦅英⦆ [여러개의 도로가 모이는] 원형 광장 [N.B.] 방사상(放射狀)의 가로(街路)가 모임 ¶①[런던]의 피카딜리 광장

cir·ri [sírai] *n.* pl. of **cirrus**.

cir·rus [sírəs] *n.* [C] (pl. **cir·ri**) a thin, narrow, white cloud very high in the air.

—[名] 권운(卷雲)

cis·tern [sístərn] *n.* [C] a tank for holding water.

—[名] 물통, 물탱크

cit·a·del [sítədl] *n.* [C] **1.** a fortress on a high place to protect a city; a strongly defended place. **2.** a safe place; a shelter.

—[名] 1. [시가가 내려다 보이는 위치에 쌓은] 요새, 성; [일반적으로] 견고한 요새 2. 피난처

ci·ta·tion [saitéiʃ(ə)n, +*Brit.* si-] *n.* [C] **1.** [C] a direct quotation or reference. **2.** (*U.S.*) a statement honoring a soldier, etc. for bravery in war. **3.** [C][U] an official order to someone to appear before a law court.

—[名] 1. 인용, 인용구 2. ⦅美⦆ 표창장 3. 소환장; 출정(出廷) 명령

•cite [sait] *vt.* **1.** quote (a passage from a book, article, etc.) **2.** bring forward or tell (facts, etc.) as proof or

—[他] 1. …을 인용하다 2. …을 증거(예)로 들다, …에 언급하다 3. …을 표창하

as an example. ¶~ *an instance from one's own experience.* **3.** praise (a soldier, etc.) for bravery in war. **4.** officially call (someone) to appear before a law court.
다, 특기(特記)하다 **4.** …을 소환하다

⁑ **cit·i·zen** [sítizn, +*U.S.* -sn] *n.* [C] **1.** a member of a state or nation. ↔alien ¶*an American* ~.① **2.** an inhabitant of a city or town; a townsman. **3.** a civilian as different from a soldier, a policeman, etc.
—[名] 1. [한 나라의] 시민, 공민, 국민 ¶①미국 국민 2. 도회인, 시민 3. [군인·경관에 대하여] 일반인, 서민

a citizen of the world, a cosmopolitan.
[熟] 세계인, 국제인

cit·i·zen·ry [sítiznri, +*U.S.* -sn-] *n.* 《*collectively*》 citizens as a group.
—[名] 시민

cit·i·zen·ship [sítiznʃìp, +*U.S.* -sn-] *n.* [U] **1.** the condition of being a citizen. **2.** the duties, rights, etc. of a citizen.
—[名] 1. 시민(공민)임 2. 시민의 의무·권리 [따위]

cit·ron [sítrən] *n.* [C] a fruit like a lemon, but larger and not so sour; a small tree bearing this fruit.
—[名] 구연(枸櫞)[의 열매], 불수감(佛手柑)

cit·rous [sítrəs] *adj.* of such fruits as lemons and oranges.
—[形] 감귤류의

cit·rus [sítrəs] *n.* [C] any tree bearing lemons, oranges, or similar fruit.
—[名] 감귤류의 식물

⁑ **cit·y** [síti] *n.* [C] (pl. **cit·ies**) **1.** a large or an important town. ¶*go to the* ~ / *the City of David*① / *the City of God*② / *the City of* [*the*] *Seven Hills*③ / *the Eternal City.*④ **2.** (*U.S.*) a legal body holding a charter from the state in which it is located and serving as a unit of local government. **3.** (*Canada*) a municipality of the highest rank. **4.** (*Brit.*) a chartered town, which is or has been the seat of a bishop. **5.** 《*the* ~》 [all] the people living in a city. **6.** 《*the C-*》 the business and financial district of London.
—[名] 1. 도시, 도회 ¶①다윗의 거리(Jerusalem 또는 Bethlehem)/②천국/③일곱 언덕의 도시(Rome을 이름)/④영원의 도시(Rome을 이름) 2. 《美》 주정부의 허가에 의한 자치체; 시(市) 3. 《캐나다》 최고의 자치체; 시 4. 《英》 주교가 있는 지역; [칙허장에 의한] 시 5. 시민[전체] 6. 런던의 구시가(상업 중심지)

city-bred [sítibrèd] *adj.* born and raised in a city.
—[形] 도시에서 자란

city hall [ˊ- ˊ] *n.* (*U.S.*) the headquarters of the officials, etc. of a city government.
—[名] 《美》 시청자

city manager [ˊ- ˊ--] *n.* (*U.S.*) a person appointed by a city council or similar body to act as manager of the city.
—[名] [선거에 의하지 않고 시의회에서 임명되는] 사무 시장

civ·ic [sívik] *adj.* of a city, citizens, or citizenship. ¶~ *rights* / ~ *pride.*
—[形] 시의; 시민의, 공민의

civ·ics [síviks] *n. pl.* 《used as *sing.*》 the science or study of the duties, rights, and privileges of citizens.
—[名] 공민학, 시정학(市政學); [학과로서의] 공민과

⁑ **civ·il** [sív(i)l] *adj.* **1.** of a citizen or citizens. ¶~ ***rights.***① **2.** not connected with the church or the military. ¶~ *aviation*② / *a* ~ *servant*③ / *enter* (or ***return***) *to* ~ *life.*④ **3.** polite; courteous; civilized. ¶*I must say something* ~ *to him.*⑤ / *keep a* ~ *tongue in one's head.*⑥ **4.** (*Law*) relating to legal proceedings in connection with private, not public, rights. ↔criminal
—[形] 1. 시민의, 공민의 ¶①공민권 2. 문관의, 민간의 ¶②민간 항공/③문관/④일반 시민의 생활로 돌아가다 3. 공손한, 예의바른; 문명의 ¶⑤그에게 무엇인가 친절한 말을 해주어야겠다/⑥말을 삼가다 4. 《法》 민사(民事)의

civil engineering [ˊ- ˋ-ˊ-] *n.* the branch of engineering dealing with the construction of bridges, roads, harbors, etc.
—[名] 토목공학

ci·vil·ian [sivíljən] *n.* [C] a person who is neither a soldier nor a sailor. —*adj.* of civilians; not military or naval.
—[名] 일반 시민, 문관 —[形] 민간의, 평민의, 일반인의, 문관의

ci·vil·i·ty [sivíliti] *n.* (pl. **-ties**) **1.** [U] politeness; good manners. **2.** 《*pl.*》 a civil act or speech. ¶*exchange civilities.*①
—[名] 1. 예의, 정중함 2. 예의바른(공손한) 언동 ¶①인사를 서로 나누다

⁑ **civ·i·li·za·tion** [sìvilizéiʃ(ə)n / -vilai-] *n.* **1.** [U] the act of civilizing; the state of being civilized; improvement in culture. **2.** [U] the civilized condition; [C] the special culture of a people or a period. ↔barbarism ¶*beyond the bounds of* ~.① **3.** 《*collectively*》 the nations and peoples which are in a high stage of social development.
—[名] 1. 개화(開化), 교화 2. 문명, 문화 ¶①문명이 미치지 않는 곳에 3. 문명 사회, 문명 국가

* **civ·i·lize** [sívilàiz] *vt.* **1.** bring (someone) out of a primitive way of life; instruct (someone) in culture, science, and art; educate. ¶~ *away.*① **2.** make (someone) better in culture and good manners. ▷**civ·i·liz·er** [-ər] *n.*
—[他] 1. …을 문명화하다, 교화하다 ¶①교화하여 [야만적인 풍습을] 없애다 2. …을 세련되게 하다, 고상하게 하다

civ·i·lized [sívilàizd] *adj.* **1.** advanced in social organi-
—[形] 1. 교화된, 문명화된 2. 예의바른,

zation, art, and science; of civilized nations or persons. ↔barbarous **2.** courteous; refined.
세련된

civil law [∠- ∠] *n.* the law having to do with private rights.
—[名] 민법(民法)

civ·il·ly [sívili] *adv.* **1.** politely; courteously. **2.** by the civil law.
—[副] 1. 공손히, 예의바르게 2. 민법에 따라서

civil marriage [∠- ∠-] *n.* a marriage not begun with a religious ceremony but still recognized by law.
—[名] [종교의식에 의하지 않고 관리가 집행하는] 계출(약식) 결혼

civil service [∠- ∠-] *n.* the departments of administration of a government concerned with public service that are not military, naval, legislative, or judicial; 《*collectively*》 the body of persons working in those branches.
—[名] 문관 근무, 행정 사무; 문관, 공무원

civil war [∠- ∠] *n.* **1.** war between two groups of citizens of one nation. **2.** 《*the C- W-*》 (*U.S.*) the war between the Northern and Southern States of the United States (1861-1865); (*Brit.*) the war between the English Parliament and the Royalists (1642-46, 1648-52).
—[名] 1. 국내 전쟁, 내란 2.《美》 남북전쟁; 《英》 Charles 1세와 의회와의 싸움

cl. **1.** centiliter. **2.** class. **3.** clause.

clack [klæk] *vi., vt.* make a short, sharp sound; talk. —*n.* [C] a short, sharp sound; a clatter; a chatter.
—[自][他] 찰깍(딸깍) 하고 소리내다; 재잘거리다 —[名] 찰깍하는 소리; 수다

***clad** [klæd] *v.* pt. and pp. of **clothe.**

‡**claim** [kleim] *vt.* **1.** ask for (something) on the ground of right; ask or insist on (something) as one's own. ¶ *~ a reward* | *~ the right to the patent*① | *Does anyone ~ this book?*② **2.** tell (something) as a fact; say. 《*~ to do; ~ that ...*》 ¶ *He claimed to have reached there; He claimed that he had reached there.* **3.** deserve. ¶ *The problem claims our attention.*③ —*vi.* insist on a right; make a claim.
—[他] 1. [당연한 권리로서] …을 요구하다, 주장하다 ¶①특허의 권리를 주장하다/②이 책의 주인은 없읍니다 2. [사실로서] …을 주장하다 3. …할 가치가 있다 ¶③그 문제는 주목할 가치가 있다 —[自] 요구하다, 주장하다

—*n.* [C] **1.** a demand for something as one's own. 《*~ for* or *to* something》 ¶ *a ~ for damages*④ | *Nobody made a ~ to this suitcase.*⑤ **2.** right to ask for something. 《*~ to* something; *~ on* or *upon* someone》 ¶ *He has no ~ to the property.* **3.** anything that is claimed, esp. a piece of public land claimed and marked out by a miner, settler, etc.
—[名] 1. 요구 ¶④손해배상의 요구/⑤이 가방의 임자는 아무도 나타나지 않았다 2. 권리 3. 청구물; 불하 청구지(請求地)

1) ***lay claim to,*** declare that one should have (something).
2) ***put in a claim for,*** say that (something) is or should be one's own.
[熟] 1)…을 요구하다 2)…에 대하여 청구권을 제출하다

claim·ant [kléimənt] *n.* [C] a person who makes a claim.
—[名] 청구자, 신청자, 원고

clair·voy·ance [klɛərvɔ́iəns] *n.* [U] **1.** the supposed power of knowing about things not seen by other persons. **2.** unusual insight.
—[名] 1. 투시[력], 천리안 2. 날카로운 통찰력

clair·voy·ant [klɛərvɔ́iənt] *adj.* **1.** having the power of seeing things not seen by other persons. **2.** unusually keen. —*n.* [C] a clairvoyant person.
—[形] 1. 투시의, 투시력이 있는, 천리안의 2. 통찰력이 있는
—[名] 천리안이 있는 사람

clam [klæm] *n.* (pl. **clams** or *collectively* **clam**) [C] **1.** a shellfish which can be eaten, like an oyster. **2.** (*U.S. colloq.*) [C] a silent, retiring person.
—[名] 1. 대합조개 2.《美口》 말수 적은 사람

shut up like a clam be silent in an unpleasant way.
[熟] 언짢은 듯이 입을 다물고 있다

clam·ber [klǽmbər] *vt., vi.* climb (something) with effort or difficulty 《*~ up* a wall》. —*n.* [C] an awkward or difficult climb.
—[他][自] [힘들여] 기어오르다 —[名] 기어 오르기

clam·mi·ly [klǽmili] *adv.* in a clammy manner.
—[副] 끈적끈적하게, 축축하게

clam·my [klǽmi] *adj.* (**-mi·er, -mi·est**) covered with something cold and wet.
—[形] 차고 끈적끈적한, 축축한

***clam·or,** *Brit.* **-our** [klǽmər] *n.* [U][C] loud noise or shouting, esp. of a crowd; a noisy demand.
—[名] [군중 따위의] 외침소리, 함성; 소동

—*vt., vi.* ask or request noisily. ¶ *~ against (for) the proposal.*①
—[他][自] 외치다; 떠들어대다 ¶①제안에 대해 시끄럽게 반대(찬성)하다

1) ***clamor down,*** trouble (a speaker) completely by speaking in loud voices.
2) ***clamor*** *someone* ***into,*** force someone to do (something) by making loud demands.
3) ***clamor*** *someone* ***out of,*** force someone to stop (some-
[熟] 1)[연설자 등을] 야유하여 말 못하게 하다 2)시끄럽게 떠들어 …에게 …시키다 3)시끄럽게 떠들어 …에게

clam·or·ous [klǽmərəs] *adj.* noisy; making noisy complaints. ¶ *be ~ for (something).*① …을 그만두게 하다
—㉠ 시끄러운, 귀찮은, 성가시게 잔소리하는 ¶①…을 시끄럽게 요구하다

clamp [klæmp] *n.* ⓒ a brace, band, or other device for fastening things together or supporting them. ⇒fig. —*vt.* fasten (something) with a clamp.
clamp down [*on*], put down (something) by force; exert pressure upon (weak people).
—㉢ 꺾쇠, 거멀못 —㉺ …을 죄다, 고정시키다

㉺ 압박하다, 단속하다, 탄압하다

clan [klæn] *n.* ⓒ **1.** a group of people in the Scottish Highlands supposed to have come from a common ancestor. **2.** a group of people united together by some common interest. ▷**clan·like** [-làik] *adj.*

[clamp]

—㉢ 1. [특히 스코틀랜드 고지(高地) 사람의] 씨족, 일족, 일문 2. 도당, 동지

clan·des·tine [klændéstin, +*Brit.* -tain] *adj.* secret.
—㉺ 비밀의, 남몰래 하는

clang [klæŋ] *n.* ⓒ a loud, ringing sound, as when metal strikes on other metal. —*vt., vi.* make or cause to make a clang. ⌜clanging.⌝
—㉢ 땡, 땡그렁(쇠붙이가 부딪쳐 울리는 소리) —㉺㉠ 땡(땡그렁)하고 울리다

clan·gor, *Brit.* -**gour** [klǽŋ(g)ər] *n.* ⓒ a continued
—㉢ 땡땡, 쨍그렁

clank [klæŋk] *n.* ⓒ a sharp, harsh metallic sound. —*vi., vt.* make a sharp, harsh sound; cause (something) to clank.
—㉢ 찰깍, 절꺽 소리 —㉺㉠ 절꺽거리(게 하)다

clan·nish [klǽniʃ] *adj.* **1.** of or related to a clan. **2.** closely united together; having a narrow view of strangers. ▷**clan·nish·ness** [-nis] *n.* ⌜of a clan.⌝
—㉺ 1. 씨족의, 일문의, 가문의 2. 당파심이 강한, 배타적인

clans·man [klǽnzmən] *n.* ⓒ (pl. **-men** [-mən]) a member
—㉢ 같은 씨족(문중)의 사람

• **clap** [klæp] *n.* ⓒ **1.** a sudden noise, such as the sound of hands struck together; a sharp blow; a slap. **2.** a sharp, explosive loud sound, as of thunder. —*vi., vt.* (**clapped, clap·ping**) **1.** strike together loudly or lightly; (of birds) move (wings) up and down. ¶ *~ one's hands* / *~ someone on the back.*① **2.** strike hands to praise (someone).
1) *clap eyes on*, (*colloq.*) catch sight of (someone); see.
2) *clap someone in prison*, put (someone) in prison.
3) *clap up*, ⓐ (of business) do business with (someone) hastily. ⓑ put (someone) in prison.
—㉢ 1. 박수 소리, 찰싹[때리기] 2. (우뢰 따위의) 쾅하는 소리 —㉠㉺ 1. 찰싹(가볍게) 때리다; [새가] 날갯짓하다 ¶①…의 등을 가볍게 두드리다 (다정한 사이의 인사) 2. 박수갈채

㉺ 1)(口)…을 보다, 우연히 발견하다 2)…을 감옥에 처넣다 3)ⓐ[거래 따위] 서둘러 결정짓다 ⓑ 투옥하다

clap·board [klǽpbɔ̀:rd] *n.* ⓒ a long, thin, overlapping board used in covering the outer walls of a wooden house; a weatherboard. —*vt.* cover (a house) with clapboards.
—㉢ 벽에 댄 판자, 비늘판 —㉺ [집]에 벽판자를 대다

clap·per [klǽpər] *n.* ⓒ **1.** a person or thing that claps. **2.** the tongue of a bell. **3.** any device for making noise.
—㉢ 1. 박수하는 사람 2. [방울종 따위의] 추(錘) 3. 딱다기

clap·trap [klǽptræp] *n.* Ⓤ empty language or insincere words used to win public attention. —*adj.* showy and insincere.
—㉢ 인기를 노린 말(수단) —㉺ 인기를 노린, 속이 빤히 들여다보이는

Clar·a [klǽrə, klɛ́ərə / klɛ́ərə] *n.* a woman's name.
—㉢ 여자 이름

Clare [klɛər] *n.* a man's name or a woman's name; a nickname for Clara, Clarence, Clarice, Clarissa.
—㉢ Clara, Clarence, Clarice, Clarissa의 애칭

clar·et [klǽrət] *n.* Ⓤ **1.** red wine of Bordeaux. **2.** rich red color.
—㉢ 1. [보르도 산의] 붉은 포도주 2. 붉은 포도주빛, 짙은 자홍색

clar·i·fi·ca·tion [klæ̀rifikéiʃ(ə)n] *n.* Ⓤ the act of clarifying; the state of being clarified.
—㉢ 깨끗이 함, 순수화

clar·i·fy [klǽrifài] *vt., vi.* (**-fied**) make or become clear, pure, or easily seen through.
—㉺㉠ 깨끗하게(맑게) 하다, 투명하게 하다(되다)

clar·i·net [klæ̀rinét] *n.* ⓒ a wooden wind musical instrument played by covering and uncovering holes and moving keys.
—㉢ 클라리넷(목관악기)

clar·i·on [klǽriən] *n.* **1.** ⓒ a trumpet with clear, sharp tones formerly used in war. **2.** Ⓤ (*poetic*) the sound made by this trumpet. —*adj.* clear and loud.
—㉢ 1. 클라리온 2. 클라리온 소리, 명쾌한 소리 —㉺ 명쾌한 음색의

clar·i·o·net [klæ̀riənét] *n.* =clarinet.

clar·i·ty [klǽriti] *n.* Ⓤ clearness.
—㉢ 맑음, 명료, 명랑, 투명

clash [klæʃ] n. ⓒ 1. a loud, broken sound like that of striking weapons or bells rung together. 2. a fight; a disagreement; (of opinions) a quarrel; discord. ¶*a ~ of opinions.* —*vi., vt.* 1. make a loud sound. 2. come into a fight; disagree strongly.
—图 1. 쟁강쟁강 [맞부딪는 소리], 땡땡 [울리는 소리] 2. 충돌, 알력, 불일치
—自⑩ 1. 땡땡 울리다 2. 충돌하다, 일치하지 않다

* **clasp** [klæsp / klɑ:sp] n. ⓒ 1. a thing to fasten two parts together, such as a buckle or brooch. 2. a grasp; an embrace. —*vi., vt.* 1. fasten (something) with a clasp. 2. hold closely; grasp; embrace. ¶~ *hands.*①
—图 1. 고리, 걸쇠, 버클, 훅 2. 꽉 쥠, 포옹; 파악 —自⑩ 1. [걸쇠로] 죄다, 고정시키다 2. 꽉 쥐다, 껴안다, 엉켜 붙다 ¶①악수하다, 세휴하다

‡ **class** [klæs / klɑ:s] n. ⓒ 1. (often *pl.*) a social rank. ¶ *the intellectual ~.*① 2. a group of students under one teacher or studying together; a classroom. 3. a meeting of such a group for study. ¶*social studies ~.*② 4. (*U.S.*) (*collectively*) a group of students in the same year in a school or college and graduating together. ¶*the ~ of 1970.*③ 5. a level according to quality, value, or rank. ¶*a first ~ hotel.*④ 6. Ⓤ kind. 7. (*the ~es*) the higher ranks of society. ↔the masses
1) *be in a class by itself* (or *oneself*), (*U.S.*) be far better than others. ⌈compared with (others).⌉
2) *be not in the same class with*, (*U.S.*) cannot be ⌋
—*vt.* put (things or persons) into groups; arrange (things or persons) according to characteristics; classify.
—*vi.* be placed or ranked, as in a class.
—图 1. [사회의] 계급 ¶①지식 계급 2. 학급 3. 수업 ¶②사회과의 수업 4. (美) 동기의 학급(졸업생) ¶③70년도 졸업반 5. 등급 ¶④일류 호텔 6. 종류 7. 상류 계급

黑 1) (美) 단연 우수하다 2) (美) …와 비교가 되지 않다

—⑩ …을 분류하다 —自 [부류·등급 따위에] 속하다

class-conscious [klǽskɑ́nʃəs / klɑ́:skɔ́n-] *adj.* aware of one's social rank.
—⑩ 계급 의식이 있는

class-fellow [klǽsfèlou / klɑ́:s-] n. =classmate.

* **clas·sic** [klǽsik] *adj.* 1. of the first class; very good. 2. of or like the art or culture of ancient Greece or Rome. —*n.* ⓒ 1. a work of literature or art which has been generally recognized to be of the first rank. 2. a writer or an artist whose works have been so regarded. 3. (*the ~s*) classical studies.
—⑩ 1. 제1급의; 일류의; 뛰어난 2. 그리이스 로마[풍]의, 고전의 —图 1. 고전 작품, 명작 2. 문호, 대예술가 3. 고전의 연구

* **clas·si·cal** [klǽsik(ə)l] *adj.* 1. first-class, esp. in literature or art. 2. of the classics. ¶*~ music.* 3. of ancient Greek or Roman art or culture.
—⑩ 1. 일류의, 규범적인 2. 고전의 3. 그리이스·로마[풍]의

clas·si·cism [klǽsisìz(ə)m] *n.* Ⓤ 1. rules of classic literature and art. 2. the following of the classic style. 3. classical learning or scholarship.
—图 1. 고전주의 2. 고전 어풍(語風)(어형) 3. 고전의 학식

clas·si·fi·ca·tion [klæ̀sifikéiʃ(ə)n] *n.* Ⓤ the act of classifying.
—图 분류[법], 등분, 유별

clas·si·fied [klǽsifàid] *adj.* 1. arranged according to classes or groups. 2. (of public documents of the United States) secret.
—⑩ 1. 분류된 2. 기밀의, 군사기밀의

* **clas·si·fy** [klǽsifài] *vt.* (**-fied**) group (books, etc.) according to classes; arrange (things or persons) in classes. ▷**class·si·fi·a·ble** [-əbl] *adj.* —**clas·si·fi·er** [-ər] *n.*
—⑩ …을 분류하다, 유별하다. 등급으로 나누다

‡ **class·mate** [klǽsmèit / klɑ́:s-] *n.* ⓒ a member of the same class in school.   ⌈where classes meet.⌉
—图 급우(級友), 동급생, 동창생

‡ **class·room** [klǽsrù(:)m / klɑ́:s-] *n.* ⓒ a room in a school⌋
—图 교실

* **clat·ter** [klǽtər] *n.* ⓒ (usu. *sing.*) 1. a loud noise like that of plates struck together. 2. noisy, confused talk and laughter. —*vi., vt.* 1. make a confused noise. 2. talk noisily.
—图 1. 덜커덕거리는 소리 2. 시끄러운 말(웃음)소리 —自⑩ 1. 덜걱덜걱 소리나다(울리다) 2. 재잘재잘 지껄이다

* **clause** [klɔ:z] *n.* ⓒ 1. (*Grammar*) a part of a sentence having a subject and predicate of its own. ¶*a principal (subordinate) ~.*① 2. a single item in a law or contract. ¶*a penal ~.*② / *a saving ~.*③
—图 1. 절(節) ¶①주(종속)절 2. [법률·조약의] 개조(箇條), 조항 ¶②벌칙/③단서(但書)

* **claw** [klɔ:] *n.* ⓒ 1. a sharp, pointed nail on a bird's or animal's foot. 2. anything like a claw. ¶*the ~ of a hammer.* —*vt.* scratch or tear (something) with claws or hands; snatch at (something).
—图 1. [새·짐승의] 발톱, [게·새우의] 집게발 2. 발톱 모양의 것 —⑩ 발톱으로 할퀴다, 잡아 찢다; 손(발)톱으로 움켜잡다

‡ **clay** [klei] *n.* Ⓤ 1. a stiff, sticky kind of earth, used for making bricks, dishes, and vases. 2. earth. ¶*die and turn to ~.*① 3. (in the Bible) the human body.
—图 1. 점토(粘土); 도토(陶土) 2. 흙 ¶①죽어서 흙이 되다 3. (聖) 육체, 인체

clay·ey [kléii] *adj.* (**clay·i·er, clay·i·est**) **1.** of or containing clay; clay-like. **2.** covered with clay.

—[形] 1. 점토가 많은, 점토질의, 점토 같은 2. 점토를 바른

‡**clean** [kli:n] *adj.* **1.** not dirty; neat. ↔dirty ¶*keep your hands ~.* **2.** pure; innocent. ¶*lead of ~ life.* **3.** well-proportioned; symmetrical. ¶*a ~ figure.* **4.** perfect; complete. ¶*lose a ~ hundred dollars.*① **5.** skillful; clever; nice. ¶*a ~ shot.* **6.** not yet used. ¶*put on a ~ collar / a ~ sheet of paper.*

—[形] 1. 깨끗한, 청결한 2. 결백한 3. 맵시있는, 균형잡힌 4. 완전한 ¶①100달러를 몽땅 잃다 5. 멋진, 익숙한 6. 신품의

1) ***make a clean breast of,*** tell (one's secret) to another frankly.
2) ***make a clean sweep of,*** take away (something) completely; win completely.

[熟] 1)…을 깨끗이 털어놓다 2)…을 일소하다

—*ad.* **1.** in a clean manner; cleanly. **2.** completely.

—[副] 1. 깨끗이 2. 완전히

—*vt.* make (something) clean; purify. ¶*Clean those dirty shoes.* —*vi.* perform the act of cleaning.

—[他] …을 깨끗이 하다 —[自] 깨끗해지다

1) ***clean down,*** brush, sweep or wipe dirt from (walls, etc.)
2) ***clean out,*** ⓐ empty (something) in order to clean it. ⓑ use up.
3) ***clean up,*** ⓐ take dirt out from (a room, etc.); put (a room, etc.) in order. ⓑ finish a piece of work. ⓒ (*U. S. colloq.*) make large profits.

[熟] 1)쓸어 내리다; [벽 따위를] 씻다 2)ⓐ…을 비우다 ⓑ…을 다 써 버리다 3)ⓐ…을 청소하다, 치우다 ⓑ…을 끝내다 ⓒ《美口》 큰돈을 벌다

clean-cut [klí:nkʌ́t] *adj.* **1.** sharply outlined or defined. **2.** well-shaped; well-formed. **3.** clear; distinct. **4.** good; innocent.

—[形] 1. 윤곽이 뚜렷한 2. 모양 있는, 맵시 좋은 3. 명확한 4. 선량한, 순진한

clean·er [klí:nər] *n.* [C] **1.** a person who cleans (offices, rooms, etc.). **2.** the owner or worker of a dry-cleaning establishment. **3.** a tool or machine for cleaning.

—[名] 1. [사무실 따위의] 청소부, 소제부 2. 세탁소[직공] 3. 청소기

clean·li·ness [klénlinis] *n.* [U] the state or habit of being clean; cleanness. habitual cleanness.

—[名] 청결; 깨끗함

***clean·ly**[1] [klénli] *adj.* (**-li·er, -li·est**) clean; habitually clean.

—[形] 깨끗한 [것을 좋아하는]

clean·ly[2] [klí:nli] *adv.* in a clean manner.

—[副] 깨끗이, 청결하게, 결백하게

clean·ness [klí:nnis] *n.* [U] the state or quality of being clean.

—[名] 깨끗함, 청결, 결백

cleanse [klenz] *vt.* **1.** make (something) clean. **2.** purify (something). ▷**cleans·er** [-ər] *n.*

—[他] 1. …을 청결하게 하다 2. …을 정화(淨化)하다

clean-shav·en [klí:nʃéivn] *adj.* with the mustache and beard shaved off.

—[形] 깨끗이 면도한

clean·up [klí:nʌ̀p / klí:nʌ́p, ˊ-] *n.* [C] the act of cleaning up.

—[名] 정화 운동; 소제, 일소

‡**clear** [kliər] *adj.* **1.** that can easily be seen through. ¶*the ~ waters of a mountain lake.* **2.** not cloudy; bright. ↔cloudy; dark ¶*a ~ day.* **3.** that can be easily seen, heard or understood; distinct; sharp. ¶*a ~ voice.*① */ a ~ photograph*② */ The meaning is ~.*③ **4.** without obstacle. ¶*a ~ space*④ */ a ~ passage.*⑤ **5.** without doubt; certain. ¶*It is ~ that …*⑥ **6.** not confused. ¶*a ~ head.* **7.** entire; net. ¶*a ~ month. / ~ profit.*

—[形] 1. 맑은 2. 갠, 밝은 3. 뚜렷한, 명확한 ¶①뚜렷한 목소리/②핀트가 잘 맞은 사진/③그 의미는 분명하다 4. 훤히 트인, 장애가 없는 ¶④빈터/⑤훤히 트인 길 5. 확실한 ¶⑥…이라는 것은 확실하다 6. 명석한 7. 에누리 없는; 완전한

1) ***clear of,*** without; free from. ¶*a person ~ of debt.*⑦
2) ***keep clear of,*** keep away from (difficulties, etc.).
3) ***The coast is clear.,*** there is no difficulty; there is nothing to be afraid of.

[熟] 1)…이 없는 ¶⑦빚 없는 사람 2)…을 피하다 3)두려워할 것은 하나도 없다

—*adv.* completely; quite; clearly. ¶*climb ~ to the top.*

—[副] 전혀

—*vt.* **1.** make (something) clear. ¶*~ muddy water.* **2.** make (someone or something) free from blame, dishonor, guilt, etc.; prove (someone) to be innocent. ¶*~ one's honor / She was cleared from the charge.* **3.** make (something) free from doubt. ¶*That clears it all up.*⑧ **4.** get rid of (obstacles); take away. ¶*~ the pavement of snow*⑨ */ ~ [dishes from] the table.* **5.** jump over (something) without touching. ¶*~ a fence.* **6.** pay. ¶*~ the debt.* **7.** earn; gain (a net profit). —*vi.* become clear; become free from fog, clouds, etc.

—[他] 1. …을 맑게(밝게) 하다, 분명히 하다 2. …의 결백을 증명하다 3. …의 의심을 풀다 ¶⑧그것으로 의심이 풀렸다 4. …을 치우다 ¶⑨포도(鋪道)의 눈을 치우다 5. …을 뛰어 넘다 6. …을 지불하다 7. [순이익]을 올리다 —[自] 개다, 맑아지다

1) ***clear away*** (or ***off***), ⓐ take away (something) to keep a place clear. ⓑ (of mist or fog) pass away.
2) ***clear out,*** ⓐ clear (a space) by emptying it. ⓑ leave or depart suddenly.
3) ***clear up,*** ⓐ make (something) clear; become clear.

[熟] 1)ⓐ…을 치우다 ⓑ[안개 따위가] 걷히다 2)[장소]를 정돈하다 ⓑ갑자기 떠나다 3) ⓐ뚜렷하게 하다(되다); 개다

ⓑ put (things) in order; make (something) tidy. ⓒ solve; explain.
b …을 정돈하다 ⓒ[문제 따위]를 해결하다

clear·ance [klíərəns] *n.* **1.** [U] the act of making clear. ¶*a ~ sale*① / *make ~ of something.*② **2.** an official certificate that a ship has been cleared at the Custom House. **3.** the act of exchanging checks and other commercial documents between different banks. **4.** [U] [C] (*Machinery*) the space between a moving object and fixed one.
—[名] 1. 치우기, 청소 ¶①재고품 염가 판매/②…을 일소하다 2. 출항 수속(허가) 3. 어음 교환 4. 《機》 간격, 틈, 여유

clear-cut [klíərkʌ́t] *adj.* **1.** with clear, sharp outlines. **2.** clear; distinct.
—[形] 1. [얼굴 따위] 윤곽이 뚜렷한 2. 뚜렷한, 명쾌한

clear-head·ed [klíərhédid] *adj.* having a clear understanding; sharp-witted.
—[形] 두뇌가 명석한, 명민한

clear·ing [klíəriŋ] *n.* **1.** [C] an open space of land in a forest which has been cleared for cultivation. **2.** [U] the act of exchanging checks, etc. between different banks.
—[名] 1. 개척[지] 2. 어음 교환

clearing house [ˊ– ˋ] *n.* a place where banks exchange checks, etc. with one another.
—[名] 어음 교환소

‡**clear·ly** [klíərli] *adv.* in a clear manner; undoubtedly.
—[副] 분명히, 의심없이

clear·ness [klíərnis] *n.* [U] **1.** the state or quality of being clear. **2.** plainness; brightness. **3.** freedom from obstacles.
—[名] 1. 명료, 맑음, 밝음 2. 명백, 명민 3. 장애가 없음, 훤히 트임

clear-sight·ed [klíərsáitid] *adj.* **1.** that can see clearly; having good eye-sight. **2.** that can understand well.
—[形] 1. 시력이 좋은 2. 총명한, 명민한

cleat [kli:t] *n.* [C] **1.** a strip of wood or iron fixed to something for support or sure footing. **2.** (*Nautical*) a piece of wood or metal having one or two projecting horns on which ropes can be fastened.
—[名] 1. 쐐기; 마개; 미끄러움을 막는 것 2. 《海》 밧줄걸이

cleav·age [klí:vidʒ] *n.* [C] **1.** the act of cleaving; the state of being cleft; split. **2.** (*Biology*) the division of an egg into smaller parts.
—[名] 1. 쪼개짐; 분열 2. 열개(裂開)

cleave¹ [kli:v] *vt., vi.* (**clove** or **cleft, clov·en** or **cleft**) **1.** split; divide. ¶*~ in two.*① **2.** cut one's way through. ¶*~ one's way through.* ▷**cleav·a·ble** [-əbl] *adj.*
—[他][自] 1. 쪼개다, 찢다 ¶①둘로 쪼개다 2. [새·배가] 공기(물)를 헤치고 나아가다

cleave² [kli:v] *vi.* cling; hold fast; be faithful to (someone). 《*~ to* someone》
—[自] 달라붙다; 애착을 느끼다, 충실하다

cleav·er [klí:vər] *n.* [C] **1.** a person or thing that cleaves. **2.** a tool used by a butcher for chopping meat or bone.
—[名] 1. 쪼개는(가르는) 기구(사람) 2. 큰 식칼

clef [klef] *n.* [C] (*Music*) a symbol placed on a staff to indicate the pitch of the notes. ¶*C ~*① / *F ~*② ⇒fig. / *G ~.*③ ⇒fig.
—[名] 《樂》 음자리표 ¶①「다」음 자리표/②「바」음 자리표/③「사」음 자리표

[G clef]

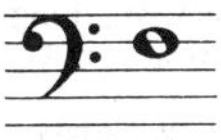
[F clef]

cleft [kleft] *adj.* split; separated; divided. ¶*in a ~ stick*① / *~ palate.*② —*n.* [C] a space or opening made by splitting.
—[形] 쪼개진, 갈라진, 분열된 ¶①진퇴유곡에 빠져서/②구개(口蓋) 파열증 —[名] 쪼개진(갈라진) 틈(조각)

clem·en·cy [klémənsi] *n.* [U] **1.** mercy; mildness of temper; gentleness. **2.** (of the weather) mildness.
—[名] 1. 인자, 관대[한 조치] 2. [기후의] 온화, 따뜻함

clem·ent [klémənt] *adj.* **1.** merciful; gentle. **2.** (of the weather) mild and pleasant; calm.
—[形] 1. 온순한, 관대한, 너그러운 2. [날씨가] 온화한, 따뜻한

clench [klentʃ] *vt.* **1.** press (something) firmly together; close (the fist, fingers, etc.) tightly. ¶*~ one's teeth.* **2.** clinch (a nail, etc.). **3.** conclude (an argument, etc.) definitely. —*vi.* (of hands, teeth, etc.) close tightly. —*n.* [C] **1.** a firm grasp. **2.** (*Boxing*) a clinch.
—[他] 1. …을 죄다; [주먹 따위]를 꽉 쥐다 2. [못 따위]의 끝을 때려 꼬부리다 3. …의 결말을 짓다 —[自] 꽉 쥐어지다 —[名] 1. 꽉 쥐기, 이를 악물기 2. 《권투》 클린치, 맞붙잡기

***cler·gy** [klə́:rdʒi] *n.* [U] 《*the ~*》 《*collectively,* used as *pl.*》 the body or group of men who have been selected by God for religious work, such as ministers, pastors, and priests.
—[名] 목사, 신부; 성직

***cler·gy·man** [klə́:rdʒimən] *n.* [C] (pl. **-men** [-mən]) a member of the clergy.
—[名] 성직자, 목사

cler·ic [klérik] *n.* [C] a clergyman. —*adj.* of a clergyman; clerical.
—[名] 성직자, 목사 —[形] 목사의, 성직의

cler·i·cal [klérik(ə)l] *adj.* **1.** of a clerk. ¶*the ~ staff*① / *~ work.*② **2.** of a clergyman. —*n.* **1.** [C] a clergyman. **2.** 《*pl.*》 clothing worn by clergymen.
—[形] 1. 서기(사무원)의 ¶①사무원/②사무 2. 성직의, 목사의 —[名] 1. 목사 2. 성직복

: clerk [klə:rk / klɑ:k] *n.* [C] **1.** an assistant in business; a salesman or saleswoman. **2.** a person who is employed in keeping records or accounts, copying letters, etc. in an office. **3.** an official who keeps records in a law court, a legislature, etc. **—*vi.*** work as a clerk.
—[名] 1. [상점의] 점원, 판매원 2. 사무원 3: 서기 —[自] 서기(점원) 노릇을 하다

: clev·er [klévər] *adj.* **1.** quick to learn; quick-witted; intelligent. **2.** skillful. ¶*be ~ at* (or *in*) / *be ~ with the pen.*① ▷**clev·er·ly** [-li] *adv.* —**clev·er·ness** [-nis] *n.*
—[形] 1. 영리한, 총명한, 재치있는, 똑똑한 2. 능숙한, 능란한, 교묘한 ¶①달필이다

clew [klu:] *n.* [C] **1.** anything that helps in solving a mystery or problem. ⇒[N.B.] **2.** a ball of thread or yarn. **3.** a lower corner of a square sail; a metal loop fastened at a corner of a sail; cords for a hammock. **—*vt.* 1.** wind (thread) into a ball. **2.** raise or lower a sail by a clew. 《~ *up, down*》.
—[名] 1. 단서, 실마리 [N.B.] 보통 clue로 씀 2. 실꾸리, 실 3. 돛귀; 돛의 아랫귀에 단 쇠고리; 해먹(hammock)을 매다는 줄 —[他] 1. …을 공 모양으로 감다 2. 돛을 끌어올리다(당겨내리다)

click [klik] *n.* [C] a light, sharp sound. **—*vi., vt.*** make or cause (*something*) to make a light, sharp sound.
—[名] 딸깍 소리 —[自][他] 딸깍 소리 나다(내다)

· cli·ent [kláiənt] *n.* [C] **1.** a person who appeals to a lawyer for advice. **2.** a customer of a tradesman.
—[名] 1. 소송(변호) 의뢰인 2. 고객, 단골

cli·en·tele [klàiəntél / klì:ɑ:ntéil] *n.* [C] 《*collectively*》 **1.** clients; customers. **2.** personal followers.
—[名] 1. 소송 의뢰인들; 고객들 2. 피(被)보호자들, 예속자들

: cliff [klif] *n.* [C] a very high and steep slope of rock.
—[名] 벼랑, [해안 따위의] 절벽

: cli·mate [kláimit] *n.* [C] **1.** the state of heat and cold, wetness and dryness, wind and calm in a certain place. **2.** a region with a particular kind of climate.
—[名] 1. [어떤 지방의] 기후, 풍토 2. [특수한 기후의] 지방, 지대

cli·mat·ic [klaimǽtik] *adj.* of or having to do with climate.
—[形] 기후[상]의, 풍토의

cli·max [kláimæks] *n.* [C] **1.** the highest point, as of excitement or interest. **2.** (*Rhetoric*) the arrangement of ideas or expressions in an ascending scale. **—*vt., vi.*** bring or come to a climax.
—[名] 1. 최고점, 절정, 최고조 2. 《修辭》 [차차로 문장의 어세를 높이는] 점층법(漸層法), 클라이맥스 —[他][自] 최고조에 달하게 하다(달하다)

: climb [klaim] *vt., vi.* **1.** go up (a mountain, wall, etc.) 《~ *up* something》. **2.** get on in the world by steady effort. **3.** (of plants) grow upward by twining around (something).
—[他][自] 1. [산·벽 따위에] 기어오르다 2. 출세하다 3. [식물이 어떤 것을] 감아 올라가다

climb down, ⓐ get down from (a tree, etc.). ⓑ abandon one's position. ⓒ give up one's opinions, attitude, etc.
[熟] ⓐ[나무 따위에서] 내려오다 ⓑ자기의 지위를 버리다 ⓒ의견 따위를 단념하다; 항복하다

climb·er [kláimər] *n.* [C] **1.** a person or thing that climbs. **2.** (*colloq.*) a person who is always trying to rise in society.
—[名] 1. 기어오르는 사람(것); 등산가 2. 《口》 야심가

clime [klaim] *n.* [C] (*poetic*) a country; a district; a climate.
—[名] 나라; 지방; 풍토

clinch [klintʃ] *vt.* **1.** fasten (a driven nail) by beating down the point. **2.** fix (something) firmly. **—*vi.*** (*Boxing*) hold one another tightly. **—*n.*** [C] **1.** the act of clinching. **2.** (*Boxing*) a tight hold.
—[他] 1. [박은 못 끝을] 꼬부리다 2. …을 고정시키다 —[自] 《권투》 맞붙들다 —[名] 1. 못 끝을 꼬부리기; 고정, 고착 2. 《권투》 클린치

clinch·er [klíntʃər] *n.* [C] **1.** a person or thing that clinches. **2.** (*colloq.*) something decisive, as in an argument.
—[名] 1. 못 끝을 꼬부리는 사람(연장) 2. 《口》 [반론의 여지가 없는] 결정적인(끝장을 내는) 말

· cling [kliŋ] *vi.* **(clung)** fix onto something closely; stick fast; adhere. 《~ *to* something》 ¶~ *together* / ~ *to the last hope*① / *Wet clothes ~ to the body.*
—[自] 들러붙다, 점착하다, 달라붙어서 떨어지지 않다; 집착하다 ¶① 끝까지 희망을 버리지 않다

clin·ic [klínik] *n.* [C] **1.** a place for medical treatment. **2.** the act of teaching medical students by treating patients in their presence. ¶*a speech ~.*①
—[名] 1. 진료소, 병원 2. 임상 강의 ¶① 발음 교정 현지 강좌

clin·i·cal [klínik(ə)l] *adj.* **1.** of or having to do with a clinic. **2.** used in a sickroom. ¶*a ~ thermometer.*①
—[形] 1. 임상[강의]의 2. 병상의 ¶① 검온기, 체온계

clink [kliŋk] *n.* [C] a light, sharp, ringing sound. **—*vi., vt.*** make or cause to make a clink.
—[名] 딸랑(찌르릉) 소리 —[自][他] 딸랑 울리다(울리게 하다)

· clip[1] [klip] *vi., vt.* **(clipped, clip·ping) 1.** cut or cut off (hair, grass, etc.) with shears or scissors. **2.** cut articles or pictures from a newspaper, magazine, etc. **3.** (*colloq.*) move rapidly. **4.** (*colloq.*) hit (someone) sharply. ¶*He clipped her on the face.*①
—[自][他] 1. [머리·잔디 따위를] 가위로 자르다, 깎다 2. [신문·잡지 따위를] 오리다 3. 《口》 날쌔게 움직이다 4. 《口》 …을 후려갈기다 ¶①그는 그녀의 얼굴을 후려갈겼다

clip someone's wings; clip the wings of, make (someone) weak.
[熟] …을 무력하게 만들다

—*n.* 1. [U] the act of clipping; [C] something clipped
—[名] 1. 깎기; 깎아낸 것

off. **2.** [U][C] the amount of wool that is cut off in one season. **3.** [C] a rapid motion. **4.** [C] (*colloq.*) a quick, sharp blow.

•clip² [klip] *vt.* (**clipped, clip·ping**) grasp or hold (something) tight. **—*n.*** [C] a thing used for holding (things) together. ¶*a paper ~.*①

clip·per [klípər] *n.* [C] **1.** a person who cuts hair, grass, etc. **2.** 《often *pl.*》 a tool for cutting or shearing. ¶*hair clippers.*① **3.** a sailing ship built for great speed. **4.** a large, fast airplane. **5.** a fast horse.

clip·ping [klípiŋ] *n.* [C] **1.** an article or picture cut out of a newspaper, magazine, etc. **2.** a thing cut out or off of something else.

clique [kli:k, +*U.S.* klik] *n.* [C] a small, closely-united group of people. ¶*an academic ~.*①

:cloak [klouk] *n.* [C] **1.** a loose outside dress. **2.** anything that covers or hides (something); a disguise.
under the cloak of, ⓐ under the mask of (something). ⓑ taking advantage of (something). ¶***attack the enemy under the ~ of darkness.***
—*vt.* **1.** cover (someone) with a cloak. **2.** hide.

cloak·room [klóukrù(:)m] *n.* [C] a room where coats, hats, etc. may be left for a time, as in a theater or hotel.

:clock [klαk / klɔk] *n.* [C] an instrument for measuring and showing time. ¶***set a ~ by the radio.***①
1) ***around the clock,*** during all 24 hours; constantly.
2) ***like a clock,*** as exactly as a clock. ⌈a race, etc.)
—*vt., vi.* measure or record the time of (a runner,

clock·wise [klάkwàiz / klɔ́k-] *adj., adv.* moving in the direction of the hands of a clock. ↔counter-clockwise

clock·work [klάkwə̀:rk / klɔ́kwə̀:k] *n.* [U] the mechanism of a clock. ¶***like ~.***①

clod [klαd / klɔd] *n.* **1.** [C] a lump of earth or clay; soil. **2.** [C] a silly person; a fool.

clog [klαg, klɔ:g / klɔg] *vt., vi.* (**clogged, clog·ging**) **1.** choke up (something); become choked up. **2.** prevent; stop. **—*n.*** [C] **1.** a thing that prevents. **2.** a block of wood used to tie a leg of an animal to prevent its movement. **3.** a shoe, usu. with a wooden sole.

clois·ter [klɔ́istər] *n.* [C] **1.** a passageway along the wall of a building, esp. a church, with an open arcade. ⇒fig. **2.** a place in which a special religious life is lived; a nunnery; a monastery. **3.** a quiet, retired place. **—*vt.*** keep (someone) in a monastery or convent.

[cloister 1.]

:close¹ [klouz] *vt.* **1.** shut. ¶*~ a door / ~ a book / ~ a shop.* **2.** fill (an opening); prevent (passage). ¶*~ a hole in a wall.* **3.** bring (something) to an end. ¶*~ a speech.*① **4.** bring (things) together; unite. **—*vi.*** **1.** become shut. ¶*The shop closes at six.* **2.** come to an end. **3.** come together; join. ¶*Her lips ~ firmly.*
1) ***close about,*** surround. ⌈thing); stop.
2) ***close down,*** put an end to the activity of (some-
3) ***close in on*** (or ***upon***), ⓐ approach (someone) to catch, attack, arrest, etc. ⓑ surround; envelope.
4) ***close out,*** (*U.S.*) sell (all goods), usu. by a bargain sale. ⌈in a line). ⓑ shut completely.
5) ***close up,*** ⓐ come nearer together (esp. of persons
6) ***close with,*** ⓐ come nearer in order to attack (someone). ⓑ accept (an offer, a bargain, etc.).

2. [한 철에] 깎아낸 양털의 분량 3. 날쌘 동작 4. 《口》 강타

—[他] …을 꽉 쥐다(붙잡다) —[名] 물건을 집는 데 쓰는 것, 집게 ¶종이집게

—[名] 1. 자르는(깎는) 사람 2. [털·풀 따위를 깎는] 큰 가위 ¶①이발기 3. 쾌속정, 쾌속 범선 4. 대형 여객기 5. 빠른 말, 준마

—[名] 1. [신문·잡지 따위에서] 오려낸 것 2. 깎아낸 것

—[名] 도당, 파벌 ¶①학파, 학벌

—[名] 1. [소매 없는] 외투, 망토 2. 덮개, 씌우개; 핑계, 구실
[熟] ⓐ…의 탈을 쓰고, …을 빙자하여 ⓑ…을 이용하여(틈타서)
—[他] 1. …에게 외투를 입히다 2. …을 덮어 감추다

—[名] [극장·호텔·역 따위의] 외투·소지품 보관소

—[名] 시계, 괘종 ¶①시계를 라디오에 맞추다
[熟] 1)24시간 내내; 끊임없이 2)시계처럼 정확하게
—[他][自] 시간을 재다(기록하다)

—[形][副] 시계바늘과 같은 방향의(으로)

—[名] 시계(태엽) 장치 ¶①정확히

—[名] 1. 흙덩이; 토양 2. 얼간이, 바보

—[他][自] 1. …을 막히게 하다, 메게 하다, 막히다, 메다 2. …을 방해하다, 멈추게 하다 —[名] 1. 장애, 방해물 2. [짐승 다리에 매는] 무거운 나무 3. 나막신

—[名] 1. 복도, 낭하, 회랑(回廊), 보랑(步廊) 2. 수도원, 수녀원 3. 은둔처 —[他] …을 수도원에 가두다

—[他] 1. …을 닫다 2. [구멍 따위]를 막다 3. …을 마감하다 ¶①연설을 끝내다 4. [대열 따위를] 좁히다 —[自] 1. 닫히다 2. 끝나다 3. 합쳐지다; 접근하다

[熟] 1)…을 둘러싸다 2)…을 폐쇄하다 3)ⓐ…에 다가가다 ⓑ…을 에워싸다 4)《美》[재고품]을 팔아 치우다 5)ⓐ [대열 따위]를 좁히다 ⓑ완료하다 6) ⓐ…에 육박하다 ⓑ…을 수락하다

—*n.* [C] **1.** a conclusion; an end. **2.** a struggle.
1) ***bring to a close,*** finish; bring to an end.
2) ***draw to a close,*** end; come to an end.

—[名] 1. 종결, 끝 2. 격투
[熟] 1)…을 끝내다 2)종말에 가까와지다

⁝ close² [klous] *adj.* **1.** fast shut. ↔open ¶*a ~ box.* **2.** confined; strictly guarded. ¶*a ~ prison.* **3.** (of space, time, etc.) near. ¶*The two houses were ~ to each other.* **4.** very friendly. ¶*a ~ friend.* **5.** not widely separated; crowded. ¶*a ~ order.*① **6.** dense; compact. ¶*a ~ fabric.*② **7.** careful; strict. ¶*~ attention.* **8.** nearly even or equal in ability, power, etc.; without much difference. ¶*a ~ election*③ */ a ~ race.*④ **9.** stingy. **10.** having little fresh air; stifling. ¶*a ~ room / ~ weather.* **11.** limited by law. ¶*a closed season for fishing.* **12.** (*colloq.*) (of money) difficult to get.
1) ***keep*** (or ***lie***) ***close,*** hide oneself.
2) ***keep something close,*** keep something secret.
3) ***press someone close,*** treat someone severely.
—*adv.* closely.

—[形] 1. 닫은 2. 감금된; 경비가 엄중한 3. 접근한 4. 친밀한, 막역한 5. 밀집한 ¶①밀집 대형(隊形) 6. 결이 촘촘한 ¶②올이 고운 피륙 7. 면밀한 8. 어슷비슷한, 호각(互角)의 ¶③어슷비슷한 투표/④접전 9. 인색한 10. 공기가 나쁜; 숨막히는 11. 금렵[금어(禁漁)]의 12. 금융이 경색한, 돈의 융통이 잘 안 되는
[熟] 1)숨어 있다 2)…을 비밀에 붙이다 3)…을 심하게 다루다
—[副] 접근하여; 밀접하게; 꼭

close call [´– ´–] *n.* (*colloq.*) a narrow escape.
—[名] 《口》 아슬아슬한 탈출, 위기일발

close-cropped [klóusklάpt / -klɔ́pt] *adj.* (of hair) cut very short.
—[形] [머리를] 짧게 깎은

close-cut [klóuskʌ́t] *adj.* =close-cropped.

closed shop [´– ´–] *n.* a shop that employs trade union members only. ↔open shop
—[名] 노동조합원만을 고용하는 공장, 비개방적 공장

close-fit·ting [klóusfítiŋ] *adj.* fitting tightly to the body.
—[形] 몸에 꼭 맞는

close-grained [klóusgréind] *adj.* having a grain which is fine and close, such as mahogany.
—[形] [마호가니 재목처럼] 나뭇결이 고운

⁝ close·ly [klóusli] *adv.* in a close manner; tightly; intently. ¶*watch (something) ~.*
—[副] 접근하여, 바싹; 꼭, 단단히; 친밀하게; 면밀하게, 주의깊게

close·ness [klóusnis] *n.* [U] the state or quality of being close; tightness; oppressiveness; intimacy; stinginess.
—[名] 치밀함; 숨막힘, 답답함; 접근; 친밀; 인색

• clos·et [klάzit / klɔ́z-] *n.* [C] **1.** a small, private room. **2.** a cupboard for storing clothes, china, linen, etc. **3.** a toilet; a water closet. —*vt.* shut up (someone) in a private room for a secret talk. ⇒[usage]
be closeted with, have a secret talk with (someone). ¶*He was closeted with the American ambassador.*

—[名] 1. 작은 방, 사실(私室) 2. 찬장, 벽장 3. 변소 —[他] 밀담하기 위해 …을 사실에 가두다 [usage] 보통 재귀적(再歸的)으로, 또는 과거분사로 씀
[熟] …와 밀담 중이다

close-up [klóusʌp] *n.* [C] **1.** (*Photography*) a picture taken at very close range. **2.** a close view.
—[名] 1. 《寫》 가까이서 크게 찍은 사진, 클로우즈업 2. 가까이에서 본 광경

clo·sure [klóuʒər] *n.* [C] **1.** the act of closing; the state of being closed; anything that closes. **2.** an end; a conclusion.
—[名] 1. 폐쇄, 폐지, 마감 2. 끝, 마지막, 종결

clot [klαt / klɔt] *n.* [C] a half-solid lump. ¶***a blood ~.***① —*vi., vt.* (**clot·ted, clot·ting**) form or cause (liquid) to form into clots.
—[名] 엉겨붙은 덩어리 ¶①핏덩어리, 응혈 —[自][他] 엉겨서 덩어리지다, …을 엉겨붙게 하다

⁝ cloth [klɔ:θ, klαθ / klɔ(:)θ] *n.* (pl. **cloths** [klɔðz, klɔθs] ⇒[N.B.]) **1.** [U] a material made by weaving wool, cotton, silk, etc. ¶*cotton ~.* **2.** [C] a piece of this material for some special purpose; a tablecloth, etc. **3.** [C] customary clothing. **4.** 《*the ~*》 the profession, esp. of clergymen. ¶*respect the ~.*
—[名] [N.B.] 복수형의 발음 [klɔðz]는 pieces of cloth, [klɔ:θs]는 kinds of cloth 로 쓰이는 일이 많음 1. 천, 피륙, 옷감 2. 천조각; 책상보, 식탁보, 걸레 따위 3. 제복 4. 성직(聖職)

⁝ clothe [klouð] *vt.* (**clothed** or **clad**) **1.** put clothes on (someone); give (someone) clothes; dress. ¶*She was clothed in wool.*① **2.** cover. ¶*a tree clothed in leaves / a garden clothed with pine trees.*② **3.** give power to (someone); give (power, etc.) to someone. ¶*~ oneself with authority.*③
—[他] 1. …에게 옷을 입히다, 옷을 주다 ¶①그녀는 털옷을 입고 있었다 2. …을 덮다 ¶②소나무로 뒤덮인 정원 3. [특히 권력]을 …에게 부여하다, 주다 ¶③권위를 가지다

⁝ clothes [klouz, klouðz / klouðz] *n. pl.* **1.** coverings for the body. ¶*a suit of ~*① */ in one's best (everyday) ~*②*. / put on (take off) one's ~*③ */ (proverb) Fine ~ make the man.*④ **2.** bedclothes.
—[名] 1. 옷, 의복 ¶①옷 한 벌/②나들이옷(평상복)을 입고/③옷을 입다(벗다)/④옷이 날개다 2. 침구

clothes bag [´– ´] *n.* a bag for holding and carrying clothes to be washed.
—[名] 빨래 자루

clothes basket [´– ´–] *n.* a basket for holding and carrying the laundry.
—[名] 빨래 바구니

clothes·brush [klóuzbrʌʃ, klóuðz- / klóuðz-] *n.* ⓒ a brush for freeing clothes from dust or mud. —愙 옷솔

clothes horse [⌃⌃] *n.* a frame on which to hang clothes for drying or airing. ⇒fig. —愙 빨래걸이, 빨래 너는 틀

clothes·line [klóuzlàin, klóuðz- / klóuðz-] *n.* ⓒ a rope or wire on which to hang clothes for drying or airing. —愙 빨랫줄

clothes peg [⌃⌃] *n.* =clothespin.

clothes·pin [klóuðzpin] *n.* ⓒ (*U.S.*) a small clip for fastening clothes on a line. —愙 (美) 빨래집게

clothes·press [klóuðzpres] *n.* ⓒ a chest, closet, etc. for storing clothes. —愙 옷장, 장롱

cloth·ier [klóuðiər] *n.* ⓒ a seller or maker of clothing; a dealer in cloth. —愙 모직물 장수, 의복상, 옷감 장수

‡**cloth·ing** [klóuðiŋ] *n.* ⓤ (*collectively*) **1.** clothes. **2.** covering. —愙 1. 옷, 의류 2. 덮개

clot·ted [klátid / klɔ́t-] *adj.* thickened; coagulated. —働 응고한

clot·ty [kláti / klɔ́ti] *adj.* full of clots; tending to clot. —働 덩어리가 많은, 엉기기 쉬운

clo·ture [klóutʃər] *n.* (*U.S.*) ⓒ a way of ending a discussion in Congress. ⇒N.B. —愙 (美) 토론 종결 [N.B. closure라고도 하며, 미국 의회의 용어]

‡**cloud** [klaud] *n.* ⓒ **1.** ⓤⓒ a white or gray mass of water vapor floating in the sky. ¶*The sun is sometimes hidden by clouds.* **2.** a mass of smoke, sand, dust, etc. ¶*a ~ of dust.* **3.** a great multitude; a cloud-like mass. ¶*a ~ of flies.* **4.** a streak or spot, as in marble. **5.** something that darkens, hides from view, dims, or threatens. ¶*the ~ of war*① / *a ~ on someone's happiness*② / *have a ~ on one's brow.*③
1) *be under a cloud,* be at a disadvantage; be under suspicion; be in trouble.
2) *in the clouds,* ⓐ far up in the sky. ⓑ absent-minded; given to daydreaming. ⓒ fanciful; imaginary.
—*vt.* **1.** cover (something) with, or as with, clouds; dim; darken. **2.** make (something) gloomy; darken (something) with trouble. —*vi.* be overcast with, or as with, clouds. ¶*The sky has clouded* [*over*]*.*
—愙 1. 구름 2. 뭉게뭉게 피어오르는 연기(모래·먼지 따위). 다수; 구름처럼 많은 떼 4. [대리석 따위의] 얼룩, 흠 5. 암영(暗影); 암운(暗雲); 어두운 그늘 ¶①전운(戰雲)/②남의 행복을 빼앗는 암운/③이마에 어두운 그림자를 짓고 있다
圈 1) 불리한 입장에 놓여 있다; 의심을 받고 있다; 곤란에 처해 있다 2) ⓐ 하늘높이 ⓑ 멀거니, 공상에 잠겨서 ⓒ 가공의, 비현실적인
—働 1. …을 흐리게 하다 2. …에 어두운 그림자를 던지다, …을 번민하게 하다 —働 흐리다

cloud-capped [kláudkæpt] *adj.* having clouds around the top. —働 구름을 인, 구름 사이로 우뚝 솟은

cloud·i·ness [kláudinis] *n.* ⓤ the state of being cloudy. —愙 흐림, 어두움, 암담

cloud·less [kláudlis] *adj.* clear; bright; without clouds. —働 맑은, 갠, 구름이 끼지 않은

•**cloud·y** [kláudi] *adj.* (**cloud·i·er, cloud·i·est**) **1.** covered with clouds. ¶*~ weather.* **2.** of or like clouds. **3.** not clear; dark; dim. ¶*a ~ picture.* **4.** spotted. ¶*~ marble.* **5.** gloomy; troubled. ¶*~ looks.* —働 1. 흐린 2. 구름의(같은) 3. 확실하지 않은, 몽롱한 4. 얼룩덜룩한, 구름무늬가 든 5. 음침한; 우울한, 침울한

clout [klaut] *n.* ⓒ **1.** (*colloq.*) a blow; a rap. ¶*give someone a ~.* **2.** a target made of white cloth; a shot that hits this. **3.** (*archaic*) a patch; a piece of cloth for cleaning a desk, the floor, etc. —*vt.* (*colloq.*) blow; rap. —愙 1. (口) 강타; 딱 치는 소리 ¶. [흰 천으로 만든] 표적, 과녁; 명중, 적중 3. (古) 헝겊 조각, 넝마, 걸레 —働 (口) …을 딱 때리다(치다)

clove¹ [klouv] *n.* ⓒ **1.** the dried flower bulbs of a tropical tree, used as a strong-smelling spice. **2.** the tree which produces cloves. [pound bulb, as in a lily.] —愙 1. [향미료로 쓰는] 정향나무의 말린 꽃 2. 정향나무

clove² [klouv] *n.* ⓒ a small, divided section of a com- [작은 인경(鱗莖)] —愙 [백합 따위의 원 뿌리에 있는]

clo·ven [klóuv(ə)n] *adj.* split; divided. ¶*a ~ hoof.* —働 쪼개진, 벌어진, 갈라진

clo·ven-foot·ed [klóuv(ə)nfútid] *adj.* **1.** having cloven feet. **2.** like a devil. —働 1. 발굽이 갈라진 2. 악마 같은

clo·ven-hoofed [klóuv(ə)nhúːft] *adj.* =cloven-footed.

•**clo·ver** [klóuvər] *n.* ⓒ a low-growing plant of the same family as the pea; any similar plant.
live (or *be*) *in clover,* live in luxury and ease.
—愙 클로우버, 토끼풀
圈 호사스럽게 살다, 안락하게 살다

clown [klaun] *n.* ⓒ **1.** a man whose business is to amuse others by jokes and foolish behavior, as in a circus. ¶*play the ~.*① **2.** an impolite person; a silly person. —*vi.* act like a clown; act silly.
—愙 1. 광대, 익살꾼 ¶①익살부리다 2. 버릇없는 사람
—働 광대노릇을 하다, 익살부리다

clown·ish [kláuniʃ] *adj.* of or like a clown; impolite; ill-mannered.
—[형] 광대 같은, 익살맞은; 버릇없는, 촌뜨기 같은

cloy [klɔi] *vt.* make (someone) weary by too much of something. 《~ someone *with*》 ¶*be cloyed with pleasure.*①
—[타] …에 싫증나게 하다, 물리게 하다 ¶①향락에 물리다

⁑**club** [klʌb] *n.* [C] **1.** a heavy stick of wood. **2.** a stick or bat used for hitting a ball in certain games. **3.** a group of people joined together for a certain purpose; a clubhouse. **4.** a playing card with one or more black marks shaped like clover leaves on it; 《*pl.*》 the suit formed by these cards. ¶*the king of clubs.*①
—[명] 1. 곤봉 2. 타구봉(打球棒) 3. 클럽; 회관 4. [트럼프의] 클럽; 클럽의 짝 ¶①클럽의 킹

—*vt.* (**clubbed, club·bing**) **1.** beat or hit (something) with a club. ¶~ *a dog to death.*② **2.** combine (people or things) for some common purpose. ¶~ *persons together.*③ —*vi.* join together for a certain purpose. 《~ *with* someone》
—[타] 1. …을 곤봉으로 때리다 ¶②개를 때려 죽이다 2. …을 모으다, 결합시키다 ¶③사람들을 집합시키다
—[자] 클럽을 만들다, 합동하다, 협력하다

club·foot [klʌ́bfùt] *n.* [C] (pl. **-feet**) an unnaturally-formed foot.
—[명] 굽은 다리

club·foot·ed [klʌ́bfútid] *adj.* having a clubfoot.
—[형] 다리가 굽은

club·house [klʌ́bháus] *n.* [C] a building used by a club.
—[명] 클럽의 회관

cluck [klʌk] *n.* [C] a cry made by a hen in calling her chickens. —*vi.* make a clucklike cry.
—[명] 꼬꼬하고 부르는 소리 —[자] [암탉이] 꼬꼬하고 울다

clue [klu:] *n.* [C] something that helps to solve a mystery, a problem, etc. ¶*I have no ~ to it.*①
—[명] 단서, 실마리 ¶①그것에 대한 단서는 전혀 없다

clump [klʌmp] *n.* [C] **1.** a group of trees, shrubs, etc. that grow closely together. ¶*a ~ of bamboos.*① **2.** a lump, as of earth. ¶*a ~ of earth.* **3.** a sound of heavy footsteps. —*vt.* plant (trees, etc.) in clusters. —*vi.* tramp heavily.
—[명] 1. [나무 따위의] 덤불 ¶①대나무 숲 2. [흙 따위의] 덩어리 3. 무거운 발소리 —[타] [나무 따위]를 군생(群生)시키다 —[자] 무거운 발걸음으로 걷다, 쿵쿵 걷다

clum·sy [klʌ́mzi] *adj.* (**-si·er, -si·est**) **1.** not skillful; lacking grace; awkward. **2.** not well-shaped or well-made; not elegant. ▷**clum·si·ly** [-li] *adv.*
—[형] 1. 서투른, 솜씨없는 2. 모양없는, 맵시없는, 투박한

clung [klʌŋ] *v.* pt. and pp. of **cling**.

***clus·ter** [klʌ́stər] *n.* [C] **1.** a number of things of the same kind growing or gathered together. ¶*a ~ of grapes.* **2.** a group of persons and things. ¶*a ~ of bees.*
—[명] 1. [과일이나 꽃 따위의] 송이 2. [사람·물건의] 떼, 무리

—*vi.* form a cluster or clusters. ¶*The girls clustered around the old man.* —*vt.* gather (things or persons) into a cluster or clusters.
—[자] 송이를 이루다, 주렁주렁 달리다, 군생하다, 떼짓다 —[타] …을 떼짓게 하다

***clutch** [klʌtʃ] *n.* [C] **1.** a strong hold. ¶*make a ~ at a cat.* **2.** 《usu. *pl.*》 control; power. ¶*be in the clutches of the police.*① **3.** a device in a machine for connecting or disconnecting the working parts; a grasping claw, hand, etc.
—[명] 1. 꽉 쥐다, 꽉 잡다 2. 손아귀, 지배력 ¶①경찰에 붙잡혀 있다 3. 연축기(連軸器), 클러치

1) ***fall*** (or ***get***) ***in the clutches of,*** get into (someone's) power.
2) ***get out of the clutches of,*** get out of (someone's) power.
[숙] 1)…의 손아귀에 들다, …의 수중에 빠지다 2)…의 마수에서 빠져나오다

—*vt.* hold tightly. ¶*She clutched her handbag to her breast.*② —*vi.* catch eagerly; snatch. 《~ *at* something》 ¶(*proverb*) *A drowning man will ~ at a straw.*③
—[타] …을 꽉 쥐다(붙잡다) ¶②그녀는 핸드백을 가슴에 꽉 껴안았다 —[자] 잡으려고 들다, 달려 붙들다 ¶③물에 빠진 사람은 지푸라기라도 잡는다

clut·ter [klʌ́tər] *n.* [C] a disorder; confused noises. ¶*be in a ~.*① —*vt.* make (a room) dirty by distributing things in a disorderly manner. ¶*His desk was cluttered* [*up*] *with books and papers.* —*vi.* make a confused noise. ¶~ *along.*②
—[명] 난잡, 소란, 소동 ¶①[실내 따위가] 어질러져 있다 —[타] …을 어지르다 —[자] 시끄러운 소리를 내다 ¶②덜커덕덜커덕 달리다

cm., cm centimeter; centimeters.

co- [kou-] *pref.* with, together, joint; equally: *cooperate* (=do something together); *coauthors* (=two authors who write one book together).
—《接頭》 함께; 공동으로; 동등하게

co. county.

Co. [kou, kʌ́mp(ə)ni] Company.

c.o., c/o **1.** in care of. **2.** carried over.

***coach** [koutʃ] *n.* [C] **1.** an old form of carriage with seats inside and often on top also. ⇒[N.B.]; a state carriage. ¶*a ~ and four*① / *a stagecoach.*② **2.** a passenger car of a railroad train; a railway carriage. **3.** an auto-
—[명] 1. 4륜 대형 마차 [N.B.] 보통 말 네 필이 끎; 공식용 마차 ¶①네 필이 끄는 대형 마차/②역마차 2. 객차 3. 세단형 자동차 4. 대형 버스 5. 코우치,

coachman

mobile like a sedan. **4.** a bus. **5.** a trainer of sports teams, etc.; a private teacher. ⌈of a coach.⌉
coach·man [kóutʃmən] *n.* ⓒ (pl. **-men** [-mən]) a driver
co·ad·ju·tor [kouædʒutər, -ədʒúː- / kouædʒutə] *n.* ⓒ **1.** an assistant; a helper. **2.** an assistant of a bishop.
co·ag·u·late [kouǽgjuléit] *vt.* cause (a liquid, etc.) to become a thickened mass. —*vi.* (of a liquid) become a thickened mass. ▷**co·ag·u·la·tor** [-tər] *n.*
co·ag·u·la·tion [kouǽgjuléi(ə)n] *n.* Ⓤ the act of coagulating; the state of being coagulated; a coagulated mass.
‡**coal** [koul] *n.* **1.** Ⓤ black mineral material that burns; ⓒ a piece of this. **2.** Ⓤ charcoal.
   1) *as black as* [*a*] *coal*, very black.
   2) *call* (or *haul, rake, take*) *someone over the coals for*, scold or blame someone for (something).
   3) *carry coals to Newcastle*, do something unnecessary. ⇒N.B. ⌈for evil.⌉
   4) *heap coals of fire on someone's head*, return good
coal-black [⌃⌃] *adj.* very black.
coal·er [kóulər] *n.* ⓒ **1.** a ship, a railroad, etc. that carries or supplies coal. **2.** a worker or merchant who supplies coal.
co·a·lesce [kòuəlés] *vi.* **1.** grow or come together. **2.** unite into one body, etc.; combine.
co·a·les·cence [kòuəlésns] *n.* Ⓤ **1.** the act of growing or coming together. **2.** 'union; combination.
co·a·li·tion [kòuəlíʃ(ə)n] *n.* **1.** Ⓤ the act of joining together. **2.** ⓒ a group of statesmen, etc. co-operating for some special purpose for a short time. ¶ *a ~ cabinet* (or *ministry*).①
coal tar [⌃⌃] *n.* a black, sticky liquid material left after gas is made from coal.
* **coarse** [kɔːrs] *adj.* **1.** not fine or small. ↔fine ¶ *~ cloth* / *~ sand.* **2.** rough; common; inferior; poor. ¶ *~ food* / *~ goods.* **3.** not delicate; not refined; not polite. ¶ *~ language* / *~ manners.*
coarse·ly [kɔ́ːrsli] *adv.* in a coarse manner.
coars·en [kɔ́ːrsn] *vt.* make (something) coarse. —*vi.* become coarse. ⌈coarse.⌉
coarse·ness[kɔ́ːrsnis] *n.* Ⓤ the quality or state of being
‡**coast** [koust] *n.* **1.** ⓒ the land along the edge of the sea; the seashore; the coastal region. **2.** (*the C-*) (*U.S.*) the region along the Pacific Ocean. **3.** ⓒ (*U.S.*) a slope on which a slide is taken; a slide or ride down a hill without the use of power.
—*vi.* **1.** sail along or near the coast; sail from port to port. **2.** (*U.S.*) ride or slide down a hill without using effort or power.
coast·al [kóustl] *adj.* of, at, near, or along a coast.
coast·er [kóustər] *n.* ⓒ **1.** a ship trading along a coast. **2.** (*U.S.*) a sled or wagon to coast (*v.* 2) on. **3.** an amusement railway, such as a roller coaster.
coast guard [⌃⌃] *n.* **1.** (*C-G-*) (*U.S.*) a group of men working to save lives and prevent secret importing or exporting along the coast. ⇒N.B. **2.** (*Brit.*) an officer on police duty along the coast; a group of such officers.
coast·guard·man [kóustgàːrdmən], **-guards-** [-gàːdz-] *n.* ⓒ (pl. **-men** [-mən]) a member of the coast guard.
coast·land [kóustlænd] *n.* ⓒ the region or land along a coast.
coast·line [kóustlàin] *n.* ⓒ the line or shape of a coast.
coast·wise [kóustwàiz] *adv., adj.* along the coast. ↔overseas
‡**coat** [kout] *n.* ⓒ **1.** a piece of outer clothing with sleeves.

지도원; 가정교사, 개인교사

—名 마부
—名 **1.** 조수, 보좌 **2.** 사교보(司教補), 감독보

—他 …을 응고시키다, 굳히다
—自 응고하다, 굳다

—名 응고, 응결, 응고물, 응괴(凝塊)

—名 **1.** 석탄 **2.** 목탄, 숯

熟 1)새까만 2)[남을 불러서] 야단치다 3)쓸데없는 짓을 하다 N.B. Newcastle은 석탄의 산지 4)원수를 은혜로 갚다

—形 새까만
—名 **1.** 석탄선, 석탄차 **2.** 석탄 인부, 석탄 장수

—自 **1.** 아물어붙다 **2.** 합동하다, 연합하다
—名 **1.** 아물어붙음, 유착(癒着) **2.** 합체, 합동, 연합
—名 **1.** 연합, 합동 **2.** [정치가들의 일시적] 결합, 제휴 ¶①연립 내각

—名 코울타르

—形 **1.** 결(알갱이)이 거친, 굵은 **2.** 조잡한, 흔한, 조악한, 열등한 **3.** 야비한; 천한; 저속한

—副 조잡하게, 천하게, 야비하게
—他 …을 거칠게 하다, 조잡하게 하다
—自 거칠어지다, 조잡해지다
—名 열등, 하등, 조잡, 거칠음, 야비함
—名 **1.** 해안, 연안, 연안 지방 **2.** 《美》 태평양 연안 지방 **3.** 《美》 썰매 타는 비탈진 언덕, [썰매 따위의] 활주

—自 **1.** 연안을 항해하다; 항구에서 항구로 항해하다 **2.** 《美》 [썰매·자전거 따위로] 미끄러져 내리다, 활강하다
—形 연안의, 행안을 따른
—名 **1.** 연안 무역선 **2.** 《美》 [언덕에서 사용하는] 썰매 **3.** [오락용] 코우스터, 활주 궤도

—名 **1.** 《美》 해안 경비대 N.B. 평시에는 재무성, 전시에는 해군성의 직할에 속함 **2.** 《英》 해안 경비대[원]

—名 해안 경비대원

—名 해안 지대

—名 해안선
—副形 연안에(의), 해안을 따라서, 근해의
—名 **1.** 웃옷, 코우트, 외투 ¶①부인복

¶*a ~ and skirt*① / *take off one's ~ to the work.*② **2.** a natural outer covering of an animal or plant; skin; fur. **3.** an outer layer of anything, as of paint or plaster.
1) ***cut one's coat according to one's cloth,*** live within one's income.
2) ***find*** (or ***pick***) ***a hole*** (or ***holes***) ***in someone's coat,*** find a fault (or faults) with someone.
3) ***turn*** (or ***change***) ***one's coat,*** change one's ways or opinions.
—*vt.* cover (something) with a coat. **2.** cover (something) with a layer of anything. ¶*~ a board with paint.*③

상하 한 벌/②웃통을 벗어 젖히고 일에 달려들다 2. 외피, 막(膜), 털가죽 3. [뼁끼 따위의] 칠, 도장(塗裝), 층(層) [熟] 1)분수에 맞는(수입에 따라) 생활을 하다 2)남의 흠을 찾다 3)변절하다
—[他] 1. …에 웃옷을 입히다 2. …에 칠하다 ¶③널빤지에 뼁끼칠을 하다

coat·ing [kóutiŋ] *n.* **1.** [C][U] a thin layer or covering. **2.** [U] material for making coats.
—[名] 1. 칠하기, 입히기 2. 코우트용 천

coat of arms [kóutəvá:rmz] *n.* (pl. **coats of arms**) **1.** a picture or design showing symbols of a family's history on a shield, used esp. by knights, noble families, etc. ⇒fig. **2.** a light garment decorated with such designs, and worn over armor.
—[名] 1. [방패 모양의] 문장(紋章) 2. 그런 문장을 넣은 겉옷의 일종

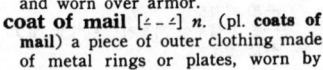

[coat of arms 1.]

coat of mail [⌐ - ⌐] *n.* (pl. **coats of mail**) a piece of outer clothing made of metal rings or plates, worn by soldiers.
—[名] 쇠사슬 갑옷

coax [kouks] *vt.* **1.** make (someone) do something by means of soft words. 《~ someone *to do* or *into doing*》 ¶*~ a child to take* (or *into taking*) *his medicine.*① **2.** get (something) by soft words. ▷**coax·er** [-ər] *n.*
—[他] 1. …을 감언으로 꾀어 …을 시키다 ¶①어린아이를 달래서 약을 먹이다 2. …을 감언으로 꾀어서…을 빼앗다

cob [kab / kɔb] *n.* [C] **1.** (*U.S.*) the center part of an ear of corn. **2.** a strong, short-legged horse for riding. **3.** a male swan, **4.** 《*pl.*》 a small mass or lump, as of coal.
—[名] 1. 《美》 옥수수의 속대 2. 다리가 짧고 튼튼한 말의 한 품종 3. 백조의 수컷 4. [석탄 따위의] 둥근 덩이

co·balt [kóubɔ:lt / kəbɔ́:lt] *n.* [U] **1.** a hard, silver-white, metallic chemical element. **2.** a dark-blue color.
—[名] 1. 코발트 2. 코발트 그림물감(짙은 청색)

cob·ble[1] [kábl / kɔ́bl] *vt.* mend (shoes, etc.); patch; put (something) together unskillfully or roughly.
—[他] [구두 따위]를 수선하다, …을 덧대어 볼품없이 고치다

cob·ble[2] [kábl / kɔ́bl] *n.* [C] 《usu. *pl.*》 a stone worn round and smooth by water. —*vt.* pave (road, etc.) with cobblestones.
—[名] 돌멩이, 조약돌 —[他] [도로 따위]에 자갈을 깔다

cob·bler [káblər / kɔ́blə] *n.* [C] **1.** a mender of shoes. **2.** an unskillful workman. **3.** (*U.S.*) a fruit pie.
—[名] 1. 구두 수선공, 2. 서투른 직공 3. 《美》 프루우트 파이[의 일종]

cob·ble·stone [káblstòun / kɔ́bl-] *n.* [C] a rounded stone, formerly often used in paving.
—[名] 조약돌, 돌멩이, 자갈

co·bra [kóubrə] *n.* [C] a very poisonous snake of India and Africa.
—[名] 코브라

cob·web [kábwèb / kɔ́b-] *n.* [C] **1.** a spider's web or a single thread of this. **2.** anything like a spider's web. **3.** 《*pl.*》 confusion; a lack of order.
—[名] 1. 거미집, 거미줄 2. [거미줄 같이] 얇은 것 3. 뒤엉킴, 혼란, 뒤죽박죽

cob·webbed [kábwèbd / kɔ́b-] *adj.* covered or filled with cobwebs.
—[形] 거미줄을 친, 거미줄투성이의

co·caine, -cain [koukéin / kə-] *n.* [U] a strong drug used to deaden pain.
—[名] 코카인

coch·i·neal [kátʃənì:l / kɔ́tʃi-] *n.* [U] a red coloring dye obtained from certain insects. ⇒[N.B.]
—[名] 코치니일 염료 [N.B.] 연지벌레를 건조하여서 뽑음

‡cock [kak / kɔk] *n.* [C] **1.** a male chicken. ↔hen; 《in *compounds*》 a male bird. ¶*a peacock / a cocksparrow.* **2.** a tap for regulating the flow of water in a pipe; a tap. **3.** a hammer of a gun. ¶*at full ~*① / *at half ~.* **4.** a weather vane in the shape of a cock. **5.** a leader; a chief; a headman. ¶*the ~ of the school.*②
live like fighting cocks, live on the best possible food; live in a very rich manner.
—*vt., vi.* **1.** set (the hammer of a gun) to fire. **2.** turn up (a hat brim); raise (the ears, the tail, etc.) stiffly; turn (the eyes) upwards or sidewards to showing attention, etc. ¶*~ one's nose.*③ / *My dog cocked its ears.* / *He cocked his eye at her.*

—[名] 1. [닭의] 수컷, 수탉; 새의 수컷 2. [수도 따위의] 꼭지 3. [총의] 공이치기, 격침 ¶①격침을 완전히 잡아당겨서; 충분히 준비하여서 4. [수탉 모양의] 풍향계 5. 두목, 우두머리, 수령 ¶②[최상급의] 수석 학생; [전교에서 제일가는] 장난꾸러기 [熟] 잘 먹고 사치스럽게 지내다, 호의호식하다
—[他][自] 1. [총의] 격침을 잡아당기다 2. [모자의 챙 따위를] 치켜올리다; [귀·꽁지 따위를] 쭈뼛이 세우다(서다);치떠보다, 치떠보며 눈짓하다 ¶③코끝을 새침하게 위로 젖히다

cock·ade [kɑkéid / kɔk-] *n.* ⓒ a knot of ribbon or a similar thing worn on the hat as a badge.
— 名 꽃 모양의 모표

cock-a-doo-dle-doo [kákədùːdlúː / kɔ́kə-] *n.* ⓒ the sound made by a cock.
— 名 [수탉 울음소리] 꼬끼오

cock-and-bull story [kákənbúlstɔ̀ːri / kɔ́k-] *n.* a foolish and unbelievable story.
— 名 엉터리 이야기, 터무니없는 이야기

cock·a·trice [kákətris / kɔ́kətràis, -tris] *n.* ⓒ a fabled large snake. ⇒ N.B.
— 名 전설상의 큰 뱀 N.B. 달걀에서 깼다고 전함

cock·crow [kákkròu / kɔ́k-] *n.* Ⓤ the time when cocks begin to crow; early morning.
— 名 닭이 울 무렵, 새벽

cock·er·el [kák(ə)rəl / kɔ́k-] *n.* ⓒ a young cock, not more than one year old.
— 名 [깬 지 1년 미만의] 수탉, 수평아리

cock·eyed [kákaid / kɔ́k-] *adj.* 1. looking sideways; cross-eyed. 2. (*slang*) twisted to one side; slanted; crooked.
— 形 1. 사팔뜨기의 2.《俗》비스듬한, 뒤틀린

cock·horse [kákhɔ̀ːrs / kɔ́khɔ̀ːs] *n.* ⓒ a child's hobbyhorse; a rocking horse.
— 名 아이들의 장난감 말, 흔들 목마

cock·le [kákl / kɔ́kl] *n.* ⓒ 1. an edible shellfish. 2. a small, light, shallow boat. 3. a wrinkle
— 名 1. 새조개 2. 작은 보우트 3. 주름, 구김살

cock·ney [kákni / kɔ́k-] *n.* (pl. **-neys**) *n.* ⓒ 1. a person born in London; a Londoner. 2. a dialect of London.
— *adj.* of Londoners; of London. ¶a ~ *accent*.
— 名 1. 런던나기 2. 런던 영어, 런던 사투리 — 形 런던나기의, 런던의

cock·pit [kákpit / kɔ́k-] *n.* ⓒ 1. an enclosed place for cockfights. 2. the scene of a great war. 3. (in an airplane) the small place where the pilot sits.
— 名 1. 투계장(鬪鷄場) 2. 전쟁터 3. 조종사석

cock·roach [kákròutʃ / kɔ́k-] *n.* ⓒ a large, black, dirty insect often found in kitchens.
— 名 진디, 바퀴

cock·sure [kákʃuər / kɔ́kʃúə] *adj.* 1. very sure; completely certain. ¶*He is ~ of* (or *about*) *it.* 2. be sure to do (something). ¶*She is ~ to come.*
— 形 1. 틀림없는, 절대 확실한 2. 꼭 …하는

cock·tail [káktèil / kɔ́k-] *n.* ⓒ 1. a mixed alcoholic drink. ¶*a ~ party.* 2. a mixture of foods served in a glass at the beginning of a meal; an appetizer.
— 名 1. 칵테일 2. 전채(前菜) 요리

cock·y [káki / kɔ́ki] *adj.* (**cock·i·er, cock·i·est**) very proud; conceited; arrogant. 「fruit or seed.」
— 形 자만심이 강한, 으스대는, 거만한

co·co [kóukou] *n.* ⓒ (pl. **co·cos**) a tropical palm tree; its
— 名 야자나무, 야자나무 열매(씨)

co·coa [kóukou] *n.* Ⓤ 1. brown powder made from crushed cacao seeds. 2. a drink made of this powder. 3. a dull brown color; a yellowish-brown color.
— 名 1. 코코아 2. 코코아 음료 3. 코코아색, 다갈색

co·co·nut, -coa- [kóukənʌ̀t] *n.* ⓒ the large, round, brown, edible nut of the coco palm.
— 名 야자나무 열매

co·coon [kəkúːn] *n.* ⓒ a silky covering spun by a silkworm, etc. to live in while in the pupa stage.
— 名 [누에 따위의] 고치

cod [kɑd / kɔd] *n.* ⓒ (pl. **cods** or *collectively* **cod**) a large edible fish with white flesh; a codfish.
— 名 대구

C.O.D., c.o.d. 1. (*Brit.*) cash on delivery; (*U.S.*) collect on delivery. 2. Concise Oxford Dictionary.

co·da [kóudə] *n.* ⓒ (*Music*) a final passage which brings a piece of music to a formal close. ⇒ N.B.
— 名 (樂) 코다 N.B. 악곡 맨 끝의 소악장

cod·dle [kádl / kɔ́dl] *vt.* 1. treat (a child, etc.) tenderly. ((~ *up*)) 2. cook (something) slowly.
— 他 1. [어린애 등을] 응석을 받다 2. 뭉근한 불로 …을 끓이다

* **code** [koud] *n.* ⓒ 1. a group of laws arranged in an orderly manner. ¶*the civil* (*criminal*) ~① / *the Code Napoleon.* 2. a set of rules or principles of conduct generally accepted by society or by a group of people. ¶*the social* ~② / *You must live up to the ~ of the school.*③ 3. a system of signs; a set of signals showing letters, etc. used in sending messages by telegraph; a system of secret writing. ¶*a ~ telegram*④ / *the International Code*⑤ / *the Morse* ~⑥ / *a telegraphic* ~.⑦
— 名 1. 법전(法典) ¶①민(형)법 법전 2. [어떤 사회의] 규칙, 규약, 관례 ¶②사회의 관례 / ③학칙에 따라 생활하지 않으면 안 된다 3. 신호; 부호; 체계; 약호, 암호 ¶④암호 전보 / ⑤국제 전신 부호 / ⑥모르스 전신 부호 / ⑦전신 암호

— *vt.* 1. put (a message, etc.) into code 2. codify.
— 他 1. …을 전신 암호로 하다 2. …을 법전으로 만들다

cod·fish [kádfiʃ / kɔ́d-] *n.* ⓒ (pl. **-fish·es** or *collectively* **-fish**) a cod or its flesh.
— 名 대구, 그 고기

cod·i·fi·ca·tion [kàdifikéiʃ(ə)n, kòud- / kɔ̀d-, kòud-] *n.* Ⓤ the act of codifying; the state of being codified.
— 名 법전 편찬; 성문화(成文化)

cod·i·fy [kádifài, kóu- / kɔ́d-, kóu-] *vt.* (**-fied**) arrange (laws, etc.) according to a system. ▷**cod·i·fi·er** [-ər] *n.* —㊌ [법률]을 법전으로 편찬하다, 법전화(化)하다

cod-liv·er oil [kádlivərɔ̀il / kɔ́d-] *n.* the oil got from the liver of cod, used as a medicine. ⇒NB. —㊇ [대구의] 간유 NB 비타민 A와 D가 많음

co·ed, co-ed [kóuéd, +*U.S.* -èd] *n.* ⓒ (*U. S. colloq.*) a girl student at a coeducational school or college. —㊇ 《美口》 남녀공학제 학교의 여학생

co·ed·u·ca·tion [kòuedʒukéiʃ(ə)n / kóuèdju(:)-] *n.* Ⓤ the education of boys and girls at the same school or college. —㊇ 남녀공학

co·ed·u·ca·tion·al [kòuedʒukéiʃ(ə)nəl / kóuèdju(:)-] *adj.* educating both boys and girls together at the same school or college. —㊎ 남녀공학의

co·ef·fi·cient [kòuifíʃ(ə)nt] *n.* ⓒ (*Mathematics*) a number or algebraic symbol placed before and multiplying another quantity. —*adj.* co-operating. —㊇ 《數》 계수(係數) —㊎ 공동 작용의

co·erce [kouə́:rs] *vt.* **1.** hold back or put down (someone) by force, esp. by legal authority. ¶ ~ *a voter.* **2.** compel; force. ¶ ~ *someone into drinking* (or *to drink*).① ▷**co·er·cer** [-sər] *n.* —㊌ 1. [법률 따위에 의하여] …을 억압하다, 구속하다 2. …을 강제하다 ¶ ①억지로 술을 먹이다

co·er·cion [kouə́:rʃ(ə)n] *n.* Ⓤ **1.** the act of coercing; the state of being coerced; the act of preventing by force. **2.** government by force. 「power to force.」 —㊇ 1. 강제; 억압 2. 탄압 정치

co·er·cive [kouə́:rsiv] *adj.* compelling; having the —㊎ 강제적인, 위압적인, 강압적인

co·e·val [kouí:v(ə)l] *adj.* of or belonging to the same age or period; present. —*n.* ⓒ a person or thing of about the same age or period. ▷**co·e·val·ly** [-vəli] *adv.* —㊎ 같은 시대의, 그 당시의 —㊇ 같은 시대의 사람(것)

co·ex·ist [kòuigzíst] *vi.* exist together, at the same time or in the same place. —㊀ 공존하다, 동시(같은 장소)에 존재하다

co·ex·ist·ence [kòuigzíst(ə)ns] *n.* Ⓤ existence together; existence at the same time or in the same place. ¶ *peaceful* ~.① 「time or in the same place.」 —㊇ 공존 ¶ ①평화공존

co·ex·ist·ent [kòuigzíst(ə)nt] *adj.* existing at the same —㊎ 공존의, 공존하는, 같은 시대의

: cof·fee [kɔ́:fi, káf- / kɔ́fi] *n.* **1.** Ⓤ a dark-brown drink made from the roasted and ground seeds of the tropical tree or shrub; ⓒ the shrub or tree itself; 《*collectively*》 the seeds. ¶ *a cup of* ~① / *black* ~ / ~ *and milk*.② **2.** Ⓤ dark brown. —㊇ 1. 코오피, 코오피 나무[열매] ¶ ①코오피 한 잔/②우유를 탄 코오피 2. 암갈색, 코오피색

coffee bean [´-´] *n.* a seed of the coffee plant. —㊇ 코오피 열매

coffee break [´-´] *n.* (*U. S.*) a short rest from work when coffee is usu. drunk. —㊇ 《美》 코오피 마시는 휴식시간

coffee cup [´-´] *n.* a cup used to drink coffee. —㊇ 코오피 잔

coffee pot [´-´] *n.* a container, usu. with a lid, in which coffee is made or served. —㊇ 코오피 끓이는 주전자, 코오피 따르는 주전자

coffee shop [´-´] *n.* a shop or restaurant where coffee, light refreshments, and usu. meals are served. —㊇ [호텔 따위의 식당을 겸한] 꺽다실, 다방

cof·fer [kɔ́:fər, káf- / kɔ́fə] *n.* ⓒ **1.** a large, strong box, chest or trunk, esp. for keeping money or valuable articles. **2.** 《*pl.*》 a place for keeping money; a treasury; funds. —㊇ 1. [귀중품을 넣어두는] 상자, 궤 2. 금고, 국고; 자금

• **cof·fin** [kɔ́fin, kɔ́:f- / kɔ́f-] *n.* ⓒ a box or case into which a dead person is placed to be buried. —*vt.* put (a dead person) into a coffin; shut up (books, etc.) tightly. —㊇ 관(棺) —㊌ …을 입관하다; [책 따위]를 사장하다

cog [kɑg, kɔ:g / kɔg] *n.* ⓒ one of a number of teeth on the edge of a wheel which enables it to move with *slip a cog,* make a mistake. 「another wheel.」 ㊇ 톱니바퀴의 톱니 「르다」 ㊁ 뜻밖의 실수를 하다, 실책을 저지

co·gent [kóudʒ(ə)nt] *adj.* (of arguments) having a powerful appeal to the mind; compelling. ¶ ~ *reasoning.*① —㊎ 설득력 있는 ¶ ①남을 수긍하게 하는 논법

cog·i·tate [kádʒitèit / kɔ́dʒ-] *vi.* reflect; consider; think seriously. ¶ ~ *upon* (or *over*) *something.*① —*vt.* think over or about (something); plan. —㊀ 생각하다, 숙고하다 ¶ ①궁리하다 —㊌ …을 숙고하다, 고안하다

cog·i·ta·tion [kàdʒitéiʃ(ə)n / kɔ̀dʒi-] *n.* Ⓤ deep thought; meditation; 《*often pl.*》 a design or plan. —㊇ 깊은 생각, 심사숙고; 고안, 계획

co·gnac [kóunjæk, +*U.S.* kánjæk] *n.* Ⓤ a kind of French brandy. ⇒NB. —㊇ 코낙 NB 프랑스의 Cognac 지방 특산

cog·nate [kágneit / kɔ́g-] *adj.* **1.** having the same origin; —㊎ 1. 기원이 같은; 같은 어족(語族)

coming from a common origin. **2.** having the same ancestor. **3.** having the same quality or nature.
—*n.* [C] **1.** a person related to another by a common ancestor. **2.** a thing or word having a common origin with another.

의 2. 같은 조상의, 동족의 3. 동종의, 동계의 —[名] 1. 친족 2. 기원이 같은 것, 동족 (언)어

cognate object [⸗⸗ ⸗⸗] *n.* (*Grammar*) an object having a common original form with the verb.

—[名]《文法》 동족 목적[어](live a happy life에 있어서의 life)

cog·ni·tion [kagníʃ(ə)n / kɔg-] *n.* [U] [C] the act of knowing; awareness; anything that is known.

—[名] 인식[력]; [인식작용의 결과로서의] 지식

cog·ni·zance [kágniz(ə)ns / kɔ́gni-] *n.* [U] **1.** the fact of being aware; knowledge or sense; notice; the scope of knowledge, etc. ¶*beyond one's ~.*① **2.** a legal hearing. **3.** the right to hold a legal heaving. ¶*within the ~ of.*② **4.** [C] a badge, the distinguishing crest.
1) ***have cognizance of,*** recognize; know.
2) ***take cognizance of,*** notice; recognize (something) officially.

—[名] 1. [보거나 하여서] 알기, 인식, 지식; 주의, 인식 범위 ¶①인식할 수 없는 2. 심리(審理) 3. 재판 관할권 ¶②…의 심리의 관할내에서 4. 기장, 문장(紋章)
[熟] 1)…을 알고 있다 2)…을 주의하다, [정식으로] 인정하다

cog·ni·zant [kágnizənt / kɔ́g-] *adj.* having cognizance of something; aware.
be cognizant of, know.

—[形] [어떤 일을] 인식하고 있는, 알고 있는
[熟] …을 알고 있다

cog·no·men [kagnóumən / kɔgnóumen] *n.* [C] (pl. **-nomens** or **-nom·i·na**) a family name; a surname; a nickname.

—[名] 성(姓), 가명(家名); 별명

cog·nom·i·na [kagnáminə / -nɔ́m-] *n.* pl. of **cognomen**.

cog·wheel [kág(h)wìːl / kɔ́g-] *n.* [C] a wheel with teeth on the rim; a gear wheel.

—[名] 톱니바퀴

co·hab·it [kouhǽbit] *vi.* live together as husband and wife.

—[自] 동서하다, 부부생활하다

co·here [kouhíər] *vi.* **1.** stick together. **2.** (of reasoning, etc.) be connected logically.

—[自] 1. 밀착하다, 결합하다 2. [이유 따위]가 앞뒤가 일치하다, 조리가 서다

co·her·ence [kouhíərəns] *n.* [U] **1.** the act of cohering. **2.** consistency; logical connection.

—[名] 1. 밀착[성] 2. [논리 따위의] 일관성, 통일성

co·her·ent [kouhíərənt] *adj.* **1.** able to stick together. **2.** logically clear and well connected. ¶*a ~ argument.*

—[形] 1. 밀착성의 2. 조리가 선, 이치에 맞는; 앞뒤가 일치하는

co·he·sion [kouhíːʒ(ə)n] *n.* [U] [C] **1.** the act of sticking together; a habit of sticking together. **2.** (*Physics*) the force by which the particles of a substance are bound together.

—[名] 1. 결합[력], 점착력 2. [분자 따위의] 응집력(凝集力), 결합력

co·he·sive [kouhíːsiv] *adj.* sticking together; apt to stick together. ▷**co·he·sive·ly** [-li] *adv.* —**co·he·sive·ness** [-nis] *n.*

—[形] 밀착력 있는, 결합력 있는

co·hort [kóuhɔːrt] *n.* [C] **1.** (in ancient Rome) a body of soldiers of from 300 to 600 men. **2.** 《often *pl.*》 a group of soldiers; a group; a band.

—[名] 1. [고대 로마의 300~600명의] 군대 2. 군대; 일대(一隊), 일단

* **coil** [kɔil] *vt., vi.* wind (a rope, etc.) around into circles; form coils. ¶*~ a rope / The snake coiled itself up.*①
—*n.* [C] **1.** anything wound in a circle. ¶*a ~ of rope*② */ a snake in a ~.* **2.** one of the circles of a spiral. **3.** a spiral of wire or pipe for conducting electricity, hot water, or the like.

—[他][自] [···을] 돌돌 감다, 뚤뚤 말다, 사리다 ¶①뱀이 사렸다 —[名] 1. 고리, 사리 ¶②밧줄의 사리 2. 한 사리, 한 마름 3. 코일, 선륜(線輪), 권선(捲線); [난방기 따위의] 나선관

: **coin** [kɔin] *n.* **1.** [C] a piece of metal used as money; 《*collectively*》 metal money. ↔paper money; notes ¶*a current ~*① */ a false ~*② */ a silver ~.* **2.** (*colloq.*) the money.
pay someone back in his own coin, treat someone as he has treated you.
—*vt.* **1.** make (metal) into coins; make (coins) by shaping pieces of metal. **2.** invent or make up (a new word, etc.) ¶*~ a word or phrase.*③

—[名] 1. 화폐; [금·은·동화 따위의] 주화 ¶①통화/②가짜돈, 위조물 2.《口》 금전
[熟] [남]에게 앙갚음하다
—[他] 1. [화폐]를 주조하다; [금속]을 화폐로 만들다 2. [신어 따위를] 만들어내다 ¶③신어를 만들다

coin·age [kɔ́inidʒ] *n.* **1.** [U] the act of making coins; a system of money. **2.** 《*collectively*》 the money made. **3.** [U] the act of making up; the invention of a new word; [C] the new word itself. ¶*the ~ of fancy (the brain).*①

—[名] 1. 화폐 주조; 화폐 제도 2. 화폐 3. 새로 만들어내기, 신조어, 신어 ¶①공상(두뇌)의 산물

co·in·cide [kòuinsáid] *vi.* **1.** (of two events) happen at the same time; (of two things) occupy the same

—[自] 1. 동시에 일어나다; [위치·외형이] 일치하다 ¶①불행하게도 그 소년

place; be the same shape and cover the same area. ¶*The unlucky boy's birthday coincided with Christmas.*① **2.** be in agreement; correspond; agree.
의 생일은 크리스마스와 일치하였다 **2.** [의견 따위가] 일치하다

co·in·ci·dence [kouínsid(ə)ns] *n.* **1.** [U] the act or state of coinciding. **2.** [C] a happening of events, ideas, etc. at the same time by chance. ¶*by a curious ~.*① **3.** [U] agreement by chance.
—[名] **1.** 동시 발생, 동시 공존 **2.** 동시 발생 사건 ¶①괴이한 일치로서 **3.** 우연의 일치, 부합

co·in·ci·dent [kouínsid(ə)nt] *adj.* happening at the same time in exact agreement. ¶*be ~ with something.*①
—[形] 동시에 일어난; 일치한, 부합된 ¶①…와 일치하다

co·in·ci·den·tal [kouìnsidéntl] *adj.* characterized by coincidence. ▷**co·in·ci·den·tal·ly** [-i] *adv.*
—[形] 부합하는, 일치의

coin·er [kɔ́inər] *n.* [C] a maker of coins, esp. one who makes false coins; an inventor, esp. of new words.
—[名] 화폐 주조자; [특히] 화폐 위조자

coke [kouk] *n.* **1.** [U] gray lumps of fuel made by heating soft coal in a closed apparatus. **2.** (*slang*) cocaine; 《*C-*》 (*U. S. colloq.*) Coca-Cola. ***—vt., vi.*** change (coal) into coke.
—[名] **1.** 코우크스, 해탄(骸炭) **2.** 《俗》 코카인; 《美口》; 코카콜라 —[他][自] …을 코우크스로 만들다; 코우크스가 되다

col [kɑl / kɔl] *n.* [C] a gap between peaks in a mountain range used as a pass.
—[名] [산봉우리 사이의] 움푹 들어간 곳, 좁은 길, [산맥 사이의] 저지(低地)

Col. [kɑl / kɔl] **1.** Colonel. **2.** Colorado.

‡**cold** [kould] *adj.* **1.** of a low temperature; very cool; chilly. ↔hot **2.** showing no feeling or passion. ¶*a ~ heart.*① **3.** feeling no warmth; indifferent; not friendly. ¶*a ~ manner.* **4.** discouraging. ¶*~ news.* **5.** not fresh. ¶*a ~ jest.* **6.** faint.
—[形] **1.** 추운; 찬 **2.** 냉정한 ¶①무정 **3.** 냉담한; 쌀쌀한 **4.** 낙심하게 하는 **5.** 낡은, 케케묵은 **6.** 희미한

1) ***make someone's blood run cold,*** fill someone with fear.
2) ***throw cold water on,*** discourage (a scheme, etc.).
[熟] 1)…을 오싹하게 하다 2)…에 찬 물을 끼얹다, …에 트집을 하다

—n. **1.** [U] a low temperature; chillness. **2.** [U] temperature below the freezing point. **3.** [C] an illness marked by a sore throat, a running nose, coughing, a headache, etc. ¶*a ~ in the head* (or *nose*)② / *a ~ on the chest* (or *lungs*)③ / *have a ~* / *catch* [*a*] *~.*
—[名] **1.** 추위 **2.** 빙점 이하 **3.** 감기 ¶②코감기/③기침감기

cold-blood·ed [kóuldblʌ́did] *adj.* **1.** having a body temperature the same as that of the surroundings. ¶*Fish and reptile are ~ animals.* ↔warm-blooded **2.** cruel; without pity. ▷**cold-blood·ed·ly** [-li] *adv.*
—[形] **1.** 냉혈의 **2.** 냉담한, 냉혹한

cold cream [⌐ ⌐] *n.* a creamy substance used for softening and cleansing the skin.
—[名] 코울드크리임

cold-heart·ed [kóuldhá:rtid] *adj.* without feeling, sympathy or love.
—[形] 냉담한, 무정한

***cold·ly** [kóuldli] *adv.* in a cold manner.
—[副] 냉정히, 쌀쌀하게

cold·ness [kóuldnis] *n.* [U] the state of being cold.
—[名] 한기, 추위, 냉담

cold war [⌐ ⌐] *n.* a sharp conflict in diplomacy, economics, etc. between states regarded as possibly leading to real war.
—[名] 냉전(무력을 쓰지 않고 외교선전에 의한 신경전)

col·ic [kɑ́lik / kɔ́l-] *n.* [U] severe pains in the stomach and bowels.
—[名] 복통, 산통(疝痛)

col·i·se·um [kɑ̀lisí:əm / kɔ̀lisí(:)əm] *n.* [C] **1.** a large building or stadium for sports, contests, etc. **2.** 《*C-*》 =Colosseum.
—[名] **1.** 대연기장(演技場); 대체육관 **2.** 콜로세움

col·lab·o·rate [kəlǽbərèit] *vi.* **1.** work together with someone, as on a literary work. ¶*Three authors collaborated on that novel.* **2.** work with, or willingly help, an enemy of one's country.
—[自] **1.** 공동으로 일하다, 합작하다 **2.** [적국에] 협력하다, 부역하다

col·lab·o·ra·tion [kəlæ̀bəréiʃ(ə)n] *n.* [U] the act of collaborating.
—[名] 공동제작, 합작, 공저(共著); [적국 따위에의] 협력, 부역

col·lab·o·ra·tor [kəlǽbərèitər] *n.* [C] a person who collaborates.
—[名] 공저자(共著者), 합작자

col·lapse** [kəlǽps] *vi.* **1.** fall down or in. ¶*The building collapsed.* **2.** fold together. ¶*The table collapses.* **3.** fail utterly; come to ruin. ¶*The scheme collapsed.* **4.** lose strength or courage; break down physically. ¶*His health collapsed.*① ***—vt. cause (something) to fail or fall in; fold. ¶*~ a bubble.*
—[自] **1.** 무너지다, 붕괴하다 **2.** 접혀 겹쳐지다 **3.** 실패하다; 파멸되다 **4.** 쇠퇴하다; 쇠약해지다 ¶①그의 건강은 쇠퇴하였다 —[他] …을 실패시키다, 좌절시키다; 접다

—n. [C] the act of collapsing. ¶*the ~ of a roof* (*a tower*)② / *the ~ of the Roman Empire*③ / *the ~ of a bank.*④
—[名] 무너짐, 붕괴, 좌절; 실패, 쇠퇴, 쇠약, 허탈 ¶②지붕(탑)의 붕괴/③로마제국의 붕괴/④은행의 파산

col·laps·i·ble [kəlǽpsibl] *adj.* that can be folded up. ¶*a ~ boat.*
—[形] [배·의자 따위] 접을 수 있는

col·lar [kɑ́lər / kɔ́lə] *n.* [C] **1.** the part of a shirt, dress or coat fitting around the neck. ¶*a turned-down ~*① / *hold* (or *seize, take*) *someone by the ~.*② **2.** a divided piece of linen, lace, etc. worn around the neck. **3.** a band of leather, etc. for the neck of a dog, a horse, etc. ¶*a dog's ~.* **4.** a metal ring used to join two pipes or rods.
—[名] 1. 칼라, 깃 ¶①접어젖힌 깃/②…의 멱살을 붙잡다 2. [훈장의] 수장(首章), 목걸이 훈장 3. 목걸이; 말의 어깨에 맨 줄 4. 고리, 접관(接管); 《建》 조임보

1) ***against the collar,*** in the face of difficulty.
2) ***in collar,*** (*colloq.*) attending to one's business.
3) ***out of collar,*** out of work.
4) ***wear*** (or ***take***) ***the collar,*** (*colloq.*) obey another's orders.

[熟] 1)곤란과 맞서서 2)사업에 종사하여, 취업하여 3)실직하여 4)《口》남의 명령에 따르다

—*vt.* **1.** put a collar on (a dog, etc.). **2.** catch (someone) by the collar. ▷**col·lar·less** [-lis] *adj.*
—[他] 1. …에 목걸이(깃)를 달다 2. …의 멱살을 잡다

col·lar·bone [kɑ́lərbòun / kɔ́lə-] *n.* [C] a bone connecting the shoulder blade and the breastbone.
—[名] 쇄골(鎖骨)

col·late [kɑléit, kəl- / kɔl-, kəl-] *vt.* compare (two or more pieces of writing) to see whether there are any differences. ▷**col·la·tor** [-ər] *n.*
—[他] [주로 책을 딴 책]과 대조하다

col·lat·er·al [kəlǽt(ə)rəl / kɔl-] *adj.* **1.** side by side; parallel. **2.** attendant or secondary; indirect; additional. ¶*~ operations.* **3.** coming from a common ancestor but in a different line. ¶*Cousins are ~ relatives.*
—[形] 1. 옆에 나란히 있는, 평행한 2. 부수된, 2차적인; 간접적인; 부차적인 3. 방계의

col·la·tion [kɑléiʃ(ə)n, kəl- / kɔl, kəl-] *n.* **1.** [C] a light meal. **2.** [U] the act of collating; a careful comparison.
—[名] 1. 가벼운 식사, 경식사 2. 대조, 조회(照會)

col·league [kɑ́li:g / kɔ́l-] *n.* [C] an associate in an office or in a profession; a fellow worker.
—[名] 동료

col·lect [kəlékt] *vt.* **1.** gather (something) together; gather (stamps, etc.) as a hobby; gather (people). ¶*~ old coins / ~ material for a dictionary.*① **2.** call for and receive pay for (debts, taxes, bills, etc.). **3.** gather together (one's thoughts, etc.); recover control of (oneself). ¶*~ one's thoughts*② / *~ one's courage*③ / *~ a horse*④ / *~ oneself.*⑤
—*vi.* **1.** gather or come together. ¶*Dust and rubbish soon ~.* **2.** meet or assemble. ¶*A crowd collects.* **3.** collect payments, etc. ¶*~ for 'Life'.*⑥
—[他] 1. …을 모으다; 수집하다; 집합시키다 ¶①사건의 자료를 수집하다 2. …을 징수하다 3. …을 집중하다 [생각]을 집중시키다; …을 가라앉히다 ¶②생각을 집중시키다/③용기를 내다/④말을 능숙하게 다루다/⑤마음을 가라앉히다 —[自] 1. 쌓이다, 모이다 2. 집합하다, 모임을 가지다 3. 수금하다 ¶⑥라이프지의 수금을 하다

col·lect·ed [kəléktid] *adj.* gathered together; calm and self-possessed; cool; quiet. ▷**col·lect·ed·ly** [-li] *adv.*
—[形] 모인, 모은, 침착한, 냉정한

col·lec·tion [kəlékʃ(ə)n] *n.* **1.** [U] the act of collecting; [C] an example of this; [C] a number of things assembled together for study or display. ¶*have a large ~ of books*① / *make a ~ of stamps.*② **2.** [U][C] a sum of money asked for and contributed for some good purpose; the act of taking in money due; the amount received. **3.** [C] a heap of things having come together.
—[名] 1. 채집, 수집; 수집물, 콜렉션 ¶①책을 많이 수집해 있다/②우표수집을 하다 2. 기부금; [세금 따위의] 징수, 수금 3. [쓰레기·종이 따위의] 더미, 퇴적

col·lec·tive [kəléktiv] *adj.* **1.** of a group. **2.** shared or done by a number of persons working together. ¶*a ~ agreement*① / *a ~ effort*② / *a ~ note*③ / *~ ownership.*④ **3.** (*Grammar*) singular in form, but plural in meaning.
—[形] 1. 집합적인; 총체의 2. 집단으로서의; 공동의 ¶①단체 협약/②총력/③공동각서/④공동 소유권 3. 《文法》 집합적인

—*n.* [C] **1.** (*Grammar*) a collective noun. **2.** any collective enterprise.
—[名] 1. 집합명사 2. 집단으로서 공동으로 하는 사업

collective bargaining [-´- ´--] *n.* talk between organized workers and their employers in order to reach an agreement on wages, hours, and working conditions.
—[名] 단체 교섭

collective farm [-´- ´] *n.* a farm formed by a group and under collective management.
—[名] [소련의] 집단농장, 콜호즈(kolkhoz)

col·lec·tive·ly [kəléktivli] *adv.* in a collective manner; in a collective sense.
—[副] 집합적으로, 집합체(총체)로서

collective noun [-´- ´] *n.* (*Grammar*) one noun used to describe a group of things.
—[名] 《文法》 집합명사 (family, class, crew 따위)

collective security [-´- -´--] *n.* a system or policy of
—[名] 집단 안전 보장

C

international peace in which all the nations taking part agree to take action against a nation that attacks any one of them.

col·lec·tor [kəléktər] *n.* [C] a person who collects; a person whose business is to collect money due.
—[名] 수집가, 채집가; 수금원, 징수원; 수세리(收稅吏)

⁑col·lege [kálidʒ / kɔ́l-] *n.* [C] **1.** (*Brit.*) a part of a university. ⇒[N.B.] **2.** (*U.S.*) an educational institution above the high school that gives degrees; a university; the academic department of a university for general study. **3.** a school of higher learning for study in the liberal arts or in professional studies. ¶*a ~ of medicine.*① **4.** the building and grounds used by a college. **5.** a body of persons having certain common rights or duties. ¶*the College of Physicians.*②
—[名] 1.《英》 대학 [N.B.] Oxford, Cambridge 대학의 자치체 2.《美》 대학(졸업하면 bachelor의 칭호를 수여함); [university 내의] [교양]학부 3. 단과대학; 특수 전문학교 ¶①약학 전문학교 4. [전문학교·대학의] 건물·운동장, 교사 5. 단체, 학회 ¶②의사회(醫師會)

col·le·gi·an [kəlí:dʒ(i)ən] *n.* [C] a college student; a member of a college.
—[名] college의 학생; 단체의 일원

col·le·gi·ate [kəlí:dʒiit, +*U.S.* -dʒit] *adj.* of or like a college; connected with a college; of or characteristic of college students. ¶*the latest ~ styles.*
—[形] college의, college 조직의; 대학생의, 대학생에 적합한

col·lide [kəláid] *vi.* come together violently; strike against each other; clash; conflict. ¶*The ships collided in the fog.*
—[自] 충돌하다; [의지·목적 따위가] 일치하지 않다

col·lie [káli / kɔ́li] *n.* [C] a Scottish sheep dog with a hairy coat.
—[名] 콜리종의 개

col·lier [káliər / kɔ́liə] *n.* [C] a coal miner; a ship for carrying coal.
—[名] [탄광의] 광부; 석탄선

col·lier·y [káliəri / kɔ́l-] *n.* [C] (pl. **-lier·ies**) a coal mine and the buildings connected with it.
—[名] 탄광, 탄갱; 채탄소(건물 기타 모든 설비를 포함)

***col·li·sion** [kəlíʒ(ə)n] *n.* [U][C] the act of colliding or meeting violently; a clash of interests, ideas, etc.
1) ***come into collision*** (=*collide* or *conflict*) ***with*** *something.*
2) ***in collision with,*** smashing into.
—[名] 충돌, 격돌; [의견·이해 따위의] 충돌
[熟] 1)…와 충돌하다 2)…와 충돌하여

col·lo·ca·tion [kàloukéiʃ(ə)n / kɔ̀l-] *n.* [U] the act of arranging or placing together; the arrangement of words in a definite order.
—[名] 배열, 배치; 낱말의 배열(배치)

col·lo·qui·al [kəlóukwiəl] *adj.* used in common conversation, not usu. used in formal or literary style. ↔literary ¶*~ language*① / *~ style.*② ▷**col·lo·qui·al·ly** [-i] *adv.*
—[形] 구어[체]의; 회화의 ¶①구어 /②구어체

col·lo·qui·al·ism [kəlóukwiəliz(ə)m] *n.* [U][C] a colloquial word or expression; a colloquial quality, style or usage.
—[名] 구어적 어구(표현); 구어체

col·lo·quy [káləkwi / kɔ́l-] *n.* [U][C] (pl. **-quies**) a talk or conversation, esp. a formal conversation.
—[名] [다소 형식적인] 대담; 자유 토의, 회화; 회담

col·lu·sion [kəlú:ʒ(ə)n] *n.* [U][C] secret agreement for an unlawful or evil purpose.
—[名] 공모, 결탁

co·logne [kəlóun] *n.* [U] a perfumed toilet water.
—[名] 콜론수, 화장수(Cologne 원산)

Co·lom·bi·a [kəlʌ́mbiə / kəlɔ́mbiə] *n.* a country in the northwest part of South America. ⇒[N.B.] ▷**Co·lom·bi·an** [-n] *adj., n.*
—[名] 남미 서북부의 공화국 [N.B.] 수도는 Bogotá

***co·lon** [kóulən] *n.* [C] a punctuation mark (:) used to introduce quotations, examples, etc.
—[名] [구둣점의] 콜론(:)

***colo·nel** [kə́:rnl] *n.* [C] **1.** the rank below that of a brigadier general in the army. **2.** the officer who commands a regiment of soldiers.
—[名] 1. 육군 대령 2. 연대장

***co·lo·ni·al** [kəlóuniəl] *adj.* **1.** of a colony or colonies. **2.** (often *C-*) of the thirteen British colonies that became the United States. —*n.* [C] a person of a colony.
—[形] 1. 식민의, 식민지의 2. 영령(英領) 식민지의 —[名] 식민지의 주민

***col·o·nist** [kálənist / kɔ́lə-] *n.* [C] **1.** a person who lives in a colony. **2.** a person who takes part in founding a colony.
—[名] 1. 식민지의 주민 2. 식민지 개척자

col·o·ni·za·tion [kàlənizéiʃ(ə)n / kɔ̀lənai-] *n.* [U] the act of founding and developing a colony or colonies or sending settlers to a colony.
—[名] 식민, 식민지 개척, 식민지화

col·o·nize [kálənàiz / kɔ́lə-] *vt.* establish a colony in (a place); send colonists to and settle in (a place). —*vi.* establish in a colony; settle in a colony.
—[他] …을 식민지로 하다, 식민지를 개척하다; [이민]을 식민지로 보내다 —[自] 식민하다; 식민지로 이주하다

col·on·nade [kɑ̀lənéid / kɔ̀l-] *n.* [C] **1.** a row of columns regularly spaced along the side or sides of a building. ⇒fig. **2.** a [double] row of trees.

—[名] 1. 줄지어 선 기둥, 주랑(柱廊) 2. [두 줄로 늘어선] 가로수

(colonnade 1.)

‡ **col·o·ny** [kɑ́ləni / kɔ́l-] *n.* [C] (pl. **-nies**) **1.** ⟪*collectively*⟫ a group of people who leave their native country and settle in another land, but remain subject to the mother country. **2.** a place or area settled in this way; any distant territory belonging to a nation. **3.** a group of people living together and closely connected by race, occupation, or the like; a place settled or occupied by any such group. ¶*the American ~ in Paris*① / *an artist's ~.*② **4.** ⟪*the Colonies*⟫ the thirteen British Colonies that became the first states of the United States. **5.** a group of animals, plants, insects, etc. living or growing together. ¶*a ~ of ants.*③

—[名] 1. 식민단(團), 이민단 2. 식민지 3. [나라 또는 도시내의] 외인(外人) 거류민단; 거류지, 조계(租界); [같은 직업인의] 집단, 부락 ¶①파리의 미국인 거리/②미술가촌 4. 독립전쟁 후 최초로 독립한 13주 5. [동·식물의] 군생(群生); 군락(群落) ¶③개미의 집단

‡ **col·or,** *Brit.* **-our** [kʌ́lər] *n.* [U] **1.** [U] [C] yellow, red, blue, and combinations of these; hue; tint. **2.** ⟪*pl.*⟫ paint. **3.** ⟪sometimes *a ~*⟫ the color of the face; complexion. ¶*have very little ~.*① **4.** the skin color of any people or race that is not white; negro. **5.** ⟪*pl.*⟫ appearance. **6.** ⟪*pl.*⟫ a flag of a nation; a flag of a military unit. **7.** (esp. in a literary work) liveliness; vividness. **8.** a special quality. ¶*a novel with local ~.*②

—[名] 1. 빛깔, 색채 2. 그림물감 3. 안색 ¶①혈색이 좋지 않다 4. 피부빛깔, 살빛; 흑인 5. 모습, 겉모양, 외관 6. 국기; 군기 7. 활기 8. 특질, 특색 ¶②지방색을 띤 소설

1) ***change color,*** grow paler or redder than usual.
2) ***give*** (or ***lend***) ***color*** (=*give an appearance of probability*) ***to something.***
3) ***give a false color to,*** change the meaning of (something) to suit one's aims.
4) ***lose color,*** turn pale.
5) ***lower one's colors,*** give up one's demand.
6) ***nail one's colors to the mast,*** show a strong determination not to change one's opinion, etc.
7) ***show one's true colors,*** show what one really is.

[熟] 1)낯빛을 바꾸다(창백해지거나 붉어지다) 2)참말같이(진짜처럼) 꾸미다 3)…의 진상을 의곡하다 4)창백해지다 5)요구를 철회하다 6)자기의 의사를 굽히지 않다 7)본성을 드러내다

—*vt.* **1.** give color to (something). **2.** express wrongly; misrepresent; exaggerate. **—*vi.*** blush.

—[他] 1. …에 착색하다 2. …을 거짓으로 표현하다, 의곡하다; 과장하다 —[自] 빛이 나다; 얼굴을 붉히다

Col·o·rad·o [kɑ̀lərǽdou, -rɑ́:dou / kɔ̀lərɑ́:dou] *n.* a western State of the United States. ⇒ [N.B.]

—[名] 미국 서부의 주 [N.B.] Colo.로 줄여 씀. 수도는 Denver

col·or·a·tion, *Brit.* **-our-** [kʌ̀ləréiʃ(ə)n] *n.* [U] the act of coloring; the arrangement of colors, as in an animal or plant. ¶*warning ~*① / *protective ~.*②

—[名] 착색법, 배색, 채색 ¶①경계색/②보호색

col·or-blind, *Brit.* **-our-** [kʌ́lərblaind] *adj.* unable to recognize or see certain colors.

—[形] 색맹의

color blindness [⏑– ⏑–] *n.* the condition of being unable to distinguish colors.

—[名] 색맹

col·or·cast [kʌ́lərkæ̀st / kʌ́ləkɑ̀:st] *n.* [C] a television broadcast in color. **—*vt.*** broadcast (a television program) in color.

—[名] 컬러 텔레비전 방송 —[他] [프로]를 컬러 텔레비전 방송하다

• **col·ored,** *Brit.* **-oured** [kʌ́lərd] *adj.* **1.** having color. ¶*~ shirts*① / *~ spectacles.* **2.** belonging to a race other than the white race, esp. the Negro race. ¶*a ~ man / a ~ race / a ~ school.*② **3.** a little influenced by emotion, prejudice, etc.

—[形] 1. 착색된, 색채가 있는 ¶①색깔이 있는 샤쓰 2. 유색[인종]의; 흑인의 ¶②흑인 학교 3. [감정 따위로] 채색된

col·or·ful, *Brit.* **-our-** [kʌ́lərf(u)l] *adj.* rich in color; interesting; exciting the imagination; vivid.

—[形] 색채가 풍부한, 다채로운, 생생한, 선명한

col·or·ing, *Brit.* **-our-** [kʌ́ləriŋ] *n.* [U] **1.** the way in which color is used by an artist. **2.** [U] [C] a substance used to give color to something, such as a pigment, a dye, etc. ¶*~ matter.*① **3.** a false appearance or look.

—[名] 1. 착색[법], 채색 2. 색깔을 내는 것, 염료, 그림물감 ¶①착색제, 색소 3. 겉치레, 외관

col·or·ist, *Brit.* **-our-** [kʌ́lərist] *n.* [C] a person using colors; an artist skillful in using colors.

—[名] 착색자, 채색자, 색칠을 능숙하게 하는 화가

col·or·less, *Brit.* **-our-** [kʌ́lərlis] *adj.* without color; pale; without interest or character. ¶*a ~ person.*

—[形] 무색의, 빛깔이 없는, 창백한, 특색이 없는, 무미건조한

C

color scheme [⌐– ⌐] *n.* a pattern, or combination of colors to produce a harmonious effect. —[名] [실내 장식·정원 따위의] 색채 배합 설계

co·los·sal [kəlásl / kəlɔ́sl] *adj.* huge; very large; splendid; incredible. ¶ ~ *dramas*① / *a man of* ~ *stature.* —[形] 거대한, 방대한; 멋진, 훌륭한; 놀랄 만한 ¶①방대한 희곡

Col·os·se·um [kɑ̀ləsí:əm / kɔ́l-] *n.* a large open-air theater built in Rome about 80 A. D. and used for games, fights, etc. —[名] 콜로세움(고대 로마의 원형 대경기장)

co·los·si [kəlásai / -lɔ́s-] *n.* pl. of **colossus.**

co·los·sus [kəlásəs / kəlɔ́s-] *n.* [C] (pl. **-los·si** or **-los·sus·es**) a very large statue; any huge person or object. —[名] 거상(巨像); 거대한 사람(것)

⁝ **col·our** [kʌ́lər] *n., v.* (*Brit.*) =color.

col·oured [kʌ́lərd] *adj.* (*Brit.*) =colored.

col·our·ful [kʌ́ləf(u)l] *adj.* (*Brit.*) =colorful.

col·our·ing [kʌ́ləriŋ] *n.* (*Brit.*) =coloring.

col·our·less [kʌ́lərlis] *adj.* (*Brit.*) =colorless.

• **colt** [koult] *n.* [C] **1.** a young horse, donkey or zebra. **2.** a young, inexperienced person. —[名] **1.** 말·당나귀·얼룩말의 새끼 **2.** 풋나기, 초심자

• **Co·lum·bi·a** [kəlʌ́mbiə] *n.* (*poetic*) the United States. —[名] 《詩》 미국, 미합중국

col·um·bine [káləmbàin / kɔ́l-] *n.* [C] a garden plant with showy flowers; the flowers of this plant. —[名] 매발톱꽃

• **Co·lum·bus** [kəlʌ́mbəs], **Christopher** *n.* (1446?-1506) an Italian who discovered America in 1492. —[名] 미국 대륙을 발견한 이탈리아인

⁝ **col·umn** [káləm / kɔ́l-] *n.* [C] **1.** a slender, upright structure; a large round post in a building. ⇒fig. **2.** anything shaped like a column. ¶*columns of smoke*① / *a* ~ *of mercury.*② **3.** a narrow division of a newspaper often used for a special subject. ¶*a contributor's* ~③ / *literary columns.* **4.** a line of soldiers or ships placed one behind another. —[名] **1.** 원주(圓柱); 기둥 **2.** 기둥 모양의 것 ¶①[기둥처럼 솟아오르는] 몇 가닥의 연기 /②수은주 **3.** [신문 따위의] 난(欄); [신문·잡지의] 특별 기고란 ¶③투고란 **4.** [군대나 군함의] 종대(縱隊), 종렬

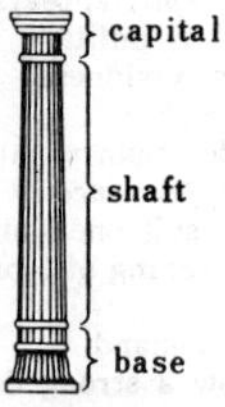
capital
shaft
base
[column 1.]

col·um·nist [káləm(n)ist / kɔ́l-] *n.* [C] a person who regularly writes a special column in a newspaper. —[名] [신문의 시사평론 따위의] 특약 기고가

co·ma [kóumə] *n.* [C] a deep, unconscious sleep caused by disease, injury, etc. —[名] 혼수(昏睡)

com·a·tose [kámətòus, kóumə- / kóumə-] *adj.* in a coma. —[形] 혼수상태에 빠진

• **comb** [koum] *n.* [C] **1.** a narrow, short piece of metal, bone, etc. with teeth, used to arrange or clean the hair. **2.** the crest of a bird. **3.** the top of a wave. **4.** a honeycomb. —*vt.* **1.** arrange or set (the hair) with a comb. **2.** search (something) thoroughly. —*vi.* (of waves) roll over or break at the top. —[名] **1.** 빗 **2.** [새의] 볏 **3.** [파도의] 물마루 **4.** 벌집 —[他] **1.** [머리]를 빗질하다, 빗다 **2.** …을 샅샅이 수색하다 —[自] [파도가] 물마루를 이루며 감아들다, 흰 물결이 일다

• **com·bat** *vt., vi.* [kəmbǽt, kámbæt / kɔ́mbət, kʌ́m- // →*n.*] (**-bat·ed, -bat·ing** or *Brit.* **-bat·ted, -bat·ting**) fight; battle; struggle. 《~ *with* or *against* someone *for*; ~ *for* something》 ¶ ~ *for a cause.*① —*n.* [kámbæt, kʌ́m- / kɔ́mbət, kʌ́m-] [C] a struggle; a battle; a fight. —[他][自] [···와] 싸우다, 투쟁하다, 격투하다, 분투하다, 항쟁하다 ¶①주의(主義)를 위해 싸우다 —[名] 격투, 싸움, 투쟁

com·bat·ant [kəmbǽt(ə)nt, kámb(ə)t-/kɔ́mb(ə)t-, kʌ́mb(ə)t-] *n.* [C] a person who fights. —*adj.* fighting. ¶*a* ~ *spirit.*① —[名] 투쟁자; 전투원 —[形] 격투하는, 싸우는, 투쟁하는 ¶①투지

com·bat·ive [kəmbǽtiv, kámbə-, kʌ́m- / kɔ́mbətiv, kʌ́m-] *adj.* ready to fight; fond of fighting. —[形] 투쟁적인, 호전적인

combe, *Brit.* **coomb** [ku:m] *n.* [C] a narrow valley. —[名] 좁고 깊은 골짜기, 협곡

⁝ **com·bi·na·tion** [kɑ̀mbinéiʃ(ə)n / kɔ̀m-] *n.* [U][C] **1.** the act or process of joining together. **2.** a thing made by combining. **3.** 《*pl.*》 a piece of underwear joining upper and lower garments in one piece. **4.** a group of persons or parties joined together for some common purpose. ¶*form a strong* ~.① **5.** the series of numbers or letters to which a dial on a lock is turned to open it. ¶*a* ~ *lock.*② **6.** the union of materials to form a chemical compound. —[名] **1.** 결합, 짝맞춤, 합동 **2.** 결합물 **3.** 콤비네이션(샤쓰와 속바지가 잇달린 내의) **4.** 한 패, 한 통속; 연합 ¶①강력한 연합을 형성하다 **5.** [자물쇠]의 짜맞춤 숫자(문자) ¶②문자 따위를 맞추어 여는 자물쇠 **6.** 화합

in combination with, joining with (someone.) —[熟] …와 합동하여(공동으로)

:com·bine *v.* [kəmbáin →*n.*] *vt.* **1.** bring (things) into union; unite. 《~ something *with*》 ¶~ *work with pleasure.*① **2.** unite (different substances) into a chemical combination. ¶*Hydrogen and oxygen are combined in water.* —*vi.* unite; mix.
—*n.* [kámbain / kɔ́mbain, kəmbáin] [C] **1.** (*U.S. colloq.*) a group of people, corporations, etc. **2.** (*U.S.*) a machine for harvesting.

com·bus·ti·ble [kəmbʌ́stibl] *adj.* **1.** apt to catch fire or burn; easily burned. **2.** easily excited. —*n.* 《usu. *pl.*》 materials which are easily set on fire.

com·bus·tion [kəmbʌ́stʃ(ə)n] *n.* [U] **1.** the act or process of burning. ¶*complete* ~.① **2.** oxidation.

:come [kʌm] *v.* (**came, come**) *vi.* **1.** move to or toward a position or place from a point farther away; move to or toward the speaker or the person addressed to. ↔go ¶*Come here.* / *Come nearer to the fireplace.* / *You must ~ and see us sometime.; You must ~ to see us sometime.*① ⇒[N.B.] / *I'll ~ to you in a moment.* / *First ~, first served.*② **2.** arrive in due course or in orderly progression. ¶*Summer comes every year.* / *Spring has* (or *is*) ~. **3.** appear. ¶*The light comes and goes.*③ / *A smile came to her lips.* **4.** arrive. ¶*Has he ~ yet?* / *The boys will ~ home tomorrow.* / *Help will ~ before long.* **5.** happen. ¶*I'm ready for whatever comes.* / *How does it ~ that you didn't know of it?*④ / *How comes it that you were there?* **6.** arrive at completion. ¶*Love will ~ in time.* / *The butter came very quickly.* **7.** occur to the mind. ¶*The solution of the problem has just ~ to me.* / *The inspiration never came.* **8.** come into being as a result of something; be born. 《~ *of* or *from* something》 ¶*No good comes of dishonesty.* / *Diseases often ~ from intemperance.* **9.** be a native of; be descended from. 《~ *from* somewhere; ~ *of* a good family, etc.》 ¶*Where do you ~ from?*⑤ ⇒[N.B.] **10.** reach; extend; amount. 《~ *to* a certain position, amount, etc.》 ¶*The dress does not ~ to my knees.* / *Your bill comes to 3,000 yen.* **11.** 《with *adj.* or *pp.*》 get or prove to be; become. ¶*His dream came true.* / *It'll ~ easy soon.*⑥ / *The shoelace came untied* (or *loose*). **12.** get into a certain state. 《~ *to do*》 ¶~ *to know someone better* / *He has ~ to see that he has lost all his fortune.*⑦ **13.** 《in *imperative*》 Look!; See here! ¶*Now ~, be patient.*⑧ **14.** 《making *an adverbial phrase*》 ¶*He will be 17 ~ Easter* (=*when Easter comes*).⑨ ⇒[N.B.] —*vt.* (*colloq.*) play the part of (someone); behave. ¶~ *the swell* / *Don't ~ the moralist over me!*⑩

1) ***come about,*** happen; occur. ¶*How did it ~ about?*
2) ***come across,*** ⓐ cross. ¶~ *across the sea.* ⓑ meet (someone) or find (something) by chance. ¶~ *across an old friend.*
3) ***come after*** (=*follow*) *someone.*
4) ***come along,*** ⓐ take one's way along (a street, etc.); move toward or with the speaker. ¶*Come along with me!* ⓑ 《in *imperative*》 Hurry up! ⓒ get along.
5) ***come and go,*** come, stay for a short time and then go away; be constantly changing.
6) ***come around*** (or ***round***), ⓐ arrive at; come in the regular course of rotation. ⓑ revive; recover. ⓒ change one's opinion and agree with another. ¶*He came around to our point of view.* ⓓ visit. ⇒[N.B.]
7) ***come at,*** ⓐ reach (some place). ⓑ make an attack on (something or someone).
8) ***come away,*** be taken away from; separate.

—[他] 1. …을 결합시키다; …을 겸하다 ¶①일과 즐거움을 겸하게 하다 2. …을 화합시키다
—[自] 결합하다

—[名] 1.《美口》[상업상의 이익 따위를 위한] 합동, 연합, 기업 연합 2.《美》콤바인, 자동 수확기(收穫機)

—[形] 1. 불타기 쉬운, 가연성의 2. 격하기 쉬운, 흥분하기 쉬운 —[名] 가연성 물질

—[名] 1. 연소 ¶①완전 연소 2. [유기체의] 산화(酸化)

—[自] 1. 오다; [말하는 사람의 입장에서 보아 상대에게로] 가다 ¶①언제고 한 번 놀러 오시오 [N.B.] 구어에서는 come and see를 쓰는 것이 보통이다/②선착순; 맨 먼저 온 자가 맨 먼저 대접 받는다 2. [차례로서] 돌아오다 3. 보이다, 나타나다 ¶③빛이 나타났다 사라졌다 하다 4. 다다르다, 도착하다 5. 일어나다, 생기다 ¶④네가 그것을 몰랐다니 어찌 된 일이냐? 6. [사물이] 이루어지다, 완성되다 7. [생각이] 떠오르다 8. [결과로서] 생기다, 태어나다 9. …의 출신이다 ¶⑤어디 출신이신지요? [N.B.] Where did(*or* have) you come from? 「어디서 오셨는지요?」와 구별할 것 10. 달하다 11. …으로 되다 ¶⑥곧 쉬워질 것이다 12. [사람이] …하게 되다 ¶⑦그는 재산을 모두 날렸다는 사실을 알게 되었다 13. 자, 이봐 ¶⑧이봐, 참게 14. …이 오면 ¶⑨부활절이 오면 그는 17살이 된다 [N.B.] 가정법 현재의 「come+주어」의 형식으로, when+주어+comes와 같음 —[他]《口》…의 역할을 하다, …인 체하다 ¶⑩나에게 대해 도덕가인 체하지 마라!

[熟] 1)일어나다, 생기다 2)ⓐ가로지르다, 건너다 ⓑ…에 우연히 마주치다, …을 우연히 찾아내다 3)…을 뒤따르다, …에 잇따르다 4)ⓐ…을 지나가다; 함께 가다; 오다 ⓑ서둘러라!, 빨리! ⓒ잘해 나가다 5)잠시 머물렀다가는 떠나가다, 오락가락하다; 쉴새없이 변하다 6)ⓐ찾아오다, 돌아오다 ⓑ[기운을] 회복하다, 소생하다 ⓒ의견을 바꾸고 동조(동의)하다 ⓓ방문하다 [N.B.] 거리상 가까운 때 쓰며, 그밖에는 come over를 쓰는 것이 보통임 7)ⓐ…에 닿다, …에 당도하다 ⓑ…을 공격하다 8)저쪽으로 가다, 떠나다, 헤어지다 9)ⓐ돌아오다 ⓑ회복하다, 복귀하다 ¶⑪권력을 다시 잡다 ⓒ기억에 되살아나

9) ***come back;*** ⓐ return. ⓑ return to a former condition or position. ¶～ *back to power.*⑪ ⓒ return to the memory.
10) ***come before,*** ⓐ come to the attention of (an authority, etc.). ⓑ have advantage over (something).
11) ***come between,*** divide or separate (two things or persons). ¶*Money came between the sisters.*
12) ***come by,*** ⓐ get; acquire. ⓑ pass by.
13) ***come clean,*** (*colloq.*) confess.
14) ***come down,*** ⓐ move to a lower position. ⓑ lose one's position, rank, or money. ¶～ *down in the world*⑫ / ～ *down in one's fortunes.*⑬ ⓒ be handed down.
15) ***come down on*** (or ***upon***), ⓐ criticize (something) strongly; scold. ⓑ make a demand on (someone) for the payment of money, etc.
16) ***come down with,*** ⓐ (*colloq.*) pay money. ⓑ (*U.S. colloq.*) begin to suffer from (an illness).
17) ***come easy*** (or ***natural***) ***to,*** be easy for (someone) to do or learn.
18) ***come forth,*** appear.
19) ***come forward,*** ⓐ approach. ⓑ stand as a candidate; offer to do.
20) ***come in,*** ⓐ enter. ¶*Come in quick!* ⓑ (of a period of time) begin; (of the tide) rise. ¶*The Christmas season came in with unwelcome heavy snowstorms.*⑭ ⓒ begin to be used or to be in fashion. ¶*The style came in five years ago.*⑮ ⓓ begin to be seasonable. ¶*At what time does the orange crop* ～ *in?*⑯ ⓔ be among the winners. ¶～ *in first* (*second, third*).⑰ ⓕ come into power. ⓖ take one's part; perform one's function.
21) ***come in for,*** (*colloq.*) receive; get a share of (money).
22) ***come in handy*** (or ***useful***), prove to be handy or useful.
23) ***come into,*** ⓐ enter (some place). ⓑ enter into (some state); enter upon (power or office). ¶～ *into existence* / ～ *into power*⑱ / ～ *into force.*⑲ ⓒ inherit; acquire.
24) ***come into one's own,*** receive fair and proper recognition; get the place or position due to one.
25) ***come near doing,*** almost do; nearly do.
26) ***come of,*** ⓐ come from (a good family, etc.) ⓑ result from (something). ⓒ happen to or become of (someone).
27) ***come off,*** ⓐ be taken away. ⓑ take place; happen. ⓒ turn out to be successful. ⓓ reach the end of a course, an event, etc. in a certain state. ¶～ *off well*⑳ / ～ *off badly*㉑ / ～ *off with flying colors*㉒ / ～ *off with honors.*㉓
28) ***come on,*** ⓐ make progress; become better. ⓑ (of night, winter, bad weather, etc.) come; begin. ⓒ meet (someone) by chance; find. ⓓ attack. ⓔ 《in *imperative*》 Hurry up!; Get started!; Please! ⓕ appear on the stage.
29) ***come out,*** ⓐ appear; become evident. ⓑ become public; be published. ¶*When will your book* ～ *out?* ⓒ be formally introduced to society. ⓓ end up in a certain way. ¶*It will* ～ *out as I expected.*㉔ / *I came out second in the race.*
30) ***come out for,*** support (someone), esp. in an election.
31) ***come out with,*** ⓐ say (something) openly. ⓑ offer (something) to the public or for sale.
32) ***come over,*** ⓐ come from a distant place. ⓑ (of a sickness, a feeling, etc.) affect; seize.
33) ***come round*** = come around.

다(다시 떠오르다) 10)ⓐ…앞에 나서다, 심의되다 ⓑ…의 상위(유리한 입장)에 서다 11)… 사이를 가르다, 이간질하다 12)ⓐ…을 손에 넣다, 얻다 ⓑ통과하다 13)《口》자백하다, 고백하다 14)ⓐ내려오다 ⓑ지위·재산 따위를 잃다 ¶⑫영락(零落)하다/⑬재산을 잃다 ⓒ전해지다 15)ⓐ…을 강력히 비판하다; 힐난하다 ⓑ[돈의 지불 따위를] …에게 요구하다 16)ⓐ《口》돈을 지불하다 ⓑ[병]에 걸리다 17)…하기가 수월하다(쉽다) 18)나타나다, 출현하다 19)ⓐ앞으로 나가다 ⓑ입후보하다, 자진해서 나서다 20)ⓐ들어가다(오다) ⓑ[계절 따위가] 시작되다, [조수가] 밀려들다 ¶⑭크리스마스 시이즌은 반갑지 않은 폭설로 시작되었다 ⓒ유행하기 시작하다 ¶⑮그 스타일은 5년 전부터 유행하기 시작했다 ⓓ먹을 만하게 되다, …철이 되다 ¶⑯오렌지 철은 언제쯤입니까? ⓔ…착(着)으로 결승에 들어가다 ¶⑰1착(2착, 3착)에 들다 ⓕ정권을 잡다 ⓖ역할을 맡아하다, 본분을 다하다 21)…을 받다; …의 몫을 받다 22)쓸모가 있게 되다, 소용이 되다 23)ⓐ에 들어가다 ⓑ…의 상태가 되다; [권력 따위의 자리]에 오르다 ¶⑱권력을 잡다/⑲효력을 발생하다 ⓒ…을 상속하다; 얻다 24)당연한 것으로서 인정받게 되다; 당연한 지위를 얻다 25)하마터면 …할 뻔하다 26)ⓐ…의 출신(태생)이다 ⓑ…에서 생기다, …의 결과이다 ⓒ…에게 일어나다; …이어떤 상태가 되다 27)ⓐ떨어지다, 빠지다, 벗겨지다 ⓑ일어나다, 발생하다, 실현되다 ⓒ잘 되어 가다 ⓓ…의 결과가 되다 ¶⑳잘 되어 가다/㉑나빠지다, 좋지 않은 결과가 되다/㉒승리를 거두다, 성공하다/㉓훌륭히 해치우다, 우등으로 나오다 28)ⓐ[순조롭게] 진행하다, 진전되다 ⓑ다가오다, 시작되다 ⓒ…에 우연히 마주치다, …을 우연히 발견하다 ⓓ…을 공격하다 ⓔ빨리빨리!; 자 가자!; 자 어서 ⓕ[무대에] 등장하다 29)ⓐ나오다, 나타나다 ⓑ세상에 나오다; 간행되다 ⓒ정식으로 사교계에 나오다 ⓓ…의 결과가 되다 ¶㉔내가 기대했던 결과가 될 것이다 30)…을 지지하다 31)ⓐ…을 공공연히 말하다, 공표하다 ⓑ…을 세상에 내놓다, 시장에 내다 32)ⓐ[먼 데서] 찾아오다 ⓑ[병·감정 따위가] 덮치다, 엄습하다 34)ⓐ성공하다 ⓑ이겨내다 ⓒ《俗》지불하다 35)ⓐ제정신이 들다 [N.B.] 발음은 [kʌ̀mtúː]로서, come to oneself의 생략형으로 생각됨. 다음의 ⓑ의 뜻으로는 [kʌ́mtə] ⓑ…에 달하다 36)일어나다, 발생하다 37)요점에 도달하다 38)사실이 되다; 실현되다 39)ⓐ…의 부류(항목)에 들다 ⓑ[영향 따위]를 받다 40)ⓐ[화제 따위에] 오르다, 문제로 되다 ⓑ다가가다, 접근하다 41)ⓐ…에 우연히 만나다, ⓑ…을 우연히 발견하다, …을 엄습하다, 공격하다 ⓒ

34) ***come through,*** ⓐ be successful. ⓑ overcome (a danger, etc.) successfully. ⓒ (*slang*) pay.
35) ***come to,*** ⓐ return to consciousness. →N.B. ⓑ reach. ¶ ~ *to an agreement* | ~ *to an end.*
36) ***come to pass,*** happen; occur. ⌈of the matter.⌉
37) ***come to the point,*** touch the most important point⌋
38) ***come true,*** prove to be correct; be realized.
39) ***come under,*** ⓐ be classed among (certain items). ⓑ be under (an influence, etc.).
40) ***come up,*** ⓐ arise, as in discussion. ¶ *The question came up at the last meeting.* ⓑ come near.
41) ***come upon,*** ⓐ meet (someone) or find (something) by chance. ⓑ attack. ⓒ ask (someone *for*).
42) ***come up to,*** ⓐ come near to (someone); reach (some place or point). ⓑ be equal to (someone or something). ¶ *This landscape doesn't ~ up to that one.*⑬
43) ***come up with,*** ⓐ overtake (someone). ⓑ present or propose (a suggestion, etc.).
44) ***come what may,*** in spite of whatever may happen.
45) ***How come?,*** (*colloq.*) Why?
come·back [kʌ́mbæk] *n.* ⓒ **1.** (*colloq.*) a return to a former position, power, etc. ¶ *make one's ~.*⑪ **2.** (*slang*) a clever answer.
co·me·di·an [kəmíːdiən] *n.* ⓒ **1.** an actor who plays in comedies; a professional entertainer who tells jokes, sings comic songs, etc. **2.** a writer of comedy.
come·down [kʌ́mdàun, +*Brit.* kʌ́mdáun] *n.* ⓒ (*colloq.*) a change for the worse; a cause of embarrassment.
• **com·e·dy** [kámidi / kɔ́m-] *n.* (pl. **-dies**) **1.** ⓒⓤ a play, movie, or show of a light and humorous character and with a happy ending. ↔tragedy ¶ *a musical ~.* **2.** ⓒ any amusing event in daily life.
come·li·ness [kʌ́mlinis] *n.* ⓤ **1.** beauty of personal appearance. **2.** fitness; suitableness; propriety.
come·ly [kʌ́mli] *adj.* (**-li·er, -li·est**) **1.** having a pleasant appearance; graceful; charming. **2.** suitable; proper.
com·er [kʌ́mər] *n.* ⓒ **1.** a person who comes. ¶ *the first ~.*⑪ **2.** a person who is likely to succeed in the future.
• **com·et** [kámit / kɔ́m-] *n.* ⓒ a bright heavenly body with a tail of light.
com·fit [kʌ́mfit] *n.* ⓒ a sweetmeat; a kind of candy.
⁑ **com·fort** [kʌ́mfərt] *vt.* **1.** ease the grief or sorrow of (someone); encourage. ¶ *~ oneself with the thought that ...*⑪ | *~ those who were crippled in the war.* **2.** make (someone) free from physical pain.
—*n.* **1.** ⓤ anything that gives cheer, hope, etc.; consolation. ¶ *a cold ~*② | *He could not give ~ to her.* | *The old man took ~ in reading.*③ **2.** ⓒ a person or thing that comforts someone. ¶ *a ~ bag.*④ **3.** ⓤ relief from pain, discomfort, etc. ¶ *live in ~.* **4.** (*pl.*) things that make life rich. **5.** ⓒ (*U.S.*) a quilted bedcover.
⁑ **com·fort·a·ble** [kʌ́mfərtəbl] *adj.* **1.** providing comfort. ¶ *feel ~.*⑪ **2.** free from pain, ache. ¶ *make oneself ~.*⑪ **3.** enough for one's needs. —*n.* ⓒ a quilted bedcover.
▷ **com·fort·a·ble·ness** [-nis] *n.* ⌈manner.⌉
com·fort·a·bly [kʌ́mfərtəbli] *adv.* in a comfortable
com·fort·er [kʌ́mfərtər] *n.* ⓒ **1.** a person or thing that comforts (someone). **2.** (*U.S.*) a padded or quilted bed covering. **3.** a long woolen scarf. **4.** (*the C-*) the Holy Spirit.
com·fort·less [kʌ́mfərtlis] *adj.* **1.** giving no comfort to the mind. **2.** without the comforts of life.

—㉠ …에게 요구하다 42)ⓐ…에게 다가가다, …에 닿다하다 ⓑ…에 필적하다, …에 맞먹다 ¶⑬이 풍경화는 저것에 미치지는 못한다 43)ⓐ…을 따라잡다 ⓑ …을 제안하다, 제출하다 44)무슨 일이 일어날지라도 45)《口》어째서 그런가?

—㉠ 1.《口》복귀, 회복 ¶①회복하다 2.《俗》재치있는 대구

—㉠ 1. 희극 배우; 코메디언 2. 희극 작가

—㉠ 《口》몰락, 영락; 곤궁의 원인

—㉠ 1. 희극 2. 희극적인 사건(장면)

—㉠ 1. [용모의] 아름다움 2. 적합; 정당
—㉠ 1. 용모가 아름다운, 어여쁜 2. 적당한, 알맞은
—㉠ 1. 오는 사람 ¶①선착자 2. 장래가 기대되는 사람, 유망한 사람

—㉠ 혜성

—㉠ 사탕 과자, 당과(糖菓)
—㉠ 1. …을 위로하다 ¶①…이라 생각하고 자위하다 2. …을 편안하게 하다

—㉠ 1. 위로, 위안 ¶②조금도 즐겁지 않은 위로/③그 노인은 독서로 자신을 위로했다 2. 위안을 주는 사람(것) ¶④위문대(袋) 3. 안락 4. 생활을 풍부하게 하는 것 5.《美》깃털 이불

—㉠ 1. 기분이 좋은 ¶①기분이 좋다 2. 안락한, 편안한 ¶②편안히 하다 3. 충분한, 넉넉한 —㉠ 깃털 이불

—㉠ 편안하게, 기분좋게
—㉠ 1. 위안자(물) 2.《美》깃털 이불 3. 털목도리 4. 성령(聖靈)

—㉠ 1. 위로가 없는 2. 위안이 없는, 낙이 없는, 쓸쓸한

com·ic [kámik / kɔ́m-] *adj.* **1.** of comedy. ↔tragic **2.** amusing. ¶*a ~ book*① / *a ~ strip.*② **—*n.*** [C] **1.** a comic actor. **2.** [U] the comic side of art, life, etc. **3.** [C] ⟪*pl.*⟫ (*colloq.*) comic strips.
—[形] 1. 희극의 2. 우스운 ¶①만화책/②[신문의] 연재 만화 —[名] 1. 희극배우 2. [인생 따위의] 희극적 측면 3. ⟪口⟫ 연재 만화

com·i·cal [kámik(ə)l / kɔ́m-] *adj.* funny; amusing. ▷ **com·i·cal·ly** [-i] *adv.*
—[形] 우스운, 익살맞은

:com·ing [kʌ́miŋ] *n.* [C][U] the act of approaching; arrival. **—*adj.*** approaching; next; promising.
—[名] 오기, 도래, 도착 —[形] 올, 다가오는, 다음의; 유망한

com·i·ty [kámiti / kɔ́m-] *n.* [U] politeness.
—[名] 예의

***com·ma** [kámə / kɔ́mə] *n.* [C] a punctuation mark(,).
—[名] 코머, 구둣점

:com·mand [kəmǽnd / -máːnd] *vt.* **1.** order. ⟪~ someone *to do; ~ that ...*⟫ ¶*~ silence*① / *I commanded that he* [*should*] *do it* (= *~ him to do it*).② **2.** be in control of (something); control or direct (something) authoritatively. ¶*~ the air*③ / *~ the sea.*④ **3.** keep control of (one's feelings, etc.); restrain. ¶*~ one's temper.* **4.** have (something) at one's disposal or use. ¶*He commands a large vocabulary.* **5.** demand to be given (something) as one's due. ¶*~ respect*⑤ / *~ sympathy.* **6.** overlook (some place), as from a height. ¶*a hill commanding the port* / *The hotel commands a fine view of the bay.* **—*vi.*** **1.** be in authority. **2.** look down on some place from a higher position.
—[他] 1. …에게 명령하다 ¶①정숙을 명령하다/②나는 그에게 그것을 하도록 명령했다 2. …을 지휘하다, …의 지배권을 잡다 ¶③제공권을 잡다/④제해권을 잡다 3. …을 억제하다 4. …을 마음대로 쓰다 5. [당연한 것으로서] …을 강요하다, 받다 ¶⑤당연한 존경을 받다 6. …을 내려다보다, [높은 데서] 굽어보다 —[自] 1. 지휘권을 가지다, 명령하다 2. 굽어보다, 내려다보다

—*n.* **1.** [C] an order; a commandment. ¶*Who is the officer in ~?*⑥ **2.** [U] ⟪sometimes *a ~*⟫ the right to command; control; ruling power. ¶*~ of one's passions.*⑦ **3.** [U] wide view; extent of vision; outlook.
—[名] 1. 명령; 지휘 ¶⑥지휘관은 누구인가? 2. 지휘권, 지배력, 제어 ¶⑦감정을 억제하는 힘 3. 널따랗게 트인 경치(조망), 전망

1) ***at the command of,*** ready to receive orders from; ready to obey.
2) ***have a good command of,*** have skill in (something). ¶*have a good ~ of words.*
3) ***in command of,*** in charge or control of.
4) ***take command of,*** begin to act as the commander of (an army, etc.).
[熟] 1)…의 명령에 따라서, …의 뜻대로 되어 2)…을 자유자재로 구사할 수 있다 3)…을 지휘하여 4)…을 지휘하다

com·man·dant [kàməndǽnt / kɔ̀m-, -dáːnt] *n.* [C] a commanding officer.
—[名] 지휘관, 사령관

com·man·deer [kàməndíər / kɔ̀m-] *vt.* **1.** take (private property such as horses and food) for military or other public use. **2.** force (men) into military service. **3.** (*colloq.*) take (something) by force.
—[他] 1. …을 징발하다 2. …을 군대에 징집하다 3. …을 강제로 빼앗다

:com·mand·er [kəmǽndər / -máːndə] *n.* [C] **1.** a person who commands. **2.** an officer commanding an army. **3.** (*U.S. Navy*) an officer ranking just below a captain.
—[名] 1. 지휘자 2. 사령관 3. ⟪美海軍⟫ 해군 중령

commander in chief [--- -] *n.* [C] (pl. **commanders ~**) **1.** an officer commanding all the armed forces of a nation. **2.** ⟪*C-*⟫ (*U.S.*) the President of the United States.
—[名] 1. [육군의] 최고 사령관; [해군의] 함대 사령관 2. ⟪美⟫ [전군(全軍)의 최고 지휘관으로서의] 미국 대통령

com·mand·ing [kəmǽndiŋ / -máːnd-] *adj.* **1.** having the power to command. **2.** authoritative. **3.** having a wide view. ¶*a ~ bluff.*①
—[形] 1. 지휘하는 2. 관록있는, 위엄있는 당당한 3. 전망이 넓은 ¶①조망이 좋은 절벽

com·mand·ment [kəmǽndmənt / -máːnd-] *n.* [C] an order; a law; a command. ¶*the Ten Commandments.*①
—[名] 계율(戒律); 명령 ¶①모세의 십계

com·mem·o·rate [kəmémərèit] *vt.* **1.** preserve the memory of (something). **2.** give honor to the memory of (something); celebrate.
—[他] 1. …을 후세에 전하다 2. …을 기념하다, 축하하다

com·mem·o·ra·tion [kəmèməréiʃ(ə)n] *n.* [U] the act of commemorating; celebration.
—[名] 기념[하기]; 축하

in commemoration of, for the memory of; in the honor of.
[熟] …을 기념하여

***com·mence** [kəméns] *vi., vt.* begin; start. ⟪*~ doing*⟫ ⇒[usage] ¶*~ a meal* / *~ the study of law; ~ studying law* / *~ with.*
—[自][他] 개시하다, …을 시작하다
[usage] 보통 commence 다음에는 부정사(不定詞)를 쓰지 않음

com·mence·ment [kəménsmənt] *n.* [U][C] **1.** a beginning; a start. **2.** ⟪*the ~*⟫ the ceremony or day of graduation in universities, etc.
—[名] 1. 시작, 개시, 착수 2. 졸업식

***com·mend** [kəménd] *vt.* **1.** praise; speak highly of (someone). ⟪~someone *for* or *to*⟫ ¶*be highly commend-*
—[他] 1. …을 칭찬하다, …을 추천하다 ¶①절찬받다/②…에게 좋은인상을 주

*ed*① / *~ oneself to ...*② / *~ someone for his good work.* **2.** give (someone or something) into the care of. ⟪~ someone *to*⟫ ¶*I ~ my child to her care.*

다 2. …에게 맡기다(위탁하다)

com·mend·a·ble [kəméndəbl] *adj.* worthy of praise.

—[形] 칭찬할 만한

com·men·da·tion [kɑ̀mendéiʃ(ə)n / kɔ̀m-] *n.* [U] **1.** praise; approval; favorable mention. **2.** the act of entrusting.

—[名] 1. 칭찬, 추천 2. 위탁

com·men·su·rate [kəménʃərit, +*U.S.* -sərit] *adj.* **1.** in the proper portion. **2.** having the same measure or size.

—[形] 1. …와 비례하는, 균형이 잘 잡힌 2. 같은 분량(면적)의

‡com·ment [kάment / kɔ́m-] *n.* [C][U] **1.** a short statement or remark; criticism; opinion. ¶*make a ~ on the subject*① / *without ~*② / *No ~.*③ **2.** an explanatory or critical note supplied to a text. —*vi.* make a comment or comments. ⟪~ *on* or *upon* something⟫ ¶*~ on someone's conduct.*④

—[名] 1. 논평; 비평; 의견 ¶①그 문제에 관해 비평하다/②아무 말도 없이, 아무 언급이 없이/③할 말 없다 2. 주석, 주해, 해설 —[自] 비평하다, 주석을 달다 ¶④남의 행실에 대해 이러니 저러니 말하다

com·men·tar·y [kάmənteri / kɔ́mənt(ə)ri] *n.* [C] (**-tar·ies**) **1.** a series of comments or explanations. ¶*a ~ on the Bible.*① **2.** an essay or treatise helping to making clear. **3.** a criticism.

—[名] 1. 주석 ¶①성서 주석, 성경 해설 2. 주해서 3. 논평, 비평

com·men·ta·tor [kάməntèitər / kɔ́mentèitə] *n.* [C] **1.** a person who makes commentaries. **2.** a person who discusses news, etc., as on the radio, etc.

—[名] 1. 주석자 2. 실황 방송[해설]자; 시사 해설자

‡com·merce [kάmə(:)rs / kɔ́mə(:)s] *n.* [U] **1.** the act of buying and selling on a large scale, esp. between different countries; business. ¶*Chamber of Commerce*① / *~ by sea*② / *domestic ~*③ / *world ~.*④ **2.** social relations.

—[名] 1. 상업, 통상, 무역 ¶①상공 회의소/②해외 무역/③국내 교역/④국제 무역 2. [사회와의] 교섭

‡com·mer·cial [kəmə́:rʃ(ə)l] *adj.* **1.** connected with commerce. ¶*~ art*① / *~ correspondence*② / *a ~ transaction*③ / *a ~ treaty.*④ **2.** made for sale. **3.** supported by an advertiser. —*n.* [C] a short announcement or visible presentation as an advertisement on the radio, T. V. etc.

—[形] 1. 상업상의 ¶①상업 미술/②상업 통신[문]/③상거래/④통상 조약 2. 판매용의, 영리적인 3. 광고·선전용의 —[名] 광고 방송

com·mer·cial·ism [kəmə́:rʃəlìz(ə)m] *n.* [U] methods and spirit of commerce; too much emphasis on profit, success, or immediate results.

—[名] 상업주의; 영리주의

com·mer·cial·ize [kəmə́:rʃəlàiz] *vt.* **1.** make (something) commercial. **2.** offer (something) for sale.

—[他] 1. …을 상업화하다 2. …을 팔려고 내놓다, 시장에 내다

com·mer·cial·ly [kəmə́:rʃəli] *adv.* from the point of view of business; in a businesslike way.

—[副] 상업적으로, 영리적으로

com·min·gle [kəmíŋgl / kɔm-] *vi., vt.* mix.

—[自][他] 뒤섞이다; …을 섞다

com·mis·er·ate [kəmízərèit] *vt.* feel or show sorrow for (something). ¶*~ the poor state of the boy.* —*vi.* sympathize. ⟪~ *with* someone⟫ ¶*~ with a boy on his grief.*①

—[他] …을 가엾게 여기다 —[自] 동정하다 ¶①소년의 슬픔에 동정하다

com·mis·sar [kɑ̀misά:r / kɔ̀misά:] *n.* [C] the head of a governmental department in the U.S.S.R. ⇒[N.B.]

—[名] [원래 소련의] 인민위원 [N.B.] 지금은 공식적으로는 minister

com·mis·sar·i·at [kɑ̀miséəriət / kɔ̀m-] *n.* [C] **1.** any of the major governmental divisions of the U. S. S. R. ⇒[N.B.] **2.** a department of an army that provides food, etc.

—[名] 1. [원래 소련의] 인민위원회 [N.B.] 지금은 공식적으로는 ministry 2. 병참부

com·mis·sar·y [kάmisèri / kɔ́misəri] *n.* [C] (pl. **-sar·ies**) **1.** a store that sells food, etc., esp. in an army. **2.** an officer of the commissariat. **3.** a person who acts for someone or a certain group; a representative.

—[名] 1. [군대 따위의] 매점 2. 병참부원 3. 대표자; 대리인

‡com·mis·sion [kəmíʃ(ə)n] *n.* **1.** [C] the act of entrusting; authority. ¶*~ sale*① / *on ~*② / *go beyond one's ~.*③ **2.** [C] a written order giving certain duties and powers, esp. in the armed forces. **3.** [C] ⟪*collectively*⟫ a group of people chosen to do things. ¶*the ~ of inquiry.*④ **4.** [C] a thing entrusted. **5.** [U] the act of performing some action, esp. a bad one. ¶*the ~ of a crime.*⑤ **6.** [U] agency; [C] a payment based on a percentage of money from sales.

1) ***in commission,*** ⓐ in service. ⓑ in operating order.
2) ***out of commission,*** ⓐ not in service. ⓑ not in working order.

—[名] 1. 위임, 위탁; [위탁된] 직권 ¶①위탁 판매/②위탁을 받고/③월권 행위를 하다 2. [장교의] 임명장; 임관 사령(任官辭令) 3. 위원, 위원회 ¶④조사 위원회 4. 위임(부탁)받은 일 5. [범죄 따위의] 저지름, 수행 ¶⑤범죄행위 6. [업무의] 대리; 수수료, 구전

[熟] 1)ⓐ현역의 ⓑ쓸 수 있는 상태의 2)ⓐ퇴역의 ⓑ쓸 수 없게 되어

C

C

—*vt.* **1.** give a commission to (someone). **2.** give (someone) a right or power. 《~ someone *to do*》 **3.** put (a warship) into service; appoint.
—[他] 1. …에게 직권을 부여하다 2. [권한 따위]를 위임하다 3. …을 취역시키다; 장교로 임명하다

com·mis·sion·aire [kəmìʃənέər] *n.* [C] a doorkeeper in uniform at an hotel, a department store, etc.; a messenger, etc.
—[名] [큰 상점 따위의] 문지기, 수위

com·mis·sioned [kəmíʃ(ə)nd] *adj.* possessing or given a commission.
—[形] 임명된

∗com·mis·sion·er [kəmíʃənər] *n.* [C] **1.** a member of a commission. **2.** a government official in charge of a department or district. ¶*High Commissioner.*①
—[名] 1. 위원 2. 지방 장관, 국장 ¶①고등 판무관

⁑com·mit [kəmít] *vt.* (**-mit·ted, -mit·ting**) **1.** give (something or someone) in trust to someone or something else. ¶*She committed her baby to the girl's care.* **2.** perform (a bad action). ¶~ *suicide.*① **3.** express one's opinion as an assurance. ¶~*oneself to do* (or *doing*).② **4.** give (oneself) wholeheartedly; undertake (something) sincerely. ¶~ *oneself to a teacher's advice*③ / ~ *oneself to reading a book.*④
—[他] 1. …을 위임하다, 위탁하다 2. [죄·잘못]을 범하다, 저지르다 ¶①자살하다 3. …에게 언질을 주다 ¶②…할 것을 약속하다 4. …에 온 성의를 다하다 전심전력하다 ¶③선생의 조언에 전심전력하다/④독서에 전렴하다

1) ***commit something to memory,*** learn something by heart.
2) ***commit something to paper,*** write something down.
[熟] 1)…을 암기하다 2)…을 써 넣다(기록하다)

com·mit·ment [kəmítmənt] *n.* **1.** [U] the act of entrusting, performing, or committing. **2.** [U][C] the act of sending someone to prison. **3.** [C] an order sending a person to prison. **4.** [C] a pledge or promise.
—[名] 1. 위탁, 위임; 수행; 범행 2. 투옥, 구류 3. 수감 명령 4. 언질, 공약,

com·mit·tal [kəmítl] *n.* =commitment.

⁑com·mit·tee [kəmíti] *n.* [C] a group of people appointed or elected to do certain things. ⇒[usage] ¶*the Committee of Supply*① / *be in* ~② / *call a meeting of the* ~.
—[名] 위원회 [usage] 구성원을 중심으로 할 때는 복수 취급 ¶①[하원] 예산 위원회/②위원회를 소집하다

com·mit·tee·man [kəmítimən] *n.* [C] (pl. **-men** [-mən]) a member of a committee.
—[名] 위원

com·mode [kəmóud] *n.* [C] **1.** a chest of drawers; a cabinet. **2.** a washstand.
—[名] 1. 옷장, 장 2. 세면대

com·mo·di·ous [kəmóudiəs] *adj.* **1.** vast; roomy. **2.** convenient; handy. ▷**com·mo·di·ous·ly** [-li] *adv.*
—[形] 1. [집·방이] 넓은, 널따란 2. 편리한, 간편한

∗com·mod·i·ty [kəmáditi / -mɔ́d-] *n.* [C] (pl. **-ties**) 《often *pl.*》 **1.** anything that is bought and sold. ¶~ *prices*① / *staple commodities.*② **2.** any useful thing.
—[名] 1. 상품, 물자, 일용품 ¶①물가/②중요 상품, 생활 필수품 2. 유용한 물건, 필수품

com·mo·dore [kámədɔ:r / kɔ́mədɔ:] *n.* [C] **1.** (*U.S. Navy*) an officer in command, ranking above a captain. **2.** a title of honor given to the head of a yacht club.
—[名] 1. 《美海軍》 [해군의] 준장 2. 요트 클럽의 회장

⁑com·mon [kámən / kɔ́m-] *a.* **1.** belonging to the community; public. ¶*a* ~ *nuisance*① / ~ *welfare.*② **2.** of all; general. ¶*a matter of* ~ *knowledge.*③ **3.** belonging equally to two or more persons or things. ¶*a* ~ *friend* / *a* ~ *kitchen* / *the* ~ *property* / *We could not find a* ~ *ground for beginning negotiations.*④ **4.** usual; ordinary; regular. ↔rare ¶*a* ~ *event* / *the* ~ *people.*⑤ **5.** not excellent or well-known in tone or quality; not polite; low. ¶*a* ~ *accent* / *a* ~ *decoration* / ~ *manners.*⑥ **6.** (*Mathematics*) belonging equally to several quantities. ¶*a* ~ *factor* / *a* ~ *denominator*⑦ / *a* ~ *fraction.* **7.** (*Grammar*) (of a noun) that can be used for any of a group or a class. ↔proper; (of gender) that is either masculine or feminine. ¶*a* ~ *noun.*
—[形] 1. 공공의, 공중의 ¶①치안 방해/②공공의 복지 2. 일반적인 ¶③상식적인 일 3. 공통의, 공동의 ¶④교섭을 개시할 공동 장소를 발견할 수가 없었다 4. 보통의, 평범한, 흔히 있는 ¶⑤서민, 일반 민중 5. 품위없는, 천한, 통속적인 ¶⑥예절(버릇)없는 태도 6. 《數》 공통의, 공약의, 통약의 ¶⑦공분모 7. 《文法》 보통[명사]의; 중성의

—*n.* **1.** 《*the* ~ or *the* ~*s*》 a tract of land considered as the property of the public, such as a park in a city. **2.** [U] a profit or right of one person in the land of another.
—[名] 1. 공유지, 공용지 2. 공유권, 공용권

1) ***in common,*** held or enjoyed equally; shared by all of a group. ¶*have something in* ~.⑧
2) ***out of the common,*** unusual; uncommon.
[熟] 1)공통으로, …와 같게 ¶⑧공통점이 있다 2)비범한, 비상한

com·mon·al·ty [kámən(ə)lti / kɔ́m-] *n.* [C] (pl. **-ties**) 《usu. *the* ~》 **1.** the common people. **2.** the people as a group.
—[名] 1. 평민, 서민, 일반 민중 2. 단체

com·mon·er [kámənər / kɔ́mənə] *n.* [C] **1.** one of the common people. **2.** (*Brit.*) a member of the House of Commons. **3.** (*Brit.*) a student who pays all his own expenses. **4.** a person who has a joint right in land.
—[名] 1. 평민 2.《英》[영국의] 하원의원 3.《英》 자비생(自費生) 4. 토지 공용권 소유자

common law [ˊ- ˊ] *n.* the unwritten law, esp. of England, based on custom or court decision. ↔statute law
—[名] 보통법, 불문법, 관습법

* **com·mon·ly** [kámənli / kɔ́m-] *adv.* usually; generally.
—[副] 일반적으로, 보통, 통속적으로

* **com·mon·place** [kámənplèis / kɔ́m-] *adj.* **1.** ordinary; usual. ¶*a ~ idea.* **2.** not new or original. — *n.* [C] **1.** a common or everyday thing. **2.** an ordinary thing.
—[形] 1. 평범한 2. 진부한 —[名] 1. 일상적인 일 2. 평범한 것

commonplace book [ˊ-- ˋ] *n.* a book in which noteworthy quotations, poems, comments, etc. are written.
—[名] 비망록

com·mons [kámənz / kɔ́m-] *n. pl.* **1.** the common people. **2.** allowance of food. ¶*be on short ~.*① **3.** (*the C-*) the House of Commons; the members of the House of Commons.
—[名] 1. 평민, 서민 2. 정량의 식사 ¶음식이 충분하지 않다 3. [영국의] 하원, 하원의원

common sense [ˊ- ˊ] *n.* good sense in everyday matters; practical judgment.
—[名] 상식, 양식

com·mon·weal [kámənwì:l / kɔ́m-] *n.* [U] the public happiness; the public good.
—[名] 복리, 공익

com·mon·wealth [kámənwèlθ / kɔ́m-] *n.* [C] **1.** the group of people who make up a nation; the state. **2.** a republic. **3.** (*C-*) a group of nations and their dependencies. ¶*the Commonwealth of Nations.*① **4.** [U] (*the C-*) the government in England under Cromwell. **5.** any State of the United States. **6.** a group of persons, etc.
—[名] 1. 국민, 국가 2. 공화국 3. 연방 ¶①영연방 4. [1649-1660년 사이의] 영국 공화정치 5. [미국의] 주 6. [공통의 이익에 의한] 단체

com·mo·tion [kəmóuʃ(ə)n] *n.* [U][C] violent movement; disorder. ¶*be in ~.*①
—[名] 격동; 동요 ¶①동요하고 있다

com·mu·nal [kəmjú:n(ə)l, kámjunl / kɔ́mjunl] *adj.* of a community; public; common.
—[形] 공동 사회의, 자치단체의, 공동의

com·mune[1] *vi.* [kəmjú:n →*n.*] **1.** talk in a very friendly manner. (*~ with* someone) ¶*~ with oneself.*① **2.** receive Holy Communion. —*n.* [kámju:n / kɔ́m-] [U] friendly talk.
—[自] 1. 친근하게 이야기하다 ¶①심사숙고하다 2. 성찬(성체)을 받다
—[名] 간담(懇談), 교제

com·mune[2] [kámju:n / kɔ́m-] *n.* [C] **1.** the smallest division for local government in France, Belgium, etc. **2.** (*the C-*) a revolutionary group that governed Paris from 1792 to 1794; the Paris Commune.
—[名] 1. [프랑스 따위의] 최소 자치구 2. [프랑스 공포시대의] 파리 혁명정부

com·mu·ni·ca·ble [kəmjú:nikəbl] *adj.* that can be communicated; that can be spread from person to person. ¶*a ~ disease*① / *Thought is ~ chiefly by words.*
—[形] 전달할 수 있는 ¶①전염병

* **com·mu·ni·cate** [kəmjú:nikèit] *vt.* **1.** give (opinions, etc.) to another; transmit. **2.** infect. —*vi.* **1.** give or exchange messages by talking, writing, etc.; correspond. (*~ with* someone) ¶*~ by telegrams.*① **2.** be connected. (*~ with* something) ¶*~ with the next room by a door.* **3.** be infected; be transmitted.
—[他] 1. [의견·열(熱) 따위를] 전하다, 전달하다 2. [병]을 감염시키다 —[自] 1. 통신하다, 연락하다 ¶①전보로 통신하다 2. [길 따위가] 통하다 3. 감염되다, 옮다, 전해지다

* **com·mu·ni·ca·tion** [kəmjù:nikéiʃ(ə)n] *n.* **1.** [U] the act of communicating. **2.** [C] information given in this way. ¶*a personal ~.*① **3.** [C][U] means of communicating. ¶*a means of ~.*② **4.** (*pl.*) a system of communicating by telephone, radio, etc.
—[名] 1. 통신, 의사 전달 2. 전갈, 편지, 전보 ¶①친서 3. 교통, 교통기관 ¶②교통기관 4. 통신기관

com·mu·ni·ca·tive [kəmjú:nikèitiv, -nikə- / -nikə-, -nikèi-] *adj.* ready to communicate; talkative.
—[形] 터놓고 이야기하는, 통신의; 이야기하기 좋아하는

com·mun·ion [kəmjú:niən] *n.* [U] **1.** the act or state of sharing. **2.** exchange of thoughts and feelings; spiritual relation; friendly talk. ¶*hold ~ with oneself.*① **3.** [C] a group of people who have the same religious beliefs. **4.** (*C-*) the act of sharing in or celebrating the Lord's Supper. ¶*Communion Service.*②
—[名] 1. 공유(共有) 2. 사상의 교환, 간담(懇談), 영적(靈的) 교섭 ¶①깊이 내성(內省)하다 3. [종교상의] 단체 4. 성찬식, 성체 배령(拜領) ¶②성찬식

com·mu·ni·que [kəmjú:nikèi] *n.* [C] an official statement or announcement. ¶*a joint ~.*①
—[名] 공보(公報), 코뮤니케 ¶①공동 코뮤니케

* **com·mu·nism** [kámjunìz(ə)m / kɔ́m-] *n.* [U] (*often C-*) a theory or system of social change directed toward the ideal of a classless society, developed by Karl Marx.
—[名] 공산주의

* **com·mu·nist** [kámjunist / kɔ́m-] *n.* [C] **1.** a person who believes in and supports communism. **2.** ⦅*C-*⦆ a member of the Communist Party. ***—adj.*** communistic.
—[名] 1. 공산주의자 2. 공산당원 —[形] 공산주의[자]의

com·mu·nis·tic [kàmjunístik / kɔ̀m-] *adj.* of or like communists or communism.
—[形] 공산주의[자]의

** **com·mu·ni·ty** [kəmjú:niti] *n.* **1.** [C] a group of people with common cultural or other conditions and living in the same place. **2.** ⦅*the* ~⦆ the public. **3.** [U] the act of sharing; the state of being the same.
—[名] 1. 공동 사회, 공동체 2. 공중(公衆) 3. 공유(共有), [사상·이해관계의] 공통; 유사(類似)

com·mu·ta·tion [kàmju(:)téiʃ(ə)n / kɔ̀m-] *n.* [U] **1.** substitution. **2.** [C] a reduction of a punishment or a penalty. **3.** (*U.S.*) regular travel over some distance between home and a work place by train.
—[名] 1. 교환, 전환 2. 감형 3. ⦅美⦆ [정기적인] 통근

com·mute [kəmjú:t] *vt.* **1.** exchange. **2.** make (a punishment, etc.) less severe. ¶*~ the death penalty to imprisonment for life.*① ***—vi.*** (*U.S.*) travel regularly or daily back and forth from one's home to one's office.
—[他] 1. …을 교환하다 2. …을 감형하다 ¶①사형에서 종신형으로 감형하다 —[自] ⦅美⦆ [정기 회수권으로] 교외에서 통근하다

com·mut·er [kəmjú:tər] *n.* [C] (*U.S.*) a person who travels back and forth from his home, usu. in the suburbs, to his work place, usu. in the city; a person who uses a commutation ticket.
—[名] ⦅美⦆ 교외로부터의 통근자; 정기(회수)권 사용자

* **com·pact**[1] [kəmpǽkt → *n.*] *adj.* **1.** closely or firmly connected; packed tightly together. **2.** condensed; short. ¶*a ~ expression.*
—[形] 1. 팽팽한, [질이] 조밀한, 촘촘한 2. 간결한

—vt. **1.** pack (things) tightly together. **2.** condense.
—[他] 1. …을 꽉 채우다 2. …을 간결하게 하다

—n. [kámpækt / kɔ́m-] [C] a small case carried by ladies containing face powder and often rouge. ▷**com·pact·ly** [-li] *adv.* —**com·pact·ness** [-nis] *n.*
—[名] 콤팩트, [휴대용] 분갑

com·pact[2] [kámpækt / kɔ́m-] *n.* [C][U] an agreement; a contract.
—[名] 계약; 약정

** **com·pan·ion**[1] [kəmpǽnjən] *n.* [C] **1.** a person who keeps company with someone; a person who travels with another or others; a comrade. **2.** one of a pair or set. ***—vt.*** accompany. ▷**com·pan·ion·less** [-lis] *adj.*
—[名] 1. 동료, 동지, 짝 2. [짝·쌍의] 한쪽 —[他] …을 동반하다, 함께 가다

com·pan·ion[2] [kəmpǽnjən] *n.* [C] (*Nautical*) **1.** a hood over the top of a companionway. **2.** a companionway.
—[名] ⦅海⦆ 1. 후갑판 천창(天窓) 2. 선실 승강구 [계단]

com·pan·ion·a·ble [kəmpǽnjənəbl] *adj.* pleasant to be with; sociable; agreeable.
—[形] 친구로 사귀기 좋은; 사교적인; 상냥한

* **com·pan·ion·ship** [kəmpǽnjənʃìp] *n.* [U] agreeable association; fellowship; company.
—[名] 교제; 사귐; 교우(交友)

com·pan·ion·way [kəmpǽnjənwèi] *n.* [C] the stairway or staircase leading from the deck of a ship to a cabin.
—[名] 선실 승강구 [계단]

** **com·pa·ny** [kʌ́mp(ə)ni] *n.* [C] (pl. **-nies**) **1.** a group of people. ¶*A great ~ came to the fair.* **2.** [U] a guest; guests. **3.** [U] ⦅*collectively*⦆ a friend; a person who goes with others; a companion or companions. ¶*He is good ~.*① / *A man is known by his ~.*② **4.** [U] companionship; society. ¶*I don't seek the ~ of him.*③ / *I cannot bear his ~.* **5.** a business firm. ¶*a publishing ~* / *John Smith and Company.*④ ⇒[N.B.] **6.** a body of 100 ~ 200 soldiers.
—[名] 1. 사람들; 일단(一團), 일행 2. 초대 손님 3. 친구; 동행자; 동료 ¶①그는 사귐성이 좋다/②사람 됨됨이는 그 친구를 보면 알 수 있다 4. 교제 ¶③그와는 사귀고 싶지 않다 5. 회사; 상회 ¶④존 스미드 상회 [N.B.] John Smith & Co.로 생략함 6. 중대(中隊)

com·pa·ra·ble [kámp(ə)rəbl / kɔ̀m-] *adj.* **1.** that can be compared. ⦅*~ with*⦆ **2.** worthy of comparison. ⦅*~ to*⦆ ¶*No other boy in our class is ~ to him.*①
—[形] 1. 비교할 수 있는 2. 필적하는 ¶①우리 학급에서 그에게 필적할 만한 소년은 없다

* **com·par·a·tive** [kəmpǽrətiv] *adj.* **1.** of comparison. **2.** using comparison as a method of study. ¶*~ literature.*① **3.** measured by comparison with something else. **4.** (*Grammar*) showing the comparative degree.
—[形] 1. 비교의 2. 비교 연구의 ¶①비교문학 3. 비교적인 4. ⦅文法⦆ 비교급의

—n. [C] ⦅*the* ~⦆ (*Grammar*) a form of an adjective or adverb used in comparisons, such as 'longer' or 'sooner'; the comparative degree.
—[名] ⦅文法⦆ 비교급

* **com·par·a·tive·ly** [kəmpǽrətivli] *adv.* in a comparative manner; relatively.
—[副] 비교적으로

compare

‡ com·pare [kəmpéər] *vt.* **1.** examine in order to find out likeness and unlikeness. ((~ one thing *with* another)) ¶ *~ a translation with the original.*① **2.** describe (one thing) as being similar to another thing. ((~ one thing *to* another)) ¶ *Life is sometimes compared to a voyage.*② **3.** (*Grammar*) give the positive, comparative, and superative degrees of (an adjective or adverb). —*vi.* be worthy of comparison.
 1) [*be*] *not to be compared with* (=[*be*] *very different* [*from*] *something.*)
 2) *compare notes,* exchange ideas.
—*n.* Ⓤ comparison.
beyond (or *past, without*) *compare,* very excellent.

• **com·par·i·son** [kəmpǽrisn] *n.* ⓤⒸ **1.** the act of comparing. ¶ *There is no ~ between the two.*① **2.** likeness. **3.** a statement that one thing is like another in some way. **4.** (*Grammar*) the change in an adjective or adverb to give degrees.
 1) *in comparison with,* [as] compared with.
 2) *without comparison,* very excellent.

com·part·ment [kəmpá:rtmənt] *n.* Ⓒ **1.** a part separated from the whole; a division; a section. ¶ *a watertight ~.*① **2.** (*U.S. Railroads*) a private bedroom; (*Brit.*) a division of a carriage.

‡ com·pass [kʌ́mpəs] *n.* **1.** Ⓒ an instrument for showing direction by means of a magnetic needle. **2.** Ⓤ the boundary of an area; range; extent. ¶ *in the ~ of a day / within the ~ of a lifetime.* **3.** Ⓤ (*Music*) the extent of a voice or of a musical instrument. **4.** the distance around any space; circuit. **5.** (usu. *pl.*) an instrument for drawing circles. ¶ *a pair of ~.*①
 1) *fetch* (or *go*) *a compass,* go a long way about.
 2) *within compass,* moderately.
—*vt.* **1.** surround. **2.** accomplish. **3.** contrive; plan. **4.** grasp (something) with the mind; understand.

com·pas·sion [kəmpǽʃən] *n.* Ⓤ sorrow and pity for the sufferings of others; sympathy. ((~ *on* or *for*))

com·pas·sion·ate [kəmpǽʃ(ə)nit] *adj.* feeling or showing compassion; merciful. [ing compatible.]

com·pat·i·bil·i·ty [kəmpæ̀təbíliti] *n.* Ⓤ the state of be-

com·pat·i·ble [kəmpǽtəbl] *adj.* able to live together in harmony. [ner; with compatibility.]

com·pat·i·bly [kəmpǽtəbli] *adv.* in a compatible man-

com·pa·tri·ot [kəmpéitriət / -pǽt-] *n.* Ⓒ a fellow countryman or countrywoman. —*adj.* of the same country.

com·peer [kəmpíər, kámpiər / kɔmpíə, kɔ́mpiə] *n.* Ⓒ **1.** an equal. **2.** a companion.

‡ com·pel [kəmpél] *vt.* (-pelled, -pel·ling) **1.** force. ((~ someone *to do*)) ¶ *The storm compelled us to stop traveling.*① **2.** get (something) by force.

com·pen·di·a [kəmpéndiə] *n.* pl. of **compendium**.

com·pen·di·ous [kəmpéndiəs] *adj.* concise.

com·pen·di·um [kəmpéndiəm] *n.* Ⓒ (pl. -di·ums or -di·a) **1.** a concise treatise. **2.** an outline.

com·pen·sate [kámpənsèit / kɔ́mpen-] *vt.* pay (someone) for his loss or service. ¶ *I will ~ you for your time.*① —*vi.* make up for something. ((~ *for* or *to* someone or something; ~ *with* or *by* something))

• **com·pen·sa·tion** [kàmpənséiʃ(ə)n / kɔ̀mpen-] *n.* ⓤⒸ **1.** the act of compensating; the state of being compensated. **2.** anything, esp. money, that makes up for a loss. **3.** (*U.S.*) salary; pay. [to compensate.]

com·pen·sa·to·ry [kəmpénsətɔ̀:ri / -t(ə)ri] *adj.* serving

• **com·pete** [kəmpí:t] *vi.* enter a contest ((~ *in* a race, etc.)); fight; be a rival. ((~ *with* someone))

compete

—他 1. …을 비교하다 ¶①번역문을 원문과 비교하다 2. …을 비유하다, …에 비기다 ¶②인생은 때로 항해에 비기는 일이 있다 3. 《文法》[형용사·부사]의 비교 변화를 나타내다 —自 필적하다

熟 1)…와는 비교가 안 되다 2) 의견을 교환하다
—名 비교
熟 비길데 없이, 무쌍하게
—名 1. 비교 ¶①그 둘은 도저히 비교가 안 된다 2. 유사(類似) 3. 비유 4. 《文法》비교 변화

熟 1)…와 비교하면 2)비길데 없이, 무쌍하게
—名 1. 구분된 부분, 구획 ¶①[배의] 방수 구획실 2.《美鐵道》[기차 따위의 개인의] 침실; 《英》[간막이한] 찻간

—名 1. 나침반 2. 한계; 범위 3. 《樂》음역(音域) 4. 둘레, 주위 5. 컴퍼스, 양각기 ¶①컴퍼스 한 개

熟 1)돌아가다 2)둘러대어 말하다
—他 1. …을 둘러싸다 2. …을 완수하다 3. …을 계획하다 4. …을 이해하다

—名 연민, 동정

—形 동정심이 많은, 자비로운

—名 양립성, 적합성
—形 양립할 수 있는, 적합한

—形 양립할 수 있게, 적합하여
—名 동포, 겨레 —形 같은 나라의

—名 1. 대등한 사람 2. 동료

—他 [남]을 억지로 …시키다 ¶①폭풍우 때문에 우리는 하는 수 없이 여행을 중지했다 2. …을 강요하다

—形 간결한, 간명한
—名 1. 개론 2. 요약, 대강

—他 …을 보상하다, 갚다 ¶①헛되이 보낸 너의 시간을 보상하겠다 —自 보상하다, 벌충하다

—名 1. 보상, 갚음 2. 보상품(금) 3. 봉급, 보수

—形 보상의, 배상의
—自 경쟁하다; [경쟁에] 참가하다; 필적하다

C

com·pe·tence [kámpit(ə)ns / kɔ́m-], **-ten·cy** [-t(ə)nsi] *n.* [U] **1.** the state of being competent; ability. 《~ *for* or *to do*》 **2.** 《usu. *a* ~》 a sufficient fortune. **3.** [U] (*Law*) legal authority.
—[名] 1. 자격; 능력 2. 상당한 재산 3. 권능, 권한

* **com·pe·tent** [kámpit(ə)nt / kɔ́m-] *adj.* having power or right to do an act; able. ▷**com·pe·tent·ly** [-li] *adv.*
—[形] 자격이 있는; 능력이 있는, 유능한

: **com·pe·ti·tion** [kàmpitíʃ(ə)n / kɔ̀m-] *n.* **1.** [U] the act of competing; the state of being a rival. **2.** [C] a contest.
—[名] 1. 경쟁; 대항 2. 시합, 경기

com·pet·i·tive [kəmpétitiv] *adj.* of competition. ▷**com·pet·i·tive·ly** [-li] *adv.*
—[形] 경쟁의

com·pet·i·tor [kəmpétitər] *n.* [C] a person or team that competes; a rival.
—[名] 경쟁자

com·pi·la·tion [kàmpiléiʃ(ə)n / kɔ̀mpi-] *n.* **1.** [U] the act of compiling. **2.** [C] anything compiled.
—[名] 1. 편집 2. 편집물, 편찬서

com·pile [kəmpáil] *vt.* collect facts, stories, etc. in one (book); make (a book) from various materials.
—[他] …을 편집하다

com·pil·er [kəmpáilər] *n.* [C] a person who compiles.
—[名] 편찬자

com·pla·cence [kəmpléisns], **-cen·cy** [-snsi] *n.* [U] a feeling of safety; self-satisfaction.
—[名] 안심, 안도감; 자기만족

com·pla·cent [kəmpléisnt] *adj.* pleased with oneself; only self-satisfied. ▷**com·pla·cent·ly** [-li] *adv.*
—[形] 흐뭇해하는; 자기만족의

: **com·plain** [kəmpléin] *vi.* **1.** express discontent with something. 《~ *of* or *about* something》 **2.** tell of one's pains. 《~ *of* a headache, etc.》 **3.** find fault; accuse.
—[自] 1. 불평을 말하다, 투덜거리다 2. [아픔을] 호소하다 3. 흠을 잡다; 비난하다

com·plain·ant [kəmpléinənt] *n.* [C] **1.** a person who complains. **2.** (*Law*) a person who charges another in a court.
—[名] 1. 불평을 말하는 사람 2. 《法》 원고, 고소인

* **com·plaint** [kəmpléint] *n.* **1.** [U][C] an expession of discontent; [C] a cause of discontent. **2.** [C] sickness. **3** [C] a formal charge.
—[名] 1. 불평[거리] 2. 병 3. 고소

com·plai·sance [kəmpléiz(ə)ns, + *U.S.* kámplizæ̀ns] *n.* [U] **1.** politeness. **2.** compliance.
—[名] 1. 공손함 2. 고분고분함, 유순함

com·plai·sant [kəmpléiz(ə)nt, + *U.S.* kámplizæ̀nt] *adj.* **1.** polite. **2.** compliant. ▷**com·plai·sant·ly** [-li] *adv.*
—[形] 1. 공손한 2. 고분고분한, 유순한

* **com·ple·ment** *n.* [kámplimənt / kɔ́m- ‖ → *v.*] [C] **1.** anything that makes an imperfect thing complete. **2.** the full number. **3.** (*Grammar*) words that complete a predicate. **4.** (*Mathematics*) the quantity needed to make an angle equal to 90°.
—[名] 1. [보충하여] 완전하게 하는 것 2. 전수(全數), 전량; 정원 3. 《文法》 보어 4. 《數》 여각(餘角)

—*vt.* [kámplimènt / kɔ́m-] make (something) perfect; complete.
—[他] …을 보충하다, 보충하여 완전하게 하다

com·ple·men·ta·ry [kàmpliméntəri / kɔ̀m-] *adj.* completing.
—[形] 보충적인

: **com·plete** [kəmplí:t] *adj.* (often **-plet·er, -plet·est**) **1.** whole; entire. ¶*a ~ set of Hemingway's novels.*① **2.** finished; ended. ¶*The work is now ~.* **3.** perfect in quality. **4.** perfect; absolute. ¶*a ~ victory.*
—[形] 1. 전부의 ¶①헤밍웨이의 소설전집 2. 완성한 3. 완전한 4. 전적인, 철저한

—*vt.* **1.** make (something) whole or perfect. **2.** finish.
—[他] 1. …을 완전하게 하다 2. …을 완성하다

: **com·plete·ly** [kəmplí:tli] *adv.* entirely; thoroughly.
—[副] 완전하게; 전적으로, 철저히

com·plete·ness [kəmplí:tnis] *n.* [U] the state of being complete.
—[名] 완전

com·ple·tion [kəmplí:ʃ(ə)n] *n.* [U] the act of completing; the state of being completed.
—[名] 완성; 만기

* **com·plex** *adj.* [kəmpléks, kámpleks → *n.* / kɔ́mpleks] **1.** made up of many parts. ¶*a ~ sentence.*① **2.** hard to understand or deal with; not simple. ¶*a ~ problem.*
—[形] 1. 복합의 ¶①복문(複文) 2. 복잡한

—*n.* [C] [*U.S.* kámpleks] **1.** a complex whole. **2.** a system of ideas that causes abnormal behavior.
—[名] 1. 합성물 2. 복합(강박) 관념

* **com·plex·ion** [kəmplékʃ(ə)n] *n.* [C] **1.** the natural color and appearance of the skin, esp. of the face. **2.** general appearance.
—[名] 1. 안색, 살빛 2. 외관, 모양, 형세

com·plex·i·ty [kəmpléksiti] *n.* (pl. **-ties**) **1.** [U] the state of being complex. **2.** [C] something complex.
—[名] 1. 복잡[함] 2. 복잡한 것

com·pli·ance [kəmpláiəns] *n.* [U] **1.** the act of complying. **2.** a tendency to obey others.
—[名] 1. 승낙 2. 굴종, 추종, 순종

in compliance with, according to. ¶*in ~ with the demands.*
[熟] …에 따라(응하여)

com·pli·ant [kəmpláiənt] *adj.* complying; yielding.
—[形] …에 응하는; 유순한, 고분고분한

* **com·pli·cate** [kámplikèit / kɔ́m-] *vt.* make (something) complex or difficult to understand.
—[他] …을 복잡하게 하다

com·pli·cat·ed [kámplikèitid / kɔ́m-] *adj.* made up of many parts ; complex ; not simple.
—[形] 복잡한

com·pli·ca·tion [kàmplikéiʃ(ə)n / kɔ̀m-] *n.* **1.** [U][C] a complex state of affairs. **2.** [C] anything that complicates ; anything that increases difficulty or confusion.
—[名] 1. 복잡 2. 복잡하게 하는 것, 분규의 씨

com·plic·i·ty [kəmplísiti] *n.* [U] partnership in crime.
—[名] 공범, 공모자

* **com·pli·ment** *n.* [kámplimənt / kɔ́m- ‖ → *v.*] **1.** [C] words of praise for a person or his work. **2.** 《*pl.*》 a formal greeting. —*vt.* [kámplimènt / kɔ́m-] **1.** pay a compliment to (someone). 《~ someone *on* his act, etc.》 **2.** congratulate. 《~ someone *on* his success, etc.》
—[名] 1. 찬사, 알랑거리는 말 2. 인사말 —[他] 1. …에게 칭송하다, 아첨의 말을 하다 2. …에게 축하의 말을 하다, 축하하다

com·pli·men·ta·ry [kàmpliméntəri / kɔ̀m-] *adj.* **1.** giving or expressing praise. **2.** given free. ¶*a ~ ticket to the play.*①
—[形] 1. 칭찬하는, 알랑거리는 2. 무료의 ¶①연극의 우대(초대)권

* **com·ply** [kəmplái] *vi.* (**-plied**) act as other's wish; agree to obey ; yield.
—[自] [요구·명령에] 응하다, 따르다

com·po·nent [kəmpóunənt] *adj.* necessary to make up a whole ; composing. ¶*~ parts.*① —*n.* [C] a component part.
—[形] 성분의 ; 구성하는 ¶①성분 —[名] 성분

com·port [kəmpɔ́:rt] *vt.* behave. 《~ oneself》 —*vi.* suit; agree. 《~ *with* something》
—[他] 처신하다, 행동하다 —[自] 적합하다, 어울리다

com·port·ment [kəmpɔ́:rtmənt] *n.* [U][C] behavior.
—[名] 태도, 행동

‡ **com·pose** [kəmpóuz] *vt.* **1.** make (something) by putting its parts together. 《~ something *of*》 **2.** create (a poem, a picture, etc.). **3.** settle (a quarrel, etc.). **4.** make (oneself) calm. **5.** (*Printing*) set up (letters). ***be composed*** (=*be made up*) ***of things.***
—[他] 1. …을 구성하다 2. …을 창작하다 3. …을 조정하다 4. …을 가라앉히다, 진정시키다 5. 《印刷》 …을 조판하다, 식자하다
[熟] …으로 이루어져 있다

com·posed [kəmpóuzd] *adj.* calm in mind ; free from anxiety. ▷**com·pos·ed·ly** [-idli] *adv.*
—[形] 침착한, 차분한, 태연한

com·pos·er [kəmpóuzər] *n.* [C] **1.** a person who composes. **2.** a person who writes music. **3.** an author.
—[名] 1. 조정자 2. 작곡가 3. 작가

com·pos·ite [kəmpázit / kɔ́mpəzit] *adj.* made up of various separate parts; compound. —*n.* [C] a compound.
—[形] 합성의, 혼합의 —[名] 합성물

* **com·po·si·tion** [kàmpəzíʃ(ə)n / kɔ̀m-] *n.* **1.** [U][C] the act of composing. **2.** [C] a work of art. **3.** [C] (*Printing*) the setting-up of type. **4.** [C] agreement.
—[名] 1. 구성 ; 창작 2. [예술]작품 3. 《印刷》 식자 4. 화해, 타협

com·pos·i·tor [kəmpázitər / -pɔ́zitə] *n.* [C] a typesetter.
—[名] 식자공 ; 식자기

com·post [kámpoust / kɔ́mpɔst] *n.* [C] **1.** a mixture of various decayed things used for fertilizing land. **2.** a compound.
—[名] 1. 혼합 비료 2. 혼합물

com·po·sure [kəmpóuʒər] *n.* [U] a peaceful state of mind ; calmness. ↔agitation
—[名] 차분함, 침착

com·pote [kámpout / kɔ́m-] *n.* **1.** [U][C] stewed fruit, usu. served as a dessert. **2.** [C] a dish with a base and stem for fruit, nuts, candy, etc.
—[名] 1. 설탕을 잰 과일 2. 과일 따위를 담는 굽 달린 접시

* **com·pound** *vt.* [kəmpáund → *adj., n.*] **1.** make (something) by combining parts or elements ; mix ; combine. ¶*~ a medicine.*① **2.** settle (a quarrel, a debt, etc.) by mutual agreement. —*vi.* agree ; compromise.
—[他] 1. …을 합성하다 ; 혼합하다 ; 섞어 합쳐서 만들다 ¶①약을 조제하다 2. 의논하여 화해하다 ; 서로 타협하여 …을 해결하다 —[自] 타협하다, 화해하다

—*adj.* [kámpaund / kɔ́m-] made up of two or more parts or elements. ¶*a ~ flower*② / *a ~ engine.*③
—[形] 합성의 ; 혼합의 ¶②집합화/③복식기관(復式機關)

—*n.* [kámpaund / kɔ́n-] [C] **1.** a substance formed by chemical combination of two or more elements. ¶*Water is a ~ of hydrogen and oxygen.* **2.** something made by mixing substances or combining parts; a mixture. ¶*Air is a ~ of several gases.* **3.** a compound word.
—[名] 1. 화합물 2. 혼합물 ; 합성물 3. 복합어

* **com·pre·hend** [kàmprihénd / kɔ̀m-] *vt.* **1.** grasp the meaning of (something) ; understand. **2.** take in ; contain.
—[他] 1. …을 이해하다 2. …을 포함하다

com·pre·hen·si·bil·i·ty [kàmprihènsibíliti / kɔ̀m-] *n.* [U] the state of being comprehensible.
—[名] 이해할 수 있음, 알기 쉬움

com·pre·hen·si·ble [kàmprihénsibl / kɔ̀m-] *adj.* that can be understood ; understandable.
—[形] 이해할 수 있는, 알기 쉬운

com·pre·hen·sion [kàmprihénʃ(ə)n / kɔ̀m-] *n.* [U] **1.** the
—[名] 1. 이해 ; 이해력 2. 포함, 함축, 내포

C

act of comprehending; the ability to understand; mental grasp. **2.** the act of taking in or including.

com·pre·hen·sive [kàmprihénsiv / kɔ́m-] *adj.* **1.** of wide scope; including much. **2.** able to understand.
—[形] 1. 범위가 넓은, 포괄적인 2. 이해력이 있는

com·pre·hen·sive·ly [kamprihénsivli / kɔ̀m-] *adv.* in a comprehensive manner; with a wide scope.
—[副] 넓게, 알기 쉽게

com·press *vt.* [kəmprés → *n.*] press (things) tightly together; make (something) smaller by pressing; condense. ¶*compressed air.* —*n.* [kámpres / kɔ́m-] [C] a wet pad applied to some part of the body to give pressure, moisture, cold, or heat.
—[他] …을 압축하다; …으로 요약하다 —[名] 압박 붕대, 습포(濕布)

com·pres·sion [kəmpréʃ(ə)n] *n.* [U] **1.** the act of compressing; the state of being compressed. **2.** summary.
—[名] 1. 압축 2. 요약

com·pres·sor [kəmprésər] *n.* [C] **1.** a person or thing that compresses. **2.** (*Surgery*) an instrument for compressing a part of the body. **3.** a machine for increasing the pressure of air, gas, etc.
—[名] 1. 압축하는 사람(것) 2.《外科》압박기 3. 압착 기계

* **com·prise, -prize** [kəmpráiz] *vt.* contain; consist of (something). ¶*This book comprises five chapters.*
—[他] …을 포함하다; …으로 이루어지다

* **com·pro·mise** [kámprəmàiz / kɔ́m-] *n.* **1.** [U][C] an agreement on something made by giving up a part of the wishes of both sides; the result of such an agreement. **2.** [C] anything existing between two different things. —*vt.* **1.** make a compromise about (something). ¶*~ a dispute.* **2.** put (something) in danger or under suspicion. ¶*~ one's name.* —*vi.* make a compromise; give way. 《*~ with* something》
—[名] 1. 타협, 화해 2. 중간물; 절충물
—[他] 1. …을 타협하여 처리하다 2. …을 위태롭게 하다; 의심스럽게 하다
—[自] 타협하다, 화해하다

comp·trol·ler [kəntróulər] *n.* =controller.

com·pul·sion [kəmpʌ́lʃ(ə)n] *n.* [U] the act of compelling; the state of being compelled.
—[名] 강제

com·pul·sive [kəmpʌ́lsiv] *adj.* forcible; that cannot be resisted. ▷**com·pul·sive·ly** [-li] *adv.*
—[形] 강제적인

com·pul·so·ry [kəmpʌ́ls(ə)ri] *adj.* that which must be done; compelled; needed. ¶*~ education.*① ↔voluntary
—[形] 강제적인; 의무적인 ¶①의무교육

com·punc·tion [kəmpʌ́ŋkʃ(ə)n] *n.* [U] the pain of the conscience; a sense of guilt; regret.
—[名] 양심의 가책; 후회, 뉘우침

com·pu·ta·tion [kàmpju(:)téiʃ(ə)n / kɔ̀m-] *n.* [U] calculation.
—[名] 계산

com·pute [kəmpjú:t] *vt.* count. ▷**com·put·a·ble** [-əbl] *adj.*
—[他] …을 계산하다, 산정하다

com·put·er [kəmpjú:tər] *n.* [C] **1.** a person or thing that computes. **2.** an electronic calculator.
—[名] 1. 계산자(者)(기) 2. 전자 계산기

* **com·rade** [kámræd, -rid / kɔ́mrid, kʌ́m-] *n.* [C] **1.** a dear companion or friend. **2.** a fellow member of a group, a political party, etc.
—[名] 1. 친구, 벗 2. 동지

com·rade·ship [kámrædʃìp, -rid- / kɔ́mrid-, kʌ́m-] *n.* [U] **1.** the state of being a comrade. **2.** the relation of comrades.
—[名] 1. 동지임 2. 동지(친구) 사이, 동지로서의 관계

con[1] [kan / kɔn] *adv.* against. ↔pro ¶*pro and ~.*① —*n.* [C] an argument against something.
the pros and cons, arguments for and against.
—[副] 반대하여 ¶①찬부 양론의, 찬반의 —[名] 반대론
[熟] 찬부 양론

con[2] [kan / kɔn] *vt.* (**conned, con·ning**) study; learn by heart.
—[他] …을 배우다, 학습하다; …을 암기하다, 외다

con·cave *adj.* [kankéiv ⌐⌐ / kɔ́nkéiv ∥ → *n.*] curved inside. ↔convex —*n.* [kánkeiv / kɔ́nkéiv] [C] a concave surface or thing.
—[形] 요면(凹面)의, 오목한 —[名] 요면, 오목한 면(것)

** **con·ceal** [kənsí:l] *vt.* **1.** hide. **2.** keep (a matter) secret.
—[他] 1. …을 감추다, 숨기다 2. …을 비밀로 하다

con·ceal·ment [kənsí:lmənt] *n.* **1.** [U] the act of concealing; the state of being concealed. **2.** [C] a place for hiding.
—[名] 1. 은폐, 은닉 2. 잠복처

* **con·cede** [kənsí:d] *vt.* **1.** admit (something) to be true; yield. ¶*~ a point in argument.*① **2.** give (a right, a privilege, etc.).
—[他] 1. …을 인정하다; …을 양보하다 ¶①토론에서 일보를 양보하다 2. [권리 따위]를 주다

* **con·ceit** [kənsí:t] *n.* **1.** [U] too much pride in one's own ability, appearance, etc. **2.** [C] a very fanciful idea.
—[名] 1. 자부심, 자만심 2. 문득 떠오른 생각, 기발한 착상

con·ceit·ed [kənsí:tid] *adj.* having high conceit about
—[形] 자만심이 강한

conceivable [237] **concerted**

one's own abiltiy, appearance, etc. [as possible.
con·ceiv·a·ble [kənsíːvəbl] *adj.* imaginable; imagined
con·ceiv·a·bly [kənsíːvəbli] *adv.* possibly.

* **con·ceive** [kənsíːv] *vt.* **1.** form (an idea, a purpose, etc.) in the mind. ¶ ~ *a hatred.*① **2.** imagine. **3.** become pregnant with (young). ¶ ~ *a child.* —*vi.* **1.** think. (~ *of something*) **2.** be with child; be pregnant.

* **con·cen·trate** [kάns(ə)ntrèit / kɔ́n-] *vt.* **1.** give all one's attention to (something); fix (one's mind) on something. ¶ ~ *one's efforts on the work* / *You must* ~ *your attention on what you are reading.*① **2.** make (something) stronger; increase the strength of (something). —*vi.* **1.** come to a center. (~ *in a place, etc.*) **2.** devote oneself; do one's best. (~ *on* or *upon something*)

con·cen·trat·ed [kάns(ə)ntrèitid / kɔ́n-] *adj.* **1.** gathered together closely in a center. **2.** made denser or stronger.

* **con·cen·tra·tion** [kὰns(ə)ntréiʃ(ə)n / kɔ̀n-] *n.* Ⓤ **1.** the act of concentrating; the state of being concentrated. **2.** close attention to one thing. **3.** thickness; density.

concentration camp [⌐-́--⌐́] *n.* a camp for prisoners of war, political enemies, etc.

con·cen·tric [kənséntrik / kɔn-] *adj.* having a common center. ¶ ~ *circles.*① ▷ **con·cen·tri·cal·ly** [-kəli] *adv.*

con·cept [kάnsept / kɔ́n-] *n.* Ⓒ a general idea.

: **con·cep·tion** [kənsépʃ(ə)n] *n.* **1.** Ⓤ the act of conceiving; the state of being conceived. **2.** Ⓤ the creation of a new life in the mother's body. **3.** Ⓒ an idea; a concept. **4.** Ⓒ a design; a plan.

: **con·cern** [kənsə́ːrn] *vt.* **1.** relate to; have to do with (someone or something). ¶ *It doesn't* ~ *you.* **2.** (usu. in *passive*) make (someone) anxious; trouble. ¶ *with a concerned air*① / *Don't let my illness* ~ *you.*②
1) *as concerns,* regarding; about; as to.
2) *as* (or *so*) *far as one be concerned,* as regards oneself. ¶ *as far as I am concerned.*
3) *be concerned about* (or *for, over*) (= *be anxious or worried about*) something. [something.
4) *be concerned with* (or *in*) (= *have relation to*)
5) *concern oneself about* (or *with*), ⓐ be worried or anxious about (someone or something). ⓑ take an interest in (someone or something).
—*n.* Ⓒ **1.** relation; connection; interest. ¶ *his* ~ *in the company.* **2.** Ⓤ anxiety; uneasiness. ¶ *a* ~ *for his safety.* **3.** (often *pl.*) affairs. ¶ *Don't busy yourself in another's concerns.* **4.** an enterprise; a business.
1) *feel concern about* (or *over*) (= *be anxious about*)
2) *of concern,* of importance. [something.

con·cerned [kənsə́ːrnd] *adj.* **1.** interested. **2.** troubled; anxious. [ner; anxiously.
con·cern·ed·ly [kənsə́ːrnidli] *adv.* in a concerned man-

: **con·cern·ing** [kənsə́ːrniŋ] *prep.* about; as to.

con·cern·ment [kənsə́ːrnmənt] *n.* Ⓤ **1.** importance. **2.** anxiety. **3.** interest.

* **con·cert** *n.* [kάnsərt / kɔ́nsət ∥ →*vt.*] **1.** Ⓤ a mutual agreement. (~ *with*) **2.** Ⓒ a musical entertainment. ¶ *attend a* ~① / *give a* ~.②
in concert, together. ¶ *act in* ~.
—*vt.* [kənsə́ːrt] plan or make (something) together with others; act in harmony with (someone or something).

con·cert·ed [kənsə́ːrtid] *adj.* **1.** agreed beforehand. ¶ ~ *schemes* / *a* ~ *action.*① **2.** arranged for several musical instruments or voices.

—ⓐ 상상할 수 있는; 있을 법한
—ⓑ 있음직하게, 아마, 어쩌면
—ⓐ **1.** [생각·의도·원한 따위]를 품다 ¶①적의를 품다 **2.** …을 상상하다 **3.** [아이]를 배다 —ⓑ **1.** 상상하다, 생각하다 **2.** 임신하다

—ⓐ **1.** …에 집중하다; …을 한 점에 모으다(쏟다) ¶너는 읽고 있는 것에 주의를 집중시켜야 한다 **2.** …을 강화하다; 농축하다 —ⓑ **1.** 집중하다 **2.** 전력하다; 전력을 기울이다

—ⓐ **1.** 집중한 **2.** 농축한

—ⓐ **1.** 집중 **2.** 전심, 전념 **3.** 농축, 농도

—ⓐ [포로 따위의] 수용소

—ⓐ 같은 중심의 ¶①동심원

—ⓐ 개념
—ⓐ **1.** 개념 작용 **2.** 임신 **3.** 관념; 개념 **4.** 착상; 계획

—ⓐ **1.** …에 관계가 있다 **2.** …을 조심시키다, 걱정시키다 ¶①근심스러운 태도로/②나의 병 때문에 걱정하지 마시오
국 1) …에 관하여는 2) …에 관한 한 3) …을 염려하다 4) …과 관계가 있다 5) ⓐ …을 걱정하다, 염려하다 ⓑ …에 관계하다; 관심이 있다

—ⓐ **1.** 관계; 이해관계 **2.** 근심, 염려, 불안 **3.** 불일, 사건; 사정 **4.** 기업; 회사

국 1) …을 조심하다 2) 중요한

—ⓐ **1.** 관계가 있는, 관계하고 있는 **2.** 근심스러운
—ⓑ 근심하여
—ⓐ …에 대하여; …에 관하여
—ⓐ **1.** 중대, 중요성 **2.** 근심, 염려 **3.** 관계, 관여

—ⓐ **1.** 협정, 협약, 일치 **2.** 음악회, 연주회 ¶①음악회에 출석하다/②음악회를 개최하다
국 일제히, 협동하여
—ⓐ …을 공동으로 생각하다; …와 협조하다

—ⓐ **1.** 협정된, 타협을 본 ¶①일치된 행동 **2.** 합주(합창)용으로 편곡된

con·cer·ti·na [kànsərtí:nə / kɔ̀nsət-] *n.* [C] a musical instrument like an accordion.
—[名] 6각형의 손풍금 (작은 아코오디온 모양)

con·cert·mas·ter [kánsərtmæ̀stər / kɔ́nsətmà:stə] *n.* [C] a leader of an orchestra, usu. the leading violinist.
—[名] 수석 주자(奏者), 합주장(合奏長)

con·cer·to [kəntʃέərtou / -tʃə́:-] *n.* [C] (pl. **-tos**) a kind of musical composition for an orchestra.
—[名] 협주곡, 콘체르토

con·ces·sion [kənséʃ(ə)n] *n.* **1.** [U][C] the act of giving way, allowing or yielding. ¶*make mutual concessions.*① **2.** [C] a right given by a government; a special right; a privilege. ¶*an oil* ~.②
—[名] 1. 양보, 양여(讓與) ¶①서로 양보하다 2. 특허, 권리 ¶②석유 채굴권

con·ces·sive [kənsésiv] *adj.* apt to give way; granting.
—[形] 양보하는

con·cil·i·ate [kənsílièit] *vt.* **1.** calm the anger of (someone); pacify. ¶~ *the child with a present.*① **2.** gain the friendship, good will, etc. of (someone).
—[他] 1. …을 달래다 ¶①어린애를 선물로 달래다 2. [남]의 [애정 따위를] 얻다, 환심을 사다

con·cil·i·a·tion [kənsìliéiʃ(ə)n] *n.* [U] the act of conciliating; the state of being conciliated. ¶*a* ~ *court.*①
—[名] 달래기, 위로, 무마; 조정 ¶①조정(調停) 재판소

con·cil·i·a·to·ry [kənsíliətɔ̀:ri / -t(ə)ri] *adj.* apt to conciliate someone or settle a quarrel.
—[形] 달래는; 조정의

con·cise [kənsáis] *adj.* short but full of meaning.
—[形] 간결(간명)한

con·clave [kánkleiv / kɔ́n-] *n.* [C] **1.** a private meeting of the cardinals for the election of a pope; a room in which such a meeting is held. **2.** a private meeting.
—[名] 1. [추기경에 의한] 교황 선거 회의[실] 2. 비밀 회의

:con·clude [kənklú:d] *vt.* **1.** bring (something) to an end. ¶~ *a speech (an argument).*① **2.** settle finally. ¶~ *a bargain*② | ~ *a peace treaty.* **3.** reach an idea of (something) by thinking; arrive at an opinion by reasoning. 《~ *that* ...》 —*vi.* **1.** end one's speech. **2.** come to an end. ¶*The meeting concluded early.*③
—[他] 1. …을 끝내다, 결말짓다 ¶①[예상대로] 연설을 끝내다 2. …을 체결하다, 맺다 ¶②거래 계약을 맺다 3. …을 추단(推斷)하다, 추정하다 —[自] 1. 말을 맺다 2. 끝나다 ¶③모임은 일찍 끝났다

:con·clu·sion [kənklú:ʒ(ə)n] *n.* [C] **1.** a final result. ¶*the* ~ *of a contest.* **2.** a final opinion reached by reasoning. ¶*form one's own* ~ *from* ...① | *jump to* (or *at*) *a* ~.② **3.** an arrangement. ¶*the* ~ *of a peace treaty.*③
—[名] 1. 종결, 결말 2. 결론 ¶①…으로 자기의 결론을 내리다/②속단하다 3. [조약의] 체결 ¶③평화조약의 체결

con·clu·sive [kənklú:siv] *adj.* decisive; final.
—[形] 결정적인; 최종적인

con·clu·sive·ly [kənklú:sivli] *adv.* decisively; finally.
—[副] 결정적으로; 최종적으로

con·coct [kankákt, kən- / kənkɔ́kt] *vt.* **1.** prepare (something) by mixing various things together. **2.** make up; undertake. ¶~ *a plan.*①
—[他] 1. …을 섞어서 만들다 2. [각색·이야기]를 꾸미다, 구성하다; [계획 따위]를 꾸미다 ¶①계획을 세우다

con·coc·tion [kankákʃ(ə)n, kən- / kənkɔ́k-] *n.* **1.** [U] the act of concocting; [C] thing prepared by mixing. **2.** [C] a plan.
—[名] 1. 조제, 조합(調合); 조제품 2. 꾸밈, 계획

con·com·i·tant [kankámit(ə)nt, kən- / kənkɔ́m-] *adj.* attendant; accompanying. ¶*a* ~ *pleasure*① | *be* ~ *to something.*② —*n.* [C] a thing which accompanies.
—[形] 부수하는, 공존의 ¶①부수하는 즐거움/②…에 부수하다 —[名] 부수물

con·cord [kánkɔ:rd / kɔ́nkɔ:d] *n.* [U] **1.** agreement; harmony. ↔discord **2.** (*Music*) a harmonious combination of melodies. **3.** (*Grammar*) agreement of words.
—[名] 1. 일치, 조화 2. 《樂》 협화음 3. 《文法》 [수(數)·격(格)·인칭·시제 따위의] 일치

con·cord·ance [kankɔ́:rd(ə)ns, kən- / kənkɔ́:d-] *n.* **1.** [U] agreement; harmony. ¶*in* ~ *with something.*① **2.** [C] a dictionary or list of words used in a certain book or by a certain author.
—[名] 1. 일치, 조화 ¶①…에 따라서, …와 일치하여 2. 용어 색인

con·cord·ant [kankɔ́:rd(ə)nt, kən- / kənkɔ́:d-] *adj.* agreeing; harmonious.
—[形] 일치된; 조화된

con·cor·dat [kankɔ́:rdæt / kɔnkɔ́:-] *n.* [C] an agreement; a contract.
—[名] 협정, 협약

con·course [kánkɔ:rs, káŋ- / kɔ́ŋkɔ:s, kɔ́n-] *n.* [C] **1.** the act or state of meeting or coming together. ¶*the* ~ *of particles*① | *the* ~ *of two rivers.*② **2.** a crowd. ¶*a large* ~ *of people.*③ **3.** (*U.S.*) a central hall in a railroad station; a central place in a park. **4.** a driveway.
—[名] 1. 모여 합침, 합류 ¶①분자의 집합/②두 강의 합류 2. 군중 ¶③대(大) 군중 3. 《美》 [정거장의] 중앙 호올; [공원의] 중앙 광장 4. 차도(車道)

·con·crete [kankrí:t, ´– / kɔ́nkri:t ‖ → *v.*, 1.] *adj.* **1.** actual; real. ¶*a* ~ *fact* | *a* ~ *idea.* **2.** solid; made of concrete. ¶*a* ~ *block.* —*n.* **1.** [C] a concrete substance. **2.** [U] a stonelike material made of cement, sand, gravel, etc. ¶*reinforced* ~① | *a* ~ *mixer.* —*vi., vt.* **1.** [kankrí:t / kən-] harden. **2.** cover (something) with concrete.
—[形] 1. 구체적인 2. 개체의; 콘크리이트로 만든 —[名] 1. 구체물(具體物), 고형체 2. 콘크리이트 ¶①철근 콘크리이트 —[自][他] 1. 굳어지[게 하]다 2. …을 콘크리이트로 씌우다

con·cre·tion [kɑnkríːʃ(ə)n / kɔn-] *n.* **1.** [U] the act of forming into a solid mass. **2.** [C] a hardened mass.
—[名] 1. 응결, 응고 2. 응고물

con·cur [kənkə́ːr] *vi.* (**-curred, -cur·ring**) **1.** agree; be in harmony. ¶~ *with him in the opinion* (*in doing*). **2.** happen at the same time; work together.
—[自] 1. 동의하다, 일치하다 2. 동시에 일어나다; 협동하다

con·cur·rence [kənkə́ːr(ə)ns / -kʌ́r-] *n.* [U] **1.** an agreement; the act of working together. ⟪~ *in*⟫ **2.** ⟪sometimes *a* ~⟫ the state of happening at the same time.
—[名] 1. 동의, 협동 2. 동시 발생

con·cur·rent [kənkə́ːr(ə)nt / -kʌ́r-] *adj.* **1.** harmonious; working together. **2.** happening at the same time.
—[形] 1. 일치의, 협력의 2. 동시 발생의

con·cus·sion [kənkʌ́ʃ(ə)n] *n.* [U][C] **1.** a sudden and violent shaking; shock. **2.** a [brain] injury caused by a blow. ¶*a ~ of the brain.*①
—[名] 1. 진동, 격동 2. 진탕(震盪) ¶①뇌진탕

:con·demn [kəndém] *vt.* **1.** blame. ⟪~ someone *for* his wrong act, etc.⟫ ¶*She condemned* [*him for*] *his foolish behavior.* **2.** pronounce punishment upon (someone); give judgment on (someone). ¶~ *someone to imprisonment*① / ~ *someone to be hanged.*② **3.** declare (someone) to be guilty. ⟪~ someone *for* or *of* his act, etc.⟫ ¶*be condemned of treason*③ / *He was condemned.*④ **4.** doom. ¶*be condemned to a life of suffering.*⑤ **5.** declare (something) to be unfit for use. **6.** declare (something) to be taken for public use.
—[他] 1. …을 비난하다, 나무라다 2. …에게 [형벌을] 선고하다 ¶①금고형을 선고하다/②교수형을 선고하다 3. …을 유죄로 판정하다 ¶③대역죄의 선고를 받다/④그는 유죄판결을 받았다 4. [비운·고난]으로 운명짓다 ¶⑤고난의 생활을 보내도록 운명지어지다 5. [물품 따위]의 사용 불능(폐기처분)을 선언하다 6. …을 접수하다, 몰수하다

con·dem·na·tion [kàndemnéiʃ(ə)n / kɔ̀n-] *n.* **1.** [U][C] the act of condemning; the state of being condemned. **2.** [C] a cause of being condemned.
—[名] 1. 비난; 유죄(부적당·몰수)의 선고 2. 비난의 이유

con·den·sa·tion [kàndenséiʃ(ə)n / kɔ̀n-] *n.* [U][C] **1.** the act of condensing; the state of being condensed. **2.** something condensed or made short. ¶*a ~ of a novel.*①
—[名] 1. 응축(凝縮), 응결 2. 응결물; [표현 따위의] 간명[화] ¶①소설의 요약

·con·dense [kəndéns] *vt., vi.* **1.** make (something) dense; become dense. ¶~ *gas to liquid.*① **2.** gather (things) to one point; concentrate. ¶*a condensing lens.*② **3.** shorten. ¶~ *a paragraph to a single sentence.*
—[他][自] 1. [···을] 응축하다, 농축시키다 ¶①기체를 응축하여 액체로 하다 2. …을 모으다 ¶②집광(集光)렌즈 3. …을 단축하다, 요약하다

con·dens·er [kəndénsər] *n.* [C] **1.** a device for holding a charge of electricity. **2.** a device for changing gas into liquid. **3.** a lens for gathering light to one point.
—[名] 1. 축전기, 콘덴서 2. 응축 장치, 응결기 3. 집광 렌즈

con·de·scend [kàndisénd / kɔ̀n-] *vi.* bring oneself down to the level of a person not so important.
—[自] [아랫사람에게] 공손히 대하다; 겸손하게 …하다

con·de·scend·ing [kàndiséndiŋ / kɔ̀n-] *adj.* having a manner which condescends. ¶*in a ~ manner.*
—[形] [아랫사람에게] 공손한, 겸손한

con·de·scen·sion [kàndisénʃ(ə)n / kɔ̀n-] *n.* [U] the act of condescending; patronizing behavior.
—[名] [아랫사람에게] 공손함, 겸손, 은혜를 베푸는 듯한 태도

con·dign [kəndáin] *adj.* (of punishment) deserved; fit; proper.
—[形] [형벌 따위가] 당연한; 응분의, 적당한

con·di·ment [kándimənt / kɔ́n-] *n.* [U][C] something that gives flavor to food.
—[名] 조미료, 양념

:con·di·tion [kəndíʃ(ə)n] *n.* **1.** [U][C] the state in which a person or thing exists. ¶*The ~ of my health prevents me from working.*① **2.** ⟪*pl.*⟫ circumstances. ¶*favorable conditions for business.*② **3.** [U] a good state, esp. of health. **4.** [C] ⟪often *pl.*⟫ something needed before something else is possible; a very important factor. **5.** [C] the social position. ¶*people of humble ~.*
—[名] 1. 상태 ¶①나는 건강상태가 나빠서 일을 못한다 2. 사정; 상황 ¶②사업에 유리한 상황 3. [주로 건강이] 좋은 상태 4. 필요 조건; 요인 5. 사회적 지위

1) ***be in*** [***good***] (***out of***) ***condition,*** be in good (poor) health; be physically prepared (unprepared).
2) ***be in no condition to do,*** be unfitted to do.
3) ***change one's condition,*** marry.
4) ***on condition*** [***that***], if only; provided [that]….

[熟] 1)건강이 좋다(나쁘다) 2)…하기에 적합하지 않다 3)결혼하다 4)…이라는 조건으로, 만약 …이라면

—*vt.* bring (someone or something) into a good condition.
—[他] …을 좋은 상태가 되게 하다

con·di·tion·al [kəndíʃ(ə)nl] *adj.* dependent on a certain condition; not perfect; not certain. ¶*a ~ promise* (*offer*) / *My stay is ~ on your plans.*① / *a ~ clause* (*mood*).
—[形] 조건부의, …나름(여하)의 ¶①나의 체류는 너의 계획 여하에 달려 있다

con·di·tion·al·ly [kəndíʃ(ə)nəli] *adv.* under or with a condition or conditions.
—[副] 조건부로

con·di·tioned [kəndíʃ(ə)nd] *adj.* subject to a condition.
—[形] …상태에 있는

con·do·la·to·ry [kəndóulətɔ̀:ri / -t(ə)ri] *adj.* expressing sorrow for another.
—[形] 조위(弔慰)의, 문상의, 조의를 표하는

con·dole [kəndóul] *vi.* express one's sympathy or sorrow for another. 《~ *with* someone *on* someone's death, etc.》
—[自] 문상하다, 조의를 표하다

con·do·lence [kəndóuləns] *n.* [U] 《often *pl.*》 a message expressing sorrow or sympathy.
—[名] 문상, 조위(弔慰), 애도

con·done [kəndóun] *vt.* pardon; excuse; overlook.
—[他] [죄]를 용서하다, 관대히 보아 주다

con·dor [kándər / kɔ́ndɔ:, -də] *n.* [C] a very large bird with a bald head and neck.
—[名] 콘도르(남미·북미 California산 큰 독수리)

con·duce [kənd(j)ú:s / -djú:s] *vi.* lead [to a good result]; contribute. 《~ *to* or *towards* something》 ¶ *Wealth does not always ~ to happiness.*①
—[自] [바람직한 결과로] 이끌어가다; […의] 도움이 되다 ¶①부귀가 반드시 행복으로 연결되는 것은 아니다

con·du·cive [kənd(j)ú:siv / -djú:siv] *adj.* helpful; favorable.
—[形] …의 도움이 되는

:**con·duct** *n.* [kándʌkt / kɔ́ndəkt ∥ → *v.*] [U] **1.** behavior; deportment. ¶ *He's quite above such ~.*① **2.** management; direction; control. **3.** leading; guidance. ¶ *under the ~ of someone.* —*v.* [kəndʌ́kt] *vt.* **1.** lead; guide. ¶ *He conducted the visitors around the museum.* **2.** manage; control. ¶ *~ a business.* **3.** behave. 《~ *oneself*》 ¶ *He conducts himself without any reserve whatever.* **4.** pass on; convey; carry. ¶ *~ water through a pipe* / *This wire conducts electricity.* —*vi.* **1.** serve as a conductor or leader. **2.** direct; lead; guide.
—[名] 1. 행위, 행실 ¶①그는 결코 그런 짓을 할 사람이 아니다 2. 경영; 관리; 통제 3. 지도, 지휘, 안내
—[他] 1. …을 지휘하다 2. …을 관리하다 3. 행동하다, 처신하다 4. …을 보내다; 전달하다; 운반하다 —[自] 1. 지도자로서 행동하다 2. 관리하다; 지휘하다

con·duc·tion [kəndʌ́kʃ(ə)n] *n.* [U] the act of carrying water through a pipe; the act of passing on heat or electricity.
—[名] [물을 파이프로] 이끌기; [열·전기 따위의] 전도(傳導)

con·duc·tive [kəndʌ́ktiv] *adj.* having the power of conducting.
—[形] 전도력이 있는

con·duc·tiv·i·ty [kɑ̀ndʌktíviti / kɔ̀n-] *n.* [U] the power of passing on heat or electricity.
—[名] 전도성(력)

***con·duc·tor** [kəndʌ́ktər] *n.* [C] **1.** a guide; a leader; a manager. **2.** a person in charge of a streetcar or bus; (*U.S.*) a person in charge of a railroad train. (cf. *Brit.* guard) **3.** a director of an orchestra or a chorus. **4.** a substance which passes on electricity, heat, or water; a lightning rod.
—[名] 1. 안내자, 지도자; 경영자, 관리인 2. [버스·전차·열차의] 차장 3. 지휘자 4. 전도체; 피뢰침

con·duit [kánd(u)it / kɔ́ndit] *n.* [C] a pipe for carrying water; a tube or subway for electric wires.
—[名] 도관(導管), 수로(水路), 도랑; 전선도관(電線導管), 선거(線渠)

cone [koun] *n.* [C] **1.** a solid body with a flat, round bottom and a pointed top; anything shaped like this. ¶ *an ice cream ~*① / *a volcanic ~.*② **2.** a seed case of the pine, cedar, and certain other evergreen trees.
—[名] 1. 원추(형); 원추형의 물건 ¶①원추형 아이스크리임 그릇/②화구구(火口丘) 2. [솔방울 모양의] 구과(毬果)

con·fab·u·late [kənfǽbjulèit] *vi.* chat or talk together in an easy way. 《~ *with* someone》 ⇒[N.B.]
—[自] […와] 담소하다 [N.B.] 구어에서는 confab의 형으로도 씀

con·fab·u·la·tion [kənfæ̀bjuléiʃ(ə)n] *n.* [U][C] the act of confabulating.
—[名] 담소, 간담

con·fec·tion [kənfékʃ(ə)n] *n.* [C] **1.** a piece of candy; a sweetmeat. **2.** a sweetened pill or drug.
—[名] 1. 과자, 당과(糖菓) 2. 당제(糖劑)

con·fec·tion·er [kənfékʃənər] *n.* [C] a person who makes or sells confections.
—[名] 과자 제조 판매인, 과자 장수(제조인)

con·fec·tion·er·y [kənfékʃənèri / -nəri] *n.* (pl. **-er·ies**) **1.** [U] 《*collectively*》 all kinds of candy, ice cream, etc. **2.** [C] a candy store.
—[名] 1. 과자류 2. 과자점

con·fed·er·a·cy [kənféd(ə)rəsi] *n.* [C] (pl. **-cies**) **1.** the act of forming a union. **2.** a union of states or nations.
—[名] 1. 연합, 동맹 2. 연합국, 동맹국

***con·fed·er·ate** [kənféd(ə)rit → *v.*] *adj.* joined together or allied. —*n.* [C] **1.** a person or state joined or allied with another. **2.** a partner in crime. —*vi.*, *vt.* [kənfédərèit] join together; ally. ¶ *~ oneself with another.*①
—[形] 동맹한, 연합의
—[名] 1. 동맹자(국) 2. 공모자
—[自][他] 동맹(연합)하다(시키다) ¶①…와 동맹(공모)하다

con·fed·er·a·tion [kənfèdəréiʃ(ə)n] *n.* [C] countries or nations joined together by agreement.
—[名] 연합(동맹)국, 연방

***con·fer** [kənfə́:r] *vt.*, *vi.* (**-ferred, -fer·ring**) **1.** give. 《~ something *on* or *upon*》 ¶ *~ a title, honor, or medal*
—[他][自] 1. …을 수여하다 2. …와 협의하다 3. …을 참조하다 [N.B.] cf.로 생

upon someone. **2.** talk over together. 《~ ***with*** someone *about*》 **3.** 《in *imperative*》 compare. ⇒[N.B.]
약합

⁑con·fer·ence [kάnf(ə)rəns / kɔ́n-] *n.* **1.** [U] the act of consulting together; consultation. **2.** [C] a meeting for discussion or for making public announcements, esp. to newspaper reporters. ¶*be in ~ with someone*① / *hold a press ~.*②
—[名] 1. 협의, 상담 2. 회의 ¶①…와 회의중이다/②기자회견을 하다

con·fer·ment [kənfə́ːrmənt] *n.* [U] the act of conferring.
—[名] [학위 따위의] 수여

⁑con·fess [kənfés] *vt., vi.* **1.** tell of (one's faults, crimes, etc.); admit; acknowledge. 《~ *that* ...》 ¶*~ one's crime* / *He confessed that he had done wrong.*① / *The prisoner refused to ~.* / *She confessed herself [to be] guilty.*② **2.** acknowledge one's belief or faith in (God, etc.). ¶*He confessed Christ.* **3.** tell of (one's sins), esp. to a priest; (of a priest) hear the confession of (someone). ¶*~ one's sins to God* / *The priest confessed a murderer.*③
—[他][自] 1. …을 고백하다, 자인(자백)하다 ¶①그는 잘못을 저질렀다는 것을 자백했다/②그 여자는 유죄를 인정했다 2. [신앙]을 고백하다 3. [신부·신]에게 참회(고해)하다; [신부가] …의 참회를 듣다 ¶③성직자는 살인범의 참회를 들었다

***confess to** something* or *doing,* acknowledge; admit.
[熟] …을 자인하다

***con·fes·sion** [kənféʃ(ə)n] *n.* [U][C] **1.** the act of confessing. ¶*make a frank ~ of one's crime* / *go to ~.*① **2.** a [written] profession of belief. ¶*a ~ of faith.*②
—[名] 1. 자백, 자인 ¶①고백하러 가다 2. [신앙의] 고백[서], 참회 ¶②신앙의 고백

con·fes·sion·al [kənféʃən(ə)l] *n.* [C] a small room where a priest hears confessions. ***—adj.*** of a confession.
—[名] 참회실, 고해실 —[形] 참회의, 신앙 고백의, 고해의

con·fes·sor [kənfésər] *n.* [C] a person who confesses; a priest who hears confessions.
—[名] 고백자, 참회자; 고해를 듣는 신부, 고해 신부

con·fi·dant [kὰnfidǽnt, ⏑⏑⏑ / kɔ̀nfidǽnt, ⏑⏑⏑] *n.* [C] a person entrusted with knowledge of one's private affairs.
—[名] 친우, 극친한 벗

con·fi·dante [kὰnfidǽnt / kɔ̀nfidǽnt, ⏑⏑⏑] *n.* [C] a close woman friend.
—[名] 여자 친구

con·fide** [kənfáid] *vi.* have trust or faith. 《~ ***in someone》 ¶*~ in each other.*① ***—vt.*** **1.** entrust. 《~ something *to*》 ¶*~ a task to one's son.*② **2.** tell (secrets, etc.) to a trusted person. ¶*~ a secret (one's trouble) to a friend.*
—[自] 신뢰(신임)하다 ¶①서로 신뢰하다 —[他] 1. …을 위탁하다, 맡기다 ¶②아들에게 일을 맡기다 2. [비밀]을 털어놓다

⁑con·fi·dence [kάnfid(ə)ns / kɔ́n-] *n.* **1.** [U] trust; firm belief. 《~ *in*》 ¶*have ~ in the future.*① **2.** [U] firm self-reliance; belief in oneself; boldness; rudeness. ¶*great ~ of success* / *be full of ~.* **3.** [C] a thing told as a secret. ¶*listen to a person's ~.*
—[名] 1. 신용, 신뢰, 신임 ¶①장래에 희망을 걸고 있다 2. 자신; 확신; 대담; 배짱 3. 터놓는 이야기, 비밀

***con·fi·dent** [kάnfid(ə)nt / kɔ́n-] *adj.* **1.** firmly believing; assured; sure. 《~ *of;* ~ *that* ...》 **2.** self-reliant. ¶*a ~ manner (smile).* **3.** bold; impolite.
—[形] 1. 확신하고 있는 2. 자신이 있는 3. 대담한; 뻔뻔스러운, 건방진

con·fi·den·tial [kὰnfidénʃ(ə)l / kɔ̀n-] *adj.* **1.** treated with confidence; trustworthy. ¶*a ~ clerk or servant.* **2.** secret. ¶*a ~ talk* / *a ~ letter*① / *a ~ agent.*② **3.** showing trust. ¶*become ~ with a stranger.*③
—[形] 1. 신임이 되는, 신뢰할 만한 2. 비밀의, 기밀의 ¶①밀서, 비밀 편지/②밀사, 스파이 3. 비밀을 터놓는, 친밀한 ¶③남과 터놓고 이야기하게 되다

con·fi·den·tial·ly [kὰnfidénʃəli / kɔ̀n-] *adv.* in a confidential manner.
—[副] 터놓고; 은밀히

con·fi·dent·ly [kάnfid(ə)ntli / kɔ́n-] *adv.* in a confident or self-assured manner; with confidence or self-assurance.
—[副] 확신을 가지고

con·fid·ing [kənfáidiŋ] *adj.* trusting.
—[形] [남을] 신뢰하는

con·fig·u·ra·tion [kənfìgjuréiʃ(ə)n] *n.* [C] the relative positions of the parts of a thing; the arrangement of parts; the external form or shape.
—[名] [부분의] 배치; 배열

⁑con·fine *n.* [kάnfain / kɔ́n- // →*v.*] 《usu. *pl.*》 **1.** a border [line]; a boundary; an edge. ¶*on the confines of night and day.* **2.** a limit. ¶*on the confines of ruin.*①
—[名] 1. 경계[선], 국경, 변경 2. [행동 따위의] 한계, 한도 ¶①파멸의 갈림길에서

—vt. [kənfáin] **1.** keep (something) within limits; restrict. ¶*His remarks are confined to the subject.* / *I shall ~ myself to saying that* ... **2.** keep (someone) within doors; shut up; imprison. ¶*be confined to one's room.*② **3.** 《usu. in *passive*》 keep (oneself) in bed at childbirth.
—[他] 1. …을 한정하다, 제한하다 2. …을 가두다; 감금하다 ¶②방안에 틀어박혀 있다 3. 해산자리에 눕다

con·fined [kənfáind] *adj.* being shut up or in childbirth.
—[形] 갇혀 있는, 감금된; 산욕(해산자리)에 누운

con·fine·ment [kənfáinmənt] *n.* **1.** [U] the act of confining; the state of being confined. **2.** [U][C] childbirth.
—[名] 1. 감금; 제한; 속박; 틀어박혀 있기 2. 해산

• **con·firm** [kənfə́:rm] *vt.* **1.** make (something) certain. ¶~ *a rumor*① / *The letter from her confirmed what you had told us before.* **2.** make (something) strong; strengthen; fortify. ¶*He was confirmed in his decision.* / *His advice confirmed my decision to go abroad.*② **3.** give a formal agreement to (something, esp. a treaty).
—[他] 1. …을 확실히 하다 ¶①풍문이 사실임을 확인하다 2. [결심 따위]를 굳히다 ¶②그의 조언으로 나는 외국으로 갈 결심을 굳혔다 3. [조약]을 비준하다

con·fir·ma·tion [kὰnfərméiʃ(ə)n] *n.* [U] [C] the act of confirming; the state of being confirmed.
—[名] 확정; 확인; 비준; 확증

con·firmed [kənfə́:rmd] *adj.* **1.** definitely or clearly proved or established; formally recognized. **2.** habitual; constant. ¶*a ~ drunkard* / *a ~ invalid.*①
—[形] 1. 확정된; 비준된 2. 습관이 되어 버린; 만성의 ¶①고질(만성병) 환자

con·fis·cate [kánfiskèit / kɔ́n-] *vt.* seize or take (someone's property) [for public use] by authority.
—[他] …을 몰수(압수 · 징발)하다

con·fis·ca·tion [kὰnfiskéiʃ(ə)n / kɔ̀n-] *n.* [U] [C] the act of confiscating; the state of being confiscated.
—[名] 몰수, 압수, 징발

con·fla·gra·tion [kὰnfləgréiʃ(ə)n / kɔ̀n-] *n.* [C] a great fire.
—[名] 큰 불, 큰 화재

: **con·flict** *n.* [kánflikt / kɔ́n- ‖ →*v.*] [C] **1.** a struggle; a fight. ¶*a ~ between two political parties.* **2.** a sharp disagreement; a collision. ¶*a ~ of opinions* / *a ~ between duty and love* / *in ~ with another opinion.*①
—[名] 1. 투쟁; 전투; 쟁의 2. [사상 · 이해 따위의] 충돌 ¶①남의 의견과 충돌(모순)하여

—*vi.* [kənflíkt] **1.** fight. 《~ *with* someone》 **2.** be in contradiction. 《~ *with* someone or something》 ¶*Our interests conflicted with theirs.*
—[自] 1. 싸우다, 다투다 2. 모순되다

con·flu·ence [kánfluəns / kɔ́n-] *n.* [C] **1.** the place where two rivers meet; the state of this. ¶*The city stands at the ~ of two rivers.*① **2.** a throng; a crowd.
—[名] 1. [강의] 합류[점] ¶①그 도시는 두 강의 합류점에 있다 2. 사람 떼, 군중

con·flu·ent [kánfluənt / kɔ́n-] *adj.* flowing together.
—[形] [강 따위가] 합류하는
—*n.* [C] a river flowing into another.
—[名] 합류하는 강, 지류(支流)

con·flux [kánflʌk / kɔ́n-] *n.* =confluence.

con·form [kənfɔ́:rm] *vt.* make (something) equal or very similar to another; adapt. ¶~ *one's manners (ideas) to those of one's associates.* —*vi.* **1.** be in harmony with what is required. **2.** act according to the law, custom, etc.
—[他] …을 [규준에] 맞추다, 순응(적응)시키다 —[自] 1. 일치하다 2. [규칙 · 관습 따위에] 따라서 행동하다

con·form·a·ble [kənfɔ́:rməbl] *adj.* similar; adapted; obedient. 《~ *to* or *with*》 ¶*be ~ to the wishes of one's parents.*
—[形] 비슷한, 적합한; 순종하는, 온순한

con·for·ma·tion [kὰnfɔ:rméiʃ(ə)n / kɔ̀nfɔ:-] *n.* [C] the act of conforming; the state of being conformed; structure; [U] adaptation.
—[名] 일치, 형상, 구조; 적합

con·form·ist [kənfɔ́:rmist] *n.* [C] **1.** a person who conforms. **2.** a member of the Church of England.
—[名] 1. 준법자 2. 영국 국교도

con·form·i·ty [kənfɔ́:rmiti] *n.* [U] **1.** likeness; agreement. ¶~ *with one's idea.*① **2.** action in agreement with what is usu. accepted, expected by custom, etc.
—[名] 1. 일치, 적합 ¶①남의 생각과의 일치 2. 복종, 준봉(遵奉)

in conformity with, in accordance with.
[熟] …에 따라서, …을 준봉하여

• **con·found** [kɑnfáund, kən- / kən- ‖ → 3.] *vt.* **1.** confuse; mix up (things). ¶*Never ~ right and wrong.*① **2.** astonish; surprise greatly. ¶*He was confounded at the sight of the busy street.*② **3.** [kánfáund / kɔ́n-] 《used to express *anger, disappointment,* etc.》 damn. ¶*Confound it* (or *you*)!③
—[他] 1. …을 혼동하다 ¶①옳고 그름을 혼동하지 마라 2. …을 어리둥절하게 하다 ¶②그는 번잡한 거리를 보고 어리둥절했다 3. …을 저주하다 ¶③제기랄!, 빌어먹을!

con·found·ed [kɑnfáundid, kən- / kən-] *adj.* **1.** confused. **2.** damned; hateful.
—[形] 1. 당황한, 어리둥절한 2. 괘씸한, 밉살스러운

con·fra·ter·ni·ty [kὰnfrətə́:rniti / kɔ̀n-] *n.* [C] (pl. **-ties**) **1.** a brotherhood. **2.** a group of men formed for some purpose, esp. religious or professional.
—[名] 1. 결사(結社) 2. [특히 종교상의] 단체; 조합

• **con·front** [kənfrʌ́nt] *vt.* **1.** stand in front of (someone); face boldly. ¶~ *danger and death.* **2.** bring face to face. **3.** stand opposite to (something).
—[他] 1. …와 마주보게 하다, …와 맞서다 2. …을 대결시키다 3. …의 맞은편에 있다

be confronted with (or ***by***) (=*face*) ***something.***
[熟] …에 직면하다

Con·fu·cian·ism [kənfjú:ʃənìz(ə)m / -ʃjən-] *n.* [U] the system of the moral teachings of Confucius and his followers.
—[名] 공자의 가르침, 유교

• **con·fuse** [kənfjú:z] *vt.* **1.** mix up (things) in the mind;
—[他] 1. …을 혼란시키다 2. …을 당황

throw (ideas, etc.) into disorder. ¶*I was confused by my errors.* **2.** puzzle. ¶*be* (or *become, get*) *confused*① / *feel confused.*② **3.** mistake (one thing) for another. ¶*~ liberty with license.*③
하게 하다 ¶①당황하다, 어리둥절하다 /②난처해하다 3. …을 혼동하다, 잘못 알다 ¶③자유와 방종을 혼동하다

con·fus·ed·ly [kənfjú:z(i)dli] *adv.* in a confused manner.
—[副] 난잡하게, 당황하여

con·fus·ing [kənfjú:ziŋ] *adj.* that confuses, puzzles, disorders, etc.
—[形] 혼란시키는 [듯한]

:con·fu·sion [kənfjú:ʒ(ə)n] *n.* [U] **1.** the act of confusing. ¶*~ of ideas.*① **2.** the state of being confused; embarrassment; disorder. ¶*be thrown into ~*② / *in ~*③ / *in the ~ of the moment.*④ **3.** the act of mistaking one thing for another.
—[名] 1. 혼란시키기, 당황하게 하기 ¶①사상의 혼란 2. 당황; 혼란, 난잡 ¶②혼란에 빠지다/③당황하여/④혼란을 틈타서 3. 혼동

con·fu·ta·tion [kànfju(:)téiʃ(ə)n / kɔ̀n-] *n.* [U] the act of confuting; something that confutes.
—[名] 설파, 논박

con·fute [kənfjú:t] *vt.* prove (something) to be false; disprove; prove (someone) to be wrong.
—[他] …을 논박하다, 꺽소리 못하게 하다

con·geal [kəndʒí:l] *vt.* freeze; make (one's blood) stiff because of horror. ¶*My blood was congealed at the sight of the scene.*① **—*vi.*** freeze; stiffen; become hard because of cold.
—[他] …을 얼리다; 오싹하게 하다 ¶①그 광경을 보고 전신의 피가 얼어붙었다 —[自] 얼다, 응결하다

con·gen·ial [kəndʒí:niəl] *adj.* **1.** having the same tastes and interests; getting on well together. ¶*~ friends.* **2.** agreeable; fit. ¶*a task ~ to one's personality.*①
—[形] 1. 마음이 맞는, 같은 성질의 2. 성미에 맞는, 쾌적한 ¶①성미에 맞는 일

con·gen·i·tal [kəndʒénit(ə)l] *adj.* (of diseases, defects, etc.) existing from one's birth; inherited; by nature. ¶*a ~ disease / ~ idiocy.*①
—[形] [병·결점 따위가] 타고난, 선천적인 ¶①선천적 백치

con·ger [káŋgər / kɔ́ŋgə] *n.* [C] a large sea eel.
—[名] 붕장어

con·gest [kəndʒést] *vt.* **1.** fill (something) too full; pack densely; ⟪usu. in *passive*⟫ overcrowd. ¶*The traffic was congested.* **2.** cause too much blood to gather in (one part of the body). ¶*The doctor said that my lungs were congested.*① **—*vi.*** become too full of blood.
—[他] 1. …을 붐비게 하다; 빽빽이 채워넣다 2. …을 충혈시키다 ¶①그 의사는 나의 폐가 울혈돼 있다고 말하였다 —[自] 충혈하다

con·gest·ed [kəndʒéstid] *adj.* **1.** too much; overcrowded. **2.** containing too much blood.
—[形] 1. 붐비는, 혼잡한 2. 충혈한

con·ges·tion [kəndʒéstʃ(ə)n] *n.* [U] **1.** the state of being congested. **2.** too much blood in one part of the body.
—[名] 1. 혼잡, 밀집 2. 충혈, 울혈

con·glom·er·ate *v.* [kənglámərèit / -glɔ́m- // → *adj., n.*] *vi.* gather into a rounded mass. **—*vt.*** gather (things) into a rounded mass.
—[自] 둥글게 뭉쳐지다 —[他] …을 둥글게 뭉치다

—*adj.* [kənglámərit / -glɔ́m-] **1.** gathered in a rounded mass. **2.** (of rock) made up of many materials gathered from various sources.
—[形] 1. 둥글게 뭉쳐진, 집괴(集塊) 모양의 2. 역암성(礫岩性)의

—*n.* [kənglámərit / -glɔ́m-] [C] **1.** a mass made up of separate substances. **2.** rock made up of small stones.
—[名] 1. 집성물(集成物) 2. 역암(礫岩)

con·glom·er·a·tion [kənglàməréiʃ(ə)n / -glɔ̀m-] *n.* **1.** [U] the act of conglomerating; the state of being conglomerated. **2.** [C] a mixed-up mass of various things; a cluster.
—[名] 1. 집성 2. 집괴물, 응괴물

·con·grat·u·late [kəngrǽtʃulèit / -grǽtju-] *vt.* express one's joy at the happiness or good fortune of another. ⟪~ someone *on* or *upon*⟫ ¶*I ~ you on your success.*①
—[他] …을 축하(경하)하다 ¶①당신의 성공을 축하합니다

congratulate** oneself **on (or ***upon***) (=*be pleased with; be proud of*) *something.*
[熟] …을 기뻐하다, 자랑하다

·con·grat·u·la·tion [kəngræ̀tʃuléiʃ(ə)n / -grætju-] *n.* **1.** [U] the act of congratulating. **2.** [C] ⟪usu. *pl.*⟫ an expression of pleasure at another's happiness or good fortune. ¶*Congratulations!*① / *offer one's congratulations.*②
—[名] 1. 축하, 경축 2. 축사, 축하의 말 ¶①축하합니다!/②축사를 말하다

con·grat·u·la·to·ry [kəngrǽtʃulətɔ̀:ri / -grǽtjulət(ə)ri] *adj.* expressing congratulations. ¶*a ~ speech.*
—[形] 축하의, 경축의

con·gre·gate [káŋgrigèit / kɔ́ŋ-] *vi.* gather; come together in a great number. **—*vt.*** gather.
—[自] [특히 대집단으로] 모이다 —[他] …을 모으다

con·gre·ga·tion [kàŋgrigéiʃ(ə)n / kɔ̀ŋ-] *n.* [C] **1.** [U] the act of congregating; the state of being congregated. **2.** a gathering of people; an assembly. **3.** ⟪*collectively*⟫
—[名] 1. 집합 2. 회합 3. [교회의] 회중(會衆) [N.B.] 음악회·강연회 따위의 청중은 audience

C

a group of people attending a church service. ⇒[N.B.]

con·gre·ga·tion·al [kàŋgrigéiʃən(ə)l / kɔ̀ŋ-] *adj.* of a meeting or congregation.
—[形] 집합의, 회중의

‡ **con·gress** [káŋgris / kɔ́ŋgres] *n.* **1.** [C] a meeting of representatives for discussion. **2.** ⦅usu. *C-*⦆ the national lawmaking body, as of the United States.
—[名] 1. [대표자의] 회의, 대회 2. [미국 등의] 국회, 의회

con·gres·sion·al [kəŋgréʃən(ə)l / kɔŋ-] *adj.* **1.** of a congress. **2.** ⦅usu. *C-*⦆ of the Congress of the United States.
—[形] 1. 회의의, 집회의 2. 미국 의회의

con·gress·man [káŋgrismən / kɔ́ŋgres-] *n.* [C] (pl. **-men** [-mən]) ⦅often *C-*⦆ **1.** a male member of Congress. **2.** a male member of the House of Representatives of the United States.
—[名] 1. 국회 의원 2. [미국의] 하원 의원

con·gru·ence [káŋgruəns / kɔ́ŋ-], **-en·cy** [-ənsi] *n.* [U] agreement; harmony.
—[名] 일치, 적합

con·gru·ent [káŋgruənt / kɔ́ŋ-] *adj.* **1.** agreeing; fit. **2.** (*Geometry*) of the same shape and size.
—[形] 1. 일치하는, 적합하는 2. 합동의

con·ic [kánik / kɔ́n-], **-i·cal** [-ik(ə)l] *adj.* of a cone; shaped like a cone. ▷**con·i·cal·ly** [-k(ə)li] *adv.*
—[形] 원추의, 원추형의

co·ni·fer [kóunifər, +*U.S.* káni-, +*Brit.* kɔ́ni-] *n.* [C] a tree such as the pine and cypress, most of which are evergreen and bear cones.
—[名] 침엽수, 구과(毬果) 식물(소나무·삼목 따위)

co·nif·er·ous [kounífərəs] *adj.* bearing cones.
—[形] 구과(毬果)를 맺는

conj. conjugation; conjunction; conjunctive.

con·jec·tur·al [kəndʒéktʃ(ə)rəl] *adj.* doubtful; having doubt.
—[形] 추측의, 억측적인

con·jec·ture [kəndʒéktʃər] *n.* [C] a guess; the act of guessing. —*vt., vi.* guess; make a guess.
—[名] 추측, 억측 —[他][自] 추측하다, 억측하다

con·join [kəndʒɔ́in] *vi., vt.* join together; become joined; unite; combine. ▷**con·join·er** [-ər] *n.*
—[自][他] 합하다, 결합하다, …을 합치다

con·joint [kəndʒɔ́int / kɔ́ndʒɔint, kɔ́ndʒɔ́int] *adj.* joined together; united; combined; associated. ¶*a ~ action.*①
—[形] 결합한, 공동의, 연합의 ¶①연대 행위, 공동 동작

con·ju·gal [kándʒug(ə)l / kɔ́n-] *adj.* **1.** married; of marriage. **2.** of husband and wife. ¶*~ affection.*① ▷**con·ju·gal·ly** [-i] *adv.*
—[形] 1. 혼인의 2. 부부의 ¶①부부애

con·ju·gate *v.* [kándʒugèit / kɔ́n- ‖ →*adj.*] *vt.* give the forms of (a verb) in regard to number, tense, etc. —*vi.* join together; unite. —*adj.* [kándʒugit, -gèit / kɔ́n-] **1.** joined together. **2.** (of words) derived from the same root. ¶*a ~ word.*①
—[他] [동사]를 활용(변화)시키다 —[自] 결합(접합)하다 —[形] 1. 결합한 2. 동근(同根)의, 어원이 같은 ¶①동근어

con·ju·ga·tion [kàndʒugéiʃ(ə)n / kɔ̀n-] *n.* **1.** [U][C] (*Grammar*) the systematic arrangement of verb forms. ¶*regular* (*irregular*) *~.*① **2.** [U][C] the act of conjugating; the state of being conjugated; connection. **3.** [U] the union of two cells of the same type.
—[名] ⦅文法⦆ 1. 동사의 활용, [어형] 변화 ¶①규칙(불규칙) 활용 2. 결합, 연결 3. 세포의 접합

* **con·junc·tion** [kəndʒʌ́ŋkʃ(ə)n] *n.* **1.** [U] the state of being joined together; union; combination. **2.** [C] (*Grammar*) a word that connects words, phrases, clauses, or sentences, such as *and, or* and *but.*
—[名] 1. 결합, 연락 2. 접속사

in conjunction with, together with.
[熟] …와 함께, 연속하여

con·junc·tive [kəndʒʌ́ŋktiv] *adj.* **1.** joining together; connecting. **2.** words, phrases, or clauses connecting in both meaning and construction. ¶*a ~ adverb.*①
—[形] 1. 연결하는, 접속하는 2. [낱말 따위가] 접속 작용이 있는, 접속의 ¶①접속부사

con·jure [kʌ́ndʒər →2.] *vt.* **1.** force (a spirit, etc.) to appear by using magic; cause (something) to appear esp. by moving the hand. ¶*~ a pigeon out of an empty hat.* **2.** [kəndʒúər] make a serious appeal to (someone); beg (someone) earnestly. ¶*I ~ you not to betray me.*① —*vi.* practice magic; perform a trick; call upon a devil by means of a spell.
—[他] 1. [영혼 따위]를 마법을 써서 나타나게 하다; …을 요술을 써서 나오게 하다; 2. …을 기원하다, 탄원하다 ¶①나를 배반하지 말기를 간청합니다 —[自] 마법을 쓰다, 요술을 부리다; [주문을 외어] 귀신을 불러내다

conjure up, cause (something) to appear as a picture in the mind.
[熟] …을 마음속에 떠오르게 하다, 상상으로 그리다

con·jur·er [kʌ́ndʒərər], **-or** *n.* [C] **1.** a magician. **2.** a person who performs tricks; a juggler.
—[名] 마술사, 요술사

Conn. Connecticut.

:con·nect [kənékt] *vt.* **1.** join (one thing) to another; unite; link. ⟪~ one thing *to* or *with*⟫ ¶*~ the cities by a railroad* / *~ someone with New York*① / *Let's ~ this wire to that one.* **2.** join in some business or by a personal relationship. ¶*He is connected with the Johnsons.*② **3.** think of (one thing) with another; associate. **—*vi.*** (of trains, etc.) run so that passengers can change from one to another without delay. ¶*This train connects with another at* Taegu.③

—[他] 1. …을 잇다, 연결하다 ¶①전화를 뉴우요오크로 연결하다 2. …와 관계를 맺다, 친척 관계에 있다 ¶②그는 존슨 집안과 친척 관계에 있다 3. …을 연상하다 —[自] [기차·버스가] 접속하다, 연락하다 ¶③이 열차는 대구에서 딴 열차와 접속한다

Con·nect·i·cut [kənétikət] *n.* a northeastern State of the United States. ⇒[N.B.]

—[名] 미국 동북부의 주 [N.B.] Conn. 이라 생략함. 주도(州都)는 Hartford

:con·nec·tion [kənékʃ(ə)n] *n.* [C] **1.** [C][U] the act of connecting; the condition of being connected; union; link. ¶*the ~ of trains.* **2.** something that joins other things together. **3.** [U] a relation; relationship; communication. ¶*I have no ~ with him.*① **4.** a relative, esp. by marriage. **5.** [U] the meeting of trains, buses, etc. that enables passengers to change vehicles within a short time. ¶*There is a bus ~ with this train.*② **6.** a group of people.

1) ***in connection with,*** in regard to.

2) ***in this connection,*** about this matter.

—[名] 1. 결합, 연락, 접속 2. 접속하는 것, 연결 기구 3. 관계; 교제 ¶①나는 그와는 관계가 없다 4. 친척 5. [열차·기선 따위의] 접속 ¶②이 열차는 버스와의 접속이 있다 6. 단체; 종파, 교파

[熟] 1)…와 관련하여 2)이 점에 있어서[는], 덧붙여 말하면

con·nec·tive [kənéktiv] *adj.* joining; serving to connect. **—*n.*** [C] **1.** a thing that connects. **2.** a word used to connect words, phrases, and clauses.

—[形] 접속의, 결합성의 —[名] 1. 연결물 2. 연결사(詞)

con·nex·ion [kənékʃ(ə)n] *n.* (*Brit.*) =connection.

con·ning tower [kániŋtàuər / kɔ́niŋtàuə] *n.* a small tower on the deck of a warship or a submarine, from which the ship is guided and observations are made.

—[名] [군함의] 사령탑, [잠수함의] 전망탑

con·niv·ance [kənáiv(ə)ns] *n.* [U] the act of conniving.

—[名] 못 본 체하기, 묵인

con·nive [kənáiv] *vi.* **1.** shut one's eyes to something wrong; pretend to be unaware of something. ⟪~ *at* something⟫ ¶*~ at the violation of the rule.*① **2.** act together secretly. ⟪~ *with* someone⟫

—[自] 1. [나쁜 일 따위를] 보고도 못 본 체하다, 묵인하다 ¶①규칙 위반을 묵인하다 2. 공모하다

con·nois·seur [kànisə́:r / kɔ̀nisə́:] *n.* [C] an expert; a fault-finding judge. ¶*a ~ of fine arts.*

—[名] 감식가, 감정가, 전문가

con·no·ta·tion [kànoutéiʃ(ə)n / kɔ̀n-] *n.* [U][C] the act of connoting; that which is connoted; an implication.

—[名] 언외(言外)의 뜻, 함축

con·note [kənóut / kɔn-] *vt.* suggest (something) in addition to the simple meaning; imply; (*colloq.*) mean.

—[他] [딴 뜻]을 의미하다, 함축하다; …을 뜻하다

con·nu·bi·al [kən(j)ú:biəl / -njú:biəl] *adj.* of marriage; married. ¶*~ rites*① / *~ love.*

—[形] 혼인의, 결혼의, 부부의 ¶①혼인의 의식

:con·quer [káŋkər / kɔ́ŋkə] *vt.* **1.** win the victory over (the enemy, etc.) in war. **2.** overcome (something) by force; gain; defeat. ¶*~ bad habits*① / *~ passions*② / *~ Mt. Everest.* **—*vi.*** be victorious; gain a victory.

—[他] 1. …와 싸워서 이기다 2. …을 정복하다, …을 극복하다 ¶①악습을 타파하다/②격정을 억제하다 —[自] 승리를 거두다

·con·quer·or [káŋkərər / kɔ́ŋkərə] *n.* **1.** [C] a person who conquers; a victor. **2.** ⟪*the C-*⟫ William I, of Normandy, who conquered England in 1066.

—[名] 1. 정복자, 승리자 2. Normandy 공 William 1세

·con·quest [kánkwest, káŋ- / kɔ́ŋ-] *n.* **1.** [U] the act of conquering; victory; subjugation. **2.** [C] anything conquered. ¶*the conquests of Napoleon.*① **3.** [C] a person whose love or favor has been won.

make a conquest of, ⓐ conquer. ⓑ win the love of (someone).

—[名] 1. 정복 2. 정복된 것, 획득한 것 (토지·사람) ¶①나폴레옹의 정복 지방 3. 애정을 획득한 사람

[熟] ⓐ…을 정복하다 ⓑ…의 사랑을 획득하다

con·san·guin·i·ty [kànsæŋgwíniti / kɔ̀n-] *n.* [U] relationship by blood or birth; kinship.

—[名] 혈족, 혈연, 동족

:con·science [kánʃ(ə)ns / kɔ́n-] *n.* [U][C] the sense of right and wrong; a moral judgment or sense. ¶*a merchant with little ~.*① ▷**con·science·less** [-lis] *adj.*

1) ***for conscience' sake,*** to satisfy one's conscience.

2) ***have something on one's conscience,*** have a sense of having done wrong.

3) ***in*** [***all***] ***conscience,*** surely; certainly; fairly.

4) ***upon one's conscience,*** ⟪used as *an oath*⟫ surely; certainly.

—[名] 양심, 선악의 관념; 도의심 ¶①비양심적인 상인

[熟] 1)마음에 걸려, 양심상, 제발 2)[어떤 일이] 양심에 걸리다 3)확실히, 공정히 4)양심에 맹세코, 꼭

con·science-strick·en [kánʃ(ə)nsstrìk(ə)n / kɔ́n-] *adj.* suffering from a feeling of having done something wrong.
—[形] 양심의 가책을 받은, 마음에 걸리는

con·sci·en·tious [kànʃiénʃəs / kɔ̀n-] *adj.* **1.** careful to act according to conscience. ¶*a ~ judge* / *a ~ worker.* **2.** done carefully and honestly.
—[形] 1. 양심적인 2. 성실한, 고지식한

conscientious objector [--ˊ- -ˊ-] *n.* a person who does not take an active part in warfare because he believes that fighting is sinful.
—[名] 양심적 참전(參戰) 거부자[종교나 주의(主義) 관계로 전쟁을 반대하는 사람]

⁑ **con·scious** [kánʃəs / kɔ́n-] *adj.* **1.** aware of something; knowing. ↔unconscious ¶*Man is a ~ being.* **2.** able to feel; sensible; sane. ¶*He became ~.*① / *Father was ~ to the last.* **3.** intentional; intended. ¶*a ~ lie.* **4.** self-conscious; shy.
be conscious of, know (someone's good points, etc.).
—[形] 1. …을 의식하고 있는, 알아차리고 있는 2. 지각이 있는, 제정신인 ¶①그는 정신이 들었다 3. 의식적인, 자각하고 있는 4. 자의식이 강한, 수줍어하는
[熟] …을 의식하다, 알아차리다

con·scious·ly [kánʃəsli / kɔ́n-] *adv.* in a conscious manner; intentionally.
—[副] 의식적으로, 자각하여

* **con·scious·ness** [kánʃəsnis / kɔ́n-] *n.* [U] **1.** 《sometimes *a ~*》 the state of being conscious; awareness. ¶*lose ~*① / *a stream of ~.*② **2.** all one's ideas and feelings.
—[名] 1. 의식, 자각 ¶①의식을 잃다/②의식의 흐름 2. 지각

con·script *vt.* [kənskrípt →*adj., n.*] force (someone) by law to serve in the army or navy; draft; take (someone) for government service. —*adj.* [kánskript / kɔ́n-] conscripted; drafted. —*n.* [kánskript / kɔ́n-] [C] a conscripted soldier or sailor.
—[他] …을 징병으로 뽑다, 징집하다 —[形] 병적에 편입된, 징집된, —[名] 징집병, 신병

con·scrip·tion [kənskrípʃ(ə)n] *n.* [U] **1.** the system by which a person is forced to serve in the army or navy; draft. **2.** the act or system of forcing contributions of money, labor, etc. to the government, esp. during wartime.
—[名] 1. 징병[제도] 2. [전시중의 금전·노동력 따위의] 징용, 징발

con·se·crate [kánsikrèit / kɔ́n-] *vt.* **1.** set (something) apart as sacred; make (something) holy or sacred. **2.** devote (something) to a special purpose.
—[他] 1. …을 신성하게 하다, 정하게 하다 2. …을 바치다, 봉헌(奉獻)하다

con·se·cra·tion [kànsikréiʃ(ə)n / kɔ̀n-] *n.* [U] **1.** the act of consecrating; the condition of having been consecrated. **2.** the ceremony of placing someone in a holy office, esp. that of a bishop.
—[名] 1. 신성화, 정화(淨化); 봉헌, 봉납 2. 성직 수임[식]

con·sec·u·tive [kənsékjutiv] *adj.* **1.** following continuously. ¶*for five ~ years* / *win four ~ victories.*① **2.** made up of parts that follow each other in regular order. ¶*~ thinking.*② ▷**con·sec·u·tive·ly** [-li] *adv.*
—[形] 1. 연속하는, 잇따른 ¶①4연승하다 2. 연락(맥락) 있는 ¶②논리적 일관성이 있는 생각

con·sen·sus [kənsénsəs] *n.* [C] a general agreement of opinion, feeling, etc. ¶*a ~ of opinion.*①
—[名] [의견·감정 따위의] 일치, 합의 ¶①다수 의견; 여론

⁑ **con·sent** [kənsént] *vi.* agree to opinions, etc. 《*~ to* something; *~ to do; ~ that …*》 ↔disapprove ¶*~ to a plan* / *the consenting party.*①
—*n.* [U] agreement; permission. ¶*with one ~*②.
1) ***age of consent,*** age at which the law recognizes one's right to marry, etc.
2) ***by common*** (or ***general, universal***) ***consent,*** as everyone agrees.
—[自] [의견에] 동의하다, 승낙하다 ¶①찬성측
—[名] 동의, 승낙 ¶②만장일치로
[熟] 1)승낙 연령(결혼이 법적으로 승인되는 나이) 2)만장일치로, 이의 없이

⁑ **con·se·quence** [kánsikwèns, -wəns / kɔ́ns(i)kwəns] *n.* **1.** [C] a result; an effect. **2.** [U] importance; value. ¶*a matter of great ~* / *a man of ~.*① **3.** [C] a logical result.
1) ***in consequence,*** as a result; therefore; hence.
2) ***in consequence of,*** as a result of; on account of.
3) ***of consequence,*** important. ¶*It is of no ~.*②
4) ***take the consequences,*** accept what happens because of one's own action.
—[名] 1. [필연의] 결과, 영향 2. [사회적] 중요성 ¶①사회적으로 중요한 사람 3. 귀결, 결론
[熟] 1)그 결과로서, 그러므로, 그런 까닭에 2)…의 결과 3)유력한, 중대한 ¶②그것은 중요하지 않다 4)[자기 행위의] 결과를 달게 받다

con·se·quent [kánsikwènt, -wənt / kɔ́ns(i)kwənt] *adj.* **1.** following as an effect or result. 《*~ on, upon, to*》 ¶*the confusion ~ upon the conflagration.*① **2.** logically consistent. —*n.* [C] a result; an effect.
—[形] 1. 결과로서 생기는 ¶①큰 화재의 결과 일어나는 당연한 혼란 2. 논리상 필연적인 —[名] 결과

con·se·quen·tial [kànsikwénʃ(ə)l / kɔ̀n-] *adj.* **1.** following as a result. ¶*~ damages.*① **2.** self-important.
—[形] 1. 결과로서 일어나는, 필연의; 간접의 ¶①간접적 손해 2. 거만한, 거드름 피우는

* **con·se·quent·ly** [kánsikwèntli, -wənt- / kɔ́nsikwənt-] *adv.* as a result; therefore.
—[副] 결과로서, 따라서

con·ser·va·tion [kànsərvéiʃ(ə)n / kɔ̀nsə(ː)-] *n.* [U] the prevention of waste, loss or damage with regard to forests, rivers, etc., esp. those under official protection and care; protection from loss or from being used up. ↔dissipation
—[名] [삼림·하천 따위의] 보호, 보존

con·serv·a·tism [kənsə́ːrvətìz(ə)m] *n.* [U] oppositon to change; the principles of a conservative party.
—[名] 보수주의, 보수 기질; 보수당의 주의

* **con·serv·a·tive** [kənsə́ːrvətiv] *adj.* **1.** opposed to change; preserving. ¶~ *policy.* **2.** 《often *C-*》 of the major political party in Great Britain or Canada. ¶*the Conservative Party.*① **3.** (*colloq.*) moderate; careful; cautious. ¶~ *estimates.*②
—[形] 1. 보수적인, 보존력이 있는 2. [영국·캐나다의] 보수당의 ¶①보수당 3.《口》온건한, 중용(中庸)의, 조심성있는, 신중한 ¶②줄잡은 어림

—*n.* [C] **1.** a conservative person. **2.** 《often *C-*》 a member of the Conservative Party in Great Britain or Canada. ▷**con·serv·a·tive·ly** [-li] *adv.*
—[名] 1. 보수주의자 2. [영국·캐나다의] 보수당원

con·ser·va·toire [kənsə̀ːrvətwáːr / kənsə́ːvətwàː] *n.* [C] a public school for teaching music and the arts.
—[名] [특히 유럽에서] 공립 예술(음악·미술)학교

con·ser·va·to·ry [kənsə́ːrvətɔ̀ːri / -sə́ːvət(ə)ri] *n.* [C] (pl. **-ries**) **1.** a greenhouse or room covered with glass, for growing and showing flowers, plants, etc. **2.** (*U.S.*) a school of music. —*adj.* preservative.
—[名] 1. 온실, 식물실 2.《美》음악학교
—[形] 보존하는, 보존성의

con·serve *vt.* [kənsə́ːrv → *n.*] **1.** keep (something) from change, loss or decay; keep (something) unchanged. ¶~ *one's health*① / ~ *money for future use.* **2.** keep (fruit) with sugar. —*n.* [kənsə́ːrv, +*U.S.* kánsəːrv, +*Brit.* kɔ́nsəːv] 《usu. *pl.*》 fruit preserved in sugar; jam.
—[他] 1. …을 보존하다 ¶①건강을 유지하다 2. [과일]을 설탕에 재다
—[名] 설탕에 잰 과일, 잼

⁑ **con·sid·er** [kənsídər] *vt.* **1.** think about (something) in order to understand it; think over. ¶~ *a problem before coming to a decision.* **2.** allow for (something); take (someone) into account. ¶~ *the feeling of others* / ~ *the poor and helpless.*① **3.** think (someone) to be something; regard as. 《~ someone [*to be*] *a fool*, etc.》 ¶*I* ~ *Shakespeare the greatest dramatist.* ⇒[usage]
all things considered, taking everything into account.
—[他] 1. …을 고찰하다, 숙고하다 2. …을 참작하다, 배려하다, 고려에 넣다 ¶①가난하고 의지할 곳 없는 사람을 생각해 주다 3. …을 […이라고] 생각하다, …이라고 여기다 (간주하다) [usage] consider Shakespeare as …와 같이 as를 쓰는 것은 틀림
[熟] 만사를 고려하여

⁑ **con·sid·er·a·ble** [kənsíd(ə)rəbl] *adj.* **1.** worth thinking about; important. ¶*The matter is* ~. **2.** not a little; much. ¶*a* ~ *distance*① / *She gets a* ~ *income.*
—[形] 1. 고려에 넣을 만한; 중요한 2. 적지 않은, 상당한 ¶①상당한 거리

* **con·sid·er·a·bly** [kənsídər(ə)bli] *adv.* a good deal; much.
—[副] 상당히, 꽤

con·sid·er·ate [kənsídərit] *adj.* thoughtful of others and their feelings; careful. ¶*It is very* ~ *of her to have said so.*① ▷**con·sid·er·ate·ly** [-li] *adv.*
—[形] 이해심(동정심) 있는, 사려깊은, 신중한 ¶①그녀가 그렇게 말했다니 참 사려깊은 일이다

⁑ **con·sid·er·a·tion** [kənsìdəréiʃ(ə)n] *n.* **1.** [U] the act of thinking in order to understand; careful thought. ¶*after due* ~.① **2.** [C] something thought of as a reason. ¶*the first* ~.② **3.** [C] money or payment; a reward. ¶*He did it for a* ~.③ **4.** [U] thoughtful care for someone or of something. ¶*show* ~ *for someone.*④ **5.** [U] importance.
1) ***in consideration of,*** ⓐ on account of. ⓑ in return for.
2) ***leave something out of consideration,*** make light of or neglect something.
3) ***on no consideration,*** in no case; not at all; never.
4) ***take something into consideration,*** think about something allow something to be a possible cause, etc.
5) ***under consideration,*** being thought about; being considered. ¶*The plan is under* ~.⑤
—[名] 1. 고려, 고찰, 숙고 ¶①심사숙고한 뒤에 2. 고려해야 할 일 ¶②제1 요건 3. 보수, 팁 ¶③그는 보수를 바라고 그것을 했다 4. 동정, 이해, 참작 ¶④…에게 동정(이해심)을 표하다 5. 중요성
[熟] 1)ⓐ…때문에, …이므로 ⓑ…의 보수(대가)로서 2)…을 도외시하다 3)결코 … 않는 4)…을 고려하다, 참작하다 5)고려중의 ¶⑤그 안은 심의중이다

* **con·sid·er·ing** [kənsíd(ə)riŋ] *prep.* taking into account; in view of something. ¶*Considering her age, she has done well.*① —*adv.* taking everything into account.
—[前] …을 고려하면, …으로서는 ¶①그녀는 나이에 비해서는 훌륭히 해냈다 —[副] [그런 대로] 비교적

con·sign [kənsáin] *vt.* **1.** hand over. ¶*The thief was consigned to jail.*① **2.** put (someone or something) into another's care; entrust. ¶~ *a child to a nurse* / ~
—[他] 1. …을 넘겨주다, 인도하다 ¶①그 도둑은 형무소에 인도되었다 2. …을 위탁하다; 맡기다 3. …을 보내다,

C

money to a bank. **3.** send; deliver. ¶~ *goods by ship.*
발송하다

con·sign·ee [kɑ̀nsainíː / kɔ̀n-] *n.* [C] a person to whom goods are consigned. ↔consignor
—[名] 하물 위탁 판매인; 하물 인수인

con·sign·ment [kənsáinmənt] *n.* **1.** [U] the act of consigning; the state of being consigned. **2.** [C] goods sent to a trader for selling.
—[名] 1. 위탁 2. 위탁 하물, 적송품(積送品), 위탁 판매품

con·sign·or [kənsáinər] *n.* [C] a person who consigns goods to another. ↔consignee
—[名] 위탁자, 하송인(荷送人), 하주

⁑**con·sist** [kənsíst] *vi.* **1.** be made up; be formed. 《~ *of* things》 ¶*Most books ~ of several chapters.* **2.** be contained. 《~ *in* something》 ¶*Happiness consists in contentment.*① **3.** agree; be in harmony. 《~ *with* something》 ¶*Health consists with temperance.*②
—[自] 1. [...으로] 이루어지다 2. [...에] 있다 ¶①행복은 만족에 있다 3. [...와] 일치하다, 양립(兩立)하다 ¶②건강은 금주(禁酒)와 양립한다

con·sist·ence [kənsíst(ə)ns], **-en·cy** [-(ə)nsi] *n.* [U] **1.** the state of firmness; stiffness. **2.** harmony; agreement; accordance. **3.** the degree of firmness or stiffness, as of a liquid.
—[名] 1. 견실[성], 견고함 2. 일치, 일관성, 모순이 없음 3. 농도, 밀도

***con·sist·ent** [kənsíst(ə)nt] *adj.* **1.** continuing without change; agreeing with the same rules, etc. ¶*This is ~ with your principles.* **2.** in agreement; in accord with something. ↔contradictory ¶*This is not ~ with what you said yesterday.* / *He is not ~ in his action.*①
—[形] 1. 시종일관한, 양립(兩立)해 있는 2. 일치하는, 모순이 없는 ¶①그의 언행에는 일치성이 없다

con·sist·ent·ly [kənsíst(ə)ntli] *adv.* in a consistent manner.
—[副] 모순 없이, 시종일관하여, 견실하게

con·so·la·tion [kɑ̀nsəléiʃ(ə)n / kɔ̀n-] *n.* **1.** [U] comfort. **2.** [C] a person or thing that consoles.
—[名] 1. 위안, 위로 2. 위안이 되는 것(사람)

con·sol·a·to·ry [kənsɑ́lətɔ̀ːri / -sɔ́lət(ə)ri] *adj.* comforting; consoling. ¶*a ~ letter.*
—[形] 위안의, 위문의

***con·sole**[1] [kənsóul] *vt.* comfort; cheer up. ¶~ *one's friend in his sorrow* / ~ *oneself by doing.*①
—[他] ...을 위로하다, 위문하다 ¶①...하여 자신을 위로하다

con·sole[2] [kɑ́nsoul / kɔ́n-] *n.* [C] **1.** the part of a pipe organ at which the organist sits, containing the keyboard, stops, and pedals. **2.** a radio or television cabinet. **3.** (of a building) a heavy, ornamental bracket. **4.** a table to be placed against a wall.
—[名] 1. [파이프 오르간의] 연주대 2. [라디오·텔레비전의] 캐비닛 3. [건물의] 운각(雲刻) 까치발 4. 벽에 기대 세운 테이블

con·sol·i·date [kənsɑ́lidèit / -sɔ́l-] *vt.* **1.** make (something) firm or strong; strengthen. **2.** unite; combine. 《~ many banks, companies, etc. *into* one》 **3.** make (something) solid. **—*vi.*** become solid or strong.
—[他] 1. ...을 굳게(튼튼하게) 하다, 강화하다 2. [회사 따위]를 합병하다, 통합하다 3. ...을 굳히다 —[自] 굳어지다, 튼튼해지다

con·sol·i·da·tion [kənsɑ̀lidéiʃ(ə)n / -sɔ̀l-] *n.* [U] the act of consolidating; the state of being consolidated; combination. ¶~ *of public loans.*①
—[名] 강화; 합병, 통합 ¶①공채(公債)의 통합

con·som·me [kɑ̀nsəméi / kənsɔ́mei] *n.* [U] a clear, strong meat soup.
—[名] 콘소메(맑은 수우프)

con·so·nance [kɑ́nsənəns / kɔ́n-] *n.* [U] **1.** harmony; agreement; accordance. ¶*act in ~ with custom.*① **2.** harmony of sounds; concordant. ↔dissonance
—[名] 1. 조화, 일치 ¶①습관대로 행동하다 2. 협화음

con·so·nant** [kɑ́nsənənt / kɔ́n-] *n.* [C] **1.** a letter of the alphabet other than ***a, e, i, o, u. (*cf.* vowel) **2.** a sound that such a letter represents. **—*adj.*** **1.** harmonious; in accordance to or with something. **2.** agreeing in sound. ▷**con·so·nant·ly** [-li] *adv.*
—[名] 1. 자음자(子音字) 2. 자음 —[形] 1. 일치하는, 조화하는 2. 협화음의

con·sort [kɑ́nsɔːrt / kɔ́n- ‖ → *v.*] *n.* [C] **1.** a husband or wife, esp. of a king, queen or ruler. **2.** a partner. **3.** a ship sailing with another. **—*vi.*** [kənsɔ́ːrt] **1.** associate with someone; go well. 《~ *with* someone》 **2.** agree; accord.
—[名] 1. [특히 국왕·여왕의] 배우자 2. 동료, 짝 3. 요선(僚船) —[自] 1. 사귀다 2. 일치하다, 조화하다

con·spec·tus [kənspéktəs] *n.* [C] a general view of a subject; an outline of a subject.
—[名] 개관(概觀); 개요

***con·spic·u·ous** [kənspíkjuəs] *adj.* **1.** easily seen; clearly visible. ↔obscure ¶*a ~ place.*① **2.** worthy of notice; remarkable. ¶*a ~ man* / *cut a ~ figure.*②
—[形] 1. 눈에 잘 띄는, 똑똑히 보이는, 남의 눈을 끄는 ¶①남의 눈에 띄는 장소 2. 현저한, 저명한 ¶②이채를 띠다

1) ***be conspicuous by*** *someone's* or *something's* ***absence,*** call attention by not being where someone or something is expected.
2) ***make oneself conspicuous,*** behave in a way that attracts attention.
[熟] 1)없으므로 오히려 눈에 띄다 2)일부러 남의 눈에 띄게 하다

con·spic·u·ous·ly [kənspíkjuəsli] *adv.* in a conspicuous manner; remarkably.
—➋ 두드러지게, 드러나게, ◾어나게, 유난히

* **con·spir·a·cy** [kənspírəsi] *n.* (pl. **-cies**) **1.** Ⓤ the act of conspiring. ¶*in ~.*⓪ **2.** Ⓒ a plot. 「spires; a plotter.」
—名 1.공모(共謀) ¶①공모하여 2. 음모, 모의

con·spir·a·tor [kənspírətər] *n.* Ⓒ a person who con-\
—名 공모자, 음모자

con·spire [kənspáiər] *vi.* **1.** form or take part in an unlawful plot. 《*~ against* the state, etc.》 **2.** act or work together; combine. ¶*All things conspired for a happy day.*⓪ —*vt.* plot. ▷**con·spir·er** [-spáiərər] *n.*
—自 1.음모를 꾸미다, 공모하다 2.함께 하다; 협력하다 ¶①만사가 잘 되어 행복한 날을 맞이하였다 —他 …을 꾀하다

con·sta·ble [kánstəbl / kʌ́n-] *n.* Ⓒ **1.** a policeman. ¶*the chief ~.*⓪ **2.** a keeper of a royal fortress or castle. ⇒N.B.
—名 1. 순경, 경관 ¶①[영국의] 경찰서장 2.성주(城主) N.B. const.; Const.; cons.; Cons.로 줄여 씀

con·stab·u·lar·y [kənstǽbjuləri / -ləri] *n.* Ⓒ (pl. **-lar·ies**) an organized body of policemen; state police.
—名 경찰대, 국가 경찰

con·stan·cy [kánst(ə)nsi / kɔ́n-] *n.* Ⓤ **1.** the state or quality of being always the same; unchangeableness. **2.** faithfulness; honesty; firmness.
—名 1. 불변, 항구성 2.성실, 충실, 견고 함

‡con·stant [kánst(ə)nt / kɔ́n-] *adj.* **1.** always the same; unchanging. ↔variable **2.** ceaseless; continuous. ¶*a ~ anxiety | ~ give-and-take.*⓪ **3.** faithful; loyal; firm. ↔false ¶*He is ~ in friendship.*
—*n.* Ⓒ a number or quality that does not change.
—彫 1. 일정 불변의, 항구적인 2. 끊임없이 계속되는, 부단한 ¶①변함없는 공정한 거래 3.절개가 굳은, 충실한, [지조가] 견고한
—名 정수(定數),불변수,정량

‡con·stant·ly [kánst(ə)ntli / kɔ́n-] *adv.* **1.** always; without change. **2.** without stopping; continuously. **3.** frequently.
—副 1.항상, 변함없이 2. 끊임없이 3. 자주

con·stel·la·tion [kànstəléiʃ(ə)n / kɔ̀n-] *n.* Ⓒ **1.** a group of stars, usu. with a name. **2.** a brilliant gathering.
—名 1.성좌, 성수(星宿) 2. 기라성 같은 (찬란한) 모임

con·ster·na·tion [kànstərnéiʃ(ə)n / kɔ̀nstə(ː)-] *n.* Ⓤ dismay; surprise and fear. ¶*in ~ | to one's ~.*⓪
—名 깜짝 놀람, 대경실색 ¶①대경실색한 일은, 놀랍게도

con·sti·pa·tion [kànstipéiʃ(ə)n / kɔ̀n-] *n.* Ⓤ a difficult condition of the bowels.
—名 변비증

con·stit·u·en·cy [kənstítʃuənsi / -stítju-] *n.* Ⓒ (pl. **-cies**) **1.** 《*collectively*》 all the voters in a district. **2.** an electoral district. **3.** 《*collectively*》 a group of supporters, customers, etc.
—名 1. 선거민 2. 선거구 3. 지지자, 단골, 고객

con·stit·u·ent [kənstítʃuənt / -stítju-] *adj.* **1.** making up a whole; that composes. ¶*the ~ parts of water.* **2.** having a right to vote; having the right to make or change a constitution. —*n.* Ⓒ **1.** a necessary part; a component; an element. **2.** a voter.
—彫 1. 구성하는 2. 선거권이 있는, 헌법 제정(개정)권이 있는
—名 1.성분, 구성물, 요소 2. 선거인

* **con·sti·tute** [kánstit(j)ùːt / kɔ́nstitjùːt] *vt.* **1.** make up (something); form; compose. ¶*The parts ~ the whole.* **2.** appoint; elect. 《*~ someone president, captain, etc.*》 ¶*be constituted representative of*⓪ | *They constituted him manager.* **3.** set up; establish. ¶*~ a committee.*
—他 1. …을 구성하다 2. …을 [...에] 선정하다, 임명하다 ¶①…의 대표자가 되다 3. …을 제정하다, 설립하다

‡con·sti·tu·tion [kànstit(j)úːʃ(ə)n / kɔ̀nstitjúː-] *n.* **1.** Ⓒ a systematic description of the fundamental laws and principles of a government. ¶*a written (an unwritten) ~.*⓪ **2.** Ⓒ the physical structure and condition of a human body. ¶*by ~*⓪ | *have a good ~.* **3.** Ⓤ the way in which a thing is composed; nature; make-up. **4.** Ⓤ establishment; appointment. **5.** 《*the C-*》 the constitution of the United States.
—名 1. 헌법 ¶①성문(불문) 헌법 2. 체격,체질 ¶①선천적으로 3. 구성, 본질,조직 4. 설립, 임명 5. 미합중국 헌법

* **con·sti·tu·tion·al** [kànstit(j)úːʃ(ə)nəl / kɔ̀nstitjúː-] *adj.* **1.** of or caused by one's constitution. ¶*a ~ disease.*⓪ **2.** of or according to the constitution of a nation, a state or a group. ¶*a ~ monarchy.* **3.** for one's health. —*n.* Ⓒ 《*colloq.*》 a walk or other exercise taken for one's health.
—彫 1. 타고난, 체질의 ¶①체질성 질환 2. 헌법의, 입헌적인 ¶②입헌군주국 3. 건강상의, 보건상의
—名 건강을 위한 산책, 보건 운동

con·sti·tu·tion·al·ism [kànstit(j)úːʃ(ə)nəlìz(ə)m / kɔ̀nstitjúː-] *n.* Ⓤ constitutional government; constitutional rules.
—名 입헌제, 입헌정치, 입헌주의

con·sti·tu·tion·al·ist [kànstit(j)úːʃ(ə)nəlist / kɔ̀nstitjúː-] *n.* Ⓒ **1.** a supporter of constitutional rules. **2.** a person who makes a special study of constitutions.
—名 1. 입헌주의자, 호헌론자 2. 헌법학자

con·sti·tu·tion·al·ly [kànstitʃ(j)úːʃ(ə)nəli / kɔ̀nstitjúː-] *adv.* 1. in or by physical constructure; naturally. 2. according to a constitution of a nation, etc.
— ㉮ 1. 체질상, 천성적으로 2. 입헌적으로, 헌법상

con·strain [kənstréin] *vt.* 1. force or compel. 《~ *someone to do*》 ¶*He constrained me to go.* 2. (usu. in *passive*) be forced to do (something). ¶*I was constrained to side with him. | I feel constrained to go.*①
— ㉯ 1. [남]에게 강요하다, 억지로 …시키다 2. 하는 수 없이 …하다 ¶①가지 않을 수 없을 것 같다

con·strained [kənstréind] *adj.* 1. forced. 2. uneasy; stiff; unnatural. ¶*a ~ voice.*
— ㉰ 1. 강제적인, 강제된 2. 불안한, 갑갑한, 부자연한

con·straint [kənstréint] *n.* ⓤ 1. the act of compelling; the state of being compelled; force. ¶*by ~*① / *under* (or *in*) *~.*② 2. the act of controlling or the state of being controlled one's natural feelings. ¶*feel ~*① / *with ~.*①
— ㉮ 1. 강제; 속박 ¶①무리하게, 억지로 ②강제되어, 부득이 2. 압박감, 옹색함, 어색함 ¶③어색함을 느끼다, 거북해하다/④거북해하여, 삼가서

con·strict [kənstríkt] *vt.* pull (things) together; contract; press together.
— ㉯ …을 죄다, 긴축하다, 압축하다

con·stric·tion [kənstríkʃ(ə)n] *n.* 1. ⓤ the act of pulling together; contraction; compression. 2. ⓤ the feeling of tightness. 3. ⓒ a constricted part.
— ㉮ 1. 긴축, 압축 2. 갑갑함, 거북함 3. 압축된 부분, 잘록한 부분

con·stric·tor [kənstríktər] *n.* ⓒ 1. something that constricts. 2. a muscle that constricts a part of the body. 3. a snake that kills by coiling around its prey.
— ㉮ 1. 긴축시키는 것, 압축기 2. 괄약근(括約筋) 3. [짐승을 졸라 죽이는] 뱀

‡ **con·struct** [kənstrʌ́kt] *vt.* 1. build; make; put or fit (things) together. ↔destroy ¶*~ a bridge.* 2. draw (something) so as to fulfil given conditions. ¶*~ a triangle.* 3. arrange or form (something) in one's mind; plan out. ¶*~ a theory.*
— ㉯ 1. …을 세우다, 짓다, 건립(건조)하다, 조립하다 2. …을 작도(作圖)하다 3. …을 생각(고안)해 내다; [글·이론 따위]를 구성하다

‡ **con·struc·tion** [kənstrʌ́kʃ(ə)n] *n.* 1. ⓤ the act of building or constructing. ¶*under ~.*① 2. ⓤ the way in which a thing is constructed. 3. ⓒ something constructed; a building. 4. ⓒ a meaning; an explanation. 5. ⓒ the arrangement, connection, or relation of words in a sentence.
— ㉮ 1. 조립, 건조, 건립 ¶①건설중, 공사중 2. 구조법 3. 건물 4. 해석 5. 구문(構文)

con·struc·tive [kənstrʌ́ktiv] *adj.* 1. helping to construct; building up; helpful. ↔destructive ¶*a ~ suggestion.* 2. of construction; structural. ¶*a ~ defect.*① 3. not directly expressed; suggested. ▷**con·struc·tive·ly** [-li] *adv.*
— ㉰ 1. 조립의, 구조상의 2. 건설적인 ¶①구조상의 결함 3. 해석에 의한, 추정적인

con·struc·tor [kənstrʌ́ktər] *n.* ⓒ a person who constructs; a builder.
— ㉮ 건설자, 건조자, 건립자

con·strue [kənstrúː] *vt.* 1. explain the meaning of (actions, etc.) 2. translate. 3. show the grammatical construction and meaning. 4. combine (words) grammatically. —*vi.* be capable of being analyzed. ¶*This sentence does not ~.*
— ㉯ 1. [행위 따위]를 해석하다 2. …을 번역하다 3. …을 문법적으로 해석(분석)하다 4. [말]을 짜맞추다, 문법적으로 연결하다 —㉲ 분석되다, 해석되다

con·sul [kánsəl / kɔ́n-] *n.* ⓒ 1. a government officer who lives in a foreign city to help his country's people and their business. ¶*an acting ~.*① 2. either of the two highest officials of the ancient Roman Republic.
— ㉮ 1. 영사(領事) ¶①대리 영사 2. [고대 로마의] 집정관(執政官)

con·su·lar [kánsjulər / kɔ́nsjulə] *adj.* of a consul.
— ㉰ 영사의, 집정관의

con·su·late [kánsjulit / kɔ́n-] *n.* 1. ⓤ a consul's position. 2. ⓒ an official residence or office of a consul.
— ㉮ 1. 영사직(領事職) 2. 영사관

con·sul·ship [káns(ə)lʃip / kɔ́n-] *n.* ⓤ 1. a consul's position. 2. a consul's term of office.
— ㉮ 1. 영사직(領事職) 2. 영사의 임기

• **con·sult** [kənsʌ́lt] *vt.* 1. seek information or advice from (someone). ¶*~ a doctor.* 2. consider; have regard to. ¶*~ one's own convenience.*① 3. refer to. ¶*~ a dictionary / Consult your watch.* —*vi.* exchange ideas with someone; take counsel. (*~ with someone*; *~ about something*) ¶*~ with someone about the matter.*②
— ㉯ 1. …에게 의견을 묻다, 진찰을 받다 2. …을 고려하다 ¶①자신의 편의만을 생각하다 3. …을 조사하다, 참고하다 —㉲ 상담하다, 협의하다 ¶②그 문제를 …에게 상담하다

con·sult·ant [kənsʌ́lt(ə)nt] *n.* ⓒ 1. a person who consults another. 2. an expert who gives professional or technical advice.
— ㉮ 1. 의논 상대 2. 고문; 고문 의사, 진찰의(醫)

con·sul·ta·tion [kàns(ə)ltéiʃ(ə)n / kɔ̀n-] *n.* 1. ⓤ the act of consulting. 2. ⓒ a meeting for consulting.
— ㉮ 1. 상담, 협의, 의논 2. [전문가의] 회의

con·sult·ing [kənsʌ́ltiŋ] *adj.* **1.** that consults. **2.** employed in giving professional advice. ¶ *a ~ lawyer.*①
— ⓗ **1.** 진찰의, 상담의 **2.** 고문의 ¶① 고문 변호사

* **con·sume** [kənsúːm / -s(j)úːm] *vt.* **1.** use up (something) completely. ¶ *~ one's time in reading.* **2.** eat or drink up. **3.** destroy; burn up. ¶ *The flames consumed the old barn.* **4.** (usu. in *passive*) get deeply into a person's mind. ¶ *He was consumed with rage.*① — *vi.* spend; waste away. ¶ *~ away with grief.*②
— ⓣ **1.** …을 써 버리다, 소비(소모)하다 **2.** …을 먹어(마셔) 버리다 **3.** …을 태워 없애다 **4.** 마음에 사무치다, 뻗히다 ¶①그는 노발대발하였다 — 自 소비되다, [써서] 없어지다, 야위다 ¶② 슬픔으로 수척해지다

* **con·sum·er** [kənsúːmər / -s(j)úː-] *n.* ⓒ a person who consumes. ↔producer ¶ *the consumer's price.*①
— ⓜ 소비자, 수요자 ¶①소비자 가격

con·sum·mate *vt.* [kánsəmèit / kɔ́n- ∥ → *adj.*] complete; finish; make (something) perfect. — *adj.* [kənsʌ́mit] complete; perfect. ¶ *~ virtue.*①
— ⓣ …을 완성하다, 완료하다
— ⓗ 완전한 ¶①완전무결한 덕(德)

con·sum·ma·tion [kànsəméiʃ(ə)n / kɔ̀nsə-] *n.* Ⓤ the act of consummating; the state of being consummated; completion.
— ⓜ 완성, 성취

* **con·sump·tion** [kənsʌ́m(p)ʃ(ə)n] *n.* Ⓤ **1.** the act of consuming; the state of being consumed; use. ↔production ¶ *~ duty* (or *tax*).① **2.** the amount used up. **3.** a disease of the lungs; tuberculosis.
— ⓜ **1.** 소비 ¶①소비세 **2.** 소비고, 소비액 **3.** 폐병, 결핵

con·sump·tive [kənsʌ́m(p)tiv] *adj.* **1.** apt to consume; wasteful. **2.** having or likely to have tuberculosis of the lungs. — *n.* ⓒ a person who has tuberculosis of the lungs. ▷**con·sump·tive·ly** [-li] *adv.*
— ⓗ **1.** 소비의, 소모성의 **2.** 폐병의
— ⓜ 폐병 환자

‡ **con·tact** *n.* [kántækt / kɔ́n- ∥ → *v.*] **1.** Ⓤ the act of touching; touch. ¶ *be in ~ with someone*① / *bring a thing into ~ with another*② / *come in ~ with something.*③ **2.** ⓒ (*U.S.*) (*pl.*) connection. ¶ *a man of many contacts.*④ **3.** ⓒ connection between two conductors of electricity. ¶ *make* (*break*) *~.*⑤ ⌈one⌉. — *vt.* [*Brit.* kɔntækt] (*colloq.*) get in touch with (some-
— ⓜ **1.** 접촉, 맞닿음 ¶①…과 접촉해 있다／②어떤 것을 딴 것에 접촉시키다／③…과 접촉하다 **2.** (美)접근, 교제 ¶④교제가 넓은 사람 **3.** 접촉, 혼선 ¶⑤ 전류를 통하다(차단하다)
— ⓣ …을 접촉시키다

con·ta·gion [kəntéidʒ(ə)n] *n.* **1.** Ⓤ the spreading of disease to others by contact. ↔infection **2.** ⓒ a disease spread in this way. **3.** Ⓒ an evil influence; a moral rottenness.
— ⓜ **1.** [접촉] 전염, 감염 **2.** 전염병 **3.** 폐풍, 타락

con·ta·gious [kəntéidʒəs] *adj.* **1.** spreading by contact. ¶ *a ~ disease.*① **2.** easily spreading from one person to another. ¶ *Laughter is ~.*②
— ⓗ **1.** [접촉] 전염의, 감염성의 ¶①접촉 전염병 **2.** 옮는, 전파하는 ¶②웃음은 옮는다

‡ **con·tain** [kəntéin] *vt.* **1.** have or hold (something) within itself; have (something) as a part; be capable of holding. ¶ *The box contains thirty apples.* **2.** be equal to (something). ¶ *A pound contains 16 ounces.* **3.** control; hold back; prevent. ¶ *~ oneself* ① / *I could not ~ myself for joy.* **4.** be divisible by (a figure).
— ⓣ **1.** …을 넣다, 속에 들어 있다, 포함(함유)하다, 넣어지다 **2.** …와 같다, …에 상당하다 **3.** …을 억제하다, 참다 ¶①참다, 자제하다 **4.** …으로 나누어지다

con·tain·er [kəntéinər] *n.* Ⓒ anything for containing something, such as a box or a can.
— ⓜ 그릇, 용기(容器)

con·tam·i·nate [kəntǽminèit] *vt.* **1.** make (something) bad or dirty by contact, etc. **2.** have a bad effect on (someone). ▷**con·tam·i·na·tor** [-ər] *n.*
— ⓣ **1.** [접촉 따위로] …을 더럽히다, 불순하게 하다, 오염시키다 **2.** …을 악에 물들이다

con·tam·i·na·tion [kəntæ̀mineíʃ(ə)n] *n.* **1.** Ⓤ the act of contaminating; the state of being contaminated. **2.** Ⓒ a thing that contaminates. **3.** a process of combining two words into one form. ⇒N.B.
— ⓜ **1.** 오염 **2.** 오물, 부패 **3.** 혼성, [언어의] 혼교(混交) N.B. 예를 들면 motel=motor+hotel; smog=smoke+fog 따위

con·temn [kəntém] *vt.* have no respect for (someone); look down on; despise; scorn.
— ⓣ …을 경멸하다, 얕보다, 깔보다

* **con·tem·plate** [kántəmplèit, kəntémpleit / kɔ́ntemplèit] *vt.* **1.** look at or think about (something) for a long time; gaze at; study carefully. ¶ *~ a problem.* **2.** meditate; look upon mentally. **3.** look forward to (something); expect. ¶ *I don't ~ any opposition from him.*① **4.** have (something) in mind; intend. (*~ doing*)
— ⓣ **1.** …을 찬찬히 보다, 응시하다, 심사숙고하다, 곰곰이 생각하다 **2.** …을 기대하다, 예기(예상)하다 ¶①그의 반대가 있으리라고는 생각지 않는다 **3.** 계획하다, …하려고 생각하다

con·tem·pla·tion [kàntəmpleíʃ(ə)n / kɔ̀ntem-] *n.* Ⓤ **1.** the act of contemplating. **2.** deep thought. **3.** expectation. **4.** intention.
— ⓜ **1.** 응시, 숙고 **2.** 명상, 묵상 **3.** 기대 **4.** 기도, 계획

con·tem·pla·tive [kəntémplətive, kɑ́ntəmplèitiv / kɔ́n-templèitiv] *adj.* thoughtful; deep in thought.
—[형] 명상의, 심사숙고하는

con·tem·po·ra·ne·ous [kəntèmpəréiniəs] *adj.* at the same period, usu. in the past.
—[형] 같은 시대의, 동기(同期)의

* **con·tem·po·rar·y** [kəntémp(ə)rèri / -rəri] *adj.* **1.** belonging to the present time. ¶*~ literature.* **2.** of the same age or date. —*n.* [C] (pl. **-rar·ies**) **1.** a person who belongs to the same period of time. ¶*our contemporaries.*① **2.** a person, a newspaper, etc. of the same age or date.
—[형] 1. 현대의, 당대의 2. …와 같은 시대의 —[명] 1. 같은 시대의 사람 ¶① 당대(현대)의 사람들 2. 같은 연배의 사람, 같은 시대의 신문

* **con·tempt** [kəntém(p)t] *n.* [U] **1.** the act of despising; the state of being despised; scorn; disgrace; disregard. ¶*in ~ of a rule*① / *Familiarity breeds ~.*② **2.** disobedience or open disrespect for the orders of a law court. ¶*~ of court.*③
1) ***bring someone into contempt,*** put shame or dishonor upon someone.
2) ***have*** (or ***hold***) ***someone in contempt,*** look down on someone; despise someone.
—[명] 1. 깔봄, 경멸, 모욕, 치욕 ¶①규칙을 무시하고/②친분이 지나치면 경멸을 사게 된다 2. 모욕죄 ¶③법정 모욕죄
[숙] 1)…에게 창피를 주다 2)…을 경멸하다

con·tempt·i·ble [kəntém(p)tibl] *adj.* deserving contempt or scorn. ¶*~ conduct / a ~ man.*
—[형] 업신여길 만한, 비열한

con·temp·tu·ous [kəntém(p)tʃuəs / -tju-] *adj.* showing or expressing contempt; scornful. ¶*a ~ smile.* ▷**contemp·tu·ous·ly** [-li] *adv.* —**con·temp·tu·ous·ness** [-nis] *n.*
—[형] [사람·태도 따위가] 경멸을 나타내는, 경멸적인, 남을 업신여기는

* **con·tend** [kənténd] *vi.* **1.** fight; struggle; take part in a contest. 《*~ with* or *against* someone》 ¶*~ with someone for a prize.*① **2.** argue; dispute; discuss. 《*~ with* someone》 ¶*He is fond of contending about everything.* —*vt.* maintain. 《*~ that …*》
—[자] 1. 다투다, 싸우다; 겨루다 ¶①…와 상을 다투다 2. 논쟁하다, 토론하다 —[타] …을 강력히 주장하다

‡ **con·tent**[1] [kɑ́ntent / kɔ́n-] *n.* **1.** 《usu. *pl.*》 what is contained in something. ¶*the contents of a house / the contents of a book.* **2.** the facts and ideas stated. ¶*the ~ of a speech.* **3.** [C][U] the power of containing; capacity; the amount contained; volume. ⇒[usage]
—[명] 1. 속에 들어 있는 것, 내용물, 목차 2. 취지, 요지 3. 수용력, 용적, 용량 [usage] 단수형은 일반적으로 추상적인 의미로, 복수형은 구체적인 의미로 쓰임

‡ **con·tent**[2] [kəntént] *vt.* satisfy; please. ¶*Nothing will ever ~ them.*
content oneself with(*=be satisfied with*) ***something.*** ¶*We have to ~ ourselves with dry bread.*
—*adj.* satisfied; pleased; willing; ready. ¶*He was never ~ with his success.*
—*n.* [U] contentment; satisfaction. ¶*in ~.*①
to one's heart's content, as much as one wants.
—[타] …에게 만족을 주다, …을 만족시키다
[숙] …을 만족하다
—[형] 만족하고 있는, 만족한, 기꺼운, 달가운
—[명] 만족 ¶①만족하여
[숙] 마음껏, 실컷, 충분히

* **con·tent·ed** [kənténtid] *adj.* satisfied with things as they are; pleased; willing. ¶*a ~ man / be ~ with one's lot / He was ~ to live in poverty.* ▷**con·tent·ed·ness** [-nis] *n.*
—[형] 만족한, 기꺼이 …하는

con·tent·ed·ly [kənténtidli] *adv.* in a contented manner.
—[부] 만족하여

con·ten·tion [kəntén∫(ə)n] *n.* **1.** [U] argument; dispute; quarrel. **2.** [C] a statement or point that a person has made or insisted on.
—[명] 1. 논쟁, 말다툼, 언쟁 2. 논점, 주장

con·ten·tious [kəntén∫əs] *adj.* fond of quarreling; apt to argue; given to disputing. ¶*a man of ~ temper.*①
—[형] 다투기 좋아하는, 논쟁적인, 이론이 있는 ¶①논쟁하기 좋아하는 사람

con·tent·ment [kənténtmənt] *n.* [U] satisfaction; the state of being pleased.
—[명] 만족, 안심, 흐뭇함

‡ **con·test** *n.* [kɑ́ntest / kɔ́n- ∥ →*v.*] [C] **1.** a fight or struggle. **2.** an argument; a discussion. **3.** a competition. ¶*an oratorical ~.*① —*v.* [kəntést] *vt.* **1.** fight for; struggle for (something). **2.** argue against; dispute about (something). **3.** try to win. —*vi.* take part in a contest. 《*~ with* someone》
—[명] 1. 싸움, 다툼 2. 논쟁, 논점 3. 경쟁 ¶①웅변대회 —[타] 1. …와 싸우다, 다투다 2. …와 논쟁하다 3. …을 겨루다 —[자] 경쟁하다

con·test·ant [kəntéstənt] *n.* [C] a person who takes part in a contest; a person who runs in an election, plays in a game, etc.
—[명] 경쟁자, [선거 따위에서] 경쟁 상대

con·text [kɑ́ntekst / kɔ́n-] *n.* [C][U] the parts just before and after a word, a sentence, etc. that fix its meaning. ¶*in this ~.*①
—[명] [문장의 뜻을 명확히 하는] 전후 관계, 문맥 ¶①이와 관련하여

con·ti·gu·i·ty [kὰntigjú(:)iti / kɔ̀n-] *n.* **1.** [U] contact. **2.** nearness. **3.** [C] a continuous mass; an unbroken stretch.
—[名] 1. 접촉 2. 인근, 인접 3. 연속

con·tig·u·ous [kəntígjuəs] *adj.* **1.** in actual contact; touching. **2.** joining; near.
—[形] 1. 접촉하는, 상접하는, 인접하는 2. 접근하는

con·ti·nence [kántinəns / kɔ́n-] *n.* [U] control of one's own desires; moderation; purity.
—[名] 자제, 절제, 정절(貞節)

⁑ **con·ti·nent**[1] [kántinənt / kɔ́n-] *n.* [C] **1.** a continuous land; a mainland. **2.** one of the six great masses of land, North America, South America, Europe, Africa, Asia, and Australia. **3.** ⦅*the C-*⦆ the mainland of Europe.
—[名] 1. 본토 2. 대륙 3. [영국과 구별하여] 유럽대륙

con·ti·nent[2] [kántinənt / kɔ́n-] *adj.* self-controlled; temperate.
—[形] 자제한, 절제 있는

∗ **con·ti·nen·tal** [kὰntinéntl / kɔ̀n-] *adj.* **1.** of or belonging to a continent; like that of a continent. ↔insular ¶*a ~ climate.* **2.** ⦅usu. *C-*⦆ of the mainland of Europe. **3.** ⦅usu. *C-*⦆ of the American colonies at the time of the American Revolution. —*n.* [C] ⦅usu. *C-*⦆ a person living on the Continent; a European.
—[形] 1. 대륙의, 대륙적인 2. 유럽대륙의 3. [미국 독립전쟁 시대의] 식민지의 —[名] 유럽대륙 사람

con·tin·gen·cy [kəntíndʒənsi] *n.* (pl. **-cies**) **1.** [U] uncertainty of occurrence. **2.** [U] chance. **3.** [C] an uncertain event. ¶*You must be ready for any ~.*①
—[名] 1. 우연성 2. 우발 3. 우발 사건 ¶①어떠한 돌발 사건에도 대비해 두지 않으면 안 된다

con·tin·gent [kəntíndʒ(ə)nt] *adj.* **1.** conditional; depending on something else. ¶*Such risks are ~ to the trade.*① / *a fee ~ on* (or *upon*) *cure.*② **2.** likely, but not certain; possible; uncertain. **3.** accidental; unexpected. ¶*a ~ fund.*③
—*n.* [C] **1.** a contingency. **2.** a body of people that is part of a larger group. **3.** an accidental or unexpected event.
—[形] 1. …여하에 달린, …나름의, …에 부수적인 ¶①그러한 위험은 그 장사에는 일어나기가 쉽다/②나았을 때 지불하는 사례금 2. 있을 법한, 있을 수 있는, …할지도 모르는 3. 우연의 ¶③긴급 준비금 —[名] 1. 부수 사건 2. 분견대 3. 뜻밖의 사건, 우발 사건

∗ **con·tin·u·al** [kəntínjuəl] *adj.* **1.** going on without stopping; endless. **2.** repeated many times; very frequent. ¶*The ~ noise gave me a headache.*
—[形] 1. 쉴새없는, 끊임없는 2. 빈번한, 자주 일어나는

∗ **con·tin·u·al·ly** [kəntínjuəli] *adv.* without stopping; again and again.
—[副] 빈번히, 끊임없이, 연속적으로

con·tin·u·ance [kəntínjuəns] *n.* [C] ⦅*sing.* only⦆ **1.** the act of going on all the time; the period of time during which a thing lasts. ¶*a ~ of bad weather*① / *of long ~.*② **2.** stay; remaining; continuing. **3.** (*Law*) postponement.
—[名] 1. 지속, 연속, 계속 기간 ¶①계속되는 악천후/②오래 지속되는 2. 체재, 존속 3. 연기

con·tin·u·a·tion [kəntìnjuéiʃ(ə)n] *n.* **1.** [U] the act of beginning again after a stop; the act or fact of not stopping; continuance. **2.** [C] an added part. ¶*build a ~ to a room.*① **3.** [C] anything by which a thing is continued.
—[名] 1. 계속, 지속, 존속 2. 잇댄 부분 ¶①방에 잇대어 증축하다 3. 계속된 것, 속편

⁑ **con·tin·ue** [kəntínju:] *vt.* **1.** go on; persist in; carry forward. ⦅*~ to do; ~ doing*⦆ ¶*~ to talk* / *How long will he ~ working?* **2.** begin again. ¶*~ a story in the following number.*① **3.** cause (something) to last or remain. ¶*~ an old servant in office.* —*vi.* **1.** last; endure. ¶*The desert continues for miles.* **2.** remain, as in a place or position. ⦅*~ in* something⦆ ¶*~ in power*② / *She still continues in weak health.*③ **3.** keep on. ¶*He continues idle.* **4.** start again.
—[他] 1. …을 계속하다; 지속하다 2. …을 다시 시작하다 ¶①계속하여 다음 번호의 이야기를 하다 3. …을 남게 하다, 존속시키다 —[自] 1. 계속되다 2. 머무르다; …채로 있다 ¶②권력의 자리에 존속하다/③그녀는 여전히 몸이 허약하다 3. … 상태를 유지하다 4. 재개하다, 다시 시작하다

con·ti·nu·i·ty [kὰntin(j)ú(:)iti / kɔ̀n-] *n.* (pl. **-ties**) [U] **1.** the state of being continuous. **2.** smooth succession. **3.** [C] an arrangement of a motion picture; a scenario. **4.** (*Radio*) the remarks made between the parts of a radio program.
—[名] 1. 계속 2. 연속 3. 영화의 촬영 대본 4. 방송 프로의 다음 차례 안내

∗ **con·tin·u·ous** [kəntínjuəs] *adj.* without a stop or break; unbroken; extended. ¶*~ labor*① / *a ~ road.*②
—[形] 끊임없는, 연속적인 ¶①계속되는 일/②외가닥길

con·tin·u·ous·ly [kəntínjuəsli] *adv.* in a continuous manner.
—[副] 끊임없이, 연속적으로

con·tort [kəntɔ́:rt] *vt.* twist or bend (something) out of its natural shape. ¶*a face contorted with pain.*①
—[他] …을 찌그러뜨리다; 뒤틀다 ¶①고통으로 일그러진 얼굴

con·tor·tion [kəntɔ́:rʃ(ə)n] *n.* [U] **1.** the act of contorting. **2.** [C] a contorted condition.
—[名] 1. 뒤틀림, 찌그러짐 2. 뒤틀린 상태

con·tour [kántuər / kɔ́ntuə] *n.* [C] **1.** an outline of a figure, a thing, etc. **2.** =contour line.
—*vt.* **1.** mark (something) with contour lines; make or form the outline of (something). **2.** build (a road, etc.) around the contour of a hill.
—*adj.* showing the outlines of mountains, etc.; of a contour line.
—[名] 1. 외형, 윤곽 —[他] 1. …에 등고선(等高線)을 그리다, …의 윤곽을 그리다(나타내다) 2. 산허리를 따라 [길]을 내다 —[形] 외형의; 등고선의

contour line [´-- ˌ-] *n.* a line drawn on a map through points all at the same height above sea level.
—[名] 등고선

con·tra- [kántrə- / kɔ́n-] *pref.* against; opposite: *contradict* (=speak against).
—《接頭》 역(逆)의, 반(反)…, 반항하는

con·tra·band [kántrəbæ̀nd / kɔ́n-] *adj.* against the law; stopped by the law or a rule. —*n.* [U] **1.** goods imported or exported unlawfully. ¶ *~ of war.*① **2.** unlawful trade of such goods.
—[形] 위법의, 금제(禁制)의 —[名] 1. 수출입 금지품 ¶①[무기·탄약 따위의] 전시 금지품 2. 밀매, 암거래

con·tra·bass [kántrəbèis / kɔ́n-] *n.* [C] (*Music*) the lowest bass voice or instrument; a double bass.
—[名] 《樂》 콘트라베이스

con·tra·cep·tion [kàntrəsépʃ(ə)n / kɔ̀n-] *n.* [U] prevention of conception; birth control.
—[名] 피임, 산아제한

:con·tract *n.* [kántrækt / kɔ́n- ‖ →*v.*] [C] **1.** an agreement; a business agreement; a promise. ¶*make* (or *enter into*) *a ~ with someone*① / *by ~.*② **2.** a written agreement enforced by law. **3.** a formal agreement of marriage.
—*v.* [kəntrǽkt] *vt.* **1.** make a legal agreement of (something). 《*~ to do*; *~* something *with*》 ¶ *~ to build a house* / *~ marriage with her.* **2.** form (a friendship, a habit, etc.). **3.** become infected with (a disease); catch. **4.** make (something) smaller; shrink; shorten. ¶ *~ one's eyebrows.*③ —*vi.* **1.** make a contract; agree formally. **2.** become smaller or shorter.
—[名] 1. 계약, 약정 ¶①…와 계약을 맺다/②청부로, 도급으로 2. 계약서 3. [정식] 약혼
—[他] 1. …을 계약하다, 약정하다 2. [친교]를 맺다; [악습 따위]가 붙다 3. [병]에 걸리다 4. …을 줄이다; 축소하다 ¶③이맛살을 찌푸리다 —[自] 1. 계약하다 2. 줄다, 수축하다

con·tract·ed [kəntrǽktid] *adj.* **1.** shortened; made smaller. **2.** narrow-minded. **3.** acquired.
—[形] 1. 수축된, 단축된 2. [마음·생각이] 좁은, 옹졸한 3. 계약한

con·trac·tile [kəntrǽkt(i)l / -tail] *adj.* that can contract or be contracted; producing contraction.
—[形] 주는, 줄일 수 있는, 수축성의

con·trac·tion [kəntrǽkʃ(ə)n] *n.* **1.** [U] the act of contracting; the state of being contracted. **2.** [C] something contracted; a shortened form. **3.** [U] the act of forming a bad habit, getting a disease, accumulating a debt, etc.
—[名] 1. 수축, 단축 2. 축약[어(語)·형] 3. [악습이] 붙기, 물들기; [병에] 걸리기; [부채를] 지기

con·trac·tor [kántræktər, kəntrǽk- / kəntrǽktə] *n.* [C] **1.** a businessman who agrees to do things for others, esp. in building houses, etc. ¶*a general ~.*① **2.** (*Anatomy*) a muscle that serves to contract.
—[名] 1. 계약자, 청부인 ¶①청부업자 2. 《解》 수축근

con·tra·dict [kàntrədíkt / kɔ̀n-] *vt.* **1.** deny; say the opposite of (what someone has said). ¶ *~ a statement.* **2.** be contrary to; disagree with (something). ¶*No truth contradicts another truth.*①
—[他] 1. …을 부정하다, 부인하다, [남의 말]에 대해 반박하다 2. [진술 따위가] …와 모순되다 ¶①진리는 서로 모순되지 않는다

con·tra·dic·tion [kàntrədíkʃ(ə)n / kɔ̀n-] *n.* [U][C] **1.** the act of contradicting; denial. **2.** contrary conditions; disagreement; opposition.
in contradiction to, to the contrary.
—[名] 1. 부정(否定), 반박 2. 모순, 자가당착
[熟] …에 정반대로

con·tra·dic·to·ry [kàntrədíkt(ə)ri / kɔ̀n-] *adj.* **1.** contradicting; in disagreement. **2.** inclined to contradict.
—[形] 1. 반박하는, 반대의 2. 모순적인, 반박적인

con·tra·dis·tinc·tion [kàntrədistíŋkʃ(ə)n / kɔ̀n-] *n.* [U] distinction by contrast. ¶*soul in ~ to body.*①
—[名] 대비(對比), 대조적 차이 ¶①육체와 대조적으로 구별한 영혼

con·tral·ti [kəntrǽlti, +*Brit.* -trá:l-] *n.* pl. of **contralto.**

con·tral·to [kəntrǽltou / -trá:l-] *n.* (pl. **-tral·tos** or **-tral·ti**) (*Music*) **1.** [U] the lowest woman's voice. **2.** [C] a person of a musical group who sings this part.
—[名] 1. 콘트랄토(여성 최저음) 2. 콘트랄토 가수

con·tra·ri·e·ty [kàntrəráiəti / kɔ̀n-] *n.* (pl. **-ties**) **1.** [U] the state or quality of being contrary. **2.** [C] something contrary.
—[名] 1. 반대, 불일치, 모순 2. 상반되는 것, 모순점

con·tra·ri·wise [kántrəriwàiz / kɔ́n-] *adv.* in the opposite way or direction; on the contrary.
—[副] 반대로, 거꾸로; 이에 반(反)하여

:con·tra·ry [kántrèri / kɔ́ntrəri // → 3.] *adj.* **1.** opposed. ¶*be ~ to one's wishes* / *hold a ~ opinion.*① **2.** opposite in direction; unfavorable. ¶*~ weather*② / *a ~ wind.*③ **3.** [+kəntréəri] (*colloq.*) always saying or doing the opposite; stubborn. ¶*a ~ child.*

—[形] 1. 반대의; …에 상반하는(어긋나는) ¶①반대 의견을 품다 2. 거꾸로, 역(逆)의; 불리한 ¶②불순한 날씨 / ③역풍 3.《口》반대로 나가는, 성미가 비뚤어진, 외고집의

—*n.* [C] (pl. **-ries**) **1.** 《*the ~*, *sing.* only》 the fact or quality that is the opposite of something else; the opposite; contradiction. ¶*neither tall nor the ~*④ / *Cold is the ~ of hot.* **2.** 《usu. *pl.*》 one of two opposing things.

—[名] 1. 반대; 모순 ¶④키가 크지도 않고 작지도 않은 2. 상반되는 사물

1) ***by contraries,*** ⓐ by way of opposition. ⓑ contrary to expectation.
2) ***on the contrary,*** exactly opposite to what has previously been said.
3) ***to the contrary,*** to the opposite effect.

[熟] 1)ⓐ반대로, 거꾸로 ⓑ기대와는 어긋나게, 뜻밖에 2)그것과는 정반대로 3)그와 반대로(의)

—*adv.* in a contrary manner. ¶*act ~ to your advice* / *~ to what I feared.*
contrary to one's expectation, to one's surprise; unexpectedly.

[熟] 의외로, 뜻밖에, 예상 밖으로

:con·trast [kántræst / kɔ́ntrɑːst // → *v.*] *n.* [C] **1.** a striking difference between things or persons compared. ¶*make a beautiful ~ with.* **2.** anything that shows difference from another thing. ¶*His white hair is in sharp ~ to* (or *with*) *his dark skin.*①

—[名] 1. 상이, 차이; 대조 2. 대상물 ¶①그의 흰 머리는 검은 피부와 두드러진 대조를 이루고 있다

—*v.* [kəntrǽst / -trɑ́ːst] *vt.* compare (things) so that the differences are made clear. 《~ something *with*》 ¶*Contrast these imported goods with the domestic products.*② —*vi.* show a difference when compared. 《~ *with* something》 ¶*His actions ~ badly with his promises.*

—[他] …을 대조하다; [대조하여] 두드러지게 하다 ¶②이 수입품들을 국산품과 대조해 보시오 —[自] […와] 좋은 대조를 이루다

con·tra·vene [kàntrəvíːn / kɔ̀n-] *vt.* **1.** disagree with (something); oppose. **2.** contradict. **3.** break; go against (a custom, a law, etc.). ¶*~ a law* (*rule*).

—[他] 1. …에 반대하다, 모순되다 2. …을 반박하다 3. [법률]을 위반하다

con·tra·ven·tion [kàntrəvénʃ(ə)n / kɔ̀n-] *n.* [U] [C] the act of contravening; opposition; conflict; violation.

—[名] 반대, 반박; 모순; 위반

:con·trib·ute [kəntríbju(ː)t] *vt., vi.* **1.** give (money, etc.) for a common purpose with others. **2.** write (articles, etc.) for a newspaper or magazine. **3.** help; aid. 《~ *to* something》 ¶*Good health contributed to his success.*①

—[他][自] 1. […을] 기부하다, 기증하다 2. […을] 투고하다, 기고하다 3. …에 공헌하다, 기여하다 ¶①건강이 그의 성공에 도움이 되었다

·con·tri·bu·tion [kàntribjúːʃ(ə)n / kɔ̀n-] *n.* **1.** [U] the act of contributing; [C] something contributed. **2.** [C] an article written for a newspaper or magazine. **3.** [C] a tax.

—[名] 1. 기부, 공헌; 기부금, 기증물 2. 투고, 기고 기사 3. 세금

con·trib·u·tor [kəntríbjutər] *n.* [C] **1.** a person who contributes. **2.** a person who writes articles for a newspaper or magazine.

—[名] 1. 기부자, 공헌자 2. 기고가, 투고가

con·trib·u·to·ry [kəntríbjutɔ̀ːri / -t(ə)ri] *adj.* contributing.

—[形] 공헌하는, …에 이바지하는

con·trite [kántrait, kəntráit / kɔ́ntrait] *adj.* **1.** very sorry for having done wrong. ¶*~ tears.*① **2.** showing deep regret and sorrow. ▷**con·trite·ly** [-li] *adv.*

—[形] 1. 죄를 뉘우치는, 회오의 ¶①회오의 눈물 2. 깊은 뉘우침(슬픔)을 나타내는

con·tri·tion [kəntríʃ(ə)n] *n.* [U] **1.** deep sorrow for sin; penitence. **2.** deep regret.

—[名] 1. 회오, 뉘우침 2. 회한(悔恨)

con·triv·ance [kəntráiv(ə)ns] *n.* **1.** [C] a thing invented; a plan or scheme; a mechanical device. **2.** [U] the act or manner of contriving.

—[名] 1. 고안, 고안물, 장치, 계획, 계략, 모략 2. 고안하기, 고안의 재간

·con·trive [kəntráiv] *vt.* **1.** invent; devise; design. ¶*~ a new kind of engine* / *~ an excuse.* **2.** plan; scheme; plot. **3.** manage. ¶*I will ~ to get there by three.* —*vi.* **1.** invent; plan; plot. **2.** manage well.

—[他] 1. …을 고안하다, 발명하다 2. …을 꾀하다, 계획하다 3. …을 잘 처리하다

:con·trol [kəntróul] *n.* **1.** [U] power or authority for ordering, ruling or guiding. **2.** [U] a holding back; a keeping down; restraint. ¶*lose ~ of one's temper.* **3.** [C] means of holding back; check. **4.** [C] 《usu. *pl.*》 a device for regulating and guiding a machine. **5.** [C] a standard of comparison for testing truth or correctness.

—[名] 1. 지배[력], 감독, 통제 2. 억제, 제어 3. 통제 수단 4. 조종 장치 5. [실험 결과의] 조사(照査) 표준, 대조부(簿)

1) ***be beyond*** (or ***out of***) *one's* ***control,*** that cannot be held back.
2) ***be in control of*** (=*have authority over*) *something.*
3) ***get*** (or ***keep***) ***under control,*** control.

[熟] 1)제어할 수가 없다, 억제하지 못하다 2)…을 관리하고 있다 3)관제하다, 제어하다 4)…의 관리하에 있다 5)제멋대로

4) ***under the control of*** (=*being governed by*) *someone.*
5) ***without control,*** freely.

—*vt.* (**-trolled, -trol·ling**) **1.** have power over (something); direct; command. **2.** hold back; keep down; restrain. ¶ ~ *oneself.*① **3.** adjust (something) so that it works well; regulate.

—[他] 1. …을 관리하다, 지배하다 2. …을 억제하다, 제어하다 ¶①자제하다 3. …을 조절(통제)하다

con·trol·la·ble [kəntróuləbl] *adj.* that can be controlled.

—[形] 제어할 수 있는, 조종할 수 있는

con·trol·ler [kəntróulər] *n.* [C] **1.** an officer who examines expenditures or accounts; a comptroller. **2.** a person who controls or directs. **3.** a device for regulating the speed of a machine.

—[名] 1. 회계 검사역(감독관 · 감사관) 2. 지배자, 관리인 3. 제어기(制御器)

con·tro·ver·sial [kàntrəvə́:rʃ(ə)l / kɔ̀ntrəvə́:-] *adj.* **1.** of controversy; debatable; disputed. **2.** fond of controversy. ▷**con·tro·ver·sial·ly** [-i] *adv.*

—[形] 1. 논쟁의, 논쟁의 대상이 되는 2. 논쟁을 좋아하는

con·tro·ver·sial·ist [kàntrəvə́:rʃ(ə)list / kɔ̀ntrəvə́:-] *n.* [C] a person who takes part in a controversy.

—[名] 논쟁자, 토론자, 논객

* **con·tro·ver·sy** [kántrəvə̀:rsi / kɔ́ntrəvə̀:-, kəntrɔ́və-] *n.* [U][C] (pl. **-sies**) **1.** an argument; a discussion. **2.** quarrel; debate.

—[名] 1. 논쟁, 논의, 토론 2. 싸움, 언쟁

con·tro·vert [kántrəvə̀:rt, kàntrəvə́:rt / kɔ́ntrəvə̀:t] *vt.* **1.** deny; oppose. **2.** dispute about (something); discuss; talk about (a question).

—[他] 1. …을 논박하다, 반론하다 2. …을 논쟁하다, 토론하다, 언쟁하다

con·tu·ma·cious [kànt(j)u(:)méiʃəs / kɔ̀ntju(:)-] *adj.* resisting authority; not willing to obey.

—[形] 복종하지 않는; 고집부리는

con·tu·ma·cy [kánt(j)uməsi / kɔ́ntjumə-] *n.* [U][C] (pl. **-cies**) going against authority; the state of being contumacious.

—[名] 불복종, 반항, 외고집

con·tu·me·ly [kánt(j)umili / kɔ́ntju(:)m(i)-] *n.* (pl. **-lies**) **1.** [U] the state of being proud, not polite, and rude. **2.** [C] severe criticism of someone; bad language or behavior to someone; an insult.

—[名] 1. 오만, 무례함 2. 모욕

co·nun·drum [kənʌ́ndrəm] *n.* [C] **1.** a puzzle. **2.** a hard problem.

—[名] 1. 수수께끼 2. 난문제

con·va·lesce [kànvəlés / kɔ̀n-] *vi.* get better; grow stronger after illness.

—[自] 건강을 회복하다, 차츰 나아가다

con·va·les·cence [kànvəlésns / kɔ̀n-] *n.* [U] a gradual recovery of health and strength after illness.

—[名] [병이] 차츰 나아감, [건강]회복

con·va·les·cent [kànvəlésnt / kɔ̀n-] *adj.* getting better; growing stronger after illness. **—*n.*** [C] a person who is getting well. ¶*a* ~ *hospital.*①

—[形] 회복기의, 차츰 나아가는 —[名] 회복기의 환자 ¶①병후 요양소

con·vec·tion [kənvékʃ(ə)n] *n.* [U] **1.** the act of conveying. **2.** (*Physics*) the transfer of heat from one place to another by means of currents of heated liquid or gas.

—[名] 1. 전달 2. [열의] 대류(對流), 환류(環流)

con·vene [kənví:n] *vi.* come together; gather. **—*vt.*** call together; send for (someone). ¶~ *a meeting.*

—[自] 모이다, 집합하다 —[他] …을 소집하다, 모이게 하다, 소환하다

* **con·ven·ience** [kənví:niəns] *n.* **1.** [U] the quality of being convenient; comfort; [C] advantage. ¶*for convenience' sake*① / *a marriage of* ~② / *It is a great* ~ *to live near a bus stop.* **2.** [C] anything handy or easy to use. ¶*modern conveniences*③ / *a house full of conveniences of every sort*④ / *Electric light is a great* ~.

—[名] 1. 편리, 편의, 형편이 좋음 ¶①편의상/②[재산을 노리는] 정략 결혼 2. 편리한 것, 편리한 설비 ¶③현대의 문명이기/④갖가지 설비가 갖춰져 있는 집

\: **con·ven·ient** [kənví:niənt] *adj.* **1.** causing no trouble; handy; easy to reach or use; suitable. ↔inconvenient ¶*a* ~ *monthly plan* / *a* ~ *tool* / *if it is* ~ *for* (or *to*) *you.*① ⇒[N.B.] **2.** (*colloq.*) near. ¶*Our house is* ~ *to the station.*

—[形] 1. 편리한, 형편이 좋은 ¶①만약 형편이 좋으시다면 [N.B.] convenient는 일반적으로 물건에 관해 씀 2. ((口)) 가까이에 있는, 손쉬운

con·ven·ient·ly [kənví:niəntli] *adv.* in a convenient manner.

—[副] 편리하게, 형편이 좋게

* **con·vent** [kánvent / kɔ́nv(ə)nt] *n.* [C] **1.** a society of women who have given themselves to a religious life; a nunnery. **2.** a building for such a society. ¶*go into a* ~.①

—[名] 1. 수녀단 2. 수도원, 수녀원 ¶①수녀가 되다

\: **con·ven·tion** [kənvénʃ(ə)n] *n.* **1.** [C] a large meeting for some special purpose; a gathering; an assembly; a conference. ¶*the annual* ~① / *the party* ~.② **2.** [C]

—[名] 1. 협의회, 회의, 대회 ¶①연례(年例) 대회/②당(黨)대회 2. 대표자 3. 조약, 협약 4. 관습, 인습, 전통 ¶③관례를

《collectively》 representatives to a meeting or assembly. **3.** [C] an agreement; a treaty. **4.** [U][C] general agreement; custom; a custom approved by general agreement; tradition. ¶*observe* ~.③ — 지키다

*** con·ven·tion·al** [kənvénʃən(ə)l] *adj.* **1.** depending on conventions. ↔legal **2.** customary; formal; commonplace; not new or original. ¶~ *phrases*① / ~ *remarks*.② — [形] 1. 회의의, 협정의 2. 관습적인, 형식적인; 상례적인, 판에 박은, 상투적인 ¶①상투적인 문구/②형식적인 말

con·ven·tion·al·i·ty [kənvènʃənǽliti] *n.* (pl. **-ties**) **1.** [U] conventional quality. **2.** 《*the -ties*》 conventional customs or rules. — [名] 1. 인습성 2. 관례, 관습

con·ven·tion·al·ly [kənvénʃ(ə)nəli] *adv.* in a conventional or usual manner. — [副] 인습적으로, 상례적으로, 관례대로

con·verge [kənvə́ːrdʒ] *vi.* meet at a point; come together. ↔diverge —*vt.* cause (something) to converge. — [自] [한 점에] 모이다; 회합하다 — [他] …을 모으다

con·ver·gence [kənvə́ːrdʒ(ə)ns] *n.* [U] the act, process, or fact of converging. ↔divergence — [名] [한 점으로] 모이기, 수렴(收斂), 귀일(歸一)

con·ver·gent [kənvə́ːrdʒ(ə)nt] *adj.* converging. — [形] 한 점에 모이는, 수렴(收斂)하는

con·ver·sant [kənvə́ːrs(ə)nt, kάnvər- / kənvə́ː-, kɔ́nvə-] *adj.* familiar with; having a knowledge of. 《~ *with*》 — [形] 정통한, 잘 알고 있는, 친밀한

: con·ver·sa·tion [kὰnvərséiʃ(ə)n / kɔ̀nvə-] *n.* **1.** [C] a talk. ¶*I had a long ~ with him.*① **2.** [U] talking. ¶*I saw him in ~ with my father.* — [名] 1. 이야기 ¶①나는 그와 오래 이야기를 하였다 2. 대화, 담화, 회화

con·ver·sa·tion·al [kὰnvərséiʃənl / kɔ̀nvə-] *adj.* **1.** of conversation. **2.** fond of conversation. **3.** good at conversation. — [形] 1. 회화의, 담화의 2. 이야기하기 좋아하는 3. 이야기를 잘하는

con·ver·sa·tion·al·ist [kὰnvərséiʃ(ə)nəlist / kɔ̀nvə-] *n.* [C] a person who likes or who is good at conversation. — [名] 이야기하기를 좋아하는 사람, 이야기를 잘하는 사람

*** con·verse**[1] [kənvə́ːrs] *vi.* talk; chat. — [自] 대담(대화)하다, 이야기를 나누다

*** con·verse**[2] *adj.* [kənvə́ːrs →*n.* / kɔ́nvəːs] opposite; contrary. —*n.* [*U.S.* kάnvəːrs] 《often *the* ~》 something that is opposite or contrary; the reverse. ¶*Converses are not always true.*① — [形] 거꾸로의, 반대의 — [名] 역(逆), 반대되는 것 ¶①역은 반드시 참(진리)은 아니다

con·verse·ly [kənvə́ːrsli / kɔ́nvəːsli, -ˊ-] *adv.* contrarily; on the contrary. — [副] 거꾸로; [먼저의 주장과는] 반대로

con·ver·sion [kənvə́ːrʒ(ə)n, -ʃ(ə)n / kənvə́ːʃ(ə)n] *n.* [U] **1.** the act of converting. **2.** change from one religion, etc. to another. **3.** exchange. ¶*a ~ table.*① — [名] 1. 전환(轉換) 2. 개종(改宗); 개심 3. 환산 ¶①환산표

*** con·vert** *vt.* [kənvə́ːrt →*n.*] **1.** change; turn 《~ one thing *into* another》; transform. ¶~ *goods into money* / ~ *water into steam.* **2.** make (someone) change from one religion, etc. to another. 《~ someone *to*》 ¶~ *the Moslems to Christianity.*① **3.** take and use (something) unlawfully. **4.** exchange (something) for another thing that is equal in value. — [他] 1. …을 바꾸다, 변하게 하다, 개조하다, 개장(改裝)하다 2. …으로 개종시키다, 개심시키다 ¶①회교도를 그리스도교로 개종시키다 3. …을 횡령하다 4. …을 환산하다

—*n.* [kάnvəːrt / kɔ́nvəːt] [C] a person who has been converted. ¶*a ~ to Christianity.*② — [名] 개종자, 개심자 ¶②그리스도교로 개종한 사람

con·vert·i·ble′ [kənvə́ːrtibl] *adj.* **1.** that can be converted or changed. ¶*Heat is ~ into electricity.* **2.** (of an automobile) having a top that can be folded down. —*n.* [C] an automobile with a folding top. ▷**con·vert·i·bly** [-i] *adv.* — [形] 1. 바꿀 수 있는, 전환할 수 있는, 환산할 수 있는 2. [자동차가] 포장 지붕의, 접는 식 포장의 — [名] 포장 지붕의(포장을 접을 수 있는) 자동차

con·vex [kənvéks, kάnveks / kɔ́nvéks] *adj.* having a surface that curves out. ↔concave — [形] 볼록한 모양의, 볼록면의

con·vex·i·ty [kənvéksiti / kɔn-] *n.* [U] the state of being convex. — [名] 볼록한 모양, 철면(凸面)

*** con·vey** [kənvéi] *vt.* **1.** take (something) from one place to another; carry. ¶*a train conveys passengers.* **2.** pass on; conduct. **3.** express; communicate. ¶*words that ~ nothing to me* / *~ an expression of grief to someone.* **4.** (*Law*) transfer (property) from one person to another by a formal written paper. — [他] 1. …을 나르다, 운반하다, 수송하다 2. [음 따위]를 전달하다, 전도하다 3. …을 나타내다(표현하다); [의미 따위]를 전달하다 4. 《法》 [정식 증서로 재산]을 양도하다

con·vey·a·ble [kənvé(i)əbl] *adj.* that can be conveyed. — [形] 운반(전달·양도)할 수 있는

con·vey·ance [kənvé(i)əns] *n.* **1.** [U] the act of carrying; transportation. **2.** [C] a thing that conveys something; a vehicle. **3.** [U] communication. **4.** [U][C] (*Law*) a transfer of property from one person to another. — [名] 1. 수송, 전송(傳送) 2. 운수 기관 3. 전달 4. 《法》 양도

con·vey·er, -vey·or [kənvéiər] *n.* [C] **1.** a person or thing that conveys goods. **2.** a mechanical device that conveys goods.
—[名] 1. 운송자, 운반하는 것 2. 운반기(장치), 콘베이어

* **con·vict** *vt.* [kənvíkt → *n.*] prove or declare (someone) to be guilty. ¶ *be convicted of theft* / *~ someone of a murder.* —*n.* [kánvikt / kɔ́n-] [C] a person convicted by a court; a person serving a prison sentence for some crime. ¶ *an ex-convict*① / *a ~ prison*②
—[他] …을 유죄로 결정하다(선언하다) —[名] 죄인, 죄수 ¶①전과자/②형무소, 교도소

* **con·vic·tion** [kənvíkʃ(ə)n] *n.* [C][U] **1.** the act of proving or declaring guilty. **2.** a strong belief; an assurance.
—[名] 1. 유죄로 결정하기, 유죄 판결 2. 신념, 확신

⁑ **con·vince** [kənvíns] *vt.* make (someone) certain; cause (someone) to believe 《~ someone *of* success, etc.; ~ *that* ...》; persuade. ¶ *~ someone of sin* / *He is convinced of the safety* (*that there is no danger*).①
—[他] …을 확신시키다, …에게 [죄·잘못 따위를] 깨우쳐 주다, 납득시키다 ¶①그는 안전하다고(위험이 없다고) 믿고 있다

con·vinc·ing [kənvínsiŋ] *adj.* that convinces; persuading by proofs. ¶ *in a ~ manner.*①
—[形] [남을] 납득시키는, 설득력 있는 ¶①납득이 가게끔, 설득하듯이

con·vinc·ing·ly [kənvínsiŋli] *adv.* in a convincing or persuading manner.
—[副] 수긍이 가도록, 확신하도록

con·viv·i·al [kənvíviəl] *adj.* **1.** gay; cheerful. **2.** fond of feasts; of a feast or an official dinner.
—[形] 1. 유쾌한, 흥겨운, 즐거운 2. 연회를 좋아하는; 연회의

con·viv·i·al·i·ty [kənvìviǽliti] *n.* [U] fondness for feasts.
—[名] 연회를 좋아하기, 환락, 주흥

con·vo·ca·tion [kànvəkéiʃ(ə)n / kɔ̀n-] *n.* **1.** [U] the act of calling together a meeting. **2.** [C] a meeting. **3.** (*Brit.*) 《usu. *C*-》 the law-making assembly of the Church of England. **4.** [C] (*Brit.*) the law-making assembly of graduates of Oxford and Durham Universities.
—[名] 1. 소집 2. 집회 3. 《英》 대주교구(大主教區) 회의 4. 《英》 [Oxford, Durham 대학의] 이사회

con·voke [kənvóuk] *vt.* call together; summon (a parliament, etc.) to assemble. ↔dissolve ▷**con·vok·er** [-ər] *n.*
—[他] [회의·의회]를 소집하다

con·vo·lu·tion [kànvəlú:ʃ(ə)n / kɔ́n-] *n.* [C] a coil; a twist.
—[名] 소용돌이; 비틀림, 뒤틀림

con·voy *vt.* [kánvɔi, kənvɔ́i → *n.* / kɔ́nvɔi] go with a ship, etc. to protect it; escort. —*n.* [*U.S.* kánvɔi] **1.** [U] escort; protection. ¶ *under ~ of destroyers.*① **2.** [C] a group of warships, soldiers, etc. led or guarded by an escort. **3.** [C] a ship, etc. that acts as an escort.
—[他] [군함 따위]를 호송(호위)하다 —[名] 1. 호송, 호위 ¶①구축함에 호송되어 2. 호송되는 함대(선단·군대) 3. 호송선

con·vulse [kənvʌ́ls] *vt.* **1.** shake violently. **2.** 《usu. *in passive*》 disturb or agitate violently. ¶ *be convulsed with pain.*① **3.** throw into a fit of laughter. ¶ *be convulsed with laughter.*②
—[他] 1. …을 진동시키다 2. …에게 경련을 일으키게 하다, …을 경련하게 하다 ¶①고통에 몸부림치다 3. …을 배꼽을 쥐고 웃다 ¶②포복절도하다

con·vul·sion [kənvʌ́lʃ(ə)n] *n.* [C] **1.** 《usu. *pl.*》 the irregular shaking of the limbs or whole body caused by illness. ¶ *be seized with convulsions*① / *fall into a fit of convulsions.*② **2.** a fit of laughter. **3.** a violent disturbance.
—[名] 1. 경련, 경풍 ¶①경련에 사로잡히다/②경련을 일으키다 2. 웃음의 발작 3. 변동, 격변, 동란

con·vul·sive [kənvʌ́lsiv] *adj.* of convulsion; having or producing convulsions. ▷**con·vul·sive·ly** [-li] *adv.*
—[形] 경련성의, 발작적인, 필사의

co·ny, co·ney [kóuni] *n.* [C] (pl. **-nies** or **-neys**) a rabbit fur.
—[名] [한 마리의] 토끼 가죽

coo [ku:] *n.* [C] a soft sound made by doves or pigeons. —*v.* (**cooed, coo·ing**) *vi.* make a soft, murmuring sound. —*vt.* murmur softly; say (something) in a soft, loving manner. ▷**coo·er** [-ər] *n.*
—[名] 국국(비둘기의 울음소리) —[自] 국국 하고 울다 —[他] …을 소곤거리듯 달콤하게 말하다

⁑ **cook** [kuk] *vt.* prepare (food, etc.) by boiling, baking, etc. ¶ *~ the dinner.* —*vi.* **1.** be cooked. **2.** act as a cook.
cook up, (*colloq.*) prepare (something) falsely; make up. ¶ *~ up a story.*①
—*n.* [C] a person whose work is cooking.
—[他] …을 요리하다; 삶거나 굽거나 하여 음식을 만들다 —[自] 1. 익다, 요리되다 2. 요리사 노릇을 하다
[熟] 《口》 …을 날조하다 ¶①이야기를 날조하다 —[名] 요리사, 쿡

cook·book [kúkbùk] *n.* [C] (*U.S.*) a book telling how to cook various kinds of foods. (cf. *Brit.* cookery book)
—[名] 《美》 요리책

cook·er [kúkər] *n.* **1.** [C] a stove for cooking. **2.** [U] kinds of fruit, etc. in relating to how well they can be cooked.
—[名] 1. 요리용 풍로 2. 요리용(요리하기 알맞은) 과일

cook·er·y [kúkəri] *n.* (pl. **-er·ies**) **1.** [U] the art of cooking. **2.** [C] a place or the tools for cooking.
—[名] 1. 요리법 2. 요리장(실), 취사 도구

cook·ie, cook·y [kúki] *n.* [C] (*U.S.*) a small, flat, sweet cake. (cf. *Brit.* biscuit)
—[名] 쿠키(작고 납작한 과자)

‡ **cool** [ku:l] *adj.* **1.** a little cold; not warm. ↔warm ¶*a ~ chamber*① / *a ~ day* / *a ~ dress.*② **2.** calm; not excited. ¶*a ~ head* / *remain ~*③ / *be ~ in the face of danger.* **3.** not friendly; indifferent. ¶*a ~ lover* / *a ~ reception.* **4.** bold; without shame. ¶*a ~ hand* (or *customer, fish*)④ / *~ insolence.*⑤ **5.** bluish, greenish, or grayish.
—[形] 1. 서늘한, 시원한; 차가운 ¶①냉동실/②시원한 옷 2. 냉정한; 침착한 ¶③당황하지 않다 3. 냉담한 4. 뻔뻔스러운 ¶④뻔뻔스러운 녀석/⑤오만불손 5. 청색(녹색·회색 따위)이 도는

—*n.* [U] 《usu. *the ~*》 something cool; a cool place or time. ¶*in the ~ of the morning.*
—[名] 냉기, 서늘한 곳(때)

—*vt., vi.* make or become cool. ¶*~ oneself.*⑥
—[他][自] 차게 하다; 차가와지다; 서늘하게 하다, 서늘해지다 ¶시원하게 하다

cool down (or ***off***), become or get cool; become calm.
[熟] 식다; 진정되다, 차분해지다

cool·er [kú:lər] *n.* [C] a device that cools foods, a room, etc.
—[名] 냉각기, 냉방 장치, 쿠울러

cool-head·ed [kú:lhédid] *adj.* calm.
—[形] 차분한, 냉정한, 침착한

coo·lie [kú:li] *n.* [C] an unskilled workman or a laborer who does hard work for little pay in China, India, etc.
—[名] [중국·인도 등지의] 막노동자, 날품팔이꾼, 쿠울리

cool·ly [kú:l(l)i] *adv.* in a cool way; calmly; in a friendly manner.
—[副] 냉담하게, 냉정히, 태연히

cool·ness [kú:lnis] *n.* [U] the state of being cool.
—[名] 서늘함; 냉정; 태연

• **coon** [ku:n] *n.* [C] (*U.S.*) **1.** a raccoon. **2.** a Negro.
—[名] 《美》 1. 너구리의 일종 2. 흑인, 검둥이

coop [ku:p] *n.* [C] a small cage or box for chickens or small animals. —*vt.* **1.** keep or put (something) in a coop. **2.** keep (someone or an animal) in a very small space. ¶*They were cooped up in a small room.*
—[名] 닭장, 닭우리 —[他] 1. …을 둥우리(우리)에 넣다 2. …을 가두다, 감금하다

co-op [kóuɑp, -́ / kóuɔp] *n.* [C] (*colloq.*) a cooperative store, society, etc.
—[名] 소비조합[매점]

coop·er [kú(:)pər / kú:pə] *n.* [C] a person who makes barrels, casks, etc.
—[名] 통 제조공

• **co·op·er·ate, co-op·er·ate** [kouάpərèit / -ɔ́p-] *vi.* work or act together for a common purpose. ¶*~ with a friend in doing the work.*
—[自] 협력하다, 협동하다

‡ **co·op·er·a·tion, co-op·er·a·tion** [kouὰpəréiʃ(ə)n / -ɔ̀p-] *n.* **1.** [U] the act of cooperating. **2.** [C] an association of people who share in both profits and losses. ¶*a consumer's* (*producer's*) *~.*①
—[名] 1. 협력, 협동 2. 협동조합 ¶①소비(생산)조합

co·op·er·a·tive, co-op·er·a·tive [kouάp(ə)rèitiv, -rətiv / -ɔ́p(ə)rətiv] *adj.* of cooperation; willing to work together with others.
—[形] 조합의; 협동의; 협력적인

co·op·er·a·tor, co-op·er·a·tor [kouάpərèitər / -ɔ́pərèitə] *n.* [C] a person who cooperates.
—[名] 협력(협동)자

co·or·di·nate, co-or·di·nate [kouɔ́:rdinit, +*U.S.* -nèit →*v.*] *adj.* **1.** of equal importance; on the same level. **2.** (*Grammar*) joining words, phrases, or clauses of equal grammatical importance. ¶*a ~ clause*① / *a ~ conjunction.*② ⇒[N.B.]
—[形] 1. 동격의, 대등한 2. 《文法》 등위(等位)의 ¶①등위절/②등위 접속사 [N.B.] and, but, or, for 따위

—*n.* [C] a coordinate person or thing.
—[名] 동등한 것, 동격자

—*vt.* [kouɔ́:rdinèit] **1.** cause (persons or things) to work together for a common purpose; bring (parts) into a proper relation; harmonize. ¶*~ the departments of a business.*③ **2.** make (things) equal in importance.
—[他] 1. …을 통합(조정)하다, [한 계통의 각 부분]을 정합(整合)하다 2. …을 대등하게 하다, 균형잡히게 하다

co·or·di·na·tion, co-or·di·na·tion [kouɔ̀:rdinéiʃ(ə)n] *n.* [U] **1.** the act of coordinating. **2.** the state or relation of being coordinated.
—[名] 1. 동등하게 하기 2. 동격, 대등한 관계

cop [kɑp / kɔp] *n.* [C] (*colloq.*) a policeman. —*vt.* (**copped, cop·ping**) **1.** steal. **2.** catch.
—[名] 《口》 순경, 경관 —[他] 1. …을 훔치다 2. …을 붙잡다

co·part·ner [kóupά:rtnər] *n.* [C] a partner; an associate.
—[名] 동료; [기업] 협동자

co·part·ner·ship [kóupά:rtnərʃip / kóupά:tnə-] *n.* [U] partnership.
—[名] 협동, 조합제도

• **cope**¹ [koup] *vi.* struggle; deal successfully. 《*~ with* a problem or a situation》 ¶*~ with the crowds* / *~ with a situation*① / *He was unable to ~ with his difficulties.*
—[自] 대등하게 싸우다; [문제·난국 따위를] 수습하다 ¶①정세에 대처하다

cope² [koup] [C] *n.* **1.** a long cape worn by priests at special times. **2.** any cover like a cope. ¶*the ~ of heaven* / *a ~ of night.* —*vt.* cover (someone) with a cope.
—[名] 1. [성직자의 망토 모양의] 법의(法衣) 2. 덮는 것 —[他] …에게 법의를 입히다

cop·i·er [kápiər / kɔ́piə] *n.* [C] **1.** a person who copies; a copyist. **2.** an imitator.
—[名] 1. 복사하는 사람, 필생(筆生) 2. 모방자

co·pi·ous [kóupiəs] *adj.* abundant; plentiful. ¶*a ~ harvest.*① ▷**co·pi·ous·ly** [-li] *adv.*
—[形] 풍부한, 많은, 방대한 ¶①풍작

:cop·per [kápər / kɔ́pə] *n.* **1.** [U] a red-brown metal. **2.** [C] a thing made of copper. **3.** [C] a copper coin, such as the U.S. cent. —*vt.* put a coat of copper on (something). —*adj.* **1.** of copper; made of copper. ¶*a ~ coin.* **2.** copper-colored.
—[名] 1. 동, 구리 2. 동제품 3. 동전(영국의 penny, 미국의 cent 따위) —[他] …에 구리를 입히다 —[形] 1. 구리의, 구리로 만든 2. 구릿빛의

cop·per·plate [kápərplèit / kɔ́pə-] *n.* **1.** [U][C] a flat plate of copper on which pictures, designs, etc. are cut. **2.** [C] a print made from such a plate. **3.** [C] copperplate printing.
—[名] 1. [인쇄하기 위해 식각(蝕刻)하거나 조각하는] 동판 2. 동판 인쇄물 3. 동판 인쇄

cop·per·smith [kápərsmìθ / kɔ́pə-] *n.* [C] a man who works in copper.
—[名] 구리 세공사

cop·per·y [kápəri / kɔ́p-] *adj.* containing copper; like copper.
—[形] 구리를 함유한, 구리 같은

cop·pice [kápis / kɔ́p-] *n.* [C] a wood of small trees, bushes, shrubs, etc.
—[名] 잡목 숲

cop·ra [káprə / kɔ́p-] *n.* [U] the dried meat of the coconut, which yields coconut oil.
—[名] 코프라[야자의 배유(胚乳)를 말린 것]

copse [kaps / kɔps] *n.* [C] =coppice.

:cop·y [kápi / kɔ́pi] *n.* [C] (pl. **cop·ies**) **1.** a thing made like another; an imitation; a reproduction. ¶*I made a ~ of the letter.* **2.** one of a number of books, magazines, newspapers, etc. made at the same printing. ¶*a ~ of "Life."* **3.** a model; a pattern. **4.** [U] typed or written material ready to be printed.
—*v.* (**cop·ied**) *vt.* **1.** make a copy of (something). ¶*I copied two pages of the book.* **2.** imitate. ¶*We should ~ his good points.*① —*vi.* make a copy. ¶*He often copies during examinations.*②
—[名] 1. 사본(寫本), 모사(模寫); [그림 따위의] 베끼기, 복사 2. [책·잡지 따위의] 1부, 권 3. [습자용] 대본, 모델 4. 원고
—[他] 1. …을 베끼다, 모사하다, 복사하다 2. …을 모방하다, 흉내내다 ¶①그의 좋은 점을 배워야 한다 —[自] 베끼다, 모사하다 ¶②그는 시험중에 남의 답안을 잘 베낀다

cop·y·book [kápibùk / kɔ́p-] *n.* [C] a book containing models of handwriting for learners to copy.
—[名] 습자책

cop·y·ist [kápiist / kɔ́p-] *n.* [C] **1.** a person who makes copies, esp. of old documents. **2.** an imitator.
—[名] 1. 복사자, 필생(筆生) 2. 모방자

cop·y·right [kápiràit / kɔ́p-] *n.* [U] the right of one person or body to publish and sell a literary or artistic work for a limited time. ¶*own the ~ on a book.* —*adj.* protected by a copyright. —*vt.* protect (a book, etc.) by a copyright.
—[名] 저작권, 판권 —[形] 저작권(판권)이 있는 —[他] …을 판권으로 보호하다

cop·y·writ·er [kápiràitər / kɔ́piràitə] *n.* [C] a writer of copy, esp. for advertisements.
—[名] 광고 원고 작성자

co·quet [koukét] *vi.* (**-quet·ted, -quet·ting**) **1.** try to attract the attention of others [usu. of the opposite set] with a pretense of fondness; flirt. **2.** act or treat something jokingly; trifle. 《~ *with* something》
—[自] 1. 남의 마음을 끌다, 아양떨다 2. 장난삼아 해 보다

co·quet·ry [kóukitri, +*U.S.* koukét-, +*Brit.* kɔ́kit-] *n.* [U][C] (pl. **-ries**) the act of coquetting; the state of being coquettish.
—[名] 교태를 부리기, 아양떨기; 요염

co·quette [koukét, +*Brit.* kɔk-] *n.* [C] a woman who tries to attract men's attention or admiration to please her vanity; a flirt.
—[名] 요염한 여자, 남자를 녹이는 여자

co·quet·tish [koukétiʃ, +*Brit.* kɔ-] *adj.* of or like a coquette; showing coquetry.
—[形] 교태부리는, 아양떠는, 요염한

cor·a·cle [kɔ́:rəkl, kar- / kɔ́r-] *n.* [C] a small fishing boat made of animal skin or oilcloth covering a wooden frame. ⇒fig.
—[名] 나무테에 짐승 가죽을 씌운 낚시배

[coracle]

·co·ral [kɔ́:rəl / kɔ́r-] *n.* **1.** [U] a hard substance made out of the skeletons of certain sea animals. **2.** [C] a sea animal whose skeleton forms coral. **3.** [C] a piece of coral used in jewelry; a toy made of coral. **4.** [U] the color of red coral; deep pink. —*adj.* **1.** of or made of coral. **2.** deep pink.
—[名] 1. 산호 2. 산호충 3. 산호 세공 4. 산호빛, 진분홍빛
—[形] 1. 산호의, 산호로 만든 2. 산호빛의

:cord [kɔ:rd] *n.* **1.** [U] a thin rope or thick string; [C] a
—[名] 1. 굵은 끈, 노끈, 가는 밧줄 2.

piece of this. **2.** [C] (*Anatomy*) a part in an animal body resembling a cord. ¶*the spinal ~*① / *the vocal cords.*② **3.** [C][U] (*Electricity*) a long, narrow device for conveying an electric current. **4.** [U] corduroy. **5.** ((*pl.*)) corduroy trousers. **6.** [U] ((often *pl.*)) any force or influence acting as a tie or bond. ¶*the cords of love.*③ **7.** [C] a measure for cutting wood.
《解》 색상(索狀) 구조(조직), 인대(靭帶) ¶①척수/②성대 **3.** 전등줄, 코오드 **4.** 코르덴(이랑지게 짠 천) **5.** 코르덴 바지 **6.** 속박, 기반(羈絆) ¶③사랑의 기반 **7.** 코오드 척(尺) 단위(장작의 체적단위)

—*vt.* fasten or connect (something) with a cord. —[他] …을 끈으로 묶다(동이다)

* **cor·dial** [kɔ́ːrdʒ(ə)l] *adj.* **1.** hearty; friendly. ¶*a ~ welcome.* **2.** encouraging the heart; reviving. ¶*a ~ drink.* —[形] **1.** 진심에서 우러나는, 성심성의의 **2.** 기력을 돋구는, 강심성(强心性)의
—*n.* [C] a stimulating medicine, drink. —[名] 강심제, 강장제

cor·dial·i·ty [kɔːrdʒǽliti / kɔ̀ːdiǽl-] *n.* **1.** [U] friendliness; sincerity. **2.** [C] a cordial act or remark. —[名] **1.** 친절, 온정 **2.** 성실한 행위; 친절한 말

cor·dial·ly [kɔ́ːrdʒəli / kɔ́ːdjəli] *adv.* in a cordial manner. —[副] 진심으로, 성의를 가지고

cor·don [kɔ́ːrd(ə)n] *n.* [C] **1.** a line or circle of policemen, soldiers, ships, etc. enclosing or guarding a place. ¶*A ~ of policemen was drawn around the hotel.*① **2.** a cord worn as an ornament. —[名] **1.** 비상선, 보초선 ¶①호텔 주위에 비상선이 쳐졌다 **2.** 수장(綬章), 장식 리본

cor·du·roy [kɔ́ːrdjurɔ̀i, kɔ́rdə-] *n.* **1.** [U] thick cotton cloth with raised lines on its surface. **2.** ((*pl.*)) trousers made of corduroy. —[名] **1.** 코르덴 **2.** 코르덴 바지

core [kɔːr] *n.* [C] **1.** the hard, central part of fruits. ¶*This pear is rotten at the ~.* **2.** the central and most important part. ¶*the ~ of a dispute*① —[名] **1.** [과실의] 속, 씨, 핵, 고갱이 **2.** 중심, 핵심, 골자 ¶①논의의 핵심
to the core, thoroughly. ¶*He is American to the ~.*② [熟] 철저히 ¶②그는 철저한 미국인이다
—*vt.* remove the core from (an apple, etc.) —[他] [과일의] 응어리를 없애다

core curriculum [´ —´——] *n.* the curriculum of a course of education in which all the subjects are based on a certain theme. —[名] 코어 커리큘럼(사회 생활에 중심을 두고 핵심적으로 편성하는 교과 과정)

Co·rin·thi·an [kərínθiən] *adj.* **1.** of Corinth. **2.** (*Architecture*) of the classical orders of Greek architecture. —[形] **1.** [옛 그리이스의 도시] 코린트의 **2.** 《建》 코린트 식의

* **cork** [kɔːrk] *n.* **1.** [U] the bark of a kind of oak. **2.** [C] a cork oak. **3.** [C] a piece of cork used as a stopper for a bottle, etc. —*vt.* stop (a bottle, etc.) with a cork. —[名] **1.** 코르크 **2.** 코르크나무 **3.** 코르크 마개 —[他] …에 코르크 마개를 하다

cork·screw [kɔ́ːrkskrùː] *n.* [C] a tool for removing corks from bottles. ⇒fig. —*adj.* shaped like a corkscrew; spiral. ¶*a ~ staircase.* —[名] 코르크 마개뽑기 —[形] 나사 모양의

[corkscrew]

cork·y [kɔ́ːrki] *adj.* (**cork·i·er, cork·i·est**) **1.** of or containing cork. **2.** like cork. —[形] **1.** 코르크의(가 들어 있는) **2.** 코르크 같은

corm [kɔːrm] *n.* [C] a bulb like underground stem of plants such as the crocus. —[名] 구경(球莖)

cor·mo·rant [kɔ́ːrm(ə)r(ə)nt] *n.* [C] **1.** a large, long-necked sea bird, used in catching fish. **2.** a person who always desires more food or more things. —[名] **1.** 가마우지 **2.** 욕심꾸러기

‡ **corn**[1] [kɔːrn] *n.* **1.** [C] a single seed of a grain such as wheat, barley or rye. **2.** [U] (*U.S.*) a tall plant that bears large grains on ears; Indian corn. **3.** [U] (*Brit.*) wheat; (*Scot.*) oats. **4.** [U] ((*collectively*)) grain in general. **5.** [U] a plant that produces such seeds. —*vt.* keep or preserve (meat, etc.) with salt in the form of grains. —[名] **1.** 곡식의 낟알 **2.** 《美》 옥수수 **3.** 《英》 밀; 《스코》 귀리 **4.** 곡류, 곡식 **5.** 곡초 —[他] …을 소금에 절이다

corn[2] [kɔːrn] *n.* [C] a hardened part of the skin, esp. on the toes. —[名] [발가락의] 티눈

corn bread [´ ´] *n.* (*U.S.*) bread made of corn meal. —[名] 《美》 옥수수 빵

corn chandler [´ ´—] *n.* (*Brit.*) a merchant dealing in grain. —[名] 《英》 잡곡상

corned [kɔːrnd] *adj.* preserved or kept with salt. ¶*~ beef.*① —[形] 소금에 절인 ¶①소금에 절인 쇠고기

‡ **cor·ner** [kɔ́ːrnər] *n.* [C] **1.** the point or angle where two lines or surfaces meet. ¶*There was a bookshelf in the ~ of the room.* **2.** the place where two streets meet. ¶*a drugstore at* (or *on*) *the ~ of the street.* **3.** a —[名] **1.** 모, 각(角) **2.** [길]모퉁이 **3.** 외딴 곳, 구석진 곳 ¶①세계 방방곡곡에서 온 관광객들 **4.** 사람 눈에 띄지 않는 곳; 지방, 지역 **5.** 궁지, 난처한 입장 ¶

C

distant or hidden place. ¶*tourists from every ~ of the earth.*① **4.** a secret place; a region. **5.** an awkward position from which escape is difficult. ¶*I was driven into a ~.*② | *I am in a tight ~.*③ **6.** a protective or ornamental piece to fit over a corner. ¶*a ~ for a photograph.* **7.** (*Commercial*) the act of buying up some stock or article so as to control its price. ¶*a ~ in wheat.*

②나는 궁지에 몰렸다/③나는 곤경에 빠져 있다 6. 모서리쇠(장식) 7. 《商》 매점(買占)

1) ***cut corners,*** ⓐ take a shorter way. ⓑ reduce the money, time or labor required.
2) ***turn the corner,*** pass the most dangerous or most important point.

[熟] 1)ⓐ 지름길로 가다 ⓑ절약하다 2)고비를 넘다, 위기를 벗어나다

—*vt.* **1.** supply (something) with a corner. **2.** drive or put (someone or something) into a corner. **3.** force (someone) into an awkward or difficult position. **4.** (*Commercial*) buy up (some stock or article) to raise its price. **—***vi.* **1.** (*Commercial*) buy up; form a corner. **2.** (of a car) turn a corner.

—[他] 1. …에 모서리를 대다(내다) 2. …을 구석에 두다(몰아넣다) 3. …을 궁지에 몰아넣다 4.《商》…을 매점하다 —[自] 1. 매점하다 2. 모퉁이를 돌아가다

—*adj.* at or on a corner. ¶*a ~ store.*

—[形] 모서리의, 구석의

cor·ner·stone [kɔ́:rnərstòun] *n.* [C] **1.** the stone at the corner of a building foundation. **2.** the most important or basic thing; a foundation. ¶*the ~ of the state.*

—[名] 1. [건물 귀퉁이의] 주춧돌 2. 중요한 것, 기초, 토대

cor·net [kɔ:rnét → 2. / kɔ́:nit, kɔ:nét] *n.* [C] **1.** a musical brass instrument like a trumpet. **2.** [*U.S.* kɔ́:rnit] a cone-shaped piece of paper for candy, etc.; (*Brit.*) a cone-shaped wafer for containing ice cream.

—[名] 1. 코오넷 2. [과자 따위의] 삼각형 종이 봉지; [아이스크리임을 담는] 원추형 웨이퍼

corn·field [kɔ́:rnfì:ld] *n.* [C] a field in which corn is grown.

—[名] 보리밭, 옥수수밭

corn·flakes [kɔ́:rnflèiks] *n. pl.* a breakfast food consisting of small toasted flakes made from corn and eaten with milk and sugar.

—[名] 코온플레이크(바삭바삭 튀긴 옥수수)

corn flour [´ ˋ] *n.* (*U.S.*) flour made from corn; (*Brit.*) flour made from grain.

—[名] 《美》 옥수숫가루; 《英》 곡식가루

cor·nice [kɔ́:rnis] *n.* [C] (*Architecture*) an ornamental molding placed along the top of a wall, a pillar, etc.

—[名] 《建》 [처마 언저리 벽의] 수평 쇠시리 장식

corn meal [kɔ́:rnmì:l] *n.* [U] **1.** (*U.S.*) meal made from corn. **2.** (*Scot.*) oatmeal.

—[名] 1.《美》 맷돌로 탄 옥수수 2.《스코》 맷돌로 탄 보리

corn·starch [kɔ́:rnstɑ̀:rtʃ] *n.* [U] (*U.S.*) a kind of flour made from corn and used in cookery.

—[名] 《美》 옥수수 녹말

co·rol·la [kərɑ́lə / -rɔ́lə] *n.* [C] the petals of a flower.

—[名] 화관(花冠)(꽃잎의 총칭)

cor·ol·lar·y [kɔ́:rəlèri, kɑ́r- / kərɔ́ləri] *n.* [C] (pl. **-la·ries**) **1.** (*Mathematics*) a statement which may be taken for granted when another has been proved. **2.** a natural result.

—[名] 1.《數》 계(系) [정리에서 추측할 수 있는 명제(命題)] 2. 필연적 귀결(결과)

co·ro·na [kəróunə] *n.* [C] (pl. **-nas** or **-nae**) **1.** a crown; something shaped like a crown. **2.** a ring of light seen around the sun or the moon.

—[名] 1. 관(冠); 관 모양의 것 2. 코로나, 햇(달)무리

co·ro·nae [kəróuni:] *n.* pl. of **corona.**

cor·o·na·tion [kɔ̀:rənéiʃ(ə)n, kɑ̀r- / kɔ̀r-] *n.* [C] the act or ceremony of crowning a king, a queen, or another ruler.

—[名] 대관식

cor·o·ner [kɔ́:rənər, kɑ́r- / kɔ́rənə] *n.* [C] a local official whose duty is to investigate any unnatural death.

—[名] 검시관(檢屍官)

cor·o·net [kɔ́:rənit, kɑ́r- / kɔ́r-] *n.* [C] **1.** a small crown worn by princes or nobles. **2.** an ornamental band worn around the head.

—[名] 1. [귀족의] 보관(寶冠), 작은 관 2. [부인용의] 관 모양의 머리 장식(띠)

cor·po·ral[1] [kɔ́:rp(ə)r(ə)l] *n.* [C] a soldier in the army below a sergeant.

—[名] 상병(上兵)(최하위의 하사관)

cor·po·ral[2] [kɔ́:rp(ə)r(ə)l] *adj.* **1.** of the body; bodily. ¶*~ punishment.*① **2.** personal. ¶*~ possession.*②

—[形] 1. 신체상의, 육체의 ¶①체형 2. 개인의 ¶②사유물

cor·po·rate [kɔ́:rp(ə)rit] *adj.* **1.** forming a corporation. ¶*~ property.*① **2.** of or related to a corporation. ¶*~ responsibility.*② **3.** united; combined.

—[形] 1. 법인 조직의 ¶①법인 재산 2. 공동의, 단체의 ¶②공동 책임 3. 단결한

:cor·po·ra·tion [kɔ̀:rpəréiʃ(ə)n] *n.* [C] **1.** a group of people permitted by law to act for purposes of business. **2.** any group of persons united in one body.

—[名] 1. 사단법인; 주식회사 2. [일반적으로] 단체, 조합

cor·po·re·al [kɔ:rpɔ́:riəl] *adj.* **1.** bodily. ↔spiritual **2.** material; physical.

—[形] 1. 신체상의 2. 물질적인; 유형(有形)의

* **corps** [kɔːr] *n.* [C] (pl. **corps** [kɔːrz]) **1.** a part of an army consisting of two or more divisions. **2.** a specialized branch of the armed forces. ¶*the Medical Corps.*① **3.** a group of people united in some special work.
—[名] 1. 군단 2. …대(隊), 특수병과 ¶①의무대 3. [일반적으로] 단체, 단(團)

corpse [kɔːrps] *n.* [C] a dead human body.
—[名] [인간의] 시체

cor·pu·lence [kɔ́ːrpjuləns], **-len·cy** [-lənsi] *n.* [U] largeness or stoutness of body; fatness.
—[名] 비만, 뚱뚱함, 비대

cor·pu·lent [kɔ́ːrpjulənt] *adj.* (of a human being) stout; fat; fleshy.
—[形] 뚱뚱한, 비대한

cor·pus·cle [kɔ́ːrpʌsl] *n.* [C] **1.** a very small particle. **2.** one of the cells which float in the blood. ¶*red* (*white*) *corpuscles.*①
—[名] 1. 미립자, 원자 2. 혈구(血球) ¶①적(백)혈구

cor·ral [kərǽl / kɔːrɑ́ːl] *n.* [C] **1.** a circular fence to hold horses, cattle, etc.; a pen. **2.** a defensive enclosure surrounded by wagons. —*vt.* **1.** drive or put (animals) into a corral. **2.** form such a circle with (wagons).
—[名] 1. 울타리가 있는 가축 우리 2. [야영할 때] 마차로 둘러 막은 원진(圓陣) —[他] 1. [소·말]을 우리에 넣다 2. [마차]로 원진을 치다

‡ **cor·rect** [kərékt] *adj.* **1.** true; right. ¶*the ~ time* / *~ pronunciation* / *~ spelling* / *You're ~ in doing so.* **2.** proper; suitable. ¶*She wore the ~ dress for a wedding.* —*vt.* **1.** make (something) right; point out the errors of (something). ¶*~ a watch* / *The teacher corrected my composition.* **2.** punish (someone) in order to correct a bad action. ¶*~ a boy for disobedience.* **3.** cure. ¶*~ a disease.*
—[形] 1. 옳은, 진실의, 정확한 2. 알맞은, 온당한, 품행방정한 —[他] 1. …을 정정하다, 바로잡다 2. …을 처벌하다 3. [병]을 치료하다

* **cor·rec·tion** [kərékʃ(ə)n] *n.* [U] [C] **1.** the act of correcting. ¶*the ~ of a composition.* **2.** a thing that is put in place of a mistake. **3.** punishment.
—[名] 1. 정정, 수정 2. 정정한 곳 3. 처벌, 교정(矯正)

cor·rect·i·tude [kəréktit(j)ùːd / -tjùːd] *n.* [U] the quality of being correct in conduct.
—[名] [품행의] 단정, 방정

cor·rec·tive [kəréktiv] *adj.* tending to correct. ¶*I have to take ~ measures.* —*n.* [C] something serving to correct.
—[形] 교정(矯正)하는 —[名] 교정하는 것(방법), 중화물(中和物)

cor·rect·ly [kəréktli] *adv.* in a correct way.
—[副] 올바르게, 정확하게

cor·rect·ness [kəréktnis] *n.* [U] the quality or state of being correct.
—[名] 정확, 품행방정

cor·re·late [kɔ́ːrilèit, kɑ́r- / kɔ́r-] *vt.* bring (something) into a common relation with another thing. ⟪~ something *with*⟫ ¶*~ the findings of geography with those of history.* —*vi.* have the same relation with a second thing toward a third thing. ⟪~ *to* or *with* something⟫ —*n.* [C] either of two closely related things. —*adj.* closely related.
—[他] …을 관련시키다 —[自] 상호관계가 있다 —[名] 상호관계가 있는 것 —[形] 관련된

cor·re·la·tion [kɔ̀ːriléiʃ(ə)n, kɑ̀r- / kɔ̀r-] *n.* [U] the same relation between two or more things toward something else.
—[名] 상호관계

cor·rel·a·tive [kərélətiv, +*Brit.* kɔr-] *adj.* **1.** having correlation. **2.** (*Grammar*) regularly used in pairs. ¶*~ conjunctions.*① —*n.* [C] (*Grammar*) a correlative word.
—[形] 1. 상호관계가 있는 2. ⟪文法⟫ 상관적인 ¶①상관 접속사 —[名] 상관어

* **cor·re·spond** [kɔ̀ːrispɑ́nd, kɑ̀r- / kɔ̀rispɔ́nd] *vi.* **1.** agree in amount, position, etc. ⟪~ *to* or *with* something⟫ ¶*His new position corresponds to his interests.* / *Let deeds ~ with words.* **2.** be like or similar. ⟪~ *to* something⟫ ¶*The American Congress corresponds to the Japanese Diet.* **3.** communicate by letters. ⟪~ *with* someone⟫ ¶*I ~ with him regularly.*
—[自] 1. 일치하다, 부합하다 2. 상당(해당)하다 3. 편지 왕래를 하다, 통신하다

* **cor·re·spond·ence** [kɔ̀ːrispɑ́ndəns, kɑ̀r- / kɔ̀rispɔ́nd-] *n.* [U] **1.** agreement; harmony. **2.** similarity. **3.** communication by exchanging letters with each other. ⟪~ *with* someone⟫ ¶*I have been in ~ with him.* / *They kept up ~ during the summer.* **4.** ⟪*collectively*⟫ letters.
—[名] 1. 일치, 부합; 조화 2. 상응(相應), 해당; 유사(類似) 3. 편지 왕래 4. 왕복서신, 편지

correspondence course [⌐–⌐– ⌐] *n.* a series of lessons given by a correspondence school on a subject.
—[名] 통신교육 [과정]

correspondence school [⌐–⌐– ⌐] *n.* a school that gives lessons by mail.
—[名] 통신교육학교

‡ **cor·re·spond·ent** [kɔ̀ːrispɑ́ndənt, kɑ̀r- / kɔ̀rispɔ́nd-] *n.* [C] **1.** a person who exchanges letters with someone. ¶*My pen pal is a good ~.* **2.** a person hired by a
—[名] 1. 편지 왕래를 하는 사람, 통신자 2. 특파원, 통신원

C

news agency, etc. to gather and send news from a distant place. ¶*our ~ in Paris.*

cor·re·spond·ing [kɔ̀:rispándiŋ, kàr- / kɔ̀rispɔ́nd-] *adj.* **1.** agreeing; equivalent. 《~ *to*》 ¶*the ~ period of last year.*① **2.** communicating by letters. ¶*a ~ clerk.*
▷ **cor·re·spond·ing·ly** [-li] *adv*
—[形] 1. 일치하는, 해당하는 ¶①작년의 같은 기간 2. 통신하는; 편지 왕래하는

* **cor·ri·dor** [kɔ́:ridər, kár-, -dɔ̀:r / kɔ́ridɔ̀:] *n.* [C] a passageway; a long hallway. ¶*I went through the ~.*
—[名] 낭하, 복도, 회랑(回廊)

cor·ri·gen·da [kɔ̀:ridʒéndə, kàr- / kɔ̀r-] *n.* pl. of **corrigendum.**

cor·ri·gen·dum [kɔ̀:ridʒéndəm, kàr- / kɔ̀r-] *n.* [C] (pl. **cor·ri·gen·da**) **1.** an error to be corrected in a manuscript, printing, etc. **2.** 《*pl.*》 a list of corrections of errors in a book.
—[名] 1. 정정해야 할 것, 오자(誤字) 2. 정오표(正誤表)

cor·ri·gi·ble [kɔ́:ridʒibl, kár- / kɔ́r-] *adj.* **1.** that can be corrected. ¶*He is a ~ criminal.*① **2.** willing to be reformed.
—[形] 1. 고칠 수 있는; 교정할 수 있는 ¶①그는 개심할 수 있는 죄인이다 2. 기꺼이 고치려고 하는

cor·rob·o·rate [kərábərèit / -rɔ́b-] *vt.* confirm; strengthen.
—[他] …을 확증하다, 확실하게 하다

cor·rob·o·ra·tion [kəràbəréiʃ(ə)n / -rɔ̀b-] *n.* [U] **1.** the act of corroborating. **2.** anything that corroborates or confirms.
—[名] 1. 확실하게 하기, 확증 2. 확증하는 것, 증거 [따위]

cor·rob·o·ra·tive [kərábərèitiv, -rət / -rɔ́b-] *adj.* corroborating; confirming.
—[形] 확증적인, 확증하는

cor·rob·o·ra·tor [kərábərèitər / -rɔ́bərèitə] *n.* [C] a person or thing that corroborates or confirms.
—[名] 확증인(물)

cor·rode [kəróud] *vt.* **1.** eat away gradually by chemical action; eat into the surface of (something); rust. ¶*Rust corroded the iron fence.* **2.** weaken or destroy (spirit, strength or force); consume; impair. ¶*Jealously corroded her character.* **—vi.** become corroded. ¶*Iron corrodes quickly.*
—[他] 1. …을 부식(腐蝕)하다 2. [마음·성격 따위]를 좀먹다 —[自] 부식하다

cor·ro·sion [kəróuʒ(ə)n] *n.* [U] the act of corroding; the state of being corroded; gradual decay.
—[名] 부식 작용; 부식; [마음 따위] 좀먹기

cor·ro·sive [kəróusiv] *adj.* having the power to corrode; eating away. ¶*Some acids are ~ to the skin.* **—n.** [C] anything that causes corrosion.
—[形] 부식성의 —[名] 부식제(腐蝕劑)

cor·ru·gate [kɔ́:rugèit, kár- / kɔ́r-] *vt.* shape (something) into wavelike folds. **—vi.** become corrugated.
—[他] …을 물결 모양이 되게(주름살지게) 하다 —[自] 주름살지다

cor·ru·gat·ed [kɔ́:rugèitid, kár- / kɔ́r-] *adj.* formed into folds; wrinkled. ¶*~ iron.*
—[形] 물결 모양의, 주름살이 진

cor·ru·ga·tion [kɔ̀:rugéiʃ(ə)n, kàr- / kɔ̀r-] *n.* [U][C] **1.** the act of corrugating; the state of being corrugated. **2.** a fold; a wrinkle; a furrow.
—[名] 1. 물결 모양으로 하기(되기), 주름살지기 2. 물결 모양의 것; 주름살

* **cor·rupt** [kərʌ́pt] *adj.* **1.** evil; wicked; taking bribes; dishonest. ¶*a ~ society / a ~ judge.* **2.** changed from a sound condition to an unsound one; impure. ¶*~ air.* **3.** (of words) different from standard usage. **4.** (of writings, text, etc.) made inferior by errors; not complete. ¶*a ~ text.*
—[形] 1. 타락한; 부도덕한; 뇌물을 받는; 부정의 2. 썩은; 더러워진 3. 표준어와 다른 4. [원고 따위] 틀린 데가 많은, 개악(改惡)된

—vt. 1. cause (someone) to be dishonest or wicked. **2.** offer money to cause (someone) to do what is wrong. ¶*~ an official.* **3.** make (something) impure; decay. **4.** make (a text, etc.) worse by changing it. **5.** cause (a form or meaning) to differ from standard usage. **—vi.** become corrupt.
—[他] 1. …을 타락시키다 2. …을 뇌물로 매수하다 3. …을 부패시키다 4. …을 개악하다 5. [언어]를 전와(轉訛)시키다 —[自] 부패하다; 타락하다

cor·rupt·i·ble [kərʌ́ptibl] *adj.* that can be corrupted.
—[形] 부패(타락)하기 쉬운; 매수할 수 있는

cor·rup·tion [kərʌ́pʃ(ə)n] *n.* [U] **1.** the act of decaying; rottenness. **2.** lack of moral principle. **3.** the act of offering money, etc. to do what is wrong; bribery; dishonesty. **4.** the act of making something impure. **5.** the act of changing for the worse; the state of being changed for the worse. **6.** the act of causing the form or meaning of a word to differ from standard usage.
—[名] 1. 부패 2. 타락 3. 독직(瀆職), 부정 4. 불순화, 오염 5. [원작의] 개악 6. 사투리, [말의] 전와(轉訛)

cor·rup·tive [kərʌ́ptiv] *adj.* tending to corrupt.
—[形] 부패성의; 타락시키는

cor·sair [kɔ́ːrsɛər] *n.* [C] **1.** a pirate. **2.** a pirate ship.
—[名] 1. 해적 2. 해적선

cor·set [kɔ́ːrsit] *n.* [C] (often *pl.*) a close-fitting kind of underclothes worn by women to give shape to the waist and hips.
—[名] 코르셋

cor·tege, -tége [kɔːrtéiʒ, -téʒ] *n.* [C] (*collectively*) **1.** a line or group of persons walking along in a ceremonial way; a ceremonial march. **2.** a group of followers, attendants, etc.
—[名] 1. 의식 행렬 2. 한 떼의 수행원(시종)

cor·tex [kɔ́ːrteks] *n.* [C] (pl. **-ti·ces** [-tisiːz]) **1.** (*Botany*) the skin on the outside of a tree; the bark. **2.** (*Anatomy*) the outer skin of an organ in an animal's body.
—[名] 1.《植》피층(皮層) 2.《解》피질(皮質), 외피(外皮)

co·si·ly [kóuzili] *adv.* =cozily.

co·si·ness [kóuzinis] *n.* =coziness.

cos·met·ic [kɑzmétik / kɔz-] *n.* [C] things used for beautifying the skin, the lips, etc. such as powder, lipstick, and face cream. **—*adj.*** beautifying the skin, the hair, the nails, etc.
—[名] 화장품 —[形] 화장용의, 미용의

cos·mic [kɑ́zmik / kɔ́z-] *adj.* **1.** of or belonging to the cosmos or the whole universe. ¶~ *laws*① / ~ *dust*② / ~ *fog* (*clouds*)③ / ~ *rays.*④ **2.** vast.
—[形] 1. 우주의 ¶①우주 법칙/②우주진(塵)/③성운(星雲)/④우주선(線) 2. 광대무변한

cos·mo·pol·i·tan [kɑ̀zməpɑ́lit(ə)n / kɔ̀zməpɔ́l-] *adj.* **1.** belonging to all parts of the world; widely spread. ¶*a ~ outlook*① / ~ *ideals.*② **2.** free from national or local thoughts. **—*n.*** [C] a cosmopolitan person; a person who feels at home in all parts of the world.
—[形] 1. 전세계에 걸친; 세계적인 ¶①세계적 시야/②세계주의적 이상 2. 한 나라(한 지방)의 생각을 초월한 —[名] 세계인, 세계주의자

cos·mos [kɑ́zməs / kɔ́zmɔs] *n.* (pl. **-mos·es**) **1.** [U] the universe considered as an orderly, harmonious system. ↔chaos **2.** [U] a complete and harmonious system. **3.** [C] a tall garden plant of the aster family that blooms in autumn.
—[名] 1. [질서정연한] 우주 2. [사상 따위의] 체계, 질서, 조화 3. 코스모스

‡cost [kɔːst / kɔst] *vt.* (**cost**) ⇒[usage] **1.** require as the price; need. ¶*The house ~ him £3,000.* / *How much does it ~ to build such a house?* / *That ~ him much time and labor.* **2.** cause a loss. (~ someone something) ¶*a victory that ~ 50,000 lives* / *The trip ~ him his life.* / *Careless driving may ~ you your life.*
—[他] [usage] 원래 cost는 자동사이므로 수동태로 할 수 없음 1. [비용·시간 따위가] 걸리다; [남에게 얼마]를 쓰게 하다; …을 필요로 하다 2. …을 희생시키다, 잃게 하다

1) ***cost someone dear*[*ly*],** make someone have a terrible experience.
2) ***cost what it may,*** by all means; at any price.

[熟] 1)…을 봉변을 당하게 하다 2)반드시, 꼭

—*n.* 1. [U][C] the price paid for anything; expense; charge. ¶*the ~ of living.* **2.** [C] sacrifice; loss; suffering.
—[名] 1. 값; 비용 2. 희생; 손실; 고통

1) ***at all costs,*** however much it may cost.
2) ***at any cost,*** by all means.
3) ***at the cost of,*** at the loss; at the expense of.
4) ***count the cost,*** consider all the circumstances.
5) ***to one's cost,*** to one's loss, injury or disadvantage.

[熟] 1)비용이 아무리 들더라도; 어떤 희생을 치르더라도 2)기어코, 꼭 3)…을 희생하고 4)온갖 사정을 고려해 보다 5)봉변을 당하여, 손해를 보고

cos·ter [kɑ́stər / kɔ́stə] *n.* (*colloq.*) =costermonger.

cos·ter·mon·ger [kɑ́stərmʌ̀ŋgər / kɔ́stəmʌ̀ŋgə] *n.* [C] (esp. *Brit.*) a person who sells fruit, vegetables, fish, etc. from a handcart or stand in the street.
—[名]《英》[과일·생선 따위를] 외치며 파는 행상인, 노점상

cos·tive [kɑ́stiv / kɔ́s-] *adj.* (of the bowls) difficult to empty.
—[形] 변비(便秘)의

cost·li·ness [kɔ́stlinis] *n.* [U] great cost; the state of being costly.
—[名] 값비쌈

‡cost·ly [kɔ́(ː)stli / kɔ́st-] *adj.* (**-li·er, -li·est**) of great value; valuable; expensive. ¶*a ~ diamond* / ~ *failures.*①
—[形] 값비싼; 귀중한; 비용이 많이 드는 ¶①값비싼 실패

•cos·tume *n.* [kɑ́st(j)uːm / kɔ́stjuːm ‖ → *v.*] [C] **1.** a complete set of clothes, esp. of a woman. **2.** clothes for a special purpose. ¶*a riding ~.*① **3.** [U] clothes of a certain place or period of time. ¶*Highland ~*② / *Victorian ~.*③
—[名] 1. [여자의] 한 벌의 의상; 옷차림 2. [특수 목적의] 의복 ¶①승마복 3. [어떤 시대·지방에 특유한] 복장, 의상 ¶②스코틀랜드 고지의 의상/③빅토리아 왕조 시대의 복장

—*vt.* [kɑst(j)úːm / kɔstjúːm] provide a costume for (someone); dress.
—[他] …에 의상을 입히다

co·sy [kóuzi] *adj.* (**-si·er, -si·est**) =cozy.

•cot¹ [kɑt / kɔt] *n.* [C] **1.** a narrow, portable bed, sometimes
—[名] 1. [즈크를 댄] 간이 침대; 2.《英》

cot — count

made of canvas stretched on a frame. **2.** (*Brit.*) a child's crib. — 名 소아용 침대

:cot² [kɑt / kɔt] *n.* Ⓒ **1.** (*poetic*) a cottage. **2.** a small place of shelter for birds, sheep, etc. — 名 1.《詩》시골집, 오두막 2. [양·새의] 우리

cote [kout] *n.* Ⓒ a shelter or shed for small animals, birds, etc. ¶*a dovecote.*① — 名 [가축·새의] 우리, 장 ¶①비둘기장

co·te·rie [kóutəri] *n.* Ⓒ a group of persons who are joined together by common interests and who often meet socially. — 名 [취미·목적이 같은] 동료, 동아리; 동인(同人)

:cot·tage [kátidʒ / kɔ́t-] *n.* Ⓒ **1.** a small house, esp. in the country. **2.** (*U.S.*) a house at a summer resort. — 名 1.시골집, 오두막집 2.《美》[피서지 따위의] 별장

cot·tag·er [kátidʒər / kɔ́tidʒə] *n.* Ⓒ a person who lives in a cottage. — 名 오두막집 주인

:cot·ton [kátn / kɔ́tn] *n.* Ⓤ **1.** soft, white fibers attached to the seeds of a certain plant. **2.** the plant that produces these fibers. **3.** thread made of cotton fibers. **4.** cloth made of cotton thread. —*adj.* made of cotton. ¶~ *cloth.* ⌈oil from cottonseeds.⌉ — 名 1. 솜, 면화 2. 목화 3. 무명실, 면사 4. 무명, 면직물 —形 면제(綿製)의, 무명의

cotton cake [⌄ ⌃] *n.* cattle food made by pressing out — 名 면화씨 깻묵

cotton wool [⌄ ⌃] *n.* raw cotton. — 名 면화, 원면

:couch [kautʃ] *n.* Ⓒ **1.** a thing on which a person lies to sleep or to rest. ⇒ NB **2.** a place to sleep or rest. —*vt.* **1.** (usu. in *passive*) lay down. **2.** put (an idea, etc.) into words; state. —*vi.* **1.** lie down on a couch; repose. **2.** lie in hiding in order to attack later. — 名 1. 잠자는 의자 NB sofa보다 낮은 침대 겸용 의자 2. 잠자리 —他 1.…을 가로 눕히다 2.…을 말로 표현하다 —自 1. 드러눕다; 쉬다 2. [짐승이 덤벼들려고] 숨어서 웅크려 기다리다

cou·gar [kú:gər] *n.* Ⓒ (pl. **-gars** or *collectively* **-gar**) a large, brownish-yellow American wildcat; a puma. — 名 퓨우머

·cough [kɔ:f / kɔf] *vt., vi.* force air with noise from the lungs in order to clear the throat. — 他自 기침하다

cough up, ⓐ force out (something) by coughing. ¶~ *up a fishbone.* ⓑ (*U.S. colloq.*) make (a secret, etc.) known carelessly; pay up (something) unwillingly. —*n.* Ⓒ the act or repeated acts of coughing. 熟 ⓐ 기침하여 …을 토해 내다 ⓑ《美》[비밀]을 무심코 말하다; …을 마지못해 지불하다 — 名 기침, 헛기침

:could [kud, kəd] *auxil. v.* pt. of **can**.
:could·n't [kúdnt] =could not. ⌈ USAGE ⌉
·couldst [kudst] *auxil. v.* (*archaic, poetic*) =could. ⇒ — 助 USAGE 주어가 thou 일 때 씀

:coun·cil [káunsi(i)l] *n.* Ⓒ a meeting or a group of elected persons for making plans or carrying out some special business. ¶*a cabinet* ~①/ *a family* ~②/ *in* ~.③ — 名 회의, 협의회, 이사회 ¶①각의(閣議)/②가족 회의/③회의중;자문기관에 의논하여

council house [⌄ ⌃] *n.* **1.** the house in which a council meeting is held; a town hall. **2.** (*Brit.*) a low-rent house or an apartment built for low-income families by the local government. ⌈a council.⌉ — 名 1.의사당; 공회당 2.《英》[저소득층의] 시영(市營)주택

coun·cil·lor, -cil·or [káunsilər] *n.* Ⓒ a member of — 名 고문관;평의원(評議員);참사(參
coun·cil·man [káuns(i)lmən] *n.* Ⓒ (pl. **-men** [-mən]) a member of the council of a city or town. — 名 시(읍·면)의회 의원 ⌈事⌉

:coun·sel [káuns(ə)l] *n.* Ⓤ **1.** the act of exchanging opinions. **2.** advice; guidance. ¶*A wise teacher gives good* ~. **3.** (pl. **-sel**) a person or a group of persons that gives advice about matters of law; a lawyer who speaks in a law court. ⌈ideas and plans.⌉
1) *keep one's own counsel,* say nothing about one's
2) *take counsel* (=*exchange ideas or opinions; consult*) *with someone.*
—*v.* (**-seled, -sel·ing** or *Brit.* **-selled, -sel·ling**) *vt.* give advice to (someone); speak favorably of (someone). ¶*I counseled her to be careful.* —*vi.* consult together. — 名 1. 협의, 상담 2. 충고, 조언 3. 변호사, 변호사단
熟 1)비밀을 지키다 2)…와 의논(협의)하다
—他 …에게 충고하다; 전하다
—自 의논하다

coun·se·lor, *Brit.* **-sel·lor** [káuns(ə)lər] *n.* Ⓒ **1.** a person who gives advice; an adviser. **2.** a lawyer. — 名 1. 상담(의논)상대 2. 변호사, 법률고문

:count¹ [kaunt] *vt.* **1.** find the number or total of (something). ¶~ *my money* / *Don't forget to* ~ *your change.* **2.** take account of (something); include. ¶*I no longer* ~ *him among my friends.* **3.** consider; think. (~ *someone happy,* etc.; ~ *that …*) ¶*I* ~ *myself fortunate in* — 他 1. …을 세다, 계산하다 2. …을 셈(계산)에 넣다 3. …이라고 생각하다; …이라 간주하다 ¶①내가 여기 있었다는 것은 운이 좋았다 —自 1. 수를 세다 2. 가치(중요성)가 있는 ¶①한

count [267] **countercheck**

being here.② / I ~ that he will come. ― vi. 1. say numbers in order. ¶~ from 1 to 50 / He can't ~ yet. 2. be of value. ¶Every vote counts.② 3. be included in counting or thinking. ¶You ~ among my best friends. 4. (Music) keep time by counting or beating.
  1) *be counted for* (or *as*), be considered as being (dead). ⌈to zero.⌉
  2) *count down*, count backward from some number
  3) *count for much*, be of much value or importance.
  4) *count in*, include.
  5) *count on* (or *upon*), rely on.
  6) *count up*, sum up; add up.
― n. Ⓤ Ⓒ the act of counting; the sum total.
  1) *keep* (*lose*) *count of*, be aware (fail to know) how many there are of a thing.
  2) *out of count*, countless.
  3) *take no count of* (=pay no attention to) something.
* **count²** [kaunt] n. Ⓒ a nobleman on the Continent, equal in rank to an English earl. ⌈↔uncountable⌉
* **count·a·ble** [káuntəbəl] adj. that can be counted.
  count·down [káuntdàun] n. Ⓒ Ⓤ the act of counting backward from some number to zero (for example 9, 8, 7, ... 1, 0) when giving a signal for starting something.
* **coun·te·nance** [káuntinəns] n. 1. Ⓤ Ⓒ the appearance or look of the face. ¶Her sad ~ worried us very much. 2. Ⓤ Ⓒ face; features. ¶The prince had a noble ~. 3. Ⓤ approval; moral support; encouragement. ¶I find no ~ in someone① / Father gave ~ to my plan. 4. Ⓤ calmness; peace of mind.
  1) *keep one's countenance*, ⓐ show no feeling; control one's expression. ⓑ keep from smiling or laughing.
  2) *lose countenance*, get excited; show one's feeling.
  3) *put someone out of countenance*, make someone uneasy, angry or perplexed.
― vt. 1. encourage; support. (~ someone *in doing*) ¶He countenanced our plan. 2. allow (something) against one's own feeling; permit.
* **count·er¹** [káuntər] n. Ⓒ 1. a thing used for counting. 2. a person who counts. 3. an imitation coin used in games for keeping score. 4. (esp. U.S.) a long table in a store, a bank, a restaurant, etc. at which goods are sold and money is handed. ⌈clerk in a store.⌉
  sit (or *serve*) *behind a counter*, work as a sales-
  coun·ter² [káuntər] adv. in the opposite direction; opposed; contrary; against. ¶His actions run ~ to the rules.① ― adj. opposite; contrary.
― vt., vi. 1. go or act counter to; oppose. 2. (Boxing) give a blow in return for that of an opponent.
― n. Ⓒ 1. that which is opposite or contrary to something else. 2. (Boxing) a blow given in return for that of an opponent.
  coun·ter·act [kàuntərǽkt] vt. act against (something); weaken the effects of (something); neutralize; hinder.
  coun·ter·ac·tion [kàuntərǽkʃ(ə)n] n. Ⓤ Ⓒ one action in opposition to another action; prevention.
  coun·ter·at·tack [káuntərətæk] n. Ⓒ an attack made in return for an enemy's attack. ― vt., vi. attack in return.
  coun·ter·bal·ance n. [káuntərbæ̀ləns → v.] Ⓒ 1. a weight balancing another. 2. an influence, a power, etc. balancing another. ― vt. [kàuntərbǽləns] act as a counterbalance to (something).
  coun·ter·check n. [káuntərtʃèk] Ⓒ 1. a check that restrains or opposes; an obstacle. 2. a check controlling another check.

표라도 중요하다 3. 셈에 들다, 계산에 포함되다 4. 《樂》박자를 맞추다

圈 1) …이라고 간주되다 2) [로켓 발사 따위에서] 초 읽기를 하다 3) 중요하다 4) …을 셈에 넣다 5) …을 기대 (의지)하다 6) [금액 따위] 총계를 내다

―몡 계산; 총계
圈 1) …의 수를 기억하고 있다 (잊어버리다) 2) 셀 수 없는 3) …을 중요시하지 않다

―몡 [영국 이외의] 백작

―휑 셀 수 있는
―몡 [로켓 발사 때의] 초 읽기

―몡 1. 얼굴 표정 2. 생김새, 용모; 안색 3. 찬조, 지지, 장려 ¶①…의 지지를 받지 못하다 4. 침착

圈 1) ⓐ 표정을 나타내지 않다 ⓑ 웃지 않고 있다 2) 흥분하다, 침착성을 잃다 3) …을 당황(불안)하게 하다, 화나게 하다
―팀 1. …을 격려하다; 원조하다 2. … 을 감정을 누르고 허락하다; 참다

―몡 1. 계기기 2. 계산자(者) 3. [노름에서 점수를 세는] 산가지; 모조화폐 4. 《美》 [상점·은행 따위의] 카운터, 계산대, 판매대

圈 점원으로 일하다
―휙 반대로, 거꾸로 ¶①그의 행동은 규칙에 위반된다 ―휑 반대의, 거꾸로의
―팀冏 1. 반대하다 2. 《권투》 되받아치다
―몡 1. 반대, 반대의 것 2. 《권투》 되받아치기

―팀 …에 반대로 작용하다, …을 방해하다; …의 효력을 약하게 하다
―몡 반대 행동, 약의 중화, 방해

―몡 역습, 반격 ―팀冏 역습하다, 반격하다

―몡 1. 평형추(平衡錘) 2. 평형력, 균형잡는 힘 ―팀 …을 평형시키다; …의 [부족]을 메우다, 벌충하다

―몡 1. 대항(방지) 수단, 방해 2. 재조회(再照會)

coun·ter·clock·wise [kàuntərklákwaiz / káuntəklɔ́k-] *adv., adj.* in the direction opposite to the normal direction of the hands of a clock. ↔clockwise
—[副][形] 시계바늘과 반대 방향으로(의)

coun·ter·feit [káuntərfit] *vt.* **1.** copy or imitate (something) in order to deceive; forge. ¶~ *ten-dollar bills* / ~ *someone's voice.* **2.** pretend. ¶~ *sorrow.*①
—*n.* [C] a copy or an imitation made to deceive.
—*adj.* **1.** not real; sham. **2.** pretended.
—[他] 1. …을 위조(모조)하다, 흉내내다 2. [감정]을 속이다, …인 체하다 ¶① 슬픈 체하다
—[名] 위조물; 모조물, 사본(寫本)
—[形] 1 모조의 2. …을 가장한

coun·ter·foil [káuntərfɔ̀il] *n.* [C] (chiefly *Brit.*) a part of a check, a money order, etc. which is kept as a record.
—[名] 《英》 [어음 따위의] 부본(副本)

coun·ter·mand [kàuntərmǽnd / -mά:nd] *vt.* **1.** (of an order, a command, etc.) withdraw; cancel. **2.** recall.
—[他] 1. [주문 따위]를 취소하다, 철회하다 2. …을 소환하다

coun·ter·march *n.* [káuntərmὰ:rtʃ → *v.*] [C] a march in the opposite direction. —*vt., vi.* [kàuntərmά:rtʃ] march back.
—[名] 뒤로 돌아가기, 반대 행진, 역전
—[他] 반대 행진하다

coun·ter·pane [káuntərpèin] *n.* [C] a coverlet for a bed; a bedspread.
—[名] [장식용] 침대 덮개

coun·ter·part [káuntərpὰ:rt] *n.* [C] **1.** a copy; a duplicate. **2.** a person or thing closely resembling another. ¶*She is her mother's* ~.① **3.** one of two parts that makes something complete when added to the other.
—[名] 1. 사본, 부본(副本), [정부(正副) 두 통 중의] 한 통 2. 아주 비슷한 사람 ¶①그녀는 어머니를 쏙 뺐다 3. [한 쌍 중의] 한쪽, 외쪽

coun·ter·plot [káuntərplὰt / káuntəplɔ̀t] *vt., vi.* (**-plot·ted, -plot·ting**) plot to defeat another plot. —*n.* [C] a plot to defeat another plot.
—[他][自] [상대의 계략을] 계략으로 이기다 —[名] 대항책

coun·ter·point [káuntərpɔ̀int] *n.* (*Music*) [C] a melody added to another as an accompaniment; [U] the art of combining melodies.
—[名] 《樂》 대위(對位) 선율; 대위법

coun·ter·poise [káuntərpɔ̀iz] *n.* **1.** [C] a weight balancing another weight; a counterbalancing weight. **2.** [U] power balancing other power. **3.** [U] balance.
—*vt.* act as a counterpoise to (something); bring (something) into balance.
—[名] 1. 평형추(錘) 2. 평형력 3. 균형, 평형
—[他] …와(을) 균형잡히게 하다

coun·ter·rev·o·lu·tion [kàuntərrevəlú:ʃ(ə)n / ⌐-----] *n.* [C] a revolution against a government itself recently established by a revolution.
—[名] 반혁명

coun·ter·vail [kàuntərvéil / káuntəvèil] *vt.* **1.** act against (another action, etc.) with equal power, effect, etc. **2.** pay for (something). —*vi.* be equal to an opposing force.
—[他] 1. …와 같은 힘(효과)을 갖게 하다, 상쇄하다 2. …을 보상하다 —[自] 필적(匹敵)하다; 균형을 이루다

count·ess [káuntis] *n.* [C] **1.** the wife or widow of an earl or a count. **2.** a lady having the rank equal to that of an earl or a count.
—[名] 1. 백작부인 2. 여자 백작

***count·less** [káuntlis] *adj.* too many to count; innumerable. ¶*the* ~ *stars.*
—[形] 셀 수 없는

coun·tri·fied [kʌ́ntrifàid] *adj.* **1.** looking or acting like a person from a rural area. countryman. **2.** countrylike; rustic; rural.
—[形] 1. 촌스러운, 시골뜨기 같은 2. 시골다운, 전원적인

⁑**coun·try** [kʌ́ntri] *n.* [C] (pl. **-tries**) **1.** the land of one nation; a nation. ¶*a small* ~. **2.** 《*sing.* only, often without *an article*》 a piece of land; a region; a district. ¶[*a*] *mountainous* ~.① **3.** 《*the* ~》 open land without many houses; a rural district. ¶*live in the* ~.② **4.** 《usu. *one's* ~》 one's home country; one's fatherland. ¶*love of one's* ~.③ **5.** 《*the*》 the people of a nation. —*adj.* of or in the country; countrylike. ¶*a* ~ *life.*
—[名] 1. 국토; 국가 2. 지역; 지방 ¶①구릉 지역; 산악지방 3. 시골; 전원지방 ¶②시골에 살다 4. 고향; 조국 ¶③향토(조국)애 5. 국민
—[形] 시골의, 시골다운

coun·try·folk [kʌ́ntrifòuk] *n.* 《*collectively,* used as *pl.*》 people living in rural areas; people who come from the same country.
—[名] 시골 사람들, 고향 사람들

***country house** [⌐-⌐] *n.* a home in the country.
—[名] 시골 저택; 별장

***coun·try·man** [kʌ́ntrimən] *n.* [C] (pl. **-men** [-mən]) a man of one's own country; a man living in a rural area.
—[名] 동포, 교포; 시골 사람

coun·try·peo·ple [kʌ́ntripì:pl] *n.* =countryfolk.

coun·try·seat [kʌ́ntrisì:t] *n.* [C] a country mansion or estate, esp. a fine one.
—[名] 시골의 대저택

coun·try·side [kʌ́ntrisàid] *n.* **1.** [C] 《usu. *the* ~》 a rural area; a certain part of the country. **2.** 《*collectively*》 the people living in a rural area.
—[名] 1. 시골; 지방 2. 지방에 살고 있는 사람들

coun·try·wom·an [kʌ́ntriwùmən] *n.* ⓒ (pl. **-wom·en** [-wìmin]) **1.** a woman of one's own country. **2.** a woman living in a rural area.

⁑**coun·ty** [káunti] *n.* ⓒ (pl. **-ties**) **1.** (*U.S.*) one part of a State forming a political unit. **2.** (*Brit.*) one part of England forming a political unit.

coup [ku:] *n.* ⓒ (pl. **coups** [ku:z]) a sudden, brilliant stroke; a master stroke. ⌈ment by force.⌉

coup d'é·tat [kú:deitá:] *n.* ⓒ a sudden change of govern-

cou·pé [kú:pei→1.] *n.* ⓒ **1.** [+*U.S.* ku:p] a closed, two-door automobile, with the seat for the driver outside. **2.** a closed carriage with a seat for two people inside.

⁑**cou·ple** [kʌ́pl] *n.* ⓒ **1.** a pair; two of the same kind. **2.** a pair of people, esp. a man and his wife, partners in a dance, etc. ¶*a married ~.*
1) *a couple of,* ⓐ two. ⓑ a few.
2) *in couples,* in pairs; two together.
—*vt.* **1.** join (things) together; link; connect. ¶*The dining car was coupled on at Osaka.* / *We ~ the name of Oxford with the idea of learning.*① **2.** marry.
—*vi.* **1.** marry. **2.** (of animals) mate. **3.** come together; unite.

cou·pling [kʌ́plin] *n.* **1.** Ⓤⓒ the act of joining together. **2.** ⓒ a device for joining parts of machinery. **3** ⓒ a link used to connect two railroad cars.

cou·pon [kú:pɔn / -pɔn] *n.* ⓒ a ticket showing that one has a right to receive goods or services.

⁑**cour·age** [kə́:ridʒ / kʌ́r-] *n.* Ⓤ the quality of being brave; the mental power of facing danger, difficulty, etc. without fear. ¶*a Man of ~*① / *pluck up ~.*②

cou·ra·geous [kəréidʒəs] *adj.* full of courage; brave; fearless. ▷**cou·ra·geous·ly** [-li] *adv.*

cour·i·er [kúriər] *n.* ⓒ **1.** a messenger sent in haste. **2.** a person hired by a group of travelers to take care of hotel reservations, tickets, etc. for them.

⁑**course** [kɔ:rs] *n.* ⓒ **1.** ⓒⓊ (often *the ~*) progress; development. ¶*the ~ of events* / *the ~ of life.* **2.** (*the ~* or *one's ~*) a route; a way; the direction to advance. ¶*the ~ of a river.* **3.** a manner of action or behavior. ¶*the best ~ to take.*① **4.** a series of studies or lessons. ¶*the ~ in French* / *college ~.* **5.** a part of a meal served at one time. ¶*a dinner of six courses.*② **6.** a piece of land marked out for a sport.
1) *as a matter of course,* as a natural thing; natu-⌉
2) *in course of,* in process of. ⌊rally.⌋
3) *in due course,* at the proper time or season; in the⌉
4) *in the course of,* during. ⌊natural order.⌋
5) *in the course of nature; in the ordinary course of things,* normally; as part of the normal or expected result of events. ⌈certainly; without doubt.⌉
6) *of course,* ⓐ as one might expect; naturally. ⓑ⌋
7) *take one's* [*own*] *course,* have one's own way; do as one wishes.
—*vt.* **1.** hunt or run after (animals) with hounds; chase. **2.** cause (a horse, etc.) to run; urge (a horse, etc.) to speed. **3.** run through or over (fields, etc.).
—*vi.* **1.** move quickly; (of liquids) run. **2.** hunt or run after animals with hounds.

cours·er [kɔ́:rsər] *n.* ⓒ (*poetic*) a swift horse.

⁑**court** [kɔ:rt] *n.* ⓒ **1.** a small open place partly or wholly surrounded by walls or buildings. **2.** a place marked with lines for playing a game. ¶*a tennis ~.* **3.** (often *C-*) a palace for a king, queen, or other ruler; a royal palace. **4.** (*collectively*) the royal family and its fol-

— 1. 같은 고향의 여자 2. 시골 여자

— 1. 군(郡)(State 아래의 행정 단위) 2. 주(州)(shire 와 같음)

— 불의의 일격; 큰 벌이, 대성공

— 쿠데타; 무력 정변(政變)
— 1. 쿠페형 자동차 2. 쿠페형 마차

— 1. 한 쌍, 둘 2. 남녀 한 쌍; 부부; 댄스하는 남녀 한 쌍

圞 1)ⓐ둘의 ⓑ두서너 개의 2)둘이서 짝을 찌어
— 1. [두 개]를 잇다, 연상(결부)시키다 ¶①옥스퍼드라는 이름으로 학문을 연상하다 2. …을 결혼시키다 —
1. 결혼하다 2. 교미(交尾)하다 3. 이어지다

— 1. 연결 2. 연결기 3. [차량의] 연결기

— 쿠우폰, 우대권, 상품권, 인환권

— 용기 ¶①용기 있는 사람/②용기를 내다

— 용감한, 용기 있는; 대담한

— 1. 급사(急使) 2. [단체]여행 안내원

— 1. 진행; 경과 2. 진로; 진행의 방향 3. [행동의] 방침, 지칠 ¶①최상의 방침 4. 과정; 학과; 단위 5. [식사의] 1품, 코오스 ¶② 6품 요리의 만찬 6. [경기 따위의] 코오스

圞 1)당연한 일로서 2)…하는 중에 3) 마침 좋은 때에; 멀지 않아 4)… 중에, …[이 지나는] 사이에 5)일이 되어 감에 따라; [일이 순조로우면] 멀지 않아 6)ⓐ[형편상] 당연히 ⓑ물론, 그렇고말고 7)자기 생각대로 하다

— 1. [사냥개에게 짐승을] 쫓게 하다 2. [말 따위를] 뛰게 하다 3. …을 가로지르다, 뛰어다니다
— 1. 빨리 달리다; 줄줄 흐르다 2. 사냥개로 사냥하다
— 준마(駿馬)
— 1. 안마당 2. [테니스] 코오트 3. 궁정, 왕궁 4. 왕족, 정신(廷臣) 5. 어전 회의 6. 법정 7. 재판관 8. 알랑거림, 아첨; 구애(求愛)

lowers living in such a place. **5.** a formal meeting held by a ruler and his officers. **6.** a place where law cases are heard; a law court. **7.** 《*collectively*》 a judge or judges in a law court. **8.** [U] the act of getting someone's favor or love.

out of court, not to be considered.

[熟] [의론 따위] 고려의 가치 없는

—*vt.* **1.** try to get the favor or love of (someone); please. **2.** try to get (something); seek. ¶~ *danger.*①

—[他] 1. …의 비위를 맞추다, …에게 구혼하다 2. …을 얻으려고 하다, 구하다 ¶①위험을 자초하다

court card [⌐⌐] *n.* (in playing cards) the king, the queen, or the jack.

—[名] [트럼프의] 그림 카아드

• **cour·te·ous** [kə́:rtiəs / kə́:tjəs] *adj.* polite; civil; thoughtful of others. ▷**cour·te·ous·ness** [-nis] *n.*

—[形] 예의바른; 친절한, 인정 있는

cour·te·ous·ly [kə́:rtiəsli / kə́:tjəs-] *adv.* in a courteous manner.

—[副] 예의바르게; 공손히, 친절히,

• **cour·te·sy** [kə́:rtisi] *n.* (pl. **-sies**) **1.** [U][C] the quality of being courteous; politeness. **2.** [C] a kind act; an example of polite behavior. **3.** [U][C] kindness; favor. ¶*by the ~ of someone.*①

—[名] 1. 예의, 공손, 정중 2. 친절한 행위, 예의바른 동작 3. 친절; 호의 ¶① ……의 호의에 의해

court·house [kɔ́:rthàus] *n.* [C] (pl. **-hous·es** [-hàuziz]) **1.** a building in which law courts are held. **2.** (*U.S.*) a building used for the government of a county.

—[名] 1. 재판소(법원 건물) 2. 《美》 군청

cour·ti·er [kɔ́:rtiər] *n.* [C] **1.** a person often present at the court of a king, etc.; a court attendant. **2.** a person who seeks the favor of another by flattering him.

—[名] 1. 조신(朝臣) 2. 아첨군, 알랑쇠

court·li·ness [kɔ́:rtlinis] *n.* [U] politeness; elegance.

—[名] 공손, 정중; 우아

court·ly [kɔ́:rtli] *adj.* (**-li·er, -li·est**) polite; elegant.

—[形] 공손한, 우아한, 품격 있는

court-mar·tial [kɔ́:rtmá:rʃ(ə)l] *n.* [C] (pl. **courts-**) a court consisting of army or navy officers for the trial of offenses against military or naval laws; a trial by such a court.

—[名] 군법회의; [군법회의에 의한] 재판

court·ship [kɔ́:rtʃip] *n.* [U] the act of trying to get a woman's love.

—[名] [남자의 여자에 대한] 구혼, 구애

• **court·yard** [kɔ́:rtjà:rd] *n.* [C] a space surrounded by walls or large buildings on all or most sides.

—[名] [성·여관 따위 큰 건물의] 안마당

⁑ **cous·in** [kʌ́zn] *n.* [C] **1.** a child of one's uncle or aunt. ⇨[N.B.] ¶*a second ~.*① **2.** a distant relative. **3.** a term of address used by a sovereign when he speaks to another sovereign or to a high-ranking nobleman.

—[名] 1. 사촌 [N.B.] first cousin, full cousin, cousin-german 이라고 함 ¶① 재종, 육촌 2. 먼 친척 3. 경(卿)(국왕의 용어)

cove [kouv] *n.* [C] a small bay; an inlet on the shore.

—[名] 작은 만(灣), 후미

cov·e·nant [kʌ́vənənt] *n.* [C] a serious promise or agreement between persons or groups.

—[名] 계약, 맹약

⁑ **cov·er** [kʌ́vər] *vt.* **1.** put over the top or surface of (something); hide (something) from view; conceal. ¶*be covered with dust | ~ a wall with paint | ~ one's mistakes.* **2.** protect. **3.** be enough to pay (a loss, etc.). ¶*My fee barely covers my expenses.*① **4.** extend over; include. ¶*~ a wild field | This clause covers all possible cases.*② **5.** travel over. ¶*~ 50 miles a day.* **6.** (in sports) protect (an area or a position).

—[他] 1. [덮개·뚜껑 따위]를 씌우다, 덮다; 가리다 2. …을 방어하다 3. [손실비용]을 충분히 메우다 ¶①내 급료로는 지출을 간신히 메운다 4. [범위가] …에 걸치다 ¶②이 조항은 모든 경우에 해당한다 5. [어떤 거리]를 가다 6. [야구 따위에서] …을 커버하다

1) *cover in,* fill (a hole, etc.) with earth.
2) *cover up,* hide; wrap up.
3) *cover oneself with* (=*win*) *glory, etc.*

[熟] 1)[구멍 따위]를 메우다 2)…을 싸 감추다 3)[영예]를 온몸에 지니다

—*n.* **1.** [C] something that covers. **2.** [C] the binding of a book, a magazine, etc. **3.** [U] disguise; pretense. **4.** [U] a shelter.

—[名] 1. 덮개 2. 책의 장정 3. 겉치레; 구실 4. 엄호물, 차폐물

1) *break cover,* come out in the open.
2) *from cover to cover,* from beginning to end.
3) *under cover,* ⓐ disguised. ⓑ secretly.

[熟] 1)[짐승이] 숨은 곳에서 뛰어나오다 2)처음부터 끝까지 3)ⓐ변장한 ⓑ몰래

cov·er·age [kʌ́vəridʒ] *n.* [U][C] the extent to which something is covered or insured.

—[名] [보험의] 보상 범위; [라디오의] 송신지역; [신문의] 취재 범위

cov·ered [kʌ́vərd] *adj.* **1.** having a cover; covering. **2.** wearing one's hat or cap.

—[形] 1. 덮개가 있는, 뚜껑 달린 2. 모자를 쓴

cov·er·ing [kʌ́vəriŋ] *n.* [C] anything that covers.

—[名] 덮개, 뚜껑, 외피(外皮)

cov·er·let [kʌ́vərlit] *n.* [C] **1.** an outside covering for a bed. **2.** a covering.

—[名] 1. 침대보 2. 덮개

cov·ert [kʌ́vərt] *adj.* secret; hidden; sheltered. ↔overt

—[形] 암암리의, 비밀의, 은밀한 —[名] 1.

¶~ *glances.* —*n.* [C] **1.** a shelter; a protected place. **2.** a small, thickly wooden area in which animals hide.
숨는 장소 2. [동물 따위가 숨는] 덤불

cov·et [kʌ́vit] *vt.* desire (esp. something that belongs to another) eagerly. ¶(*proverb*) *All ~, all lose.*①
—[他] [남의 것]을 턱없이 탐내다 ¶①《俚》대탐대실(大貪大失)

cov·et·ous [kʌ́vitəs] *adj.* very eager to get or to own something that belongs to another. ▷**cov·et·ous·ly** [-li] *adv.* —**cov·et·ous·ness** [-nis] *n.*
—[形] 턱없이 탐내는, 탐욕스러운

cov·ey [kʌ́vi] *n.* [C] **1.** a brood or a small flock of game birds, such as of partridges or quails. **2.** a group of persons.
—[名] 1. [메추라기 · 자고(鷓鴣)처럼 어미새와 사는] 새 떼 2. [사람의] 무리, 떼

‡ **cow**[1] [kau] *n.* [C] **1.** a full-grown female domestic animal that gives milk. **2.** a female of certain other animals, such as the elephant and the whale.
—[名] 1. 암소, [특히] 젖소 2. [코끼리 · 고래 따위의] 암컷

cow[2] [kau] *vt.* make (someone) afraid; frighten.
—[他] …을 으르다, 위협하다

‡ **cow·ard** [káuərd] *n.* [C] a person who lacks courage; a person who is shamefully timid. ¶ *play the ~.*①
—[名] 겁장이, 비겁한 사람 ¶①비겁한 짓을 하다
—*adj.* lacking courage.
—[形] 비겁한, 겁 많은

cow·ard·ice [káuərdis] *n.* [U] lack of courage; shameful fear.
—[名] 겁, 비겁

cow·ard·ly [káuərdli] *adj.* not brave; lacking courage. —*adv.* like a coward.
—[形] 비겁한, 겁 많은 —[副] 비겁하게도

cow·boy [káubɔ̀i] *n.* [C] (*U.S.*) a man who looks after cattle usu. on horseback.
—[名] 《美》 카우보이, 목동

cow·catch·er [káukæ̀tʃər] *n.* [C] (*U.S.*) a metal frame on the front of a locomotive, a streetcar, etc. to clear obstacles from the track. ⇒fig, [N.B.]
—[名] [기관차의] 배장기(排障器), [전차의] 구조망 [N.B.] 미국 개척 시대에 방목하는 소가 기관차 앞에 튀어나올 때 소를 보호하던 장치

[cowcatcher]

cow·er [káuər] *vi.* bend one's body in fear or shame.
—[自] 움츠리다, 위축하다

cow·herd [káuhə̀ːrd] *n.* [C] a person who looks after cows.
—[名] 소 치는 사람

cow·hide [káuhàid] *n.* **1.** [U] the skin of a cow; leather made from it. **2.** [C] (*U.S.*) a strong leather whip. —*vt.* whip (someone or something) with a cowhide.
—[名] 1. 쇠가죽 2. 《美》 쇠가죽 채찍 —[他] …을 쇠가죽 채찍으로 때리다

cowl [kaul] *n.* [C] **1.** a monk's hood, usu. attached to a gown; a hooded garment. ⇒fig. **2.** anything shaped like a cowl. **3.** a hoodlike cover for the top of a chimney. ⇒fig.
—[名] 1. [수도사의] 두건 달린 겉옷, 두건 2. 고깔 모양의 것 3. [고깔 모양의] 굴뚝갓, 불꽃막이

[cowl 1., 3.]

co-work·er [kóuwə̀ːrkər, ⌐–⌐– / ⌐⌐–] *n.* [C] a person who works with another.
—[名] 협력자

cow·pox [káupɑ̀ks / -pɔ̀ks] *n.* [U] a disease of cows causing small spots containing pus on the breasts.
—[名] 우두

cow·slip [káuslìp] *n.* [C] **1.** a wild plant with yellow flowers; an English primrose. **2.** (*U.S.*) the marsh marigold.
—[名] 1. 구륜앵초(초여름에 영국 목초지에 피는 야생화) 2. 《美》 눈동이나물

cox [kɑks / kɔks] *n.* [C] (*colloq.*) a coxswain.
—[名] 키잡이, 타수(舵手)

cox·comb [kɑ́kskòum / kɔ́ks-] *n.* [C] **1.** an empty-headed dandy; a silly man. **2.** a cockscomb.
—[名] 1. [천박한] 멋장이 2. [닭의] 볏

cox·swain [kɑ́ksən, -swèin / kɔ́kswèin, *nautical* kɔ́ksn] *n.* [C] a person who controls the course of a boat. ⇒[N.B.]
—[名] [보우트의] 키잡이; 정장(艇長) [N.B.] cox 로 줄임

coy [kɔi] *adj.* shy; modest; bashful. ¶*be ~ of* (or *about*) …
—[形] 수줍어하는, 얌전

coy·ly [kɔ́ili] *adv.* in a coy manner.
—[副] 부끄러워하여

coy·o·te [káiout, kaióuti / kɔ́iout] *n.* [C] (pl. **-tes** or *collectively* **-te**) a small wolf on the plains of western North America.
—[名] 코이요테(북미 대초원의 이리)

coz·en [kʌ́zn] *vt.* cheat; deceive.
—[他] …을 속이다

co·zy [kóuzi] *adj.* (**-zi·er, -zi·est**) warm and comfortable; snug. ¶*a ~ town.* —*n.* [C] (pl. **co·zies**) a cloth cover or cap for a teapot, used to keep the contents hot. ⇒[N.B.]
—[形] 아늑한, 기분좋은 —[名] 보온 커버 [N.B.] cosy 로도 씀

cr. **1.** credit. **2.** creditor.

• **crab**[1] [kræb] *n.* [C] **1.** a water creature with a hard outer
—[名] 1. 게 2. 감아 올리는 기계, 이동윈

crab cover and ten legs, well-known for walking sideways. **2.** a machine for lifting heavy weights. **3.** ((*the C-*)) a constellation; Cancer.
—*vi.* (**crabbed, crab·bing**) catch or hunt for crabs.
crab² [kræb] *n.* ⓒ **1.** an ill-natured person. **2.** =crab apple.
—*vt.* (**crabbed, crab·bing**) **1.** (*colloq.*) find fault. **2.** (*colloq.*) spoil.
crab apple [⌐ ⌐] *n.* a small, wild, sour apple.
crab·bed [kræbid] *adj.* **1.** ill-natured; easily showing anger; cross. **2.** hard to understand; hard to read.
:crack [kræk] *vi.* **1.** make a sharp breaking sound such as a whip or a pistol does. ¶*a cracking noise / A rifle cracked somewhere.* **2.** split or break suddenly without separation of parts. **3.** (of the voice) become harsh; change tone. —*vt.* **1.** cause (something) to make a short, sharp sound. ¶~ *a whip.*① **2.** break (something) with such a sound. **3.** cause (the voice) to become cracked or harsh. **4.** ((chiefly in *passive*)) break or crush mentally; cause to be mentally ill. ¶*He is cracked.* **5.** tell (a joke).
1) *crack down on* (=become strict with) *something.*
2) *crack up,* ⓐ lose strength. ⓑ (of an airplane) suf-
3) *crack someone up,* praise highly.   [fer damage.]
—*n.* ⓒ **1.** a sudden sharp or loud sound. ¶*the ~ of thunder.* **2.** a line between parts without a complete separation; a split; a narrow opening. ⇒NB ¶*a ~ in the cup / Open the window a ~.*① **3.** a mental or physical defect. **4.** a peculiar sound or tone of the voice.
in a crack, in a moment.
—*adj.* (*colloq.*) first-class.
—*adv.* sharply. ¶*hit him ~ in the eye.*
crack-brained [krǽkbrèind] *adj.* crazy; mad; foolish.
cracked [krækt] *adj.* **1.** having a crack or cracks. **2.** (of the voice) broken; having harsh notes. **3.** (*colloq.*) crazy.
•**crack·er** [krǽkər] *n.* ⓒ **1.** a thin, hard, and dry biscuit. **2.** a firecracker. **3.** ((*pl.*)) an instrument that cracks nuts.
crack·le [krǽkl] *vi.* make a series of short, sharp sounds.
—*n.* Ⓤ **1.** the sound of crackling. **2.** a surface or glaze of fine, irregular cracks on some kinds of china, glass, etc
crack·ling [krǽkliŋ] *n.* ⓒⓊ **1.** the hard, dry, and brown skin of roasted pork. **2.** a series of small, sharp, crackling sounds.
•**cra·dle** [kréidl] *n.* ⓒ **1.** a baby's little bed which can be gently swung or rolled. ⇒fig. **2.** a place of beginning or origin. ¶*the ~ of Western culture.* **3.** ((*the ~*)) the period of early childhood. ¶*from the ~ to the grave.*① **4.** a frame attached to a scythe for harvesting grain. **5.** a frame for supporting a ship in dry dock.
6. a box on rockers to wash gold from the earth.

[cradle 1.]

—*vt.* **1.** place or rock (a baby) in a cradle; hold (something) as in a cradle. **2.** guard or train (someone) in early life. **3.** support (a ship, etc.) in a cradle.
•**craft** [kræft / krɑːft] *n.* **1.** Ⓤ skill, esp. in making things by hand. **2.** ⓒ art or work requiring special skill. ¶*art[s] and craft[s].*① **3.** ⓒ the association of persons engaged in any trade; a labor union; a guild. **4.** Ⓤ cunning;

craft

치 **3.** 《天》 계좌(座)

—Ⓐ 게를 잡다
—Ⓐ **1.** 심술궂은 사람 **2.** 야생 사과의 일종
—Ⓐ **1.** 《口》 …의 흠을 잡다 **2.** 《口》 망쳐놓다
—Ⓐ 야생 사과의 일종
—Ⓐ **1.** 심술궂은, 심보 삐뚤어진 **2.** 난해한; 알아보기 힘든
—Ⓐ **1.** 지끈(딱)하고 소리내다 **2.** [지끈하고] 금이 가다 **3.** [목소리가] 쉬다
—Ⓐ **1.** …에 날카로운 소리를 내다 ¶①채찍을 울리다 **2.** …을 찌끈(딱)하고 부수다; 깨다 **3.** [목]을 쉬게 하다 **4.** …을 미치게 하다 **5.** [농담]을 하다

쪱 1) …을 비난하다 2) ⓐ건강이 약해지다 ⓑ[비행기가] 엉망으로 되다 3) …을 칭찬하다

—Ⓐ **1.** 쾅(딱)하는 소리; 갑작스런 날카로운 소리 **2.** 갈라진 틈, 금; 좁은 구멍 NB 흔히 부사적으로 쓰임 ¶창을 조금 열어라 **3.** 결함; 광기, 광증 **4.** 변성(變聲), 목쉼

쪱 곧, 당장
—Ⓐ 《口》 일류의
—Ⓐ 날카롭게
—Ⓐ 머리가 돈; 어리석은
—Ⓐ **1.** 금이 간, 깨진 **2.** 목이 쉰, 변한 **3.** 《口》 미친

—Ⓐ **1.** 크래커, 비스킷 **2.** 폭죽(爆竹) **3.** 호두를 깨는 기구

—Ⓐ 탁탁 소리내다
—Ⓐ **1.** 탁탁하는 소리 **2.** [도자기 따위의] 금, 잔금

—Ⓐ **1.** 구운 돼지고기의 바삭바삭하는 윗가죽 **2.** 탁탁하는 소리

—Ⓐ **1.** 요람 **2.** 발상지(發祥地), 기원 **3.** 어린 시절, 유년 시대 ¶①요람에서 무덤까지, 일생 동안 **4.** [곡식을 가지런히 베려고 낫에 댄] 덧살 **5.** [조선소의] 선가(船架), 진수(進水) 미끄름대 **6.** 선광대(選鑛臺)

—Ⓐ **1.** …을 요람에 넣어 재우다(흔들다) **2.** …을 어린 시절에 보호(훈련)하다 **3.** [배 따위]를 선가에 올려놓다

—Ⓐ **1.** 기교, 기능 **2.** 특수한 기술, 재주, 수공업, 공예 ¶①미술 공예 **3.** 동업자 조합 **4.** 교활, 못된 꾀 **5.** 배; 항공기

skill in deceiving others. **5.** (pl. **craft**) boats, ships or aircraft.

craft·i·ness [krǽftinis / krɑ́:ft-] *n.* [U] the state of being crafty; cunning.
—[名] 교활, 교묘

crafts·man [krǽftsmən / krɑ́:fts-] *n.* [C] (pl. **-men** [-mən]) **1.** a skilled workman. **2.** an artist.
—[名] **1.** 직공, 장인(匠人), 공인 **2.** 예술가

crafts·man·ship [krǽftsmənʃip / krɑ́:fts-] *n.* [U] the skill, art, or work of a craftsman.
—[名] [공인의] 기교, 기능, 기량

craft·y [krǽfti / krɑ́:f-] *adj.* (**craft·i·er, craft·i·est**) skillful in deceiving others; tricky. ¶*a ~ fox.*
—[形] 교활한, 간사한

crag [kræg] *n.* [C] a steep, rugged rock or cliff; a projecting rock.
—[名] 울퉁불퉁한 바위, 가파른 바위산

crag·gy [krǽgi] *adj.* (**-gi·er, -gi·est**) with many rocks; rugged; rough.
—[形] 바위가 많은, 울퉁불퉁한

cram [kræm] *v.* (**crammed, cram·ming**) *vt.* fill or pack tightly; press together. 《~ something ***with*** or ***into***》 ¶*~ clothes into a bag / ~ one's mouth with food / ~ one's head with knowledge.* **—*vi.*** **1.** eat too fast or too much. **2.** (*colloq.*) learn hurriedly.
—[他] …을 억지로 채워(다져) 넣다 —[自] **1.** 잔뜩(게걸스럽게) 먹다 **2.**《口》벼락으로(주입식으로) 공부하다

cram·mer [krǽmər] *n.* [C] a special teacher who crams students for examinations.
—[名] 시험 준비 교사

cramp¹ [kræmp] *n.* **1.** [C] a metal bar bent at both ends, used for holding together blocks of stone, timbers, etc. **2.** a clamp. **3.** something that restricts or confines.
—[名] **1.** 꺾쇠 **2.** 멈춤쇠, 고리쇠 **3.** 구속, 속박[하는 것]

—*vt.* **1.** fasten or hold (something) together with a cramp. **2.** keep (something) from having free action.
—[他] **1.** …을 꺾쇠로 고정시키다 **2.** [행동 따위]를 속박하다

cramp² [kræmp] *n.* [U] **1.** a sudden, sharp pain in the muscles, making movement impossible. ¶*a ~ in the calf.*① **2.** 《*pl.*》 very sharp pains in the abdomen. **—*vt.*** cause (something) to have a cramp.
—[名] **1.** 경련, 쥐 ¶①장딴지의 쥐 **2.** 급격한 복통 —[他] …에 경련을 일으키게 하다

cran·ber·ry [krǽnbèri / -b(ə)ri] *n.* [C] (pl. **-ries**) a firm, sour, red berry; the shrub on which these berries grow.
—[名] 넌출월귤[의 열매]; 그 관목

crane [krein] *n.* [C] **1.** a machine for lifting and moving heavy weights. **2.** an iron arm used for suspending pots or kettles over a fire. **3.** a large bird with very long legs and a long neck. **—*vt.*** **1.** raise (things) by a crane. **2.** stretch (the neck) to see better. **—*vi.*** stretch out one's neck.
—[名] **1.** 기중기, 크레인 **2.** [벽로에 남비 따위를 거는] 자재(自在) 갈고리 **3.** 두루미; 《美》 왜가리 —[他] **1.** …을 기중기로 나르다, 달아 올리다 **2.** [목]을 길게 뻗다 —[自] 목을 뻗다

cra·ni·a [kréiniə] *n.* pl. of **cranium.**

cra·ni·al [kréiniəl] *adj.* of the skull.
—[形] 두개(頭蓋)의

cra·ni·um [kréiniəm] *n.* [C] (pl. **-ni·ums** or **-ni·a**) the skull; the part of the skull enclosing the brain.
—[名] 두개; 두개골

crank [kræŋk] *n.* [C] **1.** a part or handle that is turned to work a machine. **2.** a sudden change of speech or thought; a strange idea or act. **3.** (*U.S. colloq.*) a person with odd ideas or one fixed idea. **4.** (*colloq.*) an ill-tempered person.
—[名] **1.** 굽은 손잡이, 크랭크 **2.** 변덕, 묘한 생각(행동) **3.**《美口》 괴짜, 기인 **4.** 심술궂은 사람

—*vt.* **1.** work or move (a motor) with a crank. **2.** bend (something) into the shape of a crank. **—*vi.*** turn a crank.
—[他] **1.** …을 크랭크로 회전시키다 **2.** …을 크랭크 모양으로 구부리다 —[自] 크랭크를 돌리다

—*adj.* loose; uneasy.
—[形] 흔들흔들하는, 불안한

crank·y [krǽŋki] *adj.* (**crank·i·er, crank·i·est**) **1.** cross; easily showing anger; ill-natured. **2.** strange; not common. **3.** apt to turn over; loose; not strong.
—[形] **1.** 심보가 삐뚤어진, 성 잘 내는 **2.** 기묘한; 괴팍한 **3.** 흔들흔들하는

cran·ny [krǽni] *n.* [C] (pl. **-nies**) a small, narrow opening in a rock, a wall, etc.; a crack.
—[名] [벽 따위의] 갈라진 틈, 금

crape [kreip] *n.* **1.** [U] crepe. **2.** [C] a piece of black cloth worn or displayed as a sign of sorrow at the death of someone.
—[名] **1.** 크레이프 **2.** 검은 상장(喪章)

:crash [kræʃ] *n.* [C] **1.** a sudden, loud noise; a falling, hitting, or breaking with force and a loud noise. ¶*The tree fell with a ~.* **2.** sudden ruin; serious failure in business. **3.** (of an airplane) a fall to the earth; a bad landing; (of cars, etc.) a violent collision.
—*vi.* **1.** make a sudden, loud noise; fall, hit, or break with force and a loud noise. ¶*~ **against*** (or ***into***) *something*① / *~ down on something.*② **2.** be suddenly
—[名] **1.** [와르르하는] 요란한 소리 **2.** 파멸, 붕괴, 파산 **3.** 불시착, 추락; [자동차의] 충돌 —[自] **1.** 요란한 소리를 내다; 와르르 부서지다(무너지다) ¶①충돌하다/②탄압하다 **2.** 파산하다 **3.** 추락하다 —[他] **1.** …을 산산이 부수다, 짜부러뜨리다 **2.** [비행기]를 파손(불시착)시키다

ruined; fail in business. **3.** (of an airplane) make a very bad landing. **—***vt.* **1.** break (something) to pieces noisily; smash. **2.** damage or destroy (an airplane) in landing. ▷**crash·er** [-ər] *n.*

crass [kræs] *adj.* **1.** dull; foolish. **2.** completely.
—[形] 1. 우둔한, 미련한 2. 철저한

crate [kreit] *n.* [C] a large frame, box, basket, etc. used for packing or carrying various articles.
—[名] [과일 · 가구 따위 포장 운반용의] 나무틀(상자 · 바구니)

cra·ter [kréitər] *n.* [C] **1.** an opening of a volcanic mountain that sends out fire and smoke. **2.** a hole in the ground caused by an explosion
—[名] 1. 분화구 2. [폭탄 따위로 생긴] 큰 구멍

cra·vat [krəvǽt] *n.* [C] **1.** a necktie. **2.** a cloth worn around the neck; a scarf.
—[名] 1. 넥타이 2. 목도리, 스카아프

* **crave** [kreiv] *vt.* **1.** have a strong desire for (something). ¶*~ water.* **2.** ask for (something) in an earnest manner; beg. ¶*~ a favor.*
—[他] 1. …을 갈망하다 2. …에 간절히 부탁하다

cra·ven [kréiv(ə)n] *adj.* cowardly. **—***n.* [C] a person who is not brave; a coward.
—[形] 겁 많은, 비겁한 —[名] 겁장이

cry craven, give in; surrender.
[熟] 항복하다

crav·ing [kréiviŋ] *n.* [C] a strong desire. ¶*have a ~ for fame.*①
—[名] 열망, 간청 ¶①명성을 열망하다

craw·fish [krɔ́:fìʃ] *n.* [C] (pl. **-fish·es** or *collectively* **-fish**) a fresh-water creature with a shell and ten legs resembling a lobster; a crayfish. **—***vi.* (*U.S. colloq.*) go back.
—[名] [바다] 가재 —[自] 《美口》 꽁무니를 빼다

‡ **crawl** [krɔ:l] *vi.* **1.** move the body slowly along the ground; creep. **2.** move or do something very slowly or carefully. ¶*~ along an icy road in a car.* **3.** be or feel as if covered with crawling things. ¶*The floor was crawling with spiders.* **4.** move in secret.
—[自] 1. 기다, 기어다니다 2. 천천히 움직이다(하다) 3. [벌레 따위가] 우글우글하다; [피부가] 근질근질하다 4. 살금살금 걷다

—*n.* [C] **1.** a slow movement along the ground. **2.** 《*the ~*》 a form of swimming.
—[名] 1. 기기, 서행 2. [수영의] 크로올

crawl·er [krɔ́:lər] *n.* [C] **1.** a person or an animal that crawls. **2.** 《often *pl.*》 a garment for a baby to wear while creeping about on the floor. **3.** (*Brit.*) a cab moving slowly in search of passengers.
—[名] 1. 기는 사람, 기는 동물 2. [갓난 아기]의 겉옷 3. 《英》 택시

crawl·y [krɔ́:li] *adj.* (**crawl·i·er, crawl·i·est**) (*colloq.*) feeling as if things are crawling over one's skin.
—[形] 《口》 근질근질한

cray·fish [kréifìʃ] *n.* [C] (pl. **-fish·es** or *collectively* **-fish**) a crawfish.
—[名] 가재

cray·on [kréiɑn, -ən] *n.* [C] **1.** a stick of soft, colored chalk, used for drawing or writing. **2.** a drawing made with crayons. **—***vt.* draw (something) with crayons.
—[名] 1. 크레용 2. 크레용화(畫) —[他] …을 크레용으로 그리다, [크레용으로] 밑그림을 그리다

craze [kreiz] *n.* [C] a very strong interest in something for a short time. **—***vt.* **1.** make (someone) mad. **2.** make tiny cracks all over the surface of (a dish, a pot, etc.) **—***vi.* become mad; be finely cracked.
—[名] [일시적] 대유행, 열광 [他] 1. …을 미치게 하다 2. [사기그릇을] 잔금을 넣어 굽다 —[自] 미치다; 잔금이 생기다

‡ **cra·zy** [kréizi] *adj.* (**-zi·er, -zi·est**) **1.** mad; foolish; showing madness. **2.** (*colloq.*) unreasonably eager. ¶*be ~ for.* **3.** not strong or sound; weak.
—[形] 1. 미친; 미친 듯한 2. 열광적인 3. [건물 · 배 따위가] 흔들흔들하는, 부서질 듯한; 병약한

creak [kri:k] *vi., vt.* make, or cause (something) to make a sharp, high sound. **—***n.* [C] a sharp, high cry or noise.
—[自][他] 삐걱거리[게 하]다 —[名] 삐걱거리는 소리

creak·y [krí:ki] *adj.* (**creak·i·er, creak·i·est**) apt to make a sharp, high sound.
—[形] 삐걱거리는

‡ **cream** [kri:m] *n.* [U] **1.** the rich, yellow, oily part of milk that comes to the top. **2.** dessert or food made of cream or like cream. **3.** a soft fat used as a medicine for the skin. **4.** a light yellow color. **5.** 《*the ~*》 the best part. ¶*the ~ of the story*① | *the ~ of the lecture.*②
—[名] 1. 크리임 2. 크리임 디저어트[식품] 3. 화장용 크리임 4. 크리임 빛 5. 가장 좋은 부분, 알짜, 정화(精華) ¶①이야기의 가경/②강연의 클라이맥스

—*vt.* **1.** add cream to (tea or coffee). **2.** take the cream from (milk); take the best part from (something). **3.** mix (things) together until the mixture has the thickness of heavy cream. **4.** cook (chicken, etc.) with cream. **—***vi.* form cream. **—***adj.* **1.** containing cream or milk; like cream. ¶*~ sauce* | *~ soup.* **2.** of the color of cream.
—[他] 1. …에 크리임을 넣다 2. [우유]에서 크리임을 채취하다; 알짜를 뽑다 3. …을 크리임 모양으로 하다 4. …을 크리임으로 요리하다 —[自] 크리임이 생기다 —[形] 1. 크리임이 함유된, 크리임 비슷한 2. 크리임 빛의

cream·er [krí:mər] *n.* [C] a small pitcher for holding cream.
—[名] 크리임 통

cream·er·y [krí:məri] *n.* [C] (pl. **-er·ies**) **1.** a place where cream, butter, and cheese are made. **2.** a store where cream, milk, and butter are sold.
—[名] **1.** 버터(치이즈) 제조공장 **2.** 크리임(우유·버터)의 판매점

cream·y [krí:mi] *adj.* (**cream·i·er, cream·i·est**) **1.** like, of, or full of cream. **2.** cream-colored.
—[形] **1.** 크리임 [모양]의; 크리임을 함유한 **2.** 크리임 빛의

crease [kri:s] *n.* [C] a line or mark made by folding cloth, paper, etc.; a fold. —*vt.* make a crease or creases in (something). —*vi.* become creased.
—[名] 접은 자국, 주름 —[他] …에 주름을 잡다 —[自] 주름이 생기다

:cre·ate [kri(:)éit] *vt.* **1.** make (something) out of nothing; bring (something) into being; produce; establish. ¶*God created the world.* **2.** be the first to act (a part) in a play. **3.** give rise to (something); cause.
—[他] **1.** …을 창조하다; 창설하다 **2.** [배우가 어떤 역]의 최초의 연기자가 되다 **3.** …을 야기하다

·cre·a·tion [kri(:)éiʃ(ə)n] *n.* **1.** [U] the act of creating; the state of being created. **2.** [U] all that God created; the world and everything in it; the universe. ¶*the Lord of Creation.*① **3.** [C] a thing created by man or by natural forces. ¶*a great ~ of art.* **4.** ((often *the C-*)) the act of creating of the world by God.
—[名] **1.** 창조 **2.** 창조물, 천지 만물, 삼라만상 ¶①만물의 영장, 인간 **3.** [인지(人知)·자연력에 의해] 창조(창작)된 것 **4.** [신에 의한] 천지 창조

cre·a·tive [kri(:)éitiv] *adj.* having the power to create; original. ¶*a ~ mind.* ▷**cre·a·tive·ly** [-li] *adv.*
—[形] 창조적인, 창작의

cre·a·tiv·i·ty [krieitíviti] *n.* [U] the state of being creative; ability to create.
—[名] 창조; 창조력

cre·a·tor [kri(:)éitər] *n.* **1.** [C] a person who creates (something). **2.** ((*the C-*)) God.
—[名] **1.** 창조자 **2.** 조물주, 신

:crea·ture [krí:tʃər] *n.* [C] **1.** anything created. **2.** a living thing; a person; an animal. ¶*a lovely ~*① */ dumb creatures*② */ Poor ~!*③ **3.** a person who is a tool of another. ¶*one of the king's creatures.*④
—[名] **1.** 창조물 **2.** 생물, 인간, 동물 ¶①여자/②말 못하는 동물/③불쌍도 해라; **3.** 앞잡이, 끄나불; 예속자, 부하 ¶④왕의 신하중 한 사람

cre·dence [krí:d(ə)ns] *n.* [U] the act of believing; belief. ¶*find ~*① */ a letter of ~*② */ give ~ to a rumor.*
—[名] 신용, 신의, 신임 ¶①…에게 신임받다/②신임장

cre·den·tials [kridénʃ(ə)lz] *n. pl.* letters of introduction.
—[名] [대·공사의] 신임장

cred·i·bil·i·ty [krèdibíliti] *n.* [U] the fact or quality of being believable.
—[名] 신용할 수 있음, 확실성

cred·i·ble [krédibl] *adj.* that can be trusted; worthy of trust; that can be believed. ▷**cred·i·bly** [-i] *adv.*
—[形] 신용할 수 있는, 믿을 만한

:cred·it [krédit] *n.* **1.** [U] trust; belief. ¶*His statement deserves no ~.*① **2.** [U] good name; honor; [C] a person or thing that adds honor. ¶*It is to his ~ that he saved a drowning child.*② */ He is a ~ to his school.* **3.** [U] belief that a person will keep a promise to pay back money. ¶*No ~ is given at this shop.*③ **4.** [U][C] (*Commercial*) a loan. **5.** [U][C] the amount of someone's money kept in an account in a bank, etc.
—[名] **1.** 신용 ¶①그의 말을 신용할 수 없다 **2.** 명성; 명예; 명예가 되는 일 ¶②물에 빠진 아이를 구한 것은 그의 명예가 되었다 **3.** [지불에 대한] 신용; 외상 ¶③이 상점은 외상 판매를 않습니다 **4.** ((商)) 융자, 대부 **5.** 예금고

1) ***do credit to someone; do someone credit,*** bring honor or a good reputation to someone.
2) ***give credit to,*** believe.
3) ***on credit,*** promising to pay later.
4) ***reflect credit on*** (=*give honor or reputation to*) ⌈*someone.*⌉

[熟] 1)…의 명예가 되다 2)…을 신용하다 3)외상으로, 신용대부로 4)…의 명예가 되다

—*vt.* believe; accept (something) as true.
—[他] …을 믿다

credit someone with (=*believe that someone has*) *something.* ¶*~ him with rare intelligence.*④
[熟] [사람]이 …을 갖고 있다고 믿다 ¶④그에게 드문 지성이 있다고 생각하다

cred·it·a·ble [kréditəbl] *adj.* bringing credit, honor, reputation, or respect. ¶*a ~ deed.*
—[形] 신용할 수 있는; 명예가 되는, 칭찬할 만한, 훌륭한

cred·it·a·bly [kréditəbli] *adv.* in a creditable manner.
—[副] 훌륭하게

·cred·i·tor [kréditər] *n.* =person to whom money or goods are owed. ↔debtor ⇒[N.B.]
—[名] 채권자 [N.B.] Cr.로 줄임

cre·do [krí:dou] *n.* (pl. **-dos**) [C] =creed.

cre·du·li·ty [krid(j)ú:liti / -djú:-] *n.* [U] willingness to believe statements too easily. ↔incredulity ¶*with ~.*①
—[名] 경신(輕信) ¶①경솔하게 믿고

cred·u·lous [krédʒuləs / -dju-] *adj.* too ready to believe things without sufficient grounds.
—[形] 쉽게 믿는, 잘 속는

·creed [kri:d] *n.* [C] **1.** a brief statement of the main points of Christian belief. **2.** any statement of faith, rules, opinions, etc. **3.** ((*the C-*)) the Apostles' Creed
—[名] **1.** [종교의] 신경(信經) **2.** 주의, 강령(綱領) **3.** 사도신경

C

creek [kri:k] n. ⓒ **1.** (esp. *U.S.*) a small stream, larger than a brook. **2.** (esp. *Brit.*) a narrow bay.
creel [kri:l] n. ⓒ **1.** a basket for carrying fish. **2.** a basket like trap for catching fish, etc.
:**creep** [kri:p] vi. (**crept** [krept]) **1.** move along close to the ground like a baby; crawl. ¶~ *under the fence.* **2.** move slowly or secretly. ¶*The cat crept silently towards the birds.* **3.** grow along a surface or a support like ivy. ¶*creeping plants.* **4.** (of time, age, etc.) come on gradually. ¶*A feeling of drowsiness crept over him.*① **5.** feel shivery; tremble with fear.
1) *creep into* (=*win*) *someone's favor.*
2) *creep on* (or *upon*), come on gradually.
——n. ⓒ **1.** the act of creeping. **2.** (*pl.*) a nervous sensation as if insects were creeping on the skin.
give someone the creeps, cause someone to shudder.
creep·er [krí:pər] n. ⓒ **1.** a person or thing that creeps. **2.** any plant that grows along the ground or over walls. **3.** (*pl.*) a baby's garment combining waist and pants.
creep·y [krí:pi] adj. (**creep·i·er, creep·i·est**) **1.** creeping. **2.** having or causing a sensation as if insects were creeping on the skin.
cre·mate [krí:meit / kriméit] vt. **1.** burn a dead body to ashes. **2.** burn.
cre·ma·tion [kriméiʃ(ə)n] n. ⓤⓒ the act of cremating.
cre·ma·to·ri·a [krèmətɔ́:riə] n. pl. of **crematorium.**
cre·ma·to·ri·um [krèmətɔ́:riəm] n. ⓒ (pl. **-ri·ums** or **-ri·a**) a building where dead human bodies are burnt to ashes.
cre·ma·to·ry [krémətɔ̀:ri, krí:m- / krémət(ə)ri] n. ⓒ (pl. **-ries**) **1.** a furnace for burning dead bodies. **2.** a building that has a furnace for burning dead bodies; a crematorium. ——adj. of cremation.
cre·o·sote [krí(:)əsòut / krí:ə-] n. ⓤ **1.** an oily liquid with a strong smell, obtained from wood tar and used to keep wood from decaying or as a medicine. **2.** a similar substance obtained got from coal tar.
crepe, crêpe [kreip] n. ⓤ a thin silk, cotton, rayon, or woolen cloth with many small folds in the surface.
* **crept** [krept] v. pt. and pp. of **creep.**
cre·scen·do [kriséndou / -ʃén-] adj., adv. (*Music*) slowly increasing in loudness or in power of tone. ⇒N.B.
——n. ⓒ (pl. **-dos**) a gradual increase in loudness, etc.
cres·cent [krésnt] n. ⓒ **1.** the shape of the moon in its first or last quarter. **2.** anything shaped like this; the national symbol of Turkey. ¶*the Cross and the Crescent.*① ——adj. **1.** shaped like a crescent. ¶*the Crescent City.*② **2.** growing; increasing.
cress [kres] n. ⓤ a plant of the mustard family.
* **crest** [krest] n. ⓒ **1.** a bunch of feathers or hair, a thick red piece, etc. on the head of a bird or an animal. **2.** a decoration, feathers, etc. on the top of a helmet. ⇒fig. **3.** a decoration at the top of a family badge. **4.** the top part; the top of a hill, a wave, etc.; a peak. ——vt. crown; top. ——vi. (of a wave, etc.) reach a crest; form a ridge.
crest·ed [kréstid] adj. having a crest. [crest 2.]
crest·fall·en [kréstfɔ̀:l(ə)n] adj. with a bowed head; in low spirits; discouraged.
cre·vasse [krivǽs] n. ⓒ **1.** a deep crack in a great mass of ice on a mountain. **2.** (*U.S.*) a break in the bank of a river, etc.

crev·ice [krévis] *n.* ⓒ a narrow opening or crack.
—ⓝ [바위 따위의] 갈라진 틈

‡crew [kru:] *n.* ⓒ ((*collectively*)) **1.** all the members belonging to one ship or aircraft, rowing a boat, etc. **2.** all the men, except the officers, belonging to one ship or aircraft. **3.** a group of persons engaged in same work. ¶ *a train ~.* **4.** (*humorous*) a group of people in general; a crowd; a gang. ¶ *a dissolute ~.*①
—ⓝ 1. [함선·비행기 따위의] 승무원 (고급 선원도 포함); [대학 따위의] 경조(競漕) 부원 2. [보통의] 선원; 승무원 3. 같은 일에 종사하는 사람 4. (戱) 한패, 동료, 떼거리, 집단 ¶ ①난봉친구

crib [krib] *n.* ⓒ **1.** a small bed with enclosed sides for a baby. **2.** a wooden container for feeding horses and cows; a stall for cattle. **3.** a box, a bin, or a building for storing grain, salt, etc. **4.** a heavy framework of logs or woods used in building. **5.** a hut or small house; a small room. **6.** (*colloq.*) the act of using another's words or ideas as one's own; a translation or key to help a student, sometimes in violation of rules.
—*v.* (**cribbed, crib·bing**) *vt.* **1.** shut up (something) in a small space. **2.** (*colloq.*) steal and use (another's ideas) as one's own. (~ *ideas,* etc. *from another*) —*vi.* use a crib, as in a test.
—ⓝ 1. [둘레에 테가 있는] 어린이 침대 2. 구유, 여물통 3. 곡물(소금) 저장통, 쌀(소금)궤 4. [건축용의] 비계, 발판 5. [통나무] 오두막; 작은 방 6. (口) 도용(盜用), 표절; 자습서

—ⓥ 1. [좁은 곳에] 몰아넣다 2. 《口》 도용(표절)하다 —ⓥ [시험에서] 자습서를 보다

crib·bage [kríbidʒ] *n.* ⓤ a game played by two, three, or four people with playing cards.
—ⓝ 카아드 놀이의 일종

crick [krik] *n.* ⓒ a sudden painful stiffness of the muscles of the neck, the back, etc. [loud, high sound.]
—ⓝ 근육의 경련

crick·et¹ [kríkit] *n.* ⓒ a small insect which makes a
—ⓝ 귀뚜라미

•**crick·et**² [kríkit] *n.* ⓤ **1.** a British outdoor game played by two teams of eleven players each with ball, bats, and two sets of three straight sticks placed in the ground. **2.** (*colloq.*) fair play; sportsmanship.
not cricket, unfair; unsportsmanlike.
—ⓝ 1. 크리켓 [영국의 국기(國技)로서 11명씩의 2개 팀이 하는 옥외 경기] 2. 《口》 공명정대
[에 위배되는]
働 공명정대하지 않은, 스포오츠 정신

cri·er [kráiər] *n.* ⓒ **1.** a person who cries. **2.** a person who shouts out announcements of goods for sale. **3.** an official who shouts out public announcements in a court of law.
—ⓝ 1. 외치는 (우는) 사람 2. [선전] 광고꾼, 길거리에서 외치는 장수 3. [공판 정의] 정리(廷吏)

‡crime [kraim] *n.* ⓒⓤ **1.** an act that is against the law; a serious sin which can be punished by law. ¶ *a capital ~.*① **2.** any evil or bad act; sinful conduct. ¶ *He is steeped in ~.*② / *It's a ~ to overfeed a dog like that.*
—ⓝ 1. [법률상의] 범죄 ¶ ①사형을 받을 만한 죄 2. [일반적으로] 죄악; 나쁜 짓 ¶ ②그는 악에 물들어 있다

‡crim·i·nal [krímin(ə)l] *n.* ⓒ a person guilty of a crime.
—*adj.* **1.** guilty of a crime; can be punished by law. ¶ *a ~ attempt.*① **2.** of crime or the punishment of crime. ¶ *a ~ court*② / *a ~ offense.*③ **3.** (*colloq.*) senseless; foolish.
—ⓝ 범죄인 —働 1. 죄를 저지른; 죄가 되는 ¶ ①범죄 미수 2. 범죄의, 형사상의 ¶ ②형사 재판소/③형사범 3. 《口》 몰상식한, 어리석은

crim·i·nal·i·ty [krìminæliti] *n.* (pl. **-ties**) **1.** ⓤ the quality or state of being criminal; guilt. **2.** ⓒ a criminal act.
—ⓝ 1. 유죄 2. 범죄 행위

crimp¹ [krimp] *vt.* press (paper or cloth) into small regular folds; make (hair, etc.) wavy. ¶ *~ one's hair.*
—*n.* **1.** ⓤ the act of crimping. **2.** ⓒ something crimped; a fold; a wave. **3.** (*pl.*) waved or curled hair.
▷**crimp·er** [-ər].
—働 …에 주름을 내다, [머리]를 곱슬거리게 하다 —ⓝ 1. 곱슬거리게 하기 2. 주름 3. 지진 머리

•**crim·son** [krímzn] *n.* ⓤ a deep red color. —*adj.* deepred. —*vt.* color (something) deep red. —*vi.* turn deep red in color; blush.
—ⓝ 진홍색 —働 진홍색의 —働 진홍색으로 하다 —ⓥ 진홍색으로 되다, 새빨개지다

cringe [krindʒ] *vi.* **1.** bend low or go down on the knees, esp. in fear or shame. **2.** behave towards another person in a very humble way in order to get favor or attention. —*n.* ⓒ the act of cringing. ▷**cring·er** [-ər] *n.*
—働 1. [무서워서] 움츠리다 2. 굽실굽실하다 —ⓝ 움츠림; 위축; 아첨

crin·kle [kríŋkl] *vi., vt.* **1.** form or move with many small folds or waves. **2.** make slight, sharp sounds. —*n.* ⓒ **1.** a small fold on the surface of material; a twist. **2.** a crinkling sound.
—働 1. 주름지(게 하)다, 오그라들(게 하)다 2. 바삭바삭 소리내다 —ⓝ 1. 주름 2. 바삭바삭 소리

crin·kly [kríŋkli] *adj.* (**-kli·er, -kli·est**) full of crinkles; wrinkled; wavy.
—働 주름진, 곱슬곱슬한

crin·o·line [krínəli(ː)n] *n.* **1.** Ⓤ a hard, rough cloth used as a lining. **2.** Ⓒ a petticoat of crinoline worn by a woman under a skirt to support it on all sides. **3.** Ⓒ a hoop skirt. ⇒fig.

[crinoline 3.]

* **crip·ple** [krípl] *n.* Ⓒ a person whose legs, arms, or body cannot be moved well; a lame person. —*vt.* **1.** make a cripple of (a person). ¶*He was crippled in World War II.* **2.** damage; make (someone or something) unable to act properly; weaken.

cri·ses [kráisiːz] *n.* pl. of **crisis**.

* **cri·sis** [kráisis] *n.* Ⓒ (pl. **-ses**) **1.** a turning point for better or worse in an illness. ¶*pass the ~.*① **2.** a time of great danger and difficulty in politics, money affairs, history, etc.; a very serious moment in any course of action; emergency. ¶*bring ... to a ~.*②

* **crisp** [krisp] *adj.* **1.** hard but easily breakable. ¶*~ toast* (or *biscuits*). **2.** (of air) fresh; sharp and clear. ¶*~ air.* **3.** (of manners, speech, etc.) active; lively; sharp; decided. ¶*a ~ manner.* **4.** (of hair, etc.) curly and wavy. ¶*~ hair.* —*vi., vt.* make or become crisp.

criss-cross [krískrɔːs / -krɔs] *n.* Ⓒ a mark or pattern made of crossed lines. —*adj.* made or marked with crossed lines; crossed; crossing. —*adv.* in different cross directions; in the form of a cross. —*vt.* mark or cover (something) with crossing lines. —*vi.* cross.

cri·te·ri·a [kraitíəriə] *n.* pl. of **criterion**.

cri·te·ri·on [kraitíəriən] *n.* Ⓒ (pl. **-ri·a** or **-ri·ons**) a standard by which to determine the correctness of a judgment.

* **crit·ic** [krítik] *n.* Ⓒ **1.** a person who judges, esp. one who judges works of art. ¶*a literary ~.* **2.** a person who points out others' faults or who judges severely.

* **crit·i·cal** [krítik(ə)l] *adj.* **1.** inclined to find fault or judge unfavorably. **2.** concerned with, busy with or skilled in criticism. ¶*~ essays.*① **3.** near a turning point or crisis. ¶*a ~ moment.*② **4.** very dangerous; causing anxiety. ¶*a ~ wound.*③

crit·i·cal·ly [krítik(ə)li] *adv.* in a critical manner; with [criticism.]

* **crit·i·cism** [krítisiz(ə)m] *n.* Ⓒ Ⓤ **1.** the act or art of judging good points and faults, esp. of works of art or literature; an opinion, spoken or written, on what is good or bad about works of art; a critical opinion. **2.** the act of pointing out faults; blame.

* **crit·i·cize,** chiefly Brit. **-cise** [krítisàiz] *vt.* **1.** judge or point out the good points and faults of (works of art or literature). ¶*He criticized three novels in one review.* **2.** find fault with (others).

cri·tique [kritíːk] *n.* **1.** Ⓒ an article or essay criticizing a work of art; a review. **2.** Ⓤ the art of criticism.

croak [krouk] *n.* Ⓒ a deep, rough sound, made by a frog, a crow, etc. —*vi.* **1.** make a deep, rough sound. **2.** predict misfortune; complain. **3.** (*slang*) die. —*vt.* say (something) in a deep, rough voice.

cro·chet [krouʃéi / króuʃei] *vi., vt.* knit (sweaters, lace, etc.) with a single long needle having a hook at one end. —*n.* Ⓤ knitting done in this way.

crock [krak / krɔk] *n.* Ⓒ **1.** a pot or jar made of baked clay. **2.** a broken piece of earthenware.

crock·er·y [krákəri / krɔ́k-] *n.* Ⓤ (*collectively*) dishes, jars, etc. made of baked clay; earthenware.

──⦿ 1.〔안감용의〕 말총 따위로 짠 빳빳한 천 2.크리놀린을 댄 페티코우트 3.둥근 테를 넣은 스커어트

──⦿ 절름발이, 앉은뱅이, 불구자, 지체(肢體)부자유자 ──⦿ 1. …을 절름거리게 하다, 병신으로 만들다 2. …을 해치다, 약하게 하다; …의 활동력을 없애다; 무능하게 하다

──⦿ 1.〔병의〕위험기, 고비 ¶①고비를 넘기다 2.〔경제·정치상의〕중대시국; 위기 ¶②…을 위기에 빠뜨리다

──⦿ 1. 바삭바삭(빠닥빠닥)하는 2. 상쾌한, 신선한 3. 팔팔한, 활발한 4. 곱슬한 ──⦿ 〔머리 따위〕 곱슬곱슬해지게 하다; 주름지게 하다

──⦿ 십자(꼴) ──⦿ 십자의, 교차한 ──⦿ 십자로, 교차하여 ──⦿ …을 십자로 교차시키다, 십자무늬를 넣다 ──⦿ 교차하다

──⦿〔판단·비판의〕 표준, 기준, 규범

──⦿ 1.〔문예·미술의〕 비평가, 평론가 2. 비판자, 일삼아 까탑는 사람

──⦿ 1. 흠을 잘 잡는, 혹평하는 2. 비평의, 평론의 ¶①평론 3. 위기의 ¶②위기 4. 위험한, 아슬아슬한; 위독한 ¶③치명상

──⦿ 비판적으로

──⦿ 1. 비평; 〔특히 문예 따위의〕 비평법(술); 평론, 강평 2. 비난, 흠잡기

──⦿ 1.〔문예 작품 따위〕의 비평을 하다, 비판을 하다 2.〔남〕을 비난하다, …의 흠을 찾다

──⦿ 1.〔문예·미술 작품 따위의〕 평론 2. 비평법
──⦿〔까마귀·개구리 따위의 우는〕소리 ──⦿ 1. 까악까악 울다 2. 불길한 예언을 하다; 투덜거리다 3. 죽다 ──⦿ …을 침울한 소리로 말하다
──⦿ 〔스웨터·레이스 따위〕 크로셰 뜨개질(편물)

──⦿ 1.〔오지〕 항아리, 독 2. 사금파리

──⦿ 오지그릇, 도자기류

croc·o·dile [krάkədàil / krɔ́k-] *n.* ⓒ **1.** a large water animal with a long head and long, sharp teeth. **2.** (*Brit. colloq.*) a group of schoolgirls out for a walk.
shed crocodile tears, pretend to be sorry.

—图 1.[아프리카·남아시아 산의] 악어 2.《英》산책 나온 여학생의 긴 행렬
熟 거짓 눈물을 흘리다

croft [krɔːft / krɔ(ː)ft] *n.* ⓒ **1.** a small field near a house. **2.** a very small rented farm.

—图 1.[집에 딸린] 작은 밭 2.소작지

Crom·well [krάmw(ə)l / krɔ́mwəl], **Oliver** *n.* (1599–1658) Lord Protecter of England.

—图 영국의 정치가

crone [kroun] *n.* ⓒ an ugly old woman.

—图 쪼그랑 할머니, 노파

cro·ny [króuni] *n.* ⓒ (pl. **-nies**) a very familiar friend.

—图 친구, 옛벗

crook [kruk] *vi., vt.* bend or curve. ¶ ~ *one's arm (finger).* —*n.* ⓒ **1.** a hook; a bend; a curve. **2.** a hooked, curved, or bent part of something. **3.** a stick with a bent or curved end. **4.** (*colloq.*) a dishonest person;
by hook or by crook, by all means.   a thief.

—自他 1.구부러지다; 구부리다 —图 구부러진 것, 갈고리 2.굴곡, 만곡(彎曲)[부] 3.자루가 구부러진 지팡이 4.《口》사기군; 도둑
熟 반드시, 꼭

crook·back [krúkbæ̀k] *n.* ⓒ a person with a crooked, rounded back.

—图 곱사등이

• **crook·ed** [krúkid] *adj.* **1.** bent; curved; twisted; not straight. ↔straight **2.** not honest; wicked. **3.** (of the body or limbs) badly formed.

—形 1.구부러진, 뒤틀린 2.[사람·행동이] 부정한, 못된 3.기형의

croon [kruːn] *vi., vt.* sing or hum in a low voice; sing in a low voice with exaggerated emotion. ¶ ~ *a lullaby* | ~ *to a baby.* —*n.* ⓒ a low, gentle singing, humming or murmuring. ▷**croon·er** [-ər] *n.*

—自他 [감상적으로] 낮은 소리로 노래하다; 콧노래하다 —图 저음의 노랫소리

‡ **crop**¹ [krɑp / krɔp] *n.* ⓒ **1.** (*the ~s*) the food plants produced in one year; a harvest of any food plant. ¶*the rice* ~ | *an abundant* (or *good*) ~ | *a bad* ~ | *an average* ~ | *What are the crops like around here?*① **2.** a group of persons or things. ¶*a* ~ *of lambs.* **3.** a short haircut. **4.** the first stomach of a bird.
—*v.* (**cropped, crop·ping**) *vt.* **1.** cut (something) short; bite off. **2.** sow; plant. ¶ ~ *the field with wheat.*
—*vi.* bear or produces a crop or crops.
crop up, appear unexpectedly.

—图 1.[한 해·한 계절의] 전 농작물; 작물; 작황(作況); 수확[고] ¶①이 근처에는 어떤 작물이 됩니까? 2.무리, 떼 3.[머리 따위의] 짧게 깎기, 중대가리 4.[새의] 멀떠구니
—他 1.[풀·줄기를] 자르다; 물어 끊다 2.…에 [작물을] 심다
—自 농작물이 되다
熟 갑자기 나타나다

crop·per [krάpər / krɔ́pər] *n.* ⓒ **1.** a person or thing that crops. **2.** a plant that produces a crop. **3.** (*colloq.*) a heavy fall. **4.** (*colloq.*) a failure; a defeat.
come a cropper, (*colloq.*) ⓐ fall heavily. ⓑ fail badly; meet with great misfortune.

—图 1.[농작물을] 베어 들이는 사람 (기구·기계) 2.수확이 있는 작물 3.《口》쿵하고 떨어지기 4.《口》실패, 추락 다, 큰 재난을 만나다
熟 ⓐ쿵하고 떨어지다 ⓑ크게 실패하

cro·quet [kroukéi / króukei, -ki] *n.* ⓤ a lawn game played by knocking wooden balls through small wire arches with hammer-like sticks.

—图 크로우케이(옥외 공놀이의 일종)

cro·quette [kroukét] *n.* ⓒ a small ball of chopped meat, potatoes, etc. cooked in fat.

—图 크로켓

cro·sier, -zier [króuʒər] *n.* ⓒ a bishop's hooked stick, serving as a sign of his position.

—图 [bishop 또는 abbot의] 홀장(笏杖)

‡ **cross** [krɔːs / krɔs] *n.* ⓒ **1.** two posts fastened across one another. **2.** a mark made by drawing one line across another; anything like a cross in shape. ⇒fig. **3.** any suffering to be borne. ¶*bear one's* ~ | *No* ~, *no crown.*① **4.** a mixture between different races; a hybrid. ¶*a* ~ *between a Malay and a Chinese.*②
on the cross, ⓐ not at right angles. ⓑ unfairly or dishonestly.
—*adj.* **1.** crossing. **2.** bad-tempered; out of humor. **3.** contrary; opposite. **4.** (of

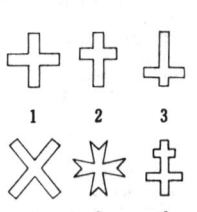

[crosse 2.]
1. Greek cross 2. Latin cross 3. St. Peter's cross 4. St. Andrew's cross 5. Maltese cross 6. patriarchal cross

—图 1.십자가 2.십자표; 십자 모양의 것 3.수난; 고난 ¶①고난 없이 영광 없다 4.혼혈; 잡종 ¶②말레이 사람과 중국인의 트기

熟 ⓐ어긋나게 ⓑ나쁜 짓을 하여

—形 1.[십자로]교차한 2.성 잘내는, 시무룩한 3.반대의 4.잡종의

blood or race) mixed.

as cross as two sticks, (*colloq.*) complaining; very irritable.

[熟] 몹시 성미가 까다로운; 안달하는

—*vt.* **1.** lay or place (something) over or across. ¶ ~ *one's arms.*③ **2.** make the sign of the cross by moving the hand upon or over (one's body). ¶ ~ *one's heart* / ~ *oneself.* **3.** go from one side to another of (something); go across (something). ¶ ~ *a road.* **4.** (of travelling persons or letters in the post) meet and pass. ¶ *Your letter crossed mine.* **5.** oppose; prevent. ¶ ~ *his plan.* **6.** occur to (the mind). ¶ *A nice idea crossed his mind.*④ **7.** mix breeds of (plants or animals). —*vi.* **1.** go across. **2.** pass, move or extend from side to side. **3.** meet and pass. **4.** breed together.

—[他] 1. …을 교차시키다 ¶③팔짱을 끼다 2. …에 십자를 긋다 3. …을 횡단하다 4. …와 스쳐 지나가다, 엇갈리다 5. …에 거스르다, …을 방해하다 6. [마음]에 떠오르다 ¶④그의 생각에 명안이 떠올랐다 7. [동식물]을 교배하다 —[自] 1. 횡단하다 2. [한 쪽에서 다른 쪽으로] 건너가다 3. 서로 엇갈리다 4. 잡종이 되다

1) *cross out* (or *off*), put crossed lines on (something) to cancel it.
2) *cross swords with someone,* ⓐ fight. ⓑ argue with someone.
3) *cross the path of someone,* ⓐ meet someone. ⓑ oppose someone's plan, wishes, etc.
4) *cross one's t's and dot one's i's,* be careful and exact in speech and conduct.

[熟] 1)선을 그어 …을 지우다 2)ⓐ…와 싸우다 ⓑ…와 논쟁하다 3)ⓐ…을 만나다 ⓑ[남의 계획 따위]를 반대(방해)하다 4. 언행에 주의하다

cross-bar [krɔ́:sbɑ̀:*r* / krɔ́sbɑ̀:] *n.* [C] **1.** a bar, line, or stripe fixed across others. **2.** a bar of wood fixed between goal posts, as in football and soccer.

—[名] 1. 빗장, 가로장 2. [축구의] 고울 포스트의 가로장

cross·bow [krɔ́:sbòu / krɔ́s-] *n.* [C] an old weapon for shooting stones and short arrows.

—[名] 석궁(石弓)

cross·bred [krɔ́:sbrèd / krɔ́s-] *v.* p. and pp. of **crossbreed.** —*adj.* of a mixed breed or race.

—[形] 잡종의

cross·breed [krɔ́:sbrì:d / krɔ́s-] *vi., vt.* (**-bred, -breed·ing**) breed by mixing kinds or races. —*n.* [C] a person, an animal, or a plant that came from parents of different races or kinds.

—[自][他] 이종(異種) 교배하다 —[名] 잡종

cross-coun·try [krɔ́:skʌ̀ntri / krɔ́skʌ́n-] *adj.* across open country or fields instead of along or over a road.

—[形] 들판을 가로지르는

cross-ex·am·i·na·tion [krɔ́:sigzæ̀minéiʃ(ə)n / krɔ́s-] *n.* [U][C] **1.** the act of cross-examining; the state of being cross-examined. **2.** a severe, close questioning.

—[名] 1. 반대 심문 2. 엄중한 힐문, 준엄한 추궁

cross-ex·am·ine [krɔ́:sigzǽmin / krɔ́s-] *vt.* **1.** question (a witness who has already been questioned by the opposing side) closely to test the truth of his evidence. **2.** question closely. ▷**cross-ex·am·in·er** [-ə*r*] *n.*

—[他] 1. …에 반대 심문하다 2. …을 엄하게 추궁하다, 힐문하다

cross-eyed [krɔ́:sàid / krɔ́s-] *adj.* having one or both eyes turned toward the nose.

—[形] 사팔뜨기의

cross-grained [krɔ́:sgrèind / krɔ́s-] *adj.* **1.** (of a board) having an irregular grain. **2.** (of a person) hard to manage; bad-tempered; ill-natured.

—[形] 1. [목재가] 결이 불규칙한 2. 성미가 까다로운, 심술궂은

cross·ing [krɔ́:siŋ / krɔ́s-] *n.* **1.** [U][C] the act of going across; a trip across a large body of water, such as a sea or a lake. ¶ *have a good* ~. **2.** [C] a place where streets, railways, rivers, etc. cross each other; a place provided for going across a street or railroad tracks. **3.** [U] the act of making a cross [over one's body]. **4.** [U][C] the act of mixing breeds.

—[名] 1. 횡단; 도항(渡航) 2. 교차점, 네거리, 횡단보도; 건널목 3. 십자를 긋기 4. 이종(異種) 교배

cross-leg·ged [krɔ́:slég(i)d / krɔ́slegd] *adj.* having one leg over the other when a person sits.

—[形] 책상다리를 한

cross·ly [krɔ́:sli / krɔ́s-] *adv.* in a cross or angry manner.

—[副] 심술궂게, 심사 사납게

cross·ness [krɔ́:snis / krɔ́s-] *n.* [U] bad temper; the state of being cross.

—[名] 심술궂음, 뿌루퉁함

cross-pur·pose [krɔ́:spə́:*r*pəs / krɔ́spə́:-] *n.* [C] an opposing purpose.

—[名] 반대의 목적(의향)

be at cross-purposes, ⓐ misunderstand each other's purpose; act so as to prevent each other's success. ⓑ act under a misunderstanding.

[熟] ⓐ서로 오해하다, 서로 성공을 방해하려고 하다 ⓑ오해하여 반대되는 짓(말)을 하다

cross-ques·tion [krɔ́:skwéstʃ(ə)n / krɔ́s-] *vt.* question closely or strictly; cross-examine. —*n.* [C] a question asked by means of cross-examination.

—[他] [상대의 증인]을 반대 심문하다; …을 엄중히 힐문하나 —[名] 반대 심문

cross reference [�´ ˴--] *n.* a reference from one part of a book, an index, etc. to another part.
—⦿ [같은 책 속에서의] 다른 항목 참조, 전후 참조

cross-road [krɔ́:sròud / krɔ́s-] *n.* ⓒ **1.** a road that crosses a main road; a road that runs from one main road to another. **2.** ((usu. *pl.*, used as *sing.*)) a place where two or more roads meet.
be at the (or *a*) *crossroads*, be at a time when a person must decide what to do.
—⦿ 1. 교차도로; [두 간선도로를 연결하는] 골목길, 샛길 2. 네거리, 십자로

▧ 기로(岐路)에 서다

cross section [˴ ˴-] *n.* **1.** the act of cutting anything across. **2.** a section cut in this way. **3.** a model selection; a sample showing all characteristic parts, relationships, etc. ¶ *a ~ of college life.*①
—⦿ 1. 가로로 자르기 2. 횡단면 3. 대표적인 면 ¶①학생 생활의 한 단면

cross-way [krɔ́:swèi / krɔ́s-] *n.* =crossroad.
cross-ways [krɔ́:swèiz / krɔ́s-] *adv.* =crosswise.
cross-wise [krɔ́:swàiz / krɔ́s-] *adv.* **1.** across. **2.** in the form of a cross. **3.** opposite to what is required; wrongly.
—⦿ 1. 비스듬히, 가로로 2. 십자로 3. 거꾸로, 반대로

cross-word puzzle [krɔ́:swə̀:rdpʌ̀zl / krɔ́swəd-] *n.* a puzzle with a set of squares to be filled in with letters.
—⦿ 글자 맞추기 퀴즈

crotch [krɑtʃ / krɔtʃ] *n.* ⓒ the point of separation of branches or legs; a fork.
—⦿ [나무의] 아귀; [인체의] 가랑이

crotch-et [krɑ́tʃit / krɔ́tʃ-] *n.* ⓒ **1.** a small hook or hook-like part. **2.** an odd notion or fancy. **3.** (chiefly *Brit.*) A quarter note in music.
—⦿ 1. 갈고리 [모양의 부분] 2. 별난 생각, 변덕 3.(英) 4분음표

* **crouch** [krautʃ] *vi.* bend low or close to the ground.
—*n.* ⓒ the act of crouching.
—⦿ 웅크리다 —⦿ 웅크리기

croup [kru:p] *n.* ⓤ a children's disease marked by a heavy cough.
—⦿ [어린이의] 위막성 후두염(僞膜性喉頭炎)

crow¹ [krou] *vi.* **1.** (*crowd* or esp. *Brit.* **crew, crowd**) (of a cock) make a loud cry. **2.** (of a baby) make a happy sound. **3.** (of persons) feel or express delight at victory over another.
crow over, rejoice at someone else's expense; boast.
—*n.* ⓒ **1.** a loud cry made by a cock. **2.** a happy sound made by a baby.
—⦿ 1. 수탉이 울다 2. [갓난애가] 좋아서 소리를 지르다 3. [사람이] 환성을 울리다

▧ …에게 이겨 뽐내다
—⦿ 1. 수탉 울음소리 2. 갓난애의 환성

‡ **crow**² [krou] *n.* ⓒ a large black bird which cries "Caw!" *as the crow flies*, in a straight line. ⌊Caw!"⌋
—⦿ 까마귀
▧ 일직선으로

crow-bar [króubɑ̀:r] *n.* ⓒ a strong iron or steel bar, used for lifting heavy things.
—⦿ 쇠지레, 쇠막대기

‡ **crowd** [kraud] *n.* ⓒ **1.** a large number of people or things gathered closely together. ¶ *large crowds in the streets*① */ in crowds.*② **2.** ((*the* ~)) people in general; the common people or the masses. ¶ *The ~ needs leadership.*③ **3.** (*colloq.*) a special group of people; a company. ¶ *a jolly ~.*④
1) *a crowd of*, a large number of.
2) *follow* (or *go with*) *the crowd*, do (something) as most people do.
—*vi.* **1.** gather in large numbers; press together. ¶ *The main street is crowded with shops.* **2.** press forward; advance by pushing. —*vt.* **1.** press (people or things) closely together; fill to excess; pack. ¶ ~ *clothes into a suitcase* / ~ *a room with furniture.* **2.** force (oneself or one's way) through; push.
crowd on sail, raise more sails to make a ship go faster.
—⦿ 1. 군중, 잡담(雜沓) ¶①도로 위의 대군중/②떼를 지어 2. 민중, 대중 ③민중은 지도자가 필요하다 3.《口》한패, 동료 ¶④유쾌한 친구

▧ 1)다수의 2)대중이 하는 대로 하다

—⦿ 1. 모여들다, 붐비다 2. 밀고 나아가다 —⦿ 1. [사람·물건]을 밀어 넣다; …을 넘칠 만큼 채우다 2. …을 밀다, 밀고 들어가다

▧ 빨리 달리려고 돛을 더 올리다

* **crowd-ed** [kráudid] *adj.* filled with a crowd; packed; close together; too close together.
—⦿ 붐비는; 만원의; 꽉 들어찬

‡ **crown** [kraun] *n.* **1.** a head covering worn by a king, a queen, etc. **2.** ⓤ ((*the* ~ or *the* C-)) the power and authority of a king, a queen, etc.; a king or queen. ¶ *succeed to the* ~.① **3.** a circle or wreath of flowers or leaves for the head, worn esp. as a sign of victory; honor; reward. **4.** the top or highest part of a thing;
—⦿ 1. 왕관 2. 왕위; 군주 ¶①왕위를 계승하다 3. [승리의] 화관, 영관, 지상의 영광(명예) 4. 꼭대기, 머리, 정수리 5. 절정, 극치 6. 치관(齒冠) 7. 영국의 5실링 은화 ¶②2실링 6펜스 은화

the top of the head; the head. ¶*the ~ of a hill.* **5.** the highest state or quality of anything. **6.** a part of a tooth above the gum or an artificial substitute for this part. ↔root **7.** a British silver coin, equal to 5 shillings. ¶*a half-crown.*②
—*vt.* **1.** make (someone) king, queen, etc.; put a crown upon the head of (someone). **2.** give honor to (someone); reward. **3.** occupy the top of (something). ¶*A wood crowns the hill.* **4.** make (something) perfect or complete; add the finishing touch to (something). ¶*The Nobel prize crowned his career as a scientist.*
—[他] 1.…에 왕관을 씌우다,…을 왕위에 앉히다 2.…에 영광을 지니게 하다 3.…의 꼭대기를 차지하다 4.…의 유종의 미를 장식하다

to crown all, to complete something.
[熟]「좋은 일·나쁜 일에 모두 써서」 그 결과, 마지막으로, 게다가

crown prince [ˊ ˊ] *n.* the heir to a king.
—[名] 황태자

crow's-feet [króuzfì:t] *n.* pl. of **crow's-foot.**

crow's-foot [króuzfùt] *n.* [C] (pl. **-feet** [-fì:t]) ⦅usu. *pl.*⦆ lines at the outside corner of the eye.
—[名] 눈초리 주름살

crow's-nest [króuznèst] *n.* [C] a small, enclosed platform near or at the top of a mast, used for looking out over the sea. ⇒fig.
—[名] 돛대 위의 망대

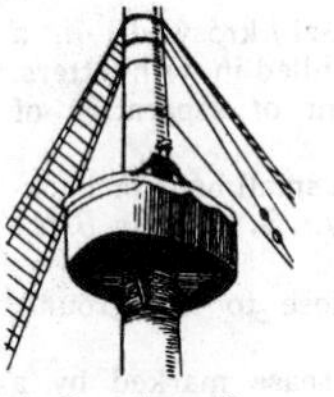
(crow's-nest)

cro·zier [króuʒər / -ʒjə] *n.* =crosier.

cru·ces [krú:si:z] *n.* pl. of **crux.**

cru·cial [krú:ʃ(ə)l] *adj.* **1.** very important; critical; decisive. **2.** severe; very hard; difficult. ▷**cru·cial·ly** [-i] *adv.*
—[形] 1. 아주 중대한; 위기의; 결정적인 2. 곤란한, 엄격한

cru·ci·ble [krú:sibl] *n.* [C] **1.** a pot for melting things that require very great heat. ¶*~ steel.*① **2.** a severe test or trial.
—[名] 1. 도가니 ¶①도가니강(鋼) 2. 가혹한 시련

cru·ci·fix [krú:sifiks] *n.* [C] **1.** a model of Christ on the cross. **2.** a cross used as a Christian symbol.
—[名] 1. 그리스도의 수난의 상(像), 고상(苦像) 2. 십자가

cru·ci·fix·ion [krù:sifíkʃ(ə)n] *n.* **1.** [U] the act of putting someone to death on a cross. **2.** [C] ⦅*the C-*⦆ the death of Christ on the cross; a picture or statue representing this scene.
—[名] 1. 책형(磔刑) 2. 그리스도의 십자가에 못박힘; 그리스도 수난의 상(그림), 고상(苦像)

cru·ci·form [krú:sifɔ̀:rm] *adj.* shaped like a cross.
—[形] 십자형의

cru·ci·fy [krú:sifài] *vt.* (**-fied, -fy·ing**) **1.** put (someone) to death by fastening him to a cross. **2.** treat severely; cause severe pain to (someone).
—[他] 1.…을 십자가에 못박다 2. 몹시 괴롭히다

***crude** [kru:d] *adj.* **1.** in a natural or raw state; not refined. ↔cultivated, refined ¶*~ oil*① / *~ materials.*② **2.** not mature; unripe. **3.** rough; coarse; bare; (of speech or work) not well finished; lacking grace, taste, or refinement. ¶*~ manners.*③ ▷**crude·ly** [-li] *adv.*
—[形] 1. 천연 그대로의, 생(生)…의 ¶①원유/②원료 2. 미숙한 3. 생경한; 조잡한, 거친; 미완성의; 조야(粗野)한 ¶③버릇없는 짓

cru·di·ty [krú:diti] *n.* (pl. **-ties**) **1.** [U] the quality or state of being crude; unripeness; roughness; lack of finish. **2.** [C] a rude or rough action; a crude thing.
—[名] 1. 날것 그대로의 상태, 미숙, 생경, 조잡 2. 미숙한 것, 버릇없는 것; 미완성품

‡**cru·el** [krú(:)əl] *adj.* (**-el·er, -el·est** or *Brit.* **-el·ler, -el·lest**) **1.** fond of causing pain to others; not caring about the pain and suffering of others. ¶*a ~ king.* **2.** causing suffering; painful. ¶*a ~ wound / a ~ sight.*
—[形] 1. [사람·행위가] 잔인한, 무자비한, 매정한 2. 무참한, 비참한, 참혹한

cru·el·ly [krú(:)əli] *adv.* in a cruel manner.
—[副] 잔인하게, 무자비하게

***cru·el·ty** [krú(:)əlti] *n.* (pl. **-ties**) **1.** [U] the quality of being cruel; the tendency to give pain to others; taking pleasure in hurting others. **2.** [C] ⦅*pl.*⦆ a cruel act.
—[名] 1. 잔혹, 무자비 2. 잔혹한 행위

cru·et [krú(:)it] *n.* [C] a small glass bottle for holding mustard, oil, etc.
—[名] [겨자·기름 따위의] 양념병

cruise [kru:z] *vi.* **1.** travel by ship with no definite end of one's journey in mind; sail about touching at a series of ports instead of going directly to one port only; make a similar trip on or over land. **2.** move or drive about slowly, looking for customers or for something remarkable. **—*vt.*** sail about (a place) with no special desti-
—[自] 1. 순항하다, 만유(漫遊)하다 2. [택시 따위가] 손님을 찾아 돌아다니다 —[他] …을 순항하다 —[名] 순항, 만유

cruis-er [krúːzər] *n.* ⓒ **1.** a warship with less armor and more speed than a battleship. ¶ *an armored (or a belted)* ~.① **2.** a motorboat, an airplane, a taxi, etc. that cruise. **3.** a police car connected with head quarters by radio; a patrol car.

— ⑧ 1. 순양함 ¶①장갑 순양함 2. 유흥용 모우터 보우트, 순항 비행기, 손님을 찾아다니는 택시 3. [경찰의]. 순찰차, 백차

* **crumb** [krʌm] *n.* **1.** (usu. *pl.*) a small piece, esp. of bread, broken or rubbed off. **2.** ⓤ the soft, inner part of bread. **3.** ⓒ a little bit; a scrap. ¶ *a ~ of hope*① */ mere crumbs of knowledge.*

— ⑧ 1. 빵부스러기 2. 빵의 부드러운 부분 3. 조금, 근소 ¶①약간의 희망

* **crum·ble** [krʌ́mbl] *vt.* break (something) into small pieces. —*vi.* fall to pieces; decay.

— ⑩ …을 가루로 만들다, 바수다 — ⑲ 부서지다; 망하다

crum·bly [krʌ́mbli] *adj.* (**-bli·er**, **-bli·est**) tending to crumble; easily crumbled. ▷**crum·bli·ness** [-nis] *n.*

— ⑲ 부서지기 쉬운, 푸석푸석한

crum·pet [krʌ́mpit] *n.* ⓒ (esp. *Brit.*) a thin, unsweetened cake eaten after it has been heated and buttered.

— ⑧ 《英》 호트케이크의 일종

crum·ple [krʌ́mpl] *vt.* press or crush (something) into irregular folds; wrinkle. ¶ *She crumpled the letter into a ball.* —*vi.* become bent into many folds.

— ⑩ …을 주름지게 하다 — ⑲ 구겨지다, 주름살지다

crunch [krʌntʃ] *vi.*, *vt.* chew noisily. **2.** crush or grind noisily. —*n.* ⓒ the act or sound of crunching.

— ⑲⑩ 1. 바삭바삭 깨물다 2. 소리내어 부수다 — ⑧ 바삭바삭 깨물기(깨무는 소리)

* **cru·sade** [kruːséid] *n.* ⓒ **1.** (often *C-*) any of the wars fought by Christians to win back their Holy City, Jerusalem. **2.** any campaign for improvement or reform. ¶ *a ~ against polio.*① —*vi.* go on or take part in a crusade.

— ⑧ 1. 십자군 원정, 성전(聖戰) 2. 개혁운동, 박멸 운동 ¶①소아마비 박멸 운동 — ⑲ 십자군(개혁 운동)에 참가하다

cru·sad·er [kruːséidər] *n.* ⓒ a person who takes part in a crusade.

— ⑧ 십자군의 전사

‡ **crush** [krʌʃ] *vt.* **1.** press together and break (something) with force; break (something) into small pieces; press (something) out of shape; force the liquid out of. (~ *down* (or *out*, *up*) *something*) ¶ ~ *down growing plants* / ~ *up beans.* **2.** destroy; conquer. ¶ ~ *a rebellion.* —*vi.* **1.** be or become crushed. **2.** press or force a way. (~ *into something*)
—*n.* **1.** ⓤ a great pressure. **2.** ⓒ a dense crowd; (*colloq.*) a crowded social gathering. ▷**crush·er** [-ər] *n.*

— ⑩ 1. …을 눌러 부수다; 분쇄하다; 구김살 투성이로 만들다; 짜내다 2. …을 압도하다; 평정하다 — ⑲ 1. 으스러지다; 구겨지다 2. 서로 밀고 들어가다, 쇄도하다

— ⑧ 1. 찌그러뜨리기 2. 쇄도, 잡담(雜沓); 군중

crush·ing [krʌ́ʃiŋ] *adj.* overcoming; final; having the power to decide. ¶ *a~ blow* / *a ~ defeat.*①

— ⑲ 압도적인, 결정적인 ¶①궤멸

* **crust** [krʌst] *n.* ⓒ **1.** the hard, outside part of bread. ↔crumb; a piece of hard, dry bread. **2.** the outside covering of a pie. **3.** any hard outside covering. ¶ *a ~ of snow.* **4.** the solid outside part of the earth. *earn one's crust,* earn one's living.
—*vt.*, *vi.* cover (something), or become covered, with a crust; form into a crust.

— ⑧ 1. 빵 껍질; 굳어진 빵조각 2. 파이 껍질 3. [물건의] 굳은 껍질 4. 지각(地殼)

熟 생계를 세우다

— ⑩⑲ 겉껍질로 덮다, 굳은 외피가 생기다, [상처에] 딱지가 앉다

crust·ed [krʌ́stid] *adj.* **1.** having a crust. **2.** (of wine) having deposited a crust in the bottle; old.

— ⑲ 1. 외피가 생긴 2. [포도주가] 버캐가 생긴; 묵은

crust·y [krʌ́sti] *adj.* (**crust·i·er**, **crust·i·est**) **1.** having a crust; like a crust; hard. ¶ ~ *bread.* **2.** ill-natured; impolite or rough in manner. ¶ *a ~ person.*

— ⑲ 1. 겉껍질이 있는, 외피 같은; 굳은 2. 성미 까다로운; 난폭한

crutch [krʌtʃ] *n.* ⓒ **1.** a stick or support to help a lame person in walking. ¶ *a pair of crutches.* **2.** anything like a crutch in shape or use. **3.** support; help. **4.** (*Brit.*) a forked support for an oar of a rowboat.

— ⑧ 1. 목발, 협장(脇杖) 2. 목발 비슷한 것; 지주(支柱) 3. 의지; 도움 4. 《英》 [보우트의] 노받이

crux [krʌks] *n.* ⓒ (*pl.* **crux·es** or **cru·ces**) **1.** the most important point. **2.** a difficult point to explain.

— ⑧ 1. 주요한 부분 2. 난점, 어려운 문제

‡ **cry** [krai] *v.* (**cried**) *vt.*, *vi.* **1.** speak in a loud voice; make loud sounds. ¶ *A baby cries when it is hungry.* / *He cried with pain.* **2.** weep. ¶ *She was crying over her misfortune.* **3.** shout out; exclaim. ¶ *The starving people cried to their chief for bread.*① **4.** announce (something) for sale; make (something) known by calling out. ¶ ~ *one's wares.*②

— ⑩⑲ 1. 외치다; [새·짐승이] 울부짖다 2. 소리내어 울다 3. 큰 소리로 말하다(부르다) ¶①굶주린 사람들은 추장에게 빵을 달라고 큰 소리로 요구했다 4. …을 소리치며 팔다, …을 큰 소리로 알리다 ¶②상품을 소리치며 팔다

1) ***cry down,*** speak ill of (someone); abuse; accuse.
2) ***cry one's eyes*** (or ***heart***) ***out,*** weep very bitterly.
3) ***cry for,*** demand; want to get (something) earnestly.
4) ***cry off,*** give up (something that one has undertaken).
5) ***cry out,*** protest; speak loudly; shout.
6) ***cry up,*** praise highly.

[熟] 1)…을 깎아내리다, 헐뜯다 2)가슴이 찢어지게 울다 3)…을 열망하다 4)[…에서] 손을 떼다 5)큰 소리를 내다 6)크게 칭찬하다

—*n.* [C] (pl. **cries**) **1.** a loud or passionate voice; a shout; a call. **2.** the act of weeping. **3.** an advertisement by calling. **4.** a public emotion; a rumor.
1) ***a far cry,*** a long distance.
2) ***hue and cry,*** ⓐ pursuit. ⓑ an expression of public anger.
3) ***in full cry,*** eagerly running after or trying to catch.
4) ***within cry*** [***of***], near enough to hear.

—[名] 1. 외침[소리], 울음소리 2. 소리내어 울기 3. 소리치며 팔기 4. 여론; 소문
[熟] 1)원거리 2)ⓐ추적 ⓑ여론의 비등 3)열심히 뒤쫓는 4)목소리가 닿는 곳에

cry·ba·by [kráibèibi] *n.* [C] (pl. **-bies**) a person who cries easily for very little reason.
—[名] 울보, 잘 우는 사람

cry·ing [kráiiŋ] *adj.* **1.** that cries; weeping. **2.** calling for attention; urgent; very bad. ¶*a ~ need.*①
—[形] 1. 울고 있는, 외치는 2. 긴급한; 심한, 지독한 ¶①긴급한 일

crypt [kript] *n.* [C] a room under the main floor of a church, frequently used for graves.
—[名] [교회당의] 지하실

cryp·tic [kríptik], **-ti·cal** [-tik(ə)l] *adj.* **1.** hidden; secret. ¶*~ writing.* **2.** mysterious. ¶*a ~ message.* **3.** suitable for concealing. ¶*~ color.*① ▷**cryp·ti·cal·ly** [-kəli] *adv.*
—[形] 1. 숨은, 비밀의 2. 신비한 3. 몸을 숨기기에 알맞은 ¶①보호색

•**crys·tal** [krístl] *n.* **1.** [U] a hard mineral (quartz) that is clear like glass. **2.** [C] a piece of crystal shaped into an ornament. **3.** [U] glass of a very superior clearness, used for making table articles; glassware made of this glass. **4.** [C] (*U.S.*) a glass cover over a watch dial. **5.** [C] a solid body formed of angles and flat surfaces. **6.** [C] a piece of quartz used in a radio.
—[名] 1. 수정 2. 수정 제품 3. 커트유리, 납유리; 납유리로 만든 식기류 4. [시계의] 뚜껑 유리 5. 결정(結晶)[체] 6. [라디오의] 검파용(檢波用) 광석

—*adj.* **1.** made of crystal. **2.** like crystal.
—[形] 1. 수정의(으로 만든) 2. 수정 같은

crys·tal·line [krístəlàin, +*U.S.* -lin] *adj.* **1.** consisting of or like crystal. **2.** very clear; transparent; of or of the nature of a crystal or crystals.
—[形] 1. 수정으로 이루어지는, 수정 같은 2. 투명한; 결정[질]의

crys·tal·li·za·tion [krìstəlizéiʃ(ə)n / -lai-] *n.* **1.** [U] the act or process of crystallizing. **2.** [C] a crystallized thing.
—[名] 1. 정화(晶化) 2. 결정[체]

crys·tal·lize, *Brit.* **-lise** [krístəlàiz] *vt.* **1.** form (something) into crystals. **2.** give a definite form to (a plan, an idea, etc.). **3.** coat (fruits, etc.) with sugar. ¶*crỳstallized fruits.* —*vi.* **1.** form into crystals. **2.** form into a definite shape. 《~ *into* something》
—[他] 1. …을 결정(結晶)시키다 2. [사상 따위]를 구체화하다 3. …을 사탕에 재다 —[自] 1. 결정하다, 정화하다 2. 구체화하다

cub [kʌb] *n.* [C] **1.** a young fox, bear, lion, etc. **2.** a rough or awkward boy.
—[名] 1. [여우·곰·사자 따위]의 새끼 2. 사나운 사내아이

Cu·ba [kjú:bə] *n.* a republic on the largest island in the West Indies. ⇒[N.B.]
—[名] 쿠바 [N.B.] 수도는 Havana

Cu·ban [kjú:bən] *adj.* of Cuba or its people. —*n.* [C] a person of Cuba.
—[形] 쿠바 섬의; 쿠바 사람의 —[名] 쿠바 사람

•**cube** [kju:b] *n.* **1.** [C] a solid figure with six equal, square faces. **2.** [U] the product that results when a number is multiplied by itself twice. —*vt.* **1.** make or form (something) into the shape of a cube. **2.** multiply (a number) by itself twice.
—[名] 1. 입방체, 정6면체 2. 세제곱, 입방 —[他] 1. …을 입방체로 만들다 2. …을 세제곱하다; …의 부피(체적)를 구하다

cu·bic [kjú:bik] *adj.* **1.** shaped like a cube. **2.** having length, breadth and height.
—[形] 1. 입방체의 2. 세제곱의, 입방의

cu·bi·cle [kjú:bikl] *n.* [C] a very small room esp. a bedroom, in a dormitory.
—[名] [간막이가 있는] 작은 침실

cub·ism [kjú:biz(ə)m] *n.* [U] (*Art*) a school of modern art in which objects are shown as cubes and other geometrical forms.
—[名] 입체파

cub·ist [kjú:bist] *n.* [C] an artist who practises cubism.
—[名] 입체파의 미술가

cu·bit [kjú:bit] *n.* [C] an ancient measure of length, about 18 to 22 inches, originally the length from the elbow to the tip of the middle finger.
—[名] 완척(腕尺)(고대의 척도)

•**cuck·oo** [kúku:, +*U.S.* kú:-] *n.* [C] (pl. **cuck·oos**) **1.** a bird whose call sounds like its name. **2.** a cry of this
—[名] 1. 뻐꾸기 2. 뻐꾸기의 울음소리 3. 《俗》 얼간이, 바보 —[形] 《俗》 미친;

bird. **3.** (*slang*) a fool. —*adj.* (*slang*) crazy; silly.
바보의

cuckoo clock [∠-∸] *n.* a clock which marks the hour by the call and the movement of a toy cuckoo.
—[名] 뻐꾹 시계

cu·cum·ber [kjú:kəmbər] *n.* [C] a vegetable that has a long green fruit, eaten in salads and as pickles.
—[名] 오이

cool as a cucumber, very cool; calm; not excited.
[熟] 태연자약한, 침착한

cud [kʌd] *n.* [U] food which some animals, like cows, bring back into the mouth from the first stomach and chew slowly again.
—[名] 새김질거리(반추동물이 제1 위에서 입으로 도로 내어 씹는 것)

chew the cud, think over and over again.
[熟] 잘 생각하다; 반성하다

cud·dle [kʌ́dl] *vt.* hold closely and tenderly; embrace lovingly. ¶*I cuddled her cute baby in my arms.* —*vi.* lie close and comfortable; lie curled. ¶*Two kittens cuddled together on a sofa.* —*n.* [U] an embrace; a caress.
—[他] …을 껴안다 —[自] 꼭 붙어 자다, 껴안다; 쪼그리고 자다 —[名] 포옹

cudg·el [kʌ́dʒ(ə)l] *n.* [C] a short, heavy stick used as a weapon; a club.
—[名] 곤봉

take up the cudgels for, strongly defend.
[熟] …을 용감하게 변호하다

—*vt.* beat (something or someone) with a cudgel.
—[他] …을 곤봉으로 때리다

cudgel one's brains, force oneself to think hard.
[熟] 머리를 짜다, 곰곰이 생각하다

cue¹ [kju:] *n.* [C] **1.** a hint; a suggestion. ¶*give someone his* (or *the*) *~*① / *take one's ~ from someone.*② **2.** the last words of an actor serving as a sign to the next actor to speak, act or enter. **3.** the part that an actor is to play. **4.** a mood; a frame of mind.
—[名] 1. 단서, 실마리, 암시 ¶①…에게 암시(힌트)를 주다/②…을 본받다 2. 대사(臺辭)의 마지막 말, 큐우 3. 역할 4. 기분

cue² [kju:] *n.* [C] **1.** a long stick used for striking the ball in billiards. **2.** a queue.
—[名] 1. [당구의] 큐우, 당구채 2. 땋은 머리, 변발(辮髮)

* **cuff** [kʌf] *n.* [C] **1.** a wristband of shirts, coats, etc. **2.** a fold around the bottom of a trouser leg.
—[名] 1. 커프스; 소매 끝동 2. [즈봉의] 접어 올린 아랫단

cui·sine [kwi(:)zí:n] *n.* **1.** [U] the manner or style of cooking. **2.** [C] the kitchen or the cooking department.
—[名] 1. 요리법 2. 부엌, 요리실

cul-de-sac [kʌ́ldəsǽk / kúl-] *n.* [C] a street or lane open at only one end; a blind alley.
—[名] 막다른골목

cu·li·nar·y [kjú:linèri, kʌ́li- / kʌ́linəri] *adj.* of cooking or the kitchen.
—[形] 요리의, 부엌의

cull [kʌl] *vt.* pick out (flowers, etc.); choose and gather; make selections out of (something). —*n.* [C] 《usu. *pl.*》 something picked out as being poor or worthless.
—[他] …을 따다, 골라 모으다; …에서 고르다 —[名] 골라 모은 것

cul·mi·nate [kʌ́lminèit] *vi.* reach the highest point or degree; reach a climax; result. 《~ *in* something》
—[自] 전성(全盛)의 극(極)에 이르다; 최고점(절정)에 달하다; 결국 …이 되다

cul·mi·na·tion [kʌ̀lminéiʃ(ə)n] *n.* [C] **1.** the highest point or position reached; the climax. **2.** the reaching of the highest point.
—[名] 1. 최고점, 정상, 극점 2. 전성, 최고점, 극치

cul·pa·ble [kʌ́lpəbl] *adj.* deserving blame; guilty.
—[形] 나무랄 만한

cul·pa·bly [kʌ́lpəbli] *adv.* in a culpable manner.
—[副] 괘씸하게[도]

cul·prit [kʌ́lprit] *n.* [C] **1.** a guilty person; an offender. **2.** a person who is accused of a crime.
—[名] 1. 죄인; 범인 2. 범죄 혐의자

cult [kʌlt] *n.* [C] **1.** a system of religious worship. **2.** great admiration or devotion for a person, or thing, esp. for only a short time; worship; craze. **3.** 《*collectively*》 a group of persons showing such admiration. ¶*the ~ of Keats.* / *the ~ of baseball.*
—[名] 1. 예배식, 의식 2. 숭배; [일시적] 열광, …열(熱) 3. 숭배자들

‡ **cul·ti·vate** [kʌ́ltivèit] *vt.* **1.** prepare and work on (land, etc.) for growing crops; (*U.S.*) loosen the soil around (growing plants). **2.** help (plants, etc.) grow by giving labor and care. **3.** improve; develop (one's ability, etc.) by education or training; devote oneself to (something). ¶*~ a hobby.* **4.** seek the acquaintance or friendship of (someone).
—[他] 1. …을 경작하다; [재배중인 작물을] 사이갈이하다 2. [초목]을 재배하다 3. …을 양성하다, 교화하다, 수양하다; …에 전념하다 4. …의 지기(知己)·교제를 구하다

cul·ti·vat·ed [kʌ́ltivèitid] *adj.* **1.** prepared for growing crops. ↔native **2.** grown with human care; not wild. ↔wild ¶*~ land.*① **3.** cultured; refined. ¶*~ taste.*②
—[形] 1. 경작된 2. 재배된 ¶①경작지 3. 교양있는, 세련된 ¶②고상한 취미

* **cul·ti·va·tion** [kʌ̀ltivéiʃ(ə)n] *n.* [U] **1.** the process or art of cultivating the soil and its products. ¶*bring waste land under ~.*① **2.** improvement of the mind; development of the body. **3.** culture; refinement.
—[名] 1. 경작, 재배; 경작 상태 ¶①황무지를 개간하다 2. 수양, 양성; [체력] 배양 3. 교양; 세련

cul·ti·va·tor [kʌ́ltivèitər] *n.* [C] **1.** a person or thing that cultivates. **2.** a tool or machine used to loosen the soil and dig up weeds around growing plants. ⇒fig.
—[名] 1. 경작자, 재배자, 양성자 2. 경운기(耕耘機)

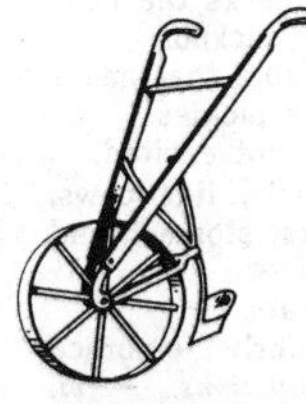
(cultivator 2.)

***cul·tur·al** [kʌ́ltʃ(ə)r(ə)l] *adj.* of culture. ▷**cul·tur·al·ly** [-i] *adv.*
—[形] 배양의; 교양의; 문화의

***cul·ture** [kʌ́ltʃər] *n.* **1.** [U] the development of the mind or body by education, training, etc. **2.** [U] the result of the careful training of the mind, training in manners, etc.; refinement. **3.** [U][C] the sum total of the ways of living built up by a race of people; the state of civilization among a group of people. **4.** [U][C] the cultivation of land; the care and breeding of bees, fish, oysters, grapes, etc. **5.** [U][C] a growth of bacteria produced in a laboratory.
—[名] 1. 수양, 교화 2. 세련, 수양 3. 문화 4. 경작; [꿀벌·물고기 따위의] 양식(養殖); 재배 5. 배양

—*vt.* cultivate.
—[他] …을 재배하다, 배양하다

cul·tured [kʌ́ltʃərd] *adj.* **1.** having or showing culture; educated; refined. **2.** produced or grown under artificial conditions. ¶*~ pearls / ~ bacteria.*
—[形] 1. 교양있는; 세련된 2. 배양된, 양식된

cul·vert [kʌ́lvərt] *n.* [C] a small channel or passage for water crossing under a road or railroad.
—[名] [철도·도로 따위의] 암거(暗渠), 지하수로, 배수지

cum·ber [kʌ́mbər] *vt.* burden; trouble; hinder; make it impossible for (someone or something) to come in or go out; block up. **—*n.*** [C] hindrance.
—[他] …을 성가시게 굴다, 골치아프게 하다; 방해하다; [장소]를 가로막다 —[名] 방해

cum·ber·some [kʌ́mbərsəm] *adj.* difficult to deal with or move; burdensome; troublesome; badly made.
—[形] 귀찮은, 성가신, 다루기 힘든; 모양 없는

cum·brous [kʌ́mbrəs] *adj.* cumbersome.
—[形] 골치아픈

cu·mu·la·tive [kjú:mjulèitiv] *adj.* growing by successive additions; heaped up; gathered together.
—[形] 누적(累積)하는, 누가(累加)하는

cu·mu·li [kjú:mjulài] *n.* pl. of **cumulus**.

cu·mu·lus [kjú:mjuləs] *n.* [C] (pl. **cu·mu·li**) **1.** a heap; a mound. **2.** [U][C] a cloud with a flat base and rounded masses often piled up like a mountain.
—[名] 1. 퇴적(堆積), 누적 2. 적운(積雲)

cu·ne·i·form [kju:ní:əfɔ̀:rm / kjú:niifɔ̀:m] *adj.* shaped like an arrowhead, as the characters in the writing of the ancient Persians, the Babylonians, etc. **—*n.*** [C] such a written character.
—[形] 쐐기 모양의 —[名] 설형(楔形)문자

‡**cun·ning** [kʌ́niŋ] *adj.* **1.** clever in deceiving; crafty; sly. **2.** (*archaic*) skillful; clever. **3.** (*U.S. colloq.*) pretty and lovable; attractive. ¶*What a ~ baby!* **—*n.*** [U] cleverness at deceiving.
—[形] 1. 교활한, 간사한 2.《古》노련한, 능숙한 3.《美口》귀여운, 매력적인 —[名] 교활, 간사함

cun·ning·ly [kʌ́niŋli] *adv.* in a cunning manner; cleverly; artfully.
—[副] 교활하게, 간사하게

‡**cup** [kʌp] *n.* [C] **1.** a small drinking vessel with a handle. ¶*a ~ and saucer.*① **2.** the contents of a full cup; a cupful. ¶*a ~ of coffee / three cups of flour.* **3.** an ornamental vessel or goblet given as a prize. ¶*win the ~.*② **4.** any object shaped like a cup. **5.** 《*the ~* or *pl.*》 wine; drinking. **6.** a mixed drink of wine, fruit, etc. ¶*have* (or *get*) *a ~ too much.*③ **7.** fate; that which we must receive or suffer. ¶*drain* (or *drink*) *the ~ of life to the bottom* (or *the dregs*)④ / *drink a bitter ~ / Her ~ of happiness was full.*⑤
—[名] 1. [코오피·홍차용의] 컵, 차종 ¶①접시 딸린 차종 2. 차종 가득 3. 상배(賞杯), 우승컵; [다리 달린] 컵 ¶②우승하다 4. 차종 모양의 것 5. 포도주; 음주 6. 포도주를 탄 음료 ¶③술 취해 있다 7. 운명, 인생의 경험 ¶④인생의 쓰고 단 맛을 다 맛보다/⑤그녀는 행복의 절정에 있다

in one's cups, drunk.
[熟] 거나해서

—*vt.* (**cupped, cup·ping**) **1.** form (something) in the shape of a cup. ¶*He cupped his hands.* **2.** take or put (something) in a cup. ¶*~ water from a stream.*
—[他] 1. …을 차종 모양으로 만들다 2. …을 차종으로 받다, 차종에 담다

***cup·board** [kʌ́bərd] *n.* [C] a piece of furniture with shelves used for storing dishes, food, etc.
—[名] 찬장

cry cupboard, cry that one is hungry; cry for food.
[熟] 배고프다고 말하다

***cup·ful** [kʌ́pfùl] *n.* [C] as much as a cup can hold; (in cooking) half a pint.
—[名] 차종 가득[한 분량]; [요리에서] 반 파인트

Cu·pid [kjúːpid] *n.* **1.** (in Roman mythology) the god of love, the son of Venus. **2.** [C] ⦅c-⦆ a picture or statue of a winged baby, used as a symbol of love; a representation of Cupid.
—[名] 1. 큐우핏(사랑의 신) 2. 큐우핏의 그림(상); 사랑의 사자(使者)

cu·pid·i·ty [kju(ː)píditi] *n.* [U] eager desire, esp. for wealth; greed.
—[名] 탐욕

cu·po·la [kjúːpələ] *n.* [C] a small dome on a building; a small tower built on top of a roof or building. ⇒fig.
—[名] 작고 둥근 지붕, 둥근 천장

〔cupola〕

cur [kəːr] *n.* [C] **1.** a worthless dog; a dog of mixed breed. **2.** a mean, worthless person.
—[名] 1. 들개; 잡종견 2. [사람의] 망종, 상놈

cur·a·ble [kjúərəbl] *adj.* that can be cured. ▷**cur·a·ble·ness** [-nis] *n.*
—[形] 치료할 수 있는

cu·ra·cy [kjúərəsi] *n.* [C] the position or office of a curate.
—[名] 목사보(補)의 직(지위)

cu·rate [kjúərit] *n.* [C] (esp. *Brit.*) a clergyman who helps a pastor, a rector, or a vicar.
—[名] ⦅英⦆ 목사보(補)

cur·a·tive [kjúərətiv] *adj.* having the power to cure. —*n.* [C] a medicine or any form of treatment that cures.
—[形] 치료의, 치료할 힘이 있는 —[名] 치료약; 치료법

cu·ra·tor [kjuəréitər] *n.* [C] a person in charge of a museum, a library, etc.
—[名] [박물관·도서관 따위의] 관리자, 관장

* **curb** [kəːrb] *n.* [C] **1.** a chain or strap under a horse's mouth, used to control the horse. **2.** anything that holds back; a check; a restraint. **3.** a line of raised stones, concrete, or wood separating a sidewalk from the street. (cf. *Brit.* kerb) —*vt.* **1.** hold (a horse) in or back by a curb. **2.** check; control.
—[名] 1. [말의] 재갈 2. 구속, 억제 3. [차도와 인도 경계의] 가장자리 돌
—[他] 1. [말]에 재갈을 물리다 2. …을 억제하다, 구속하다

curb·stone [kə́ːrbstòun] *n.* [C] a stone or the stones forming a curb.
—[名] [보도의] 가장자리 돌

curd [kəːrd] *n.* [U][C] ⦅often *pl.*⦆ the thick, soft part of milk of which cheese is made.
—[名] 응유(凝乳)

cur·dle [kə́ːrdl] *vt.* change (something) into curd; cause (something) to thicken. —*vi.* turn to curd; grow thick.
—[他] …을 굳어지게 하다, 응결(凝結)시키다 —[自] 굳어지다; 응유가 되다

⁑ **cure** [kjuər] *vt.* **1.** bring (someone) back to health ⦅~ a person *of* a disease⦆; take away (a disease). ¶ *~ a patient of a disease / This medicine cures headaches quickly.* **2.** get rid of (something bad). ⦅~ a person *of* a bad habit⦆ ¶ *~ drunkenness / ~ someone of a bad habit.* **3.** preserve (meat, fish, etc.) by salting, drying, or smoking. —*vi.* **1.** become well. **2.** be preserved by salting, etc.
—[他] 1. …을 치료하다, …을 고치다 2. …을 교정(矯正)하다 3. [건조·훈제(燻製) 또는 소금에 절여] 저장(보존)하다 —[自] 1. [병이] 낫다 2. 보존되다, 오래 가다

cure oneself of, get rid of (something) by oneself.
[熟] …을 스스로 고치다

—*n.* [C] **1.** that which recovers health or does away with an evil; a medicine; a method of curing anything. **2.** the act of curing; the state of being cured. ¶ *She is past ~ now.*① **3.** the method of preserving meat, etc. by salting, etc. **4.** religious care; the priestly office. ¶ *the ~ of souls.*② ▷**cure·less** [-lis] *adj.*
—[名] 1. 의료; 치료약; 치료법; 구제법; 교정법 2. 치료, 치유(治癒); 회복 ¶① 그녀는 이젠 회복할 가망이 없다 3. [육류·생선의] 보존[법] 4. [영혼의] 구제, 목사직 ¶② 영혼의 구제

cure-all [kjúərɔ̀ːl] *n.* [C] a medicine or any form of treatment supposed to cure all diseases.
—[名] 만병 통치약

cur·few [kə́ːrfjuː] *n.* [C] a signal, esp. by a bell, at a certain time in the evening; the time set for this; the bell itself.
—[名] 만종(晩鐘), 저녁종[의 시간]

cu·ri·o [kjúərioù] *n.* [C] (pl. **-os**) a thing which is valued because it is rare, unusual, or odd.
—[名] 골동품, 진기한 물건

⁑ **cu·ri·os·i·ty** [kjùəriásiti / -ɔ́s-] *n.* (pl. **-ties**) **1.** [U] an eager desire to know or learn. ¶ *out of* (or *from*) *~.*① **2.** [C] a strange, rare, or novel object; a curio.
—[名] 1. 호기심 ¶① 호기심에서 2. 진품, 골동품

⁑ **cu·ri·ous** [kjúəriəs] *adj.* **1.** eager to know or learn. ¶ *a ~ scholar.* **2.** strange; odd; unusual. **3.** very careful; exact. **4.** (*colloq.*) very odd; very strange.
—[形] 1. 알고 싶어하는, 호기심이 강한 2. 진기한, 호기심을 끄는 3. 면밀한, 정교한 4. ⦅口⦆ 아주 기묘한, 정상이 아닌

curious to say, strange to say; it is odd, but ….
[熟] 기묘한 일은

* **cu·ri·ous·ly** [kjúəriəsli] *adv.* in a curious manner.
—[副] 신기한 듯이, 기묘하게

⁑ **curl** [kəːrl] *vt.* make (hair, etc.) into waves or rings. ¶ ~ *one's hair* / *It curled the waves.*① **—vi.** become curved; take a spiral shape. ¶*The smoke from the camp fire curled upwards.*
—[他] …을 곱슬곱슬하게 하다; …을 물결치게 하다 ¶①물결이 인 —[自] 물결치다; 소용돌이치다; 구부러지다

—n. **1.** [C] curled hair; anything curled. **2.** [U] the state of being curled; the act of curling.
—[名] 1. 곱슬머리, 곱슬머리 모양의 것 2. 뚤뚤 말림(말기)

cur·lew [kə́ːrl(j)uː] *n.* [C] (pl. **-lews** or *collectively* **-lew**) a bird with long legs and a long curved bill.
—[名] 《鳥》 마도요

curl·ing [kə́ːrliŋ] *n.* [U] a Scottish game played by sliding large, smooth stones over ice towards a mark. **—adj.** that curls; used for curling.
—[名] 스코틀랜드의 빙상 돌던지기 놀이 —[形] 말기 쉬운, 머리털 마는 데 쓰는

curling iron [⸗- ⸗-] *n.* an iron used for curling or waving hair.
—[名] 머리 지지는 도구

* **curl·y** [kə́ːrli] *adj.* (**curl·i·er, curl·i·est**) **1.** curling; wavy; tending to curl. **2.** having curls.
—[形] 1. 곱슬머리의, 머리를 지진 2. 소용돌이가 된

cur·mudg·eon [kərmʌ́dʒ(ə)n / kəː-] *n.* [C] a bad-tempered person; a person who does not easily part with his money.
—[名] 심술궂은 사람; 구두쇠

cur·rant [kə́ːrənt / kʌ́r(ə)nt] *n.* [C] **1.** a small, dried, seedless raisin, used in cakes, etc. **2.** a small, sour, edible berry that grows in bunches.
—[名] 1. 작고 씨 없는 건포도 2. 까치밥나무

* **cur·ren·cy** [kə́ːrənsi / kʌ́r(ə)n-] *n.* (pl. **-cies**) **1.** [C][U] money in use. ¶*gold* ~ / *paper* ~. **2.** [U] a continual passing from one person to another; circulation. ¶*give ~ to a rumor*① / *These slang words have an extensive ~ in Korea.*② **3.** [U] general use; common acceptance; current value or estimation.
—[名] 1. 통화 2. 통용, 유포, 유통 ¶①소문을 퍼뜨리다/②이들 속어는 한국에서 널리 쓰이고 있다 3. 시세; 성가(聲價)

gain (or ***obtain***) ***currency,*** circulate; become widely discussed.
[熟] 널리 퍼지다

⁑ **cur·rent** [kə́ːrənt / kʌ́r(ə)nt] *n.* [C] **1.** a flow; a stream. **2.** the flow of electricity along a wire, etc. **3.** a course; a movement; the general direction; the dominant tendency.
—[名] 1. 유동(流動), 흐름 2. 전류 3. 추세, 풍조, 경향

—adj. **1.** of the present time; latest. ¶*the ~ week* / *~ English.* **2.** generally used or accepted; commonly occurring; in present use; passing from person to person. ¶*the ~ opinion* / *a ~ coin.*
—[形] 1. 현대의, 현재의 2. [일반적으로] 통용중인, 유통되는, 유포되어 있는

go (or ***pass, run***) ***current,*** circulate; become widely accepted.
[熟] 통용하다; 세상에서 인정받다

current account [⸗- -⸗] *n.* (*Economics*) an account from which money can be drawn for present use.
—[名] 당좌예금

cur·rent·ly [kə́ːrəntli / kʌ́r(ə)nt-] *adv.* **1.** at present; now. **2.** generally; commonly.
—[副] 1. 현재는, 오늘날 2. 일반적으로, 널리

cur·ric·u·la [kəríkjulə] *n.* pl. of **curriculum.**

cur·ric·u·lar [kəríkjulər] *adj.* of a curriculum.
—[形] 교과 과정의

cur·ric·u·lum [kəríkjuləm] *n.* [C] (pl. **-lums** or **-la**) a course of study in a school, a college, etc.
—[名] [학교의] 학과 과정

curriculum vi·tae [kəríkjuləmváitiː] *n.* (pl. **cur·ric·u·la ~**) an outline of one's educational career, experience, etc. used in applying for a position; a personal history.
—[名] 이력서

cur·ri·er [kə́ːriər / kʌ́riə] *n.* [C] a person who curries leather after it has been tanned.
—[名] 무두질 직공, 제혁공(製革工)

cur·rish [kə́ːriʃ] *adj.* of a worthless dog; like a cur; mean; ill-bred.
—[形] 들개의(같은), 비열한, 심술궂은

cur·ry[1] [kə́ːri / kʌ́ri] *vt.* (**-ried**) **1.** rub down or clean (a horse, etc.) with a brush or comb. **2.** prepare (tanned leather) by wetting, beating, etc.
—[他] 1. [말털 따위]를 빗질하다 2. [무두질 가죽]을 마무리하다

curry favor with, try to get (someone's) favor by flattering him.
[熟] …의 비위를 맞추다

cur·ry[2] [kə́ːri / kʌ́ri] *n.* (pl. **-ries**) **1.** [U] a peppery sauce or powder containing seeds, vegetables, etc. and flavored with various spices, used in cooking. **2.** [U][C] a dish of meat, rice, etc. flavored with curry. ¶*~ and rice.*① ⇒[usage] **—vt.** prepare or flavor (food) with curry.
—[名] 1. 카레이[가루] 2. 카레이 요리 ¶①라이스 카레이 [usage] and 로 연결되어 있으나 단수 취급 —[他] [음식]을 카레이 가루로 양념하다

⁑ **curse** [kəːrs] *v.* (**cursed** or **curst**) *vt.* **1.** ask God to punish or hurt (someone or something); wish to harm. **2.** 《usu. in *passive*》 cause great evil to (someone); torment. **3.** swear at (someone). **—vi.** swear; use bad language.
—[他] 1. …을 저주하다; …에게 재난이 일어나다; …을 괴롭히다 2. …에 욕을 퍼붓다; …에 불경(不敬)한 말을 하다 —[自] 저주하다; 욕설하다; 불경한 말을 하다

cursed

be cursed with (=*be troubled with*; *suffer from*) *someone* or *something*.
—*n.* Ⓒ **1.** a prayer that harm or injury may come to someone ; a word or words used in such a prayer. ¶(*proverb*) *Curses, like chickens, come home to roost.*② **2.** the evil or harm that comes as if in answer to a curse ; a thing that causes evil or harm. ¶*call down a ~ upon someone*③ / *Curse upon him.*④ **3.** something that is cursed. 「*to*) *something*.」
1) *do not care* (or *give*) *a curse for* (=*be indifferent*
2) *not worth a curse,* useless ; worthless.
3) *under a curse,* cursed.

curs·ed [kə́ːrsid] *adj.* **1.** under a curse ; damned. **2.** deserving a curse ; evil ; hateful. ▷**curs·ed·ly** [-li] *adv.*

cur·sive [kə́ːrsiv] *adj.* (of handwriting) with the letters joined together. —*n.* Ⓤ Ⓒ a letter made to join other letters. ▷**cur·sive·ly** [-li] *adv.*

cur·so·ry [kə́ːrs(ə)ri] *adj.* hasty ; quick and careless ; without paying attention to details. ¶*a ~ glance.*

curst [kəːrst] *adj.* cursed. —*v.* pt. and pp. of **curse.**

curt [kəːrt] *adj.* short ; rudely brief ; abrupt. ▷**curt·ly** [-li] *adv.* —**curt·ness** [-nis] *n.*

cur·tail [kəːrtéil] *vt.* cut (something) short ; cut off a part of (something) ; reduce ; shorten. 「curtailing.」

cur·tail·ment [kəːrtéilmənt] *n.* Ⓤ the act or result of

⁑ **cur·tain** [kə́ːrt(ə)n] *n.* Ⓒ **1.** a covering for a window, a cupboard, etc. ¶*draw the curtains.* **2.** a large piece of cloth or a hanging screen let down or pulled across between the stage and the audience in a theater. ¶*draw the ~*① / *The ~ rises* (*falls*).② **3.** a thing that covers, hides, or divides. ¶*a ~ of fog.*③
1) *behind the curtain,* in secret ; secretly.
2) *draw the curtain on,* ⓐ end. ⓑ show.
3) *lift the curtain on,* ⓐ begin. ⓑ reveal ; make (something) known.
—*vt.* **1.** hang or provide (something) with curtains ; decorate (something) with curtains. **2.** cover ; hide.
curtain off, separate or shut off (a room, etc.) by a curtain or curtains.

curt·sey [kə́ːrtsiː] *n.* =curtsy.

curt·sy [kə́ːrtsiː] *n.* Ⓒ (pl. **-sies**) a bow of respect or greeting by women, made by bending the knees and inclining the head and shoulders slightly.

cur·va·ture [kə́ːrvətʃər] *n.* Ⓤ the act of bending ; the state of being bent ; something curved or bent.

• **curve** [kəːrv] *n.* Ⓒ **1.** a line that has no straight part ; a rounded bend. **2.** a thing that has the shape of a curve ; a bend. ¶*a ~ in the road.* **3.** (in baseball) a ball thrown so as to curve just before it reaches the batter.
—*vt.* cause (something) to bend or turn from a straight line. —*vi.* bend ; turn. —*adj.* curved.

• **cush·ion** [kúʃ(ə)n] *n.* Ⓒ **1.** a soft bag filled with feathers, air, etc. to sit, kneel, or lie on. **2.** any soft thing which makes a shock or noise less. **3.** the soft, rubber, inner side of a billiard table. —*vt.* **1.** provide or furnish (something or someone) with cushions. **2.** protect (something or someone) with cushions.

cusp [kʌsp] *n.* Ⓒ **1.** a pointed end ; a point ; (*Astronomy*) one of the points of a crescent moon. **2.** a pointed part of the crown of a tooth or a leaf.

cus·pi·dor [kʌ́spidɔːr] *n.* Ⓒ a bowl to spit into.

cus·tard [kʌ́stərd] *n.* ⒸⓊ a yellow food made of eggs, sugar, milk, etc. boiled or baked.

cus·to·di·an [kʌstóudiən] *n.* Ⓒ **1.** a person in charge

custodian

熟 1)천벌을 받다 ; 괴로움을 당하다

—名 1. 저주 ; 저주의 말 ¶②(俚)누워서 침뱉기 2. 천벌 ; 재난 ; 재난의 원인이 되는 것 ¶③…을 저주하다/④그런 녀석은 천벌이나 받아라 3. 저주받은 것

熟 1)…을 조금도 개의하지 않다 2)전혀 가치가 없는 3)저주받은

—形 1. 저주받은 2. 저주할, 꽤씸한

—形 [필적이] 초서체의, 흘려 쓴
—名 초서

—形 되는 대로의, 대충의, 소홀한

—形 저주받은
—形 짧은, 무뚝뚝한, 퉁명스러운

—動 …을 바짝 줄이다, 생략하다, 단축하다 ; 삭감하다
—名 삭감, 절감(節減), 단축

—名 1. 커어튼, 휘장 2. [극장의] 막 ¶①막을 올리다(내리다)/②개막(폐막)이 되다 ; 이야기가 시작되다(끝나다) 3. 가로막는 것, 간막이 ¶③자욱한 안개

熟 1)배후에서, 비밀히 2)ⓐ…을 끝내다 ⓑ…을 공개하다 3)ⓐ…을 시작하다 ⓑ…을 터놓고 말하다, 공표하다

—動 1. …에 막(커어튼)을 치다 2. …을 가리다, 감추다
熟 …을 커어튼으로 가리다(가로막다)

—名 왼발을 뒤로 물리고 무릎을 굽히는 여자의 인사(절)

—名 구부리기, 구부러지기 ; 만곡(彎曲)부

—名 1. 곡선 2. 굴곡, 만곡부 3. [야구에서의] 곡구(曲球), 커어브 —動 …을 구부리다, 만곡시키다 —自 만곡하다, 구부러지다 —形 구부러진

—名 1. 쿠션, 방석 2. 쿠션 모양의 것 3. [당구대의] 쿠션 —動 1. …에 쿠션을 대다, 쿠션으로 받치다 2. …을 쿠션으로 보호하다

—名 1. 첨단, 끝 ; 초승달의 끝 2. [이·잎사귀 따위의] 끝

—名 1. 타구(唾具)
—名 커스터드[과자]

—名 1. 감시자 2. [특히 공공 건물의]

of something. **2.** a person who takes care of a public building; a janitor.

관리인, 수위

cus·to·dy [kʌ́stədi] *n.* [U] **1.** the act of keeping or guarding; the state of being guarded or watched; care; charge. **2.** imprisonment.
1) ***in custody,*** in the care of the police; in prison.
2) ***take into custody,*** arrest (someone) and put him under guard.

—[名] **1.** 보관, 보호, 관리 **2.** 감금

[熟] 1)구류되어 2)…을 수감(구속)하다

⁑ **cus·tom** [kʌ́stəm] *n.* **1.** [C][U] an ordinary or usual manner of doing or acting; habit. ¶*It was his ~ to get up early.* **2.** [C][U] a habit done for so long that it has almost the force of law. **3.** [U] support given to a business by its customers; ((*collectively*)) the customers or patrons of a shop or trader. **4.** ((*pl.*)) taxes or duties on goods brought into a country; the department of the government that gathers these taxes.
—*adj.* made to order; made esp. for each customer, etc. ↔made-to-order ¶~ *clothes.*

—[名] **1.** 습관, 풍습 **2.** 관례; 관습 **3.** 단골, 단골 손님 **4.** 관세; 세관

—[形] 주문의, 마춘; 주문품만 파는(만드는)

cus·tom·ar·i·ly [kʌ́stəmèrili / -m(ə)ri-] *adv.* in a customary manner; usually.

—[副] 습관적으로, 관례상, 일반적으로, 보통

• **cus·tom·ar·y** [kʌ́stəmèri / -m(ə)ri] *adj.* according to custom; usual; established by custom.

—[形] 통례의, 습관적인; 관례적인

⁑ **cus·tom·er** [kʌ́stəmər] *n.* [C] **1.** a person who buys regularly from the same store. **2.** (*colloq.*) a person; a fellow; a person one has to deal with. ¶*a tough ~.*

—[名] **1.** 고객, 단골[손님], 거래처 **2.** ((口)) 놈, 녀석, 곤란한 녀석

custom house [ˊ-- ˋ] *n.* a government building or office where taxes on imported, or sometimes on exported goods, are collected and where travelers' luggage is examined.

—[名] 세관

cus·tom-made [kʌ́stəmméid] *adj.* made to order; made esp. for each customer, etc.

—[形] 주문품의, 마춘

⁑ **cut** [kʌt] *v.* (**cut, cut·ting**) *vt.* **1.** separate (something) into parts with a knife, etc.; make an opening, tear, or wound in (something). ¶~ *one's finger* / ~ *a sheet of paper in three*① / ~ [*down*] *trees* / *Please ~ me a slice of bread.*② **2.** make or shape (something) by cutting; carve; engrave. ¶~ *a figure in wood* / ~ *a road through a hill*③ / ~ *one's name on a tree.* **3.** make (hair, grass, etc.) short[er] by cutting; mow; reap. ¶~ *the wheat* / ~ *one's nails* / *have one's hair ~ at the barber.* **4.** make (something) less or shorter; reduce; curtail. ¶~ *prices* / ~ *a newspaper article.*④ **5.** cause pain or suffering to (someone); pierce. ¶*The icy wind ~ me to the bone.*⑤ **6.** pretend not to see or know (someone). ¶~ *someone in the street.*⑥ **7.** (*colloq.*) be absent from (school, etc.). ¶~ *a lecture* (*a meeting*). **8.** cross. ¶*One line cuts another at right angles.*⑦ **9.** make (something) loose; dissolve. ¶~ *tar with gasoline.*⑧ **10.** hurt the feelings of (someone). —*vi.* **1.** do cutting; work as a cutter. ¶*This knife doesn't ~ well.*⑨ **2.** take cutting; be cut. ¶*The wood cuts easily.* **3.** hurt by or as by sharp piercing strokes. ¶*The wind ~ through his thin clothes.*⑩ / *The wind cuts keenly.* **4.** run away quickly. **5.** (*slang*) go by a shorter route. **6.** (*Sports*) hit a ball so that it is hit away and sometimes also made to spin. **7.** pass or go through.
1) ***cut*** (=***run***) ***about*** *some place.*
2) ***cut across,*** take a short course by going straight across (some place).
3) ***cut after*** (=***hurry after; pursue***) ***something*** or ***someone.***
4) ***cut and come again,*** have some more to eat; eat a lot, esp. of meat.
5) ***cut and run,*** get away quickly.
6) ***cut*** (=***aim a sharp blow with a sword*** or ***whip***) ***at someone.***
7) ***cut away,*** take (something) off by cutting.

—[他] **1.** …을 베다; 자르다; …에 구멍을 뚫다, 찢다, 흠(상처)을 내다 ¶①종이를 셋으로 자르다/②빵을 한 조각 잘라 주시오 **2.** 잘라서 …을 만들다; …을 파다, 새기다 ¶③산을 잘라 길을 내다 **3.** …을 깎다, 짧게 하다 **4.** …을 삭감하다, 바짝 줄이다 ¶④신문의 논설을 짧게 줄이다 **5.** …에 고통을 주다; …을 관통하다 ¶⑤찬 바람이 뼛속까지 스며들었다 **6.** …에 대하여 모르는 체하다 ¶⑥남을 길에서 만나고도 모른 체하다 **7.** …을 결석하다, 빠지다 **8.** …와 교차하다 ¶⑦한 선이 다른 선과 직각으로 교차한다 **9.** …을 용해하다 ¶⑧타르를 가솔린으로 녹이다 **10.** …의 감정을 해치다 —[自] **1.** 자르다; 베어지다 ¶⑨이 칼은 잘 들지 않는다 **2.** 잘라지다, 베어지다 **3.** …을 관통하다, 다치게 하다 ¶⑩바람이 얇은 옷 속으로 스며들었다 **4.** 급히 도망치다 **5.** 지름길로 가다 **6.** 공을 깎아 치다 **7.** 지나가다, 통과하다

[熟] 1)뛰어 다니다 2)곧장 질러가다 3)급히 쫓아가다 4)얼마든지 먹고 싶은 대로 먹다; [특히 고기를] 양껏 먹다 5)황급히 도망가다 6)…에 칼을 휘두르다; …을 몹시 때리다 7)…을 베어 버리다 8)ⓐ…을 짧게 깎다 ⓑ…을 삭감하다, 줄이다 9)ⓐ…을 베어 넘기다 ⓑ…을 칼로 베어 죽이다(상처 입히다) ⓒ[병이 사람]을 쓰러뜨리다

8) ***cut back,*** ⓐ make (something) shorter by cutting off the end. ⓑ reduce.
9) ***cut down,*** ⓐ cause (a tree, etc.) to fall by cutting it. ⓑ kill or injure (someone) by striking him with a sword, etc. ⓒ (of a disease) deprive (someone) of life or health. ⓓ make (something) less.
10) ***cut in,*** move in suddenly; interrupt.
11) ***cut off,*** ⓐ bring (something) to an end. ⓑ disconnect. ⓒ cut a part from the whole. ⓓ block.
12) ***cut on,*** hurry.
13) ***cut out,*** ⓐ take off (something) by cutting around it. ⓑ stop; finish. ⓒ promise to give up (something).
14) ***cut** something **short,*** make something shorter.
15) ***cut up,*** ⓐ cut (something) into many small pieces. ⓑ act noisily; misbehave.

ⓓ…을 바짝 줄이다, 삭감하다 10)…에 끼어들다; 방해하다 11)ⓐ…을 끝나게 하다 ⓑ…을 떼어놓다, 끊다 ⓒ…을 베어내다 ⓓ…을 막다, 방해하다 12)서둘러 나아가다 13)ⓐ…을 베어내다 ⓑ…을 그만두다 ⓒ[맹세하고]…을 끊다 14)…을 짧게 하다 15)ⓐ…을 잘게 썰다 ⓑ소동을 일으키다, 못되게 굴다

—*n.* [C] **1.** the act of cutting. **2.** a mark or traces made by cutting; a wound; a notch. **3.** a road or canal made through rock or a mountain. **4.** a stroke with a sword, a whip, etc. **5.** fashion; form; style. ¶*the ~ of a diamond.* **6.** a reduction. **7.** (*U.S.*) a snack.
give** someone **the cut direct, pretend not to see or know someone.

—[名] **1.** 자르기, 베기 **2.** 벤 자리; 벤 상처; 새긴 금 **3.** 파헤친 길(수로) **4.** [칼·채찍 따위의] 일격(一擊) **5.** 형(型) 깎는(자르는) 법 **6.** 삭제, 삭감; 에누리, 할인 **7.** 《美》 가벼운 식사
[熟] 모르는 체하다

—*adj.* **1.** formed by cutting; wounded; severed. **2.** reduced; lessened.
***cut and dry** (or **dried**),* ⓐ prepared or arranged beforehand. ⓑ lifeless; dull; boring.

—[形] **1.** 벤, 자른; 재단한; 새긴 **2.** 삭감한
[熟] ⓐ미리 준비된 ⓑ무미건조한

cut·a·way [kʌ́təwèi] *adj.* (of a coat) having a part cut away from the waist in front. **—*n.*** [C] a cutaway coat, worn by men for formal daytime occasions.

—[形] 웃옷의 앞자락을 비스듬히 재단한 —[名] 모오닝 코우트

cut·back [kʌ́tbæ̀k] *n.* [C] **1.** a return in the course of a motion picture, etc. to earlier events. **2.** a reduction in output. ¶*a ~ in orders.*①

—[名] **1.** [영화의] 장면 전환 **2.** 축소, 삭감 ¶①주문의 감소

cute [kju:t] *adj.* (*colloq.*) **1.** (*U.S.*) pleasingly pretty; charming; attractive. **2.** clever; shrewd; sharp.

—[形] 《口》 **1.** 《美》 귀여운 **2.** 영리한, 약삭빠른

cu·ti·cle [kjú:tikl] *n.* [C] the outer layer of skin, esp. that around the base of fingernails or toenails.

—[名] 표피(表皮), 외피; [손톱의 뿌리를 덮은] 엷은 피부

cut·lass, -las [kʌ́tləs] *n.* [C] a short, heavy, rather curved sword with a wide blade.

—[名] 단도; 단검

cut·ler [kʌ́tlər] *n.* [C] a person who makes, sells, or mends knives, scissors, and other cutting tools.

—[名] 칼 만드는 사람, 칼장수

cut·ler·y [kʌ́tləri] *n.* [U] **1.** 《*collectively*》 knives, scissors, and other cutting tools. **2.** knives, forks, spoons, etc. used in cutting or serving food. **3.** the business of a cutler.

—[名] **1.** 칼붙이 **2.** [식탁용의] 나이프·포오크·스푸운 따위의 기구 **3.** 칼 제조업

cut·let [kʌ́tlit] *n.* [C] **1.** a slice of meat for frying. **2.** a flat, fried piece of meat or fish.

—[名] **1.** 엷게 저민 고기 **2.** 카틀렛

cut·out [kʌ́tàut] *n.* [C] **1.** a figure cut out of something else such as a picture, a shape, or a design on paper or cardboard. **2.** a switch or device for breaking an electric current.

—[名] **1.** 도려내기, 도려낸 그림 **2.** [전류의] 개폐기(開閉器), 두꺼비집

cut·ter [kʌ́tər] *n.* [C] **1.** a person who cuts. **2.** a tool or machine for cutting. **3.** a small boat used by warships for carrying passengers and supplies to and from the shore. **4.** a kind of a small sailboat with one mast; (*U.S.*) a small, fast boat used by the Coast Guard. **5.** a small, light sleigh, usu. pulled by one horse.

—[名] **1.** 자르는 사람, 재단자 **2.** 베는 기구, 절단기 **3.** 커터(군함용 작은 보우트) **4.** 외돛을 단 배의 일종; 《美》 연안 감시선 **5.** [말 한 필이 끄는] 작은 썰매

cut·throat [kʌ́tθròut] *n.* [C] a murderer. **—*adj.*** murderous; cruel; destructive; severe.

—[名] 살인자 —[形] 살인용의; 잔인한, 파괴적인, 가혹한

cut·ting [kʌ́tiŋ] *n.* [C] **1.** [U] the act of cutting. **2.** something cut off. **3.** a small shoot or branch cut from a plant in an attempt to grow a new plant. **4.** (*Brit.*) an interesting piece cut out from a newspaper or magazine. **5.** a passage or tunnel cut through high ground for a road, a railway, etc.

—[名] **1.** 절단 **2.** 도려(잘라)내기, 잘라낸 조각 **3.** [접목에 쓰는] 접지(接枝) **4.** [신문 따위의] 오려낸 것 **5.** [도로·철도 따위의] 깎아낸 길, 개착로(開鑿路)

—*adj.* **1.** that cuts; sharp. **2.** hurting the feelings; sarcastic. ¶*a ~ remark.*① ▷**cut·ting·ly** [-li] *adv.*

—[形] **1.** 잘 드는, 예리한 **2.** 살을 에는 듯한, 신랄한, 통렬한 ¶①신랄한 말

cut·tle·fish [kʌ́tlfiʃ] *n.* ⓒ (pl. **-fish'-es** or *collectively* **-fish**) a seacreature which sends out a black, inky liquid when attacked. —명 오징어
cwt. hundredweight.
cyc·la·men [síkləmən] *n.* ⓒ a plant of the same family as the primrose, with white or red-blue flowers. —명 (植) 시클라멘
* **cy·cle** [sáikl] *n.* ⓒ **1.** a period of time, or a series of events or actions, that repeats itself regularly and in the same order. ¶*the ~ of the seasons.*① **2.** a complete set or series; a group of poems, stories, legends, etc. about a great event or hero. ¶*the Trojan ~.*② **3.** a great length of time; an age. **4.** a bicycle; a motorcycle; a tricycle. **5.** a unit of measurement of the frequency of an electric current. —명 1. 주기(週期), 순환기; 순환; 반복 ¶①계절의 순환 2. 한 때, 일단; 일단의 시가(詩歌)(이야기·전설) ¶②트로이 시사 대계(史詩大系) 3. 한 시대, 긴 세월 4. 자전거; 오오토바이; 삼륜차 5. 주파(周波), 사이클
—*vi.* **1.** ride or travel by bicycle, etc. **2.** pass through a cycle; move in a cycle. —자 1. 자전거에 타다 2. 순환하다
cy·clic [sáiklik, sík-], **-cli·cal** [-klik(ə)l] *adj.* of a cycle; moving or happening in cycles. —형 순환의; 주기적인
cy·cling [sáikliŋ] *n.* ⓤ the act or sport of riding or traveling by bicycle, etc. [bicycle, etc.] —명 자전거 타기, 사이클링
cy·clist [sáiklist] *n.* ⓒ a person who rides or travels by —명 자전거 타는 사람
cy·clone [sáikloun] *n.* ⓒ **1.** a wind blowing a roundly and around esp. in a storm. **2.** a storm moving around its center. —명 1. 선풍 2. 온대성 저기압
cy·clo·pe·di·a, -pae- [sàikləpí:diə] *n.* ⓒ a book giving classified information on all branches of knowledge; an encyclopedia. —명 백과사전
cy·clo·tron [sáiklətràn / -tròn] *n.* ⓒ an atom smasher. —명 사이클로트론(원자핵 파괴 장치)
cyg·net [sígnit] *n.* ⓒ a young swan. —명 백조의 새끼
* **cyl·in·der** [síləndər] *n.* ⓒ **1.** a solid or empty body, long and round, with its two ends equal and parallel. **2.** a round empty box in which a piston works. —명 1. 원통; 원통형의 것 2. 실린더, 기통(氣筒)
cy·lin·dri·cal [silíndrik(ə)l] *adj.* of a cylinder; shaped like a cylinder. —형 원통형의, 원기둥 모양의
cym·bal [símb(ə)l] *n.* (usu. *pl.*) (in music) one of a pair of brass plates which produce a ringing sound when clashed together. —명 심벌즈(타악기)
cyn·ic [sínik] *n.* ⓒ **1.** a person who does not believe in the goodness of human nature; an ill-natured person. **2.** ⟪*C-*⟫ a member of a group of ancient Greek philosophers who taught that the most important element of virtue is self-control. —*adj.* **1.** cynical. **2.** ⟪*C-*⟫ of the Cynics or their doctrines. —명 1. [남의 성실성을 믿지 않고] 빈정거리는 사람, 냉소가 2. 견유(犬儒)학파의 사람 —형 1. 냉소적인 2. 견유학파의
cyn·i·cal [sínik(ə)l] *adj.* doubting the honesty and goodness of human nature; like a cynic. ▷**cyn·i·cal·ly** [-kəli] *adv.* —**cyn·i·cal·ness** [-nis] *n.* —형 냉소적인; 빈정거리는
cyn·i·cism [sínisìz(ə)m] *n.* ⓤ **1.** the quality of being cynical; a cynical opinion. **2.** ⟪*C-*⟫ the doctrines or practice of the Cynics. —명 1. 냉소, 비꼬는 버릇 2. 견유철학 (犬儒哲學)
cy·pher [sáifər] *n., v.* =cipher.
cy·press [sáipris] *n.* ⓒ an evergreen tree of the pine family, having dark leaves; ⓤ the wood of this tree. —명 (植) 드린실편백; 드린실편백 재목
czar [za:r] *n.* (often *C-*) **1.** the title of the former emperors of Russia. **2.** ⓒ an emperor; an autocrat. —명 1. 옛 러시아 황제의 칭호 2. 황제, 전제군주
Czech [tʃek] *n.* **1.** ⓒ a member of a branch of the Slav races, living chiefly in Bohemia and Moravia. **2.** ⓤ their language; Bohemian. —*adj.* of Czechoslovakia, its language, or its people. —명 1. 체코 사람 2. 체코 말 —형 체코 사람(말)의
Czech·o·slo·vak, Czech·o·Slo·vak [tʃékouslóuvæk, -vɑ:k] *adj.* of Czechoslovakia, its people, or their language. —*n.* **1.** ⓒ a person of Czechoslovakia. **2.** ⓤ the language of Czechoslovakia. —형 체코슬로바키아, 체코 사람[말]의 —명 1. 체코 사람 2. 체코 말
Czech·o·slo·va·kia, Czech·o·Slo·va·kia [tʃèkousləvækiə, -vɑ́:kiə / tʃékouslou-] *n.* a country in central Europe. ⇒N.B. —명 체코슬로바키아 N.B. 수도(首都)는 Plague

D

D, d [diː] *n.* [C] (pl. **D's, Ds, d's, ds** [diːz]) **1.** the fourth letter of the English alphabet. **2.** the second note or tone of the musical scale of C major. **3.** the Roman number for 500.
—[名] 1. 영어 자모의 네째 글자 2.「라」조,「라」음 3. [로마 숫자의] 500

d. **1.** date. **2.** degree. **3.** died. **4.** English penny; pence.

dab [dæb] *vi., vt.* (**dabbed, dab·bing**) touch or tap lightly. ¶*She dabbed* [*at*] *her face with a powder puff.*① —*n.* [C] **1.** a quick, light touch. ¶*a* ~ *of powder.* **2.** a small, soft, or moist mass; a little bit. ¶*a* ~ *of cheese.*②
—[自][他] 가볍게 두드리다, 토닥거리다 ¶①소녀는 분첩으로 얼굴을 토닥거렸다 —[名] 1. 가볍게 두드리기 2. 한 덩어리; 소량 ¶②약간의 치이즈

dab·ble [dǽbl] *vt., vi.* **1.** dip (hands, feet, etc.) in and out of water; splash. **2.** do (something) as an amateur; work a little. 《~ *in* or *at* something》 ¶*He dabbled in politics.*
—[他][自] 1. [손·발 따위]를 물속에 넣다; 물을 튀기다 2. …에 손을 대다, 취미삼아 해보다

dace [deis] *n.* [C] (pl. **dac·es** or *collectively* **dace**) any small, silvery river fish.
—[名] 황어류

dachs·hund [dɑ́ːkshùnd, dǽkshʌ̀nd / dǽkshùnd] *n.* [C] a German dog with a long body and very short legs. ⇒fig.
—[名] 다크스훈트(다리가 짧고 몸통이 긴 독일종의 개)

(dachshund)

dac·tyl [dǽkt(i)l] *n.* [C] a division in verse rhythm, having one long before two short sounds.
—[名] [운율의] 장단단격(長短短格)(—◡◡), 강약약격

‡dad [dæd] *n.* [C] (*colloq.*) father.

dad·die [dǽdi] *n.* =daddy.
—[名] 아빠

•dad·dy [dǽdi] *n.* (pl. **-dies**) =dad.

dad·dy-long·legs [dæ̀dilɔ́ːŋlègz / -lɔ́ŋ-] *n. pl.* 《used as *sing.* and *pl.*》 **1.** a harmless insect with very long legs; a crane fly. **2.** (*U.S.*) a spiderlike creature usu. with very long legs.
—[名] 1. 꾸정모기 2.《美》장님거미

dae·mon [díːmən] *n.* =demon.

•daf·fo·dil [dǽfədil] *n.* [C] a yellow spring flower.
—[名] 나팔수선화

daft [dæft / dɑːft] *adj.* foolish; crazy; mad.
—[形] 어리석은; 미친

dag·ger [dǽgər] *n.* [C] **1.** a short, pointed double-edged sword or knife, used as a weapon. ⇒fig. **2.** a mark (†) of reference used in printing. ¶*a double* ~.
—[名] 1. [양날의] 단검, 단도 2. [인쇄에서 참조표시로 쓰이는] 검표 (†)

1) ***at daggers drawn,*** about to fight. ¶*be at daggers with each other.*
2) ***look daggers at,*** look at (someone) with anger or hatred.
3) ***speak daggers to,*** speak to (someone) so as to wound.

[熟] 1)[검을 빼고 서로 마주 대한 것처럼] …와 서로 노려보아; 당장 싸우려는 태세로 2)…을 무서운 눈으로 노려보다 3)에 독설(욕설)을 퍼붓다

(dagger 1.)

dahl·ia [dǽljə, dɑ́ː- / déiliə, -ljə] *n.* [C] a garden plant with bright-colored flowers. ⇒[N.B.]
—[名] 다알리아 [N.B.] 스웨덴의 식물학자 A. Dahl 의 이름에서

‡dai·ly [déili] *adj.* happening or done every day [often except Sunday]. ¶~ *life.* —*n.* [C] (pl. **-lies**) a newspaper published every day. —*adv.* every day.
—[形] 매일의, 일상의, [일요일을 제외한] 매일의 —[名] 일간신문 —[名] 매일, 날마다

dain·ti·ly [déintili] *adv.* in a dainty manner; delicately; gracefully.
—[副] 고상하게, 우아하게, 맛있게; [음식에] 까다롭게

dain·ti·ness [déintinis] *n.* [U] the state of being dainty; delicacy.
—[名] 우아함; 맛좋음; 성미 까다로움

•dain·ty [déinti] *adj.* (**-ti·er, -ti·est**) **1.** delicate and elegant in appearance. **2.** having refined or particular tastes. ¶*He was born with a* ~ *tooth.*① **3.** delicious. —*n.* [C] (pl. **-ties**) an especially nice piece of food; something delicious.
—[形] 1. 우아한 2. [특히] 음식에 까다로운; 취미가 고상한 ¶①그는 천성으로 식성이 까다롭다 3. 맛좋은, 풍미 있는 —[名] 맛있는 것; 진미

•dair·y [dέəri] *n.* [C] (pl. **dair·ies**) **1.** a place where milk and cream are kept and made into butter or cheese. **2.** a store selling milk, butter, cheese, etc. **3.** the business of making such products.
—[名] 1. 젖 짜는 곳, 낙농장 2. 낙농품 판매점, 우유 가게 3. 낙농업

D

dairy farm [∸ ∸] *n.* a farm where milk and cream are produced and butter and cheese made.
—[名] 낙농장

dair·y·maid [déərimèid] *n.* [C] a woman employed in a dairy.
—[名] 젖 짜는 여자

dair·y·man [déərimən] *n.* [C] (pl. **-men** [-mən]) a man employed in a dairy; the owner or manager of a dairy.
—[名] 낙농장의 남자 일꾼; 낙농장 경영자

da·is [déiis] *n.* [C] a raised platform in a large room or hall to hold a speaker's desk, throne, or the like.
—[名] [호올·식당의] 높은 자리, 상단; [강당의] 강단

⁑**dai·sy** [déizi] *n.* [C] (pl. **-sies**) **1.** a very common small flower, yellow in the center and white around it. **2.** (*slang*) something fine or notable.
—[名] 1. 데이지[꽃] 2.《俗》일품(逸品), 썩 좋은 것

daisy chain [∸ ∸] *n.* a string of daisies linked to form a chain.
—[名] 데이지 화환

***dale** [deil] *n.* [C] (*poetic*) a small valley.
—[名] 골짜기

dal·ly [dǽli] *vi., vt.* (**-lied**) **1.** act in a playful manner; toy; play. 《~ *with* love, temptation, etc.》 **2.** be idle; waste time. ¶*Tom dallied away the summer vacation.*
—[自][他] 1. 가지고 놀다; 장난하다; 희롱하다 2. 우물쭈물하다; [시간을] 낭비하다

***dam** [dæm] *n.* [C] **1.** a wall or bank built to keep back water. **2.** the water held back a dam. —*vt.* (**dammed, dam·ming**) hold back (water, etc.) with a dam.
—[名] 1. 댐, 둑 2. 둑으로 막은 물 —[他] [댐으로] …을 막다, 억제하다

dam up, hold back; block up; control. ¶~ *up a river* | ~ *up one's feelings.*
[熟] …을 막다, 봉쇄하다

⁑**dam·age** [dǽmidʒ] *n.* **1.** [U] harm or injury; loss. ¶*do ~ to something.*① **2.** 《*pl.*》 (*Law*) money or amount claimed or allowed by a court in return for harm or injury. **3.** (*colloq.*) cost; expense.
—[名] 1. 손해, 손상 ¶①…에 손해를 주다 2. 손해배상[금] 3. 비용; 대가(代價)

—*vt.* harm; hurt; injure; destroy. ¶*I damaged my shoes in baseball practice.*① ▷**dam·age·a·ble** [-əbl] *adj.*
—[他]…에 손해를 주다; 상처 입히다 ¶①야구 연습으로 구두가 해졌다

dam·ask [dǽməsk] *n.* [U] **1.** a species of beautiful silk or linen material with figures and designs. **2.** a tough fine steel made in Damascus, the capital of Syria. **3.** deep red color; rose-color. —*adj.* **1.** made of damask. **2.** rose-colored.
—[名] 1. 다마스커스 비단, 무늬 넣은 린네르 2. 다마스커스 강철 3. 장미빛, 담홍색 —[形] 1. 다마스커스 비단의 2. 장미빛의

***dame** [deim] *n.* [C] **1.** (*archaic*) a noble lady; the mistress of a house. **2.** 《*D-*》 (*Brit.*) a title of honor, often given to a knight's or baronet's wife. **3.** an old woman. **4.** a woman.
—[名] 1. 귀부인, 부인 2.《英》knight 또는 baronet 부인의 정식 존칭 3. 노부인 4. 여자

dame school [∸ ∸] *n.* a small private school kept by an old woman.
—[名] 노부인이 경영하는 사숙(私塾)

***damn** [dæm] *vt.* **1.** (of God) send (someone) to everlasting punishment. ¶*I'll be damned if ...*① **2.** declare or judge (something) as bad or a failure. **3.** cause (someone) to fail; ruin. **4.** express anger, dislike, etc. by using bad language. —*vi.* say 'damn'; swear.
—*n.* [C] **1.** a cry of anger or dislike; a curse. **2.** something of little value; a bit.
—[他] 1. [신이 …]을 영원히 지옥에 떨어뜨리다 ¶①죽어도 …않다 2. …을 못쓴다(나쁘다)고 말하다; 헐뜯다 3. …을 못쓰게 하다, 파탄시키다 4. …을 저주하다; …의 욕을 하다 —[自] 저주하다 —[名] 1. 저주; 욕설 2. 조금도

1) ***do not care*** (or ***give***) ***a damn,*** (*colloq.*) don't care at all.
2) ***not worth a damn,*** worthless.
[熟] 1)《口》조금도 개의치 않다 2)아무 가치도 없다

dam·na·ble [dǽmnəbl] *adj.* deserving or causing to be damned; hateful. ▷**dam·na·bly** [-bli] *adv.*
—[形] 가증한; 지옥에 떨어져야 할

dam·na·tion [dæmnéiʃ(ə)n] *n.* [U] **1.** the act of damning; the state of being damned; ruin. **2.** eternal punishment after death. **3.** curse.
—[名] 1. 지옥에 떨어지(게 하)기; 파멸 2. 영원한 벌 3. 욕설, 혹평

damned [dæmd] *adj.* **1.** condemned as bad. **2.** sent to eternal punishment. —*adv.* (*colloq.*) very.
—[形] 1. 저주받은 2. 지옥에 떨어진
—[副]《口》지독하게, 대단히

***damp** [dæmp] *adj.* slightly wet. ¶*a ~ cloth.*
—*n.* **1.** [U] a damp condition; wetness. **2.** 《*a ~*》 depression of spirits. **3.** 《usu. *pl.*》 any harmful gas in a mine.
—[形] 습기 있는, 축축한 —[名] 1. 습기 2. 낙심; 의기 소침 3. [광산 내의] 유독 가스

cast (or ***strike***) ***a damp over*** (or ***into***), cause (someone) loss of joy or hope; depress.
[熟]…의 풀이 죽게 하다, 기운을 없애다

—*vt.* **1.** make (something) slightly wet. **2.** make (someone's feelings) less strong or bright. ¶~ *one's spirits.* **3.** check; put out.
—[他] 1. …을 축축하게 하다, 적시다 2. [기]를 꺾다 3. [행동 따위]를 저지하다

1) ***damp down,*** make (a fire) slower in burning; make (sound) less loud.
2) ***damp off,*** (of a plant shoots, etc.) wither and die.
[熟] 1)[불]을 끄다;[소리]를 둔하게 하다 2)[새싹 따위가] 말라 죽다

damp·en [dǽmp(ə)n] *vt.* (chiefly *U.S.*) =damp.

damp·er [dǽmpər] *n.* [C] **1.** a person or thing that damps, dulls, or checks. **2.** a metal plate to control the current of air to a fire in a stove or furnace. **3.** a device for checking vibration, esp. of piano strings.
 cast (or ***put***) ***a damper on,*** cause (something) to be less merry.

—[名] 1. 축축하게 하는 사람(것); 흥을 깨뜨리는 사람(것) 2. [난로 따위의] 공기 조절판 3. [피아노의] 지음기(止音器)
[熟] …에 찬물을 끼얹다; …의 트집을 잡다

damp·ness [dǽmpnis] *n.* [U] the quality or state of being damp.

—[名] 습기, 축축함

∗dam·sel [dǽmz(ə)l] *n.* [C] (*archaic, poetic*) a girl; a maiden.

—[名] 《古·詩》 처녀, 소녀

dam·son [dǽmz(ə)n] *n.* [C] a small, dark, blue plum; the tree bearing it.

—[名] 서양오얏[나무]

Dan. **1.** Daniel. **2.** Danish.

‡dance [dæns / dɑːns] *vi.* **1.** move the body, esp. the feet, in rhythm, ordinarily to music. ¶ *~ to music* / *~ with someone.* **2.** move lightly and gaily about. ¶ *We danced for* (or *with*) *joy.* **3.** move up and down. ¶ *The boat danced on the waves.* / *The fallen leaves are dancing in the wind.* —*vt.* **1.** perform or take part in (a dance). ¶ *~ a waltz.* **2.** cause (someone) to dance.

—[自] 1. 춤추다, 댄스하다 2. 껑충껑충 뛰다, 뛰어 다니다 3. [물결·나뭇잎 따위가] 춤추듯 흔들리다 —[他] 1. [춤을] 추다 2. …을 춤추게 하다

 1) ***dance attendance upon*** (or ***on***), wait on (someone) often and attentively; be excessively polite and obedient to (someone).
 2) ***dance to someone's tune,*** change one's actions or opinions as a result of changed conditions.

[熟] 1)…의 비위를 맞추다 2)…의 장단에 맞추다, …의 말대로 움직이다

—*n.* [C] **1.** a rhythmic movement of the feet or body, ordinarily to music; the art of dancing. **2.** a particular kind of dance; a piece of music for dancing. ¶ *a social ~.* **3.** a dancing party. ¶ *give a ~.*①

—[名] 1. 댄스, 춤 2. 댄스의 한 종류; 댄스 곡 3. 댄스 파아티 ¶①댄스 파아티를 열다

 1) ***lead** someone **a pretty dance,*** give someone a lot of trouble; make someone follow here and there.
 2) ***lead the dance,*** take the initiative.

[熟] 1)…을 몹시 난처하게 하다; …을 이리저리 끌고 다니다 2)솔선하여 말(행동)하다

danc·er [dǽnsər / dɑ́ːnsə] *n.* [C] **1.** a person who dances. **2.** a person who makes his living by dancing.

—[名] 1. 춤추는 사람, 댄서 2. 무용가

danc·ing [dǽnsiŋ / dɑ́ːns-] *n.* [U] the art or act of dancing.

—[名] 무용, 춤, 무용법

dan·de·li·on [dǽndilàiən] *n.* [C] a common weed with small, yellow flowers.

—[名] 민들레

dan·der [dǽndər] *n.* 《*one's ~*》 (*colloq.*) anger; temper.
 get one's dander up, lose one's temper; get angry.

—[名] 《口》 화, 분노
[熟] 화내다

dan·dle [dǽndl] *vt.* **1.** move (a baby, etc.) up and down on one's knees or in one's arms. **2.** pet.

—[他] 1. [어린이]를 안고 어르다 2 …을 응석받다

dan·druff [dǽndrəf] *n.* [U] small pieces of dead skin found in the hair.

—[名] [머리의] 비듬

dan·dy [dǽndi] *n.* [C] (pl **-dies**) a man who pays great attention to his dress and looks. —*adj.* (**-di·er, -di·est**) of a dandy; very carefully dressed.

—[名] 멋장이, 쪽 빼입은 사람 —[形] 멋장이의, 쪽 빼입은

Dane [dein] *n.* [C] a person of Denmark.

—[名] 덴마아크 사람

‡dan·ger [déindʒər] *n.* ↔safety **1.** [U] the state in which there may be harm or loss of life. ¶ *A soldier at the front faces ~ every day.* **2.** [C] a thing or a person that may cause harm or death. ¶ *a ~ to peace.*①

—[名] 1. 위험, 위급 2. 위험(인)물; 장애, 위협 ¶①평화에의 위협

 1) ***at danger,*** in the position giving a signal of danger. ¶ *The signal is at ~.*②
 2) ***in danger of,*** likely to. ¶ *She is in ~ of losing her life.*③
 3) ***out of danger,*** free from danger.

[熟] 1)위험신호가 되어 ¶②위험신호가 나와 있다 2)위험하여, 위독하여 ¶③그녀는 생명이 위독하다 3)위험을 벗어나서

‡dan·ger·ous [déindʒərəs] *adj.* not safe; full of risks; likely to do harm. ↔safe ¶ *a ~ illness* / *look ~.*①
 ▷**dan·ger·ous·ness** [-nis] *n.*

—[形] 위험한, 위태로운; 겁나는 ¶①무시무시한 얼굴을 하고 있다

dan·ger·ous·ly [déindʒərəsli] *adv.* in a dangerous manner.

—[副] 위험하게

dan·gle [dǽŋgl] *vi.* **1.** hang or swing loosely. ¶ *The cord dangles.*① **2.** hang about; follow. ¶ *~ after a woman.*② —*vt.* hold (something) so that it swings and hangs loosely; cause (something) to dangle.

—[自] 1. 매달리다 ¶①코오드가 매달려 있다 2. 붙어(따라) 다니다 ¶②여자 꽁무니를 따라다니다 —[他] …을 매달다

Dan·iel [dǽnjəl] *n.* **1.** a man's name. ⇨[N.B.] **2.** (in the Bible) one of the great Hebrew prophets. **3.** a book in

—[名] 1. 남자 이름 [N.B.] 약칭은 Dan. 2. 헤브라이의 대예언자 3. 구약성경의

D

the Old Testament of the Bible. **4.** [C] a wise and honest judge.
다니엘서 **4.** 명재판관

Dan·ish [déiniʃ] *adj.* of Denmark, the Danes or their language. **—*n.*** [U] the language of the Danes.
—[形] 덴마아크의; 덴마아크 사람(말)의
—[名] 덴마아크 말

dank [dæŋk] *adj.* wet and cold; unpleasantly damp.
—[形] 축축한, 습기 있는

Dan·te [dǽnti], **Alighieri** *n.* (1265–1321) a famous Italian poet.
—[名] 단테(이탈리아의 시인)

Dan·ube [dǽnju:b], **the** *n.* the river flowing through central Europe to the Black Sea.
—[名] 다뉴브강

Daph·ne [dǽfni] *n.* **1.** (in Greek mythology) a nymph who escaped from Apollo by becoming a laurel. **2.** [C] ⟪*d-*⟫ a kind of shrub with sweet-smelling flowers; ⟪*d-*⟫ a laurel.
—[名] **1.** [그리이스 신화에서] Cupid의 장난 때문에 Apollo에게 쫓기다가 월계수로 화한 요정(妖精) **2.** 팥꽃나무; 월계수

dap·per [dǽpər] *adj.* **1.** neat; dressed with care. **2.** small and active. ▷**dap·per·ly** [-li] *adv.*
—[形] **1.** 산뜻한, 깨끗한 **2.** 작달막하고 날렵한

dap·ple [dǽpl] *n.* [C] **1.** a spot or dot. **2.** an animal marked with spots. **—*adj.*** spotted. **—*vt., vi.*** mark (something) with spots; become marked with spots.
—[名] **1.** 얼룩[무늬] **2.** 얼룩털의 짐승
—[形] 얼룩덜룩한 —[他][自][…을] 얼룩덜룩하게 하다(되다)

dap·pled [dǽpld] *adj.* spotted. ¶*a ~ horse.*①
—[形] 얼룩무늬의 ¶①얼룩말

: dare [dɛər] *auxil. v.* have enough courage or boldness for some act; be fearless; venture. ⇒[usage] ¶*He daren't do it. / They dared not tell him the truth.*
—[助] 감히 …하다, …뱃심좋게 …하다
[usage] 다음의 타동사 1.과 같은 뜻이지만, 부정·의문문에서는 조동사로 쓰임; 그러나 오늘날에는 보통 동사로 쓰이는 경향이 있음

I dare say, I suppose; probably.
[熟] 아마 …일 것이다

—*vt.* **1.** have the necessary courage. ⟪*~ to do*⟫ ¶*She does not ~ to tell him. / He dares to insult me. / He did not ~ [to] go.* **2.** venture to meet (something); face. ¶*~ any danger / I ~ anything.* **3.** challenge; defy. ⟪~ someone *to do*; ~ someone *to*⟫ ¶*I ~ you to jump. / We cannot endure to be dared by anyone.*
—[他] **1.** 감히(용기있게 뱃심좋게)…하다 **2.** …에 용감하게 맞서다 **3.** …에 도전하다, 대들다

—*n.* [C] an act of daring; challenge. ¶*take a ~.*①
—[名] 도전 ¶①도전에 응하다

dare·dev·il [dɛ́ərdèvl] *n.* [C] a reckless person.
—*adj.* reckless; bold.
—[名] 무모한 사람
—[形] 무모한

dar·ing [dɛ́əriŋ] *n.* [U] courage to take risks; bravery.
—*adj.* courageous; fearless. ▷**dar·ing·ly** [-li] *adv.*
—[名] 대담성, 용기
—[形] 대담한, 용감한

⁝ dark [dɑ:rk] *adj.* **1.** without light; with little light. ↔ light ¶*a ~ room (night) / It's getting ~.* **2.** not light-colored; of deep or blackish color. ¶*~ blue / a ~ complexion / ~ window shades.* **3.** not easily understood; secret; hidden; obscure. ¶*The meaning is still ~.*① **4.** evil; wicked. ¶*~ deeds (thoughts).* **5.** gloomy; dismal; cheerless. ¶*a ~ expression (mood) / The future looked ~.*②
—[形] **1.** 어두운, 암흑의 **2.** 검은, 거무스름한 **3.** 알기 힘든; 비밀의; 숨겨진 ¶①그 의미는 아직 분명하지 않다 **4.** 뱃속 검은, 흉악한, 못된 **5.** 음울한, 우울한, 광명이 없는 ¶②앞길은 어두웠다

—*n.* **1.** [U] the state of being dark; the absence of light. ¶*I can't see well in the ~.* **2.** [U] night; nightfall. ¶*at ~ / before ~ / after ~.* **3.** [U][C] a dark color or shade; a dark place. **4.** [U] ignorance; secrecy. ¶*I am in the ~ about what they want.*
—[名] **1.** 어둠, 암흑 **2.** 밤; 땅거미 **3.** 어두운 빛, 어두운 부분, 어두운 곳, 음영(陰影) **4.** 무지(無知), 비밀

• dark·en [dɑ́:rk(ə)n] *vt.* **1.** make (something) dark or darker. **2.** cast a shadow over (something); fill (something) with gloom. **—*vi.*** become dark or darker.
—[他] **1.** …을 어둡게(검게) 하다 **2.** [기분]을 음울하게 하다; …을 애매하게 하다 —[自] 어두워지다, 거뭇하게 되다

darken someone's door (or ***doorway***), visit.
[熟] …을 방문하다, 오다

dark horse [´ ˌ] *n.* a race horse that little is known about; an unexpected competitor.
—[名] [경마에서] 실력을 예측 못하는 말; 뜻밖의 경쟁자

dark·ish [dɑ́:rkiʃ] *adj.* somewhat dark.
—[形] 어둑어둑한; 거무스름한

dark lantern [´ ˌ–] *n.* a lantern whose light can be hidden by a cover or dark glass.
—[名] [명암 조절이 가능한] 초롱

dark·ly [dɑ́:rkli] *adv.* **1.** in a dark manner. **2.** gloomily. **3.** obscurely; secretly.
—[副] **1.** 어둡게, 검게 **2.** 음울하게 **3.** 불명료하게; 비밀히

: dark·ness [dɑ́:rknis] *n.* [U] **1.** the state of being dark. ¶*in the ~*① */ the Prince of ~.*② **2.** blindness; the absence of knowledge. **3.** gloom; secrecy.
—[名] **1.** 어둠, 암흑 ¶①어둠속에/②마왕 **2.** 맹목; 무지 **3.** 모호함; 비밀

dark·room [dɑ́:rkrù(:)m] *n.* [C] (*Photography*) a darkened room used when developing film, etc.
—[名] ⟪寫⟫ 암실

dark·some [dɑ́:rksəm] *adj.* (*poetic*) **1.** dark. **2.** gloomy.
—[形] ⟪詩⟫ **1.** 어슴프레한 **2.** 우울한

darling

‡ **dar·ling** [dáːrliŋ] *n.* ⓒ a much loved person; a favorite; a pet. ¶*My ~!* —*adj.* **1.** very dear; tenderly loved. **2.** much longed-for; much desired. ¶*one's ~ hope.*

∗ **darn** [daːrn] *vt.* mend or repair (a cloth, etc.) by weaving thread back and forth with a needle. ¶*~ a stocking.*
—*n.* ⓒ a place thus mended; the act of darning.

‡ **dart** [daːrt] *n.* ⓒ **1.** a pointed, arrow-like weapon thrown by hand. ⇒fig. **2.** (*pl.* used as *sing.*) a game in which small darts are tossed at a target. **3.** a sudden, swift movement. **4.** an insect's stinger. **5.** an extra seam to make a garment fit better. **6.** a sharp look, word, etc. —*vi.* move forward suddenly and swiftly. ¶*~ through the air.*
—*vt.* send out (something) suddenly and swiftly; shoot out. ¶*The man darted an angry glance at me.*②

[dart 1.]

dart·er [dáːrtər] *n.* ⓒ **1.** a person or thing that darts or moves suddenly. **2.** a small fresh-water fish that swims very quickly.

‡ **dash** [dæʃ] *vt.* **1.** throw or strike violently; smash; shatter. ¶*~ a cup to pieces on the floor.* **2.** splash; sprinkle. ¶*He dashed water over her* (or *in her face*). / *He was dashed with mud.* **3.** discourage; depress. ¶*All our hopes have been dashed.*① **4.** mix (something) with another substance; tinge. (*~ something with*) ¶*coffee dashed with a little brandy.* —*vi.* **1.** rush; move with violence. ¶*~ into the room* / *~ out of the room* / *I dashed back to my house.* **2.** strike violently. (*~ against* something) ¶*The huge waves dashed against the cliff.*
dash off (or *down*), ⓐ leave; hurry away. ⓑ write; {make, sketch, etc. hastily.}
—*n.* ⓒ **1.** a sudden and violent movement; a rush. ¶*the ~ of the waves on the beach.* **2.** a splash. **3.** a smash; a blow; a stroke. ¶*We heard the ~ of the rain on the windows.*② **4.** something that depresses or discourages. ¶*a ~ to his hopes.* **5.** a short race. ¶*a 100-meter ~.* **6.** a small amount. ¶*a ~ of sugar* / *yellow with a ~ of green.*③ **7.** ⓤ energy; spirit. **8.** the mark (--). **9.** ⓤ display; showy appearance.
1) *at a dash,* quickly and without rest.
2) *cut a dash,* make a striking impression; be showy.

dash·board [dǽʃbɔ̀ːrd] *n.* ⓒ **1.** an instrument board in front of the driver in an automobile, airplane, etc. **2.** a protecting shield at the front or side of a wagon, boat, etc. to keep off mud.

dash·er [dǽʃər] *n.* ⓒ **1.** a person or thing that dashes. **2.** a device for stirring cream.

dash·ing [dǽʃiŋ] *adj.* **1.** bold; lively. **2.** making much [show; gay.]

das·tard [dǽstərd] *n.* ⓒ a mean fellow without courage.
—*adj.* mean; cowardly. ▷ **das·tard·ly** [-li] *adv.*

da·ta [déitə, dáː-, +*U.S.* dǽtə] *n. pl.* (*sing.* **da·tum**) facts and figures from which conclusions can be drawn; information. ⇒usage

‡ **date**¹ [deit] *n.* ⓒ **1.** the time shown by the day, month, and year. ¶*the ~ of birth* / *What's the ~ today?*① **2.** ⓤⓒ a period of time. ¶*at an early ~.*② **3.** (*U.S. colloq.*) a promise made with someone, esp. of the opposite sex, to meet at a certain place and time; a person with whom one has made such a promise. ¶*make* (or *have*) *a ~ with her*③ / *My ~ today was Mary.*④
1) *out of date,* not in current use; old-fashioned.
2) *to date,* so far; until now; yet.
3) *up to date,* to the present time; in fashion; modern.

—名 귀여운(사랑스러운) 사람; 소중한 것 —愛 1. 귀여운, 사랑스런 2. 갈망하는, 동경하는

—他 [옷 따위]를 꿰매다, 깁다
—名꿰맨 곳; 깁기, 짜깁기, 꿰매기

—名 1. 투창(投槍), 던지는 화살 2. 화살 던지기(과녁에 화살을 던지는 실내 경기) 3. 급격한 돌진(동작) 4. [곤충의] 바늘, 침 5. 다아트(쐐기 모양의 솔기의 일종) 6. 험상궂은 표정(말)
—自 [화살처럼] 날아가다, 돌진하다 ¶①공중을 화살처럼 날아가다
—他 …을 던지다, 쏘다, 발사하다 ¶② 그 사나이는 내게 성난 눈길을 보냈다

—名 1. 투창(화살) 던지는 사람; 돌진하는 사람(것) 2. 시어(矢魚)(화살처럼 빨리 헤엄치는 민물고기)

—他 1. …을 내던지다; 때려부수다 2. [물 따위]를 끼얹다; …에 튀기다 3. …을 실망시키다, [기운·희망 따위]를 꺾다 ¶①우리의 희망은 모두 사라졌다 4. …에 가미하다, 섞다 —自 1. 매진(돌진)하다 2. [세게] 부딪치다, 충돌하다

熟 ⓐ급히 떠나다 ⓑ급히 쓰다
—名 1. 돌진 2. [물 따위] 튀기기 3. 충돌; 타격 ¶②비가 창문에 뿌리는 소리를 들었다 ¶[기운·희망 따위를] 꺾는 것, 장애 5. 단거리 경주 6. 소량, 조금 ¶③초록빛이 약간 도는 황색 7. 원기; 기력 8. 대시 기호(—) 9. 허세

熟 1)단숨에 2)허세를 부리다, 자기를 과시하다
—名 1. [자동차·비행기 조종석 앞의] 계기반(計器盤) 2. [마차의] 흙받이, [보우트 따위의] 파도 막는 널빤지

—名 1. 돌진하는 사람 2. [크리임] 교반기(攪拌機)
—形 1. 대담한, 기운찬 2. 허세부리는, 화려한
—名 비겁한 자, 겁장이
—形 비겁한

—名 자료, 데이터 [usage] 단수형 datum 은 보통 쓰이지 않음

—名 1. 날짜, 연월일, 기일 ¶①오늘은 며칠이오? 2. 시대, 연대 ¶②초기에 3. [특히 이성과의] 만날 약속, 데이트, 데이트의 상대 ¶③그녀와 데이트하다 / ④오늘의 데이트 상대는 메어리다

熟 1)시대에 뒤진 2)지금까지 3)오늘날까지; 현대적인

—*vt.* **1.** mark (something) with the date. ¶*a letter dated the 30th of September.* **2.** find out or decide the date of (something). ¶*It is very difficult to ~ this work of art.* **3.** make a promise with (someone) to have a date (*n.* 3). ¶*I'll ~ Jane for the dance.* —*vi.* **1.** be dated; have the date. **2.** be old-fashioned. ¶*This car is beginning to ~.* **3.** (*U.S. colloq.*) have a date (*n.* 3.).
—[他] 1. …에 날짜를 적다 2. …의 시일을 정하다, …의 연대를 추정하다 3. 데이트의 약속을 하다 —[自] 1. [편지 따위에] 날짜(발신지)가 적혀 있다 2. 시대에 뒤지다, 낡다 3.《美口》데이트하다

1) ***date back to,*** has existed since (a certain period). ¶*The university dates back to the 13th century.*④
2) ***date from,*** belong to or have one's origin in (a certain period). ¶*This dress dates from the 17th century.*⑤
[熟] 1)연대가 …까지 거슬러 올라가다 ¶④이 대학의 창립은 13세기까지 거슬러 올라간다 2)…에 비롯되다 ¶⑤이 의상은 17세기 것이다

date² [deit] *n.* [C] the small sweet fruit of a kind of palm tree; a tall tree bearing this fruit.
—[名] 대추, 대추나무

date·less [déitlis] *adj.* **1.** without a date. **2.** endless. **3.** of permanent interest.
—[形] 1. 날짜가 없는 2. 무제한의 3. 언제나 흥미가 있는

date line [ˊ ˋ] *n.* a line on the earth, mostly along the 180° meridian, where each calendar day first begins.
—[名] 일부(日附) 변경선(동경 또는 서경 180도의 자오선)

da·tive [déitiv] (*Grammar*) *adj.* showing the indirect object of a verb. ¶*the ~ case.*① —*n.* [C] the dative case; a word in this case.
—[形]《文法》여격(與格)의 ¶①여격, 간접목적격 —[名] 여격, 여격이 있는 말

da·tum [déitəm] *n.* sing. of **data**.

daub [dɔːb] *vt.* **1.** coat or cover (a wall, etc.) with mud, clay, etc. ¶*~ a wall with paint; ~ paint on a wall.* **2.** paint badly. —*vi.* paint crude or cheap pictures. —*n.* **1.** [C] anything daubed on; [U] the act of daubing. **2.** [C] a picture poorly painted.
—[他] 1. …에 [진흙·도료 따위]를 바르다, 발라 문지르다 2. …을 서투르게 그리다 —[自] 서투른 그림을 그리다 —[名] 1. 칠한 것; 칠하기 2. 서투른 그림

‡daugh·ter [dɔ́ːtər] *n.* [C] **1.** a female child. **2.** a female descendant.
—[名] 1. 딸 2. 여자 자손

daugh·ter-in-law [dɔ́ːtərinlɔ̀ː] *n.* [C] (pl. **daugh·ters-**) a son's wife.
—[名] 며느리

daugh·ter·ly [dɔ́ːtərli] *adj.* like or befitting a daughter.
—[形] 딸로서의; 딸 같은

daunt [dɔːnt] *vt.* frighten; make (someone) less courageous.
—[他] …의 기를 죽이다

daunt·less [dɔ́ːntlis] *adj.* brave; fearless.
—[形] 꿈쩍도 않는, 용감한

dav·en·port [dǽv(ə)npɔ̀ːrt] *n.* [C] **1.** (*U.S.*) a large sofa, often one that can be changed into a bed. **2.** (*Brit.*) a small writing desk.
—[名] 1.《美》침대 겸용의 큰 소파 2.《英》개폐식 책상의 일종

Da·vid [déivid] *n.* **1.** a man's name. **2.** (in the Bible) the second king of Israel.
—[名] 1. 남자 이름 2. 다윗(옛 이스라엘의 왕)

dav·it [dǽvit] *n.* [C] one of a pair of curved bars on a ship's side for holding or lowering small boats.
—[名] [큰 배의] 보우트 매는 기둥

daw [dɔː] *n.* [C] a kind of crow found in Europe.
—[名] 갈가마귀

daw·dle [dɔ́ːdl] *vt., vi.* waste (time); idle; move slowly. ¶*~ over work.* ▷**daw·dler** [-dlər] *n.*
—[他][自] 빈둥빈둥 시간을 보내다; 꾸물거리다

‡dawn [dɔːn] *n.* [U] **1.** the break of day; the first light in the east; daybreak. ¶*at ~ / from ~ till dusk.* **2.** beginning. ¶*the ~ of civilization.*①
—[名] 1. 새벽, 여명, 동틀녘 2. 초기, 시초 ¶①문명의 시초

—*vi.* **1.** begin to grow light in the morning. ¶*[The] day dawned.* ⇒[N.B.] / *It is just dawning.* **2.** begin to appear; develop. ¶*A new era is dawning.*
—[自] 1. 날이 새다, 동트다 [N.B.]「날이 새다」를 Night dawns.라 하지는 않음 2. [물건이] 보이기 시작하다; [서서히] 발달하기 시작하다

dawn on (or ***upon***)**,** begin to be clear to the mind of (someone). ¶*The meaning suddenly dawned on him.*
[熟] 알게(깨닫게) 되다

‡day [dei] *n.* **1.** [U] the period of light between sunrise and sunset; daylight. ↔night ¶*by ~*① / *before ~.*② **2.** [C] the 24 hours of day and night. ¶*every ~ / every other ~; every second ~*③ */ the other ~; a few days ago*④ */ some ~.*⑤ **3.** 《*sing.* without an article》 a particular or special day. ¶*Christmas Day.* **4.** 《*the ~*》 a struggle, contest, victory. ¶*win* (*lose*) *the ~.*⑥ **5.** 《often *pl.*》 period of time; epoch. ¶*the days of Queen Elizabeth / the present ~.* **6.** 《*one's ~*》 one's lifetime; a good period of one's lifetime. ¶*He has had his ~.*⑦ / (*proverb*) *Every dog has his ~.*⑧
—[名] 1. 낮, 주간; 햇볕 ¶①낮에/②날이 새기 전에 2. 하루, 일주야 ¶③하루 걸러/④전날, 며칠 전/⑤언젠가는, 멀지않아 3. 특정의 날 4. 승부, 승리, 전황 ¶⑥이기다(지다) 5. 시대 6. 일생, 번성시대 ¶⑦그에게도 좋았던 때는 있었다/⑧《俚》쥐구멍에도 볕들 날이 있다

1) ***day after day; day by day; from day to day; day in, day out,*** every day.
[熟] 1)매일 2)당시의; 오늘날의

2) ***of the day,*** of those days; of today.

day·book [déibùk] *n.* [C] **1.** a book in which each day's accounts are kept. **2.** a diary.
—[名] 1. [부기의] 일기장 2. 일기

day boy [ˊ ˋ] *n.* (*Brit.*) a student at a boy's boarding school who lives at home.
—[名] 《英》 [기숙생에 대하여] 남자 통학생

day·break [déibrèik] *n.* [U] the earliest light of day; dawn.
—[名] 새벽, 여명

day coach [ˊ ˋ] *n.* (*U.S.*) an ordinary railroad passenger car.
—[名] 《美》 보통 객차(침대차 따위와 구별하여)

day·dream [déidrì:m] *n.* [C] a dreamy thought about pleasant things; an idle fancy. —*vi.* think dreamily about pleasant things.
—[名] 백일몽; 공상 —[自] 공상에 잠기다

day laborer [ˊ ˋ–] *n.* an unskilled worker paid by the day.
—[名] 날품팔이꾼

* **day·light** [déilàit] *n.* [U] **1.** light of day. **2.** openness. **3.** daytime. ¶*in broad* ~.① **4.** dawn. ¶*at* ~.
see daylight, (*colloq.*) ⓐ understand. ⓑ approach the end of a hard job.
—[名] 1. 햇볕 2. 명백함 3. 대낮, 주간 ¶①대낮에 4. 새벽
[熟] 《口》ⓐ이해하다 ⓑ해결의 서광이 보이다

day·light-sav·ing time [déilaitséiviŋtàim] *n.* the time that is one hour faster than the standard time.
—[名] 일광 절약 시간

day·long [déilɔ̀ŋ, -lɔ̀:ŋ / -lɔ̀ŋ] *adj., adv.* through the whole day.
—[形] 종일의 —[副] 하루종일

day school [ˊ ˋ] *n.* **1.** a school held in the daytime. ↔night school **2.** a private school for students who live at home. ↔a boarding school
—[名] 1. 주간학교 2. 통학 학교

day·star [déistɑ̀:r] *n.* [C] 《usu. *the* ~》 **1.** the morning star. **2.** (*poetic*) the sun.
—[名] 1. 샛별, 금성 2. 《詩》 태양

* **day·time** [déitàim] *n.* [U] 《*the* ~》 the time when it is day.
—[名] 낮, 주간

* **daze** [deiz] *vt.* cause (someone) to feel stupid; make (someone) unable to think clearly; blind (someone) for a moment with a very bright light. —*n.* [C] a dazed condition. ¶*be in a* ~.①
—[他] …을 멍하게 하다; [광선 따위가] …의 눈을 부시게 하다 —[名] 눈부심, 흐리멍덩한 상태 ¶①얼빠져 있다

* **daz·zle** [dǽzl] *vt.* make (someone or the eyes) unable to see well with a sudden bright light; cause (someone) great admiration by a brilliant performance. —*vi.* be blinded by light; excite admiration by a brilliant performance.
—*n.* [U][C] the act of dazzling; a dazzled condition.
—[他] [눈·사람]을 눈부시게 하다; 경탄시키다 —[自] 눈이 부시다; 경탄하다
—[名] 눈이 부심; 현혹

D. C. **1.** District of Columbia. **2.** direct current.
—[略] 1. 컬럼비아 특별구 2. 직류

dea·con [dí:k(ə)n] *n.* [C] a clergyman ranking below a priest, as in the Roman Catholic Church; an officer of the church who helps a priest in various ways.
—[名] [가톨릭 교회의] 부제(副祭); 교회의 집사

‡ dead [ded] *adj.* **1.** no longer living; without life. ¶*a* ~ *body.* **2.** deathlike; insensible; without feeling. ¶~ *fingers*① / *They were* ~ *to pity.*② **3.** without power, movement, spirit, etc. ¶~ *water.*③ **4.** no longer in use. ¶*a* ~ *language.* **5.** out of play; not in the game. ¶*a* ~ *ball.* **6.** worn out; tired out. ¶*He felt* ~ *from 8 hours' walking.* **7.** complete; absolute; entirely. ¶~ *silence.* **8.** quite certain; exact. ¶*a* ~ *shot.* **9.** 《*the* ~》 dead persons. ¶*the* ~ *and the living.*④
—*adv.* absolutely; completely. ¶~ *asleep* / ~ *tired.*
—*n.* [U] the time when it is darkest or coldest. ¶*in* (or *at*) *the* ~ *of night* / *in the* ~ *of winter.*
—[形] 1. 죽은; 생명이 없는 2. 죽은 듯한; 무감각한 ¶①마비된 손가락/②그들에게는 동정심이 전혀 없었다 3. 생기(활력)가 없는; 움직이지 않는 ¶③괸 물 4. 폐지된 5. [경기 따위]가 중단된 6. 지쳐빠진 7. 전적인 8. [죽음처럼] 확실한; 정확한 9. 죽은 사람들 ¶④죽은 자와 산 자
—[副] 전혀, 아주
—[名] 가장 어두운(추운) 때

dead·en [dédn] *vt.* weaken (one's vigor, etc.); make (something) less strong. —*vi.* become dead; lose vigor.
—[他] [활기·감정 따위]를 죽이다, 약하게 하다 —[自] 죽다; 약해지다

dead letter [ˊ ˊ–] *n.* a letter that cannot be delivered because it is wrongly addressed, etc.
—[名] 배달할 수 없는 우편물

dead·line [dédlàin] *n.* [C] **1.** the time limit for finishing something, such as payment or writing stories for magazines, etc. **2.** a boundary which must not be crossed.
—[名] 1. [지불 따위의] 최종 기한, [신문·잡지 원고의] 마감 시간 2. 사선(死線)

dead·lock [dédlɑ̀k / -lɔ̀k] *n.* [C] a condition in which no one will give way; a standstill. ¶*at a* ~① / *The dispute came to a* ~. —*vt.* bring (a meeting, etc.) to a deadlock. —*vi.* come to a deadlock.
—[名] [교섭 따위의] 막다름, 교착, 정체 ¶①교착상태에 빠져 —[他] [회의 따위]를 교착상태에 빠뜨리다 —[自] 교착상태에 빠지다

‡ dead·ly [dédli] *adj.* (**-li·er, -li·est**) **1.** causing death; fatal; deathly. ¶*a* ~ *wound.*① **2.** extreme. ¶~ *dull-*
—[形] 1. 치명적인; 죽은 사람 같은 ¶①치명상 2. 극단적인, 심한

D

ness. —*adv.* **1.** as if dead. **2.** extremely.

***deaf** [def] *adj.* **1.** unable to hear. ¶*the* ~.① **2.** not willing to listen; unwilling to give attention to something. ▷**deaf·ly** [-li] *adv.*
1) ***be deaf and dumb,*** not able to hear and speak.
2) ***be deaf*** (=*not willing to listen*) ***to something.*** ¶*He is* ~ *to all advice.*②
3) ***fall on deaf ears,*** not be heard or not heeded.
4) ***turn a deaf ear*** (=*not willing to listen*) ***to something.***

deaf-and-dumb [défəndʌ́m] *adj.* unable to hear and speak. ¶*the* ~ *alphabet.*①

deaf·en [déf(ə)n] *vt.* make (someone) deaf; make (someone's hearing) impossible due to noise. ¶*The medicine deafened her for life.*①

deaf-mute [défmjú:t] *n.* [C] a person who is deaf and dumb.

deaf·ness [défnis] *n.* [U] the state of being deaf; the state of giving no attention to someone or something.

‡**deal**¹ [di:l] *v.* (**dealt**) *vi.* **1.** be concerned; be related. 《~ *with* something》 **2.** act; behave. 《~ *with* or *toward* someone》 **3.** trade. 《~ *in* or *with* something》 —*vt.* **1.** give out (something) to each; distribute. ¶~ *the cards.* **2.** give. ¶~ *him a blow.*①
1) ***deal*** (=*buy goods*) ***at a certain store.*** ¶*I* ~ *at the neighborhood market.*②
2) ***deal in,*** ⓐ be concerned in (something); have to do with (something). ¶~ *in politics.* ⓑ buy and sell; trade. ¶*He deals in oil.*
3) ***deal with,*** ⓐ keep company with (someone). ¶*He is hard to* ~ *with.*③ ⓑ manage; settle. ¶*This matter is easy to* ~ *with.* ⓒ treat; argue; discuss. ¶*a book dealing with economics.* ⓓ act or behave oneself toward others. ¶~ *fairly with everyone.*④ ⓔ do business with (someone, a firm, a store, etc.). ¶*We refuse to* ~ *with that firm any longer.*⑤

—*n.* [C] **1.** a business arrangement; a bargain; treatment. ¶*a fair* ~ / *enter into a* ~ *with him.*⑥ **2.** a policy; a plan. **3.** the distribution of cards; a player's turn to deal. (*vt.* 1) **4.** quantity; amount.
a good (or ***great***)·***deal,*** ⓐ a large amount. ¶*a great* ~ *of money.* ⓑ to a great extent or degree; much. ¶*He drinks a good* ~.

deal² [di:l] *n.* [U] a board of pine or fir wood; pine or fir wood.

***deal·er** [dí:lər] *n.* [C] a man who trades.

***deal·ing** [dí:liŋ] *n.* [U] **1.** one's behavior toward others. ¶*fair* ~.① **2.** 《*pl.*》 business; trade.

‡**dealt** [delt] *v.* pt. and pp. of **deal**¹.

***dean** [di:n] *n.* [C] **1.** the head officer in charge of a cathedral or church. **2.** the head of a department of a university. ¶*the* ~ *of a faculty.*① **3.** a very famous, older man.

‡**dear** [diər] *adj.* **1.** much loved; beloved. ¶*My* ~ *boy.* **2.** much valued; precious. ¶*my dearest wish.* **3.** high-priced; costly. ↔cheap ¶*a* ~ *shop.*
work for dear life, work very hard.
—*n.* [C] a loved one; one's sweetheart; one's darling. ⇒[N.B.] —*adv.* at a high cost. ¶*I bought it* ~. —*interj.* an expression of distress, surprise, pity, etc. ¶*Dear me!*

dear·ie [díəri] *n.* =deary.

dear·ly [díərli] *adv.* **1.** with deep love; affectionately. ¶*love someone* ~. **2.** at a high price; expensively. ¶*The peace was* ~ *won.*①

dear·ness [díərnis] *n.* [U] **1.** high price; costliness. **2.** affection; fondness.

dearth [dəːrθ] *n.* [U] 《sometimes *a* ~》 **1.** lack; too small

—[副] 1. 죽은 것처럼 2. 극단적으로
—[形] 1. 귀머거리의, 귀가 먼, ¶①귀머거리[들] 2. 들으려고 하지 않는

[熟] 1)귀머거리에 벙어리다 2)들으려고 하지 않다 ¶②그는 전혀 충고를 들으려 하지 않는다 3)근청(유의)되지 않다 4)…에 조금도 귀를 기울이지 않다

—[形] 농아(聾啞)의 ¶①농아자용 지화(指話)문자
—[他] …을 귀머거리로 만들다; [소음으로] 소리가 들리지 않게 하다 ¶①그 약으로 그녀는 평생 듣지 못하게 되었다
—[名] 농아자

—[名] 귀머거리; 귀를 기울이지 않음

—[自] 1. 관계하다; 사귀다 2. 처신(행동)하다 3. 장사(거래)하다 —[他] 1. …을 나누어 주다, 도르다 2. …을 주다; 가하다 ¶①그를 때리다

[熟] 1)…에서 구입하다, 사다 ¶②나는 이웃 시장에서 물건을 사고 있다 2)ⓐ…에 종사(관계)하다 ⓑ…을 장사하다, 취급하다 3)ⓐ…와 사귀다 ¶③그는 사귀기 힘들다 ⓑ처리하다; 수습하다 ⓒ…을 취급하다; 논하다 ⓓ…을 대하다, 처신하다 ¶④모든 사람에게 공평하게 대하다 ⓔ…와 거래하다 ¶⑤그 회사와는 더 거래하지 않겠다

—[名] 1. 거래; 처리 ¶⑥그와 거래를 하다 2. 정책; 계획 3. 카아드를 도르기; 도르는 차례 4. 분량, 액수

[熟] ⓐ다량 ⓑ많이, 대단히

—[名] 전나무(소나무) 널빤지(재목)
—[名] 상인
—[名] 1. 행동, 처신 ¶①공평한 태도 2. 거래, 장사

—[名] 1. [영국국교의] 성당의 수석 사제(司祭), 수석 목사 2. [대학의] 학[부]장 ¶①학장, 학부장 3. 장로; 고참

—[形] 1. 친애하는, 귀여운; 사랑스러운 2. 소중한, 귀중한 3. 값비싼

[熟] 열심히 일하다
—[名] 친애하는 사람, 애인, 연인 [N.B.] 호칭으로 쓰임 —[副] 값비싸게 —[感] 저런!, 어머나!

—[副] 1. 다정하게 2. 값비싸게 ¶①평화는 큰 희생을 치르고 얻은 것이었다

—[名] 1. 값비쌈 2. 애정
—[名] 1. 부족, 결핍 2. 기근 ¶①물 기근

a supply. **2.** lack of food; famine. ¶~ *of water.*①

dear·y, dear·ie [díəri] *n.* [C] (pl. **dear·ies**) (*colloq.*) a dear one; a loved one. ⇒[N.B.]
—[名] 《口》 귀여운 사람 [N.B.] 호칭으로 쓰이는 여성 용어

⁝ **death** [deθ] *n.* **1.** [U][C] the act of dying; the state of being dead. ¶*a violent* ~① / *a field of* ~② / *die a natural* ~③ / *in the hour of* ~.④ **2.** 《*D-*》 the god of death. ⇒[N.B.] **3.** 《*the* ~》 destruction; end **4.** 《*the* ~, *one's* ~》 a cause of death.
—[名] 1. 죽음 ¶①변사, 횡사/②싸움터/③천수(天壽)를 다하다/④임종에 2. 사신(死神) [N.B.] 손에 낫을 든 해골로 상징 3. 파멸, 종말 4. 죽음의 원인

1) ***as sure as death,*** surely.
2) ***at death's door,*** almost dead; in danger of dying.
3) ***be as pale as death,*** be deadly pale.
4) ***put** someone **to death,*** kill.

[熟] 1)아주 확실한 2)빈사상태에서 3)창백하다 4)…을 죽이다

death·bed [déθbèd] *n.* [C] **1.** a bed on which a person dies. **2.** the last hours of someone's life. ¶*on one's* ~.①
—[名] 1. 죽음의 자리 2. 임종 ¶①죽음에 임하여, 임종에

death·blow [déθblòu] *n.* [C] a blow that kills; a thing that destroys.
—[名] 치명적 타격

death·less [déθlis] *adj.* living forever; never dying; immortal; eternal. ¶~ *honor.*①
—[形] 죽지 않는, 불멸의 ¶①불멸의 명성

death·like [déθlàik] *adj.* like that of death; as in death. ¶~ *silence.*①
—[形] 죽음(죽은 사람) 같은 ¶①죽음과 같은 고요

death·ly [déθli] *adj.* like death or a dead person; deadly. —*adv.* as if dead.
—[形] 죽음(죽은 사람) 같은; 치명적인 —[副] 죽은 것처럼

death mask [ˊ ˋ] *n.* a clay, wax, or plaster cast of a person's face taken after his death.
—[名] 데드마스크, 사면(死面)

death rate [ˊ ˋ] *n.* the number of deaths among every 1,000 persons in one year in a given area.
—[名] 사망률

death's-head [déθshèd] *n.* [C] a human skull symbolizing death.
—[名] 해골 그림(조각)(죽음의 상징)

de·ba·cle [deibá:kl, di-, +*U.S.* -bǽkl] *n.* [C] **1.** sudden ruin. **2.** the breaking up of ice in a river.
—[名] 1. [갑작스러운] 붕괴, 대폭락; 산사태 2. [강의] 얼음이 깨지기

de·bar [dibá:*r*] *vt.* (**-barred, -bar·ring**) shut out; exclude. 《~ someone *from doing*》
—[他] …을 제외하다; 방해하다

de·bark [dibá:*r*k] *vt.* put (goods, people, etc.) on shore from a ship. —*vi.* go on shore from a ship; disembark.
—[他] …을 상륙시키다 —[自] 상륙하다

de·base [dibéis] *vt.* make (something) lower in value, character, quality, etc.; lessen the value of (something).
—[他] [인격 따위]를 떨어뜨리다; [품질·가격 따위]를 저하시키다

de·base·ment [dibéismənt] *n.* [U] the act of debasing; the state of being debased.
—[名] [품질·가격의] 저하; [품성의] 타락

de·bat·a·ble [dibéitəbl] *adj.* that can be debated; open to dispute or question; questionable. ¶~ *land.*①
—[形] 논쟁거리가 되는; 논쟁의 여지가 있는 ¶①[국경 따위의] 분쟁지; 논쟁점

⁝ **de·bate** [dibéit] *vt., vi.* **1.** talk about some question; discuss thoroughly; argue. **2.** think about; consider. —*n.* **1.** [U][C] discussion of reasons for and against a subject, etc. **2.** [C] a formal discussion between two sides, as in Parliament. ¶*a* ~ *society.*
—[他][自] 1. 논의(논쟁)하다 2. 숙고하다
—[名] 1. 토론, 논쟁 2. 토론회; [의회의] 토의

de·bat·er [dibéitə*r*] *n.* [C] a person who debates.
—[名] 토론가, 토의자

de·bauch [dibɔ́:tʃ] *vt.* lead (someone) astray; cause (someone) to be immoral. —*n.* [C] the act of taking part in sensual pleasures, etc.; immoral behavior.
—[他] …을 타락시키다 —[名] 방탕, 난봉

de·bauch·er·y [dibɔ́:tʃ(ə)ri] *n.* [U] the act of indulging excessively in sensual pleasures; seduction from duty, virtue, or morality.
—[名] 방탕, 난봉

de·ben·ture [dibéntʃə*r*] *n.* [C] a written promise of a government or of a business company to pay a debt.
—[名] 사채권(社債券), 채권

de·bil·i·tate [dibílitèit] *vt.* make (someone) weak; weaken.
—[他] …을 쇠약시키다

de·bil·i·ty [dibíliti] *n.* [U] weakness usu. of the body.
—[名] [신체의] 쇠약

deb·it [débit] *n.* [C] a statement of debt in an account book. ↔credit ¶*a* ~ *slip.*① —*vt.* enter (a sum of money) as a debt.
—[名] 차변(借邊)[기입] ¶①지불 전표 —[他] [금액]을 차변에 기입하다

deb·o·nair, -naire [dèbənέə*r*] *adj.* **1.** gay; cheerful; light-hearted. **2.** courteous; affable.
—[形] 1. 유쾌한, 쾌활한 2. 공손한

de·bouch [dibú:ʃ / -báutʃ] *vi.* **1.** (of a river) flow out. **2.** (of men, an army, etc.) come out from a small space. ¶*The soldiers debouched from the wood.*
—[自] 1. [강물이 넓은 곳으로] 흘러 나오다 2. [사람·군대가 넓은 데로] 진출하다

de·bris, dé·bris [dəbrí: / débri(:)] *n.* [U] broken, useless remains caused by destruction.
—[名] 파편, 부스러기

debt

: **debt** [det] *n.* **1.** ⓤⓒ a sum of money that has to be paid. ¶ *a national ~.*① **2.** ⓒ obligation. ¶ *owe a ~ of gratitude to someone.*②
 1) ***be out of debt***, have no debts; owing no money.
 2) ***one's debt of*** (or ***to***) ***nature***, death. ¶ *pay one's ~ to nature.*③
 3) ***keep out of debt***, live a life without debt.
 4) ***run into debt***, get into debt.
— ⓜ 1. 빚, 부채 ¶①국채 2. 신세, 은혜 ¶②남에게 신세를 지고 있다

圏 1)빚이 없다 2)죽음 ¶③죽다 3)빚지지 않고 살다 4)빚지다

debt·or [détər] *n.* ⓒ a person who owes something to another. ↔creditor
— ⓜ 빚진 사람, 채무자

de·bunk [di:bʌ́ŋk] *vt.* (*U.S. colloq.*) remove (nonsense, false sentiment or claims).
— ⓣ 《美口》…의 정체를 폭로하다, 가면을 벗기다

de·but, dé·but [dibjú: / déibu:] *n.* ⓒ **1.** the first time to take one's place in society. **2.** (of an actor) the first time to be seen on the stage.
— ⓜ 1. 정식으로 사교계에 처음 나오기 2. [배우 등의] 첫무대, 첫출연, 데뷔

deb·u·tante, dé·bu·tante [dèbjutáːnt / débju(:)tàːnt] *n.* ⓒ a young woman making her debut in society.
— ⓜ 처음 사교계에 나오는 여자

Dec. December.

de·ca- [dekə-] a word element meaning *ten*.
— 「10」을 뜻하는 연결형

dec·ade [dékeid, +U.S. dekéid] *n.* ⓒ **1.** ten years. **2.** a group of ten.
— ⓜ 1. 10년간 2. 10개 한 벌

dec·a·dence [dikéid(ə)ns, dékəd(ə)ns] *n.* ⓤ the state of being decadent; decay. ¶ *the ~ of morals.*①
— ⓜ 쇠미(衰微), 타락 ¶①도의의 퇴폐

dec·a·dent [dikéid(ə)nt, dékəd(ə)nt] *adj.* falling off in moral quality; growing worse. — *n.* ⓒ a decadent person, esp. a decadent artist or writer.
— ⓣ 쇠미하는; 퇴폐적인 — ⓜ 퇴폐적인 사람; 데카당파의 예술가(작가)

Dec·a·logue, -log [dékəlɔ̀:g / -lɔ̀g], **the** *n.* the Ten Commandments in the Bible.
— ⓜ [모세의] 십계

dec·a·me·ter [dékəmì:tər] *n.* ⓒ a measure of length equal to 10 meters.
— ⓜ 데카미터(10미터)

de·cant·er [dikǽntər] *n.* ⓒ an ornamental glass wine-bottle. ⇒fig.
— ⓜ 마개가 있는 식탁용 포도주 병

de·cap·i·tate [dikǽpitèit] *vt.* cut off the head of (someone).
— ⓣ …의 목을 자르다

: **de·cay** [dikéi] *vi.* go bad; become feeble; decline. ¶ *The old fruit decayed.* — *vt.* make (something) bad or feeble. ¶ *a decayed tooth.*① — *n.* ⓤ the act of decaying; the gradual loss of power, strength, wealth, beauty, etc. [decanter]
— ⓘ …썩다, 부패하다, 쇠퇴하다 — ⓣ …을 썩게 하다; 붕괴시키다 ¶①충치 — ⓜ 부패, 부식; 쇠퇴

[decanter]

de·cease [disí:s] *n.* ⓤ death. — *vi.* die.
— ⓜ 죽음 — ⓘ 죽다

de·ceased [disí:st] *adj.* dead. ¶ *the ~*① */ one's ~ father*② */ the family of the ~.*③
— ⓣ 죽은, [지금은] 돌아가신, 고(故) … ¶①고인/②선친/③유족

de·ceit [disí:t] *n.* ⓤⓒ the act of deceiving or lying.
— ⓜ 사기, 허위, 불성실

de·ceit·ful [disí:tf(u)l] *adj.* ready or willing to deceive; deceptive. ▷**de·ceit·ful·ly** [-fuli] *adv.*
— ⓣ 남을 속이는, 허위의, 사기적인

: **de·ceive** [disí:v] *vt.* make (someone) believe what is not true; delude. ¶ *You must not ~ him.*①
— ⓣ …을 속이다, 기만하다 ¶①그를 속여서는 안 된다

de·ceiv·er [disí:vər] *n.* ⓒ a person who deceives.
— ⓜ 속이는 사람, 사기꾼

de·cel·er·ate [di:sélərèit] *vt., vi.* cause (something) to go more slowly; slow down. ↔accelerate
— ⓣ 속력을 늦추다; [속력을] 줄이다

: **De·cem·ber** [disémbər] *n.* the twelfth and last month of the year. ⇒N.B.
— ⓜ 12월 N.B. Dec.로 줄임

de·cen·cy [dí:snsi] *n.* ⓤ the quality of being decent.
— ⓜ 예의바름; 품격

: **de·cent** [dí:snt] *adj.* **1.** (of manner, language, etc.) modest; proper and respectable. ¶ *She comes of a ~ family.*① **2.** (of dress, etc.) good enough; fitting; suitable. ¶ *wear a ~ suit of clothes.* **3.** kind; generous. ¶ *It's awfully ~ of you.* **4.** (*colloq.*) satisfactory; fair.
— ⓣ 1. [태도·언어 따위가] 고상한, 점잖은 ¶①그녀는 명문 출신이다 2. [복장 따위가] 꼴사납지 않은, 어울리는 3. 친절한 4. 《口》상당한, 만족스러운

de·cent·ly [dí:sntli] *adv.* in a decent manner.
— ⓣ 고상하게; 상당히; 상냥하게

de·cen·tral·i·za·tion [di:sèntrəlizéiʃ(ə)n / -trəlai-] *n.* ⓤ the state of being decentralized.
— ⓜ 분포, 분산; 지방 분권

de·cen·tral·ize [di:séntrəlàiz] *vt.* distribute (something) among more groups, places, local governments, etc.
— ⓣ [행정권·권력·조직 따위를] 분산시키다

deception

de·cep·tion [disépʃ(ə)n] *n.* **1.** ⓤⓒ the act of deceiving; the condition of being deceived. **2.** ⓒ a trick; a sham. ¶*There is no ~ in what he does.*①
— 图 1. 사기, 기만; 협잡 2. 가짜; 속임수 ¶①그가 하는 일에 속임수는 없다

de·cep·tive [diséptiv] *adj.* deceiving; misleading.
▷**de·cep·tive·ly** [-li] *adv.* —**de·cep·tive·ness** [-nis] *n.*
— 형 남을 속이는, 사기적인; 오해를 사게 하는; 믿을 수 없는

deci- [dési] a word element meaning *one tenth.*
— 「10분의 1」의 뜻의 연결형

de·cide [disáid] *vt.* judge and settle (a question, a doubt, etc.); choose (someone) to do something. ¶*That decided me.*① —*vi.* make up one's mind; reach a decision; resolve. ¶*I have decided to go abroad.*②
— 他 …을 결정하다, 결심하다, …을 결심시키다 ¶①그것으로 결심이 생겼다
— 自 결정(결심)하다 ¶②해외에 가기로 결정했다

de·cid·ed [disáidid] *adj.* **1.** clear; definite. ¶*a ~ difference.* **2.** firm; determined; not hesitating. ¶*give a ~ answer.*
— 형 1. 명확한, 뚜렷한 2. 결정적인; 단호한

de·cid·ed·ly [disáididli] *adv.* in a decided manner; clearly and undoubtedly. ¶*~ better.*①
— 훼 명백히, 의심할 여지 없이 ¶①확실히 더 좋은

de·cid·u·ous [disídʒuəs / -sídju-] *adj.* (of trees) losing leaves every fall; falling off at a certain time. ↔evergreen ¶*a ~ tree*① / *~ teeth.*②
— 형 낙엽성의; 탈락성의 ¶①낙엽수/②젖니

dec·i·gram, *Brit.* -gramme [désigræm] *n.* ⓒ a weight equal to one-tenth of a gram.
— 图 데시그램(1/10 그램)

dec·i·li·ter, *Brit.* -tre [désilì:tər] *n.* ⓒ a measure of volume equal to one-tenth of a liter.
— 图 데시리터(1/10 리터)

dec·i·mal [désim(ə)l] *adj.* based upon ten or tenths; progressing by tens. ¶*the ~ system*① / *the ~ point.*② —*n.* ⓒ figures at the right of a decimal point.
— 형 십진법(十進法)의, 소수(小數)의 ¶①십진법/②소숫점 — 图 소수

dec·i·me·ter, *Brit.* -tre [désimì:tər] *n.* ⓒ a measure of length equal to one-tenth of a meter.
— 图 데시미터(1/10 미터)

de·ci·pher [disáifər] *vt.* discover the meaning of (difficult or secret writing, etc.). ¶*~ an old manuscript.*①
— 他 …을 판독하다 ¶①옛 문서를 판독하다

de·ci·sion [disíʒ(ə)n] *n.* ⓤⓒ **1.** the act of making up one's mind; a resolution. **2.** a judgment reached or given. ¶*a man of ~*① / *a ~ by majority vote.*②
1) ***arrive at*** (or ***come to***) ***a decision,*** decide.
2) ***with decision,*** decisively.
— 图 1. 결정; 해결; 판정 2. 결단 ¶①결단력이 있는 사람/②다수결

熟 1)결정하다 2)과단성 있게

de·ci·sive [disáisiv] *adj.* **1.** having the quality of decision; showing decision; decided. ¶*~ ballots*① / *a ~ battle.*② **2.** definite. ¶*~ evidence.*③
de·ci·sive·ly [disáisivli] *adv.* in a decisive manner; decidedly.
— 형 1. 결정적인; [대답 따위] 단호한 ¶①결선 투표/②결전(決戰) 2. 명확한 ¶③확증
— 훼 결정적으로, 단연

deck [dek] *n.* ⓒ **1.** the floor or platform of a ship. **2.** (chiefly *U.S.*) a pack of playing cards.
clear the decks, get ready for action.
—*vt.* **1.** cover; dress; adorn. ¶*The girl was decked out in her finest clothes.* **2.** provide (a ship, etc.) with a deck.
— 图 1. 갑판, 덱 2. (美) 카아드 한 벌

熟 전투 준비를 하다
— 他 1. …을 아름답게 꾸미다; 장식하다 2. [배]에 갑판을 깔다

de·claim [dikléim] *vi.* speak or read with strong feeling. ¶*He likes to ~ before large audiences.*
declaim (=*protest*) ***against*** *someone* or *something.*
— 自 낭독하다, 열변을 토하다

熟 …을 맹렬히 비난하다, 항의하다

dec·la·ma·tion [dèkləméiʃ(ə)n] *n.* ⓤⓒ the act of declaiming; a loud and emotional talk.
— 图 [열린] 연설; 낭독[법]; 웅변

de·clam·a·to·ry [diklǽmətɔ̀:ri / -təri] *adj.* **1.** of declaiming. **2.** loud and emotional.
— 형 1. 낭독풍의 2. 웅변조의

• **dec·la·ra·tion** [dèkləréiʃ(ə)n] *n.* ⓤⓒ the act of declaring; a formal announcement. ¶*a ~ of war.*①
The Declaration of Independence, the statement made by the British colonies in North America, on July 4th, 1776.
— 图 선언, 포고, 고백 ¶①선전포고

熟 [미국의] 독립선언(1776년 7월 4일)

de·clar·a·tive [diklǽrətiv] *adj.* making a statement; explanatory. ¶*a ~ sentence.*①
— 형 선언적인; 서술적인 ¶①서술문

de·clare [diklɛ́ər] *vt.* **1.** make (something) known to the public; announce publicly and officially; proclaim. ¶*~ peace* / *~ war against* (or *upon*) *....*① **2.** say strongly; affirm. ⟪*~ that ...*; *~ someone* [*to be*] *dishonest, etc.*; *~ something* [*to be*] *true, etc.*⟫ ¶*She declared that she would never go back home again.* / *He declared me a*
— 他 1. …을 선언하다; 공표하다 ¶①…에 선전포고를 하다 2. …을 단언하다; 주장하다 ¶②그는 그 법안에 반대(찬성)임을 선언했다 3. [세관에서 과세품]을 신고하다 ¶③신고할 물건이 있읍니까? — 自 선언하다; 주장하

liar. | *He declared himself against (for, in favor of) the bill.*② **3.** make a list of (items) for taxation. ¶ *Have you anything to ~?*③ —*vi.* make a declaration; proclaim oneself for or against something. ¶ *They declared against the proposal.*④ | *..., I ~!*⑤
다 ¶④그들은 그 제안에 반대 선언을 했다/⑤정말 …이구나!, 단연 …이다

de·clen·sion [diklénʃ(ə)n] *n.* [U][C] (*Grammar*) the act of giving the different forms of a noun, a pronoun, or an adjective (e.g., who, whose, whom) according to its case. ⇒[N.B.]
—[名] 어미변화, 격변화(명사·대명사·형용사의 변화) [N.B.] 동사의 변화는 conjugation

dec·li·na·tion [dèklinéiʃ(ə)n] *n.* [U][C] **1.** the act of bending or sloping downward. **2.** a deviation of the needle of a compass east or west from true north.
—[名] 1. 기울기, 경사 2. [나침반의] 편차(偏差)

⁑ **de·cline** [dikláin] *vt.* **1.** refuse (something) politely. ↔ accept ¶ *~ an offer*① | *~ with thanks.*② **2.** (*Grammar*) give the different forms of a noun, pronoun, or adjective. —*vi.* **1.** slope downward. **2.** become increasingly less; lessen in health. ¶ *The day declines.*③ | *His health slowly declined.* —*n.* [C] a slow weakening of strength.
—[他] 1. …을 거절하다, 사퇴하다 ¶①제의를 거절하다/②고맙지만 사절하다 2. …을 격변화시키다 —[自] 1. 내리막길이 되다 2. 쇠퇴하다; 건강이 약해지다 ¶③날이 저물다 —[名] 쇠퇴

de·cliv·i·ty [diklíviti] *n.* [C] a downward slope.
—[名] 경사[면]

de·code [dikóud] *vt.* find the meaning of (secret writing, etc.) by the use of key words; translate from a code. ▷**de·co·der** [-ər] *n.*
—[他] [암호 따위]를 풀다, 보통 문장으로 번역하다

de·colle·te [deikɑ̀lətéi / -kɔ́ltei] *adj.* wearing a low-necked dress; (of a dress) having a low neck.
—[形] [여자 옷의] 어깨·목이 드러나는

de·com·pose [dì:kəmpóuz] *vt., vi.* **1.** separate (something) into basic parts; analyse. **2.** become bad; decay; rot.
—[他][自] 1. 분해하다, 분석하다 2. 썩게 하다, 부패하다

de·com·po·si·tion [dì:kɑmpəzíʃ(ə)n / -kɔm-] *n.* [U] the act of decomposing; the state of being decomposed.
—[名] 분해; 부패

* **dec·o·rate** [dékərèit] *vt.* **1.** make (something) beautiful. ¶ *We decorated the Christmas tree.*① | *We decorated the room with flowers.* **2.** give a medal to (someone) as an honor. ¶ *~ someone with the Order of the Garter.*②
—[他] 1. …을 장식하다 ¶①크리스마스트리를 장식했다 2. …에 훈장을 주다 ¶②…에 가아터 훈장을 수여하다

* **dec·o·ra·tion** [dèkəréiʃ(ə)n] *n.* **1.** [U] the act of decorating; [C] a thing used to decorate; an ornament. ¶ *interior ~*① | *~ display.*② **2.** [C] a medal.
—[名] 1. 장식; 장식물 ¶①실내 장식/②[가게의] 장식 진열 2. 훈장

Decoration Day [--ˊ- ˋ] *n.* (*U.S.*) Memorial Day.
—[名] [미국의] 전몰장병 기념일(5월 30일)

dec·o·ra·tive [dékərèitiv / -rə-] *adj.* decorating; ornamental. ¶ *~ art*① | *~ illumination.*②
—[形] 장식의, 장식적인 ¶①장식 미술/②장식 조명

* **dec·o·ra·tor** [dékərèitər] *n.* [C] a person who decorates, esp. a person who papers or paints a house. ¶ *an interior ~.*①
—[名] 장식[업]자 ¶①실내 장식가

dec·o·rous [dékərəs, +*U.S.* dikɔ́:rəs] *adj.* showing good taste; well-behaved. ▷**dec·o·rous·ly** [dékərəsli, +*U.S.* dikɔ́:rəs-] *adv.*
—[形] 고상한; 품위 있는

de·co·rum [dikɔ́:rəm] *n.* [U] the act of acting in a way suitable in good society; good and decent behavior.
—[名] 예의바름; 단정, 고상함; 예절

de·coy [dikɔ́i] *n.* [C] an artificial or real bird used to bring other birds into the range of guns; a person used to lead (someone) into a trap. —*vt.* lead (a person, bird, animal, etc.) into danger with a decoy.
—[名] 미끼, [새 따위를] 유인하는 장치 —[他] [위험한 곳으로] …을 유인하다, 꾀다

* **de·crease** [dikrí:s] *vi., vt.* become less; cause (something) to grow less. —*n.* [U] the act of decreasing; the condition of being decreased; [C] the amount by which something decreases. ↔increase
—[自][他] 줄다; 줄이다
—[名] 감소

on the decrease, gradually decreasing.
[熟] 감소하는

* **de·cree** [dikrí:] *n.* [C] **1.** an order given out by a ruler or government and having the force of law. **2.** a judgment of a court of law. —*vt., vi.* issue a decree; command by a decree.
—[名] 1. 법령, 포고 2. [법정의] 판결, 명령 —[他][自] 법령을 공포하다; 포고하다

de·crep·it [dikrépit] *adj.* weakened by old age; old and having no power.
—[形] 노쇠한, 노후한; 병약한

de·crep·i·tude [dikrépit(j)ù:d / -tjù:-] *n.* [U] the state of being decrepit; weakness, usu. from old age.
—[名] 노쇠(노후)[한 상태], 노망, 망령

de·cry [dikrái] *vt.* (**-cried**) say bad things about (something); denounce (something) openly. ▷**de·cri·er** [-ər] *n.*
—[他] …을 비난하다, 공공연히 헐뜯다

***ded·i·cate** [dédikèit] *vt.* **1.** set apart (something) for some good or holy purpose; give (something) to God. **2.** devote (one's life) to something sacred. 《~ one's life *to* science》 **3.** address (a book) to someone for expressing thanks. ¶*Dedicated to …*①
—[他] 1. …을 봉납(헌납)하다 2. [생애]를 바치다 3. …을 헌정(獻呈)하다 ¶①…에게 이 책을 바침(책머리에 쓰는 문구)

ded·i·ca·tion [dèdikéiʃ(ə)n] *n.* **1.** [U] the act of dedicating. **2.** [C] the words dedicating a book or other work to a friend, etc.
—[名] 1. 봉납, 헌납 2. [서적 따위에 쓰는] 헌정사(獻呈辭)

ded·i·ca·tor [dédikèitər] *n.* [C] a person who dedicates.
—[名] 헌납자; 헌정자

ded·i·ca·to·ry [dédikətɔ̀:ri / -kət(ə)ri] *adj.* serving as a dedication.
—[形] 봉납(봉헌)의

de·duce [did(j)ú:s / -djú:s] *vt.* reach (a conclusion) as a result of considering a general rule or principle. ↔induce 《~ something *from*》
—[他] …을 연역적(演繹的)으로 추론(推論)하다

de·duct [didʌ́kt] *vt.* take away (an amount, etc). 《~ something *from*》 ¶*~ 10% from one's salary.*
—[他] …을 공제하다, 빼다

de·duc·tion [didʌ́kʃ(ə)n] *n.* **1.** [U] the act of taking away. **2.** [C] the amount deducted. **3.** [C] a conclusion reached by considering a general rule or principle. ↔induction
—[名] 1. 공제, 빼기 2. 공제액 3. 추론, 연역(演繹)

de·duc·tive [didʌ́ktiv] *adj.* of, using, or reasoning by deduction. ▷**de·duc·tive·ly** [-li] *adv.*
—[形] 연역적인; 추론적인

⁑**deed** [di:d] *n.* [C] **1.** a thing done; an act; an action. ¶*good (evil) deeds / Deeds are better than words when people are in trouble.*① **2.** a written, printed, or signed document, containing some contract.
—[名] 1. 행위, 행동 ¶①사람이 곤경에 처해 있을 때는 말보다는 행동이 더 낫다 2. 증서

in deed, really; indeed; actually.
[熟] 실제로, 정말로

—*vt.* transfer (something) by a written or printed document.
—[他] [증서로 만들어] …을 양도하다

***deem** [di:m] *vt., vi.* think; believe; suppose. ¶*I ~ him highly.*① */ I deemed it my duty to do so.*
—[他][自] 생각하다, 믿다, …이라 여기다 ¶①나는 그를 존경한다

⁑**deep** [di:p] *adj.* **1.** going far down, back, or inward. ¶*~ snow / a ~ well / a ~ cave / a ~ shelf*① */ a ~ wound.* **2.** having a certain depth. ¶*a well ten meters ~.*② **3.** hard to understand; beyond the grasp of the ordinary mind. ¶*~ intellect / a ~ book.*③ **4.** intense; great in degree. ¶*a ~ sleep*④ */ a ~ night.*⑤ **5.** strongly felt. ¶*~ sorrow.* **6.** strong; heavy. ¶*a ~ drinker.* **7.** remote. ¶*a house ~ in the country.* **8.** low in pitch. **9.** dark and rich in color. ¶*~ blue.* **10.** cunning.
—[形] 1. 깊은, 깊숙한 ¶①깊이가 있는 시렁 2. 깊이 …의 ¶②깊이 10미터의 우물 3. 심원한, 헤아릴 수 없는 ¶③난해한 책 4. 통절한, 깊이 느끼는 ¶④숙면/⑤심야 5. 충심에서의 6. 심한 7. 외딴, 멀리 떨어진 8. [소리가] 굵고 낮은 9. [빛깔이] 짙은 10. 빈틈없는, 뱃속 검은

be deep (=*be absorbed*) ***in something.***
[熟] …에 몰두해 있다

—*n.* 《*the* ~》 **1.** the sea; the ocean. **2.** the most intense part. ¶*in the ~ of night*⑥ */ in the ~ of winter.*⑦
—[名] 1. 바다, 대양 2. 깊숙한 곳; 한창, 한가운데 ¶⑥한밤중에/⑦한겨울의

—*adv.* deeply. ¶*drink ~*⑧ */ It is found ~ in the mountains. / They talked ~ into the night.*⑨
—[副] 깊이, 깊은 곳에 ¶⑧[술을] 고래로 마시다/⑨그들은 한밤중까지 이야기했다

deep-drawn [dí:pdrɔ́:n] *adj.* deeply drawn.
—[形] 깊이 들이마신

***deep·en** [dí:p(ə)n] *vt.* make (something) deeper. ¶*~ a well / ~ one's knowledge.*① —*vi.* become deeper. ¶*The water deepened at every step.*②
—[他] …을 깊게 하다 ¶①지식을 깊게 하다 —[自] 깊어지다 ¶②강은 걸음을 옮길 때마다 깊어졌다

deep-felt [dí:pfélt] *adj.* strongly felt.
—[形] 깊이 느낀

deep-laid [dí:pléid] *adj.* secretly and carefully planned.
—[形] 주의깊게 꾸민

deep·ly [dí:pli] *adv.* **1.** to a considerable depth; strongly. ¶*feel ~.* **2.** to a great degree; thoroughly.
—[副] 1. 깊이, 강하게 2. 몹시, 철저하게

deep·ness [dí:pnis] *n.* [U] the quality of being deep; depth.
—[名] 깊음; 심원함

deep-root·ed [dí:prú:tid] *adj.* having deep roots; firmly fixed.
—[形] 깊이 뿌리박은; 뿌리깊은

deep-sea [dí:psí:] *adj.* of or in the deeper parts of the sea. ¶*~ fishery.*①
—[形] 심해의 ¶①심해 어업

deep-seat·ed [dí:psí:tid] *adj.* firmly established; firmly fixed. ¶*a ~ disease.*
—[形] 깊이 뿌리박은, 뿌리깊은

⁑**deer** [diər] *n.* [C] (pl. **deer**) a swift, graceful animal, the male of which has horns.
—[名] 사슴

deer·skin [díərskìn] *n.* [U][C] the leather made from the skin of a deer.
—[名] 사슴 가죽, 녹비

de·face [diféis] *vt.* spoil the appearance of (something) by marking or damaging the surface.
—[他] …의 외관을 더럽히다, 보기 흉하게 하다

de·face·ment [diféismənt] *n.* **1.** [U] the act of defacing; the state of being defaced. **2.** [C] a thing that defaces.
—[名] 1. 파손 2. 파손시키는 것

D

de fac·to [difǽktou / di:-] *adv., adj.* in fact, whether legal or not.
—副形 사실상(의)

de·fal·ca·tion [dìːfælkéiʃ(ə)n] *n.* 1. Ⓤ the act of stealing or misusing the money that is entrusted to one. 2. Ⓒ an amount of money stolen or misused.
—名 1. 위탁금 횡령, 부당 유용 2. 횡령(유용)액

def·a·ma·tion [dèfəméiʃ(ə)n] *n.* Ⓤ harm that is given to one's reputation. ⌜harm someone's reputation.⌝
—名 명예훼손, 중상(中傷)

de·fam·a·to·ry [difǽmətɔ̀ːri / -t(ə)ri] *adj.* intending to
—形 명예훼손의

de·fame [diféim] *vt.* harm the reputation of (someone); speak ill of (someone). ▷**de·fam·er** [-ər] *n.*
—他 …의 명예를 훼손하다; …을 중상하다

de·fault [difɔ́ːlt] *n.* Ⓤ 1. failure to do a duty ; failure to pay a debt ; failure to appear in a court of law. ¶*judgment by~.*① 2. absence ; lack.
in default of, in the absence of ; for want of.
—*vi.* fail to do a duty ; fail to pay a debt ; fail to appear in a court of law. ▷**de·fault·er** [-ər] *n.*
—名 1. [의무·채무 따위의] 불이행, 태만 ; [재판정에의] 결석 ¶①궐석재판 2. 부족 ; 결핍
熟 …이 없을 때는 ; …이 없기 때문에
—自 의무(채무)의 이행을 게을리하다, 재판에 결석하다

:**de·feat** [difíːt] *vt.* 1. overcome ; win a victory over (someone). ¶*We defeated Tokyo High School in the baseball game yesterday.* / *He has been defeated in the recent election.*① 2. make (something) useless. ¶*Our hopes were defeated.*②
defeat one's own object (or *purpose, end*), cause oneself to fail to do what one is trying to do.
—*n.* 1. Ⓤ the act of defeating. 2. ⓊⒸ the state or an instance of being defeated. ↔victory ¶*Our team has never suffered [from] ~.*③ ⌜defeatist.⌝
—他 1. …을 지우다, 쳐부수다 ¶①그는 이번 선거에서 패배했다 2. …을 무효로 하다 ¶②우리의 희망은 깨어졌다
熟 실패하다, 목적을 이루지 못하다
—名 1. 격파 2. 패배 ¶③우리 팀은 아직 패배한 일이 없다

de·feat·ism [difíːtiz(ə)m] *n.* Ⓤ the state or action of
—名 패배주의

de·feat·ist [difíːtist] *n.* Ⓒ a person who admits the inevitable defeat of his country, party, etc.
—名 패배주의자

·**de·fect** [difékt] *n.* Ⓒ the lack of something necessary to completeness ; a fault ; an imperfection. ¶*What defects can you find in this system?*①
—名 결함, 결점, 불완전 ¶①이 제도에 어떤 결함이 있다고 생각합니까?

de·fec·tion [difékʃ(ə)n] *n.* Ⓤ the act of abandoning one's loyalty, duty, religion, etc.; Ⓒ an instance of this.
—名 [충성 따위를] 버리기, 변절 ; 탈당, 탈퇴

de·fec·tive [diféktiv] *adj.* 1. having a fault ; not perfect. ↔perfect ¶*a ~ memory.* 2. lacking ; wanting. 3. below average in intelligence. ▷**de·fec·tive·ly** [-li] *adv.*
—形 1. 결함이 있는 ; 불완전한 2. […이] 없는, 결여된 3. 지능이 정상 이하의

:**de·fence** [diféns] *n.* (*Brit.*) =defense.

de·fence·less [difénslis] *adj.* (*Brit.*) =defenseless.

:**de·fend** [difénd] *vt.* 1. protect ; guard (someone or something). ¶*~ oneself*① / *They defended their country against the enemy.* 2. act, speak, or write in favor of (someone or something). ¶*~ a case*② / *He made a speech defending his ideas.*
—他 1. …을 막다, 지키다 ¶①자신을 지키다 2. …을 변호(변명)하다 ¶②사건을 변호하다

de·fend·ant [diféndənt] *n.* Ⓒ a person accused in a law court. ↔plaintiff —*adj.* of a defendant.
—名 피고 —形 피고의

de·fend·er [diféndər] *n.* Ⓒ a person who defends ; a protector. ¶*the Defender of the Faith.*①
—名 방어자 ; 옹호자 ; 변호자 ¶①신교(信敎)·옹호자

:**de·fense,** *Brit.* **-fence** [diféns] *n.* Ⓤ 1. the act of defending. ↔attack ; offense ¶*legal ~*① / *national ~*② / *offensive ~.*③ 2. Ⓒ something that defends ; a thing used to guard against attack. 3. the act of defending in boxing or fencing ; Ⓒ the group defending a goal in a game. 4. ⓊⒸ an action, speech, etc. in favor of something. ¶*make a ~.*④ 5. the answer of a defendant to a lawsuit against him.
in defense of, in order to defend.
—名 1. 방어, 방위 ¶①정당방위/②국방/③공격 방어 2. 방어물, 방위 시설 3. 수비측의 선수(팀) 4. 변호, 변명 ¶④변호하다 5. 피고의 답변
熟 …을 지키기 위해

de·fense·less, *Brit.* **-fence-** [difénslis] *adj.* having no defense. ¶*a ~ city.* ⌜gainst an attack.⌝
—形 방비가 없는

de·fen·si·ble [difénsibl] *adj.* that can be defended a-
—形 방위할 수 있는 ; 변호할 수 있는

de·fen·sive [difénsiv] *adj.* ready to defend ; for defense of defense. ↔offensive ¶*~ warfare.*① —*n.* (*the ~*) the position, attitude, etc. of defense. ¶*assume the ~ ; be on the ~.*②
—形 방어의 ; 방비용의 ; 수세(守勢)의 ; 수비의 ¶①자위(自衛) 전쟁 —名 방어, 수비 ¶②수세를 취하다

de·fer¹ [difə́:r] *vt., vi.* (**-ferred, -fer·ring**) put off; postpone; delay.

de·fer² [difə́:r] *vi.* (**-ferred, -fer·ring**) obey the judgment or opinion of another. ¶ ~ *to one's parent's opinions.*①

def·er·ence [défərəns] *n.* Ⓤ the act of obeying the judgment or opinion of another; great respect. ¶*blind* | *in deference to,* showing respect for. └~.①

def·er·en·tial [dèfərénʃ(ə)l] *adj.* showing deference; very respectful. ▷**def·er·en·tial·ly** [-ʃəli] *adv.*

de·fer·ment [difə́:rmənt] *n.* Ⓤ the act of putting off; postponing.

· **de·fi·ance** [difáiəns] *n.* Ⓤ **1.** open resistance; refusal to recognize or obey authority. **2.** a call to fight; 1) *bid defiance to,* disobey; neglect. └challenge. 2) *in defiance of,* without regard for; in spite of.

de·fi·ant [difáiənt] *adj.* showing no respect; showing the will to fight. ▷**de·fi·ant·ly** [-li] *adv.*

de·fi·cien·cy [difíʃ(ə)nsi] *n.* (pl. **-cies**) **1.** Ⓤ Ⓒ lack or absence of something needed. ¶ ~ *disease.*① **2.** Ⓒ the amount by which something falls short.

de·fi·cient [difíʃ(ə)nt] *adj.* not sufficient in quantity; incomplete; defective. ¶*be ~ in common sense.*① ▷**de·fi·cient·ly** [-li] *adv.* ┌money falls short. ↔surplus|

def·i·cit [défisit] *n.* Ⓒ the amount by which a sum of|

de·file¹ [difáil] *vt.* make (something) dirty; destroy the purity of (something). ¶*The river was defiled by waste from factories.*① ▷**de·file·ment** [-mənt] *n.*

de·file² [difáil → n.] *vi.* march in a line. —*n.* [dí:fail] Ⓒ a narrow way, passage, etc.

de·fin·a·ble [difáinəbl] *adj.* that can be defined.

· **de·fine** [difáin] *vt.* **1.** make clear the meaning of (a word). **2.** make (something) clear; make (something) distinct. ¶*ill-defined duties.*① **3.** settle the limits of (something); make clear the outline of (something). ¶ ~ *the boundary between the two countries.*②

‡ **def·i·nite** [définit] *adj.* **1.** clear; exact; certain. ↔indefinite ¶*I want a ~ answer, yes or no.*① **2.** limiting; limited; restricting. ¶*the ~ article.*②

· **def·i·nite·ly** [définitli] *adv.* **1.** clearly; in a definite manner. **2.** (*colloq.*) certainly.

def·i·ni·tion [dèfiníʃ(ə)n] *n.* Ⓤ the act of making clear the meaning of a word; Ⓒ a statement that makes clear the meaning of a word. ¶*A dictionary gives the definitions of words.*①

de·fin·i·tive [difínitiv] *adj.* **1.** decisive; conclusive; final. ¶*a ~ answer* / *a ~ statement.* **2.** limiting; defining. —*n.* Ⓒ a word that defines a noun.
▷**de·fin·i·tive·ly** [-li] *adv.* —**de·fin·i·tive·ness** [-nis] *n.*

de·flate [difléit / di(:)-] *vt.* **1.** let the air or gas out of (a balloon, tire, etc.). **2.** reduce the amount of (money) in circulation. ↔inflate

de·fla·tion [difléiʃ(ə)n / di(:)-] *n.* Ⓤ **1.** the act of deflating. **2.** a reduction in the amount of available money in circulation, causing prices to go down. ↔inflation

de·flect [diflékt] *vi.* bend or turn aside. —*vt.* change the direction of (something). ¶ ~ *rays of light.*

de·flec·tion, *Brit.* **-flex·ion** [diflékʃ(ə)n] *n.* Ⓤ Ⓒ the act of bending or turning aside. ┌to turn aside.|

de·flec·tive [difléktiv] *adj.* causing deflection; tending|

de·flex·ion [diflékʃ(ə)n] *n.* (*Brit.*) = deflection.

de·for·est [di:fɔ́:rist, -fɑr- / difɔ́rist] *vt.* cut trees off from (land). ▷**de·for·es·ta·tion** [di:fɔ̀:ristéiʃ(ə)n, -fɑ̀r- / -fɔ̀r-] *n.*

de·form [difɔ́:rm] *vt.* **1.** spoil the form or shape of (something) **2.** make (something) ugly. ¶*Pain de-*

—他自 연기하다, 미루다

—自 [남의 판단 따위에] 따르다 ¶① 부모의 의견에 따르다

—名 복종; 존경 ¶①맹종

熟 …을 존중하여, …에 따라서

—形 경의를 표하는, 공손한

—名 연기, 유예(猶豫)

—名 1. [권위에 대한] 반항, 무시 2. [경쟁 따위에의] 도전
熟 1)무시하다 2)…을 무시하고, …에 개의치 않고
—形 반항적인; 도전적인

—名 1. 부족, 결핍 ¶①비타민 결핍[증] 2. 부족분(량)

—形 [분량이] 부족한; 불완전한 ¶① 상식이 모자라다

—名 부족액, 적자
—他 …을 더럽히다;…의 신성을 모독하다 ¶①강은 공장의 폐기물로 오염되었다
—自 일렬종대로 나아가다 —名 좁은 길; 애로(隘路)

—形 정의(한정)할 수 있는
—他 1.…의 뜻을 명확히 하다 2. …을 명백히 하다 ¶①[목적 따위가] 뚜렷하지 않은 듯무 3. …의 윤곽을 명시하다, 한계를 정하다 ¶②국경을 정하다

—形 1. 명확한 ¶①나는 예스냐, 노우냐의 명확한 대답을 바란다 2. 한정적인 ¶②정관사

—副 1. 명확히; 한정적으로 2. 물론

—名 정의; 어의(語義) ¶①사전은 단어의 정의를 내린다

—形 1. 결정적인, 최종적인 2. 한정적인

—名 한정사(限定辭) (the, this 따위)

—他 1.[기구·타이어 따위]에서 공기 (가스)를 빼다 2.[통화]를 수축하다

—名 1. 공기·가스를 뽑기 2. 데플레이션, 통화수축

—自 비뚤어지다, 빗나가다 —他 …의 방향을 빗나가게 하다, 비끼게 하다
—名 빗나가기, 치우침; 편향(偏向)

—形 [옆으로] 빗나가는

—他 [토지의] 삼림(수목)을 베어 버리다

—他 1. …을 변형시키다 2. …을 보기흉하게 하다 ¶①고통으로 그의 얼굴

*formed his face.*① ▷**de·form·er** [-ər] *n.*
은 일그러졌다

de·for·ma·tion [dìːfɔːrméiʃ(ə)n] *n.* **1.** [U] the act of deforming something. **2.** [U] the state of being deformed.
—[名] 1. 변형시키기, 보기 흉하게 하기 2. 기형, 불구

de·formed [difɔ́ːrmd] *adj.* **1.** badly shaped. **2.** ugly.
—[形] 1. 기형의 2. 보기 흉한

de·form·i·ty [difɔ́ːrmiti] *n.* (pl. **-ties**) **1.** [U] the state of being badly shaped. **2.** [C] a badly shaped person or thing. **3.** [U] ugliness.
—[名] 1. 결함 2. 불구자, 기형물 3. 보기 흉함

de·fraud [difrɔ́ːd] *vt.* take away money, rights, etc. from (someone) by deception. ¶*They defrauded him of his money.; He was defrauded of his money.*① ▷**de·fraud·er** [-ər] *n.*
—[他] [돈·권리 따위를] 속여 빼앗다 ¶①그는 돈을 편취당했다

de·fray [difréi] *vt.* pay the cost or expenses of (something).
—[他] [비용·경비]를 치르다

deft [deft] *adj.* skillful or expert, esp. with fingers.
—[形] 솜씨 있는, 능숙한

deft·ly [déftli] *adv.* in a skillful manner.
—[副] 솜씨 좋게, 능숙하게

deft·ness [déftnis] *n.* [U] the quality of being deft; skillfulness.
—[名] 솜씨 있음, 능숙

de·funct [difʌ́ŋ(k)t] *adj.* dead; no longer existing.
—[形] 죽은; 소멸한, 이제는 없는

* **de·fy** [difái] *vt.* (**-fied, -fy·ing**) **1.** disobey openly. ¶*~ one's parents* | *~ the law.*① **2.** resist; withstand. ¶*~ description*② | *The problem defies solution.* **3.** show the will to fight against (someone). ⟪~ someone *to do*⟫ ¶*I ~ you to do this work.*③
—[他] 1. …에 공공연히 반항하다 ¶①법률을 무시하다 2. …을 거부하다, …에 거스르다 ¶②필설로 다할 수 없다 3. …에 도전하다 ¶③이 일을 할 테면 해봐라

de·gen·er·a·cy [didʒén(ə)rəsi] *n.* [U] the state of being degenerate.
—[名] 퇴화, 타락

de·gen·er·ate *vi.* [didʒénərèit → *adj., n.*] **1.** grow worse in quality. ⟪~ *into* something⟫ **2.** (*Biology*) sink to a lower type or state. —*adj.* [didʒénərit] showing a slow loss of good qualities; having become worse. —*n.* [didʒén(ə)rit] [C] a person having an evil character.
—[自] 1. [육체적·정신적·도덕적으로] 나빠지다, 타락하다 2 퇴화하다 —[形] 타락한, 퇴보한
—[名] 타락한 사람

de·gen·er·a·tion [didʒènəréiʃ(ə)n] *n.* [U] the act of degenerating; the state of being degenerated.
—[名] 타락, 퇴보, 퇴화

deg·ra·da·tion [dègrədéiʃ(ə)n] *n.* [U] the act of degrading; the state of being degraded.
—[名] 좌천, 파면; 타락

de·grade [digréid] *vt.* **1.** put (someone) in a lower rank, esp. as punishment. **2.** make (someone) worse; debase. ¶*You ~ yourself when you cheat at examinations.*① ▷**de·grad·er** [-ər] *n.*
—[他] 1. [특히 벌로서] 지위를 떨어뜨리다 2. …을 타락시키다 ¶①시험에서의 커닝은 네 품위를 떨어뜨리는 일이다

⁑ **de·gree** [digríː] *n.* **1.** [C] an extent; a grade. ¶*To what ~ do you want it?*① **2.** [U] position; rank. ¶*He is a man of high ~.* **3.** [C] a rank given by a college or university for completing a required course of study, or as a mark of honor. ¶*the ~ of doctor.*② **4.** [C] a unit for measuring temperature, angles, etc. **5.** [C] (*Grammar*) a grade of comparison of adjectives and adverbs. ¶*the positive (comparative, superlative) degree.*③
—[名] 1. 정도; 등급 ¶①어느 정도 그것을 바라느냐? 2. 계급, 지위, 신분 3. 학위, 칭호 ¶②박사 학위 4. [온도·각도 따위의] 도(度) 5. ⟪文法⟫[형용사·부사의] 급 ¶③원급(비교급·최상급)

1) ***by degrees,*** gradually.
2) ***in a degree,*** somewhat.
3) ***in a great degree,*** greatly.
4) ***in due degree,*** moderately.
5) ***in full degree,*** too much.
6) ***in some degree,*** to a certain extent.
7) ***not in the slightest*** (or ***least***) ***degree,*** not at all.
8) ***to a degree,*** (*colloq.*) somewhat.
9) ***to the last degree,*** extremely.

[熟] 1)차차, 점점 2)조금은 3)크게, 대단히 4)정당하게 5)충분히 6)다소 7)조금도 …않다 8)몹시, 고도로 9)극단적으로

de·hy·drate [diːháidreit] *vt.* take water or wetness from (something).
—[他] …을 탈수(脫水)하다, 건조하다

de·i·fi·ca·tion [dìːifikéiʃ(ə)n] *n.* [U] the act of deifying; the state of being deified.
—[名] 신으로 모시기, 신격화, 신성시

de·i·fy [díːifài] *vt.* (**-fied, -fy·ing**) worship (someone) as a god.
—[他] …을신과 같이 숭배하다

deign [dein] *vi.* condescend; be gracious enough. ⟪~ *to do*⟫ ¶*The queen deigned to grant an audience.* —*vt.* condescend to give (an answer, etc.).
—[自] 황송하옵게도 …하여 주시다
—[他] [대답 따위]를 주시다

de·i·ty [díːiti] *n.* (pl. **-ties**) **1.** [C] a god; a goddess. ¶*the Deity.*① **2.** [U] divine nature; the state of being a god.
—[名] 1. 신, 여신 ¶①상제(上帝); 신 2. 신성(神性); 신격

de·ject [didʒékt] *vt.* make (someone) sad or unhappy.
—[他] …을 슬퍼하게 하다, 풀이 죽게 하다

de·ject·ed [didʒéktid] *adj.* in low spirits; depressed; sad.
—[形] 기운 없는; 풀죽은

dejection

▷**de·ject·ed·ly** [-li] *adv.* —**de·ject·ed·ness** [-nis] *n.*
de·jec·tion [didʒékʃ(ə)n] *n.* ⓤ lowness of spirits; sadness.
Del. Delaware. ⌜States. ⇒**N.B.**⌝
Del·a·ware [déləwèər] *n.* an eastern State of the United⌟
* **de·lay** [diléi] *vt.* **1.** put off (something) till a later time; postpone. ¶~ *a party* / ~ *one's picnic.* **2.** make (something) late. ↔hasten ¶*Never ~ things.* / *The train was delayed three hours by the heavy snow.* —*vi.* be late; stop for a while.
—*n.* ⓒ ⓤ the act of delaying; a case or fact of being delayed. ¶*a long ~* / *avoid ~*① / *Permit no ~ in doing what is good.*②
without delay, at once; immediately.
de·lec·ta·ble [diléktəbl] *adj.* very pleasant; delightful.
de·lec·ta·tion [dì:lektéiʃ(ə)n] *n.* ⓤ pleasure; delight.
del·e·ga·cy [déligəsi] *n.* ⓒ (pl. **-cies**) a group of delegates.
* **del·e·gate** [déligit → *v.*] *n.* ⓒ a person given power to act for others. —*vt.* [déligèit] **1.** appoint or send (someone) as a delegate. ¶*They delegated him to attend the meeting.*① **2.** give over (one's power or authority) to another. ¶~ *authority to a representative.*
del·e·ga·tion [dèligéiʃ(ə)n] *n.* **1.** ⓤ the act of delegating; the state of being delegated. **2.** ⓒ a group of delegates or representatives. ⌜for printed.)⌝
de·lete [di(:)lí:t] *vt.* cross out or omit (something written⌟
del·e·te·ri·ous [dèlitíəriəs] *adj.* harmful.
Del·hi [déli] *n.* =New Delhi.
* **de·lib·er·ate** *vt., vi.* [dilíbərèit → *adj.*] think over carefully; discuss. ¶~ *on (over, about)* something⌟ ¶~ *over the question of raising taxes.*①
—*adj.* [dilíbərit] **1.** carefully thought out; done on purpose. ¶*a ~ statement.* **2.** slow and careful. **3.** slow; not hurried. ¶~ *steps.*② ⌜ly; slowly.⌝
* **de·lib·er·ate·ly** [dilíbəritli] *adv.* carefully; intentional-⌟
de·lib·er·a·tion [dilìbəréiʃ(ə)n] *n.* **1.** ⓤ careful thought. **2.** ⓤⓒ discussion. **3.** ⓤ carefulness; slowness.
de·lib·er·a·tive [dilíbərèitiv / -ətiv] *adj.* **1.** related to deliberation or discussion. ¶*a ~ assembly.*① **2.** slow and careful; thoughtful. ▷**de·lib·er·a·tive·ly** [-li] *adv.*
del·i·ca·cy [délikəsi] *n.* ⓤ (pl. **-cies**) **1.** delicate quality or nature; fineness. ¶*the ~ of a flower.*① **2.** sensitiveness. ¶~ *of hearing.* **3.** need of care or tact. ¶*a situation of extreme ~.*② **4.** (sometimes *a ~*) consideration for the feelings of others. **5.** the quality of being easily made ill; weakness. ¶*The child's ~ has always worried his parents.*③ **6.** ⓒ esp. nice food. ¶*all the delicacies of the season.*④
⁑ **del·i·cate** [délikit] *adj.* **1.** pleasing to the taste; mild; dainty. ¶~ *foods.* **2.** soft; tender; gentle. ¶*a ~ blue light.* **3.** finely sensitive; fine or precise in action; exquisite. ¶*a ~ ear for music* / *a ~ machine.* **4.** difficult to handle; requiring great care or skill. ¶*a ~ situation.* **5.** difficult to perceive or describe because of fineness; subtle. ¶~ *differences.* **6.** easily torn, broken, or made ill; frail; feeble; fragile. ¶*a ~ vase* / *~ skin* / *a ~ child.* **7.** mindful of or sensitive to the feelings of others; considerate. ¶~ *attention* / *a ~ refusal.* ▷**del·i·cate·ly** [-li] *adv.*
del·i·ca·tes·sen [dèlikətésn] *n. pl.* **1.** ⓒ (used as *sing.*) a store that sells prepared foods. **2.** ⓤ (*collectively*) cooked meats, smoked fish, cheese, salads, etc.
* **de·li·cious** [dilíʃəs] *adj.* **1.** very pleasing to taste or smell. **2.** very delightful; agreeable. —*n.* (*D-*) ⓒ a

delicious

—名 낙담; 슬픔
⌜도는 Dover⌝
—名 델러웨어 N.B. Del.로 줄임. 수⌟
—他 1. …을 연기하다 2. …을 지체시키다 —自 우물쭈물하다

—名 지연; 지체; 유예 ¶①늦지 않도록 하다/②좋은 일은 일각도 지체하지 말자
熟 즉시, 당장
—形 아주 즐거운; 유쾌한
—名 유쾌함; 기쁨
—名 대표단

—名 대표자 —他 1. …을 대표로 임명(파견)하다 ¶①그들은 그를 그 모임에 대표로 파견했다 2. [권력·권한을] 위임하다

—名 1. 대표 임명(파견) 2. 대표단

—他 …을 삭제하다, 지우다
—形 해로운

—他自 숙고하다, 토론하다 ¶①세금 인상 문제를 토의하다
—形 1. 심사숙고한; 고의의 2. 신중한 3. 침착한; 느린 ¶②느린 발걸음

—副 신중하게; 고의로; 천천히
—名 1. 심사숙고 2. 심의, 토론 3. 신중함; 느림, 완만
—形 1. 심의(토의)되는 ¶①심의회 2. 심의(숙고)를 한 끝의

—名 1. 우아, 우미(優美), 고상함 ¶①꽃의 우아한 모양 2. 민감, 예민 3. 신중함, 미묘함 ¶②아주 미묘한 상황 4. 남에게 대한 세심한 마음씨 5. 가냘픔, 연약함 ¶③아이가 연약해서 그 부모는 언제나 걱정이었다 6. 맛있는 것, 진미 ¶④계절의 온갖 진미

—形 1. [맛·향기가] 감미로운 2. 부드러운; 차분한; 침착한 3. 민감한; 정교한 4. 다루기 힘든; 신중을 요하는 5. 미묘한; 말로 나타낼 수 없는 6. 부서지기 쉬운; 약한; 허약한; 망가지기 쉬운 7. 동정심이 있는

—名 1. 조제(調製) 식품 판매점 2. 조제 식품 (요리를 한 고기·훈제한 생선·치이즈 따위)
—形 1. 맛·향기가 아주 좋은 2. 몹시 기분 좋은 —名 [미국산] 딜리셔스종

kind of red apple with a fine flavor. ▷**de·li·cious·ly** [-li] *adv.* —**de·li·cious·ness** [-nis] *n.*
의 사과

ː de·light [diláit] *n.* **1.** Ⓤ great pleasure. **2.** Ⓒ something that gives great pleasure. ¶*Dancing is her ~.*①
1) *take delight in* (=*amuse oneself with*) *something*. ¶*She takes much ~ in music.*②
2) *to one's delight,* to one's joy.
3) *with delight,* joyfully.
—*vt.* please greatly. ↔grieve ¶*~ the ear* / *I shall be delighted to go with you.*③ —*vi.* have great pleasure. (*~ in something*) ¶*Children ~ in toys.*④
be delighted at (or *with*), be pleased with (something). ¶*He was delighted at the news.*

—ⓝ 1. 큰 기쁨(즐거움) 2. 큰 기쁨을 주는 것 ¶①댄스는 그녀의 즐거움이다
熟 1)…을 즐기다 ¶②그녀는 음악을 매우 즐긴다 2)기쁘게도 3)기꺼이
—他 …을 크게 기뻐하게 하다 ¶③기꺼이 동행하겠읍니다 —自 크게 기뻐하다 ¶④어린이는 장난감을 매우 좋아한다
熟 …을 기뻐하다

de·light·ed [diláitid] *adj.* joyful; glad. ▷**de·light·ed·ly** [-li] *adv.*
—形 기뻐하는, 기쁜

ː de·light·ful [diláitf(u)l] *adj.* **1.** (of a thing) giving joy; very pleasing. ¶*~ books* / *~ holidays*. **2.** (of a person) charming. ⇨USAGE ▷**de·light·ful·ly** [-fuli] *adv.*
—形 1. 기쁨을 주는, 기쁜 2. 애교 있는 USAGE *I am delightful.*이라고는 하지 않음

de·lim·it [di(:)límit] *vt.* mark or define the boundaries of (something); describe. ⌈ing; Ⓒ a boundary.⌉
—他 …의 경계를 정하다

de·lim·i·ta·tion [dilìmitéiʃ(ə)n] *n.* Ⓤ the act of delimit-
—名 경계를 정하기; 경계

de·lin·e·ate [dilínièit] *vt.* trace or draw the outline of (something); describe. ▷**de·lin·e·a·tor** [-ər] *n.*
—他 …의 윤곽을 그리다; 기술(記述)하다

de·lin·e·a·tion [dilìniéiʃ(ə)n] *n.* Ⓤ Ⓒ the act of delineating; description; a sketch.
—名 묘사; 도형, 도해(圖解)

de·lin·quen·cy [dilíŋkwənsi] *n.* (pl. **-cies**) **1.** Ⓤ the neglect of a duty; the habit of behaving unlawfully. **2.** Ⓒ a misdeed; an offense.
—名 1. 의무 태만; 비행(非行)의 습관 2. 비행; 범죄

de·lin·quent [dilíŋkwənt] *adj.* **1.** neglecting a duty; behaving unlawfully. **2.** guilty of an offense. —*n.* Ⓒ a delinquent person; an offender.
—形 1. 의무 태만의; 비행(非行)의 2. 죄가 있는 —名 태만자, 과실자, 범죄자

de·lir·i·a [dilíriə] *n.*pl. of **delirium**. ⌈wildly excited.⌉
de·lir·i·ous [dilíriəs] *adj.* **1.** wandering in mind. **2.**
—形 1. 정신착란의 2. 매우 흥분한

de·lir·i·um [dilíriəm] *n.* (pl. **-lir·i·ums** or **-lir·i·a**) **1.** Ⓤ a temporary disorder of the mind caused by illness. **2.** Ⓒ the state of being wildly excited.
—名 1. 일시적 정신착란[상태] 2. 맹렬한 흥분

ː de·liv·er [dilívər] *vt.* **1.** take (something or someone) to a certain person or place; distribute; convey. ¶*Postmen ~ letters*. **2.** utter; speak formally. ¶*~ a speech*. **3.** strike; launch; pitch; aim. ¶*~ a blow* / *~ a curve to the batter.*① **4.** give; transfer; hand over; yield. ¶*~ oneself to the police*② / *~ him to the police.* **5.** rescue; save; relieve; set free. (*~ someone from* danger, trouble, evil, etc.) ¶*~ him from death*. **6.** assist at the birth of (a child); (*in passive*) give birth to (a child). ¶*The doctor delivered the child.* / *She was delivered of a child.*③ **7.** give forth. ¶*This well delivers much water.*
deliver oneself of, express, utter (one's opinion, etc.).

—他 1. …을 배달하다, [전갈 따위]를 전하다 2. [설교·연설]을 하다, 말하다 3. [타격·공격]을 가하다, 던지다, 투구하다 ¶①타자에게 커어브를 던지다 4. …을 넘겨 주다, 인도하다 ¶②경찰에 자수하다 5. [위험 따위에서] …을 구하다, 구해내다, 해방하다 6. [아이]를 분만시키다, 낳다 ¶③그녀는 아이를 낳았다 7. …을 내다
熟 [의견 따위]를 말하다, 공표하다

de·liv·er·ance [dilív(ə)rəns] *n.* **1.** Ⓤ the act of setting free; the state of being set free; rescue. **2.** Ⓒ a formal opinion.
—名 1. 구조; 석방 2. [의견의] 공표

de·liv·er·er [dilív(ə)rər] *n.* Ⓒ a person who delivers.
—名 구조자; 인도인(引渡人), 배달자

＊ de·liv·er·y [dilív(ə)ri] *n.* (pl. **-er·ies**) **1.** Ⓤ the act of carrying letters, goods, etc. to a person or destination. ¶*special ~.*① **2.** Ⓒ a periodical taking of letters, goods, etc. to a designated person or place. ¶*How many mail deliveries are there in this town every day?*② **3.** Ⓤ Ⓒ the act of handing over. ¶*the ~ of the ransom.*③ **4.** Ⓒ (usu. *sing.*) manner of speaking. ¶*Our teacher's ~ of the speech was excellent.*④ ⌈sides.⌉
—名 1. [편지·물품 따위의] 배달 ¶①속달 2. 정기 배달편 ¶②이 마을에는 매일 몇 번 우편을 배달해 줍니까? 3. 인도 ¶③몸값의 인도 4. 말솜씨 ¶④우리 선생의 연설 솜씨는 훌륭했다

dell [del] *n.* Ⓒ a small valley, usu. with trees on both
Del·phi [délfai, -fi] *n.* an ancient town in Greece.
del·ta [déltə] *n.* Ⓒ **1.** the fourth letter of the Greek al-

—名 [보통 양쪽에 나무가 있는] 작은
—名 고대 그리으스의 도시 ⌈끝자기⌉
—名 1. 델타(그리이스어 자모의 네째

delude [311] **democracy**

phabet (*d* or *ð*). **2.** a delta-shaped (*Δ*) piece of land at the mouth of a river between two or more branches. ¶*the Nile Delta.*①
글자) 2. [강어귀의] 삼각주 ¶①나일강 어귀의 삼각주

de·lude [dilúːd, -ljúːd] *vt.* deceive; mislead. ¶~ *oneself.*①
—他 …을 속이다, 현혹하다 ¶①잘못 「알다」

del·uge [déljudʒ] *n.* ⓒ **1.** a great flood; a heavy fall of rain; a heavy rush of water, fire, tears, words, etc. ¶*After me* (or *us*) *the* ~.① **2.** anything that comes like a flood. ¶*a* ~ *of orders.*② *the Deluge,* (in the Bible) the great flood in the days of Noah. —*vt.* **1.** flood; overflow. **2.** come down on or cover (something or someone) like a flood. ¶*He was deluged with questions.*③
—名 1. 대홍수, 큰 비; 넘치는 것, 범람 ¶①내가 없을 때 홍수가 지든말든 내 알 바가 아니다 2. 쇄도 ¶②주문의 쇄도
熟 노아의 대홍수
—他 1. …에 침수하다; 범람하다 2. …을 압도하다; 홍수처럼 뒤덮다 ¶③그에게 질문이 쇄도했다

de·lu·sion [dilúːʒ(ə)n, -ljúː-] *n.* **1.** Ⓤ the act of deluding; the state of being deluded. **2.** ⓒ a false notion or belief. *under a delusion,* mistaken.
—名 1. 현혹; 기만 2. 잘못된 생각; 망상, 착각
熟 착각을 하고

de·lu·sive [dilúːsiv, -ljúː-] *adj.* misleading; deceptive.
—形 남을 그릇 인도하는; 허위의

de luxe, de·luxe [dəlúks, -lʌ́ks] *adj.* of exceptionally fine quality; luxurious. ¶*a* ~ *hotel.*
—形 특히 질이 좋은; 호화로운; 사치스런

delve [delv] *vi.* do research. (~ *into* old books, etc.) ¶~ *in a library for information.*①
—自 주의 깊게 탐구하다 ¶①도서관에서 자료를 조사하다

dem·a·gog, -gogue [déməgɔːg, -gɑg / -gɔg] *n.* ⓒ a political leader who stirs up the people by speeches that appeal to the feelings instead of the reason.
—名 민중 선동자; 선동 정치가

:de·mand [diménd / -máːnd] *vt.* **1.** ask for (something). ((~ *to do*; ~ *that* …; ~ *something of* or *from*)) ¶~ *his money* / ~ *an answer of him* / *She demanded to know where I lived.* / *He demanded that I* [*should*] *tell him all about the accident.* ⇒USAGE **2.** (of things) need; require. ¶*The work demands great patience.* —*n.* **1.** ⓒ a request as by right or authority; requirement; need; claim. ¶*make a* ~ *for money* (on some-one) / *We have many demands on our time.*① / *I have a* ~ *to make of him.*② **2.** Ⓤⓒ desire to have or get; call. ¶~ *and supply.* / *There is a great* ~ *for typists.*
1) *in demand,* demanded or wanted.
2) *on demand,* upon request for payment.
—他 1. …을 요구하다, 강요하다, 청구하다, 힐문하다 USAGE He demanded me to tell him …처럼 demand는 사람을 목적어로 할 수 없음 2. [사물이] …을 필요로 하다, 요하다
—名 1. [권리로서의] 요구, 청구, 필요로 하는 것 ¶①여러가지로 시간을 빼앗기는 일이 많다/②그에게 요구하고 싶은 게 있다 2. [상품 따위에 대한] 수용, 요구, 판로(販路)
熟 1) 수요가 있는 2) 청구하는 대로

de·mar·cate [díːmɑːrkèit] *vt.* mark and fix the boundary of (lands, etc.); separate.
—他 [지역 따위의] 경계를 정하다; 분리하다

de·mar·ca·tion [dìːmɑːrkéiʃ(ə)n] *n.* Ⓤⓒ the act of demarcating; separation.
—名 경계 [설정]

de·mean¹ [dimíːn] *vt.* make (someone or something) mean or lower in value, quality, dignity, character, etc. ¶*She demeaned herself by begging for food.*
—他 …의 품위를 떨어뜨리다 ¶①그녀는 음식을 비럭질할 만큼 몰락했다

de·mean² [dimíːn] *vt.* behave, conduct. ¶~ *oneself well.*①
—他 처신하다 ¶①훌륭하게 처신하다
—名 행실, 품행, 태도

de·mean·or [dimíːnər] *n.* Ⓤ behavior; conduct.

de·ment·ed [diméntid] *adj.* out of one's mind; mad.
—形 미친, 발광한

de·mer·it [diːmérit] *n.* ⓒ **1.** a defect; a fault. ¶*merits and demerits.*① **2.** a mark against a pupil's record for poor work or bad behavior.
—名 1. 과실; 결점 ¶①장단점; 득실; 공과(功過) 2. [학생의 불량한 성적·행위에 대한] 벌점, 감점

de·mesne [diméin, -míːn] *n.* **1.** Ⓤ (*Law*) possession of land as one's own; land not let to others but held as one's own. **2.** ⓒ a domain; a realm.
—名 1. 《法》 토지의 소유; 자기가 소유하고 있는 토지 2. 영지(領地); [활동] 범위

De·me·ter [dimíːtər] *n.* the Greek goddess of agriculture. ⇒N.B.
—名 농업의 여신 N.B. 로마 신화의 Ceres에 해당

dem·i·god [démigɑ̀d / -gɔ̀d] *n.* ⓒ a god that is partly human.
—名 반신 반인(半神半人)

dem·i·john [démidʒɑ̀n / -dʒɔ̀n] *n.* ⓒ a large bottle enclosed in wicker.
—名 채롱에 든 목이 가는 큰 병

de·mise [dimáiz] *n.* ⓒ death.
—名 죽음, 서거, 사망

de·mo·bi·lize [diːmóubilàiz] *vt.* set (someone) free from military service.
—他 …을 제대시키다

• **de·moc·ra·cy** [dimɑ́krəsi / -mɔ́k-] *n.* (pl. **-cies**) **1.** Ⓤ government either directly by the people or through elected persons. ¶*Democracy is the government of the people, by the people, and for the people.*① **2.** ⓒ a country having such a government.
—名 1. 민주주의 ¶①민주주의란 인민의, 인민에 의한, 인민을 위한 정치이다 2. 민주국가 3. [미국의] 민주당

3. 《D-》 (*U.S.*) the Democratic Party.

* **dem·o·crat** [déməkræ̀t] *n.* [C] **1.** a person who believes or supports democracy. **2.** 《D-》 (*U.S.*) a member of the Democratic Party.
—[名] 1. 민주주의자 2.《美》 민주당원

‡ **dem·o·crat·ic** [dèməkrǽtik] *adj.* **1.** of democracy; based on democracy. **2.** 《D-》 (*U.S.*) of the Democratic Party.
—[形] 1. 민주주의의; 민주적인 2.《美》 민주당의

de·moc·ra·tize [dimákrətàiz / -mɔ́k-] *vt., vi.* make or become democratic. ▷**de·moc·ra·ti·za·tion** [dimàkrətizéiʃ(ə)n / -mɔ̀krətai-] *n.*
—[他][自] 민주화하다; 민주주의화하다

de·mol·ish [dimáliʃ / -mɔ́l-] *vt.* pull down (an old building, etc.); destroy.
—[他] [낡은 건물]을 부수다; 파괴하다

dem·o·li·tion [dèməlíʃ(ə)n] *n.* [U] destruction.
—[名] 파괴

de·mon [díːmən] *n.* [C] **1.** an evil spirit; a devil. **2.** a very wicked person. **3.** a very vigorous or energetic person. ¶*He is a ~ for work.*
—[名] 1. 악령(惡靈); 악마 2. 극악한 사람 3. 귀신 같은 사람; 정력가; 명수

de·mo·ni·ac [dimóuniæ̀k] *adj.* **1.** of a demon; like a demon; devilish. **2.** possessed by a demon. —*n.* [C] a person possessed by a demon.
—[形] 1. 악마의; 악마적인 2. 귀신들린
—[名] 귀신들린 사람

de·mon·stra·ble [démənstrəbl, +*U.S.* dimán-] *adj.* that can be proved or shown clearly by giving examples.
—[形] 증명(논증)할 수 있는

* **dem·on·strate** [démənstrèit] *vt.* **1.** show or prove (something) clearly by giving proof or examples. ¶*Magellan demonstrated that the earth is round.*① **2.** explain (something) by experiment. ¶*~ a new washing machine.* **3.** show (one's feelings) openly. —*vi.* show public feeling by a parade, meeting, etc.
—[他] 1. …을 증명(논증)하다 ¶①마젤란은 지구가 둥글다는 것을 증명했다 2. [실험으로] …을 설명하다; [상품의] 실물 선전을 하다 3. [감정]을 똑똑히 나타내다 —[自] 데모(시위)를 하다

* **dem·on·stra·tion** [dèmənstréiʃ(ə)n] *n.* [U][C] **1.** a clear proof. **2.** an explanation with the use of experiments. **3.** an open show of one's feelings. **4.** a show of public feeling by a parade, meeting, etc.
—[名] 1. 증거; 논증; 증명; 실물 2. 실험, 교수, 실연(實演) 3. [감정의] 표명 4. 시위 운동, 데모

de·mon·stra·tive [dimánstrətiv / -mɔ́n-] *adj.* **1.** showing clearly. **2.** (*Grammar*) pointing out. ¶*a ~ adjective (pronoun).*① **3.** expressing one's feelings freely and openly. ¶*~ greetings.*② —*n.* [C] (*Grammar*) a word that points out. **de·mon·stra·tive·ly** [-li] *adv.*
—[形] 1. 명시하는 2.《文法》 지시하는 ¶①지시 형용사(대명사) 3. 감정을 노골적으로 드러내는 ¶②호들갑스러운 인사 —[名]《文法》 지시사(this, that 따위)

dem·on·stra·tor [démənstrèitər] *n.* [C] **1.** a person who demonstrates. **2.** a person who takes part in a demonstration. **3.** a person who teaches and shows something by demonstration.
—[名] 1. 증명자 2. 데모 참가자 3. 실지 교수자; 실연자(實演者)

de·mor·al·ize [dimɔ́ːrəlàiz, -már- / -mɔ́r-] *vt.* **1.** weaken the morals of (someone or something); corrupt. **2.** weaken the courage of (someone).
—[他] 1. …의 풍기를 문란하게 하다 2. …의 용기를 꺾다

de·mos [díːmɑs / -mɔs] *n.* [U] the common people.
—[名] 민중

De·mos·the·nes [dimásθənìːz / -mɔ́s-] *n.* (384?–322 B.C.) the most famous orator of ancient Greece. ⇒[N.B.]
—[名] 데모스테네스 [N.B.] 고대 그리이스의 대웅변가

de·mur [dimə́ːr] *vi.* (**-murred, -mur·ring**) give a reason against something. 《~ *at* doing something》
—[自] 반대하다, 이의를 제기하다

de·mure [dimjúər] *adj.* **1.** serious; modest. **2.** assuming the air of being serious or modest. ▷**de·mure·ly** [-li] *adv.* —**de·mure·ness** [-nis] *n.*
—[形] 1. 진지한 2. 얌전(점잔)빼는

* **den** [den] *n.* [C] **1.** a place where a wild animal lives. **2.** a place where thieves live. **3.** a small, dirty room. **4.** a quite, private room for reading and work.
—[名] 1. 야수의 굴 2. 도둑의 소굴 3. 더러운 작은 방 4. [아늑한] 사실(私室)

de·ni·al [dináiəl] *n.* [U][C] **1.** a statement that something is not true. ↔affirmation **2.** refusing to acknowledge; refusing a request. ↔admittance **3.** getting along without things that one wants.
1) ***give a denial to; make a denial of,*** refuse.
2) ***take no denial,*** do not accept a refusal.
—[名] 1. 부정 2. 부인; 거절 3. 극기(克己)
[熟] 1)…을 거부하다 2)싫다는 말을 못하게 하다

den·im [dénim] *n.* [U] heavy, coarse cotton cloth.
—[名] 두꺼운 무명 천, 데님

den·i·zen [dénizn] *n.* [C] **1.** (*poetic*) an inhabitant. ¶*Birds are denizens of the forest.*① **2.** a foreigner who is given certain rights. **3.** a foreign word, plant, or animal that has been naturalized.
—[名] 1. 주민 ¶①새들은 숲의 주민이다 2. 거류 외국인 3. 외래어, 외래 동(식)물

Den·mark [dénmɑːrk] *n.* a small country in northern Europe. ⇒[N.B.]
—[名] 덴마아크 [N.B.] 수도 Copenhagen

D

de·nom·i·nate [dinámineìt / -nɔ́m-] *vt.* give a name to (someone); name (someone) as something.
—[他] …에게 명명하다; …을 …이라고 부르다

de·nom·i·na·tion [dinàminéiʃ(ə)n / -nɔ̀m-] *n.* [C] **1.** a name. **2.** a religious group or sect. **3.** a kind of unit, as of money, etc. ¶*coins of small denominations.*①
—[名] 1. 명칭 2. 종파; 교파 3. [화폐 따위의] 단위 명칭 ¶①잔돈

de·nom·i·na·tion·al [dinàminéiʃən(ə)l / -nɔ̀m-] *adj.* of a religious group.
—[形] 종파의

de·nom·i·na·tor [dinámineìtər / -nɔ́m-] *n.* [C] (*Mathematics*) the number below the line in a fraction. ⇒[N.B.]
—[名] 《數》 분모 [N.B.] 분자는 numerator

de·note [dinóut] *vt.* be the sign of (something); indicate; mean ↔connote ¶*A fever denotes sickness.*
—[他] …의 표지가 되다; …을 나타내다; 의미하다

de·noue·ment [deinú:mã:ŋ] *n.* [C] the end of a play, story, etc. where everything is made clear.
—[名] [연극·소설 따위의] 대단원, 종말

de·nounce [dináuns] *vt.* **1.** speak openly against (something); accuse. ¶*~ someone to the authorities.*① / *He was denounced as a coward.* **2.** give notice of the termination of (a treaty, etc.). ▷**de·nounc·er** [-ər] *n.*
—[他] 1. …을 공공연히 비난하다; 고발(고소)하다 ¶①…을 당국에 고발하다 2. [조약 따위의] 종결을 통고하다

***dense** [dens] *adj.* **1.** thick; crowded. ↔sparse ¶*a ~ fog.*① **2.** stupid; dull. ▷**dense·ly** [-li] *adv.*
—[形] 1. 밀집한, 조밀한; 짙은 ¶①짙은 안개 2. 우둔한, 어리석은

den·si·ty [dénsiti] *n.* (pl. **-ties**) **1.** [U] the state of being dense. ¶*the ~ of a forest.*① **2.** [U][C] (*Physics*) the quantity of matter in a unit of volume.
—[名] 1. 조밀; 밀집 상태 ¶①빽빽한 숲 2. 《理》 밀도, 농도

dent [dent] *n.* [C] a hollow made by a blow or by pressure. —*vt.* make a dent or dents in (something). —*vi.* become dented; get dented.
—[名] 움푹 팬 곳, 눌린 자국 —[他] …을 움푹 들어가게 하다 —[自] 움푹 들어가다

den·tal [déntl] *adj.* of or for the teeth or a dentist's work. ¶*a ~ office*① / *~ sounds.*② —*n.* (*Phonetics*) [C] a dental sound.
—[形] 이(齒)의; 칫과의 ¶①칫과 병원 /②치음(齒音) —[名] 《音聲》 치음([t] [d] [θ] [ð] 따위)

den·ti·frice [déntifrìs] *n.* [U] paste or powder for cleaning the teeth.
—[名] 치약, 치마분

den·tist [déntist] *n.* [C] a doctor whose work is to take care of the teeth.
—[名] 칫과 의사

den·tist·ry [déntistri] *n.* [U] the art or occupation of a dentist.
—[名] 칫과의술(업)

de·nude [din(j)ú:d / dinjú:d] *vt.* make (someone) bare; strip (something) of covering. ¶*~ someone of clothing*① / *Most trees are denuded of their leaves in winter.*②
—[他] …을 벌거벗기다; …에서 벗겨내다 ¶①…에서 옷을 벗기다/②대개의 나무들은 겨울에 잎이 다 떨어진다

de·nun·ci·a·tion [dinʌ̀nsiéiʃ(ə)n] *n.* [U][C] the act of denouncing.
—[名] 공공연한 비난; 고발; 조약의 종결 통고

⁑**de·ny** [dinái] *vt.* (**-nied**) **1.** say that something is not true. 《~ *doing*; ~ *that* …》 ↔affirm ¶*We cannot ~ the fact.* / *He denied having said so.*① / *I ~ that his statement is true.* **2.** refuse to acknowledge. ↔admit ¶*She denied her signature.*② **3.** refuse. ¶*~ oneself*③ / *He denies his son nothing.*④ / *Justice must not be denied to anyone.*
—[他] 1. …을 부정하다 ¶①그는 그렇게 말하지 않았다고 말했다 2. …을 부인하다 ¶②그녀는 자기의 서명임을 부인했다 3. …을 거부하다 ¶③자제하다/④그는 아들에게는 무엇이고 거절을 못한다

⁑**de·part** [dipá:rt] *vi.* **1.** leave; start. ↔arrive ¶*~ from one's home*① / *This train departs at 3 p.m. from Tokyo Station.* **2.** change. 《~ *from* old customs, etc.》 **3.** die.
depart [*from*] *this life,* die.
—[自] 1. 떠나다; 출발하다 ¶①고향을 떠나다 2. …에서 벗어나다 3. 죽다
[熟] 죽다

de·part·ed [dipá:rtid] *adj.* **1.** dead. **2.** gone; past.
—[形] 1. 죽은 2. 지나간; 과거의

⁑**de·part·ment** [dipá:rtmənt] *n.* [C] a separate part of a business, government, university, etc.; a division. ¶*the accounting ~*① / *the fire ~*② / *the ~ of economics*③ / *the men's clothing ~.*④
—[名] [회사·관청·대학 따위의] 부문 ¶①회계과 /②소방서 /③경제학부/④[백화점의] 신사복부

de·part·men·tal [dipà:rtméntl / dì:pa:rt-] *adj.* of a department.
—[形] 각 부문의

department store [-⌐- ⌐] *n.* a big store that sells many kinds of articles arranged in separate departments. ⇒[N.B.]
—[名] 백화점 [N.B.] 영국에서는 [big] stores라 함

***de·par·ture** [dipá:rtʃər] *n.* [C][U] **1.** the act or fact of leaving. ↔arrival ¶*the board showing arrivals and departures of buses.*① **2.** a change. ¶*a ~ from ancient ways.*② **3.** [U] (*archaic*) death.
1) ***new departure,*** a new course of action or thought.
2) ***on one's departure,*** when one starts.
3) ***take one's departure,*** start.
—[名] 1. 출발, 발차 ¶①버스의 발착을 알리는 게시판 2. 변경 ¶②구습을 버리기 3. 죽음
[熟] 1)새 방침, 신기축(新機軸) 2)출발할 때에 3)출발하다

D

depend

:de·pend [dipénd] *vi.* ((usu. with *on* or *upon*)) ⇒*depend on* (*upon*)
 1) *depend on* (or *upon*), ⓐ trust and count on. ¶*We can ~ on him.* ⓑ rely on (someone or something) as a source of help or supply. ¶*They are men to be depended upon.* / *I ~ on you for support.* ⓒ be influenced or determined by something else. ((*~ on how* (or *what*, etc.) ...)) ¶*Our trip depends upon the weather.* / *That depends on how you do it.*① ⇒USAGE
 2) *depend upon it,* ((used at the beginning or end of a sentence)): You can be quite certain. ¶*The war will ruin the country, ~ upon it.*②
 3) *That depends* (or *It* [*all*] *depends*), (*colloq.*) It is impossible to say with certainty until certain other facts are known.

de·pend·a·ble [dipéndəbl] *adj.* reliable; trustworthy.
de·pend·ant [dipéndənt] *n.* ⓒ a person who gets help or support from another.
· **de·pend·ence** [dipéndəns] *n.* Ⓤ **1.** the state of being a dependant. ↔independence ¶*He lives in ~ upon his uncle.*① **2.** trust. ¶*I have ~ on a person.*② **3.** the fact of being controlled by something else.
de·pend·en·cy [dipéndənsi] *n.* ⓒ (pl. *-cies*) a country controlled by another country.
· **de·pend·ent** [dipéndənt] *adj.* **1.** getting help or support from another. ((*~ on* or *upon*)) ↔independent ¶*He is ~ on his uncle.*① **2.** controlled by something else. ((*~* / ⎱*on* or *upon*)⎰
 ——*n.* =dependant.
de·pict [dipíkt] *vt.* show (something) with a picture; describe (something) in words. ▷**de·pict·er** [-ər] *n.*
de·pic·tion [dipíkʃ(ə)n] *n.* ⓤⓒ the act of depicting; the state of being depicted. ⎡ergy, fund, etc.⎤
de·plete [diplíːt] *vt.* empty; use up; exhaust, as of en-⎦
de·ple·tion [diplíːʃ(ə)n] *n.* Ⓤ the act of depleting; the state of being depleted.
de·plor·a·ble [diplɔ́ːrəbl] *adj.* to be deplored; lamentable; regrettable. ((*~ to someone*)) ¶*a ~ accident.*
de·plor·a·bly [diplɔ́ːrəbli] *adv.* in a deplorable manner.
de·plore [diplɔ́ːr] *vt.* **1.** be very sorry about (something); grieve over (something); lament. **2.** express regret for (something).
de·pop·u·late [diːpɑ́pjuleit / -pɔ́p-] *vt.* destroy or decrease the population of (a country, etc.).
de·pop·u·la·tion [diːpɑ̀pjuléiʃ(ə)n / -pɔ̀p-] *n.* Ⓤ the act of depopulating; the state of being depopulated.
de·port [dipɔ́ːrt] *vt.* **1.** force (someone) to leave the country; banish. ((*~ a spy, a criminal,* etc. *from* a country, etc.)) **2.** behave (oneself) in a particular manner. ¶*~ oneself like a gentleman.*①
de·por·ta·tion [dìːpɔːrtéiʃ(ə)n] *n.* Ⓤ the act of deporting; the state of being deported.
de·port·ment [dipɔ́ːrtmənt] *n.* Ⓤ behavior.
de·pose [dipóuz] *vt.* **1.** put (someone) out of a high office; remove (someone) from a throne. **2.** (*Law*) declare under oath. ((*~ that* ...)) ¶*He deposed that he had seen the prisoner on that day.*① ——*vi.* give evidence. ((*~ to something*))
· **de·pos·it** [dipázit / -pɔ́z-] *vt.* **1.** put (something) down; leave (something) lying. ¶*~ a book on the desk* / *The flood deposited a lot of mud and sand on the streets of the city.*① **2.** put (something) in a place for safekeeping. ¶*~ money in a bank.* **3.** give (a sum of money) in advance as part payment. **4.** (of birds, insects, etc.) lay. ¶*~ eggs in the ground.*

deposit

——⾃ ⇨ depend on (or upon)

🕮 1)ⓐ[…을] 신뢰하다, 신용하다 ⓑ […을] 의지(기대)하다 ⓒ[…에] 달려 있다, …나름이다 ¶①그것은 네가 하기 나름이다 USAGE 구어에서는 how 따위의 앞의 전치사가 생략됨 2)틀림 없이, 반드시 3)((口))그건 사정(때와 경우)에 달렸다

——⽥ 의지할 수 있는; 신용할 만한
——⾃ 하인; 식객(食客); 부양가족

——⾃ 1. 의존, 종속상태 ¶①그는 아저씨에 기대어 살고 있다 2. 신뢰 ¶② 남을 신뢰하다 3. 다른 것에 좌우되기

——⾃ 속국(屬國)

——⽥ 1. 남의 도움을 받는 ¶①그는 아저씨의 신세를 지고 있다 2. 다른 것에 좌우되는

——⽥ …을 그림으로 나타내다; 말로서 술하다
——⾃ 묘사, 서술

——⽥ …을 비우다; 고갈시키다
——⾃ 소모, 고갈

——⽥ 통탄스러운, 슬픈; 유감인

——⽥ 통탄스럽게
——⽥ 1. …을 슬퍼하다, 통탄하다 2. …을 유감스럽게 생각하다

——⽥ …의 주민을 절멸(絶滅)시키다; …의 주민을 줄이다
——⾃ 주민 이주; 인구 감소

——⽥ 1. …을 추방하다 2. 처신하다 ¶ ①신사답게 행동하다

——⾃ 국외 추방

——⾃ 처신, 행동
——⽥ 1. …을 면직하다; 퇴위시키다 2. (法) 선서하고 …을 증언하다 ¶①그는 그날 피고를 만났다고 증언했다
——⾃ 증언하다

——⽥ 1. …을 놓다; 퇴적(침전)시키다 ¶①홍수로 도시의 거리에는 많은 진흙과 모래가 쌓였다 2. …을 맡기다 3. [계약금]을 치르다 4. [알]을 낳다

deposition [315] depth

—*n.* ⓒ **1.** something left lying. ¶*a ~ of mud and sand.* **2.** money put in a bank; part of a payment made in advance. **3.** (*Geology*) a mass of some mineral in rocks or in the ground. ⌈*in a bank.*⓪
on deposit, in a bank. ¶*have* (or *place*) *money on ~*

de·po·si·tion [dèpəzíʃ(ə)n] *n.* **1.** ⓤ the act of putting someone out of office; removal from a throne. **2.** (*Law*) ⓤⓒ a declaration or statement made under oath. ⌈posits money in a bank, etc.

de·pos·i·tor [dipázitər / -pózitə] ⓒ a person who de-
de·pos·i·to·ry [dipázitɔ̀:ri / -pózit(ə)ri] *n.* ⓒ (pl. **-ries**) a place where a thing is put for safekeeping; a store-house.

de·pot [díːpou, dép- / dép-] *n.* ⓒ **1.** (*U. S.*) a railroad station; a bus station. **2.** a house for storing something; (*Military*) a place where military supplies are stored.

de·prave [dipréiv] *vt.* make (something) bad; corrupt.
¶*~ someone's character.*⓪

de·praved [dipréivd] *adj.* immoral; wicked; corrupt.

de·prav·i·ty [diprǽviti] *n.* (pl. **-ties**) ⓤ vice; corruption; ⓒ a corrupt or wicked act.

dep·re·cate [déprikèit] *vt.* protest or speak against (something); disapprove. ¶*We always ~ war.*

dep·re·ca·tion [dèprikéiʃ(ə)n] *n.* ⓤⓒ the act of deprecating; a protest made against something.

dep·re·ca·to·ry [déprikətɔ̀:ri / -kətəri] *adj.* deprecating;
be deprecatory of, deprecate. ⌈protesting.

de·pre·ci·ate [diprí:ʃièit] *vt.* **1.** make (something) less in value. **2.** say or think of (something) that it has little value. ¶*~ another's work*⓪ / *Don't ~ yourself.*②
—*vi.* become less in value. ↔appreciate

de·pre·ci·a·tion [diprì:ʃiéiʃ(ə)n] *n.* ⓤⓒ **1.** the act of depreciating. ↔appreciation ¶*the ~ of the yen.* **2.** the act of speaking slightingly of someone.

de·pre·ci·a·to·ry [diprí:ʃiətɔ̀:ri / -ət(ə)ri] *adj.* tending to lessen the value of (something); slighting.

dep·re·da·tion [dèpridéiʃ(ə)n] *n.* ⓤⓒ **1.** robbery; theft. **2.** (usu. *pl.*) the act of robbing.

de·press [diprés] *vt.* **1.** make the activity or power of (something) less; weaken. ¶*Trade is depressed.*⓪ **2.** make (someone) sad or gloomy; make (someone) low
▷**de·press·ing·ly** [-iŋli] *adv.* ⌊in spirits.

de·pressed [diprést] *adj.* **1.** sad; gloomy; discouraged. ¶*I feel ~.*⓪ **2.** with a low volume of business activity.

de·press·ing [diprésiŋ] *adj.* tending to depress; gloomy.

• **de·pres·sion** [dipréʃ(ə)n] *n.* **1.** ⓤ sadness; low spirits; melancholy. ¶*nervous ~*⓪ / *in a state of deep ~.* **2.** ⓒ the reduction of business activity; a bad state of trade. **3.** ⓒ a low place; a hollow. **4.** ⓒ a lowering of the atmospheric pressure.

dep·ri·va·tion [dèprivéiʃ(ə)n] *n.* ⓤⓒ **1.** the act of depriving; the state of being deprived. **2.** loss.

• **de·prive** [dipráiv] *vt.* take something away from (someone) by force; dispossess. (*~ someone of*) ¶*~ a king of his power* / *He was deprived of his sight by the traffic*
dept. 1. department. **2.** deputy. ⌊*accident.*⓪

: depth [depθ] *n.* ⓤ **1.** the quality of being deep; deepness. **2.** ⓤⓒ the distance from top to bottom. ¶*a foot in ~.*⓪ **3.** ⓤⓒ the distance from front to back. **4.** ⓒ a deep place. **5.** (usu. *pl.*) ⓒ the deepest part; a chasm; ·the sea. ¶*in the depth*[*s*] *of despair.*② **6.** the most central part; middle. ¶*in the ~ of winter.* **7.** deepness of thought; profoundness; intensity. ¶*a book of no great ~.*⓪ **8.** lowness of pitch; intensity of color, etc.

—名 **1.** 퇴적물 **2.** 은행 예금; 계약금, 보증금 **3.** 〔地質〕 광상(鑛床)

「다(하다)
熟 예금되어 ¶②은행에 예금되어 있
—名 **1.** 면직; 폐위 **2.** 〔法〕 증언; 구술서(口述書)

—名 〔은행〕 예금자; 공탁자(供託者)
—名 보관소; 창고

—名 **1.** 〔美〕 정거장; 버스 정류장 **2.** 〔軍〕 저장소; 물자 집적소

—他 …을 악화시키다; 타락시키다 ¶①…의 성격을 타락시키다
—形 타락한; 불량한
—名 타락; 비행

—他 …에 항의하다, …을 비난하다

—名 항의, 비난

—形 비난(불찬성)의; 변명조의
熟 비난하다
—他 **1.** …의 가치를 떨어뜨리다 **2.** …을 얕보다, 멸시하다 ¶①남의 일을 깔보다/②스스로 자신을 낮추다 —自 가치가 떨어지다
—名 **1.** 하락, 감가(減價) **2.** 경멸, 멸시

—形 하락 경향의, 경멸하는, 멸시하는, 감가(減價)의
—名 **1.** 약탈, 강탈 **2.** 약탈 행위, 파괴

—他 **1.** …을 약하게 하다; 부진하게 만들다 ¶①장사는 불황이다 **2.** …의 기운(의기)을 떨어뜨리다

—形 **1.** 침울한, 풀이 죽은 ¶①기분이 좋지 않다 **2.** 불경기의, 부진한
—形 우울한, 의기소침한
—名 **1.** 우울, 의기소침 ¶①신경쇠약 **2.** 불경기, 불황, 경기 후퇴 **3.** 움푹한 곳(땅) **4.** 저기압

—名 **1.** 박탈, 면직 **2.** 손실

—他 …을 박탈하다; …에서 〔물건〕을 빼앗다 ¶①그는 교통사고로 실명했다

—名 **1.** 깊음, 깊숙함 **2.** 깊이 ¶①깊이 1피이트 **3.** 안 길이 **4.** 깊은 곳; **5.** 깊이 갈라진 틈; 바다 ¶②실망의 구렁텅이에 **6.** 중심지, 한가운데 **7.** 심원, 심각함; 강도(强度) ¶③그다지 두껍지 않은 책 **8.** 〔음의〕 저조(低調), 〔빛깔의〕 농도

depth bomb [316] **derive**

1) *beyond* (or *out of*) *one's depth,* ⓐ in water too deep for one. ⓑ trying to study something that is too difficult.
2) *in depth,* completely.
depth bomb [´ ´] *n.* =depth charge.
depth charge [´ ´] *n.* a bomb dropped from a ship or airplane into the sea and arranged to explode at a certain depth to destroy enemy submarines.
dep·u·ta·tion [dèpjutéiʃ(ə)n] *n.* **1.** Ⓤ the act of deputing. **2.** Ⓒ a group of persons given the power to act for others.
de·pute [dipjúːt] *vt.* **1.** appoint (another) to do something for oneself or to act in one's place. 《~ someone *to do*》 **2.** give (one's work, etc.) to another.
dep·u·tize [dépjutàiz] *vi.* act for someone. —*vt.* (chiefly *U.S.*) appoint (someone) as a deputy; appoint (another) to act in one's place.
* **dep·u·ty** [dépjuti] *n.* Ⓒ (pl. **-ties**) **1.** a person appointed to act for another. ¶*by ~.*① **2.** 《*D-*》 an elected person in a parliament, esp. in France. ¶*a member of the Chamber of Deputies.*② —*adj.* acting as a deputy. ¶*the First Deputy Premier*③ / *a Deputy Mayor*④ / *a Deputy Speaker.*⑤
de·rail [diːréil / di(ː)-] *vt.* (usu. in *passive*) make (a train, etc.) go off the rails. ¶*be* (or *get*) *derailed.*① —*vi.* run off the rails.
de·rail·ment [diːréilmənt / di(ː)-] *n.* ⓊⒸ the act of derailing; the state of being derailed.
de·range [diréindʒ] *vt.* throw (someone) into confusion; make (someone) mad; disorder; disturb. ¶*She is deranged with worry.*① 《ance; insanity.》
de·range·ment [diréindʒmənt] *n.* Ⓤ disorder; disturb-
der·by [dáːrbi / dάːbi] *n.* Ⓒ (pl. **-bies**) (chiefly *U.S.*) a stiff felt hat with a round top and narrow brim. (cf. *Brit.* bowler) →N.B.
Der·by¹ [dáːrbi / dάːbi] *n.* a city in central England.
Der·by² [dáːrbi / dάːbi] *n.* Ⓒ (pl. **-bies**) **1.** 《*the ~*》 a famous annual horse race, at Epsom in England. **2.** any horse race of similar importance.
der·e·lict [dérilìkt] *adj.* **1.** abandoned; left; deserted. **2.** (*U.S.*) failing in one's duty; neglecting. —*n.* Ⓒ **1.** a ship abandoned at sea. **2.** a worthless person. **3.** (*U.S.*) a person who neglects his duty.
der·e·lic·tion [derilíks(ə)n] *n.* Ⓤ **1.** neglect of duty. **2.** the act of abandoning; the state of being deserted.
de·ride [diráid] *vt.* make fun of (someone); laugh at (someone); jeer. ▷**de·rid·ing·ly** [-iŋli] *adv.*
de·ri·sion [diríʒ(ə)n] *n.* **1.** Ⓤ the act of deriding; the state of being derided; ridicule; contempt. ¶*be in ~*① / *have* (or *hold*) *someone in ~*② / *They brought him into* ③ **2.** Ⓒ an object of derision.
de·ri·sive [diráisiv] *adj.* deriding.
de·ri·sive·ly [diráisivli] *adv.* in a derisive manner.
der·i·va·tion [dèrivéiʃ(ə)n] *n.* **1.** Ⓤ the act of deriving; the state of being derived. **2.** Ⓤ the source; the origin. **3.** ⒸⓊ the origination and development of a word.
de·riv·a·tive [dirívətiv] *adj.* gotten from something else; not original. —*n.* Ⓒ **1.** something derived. **2.** a word derived from another. ▷**de·riv·a·tive·ly** [-li] *adv.*
: **de·rive** [diráiv] *vt.* **1.** get; draw; receive. 《~ *something from*》 ¶~ *much pleasure from books.* **2.** trace (a word, etc.) from its origin. **3.** get knowledge of (something) by reasoning; deduce; infer. **4.** draw (one chemical compound) from another. —*vi.* come; originate. 《~ *from something*》 ¶*a word derived from*

熟 1)ⓐ깊어서 키가 모자라는 ⓑ이해할 수 없는 2)철저하게

—ⓝ [잠수함 폭파용] 수중 폭뢰

—ⓝ 1. 대리[행위], 대리 위임 2. 대리자; 대표단

—ⓥ 1. …을 자기의 대리로 지명하다 2. [일 따위의 대행]을 위임하다

—ⓥ 대리하다 —ⓥ 《美》…을 대리로 임명하다

—ⓝ 1. 대리, 대표 ¶①대리로 2. [프랑스 등지의] 국회 의원 ¶②[프랑스의] 하원의원 —ⓐ 대리의, 부(副)… ¶③ [소련의] 제1부수상/④부시장/⑤[의회의] 부의장

—ⓥ …을 탈선시키다 ¶①탈선하다
—ⓥ 탈선하다

—ⓝ 탈선

—ⓥ …을 혼란하게 하다, 미치게 하다 ¶①그녀는 걱정으로 미칠 지경이다

—ⓝ 무질서, 교란, 혼란; [정신의] 착란
—ⓝ 《美》중산모자 N.B. 더어비 경마에서 쓰는 예서

—ⓝ 더어비
—ⓝ 1. 더어비 경마(매년 영국 Epsom 에서 거행) 2. [그 밖의] 대경마

—ⓐ 1. 버림받은, 유기(遺棄)된 2. 《美》 직무태만의 —ⓝ 1. 해상에 버린 배 2. 버림받은 사람, 낙오자 3. 직무 태만자

—ⓝ 1. 직무태만 2. 포기, 유기

—ⓥ …을 조소하다, 우롱하다, 비웃다

—ⓝ 1. 조소, 비웃음 ¶①웃음거리가 되고 있다/②…을 비웃다/③그들은 그를 웃음거리로 만들었다 2. 웃음거리

—ⓐ 비웃는, 조롱하는
—ⓐ 비웃듯이, 조소하여
—ⓝ 1. 끌어내기, 유도(誘導) 2. 유래, 기원(起源) 3. [낱말의] 파생

—ⓐ 파생의, 유도적인, 유래하는 —ⓝ 1. 파생물 2. 파생어

—ⓥ 1. …을 끌어내다, 얻다 2. …의 유래를 찾다, 어원을 밝히다 3. …을 추론(推論)하다 4. …을 유도하다 —ⓥ 오다, 유래하다

Greek. ▷**de·riv·a·ble** [-əbl] *adj.*

der·o·gate [dérəgèit] *vi.* **1.** take away fame, etc.; detract. ⟪~ *from* something⟫ **2.** become worse.
—[自] 1. 명성(품위 · 가치)을 떨어뜨리다, 훼손하다 2. 타락하다

der·o·ga·tion [dèrəgéiʃ(ə)n] *n.* [U] **1.** the act of lessening power, reputation, etc. **2.** the state of becoming worse.
—[名] 1. [권력·명성 따위의] 손상, 저하 2. 타락

de·rog·a·to·ry [dirágətɔ̀:ri / dirɔ́gət(ə)ri] *adj.* tending to lessen the value of; detracting from. ¶*His conduct is ~ to his dignity.* ▷**de·rog·a·to·ri·ly** [-li] *adv.*
—[形] 손상시키는, 품위(가치)를 떨어뜨리는; 경멸적인

der·rick [dérik] *n.* [C] **1.** a large machine for lifting and moving heavy objects; a crane. ⇒fig. **2.** a framework like a tower, over an oil well, etc., to support drilling machinery.
—[名] 1. 데릭 기중기 2. [유전 따위의] 철탑, 유전탑

〔derrick 1.〕

der·vish [də́:rviʃ] *n.* [C] a Mohammedan monk.
—[名] 회교의 탁발승

des·cant *vi.* [diskǽnt → *n.*] **1.** talk at great length about something. ⟪~ *on* or *upon* something⟫ **2.** sing. —*n.* [déskænt] [C] a melody or song; a melody to be played or sung with another melody.
—[自] 1. 장황하게 이야기하다, 자세히 설명하다 2. 노래하다 —[名] 가락, 노래; 반주의 선율

:de·scend [disénd] *vi.* **1.** come or go down; slope downwards. ↔ascend ¶~ *from the hilltop* / *The road descended steeply.*① **2.** (of property, qualities, rights) be inherited; come from earlier times. ¶~ *from father to son.* **3.** lower oneself; stoop. ¶*They were surprised that he descended to cheating.*② **4.** go from generalities to particulars, as in a discussion. ¶~ *to details.*
—*vt.* go down. ↔ascend ¶~ *the hill.*
1) ***be descended from,*** have (someone) as one's ancestor. ¶*Are men descended from apes?*
2) ***descend on*** (or ***upon***)**,** make a sudden attack or visit. ¶*His anger descended on my head.*③
—[自] 1. 내려오다(가다); 아래로 경사지다 ¶①길은 가파르게 아래로 비탈지고 있었다 2. 상속되다; 유전하다 3. 몸을 낮추다, 몸을 굽혀 …하다 ¶②그가 사기를 한 것에 모두 놀랐다 4. [개론에서 각론으로] 옮기다, 세부점을 논하게 되다
—[他] …을 내려가다
[熟] 1)…의 출신(자손)이다 2)갑자기 …을 습격하다; 방문하다 ¶③그의 노여움이 내 머리 위에 떨어졌다

·de·scend·ant [diséndənt] *n.* [C] a person descended from a certain family, group, etc. ↔ancestor —*adj.* descending; coming down.
—[名] 자손 —[形] 내려가는

·de·scent [disént] *n.* **1.** [U][C] the act of coming down or going down. ↔ascent **2.** [C] a down slope. **3.** [U] the state or fact of being handed down from parent to child. **4.** [U] a family line. ¶*by* ~① / *a man of high* ~.② **5.** [U] ancestry. ¶*lineal* ~.③ **6.** [C] a sudden attack. ¶*make a ~ on the coast.*④
—[名] 1. 강하 2. 내리막길 3. 상속, 유전, 세습 4. 가문, 가계 ¶①태생은/②명문 출신 5. 자손 ¶③직계 비속(卑屬) 6. 습격 ¶④해안을 습격하다

de·scrib·a·ble [diskráibəbl] *adj.* that can be described.
—[形] 묘사할 수 있는

:de·scribe [diskráib] *vt.* **1.** tell or write about (something or someone); picture (something) in words. ¶*He describes himself as a poet.* **2.** draw; trace. ¶~ *a circle.*
—[他] 1. [특징 따위]를 말하다; 묘사하다, …을 …이라고 평하다 2. [도형 따위]를 그리다

:de·scrip·tion [diskrípʃ(ə)n] *n.* **1.** [U][C] the act of describing; an account. ¶*be beyond* ~① / *Give me a ~ of the thief.*② **2.** [C] a kind; a sort; a class. ¶*motorcars of every* ~ / *We have no food of any* ~.
—[名] 1. 기술(記述), 서술, 묘사; 설명서, 몽타아즈 ¶①형용할 수 없다/②도둑의 인상을 설명해 주시오 2. 종류, 종목, 등급

de·scrip·tive [diskríptiv] *adj.* describing. ¶*a ~ style*① / *a ~ adjective*② / *This novel is well ~ of the characters.* ▷**de·scrip·tive·ly** [-li] *adv.* —**de·scrip·tive·ness** [-nis] *n.*
—[形] 기술(서술)적인, 묘사의, 기사의 ¶①기술적인 문체/②서술 형용사

de·scry [diskrái] *vt.* (**-scried**) catch sight of (something) in the distance.
—[他] 멀리서(어렴풋이) …을 알아보다

des·e·crate [désikrèit] *vt.* treat (a holy thing) without respect. ↔consecrate
—[他] …의 신성함을 더럽히다, …을 모독하다

des·e·cra·tion [dèsikréiʃ(ə)n] *n.* [U] the act of desecrating.
—[名] 신성 모독

:des·ert¹ [dézərt] *n.* [C] a dry and sandy region, usu. without trees or water; a wilderness.
—[名] 사막, 황야
—*adj.* **1.** like a desert; having no plants. **2.** not inhabited or cultivated; wild. ¶*a ~ island.*①
—[形] 1. 사막 같은, 불모의 2. 무인의, 쓸쓸한 ¶①무인도

:de·sert² [dizə́:rt] *vt.* leave; abandon; give up. ¶*The streets were deserted.*① / *His courage deserted him.*② / *He deserted his post.* —*vi.* leave military service without
—[他] …을 버리고 돌보지 않다, 버려두다, 유기하다 ¶①거리에는 사람 그림자 하나 없었다/②그는 용기가 사라졌

desert

permission; run away from duty. 《~ *from something*》 ¶~ *to the enemy.*①

de·sert³ [dizə́:rt] *n.* **1.** ⓤ the fact of deserving reward or punishment. **2.** ⓒ 《usu. *pl.*》 suitable reward or punishment. ¶*get* (or *meet with*) *one's deserts.*① **3.** ⓒ one's valuable deed; a merit.

de·sert·ed [dizə́:rtid] *adj.* **1.** abandoned; forsaken. **2.** without any person living in it. ¶*a ~ village.*

de·sert·er [dizə́:rtər] *n.* ⓒ **1.** a person who abandons. **2.** a person who runs away from duty without permission, such as a soldier etc.

de·ser·tion [dizə́:rʃ(ə)n] *n.* ⓤⓒ the act of deserting; the state or fact of being deserted; the act or crime running away from duty without permission.

⁑ de·serve [dizə́:rv] *vt.* have a right to (do something); be worthy of (something); earn. 《~ *to do*》 ¶~ *attention* / *He deserves his promotion.* —*vi.* be worthy. ¶*He deserves well of his country.*① ▷ **de·serv·er** [-ər] *n.*

de·serv·ed·ly [dizə́:rvidli] *adv.* according to what is deserved; justly, properly.

de·serv·ing [dizə́:rviŋ] *adj.* worthy of; worth helping. ¶*He is deserving of trust.*① ▷ **de·serv·ing·ly** [-li] *adv.*

des·ic·cate [désikèit] *vt.* dry (something) thoroughly. ¶*desiccated milk.*① —*vi.* become completely dry.

⁑ de·sign [dizáin] *vt.* **1.** sketch a pattern or outline for (something). ¶~ *a new car.* **2.** plan; intend. 《~ *to do*; ~ *that …*》 ¶*The writer designed a good plot.* / *She designed to be a teacher.* **3.** destine; purpose. ¶*They designed their daughter for* (or *to be*) *an actress.* / *The room was designed to be* (or *as*) *my study.*① —*vi.* make drawings, sketches, or plans; plan and fashion the form of an object. ¶*She designs for dressmakers.* —*n.* **1.** ⓒ a pattern; a draft; a sketch; an outline. ¶*a ~ of flowers.* **2.** ⓤ idea; plan; artistic invention. ¶*the art of ~* / *This picture is poor in ~.* **3.** ⓒ a purpose; an aim; a plan. **4.** 《*pl.*》 evil intention; plot. ¶*They have designs upon* (or *against*) *her life.*②

des·ig·nate *vt.* [dézignèit → *adj.*] **1.** make out or point out (something) clearly; show. **2.** give a name to (someone); name. **3.** select (someone) for duty, etc.; appoint. 《~ *someone as*, *to* or *for*》 ¶~ *someone for the post of manager.*① —*adj.* [dézigneit / -nit] appointed; selected. ⇒ⓤⓢⓐⓖⓔ

des·ig·na·tion [dèzignéiʃ(ə)n] *n.* **1.** ⓤ the act of designating; clear indication. **2.** ⓤ the act of naming, the state of being named. **3.** ⓒ a descriptive title; a name.

de·signed [dizáind] *adj.* planned; intended.

de·sign·ed·ly [dizáinidli] *adv.* by design; on purpose; intentionally. ↔accidentally

de·sign·er [dizáinər] *n.* ⓒ **1.** a person who designs. **2.** a plotter; a person who schemes.

de·sign·ing [dizáiniŋ] *adj.* scheming; plotting; artful. —*n.* ⓤ the art of making plans, patterns, etc.

∗ de·sir·a·bil·i·ty [dizàiərəbíliti] *n.* ⓤ the state or quality of being desirable.

∗ de·sir·a·ble [dizáiərəbl] *adj.* worth wishing for; to be desired. ▷ **de·sir·a·bly** [-i] *adv.* —**de·sir·a·ble·ness** [-nis] *n.*

⁑ de·sire [dizáiər] *vt.* **1.** wish for (something); wish earnestly for (something); want. 《~ *that …*》 ¶~ *a woman for one's wife* / *leave nothing to be desired*① / *He desires that you should come back.* **2.** express a wish or ask for (someone or something); request. 《~ *someone to do*》 ¶*I ~ you to go at once.* —*n.* **1.** ⓤⓒ a wish; a strong wish. ¶*a strong ~ for*

desire

다 —㉰ 탈주(탈영)하다, 직무를 버리다 ¶③적에 투항하다

—㉤ 1. 상(벌)받을 만한 가치(자격) 2. 당연히 받아야 할 상(벌) ¶①당연한 보답(상·벌)을 받다 3. 공적; 장점

—㉤ 1. 버림받은 2. 사람이 살지 않는

—㉤ 1. 유기자 2. 탈영병, 도망자

—㉤ 유기; 탈영, 도망, 탈당

—㉤ …을 받을 만하다, …할(될) 가치가 있다 —㉰ 보답을 받을 가치가 있다 ¶①그는 국가로부터 우대받을 만한 공로가 있다

—㉤ 당연히, 정당하게

—㉤ 당연히 …을 받을 만한, …에 어울리는 ¶①그는 신용할 수 있다

—㉤ …을 건물(乾物)로 만들다, 건조시키다 —㉰ 분유 —㉰ 마르다

—㉤ 1. …의 디자인을 하다; …을 설계하다 2. …을 계획하다, …을 뜻하다 3. [어떤 목적으로] …을 예정하다 ¶①이 방은 내 서재로 만든 것이다 —㉰ 계획하다; 설계(도안)하다 —㉤ 1. 도안, 의장(意匠), 설계도 2. 디자인; 착상; 구상(構想) 3. 목적; 계획 4. 음모, 모략 ¶②그들은 그녀의 목숨을 노린다

—㉤ 1. …을 분명히 가리키다, 지적하다 2. …을 …이라고 부르다, 칭하다, 지명하다 3. …으로 임명하다 ¶①…을 지배인으로 임명하다 —㉰ 지명을 받은, 선출된 ⓤⓢⓐⓖⓔ 수식하는 명사 뒤에 옴

—㉤ 1. 지시, 지정, 명시 2. 지명, 임명 3. 존칭, 칭호

—㉤ 계획적인; 고의적인

—㉤ 계획적으로; 고의로, 일부러

—㉤ 1. 설계자, 고안자, 도안사 2. 계획자, 음모를 꾸미는 사람

—㉤ 모략을 쓰는, 속 검은 —㉰ 설계, 의장, 도안

—㉤ 바람직한

—㉤ 바람직한, 있으면 싶은, 멋진

—㉤ 1. …을 바라다, 열망하다 ¶①유감스러운 점이 조금도 없다 2. …을 요구(요망)하다

—㉤ 1. 소망, 욕망, 욕구 ¶②돈 따위는

fame / *I have no ~ for money.*② **2.** [C] 《usu. in *sing.*》 a request. ¶*at the ~ of the manager.*③ **3.** [C] a thing desired.

바라지 않는다 **2.** 희망, 요구 ¶③지배인이 바라는 대로 **3.** 바라는 것

de·sir·ous [dizáiərəs] *adj.* having or showing desire; desiring; eager. ¶*He is ~ of getting a good job.; He is ~ to get a good job.*①

—[形] 원하는, 바라는 ¶①그는 좋은 일자리를 얻기를 바란다

de·sist [dizíst] *vi.* cease; stop. 《~ *from doing*; ~ *from* something》 ¶~ *from talking.*①

—[自] 그만두다, 단념하다 ¶①그만 지껄이다

⁑ **desk** [desk] *n.* [C] a piece of furniture with a flat or sloping top for reading, writing, or drawing. ¶*be* (or *sit*) *at the* (or *one's*) *desk.*①

—[名] [사무·공부용] 책상, 데스크 ¶①글을 쓰고 있다; 사무를 보고 있다

* **des·o·late** *adj.* [désəlit → *v.*] **1.** not lived in; deserted; barren; wretched. ¶*The land is ~ of all vegetation.* **2.** left alone; solitary; lonely.

—[形] **1.** 사람이 살지 않는, 황폐한 **2.** 버림받은, 외로운, 쓸쓸한

—*vt.* [désəlèit] make (a land, etc.) desolate; make (someone) sad or lonely. ▷**des·o·late·ness** [désəlitnis] *n.*

—[他] …을 황량하게 하다, …을 살지 않게 하다; …을 외롭게 하다

des·o·late·ly [désəlitli] *adv.* lonely; sadly.

—[副] 황량하게; 쓸쓸하게

* **des·o·la·tion** [dèsəléiʃ(ə)n] *n.* **1.** [U] the act of desolating. **2.** [C] a desolate place. **3.** [U] sadness; loneliness.

—[名] **1.** 황폐 **2.** 황량한 곳, 폐허 **3.** 외로움, 쓸쓸함

⁑ **de·spair** [dispέər] *n.* **1.** [U] loss of hope; hopelessness. ¶*be driven to ~*① / *in ~*② / *in the depths of ~.*③ **2.** [C] a person or thing that causes despair. ¶*He is my ~.*④ —*vi.* lose hope; be in despair. 《~ *of* something》 ¶*We despaired of his life.; His life was despaired of.*

—[名] **1.** 절망; 자포자기 ¶①자포자기가 되다/②절망하여/③절망한 나머지 **2.** 절망시키는 사람(것) ¶④그에게는 두 손 들었다 —[自] 절망하다, 포기하다

de·spair·ing [dispέəriŋ] *adj.* feeling or showing despair; hopeless. ▷**de·spair·ing·ness** [-nis] *n.*

—[形] 자포자기의, 절망의

de·spair·ing·ly [dispέəriŋli] *adv.* in the state of having lost all hope; hopelessly.

—[副] 자포자기가 되어; 절망적으로

* **des·patch** [dispǽtʃ] *v.*, *n.* =dispatch.

des·per·a·do [dèspəréidou / -rá:-] *n.* [C] (pl. **-does** or **-dos**) a bold, reckless criminal; a person ready for any desperate and criminal deed.

—[名] 불량배, 폭한, 무법자

⁑ **des·per·ate** [désp(ə)rit] *adj.* **1.** reckless because hope is gone; ready to run any risk. ¶~ *remedy*① / *a ~ character.*② **2.** showing recklessness caused by despair; violent. **3.** with little improvement; extremely dangerous or serious. ¶*a ~ illness*③ / *a ~ fool.*④ **4.** hopeless. ▷**des·per·ate·ness** [-nis] *n.*

—[形] **1.** 자포자기의, 무모한 ¶①비상수단/②무뢰한 **2.** 목숨을 걸고 하는, 필사적인 **3.** 나아질 가망이 없는; 위험한 ¶③중병/④지독한 바보 **4.** 희망 없는

* **des·per·ate·ly** [désp(ə)ritli] *adv.* in the state of being desperate; extremely.

—[副] 무모하게, 필사적으로; 지독하게

des·per·a·tion [dèspəréiʃ(ə)n] *n.* [U] the state of being desperate; willingness to run any risk. ¶*be driven to ~*① / *in ~.*②

—[名] 무모함, 필사적임; 자포자기 ¶①자포자기가 되다/②필사적으로, 자포자기가 되어

des·pi·ca·ble [déspikəbl, dispík-] *adj.* to be looked down on; contemptible. ↔honorable

—[形] 비열한, 경멸할

des·pi·ca·bly [déspikəbli, dispík-] *adv.* in a despicable manner.

—[副] 비열하게, 비루하게

* **de·spise** [dispáiz] *vt.* look down on (someone) as worthless; feel contempt for (someone); scorn. ↔admire ¶*An honest man despises those who lie.*

—[他] …을 얕보다, 경멸하다, 깔보다

* **de·spite** [dispáit] *prep.* in spite of. ¶~ *the rain.*

—[前] …에도 불구하고

de·spoil [dispɔ́il] *vt.* steal (something) by force; rob. 《~ someone *of* something》

—[他] …을 약탈하다, 빼앗다

de·spoil·ment [dispɔ́ilmənt] *n.* [U] the act of robbing.

—[名] 약탈

de·spond [dispánd / -spɔ́nd] *vi.* lose hope.
—*n.* =despondence. ▷**de·spond·ing·ly** [-iŋli] *adv.*

—[自] 실망(낙심)하다

de·spond·ence [dispándəns / -pɔ́nd-], **-en·cy** [-ensi] *n.* [U] loss of courage or hope; discouragement; melancholy.

—[名] 낙심, 실망; 의기소침

de·spond·ent [dispándənt / -spɔ́nd-] *adj.* showing or feeling despondency; discouraged.

—[形] 낙심한; 기운 없는

des·pot [déspət, -pɑt / -pɔt] *n.* [C] a ruler who uses his power unjustly or cruelly; a tyrant.

—[名] 전제군주, 독재자, 폭군

des·pot·ic [dispátik / despɔ́t-] *adj.* of a despot or tyrant; cruel; unjust.

—[形] 전제(독재)적인; 횡포한

des·pot·ism [déspətìz(ə)m] *n.* **1.** [U] the rule of a despot; tyranny. **2.** [C] a country or government ruled by a

—[名] **1.** 전제(독재)정치, 폭정 **2.** 독재군주국, 전제 정부

D

dessert [320] **detail**

despot. ⌈meal. ¶serve ~.⌉
- **des·sert** [dizə́ːrt] *n.* ⓒ a course served at the end of a meal. ¶serve ~.
  des·sert·spoon [dizə́ːrtspùːn] *n.* ⓒ a spoon for dessert.
- **des·ti·na·tion** [dèstinéiʃ(ə)n] *n.* ⓒ **1.** the place to which a person is going or a thing is being sent. **2.** an intention; one's ultimate end.
- **des·tine** [déstin] *vt.* (usu. in *passive*) set (something) apart for a particular purpose; determine the future of (someone); intend. (*~ for* something) ¶*be destined to be a queen*① / *be destined never to meet.*②
  [*be*] *destined for,* ⓐ intended to go to (a place). ¶*a plane destined for New York.* ⓑ intended for (something). ¶*He was destined for the church.*③
- **des·ti·ny** [déstini] *n.* (pl. **-nies**) **1.** ⓤⓒ a person's lot or fate. ¶*a man of ~.* **2.** ⓤ (*D-*) the goddess of destiny; Providence. **3.** (*the Destinies*) the three Fates.
  des·ti·tute [déstit(j)ùːt / -tjùːt] *adj.* lacking the things necessary to sustain life; needy. ¶*be ~ of brains*① / *the ~.*
- **des·ti·tu·tion** [dèstit(j)úːʃ(ə)n / -tjúː-] *n.* ⓤ the state of being destitute; lack; extreme poverty.
- :**de·stroy** [distrɔ́i] *vt.* **1.** break (something) to pieces; make (something) useless; ruin; spoil. ¶*~ construct* **2.** put an end to (something); kill. ¶*~ oneself.*② **3.** make (something) powerless.
- **de·stroy·er** [distrɔ́iər] *n.* ⓒ **1.** a person or thing that destroys. **2.** a small, fast, powerful warship with guns, torpedoes, etc.
  de·struct·i·ble [distrʌ́ktəbl] *adj.* that can be destroyed.
- :**de·struc·tion** [distrʌ́kʃ(ə)n] *n.* ⓤ the act of destroying; the state of being destroyed. ↔construction
- **de·struc·tive** [distrʌ́ktiv] *adj.* causing destruction; fond of destroying. ↔constructive ¶*be ~ of health*① / *be ~ to morals.*② ▷**de·struc·tive·ly** [-li] *adv.*
  des·ue·tude [déswit(j)ùːd / disjúː(ː)itjùːd] *n.* ⓤ the state of being no longer used; disuse. ¶*fall into ~.*①
  des·ul·to·ry [dés(ə)ltɔ̀ːri / -t(ə)ri] *adj.* jumping from one thing to another; disconnected; without aim or method; random. ¶*~ reading.*① ▷**des·ul·to·ri·ly** [-li] *adv.*
  de·tach [ditǽtʃ] *vt.* **1.** loosen and remove; unfasten; separate; disconnect. ↔attach (*~ something from*) ¶*~ a sheet from a looseleaf notebook.* **2.** send away (someone) on a special mission.
  de·tach·a·ble [ditǽtʃəbl] *adj.* that can be detached.
  de·tached [ditǽtʃt] *adj.* **1.** separate from others; disconnected; isolated. ¶*a ~ house.*① **2.** not moved by others or by one's own interests, etc.; fair. ¶*a ~ view.*
  de·tach·ment [ditǽtʃmənt] *n.* **1.** ⓤ the act of detaching; separation. **2.** ⓒ (*Military*) a unit of troops or ships sent on some special duty. **3.** ⓤ the act of standing apart; aloofness.
- :**de·tail** *n.* [díːteil, ditéil→*v.*] ⓒ **1.** a small, unimportant part; a tiny item; (usu. *pl.*) particulars. ¶*a matter of ~* / *give the full details of a thing* / *go (or enter) into detail[s].*① / *I cannot tell you any details.*② **2.** ⓤ a small decoration or accessory in a building, picture, machine, etc. **3.** ⓒ a small group chosen for or sent on some special duty.
  in detail, item by item; thoroughly; with particulars. ¶*I had no time to explain it in ~.*
  —*vt.* [ditéil / díːteil] **1.** tell (something) fully; give a minute report on (something). **2.** (*Military*) choose (someone) for or send on a special mission. ¶*The captain detailed ten men to guard the station.*

—名 [식사 끝에 먹는] 디저어트
—名 디저어트용 스푸운
—名 1.목적지,도착지 2.목표; 궁극적인 목적

—他 …을 예정하다; 운명지우다 ¶①여왕이 되기로 되어 있다/②두 번 다시 못 만날 운명이다

熟 ⓐ…행의 ⓑ…이 될 운명이다 ¶③그는 성직자가 될 운명이었다

—名 1.운명,운,숙명 2.운명의 여신; 신의(神意) 3.운명의 세 여신

—形 결핍되는,없는; 빈곤한 ¶①두뇌가 없다/②가난한 사람들

—名 빈곤; 결핍; 빈궁

—他 1. …을 파괴하다, 망치다, 못쓰게 하다 2. …을 박멸하다, 멸망시키다, 죽이다 ¶①자살하다 3. …을 무효로 하다

—名 1.파괴자,박멸하는 사람 2.구축함

—形 파괴할 수 있는
—名 파괴, [문서의] 파기[죄]; 박멸, 섬멸; 멸망,파멸
—形 파괴적인,해로운 ¶①건강에 해롭다/②풍기를 해치다

—名 폐지,폐절(廢絶); 폐지 상태 ¶①폐지되다
—形 종잡을 수 없는, 산만한, 닥치는 대로의 ¶①띄엄띄엄 읽는 독서

—他 1. …을 떼어놓다, 떼어내다 2. [군대·군함을] 분견(分遣)하다

⌈수 있는⌉
—形 분리할 수 있는; 분견(分遣)할
—形 1.분리한; 떨어진,고립한 ¶①외딴집 2.공평한,초연한,사심이 없는

—名 1.분리 2.(軍)[부대·함선 따위의] 분견(分遣),파견대 3.고립,초연해 있기

—名 1.세부,세목,상세 ¶①상술(詳述)하다/②자세한 것은 말할 수 없다 2.[건축·미술의] 세부,세부 묘사 3.분견,특파부대,선발대

熟 상세하게

—他 1. …을 자세히 말하다 2.(軍)[특수 임무를 주어] …을 파견(분견)하다

de·tailed [ditéild / dí:teild] *adj.* having many details; described minutely. ¶*give a ~ report.*①
—[形] 상세한, 자세한 ¶①상세하게 보도하다

de·tain [ditéin] *vt.* **1.** keep (someone) from going; delay. ¶*be detained by business.* **2.** confine; keep.
—[他] 1. …을 붙들다, 기다리게 하다 2. …을 감금(구류)하다

***de·tect** [ditékt] *vt.* **1.** find out; discover. ¶*~ someone in the act of stealing.* **2.** discover the existence of (something). ¶*~ a sound in the distance.*
—[他] 1. …을 발견하다, 찾아내다 2. …을 탐지하다

de·tec·tion [ditékʃ(ə)n] *n.* [U] **1.** the act of detecting; discovery. ¶*the ~ of theft.* **2.** (*Electronics*) changing of an alternating current into a direct current.
—[名] 1. 발견, 간파, 탐지 2.《電子工學》 검파(檢波)

***de·tec·tive** [ditéktiv] *n.* [C] a person whose work is to find information secretly or to discover who committed a crime. ¶*a private ~.*① —*adj.* of or for detection.
—[名] 탐정, 형사 ¶①사립(비밀) 탐정 —[形] 탐정의, 탐지하기 위한

de·tec·tor [ditéktər] *n.* [C] **1.** a person or thing that detects. **2.** (*Electronics*) a device, usu. a vacuum tube or crystal in a radio, which changes an alternating current into a direct current; a rectifier.
—[名] 1. 발견자, 간파하는 사람 2.《電子工學》 검파기

de·ten·tion [diténʃ(ə)n] *n.* [U] **1.** the act of detaining; the state of being detained; delay. **2.** the act of keeping someone in confinement. ¶*be under ~ / a ~ camp*① */ a ~ hospital*② */ a house of ~.*③
—[名] 1. 붙들기, 억류; 지체 2. 유치, 구류, 감금 ¶①임시 수용소/②격리 병원/③미결수 감방

de·ter [ditə́:r] *vt.* (**-terred, -ter·ring**) prevent (someone) by discouraging; keep back; hinder; check. 《~ someone *from*》 ¶*Nothing could ~ him from attempting to reach the unconquered peak.*
—[他] …을 단념하게 하다, 그만두게 하다, 주저하게 하다

de·te·ri·o·rate [ditíəriərèit] *vi.* become worse; lessen in value. —*vt.* make (something or someone) worse.
—[自] [질이] 나빠지다, 저하되다 —[他] …을 악화시키다, 저하시키다

de·te·ri·o·ra·tion [ditìəriəréiʃ(ə)n] *n.* [U] the act of deteriorating; the state of being deteriorated.
—[名] 악화, 저하, 타락

de·ter·mi·nant [ditə́:rminənt] *n.* [C] a thing that determines. —*adj.* determining.
—[名] 결정하는 사람(것) —[形] 결정하는

de·ter·mi·nate [ditə́:rm(i)nit] *adj.* **1.** limited; fixed; definite. **2.** determined; resolute.
—[形] 1. 한정된, 확정된, 명확한 2. 결정적인, 단호한

***de·ter·mi·na·tion** [ditə̀:rminéiʃ(ə)n] *n.* [U] **1.** the act of determining; the state of being determined; resolution. **2.** a firm intention. **3.** (*Physics*) the act of finding out the exact amount; calculation.
—[名] 1. 결심, 결정 2. 결단력 3. [길이·비율 따위의] 측정[법]

de·ter·mi·na·tive [ditə́:rminèitiv, ditə́:rminətiv / -tə́:min-] *adj.* determining; defining. —*n.* [C] a thing that determines.
—[形] 결정력이 있는, 한정적인 —[名] 결정(한정)하는 것

‡**de·ter·mine** [ditə́:rmin] *vt.* **1.** resolve; decide. 《~ *to do*》. ¶*I determined to go. / This determined me to act at once. / He is determined to explain the matter to them.* **2.** find out exactly; fix the position of (something); ascertain. **3.** fix or settle beforehand. **4.** (*Logic*) limit (a notion); define. —*vi.* **1.** make up one's mind. 《~ *on* or *upon* something》 ¶*I determined on going.* **2.** (*Law*) come to an end; close.
—[他] 1. …을 결심하다, 결정하다 2. …을 분명히 정하다, 확정하다 3. …을 예정하다 4.《論》 …을 한정하다 —[自] 1. 결정하다, 결심하다 2.《法》 [효력 따위가] 종결되다

***de·ter·mined** [ditə́:rmind] *adj.* with one's mind firmly made up; resolved; firm; resolute. ¶*I am determined not to ask you. / He faced me with a ~ look.*①
—[形] 굳게 결심한; 단호한; 결정된 ¶①그는 단호한 표정으로 나를 직시했다

de·ter·rent [ditə́:rənt, -tér- / -tér-] *adj.* deterring; restraining. —*n.* [C] a thing that deters.
—[形] 방해하는, 저지하는 —[名] 억제하는 사물

de·test [ditést] *vt.* dislike very much; hate deeply. ↔ love
—[他] …을 몹시 싫어(미워)하다

de·test·a·ble [ditéstəbl] *adj.* deserving to be detested; hateful. ▷**de·test·a·ble·ness** [-nis] *n.*
—[形] 몹시 싫은

de·tes·ta·tion [dì:testéiʃ(ə)n] *n.* **1.** [U] very strong dislike; hatred. ¶*His ~ for me was very strong.*① **2.** [C] a detested person or thing; an object of hatred.
—[名] 1. 몹시 싫음, 증오, 염오 ¶①그는 나를 몹시 싫어했다 2. 미움받는 것

have (or ***hold***) *something* ***in detestation,*** dislike strongly.
[熟] 몹시 싫어하다

de·throne [diθróun] *vt.* remove (someone) from a throne; depose (someone) from an important position. 《~ someone *from*》
—[他] [왕]을 퇴위시키다; …을 [중요한 지위에서] 면직시키다, 끌어내리다

D

de·throne·ment [diθróunmənt] *n.* [U] the act of dethroning; the state or fact of being dethroned.
—[名] 폐위; 퇴위

det·o·nate [détounèit] *vt.* cause (something) to explode with a loud noise. —*vi.* explode with a sudden loud noise. ¶*A powder magazine detonated.*
—[他] [큰 소리를 내며] …을 폭발시키다 —[自] [큰 소리를 내며] 폭발하다

det·o·na·tion [dètounéiʃ(ə)n] *n.* [U][C] the act of detonating; the state of being detonated; a loud noise.
—[名] 폭발, 폭음

de·tour [dí:tuər, ditúər / déituə] *n.* [C] **1.** a road that is used when the regular or direct road cannot be traveled. ¶*make a* ~.① **2.** a roundabout way. —*vi.* use a detour. —*vt.* **1.** cause (someone or something) to make a detour. **2.** avoid. ¶*We detoured the hill.*
—[名] 1. 우회(迂回) ¶①우회하다 2. 돌아가는 길, 우회로 —[自] [멀리] 돌아가다 —[他] 1. …을 우회시키다 2. …을 피하다

de·tract [ditrǽkt] *vt.* take away. 《~ someone or something *from*》 —*vi.* make something less in value. 《~ *from* something》 ¶~ *from the beauty of a picture.*①
—[他] [가치 따위]를 떨어뜨리다 —[自] [가치를] 감하다, 줄다 ¶①그림의 아름다움을 해치다

de·trac·tion [ditrǽkʃ(ə)n] *n.* [U] **1.** the act of detracting. **2.** the act of speaking ill of another.
—[名] 1. 감손(減損) 2. 욕설, 비방

de·trac·tor [ditrǽktər] *n.* [C] a person who detracts or speaks ill of another.
—[名] 욕설을 하는 사람, 중상자

det·ri·ment [détrimənt] *n.* [U] damage; loss; injury; harm. ¶*without ~ to someone's character*① / *He always overeats to the ~ of his health.*②
—[名] 손해; 상해(傷害) ¶①남의 인격을 손상하지 않고/②그는 언제나 과식으로 건강을 해친다

det·ri·men·tal [dètriméntl] *adj.* damaging; injurious; harmful. ▷**det·ri·men·tal·ly** [-i] *adv.*
—[形] 해로운, 이익이 없는

* **De·troit** [ditrɔ́it] *n.* a city in southeastern Michigan.
—[名] 미국 Michigan 주 동남부의 도시

deuce[1] [d(j)u:s / dju:s] *n.* [C] **1.** a card or the side of a die having two spots. ¶*the ~ of hearts.*① **2.** (*Tennis*) a tie score of 40–40.
—[名] 1. [카아드] 두 끗, [주사위의] 두점 눈 ¶①하아트의 2 2.《테니스》 듀우스

deuce[2] [d(j)u:s / dju:s] *n.* 《*the* ~》 (*colloq.*) bad luck; devil. ¶*go to the* ~① / *like the* ~② / *The weather played the ~ with our plans.* / *There will be the ~ to pay.*③
—[名] 《口》 재난, 불운, 악마 ¶①멸망하다/②맹렬한 기세로/③뒷일이 무섭다

deuced [d(j)u:st, d(j)ú:sid / dju:st, djú:sid] *adj.* (chiefly *Brit. colloq.*) devilish; damned.
—[形] 《英》 아주 괘씸한, 지독한

Deu·ter·on·o·my [d(j)ù:tərɑ́nəmi / djù:tərɔ́n-] *n.* the fifth book of the Old Testament. ⇒[N.B.]
—[名] 신명기(申命記) [N.B.] 구약성서 중의 Moses 5서 중의 한 서(書)

de·val·u·ate [di:vǽljuèit] *vt.* lessen the value of (something).
—[他] …의 가치를 내리다

de·val·u·a·tion [di:væ̀ljuéiʃ(ə)n] *n.* [U] the act of devaluating; the state of being devaluated.
—[名] 평가절하

dev·as·tate [dévəstèit] *vt.* ruin; destroy. ¶*a town devastated by war.*
—[他] …을 황폐하게 하다; 파괴하다

dev·as·ta·tion [dèvəstéiʃ(ə)n] *n.* [U][C] destruction; desolation.
—[名] 파괴; 황폐

⁑ **de·vel·op** [divéləp] *vt.* **1.** make (something) larger or better; strengthen. ¶~ *one's body.* **2.** work out (something) in greater detail; explain more fully. **3.** (*Photography*) treat (a film) with chemicals to bring out a picture. —*vi.* grow up; become larger, better, or more complete. ¶*Plants ~ from seeds.* / *Seeds ~ into plants.*① / *The story gradually developed in his mind.*②
—[他] 1. …을 발육시키다, 발전시키다; 강하게 하다 2. …을 자세하게 설명하다 3.《寫》 …을 현상하다 —[自] 발육하다, 발전하다; 전개하다 ¶①종자가 자라서 식물이 된다/②이야기 줄거리가 차츰 그의 머릿속에 전개되었다

de·vel·op·er [divéləpər] *n.* [C] **1.** a person or thing that develops. **2.** (*Photography*) a chemical used to make a picture visible on a film, plate, print, etc.
—[名] 1. 개발자, 개발물 2.《寫》 현상액(약)

⁑ **de·vel·op·ment** [divéləpmənt] *n.* **1.** [U] the act of developing; growth; evolution. **2.** [U][C] a stage of advancement; an outcome; a result. ¶*the latest developments in the stock market.* **3.** [U] (*Photography*) the act of developing a picture.
—[名] 1. 발육, 발달 2. 개발; 발달(발전)된 것, 발달(발전)단계, 정세; 결과 3.《寫》 현상

de·vi·ate [dí:vièit] *vi.* turn aside from something. ¶~ *from the right way* / *In his statements, the witness deviated from the truth.*① ▷**de·vi·a·tor** [-ər] *n.*
—[自] 빗나가다, 이탈하다 ¶①증인은 진술에 있어서 사실에서 벗어났다

de·vi·a·tion [dì:viéiʃ(ə)n] *n.* [U][C] the act of deviating; the act of turning aside. ¶*standard* ~.①
—[名] 빗나가기, 탈선, 편차(偏差), 치우침 ¶①표준 편차

⁑ **de·vice** [diváis] *n.* [C] **1.** a plan; a design; a scheme. **2.** 《often *pl.*》 a trick. **3.** a mechanical invention for a special purpose; a machine; an apparatus. ¶*a ~ for*
—[名] 1. 고안, 안(案), 취향 2. 책략 3. 발명품, 고안물, 장치 4. 도안, 의장(意匠) 5. 상표

catching flies. **4.** an ornamental picture or design. **5.** a trade mark.
leave someone to his own devices, let someone do as he wishes.

[熟] [충고나 원조를 하지 않고] …에게 제멋대로 하게 하다

: dev·il [dévl] *n.* [C] **1.** a wicked spirit; a demon; ⟪*the D-*⟫ Satan. ¶(*proverb*) *Talk of the ~, and he is sure to appear.*① **2.** a wicked or cruel person. **3.** an unfortunate or pitiful person. ¶*a poor ~.* **4.** ⟪*the ~*⟫ (*colloq.*) ⟪used in *exclamations,* expressing *disgust, anger, surprise,* etc.⟫ the deuce. ¶*What the ~ is he doing?*②

—[名] **1.** 악마; 악귀; 마왕 ¶①⟪俚⟫ 호랑이도 제 말하면 온다 **2.** 극악한 사람 **3.** 불쌍한 사람 **4.** 제기랄!, 도대체 ¶②도대체 그 녀석은 무엇을 하고 있느냐?

1) ***a*** (or ***the***) ***devil of a ...,*** hellish; damned. ¶*He is a ~ of a boy.*③
2) ***the devil to pay,*** much trouble ahead.
3) ***give the devil his due,*** be fair even to a bad or disliked person.
4) ***go to the devil,*** be ruined; ⟪as *imperative*⟫ Be off! Go to hell!
5) ***like the devil,*** with great energy, etc.
6) ***paint the devil blacker than he is,*** exaggerate one's sinful deeds.
7) ***play the devil with,*** (*colloq.*) do much harm to (something); ruin.
8) ***raise the devil,*** (*colloq.*) make a great disturbance.

[熟] 1)싫은… ¶③정말 싫은 아이이다 2)앞으로의 곤란 3)[보잘것 없는 사람에 대해서도] 공평하게 대하다 4)멸망하다; 뒈져라!, 꺼져라! 5)맹렬히, 필사적으로 6)한 술 더 떠서 나쁘게 말하다 7)⟪口⟫…을 엉망으로 만들다 8)⟪口⟫ 큰 소동을 일으키다

dev·il·fish [dévlfiʃ] *n.* [C] (pl. **-fish·es** or *collectively* **-fish**) **1.** a giant ray. **2.** an octopus.

—[名] **1.** 큰 가오리 **2.** 문어, 오징어

dev·il·ish [dévliʃ] *adj.* **1.** like a devil; very cruel. **2.** (*colloq.*) extreme. —*adv.* (*colloq.*) extremely.

—[形] **1.** 악마 같은, 극악한 **2.** ⟪口⟫ 극단적인 —[副] 극단적으로

de·vi·ous [dí:viəs] *adj.* **1.** winding; round-about; indirect ¶*take a ~ course.* **2.** straying from the proper course. ¶*a man of ~ nature.* ▷**de·vi·ous·ness** [-nis] *n.*

—[形] **1.** 꾸불꾸불한; 멀리 돌아가는 **2.** 정도(正道)에서 벗어난

• de·vise [diváiz] *vt.* **1.** think out; plan; invent. ¶*~ a plan.* **2.** (*Law*) give or leave (something) by a will. —*n.* (*Law*) **1.** [U] a gift or real property left by a will. **2.** [C] a will or part of a will doing this.

—[他] **1.** …을 고안하다, 궁리하다; 발명하다 **2.** ⟪法⟫ [부동산 따위]를 유증(遺贈)하다 —[名] **1.** 유증 **2.** 유언 조항

de·vi·tal·ize [di:váitəlàiz] *vt.* **1.** take the life of (something); kill. **2.** make (someone) less vital.

—[他] **1.** …을 죽이다 **2.** …에서 활력을 빼앗다

de·void [divɔ́id] *adj.* lacking; completely without. ¶*be ~ of courage.* ⇒[usage]

—[形] …이 없는, 결핍된 [usage] 명사 앞에는 쓰지 않음

de·volve [diválv / -vɔ́lv] *vt.* transfer. ⟪*~* something *on* or *upon*⟫ ¶*~ work upon* (or *on*) *an assistant.* —*vi.* be passed to someone else; be handed down. ⟪*~ on* or *upon* someone⟫ ¶*It devolved upon me to ...*①

—[他] …을 양도(위임)하다, 넘기다
—[自] 귀속하다, 넘어가다 ¶①내가 …하기로 되었다

: de·vote [divóut] *vt.* give (oneself) completely to something or someone. ¶*be deeply devoted to each other*① / *He devoted his life to the study of literature.*

—[他] …을 바치다, 맡기다 ¶①서로 깊이 사랑하고 있다

de·vot·ed [divóutid] *adj.* loyal; faithful; very loving; deeply attached to someone. ¶*a ~ wife / She is ~ to her children.*①

—[形] 헌신적인; 충실한; 열렬히 사랑하는 ¶①그녀는 아이들을 헌신적으로 사랑한다

de·vot·ed·ly [divóutidli] *adv.* in a devoted manner; loyally; faithfully.

—[副] 헌신적으로; 충실히; 열애하여

dev·o·tee [dèvoutí:] *n.* [C] **1.** a person deeply devoted to something; an enthusiastic fan or supporter. **2.** a person deeply devoted to religion.

—[名] **1.** 열애하는 사람 **2.** 광신적 신봉자

de·vo·tion [divóuʃ(ə)n] *n.* [U] **1.** deep, strong love; loyalty; faithfulness. ¶*the ~ of a mother to her child.*① **2.** the act of devoting; the state of being devoted. ¶*~ to study.* **3.** religious worship. **4.** ⟪*pl.*⟫ prayers.

—[名] **1.** 열렬한 사랑; 헌신; 충실 ¶①자식에 대한 어머니의 강한 사랑 **2.** 애착, 열심 **3.** 신앙 **4.** 기도

de·vo·tion·al [divóuʃənəl] *adj.* characterized by devotion; having to do with worship. ▷**de·vo·tion·al·ly** [-li] *adv.*

—[形] 신앙심의, 경건한, 기도의

: de·vour [diváuər] *vt.* **1.** eat (something) greedily or hungrily. **2.** consume; waste; destroy; swallow up. **3.** take in (something) greedily with the eyes or ears. **4.** absorb (something) wholly. ¶*I am devoured by* (or *with*) *anxiety.* ▷**de·vour·ing·ly** [-iŋli] *adv.*

—[他] **1.** …을 게걸스럽게 먹다 **2.** [불길이] …을 핥아 없애다; 망치다; 삼켜버리다 **3.** …을 뚫어질 듯이 보다; 넋을 잃고 듣다 **4.** …에 열중하다

de·vout [diváut] *adj.* **1.** very religious; pious. **2.** earnest; sincere; hearty. ▷**de·vout·ly** [-li] *adv.*

—[形] **1.** 신앙심 깊은 **2.** 열심인; 성실한, 선량한

: dew [d(j)u: / dju:] *n.* [U] [C] **1.** the moisture from the air that condenses and appears in small drops on cool sur-

—[名] **1.** 이슬 **2.** [땀·눈물] 방울 ¶①구슬 같은 땀 **3.** 상쾌함 ¶②젊음의 신

faces during the night. **2.** any moisture in small drops. ¶*the ~ of sweat.*① **3.** anything regarded as refreshing like dew. ¶*the ~ of youth*② | *the golden ~ of sleep.*③
—*vt., vi.* wet with dew; fall as dew.
선함/③기분 좋은 숙면
—[他][自] …을 이슬로 적시다; 이슬이 내리다

dew·drop [d(j)ú:dràp / djú:drɔ̀p] *n.* [C] a small drop of dew.
—[名] 이슬[방울]

dew·fall [d(j)ú:fɔ̀:l / djú:-] *n.* **1.** [U][C] the formation of dew. **2.** [U] the time at which dew begins to form.
—[名] 1. 이슬맺이 2. 이슬이 내리는 시각, 땅거미질 때

* **dew·y** [d(j)ú:i / djú:i] *adj.* (**dew i er, dew i est**) **1.** wet with dew. ¶*~ grass.* **2.** like dew; refreshing. ¶*~ tears.*
—[形] 1. 이슬에 젖은 2. 이슬 같은; 상쾌한

dex·ter·i·ty [dekstériti] *n.* [U] skill, esp. in handling something; cleverness.
—[名] 솜씨 좋음; 총명

dex·ter·ous [dékst(ə)rəs] *adj.* **1.** skillful in using one's hands. ¶*a ~ typist.* **2.** clever.
—[形] 1. 솜씨 좋은 2. 총명한

dex·ter·ous·ly [dékst(ə)rəsli] *adv.* **1.** skillfully. **2.** cleverly.
—[副] 1. 솜씨 좋게 2. 총명하게

dex·trous [dékstrəs] *adj.* =dexterous.

dex·trous·ly [dékstrəsli] *adv.* =dexterously.

di·a·be·tes [dàiəbí:ti:z] *n.* [U] (*Medicine*) a disease in which there is an excessive amount of sugar in the urine.
—[名] 《醫》 당뇨병

di·a·bet·ic [dàiəbétik, -bí:-] *adj.* of or having to do with diabetes. —*n.* [C] a person suffering from diabetes.
—[形] 당뇨병의(에 걸린) —[名] 당뇨병 환자

di·a·bol·ic [dàiəbálik / -bɔ́l-], **-i·cal** [-ik(ə)l] *adj.* like the devil; devilish; very cruel.
—[形] 악마 같은; 극악무도한

di·a·bol·i·cal·ly [dàiəbálikəli / -bɔ́l-] *adv.* in a diabolical manner; devilishly; cruelly.
—[副] 악마처럼; 극악무도하게

di·a·dem [dáiədèm] *n.* [C] a crown; a headband of cloth. ⇒fig.
—[名] 왕관, [왕·여왕의] 머리띠

(diadem)

di·ag·nose [dáiəgnòus, -nòuz / -nouz, -nóuz] *vt.* find out the nature of (something) by an examination. ¶*The doctor diagnosed her illness as influenza.*
—[他] …을 진단하다.

di·ag·no·ses [dàiəgnóusi:z] *n.* pl. of **diagnosis.**

di·ag·no·sis [dàiəgnóusis] *n.* [C][U] (pl. **-ses**) the act of diagnosing.
—[名] 진단

di·ag·o·nal [daiǽgən(ə)l] *n.* [C] a straight line cutting across in a slanting direction. —*adj.* going across in a diagonal direction. ¶*~ cloth*① | *~ lines.*②
—[名] 대각선 —[形] 대각선의 ¶①능직(綾織)/②대각선

di·ag·o·nal·ly [daiǽgənəli] *adv.* in a diagonal direction.
—[副] 비스듬히, 엇갈려서

di·a·gram [dáiəgræ̀m] *n.* [C] a drawing or sketch showing the important parts of something. —*vt.* (**-gramed, -gram·ing** or *Brit.* **-grammed, -gram·ming**) make a diagram of (something); show (something) by a diagram.
—[名] 도표, 도식(圖式), 일람표 —[他] …을 도해하다; 도표로 나타내다

di·al [dái(ə)l] *n.* [C] **1.** a clocklike face on which an indicator shows the amount of something. **2.** a plate, disk, etc., on a radio or television set for locating stations; such a plate on an automatic telephone with numbers, letters, etc. **3.** a sundial.
—[名] 1. 지침면(指針面), 문자반 2. [라디오·텔레비전·자동식 전화의] 다이얼 3. 해시계

—*vt.* (**-aled, -al·ing** or *Brit.* **-alled, -al·ling**) **1.** tune in (a radio station, program, etc.) by using a radio dial. **2.** call (someone) by means of a telephone dial. ¶*~ the fire station* | *~ 03 for long distance to Tokyo.*
—[他] 1. [라디오·텔레비전을] …에 맞추다 2. …에 전화를 걸다

di·a·lect [dáiəlèkt] *n.* [C][U] **1.** a form of speech used in a fairly definite region of a country. ¶*Kyushu dialects.* **2.** words or pronunciations of certain professions or classes of people. ¶*a literary ~.*
—[名] 1. 방언 2. [어떤 직업·계급의] 관용어, 사투리

di·a·lec·tal [dàiəléktl] *adj.* of a dialect.
—[形] 방언의

di·a·lec·tic [dàiəléktik], **-ti·cal** [-tik(ə)l] *n.* [C] **1.** the art or practice of logical discussion to find out the truth of a theory or opinion. **2.** 《often *pl.*》 a discussion of the logical truth of an opinion or theory. —*adj.* **1.** of logical discussion. **2.** =dialectal.
—[名] 1. 변증법 2. 논리적 토론[술]
—[形] 1. 변증법적인

di·a·log, -logue [dáiəlɔ̀:g, -lág / -lɔ̀g] *n.* **1.** [C] a conversation or talk. **2.** [C] a written work in the form of a
—[名] 1. 대화, 회화 2. 대화체의 작품 3. [극·소설 따위의] 대화 부분

conversation. **3.** [U] [C] a conversation in a play, story, etc. ¶*The ~ in this novel is poor.*

* **di·am·e·ter** [daiǽmitər] *n.* [C] [U] a straight line passing through the center of a circle; the length of such a line. ¶*the ~ of a tree trunk / 5 feet in ~.*
—[名] 직경

di·a·met·ric [dàiəmétrik], **-ri·cal** [-rik(ə)l] *adj.* **1.** of or along a diameter. **2.** exactly opposite.
—[形] 1. 직경의 2. 정반대의

di·a·met·ri·cal·ly [dàiəmétrikəli] *adv.* **1.** in a diametric direction. **2.** directly opposite. **3.** entirely. ¶*be ~ opposed.*①
—[副] 1. 직경으로 2. 정반대로 3. 전혀 ¶①전혀 정반대이다

⁑ **dia·mond** [dáiəmənd] *n.* [C] **1.** [C] [U] a brilliant precious stone formed in crystals of nearly pure carbon, of great value and hardness. ¶*a ~ field.*① **2.** a figure shaped like this. **3.** a playing card with this figure; 《*pl.*》 the suit of playing cards with this figure. **4.** (*Baseball*) the infield; the whole playing field. **5.** a tool with a diamond tip for cutting glass.
1) ***black diamond,*** coal.
2) ***diamond anniversary,*** the sixtieth (or seventy-fifth) celebration of an event.
3) ***diamond cut diamond,*** two well-matched persons disputing or struggling against each other.
4) ***diamond in the rough; rough diamond,*** ⓐ an uncut diamond. ⓑ a person who is worthy, though having poor manners.
—[名] 1. 다이아몬드, 금강석 ¶①다이아몬드 산지 2. 다이아몬드꼴, 마름모꼴 3. [카아드의] 다이아몬드 패[들] 4. [야구의] 내야; 야구장 5. 유리 끊는 칼
[熟] 1)석탄 2)제60(75)회 기념일 3)[논쟁·싸움 따위] 막상막하의, 불을 뿜는 4)ⓐ천연 그대로의 금강석 ⓑ거칠기는 하나 바탕은 좋은 사람

diamond wedding, [´–––, ––´–] *n.* the sixtieth or seventy-fifth anniversary of a wedding.
—[名] 다이아몬드혼식(婚式)(결혼 60 또는 75년 기념일)

Di·an·a [daiǽnə] *n.* the Roman goddess of the hunt and of the moon, worshipped esp. as the protectress of women. ⇒[N.B.]
—[名] 다이아나(달과 사냥의 여신) [N.B.] Artemis 참조

di·a·per [dáiəpər] *n.* **1.** [C] a small cloth used as a sanitary towel for babies. **2.** [U] a pattern of small repeated geometric figures. ⇒fig. **3.** a white cotton or linen cloth with such a pattern. **—*vt.*** ornament (something) with a diaper pattern.

〔diaper 2.〕

—[名] 1. 기저귀 2. 마름모꼴 무늬 3. 마름모꼴 무늬의 린네르 —[他] …을 마름모꼴 무늬로 장식하다

di·aph·a·nous [daiǽfənəs] *adj.* transparent. ¶*~ cloth.*
—[形] 투명한

di·a·phragm [dáiəfræ̀m] *n.* [C] **1.** a wall of muscle between the chest and the abdomen. **2.** a vibrating disk in a telephone. **3.** a device to control the amount of light entering a camera, microscope, etc.
—[名] 1. 횡격막(橫隔膜) 2. [전화의] 진동판 3. [카메라·현미경 따위의] 조리개

di·a·rist [dáiərist] *n.* [C] a person who keeps a diary.
—[名] 일기를 쓰는 사람

di·ar·rhe·a, -rhoe·a [dàiəríːə] *n.* [U] (*Medicine*) too frequent and too loose movements of the bowels.
—[名] 《醫》 설사

⁑ **di·a·ry** [dáiəri] *n.* [C] (pl. **-ries**) a daily record of what one has done or thought about, or of the events during the day; a book for keeping this record. ¶*keep a ~.*①
—[名] 일기; 일기장 ¶①일기를 쓰다

di·a·stase [dáiəstèis] *n.* [U] an organic chemical substance that changes a white, tasteless food substance into sugar.
—[名] 디아스타아제, 전분당화소(澱粉糖化素)

di·a·tribe [dáiətràib] *n.* [C] [U] a bitter and violent attack in words against something or someone.
—[名] 맹렬한 비난

dib·ble [díbl] *n.* [C] a small curved, pointed tool for making holes in the ground.
—[名] [파종 또는 모종용의] 작은 삽

dice [dais] *n. pl.* (pl. of **die**²) **1.** small cubes with each side marked with from one to six spots. ¶*play at ~.* **2.** a game played with dice. **—*vi.*** play dice **—*vt.*** **1.** cut (something) into small cubes. ¶*~ carrots.* **2.** lose (something) by gambling with dice. ¶*~ away one's fortune.*①
—[名] 1. 주사위 2. 주사위 놀이, 도박 —[自] 주사위로 놀다 —[他] 1. …을 주사위 모양으로 자르다 2. 주사위 노름(도박)에서 [돈 따위]를 잃다 ¶①도박으로 재산을 잃다

dice·box [dáisbɑ̀ks / -bɔ̀ks] *n.* [C] a box from which dice are thrown.
—[名] [주사위를 흔드는] 주사위 통

Dick [dik] *n.* a nickname of Richard.
—[名] Richard의 애칭

dick·ens [díkinz] *n.* [C] **1.** devil. **2.** 《*the ~*》 exclamation expressing surprise. **3.** 《*the ~*》 often used as a mild curse. ¶*What the ~ is it?*①
—[名] 1. 악마 2. [놀람 따위를 나타내어] 이런!, 제기랄! 3. 도대체 ¶①도대체 그건 뭐냐?

dick·er [díkər] *vi.* (*U.S.*) trade on a small scale; bargain; barter. —*n.* ⓒ **1.** the number or quantity ten. **2.** a small bargain. —自 (美) 작은 거래를 하다, [값을] 깎다 —名 **1.** 열 [개] **2.** 작은 거래

dic·ta [díktə] *n.* pl. of **dictum**.

• **dic·tate** *v.* [díkteit, -´-→ n.] *vt.* **1.** say or read (something) aloud to be written down by another person. ¶ ~ *a letter to a person.* **2.** order; command. ¶ ~ *terms to the vanquished enemy.* —*vi.* **1.** say or read something aloud to be taken down. ¶ ~ *to a class.* **2.** give orders. ¶ ~ *to me.* —*n.* [díkteit] ⓒ (often *pl.*) an order by an authoritative person; a command. —他 **1.** ...을 받아쓰게 하다, 구술(口述) 하다 **2.** ...을 명령하다 ¶①패한 적에게 강화 조건을 명령하다 —自 **1.** [구술하여] 받아쓰게 하다 **2.** 명령하다, 지시하다

—名 명령, 지시

• **dic·ta·tion** [diktéi∫(ə)n] *n.* Ⓤ **1.** the act of dictating; ⓒ the words to be taken down. **2.** the act of giving orders. —名 **1.** 받아쓰기, 구술(口述); ⓒ 받아쓴 구절 **2.** 명령, 지시

dic·ta·tor [díkteitər, diktéitər / diktéitə] *n.* ⓒ **1.** a ruler with absolute power and authority. **2.** a person who dictates. —名 **1.** 독재자, 명령자 **2.** 받아쓰게 하는 사람, 구술자

dic·ta·to·ri·al [dìktətɔ́:riəl] *adj.* **1.** of or like a dictator. **2.** behaving like a dictator; imperious. —形 **1.** 독재자의, 독재적인 **2.** 오만한, 권세를 부리는

dic·ta·tor·ship [díkteitərʃìp, diktéitər- / diktéitə-] *n.* Ⓤ **1.** the position or rank of a dictator; the period that a dictator's rule lasts. **2.** absolute authority. —名 **1.** 독재자의 직(임기) **2.** 독재권, 절대권

dic·tion [díkʃ(ə)n] *n.* Ⓤ the way of expressing ideas in words; the style of speaking or writing; the choice of words. ¶ *poetic* ~. —名 말씨, 어법; 용어 선택 ¶①시어 (詩語)

: dic·tion·ar·y [díkʃənèri / -(ə)n(ə)ri] *n.* ⓒ (pl. **-ar·ies**) a book containing the words of a language, usu. arranged alphabetically, with explanations of their meanings. —名 사서, 사전, 자전

dic·tum [díktəm] *n.* ⓒ (pl. **-tums** or **-ta**) **1.** a saying; a maxim; a comment; an authoritative opinion. **2.** a formal assertion. —名 **1.** 격언, 금언 **2.** [유권적] 단언

‡ did [did] *v.* pt. of **do**.

di·dac·tic [daidǽktik / di-], **-ti·cal** [-tik(ə)l] *adj.* intended to be instructive. —形 교훈적인, 교사(教師)인 체하는

‡ did·n't [dídnt] =did not.

didst [didst] *v.* (*archaic*) =did. ⇒usage —他 usage 주어는 thou

‡ die¹ [dai] (ppr. **dy·ing**) *vi.* **1.** come to the end of life; stop living; become dead. ¶ ~ *by violence* | ~ *in battle* | ~ *for his country* | ~ *from drinking too much whisky* | ~ *from a wound* (*weakness, carelessness, an accident*) | ~ *of an illness* (*a disease, hunger, cold, grief, fever, heat, old age, the bite of a snake*) | ~ *with joy* (*shame*) ⇒ usage | *My mother died in 1964.* | *He died the death of a hero.*; *He died a hero's death.* | *He was born poor but died rich.* | *He died a beggar.* **2.** (in the Bible) suffer the agony of death. **3.** come to an end; lose force or strength; stop. ¶ *Reading his letter, her hopes died within her.* | *The day died into night.* | *The sound* (*noise*) *died away.* **4.** (*colloq.*) (usu. in *participle*) want very much; be very desirous. (~ *to do*; ~ *for* something) ¶ *I am dying to do it.* | *I am dying for a glass of beer.* weaker until ceasing.

—自 **1.** 죽다, 말라 죽다 ¶①비명에 죽다 usage die of는 질병·부상·노령·낙심 따위 사인일 때 가장 흔히 쓰이며 die from 다센으로 쓰이는 일도 있음. die with는 감정적인 것 때문에 죽을 때 쓰임 **2.** 《聖》죽을 고생을 하다 **3.** 사라지다, 꺼지다, 없어지다, 희미해지다, 약해지다 **4.** 《口》...이 탐나서 못견디다, 갈망하다

1) **die away**, (of wind, sound) gradually become
2) **die back** (or **down**), (of a plant) wither to the roots.
3) **die hard**, resist to the end; struggle until death.
4) **die in one's boots**, die by violence, esp. in battle.
5) **die off**, die one after another until all are dead.
6) **die out**, become extinct; come to a complete end.
7) *Never say die!,* Keep up your courage!

圞 1)[바람·소리 따위가] 차츰 조용해지다 2)[초목이] 뿌리까지 말라 죽다 3)완강히 저항하다, 죽을 때까지 싸우다 4)변사하다 5)차례차례 모두 죽어 없어지다 6)멸종(사멸)하다 7) 죽는 소리 하지 말라!, 기운을 내라!

: die² [dai] *n.* ⓒ **1.** (pl. **dice** →2.) a small cube marked with figures from one to six. ¶ *as level* (or *straight,*

[die² 2.]

—名 **1.** 주사위 ¶①똑바른, 정직한, 결코 틀림없는/②주사위는 이미 던져졌다(일은 이미 결정되었다) NB Julius Caesar (B.C.102 –B.C. 44)의 유명한

*true) as a die*① */ The ~ is cast.*② ⇒[N.B.] **2.** (pl. **dies**) (*Machinery*) any tool or apparatus used for molding, shaping, cutting, or stamping something. ⇒p. 326 fig.

die-hard [dáihɑ̀:rd] *adj.* resisting to the last. **—*n.*** [C] a person who resists vigorously to the last.

Die·sel [dí:z(ə)l] *n.* **1., Rudolf** (1858–1913) a German engineer who invented the Diesel engine. **2.** [C] a Diesel (or diesel) engine.

* **di·et**¹ [dáiət] *n.* [C] **1.** what a person or animal usu. eats and drinks; daily fare. **2.** a special selection of food for health, usu. to reduce one's weight. ¶*put someone on a special ~.*① **—*vt., vi.*** have (someone) take special food and drink. 《~ oneself *on*》

* **di·et**² [dáiət] *n.* **1.** [C] a formal assembly. **2.** 《often *D-*》 the national parliamentary assembly, as in Japan, Denmark, Sweden, etc. ¶*the Japanese Diet.* ⇒[N.B.]

di·e·tar·y [dáiətèri / -t(ə)ri] *adj.* having to do with diet. ¶*a ~ cure*① **—*n.*** (pl. **-tar·ies**) **1.** [U] allowance of daily food in a hospital, prison, etc. **2.** [C] a system of diet.

di·e·tet·ic [dàiitétik], **-i·cal** [-ik(ə)l] *adj.* of diet.

di·e·tet·ics [dàiitétiks] *n. pl.* 《used as *sing.*》 the study of the amount and kinds of food needed for health.

di·e·ti·cian [dàiitíʃ(ə)n] *n.* =dietitian.

di·e·ti·tian [dàiitíʃ(ə)n] *n.* [C] an expert in dietetics.

⁑ **dif·fer** [dífər] *vi.* **1.** be different; be unlike. 《~ *from* someone or something; ~ *in* something》 ¶*~ in habit / French differs from English in many points.* **2.** have a different opinion; disagree. 《~ *with* or *from* someone》 ↔agree ¶*I beg to ~.*① */ He differs with me entirely.*

agree to differ, give up trying to persuade each other.

⁑ **dif·fer·ence** [díf(ə)rəns] *n.* [C][U] **1.** the state of being unlike. ¶*a ~ in quality.* **2.** the way or point in which people or things are different; distinction. **3.** the condition of having a different opinion; disagreement; quarrel. ↔agreement ¶*They have had differences.*① **4.** (*Mathematics*) the amount by which one quantity is greater or less than another; the remainder left when one quantity is subtracted from another.

1) ***make a difference,*** ⓐ 《usu. in *negative*》 give different treatment. ¶*make no ~ between them.*② ⓑ matter; be important; have an effect. ¶*It makes a ~ to us.*③ */ One false step will make a great ~.*④

2) ***split the difference,*** compromise; meet halfway.

3) ***What's the difference?,*** (*colloq.*) What does it matter?

⁑ **dif·fer·ent** [díf(ə)rənt] *adj.* ↔same **1.** not alike; not like; not the same; separate. 《~ *from, to* or *than*》 ¶*~ people with the same name.*① **2.** various; unusual.

dif·fer·en·tial [dìfərénʃ(ə)l] *adj.* **1.** of a difference; having, showing, or depending on a difference; distinctive. ¶*~ rates*① */ a ~ character*② */ ~ calculus.*③ **2.** (*Mechanics*) making use of the differences of two or more motions. **—*n.* 1.** [U] the amount of difference in pay. **2.** [C] (*Machinery*) a differential gear.

dif·fer·en·ti·ate [dìfərénʃièit] *vt.* make a difference between (things or persons); find out the difference between (things). 《~ something *from*》 ¶*~ two materials.* **—*vi.*** become different.

dif·fer·en·ti·a·tion [dìfərènʃiéiʃ(ə)n] *n.* [U] the act of differentiating; the state of being differentiated.

dif·fer·ent·ly [díf(ə)rəntli] *adv.* in a different manner.

⁑ **dif·fi·cult** [dífikʌ̀lt / -k(ə)lt] *adj.* ↔easy **1.** hard to do or understand; not easy. ¶*be ~ of access*① */ be ~ to answer / The food is ~ to digest. / The problem is ~ to*

말 2.《機》 철판을 찍어내는 틀, 수나사 깎는 기구

—[形] 최후까지 버티는 —[名] 끝까지 버티는 사람, 완고한 사람

—[名] 1. 독일의 디이젤기관 발명자 2. 디이젤 엔진(내연 기관)

—[名] 1. 음식물 2. [건강을 위한] 규정식, 식이(食餌) ¶①…에 규정식을 먹게 하다 —[他][自] 규정된 음식을 먹(게 하)다

—[名] 1. 정식 회의 2. 국회 [N.B.] 미국은 Congress, 영국은 Parliament, 한국은 National Assembly라 함

—[形] 식사의 ¶①식이요법 —[名] 1. [병원·교도소 따위의] 규정 식이 2. 규정식

—[形] 식사의, 식이요법의

—[名] 영양학, 식이요법

—[名] 영양학자, 영양사(士)

—[自] 1. 다르다, 틀리다 2. 의견이 다르다 ¶①실례지만 내 의견은 다르오

[熟] 의견 차이가 있음을 인정하다

—[名] 1. 다름, 상위 2. 차별 3. 의견의 불일치, 불화; 싸움 ¶①그들은 사이가 틀어졌다 4.《數》 차(差); 나머지

[熟] 1)ⓐ차별하다 ¶②양자 사이에 구별을 짓지 않다 ⓑ관계하다, 중요하다, 영향을 미치다 ¶③우리에게는 관계가 있다/④한 발자국 잘못하면 큰 일이 난다 2)절충하다, 타협하다 3)《口》 그것이 어쨌다는 거냐?

—[形] 1. 다른; 틀린; 별개의 ¶①동명이인 2. 여러가지의, 각종의; 색다른

—[形] 1. 차별적인, 특정의, 특이한 ¶①[철도 따위의] 특정 운임률/②특이한 성격/③미분(微分) 2.《機》 차동(差動)의 —[名] 1. 요금차, 차별 요금 2.《機》 차동 톱니바퀴

—[他] …을 차별하다; 구별하다

—[自] 구별이 생기다

—[名] 구별, 판별, 차별

—[副] 다르게, 따로따로

—[形] 1. …하기 어려운, 알기 힘든, 곤란한 ¶①가까이 하기 어렵다 2. 성미 까다로운, 다루기 힘든 ¶②까다로운 사람

D

solve. **2.** hard to deal with; stubborn. ¶*a ~ person.*②

⁑ dif·fi·cul·ty [dífikʌlti / -k(ə)lti] *n.* [U][C] **(pl. -ties) 1.** the state or condition of being difficult. ¶*without ~*① / *with ~.*② **2.** something that is difficult; an obstacle. ¶*be under a ~*③ / *find no ~ in doing something.*④ **3.** 《usu. *pl.*》 financial troubles. ¶*be in difficulties.*⑤
make a difficulty, object to someone or something.

—[名] 1. 어려움, 곤란 ¶①쉽게/②간신히 2. 어려운 일, 난국; 장애, 방해, 지장, 이의 ¶③어려운 처지에 있다/④쉽게…하다 3. 재정곤란 ¶⑤돈에 쪼들리고 있다
[熟] 반대하다, 애로를 말하다

dif·fi·dence [dífid(ə)ns] *n.* [U] the state of being diffident; lack of self-confidence; shyness.
—[名] 자신이 없음; 기가 약함; 수줍음

dif·fi·dent [dífid(ə)nt] *adj.* lacking in self-confidence; shy.
—[形] 자신이 없는; 수줍은

dif·fi·dent·ly [dífid(ə)ntli] *adv.* in a diffident manner.
—[副] 자신없이, 수줍게

dif·frac·tion [difrǽkʃ(ə)n] *n.* [U] (*Physics*) the act of breaking up sound waves, electricity, etc. around obstacles.
—[名] 《理》 [음파 따위의] 회절(回折)

dif·fuse *v.* [difjú:z → *adj.*] *vt.* spread out; scatter widely. —*vi.* mix together by spreading into one another. —*adj.* [difjú:s] **1.** widely spread; scattered. **2.** wordy; not concise. ¶*a ~ writer.* ▷**dif·fuse·ness** [-nis] *n.*
—[他] …을 뿌리다, 보급시키다 —[自] 뿌려지다, 유포하다 —[形] 1. 널리 퍼진, 흩어진 2. [표현 따위가] 장황한, 산만한

dif·fuse·ly [difjú:sli] *adv.* in a diffuse manner.
—[副] 장황하게, 수다스럽게

dif·fu·sion [difjú:ʒ(ə)n] *n.* [U] **1.** the act of diffusing; the state of being diffused. **2.** wordiness.
—[名] 1. 보급, 살포 2. 산만

dif·fu·sive [difjú:siv] *adj.* **1.** having a tendency to diffuse; showing diffusion. **2.** wordy.
—[形] 1. 살포되는, 보급하는 2. 장황한, 수다스러운

⁑ dig [dig] *v.* **(dug, dig·ging)** *vt.* **1.** break up or loosen (earth, sand, etc.), as with a spade. ¶*~ the ground.* **2.** make (a hole) in the ground. ¶*~ a hole / ~ a tunnel through the hill.* **3.** (*colloq.*) poke; thrust. ¶*~ a horse with spurs / ~ one's fingers into the mud / ~ someone in the ribs.*① —*vi.* **1.** break up, turn over, or remove (earth, sand, etc.) as with a spade. 《*~ into, ~ through* something》 ¶*~ deep / ~ for gold.* **2.** make one's way as by removing or turning over material. ¶*~ under the mountain / ~ through the hill.* **3.** search; study hard. ¶*~ for information / ~ into a writer's diary / He is digging at mathematics.*

—[他] 1. …을 파다, [토지 따위]를 파헤치다 2. [구멍 따위]를 뚫다 3. 《口》 …을 쿡 찌르다, 찔러 넣다 ¶①[손가락 또는 팔꿈치로] 남의 옆구리를 쿡 찌르다 —[自] 1. 흙을 파다 2. 파면서 나아가다, 파서 뚫다 3. 탐구하다

1) ***dig in,*** ⓐ dig trenches for protection. ⓑ work hard.
2) ***dig out,*** find or discover (something) by an effort or search; make a careful inquiry. ¶*We dug out the truth from many reports.*
3) ***dig up,*** ⓐ break up earth by digging; remove (something) from the ground by digging. ⓑ find out.

[熟] 1)ⓐ참호를 파다 ⓑ열심히 공부(일)하다 2)…을 탐구하다, 찾아내다, 조사하다 3)ⓐ흙을 파 일으키다, …을 파내다 ⓑ…을 발견하다

—*n.* [C] the act of digging; a thrust or poke; a remark against someone. ¶*give him a ~ in the ribs.*②
—[名] 파내기, 쿡 찌르기, 빈정대기 ¶②그의 옆구리를 쿡 찌르다

• di·gest [didʒést, daidʒést → *n.*] *vt.* **1.** change (food) into a state in which the body can absorb it. **2.** think (something) over; understand and absorb mentally. **3.** arrange (something) according to some system. **4.** (*Chemistry*) dissolve. **5.** bear; endure. —*vi.* be digested; digest food. —*n.* [dáidʒest] [C] summary.
—[他] 1. …을 소화하다 2. …을 숙고하다, 이해하여 자기 것으로 만들다 3. [계통적으로] 정리하다, 적요(摘要)하다 4. 《化》 …을 침지(浸漬)하다 5. …을 참다 —[自] 소화하다, 삭여지다 —[名] 적요, 총람(總覽)

di·gest·i·ble [didʒéstibl, dai-] *adj.* that can be digested.
—[形] 소화할 수 있는, 간추릴 수 있는

di·ges·tion [didʒéstʃ(ə)n, dai-] *n.* [U] the act of digesting; the condition of being digested; 《*a ~*》 the power of digesting.
—[名] 소화[작용, 력]; 동화력; 《化》 침지(浸漬)

di·ges·tive [didʒéstiv, dai-] *adj.* of, for, or helping digestion; having the power to digest. —*n.* [C] something that aids digestion.
—[形] 소화의, 소화를 촉진하는; 소화력이 있는 —[名] 소화제

dig·ger [dígər] *n.* [C] **1.** a person that digs. **2.** any tool or machine for digging.
—[名] 1. 파는 사람 2. 파는 연장(기계)

dig·it [dídʒit] *n.* **1.** [U] a finger or toe. **2.** any of the figures from 0 to 9.
—[名] 1. 손(발)가락 2. 아라비아 숫자 (0, 1, 2…9)

dig·i·tal·is [dìdʒitéilis] *n.* **1.** [U] a medicine made from foxglove and used for stimulating the heart. **2.** [C] a kind of plant; foxglove.
—[名] 1. 강심제의 일종(디기탈리스의 마른 잎으로 만듦) 2. 디기탈리스

dig·ni·fied [dígnifàid] *adj.* having and showing dignity; majestic; noble.
—[形] 품위있는; 고귀한

dig·ni·fy [dígnifài] *vt.* **(-fied) 1.** give dignity to (some-
—[他] 1. …에 위엄을 갖추다; …을 고귀

one or something); make (someone or something) noble or worthy. **2.** give a high-sounding name to (someone or something). ¶~ *cowardice with the name of prudence.*①
하게 하다; …에 가치를 주다 **2.** …에 어마어마한 이름을 붙이다 ¶①비겁한 것을 신중한 것이라고 하면서 거드름 피우다

dig·ni·tar·y [dígnitèri / -t(ə)ri] *n.* [C] (pl. **-tar·ies**) a person holding a position of honor, esp. in a church.
—[명] 고관, 저명 인사; 고승(高僧)

* **dig·ni·ty** [dígniti] *n.* (pl. **-ties**) **1.** [U] stateliness; worth; nobleness. ¶*with* ~.① **2.** [C] a high rank, office, or title. **3.** [C] a person of high rank, office, or title.
—[명] **1.** 위엄, 거룩함; 존엄성 ¶①위엄 있게, 점잔빼고 **2.** 높은 지위(벼슬) **3.** 고위 인사, 고관

1) ***be beneath one's dignity,*** be unsuitable for one to do.
2) ***stand*** (or ***be***) ***upon one's dignity,*** assume an air of importance; refuse to do what one considers to be undignified.
[熟] 1)[…하기는] 체면에 관계되다 2) 젠체하다, 뽐내다

di·graph [dáigræf / -grɑ:f] *n.* [C] two letters to represent a single sound, such as sh, ea, etc.
—[명] 이중 글자(두 자로 한 음이 나는 sh, ea 따위)

di·gress [digrés, dai-] *vi.* turn away from the main subject in talking or writing. 《~ *from* the main topic, subject, etc.》
—[자] 옆길로 빗나가다, 탈선하다

di·gres·sion [digréʃ(ə)n, dai-] *n.* [U][C] the act of getting away from the main subject in talking or writing.
—[명] 본론에서 벗어나기, 여담(餘談), 탈선

di·gres·sive [digrésiv, dai-] *adj.* being digressed; digressing. ▷**di·gres·sive·ness** [-nis] *n.*
—[형] 지엽적인, 본론에서 벗어난

dike [daik] *n.* [C] **1.** a bank of earth built as a defense against flooding. **2.** a ditch. —*vt.* **1.** provide or protect (something) with dikes. **2.** drain with a ditch. ⇒[N.B.]
—[명] **1.** 방벽(防壁) **2.** 도랑, 개천 —[타] **1.** …에 둑을 쌓다 **2.** …에 도랑을 두르다 [N.B.] dyke 로도 씀

di·lap·i·dat·ed [dilǽpidèitid] *adj.* falling to pieces; ruined; shabby. ¶*a ~ house.*
—[형] 헐어빠진, 황폐한; 초라한

di·late [dailéit, di-] *vi.* **1.** become larger or wider. **2.** speak or write in detail. 《~ *on* or *upon* one's view, etc.》 —*vt.* make (something) larger or wider; enlarge.
—[자] **1.** 퍼지다, 커지다 **2.** 부연(敷衍)하다, 자세히 설명하다 —[타] …을 펼치다, 크게 하다

di·lat·ed [dailéitid, di-] *adj.* widened; expanded.
—[형] 퍼진, 커진, 확장된

di·la·tion [dailéiʃ(ə)n, di-] *n.* [U] the act of dilating; the state of being dilated; enlargement.
—[명] 팽창, 확대

dil·a·to·ry [dílətɔ̀:ri / -t(ə)ri] *adj.* given to delay; not prompt; causing delay.
—[형] 느린, 지체되는; 시간을 끄는

di·lem·ma [dilémə, +*Brit.* dai-] *n.* [C] **1.** any situation requiring a choice; a difficult situation. ¶*in a ~.*① **2.** an argument forcing an opponent to choose between equally unfavorable alternatives.
—[명] **1.** 진퇴양난, 궁지 ¶①진퇴유곡에 빠져 **2.** 양도논법(兩刀論法), 딜레마

on the horns of a dilemma, faced with a choice between equally unfavorable alternatives.
[熟] 진퇴유곡에 빠져

dil·et·tan·te [dìlitǽnti] *n.* [C] (pl. **-tes** or **-ti**) **1.** a lover of the fine arts. **2.** a person who follows an art or science only for amusement.
—[명] **1.** 예술 애호가 **2.** 아마튜어 예술가

dil·et·tan·ti [dìlitǽnti:] *n.* pl. of **dilettante.**

* **dil·i·gence**[1] [dílidʒ(ə)ns] *n.* [U] the state of being diligent; hard work; careful effort; industry.
—[명] 부지런함, 근면; 열심; 공들임

dil·i·gence[2] [dílidʒ(ə)ns] *n.* [C] a public stagecoach formerly used in France.
—[명] [옛날 프랑스의] 합승 마차

* **dil·i·gent** [dílidʒ(ə)nt] *adj.* hard-working; industrious; attentive to one's duties; careful and steady. ↔idle
—[형] 부지런한, 근면한; 힘들인

dil·i·gent·ly [dílidʒ(ə)ntli] *adv.* in a diligent manner.
—[부] 부지런히, 애써서, 공들여

dil·ly-dal·ly [dílidæ̀li] *vi.* (**-lied**) waste time; act in an indecisive manner; loiter.
—[자] 꾸물거리다, 망설이다, 빈들빈들하다

di·lute [dil(j)ú:t, dai-] *vt.* **1.** make (a liquid) weaker or thinner by adding water or some other liquid. 《~ milk *with* water》 **2.** weaken or lessen. —*adj.* weakened or thinned by the addition of water, etc.
—[타] **1.** [액체]에 물을 타다, …을 묽게 하다 **2.** …을 약하게 하다, 희박하게 하다 —[형] 물을 탄, 묽은; 희미한

di·lu·tion [dil(j)ú:ʃ(ə)n, dai-] *n.* **1.** [U] the act of diluting; the state of being diluted. **2.** [C] something diluted.
—[명] **1.** 묽게 하기, 희석(稀釋)[도] **2.** 희석물(액)

‡ **dim** [dim] *adj.* (**dim·mer, dim·mest**) **1.** not bright; not clear; shadowy; dark. ¶*in the ~ light.*① **2.** not clearly seen, heard, or understood; vague. **3.** not seeing. ¶~ *with tears / grow ~.* **4.** stupid; dull. —*vi.* (**dimmed, dim·ming**) *vi.* become dim; fade. —*vt.* make
—[형] **1.** 어둠침침한; 희미한 ¶①희미한 불빛 아래 **2.** 뚜렷하지 않은, 몽롱한 **3.** 보이지 않는, 흐린 **4.** 어리석은, 우둔한 —[자] 어둠침침해지다, 흐릿해지다 —[타] …을 어둠침침하게 하다, …을 흐

dime

(something) dim.
dime [daim] *n.* ⓒ a silver coin of the United States and of Canada, equal to 10 cents. ——ⓝ [미국·캐나다의] 10센트 은화(1/10달러)
di·men·sion [diménʃ(ə)n, +*Brit.* dai-] *n.* ⓒ **1.** any measurement of length, breadth, or thickness. ¶*of one ~*① / *of two dimensions*② / *of three dimensions.*③ **2.** (usu. *pl.*) size; extent. ¶*in dimensions*④ / *of great* (or *vast*) *dimensions.*⑤ ——ⓝ 1.[길이·폭·두께 따위의] 치수 ¶①선(線)의/②길이의/②평면의, 길이와 폭의/③입체의 2. 크기; 범위 ¶④치수는/⑤아주 큰
di·men·sion·al [dɪmenʃən(ə)l, +*Brit.* dai-] *adj.* of dimension or dimensions. ——ⓟ 치수의, 치수로 잴 수 있는
* **di·min·ish** [dimíniʃ] *vt.* make (something) smaller in size, amount, etc.; lessen; reduce; decrease. ——*vi.* become smaller or less. ——ⓣ [크기·분량 따위]를 축소하다, 작게 하다, 줄이다 ——ⓘ 작아지다, 감소하다
di·min·u·en·do [dimìnjuéndou] *n.* ⓒ (pl. **-dos**) (*Music*) a gradual lessening of loudness. ——*adj., adv.* (*Music*) with diminuendo. ——ⓝ (樂) 점점 약해지는 음 ——ⓟⓑ (樂) 점점 약한(약하게)
dim·i·nu·tion [dìmin(j)ú:ʃ(ə)n / -njú:ʃ(ə)n] *n.* ⓤⓒ the act of diminishing; the state of being diminished; the condition of lessening in quantity, quality, etc.; decrease. ——ⓝ 감소, 축소, 감손(減損)
di·min·u·tive [dimínjutiv] *adj.* **1.** very small; tiny. **2.** (*Grammar*) expressing smallness. ——*n.* ⓒ **1.** a small person or thing. **2.** (*Grammar*) a word formed from another by the addition of a suffix expressing smallness. ——ⓟ 1. 작은, 소형의 2. 《文法》 지소(指小)의 ——ⓝ 1. 작은 사람(것) 2. 《文法》 지소사 ⓝⒷ duck*ling*, stream*let*의 -ling, -let 따위
dim·ly [dímli] *adv.* in a dim manner. ——ⓑ 어둠침침하게, 희미하게
dim·ness [dímnis] *n.* ⓤ the state of being dim. ——ⓝ 어둠침침함, 희미함
dim·ple [dímpl] *n.* ⓒ **1.** a small natural hollow in the cheek or chin. **2.** any small, hollow place; a ripple. ——*vt.* make dimples in (something). ——*vi.* show or form dimples. ——ⓝ 1. 보조개 2. 움푹한 곳; 잔물결 ——ⓣ …에 보조개를 만들다, 잔물결을 일으키다 ——ⓘ 보조개가 생기다, 잔물결이 일다
din [din] *n.* ⓤ (sometimes *a ~*) a loud, confused noise. ——*vt.* (**dinned, din·ning**) strike (something) with a din; say over and over; repeat noisily. ¶*~ ideas into someone's ears.* ——*vi.* make a din. ——ⓝ 소음, 시끄러운 소리 ——ⓣ …을 울려 퍼지게 하다, 시끄럽게 되풀이하다 ——ⓘ 울려 퍼지다
:**dine** [dain] *vi.* eat dinner. ——*vt.* give a dinner to or for (someone).
dine out, eat dinner away from home. ——ⓘ 정찬을 먹다, 식사를 하다 ——ⓣ …을 정찬에 초대하다
熟 밖에서 식사하다
din·er [dáinər] *n.* ⓒ **1.** a person who dines. **2.** a railroad dining-car. ——ⓝ 1. 식사하는 사람 2. 식당차
ding-dong [díŋdɔ̀ːŋ / -dɔ́ŋ] *n.* ⓒ the sound made by a bell; any similar sound; the continuous ringing of a bell. ——ⓝ 땡땡, 뎅뎅, 계속 울리는 소리
din·gi·ly [díndʒili] *adv.* in a dingy manner. ——ⓑ 거무칙칙하게, 그을어
din·gi·ness [díndʒinis] *n.* ⓤ the condition of being dingy. ——ⓝ 거무칙칙함, 그을음
din·gy [díndʒi] *adj.* (**-gi·er, -gi·est**) dirty-looking; dull. ——ⓟ 더러워진; 거무칙칙한
din·ing car [dáiniŋ kɑ̀ːr] *n.* a railroad car in which meals are served. ——ⓝ 식당차
dining room [⌐ ⌐ ⌐] *n.* a room in which people eat their meals. ——ⓝ 식당
dining table [⌐ ⌐ ⌐] *n.* a table on which meals are served. ——ⓝ 식탁
:**din·ner** [dínər] *n.* **1.** ⓤⓒ the main meal of the day, usu. taken in the evening. **2.** ⓒ a formal meal in honor of someone or on some special occasion. ——ⓝ 1. 정찬 2. [공식적인] 만찬회, 오찬회
dinner jacket [⌐ ⌐ ⌐] *n.* a tuxedo jacket. ——ⓝ 약식 야회복
dinner service [⌐ ⌐ ⌐] *n.* a special set of plates; dishes used at dinner. ——ⓝ 정찬용 식기류 한 벌
dinner set [⌐ ⌐] *n.* =dinner service.
di·no·saur [dáinəsɔ̀ːr] *n.* ⓒ any of a group of very large reptiles that lived a long time ago. ——ⓝ [중생대(中生代)의] 공룡(恐龍)
dint [dint] *n.* ⓒ a mark or slight hollow in a hard surface made by a blow or pressure; a dent.
by dint of, by means of something. ¶*He succeeded by ~ of hard work.*①
——*vt.* make a dent in (something). ——ⓝ [치거나 밀거나 하여 생긴] 움푹 팬 곳, 맞은 자국
熟 …에 의하여 ¶①그는 열심히 일한 덕으로 성공했다
——ⓣ …을 움푹 들어가게 하다
di·o·cese [dáiəsi:s / -si(ː)s] *n.* ⓒ the district under a bishop's authority. ——ⓝ bishop의 감독 관구(管區)
:**dip** [dip] *v.* (**dipped, dip·ping**) *vt.* **1.** put (something) into a liquid for a moment, as to wet or to color it. ——ⓣ 1. …을 살짝 담그다, 담가서 염색하다 2. …을 액체에 적셔서 씻다 3.

diphtheria

¶~ *a pen in ink.* **2.** wash or clean (something) by putting in a liquid. ¶~ *a dress.* **3.** put (one's hand, a spoon, etc.) into something to take something else out; get or take out (something) by scooping up with a container, the hand, etc. ¶~ *fresh water from a stream.* **4.** lower and quickly raise (a flag, etc.) again. ¶~ *one's headlights*① / ~ *a flag.* —*vi.* **1.** plunge into water or other liquid and emerge quickly. ¶*The boat dipped into the waves.* **2.** (*Geology*) sink; descend gradually; incline or slope downward. ¶*The road dips.* / *The sun dipped below the horizon.* **3.** read random passages of a book; study superficially. [melted fat.]
1) *dip candles,* make candles by dipping wicks into
2) *dip deep into the future,* think over one's future deeply.
3) *dip one's hand into one's purse,* spend money freely.
—*n.* **1.** ⓒ the act of dipping of any kind, esp. of plunging into water. ¶*have* (or *take*) *a ~ in the sea.* **2.** Ⓤ a liquid in which something is dipped for cleaning, dyeing, etc. ¶*sheep-dip.*① **3.** ⓒ an act of sinking down; a short downward slope; a slight hollow. ¶*a ~ in the stock-market prices*② / *a ~ in the road* / *a ~ among the hills.* **4.** ⓒ a candle made by dipping.
diph·the·ri·a [difθíəriə, dif-/dif-] *n.* Ⓤ (*Medicine*) a dangerous, quickly spreading disease of the throat.
diph·thong [dífθɔːŋ, dífθ-/-θɒŋ] *n.* ⓒ **1.** a combination of two vowel sounds pronounced in one syllable. **2.** two vowel letters joined together.
di·plo·ma [diplóumə] *n.* ⓒ (pl. **-mas** or **-ma·ta**) **1.** a certificate given to a student by a school, college, or university. **2.** any official document showing honors, privileges, etc.
di·plo·ma·cy [diplóuməsi] *n.* Ⓤ **1.** the management of relations between nations. **2.** tactful skill in handling others; tact.
dip·lo·mat [díplэmæt] *n.* ⓒ **1.** a representative of a government whose work is to look after the interests of his own nation in a foreign country. **2.** a tactful person.
di·plo·ma·ta [diplóumətə] *n.* pl. of **diploma.**
dip·lo·mat·ic [dìpləmǽtik] *adj.* of diplomacy; tactful and skillful in dealing with people. ¶*the ~ service*① / ~ *corps* / *a ~ answer* / *settle by ~ means.*
dip·lo·mat·i·cal·ly [dìpləmǽtikəli] *adv.* in a diplomatic manner; according to the rules of diplomacy.
di·plo·ma·tist [diplóumətist] *n.* ⓒ a diplomat.
dip·per [dípər] *n.* ⓒ **1.** a person or a thing that dips; a cup with a long handle used to dip water. **2.** (*the D*-) either of two groups of stars in the northern sky in the shape of a dipper. ¶*the Big Dipper*① / *the Little Dipper.*② [~ *need of help.*]
dire [dáiər] *adj.* horrible; terrible; dreadful. ¶*He is in*
: **di·rect** [dirékt, dai-] *vt.* **1.** control; guide. ¶~ *a company*① / *Policemen ~ traffic.*② **2.** order; command. ((~ someone *to do*; ~ *that* ...)) ¶*The teacher directed the pupils to form a line.*③ / *He directed that you should start at once.*④ **3.** aim at (something); turn (one's attention, efforts, etc.) to something. **4.** tell (someone) the way. ¶*Can you direct me to the station?* **5.** send (a letter, etc.) to someone. ¶*a letter directed to him.*
—*adj.* **1.** straight. ¶*a ~ road.* **2.** frank; clear. ¶*a ~ answer.* **3.** with nothing or no one between; immediate. ¶*a ~ tax*⑤ / *make ~ contacts with him.*⑥ **4.** without stopping. **5.** in an unbroken line. ¶*a ~ hit.*⑦
direct current [-́ -́ -́] *n.* electricity that flows in one

direct current

[손·스푼 따위]를 무엇인가 건져내기 위하여 넣다; 손·그릇으로 …을 건져내다, 퍼내다 **4.** [깃발 따위를] 잠깐 내렸다 올리다 ¶①[눈부시지 않도록] 헤드라이트를 내리다 —自 **1.** 살짝 물속에 들어갔다 나오다 **2.** (*地質*) 침하(沈下)하다; 천천히 기울다, 아래 쪽으로 기울다 **3.** [책 따위를] 대충(띄엄띄엄) 읽다; 장난삼아 조금 해보다

團 1)녹인 초에 심지를 넣어 양초를 만들다 2)장래를 깊이 생각하다 3)돈을 물 쓰듯 하다

—名 **1.** 담그기, 살짝 잠기기, 목욕하기 **2.** 침액(浸液) ¶①세양액(洗羊液) **3.** 침하; 경사; 움푹한 데 ¶②증권 시세의 하락 **4.** 양초

—名 (*醫*) 디프테리아

—名 **1.** 이중모음(ai, ɔi, ei 따위) **2.** 이중 모음자[æ, œ 따위]

—名 **1.** [대학 따위의] 졸업증서, 면허장 **2.** 공문서, 특허장

—名 **1.** 외교 **2.** 외교 수완; 교제술

—名 **1.** 외교관 **2.** 외교가

—動 외교의; 외교 수완이 있는; 사람을 잘 다루는 ¶①대(공)사관원, 외교관 근무

—副 외교적으로, 외교상

—名 외교관, 외교가

—名 **1.** 퍼내는 사람(기구), 국자 **2.** 북두칠성 ¶①대웅좌(大熊座)/②소웅좌

—動 무서운, 비참한; 심한
—動 **1.** …을 지휘하다; 인도하다 ¶①회사를 경영하다/②순경이 교통정리를 한다 **2.** …에게 명령하다 ¶③선생은 학생들에게 일렬로 서라고 명령했다/④너는 곧 떠나라는 그의 명령이다 **3.** …을 겨냥하다; 돌리다 **4.** …에 길을 가르쳐 주다 **5.** [편지 따위를] 보내다

—動 **1.** 똑바른 **2.** 솔직한; 분명한 **3.** 직접의 ¶⑤직접세/⑥그와 직접 접촉하다 **4.** 직통의 **5.** 직제(直系)의 ¶⑦명중

—名 [전기의] 직류

direction [332] **disaffection**

direction only. ↔alternating current

: **di·rec·tion** [dirékʃ(ə)n, dai-] *n.* **1.** ⓤ instruction; guidance. ¶*work under the ~ of a leader.*① **2.** ⓒ (usu. *pl.*) information about what to do, how to do something, etc.; an order; a command. **3.** ⓒ (usu. *pl.*) the address on a letter or parcel. **4.** ⓒⓤ the way a person or thing faces. ¶*in every directions; in all directions*② / *a ~ finder*③ / *a sense of ~.*④ ―名 1.지휘;지도;감독 ¶①지도자의 지휘하에 일하다 2.지시;명령,명령 3.[편지의] 주소 성명,겉봉 4.방향,방위(方位) ¶②사방팔방으로/③방향 탐지기/④방향 감각

: **di·rect·ly** [diréktli, dai-] *adv.* **1.** in a direct manner; straight. ¶*This road leads ~ to the lake.*① **2.** at once; right away; immediately. ¶*Go there ~.* ――*conj.* as soon as … ¶*He gets up ~ the bell rings.* [direct.] ―副 1.똑바로,직접 ¶①이 길은 똑바로 호수에 이른다 2.[…하자] 동시에,즉시 ―接 …하자마자

di·rect·ness [diréktnis, dai-] *n.* ⓤ the state of being ―名 직접적임,똑바름; 솔직함

: **di·rec·tor** [diréktər, dai-] *n.* ⓒ **1.** a manager; a leader; a person who directs the production of a play, film, dancing, or television. **2.** a member of a board chosen to carry on the affairs of a company or society. ¶*a board of directors*① / *a personnel ~*② / *a managing ~.*③ ―名 1.지휘자,지도차 [영화 따위의] 감독,[연극의] 연출가 2.이사(理事), 지배인,중역; 교장,장관,국장 ¶①이사회/②인사국장/③전무이사

di·rec·to·rate [dirékt(ə)rit, dai-] *n.* ⓒ **1.** the office of a director. **2.** a group of directors. ―名 1.이사·감독의 직위 2.이사회,간부회

di·rec·tor·ship [diréktərʃip, dai-] *n.* ⓤ the position or term of office of a director. ―名 이사의 직(임기)

di·rec·to·ry [dirékt(ə)ri, dai-] *n.* ⓒ (pl. **-ries**) **1.** a book of names and addresses. ¶*a telephone ~*① / *a business ~.*② **2.** a book of rules or directions. ――*adj.* directing; leading; instructing. [*~ misfortune.*] ―名 1.주소 성명록,인명록 ¶①전화번호부/②상공인1명부 2.규칙서 ―形 지휘의,관리의

dire·ful [dáiərf(u)l] *adj.* dreadful; awful; terrible. ¶*a* ―形 무서운,무시무시한

dirge [də:rdʒ] *n.* ⓒ a song of grief or sorrow; a lament. ―名 비가(悲歌),장송가

dir·i·gi·ble [dírɪdʒibl, +*Brit.* dirídʒəbl] *n.* ⓒ an airship. ――*adj.* that can be controlled. ¶*a ~ balloon.* ―名 비행선 ―形 조종할 수 있는 ¶①비행선

dirk [də:rk] *n.* ⓒ a dagger. ――*vt.* wound (someone) with a dirk. [clean action.] ―名 단검 ―他 …을 단검으로 찌르다

*** dirt** [də:rt] *n.* ⓤ **1.** unclean matter; dust; mud. **2.** un― ―名 1.오물;먼지,쓰레기,진흙 2.비

dirt-cheap [də́:rttʃí:p] *adj.* very cheap. ¶*This hou―* ―形 굉장히 싼 [열한 행위]

dirt·i·ly [də́:rtili] *adv.* in a dirty manner. [was] ―副 불결하게,상스럽게

dirt·i·ness [də́:rtinis] *n.* ⓤ the state of being dirty ―名 불결,상스러움,비열

: **dirt·y** [də́:rti] *adj.* (**dirt·i·er, dirt·i·est**) **1.** soiled with dirt; unclean. ¶*a ~ bomb*① / *a ~ road.* **2.** unclean in color; grayish. ¶*a ~ green.* **3.** not clean in speech, action, or thought; crude. ¶*~ money*② / *do one's ~ work for someone.*③ **4.** rough; stormy. ―形 1.더러운,불결한 ¶①더러운 폭탄(방사낙진이 있는 원자탄 따위) 2.[빛깔이] 칙칙한 3.상스러운;비열한 ¶②부정한 돈/③…을 위해 궂은 일을 하다 4.[날씨가] 험악한

――*vt., vi.* (**dirt·ied**) make (something or someone) dirty; become dirty; put (someone) to shame. ―他自 …을 더럽히다;더러워지다;에게 창피를 주다

dis- [dis-] *pref.* **1.** opposition: *disagree* (=don't agree). **2.** reverse: *discourage* (=lose one's courage). **3.** apart; away: *dismiss* (=permit to go). ―《接頭》1.취소 2.반대 3.분리,제거

dis·a·bil·i·ty [dìsəbíliti] *n.* ⓤ lack of physical or mental ability. ¶*be excused because of mental ~.*① ―名 무력,무능; 무자격 ¶①정신장애로 용서를 받다

dis·a·ble [diséibl] *vt.* **1.** make (something or someone) unable or unfit; make (something or someone) useless; cripple. 《*~ someone from doing; ~ someone for*》 ¶*a disabled soldier*① / *His old age disabled him from working.*② **2.** disqualify legally. ―他 1.…을 쓸모없게 만들다,무력하게 하다;불구로 만들다 ¶①상이군인/②그는 노령으로 일할 수 없었다 2. …을 법률상 무능력하게 하다

dis·a·buse [dìsəbjú:z] *vt.* free (someone) from wrong ideas or mistakes. 《*~ someone of*》 ¶*Education should ~ people of superstition.*① ―他 …의 잘못〔그릇된 생각〕을 없애다 ¶①교육은 인간의 미신을 없애야 한다

dis·ad·van·tage [dìsədvǽntidʒ / -vɑ́:n-] *n.* **1.** ⓒ something that prevents success; an unfavorable situation. ¶*He sold goods at a ~.*① **2.** ⓤ loss. ―名 1.불리한 입장·조건 ¶①그는 손해를 보고 물건을 팔았다 2.불이익,손실

dis·ad·van·ta·geous [dìsædvəntéidʒəs / dìsædvɑ:n-] *adj.* unfavorable to success; inconvenient. ―形 불리한;형편이 좋지 않은

dis·af·fect·ed [dìsəféktid] *adj.* unfriendly; discontented. ―形 불만이 있는,정떨어진

dis·af·fec·tion [dìsəfékʃ(ə)n] *n.* ⓤ lack of affection or good will; discontent. ¶*Lack of food caused ~ against* ―名 인심이 이탈;불만,불평 ¶①식량 부족이 정부에 대한 불만을 낳았다

*the government.*①

dis·a·gree [dìsəgríː] *vi.* **1.** fail to agree. 《~ *with* someone or something *in*》 ¶*She disagrees with her mother-in-law.*① **2.** quarrel; talk angrily. 《~ *with* someone》 ¶*Whenever we meet, we ~.* **3.** cause physical pain or discomfort. 《~ *with* someone》 ¶*Hot weather disagrees with me.*②

—[自] 1. 일치하지 않다 ¶①그녀는 시어머니와 의가 좋지 않다 2. 싸우다, 의견이 다르다 3. [풍토·음식이] 맞지 않다 ¶②더운 기후는 나에게 맞지 않는다

dis·a·gree·a·ble [dìsəgríəbl] *adj.* **1.** unpleasant; offensive. ¶*Advice sometimes sounds ~.* **2.** unpleasant in manner; bad-tempered. ¶*He is a ~ man.*①

—[形] 1. 불쾌한, 싫은 2. [성질 따위] 나쁜, 심술궂은 ¶①그는 마음에 안 맞는 녀석이다

dis·a·gree·a·bly [dìsəgríəbli] *adv.* in a disagreeable manner.

—[副] 불쾌하게

dis·a·gree·ment [dìsəgríːmənt] *n.* **1.** [U] difference of opinion; lack of agreement. **2.** [C] an argument; a quarrel. ¶*have a ~ with one's wife.*①

—[名] 1. [의견 따위의] 불일치 2. 논쟁, 싸움 ¶①아내와 싸움을 하다

dis·al·low [dìsəláu] *vt.* refuse to permit (something); reject. ¶*Father disallowed my proposal.*

—[他] [요구 따위]를 불허하다; 거부하다; 각하하다

⁑dis·ap·pear [dìsəpíər] *vi.* go out of sight; be no longer seen; become lost. ↔appear ¶*The sun disappeared behind a cloud.* / *My books have disappeared.* / *The money disappeared mysteriously from the safe.*①

—[自] 보이지 않게 되다; 사라지다 ¶①이상하게도 그 돈은 금고에서 사라졌다

dis·ap·pear·ance [dìsəpíərəns] *n.* [U][C] the act of disappearing. ↔appearance

—[名] 소실(消失); 실종, 행방불명

⁑dis·ap·point [dìsəpɔ́int] *vt.* **1.** cause (someone) sorrow by failing to satisfy his expectation, desire, hope, etc. ¶*The result disappointed me.* / *We were disappointed at the news.*① / *I was disappointed in my new teacher.*② / *They were disappointed that she did not come.* **2.** break one's promise to (someone). **3.** upset.

—[他] 1. …을 실망시키다, …의 기대를 배반하다 ¶①우리는 그 소식을 듣고 실망했다/②나는 새로운 선생에 실망했다 2. …와의 약속을 저버리다 3. [목적·희망 따위]를 꺾다, 좌절시키다

be disappointed of (=*fail to get*) *what one has desired.* ¶*He was disappointed of the first prize.*③

[熟] …의 기대가 어긋나다 ¶③그는 1등의 기대가 어긋났다

***dis·ap·point·ment** [dìsəpɔ́intmənt] *n.* **1.** [U] the state of being disappointed. ¶*to one's ~.*① **2.** [C] a person or thing that disappoints.

—[名] 1. 실망 ¶①낙심천만하게도 2. 실망시키는 사람(일·것)

dis·ap·pro·ba·tion [dìsæproubéiʃ(ə)n] *n.* =disapproval.

dis·ap·prov·al [dìsəprúːv(ə)l] *n.* [U] the act of disapproving; failure to approve.

—[名] 불찬성, 안 된다고 하기

dis·ap·prove [dìsəprúːv] *vt., vi.* **1.** have or express an unfavorable opinion of (something); think (something) wrong. 《~ *of* something》 ¶*I wholly ~ of his attitude.*① **2.** refuse to approve; reject. ¶*The court disapproved the verdict.*②

—[他][自] 1. [의견·행위 따위를] 안 된다고 하다, 찬성(동의)하지 않다 ¶①그의 태도에는 전적으로 불찬성이다 2. [안을] 인가하지 않다 ¶②법정은 배심원의 평결(評決)을 받아들이지 않았다

dis·ap·prov·ing·ly [dìsəprúːviŋli] *adv.* in a disapproving manner; showing disapproval. ¶*He looked at me ~.*

—[副] 불찬성하여; 비난하여

dis·arm [disáːrm] *vt.* **1.** take weapons from (someone). 《~ someone *of* his weapon》 **2.** get rid of ill-feeling or suspicion in (someone); make (someone) friendly. ¶*Religion disarms death of its terror.*① —*vi.* abandon or reduce the quantity of military equipment.

—[他] 1. …의 무기를 빼앗다, 무장을 해제하다 2. …의 노여움(의심)을 없애다 ¶①종교는 죽음의 공포를 없애 준다 —[自] 군비를 해제하다; 군비를 축소하다

dis·ar·ma·ment [disáːrməmənt] *n.* [U] the act of disarming; the reduction of armed forces. ¶*a ~ conference.*①

—[名] 무장해제; 군비축소 ¶①군축회의

dis·ar·range [dìsəréindʒ] *vt.* break up the proper arrangement of (something); disorder. ¶*The wind disarranged the papers on the desk.*

—[他] …을 어지럽히다, 혼란케 하다

dis·ar·range·ment [dìsəréindʒmənt] *n.* [U] the act of disarranging; the state of being disarranged; disorder.

—[名] 혼란, 교란, 난맥, 무질서

***dis·as·ter** [dizǽstər / -áːstə] *n.* [C][U] a sudden event which causes great unhappiness, such as a big fire, an earthquake, or a flood. ¶*victims of a railroad ~* / *This temple has had many disasters since 1600.*

—[名] 천재(天災), 재난, 불행

dis·as·trous [dizǽstrəs / -áːs-] *adj.* causing great loss or injury; very unhappy. ¶*a ~ war.*

—[形] 재해의, 비참한, 손해가 큰; 불행한

dis·as·trous·ly [dizǽstrəsli / -áːs-] *adv.* in a disastrous manner.

—[副] 비참하게

dis·a·vow [dìsəváu] *vt.* deny; refuse. ¶*The king disavowed the statement bearing his signature.*

—[他] …을 부인하다, 거부하다

D

dis·a·vow·al [dìsəváuəl] *n.* Ⓤ Ⓒ the act of disavowing; refusal to approve; denial.
—Ⓢ 부인; 거절

dis·band [disbǽnd] *vt., vi.* 1. discharge (someone) or retire from military service. 2. break up (an organization, etc.). ¶*They disbanded their company.*
—⑩ⓐ 1. …을 제대시키다 2. …을 해산(해체)시키다

dis·be·lief [dìsbilíːf] *n.* Ⓤ the act of disbelieving; denial of belief; unbelief. [distrust.
—Ⓢ 불신; 의혹; 신앙을 부인하기; 의심하다

dis·be·lieve [dìsbilíːv] *vi., vt.* fail to believe; doubt; *disbelieve in,* distrust. ¶~ *in a religion.*
—ⓐ 신용하지 않다; 신앙하지 않 熟 …을 신앙하지 않다

dis·bur·den [disbə́ːrdn] *vt., vi.* take away a burden from (something); unload; get rid of a burden. ¶~ *one's mind*① / *They disburdened me of my grief.*
—⑩ⓐ […에서] 무거운 짐을 내리다, […을] 안심하(게 하)다 ¶①마음의 무거운 짐을 풀다

dis·burse [disbə́ːrs] *vt., vi.* pay money.
—⑩ⓐ 지불하다

dis·burse·ment [disbə́ːrsmənt] *n.* 1. Ⓤ the act of disbursing; payment. ¶*We advanced ~.*① 2. Ⓒ the money that is so paid.
—Ⓢ 1. 지불 ¶①우리는 지불을 선불했다 2. 지불금

disc [disk] *n.* =disk.

dis·card [diskáːrd] *vt.* throw away (something useless); give up; dismiss. ¶*He discarded his old shoes.* —*n.* 1. Ⓤ abandonment. 2. Ⓒ something or someone discarded. ¶*throw into the ~.*①
—⑩ (필요없다고) …을 버리다; 해고하다 —Ⓢ 1. 버리기 2. 버림받은 것(사람) ¶①버리다

dis·cern [disə́ːrn, -zə́ːrn] *vt.* see or understand clearly. ¶~ *good and evil;* ~ *good from evil*① / ~ *a distant object.*② —*vi.* see a difference. ¶~ *between good and evil.* [clearly; distinguishable.
—⑩ …을 똑똑히 알아 보다, 식별하다 ¶①선악을 식별하다/②먼곳에 있는 것을 알아 보다 —ⓐ 식별하다

dis·cern·i·ble [disə́ːrnibl, -zə́ːrn-] *adj.* that can be seen
—Ⓢ 식별할 수 있는; 분간할 수 있는

dis·cern·ing [disə́ːrniŋ, -zə́ːrn-] *adj.* able to see and judge; having sound common sense. [of discerning.
—Ⓢ 식별력이 있는; 명민한

dis·cern·ment [disə́ːrnmənt, -zə́ːrn-] *n.* Ⓤ the power
—Ⓢ 식별력, 안식의 날카로움, 통찰력

: dis·charge [distʃáːrdʒ →*n.*] *vt.* 1. take off (a load) from a ship; unload. ¶~ *a cargo* / ~ *a ship of her cargo.*① 2. shoot; fire. ¶~ *a gun* / ~ *a shot from a gun.* 3. send out; give out; emit. ¶~ *smoke* / *The wound is still discharging pus.* 4. set (someone) free; release. ¶~ *a patient from* [the] *hospital.*② 5. send (someone) away from his employment; dismiss; fire. 6. do; perform. ¶~ *one's duties.* —*vi.* get rid of a burden; (of water, color, etc.) pour forth; run; (of a gun) fire. ¶*The river discharges into Yellow Sea.*
—⑩ 1. …을 내리다, [배에서 양륙(揚陸)하다 ¶①배에서 짐을 부리다 2. …을 발사(발포)하다; 방출하다 3. …을 배출하다, 토해 내다 4. …을 자유로 해주다; 방면하다 ¶②환자를 퇴원시키다 5. …을 해고하다 6. 이행하다 —ⓐ 짐을 부리다; 흘러 들어가다, 번지다; 발사하다

—*n.* [-,́ -,́] 1. Ⓤ Ⓒ the act of discharging. ¶*a ~ fo shots* / *a port of ~* / *the ~ of prisoners* / ~ *from service.* 2. Ⓒ a flow of electricity. 3. Ⓒ a writing that shows someone's release.
—Ⓢ 1. 짐을 부리기, 양륙; 발사, 발포; 방출, 유출; 제대; 해임, 해고; 해방, 면제; 지불 의무의 수행, 이행 2. 방전(放電) 3. 제대 증명서; 해임장

dis·ci·ple [disáipl] *n.* Ⓒ 1. a student; a follower. 2. a follower of Jesus, esp. one of the twelve apostles.
—Ⓢ 1. 제자, 문하생 2. 그리스도의 12사도의 한 사람

dis·ci·pli·nar·i·an [dìsiplinέəriən] *n.* Ⓒ a person who supports strict discipline.
—Ⓢ 엄격히 규율을 지키(게 하)는 사람

dis·ci·pli·nar·y [dísiplinèri / -nəri] *adj.* 1. of or for discipline. 2. intended to punish the violation of order or discipline. ¶~ *punishment.*①
—⑩ 1. 훈련(훈육)의 2. 징계의 ¶①징계처분

• **dis·ci·pline** [dísiplin] *n.* Ⓤ 1. training. ¶*mental ~*① / *courage without ~.*② 2. orderly conduct among school children, soldiers, etc. ¶*military ~.* 3. punishment. 4. Ⓒ a branch of knowledge. —*vt.* 1. train; instruct; educate. 2. punish.
—Ⓢ 1. 훈련, 훈육 ¶①두뇌의 훈련/②만용 2. 수양, 규율 3. 징계, 징벌 4. 학문; 학과 —⑩ 1. …을 훈련하다, 훈육하다 2. …을 처벌하다

dis·claim [diskléim] *vt.* 1. disapprove; deny. ¶*They ~ the authority of Jesus Christ.* 2. reject as not belonging to oneself; disown. ¶*He disclaimed his only son.*
—⑩ 1. [권위 따위]를 부인하다 2. [관계·권리 따위]를 포기하다, 기권하다

• **dis·close** [disklóuz] *vt.* show; make (something) known. ¶~ *one's plan* / ~ *a secret.*
—⑩ …을 나타내다, 폭로하다, 노출시키다, 발표하다

dis·clo·sure [disklóuʒər] *n.* 1. Ⓤ the act of disclosing; the state of being disclosed. 2. Ⓒ a thing which is disclosed.
make a disclosure of, disclose or tell of (something).
—Ⓢ 1. 폭로, 발각, 발표 2. 폭로된 사물

熟 폭로하다

dis·col·or, *Brit.* **-our** [diskʎlər] *vt.* change the color of
—⑩ …을 변색시키다 —ⓐ 변색하다

discoloration　[335]　discount

(something). ¶*Dyes discolored the water.* —*vi.* change in color; lose freshness; fade.

dis·col·or·a·tion, *Brit.* **-our-** [dìskʌləréiʃ(ə)n] *n.* **1.** Ⓤ the act of discoloring; the state of being discolored. **2.** Ⓒ a stain. ——名 1. 변색 2. 더럼, 얼룩

dis·com·fit [diskʌ́mfit] *vt.* **1.** defeat (the enemy) completely. **2.** overthrow; upset. **3.** make (someone) uneasy or confused; embarrass. ——동 1. …을 완패시키다 2. [계획 따위]를 뒤엎다, 좌절시키다 3. …을 당황케 하다, 허둥거리게 하다

dis·com·fi·ture [diskʌ́mfitʃər] *n.* Ⓤ the act of discomfiting; the state of being discomfited; a complete defeat; failure of plans or hopes; confusion. ——명 완패(完敗), 패배; 좌절, 실패; 낭패, 당황

dis·com·fort [diskʌ́mfərt] *n.* **1.** Ⓤ lack of comfort or pleasantness; uneasiness. ¶*at personal* ~① / *without* ~.② **2.** Ⓒ anything causing discomfort. ——명 1. 불쾌, 불안; 불편 ¶①불편을 참고서/②불편없이 2. 불쾌하게 하는 것

dis·com·mode [dìskəmóud] *vt.* annoy; trouble. ——동 …을 불편하게 하다, 괴롭히다

dis·com·pose [dìskəmpóuz] *vt.* disturb the peace and quietness of (someone); make (someone) anxious. ——동 …의 침착성(안정감)을 잃게 하다; 불안하게 하다

dis·com·po·sure [dìskəmpóuʒər] *n.* Ⓤ the act of discomposing; the state of being discomposed; agitation; anxiety; uneasiness. ——명 마음의 동요, 불안, 당황

dis·con·cert [dìskənsə́:rt] *vt.* **1.** disturb; embarrass; confuse. ¶*His late arrival disconcerted us.* **2.** upset. ¶*Our plans were disconcerted by him.* ——동 1. …을 당황하게 하다, 어리둥절하게 하다 2. [계략]을 뒤집어엎다, 좌절시키다

dis·con·cert·ment [dìskənsə́:rtmənt] *n.* Ⓤ the act of disconcerting; the state of being disconcerted; embarrasment; confusion. ——명 당황, 낭패; 교란

dis·con·nect [dìskənékt] *vt.* separate; cut off (a telephone, etc.). ¶~ *an electric fan* / ~ *oneself from a bad companion*① / ~ *a machine.*② ——동 …을 끊다, 분리하다 ¶①나쁜 친구와 손을 끊다/②기계를 분해하다

dis·con·nect·ed [dìskənéktid] *adj.* **1.** separated. **2.** unrelated; unreasonable; not logical. ¶*a* ~ *argument.* ——형 1. 따로따로 떨어진, 연락이 끊긴 2. 질서 없는, 지리멸렬의

dis·con·nec·tion, *Brit.* **-nex·ion** [dìskənékʃ(ə)n] *n.* Ⓤ the act of disconnecting; the state of being disconnected. ——명 분리, 절단, 지리멸렬

dis·con·so·late [diskɑ́ns(ə)lit / -kɔ́n-] *adj.* comfortless; hopeless; sad; gloomy; melancholy. ——형 울적한, 마음 둘 곳 없는, 쓸쓸한

・**dis·con·tent** [dìskəntént] *n.* Ⓤ dissatisfaction; discontent; uneasiness; Ⓒ a cause of this. —*vt.* (usu. in *passive*) make discontented or dissatisfied. ¶*She was discontented with the result.*① ——명 불평, 불만 ——동 …에게 불만을 품게 하다 ¶①그녀는 그 결과에 불만이었다

・**dis·con·tent·ed** [dìskənténtid] *adj.* dissatisfied; unhappy. ¶*I am* ~ *with my position.*① ——형 불만의, 불평의 ¶①나는 내 지위에 싫증이 났다 [dissatisfaction.]

dis·con·tent·ment [dìskənténtmənt] *n.* Ⓤ discontent; ——명 불평, 불만

dis·con·tin·u·ance [dìskəntínjuəns] *n.* Ⓤ the act of discontinuing; the state of being discontinued; stoppage; interruption. [uance.] ——명 중지, 중절(中絶), 중단

dis·con·tin·u·a·tion [dìskəntìnjuéiʃ(ə)n] *n.* =discontin-

dis·con·tin·ue [dìskəntínju:] *vt.* put an end to (something); stop. ¶~ *a business.*① —*vi.* come to an end; cease. ¶*The publication of this magazine will* ~.② ——동 …을 그만두다, 중지하다 ¶①장사를 그만두다 ——자 중지되다 ¶②이 잡지는 폐간될 것이다

dis·con·ti·nu·i·ty [dìskɑ̀ntinjú(:)iti / -kɔ̀n-] *n.* Ⓤ the state of being discontinuous; interruption. [interrupted.] ——명 중단, 단절

dis·con·tin·u·ous [dìskəntínjuəs] *adj.* not continuous; ——형 중단된, 끊어진

dis·cord [dískɔ:rd] *n.* **1.** Ⓤ difference of opinion; disagreement. ¶*domestic* ~.① ↔concord **2.** Ⓤ Ⓒ (*Music*) lack of harmony. ↔harmony ——명 1. 의견 차이, 불일치 ¶①가정불화 2. 《樂》 불협화음

be in discord with, do not agree or be not in harmony with (someone or something). 熟 …와 사이가 나쁘다, 조화하지 않다

dis·cord·ance [diskɔ́:rd(ə)ns], **-an·cy** [-(ə)nsi] *n.* Ⓤ **1.** disagreement. **2.** (*Music*) lack of harmony. ——명 1. 부조화, 불일치 2. 《樂》 불협화음

dis·cord·ant [diskɔ́:rd(ə)nt] *adj.* **1.** not harmonious; harsh. ¶*a* ~ *sound.*① **2.** disagreeing; incongruous. ¶*There are many* ~ *points in this book.* [manner.] ——형 1. 조화되지 않는; 귀에 거슬리는 ¶①귀에 거슬리는 소리 2. 일치하지 않는

dis·cord·ant·ly [diskɔ́:rd(ə)ntli] *adv.* in a discordant ——동 조화를 안 이루어

dis·count [dískaunt -́- / -́- ∥ → *n.*] *vt.* **1.** take away (a cer- ——동 1. …을 할인하다 ¶①판매중인

discountenance [336] **discriminate**

tain amount) from a price ; reduce a price by a certain percentage. ¶~ *all the electric fans for sale.*① **2.** take (a story, etc.) at less than face value. **3.** sell or buy (a bill, etc.) at a reduction of a certain percentage.
—*n.* [´–] ⓒ ⓤ **1.** a reduction from an original price. ¶*bank* (or *banker's*) ~② / *cash* ~③ / *allow a 10 percent* ~.④ **2.** the rate of interest charged for discounting a bill. ¶*give 5% ~ for cash.*⑤ **3.** an allowance for exaggeration. ¶*accept a story with some ~.*
1) *at a discount,* ⓐ below face value. ↔at a premium ⓑ unwanted and easily obtained.
2) *give* (or *allow*) *a discount on,* make the price of (something) lower.

dis·coun·te·nance [diskáuntinəns] *vt.* **1.** discourage; disapprove. **2.** put (someone) to shame.

• **dis·cour·age** [diskə́:ridʒ / -kʌ́r-] *vt.* **1.** make (someone) lose courage ; disappoint. ↔encourage ¶*be discouraged at the news*① / *The news discouraged me.* **2.** persuade (someone) not to do ; prevent. ((~ someone *from doing*)) ¶~ *him from going out* / ~ *all attempts at study.*

dis·cour·age·ment [diskə́:ridʒmənt / -kʌ́r-] *n.* **1.** ⓤ the act of discouraging ; the state of being discouraged ; disappointment. **2.** ⓒ something that discourages.

dis·cour·ag·ing [diskə́:ridʒiŋ / -kʌ́r-] *adj.* apt to discourage ; depressing. ¶~ *prospects.*①

• **dis·course** *n.* [dísko:rs,´–´→*v.*] ⓒ **1.** a lecture ; a speech. **2.** a talk ; a conversation. —*vi.* [–´] give a lecture ; talk ; speak. ¶~ *on* (or *about, of*) *politics.*

dis·cour·te·ous [diskə́:rtiəs] *adj.* impolite ; rude.

dis·cour·te·sy [diskə́:rtisi] *n.* (pl. **-sies**) **1.** ⓤ impoliteness ; bad manners. **2.** ⓒ an impolite act or opinion.

⁑ **dis·cov·er** [diskʌ́vər] *vt.* **1.** find or find out (something) for the first time. ¶~ *a new star.* **2.** be aware of (something); realize. ((~ someone *to be ;* ~ *that ... ;* ~ *what...*)) ¶*I discovered him to be dishonest.; I discovered that he was dishonest.*①

dis·cov·er·er [diskʌ́vərər] *n.* ⓒ a person who discovers.

• **dis·cov·er·y** [diskʌ́v(ə)ri] *n.* (pl. **-er·ies**) **1.** ⓤ the act of discovering or finding. ¶*make a new ~*① / *an epoch-making ~ of science.*② **2.** ⓒ a thing that is discovered.

dis·cred·it [diskrédit] *vt.* disbelieve ; doubt. ¶*The report is discredited.*① —*n.* **1.** ⓤ disbelief ; doubt. **2.** ⓤ loss of respect ; disgrace ; dishonor. ⓒ (usu. *a ~*) a person or thing causing such loss. ¶*a thing to one's ~* / *a ~ to our family*② / *bring someone into ~*③ / *fall into ~.*④ 〔orable ; shameful.〕

dis·cred·it·a·ble [diskréditəbl] *adj.* disgraceful ; dishon-
dis·creet [diskrí:t] *adj.* careful ; prudent. 〔fully.〕
dis·creet·ly [diskrí:tli] *adv.* in a discreet manner ; care-
dis·crep·an·cy [diskrépənsi] *n.* (pl. **-cies**) **1.** ⓤ difference ; disagreement. ¶~ *between two reports*① / ~ *in ability.* **2.** ⓒ an example of disagreement.
dis·crep·ant [diskrépənt] *adj.* different ; disagreeing.
dis·crete [diskrí:t] *adj.* **1.** separate ; discontinuous. **2.** made up of different parts. ▷ **dis·crete·ly** [-li] *adv.*
dis·cre·tion [diskréʃ(ə)n] *n.* **1.** freedom of judgment or choice. ¶*at ~*① / *leave to someone's ~.*② **2.** carefulness ; prudence.
dis·cre·tion·ar·y [diskréʃ(ə)nèri / -əri] *adj.* left to individual judgment or choice ; voluntary. ↔compulsory ¶*a ~ order*① / *a ~ principle.*②
dis·crim·i·nate [diskrímineìt] *vt., vi.* **1.** observe the difference ; see clearly. ((~ *between* two things ; ~ one-thing *from* another)) ¶*It is difficult to ~ between good*

—ⓢ 모든 선풍기를 할인하다 **2.** …을 에누리하여 듣다(생각하다) **3.** [어음 따위를] 할인하여 사다(팔다)

—ⓢ **1.** 할인 ¶②할인 은행/③현금 할인/④10퍼어센트의 할인을 하다 **2.** 어음 할인으로 지불하면 5푼 할인을 하다 **3.** 에누리, 참작

📖 1)ⓐ할인하여 ⓑ값이 떨어져, 팔리지 않는 2)…의 할인을 하다

—ⓣ **1.** …을 좌절시키다 ; …에 반대하다 **2.** …을 창피당하게 하다
—ⓣ **1.** …의 용기를 잃게 하다, …을 낙심시키다 ¶①뉴우스를 듣고 낙심하다 **2.** …을 하지 않도록 말리다, 막다

—ⓢ **1.** 낙심, 낙담 **2.** 낙심시키는 것(사정)

—ⓣ 낙담시키는 ; 기운을 꺾는 ¶①비관적인 전망
—ⓢ **1.** 강연, 연설, 설교 **2.** 이야기 ; 담화 —ⓣ 강연하다 ; 설교하다 ; 이야기 (말)하다
—ⓣ 무례한, 버릇없는
—ⓢ **1.** 실례, 무례 **2.** 무례한 짓, 버릇없음

—ⓣ **1.** …을 발견하다 **2.** …을 알아차리다, 깨닫다 ¶①그가 정직하지 않다는 것을 알았다

—ⓢ 발견자

—ⓢ **1.** 발견 ¶①새로운 발견을 하다/②과학상의 획기적 발견 **2.** 발견물

—ⓣ …을 신용하지 않다 ; 의심하다 ¶①그 보고는 신용되지 않는다 —ⓢ **1.** 불신, 불신임 ; 의심 **2.** 불명예, 창피 ¶②집안의 창피/③…의 신용을 떨어뜨리다/④망신을 당하다

—ⓣ 신용을 해치는 ; 불명예의, 창피한
—ⓣ 조심성 있는, 분별있는
—ⓣ 신중하게, 주의 깊게
—ⓢ **1.** 차이, 모순 ¶①두 보고서의 차이 **2.** 차이(모순)가 있는 문제

—ⓣ 차이가 있는, 모순된
—ⓣ **1.** 별개의, 연속되지 않은 **2.** 별개의 부분으로 이루어진
—ⓢ **1.** 자유 재량, 행동(선택)의 자유 ¶①마음대로/②…의 재량에 맡기다 **2.** 분별, 신중성
—ⓣ 임의의, 마음대로의 ¶①임의 주문/②독단주의

—ⓣⓘ **1.** 구별하다, 식별하다 ¶①좋은 책과 무가치한 책을 구별하기란 힘들다 **2.** 차별대우하다

*books and poor ones.*① **2.** make a difference in treatment.
discriminate in favor of (against), treat (someone) well (badly).
[熟] …을 우대(냉대)하다
—*adj.* marked by discrimination; clear; distinct.
—[形] 식별된; 명료한

dis·crim·i·nat·ing [diskrímineìtiŋ] *adj.* **1.** able to discriminate; seeing a difference clearly. **2.** treating something differently. ¶~ *tariff.*①
—[形] 1. 식별력이 있는, 분별있는 2. 차별적인 ¶①차별 세율

dis·crim·i·na·tion [diskrìminéiʃ(ə)n] *n.* [U] **1.** the act of discriminating; distinction. ¶*without* ~.① **2.** the ability to observe a difference; judgment. **3.** the act of making a difference in treatment. ¶*racial* ~.②
—[名] 1. 구별 ¶①구별 없이 2. 식별력 3. 차별대우 ¶②인종차별

dis·crim·i·na·tive [diskrímineìtiv / -krímina-] *adj.* **1.** (of persons) observing discrimination. **2.** (of things) making or showing distinction.
—[形] 1. [사람이] 식별력이 있는 2. [물건이] 구별을 나타내는 데에 쓸모있는, 특수한

dis·crim·i·na·to·ry [diskrímìnətɔ̀:ri / -təri] *adj.* =discriminative.

dis·cur·sive [diskə́:rsiv] *adj.* moving about from one topic to another; wandering.
—[形] 산만한, 갈피를 못 잡는, 화제가 왔다갔다하는

dis·cus [dískəs] *n.* [C] a heavy, round plate of stone or metal, thrown for distance as a test of strength and skill. ¶*the* ~ *throw.*①
—[名] 원반, 원반 던지기 ¶①원반 던지기

dis·cuss [diskʌ́s] *vt.* talk over (something) together; argue; debate; examine. 《~ *how* (or *what,* etc.) *to do*; ~ *how* (or *what,* etc.) …》 ¶*I discussed politics with my friends.* / *We discussed what to do next.* ⇒[N.B.]
—[他] …을 논의하다, 토론하다; 검토하다
[N.B.] discuss는 타동사이므로 전치사를 쓰지 않음. discuss about a problem은 잘못

dis·cus·sion [diskʌ́ʃ(ə)n] *n.* [U][C] the act of discussing; argument; debate. ¶*a question under* ~① / *have a* ~ *on* (or *about*) *the question.*②
—[名] 토의, 변론, 토론 ¶①심의중인 문제/②그 문제에 관해 토론하다

dis·dain [disdéin] *vt.* **1.** look down on (someone or something); scorn. **2.** be too proud to do (something). 《~ *to do*; ~ *doing*》 ¶~ *to notice* (or *noticing*) *an insult.*①
—[他] 1. …을 경멸하다 2. […함을] 떳떳이 여기지 않다 ¶①모욕 따위에 별로 마음쓰지 않다
—*n.* [U] an attitude or feeling of scorn.
—[名] 경멸, 모멸

dis·dain·ful [disdéinf(u)l] *adj.* expressing scorn or contempt; proud. ¶*be* ~ *of someone.*①
—[形] 경멸적인, 거만한 ¶①…을 경멸하다

dis·ease [dizí:z] *n.* [U][C] **1.** illness; sickness. ¶*a serious* ~① / *a family* ~② / *catch* (or *suffer from*) *a* ~. **2.** an abnormal condition of a plant. **3.** a bad condition of the mind, public affairs, etc. ¶*Poverty is a social* ~.③
—[名] 1. 병, 질병 ¶①중병/②유전병 2. [식물 따위의] 병해 3. [정신・사회 따위의] 폐해; 해악 ¶③빈곤은 사회적 병폐이다

dis·eased [dizí:zd] *adj.* sick; unhealthy. ¶*a* ~ *part.*
—[形] 병에 걸린, 병적인

dis·em·bark [dìsimbá:rk] *vt.* take (something) away from a ship to the land; unload. **—***vi.* leave a ship for the land; land.
—[他] …을 양륙(揚陸)하다; 상륙시키다
—[自] 상륙하다

dis·em·bar·ka·tion [dìsembɑ:rkéiʃ(ə)n] *n.* [U] the act of landing or unloading.
—[名] 상륙; 양륙

dis·em·bod·y [dìsimbádi / -bɔ́di] *vt.* (**-bod·ied**) make (a spirit, etc.) free from the body. ¶*a disembodied spirit.*①
—[他] [영혼 따위]를 육체에서 분리시키다 ¶①육체를 떠난 영혼

dis·em·bow·el [dìsimbáuəl] *vt.* (**-eled, -el·ing** or *Brit.* **-elled, -el·ling**) take out the bowels of (an animal, etc.).
—[他] …의 창자를 꺼내다

dis·en·chant [dìsintʃǽnt / -tʃá:nt] *vt.* set (something) free from the power of magic or illusion. ¶*be disenchanted.*① ▷**dis·en·chant·ment** [-mənt] *n.*
—[他] …의 마법을 풀다, 환상에서 깨우다 ¶①환상에서 깨어나다

dis·en·cum·ber [dìsinkʌ́mbər] *vt.* free from (a trouble or burden); disburden.
—[他] …을 제거하다; 귀찮은 것을 없애다

dis·en·gage [dìsingéidʒ] *vt.* **1.** set (someone) free from an engagement, duty, etc. ¶~ *oneself from.*① **2.** unfasten; loosen.
—[他] 1. …을 약속・일에서 해방시키다 ¶①…에서 떠나다 2. …을 해방하다; 떨어지다

dis·en·gaged [dìsingéidʒd] *adj.* **1.** having no appointments; not busy. **2.** unoccupied; empty.
—[形] 1. 약속이 없는, 한가한 2. [장소 따위가] 비어 있는

dis·en·gage·ment [dìsingéidʒmənt] *n.* [U] the act or process of disengaging; freedom from duty.
—[名] 해방; 자유

dis·en·tan·gle [dìsintǽŋgl] *vt.* make (something) free from what is confused; untwist.
—[他] [혼란에서] …을 풀어 놓다; [얽힌 것]을 풀다

dis·es·teem [dìsistí:m] *vt.* scorn; pay little attention to (someone). **—***n.* [U] scorn; dislike.
—[他] …을 경멸(경시)하다 —[名] 경멸; 혐오

dis·fa·vor, *Brit.* **-vour** [disféivər] *n.* [U] **1.** dislike; displeasure. **2.** a state in which a person is unpopular.
—[名] 1. 혐오, 푸대접, 싫어함 2. 인망(인기)이 없음, 평판이 나쁨 ¶①…의 눈

disfigure / dishonor

¶ *be in ~ with someone*① / *fall* (or *come*) *into ~.*②
— *vt.* treat unkindly; dislike.

dis·fig·ure [disfígjər / -fígə] *vt.* spoil the appearance, shape, or value of (something). ¶ *Large buildings disfigured the countryside.* 「pearance or shape.」

dis·fig·ured [disfígjərd / -fígəd] *adj.* with a spoiled ap-

dis·fig·ure·ment [disfígjərmənt / -fígə-] *n.* Ⓤ the act of disfiguring; the state of being disfigured.

dis·fran·chise [disfræntʃaiz] *vt.* 1. take away a right of citizenship, esp. the right to vote, from (someone). 2. take away from (someone) a right, privilege, or power.

dis·gorge [disgɔ́:rdʒ] *vt.* 1. throw out (something) from the throat. 2. pour forth. ¶ *That river disgorges its water into the Pacific Ocean.* 3. give up unwillingly.

• **dis·grace** [disgréis] *n.* 1. Ⓤ dishonor; shame. ¶ *bring ~ on someone.*① 2. Ⓒ a cause of disgrace. ¶ *The affair is a ~ to him.* 3. Ⓤ loss of favor or good name. ¶ *fall into ~*② / *He is now in ~.*③
— *vt.* 1. bring a bad name to (someone or something). ¶ *Don't ~ the school name.* 2. remove (someone) from a position.

dis·grace·ful [disgréisf(u)l] *adj.* shameful; dishonorable.
▷ **dis·grace·ful·ly** [-fuli] *adv.*

dis·grun·tled [disgrʌ́ntld] *adj.* discontented; displeased.

• **dis·guise** [disgáiz] *vt.* 1. hide the real appearance of (someone). ¶ *He disguised himself as a lady.* 2. hide the true nature of (something). ¶ *~ one's intentions*① / *~ one's voice*② / *cannot ~ the fact that* ...③
— *n.* Ⓤ Ⓒ 1. a change of appearance. ¶ *attend a party in ~.* 2. false show; pretense. ¶ *without ~*④ / *throw off one's ~*⑤ / *His anger was all ~.*

• **dis·gust** [disgʌ́st] *n.* Ⓤ very strong and sickening dislike. ¶ *have a ~ for snakes.* — *vt.* cause strong dislike in (someone); sicken. ¶ *be disgusted at* (or *by, with*) *her chatter* / *His rudeness disgusted everybody.*

dis·gust·ed [disgʌ́stid] *adj.* be sick and tired. ¶ *a ~ look.*
dis·gust·ed·ly [-li] *adv.*

dis·gust·ful [disgʌ́stf(u)l] *adj.* causing disgust; disagree-

• **dis·gust·ing** [disgʌ́stiŋ] *adj.* causing a strong dislike.

dis·gust·ing·ly [disgʌ́stiŋli] *adv.* in a disgusting manner.

‡ **dish** [diʃ] *n.* Ⓒ 1. a plate, bowl, etc. used for serving food. 2. the food in a dish. ¶ *one's favorite ~*① / *three dishes of beans.*② 3. a dish-shaped thing. — *vt.* 1. serve (food) in a dish. 2. shape (something) like a dish. 「day clothes.」

dish·a·bille [dìsæbí:l, dìsə-] *n.* Ⓤ informal dress; every-

dis·har·mo·ni·ous [dìshɑ:rmóuniəs] *adj.* lacking harmony.

dis·har·mo·ny [dishɑ́:rməni] *n.* Ⓤ Ⓒ (pl. **-nies**) the state of having no harmony; disagreement.

dish·cloth [díʃklɔ̀:θ / -klɔ̀θ] *n.* Ⓒ a cloth used for washing dishes; a dishtowel.

dis·heart·en [dishɑ́:rtn] *vt.* discourage; disappoint.

di·shev·eled, *Brit.* **-elled** [diʃévəld] *adj.* (of clothes or hair) not arranged; untidy.

‡ **dis·hon·est** [disɑ́nist / -ɔ́nist] *adj.* not honest; unfair; faithless. 「manner.」

• **dis·hon·est·ly** [disɑ́nistli / -ɔ́nist-] *adv.* in a dishonest

dis·hon·es·ty [disɑ́nisti / -ɔ́nist-] *n.* (pl. **-ties**) 1. Ⓤ lack of honesty. 2. Ⓒ a dishonest act; a cheat.

• **dis·hon·or**, *Brit.* **-our** [disɑ́nər / -ɔ́nə] *n.* 1. Ⓤ loss of honor; disgrace; shame. 2. Ⓒ a cause of dishonor. ¶ *be a ~ to.*① 3. Ⓤ insult. ¶ *I offered him no ~.* 4.

—밖에 나다/②미움을 사다; 인기를 잃다 —㉧ …을 푸대접하다; 싫어하다
—㉧ …의 모양을 해치다; …을 보기 흉하게 하다; …의 가치를 떨어뜨리다

—㉴ 모양이 망가진
—㉵ 모양을 망가뜨림, 보기 흉함

—㉧ 1. …한테서 공민(선거)권을 빼앗다 2. …한테서 권리(특권)를 빼앗다

—㉧ 1 …을 토해내다 2. …을 쏟다 3. [부정 소득 따위]를 게워내다

—㉵ 1. 불명예; 오명 ¶①…의 명예를 더럽히다 2. 치욕, 망신거리 3. 눈밖에 남, 인기 없음 ¶②총애를 잃다/③그는 미움을 받고 있다
—㉧ 1. …을 망신시키다; 더럽히다 2. …의 지위를 빼앗다

—㉴ 창피한; 불명예스러운

—㉴ 불만을 품은; 시무룩한
—㉧ 1. …을 변장시키다 2. …의 본성을 감추다 ¶①의도를 숨기다/②목소리를 속이다/③…이라는 사실을 감출 수 없다
—㉵ 1. 변장 2. 겉치레; 핑계, 구실 ¶④숨김없이/⑤정체를 드러내다

—㉵ 혐오; 메스꺼움 ¶①뱀을 몹시 싫어하다 —㉧ 메스껍게 하다; …을 넌더리나게 하다

—㉴ 넌더리가 난; 싫증난

—㉴ 구역질나는, 지긋지긋한, 아주 싫은
—㉴ 구역질나는, 싫은
—㉳ 구역질나게, 메스껍게
—㉵ 1. 접시 2. 접시에 담은 음식 ¶①좋아하는 음식/②세 접시의 콩 3. 접시 모양의 것 —㉧ 1. …을 접시에 담아 내다 2. …을 접시 모양으로 하다

—㉵ 평상복; 약장(略裝)
—㉴ 조화되지 않은; 불일치의; 불협화의

—㉵ 부조화; 불협화음

—㉵ 행주

—㉧ …을 낙심(실망)시키다
—㉴ 헝클어진, 덥수룩한, 단정치 못한

—㉴ 부정직한; 불성실한

—㉳ 부정직하게; 불성실하게
—㉵ 1. 부정직; 불성실 2. 부정행위; 사기
—㉵ 1. 불명예, 면목없음 2. 망신(수치)거리 ¶①…의 망신이다 3. 굴욕 4. [어음의] 부도

dishonorable

Ⓤ failure to pay a check.
— *vt.* **1.** bring shame to (someone); disgrace. ¶ ~ *oneself.*① **2.** refuse to pay (a check). ¶ *a dishonored check.*②
— 他 1. …의 이름을 더럽히다 ¶②자신의 명예를 더럽히다 2. [어음]의 지불을 거절하다 ¶③부도수표
— 形 창피한; 불명예스러운

dis·hon·or·a·ble [disánərəbl / -ɔ́nə-] *adj.* shameful; disgraceful; having no honor.

dis·il·lu·sion [dìsilúːʒ(ə)n] *n.* Ⓤ the state of being free from illusion; disenchantment. — *vt.* make (someone) free from a mistaken belief; disenchant. ¶ *be* (or *become*) *disillusioned.*①
— 名 환상에서 깨어나게 함; 환멸
— 他 …의 미몽(迷夢)(환상)에서 깨어나게 하다, …에 환멸을 느끼게 하다 ¶①환멸을 느끼다

dis·il·lu·sion·ment [dìsilúːʒ(ə)nmənt] *n.* Ⓤ the state of being disillusioned.
— 名 환멸

dis·in·cli·na·tion [dìsinklinéiʃ(ə)n] *n.* ⓒⓊ (usu. *a* ~ or *one's* ~) a dislike; the state of being unwilling. ¶ *have a* ~ *to work.*①
— 名 싫증; 마음내키지 않음 ¶①일할 생각이 나지 않다

dis·in·cline [dìsinkláin] *vt.* make (someone) unwilling to do something. ¶ *He is disinclined to study.*① —*vi.* be unwilling. ⌈of (something).
— 他 …에 싫증이 나게 하다 ¶①그는 공부를 싫어한다 —自 싫어하다

dis·in·fect [dìsinfékt] *vt.* destroy the harmful bacteria
dis·in·fect·ant [dìsinféktənt] *n.* ⓒ a thing used for disinfecting. —*adj.* disinfecting. ⌈fecting.
— 他 …을 살균·소독하다
— 名 소독(살균)제 —形 소독의

dis·in·fec·tion [dìsinfékʃ(ə)n] *n.* Ⓤ the act of disin-
— 名 소독

dis·in·gen·u·ous [dìsindʒénjuəs] *adj.* dishonest; unfair; insincere. ⌈heir from (someone).
— 形 부정직한; 성의 없는; 솔직하지 못한 「폐적(廢嫡)하다」

dis·in·her·it [dìsinhérit] *vt.* take away the right as a
— 他 …에게서 상속권을 빼앗다; …을

dis·in·te·grate [disíntigrèit] *vt., vi.* break up into pieces; disunite. ¶ *Rocks are disintegrated by weathering.*
— 他自 붕괴하다(시키다); 분해하다(시키다)

dis·in·te·gra·tion [disìntigréiʃ(ə)n] *n.* Ⓤ the process of disintegrating. ¶ *the* ~ *of an empire.*①
— 名 붕괴, 분해 ¶①제국의 붕괴

dis·in·ter·est·ed [disínt(ə)ristid] *adj.* fair; just; unselfish ¶ *All judges should be disinterested.*①
— 形 공평한; 사심이 없는 ¶①재판관은 모두 공평해야 한다

dis·join [disdʒɔ́in] *vt., vi.* divide; separate.
— 他自 분리시키다(하다); 떼다

dis·joint [disdʒɔ́int] *vt., vi.* put out of place; separate. ¶ *He disjointed a chicken for cooking.*
— 他自 탈구(脫臼)시키다(하다); 낱낱이 헤뜨리다

dis·joint·ed [disdʒɔ́intid] *adj.* **1.** separated; broken up; deprived of order. ¶ *a* ~ *discourse.* **2.** out of joint.
— 形 1. 흐트러진, 관절을 뺀 2. [사상·문체가] 조리가 서지 않는

dis·junc·tion [disdʒʌ́ŋkʃ(ə)n] *n.* Ⓤⓒ separation.
— 名 분리; 분열

disk [disk] *n.* ⓒ **1.** a thin, flat, round thing. **2.** a flat and round surface. ¶ *the moon's* ~.① **3.** a phonograph record.
— 名 1. 원반(圓盤), 평원판(平圓板) 2. 평원판의 표면 ¶①달의 표면 3. [축음기의] 레코오드

disk jockey [⌐ ⌐-] *n.* (*U.S. colloq.*) an announcer who carries on a radio program of recorded music.
— 名 《美口》 디스크 조키

• **dis·like** [disláik] *n.* ⓒ (usu. *a* ~) a feeling of not liking; distaste. ¶ *She has a strong* ~ *for* (or *of*) *insects.*① / *He took a* ~ *to us.*② — *vt.* have a feeling against (someone or something); hate.
— 名 싫어함; 미움 ¶①그녀는 벌레를 아주 싫어한다/②그는 우리들을 미워했다 — 他 …을 싫어하다, 미워하다

dis·lo·cate [dísləkèit] *vt.* **1.** put (bones) out of joint. ¶ *have* (or *get*) *one's knee dislocated.*① **2.** disarrange; disturb. ¶ ~ *traffic.* ⌈dislocated.
— 他 1. …을 탈구(脫臼)시키다 ¶①무릎관절을 삐다 2. [순서·위치 따위]를 어지럽히다; 혼란시키다

dis·lo·ca·tion [dìsləkéiʃ(ə)n] *n.* Ⓤⓒ the state of being
— 名 탈구; 혼란

dis·lodge [dislάdʒ / -lɔ́dʒ] *vt.* send out (someone or something) from a place; force out. ¶ ~ *the enemy from a hill.*① ▷ **dis·lodge·ment** [-mənt] *n.*
— 他 …을 제거하다; 이동시키다; 쫓아버리다, 격퇴하다 ¶①적을 언덕에서 물리치다

dis·loy·al [dislɔ́iəl] *adj.* unfaithful; false; dishonest. ¶ *a* ~ *wife.*① ▷ **dis·loy·al·ly** [-i] *adv.*
— 形 불충실한; 신의 없는 ¶①부정(不貞)한 아내

dis·loy·al·ty [dislɔ́iəlti] *n.* (pl. **-ties**) **1.** Ⓤ the state of being disloyal. **2.** ⓒ a disloyal act. ¶ *He was killed for* ~ *to his country.*①
— 名 1. 불충(不忠), 신의 없음 2. 불충스러운(신의 없는) 짓 ¶①그는 조국을 배반해서 사형당했다

• **dis·mal** [dízməl] *adj.* **1.** gloomy; dark. ¶ ~ *weather* / ~ *prospects.* **2.** unhappy; depressed; not cheerful.
— 形 1. 음울한; 어두운 2. 쓸쓸한, 무시무시한, 스산한

dis·mal·ly [dízməli] *adv.* in a dismal manner.
— 副 무시무시하게; 음울하게; 쓸쓸히

dis·man·tle [dismǽntl] *vt.* **1.** take away all the sails, furniture, accessories, etc. from (a ship, house, etc.). ¶ ~ *a ship*① / ~ *a house of its roof.*② **2.** take (a ma-
— 他 1. [가구·장비 따위]를 …에서 거두어 치우다(없애다) ¶①배의 장비를 제거하다/②집의 지붕을 벗기다 2. …

chine) to pieces.
을 분해하다

***dis·may** [disméi] *n.* [U] fright; discouragement. ¶*in* ~① / *to one's* ~.② —*vt.* terrify; dishearten. ¶*I was dismayed at the news.*
—[名] 놀람; 당황 ¶①당황하여/②놀라운 일은 —[他] …을 깜짝 놀라게 하다

dis·mem·ber [dismémbər] *vt.* **1.** cut away the limbs of (a dead body). **2.** separate (a nation) into two or more parts; divide. ¶*The war dismembered the country.*①
—[他] 1. [시체]의 손발을 절단하다 2. [나라]를 분할하다 ¶①전쟁으로 그 나라는 분할되었다

***dis·miss** [dismís] *vt.* **1.** permit all persons in (a meeting, etc.) to go away. ¶~ *the assembly* / *Dismissed!*① **2.** send (someone) away from an office; discharge. ¶~ *an officer from his position.*② **3.** stop thinking about (something). ¶~ *an anxiety from one's thoughts.*③ **4.** (*Law*) not accept (a claim) in a court.
—[他] 1. [모임 따위]를 해산시키다 ¶①해산!(구령) 2. …을 해고하다, 면직하다 ¶②관리를 면직시키다 3. [생각]을 버리다 ¶③근심을 잊다 4. [소송]을 기각하다

dis·miss·al [dismís(ə)l] *n.* [U] the act of dismissing; the state of being dismissed; discharge; release.
—[名] 해고; 면직; 추방

dis·mount [dismáunt] *vi.* get off a horse, etc. —*vt.* **1.** throw or take away (someone or something) from a horse, etc. **2.** take away (something) from its mounting.
—[自] 말 따위에서 내리다 —[他] 1. …을 말 따위에서 내던지다(내리다) 2. …을 [받침·틀 따위에서] 떼어내다

dis·o·be·di·ence [dìsəbí:diəns] *n.* [U] the act of disobeying; refusal to obey orders.
—[名] 불복종, 불효

dis·o·be·dient [dìsəbí:djənt] *adj.* refusing to obey orders. ¶~ *to the law.*①
—[形] 명령 불복종의, 불효의 ¶①법률에 따르지 않다

***dis·o·bey** [dìsəbéi] *vt., vi.* refuse or fail to obey (orders, rules etc.).
—[他][自] […에] 따르지 않다, 어기다

dis·o·blige [dìsəbláidʒ] *vt.* **1.** refuse to oblige (someone). **2.** disregard the wishes of (someone); offend; give inconvenience to (someone). ¶*She is* ~ *to me.*①
—[他] 1. …에게 불친절하게 하다 2. …의 뜻을 어기다; …에게 폐를 끼치다 ¶①그녀는 내게 불친절하다

dis·o·blig·ing [dìsəbláidʒiŋ] *adj.* unkind; unhelpful.
—[形] 불친절한; 도움이 안 되는

***dis·or·der** [disɔ́:rdər] *n.* **1.** [U] disarrangement; confusion. **2.** [U] abnormal political confusion. ¶*be in* ~① / *fall into* ~.② **3.** [C][U] an illness. ¶*a* ~ *of the stomach.* —*vt.* **1.** break the order of (something); confuse; disturb. **2.** lose the health of (a body).
—[名] 1. 무질서, 혼란 2. [사회·정치상의] 불온, 소동 ¶①혼란상태이다/②혼란에 빠지다 3. [가벼운] 병, [심신의] 불편함 —[他] 1. …을 어지럽히다; 혼란케 하다 2. …을 병나게 하다

dis·or·dered [disɔ́:rdərd] *adj.* in confusion; out of order; ill. ¶*a* ~ *mind*① / ~ *digestion.*
—[形] 혼란된, 어지러운; 고장난; 병이 난 ¶①정신착란

dis·or·der·ly [disɔ́:rdərli] *adj.* **1.** out of order. ¶*a* ~ *conduct.*① **2.** (*Law*) against public peace or order.
—[形] 1. 무질서한 ¶①풍기문란 행위 2. (法) 치안 방해의, 풍기문란의

dis·or·gan·i·za·tion [disɔ̀:rgənizéiʃ(ə)n / -ɔ̀:gənai-] *n.* [U] the act of disorganizing; disunion; disarrangement.
—[名] [조직체의] 해체; 분열; 질서 혼란

dis·or·gan·ize [disɔ́:rgənàiz] *vt.* break up the order or system of (something); confuse. ¶~ *a labor union.*
—[他] …의 조직을 파괴하다, …을 와해시키다, …을 혼란케 하다

dis·own [disóun] *vt.* refuse to admit (someone or something) as one's own. ¶*He disowned his son.*
—[他] [소유권·의무·관계 따위]를 부인하다

dis·par·age [dispǽridʒ] *vt.* speak ill of (someone); say that something or someone is valueless.
—[他] 깔보다, …을 헐뜯다, 험담하다

dis·par·age·ment [dispǽridʒmənt] *n.* [U] the act of disparaging. ¶*Poverty is no* ~ *to greatness.*①
—[名] 경멸, 비난, 치욕 ¶①빈곤이 위대함에 대한 치욕은 아니다

dis·par·i·ty [dispǽriti] *n.* [U][C] (pl. **-ties**) inequality; unlikeness. ¶~ *of years*① / ~ *in their reports.*②
—[名] 같지 않음, 부등(不等), 차이 ¶①나이가 같지 않음/②보고의 차이

dis·pas·sion·ate [dispǽʃ(ə)nit] *adj.* free from passion; calm; fair. ¶*a* ~ *judge.*①
—[形] 감정에 흔들리지 않는; 냉정한; 공평한 ¶①공정한 재판관

***dis·patch, des-** [dispǽtʃ] *vt.* **1.** send out (something) with speed or at once; send (someone) off carrying a very important message. ¶~ *someone on an errand.*① **2.** finish (a job) quickly. ¶~ *business.* **3.** kill.
—[他] 1. …을 급송(급파)하다 ¶①…을 심부름 보내다 2. [일]을 재빨리 해치우다 3. …을 죽이다

—*n.* **1.** [U] the act of dispatching; the state of being dispatched. **2.** [C] something dispatched; a very important message or report. **3.** [U] speed. **4.** [U][C] the act of killing.
with dispatch, in haste.
—[名] 1. 급송, 급파 2. 급송(급파)된 것; 지급편, 지급보(至急報); 특보 3. 민속 4. 살해
[熟] 지급으로

dis·pel [dispél] *vt.* (**-pelled, -pel·ling**) drive (doubt, fears, etc.) away. ¶~ *fears.*
—[他] [의심·근심 따위]를 쫓아(털어) 버리다, 없애다

dis·pen·sa·ble [dispénsəbl] *adj.* not important; needless; unnecessary. ↔indispensable
—[形] 중요하지 않은; 없어도 상관없는

dis·pen·sa·ry [dispéns(ə)ri] *n.* [C] (pl. **-ries**) a place where medicines are given; an institution where medicines
—[名] 약국; 보건소, 시료소(施療所)

D

dispensation [341] disposed

and medical treatment are given free or for a small fee.

dis·pen·sa·tion [dìspenséiʃ(ə)n] *n.* **1.** Ⓤ the act of giving out; distribution. ¶*the ~ of food.* **2.** Ⓒ a thing which is given out or distributed. **3.** Ⓒ a rule; a principle. ¶*under the old ~.*① **4.** Ⓒ something that is ordered by Providence. **5.** Ⓒ (*Theology*) any religious system. ¶*the Christian ~.*① **6.** Ⓤ Ⓒ (*Catholic*) official permission to dericate from the provisions of a special church law.

— 图 1. 분배 2. 나누어 준 것 3. 통치, 관리 ¶①낡은 통치제도하에서 4. 하늘의 뜻, 섭리 5. 율법 ¶②그리스도교 법규 6. 《가톨릭》 특면(特免)[장]

dis·pense [dispéns] *vt.* **1.** give out; distribute. ¶*~ food and clothing to the war-suferers.* **2.** carry out (a law); administer. ¶*~ justice.*① **3.** make up (a new medicine) by mixing several kinds.

dispense with, ⓐ make (a thing) unnecessary. ¶*Machinery dispenses with much labor.*② ⓑ do without.

▷**dis·pens·er** [-ər] *n.*

— 他 1. …을 분배하다, 나누어 주다 2. [법]을 시행하다 ¶①법을 시행하다 3. [약]을 조제하다

熟 ⓐ …을 불필요하게 하다 ¶②기계는 노동력을 크게 줄여 준다 ⓑ … 없이 지내다

dis·per·sal [dispə́:rs(ə)l] *n.* Ⓤ the act of dispersing; the state of being dispersed. ¶*the ~ of population.*①

— 图 1. 살포, 소산(消散), 해산, 분산, 소개(疎開) ¶①인구의 분산

dis·perse [dispə́:rs] *vt.* **1.** scatter (something) in all directions. ¶*~ a crowd.* **2.** break up (light) into its colored rays by means of a prism; dispel (clouds, fog, etc.) —*vi.* scatter; break up; spread in all directions.

— 他 1. …을 흩뜨리다; 해산시키다 2. [광선]을 분광(分光)하다; [구름·안개 따위]를 흩어지게 하다 —自 흩어지다; 해산하다; 흩어 없어지다

dis·per·sion [dispə́:rʃ(ə)n] *n.* Ⓤ **1.** the act of dispersing; the state of being dispersed. **2.** the breaking up of light into its color rays by a prism.

— 图 1. 분산, 산란(散亂), 해방 2. [광선의] 분광

dis·pir·it [dispírit] *vt.* discourage; disappoint.

— 他 …의 기를 꺾다, 낙심시키다

dis·place [displéis] *vt.* **1.** remove (something) from its place; shift. ¶*a displaced person*① **2.** remove (someone) from a position; discharge. ¶*~ an officer.* **3.** replace. ¶*The streetcar was displaced by the bus.*

— 他 1. …을 바꿔 놓다, 이동하다 ¶① [특히 전쟁 중의] 난민(難民) 2. …을 면직하다 3. …의 대신 들어서다

dis·place·ment [displéismənt] *n.* Ⓤ **1.** the act of displacing; the state of being displaced. **2.** the weight of the volume of water. ¶*a ship of 10,000 tons ~.*①

— 图 1. 옮겨 놓기; 바꿔 놓기; 면직 2. [선박의] 배수량 ¶①[배수 톤수] 1만 톤의 배

‡**dis·play** [displéi] *vt.* **1.** spread (goods) before people; show; exhibit; hoist. ¶*~ goods* / *~ the national flag.* **2.** show (one's feelings, ability, etc.); make known. ¶*~ no fear.*① **3.** open out (newspapers, etc.); unfold. —*n.* Ⓒ Ⓤ **1.** an exhibition; a show. ¶*a ~ of fireworks*② / *the fine vases on ~.*③ **2.** the act of showing one's knowledge, wealth, etc.. ¶*make a ~ of one's skill* / *out of ~.*④

— 他 1. …을 꾸미다, 전시하다; 올리다 2. [감정·능력 따위]를 나타내다, 발휘하다 ¶①두려움을 보이지 않다 3. [신문 따위]를 펼치다

— 图 1. 전시 ¶②불꽃놀이 / ③진열된 꽃병 2. 자랑삼아 보이기, 과시 ¶④ 것 보라는 듯이

dis·please [displí:z] *vt.* make (someone) angry or annoyed; dissatisfy. ¶*be displeased at something*① / *She is displeased with me.*②

— 他 …을 불쾌하게 하다; 성나게 하다 ¶①…에 기분이 나빠지다 / ②그녀는 내게 화를 냈다

dis·pleas·ing [displí:ziŋ] *adj.* not pleasing to someone; disagreeable. ¶*That is ~ to me.*①

— 形 [사물이] 불쾌한 ¶①그것은 나로서는 불쾌하다

dis·pleas·ure [displéʒər] *n.* Ⓤ (sometimes *a~*) the state of being displeased; dissatisfaction; anger; annoyance; pain. ¶*incur the ~ of someone*① / *take* [*a*] *~ in.*②

— 图 불만, 불쾌; 기분 나쁨, 성냄 ¶① …의 기분을 상하다 / ②불쾌하게 생각하다, 성내다

dis·port [dispó:rt] *vt., vi.* play; amuse (oneself).

— 他自 …와 놀다, 즐기게 하다

dis·po·sal [dispóuz(ə)l] *n.* Ⓤ **1.** the act of disposing. ¶*the ~ of business affairs.*① **2.** the act of giving away; transfer. ¶*the ~ of an old house.*② **3.** arrangement. ¶*the ~ of troops.*③

at (or *in*) *one's disposal,* at one's service. ¶*I have all the money at my ~.*④

— 图 1. 정리, 처리, 처분 ¶①사무의 처리 2. 양도, 매도(賣渡) ¶②낡은 집을 팔아치우기 3. 배치, 배열 ¶③군대의 배치

熟 뜻대로, 자유로 ¶④이 돈은 모두 내 마음대로 할 수 있는

‡**dis·pose** [dispóuz] *vt.* **1.** arrange. ¶*~ troops.* **2.** deal with or settle (affairs). **3.** make (someone) willing; incline. ((*~ someone to do*; *~ someone for*)) ¶*His advice disposed me to read it.*

dispose of, ⓐ put (something) away; get rid of (something). ¶*~ of oneself.*① ⓑ give away (something); transfer; sell. ⓒ (*colloq.*) eat or drink.

— 他 1. …을 배열하다, 배치하다 2. [사물]을 처리하다 3. …을 …하고 싶은 생각이 들다

熟 ⓐ …을 치우다 ¶①거취를 결정하다 ⓑ …을 팔아 치우다, …을 처분하다 ⓒ먹다, 마시다

dis·posed [dispóuzd] *adj.* inclined; liable; tending. ¶

— 形 …할 생각이 있는, 경향이 있는

Are you ~ for a walk?
be well disposed, ⓐ be good-natured. ⓑ 《usu. with *toward*》 be friendly. ¶*she is well ~ toward him.*

[熟] ⓐ성질이 좋다 ⓑ호감을 품고 있다

***dis·po·si·tion** [dìspəzíʃ(ə)n] *n.* [C] 《*usu. sing., a ~*》 **1.** a natural tendency; a nature; a personal character. ¶*a mild ~.* **2.** a tendency. ¶*show a ~ to put it off.*① **3.** arrangement. ¶*the ~ of furniture / make one's ~.*② **4.** management; (*Law*) the act of giving money, etc. by means of a will.

—[名] 1. 성질, 성벽 2. 경향, 의향 ¶①그것을 연기할 의향을 보이다 3. 배치, 배열 ¶②만반의 준비를 갖추다 4. 처치; 처분; 양도; 《法》 유증(遺贈)

at one's disposition, as one likes.

[熟] 자기 마음대로, 자유로

dis·pos·sess [dìspəzés] *vt.* take away a house, etc. from (someone). 《~ someone *of*》 ¶*~ the king of his crown.*①

—[他] [재산 따위를 남]에게서 빼앗다, 박탈하다 ¶①왕위를 빼앗다

dis·praise [dispréiz] *vt.* find fault with; blame. —*n.* [U] blame; criticism. ¶*speak in ~ of someone.*①

—[他] …을 비난하다, 헐뜯다 —[名] 비난; 욕설 ¶①…을 헐뜯다

dis·proof [disprú:f] *n.* **1.** [U] the act of disproving; refutation. **2.** [C] a piece of evidence or fact that disproves.

—[名] 1. 반증(反證), 논박, 반박 2. 반증 물건(反證物件)

dis·pro·por·tion [dìsprəpɔ́:rʃ(ə)n] *n.* [U] the state of being out of proportion; a lack of proportion; inequality.

—[名] 불균형, 어울리지 않음

dis·pro·por·tion·ate [dìsprəpɔ́:rʃ(ə)nit] *adj.* not in proportion; out of balance. ¶*The windows are ~ to the height of this house.*①

—[形] 어울리지 않는 ¶①그 창은 이 집의 높이와 어울리지 않는다

dis·prove [disprú:v] *vt.* prove (something or someone) to be false.

—[他] …의 반증을 들다

dis·pu·ta·ble [dispjú:təbl] *adj.* not yet decided; questionable. ↔indisputable ¶*~ opinions.*①

—[形] 논의할 여지가 있는; 불확실한 ¶①논의해 봐야 할 의견

dis·pu·tant [dispjú:t(ə)nt] *n.* [C] a person who talks about a question.

—[名] 논쟁자

dis·pu·ta·tion [dìspju(:)téiʃ(ə)n] *n.* [U][C] the act of disputing; argument; discussion.

—[名] 논쟁, 논의

dis·pu·ta·tious [dìspju(:)téiʃəs] *adj.* fond of arguing; apt to dispute. ¶*a ~ person.*①

—[形] 논쟁을 좋아하는; 논쟁적인 ¶①논쟁을 좋아하는 사람

‡**dis·pute** [dispjú:t] *vi.* debate; argue. 《~ *about* something; ~ *with* or *against* someone》 —*vt.* **1.** question the truth of (something); discuss. ¶*~ a statement.* **2.** contend for (something); oppose; resist. ¶*~ every inch of ground*① */ ~ the enemy's passage.*②

—[自] 논쟁하다, 말다툼하다 —[他] 1. …의 진위(眞僞)를 문제삼다, 논쟁하다 2. …을 다투다; 반대하다, 거스르다 ¶①한 뼘의 땅도 잃지 않으려고 다투다/②적의 통과를 저지하다

—*n.* [U][C] the act of disputing; argument; quarrel. ¶*in ~*③ */ beyond* (or *without*) *~.*④

—[名] 토의, 논쟁, 말다툼 ¶③논쟁 중인/④의론의 여지 없이

dis·qual·i·fi·ca·tion [diskwὰlifikéiʃ(ə)n / -kwɔ̀l-] *n.* **1.** [U] the act of disqualifying; the state of being disqualified. **2.** [C] a cause that disqualifies something.

—[名] 1. 자격 박탈, 무자격, 실격 2. 무자격이 되는 이유, 결격 조항

dis·qual·i·fy [diskwάlifài / -kwɔ́l-] *vt.* (**-fied**) **1.** make (someone) unable to do something. 《~ someone *for*》 ¶*a disqualified person / ~ someone for the job.*① **2.** take a right or privilege away from (someone) legally. ¶*be disqualified from competing in a race*② */ I am disqualified by my weak heart from serving in the army.*③

—[他] 1. …의 자격을 빼앗다 ¶①…에게 그 일을 할 수 없게 하다 2. [법률상] …을 무능력하게 하다 ¶②경주에 출전 자격을 박탈당하다/③나는 심장병으로 군에 복무할 수 없다

dis·qui·et [diskwáiət] *vt.* make (someone) anxious or uneasy. ¶*My heart is disquieted.*① —*n.* [U] anxiety; uneasiness.

—[他] …을 불안하게 하다, …에게 안달나게 하다 ¶①나는 마음이 불안하다 —[名] 불안, 근심, 동요

dis·qui·e·tude [diskwáiit(j)ù:d / -tjù:d] *n.* [U] anxiety; uneasiness; trouble.

—[名] 불안, 불온

dis·qui·si·tion [dìskwizíʃ(ə)n] *n.* [C] a long, formal speech or writing on some subject; a discourse; a treatise.

—[名] 논문, 논설; 논고(論考)

dis·re·gard [dìsrigά:rd] *vt.* pay no attention to (someone or something); treat (someone) without proper respect; ignore. ¶*Don't ~ the footnotes.*① —*n.* [U] 《sometimes *a ~*》 lack of attention or respect; indifference. ¶*~ of traffic rules*② */ have a ~ for money.*③

—[他] …을 무시하다, 등한히 하다; 경시하다 ¶①각주를 무시하지 마라 —[名] 무시; 무관심 ¶②교통 규칙의 무시/③돈에 무관심하다

dis·re·pair [dìsripέər] *n.* [U] the condition of needing repairs; ruin. ¶*be in ~.*①

—[名] 파손; 황폐 ¶①[수리할 수 없을 정도로] 망가져 있다

dis·rep·u·ta·ble [dìsrépjutəbl] *adj.* unpopular; disgraceful; shameful.

—[形] 평판이 나쁜; 창피한

dis·re·pute [dìsripjú:t] *n.* [U] lack of repute; bad reputation; dishonor; disfavor. ¶*fall into general ~.*①

—[名] 평판이 나쁨, 악평; 불명예 ¶①세상의 평이 나빠지다

dis·re·spect [dìsrispékt] *n.* [U] lack of respect; rudeness; impoliteness. ¶*one's ~ to one's teacher.*①

—[名] 무례, 실례, 불경(不敬) ¶①교사에 대한 무례

dis·re·spect·ful [dìsrispéktf(u)l] *adj.* showing lack of respect; rude; discourteous; impolite.

—[形] 무례한, 실례되는

dis·robe [dìsróub] *vi., vt.* take off the clothes (of oneself or someone else).

dis·rupt [disrʌ́pt] *vt., vi.* break up; split up. ¶ ~ *the state.*

dis·rup·tion [disrʌ́pʃ(ə)n] *n.* Ⓤ the act of disrupting; the state of being disrupted. ¶ *the ~ of the state.*①

dis·sat·is·fac·tion [dìs(s)sætisfǽkʃ(ə)n] *n.* Ⓤ the state of not being satisfied; discontent; Ⓒ something that causes dissatisfaction. ¶ *express ~ at* (or *with*) *something.*①

dis·sat·is·fied [dís(s)sætisfàid] *v.* pp. of **dissatisfy**.
—*adj.* not satisfied; discontented; displeased. ¶ *a ~ look.*①

dis·sat·is·fy [dís(s)sætisfài] *vt.* (**-fied**) fail to satisfy (someone); discontent; displease. ¶ *I am dissatisfied with* (or *at*) *my position.*①

dis·sect [disékt] *vt.* **1.** cut (something) in pieces. **2.** separate (a dead body, animals, plants, etc.) to examine; anatomize. ¶ *a dissecting knife* (*room*).① **3.** criticize (something) in detail; analyze. ¶ ~ *a problem.*②

dis·sec·tion [disékʃ(ə)n] *n.* Ⓤ **1.** the act of dissecting; analysis; Ⓒ something that has been dissected. **2.** a detailed examination.

dis·sem·ble [disémbl] *vt.* hide (one's feeling, intentions, etc.). —*vi.* pretend not to notice.

dis·sem·i·nate [disémineìt] *vt.* scatter; spread; propagate. ¶ ~ *Christianity among the villages.*

dis·sem·i·na·tion [dìseminéiʃ(ə)n] *n.* Ⓤ the act of disseminating; the state of being disseminated; wide distribution (of ideas or doctrines).

dis·sen·sion [disénʃ(ə)n] *n.* Ⓤ disagreement in opinion; difference; Ⓒ a quarrel. ¶ *family ~.*①

dis·sent [disént] *vi.* **1.** disagree in opinion. ↔consent 《~ *from* someone or something》 ¶ *They dissented from each other.*① **2.** (*Brit.*) reject the rules and beliefs of present churches. —*n.* Ⓤ **1.** disagreement or difference in opinion. **2.** (*Brit.*) separation from the Church of England; (《*collectively*》) nonconformity.

dis·sent·er [diséntər] *n.* Ⓒ **1.** a person who is different in opinion. **2.** a nonconformist.

dis·sen·tient [disénʃ(i)ənt] *adj.* disagreeing in opinion; objecting. —*n.* Ⓒ a person who disagrees.

dis·ser·ta·tion [dìsə(ː)rtéiʃ(ə)n] *n.* Ⓒ a treatise or thesis, esp. one required for a university degree.

dis·serv·ice [di(s)sə́ːrvis] *n.* Ⓤ (often *a ~*) an ill treatment; a harmful action. ¶ *do someone a ~.*①

dis·sev·er [di(s)sévər] *vt.* separate; disunite.

dis·sim·i·lar [di(s)símilər] *adj.* not similar; different. ¶ *They are ~ to each other.*①

dis·sim·i·lar·i·ty [dì(s)similǽriti] *n.* (pl. *-ties*) Ⓤ the state of dissimilar; difference Ⓒ a point of difference.

dis·sim·u·late [disímjulèit] *vt., vi.* hide (one's feelings, intentions, etc.) by pretense; pretend.

dis·sim·u·la·tion [disìmjuléiʃ(ə)n] *n.* Ⓤ the act of dissimulating; pretense; hypocrisy; disguise.

dis·si·pate [dísipèit] *vt.* **1.** scatter (something) in all directions. ¶ *The wind dissipated the fog.*① **2.** drive (something) completely away. ¶ ~ *anxiety.*②. **3.** waste. ¶ ~ *someone's energies.*② —*vi.* **1.** vanish. ¶ *The mists gradually dissipated.* **2.** lead a wasteful life.

dis·si·pat·ed [dísipèitid] *adj.* **1.** scattered. **2.** indulging in pleasure to excess; wasted.

dis·si·pa·tion [dìsipéiʃ(ə)n] *n.* **1.** Ⓤ the act of dissipating; dispersion. ¶ *the ~ of fog.*① **2.** Ⓒ a pastime; an amusement. **3.** Ⓤ excessive indulgence in pleasure.

dis·so·ci·ate [disóuʃièit] *vt.* **1.** break the connection

—自他 옷을 벗[기]다

「(하다)
—他自 분열시키다(하다);와해시키다
—名 [국가·제도 따위의] 분열; 와해 ¶①국가의 파멸

—名 불만,불평; 불만의 원인 ¶①…에게 불만을 말하다

—形 불만스러운 ¶①불만스러운 눈초리

—他 …을 만족시키지 않다; 불만(불평)을 품게 하다 ¶①나는 내 지위에 불만이다

—他 1. …을 잘게 자르다 2. …을 해부하다 ¶①해부도(刀)(실) 3. …을 상세히 비평하다; 분석하다 ¶②문제를 검토하다

—名 1. 절개(切開),해부(체) 2. 분석적(면밀한) 연구

—他 [감정·의도 따위]를 감추다
—自 모르는 체하다
—他 …을 뿌리다,살포하다; [교리 따위]를 퍼뜨리다,선전하다
—名 씨뿌리기; 살포, [보도·가르침 따위의] 전파, 유포

—名 의견 차이; 불화, 알력, 싸움 ¶①가정불화
—自 1. 의견을 달리하다 ¶①그들은 서로 의견이 달랐다 2. 《英》 국교에 반대하다 —名 1. 부동의(不同意), 이의 2. 《英》 국교 반대; 비국교도

—名 1. 반대자, 이의를 가진 사람 2. 영국 국교 반대자
—形 의견이 다른; 이의를 제기하는
—名 반대자, 이의 제기자
—名 논설; 학위 논문

—名 심한 처사(대우), 이롭지 못한 일 ¶①…에게 이롭지 못한 일을 하다
—他 …을 분리(분할)하다
—形 같지 않은, 다른 ¶①그들은 서로 닮지 않았다
—名 닮지 않음; 상이점

—他自 [감정·의지 따위를] 감추다, 숨기다, 시치미떼다
—名 시치미떼기, 은폐, 허위

—他 1. …을 흩뜨리다 ¶①바람으로 안개가 흩어졌다 2. …을 없애다, 씻어버리다 3. …을 낭비하다 ¶②정력을 헛되이 쓰다 —自 1. 흩어지다 2. 방탕하다

—形 1. 분산된 2. 방탕한; 낭비적인

—名 1. 분산, 흩어져 사라짐 ¶①안개의 걷힘 2. 기분전환, 심심풀이; 오락 3. 방탕

—他 1. …을 분리하다, 떼어놓다

with (someone); disunite. ¶*dissociated personality*① / *~ oneself from (someone)*.② **2.** (*Chemistry*) separate.
¶①분열 인격(分裂人格)/②…와의 관계를 끊다 2.《化》해리(解離)하다

dis·sol·u·bil·i·ty [disɑ̀ljubíliti / -sɔ̀l-] *n.* [U] the quality of being dissoluble; solubility.
—[명] 용해성, 분해성

dis·sol·u·ble [disɑ́ljubl / -sɔ́l-] *adj.* that can be divided into parts; dissolvable.
—[형] 용해(분해)할 수 있는

dis·so·lute [dísəl(j)ù:t] *adj.* loose in behavior and morals; immoral; dissipated.
—[형] 행실이 나쁜; 방탕한

dis·so·lu·tion [dìsəl(j)ú:ʃ(ə)n] *n.* [U] [C] **1.** the act of breaking up; decomposition **2.** an ending; finish. ¶*the ~ of the National Diet.*① **3.** destruction; ruin. **4.** death.
—[명] 1. 분해, 분리 2. 해소, 해산 ¶①국회의 해산 3. 괴멸, 소실(消失) 4. 죽음

:dis·solve [dizɑ́lv / -zɔ́lv] *vt.* **1.** make (something) liquid; melt. ¶*The sun dissolves the snow.* **2.** break up; disunite ¶*~ the National Diet.*① **3.** clear up (something); solve; explain. ¶*~ doubts.*② —*vi.* **1.** become liquid; melt away. ¶*Sugar dissolves in water.* **2.** disunite. ¶*The House of Councilors dissolved.*③ **3.** fade away; vanish. ¶*be dissolved in tears.*④
—[타] 1. …을 녹이다 2. …을 해산시키다, 해소시키다 ¶①국회를 해산하다 3. …을 해결하다, 해설하다 ¶②미심스러운 점을 설명하다 —[자] 1. 녹이다, 분해하다 2. 해산하다, 해소하다 ¶③참의원을 해산했다 3. 차츰 사라져 없어지다 ¶④훌쩍훌쩍 울다

—*n.* [U] (*Motion pictures, Television*) the gradual disappearing or appearing of figures in a scene; a fade-out; a fade-in.
—[명] 《映畫·텔레비전》 용암(溶暗)

dis·so·nance [dísənəns] *n.* **1.** [U] disagreement; disharmony. **2.** [U] [C] (*Music*) a disharmonious sound; a lack of harmony. ↔consonance
—[명] 1. 불화, 부조화 2. 《樂》 불협화음

dis·so·nant [dísənənt] *adj.* **1.** unpleasant to the ear; harsh. ¶*~ sounds.*① **2.** disharmonious; disagreeing.
—[형] 1. 귀에 거슬리는 ¶①귀에 거슬리는 소리 2. 부조화의, 불일치의

dis·suade [diswéid] *vt.* advise (someone) not to do something wrong. 《~ someone *from doing* a bad action, etc.》 ↔persuade ¶*~ someone from going alone to a dangerous zone.*①
—[타] …에게 …을 그만두게 하다 ¶①…을 타일러서 위험지대에 혼자 가지 않게 하다

dis·sua·sion [diswéiʒ(ə)n] *n.* [U] the act of dissuading; advice.
—[명] 타일러서 말리기; 충고, 권고

.**dis·taff** [dístæf / -tɑ:f] *n.* [C] **1.** a stick to hold wool, etc. for spinning into thread. **2.** 《*the ~*》 woman's work. **3.** 《*the ~*》 the female sex.
—[명] 1. [물레용의] 실패 2. 여성의 일 3. 여성

the distaff side, the female members of a family.
[熟] 모계(母系); [집안의] 여자 식구

⁝dis·tance [díst(ə)ns] *n.* [C] **1.** [C] [U] the space between one and another. ¶*the ~ between Japan and America* / *within hearing ~.*① **2.** the place far away. ¶*The plane flew away into the ~.*② / *We saw a light in the ~.* **3.** space of time; interval. ¶*a ~ of three years.*③ **4.** coldness of manner; lack of friendship. ¶*keep someone at a ~.*④
—[명] 1. 거리, 간격 ¶①부르면 들리는 거리에 2. 먼 곳 ¶②비행기는 멀리 날아갔다 3. [시일의] 간격, 기간, 동안 ¶③3년 동안 4. 냉담, 쌀쌀함 ¶④…을 멀리하다

:dis·tant [díst(ə)nt] *adj.* **1.** far away in time or space. ¶*a ~ view*① / *a ~ signal*② / *The town is ten miles ~ from Paris.* **2.** far off in relationship, likeness, etc. ¶*a ~ likeness*③ / *a ~ relative.*④ **3.** not friendly; cool in manner; reserved. ¶*a ~ air.*⑤
—[형] 1. 먼, 떨어져 있는 ¶①원경(遠景)/②원격(遠隔) 신호기 2. [관계·닮는 정도 따위가] 먼, 얼마 안 되는 ¶③얼마 안 되는 유사점/④먼 친척 3. 쌀쌀한; 냉담한 ¶⑤냉담한 태도

dis·taste [distéist] *n.* [U] 《often *a ~*》 dislike. ¶*have a ~ for cooking.*①
—[명] 싫증, 염증 ¶①요리를 좋아하지 않다

dis·taste·ful [distéistf(u)l] *adj.* tasteless; poor; unpleasant; disagreeable. ¶*Work is ~ to him.*①
—[형] 맛없는; 싫은 ¶①그는 일을 싫어한다

dis·tem·per[1] [distémpər] *n.* [U] **1.** an easily-spread disease, chiefly of young dogs. **2.** a disorder in the body or the mind; disease. **3.** social disorder or confusion. —*vt.* disorder; confuse. ¶*a distempered mind.*①
—[명] 1. 디스템퍼(강아지의 전염병) 2. [정신·육체의] 이상; 병 3. 사회적 불안 —[타] [심신]이 탈이 나게 하다 ¶①정신이상

dis·tem·per[2] [distémpər] *n.* **1.** [U] paint made by using eggs or glue instead of oil. **2.** [C] a tempera paint. —*vt.* paint (something) in distemper.
—[명] 1. 갖풀 그림물감 2. 템페라 그림 —[타] …을 갖풀 그림물감으로 그리다

dis·tend [disténd] *vt., vi.* swell; enlarge; expand.
—[타][자] 팽창시키다(하다); 펼치다

dis·ten·sion, -tion [disténʃ(ə)n] *n.* [U] the act of distending; the state of being distended; enlargement; expansion. ¶*the ~ of the lungs.*①
—[명] 확대; 팽창; 확장 ¶①폐의 팽창

dis·till, *Brit.* **-til** [distíl] *vt.* **1.** heat (a liquid) until it is changed to steam. **2.** get (something) by the process of distillation. ¶*distilled water*① / *~ fresh water from*
—[타] 1. [액체]를 증류하다 2. 증류하여 …을 만들다 ¶①증류수/②바닷물을 증류하여 담수(淡水)를 만들다 3. …을

D

*sea water.*② **3.** extract the essence of (something). **—***vi.* **1.** fall in drops; drip. **2.** practice distillation; purify; refine.
발췌하다, 순화(純化)하다 —[自] 1. [방울이] 떨어지다, 스며나오다 2. 증류하다

dis·til·la·tion [dìstiléiʃ(ə)n] *n.* **1.** [U] the act of distilling. **2.** [C] a thing distilled.
—[名] 1. 증류 2. 증류물

dis·tilled [distíld] *adj.* produced by distilling. ¶ *~ water.*①
—[形] 증류하여 만든 ¶①증류수

dis·till·er [distílər] *n.* [C] **1.** a person or an apparatus that distills. **2.** a person or company that makes alcoholic liquors, esp. whisky.
—[名] 1. 증류자, 증류기 2. 양조자(회사)

dis·till·er·y [distíləri] *n.* [C] (pl. **-er·ies**) a place where distillation is carried on.
—[名] 증류소, 양조장

: dis·tinct [distíŋ(k)t] *adj.* **1.** not exactly the same; separate. ¶*keep two things ~*① / *White bears are ~ from pandas.*② **2.** different in nature or quality. ¶*Iron is ~ from gold.*③ **3.** clear; plain. ¶*~ pronunciation.* **4.** definite; unmistakable. ▷**dis·tinct·ness** [-nis] *n.*
—[形] 1. 별개의 ¶①양자를 구별하다/②흰 곰은 팬더와는 다르다 2. 다른 ¶③쇠와 금은 다르다 3. 명백한, 명료한 4. 명확한, 틀림이 없는

: dis·tinc·tion [distíŋ(k)ʃ(ə)n] *n.* **1.** [U] the act of making a distinct separation; division. ¶*without ~*① / *~ of birth*② / *make no ~ between A and B.*③ **2.** [C] a difference. ¶*a ~ without a difference.*④ **3.** [C] a characteristic difference. **4.** [U] [C] honor; fame. **5.** excellence.
—[名] 1. 구별, 차별 ¶①차별 없이/②출생의 차이/③A와 B를 구별하지 않다 2. 상이 ¶④차별없는 구별 3. 특이성 4. 영예, 명성 5. 탁월, 우수성

dis·tinc·tive [distíŋ(k)tiv] *adj.* marking a difference; remarkable; special.
—[形] 구별적인, 구별이 있는; 특수한, 독특한

• dis·tinct·ly [distíŋ(k)tli] *adv.* in a distinct manner; clearly; precisely.
—[副] 뚜렷이; 명확히

• dis·tin·guish [distíŋgwiʃ] *vt.* **1.** see or show the difference between (two things). ⟪~ one *from* another⟫ ¶*~ right from wrong.*① **2.** admit clearly. ¶*~ someone at a distance.*② **3.** make (someone) famous; characterize. ¶*~ oneself in literature (by scholarship)*③ / *a man distinguished for courage.*④ **4.** separate (persons or things) into groups according to kind; classify. ¶*~ sounds into high and low.*⑤ **—***vi.* see or show the difference. ¶*~ between right and wrong.*
—[他] 1. …을 구별하다 ¶①옳고 그른 것을 구별하다 2. …을 식별(판별)하다 ¶②먼 곳에 있는 사람을 알아보다 3. …을 유명하게 하다 ¶③문학으로 이름을 높이다(학식으로 알려지다)/④용기로서 알려진 사람 4. …을 분류하다 ¶⑤음을 높고 낮은 것으로 나누다 —[自] 구별하다

dis·tin·guish·a·ble [distíŋgwiʃəbl] *adj.* that can be distinguished.
—[形] 구별(분간)할 수 있는

• dis·tin·guished [distíŋgwiʃt] *adj.* **1.** famous; well-known; admirable. ¶*a ~ family.*① **2.** noble.
—[形] 1. 유명한 ¶①명문 2. 고귀한, 품위 있는

dis·tort [distɔ́:rt] *vt.* **1.** change the natural shape of (something); twist. ¶*~ one's face.*① **2.** change the truth or original meaning of (something). ¶*~ the facts.*
—[他] 1. …을 찌그러뜨리다; 비틀다 ¶①얼굴을 찡그리다 2. [사실]을 의곡하다; 곡해하다

dis·tor·tion [distɔ́:rʃ(ə)n] *n.* **1.** [U] the act of distorting; the state of being distorted. ¶*the ~ of the face.* **2.** [C] anything distorted.
—[名] 1. 찌그러뜨리기; 비틀림; 견강부회(牽强附會); 곡해 2. 찌그러진 것

dis·tract [distrǽkt] *vt.* **1.** turn (the mind, attention, etc.) in a different direction; divert. ¶*Reading distracts the mind from grief.*① **2.** make trouble for; confuse. ¶*Her mind was distracted by grief.* **3.** drive (someone) mad.
—[他] 1. [마음 따위를] 흩어지게 하다, 딴곳으로 돌리다 ¶①독서는 슬픔을 잊게 해준다 2. …을 괴롭히다; 혼란하게 하다 3. …을 미치게 하다

dis·tract·ed [distrǽktid] *adj.* (of the mind) confused; troubled.
—[形] 혼란된; 미친

dis·trac·tion [distrǽkʃ(ə)n] *n.* **1.** [U] the act of distracting; the state of being distracted. ¶*drive to ~*① / *to ~.*② **2.** [C] anything that distracts. **3.** [C] a diversion; an amusement. ¶*We need some distractions after work.*③
—[名] 1. 마음이 흩어짐; 마음의 혼란; 정신착란 ¶①미치게 하다/②미칠 듯이 2. 마음을 흩어지게 하는 것 3. 기분전환; 오락

dis·train [distréin] *vt., vi.* seize and hold (someone's property) for debt. ¶*~ property from someone.*①
—[他][自] 차압하다 ¶①…의 재산을 차압하다

dis·traught [distrɔ́:t] *adj.* **1.** in a state of confusion; mentally confused. **2.** driven mad; crazed.
—[形] 1. 마음이 산란한 2. 미친 [듯한]

: dis·tress [distrés] *n.* **1.** [U] great pain or sorrow. **2.** [C] a cause of distress. ¶*He is a great ~ to his father.* **3.** [U] danger; difficulty; trouble. ¶*a ship in ~* / *be in ~.*① **—***vt.* trouble; embarrass. ¶*~ oneself* / *be distressed at* (or *to hear*) *the news.*
—[名] 1. 고통; 비탄, 근심 2. 걱정거리 3. 곤궁, 빈곤, 재난, 난파 ¶①곤란받고 있다; 조난 상태이다 —[他] …을 괴롭히다; 고민시키다; 슬퍼하게 하다

dis·tress·ful [distrésf(u)l] *adj.* **1.** painful. **2.** unhappy; miserable.
—[形] 1. 고통스러운 2. 불행한; 비참한

: dis·trib·ute [distríbju(:)t] *vt.* **1.** give (things) to each; hand out. ¶*~ pamphlets to the audience.*① **2.** spread
—[他] 1. …을 분배하다; 배급하다 ¶①청중에게 팜플렛을 돌리다 2. …을 분

D

distribution
[346]
divergence

out; scatter. ¶ *a widely-distributed animal.*② **3.** divide (things) into groups; classify. ¶ *~ books according to subject.*

* **dis·tri·bu·tion** [dìstribjúːʃ(ə)n] *n.* ⓤ the act or manner of distributing; ⓒ an instance of this. ¶ *the ~ of wealth*① / *the equal ~ of property.*②

dis·trib·u·tive [distríbjutiv] *adj.* **1.** of distribution. **2.** of each member of a group. ——*n.* ⓒ a distributive word. ⇒N.B. ┌company that distributes.┐

dis·trib·u·tor [distríbjutər] *n.* ⓒ a person, thing, or ┘

: **dis·trict** [dístrikt] *n.* ⓒ **1.** any region; a part of a country. ¶ *an agricultural ~ / the Kanto District.* **2.** a part of a country divided for a special purpose. ¶ *a police ~ / a school ~*① / *an election ~.*②

* **dis·trust** [distrʌ́st] *vt.* disbelieve; doubt; suspect. ——*n.* ⓤ (sometimes *a ~*) disbelief; doubt; suspicion.

dis·trust·ful [distrʌ́stf(u)l] *adj.* not trusting; not being trusted; doubtful.

: **dis·turb** [distə́ːrb] *vt.* **1.** break the calm condition of (something); stir up. ¶ *~ the peace.*① **2.** make (someone) uneasy or anxious; bother; interrupt. ¶ *~ a sleeping baby*② / *I'm sorry to ~ you.* **3.** put (something) out of order. ¶ *Don't ~ the cards in this case.*

* **dis·turb·ance** [distə́ːrb(ə)ns] *n.* **1.** ⓤ the act of disturbing; the state of being disturbed. **2.** ⓒ a thing that disturbs something. ┌greement; discord.┐

dis·un·ion [disjúːnjən] *n.* ⓤ **1.** separation. **2.** disa-┘

dis·u·nite [dìsjuːnáit] *vt., vi.* **1.** separate; disjoin. **2.** make (things or persons) disagree.

dis·use *vt.* [disjúːz→*n.*] (chiefly in *passive*) cease to use. ¶ *a disused word.* ——*n.* ⓤ [disjúːs] disusage; abandonment. ¶ *fall into ~.*①

* **ditch** [ditʃ] *n.* ⓒ a long, narrow channel dug in the earth; a channel; a gutter. ┌tion.┐
  1) *be driven to the last ditch,* be in a difficult situa-┘
  2) *die in a ditch,* die on the road; die poor.
  ——*vi., vt.* **1.** dig a ditch. **2.** throw (something) into a ditch; fall into a ditch.

dit·to [dítou] *n.* ⓒ (pl. **-tos**) the same. ⇒N.B. ¶ *a ~ mark / say ~ to someone.* ——*adv.* as before.

dit·ty [díti] *n.* ⓒ (pl. **-ties**) a short, simple song.

di·ur·nal [daiə́ːrn(ə)l] *adj.* **1.** daily. **2.** work. **2.** belonging to the daytime. ¶ *~ heat.*① **3.** performed in twenty-four hours. ¶ *the earth's ~ revolution.*②

di·van [diváen, dáivæn] *n.* ⓒ **1.** a long, low sofa with cushions, usu. against a wall. **2.** a court or council room as in Turkey. **3.** a smoking room.

* **dive** [daiv] *vi.* (**dived** or *U.S.* **dove**) **1.** go down head first into water; go into water suddenly. ¶ *~ in the water / He dived into the sea.*① **2.** go out of sight suddenly. ¶ *~ into the bushes.* **3.** thrust the hand suddenly into something. ¶ *She dived into her pockets.*② **4.** go down in the air at a steep angle; nose-dive. **5.** enter into a subject. ¶ *~ into economics.*③
——*n.* ⓒ **1.** an act of diving. ¶ *a fancy ~.*④ **2.** a cheap drinking-place, esp. one in a basement. ¶ *an opium ~.*⑤

div·er [dáivər] *n.* ⓒ **1.** a person or thing that dives. **2.** a person whose job is diving. **3.** a diving bird, as the grebe or loon.

di·verge [divə́ːrdʒ, dai-] *vi.* **1.** (of roads, etc.) go in different directions from the same point. ¶ *~ from the main road.*① **2.** (of opinions, etc.) differ; become different.

di·ver·gence [divə́ːrdʒ(ə)ns, dai-] *n.* ⓤⓒ the act of di-

포하다, 살포하다 ¶②널리 분포된 동물 **3.** ⋯을 구분하다; 분류하다

——ⓝ 분배, 배포 ¶①부(富)의 배분/② 재산의 평등한 분배

——ⓐ 1. 배급의; 분배의 2. 개체적인 ——ⓝ 개별적 대명사(형용사) N.B. each, every 따위

——ⓝ 분배자; 배급자; 분배기

——ⓝ 1. 〔한 나라 안의〕 지방; 지역 2. 행정구; 관할구 ¶①학구/②선거구

——ⓥ ⋯을 신용하지 않다; 의심하다, 수상히 여기다 ——ⓝ 불신; 의혹; 의심

——ⓐ 남을 신용하지 않는; 자신이 없는; 의심 깊은

——ⓥ 1. ⋯을 흐트러뜨리다; 교란하다 ¶①치안을 교란하다 2. ⋯을 불안하게 하다; 방해하다; 소란하게 하다 ¶②잠자는 아이를 깨우다 3. ⋯의 순서 따위를 어지럽히다

——ⓝ 1. 교란; 방해; 불안 2. 흐트러뜨리는 것

——ⓝ 1. 분리; 분열 2. 불화, 내분; 불통일

——ⓝ 1. 분리(분열)하다 2. 불화하게 하다, 의견이 갈라지게 하다

——ⓥ ⋯의 사용을 중지하다 ——ⓝ 쓰지 않음, 폐기 ¶①폐지되다

——ⓝ 도랑, 시궁창, 배수구

圏 1)궁지에 빠지다 2)객사하다

——ⓥⓘ 1. 도랑을 파다 2. 도랑에 ⋯을 던져넣다; 도랑에 빠지다

——ⓝ 같음, 위(앞)와 같음 N.B. d°, do 로 줄임 〔앞에서와〕 마찬가지로

——ⓝ 소곡가, 민요

——ⓐ 1. 매일의 2. 대낮의 ¶①대낮의 더위 3. 24시간의 ¶②지구의 공전(公轉)

——ⓝ 1. 벽에다 붙인 긴 의자 2. 〔터어키 따위의〕 국정(國政)회의; 회의실 3. 끽연실

——ⓘ 1. 물속에 뛰어들다, 잠수하다 ¶①바다에 뛰어들다 2. 갑자기 자취를 감추다 3. 손을 찔러 넣다 ¶②주머니에 손을 넣었다 4. 급강하하다 5. 탐구(몰두)하다 ¶③경제학을 파고들다 ——ⓝ 1. 잠수; 급강하 ¶④〔수영의〕 곡예 다이빙 2. 〔특히〕 지하의 싸구려 술집 ¶⑤아편굴

——ⓝ 1. 뛰어드는 사람(것) 2. 잠수부 3. 〔鳥〕 아비·농병아리류

——ⓘ 1. 분기(分岐)하다 ¶①한길에서 벗어나다 2. 〔의견 따위가〕 갈라지다

——ⓝ 분기, 갈라짐; 상이(相異) ¶①커

verging; the state of being diverged; separation; difference. ¶*a wide ~ of opinion.*① — 다란 의견의 차이

di·ver·gent [divə́:rdʒ(ə)nt, dai-] *adj.* separating; different. —[形] 분기하는, 갈라지는; 다른, 가지각색의

di·vers [dáivə(:)rz] *adj.* various; several; different. —[形] 여러가지의, 잡다한; 다른

di·verse [divə́:rs, daivə́:s] *adj.* **1.** unlike in character; different. **2.** various. —[形] 1. 다른, 틀리는 2. 여러가지의

di·ver·si·fi·ca·tion [divə̀:rsifikéiʃ(ə)n, dai- / daivə̀:sifikéiʃ(ə)n] *n.* [U] [C] the act of diversifying; the state of being diversified; variation; change. —[名] 다종다양[하게 하기]; 변화

di·ver·si·fy [divə́:rsifài / daivə́:si-] *vt.* (**-fied**) give variety to (something); vary; change. ¶*be diversified.*① —[他] …에 변화를 주다, …을 변화시키다 ¶①변화가 풍부하다

di·ver·sion [divə́:rʒ(ə)n, dai-, -ʃ(ə)n / daivə́:ʃ(ə)n, di-] *n.* **1.** [U] the act of turning aside. ¶*the ~ of the mind from one's study.*① **2.** [C] a recreation; an amusement. —[名] 1. 다른 쪽으로 쏠리게 하기, [주의의] 전환 ¶①공부에서 마음을 다른 데로 돌리다 2. 오락, 기분전환

di·ver·si·ty [divə́:rsiti, dai- / daivə́:siti, di-] *n.* [U] [C] (pl. **-ties**) remarkable difference; unlikeness; variety. —[名] 상이, 잡다함, 다양성

di·vert [divə́:rt, dai- / daivə́:t, di-] *vt.* **1.** turn (someone or something) aside. ¶*~ someone from his cares*① / *be diverted into a side issue.*② **2.** please; amuse. ¶*~ oneself by dancing.* —[他] 1. …을 다른 곳으로 돌리다, 전환시키다 ¶①기분전환으로 근심을 잊게 하다/②지엽적 문제에 이르다 2. 기분을 풀다

di·vert·ing [divə́:rtiŋ, dai- / daivə́:tiŋ, di-] *adj.* amusing; entertaining. ¶*a ~ sport.* —[形] 재미있는, 기분전환이 되는

di·vest [divést, dai-] *vt.* take something away from (someone); strip. 《~ someone *of* his purse, etc.》 ¶*be divested of something*① / *~ oneself of something*② / *~ someone of his office*③ / *I was divested of my coat.*④ —[他] …을 벗기다, 빼앗다, 박탈하다 ¶①…을 잃다/②…을 벗다, 버리다/③…의 지위를 빼앗다/④나는 웃옷을 빼앗겼다

:di·vide [diváid] *vt.* **1.** split up; separate (something) into parts. ¶*The school year is divided into three terms.* **2.** distribute; share. ¶*~ the profits with a friend* / *They divided the cake among them.* **3.** differ from (something) in feeling, opinion, etc.; disagree. ¶*Our opinions were divided on the point.*① **4.** (*Mathematics*) separate into equal parts. ¶*~ 8 by 2, and you get 4; 8 divided by 2 is* (or *equals, gives*) *4.* / *7 divides 42.*② —[他] 1. …을 나누다, 쪼개다, 분리(분류)하다 2. …을 분배하다, 나누다 3. [감정·의견 따위]를 분열시키다 ¶①우리의 의견은 그 점에서 갈라졌다 4. 《數》[수]를 나누다, 우수리 없이 나뉘게 하다 ¶②42는 7로 나눌 수 있다

—*vi.* **1.** become separate; part. ¶*~ into 4 groups.* **2.** separate into groups in voting on a question. **3.** (*Mathematics*) separate into equal parts. ¶*49 divides by 7.* —[自] 1. 나누어지다, 쪼개지다, 의견이 갈라지다 2. 표결하다, 찬반으로 나누다 3. 《數》 나눗셈하다, 나뉘다

—*n.* [C] **1.** a division; distribution. **2.** something that divides, esp. a watershed or ridge. —[名] 1. 분할, 분배 2. 분수령, 분수계(分水界)

div·i·dend [dívidènd] *n.* [C] **1.** a number to be divided by a divisor. ↔divisor **2.** a sum of money to be divided among stockholders. ¶*declare a ~.*① —[名] 1. 나뉨수, 피제수(被除數) 2. 배당금 ¶①배당 지불을 발표하다

di·vid·ers [diváidərz] *n. pl.* a pair of small compasses used for dividing lines. ⇒[usage] —[名] 분할 컴퍼스 [usage] a pair of dividers 로 씀

div·i·na·tion [dìvinéiʃ(ə)n] *n.* **1.** [U] the act of foretelling the future. **2.** [C] a skillful guess; a prediction. —[名] 1. 점(占) 2. 예언; 예견, 예측

:di·vine [diváin] *adj.* **1.** of God; Godlike. ¶*~ judgment*① / *the ~ Being* (or *Father*).② **2.** given by God. ¶*the ~ right of kings.*③ **3.** for or to God; holy. ¶*a ~ service.*④ **4.** very excellent. ¶*What ~ weather!*⑤ —[形] 1. 신(神)의(같은) ¶①신의 심판/②신, 하나님 2. 신이 주신 ¶③신이 주신 왕권 3. 신에게 바친; 신성한 ¶④예배식 4. 비범한 ¶⑤참 좋은 날씨로구나!

—*n.* [C] a priest; a scholar of Christianity. **—*vt., vi.*** tell something about the future; find out (something) by inspiration; guess. —[名] 목사; 신학자 —[他][自] 점치다; 간파하다, 미리 알다

di·vine·ly [diváinli] *adv.* in a divine manner; by the influence of God; excellently. —[副] 신과 같은; 신의 힘으로; 절묘하게

di·vin·er [diváinər] *n.* [C] a magician; a fortuneteller; a predictor; a guesser. —[名] 점장이; 예언자

div·ing bell [dáiviŋbèl] *n.* a steel room shaped like a bell, in which men can work under water. —[名] 종 모양의 잠수기

diving board [⌐-⌐] *n.* a springboard. —[名] [수영의] 다이빙대

di·vin·i·ty [divíniti] *n.* (pl. **-ties**) **1.** [C] a divine being; 《*the D-*》 God, the Lord. **2.** [U] a divine quality; godhood. **3.** [U] the study of Christianity. ¶*a doctor of ~.*① —[名] 1. 신; 그리스도교의 신 2. 신성(神性) 3. 신학 ¶①신학박사

di·vis·i·ble [divízibl] *adj.* **1.** that can be divided. **2.** —[形] 1. 나눌 수 있는 2. 《數》 [우수리

(*Mathematics*) that can be divided without leaving a remainder.

‡ **div·i·sion** [divíʒ(ə)n] *n.* **1.** [C][U] the act of dividing; the state of being divided; separation into parts. **2.** [C][U] the act of sharing; distribution. **3.** [C][U] (*Mathematics*) the process of dividing one number by another. **4.** [C] something that divides; a boundary; a separating wall. **5.** [C] a part; a department; a section. **6.** [C] (*Military*) a section of an army. ⇒[N.B.] **7.** [C][U] a difference of opinion, etc.; disagreement.

di·vi·sion·al [divíʒən(ə)l] *adj.* that divides; of a division. ¶*a ~ commander.*①

di·vi·sor [diváizər] *n.* [C] (*Mathematics*) the number or quantity by which another number or quantity is divided. ↔dividend ¶*a common ~.*①

* **di·vorce** [divɔ́:rs] *n.* **1.** [C][U] the legal or formal ending of a marriage. **2.** [C] a complete separation. —*vt.* **1.** put an end to a marriage of (someone) legally or formally. ¶*The judge divorced Mr. & Mrs. Johnson.*① **2.** get rid of (a husband or wife) by a divorce. ¶*~ one's husband / be divorced from one's husband*② */ ~ oneself from one's husband.*③ **3.** separate. 《~something *from*》 ¶*~ one's conduct from one's principles.*④

di·vulge [divʌ́ldʒ / dai-] *vt.* make (something) known; tell; reveal. ¶*~ a secret plan to the enemy.*①

diz·zi·ness [dízinis] [U] *n.* the state of being dizzy.

diz·zy [dízi] *adj.* (**-zi·er, -zi·est**) **1.** feeling as if everything were turning around; not steady; likely to make dizzy. ¶*a ~ height.*① **2.** confused; bewildered. —*vt.* (**-zied**) make (someone) dizzy. ▷**diz·zi·ly** [-li] *adv.*

‡ **do** [du:, du, də] *v.* (**did, done**) *vt.* **1.** perform; fulfil; carry out. ¶*I have nothing to ~. / I have already done it. / Do your duty.* **2.** finish; complete. 《*~ doing*》 ⇒[usage] ¶*What is done cannot be undone.*① **3.** bring about; cause; give. ¶*Will you ~ me a favor?*② **4.** produce; create. ¶*He does oil portraits.* **5.** adapt; translate. ¶*~ Shakespeare into Korean. / Walt Disney did the book into a movie.* **6.** put (something) in order; arrange. ¶*~ the flowers*③ */ ~ the bedroom / She did her hair.* **7.** work; study; solve. ¶*~ a problem.* **8.** serve; suit. ¶*That will ~ you very well.* **9.** act (a play, etc.); play the part of (something). ¶*They are doing "Hamlet." / She did the hostess admirably.* **10.** exhaust; tire; wear out. ¶*That last set of the game did me. / I'm done—I can walk no farther.* **11.** visit; travel as a sightseer. ¶*~ the sights of Seoul / ~ Korea in twenty days.* **12.** travel (a certain distance); travel at the rate of (a certain speed); cover. ¶*They did twenty miles a day. / My car is doing 60 kilometers an hour.* **13.** 《usu. in *pp.*》 cook; prepare. ¶*I like my meat well-done.*④ **14.** entertain; treat. ¶*They did me well at that hotel.* **15.** (*colloq.*) cheat; trick. 《~ someone *out of*》 ¶*He did her out of her money.* —*vi.* **1.** behave; act; work. ¶*~ right / Let us be up and doing.*⑤ **2.** 《used in *pp.*》 finish; be finished. 《*~ with* something》 ¶*I have done with him.*⑥ */ Have done!*⑦ **3.** get along; live. ¶*How do you ~? / Mother and child are doing well.* **4.** grow well. ¶*The patient will ~ now.* **5.** be suitable; serve; suit. ¶*Any time after five will ~. / This won't ~.*⑧

1) ***do away with,*** ⓐ get rid of (something); abolish. ⓑ kill.
2) ***do by,*** deal with (something); treat.
3) ***do for,*** ⓐ ruin; destroy; kill. ⓑ act for (something). ⓒ manage or provide for (something).

없이] 나누어지는

—[名] 1. 분할, 구분 2. 분배 3.《數》 나눗셈 4. 간막이; 경계선; 간막이벽 5. 부분; 한 구획 6.《軍》 사단 [N.B.] 보병 2~3개 연대와 그 밖의 보조 부대로 편성됨 7. 의견 차이, 불화

—[形] 구분하는, 분할상의, 일부의, 나눗셈의, 사단(師團)의 ¶①사단장

—[名] 《數》 제수(除數) ¶①공약수

—[名] 1. 이혼 2. 분리

—[他] 1. …을 이혼시키다 ¶①판사는 존슨 부부를 이혼시켰다 2. [남편 또는 아내]를 이혼하다 ¶②남편과 이혼하다/③남편과 이혼하다 3. …을 분리하다, 절연하다 ¶④자기의 행동을 주의(主義)와 분리시키다

—[他] …을 입밖에 내다, 누설하다 ¶①적에게 비밀계획을 누설하다

—[名] 현기증

—[形] 1. 현기증이 나는, 어지러운 ¶①어지러울 정도의 높이 2. 혼란된, 얼빠진 —[他] …에게 현기증이 나게 하다

—[他] 1. …을 하다; 다하다; 수행하다 2. …을 해치우다, 끝내다 [usage] 보통 be done, have done의 형태로 씀 ¶①이미 끝난 일을 돌이킬 수 없다 3. …을 가져오다; 주다 ¶②부탁 좀 들어 주겠읍니까? 4. …을 제작하다, 만들어 내다 5. …을 각색하다, 번역하다 6. …을 정돈하다; 가지런히 하다 ¶③꽃꽂이 하다 7. …에 종사하다; …의 공부를 하다; …을 해결하다 8. …에 쓸모가 있다; 알맞다 9. …의 배역을 맡아 하다 10. …을 피로하게 하다 11. …을 여행하다; 구경하다 12. [어떤 거리]를 가다; …의 속력으로 가다 13. …을 요리하다; [음식]을 장만하다 ¶④내 고기는 잘 익혀 주시오 14. …을 대접하다, 대우하다 15.《口》 …을 속이다, 기만하다 —[自] 1. 처신하다; 하다; 일을 하다 ¶⑤일어나서 잘 해보자; 자아 열심히 일하자 2. 끝내다, 마치다 ¶⑥그와는 손을 끊었다/⑦그만 둬라!, 아서라! 3. 살아가다, 지내다 4. [환자가] 나아지다 5. [어떤 목적에] 알맞다; 쓸모 있다; 소용에 닿다 ¶⑧이것은 소용 없다

[熟] 1)ⓐ…을 없애다; 폐지하다 ⓑ…을 죽이다 2)대우하다 3)ⓐ…을 망쳐 놓다; 죽이다 ⓑ…의 대신(대리) 노릇을 하다 ⓒ…을 보살피다 4)…의 도움

do. [349] **document**

4) *do someone good,* benefit.
5) *do in,* ⓐ cheat. ⓑ (*slang*) kill; ruin. ⓒ exhaust.
6) *do or die,* make a supreme effort.
7) *do someone out of,* (*slang*) cheat; deceive.
8) *do over,* ⓐ repeat. ⓑ (*colloq.*) redecorate.
9) *do up,* ⓐ wrap and tie up. ⓑ pin up or arrange (the hair); clean and prepare. ⓒ (*colloq.*) (in *passive*) tire out; exhaust. 「very well.」
10) *do something up brown,* (*slang*) do completely or
11) *do with,* ⓐ deal with (something). ⓑ endure; be satisfied with (something). 「thing).」
12) *do without,* get along without; dispense with (some-
13) *have* (or *be*) *done with,* ⓐ cease to have any connection with (someone). ⓑ finish doing or using (something).
14) *have to do with* (=*have relation with or to*) something.
15) *make do* (=*get along or manage*) *with* something.
——*auxil. v.* 1. (in *interrogative*) ¶*Do you like apples?* 2. (in *emphasizing a verb*) ¶*I ~ want to go.* 3. (in *negative*) ¶*I ~ not know it. / Little did I dream that you would return.* ⇒USAGE
——*substitute v.* (used as *substitute* for other *verbs*)
do. ditto. ¶*"Do you like sports?" "Yes, I do."*
doat [dout] *v.* =dote. 「gentle horse.」
dob·bin [dábin / dɔ́b-] *n.* ⓒ a nickname for a slow,
doc·ile [dás(i)l / dóusail] *adj.* 1. obedient. 2. easy to teach; teachable. ▷**doc·ile·ly** [-i] *adv.* 「being docile.」
do·cil·i·ty [dousíliti, +*U.S.* dɑsíliti] *n.* Ⓤ the state of
• **dock**[1] [dɑk / dɔk] *n.* ⓒ 1. a platform where a ship may be repaired, built, or loaded. 2. a wharf; a pier. ——*vt.* bring (a ship) into a dock. ——*vi.* 1. come into a dock. 2. (of two spaceships) join together in outer space.
dock[2] [dɑk / dɔk] *n.* ⓒ the solid part of an animal's tail. ——*vt.* 1. cut (a tail, etc.) short. 2. reduce (wages, etc.), usu. temporarily.
dock[3] [dɑk / dɔk] *n.* ⓒ (*the ~*) a place in a law court where a prisoner stands or sits.
• **dock·yard** [dɑ́kjɑːrd / dɔ́kjɑːd] *n.* ⓒ (*U.S.*) a place where war ships are built and repaired. (cf. *Brit.* navy yard)
‡ **doc·tor** [dɑ́ktər / dɔ́ktə] *n.* ⓒ 1. a person who practices medicine; a physician; a surgeon. ¶*one's family ~*① / *see* (or *consult*) *a ~*② / *be under the ~*③ / *send for the ~.*④ 2. the highest degree given by a university or college; a person who has received such a degree. ⇒N.B. ¶*Doctor of Law / a Doctor of the Church.* 3. (*archaic*) a learned man.
——*vt.* (*colloq.*) 1. treat diseases in (someone). 2. repair; mend. ——*vi.* (*colloq.*) 1. be a doctor. 2. take medicine.
doctor up, make (something) inferior, etc. by adding a poor ingredient.
doc·tor·ate [dɑ́kt(ə)rit / dɔ́k-] *n.* ⓒ a degree of doctor given by a university or college. 「instructive.」
doc·tri·nal [dɑ́ktrin(ə)l / dɔktráin(ə)l] *adj.* of doctrine;
‡ **doc·trine** [dɑ́ktrin / dɔ́k-] *n.* ⓒⓊ 1. something taught as the belief of a church, nation, etc.; belief; principle. 2. what is taught; teachings.
• **doc·u·ment** [dɑ́kjumənt / dɔ́k-] ‖→*vt.*] *n.* ⓒ anything written, printed, etc., that gives information or proof; anything served as evidence. ¶*human documents*① / *official documents*② ——*vt.* [dɑ́kjument / dɔ́k-] 1. provide (someone) with documents. 2. prove or guarantee (some-

이 되다 5)ⓐ…을 속이다 ⓑ(俗)…을 해치우다, 죽이다 ⓒ…을 지쳐빠지게 하다 6)죽을 각오로 하다 7)(俗)속여서 …을 빼앗다 8)ⓐ…을 다시 하다 ⓑ (口)…에 겉칠을 하다 9)ⓐ…을 꾸리다, 싸다 ⓑ[머리]를 땋아 올리다, …을 손질하다, 치우다 ⓒ(口)…을 지쳐빠지게 하다 10)(俗)…을 완전히 하다 11)ⓐ…을 처리하다 ⓑ…으로 그럭저럭 참다(만족하다) 12)… 없이 견디다 13)ⓐ…와 관계를 끊다 ⓑ…을 끝내다 14)…와 관계가 있다 15)…으로 그럭저럭 해나가다(견디다) ——⒈ 1.[의문문에 써서] 2.[긍정문을 강조하여] 3.[부정문에 써서] USAGE not 이외의 부정어일 때에는 도치(倒置)됨

——(代動詞) [동일한 동사 및 그에 따른 어군(語群)의 반복을 피하여 대동사로 씀]
——图 농사짓는 말
——働 1. 유순한 2. 가르치기 쉬운

——图 유순함, 가르치기 쉬움
——图 1. 선거(船渠), 독 2. 부두, 선창, 잔교(棧橋) ——働 [배]를 독에 넣다 ——⒈ 1.[배가] 독에 들어가다 2.[두 우주선이] 도킹하다

——图 [짐승 꼬리의] 줄기 부분 ——働 1.[꼬리 따위]를 짧게 자르다 2.[임금 따위]를 바짝 줄이다, 삭감하다
——图 [법정의] 피고석

——图 조선소; 해군 공창(工廠)

——图 1. 의사 ¶①가족 의사/②의사의 진찰을 받다/③치료를 받는 중이다/④의사를 부르러 보내다 2. 박사 학위;박사 N.B. Dr.로 줄임 3. 학자

——働 (口) 1. …을 치료하다 2. …을 수리하다 ——働 (口) 1. [의사가] 개업하다 2. 약을 먹다
魘 [음식]에 다른 것을 섞다

——图 박사 학위

——働 교리의, 학리(學理)적인;교훈적인
——图 1. 교리, 주의, 학설 2. 가르침; 교훈

——图 문서, 서류, 증서 ¶①인간 기록/②공문서 ——働 1. …에 서류를 제출하다 2. …을 문서로 증명하다

thing or someone) by documents. ▷**doc·u·men·ta·tion** [dɑ̀kjumentéiʃ(ə)n / dɔ̀k-] *n.*

doc·u·men·ta·ry [dɑ̀kjuméntəri / dɔ̀k-] *adj.* **1.** in the form of a document. ¶~ *evidence.*① **2.** recording an actual event in an artistic fashion. **—***n.* [C] (pl. **-ries**) a documentary motion picture.
—[形] 1. 문서의, 서류의, 증서의 ¶①증거 서류 2. [영화 따위가] 사실을 기록한, 기록영화의 —[名] 기록영화

dod·der [dɑ́dər / dɔ́də] *vi.* shake or tremble as from old age or weakness.
—[自] 비틀거리다, 떨다

•**dodge** [dɑdʒ / dɔdʒ] *vi.* **1.** move quickly aside. ¶*He dodged about.*① / *They dodged around the corner.* **2.** escape by some trick. **—***vt.* **1.** move quickly to avoid (a blow, someone, etc.). **2.** avoid (a question, etc.) by some trick. **—***n.* [C] **1.** a quick movement to one side. **2.** (*colloq.*) a trick.
—[自] 1. 날쌔게 움직이다(몸을 비키다) ¶①그는 날쌔게 몸을 비켰다 2. 교묘히 받아 넘기다(빠져나가다) —[他] 1. 몸을 비켜 …을 피하다 2. 교묘히 …을 피하다 —[名] 1. 몸을 비키기 2. 《口》 속임수, 발뺌; 술책

dodg·er [dɑ́dʒər / dɔ́dʒə] *n.* [C] **1.** a person who dodges. **2.** a dishonest person. **3.** (*U.S.*) a small handbill.
—[名] 1. 날쌔게 몸을 비키는 사람 2. [의무의] 기피자 3. 《美》 삐라[쪽지]

doe [dou] *n.* [C] a female deer, rabbit, or hare.
—[名] 암사슴; [토끼 따위의] 암컷

do·er [dú(:)ər] *n.* [C] a person who does something.
—[名] 행하는 사람, 행위자

⁝**does** [dʌz] *v.* the third person, singular, present, indicative form of **do**¹.

doe·skin [dóuskìn] *n.* **1.** [C] the skin of a female deer. **2.** [U] a fine, smooth woolen cloth.
—[名] 1. 암사슴의 가죽 2. 암사슴 가죽 비슷한 모직물

:**does·n't** [dʌ́znt] =does not.

doff [dɑf, dɔ:f / dɔf] *vt.* **1.** take off or remove (one's hat, clothing, etc.). ↔don **2.** throw (one's habit, etc.) aside; give up.
—[他] 1. …을 벗다 2. …을 버리다

⁝**dog** [dɔ:g / dɔg] *n.* [C] **1.** a common domestic animal, kept as a pet, for hunting, etc. ¶(*proverb*) *Every ~ has day.*① / (*proverb*) *Give a ~ a bad name and hang him.*② / (*proverb*) *Love me, love my ~.*③ **2.** any animal of the same family as the dog; a male dog, fox, wolf, etc. **3.** a low, worthless man; a fellow. ¶*You ~ !*④ / *a lucky ~.*⑤ **4.** 《*pl.*》 any device to hold or grip something. **5.** 《*the D-*》 either of two star groups near Orion, Canis Major (the Great Dog) or Canis Minor (the Little Dog).
—[名] 1. 개 ¶①《俚》쥐구멍에도 볕 들 날이 있다/②《俚》한 번 누명을 쓰면 벗기 어렵다/③《俚》 나를 사랑한다면 내 개도 사랑해라 2. 개과(科)의 동물; [여우·늑대·개 따위의] 수컷 3. 못난 녀석; 놈, 망나니 ¶④망할 자식!/⑤운이 좋은 녀석 4. 쇠갈고리, 쇠집게 5. 큰개좌(座), 작은개좌

1) ***a dead dog,*** a useless thing.
2) ***die a dog's death*** (or ***the death of a dog***), die in misery.
3) ***dog eat dog,*** killing or injuring one another.
4) ***dog in the manger,*** a person who prevents others from enjoying something.
5) ***a dog's age,*** (*colloq.*) a long time.
6) ***a dog's chance,*** a chance with little probability of being realized.
7) ***give*** (*or* ***throw***) ***something to the dogs,*** throw something aside as worthless.
8) ***go to the dogs,*** be ruined.
9) ***help a lame dog over a stile,*** help (someone) in trouble.
10) ***lead a dog's life,*** (*colloq.*) live or exist unhappily.
11) ***Let sleeping dogs lie,*** (*proverb*) let matters stand as they are.
12) ***put on the dog,*** (*colloq.*) make a show of being elegant, etc.
13) ***teach an old dog new tricks,*** induce an old person to adopt new methods, etc.

[熟] 1)무용지물 2)비참한 죽음을 하다 3)동족 상잔, 공동 파멸 4)심술장이 5)《口》오랫동안 6)얼마 안되는 가망 7)[가치없는 것이라 하여] 던져 버리다 8)파멸하다 9)남이 곤란할 때 도와주다 10)《口》 비참한 생활을 하다 11)《俚》잠자는 개를 깨우지 말라, 벌집을 쑤시지 말라 12)《口》젠체하다, 뽐내다 13) 노인에게 새로운 방식(사상)을 가르치다, 때늦은 짓을 하다

—*vt.* (**dogged, dog·ging**) follow or hunt (a person or an animal) like a dog.
—[他] [개처럼] …을 미행하다, …에 어디까지나 따라다니다

dog someone's steps, follow someone closely.
[熟] …의 뒤를 밟다

dog·cart [dɔ́:gkɑ̀:rt / dɔ́gkɑ̀:t] *n.* [C] **1.** a small cart pulled by dogs. **2.** a small, open carriage, usu. with two wheels.
—[名] 1. 개가 끄는 수레 2. 경장(輕裝) 2륜 마차(등을 맞대고 앉는 두 개의 좌석이 있음)

dog days [ˊ ˋ] *n. pl.* the very hot and uncomfortable days in July and August.
—[名] 복중, 삼복더위의 계절

dog-ear [dɔ́:gìər / dɔ́gìə] *n.* [C] a turned-down corner of a page in a book. **—***vt.* turn down the corner of (a page of a book). ⇒[N.B.]
—[名] 책장 모서리의 접힌 데 —[他] 책장의 귀를 접다 [N.B.] dog's-ear로도 씀

dog-eared [dɔ́:gìərd / dɔ́gìəd] *adj.* in the state of having dog-ears; (of a book) well worn or well-used.
—[形] 책장의 귀가 접힌; 낡은, 초라한

dog·ged [dɔ́:gid / dɔ́g-] *adj.* not easily giving up; steady; fixed in opinion; stubborn. ▷**dog·ged·ly** [-li] *adv.*
—[形] 쉽게 굽히지 않는; 완고한, 끈기 있는

dog·ger·el [dɔ́:g(ə)r(ə)l / dɔ́g-] *n.* [U] very poor poetry; irregular verse. **—*adj.*** of or like doggerel.
—[名] [운율이 맞지 않는] 엉터리 시 —[形] 서투른. 졸렬한

dog·gie [dɔ́:gi / dɔ́gi] *n.* [C] a little dog; a pet name for a dog.
—[名] 강아지; 멍멍(애칭)

dog·gy [dɔ́:gi / dɔ́gi] *adj.* (**-gi·er, -gi·est**) like a dog; fond of a dog. **—*n.*** [C] (pl. **-gies**) a little dog; a doggie.
—[形] 개 같은; 개를 좋아하는 —[名] 강아지; 멍멍(애칭)

dog·ma [dɔ́:gmə, dάg- / dɔ́g-] *n.* [C] (pl. **-mas** or **-ma·ta**) **1.** a belief, principle, or doctrine taught or held as truth by some authority. **2.** an opinion strongly supported by those who believe it.
—[名] 1. 교의(敎義), 교리; 정리(定理), 정설 2. 독단[설], 도그마

dog·ma·ta [dɔ́:gmətə, dάg- / dɔ́g-] *n.* pl. of **dogma.**

dog·mat·ic [dɔ:gmǽtik, dɑg- / dɔg-] *adj.* **1.** of or like dogma; very strong in support of and belief in one's opinions. **2.** believed as truth without proof.
—[形] 1. 교의의, 교리에 관한 2. 독단적인

dog·ma·tism [dɔ́:gmətìz(ə)m, dάg- / dɔ́g-] *n.* [U] the quality of being dogmatic.
—[名] 독단론, 독단주의

dog·ma·tist [dɔ́:gmətist, dάg- / dɔ́g-] *n.* [C] a person who is dogmatic or who states dogmas.
—[名] 독단론자, 독단주의자

dog·wood [dɔ́:gwùd / dɔ́g-] *n.* [C] a tree with white or pink flowers in the spring and red fruit in the autumn.
—[名] 산딸나무류

doi·ly [dɔ́ili] *n.* [C] (pl. **-lies**) a small napkin or mat of linen, paper, etc., used under plates, vases, etc.
—[名] 작은 냅킨

do·ings [dú(:)iŋz] *n. pl.* deeds; actions; behavior; conduct.
—[名] 행위; 행동, 행실; 처신

dol·drums [dάldrəmz / dɔ́l-], **the** *n. pl.* **1.** the part of the ocean near the equator with very little wind. **2.** dullness; low spirits.
—[名] 1. [적도 부근 해상의] 열대 무풍대 2. 무기력, 우울

in the doldrums, in a low and sad state of mind.
[熟] 침울해 있는

dole[1] [doul] *n.* [C] **1.** a portion of money, food, etc., given in charity; alms. **2.** (*Brit.*) a weekly payment given by the government to unemployed workers.
—[名] 1. 시주, 의연품(義捐品) 2. 《英》 실업수당

be (or ***go***) ***on the dole,*** receive these weekly payments from the government.
[熟] 실업수당을 받다

—*vt.* give out (something) in portions to the poor, etc.; give (something) in small portions.
—[他] [빈민에게] …을 나누어 주다; 조금씩(아까운 듯이) 주다

dole out, measure out sparingly.
[熟] 조금씩 내다

dole[2] [doul] *n.* [U] (*poetic*) sorrow; grief.
—[名] 슬픔

dole·ful [dóulf(u)l] *adj.* sad; mournful; melancholy.
—[形] 슬픈, 애처로운, 우울한

⁑**doll** [dɑl / dɔl] *n.* [C] **1.** a child's toy made to look like a baby, a child, etc. ¶*the Doll's Festival* (or *the Festival of Dolls*).① **2.** a pretty but rather stupid girl or woman.
—[名] 1. 인형 ¶①인형 축제 2. 아름답지만 백치 같은 소녀(여자)

—*vi., vt.* (*slang*) dress smartly 《~ *up*》. ¶*be dolled up*② / ~ [*oneself*] *up*.③ ▷**doll·like** [-làik] *adj.*
—[自][他] 《俗》 아름답게 차려 입다 ¶②쪽 빼 입고 있다/③쪽 빼 입다

⁑**dol·lar** [dάlər / dɔ́lə] *n.* [C] **1.** a unit of money in the United States and some other countries; a hundred cents. ⇒[N.B.] **2.** a coin or piece of paper money worth one dollar.
—[名] 1. 달러 [N.B.] 기호는 $, $ 2. 달러 화폐(지폐)

dol·ly [dάli / dɔ́li] *n.* [C] (pl. **dol·lies**) **1.** a child's word for a doll. **2.** a small, low frame with wheels, used to carry heavy objects.
—[名] 1. 《小兒》 인형, 각시님 2. 바퀴 달린 짐 나르는 대(臺)

dol·or·ous [dάlərəs / dɔ́l-] *adj.* sad; mournful; painful.
—[形] 슬픈; 애처로운; 괴로운

dol·phin [dάlfin / dɔ́l-] *n.* [C] a sea animal related to the whale, but smaller.
—[名] 돌고래류

dolt [doult] *n.* [C] a dull, stupid fellow.
—[名] 바보, 멍청이, 얼간이

do·main [dəméin] *n.* [C] **1.** the territory under the control of one government or ruler. **2.** the land owned by one person or family; an estate. **3.** a field or sphere of thought, activity, etc.
—[名] 1. 영토, 영지(領地) 2. [개인의] 소유지 3. [사상·활동 따위의] 범위, …계(界), 영역

⁎**dome** [doum] *n.* [C] **1.** a large, rounded roof. **2.** something high and rounded like a dome. **—*vt.*** cover (something) with a dome; shape (something) like a dome.
—[名] 1. 둥근 지붕 2. 둥근 지붕 모양의 것 —[他] …에 둥근 지붕을 달다; …을 반구(半球) 모양으로 하다

—*vi.* rise or swell out like a dome.
—[自] 반구형으로 부풀다

domed [doumd] *adj.* rounded; of or like a dome. ¶*a ~ forehead.*
—[形] 반구형의, 둥근 지붕(천장)의

⁑**do·mes·tic** [dəméstik] *adj.* **1.** of the home, family, or household affairs. ¶~ *affairs*① / ~*science*② / ~*industry*.③
—[形] 1. 가정의, 가족의, 가사의 ¶①가사/②[학과로서] 가정과/③가내 공업/

domesticate [352] **donate**

2. of one's own country ; not foreign. ↔foreign **3.** made in one's own country ; native ; home-made. ↔imported **4.** not wild ; tame. ↔wild ¶ *a ~ animal.*ⓐ **5.** fond of home and family life or household affairs. ¶ *a ~ man.*ⓑ —*n.* ⓒ **1.** a servant in a household. **2.** (*pl.*) native products.

do·mes·ti·cate [dəméstikèit] *vt.* **1.** tame (animals, etc.) for domestic use ; civilize. **2.** make (someone) fond of family life ; make (someone) domestic. **3.** naturalize.

do·mes·ti·ca·tion [dəmèstikéiʃ(ə)n] *n.* ⓤ the action of domesticating, the state of being domesticated.

do·mes·tic·i·ty [dòumestísiti] *n.* (pl. **-ties**) **1.** ⓤ home and family life ; love of home and family life. **2.** ((usu. *pl.*) domestic affairs.

dom·i·cile [dámis(i)l / dóumisail] *n.* ⓒ **1.** house ; home ; residence. **2.** (*Law*) the place of permanent residence. —*vt.* settle (someone) in a domicile. ¶ *be domiciled at* (or *in*) *a place.* —*vi.* dwell ; reside.

dom·i·nance [dámənəns / dɔ́m-] *n.* ⓤ the state of being dominant ; rule ; control.

dom·i·nant [dámənənt / dɔ́m-] *adj.* **1.** most influential ; ruling ; governing. **2.** rising high above others. **3.** (*Music*) based on or having to do with the fifth note of a scale. —*n.* ⓒ (*Music*) the fifth note in a scale. ▷**dom·i·nant·ly** [-li] *adv.*

dom·i·nate [dámənèit / dɔ́m-] *vt.* **1.** control or rule (someone, etc.) by strength or will. **2.** rise high above (others). —*vi.* occupy a commanding position. ((*~ over* someone, etc.) ¶ *~ over the weak.*

dom·i·na·tion [dàmənéiʃ(ə)n / dɔ̀m-] *n.* ⓤ control ; rule.

dom·i·neer [dàmənίər / dɔ̀mənίə] *vi.* rule at one's own will ; behave like a tyrant (*~ over* someone, etc.). ¶ *~ over the inferior.*ⓓ 「domineer ; masterful.」

dom·i·neer·ing [dàmənίəriŋ / dɔ̀m-] *adj.* inclined to

Dom·i·nic [dámnik / dɔ́m-], **Saint** *n.* (1170-1221) a Spanish priest. ⇒N.B.

Do·min·i·can [dəmínikən] *adj.* of Saint Dominic. ¶ *the ~ order.*ⓓ —*n.* ⓒ **1.** a friar or nun of the Dominican order. **2.** a person of the Dominican Republic.

Dominican Republic [-´--- -´-] **the,** *n.* a country in the West Indies. ⇒N.B.

∗**do·min·ion** [dəmínjən] *n.* **1.** ⓤ power to rule ; sovereignty. ¶ *bring someone under ~.*ⓓ / *excercise ~ over a country.*ⓐ **2.** ⓤⓒ a territory under the control of a ruler or government. **3.** (*the D-*) a self-governing part of the British Empire.

dom·i·no [dámənòu / dɔ́m-] *n.* **1.** ⓒ (pl. **-noes** or **-nos**) a loose cloak with a mask, worn at masquarades. **2.** a person wearing a domino.

dom·i·noes [dámənòuz / dɔ́n-] *n. pl.* **1.** flat pieces of bone, wood, etc. with dots on one side and used in playing dominoes. **2.** (used as *sing.*) a game played with such pieces.

∗**don**¹ [dan / dɔn] *n.* ⓒ **1.** ((*D-*)) Mr. ; Sir. ⇒N.B. **2.** a Spanish gentleman ; a Spaniard. **3.** an important man. **4.** (*colloq.*) a head, tutor, or fellow of any college as at Oxford or Cambridge University.

don² [dan / dɔn] *vt.* (**donned, don·ning**) put on (clothing, etc.). ↔doff ⇒N.B.

Don [dan / dɔn] *n.* **1.** a nickname for **Donald. 2.** ((*the ~*)) the river flowing through the European part of the U.S.S.R. ⇒N.B.

Don·ald [dán(ə)ld / dɔ́n-] *n.* a man's name. ⇒N.B.

do·nate [dóuneit, -´- / -´-] *vt.* (*U.S.*) give ; contribute.

2. 자기 나라의, 국내의 3. 국산의, 자기 집에서 만든 4. 길들여진 ¶④가축, 가금(家禽) 5. 가정적인, 집안 일을 좋아하는 ¶⑤가정적인 사내, 외출을 싫어하는 남자
—ⓝ 1. 하인, 사용인 2. 가내(국내)제품
—ⓥ 1. …을 길들이다, 교화(敎化)하다 2. …을 가정에 정들게 하다 3. …을 토지에 정들게 하다
—ⓝ 길들이기, 교화

—ⓝ 1. 가정생활 ; 가정에의 애착, 가정적임 2. 가사(家事)

—ⓝ 1. 주소, 주거(住居) 2. (法) 본적지, 기류지 —ⓥ…의 주소를 정하다, …을 정주시키다 —ⓥ 거주(정주)하다

—ⓝ 권세, 우세 ; 지배

—ⓥ 1. [가장] 우세한, 지배적인 2. 우뚝 솟은, 높은 3. (樂) 제5음의, 속음(屬音)의 —ⓝ 제5음

—ⓥ 1. …을 지배하다, 제어하다, 좌우하다 2. …의 위로 우뚝 솟다, …을 굽어다보다 —ⓥ 지배하다, 우위(優位)를 차지하다
—ⓝ 통치, 지배
—ⓥ 권세를 휘두르다 ; 거만하게 굴다, 압제하다 ¶①신분 낮은 사람에게 뽐내다
—ⓥ 거만한, 뽐내는, 압제적인
—ⓝ 스페인의 성직자 N.B. 도미니코 수도회의 창시자
—ⓥ 성(聖) 도미니코의 ¶①도미니회 —ⓝ 1. 도미니코회의 수도사 2. 도미니카 공화국의 사람
—ⓝ 도미니카 공화국 N.B. 수도는 Santo Domingo
—ⓝ 1. 지배권, 주권 ¶①…을 복종시키다/②나라를 지배하다 2. 영토 3. [영국의] 자치령

—ⓝ 1. 가장 무도회의 가면이 달린 겉옷 2. 도미노 가장복 착용자

—ⓝ 1. 도미노 패(牌) 2. 도미노 놀이

—ⓝ 1. 님, 씨, 선생 N.B. 스페인에서 세례명에 붙이는 존칭 2. 스페인 신사(사람) 3. 큰 인물 4. (口) 학감(學監), 지도교사, 특별 연구원
—ⓥ [옷 따위]를 입다, 착용하다 N.B. do on의 단축형
—ⓝ 1. Donald 의 애칭 2. [소련의] 돈 강

—ⓝ 남자 이름 N.B. 애칭 Don
—ⓥ (美) …을 기부(기증)하다

do·na·tion [dounéiʃ(ə)n] *n.* **1.** Ⓤ the act of giving **2.** Ⓒ a gift; a contribution. ¶*donations to the school.*
— 图 1. 기부, 기증, 증여 2. 기부금, 기증물

done [dʌn] *v.* pp. of **do**.
— *adj.* **1.** completed; finished. ¶*be ~ with something.* **2.** (*colloq.*) tired out. ¶*You look ~.* **3.** cooked enough. ¶*under-done*① / *half-done*② / *over-done.*
— 形 1. 완성된, 끝난 2. 《口》지쳐빠진 3. [음식이] 익은, 구워진 ¶①덜 익은 (구워진) / ②반쯤 익은

don·jon [dándʒən, dʌ́n- / dɔ́n-, dʌ́n-] *n.* Ⓒ the keep of a castle or a large, strongly-built tower [of a castle].
— 图 [성곽의] 탑, 내성(內城)

* **don·key** [dáŋki / dɔ́ŋ-] *n.* Ⓒ **1.** a small animal like a horse; an ass. **2.** a silly or foolish person.
— 图 1. 당나귀 2. 바보, 얼간이

do·nor [dóunər] *n.* Ⓒ a person who donates; a giver.
— 图 기부자, 기증자, 시주(施主)

don't [dount] =do not.
— *n.* (usu. *pl.*) rules or customs that forbid something.
— 图 금지 조항, 금제(禁制)

* **doom** [du:m] *n.* Ⓤ **1.** an unhappy or tragic fate; ruin; death. ¶*go to* (or *meet, know*) *one's ~.*① **2.** a judgment; a sentence. **3.** God's Last Judgment of mankind; the end of the world. ¶*till the crack of ~.*② — *vt.* **1.** sentence. (*~ someone to*) ¶*~ someone to death.*③ **2.** (chiefly in *passive*) destine. (*~ someone to*) ¶*be doomed to fail* (or *to failure*).④
— 图 1. [나쁜] 운명, 파멸, 죽음 ¶①죽다 2. 재판, 판결 3. 신이 내리는 최후의 심판; 이 세상의 마지막 날 ¶②이 세상 끝까지 — 働 1. [형을] …에게 선고하다 ¶③사형을 선고하다 2. …을 운명짓다 ¶④실패할 운명이다

dooms·day [dú:mzdèi] *n.* Ⓒ (often *D*-) the end of the world; the day of God's Last Judgment of mankind.
— 图 세상의 마지막 날; 최후의 심판일

door [dɔːr] *n.* Ⓒ **1.** an entrance to a building or room; a doorway. ¶*enter by* (or *at*) *the front ~.*① **2.** a thing which shuts the entrance. ¶*shut* (*open*) *the ~.* **3.** a room, house, or building that a door belongs to. ¶*from ~ to ~*② / *My house is next ~ but one to his.*③ **4.** any means of entrance. ¶*a ~ to success.*
 1) *lay a mistake at someone's door,* blame someone for a mistake
 2) *out of doors,* in the open air; outside.
 3) *show someone the door,* tell someone to leave.
 4) *with an open door,* in public.
— 图 1. 문간, 출입구, 현관 ¶①현관으로 들어가다 2. 문, 문짝 3. [문이 있는] 방, 집; 한 집 ¶②집집마다 / ③우리 집은 그의 집에서 한 집 걸러 이웃이다 4. 문호, …에 이르는 길

熟 1)…을 남의 탓으로 하다 2)문밖(옥외)에서 3)…에게 나가라고 말하다 4)공공연히

door·bell [dɔ́ːrbèl] *n.* Ⓒ a bell at or near a door, rung by someone wishing to have the door opened.
— 图 현관의 벨(초인종)

door-frame [dɔ́ːrfreim] *n.* Ⓒ a wooden frame within which a door (*n.* 2.) is hung.
— 图 문틀

door·keep·er [dɔ́ːrkìːpər] *n.* Ⓒ a person who guards a door; a doorman. ⌜handle on a door.⌝
— 图 수위, 문지기

door·knob [dɔ́ːrnàb / dɔ́ːrnɔ̀b] *n.* Ⓒ a small knob or
— 图 문의 손잡이

door·man [dɔ́ːrmæ̀n, -mən] *n.* Ⓒ (pl. **-men** [-mèn, -mən]) **1.** a man whose work is opening the door of a hotel, store, etc. for those who enter or leave. ⇒N.B. **2.** a doorkeeper. ⌜door on which one can wipe one's shoes.⌝
— 图 1. 문지기, 도어맨 N.B. 짐을 나르거나 택시를 불러 주는 사람 2. 수위

door·mat [dɔ́ːrmæ̀t] *n.* Ⓒ a mat usu. placed before a
— 图 [현관의] 구두 흙을 터는 매트

door·nail [dɔ́ːrnèil] *n.* Ⓒ a nail with a large head used for decorating doors.
dead as a doornail, entirely dead.
— 图 [문의] 장식용 대갈못
熟 완전히 죽은

door·plate [dɔ́ːrplèit] *n.* Ⓒ a metal plate on a door with a name, house number, etc. on it.
— 图 문패

door·post [dɔ́ːrpòust] *n.* Ⓒ either of the two sidepieces of a doorframe. ⌜door of a house.⌝
— 图 [문 양쪽의] 옆기둥

door·step [dɔ́ːrstèp] *n.* Ⓒ a step leading to the outer
— 图 문앞의 층계

* **door·way** [dɔ́ːrwèi] *n.* Ⓒ the entrance to a building, room, etc. closed and opened by a door.
— 图 대문간, 출입구; 문호

door·yard [dɔ́ːrjàːrd] *n.* Ⓒ (*U.S.*) a yard in front of the door of a house.
— 图 《美》현관(대문간)의 앞마당

dope [doup] *n.* Ⓤ **1.** a harmful drug which makes a person feel dull or sleepy; Ⓒ a person who takes such drugs. **2.** oil, grease, etc. used to make something run smoothly. **3.** a thick liquid used as protection on the cloth parts of an airplane. ⇒N.B. **4.** (*slang*) information. **5.** Ⓒ (*U.S. slang*) a very stupid person. — *vt.* **1.** (*slang*) give dope (*n.* 1.) to (someone). **2.** (*slang*) pre-
— 图 1. 마약; 마약 중독자 2. 윤활제 3. 도우프 도료 N.B. 비행기의 날개 따위에 바르는 일종의 와니스 4. 《俗》정보 5. 《美俗》얼간이
— 働 1. 《俗》…에 마약을 먹이다 2. 《俗》…의 예상을 하다 3. …에 도우프 도료를 칠하다

dict; forecast. **3.** apply dope (*n.* 2., 3.) to (something).
dope out, (*slang*) understand; figure out.
[熟]《俗》…을 이해하다, 생각해 내다

Do·ra [dɔ́:rə] *n.* a nickname for Dorothea, Dorothy, or Theodora.
—[名] Dorothea, Dorothy, Theodora의 애칭

Dor·ic [dɔ́:rik / dɔ́r-] *adj.* **1.** of Doris or its people (*n.* 1.). **2.** (*Architecture*) of the architectural style of Doris or its people (*n.* 1.).
—[形] 1. 도리스 지방의, 도리아 사람의 2.《建》도리아식의

Dor·is *n.* **1.** [dɔ́ris / dɔ́:r- →2.] a country in ancient Greece. **2.** [dɔ́:ris, dɑ́r- / dɔ́ris] a woman's name.
—[形] 1. 고대 그리이스의 한 지방, 도리스 2. 여자 이름

dor·mant [dɔ́:rmənt] *adj.* **1.** sleeping, or as if asleep. **2.** inactive. ¶*a ~ volcano.*①
—[形] 1. 잠자는 [듯한] 2. 휴지(休止)하고 있는, 잠복한 ¶①휴화산

dor·mer [dɔ́:rmər] *n.* [C] an upright window in a sloping roof.
—[名] 지붕창

dor·mice [dɔ́:rmàis] *n.* pl. of **dormouse**.

* **dor·mi·to·ry** [dɔ́:rmitɔ̀:ri / dɔ́:mit(ə)ri] *n.* [C] (pl. **-ries**) **1.** (*U.S.*) a building containing a number of sleeping rooms. **2.** (*Brit.*) a sleeping room containing a number of beds.
—[名] 1.《美》기숙사 2.《英》공공침실, 합숙실

dor·mouse [dɔ́:rmàus] *n.* [C] (pl. **-mice**) a small animal that looks somewhat like a squirrel.
—[名] 다람쥐 비슷한 쥐의 일종

Dor·o·thea [dɔ̀:rəθíə, dɑ̀r- / dɔ̀r-] *n.* a woman's name.
—[名] 여자 이름

Dor·o·thy [dɔ́:rəθi, dɑ́r- / dɔ́r-] *n.* a woman's name.
—[名] 여자 이름

dor·sal [dɔ́:rs(ə)l] *adj.* of or on the back. ¶*a ~ fin*①
—[形] 등의, 등에 가까운 ¶①등지느러미

do·ry[1] [dɔ́:ri] *n.* [C] (pl. **-ries**) a rowboat with a flat bottom. ⇒[N.B.]
—[名] 밑이 판판한 배 [N.B.] 미국 New England 지방에 많음

do·ry[2] [dɔ́:ri] *n.* [C] (pl. **-ries**) a small sea fish that can be eaten.
—[名] 달고기류의 식용어

dos·age [dóusidʒ] *n.* [C][U] the quantity of a medicine to be taken at one time.
—[名] 1회분의 투약량(投藥量)

dose [dous] *n.* [C] the quantity of a medicine to be taken at one time; dosage.
—[名] [약의] 한 첩, 1회 복용량
a dose of, a bit of.
[熟] 소량의
—*vt.* **1.** give medicine to (someone) in doses. 《~ someone *with*; ~ a medicine *to*》. ¶*~ aspirin to a patient; ~ a patient with aspirin.*① **2.** blend. 《~ something *with*》 ¶*~ wine with sugar.*
—[他] 1. …에 약을 주다 ¶①환자에게 아스피린을 주다 2. …에 섞다

* **dost** [dʌst] *v.* (*archaic*) =do. ¶*Thou ~.*

‡ **dot**[1] [dɑt / dɔt] *n.* [C] **1.** a small round mark; a point; a period. **2.** a short sound used in telegraphy.
—[名] 1. 점(點); 마침표, 종지부 2. [모르스 부호의] 점
on the dot, (*colloq.*) at the exact time.
[熟] 꼭 제 시간에
—*vt.* (**dot·ted, dot·ting**) mark (something) with a dot; cover (something) with dots. ¶*a field dotted with sheep.*①
—[他] …에 점을 찍다; 점점이 산재시키다 ¶①양이 산재한 들판

dot[2] [dɑt / dɔt] *n.* [C] money, land, etc. that a woman brings to her husband at marriage; dowry.
—[名] 아내의 지참금(물), 아내의 자산

dot·age [dóutidʒ] *n.* [U] a feeble and childish condition caused by old age. ¶*in one's ~.*①
—[名] 망령, 노망 ¶①망령이 들어

do·tard [dóutərd] *n.* [C] a person who is feeble and childish because of old age.
—[名] 노망한 늙은이

dote [dout] *vi.* **1.** be feeble and childish because of old age. **2.** be foolishly fond of someone. ¶*~ on* (or *upon*) *one's son.*
—[自] 1. 노망들다 2. 맹목적으로 사랑하다

* **doth** [dəθ, dʌθ] *v.* (*archaic*) =does.

dot·ing [dóutiŋ] *adj.* foolishly fond. ▷**dot·ing·ly** [-li] *adv.*
—[形] 사랑에 빠진, 주착없는

‡ **dou·ble** [dʌ́bl] *adj.* **1.** twice as much or as many. ¶*a ~ portion*① / *~ pay* ⇒[N.B.] **2.** in pairs; of two equal parts. ¶*a ~ room / a ~ track.*② **3.** twofold. ¶*a ~ chin / a ~ bottom.*③ **4.** for two persons or things; used for two purposes. ¶*a ~ bed.* **5.** having two meanings or characters. ¶*a ~ character / a ~ life.*④ **6.** (of flowers) having more than one set of petals. ¶*a ~ rose.*
—[形] 1. 두 곱의 ¶①두 사람 몫 [N.B.] 원래는 명사로서 double of의 형태로 쓰였음 2. 쌍으로 된; 두 개 한 벌의 ¶②[철도의] 복선(複線) 3. 이중의 ¶③[선박의] 이중 선저(船底) 4. 2인용의; 두 가지 용도의 5. 두 가지로 해석되는; 표리 있는 ¶④표리 있는 생활 6. [꽃잎이] 여러 겹의
—*adv.* **1.** twice. **2.** in two; in a pair; two together.
—[副] 1. 이중으로, 두 배로 2. 두 가지로, 한 쌍으로
—*n.* [C] **1.** an amount that is twice as much. **2.** a thing or person that looks like another. **3.** 《*pl.*》 a game played by two players on each side.
—[名] 1. 곱, 두 배의 수(양) 2. 흡사한 사람(것) 3. [경기의] 복식 시합
on the double, (*U.S.*) quickly; in a slow run.
[熟]《美》구보로; 재빨리
—*vt.* **1.** make (something) twice as much or as many; add an equal amount to (something). ¶*~ one's fortune.* **2.** fold or bend (something) in two. ¶*~ a piece of*
—[他] 1. …을 두 배로 하다 2. …을 둘로

double-barreled [355] **doughty**

paper. **3.** close tightly together. ¶*~ one's fists in anger* / *~ up one's legs.* **4.** act (two parts). ¶*~ the parts of a maid and a cook.* —*vi.* **1.** increase twice as much or as many. ¶*The money doubled in three years.* **2.** be folded or bent in two. **3.** turn back suddenly on the same course. **4.** play two parts. ¶*The maid doubled as cook.*
 1) ***double back,*** ⓐ fold over. ⓑ go back the same way that one came.
 2) ***double for,*** take the place of (someone); substitute for (someone).
 3) ***double up,*** ⓐ fold up; curl up. ⓑ draw the knees up to the chest. ¶*be doubled up with pain.*

dou·ble-bar·reled [dʌ́blbǽrəld] *adj.* **1.** having two barrels. **2.** having two purposes. 「family. ⇒N.B.

double bass [´-´] *n.* a musical instrument of the violin

dou·ble-breast·ed [dʌ́blbréstid] *adj.* (of a coat) overlapping at the front and having two rows of buttons. ↔single-breasted

dou·ble-deal·er [dʌ́bldí:lər] *n.* ⓒ a deceiver.

dou·ble-deal·ing [dʌ́bldí:liŋ] *n.* Ⓤⓒ the act of cheating or deceiving. —*adj.* deceitful.

dou·ble-deck·er [dʌ́bldékər] *n.* ⓒ a ship or a bus with an upper deck or floor.

dou·ble-edged [dʌ́bléd͡ʒd] *adj.* **1.** having two edges; two-edged. **2.** that can be understood in two ways.

double entry [´-´-´] *n.* a method of bookkeeping in which each transaction is written twice.

dou·ble-faced [dʌ́blféist] *adj.* **1.** deceitful; insincere. **2.** having two faces or aspects.

dou·ble-quick [dʌ́blkwík] *n.* Ⓤⓒ a very fast step in marching. —*adj., adv.* very quick[ly]. —*vi., vt.* march in double-quick step.

dou·blet [dʌ́blit] *n.* ⓒ **1.** a man's close-fitting jacket worn from 15th century to 17th century. **2.** one of a pair of two similar things; a pair. **3.** one of two or more words in a language having the same original but a different form or meaning. ⇒N.B.

dou·bly [dʌ́bli] *adv.* twice.

‡doubt [daut] *vt.* be difficult to believe; be not sure of (something). 《*~ that* (or *if, whether, when, what,* etc.) *...*; *~ doing*》 ⇒usage ¶*The money in my own eyes* / *I ~ if he will succeed.*⁽¹⁾ / *I don't ~ that he is honest.* —*vi.* be not sure; be not decided. 《*~ of something*》 ¶*He doubted of his son's ability.* / *I have never doubted of her success.* —*n.* Ⓤⓒ a feeling of doubting; lack of belief. ¶*I have grave doubts about it.*
 1) *beyond* (or *no, without*) *doubt,* surely; certainly.
 2) *in doubt,* not sure; uncertain.

•**doubt·ful** [dáutf(u)l] *adj.* **1.** in doubt; uncertain. ¶*I am ~ of the fact.* / *He was ~ about her ability to do the work.* **2.** causing or feeling doubt. ¶*a ~ future.*⁽¹⁾
 ▷ **doubt·ful·ness** [-nis] *n.*   「doubtful.

doubt·ful·ly [dáutfuli] *adv.* in the manner of being

‡**doubt·less** [dáutlis] *adv.* certainly; without doubt; very probably. —*adj.* having no doubts; sure.

dough [dou] *n.* Ⓤ **1.** the mixture of flour, water, etc. for baking; any soft mass like this. **2.** (*slang*) money.

dough·boy [dóubɔ̀i] *n.* ⓒ (*U.S. colloq.*) a foot soldier in the United States army.

dough·nut [dóunət, dóunʌ̀t] *n.* ⓒ a small, brown cake fried in deep fat, usu. in the shape of a ring or a ball. ⇒N.B.   [▷**dough·ti·ness** [-nis] *n.*

dough·ty [dáuti] *adj.* (**-ti·er, -ti·est**) brave; strong.

─접어 겹치다 3. …을 단단히 쥐다 4. …의 두 가지 역할을 하다 ─自 1. 2배가 되다 2. 두 겹이 되다, 둘로 겹치다 3. 갑자기 되돌아오다 4. 두 가지 배역(구실)을 맡아 하다

熟 1)ⓐ접어 겹치다 ⓑ오던 길을 되돌아가다 2)…의 대역을 하다 3)ⓐ접어 올리다, 접혀지다 ⓑ몸을 굽히[게 하]다

─形 1. [총이] 쌍발식의, [망원경이] 쌍통(雙筒)식의 2. 이중 목적의
─名·더블 베이스 N.B. 최저음 현악기
─形 [코우트의] 앞가슴에 단추가 두 줄 있는

─名 두 마음을 품은 사람
─名 표리 있는 언행 ─形 두 마음이 있는, 표리 있는
─名 이층 갑판의 배, 이층 버스(객차·전차 따위)
─形 1. 쌍날의 2. [의견 따위가] 찬반 어느 쪽으로도 해석될 수 있는
─名 복식 기장법

─形 1. 두 마음이 있는 2. 양면(兩面)이 있는
─名 [군대의] 구보 ─形 구보의(로), 급속한(하게) ─自他 구보로 나아가(게 하)다
─形 1. [15-17세기의 허리가 잘록한] 남자용 웃옷 2. 흡사한 것의 한 쪽; 쌍을 이룬 것의 한쪽 3. 자매어(姉妹語) N.B. fashion 과 faction 따위

─副 두 배로, 두 겹으로, 두 가지로
─他 …을 의심하다, 미심쩍게 여기다
usage 의문문·부정문에는 that절, 긍정문에는 if, whether, when 절 따위를 씀 ¶①그가 성공할지 의심스럽다

─自 의심하다; 수상히 여기다
─名 의문, 불신

熟 1)확실히; 의심없이 2)의심하여; 불확실하여

─形 1. [사람이] 의심을 품은; 불확실한 2. 못 미더운, 분명하지 않은 ¶①불안한 장래

─副 의심스럽게, 수상쩍게
─副 확실히, 의심 없이; 아마 ─形 의심 없는; 확실한
─名 1. 가루반죽, 설익은 빵; 부드러운 덩어리 2. 《俗》 돈
─名 《美口》 보병

─名 도우넛 N.B. 미국에서는 고리 모양, 영국에서는 만두 모양

─形 용맹스런; 힘센

Doug·las [dʌ́gləs] *n.* a man's name. ⇒[N.B.]

dour [dúər] *adj.* **1.** gloomy; sullen. **2.** (*Scot.*) severe; stubborn. ▷**dour·ly** [-li] *adv.* —**dour·ness** [-nis] *n.*

douse [daus] *vt.* **1.** put (something) into water. **2.** throw water over (something or someone). ¶~ *someone with water.* **3.** (*colloq.*) put out (a light).

•**dove** [dʌv] *n.* [C] **1.** a bird of the pigeon family, but smaller than a pigeon. **2.** a gentle or loving person. ¶*My* ~.① **3.** 《*D-*》 the Holy Ghost.

dove·cot [dʌ́vkɑ̀t / -kɔ̀t] *n.* =dovecote.

dove·cote [dʌ́vkòut] *n.* [C] a small house for doves or pigeons.

Do·ver [dóuvər] *n.* a seaport in southeast England.
the Strait[*s*] *of Dover,* a narrow channel between France and England.

dove·tail [dʌ́vtèil] *n.* [C] (*Architecture*) a part or joint shaped like a dove's tail. —*vt.* fasten or join (something) together by means of dovetails. —*vi.* fit together exactly. ¶*Your plans ~ with mine.*①

dow·a·ger [dáuədʒər] *n.* [C] **1.** (*Law*) a woman who holds a title or property from her dead husband. ¶~ *duchess*① / *the Empress Dowager*② **2.** an elderly lady with dignity.

dow·dy [dáudi] *adj.* (**-di·er, -di·est**) badly dressed; not neat; shabby. —*n.* [C] (pl. **-dies**) a dowdy woman. ▷**dow·di·ly** [-li] *adv.* —**dow·di·ness** [-nis] *n.*

dow·er [dáuər] *n.* [U][C] **1.** a woman's share of her dead husband's property. **2.** a natural gift. —*vt.* provide (someone) with a dower. ▷**dow·er·less** [-lis] *adj.*

⁝**down**[1] [daun] *adv.* **1.** to a lower place; toward the ground. ¶*knock ~ / come ~.* **2.** in a lower place. ¶*Down in the valley the fog still lingers.* **3.** to the lower course of a river. ¶*flow ~ the river.* **4.** from a city to the country. ¶*go ~ to the country.* **5.** southward. ¶*go ~ south.* **6.** to a later period. ¶*be handed ~ from father to son.* **7.** to a smaller quantity, value, etc. ¶*Bread is ~.*① **8.** really; seriously. ¶*get ~ to work.*② **9.** on paper. ¶*write ~ the address.* **10.** in cash. ¶*pay ~.*
1) ***down and out,*** without money, friends, health, etc.
2) ***down on,*** angry at; feeling ill-will toward.
3) ***Down with!,*** Overthrow! ¶*Down with the Cabinet!*③
4) ***up and down,*** to and fro; from side to side.
—*prep.* down, toward, on, through, along etc. ¶*live further ~ the river*④ / ~ *the ages / I went ~ the road.*
—*adj.* **1.** in a lower place. ¶*a ~ leap.*⑤ **2.** (of a train, etc.) downward; going down. ¶*a ~ train.*⑥ **3.** ill; sick; not active. ¶*He is ~ with influenza.*⑦
—*vt.* **1.** defeat; overcome; beat. ¶~ *one's opponent.* **2.** cause (something) to fall down. **3.** drink down.
—*n.* **1.** [U] a downward movement. **2.** 《usu. *pl.*》 a misfortune; what is unlucky. ¶*the ups and downs of life.*⑧

down[2] [daun] *n.* [U] the first soft feathers of young birds, etc. ¶*a bed of ~.*①

down[3] [daun] *n.* **1.** 《usu. *pl.*》 rolling, grassy, open land. **2.** [C] a treeless mound of sand made by the wind.

down·cast [dáunkæ̀st / -kɑ̀:st] *adj.* looking downward; sad; discouraged. —*n.* [C] a downcast look; ruin.

down·fall [dáunfɔ̀:l] *n.* [C] **1.** ruin; a heavy fall. **2.** a heavy rain, etc.

down·grade [dáungréid] *n.* [C] a downward slope. —*vt.* move (someone) to a lower rank with a smaller salary; view (something) in a less favorable way.

down·heart·ed [dáunhɑ́:rtid] *adj.* discouraged.

down·hill [dáunhíl] *adv.* downward. —*adj.* going

—[名] 남자 이름 [N.B.] 애칭 Doug
—[形] 1. 침울한, 시무룩한 2. 《스코》 엄한; 완고한
—[他] 1. …을 물속에 처박다 2. …에 물을 끼얹다 3. 《口》 [등불]을 끄다
—[名] 1. 비둘기 2. 귀여운(상냥한) 사람 ¶①[호칭으로] 오오, 귀여운 애야 3. 성령(聖靈)
—[名] 비둘기장
—[名] 영국 동남부의 항구
[熟] 도우버 해협
—[名] 《建》 열장 장부촉 이음 —[他] …을 열장 장부촉으로 맞추다, 꼭 들어맞게 하다 —[自] 꼭 들어맞다 ¶①네 계획은 내것과 꼭 들어맞는다
—[名] 1. 죽은 남편의 재산·작위를 이어받은 과부 ¶①[영국의] 공작 미망인/②황태후 2. 품위(위엄)있는 노부인
—[形] [복장이] 단정하지 못한, 촌스러운; 초라한 —[名] 옷차림이 단정하지 못한 여자
—[名] 1. 과부산(寡婦產) 2. 천부의 재능 —[他] [과부산·재능을 남]에게 주다
—[副] 1. 아래로; 지상으로 2. 아래[쪽]에서 3. 하류로 4. 시골로 5. 남쪽으로 6. [시대가] 내려와서 7. [분량·가치·정도 따위가] 내려서, 떨어져서 ¶①빵값이 내렸다 8. 실제로; 진심으로 ¶②본격적으로 일에 착수하다 9. 종이[따위]에 10. 현금으로
[熟] 1)완전히 몰락하여 2)성나서; 원한을 품고 3)타도하다 ¶③내각은 물러가다 4)여기저기, 왔다갔다
—[前] …을 내려와서; …의 아래쪽에; …을 따라서 ¶④강의 훨씬 하류에 살다
—[形] 1. 아래쪽의 ¶⑤뛰어내리기 2. 아래쪽으로의; 내려가는 ¶⑥하행 열차 3. 병이 든; 기운 없는 ¶⑦그는 감기에 걸려 있다
—[他] 1. …을 타도하다 2. …을 떨어뜨리다 3. …을 삼키다, 마시다
—[名] 1. 하강 2. 불행; 불운 ¶⑧인생의 기복
—[名] 솜털, 부드러운 털 ¶①깃털 이불, 안락한 생활
—[名] 1. [양치기에 알맞은] 언덕진 초원지 2. 모래언덕
—[形] 눈을 내리뜬, 풀이 죽은 —[名] 눈을 내리뜨기; 파멸, 멸망
—[名] 1. 몰락, 멸망, 급격한 낙하 2. [비 따위가] 많이 내림
—[名] 내리받이 —[他] …을 강등시키다; …의 품질(지위)를 떨어뜨리다
—[形] 낙심한, 기가 죽은
—[副] 내려가서, 아래쪽으로 —[形] 내리

downward; worse.

Down·ing Street [dáuniŋstrì:t] *n.* **1.** a street in London, where government offices and the residence of the prime minister stand. **2.** the British government.

down·pour [dáunpɔ̀:r] *n.* [C] a heavy rain.

down·right [dáunràit] *adj.* **1.** absolute; thorough. **2.** plain; frank; honest; straightforward. **—*adv.*** absolutely; thoroughly.

down·stage [dáunstéidʒ] *adv.* toward the front of the stage.

down·stairs [dáunstέərz] *adv.* down the stairs; on or to a lower floor. **—*adj.*** on a lower floor. **—*n.*** ⦅*pl.*⦆ the lower floor or floors.

down·stream [dáunstrí:m] *adv.* in or with the current of a stream.

down·town [dáuntàun →*adv.*] *n.* [C] the main business section of a town. ↔uptown **—*adj.*** of or in the main business section of a town. **—*adv.*** [∸ ∸] to, toward, or in the main business section of a town.

down·trod·den [dáuntràdn / -trɔ̀dn] *adj.* oppressed; trodden down.

down·ward [dáunwərd] *adj., adv.* toward what is lower; toward a later time. ↔upward

down·wards [dáunwərdz] *adv.* =downward.

down·y [dáuni] *adj.* (**down·i·er, down·i·est**) of or like the first soft feathers or hair. ▷**down·i·ness** [-nis] *n.*

dow·ry [dáuri] *n.* [C] (pl. **-ries**) **1.** the money, property, etc. that a woman brings to her husband at marriage. **2.** a natural gift.

dox·ol·o·gy [dɑksálədʒi / dɔksɔ́l-] *n.* [C] (pl. **-gies**) a hymn or prayer praising God.

doy·en [dɔ́iən, -en] *n.* [C] the senior member of a group. ¶*the ~ of the diplomatic corps.*①

doz. dozen; dozens.

doze [douz] *vi.* sleep lightly. ¶*~ off*① / *~ over a book.* **—*n.*** [C] a light sleep; a nap.

doz·en [dʌ́zn] *n.* [C] (pl. **-ens** or **-en**) a group of 12. ¶***three** ~ eggs / some ~ of eggs*① / *some dozens of eggs*② /*sell by the ~* / *in dozens*③ / *a baker's* (or *devil's, long, printer's*) ~.④

1) ***dozens of times,*** many times.

2) ***talk nineteen*** (or ***thirteen***) ***to the dozen,*** (*slang*) talk incessantly.

Dr. Dr, Doctor.

drab[1] [dræb] *adj.* (**drab·ber, drab·best**) **1.** dull; monotonous. **2.** dull brownish or yellowish gray. **—*n.*** [U] a dull, brownish gray. ▷**drab·ly** [-li] *adv.*

drab[2] [dræb] *n.* [C] a dirty, untidy woman.

drachm [dræm] *n.* **1.** (*Brit.*) dram. **2.** drachma.

drach·ma [drǽkmə] *n.* [C] (pl. **-mas** or **-mae**) **1.** a unit of Greek money. **2.** an ancient Greek silver coin.

drach·mae [drǽkmi:] *n.* pl. of **drachma.**

draft, draught [dræft / drɑ:ft] *n.* **1.** [U][C] a current of air, esp. in a room. ¶*feel the ~.*① **2.** [C] a device for regulating the current of air in a stove, etc. [C] **3.** a plan; a sketch; a rough copy. ¶*make out a ~ of.*② **4.** [U] (*U.S.*) a selection of persons for military service. **5.** [C] persons selected for military service. **6.** [U] the act or quantity of pulling loads, etc. **7.** [C] ⦅usu. *draught*⦆ the pulling in of a fish net; the quantity of fish caught in a net, etc. **8.** [C] a written order from one person, bank, etc. to another, ordering the payment of money. ¶*a ~ of demand*③ / *make a ~ of money*④ / *make a ~ on a bank* (or *fund*).⑤ **9.** [U] ⦅usu. *draught*⦆ the depth of water needed to float a ship. **10.** [C] ⦅usu. *draught*⦆ the amount taken at one drink; an act of breathing in air, smoke, etc. ¶*at a ~.*

—*vt.* **1.** make a sketch of, plan for, or a rough copy of

받이의; 한층 나빠진

—[名] 1. 영국 런던의 다우닝가 2. 영국 정부

—[名] 억수, 폭우

—[形] 1. 절대한; 철저한 2. 노골적인; 솔직한 —[副] 절대로; 철저하게

—[副] 무대 앞쪽에

—[副] 아래층에[서] —[形] 아래층의 —[名] 아래층

—[副] 하류에, 강을 내려가서

—[名] 상업지구 —[形] 상업지구의 —[副] 상업지구에(로·에서)

—[形] 학대받은; 짓밟힌

—[形][副] 아래쪽으로의(에), 내려가는;…이후의(에)

—[形] 솜털의, 폭신폭신한

—[名] 1. 신부 지참금 2. 천부의 재능

—[名] 송영가(頌榮歌), 찬가; 영광의 찬가

—[名] 고참자; 수석 ¶①외교단의 수석 대사

—[自] 졸다 ¶①꾸벅꾸벅 졸다 —[名] 졸기, 선잠, 풋잠

—[名] 12개, 다스, 타(打) ¶①달걀 한 다스/②달걀 몇 다스/③한 타씩/④13개

[熟] 1)몇 번이고 몇 번이고 2)⦅俗⦆쉴새 없이 지껄이다

—[形] 1. 우중충한; 단조로운 2. 황갈색의, 다색(茶色)의 —[名] 황갈색

—[名] 행실 나쁜 여자, 매춘부

—[名] 1. ⦅英⦆ 드램 2. 드라크마(은화)

—[名] 1. 드라크마(화폐 단위) 2. [옛 그리이스의] 드라크마 은화

—[名] 1. 틈으로 들어오는 바람, 통풍 ¶①주머니가 비어 있다 2. [난로 따위의] 통풍장치 3. 설계도; 도안, 초안 ¶②…을 기초하다 4. ⦅美⦆ 징병 5. 분견(특파)대 6. [짐 따위를] 끌기, 견인량(牽引量) 7. [그물의] 한 번 당기기; 한 그물의 어획고 8. 어음 발행, 환어음, 지불 명령서, 수표 ¶③요구불 환어음/④돈을 인출하다/⑤은행(자금)에서 꺼내다 9. [배의] 흘수(吃水) 10. [약 따위의] 1회분, 한 모금[의 분량], [공기·연기 따위의] 한 번 들이마시기

—[他] 1. …을 기초하다; …의 밑그림을

D

draftsman [358] **dramatics**

(something). **2.** select (someone) for military service.
drafts·man [dræftsmən / drɑ́ːfts-] *n.* ⓒ (pl. **-men** [mən])
1. a person who draws plans or sketches. **2.** a person who writes out documents, speeches, etc.
draft·y [dræfti / drɑ́ːfti] *adj.* (**draft·i·er, draft·i·est**) causing a current of air. ▷ **draft·i·ly** [-li] *adv.*
‡ **drag** [dræg] *v.* (**dragged, drag·ging**) *vt.* **1.** pull or draw (a heavy thing) slowly along the ground; trail (something) on the ground. ¶ *They dragged the log out of the forest. | ~ one's skirt.* **2.** search the bottom of (a river, lake, etc.) for something with a net or a hook. ¶ *They dragged the lake for his body.* **3.** level and smooth (land) with a harrow. ── *vi.* **1.** trail on the ground; be dragged. **2.** move slowly; (of time) pass slowly and tediously. ¶ *Time dragged on. | The day dragged by.*
1) ***drag in***, bring in.
2) ***drag on*** (or ***out***), make (something) too slow or too long; be too slow; last too long.
── *n.* ⓒ **1.** a net, hook, etc. used in dragging (*vt.* 2.). **2.** the act of dragging (*vt.* 1.). **3.** anything that hinders; an obstruction. ¶ *She is a ~ on my career.*
drag·ging [drǽgiŋ] *adj.* very slow in walking, developing, etc. ¶ *She walked with ~ feet.*
drag·gle [drǽgl] *vt.* make (something) wet or dirty by dragging through mud, water, etc. ── *vi.* **1.** be draggled. **2.** follow slowly.
drag·net [drǽgnèt] *n.* ⓒ **1.** a net pulled over the bottom of a river, etc. **2.** a network for catching criminals by the police.
* **drag·on** [drǽg(ə)n] *n.* ⓒ **1.** a terrible animal supposed to look like a huge snake. ⇒ N.B. **2.** a very severe and watchful woman.
* **drag·on·fly** [drǽg(ə)nflài] *n.* ⓒ (pl. **-flies**) a large insect, with a long, thin body and two pairs of large wings.
dra·goon [drəgúːn] *n.* ⓒ a horse-soldier.
‡ **drain** [drein] *vt.* **1.** draw off (water) from a place; make (a place) dry by drawing off water. ¶ *~ water from the road.* **2.** drink up. ¶ *~ a pint of beer.* **3.** exhaust; use up; deprive. (*~ something of*) ¶ *The war drained the land of its people and wealth.* ── *vi.* **1.** flow gradually. ¶ *~ away | The water drains into a river.* **2.** become empty or dry by draining. ¶ *The land drains into the river.* **3.** exhaust gradually. ── *n.* ⓒ **1.** a ditch or pipe for carrying off water. **2.** anything that gradually use up money, etc.
drain·age [dréinidʒ] *n.* **1.** ⓤ the act or process of draining. ¶ *~ work.* **2.** ⓒ a system of drains. **3.** ⓒ that which is drained off. **4.** ⓒ an area that is drained.
drain·pipe [dréinpàip] *n.* ⓒ a large pipe for carrying off water, etc.
drake [dreik] *n.* ⓒ a male duck.
dram [dræm] *n.* ⓒ **1.** a unit of weight. **2.** a small drink of liquor. ¶ *be fond of a ~.*
* **dra·ma** [drɑ́ːmə, +U.S. drǽmə] *n.* **1.** ⓒ a play for the theater. **2.** ⓒ a series of happenings as interesting as such a play. **3.** ⓤ (often *the ~*) the branch of literature having to do with plays. ¶ *Elizabethan ~.*
* **dra·mat·ic** [drəmǽtik] *adj.* **1.** of drama; having to do with plays. ¶ *a ~ performance | a ~ right.* **2.** seeming like a drama; exciting; impressive. ¶ *a ~ event.*
dra·mat·i·cal·ly [drəmǽtikəli] *adv.* **1.** in a dramatic manner. **2.** from a dramatic point of view.
dra·mat·ics [drəmǽtiks] *n. pl.* **1.** (used as *sing.*) the art of acting or producing plays. **2.** plays produced by amateurs.

그리다 2. …을 징병으로 뽑다
── ⓝ 1. 제도자 2. [공문서·연설 따위의] 기초자

── ⓐ 틈으로 바람이 들어오는

── ⓥ 1. [무거운 것을] 끌다; 질질 끌다 ¶ ①스커어트자락을 질질 끌다 2. [강·호수 따위]의 바닥을 훑다 ¶ ②그들은 그의 시체를 찾기 위해 호수 바닥을 뒤졌다 3. 써레로 [토지]를 고르다
── ⓘ 1. 질질 끌다 2. 천천히 움직이다; [시간이] 천천히 지나가다

熟 1) 끌어들이다 2) 질질 오래 끌다

── ⓝ 1. [물밑을 훑는] 그물, 저인망(底引網); 갈고리 2. [질질] 끌기 3. 방해, 장애 ¶ ③그녀는 내 출세에 방해가 됐다
── ⓐ 아주 느린; 질질 끄는 ¶ ①그녀는 발을 질질 끌며 걸었다
── ⓥ [물건]을 질질 끌어 적시다(더럽히다) ── ⓘ 1. 질질 끌려 더러워지다 2. 천천히 따라가다
── ⓝ 1. 저인망(底引網) 2. 수사망

── ⓝ 1. 용 N.B. 날개와 발톱이 있고 불과 연기를 뿜는다는 전설상의 괴물 2. 엄중한 감시인, 시중드는 부인
── ⓝ 잠자리

── ⓝ 기병
── ⓥ 1. [물]을 빼다; …에서 배수(排水)하다 2. …을 마셔 비우다 3. …을 소모시키다; 빼앗다 ¶ ①전쟁이 그곳의 인명과 재산을 빼앗아 갔다 ── ⓘ 1. 천천히 흐르다 2. 배수되어 말라 버리다 ¶ ②그 토지의 물은 강으로 빠진다 3. 서서히 소모하다 ── ⓝ 1. 배수거(渠), 수채, 하수도 2. 낭비, 지출; 끊임없는 유출

── ⓝ 1. 배수, 방수(放水) 2. 배수 조직 3. 하수, 구정물 4. [하천의] 배수 구역, 유역

── ⓝ 배수관, 하수관
── ⓝ 오리의 수컷
── ⓝ 1. 드램(형량 단위) 2. 한 입, 소량 ¶ ①술을 좋아하다
── ⓝ 1. 희곡, 각본 2. 극적인 사건 3. 극문학, 극 ¶ ①엘리자베드 왕조의 극

── ⓝ 1. 극의, 희곡의 ¶ ①연기, 연극/② 흥행권 2. 극적인, 눈부신 ¶ ③극적인 사건
── ⓐ 1. 극적으로 2. 극의 관점에서

── ⓝ 1. 연출법, 연기 2. 소인극(素人劇)

dram·a·tist [drǽmətist] *n.* [C] a writer of plays.
—[名] 극작가, 희곡 작자

dram·a·ti·za·tion [drӕmətizéiʃ(ə)n / -taiz-] *n.* [U][C] the act of dramatizing; that which is dramatized.
—[名] 각색, 희곡화; 각색 작품

dram·a·tize [drǽmətàiz] *vt.* **1.** put (a story, etc.) into the form of a play. **2.** express (something) in a dramatic way.
—[他] 1. …을 극화하다, 각색하다 2. …을 극적으로 표현하다

* **drank** [drӕŋk] *v.* pt. of **drink**.

drape [dreip] *vt.* **1.** cover (something) with cloth or hang cloth around (something) in loose folds. ¶ *~ with red hangings.*① **2.** arrange (clothes, etc.) in graceful folds. ¶ *~ the robe around the model's shoulder.* —*n.* [C] ⦅often *pl.*⦆ cloth hung in folds; a curtain.
—[他] 1. [옷·포장 따위]로 주름을 잡아 가리다 ¶①붉은 휘장으로 [아름답게] 꾸미다 2. …을 우아하게 걸치다 —[名] 포장, 휘장; 커어튼

drap·er [dréipər] *n.* [C] (*Brit.*) a dealer in cloth or dry goods.
—[名] ⦅英⦆ 포목상, 포목상인

dra·per·y [dréipəri] *n.* (pl. **-per·ies**) **1.** ⦅often *pl.*⦆ clothing or hangings arranged in graceful folds. **2.** [U] materials used for curtains, garments, etc. **3.** [U] (*Brit.*) the business of a draper.
—[名] 1. [주름이 있는] 휘장, 포장, 커어튼 2. 피륙, 직물 3. ⦅英⦆ 직물업, 포목상

dras·tic [drǽstik] *adj.* acting with a strong or violent effect; violent. ¶ *~ measures*① / *a ~ reform*② / *apply a ~ remedy.*③ ▷**dras·ti·cal·ly** [-kəli] *adv.*
—[形] 격렬한, 맹렬한, 철저한 ¶①비상수단/②근본적 개혁/③강제 치료법을 쓰다

* **draught** [drӕft / drɑːft] *n.*, *v.* =draft. ▷**draught·er** [-ər] *n.*

draughts·man [drǽftsmən / dɑ́ːfts-] *n.* (pl. **-men** [-mən]) =draftsman.

draught·y [drǽfti / drɑ́ːfti] *adj.* (**draught·i·er**, **draught·i·est**) =drafty.

** **draw** [drɔː] *v.* (**drew**, **drawn**) *vt.* **1.** pull. ¶ *~ the curtains* / *~ a hat over the face*① / *They drew her aside.*② **2.** pull out. ¶ *~ a sword*③ / *~ a cork from a bottle.* **3.** take out; get; receive. ¶ *~ money from a bank* / *~ a conclusion.*④ **4.** attract. ¶ *~ our attention to the fact.* **5.** bring [about]; cause. ¶ *~ applause*⑤ / *~ ruin upon oneself.* **6.** make (a picture, figure, etc.) with a pen, a pencil, chalk, etc. ¶ *~ a circle* / *Draw me a rough sketch.* **7.** finish (a game) undecided. ¶ *a drawn game* / *The game was drawn.* **8.** take in (breath). ¶ *~ a deep breath.* **9.** write out. ¶ *~ a check.* **10.** (of a ship) need (a certain depth of water) to float in. ¶ *This boat draws two feet.*⑥ —*vi.* **1.** move; be moved. ¶ *This cart draws easily.* **2.** approach; come near. ¶ *~ together*⑦ / *Winter is drawing near.* / *This year drew to its close.* **3.** make a picture with a pen, a pencil, chalk, etc. **4.** finish a game undecided. **5.** cause air to flow. **6.** take out a pistol, sword, etc. **7.** attract people. ¶ *The play is drawing very well.*⑧
—[他] 1. …을 끌다 ¶①모자를 푹 눌러 쓰다/②그들은 그녀를 옆으로 당겼다 2. …을 잡아 빼다(뽑다) ¶③칼을 뽑다 3. …을 얻다; 받다 ¶④결론을 얻다 4. …을 끌어당기다 5. …을 초래하다; 야기하다 ¶⑤갈채를 받다 6. …을 그리다 7. …을 무승부로 하다 8. [숨]을 들이쉬다 9. [증서·문서]를 쓰다 10. …피이트의 흘수(吃水)다 ¶⑥이 배는 흘수가 2피이트이다 —[自] 1. 움직이다 2. 가까이 가다 ¶⑦모여들다 3. 그리다 4. 무승부로 끝나다 5. 바람이 통하다 6. 권총·칼 따위를 뽑다 7. 사람을 끌어당기다 ¶⑧이 연극은 관중을 많이 끈다

1) ***draw out,*** ⓐ make (someone) talk. ⓑ extend; prolong.
2) ***draw up,*** ⓐ write out formally. ⓑ stop.
[熟] 1)ⓐ…에게 말을 시키다 ⓑ질질 끌다 2)ⓐ정식으로 쓰다 ⓑ멈추다, 서다

—*n.* [C] **1.** the act of drawing. **2.** something that attracts; an attraction. ¶ *The new play is a great ~.* **3.** a game that ends in a tie.
—[名] 1. 끌기; 뽑기 2. 끌어당기는 것; 인깃거리 3. 무승부의 게임

draw·back [drɔ́ːbӕk] *n.* [C] **1.** something that causes trouble; a disadvantage; a hindrance. ¶ *a ~ to success.*① **2.** money paid back from a charge previously made.
—[名] 1. 장애, 고장; 결점; 불이익 ¶①성공에의 장애 2. 환불금, 환불받은 세금, 공제

draw·bridge [drɔ́ːbrìdʒ] *n.* [C] a bridge that can be lifted, lowered, or moved to one side.
—[名] 도개교(跳開橋), 가동교(可動橋); [성곽의] 들어올리는 다리

draw·ee [drɔːíː] *n.* [C] a person for whom an order or draft to pay money is written. ↔drawer
—[名] 어음 수취인

* **draw·er** [drɔ́ːər →3., 4.] *n.* [C] **1.** a person or thing that draws. **2.** a person who draws an order to pay money. ↔drawee **3.** [drɔːr] a box that slides in and out of a chest, table, etc. **4.** ⦅*pl.*⦆ [drɔːrz] an undergarment for the lower part of the body.
—[名] 1. 끄는 사람(것), 제도자 2. 어음 발행인 3. 서랍 4. 팬츠, 드로오즈

draw·ing [drɔ́ːiŋ] *n.* **1.** [U] the act of a person or thing that draws. **2.** [U] the art of representing objects by lines. **3.** [C] a picture, design, sketch, etc. drawn with a pencil, chalk, etc.
—[名] 1. 끌어내기 2. 제도 3. 그림, 도화, 도면

drawing board [ˊ-ˋ] *n.* a board on which paper is placed for drawing.
—[名] 제도판, 화판(畫板)

D

drawing room

drawing room [≤ ≥] *n.* **1.** a room in which guests are received. **2.** (*U.S.*) a private compartment in a sleeping car.
drawl [drɔːl] *vi., vt.* speak in a slow, lazy way. —*n.* ⓒ a slow, lazy way of speaking. ▷**drawl·er** [-ər] *n.*
:drawn [drɔːn] *v.* pp. of **draw**.
dray [drei] *n.* ⓒ a low, strong cart for carrying heavy loads. —*vt.* carry (something) on a dray.
dray·man [dréimən] *n.* ⓒ (pl. **-men** [-mən]) a man who drives a dray.
:dread [dred] *vt.* fear greatly. (*~ to do; ~ that ...*) ¶*~ visits to the dentist* / *~ to think what may happen* / *I ~ that he might come.*① —*n.* Ⓤ (sometimes *a ~*) fear; anxiety. ¶*be in ~ of*② / *have a ~ of.*③ —*adj.* dreadful; dreaded; awful. ⌈greatly feared.⌉
dread·ed [drédid] *adj.* looked with fear or anxiety;
:dread·ful [drédf(u)l] *adj.* **1.** causing dread; fearful; terrible. **2.** (*colloq.*) very bad; very disagreeable.
dread·ful·ly [drédfuli] *adv.* **1.** in a dreadful manner. **2.** very. ¶*be ~ tired.*①
:dream [driːm] *n.* ⓒ **1.** an image or a thought passing through a sleeping person's mind. ¶*have a dreadful ~.* **2.** a fancy; an imagination; a vision; a daydream. **3.** a hope for the future; what one wants to realize. ¶*He realized his ~ of becoming a professor.*① **4.** anything so charming that it seems dreamlike. ¶*She looked a perfect ~.*②
—*vi., vt.* (**dreamed** or **dreamt**) **1.** have dreams during sleep. **2.** (in *negative*) suppose; think of (something) as possible. (*~ that ..., ~ of* something) ¶*He little dreamed that he would hurt her.*③ **3.** imagine; hope.
1) *dream away,* pass one's time idly.
2) *dream of,* ⓐ have dreams of (something). ⓑ indulge in daydreams of (something). ⓒ (in *negative*) think of (something) as possible. ¶*Little did I ~ of meeting you.*④
dream·er [dríːmər] *n.* ⓒ a person who dreams; a person who does not have practical ideas or plans.
dream·land [dríːmlænd] *n.* **1.** ⓤⓒ a place which a person feels to be unreal. **2.** ⓤⓒ a utopia. **3.** ⓤ sleep.
dream·less [dríːmlis] *adj.* without dreams.
dream·like [dríːmlaik] *adj.* like a dream.
dreamt [dremt] *v.* pt. and pp. of **dream**.
dream·y [dríːmi] *adj.* (**dream·i·er, dream·i·est**) **1.** full of dreams. **2.** like something in a dream; vague; dim. **3.** unreal; impractical. ▷**dream·i·ly** [-li] *adv.* ⌈ness [-nis] *n.*⌉
drear [driər] *adj.* (*poetic*) =dreary.
*****drear·y** [dríəri] *adj.* (**drear·i·er, drear·i·est**) **1.** dull; cheerless; gloomy; making low-spirited. **2.** sad; sorrowful. ▷**drear·i·ly** [-li] *adv.* —**drear·i·ness** [-nis] *n.*
dredge¹ [dredʒ] *n.* ⓒ **1.** a machine for digging out the bottom of a river, harbor, etc. **2.** a device with a net for catching shellfish, etc. from the bottom of the sea.
—*vt.* **1.** clean out (a harbor, etc.) with a dredge. ¶*~ up the river.* **2.** gather (shellfish, etc.) with a dredge.
dredge² [dredʒ] *vt.* scatter; ((*~ something with*)); sprinkle. ((*~ sugar, etc. over*)) ¶*~ meat with flour.*①
dredg·er [drédʒər] *n.* ⓒ **1.** a person who operates a dredge. **2.** a ship with a dredge; a dredging machine. ⇒fig.

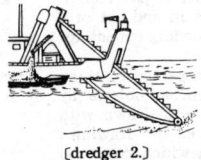
[dredger 2.]

dredger

—ⓢ **1.** 객실, 응접실 **2.** 《美》[침대차의] 특별 전용실

—⃝ⓘ 느리게(점잔빼어) 말하다 —ⓢ 느린 말씨

—ⓢ 큰 짐마차 —ⓘ …을 큰 짐마차로 나르다
—ⓢ 짐마차 마부, 짐마차꾼

—ⓘ …을 몹시 두려워하다, 염려하다 ¶①그가 오지 않을까 염려된다 —ⓢ 공포, 불안, 근심 ¶②…을 끊임없이 두려워하다/③…을 근심하다 —ⓐ 몹시 두려운

—ⓐ 무서워한, 염려하던
—ⓐ **1.** 무서운; 무시무시한 **2.** 《口》 아주 심한, 몹시 싫은
—ⓓ **1.** 무섭게, 무시무시하게 **2.** 몹시 ¶①몹시 지치다

—ⓢ **1.** 꿈 **2.** 환상; 공상; 백일몽 **3.** 희망; 이상 ¶①그는 교수가 되겠다는 꿈을 실현했다 **4.** 꿈처럼 아름다운 것 ¶②그녀는 꿈처럼 아름다웠다

—⃝ⓘ **1.** 꿈을 꾸다 **2.** 생각하다; 있을 수 있다고 생각하다 ¶③그는 그녀를 상처 입히리라고는 꿈에도 생각 못했다 **3.** 공상하다; 희망하다
圏 1)빈둥빈둥 시간을 보내다 2)ⓐ …의 꿈을 꾸다 ⓑ몽상에 잠기다 ⓒ…이 있을 수 있다고 생각하다 ¶④당신을 만나리라고는 꿈에도 생각 못했다

—ⓢ 꿈꾸는 사람; 몽상가

—ⓢ **1.** 꿈나라 **2.** 이상향, 도원경 **3.** 잠

—ⓐ 꿈을 꾸지 않는
—ⓐ 꿈 같은, 어렴풋한

—ⓐ **1.** 꿈이 많은 **2.** 꿈과 같은, 막연한 어렴풋한 **3.** 비현실적인; 환상적인

—ⓐ **1.** 지루한; 쓸쓸한; 음울한; 적막한 **2.** 슬픈

—ⓢ **1.** 준설기 **2.** 저인망(底引網) —ⓘ **1.** [항구 따위를] 준설하다 **2.** 저인망으로 …을 잡다

—ⓘ [가루 따위를] 뿌리다; 살포하다 ¶①고기에 밀가루를 뿌리다

—ⓢ **1.** 준설 인부, 저인망 사용자 **2.** 준설선; 준설기

dreg [dreg] *n.* ⓒ ((usu. *pl.*)) matter which is found at the bottom of a liquid; the most worthless part of anything. ¶*the dregs of society.*①

—名 [밑에 남는] 찌꺼기, 앙금, 재강; 쓰레기, 보잘것 없는 것 ¶①사회의 최하층, 인간의 쓰레기

drench [drentʃ] *vt.* make (something) thoroughly wet; soak. ¶*be drenched [to the skin] with* (or *by*) *rain.*①
—*n.* ⓒ **1.** the act of drenching. ¶*a ~ of rain.*② **2.** a draft of medicine given to a sick animal.

—他 …을 흠뻑 적시다; 물에 담그다 ¶①비에 흠뻑 젖다 —名 1.함빡 젖기; 물에 담그기 ¶②억수, 호우 2.물약

‡**dress** [dres] *n.* **1.** Ⓤ clothes; costume. ¶*spend much money on ~.* **2.** Ⓤ formal clothes. ¶*in full ~*① / *in evening ~.* **3.** ⓒ an outer garment for women, girls, and babies; a gown.
—*vt.* **1.** put clothes on (someone). ¶*She dressed herself in her Sunday best.* / *She is dressing her dolls.* **2.** adorn; decorate. ¶*~ the store windows for Christmas* / *~ the street with flags.* **3.** brush and arrange (hair); comb. ¶*She dressed her hair.* **4.** put a medicine and bandage on (a wound). ¶*The nurse cleaned and dressed the wound.* **5.** make (something) ready for use; prepare. —*vi.* **1.** put on clothes; wear clothes. ¶*He dressed quickly.* **2.** put on formal clothes. ¶*Now they don't ~ for dinner.* **3.** (*Military*) get into a straight line. ¶*~ to* (or *by*) *the right.*②
1) *dress down,* (*colloq.*) scold; beat; thrash.
2) *dress up* (or *out*), put on one's best clothes; put on formal clothes.

—名 1. 복장, 의복, 의장 2. 정장(正裝) ¶①정장으로 3. [여자·아동용] 원피이스식 웃옷
—他 1. …에 옷을 입히다 2. …을 아름답게 꾸미다 3. [머리]를 빗질하다, 조발하다 4. [상처]의 치료를 하다 5. …의 준비를 하다 —自 1. 몸차림을 하다; 옷을 입다 2. 정장하다 3. 〖軍〗정렬하다 ¶②우로 나란히 서다

熟 1)꾸짖다; 채찍질하다 2)쭉 ■입다; 정장하다

dress circle [ˊ ˰ˊ] *n.* the section of seats in a theater, etc., which has the best, most expensive seats. ⇒Ⓝ.Ⓑ.
dress coat [ˊ ˊ] *n.* an evening coat.
dress·er¹ [drésər] *n.* ⓒ **1.** a person who dresses himself. **2.** a person who assists another person to dress. **3.** a person or thing that dresses stone, wood, etc.
dress·er² [drésər] *n.* ⓒ **1.** a piece of furniture with drawers for clothes and with a mirror; bureau. **2.** a piece of kitchen furniture with shelves for dishes.
dress·ing [drésiŋ] *n.* **1.** Ⓤ the act of putting on clothes. **2.** Ⓤ ⓒ the material used to dress. **3.** Ⓤ ⓒ a sauce for salads, fish, etc. **4.** Ⓤ ⓒ medicines and bandages to put on wounds, etc. **5.** Ⓤ chemical plant food.
dressing gown [ˊ ˰ ˊ] *n.* a loose gown worn over night clothes.
dressing room [ˊ ˰ ˊ] *n.* a room for dressing.
dressing table [ˊ ˰ ˰ ˊ] *n.* a low table with a mirror; a dresser.
dress·mak·er [drésmèikər] *n.* ⓒ a person who makes women's dresses, etc. ↔tailor —*adj.* (of women's clothing) having soft lines and subdued decoration.
dress rehearsal [ˊ ˰ˊ] *n.* the final rehearsal of a play with costumes.   ⌈*lets.*①
dress suit [ˊ ˊ] *n.* men's formal suit worn in the even-⌊
dress·y [drési] *adj.* (**dress·i·er, dress·i·est**) fond of wearing showy clothes; stylish. ▷**dress·i·ness** [-nis] *n.*
*· **drew** [dru:] *v.* pt. of **draw**.
drib·ble [dríbl] *vi.* **1.** fall drop by drop; trickle. ¶*~ from the leak in the tank.*① **2.** let saliva run from the mouth. —*vt.* **1.** let (liquid) fall drop by drop. **2.** move (a ball) forward by repeated bounces. —*n.* Ⓤ ⓒ **1.** the act of dropping; trickle. **2.** a very light rain. **3.** the act of dribbling a ball.
drib·let [dríblit] *n.* ⓒ a small amount. ¶*by* (or *in*) *drib-*⌊
dri·er [dráiər] *n.* ⓒ **1.** a person or thing that dries. **2.** a device that removes water by heat, etc.; a dryer. **3.** a substance that makes something dry quickly.
‡**drift** [drift] *vi.* **1.** be carried along by an air or water current. ¶*The boat drifted out to sea.* **2.** be carried

—名 극장 특등석 Ⓝ.Ⓑ. 이 자리에서는 evening dress를 입는 데서
—名 남자용 야회복의 웃옷
—名 1. [어떤] 복장을 하는 사람 2. 의상 담당자 3. 마무리하는 사람(도구); 장식자
—名 1. 거울 달린 화장대 2. 찬장이 달린 조리대; 식기 선반
—名 1.옷 입기 2. 마무리 재료 3. [샐러드용] 흰 소스 4. [상처에 바르는] 고약, 붕대 5. 화학 비료

—名 화장옷, 실내복

—名 화장실
—名 경대, 화장대

—名 [부인복 따위의] 재봉사, 양재사
—形 [부인복의] 선이 부드럽고 장식이 야하지 않은
—名 [의상을 입고 하는] 마지막 무대 연습, 총연습
—名 [남자] 야회복
—形 옷차림에 마음을 쓰는; 옷맵시가 좋은

—自 1. 방울져 떨어지다; 줄줄 흐르다 ¶①탱크의 구멍에서 줄줄 새다 2. 침을 흘리다 —他 1. …을 똑똑 떨어뜨리다 2. [공]을 드리블하다 —名 1.방울져 떨어지기 2. 가랑비 3. 드리블

—名 소량, 소액 ¶①조금씩
—名 1. 말리는 사람(것) 2. 건조기(乾燥器), 드라이어 3. 건조제

—自 1. 떠돌다; 표류하다 2. 돼가는 대로 놔두다; 정처 없이 헤매다 ¶①한

driftwood / drive

along by circumstances; go along without aim. ¶~ *along through life*① / ~ *into war*.② **3.** be heaped by force of wind or water. ¶*The snow has drifted badly.* —*vt.* cause (something) to drift. ¶~ *a boat out to sea.* —*n.* ⓒ **1.** ⓤⓒ the state of being drifted; the direction of drifting. **2.** tendency; trend. ¶*the ~ of opinion.* **3.** general meaning; intent. ¶*the ~ of an argument.* **4.** snow, sand, etc. heaped up by the wind or water. ¶*a ~ of snow.*

drift·wood [dríftwùd] *n.* ⓤ wood drifting in the water or washed up on beaches.

* **drill**¹ [dril] *n.* ⓒ **1.** a tool or a machine for making holes. **2.** military or physical exercises. **3.** the process of teaching or training by repetition.
—*vt.* **1.** make a hole in (something) with a drill. **2.** train; teach (someone) by repetition. ¶~ *boys in grammar*.① —*vi.* **1.** make a hole with a drill. **2.** be taught or trained by repetition. ▷**drill·er** [-ər] *n.*

drill² [dril] *n.* ⓒ **1.** a machine for planting seeds. **2.** a small and long cut made in the ground to plant seeds in; a row of planted seeds —*vt.* plant (seeds, etc.) in drills (*n.* 2.). ¶~ *wheat* / ~ *a field with wheat.*

drill·mas·ter [drílmæstər / -mɑ̀:stə] *n.* ⓒ **1.** an officer who leads military drill. **2.** a person who teaches by

dri·ly [dráili] *adv.* =dryly. ⎰drilling.⎱

: **drink** [driŋk] *v.* (**drank, drunk**) *vt.* **1.** swallow (liquid). ¶~ *off* (or *up*) *a glass of beer*① / ~ *a glass dry.*② **2.** drink in order to show one's hope for (something); drink for the good of (someone). ¶~ *his health* / ~ *success to him* / ~ *the Queen.* **3.** absorb. —*vi.* **1.** swallow liquid. **2.** drink alcoholic liquor habitually or too much. **3.** absorb. **4.** (of liquid) taste. ¶*This wine drinks pretty well.*③
1) ***drink away***, lose or spend (money, etc.) by drinking. ¶~ *away one's fortune.*
2) ***drink down***, ⓐ swallow. ⓑ make oneself forget (an unpleasant matter) by drinking wine.
3) ***drink in***, ⓐ absorb. ⓑ take in (something) eagerly through the eyes, etc. ⓒ be charmed with (beauty).
4) ***drink to***, drink in order to show one's respect or hope to (someone or something).
—*n.* ⓤⓒ **1.** any liquid for drinking; alcoholic liquors. **2.** ⓤ the state of being drunk. ¶*be on the ~.*④
a drink of, a mouthful of; a cup, glass, etc. of.

drink·a·ble [dríŋkəbl] *adj.* suitable for drinking. —*n.* ⎱usu. *pl.*⎰ something to drink.

drink·er [dríŋkər] *n.* ⓒ **1.** a person who drinks. **2.** a person who drinks alcoholic liquor habitually or too much. ¶*a hard* (or *heavy*) ~ ① ⎱liquor.⎰

drink·ing [dríŋkiŋ] *n.* ⓤ the habit of taking alcoholic

* **drip** [drip] *v.* (**dripped** or **dript, drip·ping**) *vi.* let drops fall; fall in drops. ¶~ *from the trees.* —*vt.* let (liquid) fall in drops. —*n.* ⓒ a falling in drops; ⎱often *pl.*⎰ liquid that falls in drops.

drip·ping [drípiŋ] *n.* ⓒ anything that drops; ⎱often *pl.*⎰ the fat and juices melted from roasted meat.

: **drive** [draiv] *v.* (**drove, driv·en**) *vt.* **1.** make (a horse, etc.) go. ¶~ *the cattle to* [*the*] *pasture.*① **2.** put (a car, carriage, etc.) in motion; operate; control. ¶~ *a car around the corner.* **3.** carry (someone) in a car. ¶*Will you ~ me home* (*to the station*)?② **4.** force; compel. ((~ someone *to*; ~ someone *to do*)) ¶*Ambition drove him to crime.*③ / *Hunger drove her to steal.* **5.** ⎱usu. in *passive*⎰ (of steam, gasoline, etc.) make (a

평생을 되는 대로 살다/②어느 사이에 전쟁에 말려들다 **3.** 바람에 불리어 쌓이다; 퇴적하다 —他 …을 표류시키다; 불어서 내려보내다, 휘몰아치다 —名 1. 표류; 흐름의 방향 2. 경향, 동향 3. 취지; 대세의 흐름 4. 바람에 불리어 쌓인 것; 퇴적물

—名 유목(流木)

—名 1. 송곳, 천공기(穿孔機) 2. 교련; 체육 훈련 3. 연습, 훈련
—他 1. …에 송곳으로 구멍을 뚫다 2. …을 훈련하다; …에게 가르치다 ¶① 학생들에게 문법을 가르치다 —自 1. 구멍을 뚫다 2. 교련을 받다, 맹연습하다

—名 1. 조파기(條播機) 2. [씨를 뿌리는] 작은 이랑; [뿌린 씨앗·농작물의] 줄 —他 [씨]를 이랑에 뿌리다

—名 1. 교련 교관 2. 엄하게 가르치는 사람

—他 1. …을 마시다, 다 들이키다 ¶① 맥주를 단숨에 마시다/②마셔서 비우다 2. …을 위해 축배를 들다 3. …을 흡수하다 —自 1. 음료를 마시다 2. 술을 고래로 마시다; 술 마시는 버릇이 있다 3. 빨아들이다 4. [음료가] …한 맛이 나다 ¶③이 포도주는 꽤 맛이 좋다
圞 1) …을 술로 잃다 2)ⓐ …을 삼키다 ⓑ 술을 마셔 …을 잊다 3)ⓐ …을 흡수하다 ⓑ [감각을 통해] …을 받아들이다 ⓒ …에 넋을 잃다 4) …을 위해 축배를 들다

—名 1. 마실 것; 술 2. 술 마신 상태 ¶ ①취해 있다
圞 한 모금의, 한 잔의
—形 마실 수 있는, 마시기 알맞은
—名 음료
—名 1. 마시는 사람 2. 술고래 ¶① 술꾼, 술고래

—名 음주
—自 [액체가] 방울져 (똑똑) 떨어지다
—他 …을 똑똑 떨어지게 하다
—名 방울져 떨어지기; 물방울

—名 방울져 떨어지기; 물방울

—他 1. [동물 따위]를 몰다; 몰고 가다 ¶①소를 목장까지 몰고 가다 2. …을 운전하다 3. …을 차로 나르다 ¶②집(역)까지 태워다 주시겠습니까? 4. …을 억지로 시키다 ¶③야심 때문에 그는 범죄를 저지르게 되었다 5. …을 움직이다; …의 동력원이 되다 6. …을 몰아치다; 내던지다 7. …을 쳐

machine) move. ¶*A motorboat is driven by a gasoline engine.* **6.** dash; throw. ¶*The wind drove the ship onto the rocks.* **7.** move (something) by hitting. ¶~ *a ball* / ~ *a nail into a board.*④ **8.** make (someone) work too hard. **9.** carry on. ¶~ *a good bargain.*⑤ **—*vi.*** **1.** go in a car, etc. ¶~ *to the lake.* **2.** dash; rush; go forward violently. ¶*The ship drove across the waves.*

날리다; 때려 박다 ¶④못을 판자에 때려 박다 8. …을 혹사하다 9. …을 영위하다, [거래]를 하다 ¶⑤수지가 맞는 거래를 하다 —[自] 1. 자동차로 가다; 드라이브하다 2. 돌진하다

drive at mean; intend; aim at.

[熟] …을 뜻하다; 의도하다, 노리다

—*n.* **1.** [U] the act of driving. **2.** [U][C] a fast, hard blow. **3.** [C] a trip in a car, carriage, etc. ¶*a three hours'* ~. **4.** [C] a short road for cars. ⇒[N.B.] **5.** [U] energy; vigor. ¶*a man with* ~. **6.** [U] an effort for some special purpose; [C] a campaign. ¶*a Red Cross* ~.

—[名] 1. 차를 몰기 2. 타격 3. 드라이브 [여행] 4. 차도 [N.B.] 대문과 현관 사이처럼 거리가 짧은 것 5. 기력; 활력 6. [특별한 목적을 위한] 노력; …운동

drive-in [dráivìn] *n.* [C] a place where people can eat, shop, attend movies, etc. while in their cars. ¶*a* ~ *theater (bank).*①

—[名] 드라이브인(자동차를 타고 들어가는 각종 시설) ¶①드라이브인 극장(은행)

driv·el [drív(ə)l] *vi.* (**-eled, -el·ing** or *Brit.* **-elled, -el·ling**) **1.** let liquid run from the mouth; flow from the mouth like liquid. **2.** talk childish nonsense. **—*n.*** [U] **1.** liquid running from the mouth. **2.** stupid, foolish talk.

—[自] 1. 침을 흘리다; 침처럼 흐르다 2. 철없는 소리를 하다 —[名] 1. 침 2. 철없는 소리

‡driv·en [drív(ə)n] *v.* pp. of **drive**.

‡driv·er [dráivər] *n.* [C] **1.** a person who drives a car, carriage, railway engine, etc. **2.** a person who makes other people work hard. **3.** a golf club with a wooden head.

—[名] 1. 운전수, 마부, 조종사, 기관수 2. [부하를 마구 부려먹는] 감독, 십장 3. 장타용 골프채

drive·way [dráivwèi] *n.* [C] (chiefly *U.S.*) a road for automobiles to drive on.

—[名] [美] 자동차 도로

driv·ing belt [dráiviŋbèlt] *n.* [C] (*Machinery*) a belt that carries motion from an engine to machinery.

—[名] [기계의] 벨트

driz·zle [drízl] *vi.* rain in as small drops as mist. **—*n.*** [U] a rain of this kind. ▷**driz·zly** [-i] *adv.*

—[自] 이슬비가 내리다 —[名] 이슬비, 가랑비

droll [droul] *adj.* queer; funny; amusing. **—*n.*** [C] a droll person.

—[形] 익살맞은, 기묘한; 재미있는 —[名] 익살꾸러기

drom·e·dar·y [drámədèri, drʌ́m- / drʌ́məd(ə)ri, drɔ́m-] *n.* [C] (pl. **-dar·ies**) a swift camel for riding, usu. with one hump.

—[名] [아라비아산] 단봉(單峰)낙타

drone¹ [droun] *n.* [C] **1.** a male honeybee. **2.** a person who does not like to work. **—*vi.*** spend time idly.

—[名] 1. 수벌 2. 게으름뱅이 —[自] 무위도식하다

drone² [droun] *vi.* **1.** make a low, continuous, humming sound. **2.** talk in a monotonous voice. **—*vt.*** utter (words) in a low, monotonous voice. **—*n.*** [C] a low, continuous humming sound.

—[自] 1. 윙윙 울리다 2. 단조롭게 말하다 —[他] …을 단조롭게 말(노래)하다 —[名] 윙윙거리는 소리; 단조로운 저음

•droop [dru:p] *vi.* **1.** hang down; sink down. **2.** become weak; lose strength; become discouraged. **—*vt.*** let (one's eyes, neck, etc.) hang or sink down. **—*n.*** [C] the state of drooping. ▷**droop·ing·ly** [-iŋli] *adv.*

—[自] 1. 수그러지다, 눈을 내리 깔다 2. 약해지다; 원기가 없어지다 —[他] [눈·목 따위]를 숙이다, 수그리다 —[名] 수그림, 의기소침

‡drop [drap / drɔp] *v.* (**dropped, drop·ping**) ***vi.*** **1.** fall. ¶*An apple dropped from the tree.* **2.** fall in drops. ¶*The tears dropped from her eyes.* **3.** fall suddenly; fall dead, wounded, exhausted, etc. ¶~ *to* (or *on*) *one's knees*① / ~ *into the chair*② / *The wounded man dropped dead.*③ **4.** go down. ¶*He dropped from the window to the ground.* **5.** become lower. ¶*The temperature suddenly dropped.* **6.** come to an end; stop. **7.** come into a certain state. ¶~ *asleep*④ / ~ *into slumber* (*oblivion*).⑤ **—*vt.*** **1.** let (something) fall. ¶*I dropped a teacup.* **2.** let (liquid) fall in drops. ¶*She dropped tears over his death.*⑥ **3.** knock down, shoot down. ¶~ *a pigeon.* **4.** put an end to (something); stop. ¶~ *a discussion.* **5.** send. ¶~ *a line.*⑦ **6.** suggest; hint. **7.** make (something) lower. ¶~ *one's voice.* **8.** let (someone) out of a car. ¶*Drop me at the next corner.*⑧ **9.** omit; give up; dismiss. ¶~ *one's bad habit.*

—[自] 1. 떨어지다 2. 방울져 떨어지다 3. [죽음·피로 따위로] 픽 쓰러지다 ¶①털썩 주저앉다/②털썩 의자에 앉다/③부상자는 픽 쓰러져 죽었다 4. 내리다 5. 내려가다 6. 끝나다; 멈추다 7. [어떤 상태로] 되다 ¶④잠들다/⑤잠들다(잊다) —[他] 1. …을 떨어뜨리다 2. …을 방울져 떨어지게 하다 ¶⑥그녀는 그의 죽음에 눈물을 흘렸다 3. …을 타도하다; 쏘아 떨어뜨리다 4. …을 끝내다; 그만두다 5. …을 [써서] 보내다 ¶⑦한 줄 써 보내다 6. …을 암시하다 7. …을 내리다 8. …을 하차시키다 ¶⑧다음 모퉁이에서 내려 주시오 9. …을 생략하다; 단념하다; 버리다

1) ***drop across,*** ⓐ meet (someone) by chance; come across (someone). ⓑ scold.

[熟] 1)ⓐ…와 마주치다 ⓑ…을 꾸짖다

D

dropping

2) *drop in* (=call) *at a place.*
3) *drop in* (=call) *on someone.*
4) *drop in with,* meet (*someone*) by chance.
5) *drop off,* ⓐ disappear. ⓑ become less. ⓒ fall asleep; die.
6) *drop on* (or *upon*), scold (someone) severely.
—*n.* ⓒ 1. a small fall of liquid. ¶ *~ by ~.*② 2. a very small quantity. ¶ *a ~ of mercy.* 3. anything like a drop in shape. ¶ *fruit drops.* 4. a sudden fall. ¶ *a ~ in prices.* 5. the length of a fall. ¶ *a ~ of 250 feet.*

drop·ping [drɔ́piŋ / drɔ́p-] *n.* ((*pl.*)) 1. something which is dropped. 2. dung of animals.

drop·sy [drɑ́psi / drɔ́p-] *n.* ⓤ (*Medicine*) an unnatural collection of watery fluid in some part of the body.

dross [drɔːs / drɔs] *n.* 1. ⓤ waste material formed on the surface of melting metals. 2. worthless stuff.

drought [draut] *n.* ⓤⓒ 1. a long period of dry weather. 2. ⓤ lack of water; dryness.

drought·y [dráuti] *adj.* (**drought·i·er, drought·i·est**) 1. suffering from drought. 2. dry; lacking water.

: drove¹ [drouv] *v.* pt. of **drive**.

drove² [drouv] *n.* ⓒ 1. a large group of cattle, sheep, etc. moving together. 2. a crowd of people.

dro·ver [dróuvər] *n.* ⓒ a man who takes cattle, sheep, etc., to market; a dealer in cattle.

: drown [draun] *vi.* die under water. —*vt.* 1. kill (someone) by keeping him under water. ¶ *be drowned*① *∣ ~ oneself.*② 2. cause (a sound) not to be heard by making a larger sound. 3. cause oneself to forget (something) by drinking.

drowse [drauz] *vi.* be sleepy; be half asleep; doze. —*vt.* make (someone) sleepy; spend (time) in drowsing. —*n.* ⓤ (sometimes *a ~*) the condition of being half asleep; doze.

* **drow·sy** [dráuzi] *adj.* (**-si·er, -si·est**) 1. half asleep; sleepy. 2. making half asleep. 3. caused by sleepiness. ▷**drow·si·ly** [-li] *adv.* —**drow·si·ness** [-nis] *n.*

drub [drʌb] *vt.* (**drubbed, drub·bing**) 1. beat (someone) with a stick; beat. 2. defeat (someone) soundly in a fight, game, etc. ▷**drub·ber** [drʌ́bər] *n.*

drudge [drʌdʒ] *n.* ⓒ a person who works hard at tiresome, unpleasant tasks. —*vi.* work like a drudge. ¶ *~ at dictionary-making.*①

drudg·er·y [drʌ́dʒ(ə)ri] *n.* ⓤ (pl. **-er·ies**) hard, uninteresting, or unpleasant work.

* **drug** [drʌg] *n.* ⓒ 1. any substance used as a medicine. 2. a habit-forming medical substance used to lessen pain or cause sleep.
—*vt.* (**drugged, drug·ging**) 1. mix harmful drugs in (food, etc.). 2. give [harmful] drugs to (someone). 3. affect (the body or senses) in an unnatural way.

drug·gist [drʌ́gist] *n.* ⓒ 1. a person who sells drugs, medicines, etc. 2. (*U.S.*) a person who has a license to make medicine according to a doctor's direction. (cf. *Brit.* chemist)

drug·store [drʌ́gstɔːr] *n.* ⓒ (*U. S.*) a store where drugs, cigarettes, ice cream, etc. are sold.

: drum [drʌm] *n.* ⓒ 1. a musical instrument that makes a sound when beaten. ¶ *beat a march on the ~.*① 2. the sound made by a drum; any sound like this. 3. any drumlike object. 4. a drumlike part of a machine. —*vt.* (**drummed, drum·ming**) 1. play (music, etc.) on a drum. 2. beat, tap, or strike again and again. ¶ *~ the table with one's fingers.*② 3. train by repeating.

drum

2)[장소]에 들르다 3)[남]에게 들르다 4)…와 마주치다 5)ⓐ사라지다 ⓑ줄다 ⓒ잠자다; 죽다 6)…을 몹시 꾸짖다

—ⓝ 1. 물방울 ¶⑨한 방울씩 2. 소량, 미량 3. 물방울 모양의 것 4. 급락, 하락 5. 낙하 거리

—ⓝ 1. 방울져 떨어지는 것 2.[짐승의] 똥

—ⓝ 수종증(水腫症)

—ⓝ 1. 쇠찌꺼기; 쇠똥 2. 가치 없는 것

—ⓝ 1. 한발, 가뭄 2.[대기 따위의] 건조, 수분 부족

—ⓐ 1. 한발의 2. 바싹 마른

—ⓝ 1.[떼를 지어 움직이는] 가축 떼 2. 군중

—ⓝ 가축을 시장으로 몰고 가는 사람, 가축 장수

—ⓥ 물에 빠져 죽다 —ⓥ 1. …을 익사시키다 ¶①익사하다/②투신 자살하다 2. …을 들리지 않게 하다 3. …을 술로 잊어버리다

—ⓥ 졸다 —ⓥ …을 꾸벅꾸벅 졸게 하다; [세월]을 부질없이 보내다 —ⓝ 졸음; 선잠, 풋잠

—ⓐ 1. 졸린, 졸리는 듯한 2. 졸음이 오는 3. 꾸벅꾸벅 조는

—ⓥ 1. …을 몽둥이로 치다; 때리다 2. …을 패배시키다

—ⓝ 악착스럽게 일하는 사람 —ⓥ 싫은 일을 악착같이 일하다 ¶①사전 만드는 일에 애를 쓰다

—ⓝ 단조롭고 기계적인 일

—ⓝ 1. 약[품] 2. 마약

—ⓥ 1.[음식]에 독약(마약)을 섞다 2. …에 독약(마약)을 먹이다 3. …을 취(마비)시키다

—ⓝ 1. 약종상 2.《美》약제사

—ⓝ《美》드러그스토어(약 이외에도 담배·아이스크림 따위도 제공)

—ⓝ 1. 북 ¶①진군의 북을 울리다 2. 북소리; 그와 비슷한 소리 3. 북 같은 것 4.[기계의] 원통형 부분

—ⓥ 1.[북으로 곡]을 연주하다 2. …을 둥둥 두드리다 ¶②손가락으로 이불을 똑똑 두드리다 3. …을 되풀이

(~ something *into*) ¶~ *complaints into someone's ears*③ / ~ *a lesson into someone.*④ —*vi.* **1.** beat a drum. **2.** beat rhythmically over and over again. **3.** make a sound like that of a drum. 1) ***drum someone out of,*** send someone away from (a club, etc.) in disgrace. 2) ***drum up,*** call (customers, etc.) together by drumming; collect; gather.

하여 가르치다 ¶③…에게 잔소리를 쉴새없이 하다/④학과를 …에게 되풀이 가르치다. —[自] 1. 북을 치다 2. 둥둥 치다(두드리다) 3. 북 같은 소리를 내다 [熟] 1)…을 …에서 몰아내다; 추방(제명)하다 2)북을 쳐서 …을 모으다

drum·beat [drʌ́mbìːt] *n.* [C] a sound produced by beating a drum.
—[名] 북소리

drum major [∠ ∠–] *n.* a person who leads a marching band.
—[名] [연대의] 고수장(鼓手長), 군악대장

drum·mer [drʌ́mər] *n.* [C] **1.** a person who plays a drum. **2.** (*U.S.*) a traveling salesman.
—[名] 1. 고수(鼓手) 2. 《美》 [지방] 순회 외판원

drum·stick [drʌ́mstìk] *n.* [C] a stick for beating a drum.
—[名] 북채

***drunk** [drʌŋk] *v.* pp. of **drink.**
—*adj.* (in *predicative*) **1.** overcome by alcoholic drink; intoxicated. ¶*get* ~① / *be beastly* (or *blind, dead*) ~.② **2.** deeply moved; very excited. ¶*be* ~ *with success.* —*n.* [C] **1.** a drunken person. **2.** a drinking party.
—[形] 1. 술취한 ¶①취하다/②곤드레만드레 취해 있다 2. 흥분한, 열중한 —[名] 1. 술주정뱅이 2. 술잔치

drunk·ard [drʌ́ŋkərd] *n.* [C] a person who is often drunk or who drinks too much.
—[名] 술고래, 술주정뱅이

*drunk·en** [drʌ́ŋk(ə)n] *adj.* (in *attributive*) **1.** drunk. ↔sober **2.** caused by or resulting from a drunken condition. ¶*a* ~ *brawl.*① ▷**drunk·en·ly** [-li] *adv.*
—[形] 1. 술취한, 술고래의 2. 술로 인한 ¶①술김의 싸움

drunk·en·ness [drʌ́ŋk(ə)nnis] *n.* [U] the state or habit of being drunk.
—[名] 술취함, 명정(酩酊)

drupe [druːp] *n.* [C] a fruit with a hard, stone-like seed surrounded by a soft, fleshy part, such as plums and peaches.
—[名] 핵과(核果); 다육과(多肉果)

⁑dry [drai] *adj.* (**dri·er, dri·est**) **1.** not wet; not moist. ¶*a* ~ *towel.* **2.** having little or no water. ¶*a* ~ *well.* **3.** having little or no rain. ¶*a* ~ *season.* **4.** thirsty. ¶*feel* ~. **5.** not giving milk. ¶*a* ~ *cow.* **6.** not shedding tears; showing no feeling. ¶*a* ~ *laugh* / ~ *thanks.* **7.** not interesting; dull. **8.** not sweet. ¶~ *wine.* **9.** without butter, jam, etc. on it. ¶~ *toast.*
—[形] 1. 마른 2. 물기 없는 3. 비가 오지 않는 4. 목마른 5. 젖이 안 나오는 6. 눈물을 흘리지 않는; 감정을 나타내지 않는 7. 시시한 8. 단맛이 없는 9. 버터(잼 따위)를 바르지 않은

—*vt.* make (something) dry; wipe away moisture from (something). ¶~ *your eyes* / ~ *oneself*① / ~ *your hands on this towel.* —*vi.* become dry; lose moisture. ***dry up,*** ⓐ become completely dry; become intellectually unable to produce. ⓑ (*colloq.*) stop talking.
—[他] …을 말리다; …의 수분을 닦아내다 ¶①몸의 물기를 닦다
—[自] 마르다
[熟] ⓐ바싹 마르다; [지식 따위가] 고갈되다 ⓑ《口》이야기를 그치다

dry·ad, Dry- [dráiəd / -æd] *n.* [C] (pl. **-ads** or **-a·des** [-diːz]) (in Greek mythology) a goddess who lives in a tree; a spirit of the forest.
—[名] 숲의 여신, 나무의 요정(妖精)

dry battery [∠ ∠––] *n.* a dry electric battery.
—[名] 건전지

dry cleaning [∠ ∠–] *n.* the cleaning of cloth without water.
—[名] 드라이 클리이닝, 건식(乾式) 세탁법

dry·er [dráiər] *n.* =drier.

dry·ly [dráili] *adv.* without emotion; in a dry manner.
—[副] 냉담하게; 무미건조하게

dry·ness [dráinis] *n.* [U] the state of being dry; lack of emotion.
—[名] 건조; 냉담, 무미건조

dry rot [∠ ∠] *n.* [U] **1.** a decay of wood, causing it to become a dry powder. **2.** any moral decay.
—[名] 1. [목재의] 건조 부패 2. [도덕의] 퇴폐, 타락

dry-shod [dráiʃɑ́d / -ʃɔ́d] *adj.* without wetting the feet or shoes.
—[形] 발(신)을 적시지 않는

du·al [d(j)úːəl / djú(ː)-] *adj.* of two; showing two; having two parts; double; twofold. ¶~ *control.*①
—[形] 둘의, 이중의, 이중성의, 이원적(二元的)인 ¶①이중 제어(二重制御)

du·al·ism [d(j)úːəliz(ə)m / djú(ː)-] *n.* **1.** [U] the state of being dual; duality. **2.** (*Philosophy*) the theory that the world can be explained in terms of two basic substances or principles, such as mind and body.
—[名] 1. 이중성, 이원성 2. 《哲》 이원론

du·al·i·ty [d(j)uːǽliti / dju(ː)-] *n.* [U][C] (pl. **-ties**) a dual condition or quality.
—[名] 이중성, 이원성

dub¹ [dʌb] *vt.* (**dubbed, dub·bing**) **1.** make (someone) a knight by touching him on the shoulder lightly with a
—[他] 1. 검으로 어깨를 가볍게 두드리고 …에게 나이트 작위를 수여하다 2.

sword. **2.** give (someone) a title, nickname, etc.; call. ¶~ *someone a scholar.*
…에게 직함(별명)을 주다(붙이다); …을 …이라고 부르다

dub² [dʌb] *n.* [C] (*slang*) an awkward, unskillful person.
—[名] 서투른(손재주 없는) 사람

dub³ [dʌb] *vt.* (**dubbed, dub·bing**) make a new recording on or for (a film) by adding music, speech, etc. —*n.* [U] the sound thus added or altered.
—[他] [필름에 음악 따위의] 새로운 녹음을 하다 —[名] [필름에] 새로 넣은 녹음

du·bi·ous [d(j)ú:biəs / djú:bi-] *adj.* **1.** doubtful; uncertain; ambiguous. ↔clear, simple ¶*a ~ answer* / *~ weather* / *He felt ~ what to do.*① **2.** questionable; causing suspicion. ¶*a ~ character.*② ▷**du·bi·ous·ly** [-li] *adv.*
—[形] 1. 미심쩍은; 분명하지 않은; 애매한 ¶①그는 어떻게 할지 망설였다 2. 수상한; 의혹이 생기는 ¶②수상한 인물

Dub·lin [dʌ́blin] *n.* the capital of the Irish Republic.
—[名] 아일란드 공화국의 수도

du·cal [d(j)ú:k(ə)l / djú:-] *adj.* of a duke or dukedom.
—[形] 공작의; 공작령(公爵領)의

•**duch·ess** [dʌ́tʃis] *n.* [C] **1.** the wife or widow of a duke. **2.** a woman with a rank equal to a duke's.
—[名] 1. 공작 부인, 공작 미망인 2. 여자 공작

duch·y [dʌ́tʃi] *n.* [C] (pl. **duch·ies**) the land ruled by a duke or duchess; dukedom.
—[名] 공국(公國), 공작령(公爵領)

:duck¹ [dʌk] *n.* [C] **1.** a wild or domestic swimming bird; the female duck. ↔drake **2.** [U] the flesh of a duck. **3.** a term of affection. **4.** (*slang*) a person; a fellow.
1) ***duck*[*s*] *and drake*[*s*],** a game in which flat stones are made to skip along the water.
2) ***a fine day for* [*young*] *ducks,*** rainy weather.
3) ***like water off a duck's back,*** with no effect.
4) ***make ducks and drakes of money,*** waste money foolishly.
5) ***take to something like a duck to water,*** learn something naturally and very easily.

—[名] 1. 오리; 집오리; 오리의 암컷 2. 오리(집오리)의 고기 3. 귀여운 사람; 애인 4. 《俗》 사람, 녀석
[熟] 1)물수제비 뜨기 2)비오는 날 3)쓸모없는, 마이동풍격으로 4)돈을 낭비하다 5)…을 아주 자연스럽게(쉽게) 배우다

:duck² [dʌk] *vi.* **1.** dip suddenly [under water etc.] for a short time. ¶~ *under a desk.* **2.** lower or move to one side suddenly. —*vt.* **1.** dip (the body, head, etc.) under water for a short time. **2.** lower (the head, body, etc.) suddenly. —*n.* [C] the act of ducking.
—[自] 1. 쏙 [물속으로] 들어가다 2. 머리를 홱 숙이다(몸을 비키다) —[他] 1. …을 홱 물속에 처박다 2. …을 홱 내리다 —[名] 머리(몸)을 홱 숙이기(내리기)

duck³ [dʌk] *n.* **1.** [U] strong cotton or linen cloth. **2.** 《*pl.*》 trousers or slacks made of duck.
—[名] 1. 일종의 즈크, 돛베 2. 즈크 즈봉(바지)

duck⁴ [dʌk] *n.* [C] an army truck which can be used both on land and in water.
—[名] [수륙 양용의] 군용 수송 트럭

duck·bill [dʌ́kbìl] *n.* [C] a small, bird-like water mammal of Australia that lays eggs.
—[名] 오리너구리

duck·ing [dʌ́kiŋ] *n.* [U] **1.** the manner of ducking. **2.** the sport of hunting wild ducks.
—[名] 1. 머리(몸)를 갑자기 숙이기 2. 오리 사냥

duck·ling [dʌ́kliŋ] *n.* [C] a young duck.
—[名] 오리 새끼

duct [dʌkt] *n.* [C] **1.** a tube for carrying water, air, wires, etc. **2.** a tube in the body carrying a bodily liquid like tears. ¶*a tear ~.*①
—[名] 1. 수송관(管), 도관(導管) 2. 선(腺) ¶①누선(淚腺)

duc·tile [dʌ́ktil / -ta(i)l] *adj.* **1.** that can be drawn out into the form of a wire. ¶*Copper is highly ~.* **2.** that can be easily shaped. **3.** easily influenced or led.
—[形] 1. 잡아 늘일 수 있는 2. [점토 따위가] 어떤 모양으로도 되는 3. [성질이] 유순한

duc·til·i·ty [dʌktíliti] *n.* [U] the quality of being ductile.
—[名] 연성(延性); 유연성; 유순함

dudg·eon [dʌ́dʒ(ə)n] *n.* [U] anger. ¶*be in high* (or *great, deep*) *~.*①
—[名] 노여움, 화 ¶①몹시 화가 나 있다

:due [d(j)u: / dju:] *adj.* **1.** (of a debt, bill, etc.) scheduled or expected to be paid or to be ready; (of a train, etc.) scheduled to arrive. ¶*the ~ date* / *The bill is ~ on the 25th inst.* / *The train is ~ at 7:30 p.m.* **2.** proper; suitable. ¶*a ~ reward for the work*① / *in ~ time.* **3.** fair; considerable. ¶*after ~ consideration.*②
1) ***be due to*** ⓐ be owing to; be caused by (something). ¶*The accident was ~ to his carelessness.*③ / *Poor harvest* [*which is*] *~ to bad weather.* ⓑ should be given to (someone). ¶*Half the money is ~ to me.* / *Punishment is ~ to him.*④
2) ***be due*** (=*be appointed* or *scheduled*) ***to do.*** ¶*He is ~ to come here tonight.*
3) ***in due course,*** in good time; at the proper time.

—[形] 1. [부채 따위] 지불하기로 되어 있는; 지불 기일이 된; [열차 따위] 도착 예정의 2. 상응하는; 당연한 ¶①노동에 대한 당연한 보수 3. 상당한 ¶②잘 생각한 끝에
[熟] 1)ⓐ…의 탓이다 ¶③그 사고는 그의 부주의의 탓이었다 ⓑ당연히 …에게 주어야 하다 ¶④그에게 벌을 주어야 한다 2)…할 예정이다 3)마침 좋은 때에

duel [367] **dump**

—*n.* **1.** ⓒ (*sing.* only) that which is owed, or which is required as a right. ¶*Courtesy is his ~ while he is your guest.*⑤ **2.** (usu. *pl.*) a regular fee; tax; charge. ¶*harbor dues.* ⌈*wind is ~ west.*⌉
—*adv.* (of direction) exactly. ¶*sail ~ south / The*

du·el [d(j)uːəl / djúː(ː)əl] *n.* ⓒ **1.** a private fight between two men with swords or pistols. ¶*fight a ~ with someone.* **2.** any fight between two persons. ¶*a ~ of wits*① */ a ~ of words.*② —*vi., vt.* (-eled, -el·ing or *Brit.* -elled, -el·ling) fight a duel; fight in a duel.

du·el·ist, esp. *Brit.* **-el·list** [d(j)úːəlist / djúː(ː)-] *n.* ⓒ a man who fights a duel. ⌈two players or singers.⌉

du·et [d(j)uːét / djuː(ː)-] *n.* ⓒ (*Music*) a tune or song for

duff·er [dʌ́fər] *n.* ⓒ (*Brit. slang*) a useless or foolish

:**dug** [dʌg] *v.* pt. and pp. of **dig**. ⌊person.⌋

du·gong [dúːgɔŋ, -gɔːŋ / d(j)úːgɔŋ] *n.* ⓒ a large fish-like animal living in tropical seas.

dug·out [dʌ́gàut] *n.* ⓒ **1.** (*Military*) a shelter dug in a hillside or the ground. **2.** a small shelter at the side of a baseball field, used by the players when not playing. **3.** a boat made of a large log.

:**duke** [d(j)uːk / djuːk] *n.* ⓒ **1.** (*Brit.*) a nobleman of the highest order, next below a prince. ↔**duchess 2.** a prince who rules a small state in some parts of Europe.

duke·dom [d(j)úːkdəm / djúːk-] *n.* **1.** ⓒ a small state ruled by a duke. **2.** Ⓤ the title or rank of a duke.

dul·cet [dʌ́lsit] *adj.* sweet; pleasing, esp. to the ear.

:**dull** [dʌl] *adj.* **1.** not sharp. ¶*a ~ pencil / a ~ knife.* **2.** stupid; slow to learn or understand. ¶*a ~ pupil / a ~ student.* **3.** not bright or clear. ¶*a ~ color / a ~ sound.* **4.** not interesting. ¶*a ~ book.* **5.** not sensitive. **6.** not active. ¶*Business is ~ this winter.* **7.** not felt keenly. ¶*a ~ pain.* ⌈*blade.* —*vi.* become dull.⌉
—*vt.* make (something) dull. ¶*~ the pain / the*

dull·ard [dʌ́lərd] *n.* ⓒ a dull or stupid person.

dull·ness [dʌ́lnis] *n.* Ⓤ the state of being dull.

dul·ly [dʌ́l(l)i] *adv.* in a dull manner.

du·ly [d(j)úːli / djúː-] *adv.* **1.** properly. **2.** sufficiently. **3.** on time. ⌈*to hand.*①⌉
duly to hand, properly received. ¶*Your letter is ~*

:**dumb** [dʌm] *adj.* **1.** having no power of speech. **2.** silent. ¶*a ~ show.*① **3.** (*U. S. colloq.*) stupid; dull.
1) *be struck dumb with* (=cannot speak for the moment because of) *horror, surprise, etc.*
2) *strike someone dumb,* make someone speechless with surprise.

dumb·bell [dʌ́mbèl] *n.* ⓒ a short bar with a heavy ball at each end, used for exercising. ¶*~ exercise*①.

dumb·found [dʌmfáund] *vt.* =dumfound

dumb show [´ `] *n.* **1.** a gesture without speech. **2.** a part of a play given in gestures; a pantomime.

dum·found [dʌmfáund] *vt.* make (someone) unable to speak because of surprise.

dum·my [dʌ́mi] *n.* ⓒ (pl. **-mies**) **1.** (*slang*) a person who is dumb. **2.** a figure made in human form, used for showing clothes, etc. **3.** a person who acts for another. **4.** an imitation; a sham.
—*adj.* (**-mi·er, -mi·est**) sham; looking like a real one.

dump [dʌmp] *vt.* **1.** let (something) fall in a mass; throw (something) down. **2.** (*Commerce*) sell (large quantities of goods) at excessively low prices, esp. in a foreign country. —*vi.* fall in a mass.
—*n.* ⓒ **1.** a place where rubbish is thrown away; a heap of rubbish; a place where loads are emptied out.

—名 1. 당연히 지불되어야 할 것 ¶⑤ 그가 네 손님인 이상 당연히 그에게는 예절을 다해야 한다 2. 회비; 세금; 사용료
—副 똑바로 …, 정(正)…
—名 1. 결투 2. 두 사람 사이의 싸움; 경기 ¶①지혜의 시합/②말다툼
—自他 결투하다

—名 결투자

—名〔樂〕이중창(주), 이중창(주)곡

—名〔英俗〕바보, 얼간이; 건달

—動 …을 파다, 땅을 파다의 과거·과거분사

—名 듀우공(인도양에 사는 포유동물)

—名 1.〔軍〕대피호 2. [야구장의] 선수 대기소 3. 통나무배

—名 1. 공작 2. 대공(大公)

—名 1. 군주의 영토; 공국(公國) 2. 공작의 지위(신분) ⌈좋은⌉
—形 [특히 음색이] 아름다운; 기분
—形 1. 무딘; 잘 들지 않는 2. [머리가] 둔한; 어리석은 3. 밝지(맑지) 못한, 흐린 4. 재미없는, 지루한 5. 감각이 둔한; 무감각의 6. 활발하지 못한; 부진한 7. [아픔이] 무지근하게 느껴지는
—他 …을 무디게 하다 —自 무디어
—名 둔재, 바보 ⌊지다.⌋
—名 무딤; 활기 없음; 단조로움
—副 둔하게, 활기 없게
—副 1. 정당하게, 적당히 2. 충분히 3. 때에 알맞게 ⌈을 받았읍니다.⌉
熟 어김없이 받았음 ¶①귀하의 서한
—形 1. 말을 못하는, 벙어리의 2. 침묵의; 말수 적은 ¶①무언극 3. 어리석은, 저능한
熟 1) …에 깜짝 놀라다 2) …을 깜짝 놀라게 하다

—名 아령 ¶①아령 체조

—名 1. 몸짓 2. 무언극

—他 …을 아연실색케 하다

—名 1.〔俗〕벙어리 2. [양품점 따위의] 모델 인형, [사격 연습용의] 표적 인형 3. 남의 대신 노릇을 하는 사람 4. 가짜, 모조품
—形 가짜의, 간판뿐인
—他 1. …을 쿵하고 내리다(떨어뜨리다), [쓰레기 따위]를 버리다 2.〔商〕투매(덤핑)하다 —自 쿵하고 떨어지다

—名 1. 쓰레기장; 쓰레기 더미; 짐 내리는 곳 2. 쿵(털썩)하는 소리

2. a sound which is made when something falls down in a mass.
do not care a dump, do not care at all.
[熟] 조금도 개의치 않다

dump·ing [dʌ́mpiŋ] *n.* [U] the act of selling goods at excessively low prices.
—[名] 투매, 덤핑

dump·ling [dʌ́mpliŋ] *n.* [C] a pudding of dough, often folded over and containing fruit or meat.
—[名] 고기·사과를 넣고 구운 경단

dumps [dʌmps] *n. pl.* a gloomy state of mind; melancholy. ¶*be in the* ~.①
—[名] 우울 ¶①우울해하고 있다

dump·y [dʌ́mpi] *adj.* (**dump·i·er, dump·i·est**) short and thick.
—[形] 땅딸막한, 굵고 짧은

dun[1] [dʌn] *vt.* (**dunned, dun·ning**) repeatedly demand that (someone) pay a debt. —*n.* [C] a person who duns.
—[他] …에게 귀찮게 빚을 독촉하다
—[名] 재촉이 심한 빚장이

dun[2] [dʌn] *n.* [U] a dull grayish-brown. —*adj.* of a dull grayish-brown.
—[名] 암갈색 —[形] 암갈색의

dunce [dʌns] *n.* [C] a stupid person who is not clever at learning; a stupid pupil.
—[名] 바보[학생]; 열등생

dun·der·head [dʌ́ndərhèd] *n.* [C] a stupid person.
—[名] 바보, 얼간이

dune [d(j)u:n / dju:n] *n.* [C] a low sand hill heaped up by the wind, esp. near a shore.
—[名] 모래언덕

dung [dʌŋ] *n.* [U] the waste matter of animals; manure. —*vt.* manure (the ground) with dung.
—[名] [마소의] 똥; 거름 —[他] [토지]에 비료를 주다

dun·geon [dʌ́ndʒ(ə)n] *n.* [C] **1.** a dark underground prison, esp. in an old castle. **2.** a great tower of a castle.
—[名] 1. 지하 감옥 2. [성곽의] 내성(內城)

dung·hill [dʌ́ŋhìl] *n.* [C] **1.** a heap of waste matter from animals. **2.** a wicked place or person.
—[名] 1. 똥(거름) 더미 2. 더러운 곳(사람)

dupe [d(j)u:p / dju:p] *n.* [C] a person who is easily tricked or who believes everything. —*vt.* trick; deceive; cheat.
—[名] 잘 속는 사람 —[他] …을 속이다, 기만하다

du·plex [d(j)ú:pleks / djú:-] *adj.* double; twofold.
—[形] 이중의

du·pli·cate [d(j)ú:plikit / djú:- ∥ →*v.*] *adj.* **1.** double; consisting of two equal parts. ¶*Man's lungs are* ~.① **2.** exactly like another. ¶*a* ~ *copy* / *a* ~ *key.*②
—[形] 1. 이중의; 한 쌍의 ¶①사람의 폐는 쌍을 이루고 있다 2. 아주 똑같은; 사본(寫本)의, 부(副)의, 복제(複製)의 ¶②같은 열쇠

—*n.* [C] something made exactly like another; a copy.
—[名] 부본(副本), 사본, 복제

in duplicate, in two copies. ¶*type a letter in* ~.
[熟] 정부(正副) 2통으로

—*vt.* [-kèit] make an exact copy of (something).
—[他] …을 복사하다

du·pli·ca·tion [d(j)ù:plikéiʃ(ə)n / djù:-] *n.* **1.** [U] the act of duplicating; the state of being duplicated. **2.** [C] a copy.
—[名] 1. 복제, 복사; 이중 2. 복제물, 복사물

du·pli·ca·tor [d(j)ú:plikèitər / djú:plikèitə] *n.* [C] a machine or person that makes copies.
—[名] 복사기; 복사하는 사람

du·plic·i·ty [d(j)u(:)plísiti / djù:-] *n.* [U] the act of doing something in two different manners to deceive others.
—[名] [언행 따위의] 표리부동, 겉과 속이 다름; 딴 속셈

du·ra·bil·i·ty [d(j)uərəbíliti / djùərə-] *n.* [U] the quality of lasting long; ability to continue long in the same state.
—[名] 영속성; 내구성(耐久性)

du·ra·ble [d(j)úərəbl / djúər-] *adj.* lasting a long time; able to continue long in the same state.
—[形] 오래 견디는; 내구성이 있는

du·ral·u·min [d(j)uərǽljumin / djuər-] *n.* [U] a light, strong metal that is a mixture of aluminum, copper, manganese, etc., used in aircraft, etc.
—[名] 듀랄루민

du·ra·tion [d(j)uəréiʃ(ə)n / djuər-] *n.* [U] **1.** the state of continuing in time. **2.** the period of time during which anything lasts. ¶*be of long* (*short*) ~.①
—[名] 1. 지속 2. 지속 기간 ¶①오래 지속하다(지속 못 하다)

du·ress [d(j)úəris / djuərés, djúəres] *n.* [U] **1.** imprisonment. **2.** threats used to force someone to do something. ¶*under* ~.①
—[名] 1. 감금 2. 강제, 협박 ¶①협박 받아

⁑**dur·ing** [d(j)úəriŋ / djúər-] *prep.* **1.** throughout the time of. ¶~ *the day.*① **2.** at some point of time in. ¶*He called on me sometime* ~ *the week.*
—[前] 1. … 동안 [죽] ¶①하루종일 2. …사이에, 사이

durst [də:rst] *v.* (*archaic*) pt. of **dare.**

*·**dusk** [dʌsk] *n.* [U] a state between darkness and light; time just before it gets quite dark. ↔dawn
—[名] 땅거미; 황혼; 어둠

at dusk, at the time just before dark.
[熟] 땅거미질 때

—*adj.* dark; dusky. —*vt., vi.* make (something) dim or dark; become or look dark.
—[形] 어스레한 —[他][自] 어둑어둑해지[게 하]다

dusk·i·ness [dʌ́skinis] *n.* [U] the state of being dusky.
—[名] 어둑어둑함

dusk·y [dʌ́ski] *adj.* (**-i·er, -i·est**) somewhat dark.
—[形] 어둑어둑한, 어스레한

⁑**dust** [dʌst] *n.* [U] **1.** very small pieces of waste matter;
—[名] 1. 먼지, 티끌 ¶①구름 같은 먼지

dust bin [369] **duty-free**

powder of earth. ¶*a cloud of* ~.① **2.** earth; soil. **3.** any powder. ¶*be crushed into* ~.② **4.** ((*the* ~)) (*poetic*) a dead and decayed human body. **5.** (*Brit.*) rubbish.
1) *bite the dust*, die; get wounded.
2) *lick the dust*, ⓐ =bite the dust. ⓑ humble oneself like a slave.
3) *shake the dust off one's feet*, go away in anger.
4) *throw dust in someone's eyes*, deceive; mislead.
—*vt.* **1.** cover (something) with powder; sprinkle (powder) over something. ¶~ *a cake with sugar* / ~ *sand over the ground*.③ **2.** take the dust off (something). ¶~ *a room*. ⌈and household rubbish are kept.⌉
dust bin [´-´] *n.* (*Brit.*) a can or box in which ashes
dust·er [dʌ́stər] *n.* ⓒ **1.** a person who takes off dust. **2.** a thing which takes off dust; a cloth or brush for removing dust. **3.** a long, light, coat worn to keep dust off or out. **4.** a machine for scattering dust or powder on something.
dust·man [dʌ́stmən] *n.* ⓒ (**-men** [-mən]) (*Brit.*) a man employed to remove rubbish.
dust·pan [dʌ́stpæn] *n.* ⓒ a flat, broad pan in which dust is collected and removed.
dust·y [dʌ́sti] *adj.* (**dust·i·er, dust·i·est**) **1.** covered with dust. **2.** like dust in appearance. **3.** having a color ⌉ *not so dusty*, not so bad. ⌊similar to that of dust.⌋ ▷**dust·i·ly** [-li] *adv.* —**dust·i·ness** [-nis] *n.*
Dutch [dʌtʃ] *adj.* of the Netherlands, its people, or their language. ⌈(someone) severely.⌉ *talk to someone like a Dutch uncle*, preach to or scold
—*n.* **1.** ⓤ the language of the Netherlands. **2.** ((*the* ~)) the people of the Netherlands.
1) *beat the Dutch*, be very surprising.
2) *double Dutch*, a language that cannot be understood at all. ⌈penses for) a meal, etc.⌉
3) *go Dutch on* (=*have each person pay his own ex-*
4) *in Dutch*, (*slang*) in trouble, in disgrace.
Dutch auction [´ ´-´] *n.* a sale where the price gradually comes down until a buyer is found.
Dutch bargain [´ ´-´] *n.* an agreement about buying and selling settled while drinking; a wet bargain.
Dutch comfort [´ ´-´] *n.* a comfort which is not really a comfort to the person to whom it is given.
Dutch courage [´ ´-´] *n.* courage produced under the influence of alcohol.
Dutch door [´ ´-´] *n.* a door consisting of two units.
Dutch·man [dʌ́tʃmən] *n.* ⓒ (pl. **-men** [-mən]) **1.** a person of the Netherlands; a Hollander. **2.** a Dutch ship. **3.** (*slang*) a German.
Dutch treat [´ ´-´] *n.* (*U. S. colloq.*) a meal or entertainment in which each person pays for himself.
du·te·ous [d(j)úːtiəs / djúː-] *adj.* (*poetic*) obedient; dutiful. ¶*a* ~ *servant*. ⌈on which a tax must be paid.⌉
du·ti·a·ble [d(j)úːtiəbl / djúː-] *adj.* (of imported goods)
du·ti·ful [d(j)úːtif(u)l / djúː-] *adj.* performing the duties of one's position; obedient to one's parents or elders. ¶*a* ~ *son*. ▷**du·ti·ful·ly** [-fuli] *adv.* —**du·ti·ful·ness** [-nis] *n.*
du·ty [d(j)úːti / djúːti] *n.* (pl. **-ties**) **1.** ⓒ what a person ought to do; an obligation. ¶*It's your* ~ *to do this work*. **2.** (often *pl.*) service that a person ought to do in his position. ¶*a* ~ *of a policeman*.① **3.** ⓤ respect; obedience. ¶*pay one's* ~ *to one's teacher*. **4.** ⓒ a tax; ((usu. *pl.*)) tax, on articles of foreign trade.
on (*off*) *duty*, at (not at) one's work.
du·ty-free [d(j)úːtifríː / djúːti-] *adj.* (of goods) free of

2. 흙 3. 가루, 분말 ¶②가루로 빻다 4. 《詩》 시체; 인간 5. 《英》 쓰레기, 재

图 1)죽다; 상처입다 2)ⓑ굴욕을 참다 3)자리를 박차고 가 버리다 4)속이다

—⑪ 1. …을 가루로 덮다; …에 [가루] 를 뿌리다 ¶③지면에 모래를 뿌리다 2. …의 먼지를 없애다

—⑫ 《英》 쓰레기통
—⑫ 1. 소제부, 먼지를 터는 사람 2. 총채; 청소기; 걸레 3. 먼지 막이로 입는 웃옷 4. [살충제 따위의] 살포기

—⑫ 《英》 쓰레기 인부

—⑫ 쓰레받기

—⑬ 1. 먼지투성이의, 먼지가 많은 2. 먼지 같은, 가루 모양의 3. 먼지 빛깔의, 회색의
图 그다지 나쁘지 않은
—⑬ 네덜란드의, 네덜란드 사람(말)의

图 엄하게 타이르다(꾸짖다)
—⑫ 1. 네덜란드 말 2. 네덜란드 사람 (국민)

图 1)깜짝 놀랄 만하다 2)횡설수설 3) [식사 따위] 비용을 각자 부담으로 하다 4)《俗》곤경에 빠져; 미움을 사서

—⑫ 값을 깎아 내려가는 경매

—⑫ 한 잔 마시면서 맺는 매매계약

—⑫ 전혀 위로가 되지 않는 위로

—⑫ 술김에 내는 용기

—⑫ 상하 2단으로 된 문짝
—⑫ 1. 네덜란드 사람 2. 네덜란드 배 3. 《俗》 독일인

—⑫ 《美口》 회비를 각자 부담하는 회식

—⑬ 《詩》 본분을 지키는, 순종하는

—⑬ 관세가 부과되는, 세금이 붙는
—⑬ 충실한; 효성스러운

—⑫ 1. 의무 2. 임무; 직무 ¶①경찰관으로서의 임무 3. 존경; 복종 4. 세금; 관세

图 당번(비번)의
—⑬ 면세의

dwarf [dwɔːrf] *n.* ⓒ (pl. **dwarfs**) **1.** a person, an animal, a plant, etc. much smaller than the usual size. **2.** (in fairy tales) a small ugly man with magic powers. ↔giant 「growth.」
　—*adj.* much smaller than the usual size; checked in
　—*vt., vi.* become smaller; make (something) smaller; keep (something) from growing large.
dwarf·ish [dwɔ́ːrfiʃ] *adj.* like a dwarf; much smaller than usual. 「its growth.」
dwarf tree [⌣ ⌣] *n.* a tree which has been checked in
‡**dwell** [dwel] *vi.* (**dwelt** or **dwelled**) (*archaic*) live; make one's home. (~ *at* or *in* some place)
　dwell on (or ***upon***), think, write, or speak about (something) for a long time; put emphasis on (something). ¶~ *on one's past failures*① / ~ *on the necessity of something.*②
dwell·er [dwélər] *n.* ⓒ a person who lives in a place. ¶*town dwellers.* 「lives.」
・**dwell·ing** [dwéliŋ] *n.* ⓒ a house; a place in which one
dwelling house [⌣⌣ ⌣] *n.* a house in which one lives.
・**dwelt** [dwelt] *v.* pt. and pp. of **dwell**.
dwin·dle [dwíndl] *vi.* become smaller and smaller; waste away; lose importance.
　dwindle away into nothing, waste away into nothing.
・**dye** [dai] *n.* Ⓤⓒ the material used to color cloth, hair, etc.; a color produced by such matter.
　a crime of the blackest (or ***deepest***) ***dye,*** a crime of the worst kind.
　—*vt.* color (something) with a dye. ¶~ *a white dress blue*①. —*vi.* become colored. ¶~ *well* (*badly*).②
　dye something in the grain; (*U.S.*) ***dye something in the wool,*** dye something before weaving; make something fixed or unchangeable.
・**dy·er** [dáiər] *n.* ⓒ a person whose business is to dye cloth.
dye·stuff [dáistʌf] *n.* Ⓤⓒ a material giving, or used as, a dye. 「factory where cloth is dyed.」
dye·works [dáiwə̀ːrks] *n. pl.* (used as *sing.* and *pl.*) a
‡**dy·ing** [dáiiŋ] *adj.* **1.** near to death; (of the sun) about to sink; about to disappear. **2.** (*slang*) anxious. ¶*She is ~ to go.*① 「about to die.」
　1) *one's dying words,* words spoken by one who is
　2) *till* (or *to*) *one's dying day,* till (or to) the day
　—*n.* death. 「when one dies.」
dyke [daik] *n., v.* =**dike**.
dy·nam·ic [dainǽmik] *adj.* **1.** (of force) in actual motion. ↔static; (of a person) active; forceful. **2.** of dynamics.
dy·nam·ics [dainǽmiks] *n. pl.* (used as *sing.*) **1.** a science that treats of motion. **2.** moving forces, physical or moral.
dy·na·mite [dáinəmàit] *n.* Ⓤ a kind of high explosive used in blasting rock, hard earth, etc. —*vt.* blow up (something) with dynamite.
dy·na·mo [dáinəmòu] *n.* ⓒ (pl. **-mos**) a machine for changing mechanical power into electric current.
dy·nas·tic [dainǽstik / dinǽstik, dai-] *adj.* of a dynasty.
dy·nas·ty [dáinəsti / dí-] *n.* ⓒ (pl. **-ties**) a series of rulers of the same family.
dys·en·ter·y [dís(ə)ntéri / dís(ə)ntri] *n.* Ⓤ (*Medical*) a disease of the bowels, accompanied by bloody discharges.
dys·pep·si·a [dispépsiə] *n.* Ⓤ poor digestion.
dys·pep·tic [dispéptik] *adj.* suffering from dyspepsia.
　—*n.* ⓒ a person suffering from dyspepsia.

—❷ 1. 난쟁이, 보통보다 작은 동(식) 물 2. [동화의] 난쟁이·마술사

—❸ 왜소한; 발육이 잘 안 된
—❸⾃ 작게 하다(되다); …의 발육을 방해하다, …을 위축시키다
—❸ 난쟁이 같은, 왜소한

—❷ 분재(盆栽)
—❸⾃ 거주하다
熟 …을 곰곰이 생각(궁리)하다; 자세히 설명하다; 강조(역설)하다 ¶①과거의 실패를 자꾸만 생각하다/②…의 필요성을 역설하다

—❷ 거주자; 주민

—❷ 집; 주소
—❷ 주택

—❸⾃ [점점] 작아지다, 감소하다; [명성 따위가] 줄어들다
熟 점점 줄어져 없어지다
—❷ 염료; 염색; 색조

熟 극악의 범죄

—❸ …을 물들이다 ¶①흰 옷을 푸르게 염색하다 —❸ 물들다 ¶②염색이 잘 되다(안 되다)
熟 [짜기 전에] 실에 물들이다; [사상 따위를] 깊이 스며들게 하다
—❷ 염색 업자

—❷ 물감, 염료

—❷ 염색 공장
—❸ 1. 죽어 가는, 빈사상태의; 저물어 가는; 사라질 듯한 2. (俗) 간절히 …하고 싶어하는 ¶①그녀는 몹시 가고 싶어한다
熟 1) 유언 2) 죽는 날까지
—❷ 죽음

—❸ 1. 동적인; 활력이 있는; 힘찬 2. 역학[상]의
—❷ 1. 동력학, 역학 2. 동력; 활력

—❷ 다이너마이트 —❸ …을 다이너마이트로 폭파하다

—❷ 다이너모우, 발전기

—❸ 왕조의
—❷ 왕조

—❷ (醫) 이질, 적리

—❷ 소화불량
—❸ 소화불량의, 위가 약한 —❷ 위가 약한 사람, 소화불량의 사람

E

E, e [i:] *n.* ⓒ (pl. **E's, Es, e's, es** [i:z]) **1.** The fifth letter of the English alphabet. **2.** (*Music*) the third tone or note in the C major scale.

E, E., e, e. [i:] east.

‡each [i:tʃ] *adj.* every one of. ¶ ~ *person* | *on* ~ *occasion.*
—*pron.* **1.** each person; each thing. ¶ ~ *of us* | *They hate* ~ *other.; Each hates the other.* **2.** all. ¶ *We* ~ *tried, but in vain.*① —*adv.* to or for each. ¶ *They cost a penny each.*

‡ea·ger [í:gər] *adj.* desiring very much; anxious; zealous. ¶ *an* ~ *contest* | *He is* ~ *to work.* | *We are* ~ *for (or after) peace.*①

·ea·ger·ly [í:gərli] *adv.* in a desirous manner; zealously.

·ea·ger·ness [í:gərnis] *n.* Ⓤ the state of being eager. ¶ *In his* ~ *to go abroad, he violated the law.*①
be all eagerness (= *be anxious*) **to do.**

‡ea·gle [í:gl] *n.* ⓒ **1.** a large bird with sharp eyes, powerful wings and hooked bill. **2.** a symbol using the eagle. **3.** (*U.S.*) an old gold coin worth 10 dollars.

ea·glet [í:glit] *n.* ⓒ a young eagle.

‡ear[1] [iər] *n.* ⓒ **1.** the organ, power, or sense of hearing. ¶ *the external* (*internal, middle*) ~① | *cover* (or *stop*) *one's ears*② | *A word in your* ~.③ | (*proverb*) *Walls have ears.*④ **2.** anything shaped like an ear. ¶ (*proverb*) *Little pitchers have long* (or *wide*) *ears.*⑤
1) **be all ears,** listen eagerly or attentively.
2) **fall on deaf ears,** not to be listened to; be ignored.
3) **go in one ear and out the other,** have no effect or make no impression.
4) **have an** (**no**) **ear for,** can (cannot) judge the worth of [music].
5) **have itching ears,** be very eager to near a rumor,
6) **have** (or **keep, hold**) **an ear to the ground,** pay careful attention to public opinion or situation of something.
7) **lend** (or **give**) **an ear,** listen; pay attention. ((~ *to*
8) **set by the ears,** cause disagreement or quarrel in or between (persons).
9) **turn a deaf ear,** refuse to listen; ignore.
10) **up to the ears,** deeply engaged, esp. in debt, etc.
▷**earlike** [-làik] *adj.*

ear[2] [iər] *n.* ⓒ the head or spike of grains. ¶ ~ *of wheat*① | *in* ~.② —*vi.* grow or form ears.

ear·ache [íərèik] *n.* ⓒⓊ pain in the ear.

·earl [əːrl] *n.* ⓒ (*Brit.*) a nobleman ranking between marquis and viscount. ⇒**N.B.**

earl·dom [ə́ːrldəm] *n.* **1.** ⓒ the land owned or ruled by an earl. **2.** Ⓤ the rank or title of an earl.

‡ear·ly [ə́ːrli] *adj.* (**-li·er, -li·est**) **1.** before the usual time. **2.** near the beginning of. ¶ ~ *fruits*① | ~ *spring*② | ~ *Christians.* **3.** in the near future. ¶ *at the earliest.*③
1) **an early bird,** an early riser.
2) **keep early hours,** rise and go to bed early.
—*adv.* **1.** before the usual time. ¶ *go to school* ~. **2.** near to the beginning of a period of time. ¶ *He had* ~ *learned.; He had learned early in life.*

ear·mark [íərmàːrk] *n.* **1.** ⓒ a mark put on the ear of

—⒩ 1. 영어 자모의 다섯째 글자 2. 《樂》「마」음

—⒫ 각각의,제각기의, 각자의 —⒭ 1. 각자; 각각 2.제각기 모두 ¶①우리들 모두가 해보았으나 허사였다 —⒜ 각자에게, 각자를 위하여

—⒫ 열심인, 열렬한; 열망하는 ¶①우리는 평화를 열망하고 있다

—⒜ 열심히, 열렬히

—⒩ 열심, 갈망, 열망 ¶①외국에 가려고 열망한 나머지 그는 법을 어겼다 🅟 ⋯하고 싶어 못견디다

—⒩ 1. 수리, 독수리 2. 독수리표 3. 《美》옛날의 10달러 금화

—⒩ 새끼 수리

—⒩ 1. 귀, 청력(聽力); 음감(音感); 청각 ¶①외(중・내)이/②귀를 막다, 들으려 하지 않다/③한 마디 할 말이 있네/④(俚)벽에도 귀가 있다, 낮 말은 새가 듣고 밤 말은 쥐가 듣는다 2. 귀 모양의 것 ¶⑤(俚)아이들은 귀는 밝다 🅟 1)열심히 귀를 기울이[고 있]다 2)들어 주지 않다; 무시당하다 3)한 쪽 귀로 들어가서 한 쪽 귀로 나가다, 쇠귀에 경 읽기다 4)[음악]을 알다(모르다) 5)[소문 따위를] 몹시 듣고 싶어 하다 6)여론에 귀를 기울이다; 정세에 주의를 기울이다 7)⋯에 귀를 기울이다, 경청하다 8)⋯을 다투게 하다, 불화하게 하다 9)⋯을 들으려 하지 않다; 무시하다 10)[빚 따위에 몰려] 꼼짝 못하여, 깊이 빠져

—⒩ [곡식의] 이삭 ¶①밀 이삭/②이삭이 패어 —⒱ 이삭이 [패어]나다

—⒩ 귀앓이

—⒩ 《英》백작 N.B. 유럽대륙의 count 에 상당함

—⒩ 1. 백작의 영지(領地) 2. 백작의 작위(신분)

—⒫ 1. 이른, 빠른 2. 초기의, 일찍되는, 올리는 ¶①맏물 과일/②이른봄 3. 가까운 장래의 ¶③일리도, 빨라도 🅟 1)일찍 일어나는 사람 2)일찍 자고 일찍 일어나다

—⒜ 1. 일찌기, 일찍감치 2. 초기에

—⒩ 1. [가축 따위의 귀에 다는] 표 2.

a domestic animal to show the owner of it. **2.** any mark put to show what the thing is; a sign. **—***vt.* **1.** make an earmark on (animals). **2.** set aside or reserve (something) for special purposes. ¶*~ the money for traveling.*①
[일반적으로] 표, 소유 기호 **—**[他] **1.** …의 귀에 표를 달다 **2.** …을 따로 젖혀놓다, [일정한 용도에 쓰려고] 따로 떼어두다 ¶①여행하려고 돈을 따로 떼어두다

:earn [ə:rn] *vt.* **1.** receive (money) for work, service, etc. ¶*~ 1,000 yen a day.* **2.** get (a good name, fame, etc.). **3.** be worthy of (something); deserve. ¶*You have earned our praise.*①
—[他] **1.** [돈]을 벌다, …의 수입을 얻다 **2.** [명성 따위]를 얻다 **3.** …을 받을 만하다 ¶①너의 행위는 칭찬받을 만하다

:ear·nest¹ [ə́:rnist] *adj.* **1.** serious and intense; sincerely zealous. **2.** important.
in earnest, serious[ly]; not joking[ly]; sincere[ly] and zealous[ly].
—[形] **1.** 진지한, 열심인, 열렬한 **2.** 중요한
[熟] 진지하게, 진심으로; 본격적으로

ear·nest² [ə́:rnist] *n.* [C] 《usu. *an ~*》 **1.** money partly paid in advance. **2.** a sign of what is to come; a token.
—[名] **1.** 착수금, 약조금, 보증금 **2.** 징조, 전조

ear·nest·ly [ə́:rnistli] *adv.* in an earnest manner.
—[副] 진지하게, 열심히

ear·nest·ness [ə́:rnistnis] *n.* [U] the state of being earnest.
—[名] 진지함, 진심, 열심

earn·ing [ə́:rniŋ] *n.* **1.** [U] the act of earning. **2.** 《*pl.*》 money earned by labor, etc.; gains; profits.
—[名] **1.** 벌기, 벌이 **2.** 소득, 수입

ear·phone [íərfòun] *n.* [C] a headphone.
—[名] 이어포운

ear·ring [íərrìŋ] *n.* [C] an ornament for the ear.
—[名] 귀고리, 귀엣고리

ear·shot [íərʃɑ̀t / -ʃɔ̀t] *n.* [U] the distance over which a sound, esp. of the human voice, can be heard; the range of hearing. ¶*be out of (within) ~.*①
—[名] [목소리・음 따위가] 들리는 거리, 부르면 들리는 거리 ¶①불러도 들리지 않는(들리는) 곳에 있다

:earth [ə:rθ] *n.* (pl. **earths** [ə:rθs, +*Brit.* ə:ðz] **1.** 《*the ~*》 the planet we live on. ¶*on the surface of the ~.* **2.** [U] the world we live in. ¶*while he was on ~.*① **3.** 《*the ~*》 the people who live on the earth. **4.** 《*the ~*》 land; ground. **5.** [U] soil. ¶*carry ~ in a car.*
1) ***come back*** (or ***down***) ***to earth,*** return to reality; stop dreaming.
2) ***move heaven and earth,*** make every effort to gain some aim.
3) ***run to earth,*** discover after a long search.
4) ***What on earth,*** What in the world … ¶*What on ~ was that?*
—*vt.* cover (roots) with earth.
—[名] **1.** 지구 **2.** 이 세상, 이승, 현세 ¶①그가 살아 있던 때 **3.** 지구상의 주민 **4.** 육지; 대지, 땅 **5.** 흙
[熟] 1)[꿈에서 깨어] 현실로 돌아오다; 몽상(환상)을 버리다 2)온갖 노력을 다하다 3)겨우 찾아(밝혀)내다 4) 도대체
—[他] [뿌리]에 흙을 덮다

earth·en [ə́:rθ(ə)n] *adj.* made of earth or baked clay.
—[形] 흙으로 만든; 오지로 만든

earth·en·ware [ə́:rθ(ə)nwɛ̀ər] *n.* [U] anything made of baked clay.
—[名] 토기, 도기(陶器), 오지그릇

·earth·ly [ə́:rθli] *adj.* (**-li·er, -li·est**) **1.** of the earth. ↔heavenly **2.** of this world; worldly. ¶*~ joys.* **3.** (*colloq.*) that may be thought or expected; possible. ¶*have no* (or *not an*) *~ chance*① / *something of no ~ use*② / *What ~ use can it be?*③
—[形] **1.** 지구의, 지상의 **2.** 현세의, 속세의, 이승의 **3.** 가능한 ¶①전혀 가망이 없다/②전혀 쓸모없는 것/③도대체 그것이 무슨 소용이 있단 말인가?

·earth·quake [ə́:rθkwèik] *n.* [C] a sudden violent shaking of the earth's surface.
—[名] 지진

earth·worm [ə́:rθwə̀:rm] *n.* [C] a worm living in the soil.
—[名] 지렁이

earth·y [ə́:rθi] *adj.* (**earth·i·er, earth·i·est**) **1.** of or like earth. **2.** of this world; worldly. **3.** unrefined; coarse.
—[形] **1.** 흙의, 지구(상)의 **2.** 세속(현세)의 **3.** 흙냄새 나는, 투박한, 조잡한

ear trumpet [´ ˘–] *n.* a trumpet-shaped tube held to the ear, used by a partially deaf person as a hearing aid.
—[名] 나팔형 보청기

:ease [i:z] *n.* [U] the state of being free from pain, worry, trouble, difficulty, etc.
1) ***at*** [*one's*] ***ease,*** comfortable, relaxed. ¶*Stand at ~.*①
2) ***take one's ease,*** relax and make oneself comfortable.
3) ***with ease,*** easily. ¶*He speaks English with ~.*
—*vt.* **1.** make (someone) free from pain, etc.; make (pain, difficulty, etc.) less. 《*~* someone *of*》 ¶*~ oneself.*② **2.** make (a belt, etc.) loose; loosen. 《*~ away* (or *down, off*) something》 **3.** move carefully. ¶*~ one's car into a narrow street.* **—***vi.* (of pain, speed, etc.) become less gradually; relax slowly.
ease out, (*U.S.*) gradually force (someone) out of a job; (*Sports*) win easily.
—[名] 안락, 편안함; 안심, 안이함, 안일, 용이함
[熟] 1)편안히, 마음놓고 ¶①쉬엇! 2)몸을 편안히 하다 3)쉽게, 수월하게
—[他] **1.** …을 편하게 하다; [고통 따위]를 완화시키다, 덜다 ¶②마음을 풀다(개운하게 하다); 뒤를 보다 **2.** …을 늦추다, 느슨하게 하다 **3.** …을 조심스럽게 움직이다 **—**[自] [고통 따위가] 덜해지다, 완화하다, [속도가] 떨어지다
[熟] 《美》 …을 사직시키다; 《스포오츠》 쉽게 이기다, 낙승하다

ea·sel [í:zl] *n.* [C] an upright frame to hold a canvas for
—[名] 화가(畫架), 칠판틀, 이이즐

easily

painting, a blackboard, etc.
‡ **eas·i·ly** [í:zili] *adv.* **1.** in an easy manner; with ease; without effort; smoothly. **2.** very likely.
eas·i·ness [í:zinis] *n.* Ⓤ **1.** the state of being easy. **2.** carelessness; indifference; ease of manner.
‡ **east** [i:st] *n.* 《usu. *the* ~》 **1.** the direction where the sun rises. **2.** 《also *E*-》 an eastern region or district in the world, in a country, etc. ¶ *the Far East*① / *the Middle East*② / *the Near East*.③ **3.** 《*the E*-》 the Asiatic countries; the Orient; (*U.S.*) the eastern part of the United States. —*adj.* of, to, from, or in the east. —*adv.* toward the east.
East·er [í:stər] *n.* a Christian festival celebrating Christ's coming to life again. ¶ *Easter Day* (or *Sunday*). ⇒N.B.
east·er·ly [í:stərli] *adj., adv.* of, toward, or from the east. ¶ *an* ~ *wind*① / *The wind blows* ~.②
‡ **east·ern** [í:stərn] *adj.* of, toward, from, or in the east.
east·ward [í:stwərd] *adj., adv.* toward the east.
east·wards [í:stwərdz] *adv.* =eastward.
‡ **eas·y** [í:zi] *adj.* (**eas·i·er, eas·i·est**) **1.** not difficult. ¶ *an* ~ *problem.* **2.** free from pain, worry, etc. ¶ *I feel* ~ *about the matter.* **3.** pleasing; pleasant. **4.** not strict. ¶ *an* ~ *master.* **5.** loose. ¶ *an* ~ *coat.* —*adv.* in a comfortable manner.
Take it easy! ⓐ Be easy! (*adj.* 2.) ⓑ Good-by!
easy chair [⸺ ⸺] *n.* an arm chair designed for comfort.
eas·y-go·ing [í:zigóuiŋ] *adj.* not worrying; taking matters easily.
‡ **eat** [i:t] *v.* (**ate, eaten**) *vt.* **1.** take (food) in through the mouth. **2.** waste, consume, or destroy as if by eating. ¶ *Acids* ~ *metals.* **3.** annoy; trouble. ¶ 《*colloq.*》 *What's eating Tom?* —*vi.* **1..** take food or a meal. **2.** consume something gradually. ⌜secretly.⌝
 1) *eat one's heart out,* be very sad; worry oneself
 2) *eat one's words,* take back what one has said.
 3) ⓐ *eat out,* use up. ⓑ take a meal at a restaurant, etc.; dine away from home.
 4) *eat out of one's hand,* do whatever one wishes.
 5) *eat up,* ⓐ eat completely. ⓑ 《usu. in *passive*》 make (someone) interested in something. ¶ *He is eaten up with curiosity.*
eat·a·ble [í:təbl] *adj.* fit to eat. —*n.* 《*pl.*》 anything ⌜fit to eat; food.⌝
‡ **eat·en** [í:tn] *v.* pp. of **eat**.
eat·er [í:tər] *n.* Ⓒ a person who eats. ¶ *a big* ~.①
eau de Co·logne [óu də kəlóun] *n.* a sweet-smelling toilet water; cologne. ⌜the sides of a building.⌝
eaves [i:vz] *n. pl.* the edges of a roof projecting beyond
eaves·drop [í:vzdrɑp / -drɔp] *vi.* (**-dropped, -drop·ping**) listen secretly to the private talk of other people.
ebb [eb] *n.* Ⓒ **1.** the flowing back of the tide away from the shore toward the sea; the low tide. ↔flood **2.** decline; decay. ¶ *be at an* ~.① —*vi.* **1.** flow back or out; go back. **2.** (of power, etc.) weaken; decline.
ebb tide [⸺ ⸺] *n.* the tide at ebb. ↔flood tide
eb·on·ite [ébənàit] *n.* Ⓤ black material used for combs, fountain pens, etc.; hard rubber.
eb·on·y [ébəni] *n.* Ⓤ the hard black wood used for furniture, etc.; Ⓒ tropical trees that yield this wood. —*adj.* **1.** made of or like ebony. **2.** deep black.
e·bul·lient [ibʌ́liənt] *adj.* **1.** boiling. **2.** full of a happy feeling, enthusiasm, etc.; high-spirited.
eb·ul·li·tion [èbəlíʃ(ə)n] *n.* Ⓤ Ⓒ **1.** the state of boiling or bubbling up. **2.** a sudden outburst of feeling, etc.
ec·cen·tric [ikséntrik, ek-] *adj.* **1.** unusual; queer; odd.

eccentric

—⦿ 1. 쉽게, 용이하게, 수월하게, 거뜬히, 술술, 거침없이 2. 아마, 필시
—⦿ 1. 쉬움, 용이함 2. 마음 가벼움, 태평; 부주의, 불찰; 무관심; 침착
—⦿ 1. 동쪽 2. 동부 ¶①극동/②중동/③근동 3. 동양; 〔美〕 [미국의] 동부 —⦿ 동쪽[으로, 으로부터]의 —⦿ 동쪽으로

—⦿ 부활절 N.B. 3월 21일 이후 28일 간의 만월(滿月) 다음 일요일
—⦿⦿ 동쪽의, 동쪽으로, 동쪽에서 ¶①동풍/②바람이 동쪽에서 분다
—⦿ 동쪽[으로, 으로부터]의
—⦿⦿ 동쪽으로[의]

—⦿ 1. 쉬운, 수월한, 용이한 2. 고통이나 고민이 없는; 마음편한 3. 쾌적한, 기분좋은, 안락한 4. 엄하지 않은, 관대한 5. 헐렁헐렁한, 낙낙한 —⦿ 쉽게; 편안히 「하게!」 ⓐ안녕!, 잘 가게!」
熟 ⓐ마음을 푹 놓게!, 서둘지 말고」
—⦿ 안락의자
—⦿ 태평스러운; 안일한

—⦿ 1. …을 먹다 2. …을 부식(腐蝕)(침식)하다 3. …을 귀찮게 굴다, 괴롭히다, 난처하게 하다 —⦿ 1. 식사하다 2. 부식(침식)하다

熟 1)몹시 슬퍼하다; 남 몰래 고민하다 2)식언하다, 앞서 한 말을 어기다 3) ⓐ…을 다 써버리다, 먹어 없애다 ⓑ외식(外食)하다 4)남이 바라는 대로 하다, 굴종하다 5)ⓐ…을 먹어 없애다, 깨끗이 먹어 치우다 ⓑ[남]을 열중하게 하다

—⦿ 먹을 수 있는, 식용에 알맞은
—⦿ 먹을 수 있는 것, 음식물
—⦿ 먹는 사람 —⦿ 대식가
—⦿ 오 드 콜로뉴(일종의 향수)

—⦿ 처마
—⦿ 엿듣다

—⦿ 1. 썰물, 간조 2. 쇠퇴, 감퇴 ¶①쇠퇴기에 있다 —⦿ 1. [조수가] 빠지다 2. [세력 따위가] 쇠퇴하다

—⦿ 썰물, 간조
—⦿ 에보나이트; 경화(硬化)고무

—⦿ 흑단(黑檀); 흑단나무
—⦿ 1. 흑단으로 만든, 흑단 같은 2. 새까만

—⦿ 1. 끓어 넘치는, 비등(沸騰)하는 2. 열광적인; 원기가 넘쳐흐르는
—⦿ 1. 비등 2. [감정 따위의] 격발, 폭발

—⦿ 1. 보통이 아닌, 괴상(괴이)한 2.

eccentricity — economy

2. (of the two circles) not having the same center. **3.** not placed in the center. ↔concentric —*n.* ⓒ **1.** an eccentric person. **2.** the device for changing round motion into back-and-forth motion.
—名 **1.** 괴벽한 사람, 괴짜 **2.** 편심기(偏心機)

ec·cen·tric·i·ty [èksentrísiti] *n.* (pl. **-ties**) **1.** ⓤ the state of being eccentric; oddity. **2.** ⓒ an odd act or characteristic. ⌈—*adj.* =ecclesiastical.⌉
—名 **1.** 피벽스러움, 괴상함 **2.** 피이한 버릇, 기벽; 피이한 것, 기행(奇行)

ec·cle·si·as·tic [iklì:ziǽstik] *n.* ⓒ a clergyman or priest.
—名 성직자

ec·cle·si·as·ti·cal [iklì:ziǽstik(ə)l] *adj.* of the church or the clergy. ¶~ *principles.*
—形 교회의, 성직의

ech·e·lon [éʃəlàn / -lɔ̀n] *n.* ⓒ the troops, airplanes, etc., arranged like steps. ⇒fig. ¶*an airplane* ~. —*vt.* form or move (airplanes, etc.) in echelon.
—名 제형(梯形) 편성, 제단(梯團), 제진(梯陣) —他 [비행기 따위]를 제진으로 편성하다 (움직이게 하다)

: ech·o [ékou] *n.* ⓒ (pl. **-oes**) **1.** the state of repeating a sound by reflection. **2.** the act of repeating or imitating another person's thoughts or views. **3.** a person who imitates another person's acts, etc. closely. —*vi.* repeat in sound; sound again. 《~ *with* someone's voice, etc.》 —*vt.* **1.** reflect (sounds). **2.** repeat (another person's words); imitate (another person's acts, etc.).
[echelon]
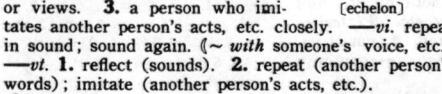
—名 **1.** 반향; 메아리 **2.** 흉내, 모방 **3.** 모방자 —自 반향하다, 메아리치다 —他 **1.** …을 반향시키다 **2.** [남의 언동]을 모방하다, 흉내내다

Ech·o [ékou] *n.* (in Greek legend) a nymph who loved Narcissus. ⌈filled with cream.⌉
—名 [그리이스 신화의] 숲의 여신

e·clair [eikléər, +U.S. -́-] *n.* ⓒ a finger-shaped cake
⌈과자⌉
—名 크리임을 넣은 손가락 모양의

ec·lec·tic [ekléktik] *adj.* choosing and using the best from various sources; made up of things selected from various sources; selecting. —*n.* ⓒ a person who uses eclectic methods in philosophy, etc.
—形 선택하는; 절충하는; 절충적인
—名 절충학파(주의)의 사람

e·clipse [iklíps] *n.* ⓒ entire or partial cutting off of the light of the sun, moon, etc. by some other heavenly body. ¶*solar* ~①/*lunar* ~.② —*vt.* **1.** cause an eclipse of (the sun, moon, etc.); darken. **2.** obscure the fame of (someone).
—名 [해·달의] 식(蝕) ¶①일식/②월식 —他 **1.** [천체가] …을 먹어 들어가다; 어둡게 하다 **2.** [남]의 명성 따위를 빼앗다

e·clip·tic [ikliptik] *n.* 《*the* ~》 the path which the sun appears to follow among the stars in a year. —*adj.* of eclipses or the ecliptic.
—名 황도(黃道) —形 식(蝕)의; 황도의

ec·logue [éklɔ:g, -lɑg / -lɔg] *n.* ⓒ a short poem of shepherds and their life, often in the form of a conversation between shepherds.
—名 목가, 전원시

: e·co·nom·ic [ì:kənámik, èkə- / -nɔ́m-] *adj.* **1.** of economics. **2.** of the management of income, expenses, etc.
—形 **1.** 경제학의 **2.** 경제상의

• e·co·nom·i·cal [ì:kənámik(ə)l, èkə- / -nɔ́m-] *adj.* **1.** careful not to waste money, time, goods, etc.; thrifty. ↔ extravagant **2.** not wasteful. **3.** of economics.
—形 **1.** [사람이] 검소한, 검약하는 **2.** [사물이] 경제적인 **3.** 경제[학]의

e·co·nom·i·cal·ly [ì:kənámikəli, èkə- / -nɔ́m-] *adv.* **1.** in an economical manner. **2.** from the viewpoint of economics.
—副 **1.** 경제적으로 **2.** 경제[학]상으로 보아

e·co·nom·ics [ì:kənámiks, èkə- / -nɔ́m-] *n. pl.* 《used as *sing.*》 the social science that treats of the production, distribution, and consumption of wealth.
—名 경제학

e·con·o·mist [i(:)kánəmist / -kɔ́n-] *n.* ⓒ **1.** a person who studies economics. **2.** an economical person.
—名 **1.** 경제학자 **2.** 검약자, 절약가

e·con·o·mize [i(:)kánəmàiz / -kɔ́n-] *vi.* be economical or careful in spending money. —*vt.* spend (money, time, etc.) or use (goods, etc.) without waste.
—自 절약하다 —他 …을 경제적으로 쓰다

• e·con·o·my [i(:)kánəmi / -kɔ́n-] *n.* (pl. **-mies**) **1.** ⓤ the management of the income, expense, goods, etc. of a household, private business, community, society, etc. ¶*national* ~. **2.** ⓤⓒ the state of being free from waste of money, time, labor, etc. by careful planning and use. ¶*It is an* ~ *of labor and time to work hard*
—名 **1.** 경제 **2.** 절약, 검약 ¶①제한된 시간에 열심히 일하는 것은 노력과 시간의 절약이 된다 **3.** 조직체

ecstasy [375] **editorialize**

*for a limited time.*① **3.** ⓒ an organization; a system.
ec·sta·sy [ékstəsi] *n.* ⓒ (pl. **-sies**) **1.** a feeling of great joy; great delight; rapture. ¶*with* ~. **2.** the state of being beside oneself with some emotion, esp. joy.
 in an ecstasy of joy, beside oneself with joy; absorbed in joy.

—名 1. 열광, 광희(狂喜) 2. 무아의 경지, 황홀 상태
熟 기쁜 나머지 자신을 잊고

ec·stat·ic [ekstǽtik, ik-] *adj.* of or in ecstasy; rapturous. —*n.* ⓒ a person who is in the state of ecstasy. ▷**ec·stat·i·cal·ly** [-kəli] *adv.*

—形 광희의, 기뻐 날뛰는 —名 황홀경에 빠져 있는 사람, 광희하는 사람

Ec·ua·dor [èkwədɔ́:r] *n.* a country on the northwestern coast of South America. ⇒[N.B.] 「a person of Ecuador.」
Ec·ua·do·ri·an [èkwədɔ́:riən] *adj.* of Ecuador. —*n.* ⓒ

—名 남미 서북 해안의 공화국 [N.B.] 수도는 Quito 「사람」
—形 에쿠아도르의 —名 에쿠아도르 사람

ec·ze·ma [éksimə, égzi-] *n.* Ⓤ a disease of the skin with pain, itching, fever, swelling, etc.

—名 습진

ed. editor; edition; edited. 「ward, and Edwin.」
Ed [ed] a petname of Edgar, Edmond, Edmund, Ed-

—名 Edgar 따위의 애칭

ed·dy [édi] *n.* ⓒ (pl. **-dies**) (of water, smoke, etc.) a round or coiled movement against the main current. ¶*get into* (or *get caught up by*) *an* ~.① —*vi., vt.* (**-died**) move round and round in small circles; whirl or cause (water, etc.) to whirl.

—名 회오리, 소용돌이 ¶①소용돌이치 [게 하]다

E·den [í:dn] *n.* **1.** (in the Bible) the garden where Adam and Eve lived at first. **2.** a delightful place.

—名 1. 에덴동산 2. 낙원

Ed·gar [édgər] *n.* a man's name. ⇒[N.B.]

—名 남자 이름 [N.B.] 애칭은 Ed

edge [edʒ] *n.* ⓒ **1.** a sharp, cutting side of a blade. ¶*This knife has a keen* ~.① **2.** the border. ¶*the* ~
 1) *be on edge*, be very excited. 「*of a table.*」
 2) *on the edge of doing*, be about to do. 「*on edge.*」
 3) *set something on edge*, irritate. ¶*set one's nerves*
—*vt.* **1.** give an edge to (a knife); sharpen. **2.** put a border on (something). ¶~ *a curtain with lace.* **3.** cause (something) to move carefully. —*vi.* move carefully.

—名 1. [칼 따위의] 날 ¶①이 칼은 예리하다(잘든다) 2. 가장자리; 테
熟 1)몹시 흥분하고 있다 2)…하려 하고 있다 3)…을 짜증나게 하다
—他 1. …에 날을 세우다; 날카롭게 (예리하게) 하다 2. …에 가장자리(테)를 붙이다 3. …을 조심스럽게 움직이다
—自 조심스럽게 움직이다

edge·ways [édʒwèiz] *adv.* with the edge forward; on, by, with, or toward the edge.
 get a word in edgeways, say a few words in a conversation when the other person is, for a moment, silent.

—副 칼날을 들이대고; 가장자리(테)를 따라(붙여)
熟 [틈을 타서] 한 마디 참견하다

edge·wise [édʒwàiz] *adv.* =edgeways. 「edge.」
edg·ing [édʒiŋ] *n.* Ⓤⓒ narrow border which forms an
ed·i·ble [édibl] *adj.* fit to eat; eatable. —*n.* (*pl.*) eatable things; food. 「authority; decree.」
e·dict [í:dikt] *n.* ⓒ the official public order sent out by
ed·i·fi·ca·tion [èdifikéiʃ(ə)n] *n.* Ⓤ spiritual instruction; moral improvement.
ed·i·fice [édifis] *n.* ⓒ a large building.
ed·i·fy [édifài] *vt.* (**-fied**) improve morally; instruct.
Ed·in·burgh [éd(i)nbə̀:rou / -b(ə)rə] *n.* the capital of Scotland. 「can inventor.」
Ed·i·son [édisn], **Thomas Alva** *n.* (1847-1931) an Ameri-
ed·it [édit] *vt.* read, correct, and put (an author's writings, etc.) into a suitable form for publication.
ed·it. [édit] edition; edited; editor.

—名 가장자리를 달기, 테를 붙이기
—名 식용의; 먹을 수 있는 —名 식용품
—名 칙령(勅令); 포고(布告)
—名 교훈; 교화
—名 큰 건물, 대건축물 「하다」
—他 …의 덕성을 기르다; …을 교화
—名 스코틀랜드의 수도
—名 미국의 발명가
—他 …을 편집하다

* **e·di·tion** [idíʃ(ə)n] *n.* ⓒ **1.** (of a magazine, book, newspaper, etc.) the number of copies printed at one time; an issue. ¶*the first* (*second*) ~.① **2.** the form in which a book, etc. is published. ¶*a cheap* ~.②

—名 1. 간행물, 판(版) ¶①제1(제2)판 2. …판 ¶②염가판

‡ **ed·i·tor** [éditər] *n.* ⓒ **1.** a person who edits a newspaper, etc. **2.** a person who writes editorials.
* **ed·i·to·ri·al** [èditɔ́:riəl] *adj.* of or by an editor. —*n.* ⓒ a leading article in a newspaper, etc. in which an editor gives opinions.

—名 1. 편집자(인) 2. 사설 담당 기자, 논설 위원
—形 편집인의(에 인한) —名 논설, 사설

ed·i·to·ri·al·ize [èditɔ́:riəlàiz] *vi., vt.* **1.** express editorial opinions in a newspaper, etc. **2.** put (editorial opinions) into an article, etc.

—自他 1. 사설로 논하다, 논설하다 2. [논설을] 싣다, 게재하다

Ed·mond, -mund [édmənd] *n.* a man's name. ⇒[N.B.]
—[名] 남자 이름 [N.B.] 애칭은 Ed

•**ed·u·cate** [édʒukèit / édju(:)-] *vt.* **1.** teach; train. **2.** send (someone) to school.
—[他] 1. …을 교육하다, 가르치다; 훈련하다 2. …을 학교에 보내다

ed·u·cat·ed [édʒukèitid / édju(:)-] *adj.* having education or a cultivated mind, etc.; trained.
—[形] 교육을 받은, 교육(교양)이 있는; 훈련된

⁑**ed·u·ca·tion** [èdʒukéiʃ(ə)n / èdju(:)-] *n.* **1.** [U][C] the process of developing knowledge, skill, ability, character, etc. by teaching or training. **2.** [U] the knowledge, skill, etc. developed by such training. **3.** [U] science that deals with the principles, etc., of teaching and learning.
—[名] 1. 교육 2. 교양 3. 교육학

•**ed·u·ca·tion·al** [èdʒukéiʃən(ə)l / èdju(:)-] *adj.* of education; instructive. ¶*an ~ film.* ▷**ed·u·ca·tion·al·ly** [-i] *adv.*
—[形] 교육의; 교육적인

ed·u·ca·tor [édʒukèitər / édju(:)kèitə] *n.* [C] a person who educates; a teacher.
—[名] 교육자, 교사

e·duce [id(j)ú:s / -djú:s] *vt.* bring out; draw forth; develop (talent, etc.).
—[他] [재능 따위]를 끌어내다, 나타나게 하다

Ed·ward [édwərd] *n.* a man's name. ⇒[N.B.]
—[名] 남자 이름 [N.B.] 애칭은 Ed, Ned

eel [i:l] *n.* [C] a long, smooth, snake-like fish living in a lake or the sea.
—[名] 뱀장어

e'en [i:n] (*poetic*) *adv.* =even. **—*n.*** =evening.

e'er [εər] *adv.* (*poetic*) =ever.

ee·rie [íəri] *adj.* **1.** causing a mysterious feeling or fear; strange. **2.** timid or uneasy because of superstition. ▷**ee·ri·ly** [-li] *adv.* —**ee·ri·ness** [-nis] *n.*
—[形] 1. 무시무시한, 등골이 오싹하는, 기분나쁜 2. 무서워하는, 겁먹은

ee·ry [íəri] (**-ri·er, -ri·est**) *adj.* =eerie.

ef·face [iféis] *vt.* **1.** rub or wipe out (bad memories, etc.). **2.** keep (oneself) from being noticed. ¶*~ oneself.*① ▷**ef·face·a·ble** [-əbl] *adj.*
—[他] 1. …을 지워 없애다 2. …을 눈에 띄지 않게 하다 ¶①자신을 매장하다

⁑**ef·fect** [ifékt] *n.* **1.** [C][U] the result of a cause. ¶*His failure is the ~ of idleness.* **2.** [C][U] an impression on the mind. ¶*a dramatic ~.*① **3.** [U] the power which produces some results. ¶*The medicine had no ~.*② **4.** [C][U] influence; the state of being influenced. ¶*the effects of heat.*③ **5.** [U] the main idea; meaning. **6.** ⦅*pl.*⦆ goods or things belonging to someone.
1) ***bring to effect; carry into effect,*** put into practice; carry out.
2) ***for effect,*** in order to produce an effect; for show.
3) ***give effect to,*** put (a plan) into practice.
4) ***in effect,*** ⓐ in fact; really. ⓑ having legal force.
5) ***of no effect,*** in vain.
6) ***to the effect that,*** having the essential meaning that …
—*vt.* produce (something) as a result; cause; bring about.
—[名] 1. 결과 2. 인상; [심적] 효과 ¶①극적 효과 3. 효력; 효험, 효능 ¶②그 약은 효험이 없었다 4. 영향 ¶③더위[먹음] 5. 취지; 의미 6. 동산물건(動產物件)
[熟] 1)실행에 옮기다 2)효과를 노리고; 그럴 듯하게 보이기 위하여 3)…을 실행에 옮기다 4)ⓐ실제로는; 사실상 ⓑ[법적] 효력으로써 5)효과 없이, 헛되이 6)…이라는 뜻의
—[他] 결과로 …을 낳다; 초래하다

•**ef·fec·tive** [iféktiv] *adj.* **1.** having an effect; producing the expected or desired effect. ¶*~ steps toward world peace / take ~ measures*① */ The medicine was ~*②. **2.** producing a remarkable or striking impression. ¶*The dress is ~.*③ **3.** actual or existing.
become effective, come into effect. ¶*The peace treaty is expected to become ~ on May 1.*
—*n.* ⦅*pl.*⦆ soldiers equipped and ready for fighting.
—[形] 1. 유효한, 효과가 있는 ¶①유효한 수단을 취하다/②약은 효험이 있었다 2. 효과적인; 눈에 띄는, 두드러지는 ¶③그 옷은 남의 눈을 끈다 3. 실제의, 사실상의
[熟] 효력을 발생하는
—[名] 동원할 수 있는 군인, 실제 병력

ef·fec·tive·ly [iféktivli] *adv.* in an effective manner.
—[副] 유효하게, 효과적으로; 사실상

ef·fec·tu·al [ifékt∫u(ə)l / -tju-] *adj.* **1.** able to produce the expected effect. **2.** having legal force.
—[形] 1. 효과적인; 효력이 있는 2. [법령이] 유효한

ef·fec·tu·al·ly [ifékt∫u(ə)li / -tju-] *adv.* in an effectual manner; effectively.
—[副] 유효하게; 효과적으로

ef·fem·i·na·cy [iféminəsi] *n.* [U] the state of being effeminate; unmanly weakness.
—[名] 나약, 사내답지 못함

ef·fem·i·nate *adj.* [iféminit → *v.*] lacking in manly qualities; unmanly. **—*vt., vi.*** [iféminèit] make (someone) effeminate; become effeminate.
—[形] 사내답지 못한; 나약한 —[他][自] 나약하게 하다(되다)

ef·fer·vesce [èfərvés] *vi.* **1.** give or send out bubbles of gas; bubble up. **2.** be excited.
—[自] 1. 거품 일다; 비등(沸騰)하다 2. 흥분하다

ef·fer·ves·cence [èfərvésns] *n.* [U] the act of bubbling; the state of being effervesced; excitement; liveliness.
—[名] 비등; 흥분

ef·fer·ves·cent [èfərvésnt] *adj.* sending out bubbles of
—[形] 비등성(沸騰性)의; 흥분한

effete [eff:t] *adj.* worn out; tired out; not able to produce. 「pected results; effective.
—형 정력이 다한, 기진맥진한; 쇠퇴한; 생산력이 없는 「능)이 있는

ef·fi·ca·cious [èfikéiʃəs] *adj.* able to produce the ex-
—형 유효한; 효력이 있는; 효험(효

ef·fi·ca·cy [éfikəsi] *n.* Ⓤ the state of being efficacious.
—명 유효, 효능

ef·fi·cien·cy [ifíʃ(ə)nsi] *n.* Ⓤ the state of being efficient; effectiveness.
—명 유능; 유효; 능률

ef·fi·cient [ifíʃ(ə)nt] *adj.* able to produce the desired results; able. ¶ *an ~ man* / *(Philosophy) the ~ cause.*①
—형 효과 있는; 능률적인; 유능한 ¶ ①[哲] 동인(動因), 작인(作因)

ef·fi·cient·ly [ifíʃ(ə)ntli] *adv.* in an efficient manner.
—부 유효하게; 능률적으로

ef·fi·gy [éfidʒi] *n.* Ⓒ (pl. **-gies**) a portrait, statue, or image of a person.
—명 초상, 상(像), 우상

ef·flo·resce [èflɔːrés] *vi.* blossom out; flower.
—자 꽃이 피다, 개화하다

ef·flo·res·cence [èflɔːrésns] *n.* Ⓤ the act of efflorescing; the time of flowering.
—명 개화; 개화기

ef·flu·ence [éfluəns] *n.* Ⓤ the act of flowing out or forth; Ⓒ a thing that flows out or forth.
—명 방출(放出), 유출(流出); 방출물, 유출물

ef·flux [éflʌks] *n.* Ⓤ the act of flowing out; Ⓒ a thing that flows out.
—명 유출; 유출물

ef·fort [éfərt] *n.* Ⓒ Ⓤ 1. the act of putting forth energy and strength; vigorous attempt. ¶ *by ~*① / *after all one's ~*② / *make an effort* (or *efforts*) *to do something.*③ 2. Ⓒ a result of effort; a thing done with effort. ¶ *a wonderful literary ~.*
  1) *make every effort,* do all one can.
  2) *with* [*an*] *effort,* with great pains; with difficulty.
  3) *without effort,* quite easily.
—명 1. 노력; 수고 ¶ ①노력하여 /②온갖 노력에도 불구하고/③…하려고 노력하다 2. 노력의 결과; 역작

圖 1)온갖 노력을 다하다 2)힘들여, 애써서 3)쉽사리, 수월하게
「쉬운」

ef·fort·less [éfərtlis] *adj.* making no effort; easy.
—형 노력하지 않는, 힘들이지 않는;

ef·fron·ter·y [efrʌ́ntəri] *n.* Ⓤ Ⓒ (pl. **-ter·ies**) shamelessness; boldness; a ˆhameless. ¶ *have the ~ to do something.*①
—명 뻔뻔스러움, 몰염치, 철면피한 행위 ¶①뻔뻔스럽게도 …하다
「gent; brightness; radiance:」

ef·ful·gence [efʌ́ldʒ(ə)ns] *n.* Ⓤ the state of being efful-
—명 광채; 찬란한 광채

ef·ful·gent [efʌ́ldʒ(ə)nt] *adj.* shining brightly; radiant.
—형 눈부시게 빛나는, 찬란한

ef·fuse [efjúːz] *vt., vi.* pour out or forth; gush out.
—타자 쏟아 나오다, 방출하다

ef·fu·sion [efjúːʒ(ə)n] *n.* 1. Ⓤ the act of effusing; Ⓒ something that effuses. 2. Ⓤ Ⓒ a free outpouring of thought or feeling.
—명 1. 유출(流出), 방출; 유출물 2. [감정·언어의] 토로, 발로

ef·fu·sive [ifjúːsiv] *adj.* expressing too much feeling or emotion; demonstrative; poured out.
—형 심정을 토로하는, 넘쳐흐르는, 쏟아나오는

e.g. [íːdʒíː, f(ə)rigzǽmpl / -záːm-] for example.
—(略) 예를 들면

egg [eg] *n.* Ⓒ a round body laid by birds or other animals, from which the young come out. 「attempt.
  1) *put all one's eggs in one basket,* risk all on a single
  2) *teach one's grandmother to suck eggs,* teach someone who is wiser than oneself.
—명 알, 달걀

圖 1)한 사업에 전재산을 투자하다 2) 부처님에게 설법하다

egg·beat·er [égbìːtər] *n.* Ⓒ an instrument used for beating eggs. 「egg.
—명 달걀을 저어 거품을 일게 하는 기구

egg·cup [égkʌp] *n.* Ⓒ a small cup for holding a boiled
—명 삶은 달걀을 넣는 컵

egg·plant [égplæ̀nt / -plàːnt] *n.* Ⓒ a plant with eatable egg-shaped, purple fruit; the fruit of this plant.
—명 가지 나무

egg·shell [égʃèl] *n.* Ⓒ the shell of an egg.
—명 달걀 껍질

eg·lan·tine [égləntàin, +*U.S.* -tìːn] *n.* Ⓒ a sweet-smelling wild rose with pink flowers and a prickly stem.
—명 들장미의 일종

e·go [íːgou, égou / égou] *n.* Ⓒ (pl. **-gos**) the self.
—명 자아(自我), 자기

e·go·ism [íːgouìz(ə)m / égou-] *n.* Ⓤ 1. (*Philosophy*) the theory that self-interest is the proper goal of all human actions. ↔altruism 2. selfishness.
—명 1. 이기주의 2. 이기심, 아욕(我慾), 자기 본위, 제멋대로임

e·go·ist [íːgouist / égou-] *n.* Ⓒ 1. a believer in egoism. 2. a selfish person. 「centered; selfish.
—명 1. 이기주의자 2. 제멋대로 하는 사람, 자기중심적인 사람

e·go·is·tic [ìːgouístik / ègou-]**, -ti·cal** [-tik(ə)l] *adj.* self-
—형 이기적인, 제멋대로 하는

e·go·tism [íːgətìz(ə)m / égou-] *n.* Ⓤ 1. the habit of talking or writing too much about oneself. 2. self-conceit; selfishness. 「tism; a selfish person.
—명 1.자기 중심벽(癖) 2.자만심, 자부심; 아욕(我慾)

e·go·tist [íːgətist / égou-] *n.* Ⓒ a person who shows ego-
—명 자기중심 주의자; 제멋대로 하
「는 사람

e·go·tis·tic [ìːgətístik, ìːgə-/ égou-], **-ti·cal** [-tik(ə)l] *adj.* showing or characterized by egotism; selfish. —형 자기중심의; 이기적인

e·gre·gious [igríːdʒəs] *adj.* remarkably bad; shocking; notorious. ▷**e·gre·gious·ly** [-li] *adv.* —형 지독한; 터무니없는, 언어도단의; 악명높은

e·gress [íːgres] *n.* **1.** Ⓤ the act of going out. **2.** Ⓒ a way out; an exit. **3.** Ⓤ the right to go out. ↔ingress —명 1. 밖으로 나가기 2. 출구 3. 밖으로 나가는 권리

e·gret [íːgret] *n.* Ⓒ a large wading bird of the heron family; its long, beautiful plumes. —명 큰백로; 백로의 깃털

• **E·gypt** [íːdʒipt] *n.* a country in northeastern Africa. ⇒ —명 아프리카 북부의 공화국 [N.B.] 「수도는 Cairo」

• **E·gyp·tian** [idʒípʃ(ə)n] *adj.* of Egypt or its people or their language. —*n.* **1.** Ⓒ a person of Egypt. **2.** Ⓤ the language of the ancient Egyptians. —형 이집트[사람·말]의 —명 1. 이집트 사람 2. 이집트 말

• **eh** [ei] *interj.* an exclamation to express surprise or doubt, or to invite agreement. ¶ *You're angry with me,* ~ ? —감 뭐?, 뭐라고?

ei·der [áidər] *n.* Ⓒ a large, northern sea duck with soft, downy breast feathers. —명 [북유럽 연안산] 솜털오리

‡ **eight** [eit] *n.* **1.** Ⓤ the number between seven and nine; 8. **2.** Ⓒ any group or set of eight persons or things. ¶ *the Eights.*① **3.** Ⓒ anything shaped like 8. *a figure* [*of*] *eight,* (*Skating*) movement following —*adj.* of 8. [the shape of an 8.] —명 1. 여덟, 8 2. 여덟 사람(개) 한 조 ¶①Oxford대학 대 Cambridge대학 보우트 레이스 3. 8자형의 것 熟《스케이트》 8자형 활주(滑走) —형 여덟의, 8의

‡ **eight·een** [éitíːn] *n.* Ⓤ the number between seventeen and nineteen. —*adj.* of 18. —명 열 여덟, 18 —형 열 여덟의, 18의

‡ **eight·eenth** [éitíːnθ] *n.* **1.** (*the* ~) number 18; 18th. **2.** Ⓒ one of 18 equal parts of anything. —*adj.* of 18th. —명 1. 제18 2. 18분의 1 —형 제18의, 열 여덟째; 18분의 1의

eight·fold [éitfòuld] *adj.* having eight times as much or as many. —*adv.* eight times as much or as many. —형 8배의; 여덟 겹의 —부 8배로; 여덟 겹으로

‡ **eighth** [eitθ] *n.* **1.** (*the* ~) number 8; 8th. **2.** Ⓒ one of 8 equal parts of anything. —*adj.* of 8th. —명 1. 제8, 여덟째 2. 8분의 1 —형 제8의, 여덟째의; 8분의 1의

‡ **eight·i·eth** [éitiiθ] *n.* **1.** (*the* ~) number 80; 80th. **2.** Ⓒ one of 80 equal parts of anything. —*adj.* of 80th. —명 1. 제80, 여든째 2. 80분의 1 —형 제80의, 여든째의 「80개의」

‡ **eight·y** [éiti] *n.* Ⓒ eight times ten; 80. —*adj.* of 80. —명 여든, 80 —형 80의; 여든 살의,

Ein·stein [áinstain], **Albert** *n.* (1879-1955) a German-American physicist.① —명 독일 태생의 미국 물리학자 [land.]

Eir·e [έərə] *n.* the former name of the Republic of Ire- —명 아일랜드 공화국의 구칭

‡ **ei·ther** [íːðər / áiðə] *adj., pron.* **1.** one or the other of two. ¶ *take* ~ *road.*① **2.** one and the other of two; each. ¶ *The flowers are blooming on* ~ *side of the walk.* / *I have not read* ~ *book.*② —*pron.* one or the other. ¶ *Either of the pencils is mine.*③ —형 ①[둘 중의] 어느 한쪽의 ¶①어느 한쪽 길을 택하다 2. 양쪽의, 어느 쪽의 ¶②어느 쪽 책도 읽지 못했다 —대 어느 한쪽 ¶③그 연필 중 어느 하나는 내것이다

—*conj., adv.* **1.** (used as *either ... or*) ¶ *Either you or I am to go.*④ ⇒ [usage] / *I want to go to* ~ *America or England.* / *not wise or handsome* ~. **2.** (used after a *negative*) also. ¶ *If you don't go, I shall not go,* ~. —접·부 1. …이든 또는 …이든 ¶④너든지 나든지 누가 가야 한다 [usage] 동사는 가까운 쪽의 주어에 일치한다 2. …도 역시 … 않는

e·jac·u·late [idʒǽkjulèit] *vt.* **1.** say suddenly and briefly. **2.** eject. —타 1. …을 별안간 외치다 2. [액체를] 사출(射出)하다

e·jac·u·la·tion [idʒǽkjuléiʃ(ə)n] *n.* Ⓤ Ⓒ **1.** something said suddenly and briefly; exclamation. **2.** ejection. —명 1. 갑작스러운 외침 2. 사출

e·ject [i(ː)dʒékt] *vt.* throw out; force out; emit; discharge. —타 …을 쫓아내다, 추방하다; 배출하다

e·jec·tion [i(ː)dʒékʃ(ə)n] *n.* **1.** Ⓤ Ⓒ the act of ejecting; the state of being ejected. **2.** Ⓒ something ejected. —명 1. 방출; 배출 2. 배출물

eke [iːk] *adv.* (*archaic*) also. —부 《古》 또한, 역시

• **e·lab·o·rate** *adj.* [ilǽb(ə)rit → *v.*] worked out with great care and in great detail; complicated. —*v.* [ilǽbərèit] *vt.* work out (something) with great care; produce (something) by effort. —*vi.* talk or write in detail. (~ *on* or *upon* something) —형 애써서 만든, 공들인, 정교한; 복잡한 —타 …을 공들여 만들다; 애써서 만들어내다 —자 자세하게 말하다(쓰다)

e·lab·o·rate·ly [ilǽb(ə)ritli] *adv.* in an elaborate manner. —부 정성들여, 공들여; 정교하게

e·lab·o·ra·tion [ilæ̀bəréiʃ(ə)n] *n.* **1.** Ⓤ the act of elaborating; the state of being elaborated. **2.** Ⓒ something elaborated. —명 1. 공들여 만들기, 정교 2. 애써서 만든 것, 노작(勞作), 역작

e·lapse [ilǽps] *vi.* slip away; pass. —자 [시간이] 경과하다, 지나다

• **e·las·tic** [ilǽstik] *adj.* **1.** able to spring back to its original size, shape, or position after being pulled or —형 1. 탄력성 있는 ¶①탄력/②탄력한도 2. 활달한; 융통성 있는 ¶③활

elasticity

pressed. ¶~ *force*① / ~ *limit*.② **2.** able to recover quickly from depression; flexible; adaptable. ¶*an ~ conscience*③ / *an ~ rule*.④ —*n.* Ⓤ tape, cloth, etc. given an elastic quality by partly weaving rubber into it; Ⓒ a rubber band.

—名 달한 마음/④융통성 있는 규칙 —名 고무 끈; 둥근 고무줄

e·las·tic·i·ty [ilæstísti, ì:læs- / élæs-] *n.* Ⓤ **1.** the state or quality of being elastic. **2.** flexibility; adaptability.

—名 1. 탄력[성] 2. 융통성; 순응성

e·late [iléit] *vt.* make (someone) high-spirited; make (someone) proud or joyful. ¶*be elated by one's success.*

—他 …의 원기를 돋구어 주다; …을 의기양양하게 하다

e·lat·ed [iléitid] *adj.* in high spirits; proud; joyful.

—形 의기왕성한; 의기양양한

e·la·tion [iléiʃ(ə)n] *n.* Ⓤ high spirits; joyous pride.

—名 왕성한 원기; 의기양양함

· **el·bow** [élbou] *n.* Ⓒ **1.** the joint between the upper and lower arm. **2.** anything bent like an elbow, as a sharp turn in a road, etc.

—名 1. 팔꿈치 2. 팔꿈치 모양의 것

1) *at someone's elbow,* close to someone.
2) *out at [the] elbows,* ⓐ (of clothes) worn out; ragged. ⓑ poor.
3) *rub elbows with,* associate with (famous people).
4) *up to the elbows,* (in work) very busy; deeply engaged.

熟 1)팔 닿는 곳에, 가까이에 2)ⓐ[옷의] 팔꿈치가 떨어져서 ⓑ가난한 3)[명사]와 교제하다 4)[일에] 몰두하여

—*vt.* push (something) with the elbows. ¶~ *oneself into the room*① / ~ *one's way through a crowd.* —*vi.* make one's way by pushing.

—他 …을 팔꿈치로 밀다 ¶①팔꿈치로 밀어 젖히고 방안으로 들어가다
—自 밀어젖히고 나아가다

el·bow-chair [élbout ʃéər] *n.* Ⓒ a chair with supports on which the elbows may rest.

—名 팔걸이 의자

el·bow-room [élbouruː(ː)m] *n.* Ⓤ enough space to move or work in.

—名 활동할 수 있는 여지; 여유

‡ **eld·er**¹ [éldər] *adj.* (*compar.* of **old**) older; senior. ¶*my ~ sister* / *My ~ brother is two years older than I.* ↔younger ⇒Usage —*n.* Ⓒ **1.** an older person; an aged person. **2.** an ancestor. **3.** one of the older and more powerful men in a community, etc. **4.** an official of certain churches.

—形 손위의, 연상(年上)의, 고참의
Usage elder는 형제자매의 관계를 나타내며, older는 일반적으로 연상을 나타냄 —名 1. 연장자, 손윗사람; 노인 2. 조상 3. 원로 4. [장로교회의] 장로

el·der² [éldər] *n.* Ⓒ a low tree with white flowers and purple berries.

—名 넙은잎딱총나무의 일종

el·der·ly [éldərli] *adj.* somewhat old; past middle age.

—形 연세가 지긋한; 초로(初老)의

· **eld·est** [éldist] *adj.* (*superl.* of **old**) oldest; first born. ¶*my ~ son.*

—形 가장 손위(연상)의; 맏아들(장자)의

El Do·ra·do [èldərá:dou, +*U.S.* -réi-] *n.* (pl. **-dos**) Ⓤ an imaginary country with much gold in South America, sought by early Spanish explorers; Ⓒ (also *Eldorado*) any unbelievably rich place.

—名 황금의 나라; 보물의 산

‡ **e·lect** [ilékt] *vt.* **1.** choose; select by vote. ¶~ *a President* / *He was elected mayor.*① **2.** decide. (~ *to do*) ¶*He elected to stay at home.* —*adj.* chosen; elected but not yet in office. ¶*the bride ~*② / *the mayor ~.* ⇒Usage —*n.* (*the ~*) **1.** persons belonging to a group with special rights. **2.** those chosen by God for eternal life because of their merit. ¶*God's ~.*③

—他 1. …을 선거하다 ¶①그는 시장으로 당선되었다 2. …을 결정하다 —形 뽑힌, 선출된 ¶②뽑힌 신부, 약혼녀 Usage 흔히 명사 다음에 옴
—名 1. 뽑힌 사람 2. 신의 선민(選民) ¶③신의 선민(이스라엘 사람)

‡ **e·lec·tion** [ilékʃ(ə)n] *n.* Ⓒ Ⓤ the act of electing, esp. by vote. ¶*an ~ for the Diet* / *carry an ~*① / *stand for ~.*②

—名 선거, 선임 ¶①당선되다/②입후보하다

e·lec·tive [iléktiv] *adj.* **1.** chosen or appointed by election. **2.** having the right or power to elect. ¶~ *body.*① **3.** (*U.S.*) open to choice; not required; optional. ↔compulsory, required ¶*an ~ subject.*② —*n.* Ⓒ (*U.S.*) an elective subject or course of study.

—形 1. 선거에 의한 2. 선거권이 있는 ¶①선거 모체 3. (美) 선택의 ¶②선택 과목 —名 (美) 선택 과목

e·lec·tor [iléktər] *n.* Ⓒ a person who has the right or power to elect.

—名 선거인, 유권자

e·lec·tor·al [iléktərəl] *adj.* **1.** of an election or electors. ¶*an ~ district.*① **2.** made up of electors.

—形 1. 선거[인]의 ¶①선거구 2. 선거인으로 이루어진

elector·al college [-́-́-- -́-] *n.* (*U.S.*) an assembly of electors chosen by the voters to elect the President and the Vice-President of the United States.

—名 (美) 대통령(부통령) 선거인단

e·lec·tor·ate [iléktərit] *n.* Ⓒ (*collectively*) the body of persons having the right to vote in an election.

—名 선거민, 유권자 [전체]

‡ **e·lec·tric** [iléktrik] *adj.* **1.** of electricity. ¶*an ~ current*

—形 1. 전기의 2. 전격적인; 자극적인

electrical [380] **elementary**

(shock, wave, wire) / ~ power. **2.** exciting; thrilling.
e·lec·tri·cal [iléktrik(ə)l] *adj.* =electric.
e·lec·tri·cal·ly [iléktrikəli] *adv.* by or with electricity. —圖 전기로, 전기학상
e·lec·tri·cian [ilèktríʃ(ə)n] *n.* ⓒ a person who makes, —名 전기 기사; 전기학자
repairs, or sells electric apparatus; an expert in the
science of electricity.
* **e·lec·tric·i·ty** [ilèktrísiti] *n.* Ⓤ **1.** a form of energy that —名 1.전기 2.전류 3.전기학
is produced by the flow of electrons. **2.** an electric
current. **3.** the science of electricity.
e·lec·tri·fi·ca·tion [ilèktrifikéiʃ(ə)n] *n.* Ⓤ the act of e- —名 대전(帶電),충전; 전화(電化); 감
lectrifying; the state of being electrified; the state of 전
being struck by electricity.
e·lec·tri·fy [iléktrifài] *vt.* (**-fied**) **1.** put electricity into —他 1. …에 전기를 통하다; 대전(帶
(something). ¶*an electrified body.*① **2.** make (a rail- 電)시키다 ¶①대전체 2. …을 전화(電
way, etc.) able to use electricity. ¶~ *a railway system.* 化)하다 3. …을 감동시키다
3. excite; thrill.
e·lec·tro- [iléktrou-] a word element meaning *electricity*. —「전기」를 뜻하는 연결형
e·lec·tro·cute [iléktrəkjùːt] *vt.* kill (a criminal, etc.) by —他 …을 전기 사형에 처하다
an electric current, as in an electric chair.
e·lec·tro·cu·tion [ilèktrəkjúːʃ(ə)n] *n.* Ⓤ the act of elec- —名 전기 사형
trocuting; the state of being electrocuted.
e·lec·trode [iléktroud] *n.* ⓒ either of the two terminals —名 전극(電極)
of a battery, etc.
e·lec·trol·y·sis [ilèktrálisis / -tról-] *n.* Ⓤ the separation —名 전기분해,전해(電解)
of a substance into its chemical elements by electricity.
e·lec·tro·mag·net [ilèktroumǽgnit] *n.* ⓒ a piece of —名 전자석(電磁石)
iron that becomes a strong magnet when an electric
current is passed through wire coiled around it.
e·lec·tron [iléktran / -trɔn] *n.* ⓒ the smallest unit of —名 전자(電子)
matter having negative electricity.
e·lec·tron·ic [ilèktránik / -trón-] *adj.* of an electron, —形 전자[공학]의
electrons or electronics. ¶*an ~ calculator* (or *comput-
er*) / *~ music.*
e·lec·tron·ics [ilèktróniks / -trón-] *n. pl.* (used as *sing.*) —名 전자공학
the science of the systems and phenomena of electrons.
e·lec·tro·plate [iléktrouplèit] *vt.* cover (something) with —他 …에 전기도금을 하다 —名 전기
a thin coating of metal by electrolysis. —*n.* ⓒ some- 도금 제품
thing covered in this way.
el·e·gance [éligəns] *n.* **1.** Ⓤ the quality of being elegant —名 1.우아함; 고상함 2.우아한 것
or refined. **2.** ⓒ something elegant.
el·e·gan·cy [éligənsi] *n.* (pl. **-cies**) =elegance.
* **el·e·gant** [éligənt] *adj.* having or showing good taste; —形 우아한; 고상한,품위있는 ¶①고
refined; graceful. ¶*~ dress* / *an ~ young woman* / *an* 아(高雅)한 예술
~ style / *~ manners* / *~ arts.*① ▷**el·e·gant·ly** [-li] *adv.*
el·e·gi·ac [èlidʒáiæk, ilːdʒiæk / èlidʒáiək] *adj.* **1.** of or —形 1.만가(挽歌)의, 애가조(哀歌調)
fit for an elegy. **2.** sad; mournful. —*n.* ((*pl.*)) a series 의 2.애수적인 —名 비가, 애가
of elegiac verses. ⌜row, esp. for the dead.⌝
el·e·gy [élidʒi] *n.* ⓒ (pl. **-gies**) a poem expressing sor-⌟ —名 비가,애가; 만가
:**el·e·ment** [éləmənt] *n.* ⓒ **1.** (*Chemistry*) a substance —名 1.《化》원소 2.요소;성분 3. 4대
that cannot be separated into simpler substances. **2.** 요소의 하나(흙·공기·불·물) NB
a simple and essential thing of which anything is made 고대철학에서 자연을 구성하는 근본요
up. **3.** earth, air, fire, or water. ⇨NB **4.** ((*the* ~*s*)) 소로 생각되었음 4.자연의 힘 ¶①자
the forces of nature, such as rain and wind. ¶*the fury* 연의 맹위/②풍우에 노출된 5.초보;기
*of the elements*① / *exposed to the elements.*② **5.** ((*the* 초; 기본 ¶③물리학의 초보 6.생존
~*s*)) the steps that must be learnt first. ¶*the elements* 에 알맞은 자연환경
*of physics.*① **6.** natural or fitting surroundings.
be in (*out of*) *one's element,* be (be not) in the sur- 圖 자기가 뜻대로 할 수 있는 환경내
roundings where one can show at one's best. (밖)에 있다
el·e·men·tal [èliméntl] *adj.* **1.** of an element; essential; —形 1.원소의;요소의;기본적인 2. 4대
basic. **2.** of the four elements; of the forces of nature. 요소의; 자연력의 ¶①대폭풍우/②자
¶*~ forces* / *~ grandeur* / *~ strife*① / *~ worship.*② **3.** 연력 숭배 3. 단순하지만 힘센,투박한
simple but powerful. **4.** =elementary.
* **el·e·men·ta·ry** [èlimént(ə)ri] *adj.* **1.** of the first steps; —形 1.초보의, 초등의; 기본의 ¶①국
necessary to be learned first; of the beginning. ¶*~* 민학교 2.원소의

education (knowledge) | *an* ~ *school.*① **2.** of a chemical element or elements.

‡el·e·phant [élifənt] *n.* [C] (pl. **-phants** or *collectively* **-phant**) a large, heavy animal with a thick skin, long nose, and tusks. —[名] 코끼리

a white elephant, something costly but troublesome and useless to its owner. [熟] 귀찮은(주체하기 힘든) 소유물

•el·e·vate [élivèit] *vt.* **1.** lift up; raise. ¶*He was elevated to the peerage.*① | *This book will* ~ *the minds of young people.* **2.** put (someone) in high spirits; encourage. —[他] 1. …을 올리다, …을 높이다 ¶① 그는 귀족으로 승격되었다 2. …의 기운을 북돋우다, 사기를 높이다

el·e·vat·ed [élivèitid] *adj.* **1.** raised; high. ¶*an* ~ *railroad* (or *railway*). **2.** noble; lofty. **3.** in high spirits. —[形] 1. 높아진, 높은 2. 고상(고결)한 3. 의기왕성한

el·e·va·tion [èlivéiʃ(ə)n] *n.* **1.** [U] the act of elevating; the state of being elevated. **2.** [C] a raised place; a high place. **3.** [C] a height; a height above sea level. ¶*an* ~ *of 3,000 feet.*① **4.** [U] dignity; nobility. —[名] 1. 높이기, 향상, 승진 2. 고지(高地), 높직한 언덕 3. 고도; 해발 ¶①해발 3,000 피이트 4. 위엄, 고상(고결)함

‡el·e·va·tor [élivèitər] *n.* [C] (*U.S.*) a machine to carry people and things up and down in a building. (cf. *Brit.* lift) —[名] 엘리베이터, 승강기

‡e·lev·en [ilév(ə)n] *n.* [C] **1.** [U] the number between ten and twelve; 11. **2.** [C] any group or set of eleven persons or things; a football or cricket team. ¶*be in the* ~.① —*adj.* of 11. —[名] 1. 열 하나, 11 2. 축구·크리켓의 티임 ¶①축구(크리켓) 선수다 —[形] 11의

‡e·lev·enth [ilév(ə)nθ] *n.* **1.** 《*the* ~》 number 11; 11th. **2.** [C] one of 11 equal parts of anything. —*adj.* of 11th. —[名] 1. 제 11, 열 한째 2. 11 분의 1 —[形] 제 11 의, 열한째의, 11 분의 1 의

at the eleventh hour, at the last possible moment. ¶*change a plan at the* ~ *hour.* [熟] 아슬아슬한 고비에, 마지막 순간에

elf [elf] *n.* [C] (pl. **elves**) **1.** a tiny, harmful fairy. **2.** a harmful or mischievous child. ▷**elf·like** [-làik] *adj.* —[名] 1. 꼬마 요정 2. 장난꾸러기 아이, 개구장이

elf·in [élfin] *adj.* =elfish. —*n.* =elf.

elf·ish [élfiʃ] *adj.* like an elf; mischievous. —[形] 꼬마 요정 같은, 장난이 심한, 짓궂은

e·lic·it [ilísit] *vt.* draw forth; cause. 《~ something *from*》 ¶*His fine acting elicited applause from the audience.* —[他] …을 끌어내다

el·i·gi·bil·i·ty [èlidʒibíliti] *n.* [U] the state of being eligible. —[名] 적격[성]

el·i·gi·ble [élidʒəbl] *adj.* fit to be chosen; suitable. ¶*He is* ~ *for the position.* —*n.* [C] an eligible person. —[形] 뽑힐 자격이 있는, 적격의 —[名] 적격자, 적임자

•e·lim·i·nate [ilíminèit] *vt.* get rid of (something); remove; take out. ¶~ *danger.* —[他] …을 제거(삭제)하다, 지워 없애다, 삭제하다

e·lim·i·na·tion [ilìminéiʃ(ə)n] *n.* [U] the act of eliminating; the state of being eliminated. ¶*an* ~ *match.*① —[名] 제거, 삭제 ¶①예선 시합

e·lim·i·na·tor [ilíminèitər] *n.* [C] a person who eliminates. —[名] 제거하는 사람

e·lite, é·lite [eilí:t, +*U.S.* il-, +*Brit.* el-] *n.* 《*the* ~, *collectively*》 chosen people; the best people. ¶*the* ~ *of society.*① —[名] 뽑힌 사람들, 정예(精銳), 엘리트, 선량(選良) ¶①명사, 상류 인사

e·lix·ir [ilíksər] *n.* [C] a medicine that cures all ills. ¶*the* ~ *of life.*① —[名] 만병 통치약, 영약(靈藥) ¶①불로장수의 영약

•E·liz·a·beth [ilízəbəθ] *n.* a woman's name. ⇨[N.B.] —[名] 여자 이름 [N.B.] 애칭은 Beth, Betty, Liz 따위

E·liz·a·be·than [ilìzəbí:θ(ə)n] *adj.* of the time of Queen Elizabeth I (1558–1603). ¶~ *literature.* —*n.* [C] a person, esp. a writer or an artist, of the Elizabethan time. —[形] 엘리자베드 여왕 시대의, 엘리자베드조(朝)의 —[名] 엘리자베드 시대의 문학자·예술가

elk [elk] *n.* [C] (pl. **elks** or *collectively* **elk**) a large deer of northern Europe, Asia, and America. —[名] 뿔이 큰 사슴의 일종

ell¹ [el] *n.* [C] an old measure of length, used chiefly in measuring cloth, equal to 114.3 meters. ¶(*proverb*) *Give him an inch and he'll take an* ~.① —[名] 엘(척도) ¶①《俚》한 치를 주니 한 자를 달란다, 봉당을 빌려 주니 안방까지 달란다

ell² [el] *n.* [C] **1.** the letter L, l. **2.** something shaped like L. —[名] 1. L자 2. L자형의 것

El·len [élin] *n.* a woman's name. —[名] 여자 이름

el·lipse [ilíps] *n.* [C] a shape like an egg; an oval. —[名] 타원[형]

el·lip·ses [ilípsi:z] *n.* pl. of **ellipsis**.

el·lip·sis [ilípsis] *n.* [U][C] (pl. **-ses**) the omission of a word or phrase; (*Printing*) marks showing omission. —[名] 생략[법]; 《印刷》 생략부호

el·lip·tic [ilíptik], **-ti·cal** [-tik(ə)l] *adj.* **1.** shaped like an ellipse. **2.** (*Grammar*) having a word or phrase omitted. —[形] 1. 타원[형]의 2. 《文法》 생략적인

•elm [elm] *n.* [C] a tall, graceful tree planted chiefly for shade; [U] the hard, heavy wood of this tree. —[名] 느릅나무; 느릅나무 재목

el·o·cu·tion [èləkjú:ʃ(ə)n] *n.* [U] the art or manner of speaking or reading clearly and effectively in public.
—[名] 웅변술, 낭독법; 이야기투, 연설투

el·o·cu·tion·ar·y [èləkjú:ʃ(ə)nèri / -əri] *adj.* of elocution.
—[形] 웅변술의, 낭독법의

el·o·cu·tion·ist [èləkjú:ʃ(ə)nist] *n.* [C] a person skilled in elocution; a person who teaches elocution.
—[名] 웅변가, 낭독가; 연설(낭독)법의 교사

e·lon·gate [ilɔ́:ŋgèit / í:lɔŋgèit] *vt.* make (something) longer; lengthen; stretch. **—*vi.*** become longer. **—*adj.*** lengthened; long.
—[他] …을 늘이다, 연장하다 —[自] 늘어나다, 길어지다
—[形] 늘어난, 길어진, 긴

e·lon·ga·tion [ilɔ̀:ŋgéiʃ(ə)n / ì:lɔŋ-] *n.* **1.** [U] the act of lengthening; extension. **2.** [C] a lengthened part.
—[名] 1. 늘어나기, 연장, 신장(伸長) 2. 연장선, 늘어난 부분

e·lope [ilóup] *vi.* **1.** run away with a lover. **2.** escape secretly. ▷**e·lop·er** [-ər] *n.*
—[自] 1. [애인과 함께] 집을 뛰쳐나오다 2. 도망치다 「기, 도망

e·lope·ment [ilóupmənt] *n.* [U] the act of eloping.
—[名] [애인과 함께] 집을 뛰쳐나오기, 도망

*** el·o·quence** [éləkwəns] *n.* [U] fluent and forceful speaking; the art or power to win something by speaking.
—[名] 웅변; 웅변술

*** el·o·quent** [éləkwənt] *adj.* having or showing eloquence; fluent; very expressive. ▷**el·o·quent·ly** [-li] *adv.*
—[形] 웅변의, 변설이 능숙한; 남을 감동시키는

El Sal·va·dor [elsǽlvədɔ̀:r / ⌐ ⌐⌐⌐] *n.* a small country in western Central America, on the Pacific side. ⇒[N.B.]
—[名] 중미 서부의 작은 공화국 [N.B.] 수도는 San Salvador

⁑ else [els] *adj.* ⇒[usage] **1.** other; different. ¶*anybody ~ / This is somebody else's coat. / What ~ could I say?* **2.** additional; more. ¶*Who ~ is there in the room? / There is no one ~ who knows about it.*
—[形] [usage] some-, any-, no- 가 붙는 말, 또는 의문 대명사 다음에 옴 1. 다른, 딴 2. 그밖의

—*adv.* **1.** in a different way. ¶*How ~ can I solve the problem?* **2.** besides; in addition. ¶*Where ~ did you go?*
—[副] 1. 그밖에, 달리, 따로이 2. 게다가, 그 위에

or else, otherwise; if not. ¶*Take care, or ~ you will fall.*
[熟] 그렇지 않으면

⁑ else·where [élsw(h)èər / ⌐⌐] *adv.* in, at, or to some other place. ¶*as ~.*①
—[副] 다른 곳에(으로), 어딘가 딴 곳에 ¶①다른 장소와 마찬가지로

e·lu·ci·date [ilú:sidèit / il(j)ú:si-] *vt.* make (something) clear; clarify; explain.
—[他] …을 명백히 하다, 밝히다; 설명하다

e·lu·ci·da·tion [ilù:sidéiʃ(ə)n / il(j)ù:si-] *n.* [U] the act of making clear; explanation.
—[名] 명시, 설명, 해설

e·lude [ilú:d / il(j)ú:d] *vt.* get away from (something); escape; avoid. ¶*The meaning eludes me.*①
—[他] …에서 벗어나다, …을 비키다 ¶①그 뜻을 도저히 알 수 없다

e·lu·sion [ilú:ʒ(ə)n / il(j)ú:-] *n.* [U] the act of eluding; escape.
—[名] 피하기, 회피

e·lu·sive [ilú:siv / il(j)ú:-] *adj.* **1.** (of words, etc.) difficult to understand or remember. **2.** inclined to escape. ▷**e·lu·sive·ly** [-li] *adv.* —**e·lu·sive·ness** [-nis] *n.*
—[形] 1. 이해하기 어려운; 외기 힘든 2. 잘 도망치는

elves [elvz] *n.* pl. of **elf.**

E·ly·sian [ilíʒən / -ziən] *adj.* of or like Elysium; heavenly; happy; delightful. ¶*the ~ fields.*①
—[形] 극락의(같은); 행복한; 즐거운 ¶①극락 정토, 낙원

E·ly·sium [ilíʒiəm / -ziəm] *n.* (in Greek mythology) a place where virtuous people went after death; paradise; the place of perfect happiness.
—[名] 극락, 낙원, 이상향; 더 없이 행복한 장소

'em, em [əm] *pron.* (*colloq.*) them.

e·ma·ci·ate [iméiʃièit] *vt.* make (someone or something) thin. **—*vi.*** become thin.
—[他] …을 야위게 하다, 수척하게 하다
—[自] 야위다, 수척해지다

em·a·nate [émənèit] *vi.* come out; issue. 《~ *from* something》 ¶*Various ideas ~ from the brain.*①
—[自] 흘러나오다, 유출되다; 나오다 ¶①갖가지 생각이 머리에서 나온다

em·a·na·tion [èmənéiʃ(ə)n] *n.* [U] **1.** the act of emanating. **2.** [C] something emanated.
—[名] 1. 유출 2. 유출물, 방사물(放射物)

e·man·ci·pate [imǽnsipèit] *vt.* set (someone) free; release. 《~ someone *from*》
—[他] …을 해방하다, 석방하다

e·man·ci·pa·tion [imæ̀nsipéiʃ(ə)n] *n.* [U] the act of emancipating; the state of being emancipated.
—[名] [노예 따위의] 해방, 석방

e·man·ci·pa·tor [imǽnsipèitər] *n.* [C] a person who emancipates. ¶*the great ~.*① ⇒[N.B.]
—[名] 해방자 ¶①위대한 해방자 [N.B.] Abraham Lincoln 을 가리킴

e·mas·cu·late [imǽskjulèit → *adj.*] *vt.* **1.** remove the male organs of (an animal). **2.** weaken. **—*adj.*** [imǽskjulit] weakened.
—[他] 1. …의 불알을 까다, 거세하다 2. …을 무기력하게(약하게) 하다 —[形] 힘없는, 무기력한, 쇠약해진

e·mas·cu·la·tion [imæ̀skjuléiʃ(ə)n] *n.* [U] the act of emasculating; the state of being emasculated.
—[名] 불알까기, 거세; 무기력, 나약

em·balm [imbɑ́:m] *vt.* **1.** keep (a dead body) from decaying. **2.** keep (something) in memory. **3.** fill
—[他] 1. [시체]를 방부하다 2. …을 오래 기억에 남기다 3. …에 향기를 채우

embankment [383] **embrace**

(something) with a sweet scent. ▷**em·balm·er** [-ər] n.
em·bank·ment [imbǽŋkmənt] n. ⓒ a bank or wall of earth, stones, etc. used to keep back water.
em·bar·go [embá:rgou / im-] n. ⓒ (pl. **-goes**) **1.** a government order that ships must not enter or leave its ports; a restriction put on trade by law. ¶*gold ~ / lay (or put) an ~ on trade① / lift (or take off, remove) an ~ / under an ~.* **2.** any restriction. —*vt.* lay (ships, etc.) under an embargo; put an embargo on (trade).
em·bark [imbá:rk] *vi.* **1.** go on board a ship. 《*~ for Europe, etc.*》 ¶*~ for England.①* **2.** set out; start. 《*~ in, on* or *upon* something》 ¶*~ upon a venture.* —*vt.* **1.** take (someone or something) on board a ship. **2.** engage. ¶*~ oneself in an enterprise.②*
em·bar·ka·tion [èmba:rkéiʃ(ə)n] n. Ⓤ the act of embarking.
∗**em·bar·rass** [imbǽrəs, +U.S. em-] *vt.* disturb (someone); confuse ¶*I feel (or be) embarrassed① / Don't me with difficult questions.* 「ing; difficult.」
em·bar·rass·ing [imbǽrəsiŋ, +U.S. em-] *adj.* confus-
em·bar·rass·ment [imbǽrəsmənt / em-] n. **1.** Ⓤ the state of being embarrassed. ¶*to one's ~.②* **2.** ⓒ a thing that embarrasses.
em·bas·sy [émbəsi] n. ⓒ (pl. **-sies**) **1.** an ambassador and his assistants. **2.** the official building where an ambassador lives. **3.** a position or duties of an ambassador. 「thing） for battle.」
em·bat·tle [imbǽtl / em-] *vt.* prepare or arrange (some-
em·bed [imbéd / em-] *vt.* (**-bed·ded, -bed·ding**) 《usu. in *passive*》 put (something) in a bed; fix or set deeply. ¶*The incident is embedded in my memory.*
em·bel·lish [imbéliʃ / em-] *vt.* **1.** make (something) more beautiful; decorate. ¶*~ a dress with lace and ribbons.* **2.** make (a story, etc.) more interesting.
em·bel·lish·ment [imbéliʃmənt / em-] n. ⓊⒸ **1.** decoration. **2.** addition to make (a story, etc.) interesting.
em·ber [émbər] n. 《usu. *pl.*》 pieces of wood or coal still glowing in the dying fire; ashes in which there is still some fire.
em·bez·zle [imbézl / em-] *vt.* steal (money, etc. given into one's care). 「of embezzling.」
em·bez·zle·ment [imbézlmənt / em-] n. ⓊⒸ the act
em·bit·ter [imbítər / em-] *vt.* make (someone) bitter.
em·blem [émbləm] n. ⓒ a symbol; a badge.
em·blem·at·ic [èmblimǽtik], **-i·cal** [-ik(ə)l] *adj.* symbolical. ¶*The cross is ~ of Christianity.①*
em·bod·i·ment [imbádimənt / -bɔ́d-] n. **1.** Ⓤ the act of embodying; the state of being embodied. **2.** ⓒ something embodied; something that embodies.
em·bod·y [imbádi / -bɔ́d-] *vt.* (**-bod·ied**) **1.** express (ideas, etc.) in a real form. ¶*This book embodies democratic ideals.* **2.** collect (matters) into a book, etc.; include (things) in a body.
em·bold·en [imbóuld(ə)n] *vt.* make (someone) bold.
em·bos·om [imbúzəm, +U.S. em-] *vt.* 《usu. in *passive*》 surround. ¶*a small village embosomed in hills.①*
em·boss [imbɔ́:s, -bás, em- / imbɔ́s] *vt.* decorate (paper, leather, etc.) with a design, figures, etc., that are raised on the surface; cause (a design, figure, etc.) to raise on the surface.
∗**em·brace** [imbréis / em-] *vt.* **1.** hold (someone) in one's arms. **2.** surround; enclose. ¶*a house embraced by trees.* **3.** include. **4.** accept. ¶*~ Christianity.* —*vi.* hold one another in the arms. —n. ⓒ the act of embracing. ▷**em·brace·a·ble** [-əbl] *adj.*

—다
—⊛ 둑 쌓기; 둑, 제방

—⊛ 1. [선박의] 출항(입항) 금지, 수출 (수입) 금지, 통상 금지 ¶①통상을 금 지하다 2. 금지 —⊕ [선박]의 출항(입 항)을 금지하다; [통상]을 금지하다

—⊜ 1. 배에 타다, 출항하다 ¶①영국 을 향하여 출항하다 2. 출발하다, 시작 하다 —⊕ 1. …을 배에 태우다, 승선시 키다, 싣다, 탑재하다 2. …에 종사시키 다 ¶②사업에 착수하다
—⊛ 화물 적재, 선적
—⊕ …을 난처하게 하다, 당황하게 하 다, 혼란시키다 ¶①어쩔 줄 모르다, 쩔 쩔매다
—⊜ 난처하게 하는; 귀찮은, 성가신
—⊛ 1. 당황, 곤혹, 수줍음, 어색함, 어쩔 줄 모름 ¶①난처하게도, 당황한 일은 2. 당황하게 하는 일(것)
—⊛ 1. 대사, 대사관원 2. 대사관 3. 대 사의 임무(직위)

—⊕ …을 전투태세를 갖추게 하다
—⊕ …을 파묻다, 끼워넣다; …을 [기 억 따위에] 깊이 간직하다

—⊕ 1. …을 아름답게 하다; 장식하다 2. [소설 따위]를 재미있게 꾸미다, 윤 색하다
—⊛ 1. 장식 2. 윤색, 수식

—⊛ 타다 남은 불, 등걸불

—⊕ [돈 따위]를 착복하다, 횡령하다

—⊛ 착복, 횡령
—⊕ …을 쓰라리게 하다, 고통을 주다
—⊛ 상징, 표상; 기장, 휘장
—⊜ 상징적인 ¶①십자가는 그리스도 의 상징이다
—⊛ 1. 형상을 부여하기, 구체화, 구 현 2. 화신(化身), 권화(權化), 구체화한 것; 구체화하는 것
—⊕ 1. …을 구체적으로 나타내다; 구 체화하다 2. …을 책 따위에 수록하다; …을 포함하다

—⊕ …을 대담하게 하다
—⊕ …을 둘러싸다; 품에 안다 ¶①작 은 산들로 둘러싸인 마을
—⊕ …을 돋을새김하다, 양각으로 새기 다; 볼록 나오게 하다

—⊕ 1. …을 껴안다, 포옹하다 2. …을 둘러싸다, 에워싸다 3. …을 포함하다 4. …을 받아들이다 —⊜ 서로 껴안다
—⊛ 포옹

em·bra·sure [imbréiʒər / em-] n. ⓒ
1. an opening in a wall for a gun.
2. a window or door with sloping sides, as in an old stone castle. ⇒fig.

[embrasure 2.]

— ⓝ 1. 총안(銃眼) 2. [문·창 둘레의] 나팔꽃 모양[의 구멍]

* **em·broi·der** [imbrɔ́idər, +U.S. em-] vt. 1. decorate (cloth, leather, etc.) with a needlework design; put (a figure) on cloth, etc. 2. add something untrue to (a story, etc.); exaggerate. —vi. do embroidery.
▷ **em·broi·der·er** [-rər] n.

— ⓥ 1. …에 […을] 수놓다 2. …을 과장하다 — ⓥ 수를 놓다, 자수하다

em·broi·der·y [imbrɔ́id(ə)ri, +U.S. em-] n. (pl. **-der·ies**)
1. Ⓤ the act or art of embroidering; an ornamental needlework. 2. ⓒ an embroidered work or material.

— ⓝ 1. 수놓기, 자수 2. 자수품

em·broil [imbrɔ́il, +U.S. em-] vt. 1. make (someone) take part in a quarrel, etc. ¶*become embroiled in a dispute*.① 2. throw (something) into a confusion.
▷ **em·broil·ment** [-mənt] n.

— ⓥ 1. …을 휩쓸어 넣다 ¶①싸움에 휩쓸려 들다 2. …을 혼란시키다(분규시키다); 끝내디아프게 하다

em·bry·o [émbriòu] n. ⓒ (pl. **-os**) 1. an animal before birth. 2. a plant within a seed. ¶*in* ~.① —*adj.* undeveloped; not mature.

— ⓝ 1. 태아 2. 배(胚), 배아(胚芽) ¶①발달이 덜 된, 미숙한

em·bry·ol·o·gist [èmbriɑ́ləʒist / -ɔ́l-] n. ⓒ a specialist in embryology. 「embryos.」

— ⓝ 태생학자, 발생학자

em·bry·ol·o·gy [èmbriɑ́lədʒi / -ɔ́l-] n. Ⓤ the science of

— ⓝ 태생학, 발생학

em·bry·on·ic [èmbriɑ́nik / -ɔ́n-] *adj.* 1. of or like the embryo. 2. undeveloped; not mature.

— ⓐ 1. 태아의(같은); 배(胚)의, 배아의(같은) 2. 미발달의, 미숙한

em·cee [émsí:] (U.S. *colloq.*) n. ⓒ a master of ceremonies. —vt. act as a master of ceremonies for (a radio program, television show, etc.). —vi. act as a master of ceremonies. ⇒ⓃⒷ

— ⓝ 《美口》 사회자 — ⓥ …의 사회를 맡아 보다, 사회하다 — ⓥ 사회보다
ⓃⒷ Master of Ceremonies 의 약자 M.C.에서

em·er·ald [ém(ə)rəld] n. 1. ⓒ a bright-green precious stone. 2. Ⓤ bright green. —*adj.* of or like emerald; bright-green. 「*hind the clouds*.」

— ⓝ 1.에메랄드, 취옥(翠玉) 2. 밝은 초록빛, 에메랄드색 — ⓐ 에메랄드[색]의

* **e·merge** [imə́:rdʒ] vi. come out; appear. ¶~ *from be-*

— ⓥ 나오다; 나타나다

e·mer·gence [imə́:rdʒ(ə)ns] n. Ⓤ the act of emerging; appearance.

— ⓝ 출현

* **e·mer·gen·cy** [imə́:rdʒ(ə)nsi] n. ⓒⓊ (pl. **-cies**) a sudden, unexpected happening. ¶*an* ~ *case* (or *box*)① / *an* ~ *door*② / *an* ~ *landing*③ / *an* ~ *measures*④ / *in case of* (or *in an*) ~.⑤ 「*unexpectedly*.」

— ⓝ 비상사태, 돌발사고 ¶①구급상자/②비상구/③비상착/④비상수단, 응급조치/⑤위급한 경우에는, 비상시에는

e·mer·gent [imə́:rdʒ(ə)nt] *adj.* happening suddenly and

— ⓐ 돌발적인, 불의의

e·mer·i·tus [imérətəs, +Brit. i:-] *adj.* retired but holding one's rank or title. ¶*an* ~ *professor; a professor* ~.①

— ⓐ 명예 퇴직의 ¶①명예교수

Em·er·son [émərsn], **Ralph Waldo** n. (1803-1882) an American essayist, poet, and philosopher.

— ⓝ 미국의 평론가·시인·철학자

em·er·y [éməri, +U.S. émri] n. Ⓤ a hard mineral, used for grinding, smoothing, and polishing.

— ⓝ 금강사(金剛砂)

e·met·ic [imétik] *adj.* causing to throw up food. —n. ⓒ a medicine that causes someone to throw up food.

— ⓐ 구역질나게 하는, 메스꺼워지는
— ⓝ 구토제

em·i·grant [émigr(ə)nt] n. ⓒ a person who emigrates. ↔immigrant —*adj.* emigrating.

— ⓝ 이민 — ⓐ 이민의, 이주하는

em·i·grate [émigrèit] vi. leave one's own country to live in another. ↔immigrate ¶~ *from England to America*. —vt. cause (someone) to emigrate.

— ⓥ 이주하다 — ⓥ …을 이주시키다

em·i·gra·tion [èmigréiʃ(ə)n] n. 1. Ⓤ the act of emigrating. 2. ⓒ a group of emigrants.

— ⓝ 1. 이주, 이민 2. 이민[단]

Em·i·ly [ém(i)li] n. a woman's name.

— ⓝ 여자 이름

em·i·nence [émināns], **-nen·cy** [-nənsi] n. 1. Ⓤ highness in rank or position; greatness. ¶*a man of* ~.① 2. ⓒ a high place. ¶*on an* ~.

— ⓝ 1.[지위 따위가] 높음; 탁월, 명성, 저명 ¶①명사 2. 높은 곳, 고소(高所)

* **em·i·nent** [éminənt] *adj.* high; great; remarkable; famous. ¶*an* ~ *position* / *an* ~ *soldier* / *a man* ~ *for deeds* / *men* ~ *in science*.

— ⓐ 높은; 탁월한, 저명한

em·i·nent·ly [éminəntli] *adv.* in an eminent manner.
—[副] 뛰어나게, 탁월하게, 현저히

e·mir [əmíər] *n.* Ⓒ **1.** an Arabian ruler, prince, etc. **2.** a title of the descendants of Mohammed.
—[名] 1. [아라비아의] 추장, 왕족 2. 모하멧 자손의 존칭

em·is·sar·y [émisèri / -s(ə)ri] *n.* Ⓒ (pl. **-sar·ies**) a person or secret agent sent on a special mission; a spy.
—[名] 밀사, 밀정, 간첩, 스파이

e·mis·sion [imíʃ(ə)n] *n.* **1.** Ⓤ the act of emitting. **2.** Ⓒ something emitted.
—[名] 1. 방사(放射), 방출, 발행 2. 방사물, 방출물

e·mit [imít] *vt.* (**e·mit·ted, e·mit·ting**) **1.** give off; send forth (light, smell, etc.); discharge. **2.** issue (paper money, etc.).
—[他] 1. [빛 따위]를 방사하다, 내다 2. [지폐 따위]를 발행하다

e·mol·u·ment [imáljumənt / -mɔ́l-] *n.* Ⓒ 《usu. *pl.*》 profit from a job; gain; payment; salary; fees.
—[名] 보수, 수당, 이득; 급료, 임금, 봉급

‡ **e·mo·tion** [imóuʃ(ə)n] *n.* ⓊⒸ a strong feeling; an excitement. ¶ *with* ~① / *without* ~.②
—[名] 흥분; 정서, 감격, 감동 ¶①감동하여/②냉정히, 태연히

* **e·mo·tion·al** [imóuʃ(ə)n(ə)l] *adj.* **1.** of or showing the emotions; appealing to the emotions. **2.** easily excited.
—[形] 1. 감정(정서)의; 감정에 호소하는 2. 흥분하기 쉬운, 감동하기 쉬운

e·mo·tion·al·ly [imóuʃ(ə)n(ə)li] *adv.* in an emotional manner.
—[副] 정서적으로; 감정에 호소하여

e·mo·tion·less [imóuʃ(ə)nlis] *adj.* expressing no emotion.
—[形] 감정이 없는, 무감정의

‡ **em·per·or** [émp(ə)rər] *n.* Ⓒ a man who rules an empire. ↔empress ¶ *His Majesty the Emperor.*①
—[名] 황제, 제왕, 천황 ¶①황제폐하

em·pha·ses [émfəsì:z] *n.* pl. of **emphasis**.

* **em·pha·sis** [émfəsis] *n.* ⓊⒸ (pl. **-ses**) **1.** (of expression, thought, etc.) special force; importance. ¶ *lay* (or *place, put*) *great* ~ *on* (or *upon*) *something.*① **2.** special force given to syllables, words, or phrases, etc.; an accent.
—[名] 1. 강조, 힘줌; 중요함, 중요시 ¶①…에 중점을 두다, …을 크게 강조하다 2. 강세, 어세

* **em·pha·size** [émfəsàiz] *vt.* put emphasis on (something).
—[他] …을 강조하다

em·phat·ic [imfǽtik] *adj.* strongly expressed; stressed; speaking with force; striking.
—[形] 강조된; 어세가 강한, 악센트가 있는; 두드러진, 현저한

em·phat·i·cal·ly [imfǽtikəli] *adv.* in an emphatic manner; decidedly.
—[副] 강조하여, 힘주어; 단호히, 강력히

‡ **em·pire** [émpaiər] *n.* **1.** Ⓒ a group of countries under one ruler. ¶ *Empire City (State)*① / *Empire Day.*② **2.** Ⓤ absolute power or control.
—[名] 1. 제국 ¶①New York 시(주)의 별명/②대영제국 경축일(5월24일) 2. 절대권, 절대 지배권

em·pir·ic [empírik] *n.* Ⓒ **1.** a person who does not believe in theory and who relies on practical experience. **2.** a person who has no regular or proper training; a quack.
—[名] 1. 경험주의자 2. 야바위꾼, 협잡꾼; 돌팔이 의사

em·pir·i·cal [empírik(ə)l] *adj.* based entirely on experiment or practical experience. ▷**em·pir·i·cal·ly** [-kəli] *adv.*
—[形] 실험에 근거를 두는, 경험상의

‡ **em·ploy** [emplɔ́i] *vt.* **1.** get (someone) to work by paying wages or a salary; hire; give work to (someone). ¶ ~ *a new secretary* / *I am employed at a trading company.*① **2.** use; spend; take up. ¶ ~ *one's spare time in reading books*② / *Reading books employs much of his time.* —*n.* Ⓤ the act of employing; the state of being employed; service; use. ¶ *I'm in his* ~.③ / *I have him in my* ~.④
—[他] 1. …을 고용하다; …에게 일(직업)을 주다 ¶①나는 무역회사에 근무하고 있다 2. …을 이용하다; [물건을] 쓰다, 소비하다; 차지하다, [시간·장소를] 잡다 ¶②여가를 독서로 보내다 —[名] 고용; 근무; 이용 ¶③나는 그에게 고용돼 있다/④나는 그를 고용하고 있다

* **em·ploy·ee** [implɔ́ii:, èmplɔií:] *n.* Ⓒ a person who is employed by another and paid wages. ↔employer
—[名] 고용인, 사용인, 종업원

* **em·ploy·er** [implɔ́iər] *n.* Ⓒ a person or firm that employs others. ↔employee
—[名] 고용주, 사용자, 주인; 상회, 회사

‡ **em·ploy·ment** [implɔ́imənt] *n.* **1.** Ⓤ the act of employing; the state of being employed. **2.** ⓊⒸ work; occupation. ¶ *an* ~ *agency* (or *bureau, office*)① / *be out of* ~② / *in the* ~ *of someone*③ / *take someone into* ~④ / *throw someone out of* ~.⑤
—[名] 1. 사용, 고용; 근무 2. 일, 직업 ¶①직업 소개소(안정소)/②실직하여 있다, 실업자로 있다/③…에게 고용되어/④…을 고용하다/⑤…을 해고하다(실직시키다)

em·pow·er [impáuər] *vt.* give power or authority to (someone); enable; permit. 《~ someone *to do*》 ¶ ~ *man to control nature.*
—[他] …에게 힘(권한)을 주다

‡ **em·press** [émpris] *n.* Ⓒ the wife of an emperor; a woman ruler of an empire. ¶ *Her Majesty the Empress.*①
—[名] 황후(皇后); 여제(女帝) ¶①황후폐하

emp·ti·ness [ém(p)tinis] *n.* Ⓤ the state of being empty.
—[名] 빔, 공허; 무지(無知)

‡ **emp·ty** [ém(p)ti] *adj.* (**-ti·er, -ti·est**) **1.** holding nothing within itself; unoccupied. ¶ *an* ~ *bottle.* **2.** with-
—[形] 1. 비어 있는; 사람이 없는 2. 무의미한, 공허한 3. 《口》 배고픈, 공복의

E

empty-handed [386] **enclosure**

out meaning; vain. ¶*an ~ promise.* **3.** (*colloq.*) hungry. **empty of,** lacking; without. ¶*a life ~ of happiness.*
—*n.* ⓒ (pl. **-ties**) anything empty.
—*v.* (**-tied**) *vt.* make (something) empty or vacant. ¶*~ a purse upon a table*① / *~ a bottle into a cup.* —*vi.*
1. become empty or vacant. **2.** (of a river) flow out. ¶*The Sumida empties into the Bay of Tokyo.*
emp·ty-hand·ed [ém(p)tiháendid] *adj.* having or carrying nothing in the hands.
emp·ty-head·ed [ém(p)tihédid] *adj.* stupid; silly; ignorant.
e·mu [í:mju:] *n.* ⓒ a large Australian bird closely resembling the ostrich, but smaller.
em·u·late [émjuléit] *vt.* try to equal or be better than (someone). ⌈an imitation. ¶*in a spirit of ~.*①
em·u·la·tion [èmjuléiʃ(ə)n] *n.* Ⓤ the act of emulating;
e·mul·si·fy [imʎlsifài] *vt.* (**-fied**) change (something) into an emulsion. ▷**e·mul·si·fi·er** [-*ər*] *n.*
e·mul·sion [imʎlʃ(ə)n] *n.* ⓊⒸ an oily, milky liquid, containing very tiny drops of fat, oil, etc.
:en·a·ble [inéibl] *vt.* make (someone or something) able; give (someone or something) ability, means, etc. 《*~ someone to do*》 ¶*His help enabled me to finish the work.*
en·act [inǽkt] *vt.* **1.** make (a bill) into a law. ¶*an enacting clause*① / *as by law enacted.* **2.** play the part of (someone); act. **3.** 《chiefly in *passive*》 take place.
en·act·ment [inǽktmənt] *n.* **1.** Ⓤ the act of enacting; the state of being enacted. **2.** ⓒ a law.
e·nam·el [inǽm(ə)l] *n.* Ⓤ **1.** a hard glasslike substance; a smooth, hard, glossy coating. ¶*~ paint.*① **2.** any smooth, hard, enamel-like substance. —*vt.* (**-eled, -el·ing** or *Brit.* **-elled, -el·ling**) cover or decorate (something) with enamel. ¶*enameled leather.*
en·am·or, *Brit.* **-our** [inǽmər] *vt.* 《chiefly in *passive*》 charm; fascinate; fall in love with (someone). ¶*be enamored of a girl* / *be enamored with a story.*
en·camp [inkǽmp] *vi.* stay or settle in a camp. 《*~ in a place*》 —*vt.* put (someone) in a camp.
en·camp·ment [inkǽmpmənt] *n.* **1.** Ⓤ the act of encamping; the state of being encamped. **2.** ⓒ a camp.
en·case [inkéis] *vt.* put (something) into a case; enclose.
en·chain [intʃéin-] *vt.* **1.** put or bind (something) with a chain. **2.** attract the complete attention of (someone)
・**en·chant** [intʃǽnt / -tʃá:nt] *vt.* **1.** use magic on (someone); bewitch. **2.** delight; charm; fascinate. ¶*be enchanted by her singing* / *be enchanted with the flowers.*
en·chant·er [intʃǽntər / -tʃá:ntə] *n.* ⓒ a person who enchants; a magician. ↔**enchantress**
en·chant·ing [intʃǽntiŋ / -tʃá:nt-] *adj.* delightful; very attractive; charming.
en·chant·ment [intʃǽntmənt / -tʃá:nt-] *n.* **1.** Ⓤ the act of enchanting; the state of being enchanted. **2.** ⓒ a thing that enchants.
en·chan·tress [intʃǽntris / -tʃá:nt-] *n.* ⓒ **1.** a woman who enchants; a witch. ↔**enchanter** **2.** a very fascinating, charming woman.
en·cir·cle [insə́:rkl] *vt.* **1.** make a circle around (someone or something); surround. **2.** move in a circle around (someone or something).
・**en·close** [inklóuz] *vt.* **1.** shut (a place) in on all sides; surround. ¶*The orchard is enclosed with hedges.* **2.** put (something) in an envelope. ¶*~ a check for $300.* **3.** contain; hold; shut up.
en·clo·sure [inklóuʒər] *n.* **1.** Ⓤ the act of enclosing;

蓺 …이 없는; 결여된
—옴 빈 것
—㉰ 비우다, 내다 ¶①지갑에 든 것을 비워 탁상에 놓다 —㉯ 1. 비다 2. [강이] 흘러들다

—㉱ 빈손의, 맨 손의

—㉱ 머리가 텅 빈, 무식한, 무지한
—㉵ 에뮤(호주산 타조 비슷한 큰 새)

—㉰ …에게 지지 않도록 하다

—㉵ 경쟁, 겨룸 ¶①경쟁심에서
—㉰ …을 젖같이 만들다, 유화(乳化)하다

—㉵ 유탁액(乳濁液); 유제(乳劑)

—㉰ …을 가능하게 하다, …에게 힘 (수단 따위)을 주다

—㉰ 1. [법률]을 제정하다 ¶①제정 조항 2. …의 역을 맡아 하다, 상연하다 3. 일어나다
—㉵ 1. [법의] 제정 2. 법령, 법규

—㉵ 1. 에나멜; [오지그릇의] 유약, 오 짓물, 법랑(琺瑯) ¶①광택 페인트 2. [이 따위의] 법랑질 —㉰ …에 유약을 입히다, 에나멜을 칠하다

—㉰ …을 매혹시키다; …에게 반하게 하다

—㉯ 야영하다 —㉰ …을 야영시키다

—㉵ 1. 야영, 노영[하기] 2. 야영, 노영[지]
—㉰ …을 상자에 넣다; 싸다
—㉰ 1. …을 쇠사슬로 매다 2. …의 주 의 따위를 끌다
—㉰ 1. …에게 요술(마술)을 걸다 2. …을 기쁘게 하다; 반하게 하다, 황홀하게 하다

—㉵ 마법사, 요술장이

—㉱ 기쁜; 매혹적인, 황홀하게 하는

—㉵ 1. 마법을 쓰기; 마법; 매혹, 매력 2. 반하게 하는 것

—㉵ 1. 여자 마법사(요술장이) 2. 매혹적인 여자

—㉰ 1. …을 둥글게 둘러싸다; 에워싸다 2. …의 둘레를 돌다, 일주하다

—㉰ 1. …을 둘러싸다; 에워싸다 2. … 을 봉투에 넣다, 동봉하다 3. …을 넣다, 밀폐하다

—㉵ 1. 포위, 둘러싸기 2. 동봉(봉입)한

the state of being enclosed. **2.** [C] something that is enclosed; something that encloses, as a wall or fence.
것; 울타리, 울, 담

en·com·pass [inkʌ́mpəs] *vt.* **1.** surround entirely; encircle. **2.** enclose; contain. ▷**en·com·pass·ment** [-mənt] *n.*
—[他] 1. …을 둘러싸다; 에워싸다; 포위하다 2. …을 봉입하다; 포함하다

en·core [ɑ́ŋkɔːr / ɔŋkɔ́ː] *interj.* Once more!; Again! —*n.* [C] **1.** a demand of "Encore!". **2.** an additional song, etc., given in reply to such a demand. —*vt.* call for an encore to (someone).
—[感] 1. 재청이오!, 앙코오르! —[名] 재청이오(앙코오르)!하는 외침, 재청의 요구 2. 재청에 응하는 연주(노래) —[他] …을 재청하다

‡**en·coun·ter** [inkáuntər] *vt.* **1.** come upon (someone). **2.** meet (an enemy, etc.). **3.** meet with (difficulties, etc.). —*vi.* **1.** meet unexpectedly with someone. **2.** meet in a fight. 《~ *with* an enemy》 —*n.* [C] a sudden, unexpected meeting with someone or something.
—[他] 1. …와 우연히 만나다(마주치다) 2. …와 교전하다 3. [곤란 따위]에 부닥치다 —[自] 1. 마주치다, 만나다 2. 회전(會戰)하다 —[名] 뜻밖의 만남, 조우, 조우전(戰), 충돌

‡**en·cour·age** [inkə́ːridʒ / -kʌ́ridʒ] *vt.* **1.** give courage to (someone); inspire. ↔discourage 《~ someone *to do*》 ¶~ *a boy to study* (or *in his studies*)① / *be encouraged by someone's success.* **2.** help; support; promote. ¶*Our school encourages sports.* ▷**en·cour·ag·er** [-ər] *n.* —**en·cour·ag·ing·ly** [-li] *adv.*
—[他] 1. …의 용기를 북돋우다 ¶①소년을 격려하여 공부하게 하다 2. …을 조장하다; 촉진하다; 장려하다

en·cour·age·ment [inkə́ːridʒmənt / -kʌ́ridʒ-] *n.* [U] the act of encouraging; the state of being encouraged; [C] something that encourages. ¶*take ~ from his words*① / *There is some ~ in doing it.*②
—[名] 격려; 장려; 격려가 되는 것 ¶①그의 말로 힘을 얻다/②그것을 하는 데 다소 신바람이 난다

en·cour·ag·ing [inkə́ːridʒiŋ / -kʌ́ridʒ-] *adj.* giving courage.
—[形] 용기를 북돋우는; 장려하는, 고무적인

en·croach [inkróutʃ] *vi.* go beyond proper limits. 《~ *on* or *upon* something》 ¶*The sea encroaches on* (or *upon*) *the land.*① / ~ *on* (or *upon*) *a neighboring land.*
—[自] 침입하다, 침식하다, 침해하다 ¶①바다가 육지를 침식한다

en·croach·ment [inkróutʃmənt] *n.* [U][C] the act of encroaching; something taken by encroaching.
—[名] 침입[지], 침식[지], 침해

en·crust [inkrʌ́st] *vt., vi.* =incrust.

en·cum·ber [inkʌ́mbər] *vt.* **1.** get in the way of (someone or something); hinder. ¶*She was encumbered by her long skirts while running.* **2.** choke up; fill. **3.** burden. ¶*be encumbered with debts.*①
—[他] 1. …을 방해하다; 훼방놓다 2. [장소를] 막다 3. [부채 따위]를 지게 하다 ¶①빚을 지고 고민하다

en·cum·brance [inkʌ́mbr(ə)ns] *n.* [C] anything that encumbers; obstruction; burden.
—[名] 방해물, 거추장스러운 것, 말썽거리; 짐

en·cy·clo·pe·di·a, -pae- [insàikloupíːdiə, en-] *n.* [C] a book or series of books about all branches of knowledge. ¶*Encyclopaedia Britannica.*
—[名] 백과사전, 백과전서

en·cy·clo·pe·dic, -pae- [insàikloupíːdik, en-] *adj.* **1.** of or like an encyclopedia. **2.** about all branches of knowledge.
—[形] 1. 백과사전 같은 2. 지식이 해박한, 박식한, 박학의

‡**end** [end] *n.* [C] 《often *the* ~》 **1.** the last point or part; the finish. ¶*journey's ~ / the ~ of the year / the ~ of the street.* **2.** an aim; a purpose. ¶*gain one's end*[*s*]. **3.** death; ruin. ¶*an early ~ / It was the ~ of him.*① **4.** conclusion. **5.** a small part that remains. ¶*a cigarette ~.*②
—[名] 1. 끝; 마지막; 종말 2. 목적 3. 죽음, 최후; 파멸, 멸망 ¶①그것이 그의 파멸이었다 4. 결론 5. 나부랑이, 동강이, 쪼가리 ¶②담배 꽁초

1) ***at a loose end; at loose ends,*** (*colloq.*) unoccupied; having nothing to do.
2) ***at one's wit's end,*** not knowing what to do; very anxious.
3) ***be at an end,*** have finished.
4) ***come to an end,*** end.
5) ***in the end,*** finally; at last.
6) ***make an end of*** (=*stop; abolish*) *something.*
7) ***make both ends meet,*** live within one's income.
8) ***no end,*** very much.
9) ***no end of,*** a large number (or amount) of.
10) ***on end,*** upright. ¶*put a bottle on ~.*
11) ***put an end to*** (=*stop; abolish*) *something.*
12) ***to the end,*** until the end arrives; until someone reaches the end.

[熟] 1)《口》 직업이 없는; 할 일이 없는 2)어찌 할 바를 몰라; 몹시 근심하여 3)…을 다하다, 끝나다 4)끝나다 5)결국; 마침내 6)…을 그만두다; 폐지하다 7)수입 범위내에서 생활하다, 수지를 맞추다 8)몹시, 대단히 9)무척 많은, 한없는 10)곧추 서서 11)…을 그만두다; 폐지하다 12)끝까지, 최후까지

—*vt.* bring (something) to an end; put an end to (something). —*vi.* come to an end.
—[他] …을 끝내다, 마치다 —[自] 끝나다, 결말이 나다

1) ***end by doing,*** do something last.
[熟] 1)마지막으로 …하다, …하는 것으

2) ***end in,*** have (something) as a result; lead to (something) at the end. ¶*The argument between the two men ended in a fight.*③
3) ***end up,*** finish; die. ¶*~ up in prison.*④
4) ***end*** (=*be finished*) ***with something.***

로 끝맺다 2)결국 …이 되다 ¶③두 사람 사이의 언쟁은 결국 싸움으로 번졌다 3)끝나다; 죽다 ¶④옥사(獄死)하다 4)…으로 끝나다

en·dan·ger [indéindʒər] *vt.* put (someone or something) in danger; expose (someone or something) to danger.
—[他] …을 위험에 빠뜨리다, 위태롭게 하다, 위험에 처하게 하다

en·dear [indíər] *vt.* ⟪*reflexively*⟫ make (oneself) dear; cause (oneself)) to be loved. ¶*She endeared herself to the children. / Her kindness endeared her to all.*①
—[他] …을 그리워하게 하다; 사모하게(사랑하게) 하다 ¶①그녀는 친절하였으므로 모든 사람이 따랐다

en·dear·ment [indíərmənt] *n.* **1.** [U] the act of endearing; the state of being endeared. **2.** [C] something that endears; an act or word that expresses affection.
—[名] 1. 친애, 사모, 애모 2. 사모하게 하는 것; 애정의 표시, 애무

⁑**en·deav·or,** *Brit.* **-our** [indévər] *vi.* try hard; make an effort; strive. ¶*~ after more riches / He endeavored to call back his dog.* —*n.* [C] an earnest attempt.
—[自] 노력하다 —[名] 열성; 노력

en·dem·ic [endémik] *adj.* found in a certain nation or area. —*n.* [C] an endemic disease.
—[形] 풍토의, 한 지방에 특유한 —[名] 풍토병, 지방병

***end·ing** [éndiŋ] *n.* **1.** the end; the last part. **2.** death.
—[名] 1. 끝, 종말, 결말; 말미(末尾), 결미(結尾), 2. 죽음

***end·less** [éndlis] *adj.* **1.** having no end; lasting or going on forever. ↔limited **2.** very frequent. ¶*~ trouble.*① ▷**end·less·ness** [-nis] *n.*
—[形] 1. 끝없는, 한없는; 영원히 계속되는 2. 끊임없는, 쉴새없는 ¶①쉴새없는 고생

end·less·ly [éndlisli] *adv.* in an endless manner.
—[副] 끝없이, 한없이; 끊임없이

en·dorse [indɔ́:rs] *vt.* **1.** write one's name, comment, etc. on the back of a check, etc. **2.** approve.
—[他] 1. [수표 따위]에 이서(裏書)하다 2. …을 인정하다, 승인하다

en·dor·see [èndɔ:rsí:, +*U.S.* indɔ:rsí:] *n.* [C] a person to whom a check, note, etc. is assigned by endorsement.
—[名] 피이서인(被裏書人)

en·dorse·ment [indɔ́:rsmənt] *n.* [U] [C] **1.** the act of endorsing. **2.** approval; support.
—[名] 1. 이서(裏書), 배서(背書) 2. 시인, 확인; 지지

en·dor·ser, -sor [indɔ́:rsər] *n.* [C] a person who endorses.
—[名] 이서인, 보증인

en·dow** [indáu] *vt.* **1.** give a large sum of money to (a school, etc.) as the source of permanent income. ¶*~ a college.* **2.** ⟪in *passive*⟫ provide. ⟪~ someone ***with⟫ ¶*He is endowed with genius in music.*
—[他] 1. …에 기금으로서 기부하다 2. [재능 따위]를 부여하다

en·dow·ment [indáumənt] *n.* **1.** [U] the act of endowing. **2.** [C] money or property endowed. **3.** ⟪usu. *pl.*⟫ a gift of nature; talent. ¶*natural* endowments.①
—[名] 1. 기금, 기부, 기증 2. 기부금, 기본재산 3. 천성; 자질, 재능 ¶①천부의 재능

en·dur·a·ble [ind(j)úərəbl / -djúər-] *adj.* that can be endured.
—[形] 참을(견딜) 수 있는

en·dur·ance [ind(j)úərəns / -djúər-] *n.* [U] the act or power of enduring; patience. ¶*~ flying*① / *with ~.*
beyond (or ***past***) ***endurance,*** to an extent that one can no longer endure.
—[名] 지구력, 내구성; 인내[력], 참을성 ¶①내구비행(耐久飛行)
[熟] 참을 수 없을 만큼

⁑**en·dure** [ind(j)úər / -djúə] *vt.* suffer (pain, etc.) without expressing dislike; bear. ⟪*~ to do; ~ doing; ~ that …*⟫ ¶*~ much pain / I cannot ~ being disturbed.* —*vi.* **1.** last; continue. **2.** bear or put up with pain, etc. ¶*~ to the last.*
—[他] [고통 따위]에 견디다, 참다; [고난 따위]를 달게 받다 —[自] 1. 견디어내다; 계속하다 2. 참다, 견디다

en·dur·ing [ind(j)úəriŋ / -djúər-] *adj.* long-suffering; lasting.
—[形] 참는, 견디는; 지속하는

⁑**en·e·my** [énimi] *n.* (pl. **-mies**) [C] **1.** a person or group that fights against another. ¶*a lifelong ~.*① **2.** ⟪*the ~*⟫ a military force, nation, etc. at war with another. ¶*The ~ was forced to retreat.* **3.** anything harmful like an enemy. ↔friend ¶*an ~ of freedom / an ~ to success.*
1) ***be an enemy to,*** do harm to (someone); hate.
2) ***be one's own enemy,*** injure oneself.
3) ***the*** [***old***] ***Enemy,*** the Devil.
—[名] 1. 적, 적병 ¶①철천지 원수 2. 적군, 적국 3. 해를 끼치는 것, […의] 적
[熟] 1)…을 해치다; 미워하다 2)자기자신을 해치다 3)악마

en·er·get·ic [ènərdʒétik], **-i·cal** [-ik(ə)l] *adj.* full of energy; vigorous; forceful.
—[形] 정력적인; 원기왕성한; 힘센

en·er·get·i·cal·ly [ènərdʒétik(ə)li] *adv.* with energy.
—[副] 정력적으로, 원기왕성하게, 힘차게

en·er·gize [énərdʒàiz] *vt.* give energy to (someone or something); make (someone or something) active. ¶*~ the spirit with brave words.* —*vi.* show energy; be active. ▷**en·er·giz·er** [-ər] *n.*
—[他] …에 정력을 주다; …을 활동적으로 하다 —[自] 힘을 내다; 정력적으로 활동하다

E

:en·er·gy [énərdʒi] *n.* [U] **1.** strength; force; power; vigor. ¶*be full of* ~.① / *with* ~.② **2.** ⦅*pl.*⦆ a person's active power. **3.** (*Physics*) the capacity for doing work. ¶*conservation of* ~③ / *latent* (or *potential*) ~.④
devote (or ***apply***) *one's* ***energies*** (=*give one's all active power*) ***to*** *something.*

—[名] 1. 힘; 세력; 정력; 원기 ¶①정력이 왕성하다/②정력적으로, 힘차게 2. 활동력 3. ⦅理⦆ 에네르기 ¶③에네르기의 불멸/④잠재 에네르기
[熟] …에 온 정력을 쏟다

en·er·vate [énərvèit] *vt.* lessen the vigor or strength of (someone or something); weaken physically or mentally. ▷**en·er·va·tion** [ènərvéiʃ(ə)n] *n.*

—[他] …에서 기운(활력)을 빼앗다; …을 약하게 하다

en·fold [infóuld] *vt.* **1.** wrap up. ¶~ *someone in a cloak.* **2.** embrace.

—[他] 1. …을 싸다 2. …을 포옹하다

•en·force [infɔ́ːrs] *vt.* **1.** put (something) into force; make (a law, etc.) effective. **2.** force; compel. ⦅~ an action *upon*⦆ ▷**en·force·a·ble** [-əbl] *adj.*

—[他] 1. …을 시행하다; [법률 따위]를 실시하다 2. …을 강요하다, 강제하다

en·force·ment [infɔ́ːrsmənt] *n.* [U] enforcing or putting into force.

—[名] 시행, 실시, 강제

:en·gage [ingéidʒ] *vt., vi.* **1.** promise. ⦅~ [oneself] *to do*⦆ ¶*I'll* ~ *to finish it by six.*① **2.** say firmly; assure. ⦅~ *that* …⦆ ¶*I'll* ~ *that he is very faithful.* **3.** reserve. ¶*We engaged two seats.* **4.** employ; hire. ¶*We engaged him as a translator.* **5.** ⦅usu. in *passive*⦆ make (someone) busy; fill the time of (someone). ⦅~ someone *in*⦆ ¶(*Brit.*) *The line is engaged.*② (cf. *U.S.* The line is busy.) / *I'm engaged* [*for*] *this evening.*③ / *We engaged him in conversation.* / *He is engaged in writing a letter.* / *They were engaged in conversation.*④ **6.** attract (someone's attention).
1) ***engage on*** (=*start; begin*) *something.*
2) ***be engaged*** (=***have promised to marry***) ***to someone.***
3) ***engage*** *oneself* ***to*** *someone,* promise to marry.

—[他][自] 1. 약속하다; 꼭 …하다 ¶①여섯 시까지 꼭 끝마치겠다 2. …을 단언하다;보증하다 3. 예약하다 4. 고용하다 5. […의] 시간을 차게 하다 ¶② ⦅英⦆ [전화에서] 통화중입니다/③오늘 밤은 시간이 꽉 차 있다(사이가 없다) /④그들은 이야기의 꽃을 피우고 있었다 6. [남의 주의 따위를] 끌다
[熟] 1)…에 착수하다 2)…와 약혼해 있다(약혼중이다) 3)…와 약혼하다

en·gaged [ingéidʒd] *adj.* **1.** promised to marry. ¶*an* ~ *girl.* **2.** busy; occupied. **3.** hired. **4.** fitted together. **5.** fighting.

—[形] 1. 약혼중의 2. 바쁜, 여가가 없는; 사용중의 3. 고용된 4. 맞물린, 연동(連動)의 5. 교전중의

•en·gage·ment [ingéidʒmənt] *n.* [C] **1.** a promise; a promise to marry. ¶*break off an* ~.① **2.** employment; a period of being employed; time of use. ¶*six months'* ~. **3.** fight; battle.
1) ***be under engagement,*** have a contract.
2) ***enter into*** (or ***make***) ***an engagement with,*** promise; contract.
3) ***meet*** *one's* ***engagements,*** pay one's debts.

—[名] 1. 약속; 약혼 ¶①해약하다; 파혼하다 2. 고용;고용 기간; 사용 기간 3. 교전
[熟] 1)계약되어 있다 2)…와 약속하다; 계약하다 3)채무를 청산하다

en·gag·ing [ingéidʒiŋ] *adj.* attractive; pleasing; charming. ¶*her* ~ *look.* ▷**en·gag·ing·ly** [-li] *adv.*

—[形] 마음을 끄는, 상냥한, 애교있는, 매력있는

en·gen·der [indʒéndər] *vt.* produce; cause. ¶*Sympathy often engenders love.*

—[他] …을 생기게 하다, 발생시키다

:en·gine [éndʒin] *n.* [C] **1.** a machine that produces power or motion. ¶*internal combustion* ~.① **2.** a machine that pulls a train, etc.; a locomotive. **3.** a machine; a device. ¶*a dental* ~.②

—[名] 1. 기관, 엔진, 발동기 ¶①내연기관 2. 기관차 3. 기계; 장치 ¶②칫과용 엔진

engine driver [ˊ- ˋ-] *n.* (*Brit.*) an engineer on a machine. (cf. *U.S.* engineer)

—[名] ⦅英⦆ 기관사, 운전수

:en·gi·neer [èndʒiníər] *n.* [C] **1.** a person who designs machines, roads, bridges, etc. ¶*an electrical* ~.① **2.** (*U.S.*) a driver; a mechanic. (cf. *Brit.* engine driver) **3.** (*Military*) a member of a group that does engineering work. —*vt.* manage or guide skillfully. —*vi.* work as an engineer.

—[名] 1. 기사(技師), 공학자 ¶①전기기사 2. 기관사, 기관공 3. 공병(工兵) —[他] …을 공작하다, 솜씨있게 처리하다 —[自] 기사로서 일하다

•en·gi·neer·ing [èndʒiníəriŋ] *n.* [U] the science, work, or job of an engineer. ¶*civil* (*electrical, mechanical*) ~.①

—[名] 공학, 공사, 기관학 ¶①토목(전기·기계)공학

:Eng·land [íŋglənd] *n.* **1.** the largest division of Great Britain. **2.** Great Britain.

—[名] 1. 잉글랜드 2. 영국

:Eng·lish [íŋgliʃ] *adj.* of England, its people, or their language. —*n.* **1.** ⦅*the* ~, *collectively*⦆ the people of England. **2.** [U] the English language.

—[形] 영국[인]의, 잉글랜드[사람]의, 영국의, 영어의 —[名] 1. 영국인, 영국 국민 2. 영어

:Eng·lish·man [íŋgliʃmən] *n.* (pl. **-men** [-mən]) [C] **1.** a person of England. **2.** an English ship.

—[名] 1. 영국인 2. 영국 배

Eng·lish·wom·an [íŋgliʃwùmən] *n.* [C] (pl. **-wom·en**

—[名] 영국 여자(부인)

E

[-wìmin]) a woman of England.

en·graft [engrǽft, in- / -grá:ft] *vt.* **1.** insert (a part of one tree) into another tree; implant. ¶~ *peach upon the plum.* **2.** fix (something) in someone's mind, soul, etc. ¶*Patriotism was engrafted in his soul.*① —[他] 1. …을 접붙이다, 접목하다 2. …을 마음속에 심어 주다, 주입하다, 붙어넣다 ¶①그의 마음속에 애국심이 심어졌다

en·grave [ingréiv] *vt.* **1.** cut (letters, figures, etc.) on metal, stone, or wood. ¶~ *a name on a stone;* ~ *a stone with a name.*① **2.** impress deeply. 《~ something *on* one's mind》 ¶~ *the sight on one's memory.*② —[名] 1. …을 새기다, …에 새겨넣다, 조각하다 ¶①돌에 이름을 새기다 2. …을 마음속에 새기다, 명심하다 ¶②그 광경을 깊이 마음에 새겨두다

en·grav·er [ingréivər] *n.* [C] a person who engraves. —[名] 조각가, 조판공(彫版工)

en·grav·ing [ingréiviŋ] *n.* **1.** [U] the art of an engraver. **2.** [C] an engraved design, plate, etc.; a picture printed from an engraved block or plate, etc. —[名] 1. 조각, 조각술 2. 조판(彫版), 판화(版畫)

en·gross [ingróus] *vt.* 《chiefly in *passive*》 **1.** occupy or absorb wholly (someone's time, etc.). ¶*be engrossed in an exciting story.*① **2.** write (something) in large letters or in legal form. ▷**en·gross·ment** [-mənt] *n.* —[他] 1. [시간 따위]를 빼앗다, …을 열중(몰두)하게 하다 ¶①재미있는 이야기에 열중하다 2. …을 큰 글씨로 쓰다, 정식으로 쓰다, 정서하다

en·gulf [ingʌ́lf] *vt.* swallow up; submerge. —[他] …을 감아들이다, 빨아들이다

en·hance [inhǽns / -há:ns] *vt.* heighten or increase (the value, etc.). ▷**en·hance·ment** [-mənt] *n.* —[他] [가치 따위]를 높이다, 올리다, 더하다

e·nig·ma [inígmə] *n.* [C] **1.** a riddle. **2.** a puzzling person or thing. —[名] 1. 수수께끼 2. 불가사의한 사람(사물)

en·ig·mat·ic [ènigmǽtik], **-i·cal** [-ik(ə)l] *adj.* puzzling; mysterious; perplexing. —[形] 수수께끼 같은, 불가사의한, 풀기 어려운

en·join [indʒɔ́in] *vt.* **1.** command; order. 《~ someone *to do*》 ¶~ *silence on the children* / ~ *a student to be diligent.*① **2.** (*Law*) prohibit. 《~ someone *from doing*》 —[他] 1. …에게 명령하다, 분부하다 ¶①학생에게 부지런히 공부하도록 말하다 2. …을 금하다, 금지하다

⁑**en·joy** [indʒɔ́i] *vt.* **1.** be happy with (something); take delight in (something); make (someone) pleased. ¶~ *oneself*① / *How did you ~ your trip?*② **2.** have (something) as one's strong point; have the use of (something). ¶~ *good health.*③ —[他] 1. …을 기뻐하다, 즐기다; [남]을 기쁘게 하다 ¶①즐기다; 즐겁게 지내다/②여행은 재미있었느냐? 2. 향유(享有)하다, 누리다 ¶③건강을 누리다

en·joy·a·ble [indʒɔ́iəbl] *adj.* giving joy; able to be enjoyed; pleasant. ▷**en·joy·a·bly** [-əbli] *adv.* —[形] 즐거운; 즐길 수 있는; 유쾌한

***en·joy·ment** [indʒɔ́imənt] *n.* [U] **1.** the act of enjoying; happiness; joy; pleasure. ¶*take ~ in* (*something*).① **2.** the state of having as one's strong point; use. ¶*be in the ~ of good health.*② —[名] 1. 즐거움, 향락, 쾌락 ¶①…을 즐기다 2. 향유, 향수(享受) ¶②건강을 누리고 있다

en·kin·dle [enkíndl, in-] *vt.* **1.** light up; set (something) on fire. **2.** make (passion, etc.) active; excite. —[他] 1. …에 불을 붙이다; …을 타오르게 하다 2. [정열]을 불러 일으키다

***en·large** [inlá:rdʒ] *vt.* **1.** make (something) larger; increase (something) in size; expand. ¶*a revised and enlarged edition.*① **2.** (*Photography*) reproduce (a print) on a larger scale. ¶*an enlarged photograph.* —[他] 1. …을 크게 하다, 확대(확장)하다 ¶①[책의] 개정 증보판 2. [사진]을 확대하다
—*vi.* become larger. —[自] 커지다, 퍼지다, 확대되다
enlarge on (or ***upon***), speak or write more about (something). ¶*I need not ~ further on* (or *upon*) *this point.*② [熟] …을 자세히 설명하다 ¶②이 점에 관해 더 이상 자세히 설명할 필요는 없다

en·large·ment [inlá:rdʒmənt] *n.* **1.** [U] the act of enlarging; the state of being enlarged. **2.** [C] anything enlarged; an addition. —[名] 1. 확대, 확장 2. 증가물, 증축, [사진의] 확대판, 증보판

***en·light·en** [inláitn] *vt.* give more knowledge to (someone); instruct; inform. ¶*Will you ~ me on this subject?* ▷**en·light·en·er** [-ər] *n.* —[他] …에게 지식을 부여하다, …을 교화하다, 계몽하다, 알리다, 가르쳐 주다

en·ligh·tened [inláitnd] *adj.* cultivated; civilized; well-informed. —[形] 계몽된, 깬, 진보된, 개화된, 문명의

en·light·en·ment [inláitnmənt] *n.* [U] the act of enlightening; the state of being enlightened. —[名] 계몽, 개화, 교화

en·list [inlíst] *vt.* **1.** get (someone) to join the military service. **2.** get the support or help of (someone). —[他] 1. …을 병적에 넣다, 징모(徵募)하다 2. …의 지지(협력)를 얻다
—*vi.* **1.** join the military service. ¶~ *in the army.* **2.** give one's support to something; join a movement. 《~ *in* something》 ¶~ *under the banner of freedom*① / ~ *in a cause.*② —[自] 1. 징병에 응하다, 응모하다 2. 협력(참가)하다 ¶①자유의 깃발 아래 참가하다/②어떤 주의에 가담하다

en·list·ed man [inlístidmæ̀n] *n.* (*U.S.*) a man in the armed forces who is not a commissioned officer or a warrant officer. ⇒[N.B.] —[名] [장교 이하의] 하사관, 사병 [N.B.] E.M.으로 생략함

en·list·ment [inlístmənt] *n.* [U][C] **1.** the act of enlisting; the state of being enlisted. **2.** the period for which a man enlists.
—[名] 1. [병사의] 징모, 병적 편입, 모병 2. 군 복무 연한(기간)

en·liv·en [inláivn] *vt.* make (someone) lively or cheerful.
—[他] …에게 활기를 띠게 하다

en·mi·ty [énmiti] *n.* [U] strong dislike; hatred. ¶*be at ~ with someone*① / *have ~ against someone.*②
—[名] 적의(敵意), 증오, 원한 ¶①…와 반목하고 있다/②…에게 적의를 품다

en·no·ble [inóubl, ennóu-] *vt.* **1.** give (someone) a rank or title of nobility. **2.** make (someone) noble in nature, etc.
—[他] 1. …에게 작위(爵位)를 수여하다, 귀족에 봉하다 2. [품위 따위]를 고상하게 하다

en·nui [ɑːnwíː] *n.* [U] weariness of mind; boredom.
—[名] 권태, 지루함, 심심함

e·nor·mi·ty [inɔ́ːrmiti] *n.* [U][C] (pl. **-ties**) extreme wickedness; a serious crime.
—[名] 극악성, 흉악; 흉악 범죄

‡ e·nor·mous [inɔ́ːrməs] *adj.* very large; huge; immense. ¶*~ profits* / *a man of ~ strength* / *the ~ sum of money*① / *Long ago ~ animals lived on the earth.*②
—[形] 거대한, 방대한, 막대한 ¶①막대한 금액(거액)의 돈, 거금/②태고에는 거대한 동물이 지상에 살고 있었다

e·nor·mous·ly [inɔ́ːrməsli] *adv.* in an enormous manner; extremely; vastly; unreasonably.
—[副] 몹시, 엄청나게, 막대하게, 어마어마하게

‡ e·nough [inʌ́f] *adj.* as much or many as necessary; sufficient. ¶*I have ~ money to buy the car.; I have money ~ to buy the car.*① ⇒[usage]
—*adv.* **1.** to the necessary degree. ¶*This meat is not baked ~.* / *He was old ~ to have walked all the way.*② **2.** quite; fully. ¶*This is good ~.*③
well enough, fairly; perfectly. *You know well ~ what I mean.*
—*n.* [U] the amount necessary. ¶*She had ~ of everything.* / *Enough of that!*④
1) ***have had enough*** (=*be sick; be tired*) ***of something.***
2) ***have enough to do,*** can barely do.
—[形] 충분한, 족한, 넉넉한 ¶①자동차를 살 만한 돈은 충분하다 [usage] 명사 다음에 오는 쪽이 더 강조적임
—[副] 1. 충분히 ¶②그는 내처 걸어갈 수 있을 만한 나이였다 2. 아주; 무척 ¶③아주 좋다
[熟] 꽤 좋게; 완전하게
—[名] 충분한 양(수) ¶④인제 그만!, 됐어!
[熟] 1)…에 물려(싫증나) 있다 2)겨우 …할 수 있다

‡ en·quire [inkwáiər] *v.* =inquire.

• en·quir·y [inkwáiəri] *n.* (pl. **-quir·ies**) =inquiry.

en·rage [inréidʒ] *vt.* put (someone) into a rage; make (someone) very angry. ¶*be enraged at an insult*① / *be enraged with* (or *against*) *a haughty person.*②
—[他] …을 화나게 하다, 격분시키다 ¶①모욕을 받고 화가 나 있다/②거만한 사람에게 격분하고 있다

en·rap·ture [inrǽptʃər] *vt.* fill (someone) with great delight or joy. ¶*be enraptured with* (or *over*) *good fortune.*①
—[他] …을 몹시 기쁘게 하다, 기뻐서 어쩔 줄 모르게 하다 ¶①행운을 미칠 듯이 기뻐하다

• en·rich [inrítʃ] *vt.* **1.** make (someone or something) rich or splendid; (of land) fertilize. **2.** improve or raise the value of (something). ¶*~ a food with a seasoning.*①
—[他] 1. …을 부유하게 하다, 풍부하게 하다, [땅]을 기름지게 하다 2. …의 가치를 높이다 ¶①조미료로 음식 맛을 좋게 하다

en·rich·ment [inrítʃmənt] *n.* **1.** [U] the act of enriching; the state of being enriched. **2.** [C] a thing that enriches.
—[名] 1. 풍부, 비옥 2. 풍부하게 하는 것

en·roll, *Brit.* **-rol** [inróul] *vt.* (**-rolled, -roll·ing**) **1.** write (someone's name) in a list; enlist. **2.** make (someone) a member. ¶*be enrolled in a school.*
—[名] 1. …을 명부에 올리다; 등록하다 2. …을 회원이 되게 하다

en·roll·ment, *Brit.* **-rol-** [inróulmənt] *n.* [U][C] the act of enrolling; the state of being enrolled; a number enrolled.
—[名] 명부 기입(등록); 기재; 입학; 입대; 등록자 수

en route [ɑːnrúːt] *adv.* on the way. ¶*be ~ to* (or *for*) *New York.*①
—[副] 도중에, 도상(途上)에 ¶①뉴욕으로 가는 도중에

en·sem·ble [ɑːnsɑ́ːmbl] *n.* [C] **1.** all the parts of a thing viewed together; the total effect. **2.** (*Music*) a performance of the entire group of singers, musicians, etc. **3.** all the parts of a woman's harmonious costume designed to be worn together.
—[名] 1. 총체(總體); 전체적인 효과 2. 《樂》 협주곡, 앙상블 3. 전체적 조화를 이룬 한 벌의 부인복

en·shrine [inʃráin] *vt.* **1.** keep (someone or something) in a shrine. **2.** keep (something) sacred; cherish.
—[他] 1. …을 사당에 모시다, 안치하다 2. …을 마음속에 몰래 간직하다,

en·sign [énsain] *n.* [C] **1.** a flag; a banner. ¶*the national ~.*① **2.** [énsn] (*U.S.*) a navy officer who ranks next below a lieutenant junior grade. **3.** (*Brit.*) a former army officer carrying a flag. **4.** a badge showing one's rank, position, etc.
—[名] 1. 기, 국기 ¶①국기 2. 《美》 해군 소위 3. 《英》 기수(旗手) 4. 기장(記章)

en·slave [insléiv] *vt.* make (someone) a slave; take
—[他] …을 노예로 만들다; 사로잡다

away freedom from (someone). ¶~ *someone to superstition*① | *be enslaved by passion.*②
¶①…을 미신에 사로잡히게 하다/②정욕의 노예가 되다

en·snare [ensnέər, in-] *vt.* catch (an animal) in a trap; capture (someone) by a trick.
—[他] …을 함정에 빠뜨리다, 덫으로 잡다

∗**en·sue** [ens(j)úː, in-] *vi.* come after; follow; result. 《~ *from* or *on* something》 ¶*What will ~ from* (or *on*) *this?*
—[自] 후에 일어나다; 잇따라 일어나다, …의 결과로서 일어나다

en·sure [inʃúər] *vt.* **1.** make (something) sure or certain. **2.** make (someone or something) safe; protect. 《~ something *against* or *from*》 ¶*I could have ensured myself against* (or *from*) *the risk.*①
—[他] 1. …을 보증하다, 확실하게 하다 2. …을 안전하게 하다, 지키다, 보호하다 ¶①그 위험으로부터 자신을 보호할 수가 있었다

en·tab·la·ture [entǽblətʃər] *n.* [C] a horizontal part of a building supported by the top of columns.
—[名] 기둥 상부에 걸친 수평 부분

en·tail [intéil] *vt.* make (something) necessary; impose; require. 《~ expense, etc. *on* or *upon*》 ¶*It is entailed on man to observe the law.*①
—[他] …을 과(課)하다, 필요로 하다 ¶①사람은 법률을 지키지 않으면 안된다

en·tan·gle [intǽŋgl] *vt.* **1.** catch (something) in a net, vine, etc. 《~ something *in*》 ¶*He entangled his feet in a net.* **2.** put (someone) into difficulty; involve. ¶*be entangled with someone.*①
—[他] 1. …을 얽히게 하다, 얽히어 감기게(걸리게) 하다 2. …을 곤란에 빠뜨리다; 걸려들게 하다 ¶①남과 복잡한 관계에 빠지다

en·tan·gle·ment [intǽŋglmənt] *n.* [U] **1.** the act of entangling; [C] the state of being entangled; something that entangles. **2.** 《use. *pl.*》 a barrier of barbed wire.
—[名] 1. 뒤얽힘, 분규, 혼란, 휩쓸려(말려)듦 2. 철조망

en·tente [ɑːntɑ́ːnt] *n.* [C] an agreement between two or more governments.
—[名] [국가간의] 협정, 협상

⁑**en·ter** [éntər] *vt.* **1.** come or go into (a room, etc.). **2.** become a member of (a club, etc.). **3.** begin; start. **4.** write (something) in a list, book, etc. —*vi.* **1.** come or go in. **2.** come into a group; join. **3.** make a beginning.
1) ***enter into,*** ⓐ take part in (a conversation, an agreement, etc.). ⓑ feel sympathy with (others' feelings). ⓒ bind oneself by (a promise, etc.).
2) ***enter on*** (or ***upon***), ⓐ take possession of (something). ⓑ begin; start.
—[他] 1. …에 들어가다 2. …에 입회하다; 참가하다 3. …을 시작하다 4. …을 등록하다; 기입하다 —[自] 1. 들어가다 2. 참가하다 3. 시작하다, 착수하다
[熟] 1)ⓐ…에 참가하다 ⓑ[감정]을 알아주다, …에게 동정하다 ⓒ…의 계약을 맺다 2)ⓐ…의 소유권을 얻다 ⓑ…을 시작하다, …에 착수하다

en·ter·ic [entérik] *adj.* of the bowels. ¶~ *fever.*①
—[形] 장(腸)의 ¶①장티푸스

⁑**en·ter·prise** [éntərpràiz] *n.* **1.** [C] a plan that requires much money and courage to carry it out; a project. ¶*a private ~.*① **2.** [U] courage and willingness to start such projects. ¶*a spirit of ~*② | *have no ~.*③
—[名] 1. 기업, 기획, 모험적인 사업 ¶①사(민간)기업 2. 모험심, 기업심, 진취의 기상 ¶②기업심/③진취의 기상이 없다

en·ter·pris·ing [éntərpràiziŋ] *adj.* showing enterprise; courageous; willing to take risks. ¶*an ~ man*① | *an ~ spirit.*②
—[形] 기업적인, 기업심이 있는; 용감한; 진취의 기상이 왕성한 ¶①기업가/②진취의 기상

⁑**en·ter·tain** [èntərtéin] *vt.* **1.** please; amuse. ¶*The play entertained us very much.* **2.** receive (someone) as a guest; give food and drink to (guests). 《~ someone *with*》 ¶*She entertained five people at* (or *to*) *dinner.*① | *I was entertained with fruit.*② **3.** hold (something) in mind; consider.
—[他] 1. …을 즐겁게 하다, 위안하다 2. …을 대접하다, 환대하다; …에게 음식을 대접하다 ¶①그녀는 다섯 사람을 만찬에 초대하였다/②나는 과일 대접을 받았다 3. …을 생각하다; 마음에 품다

en·ter·tain·er [èntərtéinər] *n.* [C] a person who entertains, esp. a dancer, singer, etc. at night clubs, etc.
—[名] 즐겁게 하는 사람, 접대자, 연예인

en·ter·tain·ing [èntərtéiniŋ] *adj.* interesting; amusing.
—[形] 재미있는, 즐거운, 유쾌한

∗**en·ter·tain·ment** [èntərtéinmənt] *n.* **1.** [U][C] the act of entertaining; the state of being entertained; hospitality. ¶~ *expenses*① | *a house of ~.*② **2.** [C] something that interests, pleases, or amuses. ¶*an ~ tax.*③ **3.** [U] amusement.
—[名] 1. 향응, 환대, 접대, 연회 ¶①접대비/②여관, 선술집 2. 여흥, 연예 ¶③흥행세 3. 오락

en·thrall, -thral [inθrɔ́ːl] *vt.* charm; captivate; enslave. ▷**en·thrall·ment** [-mənt] *n.*
—[他] …을 매혹시키다; 노예로 만들다

en·throne [inθróun] *vt.* **1.** place (a king, bishop, etc.) on a throne. **2.** place (someone) highest of all. ¶*a queen enthroned in the hearts of her people.*
—[他] 1. …을 왕위[사교(司敎)의 자리]에 앉히다 2. …을 숭상하다, 떠받들다

en·throne·ment [inθróunmənt] *n.* [U][C] the act of enthroning; the state of being enthroned.
—[名] 즉위[식], 사교(司敎) 취임[식]; 숭배

⁑**en·thu·si·asm** [inθ(j)úːziæ̀z(ə)m] *n.* [U] very strong interest; eagerness; zeal. ↔indifference ¶*an ~ for base-*
—[名] 열광, 열중, 감격 ¶①열광(열중)하여

enthusiast

ball | with ~.

en·thu·si·ast [inθ(j)ú:ziæst] *n.* ⓒ a person full of enthusiasm. ¶*an ~ about politics | an ~ for baseball.*
— 열중하는 사람, 열광자, …팬, …광 (狂)

* **en·thu·si·as·tic** [inθ(j)ù:ziǽstik] *adj.* full of enthusiasm; zealous; eager. ¶*an ~ admirer of music.* [thusiasm.]
— 열렬한, 열심인, 열광적인

en·thu·si·as·ti·cal·ly [inθ(j)ù:ziǽstik(ə)li] *adv.* with en-]
— 열심히, 열렬히, 열광적으로

en·tice [intáis] *vt.* tempt (someone) away by arousing hopes or desires; allure. ⟨*~ someone to do*⟩ ¶*~ a girl away from home* | *~ a dog in the garden.*
— 他 …을 유혹하다, 꾀어서 …하게 하다 ¶①처녀를 집에서 꾀어내다/②개를 정원 안으로 끌어들이다

en·tice·ment [intáismənt] *n.* **1.** Ⓤ the act of enticing; the state of being enticed. **2.** ⓒ something that entices.
— 名 1.유혹, 꾐 2. 유혹물, 미끼

‡en·tire [intáiər] *adj.* **1.** not lacking anything; whole; not broken. ¶*~ affection | The vase was found ~.* **2.** complete; utter. ¶*~ ignorance.*
— 形 1. 모두 갖추어진, 전체의, 완전한, 흠이 없는 ¶①꽃병은 손상된 데 없이 발견되었다 2. 완전한, 순전한

‡en·tire·ly [intáiərli] *adv.* wholly; completely; fully.
— 副 전혀, 고스란히, 완전히

en·tire·ty [intáiərti] *n.* ⓒ (*pl.* **-ties**) ⟨usu. *the ~* or *its ~*⟩ Ⓤ the state of being entire; wholeness; completeness; a complete thing.

in its entirety, wholly; completely.
— 名 전체; 완전[한 상태, 한 것]

熟 고스란히 그대로, 온전히, 전면적으로

* **en·ti·tle** [intáitl] *vt.* **1.** give a title to (someone or something); call (someone or something) by name. ¶*a book entitled 'On Liberty'.* **2.** give a right to ⟨someone⟩. ¶*His learning entitles him to respect.*
— 他 1. …을…이라고 이름붙이다, …이라고 표제를 붙이다 2. …에게 권리(자격)를 주다 ¶①그는 그 학문에 의해 존경받을 만한 자격이 있다

en·ti·ty [éntiti] *n.* (*pl.* **-ties**) ⓒ something that has a real existence; Ⓤ being; existence.
— 名 실재(實在)[물], 실체, 본질

en·tomb [intú:m] *vt.* place (someone) in a tomb; bury. ▷**en·tomb·ment** [-mənt] *n.*
— 他 …을 무덤에 파묻다, 매장하다

en·to·mol·o·gy [èntəmάlədʒi / -mɔ́l-] *n.* Ⓤ the science [of insects.]
— 名 곤충학

en·trails [éntreilz, +U.S. -trəlz] *n. pl.* the inner parts of a man or animal; bowels; inner parts.
— 名 내장; 창자; 내부

‡en·trance¹ [éntr(ə)ns] *n.* **1.** ⓊⓈ the act of entering. ¶*~ into life | ~ upon an office | Entrance Free | No Entrance.* **2.** ⓒ a place by which to enter; a gate; a door. **3.** Ⓤⓒ a right or permission to enter.
— 名 1. 들어가기, 입장 ¶①입장 무료 /②입장 사절 2. 입구 3. 입장권(權), 입장 허가

en·trance² [intrǽns / -trá:ns] *vt.* put (someone) into a wonderful state; fill (someone) with joy or delight; charm. ¶*be entranced with music | be entranced at the sight.* ▷**en·tranc·ing·ly** [-iŋli] *adv.*
— 他 …을 황홀하게 하다; 기뻐 어쩔 줄 모르게 하다; 넋을 잃게 하다

en·trant [éntr(ə)nt] *n.* ⓒ a person who enters; a new member in a club, university, etc.; a person taking part in a contest.
— 名 들어가는 사람, 입장자; 입회자; 입학자; 참가자

en·trap [intrǽp] *vt.* (**-trapped, -trap·ping**) catch (someone) in a trap; bring (someone) into difficulty or danger; deceive. ¶*~ someone to destruction.*
— 他 …을 함정에 빠뜨리다, 덫에 걸리게 하다, …을 속이다 ¶①남을 속여서 파멸에 빠뜨리다

* **en·treat** [intrí:t] *vt.* ask earnestly; beg; implore. ¶*~ someone for* (or *to show*) *mercy. | I ~ [of] you to go. | I ~ this favor of you.*
— 他 …에게 간청(탄원)하다 ¶①제발 이 소원을 들어 주시기 바랍니다

en·treat·y [intrí:ti] *n.* Ⓤⓒ (*pl.* **-treat·ies**) an earnest request; prayer; appeal. ¶*make entreaties | deaf to all entreaties.*
— 名 간청, 탄원, 애원 ¶①몇 번이고 탄원하다/②어떤 애원도 들어 주려 하지 않다

en·tree, en·trée [á:ntrei / ɔ́(:)n-] *n.* **1.** Ⓤ a right or freedom to enter. **2.** ⓒ (*U.S.*) the main dish of food in a meal. **3.** ⓒ a dish of food served before the roast or between the main courses.
— 名 1. 입장권(權), 입장 허가 2. 〔美〕 [불고기 이외의] 주요 요리 3. 앙트레 (불고기가 나오기 전에, 또는 메인 코오스 중간에 나오는 요리)

en·trench [intréntʃ] *vt.* **1.** surround (something) with a trench; protect; defend. ¶*~oneself.* **2.** establish firmly.
— 他 1. …을 참호로 둘러싸다, 지키다 2. …을 확립하다

en·trench·ment [intréntʃmənt] *n.* Ⓤⓒ the act of entrenching; the state of being entrenched; a trench made for defense.
— 名 참호 파기; 참호

en·tre·pre·neur [à:ntrəprənə́:r / ɔ́(:)ntrəprənə́:r] *n.* ⓒ a person who organizes and manages an enterprise.
— 名 기업가, 흥업주(興業主)

en·trust [intrʌ́st] *vt.* charge (someone) with a trust. ⟨*~ business to someone; ~ someone with business*⟩
— 他 …을 [남에게] 맡기다, 위탁하다

* **en·try** [éntri] *n.* [C] (pl. **-tries**) **1.** [C][U] the act of entering; entrance. ¶*Japan's ~ into the UN.* **2.** a place or way by which to enter. **3.** [C][U] the act of recording something in a book, etc.; something written or printed in a book, etc. ¶*double (single) ~*① / *an ~ in the family register.*② **4.** a person or thing taking part in a contest. **5.** (*Law*) the act of taking possession of lands, buildings, etc. by entering or setting foot in or on them.

—[名] 1. 들어가기; 입장, 등장, 가입 2. 입구, 현관 3. 기입; 기입 사항 표제어 ¶①부기의 복(단)식 기입/②입적 4. [경기의] 참가자, 출품물 5. 《法》 [토지·가옥에의] 침입, 점유

1) ***make an entry of*** (=*write down; record*) ***something.***
2) ***make one's entry,*** enter.

[熟] 1)[어떤 사항]을 기입(등록)하다 2)입장(등장)하다

en·twine [intwáin] *vt.* twine; twist; wind. 《~ something *round* or *with*》 ¶*~ a creeper round a pillar.*

—[他] …을 얽히게 하다, 감겨들게 하다

en·twist [intwíst, en-] *vt.* twist (things) together.

—[他] …을 꼬아서 합치다, 꼬다

e·nu·mer·ate [in(j)ú:mərèit / -njú:-] *vt.* name (persons or things) one by one; mention; count. ¶*~ someone's weak points.* ▷**e·nu·mer·a·tor** [-ər] *n.*

—[他] …을 열거하다, 들다; 세다 ¶남의 약점을 낱낱이 열거하다

e·nu·mer·a·tion [in(j)ù:məréiʃ(ə)n / -njù:-] *n.* **1.** [U] the act of enumerating. **2.** [C] a list; catalogue.

—[名] 1. 낱낱이 세기(들기), 열거 2. 목록, 일람표

e·nun·ci·ate [inʌ́nsièit, -ʃi-] *vt.* state definitely; pronounce (words) clearly. ▷**e·nun·ci·a·tor** [-ər] *n.*

—[他] …을 명확히 말하다; …을 똑똑히 발음하다

e·nun·ci·a·tion [inʌ̀nsiéiʃ(ə)n, -ʃi-] *n.* [U][C] the act of enunciating; the state of being enunciated; a definite statement; announcement.

—[名] 발음[하는 투]; 언명; 선언

en·vel·op [invéləp] *vt.* wrap up; cover up; surround. ¶*be enveloped in flames* / *be enveloped in blankets.*

—[他] …을 싸다, 봉하다, 덮어 가리다; 에워싸다

E

* **en·ve·lope** [énviloup, +*U.S.* ɑ́:n-] *n.* [C] **1.** a paper cover for letters, etc. **2.** covering; wrapper. **3.** the bag that holds the gas in a balloon.

—[名] 1. 봉투 2. 씌우개; 싸개 3. [기구(氣球)의] 기낭(氣囊)

en·vel·op·ment [invéləpmənt] *n.* **1.** [U] the act of enveloping; the state of being enveloped. **2.** [C] something that envelops; a wrapper.

—[名] 1. 봉하기, 싸기, 포위 2. 싸개, 포장지

en·ven·om [invénəm, en-] *vt.* **1.** put poison on or into (something). **2.** fill (something) with hate. ¶*envenomed words.*①

—[他] 1. …에 독약을 넣다 2. …에 독기를 띠게 하다 ¶①독설

en·vi·a·ble [énviəbl] *adj.* to be envied; very desirable. ▷**en·vi·a·ble·ness** [-nis] *n.* —**en·vi·a·bly** [-bli] *adv.*

—[形] 샘나는; 부러운

en·vi·ous [énviəs] *adj.* full of envy; feeling or expressing envy. ¶*an ~ glance.* ▷**en·vi·ous·ness** [-nis] *n.*

—[形] 부러워하는; 시기심을 품고 있는 시기에 찬

en·vi·ous·ly [énviəsli] *adv.* in an envious manner.

—[副] 샘내어, 부러워하여

en·vi·ron [inváiər(ə)n] *vt.* surround; encircle. ¶*be environed with* (or *by*) *the enemy.*

—[他] …을 둘러싸다, 포위하다, 에워싸다

* **en·vi·ron·ment** [inváiərənmənt] *n.* [U][C] **1.** the act of surrounding; the state of being surrounded. **2.** all the conditions that influence something; surroundings. ¶*social (moral) ~.*①

—[名] 1. 둘러싸기, 포위 2. 주위, 환경 ¶①사회적(도덕적) 환경

* **en·vi·rons** [inváiər(ə)nz / énvir(ə)nz] *n. pl.* the districts surrounding a town or city; suburbs. ¶*Paris and its ~.*①

—[名] [도시의] 주위, 부근; 교외, 근교(近郊) ¶①파리와 그 근교

en·vis·age [envízidʒ, in-] *vt.* **1.** face (danger, etc.). **2.** form an image of (something or someone) in one's mind.

—[他] 1. [위험 따위]에 직면하다 2. …을 마음속에 그리다

en·voy[1] [énvɔi] *n.* [C] a messenger sent from one government to another. ⇒[N.B.]

—[名] 외교사절 [N.B.] 대사의 아래이며 공사의 위에 속함

en·voy[2] [énvɔi] *n.* [C] (*poetic*) a short concluding section in a poem.

—[名] 《詩》 결구(結句)

* **en·vy** [énvi] *n.* (pl. **-vies**) **1.** [U] a feeling of discontent or ill will against another's good fortune; jealousy. **2.** [C] 《usu. *the ~*》 the object of such feeling. ¶*She was the ~ of the young girls.*

—[名] 1. 시기, 샘, 질투 2. 선망의 대상

1) ***be in envy*** (=*be jealous*) ***of something.***
2) ***out of envy,*** driven by jealousy.

[熟] 1)…을 부러워하다 2)질투한 나머지

—*vt.* (**-vied**) feel envy toward (someone). ¶*I don't ~ you your fortune.*① / *I ~ [you] your many books.* / *How I ~ you!*②

—[他] …을 시기하다, 부러워하다 ¶①나는 너의 재산을 부러워하지는 않는다/②네가 얼마나 부러운지 모르겠다

en·zyme [énzaim] *n.* (*Chemistry*) [C] a chemical sub-

—[名] 《化》 효소(酵素)

E·os [í:as / -ɔs] *n.* (in Greek mythology) the goddess of the dawn. ⇒ [N.B.] —名 새벽의 여신 [N.B.] 로마 신화의 Aurora에 해당

ep·au·let, -lette [épəlèt / épou-] *n.* ⓒ the shoulder ornament of a uniform. ⇒fig. ¶*win one's epaulets.*① —名 견장(肩章) ¶①[하사관이] 장교로 승진하다

[epaulet]

e·phem·er·al [ifémər(ə)l] *adj.* lasting only a day; very short-lived. —形 하루살이 목숨의; 생명이 짧은, 단명한

ep·ic [épik] *n.* ⓒ a long poem of the adventures of a hero. —*adj.* of or like an epic. —名 서사시, 사시(史詩) —形 서사시의; 서사시적인

ep·i·cen·ter, *Brit.* **-tre** [épisèntər] *n.* ⓒ a point directly above the true center of the earthquake. —名 진앙(震央)[진원(震源) 바로 위에 있는 지점], 진원지

ep·i·cure [épikjùər] *n.* ⓒ a person who finds pleasure in eating and drinking. —名 식도락가, 미식가(美食家)

ep·i·cu·re·an [èpikjurí:ən] *adj.* **1.** of or like an epicure; fond of pleasure and luxury. **2.** ((*E-*)) of Epicurus or his philosophy. —*n.* ⓒ **1.** a person who likes pleasure and luxury; an epicure. **2.** ((*E-*)) a person who believes in the philosophy of Epicurus. —形 1. 식도락의, 쾌락주의의 2. 에피큐로스의; 에피큐리안의 —名 1. 쾌락주의자; 미식가(美食家) 2. 에피큐로스설 신봉자

Ep·i·cu·re·an·ism [èpikjurí:ənìz(ə)m] *n.* ⓤ **1.** the philosophy or principles of Epicurus (342 ?-270 B.C.) or his followers. ⇒[N.B.] **2.** ((*e-*)) the taste of an epicurean. —名 1. 에피큐로스의 철학 [N.B.] 쾌락을 인생의 최고선(最高善)으로 삼음 2. 미식주의, 식도락, 쾌락주의

ep·i·dem·ic [èpidémik] *n.* ⓒ a disease that spreads rapidly among many people in one area. —*adj.* (of a disease) spreading rapidly and widely. —名 유행(전염)병 —形 전염성의, 유행성의

ep·i·gram [épigræm] *n.* ⓒ a short, witty saying or poem. —名 경구(警句), 짧고 날카로운 말; 풍자시

ep·i·gram·mat·ic [èpigrəmǽtik] *adj.* of or like an epigram; short and witty. —形 경구의, 경구적인; 풍자적인

ep·i·graph [épigræf / -grɑ̀:f] *n.* ⓒ **1.** carved words on a statue or building. **2.** a quotation or motto at the beginning of a book or chapter. —名 1. 비명(碑銘), 비문, 제명(題銘) 2. [권두(卷頭)의] 제사(題詞), 표어

ep·i·lep·sy [épilèpsi] *n.* ⓤ a nervous disease in which a person loses consciousness for a while. —名 간질, 지랄병

ep·i·lep·tic [èpiléptik] *adj.* of epilepsy. —*n.* ⓒ a person who has epilepsy. —形 간질병의 —名 간질병 환자

ep·i·log, *Brit.* **-logue** [épilɔ̀:g, -làg / -lɔ̀g] *n.* ⓒ **1.** the last part of a novel, poem, etc. **2.** a speech given to the audience at the end of a play. ↔prologue —名 1. [책의] 끝맺는 말, 발문(跋文) 2. 연극의 끝말, 폐막사

e·pis·co·pa·cy [ipískəpəsi] *n.* ⓤⓒ **1.** the government of a church by bishops. **2.** the position of a bishop. —名 1. [영국 국교의] 감독 제도 2. 감독의 직

e·pis·co·pal [ipískəp(ə)l] *adj.* **1.** of bishops; governed by bishops. **2.** ((*E-*)) of the Church of England, or of certain Protestant churches of the United States. ¶*the ~ Church*① / *the Protestant ~ Church.*② —形 1. 주교(主教)의, 감독[제도]의 2. 감독파의 ¶①영국 성공회(聖公會)/② 미국 성공회

E·pis·co·pa·li·an [ipìskəpéiliən] *n.* ⓒ a member of the Protestant Episcopal Church. —*adj.* =Episcopal; ((*e-*)) =episcopal. —名 미국 성공회 회원

ep·i·sode [épisòud] *n.* ⓒ **1.** an interesting event or experience in someone's life or history. **2.** an event or action separate from the main plot of a novel or play. —名 1. 삽화적인 사건, 에피소우드 2. [소설·연극 중의] 삽화

e·pis·tle [ipísl] *n.* ⓒ **1.** a letter, usu. a long, instructive letter. ⇒[N.B.] **2.** ((*E-*)) a letter written by one of Christ's Apostles. —名 1. 편지, 서한 [N.B.] 지금은 익살스러운 뜻으로 쓰임 2. 사도(使徒) 서한

ep·i·taph [épitæf / -tɑ̀:f] *n.* ⓒ words written on a tombstone in memory of a dead person. —名 묘비명(墓碑銘), 비문

ep·i·thet [épiθèt] *n.* ⓒ an adjective, or a phrase expressing some quality, as in 'Ivan *the Terrible*'. —名 [성질을 나타내는] 형용사[구], 별명, 통칭

e·pit·o·me [ipítəmi] *n.* ⓒ **1.** a summary; an outline. **2.** a representative of some quality. —名 1. 대요, 개요, 개략 2. […의] 축도(縮圖)

* **ep·och** [épək / í:pɔk] *n.* ⓒ a period of time, esp. when some important events happened; the beginning of such a period. ¶*make* (or *mark*) *an ~ in something.*① —名 [획기적인] 시대; 신기원(新紀元) ¶①…에 하나의 신기원을 이루다

ep·och-mak·ing [épəkmèikiŋ / í:pɔk-] *adj.* beginning an epoch; very important.

eq·ua·bil·i·ty [èkwəbíliti, ì:kwə-] *n.* [U] the state of being equable.

eq·ua·ble [ékwəbl, í:k-] *adj.* changing little; unvarying; even; calm. ▷**eq·ua·bly** [-bli] *adv.*

⁑ **e·qual** [í:kw(ə)l] *adj.* **1.** same in number, size, degree, etc.; identical. ¶*Twice 3 is ~ to 6.*① / *The totals are ~.*② / *He speaks French and Dutch with ~ ease.* **2.** able to; fit for. ¶*He is ~ to this work.*③
—*n.* [C] a person or thing equal to another; a rival. ¶*He has no ~.*④
—*vt.* (**e·qualed, e·qual·ing** or *Brit.* **e·qualled, e·qual·ling**) be equal to (someone or something). ¶*Three and two equal[s] five.*

e·qual·i·ty [i(:)kwáliti / i:kwɔ́l-] *n.* [U] the state of being equal.

e·qual·i·za·tion [ì:kwəlizéiʃ(ə)n / -laiz-] *n.* [U] the act of equalizing; the state of being equalized.

e·qual·ize, *Brit.* **-ise** [í:kwəlàiz] *vt.* make (something) equal or uniform.

⁑ **e·qual·ly** [í:kwəli] *adv.* in an equal manner; uniformly.

e·qua·nim·i·ty [ì:kwənímiti, èk-] *n.* [U] calmness.

e·quate [i(:)kwéit] *vt.* **1.** make (something) equal. **2.** consider or treat (something) as equal.

e·qua·tion [ikwéiʃ(ə)n, -ʒ(ə)n] *n.* **1.** [U] the act of equating; the state of being equated. **2.** [C] a statement that two quantities are equal. ¶*an algebraic ~*①

e·qua·tor [ikwéitər] *n.* ⟪*the ~*⟫ an imaginary line lying around the middle of the earth, equally distant from the North Pole and the South Pole.

e·qua·to·ri·al [ì:kwətɔ́:riəl, èkwə-] *adj.* of, near, or at the equator.

e·ques·tri·an [ikwéstriən] *adj.* **1.** of horses or horse-riding. **2.** on horseback. —*n.* [C] a person skilled in horse-riding.

e·qui·dis·tant [í:kwidíst(ə)nt] *adj.* equally distant.

e·qui·lat·er·al [í:kwilǽt(ə)r(ə)l] *adj.* having all sides equal. —*n.* [C] a figure having all sides equal.

e·qui·lib·ri·um [ì:kwilíbriəm] *n.* **1.** [U][C] a balanced state or condition. **2.** [U] calmness of mind.

e·qui·noc·tial [ì:kwinákʃ(ə)l / -nɔ́k-] *adj.* **1.** of the equinox. ¶*the ~ line.*① **2.** near or at the equinox. —*n.* [C] a storm occurring near or at the equinox.

e·qui·nox [í:kwinàks / -nɔ̀ks] *n.* [C] ⟪usu. *the ~*⟫ the time in a year when night and day are equal of length. ¶*the spring (autumnal) ~.*①

• **e·quip** [ikwíp] *vt.* (**e·quipped, e·quip·ping**) cause (someone or something) to have necessary things. ⟪*~ someone or something with*⟫ ¶*~ oneself*① / *~ someone for a journey*② / *I equipped my son with a sound education.*③

⁑ **e·quip·ment** [ikwípmənt] *n.* [U] **1.** the act of equipping; the state of being equipped. **2.** ⟪often *pl.*⟫ a collection of necessary things furnished for some purpose.

e·qui·poise [ékwipɔ̀iz, í:kwi-] *n.* [U] the state of being balanced.

eq·ui·ta·ble [ékwitəbl] *adj.* fair; just. ▷**eq·ui·ta·ble·ness** [-nis] *n.* —**eq·ui·ta·bly** [-bli] *adv.*

eq·ui·ty [ékwiti] *n.* [U] fairness; justice.

e·quiv·a·lence [ikwívələns] *n.* [U] the state of being equivalent.

• **e·quiv·a·lent** [ikwívələnt] *adj.* equal in value, measure, amount, force, meaning, etc. ¶*What is $ 1 ~ to in Japanese money?*① —*n.* [C] something equivalent. ▷**e·quiv·a·lent·ly** [-li] *adv.*

e·quiv·o·cal [ikwívək(ə)l] *adj.* **1.** having two or more meanings; not clear; vague. ¶*an ~ answer.* **2.** uncertain; doubtful. ▷**e·quiv·o·cal·ly** [-kəli] *adv.*

—[형] 획기적인, 매우 중대한
—[명] 한결같음, 평등, 균등; 평온, 침착
—[형] 변화가 적은; 한결같은, 평온한, 침착한
—[형] 1. 같은, 동등한 ¶①3 곱하기 2는 6/②합계가 맞는다 2. …할 능력이 있는; …에 맞는, 맞먹는, 감당할 수 있는 ¶③그이라면 이 일을 할 수 있다
—[명] 대등한 것, 필적하는 것 ¶④그와 겨룰 만한 사람은 없다
—[타] …에 필적하다, …와 맞먹다
—[명] 동등, 평등, 한결같음
—[명] 동등[화], 평등[화], 균등[화]
—[타] …을 평등하게 하다, …을 한결같게 하다
—[부] 같게; 동등하게, 평등하게
—[명] 평온, 침착
—[타] 1. …을 같게 하다, 동등하게 하다 2. …을 동등(평등)시하다
—[명] 1. 같게(동등하게) 하기, 동등 2. 방정식, 등식(等式) ¶①대수 방정식
—[명] 적도(赤道)
—[형] 적도[부근]의
—[형] 1. 말의; 승마의 2. 마상(馬上)의
—[명] 마술가(馬術家)
—[형] 등거리(等距離)의
—[형] 등변(等邊)의 —[명] 등변형
—[명] 1. 평형(平衡), 균형 2. [마음의] 평온, 평정
—[형] 1. 주야 평분시(平分時)의, 춘분·추분의 ¶①주야 평분선 2. 춘분(추분)[무렵]의 —[명] 춘·추분 때의 모진 바람
—[명] 춘분(추분)[점] ¶①춘분(추분)
—[타] …에 [필요한 것을] 장비하다, 채비를 차리다 ¶①몸차림하다, 채비하다/②남에게 여행 준비를 시키다/③나는 내 아들에게 훌륭한 교육을 시켰다
—[명] 1. 준비, 채비 2. 장비; 설비; 비품
—[명] 균형, 평형
—[형] 공평한, 정당한
—[명] 공평, 공정, 정당
—[명] 동등, 등가(等價), 등치(等値)
—[형] 같은, …와 동등한 ¶①1달러는 한화로 얼마에 상당하는가? —[명] 동등물
—[형] 1. 두 가지 뜻을 지닌, 다의적(多義的)인; 뜻이 모호한 2. 확실치 않은; 의심스러운, 수상쩍은

equivocate

e·quiv·o·cate [ikwívəkèit] *vi.* use vague expressions.
—自 애매한 말을 쓰다, 얼버무리다

e·quiv·o·ca·tion [ikwìvəkéiʃ(ə)n] *n.* ⓒⓤ **1.** the use of equivocal expressions. **2.** an equivocal expression.
—名 1. 애매한 말을 쓰기, 얼버무림 2. 모호한 표현

*** e·ra** [íərə] *n.* ⓒ an age or a period in history. ¶ *the Christian ~①*
—名 기원(紀元), 연대, 시대 ¶① 서력 기원

e·rad·i·cate [irǽdikèit] *vt.* get rid of (something) completely; destroy. ▷**e·rad·i·ca·tor** [-ər] *n.*
—他 …을 근절하다, 박멸하다

e·rad·i·ca·tion [irædikéiʃ(ə)n] *n.* ⓤ the act of eradicating; destruction.
—名 근절, 박멸

e·rase [iréis / iréiz] *vt.* rub out. ¶ *~ chalk marks from a blackboard.* ▷**e·ras·a·ble** [-əbl] *adj.*
—他 …을 지우다, 삭제하다

e·ras·er [iréisər / -réizər] *n.* ⓒ a thing that erases; a wiper. ¶ *a pencil ~① / a blackboard ~.②*
—名 지우개 ¶① 고무 지우개 /② 칠판 지우개

e·ra·sure [iréiʒər, +U.S. -ʃər] *n.* ⓤ the act of erasing.
—名 지워 없앰, 말소, 삭제

*** ere** [ɛər] *prep., conj. (poetic, archaic)* before.
—前接 …(하기)전에

: e·rect [irékt] *adj.* **1.** straight up; upright; directed upward. ¶ *an ~ figure① / stand ~.②* —*vt.* **1.** put (someone or something) straight up. ¶ *~ oneself.* **2.** build. ¶ *~ a house.* **3.** set up. ¶ *~ a machine.* ▷**e·rect·ly** [-li] *adv.* —**e·rect·ness** [-nis] *n.*
—形 곧추 선, 똑바로 선, 직립(直立)의 ¶① 직립상(像)/② 똑바로 서다 —他 1. …을 곧추(똑바로) 세우다 2. …을 짓다, 건립하다 3. …을 조립하다

e·rec·tion [irékʃ(ə)n] *n.* **1.** ⓤ the act of erecting; the state of being erected. **2.** ⓒ a thing which is erected; a building.
—名 1. 직립(直立) 2. 직립물; 건설물, 건물

E·rie [íəri], **Lake** *n.* one of the five Great Lakes, between the United States and Canada.
—名 에리호(湖)(미국과 캐나다 사이에 있는 5대호의 하나)

er·mine [ə́:rmin] *n.* (pl. **-mines** or *collectively* **-mine**) **1.** ⓒ a kind of weasel whose fur turns white in winter. **2.** ⓤ the soft, white fur of this animal.
—名 1. 어어민, 흰 담비 2. 흰 담비의 모피

Er·nest [ə́:rnist] *n.* a man's name.
—名 남자 이름

e·rode [iróud] *vt.* eat or wear away gradually.
—他 …을 침식(浸蝕)하다

E·ros [íərɑs, érɑs / érɔs] *n.* (in Greek mythology) the god of love. ⇒N.B.
—名 [그리이스 신화의] 사랑의 신 N.B. 로마 신화의 Cupid에 해당함

e·ro·sion [iróuʒ(ə)n] *n.* ⓤⓒ the act of eroding; the state of being eroded.
—名 침식(浸蝕), 부식(腐蝕)

e·ro·sive [iróusiv] *adj.* eroding; causing erosion.
—形 침식성의; 부식성의

err [ə:r] *vi.* **1.** make mistakes; be wrong. **2.** do wrong; sin. ¶ *To err is human, to forgive divine.*
—自 1. 그르치다; 틀리다 2. 죄를 범하다, 잘못을 저지르다

*** er·rand** [ér(ə)nd] *n.* ⓒ **1.** a short trip for a special purpose, esp. for someone else. ¶ *The boy was sent on an ~ to the office.* **2.** the purpose of such a trip.
—名 1. 심부름 2. [심부름의] 용무, 목적

er·ra·ta [iréitə, erá:-, eréi-] *n.* pl. of **erratum**.

er·rat·ic [irǽtik] *adj.* **1.** not steady; wandering; irregular. **2.** unusual; queer. ¶ *~ behavior.*
—形 1. 일정하지 않은; 변덕스러운 2. 별난, 엉뚱한

er·ra·tum [iréitəm, erá:-, eréi-] *n.* ⓒ (pl. **-ta**) an error or mistake in writing or printing.
—名 오자(誤字), 오식(誤植)

er·ro·ne·ous [iróuniəs, er-] *adj.* mistaken; incorrect.
—形 틀린; 그릇된

: er·ror [érər] *n.* ⓒⓤ **1.** something wrong; a mistake; the state of being wrong or mistaken. ¶ *do* (or *commit, make*) *an ~① / be in ~.②* **2.** a misplay in baseball.
—名 1. 잘못; 틀림, 오류 ¶① 잘못을 저지르다 /② 잘못 생각하고 있다 2. [야구에서] 에러, 실책

er·u·dite [éru(:)dàit, érju(:)-] *adj.* of knowledge; learned. ▷**er·u·dite·ly** [-li] *adv.*
—形 학식이 있는, 박식한

er·u·di·tion [èru(:)díʃ(ə)n, èrju(:)-] *n.* ⓤ wide knowledge or learning.
—名 박식, 박학, 학식

e·rupt [irʌ́pt] *vi.* (of a volcano) burst out.
—自 [화산이] 분출(噴火)하다

e·rup·tion [irʌ́pʃ(ə)n] *n.* ⓤⓒ **1.** the act of erupting. **2.** smoke, ashes, etc. which is erupted from a volcano. **3.** red spots on the skin. ¶ *an ~ on the face.*
—名 1. 분출, 분화 2. 분출물, 분연(噴煙), 화산재 3. 발진(發疹)

e·rup·tive [irʌ́ptiv] *adj.* **1.** tending to erupt. **2.** of or caused by eruptions.
—形 1. 분화성(噴火性)의 2. 분화에 의한

es·ca·late [éskəlèit] *vt., vi.* make or become larger in degree, scale, etc.; increase. ¶ *~ a war.*
—他自 확대시키다, 확대하다

es·ca·la·tion [èskəléiʃ(ə)n] *n.* ⓤⓒ the act of increasing; a gradual increase in military forces, etc. ¶ *~ of a war.*
—名 증가; [군사력 따위의] 단계적 확대

es·ca·la·tor [éskəlèitər] *n.* ⓒ a moving stairway for carrying people up or down.
—名 에스컬레이터, 자동식 계단

es·ca·pade [éskəpèid, ⌐⌐⌐] *n.* ⓒ an escape from rules
—名 탈선 행위; 자유분방한 행위, 방종

or restraint; a mischievous or wild adventure.

: es·cape [iskéip] *vi.* **1.** get free; slip. ⟪~ *from* or *out of* a place⟫ ¶*Three prisoners escaped from the prison.* **2.** come out through a hole; leak. ⟪~ *from* a pipe, etc.⟫ ¶*The gas is escaping.* —*vt.* **1.** keep away from (danger, etc.); avoid; elude. ⟪~ *doing*⟫ ¶~ *the danger* | ~ *a task* | *He escaped being killed in the battle.*① **2.** (of a word, sign, etc.) come out from (lips, etc.) carelessly. ¶*Angry words escaped his lips.*② **3.** do not come into the notice or memory of (someone). ¶*His name escaped her.*③

—[自] **1.** 달아나다, 도망치다, 탈출하다 **2.** 새[어 나오]다 —[他] **1.** …을(에서) 벗어나다, 모면하다; 피하다 ¶①그는 전사를 모면했다 **2.** [입에서] 무심코 새나오다 ¶②분노의 말이 무심코 그의 입에서 튀어나왔다 **3.** [남]의 기억 따위에서 사라지게 하다 ¶③그녀는 그의 이름이 생각나지 않았다

1) ***cannot escape,*** cannot help; cannot avoid.
2) ***escape** someone's **memory,*** to be forgotten; cannot be remembered.

[熟] 1)…하지 않을 수가 없다 2)잊혀지다; 생각나지 않다

—*n.* **1.** [C][U] the act or fact of escaping. **2.** [C] (of water, gas, etc.) the act of escaping from a pipe, etc.

—[名] **1.** 도망, 탈출 **2.** 새어나오기, 누출(漏出)

es·cape·ment [iskéipmənt] *n.* [C] a device in a clock or watch for controlling the movement. ⇒fig.

—[名] [시계 톱니바퀴의] 방탈(防脫)장치

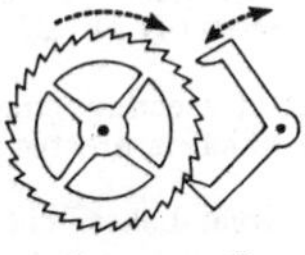
〔escapement〕

es·carp·ment [iská:rpmənt] *n.* [C] a steep slope; a cliff.

—[名] 급경사면; 단애(斷崖)

es·chew [estʃúː, is-] *vt.* keep away from (something); avoid.

—[他] …을 멀리하다; 피하다

· es·cort *n.* [éskɔːrt → *v.*] [C] **1.** a person or persons going along with another or others to protect or guide. **2.** a group of warships or airplanes protecting unarmed ships.

—[名] **1.** 호위자, 호송원, 경호원 **2.** 호위함(艦); 호위[비행]기

under escort, accompanied by police for protection.

[熟] 호위 아래, 호위를 받고

—*vt.* [iskɔ́ːrt] go along with (someone) as an escort. ¶~ *a young girl.*

—[他] …을 호위하다, 호송하다, 수행하다

es·cutch·eon [iskʌ́tʃ(ə)n] *n.* [C] a shield on which a family mark is put.

—[名] 방패 모양의 문장(紋章) 바탕

Es·ki·mo [éskimòu] *n.* (pl. **-mos** or **-mo**) **1.** [C] a member of a North American Indian race living in the extreme north of America and Greenland. **2.** [U] the language of this race.

—[名] **1.** 에스키모 사람 **2.** 에스키모 말

es·o·ter·ic [èsoutérik] *adj.* understood only by a small number of people.

—[形] 비전(秘傳)의; 비결(비법)의; 비밀의

· es·pe·cial [ispéʃ(ə)l] *adj.* special; exceptional; particular.

—[形] 특별한, 각별한; 특수한

: es·pe·cial·ly [ispéʃ(ə)li] *adv.* particularly; chiefly.

—[副] 특히, 각별히; 유달리

Es·pe·ran·to [èspəræ̀ntou, -ráːn-] *n.* [U] an artificial language for international use. ⇒[N.B.]

—[名] 에스페란토어 [N.B.] 폴란드 Dr.L. L. Zemenhof 가 창안

es·pi·o·nage [éspiənidʒ, espáiə-, èspiənáːʒ] *n.* [U] **1.** the act of spying. **2.** the systematic use of spies by a government to learn the secrets of other nations.

—[名] **1.** 염탐, 스파이 행위 **2.** 스파이 조직[망]

es·pla·nade [èsplənéid, -náːd] *n.* [C] a level space used for public walks or drives.

—[名] [평탄한] 산책길, 드라이브 길

es·pous·al [ispáuz(ə)l] *n.* **1.** [U] the act of espousing. **2.** [C] ⟪usu. *pl.*⟫ a marriage ceremony.

—[名] **1.** [주의·주장 따위의] 옹호 **2.** 결혼[식]

es·pouse [ispáuz] *vt.* **1.** give support to (something); take (an idea, etc.) as one's own; adopt. ¶~ *a democratic principle.* **2.** marry.

—[他] **1.** …을 지지하다; 채용(채택)하다 **2.** …을 아내로 맞이하다, 시집보내다

es·py [ispái] *vt.* (**-pied**) see; catch sight of.

—[他] …을 찾아내다; 발견하다

Esq. Esquire.

es·quire [iskwáiər, es-] *n.* (*Brit.*) **1.** ⟪*E-*⟫ the title of respect, placed after a man's last name. ⇒[usage] **2.** a member of the upper class ranking next below a knight.

—[名] ⟪英⟫ **1.** …씨, …님, 귀하 [usage] 특히 편지에서 Esq.로 줄여서 사용함 **2.** 기사(나이트) 다음가는 지위의 사람

· es·say *n.* [ései, ési → *v.*] [C] a short literary composition. ¶*an ~ on modern music.* —*vi., vt.* [eséi] try; attempt. ⟪~ *to do*⟫

—[名] 수필, 평론, 소론(小論) —[自][他] 시도하다, 꾀하다

es·say·ist [éseiist] *n.* [C] a person who writes essays.

—[名] 수필가

· es·sence [ésns] *n.* [U] **1.** the fundamental nature of a thing. ¶*Health is the ~ of happiness.* **2.** (*Philosophy*) true substance. **3.** [C][U] extract. **4.** [C][U] a pleasant-smelling liquid; a perfume.

—[名] **1.** 본질; 요소 **2.** ⟪哲⟫ [현상에 대하여] 실재, 실체, 본체 **3.** 정(精), 엑스 **4.** 향수, 향료

in essence, essentially; in fact.

[熟] 본질에 있어서, 요는

: es·sen·tial [isénʃ(ə)l] *adj.* absolutely necessary; very

—[形] 없어서는 안될, 필수의; 본질적인

essentially [399] **ether**

important; fundamental. ¶*things ~ for daily life* / *Health is ~ to happiness.* —*n.* Ⓒ (usu. *pl.*) absolutely necessary elements or qualities. ¶*the essentials of life* / *~ to happiness.*

es·sen·tial·ly [isénʃ(ə)li] *adv.* in essence; in essentials; fundamentally.

‡es·tab·lish [istǽbliʃ] *vt.* **1.** found; build up. ¶*~ a school* / *~ a ship.* **2.** set up (something) on a permanent basis; constitute. ¶*~ a theory* / *~ the constitution.* **3.** cause (someone) to settle down to something. 《*~ someone in a postition, etc.*》 ¶*He established his son in trade.* **4.** get (something) generally accepted; prove. 《*~ that ...*》 ¶*He established that what he said was true.*

es·tab·lish·ment [istǽbliʃmənt] *n.* **1.** Ⓤ the act of establishing; the state of being established. **2.** Ⓒ something established, such as a household, a business, etc. ¶*keep a large ~.* **3.** 《*the E-*》 the Church of England.

es·tate [istéit] *n.* Ⓒ **1.** a large house and lands as one's property. **2.** everything belonging to someone; property; possessions. ¶*real (personal) ~.* **3.** Ⓤ a certain period in life. ¶*attains man's (or woman's) ~.* **4.** a class or group of people in a nation.

es·teem [istí:m] *vt.* **1.** have a very favorable opinion of (something); value highly; respect. ¶*I ~ him for his honesty.* **2.** think; consider. ¶*I ~ it worthy.* —*n.* Ⓤ an opinion, usu. very favorable; high regard. ¶*hold him in high (or great) ~.*

es·ti·ma·ble [éstiməbl] *adj.* **1.** worthy of esteem. **2.** can be estimated or calculated; calculable.

‡es·ti·mate [éstimèit] *vt.* **1.** determine the value of (something); judge. **2.** find out the value, size, cost, etc. of (something). ¶*He estimated his losses at a hundred dollars.* —*vi.* calculate the value, size, cost, etc. —*n.* [éstimit, -mèit] Ⓒ the act of estimating; a rough calculation; a statement of the probable cost of a job.

es·ti·ma·tion [èstiméiʃ(ə)n] *n.* **1.** Ⓤ Ⓒ the act of estimating; judgment; opinion. ¶*in my ~.* **2.** Ⓤ esteem; respect. ¶*hold someone in high ~* / *stand high in ~.*

es·trange [istréindʒ] *vt.* **1.** separate (someone) because of a loss of feeling or affection. ¶*Their quarrel estranged the two lovers.* **2.** keep (someone) apart or away. 《*~ someone from a bad companion, etc.*》

es·trange·ment [istréindʒmənt] *n.* Ⓤ Ⓒ the act of estranging; the state of being estranged.

es·tu·ar·y [éstʃuèri, -tjuəri] *n.* Ⓒ (pl. **-ar·ies**) **1.** a wide mouth of a river into which the tide flows. **2.** an inlet of the sea.

‡etc. [etsét(ə)rə, +*Brit.* it-] =et cetera.

et cet·er·a [et-sét(ə)rə, +*Brit.* it-] and so on; and so forth.

etch [etʃ] *vt., vi.* make (pictures, etc.) by engraving designs on a metal plate with acids. ▷**etch·er** [-ər] *n.*

etch·ing [étʃiŋ] *n.* Ⓒ **1.** a picture, design, etc. printed from an etched plate. **2.** Ⓤ the art of an etcher.

•e·ter·nal [itə́:rn(ə)l] *adj.* **1.** everlasting; timeless; unchangeable. ¶*~ truth* / *the Eternal City.* **2.** (*colloq.*) too frequent; endless. ¶*~ chatter.* —*n.* 《*the E-*》 God.

e·ter·nal·ly [itə́:rn(ə)li] *adv.* **1.** forever. **2.** unchangeably. **3.** constantly.

e·ter·ni·ty [itə́:rniti] *n.* (pl. **-ties**) Ⓤ **1.** the state of being eternal; all time; endlessness. **2.** the endless period after death; future life. **3.** Ⓒ a period of time that seems endless. **4.** 《*the -ties*》 the eternal truths.

e·ther [í:θər] *n.* Ⓤ **1.** (*Chemistry*) a colorless, strong-smelling liquid produced from alcohol. **2.** an assumed

—⦿ 본질적 요소, 주요점

—⦿ 본질적으로, 근본적으로, 본래
—⦾ 1. …을 설립하다, 창설하다, 창립하다; 건조(建造)하다 2. …을 확립하다; 제정하다 ¶①헌법을 제정하다 3. …을 [지위·직업 따위에] 앉히다; 자리잡게 하다 4. …을 납득시키다; 입증(확증)하다

—⦿ 1. 확립, 확정, 개설(開設), 설립, 창립 2. 설립물, 세대(世帶), 회사 ¶①큰 살림을 꾸려 나가고 있다 3. 영국 국교

—⦿ 1. 가옥, 땅, 지소(地所) 2. 소유물; 재산 ¶①부동산(동산) 3. [인생의] 시기, 시대 ¶②성년에 달하다 4. [정치상·사회상의] 계급

—⦾ 1. …을 존경하다, 존중하다 2. …을 […이라고] 여기다, 생각하다 —⦿ 존중, 존경, 경의 ¶①그를 높이 존경하다

—⦿ 1. 존경할 만한, 존중할 만한 2. 평가(견적)할 수 있는
—⦾ 1. …을 평가하다, 판단하다 2. …을 견적하다, 개산(槪算)하다 ¶①그는 손실을 100 달러로 추산했다 —⦿ 평가; 견적[서]

—⦿ 1. 견적, 평가; 판단, 의견 ¶①나의 견해로는 2. 존중, 존경 ¶②…을 높이 평가하다, 크게 존경하다
—⦾ 1. …을 멀어지게 하다, 정떨어지게 하다, 소원히 하다 ¶①그 싸움으로 두 애인은 사이가 서먹서먹해졌다 2. …을 멀리하다

—⦿ 소원; 이간

—⦿ 1. [폭이 넓은] 강어귀 2. [바다의] 작은 만(灣)

— …따위, 기타, 등등

—⦾ [산류(酸類)로 금속판에 그림 따위를] 식각(蝕刻)하다, 식각법을 쓰다
—⦿ 1. 동판화; 부식 동판화(術), 에칭 2. 부식법, 식각법
—⦿ 1. 영구(영원)한; 불멸의, 불후의 ¶①영원한 도시, 로마 2. (口) 쉴새없는; 끊임없는; 끝없는 ¶②그칠 줄 모르는 수다 —⦿ 〖신(神)〗

—⦾ 1. 영원히 2. 변함없이 3. 끊임없이, 부단히

—⦿ 1. 영원, 영구; 무궁; 불멸 2. 영세(永世), 내세 3. 끝없는 계속, [영원한 것처럼 생각되는] 긴 기간 4. 불변의 사실(진리)

—⦿ 1.(化) 에에테르 2. 에에테르 [빛·열·전기·자기의 가상적 매체(媒體)]

medium filling all space, through which light waves and wireless waves are transmitted. **3.** (*poetic*) the upper sky.
3. 《詩》 하늘, 창공

e·the·re·al [iθíəri(:)əl] *adj.* **1.** light; airy. **2.** extremely delicate or refined. ¶ ~ *beauty.* **3.** heavenly.
—[形] 1. 가벼운, 공기 같은 2. 미묘한, 영묘(靈妙)한 3. 하늘의, 천상의

eth·ic [éθik], **-i·cal** [-ik(ə)l] *adj.* of ethics; moral.
—[形] 윤리[학]의; 도덕상의

eth·ics [éθiks] *n. pl.* **1.** 《used as *sing.*》 the study of standards of right and wrong in human behavior. ¶*Ethics deals with moral conduct.* **2.** individual or professional morals.
—[名] 1. 윤리학 2. [개인의] 도덕; [직업상의] 도덕

eth·nic [éθnik], **-ni·cal** [-nik(ə)l] *adj.* **1.** of racial groups. **2.** neither Christian nor Jewish; pagan.
—[形] 1. 인종(종족)의 2. 이교도의; 이방인의

eth·nol·o·gy [eθnálədʒi / -nɔ́l-] *n.* [U] the science of the various races of mankind.
—[名] 인류학, 민족학

et·i·quette [étikèt, -kit, +*Brit.* ⩥-⩤] *n.* [U] the customs or formal rules of behavior in polite society, a profession, an official ceremony, etc.
—[名] 예식, 예법, 예의범절, 에티켓

E·ton [í:tn] *n.* a town in South Buckinghamshire, in south England, on the Thames River. ⇨[N.B.]
—[名] 잉글란드 남부 버킹엄시어에 있는 도시 [N.B.] Eton College의 소재지

é·tude [eit(j)ú:d, -tú:d, +*U.S.* ⩤-] *n.* [C] (*Music*) a piece of music intended to give some technical practice. ¶*a concert* ~.
—[名] 《樂》 연습곡, 에튀드

et·y·mo·log·i·cal [ètimələ́dʒik(ə)l / -lɔ́dʒ-] *adj.* of etymology.
—[形] 어원의, 어원학[상]의

et·y·mol·o·gist [ètimálədʒist / -mɔ́l-] *n.* [C] a person skilled in etymology.
—[名] 어원학자

et·y·mol·o·gy [ètimálədʒi / -mɔ́l-] *n.* (pl. **-gies**) **1.** [U] the study of linguistic changes, esp. of word origins. **2.** [C] an account or explanation of the origin and history of a word.
—[名] 1. 어원학 2. [어떤 말의] 어원, 어원의 설명

eu·ca·lyp·ti [jù:kəlíptai] *n.* pl. of **eucalyptus**.

eu·ca·lyp·tus [jù:kəlíptəs] *n.* [C] (pl. **-tus·es** or **-ti**) any of the tall, evergeen trees.
—[名] 유우칼립터스(호주산의 큰 상록수)

Eu·cha·rist [jú:kərist] *n.* 《*the* ~》 **1.** the Lord's Supper. **2.** the bread and wine taken at the Lord's Supper.
—[名] 1. 성찬 2. [성찬용] 빵과 포도주

Eu·clid [jú:klid] *n.* (300 B.C.?) a Greek mathematician.
—[名] 그리이스의 수학자

eu·gen·ics [ju(:)dʒéniks] *n. pl.* 《used as *sing.*》 the science of improving the human race.
—[名] 우생학

eu·lo·gize [jú:lədʒàiz] *vt.* praise highly.
—[他] …을 칭찬하다, 찬양하다

eu·lo·gy [jú:lədʒi] *n.* (pl. **-gies**) **1.** [C] a speech or writing in praise of a person, esp. a dead person, a thing, etc. **2.** [U] high praise.
—[名] 1. 찬사 2. 칭찬, 찬양

eu·phe·mism [jú:fimìz(ə)m] *n.* [U] the use of a mild or indirect expression or word instead of a coarse or unpleasant one; [C] an example of this.
—[名] [노골적으로 말하기를 피하는] 완곡[어]법; 완곡한 어구

eu·phe·mis·tic [jù:fimístik] *adj.* of or showing euphemism.
—[形] 완곡어법의, 완곡한

eu·pho·ny [jú:fəni] *n.* [U][C] (pl. **-nies**) the state of having a pleasant sound; agreeableness of sound; a pleasing sound.
—[名] 듣기 좋은 음조; 악음(樂音)

Eu·phra·tes [ju:fréiti:z], **the** *n.* a river flowing through Mesopotamia. ⇨[N.B.]
—[名] 유프라테스강 [N.B.] 그 유역은 고대문명의 발상지

Eur·a·sia [juəréiʒə, -ʃə] *n.* Europe and Asia.
—[名] 유우라시아, 구아(歐亞)[대륙]

Eur·a·sian [juəréiʒən, -ʃən] *adj.* **1.** of Eurasia or its people. **2.** of mixed European and Asiatic blood. —*n.* [C] a person of mixed European and Asiatic blood.
—[形] 1. 유우라시아의, 구아[인]의 2. 구아 잡종의 —[名] 구아 혼혈아

eu·re·ka [juərí:kə] *interj.* I have found it!
—[感] 알았다!; 됐다!

‡**Eu·rope** [júərəp] *n.* a continent to the west of Asia.
—[名] 유럽, 구주

‡**Eu·ro·pe·an** [jùərəpí(:)ən] *adj.* of Europe or its people. —*n.* [C] a person of Europe.
—[形] 유럽[인]의 —[名] 유럽인

Eu·ro·pe·an·ize [jùərəpí(:)ənàiz] *vt.* make (something) European style.
—[他] …을 유럽풍(식)으로 하다, 유럽화하다

eu·tha·na·sia [jù:θənéiʒə, -ʒiə / -ziə] *n.* [U] the method of causing death easily and painlessly; an easy, painless death.
—[名] 안사술(安死術); 안락사

e·vac·u·ate [ivǽkjuèit] *vt.* **1.** move (someone or something) to a safe place. **2.** make (a house etc.) vacant;
—[他] 1. [군대]를 철수(철병)시키다; …을 소개(疎開)시키다 2. [집 따위]를

make (something) empty. **3.** let (waste matter) out from the body.
비우다, 명도(明渡)하다; [속에 든 것]을 비우다 **3.** [대변]을 배설하다

e·vac·u·a·tion [ivæ̀kjuéiʃ(ə)n] *n.* [U] [C] the act of evacuating; withdrawal; removal; discharge.
—[名] [군대의] 철수, 철병, 소개(疏開); 명도(明渡); 배설[물]

e·vac·u·ee [ivæ̀kju(:)í:, +*U.S.* ivǽkjuì:] *n.* [C] a person who is moved to a safe place in war time.
—[名] [위험지대로부터의] 소개자, 피난자

e·vade [ivéid] *vt.* get away from (something); escape; avoid.
—[他] …을 벗어나다, 모면하다; 회피하다

e·val·u·ate [ivǽljuèit] *vt.* find or decide the value or the amount of (something). ¶~ *an old house.*
—[他] …의 가치를 검토하다; …을 평가하다

e·va·l·u·a·tion [ivæ̀ljuéiʃ(ə)n] *n.* [U] the act of evaluating; the state of being evaluated; valuation.
—[名] 평가, 감정

e·van·gel·ic [ì:vændʒélik, èvæn-] **-i·cal** [-ik(ə)l] *adj.* of, based on, or according to the teachings of the Gospels or the New Testament.
—[形] 복음(전도)의; 복음주의의

e·van·gel·ist [ivǽndʒilist] *n.* [C] **1.** a preacher of the Gospel, esp. a traveling preacher. **2.** 《*E*-》 one of the four writers of the Gospels, Matthew, Mark, Luke, or John.
—[名] **1.** 복음의 선교자; 전도자 **2.** 복음서 저자

e·vap·o·rate [ivǽpərèit] *vi.* **1.** change into vapor. **2.** vanish; disappear. —*vt.* **1.** cause (a liquid) to change into gas. **2.** remove water from (fruit, etc.). ¶*evaporated milk.*①
—[自] **1.** 증발하다 **2.** 사라지게(없어지게) 하다 —[他] **1.** …을 증발시키다 **2.** [과일 따위]의 수분을 빼다 ¶①[통조림으로 된] 농축(濃縮) 우유

e·vap·o·ra·tion [ivæ̀pəréiʃ(ə)n] *n.* [U] [C] the act of evaporating.
—[名] 증발; 탈수

e·va·sion [ivéiʒ(ə)n] *n.* **1.** [U] the act of evading. **2.** [C] a means of evading; a trick to avoid something.
—[名] **1.** 도피; [책임의] 회피 **2.** 핑계; 발뺌

e·va·sive [ivéisiv] *adj.* tending or trying to evade. ▷**e·va·sive·ly** [-li] *adv.* —**e·va·sive·ness** [-nis] *n.*
—[形] 회피적인, 핑계(발뺌)의

***eve** [i:v] *n.* [C] **1.** evening or day before a holiday or some other special day. ¶*Christmas Eve / New Year's Eve.* **2.** time just before some event. ¶*on the ~ of the event.*① **3.** (*poetic*) evening.
—[名] **1.** 축제일의 전날[밤] **2.** [무슨 사건의] 직전 ¶①그 사건의 직전에 **3.** 《詩》 저녁, 밤

Eve [i:v] *n.* (in the Bible) the first woman, Adam's wife.
—[名] 이브(Adam의 아내)

‡**e·ven**[1] [í:v(ə)n] *adj.* **1.** flat; smooth. ¶*as ~ as glass.* **2.** at the same level; on the same surface. ¶*The snow was ~ with the roof.*① **3.** always the same; regular; uniform. ¶*an ~ color*② / *an ~ tempo.*③ **4.** equal; equally balanced. ¶*an ~ bargain*④ / *~ scores.* **5.** calm. ¶*an ~ temper.* **6.** exact; precise. **7.** (of numbers) that can be divided by 2. ↔odd
—[形] **1.** 판판한, 평탄한; 반드러운 **2.** 같은 높이의; 같은 평면상의 ¶①눈이 지붕 높이까지 쌓였다 **3.** 한결같은, 불변의; 규칙적인 ¶②한결같은 색깔/③일정한 박자 **4.** 동등한; 균등의 ¶④득실이 없는 거래 **5.** 차분한, 고요한 **6.** 정확한; 엄밀한 **7.** 우수(偶數)의

be even with (=*have one's revenge on*) *someone.*
[熟] …에게 복수하다, 앙갚음하다

—*vt.* make (something) level, equal, or balanced.
—*vi.* become level, equal, or balanced.
—[他] …을 판판하게(동등하게, 균등하게) 하다 —[自] 판판해지다, 동등해지다

—*adv.* **1.** though it would not be expected; truly; indeed. ¶*He never ~ opened the book.*⑤ / *Even children could understand it.*⑥ **2.** 《with *comparative degree*》 still; yet. ¶*His error was ~ worse.*
—[副] **1.** …조차, …까지도; 확실히, 과연, 정말 ¶⑤그는 책을 펼치기조차도 안 한다/⑥아이들이라도 알 수 있다 **2.** 한층, 더욱

1) ***even as,*** ⓐ just as; just like. ⓑ at the very time. ¶*She left ~ as you came.*
2) ***even if*** (or ***though***)***,*** in spite of the fact that …
[熟] 1)ⓐ…와 같이 ⓑ바로 그때 2)비록 …일지라도

e·ven[2] [í:v(ə)n] *n.* [C] (*poetic*) evening.
—[名] 《詩》 저녁, 밤

e·ven-hand·ed [ív(ə)nhǽndid] *adj.* fair; just.
—[形] 공평한; 공명정대한

‡**eve·ning** [í:vniŋ] *n.* [C] 《sometimes *sing.* without *art.*》 **1.** the last part of a day; time between sunset and night. ¶*early* (*late*) *in the ~ / musical evenings*① / *this* (*tomorrow, yesterday*) *~ / on Friday ~.*② **2.** the last part of one's life, etc. ¶*the ~ of one's life.*③ —*adj.* in, of, or for the evening.
—[名] **1.** 해질 무렵, 해거름; 저녁, 밤 ¶①음악의 밤/②금요일 밤에 **2.** 만년(晩年), 쇠퇴기 ¶③만년 —[形] 저녁때(해거름)의

evening dress [⌐-⌐] *n.* formal clothes worn in the evening.
—[名] 야회복

e·ven·ly [í:v(ə)nli] *adv.* in an even manner.
—[副] 판판하게; 평등하게, 균등히

‡**e·vent** [ivént] *n.* [C] **1.** an important happening; an occurrence. ¶*a historical ~ / It was quite an ~.*① **2.** a result; an outcome. **3.** one of a series of matches in a program of sports. ¶*a main ~.*②
—[名] **1.** 사건, 우발 사건 ¶①그것은 정말 대사건이었다 **2.** 결과, 성과 **3.** [경기 순서 중의] 한 게임, 한 시합 ¶②주요 종목(경기)

1) ***at all events; in any event,*** in any case; no matter what happens.
2) ***in the event of,*** in case of; if there is; if there should happen to be.

[熟] 1)아뭏든,좌우간,어떻든 2)만일 …의 경우에는

e·vent·ful [ivéntf(u)l] *adj.* **1.** full of events, esp. important events. **2.** having important results; important.

— [形] 1. 사건이 많은,다사한,파란 많은 2. 중요(중대)한

e·ven·tide [íːv(ə)ntàid] *n.* [U] (*poetic*) evening.

— [名] 《詩》 땅거미질 무렵,해거름,저녁

e·ven·tu·al [ivéntʃuəl] *adj.* **1.** coming as a result of a series of events; final. **2.** depending on future events; possible.

— [形] 1. 결과로서 올; 최후(종국)의 2. 장차 일어날지도 모를

e·ven·tu·al·i·ty [ivèntʃuǽliti] *n.* (pl. **-ties**) **1.** [C] an event or a condition that may happen. **2.** [U] the state of being eventual; possibility.

— [名] 1. 불의의(예측할 수 없는) 사건; 장차 일어날지도 모를 사건 2. 우발성

* **e·ven·tu·al·ly** [ivéntʃuəli] *adv.* in the end; at last; finally.

— [副] 결국,마침내

‡ **ev·er** [évər] *adv.* **1.** at any time; until now. ¶ *Nothing ~ happens.*① / *Did you ~ hear such stuff?*② / *It was the best thing I ~ saw.* **2.** at all times; always. ¶ *He is ~ the same.*
1) ***ever after,*** continuously from that time.
2) ***ever and anon,*** sometimes.
3) ***ever since,*** from that time on.
4) ***ever so,*** (*colloq.*) very.
5) ***for ever,*** for all future time; continuously.

— [副] 1. 언젠가,여태껏,지금까지 ¶①결코 아무 일도 일어나지 않는다/②그런 소리를 들어 본 일이 있는가? 2. 언제나,늘,항상
[熟] 1)그때부터 죽, 그후 줄곧 2)이따금,때때로 3)그 뒤로는,그때 이후 4)매우,대단히 5)영원(영구)히, 끊임없이

Ev·er·est [év(ə)rist], **Mount** *n.* the highest mountain in the world, in Nepal and Tibet. ⇒[N.B.]

— [名] 에베레스트 산 [N.B.] 8,848m

ev·er·green [évərgrìːn] *adj.* (of trees, shrubs, etc.) having green leaves throughout the year. **—*n.*** [C] **1.** an evergreen plant. **2.** (*pl.*) evergreen twigs or branches used for decoration, esp. at Christmas.

— [形] 상록의 — [名] 1. 상록수,늘푸른 나무 2. [크리스마스 장식용의] 상록수 가지

* **ev·er·last·ing** [èvərlǽstiŋ / èvəlɑ́ːstiŋ] *adj.* **1.** lasting forever; eternal. ¶ *~ fame.* **2.** lasting a long time. **3.** lasting indefinitely; repeated too often; tiresome. ¶ *~ jokes.* **—*n.*** **1.** [U] eternity. **2.** (*the E-*) God.

— [形] 1. 영원한 2. 영원히 계속되는,영속의 3. 끝없는; 끊임없는; 지루한 — [名] 1. 영구,영원 2. 신(神)

ever·last·ing·ly [èvərlǽstiŋli / èvəlɑ́ːst-] *adv.* in an everlasting manner.

— [副] 영구(영원)히,한없이

ev·er·more [èvərmɔ́ər] *adv.* always; continuously; forever.

— [副] 늘,항상; 영원(영구)히

‡ **ev·ery** [évri] *adj.* **1.** each of all. ¶ *~ one of you*① / *They listened to ~ word of his lecture.* / *Every man cannot be a Newton at will.* **2.** each. ¶ *~ other day*② / *He comes ~ third day.*
1) ***every bit,*** quite.
2) ***every now and then,*** sometimes.
3) ***every time,*** whenever.

— [形] 1. 모든,하나도 남김없는 ¶①너희들 모두 2. 각각의,제각기의,매(每)…,…마다 ¶②이틀마다,하루 걸러
[熟] 1)아주; 어느 점으로 보나 2)때때로,가끔 3)[…할] 때마다,[…할] 때는 언제나

‡ **eve·ry·bod·y** [évribàdi / -bɔ̀di] *pron.* everyone; every person.

— [代] 누구든지 모두,사람마다

‡ **eve·ry·day** [évridèi] *adj.* **1.** daily; of every day. ¶ *~ life.* **2.** for ordinary days. ¶ *~ clothes.*① **3.** ordinary; not new. ¶ *~ affairs.*

— [形] 1. 매일의,나날의 2. 일상의,평상시의 ¶①평상복 3. 흔히 있는,흔해빠진,평범한

‡ **eve·ry·one** [évriwʌ̀n] *pron.* everybody; each person.

— [代] 누구든지 모두

‡ **eve·ry·thing** [évriθìŋ] *pron.* **1.** all things. **2.** the most important thing. ¶ *Honor is ~ to him.*①
before everything, first of all.

— [代] 1. 무엇이든지 모두,만사 2. 가장 중한 것 ¶①그에게는 명예보다 더 중요한 것은 없다
[熟] 무엇보다도 우선

‡ **eve·ry·where** [évri(h)wèər / -wèə] *adv.* in all places; wherever. ¶ *He was welcomed ~ he went.*①

— [副] 어디든지,도처에 ¶①그는 가는 곳마다 환영을 받았다

e·vict [i(ː)víkt] *vt.* make (someone) go away from land, a building, etc. by the power of law; expel.

— [他] …에서 퇴거시키다,쫓아내다,축출하다

e·vic·tion [i(ː)víkʃ(ə)n] *n.* [U] [C] the act of evicting; the state of being evicted; expulsion.

— [名] 쫓아냄,추방,축출

‡ **ev·i·dence** [évid(ə)ns] *n.* [U] [C] anything that makes clear the truth; ground for belief; a proof. ¶ *false ~* / *collect ~* / *There is enough ~ to prove him innocent.*① / *Her flushed look was visible ~ of her fever.*
1) ***bear*** (or ***give***) ***evidence*** (=*show signs*) ***of something.***
2) ***in evidence,*** easily seen or noticed; clear.
—*vt.* make (something) clear by evidence; prove.

— [名] 증거[물] ¶①그의 무죄를 증명할 만한 증거는 충분히 있다
[熟] 1)…의 자취가 있다 2)뚜렷이,분명히,눈에 띄게
— [他] …을 입증하다

* **ev·i·dent** [évid(ə)nt] *adj.* easy to see or understand; plain; clear.

— [形] 명백한,분명한

ev·i·dent·ly [évid(ə)ntli] *adv.* plainly ; clearly.
—卿 분명(명백)히

e·vil [í:vl] *adj.* **1.** morally bad or wrong ; sinful ; wicked. ¶ ~ *conduct.*① **2.** harmful ; injurious. ¶ ~ *laws.* **3.** unfortunate.
1) *fall upon* (or *on*) *evil days,* have ill luck.
2) *in an evil hour,* unfortunately.
—*n.* **1.** Ⓤ something bad ; sin ; wickedness. **2.** Ⓒ a thing that causes harm or injury.
▷**e·vil·ly** [-vili] *adv.* —**e·vil·ness** [-nis] *n.*
—形 1. 나쁜, 못된, 사악한 ¶①못된 짓, 비행(非行) 2.해로운 3.불길한, 불운(不運)한
熟 1. 불운을 만나다. 2)운수 사납게, 불행히도
—名 1. 악, 사악, 악행 2. 해악, 악폐, 재앙

e·vil·do·er [í:vldú(:)ər] *n.* Ⓒ a person who does evil.
—名 나쁜 짓을 하는 사람, 악인

e·vil-look·ing [í:vllúkiŋ] *adj.* having a disagreeable appearance ; ill-looking.
—形 험상궂게 생긴

e·vil-mind·ed [í:vlmáindid] *adj.* having an evil mind ; 「wicked.」
—形 나쁜 마음을 품은, 사심이 있는 ;

Evil One [´- ´-], **the** *n.* the Devil ; Satan.
—名 악마 「사악한, 심술궂은」

e·vince [ivíns] *vt.* show clearly (one's quality, feeling, etc.) ; prove.
—他 …을 분명히 나타내다, 명시하다

e·voke [ivóuk] *vt.* call forth ; bring out ; summon.
—他 …을 불러일으키다, 환기시키다

ev·o·lu·tion [èvəlú:ʃ(ə)n, +*Brit.* ì:və-] *n.* Ⓤ **1.** the process of being formed ; growth ; development. ¶ *the ~ of the drama*① / *the ~ of a chicken from an egg.*② **2.** (*Biology*) the process that all living things have developed from lower and simpler forms of life. ¶ *the ~ of man* / *the theory of ~.*③ 「tionary.」
—名 1. 전전, 발전, 전개 ; 성장 ¶①극의 전개/②달걀로부터 병아리로의 성장 2.《生》진화(론) ¶③진화론

ev·o·lu·tion·al [èvəlú:ʃən(ə)l, +*Brit.* ì:və-] *adj.* =evolu-」

ev·o·lu·tion·ar·y [èvəlú:ʃənèri / -ʃ(ə)nəri, ì:və-] *adj.* **1.** of evolution ; developed step by step. **2.** agreeing with the theory of evolution.
—形 1. 전개적인, 발달의 2. 진화(론)의

ev·o·lu·tion·ist [èvəlú:ʃ(ə)nist, +*Brit.* ì:və-] *n.* Ⓒ a person who believes the theory of evolution.
—名 진화론자

e·volve [iválv / ivɔ́lv] *vt.* **1.** develop gradually. **2.** develop (a living thing) to a higher state. **3.** give off (heat, gas, etc.). —*vi.* **1.** be developed. **2.** reach a more highly organized state by a process of growth and change.
—他 1. …을 전개하다, 발전시키다 2. …을 진화시키다 3. [열 따위]를 방출하다 —自 1. 전개하다, 진전되다 2. 진화하다

ewe [ju:] *n.* Ⓒ a female sheep. ↔ram
—名 암양(羊)

ew·er [jú(:)ər] *n.* Ⓒ a wide-mouthed water pitcher.
—名 [아가리가 큰] 물항아리

ex- [eks-] *pref.* **1.** out of ; from ; out : *exit* (=go out). **2.** utterly ; thorough : *exterminate* (=destroy utterly). **3.** beyond : *excess* (=conduct that goes beyond the usual limit). **4.** former ; formerly : *ex-governor* (=the former governor).
—《接頭》1. …으로부터, 밖으로 2. 철저히 3. …의 한계 이상으로 4. 이전의, 전(前)…

ex·act [igzǽkt] *adj.* accurate ; strictly correct ; precise.
—*vt.* require ; claim ; insist upon.
—形 정확한, 틀림없는 ; 정밀(엄밀)한
—他 …을 요구하다 ; 강요하다

ex·act·ing [igzǽktiŋ] *adj.* **1.** requiring much ; severe ; strict. ¶ *an ~ teacher.* **2.** requiring great care, effort, or patience. ¶ *an ~ task.*
—形 1. 가혹한 ; 엄한 2. 힘드는, 고된

ex·ac·tion [igzǽkʃ(ə)n] *n.* **1.** Ⓤ the act of exacting. **2.** Ⓒ something exacted, esp. a tax, etc. which a person is forced to pay.
—名 1. 강제, 강요, 가혹한 요구 2. 강제 징수, 가혹한 세금

ex·act·i·tude [igzǽktit(j)ù:d / -tju:d] *n.* =exactness.

ex·act·ly [igzǽktli] *adv.* **1.** in an exact manner ; accurately ; precisely. **2.** yes ; indeed ; just so ; quite right.
—卿 1. 정확히 ; 엄밀히 2. 과연, 암 그렇고말고

ex·act·ness [igzǽktnis] *n.* Ⓤ the quality of being exact ; precision.
—名 정확 ; 엄정(嚴正)

ex·ag·ger·ate [igzǽdʒərèit] *vt.* **1.** think of or express (something) as greater than it really is ; go beyond the truth ; overstate. ¶ *It is impossible to ~ the importance of health.*① **2.** increase or enlarge abnormally. —*vi.* give an exaggerated thought or expression of something. ▷**ex·ag·ger·a·tor** [-ər] *n.*
—他 1. …을 과대시하다 ; 과장하다, 허풍치다 ¶①건강이 중요하다는 것은 아무리 과장하여 말하여도 지나친 일은 아니다 2. [기관(器官) 따위]를 비대시키다 —自 과장하여 생각하다(말하다, 쓰다)

ex·ag·ger·a·tion [igzæ̀dʒəréiʃ(ə)n] *n.* **1.** Ⓤ the act of exaggerating ; the state of being exaggerated. **2.** Ⓒ an exaggerated statement.
—名 1. 과장, 허풍, 과대시 2. 과장된 말, 침소봉대의 표현

ex·alt [igzɔ́:lt] *vt.* **1.** make (someone) higher in rank,
—他 1. …을 높이다, 승진시키다 2. …

honor, power, character, quality, etc. **2.** fill (someone) with pride, joy, or noble feeling; praise. — 을 의기양양하게 하다; 칭찬하다, 추어올리다

ex·al·ta·tion [ègzɔ:ltéiʃ(ə)n] *n.* [U] **1.** the act of exalting; the state of being exalted. **2.** feeling of great joy, pride, etc.; rapture. —[名] 1. 높이기, 올리기, 고양(高揚) 2. 의기양양, 기고만장; 광희(狂喜)

ex·alt·ed [igzɔ́:ltid] *adj.* **1.** elevated in rank, honor, etc. ¶*an ~ personage.*① **2.** noble; elevated; lofty. ¶*an ~ style of writing.* —[形] 1. [지위·신분이] 높은, 고귀한 ¶①고귀한 사람 2. 고상한; 숭고한

ex·am [igzǽm] *n.* [C] (*colloq.*) examination. —[名] 시험

⁑**ex·am·i·na·tion** [igzæ̀minéiʃ(ə)n] *n.* **1.** [U] the act of examining; the state of being examined. **2.** [C] a careful test of someone's knowledge, ability, etc.; an inquiry into someone's physical condition. ¶*an ~ in English / an entrance ~ / a medical ~.*① —[名] 1. 검사, 검열 2. 시험; 진단; 진찰 ¶①건강진단

⁑**ex·am·ine** [igzǽmin] *vt.* **1.** look at or into (something) carefully to find out the facts and learn about them; inspect; investigate. ¶*~ oneself*① */ have one's health examined*② */ ~ old records.*③ **2.** test (a pupil, etc.) by questions. 《~ someone *in* knowledge, ability, etc.》 ¶*~ pupils in history.* —[他] 1. …을 조사하다; 검사하다; 심사하다 ¶①반성해 보다/②건강진단을 받다/③옛 기록을 조사하다 2. …을 시험하다

ex·am·i·nee [igzæ̀miní:] *n.* [C] a person who is being examined. —[名] 수험자

ex·am·in·er [igzǽminər] *n.* [C] a person who examines. —[名] 시험관, 심사관, 검사관

⁑**ex·am·ple** [igzǽmpl / -zá:m-] *n.* [C] **1.** one part that shows what the whole is like; a sample; a specimen. ¶*This is a good ~ of Shakespeare's verse.*① **2.** one thing or event that agrees with the general rule. **3.** a fact in the past used as a key to decide matters in the present. **4.** a person or thing to be imitated; a model. ¶*follow someone's ~*② */ He is an ~ for all of us.* **5.** a warning; a lesson. ¶*make an ~ of someone.*③ —[名] 1. 보기 ¶①이것은 셰익스피어 시의 한 좋은 보기이다 2. 실례(實例) 3. 전례 4. 모범; 귀감 ¶②남을 본보기로 하다 5. 본보기, 훈계 ¶③남을 본보기로 처벌하다

1) ***beyond*** (or ***without***) ***example,*** having no example in the past.
2) ***for example,*** for instance.
[熟] 1)전례가 없는 2)예를 들면

ex·as·per·ate [igzǽsp(ə)rèit / -á:s-] *vt.* **1.** irritate very much; make (someone) angry. 《~ someone *against*》 **2.** make (disease, ill feeling, etc.) worse. —[他] 1. …을 짜증나게(안달나게) 하다; 성나게 하다 2. …을 더 악화시키다

ex·as·per·a·tion [igzæ̀spəréiʃ(ə)n / -à:s-] *n.* [C] extreme annoyance or irritation; anger. —[名] 격노, 분격, 격분

ex·ca·vate [ékskəvèit] *vt.* make (a hole) in the ground, etc.; dig; make (something) hollow by taking out the inner part; get or uncover (something) by digging. —[他] [구멍]을 파다; …에 구멍(굴)을 파다, …을 파서 동굴로 만들다; …을 파 일으키다, 발굴하다

ex·ca·va·tion [èkskəvéiʃ(ə)n] *n.* **1.** [U] the act of excavating. **2.** [C] a hole or hollow made by digging. —[名] 1. 발굴, 구멍파기 2. [파서 만든] 구멍, 동굴, 공동(空洞)

ex·ca·va·tor [ékskəvèitər] *n.* [C] a person or thing that excavates. —[名] 발굴자, 굴착자; 굴착기

•**ex·ceed** [iksí:d] *vt.* **1.** go beyond the limit of (something). ¶*~ the speed limit.* **2.** be more or greater than (someone); excel; surpass. ¶*~ someone in knowledge.*① —[他] 1. …의 한도를 넘다 2. …을 능가하다, …보다 우월하다 ¶①지식에 있어서 남을 능가하다

ex·ceed·ing [iksí:diŋ] *adj.* very great; extreme; unusual. —[形] 과도한, 대단한, 굉장한

•**ex·ceed·ing·ly** [iksí:diŋli] *adv.* more than others; very greatly; extremely; unusually. —[副] 굉장히, 엄청나게

•**ex·cel** [iksél] *v.* (**-celled, -cel·ling**) *vt.* do better than (someone); surpass. 《~ someone *in* courage, etc.》 ¶*You ~ me in historical knowledge.* —*vi.* be remarkably good. 《~ *in* (or *at, as*) something》 ¶*He excels in mathematics.*① —[他] …을 능가하다, […보다] 탁월하다 —[自] 뛰어나다, 탁월하다 ¶①그는 수학에 월등히 뛰어나 있다

ex·cel·lence [éks(ə)ləns] *n.* **1.** [U] the state of being excellent; superiority. **2.** [C] an excellent quality or feature. —[名] 1. 탁월, 우수, 걸출 2. 장점, 미점, 미덕

ex·cel·len·cy [éks(ə)lənsi] *n.* [U] **1.** (*archaic*) =excellence. **2.** 《*E-*》 a title of honor given to an ambassador, governor, president, bishop, etc. ⇒[usage] —[名] 2. 각하 [usage] Your (His, Her) Excellency와 같이 씀

⁑**ex·cel·lent** [éks(ə)lənt] *adj.* unusually good; better than others; superior. ▷**ex·cel·lent·ly** [-li] *adv.* —[形] 우수한, 탁월한, 뛰어난, 빼어난

ex·cel·si·or [iksélsiər, ek- / -siɔ̀ː, -siə] *adj.* ever upward; higher still. ⇒[N.B.] —*n.* [U] (*U.S.*) soft, fine, curled shavings of wood used for stuffing or packing.
—[形] 한층 더 높이 [N.B.] New York주의 표어 —[名] 《美》 [속을 채우거나 포장용의] 대팻밥

‡ex·cept [iksépt] *prep.* other than; not including; but. ¶*Everyone ~ him answered the question correctly.* / *Nothing remains for us to do, ~ to enjoy the fruits of our labors.*①
—[前] …을 제외하고는, …이외는 ¶①우리 노력의 성과를 거두는 이외는 인제 더 할 일은 없다

1) ***except for,*** but for; if it were not for.
2) ***except that,*** if not; unless.
[熟] 1)…이 없으면, …만 아니라면, 2) …을 빼고는, …이외는

—*vt.* leave out; omit; exclude.
—[他] …을 제외하다, 빼다

ex·cept·ing [ikséptiŋ] *prep.* except; leaving out.
—[前] …을 제외하고는; …이외는

‡ex·cep·tion [iksépʃ(ə)n] *n.* **1.** [C][U] the act of leaving out. ¶*by way of ~*① / *liable* (or *subject*) *to ~*② / *make an ~ of*③ / *make no exceptions*④ / *with the ~ of.*⑤ **2.** [C] a person or thing left out; an unusual instance. **3.** objection.
—[名] **1.** 제외 ¶①예외로서/②이의를 신립할 만한, 반대할 수 있는/③…을 제외하다, 예외로 하다, 각별히 취급하다/④예외로 하지 않다, 특별 취급하지 않다/⑤…을 제외하고, …이외는 **2.** 예외; 이례(異例) **3.** 이의

take exception (=*object; do not agree*) ***to*** (or ***against***) *something.* ¶*He took ~ to* (or *against*) *my proposal.*
[熟] …에 이의를 신립하다, 불복하다

ex·cep·tion·a·ble [iksépʃ(ə)nəbl] *adj.* liable to exception; objectionable.
—[形] 반대할 수 있는, 이의를 말할 수 있는

ex·cep·tion·al [iksépʃən(ə)l] *adj.* out of the ordinary; unusual; uncommon.
—[形] 예외의, 이례적인

ex·cep·tion·al·ly [iksépʃ(ə)nəli, -ʃənli] *adv.* in an exceptional manner or way.
—[副] 예외적으로, 파격적으로, 이례적으로

ex·cerpt *vt.* [iksə́ːrpt →*n.*] take (a passage) from a book, film, etc.; quote. —*n.* [éksəːrpt] [C] a selected passage; a quotation; an extract.
—[他] [책에서] …을 발췌하다, 인용하다
—[名] 발췌, 초록(抄錄)

•ex·cess *n.* [iksés →*adj.*] **1.** [U] too much; more than enough. **2.** [C] the amount greater than is necessary; surplus. ↔lack **3.** [U] 《often *pl.*》 eating or drinking too much; immoderation.
—[名] **1.** 초과, 과다, 과잉 **2.** 초과액, 여분 **3.** 부절제, 불근신, 불손

1) ***in excess of,*** more than.
2) ***to*** (or ***in***) ***excess,*** too much.
[熟] 1)…보다 이상으로, …을 초과하여 2)극단으로, 지나치게

—*adj.* [iksés, ékses] beyond what is allowed; extra. ¶*~ baggage*① / *an ~ fare.*②
—[形] 제한 외의, 여분의 ¶①제한 초과 수하물/②초과 추징금, 부족 요금

•ex·ces·sive [iksésiv] *adj.* too much; beyond due measure; immoderate; extreme.
—[形] 과도한, 지나친; 극단적인

ex·ces·sive·ly [iksésivli] *adv.* in an excessive manner; too much; too greatly.
—[副] 과도하게, 지나치게; 몹시 극단으로

‡ex·change [ikstʃéindʒ] *vt.* give and receive; barter. 《~ something *for*》 ¶*~ clothing for food*① / *~ opinions.*② —*n.* **1.** [U] the act of exchanging. **2.** [U] a money-changer's trade. **3.** [C] something exchanged for another thing. **4.** [C] a building where merchants assemble for business.
—[他] …을 교환하다 ¶①옷을 음식과 바꾸다/②의견을 교환하다
—[名] **1.** 교환 **2.** 환전업(換錢業) **3.** 교환물 **4.** 교환소, 거래소

ex·change·a·ble [ikstʃéindʒəbl] *adj.* can be exchanged.
—[形] 교환할 수 있는

ex·cheq·uer [ékstʃekər / ikstʃékə] *n.* [C] **1.** a place where public money is kept; the Treasury. **2.** (*colloq.*) finances; funds. **3.** 《*the E-*》 (*Brit.*) a department of the government which deals with public money. ¶*Chancellor of the Exchequer.*
—[名] **1.** 국고 **2.** 《口》 재정, 자력 **3.** 《英》 재무성 ¶[영국의] 재무상

ex·cise[1] [iksáiz, ék-] *n.* [U][C] tax on certain articles made, sold, or consumed within a country. ¶*the ~ on tobacco.*
—[名] [국내] 물품세

ex·cise[2] [iksáiz, ek-] *vt.* cut out; remove.
—[他] …을 베어내다; 삭제하다

ex·ci·sion [iksíʒ(ə)n / eks-] *n.* [U] the act of excising; removal; [C] something excised.
—[名] 절제(切除), 절단; 삭제; 베어낸 것, 절제(삭제)된 것

ex·cit·a·ble [iksáitəbl] *adj.* can be excited; easily excited.
—[形] 격하기 쉬운, 흥분하기 잘 하는

‡ex·cite [iksáit] *vt.* **1.** stir up the feelings of (someone); stimulate. ¶*~ the audience* / *~ oneself*① / *become* (or *get*) *excited at* (or *by, about, over*) *his words.*② **2.** cause (something) to awake; make (something) active. ¶*The news excited envy in her.* ▷**ex·cit·er** [-ər] *n.*
—[他] **1.** …을 흥분시키다, 자극하다 ¶①흥분하다/②그의 언사에 격분하다 **2.** …을 분기시키다, 환기시키다; …을 선동하다

ex·cit·ed·ly [iksáitidli] *adv.* in an excited manner.
—[副] 흥분하여

‡ex·cite·ment [iksáitmənt] *n.* **1.** [U] the act of exciting;
—[名] **1.** 자극, 격려; 흥분 ¶①흥분하여

the state of being excited. ¶*in* ~[1] / *throw someone into* ~.[2] **2.** [C] a thing that excites.
/②…을 흥분시키다 2. 자극물

***ex·cit·ing** [iksáitiŋ] *adj.* stirring; stimulating; thrilling.
—[形] 자극적인, 흥분시키는

‡**ex·claim** [ikskléim] *vi., vt.* cry out suddenly in surprise, fear, etc.; shout.
—[自][他] 외치다, 부르짖다, 절규하다

exclaim against, criticize (something) loudly.
[熟] 큰 소리로 …을 비난하다

ex·cla·ma·tion [èkskləméiʃ(ə)n] *n.* **1.** [U][C] the act of exclaiming. **2.** [C] a thing exclaimed.
—[名] 1. 절규 2. [감탄의] 외침

***exclamation mark** [--ˊ-ˋ] *n.* a mark (!) in writing or printing to show surprise, sorrow or other strong feeling. ⇒[N.B.]
—[名] 감탄부호 [N.B.] exclamation point 라고도 함

ex·clam·a·to·ry [iksklǽmətɔ̀:ri / -t(ə)ri] *adj.* of, expressing, using, or containing exclamation.
—[形] 감탄의, 절규적인

***ex·clude** [iksklú:d] *vt.* **1.** shut out; keep out. 《~ someone *from*》 ¶*a nation excluded from the United Nations.* **2.** force out; expel; reject. ¶~ *the possibility of going back.*[1]
—[他] 1. …을 제외하다, 내쫓다; 배제하다 2. …을 몰아내다; 각하(거절)하다 ¶①돌아갈 가능성을 허용하지 않다

ex·clu·sion [iksklú:ʒ(ə)n] *n.* [U] the act of excluding; the state of being excluded.
—[名] 제외; 배제, 추방; 배척, 거절

to the exclusion of (=*so as to shut out*) ***something.***
[熟] …을 제외하고

***ex·clu·sive** [iksklú:siv] *adj.* **1.** shutting out others; trying to shut out others. **2.** not shared or divided with others; single; sole. ¶~ *rights*[1] / ~ *use.*[2]
—[形] 1. 제외적인, 서로 용납하지 않는; 배타적인 2. 독점적인, 점유적인 ¶①점유권/②전용(專用)

exclusive of, excluding; excepting.
[熟] …을 제외하여

ex·clu·sive·ly [iksklú:sivli] *adv.* in an exclusive manner; solely.
—[副] 배타적으로; 독점적으로

E

ex·com·mu·ni·cate [èkskəmjú:nikèit] *vt.* shut out(someone) from membership in a church.
—[他] …을 파문(破門)하다

ex·com·mu·ni·ca·tion [èkskəmjù:nikéiʃ(ə)n] *n.* **1.** [U] the act of excommunicating; the state of being excommunicated. **2.** [C] a formal statement announcing this.
—[名] 1. 파문(破門) 2. 파문 선언

ex-con·vict [ékskánvikt / -kɔ́n-] *n.* [C] a person with a criminal record; an old offender.
—[名] 전과자

ex·cre·ment [ékskrimənt] *n.* [U] waste matter that is sent out from the body.
—[名] 배설물, 대변

ex·crete [ekskrí:t, iks-] *vt.* **1.** send out (waste matter) from the body. **2.** take away (waste matter) from the blood or tissues.
—[他] 1. …을 배설하다 2. …을 분비하다

ex·cre·tion [ekskrí:ʃ(ə)n, iks-] *n.* **1.** [U] the act of excreting. **2.** [C][U] that which is excreted.
—[名] 1. 배설, 분비 2. 배설물, 분비물

ex·cre·to·ry [ékskritɔ̀:ri / ekskrí:təri] *adj.* of excretion.
—[形] 배설의, 분비의

ex·cru·ci·at·ing [ikskrú:ʃièitiŋ] *adj.* very painful; agonizing; torturing.
—[形] 괴롭히는, 고통을 주는, 고문당하는 듯한

***ex·cur·sion** [ikskə́:rʒ(ə)n, -ʃ(ə)n] *n.* [C] a short journey or trip, esp. for pleasure. ¶*go on* (or *for*) *an* ~[1] / *make* (or *take*) *an* ~ *to the lake.*[2]
—[名] 소풍, 짧은 여행, 유람 여행 ¶①소풍가다/②호수로 소풍가다

ex·cur·sive [ikskə́:rsiv] *adj.* **1.** of excursions. ¶~ *trips.*[1] **2.** off the subject; wandering. ¶~ *reading.*[2] ▷**ex·cur·sive·ly** [-li] *adv.*
—[形] 1. 유람의 ¶①유람 여행 2. 주제(主題)를 벗어난; 산만한, 종작없는 ¶②난독(亂讀)

ex·cus·a·ble [ikskjú:zəbl] *adj.* pardonable; permissible.
—[形] 용서할 수 있는; 변명이 서는

‡**ex·cuse** *vt.* [ikskjú:z →*n.*] **1.** pardon; forgive. ¶*She excused his mistake.* **2.** make (someone) free from duty, etc. ¶*I was excused from the examination.*[1] **3.** give reasons to (one's conduct); explain. ¶*I do not mean to* ~ *my fault.* / *Ignorance does not* ~ *his mistake.*[2] **4.** 《*reflexively*》 ask to be forgiven; apologize. ¶*I excused myself for my rudeness.*
—[他] 1. …을 용서하다; [관대히] 보아주다 2. …을 면제하다 ¶①나는 시험을 면제받았다 3. …의 핑계를 대다, 변명하다; [행동]의 설명을 하다 ¶②몰랐다는 것은 그의 잘못에 대한 변명이 되지 않는다 4. …의 용서를 빌다, …을 사죄하다

—*n.* [ikskjú:s] [C] **1.** an explanation of one's conduct; an apology. **2.** a pardon. **3.** release from duty, etc.
—[名] 1. 변명, 해명; 사죄, 사과 2. 용서 3. 면제

***ex·e·cute** [éksikjù:t] *vt.* **1.** carry out (a job, etc.); do. **2.** put (a law, etc.) into effect; enforce. **3.** put (someone) to death according to law. ¶*The criminal was executed.* **4.** make (fine arts, etc.) according to a plan; play or perform (a piece of music, etc.)
—[他] 1. …을 집행하다, 수행하다 2. …을 실행(실시)하다 3. …을 사형에 처하다 4. [미술품 따위]를 제작하다; [악곡 따위]를 연주하다

***ex·e·cu·tion** [èksikjú:ʃ(ə)n] *n.* Ⓤ **1.** the act of executing; the state of being executed; performance. **2.** the way of executing; skill. **3.** Ⓒ a written order issued by a court to put a judgment into effect.
—[名] 1. 집행, 수행; 사형 집행; 실시, 실행 2. 실행 방법, 수법; 솜씨, 기술 3. 집행 영장(令狀)

do execution, have an effective action; take effect.
[熟] 위력을 발휘하다; 효과를 나타내다

ex·e·cu·tion·er [èksikjú:ʃ(ə)nər] *n.* Ⓒ a person whose job is to put criminals to death according to law.
—[名] 사형 집행인

‡ex·ec·u·tive [igzékjutiv] *adj.* of or carrying out management; having the power of putting the laws into effect. ¶*~ ability*① / *an ~ committee*② / *the Executive Mansion.*③ —*n.* Ⓒ a person who carries out or manages affairs; the branch of a government that carries out the laws. ¶*the* [*Chief*] *Executive.*④
—[形] 사무 집행의; 집행권(력)이 있는 ¶①실무의 재능, 실행 능력/②집행 위원회/③[미국의] 대통령 관저; 주(州) 지사 관사 —[名] 지배인; 중역; 행정관; 행정부 ¶④[미국의] 대통령; 주지사

ex·ec·u·tor *n.* Ⓒ **1.** [igzékjutər →2.] a person who is named to carry out the provisions of another's will. **2.** [éksikjù:tər] a person who performs things.
—[名] 1. [지정] 유언 집행자 2. 집행자

ex·em·plar [igzémplər] *n.* Ⓒ **1.** a person or thing worth imitating; a model. **2.** a sample; an example.
—[名] 1. 모범; 본보기, 귀감 2. 표본, 유례(類例)

ex·em·pla·ry [igzémpləri] *adj.* **1.** worth imitating; serving as a model or pattern. ¶*~ conduct.* **2.** serving as a warning to others. ¶*~ punishment.*①
—[形] 1. 모범으로 삼을 만한, 모범(전형)적인, 본보기의 2. 경고가 되는 ¶①[본보기로서의] 징계처벌

ex·em·pli·fi·ca·tion [igzèmplifikéiʃ(ə)n] *n.* **1.** Ⓤ the act of showing by example. **2.** Ⓒ an example; an illustration.
—[名] 1. 예증(例證), 예시(例示) 2. 좋은 예, 적례(適例)

ex·em·pli·fy [igzémplifài] *vt.* (**-fied**) show or illustrate (something) by example; be an example of (something).
—[他] …을 예증하다, 예시하다

ex·empt [igzém(p)t] *vt.* make (someone) free from a duty, rule, etc.; release. ⟪~ someone *from* an obligation, etc.⟫ ¶*~ foreign tourists from taxes.*① —*adj.* free from a duty, an obligation, a rule, etc.; released. —*n.* Ⓒ an exempt person.
—[他] …을 면제하다 ¶①외국 관광객의 세금을 면제하다 —[形] 면제된, 면제의 —[名] 면세자, 면제된 사람

ex·emp·tion [igzém(p)ʃ(ə)n] *n.* ⓊⒸ the act of exempting; the state of being exempted.
—[名] 면제, 해제

‡ex·er·cise [éksərsàiz] *n.* **1.** Ⓤ the use of body or mind in order to improve it. **2.** Ⓒ a lesson for practice; a drill. ¶*an ~ in English grammar.* **3.** ⟪*pl.*⟫ ceremonies. ¶*opening exercises.*
—[名] 1. [심신의] 연마 2. 연습 문제 3. 식, 의식(儀式)

—*vt.* **1.** use (one's body or mind) to improve it. **2.** give exercise to (one's body, a horse, etc.); drill. **3.** carry out (duty, etc.). **4.** ⟪usu. in *passive*⟫ perplex; worry. —*vi.* take exercise.
—[他] 1. [심신]을 연마하다 2. …을 훈련하다 3. …을 이행하다 4. …을 괴롭히다, 번민하게 하다 —[自] 연습하다; 운동(체조)하다

***ex·ert** [igzə́:rt] *vt.* use actively; put (something) into action; make (something) active; have (an influence) on someone. ⟪~ an influence *on*⟫ ¶*~ every effort*① / *~ oneself for an object.*②
—[他] [지력(知力)·따위]를 쓰다; [힘 따위]를 발휘하다; [영향]을 미치다 ¶①온갖 노력을 다하다/②목적을 위하여 노력하다

ex·er·tion [igzə́:rʃ(ə)n] *n.* ⓊⒸ **1.** the act of exerting; effort. **2.** exercise; active use; use.
—[名] 1. 노력, 진력 2. 연마; 행사(行使)

Ex·e·ter [éksitər] *n.* a city in Devonshire, England.
—[名] 잉글란드 Devonshire의 도시

ex·e·unt [éksiʌnt] *vi.* (in stage direction) they go out.
—[自] 퇴장하다

ex·ha·la·tion [èkʃ(h)əléiʃ(ə)n, ègzə-] *n.* ⓊⒸ **1.** the act of exhaling. **2.** something exhaled, as air, vapor, steam, etc.
—[名] 1. 숨을 내쉬기, 증발, 발산 2. 발산물; 증기(수증기·안개 따위)

ex·hale [ekshéil, egzéil] *vt., vi.* breathe out; give forth (air, vapor, sound, etc.). ↔inhale ¶*~ a sigh*① / *The engine exhaled steam.*
—[他][自] [숨을] 내쉬다; [증기 따위를] 발산시키다(하다) ¶①한숨을 내쉬다

‡ex·haust [igzɔ́:st] *vt.* **1.** make (something) completely empty; use up; expend completely. ¶*~ a well* / *~ a fortune.* **2.** tire out; make (someone) very tired. ¶*I am exhausted with toil.*① **3.** discuss or study thoroughly. —*vi.* pass out; escape. ¶*Steam exhausts.* —*n.* ⓊⒸ **1.** the act of sending out used steam, such gas, gasoline, etc., from a machine. **2.** a pipe for sending out steam, gas, gasoline, etc. **3.** the used steam, gas, gasoline, etc., that is sent out.
—[他] 1. …을 비우다; 다 써 버리다 2. [체력 따위]를 소모하다; [남]을 지치게 하다 ¶①힘든 일을 하였더니 지쳤다 3. [문제 따위]를 철저히 연구하다(토론하다) —[自] 빠져나가다, 새다, 유출(流出)하다 —[名] 1. 배출(排出) 2. 배기(排氣) 장치 3. 배출물

ex·haust·ing [igzɔ́:stiŋ] *adj.* producing much tiredness. —[形] [심신]을 피로하게(지치게) 하다

ex·haus·tion [igzɔ́:stʃ(ə)n] *n.* [U] **1.** the act of exhausting; the state of being exhausted. **2.** great tiredness. —[名] 1. 배출; 소모, 고갈(枯渴) 2. 극도의 피로

ex·haus·tive [igzɔ́:stiv] *adj.* leaving nothing out; thorough; complete. ¶*an ~ study.* —[形] 남김없는, 고갈시키는; 철저한

ex·haust·less [igzɔ́:stlis] *adj.* that can not be exhausted. —[形] 다함이 없는, 무진장의

‡**ex·hib·it** [igzíbit] *vt., vi.* **1.** show; display. **2.** show (pictures, etc.) publicly. **3.** (*Law*) show (an evidence, etc.) in court. —*n.* [C] **1.** a thing or things shown publicly. **2.** something shown in court as evidence. —[他][自] 1. …을 보이다, 나타내다 2. [전람회 따위에] …을 진열하다, 출품하다 3. 《法》…을 제출하다 —[名] 1. 출품물, 진열품 2. 증거 서류(물건)

***ex·hi·bi·tion** [èksibíʃ(ə)n] *n.* [C] **1.** the act or fact of showing publicly. **2.** a public show of pictures, goods, etc. **3.** pictures, goods, etc. shown publicly. —[名] 1. 공시(公示), 전시, 전람 2. 전람회, 박람회 3. 진열품, 전시품

make an (or *a regular*) *exhibition of oneself,* act so badly in public that one receives contempt. [熟] 웃음거리가 되다

ex·hil·a·rate [igzílərèit] *vt.* fill (someone) with high spirits; make (someone) cheerful or merry. —[他] …의 기분을 돋구다; …을 쾌활하게 하다

ex·hil·a·ra·tion [igzìləréiʃ(ə)n] *n.* [U] **1.** the act of exhilarating. **2.** the state of being exhilarated; high spirits; liveliness. —[名] 1. 기분을 돋구기 2. 유쾌, 흥겨움

ex·hort [igzɔ́:rt] *vt., vi.* urge strongly; advise or warn earnestly. ▷**ex·hort·er** [-ər] *n.* —[他][自] 권고하다; 충고하다, 훈계하다

ex·hor·ta·tion [ègzɔ:rtéiʃ(ə)n, èks-] *n.* [U][C] **1.** the act of exhorting. **2.** a speech, sermon, etc., that exhorts. —[名] 1. 권고, 장려 2. 훈계

ex·hume [igz(j)ú:m, +*U.S.* iks(j)ú:m, +*Brit.* ekshjú:m] *vt.* **1.** take out (a dead body) from a grave, etc.; dig up. **2.** reveal; disclose. —[他] 1. [묘 따위]를 파내다, 발굴하다 2. …을 폭로하다, 밝히다

ex·i·gence [éksidʒ(ə)ns] *n.* =exigency.

ex·i·gen·cy [éksidʒ(ə)nsi] *n.* [C] (pl. **-cies**) **1.** a situation demanding urgent action or attention; an urgent case. **2.** 《usu. *pl.*》 urgent needs or demands. —[名] 1. 긴급, 급박; 긴급(절박)한 사정 2. 급무(急務), 긴급 사태

ex·i·gent [éksidʒ(ə)nt] *adj.* demanding to act or pay attention at once; urgent; pressing. —[形] 긴급한, 절박한

***ex·ile** [éksail, égz-] *vt.* force (someone) to leave his country or home; banish. ¶*~ oneself*① / *They exiled him from his own country.* —*n.* **1.** [U] the state of being exiled; banishment. **2.** [C] an exiled person. —[他] …을 추방하다 ¶①유랑하다, 망명하다 —[名] 1. 추방 2. 추방인

‡**ex·ist** [igzíst] *vi.* **1.** have actual existence; be. ¶*Do you believe that God exists?* **2.** continue to be; live. ¶*~ on one's salary / No man can ~ without air.* —[自] 1. 존재하다, 있다 2. 생존하다, 살아 있다

‡**ex·ist·ence** [igzíst(ə)ns] *n.* [U] **1.** the state of being; existing; real or actual being; being. **2.** [U][C] living; life. ¶*a struggle for ~*① / *daily ~.*② **3.** [C] a thing that exists. —[名] 1. 존재 2. 생존; 생활 ¶①생존 경쟁/②일상 생활 3. 생존물

ex·it [éksit, égzit] *n.* [C] **1.** a way out; a doorway. ↔ entrance. **2.** the act of going out; departure. **3.** (of actors) the act of leaving the stage. —*vi.* (of actors) go out; depart. ¶*Exit Macbeth.* —[名] 1. 출구(出口) 2. 외출, 퇴거 3. 퇴장 —[自] [등장 인물이] 퇴장하다

ex·o·dus [éksədəs] *n.* **1.** [C] the act of going out; departure. ¶*the summer ~ to the country.*① **2.** 《*E-*》 (in the Bible) the departure of the Israelites from Egypt. **3.** 《*E-*》 the second book of the Old Testament, that tells of this departure. —[名] 1. [많은 사람이] 몰려 나가기, 출발; [이민 따위의] 출국 ¶①시골로 가는 여름철의 피서 2. 이스라엘 사람들의 이집트 출국 3. 《聖》 출애급기

ex·on·er·ate [igzánərèit] *vt.* **1.** make (someone) free from blame. **2.** make (someone) free from obligation, duty, etc. —[他] 1. [남을] 결백함을(죄가 없음을) 밝혀 주다 2. [의무·책임 따위]를 면제하다

ex·or·bi·tant [igzɔ́:rbit(ə)nt] *adj.* (of a price, charge, demand, etc.) unreasonable or extraordinary. ¶*an ~ price.* —[形] [요구가] 엄청난, [값 따위가] 터무니없는

ex·or·cise, -cize [éksɔ:rsàiz] *vt.* drive out (an evil spirit) by prayers, ceremonies, etc. ▷**ex·or·cis·er** [-ər] *n.* —[他] …으로 마귀를 쫓다, 액막이하다

ex·ot·ic [igzátik / igzɔ́t-, eks-] *adj.* **1.** introduced from a foreign country; not native. ¶*~ foods / ~ manners.* **2.** striking or unusual in effect or style; strange. ¶*the ~ dress of traditional Japan.* —*n.* [C] anything exotic. —[形] 1. 외래의; 외국산의 2. 이국풍(異國風)의, 이국 정조(情調)의 —[名] 외래의 것(식물·외래어 따위)

▷**ex·ot·i·cal·ly** [-kəli] *adv.*

• **ex·pand** [ikspǽnd] *vt., vi.* **1.** make or become larger or wider; spread out; unfold. ¶*Heat expanded the metal.* / *A bird expands its wings.* **2.** develop (something) by adding details. ¶*He expanded a short story into a novel.*
—[他][自] 1. …을 확대하다, 확장하다, 팽창시키다(하다); 펴다, 펼치다, 퍼지다 2. [토론 따위를] 발전시키다

ex·panse [ikspǽns] *n.* [C] a large, open space or surface. ¶*an ~ of water.*①
—[名] 넓게 퍼진 것, 넓이, 공간 ¶①넓고 넓은 수면

ex·pan·si·ble [ikspǽnsibl] *adj.* that can be expanded.
—[形] 넓게 펼 수 있는, 팽창시킬 수 있는

• **ex·pan·sion** [ikspǽnʃ(ə)n] *n.* [U][C] **1.** the act or process of expanding; the state of being expanded. **2.** development.
—[名] 1. 팽창, 확장, 확대 2. 발전

ex·pan·sive [ikspǽnsiv] *adj.* **1.** tending to expand. **2.** wide; vast; spacious. **3.** showing one's feelings freely and openly. ▷**ex·pan·sive·ly** [-li] *adv.* —**ex·pan·sive·ness** [-nis] *n.*
—[形] 1. 넓게 퍼지는 2. 넓디넓은, 란 3. 개방적인, 마음이 넓은, 대범한

ex·pa·ti·ate [ekspéiʃièit, iks-] *vi.* write or speak much. 《~ *on* or *upon* a story, etc.》 ▷**ex·pa·ti·a·tor** [-ər] *n.*
—[自] 상세히 말하다(쓰다), 상술(詳述)하다

ex·pa·tri·ate [ekspéitrièit / -pǽ-] *vt.* send (someone) out of his native country; give up (one's citizenship); banish; exile. ¶~ *oneself.*① —*n.* [C] an expatriated person.
—[他] …을 국외로 추방하다; 국적을 이탈하다 ¶①자기 나라를 떠나다, 국적을 버리다 —[名] 국외 추방자

ex·pa·tri·a·tion [ekspèitriéiʃ(ə)n / -pætri-] *n.* [U] the act of expatriating; the state of being expatriated.
—[名] 국외 추방; 국적 이탈

⁑ **ex·pect** [ikspékt] *vt.* **1.** think of (something) that it will probably happen; look forward to (something); hope. 《~ *to do*; ~ someone *to do*》 ¶*I ~ you to help me.* **2.** think of (someone) that it will probably come. ¶*I expected you yesterday.* **3.** (*colloq.*) think; suppose.
—[他] 1. …을 기대하다; 추구하다; 바라다 2. [오는 것]을 기다리다 3. 《口》 …을(이라고) 생각하다

ex·pect·an·cy [ikspékt(ə)nsi] *n.* (pl. **-cies**) =expectation.

ex·pect·ant [ikspékt(ə)nt] *adj.* looking forward to something. ¶*an ~ mother*① / *an ~ heir.*② —*n.* [C] a person who expects something. ▷**ex·pect·ant·ly** [-li] *adv.*
—[形] 예기하는, 기대하는, 기다리고 있는 ¶①임신부/②추정(推定) 재산 상속인 —[名] 예기자, 기대자

• **ex·pec·ta·tion** [èkspektéiʃ(ə)n] *n.* **1.** [U] the state of expecting or being expected; anticipation. **2.** [C] something expected. **3.** 《*pl.*》 a prospect of the future, esp. something to be inherited. ¶*She has expectations from a rich uncle.*
—[名] 1. 예기, 기대 2. 기대되는 것 3. [전도가] 유망한 가망; [재산 상속의] 가망

ex·pe·di·ence [ikspíːdiəns] *n.* =expediency.

ex·pe·di·en·cy [ikspíːdiənsi] *n.* [U][C] (pl. **-cies**) the state of being expedient; self-interest.
—[名] 편의, 방편, 편법; 사리(私利)

ex·pe·di·ent [ikspíːdiənt] *adj.* suitable for the purpose; convenient; advisable. ¶*It is ~ that you go.* —*n.* [C] a means to a purpose. ▷**ex·pe·di·ent·ly** [-li] *adv.*
—[形] 편의의, 편리한; 형편이 좋은; 유리한 —[名] 방책, 수단, 편법

ex·pe·dite [ékspidàit] *vt.* **1.** make (a business, etc.) easy and quick. **2.** issue or dispatch (an official document).
—[他] 1. …을 촉진하다, 진척시키다 2. [공문서]를 급송하다

⁑ **ex·pe·di·tion** [èkspidíʃ(ə)n] *n.* **1.** [C] a journey for some special purpose, as discovery or battle. **2.** [C] a group of people, ships, etc., that make such a journey or voyage. **3.** [U] efficient and prompt action or speed.
—[名] 1. 원정, 탐험 2. 탐험대; 원정대 3. 신속, 급속

ex·pe·di·tion·ar·y [èkspidíʃənèri / -ʃən(ə)ri] *adj.* of an expedition.
—[形] 원정의, 토벌의, 탐험의

ex·pe·di·tious [èkspidíʃəs] *adj.* quick; speedy; effective and prompt. ▷**ex·pe·di·tious·ly** [-li] *adv.*
—[形] 신속한, 급속한; 속효가 있는

ex·pel [ikspél] *vt.* (**-pelled, -pel·ling**) drive (someone) out by force; dismiss. ¶*be expelled from school.*①
—[他] …을 내쫓다, 축출하다, 제명하다 ¶①퇴학당하다

ex·pend [ikspénd] *vt.* **1.** spend (money, time, etc.). ⇒ [usage] **2.** use up (energy, etc.). 《~ something *on, in*》 ¶~ *enormous energy and time on work.*
—[他] 1. [돈·시간]을 쓰다, 소비하다 [usage] 이 뜻으로는 보통 spend를 씀 2. [노력 따위]를 들이다, 소비하다

• **ex·pend·i·ture** [ikspénditʃər, +*U.S.* -tʃuər] *n.* [U] **1.** the act of expending. **2.** [U][C] the amount of money expended. ↔income ¶*annual ~*① / *current ~.*②
—[名] 1. 지출 2. 지출액, 비용 ¶①세출/②경상비(經常費)

⁑ **ex·pense** [ikspéns] *n.* **1.** [U] 《sometimes *an* ~》 money paid or needed to do something; cost. ¶*household ~* / *at one's [own] ~*① / *at an ~ of 1,000 won.*② **2.** [C] 《usu. *pl.*》 a cause of expense. ¶*living expenses.*③ **3.**
—[名] 1. 지출, 비용 ¶①자비로/②천원의 비용을 들이고 2. 경비, …비 ¶③생활비 3. 손실; 희생 ¶④그는 건강을 희생시키고 재산을 벌었다

E

expensive

⒰ loss; sacrifice. ¶*He made a fortune at the ~ of his health.*①
1) **go to the expense of** (=*willingly spend money on*) something. ¶*go to the ~ of traveling abroad.*
2) **put someone to expense**, force someone to pay expenses.

: **ex·pen·sive** [ikspénsiv] *adj.* costly; causing expense.
  come expensive, prove to be expensive.
  ex·pen·sive·ly [ikspénsivli] *adv.* in an expensive manner.

: **ex·pe·ri·ence** [ikspíəriəns] *n.* **1.** ⒰ the act of gaining knowledge, skill, wisdom, etc. by one's own actions or by practice. ¶*a man of ~*① / *learn something by ~*② / *gain ~ in teaching.*③ **2.** ⓒ something experienced.
  —*vt.* have experience of (something). ¶*~ difficulties* / *be experienced in leading students.*④

• **ex·pe·ri·enced** [ikspíəriənst] *adj.* having much experience; skillful; expert. ¶*an ~ teacher* / *have an ~ eye.*①

: **ex·per·i·ment** *n.* [ikspérimənt → *v.*] ⓒ⒰ a trial or a test to find out something. ¶*an ~ in physics*① / *make* (or *try*) *an ~ in* (or *on*) *chemical action.*②
  —*vi.* [ikspérimènt] try tests to find out something. (*~ on* (or *in*) something)

ex·per·i·men·tal [ikspèriméntl, eks-] *adj.* of or based on experiments. ¶*in the ~ stage.*①

ex·per·i·men·tal·ly [ikspèrimén təli, eks-] *adv.* in an experimental manner.

ex·per·i·men·ta·tion [ikspèrimentéiʃ(ə)n, eks-] *n.* ⒰ the act of experimenting; the practice of experiments.

ex·per·i·ment·er, -ment·or [ikspérimèntər] *n.* ⓒ a person who carries out experiments.

: **ex·pert** *n.* [ékspərt → *adj.*] ⓒ a person who has special knowledge or skill; a specialist. ¶*a technical ~*① / *an ~ at one's work.*② —*adj.* [+ ⌐] very skillful; having special skill. ¶*an ~ swimmer* / *be ~ in* (or *at*) *skiing.*③

ex·pi·ate [ékspièit] *vt.* pay for (one's wrong act) by receiving punishment.

ex·pi·a·tion [èkspiéiʃ(ə)n] *n.* ⒰ the act of expiating. ¶*in ~ of one's sin* (or *crime*).

ex·pi·ra·tion [èkspiréiʃ(ə)n] *n.* ⒰ **1.** the act of breathing out. **2.** end; close. ¶*at the ~ of one's term of office.*①

ex·pire [ikspáiər] *vi.* **1.** breathe out. **2.** die; (of fire, etc.) go out. **3.** (of a license, etc.) come to an end.
  —*vt.* breathe out (air) from the lungs.

: **ex·plain** [ikspléin] *vt.* **1.** tell the meaning of (something); make (something) clear. (*~ that, why, how, etc. ...*) ¶*She explained why she was late in getting home.*① **2.** give reasons for or causes of (something); account for; excuse. ¶*How do you ~ your behavior?*

ex·plain·a·ble [ikspléinəbl] *adj.* that can be explained.

: **ex·pla·na·tion** [èksplənéiʃ(ə)n] *n.* ⓒ⒰ **1.** the act of explaining. ¶*by way of ~*① / *Can you say anything in ~ of your conduct?*② **2.** a statement.
  come to an explanation (=*come to a mutual understanding*) **with someone.**

ex·plan·a·to·ry [ikspl金nətɔ:ri | -t(ə)ri] *adj.* serving to make something clear; explaining.

ex·pli·ca·ble [éksplikəbl] *adj.* that can be explained.

ex·plic·it [iksplísit] *adj.* **1.** clearly expressed. **2.** frank. ¶*Be ~.* ▷**ex·plic·it·ly** [-li] *adv.* —**ex·plic·it·ness** [-nis] *n.*

• **ex·plode** [iksplóud] *vt.* **1.** cause (something) to burst suddenly. **2.** destroy (a theory, etc.) —*vi.* burst suddenly and noisily; burst forth. ¶*He exploded with anger.*①

explode

🅶 1) …에 비용을 들이다 2) …에게 비용을 분담시키다

—⒜ 값비싼; 비용이 드는
🅶 비싸게 치이다
—⒜ 비용을 들여서; 사치스럽게

—⒜ 1.경험,체험 ¶①경험이 풍부한 사람/②경험에 의하여 …을 배우다/③교편의 경험을 쌓다 2.경험한 것

—⒜ …을 경험(체험)하다 ¶④학생을 지도하는 데 익숙하다

—⒜ 경험이 있는, 노련한 ¶①안식이 높다

—⒜ [과학상의] 실험,시험 ¶①물리의 실험/②화학작용의 실험을 하다

—⒜ 실험하다

—⒜ 실험의; 실험에 근거를 둔 ¶①실험중인

—⒜ 실험적으로, 실험상

—⒜ 실험, 실지 연습

—⒜ 실험자

—⒜ 숙련자; 전문가 ¶①공예의 전문가,기술자/②일에 숙달된 사람 —⒜ 숙련된,노련한; 전문적인 ¶③스키이에 능숙하다

—⒜ …의 죄를 갚다, …을 보상하다, 속죄하다

—⒜ 죄갚음,속죄,보상

—⒜ 1.숨을 내쉬기, 호기(呼氣) 2.종료, 만기 ¶①임기를 마치고

—⒜ 1.숨을 내쉬다 2.숨을 거두다, 죽다; [불 따위가] 꺼지다 3.만기가 되다,끝나다 —⒜ [숨]을 내쉬다

—⒜ 1.…을 설명하다; 명백히하다 ¶①그녀는 집에 늦게 돌아온 이유를 설명했다 2.…을 변명하다

—⒜ 설명할 수 있는
—⒜ 1.설명 ¶①설명으로서/②너의 행위에 대해 해명할 수 있는가? 2.변명
🅶 …와 화해가 되다, 양해가 이루어지다

—⒜ 설명의,변명의; 해명하는

—⒜ 설명할 수 있는,해명할 수 있는
—⒜ 1.명백한,명확한 2.숨김없는,솔직한

—⒜ 1.…을 폭발시키다 2.…을 타파하다,논파(論破)하다 —⒜ 폭발하다; [감정 따위가] 격발하다 ¶①그는 울화통을 터뜨렸다(발끈 성을 냈다)

*** ex·ploit** *n.* [éksplɔit, iksplɔ́it →*v.*] [C] a bold or heroic act. **—***vt.* [iksplɔ́it] **1.** develop. ¶ ~ *natural resources.*① **2.** use (something) for one's own purpose; use (something) selfishly. ¶ ~ *the working classes.*②
—[名] 1. 공훈, 공적 —[他] …을 개발하다 ¶①천연자원을 개발하다 2. …을 먹이로 삼다; 착취하다 ¶②노동자 계급을 착취하다

ex·ploi·ta·tion [èksplɔitéiʃ(ə)n] *n.* [U] **1.** the act of exploiting; the state of being exploited. **2.** selfish use.
—[名] 1. 개발, 개척 2. 이기적인 이용; 착취

*** ex·plo·ra·tion** [èksplɔ:réiʃ(ə)n] *n.* [U][C] the act of exploring.
—[名] 탐험, [실지]답사

*** ex·plore** [iksplɔ́:*r*] *vt.* **1.** travel through (a little-known land or sea) in order to study it. ¶ ~ *an uninhabited island.*① **2.** examine closely.
—[他] 1. …을 탐험하다 ¶①무인도를 탐험하다 2. …을 조사하다

*** ex·plor·er** [iksplɔ́:rə*r*] *n.* [C] a person who explores.
—[名] 탐험가

‡ ex·plo·sion [iksplóuʒ(ə)n] *n.* [C] the act of exploding; the state of being exploded. ¶*an* ~ *of laughter.*①
—[名] 폭발; 파열; [감정의] 격발 ¶①폭소

ex·plo·sive [iksplóusiv] *adj.* of explosion; tending to burst out with emotion. **—***n.* [C] an explosive substance.
—[形] 폭발의; [감정이] 격하기 쉬운 —[名] 폭발물

ex·po·nent [ekspóunənt] *n.* [C] **1.** a person or thing that explains. **2.** a symbol; an example. ¶*Lincoln is an* ~ *of self-education.*① **—***adj.* explaining.
—[名] 1. 설명자, 해명하는 것 2. 전형(典型); [본]보기 ¶①링컨은 독학의 전형(대표자)이다 —[形] 설명적인

*** ex·port** *vt.* [ekspɔ́:rt →*n.*] send (goods) to another country for sale. ↔import **—***n.* [ˊ–] **1.** [U] the act of exporting goods. **2.** [C] something exported.
—[他] [물품]을 수출하다 —[名] 1. 수출 2. 수출품

ex·por·ta·tion [èkspɔ:*r*téiʃ(ə)n] *n.* [U] the act of exporting. ↔importation
—[名] 수출

ex·port·er [ikspɔ́:*r*tə*r*, ˊ––] *n.* [C] a person or company that exports.
—[名] 수출업자; 수출 회사

‡ ex·pose [ikspóuz] *vt.* **1.** leave (someone or something) unprotected. ¶ ~ *someone to danger*① / ~ *one's skin to the sunlight.*② **2.** make (something) known; disclose. ¶ ~ *a secret.* **3.** show openly; display. ¶ ~ *new books in a shop-window.* **4.** leave (something) open to view; uncover; bare. **5.** (*Photography*) cause light to act on (a film). **6.** abandon.
—[他] 1. …을 쐬다, 드러내다 ¶①남을 위험에 드러내다/②햇볕에 피부를 쬐다 2. …을 알리다; 들추어내다, 폭로하다 3. …을 진열하다 4. …을 노출하다 5. 《寫》 …을 감광(感光)시키다 6. …을 버리다

ex·po·si·tion [èkspəzíʃ(ə)n] *n.* **1.** [U][C] the act of exposing; explanation. **2.** [C] (*U.S.*) an exhibition of art, industrial products, etc.
—[名] 1. 설명, 해설 2. 《美》 박람회

ex·pos·i·tive [ikspázitiv / ekspɔ́z-] *adj.* descriptive; explanatory.
—[形] 설명적인; 해설적인

ex·pos·i·tor [ikspázitə*r* / ekspɔ́zitə] *n.* [C] a person who explains; an interpreter.
—[名] 설명자; 해설자

ex·pos·i·to·ry [ikspázitɔ̀:ri / ekspɔ́zit(ə)ri] *adj.* explanatory; expositive.
—[形] 설명적인; 해설적인

ex·pos·tu·late [ikspástʃulèit / -pɔ́stju-] *vi.* advise earnestly not to do; protest against someone's act.
—[自] 간(諫)하다, 충고하다

ex·pos·tu·la·tion [ikspàstʃuléiʃ(ə)n / -pɔ̀stju-] *n.* [U] the act of expostulating; [C] words used in expostulating.
—[名] 충고, 타이름; 충고의 말, 간언(諫言)

‡ ex·po·sure [ikspóuʒə*r*] *n.* **1.** [U][C] the act of exposing; the state of being exposed; disclosure of something secret or private, etc. ¶ ~ *to the rain.*① **2.** [C] (of a house, etc.) direction or location. ¶*a house with a southern* ~.② **3.** [C] (*Photography*) the length of time during which film is exposed. ¶*an* ~ *meter.*③ **4.** [U][C] the act of abandoning a baby, etc.
—[名] 1. [햇볕·비바람 따위에] 쐬기, 쬐기, 맞히기; [비밀 따위의] 폭로 ¶①비를 맞히기 2. [집 따위의] 방위, …향(向) ¶②남향집 3. 《寫》 노출 ¶③노출계 4. [어린애 따위의] 유기

die of exposure, die outdoors because of having no protection from the weather.
[熟] [집 없이] 길바닥에서 죽다

ex·pound [ikspáund] *vt.* explain (something) in detail.
—[他] …을 자세히 설명하다

ex·pres·i·dent [ékspréziḍ(ə)nt] *n.* [C] a former president.
—[名] 전(前)대통령

‡ ex·press [iksprés] *vt.* **1.** say or show (a meaning, thought, etc.); make (something) known. ¶ ~ *oneself*① / *Words cannot* ~ *it.* / *Her smile expressed joy.* **2.** get (juice, etc.) by pressing; squeeze out. **3.** send (letters, etc.) by express mail.
—[他] 1. …을 나타내다, 표현하다; 발표하다 ¶①의견을 말하다 2. [과즙 따위]를 짜다 3. 속달편으로 부치다

—*adj.* **1.** clearly stated; definite. ¶*an* ~ *command (wish).* **2.** speedy; with few stops. ¶*an* ~ *train.*
—[形] 1. 명확한; 명시된, 표명된 2. 지급[편]의; 급행의

—*n.* [C] **1.** an express train, bus, etc. **2.** a special messenger. **3.** a means of carrying mails, etc. speedily.
—[名] 1. 급행 2. 급사(急使); 특사 3. 속달편

‡ ex·pres·sion [ikspréʃ(ə)n] *n.* **1.** [U] the act of expressing;
—[名] 1. 표현; 말투; 언사; 어구 ¶①교

E

[C] a particular word or phrase; a saying. ¶*a happy ~.*① **2.** [C] a look that expresses the feelings; the tone in which a person speaks, reads, or sings. ¶*a sad ~.*
묘한 표현(말솜씨) **2.** 표정; 음조(音調)

1) ***beyond*** (or ***past***) ***expression,*** beyond description; cannot be said in words.
2) ***find expession*** (=*be expressed*) ***in*** *something.*
3) ***give expression to*** (=*express; manifest*) *something.* ¶*He gave ~ to his thoughts.*②

[熟] 1)형언할 수 없는 2)…에 나타나다 3)…을 표현하다 ¶②그는 자기의 사상을 표현했다

ex·pres·sion·less [ikspréʃ(ə)nlis] *adj.* having no expression.
—[形] 표정이 없는; 무표정한

ex·pres·sive [iksprésiv] *adj.* **1.** (of the feelings, etc.) expressing. ¶*a look ~ of joy.* **2.** full of meaning; significant. ¶*an ~ face.* ▷**ex·pres·sive·ly** [-li] *adv.*
—[形] 1. [감정 따위]를 나타내는 2. 의미심장한

ex·press·ly [iksprésli] *adv.* **1.** clearly. **2.** particularly; on purpose. ¶*He came ~ to bring the book to me.*
—[副] 1. 명백히 2. 특별히; 일부러

ex·pro·pri·ate [ekspróuprièit] *vt.* deprive (someone) of property, etc; take land, etc. from (someone).
—[他] [재산 따위]를 징발하다; [토지 따위]를 몰수하다

ex·pul·sion [ikspʌ́lʃ(ə)n] *n.* [U][C] the act of expelling; the state of being expelled. ¶*~ from school.*①
—[名] 추방, 축출; 제명 ¶①퇴학, 방교(放校)

ex·punge [ekspʌ́ndʒ] *vt.* wipe or strike out (words, etc.).
—[名] …을 지우다; 삭제하다

ex·pur·gate [ékspə(:)rgèit, ekspə́:rgeit] *vt.* remove parts considered improper or objectionable from (a book, etc.). ▷**ex·pur·ga·tor** [-ər] *n.*
—[他] [서적의 부적당한 대목]을 삭제하다

* **ex·qui·site** [ékskwizit, ikskwízit] *adj.* **1.** delicately beautiful; excellent; carefully or elaborately made. ¶*~ beauty / ~ designs.* **2.** keenly or intensely felt. ¶*an ~ ear for music / ~ pain.* ▷**ex·qui·site·ness** [-nis] *n.*
—[形] 1. 절묘한; 더할나위 없는; 정교한, 공들인 2. 예민한, 격렬한

ex·qui·site·ly [ékskwizitli, ikskwízit-] *adv.* in an exquisite manner.
—[副] 더할나위 없이, 절묘하게; 날카롭게; 정교하게

ex·tant [ekstǽnt, ékstənt] *adj.* (esp. of old books, etc.) still in existence; existing. ↔extinct.
—[形] [오래된 서적 따위가] 현존하는, 남아 있는

ex·tem·po·ra·ne·ous [ekstèmpəréiniəs] *adj.* spoken or made without any preparation. ▷**ex·tem·po·ra·ne·ous·ly** [-li] *adv.* —**ex·tem·po·ra·ne·ous·ness** [-nis] *n.*
—[形] 즉석의, 임시변통의

ex·tem·po·re [ekstémpəri] *adj., adv.* without any preparation; offhand. ¶*speak ~.*
—[形][副] 즉석의(에서), 즉흥적인(으로)

ex·tem·po·rize [ekstémpəràiz] *vt., vi.* speak, sing, etc. extempore. ▷**ex·tem·po·ri·za·tion** [-rizéiʃ(ə)n / -raizéi-] *n.*
—[他][自] 즉석에서 연설 따위를 하다

: **ex·tend** [iksténd] *vt.* **1.** make (something) longer; stretch or spread out. ¶*~ one's hand to one's neighbors / ~ a wire between two posts*① */ ~ the road to the next village.* **2.** make (something) wider; enlarge; increase (power, influence, etc.). ¶*~ the park / ~ the power of the country.*② **3.** give; offer. ¶*~ help to the poor.* **—*vi.*** **1.** stretch; reach. **2.** continue. ¶*My garden extends as far as the woods.*
—[他] 1. …을 늘이다, 연장하다; 뻗다, 펴다 ¶①두 기둥에 철사를 치다 2. …을 확대하다; [세력 따위]를 뻗치다 3. [은혜·친절 따위]를 베풀다 —[自] 1. 퍼지다; 이르다, 달하다 2. …에 걸치다, 계속되다

ex·tend·ed [iksténdid] *adj.* stretched out; spread out; prolonged.
—[形] 넓은; 확장한; 연장한

* **ex·ten·sion** [iksténʃ(ə)n] *n.* **1.** [U] the act of extending; the state of being extended. ¶*the ~ of knowledge / the ~ of a railway line.* **2.** [C] an additional part (of a building, railway line, etc.); an inner telephone line. ¶*an ~ lecture*① */ an ~ ladder*② */ an ~ table.*③
—[名] 1. 연장, 신장(伸張); 펴기, 연기 2. 연장 부분, 연장선; [전화의] 내선(內線) ¶①대학 공개 강좌/②신축(伸縮) 사다리/③신축자재의 탁자

* **ex·ten·sive** [iksténsiv] *adj.* **1.** wide; large; on a large scale. ¶*~ knowledge / an ~ plan.* **2.** covering a wide space; coarse. ¶*~ reading / ~ agriculture.*① ▷**ex·ten·sive·ness** [-nis] *n.*
—[形] 1. 넓은, 광대한; 광범위한; 대규모의 2. 다방면에 걸친; [광대한 농토를 사용하는] 조방적(粗放的)인 ¶①조방농업

ex·ten·sive·ly [iksténsivli] *adv.* in an extensive manner; widely.
—[副] 넓게; 광범위하게

* **ex·tent** [ikstént] *n.* **1.** [U][C] size; length; space; amount. ¶*a vast ~ of land.* **2.** [C] the degree; limit. ¶*This is the ~ of my ability. / Who is not amazed at the ~ of his knowledge?*
—[名] 1. 크기; 길이; 넓이; 양(量) 2. 정도; 범위, 한계

1) ***to a great extent,*** for the most part; largely.
2) ***to some*** (or ***a certain***) ***extent,*** up to a certain degree.

[熟] 1)대부분은; 크게 2)어느 정도까지, 다소 3)…정도(범위)까지 ¶①힘자라는 데까지

extenuate [413] **extraction**

3) *to the extent of,* to a certain degree of. ¶*to the full ~ of one's power.*① / *to the utmost ~.*

ex·ten·u·ate [eksténjuèit, iks-] *vt.* make (a crime, etc.) seem less serious by making excuses. ¶*Nothing can ~ his wrong.*

— 働 [범죄 따위]를 가볍게 하다, [정상을] 참작하다

ex·ten·u·a·tion [ikstènjuéiʃ(ə)n] *n.* Ⓤ Ⓒ the act of extenuating; the state of being extenuated.

— 图 정상 참작, [죄의] 경감

ex·te·ri·or [ikstíəriə] *adj.* **1.** of an outer surface; external; outward. ↔interior. ¶*the ~ wall of the castle.* **2.** belonging to the outside. ¶*His recent behavior is ~ to his real character.*① **3.** foreign. ¶*an ~ policy.*② —*n.* Ⓒ the outside; an outer surface; a visible appearance. ⌈*completely*; *root out.*⌉

— 働 1. 외부(외면)의; 밖의 2. 상관이 없는 ¶①그의 최근의 행동은 그의 본래의 성격과는 무관하다 3. 대외적인, 외교상의 ¶②외교 정책 — 图 외부; 외면; 외관

ex·ter·mi·nate [ikstə́:rminèit] *vt.* destroy (something)
ex·ter·mi·na·tion [ikstə̀:rminéiʃ(ə)n] *n.* Ⓤ Ⓒ the act of exterminating; the state of being exterminated.

— 働 …을 전멸시키다; 근절하다
— 图 근절, 전멸, 멸종

* **ex·ter·nal** [ikstə́:rn(ə)l] *adj.* **1.** on, of, or for the outer part; outward. ↔internal. ¶*~ evidence* / *the ~ world.*① **2.** outwardly visible; superficial. ¶*~ religion.* **3.** foreign. ¶*an ~ policy.*② **4.** (*Medical*) used on the outside of the body. ¶*The lotion is for ~ application.*③ —*n.* Ⓒ **1.** an outer part. **2.** (*pl.*) the outward form or appearance. ¶*judge by externals.*④ ⌈*part.*⌉

— 働 1. 밖의, 외부의, 외적인 ¶①외계 (外界) 2. 표면의; 피상적인 3. 외래 (外來)의, 대외적인 ¶②대외 정책 4. (图) 외용(外用)의 ¶③그 세척제는 외용이다 — 图 1. 외부, 2. 외형, 외관 ¶④외관 (외모)으로 판단하다

ex·ter·nal·ly [ikstə́:rnəli] *adv.* from or on the outer

— 働 외부에서(로부터); 외관상

ex·tinct [ikstíŋ(k)t] *adj.* (of a light or fire) no longer burning; gone out; dead; no longer existing. ¶*an ~ volcano* / *an ~ animal.*

— 働 [불이] 꺼진; 끊어진; 사멸한, 멸종된; 없어진, 폐지된

ex·tinc·tion [ikstíŋ(k)ʃ(ə)n] *n.* Ⓤ Ⓒ the act of extinguishing; the state of being extinct.

— 图 소화(消火), 진화; 사멸, 멸종; 소멸

* **ex·tin·guish** [ikstíŋgwiʃ] *vt.* **1.** put out (a light, fire, etc.). **2.** destroy (hopes, love, life, passions, etc.). **3.** overcome; make (someone) silent. **4.** pay (one's debts).
ex·tin·guish·er [ikstíŋgwiʃər] *n.* Ⓒ an apparatus for putting out a light, fire, etc.

— 働 1. …을 끄다 2. …을 소멸시키다 3. …을 압도하다; 입을 다물게 하다 4. [부채]를 상각(償却)하다, 갚다
— 图 끄는 것; 소화기(消火器), 촛불 끄는 기구

ex·tir·pate [ékstə(:)rpèit, ikstə́:(r)-] *vt.* destroy completely; root out. ¶*~ weeds* / *~ a social evil.*
ex·tir·pa·tion [èkstə(:)rpéiʃ(ə)n] *n.* Ⓤ Ⓒ the act of extirpating; the state of being extirpated.

— 働 …을 박멸하다; 근절시키다
— 图 박멸; 근절, 절멸(絶滅)

ex·tol, ex·toll [ikstál, -tóul / -tóul] *vt.* praise (someone) highly. ⌈*someone.*⌉
extol someone to the skies, speak very highly of

— 働 …을 극구 칭찬하다, 격찬하다
圜 …을 극구 칭찬하다

ex·tort [ikstɔ́:rt] *vt.* **1.** obtain (money, etc.) from someone by threats, force, etc. **2.** compel (someone) to do something by force. ▷**ex·tort·er** [-ər] *n.*

— 働 1. …을 읊아내다, 강탈하다 2. …을 강요하다

ex·tor·tion [ikstɔ́:rʃ(ə)n] *n.* Ⓤ Ⓒ **1.** the act of extorting. **2.** money, etc. obtained in this way.

— 图 1. 착취, 강탈, 강요 2. 강탈물

ex·tor·tion·ate [ikstɔ́:rʃ(ə)nit] *adj.* demanding unreasonable payment; much too high. ¶*an ~ price.* ▷**ex·tor·tion·ate·ly** [-li] *adv.*

— 働 강탈적인; [값 따위가] 터무니없는, 엄청나게 비싼

ex·tor·tion·er [ikstɔ́:rʃ(ə)nər] *n.* Ⓒ a person who extorts.

— 图 강탈자, 강청자(强請者), 착취자

: **ex·tra** [ékstrə] *adj.* more than usual or expected; additional. ¶*an ~ edition*① / *an ~ inning* / *an ~ train.* —*adv.* more than usually; especially. —*n.* Ⓒ money, newspapers, persons, etc. that are added to the usual number or amount.

— 働 여분의, 임시의, 특별한 ¶①임시 증간(增刊) 2. 여분으로; 특별히 — 图 할증금(割增金), 호외(號外), 임시 고용 배우, 엑스트라

* **ex·tract** *vt.* [ikstrǽkt→*n.*] **1.** pull out or take out (something), usu. with effort. ¶*~ a tooth* / *~ a confession.*① **2.** obtain (juice, etc.) by boiling, pressing, etc. ¶*~ oil from olives.*② **3.** choose or copy out (a passage) from a book, etc; quote. ¶*~ examples from a story.* —*n.* [ékstrækt] **1.** Ⓤ Ⓒ something extracted. **2.** Ⓒ a passage taken or quoted from a book, etc. ▷**ex·trac·tor** [ikstrǽktər] *n.*

— 働 1. …을 빼다, 뽑다, 적출(摘出)하다, 끌어내다 ¶①자백시키다 2. …을 증류해서 뽑다, 추출(抽出)하다 3. …을 발췌하다, 초록(抄錄)하다

— 图 1. 추출물, 엑스 2. [서적 따위에서의] 발췌, 인용구

ex·trac·tion [ikstrǽkʃ(ə)n] *n.* Ⓤ Ⓒ **1.** the act of extract-

— 图 1. 뽑아내기, 빼내기 2. 추출물, 엑

ing; the state of being extracted. **2.** something extracted. **3.** origin; birth. ¶*people of humble ~.*
— 스; 발췌 **3.** 혈통, 계통, 태생

ex·tra·ne·ous [ikstréiniəs] *adj.* not related to the matter which is being considered; coming from foreign countries.
—[形] 무관계한; 외래의

ex·traor·di·nar·i·ly [ikstrɔ́:rdinèrili / -trɔ́:d(i)n(ə)ri-] *adv.* in an extraordinary manner.
—[副] 비상하게, 엄청나게

⁑ex·traor·di·nar·y [ikstrɔ́:rdinèri / -trɔ́:d(i)n(ə)ri] *adj.* **1.** beyond the usual order; unusual; eccentric; remarkable. ¶*an ~ genius / an ~ man / ~ weather.* **2.** additional to the regular staff; special; extra. ¶*an ~ general meeting*① */ an ambassador ~.*②
—[形] **1.** 비상한; 비범한; 보통이 아닌, 별난; 놀랄 만한 **2.** 임시의; 특명의 ¶①임시 총회/②특명 전권 대사

ex·tra·ter·ri·to·ri·al [ékstrətèritɔ́:riəl] *adj.* free from the laws of the country that one lives in.
—[形] 치외법권의

ex·trav·a·gance [ikstrǽvəgəns] *n.* **1.** [U] the act of being extravagant. **2.** [C] a careless or absurd action, idea, speech, etc.
—[名] **1.** 사치; 낭비 **2.** 엉뚱한 언행

ex·trav·a·gant [ikstrǽvəgənt] *adj.* **1.** spending money, things, etc. carelessly or unreasonably. ¶*an ~ person.* **2.** (of speech, action, etc.) beyond the limits of reason.
—[形] **1.** 사치한, 낭비하는 **2.** 엄청난, 터무니없는

load someone with extravagant praise, praise someone to an excessive degree.
[熟] …을 과찬(過讚)하다

▷**ex·trav·a·gant·ly** [-li] *adv.*

⁑ex·treme [ikstrí:m] *adj.* (sometimes **-trem·er, -trem·est**) **1.** of the highest degree; very great; excessive. ¶*~ old age / ~ poverty / the ~ penalty.*① **2.** (of ideas, etc.) radical; advanced. **3.** at the very end; farthest away. ¶*the ~ end of the ocean.* **4.** last.
—[形] **1.** 비상한; 극단적인; 과도한 ¶①극형 **2.** 과격한 **3.** 맨 끝의, 가장 먼 **4.** 최후(최종)의

in one's extreme moments; at the extreme hour of life, at the end of life.
[熟] 죽는 순간에, 임종 때에

—*n.* **1.** [C] an extreme degree, state or act. **2.** 《*pl.*》 things as different in qualities, etc. as possible. ¶*the extremes of heat and cold / (Proverb) Extremes meet.*②
—[名] **1.** 극도, 극단 **2.** 양(兩)극단 ¶②《俚》양극단은 일치한다

1) ***go to extremes; run to an extreme,*** take excessive measures; be excessive in speech, action, etc.
2) ***in [the] extreme,*** to the utmost degree; very.
[熟] 1)극단적인 수단을 쓰다, 극단으로 흐르다 2)극단으로; 몹시, 극히

▷**ex·treme·ness** [-nis] *n.*

⁑ex·treme·ly [ikstrí:mli] *adv.* to an extreme degree; very.
—[副] 극단으로, 극도로; 몹시, 극히

ex·trem·i·ty [ikstrémiti] *n.* [C] (pl. **-ties**) **1.** the point or end farthest away from the main part. ¶*at the ~ of the bridge.* **2.** the state of extreme pain or need; the last stage. ¶*the ~ of poverty / be in dire ~*① */ expect the ~*② */ to the last ~.*③ **3.** 《sometimes *pl.*》 an extreme measure. ¶*go to eytremities*④ **4.** 《usu. *pl.*》 the hands and feet.
—[名] **1.** 끝, 말단 **2.** 극도, 궁지 ¶①비참한 궁지에 처해 있다/②만일의 경우를 각오하다/③최후까지, 죽을 때까지 **3.** 비상 수단 ¶④최후 수단에 호소하다 **4.** 손발, 사지

ex·tri·cate [ékstrikèit] *vt.* set (someone) free from danger, difficulty, etc; release (an animal) from a trap, etc. ¶*He managed to ~ himself from the difficulties.*①
—[他] …을 구해내다, 구출하다, 탈출시키다 ¶①그는 용케 그 난국으로부터 탈출하였다

ex·tri·ca·tion [èkstrikéiʃ(ə)n] *n.* [U] [C] the act of extricating; the state of being extricated.
—[名] 구출, 탈출; 유리(遊離)

ex·trude [ekstrú:d, iks-] *vt.* push out; drive out.
—[他] …을 밀어내다; 쫓아내다

ex·u·ber·ance [igzú:bər(ə)ns / -z(j)ú:-], **-an·cy** [-ənsi] *n.* 《usu. *an ~*》 the state of being exuberant; abundance. ¶*an ~ of health.*①
—[名] 무성; 충만 ¶①넘쳐흐를 듯한 건강

ex·u·ber·ant [igzú:bər(ə)nt / -z(j)ú:-] *adj.* **1.** growing plentifully; abundant. ¶*The trees have ~ foliage.* **2.** filled with good health and spirits; full of vitality. ¶*The children are in ~ spirits.*①
—[形] **1.** 우거진, 무성한; 풍부한 **2.** 기운이 넘쳐흐르는, 기운찬 ¶①아이들은 활기에 차 있다

ex·ude [igz(j)ú:d, iks(j)ú:d] *vt., vi.* send out (something) in drops; (of sweat, etc.) flow out softly.
—[他][自] …을 스며(배어)나오게 하다; …에 스며(배어)나오다

ex·ult [igzʌ́lt] *vi.* be very glad. 《*~ at* (or *in, over*) something》 ¶*They exulted in the victory.*①
—[自] 기뻐 날뛰다, 환희하다 ¶①그들은 승리에 환희하였다

ex·ult·ant [igzʌ́lt(ə)nt] *adj.* feeling great joy; triumphant.
—[形] 기뻐 날뛰는, 환희하는; 의기양양한

ex·ul·ta·tion [ègzʌltéiʃ(ə)n] *n.* [U] the act of exulting; great joy.
—[名] 환희, 광희(狂喜)

‡ **eye** [ai] *n.* [C] **1.** an organ of the body with which things are seen. ¶*the naked* ~ / *compound eyes*① / *blue eyes.* **2.** a look; a gaze. ¶*cast* (or *fix*) *one's* ~ *on something*② / *keep an* ~ (or *one's eyes*) *on a baby.*③ **3.** the power or sense of seeing; eyesight. **4.** the power of judgng; judgement. ¶*He has a keen* ~ *for coloring.* **5.** ⦅usu. *pl.*⦆ opinion; point of view. ¶*in the eyes of the law*④ / *You are wrong in my eyes.*⑤ **6.** an eye-like thing. ¶*an* ~ *of a needle* / *an* ~ *of a potato.*⑥ **7.** something central. ¶*an* ~ *of a typhoon*⑦ / *bull's* ~.⑧

—[名] 1. 눈 ¶①복안(複眼) 2. 보기; 주시; 감시 ¶②흘끗 보다(주시하다)/③아기를 지켜보다 3. 시각 4. 판단력; 식별 능력 5. 의견; 견해 ¶④법률에 비추어보아/⑤내가 보기에는 네가 잘못이다 6. 눈 같은 것 ¶⑥감자의 눈(싹) 7. 중심 ¶⑦태풍의 눈/⑧과녁 복판의 흑점

1) ***the apple of one's eye,*** the dearest person or thing that one has.
2) ***clap eyes on*** (=*happen to see*) *something.*
3) ***close*** (or ***shut***) *one's* ***eyes to*** (=*refuse to see or think about*) *something.*
4) ***give an eye to*** (=*keep an occasional watch on*) *something.*
5) ***have an eye to,*** watch for (something) to get.
6) ***in the mind's eye,*** in imagination.
7) ***look someone straight in the eye,*** be quite frank with someone.
8) ***make eyes at,*** look at (someone) lovingly.
9) ***open someone's eyes to,*** make someone understand or realize the true state of (something).
10) ***see eye to eye,*** be in complete agreement.
11) ***set eyes on*** (=*look at*) *something.*
12) ***turn a blind eye to*** (=*pretend not to see*) *something.*

[熟] 1)가장 사랑하는(소중한) 것 2)…을 보다, 눈에 띄다 3)…에서 눈길을 돌리다, 보지 않다; 무시하다 4)…을 때때로 돌보아 주다, …에 주목하다 5)…에 눈독을 들이다 6)상상으로, 마음속으로 7)…와 흉금을 털어놓다 8)…에 추파를 던지다 9)…의 진상(사실)을 알게 하다 10)의견이 완전 일치하다 11)…을 보다 12)…을 보고도 못 본 체하다

—*vt.* (**eyed, ey·ing** or **eye·ing**) look at; watch. —[他] …을 보다; 주시하다

eye·ball [áibɔ̀:l] *n.* [C] the ball-shaped part of the eye. —[名] 눈알, 안구

• **eye·brow** [áibràu] *n.* [C] the hair above the eye. —[名] 눈썹
knit the eyebrows, bend one's brows. [熟] 눈살을 찌푸리다

eye·glass [áiglæ̀s / -glɑ̀:s] *n.* [C] **1.** a lens used to help eyesight. **2.** a cup used for washing eyes. **3.** an eyepiece. **4.** ⦅*pl.*⦆ a pair of glass lenses used to improve eyesight. —[名] 1. 안경 알 2. 눈 씻는 컵, 세안용 컵 3. 대안(對眼)렌즈, 접안(接眼)렌즈 4. 안경

eye·lash [áilæʃ] *n.* [C] a hair or hairs growing on the edge of the eyelid. —[名] 속눈썹

eye·less [áilis] *adj.* blind; without eyes. —[形] 소경의, 장님의; 눈이 없는

eye·let [áilit] *n.* [C] **1.** a small hole to receive a cord, lace, rope, etc. **2.** a metal ring set in a hole. **3.** a hole to peep through; a loophole. —[名] 1. 작은 구멍 2. 구멍 가장자리에 해 박은 쇠고리 3. 들여다보는 구멍

eye·lid [áilìd] *n.* [C] the upper or lower cover of the skin over the eye. ¶*the upper* (*the lower*) ~.① —[名] 눈까풀 ¶①윗(아랫)눈까풀
hang [***on***] ***by the eyelids,*** just cling to (something). [熟] 간신히 매달려 있다

eye opener [∠ ∸–] *n.* [C] (*colloq.*) **1.** something that makes the eyes open in surprise, wonder, etc., such as a piece of news, or a discovery. **2.** a drink of alcohol for waking a person up. —[名] 1. 괄목할 만한 일, 놀랄 만한 사건 2. [아침의] 해장술

eye·piece [áipì:s] *n.* [C] the lens nearest to the eye in a microscope, telescope, etc. —[名] 대안(對眼)렌즈, 접안경(接眼鏡)

eye·shot [áiʃɑ̀t / -ʃɔ̀t] *n.* [U] the distance at which one can see; the field of vision. ¶*beyond* (or *out of*) ~① / *within* (or *in*) ~.② —[名] 눈길이 미치는(눈에 보이는) 곳, 시계(視界) ¶①보이지 않는 곳에/②보이는 곳에

eye·sight [áisàit] *n.* [U] **1.** the power of seeing. ¶*lose one's* ~. **2.** the range of sight. ¶*in one's* ~.① —[名] 1. 시각, 시력 2. 시계, 시야 ¶①눈앞에서

eye·sore [áisɔ̀:*r*] *n.* [C] a thing unpleasant to look at. —[名] 눈에 거슬리는 것

eye·teeth [áiti:θ] *n.* pl. of **eyetooth.**

eye·tooth [áitù:θ] *n.* [C] (pl. **-teeth**) either of the two pointed teeth in the upper jaw; the canine tooth. —[名] [특히 위턱의] 송곳니, 견치(犬齒)
cut one's eyeteeth, grow up; become experienced. [熟] 어른이 되다; 세상 물정을 알게 되다

eye·wash [áiwɑ̀ʃ / -wɔ̀ʃ] *n.* [U] **1.** a lotion for washing the eyes. **2.** (*colloq.*) a dishonest statement; flattery. —[名] 1. 안약, 세안수 2. ⦅口⦆ 엉터리 수작; 아첨

eye·wit·ness [áiwítnis, ∠∸–] *n.* [C] a person who has actually seen an event and can testify to it. —[名] 목격자; 실지 증인

ey·rie, ey·ry [ɛ́əri, íəri / áiəri, ɛ́əri] *n.* (pl. **-ries**) =aerie.

F

F, f [ef] *n.* [C] (pl. **F's, Fs, f's, fs** [efs]) **1.** the sixth letter of the English alphabet. **2.** (*Music*) the fourth note of the musical scale of C major.
—[名] 1. 영어 자모의 여섯째 글자 2. 《樂》「바」음

F. 1. Fahrenheit. **2.** February. **3.** French. **4.** Friday.

Fa·bi·an [féibiən] *adj.* cleverly firing out an enemy by slowness and caution. ¶~ *tactics.*
—[形] [로마의 장군 Fabius가 취한 것과 같은] 지구전법(持久戰法)의

• fa·ble [féibl] *n.* **1.** [C] a story made up in order to teach a moral. ¶*Aesop's Fables.* **2.** [U] 《*collectively*》 legends; myths. **3.** [C] an untrue story; a lie.
—[名] 1. 우화 2. 전설, 신화 3. 지어낸(꾸며낸) 이야기, 거짓말

fa·bled [féibld] *adj.* told about in fables, legends or myths; having no real existence; fictitious.
—[形] 우화(전설·신화)로 전해지는; 지어낸(꾸며낸) 이야기의

• fab·ric [fǽbrik] *n.* **1.** [C] a cloth made by weaving. ¶*cotton (silk, woolen) fabrics.*① **2.** [U] the style or pattern of weaving; texture. ¶*cloths of different ~.* **3.** [U] [C] a framework; a structure; [C] a building. ¶*the social ~*② / *the ~ of an argument.*③
—[名] 1. 직물 ¶①면(견·모)직물 2. [직물의] 짜임새, 바탕 3. 골조(骨組), 구조; 구조물, 건물 ¶②사회 조직/③토론의 구성법

fab·ri·cate [fǽbrikèit] *vt.* **1.** make; build; construct. ¶~ *automobiles* / ~ *a bridge.* **2.** make up (stories, lies, etc.); make (a false document)
—[他] 1. …을 만들다, 건조(建造)하다, 조립하다 2. …을 날조하다; 위조하다

fab·ri·ca·tion [fæ̀brikéiʃ(ə)n] *n.* **1.** [U] the act of fabricating. **2.** [C] something fabricated.
—[名] 1. 제조, 날조 2. 지어낸 일

fab·u·list [fǽbjulist] *n.* [C] a person who writes or tells fables.
—[名] 우화 작가; 거짓말장이

fab·u·lous [fǽbjuləs] *adj.* **1.** of or belonging to legends or myths. ¶*a ~ hero.* **2.** hard to believe; enormous.
—[形] 1. 전설(신화)상의, 전설적인 2. 믿어지지 않는, 터무니없는

fab·u·lous·ly [fǽbjuləsli] *adv.* extremely; incredibly.
—[副] 어마어마하게; 믿어지지 않을 만큼

fa·cade [fəsɑ́:d] *n.* [C] the front part of a building. ⇒fig.
—[名] 건물의 정면

[facade]

⁝ face [feis] *n.* [C] **1.** the front part of the head. **2.** a look or expression. ¶*wear a sad ~.* **3.** 《*often pl.*》 (*colloq.*) an ugly or peculiar look made by moving the mouth, eyes, etc. ¶*make a ~ at someone.*① **4.** the outward appearance or aspect. **5.** the surface of something, esp. the front, upper, or outer part. ¶*the ~ of a card.*② **6.** 《*the ~*》 (*colloq.*) boldness; impudence. **7.** [U] dignity. ¶*lose [one's] ~*③ / *save [one's] ~.*④
—[名] 1. 얼굴 2. 안색, 표정 3. 《口》 찌푸린 얼굴 ¶①남에게 상을 찌푸리다 4. 외견, 외관, 겉보기 5. 정면, 표면, 거죽, 앞면 ¶②카아드의 겉면 6. 《口》 뻔뻔스러움, 염치없음 7. 체면, 면목 ¶③면목을 잃다/④체면을 세우다

1) ***face down (up),*** with the head or face turned downwards (upwards).
2) ***face to face,*** ⓐ with faces turned toward each other. ⓑ in the presence of. 《~ *with*》
3) ***have the face,*** be shameless or bold enough. 《~ *to do* something》
4) ***in someone's face,*** ⓐ in the presence of. ⓑ openly.
5) ***in [the] face of,*** ⓐ in the presence of. ⓑ in spite of.
6) ***make*** (or ***pull***) ***a face*** (or ***faces***), show an expression of disgust, pain, etc. 《~ *at* or *in* something》
7) ***make*** (or ***pull***) ***a long face,*** look sad or unhappy.
8) ***put a new face on*** (=*change the aspect of*) something.
9) ***set*** (or ***put***) ***one's face against*** (=*oppose, resist*) someone or something.
10) ***show one's face,*** appear.
11) ***to someone's face,*** ⓐ openly; boldly. ⓑ in someone's presence.

[熟] 1)얼굴을 숙이고(쳐들고); 겉을 아래로(위로) 하고 2)ⓐ[…와] 마주 보고 ⓑ[…의] 면전에서 3)뻔뻔스럽게도 […하다] 4)ⓐ…의 면전에서 ⓑ공공연하게 5)ⓐ…의 면전에서 ⓑ…에도 불구하고 6)얼굴을 찡그리다 7)침울한(실망한) 얼굴을 하다 8)…의 국면(면목)을 일신하다 9)…에 단호히 반대하다, 반항하다 10)얼굴을 내밀다, 모습을 나타내다 11)ⓐ공공연히 맞대놓고 ⓑ…의 면전에서

—*vt.* **1.** look or be turned toward or be opposite to (someone or something). ¶*My house faces a main*
—[他] 1. …쪽을 향하다, …에 면하다 ¶⑤나의 집은 번화가에 면해 있다 2.

facet [417] **factory**

*street.*⑤ **2.** meet bravely or boldly; confront. ¶ *~ danger / I cannot ~ him.*⑥ **3.** cover or line (something) with a different material. 《~ something *with*》 ¶*They faced the wooden house with brick.* —*vi.* be turned; look. ¶*~* [*to the*] *north / Right ~!*⑦
 face up to, face (something) with courage; admit (something).

fac·et [fǽsit] *n.* ⓒ **1.** one of the small, flat, polished surfaces of a cut gem or stone. ⇒fig. **2.** an aspect.

fa·ce·tious [fəsíːʃəs] *adj.* fond of joking; humorous. ¶ *a ~ remark.*① ▷**fa·ce·tious·ness** [-nis] *n.*

fa·ce·tious·ly [fəsíːʃəsli] *adv.* in a face- [facet 1.] tious manner; jokingly. [each other.]

face-to-face [féistəféis] *adv., adj.* in the presence of

fa·cial [féiʃ(ə)l] *adj.* of or for the face. ¶ *a ~ expression*① */ ~ cream.*② —*n.* ⓊⒸ (*colloq.*) a treatment of the face, esp. by massage.

fac·ile [fǽsil / fǽsail] *adj.* **1.** easy to do. ↔difficult ¶*a ~ task.* **2.** moving or working easily. ¶*have a ~ tongue.* **3.** gentle; mild. ¶*She has a ~ nature.*

fa·cil·i·tate [fəsílitèit] *vt.* make (something) easy. ¶ *Airplanes ~ travel.* ⇒USAGE

fa·cil·i·ty [fəsíliti] *n.* (pl. **-ties**) **1.** Ⓤ ease. ↔difficulty ¶*play the piano with ~.*① **2.** Ⓤ the ability to do something easily. ¶*He has great ~ in English conversation.* **3.** (*pl.*) the means which makes an action, etc. easier; something designed to serve a certain function. 《*~ for*》 ¶*kitchen facilities*② */ facilities for travel.*③
 1) *give* (or *afford, accord*) *someone every facility for,* smooth someone's way for doing something.
 2) *with facility,* with ease.

fac·ing [féisiŋ] *n.* **1.** Ⓒ a covering for the decoration or protection of a building. ¶*a wooden house with a brick ~.*① **2.** Ⓤ material applied along an edge of a garment.

fac·sim·i·le [fæksímili] *n.* Ⓒ an exact copy or reproduction of writing, a manuscript, etc.

‡ fact [fǽkt] *n.* **1.** Ⓒ something that has happened or been done; an actual event or deed. ¶*a historic ~ / Tell me the facts of the case.* **2.** Ⓒ something known to be true or accepted to be true. ¶*No one can deny the ~ that fire burns.* **3.** Ⓤ the quality of being real; truth. ¶*a question of ~ / Fact is stranger than fiction.*① **4.** Ⓒ (*Law*) the statement of something that has been done, etc. ¶*His facts are doubtful.*
 1) *as a matter of fact; in point of fact,* truly; really.
 2) *in fact,* ⓐ =as a matter of fact. ⓑ in brief.

fac·tion [fǽkʃ(ə)n] *n.* **1.** Ⓒ a group of people in a political party, etc. **2.** Ⓤ the act of quarreling among the members of a political party, etc.

fac·tion·al [fǽkʃən(ə)l] *adj.* of factions.

fac·tious [fǽkʃəs] *adj.* **1.** tending to form factions. **2.** fond of causing trouble. ▷**fac·tious·ly** [-li] *adv.*

fac·ti·tious [fæktíʃəs] *adj.* artificial; produced by design. ↔natural ▷**fac·ti·tious·ly** [-li] *adv.*

‡ fac·tor [fǽktər] *n.* Ⓒ **1.** something that helps to bring about a result; an element. ¶*Effort is an important ~ in success.*① **2.** (*Mathematics*) any of the numbers that produce a given number when multiplied together. **3.** a person who does business for another; an agent.

‡ fac·to·ry [fǽkt(ə)ri] *n.* Ⓒ (pl. **-ries**) a building or group of buildings where goods are manufactured.

…에 대항하다; …에 정면으로 맞서다 ¶⑥나는 그를 대항할 수가 없다 **3.** …의 겉칠(걸치장)을 하다 ¶⑦향하다, 면(面)하다 ¶⑦우향우!

圈 …에 대담하게 맞서다; …을 인정하다

—⑧ **1.** 보석의 작은 평면 **2.** [사물의] 면

—⑲ 익살맞은, 우스꽝스러운 ¶①익살스러운 말

—⑲ 익살맞게, 우스꽝스럽게

—⑳⑲ 정면으로 마주보고(마주보는)
—⑲ 얼굴의 ¶①얼굴 표정/②화장 크림 —⑧《口》미안술(美顔術)

—⑲ **1.** 쉬운, 수월한 **2.** 술술 움직이는, 척척 해내는, 유창한 **3.** 유순한, 말 잘 듣는

—⑩ …을 용이하게 하다 USAGE 반드시 사물을 나타내는 말이 주어가 됨
—⑧ **1.** 용이함 ¶①피아노를 쉽게 치고 있다 **2.** 손쉽게 하는 능력, 능란한 솜씨, 숙련 **3.** [편의를 제공하는] 설비; 기관; 시설 ¶②취사 시설/③여행 기관

圈 1)남에게 …의 모든 편의를 제공하다 2) 술술, 손쉽게

—⑧ **1.** 표면을 단장하기, 표면 화장 ¶①벽돌로 표면을 쌓은 목조 가옥 **2.** [옷의] 단(가장자리)의 옷감

—⑧ [필적·원고 따위의] 정교한 복사, 모사(模寫)
—⑧ **1.** 실제로 일어났던 일, 사실 **2.** 실제로 있는 일, 진상 **3.** [이론·의견·상상 따위의] 대하여] 현실성; 진실 ¶①사실은 소설보다도 기묘하다 **4.**《法》신립(申立)의 사실

圈 1)실제로; 사실상 2)ⓑ요는, 요컨대

—⑧ **1.** 당파, 파벌 **2.** 파벌 싸움, 당쟁, 내분

—⑲ 당파의; 파벌적인
—⑲ **1.** 당파를 만들기 좋아하는, 당파심의 **2.** 파벌 싸움을 일삼는
—⑲ 인위적인, 지어낸, 꾸며낸

—⑧ **1.** [결과를 가져오는] 요인, 요소 ¶①노력은 성공의 중요한 요인이다 **2.**《數》인수(因數) **3.** 대리인

—⑧ [제조]공장, 제조소

fac·to·tum [fæktóutəm] *n.* [C] a man who is employed to do all kinds of work.

fac·tu·al [fæktʃuəl] *adj.* concerned with fact; based on facts. ↔theoretical

* **fac·ul·ty** [fæk(ə)lti] *n.* [C] (pl. **-ties**) **1.** ability to do some special thing. ¶*She has a great ~ for mathematics.*① **2.** a power of the mind or body. ¶*the ~ of sight.*② **3.** a department of learning in a university. ¶*the ~ of law (medicine).*③ **4.** 《*the ~, collectively*》 the teaching staff in any school.

fad [fæd] *n.* [C] something everybody does or is interested in for a short time.

* **fade** [feid] *vi.* **1.** (of a color, a light, etc.) grow pale; (of a sound) grow faint. ¶*The sound of drums faded away.*① **2.** lose freshness or strength. ¶*The flowers ~ in autumn.*② **3.** go out of sight slowly. —*vt.* cause (something) to lose color.
1) ***fade in (out),*** (of motion pictures, radio, television, etc.) slowly become more (less) distinct.
2) ***fade into,*** lose color or strength and become (something else).

fad·ed [féidid] *adj.* having lost color or freshness.

fade-in [féidìn] *n.* [C] (of motion pictures, etc.) a scene that slowly appears.

fade-out [féidàut] *n.* [C] (of motion pictures, etc.) a scene that slowly disappears.

fa·er·y [féiəri, fέəri] *n.* [C] (pl. **-er·ies**) (*archaic*) **1.** fairyland. **2.** a fairy. —*adj.* (*archaic*) fairy.

fag [fæg] *v.* (**fagged, fag·ging**) *vi.* work hard until tired. 《~ *at* something》 ¶*He fagged away at physics.*① —*vt.* 《usu. in *passive*》 make (someone) tired out by hard work. —*n.* **1.** [U] 《often *a* ~》 (chiefly *Brit.*) a piece of hard, uninteresting work. **2.** [C] (*Brit.*) a pupil who serves a senior pupil in public schools.

fag end [ˊ ˊ] *n.* the last, useless part of something.

fag·ot, *Brit.* **fag·got** [fægət] *n.* [C] a bundle of sticks bound together and used for firewood.

Fahr. Fahrenheit.

Fahr·en·heit [fær(ə)nhàit] *adj.* of or according to the Fahrenheit scale on which the freezing point is 32° and boiling point of water is 212°. ↔Celsius ⇒[N.B.]

‡ **fail** [feil] *vi.* **1.** not succeed; be unable to do. 《~ *in* a test, etc.》 ↔succeed ¶~ *in mathematics.* **2.** be not enough; be wanting; lack. 《~ *in* something》 ¶~ *in truthfulness* / *Our water supply failed again.*① **3.** lose power (*or* strength); grow weak. 《~ *in* something》 ¶*The patient failed rapidly.* / *The engine failed.*② **4.** lose all one's money in business. —*vt.* **1.** disappoint utterly; neglect to support or help (someone). ¶*I failed her.*③ **2.** not do; neglect. 《~ *to do* something》 ¶*Don't ~ to come.* **3.** (*colloq.*) be unsuccessful in (a test, etc.); give the mark of failure to (someone).
fail of, be unable to have or get; lack.
—*n.* [U] failure. ⇒[usage]
without fail, certainly; surely.

fail·ing [féiliŋ] *n.* [C] a fault or weak point; [U] a failure. —*prep.* in the absence of; without. ¶*Failing good weather, the picnic will be postponed.*①

‡ **fail·ure** [féiljər] *n.* [U][C] **1.** lack of success. ↔success ¶~ *in a test* / *end in* ~.① **2.** the state of being not enough. ¶*Crop failures resulted in famine.*② **3.** the act of becoming weak or losing strength. ¶*heart* ~③ / *the ~ of one's health.*④ **4.** [C] bankruptcy. **5.** [C] an unsuccessful person or thing. **6.** the act of not doing or failing to do. ¶*a ~ in duty* / *~ to be on time.*

fain [fein] *adv.* (*poetic*) willingly; gladly.
would fain, willingly. ¶*I would ~ go.*

—[名] 잡역부, 막일군

—[形] 사실[상]의; 사실에 근거를 둔

—[名] 1. 재능 ¶①그녀는 수학에 대단한 재능을 갖고 있다 2. [신체의] 기능, 구실 ¶②시각(視覺) 3. [대학의] 학부 ¶③법(의)학부 4. 교직원, 교수진

—[名] 일시적 유행; 변덕

—[自] 1. 점점 빛을 잃다, 바래다, 사라지다 ¶①북소리가 점점 멀어져 갔다 2. 쇠퇴하다, 시들다 ¶②꽃은 가을이 되면 시든다 3. [서서히] 그 자취를 감추다
—[他] …빛깔을 바래게 하다
[熟] 1)[소리·영상이] 차차 분명해(희미해)지다 2)엷어(약해)져서 …이 되다

—[形] 빛이 바랜; 시든

—[名] 차차로 나타나는 장면

—[名] 차차로 사라지는 장면

—[名] 《古》 1. 요정의 나라 2. 요정
—[形] 《古》 요정의(같은)

—[自] 열심히(지칠 때까지) 일하다 ¶①그는 부지런히 물리학을 공부했다
—[他] [일 따위로] …을 지치게 하다
—[名] 1. 《英》 고된 일 2. 《英》 상급생의 잔심부름하는 하급생

—[名] 나부랑이, 끄트머리; 찌끼

—[名] 나뭇단, 동나무

—[形] 화씨(華氏)의 [N.B.] F., Fahr.로 줄여 씀. 고안자 G.D.Fahrenheit(1686-1736)의 이름에서

—[自] 1. 실패하다; 낙제하다 2. 부족되다, 결핍되다 ¶①우리의 급수(給水)가 또 끊겼다 3. 쇠퇴하다; 약해지다 ¶②엔진이 꺼졌다 4. 파산하다 —[他] 1. …을 실망시키다, 저버리다 ¶③나는 그녀를 저버렸다 2. …을 하지 않다; …을 게을리하다 3. 《口》 …에 낙제하다, [시험에서] …을 떨어뜨리다
[熟] 달성 못하다; …이 없다
—[名] 실패 [usage] 다음 숙어로만 씀
[熟] 어김없이, 꼭

—[名] 결점, 약점; 실패 —[前] …이 없어서(없을 경우에는) ¶①날씨가 궂으면 피크닉은 연기된다

—[名] 1. 실패 ¶①실패로 돌아가다 2. 부족, 결핍 ¶②흉작으로 기근이 들었다 3. 쇠약; 힘의 감퇴 ¶③심장마비 /④건강의 쇠퇴 4. 파산 5. 실패자; 실패로 돌아간 것 6. 불이행, 태만

—[副] 기꺼이
[熟] 기꺼이 …하다

:faint [feint] *adj.* **1.** dim; indistinct; vague. ¶*a ~ light* / *I have not the faintest idea about it.*① **2.** (of mental or physical force) weak; almost used up. ¶*a ~ voice* / *The traveler was ~ from hunger and cold.* **3.** done without eager interest. ¶*make a ~ attempt.* **4.** likely to lose consciousness. ¶*She felt ~.* **—*vi.*** lose consciousness.
—[形] 1. 희미한, 어렴풋한, 몽롱한 ¶①그 일에 관해서는 통 모르겠다 2. [체력·기력 따위가] 가냘픈; 노곤한 3. 무기력한; 열성이 없는 4. 정신이 아찔한, 어질어질한 —[自] 기절하다; 정신이 아찔해지다

—*n.* [C] a loss of consciousness. ¶*go down in a ~.*②
—[名] 기절, 실신 ¶②기절하다

faint-heart·ed [féinthá:rtid] *adj.* lacking courage; timid.
—[形] 용기가 없는, 겁 많은, 심약한

***faint·ly** [féintli] *adv.* in a faint manner; vaguely; indistinctly.
—[副] 힘없이, 가냘프게; 희미하게; 어렴풋이

faint·ness [féintnis] *n.* [U] the state of being faint; the act of fainting.
—[名] 희미함, 약함, 가냘픔; 실신, 정신이 아찔함

:fair¹ [fεər] *n.* [C] **1.** (chiefly *Brit.*) a gathering to buy and sell things that is held in a particular place at a regular time; a market. **2.** an entertainment and a sale of articles, esp. for charitable purposes; a bazaar. ¶*a church ~.* **3.** a display of goods, products, etc. ¶*an international trade ~*① / (*U.S.*) *a World's Fair.*②
—[名] 1. 《英》 정기적으로 서는 장 2. 자선시(慈善市) 3. 공진회(共進會), 품평회; 견본시(見本市) ¶①국제 견본시/②《美》 만국 박람회

a day after the fair, too late.
[熟] 사후 약방문

:fair² [fεər] *adj.* **1.** just, honest or right according to the rules. ¶*~ play* / *a ~ judge.*① **2.** pretty good; average; not bad. ¶*a ~ crop*② / *make a ~ grade in arithmetic.* **3.** (of weather) clear; not rainy or stormy; (of a wind) favorable. ¶*a ~ sky.* **4.** promising, likely. ¶*a ~ chance of success.* **5.** light in color; blond. ↔dark ¶*~ hair.* **6.** clean; plain. ¶*a ~ copy.* **7.** gentle; polite. ¶*~ words.* **8.** (chiefly *poetic*) beautiful; lovely.
—[形] 1. 올바른, 공평한, 규칙에 따른(맞는) ¶①공정한 재판관 2. 꽤 좋은, 적당한, 쓸쓸한 ¶②상당한 풍작 3. [날씨가] 맑은, 순조로운; 순풍의 4. 유망한, 가망이 있는 5. 살결이 흰, 금발의 6. 깨끗한, 명료한 7. 얌전한, 공손한 8. 《詩》 아름다운, 귀여운

—*adv.* in a fair manner; honestly. ¶*play ~.*
—[副] 공정하게, 공평히; 정직하게

1) ***bid fair*** (*=seem likely; have a good chance.*) *to do.*
2) ***fair and square,*** (*colloq.*) just; honest.
[熟] 1)…할 가망이 충분히 있다 2)공정한, 정직한

fair-haired [fέərhέərd] *adj.* having light-colored hair; blond.
—[形] 금발의

:fair·ly [fέərli] *adv.* **1.** justly; honestly. ¶*The games were judged ~.* / *It may ~ be said that…*① **2.** somewhat. ¶*Mary plays the piano ~ well.* **3.** (*colloq.*) completely; clearly. ¶*He was ~ caught in the trap.*
—[副] 1. 공정하게, 공평히 ¶① …이라 말해도 과언은 아니다 2. 상당히, 꽤 3. 《口》 완전히, 아주

fair·ness [fέərnis] *n.* [U] the state of being fair.
—[名] 공명정대; 살결이 흼; 아름다움

fair-spo·ken [fέərspóuk(ə)n] *adj.* courteous in speech.
—[形] 말씨가 정중한(공손한)

fair·way [fέərwèi] *n.* [C] a passage where ships sail in a river or a harbor.
—[名] 항로, 뱃길

fair-weath·er [fέərwèðər] *adj.* suitable only for fair weather; not helpful in time of need.
—[形] 좋은 날씨에만 적합한; 정작 위급할 때에는 도움이 안 되는

:fair·y [fέəri] *n.* [C] (pl. **fair·ies**) a tiny imaginary being with magic powers. **—*adj.*** of or like fairies; lovely.
—[名] 요정(妖精) —[形] 요정의, 요정 같은; 사랑스러운, 귀여운

fair·y·land [fέərilæ̀nd] *n.* **1.** [U] the country of the fairies. **2.** [C] an enchanting, pleasant and beautiful place.
—[名] 1. 요정의 나라 2. 선경(仙境), 도원경(桃源境)

fairy tale [ˊ- ˋ] *n.* **1.** a story about fairies. **2.** an untrue story; a lie.
—[名] 1. 요정들의 이야기; 동화 2. 지어낸 이야기; 거짓말

:faith [feiθ] *n.* [U] **1.** trust; confidence. ¶*lose ~ in*① / *have ~ in a friend.* **2.** belief in God or in the truths of religion; firm belief. ¶*have ~ in Christianity.*② **3.** [C] a system of religious belief; a doctrine. **4.** promise to be loyal; loyalty; sincerity.
—[名] 1. 신용; 신뢰 ¶①…을 신뢰(신용)하지 않게 되다 2. 신앙; 신념 ¶②그리스도교를 믿다 3. 교리; 신조 4. 충실; 성실; 서약

1) ***in good*** (***bad***) ***faith,*** honestly (dishonestly).
2) ***keep*** (***break***) ***faith with*** (*=remain* (*cease to remain*) *loyal to*) *someone* or *something.*
[熟] 1)선의(악의)로써, 성실히(불성실하게) 2)…에 대하여 신의를 지키다(어기다)

:faith·ful [féiθf(u)l] *adj.* **1.** true to one's word, promise, etc; loyal to someone or something; doing one's duty; reliable. 《~ to》 ¶*a ~ friend* / *be ~ to one's duty*① / *be ~ to God.*② **2.** accurate; without mistakes. ¶*a ~ copy.* **—*n.*** 《*the ~*》 the people who believe truly or who support loyally.
—[形] 1. 성실한; 충실한; 신뢰할 만한, 믿을 만한 ¶①임무에 충실하다/②신을 충실히 믿다 2. 정확한; 틀림이 없는 —[名] 참된(충실한) 신자; 충실한 지지자

***faith·ful·ly** [féiθfuli] *adv.* in a faithful manner. ¶*Yours faithfully; Faithfully yours.*①
—[副] 성실히; 충실히; 정확히 ¶①경구(敬具), 재배(再拜)

faith·ful·ness [féiθf(u)lnis] *n.* [U] the state of being faithful; honesty.
—[名] 성실; 충실; 정확

faith·less [féiθlis] *adj.* not reliable; unworthy of trust; false.
—[形] 믿지 못할; 신의 없는, 불[성]실한

fake [feik] *vt.* **1.** make (something) for the purpose of deceiving. ¶~ *a Picasso.*① **2.** pretend. ¶~ *blindness.* —*n.* [C] **1.** something that seems genuine but is not. ¶*His illness was a*~. **2.** a person who tries to deceive; a person who pretends to be what he isn't.
—[他] 1. …을 위조하다 ¶①피카소의 그림을 위조하다 2. …인 체하다 —[名] 1. 위조품, 모조품, 가짜 물건 2. 사기꾼, 협잡꾼

fal·chion [fɔ́:l(t)ʃ(ə)n] *n.* [C] a broad, short sword with an edge that curves to a point. ⇒fig.; (*poetic*) a sword.
—[名] 언월도(偃月刀); 칼, 검

(falchion)

fal·con [fɔ́:lkən, +*U.S.* fǽl-] *n.* [C] a hawk trained to hunt other birds and small animals.
—[名] [사냥용] 매, 새매

fal·con·er [fɔ́:lkənər, +*U.S.* fǽl-] *n.* [C] a person who hunts with falcons; a trainer of falcons.
—[名] 매를 부리는 사람, 매부리

fal·con·ry [fɔ́:lk(ə)nri, +*U.S.* fǽl-] *n.* [U] **1.** the sport of hunting with falcons. **2.** the art of training a falcon.
—[名] 1. 매사냥 2. 매 길들이는 법

‡**fall** [fɔ:l] *vi.* (**fell, fall·en**) **1.** drop from a higher place or position; come down. ↔rise 《~ *from* or *down* some place》 ¶~ *from a tree* / ~ *down a bank.* **2.** come down suddenly from a standing or sitting position; (of a building) break into pieces. ¶*I nearly fell down.*① **3.** (of hair, curtains, etc.) hang down. 《~ *over* or *upon* something》 ¶*Her curls fell* [*up*]*on her shoulders.* **4.** become lower or less in number, amount, degree, value, etc. ¶*Prices will* ~. / *The wind fell.*② **5.** (of land) slope; (of rivers) flow. 《~ *down* or *into* some place》 ¶*The Mississippi falls into the Gulf of Mexico.* **6.** be wounded or killed: die. ¶~ *in battle.*③ **7.** be overthrown or captured; give up; yield to (temptation, sin, etc.) ¶~ *into bad habits* / *The fortress fell.* **8.** lose position, reputation, etc. ¶~ *from the people's favor.* **9.** become or pass into a certain mental or physical state. ⇒[usage] ¶~ *in love.* **10.** happen; occur; come by chance 《~ *on* or *to* something》; come as a right or inheritance. ¶*On what day does Christmas* ~ *this year?*④ / *The estate fell to her.*⑤ **11.** come upon or reach as if by dropping down. ¶*Night fell.* / *Light fell upon my eyes.* **12.** be placed; (of the eyes) be directed. 《~ *on* something》; (of speech) be spoken. 《~ *from* something》 ¶*The accent falls on the first syllable.*⑥ / *Words fell from his lips.*
—[自] 1. 떨어지다, 낙하하다, [꽃·낙엽 따위가] 지다, 내리다 2. 넘어지다, 쓰러지다; [건물 따위가] 무너지다, 붕괴하다 ¶①자칫하면 넘어질 뻔했다 3. 늘어지다 4. [값 따위가] 떨어지다, 하락하다, 저하하다; 감퇴하다, 줄다 ¶②바람이 잤다 5. [땅이] 경사지다; [강·물줄기가] 흘러들다 6. 부상하다; [상처를 입고] 죽다 ¶③전사하다 7. 함락하다; 단념하다; [유혹 따위에] 굴복하다, 타락하다 8. [지위·명성 따위가] 떨어지다, 저하하다 9. [어떤 상태에] 빠지다; …이 되다 [usage] 보어 또는 구를 수반함 10. [사건 따위가] 일어나다, 발생하다; [우연히 …에게] 굴러들다; [권리·유산 따위가] 손에 들어오다 ¶④금년에는 크리스마스가 무슨 요일에 들었는가?/⑤재산은 그녀에게로 돌아갔다 11. [떨어지듯이] 닥쳐(다가)오다 12. …에 두어지다; [시선이] 향하다, 쏠리다; [말이] 새어나오다 ¶⑥악센트는 첫음절에 온다

1) ***fall among,*** come among by chance.
2) ***fall away,*** ⓐ take away support, etc.; desert. ⓑ disappear. ⓒ grow thin and weak.
3) ***fall back,*** move back or away; withdraw.
4) ***fall back on*** (or ***upon***), ⓐ depend on (someone) for support. ⓑ go back to (some place) for safety.
5) ***fall behind,*** fail to keep pace with.
6) ***fall down on*** (=*fail to accomplish*) *a job.*
7) ***fall flat,*** (of a joke, etc.) fail to entertain or interest.
8) ***fall in,*** ⓐ fall or break down. ⓑ (*Military*) form ranks.
9) ***fall in with,*** ⓐ become associated with (someone). ⓑ meet or join by chance. ⓒ agree with (someone).
10) ***fall off,*** start to decrease; decline.
11) ***fall on*** (or ***upon***), ⓐ attack. ⓑ take place on (something).
12) ***fall out,*** ⓐ quarrel; stop being friends. ⓑ (*Military*) break ranks.
13) ***fall short,*** ⓐ be not enough. ⓑ fail to fulfill. 《~ *of*》
14) ***fall through,*** (of a plan, etc.) fail to materialize.
15) ***fall to,*** ⓐ begin. ⓑ begin to eat, fight, etc. ⓒ close by itself. ⓓ be assigned to.

[熟] 1)우연히 …의 속에 들다 2)ⓐ저버리다 ⓑ사라지다 ⓒ약해지다, 야위다 3)물러나다 4)ⓐ…에 의지하다 ⓑ[…으로 무사히 철수하다 5)뒤떨어지다, 낙오하다 6)…을 마치지(다하지) 못하다 7)[농담 따위가] 실패로 돌아가다 8)ⓐ붕괴하다 ⓑ《軍》 정렬하다 9)ⓐ…와 사귀다, 교제하다 ⓑ…와 우연히 만나다, …에 참가하다 ⓒ…와 일치하다, …에 동의하다 10)줄기 시작하다, 쇠퇴하다 11)ⓐ…을 공격하다 ⓑ…에 맞다, 닥치다, 덮치다 12)ⓐ싸우다; 사이가 틀어지다 ⓑ《軍》 열을 흐트리다, 대열을 떠나다 13)ⓐ[…에] 부족하다 ⓑ[…에] 미달하다, 미치지 못하다 14)[계획 따위가] 실패(수포)로 돌아가다 15)ⓐ…을 시작하다 ⓑ식사나 싸움을 시작하다 ⓒ[문 따위가] 저절로 닫히다 ⓓ…의 임무로 되다 16)ⓐ…을 떨어뜨리다 ⓑ[비밀 따위]를 누설하다

F

16) ***let something fall,*** ⓐ drop. ⓑ reveal (a secret, etc).
—*n.* [C] **1.** the act of falling, dropping or coming down. ¶*a ~ from a horse.*⑦ **2.** the amount that falls; a distance fallen; that which falls or has fallen. ¶*a heavy ~ of snow*⑧ / *a ~ of eight feet.*⑨ **3.** a decrease; a decline; a reduction in value, price, etc.; (of land) a downward slope. ¶*a ~ in prices.*⑩ **4.** ruin; destruction. ¶*the ~ of Rome.* **5.** 《usu. *pl.*》 water coming over a cliff; a waterfall. ¶*Niagara Falls.* **6.** [U][C] 《~ or *the* ~》 (chiefly *U.S.*) autumn. **7.** 《*the F-*》 Adam's sin and its result.
—[名] 1. 떨어짐, 낙하, 추락; 타락; 쓰러짐, 넘어짐, 전도(轉倒) ¶⑦낙마(落馬) 2. 강우(강설)량; 낙차(落差); 낙하물 ¶⑧폭설(暴雪)/⑨8피이트의 낙차 3. 저하, 쇠약, 하락, 감소; [명예 따위의] 실추(失墜); [땅 위의] 경사 ¶⑩물가의 하락 4. 함락, 몰락 5. 폭포 6. 가을 7. 인간의 타락

—*adj.* of, for or in the autumn.
—[形] 가을의, 가을용의, 가을에 알맞은

fal·la·cious [fəléiʃəs] *adj.* misleading; erroneous; logically unsound. ▷**fal·la·cious·ly** [-li] *adv.*
—[形] 남을 현혹시키는; 그릇된; 불합리한

fal·la·cy [fǽləsi] *n.* (pl. **-cies**) **1.** [C] a mistaken idea or belief. ¶*It is a ~ that the rich are always happy.* **2.** [U] unsound or false reasoning.
—[名] 1. 그릇된 생각(신념) 2. 불합리한(틀린) 추론

fall·en [fɔ́:l(ə)n] *v.* pp. of **fall.**
—*adj.* **1.** dropped. ¶*~ leaves.* **2.** down flat. ¶*a ~ tree.* **3.** degraded. ¶*a ~ woman.* **4.** ruined. ¶*a ~ nation.* **5.** killed in battle. ¶*the ~.*①
—[形] 1. 떨어진 2. 쓰러진 3. 타락한 4. 멸망한 5. 전사한 ¶①전사자

fal·li·bil·i·ty [fæ̀libíliti] *n.* [U][C] the state or quality of being fallible; a fallible quality.
—[名] 오류에 빠지기 쉬움

fal·li·ble [fǽlibl] *adj.* liable to err. ¶*All men are ~.*
—[形]오류에 빠지기 쉬운

fall·ing [fɔ́:liŋ] *n.* [U][C] the act of coming down. —*adj.* descending. ¶*a ~ star.*① ↔rising
—[名] 낙하; 타락
—[形] 떨어지는, 내리는 ¶①유성(流星)

fall-out [fɔ́:làut] *n.* [U] the radioactive particles and dust that fall to the earth after a nuclear explosion.
—[名] 방사성 낙진, 죽음의 재

fal·low [fǽlou] *adj.* (of land) plowed, but left unseeded.
—*n.* [U] land plowed, but left unseeded for a season.
—[形] [토지가] 묵어 있는, 휴한중인
—[名] 휴한지

false [fɔ:ls] *adj.* **1.** not true; not correct; wrong. ¶*a ~ report.* **2.** not trustful; lying. **3.** not faithful or loyal. ¶*a ~ friend.* **4.** not natural; artificial; not real. ¶*~ teeth.*① **5.** supplemental. ¶*a ~ deck.*
—[形] 1. 틀린, 그릇된, 부정의 2. 신용할 수 없는, 허위의 3. 불성실한 4. 모조의; 인조의; 가짜의 ¶①의치(義齒) 5. 임시의, 일시적인, 보조의

—*adv.* in a false manner.
—[副] 부실하게, 부정으로

false-heart·ed [fɔ́:lshá:rtid] *adj.* unfaithful; disloyal.
—[形] 부실한, 불성실한; 성실치 못한

false·hood [fɔ́:lshùd] *n.* **1.** [U] the act of telling lies. **2.** [C] a lie. ¶*utter falsehoods.*①
—[名] 1. 거짓말하기 2. 거짓말 ¶①거짓말하다

false·ly [fɔ́:lsli] *adv.* in a false manner.
—[副] 거짓으로; 부정하게; 불실하게

false·ness [fɔ́:lsnis] *n.* [U] the state or quality of being false.
—[名] 허위; 부정; 불실, 불성실

fal·set·to [fɔ:lsétou] *n.* [C] (pl. **-tos**) (*Music*) an unnaturally high-pitched voice in a man; a person who sings with such a voice.
—[名] 《樂》 가성(假聲); 가성 가수

fal·si·fi·ca·tion [fɔ̀:lsifikéiʃ(ə)n] *n.* [U][C] the act of falsifying; the state of being falsified.
—[名] 위조; 변조; [사실의] 곡해, 의곡; [기대를] 배반당하기

fal·si·fy [fɔ́:lsifài] *v.* (**-fied**) *vt.* **1.** change (something) in order to deceive. ¶*~ documents*① / *~ records.* **2.** prove (something) to be false. —*vi.* make false statements. ▷**fal·si·fi·er** [-ər] *n.*
—[他] 1. …을 위조하다; [사실을] 의곡하다 ¶①서류를 위조하다 2. …이 거짓임(그릇됨)을 증명하다 —[自] 거짓말하다

fal·si·ty [fɔ́:lsiti] *n.* (pl. **-ties**) [U] the state of being false; [C] an error.
—[名] 허위; 틀림, 오류

fal·ter [fɔ́:ltər] *vi.* **1.** hesitate; lose courage. ¶*She faltered for a moment at the door.* **2.** move or act unsteadily; stumble. ¶*The man faltered away.* **3.** speak hesitatingly or stammeringly; (of the voice) waver. —*vt.* utter hesitatingly or brokenly.
—[自] 1. 망설이다, 주저하다;머뭇거리다 2. 비틀거리다; [돌 따위에 채어] 넘어지다 3. 우물거리다; 말을 더듬다; [목소리가] 떨리다 —[他] …을 머뭇거리며(더듬거리며) 말하다

fal·ter·ing [fɔ́:lt(ə)riŋ] *adj.* hesitating; stumbling; stammering. ▷**fal·ter·ing·ly** [-li] *adv.*
—[形] 망설이는; 비틀거리는; 말을 더듬는

fame [feim] *n.* **1.** [U] high reputation; renown. ↔notoriety **2.** [U] common or public opinion or estimation of someone.
—[名] 1. 명성; 고명(高名) 2. 여론, 세평; 평판

come to fame; gain (or ***win***) ***fame,*** become famous.
[熟] 유명해지다

famed [feimd] *adj.* well-known; famous.
—[形] 유명한, 이름난, 소문이 자자한

fa·mil·iar [fəmíljər] *adj.* **1.** well-known; common; seen often. ¶*a ~ scene / be ~ to people.* **2.** having a good
—[形] 1. 잘 알려져 있는; 통속적인, 흔한, 눈에 익은 2. 잘 알고 있는; 정통한

F

familiarity [422] **fancy**

knowledge of; well-acquainted. ¶*He is ~ with the classics.*① **3.** friendly; close; intimate. ¶*a ~ friend / be ~ with someone.* **4.** not formal; easy. ¶*in ~ English.* **5.** too informal; bold. ¶*too ~ with a stranger.*

fa·mil·iar·i·ty [fəmìliǽriti] *n.* (pl. **-ties**) **1.** Ⓤ the state of being familiar; intimacy; friendship. ¶*I am on terms of ~ with him.*① **2.** Ⓤ close acquaintance. ¶*His ~ with Shakespeare surprised me.* **3.** Ⓤ lack of formality or ceremony. ¶(*proverb*) *Familiarity breeds contempt.*② **4.** Ⓤ (often *pl.*) an unduly informal act or expression. ¶*I don't like such familiarities.*③

—❸ 1. 그는 고전에 정통하다 3. 친한, 허물없는 4. 화기애애한, 딱딱하지 않은 5. 치근거리는, 뻔뻔스러운

—❸ 1. 친밀; 친교 ¶①나는 그와는 친밀한 사이다 2. 정통함 3. 치근치근함; 버릇없음 ¶②(俚) 친분이 지나치면 경멸金. 산다 4. 치근치근한 언행 ¶③나는 그 따위 치근치근한 태도는 싫다

fa·mil·iar·i·za·tion [fəmìljərizéiʃ(ə)n / -rai-] *n.* Ⓤ the act of familiarizing; the state of being familiarized.

—❸ 친밀, 정통, 익숙함

fa·mil·iar·ize [fəmíljəràiz] *vt.* **1.** make (someone) well acquainted with something. ((~ someone *with*)) ¶*~ oneself with something*① / *~ a girl with the use of a sewing machine.*② **2.** make (something) well known to people; popularize. 「intimately.」

—⓽ 1. …을 익숙(친숙)하게 하다 ①…에 정통하다 / ②소녀에게 재봉틀 사용법을 익숙하도록 가르치다 2. …을 잘 알게 하다

fa·mil·iar·ly [fəmíljərli] *adv.* in a familiar mannar;」

—⓽ 친하게; 친밀하게

‡**fam·i·ly** [fǽm(i)li] *n.* Ⓒ (pl. **-lies**) **1.** a group of people consisting of parents and their children. ¶*My ~ are all early risers.* ⇒ⓤsage 2. (collectively) the children of two parents. ¶*Does he have any ~?* **3.** a group of persons who are related; all persons descended from a common ancestor. **4.** Ⓤ (esp. *Brit.*) good or noble descent. ¶*a man of ~.*④ **5.** race. **6.** a group of related plants or animals; a group of closely related things. ¶*the rose ~ / a ~ of languages.*② —*adj.* of a family.

—❸ 1. 가족, 식구 Usage 전원을 한 집합체로 볼 때는 단수 동사, 가족의 각 개인에 중점을 둘 때에는 복수 동사를 받음 2. (양친과 구별하여) 아이들 3. 일족; 문중(門中) 4. 좋은 가문 ¶①명문의 출신 5. 종족 6. (동·식물의) 과(科); (분류상의) 계통, 유(類) ¶②어족(語族)

—⓽ 가족의, 한 집안의; 가정의

fam·ine [fǽmin] *n.* **1.** Ⓤ extreme lack of food; starvation. ¶*Thousands of people died of ~.*① **2.** Ⓒ a serious shortage of anything. ¶*a water* (*coal*) *~.*②

—❸ 1. 기근(飢饉) ¶①수천 명의 사람들이 기근으로 죽었다 2. 큰 부족(결핍) ¶②물(석탄)기근

fam·ish [fǽmiʃ] *vi.* suffer from extreme hunger. ¶*be famished* [*to death*]① / (*colloq.*) *I am famishing.*② —*vt.* cause (someone) to suffer from hunger.

—⓲ 굶주리다 ¶①굶어죽다 / ②(口)몹시 시장하다 —⓽ …을 굶주리게 하다

‡**fa·mous** [féiməs] *adj.* **1.** very well-known; noted. ↔unknown ¶*This place is ~ for its hot springs.*① **2.** (*colloq.*) excellent; first-rate. ¶*That's ~!*

—⓽ 1. 유명한, 이름난 ¶①이 곳은 온천으로 유명하다 2. (口) 훌륭한, 굉장한, 최고의

‡**fan**¹ [fæn] *n.* Ⓒ **1.** an instrument to make a current of air. ¶*an electric ~.*② **2.** something resembling a fan. —*vt.* (**fanned, fan·ning**) **1.** make a current of air flow onto (something). ¶*~ oneself*② / *~ a fire.*② **2.** drive away (something) with a fan, etc. ¶*~ away flies.* **3.** stir up; excite.

—❸ 1. 부채 ¶①선풍기 2. 부채 모양의 물건
—⓲ 1. …을 부치다, 부채질하다 ¶②부채질하다, 부치다 / ③부채질하여 불을 피우다 2. …을 부채 따위로 쫓다 3. …을 부추기다; 선동하다

‡**fan**² [fæn] *n.* Ⓒ (*colloq.*) an enthusiastic supporter; a fanatic. ¶*a baseball ~ / a movie ~.*

—❸ (口) 열성적인 애호가, 팬

fa·nat·ic [fənǽtik] *n.* Ⓒ a person who is possessed by excessive and unreasonable feelings or beliefs. —*adj.* fanatical. 「yond reason.」

—❸ 열광자; 광신자 —⓽ 열광적인; 광신적인

fa·nat·i·cal [fənǽtik(ə)l] *adj.* enthusiastic or zealous be-」

—⓽ 열광적인; 광신적인

fa·nat·i·cal·ly [fənǽtik(ə)li] *adv.* in a fanatical manner; frantically 「beyond reason.」

—⓲ 열광하여; 광신적으로

fa·nat·i·cism [fənǽtisìz(ə)m] *n.* Ⓤ enthusiasm or zeal」

—❸ 열광; 광신

fan·ci·er [fǽnsiər] *n.* Ⓒ a person who has a special interest in something. ¶*a bird* (*dog, rose*) *~.*②

—❸ 애호가 ¶①새(개·장미) 애호가

fan·ci·ful [fǽnsif(u)l] *adj.* **1.** imaginary; unreal. ¶*a ~ story.*① **2.** led by imagination; imaginative. ¶*a ~ writer.*② **3.** (of clothes, decoration, etc.) curiously designed; quaint. ▷**fan·ci·ful·ly** [-fuli] *adv.*

—⓽ 1. 상상의; 가공(架空)의 ¶①가공의 소설 2. 상상에 의해 움직이는, 공상적인 ¶②공상적인 작가 3. 별난, 기발한, 기상천외의

‡**fan·cy** [fǽnsi] *n.* (pl. **fan·cies**) **1.** Ⓤ Ⓒ the power of the mind to imagine things not present; imagination. **2.** Ⓒ an idea, image, or thought so formed. ¶*a pleasing ~.* **3.** (usu. *a ~*) an example of taste or judgment in art, literature, dress, etc.; a liking; a fondness. ¶*have*

—❸ 1. 공상력; 상상력 2. 심상(心像); 착상; 고안, 생각 3. 애호, 취미, 도락 ¶①고양이새끼를 애완하다 4. 갑자기 내킨 생각, 변덕

*a ~ for kittens.*① **4.** [C] an idea; caprice; whim.
—*adj.* **(-ci·er, -ci·est) 1.** decorated; ornamental; made to please the eye. ¶*a ~ dress.* **2.** based on the fancy; imaginary. ¶*a ~ picture.* **3.** requiring unusual skill. ¶*~ skating.* **4.** extravagant; above the real value. ¶*a ~ price.* **5.** (*U.S.*) particularly excellent.

—[形] **1.** 장식적인 **2.** 변덕스러운;공상적인 **3.** 곡예의, 묘기의 **4.** 엄청난, 터무니없는 **5.** 특선(特選)의

—*vt.* **(fan·cied) 1.** picture to oneself; imagine. 《~ *doing*; ~ *that* ...》 ¶*I can't ~ his saying such a thing.* **2.** believe (something or someone) without being certain; suppose. 《~ *that*...; ~ someone *to be*》 ¶*I ~ [that] I've met him somewhere. / They fancied Tom [to be] dead. / She fancies herself beautiful.*② **3.** have liking for (something or someone); like. 《~ *doing*》 ¶*I ~ rowing more than riding.*

—[他] **1.** …을 공상(상상)으로 그리다 **2.** …이라고 생각하다, [어쩐지] …이라는 생각이 들다; …이라고 자부하다 ¶②그녀는 자기가 미인이라고 자부하고 있다 **3.** …에 취미를 가지다, …을 좋아하다

fan·cy·work [fǽnsiwə̀:rk] *n.* [U] ornamental needlework; embroidery.

—[名] 수예, 자수

fan·fare [fǽnfɛər] *n.* [C] a short flourish, tune or call sounded by trumpets or bugles.

—[名] 화려한 트럼펫(나팔)의 취주, 팡파아르

fang [fæŋ] *n.* [C] a long, pointed tooth of a wild beast, a poisonous snake, etc.

—[名] [짐승의] 송곳니, [뱀의] 독아(毒牙)

fan·light [fǽnlàit] *n.* [C] a fan-shaped window or sash over a door. ⇒fig.

—[名] [문 위의] 부채꼴 창

[fanlight]

fan·ta·si·a [fæntéiʒə, -zjə] *n.* [C] a free musical composition not fixed in form or style.

—[名] 환상곡

***fan·tas·tic** [fæntǽstik], **-cal** [-k(ə)l] *adj.* **1.** odd; queer; grotesque. ¶*Fashions in dress are very ~ nowadays.* **2.** imaginary; unreal; irrational. ¶*~ fears.*①

—[形] **1.** 별난; 괴상한; 괴기한 **2.** 상상의; 비현실적인 ¶①근거없는 공포

fan·tas·ti·cal·ly [fæntǽstik(ə)li] *adv.* in a fantastic manner.

—[副] 괴상하게; 공상적으로

fan·ta·sy [fǽntəsi, -zi] *n.* (pl. **-sies**) **1.** [U] fancy; imagination. **2.** [C] a product of the fancy; a daydream. **3.** [C] (*Music*) a fantasia. ⇒[N.B.]

—[名] **1.** 공상; 상상 **2.** 공상의 산물(產物); 백일몽 **3.** 환상곡 [N.B.] phantasy로도 씀

‡far [fɑ:r] **(far·ther** or **fur·ther, far·thest** or **fur·thest)** *adv.* **1.** a long way off or at a great distance in time or space. ¶*~ away from the house / ~ back in history.* ⇒[usage] **2.** very much; to a great degree. ¶*This box is ~ better than that one.*

—[副] **1.** [시간이] 아득히, 오래; [장소가] 멀리 [usage] 구어에서는 의문문·부정문으로 쓰며, 긍정문에서는 a long way를 씀 **2.** 훨씬, 대단히

1) ***as*** (or ***so***) ***far as,*** to the distance, extent or degree that. ¶*walk as ~ as the river*① */ as ~ as I know.*②
2) ***by far,*** very much. ¶*by ~ the best.*③
3) ***far and away,*** very much.
4) ***far and near,*** everywhere.
5) ***far and wide,*** everywhere.
6) ***far be it from me*** (=*I do not want*) *to do.*
7) ***far from it,*** not in the least.
8) ***go far,*** be successful; accomplish a great deal.
9) ***How far...?,*** to what extent?; at what distance? ¶*How ~ can she be trusted?*④
10) ***so far,*** to the extent that; up to now.

[熟] 1)[장소가] …까지, [범위가] …한(限) ¶①강까지 걸어가다/②내가 아는 한 2)훨씬, 단연 ¶③최상의 것 3)훨씬, 단연 4)도처에 5)널리, 도처에, 두루 6)…할 생각은 추호도 없다 7)그런 일은 결코 없다 8)성공하다 9)[거리·정도가] 얼마인가? ¶④그녀를 어느만큼 신용할 수 있는가? 10)거기(여기)까지는

—*adj.* **1.** distant; not near; remote. ⇒[usage] ¶*a ~ country.* **2.** more distant of the two. ¶*The ~ side of the building was dark.* **3.** advanced. ¶*She is ~ on in years.*⑤

—[形] **1.** 먼 [usage] 구어에서는 특정한 구에만 명사 바로 앞에 씀 **2.** 보다 더 먼 **3.** 훨씬 앞선 ¶①그녀는 나이가 많다

far·a·way [fɑ́:rəwéi / ⌐–⌐] *adj.* **1.** distant; remote. ¶*~ places / ~ times.* **2.** dreamy; vague. ¶*a ~ look.*

—[形] **1.** 먼; 먼 옛날의 **2.** 꿈꾸는 듯한; 어렴풋한

farce [fɑ:rs] *n.* [C] **1.** a play intended merely to cause people to laugh. **2.** an absurd and useless affair.

—[名] **1.** 소극(笑劇); 광대극 **2.** 익살, 웃음거리, 우스꽝스러운 것

far·ci·cal [fɑ́:rsik(ə)l] *adj.* of or like a farce; absurd; ridiculous. ▷**far·ci·cal·ly** [-k(ə)li] *adv.*

—[形] 광대극의(같은); 우스꽝스러운; 익살맞은

‡fare [fɛər] *n.* **1.** [C] the money paid to ride on a train, car, bus, etc. ¶*I paid the taxi ~.* **2.** [C] a passenger.

—[名] **1.** 운임, 요금 **2.** 승객 **3.** 음식물 ¶①메뉴, 식단표

F

Far East [424] **fascination**

¶*There was only one ~ on the train.* **3.** Ⓤ food and drink. ¶*That was good ~. / a bill of ~.*①
—*vi.* **1.** get along; do. ¶*How did you ~ in Hawaii?* **2.** turn out; happen. (*~ with someone*) ⇒ⓤⓢⓐⓖⓔ ¶*~ well in business / It fared ill with them.*② **3.** eat food or be entertained. ¶*~ ill* (*well*). **4.** (*archaic*) go; journey. ¶*~ forth on one's travels.* 「China, India, etc.」
Far East [⌣ ⌣] *n.* the part of Asia that includes Japan,
: fare·well [fέərwél] *interj.* good-by.
—*n.* **1.** Ⓒ a salutation at parting. **2.** ⓊⒸ the act of parting. ¶*a sad ~*
bid (or *say*) *farewell to; bid farewell; take one's farewell of; make one's farewell to,* say good-by to (someone). 「*~ address.*②」
—*adj.* parting; last. ¶*a ~ kiss / a ~ party*① */ make a*
far·famed [fá:rfèimd] *adj.* widely-known; well-known.
far·fetched [fá:rfétʃt] *adj.* forced; unnatural.
far·flung [fá:rflʌ́ŋ] *adj.* widely-spread; extensive.
far·gone [fá:rgɔ́:n / -gɔ́n] *adj.* far advanced in a certain condition; very ill; very drunk; very much in debt.
: farm [fɑ:rm] *n.* Ⓒ **1.** a piece of land used to raise crops or animals, usu. plus a house and the other necessary buildings belonging to it. ¶*a dairy ~*① */ work* (*live*) *on a ~.*② **2.** a place like a farm. ¶*a chicken ~*③ */ an oyster ~.*④ **3.** a farm house.
—*vi.* raise crops or animals on a farm. ¶*My uncle is farming in Hokkaido.* —*vt.* cultivate. ¶*He farms 250 acres.* 「on a farm.」
: farm·er [fá:rmər] *n.* Ⓒ a person who owns or works
farm hand [⌣ ⌣] *n.* a person who works on someone else's farm. 「farm.」
· **farm·house** [fá:rmhàus] *n.* Ⓒ a dwelling house on a
farm·ing [fá:rmiŋ] *n.* Ⓤ the business or management of operating a farm; agriculture.
farm·stead [fá:rmstèd] *n.* (*Brit.*) Ⓒ a farm with its buildings.
farm·yard [fá:rmjà:rd] *n.* Ⓒ an area around farm buildings or enclosed by them.
far-off [fá:rɔ́:f / -ɔ́f] *adj.* remote; distant.
far-reach·ing [fá:rí:tʃiŋ] *adj.* **1.** extending far in influence or effect. **2.** extending a great distance.
far·ri·er [fǽriər] *n.* Ⓒ (*esp. Brit.*) **1.** a person who shoes horses. **2.** a horse doctor.
far·row [fǽrou] *n.* Ⓒ a family of baby pigs.
far·see·ing [fá:rsí:iŋ] *adj.* able to see far into the future.
far·sight·ed [fá:rsáitid] *adj.* **1.** able to see far; seeing distant objects more clearly than near objects. **2.** farseeing; well-planned. ▷**far-sight·ed·ly** [-li] *adv.*
: far·ther [fá:rðər] *adj.* compar. of **far**. **1.** more distant; or remoter. **2.** additional; more; further. ¶*until ~ notice.*① —*adv.* **1.** to or at a greater distance. **2.** to or at a more advanced point. **3.** in addition; moreover; also; further. 「tant; farthest.」
far·ther·most [fá:rðərmòust] *adj.* most remote or dis-
: far·thest [fá:rðist] *adj.* (superl. of **far**) most remote or distant. —*adv.* to or at the greatest distance.
far·thing [fá:rðiŋ] *n.* Ⓒ (*Brit.*) a coin worth a quarter of a penny.
fas·ci·nate [fǽsinèit] *vt.* **1.** (of snakes, etc.) hold (frogs, etc.) motionless or powerless by a fixed stare or through terror. **2.** charm or attract greatly.
fas·ci·nat·ing [fǽsinèitiŋ] *adj.* charming; enchanting. ▷**fas·ci·nat·ing·ly** [-li] *adv.*
fas·ci·na·tion [fæ̀sinéiʃ(ə)n, +*U.S.* fæ̀snéi-] *n.* Ⓤ **1.** the

—ⓐ 1.지내다, 살아가다 2.되어가다, …이 되다 ⓤⓢⓐⓖⓔ it를 주어로 함 ¶② 그들은 신통치 않았다(실패했다) 3. 먹다, 음식 대접을 받다 4.(古) 가다; 여행하다
—ⓝ 극동
—ⓘ 안녕!, 잘 가거라(있거라)!
—ⓝ 1.작별 인사 2.작별, 고별

🖼 …에게 작별을 고하다

「고별사(辭)를 말하다」
—ⓐ 작별의; 고별의 ¶①송별회/②
—ⓐ 널리 알려진; 유명한 「연한」
—ⓐ 억지로 갖다붙인, 억설의; 부자
—ⓐ 널리 퍼져 있는, 광범위한
—ⓐ [어떤 상태가] 퍽 진전된; 병세가 퍽 심해진; 몹시 취한; 빚이 늘어선
—ⓝ 1.농장, 농원 ¶①낙농장/②농장에서 일하다(살다) 2.사육장, 양식장 ¶③양계장/④굴 양식장 3.농가

—ⓥ 농사를 짓다, 농업을 하다
—ⓥ …을 경작하다

—ⓝ 농업(농장) 경영자; 농부, 농사꾼
—ⓝ 농장 노동자, 머슴

—ⓝ 농장에 있는 주택; 농가
—ⓝ 농장 경영; 농업

—ⓝ (英) 농장

—ⓝ 농가의 마당

—ⓐ 아득히 먼, 멀리 멀어진
—ⓐ 1.[효과·영향 따위가] 멀리까지 미치는, 원대한 2.널리 퍼지는
—ⓝ (英) 1.제철공(蹄鐵工) 2.말의사, 수의(獸醫)
—ⓝ 돼지의 한 배 새끼 「다보는」
—ⓐ 선견지명이 있는, 앞일을 잘 내
—ⓐ 1.먼데를 잘 보는; 원시안의 2.선견지명이 있는; 신중한

—ⓐ 1.더 먼, 더 저쪽의 2.그 위의, 그 이상의, 그밖의 ¶①추후 통지가 있을 때까지 —ⓐ 1.더 멀리 2.더 나아가서 3.그 위에, 게다가, 더우기

—ⓐ 가장 먼
—ⓐ 가장 먼 —ⓐ 가장 멀리, 훨씬 저쪽에
—ⓝ (英) 영국의 최소 화폐(1/4페니), 그 동전
—ⓥ 1.…을 움츠리게 하다, 노려보아 꼼짝못하게 하다 2.…의 넋을 빼앗다, 매혹시키다, 뇌쇄하다
—ⓐ 매혹적인, 황홀하게 하는, 요염한

—ⓝ 1.매혹; 황홀한 상태 2.매력; 매

act of fascinating; the state of being fascinated. **2.** very strong attraction; the power to fascinate; charm.
혹[력]

fas·cism [fǽʃiz(ə)m] *n.* [U] **1.** 《also *F-*》 a repressive system of government and society established in Italy under the leadership of Mussolini in 1922. **2.** any principles or methods like fascism.
—[名] **1.** 파시즘[이탈리아 국수당(國粹黨)의 주의] **2.** 파쇼적 지도정신; 국수주의

fas·cist [fǽʃist] *n.* [C] **1.** 《*F-*》 a member of the political party established by Mussolini. **2.** anyone who believes in fascism.
—[名] **1.** 이탈리아의 국수당원, 파시스트 **2.** 국수주의자, 파쇼

‡ fash·ion [fǽʃ(ə)n] *n.* **1.** [C][U] 《often *the* ~》 the accepted style or custom of a certain time, esp. in dress; the current mode or vogue. ¶*be in* (*out of*) ~① / *bring* (*something*) *into* ~② / *come into* ~③ / *go out of* ~④ / *lead* (or *set*) *the* ~.⑤ **2.** [C] a manner; a way. ¶*She walks in a peculiar* ~.⑥ / *I paint in my own* ~.⑦ **3.** 《*collectively*》 those people who act in accord with the current preferences of society; 《*the* ~》 the fashionable wórld.
—[名] **1.** 유행[형]; 유행 풍습, 패션 ¶①유행하고 있다(유행에 뒤떨어져 있다)/②…을 유행시키다/③유행하게 되다/④유행하지 않게 되다/⑤유행을 만들어내다 **2.** 양식, 방법, 형, 스타일 ¶⑥그녀는 이상한 모양으로 걷는다/⑦나는 내 나름대로 그림을 그린다 **3.** 사교(유행)계의 사람들; 상류사회

1) ***after*** (or ***in***) ***a fashion,*** in some manner; not very well; to some extent.
2) ***after the fashion*** (=*following the example*) ***of*** *something.*
3) ***be all the fashion,*** (of a way of dressing, a custom, etc.) be very popular.
[熟] 1)어느 정도, 그럭저럭 2)…에 따라서, …식으로 3)대단한 인기다

—*vt.* **1.** form; shape. ¶~ *a doll from a piece of wood.* **2.** fit. 《~ someone *to*》 ¶~ *a student to modern ideas.*
—[他] **1.** …을 만들다, 형성하다 **2.** …을 적응시키다, 적합하게 하다

• fash·ion·a·ble [fǽʃ(ə)nəbl] *adj.* **1.** in accord with the current style; in fashion; up-to-date. **2.** used by rich, elegant people.
—[形] **1.** 유행의, 현대식의 **2.** 상류사회의

fash·ion·a·bly [fǽʃ(ə)nəbli] *adv.* in a fashionable manner.
—[副] 유행에 따라서, 현대식으로

‡ fast[1] [fæst / fɑːst] *adj.* **1.** quick; rapid. ↔slow **2.** (of a clock or watch) showing a time ahead of the correct time. ¶*My watch is two minutes* ~. **3.** firmly fixed. ↔loose ¶*take* [*a*] ~ *hold of something.*① **4.** not losing color; unfading. **5.** not changing one's mind; loyal. ¶*a* ~ *friend.* **6.** wild.
—[形] **1.** 빠른, 날랜 **2.** [시계가] 빠른, 더 가는 **3.** 단단한, 정착한, 움직이지 않는 ¶①무엇을 꽉(단단히) 쥐다 **4.** [색깔이] 바래지 않는 **5.** 성실한; 충실한 **6.** 방탕한; 방종한

—*adv.* **1.** firmly; fixedly. **2.** soundly. ¶*The child is* ~ *asleep.* **3.** quickly; rapidly **4.** wildly. ¶*live* ~.②
—[副] **1.** 단단히, 굳게 **2.** [잠이] 깊게, 푹 **3.** 빠르게, 날래게 **4.** 방탕(방종)하게 ¶①방탕한 생활을 하다

play fast and loose, say one thing and do another.
[熟] 이랬다저랬다하다, 언행이 일치하지 않다

fast[2] [fæst / fɑːst] *vi., vt.* eat no food for a time, esp. as a religious duty. ¶~ *on bread and water*① / ~ *an illness off.*② —*n.* [C] **1.** the act of fasting. **2.** a day or period of fasting.
—[自][他] 단식하다, 절식하다, 정진(精進)하다 ¶①빵과 물만으로 정진 생활을 하다/②절식하여 병을 고치다 —[名] **1.** 단식 **2.** 단식일, 단식 기간

break one's fast, take a meal for the first time after fasting; eat breakfast.
[熟] 단식을 그치다; 조반을 만들다

‡ fas·ten [fǽsn / fɑ́ːsn] *vt.* **1.** fix or attach firmly; tie. **2.** shut; close. ¶*I fastened the front door.* **3.** direct; fix. 《~ something *upon*》 ¶~ *one's eyes on* (or *upon*) *her face* / *We fixed the nickname upon him.* —*vi.* become fast. ¶*The door didn't* ~.
—[他] **1.** …을 단단히 고정시키다, 꽉 동여매다 **2.** …을 닫다, 잠그나 **3.** …을 향하게 하다; [시선 따위를] …에 쏟다 —[自] 잠기다; 닫히다

fasten something up, close something and make it fast; tie firmly.
[熟] …을 꽉 폐쇄하다; 단단히 동여매다

fas·ten·er [fǽsnər / fɑ́ːsnə] *n.* [C] **1.** a person who fastens. **2.** a thing used to fasten a door, a garment, etc.
—[名] **1.** 잠그는 사람 **2.** 잠그는 물건, 걸쇠, 죔쇠, 척(chuck)

fas·ten·ing [fǽsniŋ / fɑ́ːsniŋ] *n.* [C] a thing used to fasten, such as a lock, a bolt, or a clasp.
—[名] 잠그는(걸어매는) 것(걸쇠·빗장·자물쇠 따위)

fas·tid·i·ous [fæstídiəs] *adj.* hard to please; very careful; very critical. ¶*She is* ~ *about her clothes.*
—[形] 가리는 것이 많은, 까다로운, 괴팍스러운; 몹시 비판적인

fas·tid·i·ous·ly [fæstídiəsli] *adv.* in a fastidious manner.
—[副] 괴까다롭게, 괴팍스럽게

fast·ness [fǽstnis / fɑ́ːst-] *n.* [U] **1.** a strong, secure place; a fortress. **2.** the quality or state of being fast.
—[名] **1.** 요새, 성채 **2.** 견고함, 고정; 신속

‡ fat [fæt] *n.* [U] **1.** the oily white or yellow part of meat. **2.** the richest part of anything. ¶*live on the* ~ *of the land.*①
—[名] **1.** 비계; 지방(脂肪) **2.** 가장 좋은 부분, 알짜 ¶①호화롭게 살다

—*adj.* (**fat·ter, fat·test**) **1.** having a lot of fat; fleshy. ↔lean ¶*get* ~.② **2.** thick; well-filled; rich. ¶*a* ~ *purse.* **3.** oily; greasy. **4.** productive; fertile.
—[形] **1.** 살찐, 뚱뚱한, ¶②살찌다 **2.** 부푼, 풍만(풍요)한 **3.** 기름진 **4.** [땅이] 비옥한

a fat lot, (*colloq.*) not at all. ¶*A* ~ *lot you care!*③
[熟] 《口》 조금도 …않는 ¶③조금도 걱정해 주지 않으면서 !

F

—*vt.* make (someone or something) fat. —*vi.* become fat.
—[他] …을 살찌우다 —[自] 살찌다

* **fa·tal** [féitl] *adj.* **1.** causing death or ruin. ¶ *~ accidents* / *a ~ disease* / *The wound proved ~ to him.*① **2.** decisive; fateful. ¶ *The ~ day arrived at last.*
—[形] **1.** 생명에 관계되는, 치명적인; 파멸적인 ¶①그 상처가 그의 치명상이 되었다 **2.** 숙명의

fa·tal·ism [féitəliz(ə)m] *n.* [U] the belief that everything is determined or controlled by fate.
—[名] 숙명론, 운명론

fa·tal·ist [féitəlist] *n.* [C] a person who believes in fatalism.
—[名] 숙명론자, 운명론자

fa·tal·is·tic [fèitəlístik] *adj.* of or based on fatalism.
—[形] 숙명론적인, 숙명적인

fa·tal·i·ty [feitǽliti, fə-] *n.* (pl. **-ties**) **1.** [C] a fatal accident; a misfortune **2.** [U] the condition or state of being fated; the inevitable course of destiny. **3.** [C] death in war or as a result of an accident or a disaster; [U] a person killed in an accident or a disaster.
—[名] **1.** [숙명적인] 불행, 재난, 참사 **2.** 인과, 운명, 숙명 **3.** [전쟁·사고 따위로 말미암은] 죽음, 사망자

fa·tal·ly [féitəli] *adv.* in a fatal manner; according to fate.
—[副] 치명적으로, 불운하게; 숙명적으로, 필연적으로

‡ **fate** [feit] *n.* [U] **1.** the power supposed to guide all events beyond any person's control. **2.** death; ruin. **3.** 《*the Fates*》 (in Greek mythology) the three Goddesses of destiny. ⇒[N.B.]
1) ***as sure as fate,*** certainly.
2) ***meet one's fate,*** die.
—[名] **1.** 숙명, 운명, 운 **2.** 죽음, 파멸 **3.** 운명의 여신 [N.B.] 생명의 실을 잣는 Cloths, 그 실을 재는 Lachesis, 그 실을 끊는 Atropos의 세 신
[熟] 1)확실히, 반드시 2)죽다

fat·ed [féitid] *adj.* **1.** controlled by fate. **2.** destined, esp. to destruction.
—[形] **1.** 숙명적인 **2.** 운이 다한, 파멸의 운명에 놓인

fate·ful [féitf(u)l] *adj.* **1.** controlled by fate. **2.** having important results; decisive. **3.** causing death.
—[形] **1.** 숙명적인 **2.** 중대한; 결정적인 **3.** 치명적인

fate·ful·ly [féitfuli] *adv.* in a fateful manner.
—[副] 숙명적으로, 결정적으로

‡ **fa·ther** [fɑ́:ðər] *n.* [C] **1.** a man parent; 《often *F-*》 one's own father. **2.** a man like a father. ¶ *He was a ~ to the weak.* **3.** a founder; an important leader. ¶ *the ~ of our school.* **4.** 《often *F-*》 a priest, esp. one who belongs to a certain order in the church; a title of such a man; the head of a monastery. **5.** 《*Our F-*》 God.
—[名] **1.** 아버지; 부친 **2.** 아버지 같은 사람 **3.** 창시자; 창도자 **4.** 신부[의 직함], 수도원장 **5.** 신, 하나님 아버지

—*adj.* **1.** that is a father. ¶ *a ~ bird.* **2.** of or like a father. ¶ *~ love.* **3.** native.
—[形] **1.** 아버지인 **2.** 아버지의, 아버지 같은 **3.** 조국의

—*vt.* **1.** be the father of (someone); care for (someone) as a father. **2.** create; invent.
—[他] **1.** …의 아버지이다; 아버지로서 …을 부양하다 **2.** …을 창조하다; 발명하다

fa·ther·hood [fɑ́:ðərhùd] *n.* [U] the state of being a father.
—[名] 아버지임

fa·ther-in-law [fɑ́:ðərinlɔ̀:] *n.* [C] (pl. **fa·thers-**) the father of one's husband or wife.
—[名] 장인; 시아버지

fa·ther·land [fɑ́:ðərlæ̀nd] *n.* [C] a person's native country.
—[名] 조국

fa·ther·less [fɑ́:ðərlis] *adj.* without a father living.
—[形] 아버지가 없는

fa·ther·ly [fɑ́:ðərli] *adj.* **1.** of a father. **2.** like a father; kindly. ▷**fa·ther·li·ness** [-nis] *n.*
—[形] **1.** 아버지의 **2.** 아버지다운, 자애로운

fath·om [fǽðəm] *n.* [C] (pl. **fath·oms** or *collectively* **fath·om**) a unit of measure equal to 6 feet, used in measuring the depth of water. —*vt.* **1.** measure the depth of (water). **2.** reach the bottom of (something); understand completely.
—[名] 길(6피이트) —[他] **1.** [물의] 깊이를 재다 **2.** …의 밑바닥까지 닿다; …의 속을 헤아리다; …을 납득하다

fath·om·less [fǽðəmlis] *adj.* too deep to be measured; not easily understood; incomprehensible.
—[形] 잴 수 없는, 깊이를 알 수 없는; 이해할 수 없는, 불가해한

* **fa·tigue** [fətí:g] *n.* [U] **1.** the state of being very tired; weariness. **2.** the cause of weariness; labor. **3.** a condition of weakening in metal, wood, etc. after long strain or use. **4.** [C] (in the army, etc.) the work of cleaning, cooking, etc. —*vt.* make (someone) weary; tire. ¶ *I am fatigued with my long journey.*①
—[名] **1.** [심신의] 피로 **2.** 피로의 원인, 노고, 노역(勞役) **3.** [금속·목재 따위의] 약화(弱化) **4.** [군무(軍務) 이외의] 잡역, 작업 —[他] …을 피로하게 하다 ¶①나는 오랜 여행에 지쳤다

fat·ten [fǽtn] *vt.* make (someone) fat. —*vi.* become fat.
—[他] …을 살찌게 하다 —[自] 살찌다

fat·tish [fǽtiʃ] *adj.* rather or somewhat fat.
—[形] 좀 살찐, 약간 뚱뚱한

fat·ty [fǽti] *adj.* (**-ti·er**, **-ti·est**) of fat; containing fat; like fat. ▷**fat·ti·ness** [-nis] *n.*
—[形] 지방질의, 지방이 많은; 지방 같은, 지방 모양의

fa·tu·i·ty [fət(j)ú:iti / fətjú(:)i-] *n.* [U] (pl. **-ties**) the state of being foolish; stupidity; foolishness; [C] an example of foolishness, etc.
—[名] 어리석음, 우둔; 어리석은 언동

fat·u·ous [fǽtʃuəs / -tju-] *adj.* foolish but self-satisfied; silly; foolish.
—[形] 어리석은, 얼빠진

faucet [fɔ́:sit] *n.* ⓒ an instrument containing a valve for controlling the flow of liquid from a pipe, a cask, etc.

—ⓝ [통 따위의] 물꼭지, 마개

‡**fault** [fɔ:lt] *n.* ⓒ **1.** a mistake. ¶ *There are a lot of faults in your composition.* **2.** a bad part; a weak point in one's character. ¶ *Carelessness is his ~.* **3.** (*sing.* only) blame; responsibility. ¶ *It's not your ~.*① **4.** (in tennis, etc.) a failure to serve the ball correctly.
1) *be at fault*, not know what to do next; be at a loss.
2) *find fault with* (=*try to find the bad point of*) *someone* or *something*.
3) *to a fault*, too much; excessively.

—ⓝ 1. 잘못, 과실 ; 실수 2. 결점, 흠 ; 약점 3. [과실의] 책임 ¶①그것은 너의 잘못은 아니다 4. [정구 따위에서] 서어브의 실수

圈 1)어찌 할 바를 모르다, 당황하다 2)…의 흠을 잡다 3)지나치게, 극단으로

fault-find·er [fɔ́:ltfàində*r*] *n.* ⓒ a tiresome person who likes to criticize.

—ⓝ 흠잡는 사람, 잔소리꾼

fault·find·ing [fɔ́:ltfàindiŋ] *adj., n.* Ⓤ [the act of] finding fault or criticizing.

—圈ⓝ 흠잡는 ; 흠잡기, 트집잡기

fault·i·ly [fɔ́:ltili] *adv.* in a faulty manner.

—圖 실수하여 ; 불완전하게

fault·less [fɔ́:ltlis] *adj.* having no fault at all; perfect.
fault·less·ly [fɔ́:ltlisli] *adv.* in a faultless manner; perfectly.

—圈 과실이 없는 ; 완전무결한
—圖 과실이 없이, 완전히

fault·y [fɔ́:lti] *adj.* (**fault·i·er, fault·i·est**) having faults; wrong; imperfect. ▷**fault·i·ness** [-nis] *n.*

—圈 과실이 있는, 잘못된, 불완전한

faun [fɔ:n] *n.* ⓒ (in Roman mythology) a spirit of the woods, with a goat's horns, feet and pointed ears, that helped farmers and shepherds. ⇒fig.

—ⓝ 포온 [숲·목축의 신으로 반인반양 (半人半羊)]

fau·na [fɔ́:nə] *n.* ⓒ (pl. **-nas** or collectively **-nae**) all the animals found in a certain region or period.

—ⓝ [한 지방 또는 한 시대의] 동물군(群), 동물구계(區系)

fau·nae [fɔ́:ni] *n.* pl. of **fauna**.

Faust [faust] *n.* (in German legends) a man who sold his soul to the devil in return for power and knowledge.

—ⓝ 파우스트 (Goethe 작 비극의 주인공)

[faun]

‡**fa·vor,** *Brit.* **-vour** [féivə*r*] *n.* **1.** ⓒⓊ [an act of] kindness; special will. ¶ *treat someone with ~.* **2.** ⓒⓊ an approval; a consent; an agreement. ¶ *grant someone a ~ | May I ask a ~ of you?*① **3.** Ⓤ special kindness to a particular person. ¶ *win the ~ of someone | She was in high ~ with the king.*② **4.** ⓒ a small gift [given as a love token].
—*vt.* **1.** agree to (something); approve. ¶ *I ~ your opinion.* **2.** show a special kindness to (a particular person); prefer unfairly. ¶ *A teacher should not ~ one pupil over others in her class.*③ **3.** help ; aid ; assist. ¶ *Fortune favors the brave.* **4.** do a kindness to (someone); oblige. (*~ someone with*) ¶ *Will you ~ me with a song?*④ **5.** (*colloq.*) resemble (someone) in looks.

—ⓝ 1. 친절, 호의 2. 허가 ; 동의, 찬성 ¶①한 가지 부탁이 있는데요 3. 총애 ; 편애 ¶②그녀는 왕의 두터운 총애를 받았다 4. 선물, [애정의 표시로 주는] 작은 기념품
—他 1. …에 찬성하다 2. …을 편애하다 ; 편들다 ¶③선생은 학급내의 특정한 아동을 편애해서는 안 된다 3. …을 도와주다 ; …을 두둔하다 (편들다) 4. …을 친절히 대하다 5. …을 닮다

•**fa·vor·a·ble,** *Brit.* **-vour-** [féiv(ə)rəbl] *adj.* **1.** favoring ; approving. **2.** affording convenience ; suitable ; helpful. ¶ *a ~ wind.* **3.** promising.

—圈 1. 호의적인, 승낙하는 2. 형편 좋은, …에 알맞은, 도움이 되는 3. 유망한

fa·vor·a·bly, *Brit.* **-vour-** [féivərəbli] *adv.* in a favorable manner.

—圖 형편 좋게 ; 유망하게 ; 호의를 가지고, 친절히

fa·vored, *Brit.* **-voured** [féivə*r*d] *adj.* **1.** treated with favor ; with special advantages. ¶ *the most-favored-nation clause.*① **2.** (often in *compounds*) with a certain appearance. ¶ *hard-favored*② *| well-favored.*③

—圈 1. 혜택을 받은, 행운의 ¶①최혜국조관(最惠國條款) (국제법) 2. 용모가 …한 ¶②무서운 얼굴을 한/③용모가 아름다운

fa·vor·ite, *Brit.* **-vour-** [féivə*r*it] *adj.* liked above all others. ¶ *one's ~ daughter.*① —*n.* ⓒ **1.** a person or thing liked above all others. ¶ *fortune's ~*② */ be a ~ with someone.*③ **2.** a person, a horse, etc. expected to win.

—圈 마음에 드는, 총애하는 ¶①총애하는 딸 —ⓝ 1. 마음에 든 (인기 있는) 사람 (것) ; 총아 ; 좋아하는 것 ¶②행운아/③…에게 인기가 있다 2. [경마의] 인기있는 말, [경기의] 인기있는 선수

fa·vor·it·ism, *Brit.* **-vour-** [féivəritìz(ə)m] *n.* Ⓤ the act of favoring one person or group above all others ; partiality.

—ⓝ 편애

‡**fa·vour** [féivə*r*] *n.* (*Brit.*) =favor.

fawn¹ [fɔ:n] *n.* **1.** ⓒ a deer less than one year old. **2.**

—ⓝ 1. 새끼사슴 2. 엷은 황갈색

fawn

Ⓤ a light, yellowish brown color. —*adj.* light yellowish-brown. —*vi.* (of a deer) bear a fawn.
* **fawn**² [fɔːn] *vi.* **1.** seek favor by acting slavishly. 《~ *on* or *up* someone》 **2.** (of dogs, etc.) show fondness by moving the tail. 《~ *on* or *upon* someone》
fay [fei] *n.* Ⓒ (*poetic*) a fairy.
fe·al·ty [fíː(ə)lti] *n.* (pl. **-ties**) Ⓤ **1.** loyalty to one's ruler. **2.** (*poetic*) loyalty ; faithfulness.
: **fear** [fiər] *n.* Ⓤ **1.** a feeling caused by danger; terror; dread. ¶ *the ~ of death.* **2.** anxiety; uneasiness; Ⓒ that which one fears. ¶ *I feel no ~ for my future.* **3.** awe ; great respect. ¶ *a ~ of God.*
   for fear of something ; *for fear* [*that*] ... *should* (or *might*) *do*, lest ... should do; so as not to do.
   —*vt.* **1.** be afraid of ; be frightened by (something). 《~ [*that*] ...》 **2.** have great respect for (God, etc.).
* **fear·ful** [fíərf(u)l] *adj.* **1.** terrible ; dreadful. ¶ *a ~ accident.* **2.** full of fear ; afraid. ¶ *He was ~ of the consequences.*
fear·ful·ly [fíərf(ə)li] *adv.* in a fearful manner; very much. ¶ *I am ~ busy now.*①
* **fear·less** [fíərlis] *adj.* without fear ; brave. ▷ **fear·less·ly**
fear·some [fíərsəm] *adj.* **1.** frightful ; horrible ; terrifying. **2.** afraid ; timid. ▷ **fear·some·ly** [-li] *adv.*
fea·si·bil·i·ty [fìːzəbíliti] *n.* Ⓤ the quality of being feasible.
fea·si·ble [fíːzibl] *adj.* **1.** capable of being done or carried out ; possible ; practicable. ¶ *a ~ plan.* **2.** likely ; probable. ¶ *a ~ rumor.* **3.** suitable ; convenient. ¶ *a road ~ for driving.* ▷ **fea·si·bly** [-i] *adv.*
: **feast** [fiːst] *n.* Ⓒ **1.** a rich and plentiful meal for some special occasion ; a banquet. **2.** anything pleasant ; a delight ; a pleasure. **3.** a festival, esp. a religious festival or anniversary. —*vi.* have a feast. —*vt.* **1.** entertain (someone) with a rich meal. **2.** give pleasure to (something). ¶ *~ one's ears with good music*① / *~ one's eyes on rare books.* ▷ **feast·er** [-ər] *n.*
* **feat** [fiːt] *n.* Ⓒ **1.** a great deed done by extraordinary skill, strength, etc.; a remarkable act. ¶ *a ~ of arms.*①
: **feath·er** [féðər] *n.* Ⓒ **1.** one of the light coverings which grow on a bird's skin; 《*collectively*》 the feathers of a bird. ¶ *as light as a ~*① / (*proverb*) *Birds of a ~ flock together.*② / *Fine feathers make fine birds.*③ **2.** 《*collectively*》 birds, esp. game birds. ¶ *fur and ~.*④ **3.** anything light like a feather.
   1) *crop someone's feathers,* humble someone's pride.
   2) *do not care a feather,* do not care a bit.
   3) *a feather in one's cap* (or *hat*), something to be proud of ; an honor. 「humor; in high spirits.」
   4) *in fine* (or *good, high*) *feather,* in very good
   5) *in full feather,* ⓐ with all the feathers grown. ⓑ in full dress. ⓒ in high spirits. 「coward.」
   6) *show the white feather,* show signs of being a
   —*vt.* **1.** cover or adorn (something) with feathers. **2.** make (an oar) go flat over the face of water. —*vi.* grow feathers. 「one else's expense.」
   feather one's nest, make oneself rich, usu. at some-
feather bed [-∠-∠] *n.* a mattress that is filled with feathers.
feath·er·weight [féðərwèit] *n.* Ⓒ **1.** a very light or unimportant person or thing. **2.** a boxer who weighs between 118 and 126 pounds.
feath·er·y [féðəri] *adj.* (sometimes **-er·i·er**, **-er·i·est**) **1.** covered with feathers. **2.** soft like feathers.
: **fea·ture** [fíːtʃər] *n.* Ⓒ **1.** a part of the face, such as the

feature

—❀ 엷은 황갈색의 —⊕ [사슴이] 새끼를 낳다
—⽬ **1.** 아첨하다, 알랑거리다, 머리굽히다 **2.** [개 따위가] 꼬리를 흔들며 매달리다
—⊕ 《詩》 요정(妖精)
—⊕ **1.** [영주에 대한] 충성; 의무 **2.** 신의(信義), 성실
—⊕ **1.** 두려움 ; 공포 **2.** 근심, 걱정, 불안 ; 걱정거리 **3.** [특히 신에 대한] 두려움, 외경(畏敬) ; 숭상(崇尙)

🔲 ...하지 않도록

—⊕ **1.** ...을 두려워하다 ; 걱정하다 **2.** 외구(畏懼)하다 ; 숭상하다
—❀ **1.** 무서운, 무시무시한 **2.** 두려워하는, 염려(근심)하는

—⊕ 무서워하며, 벌벌 떨며 ; 대단히, 굉장히 ①지금 굉장히 바쁘다
—❀ 겁내지 않는 ; 대담한
—❀ **1.** 무서운, 무시무시한 **2.** 무서워하는, 겁내는 ; 벌벌 떠는
—⊕ 가능성, 실행할 수 있음
—❀ **1.** 실행할 수 있는, 가능성이 있는 **2.** 그럴 듯한 **3.** 알맞은, 편리한

—⊕ **1.** 향연, 잔치, 연회 **2.** [귀·눈을] 즐겁게 하는 것, 환락 **3.** [특히 종교상의] 축제일, 축일, 기념제, 제례(祭禮)
—⽬ 성찬을 먹다 —⊕ **1.** ...에게 성찬을 대접하다 **2.** [귀·눈을] 즐겁게 하다 ①음악을 듣고 귀를 즐겁게 하다

—❀ 공적, 업적 ; 뛰어난 재주, 묘기 ¶ ①무공, 무훈
—⊕ **1.** 깃 ; 깃털 ¶①아주 가벼운/②《俚》유유상종(類類相從)/《俚》③옷이 날개 **2.** 새, 조류, [특히] 엽조(獵鳥) ¶④[사냥용] 짐승과 새 **3.** 깃털같이 가벼운 것

🔲 1)...의 오만한 콧대를 꺾어 주다 2) 털끝만치도 개의하지 않다 3) 자랑거리, 영광이 되는 것 ; 명예 4) 신바람이 나서 ; 원기왕성하여 5)ⓐ[새가] 깃털이 다 자란 ⓑ성장(盛裝)하여 ⓒ원기왕성하여 6) 겁을 내다, 꽁무니를 빼다

—⊕ **1.** ...을 깃털로 덮다(장식하다) **2.** [노]를 수평으로 젖히다
—⽬ 깃털이 나다(자라다)
🔲 사복을 채우다
—⊕ 깃털을 넣은 요

—⊕ **1.** 매우 가벼운 사람(것) ; 하찮은 사람(것) **2.** [권투의] 페더급 선수

—⊕ **1.** 깃털이 난, 깃털로 덮인 **2.** 깃털처럼 부드러운
—⊕ **1.** 얼굴의 한 부분(눈·코·

eyes, the nose, the mouth, etc. **2.** ⦅*pl.*⦆ the face. **3.** a characteristic or distinct part that attracts attention. **4.** (*U. S.*) a long, principal, motion picture. **5.** a prominent, special item in a newspaper, magazine, etc.; a popular program on the radio or on television. ¶*make a ~ of (something).*① **—*vt.*** **1.** portray or make the features of (something); emphasize. **2.** present (someone) as the star actor or actress.

귀 따위) 2. 용모, 얼굴 생김새 3. 특징, 특색, 욧점 4. ⦅美⦆ 특작(장편) 영화 5. 특종(특집)기사; 인기 프로 ¶①…을 인깃거리로 하다
—[他] 1. …의 특징을 그리다; …을 인깃거리로 하다; …을 두드러지게 하다 2. …을 주연(主演)시키다

fea·ture·less [fíːtʃərlis] *adj.* without characteristic features; not impressive.
—[形] 특색이 없는; 신기할 것 없는

Feb. February.

⁑ **Feb·ru·ar·y** [fébruèri / -ruəri] *n.* the second month of the year. ⇒[N.B.]
—[名] 2월 [N.B.] Feb.로 줄여 씀

feck·less [féklis] *adj.* spiritless; weak; of no use.
—[形] 무기력한; 약한; 쓸모없는

fe·cund [fíːkənd, fékʌnd] *adj.* productive; fruitful.
—[形] 다산(多産)의; [토지가] 기름진

fe·cun·di·ty [fi(ː)kʌ́nditi] *n.* [U] the quality of being fecund.
—[名] 다산성; 비옥

⁑ **fed** [fed] *v.* pt. and pp. of **feed**.

* **fed·er·al** [fédər(ə)l] *adj.* **1.** of or based upon federation, esp. between nations or states. **2.** ⦅usu. *F-*⦆ (*U.S.*) of or supporting the central government as opposed to the individual governments of the separate states. ¶*The Federal Bureau of Investigation.*①
—[形] 1. 연합(동맹)의 2. ⦅美⦆ 연방의, 연방정부의 ¶①[미국의] 연방 수사국(FBI로 줄여 씀)

fed·er·ate *vi., vt.* [fédərèit → *adj.*] unite into a federation. **—*adj.*** [fédərit] united into a federation.
—[自][他] [···을] 연합하다(시키다) —[形] 동맹의, 연합한

* **fed·er·a·tion** [fèdəréiʃ(ə)n] *n.* **1.** [U] the act of federating; [C] a political unity composed of a number of separate states, etc. ¶*the Federation of Labor.*① **2.** a group of nations united into a league.
—[名] 1. 연맹, 연합, 동맹 ¶①노동 총동맹 2. 연방[정부]

* **fee** [fiː] *n.* [C] **1.** money paid for a service or for a right to do something. ¶*an admission ~*① / *school fees.*② **2.** tip. **3.** [U] the right to keep and use land.
—*vt.* give a fee or tip to (someone).
—[名] 1. 사례, 입회금, 수수료 ¶①입장료/②수업료 2. 팁, 행하(行下) 3. 영대차지권(永代借地權)
—[他] 요금을 지불하다, 사례하다

* **fee·ble** [fíːbl] *adj.* (**-bler, -blest**) lacking strength, distinctness, brightness, etc.; weak. ¶*a ~ voice (light).*①
—[形] 약한, 불명료한, 희미한, 가냘픈 ¶①가냘픈 목소리(희미한 빛)

fee·bly [fíːbli] *adv.* in a feeble manner.
—[副] 약하게, 미약하게, 힘없이, 가냘프게

fee·ble-mind·ed [fíːblmáindid] *adj.* lacking normal mental powers or firmness of mind.
—[形] 의지가 박약한, 정신 박약의, 저능의

⁑ **feed** [fiːd] *v.* (**fed**) *vt.* **1.** give food to (a baby or an animal). ¶*~ children / It's time to ~ horses.* **2.** give (something) as food. ¶*~ corn to horses.* **3.** supply. ⦅~ something *with* water, oil, coal, etc.⦆ ¶*~ the engine with gasoline.*① **—*vi.*** eat food.
***feed (=live) on** something.* ¶*We Japanese ~ on rice.*
—*n.* [U] **1.** food for animals. **2.** [C] an act of feeding.
—[他] 1. …에 먹이(모이)를 주다, 음식을 먹이다 2. …을 먹이(음식)로서 주다 3. …을 공급하다 ¶①엔진에 급유(給油)하다
—[自] 먹이(음식)를 먹다
[熟] …을 먹이(주식)로 하다
—[名] 1. 먹이, 사료 2. 사육(飼育); 공급

feed·er [fíːdər] *n.* [C] **1.** a person or an animal that feeds. **2.** a device supplying material or fuel to a machine. **3.** a stream flowing into the main river; a branch railway, airline, etc. **4.** a baby's feeding bottle.
—[名] 1. 먹는 사람(짐승), 사육자, 공급자 2. [기계의] 공급 장치 3. [강의] 지류; [철도·항공의] 지선(支線) 4. [유아용] 젖병

feeding bottle [ˊ-- ˋ-] *n.* a bottle from which babies are given milk; a feeder.
—[名] [유아용] 젖병

⁑ **feel** [fiːl] *v.* (**felt**) *vt.* **1.** touch; know or find (something) by touching. ⦅~ *whether* (or *how*, etc.)…⦆ ¶*The doctor felt Bill's pulse. / Feel how cold the water is.*① **2.** know (something) through the senses. ⦅~ someone or something *do* or *doing*⦆ ¶*~ the cold (the heat) / Did you ~ the earthquake? / I felt someone gazing at me. / We felt the ground sinking.* **3.** have a sense of; be moved by (something). ¶*I don't ~ much pity for him.*② **4.** think. ⦅~ *that*…; ~ someone or something *to do*⦆ **—*vi.*** **1.** have a sense of being; be. ¶*Both of them felt comfortable.* **2.** give a sense of being. ¶*Velvet feels smooth.*③ **3.** search by touching. ⦅~ *for* something⦆ ¶*I felt in my pocket for a coin.* **4.** have sympathy with someone. ⦅~ *for* someone⦆ ¶*I felt for her deeply.*
—[他] 1. …을 만져보다; …을 만져보고 알다(찾아내다); 더듬다 ¶①물이 얼마나 찬지 만져보아라 2. …을 느끼다, 감지(感知)하다 3. …에 감동하다; 마음속으로 …을 느끼다 ¶②그가 그다지 불쌍하다고는 생각지 않는다 4. …이라고 생각하다 —[自] 1. 느낌(감각)이 있다; …하다 2. […한] 느낌이 들다 ¶③우단은 매끄럽다 3. 더듬어 찾다 4. 동정하다, 가엾게 여기다

feeler [430] **fellowship**

1) *feel as if* (or *though*), have the impression that... ¶*She felt as if her head were* (or *was*) *burning.*①
2) *feel for*, search for (something) blindly with the hand.
3) *feel like*, want; wish. ¶*I don't ~ like eating now.*①
4) *feel up to* (=*feel fit for*) something, (*colloq.*). ¶*~ up to a long walk.*
—*n.* ⓒ (usu. *the ~*) 1. the act of feeling. 2. the sense of touch.

feel·er [fí:lər] *n.* ⓒ 1. a specialized organ for touching on an animal's body, esp. an insect's antenna. 2. a proposal, a hint, etc. made in order to find out the opinions or plans of others.

‡ **feel·ing** [fí:liŋ] *n.* 1. ⓤⓒ the condition of touching; the power of physical sensation. ¶*a ~ of joy* (*sadness*).① 2. ⓤⓒ the sense of touch. 3. ⓤ an emotion; emotional excitement. ¶*with ~.*② 4. ⓤ sympathy; pity. ¶*show a ~ for the poor.*③ 5. ⓒ an opinion. ¶*What's your ~ about this idea?*④ 6. ⓤ understanding; sensibility. ¶*She has a keen ~ for beauty.* 7. (*pl.*) emotions; sensibilities. ¶*a man of feelings*④ / *enter into someone's feelings.*⑤
—*adj.* sensitive; emotional; sympathetic.

feel·ing·ly [fí:liŋli] *adv.* in a manner showing strong feeling; with emotion.

‡ **feet** [fi:t] *n.* pl. of **foot**.

feign [fein] *vt.* 1. pretend. (*~ that...*) ¶*~ illness*① / *He feigned himself* [*to be*] *mad.*; *He feigned that he was mad.* 2. make up (something) to deceive. ¶*~ an excuse.*

feint [feint] *n.* ⓒ 1. a false appearance. ¶*Jack made a ~ of working hard.* 2. (*Boxing, Fencing*) a pretended blow. —*vi.* (*Boxing, Fencing*) make a pretended blow.

feld·spar [féld)spɑ̀:r] *n.* ⓤⓒ any of several white or light-red minerals. ⇒N.B.

fe·lic·i·tate [filísiteit] *vt.* congratulate; express good wishes to someone. (*~ someone on* or *upon*)

fe·lic·i·ta·tion [filìsitéiʃ(ə)n] *n.* ⓤ congratulation; (usu. *pl.*) an expression of good wishes.

fe·lic·i·tous [filísitəs] *adj.* (of words, etc.) well-chosen; appropriate. ¶*a ~ remark* (*quotation*).

fe·lic·i·ty [filísiti] *n.* (pl. **-ties**) 1. ⓤ happiness; good fortune. 2. ⓤ a pleasing aptness in expression; ⓒ a well-chosen expression.

fe·line [fí:lain] *adj.* 1. belonging to the cat family. 2. catlike; sly; stealthy. —*n.* ⓒ any animal belonging to the cat family, such as a lion, a tiger or a leopard.

‡ **fell**¹ [fel] *vi.* pt. of **fall**.

fell² [fel] *vt.* knock down; cut down (a tree).
—*n.* ⓒ all the trees cut down in one season.

fell³ [fel] *adj.* 1. cruel; terrible. 2. deadly; destructive.

fell⁴ [fel] *n.* ⓤ an animal's skin with the hair.

fel·loe [félou] *n.* ⓒ the circular edge of the framework of a wheel. ⇒N.B.

‡ **fel·low** [félou, félə] *n.* ⓒ 1. (often *pl.*) a companion; an associate; a partner. ¶*fellows in arms.*① 2. (*colloq.*) a man or boy; a person. ¶*My dear ~.*② / *Poor ~!*③ / *He is not a bad ~.* 3. a person of the same class or rank; an equal. ¶*I never saw his ~.*④ 4. one of a pair. ¶*Where is the ~ of this glove?* 5. a graduate student who is given money to continue his studies, often with teaching duties. 6. (*F-*) an honored member of a learned society. ¶*a Fellow of the British Academy.*⑤
—*adj.* belonging to the same class or group; having a similar background. ¶*~ workers* / *a ~ student.*

fellow feeling [⌣ ⌣⌣] *n.* sympathy.

· **fel·low·ship** [félouʃìp] *n.* 1. ⓤ companionship; friendly association. ¶*I enjoy his ~.*① / *~ in misfortune.*②

felon [431] **ferment**

2. ⓒ a group of people having similar tastes, interests, etc.; ⓤ membership in such a group. ¶ *admit someone to (into)* ~. **3.** ⓒ a position or sum of money given to a graduate student in a university to further his studies.
fel·on¹ [félən] *n.* ⓒ (*Law*) a person who has committed ⌈a serious crime.⌉
fel·on² [félən] *n.* ⓤ a very painful poisoned place on a finger or toe, usu. near the nail.
fe·lo·ni·ous [filóuniəs] *adj.* (*Law*) of the nature of a felony; very wicked.
fel·o·ny [féləni] *n.* (pl. **-nies**) (*Law*) ⓤ very serious crime such as murder; ⓒ an instance of this.
fel·spar [félspɑ:r] *n.* (chiefly *Brit*) =feldspar.
* **felt**¹ [felt] *v.* pt. and pp. of **feel**.
: **felt**² [felt] *n.* ⓤ cloth made by pressing closely together wool, hair, or fur. —*adj.* made of felt. ¶ *a* ~ *hat.*
: **fe·male** [fí:meil] *adj.* **1.** of the sex that gives birth to young or eggs; (of plants) fruit-bearing. ↔male ¶ *a* ~ *child | a* ~ *flower.* **2.** of women or girls. ¶ ~ *education.* —*n.* ⓒ a person or animal of this sex.
fem·i·nine [féminin] *adj.* **1.** of or like women. ¶ ~ *beauty | a* ~ *fashion.*① **2.** (*Grammar*) of the gender to which the names of females belong. ↔masculine
fem·i·nism [féminìz(ə)m] *n.* ⓤ **1.** the theory that women should have rights equal to those of men in all points. **2.** the doctrine that favors more rights and activities for women. ⌈nism.⌉
fem·i·nist [féminist] *n.* ⓒ a person who supports femi-⌋
fen [fen] *n.* ⓒ (*Brit.*) a low, wet piece of land; a marsh.
fence [fens] *n.* **1.** ⓒ a wall of stone, wood, wire, etc. to enclose a garden, a farm, etc. **2.** ⓤ fencing.
sit on the fence, have not made up one's mind which side to take; remain neutral.
—*vt.* enclose (a garden, etc.) with a fence. —*vi.* fight with swords in the sport of fencing.
  1) *fence about* (or *in, round, up*), enclose (a garden, etc.) with a fence. ⌈thing from or against.⌉
  2) *fence something from* (or *against*), protect some-⌋
  3) *fence off,* avoid; keep off.
fenc·er [fénsər] *n.* ⓒ a person who knows how to fight with a sword in the sport of fencing.
fenc·ing [fénsiŋ] *n.* ⓤ **1.** the sport of fighting with swords. **2.** ((*collectively*)) fences. **3.** material for fences.
fend [fend] *vt.* defend.
  1) *fend for oneself,* get along by one's own efforts.
  2) *fend off,* avoid (a blow, etc.).
fend·er [féndər] *n.* ⓒ **1.** (*U.S.*) a guard over the wheel of an automobile against splashing mud. (cf. *Brit.* a mud guard) **2.** a part on an automobile, ship, locomotive, etc. for preventing damage caused by striking against another thing. ⇒fig. **3.** (*U.S.*) a frame on the lower part of a locomotive or streetcar to catch or push aside anything hit. **4.** a metal guard or screen in front of a fireplace.

[fender 2.]

Fer·di·nand [fə́:rdinænd / -nənd] *n.* a man's name.
fer·ment *v.* [fə(:)rmént → *n.*] *vi.* (of wine) go through a chemical change in which bubbles of gas are given off because of the presence of yeast or bacteria. **2.** become excited. —*vt.* **1.** make (something) undergo this chemical change. **2.** excite. —*n.* [fə́:rment] **1.** ⓒ a substance that produces this chemical change, such as

함께 하기 2. 조합, 단체;회원임 3. 대학의 특별 연구원의 지위; 그 특별 연구원이 받는 장학금

—⊛ (法) 중죄인(重罪人)
—⊛ 표저(瘭疽)

—⊛ (法) 중죄의; 흉악한

—⊛ (法) 중죄

—⊛ 펠트, 모전(毛氈) —⊛ 펠트로 만든
—⊛ 1. 여자(여성)의; 암컷의; [식물의] 자성(雌性)의 2. 부인의; 여자의
—⊛ 여성; 동물의 암컷 [N.B.] 경멸적으로도 씀
—⊛ 1. 여성의; 여자 같은 ¶①여성적 유형 2. (文法) 여성의

—⊛ 1. 남녀 동등권주의 2. 여권 신장론

—⊛ 남녀 동등권론자; 여권 신장론자
—⊛ (英) 늪, 소택지(沼澤地)
—⊛ 1. 울, 울타리; 담 2. 펜싱, 검술

圏 형세를 살피다, 유리한 편에 붙으려고 중간 입장을 취하다
—⊛ …에 울타리(담)를 두르다
—⊛ 펜싱(검술)을 하다
圏 1) [정원 따위]에 울타리를 두르다
2) …을 …에서 지키다(보호하다) 3) …을 피하다; …을 막다

—⊛ 검객, 검술가

—⊛ 1. 펜싱, 검술 2. 울타리; 담 3. 울타리(담)의 재료
—⊛ …을 막다, 방위하다
圏 1) 자활하다, 혼자서 이럭저럭 해나가다 2) [공격]을 피하다
—⊛ 1. (美) [자동차의] 흙받이, 펜더 2. [기관차 따위의] 완충 장치; [배의] 방현물(防舷物)(완충재) 3. (美) [전차 따위의] 구난기(救難器) 4. [벽난로 앞에 놓는 낮은] 난로망(網), 철사망

—⊛ 남자 이름
—⊛ 1. 발효하다 2. 흥분하다
—⊛ 1. …을 발효시키다 2. …을 흥분시키다 —⊛ 1. 효소 2. 흥분

yeast, bacteria, etc. **2.** [U] a state of unrest or excitement.

fer·men·ta·tion [fə̀ːrmentéiʃ(ə)n] *n.* [U] **1.** the act or process of fermenting. **2.** excitement.
—[名] 1. 발효[작용] 2. 흥분

***fern** [fəːrn] *n.* [C] any of a group of plants with no flowers but forming their seeds on the back of featherlike leaves.
—[名] 양치(羊齒)[류]

fe·ro·cious [fəróuʃəs] *adj.* savagely cruel. ¶*a ~ lion.* ▷**fe·ro·cious·ly** [-li] *adv.*
—[形] 사나운, 흉포한, 잔인한

fe·roc·i·ty [fərásiti / -rɔ́s-] *n.* (pl. **-ties**) [U] savage cruelty; [C] a savagely cruel act.
—[名] 사나움, 잔인[성], 광포[성]; 광포한 행위, 만행

fer·ret [férit] *n.* [C] a white, catlike animal used to hunt rats and rabbits.
—[名] 흰담비

fer·ro·con·crete [fèroukánkriːt / féroukɔ́ŋ-] *n.* [U] concrete strengthened by a metal framework inside it.
—[名] 철근 콘크리이트

fer·rous [férəs] *adj.* of or containing iron.
—[形] 철의, 쇠의, 철을 함유하는

fer·rule [férəl / féruːl] *n.* [C] a metal cap put around the end of a stick, an umbrella, etc. to prevent wear or slipping; a metal ring used to strengthen any joint.
—[名] [지팡이·우산 따위의 손잡이 끝에 있는] 쇠끝, 물미

***fer·ry** [féri] *n.* [C] (pl. **-ries**) **1.** a place where boats carry people and goods across a river, a lake, etc. **2.** a boat used for carrying people and goods; a ferryboat. —*v.* (**-ried**) *vt.* **1.** carry (people and goods) in a ferryboat. 《~ someone or something *across*》 **2.** cross (a river) in a boat. **3.** deliver (an aircraft, a motorcar, etc.) under its own power. —*vi.* go across in a ferryboat. ¶*We ferried over to the island.*①
—[名] 1. 나루터 2. 나룻배; 페리보우트 —[他] 1. …을 나룻배로 나르다 2. [강 따위]를 나룻배를 타고 건너다 3. [항공기 따위]를 자력(自力) 수송하다 —[自] 나룻배로 건너다 ¶①우리는 나룻배를 타고 섬으로 건너갔다

fer·ry·boat [féribòut] *n.* [C] a boat used for ferrying.
—[名] 나룻배, 페리보우트

fer·ry·man [férimən] *n.* [C] (pl. **-men** [-mən]) **1.** a man who owns a ferryboat. **2.** a man who works on a ferryboat.
—[名] 1. 도선업자 2. 나룻배 사공

F

***fer·tile** [fə́ːrtl / fə́ːtail] *adj.* **1.** (of land) able to produce large of crops. ¶*~ soil.* **2.** (of a plant) able to produce seeds or fruit; (of an animal) able to produce young. ¶*a ~ flower / a ~ egg.*①
—[形] 1. [땅이] 기름진, 비옥한 2. 열매를 맺는; 번식력이 있는 ¶①수정란(受精卵)

be fertile in (or *of*), produce much.
[熟] …이 풍부하다, …이 많이 나다

fer·til·i·ty [fəːrtíliti] *n.* [U] the state or quality of being fertile.
—[名] 비옥; 결실; 번식력

fer·ti·li·za·tion [fəːrtilizéiʃ(ə)n / fəːtilai-] *n.* [U] **1.** the act of fertilizing; the state of being fertilized. **2.** (of a plant or an animal) the change that takes place in a cell or a seed before it starts to grow.
—[名] 1. 비옥[하게 하기] 2. 수화(受花), 수정(受精)

fer·ti·lize [fə́ːrtilàiz] *vt.* **1.** cause (land) to produce much. ¶*~ soil.* **2.** make (a flower or an egg cell) start to grow by combining it with a male flower or a male egg cell.
—[他] 1. [땅]을 비옥하게 하다 2. [식물]에 수화(受花)시키다, [동물]에게 수정(受精)시키다

fer·ti·liz·er [fə́ːrtilàizər] *n.* [U][C] material used to make land able to produce more.
—[名] 비료

fer·ven·cy [fə́ːrvənsi] *n.* [U] earnestness; enthusiasm.
—[名] 열심; 열렬

fer·vent [fə́ːrvənt] *adj.* **1.** earnest; enthusiastic. ¶*receive a ~ welcome.* **2.** hot. ▷**fer·vent·ly** [-li] *adv.*
—[形] 1. 열심한, 열렬한 2. 뜨거운

fer·vid [fə́ːrvid] *adj.* intensely emotional; very ardent. ¶*a ~ speech*① / *~ devotion.*② ▷**fer·vid·ly** [-li] *adv.*
—[形] 열정적인, 열렬한 ¶①열정적인 연설/②열렬한 애착

fer·vor, *Brit.* **-vour** [fə́ːrvər] *n.* [U] intense emotion; ardor. ¶*speak with ~.*①
—[名] 열정, 열렬 ¶①열정을 가지고 이야기하다

fes·tal [féstl] *adj.* of a feast or festival; gay; joyous.
—[形] 경축의, 축제의; 흥겨운, 즐거운

fes·ter [féstər] *vi.* **1.** become filled with poisonous matter. ¶*My wound has festered.*① **2.** cause a sore or painful feeling. ¶*Anger festered in his mind.*②
—[自] 1. 곪다 ¶①나의 상처가 곪았다 2. 쑤시다, 아프다, 사무치다 ¶②그는 화가 나서 속이 들끓었다

***fes·ti·val** [féstəv(ə)l] *n.* [C] **1.** a day or special time of rejoicing and celebration. ¶*a Thanksgiving ~*① / *Christmas and Easter are two festivals of the Christian church.* **2.** a season of cultural entertainments, often annual. ¶*a music ~*② / *the Edinburgh International Festival.*③
—[名] 1. 축일; 축제 ¶①추수 감사절의 축제 2. [정기적으로 개최되는] …제 ¶②음악제/③에딘버러 국제 예술제

fes·tive [féstiv] *adj.* of a festival; gay; joyous; merry. ¶*a ~ occasion / a ~ scene.*① ▷**fes·tive·ly** [-li] *adv.*
—[形] 축제의; 흥겨운; 즐거운; 유쾌한 ¶①즐거운 광경

fes·tiv·i·ty [festíviti] *n.* (pl. **-ties**) **1.** [U] merrymaking;
—[名] 1. 축제 기분; 축제 소동 2. 경축

gaiety. **2.** 《*pl.*》 festive events or activities.
행사

fes·toon [festúːn] *n.* [C] a chain of flowers, leaves, ribbons, etc. which hangs between two points as a decoration. ⇒fig. ¶*a ~ of roses.* **—*vt.*** **1.** decorate (something) with festoons. ¶*The Christmas tree was festooned with colored paper and fairy lamps.* **2.** form (something) into festoons.
—[名] [장식용] 꽃줄 —[他] 1.…을 꽃줄로 장식하다 2.…을 꽃줄로 만들다

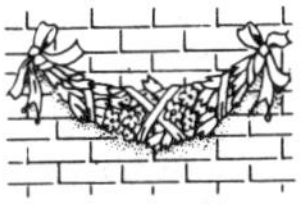
〔festoon〕

fetch [fetʃ] *vt.* **1.** go to get and bring back. 《~ some-thing *for* or *to*》 ¶*Fetch me a glass of water. / I'll ~ the letter for you. / Please ~ the dictionary to me.* **2.** (of goods) bring (a price, etc.); sell for. ¶*This house will ~ [you] a good price.* **3.** (*colloq.*) strike. ¶*He fetched me a blow on the head.* **4.** utter (a sigh, a groan, etc.); cause (tears, blood, etc.) to come out. ¶*~ a deep sigh.* **5.** (*colloq.*) attract; charm. ¶*~ the public.*
—[他] 1.…을 가서 가지고(데리고) 오다 2.[값 따위가 얼마] 나가다; [얼마]에 팔리다 3.《口》…에게 [타격을] 가하다 4.[한숨·신음소리 따위]를 내다; [피·눈물 따위]를 나오게 하다 5.《口》매혹하다, 마음을 사로잡다

1) ***fetch and carry,*** do small jobs; run errands.
2) ***fetch up,*** ⓐ (*nautical, colloq.*) stop; arrive. 《~ *at* a place》 ⓑ (*Brit. colloq.*) throw up food, etc. from the stomach through the mouth.
[熟] 1)허드렛일을 하다, 바쁘게 심부름 다니다 2)ⓐ《海, 口》…에 멈추다, 서다; 도착하다 ⓑ《英口》…을 토하다, 게우다

fetch·ing [fétʃiŋ] *adj.* (*colloq.*) attractive; charming.
—[形] 매력이 있는, 매혹적인

fete, fête [feit] *n.* [C] a festival; an outdoor entertainment. ¶*held a great ~ / ~ day.* **—*vt.*** honor (someone) with a fete or party. ¶*~ the engaged couple.*①
—[名] 축제; 야외의 축하연 —[他] 축하연을 베풀어 [남]을 축하하다

fet·id [fétid, fíːt-] *adj.* smelling very bad; stinking.
—[形] 악취가 나는, 구린, 냄새가 고약한

fe·tish [fíːtiʃ, fét-] *n.* [C] **1.** an object supposed to have supernatural or magic power. **2.** anything respected or loved to an abnormal degree.
—[名] 1. 주물(呪物), 물신(物神) 2. 맹목적 숭배물

fet·lock [fétlàk / -lɔ̀k] *n.* [C] **1.** the back part of a horse's leg just above the foot. ⇒fig. **2.** a tuft of hair on that area.
—[名] 1. 구절(球節)(말발굽의 관절) 2. 거모(距毛)(말발굽 위 뒤쪽에 난 털)

〔fetlock 1.〕

fet·ter [fétər] *n.* **1.** [C] a chain to bind the feet and so prevent escape. **2.** 《usu. *pl.*》 anything that binds; a restraint.
—[名] 1. 족쇄 2. 구속물, 속박

in fetters, fettered; restrained.
[熟] 족쇄를 채운; 속박된

—*vt.* **1.** bind (the feet) with fetters. **2.** bind; restrain.
—[他] 1. …을 족쇄로 채우다 2. …을 구속하다

fet·tle [fétl] *n.* [U] physical or mental condition.
—[名] [심신의] 상태

fe·tus [fíːtəs] *n.* [C] a young animal not yet born.
—[名] 태아

feud¹ [fjuːd] *n.* [C] a bitter quarrel between families, tribes, etc., often passed down from generation to generation.
—[名] [가족·민족 사이 따위에서 대대로 내려오는] 불화; 원한; 숙원(宿怨)

feud² [fjuːd] *n.* [C] an estate granted to a tenant.
—[名] 영지, 봉토(封土)

feu·dal [fjúːdl] *adj.* of feudalism. ¶*the ~ age.*①
—[形] 봉건제도의 ¶①봉건시대

feu·dal·ism [fjúːd(ə)lìz(ə)m] *n.* [U] the social, economic, and political system in Europe during the Middle Ages.
—[名] [중세 유럽의] 봉건제도

feu·da·to·ry [fjúːdətɔ̀ːri / -dət(ə)ri] *adj.* owing feudal services to a lord. **—*n.*** [C] (pl. **-ries**) a person owing feudal services to a lord; a vassal.
—[形] 영주에게 봉건적 역무(役務)를 지고 있는 —[名] 봉건 가신(家臣)

fe·ver [fíːvər] *n.* [U] **1.** 《often *a ~*》 a diseased condition with the body temperature higher than usual. ¶*bring the ~ down*① / *A sick person of ten has a ~.* ⇒[usage] **2.** any disease that causes a high body temperature. ¶*scarlet ~*② / *typhoid ~.*③ **3.** 《usu. *a ~*, *sing.* only》 great nervous excitement. ¶*be in a ~ of anxiety.*④
—[名] 1. 열, 발열 ¶①열을 내리게 하다 [usage] 이 경우의 a는 one의 뜻이 아니고 some의 뜻 2. 열병 ¶②성홍열 /③장티푸스 3. 흥분, 열광 ¶④걱정이 되어 자신을 잊고 있다

fe·vered [fíːvərd] *adj.* having fever; excited.
—[形] 열이 있는; 흥분한

fever heat [ˊ- ˋ] *n.* a body temperature higher than normal.
—[名] [평상시 체온 이상의] 열

fe·ver·ish [fíːvəriʃ] *adj.* **1.** having fever. ¶*I am ~ from my cold.* **2.** causing or caused by fever. ¶*a ~ swamp*① / *a ~ dream.* **3.** excited; restless. ¶*~ activities / in ~ haste.* ▷**fe·ver·ish·ly** [-li] *adv.* —**fe·ver·ness** [-nis] *n.*
—[形] 1. 열이 있는 2. 열병에 걸리게 하는, 열병으로 말미암은 ¶①열병을 일으키게 하는 소택지 3. 흥분한; 침착하지 못한, 들뜬

F

few [fju:] *adj.* **1.** ((used without *a*)) not many; a small, indefinite number of. ↔many ¶*a man of ~ words*① / *He has ~ friends in this city.* **2.** ((used with *a*)) not many but some; a small number of. ↔none ¶*in a ~ days* / *I have a ~ friends.* / *A ~ people were present.* ⇒[usage] —*n., pron.* **1.** a small, indefinite number of people, things, etc. ⇒[usage] ¶*Few believed her story.* / *A faithful ~ remained.* / *A ~ of the eggs were broken.* **2.** ((*the* ~)) the minority of people.
1) ***every few minutes (hours, days, etc.),*** at intervals of a few minutes (hours, days, etc.)
2) ***few and far between,*** very few in number; widely separated. ¶*Travelers in the desert are ~ and far between.*
3) ***a good few; not a few; quite a few,*** a fairly large number [of].
4) ***no fewer than,*** as many as. ¶*There were no ~ than fifty students present.*
5) ***some few,*** a fair but not large number of.

—[형] **1.** 조금밖에 없는, [부정적으로] 거의 없는 ¶①과묵한 사람 **2.** [긍정적으로] 조금은 있는, 소수의 [usage] few, a few 다 복수명사를 수반함. [a] few는 수에 관해 쓰며, [a] little은 양에 씀 —[명][대] **1.** 소수의 사람(물건) [usage] 부정관사의 유무에 의한 뜻의 차이는 형용사와 같음. 또 구문상 few, a few 다 항상 복수 **2.** [다수에 대하여] 소수 [숙] 1)2·3분(2·3시간, 2·3일)마다 2)극히 드물게; 드문드문; 오랜 동안을 두고 3)꽤 많은(적지 않은) 수[의], 다수[의] 4)…만큼, …이나 5)소수의 [것], 얼마간

fez [fez] *n.* (pl. **fez·zes** [féziz]) [C] a red felt cap ornamented with a long, black tassel. —[명] 터어키 모자

fi·an·cé [fì:ɑ:nséi, fi:ɑ́:nsei / fiɑ́:(n)sei] *n.* [C] a man engaged to be married. —[명] 약혼자(남자)

fi·an·cée [fì:ɑ:nséi, fi:ɑ́:nsei / fiɑ́:(n)sei] *n.* [C] a woman engaged to be married. —[명] 약혼자(여자)

fi·as·co [fiǽskou] *n.* [C] (pl. **-cos** or **-coes**) a complete failure. —[명] 대실패

fi·at [fáiət, fáiæt] *n.* [C] an authoritative order or command. —[명] 명령, 엄명

fib [fib] *n.* [C] a lie about something unimportant. —*vi.* (**fibbed, fib·bing**) tell such a lie. ▷**fib·ber** [fíbər] *n.* —[명] 악의없는 거짓말 —[자] 악의없는 거짓말을 하다

·**fi·ber,** *Brit.* **-bre** [fáibər] *n.* **1.** [C] a single thread of any kind. ¶*nerve (muscle) fibers.*① **2.** [U] a substance composed of threads. ¶*cotton (hemp) ~.*② **3.** [U] ((sometimes *pl.*)) character; nature. ¶*a man of tough ~.*③ —[명] **1.** 섬유 ¶①신경(근)섬유 **2.** 섬유 제품 ¶②면(대마)섬유 **3.** 성격, 기질 ¶③기질이 끈질긴 사람

fi·brous [fáibrəs] *adj.* having, made up of, or like fibers. —[형] 섬유[질]의, 섬유 모양의

fick·le [fíkl] *adj.* (sometimes **-ler, -lest**) changing; not constant. ¶*~ weather.* —[형] 변하기 쉬운, 변덕스러운

·**fic·tion** [fíkʃ(ə)n] *n.* **1.** [U] anything imagined or made up; [C] a made-up story. ↔fact ¶*separate fact from ~*① / *The story is pure ~.*② **2.** [U] literary writings about imaginary people and events. ↔nonfiction ¶*Fact is stranger than ~.*③ ▷**fic·tion·al** [-ʃən(ə)l] *adj.* —[명] **1.** 지어낸 것; 꾸며낸 이야기, 허구(虛構) ¶①사실을 허구와 분간하다 /②그 이야기는 순전히 꾸며낸 것이었다 **2.** 소설 ¶③사실은 소설보다도 기묘하다

fic·ti·tious [fiktíʃəs] *adj.* **1.** imaginary; made-up. ¶*a ~ character.*① **2.** false; not real. ¶*a ~ name.* ▷**fic·ti·tious·ly** [-li] *adv.* —[형] **1.** 가공(架空)의, 꾸며낸 이야기의 ¶①가공의 인물 **2.** 허위의, 거짓의

fid·dle [fídl] *n.* (*colloq.*) [C] a violin.
1) ***fit as a fiddle,*** in good health.
2) ***play second fiddle,*** take a secondary part.
—*vi.* **1.** (*colloq.*) play the violin. **2.** handle aimlessly. ((~ *with* something)) —*vt.* (*colloq.*) play (a tune) on the violin. ***fiddle away,*** idle away.
—[명] ((口)) 바이올린 [숙] 1)원기왕성한 2)단역을 맡다, 부하 노릇을 하다 —[자] **1.** ((口)) 바이올린을 켜다 **2.** 만지작거리다, 가지고 놀다 —[타] [곡]을 바이올린으로 켜다 [숙] 허송세월하다

fid·dle·stick [fídlstìk] *n.* [C] **1.** a violin bow. **2.** ((in *negative*)) something unimportant. ¶*not care a ~.*① —[명] **1.** 바이올린의 활 **2.** 하찮은 것 ¶①조금도 개의치 않다

fid·dl·ing [fídliŋ] *adj.* trifling; useless. —[형] 보잘것 없는, 하찮은

fi·del·i·ty [fidéliti, fai-] [U] *n.* **1.** faithfulness; loyalty. ¶*~ to one's master (principles).* **2.** accuracy; exactness. ¶*report the news with ~*① / *a high ~ radio.*② —[명] **1.** 충실, 충성 **2.** 정확, 정밀 ¶①뉴우스를 정확히 전하다/②하이파이(고충실도) 라디오

fidg·et [fídʒit] *vi.* be restless and uneasy. ((~ *about* something or oneself)) ¶*~ about oneself.* —*vt.* make (someone) uneasy; worry. ¶*The heat fidgeted me.* —*n.* **1.** [C] a restless person. **2.** ((often *pl.*)) restlessness. —[자] 안절부절 못하다, 애타다 —[타] 안절부절 못하게 하다, 애태우다 —[명] **1.** 안절부절 못하는(조바심하는) 사람 **2.** 안절부절 못함

fidg·et·y [fídʒiti] *adj.* restless; uneasy. —[형] 안절부절 못하는, 조바심하는

fie [fai] *interj.* for shame!; shame! ¶*Fie, for shame!* / *Oh, ~ upon you for lying!*① —[감] 체!, 제기!, 보기 싫다! ¶①밉살스럽게도 거짓말하다니!

fief [fi:f] *n.* [C] a piece of land held as a feudal estate. —[명] 영토, 봉토(封土)

field [fi:ld] *n.* [C] **1.** an open land with few or no trees. **2.** an enclosed piece of land used for planting, pasture, —[명] **1.** 들, 벌판 **2.** 밭, 전답; 목초지 **3.** [하늘 따위] 넓디넓게 퍼진 곳 **4.** 광장;

etc. **3.** a wide area or expanse. **4.** a piece of land used for sports or an other special purpose. ¶*a flying ~.*① **5.** a piece of land where some natural product is obtained. ¶*a coal ~.*② **6.** a battlefield. **7.** the general kind of studies which one is studying; the general type of work which one is doing. **8.** the inside part of an athletic field surrounded by a running track. **9.** (in baseball) the outfield.
경기장 ¶①비행장 **5.** [광물 따위의] 산지 ¶②탄전 **6.** 전쟁터 **7.** 분야 **8.** 피일드 경기장 **9.** 외야

1) ***be in the field,*** ⓐ be at the front. ⓑ be taking part ⌈in a game, etc.
2) ***hold the field,*** maintain one's position. ⌈etc.
3) ***take the field,*** begin a battle, a campaign, a game,
[熟] 1)ⓐ싸움터에 나가 있다, 종군중이다 ⓑ경기중이다 2)유리한 위치를 차지하다; 일보도 물러서지 않다 3)전투(운동, 경기)를 시작하다

—*vt.* (in baseball, cricket, etc.) stop or catch and return (a ball). —*vi.* (in baseball, cricket, etc.) play as a fielder.
—[他] [공]을 받아서 되던지다 —[自][야수(野手)로서] 수비를 하다

field day [ˊ ˋ] *n.* [C] **1.** a day when military drills, mock fights, etc. are done, usu. as entertainment. **2.** (*U.S.*) a day of unusual activity. **3.** (*U.S.*) a day for outdoor sports, esp. on a large scale.
—[名] **1.** 야외 연습일 **2.** 특별한 행사가 있는 날 **3.** 《美》 야외 운동회의 날

field·er [fíːldər] *n.* [C] (of baseball or cricket) a player.
—[名] 선수, 야수(野手)

field glass [ˊ ˋ] *n.* 《usu. *pl.*》 a pair of small telescopes.
—[名] 쌍안경

field hospital [ˊ ˋ-‐] *n.* a temporary hospital near a battlefield.
—[名] 야전병원

field marshal [ˊ ˋ-] *n.* (*Brit.*) an army officer ranked just below the commander in chief. (cf. *U.S.* General of the Army)
—[名] 《英》 육군 원수

field work [ˊ ˋ] *n.* scientific or technical exploration done outside the school, the office, etc.
—[名] 현지 조사, 야외 연구

fiend [fiːnd] *n.* [C] **1.** a devil or demon. **2.** a very cruel or wicked person. **3.** (*colloq.*) a person much given to some habit. ¶*an opium ~.*
—[名] **1.** 악마 **2.** 악귀 같은(잔인한) 사람 **3.** 《口》 …광(狂), …에 미친 사람

fiend·ish [fíːndiʃ] *adj.* very cruel; devilish.
—[形] 잔인한; 악마 같은

‡**fierce** [fiərs] *adj.* **1.** savage; wild. ¶*as ~ as a tiger.* **2.** violent; raging. ¶*the ~ heat / be ~ with anger.* **3.** very eager or active. ¶*make ~ efforts to win.* ▷**fierce·ness** [-nis] *n.*
—[形] **1.** 사나운; 야만적인 **2.** [비바람 따위가] 거센; 격렬한 **3.** 열렬한, 열심인

***fierce·ly** [fíərsli] *adv.* violently; wildly.
—[副] 사납게, 거칠게; 맹렬히

***fier·y** [fáiəri] *adj.* (**fier·i·er, fier·i·est**) **1.** like fire; burning; glowing. ¶*a ~ sunset.* **2.** full of feeling; intensely passionate. ¶*a ~ speech.* **3.** easily excited or angered. ¶*a ~ nature / a ~ temper.*
—[形] **1.** 불 같은, 불타는 듯한, 작열하는 **2.** 격한; 열렬한 **3.** 격하기 쉬운, 성을 잘 내는, 성마른

fife [faif] *n.* [C] a small, shrill-toned musical instrument like a flute. —*vt., vi.* play on a fife. ▷**fif·er** [-ər] *n.*
—[名] 횡적(橫笛) —[自][他] 횡적을 불다

‡**fif·teen** [fíftíːn] *n.* [U] the number between fourteen and sixteen; 15. —*adj.* of 15.
—[名] 15 —[形] 15의

‡**fif·teenth** [fíftíːnθ] *n.* **1.** 《usu. *the ~*》 the number 15; 15th. **2.** [C] one of 15 equal parts of anything. —*adj.* of the 15th.
—[名] **1.** 제15, 열 다섯[번]째 **2.** 15 분의 1 —[形] 열 다섯[번]째의; 15 분의 1의

‡**fifth** [fifθ] *n.* **1.** 《usu. *the ~*》 the number 5; 5th. **2.** [C] one of 5 equal parts of anything. —*adj.* of 5th.
—[名] **1.** 제5, 다섯[번]째 **2.** 5 분의 1 —[形] 다섯[번]째의; 5 분의 1의

‡**fif·ti·eth** [fíftiiθ] *n.* **1.** 《usu. *the ~*》 the number 50; 50th. **2.** [C] one of 50 equal parts of anything. —*adj.* of the 50th.
—[名] **1.** 제50, 쉰[번]째 **2.** 50분의 1 —[形] 쉰[번]째의; 50 분의 1의

‡**fif·ty** [fífti] *n.* [U] five times ten; 50. —*adj.* of 50.
—[名] 50 —[形] 50의

fif·ty-fif·ty [fíftifífti] (*colloq.*) *adv.* with equal shares. —*adj.* shared equally; half likely and half unlikely.
—[副] 50 대 50 으로, 반반으로, 균등하게 —[形] 균등하게 나눈; 반반의

***fig** [fig] *n.* [C] **1.** a small, sweet fruit grown in warm countries. **2.** 《in *negative*》 a very small amount; a little bit.
—[名] **1.** 무화과 **2.** 조금, 미량(微量); 보잘것 없는 것; 하찮은 것

not care a fig for, not care at all; consider (something) as valueless.
[熟] …을 전혀 문제삼지 않다

fig. 1. figure. **2.** figurative. **3.** figuratively.

‡**fight** [fait] *v.* (**fought**) *vt.* **1.** try to overcome; struggle against (someone or something). ¶*~ disease*① / *~ a rival for the business.*② **2.** try to win (something); take part in (a struggle, etc.) ¶*~ a battle / ~ a prize fight.* **3.** cause (dogs, etc.) to fight. —*vi.* struggle;
—[他] **1.** …와 싸우다 ¶①병마와 싸우다/②사업 경쟁자와 싸우다 **2.** …을 싸워서 획득하려 하다, 겨루다; [싸움]에 참가하다 **3.** …을 싸우게 하다 —[自] 싸우다; 격투하다

F

combat. 《~ *against* or *with* someone or something》
1) ***fight it out,*** continue fighting until one wins; settle by fighting.
2) ***fight shy of*** (=*keep away from; avoid*) *something.*
—*n.* [C] **1.** an act of fighting. **2.** a battle; a contest. **3.** a boxing match. **4.** [U] will or power to fight; fighting spirit.

[熟] 1)최후까지 싸우다; 싸워서 결말을 짓다 2)…을 피하다
—[名] **1.** 싸움 **2.** 전투, 투쟁 **3.** 권투 시합 **4.** 전투력, 투지

* **fight·er** [fáitər] *n.* [C] **1.** a person who fights, struggles, resists, etc. ¶*a ~ for liberty.*① **2.** an airplane designed for attacking enemy airplanes.
—[名] **1.** 전사, 투사 ¶①자유의 투사 **2.** 전투기

fig·ment [fígmənt] *n.* [C] something imagined.
—[名] 꾸며낸 이야기, 허구(虛構)

fig·ur·a·tive [fígjurətiv] *adj.* **1.** involving a figure of speech, esp. a metaphor; not literal. **2.** with many figures of speech. **3.** representing by a symbol or likeness; symbolic. ▷**fig·ur·a·tive·ly** [-li] *adv.*
—[形] **1.** 비유적인; 전의(轉意)의 **2.** 형용이 많은; 수식이 풍부한 **3.** 상징적인

‡ **fig·ure** [fígjər / fígə] *n.* [C] **1.** an outer shape; an outline; a form. **2.** a form of the human body; an appearance. **3.** an image; a statue. **4.** a person, esp. an important one. **5.** a drawing; an illustration; a design. **6.** a symbol which indicates a number, such as 1, 2, 3, etc. **7.** an amount or value expressed in figures; a price. **8.** 《*pl.*》 calculation. ¶*I'm poor at figures.*
1) ***cut*** (or ***make***) ***a fine*** (*poor, etc.*) ***figure,*** produce a certain impression.
2) ***do figures,*** calculate; reckon.
—*vt.* **1.** show (something) by a figure. **2.** imagine; think. ¶*I ~ it like this.*① **3.** decorate (something) with a figure or pattern. **4.** calculate. **—*vi.*** appear as an important part.
1) ***figure as*** (=*play the part of*) *Hamlet.*
2) ***figure*** (=*plan*) ***for*** *something.*
3) ***figure on,*** ⓐ take (something) into consideration. ⓑ rely on (something).
4) ***figure out*** (=*think out; determine; solve*) *something.*
—[名] **1.** 형태, 외형 **2.** 모습, 풍채; 외관 **3.** 상(像) **4.** [두드러진] 인물; 명사 **5.** 그림, 도해; 도안 **6.** 숫자 **7.** 수치(數値); 값 **8.** 계산, 산수
[熟] 1)두각을 나타내다(초라하게 보이다) 2)셈하다, 계산하다
—[他] **1.** …을 그림(수)으로 나타내다 **2.** …을 상상하다; 생각하다 ¶①나는 그것을 이렇게 생각한다 **3.** …을 그림(도안)으로 장식하다 **4.** …을 계산하다
—[自] 두각을 나타내다, 이채를 띠다
[熟] 1)[햄릿]의 역할을 하다 2)…을 계획하다 3)ⓐ…을 계산에 넣다 ⓑ…을 의지하다 4)…을 생각해 내다; 결정하다; 해결하다

fig·ured [fígjərd / fígəd] *adj.* having a design or pattern.
—[形] 무늬가 있는, 의장도안(意匠圖案)이 있는

fig·ure·head [fígjərhèd / fígə-] *n.* [C] **1.** a person who is important only in name but has no real authority. **2.** a statue or carving on the bow of a ship. ⇒fig.
—[名] **1.** 명목상의 수령(우두머리) **2.** 선수상(船首像)

〔figurehead 2.〕

fig·u·rine [fìgjurí:n / ∸-∸] *n.* [C] a small ornamental figure; a statuette.
—[名] 작은 입상(立像)

fil·a·ment [fíləmənt] *n.* [C] **1.** a very fine thread. **2.** a fine metal thread which lights up in an electric bulb. **3.** (*Botany*) a slender stalk of a flower stamen.
—[名] **1.** 가는 섬유 **2.** [전구의] 백열선(白熱線), 섬조(纖條), 필라멘트 **3.** 《植》 화사(花絲)

fil·a·ture [fílətʃər] *n.* **1.** [U] the act of reeling silk from cocoons. **2.** [C] a machine for reeling silk; a factory for reeling silk.
—[名] **1.** 고치에서 실을 뽑기; 물레질, 제사(製絲) **2.** 물레; 제사 공장

fil·bert [fílbə(:)rt] *n.* [C] a hazelnut.
—[名] 개암나무의 열매, 개암

filch [filtʃ] *vt.* steal (something of little value).
—[他] …을 좀도둑질하다, 훔치다

‡ **file**[1] [fail] *n.* [C] **1.** a folder or a case for keeping papers in order. **2.** a set of papers kept in order. ¶*keep on ~.*① **3.** a line of people or things one behind another. ↔rank
—*vt.* arrange (papers) in order.
—*vi.* march in a file.
—[名] **1.** 종이끼우개 **2.** 서류철, 문서철 ¶①철해 두다 **3.** 종대(縱隊), 열, 줄
—[他] [서류]를 철하다 —[自] 종대로 행진하다

file[2] [fail] *n.* [C] a steel tool for smoothing wood or metal. ⇒fig.
—[名] 줄[칼]

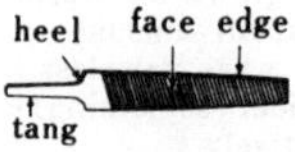

〔file[2]〕

fil·i·al [fíliəl] *adj.* due from a child to his parents. ¶*~ piety.*①
—[形] 자식으로서 ¶①효도

fil·i·bus·ter [fílibʌstər] *n.* [C] **1.** (*U.S.*) a person who hinders the passage of a bill by making long speeches; a series of such speeches. **2.** a person who engages in an unlawful fight against another country.
—[名] **1.** 의사 방해[의 장시간 연설]자; 의사 방해의 긴 연설 **2.** 불법 전사(戰士); 약탈병

filigree

fil·i·gree [fíligrì:] *n.* ⓤ ornamental work of gold or silver wire. ―⑲ 금·은 따위의 선조(線條) 세공, 철사 세공

fil·ings [fáiliŋz] *n. pl.* small pieces rubbed off by a file. ―⑲ 줄밥(줄에 쓸려 떨어진 부스러기)

Fil·i·pi·no [fílipí:nou] *n.* ⓒ (pl. **-nos**) a person of the Philippines. ―*adj.* Philippine. ―⑲ 필리핀 사람 ―⑱ 필리핀의

⁑fill [fil] *vt.* **1.** take up all the space in (something); make (a box, a room, etc.) full. ¶ *~ the bottle with wine* / *Her heart was filled with joy.* / *His huge body filled the chair.*① **2.** stop up or close a hole in (something). ¶ *~ a tooth.* **3.** satisfy; fulfill. ¶ *~ an order.* ―*vi.* **1.** become full. **2.** (of sails) swell.
1) *fill in,* ⓐ fill (a hole, etc.) with something. ⓑ make (a document, etc.) complete by putting it the necessary information.
2) *fill out,* ⓐ make or grow larger; expand. ⓑ make (a document, etc.) complete by filling it in; fill it.
3) *fill up,* ⓐ fill completely or excessively. ⓑ make (something) complete by filling it in; fill out.
―*n.* **1.** ⓒ (*a ~*) an amount enough to fill. ¶ *a ~ of tobacco.*② **2.** (*one's ~*) an amount enough to satisfy. ¶ *eat (drink, have, etc.) one's ~.*③ **3.** anything to fill in a hole, etc.
―⑲ 1. …을 가득하게 하다; 채우다 ¶①그의 큰 몸집은 의자에 꽉 찼다 2. …의 구멍을 메우다 3.[직무 따위]를 다하다; 수행하다 ―⑥ 1.[가득]차다 2.[바람을 안고] 불룩해지다
圝 1)ⓐ[구멍]을 메우다 ⓑ[서류 따위]에 필요 사항을 적어 넣다 2)ⓐ…을 부풀게 하다(부풀다); 확장하다 ⓑ[서류 따위]에 빽빽이 써 넣다 3)ⓐ…을 채우다, …에 충만하다 ⓑ…의 빈곳을 채우다
―⑳ 1. …그릇에 가득한 분량 ¶②파이프 하나 가득한 담배 2.필요량 ¶③배불리 먹다(마시다) 3.채우는(메우는) 것

fil·let [filit→*n.* 2, *v.* 2.] *n.* ⓒ **1.** a ribbon or a narrow band worn around the head. **2.** [+*U.S.* filéi, fílei] a slice of fish or meat without bones. ―*vt.* **1.** bind (a head) with a ribbon or a narrow band. **2.** [+*U.S.* filéi, fílei] cut (fish or meat) into fillets; cut fillets from (fish or meat). ―⑳ 1.머리끈, 머리에 띠는 리본 2.필레 살코기;[생선의 가시를 바른] 저민 고기 ―⑲ 1. [머리] 를 끈으로 매다(동이다) 2.[고기·생선]을 저미다, …에서 필레 살코기를 저며 내다

fill·ing [fíliŋ] *n.* ⓒ a thing used to fill something else. ―⑳ 메워 넣는 것, 충전물

filling station [⌐⌐⌐] *n.* (*U.S.*) a place where gasoline and oil for automobiles are sold; a gas station. ―⑳ 《美》[자동차의] 주유소, 급유소

fil·lip [fílip] *n.* ⓒ **1.** a quick, smart blow with a fingernail. **2.** a thing that gives excitements. ―*vt.* **1.** strike (someone or something) with a fingernail. **2.** arouse. ―⑳ 1.손가락으로 튀기기 2.자극물 ―⑲ 1. …을 손가락으로 튀기다 2. …을 자극하다

fil·ly [fíli] *n.* ⓒ (pl. **-lies**) a young female horse. ―⑳ 암망아지

⁑film [film] *n.* **1.** ⓒ a very thin skin or coating. **2.** ⓤⓒ a strip of thin, flexible material coated with a substance sensitive to light, used in taking photographs. **3.** ⓒ a motion picture. ―*vt.*,*vi.* **1.** cover (something) or become covered with a film. **2.** photograph or be photographed for motion pictures. **3.** make a motion picture of (something); become a motion picture. ―⑳ 1.엷은 껍질, 박막(薄膜), 피막(被膜) 2.[사진의] 필름 3. 영화 ―⑲⑥ 1. …을 얇은 껍질로 덮다, 얇은 껍질로 덮이다, 2. …을 촬영하다; [영화에] 찍히다 3. …을 영화화하다; 영화로 되다

film·y [fílmi] *adj.* (**-i·er, -i·est**) like a film; very thin. ―⑱ 얇은 껍질(막) 모양의, 매우 얇은

fil·ter [fíltər] *n.* ⓒ **1.** a device for purifying liquid or gas by separating out any impurities. **2.** a material used in such a device. **3.** a device for shutting out certain kinds of lights, electric currents, etc.
―*vt.* purify (liquid or gas) by a filter (*n.* 1.) ¶ *~ water through sand.* ―*vi.* move or pass very slowly.
―⑳ 1.여과기(濾過器),여과 장치 2.여과물 3.여광기(濾光器), 필터, 여과기 (濾波器)
―⑲ …을 거르다,여과하다 ―⑥ 침투하다, 스며들다(나오다)

filth [filθ] *n.* **1.** ⓤ disgusting dirt. **2.** ⓒ dirty words or thoughts. ▷**filth·i·ness** [-inis] *n.* ―⑳ 1.오물,불결한 것 2.음탕한 말 (생각)

filth·y [fílθi] *adj.* (**filth·i·er, filth·i·est**) disgustingly dirty. ▷**filth·i·ly** [-li] *adv.* ―⑱ 더러운, 불결한, 추악한

fil·tra·tion [filtréiʃ(ə)n] *n.* ⓤ the act of filtering. ―⑳ 여과[작용]

fin [fin] *n.* ⓒ **1.** a winglike part of a fish's body which enables the fish to swim and to balance itself in the water. **2.** anything used like a fin. ¶ *an airplane ~.* ―⑳ 1.지느러미 2.지느러미 모양의 것

⁑fi·nal [fáin(ə)l] *adj.* **1.** of, coming or happening at the end; last. **2.** not to be changed; decisive. **3.** related to something's purpose. ―*n.* ⓒ **1.** (usu. *the ~*) something final. **2.** (*pl.*) the last event or game in a series. ―⑱ 1.최후의, 종국의 2. 종국적인, 결정적인 3.목적을 나타내는 ―⑳ 1.최후의 것 2.최종 시험; 결승전

fi·na·le [finǽli, -nɑ́:li / -nɑ́:li] *n.* ⓒ **1.** the last part of a long piece of music or a play. **2.** the last part. ―⑳ 1.종곡(終曲), 종악장; 종막(終幕), 대단원(大團圓) 2.종국, 결말

finale

fi·nal·i·ty [fainǽliti] *n.* (pl. **-ties**) **1.** [U] the state of being final; conclusiveness. ¶*an air of ~ / speak with ~.* **2.** [C] something final.
—[名] 1. 종국, 결말, 최후 2. 결정적인 언동(것)

‡ **fi·nal·ly** [fáin(ə)li] *adv.* **1.** at last. **2.** in a final manner; conclusively.
—[副] 1. 최후로, 마침내, 결국 2. 최종적으로, 결정적으로

‡ **fi·nance** [finǽns, fáinæns / fainǽns] *n.* **1.** [U] [the science of] the management of large amounts of money. **2.** 《*pl.*》 funds; income. —*vt.* provide money for (a plan, etc.). —*vi.* manage money.
—[名] 1. 재정; 재무; 재정학 2. 세입(歲入), 재원, 수입 —[他] …에 융자하다, 자본을 제공하다 —[自] 재정을 처리하다

‡ **fi·nan·cial** [finǽnʃ(ə)l, fai- / fai-, fi-] *adj.* of finance or the management of money. ¶*~ affairs*① */ ~ circles*② */ ~ difficulties.*③ */ the ~ year.*④
—[形] 재정[상]의, 재무의, 금융상의 ¶①재무 사정/②재계(財界)/③재정 곤란/④재정(회계) 연도

fi·nan·cial·ly [finǽnʃəli, fai- / fai-, fi-] *adv.* in relation to finances.
—[副] 재정상, 재정적으로

fin·an·cier [finənsíər, fài- / fainǽnsiə] *n.* [C] **1.** a person who is skilled in finance. **2.** a person who engages in a financial operation.
—[名] 1. 재정가, 재무관 2. [금융]자본가

finch [fintʃ] *n.* [C] any of various small songbirds such as sparrows, canaries, and cardinals.
—[名] 참새과의 작은 새

‡ **find** [faind] *vt.* (**found**) **1.** come upon or meet with (something or someone) by chance; discover. ¶*He found a coin on the train. / You will ~ a funny boy in this class.* **2.** look for and get back. ¶*He found his purse under the table.* **3.** learn (something) by experience, trial, or study; see; know. 《~ something *good*, etc; ~ *that* ...》 ¶*I found him a very sensible man.; I found that he was a very sensible man.*① */ I found it difficult to explain.; I found [that] it was difficult to explain.*② **4.** get; obtain. ¶*Will you ~ me a job?*③ */ He found the courage to face the trial.*④ **5.** reach. ¶*The arrow found its target.* **6.** arrive at (a conclusion); decide and declare. 《~ someone *honest*, etc.》 ¶*He was found guilty.*⑤ **7.** provide; supply. 《~ someone *in* or *with*》 ¶*The hotel is well found.*⑥
1) ***find oneself,*** discover one's power or abilities.
2) ***find out,*** discover; solve; learn.
—*n.* [C] a thing found, esp. a valuable thing.
—[他] 1. [우연히] …을 발견하다; 눈에 띄다; …을 만나다 2. [찾아서] …을 발견해내다, 찾아내다 3. …을 알다, …이라고 깨닫다 ¶①나는 그가 상당히 분별있는 사람이라는 것을 알았다/②그것을 설명하기란 힘들다는 것을 알았다 4. …을 [노력하여] 얻다 ¶③일자리를 좀 구해 주시겠읍니까?/④그는 용기를 내어 시련과 맞섰다 5. …에 다다르다, 미치다 6. [결론 따위]에 달하다; …이라고 판결하다 ¶⑤그는 유죄 판결을 받았다 7. …을 공급하다; 마련하다, 준비하다 ¶⑥그 호텔은 설비가 좋다
[熟] 1)자기의 천분을 알다 2)…을 발견하다; [수수께끼를] 풀다; 배우다
—[名] 발견; 우연히 발견한 값진 물건

find·er [fáindər] *n.* [C] **1.** a person who finds. **2.** a small lens on a camera to help find objects more easily.
—[名] 1. 발견자 2. [카메라·망원경의] 파인더

* **find·ing** [fáindiŋ] *n.* **1.** [U] discovery. **2.** [C] 《often *pl.*》 something found. **3.** [C] a decision reached after an examination. **4.** 《*pl.*》 tools, supplies, etc.
—[名] 1. 발견, 찾아내기 2. 발견물 3. 판결, 판정 4. 부속품류, 부속물, [직공 등의] 여러가지 연장

‡ **fine**[1] [fain] *adj.* **1.** very good; excellent. ⇨[N.B.] ¶*A ~ pal you are!*① **2.** clear; bright. ¶ *a ~ day.* **3.** very small or thin. ¶*~ thread / ~ sand / a ~ pen.* **4.** delicate. ¶*a ~ question.* **5.** sharp; sensitive. ¶*He has a ~ ear for music.* **6.** elegant; refined. ¶*a ~ manner.* **7.** handsome; good-looking.
—*adv.* (*colloq.*) very well; splendidly.
—[形] 1. 훌륭한, 멋진; 좋은 [N.B.] 반어적(反語的)인 뜻으로도 씀 ¶①친구 한번 좋다 2. 맑게 갠 3. 작은; 가는; 보드라운; 고운 4. 미묘한 5. 날카로운, 예민한; 감수성이 강한 6. 세련된 7. 아름다운, 미모의
—[副] 훌륭히, 잘

fine[2] [fain] *n.* [C] a sum of money paid as a punishment. —*vt.* cause (someone) to pay a fine.
—[名] 벌금, 과료 —[他] …에 벌금을 과하다

fine-drawn [fáindrɔ́:n] *adj.* **1.** drawn out very thin. ¶*a ~ wire.* **2.** very subtle; too subtle.
—[形] 1. 아주 가늘게 뽑은 2. [토론 따위가] 세밀한 데까지 미친

* **fine·ly** [fáinli] *adv.* in a fine manner.
—[副] 훌륭히, 멋지게; 가늘게; 정교하게

fine·ness [fáinnis] *n.* [U] **1.** the state or quality of being fine. **2.** the proportion of pure gold or silver in a mixture of metals.
—[名] 1. 훌륭함, 멋짐, 아름다움 2. 순도(純度), [합금 중의] 함유량의 비율

fin·er·y [fáinəri] *n.* [U] gay clothes or ornaments.
—[名] 아름다운(화려한) 옷(장식품)

fine-spun [fáinspʌ́n] *adj.* **1.** spun until very thin. **2.** very subtle.
—[形] 1. 아주 가늘게 짠 2. 미묘한, 치밀한

‡ **fin·ger** [fíŋgər] *n.* [C] **1.** one of the five end parts of the hand, usu. except the thumb. **2.** the part of a glove that covers a finger. **3.** something like a finger in shape or use. ¶*the fingers of a clock.*①
—*vt.* touch or hold (something) with the fingers; turn about (something) in the fingers.
—[名] 1. 손가락 2. [장갑의] 손가락 3. 손가락 모양의 것 ¶①시계의 바늘
—[他] …을 손가락으로 만지다(만지작거리다, 장난하다)

F

finger bowl [⌐-⌐] *n.* a bowl to hold water for rinsing the fingers at table after eating.
—[名] [식탁 위의] 손가락 씻는 그릇

fin·ger·ing [fíŋg(ə)riŋ] *n.* [U] **1.** the act of handling with the fingers. **2.** the act or technique of using the fingers in playing a musical instrument. **3.** signs to show how the fingers are to be used.
—[名] 1. 손가락으로 만지작거리기, 손장난 2. 운지법(運指法) 3. 운지 기호

finger post [⌐-⌐] *n.* a post, often shaped like a finger, to show the direction.
—[名] 길을 가리키는 손가락표

fin·ger·print [fíŋgərprìnt] *n.* [C] an impression of the lines on the end of a finger used for identifying a person. —*vt.* take the fingerprints of (someone).
—[名] 지문 —[他] …의 지문을 채취하다

fin·ger·stall [fíŋgərstɔ̀:l] *n.* [C] a cover for a injured finger made of leather or rubber.
—[名] 손가락 싸개(고무·가죽 따위로 만들어 다친 손가락을 싸는 것)

fin·ger·tip [fíŋgərtìp] *n.* [C] the tip of a finger.
—[名] 손가락 끝

fin·i·cal [fínik(ə)l] *adj.* too particular or precise.
—[形] 지나치게 신경을 쓰는, 너무 꼼꼼한

fi·nis [fínis / fáinis] *n.* [C] ⦅*sing.* only⦆ the end.
—[名] 끝, 종결, 죽음

‡ **fin·ish** [fíniʃ] *vt.* **1.** bring (something) to the end; come to the end of (something). ⦅~ *doing*⦆ ¶ ~ *one's work* / ~ *writing a letter*. **2.** make (something) perfect; complete. **3.** overcome; destroy; kill —*vi.* come to an end; end.
—[他] 1. …을 끝마치다 2. …을 완성하다; 마무리하다 3. …을 해치우다; 죽이다 —[自] 끝나다; 그치다

1) ***finish off,*** bring (something) to the end; give final touches to (something); kill.
2) ***finish up,*** complete; use up completely; eat the whole of (something).
3) ***finish with,*** end; complete; stop being friends with (someone).
[熟] 1)…을 끝내다; 죽이다 2)…을 마무리하다; 다 써 버리다; [음식]을 먹어치우다 3)…으로 끝장을 내다; …와 절교하다

—*n.* [C] **1.** an end; the last stage. **2.** a completed state. **3.** a way of finishing.
—[名] 1. 끝, 종결; 최후 2. 완성 3. 마무리

‡ **fin·ished** [fíniʃt] *adj.* **1.** completed; perfect. **2.** refined; fine.
—[形] 1. 완성된, 완전한 2. 세련된

fi·nite [fáinait] *adj.* having limits; (*Grammar*) having definite person, number and tense. ↔infinite
—[形] 한이 있는; 한정된; ⦅文法⦆ 정형(定形)의, 인칭·수에 제한되는

Fin·land [fínlənd] *n.* a country in northern Europe. ⇒[N.B.]
—[名] 핀란드 [N.B.] 수도는 Helsinki

Finn [fin] *n.* [C] a person of Finland.
—[名] 핀란드 사람

Finn·ish [fíniʃ] *adj.* of Finland, its people, or their language. —*n.* [U] the language of Finland.
—[形] 핀란드[사람·말]의 —[名] 핀란드 말

fin·ny [fíni] *adj.* having fins; like a fin; of fish.
—[形] 지느러미가 있는(것 같은); 물고기의

fiord, fjord [fjɔ:rd] *n.* [C] a long, narrow inlet of the sea between high banks, esp. in Norway.
—[名] 협만(峽灣), 협강(峽江), 피요르드

• **fir** [fə:r] *n.* [C] an evergreen tree which has cones and needlelike leaves like the pine; [U] its wood.
—[名] 전나무; 전나무 재목

‡ **fire** [fáiər] *n.* **1.** [U] the heat or light produced by burning flame. **2.** [C] something burning; burning material in a stove, etc. **3.** [C] a destructive burning. ¶ *A ~ broke out in* Chongro *last night.*① **4.** [U] ⦅often *a* ~⦆ the shooting of guns, etc. **5.** [U] strong feeling; excitement.
—[名] 1. 불, 불꽃 2. [모닥불·난로 따위의] 불 3. 화재, 불 ¶①어젯밤 종로에서 불이 났다 4. [총포의] 발사, 포화; 사격 5. 정열, 열정

1) ***catch*** (or ***take***) ***fire,*** begin to burn.
2) ***lay a fire,*** prepare a fire in a fireplace, etc.
3) ***on fire,*** burning.
4) ***play with fire,*** take unnecessary risks.
5) ***set fire to something; set something on fire,*** cause something to burn.
[熟] 1)불붙다 2)불 땔 준비를 하다 3)불타는, 불붙고 있는 4)불장난하다, 경솔하게도 위험한 짓을 하다 5)…에 불을 붙이다

—*vt.* **1.** cause (something) to burn. **2.** supply fuel to (something). **3.** dry (something) by heat; bake. ¶ ~ *bricks.* **4.** excite. ¶ ~ *someone's blood.* **5.** shoot (guns, etc.) **6.** (*colloq.*) dismiss (someone) from a post. —*vi.* **1.** burst into flame. **2.** grow hot, red, or excited. **3.** (of guns) go off; shoot. ⦅~ *at* something⦆
—[他] 1. …에 불을 붙이다 2. …에 연료를 지피다 3. …을 불에 쬐어 말리다; 굽다 4. [감정]을 자극하다 5. …을 발사하다 6. …을 해고하다 —[自] 1. 불이 붙다 2. 흥분하다, 격하다 3. 발사하다

fire up, ⓐ set on fire. ⓑ become angry.
[熟] ⓐ불을 붙이다(때다) ⓑ분격하다

fire alarm [⌐-⌐] *n.* a signal that a fire has broken out; an apparatus that gives such a signal.
—[名] 화재 경보; 화재 경보기

fire·arm [fáiərà:rm] *n.* ⦅usu. *pl.*⦆ a small weapon, such as a gun, a pistol, a rifle, etc.
—[名] 화기, 총포

fire bomb [⌐⌐] *n.* a bomb that burns violently for the purpose of destruction.
—[名] 소이탄

fire·brand [fáiərbrænd] *n.* [C] **1.** a piece of burning wood. **2.** a person who stirs up strife among a crowd.
—[名] 1. 관솔, 불붙이는 나무토막 2. 소란 따위의] 선동자

F

fire·brick [fáiərbrìk] *n.* ⓒ a piece of brick made of a special clay that can withstand great heat. —몡 내화(耐火) 벽돌

fire brigade [´-`] *n.* an organized body of firemen. —몡 소방대

fire company [´-`-] *n.* an organized body of firemen. —몡 소방대

fire·crack·er [fáiərkrækər] *n.* ⓒ a roll of paper which contains gunpowder and a fuse. —몡 폭죽(爆竹), 딱총

fire·damp [fáiərdæmp] *n.* ⓤ a gas formed in coal mines which is sometimes explosive. —몡 탄갱(炭坑) 내의 폭발 가스

fire·dog [fáiərdɔ̀:g / fáiədɔ̀g] *n.* ⓒ an iron support for logs in a fireplace; an andiron. —몡 [벽난로의] 장작 받침쇠

fire engine [´-`] *n.* a machine to put out fires, usu. with hoses for throwing water; a truck equipped with such a machine. —몡 소방 펌프; 소방차

fire escape [´-`] *n.* a stairway, ladder, etc. to give a way of escape from a burning building. —몡 화재 피난 장치, 피난 사닥다리

fire extinguisher [´-`---] *n.* a portable metal tank filled with chemicals which extinguish fire. —몡 소화기(消火器)

fire·fly [fáiərflài] *n.* ⓒ (pl. **-flies**) a small insect that emits flashes of soft light. —몡 반디

fire·guard [fáiərgà:rd] *n.* ⓒ a metal screen placed in front of a fireplace as a protection. ⇒fig. —몡 난롯가에 두른 철망

fire hose [´-`] *n.* a tube to carry water to put out fires. —몡 소방용 호오스

fire irons [´-`] *n. pl.* the poker, tongs, shovel, etc. which are used in tending for a domestic fireplace. —몡 [부지깽이·부젓가락·부삽 따위] 난로용 연장

[fireguard]

fire·less [fáiərlis] *adj.* without a fire; lacking fire. —몝 불이 없는

fire·light [fáiərlàit] *n.* ⓤⓒ the light cast by a fire. —몡 난로의 불빛, 불빛

fire·lock [fáiərlɔ̀k / fáiəlɔ̀k] *n.* ⓒ an early type of gun that was fired by sparks. —몡 화승총(火繩銃)

fire·man [fáiərmən] *n.* ⓒ (pl. **-men** [-mən]) 1. a person who is trained to put out fires. 2. a person who takes care of the fire in a furnace, a boiler, etc. —몡 1. 소방수 2. 화기 감시원, 화부

·**fire·place** [fáiərplèis] *n.* ⓒ a place to hold a fire, esp. one built at the base of a chimney. —몡 벽난로, 난로

fire·proof [fáiərprù:f] *adj.* made of material that will not burn; fire-resisting. ¶a ~ *building*. —몝 내화(耐火)의, 방화(防火)의

fire·side [fáiərsàid] *n.* ⓒ 1. (usu. *the* ~) the place near a fireplace or hearth. 2. home; home or family life. —몡 1. 난롯가, 노변(爐邊) 2. 가정[생활]

fire tower [´-`] *n.* a tower for watching for fires. —몡 화재 감시탑

fire·wood [fáiərwùd] *n.* ⓤ wood for use as fuel. —몡 장작, 땔나무

fire·works [fáiərwə̀:rks] *n. pl.* firecrackers, rockets, etc. used in celebrations to make a loud noise or a brilliant fiery display of light. ¶*let* (*set*) *off* ~.① —몡 꽃불 ¶①꽃불을 쏘아 올리다

fir·ing [fáiəriŋ] *n.* ⓤ 1. the act of setting on fire; the act of shooting guns. 2. material for fuel. —몡 1. 불을 붙이기(때기), 점화, 발포, 발사 2. 연료, 땔감

‡**firm¹** [fə:rm] *adj.* 1. (of the body, a building, etc.) strong and hard; solid; fixed. ¶*a* ~ *muscle* / *a* ~ *building*. 2. (of one's faith, will, etc.) not easily changed; decided; resolute. ¶*a* ~ *conviction*. 3. (*Commerce*) steady; constant. ¶*be* ~ *in price*.① —몝 1. 굳은, 단단한, 튼튼한 2. 단호한, 확고한, 강력한 3.(商)[시세가] 견조(堅調)의, 보합(步合)의 ¶①시세가 보합상태에 있다

firm² [fə:rm] *n.* ⓒ a business company or partnership of two or more people. —몡 상회, 회사

fir·ma·ment [fə́:rməmənt] *n.* (*the* ~) the sky; the heavens. —몡 하늘, 창공; 천계(天界)

‡**firm·ly** [fə́:rmli] *adv.* in a firm manner. —몜 굳게, 단단히, 확고히, 단호히

firm·ness [fə́:rmnis] *n.* ⓤ the state or quality of being firm. —몡 견고, 확고부동

‡**first** [fə:rst] *adj.* 1. before all others in order, time, or place; earliest. ↔last ¶*a* ~ *edition* / *the* ~ *frost of the winter*. 2. most important or highest in rank, quality, etc. ¶*a* ~ *secretary* / *the* ~ *lady*. —몝 1. 제 1의, 첫째의, 처음의, 최초의 2. 제 1위의; 가장 중요한; 최상의; 제 1류의

1) *at first hand,* directly; from personal knowledge. —囝 1) 직접, 손수; 개인적으로 2) 첫눈

2) ***at first sight,*** at the first glance; upon being first seen. 3) ***first thing,*** (*colloq.*) before anything else, at once. 4) ***for the first time,*** before one does anything else. 5) ***in the first place,*** to begin with; firstly.
에; 언뜻 보아서는 3)우선, 맨처음에; 즉시 4)처음으로 5)위선, 맨 먼저

—*adv.* **1.** ahead of any other person or thing in time, rank, or space; to begin with. ¶*We must finish our work ~.* **2.** for the first time. ¶*I ~ met her two years ago.* **3.** rather than anything else. ¶*We will die ~.*①
—[副] **1.** 첫째로, 최초로; 우선, 먼저 **2.** 처음으로 **3.** 오히려, 차라리 ¶①차라리 죽는 편이 낫다(죽어 버리겠다)

1) ***first and foremost,*** before all others; first of all. 2) ***first and last,*** altogether; on the whole.
[熟] 1)[무엇보다도] 맨 먼저 2)전후를 통하여; 통틀어서

—*n.* [C] 《usu. *the ~*》 **1.** the person, thing, place, etc. that is first. ¶*the ~ of the speakers.* **2.** the first day of a month. ¶*the ~ of June.* **3.** a first prize in a race, etc. **4.** 《*pl.*》 articles of the best quality.
—[名] **1.** 제 1, 처음, 제 1 위 **2.** 달의 첫째 날 **3.** 1 등상 **4.** 1 등품, 최우량품

1) ***at*** [***the***] ***first,*** in the beginning. 2) ***be the first*** (=*do willingly* or eagerly) ***to do something.*** 3) ***from the first,*** from the beginning.
[熟] 1)처음에는 2)솔선하여 …하다 3)처음부터

first-aid [fə́ːrstéid] *adj.* of the first aid.
—[形] 응급치료의

first aid [⌐ ⌐] *n.* temporary or emergency treatment given to an injured person before regular medical treatment.
—[名] 응급치료

first-born [fə́ːrstbɔ̀ːrn] *adj.* born first; eldest. ¶*one's ~ child.* —*n.* [C] the first-born child; the eldest.
—[形] 맨 먼저 [태어]난 —[名] 장자, 장녀, 첫아이

first-class [fə́ːrstklǽs / fə́ːs(t)kláːs] *adj.* of the highest, finest or best quality; (*colloq.*) excellent. ¶*a ~ hotel.* —*adv.* with the best accommodations. ¶*travel ~.*
—[形] 제 1 급의, 제 1 류의, 최상의; 《口》 아주 훌륭한 —[副] 1 등으로

first class [⌐ ⌐] *n.* **1.** the highest, finest or best class or rank. **2.** (of trains, ships, airplanes, etc.) the most expensive and luxurious class of accommodation.
—[名] **1.** 1 류, 1 급, 제 1 류 **2.** [기차·배·비행기 따위의] 1 등

first floor [⌐ ⌐] *n.* (*Brit.*) the floor just above the ground floor of a building; (*U.S.*) the ground floor.
—[名] [영국의] 2 층, [미국의] 1 층

first fruits [⌐ ⌐] *n. pl.* **1.** the earliest products of a harvest or a season. **2.** the first products or results of one's work or activity.
—[名] **1.** 만물, 햇것, 햇곡식 **2.** 첫수확, 최초의 성과

first-hand [fə́ːrsthǽnd] *adj.* obtained directly from the original source; direct. —*adv.* directly.
—[形] 직접의, 바로 얻은 —[副] 직접으로

first·ling [fə́ːrstliŋ] *n.* [C] **1.** the first product or result of a harvest or a season. **2.** the first offspring of an animal. **3.** the first result.
—[名] **1.** 만물, 햇것, 햇곡식 **2.** [가축의] 첫배 **3.** 최초의 결과

first·ly [fə́ːrstli] *adv.* in the first place; first of all.
—[副] 우선, 첫째로

first name [⌐ ⌐] *n.* Christian name; given name.
—[名] 세례명

first-rate [fə́ːrstréit] *adj.* of the highest, best class or rank; excellent. —*adv.* (*colloq.*) very good; excellently; very well.
—[形] 제 1 급의, 제 1 류의; 우수한 —[副] 《口》 훌륭하게, 아주 멋지게(잘)

firth [fəːrθ] *n.* [C] a narrow arm of the sea; a river mouth.
—[名] 작은 만(灣), 후미

fis·cal [físk(ə)l] *adj.* of the financial matters of a government; financial. ¶*a ~ year.*①
—[形] 국고의, 재정의, 회계의 ¶①회계 연도

‡**fish** [fiʃ] *n.* (pl. **fish·es** or *collectively* **fish**) **1.** [C] a cold-blooded animal which lives in water. **2.** [U] the flesh of such animals when used for food.
—[名] **1.** 물고기, 어류 **2.** 생선, 고기, 어육(魚肉)

1) ***drink like a fish,*** drink a great deal of alcohol. 2) ***feed the fishes,*** ⓐ be seasick. ⓑ drown. 3) ***feel like a fish out of water,*** feel uncomfortable in unsuitable surroundings.
[熟] 1)술을 고래로 마시다 2)ⓐ뱃멀미하다 ⓑ물고기 밥이 되다, 익사하다 3)[뭍에 오른 물고기처럼] 불편하다, 거북하다, 환경이 알맞지 않다

—*vi.* **1.** try to catch fish. ¶*~ with a rod and line.* **2.** search for pearls, etc. in water; try to find anything hidden, buried, etc. 《*~ for* something》 ¶*~ in a pocket for a coin.* **3.** try to get information, etc., usu. by indirect methods. 《*~ for* something》 ¶*~ for compliments.* —*vt.* **1.** catch (fish); try to catch fish in (a lake, etc.) ¶*~ salmon / ~ a river.* **2.** pull or draw out (something or someone) from water or as if from water. 《*~* someone or something *from* or *out of*》 ¶*~ someone from the water.*
—[自] **1.** 고기잡이하다, 낚시질하다 **2.** [진주 따위를] 채취하다; [숨겨져 있는 것을] 찾다 **3.** [정보 따위를] 넌지시(완곡한 방법으로) 캐내다 —[他] **1.** [물고기]를 낚다(잡다); [강]에서 낚시질하다 **2.** …을 물 속에서 끌어올리다; 끌어내다

F

fish out (=*exhaust the fish of; catch all the fish of*) *a pond, etc.*
[熟] [연못 따위]에서 물고기를 몽땅 잡아 버리다, 물고기의 씨가 마르게 하다

fish·er [fíʃər] *n.* [C] **1.** a fisherman. **2.** an animal that catches fish for food. **3.** a fishing-boat.
—[名] 1. 어부; 고기잡이하는 사람, 낚시꾼 2. 물고기를 잡아먹는 동물 3. 어선

* **fish·er·man** [fíʃərmən] *n.* [C] (pl. **-men** [-mən]) **1.** a man who fishes for a living or for sport. **2.** a ship used in fishing.
—[名] 1. 어부, 낚시꾼 2. 어선

fish·er·y [fíʃəri] *n.* (pl. **-er·ies**) **1.** [U] business of catching fish. **2.** [C] a fishing ground.
—[名] 1. 어업 2. 어장

fish·hook [fíʃhùk] *n.* [C] a barbed hook for catching fish.
—[名] 낚시[바늘]

* **fish·ing** [fíʃiŋ] *n.* [U] the act of catching fish for a living or for sport.
—[名] 낚시질; 고기잡이, 어업

fish·mon·ger [fíʃmʌ̀ŋgər] *n.* [C] (esp. *Brit.*) a person who sells fish; a dealer in fish.
—[名] 《英》 생선장수

fish pond [ˊ ˊ] *n.* a pond in which fish are kept or bred.
—[名] 양어못, 양어장

fish·wife [fíʃwàif] *n.* [C] (pl. **-wives**) **1.** a woman who sells fish. **2.** a vulgar, scolding woman.
—[名] 1. 여자 생선장수 2. 입심사나운 (입이 건) 여자

fish·wives [fíʃwàivz] *n.* pl. of **fishwife.**

fish·y [fíʃi] *adj.* (**fish·i·er, fish·i·est**) **1.** like a fish. **2.** full of fish. **3.** (*colloq.*) arousing suspicion; unlikely. ¶*His story sounds ~.* ▷**fish·i·ly** [-li] *adv.*
—[形] 1. 물고기 같은 2. 물고기가 많은 3. 《口》 의심스러운, 미심쩍은; 있을성 싶지 않은

fis·sion [fíʃ(ə)n] *n.* [U] [C] **1.** the act of splitting into parts. ¶*atomic (nuclear) ~.*① **2.** (*Biology*) a process of reproduction by splitting. ¶*grow by ~.*②
—[名] 1. 열개(裂開), 분열 ¶①원자핵(핵)분열 2. 《生》 분열, 분체(分體) ¶②분열 증식(增殖)하다

fis·sure [fíʃər] *n.* [C] a long, narrow opening; a crack.
—[名] 갈라진 틈, 째진 금, 균열

* **fist** [fist] *n.* [C] **1.** a clenched hand. **2.** (*colloq.*) a hand. ¶*Give us your ~.*① **3.** (*colloq.*) handwriting. ¶*He writes a good ~.* —*vt.* strike (something) with the fist.
—[名] 1. 주먹 2. 《口》 손 ¶①악수하자, 손을 내밀게 3. 《口》 필적(筆跡) —[他] …을 주먹으로 치다(때리다)

‡ **fit¹** [fit] *adj.* (**fit·ter, fit·test**) **1.** suitable or suited for; good enough. 《*~ for; ~ to do*》 ¶*~ food for dogs / ~ to drink / ~ for a king.* **2.** proper; right. ¶*It is not ~ for me to do such a thing.* **3.** ready; in suitable condition. ¶*The ship is now ~ for sea.*① **4.** in good health; sound mentally and physically. ¶*He keeps ~ by playing tennis.*②
—[形] 1. 적합한, 알맞은, 어울리는 2. 적절한 3. 준비가 되어 있는 ¶①배는 떠날 준비가 되어 있다 4. 건강 상태가 좋은 ¶②그는 정구를 하여 건강을 유지하고 있다

see (or ***think***) ***fit*** (=*consider proper* or *advisable; decide*) *to do.*
[熟] […하는 것이] 적당하다고 …생각하기로 작정하다

—*v.* (**fit·ted** or **fit, fit·ting**) *vt.* **1.** be suitable for or to (something or someone); suit. ¶*The name fits him perfectly. / He fits the description. / This coat doesn't ~ him well.* **2.** make (someone or something) suitable; adapt; prepare. 《~ something *to* (or *in*); ~ someone *for*; ~ someone *to do*》 ¶*~ oneself for a new job / ~ the punishment to the crime / This school fits students for college.*③ */ The hard training fitted us to win the championship.* **3.** furnish; supply; equip. 《~ someone or something *with*》 ¶*~ a library with shelves.* —*vi.* be suitable or proper; agree. ¶*~ like a glove*④ */ The door fits badly.*⑤
—[他] 1. …에 적합하다, 맞다 2. …을 적합하게(맞게) 하다; [할 수 있도록] …에게 준비시키다 ¶③이 학교는 대학 진학을 위한 준비 교육을 한다 3. …에 공급하다; …에 갖추다, 설비하다 —[自] 맞다, 적합하다 ¶④꼭 맞다/⑤그 문은 잘 맞지 않는다

1) ***fit in,*** be in harmony; accord. 《*~ with*》 ¶*She doesn't ~ in with others.*
2) ***fit out*** (or ***up***), supply; equip.
[熟] 1)[…와] 일치하다, 조화하다 2)…공급(장비)하다

—*n.* **1.** [U] the state or quality of being fit. ¶*The ~ of this coat is perfect.* **2.** a thing that fits.
—[名] 1. 적합[성] 2. 잘 맞는 것(몸에 맞는 옷 따위)

* **fit²** [fit] *n.* [C] **1.** a sudden, violent attack of disease; loss of consciousness; convulsions. ¶*go into fits.*① **2.** a sudden, temporary outburst of emotion. **3.** a short period of doing one thing. ¶*when the ~ is on.*②
—[名] 1. [병의] 발작; 경련 ¶①졸도(기절)하다 2. [감정의] 격발 3. [일시적인] 기분, 변덕 ¶②[어쩌다가] 마음이 내키면

fit·ful [fítf(ə)l] *adj.* irregular; changeable. ¶*a baby's ~ crying.* ▷**fit·ful·ly** [-fuli] *adv.* —**fit·ful·ness** [-nis] *n.*
—[形] 발작적인; 변덕스러운

fit·ly [fítli] *adv.* in a suitable manner; at a proper time.
—[副] 적당히, 적절하게, 꼭 맞게; 적시에

fit·ness [fítnis] *n.* [U] good condition; suitability.
—[名] 적당, 적절, 적합성, 건강

fit·ter [fítər] *n.* [C] **1.** a person who fits. **2.** a person who fits dresses, suits, etc. on people. **3.** a man who fits together or adjusts the parts of a machine.
—[名] 1. 적합자 2. [옷을 가봉하여] 입혀 보는 사람 3. [기계의] 조립공, 정비사

fit·ting [fítiŋ] *adj.* suitable; proper. **—*n.* 1.** [C] the act of trying on clothes to see if they fit. **2.** ⟪*pl.*⟫ necessary fixtures of a house, shop, etc.; furnishings.
—[形] 어울리는, 적당한 —[名] 1. 가봉 2. 비품; 가구(도구)류, 부속품

⁑five [faiv] *n.* **1.** [U] the number between four and six; 5. **2.** [C] a group of 5 persons, esp. on a basketball team. **—*adj.*** of 5.
—[名] 1. 다섯, 5 2. 다섯 개 한벌; 5인조, [특히 농구의] 티임 —[形] 5의, 다섯 개(사람)의

fiv·er [fáivər] *n.* [C] (*U.S. colloq.*) a five-dollar bill. (*Brit. colloq.*) a five-pound note.
—[名] ⟪美口⟫ 5달러 지폐; 5파운드 지폐

⁑fix [fiks] *vt.* **1.** make (something) firm; fasten. ¶*~ a handle to an ax* | *~ the date in my mind* (or *memory*).① **2.** set definitely; determine; establish (one's residence, etc.). ¶*~ a price* | *~ a day for a meeting* | *He fixed himself in the city.* **3.** direct (the eyes, one's attention, etc.) steadily; (of an object) attract and hold (one's attention). ¶*~ the mind on a book* | *The sight fixed my attention.* **4.** (esp. *U.S.*) arrange; (*U.S.*) prepare. ¶*~ one's hair* | *~ some refreshments.* **5.** (*U.S.*) repair. ¶*~ a clock.* **6.** put or place (blame, etc.) on someone. ¶*~ our hopes on her.* **7.** (*Chemistry*) make (a gas, etc.) solid; (*Photography*) make (a negative) permanent; (*Dyeing*) make (a color) fast. **—*vi.*** become fixed.
1) ***fix on*** (or ***upon***) (=*decide on; choose*) *something* or *someone.*
2) ***fix up,*** ⓐ arrange; put (something) in order. ⓑ (*U.S.*) repair. ⓒ furnish; provide (someone) with something.
—*n.* [C] (*colloq.*) a difficult position. ¶*I'm in a ~.*
—[他] 1. [사물]을 고정시키다; 장치하다 ¶①그 연대를 단단히 머릿속에 새겨 두다(기억해 두다) 2. …을 결정하다; [주소 따위]를 정하다 3. [주의]를 기울이다, [시선]을 …에 쏟다; [주의]를 끌다, 4. ⟪美⟫ …을 정돈하다; ⟪美⟫ [식사 따위]의 채비를 하다, 준비하다 5. ⟪美⟫ …을 고치다, 조정하다 6. [죄 따위]를 지우다; 뒤집어씌우다, …에게 돌리다 7. ⟪化⟫ [가스 따위]를 응고(凝固)시키다; [사진]을 정착시키다; [빛깔]을 고정시키다
—[自] 고정하다; 고착하다; 응고하다
[熟] 1) …으로 결정하다; …을 선정하다
2) ⓐ …의 준비를 갖추다, …을 정리하다 ⓑ⟪美⟫ …을 수리(수선)하다 ⓒ …으로 비치하다, 설비하다
—[名] ⟪口⟫ 곤란한 처지, 곤경

fix·a·tion [fikséiʃ(ə)n] *n.* [U] the act of fixing; the state of being fixed.
—[名] 고착, 정착

fix·a·tive [fíksətiv] *adj.* serving to prevent fading or change. **—*n.*** [C] a substance for keeping something from fading or changing.
—[形] 정착하는, 고정하는 —[名] 정착제(액)

***fixed** [fikst] *adj.* firmly established; not movable; settled; steady. ¶*a ~ price*① | *a ~ fact* | *with a ~ look.*
—[形] 고정된; 정착된; 확고한 ¶①정가

fix·ture [fíkstʃər] *n.* [C] something permanently put in place. ¶*electric-light fixtures.*①
—[名] 정착물; 설치물, 비품 ¶①전등 설비

fizz [fiz] *vi.* make a hissing sound. **—*n.* 1.** [C] a hissing sound. **2.** [U] a bubbling drink, such as champagne or soda water.
—[自] 쉭 소리내다, 쉭쉭하다 —[名] 1. 슈욱하는 소리 2. 거품 나는 음료

fiz·zle [fízl] *vi.* **1.** make a hissing sound. **2.** (*colloq.*) fail. **—*n.*** [C] **1.** a hissing sound. **2.** (*colloq.*) a failure.
—[自] 1. 슈욱하고 소리내다 2. ⟪口⟫ 실패하다 —[名] 1. 쉭쉭[하는 소리] 2. ⟪口⟫ 실패

fjord [fjɔ́:rd] *n.* =fiord.

flab·ber·gast [flǽbərgæ̀st / -bəgɑ̀:st] *vt.* (*colloq.*) astonish greatly; amaze.
—[他] …을 어리벙벙하게 하다, 깜짝 놀라게 하다

flab·by [flǽbi] *adj.* (**-bi·er, -bi·est**) not firm; soft; weak. ¶*~ muscles* | *~ will.* ▷**flab·bi·ly** [-li] *adv.*
—[形] 연약한; [근육이] 축 늘어진; 맥없는 「늘호늘한

flac·cid [flǽksid] *adj.* feeble; weak. ¶*~ muscles.*
—[形] 연약한; [근육이] 축 늘어진, 호늘호늘한

⁑flag¹ [flæg] *n.* [C] **1.** a piece of cloth with marks or patterns, used as a symbol of a nation, a state, etc. ¶*a national ~* | *strike one's* (or *the*) *~.*① **2.** a piece of cloth with or without a symbol, used to give information. ¶*hang the white ~.*② **—*vt.*** (**flagged, flag·ging**) **1.** put a flag on (something); decorate (something) with flags. **2.** signal or communicate (orders, etc.) by flags.
—[名] 1. 기(旗) ¶①기를 내리다; 항복하다 2. [신호]기 ¶②백기를 올리다, 항복하다 —[他] 1. …에 기를 달다; …을 기로 장식하다 2. …을 기로 신호하다

flag² [flæg] *n.* [C] a plant with large, showy flowers and sword-shaped leaves; the iris.
—[名] 붓꽃·제비붓 따위 붓꽃속(屬)의 식물

flag³ [flæg] *vi.* (**flagged, flag·ging**) get tired; grow weak.
—[自] 시들다; 쇠퇴하다

flag⁴ [flæg] *n.* [C] a flat stone for pavement; a flagstone. **—*vt.*** (**flagged, flag·ging**) pave (a road, etc.) with flagstones.
—[名] [포석(鋪石)용] 판석(板石) —[他] …에 판석을 깔다, 판석으로 포장하다

flag·ging [flǽgiŋ] *n.* **1.** [U] flagstones. **2.** [C] a pavement made of flagstones.
—[名] 1. 판석 2. 판석 포장도로

fla·gi·tious [flədʒíʃəs] *adj.* shamefully wicked.
—[形] 흉악한; 극악무도한, 천인공노할

flag·man [flǽgmən] *n.* [C] (pl. **-men** [-mən]) **1.** a person who carries a flag. **2.** a person who signals at a railroad crossing, etc.
—[名] 1. 기수(旗手) 2. 신호기수

F

flag·on [flǽgən] *n.* ⓒ a vessel for liquids, usu. having a handle and a spout, and often a lid; a large bottle. ⇒fig. —⒠ 목이 가는 병(탁상용·성찬식 ♡⸳ 큰 포도줏병
flag·pole [flǽgpòul] *n.* ⓒ a pole from which a flag is flown. —⒠ 깃대
fla·grant [fléigr(ə)nt] *adj.* outrageous; very wicked; scandalous. ▷**fla·grant·ly** [-li] *adv.* —⒣ 언어도단의; 극악무도한; 악명높은

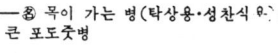
(flagon)

flag·ship [flǽgʃip] *n.* ⓒ a ship that carries the commander of a fleet. —⒠ 기함(旗艦)
flag·staff [flǽgstæf / -stɑ:f] *n.* =flagpole.
flag station [⸳ ⸳⸳] *n.* ⓒ a railroad station at which trains stop only when a signal is given. —⒠ 간이(임시) 정거장(신호가 있을 때에만 정차함)
flag·stone [flǽgstòun] *n.* ⓒ a large, flat stone for pavements, etc. —⒠ 판석(板石), 포석(鋪石)
flail [fleil] *n.* ⓒ an old-fashioned instrument for beating grain by hand. —⒠ [보리타작 따위에 쓰는] 도리깨
flair [flɛər] *n.* **1.** ⓒ keen perception. **2.** ⓤ natural talent or ability. —⒠ 1.직각적 식별력, 예민한 안식(眼識) 2.재능, 재간

• **flake** [fleik] *n.* ⓒ a small, light mass. *¶flakes of snow.* —*vi.* **1.** come off in flakes. **2.** break into flakes. —*vt.* **1.** make (snow, etc.) fall in flakes. **2.** separate (something) into flakes. ▷**flake·like** [-làik] *adj.* —⒠ [눈·깃털의] 작은 조각 —⒤ 1. 펄펄 내리다 2.얇은 조각으로 떨어지다 —⒣ 1. …을 펄펄 흩날리다(내리게 하다) 2. …을 얇은 조각으로 벗기다
flak·y [fléiki] *adj.* (**flak·i·er, flak·i·est**) **1.** consisting of flakes. **2.** easily broken into flakes. —⒣ 1. 얇은 조각의, 조각조각의 2. 벗겨지기 쉬운
flam·boy·ant [flæmbɔ́iənt] *adj.* **1.** gorgeously brilliant; excessively decorated. **2.** of or having the style of late French Gothic architecture. ▷**flam·boy·ant·ly** [-li] *adv.* —⒣ 1. [문체(文體)·몸차림이] 눈부시게 화려한, 현란한 2.《建》플랑보양 양식의, 불꽃 모양의, 화염(火焰)의
: **flame** [fleim] *n.* **1.** ⓤⓒ glowing, red or yellow tongues of light from a blazing fire. **2.** ⓒ a thing or condition like flame. **3.** ⓒ a burning feeling; passion. **4.** ⓒ (*slang*) a sweetheart. —⒠ 1.불꽃, 화염 2.불꽃 같은 광채, 휘황한 광채 3.정염(情炎), 정열, 격정 4.《俗》애인, 연인

1) *burst into flame[s],* burst out in flames; begin to burn.
2) *commit to the flames,* burn up; reduce to ashes.
3) *fan the flame,* stir up someone's feelings or passions.
4) *in flames,* bursting into flames; burning.

☒ 1)확 타오르다 2)소각하다 3)정열을 부채질하다 4)불타오르다

—*vi.* **1.** burn with flames. **2.** grow hot, red, etc. **3.** give out a bright light. **4.** have or show a burning feeling; burst out quickly and hotly [with anger, etc.]. *flame out* (or *up*), burst out in flame or with anger. —⒤ 1. 불길을 내다(뿜다), 불타오르다 2.[얼굴이] 확 붉어지다 3.[불꽃처럼] 빛나다, 번쩍이다 4.[정열 따위가] 불타오르다; 불끈 성내다, 분격하다
☒ 확 타오르다; 분노(격분)하다

flam·ing [fléimiŋ] *adj.* **1.** burning. **2.** very bright. **3.** passionate; ardent. —⒣ 1. 불타는, 타오르는 2. [빛같이] 불타는 듯한 3. 열렬한, 정열에 불타는
fla·min·go [fləmíŋgou] *n.* ⓒ (*pl.* **-gos** or **-goes**) a tropical wading bird with long legs, a long neck and webbed feet. —⒠ 플라밍고, 홍학(紅鶴)
flange [flændʒ] *n.* ⓒ a projecting rim on a wheel for keeping it in place. ⇒fig. —⒠ 플랜지, 불쑥 나온 테두리, [차바퀴의] 테두리, 가장자리
• **flank** [flæŋk] *n.* ⓒ **1.** the fleshy side of an animal or a person between the ribs and the hip; a piece of meat cut from this part. **2.** (of a building, a mountain, etc.) the side. **3.** The right or left side of an army, a fleet, etc. *¶cover a ~*① */ turn the ~ of the enemy.*②
in flank, at, on or from side. *¶take in ~.*③
—⒠ 1. 옆구리; 옆구릿살 2. [건물·산 따위의] 측면 3. [대열의] 측면; [좌우의] 익(翼) ¶①측면을 엄호하다/②적의 측면을 돌아 뒤로 나가다

☒ 측면으로(에서) ¶③측면을 찌르다

—*vt.* **1.** be at the side of (someone or something). **2.** get around the right or left side of (someone or something). **3.** attack (an enemy, etc.) from the side. ▷**flank·er** [-ər] *n.*
(flange)
—⒣ 1. …의 측면에 서다 2. …의 측면을 돌다 3. …의 측면을 공격하다

flan·nel [flǽn(ə)l] *n.* ⓤ **1.** a soft, warm woolen cloth. **2.** (*pl.*) clothes made of flannel; woolen underwear —*adj.* made of flannel. —⒠ 1.플란넬 2.플란넬 옷가지; 모직으로 만든 두꺼운 속옷
—⒣ 플란넬로 만든

• **flap** [flæp] *v.* (**flapped, flap·ping**) *vi.* **1.** (of wings) move up and down. **2.** (of a wide, flat object) move lightly with a slight noise. *¶The curtains flapped in the* —⒤ 1. [새가 날개를] 푸드덕거리다, 날개치다 2. 펄럭이다, 나부끼다 —⒣ 1. [새가 깃을] 푸드덕거리다, 날개치

breeze. —*vt.* **1.** move (the wings) up and down. **2.** cause (a wide, flat object) to move lightly with a slight noise. **3.** strike (someone or something) with something broad and flat. ¶~ *flies away* (or *off*).①

다 2. …을 펄럭이게(나부끼게) 하다 3. …을 가볍게 치다, 찰싹찰싹 치다 ¶①쳐서 파리를 쫓다

—*n.* [C] **1.** a broad and flat object that hangs loosely, attached at one side only. ¶*the* ~ *of an envelope*. **2.** a flapping motion or noise.

—[名] 1. 늘어져서 펄렁거리는 것, [봉투·호주머니 따위의] 늘어진 부분, 뚜껑 2. 펄럭이기, 나부낌, 펄럭이는 소리

flap·per [flǽpər] *n.* [C] **1.** something broad and flat used for striking with. **2.** a flap.

—[名] 1. 찰싹찰싹 치는 것 2. 파리채

flare [flɛər] *vi.* **1.** burn unsteadily. **2.** signal by lights. **3.** spread out in the shape of a bell. —*vt.* **1.** signal (something) by lights. **2.** spread out.

—[自] 1. 불길이 너울거리다 2. 빛으로 신호하다 3. 나팔꽃 모양으로 벌어지다 —[他] 1. …을 빛(화염)으로 신호하다 2. …을 튀어(뻗어)나오게 하다

flare up (or ***out***), ⓐ burst into flames. ⓑ get angry suddenly.

[熟] ⓐ확 타오르다 ⓑ불끈 성내다

—*n.* [C] **1.** an unsteady, bright light. **2.** a dazzling light used for a signal. **3.** (of anger, etc.) an outburst. **4.** a part spreading out into a bell shape. **5.** a part that spreads out or curves. ¶*a* ~ *skirt*.

—[名] 1. 너울거리는 불꽃, 휘황한 불빛 2. 섬광 신호 3. [노염 따위의] 폭발 4. 나팔꽃 모양의 벌어짐 5. [스커어트 따위의] 플레어

flar·ing [flɛ́əriŋ] *adj.* **1.** flaming. **2.** very bright or showy. **3.** gradually spreading outward.

—[形] 1. 훨훨 타는 2. 현란한, 화려한 3. 나팔꽃 모양의

⁑**flash** [flæʃ] *n.* [C] **1.** a sudden bright light. ¶*a* ~ *of lightning*. **2.** (of wit, anger, genius, etc.) a sudden and brilliant burst. ¶*a* ~ *of hope* | *a* ~ *of genius*.① **3.** a brief news report, esp. one given by radio. **4.** [U] showy display.

—[名] 1. 섬광, 번쩍임 2. [기지 따위의] 번득임 ¶①천재의 번득임 3. [라디오 따위의] 짤막한 뉴우스 4. 속된(야한) 꾸밈

in a flash, in a very short time; suddenly.

[熟] 순식간에, 금시에, 별안간

—*vi.* **1.** appear with sudden brightness; gleam; glitter. ¶*Lightning flashed.* | *His eyes flashed with rage.* **2.** come suddenly into the mind; move quickly. 《~ *by*》 ¶*A car flashed by.* —*vt.* **1.** give out (fire, light, etc.) in sudden flashes; cause (something) to flash. ¶~ *gunpowder* | *Her eyes flashed anger.* **2.** send (a signal, etc.) by flashes of light; communicate (news, etc.) in a short period. **3.** rapidly direct (a glance, a smile, etc.) at someone. **4.** (*colloq.*) display showily.

—[自] 1. 확 비추다, 번쩍이다; 빛나다 2. [생각 따위가] 문득(퍼뜩) 떠오르다; 휙 지나가다 —[他] 1. …을 번쩍이게 하다(발화시키다); 번득이게 하다 2. [신호]를 점멸광(點滅光)으로 보내다; [뉴우스]를 속보하다 3. [미소 따위]를 얼핏 보내다 4. 《口》 …을 자랑해 보이다, 과시하다

flash·i·ly [flǽʃili] *adv.* in a flashy manner.

—[副] 야하게, 난하게

flash·light [flǽʃlàit] *n.* [C] **1.** the light sent out by a lighthouse. **2.** a portable electric light. **3.** a sudden, very bright light for taking photographs.

—[名] 1. [등대의] 회전등 2. 회중전등 3. 섬광; 섬광등

flash·y [flǽʃi] *adj.* (**flash·i·er, flash·i·est**) **1.** very bright for a moment. **2.** looking very bright and good, but worthless. ▷**flash·i·ly** [-li] *adv.*

—[形] 1. 일시적으로 화려한 2. 야한; 거죽만 번드르르한

flask [flæsk / flɑːsk] *n.* [C] **1.** a glass bottle with a narrow neck used in chemical laboratories for holding or heating liquids, etc. **2.** a small metal or leather bottle for holding liquids or powder.

—[名] 1. 플라스크, [화학 실험용] 유리병 2. 물통, 수통(水筒); 탄약통

⁑**flat**[1] [flæt] *adj.* (**flat·ter, flat·test**) **1.** having an even surface; smooth and even; level. ¶*a* ~ *piece of land*. **2.** not very deep or thick. ¶*a* ~ *pan* | *a* ~ *coin*. **3.** 《as *predicative*》 lying at full length; spread out. ¶*I laid him* ~ *on the ground*. **4.** (of a price, etc.) at a fixed rate; uniform. ¶*a* ~ *service charge*.① **5.** (of life, commerce, etc.) inactive; lifeless; dull. ¶*a* ~ *stock market*. **6.** (of drink, food, etc.) having little or no taste or flavor. ¶~ *beer*. **7.** (of a tire) empty of air; deflated. ¶*a* ~ *tire*. **8.** (*Music*) lowered a half step below the true pitch; (of painting) lacking depth or distance; without gloss. **9.** exact; absolute; complete. ¶*a* ~ *refusal*② | *That's* ~.③ **10.** (*colloq.*) without money; penniless.

—[形] 1. 납작한, 평평한, 판판한 2. [접시 따위가] 얇은, 두껍지 않은 3. 납작 엎드린, 발딱 쓰러진 4. 균일의 ¶①균일 서어비스 요금 5. 활발하지 못한, 활기 없는; 따분한 6. 김빠진, 맛없는 7. [타이어가] 바람이 빠진, 빵꾸난 8. 《樂》 반음 낮은, 변음의; [그림이] 단조로운; 광택이 없는 9. 어김없는; 단호한; 전적인 ¶②단호한 거절/③말한 그대로다, 단연 그렇다 10. 《口》 무일푼의

—*adv.* **1.** in a flat manner; evenly. **2.** exactly; absolutely; completely. ¶*10 seconds* ~④ | *I tell you* ~.⑤ **3.** (*Music*) half a step below the true pitch.

—[副] 1. 납작하게, 판판하게 2. 꼭, 정확히; 딱 잘라, 단호히; 완전히, 전적으로 ¶④10초 플랫(경기 기록)/⑤솔직히 말씀드립니다 3. 《樂》 반음 내려서

fall flat, ⓐ fall suddenly and at full length. ⓑ (of a joke, etc.) fail to have the desired effect or to impress.

[熟] ⓐ팍(발딱) 쓰러지다 ⓑ실패하다; 흥미를 끌지 못하다

—*n.* [C] **1.** something flat; a flat part or side. **2.** a

—[名] 1. 납작한(판판한) 것; 판판한 쪽

flat piece of land; a plain; a marsh; ⦅*pl.*⦆ shallows. **3.** (*Music*) a tone a half step below the true pitch; the sign (♭) showing this. ↔sharp
(면) 2. 평지; 평원; 늪; 얕은 갯바닥, 개펄 3. ⦅樂⦆ 내림음; 내림표, 플랫

* **flat²** [flæt] *n.* [C] (*Brit.*) an apartment or a set of rooms on the same floor for a single family.
—[名] ⦅英⦆ 같은 층의 여러 방을 한 가족이 쓰게 된 주택; 아파아트

flat·boat [flǽtbòut] *n.* [C] a large flat-bottomed boat used on a river.
—[名] [대형의] 너벅선, 바닥이 평평한 배

flat·feet [flǽtfì:t] *n.* pl. of **flatfoot**.

flat·fish [flǽtfìʃ] *n.* [C] (pl. **-fish·es** or *collectively* **-fish**) any of a group of fishes with flat bodies and with both eyes on the upper side, such as the flounder.
—[名] 넙치 가자미류의 물고기

flat·foot [flǽtfùt] *n.* [C] (pl. **-feet**) a foot with a flattened arch.
—[名] 편평족(扁平足), 마당발

flat·foot·ed [flǽtfùtid] *adj.* of a flatfoot; with flatfeet.
—[形] 편평족의

flat·i·ron [flǽtàiərn / -àiən] *n.* [C] an iron with a flat surface, heated for use in pressing or smoothing cloth.
—[名] 다리미, 인두

flat·ten [flǽtn] *vt., vi.* make (something) or become flat.
—[他][自] 평평하게 하다(되다)

* **flat·ter** [flǽtər] *vt.* **1.** praise too much; try to please (someone) with compliments. ¶*Oh, you ~ me!*① **2.** make (someone) look better than what is true. ¶*The picture flatters her.*② **3.** satisfy the vanity of (someone). ¶*He was flattered by her invitation.* **4.** please (the senses, the eye, the ear, etc.) ¶*The music flattered her ears.*
flatter oneself (=*venture to think; be pleased to know or think*) ***that…***
—[他] 1. …에게 아첨하다, 알랑거리다, 추어주다 ¶①비행기 태우시네요 2. …을 실물보다 좋게 보이게 하다 ¶②이 사진은 실제의 그녀보다 낫게 찍혔다 3. …을 의기양양하게(우쭐하게) 하다 4. [오감(五感)을] 즐겁게 하다
[熟] 제딴에는 …이라고 믿다, 자부하다

* **flat·ter·y** [flǽtəri] *n.* (pl. **-ter·ies**) **1.** [U] the act of flattering. **2.** [C] praise, usu. insincere and false.
—[名] 1. 아첨, 아부 2. 감언[이설]

flaunt [flɔ:nt] *vt., vi.* **1.** display proudly; parade. ¶~ *[one's] new clothes.* **2.** wave or flutter in the wind. ¶*flags flaunting in the wind.*
—[他][自] 1. [···을] 자랑해 보이다 2. [기 따위]를 휘날리다; [기 따위가] 휘날리다

* **fla·vor,** *Brit.* **-vour** [fléivər] *n.* [U][C] **1.** taste. **2.** a characteristic quality. **3.** odor. **—***vt.* **1.** give taste to (something); season. ⦅~ something *with*⦆ **2.** give a characteristic quality to (something).
—[名] 1. 맛, 풍미, 향미 2. 풍취, 운치, 정취, 향기 —[他] 1. …에 맛을 내다 2. …에 풍취를 곁들이다

fla·vor·ing, *Brit.* **-vour-** [fléivəriŋ] *n.* [C] a thing used to give a special taste to food or drink.
—[名] 조미료, 양념

* **fla·vour** [fléivər] *n.* (*Brit.*) =flavor.

flaw [flɔ:] *n.* [C] a crack; a fault; an imperfect point. ¶*a ~ in one's character.*
—[名] 금; 흠; 결점, 결함

flaw·less [flɔ́:lis] *adj.* without a flaw; perfect.
—[形] 흠이 없는; 완전한

* **flax** [flæks] *n.* [U] **1.** a slender, blue-flowered plant grown for its fiber and seeds. **2.** the threadlike fibers from the stem of this plant.
—[名] 1. 아마(亞麻) 2. 아마 섬유

flax·en [flǽksn] *adj.* **1.** like flax; of flax. **2.** like the color of flax; pale-yellow.
—[形] 1. 아마 같은; 아마의, 아마로 만든 2. 아마 빛깔(엷은 황갈색)의

flay [flei] *vt.* **1.** strip off the skin from (something). **2.** scold or criticize severely.
—[他] 1. [껍질]을 벗기다(까다) 2. …을 혹평하다, 몹시 꾸짖다

flea [fli:] *n.* [C] a small, wingless insect which can jump and which sucks the blood of man and other animals.
—[名] 벼룩

flea·bite [flí:bàit] *n.* [C] **1.** a bite of the flea; a trifling wound. **2.** a small inconvenience.
—[名] 1. 벼룩에 물린 자국; 조그마한 상처 2. 사소한 일

fleck [flek] *n.* [C] a spot or streak of color, light, etc., esp. one on the skin. **—***vt.* spot (something) with flecks.
—[名] 반점, 광선; 주근깨 —[他] …에 반점을 넣다

fled [fled] *v.* pt. and pp. of **flee**.

fledge [fledʒ] *vt.* **1.** bring up (a young bird) until it is able to fly. **2.** cover (something) with feathers. **—***vi.* (of birds) grow the feathers necessary for flying.
—[他] 1. [새새끼]를 기르다 2. …을 깃털로 덮다 —[自] 깃털이 다 나다; 날 수 있게 되다

fledged [fledʒd] *adj.* with wings fully developed for flight; able to fly; experienced or capable.
—[形] 깃털이 다 난; 날 수 있게 된; 제 구실을 할 수 있게 된

fledg·ling, *Brit.* **fledge-** [flédʒliŋ] *n.* [C] **1.** a young bird just able to fly. **2.** an inexperienced person.
—[名] 1. 깃털이 갓난 새새끼 2. 풋나기, 애숭이

* **flee** [fli:] *v.* (**fled**) *vi.* **1.** run away. ⦅~ *from* or *to* a place⦆ ¶~ *from the angry tiger* / ~ *for one's life.*① **2.** vanish; disappear swiftly. **—***vt.* run away from (some place). ¶*He fled the country.*
—[自] 1. 달아나다, 도망치다 ¶①간신히 목숨을 건지고 도망치다 2. 사라지다, 소산(消散)하다
—[他] …에서 도망치다, …을 피하다

fleece — flight

fleece [fli:s] *n.* **1.** ⓤ the woolly coat covering a sheep or a similar animal. **2.** ⓒ the amount of wool cut from a sheep at one time. **3.** ⓒ something like wool. —*vt.* **1.** rob; cheat. 《~ someone *of*》 **2.** remove the fleece of (a sheep).

—⓽ 1. [양 따위의] 털 2. 한 마리에서 한 번 깎는 분량의 양털 3. 양털 같은 것 —⓽ 1. [남]에게서 훔쳐내다, 깎대기 벗기다 2. [양]의 털을 깎다

fleec·y [flí:si] *adj.* (**fleec·i·er, fleec·i·est**) **1.** like a fleece. **2.** covered with fleece. **3.** made of fleece.

—⓽ 1. 양털 같은 2. 양털로 덮은 3. 양털로 만든

· fleet¹ [fli:t] *n.* ⓒ **1.** a group of warships under one command. ¶*a combined ~.*① **2.** a large group of ships, airplanes, automobiles, etc. moving or working together or under a single ownership.

—⓽ 1. 함대 ¶①연합 함대 2. [배·비행기·차 따위의] 대(隊)

· fleet² [fli:t] *adj.* swift; rapid. ¶*a fleeting glance.*① —*vi.* (*poetic*) move rapidly. —*vt.* cause (time) to pass swiftly. ¶*Many young gentlemen ~ the time carelessly.*

—⓽ 빠른, 민속한, 쾌속의 ¶①일별(一瞥) —⓼ (詩) 빨리 지나가다, 날아가 버리다 —⓽ [때]를 보내다

: flesh [fleʃ] *n.* ⓤ **1.** the soft parts of the body that are between the skin and the bones. ¶*gain* (or *put on*) *~*① / *in ~ and blood.*② **2.** meat. ⇒NB. **3.** (*the ~*) body, not the soul or spirit. **4.** (*the ~*) physical desires. **5.** the soft part of fruit.
 1) ***flesh and blood,*** ⓐ the human body; human nature. ⓑ a person closely related to one.
 2) ***go the way of all flesh,*** die.
 3) ***in the flesh,*** ⓐ alive; in bodily form. ⓑ in person.

—⓽ 1. 고기, 살 ¶①살찌다/②육체로서 2. 식용의 고기 NB 이 뜻으로는 보통 meat을 씀 3. 육체 4. 육욕; 수성 (獸性) 5. 과육(果肉)

圞 1)ⓐ[피가 통하는] 육체, 인간; 인정 ⓑ육친, 혈육 2)죽다 3)ⓐ산 몸이 되어, 육체의 형상으로 ⓑ직접 본인이

flesh·ly [fléʃli] *adj.* (**-li·er, -li·est**) **1.** of the flesh; bodily. **2.** sensual. ▷**flesh·li·ness** [-nis] *n.*

—⓽ 1. 육체의, 육체적인 2. 육욕에 빠진

flesh·y [fléʃi] *adj.* (**flesh·i·er, flesh·i·est**) **1.** fat. **2.** of or like flesh. **3.** pulpy; very soft. ▷**flesh·i·ness** [-nis] *n.*

—⓽ 1. 살찐, 뚱뚱한 2. 육체의 3. 과육[모양]의; 다육질의; 연한, 말랑말랑한

fleur-de-lis [flə̀:rdəlíː, -líːs] *n.* ⓒ (pl. **fleurs-de-lis** [flə̀:rdəlíːz]) **1.** an iris [flower or plant]. **2.** an ornament like an iris. ⇒fig.

—⓽ 1. 붓꽃[의 꽃] 2. 붓꽃 모양의 무늬[문장(紋章)]

: flew [flu:] *v.* pt. of **fly**¹.

flex [fleks] *vt., vi.* bend or curve (a joint, a finger, etc.).

[fleur-de-lis 2.]

—⓽⓼ …을 구부리다; 구부러지다

flex·i·bil·i·ty [flèksibíləti] *n.* ⓤ the quality of being flexible.

—⓽ 구부리기 쉬움, 유연[성]

flex·i·ble [fléksibl] *adj.* **1.** easily bent without breaking. **2.** easily managed or led; adaptable.

—⓽ 1. 구부리기 쉬운, 유연한 2. 다루기 쉬운, 유순한; 융통성 있는

flick [flik] *n.* ⓒ **1.** a quick, light stroke, as of a whip. **2.** the light, snapping sound of such a stroke. **3.** the act of moving suddenly. —*vt.* **1.** strike lightly. **2.** move quickly and lightly.

—⓽ 1. 가볍게 때리기, 경타(輕打) 2. 획, 딱[하는 소리] 3. 쾌 움직이기 —⓽ 1. …을 가볍게 톡 때리다 2. 쾌 움직이다

· flick·er¹ [flíkər] *vi.* **1.** shine or burn unsteadily. **2.** move back and forth; quiver. —*n.* ⓒ **1.** an unsteady light or flame. **2.** (of leaves, etc.) a quick and light movement.

—⓼ 1. 깜박깜박하다, 명멸(明滅)하다 2. 한들거리다, 떨다 —⓽ 1. 깜박이는 빛[불꽃] 2. 깜박임, 한들거림

flick·er² [flíkər] *n.* ⓒ a kind of woodpecker of North America with golden-yellow feathers.

—⓽ 딱다구리의 일종

fli·er [fláiər] *n.* ⓒ **1.** a person or a thing that flies; an airplane pilot. **2.** a very fast train, ship, bus, etc.

—⓽ 1. 하늘을 나는 사람(것); 비행사 2. 급행 열차; 쾌속선

: flight¹ [flait] *n.* ⓒ **1.** ⓤⓒ the act or the manner of flying. **2.** a distance that a bullet, an airplane, etc. can fly over. **3.** a group of birds, insects, etc. flying through the air together. **4.** the state of swift passing; (of time) a swift passage. **5.** an act of passing over or beyond what is ordinary. ¶*a ~ of fancy.* **6.** a group or series of stairs. ⇒fig.
 1) ***make*** (or ***take***) ***a flight,*** fly.
 2) ***take*** (or ***wing***) ***its*** (or ***one's***) ***flight,*** fly [off].

[flight¹ 6.]

—⓽ 1. 비행, 날기 2. [탄알 따위의] 비행 거리, 비정(飛程) 3. 메지어 날아가는 철새[따위] 4. 신속한 움직임; [때의] 빠른 경과, 빨리 지나감 5. [공상·야심의] 비약 6. 계단의 한 연속, 연속된 한 줄의 계단

圞 1)비행하다 2)날다; [영혼 따위가] 육체를 떠나다

flight² [flait] *n.* ⓤⓒ the act of fleeing or running away.
 1) ***put the enemy, etc. to flight,*** force the enemy, etc. to run away.

—⓽ 패주, 도주, 탈주, 탈출

圞 1)[적 따위]를 패주시키다 2)도망치다

2) ***take to flight; betake oneself to flight,*** run away.

flight·y [fláiti] *adj.* (**flight·i·er, flight·i·est**) **1.** unsteady in character; changeable. **2.** slightly crazy.
—[形] 1. 들뜬; 변덕스러운 2. 엉뚱한, 경솔한

flim·sy [flímzi] *adj.* (**-si·er, -si·est**) **1.** light and thin; weak. **2.** lacking seriousness; shallow. —*n.* [U] a thin piece of paper used by reporters.
—[形] 1. 얄팍한, 부서지기 쉬운 2. 천박한, 보잘것 없는 —[名] 얇은 종이, 복사용지

flinch [flintʃ] *vi.* move back. 《~ *from* difficulty, danger, pain, etc.》
—[自] 주춤하다, 움찔하다

* **fling** [fliŋ] *v.* (**flung**) *vt.* **1.** throw violently or forcibly. 《~ something *at*》 ¶~ *a stone at a dog.* **2.** move, send, or cast suddenly or angrily. ¶~ *one's clothes on*① / ~ *the door open*② / *The king flung his brother into prison.*③ —*vi.* **1.** go or rush violently. 《~ *away* or *off* someone or something》 ¶*She flung away from him.*④ **2.** (of a horse, etc.) kick or plunge violently. 《~ *about something*》
—[他] 1. …을 세게 던지다, …을 향해 던지다 2. …을 갑자기 움직이다; 내동댕이치다; 내던지다 ¶①옷을 후딱 걸치다/②문을 후닥닥 열다/③그 왕은 동생을 감옥에 처넣었다 —[自] 1. 돌진하다, 내닫다 ¶④그녀는 그를 뿌리치고 가 버렸다 2. [말 따위가] 날뛰다

1) ***fling oneself into an enterprise,*** take up an enterprise vigorously or ardently.
2) ***fling oneself*** (=*depend*) ***on*** (or ***upon***) *someone.*
3) ***fling out,*** ⓐ (of a horse) kick violently. ⓑ (of a person) act or talk wildly; abuse.
[熟] 1)[사업]에 투신(헌신)하다 2)…에 의지하다 3)ⓐ[말이] 날뛰다 ⓑ난폭하게 행동하다; 욕설을 퍼붓다

—*n.* [C] **1.** the act of flinging; a sudden throw or movement. ¶*at one* ~⑤ / *give a* ~.⑥ **2.** (of a horse) the act of kicking or plunging. **3.** a period of self-indulgent or unrestrained activity. **4.** a scornful or abusive remark.
—[名] 1. 내던지기, 휘두르기 ¶⑤단숨(단번)에/⑥내던지다, 걷어차다 2. [말이] 날뛰기; 걷어차기; 발길질 3. 방탕[의 기간] 4. 폭언, 욕설

1) ***have a fling at,*** ⓐ jeer at (someone); abuse. ⓑ make an attempt at (something).
2) ***in full fling,*** at its height.
[熟] 1)ⓐ…을 비웃다 ⓑ…을 꾀하다, 시도하다 2)최고조로

flint [flint] *n.* **1.** [U][C] a very hard stone that makes a spark when struck against steel; a piece of alloy used in a lighter. **2.** [U] anything that is very hard.
—[名] 1. 부싯돌, 라이터 돌 2. 아주 단단한 물건

flint·y [flínti] *adj.* (**flint·i·er, flint·i·est**) **1.** consisting of or like flint. **2.** very hard like flint.
—[形] 1. 부싯돌의(같은) 2. 단단한; 무정한; 완고한

flip [flip] *vt., vi.* (**flipped, flip·ping**) **1.** toss or move (something) with the fingers; strike lightly. ¶~ *up.* **2.** pull suddenly. —*n.* [C] **1.** a light stroke or tap with the fingers. **2.** a sudden, quick movement.
—[他][自] 1. […을] 손가락으로 튀기다; […을] 톡 치다 2. […을] 홱 잡아당기다 —[名] 1. 손가락으로 튀기기 2. 홱 움직이기

flip-flap [flípflæ̀p], **-flop** [-flɑ̀p / -flɔ̀p] *n.* [C] **1.** the sound made when a long, loose thing repeatedly hits another object. **2.** a kind of jumping; a machine with cars for passengers hung at ends of moving arms.
—[名] 1. 파닥파닥[하는 소리] 2. 공중제비; [놀이터의] 공중 회전 시이소

flip·pan·cy [flípənsi] *n.* [U] the state of being flippant.
—[名] 경솔, 경박

flip·pant [flípənt] *adj.* not serious; disrespectful to elders. ¶*a* ~ *answer.* ▷**flip·pant·ly** [-li] *adv.*
—[形] 경솔한, 경망스러운; 주제넘은, 건방진

flip·per [flípər] *n.* [C] a broad, flat limb of certain sea animals used in swimming. ¶*Sea turtles have flippers.*
—[名] 지느러미 모양의 발, [거북·펭귄새 따위의] 물갈퀴, 오리발

flirt [flə:rt] *vt.* **1.** throw suddenly. **2.** move (a fan) to and fro quickly. —*vi.* **1.** make love in a playful way. **2.** think playfully. —*n.* [C] **1.** a person who makes love in a playful way. **2.** a sudden toss; a quick movement of a fan.
—[他] 1. …을 홱 던지다 2. …을 팩팩 움직이다, —[自] 1. 시시덕거리다 2. 장난으로 생각하다, 가지고 놀다 —[名] 1. 사랑장난을 하는 사람 2. 홱 던지기; [부채 따위의] 펄럭거림

flir·ta·tion [flə:rtéiʃ(ə)n] *n.* [U][C] a love affair that is not serious.
—[名] [남녀의] 희롱, 연애 유희

flir·ta·tious [flə:rtéiʃəs] *adj.* inclined to flirt.
—[形] 시시덕거리는, 희롱하기 좋아하는

* **flit** [flit] *vi.* (**flit·ted, flit·ting**) **1.** fly lightly and quickly from place to place. **2.** pass lightly and quickly. —*n.* [C] a light, quick movement.
—[自] 1. 훨훨 날아가다 2. [사람이] 경쾌하게 지나가다, [환상 따위가] 스쳐 지나가다 —[名] 경쾌한 움직임

flit·ter [flítər] *vi.* fly about in an irregular way.
—[自] 훨훨 날아다니다

‡ **float** [flout] *vi.* rest or drift on the surface of water or another liquid; be held up or carried along by air, water, etc. ¶*a leaf floating on the water* / *An adballoon is floating in the sky.*① —*vt.* **1.** cause (something) to float; set (something) afloat; cover (something) with liquid. ¶~ *oil over the swamp to destroy mosquitoes.*② **2.** circulate (rumors, etc.). **3.** (*Commercial*) support (a company, a scheme, etc.); circulate (securities, etc.).
—[自] [물위·하늘 따위에] 뜨다; 떠돌다 ¶①애드발루운이 하늘에 떠 있다 —[他] 1. …을 띄우다; 떠돌게 하다, 표류시키다; …에 액체를 흐르게 하다 ¶②모기를 죽이려고 늪에 기름을 붓다 2. [소문 따위]를 퍼뜨리다 3. [商] …을 성립시키다, 설립하다, 세우다; 유통시키다

floatage

—*n.* ⓒ **1.** something that floats; a buoy. ¶ *a ~ on a fishline.* **2.** a raft; a flat-bottomed boat. **3.** a low, flat car used in a parade or pageant.

float·age [flóutidʒ] *n.* = flotage.

floa·ta·tion [floutéiʃ(ə)n] *n.* = flotation.

float·ing [flóutiŋ] *adj.* **1.** that floats. **2.** not fixed ¶ *a vote.*

flock¹ [flak / flɔk] *n.* ⓒ **1.** a group of sheep, goats, or birds living, traveling, or feeding together. ¶ *flocks and herds.* **2.** a crowd. **3.** the people of the same church group. *in flocks,* in large groups.
—*vi.* gather or move in a flock.

flock² [flak / flɔk] *n.* ⓒ **1.** a tuft of wool. **2.** (*pl.*) waste wool or cotton for stuffing mattresses and cushions.

floe [flou] *n.* ⓒ a large sheet or mass of floating ice.

flog [flag / flɔg] *vt.* (**flogged, flog·ging**) beat (someone) very hard with a whip or a stick. [hard.

flog·ging [flágiŋ / flɔ́g-]. *n.* ⓤⓒ punishment by beating

flood [flʌd] *n.* ⓒ **1.** a large amount of water covering land that is usu. dry. **2.** the tide flowing toward the shore; the rising tide. ↔ebb **3.** a great quantity of something. ¶ *a ~ of tears* / *floods of fan letters.* **4.** (*poetic*) the ocean; the sea; a lake; a river. **5.** (*the F-*) (in the Bible) the great flood that covered the earth in the time of Noah; the Deluge.
—*vt.* **1.** cover (something) with a large amount of water; discharge much water into (something). **2.** cover (something) like a flood; fill. —*vi.* **1.** (of a river, etc.) rise in a flood; become covered with water. **2.** (of the tide) rise. **3.** flow or pour in like a flood. ¶ *People flooded into the theater.*
flood out, force to leave a house because of floods.

flood·gate [flʌ́dgèit] *n.* ⓒ a gate in a canal, a river, etc. to control the water.

flood·light [flʌ́dlàit] *n.* ⓒ a lamp that gives a broad beam of light covering a large area; the light provided by such lamps. —*vt.* (**-light·ed** or **-lit**) light (something) by a floodlight.

floor [flɔːr] *n.* ⓒ **1.** the bottom surface of a room; the part of a room on which people walk. **2.** a story of a building. ¶ *the first ~.* **3.** the bottom of the ocean or of a cave. **4.** a part of a room or hall where members of a lawmaking body sit. **5.** (*the ~*) the right to speak. **6.** (*colloq.*) (of prices) the lowest level.
take the floor, (*U.S.*) stand up to speak in a discussion or at a public meeting.
—*vt.* **1.** put a floor in (a building). **2.** knock down.

floor·ing [flɔ́ːriŋ] *n.* **1.** ⓒ a floor. **2.** ⓤ (*collectively*) floors; material for making floors.

floor show [´-´] *n.* an entertainment of music, singing, dancing, etc. at a night club.

floor·walk·er [flɔ́ːrwɔ̀ːkər] *n.* ⓒ a person who oversees sales and direct customers in a large store.

flop [flap / flɔp] *v.* (**flopped, flop·ping**) *vt.* drop or throw noisily. —*vi.* **1.** move around heavily and noisily. **2.** fall or drop in this way. **3.** change suddenly. **4.** (*colloq.*) fail. —*n.* ⓒ **1.** the act or sound of flopping. **2.** (*colloq.*) a failure. [period of time.

flo·ra [flɔ́ːrə] *n.* ⓤ the plants of a particular area or

flo·ral [flɔ́ːrəl] *adj.* of, made of or like flowers.

floral em·blem [´-- ´-] *n.* a flower or a plant which is the symbol of a country, a state, a city, etc.

flo·res·cence [flɔːrésns] *n.* ⓤ **1.** the state of blossoming. **2.** the period of blossoming.

---

florescence

—몡 1.뜨는 물건, 부표(浮標), 부대(浮袋); 낚시 찌 2.뗏목;부주(浮舟) 3. [행렬 때 장식하여 끄는] 나지막하고 판판한 차(車)

—몡 1.떠 있는,떠도는 2.유동성의,일정하지 않은 ¶①부동표(浮動票)
—몡 [특히 양·염소·새 따위의] 떼 ¶①양떼와 소떼 2.군중 3.그리스도교도
圈 떼지어, 우르르 몰려서
—囘 떼짓다, 모이다
—몡 1.털뭉치 2.털부스러기, 솜부스러기

—몡 큰 부빙(浮氷)

—태 …을 몹시 매질하다(채찍질하다)

—몡 채찍질, 태형(笞刑)

—몡 1.홍수, 큰 물 2.밀물, 만조 3.[홍수와도 같은] 범람, 쇄도, 다량의 유출 ¶①쏟아지는 눈물/②뗀 레터의 쇄도 4.(詩) 대양, 바다; 호수; 강 5.(聖) 노아의 홍수

—태 1.…을 홍수지게 하다, 물에 잠기게 하다 2.…을 범람시키다 —囘 1.홍수지다, 범람하다 2.[조수가] 밀려들다, 만조가 되다 3.[홍수처럼] 밀어닥치다, 쇄도하다

圈 홍수로 철거시키다
—몡 수문(水門)

—몡 일광(溢光)(건물 따위에 여러 방면에서 광선을 비추어 그늘지지 않게 하는 조명) —태 …을 일광으로 비추다

—몡 1.마루,(방)바닥 2.[건물의] 층 ¶①(美) 1층, (英) 2층 3.[바다·동굴 따위의] 밑바닥 4.의원석 5.[의원의] 발언권 6.(口) [가격의] 최저

圈 (美) 발언하기 위해 기립하다 「을 때려눕히다」
—태 1.…에 마루를 깔다(놓다) 2.…
—몡 1.마루 2.(총칭)마루; 마루 재목(재료)

—몡 [나이트클럽·호텔·카바레의] 쇼우, 여흥(餘興)

—몡 [백화점 따위의] 판매장 감독

—태 …을 툭 떨어뜨리다, 철썩 던지다
—囘 1.퍼덕퍼덕 움직이다; 어슬렁어슬렁 걷다 2.털썩 떨어지다 3.갑자기 변하다 4.실패하다 —몡 1.털썩(툭) 떨어뜨리기(떨어지는 소리) 2.실패

—몡 [한 지방·한 시대의] 식물군
—형 꽃의, 꽃 같은 [식물구계(區系)
—몡 [나라·주(州)·시(市) 따위를] 상징하는 꽃

—몡 1.개화(開花) 2.개화기, 꽃시절

flo·ret [flɔ́:rit] *n.* ⓒ one of the small flowers which make up the flower head of an aster, a daisy, a dandelion, etc.
—ⓝ [국화과 식물의] 작은 통화(筒花)

flo·ri·cul·ture [flɔ́:rikʌ̀ltʃər] *n.* Ⓤ the science or practice of growing flowers.
—ⓝ 화초 재배

flor·id [flɔ́:rid / flɔ́rid] *adj.* 1. (of a face) bright in color; naturally very red. 2. flowery; richly ornamented. ▷**flor·id·ly** [-li] *adv.* —**flor·id·ness** [-nis] *n.*
—ⓝ 1.[안색이] 불그스름한, 혈색이 좋은 2. 화려한, 현란한, 야한

Flor·i·da [flɔ́:ridə, flɑ́ri- / flɔ́ri-] *n.* the extreme southeastern State of the United States. ⇒N.B.
—ⓝ 미국 동남단의 주 N.B. Fla.,Flor.로 줄여 씀. 수도는 Tallahassee

flor·in [flɔ́:rin, flɑ́r- / flɔ́rin] *n.* ⓒ a former English silver coin.
—ⓝ 플로린(2실링에 상당)

flo·rist [flɔ́:rist, flɑ́- / flɔ́rist] *n.* ⓒ a person who grows or sells flowers as a business.
—ⓝ 꽃장수; 화초 재배자

floss [flɔ:s / flɔs] *n.* Ⓤ 1. a shiny, untwisted silk thread used for embroidery. 2. (of plant) the soft, silky fibers of certain pods.
—ⓝ 1. [고치의] 풀솜; 명주솜; [꼬지 않은] 명주실 2. [식물의] 풀솜 모양의 털; [옥수수 따위의] 수염

flo·tage [flóutidʒ] *n.* Ⓤ 1. the act of floating. 2. the power of floating; anything that floats. 3. (collectively) the ships, etc. floating on a river, the sea, etc. 4. the part of a ship above the water line.
—ⓝ 1. 뜨기 2. 부력(浮力); 부유물, 표류물 3. [하천에 뜨는] 배, 뗏목 4. 흘수선 위의 선체

flo·ta·tion [floutéiʃ(ə)n] *n.* Ⓤ 1. the act of floating. 2. (in commercial) the act of beginning a business; the act of selling bonds, securities, etc.
—ⓝ 1. 뜨기, 부양(浮揚) 2. [회사의] 설립; [채권 따위의] 발행

flo·til·la [floutílə] *n.* ⓒ a small fleet; a fleet of small ships.
—ⓝ 소함대, 소형 선대(船隊)

flounce[1] [flauns] *vi.* move suddenly showing anger or impatience; struggle. (~ *about* or *away* from some place) —*n.* ⓒ a sudden or jerky movement showing anger or impatience.
—ⓥ 몸부림치다, 버둥거리다, 버둥질하다 —ⓝ 몸부림, 버둥질

flounce[2] [flauns] *n.* ⓒ an ornamental strip of cloth, gathered and sewed to a dress, a skirt, etc. as trimming. ⇒fig. —*vt.* trim (something) with a flounce.
—ⓝ [부인복의] 주름 장식
—ⓥ …에 주름 장식을 달다

floun·der[1] [fláundər] *vi.* 1. struggle awkwardly and violently, as in mud, water, or snow. ¶*The horse floundered in the deep mud.* 2. make mistakes or stumble, esp. in speaking; hesitate. —*n.* ⓒ the act of floundering.
[flounce[2]]
—ⓥ 1. 몸부림치다, 버둥거리다, 발버둥질치다, 버둥거리다가 수렁에 빠지다 2. [연설 따위에서] 실수하다; 더듬거리다, 횡설수설하다; 망설거리다 —ⓝ 몸부림, 버둥거림, 초조

floun·der[2] [fláundər] *n.* ⓒ (pl. **-ders** or *collectively* **-der**) any flatfish.
—ⓝ 가자미류의 식용어

‡**flour** [fláuər] *n.* Ⓤ 1. the fine powder made by grinding wheat or grain. ⇒N.B. ¶*a ~ mill.* 2. any fine powder. —*vt.* 1. put flour on (something); cover (something) with flour. ¶*~ the fish before frying it.* 2. (*U.S.*) make (grain) into flour.
—ⓝ 1. 밀가루, 소맥분 N.B. 밀가루 이외의 것은 buckwheat flour, rye flour 따위처럼 씀 2. 분말, 고운 가루
—ⓥ 1. …에 가루를 뿌리다 2.(美) …을 가루로 빻다

•**flour·ish** [flə́:riʃ / flʌ́riʃ] *vi.* 1. (of plants) grow thick; thrive. ¶*Palm trees do not ~ in cold countries.* 2. be at the peak of life or activity; prosper. ¶*My business is flourishing.*① 3. write in a decorative style; speak or write with ornamental phrases. 4. (*Music*) perform a fanfare; play a gay, flowery passage. —*vt.* 1. wave (something) in a showy way. ¶*John flourished the letters.*② 2. write, speak or play ornamentally.
—*n.* ⓒ 1. the waving motion of a sword, an arm, etc. ¶*She laughed with a ~ of her hand.*③ 2. an extra curved line for decoration in writing. 3. a showy word or phrase in speech or writing. ¶*a letter full of flourishes.*④ 4. (*Music*) a showy passage or performance.
—ⓥ 1. 우거지다, 무성하다 2. 최고조로 번창하다; 번영하다 ¶①나의 사업은 번창하고 있다 3. 멋부려 쓰다(말하다) 4.(樂) 화려하게 취주하다; 화려하게 연주하다 —ⓥ 1. …을 자랑삼아 흔들어 보이다 ¶②존은 편지를 자랑해 보였다 2. …을 멋부려 쓰다(말하다, 연주하다)
—ⓝ 1. [손·칼 따위를] 흔들기, 휘두르기 ¶③그녀는 손을 흔들면서 웃었다 2. [서명(署名) 따위의] 화려하게 쓰기 3. 미사여구(美辭麗句) ¶④미사여구성이의 편지 4.(樂) 화려한 연주

•**flour·y** [fláuəri] *adj.* 1. of or like flour. 2. covered with flour. 3. white like flour.
—ⓝ 1. 가루(모양)의 2. 가루투성이의 3. 하얀, 흰

flout [flaut] *vt.* show contempt for (someone or something). ¶*~ a person's advice.*① —*vi.* show contempt. (*~ at* something) —*n.* ⓒ an act or a speech filled with contempt and insults. ▷**flout·er** [-ər]
—ⓥ …을 조롱하다, 모욕하다 ¶①남의 충고를 비웃다 —ⓥ 우롱하다 —ⓝ 우롱, 모욕, 비웃음

flow [flou] *vi.* **1.** run along, as a stream does. ¶*The Sumida flows into Tokyo Bay.* **2.** move easily or smoothly. **3.** continue smoothly. ¶*His speech flowed on.* **4.** hang loose. ¶*Her hair flowed over her shoulders.* **5.** (of the tide) rise. ↔ebb ¶*The tide began to flow.* **6.** be full; be plentiful; abound. ¶*rivers flowing with fish | Her heart flowed with gratitude.*①
—*n.* ⓒ (*sing.* only) **1.** the act or manner of flowing. **2.** any continuous movement like water in a river; anything that suggests this. ¶*a rapid ~ of speech | the ~ of her hair over her shoulders.* **3.** the amount that flows. ¶*a ~ of 100 gallons of oil a second.*② **4.** rise of the tide. ¶*The tide is on the ~.*

—⾃ 1. 흐르다 2. 흐르듯이 움직이다 (나아가다) 3. 물 흐르듯이 잇따라 나오다, 술술 흘러·나오다 4. 척 늘어지다 5. [조수가] 밀다, 차다 6. 넘치다; 가득 차 있다 ¶①그녀의 가슴은 감사하는 마음으로 가득하였다

—名 1. 유동(流動); 흐르기 2. 강물 [같은] 흐름; [동작의] 연속 3. 흐르는 양, 유출량 ¶②1초 동안에 100갈론의 기름의 흐름 4. 밀물, 만조

flow·er [fláuər] *n.* **1.** ⓒ the part of a plant which produces the seeds; a bloom; a blossom. **2.** ⓒ a flowering plant. **3.** ((*the ~*)) the best part or period. ¶*the ~ of chivalry*① *| in the ~ of his age.*
in flower, bearing flowers; blooming.
—*vi.* **1.** bear flowers; bloom; blossom. ¶*Some roses ~ throughout the growing season.* **2.** come into the finest or fairest condition; flourish. ¶*Girls tend to ~ early in the tropics.*②

—名 1. 꽃 2. 화초; 꽃이 피는 식물 3. 정화(精華), 정수(精髓); 한창 때, 청춘기 ¶①기사도의 귀감

🔳 꽃피어, 만발하여
—⾃ 1. 꽃피다 2. 전성기에 이르다, 번영하다, 성숙하다 ¶②열대 지방에서는 여성은 조숙하는 경향이 있다

flow·ered [fláuərd] *adj.* **1.** having flowers. **2.** decorated with flowers or patterns of flowers.

—形 1. 꽃핀 2. 꽃으로 장식한, 꽃무늬를 단

flow·er·er [fláuərər] *n.* ⓒ a plant that flowers at a particular time or in a certain manner. ¶*an early (a late) ~.*①

—名 꽃이 피는 식물 ¶①꽃이 빨리 (늦게) 피는 식물

flow·er·et [fláuərit] *n.* ⓒ a small flower.
flow·er·ing [fláuəriŋ] *adj.* bearing flowers.
flow·er·pot [fláuərpàt / fláuəpɔ̀t] *n.* ⓒ a container, usu. made of clay, in which plants can be grown.

—名 작은 꽃
—形 꽃이 피는
—名 화분

flower vase [²⁻ ˴] *n.* an ornamental vessel of glass, pottery, metal, etc. for containing cut flowers.

—名 꽃병

flow·er·y [fláuəri] *adj.* (**-er·i·er, -er·i·est**) **1.** full of flowers. **2.** like flowers. **3.** decorated with flowers or patterns of flowers. **4.** filled with fine words and phrases. ¶*a ~ speech.* ▷**flow·er·i·ness** [-nis] *n.*

—形 1. 꽃이 많은 2. 꽃 같은, 꽃 모양의 3. 꽃으로 장식한; 꽃무늬가 있는 4. 화려한

flown [floun] *v.* pp. of *fly*.
flu [flu:] *n.* (*colloq.*) =influenza.
fluc·tu·ate [flʌ́ktʃuèit / -tju-] *vi.* **1.** rise and fall, like waves. **2.** change continually and irregularly.

—⾃ 1. 파동(波動)하다 2. 동요하다, 변동하다

fluc·tu·a·tion [flʌ̀ktʃuéiʃ(ə)n / -tju-] *n.* ⓤⓒ the act of fluctuating; a motion like a wave; continual, irregular change. ¶*the ~ of the stock market.*①

—名 파동, 변동 ¶①증권 시세의 변동

flue [flu:] *n.* **1.** ⓒ a tube, pipe or other passage for the conveyance of air, smoke, flame, hot air, etc. **2.** =influenza.

—名 1. 작은 굴뚝, 연기 송(送)하는 길, 염관(炎管)

flu·en·cy [flú(:)ənsi] *n.* ⓤ the state or quality of being fluent; the ability to speak easily and well. ¶*with ~.*①

—名 유창함; 능변 ¶①유창하게, 막힘없이

• **flu·ent** [flú(:)ənt] *adj.* **1.** flowing smoothly and rapidly. **2.** able to speak easily and well. ¶*a ~ speech (speaker).*①

—形 1. 유창한, 막힘없는 2. 능변의 ¶①능변(능변가)

flu·ent·ly [flú(:)əntli] *adv.* in a fluent manner.

—形 유창하게

fluff [flʌf] *n.* ⓤ **1.** very soft and light particles like feathers or hair. **2.** first soft hair or beard. —*vt.* shake (something) into the state of fluff. —*vi.* become fluffy.

—名 1. 보풀 2. 솜털, 갓난 털 —他 …을 보풀이 일게 하다 —⾃ 보풀이 일다

fluff·i·ness [flʌ́finis] *n.* ⓤ the state or quality of being fluffy.
fluff·y [flʌ́fi] *adj.* (**fluff·i·er, fluff·i·est**) of fluff; like fluff; covered with fluff.

—名 보풀이 일기; 솜[털] 모양
—形 보풀의; 푹신푹신한, 솜털로 덮인

• **flu·id** [flú(:)id] *adj.* **1.** flowing easily, like water or gas. ¶*~ matter.*① **2.** changing easily and rapidly. ¶*~ opinions.*② —*n.* ⓤⓒ (*Physics*) a substance that flows like water, gas, etc. ▷**flu·id·ly** [-li] *adv.*

—形 1. 유동하는 ¶①유동체 2. 변하기 쉬운 ¶②변하기 쉬운 의견 —名 (理) 유체(流體); 유동체

flu·id·i·ty [flu(:)íditi] *n.* ⓤ the state of being fluid.

—名 유동성, 유체성(流體性)

fluke¹ [flu:k] *n.* ⓒ **1.** a sharp, triangular blade at the end of each arm of an anchor. ⇒fig. **2.** the barbed head of a spear, a harpoon, an arrow, etc. **3.** ((*pl.*)) a whale's tail.

[fluke¹ 1.]

fluke² [flu:k] *n.* ⓒ **1.** (*colloq.*) a lucky chance or accident. ¶*win a game by* ~.① **2.** (of billiards, etc.) a lucky stroke or shot.

flung [flʌŋ] *v.* pt. and pp. of **fling**.

flunk [flʌŋk] *vi.* **1.** (*U.S. colloq.*) get an unsuccessful mark in schoolwork. ((~ *in* an examination)) **2.** give up. —*vt.* **1.** fail in (schoolwork). ¶*~ a student* / *~ a math examination.*① **2.** cause (a student) to fail; give a grade of failure to (a student).

flunk·ey [flʌ́ŋki] *n.* (*Brit.*) =flunky.

flunk·y [flʌ́ŋki] *n.* ⓒ (pl. **flunk·ies**) **1.** a manservant dressed in a special uniform; a footman. ⇒**N.B. 2.** a person who flatters.

flu·o·resce [flù(:)ərés] *vi.* emit light by fluorescence.

flu·o·res·cence [flù(:)ərésns] *n.* ⓤ (*Physics*) **1.** the property of a substance of emitting visible light while exposed to light or X-rays. **2.** light emitted from such a substance.

flu·o·res·cent [flù(:)ərésnt] *adj.* **1.** emitting fluorescence. **2.** having the property of fluorescence.

flu·o·rine [flú(:)ərli:n, +*U.S.* -rin] *n.* ⓤ (*Chemistry*) a greenish-yellow gas that is a very active chemical element.

flu·o·rite [flú(:)əràit] *n.* ⓤⓒ a transparent mineral of various colors, used in glassmaking, etc.

flur·ry [flə́:ri / flʌ́ri] *n.* ⓒ (pl. **-ries**) **1.** a sudden rush of wind. **2.** a sudden gust of rain or snow. **3.** a sudden confusion of the mind.
  in a flurry, in a state of hurry and confusion.
  —*vt.* (-ried) confuse. ¶*be flurried with the preparations for the party.*

• **flush**¹ [flʌʃ] *vi.* **1.** become red in one's face; blush. ¶*She (or Her face) flushed when she heard the news.* **2.** rush suddenly; flow rapidly. ¶*The tide flushed through the narrow inlet.* —*vt.* **1.** make (someone or someone's face) red. ¶*The story flushed her cheeks with shame.* **2.** cause (something) to rush or flow rapidly. ¶*~ the water away.* **3.** wash away (something) with a rapid flow of water. ¶*~ the toilet* / *~ the floor with a hose.*① **4.** (usu. in *passive*) excite; make (someone) joyful too much. ¶*She was flushed with pride at her son's success.*②
  —*n.* ⓒ **1.** a blush; a sudden glow. **2.** a sudden rush; a rapid flow (as of water). **3.** fresh growth. ¶*the spring ~ of grass* / *a second ~ of bloom.*③ **4.** glowing vigor. ¶*a ~ of youthful ardor.* **5.** an excited condition of feeling. ¶*a quick ~ of anger.*

flush² [flʌʃ] *adj.* **1.** in a full flow. **2.** (*colloq.*) having plenty of money; abundant; lavish. ¶*be ~ with money.* **3.** making a level surface; even.

flush³ [flʌʃ] *vi.* (of birds) fly away suddenly. —*vt.* cause (a bird, etc.) to fly away. ▷**flush·er** [-ər] *n.*

flus·ter [flʌ́stər] *vt.* make (someone) nervous and confused. ¶*~ oneself.*① —*vi.* become nervous and confused. ¶*She was utterly flustered by his sudden appearance.*② —*n.* ⓒ (usu. *a ~*) the state of being flustered; confusion.
  all in a fluster, in an extremely confused manner.

flute [flu:t] *n.* ⓒ **1.** a long, slender musical instrument with many finger holes, played by blowing into a hole near the upper end. **2.** (*Architecture*) a long round groove in a column or a pillar.
— *vi., vt.* **1.** play a flute; speak, sing or whistle in a flutelike tone. **2.** (*Architecture*) make a long round groove in a column, a pillar, etc.

flut·ing [flú:tiŋ] *n.* ⓒ **1.** a sound as if produced by a flute. **2.** a decoration made of long round grooves or cords.

flut·ist [flú:tist] *n.* ⓒ a person who plays on the flute.

flut·ter [flʌ́tər] *vi.* **1.** (of birds) move the wings lightly up and down. **2.** wave back and forth lightly and irregularly. ¶*The curtain fluttered in the breeze.*① **3.** beat quickly and irregularly. **4.** be confused or nervous.
— *vt.* **1.** cause (something) to move lightly. ¶*The bird fluttered its wings in the cage.*② **2.** put (someone) into a state of excitement and confusion.
— *n.* ⓒ **1.** a quick, fluttering movement. ¶*the ~ of wings.* **2.** confusion; excitement. ¶*be in a ~ over something.*③ ▷ **flut·ter·er** [-tərər] *n.*

flux [flʌks] *n.* **1.** ⓒ (*sing.* only) the act of flowing. **2.** ⓤ the rising movement of the tide. ↔reflux **3.** ⓤ constant change or movement. ¶*All things are in a state of ~.*① **4.** ⓒ (*Medicine*) an unnatural and abnormal discharge of blood or fluid from the body.

‡**fly**¹ [flai] *vi.* (**flew, flown** → 6.) **1.** move through the air. ¶*A crow is flying.* / *An arrow flew toward the target.*① / *Fireworks flew up.*② **2.** float or wave in the air. ¶*a flag flying from the tall pole.* **3.** operate or travel in an airplane. ¶*He flew to Osaka.* **4.** move or pass swiftly. ¶*The hours flew as she busied herself about the house.* **5.** move or change one's state suddenly. ¶*The door flew open.*③ *He flew into a rage.*④ **6.** (in Brit. **fled**) run away; flee. — *vt.* **1.** cause (something) to move or float through the air. ¶*~ a kite*⑤ / *~ a carrier pigeon.*⑥ **2.** operate (an airplane); go across or over (some place) by airplane. ¶*~ the Pacific.* **3.** carry (something) by air. **4.** escape from (some place). ¶*The bird has flown its cage.*
fly high, be ambitious.
— *n.* ⓒ (pl. **flies**) **1.** the act or process of flying; flight. **2.** a baseball hit high into the air.
on the fly, ⓐ very busily; without resting. ⓑ while still in the air; before touching the ground.

‡**fly**² [flai] *n.* ⓒ (pl. **flies**) **1.** a small, two-winged insect, esp. a housefly. **2.** a fishhook with feathers, silk, etc. on it to make it look like a fly.

fly·er [fláiər] *n.* =flier.

fly·flap [fláiflæp] *n.* ⓒ an instrument used to kill flies.

•**fly·ing** [fláiiŋ] *adj.* very quick. ¶*a ~ visit* / *a ~ fish.*

fly·leaf [fláilì:f] *n.* ⓒ (pl. **-leaves**) a blank leaf or page at the beginning or the end of a book, a pamphlet, etc.

fly·leaves [fláilì:vz] *n.* pl. of **flyleaf**.

•**fly·o·ver** [fláiòuvər] *n.* ⓒ **1.** a low flight by airplanes over a public place. **2.** (*Brit.*) a highway over or across a road or railway. (cf. *U. S.* overpass) =fig.

fly·pa·per [fláipèipər] *n.* ⓤ ⓒ sticky paper to catch flies.

fly·trap [fláitræp] *n.* ⓒ **1.** a trap to catch flies. **2.** a plant that catches insects in its flower.

[flyover 2.]

— 图 1. 플루우트, 피리 2. 《建》 [기둥의] 세로홈

— 自 他 1. 플루우트를 불다; 플루우트 같은 소리로 말하다(노래부르다, 휘파람 불다) 2. 《建》 기둥 따위에 세로홈을 파다

— 图 1. 플루우트 [같은] 소리, 피릿소리 2. 세로홈

— 图 플루우트 취주자, 피리 부는 사람

— 自 1. 날개치다 2. 펄럭이다, 펄럭거리다 ¶①커어튼이 미풍에 펄럭거렸다 3. 불규칙하게 치다 4. 당황하다, 안절부절 못하다 — 他 1. …을 펄럭이게 하다 ¶②새가 새장 속에서 날개를 푸드덕거렸다 2. …을 당황하게(안절부절 못하게) 하다

— 图 1. 날개치기, 펄럭임 2. 당황, 동요, 설렘 ¶③…으로 당황하고 있다

— 图 1. 흐름, 유출(流出) 2. 밀물 3. 끊임없는 변화, 유전(流轉) ¶①만물은 끊임없이 변화하고 있다 4. 《醫》 [혈액·배설물 따위의] 이상 배출

— 自 1. 날다 ¶①화살이 과녁을 향해 날아갔다/②꽃불이 날아 올라갔다 2. 하늘에 떠오르다; 나부끼다 3. [비행기로] 가다; [비행기를] 조종하다 4. [나는 듯이] 질주하다, 지나가다 5. 갑자기 움직이다; 별안간 상태가 변화하다 ¶③문이 홱 열리다/④그는 발끈 성을 냈다 6. 달아나다, 도망치다 — 他 1. …을 날리다; …을 공중에 띄우다 ¶⑤연을 띄우다/⑥전서구(傳書鳩)를 날리다 2. [비행기를] 조종하다; …을 비행하다 3. …을 공수(空輸)하다 4. …에서 도망치다

熟 큰 뜻을 품다
— 图 1. 날기, 비행 2. [야구에서] 플라이, 비구(飛球)
熟 ⓐ급히 서둘러서, 허겁지겁 ⓑ비행중인; [비구가] 땅에 떨어지기 전에
— 图 1. 파리; 날벌레 2. 파리낚시, 제물낚시

— 图 파리채 [한
— 形 나는 듯이 빠른; 몹시 급한, 황급
— 图 [책의 권두·권말에 붙이는] 표지 안쪽의 면지; 여백 페이지

— 图 1. 의례비행(儀禮飛行) 2. 《英》 고가도로

— 图 파리 잡는 끈끈이 종이

— 图 1. 파리통 2. 파리잡이풀

fly·wheel [flái(h)wì:l] *n.* ⓒ a heavy metal wheel to keep the speed of the machine constant.
—名 플라이휘일(속도를 조정하는 바퀴)

foal [foul] *n.* ⓒ a very young horse or donkey.
—名 망아지, 당나귀(노새) 새끼

*** foam** [foum] *n.* ⓤ ((sometimes *a* ~)) the mass of small bubbles which forms on the surface of a liquid. —*vi.* **1.** produce foam. **2.** form bubbles on water, etc.
—名 거품 —自 1. 거품을 내다 2. 거품이 일다

foam·y [fóumi] *adj.* (**foam·i·er, foam·i·est**) **1.** foaming. **2.** filled with foam. **3.** like foam. ▷**foam·i·ly** [-li] *adv.*
—形 1. 거품 이는 2. 거품투성이의 3. 거품 같은

fob [fɑb / fɔb] *n.* **1.** ⓒ a small pocket below the waistline of a man's trousers for carrying a watch, etc.; a watch pocket. **2.** a short chain attached to a watch and hanging from such a pocket.
—名 1. [바지 위쪽의] 시계 넣는 작은 주머니 2. 회중시계의 줄(끈)

fo·cal [fóuk(ə)l] *adj.* of a focus. ¶*the* ~ *length of a lens.*①
—形 촛점의 ¶①렌즈의 촛점 거리

fo·ci [fóusai] *n.* pl. of **focus**.

*** fo·cus** [fóukəs] *n.* ⓒ (pl. **-cus·es** or **fo·ci**) **1.** a point where rays of light meet after being reflected by a mirror or refracted by a lens. ¶*a real* ~① / *a virtual* ~.② **2.** the distance to such a point from the center of a lens. **3.** an adjustment of a person's eyes or a camera lens to make an outline into a clear image. **4.** a center of attention, interest, etc.
—名 1. 촛점 ¶①실(實)촛점/②허(虛)촛점 2. 촛점 거리 3. 촛점을 맞추기 위한 조정 4. 흥미의 중심

—*v.* (**-cused, -cus·ing** or *Brit.* **-cussed, -cus·sing**) *vt.* **1.** bring (something) into focus. **2.** adjust the distance of (a lens) to make a clear image. **3.** fix (all one's attention) on one thing. ¶~ *one's mind on the political problem.*③ —*vi.* **1.** come to a focus. **2.** adjust one's camera or eyes to make a clear image.
—他 1. …을 촛점에 모으다 2. [렌즈]의 촛점을 맞추다 3. [주의]를 집중하다 ¶③정치 문제에 관심을 집중하다
—自 1. 촛점에 모이다 2. 렌즈 따위의 촛점을 맞추다

*** foe** [fou] *n.* ⓒ (*poetic*) an enemy, esp. an enemy in war.
—名 (詩) 적, 원수

foe·tus [fí:təs] *n.* =**fetus**.

*** fog** [fɑg / fɔg] *n.* **1.** ⓤⓒ very thick mist; a mass of fine drops of water near the earth's surface; a cloud-like mass of smoke, dust, etc. in the air. ¶*a* ~ *warning*① / *The* ~ *has cleared* [*off*].② **2.** ⓒ mental confusion. ¶*I'm quite in a* ~ *as to what you mean.*③ **3.** ⓤⓒ (*Photography*) a cloud on a print of a photograph.
—名 1. 안개 ¶①농무(濃霧) 경보/②안개가 걷혔다 2. 혼미(混迷), 당황 ¶③무슨 말씀인지 통 납득이 안 갑니다 3. (寫) 사진의 흐림

—*v.* (**fogged, fog·ging**) *vt.* **1.** cover (something) with fog. **2.** confuse (one's mind). **3.** produce a cloud in (a photograph). —*vi.* **1.** become covered with fog. **2.** (of a photograph) become fogged. 「of heavy fog.」
—他 1. …을 안개로 덮다 2. [마음]을 혼미(당황)하게 하다 3. [사진]을 흐리게 하다
—自 1. 안개에 덮이다 2. [사진이] 흐려지다

fog·bound [fɑ́gbàund / fɔ́g-] *adj.* unable to sail because
—形 [배가] 안개에 갇힌

fog·gy [fɑ́gi / fɔ́gi] *adj.* (**-gi·er, -gi·est**) **1.** covered with fog. **2.** not clear. **3.** confused. 「ships in a fog.」
—形 1. 안개가 자욱이 낀 2. 몽롱한 3. 혼미(당황)한

fog·horn [fɑ́ghɔ̀ːrn / fɔ́ghɔ̀ːrn] *n.* ⓒ a horn blown to warn
—名 농무 경적

fo·gy [fóugi] *n.* ⓒ (pl. **fo·gies**) ((usu. *old* ~)) a person who is out of date in thought and action.
—名 시대에 뒤진 사람

foi·ble [fɔ́ibl] *n.* ⓒ a weak point in a person's character.
—名 [성격의] 약점

foil¹ [fɔil] *vt.* prevent someone from being successful in (plans, etc.).
—他 [계획 따위]를 좌절시키다

foil² [fɔil] *n.* **1.** ⓤ a very thin, paperlike sheet of metal. ¶*gold* ~.① **2.** ⓒ a person or thing that makes another seem better by contrast. ¶*play the* ~ *to someone.*②
—名 1. 박(箔) ¶①금박 2. 돋보이게 하는 사람(것) ¶②남을 돋보이게 하는 역할을 하다(연기하다)

foil³ [fɔil] *n.* ⓒ a long light sword with a button on the point, used in fencing; ((*pl.*)) the act of fencing.
—名 [칼끝에 솜뭉치를 댄] 펜싱 연습용 칼; 펜싱

foist [fɔist] *vt.* sell (something worthless) to someone by a dirty trick. ((~ *something* [*off*] *on*))
—他 [가짜 물건]을 떠맡기다, 속여 팔다

‡ fold¹ [fould] *vt.* **1.** bend and press one part of (something) over another part. **2.** hold (one's arms, hands, etc.) over one another. **3.** put the arms around (something) to hold it. ¶*She folded the baby in her arms.*① **4.** wrap.
fold up, ⓐ make (something) compact by folding. ⓑ (*colloq.*) fail; collapse.
—*n.* ⓒ **1.** a part that is folded. **2.** a mark made by folding; a hollow made by folded parts. ¶*a* ~ *in a blanket.*②
—他 1. …을 겹치다 2. [손·팔 따위]를 끼다 3. …을 껴안다 ¶①그녀는 아기를 껴안았다 4. …을 싸다, 둥치다
薰 ⓐ …을 차곡차곡 접다 ⓑ [연극 따위가] 실패하다
—名 1. 겹쳐진 것, 층(層) 2. 접었던 자국; 주름 ¶②담요를 개었던 주름

fold² [fould] *n.* [C] **1.** a small enclosure for sheep. **2.** 《*the* ~》 the sheep kept in a fold. **3.** the Christian church; the members of a church. **—***vt.* keep (sheep) in a fold.
—[名] 1. 양(羊)우리 2. [우릿속의] 양떼 3. 그리스도 교회; 신도들, 회중(會衆) —[他] [양]을 [우리에] 가두다

-fold [-fould] *suf.* times as many, as much, as great; having many parts: *manifold* (=having many parts; many and various) / *threefold* (=having three parts; having three times as much or as many).
—《接尾》 …배(倍)의, …겹의

fold·er [fóuldər] *n.* [C] **1.** a person or thing that folds. **2.** a sheet of stiff paper used to cover or hold loose papers. **3.** a booklet or pamphlet folded up but not stitched.
—[名] 1. 접는 사람(기구) 2. 종이(서류)끼우개 3. 접었다폈다하는 책(팜플렛)

fold·ing [fóuldiŋ] *adj.* that can be folded. ¶*a ~ bed.*
—[形] 접을(갤) 수 있게 된

folding doors [ˊ- ˊ] *n. pl.* doors with hinged parts so that they can be folded or unfolded. ⇒fig.
—[名] 접게 된 문, 쌍창문

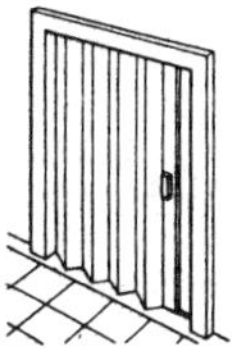
〔folding doors〕

·fo·li·age [fóuliidʒ] *n.* [U] 《*collectively*》 all the leaves of a plant or a tree.
—[名] [나무의] 잎

fo·li·ate *adj.* [fóuliit, -lièit →*v.*] having leaves; covered with leaves. **—***vi.* [fóulièit] send out leaves.
—[形] 잎이 있는 —[自] 잎을 피우다

fo·li·o [fóuliòu] *n.* [C] (pl. **-li·os**) **1.** a large sheet of paper folded once to make two leaves, or four pages, of a book, etc. **2.** a large book made of sheets of paper folded in this way. **3.** a page number of a book.
—[名] 1. [전지(全紙)의] 2절(4페이지분) 2. 2절판의 책(전지 절반 크기의 책) 3. [책의] 페이지 수

:folk [fouk] *n.* [C] (pl. **folks** or *collectively* **folk**) **1.** 《often *pl.*》 people in general. **2.** 《usu. *pl.*》 (*colloq.*) the members of one's family. ¶*my folks.*①
—[名] 1. 사람들 2. 《口》 가족, 친척, 일가 ¶①우리집 사람들(친척)

folk dance [ˊ ˋ] *n.* a dance originating among the common people and handed down from age to age; a piece of music for such a dance.
—[名] 민속(향토) 무용; 그 음악

folk·lore [fóuklɔ̀ːr] *n.* [U] the beliefs, customs and sayings of a people handed down from age to age; the study of these.
—[名] 민간 전승(傳承), 민속학

folk song [ˊ ˋ] *n.* a song made and handed down among the common people; a song composed in the style of such a song.
—[名] 민요, 포우크송

folk tale [ˊ ˋ] *n.* a story originating among the common people and handed down from age to age.
—[名] 민간 전설(설화)

:fol·low [fálou / fɔ́l-] *vt.* **1.** go or come after; succeed to (something). ¶*Spring follows winter.* **2.** result from (something). ¶*Misery follows war.*① **3.** go along (a road, etc.). ¶*Follow this street to the station.* **4.** go along with (someone); accompany. ¶*He followed her home from the party.*② **5.** pursue; chase. ¶*~ an enemy / ~ hounds.*③ **6.** act according to (something); take (something) as a guide; obey. ¶*~ instructions*④ / *~ a policy.* **7.** look at (something) carefully; pay attention to (something). ¶*fail to ~ the ball.*⑤ **8.** understand. ¶*~ a speech / ~ a play.* **9.** take (something) as one's work. ¶*~ the sea*⑥ / *~ the law.* **—***vi.* **1.** go or come after. 《*~ after* someone or something》 ¶*The policeman followed after the man.* **2.** result logically. 《*~ that* ...》 ¶*They are rich, but it doesn't ~ that they must be happy.*⑦

1) ***as follows,*** as is written below.
2) ***follow one's nose,*** go in a straight course.
3) ***follow out,*** carry out (something) to the end.
4) ***follow through,*** swing (a bat, racket, etc.) fully.
5) ***follow up,*** ⓐ follow closely. ⓑ carry out (something) to the end. ⓒ increase the effect of (something) by doing it more.

—*n.* [C] the act or process of following.

—[他] 1. …을 뒤따르다; …을 잇따르다; …의 뒤를 잇다 2. …의 결과로서 일어나다 ¶①전쟁 뒤에는 비참이 뒤따른다 3. …을 따라서 가다 4. …와 함께 가다 ¶②그는 파아티가 끝난 다음 그녀를 집까지 바래다 주었다 5. …을 뒤쫓다, 쫓아가다, 추구하다 ¶③…사냥개를 따라 사냥감을 뒤쫓다 6. …에 따르다, …을 지키다 ¶④교훈을 지키다 7. …을 지켜보다; …에 주의를 기울이다 ¶⑤공의 행방을 놓치다 8. …을 알다, 이해하다 9. …에 종사하다; …을 업으로 삼다 ¶⑥선원이 되다
—[自] 1. 뒤따라 가다(오다) 2. 결과로서 …이 되다 ¶⑦그들은 부자이지만 반드시 행복할 것이라고는 말할 수 없다
[熟] 1)다음과 같이, 아래와 같이 2)곧장 나아가다 3)…을 끝까지(철저히) 해내다 4)[야구 배트·정구채 따위]를 공을 친 후에도 끝까지 휘두르다 5)ⓐ바싹 뒤따르다 ⓑ…을 철저히 추구하다; 끝까지 해내다 ⓒ더 효과를 올리기 위하여 한층 노력하다
—[名] 뒤따르기, 뒤쫓기,

F

:fol·low·er [fálouər / fɔ́l-] *n.* [C] **1.** a person who follows; a servant. **2.** a supporter of the beliefs or teachings of another.
—[名] 1. 종자(從者), 수행원, 부하 2. [신앙·학설 따위의] 신봉자, 지지자, 추종자

:fol·low·ing [fálouiŋ / fɔ́l-] *adj.* going or coming after; next. —*n.* [C] 《*collectively*》 a group of followers.
—[形] 다음의, 이하의 —[名] 전(全)수행원, 부하

:fol·ly [fáli / fɔ́li] *n.* (pl. **-lies**) **1.** [U] the state of being foolish. **2.** [C] a foolish action.
—[名] 1. 어리석음, 우매 2. 어리석은 짓, 우행(愚行)

fo·ment [foumént] *vt.* **1.** bathe (a hurt or a painful place) with warm water or medical lotion. **2.** help the growth or development of (usu. something undesirable).
—[他] 1 [환부]를 찜질하다 2. …을 조장하다

fo·men·ta·tion [fòumentéiʃ(ə)n] *n.* [U] **1.** treatment of a hurt or a painful place with warm water or medical lotion. **2.** the act of stirring up; encouragement.
—[名] 1. 찜질 2. 조장, 자극, 도발

:fond [fand / fɔnd] *adj.* **1.** liking. **2.** affectionate; tender. ¶*a ~ mother.* **3.** loving too much; foolishly loving.
be fond of, like; love. ¶*He is ~ of drinking.*
—[形] 1. 좋아하는 2. 다정한, 정다운 3. 사랑에 빠진, 맹목적으로 좋아하는
[熟] …을 좋아하다

fon·dle [fándl / fɔ́ndl] *vt.* touch or stroke (someone or something) gently with love or affection. ¶*~ a kitten.*
—[他] …을 귀여워하다, 애무하다, 희롱하다

fond·ly [fándli / fɔ́nd-] *adv.* **1.** affectionately; lovingly. **2.** foolishly; ignorantly.
—[副] 1. 다정하게 2. 어리석게도, 무지하게도

fond·ness [fándnis / fɔ́nd-] *n.* [U] tender liking; doting affection.
—[名] 애호; 지나치게 귀여워함(사랑함)

fon·due [fándu:, fandú: / fɔ́ndu:, fɔndú:] *n.* [U][C] a dish made of eggs, butter, etc., plus melted cheese.
—[名] 퐁뒤(계란·버터 따위에 녹인 치이즈를 넣어 만든 요리)

font [fant / fɔnt] *n.* [C] **1.** a basin to contain the water for baptism. **2.** (*poetic*) a fountain.
—[名] 1. 세례반(洗禮盤), 성수반(聖水盤) 2. (詩) 샘

:food [fu:d] *n.* [U] **1.** anything eaten or drunk by a person or an animal, or taken in by a plant to live and grow. ¶*~ and drink*① / *~, clothing, and shelter.*② **2.** something that serves in any way. ¶*~ of fancy*③ / *~ for thought.*④
—[名] 1. 식량, 영양 ¶①음식물/②의식주 2. [마음의] 양식 ¶③공상의 재료/④사색의 양식

food·stuff [fú:dstʌf] *n.* [C] 《often *pl.*》 a material used as food.
—[名] 식료품

:fool [fu:l] *n.* [C] **1.** a foolish person. **2.** a person who is tricked. ¶*an April ~.*① **3.** a person formerly kept by a king or nobleman to provide amusement.
1) ***be a fool for one's pains,*** make an effort in vain.
2) ***be fool enough to do,*** do (something) in a very foolish way; do a foolish thing.
3) ***be no fool,*** be clever and capable.
4) ***make a fool of*** (=*deceive* or *make fun of*) someone.
5) ***play the fool with*** (=*cheat*) someone.
—[名] 1. 바보, 얼간이 2. 바보 취급당하는 사람 ¶①4월 바보(만우절에 속은 사람) 3. [옛날 궁중의] 어릿광대
[熟] 1)헛수고하다 2)어리석게도 …하다 3)조금도 빈틈이 없다, 매우 약삭빠르다 4)남을 바보 취급하다 5)…을 속이다

—*vi.* **1.** act like a fool. **2.** joke. ¶*Don't ~ with the pistol.* —*vt.* make a fool of (someone).
1) ***fool around,*** spend time idling.
2) ***fool away,*** spend (time, money, etc.) foolishly.
3) ***fool** someone **into doing,*** deceive and so make someone do something.
—[自] 1. 바보짓하다 2. 익살떨다, 까불다
—[他] …을 바보 취급하다
[熟] 1)빈들빈들 놀다, 핀둥핀둥 시간을 보내다 2)[시간·돈을] 어리석게[헛되이] 소비하다 3)…을 속여서 …시키다

fool·er·y [fú:ləri] *n.* [U][C] (pl. **-er·ies**) a foolish act.
—[名] 어리석은 짓, 바보짓,

fool·har·dy [fú:lhɑ̀:rdi] *adj.* (**-di·er, -di·est**) without thought; bold
—[形] 무모한, 저돌적인

:fool·ish [fú:liʃ] *adj.* without good sense; silly; stupid. ▷**fool·ish·ly** [-li] *adv.* —**fool·ish·ness** [-nis] *n.*
—[形] 어리석은, 바보 같은

fool·proof [fú:lprù:f] *adj.* (*colloq.*) so safe or simple that even a fool can use, handle, and understand it correctly.
—[形] 《口》 [바보라도 할 수 있을 만큼] 간단한, 아주 손쉬운, 식은 죽 먹기의

fools·cap [fú:lskæ̀p] *n.* [C] a size of writing paper, usu. 13×17 inches.
—[名] 푸울스캡판(判) (13×17 인치의 인쇄용지 판)

fool's cap [fú:lzkæ̀p] *n.* a cap formerly worn by a clown. ⇒fig.
—[名] [원뿔꼴의] 광대 모자

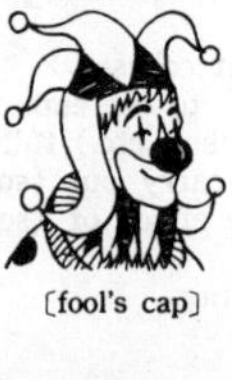
〔fool's cap〕

:foot [fut] *n.* [C] (pl. **feet**) **1.** the end part of a leg on which a person or an animal stands or walks. ¶*A cat's feet are called paws.* **2.** the lowest part, place, or end of anything; the bottom; the base. ¶*the ~ of a mountain*① / *the feet of a table.*② **3.** 《*collectively*》 sol-
—[名] 1. 발 2. [온갖 물건의] 발에 해당하는 부분; 최하부, 최저부; 말단 부분; 기부(基部); [산 따위의] 기슭 ¶①산기슭/②책상(탁자)다리 3. 보병 ¶③보병과 기병 4. 피이트 [N.B.] 12인치, 약 30센티 5. 운각(韻脚)

F

diers who fight on foot; the infantry. ¶ ~ *and horse.*③ **4.** a measure of length. ⇒[N.B.] **5.** one of the parts into which a line of poetry is divided.

1) ***at someone's feet,*** under the control of someone; as someone's disciple.
2) ***carry someone off his feet,*** make someone very enthusiastic; rouse someone's enthusiasm.
3) ***find one's feet,*** learn to manage well.
4) ***find*** (or ***get, have, know***) ***the length of someone's foot,*** learn someone's weak points.
5) ***have one foot in the grave,*** be near death.
6) ***keep one's feet,*** ⓐ continue standing. ⓑ act carefully.
7) ***on foot,*** ⓐ standing or walking. ¶*go on ~.* ⓑ (of an enterprise, etc.) going on; in progress. ¶*set an enterprise on ~.*④
8) ***put one's best foot forward,*** ⓐ walk or run as fast as possible. ⓑ do one's utmost.
9) ***put one's foot down,*** act firmly or decisively, esp. to stop someone else's action.
10) ***put one's foot in it,*** make a blunder.
11) ***trample*** (or ***tread***) ***someone*** or ***something under foot,*** override; oppress. ¶*trample the will of the people under ~.*⑤

[熟] 1)…의 뜻대로(하자는 대로) 하여, …의 부하(제자)가 되어 2)…을 열중시키다 3)본령(本領)을 발휘하다 4)…의 약점을 잡다 5)한 발을 무덤 속에 넣고 있다, 다 죽어 가고 있다 6)ⓐ[쓰러지지 않고] 똑바로 서 있다 ⓑ신중히 행동하는 7)ⓐ서서; 걸어서, 도보로 ⓑ움직여; 진행중인 ¶④사업을 발족시키다 8)ⓐ될 수 있는 대로 빨리 걷다(서두르다) ⓑ최선을 다하다 9)단호히 행동하다 10)실수하다, 실책을 저지르다 11)짓밟다, 유린하다, 억압하다 ¶⑤민의를 짓밟다

—*vt., vi.* **1.** walk. ¶ ~ *the bad road.*⑥ **2.** dance; kick. ¶ ~ *the stage.*⑦ **3.** make the foot of (a stocking, etc.). **4.** add up. 《~ *up* accounts, etc.》 **5.** pay (a bill, expenses, etc.). ¶*I'll ~ the bill.*⑧

—[他][自] **1.** 걷다 ¶⑥나쁜 길을 걷다 **2.** 춤추다; 차다 ¶⑦무대에서 춤추다 **3.** [양말 따위의] 발 부분을 만들다 **4.** 합계하다 **5.** [계산·비용 따위]를 지불하다 ¶⑧그 계산은 내가 치르겠다

***foot·ball** [fútbɔ̀:l] *n.* **1.** [U] a field game played with a large leather ball by two teams of 11 players. **2.** [C] a ball of leather used in this game. ¶*American ~*① / *Association ~.*②

—[名] **1.** 축구, 풋보올 **2.** 축구 공 ¶①미식 축구/②아식 축구(soccer)

foot·board [fútbɔ̀:rd] *n.* [C] a board or small platform to support the feet.

—[名] 발판, 디딤널

foot·bridge [fútbrìdʒ] *n.* [C] a narrow bridge for persons who are walking.

—[名] [보행자용] 인도교

foot·fall [fútfɔ̀:l] *n.* [C] **1.** a footstep. **2.** the sound of a footstep.

—[名] **1.** 걸음 **2.** 발소리

foot·gear [fútgìər] *n.* [U] 《*collectively*》 covering for the feet, such as shoes, boots, and slippers.

—[名] 신는 것[구두·양말 따위]

foot·hill [fúthìl] *n.* [C] 《usu. *pl.*》 a low hill near the base of a mountain or mountain range.

—[名] 산기슭의 작은 언덕

foot·hold [fúthòuld] *n.* [C] **1.** a place for supporting the feet. **2.** a firm position.

—[名] **1.** 발 딛는 곳, 발판 **2.** 확고한 지위

foot·ing [fútiŋ] *n.* [C] 《usu. *sing.*》 **1.** [U][C] a place supporting the feet. ¶*He lost his ~ and fell.*① / *Mind your ~ !*② **2.** an established position. **3.** a relationship to others. ¶*He is on a friendly ~ with many people.*③ **4.** (*Commercial*) the amount obtained by adding up figures. **5.** the part of a building, etc. which touches the earth. **6.** the act of moving on the feet in dancing.

—[名] **1.** 발판, 발디딤 ¶①그는 발을 헛디뎌서 떨어졌다/②발밑을 조심하게! **2.** 입장, 지위 **3.** 관계 ¶③그는 많은 사람들과 친한 사이이다 **4.**《商》[숫자의] 합계, 총계 **5.** 기초 **6.** 댄스의 스텝

foot·lights [fútlàits] *n. pl.* a row of lights in the front of a stage, nearly on a level with the feet of actors.

—[名] 각광(脚光)

appear (or ***come***) ***before the footlights,*** attract the attention of people; appear on the stage; be an actor.

[熟] 각광을 받고 등장하다; 무대에 서다

foot·man [fútmən] *n.* [C] (pl. **-men** [-mən]) a man servant, usu. in a uniform, who waits on the table, opens the doors, attends his master when driving, etc.

—[名] [흔히 제복을 입은] 종복(從僕), 사환, 급사

foot·mark [fútmɑ̀:rk] *n.* [C] a footprint.

—[名] 발자국

foot·note [fútnòut] *n.* [C] a note at the bottom of a page. **—*vt.*** add such a note to (a text, etc.).

—[名] 각주(脚註) —[他] …에 각주를 달다

foot·pad [fútpæ̀d] *n.* [C] a highway robber who goes on foot. ⇒[N.B.]

—[名] [걸어다니는] 노상 강도 [N.B.] highwayman (말 타고 다니던 노상 강도)

foot·path [fútpæ̀θ / -pɑ̀:θ] *n.* [C] (pl. **-paths** [-pæ̀ðz ·pæ̀θz / ·pɑ:ðz]) a narrow path for persons on foot; a sidewalk.

—[名] 보도(步道)

foot·print [fútprìnt] *n.* [C] a mark or print made by a foot.

—[名] 발자국

foot race [ㅗ ㅗ] *n.* a contest of speed in running or walking. —[名] 도보 경주; 달리기 경주

foot soldier [ㅗ ㅗ-] *n.* a soldier who fights on foot; an infantryman. —[名] 보병

foot·sore [fút-sɔ̀:r] *adj.* having sore feet [from excessive walking]. —[形] 발이 아픈, 발병이 난

⁎ **foot·step** [fút-stèp] *n.* [C] **1.** a person's step. **2.** the distance covered by a step. **3.** the sound made by stepping. **4.** a footprint. —[名] **1.** 걸음[걸이] **2.** 보폭(步幅) **3.** 발소리 **4.** 발자국

follow (or *walk*) *someone's **footsteps**,* succeed; imitate what someone else has done. [熟] …을 본받다, 선례를 좇다; …의 유지(遺志)를 잇다

foot·stool [fút-stù:l] *n.* [C] a low stool on which to rest the feet. —[名] [쉴 때 발을 올려놓는] 발판

foot·way [fútwèi] *n.* [C] a footpath; a sidewalk. —[名] 보도, 인도

foot·wear [fútwɛ̀ər] *n.* [U] 《*collectively*》 anything to be worn on the feet, such as shoes, slippers and boots; footgear. —[名] 신는 것[구두·슬리퍼 따위를 통틀어 일컫는 상용어(商用語)]

foot·work [fútwə̀:rk] *n.* [U] the use of the feet, as in boxing, tennis, dancing, etc. —[名] 「경기·권투 따위의」 발놀림, 풋워어크

fop [fɑp / fɔp] *n.* [C] a man who pays too much attention to his clothes, appearance, etc. —[名] 맵시꾼, 멋장이

fop·per·y [fápəri / fɔ́p-] *n.* [U][C] (pl. **-per·ies**) the behavior, clothes, etc. of a fop. —[名] 멋부리기, 맵시내기

fop·pish [fápiʃ / fɔ́p-] *adj.* having the characteristics of a fop; like a fop. —[形] 모양낸, 멋부리는

⁑ **for** [fɔ:r, fər] *prep.* **1.** in support or in favor of; in the interest of. ¶ *fight ~ one's country* / *He voted ~ Mr. Smith.*① / *I am ~ the proposal.*② ↔against **2.** in place of; representing. ¶ *use a box ~ a desk* / *speak ~ the classmates*③ / *A lawyer acts ~ his client.* **3.** in exchange for; in return for; to the amount of. ¶ *a check ~ $500* / *give a cat ~ a dog*④ / *These apples are twelve ~ a dollar.* **4.** preparing for. ¶ *study ~ examinations* / *save ~ a rainy day.*⑤ **5.** with the purpose of; as being. ¶ *build a building ~ a church* / *We chose him ~ our leader.* **6.** toward. ¶ *the 11:30 train ~ Pusan*⑥ / *He left ~ Osaka.* / *The plane ~ London took off just now.*⑦ **7.** being used by or with; suitable to. ¶ *a book ~ children* / *suits ~ big men.* **8.** because of; by reason of. ¶ *We shouted ~ joy.*⑧ / *He was punished ~ stealing.*⑨ **9.** taking into account; in comparison with. ¶ *It is very warm ~ March.* / *He is tall ~ his age.*⑩ **10.** as far or long as; during. ¶ *walk ~ a mile* / *He stayed here ~ two weeks.* **11.** in spite of. ¶ *For all her faults, I like her.*⑪ **12.** in or with regard to; as concerns. ¶ *as ~ me*⑫ / [*as*] *~ the rest*⑬ / *So much ~ today.*⑭ **13.** that one will, should, might, must ... 《*~ someone to do*》 ¶ *It is time ~ you to go.* / *French is difficult ~ me to learn.*

—[前] **1.** …을 지지하여, …을 위하여 ¶ ①그는 스미드씨에게 투표하였다 / ②나는 그 제안에 찬성이다 **2.** …의 대신에; …을 대표하여 ¶③동급생을 대변하다 **3.** …의 교환으로서, …에 대하여; …에 달하는 ¶④개와 교환으로 고양이를 주다 **4.** …에 대비하여 ¶⑤만약의 경우에 대비하여 저축하다 **5.** …의 목적으로; …으로서 **6.** …을 향하여, …행(行)의 ¶⑥부산행 11시 30분발 열차 / ⑦런던행 비행기는 방금 이륙하였다 **7.** …용(用)의; …에 알맞은, 어울리는 **8.** …의 이유로, …이므로 ¶⑧우리는 기뻐서 소리질렀다(환성을 올렸다) ¶⑨그는 도둑질하였기 때문에 처벌받았다 **9.** …을 고려하면, …에 비하여, …치고는 ¶⑩그는 나이에 비해서는 키가 크다 **10.** …동안; 기간중 **11.** …에도 불구하고 ¶⑪결점은 있지만 나는 그녀가 좋다 **12.** …에 관해서는, 에 대해서는 ¶⑫나로서는 / ⑬나머지에 대해서는 / ⑭오늘은 이만큼 해두자 **13.** …에게 있어서는

1) ***for oneself,*** in order to benefit oneself; having no help from others; by one's own efforts. ¶ *You must do it ~ yourself.*
2) ***for good,*** permanently.
3) ***Oh,*** (or ***O***) ***for ... !,*** I wish I had! ¶ *Oh, ~ a glass of water!*

[熟] 1) 자신을 위해서; 스스로; 혼자서, 혼자 힘으로 2) 영구히 3) [갈망을 나타내어] …였으면!

—*conj.* because; since. ¶ *We can't start out, ~ it is raining hard.* —[接] 그 이유는, 왜 그런가 하면; …이므로

fo·ra [fɔ́:rə] *n.* pl. of **forum.**

for·age [fɔ́:ridʒ, fár- / fɔ́r-] *n.* **1.** [U] food for horses or cattle. **2.** [U][C] the act of searching for such food. —[名] **1.** [마소의] 먹이, 꼴, 사료 **2.** 마량(馬糧) 징발

—*vi.* **1.** wander in search for food. **2.** search for something one wants. 《*~ for* something》 —[自] **1.** 식량을 찾아 돌아다니다 **2.** 먹이를 찾다

—*vt.* **1.** get food from (someone); plunder. **2.** supply (horses) with food; feed. ▷**for·ag·er** [-ər] *n.* —[他] **1.** …에서 먹이(식량)를 얻다; 약탈하다 **2.** [말]에게 꼴을 주다, 마초를 먹이다

for·ay [fɔ́:rei, -ㅗ / fɔ́r-] *n.* [C] a sudden attack to steal things by force. —*vt., vi.* make a raid. —[名] 침략, 약탈 —[他][自] […을] 침략하다, 약탈하다

⁎ **for·bad** [fərbǽd] *v.* pt. of **forbid.**

⁎ **for·bade** [fə:rbǽd, -béd] *v.* pt. of **forbid.**

for·bear¹ [fɔ:rbɛ́ər] *v.* (**-bore, -borne**) *vt.* keep oneself from (something); endure. 《*~ to do* something》 —[他] …을 삼가다, 참다, 견디다

—*vi.* —[自] **1.** …을 피하다, 삼가다 **2.** 참다

F

1. hold back. (~ *from* something) 2. control oneself.

for·bear[2] [fɔ́:rbɛ̀ər] *n.* =forebear.

for·bear·ance [fɔ:rbɛ́ərəns] *n.* [U] (*Law*) **1.** the act of forbearing. **2.** self-control.

—[名] 1. 인내 2. 자제

⁑ for·bid [fərbíd] *vt.* (**-bade** or **-bad, -bid·den** or **-bid, -bid·ding**) **1.** order (someone) not to do. ¶ ~ *someone* [*to enter*] *the house* / *Her father forbade her marriage.* / *The doctor forbids him wine.* / *God ~ !*① **2.** make (something) impossible; prevent. ¶ *Time forbids that ...*② / *High walls ~ all approach.* / *Smoking is forbidden here.*③

—[他] 1. …을 허락하지 않다 ¶①단연코 [그런 일은] 없다! 2. [사정이] …을 허락하지 않다 ¶②시간이 …을 허락하지 않는다/③여기서는 금연이다

∗ for·bid·den [fərbídn] *v.* pp. of **forbid**.

for·bid·ding [fərbídiŋ] *adj.* **1.** looking dangerous and disagreeable. **2.** stern. ¶ *a ~ look.*

—[形] 1. 가까이하기 어려운 2. 험악한, 엄격한

for·bore [fɔ:rbɔ́:r] *v.* pt. of **forbear**.

for·borne [fɔ:rbɔ́:rn] *v.* pp. of **forbear**.

⁑ force [fɔ:rs] *n.* [U] **1.** strength; energy; power. ¶ *the ~ of the wind*① / *the ~ of the explosion.*② **2.** the strength used upon or against someone or something. ¶ *use ~ on someone*③ / *Don't resort to ~.*④ **3.** [U][C] the power to influence, control or persuade; effectiveness. ¶ *a debater with much ~*⑤ / *with all one's ~.*⑥ **4.** [C] an organized body of persons for action; the military power; (often *pl.*) a body of armed men; troops. ¶ *the police ~*⑦ / *the Air Force* / *the labor ~*⑧ / *in full ~.*⑨

1) ***by force,*** forcibly. ¶ *They made him do it by ~.*

2) ***by force of*** (=*by means of*) *a habit, etc.*

3) ***in force,*** ⓐ in great numbers. ⓑ in effect or operation; valid. ¶ *put in ~*⑩ / *The law is still in ~.*

—*vt.* **1.** make (someone) do something by force; compel; impose. (~ someone *to do*; ~ someone *into*) ¶ *He forced her to confess.*⑪ / *Hunger forced him into a crime.* **2.** get or take (something) by force. ¶ ~ *a bag out of someone's hand.*⑫ **3.** produce or effect (something) by force. ¶ ~ *a smile* (*a laugh, tears*)⑬ / ~ *cucumbers.* **4.** hasten the growth or development of (plants, etc.).

—[名] 1. 힘, 세력 ¶①풍력(風力)/②폭발력 2. 폭력, 폭행 ¶③…에게 폭력을 쓰다/④완력에 의지하지 마라! 3. 세력, 영향력, 지배력, 설득력; 효과 ¶⑤매우 설득력 있는 토론가/⑥전력을 다하여 4. [협동 동작을 하는] 집단, 총력; 병력, 부대, 군대 ¶⑦경찰/⑧노동력/⑨총력으로, 총동원하여

[熟] 1)강제적으로, 억지로 2)[습관]의 힘으로(에 의하여) 3)ⓐ대거하여 ⓑ실시중인; 유효한 ¶⑩실시하다

—[他] 1. …에게 억지로 …시키다; …을 강요(강제)하다 ¶⑪그는 억지로 그녀를 자백시켰다 2. …을 완력으로 빼앗다, 강탈하다 ¶⑫ …의 손에서 백을 강탈했다. 3. …을 억지로 짓다(내다) ¶⑬억지로 미소짓다(웃다, 울다) 4. [야채 따위의] 촉성 재배를 하다

forced [fɔ:rst] *adj.* **1.** brought about or made by force. ¶ ~ *labor*① / ~ *insurance*② / *a ~ march.*③ **2.** made or kept up by an unnatural effort. ¶ *a ~ smile*④ / ~ *tears.*⑤

—[形] 1. 강제적인 ¶①강제노동/②강제보험/③강행군 2. 부자연한 ¶④억지웃음/⑤거짓 눈물

force·ful [fɔ́:rsf(u)l] *adj.* full of force; powerful. ▷**force·ful·ly** [-fuli] *adj.* **—force·ful·ness** [-nis] *n.*

—[形] 힘센, 힘찬; 격렬한

for·ceps [fɔ́:rseps] *n.* [C] (pl. **-ceps** or **-ci·pes**) a pair of small tongs or pincers used by surgeons, dentists, etc. ⇒fig.

—[名] [외과·치과용의] 겸자(鉗子), 핀셋

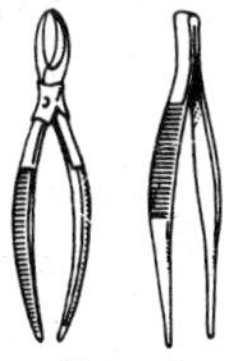

〔forceps〕

for·ci·ble [fɔ́:rsibl] *adj.* **1.** carried out by force. ¶ *a ~ detention*① / *a ~ execution.*② **2.** having force; powerful. ¶ *a ~ style.*③ ▷**for·ci·bly** [-i] *adv.*

—[形] 1. 강제적인 ¶①억류(抑留)/②강제 집행 2. 힘이 있는, 힘찬 ¶③힘있는 문체

for·ci·pis [fɔ́:rsipì:z] *n.* pl. of **forceps**.

∗ ford [fɔ:rd] *n.* [C] a shallow place in a river where a person can cross by walking. **—*vt., vi.*** cross (a stream, a river, etc.) by walking; wade.

—[名] 여울, [걸어서 건널 수 있는] 강의 얕은 곳 —[他][自] […의] 여울을 건너다

fore [fɔ:r] *adj.* **1.** situated at the front. **2.** being or coming first in time, place, etc. **—*adv.*** in the front part, esp. of a ship. **—*n.*** [C] (*the ~*) a forward part.

to the fore, ⓐ at the front. ⓑ at hand. ⓒ into a prominent place or position. ¶ *He has come to the ~.*① ⓓ alive.

—*interj.* (*Golf*) a warning shout to someone in the way.

—[形] 1. 앞의, 전방의 2. 최초의 —[副] 전방에서, 앞쪽에; 이물에(쪽으로) —[名] 앞부분

[熟] ⓐ전면에 ⓑ금방 쓸 수 있게 되어 ⓒ눈에 띄는 곳에 ¶①그는 최근 세인의 이목을 끌게 되었다 ⓓ살아 있는

—[感] 《골프》 공이 간다!, 위험하다!

fore-and-aft [fɔ́:rəndǽft / -á:ft] *adj.* (of a ship) from bow to stern. ¶ *a ~ sail*① / ~ *rigged.*②

—[形] 이물에서 고물로의 ¶①종범(縱帆)/②종범 장치의

fore·arm[1] [fɔ́:rà:rm] *n.* [C] the part of an arm between the elbow and the wrist.

—[名] 앞팔, 전박(前膊)

F

fore·arm² [fɔ:rá:rm] *vt.* arm (someone or oneself) for a fight or for trouble beforehand. —[他] …을 미리 무장하다

fore·bear [fɔ́:bὲər] *n.* [C] 《usu. *pl.*》 an ancestor; a forbear. —[名] 조상, 선조

fore·bode [fɔ:rbóud] *vt.* **1.** give (someone) warning of something bad that is going to happen; predict. **2.** show a sign of (something bad). ▷**fore·bod·er** [-ər] *n.* —[他] 1. …의 전조를 보이다; …을 미리 알리다, 예언하다 2. …을 예감하다

***fore·cast** [fɔ́:rkæ̀st / -kὰ:st] *n.* [C] a description of an event which is going to happen in the future. ¶*a weather* ~.① —*vt.* say in advance (what is going to happen in the future.) —[名] 예보 ¶①일기예보 —[他] …을 예보하다

fore·cas·tle [fóuksl] *n.* [C] **1.** the upper deck in the bow of a ship. **2.** the front part of a ship where the sailors live. ⇒[N.B.] —[名] 1. 앞갑판 2. 앞갑판 밑의 선원실 [N.B.] fo'c'sle이라고도 씀

fore·close [fɔ:rklóuz] *vt.* **1.** shut out. **2.** (*Law*) take away someone's right to take back a mortgage. —[他] 1. …을 제외하다 2. 《法》 [저당물을 찾을 권리]를 상실하게 하다

fore·doom [fɔ:rdú:m] *vt.* doom beforehand. —[他] …의 운명을 미리 정하다

***fore·fa·ther** [fɔ́:rfὰ:ðər] *n.* [C] 《usu. *pl.*》 an ancestor. ¶*Forefathers' Day.*① —[名] 조상, 선조 ¶①청교도 미대륙 상륙 기념일(12월 21일)

fore·fin·ger [fɔ́:rfiŋgər] *n.* [C] the finger next to the thumb; the index finger. —[名] 집게손가락

fore·foot [fɔ́:rfùt] *n.* [C] (pl. **-feet** [-fi:t]) **1.** one of the front feet of a four-footed animal, insect, etc. **2.** the forward end of a keel. —[名] 1. [짐승·곤충의] 앞발 2. 용골(龍骨)의 앞끝

fore·front [fɔ́:rfrʌ̀nt] *n.* [C] **1.** the foremost position. **2.** the center of activity. —[名] 1. 맨 앞 2. [활동 따위의] 중심

fore·gath·er [fɔ:rgǽðər] *v.* =forgather.

fore·go¹ [fɔ:rgóu] *v.* (**-went, -gone**) =forgo.

fore·go² [fɔ:rgóu] *vt., vi.* (of degree, time, etc.) go before; precede. —[他][自] [···에] 앞서가다, 앞장서다; 앞서다, 먼저 일어나다

fore·go·ing [fɔ:rgóuiŋ] *adj.* previously; just before. ¶*the* ~ *chapter.*① —[形] 전술(前述)한 ¶①전장(前章)

fore·gone [fɔ:rgɔ́:n / fɔ́:gɔn] *v.* pp. of **forego**.
—*adj.* that has gone before. —[形] 앞선, 기왕의, 기지(旣知)의

foregone conclusion [⌐-- ⌐-⌐-] *n.* a thing that was never in doubt from the start; an inevitable result. —[名] 처음부터 다 알고 있는 결론; 피할 수 없는 결과

fore·ground [fɔ́:rgràund] *n.* [C] **1.** the part of a scene, picture, etc. nearest to a spectator. ↔background **2.** the most noticeable position. —[名] 1. [풍경·그림의] 전경(前景) 2. 표면, 눈에 띄는 위치

fore·hand [fɔ́:rhæ̀nd] *adj.* (in tennis, etc.) struck from the racket-holding side of the body. ↔backhand —*n.* [C] **1.** a forehand stroke in tennis. **2.** the part of a horse in front of the rider. —[形] [정구 따위에서] 앞으로 (바로) 치는 —[名] 1. 앞으로 치기, 정타(正打) 2. 말의 앞쪽 몸뚱이

⁑**fore·head** [fɔ́:rid, fάr- / fɔ́rid] *n.* [C] the part of the face between the eyebrows and the beginning of the hair. —[名] 이마

⁂**for·eign** [fɔ́:rin, fάr- / fɔ́r-] *adj.* **1.** of or belonging to another country. ¶*a* ~ *language* / *discuss* ~ *affairs.* **2.** of another country. ¶*a* ~ *policy* / *the Foreign Ministry.*① **3.** not natural; not related. 《~ *to*》 ¶*Keeping silence is* ~ *to my nature.*② **4.** from outside. —[形] 1. 외국의 2. 외국에 관한; 외교의 ¶①외무부 3. 성미에 맞지 않는; 아무 관련이 없는 ¶②침묵을 지킨다는 것은 나의 성미에 맞지 않는다 4. 외부로부터의

***for·eign·er** [fɔ́:rinər, fάr- / fɔ́rinə] *n.* [C] a person who belongs to another country; an alien. —[名] 외국인

fore·judge [fɔ:rdʒʌ́dʒ] *vt.* judge or decide beforehand. —[他] …을 미리 판단하다, 예단(豫斷)하다

fore·know [fɔ:rnóu] *vt.* (**-knew** [-njú:], **-known** [-nóun]) have knowledge of (something) beforehand. —[他] …을 미리 알다, 예지(豫知)하다

fore·knowl·edge [fɔ́:rnάlidʒ / fɔ́:nɔ́l-] *n.* [U] knowledge of something before it exists or happens. —[名] 예지(豫知), 선견(先見)

fore·land [fɔ́:rlənd] *n.* [C] **1.** a point of land projecting into the sea; a cape. **2.** the land along the coast. ↔hinterland —[名] 1. 갑(岬) 2. 해안지방

fore·leg [fɔ́:rlèg] *n.* [C] one of the front legs of a four-legged animal or insect. —[名] [짐승·곤충의] 앞발

fore·lock [fɔ́:rlὰk / fɔ́:lɔ̀k] *n.* [C] a lock of hair growing above the forehead. —[名] 앞머리

fore·man [fɔ́:rmən] *n.* [C] (pl. **-men** [-mən]) **1.** a man in charge of a group of workers in a factory, etc. **2.** the chairman of a jury. —[名] 1. 직공장, 십장 2. 배심장(陪審長)

fore·mast [fɔ́ːrmæst / fɔ́ːmɑ̀ːst] *n.* ⓒ the mast nearest the front of a ship. —⑱ 앞돛대

* **fore·most** [fɔ́ːrmòust] *adj.* **1.** first in place. **2.** first in degree, activity, importance, etc. —*adv.* first.
first and foremost, first; before all else.
—⑲ 1. 맨 앞의 2. 제1급의, 1류의
—⑭ 맨 먼저
圞 맨 먼저

fore·noon [fɔ́ːrnùːn] *n.* Ⓤ morning. —⑱ 오전

fo·ren·sic [fərénsik] *adj.* **1.** of a law court. ¶ ~ *medicine.*① **2.** of a public debate.
—⑲ 1. 법정의 ¶①법의학 2. 변론의, 토론의

fore·or·dain [fɔ̀ːrɔːrdéin / fɔ̀ːrɔːdéin] *vt.* determine the future or fate of (something or someone) beforehand.
—⑭ …의 운명을 미리 정하다

fore·part [fɔ́ːrpɑ̀ːrt] *n.* ⓒ the front part. —⑱ 앞부분

fore·paw [fɔ́ːrpɔ̀ː] *n.* ⓒ a front paw of an animal.
—⑱ [개·고양이 따위의] 앞발

fore·run·ner [fɔ́ːrrʌ̀nər] *n.* ⓒ **1.** a person who goes or is sent before to pronounce the coming of another. **2.** a sign that something is to come; an omen. **3.** an ancestor; a predecessor.
—⑱ 1. 선구자 2. 전조, 조짐 3. 조상, 선조; 전임자, 선배

fore·sail [fɔ́ːrsèil] *n.* ⓒ the main sail on the foremast of a ship.
—⑱ 앞돛대의 큰 돛

* **fore·see** [fɔːrsíː] *vt.* (**-saw** [-sɔ́ː], **-seen** [-síːn]) see or know (something) beforehand. ¶ ~ *trouble.*①
—⑭ …을 미리 알다, 예지(豫知)하다 ¶①곤란을 미리 알다

fore·shad·ow [fɔːrʃǽdou] *vt.* suggest (something) in advance; indicate (something is going to happen) beforehand.
—⑭ …을 미리 암시하다, 징후를 보이다

fore·short·en [fɔːrʃɔ́ːrtn] *vt.* (in drawing or painting) make the lines of (an object) shorter than they really are.
—⑭ …을 원근법(遠近法)에 의하여 그리다

fore·show [fɔːrʃóu] *vt.* (**-showed, -shown** [-ʃóun]) show (something) beforehand; foretell.
—⑭ …을 예시하다, 전조를 보이다

fore·sight [fɔ́ːrsàit] *n.* Ⓤ **1.** the power to see the future. ¶ *a man of* ~.① **2.** careful thought or regard for the future.
—⑱ 1. 선견지명 ¶①선견지명이 있는 사람 2. [장래에 대한] 깊은 사려

‡ **for·est** [fɔ́ːrist, fɑ́r- / fɔ́r-] *n.* **1.** ⓤⓒ a large area covered with trees. ¶ *forests stretching for miles*① / *a deep* ~② / *primeval forests.*③ **2.** ⓒ a large group of trees. ¶ *land covered with forest*[*s*] / *cut down a* ~. **3.** ⓒ something which looks like a forest. ¶ *a* ~ *of chimneys.*④
—*vt.* plant (a place) with trees.
—⑱ 1. 숲, 삼림, 삼림지 ¶①몇 마일이나 뻗어 있는 삼림 /②깊은 숲 /③원시림 2. 수목 3. 임립(林立)한 것 ¶④임립한 굴뚝
—⑭ …을 수목으로 덮다, 식림(植林)하다

fore·stall [fɔːrstɔ́ːl] *vt.* go ahead of or do something before (another) and so prevent another's doing it first; upset a previous plan by doing something before (another).
—⑭ …에 앞서다; 선수를 치다, 기선(機先)을 제하다

for·est·er [fɔ́ːristər, fɑ́r- / fɔ́ristə] *n.* ⓒ **1.** a person who looks after a forest and the animals there. **2.** a person or an animal living in a forest.
—⑱ 1. 삼림관(森林官) 2. 삼림지 거주자, 숲속에 사는 동물

for·est·ry [fɔ́ːristri, fɑ́r- / fɔ́r-] *n.* Ⓤ **1.** the science of planting and caring for forests. **2.** the management of forests. **3.** (*collectively*) forest land.
—⑱ 1. 삼림학(森林學) 2. 삼림 관리 3. 삼림지

fore·taste *n.* [fɔ́ːrtèist → *v.*] ⓒ a previous experience of something that one is to enjoy or suffer in the future; an anticipation. —*vt.* [fɔːrtéist] anticipate; enjoy (something) by looking forward to it.
—⑱ 미리 맛보기, 시식(試食); 예상
—⑭ …을 예기하다; 예기하고 기뻐하다(즐거워하다)

fore·tell [fɔːrtél] *vt.* (**-told**) tell of (something) beforehand.
—⑭ …을 예고하다

fore·thought [fɔ́ːrθɔ̀ːt] *n.* Ⓤ **1.** careful thoughts for the future. **2.** previous planning.
—⑱ 1. 장래에 대한 고려 2. 계획

fore·to·ken *vt.* [fɔːrtóukn → *n.*] be a sign of (something).
—*n.* [fɔ́ːrtòuk(ə)n] ⓒ a sign that something is to happen; an omen.
—⑭ …의 전조가 되다 —⑱ 전조

fore·told [fɔːrtóuld] *v.* pt. and pp. of foretell.

‡ **for·ev·er** [fərévər] *adv.* **1.** for an endless time; for ever. **2.** all the time. ⇒N.B. —*n.* Ⓤ eternity.
—⑭ 1. 영원히, 영구히 2. 끊임없이
N.B. 영국에서는 for ever —⑱ 영원
—⑭ 영구히, 영원히

for·ev·er·more [fərèvərmɔ́ːr] *adv.* forever; ever.
—⑭ …을 미리 경고(주의)하다

fore·warn [fɔːrwɔ́ːrn] *vt.* give a previous warning to (someone or something).

fore·word [fɔ́ːrwə̀ːrd] *n.* ⓒ introductory remarks to a book; a preface.
—⑱ 서문, 머리말

for·feit [fɔ́ːrfit] *n.* **1.** ⓒ something that is lost or given up because of one's crime, fault, etc.; a fine; a penalty.
—⑱ 1. 몰수물; 벌금, 과료 2. [권리 따위의] 상실

2. [U] loss of rights, etc. as a penalty.
—*adj.* taken away as a forfeit. —[形] 몰수당한
—*vt.* be deprived of (something) as a forfeit. ¶ ~ *one's licence.*① ▷**for·feit·er** [-ər] *n.* —[他] …을 몰수(박탈)당하다 ¶①면허장을 압수당하다

for·fei·ture [fɔ́:rfitʃər] *n.* **1.** [C] something that is lost as a forfeit; penalty. **2.** [U] loss of rights, etc. —[名] 1. 몰수물, 벌금, 과료 2. [권리 따위의] 상실

for·gath·er [fɔ:rgǽðər] *vi.* **1.** meet together; assemble. **2.** be friendly. ⟪~ *with* someone⟫ **3.** meet (someone) by chance. —[自] 1. 모이다, 회합하다 2. 친하게 지내다, 교제하다 3. [우연히] 만나다

⁑ **for·gave** [fərgéiv] *v.* pt. of **forgive**.

* **forge**[1] [fɔ:rdʒ] *n.* [C] **1.** a fireplace where metal is heated and hammered into shape. **2.** a place where iron, etc. is melted and hammered into shape. —[名] 1. [대장간의] 노(爐) 2. 대장간, 철공장
—*vt.* **1.** heat and hammer (metal) into shape. ¶ ~ *an anchor.*① **2.** produce; invent. **3.** imitate. ¶ ~ *a banknote.* —*vi.* **1.** shape metal or iron, as a blacksmith does. **2.** make something false to deceive others. —[他] 1. [쇠]를 벼리다 ¶①닻을 [벼려서] 만들다 2. [거짓말·계획 따위]를 꾸며내다, 날조하다 3. …을 위조하다 —[自] 1. 대장일을 하다 2. 위조하다

forge[2] [fɔ:rdʒ] *vi.* go forward slowly and steadily. —[自] [말·사람이] 서서히 나아가다

forg·er [fɔ́:rdʒər] *n.* [C] a person who imitates something to deceive others. —[名] 위조자, 날조자

for·ger·y [fɔ́:rdʒəri] *n.* (pl. **-ger·ies**) **1.** [U] the act of forging a signature, a coin, etc. **2.** [C] something produced falsely to deceive. —[名] 1. 위조 2. 위조물

⁑ **for·get** [fərgét] *v.* (**-got, -got·ten** or **-got, -get·ting**) *vt.* **1.** fail to remember; lose memory of (something). ¶ *He soon forgets his father's advice.* **2.** omit or neglect (something) without meaning to. ¶ *I forgot to close the window.*① **3.** leave (something) behind unintentionally. ¶ ~ *one's umbrella on a bus.* **4.** banish (bad memories, etc.) from the mind. ¶ ~ *and forgive*② / *Forget it!*③ —*vi.* fail or cease to remember; be forgetful. ⟪~ *about* something⟫ ¶ *I quite forgot about it.*
—[他] 1. …을 잊다; 망각하다 2. …을 게을리하다, 등한히 하다 ¶①나는 창문을 닫는 것을 잊어버렸다 3. …을 놓고 잊어버리다, 놓아둔 채 잊고 떠나다 4. [나쁜 기억 따위]를 털어버리다; 마음쓰지 않다 ¶②[원한 따위를] 깨끗이 잊어버리다/③그런 일로 신경 쓰지 말게!, 잊어버리게! —[自] 잊다, 잊어버리기를 잘 하다
forget oneself, ⓐ behave in an improper manner; lose one's dignity. ⓑ act unselfishly, not thinking of one's own interests. [熟] ⓐ자기 분수를 잊다, 자제력을 잃다 ⓑ자기를 돌보지 않다, 사리(私利)를 생각지 않고 행동하다

for·get·ful [fərgétf(u)l] *adj.* **1.** having a poor memory. ⟪~ *of*⟫ ¶ *He is very ~ of things.*① **2.** apt to neglect. ▷**for·get·ful·ly** [-fuli] *adv.* —[形] 1. 잊기 쉬운, 잊기 일쑤인 ¶①그는 무엇을 잊기를 잘한다 2. 게을리하기 쉬운

for·get·ful·ness [fərgétf(u)lnis] *n.* [U] **1.** poor memory. **2.** carelessness; neglect. —[名] 1. 잊기 쉬움, 건망증 2. 부주의; 태만

for·get-me-not [fərgétminɑ̀t / fəgétminɔ̀t] *n.* [C] a small plant with small blue or white flowers. —[名] 물망초(신의와 우애의 상징)

for·giv·a·ble [fərgívəbl] *adj.* that can be forgiven. —[形] 용서할 수 있는

⁑ **for·give** [fərgív] *v.* (**-gave, -giv·en**) *vt.* **1.** give up the desire to punish (someone). ⟪~ someone *for*; ~ someone *his crime,* etc.⟫ ¶ *Will you ~ me? / They forgave him his failure.* **2.** do not demand payment for (a debt etc.). ¶ ~ *a debt.*① —*vi.* show forgiveness. —[他] 1. …을 용서하다 2. …을 면제하다 ¶①빚을 면제하다 —[自] 용서하다

* **for·giv·en** [fərgív(ə)n] *v.* pp. of **forgive**.

for·give·ness [fərgívnis] *n.* [U] the act of forgiving; the state of being forgiven; willingness to forgive. —[名] 용서, 관용, 관대함; 면제

for·giv·ing [fərgíviŋ] *adj.* ready to forgive. —[形] [쾌히] 용서하는, 관대한

for·go [fɔ:rgóu] *vt.* (**-went, -gone**) do without (something); refrain from (something). —[他] …없이 때우다, …을 삼가다

⁑ **for·got** [fərgɑ́t / fəgɔ́t] *v.* pt. and pp. of **forget**.

⁑ **for·got·ten** [fərgɑ́tn / fəgɔ́tn] *v.* pp. of **forget**.

⁑ **fork** [fɔ:rk] *n.* [C] **1.** an instrument with a handle and two or more pointed parts, used for picking up or holding something to eat. ¶ *a knife and ~.*① ⇒[usage] **2.** an instrument like a fork; a garden fork. ⇒fig. **3.** —[名] 1. [식탁용] 포오크 ¶①나이프와 포오크 [N.B.] 한 벌로 취급되므로 fork 앞의 a는 불필요 2. 포오크 모양의 기구; 갈퀴, 쇠스랑 3. 분기점(分岐點) —[自] 갈래지다, 분기하다 —[他] [갈퀴

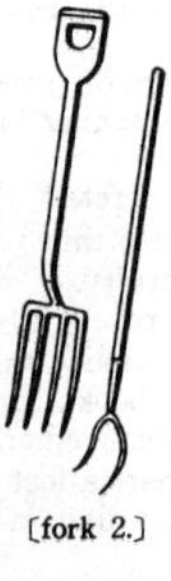
[fork 2.]

forked [fɔːrkt] *adj.* in the shape of a fork; divided into branches. ¶ *a* ~ *lightning* / *a* ~ *road*.

for·lorn [fərlɔ́ːrn] *adj.* (sometimes ~·**er**, ~·**est**) **1.** miserable and unhappy. **2.** left alone; deserted.

forlorn hope [-́ -́] *n.* **1.** a very faint hope. **2.** a very dangerous plan or enterprise that has little chance of success.

‡**form** [fɔːrm] *n.* **1.** ⓤ ⓒ shape; outward appearance; the figure of a person or an animal. ¶ *the* ~ *of a cross* / *A* ~ *moved in the mist.* **2.** ⓒ a kind or type; a particular structural condition. ¶ *a lower* ~ *of animal life.* **3.** ⓒ a thing that gives shape to something; a mold. **4.** ⓤ set order; method. ¶ *certain forms of worship.* **5.** ⓤ orderly arrangement of parts in a work of art; style; pattern. ¶ *in the* ~ *of a drama.* **6.** ⓤ behavior according to rule, custom, or etiquette. ¶ *good (bad)* ~. **7.** ⓤ ⓒ (*Grammar*) a shape taken by a word in spelling, sound, or inflection. **8.** ⓒ (*Brit.*) a grade or class of pupils in a school. (cf. *U. S.* grade) **9.** ⓒ a set order of words; a printed paper with spaces to be written in. ¶ *fill in the* ~. **10.** ⓤ (of a horse, a runner etc.) good condition. ¶ *be in (out of)* ~.
— *vt.* **1.** shape; make. ¶ ~ *a cup out of clay* / *Water forms ice when it freezes.* **2.** build up (character, etc.); train; develop (habits, etc.). **3.** compose; organize; make up. ¶ ~ *a club* / ~ *a committee.* **4.** frame (ideas, opinions, etc.) in the mind; arrange (someone or something) in some order. — *vi.* take shape; be formed.

•**for·mal** [fɔ́ːrm(ə)l] *adj.* **1.** of the outward form rather than the content. ¶ ~ *resemblance* / ~ *logic* / ~ *obedience.* **2.** according to strict forms, rules, etc.; regular. ¶ *a* ~ *receipt.* **3.** according to the forms, ceremonies, customs, etc. ¶ *a* ~ *call* / *a* ~ *man.*

for·ma·lin [fɔ́ːrmalin] *n.* ⓤ a liquid used to do away with germs and bad smells.

for·mal·ism [fɔ́ːrməlìz(ə)m] *n.* ⓤ excessive attention to forms and customs.

for·mal·i·ty [fɔːrmǽliti] *n.* ⓤ (pl. -**ties**) **1.** the state or quality of being formal; strict adherence to established rules, customs, procedure, etc.; rigidity. ¶ *No* ~, *please.* **2.** (usu. *pl.*) a formal act; a ceremony. ¶ *the formalities of a wedding.* **3.** (usu. *pl.*) an established method of procedure required by custom or rule. ¶ *the legal formalities* / *go through due formalities.*

for·mal·ly [fɔ́ːrməli] *adv.* in a formal manner; in form.

•**for·ma·tion** [fɔːrméiʃ(ə)n] *n.* **1.** ⓤ the process or act of forming; the state of being formed. ¶ *the* ~ *of character* / *the* ~ *of a Cabinet.* **2.** ⓤ a way in which something is formed; structure. **3.** ⓤ an arrangement of troops, airplanes, ships, etc. ¶ *a battle* ~ / ~ *flying.* **4.** ⓒ (*Geology*) a series of layers of the same kind of rock or mineral.

form·a·tive [fɔ́ːrmətiv] *adj.* of forming or developing; forming; shaping. ¶ ~ *arts* / ~ *elements.*

‡**for·mer** [fɔ́ːrmər] *adj.* **1.** earlier; previous; long past. **2.** first of two which were mentioned before. ¶ *Of the two men, I prefer the latter to the* ~.

‡**for·mer·ly** [fɔ́ːrmərli] *adv.* in the past; in former times; previously.

for·mic [fɔ́ːrmik] *adj.* of ants; found in ants. ¶ ~ *acid.*

•**for·mi·da·ble** [fɔ́ːrmidəbl] *adj.* **1.** causing fear, dread or awe. ¶ *a* ~ *enemy.* **2.** difficult to overcome or

---

쇠스랑 따위로] …을 적어(긁어)올리다(파다)

— ⓐ 갈래진, 가랑이 모양의 ¶①갈래 모양의 전광(電光)/②두 갈랫길

— ⓐ 1. 비참한, 절망적 2. 고독한; 버림받은, 저버려진

— ⓐ 1. 가냘픈 희망 2. 절망적인 계획 (기획)

— ⓐ 1. 모양; 형상; 외관; 사람의 형상 (그림자); 모습,자태 2. 종류; 형(型); 형태 ¶①하등 동물 3. 형(型); 원형 (原型) 4. 정해진 방법; 방식 ¶②예배의 여러 형식 5. [표현의] 양식,형태; 형식 6. 예식, 예의,예법 ¶⑦《文法》[의미에 대하여] 형식, 어형(語形) 8. [영국의] 학급 9. 서식(書式); 신청 용지 10. 심신의 상태,컨디션 ¶③컨디션이 좋다(나쁘다)

— ⓥ 1. …을 형성하다, 형태를 이루다; 짓다; 만들다 2. [성품 따위를] 길러내다; …을 단련하다; [습관 따위를] 붙이다 3. …을 구성하다; 조직하다; 형성하다 4. [생각 따위를] 구성하다, 짜다; …을 정리하다, 정렬시키다
— ⓥ 모양을 이루다, 모양이 되다
— ⓐ 1. 형식의, 형식적인; 표면적인 ¶①표면상의 유사(類似)/②형식 논리/③표면상의 복종 2. 정식의 ¶④정식 영수증 3. 형식에 치우친, 의례적인, 격식 차리는 ¶⑤의례적인 방문/⑥형식적인
— ⓐ 포르말린(살균·소독제) [주의자]

— ⓐ 형식주의; 형식론; 허례

— ⓐ 1. 형식적임, 형식에 구애됨; 딱딱함 ¶①편안히 하십시오 2. 의례(儀禮) ¶②혼례의 의식 3. 절차, 수속 ¶③법률상의 절차/④정식 절차를 밟다

— ⓐⓓ 형식적으로; 정식으로
— ⓐ 1. 형성, 구성 ¶①인격의 도야/②조각(組閣) 2. 구조 3. 대형(隊形); 편대 ¶③전투 대형/④편대 비행 4.《地質》암층(岩層)

— ⓐ 형성(발달)의 ¶①조형 미술/②[말의] 구성 요소
— ⓐ 1. 이전의,전의,먼저의 2. 전자의 ¶①두 사람 중 전자보다는 후자가 좋다

— ⓐⓓ 옛날에는, 전에는

— ⓐ 개미의 ¶①의산(蟻酸)
— ⓐ 1. 무서운, 가공할 ¶①강적 2. 얕잡을 수 없는, 만만치 않은 ¶②만만치

handle. ¶*a ~ task.*② **3.** of a surprising number, amount, difficulty, etc. ¶*a ~ pile of letters.*③ ▷**for·mi·da·bly** [-i] *adv.*
않은 일 **3.** 엄청나게 많은, 방대한 ¶③엄청나게 많은 편지더미

form·less [fɔ́:rmlis] *adj.* having no definite or regular form; shapeless.
—[形] 형태가 없는, 무형의

For·mo·sa [fɔ:rmóusə] *n.* a Chinese island off southeastern China; Taiwan.
—[名] 대만

For·mo·san [fɔ:rmóusən] *adj.* of Formosa. —*n.* **1.** [C] a person of Formosa. **2.** [U] the language of Formosa.
—[形] 대만의 —[名] **1.** 대만 사람 **2.** 대만 말

• **for·mu·la** [fɔ́:rmjulə] *n.* [C] (pl. **-las** or **-lae**) **1.** a fixed form of words used on certain occasion. **2.** (*Medicine*) a prescription. ¶*a ~ for a cough.*① **3.** (*Mathematics*) a rule expressed in algebraic symbols. **4.** (*Chemistry*) an expression of the composition of a compound by chemical symbols. ¶*a molecular ~*② / *a structural ~.*③
—[名] **1.** [인사말 따위] 판에 박은 말, 상투어 **2.** 《醫》 처방전 ¶①기침에 대한 처방전 **3.** 《數》 공식 **4.** 《化》 식(式) ¶②분자식/③구조식

for·mu·lae [fɔ́:rmjulì:] *n.* pl. of **formula**.

for·mu·late [fɔ́:rmjulèit] *vt.* **1.** express (something) in the form of a formula; reduce (something) to a formula. **2.** express (something) precisely and systematically.
—[他] **1.** …을 공식으로 나타내다; 공식화(化)하다 **2.** …을 정확히 계통적으로 말하다

for·mu·la·tion [fɔ:rmjuléiʃ(ə)n] *n.* **1.** [U] the act of formulating. **2.** [C] an exact and clear expression.
—[名] **1.** 공식화; 계통적 표시 **2.** 명확한 표현

• **for·sake** [fərséik] *vt.* (**-sook, -sak·en**) **1.** leave (someone) alone; desert. **2.** give up (a habit, an idea, etc.).
—[他] **1.** 을 저버리다 **2.** [습관 따위]를 버리다

for·sak·en [fərséik(ə)n] *v.* pp. of **forsake**.

for·sook [fərsúk] *v.* pt. of **forsake**.

for·swear [fɔ:rswέər] *v.* (**-swore, -sworn**) *vt.* pledge oneself to give up (something). ¶*~ smoking.* —*vi.* make a false statement under oath.
—[他] [맹세코] …을 그만두다
—[自] 거짓 맹세를 하다

for·swore [fɔ:rswɔ́:r] *v.* pt. of **forswear**.

for·sworn [fɔ:rswɔ́:rn] *v.* pp. of **forswear**.

F

• **fort** [fɔ:rt] *n.* [C] a strong building or place surrounded with defenses against enemies.
—[名] 성채, 보루(堡壘), 요새

forte[1] [fɔ:rt] *n.* [C] one's strong point; anything in which one excels or shows particular power.
—[名] 장점, 특기

for·te[2] [fɔ́:rti] *adj.* (*Music*) loud. —*adv.* loudly. ⇒[N.B.] ｢f.로 줄여 씀｣
—[形] 《樂》 강음의 —[副] 강하게 [N.B.]

⁑ **forth** [fɔ:rθ] *adv.* **1.** forward; onward. ↔backward **2.** 《usu. connected with *a verb*》 out into view. ¶*bring ~*① / *Trees put ~ new leaves in spring.*②
1) ***and so forth,*** and so on.
2) ***back and forth,*** to and fro.
3) ***so far forth,*** so far.
—[副] **1.** 앞으로, 전방으로 **2.** 밖으로, 나타나서 ¶①낳다; 일으키다/②나무들은 봄에 새싹이 튼다
[熟] 1)…따위, …등등 2)여기저기에, 이리저리 3)거기까지는, 그만큼은

forth·com·ing [fɔ́:rθkʌ́miŋ] *adj.* **1.** about to come; approaching. ¶*a list of ~ books.*① **2.** at hand when expected or needed.
—[形] **1.** 장차 오려고 하는, 다가오는 ¶①근간 도서 목록 **2.** [준비되어 있어서] 곧 손에 넣을 수 있는

forth·right *adj.* [fɔ́:rθràit → *adv.*] **1.** frank; straightforward. **2.** going straight ahead. —*adv.* [fɔ:rθráit] straight; at once. ▷**forth·right·ness** [-nis] *n.*
—[形] **1.** 솔직한 **2.** 똑바로 나아가는
—[副] 똑바로; 즉시

forth·with [fɔ́:rθwíð, -wíθ] *adv.* at once; without delay.
—[副] 곧, 당장

⁑ **for·ti·eth** [fɔ́:rtiiθ] *n.* **1.** 《usu. *the ~*》 the number 40; 40th. **2.** [C] one of 40 equal parts of anything. —*adj.* of the 40th.
—[名] **1.** 제 40, 마흔[번]째 **2.** 40분의 1
—[形] 40번째의; 40분의 1의

for·ti·fi·ca·tion [fɔ:rtifikéiʃ(ə)n] *n.* **1.** [U] the act or science of fortifying. **2.** [C] 《usu. *pl.*》 works for defense, such as walls and towers; a fortified place.
—[名] **1.** 성채 구축, 축성술(築城術), 요새화, 강화 **2.** 방어 공사; 성채, 요새

for·ti·fy [fɔ́:rtifài] *vt.* (**-fied**) **1.** (*Military*) strengthen (a place) with forts, walls, etc. for defense against attack. **2.** strengthen (someone) physically or mentally. ¶*~ oneself against the cold*① / *~ one's courage.*② **3.** strengthen (wine) by adding alcohol. **4.** enrich (food) by adding vitamins and minerals.
—[他] **1.** 《軍》 …을 요새화하다 **2.** …을 [육체적·정신적으로] 강하게 하다 ¶①추위에 대비하여 몸을 튼튼히 하다/②용기를 불러일으키다 **3.** [술에] 알코올을 타서 독하게 하다 **4.** 음식물의 영양가를 높이다

for·tis·si·mo [fɔ:rtísimou] *adj.* (*Music*) very loud. ↔ pianissimo —*adv.* (*Music*) very loudly.
—[形] 《樂》 아주 강한 —[副] 《樂》 아주 강하게 (*ff.* *ffor.* *fortiss*로 줄여 씀)

for·ti·tude [fɔ́:rtit(j)ù:d / -tjù:d] *n.* [U] firm courage and endurance in the face of danger, trouble, misfortune, etc.
—[名] [불행 따위에 견디는] 용기

• **fort·night** [fɔ́:rtnàit] *n.* [C] (chiefly *Brit.*) two weeks.
—[名] 《英》 2주간 ¶①2주일 후(전)의

¶ *Monday* ~.①
fort·night·ly [fɔ́ːrtnàitli] *adv.* once a fortnight. —*adj.* appearing once a fortnight.
* **for·tress** [fɔ́ːrtris] *n.* ⓒ a place strengthened by military defenses.
for·tu·i·tous [fɔːrt(j)úːitəs / -tjúː(ː)i-] *adj.* happening accidentally ; casual. ▷**for·tu·i·tous·ly** [-li] *adv.*
for·tu·i·ty [fɔːrt(j)úːiti / -tjúː(ː)i-] *n.* (pl. **-ties**) Ⓤ chance or accident ; ⓒ an accidental happening.
for·tu·nate [fɔ́ːrtʃ(ə)nit] *adj.* **1.** having good luck ; receiving some unexpected good ; lucky. **2.** bringing good luck that was not expected.
for·tu·nate·ly [fɔ́ːrtʃ(ə)nitli] *adv.* by good fortune ; luckily.
‡ **for·tune** [fɔ́ːrtʃ(ə)n] *n.* **1.** Ⓤ ⓒ great wealth ; riches ; a great sum of money or property. ¶*make a* ~ / *She has a large* ~. **2.** Ⓤ ⓒ what happens [good or bad] to someone ; luck ; chance ; destiny ; lot. ¶*have one's* ~ *told*① / *tell someone's* ~.② **3.** ⓒ good luck ; success in general ; prosperity. ¶*seek one's* ~.③
for·tune-tell·er [fɔ́ːrtʃ(ə)ntèlər] *n.* ⓒ a person who foretells what will happen to other people in the future.
for·tune-tell·ing [fɔ́ːrtʃ(ə)ntèliŋ] *n.* Ⓤ the act of foretelling the future events of other people.
‡ **for·ty** [fɔ́ːrti] *n.* Ⓤ four times ten ; 40. —*adj.* of 40.
fo·rum [fɔ́ːrəm] *n.* ⓒ (pl. **-rums** or **-ra**) **1.** the public square or market place for meeting in an ancient Roman city. **2.** a law court. **3.** an assembly for the discussion of a subject of current interest. ¶*an open* ~.①
‡ **for·ward** [fɔ́ːrwərd] *adj.* **1.** situated in the front ; moving ahead ; onward. ↔backward ¶*a* ~ *movement.* **2.** advanced ; (of plants, children, etc.) well-advanced ; early. ¶*She is* ~ *for her age.*① **3.** bold ; impudent. **4.** ready ; eager. (~ *to do*)
—*adv.* **1.** to or toward the front ; onward ; ahead ; toward the future. ↔backward ¶*run* ~. **2.** out ; into view. ¶*come* ~.② *look forward to,* wait for or expect (something) with pleasure. —*vt.* **1.** send (a letter, etc.) to a new address ; dispatch (cargo, etc.). ¶~ *letters to a new address.* **2.** advance ; promote ; hasten. ¶~ *a plan.* —*n.* ⓒ (*Sports*) a player stationed in a scoring position.
for·ward·ness [fɔ́ːrwərdnis] *n.* Ⓤ **1.** advanced state of development. **2.** eagerness. **3.** lack of modesty ; boldness.
‡ **for·wards** [fɔ́ːrwərdz] *adv.* =forward.
for·went [fɔːrwént] *v.* pt. of **forgo.**
fos·sil [fásl / fɔ́sl] *n.* ⓒ the hardened remains or traces of animals or plants of prehistoric ages found in rock formations in the earth.
fos·sil·i·za·tion [fàsiləzéiʃ(ə)n / fɔ̀silai-] *n.* Ⓤ the act of fossilizing ; the state of being fossilized ; ⓒ something fossilized.
fos·sil·ize [fásilàiz / fɔ́sil-] *vt.* **1.** make (something) into a fossil. **2.** make (ideas or opinions) out-of-date. —*vi.* **1.** become fossilized. **2.** grow old-fashioned.
* **fos·ter** [fɔ́ːstər, fás- / fɔ́stə] *vt.* **1.** help (someone or something) to grow or develop. ¶~ *a child*① / ~ *foreign trade.*② **2.** promote the growth of (plants, feelings, etc.). ¶~ *musical ability.* **3.** keep (ambitions, etc.) in one's mind. ¶~ *evil thoughts.*③ —*adj.* (*U.S.*) being or having been brought up in the same family, though not related by blood. ¶*a* ~ *parent.*④
Fos·ter [fɔ́ːstər, fás- / fɔ́stə], **Stephen Collins** *n.* (1826-1864) an American composer who is famous for "My Old Kentucky Home", "Old Folks at Home", etc.

—❶ 월요일
—❶ 2 주일마다, 2 주일에 한 번
—❶ 격주(隔週)[발간]의
—❷ 요새(要塞)

—❶ 우연한, 뜻밖의

—❷ 우연, 우연성 ; 우연한 일

—❶ 1. 운이 좋은, 행운의, 다행한 2. 행운을 가져오는

—❶ 운 좋게도, 다행히
—❷ 1. 부(富) ; 재산 ; 큰 재산, 거액의 돈 2. 운 ; 운수 ; 운명 ①…의 운수를 점치게 하다/②…의 운수를 점치다 3. 행운 ; 성공 ; 번영 ¶③행운을 찾다, 출세의 길을 찾다

—❷ 점장이

—❷ 점, 길흉 판단

—❷ 40 —❶ 40의
—❷ 1. [고대 로마의] 집회 광장 2. 법정 3. 토론회 ¶①공개 토론회

—❶ 1. 앞(전방)의, 앞쪽의 2. 진보된 ; 진보적인 ; 조숙한 ; 계절에 앞선 ¶①그녀는 나이에 비해 조숙하다 3. 뻔뻔스러운, 주제넘은 ; 건방진 4. 자진해서 […하다]
—❶ 1. 앞(전방)으로(에), 앞쪽에 ; 장래에 2. 밖에(으로) ; 보이는 곳에(으로) ¶②앞으로 나오다 ; [표면에] 나서다
📖 …을 기대하다
—❶ 1. [편지]를 전송(轉送)하다, 송달하다 2. …을 나아가게 하다 ; 촉진(조성)하다 —❷ 전위(前衛)

—❷ 1. 진보의 속도 2. 마음내킴, 열심 3. 촐싹거림, 주제넘음, 건방짐

—❷ 화석(化石)

—❷ 화석 작용, 화석화(化) ; 화석

—❶ 1. …을 화석이 되게 하다 2. …을 시대에 뒤떨어지게 하다 —❶ 1. 화석이 되다 2. 시대(유행)에 뒤떨어지다
—❶ 1. …을 기르다 ¶①수양아들을 양육하다/②외국 무역을 육성하다 · 2. [재능 따위]를 육성하다 3. [야심 따위]를 마음에 품다 ¶③사악한 생각(사심)을 품다 —❶ 기르는, 양육의 ¶④수양 부모

—❷ 미국의 작곡가

:fought [fɔːt] *v.* pt. and pp. of **fight**.

∗foul [faul] *adj.* **1.** very dirty; smelling bad; unpleasant. ¶~ *water.* **2.** (of language, etc.) bad or rude; against the rules; unfair. ¶~ *play.*① **3.** wicked; evil. **4.** (of weather) rough or stormy; (of wind or tide) contrary. **5.** choked with dirt, soot, etc.; entangled.

—[形] 1. 불결한, 더러운; 불쾌한, 구역질 나는; 괘씸한 2. 추잡한; 상스러운; 반칙의; 부정한 ¶①부정; 반칙 3. 부정한; 사악한 4. [날씨가] 궂은, 사나운, 음산한; [바람·조수가] 반대의 5. [진흙·검댕 따위로] 막힌; 뒤얽힌

fall (or ***run, go***) ***foul,*** ⓐ (of a ship) strike against (something). ⓑ (of a person) quarrel with (someone).

[熟] ⓐ[배가] …와 충돌하다 ⓑ …와 싸우다, 말다툼하다

—*n.* [C] **1.** (*Sports*) a play or an action which breaks the rules. **2.** (*Baseball*) a ball knocked outside the base line.

—[名] 1. 《스포오츠》 규칙 위반, 부정행위 2. 《野球》 파울보올

—*vt.* **1.** make (someone or something) foul; dishonor. ¶~ *the air.* **2.** (*Sports*) commit a foul against (an opponent). **3.** block or choke (a chimney, etc.) with soot, etc. **4.** (of ships, etc.) go violently against (something); cause (anchors, nets, etc.) to become entangled; jam (a road crossing, etc.). **—*vi.*** **1.** become foul; become entangled; strike against each other. **2.** (*Sports*) commit a foul; break rules; (*Baseball*) hit a foul.

—[他] 1. …을 더럽히다; …을 불명예스럽게 하다 2. 《스포오츠》 …을 방해하다 3. …을 막히게 하다 4. [배 따위가] …와 충돌하다; [닻 따위]를 얽히게 하다; [통로 따위]를 막히게 하다, 두절시키다 —[自] 1. 더러워지다; 엉클어지다; 부딪치다 2. 《스포오츠》 반칙을 범하다; 《野球》 파울을 치다

foul up, (*colloq.*) make a mess of something; cause disorder.

[熟] 《口》 망쳐놓다; 혼란에 빠뜨리다

fou·lard [fuːláːrd, fəl- / fúːlaːd] ***n.*** [U] a soft, light material of silk, usu. with printed patterns; an article made of foulard, such as a necktie, scarf or handkerchief.

—[名] 플라아르 천; 플라아르 천으로 만든 것

foul line [⸗ ⸗] ***n.*** (*Baseball*) either of the two lines extending from the home plate through the first or the third base to the end of the outfield.

—[名] 《野球》 파울 라인, 파울선(線)

foul·ly [fáuli] *adv.* in a dirty or immoral manner.

—[副] 더럽게; 부정하게

foul·ness [fáulnis] ***n.*** [U] the quality of being foul; [C] an immoral act.

—[名] 불결, 더러움, 악취; 부정[행위]

foul play [⸗ ⸗] ***n.*** play against the rules; an unfair action. ↔fair play

—[名] 경기의 반칙

foul-spo·ken [fáulspòuk(ə)n] *adj.* using indelicate language.

—[形] 입심사나운, 입이 건, 상소리를 쓰는

:found¹ [faund] *v.* pt. and pp. of **find**.

:found² [faund] *vt.* **1.** start the construction of (something). ¶~ *a new city.*① **2.** lay the base of (something). 《~ *on* something》 ¶*write a story founded on facts.*②

—[他] 1. …을 창립하다 ¶①새 도시를 건설하다 2. …을 근거로 삼다 ¶②사실에 입각하여 소설을 쓰다

found³ [faund] *vt.* melt (metal) and form it into some shape by a mold.

—[他] …을 주조(鑄造)하다

:foun·da·tion [faundéiʃ(ə)n] ***n.*** **1.** [U] the act of establishing something. **2.** [C] 《often *pl.*》 a base to support the whole of a building. ¶*the ~ of a house.* **3.** [C][U] that on which some belief, idea, etc. is based. ¶*the foundations of his belief* | *The rumor has no ~.*① **4.** [C] a fund to support a school, a hospital, etc.

—[名] 1. 창립 2. 토대, 기초 3. 근거 ¶①그 소문은 사실무근이다 4. 기금, 재단

be on the foundation, receive one's money from some institution.

[熟] 재단으로부터 장학금을 받고 있다

∗foun·der¹ [fáundər] ***n.*** [C] a person who founds or establishes something.

—[名] 창립자, 설립자

foun·der² [fáundər] *vi.* **1.** fall in. **2.** break down. **3.** (of a ship) fill with water and sink. **—*vt.*** **1.** cause (a house) to fall in. **2.** cause (a horse) to break down. **3.** fill (something) with water and sink (it).

—[自] 1. [집 따위가] 무너지다 2. [말이] 쓰러지다 3. [배가] 침수하여 가라앉다 —[他] 1. [집 따위]를 무너뜨리다 2. [말]을 쓰러뜨리다 3. …을 물이 차서 가라앉게 하다

found·er³ [fáundər] ***n.*** [C] a person who casts metal.

—[名] 주조공(鑄造工)

found·ling [fáundliŋ] ***n.*** [C] a baby or child found abandoned, whose parents are unknown.

—[名] 버린 아이, 기아

foundling hospital [⸗-⸗--] ***n.*** an institution where abandoned babies or children are taken in and looked after.

—[名] 기아 양육원

found·ry [fáundri] ***n.*** (pl. **-ries**) **1.** [U] the process or act of melting and molding metal; [C] things made by this process. **2.** [C] a place where metal is melted to be put into a mold. ¶*an iron ~.*①

—[名] 1. 주조; 주조물 2. 주조 공장 ¶①철공소

fount [faunt] ***n.*** [C] (*poetic*) **1.** a fountain. **2.** a source.

—[名] 《詩》 1. 샘 2. 원천, 근원

foun·tain [fáunt(i)n] *n.* ⓒ **1.** a stream of water rising up into the air. **2.** an artificial spring of water forced out through pipes and falling into a basin. **3.** a device for supplying water. **4.** a natural spring of water. **5.** a source of anything. ¶*a ~ of information.*①

foun·tain·head [fáunt(i)nhèd] *n.* ⓒ **1.** a spring from which a stream begins. **2.** an original source of anything.

fountain pen [´-- ´] *n.* a pen for writing with a constant supply of ink within its holder.

four [fɔːr] *n.* Ⓤ the number between three and five; 4. *on all fours*, on hands and knees.
—*adj.* of four. ¶(*Baseball*) *~ balls*① / *a four-cycle engine*② / *four-dimensional.*③

four·fold [fɔ́ːrfòuld] *adj.* **1.** four times as much or as many. **2.** having four folds or parts. —*adv.* four times as much or as many.

four-o'clock [fɔ́ːrəklɑ̀k / -klɔ̀k] *n.* ⓒ a small garden plant with long red, white, or yellow flowers.

four·pence [fɔ́ːrp(ə)ns] *n.* Ⓤ (*Brit.*) the sum of four pence. ⇒N.B.

four·pen·ny [fɔ́ːrp(ə)ni] *adj.* totaling or costing four-pence.

four·square [fɔ́ːrskwɛ́ər] *adj.* **1.** square. **2.** firm; steady. **3.** frank.

four·teen [fɔ́ːrtíːn] *n.* Ⓤ the number between thirteen and fifteen; 14. —*adj.* of 14.

four·teenth [fɔ́ːrtíːnθ] *n.* **1.** (*the ~*) the number 14. **2.** ⓒ one of 14 equal parts of anything. —*adj.* of 14th.

fourth [fɔːrθ] *n.* **1.** (*the ~*) the number 4; 4th. **2.** ⓒ one of four equal parts. —*adj.* of 4th.

fourth·ly [fɔ́ːrθli] *adv.* in the fourth place.

fowl [faul] *n.* (*pl.* **fowls** or *collectively* **fowl**) **1.** ⓒ (*archaic, poetic*) a bird. ¶*the fowls of the air.*① **2.** Ⓤ (*collectively*) any of the larger birds. ¶*game ~.*② **3.** ⓒ a domestic bird used for food; a cock or hen. ¶*domestic ~.* **4.** Ⓤ the flesh of these birds.

fowl·er [fáulər] *n.* ⓒ a person who shoots or catches wild birds.

fowl·ing [fáuliŋ] *n.* Ⓤ the act of hunting wild birds.

fowling piece [´- ´] *n.* a light gun for shooting wild birds.

fox [fɑks / fɔks] *n.* **1.** ⓒ a wild animal of the dog family with a bushy tail. ⇒N.B. **2.** Ⓤ its fur. **3.** ⓒ a sly and cunning person.

fox·glove [fɑ́ksglʌ̀v / fɔ́ks-] *n.* ⓒ a plant with large, bell-shaped purple or white flowers.

fox·hound [fɑ́kshàund / fɔ́ks-] *n* a kind of dog with a keen sense of smell trained to hunt foxes. ⇒fig.

fox terrier [´ ´--] *n.* a small dog, formerly used for driving foxes out of holes, but now kept as a pet. ⇒fig.

[foxhound]

fox trot [´ ´] *n.* a dance with a variety of short, quick steps; a piece of music for it.

fox·y [fɑ́ksi / fɔ́ks-] *adj.* (**fox·i·er, fox·i·est**) **1.** like a fox; cunning. **2.** of the color of a fox.

foy·er [fɔ́iər / fɔ́iei] *n.* ⓒ **1.** a lobby in a theater or hotel. **2.** an entrance hall in a house.

[fox terrier]

—@ 1. 분수 2. 분수지(池), 분수탑 3. 음료수전(栓) 4. 샘 5. 원천, 근원 ¶① 지식의 샘

—@ 1. 수원(水源) 2. 원천, 본원(本源)

—@ 만년필

—@ 4, 넷
圖 네 발로 기어
—@ 네 개의, 넷의, 4의 ¶①(野球) 4구 / ②4 주기식 엔진 / ③4 차원의

—@ 1. 4 배의 2. 네 겹의 —@ 4 배로; 네 겹으로

—@ 분꽃

—@ 4 펜스 N.B. 4d., 4d로 줄여 씀

—@ 4 펜스의

—@ 1. 4 각의, 정방형의 2. 튼튼한, 견고한 3. 솔직한

—@ 14, 열 넷 —@ 14의

—@ 제14, 열 네 번째 2. 14분의 1
—@ 제14의, 열 네 번째의; 14분의 1의
—@ 1. 제4, 네 번째 2. 4분의 1 —@ 제4의, 네 번째의; 4분의 1의

—@ 네 번째로

—@ 1. 새 ¶①공중의 새 2. 큰 조류 ¶②엽조(獵鳥) 3. 가금; 닭 4. 새고기; 닭고기

—@ 들새를 잡는 사람, 새 사냥꾼

—@ 들새를 잡는 일
—@ 엽총, 새총

—@ 1. 여우 N.B. fox는 수여우, 암여우는 vixen 2. 여우의 모피 3. 교활한 사람

—@ 디기탈리스

—@ 폭스하운드 종의 개(여우 사냥용)

—@ 폭스테리어 개(원래는 여우 사냥에 썼으나 지금은 애완용)

—@ 폭스트롯(짧고 빠른 스텝의 사교춤); 그 춤곡

—@ 1. 여우 같은; 교활한 2. 여우 빛깔의

—@ 1. [극장 따위의] 휴게실 2. 현관 호올

fr. 1. franc. **2.** from. **3.** fragment.
Fr. 1. France. **2.** French. **3.** Father. **4.** Friday.
* **frac·tion** [frǽkʃ(ə)n] *n.* ⓒ **1.** a very small piece broken off; a fragment. ¶*in a ~ of a second.*① **2.** a number less than a whole number. ¶*A half is a ~, and so is a fourth.*② */ a decimal ~*③ */ an improper ~.*④

—❸ **1.** 단편(斷片), 파편 ¶①순식간에 **2.** 분수(分數) ¶②2분의 1은 분수이며 4분의 1도 그렇다/③소수/④가분수

frac·tion·al [frǽkʃən(ə)l] *adj.* of a fraction.

—❸ 얼마 안 되는, 미소한; 분수의

frac·tious [frǽkʃəs] *adj.* **1.** easily made angry. **2.** hard to control. ¶*a ~ child.* ▷**frac·tious·ly** [-li] *adv.*

—❸ **1.** 성 잘 내는, 성마른 **2.** 다루기 힘든

frac·ture [frǽktʃər] *n.* **1.** ⓊⒺ the state or process of being broken; ⓒ a break in a bone. ¶*He suffered a ~ in the fall.*① **2.** ⓒ a break; a crack. —*vi., vt.* break; crack. ¶*~ one's leg.*

—❸ **1.** 부서짐, 깨짐; 골절 ¶①그는 떨어져서 뼈가 부러졌다 **2.** 갈라진 금(틈) —ⒺⓌ 부수다; 부러지다, [뼈따위를] 부러뜨리다

frag·ile [frǽdʒil / -dʒail] *adj.* easily broken or destroyed. ↔strong; elastic ¶*~ china.*① ▷**frag·ile·ly** [-aili] *adv.*

—❸ 부서지기 쉬운; 약한 ¶①깨지기 쉬운 도자기

fra·gil·i·ty [frədʒíliti] *n.* Ⓤ the quality or state of being fragile.

—❸ 부서지기 쉬움; 허약함

* **frag·ment** [frǽgmənt] *n.* ⓒ **1.** a part; a part that is broken off from a thing. ¶*overhear fragments of a conversation.*① **2.** an unfinished work.

—❸ **1.** 파편, 단편 ¶①회화의 단편을 우연히 듣다 **2.** 단장(斷章)

frag·men·tar·y [frǽgməntèri / -t(ə)ri] *adj.* made up of fragments; not complete.

—❸ 단편의; 미완성의

* **fra·grance** [fréigr(ə)ns] *n.* Ⓤ sweetness of smell; a sweet smell.

—❸ 향기로움; 방향

* **fra·grant** [fréigr(ə)nt] *adj.* **1.** having or giving off a sweet smell. ¶*be ~ with flowers.*① **2.** pleasant.

—❸ **1.** 향기로운, 향기가 좋은 ¶①꽃향기가 그윽하다 **2.** 기분 좋은, 유쾌한

fra·grant·ly [fréigr(ə)ntli] *adv.* in a fragrant state.

—❹ 향기롭게, 그윽하게

* **frail** [freil] *adj.* **1.** fragile. **2.** having a delicate structure. **3.** apt to be tempted easily. ▷**frail·ness** [-nis] *n.*

—❸ **1.** 부서지기 쉬운, 약한 **2.** [몸이] 허약한 **3.** 지조가 약한, 부정(不貞)한

frail·ty [fréilti] *n.* (pl. -ties) **1.** Ⓤ the quality of being frail; moral weakness. **2.** ⓒ a fault; a defect.

—❸ **1.** 부서지기 쉬움, 약함; 의지 박약 **2.** 약점, 단점, 결점

: **frame** [freim] *n.* ⓒ **1.** a supporting or shaping structure. ¶*the ~ of a house.* **2.** the body structure. ¶*a man of large ~.* **3.** a border surrounding of a picture, etc. ¶*a window ~.* **4.** the way something is put together; a structure; a system. ¶*a ~ of government.* **5.** a state of mind. ¶*in a happy ~ of mind.*
—*vt.* **1.** shape; put together; construct. ¶*~ a boat.* **2.** compose; plan; invent; imagine. ¶*~ a constitution.* **3.** surround with or put (a picture, etc.) into a frame. **4.** adapted; fit; suitable. ¶*They are not framed for business.* **5.** (*colloq.*) cause (someone) to appear guilty.

—❸ **1.** [건조물의] 뼈대, 골조 **2.** 골격, 체격 **3.** 틀, 얼개, 사진틀 **4.** 구조; 구성; 조직 **5.** 기분; [마음의] 상태

—ⒺⓌ **1.** …의 형태를 이루다, 뼈대를 짜다, 조립하다 **2.** …을 구성하다; 고안하다; 상상하다 **3.** …을 틀에 끼우다, …에 가장자리를 대다 **4.** …을 알맞게 하다 **5.** …을 유죄가 되게 하다

fram·er [fréimər] *n.* ⓒ **1.** a person who builds up a plan, etc. **2.** a person who makes frames for pictures.

—❸ **1.** 구성(기획)자 **2.** 사진틀 세공자

frame-up [fréimλp] *n.* ⓒ (*U.S. colloq.*) **1.** a secret plan for an evil purpose. **2.** an arrangement to make an innocent person seem guilty.

—❸ **1.** (美口) 야바위 **2.** 음모, 흉계

frame·work [fréimwə̀ːrk] *n.* ⓒ **1.** a support to which a thing is fixed. **2.** a way in which something is constructed. ¶*the ~ of society.*①

—❸ **1.** 뼈대 구조 **2.** 골조, 기구(機構) ¶①사회의 기구

* **franc** [frǽŋk] *n.* ⓒ a unit of money in France, Belgium and Switzerland. ⇒NB

—❸ 프랑(프랑스 등지의 화폐 단위)

: **France** [frǽns / frɑːns] *n.* a country in western Europe.

—❸ 프랑스 NB 수도는 Paris

Fran·ces [frǽnsis / frɑ́ːn-] *n.* a woman's name.

—❸ 여자 이름

fran·chise [frǽntʃaiz] *n.* ⓒ **1.** a right granted by a government. **2.** (*usu. the ~*) the right to vote; the right of citizenship.

—❸ **1.** 특권 **2.** 선거권; 시민권

Fran·cis [frǽnsis / frɑ́ːn-] *n.* **1.** a man's name. ⇒NB **2.** , **Saint** (1182-1226) an Italian monk who founded the Franciscan order.

—❸ **1.** 남자 이름 NB 애칭은 Frank **2.** 성(聖) 프란체스코(프란체스코 수도회의 창시자)

: **frank** [frǽŋk] *adj.* free in expressing one's feelings, thoughts, etc.; straightforward; honest. ▷**frank·ness** [-nis] *n.*

—❸ 꾸밈(숨김)없는, 솔직한

frank·furt·er [frǽŋkfərtər] *n.* ⓒ a reddish sausage

—❸ 프랑크푸르트 소시지(쇠고기·돼

made of beef and pork; frankfurt sausage. 지고기로 만든 소시지); 비엔나 소시지

Frank·lin [frǽŋklin], **Benjamin** *n.* (1706–90) an American statesman, author, scientist, and inventor. —[名] 미국의 정치가・저술가・물리학자・발명가

‡**frank·ly** [frǽŋkli] *adv.* in a frank manner. —[副] 솔직히, 터놓고

•**fran·tic** [frǽntik] *adj.* very much excited; wild with excitement, pain, etc. ▷**fran·ti·cal·ly** [-k(ə)li] *adv.* —[形] 광란(狂亂)의; 열광적인

fra·ter·nal [frətə́:rn(ə)l] *adj.* of brothers; like brothers; of a society of men banded together like brothers. ¶ ~ *love.*① —[形] 형제의; 형제다운, 우애의; 우애조합(友愛組合)의 ¶①형제의 사랑

fra·ter·ni·ty [frətə́:rniti] *n.* (pl. **-ties**) **1.** [U] the state of being brothers; brotherhood. **2.** [C] (*U.S.*) a social group of young men in a college. ↔sorority —[名] 1. 형제 관계 2. 《美》 대학의 남학생 사교클럽, 우애회

frat·er·nize [frǽtərnàiz] *vi.* meet together in a friendly way. 《~ *with* someone; ~ *together*》 —[自] [형제처럼] 친하게 사귀다

frat·ri·cide [frǽtrisàid] *n.* **1.** [U] the act of killing one's own brother or sister. **2.** [C] a person who kills his own brother or sister. —[名] 1. 형제(자매) 살해 2. 형제(자매)를 죽이는 사람, 형제(자매) 살해범

fraud [frɔ:d] *n.* **1.** [U] trickery practiced to gain an unfair profit; dishonesty. ¶ *pious* ~.① **2.** [C] an act of fraud; a dishonest act; a person who practices fraud. —[名] 1. 협잡, 기만 ¶①위선(僞善) 2. 사기, 부정행위; 사기꾼, 협잡꾼

fraud·u·lent [frɔ́:dʒulənt / -dju-] *adj.* dishonest; deceitful. —[形] 사기의, 부정의

fraught [frɔ:t] *adj.* filled; involving. —[形] 충만한; 포함(함유)하는

fray[1] [frei] *n.* [C] a quarrel; a fight. —[名] 다툼; 싸움

fray[2] [frei] *vt.* wear or rub off (cloth, rope, etc.) to threads or fibers at the end or the edge. —*vi.* become frayed. —[他] …을 문지르다; 닳아 해지게 하다(끊어뜨리다), [누더기가 되게] 해뜨리다 —[自] 닳아 해지다

freak [fri:k] *n.* **1.** [C] an unusual or abnormal person or thing. ¶ *a* ~ *of nature.*① **2.** [C][U] a causeless, sudden fancy or change of mind. ¶ *out of mere* ~② —*adj.* unusual. —[名] 1. 기형(畸形); 변형 ¶①조화(造化)의 장난 2. 변덕, 일시적 기분 ¶②그저 일시적 기분으로 —[形] 별난, 진기한

freak·ish [frí:kiʃ] *adj.* of or like a freak. —[形] 별난, 기형적인; 변덕스러운, 일시적 기분의

freck·le [frékl] *n.* [C] a small brownish spot on the skin. —*vt.* cover (the face, the hands, etc.) with freckles. ¶ *His face is freckled all over.* —*vi.* become spotted with freckles. —[名] 작은 얼룩(점); 주근깨 —[他] [얼굴・팔 따위]에 주근깨가 생기게 하다 —[自] 주근깨가 생기다

Fred [fred] *n.* a nickname of Frederick. —[名] Frederick의 애칭

Fred·er·ick [fréd(ə)rik] *n.* a man's name. —[名] 남자 이름

‡**free** [fri:] *adj.* **1.** not under any control; independent. ¶ *a* ~ *country* / ~ *will.* **2.** not imprisoned; released. ↔captive **3.** able to act or think as one pleases. ¶ *You are* ~ *to think so.* **4.** open to all; allowable. ¶ *He is* ~ *of the library.*① **5.** without anything to stop; not hindered. ¶ *along the* ~ *and open highway* / *The ship had* ~ *passage through the canal.*② **6.** given without payment. ¶ *a* ~ *pass*③ / *Admission Free.*④ **7.** not busy; at leisure. ¶ *Will you be* ~ *tonight?* **8.** not fixed or fastened; loose. ¶ *One end of the rope was left* ~. —[形] 1. 자유로운; 속박이 없는; 독립된 2. 붙잡혀(갇혀) 있지 않은 3. 자유로이 …할 수 있는; 마음대로의 4. 개방된; 자유로 출입할 수 있는 ¶①그는 도서관에 자유로 출입할 수 있다 5. 장해가 없는, 방해받지 않는 ¶②그 배는 운하를 자유로이 통행할 수 있었다 6. 무료의 ¶③무료 입장권/④입장무료(게시 문구) 7. 한가로운, 손이 빈 8. 고정되어 있지 않은

1) ***free from*** (or ***of***), without; not having; lacking.
2) ***free with,*** giving or using much of.
3) ***set free,*** make (someone) free; let (someone) loose; release.

[熟] 1)…이 없는 2)…에 후한, 아낌없이 주는(쓰는) 3) …을 해방(석방)하다, 놓아주다

—*adv.* **1.** in a free manner. **2.** without cost; paying nothing. —[副] 1. 자유로 2. 무료로

—*vt.* (**freed**) **1.** make (someone or something) free; release. **2.** take pains, etc. from (someone). 《~ someone *from* or *of*》 ¶ ~ *oneself from responsibility.*⑤ —[他] 1. …을 해방(석방)하다 2. …을 구하다; 벗어나게 하다 ¶⑤책임을 면하다(벗다)

free·born [frí:bɔ̀:rn] *adj.* born free, not in slavery. —[形] 자유의 몸으로 태어난

free city [ˊ ˊ] *n.* a city forming an independent state. —[名] 자유시(自由市)

freed·man [frí:dmən / -mæ̀n] *n.* [C] (pl. **-men** [-mən / -mèn]) a man freed from slavery. ↔freedwoman —[名] [노예신분에서 해방된] 자유민

‡**free·dom** [frí:dəm] *n.* **1.** [C][U] the state of being free; liberty. ¶ ~ *of speech.*① **2.** [U] the state of being free from burdens, duties, another's control, etc. ¶ ~ *from fear.*② **3.** [U] frankness. ¶ *speak with* ~. **4.** [C] free use. ¶ *the* ~ *of a library* / *She has* ~ *of the house.* —[名] 1. 자유 ¶①언론의 자유 2. 구애받지 않음, 속박되지 않음 ¶②공포로부터의 자유 3. 흉허물 없음, 소탈함, 솔직함 4. 자유로 쓸 수 있음, 출입의 자유, 자유 사용권

F

free-for-all [fríːfərɔːl] *n.* ⓒ a fight, a contest, etc. open to everyone or in which everyone may take part. —*adj.* open to all.
— 영 참가 자유의 경기 — 영 자유로 참가할 수 있는, 입장(참가) 자유의

free·hand [fríːhænd] *adj.* done by hand, without any instruments.
— 영 손으로 그린

free·hand·ed [fríːhændid] *adj.* generous; liberal.
— 영 통이 큰, 돈 잘 쓰는, 활수(滑手)의

free·hold [fríːhòuld] *n.* ⓤ complete ownership of land; ⓒ a piece of land so owned. ▷**free·hold·er** [-ər] *n.*
— 영 종신(자유) 부동산 보유권; 자유 보유지

free lance [≤ ≤] *n.* 1. a writer, an artist, etc. who does not work for one regular employer. 2. a soldier in the Middle Ages who sold his service to any ruler
— 영 1. 자유 계약 기고가(寄稿家), 자유 작가 2. 용병(傭兵)

:free·ly [fríːli] *adv.* in a free manner. 「활달하게」 or state.
— 부 1. 자유로, 마음대로; 통이 크게,

free·man [fríːmən] *n.* ⓒ (*pl.* **-men** [-mən]) 1. a person who is not a slave. 2. a person who has civil and political rights; a citizen. 「to traders of all countries.」
— 영 1. 자유민 2. 시민, 공민(公民)

free port [≤ ≤] *n.* a part of or all of a port open equally
— 영 자유 무역항

free·si·a [fríːʒ(i)ə / -ʒjə] *n.* ⓒ a plant with clusters of white or yellow flowers. 「spoken.」
— 영 프리지어(붓꽃과의 구근 식물)

free·spo·ken [fríːspóuk(ə)n] *adj.* speaking freely; out-
— 영 솔직한, 숨김없이(터놓고) 말하는

free·think·er [fríːθíŋkər] *n.* ⓒ a person who forms his religious opinions independently of authority or tradition.
— 영 [종교상의] 자유 사상가

free trade [≤ ≤] *n.* trade free from governmental restrictions, taxes, protective duties, etc.
— 영 자유무역

free·way [fríːwei] *n.* ⓒ an express highway.
— 영 [자동차용] 고속도로

free·will [fríːwíl] *adj.* of one's own will; voluntary.
— 형 자유의사의

free will [≤ ≤] *n.* the human will free from any restraints.
— 영 자유의사

:freeze [friːz] *v.* (**froze, fro·zen**) *vi.* 1. change into ice. 2. become hard or rigid with cold; be killed or damaged with cold. 3. be covered with ice. 4. feel very cold. ¶*I'm freezing!* 5. become rigid or motionless with fear, etc. ¶*His smile froze suddenly.* / *She froze in terror at the sight.* —*vt.* 1. change (water) into ice; cover (something) with ice. 2. harden (something) by cold. 3. kill or damage (something living) by cold. 4. cause (someone) to freeze with fear, etc.; horrify. 5. fix (prices, etc.) at a given level.
1) *freeze out*, force (someone) out.
2) *freeze up*, stiffen (something) through cold.
—*n.* ⓤⓒ 1. the state of freezing or being frozen. 2. a period of freezing weather.
— 자 1. 얼다 2. 추위서 [몸이] 굳어지다; 얼어죽다, 동사하다; 추위로 동상을 입다 3. 얼음으로 뒤덮이다 4. 매우 춥다 5. 소름끼치다, 몸서리치다; [표정 따위가] 굳어지다; [얼어붙은 듯이] 꼼짝 않다 — 타 1. …을 얼리다, 동결시키다 2. …을 추위로 굳어지게 하다; 냉동하다 3. …을 얼어죽게 하다; 동상을 입게 하다 4. …을 소름끼치게(오싹하게) 하다 5. [물가 따위]를 동결시키다 熟 1) …을 내쫓다 2) …을 동결하다
— 영 1. 결빙 2. 결빙기, 혹한

freez·er [fríːzər] *n.* ⓒ 1. a machine to make ice cream or sherbet. 2. a refrigerator cabinet for quick-freezing and storage.
— 영 1. 아이스크림 제조기 2. 냉동기, 냉장고

freez·ing point [fríːziŋpɔ̀int] *n.* the temperature at which a liquid freezes.
— 영 빙점

·freight [freit] *n.* ⓤ 1. the ordinary transportation of goods by water, road or air. ↔express 2. the amount paid for carrying goods. 3. the goods transported. 4. (esp. *Brit.*) the cargo of a vessel; the transportation of goods by water. 5. ⓒ (*U.S.*) a freight train.
— 영 1. [보통의] 화물 운송 2. 운송료, 운임 3. 운송 화물, 적하(積荷) 4. 뱃짐, 선하(船荷); 수상 운송 5. 화물열차

freight·er [fréitər] *n.* ⓒ 1. a ship for carrying cargo; a cargo vessel. 2. a person who receives and forwards freight.
— 영 1. 수송선, 화물선 2. 운송업자

:French [frentʃ] *adj.* of France. —*n.* 1. (*the* ~, collectively, used as pl.*) the people of France. 2. the language of France.
— 형 프랑스의 — 영 1. 프랑스 사람 2. 프랑스어

French horn [≤ ≤] *n.* a brass wind instrument with a long, coiled tube which has a soft tone. ⇒fig.
— 영 프렌치 호른(소용돌이꼴의 금관 악기)

·French·man [fréntʃmən] *n.* ⓒ (*pl.* **-men** [-mən]) a person of France.
— 영 프랑스 사람

French·wom·an [fréntʃwùmən] *n.* ⓒ (*pl.* **-wom·en** [-wìmin]) a woman of France.
— 영 프랑스 여자(부인)

fren·zied [frénzid] *adj.* wildly excited or [French horn]
— 형 열광적인

uncontrolled with joy, fear, pain, etc.

fren·zy [frénzi] *n.* [U] the state near madness or of wild feeling. —[名] 광포(狂暴), 광란, 극도의 흥분

fre·quen·cy [fríːkwənsi] *n.* [U] the state of being repeated often. —[名] 자주 일어남, 빈번함; 빈도

‡fre·quent *adj.* [fríːkwənt → *vt.*] **1.** repeated often. ¶~ *visits.* **2.** regular; habitual. ¶*a ~ theatergoer.*① —*vt.* [fri(ː)kwént] visit often. —[形] 1. 자주 일어나는, 잦은, 빈번한 2. 상습적인 ¶①영화구경을 자주 가는 사람 —[他] …을 자주 방문하다

fre·quent·er [fri(ː)kwéntər] *n.* [C] a habitual visitor. —[名] 자주 가는 사람, 늘 오는 사람

‡fre·quent·ly [fríː(ː)kwəntli] *adv.* often. —[副] 자주, 때때로, 빈번히

fres·co [fréskou] *n.* [C] (pl. **-coes** or **-cos**) a picture painted on a wall of a church, etc.; [U] the method of painting on walls. —[名] [교회 따위의] 프레스코 벽화; 프레스코 화법

‡fresh [freʃ] *adj.* **1.** new; newly made or obtained. ¶~ *bread* / ~ *eggs* / ~ *herring.* **2.** not known or used before. ¶*break ~ ground*① / *Do you have any ~ news?*② **3.** lively; vigorous. ¶*a ~ complexion.* **4.** (of colors, etc.) clear; bright. ¶*a ~ red.*③ **5.** (of air, water, etc.) clean and new; pure. ¶~ *air.* **6.** not salty. ¶~ *butter.* **7.** another; different; additional. ¶*make a ~ start* / *begin a ~ paragraph.* **8.** not experienced. ¶*a ~ hand.*④ —[形] 1. 신선한, 싱싱한; 방금 만든, 갓 잡은 2. 미지의, 아직 이용하지 않은; 처음의, 새로운 ¶①처녀지를 개척하다/②뭐 새로운 소식이 있는가? 3. 생기 있는, 팔팔한, 기운찬 4. 선명한, 산뜻한 ¶③산뜻한 빨강 5. 상쾌한; 맑은 6. 소금기 없는 7. 신규의, 새로이 하는; 딴 8. 경험없는, 미숙한 ¶④풋나기, 신출내기

fresh·en [fréʃn] *vt.* make (something) fresh. —*vi.* become fresh. —[他] …을 신선하게(새롭게) 하다 —[自] 신선해지다, 새로와지다

fresh·et [fréʃit] *n.* [C] **1.** an overflow of a river caused by heavy rain or melted snow. **2.** a stream of fresh water flowing into the sea. —[名] 1. [빗물·눈석임물 따위에 의한] 홍수 2. [바다로 흐르는] 민물의 흐름

fresh·man [fréʃmən] *n.* [C] (pl. **-men** [-mən]) a student in the first year of high school or college; a beginner. —[名] 신입생, 신참자, 초년생

fresh·wa·ter [fréʃwɔ̀ːtər, +*U.S.* -wɑ̀-] *adj.* of or living in water that is not salty. ↔salt-water —[形] 민물의, 담수의

***fret¹** [fret] *v.* (**fret·ted, fret·ting**) *vt.* **1.** worry; irritate. **2.** eat away; rub away. —*vi.* be worried; be anxious. ¶~ *over the problem.* —[他] 1. …을 애태우다, 짜증나게 하다 2. …을 먹어들어가다; 닳아 없어지게 하다 —[自] 애타다, 안달하다, 짜증내다

fret² [fret] *n.* [C] a bit of wood on the finger board of some musical instruments. —[名] 프렛(현악기의 줄받이)

fret³ [fret] *n.* [C] a decorative design made of straight lines bent or combined at angles. —[名] 뇌문(雷紋) 격자 세공, 연속된 만자(卍字) 무늬

fret·ful [frétf(u)l] *adj.* ill-humored; irritable. —[形] 짜증내는, 성 잘 내는, 까다로운

fret saw [ㅅ ㅅ] *n.* a saw with a long, slender blade and fine teeth, used to cut ornamental work from thin wood. —[名] [뇌문(雷紋) 세공용] 실톱

fret·work [frétwəːrk] *n.* [U] ornamental work with frets in wood. ⇒fig. —[名] 뇌문 장식, 뇌문 세공

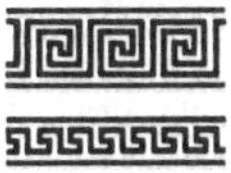
(fretwork)

‡Fri. =Friday.

fri·a·ble [fráiəbl] *adj.* easily broken into powder. —[形] 부서지기 쉬운, 약한

***fri·ar** [fráiər] *n.* [C] a member of certain religious orders; a monk. —[名] [탁발(托鉢) 수도회의] 수도사

fric·a·tive [fríkətiv] *n.* [C] a fricative sound. —[名] 마찰음([f] [v] [θ] [ð] 따위)

fric·tion [fríkʃ(ə)n] *n.* **1.** [U] the rubbing of one thing against another. **2.** [U] [C] disagreement because of differences in ideas, opinions, etc. —[名] 1. 마찰 2. 알력, 불화

‡Fri·day [fráidi, -dei] *n.* the sixth day of the week. ⇒[N.B.] —[名] 금요일 [N.B.] Fri.로 줄여 씀

fried [fraid] *v.* pt. and pp. of **fry**. —*adj.* cooked in hot oil. —[形] 기름에 튀긴, 프라이한

‡friend [frend] *n.* [C] **1.** a person whom one knows and likes and who is not a lover or relative. ¶*a ~ of mine.*① ⇒[N.B.] / *They are good* (or *great*) *friends.*② **2.** a person who favors and supports; a helper; a patron. ¶*a ~ of democracy*③ / *a ~ of the poor.* **3.** a person who belongs to the same group or side; an ally. ↔a foe; an enemy **4.** (*a F-*) a member of a certain religious group called Quakers. —[名] 1. 친구, 벗 ¶①나의 친구 [N.B.] one of my friends는 「나의 친구들 중의 한 사람」의 뜻/②그들은 막역한 사이이다 2. 후원자, 지지자, 찬성자, 동조자 ¶③민주주의의 지지자 3. 편, 동지, 동료, 짝패 4. 프렌드회의 일원, 퀘이커교도

***be* (*make*) *friends with* (=*be* (*become*) *a friend of*) someone.** [熟] …와 친구 사이이다(친구가 되다)

friend·less [fréndlis] *adj.* without friends. —[形] 친구가 없는, 의지할 곳 없는

‡friend·ly [fréndli] *adj.* (**-li·er, -li·est**) **1.** having the nature of a friend; like a friend; kindly. ¶*a ~ game*① / *have ~ relations with.*② **2.** favoring and supporting. —[形] 1. 우정 있는, 친절한 ¶①친선 경기(시합)/②…와 친한 사이이다 2. 자기편의, 지지하는

‡ friend·ship [fréndʃìp] *n.* [U] the state of being friends; the feeling that exists between friends.
—[名] 친구의 사이, 우정

frieze [fri:z] *n.* [C] an ornamented band along a part of wall just below the ceiling.
—[名] 띠 모양의 장식벽(壁)

frig·ate [frígit] *n.* [C] a fast warship; a fast sailing warship used from 1750 to 1850. ⇒fig.
—[名] 프리깃함(艦); 고대의 쾌속 범선

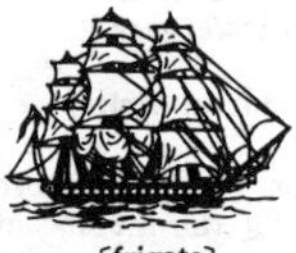
〔frigate〕

‡ fright [frait] *n.* **1.** [U] sudden fear; [C] a state of sudden fear. ¶*have a ~.*① **2.** (*colloq.*) a person or thing that is very ugly or ridiculous.
take fright at, be surprised at.
—[名] 1. 놀람, 경악; 공포[의 상태] ¶① 겁(공포)에 질리다 2.《口》[소름끼칠 만큼] 흉한(추악한) 사람(것)
[熟] …에 놀라다, 겁을 집어먹다

‡ fright·en [fráitn] *vt.* **1.** throw (a person or an animal) into a fright; terrify. ¶*The large noise frightened everyone. / The boy was frightened at the sudden appearance of the big dog.*① **2.** set (a person or an animal) in motion by frightening; move (a person or an animal) away by frightening. ¶*The speeding car frightened away a cat sitting on the road.*②
—[他] 1. …을 깜짝 놀라게 하다, 간담을 서늘하게 하다 ¶①그 소년은 커다란 개가 갑자기 나타나는 바람에 깜짝 놀랐다 2. …을 위협하여 …하게 하다 ¶②전속력으로 달리던 그 자동차는 길 위에 앉아 있던 고양이를 깜짝 놀라게 하여 쫓아버렸다

fright·ful [fráitf(u)l] *adj.* **1.** causing great fear; fearful. ¶*a ~ accident.* **2.** ugly; unpleasant. **3.** (*colloq.*) very.
—[形] 1. 놀라운, 무시무시한, 무서운 2. 몹시 추악한; 불쾌한

fright·ful·ly [fráitf(u)li] *adv.* **1.** in a frightening way. **2.** (*colloq.*) very.
—[副] 1. 무섭게 2.《口》 지독하게, 몹시

frig·id [frídʒid] *adj.* **1.** very cold. ¶*the ~ zone.*① **2.** (of manners, etc.) indifferent; (of an expression, etc.) stiff.
—[形] 1. [날씨가] 몹시 추운, 한랭한 ¶①한대(寒帶) 2. 냉담한, 쌀쌀한; 딱딱한

frill [fril] *n.* **1.** [C] an ornamental edge on a garment. **2.** 《*pl.*》 useless ornamentation; affectation.
—[名] 1. 주름잡은 가장자리 장식, 프릴 2. 허식, 거드름, 젠체하기

• fringe [frindʒ] *n.* [C] **1.** an ornamental edge of loose threads. **2.** the edge of something.
—[名] 1. [옷단 따위의] 술; 가두리 장식 2. 가장자리, 변두리

frip·per·y [frípəri] *n.* (pl. **-per·ies**) [U] unnecessary ornament on a dress, etc.; [C] a cheap decoration.
—[名] [옷 따위의] 야한 장식품; 값싼(번드르르한) 물건

frisk [frisk] *vi.* jump and run about playfully; behave in a joyful way. **—*vt.*** move (something) in a playful manner.
—[自] 뛰어 돌아다니다; 까불다, 장난치다 —[他] …을 가볍게 움직이다(흔들다)

frisk·y [fríski] *adj.* (**frisk·i·er, frisk·i·est**) lively.
—[形] 뛰어 돌아다니는; 쾌활한

frit·ter [frítər] *vt.* cut (something) into small pieces.
—[他] …을 잘게 쪼개다

fri·vol·i·ty [friváliti / -vɔ́l-] *n.* (pl. **-ties**) [U] the state of being frivolous; [C] a frivolous act.
—[名] 천박, 경솔; 경박한 행동

friv·o·lous [frívələs] *adj.* not serious; trifling.
—[形] 경솔(경박)한; 하찮은, 보잘것없는

friz, frizz [friz] *vt.* (**frizzed, friz·zing**) form (hair) into small curls. **—*n.*** [C] (pl. **friz·zes** [fríziz]) curled hair.
—[他] [머리]를 곱슬곱슬하게 하다, 고수머리로 하다 —[名] 고수머리

friz·zle¹ [frízl] *vt.* form (something) into small, crisp curls; curl. **—*n.*** [C] a small, crisp curl.
—[他] …을 곱슬곱슬하게 하다, 지지다 —[名] 고수머리

friz·zle² [frízl] *vt.* fry or broil. **—*vi.*** make a noise while frying or broiling.
—[他] …을 기름에 지글지글 튀기다 —[自] 지글지글 소리나다

friz·zly [frízli] *adj.* full of small, crisp curls; curly.
—[形] 곱슬곱슬하게 지진, 곱슬곱슬한

• fro [frou] *adv.* away. ⇒[usage]
to and fro, forward and back again.
—[副] 저쪽에, 저리로 [usage] 숙어에만 쓴
[熟] 여기저기에, 이리저리

• frock [frɑk / frɔk] *n.* [C] a long outer garment; a woman's dress.
—[名] [여자용]원피이스로 된 드레스

frock coat [´ ´] *n.* a long black coat for men.
—[名] 프록코우트 (남자용 예복)

• frog [frɑg / frɔg] *n.* [C] **1.** a small green or brown jumping animal that lives in water and on land. **2.** an ornamental or fastening button on a garment.
—[名] 1. 개구리 2. 장식 단추

frol·ic [frálik / frɔ́l-] *n.* [C] a piece of fun; a mischievous act. **—*vi.*** (**-icked, -ick·ing**) play or jump about happily. ▷**frol·ick·er** [-ər] *n.*
—[名] 까불기, 장난, 떠들며 놀기
—[自] 까불며 뛰노는, 떠들며 장난치는

frol·ic·some [fráliksəm / frɔ́l-] *adj.* full of fun; merry.
—[形] 까불며 뛰노는; 유쾌한

‡ from [frɑm, frʌm, frəm / frɔm, frəm] *prep.* **1.** (of place or time) starting at. ¶*~ here to the station / a train ~ New York / ~ that time onward*① */ ~ June 1.* **2.** beginning with. ¶*There were ~ 10 to 20 boys there.*② **3.** out of. ¶*take a fountain pen ~ one's pocket.* **4.** sent by. ¶*letters ~ friends.* **5.** having the origin or source in. ¶*words ~ Shakespeare.* **6.** out of the reach
—[前] 1. …에서, 으로부터; …이후 ¶①그때 이후 죽 2. …이하, 이상 ¶②거기에는 10명에서 20명의 소년들이 있었다 3. …에서 밖으로 4. …에게서 보내온 5. …에 근원을 둔; …에서 인용한 6. 떨어져서, 거리를 두고; [힘·손]이 닿는 범위에서 7. …의 원인(이유)

or possession of. ¶*Take his sword ~ him.* **7.** caused by; because of; by reason of. ¶*suffer ~ malaria.*③ **8.** being different. ¶*Anyone can tell black ~ white.*④ **9.** in imitation of. ¶*paint ~ nature.*⑤ **10.** using as material. ¶*Wine is made ~ grapes.*

으로 ¶③말라리아로 고생하다 **8.** …와 구별하여 ¶④누구든지 흑백을 분간할 수 있다 **9.** …을 모방하여 ¶⑤실물을 사생(寫生)하다 **10.** …을 재료로 하여, …으로

‡**front** [frʌnt] *n.* [C] **1.** ⟪usu. *the ~*⟫ the foremost part; the part that faces forward. **2.** the land that faces a sea, a river, a lake, etc. **3.** the place where actual fighting is going on. **4.** a political movement on a large scale; the forces fighting for some political or social aim. ¶*the people's ~.*① **5.** a line between cold and warm air masses. ¶*a cold (warm) ~.*② **6.** a manner or kind of appearance, esp. one not showing proper respect. **7.** the forehead.

—[名] **1.** 앞부분; 전방; 정면 **2.** [바다·호수 따위에 면한] 지역 **3.** 전선(前線), 일선; 전쟁터 **4.** 정치 투쟁; 전선(戰線) ¶①인민 전선 **5.** 전선(前線) ¶②한랭(온난) 전선 **6.** [뻔뻔스러운] 행동, 태도 **7.** 이마

1) ***come to the front,*** become very noticeable or important.
2) ***put a bold front on,*** face (someone) boldly.

[熟] 1)정면으로 나타나다; 뚜렷해지다 2)…에 대해 대담하게 맞서다

—*adj.* of, in, on, or at the front. ¶*a ~ door.*

—[形] 앞의, 전면의, 선두의

—*vt., vi.* stand opposite to (something); face. ¶*The hotel fronts [on] the lake.*

—[他][自] …에 면하다; 향하다

front·age [frʌ́ntidʒ] *n.* [C] **1.** the front of a building. **2.** the land facing a street, a sea, a river, etc.

—[名] **1.** [건물의] 정면 **2.** [거리나 바다로 면한] 지역, 임계지(臨界地)

fron·tal [frʌ́nt(ə)l] *adj.* **1.** of, on, in or at the front. **2.** of the forehead.

—[形] **1.** 정면의, 정면으로 향한 **2.** 이마의, 앞이마의

•**fron·tier** [frʌntíər / frʌ́ntiə] *n.* [C] **1.** the part of a country nearest another country. **2.** (*U.S.*) the farthest edge of a country. **3.** a limit; an undeveloped region.

—[名] **1.** 국경지방 **2.** 변경지방 **3.** 한계; 미지의 영역

fron·tiers·man [frʌntíərzmən / frʌ́ntiəz-] *n.* [C] (pl. **-men** [-mən]) a man who lives on the frontier.

—[名] 국경지방의 주민

fron·tis·piece [frʌ́ntispìːs] *n.* [C] a picture facing the first page or the title page of a book.

—[名] [책의] 머리 그림; [책의] 안표지

‡**frost** [frɔːst / frɔst] *n.* **1.** [U] white frozen vapor; [C] a period of cold weather that makes such vapor. **2.** [U] the state of being frozen. **3.** [U] coldness of manner, etc. **4.** [C] (*colloq.*) a failure. —*vt.* **1.** cover (something) with frost. **2.** cover (a cake, etc.) with white sugar. —*vi.* cover with frost.

—[名] **1.** 서리; 서리가 내리는 시기 **2.** 결빙(結氷) **3.** 냉혹, 냉담 **4.** ⟪口⟫ 실패
—[他] **1.** …을 서리로 뒤덮다 **2.** [케이크 따위]에 설탕을 뿌리다(입히다)
—[自] 서리가 내리다

frost·bite [frɔ́ːstbàit / frɔ́st-] *n.* [U] injury caused by cold to a part of the body.

—[名] 얼음박힘, 동상

frost·bit·ten [frɔ́ːstbìtn / frɔ́st-] *adj.* injured by severe cold.

—[形] 동상에 걸린, 상해(霜害)를 입은

frost·ing [frɔ́ːstiŋ / frɔ́st-] *n.* [U] **1.** a mixture of sugar and some liquid used to cover a cake. **2.** a dull finish on glass, metal, etc.

—[名] **1.** 케이크 겉에 입히는 설탕 **2.** [유리·금속면 따위의] 윤을 없앰

frost·y [frɔ́sti] *adj.* (**frost·i·er, frost·i·est**) **1.** covered with frost; cold enough for frost. **2.** unfriendly.

—[形] **1.** 서리가 내리는; 혹한의 **2.** 냉담한, 쌀쌀한

froth [frɔːθ, frɑθ / frɔθ] *n.* [U] **1.** ⟪*collectively*⟫ foam on a liquid; a foam of saliva caused by disease or excitement. ¶*~ on beer.* **2.** anything trifling or worthless.

—[名] **1.** 거품; 포말(泡沫) **2.** 하찮은 것, 보잘것 없는 것

froth·y [frɔ́ːθi, frɑ́θi / frɔ́θi] *adj.* (**froth·i·er, froth·i·est**) **1.** of, like or covered with froth. **2.** trifling; empty; worthless. ▷**froth·i·ness** [-nis] *n.*

—[形] **1.** 거품의, 거품 같은; 거품투성이의 **2.** 하찮은, 보잘것 없는; 텅 빈, 공허한

‡**frown** [fraun] *vi.* **1.** bend one's brows in deep thought, strong feeling, displeasure, etc. **2.** look disapprovingly; have a displeased look. ⟪~ *at* (or *on, upon*) something⟫ ¶*They ~ at the villain.* —*vt.* **1.** express (displeasure, disapproval, etc.) by frowning. **2.** reject or force (someone or something) to retire by frowning. ⟪~ something or someone *away* (or *back, off, down*)⟫ ¶*~ down the request.*

—[自] **1.** 눈살을 찌푸리다, 상을 찡그리다 **2.** 비난하듯이 보다; 불쾌한 표정을 짓다 —[他] **1.** 상을 찡그리고 불쾌한(비난의) 내색을 하다 **2.** 눈살을 찌푸려 …을 물리치다(위압하다)

—*n.* [C] an act of frowning.

—[名] 눈살을 찌푸리기; 우거지상

frowz·y [fráuzi] *adj.* (**frowz·i·er, frowz·i·est**) **1.** dirty; slovenly. **2.** smelling bad; musty.

—[形] **1.** 지저분한, 누추한; 게으른, 단정하지 못한 **2.** 악취를 풍기는, 곰팡내 나는

•**froze** [frouz] *v.* pt. of **freeze.**

•**fro·zen** [fróuzn] *v.* pp. of **freeze.**
—*adj.* **1.** turned into ice; hardened by cold. **2.** very cold. **3.** cold-hearted; unfeeling.

—[形] **1.** 언, 동결한, 결빙한 **2.** 찬, 차가운 **3.** 쌀쌀한, 냉담한

fruc·ti·fy [fráktifài] *v.* (**-fied**) *vi.* bear fruit. ——*vt.* make (something) bear fruit; make (a tree, a plant, a soil, etc.) fruitful.

fru·gal [frú:g(ə)l] *adj.* **1.** avoiding waste; saving; economical. ¶*a ~ housekeeper* / *She is ~ with her money.* **2.** costing little. ▷**fru·gal·ly** [-gəli] *adv.*

fru·gal·i·ty [fru:gǽliti] *n.* ⓤ the avoidance of waste.

‡**fruit** [fru:t] *n.* ⓤ **1.** ((usu. *sing.*, *collectively*)) the edible or juicy part of a plant or a tree containing the seeds. ⇒usage ¶*fresh ~* / *grow ~*① / *pare a piece of ~* / *fruits in season*① / *I want to eat more ~.* **2.** ((*collectively*)) (*Botany*) the part of a plant where seeds are formed. **3.** ((usu. *pl.*)) any product of a plant, such as grain, vegetables, etc. ¶*the fruits of the earth.*① **4.** ((often *pl.*)) the result or reward of any action; product; profit. ¶*the fruits of study* / *bear ~.*
——*vi.* produce fruit.

fruit·er·er [frú:tərər] *n.* ⓒ a dealer in fruit.

•**fruit·ful** [frú:tf(u)l] *adj.* producing fruit or good results abundantly. ¶*a ~ tree* / *a ~ soil*① / *a study ~ of effect.*

fru·i·tion [fru(:)íʃ(ə)n] *n.* ⓤ **1.** realization of anything desired ; fulfillment; attainment. ¶*come* (*or be brought*) *to ~*① / *~ of my long-standing hope.* **2.** use or possession accompanied by pleasure. ¶*the ~ of modern life.* **3.** the state of bearing fruit.

fruit·less [frú:tlis] *adj.* **1.** bearing no fruit; barren. **2.** having no results; useless; vain.

fruit·y [frú:ti] *adj.* (**fruit·i·er**, **fruit·i·est**) **1.** of fruit. **2.** like fruit in taste or smell. **3.** rich.

frus·trate [frástreit / frastréit] *vt.* bring (plans, efforts, etc.) to nothing; prevent (someone) from carrying out a purpose. ¶*The prisoners were frustrated in their attempt to escape.*①

frus·tra·tion [frʌstréiʃ(ə)n] *n.* ⓤⓒ **1.** the act of frustrating; the state of being frustrated. **2.** (*Psychology*) a condition of insecurity or dissatisfaction caused by frustrated desires, inner conflicts, etc.

•**fry**¹ [frai] *vt.* (**fried**) cook in hot fat, oil, etc. ——*n.* ⓒ (*pl.* **fries**) a dish of something fried.

fry² [frai] *n.* ⓤ (*collectively*) **1.** the young of fish or of certain other animals. **2.** small adult fish which swim in groups.

fry·ing pan [fráiiŋpæn] *n.* a flat iron pan with a long handle, used for cooking.

ft. foot; feet.

fud·dle [fʌdl] *vt.* make (someone) stupid with drink; intoxicate. ——*vi.* drink to excess.

•**fu·el** [fjú(:)əl] *n.* ⓤ **1.** any material that can be burned to produce heat or power. **2.** ⓒ anything that keeps or increases a feeling. ——*vt.* (**-eled**, **-el·ing** *or Brit.* **-elled**, **-el·ling**) supply (a car, a ship, etc.) with fuel.

fu·gi·tive [fjú:dʒitiv] *n.* ⓒ a person who is running away. ¶*a ~ from justice.* ——*adj.* **1.** running away; fleeing. **2.** wandering; roving.

fugue [fju:g] *n.* ⓒ a piece of music in which the same melody is repeated with variations.

-ful [-fəl, -ful] *suf.* **1.** full of; abounding in; characterized by: *beautiful* (=abounding in beauty). **2.** able to: *helpful* (=able to help). **3.** [of] a quantity that fills: *spoonful* (=a quantity that fills a spoon).

•**ful·fill**, *Brit.* **-fil** [fulfíl] *v.* (**-filled**, **-fil·ling**) *vt.* **1.** carry out (a promise, duties, etc.). **2.** satisfy (a requirement, a condition, etc.). **3.** finish; complete (a period of time, a term of office, etc.). ▷**ful·fill·ment**, **ful·fil·ment** [-mənt] *n.*

⁑ full [ful] *adj.* **1.** holding as much as it can; filled. 《~ *of*》 ¶*fill the glass ~*① | *a basket ~ of flowers.* **2.** complete; entire. ¶*walk a ~ mile* | *I waited a ~ hour.* | *in ~ bloom.*② **3.** at the highest degree; reaching the limit. ¶*~ speed* | *~ strength* | *~ summer* | *~ daylight* | *~ moon.* **4.** moved with deep feeling. ¶*My heart was too ~ for words.*③ **5.** not tight. ¶*a ~ sleeve.* **6.** plump; round. ¶*be ~ in the face.* **7.** strong; rich. ¶*a ~ voice.*④
—[形] 1. 가득 찬; 하나 가득의, 충만한 ¶①잔을 가득 채우다 2. 완전한; 충분한 ¶②[꽃이] 만개한, 활짝 핀 3. 최대한의; 힘껏의; 최고의; 한창인 4. 가슴이 벅찬 ¶③나는 가슴이 벅차서 말할 수가 없었다 5. 헐렁한, 낙낙한 6. 불룩한 7. 힘찬, 강한; 풍부한 ¶④낭랑한 목소리

—*adv.* **1.** completely; entirely; quite. **2.** exactly. ¶*hit him ~ on the nose.*
—[副] 1. 완전히; 아주 2. 꼭, 정확히

—*n.* [U] **1.** the whole. ¶*Tell me the ~ of it.* **2.** the utmost extent, degree, length, etc.
—[名] 1. 전부 2. 최고점, 절정, 한창임

1) ***at the full,*** at the time or point of fullness.
2) ***in full,*** completely; (written or said) with all the words.
3) ***to the full,*** completely; to the utmost extent; fully.
[熟] 1)절정에; 한창 때에 2)완전히, 전부, 줄이지 않고 3)충분히, 마음껏

full·back [fúlbæ̀k] *n.* [C] (in football) a player whose position is farthest from the opponent's goal.
—[名] 《蹴球》 풀백, 후위(後衛)

full-blown [fúlblóun] *adj.* in full bloom; fully expanded; fully developed. ¶*a ~ flower* | *a ~ sail.*
—[形] 만발한, 만개의; 터질 듯한, [돛이] 바람을 가득 안은; 완전히 성숙한

full dress [⌐ ⌐] *n.* the formal style of clothes for ceremonial occasions; formal attire. ¶*in ~.*
—[名] 정장(正裝)

full-fash·ioned [fúlfæ̀ʃ(ə)nd] *adj.* knitted to fit the shape of a body part, esp. of a foot or a leg.
—[形] 몸에 꼭 맞게 짠

full-fledged [fúlflédʒd] *adj.* **1.** fully developed. **2.** (of a bird) with the feathers fully grown; able to fly.
—[形] 1. 완전히 자립할 수 있게 된 2. [새가] 깃털이 다 난, 날 수 있는

full-grown [fúlgróun] *adj.* fully grown.
—[形] 충분히 성장한

full-length [fúlléŋθ] *adj.* as large as the human body.
—[形] 등신대(等身大)의

full·ness [fúlnis] *n.* [U] the state of being full.
—[名] 충만, 가득 참; 풍부, 풍만

full stop [⌐ ⌐] *n.* a period.
—[名] 종지부, 종지점

full-time [fúltáim] *adj.* during all normal working hours. ¶*a ~ nurse.* ↔part-time, half-time
—[形] 전(全)시간의, 전시간 취업의

⁑ ful·ly [fúli] *adv.* completely; entirely; wholly.
—[副] 아주; 충분히; 완전히

ful·mi·nate [fʌ́lminèit] *vt., vi.* **1.** protest or blame violently. 《~ *against* something or someone》 **2.** speak loudly and angrily. **3.** burst suddenly.
—[他][自] 1. …에게 비난을 퍼붓다 2. 호통치다, 야단치다 3. 폭발하다(시키다)

ful·mi·na·tion [fʌ̀lminéiʃ(ə)n] *n.* [U][C] **1.** the act of fulminating; strong criticism; bitter protest. **2.** a violent explosion.
—[名] 1. 비난, 힐난하는 말, 폭언 2. 폭발

ful·some [fúlsəm] *adj.* (of flattery) so much as to be unpleasant.
—[形] [아첨이] 비위에 거슬리는, 정도에 지나쳐서 불쾌한

fum·ble [fʌ́mbl] *vi., vt.* **1.** use one's hands uncertainly when looking for (something). 《~ *for* something》 ¶*He fumbled in the darkness for the doorknob.*① **2.** deal with (a ball) unskillfully. —*n.* [C] (of baseball, etc.) failure to hold or catch a ball properly.
—[自][他] 1. 손으로 더듬다 ¶①그는 어둠 속에서 더듬어서 문의 손잡이를 찾았다 2. 어설프게(서투르게) 다루다 —[名] [야구 따위의] 펌블(공을 잡았다가 실수하여 놓치기)

fume [fjuːm] *n.* [C] **1.** 《usu. *pl.*》 smoke or gas, esp. that having a strong, unpleasant smell. ¶*the fumes of tobacco.* **2.** a fit of anger; excitement. —*vi.* **1.** give off gas or smoke. **2.** pass off in fumes. —*vt.* treat (something) with smoke, etc.
—[名] 1. 연기; 증기; 확 풍기는 훈김 2. 흥분 상태, 노기, 배알 —[自] 1. 연기를 내다, 그을리다 2. 연기로 사라지다, 증발하다 —[他] …을 그을리다, 연기에 쐬다

fu·mi·gate [fjúːmigèit] *vt.* smoke (something) heavily.
—[他] …을 그을리다, 연기를 쐬다

fu·mi·ga·tion [fjùːmigéiʃ(ə)n] *n.* [U] the act of smoking (something) heavily.
—[名] 연기를 쐬기; 훈증[소독]

⁑ fun [fʌn] *n.* [U] merriment; joking; amusement; a person or thing which causes amusement or merriment. ¶*We had a lot of ~ at a swimming pool.*①
—[名] 장난, 농; 재미있는 사람(일) ¶①우리는 수영 풀에서 아주 재미있게 놀았다

make fun of, ⓐ laugh at (someone). ⓑ bring (someone) into ridicule.
[熟] ⓐ…을 비웃다 ⓑ…을 놀려대다, 조롱하다

⁑ func·tion [fʌ́ŋkʃ(ə)n] *n.* [C] **1.** natural and proper work; a particular purpose. ¶*The ~ of the stomach is to digest food.*① | *The ~ of education is to develop the mind.*② **2.** a formal public ceremony. **3.** (*Mathematics*) a mathematical amount whose value is related to the changing value of some other amount.
—[名] 1. 기능, 작용, 구실, 직무; [본래의] 목적 ¶①위는 음식을 소화시키는 구실을 한다/②교육의 본래의 목적은 정신을 발달시키는 데 있다 2. 의식(儀式); 축제, 제전(祭典) 3. 《數》 함수

F

—*vi.* work; act.
—[自] 구실을 하다, 작용하다; 직분을 다하다

func·tion·al [fʌ́ŋkʃən(ə)l] *adj.* **1.** having a function; relating to a function. **2.** working; acting.
—[形] 1. 기능상의 2. 작용하는

func·tion·ar·y [fʌ́ŋkʃənèri / -ʃən(ə)ri] *n.* [C] (pl. **-ar·ies**) an official.
—[名] 직원, 관리

:fund [fʌnd] *n.* [C] **1.** the amount of money put aside for a particular purpose. ¶*scholarship ~*① / *A relief ~ was collected for the sufferers of the flood.*② **2.** ⟪*pl.*⟫ money in one's possession ready to use. **3.** a stock; a supply. ¶*The old man has a ~ of interesting stories.*③
—[名] 1. 자금, 기금 ¶①장학 기금/②수재민을 위한 구호 자금이 거두어졌다 2. 재원(財源) 3. 축적, 비축, 온축(蘊蓄) ¶③그 노인은 재미있는 이야기를 많이 알고 있다

·fun·da·men·tal [fʌ̀ndəméntl] *adj.* of, relating to or forming the foundation; very important; most necessary. ¶*~ law*① / *~ principle.*② ▷**fun·da·men·tal·ly** [-təli] *adv.* —**fun·da·men·tal·ism** [-təlìz(ə)m] *n.*
—[形] 기초의; 근본적인; 중요한 ¶①기본법/②원칙, 원리

:fu·ner·al [fjú:n(ə)r(ə)l] *n.* [C] a ceremony performed when a dead person's body is buried or burned. ¶*a state ~.*① —*adj.* of a funeral. ¶*a ~ director*② / *a ~ march.*③
—[名] 장례식 ¶①국장(國葬) —[形] 장례식의 ¶②장의사/③장송 행진곡

fu·ne·re·al [fju:níəriəl] *adj.* of a funeral; like a funeral; sad and solemn; gloomy. ¶*a ~ expression.*
—[形] 장례식의, 장송(葬送)의; 장례식 같은; 구슬픈; 침울한

fu·nic·u·lar [fju(:)níkjulər] *adj.* of a rope.
—[形] 끈 모양의, 색조(索條)의

funk [fʌŋk] *n.* [C] (*colloq.*) **1.** a great fear. **2.** a coward.
—[名] ⟪口⟫ 1. 공포, 무서움, 겁 2. 겁장이

fun·nel [fʌ́nl] *n.* [C] **1.** a cone-shaped pipe with a wide mouth, for putting liquid or powder into a small opening. **2.** anything shaped like a funnel. **3.** a pipe for letting out smoke.
—[名] 1. 깔때기 2. 깔때기 모양의 것 3. 굴뚝, 연통

:fun·ny [fʌ́ni] *adj.* (**-ni·er, -ni·est**) **1.** causing laughter; comical; amusing. ¶*a ~ story.* **2.** (*colloq.*) strange; odd. ¶*a ~ affair.* ▷**fun·ni·ly** [-li] *adv.*
—[形] 1. 재미있는, 우스꽝스러운 2. ⟪口⟫ 기묘한, 별난

:fur [fəːr] *n.* [U] **1.** the soft, thick hair covering the skin of certain animals. **2.** [C] the skin of an animal with such hair; ⟪usu. *pl.*⟫ an article of clothing made of or trimmed with such skin. **3.** [U] ⟪*collectively*⟫ the animals with such skin.
—[名] 1. 부드러운 털 2. 모피; 모피 제품 3. 부드러운 털이 난 짐승, 모피수(獸)(밍크·여우 따위)

—*vt.* (**furred, fur·ring**) make or cover (something) with fur. ¶*~ a coat.*
—[他] …을 모피로 만들다, …을 모피로 씌우다

fur·bish [fə́:rbiʃ] *vt.* polish; make an old thing like a new one by polishing it. ¶*~ up old furniture.*①
—[他] …을 닦다, 윤을 내다 ¶①낡은 가구를 반들반들하게 닦다

·fu·ri·ous [fjúəriəs] *adj.* very violent and angry; strong and uncontrolled. ¶*a ~ quarrel*① / *a ~ storm.*② ▷**fu·ri·ous·ly** [-li] *adv.* —**fu·ri·ous·ness** [-nis] *n.*
—[形] 성나서 날뛰는; 광포한 ¶①맹렬한 싸움(아귀다툼)/②사나운 폭풍

furl [fəːrl] *vt.* roll up; fold up. ¶*~ a sail.*
—[他] …을 감[아 올리]다, 접다

fur·long [fə́:rlɔ:ŋ / -lɔŋ] *n.* [C] a measure of distance equal to 1/8 th of a mile.
—[名] 길이의 단위(8분의 1 마일)

fur·lough [fə́:rlou] *n.* [U][C] time of rest from one's work, esp. for a soldier.
—[名] 휴가

·fur·nace [fə́:rnis] *n.* [C] a large enclosed fire used to heat a building or to melt metals.
—[名] 노(爐), 용광로

:fur·nish [fə́:rniʃ] *vt.* **1.** supply; provide. ¶*~ servants with money; ~ money to servants.* **2.** supply (a room, a house, etc.) with furniture, etc. ¶*~ a room with a beautiful picture.*① ▷**fur·nish·er** [-ər] *n.*
—[他] 1. …에 비치(설비)하다; …을 공급하다 2. …에 [가구 따위]를 장치하다 ¶①방에 아름다운 그림을 장식하다

fur·nished [fə́:rniʃt] *adj.* with furniture. ¶(*Advertisement*) *Furnished House to Let.*①
—[形] 가구가 비치된 ¶①가구를 비치한 셋집

fur·nish·ings [fə́:rniʃiŋz] *n. pl.* the furniture of a room, a house, etc.
—[名] [집·방의] 비품, 가구, 세간

:fur·ni·ture [fə́:rnitʃər] *n.* [U] **1.** ⟪*collectively*⟫ things of daily use in a home, such as beds, tables, chairs, and desks. **2.** any needed item for a machine, etc.
—[名] 1. 가구 2. 부속 설비, 부속품

fu·ror [fjúərɔ:r], **fu·ro·re** [fjuərɔ́:ri] *n.* [C] enthusiastic admiration; excitement; an example of such excitement, etc.
—[名] 열광적인 찬양, 절찬; 열광, 열중

fur·ri·er [fə́:riər / fʌ́riə] *n.* [C] a person who buys and sells furs.
—[名] 모피 상인

fur·row [fə́:rou / fʌ́r-] *n.* [C] **1.** a long, narrow line cut in the earth by a plow. **2.** a wrinkle of a face. —*vt.* **1.** make furrows in (land). **2.** wrinkle.
—[名] 1. [밭]고랑; 도랑 2. [얼굴의] 주름살 —[他] 1. …에 고랑을 내다 2. …에 주름살지게 하다

F

fur·ry [fə́:ri] *adj.* (**-ri·er, -ri·est**) **1.** covered or trimmed with fur. **2.** of or made of fur. ▷**fur·ri·ness** [-nis] *n.*
—[形] **1.** 모피로 덮인(장식한) **2.** 모피로 만든, 모피가 붙은

‡ fur·ther [fə́:rðər] *adj.* compar. of **far. 1.** more; moreover. **2.** farther; more distant.
—[形] **1.** 그 위의, 더 한층의 **2.** 더 먼
1) ***for further details,*** about more details. 2) ***until further notice,*** until [we] tell or inform you later.
[熟] 1)더 자세히, 상세한 것은 2)추후 통지가 있을 때까지
—*adv.* **1.** at or to a greater extent. **2.** besides; in addition. **3.** at or to a greater distance.
—[副] **1.** 더 한층 나아가서 **2.** 게다가 또, 더우기 **3.** 더 멀리
—*vt.* promote; put forward.
—[他] …을 진행시키다, 조성(촉진)하다

fur·ther·ance [fə́:rðər(ə)ns] *n.* [U] the act of helping forward; advancement.
—[名] 조장, 조성, 촉진

*** fur·ther·more** [fə́:rðərmɔ́:r] *adv.* moreover; besides.
—[副] 더우기, 게다가, 더군다나

fur·ther·most [fə́:rðərmòust] *adj.* furthest; most distant.
—[形] 가장 먼

fur·thest [fə́:rðist] *adj., adv.* =farthest.

fur·tive [fə́:rtiv] *adj.* **1.** done secretly; stealthy. ¶*a ~ glance.*① **2.** sly. ▷**fur·tive·ness** [-nis] *n.*
—[形] **1.** 몰래 하는, 남의 눈을 피해서 하는, 은밀한 ¶①슬쩍 엿보기 **2.** 교활한, 능갈친

fur·tive·ly [fə́:rtivli] *adv.* secretly.
—[副] 남몰래, 은밀히, 슬쩍

*** fu·ry** [fjúəri] *n.* (pl. **-ries**) **1.** [U] fierce anger; violence. **2.** [C] an outburst of anger. **3.** ⟪*F-*⟫ (in Greek mythology) one of the three goddesses of revenge.
—[名] **1.** 격분, 격노; 광포(狂暴) **2.** 분노의 폭발 **3.** [그리이스 신화에 나오는] 복수의 세 여신 중의 하나
in a fury, in anger; fiercely.
[熟] 격분하여, 노발대발하여

furze [fə:rz] *n.* [U] a low, evergreen shrub on waste land.
—[名] 가시금작화

fuse¹ [fju:z] *n.* [C] **1.** (*Electricity*) a piece of wire forming a part of an electric circuit to prevent the formation of an excessive current. **2.** a tube or cord of explosives for carrying the spark.
—[名] **1.**⟪電⟫ 퓨우즈 **2.** 도화선, 신관(信管)

fuse² [fju:z] *vt., vi.* melt; melt together.
—[他][自] 녹(이)다; 융합시키다(하다)

fu·se·lage [fjú:səlà:ʒ / -zilà:ʒ] *n.* [C] the body of an airplane.
—[名] 비행기의 동체, 기체

fu·si·ble [fjú:zibl] *adj.* that can be melted.
—[形] 녹기 쉬운, 융해하는, 가용성의

fu·sil·ier [fjù:zilíər] *n.* [C] formerly, a soldier who carried a light gun called a fusil.
—[名] 수발총병(燧發銃兵) (수발총을 쓰던 옛날 병정)

fu·sil·lade [fjú:səlèid / -zilèid] *n.* [C] the act of continuously firing guns for a long time; something like this. —*vt.* shoot or attack (something or someone) by a fusillade.
—[名] 일제 사격; [야구의] 집중 안타 —[他] …을 일제 사격(공격)하다

fu·sion [fjú:ʒ(ə)n] *n.* **1.** [U] the act of melting by heat [into one]; the state of being melted [into one]. **2.** [C] something that has been melted [into one]. **3** [C] union.
—[名] **1.** 용해, 융해; 융합 **2.** 용해(융해)한 것 **3.** 결합, 합동, 연합

*** fuss** [fʌs] *n.* [U][C] excitement about an unimportant matter; an excited and anxious state of mind; [C] ⟪*a ~*⟫ an example of excitement, confusion, etc. —*vi.* make a fuss. —*vt.* cause (someone) to get into a fuss.
—[名] 공연한 소동; 안달; 대소동 —[自] 법석대다 —[他] …을 떠들게 하다

fuss·y [fʌ́si] *adj.* (**fuss·i·er, fuss·i·est**) **1.** full of fuss. **2.** (of clothes, etc.) decorated too much. ▷**fuss·i·ly** [-li] *adv.* —**fuss·i·ness** [-nis] *n.*
—[形] **1.** 법석대는, 야단법석의 **2.** [옷 따위] 야단스럽게 꾸민, 지나치게 모양을 낸

fus·tian [fʌ́stʃən / fʌ́stiən] *n.* [U] **1.** thick cotton cloth. **2.** high-sounding but empty language.
—[名] **1.** 퍼스티언 천(두꺼운 면직물) **2.** 과장된 말, 허풍

fust·y [fʌ́sti] *adj.* (**fust·i·er, fust·i·est**) having a stale smell; old-fashioned.
—[形] 곰팡내나는, 퀴퀴묵은, 진부한

fu·tile [fjú:t(ə)il / -tail] *adj.* useless; worthless; frivolous.
—[形] 무익한, 쓸모없는; 하찮은; 천박한

fu·til·i·ty [fju(:)tíliti] *n.* (pl. **-ties**) [U] uselessness; [C] a futile action, etc.
—[名] 무익[한 것], 경망스러운 행동

‡ fu·ture [fjú:tʃər] *n.* [C] **1.** ⟪usu. *the ~*⟫ the time that is to come after the present; what is to come. **2.** a hopeful prospect. **3.** (*Grammar*) the future tense.
—[名] **1.** 미래, 장래, 앞날 **2.** [유망한] 전도, 장래성 **3.**⟪文法⟫ 미래 시제(時制)

fu·tu·ri·ty [fju(:)t(j)úəriti / -tjúəriti] *n.* (pl. **-ties**) **1.** [U] the future. **2.** ⟪*pl.*⟫ a future event.
—[名] **1.** 미래, 장래 **2.** 미래의 사건

fuze [fju:z] *n.* =fuse¹.

fuzz [fʌz] *n.* [U] light, soft fiber of cloth, down or hair. —*vt.* cover (something) with fuzz; make (something) fuzzy. —*vi.* become covered with fuzz.
—[名] 보풀, 솜털 —[他] …을 보풀 일게 하다 —[自] 보풀이 일다

fuzz·y [fʌ́zi] *adj.* (**fuzz·i·er, fuzz·i·est**) **1.** of or covered with fuzz. **2.** not clear.
—[形] **1.** 보풀의, 보풀이 인 **2.** 흐린, 흐릿한

F

G

G, g [dʒiː] *n.* ⓒ (*pl.* **G's, Gs, g's, gs** [dʒiːz]) **1.** the seventh letter of the English alphabet. **2.** (*Music*) the fifth note in the major scale of C. ¶ ~ *flat* (*sharp*).①
— ⓝ 1. 알파벳의 일곱째 글자 2.(樂)「사」음 ¶①내림(올림)「사」조

gab [gæb] *n.* ⓒ (*colloq.*) chatter; idle talk. ¶*the gift of the* ~ ① — *vi.* (**gabbed, gab·bing**) talk very much; chatter.
— ⓝ (口) 수다, 잡담 ¶①말주변. 수다
— ⓥ 수다떨다

gab·ar·dine [gǽbərdìːn, ⹁–⹁] *n.* **1.** Ⓤ a kind of woolen, cotton, or rayon cloth used for raincoats, suits, etc. **2.** ⓒ a long cloak worn by the Jews in the Middle Ages.
— ⓝ 1. 개버딘 천(이랑지게 짠 방수웃감) 2. 헐겁고 긴 웃옷

gab·ble [gǽbl] *vi., vt.* talk fast without meaning. ¶ ~ *out an apology.* — *n.* Ⓤ rapid talk without meaning.
— ⓥⓘ 재잘거리다 — ⓝ 알아들을 수 없는 소리

gab·er·dine [gǽbərdìːn, ⹁–⹁] *n.* =gabardine.

ga·ble [géibl] *n.* ⓒ the triangular part of a building, formed by two opposite slopes of a roof.
— ⓝ 박공(牔栱), 박풍(牔風)

ga·bled [géibld] *adj.* built in the form of a gable; having gables.
— ⓐ 박공이 있는, 박공 구조의

Ga·bri·el [géibriəl] *n.* **1.** a man's name. **2.** (in the Bible) one of the archangels, usu. God's messenger of good news or comfort. ⇒ⓃⒷ
— ⓝ 1. 남자 이름 2. 천사 가브리엘 ⓃⒷ 성모 마리아에게 수태(受胎)를 고지(告知)

gad [gæd] *vi.* (**gad·ded, gad·ding**) go about restlessly without purpose.
— ⓥ 나다니다, 어슬렁거리다

gad·fly [gǽdflài] *n.* ⓒ (*pl.* **-flies**) **1.** a fly that stings cattle and horses. **2.** an annoying person.
— ⓝ 1. 등에 2. 귀찮은 사람

gadg·et [gǽdʒit] *n.* ⓒ a small mechanical instrument, device, accessory, etc.
— ⓝ 장치. 부속품; 작은 기계; 자질구레한 물건

Gael [geil] *n.* ⓒ a Celt born or living in Scotland or in Ireland.
— ⓝ 게일 사람

Gael·ic [géilik] *adj.* of the Gaels or their language. — *n.* Ⓤ language of the Gaels.
— ⓐ 게일 사람의, 게일 말의
— ⓝ 게일 말

gag [gæg] *n.* ⓒ **1.** something put in or on the mouth to keep silent. **2.** (*colloq.*) any humorous joke or trick told or done by an actor to get a laugh.
— *vt.* (**gagged, gag·ging**) **1.** put a gag into or on the mouth of (someone). **2.** prevent (someone) from speaking freely by force or authority.
— ⓝ 1. 입마개, 재갈 2.(口) 익살, 익살스런 몸짓(장치)
— ⓥⓘ 1. …에게 재갈을 물리다 2. …의 언론을 탄압하다

gage¹ [geidʒ] *n.* ⓒ **1.** a glove thrown down in challenge; a challenge. **2.** a thing given to make a promise sure; a pledge. ¶*throw down a gage*, challenge.
— ⓝ 1. 도전의 표시로서 던진 장갑; 도전 2. 저당물
⊛ 도전하다

gage² [geidʒ] *n., v.* (*U.S.*) =gauge.

gai·e·ty [géiəti] *n.* (*pl.* **-ties**) **1.** Ⓤ the state of being gay; cheerfulness; merriment. **2.** (often *pl.*) gay entertainment; festivities.
— ⓝ 1. 명랑, 유쾌 2. 즐거운 일, 잔치놀이, 환락

gai·ly [géili] *adv.* **1.** happily; merrily. **2.** (of dress, color, etc.) brightly; showily.
— ⓐⓓ 1. 유쾌하게, 명랑하게, 쾌활하게 2. 화려하게, 호화롭게

‡ **gain** [gein] *vt.* **1.** get (something) by effort; earn; win. ¶ ~ *one's living*① | ~ *possession of an object*② | ~ *the prize.* **2.** reach; get to; arrive at (a place). ¶ ~ *one's ends.*③ **3.** increase; improve. ¶ ~ *weight* (*speed*). **4.** (of a watch or clock) become fast by (some minutes, etc.). ↔lose ¶*My watch gains two minutes a day.*④
— *vi.* **1.** make progress; increase; improve. ¶*She is gaining in weight.*⑤ **2.** (of a watch or clock) go fast. ¶*My watch gains by five minutes a day.*
 1) *gain on* (=*get nearer to*) someone or something.
 2) *gain someone over*, persuade someone to take one's side.
— *n.* **1.** ⓒⓤ profit; advantage; (often *pl.*) something gained. ¶*No gains without pains.*⑥ **2.** ⓒ increase; improvement; addition. ¶*a* ~ *to knowledge.*⑦
— ⓥⓘ 1. …을 얻다; 벌다 ¶①생활비를 벌다/②물건을 입수하다 2. …에 도달하다 ¶③목적을 달성하다 3. …을 증대하다 4.[시계가] …만큼 더 가다 ¶④내 시계는 하루에 2분 더 간다

— ⓥⓘ 1. 진보하다; 늘다 ¶⑤그녀는 체중이 늘고 있다 2.[시계가] 더 가다

▨ 1)…에 쫓아가다 2)…을 같은 편으로 끌어들이다

— ⓝ 1. 벌이; 이익; 이득 ¶⑥노력 없이 이득 없다 2. 증가; 증진 ¶⑦지식의 증대

gain·er [géinər] *n.* ⓒ a person who gains. *come off a gainer,* make a profit; win.
　—ⓒ 획득자, 승리자
　熟 이익을 보다, 이기다

gain·ful [géinf(u)l] *adj.* profitable; paying.
　—⒜ 이익이 있는, 유리한

gain·ings [géiniŋz] *n. pl.* earnings; profits.
　—ⓒ 소득, 수익

gainst, 'gainst [genst, +*Brit.* geinst] *prep., conj.* (*poetic*) =against.

gait [geit] *n.* ⓒ a manner of walking or running. ¶*The old man walked with a shuffling ~.*①
　—ⓒ 걸음걸이, 걷는 모양; 보조 ¶① 노인은 발을 질질 끌며 걸었다

gai·ter [géitər] *n.* ⓒ (usu. *pl.*) a covering of cloth or leather for the lower leg or ankle.
　—ⓒ 각반(脚絆)

gal. gallon; gallons.

ga·la [géilə, gǽ-/gáː-] *n.* ⓒ celebration; festival. ¶*in ~.*① —*adj.* festive; showy. ¶*a ~ dinner.*
　—ⓒ 축제, 제례 ¶①나들이옷을 차려 입고 ①축제의; 쾌활한

ga·lac·tic [gəlǽktik] *adj.* of the Milky Way.
　—⒜ 은하의

gal·ax·y [gǽləksi] *n.* ⓒ (pl. **-ax·ies**) 1. a brilliant group of people. ¶*a ~ of movie actresses.*① 2. (*the G-*) a huge group of stars; the Milky Way.
　—ⓒ 1. [미인·재원(才媛)들의] 모임, 기라성 ¶①기라성 같은 여배우들 2. 은하 은하수

* **gale**¹ [geil] *n.* ⓒ 1. a strong wind. 2. (*poetic*) breeze. 3. an outburst. ¶*a ~ of laughter from the spectators.*
　—ⓒ 1. 강풍, 질풍 2. 산들바람 3. [웃음·노여움 따위의] 폭발

gall¹ [gɔːl] *n.* Ⓤ 1. a bitter fluid made by the liver. 2. anything bitter or distasteful; hate. 3. (*U.S. colloq.*) impudence. ¶*I have the ~ to do ...*①
　dip one's pen in gall, write with bitterness.
　—ⓒ 1. 쓸개즙; 담낭(膽囊) 2. 몹시 쓴 것, 증오, 악의 3. 뻔뻔스러움 ¶①뻔뻔 스럽게도 …하다
　熟 독필(毒筆)을 휘두르다

gall² [gɔːl] *vt., vi.* 1. make or become sore by rubbing hard. 2. make (someone) angry; annoy. ¶*She was galled by his constant criticism.*① —*n.* 1. ⓒ a sore spot on the skin caused by rubbing. 2. Ⓤ something irritating; annoyance.
　—ⓣⓘ 1. 스쳐 벗기다 2. …을 초조하게 하다; 성나게 하다 ¶①그녀는 그의 끊임없는 비판에 화가 났다 —ⓒ 1. 찰상(擦傷), 생채기 2. 초조, 안달; 고뇌

gall³ [gɔːl] *n.* ⓒ something like a ball that is formed on leaves by insects, bacteria, etc.
　—ⓒ 몰식자(沒食子), 충영(蟲癭), 오배자(五倍子)

* **gal·lant** *adj.* [gǽlənt →*adj.* 4., *n.*] 1. brave; daring. ¶*a ~ knight | the honorable and ~ member.*① 2. grand and noble in appearance. 3. gay; showy. 4. [+*U.S.* gəlǽnt] very polite and kind to women.
　—*n.* [gǽlənt, gəlǽnt] ⓒ 1. a high-spirited or brave man. 2. a man of fashion. 3. a man who is very polite and kind to women; a lover. ▷**gal·lant·ness** [-nis] *n.*
　—⒜ 1. 씩씩한, 용감한 ¶①군인 출신의 의원 2. 당당한 3. 쪽 빼입은, 화려한 4. [부인에 대하여] 친절한, 상냥한
　—ⓒ 1. 씩씩한 사람 2. 멋장이 3. 부인에게 은근한 사내; 애인 「manner.」

gal·lant·ly [gǽləntli, +*U.S.* gəlǽntli] *adv.* in a gallant
　—⒜ 용감하기; 화려하게; 은근히

gal·lant·ry [gǽləntri] *n.* (pl. **-ries**) 1. Ⓤ a noble spirit or action; bravery; ⓒ gallant conduct or speech. 2. Ⓤ very great politeness or kindness to women.
　—ⓒ 1. 용감, 용맹; 무용, 용감한 언동 2. 부인에게 은근함

gal·le·on [gǽliən] *n.* ⓒ a large sailing ship, formerly used as a warship by the Spaniards.
　—ⓒ 갈레온 배(옛날 스페인의 전함)

: gal·ler·y [gǽləri] *n.* ⓒ (pl. **-ler·ies**) 1. a long, narrow hall or passage, often with windows on one side only. 2. the highest floor of a theater or hall; the people who sit there. 3. a room or building for showing works of art.
　1) *bring down the gallery,* excite the admiration of the audience. 「people.」
　2) *play to the gallery,* seek the praise of the common
　—ⓒ 1. 회랑, 보랑(步廊) 2. [극장의] 맨 위층; 보통 관람석[의 관객] 3. 화랑, 미술품 진열실(관)
　熟 1)일반 관중의 갈채를 받다 2)대중의 취미에 영합하다

gal·ley [gǽli] *n.* ⓒ 1. a warship moved by oars and sails, used in ancient times. ⇒N.B. 2. (*Printing*) a tray for holding set-up type; a proof printed from such type.
　—ⓒ 1. 갤리 배 N.B. 옛날 노예·죄수에게 젓게 한 전함 2. (印刷) 게라(조판한 활자를 담는 목판); 교정쇄

galley proof [-⌒] *n.* (*Printing*) a proof printed from type in a galley so that errors can be corrected.
　—ⓒ (印刷) 조판 교정쇄

galley slave [-⌒] *n.* 1. a slave or prisoner forced to row a galley. 2. anyone who does very hard work.
　—ⓒ 1. 갤리 배의 노예 2. 힘드는 일을 하는 사람

Gal·lic [gǽlik] *adj.* 1. of Gaul or its people. 2. French.
　—⒜ 1. 고올[사람]의 2. 프랑스의

gall·ing [gɔ́ːliŋ] *adj.* vexing; irritating.
　—⒜ 괴롭히는, 비위에 거슬리는

* **gal·lon** [gǽlən] *n.* ⓒ a unit of measure for liquids, being equal to 3.785 liters (=the U.S. gallon) and 4.546 liters (=the British gallon).
　—ⓒ 갈론(용량의 단위)

gal·lop [gǽləp] *n.* ⓒ the fastest speed at which horses can run.
at a (or *full*) *gallop,* at great speed.
—*vt.* cause (a horse) to run at full speed. —*vi.* **1.** (of a horse) go or move at a gallop. **2.** read or speak in a hurry. (*~ over* or *through*)
gallop off, run away on horseback.

gal·lows [gǽlouz, +U.S. -ləz] *n.* ⓒ (pl. **-lows·es** or **-lows**) **1.** an upright wooden framework where people are hanged. **2.** (usu. *the ~*) death by hanging. ¶*cheat the ~*① / *come to the ~*② / *have a ~ look.*③

ga·losh [gəláʃ / -lɔ́ʃ] *n.* ⓒ (usu. *pl.*) a pair of overshoes, usu. made of rubber or plastic, used on a wet day.

gal·van·ic [gælvǽnik] *adj.* **1.** producing or caused by an electric current. **2.** affecting or affected as if by an electric shock.

gal·va·nism [gǽlvənìz(ə)m] *n.* Ⓤ **1.** electricity, esp. produced by chemical action. **2.** application of such electricity to the body as medical treatment.

gal·va·ni·za·tion [gæ̀lvənizéiʃ(ə)n / -nai-] *n.* Ⓤ the act of galvanizing; the state of being galvanized.

gal·va·nize [gǽlvənàiz] *vt.* **1.** give an electric shock to (something). **2.** stir up; excite. ¶*~ someone to* (or *into*) *life.*① **3.** cover (iron, etc.) with metal to prevent rusting. ¶*galvanized iron.*

gam·ble [gǽmbl] *vi., vt.* **1.** play for money or some other prize; bet. ¶*~ away one's fortune.*① **2.** risk (something) for some uncertain gain. —*n.* ⓒ (*colloq.*) anything that involves risk. ¶*on the ~.*②

gam·bler [gǽmblər] *n.* ⓒ a person who gambles.

gam·bol [gǽmb(ə)l] *n.* ⓒ (usu. *pl.*) the act of dáncing and jumping about for sport or joy. —*vi.* (**-boled, -bol·**ing or esp. *Brit.* **-bolled, -bol·ling**) run and jump about. ¶*Young lambs ~ in the spring sunshine.*

gam·brel [gǽmbrəl] *n.* ⓒ a roof having two slopes on each side. ⇒fig.

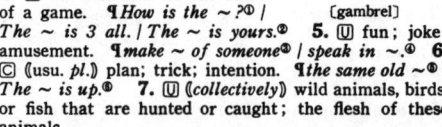
[gambrel]

game [geim] *n.* **1.** ⓒ a play or contest with rules; a sport. **2.** ⓒ things needed to play a game. ¶*toys and games.* **3.** ⓒ a single round of a series of contests. ¶*He won four games out of six.* **4.** ⓒ the condition or the score of a game. ¶*How is the ~?*① / *The ~ is 3 all.* / *The ~ is yours.*② **5.** Ⓤ fun; joke; amusement. ¶*make ~ of someone*③ / *speak in ~.*④ **6.** ⓒ (usu. *pl.*) plan; trick; intention. ¶*the same old ~*⑤ / *The ~ is up.*⑥ **7.** Ⓤ (*collectively*) wild animals, birds, or fish that are hunted or caught; the flesh of these animals.
play the game, play fair; follow the rules.
—*adj.* having enough spirit; ready; willing. ¶*They are ~ for any adventure.*⑦

game bag [∠⌣] *n.* a bag used for carrying game (*n.* 7.) that has been killed.

game·cock [géimkàk / -kɔ̀k] *n.* ⓒ a rooster trained for fighting.

game·keep·er [géimkì:pər] *n.* ⓒ (*Brit.*) a person who protects and takes care of wild animals and birds.

game·ly [géimli] *adv.* like a gamecock; bravely.

game·some [géimsəm] *adj.* full of play; ready to play.

gam·ma [gǽmə] *n.* ⓒ the third letter of the Greek alphabet (*Γ, γ*=English G, g).

gam·mon¹ [gǽmən] *n.* Ⓤ (*Brit. colloq.*) nonsense. —ⓝ 〈英口〉헛소리, 엉터리

gam·mon² [gǽmən] *n.* Ⓒ a pig's thigh which is salted and smoked. —ⓝ 훈제(燻製)한 돼지 넓적다리 고기

gam·ut [gǽmət] *n.* Ⓒ 1. the whole series of musical notes that can be produced by the human voice or musical instrument. 2. the major scale. 3. the whole range of anything. ¶*run* (or *go*) *the* [*whole*] ~ *of experience.*① —ⓝ 1. 전음역(全音域) 2. 장음계 3. 전범위, 전반 ¶①온갖 경험을 다하다

* **gang** [gæŋ] *n.* Ⓒ 1. a group of people working together for a bad purpose. ¶*a ~ of robbers.*① 2. a group of workmen under one foreman. 3. a set of tools or machines arranged for use together. —*vi., vt.* (*colloq.*) 1. form (a gang). 2. attack in a group. —ⓝ 1. [악한 등의] 일단, 일대 ¶①폭력단 2. [노동자·노예 등의] 한 떼 3. [도구의] 한 벌 —ⓥ 1. 폭력단을 만들다 2. 떼지어 공격하다

Gan·ges [gǽndʒi:z], **the** *n.* a river which flows across North India into the Bay of Bengal. —ⓝ 갠지스 강(벵골만으로 흘러드는 인도의 강)

gang·plank [gǽŋplæŋk] *n.* Ⓒ a movable bridge by which people get on and off a ship. [gang of criminals.] —ⓝ [배에서 부두에 걸쳐 놓은] 좁은 통로, 건널판

gang·ster [gǽŋstər] *n.* Ⓒ (*U.S. colloq.*) a member of a —ⓝ 〈美口〉악한, 갱

gang·way [gǽŋwèi] *n.* Ⓒ 1. a passage between the seats in a theater, etc. 2. a gangplank. —*interj.* Stand aside and make room! —ⓝ 1. 좌석 사이의 통로 2. 건널판 —ⓘ 비켜라!

* **gaol** [dʒeil] *n., vt.* (*Brit.*) =jail. —ⓝ ⓥ = jail

* **gap** [gæp] *n.* Ⓒ 1. an opening. 2. a period of time which is characterized by silence. ¶*a ~ in the conversation.*① 3. a difference of opinion, character, etc. 4. a mountain pass. —ⓝ 1. 갈라진 (쪼개진) 틈 2. 터진 곳; 중단 ¶①대화의 중단 3. 의견차이, 격차 4. 산길, 산골짜기

gape [geip] *vi.* 1. open the mouth wide; yawn. 2. stare with the mouth open as in amazement. —*n.* Ⓒ the act of gaping; a yawn. ▷**gap·er** [-ər] *n.* —ⓥ 1. 입을 크게 벌리다; 하품하다 2. 입을 벌리고 바라보다 —ⓝ 입을 벌리고 바라보기; 하품

* **ga·rage** [gərá:(d)ʒ / gǽra(d)ʒ, -ridʒ] *n.* Ⓒ a building or place where automobiles and airplanes are kept or repaired. —*vt.* put or keep (an automobile or airplane) in a garage. —ⓝ 자동차 차고, 자동차 수리공장; [비행기의] 격납고 —ⓥ …을 차고(격납고)에 넣다

garb [ga:rb] *n.* Ⓤ dress, esp. of a priest, judge, or prisoner. —*vt.* (usu. in *passive* or *reflexively*) clothe. ¶*be garbed in convict clothes*① / ~ *oneself in.* —ⓝ [특징이 있는] 복장, 의상 —ⓥ …한 복장을 시키다 ¶①죄수옷을 입게 되다

gar·bage [gá:rbidʒ] *n.* Ⓤ things, esp. food, thrown away from a kitchen, store, etc. —ⓝ [주방의] 쓰레기, 찌꺼기, 폐물, 드물

gar·ble [gá:rbl] *vt.* 1. change (facts, stories, etc.) in a misleading way. ¶*a garbled account.* 2. quote wrongly from (someone's statements or writings) without ill-will. —ⓥ 1. [사실]을 왜곡하다 2. …을 잘못 전하다

‡ **gar·den** [gá:rdn] *n.* Ⓒ 1. a place, usu. close to a house for growing vegetables, flowers, fruit, etc. ¶*a flower* ~ / *a back* ~.① 2. (often *pl.*) a park or place for public enjoyment where trees or flowers are planted and often animals are displayed. ¶*a zoological* ~.② —*vt., vi.* take care of a garden; work in a garden. —ⓝ 1. 채소밭; 화단; 과수원; 정원 ¶①뒤뜰 2. 공원; 유원지 ¶②동물원

—ⓥⓘ 정원의 손질을 하다; 원예를 하다

* **gar·den·er** [gá:rdnər] *n.* Ⓒ a person who works in a garden or who is hired to take care of it. —ⓝ 정원사, 원예사

gar·de·ni·a [ga:rdí:niə] *n.* Ⓒ a sweet-smelling white flower with waxy petals. —ⓝ 치자나무

gar·gle [gá:rgl] *vi., vt.* wash and make clean (the throat) with a liquid which is kept moving at the back of it. —*n.* Ⓒ a liquid that is used for this purpose. —ⓘⓥ 양치질하다 —ⓝ 양치질하는 약

gar·goyle [gá:rgɔil] *n.* Ⓒ a pipe for carrying off rain water, often in the form of a grotesque human being or animal. ⇒fig., N.B. —ⓝ 지붕에서 물이 떨어지는 홈통의 주둥이 N.B. 고딕 건축에 많음

gar·ish [gɛ́əriʃ] *adj.* too bright; showy. ▷**gar·ish·ly** [-li] *adv.* —**gar·ish·ness** [-nis] *n.* —ⓐ 번쩍거리는, 야한, 화려한

gar·land [gá:rlənd] *n.* Ⓒ a circle of flowers or leaves to be worn on the head as an honor. ¶*gain* (or *carry* [gargoyle] —ⓝ 화환, 화관 ¶①승리를 얻다 —ⓥ …에 화환을 씌우다, …을 화환으로 장식하다

away, win) *the* ~.① —*vt.* crown or decorate (someone) with garlands.

gar·lic [gá:rlik] *n.* [U] a strong-smelling plant of the lily family, used to flavor meats or salads.
—[名] 마늘

* **gar·ment** [gá:rmənt] *n.* [C] **1.** any article of clothing, as a dress, coat, or hat. **2.** an outer covering. —*vt.* clothe.
—[名] 1. 옷, 의복 2. 겉옷, 외투 —[他] …에게 입히다

gar·ner [gá:rnər] *vt.* gather and store away. —*n.* [C] a storehouse for grain.
—[他] …을 저장하다 —[名] 곡물 창고

gar·net [gá:rnit] *n.* [U][C] a precious stone, usu. with a deep-red color.
—[名] 석류석(石榴石); 가아넷(보석)

gar·nish [gá:rniʃ] *n.* **1.** [U] something laid around food in a dish as a decoration. **2.** [C] a decoration. —*vt.* decorate (esp. food). ¶~ *the steak with parsley.*
—[名] 1. [요리의] 장식 고명, 곁들임 2. 장식, 장식물 —[他] [음식물]에 고명을 곁들이다

gar·nish·ment [gá:rniʃmənt] *n.* [U][C] decoration.
—[名] 장식

gar·ni·ture [gá:rnitʃər] *n.* [U][C] decoration; garnish.
—[名] 부속품, 장식물

gar·ret [gǽrit] *n.* [C] a room just below the roof of a house; an attic.
—[名] 고미다락방

1) ***be wrong in the garret,*** be crazy; be queer in the head.
2) ***from cellar to garret; from garret to kitchen,*** everywhere in the house.
[熟] 1)머리가 돌았다 2)집안 구석구석에

* **gar·ri·son** [gǽrisn] *n.* [C] **1.** a group of soldiers placed in a fort or town. **2.** a place that has a garrison. ¶*go* (*or be sent*) *into* ~.① —*vt.* **1.** place soldiers in (a fort or town). **2.** defend (a place) by a garrison.
—[名] 1. 수비대(병), 주둔군 2. 주둔지 ¶①수비를 하다 —[他] 1. …에 수비대를 두다 2. …을 수비대로 지키다

gar·ru·li·ty [gərú:liti, +*Brit.* gær-] *n.* [U] the quality of being garrulous.
—[名] 수다, 다변(多辯)

gar·ru·lous [gǽr(j)uləs] *adj.* talking too much usu. about unimportant things. ▷**gar·ru·lous·ness** [-nis] *n.*
—[形] 수다스러운

gar·ru·lous·ly [gǽr(j)uləsli] *adv.* in a garrulous manner.
—[副] 재잘재잘

gar·ter [gá:rtər] *n.* [C] **1.** (*usu. pl.*) a pair of elastic bands or straps, used to hold up stockings or socks. **2.** (*the G-*) (*Brit.*) the highest order of knighthood. ¶*a knight of the Garter*① / *the Order of the Garter.*② —*vt.* fasten (a stocking or sock) with a garter.
—[名] 1. 양말 대님, 가아터 2. 《英》 가아터 훈장 ¶①가아터 훈작사(勳爵士)/②가아터 훈위(勳位) —[他] 양말 대님으로 [양말]을 묶다

G

⁝ **gas** [gæs] *n.* [U] **1.** any airlike substance. **2.** any kind of gas or a mixture of gases, used for lighting or heating. ⇒[usage] ¶*a* ~ *lamp* / *turn down the* ~① / *turn on* (*off*) *the* ~.② **3.** (*Coal mining*) a mixture of explosive gas and air. **4.** poisonous gas used in warfare. **5.** (*U.S. colloq.*) gasoline.
—[名] 1. 가스, 기체 2. [등화·온열용의] 가스 [usage] 종류를 나타낼 때는 부정관사 또는 복수형을 취함 ¶①가스[등]의 빛을 줄이다/②가스를 틀다(끄다) 3. [탄갱의] 폭발 가스 4. 독가스 5. 《美口》 휘발유

step on the gas, accelerate; speed up.
[熟] 속력을 내다; 서두르다

—*vt.* (**gassed, gas·sing**) **1.** supply (something) with gas. **2.** attack (the enemy) by poisonous gas. **3.** (*colloq.*) supply (something) with gasoline. —*vi.* (*colloq.*) talk in an empty way; boast.
—[他] 1. …에 가스를 공급하다 2. [적]을 독가스로 공격하다 3. 《口》 …에 가솔린을 보급하다 —[自] 《口》 잡담을 하다, 허풍떨다

gas·bag [gǽsbæ̀g] *n.* [C] **1.** a bag for holding gas. **2.** (*colloq.*) a person who talks in an empty way.
—[名] 1. [비행기·기구 따위의] 가스 주머니 2. 《口》 수다장이

ga·se·ous [gǽsiəs] *adj.* of or like gas.
—[形] 가스의, 가스 모양의

gas fire [⌐ ⌐] *n.* [a stove for] a fire burning gas to heat a room.
—[名] 가스의 불, 가스 난로

gas fittings [⌐ ⌐–] *n., pl.* the apparatus such as pipes, burners, etc., for heating or lighting with gas.
—[名] 가스 기구; 가스등

gash [gæʃ] *n.* [C] a long, deep cut. —*vt.* make a long, deep cut in (something).
—[名] 깊은 상처 —[他] …에 깊은 상처를 입히다

gas·i·fy [gǽsifài] *vt.* (**-fied**) change (something) into gas.
—[他] …을 기체(가스)화하다

* **gas·o·line, -lene** [gæ̀soulí:n / ⌐––] *n.* [U] a colorless liquid which catches fire very easily, used as fuel for an automobile, etc. ⇒[N.B.]
—[名] 가솔린, 휘발유 [N.B.] 영국에서는 petrol을 씀. 또 미국에서는 gas라고도 씀

gas·om·e·ter [gæsámitər / -ɔ́mitə] *n.* [C] **1.** an apparatus for holding and measuring gas. **2.** (*Brit.*) a tank for holding gas. ⇒[N.B.]
—[名] 1. 가스 계량기 2. 《英》 가스 탱크 [N.B.] gas holder라고도 함

* **gasp** [gæsp / gɑ:sp] *n.* [C] the act of breathing with a quick, painful effort.
—[名] 헐떡거림, 숨참

at the last gasp, at the last moment; about to die.
[熟] 마지막 순간에, 임종 때에

—*vi.* breathe hard; pant. **—*vt.*** speak breathlessly. 《~ *out* something》 ¶~ *out the outline.*
—[自] 헐떡이다 —[他] 헐떡이며 말하다

gasp out (or ***away***) ***one's life; gasp one's last,*** breathe one's last; die.
[熟] 마지막 숨을 쉬다, 죽다

gas·sy [gǽsi] *adj.* (**-si·er, -si·est**) **1.** full of gas. **2.** like gas.
—[形] 1. 가스가 가득찬 2. 가스질(모양)의

gas·tric [gǽstrik] *adj.* of the stomach. ¶~ *juice*① / ~ *ulcer.*②
—[形] 위(胃)의 ¶①위액/②위궤양

gas·works [gǽswə:rks] *n. pl.* 《usu. used as *sing.*》 a place where gas is made.
—[名] 가스 제조소

⁑**gate** [geit] *n.* [C] **1.** a part in a wall or fence which can be opened and closed. ¶*enter the front* ~① / *at the* ~ *of death.*② **2.** a door or valve to control or stop the flow of water in a pipe, canal, etc. **3.** the number of people who pay to see a contest; the amount of money received at the entrance gate.
—[名] 1. 문, 출입문, 개찰구 ¶①정면 입구로 들어가다/②죽음의 문턱에서 2. 수문, 갑문(閘門) 3. 입장자 수; 입장료 총액

1) ***get the gate,*** (*U.S. colloq.*) be discharged.
2) ***give someone the gate,*** (*U.S. colloq.*) discharge.
[熟] 1)《美口》해고당하다 2)《美口》…을 해고하다

gate·house [géithàus] *n.* [C] a house built at or over a gate.
—[名] 수위실, 문지기 집

gate-keep·er [géitkì:pər] *n.* [C] a person who is in charge of a gate.
—[名] 문지기, 수위

gate·post [géitpòust] *n.* [C] the post on the side of a gate.
—[名] 문기둥

***gate·way** [géitwèi] *n.* [C] **1.** an entrance in a wall or fence. **2.** a way or means of entering. ¶*New York is a* ~ *to the United States.*①
—[名] 1. 문, 출입구 2. …에 이르는 길, 입구, 수단 ¶①뉴욕은 미국의 입구이다

⁑**gath·er** [gǽðər] *vt.* **1.** cause (persons or things) to come together in one place. ¶~ *an army* / *He gathered a crowd about him.* **2.** pick up and collect. ¶~ *flowers.* **3.** gain slowly; make (someting) greater in amount. ¶~ *speed*① / ~ *a million dollars.* **4.** conclude; understand. 《~ *that* ...; ~ something *from*》 ¶*From what I hear I* ~ *that he disagrees.*② **5.** draw (cloth) in small folds. ¶~ *a skirt.* **6.** wrinkle (one's brow). **—*vi.* 1.** come together; assemble. ¶*We gathered around the fire.* **2.** become greater in amount; increase. ¶*Suspicion was gathering rapidly in his mind.* **3.** become wrinkled.
—[他] 1. …을 모으다, 소집하다 2. …을 따 모으다; 채집하다 3. …을 천천히 늘리다; 조금씩 모으다 ¶①차츰 속력을 내다 4. …을 추측하다; …을 알다 ¶②들은 바로써 그가 반대라는 것을 알겠다 5. [천]에 주름을 잡다 6. [얼굴]을 찡그리다; …에 주름지게 하다 —[自] 1. 모이다 2. 증대하다; 강화하다 3. 주름살지다

—*n.* [C] a small fold or pleat made when cloth is gathered (→ *vt.* 5.)
—[名] 주름

***gath·er·ing** [gǽðəriŋ] *n.* [C] **1.** a meeting in a group or team. **2.** a collection of money, things, etc. **3.** a swelling on the body with pus in it.
—[名] 1. 집회, 모임 2. 채집, 수금, 집적(集積) 3. 화농(化膿), 부스럼

gaud [gɔ:d] *n.* [C] a cheap, showy ornament.
—[名] 번지르르한 싸구려 장식품

gaud·i·ly [gɔ́:dili] *adv.* in a gaudy manner.
—[副] 야단스럽게, 상스럽게

gaud·y [gɔ́:di] *adj.* (**gaud·i·er, gaud·i·est**) too bright and gay; showy. ▷**gaud·i·ness** [-nis] *n.*
—[形] 야단스러운, 야한; 천한, 상스러운

gauge [geidʒ] *n.* [C] **1.** a standard measurement. **2.** an instrument for measuring size, amount, etc. ¶*a rain* (*wind*) ~.① **3.** the distance between railroad rails. ¶*broad* (*narrow*) ~.② **4.** the depth to which a fully loaded ship goes down to in water.
—[名] 1. [대포 따위의 구경의] 표준 치수, 규격 2. 자, 저울, 말, 계기 ¶①우량(풍속)계 3. [철도의] 표준 궤간(軌間) ¶②광(협)궤(軌) 4. [배의] 만재 흘수

take the gauge of, measure; estimate.
[熟] …을 재다; 평가하다

—*vt.* 1. measure accurately. **2.** estimate; judge.
—[他] 1. …을 정확히 재다 2. …을 평가하다, 판단하다

gaunt [gɔ:nt] *adj.* **1.** very thin; lean. **2.** desolate; bleak.
—[形] 1. 여윈, 마른 2. 황량한

gaunt·let [gɔ́:ntlit, gɑ́:nt-] *n.* [C] **1.** an iron glove used by soldiers in the Middle Ages to protect the hand. ⇨fig. **2.** (*Fencing, Riding*) a heavy glove with a long cuff.
—[名] 1. [철제의] 긴 장갑 2. [승마·펜싱용의] 긴 장갑

1) ***fling*** (or ***throw***) ***down the gauntlet,*** challenge.
2) ***take*** (or ***pick***) ***up the gauntlet,*** accept a challenge.
[熟] 1)도전하다 2)도전에 응하다

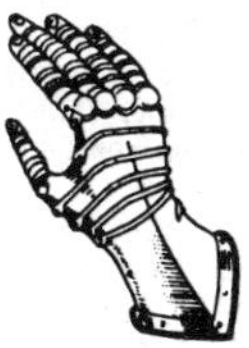
[gauntlet 1.]

gauze [gɔ:z] *n.* [U] **1.** a thin, light cloth which can be seen through. **2.** a thin haze.
—[名] 1. 가아제 2. 엷은 안개, 아지랭이

gauz·y [gɔ́:zi] *adj.* (**gauz·i·er, gauz·i·est**) like gauze; thin and light. ¶*a ~ mist.*①
— 가아제 같은, 엷은, 투명한 ¶①엷은 안개

: **gave** [geiv] *v.* pt. of **give**.

gav·el [gǽv(ə)l] *n.* ⓒ a small hammer used by a chairman or an auctioneer to signal for attention or order.
— ⓝ [경매인의] 망치, [의장·사회자의] 의사봉, 사회봉

ga·votte [gəvát / -vɔ́t] *n.* ⓒ a lively old French dance; music for this dance.
— ⓝ 가보트; 가보트곡

gawk [gɔ:k] *n.* ⓒ an awkward, stupid, or bashful person.
— ⓝ 얼간이, 멍청이

gawk·y [gɔ́:ki] *adj.* (**gawk·i·er, gawk·i·est**) awkward; stupid; bashful. ▷**gawk·i·ly** [-li] *adv.* —**gawk·i·ness** [-nis] *n.*
— ⓐ 바보의, 서투른; 수줍어하는

: **gay** [gei] *adj.* **1.** cheerful; merry. ¶*She is as ~ as a lark.* **2.** bright-colored; showy. **3.** fond of pleasures; not moral. ¶*He is leading a ~ life.*①
— ⓐ 1. 즐거운, 쾌활한 2. 화려한, 번지르르한 3. 방탕한 ¶①그는 방탕한 생활을 하고 있다

gay·e·ty [géiəti] *n.* =gaiety.
gay·ly [géili] *adv.* =gaily.

: **gaze** [geiz] *vi.* look long and steadily. 《~ *into* (or *at, on, upon*) something》 —*n.* ⓒ a steady look. ¶*fix one's ~ on someone*① / *stand at ~.*②
— ⓥ 빤히 바라보다, 응시하다 —ⓝ 응시, 주시, 주목 ¶①…을 바라보다/②응시하고 있다

ga·zette [gəzét] *n.* ⓒ **1.** a newspaper. **2.** (*Brit.*) a government journal or news sheet. —*vt.* publish (something) in a gazette. ¶*be gazetted out.*①
— ⓝ 1. 신문 2. (英) 관보(官報) —ⓥ …을 관보로 공고하다 ¶①관보로 사임이 발표되다

gaz·et·teer [gæ̀zitíər] *n.* ⓒ **1.** a dictionary or an index of geographical names. **2.** a person who writes for a gazette.
— ⓝ 1. 지명 사전, 지명 색인(索引) 2. 관보(신문)기자

• **gear** [giər] *n.* ⓒ **1.** a set of metal wheels with teeth in a machine which makes it go faster or slower. ⇒fig. ¶*a high* (*top*) *~.*① **2.** 《*collectively*》 a set of things used for some special purpose. ¶*fishing ~.*② **3.** working order or condition.
  1) *in gear,* in order; working well.
  2) *out of gear,* out of order; not working well.
—*vt.* furnish (something) with gear; connect (something) by gears. —*vi.* (of gears) fit together.
— ⓝ 1. 전동(傳動)장치, 톱니바퀴, 기어 ¶①고속 기어 2. [기계의] 장치, 도구 ¶②낚시 도구, 낚시 도구 한 벌 3. 형편, 상태

[gear 1.]

圖 1)기계가 연동(連動)하여; 원활히 잘 되어 2)기어가 빠져; 원활히 되지 않아
—ⓥ …에 전동 장치(기어)를 걸다 —ⓥ [톱니바퀴]가 서로 맞물다

gee [dʒi:] *interj.* **1.** a word of command to horses, oxen, etc. to turn to the right or go ahead. **2.** (*U.S.*) an exclamation of surprise, etc.
— ⓘ 1. [말·소에게] 우로 [돌아]! 2. (美) 저런!, 제기랄!

: **geese** [gi:s] *n.* pl. of **goose**.

gel·a·tin, -tine [dʒélət(i)n / dʒèlətí:n] *n.* Ⓤ clear, jellylike substance made from animal bones or hoofs or from vegetables. ¶*~ paper*① / *vegetable ~.*②
— ⓝ 젤라틴 ¶①[사진의] 젤라틴 감광지/②한천(寒天)

ge·lat·i·nous [dʒilǽtinəs] *adj.* jellylike; containing gelatin.
— ⓐ 젤라틴 모양의; 젤라틴을 함유한

geld [geld] *vt.* (**geld·ed** or **gelt**) get rid of the male glands of (a horse or other animal).
— ⓥ …을 거세하다, 불까다

gel·id [dʒélid] *adj.* cold as ice; frozen.
— ⓐ 얼음 같은; 혹한의

gelt [gelt] *v.* pt. and pp. of **geld**.

• **gem** [dʒem] *n.* ⓒ **1.** a precious stone; a jewel. **2.** anything very valuable and beautiful. —*vt.* (**gemmed, gem·ming**) set or adorn (something) with gems.
— ⓝ 1. 보석 2. 귀중한 (아름다운) 사람 (것) —ⓥ …을 보석으로 장식하다, …에 보석을 박다

gen·der [dʒéndər] *n.* Ⓤ **1.** (*Grammar*) the grouping of nouns into three classes, such as masculine, feminine, neuter; ⓒ one of these classes. ¶*the common* (*masculine, feminine, neuter*) *~.*① **2.** (*colloq.*) sex.
— ⓝ 1. (文法) 성(性) ¶①통(通)(남·여·중)성 2. (口) 성

gene [dʒi:n] *n.* ⓒ a small unit in a cell that causes a special characteristic of the parent to pass on to the child.
— ⓝ 유전자(遺傳子), 유전 단위(인자)

ge·ne·a·log·i·cal [dʒì:niəládʒik(ə)l / -lɔ́dʒ-] *adj.* of genealogy.
— ⓐ 가계(家系)의, 계통의, 족보의

ge·ne·al·o·gist [dʒì:niǽlədʒist] *n.* ⓒ a person who studies genealogy.
— ⓝ 족보학자

ge·ne·al·o·gy [dʒìːniǽlədʒi] n. ⓊⒸ (pl. **-gies**) the [science of the] historical development of families and also of animals and plants. —ⓝ 족보, 계통, 가계, 혈통; 족보학

gen·er·a [dʒénərə] n. pl. of **genus**.

gen·er·al [dʒén(ə)r(ə)l] adj. **1.** of all; for all; common to many or most. ¶*a ~ opinion*① / *a ~ strike.*② **2.** not special. ¶*a ~ education* / *a ~ magazine.*③ **3.** common; usual; ordinary. ¶*~ pronunciation* / *a ~ custom.*④ **4.** not exact; not definite; vague. ¶*a ~ sense* / *His statement is too ~.* **5.** chief; of the highest rank. ¶*a ~ officer*⑤ / *a governor ~.*⑥
—ⓝ. Ⓒ **1.** an army officer of high rank who commands many soldiers. **2.** a chief; a head.
in [the] general, usually; for the most part; generally.
—ⓐ 1. 전반적인; 보편적인 ¶①여론 / ②총파업 2. 전문적이 아닌; 일반적인 ¶③종합잡지 3. 보통의; 통상의 ¶④널리 행하여지는 습관 4. 대체의; 개략의; 막연한 5. …장(長), 총(總)… ¶⑤육군 장성 / ⑥총독
—ⓝ 1. 장군 2. 우두머리
熟 보통; 대체로, 일반적으로

gen·er·al·i·ty [dʒènərǽləti] n. (pl. **-ties**) **1.** Ⓤ the state of being general. **2.** Ⓤ a general and rather vague statement. **3.** Ⓒ a general principle or rule. **4.** Ⓤ the great part; the mass. ¶*the ~ of people.*①
—ⓝ 1. 일반성, 보편성 2. 개략, 개설 3. 통칙, 통상(通性), 보편적 진리 4. 태반, 대다수 ¶①대개의 사람들

gen·er·al·i·za·tion [dʒèn(ə)rəlizéiʃ(ə)n / -lai-] n. **1.** Ⓤ the act of generalizing. **2.** Ⓒ a general idea or rule.
—ⓝ 1. 종합, 개괄, 귀납(歸納) 2. 개념, 통칙

gen·er·al·ize [dʒén(ə)rəlàiz] vt. **1.** treat (something) as a whole. **2.** form (a general idea or rule) from particular facts.
—ⓥ 1. …을 일반화하다; 일반론으로서 다루다 2. [일반적 법칙]을 얻다; 귀납하다

gen·er·al·ly [dʒén(ə)rəli] adv. **1.** most of the time; usually. **2.** in most cases; widely. **3.** in a general sense. ¶*~ speaking.*①
—ⓐ 1. 일반적으로; 대개는 2. 대개; 널리 3. 보편적으로 ¶①보편적으로 말하면

gen·er·al·ship [dʒén(ə)r(ə)lʃìp] n. Ⓤ **1.** the military skill or ability of a general. **2.** the authority of a general. **3.** the rank or position of a general.
—ⓝ 1. 대장다운 바탕(그릇), 지휘 수완 2. 통솔력 3. 대장·장군의 직위(신분)

gen·er·ate [dʒénərèit] vt. **1.** produce. ¶*Fire generates heat.*① **2.** bring (something) into life; bear. **3.** (*Mathematics*) form (a line, figure, surface, etc.) by moving a point, line, etc.
—ⓥ 1. …을 발생시키다 ¶①불은 열을 발생시킨다 2. …에 생명을 주다, …을 낳다 3. (數) [점이나 선이] …을 형성하다; 그리다

gen·er·a·tion [dʒènəréiʃ(ə)n] n. **1.** Ⓒ all the people that are born about the same time. ¶*the younger ~.*① **2.** Ⓒ a period of time between the birth of one generation and the next; about 30 years. ¶*for generations*② / *from ~ to ~.*③ **3.** Ⓒ one step in the descent of a family. ¶*three generations—grandfather, father, and son.*④ **4.** Ⓤ the act of producing.
—ⓝ 1. 같은 시대의 사람들 ¶①젊은 세대의 사람들 2. 한 세대(부모의 대를 이어 자식에게 양도할 때까지의 약 30년간) ¶②몇 세대에 걸쳐서 / ③세대에서 세대로 3. 일대 ¶④조부, 부친, 아들의 삼대 4. 산출; 생식(生殖), 발생

gen·er·a·tive [dʒénərèitiv, -rətiv] adj. **1.** producing a child or children. **2.** having the power of producing.
—ⓐ 1. 생식의 2. 생산력이 있는; 생식력이 있는

gen·er·a·tor [dʒénərèitər] n. Ⓒ a machine that produces electricity, gas, or steam.
—ⓝ [가스·증기 따위의] 발생기; 발전기

ge·ner·ic [dʒinérik] adj. **1.** of a genus. **2.** of or common to a class or group; not special.
—ⓐ 1. 속(屬)의, 유(類)의 2. 전체에 관한, 포괄적인

gen·er·os·i·ty [dʒènərásiti / -rɔ́s-] n. (pl. **-ties**) **1.** Ⓤ the quality of being generous. **2.** Ⓒ a generous act.
—ⓝ 1. 관대, 관용 2. 관대한 행위

gen·er·ous [dʒén(ə)rəs] adj. **1.** willing to give; unselfish. ¶*be ~ with one's money.*① **2.** willing to forgive; noble. **3.** large in amount; plentiful. ¶*a ~ supply of meat.*②
▷**gen·er·ous·ness** [-nis] n.
—ⓐ 1. 아낌없는, 통이 큰, 인심 좋은 ¶①돈을 잘 쓰다 2. 관대한 3. 충분한; 풍부한 ¶②고기의 풍부한 공급

gen·er·ous·ly [dʒén(ə)rəsli] adv. in a generous manner.
—ⓥ 관대하게; 인심 좋게; 충분히

gen·e·ses [dʒénisìːz] n. pl. of **genesis**.

gen·e·sis [dʒénisis] n. Ⓒ (pl. **-ses**) **1.** origin; creation. **2.** (*the G-*) the first book of the Bible, which includes the story of the creation of the world by God.
—ⓝ 1. 기원; 발생; 창생(創生); 창시 2. 창세기

ge·net·ic [dʒinétik] adj. of origin or natural growth.
—ⓐ 기원의; 발생의

ge·net·ics [dʒinétiks] n. pl. (used as sing.) the science of heredity.
—ⓝ 발생학, 유전학

Ge·ne·va [dʒiníːvə] n. a city in southwest Switzerland.
—ⓝ 제네바

ge·ni·al [dʒíːniəl] adj. **1.** warm and friendly; kindly. ¶*a ~ welcome.* **2.** fit for growth; mild. ¶*a ~ climate.*
▷**ge·ni·al·ly** [-i] adv. —**ge·ni·al·i·ty** [dʒìːniǽliti] n.
—ⓐ 1. 친절한, 인정 있는 2. 발육에 알맞은; 온화한

ge·nie [dʒíːni] n. Ⓒ (pl. **-nies** or **ge·ni·i**) (in Arabian
—ⓝ 마귀, 요괴, 도깨비

fairy tales) a spirit with magical powers.

ge·ni·i [dʒíːniài] *n.* pl. of **genius** or **genie**.

gen·i·tive [dʒénitiv] *n.* [C] (*Grammer*) a case indicating possession, origin or source. **—***adj.* of this case; in this case. — [名] 속격(屬格), 소유격 — [形] 속격의; 소유격의

: ge·ni·us [dʒíːniəs] *n.* [C] **1.** [U] very great natural ability. **2.** a person who has such ability. **3.** the special character of a nation, language, or age. ¶*the ~ of the English language.*① **4.** (pl. **ge·ni·i**) a guardian spirit of a place or person. — [名] 1. 비범한 재능 2. 천재 3. 특질; 정신 ¶①영어의 특질 4. 수호신

gen·re [ʒáːnr(ə)] *n.* [C] a kind; a style. — [名] 유형, 형식, 양식, 장르

gen·teel [dʒentíːl] *adj.* **1.** polite; well-bred. **2.** pretending to be aristocratic. ¶*do the ~.*① ▷**gen·teel·ly** [-i] *adv.* —**gen·teel·ness** [-nis] *n.* — [形] 1. 예의바른; 가문이 좋은 2. 젠체하는, 점잔 빼는 ¶①점잔 빼다

gen·tian [dʒénʃ(i)ən] *n.* [C] tall plants with blue, white, red, or yellow flowers. — [名] 《植》 용담(龍膽)

gen·tile, Gen- [dʒéntail] *n.* [C] **1.** a person who is not Jewish. **2.** a person who does not believe in the Jewish, Christian, or Mohammedan god. **3.** a person who is not a Mormon. **—***adj.* **1.** not Jewish (and, in some cases, not Christian, not Mohammedan). **2.** (*U.S.*) of persons who are not Mormons. — [名] 1. 유대인이 아닌 사람, 이방인 2. [일반적으로] 이교도 3. 비(非)모르몬교도 — [形] 1. 유대인이 아닌, [일반적으로] 이교도의 2. 《美》 비모르몬 교도의

gen·til·i·ty [dʒentíliti] *n.* [U] (pl. **-ties**) **1.** the state of belonging to the upper class. **2.** good manners; refinement. **3.** 《usu. *pl.*》 pretended refinements. ¶*shabby ~.*① **4.** 《*the ~*》 the upper class. — [名] 1. 명문 태생 2. 고상, 우아 3. 점잔 빼기 ¶①[가난을 애써 감추는] 억지 체면 유지 4. 상류계급

: gen·tle [dʒéntl] *adj.* (**-tler, -tlest**) **1.** mild in manner; kindly. ¶*He is ~ to his students.* **2.** not rough; not hard; soft. ¶*a ~ breeze | a ~ blow.* **3.** not steep. ¶*a ~ slope.* **4.** of good birth; refined; polite. ¶*~ manners | a man of ~ birth.*① **5.** tame. ¶*a ~ dog.* — [形] 1. 부드러운, 친절한 2. 온화한, 심하지 않은 3. 완만한 4. 명문 태생의; 고상한; 공손한, 예의 바른 ¶①가문이 좋은 사람 5. 길든

gen·tle·folk [dʒéntlfòuk], **-folks** [-fòuks] *n.* pl. people of good family. — [名] 지체(문벌) 좋은 사람들

: gen·tle·man [dʒéntlmən] *n.* [C] (pl. **-men** [-mən]) **1.** a man of good taste and manners; a well-bred man; a man of good family. **2.** a man. — [名] 1. 신사 2. 남자

gen·tle·man·like [dʒéntlmənlàik] *adj.* like a gentleman; polite. — [形] 신사적인, 예의 바른

gen·tle·man·ly [dʒéntlmənli] *adj.* gentlemanlike. — [形] 신사적인, 예의 바른

gen·tle·ness [dʒéntlnis] *n.* [U] the quality of being gentle. — [名] 온순, 친절, 얌전함

gen·tle·wom·an [dʒéntlwùmən] *n.* [C] (pl. **-wom·en** [-wìmin]) a woman of good family; a lady. — [名] 양가의 부인; 귀부인, 숙녀

: gen·tly [dʒéntli] *adv.* **1.** in a gentle manner. **2.** moderately. — [副] 1. 부드럽게, 친절하게, 조용히 2. 알맞게

gen·try [dʒéntri] *n.* [U] **1.** 《*the ~*》 (*Brit.*) people of good family. ⇒[N.B.] **2.** people [of any class]; fellows. ¶*these ~.*① — [名] 1. 《英》 신사 계급 [N.B.] 귀족 다음가는 상류계급 2. 사회, 계급, 무리 ¶①이 사람들

· gen·u·ine [dʒénjuin] *adj.* **1.** real; true. ¶*a ~ diamond | ~ writing.*① **2.** sincere. ¶*~ repentance.* — [形] 1. 진짜의, 진품의 ¶①친필 2. 성실한, 진심에서의

gen·u·ine·ly [dʒénjuinli] *adv.* in a genuine manner. — [副] 진심에서, 성실히

ge·nus [dʒíːnəs] *n.* [C] (pl. **gen·er·a** or **ge·nus·es**) **1.** a kind; a class. **2.** (*Biology*) a group of animals or plants which have a common structure, but are different in important points. ⇒[N.B.] ¶*The tiger and cat belong to different species of the same ~.*① — [名] 1. 종류 2. 《生》 속(屬) [N.B.] family(과)와 species(종)의 중간 ¶①호랑이와 고양이는 속은 같으나 종이 다르다

ge·og·ra·pher [dʒiːágrəfər / dʒiɔ́grəfə] *n.* [C] a person who specializes in geography. — [名] 지리학자

ge·o·graph·ic [dʒìːəgrǽfik / dʒiə-], **-i·cal** [-ik(ə)l] *adj.* of geography. — [形] 지리학의; 지리의

ge·o·graph·i·cal·ly [dʒìːəgrǽfikəli / dʒiə-] *adv.* according to geography. — [副] 지리적으로; 지리학상

: ge·og·ra·phy [dʒiːágrəfi / dʒiɔ́g-] *n.* [U] **1.** the study of the earth's surface and everything connected with it. ¶*human ~*① *| physical ~.*② **2.** the natural features of a place or region. — [名] 1. 지리학 ¶①인문 지리학/②자연 지리학 2. 지세(地勢), 지형

ge·o·log·ic [dʒìːəládʒik / dʒiəlɔ́dʒ-], **-i·cal** [-ik(ə)l] *adj.* — [形] 지질학상의

ge·ol·o·gist [dʒi:áladʒist / dʒiɔ́l-] *n.* ⓒ a person who specializes in geology.
ge·ol·o·gy [dʒi:áladʒi / dʒiɔ́l-] *n.* ⓤ **1.** the study of the earth's layers and rocks in order to learn their changes and history. **2.** the earth's features in a special area.
ge·o·met·ric [dʒi:əmétrik / dʒiə-], **-ri·cal** [-rik(ə)l] *adj.* of geometry. ¶ ~ *progression*① / ~ *proportion*.
ge·om·e·try [dʒi:ámitri / dʒiɔ́m-] *n.* ⓤ the branch of mathematics that deals with lines, angles, and solids. ¶*analytical* ~① / *descriptive* ~.②
George [dʒɔːrdʒ] *n.* a man's name.
by George, (usu. *Brit.*) an exclamation of surprise, etc.
Geor·gia [dʒɔ́:rdʒə / dʒɔ́:dʒiə] *n.* a southern State of the United States, on the Atlantic coast. ⇒N.B.
Geor·gian [dʒɔ́:rdʒən / dʒɔ́:dʒiən] *adj.* **1.** of the period of the four Georges who were kings of England from 1714 to 1830. **2.** of Georgia or its people. —*n.* ⓒ a person of Georgia.
ge·ra·ni·um [dʒiréiniəm] *n.* ⓒ a plant with rose-colored flowers.
germ [dʒəːrm] *n.* ⓒ **1.** a very tiny animal or plant that may cause disease; a microbe. **2.** a seed; a bud. **3.** a beginning of anything; an origin. ¶*the ~ of life* / *be in* ~.①
‡**Ger·man** [dʒə́ːrmən] *adj.* of Germany, its people, or their language. —*n.* **1.** ⓒ a person of Germany. **2.** ⓤ the language of Germany.
Ger·man·ic [dʒə(ː)rmǽnik] *adj.* German; Teutonic.
—*n.* ⓤ the language of Teutonic races.
‡**Ger·ma·ny** [dʒə́ːrməni] *n.* a country in north central Europe, on the North Sea and the Baltic Sea. ⇒N.B.
ger·mi·cide [dʒə́ːrmisàid] *n.* ⓒ a substance that is used to kill disease germs.
ger·mi·nate [dʒə́ːrminèit] *vi.* start growing. —*vt.* cause (something) to grow or develop. ¶ ~ *seeds*.
ger·mi·na·tion [dʒə̀ːrminéiʃ(ə)n] *n.* ⓤ the act of germinating; the state of being germinated.
ger·und [dʒérənd] *n.* ⓒ (*Grammar*) a verb form used as a noun; a verbal noun.
ges·tic·u·late [dʒestíkjulèit] *vi., vt.* make gestures; express (something) by gestures. gesticulating.
ges·tic·u·la·tion [dʒestìkjuléiʃ(ə)n] *n.* ⓤⓒ the act of
‡**ges·ture** [dʒéstʃər] *n.* **1.** ⓒⓤ the movement of the body, esp. the hands and arms, to express an idea or feeling. ¶*speak by* ~.① **2.** ⓒ something said or done to impress others. ¶*a ~ of friendship.*② —*vi., vt.* =gesticulate.
‡**get** [get] *v.* (**got, got** or **got·ten**) *vt.* **1.** obtain; gain; receive; be given. ¶ ~ *a prize* / ~ *a letter* / ~ *permission from the government.* **2.** go and take; bring; fetch. ¶*Get me a chair.*① **3.** buy. ¶*He got me a dictionary.*; *He got a dictionary for me.* **4.** catch. ¶*She got a bad cold.* / *The policemen got a suspect.* **5.** earn. ¶ ~ *one's living.* **6.** understand. ¶*I don't* ~ *what you mean.* **7.** cause; persuade. ((~ *someone or something to do*)) ¶*Please* ~ *her to come here.* **8.** cause (something) to be done. ((~ *something done*)) ¶*I got my hair cut yesterday.*② **9.** cause (something) to be in a certain condition. ¶*I'll get the breakfast ready.* / *Get your hands clean.* / *Can you* ~ *the clock going again?*② / *I have to* ~ *my work finished by noon.*③ **10.** ((have got to)) have to. ¶*She has got to go.* —*vi.* **1.** arrive; reach. ¶ ~ *home late* / ~ *to the station.* **2.** become; grow. ¶ ~ *angry* / ~ *wet.* **3.** be; come to be. ⇒USAGE ¶*They got caught in the shower.*② / *She got married last month.*

get

—⊛ 지질학자
—⊛ 1. 지질학 2. 지질

—⊛ 기하학[상]의, 기하학적인 ¶①기하[동비(等比)] 급수
—⊛ 기하학 ¶①해석 기하학/②도형(화법) 기하학

—⊛ 남자 이름
𝕰 (英) 정말로
—⊛ 미국 남부의 주 N.B. Ga.로 줄임. 수도 Atlanta
—⊛ 1. 영국의 조오지 1세부터 4세까지의 시대의 2. 조오지아 주[민]의
—⊛ 조오지아 주의 주민

—⊛ 제라늄, 양아욱
—⊛ 1. 세균, 병균 2. 배종(胚種), 유아(幼芽) 3. 싹틈, 기원; 근원 ¶①아직 싹트는 상태이다, 발전 단계이다

—⊛ 독일[인·어]의 —⊛ 1. 독일인 2. 독일어

—⊛ 독일인의; 튜우튼 민족의 —⊛ 튜우튼 말
—⊛ 독일 N.B. 현재 East Germany 와 West Germany 로 분열

—⊛ 살균제.

—⊜ 싹트다, 발생하다 —⊛ …을 싹트게 하다, 발달시키다
—⊛ 싹틈, 발아(發芽)

—⊛ 《文法》 동명사

—⊜⊛ 몸짓(손짓)을 하다, 손짓으로 말하다(…을 나타내다)
—⊛ 몸짓, 손짓
—⊛ 1. 몸짓, 손짓 ¶①손짓으로 말하는 2. 거동, 태도 ¶②우정 있는 태도

—⊛ 1. …을 얻다; 받다; 획득하다 2. …을 가져오다 ¶①의자를 갖다 주시오 3. …을 사다; …에게 사 주다 4. …을 잡다; [병]에 걸리다 5. …을 벌다 6. …을 이해하다 7. [남]에게 …시키다 8. …하여 받다 ¶②어제 머리를 깎았다 9. …을 어떤 상태로 하다 ¶③시계를 다시 가게 할 수 있읍니까? / ④낮 12시까지 일을 끝내야 한다 10. …해야 하다 —⊜ 1. 도착하다 2. …이 되다 3. …당하다 USAGE be동사 대신으로 수동태를 만듦 ¶⑤그들은 소나기를 만났다 4. …하기 시작하다; …하게 되다

4. begin. 《~ *to do*, ~ *doing*》 ¶~ *talking* | ~ *to know him.*

1) ***get about*** (or ***around***), ⓐ move from place to place. ⓑ become widely known.
2) ***get** something* ***across,*** make something clear or understood.
3) ***get along,*** ⓐ manage to make a living. ¶*I can't ~ along without his help.* ⓑ make progress; proceed. 《~ along *with* something》 ¶*How is he getting along with his English?*⑥ ⓒ succeed. ⓓ be on good terms. 《~ along *with* someone》
4) ***get at,*** ⓐ reach; approach. ⓑ find out; obtain. ⓒ mean; imply. ¶*I can't see what you are getting at.*⑦ ⓓ be engaged in (work).
5) ***get away,*** go away; leave; escape.
6) ***get away with,*** do (something) without being punished.
7) ***get back,*** return; recover.
8) ***get by,*** ⓐ pass. ¶*I moved aside to let the car ~ by.*⑧ ⓑ =get away with. ⓒ =get along ⓐ.
9) ***get down,*** ⓐ descend. ⓑ (*colloq.*) become depressed.
10) ***get** someone or something* ***down,*** ⓐ cause something to be down; swallow. ⓑ make someone depressed or annoyed.
11) ***get down to*** (=*begin to consider or act on*) *something.*
12) ***get in,*** ⓐ enter. ⓑ arrive. ⓒ put (words) in; interrupt.
13) ***get off,*** ⓐ get down; descend. ⓑ start. 《~ off *from* school, etc.》 ⓒ escape. 《~ off *from* an accident, etc.》
14) ***get on,*** ⓐ mount. ¶~ *on a bicycle.* ⓑ continue. ⓒ =get along.
15) ***get out,*** ⓐ go; leave. ⓑ become known; publish.
16) ***get out of,*** escape; avoid.
17) ***get over,*** ⓐ recover from (illness, etc.). ⓑ overcome.
18) ***get through,*** ⓐ finish. ⓑ manage to survive.
19) ***get to,*** ⓐ arrive at (a place). ⓑ begin.
20) ***get up,*** get out of bed; stand up.
21) ***get up to,*** arrive at; reach; catch up.

[熟] 1)ⓐ돌아다니다 ⓑ퍼지다 2)…을 알게 하다 3)ⓐ살아가다 ⓑ진보시키다 ¶⑥그의 영어는 어느 정도나 나아갔느냐? ⓒ성공하다 ⓓ사이좋게 지내다 4)ⓐ…에 도착하다 ⓑ…을 찾아내다; 손에 넣다 ⓒ…을 의미하다 ¶⑦나는 당신의 진의가 무엇인지 모르겠소 ⓓ…에 종사하다 5)가 버리다; 도망치다 6)처벌 받지 않고 …을 하다 7)…을 되돌리다; 회복하다 8)ⓐ통과하다 ¶⑧차를 보내기 위해 나는 옆으로 비켰다 9) ⓐ내리다 ⓑ《口》 풀이 죽다 10) ⓐ…을 내리다;[약 따위]를 삼키다 ⓑ…을 풀이 죽게 하다 11)…을 시작하다; …에 본격적으로 달려 들다 12)ⓐ들어가다 ⓑ도착하다 ⓒ말참견하다 13)ⓐ내리다 ⓑ출발하다 ⓒ도망치다 14)ⓐ…에 타다 ⓑ…을 계속하다 15)ⓐ가다; 떠나다 ⓑ알려지다; 출판하다 16)…에서 도망치다; 피하다 17)ⓐ에서 회복하다 ⓑ…을 압도하다 18)ⓐ…을 끝내다 ⓑ살아 남다 19)ⓐ…에 도착하다 ⓑ…을 시작하다 20)기상하다; 일어서다 21)…에 도착하다; …을 잡다

Geth·sem·a·ne [geθsémәni] *n.* (in the Bible) a garden east of Jerusalem where Jesus was finally caught by the Romans.
—[名] 겟세마네(그리스도가 고난을 받은 땅)

get-up [gétʌp] *n.* Ⓒ (*colloq.*) an arrangement; dress; a style.
—[名] 《口》 몸치장, 옷차림, 옷맵시

gey·ser *n.* Ⓒ **1.** [gáizәr →2.] a hot spring that frequently sends jets of hot water and steam into the air. **2.** [gí:zәr] (*Brit.*) an apparatus to heat water quickly by gas. (cf. *U.S.* a water heater)
—[名] **1.** 간헐천(間歇泉) **2.**《英》 물 끓이는 가스 장치

Gha·na [gá:nә] *n.* a country on the coast of West Africa. ⇒[N.B.]
—[名] 서부 아프리카의 공화국 [N.B.] 수도 Accra

* **ghast·ly** [gǽstli / gá:st-] *adj.* (**-li·er, -li·est**) **1.** horrible; dreadful. **2.** like a ghost; pale. ¶*The sick man looked ~.* **3.** (*colloq.*) shocking; very bad. ¶*a ~ mistake.*
—*adv.* in a ghastly manner; horribly.
—[形] **1.** 무서운, 무시무시한, 오싹하는 **2.** 유령 같은, 창백한 **3.** 심한; 싫은
—[副] 무시무시하게

ghet·to [gétou] *n.* Ⓒ (pl. **-tos**) a special part of a city where Jews live; (*U.S.*) the Negro quarter.
—[名] 유대인 지구(가); 《美》 흑인 지구

: **ghost** [goust] *n.* Ⓒ **1.** the spirit of a dead person, supposed to appear before living persons. ¶*Do you believe in ghosts?* **2.** a shadowy image; a slight suggestion. **3.** a secondary abnormal image or picture which appears on a TV screen, etc.
1) ***give up the ghost,*** die.
2) ***have not the ghost of a chance,*** have no chance at all.
—[名] **1.** 유령, 망령; 요괴 **2.** 그림자; 흔적, 희미한 기색 **3.** [텔레비전의] 복상(複像)
[熟] 1)죽다 2)전혀 기회(가망)가 없다

ghost·ly [góustli] *adj.* (**-li·er, -li·est**) **1.** of or like a ghost; faint; shadowy. ¶*our ~ enemy.*① **2.** spiritual.
▷**ghost·li·ness** [-nis] *n.*
—[形] **1.** 유령의(같은); 희미한; 그림자 같은 ¶①악마 **2.** 정신적인, 영혼의

ghoul [gu:l] *n.* Ⓒ **1.** (in Oriental folklore) an evil spirit that eats dead bodies. **2.** a horrible man.
—[名] **1.** 무덤을 파고 시체를 먹는 악귀 **2.** 잔인한 사람

GI, G.I. [dʒí:ái] *n.* Ⓒ (pl. **GI's, G.I's, GIs**) (*colloq.*) an
—[名] [여군도 포함하여] 미군 병사

G

enlisted soldier in the United States army. ⇒[N.B.] —*adj.* issued by the government; (*colloq.*) standardized by the Army. ¶*a ~ uniform.*

[N.B.] *G*overnment *I*ssue(정부 지급)의 준말 —[形] 관급(官給)의; 군대 규격의

:gi·ant [dʒáiənt] *n.* [C] **1.** an imaginary person who has great size and power. **2.** a very large person or thing. —*adj.* very large; huge.

—[名] **1.** 거인 **2.** 거한(巨漢), 큰 사나이; 거대한 것 —[形] 거대한, 아주 큰

gib·ber [dʒíbər] *vi.* talk fast and meaninglessly. ¶*Monkeys ~.*

—[自] 뜻 모를 말을 빨리 지껄이다

gib·ber·ish [dʒíbəriʃ, gíbə-] *n.* [U] rapid and not clear talk; meaningless talk.

—[名] 입싸게 지껄이는 뜻 모를 말

gib·bet [dʒíbit] *n.* [C] a kind of machine with a post and an arm used for hanging a man. —*vt.* **1.** kill (someone) by hanging on a gibbet. **2.** expose (someone) to criticism by the public.

—[名] 교수대 —[他] **1.** …을 교수형에 처하다 **2.** …을 창피를 주다, 모욕하다

gib·bon [gíbən] *n.* [C] a kind of small, long-armed monkey living in southeastern Asia.

—[名] 긴팔원숭이

gib·bous [gíbəs] *adj.* **1.** convex; curved out. **2.** (of the moon) between half and full. ¶*a ~ moon.*

—[形] **1.** 철면(凸面)의, 불룩한 **2.** 반달과 보름달 사이의

gibe [dʒaib] *vi., vt.* sneer at (someone); make fun of (someone). —*n.* [C] the act of sneering.

—[自][他] [···을] 조롱하다, 업신여기다 —[名] 조롱, 비웃음

gid·di·ly [gídili] *adv.* in a giddy manner.

—[副] 현기증나게, 경솔하게

gid·di·ness [gídinis] *n.* [U] the state of being giddy.

—[名] 현기증; 경솔

gid·dy [gídi] *adj.* (**-di·er, -di·est**) **1.** dizzy. **2.** causing dizziness. ¶*~ height.* **3.** not serious; heedless.
act (or *play*) ***the giddy goat,*** act foolishly.

—[形] **1.** 현기증이 나는 **2.** 어질어질한 **3.** 부박(浮薄)한, 경솔한
[熟] 바보짓하다

:gift [gift] *n.* **1.** [C] a present. ¶*a Christmas ~ / He made a ~ of one million won to the old people's home.*① **2.** [U] the power or right to give. ¶*The position is within his ~.*② **3.** [C] something one is born with; a natural talent. ¶*the ~ of tongues.*③
1) ***at a gift,*** even as a gift. ¶*I would not take it at a ~.*④
2) ***by*** (or ***of***) ***free gift,*** for nothing; free of charge.

—[名] **1.** 선물 ¶①그는 양로원에 100만 원을 기증했다 **2.** 수여권 ¶②그 지위를 줄 권리는 그에게 있다 **3.** [천부의] 재능, 자질 ¶③어학의 재능
[熟] 1)공짜라도 ¶④공짜라도 그건 안 받겠다 2)공짜로

gift·ed [gíftid] *adj.* having great natural ability; talented.

—[形] 천부의 재능이 있는

gig [gig] *n.* [C] **1.** an open, light, two-wheeled carriage drawn by one horse. **2.** a long, light boat attached to a ship for the captain's use.

—[名] **1.** 한 필이 끄는 2륜 마차 **2.** 배에 실은 선장용 보우트

·gi·gan·tic [dʒaigǽntik] *adj.* very big like a giant; enormous; immense.

—[形] 거대한, 방대한, 대규모의

gig·gle [gígl] *vi.* laugh in a silly manner. —*n.* [C] a silly laugh. ▷**gig·gler** [-ər] *n.* —**gig·gling·ly** [-iŋli] *adv.*

—[自] 껄껄 웃다 —[名] 껄껄 웃음

·gild¹ [gild] *vt.* (**gild·ed** or **gilt**) **1.** coat or cover (something) with thin gold. **2.** make (something) shine like gold. **3.** make (something) seem better and more attractive than it really is.
gild the pill, make an unpleasant thing seem acceptable.

—[他] **1.** …에 도금(鍍金)하다, …에 금박을 입히다 **2.** …을 황금빛으로 빛나게 하다 **3.** …을 실제보다 좋게 보이게 하다
[熟] 흉한 것을 보기 좋게 만들다

gild² [gild] *n.* =guild.

gild·ed [gíldid] *adj.* covered with thin gold.

—[形] 금박을 씌운, 도금한

gild·ing [gíldiŋ] *n.* [U] the gold leaf or similar material with which a thing is gilded. ¶*chemical* (or *electric*) *~.*①

—[名] 도금, 금박 ¶①전기 도금

gill [gil] *n.* [C] 《usu. *pl.*》 **1.** the part of a fish's body for breathing under water. **2.** the flesh under the chin and jaws of a person. **3.** the hanging flesh under a fowl's throat.

—[名] **1.** 아가미 **2.** 사람의 턱밑의 살 **3.** [닭 따위의] 턱밑에 처진 살

gilt [gilt] *v.* pt. and pp. of **gild¹**.
—*adj.* covered with thin gold; gilded. ¶*~ top.*① —*n.* [U] a thin layer of gold or gold-colored substance.

—[形] 도금한, 금박을 입힌 ¶①[서적의] 금박을 입힌 꼭대기 —[名] 도금, 금박

gilt-edged [gíltèdʒd] *adj.* **1.** covered with gold. **2.** of the best quality. ¶*~ securities.*①

—[形] **1.** [종이·서적 따위의] 금테를 두른 **2.** 최상의 ¶①일류 증권

gim·crack [dʒímkrӕk] *n.* [C] a pretty but worthless thing. —*adj.* pretty but worthless.

—[名] 번지르르한 싸구려 물건 —[形] 번지르르하고 값싼, 속임수의

gim·let [gímlit] *n.* [C] a small tool with a screw point for making small holes.

—[名] 나사송곳

·gin¹ [dʒin] *n.* [U] a strong, colorless alcoholic drink.

—[名] 진(술의 일종)

·gin² [dʒin] *n.* [C] **1.** a machine to separate cotton from

—[名] **1.** 씨아 **2.** 덫 —[他] **1.** [목화의 씨]

G

its seeds. 2. a trap; a snare. —*vt.* (**ginned, gin·ning**) 1. clear (cotton) of seeds. 2. trap; snare.

— 명 1. 씨를 빼다 2. …을 덫으로 잡다

* **gin·ger** [dʒíndʒər] *n.* ⓤ 1. a tropical plant from which a strong spicy powder is obtained; its powder. 2. (*colloq.*) energy. 3. reddish or brownish yellow color.

—명 1. 생강, 생강 2. (口) 정력 3. 붉은 색, 적황색

gin·ger·bread [dʒíndʒərbrèd] *n.* 1. ⓤ a cake or cookie flavored with ginger. 2. ⓒ a pretty but worthless thing. —*a.* showy. ¶ ~ work.① [cautious[ly].

—명 1. 생강이 든 케이크 2. 싸구려 장식 —형 허울만 좋고 쓸모 없는, 겉뿐인 ¶①번지르르한 싸구려 장식

gin·ger·ly [dʒíndʒərli] *adj., adv.* very careful[ly];

—형⑨ 조심성 깊은(깊게)

ging·ham [gíŋəm] *n.* ⓤ a cotton cloth which is usu. designed in stripes or checks.

—명 깅검(줄 무늬·바둑판 무늬의 무명천)

ging·ko [gíŋkou] *n.* (pl. **-kos** or **-koes**) =ginkgo.

gink·go [gíŋkgou, +*U.S.* dʒíŋk-] *n.* ⓒ (pl. **-goes**) a tree found in China and Korea that has fan-shaped leaves and bears eatable nuts. ¶*a ~ nut.*①

—명 은행나무 ¶①은행[열매]

gin·seng [dʒínseŋ] *n.* ⓒ a plant found in China or Korea, whose root is used for medicine.

—명 인삼

gip·sy, Gip·sy [dʒípsi] *n., adj.* (esp. *Brit.*) =gypsy.

gi·raffe [dʒiræf / -ráːf] *n.* ⓒ an African animal with a very long neck and legs and a spotted skin.

—명 기린

gird [gəːrd] *vt.* (**girt** or **gird·ed**) 1. put a belt around (something). 2. surround; encircle.

—타 1. 띠로 …을 두르다 2. …을 둘러싸다

gird·er [gə́ːrdər] *n.* ⓒ a bar of wood or steel supporting a building, bridge, etc.

—명 도리, 대들보

* **gir·dle** [gə́ːrdl] *n.* ⓒ 1. something worn around the waist, such as a sash or belt. 2. anything that surrounds like a girdle. 3. a support like a corset worn about the hips or waist. —*vt.* 1. encircle. 2. put a girdle around (the waist).

—명 1. 띠; 벨트 2. 띠 모양의 것 3. 거어들(코르셋 비슷한 여자옷의 안받침) —타 1. …을 둘러싸다 2. …을 띠로 두르다

‡ **girl** [gəːrl] *n.* ⓒ 1. a female child; a young unmarried woman. 2. a female servant. 3. (*colloq.*) a sweetheart. 4. (*colloq.*) a woman of any age.

—명 1. 소녀, 계집아이, 딸 2. 하녀 3. 연인, 애인 4. 여자

girl·hood [gə́ːrlhùd] *n.* ⓤ the time of being a girl.
girl·ish [gə́ːrliʃ] *adj.* 1. of a girl. 2. like a girl; suitable for girls. ▷ **girl·ish·ly** [-li] *adv.* —**girl·ish·ness**

—명 소녀(처녀)시절
—형 1. 소녀의 2. 소녀다운, 소녀에 어울리는

girt [gəːrt] *v.* pt. and pp. of **gird**.
girth [gəːrθ] *n.* ⓒ 1. the distance around anything. ¶*the ~ of a tree.* 2. a band around an animal for holding a saddle, pack, etc. in place. [speech.

—명 1. 둘레의 치수 2. [말 따위의] 뱃대끈

gist [dʒist] *n.* ⓒ the essential point. ¶*the ~ of his*

—명 요점, 요지; 골자

‡ **give** [giv] *vt.* (**gave, giv·en**) 1. cause (someone) to have; hand over; present. ¶*~ him a book; ~ a book to him.* 2. pay. ¶*~ 1,000 yen for this book.* 3. grant; allow; permit. ¶*God ~ me wisdom.*① 4. furnish; provide; supply. ¶*~ a medicine to a patient*② | *Cows ~ us milk.* 5. pass on; communicate. ¶*~ a message.* 6. show; exhibit. ¶*~ an example* | *The thermometer gives 30°C now.* 7. devote. ¶*~ one's mind to one's study* | *He gave his life to his country.* 8. perform; do. ¶*~ a kick* | *~ a cry* | *~ a push* | *~ a party* | *~ a play.*③ —*vi.* 1. make a gift. 2. bend; break down; yield. ¶*The old chair gave when I sat on it.*④ 3. become mild; melt. ¶*The winter is giving.*⑤ | *The frost didn't ~ all*
1) *give and take,* exchange on an equal basis. [day.
2) *give away,* ⓐ give (something) as a present. ⓑ make known (something secret); reveal; betray.
3) *give back,* return (something) to its owner; restore;
4) *give forth,* emit; spread. [reply.
5) *give in,* ⓐ stop fighting and admit defeat; yield. ⓑ hand over.
6) *give it to,* (*colloq.*) punish.
7) *give off,* put forth; emit.
8) *give out,* ⓐ become very tired; become used up. ⓑ give (things) to others. ⓒ publish; make known. ⓓ emit; put forth.

—명 웃점; 요지; 골자
—타 1. …에게 주다 2. …을 지불하다 3. …을 수여하다; 인가하다 ¶①하나님, 나에게 지혜를 주소서 4. …을 공급하다; 투약(投藥)하다 ¶②환자에게 약을 주다 5. …을 전달하다 6. …을 보이다, 나타내다 7. …을 바치다, …에게 몰두하다 8. …하다; 행하다 ¶③극을 상연하다 —자 1. 주다; 선물하다 2. 휘다, 비틀다, 부서지다 ¶④낡은 의자는 내가 올라앉자 부서졌다 3. [기후가] 온화해지다, 풀리다 ¶⑤겨울 추위가 풀리고 있다

圖 1) 대등한 입장에서 거래하다 2) ⓐ …을 선물하다 ⓑ [비밀]을 누설하다 3) …을 돌려주다; 원상 복귀하다; 대답하다 4) 방사(放射)하다; 내다; 퍼뜨리다 5) ⓐ 굴복하다 ⓑ 제출하다 6) …을 벌주다 7) ⓐ 을 내다, 풍기다 ¶⑥몹시 지치다; 다 써 버리다 ⓑ …을 분배하다 ⓒ …을 발행하다; 알리다 ⓓ …을 발산하다, 내다 9) ⓐ 제출하다 ⓑ 그만두다 10) ⓐ 단념하다 ¶⑥문제가 너무 어려워서 도중에 던져 버리고 말았다

give-and-take [491] **glaring**

9) *give over*, ⓐ hand over. ⓑ stop; cease.
10) *give up*, ⓐ stop trying. ¶*I have given up smoking.* / *The problem was too difficult for me, so I gave up.*ⓑ ⓑ abandon hope; despair. ¶*The doctor has given him up.*ⓒ ⓒ surrender. ⓓ devote oneself to; indulge in (something).

give-and-take [gívəntéik] *n.* Ⓤ **1.** an exchange on an equal basis; mutual cooperation. **2.** good-natured exchange of talk, ideas, etc.

give·a·way [gívəwèi] *n.* **1.** Ⓤ the act of telling a secret carelessly; betrayal. **2.** Ⓒ a premium given for promoting sales. **3.** Ⓒ a question-and-answer game as a radio or television show in which prizes are given away.

‡ **giv·en** [gívn] *v.* pp. of **give**.
—*adj.* **1.** stated; fixed; appointed. ¶*a ~ condition* / *finish the work in a ~ time.* **2.** taken as a basis of reasoning; assumed; granted. ¶*a ~ factor* / *a ~ circle.*ⓐ **3.** inclined; accustomed. ¶*He is ~ to drinking.*ⓑ

giv·er [gívər] *n.* Ⓒ a person who gives.

gla·cial [gléiʃəl, +Brit. gléisjəl] *adj.* **1.** of or like ice; very cold; icy. **2.** of glaciers or the glacial period.

gla·cier [gléiʃər / glǽsjə] *n.* Ⓒ a large riverlike mass of ice which moves slowly down a mountain.

‡ **glad** [glæd] *adj.* (**glad·der, glad·dest**) **1.** happy; pleased. ¶*I'm very ~ to see you.* **2.** pleasant; joyful. ¶*~ news.*

glad·den [glǽdn] *vi., vt.* become or make happy.

glade [gleid] *n.* Ⓒ an open space in a forest.

glad·i·a·tor [glǽdièitər] *n.* Ⓒ **1.** (in Ancient Rome) a man trained or hired to fight before the public to entertain them. **2.** a person who argues with great skill.

glad·i·o·li [glædióulai] *n.* pl. of **gladiolus**.

glad·i·o·lus [glædióuləs] *n.* Ⓒ (pl. **-lus·es** or **-li**) a garden plant of the iris family with swordshaped leaves and beautiful flowers.

* **glad·ly** [glǽdli] *adv.* in a glad manner.

glad·ness [glǽdnis] *n.* Ⓤ the state of being glad.

glad·some [glǽdsəm] *adj.* joyful; cheerful; delightful.

glam·or [glǽmər] *n.* =**glamour**.

glam·or·ous [glǽmərəs] *adj.* charming; fascinating.
▷**glam·or·ous·ly** [-li] *adv.*

glam·our [glǽmər] *n.* Ⓤ (sometimes *a ~*) mysterious charm or fascination; enchantment.
cast a glamour over, enchant.

‡ **glance** [glæns / glɑːns] *n.* Ⓒ **1.** a swift look. ¶*at a ~*ⓐ / *cast a ~ at a report*ⓑ / *steal a ~ at a pretty girl*ⓒ / *He took a ~ at the book.* / *They exchanged glances.*ⓓ **2.** a gleam; a flash.
—*vi.* **1.** look quickly. ⟨*~ at something or someone*⟩ **2.** gleam; flash. **3.** (of a bullet, etc.) slide off (something); (of a speech, etc.) turn away from the subject. ⟨*~ away or off something*⟩
glance back, reflect. ¶*~ back the light.*

gland [glænd] *n.* Ⓒ an organ in the body which gives out some substance.

glan·du·lar [glǽndʒulər / -dju-] *adj.* of or like a gland.

* **glare** [glɛər] *n.* Ⓒ (usu. *sing.*) **1.** a bright and dazzling light. ¶*the ~ of the sun.* **2.** a fierce and angry look. ¶*the ~ of the lion.* **3.** Ⓤ showy appearance or display.
—*vi.* **1.** shine with a dazzling light. ¶*The hot sun glared down on us.* **2.** stare angrily. ⟨*~ at* or *upon* someone⟩ ¶*The woman glared at me.* —*vt.* express (something) with a fierce look. ¶*He glared hatred at me.*

glar·ing [glɛ́əriŋ] *adj.* **1.** dazzlingly bright. **2.** fierce

ⓑ절망하다 ¶ⓒ의사는 그를 포기해 버렸다 ⓒ[직업 따위]를 버리다 ⓓ…에 몰두하다; 몸을 바치다

—ⓝ 1. 대등한 조건하의 거래(교환); 협조 2. 의견 교환

—ⓝ 1. 무심코 비밀을 말하기 2. 경품, 덤 3. [라디오·텔레비전의] 퀴즈 프로

—ⓐ 1. 정해진, 일정한 2. 주어진, 전체의; 가설(假說)의 ¶①주어진 원 3. …하고 싶어하는, 에 빠진; …하는 버릇이 있는 ¶②그에게는 음주벽이 있다

—ⓝ 주는 사람, 기증자
—ⓐ 1. 얼음의, 얼음 같은, 몹시 차가운 2. 빙하[시대]의
—ⓝ 빙하

—ⓐ 1. 기쁜, 즐거운 2. 반가운

—ⓥ 기뻐하[게 하]다
—ⓝ 숲 사이의 빈터
—ⓝ 1. 검투사(劍鬪士) 2. 논쟁자

—ⓝ 글라디올러스

—ⓐⓓ 기쁘게, 기꺼이
—ⓝ 기쁨, 즐거움
—ⓐ 기쁜; 유쾌한

—ⓐ 매력적인

—ⓝ 매력

ⓥ …을 매혹하다
—ⓝ 1. 힐끗 보기, 일별 ¶①얼핏 보아 /②보고서를 쭉 훑어보다/③예쁜 소녀를 몰래 훔쳐 보다/④그들은 서로 눈짓을 했다 2. 번득임
—ⓥ 1. 힐끗 보다 2. 번득이다 3. 옆으로 빗나가다

ⓥ …을 반사하다
—ⓝ 선(腺)

—ⓐ 선의; 선성(腺性)의
—ⓝ 1. 섬광 2. 노려봄 3. 야단스러움, 야함

—ⓥ 1. 반짝반짝 빛나다 2. 노려보다
—ⓥ 노려보아 …을 나타내다 ¶①그는 혐오의 눈초리로 나를 보았다

—ⓐ 1. 반짝반짝 빛나는; 눈부신; 2. 몹

and angry. ¶ ~ *eyes.* **3.** too bright; showy. **4.** evident. ¶ *a ~ mistake.*
시 성난 **3.** 야한, 야단스러운 **4.** 분명한

Glas·gow [glǽsgou / glɑ́:s-] *n.* a large seaport in southwest Scotland. ⇒[N.B.]
—[名] 스코틀랜드의 도시 [N.B.] 섬유·조선·제강 따위의 중심지

⁑ **glass** [glæs / glɑ:s] *n.* **1.** [U] a hard substance which is usu. clear and easily broken. **2.** [U] ⟪*collectively*⟫ things made of glass. **3.** [C] an object made of glass, such as a drinking vessel, mirror, etc. **4.** ⟪*pl.*⟫ spectacles; eyeglasses.
—[名] **1.** 유리 **2.** 유리 제품 **3.** 컵, 거울 [따위] **4.** 안경

glass·ful [glǽsfùl / glɑ́:s-] *n.* [C] as much as a glass can hold.
—[名] 컵 가득[한 분량]

glass·house [glǽshàus / glɑ́:s-] *n.* [C] (pl. **-houses** [-hàuziz]) **1.** a place where glass is made; glassworks. **2.** a hothouse; a greenhouse.
—[名] **1.** 유리 공장 **2.** 온실

glass·ware [glǽswɛ̀ər / glɑ́:swɛ̀ə] *n.* [U] ⟪*collectively*⟫ articles made of glass, such as glass dishes, pitchers, etc.
—[名] 유리 제품

glass·work [glǽswə̀:rk / glɑ́:swə̀:k] *n.* [U] **1.** the industry manufacturing glass and glassware. **2.** glassware. **3.** ⟪usu. *pl.* used as *sing.*⟫ a factory where glass is made.
—[名] **1.** 유리 제조업 **2.** 유리 제품 **3.** 유리 공장

glass·y [glǽsi / glɑ́:si] *adj.* (**glass·i·er, glass·i·est**) **1.** like glass; smooth. **2.** (of the eye or look) lifeless; expressionless.
—[形] **1.** 유리 같은; 매끄러운 **2.** 생기 없는, 멍하니 있는

glau·co·ma [glɔ:kóumə] *n.* [U] a disease of the eye.
—[名] 녹내장(綠內障)(눈병의 일종)

glaze [gleiz] *vt.* **1.** put glass in (something). **2.** cover (something) with a glassy surface. ¶ ~ *pottery.* —*vi.* become glassy. —*n.* **1.** [C] a smooth, glasslike surface. **2.** [U] substance used for glazing.
—[他] **1.** …에 유리를 끼우다 **2.** …의 표면에 광택이 나게 하다 —[自] 유리처럼 되다 —[名] **1.** 반들반들한 표면 **2.** 유약(釉藥)

gla·zier [gléiziər] *n.* [C] a person whose job is to put glass in picture frames, windows, etc.
—[名] 유리장수

⁑ **gleam** [gli:m] *n.* [C] **1.** a brief beam or flash of light. ¶ *a ~ of the distant sea.* **2.** a brief show of feeling or emotion. ¶ *a faint ~ of hope.* —*vi.* **1.** flash with light. ¶ *Stars gleamed.* **2.** (of emotion, wit, etc.) appear suddenly. ¶ *Wit gleamed in his speech.*①
—[名] **1.** 희미한 빛, 반짝임 **2.** [감정 따위의] 번득임 —[自] **1.** 반짝 빛나다 **2.** 번득이다 ¶①그의 연설에는 재치가 번득인다

glean [gli:n] *vi., vt.* **1.** gather what the reapers have left after the harvest in a field. ¶ ~ *corn.* **2.** collect (information, news etc.) little by little. ¶ *He gleaned all the news of his missing father he could.*
—[自][他] **1.** 이삭을 줍다 **2.** [···을] 조금씩 수집하다

glean·ings [glí:niŋz] *n. pl.* things gleaned; collection.
—[名] 수집한 것

glebe [gli:b] *n.* **1.** [U] (*poetic*) soil; field. **2.** (*Brit.*) [C] a portion of land owned by a clergyman as part of his living.
—[名] **1.** ⟪詩⟫ 토지, 밭 **2.** ⟪英⟫ 교회에 속하는 논밭

glee [gli:] *n.* [U] **1.** joy; delight. **2.** (*Music*) [C] a part song for three or more voices, usu. without accompaniment of musical instruments.
—[名] **1.** 기쁨; 환희 **2.** ⟪樂⟫ 합창곡

in high glee, with great joy.
[熟] 아주 기뻐서

glee·ful [glí:f(u)l] *adj.* filled with glee; joyous; gay.
▷**glee·ful·ly** [-i] *adv.* —**glee·ful·ness** [-nis] *n.*
—[形] 몹시 기뻐하는; 즐거운

* **glen** [glen] *n.* [C] a small, narrow valley.
—[名] 협곡, 골짜기

glen·gar·ry [glengǽri] *n.* [C] (pl. **-ries**) a cap worn by Highlanders in Scotland.
—[名] [스코틀랜드 고지 사람의] 모자

glib [glib] *adj.* (**glib·ber, glib·best**) speaking smoothly but without much thought or truth. ¶ *a ~ speech* / *a ~ excuse* / *be of ~ tongue.*①
—[形] 잘 조잘거리는, 입심 좋은 ¶①입심이 좋다

glib·ly [glíbli] *adv.* in a glib manner.
—[副] 재잘재잘, 유창하게

* **glide** [glaid] *vi.* **1.** move along smoothly and easily; slide. ¶ *Many skaters were gliding on the ice.* **2.** pass gradually. ¶ *The hours glided past.* **3.** travel through the air without using an engine. —*vt.* cause (something) to glide. —*n.* [C] **1.** a smooth and easy movement. **2.** (of an airplane) a slow downward movement without using an engine.
—[自] **1.** 미끄러지다 **2.** 천천히 지나가다 **3.** 활공하다 —[他] …을 미끄러지게 하다 —[名] **1.** 미끄러지기, 활주 **2.** 활공

glid·er [gláidər] *n.* [C] an aircraft like an airplane but without an engine.
—[名] 글라이더

G

glim·mer [glímər] *n.* ⓒ **1.** a faint, wavering light. **2.** a hint; a faint glimpse. ¶*a ~ of hope.* —*vi.* **1.** shine faintly and waveringly; flicker. ¶*The lights glimmered in the fog.* **2.** appear faintly.

: glimpse [glimps] *n.* ⓒ **1.** a brief, quick view. ¶*see someone by glimpses* / *I caught* (or *get*) *a ~ of her in the crowd.*① **2.** a brief appearance; a hint. ¶*a ~ of what is to come.* —*vt., vi.* catch a quick view of (something); look briefly.

glint [glint] *vi.* flash; spark. —*n.* ⓒ a flash; a gleam. ¶*the ~ of gold.*

* **glis·ten** [glísn] *vi.* sparkle; gleam; shine. ¶*The dewdrops glistened in the sun.* —*n.* ⓒ a gleam.

: glit·ter [glítər] *vi.* **1.** shine brightly and at intervals; sparkle. ¶(*proverb*) *All is not gold that glitters.*① **2.** (of clothes, etc.) be bright and showy. —*n.* ⓒⓤ **1.** a bright, sparkling light. **2.** brightness.

gloam·ing [glóumiŋ] *n.* ((*the ~*)) twilight; dusk.

gloat [glout] *vi.* look contentedly; feel or show selfish pleasure. ((*~ upon* or *over something*)) ¶*They gloated over the stolen jewels.*

glob·al [glóub(ə)l] *adj.* **1.** of the earth; worldwide. **2.** globe-shaped.

: globe [gloub] *n.* ⓒ **1.** anything shaped like a ball; a sphere. **2.** ((*the ~*)) the earth. **3.** a sphere showing a map of the earth or sky on it. ¶*a celestial* (*a terrestrial*) *~.*①

globe·fish [glóubfiʃ] *n.* ⓒ (pl. **-fish·es** or *collectively* **-fish**) a fish that can make itself globe-shaped by taking in air.

glob·u·lar [glábjulər / glɔ́bjulə] *adj.* **1.** shaped like a globe; round. **2.** consisting of globules.

glob·ule [glábju:l / glɔ́b-] *n.* ⓒ a very small ball; a tiny drop of liquid. ¶*a ~ of sweat.*①

* **gloom** [glu:m] *n.* ⓤ **1.** dimness; darkness. ¶*The scenery was enveloped in ~.* **2.** ((sometimes *a ~*)) sadness; melancholy. ¶*cast ~ over* (or *upon*) *married life* / *chase one's ~ away.*① —*vt., vi.* make (something) dark; become dark.

gloom·i·ly [glú:mili] *adv.* **1.** darkly. **2.** melancholily.

* **gloom·y** [glú:mi] *adj.* (**gloom·i·er, gloom·i·est**) **1.** dark; dim. **2.** sad; melancholy. **3.** discouraging. ▷**gloom·i·ness** [-nis] *n.*

glo·ri·a [glɔ́:riə] *n.* ⓒ **1.** a song of praise to God. **2.** ((*G-*)) one of three Latin hymns of praise to God. **3.** a halo.

glo·ri·fi·ca·tion [glɔ̀:rifikéiʃ(ə)n] *n.* ⓤ **1.** the act of glorifying; the state of being glorified. **2.** (*colloq.*) celebration; festivity.

glo·ri·fy [glɔ́:rifài] *vt.* (**-fied**) **1.** give glory to (someone); make (someone) glorious. ¶*~ God.* **2.** praise; honor. ¶*~ the hero.* **3.** make (something) more beautiful or splendid. ¶*Moonlight glorified the running water.*

: glo·ri·ous [glɔ́:riəs] *adj.* **1.** full of glory. ¶*a ~ victory.* **2.** giving glory. **3.** magnificient; splendid. ¶*a ~ sunset.* **4.** (*colloq.*) delightful. ¶*We had a ~ time.*

glo·ri·ous·ly [glɔ́:riəsli] *adv.* **1.** magnificently. **2.** (*colloq.*) delightfully.

: glo·ry [glɔ́:ri] *n.* ⓤ (pl. **-ries**) **1.** great praise and honor. **2.** ⓒ anything bringing this. **3.** great beauty; splendor. ¶*the ~ of the sunset.* **4.** ⓤⓒ the best state. ¶*Greece in her ~.*① **5.** praise given in worship, esp. of God. ¶*a hymn to God's ~.* **6.** ⓒ a halo.
 1) *be in one's glory,* be at the best state of one's life.

—ⓝ **1.** 희미한 빛, 깜박임 **2.** 어렴풋한 기억(인식) —ⓥ **1.** 가물가물 비추다 **2.** 희미하게 보이다

—ⓝ **1.** 힐끗 보기 ¶①군중 속에서 그녀를 힐끗 보았다 **2.** 어렴풋이 알기 —타자 [⋯을] 힐끗 보다

—ⓥ 번쩍 빛나다, 번득이다 —ⓝ 번득임, 섬광 ¶the ~ of gold.

—ⓥ 반짝반짝 빛나다, 번쩍이다 —ⓝ 번쩍임

—ⓥ **1.** 반짝반짝 빛나다 ¶①(俚)빛나는 것이라고 반드시 금은 아니다 **2.** [옷 따위가] 번지르르하다 —ⓝ **1.** 번쩍임 **2.** 휘황찬란함, 화려

—ⓝ 황혼; 땅거미

—ⓥ 흡족한 듯이 바라보다; 고소한 듯이 바라보다

—ⓐ **1.** 지구의; 전세계의 **2.** 공 모양의

—ⓝ **1.** 공, 구체(球體) **2.** 지구 **3.** 지(천)구의(儀) ¶①천(지)구의

—ⓝ 복어

—ⓐ **1.** 공 모양의 **2.** 작은 구체(球體)로 된

—ⓝ 작은 구체; 물방울 ¶①땀방울

—ⓝ **1.** 어둠; 암흑 **2.** 슬픔; 우울 ¶①우울한 기분을 풀다 —ⓥ타 어둡게(우울하게) 하다(되다)

—ⓐⓓ **1.** 어둡게 **2.** 음침하게
—ⓐ **1.** 어두운 **2.** 우울한, 슬픈 **3.** 풀이 죽은, 의기소침한

—ⓝ **1.** 신의 영광을 칭송하는 노래 **2.** 송영가(頌榮歌) **3.** 광륜(光輪)

—ⓝ **1.** 신의 영광 찬미; 찬미 받음 **2.** (口) 축하 잔치, 축제

—ⓥ **1.** ⋯에 영광을 더하다, ⋯을 숭상하다 **2.** ⋯을 칭찬하다 **3.** ⋯을 미화(美化)하다

—ⓐ **1.** 영광스러운 **2.** 명예로운 **3.** 장려한, 찬란한 **4.** (口) 유쾌한

—ⓐⓓ **1.** 장려하게 **2.** 유쾌하게

—ⓝ **1.** 명예 **2.** 명예를 가져오는 것 **3.** 장려함, 장관 **4.** 전성(全盛), 절정 ¶①전성기의 그리이스 **5.** 찬미, 송영 **6.** 후광(後光), 광배(光背), 광륜

熟 1)전성기에 있다 2)신을 찬미하다

gloss

2) ***give glory to God***, worship God.
3) ***go to glory***, die.
4) ***Old Glory***, the Stars and Stripes, the national flag of the United States.
5) ***return with glory***, return in triumph.
6) ***send someone to glory***, kill.
—*vi.* (-ried) be proud. 《~ *in* something》
— ⓐ 자랑으로 생각하다

gloss [glɔːs / glɔs] *n.* ⓒ brightness on the surface; a smooth, shining surface. ¶*the ~ of satin.* —*vt.* **1.** make (something) smooth and shining. **2.** make (an error, a fault, etc.) seem right; make (something) seem better than it really is. ¶*~ over one's errors.*① —*vi.* become shiny.
— ⓝ 광택, 윤 — ⓥ 1. …의 광택을 내다 2. …을 그럴싸하게 꾸며대다, 보기 좋게 겉치레하다 ¶①과오를 그럴싸하게 꾸며대다 — ⓐ 윤이 나다

glos·sa·ry [ɡlɑ́səri / ɡlɔ́s-] *n.* (pl. **-ries**) ⓒ a small dictionary or list of special words. ¶*a ~ to Shakespeare.*
— ⓝ [특수어·술어의] 용어 사전, 어해(語解)

gloss·y [ɡlɔ́ːsi / ɡlɔ́si] *adj.* (**gloss·i·er, gloss·i·est**) smooth and shiny. ▷**gloss·i·ly** [-li] *adv.* —**gloss·i·ness** [-nis] *n.*
— ⓐ 광택이 있는

glot·ti·des [ɡlɑ́tidiːz / ɡlɔ́t-] *n.* pl. of **glottis**.

glot·tis [ɡlɑ́tis / ɡlɔ́t-] *n.* ⓒ (pl. **-tis·es** or **-ti·des**) an opening between the vocal cords.
— ⓝ 성문(聲門)

:**glove** [ɡlʌv] *n.* ⓒ **1.** a covering for the hand to keep it warm. **2.** a padded covering to protect the hand in some sports, such as boxing, baseball, etc.
— ⓝ 1. 장갑 2. [야구·복싱의] 글러브

1) ***be hand in*** (or ***and***) ***glove*** (=*be very intimate*) ***with*** *someone*.
2) ***fit like a glove***, fit perfectly.
3) ***handle with*** (***without***) ***gloves***, treat gently (roughly). ¶*I handled her with gloves, because she was in deep grief.*①
4) ***take off the gloves***, argue or contend seriously.
5) ***throw down the glove***, challenge.
—*vt.* cover (a hand) with a glove.
圖 1)…와 밀접한 관계가 있다 2)꼭 맞다 3)…을 부드럽게(거칠게) 다루다 ¶①그녀는 슬픔에 잠겨 있어서 나는 부드럽게 대했다 4)[싸움·언쟁]에 기를 쓰고 대들다 5)…에 도전하다
— ⓥ …에 장갑을 끼다

:**glow** [ɡlou] *n.* ⓒ 《usu. *sing.*》 **1.** brightness. ¶*the ~ of sunset.* **2.** warmth of the body. **3.** flushed look; rosy color of the face. ¶*the ~ of good health on his cheeks.*
all in (or ***of***) ***a glow***, with a flushed look.
—*vi.* **1.** shine with a strong color. **2.** become warm and flushed. **3.** give off light and heat. **4.** burn with the passion of excitement. ¶*~ with anger.*
— ⓝ 1. 빛남 2. 후끈후끈함 3. 얼굴을 붉힘, 홍조(紅潮)
圖 새빨개져서
— ⓐ 1. [빛깔이 타오르듯] 빛나다 2. 기열되어 빛나다; 홍조를 띠다 3. 광선(열)을 내다 4. [감정이] 불타오르다

glow·er [ɡláuər] *vi.* stare angrily. 《~ *at someone*》 ¶*The detective glowered at the robber.*① —*n.* ⓒ an angry look. ▷**glow·er·ing·ly** [-əriŋli] *adv.*
— ⓐ 노려보다 ¶①형사는 도둑을 노려보았다 — ⓝ 성난 얼굴

glow·ing [ɡlóuiŋ] *adj.* **1.** shining with a red or white color of hot metal, etc. **2.** bright. **3.** appearing warm. ¶*~ cheeks.* **4.** eager; animated. ▷**glow·ing·ly** [-li] *adv.*
— ⓐ 1. 백열(白熱)의;새빨갛게 달아오른 2. 선명한, 뚜렷한 3. 홍조를 띤 4. 열중한

glow·worm [ɡlóuwəːrm] *n.* ⓒ an insect that glows in the dark.
— ⓝ 개똥벌레류의 유충

gloze [ɡlouz] *vt.* **1.** explain away. **2.** talk flatteringly.
— ⓥ 1. …을 말로 얼버무리다 2. 아첨하다

glu·cose [ɡlúːkous] *n.* Ⓤ a kind of sugar found in fruit or honey.
— ⓝ 포도당

•**glue** [ɡluː] *n.* Ⓤ **1.** a sticky substance made by boiling the skins and bones of animals. **2.** any similar sticky substance. —*vt.* **1.** stick (things) with glue. 《~ *one thing to another*》 ¶*~ a map to a piece of paper.* **2.** attach firmly.
— ⓝ 1. 아교 2. 접착제 — ⓥ 1. …을 아교로 붙이다 2. 붙어서 떨어지지 않다

glum [ɡlʌm] *adj.* (**glum·mer, glum·mest**) gloomy; sullen.
— ⓐ 우울한; 뚱한, 무뚝뚝한

glut [ɡlʌt] *vt.* (**glut·ted, glut·ting**) fill too full; oversupply. ¶*~ the appetite* / *~ one's eyes*① / *~ the market.* —*n.* ⓒ a full supply; too large a supply.
— ⓥ 잔뜩 먹이다; 지나치게 공급하다 ¶①실컷 …이 나도록 바라보다
— ⓝ 충분; 공급 과다

glu·ten [ɡlúːtn] *n.* Ⓤ a tough, sticky substance found in the flour of wheat.
— ⓝ 부질(麩質)

glu·ti·nous [ɡlúːtinəs] *adj.* sticky.
— ⓐ 끈적끈적한

glut·ton [ɡlʌ́tn] *n.* ⓒ **1.** a person who eats too much. **2.** a person who has a great desire for something. ¶*a*
— ⓝ 1. 대식가 2. 열중하는 사람

~ *of books.*

glut·ton·ous [glʌ́tnəs] *adj.* fond of eating too much. ***be gluttonous of,*** ⓐ eat greedily. ⓑ be absorbed in (something).

—[形] 게걸든, 잘 먹는
[熟] ⓐ…을 게걸스럽게 먹다 ⓑ…에 열중하다, 에 정신을 빼앗기다

glut·ton·ous·ly [glʌ́tnəsli] *adv.* greedily.

—[副] 욕심을 부려

glut·ton·y [glʌ́tni] *n.* [U][C] (pl. **-ton·ies**) the act of eating greedily; the habit of eating too much.

—[名] 대식, 폭식(暴食)

glyc·er·in, -ine [glísərin / glìsəríːn] *n.* [U] a sweet, colorless, thick liquid used in medicines, explosives, etc.

—[名] 글리세린

glyc·er·ol [glísərɔ̀ul, -rɑ̀l / -rɔ̀l] *n.* [U] glycerin. ⇒[N.B.]

—[名] 글리세롤 [N.B.] 글리세린의 학명

gly·co·gen [gláikoudʒèn, +*Brit.* glík-] *n.* [U] a substance found in an animal's body which is changed into sugar when needed.

—[名] 글리코겐

gm., gram[s]; (*Brit.*) gramme[s].

G-man [dʒíːmæ̀n] *n.* [C] (pl. **G-men** [-mèn]) (*U.S. colloq.*) a member of the FBI (=Federal Bureau of Investigation).

—[名]《美口》연방 검찰국 형사, 비밀 경찰원

gnarl [nɑːrl] *n.* [C] a knot on a tree or in wood; a hard, rough lump.

—[名] 나무의 옹이(혹·마디)

gnarled [nɑːrld] *adj.* knotted and twisted; full of knots.

—[形] 비꼬인; 옹이투성이의

gnash [næʃ] *vi., vt.* **1.** strike or grind (the teeth) together. ¶~ *the teeth.*① **2.** bite by grinding the teeth.

—[自][他] **1.** 이를 갈다 ¶①이를 갈다 **2.** 이를 악물다

gnat [næt] *n.* [C] **1.** a small, two-winged insect that has an itch-causing bite. **2.** (*Brit.*) a mosquito.

—[名] **1.** 각다귀 **2.**《英》모기

* **gnaw** [nɔː] *vi., vt.* (**gnawed, gnawed** or **gnawn**) **1.** bite off or eat away with teeth bit by bit. **2.** wear away. **3.** torment.

—[自][他] **1.** 조금씩 물어끊다 **2.** 닳려 없애다 **3.** 괴롭히다

gnawn [nɔːn] *v.* pp. of **gnaw.**

gnome [noum] *n.* [C] an imaginary dwarf who guards treasures of gold, silver, and jewels.

—[名] [지하의 보물을 지킨다고 하는] 난장이

‡ **go** [gou] *vi.* (**went, gone**) **1.** move from one place to another. ¶~ *to the station.* **2.** move away; leave. ¶~ *on a journey* | *She came in the morning and went in the evening.* | *It is time for you to* ~.① **3.** proceed; advance. ¶*This car can* ~ *70 kilometers an hour.*② **4.** pass; pass away. ¶*Summer is going.* **5.** be spent; be used up. ¶*His money goes for drink.*③ **6.** extend; reach. ¶*How far does this road* ~*?* | *Her memory does not* ~ *back that far.*④ **7.** be in motion or action; work. ¶*Can you make this watch* ~*?*⑤ | *There goes the bell.*⑥ **8.** pass from one state to another; become. ¶~ *mad* | ~ *to sleep.* **9.** be broken suddenly; stop being; die. ¶*The mast went in the storm.*⑦ | *She is dead and gone.* **10.** be known; be current. ¶*He goes by the name of Jack.*⑧ | *The rumor went through the village.* **11.** be placed; belong. ¶*This book goes on the top shelf.* **12.** be given. ¶*First prize went to John.*

—[自] **1.** 가다 **2.** 가 버리다, 떠나다, 출발하다 ¶①이제 가실 시간입니다 **3.** 나아가다 ¶②이 차는 시속 70 킬로를 낼 수 있다 **4.** 지나가다 **5.** 쓰이다; 소비되다 ¶③그의 돈은 술값으로 나간다 **6.** 이르다, 미치다; 통하다 ¶④그녀의 기억은 거기까지 미치지 못한다 **7.** 움직이다; 일하다 ¶⑤이 시계를 가게 할 수 있소?/⑥벨이 울리고 있다 **8.** …이 되다 **9.** 뚝 부러지다; 소멸하다; 죽다 ¶⑦폭풍으로 돛대가 부러졌다 **10.** 알려지다; 유포되다 ¶⑧그는 잭이라는 이름으로 알려져 있다 **11.** 놓여지다; 속하다 **12.** 주어지다

1) ***be going to do,*** ⓐ be about to do. ¶*It is going to rain.* ⓑ intend to do; be scheduled to do. ¶*I am going to see him this afternoon.*

2) ***go about,*** ⓐ go here and there. ⓑ begin; start. ¶~ *about one's work.*

3) ***go about to do,*** try to do; make an effort to do.

4) ***go after*** (=*try to get*) *something.*

5) ***go against,*** ⓐ resist; oppose. ⓑ be contrary to (something).

6) ***go ahead,*** go on; proceed.

7) ***go along with,*** (*U.S.*) ⓐ cooperate with; work together with (someone). ⓑ carry out; fulfill.

8) ***go around,*** ⓐ be enough for all. ¶*The food will just* ~ *around.*⑨ ⓑ reach one's destination by a way other than the nearest road.

9) ***go at,*** ⓐ begin; start (work). ⓑ attack.

10) ***go back on,*** (*colloq.*) break (a promise, etc.); betray (one's friend, etc.).

[熟] 1)ⓐ…하려 하고 있다 ⓑ…의 예정(작정)이다 2)ⓐ이리저리 가다 ⓑ…을 시작하다 3)…을 시도하다; …하려고 노력하다 4)…을 얻으려고 하다 5)ⓐ…에 반항하다 ⓑ…와 상반되다 6)앞으로 나아가다; 선행하다 7)《美》ⓐ…와 함께 일하다 ⓑ실행하다 8)ⓐ…에게 모두 돌아가다 ¶⑨음식은 모두에게 돌아갈 만큼 있다 ⓑ멀리 돌아가다 9)ⓐ…을 시작하다 ⓑ…을 공격하다 10)《口》…을 어기다; 배반하다 11)…의 배후(진상)를 조사하다 12)…을 넘다; …을 능가하다 13)ⓐ지나다 ⓑ…에 이끌리다 14)ⓐ가라앉다; 내리다 ⓑ기록되다; 기억되다 ¶⑩그의 이름은 대발명가로서 역사에 남을 것이다 ⓒ조용해지다 ¶⑪바람이 자다 ⓓ패배당하다 15)ⓐ…을 얻으려고 하다

11) ***go behind,*** search for a real or hidden meaning of (someone's words).
12) ***go beyond,*** exceed.
13) ***go by,*** ⓐ pass. ¶*Years ~ by.* ⓑ be guided or led by (something).
14) ***go down,*** ⓐ sink; descend; (of the sun, etc.) set. ⓑ be written as a record; be remembered. ¶*His name will ~ down in history as a great inventor.*⑩ ⓒ calm down. ¶*The wind has gone down.*⑪ ⓓ be defeated.
15) ***go for,*** ⓐ try to get; aim at (something). ⓑ be taken as (something). ⓒ attack.
16) ***go forth,*** be published.
17) ***go in,*** enter; take part in (a game, etc.).
18) ***go in for,*** take up (something) as one's business, hobby, etc.
19) ***go in on*** (or ***with***), take part in (something); join.
20) ***go into,*** ⓐ join; enter. ¶*~ into Parliament.*⑫ ⓑ research; examine; study.
21) ***go off,*** ⓐ burst out; explode. ¶*Firecrackers went off.* ⓑ be held; be done. ⓒ cease; depart.
22) ***go on*** (or ***upon***), continue; proceed. ¶*~ on walking.*
23) ***go out,*** ⓐ come to an end. ⓑ stop burning; be extinguished. ⓒ become outdated.
24) ***go over,*** examine; inspect.
25) ***go through,*** ⓐ experience; endure. ¶*~ through great hardship.*⑬ ⓑ search.
26) ***go through with,*** complete; finish.
27) ***go together,*** harmonize; match.
28) ***go under,*** ⓐ sink. ⓑ fail; be defeated.
29) ***go up,*** rise; mount; increase.
30) ***go with,*** ⓐ accompany; associate. ⓑ match.
31) ***go without*** (=*manage* or *do without*) *something.* ¶*Man cannot ~ without water.*⑭
32) ***It goes without saying that ...,*** It is needless to say that ...

ⓑ…이라 간주되나 ⓒ…을 공격하다 16)출판되다 17)…으로 들어가다; …에 참가하다 18)…에 종사하다; 열중하다 19)…에 참가하다 20)ⓐ…에 끼다, 들어가다 ¶⑫국회의원이 되다 ⓑ조사하다 21)ⓐ폭발하다 ⓑ거행되다 ⓒ끝내다; 가 버리다 22)…을 계속하다; 추진하다 23)ⓐ끝나다 ⓑ꺼지다 ⓒ구식이 되다 24)…을 조사하다 25)ⓐ[괴로움을] 경험하다; 견디다, 참다 ¶⑬큰 곤란을 겪다 ⓑ…을 찾다 26)…을 해내다; 완성하다 27)어울리다; 조화하다 28)ⓐ가라앉다 ⓑ실패하다; 지다 29) 올라가다, 늘다 30)ⓐ…에 수반(동반)하다; 동행하다 ⓑ…에 조화하다 31)…없이 지내다(견디다) ¶⑭인간은 물 없이 살 수 없다 32)…은 말할 것도 없다

—*n.* [U] **1.** the act of going. ¶*the come and ~ of the seasons.*⑮ **2.** energy; spirit. ¶*be full of ~.*
on the go, busy; active.

—[명] **1.** 가기 ¶⑮사철의 바뀜 **2.** 정력, 기력
[熟] 바쁘게; 활발하게

goad [goud] *n.* [C] **1.** a pointed stick for driving cattle. **2.** anything that drives or urges someone to action. **—*vt.*** **1.** drive (cattle) with a goad. **2.** urge (someone) to action. 《~ someone *into doing*; ~ someone *to do*》 ¶*Hunger goaded her into stealing a loaf of bread.*① | *His laughter goaded me to try.*

—[명] **1.** [가축을 모는] 막대기 **2.** 자극물, 격려(물)
—[타] **1.** [가축]을 막대기로 찌르다 **2.** …을 자극(격려)하여 …시키다 ¶①그녀는 배가 고파 한 덩어리의 빵을 훔쳤다

go·a·head [góuəhèd] *adj.* (*colloq.*) pushing; eager.

—[형] 《口》 진취적인

***goal** [goul] *n.* [C] **1.** a place where the course of a race ends. ¶*He will be the first runner to cross the ~.*① **2.** a place through which a ball must be sent in order to score in games, such as football and soccer. **3.** the score thus made. ¶*Our team made a ~.*② **4.** an aim or purpose for which an effort is made. ¶*What is your ~ in life?*③ ▷**goal·less** [-lis] *adj.*

—[명] **1.** 결승점(선) ¶①그가 1착으로 결승점에 들어올 것이다 **2.** [축구 따위의] 고울 **3.** 득점 ¶②우리 티임이 득점을 했다 **4.** 목적, 목표 ¶③당신의 인생 목표는 뭐요?

goal·keep·er [góulkì:pər] *n.* [C] a player who guards a goal in football, soccer, etc.

—[명] [축구 따위의] 고울키이퍼, 문지기

‡goat [gout] *n.* [C] (pl. **goats** or *collectively* **goat**) **1.** a hairy animal with horns and a beard. **2.** (*U.S. colloq.*) a person who is forced to take the blame or punishment for another's deed. ▷**goat·like** [-làik] *adj.*
1) ***act*** (or ***play***) ***the*** [***giddy***] ***goat,*** do a foolish thing.
2) ***get one's goat,*** torment; make (someone) angry. ¶*The constant noisy sounds get my ~.*①
3) ***separate the sheep from the goats,*** distinguish the good from the bad.

—[명] **1.** 염소 **2.** 《美口》 남의 죄를 뒤집어쓰는 사람, 희생
[熟] 1)바보짓을 하다 2)…을 괴롭히다; 성나게 하다 ¶①쉴새 없는 소음이 나를 괴롭혔다 3)선인과 악인을 구별하다

G

goat·ee [goutí:] *n.* [C] a pointed hair on a man's chin like a goat's beard.
—[名] [턱 밑의] 염소수염

goat·skin [góutskìn] *n.* [U] the skin of a goat; leather made from the skin of a goat.
—[名] 염소 가죽

gob·ble¹ [gábl / gɔ́bl] *vi., vt.* swallow quickly or greedily.
gobble up, (*U.S.*) eat up.
—[自][他] 게걸스럽게 먹다(삼키다)
[熟] 《美》 다 먹어 치우다

gob·ble² [gábl / gɔ́bl] *n.* [C] a noise that a male turkey makes in the throat. —*vi.* make this noise.
—[名] 칠면조의 울음 소리 —[自] 칠면조가 울다

gob·bler [gáblər / gɔ́blə] *n.* [C] a male turkey.
—[名] 칠면조의 수컷

go-be·tween [góubitwì:n] *n.* [C] a person who does business for two persons or parties that do not meet each other.
—[名] 매개인, 중개인; 알선자, 거간꾼

gob·let [gáblit / gɔ́b-] *n.* [C] a drinking glass with a base and stem, but with no handle. ⇒fig.
—[名] 굽이 달린 납작한 잔

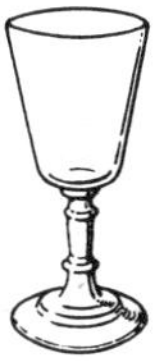
〔goblet〕

gob·lin [gáblin / gɔ́b-] *n.* [C] (in a fable or myth) a mischievous or evil spirit in the form of an ugly-looking dwarf.
—[名] [사람을 해치는] 난장이 마귀

go-by [góubài] *n.* 《usu. *the* ~》 (*colloq.*) the act of going by without notice.
*give someone **the go-by,*** disregard or neglect intentionally.
—[名] 《口》 보고도 못 본 체하고 지나치기
[熟] …을 보고도 못 본 체하다

go·cart [góukà:rt] *n.* [C] **1.** a baby carriage pushed by hand. **2.** a small structure for teaching children to walk. **3.** a light carriage.
—[名] **1.** 유모차 **2.** 보행기 **3.** 소형 자동차

god [gad / gɔd] *n.* [C] **1.** 《*G*-》 the maker and ruler of the universe; Supreme Being; Creator. ¶*Almighty God.* **2.** a being worshiped as having supernatural powers; a deity; a divinity: a male god. ↔goddess ¶*the ~ of day*① / *the ~ of heaven* / *the ~ of the sea*② / *God knows.*③ **3.** an image of a god; an idol. **4.** [C] a person or thing worshipped like a god.
—[名] **1.** 창조주; 하나님 **2.** 신 ¶①태양신 (=Apollo)/②바다의 신(=Neptune)/③신만이 안다, 아무도 모른다 **3.** 신상(神像); 우상 **4.** 숭배받는 사람(것)

god·child [gádtʃàild / gɔ́d-] *n.* [C] (pl. **-chil·dren** [-tʃìldr(ə)n]) a child whom a grown-up person promises, at its baptism, to help in its religious training.
—[名] 대자(代子)(세례식 때에 종교 교육을 보증해 주는 아이)

god·daugh·ter [gáddɔ̀:tər / gɔ́ddɔ̀:tə] *n.* [C] a female godchild.
—[名] 대녀(代女)

god·dess [gádis / gɔ́d-] *n.* [C] **1.** a female god. **2.** a very beautiful or charming woman.
—[名] **1.** 여신 **2.** 절세의 미녀

god·fa·ther [gádfà:ðər / gɔ́dfà:ðə] *n.* [C] a man who promises to help someone else's child in its religious training when the child is baptized.
—[名] 대부(代父)(남의 아이의 세례식 때 종교 교육을 보증하는 사람)

God-fear·ing [gádfìəriŋ] *adj.* fearing God; deeply respectful of God; religious.
—[形] 신을 두려워하는; 경건한

God-for·sak·en [gádfərsèikn] *adj.* **1.** (of a person) abandoned by God; spoiled in character. **2.** (of a place) desolate; lonely.
—[形] **1.** 신에게 버림받은; 타락한 **2.** 황량한

God-giv·en [gádgiv(ə)n / gɔ́d-] *adj.* **1.** given by God. **2.** very welcome.
—[形] **1.** 천부의, 하늘이 내린 **2.** 절호의

God·head [gádhèd / gɔ́d-] *n.* **1.** 《*the* ~》 God. **2.** [U] 《*g*-》 divine nature.
—[名] **1.** 신 **2.** 신성(神性)

god·less [gádlis / gɔ́d-] *adj.* **1.** not believing in God; not religious. **2.** wicked. ▷**god·less·ness** [-nis] *n.*
—[形] **1.** 신앙심이 없는, 신을 믿지 않는 **2.** 사악한

god·like [gádlàik / gɔ́d-] *adj.* **1.** like God or a god; divine. **2.** suitable for God or a god.
—[形] **1.** 신과 같은; 신성(神性)의 **2.** 신에게 어울리는

god·ly [gádli / gɔ́d-] *adj.* (**-li·er, -li·est**) obeying God; pious; divine. ▷**god·li·ness** [-nis] *n.*
—[形] 신을 공경하는, 믿음이 두터운

god·moth·er [gádmʌ̀ðər / gɔ́dmʌ̀ðə] *n.* [C] a woman who promises, at the baptism of a child, to help in its religious training.
—[名] 대모(代母)

god·par·ent [gádpɛ̀ərənt / gɔ́d-] *n.* [C] a godfather or godmother.
—[名] 대부모(代父母)

god·send [gádsènd / gɔ́d-] *n.* [C] a piece of good fortune that comes unexpectedly as if sent by God.
—[名] 하나님의 선물, 뜻밖의 행운, 횡재

god·son [gádsʌ̀n / gɔ́d-] *n.* [C] a male godchild.
—[名] 대자(代子)

God·speed [gádspí:d / gɔ́d-] *n.* [U] [wish for] good fortune of a person going on a journey; success. ⇒[N.B.]
—[名] 성공(행운)의 축원(기도) [N.B.] God speed you.의 준말 ¶①…의 행운

¶*wish* (or *bid*) *someone* ~.①
(안전)을 빌다

go·er [góuər] *n.* [C] a person or thing that goes.
—[名] 가는 사람(것)

Goe·the [gə́:tə], **Johann Wolfgang von** *n.* (1749-1832) a German poet, novelist, dramatist and philosopher.
—[名] 독일의 시인・소설가・극작가・철학자

gog·gle [gágl / gɔ́gl] *n.* **1.** ⟪usu. *pl.*⟫ large eye-glasses to protect the eyes from light, dust, etc. **2.** [C] the act of rolling the eyes to express surprise, fear, etc. —*vi., vt.* roll the eyes.
—[名] 1. 먼지를 막는 안경, 보호 안경 2. [놀라서] 눈을 부릅뜨기 —[自][他] [눈을] 부릅뜨다, 희번덕거리다

⁑**go·ing** [góuiŋ] *n.* [U] **1.** departure. ¶*His ~ was unexpected.* **2.** the condition of ground or land for travelling, walking, riding, etc. **3.** the speed or method of traveling.
—[名] 1. 출발 2. 길의 상태 3. 여행의 속도(방법)

—*adj.* **1.** moving; working. ¶*keep a machine ~ / set a clock ~*① / *It easily got ~.*② **2.** current; (*colloq.*) existing. ¶*the ~ rate.*③
1) ***going on,*** (of time etc.) nearly; almost.
2) ***in going order,*** in a normal condition.
—[形] 1. 진행중인; 활동중인 ¶①시계를 가게 하다/②그것을 쉽게 움직였다 2. 현행의; ⟪口⟫ 현재 있는 ¶③현행 운임(비율)
[熟] 1)[시간 따위] 거의 [다 되어] 2) 이상없이

⁑**gold** [gould] *n.* [U] **1.** a shiny, precious metal of bright-yellow color, used for making coins or jewelry. **2.** coins made of gold. **3.** a large sum of money; wealth. **4.** a precious or pure quality. **5.** the color of gold.
1) ***the age of gold,*** the most flourishing age; the golden age.
2) ***as good as gold,*** (usu. of children) very obedient.
3) ***a heart of gold,*** [a man of] noble, pure heart.
—[名] 1. 금 2. 금화 3. 부(富), 막대한 돈 4. 귀중한 것; 순수한 것 5. 황금빛
[熟] 1)황금 시대 2)아주 유순한 3)아름다운 마음씨(순정)[를 가진 사람]

—*adj.* [made] of gold; like gold; of the color of gold. ¶~ *embargo*① / *the ~ standard.*②
—[形] 금의, 금으로 만든; 금 같은; 황금빛의 ¶①금 수출금지/②금본위

gold digger [⁄ ⁄‿] *n.* **1.** (*colloq.*) a person who digs or seeks for gold. **2.** a woman who tries to get money from men by tricks.
—[名] 1. 금광 탐색자, 사금(砂金)장이 2. 남자를 속여 돈을 후려먹는 여자

gold-dust [góulddʌst] *n.* [U] gold in the form of a fine powder.
—[名] 사금

⁑**gold·en** [góuld(ə)n] *adj.* **1.** [made] of gold. ¶*a ~ chair.* **2.** yielding or containing gold. ¶*The Golden State.*① **3.** having the color of gold; shining like gold. ¶~ *hair.* **4.** excellent; beautiful. ¶*a ~ saying*② / *a ~ voice.* **5.** best; most flourishing. ¶*the ~ age of baseball.*
—[形] 1. 금의, 금으로 만든 2. 금이 나는; 금을 함유하는 ¶①캘리포오니아 주의 별명 3. 금빛의(으로 빛나는) 4. 우수한; 아름다운 ¶②금언(金言) 5. 전성기의; 번영하는

gold·en·rod [góuld(ə)nràd / -rɔ̀d] *n.* [C] a tall autumn-blooming plant with many small yellow flowers.
—[名] 메역취속(屬)의 식물

gold·finch [góuldfìntʃ] *n.* [C] a small bright-colored song-bird.
—[名] 방울새류

gold·fish [góuldfìʃ] *n.* [C] (pl. **-fish·es** or *collectively* **-fish**) a reddish-golden-colored fish living in fresh water.
—[名] 금붕어

gold leaf [⁄ ⁄] *n.* gold beaten into very thin sheets.
—[名] 금박

gold mine [⁄ ⁄] *n.* **1.** a mine that yields gold. **2.** a source of something profitable.
—[名] 1. 금광 2. 보고(寶庫)

gold·smith [góuldsmìθ] *n.* [C] a person whose work is making things of gold.
—[名] 금 세공인

***golf** [gɑlf, gɔ:lf / gɔlf] *n.* [U] an outdoor game played with a small, hard, rubber ball and a set of long-handled clubs. —*vi.* play this game.
—[名] 골프 —[自] 골프를 하다

golf·er [gálfər, gɔ́:l- / gɔ́lfə] *n.* [C] a person who plays golf.
—[名] 골프를 하는 사람

Gol·go·tha [gálgəθə / gɔ́l-] *n.* **1.** the place where Jesus Christ was killed on a cross. **2.** [C] ⟪*g*-⟫ a burial place.
—[名] 1. 골고다의 언덕 2. 묘지

go·losh [gəláʃ / -lɔ́ʃ] *n.* =galosh.

gon·do·la [gándələ / gɔ́n-] *n.* [C] a long, narrow boat with high, pointed ends, rowed with an oar, used in Venice. ⇒fig.
—[名] 곤돌라

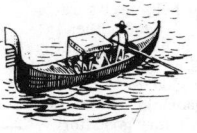

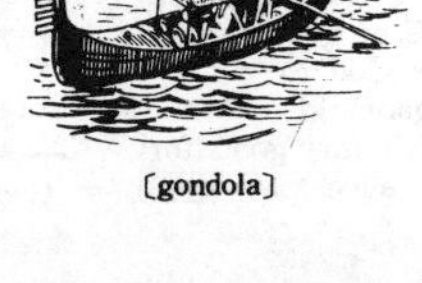
〔gondola〕

gon·do·lier [gàndəlíər / gɔ̀ndəlíə] *n.* [C] a person who rows a gondola.
—[名] 곤돌라의 사공

⁑**gone** [gɔ(:)n] *v.* pp. of **go.**

G

gong

—*adj.* **1.** past; lost. ¶*a man ~ forty years of age.* **2.** deceased; dead. **3.** ruined; hopeless. ¶*a ~ case.*① **4.** weak and faint. ¶*a ~ feeling.*
be gone on (=*be in love with*) *someone.* (*colloq.*) ¶*He is ~ on her.*

gong [gɔːŋ, gɑŋ / gɔŋ] *n.* ⓒ a bell, shaped like a disc.

: good [gud] *adj.* (**bet·ter, best**) ↔bad **1.** excellent; having fine qualities. ¶*~ tea.* **2.** well-behaved; honest. ¶*a ~ boy / a ~ wife / lead a ~ life.* **3.** kind. ¶*be ~ to one's neighbors.* **4.** useful; efficient; suitable. ¶*~ for the health / ~ for nothing.*① **5.** happy; enjoyable; agreeable. ¶*~ news / have a ~ time [of it].*② **6.** clever; able; skillful. ¶*a ~ dancer / be ~ at tennis.* **7.** healthy; strong; well. ¶*~ eyesight / feel ~.* **8.** real; reasonable. ¶*a ~ excuse / She had indeed ~ reason to get up early this morning.* **9.** reliable; dependable; responsible. ¶*~ advice / ~ sense.* **10.** sufficient; considerable. ¶*a ~ day's work*③ */ make ~ progress.* **11.** 《the ~》 well-behaved people.
1) *as good as,* almost; practically. ¶*He is as ~ as dead.*④ 　　　　　　　　　　　[*~ and wise.*]
2) *good and,* very; completely; thoroughly. ¶*She is*
3) *make good,* ⓐ repay; replace. ⓑ fulfill; succeed in doing.
—*n.* ⓤ **1.** an act that is helpful; benefit; advantage. ¶*do ~ / I am saying this for your ~.* **2.** merit; good point. **3.** 《*pl.*》 things for selling or buying; merchandise. ¶*goods in stock / dress goods.* **4.** 《*pl.*》 things owned; possessions; property.
1) *for good [and all],* forever; permanently; finally.
2) *to the good,* as a profit, benefit, or advantage.

: good-by, -bye [gùdbái] *interj.* farewell! —*n.* ⓒ a word spoken when parting from another; a farewell.
say good-by, take leave. ¶*I must say ~ now.*

good-for-noth·ing [gúdfərnʌθiŋ] *adj.* worthless; useless. —*n.* ⓒ a worthless or useless person.

good-heart·ed [gúdháːrtid] *adj.* kind; generous. ▷**good-heart·ed·ly** [-li] *adv.* —**good-heart·ed·ness** [-nis] *n.*

good-hu·mored, *Brit.* **-moured** [gúdhjúːmərd] *adj.* cheerful; amiable. ▷**good-hu·mored·ly** [-li] *adv.*

good·ish [gúdiʃ] *adj.* pretty good; fairly great; considerable. 　　　　　　　　　　　　　　　　[beauty.]

good·li·ness [gúdlinis] *n.* ⓤ the state of being goodly;

good-look·ing [gúdlúkiŋ] *adj.* attractive; beautiful; handsome in appearance.

* **good·ly** [gúdli] *adj.* (**-li·er, -li·est**) **1.** excellent; fine. **2.** good-looking; handsome. ¶*a ~ gentleman.* **3.** considerable. ¶*a ~ sum of money.*

* **good-na·tured** [gúdnéitʃərd] *adj.* kindly; cheerful; agreeable. ▷**good-na·tured·ly** [-li] *adv.*

: good·ness [gúdnis] *n.* ⓤ **1.** the state of being good; virtue. **2.** kindness; friendliness. ¶*She had the ~ to lend me the money.*① **3.** the best part. ¶*the ~ of meat.*
1) *for goodness' sake,* for God's (Heaven's) sake.
2) *Goodness knows,* Nobody knows.
—*interj.* an exclamation of surprise. ⇒[N.B.] ¶*Goodness [gracious]! ; Oh my ~!*② 　　　　　　　　[able.]

good-tem·pered [gúdtémpərd] *adj.* good-natured; ami-

* **good will** [⌒ ⌒] *n.* **1.** kindly or friendly feeling; kindness; willingness. **2.** (*Commercial*) the popularity or reputation of a business, shop, etc.

good·y [gúdi] *n.* ⓒ (*pl.* **good·ies**) **1.** 《usu. *pl.*》 sweetmeat; candy. **2.** a person who pretends to be virtuous.

goody

—⊛ **1.** 지나간; 사라진 **2.** 죽은 **3.** 영락한, 가망없는; 틀린 ¶①절망적인 것; 가망없는 환자 **4.** 정신을 잃은, 까라진

⊚ (口)…에 홀딱 반하다
—⊛ 징; 접시 모양의 초인종

—⊛ **1.** 훌륭한; 좋은 **2.** 행실 바른; 성실한, 선량한 **3.** 친절한 **4.** 쓸모 있는, 알맞은 ¶①아무 쓸모도 없는 **5.** 행복한; 유쾌한, 기분 좋은 ¶②즐거운 시간을 보내다 **6.** 영리한; 능숙한; 솜씨 있는 **7.** 건강한; 힘센, 튼튼한 **8.** 그럴듯한, 정당한 **9.** 신용할 수 있는 **10.** 풍부한; 충분한; 상당한 ¶③꼬박 하루 걸리는 일 **11.** 선인(善人)

照 1) 거의 …이나 마찬가지 ¶④그는 죽은 거나 마찬가지다 2) 충분히; 완전히; 매우 3) ⓐ메우다, 보충하다; 지불하다 ⓑ이행하다; 성공하다

—⊛ **1.** 이익; 득 **2.** 장점 **3.** 상품; 물품 **4.** 재산; 동산

照 1) 영원히; 이것을 마지막으로 2) 이익으로서

—⊛ 안녕히 —⊛ 작별 인사, 하직

照 작별을 고하다
—⊛ 쓸모없는, 무용의 —⊛ 건달

—⊛ 친절한, 관대한

—⊛ 기분이 좋은

—⊛ 꽤 좋은; 상당한

—⊛ 꽤 좋음; 아름다움
—⊛ 매력적인; 미모의

—⊛ **1.** 훌륭한, 뛰어난 **2.** 미모의 **3.** 상당한, 꽤 많은

—⊛ 친절한, 상냥한, 기분이 좋은

—⊛ **1.** 좋음, 선량, 미덕 **2.** 친절 ¶① 그녀는 친절하게도 돈을 빌려주었다 **3.** 가장 좋은 곳

照 1) 제발, 부탁이니 2) 아무도 모른다, 누가 알 게 뭐냐
—⊛ 어렵쇼!, 저런! [N.B.] God 대신으로 씀 ¶②저런!, 어렵쇼!
—⊛ 얌전한, 상냥한
—⊛ **1.** 호의; 친절; 친선 **2.** (商) 신용

—⊛ **1.** 캔디, 과자 **2.** 도덕가(선인)인 체하는 사람

—*interj.* an exclamation of pleasure. —*adj.* (**good·i·er, good·i·est**) pretending to be virtuous.
—[감] 야아, 근사하다!, 신난다! —[형] 도덕가(선인)인 체하는

⁑ **goose** [gu:s] *n.* [C] (pl. **geese** →3.) **1.** a web-footed, flat-billed water bird with a long neck; a female goose. ⇒[N.B.] ¶*a wild* ~① / (*proverb*) *kill the* ~ *that lays the golden eggs*② / (*proverb*) *The* ~ *hangs high.*③ **2.** a silly person. **3.** (pl. **gooses**) a tailor's smoothing iron with a long curved handle like a goose's neck.
—[명] **1.** 거위; 거위 암컷 [N.B.] 수컷은 gander ¶①기러기/②(俚)목전의 이익을 탐하다가 장래의 큰 이익을 망치다/③(俚)만사가 잘 돼 간다 **2.** 바보, 얼간이 **3.** 양복점의 다리미

cook someone's ***goose,*** ruin someone's reputation, plan, etc. ¶*The scandal will cook her* ~.
[숙] …의 기회(계획·희망)를 망쳐 놓다

goose·ber·ry [gú:sbèri, gú:z- / gúzb(ə)ri] *n.* [C] (pl. **-ries**) a small, sour berry, used to make pies, jam, etc.; the thorny bush that this berry grows on.
—[명] (植) 구즈베리[나무]

goose flesh [ˊ ˋ] *n.* a rough condition of the skin caused by cold, fear, shock, etc.
—[명] 소름

G.O.P. Grand Old Party; the Republican Party.
—(略) 미국 공화당

go·pher [góufər] *n.* [C] **1.** a ratlike animal with large cheek bags. **2.** a ground tortoise.
—[명] **1.** [미국산] 뒤쥐 **2.** 땅거북의 일종

gore¹ [gɔ:r] *n.* [U] thick or clotted blood.
—[명] 엉긴 피, 핏덩어리

gore² [gɔ:r] *vt.* wound (someone) with a horn or tusk.
—[타] …을 찌르다

gore³ [gɔ:r] *n.* [C] a long, triangular piece of cloth put or made in a garment, sail, etc., to change its width or shape. —*vt.* put or make a gore in (something).
—[명] [돛·스커어트·우산 따위의] 삼각천 —[타] …에 삼각천을 대다

gorge [gɔ:rdʒ] *n.* [C] **1.** a deep, narrow valley, usu. with steep, rocky walls. **2.** the act of eating greedily. **3.** contents of the stomach. **4.** a feeling of disgust. **5.** a mass blocking up a passage.
—[명] **1.** 협곡 **2.** 폭식(暴食), 대식 **3.** 위 속의 음식물 **4.** 불쾌, 메스꺼움 **5.** 통로를 막는 것

1) ***make someone's gorge rise,*** cause someone to feel sick with disgust or to feel angry.
2) ***rouse*** (or ***stir***) ***the gorge,*** make (someone) angry.
[숙] 1)…을 메스껍게 하다, 불쾌한 느낌을 갖게 하다 2)…을 성나게 하다

—*vi.* eat greedily. —*vt.* (usu. *in passive* or *reflexively*) stuff (one's stomach) with food; swallow (something) greedily. ¶~ *oneself with beefsteak.*
—[자] 게걸스럽게 먹다 —[타] 잔뜩 먹이다; …을 게걸스럽게 쑤셔 넣다

• **gor·geous** [gɔ́:rdʒəs] *adj.* rich in color; magnificent. ¶*a* ~ *sunset.* ▷**gor·geous·ness** [-nis] *n.*
—[형] 화려한, 호화로운, 눈부신, 찬란한, 훌륭한

gor·geous·ly [gɔ́:rdʒəsli] *adv.* in a gorgeous manner; splendidly; beautifully.
—[부] 멋지게, 호화롭게, 아름답게

gor·get [gɔ́:rdʒit] *n.* [C] **1.** a piece of armor to protect the throat. **2.** a veil to protect the neck and breast worn by women in the Middle Ages.
—[명] **1.** [갑옷의] 목가림 **2.** 목·가슴 가리개

go·ril·la [gəríla] *n.* [C] the largest of the manlike apes, living in Africa.
—[명] 고릴라

gor·mand [gɔ́:rmənd] *n.* =gourmand.

gor·mand·ize [gɔ́:rməndàiz] *vi., vt.* eat very greedily; gorge.
—[자][타] [···을] 게걸스럽게 먹다

gorse [gɔ:rs] *n.* [U] (esp. *Brit.*) a prickly shrub with yellow flowers.
—[명] (英) 가시금작화

gor·y [gɔ́:ri] *adj.* (**gor·i·er, gor·i·est**) bloody. ▷**gori·ly** [-li] *adv.* —**gor·i·ness** [-nis] *n.*
—[형] 피투성이의

gosh [gɑʃ / gɔʃ] *interj.* an exclamation of surprise; by God.
—[감] 이크!, 아뿔싸!, 맹세코!

gos·ling [gázliŋ / gɔ́z-] *n.* [C] **1.** a young goose. **2.** a foolish, inexperienced person.
—[명] **1.** 거위 새끼 **2.** 애송이, 풋나기

• **gos·pel** [gásp(ə)l / gɔ́s-] *n.* [C] **1.** the teaching of Jesus and the Apostles. **2.** (usu. *the G-*) any one of the first four books of the New Testament. ⇒[N.B.] **3.** (usu. *the G-*) any selected part of these books. **4.** (*colloq.*) anything earnestly believed as a guide for action. ¶*the* ~ *of temperance.*① **5.** absolute truth.
—[명] **1.** 복음, 그리스도교의 교리 **2.** 복음서 [N.B.] 마태복음·마가복음·누가복음·요한복음 중의 하나 **3.** 복음서 중의 일절 **4.** 행동에 대한 신조 ¶①금주주의 **5.** 절대적 진리

1) ***preach the gospel,*** give a religious sermon.
2) ***take something as gospel,*** believe something to be true.
[숙] 1)전도하다 2)…을 진실이라 여기다

gos·sa·mer [gásəmər / gɔ́səmə] *n.* **1.** [C] a thread of cobweb on grass or in the air. **2.** [U][C] a very thin, light, soft cloth. **3.** [C] a coat made of this cloth. **4.** [U][C] anything very light and thin. —*adj.* very
—[명] **1.** 거미줄 **2.** 얇고 가벼운 천; 사(紗) **3.** 얇은 천의 외투 **4.** 섬세한 것 —[형] 얇고 가벼운

light and thin.

* **gos·sip** [gɑ́sip / gɔ́s-] *n.* **1.** [U] idle talk and rumors about other people. **2.** [C] a person who talks idly about other people. **—***vi.* talk or chatter idly about other people. ¶ *~ about the neighbors.* ▷**gos·sip·er** [-ər] *n.*

—[名] 1. 세상 이야기, 남의 소문, 잡담 2. 남의 소문을 좋아하는 사람 —[自] 소문 이야기(잡담)를 하다

⁑ **got** [gɑt / gɔt] *v.* pt. and pp. of **get**.

Goth [gɑθ / gɔθ] *n.* [C] **1.** a member of a Teutonic tribe that conquered the Roman Empire in the third, fourth, and fifth centuries. **2.** an uncivilized person; a barbarian.

—[名] 1. 고오트 사람 2. 야만인

Goth·am *n.* **1.** [gɑ́θəm, góuθəm / góuθəm, gɔ́θəm // → 2.] (*U.S.*) New York City. **2.** [gɑ́təm / góutəm] an English village whose inhabitants were said to be very foolish. ***wise men of Gotham,*** foolish people.

—[名] 1.《美》 뉴욕시 2. 바보의 마을(주민이 모두 바보였다는 영국의 전설상의 마을)
[熟] 바보들

Goth·ic [gɑ́θik / gɔ́θ-] *n.* [U] **1.** a style of architecture with pointed arches and high, steep roofs. **2.** the language of the Goths. **3.** (*U.S.*) a kind of type used in printing. **—***adj.* **1.** of Gothic architecture. **2.** of the Goths or their language. **3.** uncivilized; barbarous. **4.** medieval.

—[名] 1. 고딕식 건축 2. 고오트 말 3. 고딕체 활자 —[形] 1. 고딕 건축의 2. 고오트[사람 · 말]의 3. 미개한; 야만의 4. 중세의

got·ten [gɑ́tn / gɔ́tn] *v.* pp. of **get**.

gouge [gaudʒ] *n.* [C] **1.** an instrument with a curved blade for cutting holes. **2.** a hole made by a gouge. **3.** (*U.S. colloq.*) a trick. **—***vt.* **1.** cut with a gouge. **2.** dig out. 《*~ out* something》 **3.** (*U.S. colloq.*) trick.

—[名] 1. 둥근 끌 2. 둥근 끌로 판 구멍 3.《美口》 사기 —[他] 1. …을 둥근 끌로 파다 2. …을 도려내다 3.《美口》 …을 속이다

gourd [guərd] *n.* [C] a hard-shelled fruit of the melon family; the dried shell of this fruit, used for cups, etc.

—[名] 호리병박[의 열매]; 그것을 말려 만든 그릇

gour·mand [gúərmənd] *n.* [C] a person who is fond of good eating.

—[名] 미식가

gout [gaut] *n.* [U] 《often *the ~*》 a painful swelling of the joints, esp. of the foot.

—[名] 통풍(痛風)

gout·y [gáuti] *adj.* (**gout·i·er, gout·i·est**) **1.** suffering from gout. **2.** of gout. **3.** causing gout. ▷**gout·i·ness** [-nis] *n.*

—[形] 1. 통풍에 걸린 2. 통풍의 3. 통풍을 일으키는

⁑ **gov·ern** [gʌ́vərn] *vt.* **1.** rule; manage; direct. ¶ *~ the people / ~ a school.* **2.** influence; guide; determine. ¶ *~ someone's choice.* **3.** control; restrain. ¶ *~ one's passions.* **—***vi.* be a ruler. ¶ *The queen reigns, but does not ~.*

—[他] 1. …을 통치하다; 관리하다; 제어하다 2. …에 영향을 미치다; …을 좌우하다; 결정하다 3. …을 억제하다 —[自] 지배 통치하다, 관리하다

gov·ern·a·ble [gʌ́vərnəbl] *adj.* able to govern.

—[形] 다스릴 수 있는

gov·ern·ess [gʌ́vərnis] *n.* [C] a woman who teaches children in their own home.

—[名] 여자 가정교사

gov·ern·ing [gʌ́vərniŋ] *adj.* having the right to govern.

—[形] 통치권을 가진

⁑ **gov·ern·ment** [gʌ́vər(n)mənt] *n.* **1.** [U] control; management. ¶ *good* (*bad*) *~ / school ~.* **2.** [C] 《sometimes *G-*》 the body of persons ruling a country. ¶ *a ~ officer / the United States ~.* **3.** [C] a system of ruling. ¶ *a democratic ~.* **4.** [U] (*Grammar*) the influence of one word which determines the case or mood of another.

—[名] 1. 관리; 통치; 경영 2. 정부 3. 정체(政體) 4.《文法》 지배

gov·ern·men·tal [gʌ̀vərnméntl] *adj.* of government.

—[形] 정치의; 정부의

⁑ **gov·er·nor** [gʌ́vərnər] *n.* [C] **1.** a person who is elected as head of a state of the United States or is appointed head of a British colony. **2.** a person who manages or directs a club, society, etc. **3.** the part of a machine that controls the speed of motion. ¶ *an electric ~.*

—[名] 1. [주]지사; 총독 2. 총재; 관리자 3. 속도 조절기

governor general [ˊ-- ˊ--] *n.* (pl. **governors ~** or **~ generals**) a chief of governors.

—[名] 총독

gov·er·nor·ship [gʌ́vərn(ə)ʃip] *n.* [U] the position of a governor.

—[名] 지사(장관 · 총재 등)의 직위(지위)

⁑ **gown** [gaun] *n.* [C] **1.** a woman's dress. ¶ *an evening ~.* **2.** a long, loose robe which judges, priests, scholars, etc. wear to show their position, profession, etc. **3.** a nightgown or a dressing gown. **4.** 《*collectively*》 members of a university.

—[名] 1. 부인복 2. 정복, 성직복, 법관복, 가운 3. 잠옷; 화장복; 실내복 4. 대학의 사람들(교수 · 학생 따위)

G

1) ***arms and gown,*** war and peace.
2) ***take the gown,*** become a priest or a lawyer.
—*vi., vt.* put on a gown.

[熟] 1)전쟁과 평화 2)목사(변호사)가 되다
—[自][他] 가운을 입다

* **grab** [græb] *vt., vi.* (**grabbed, grab·bing**) **1.** seize suddenly; snatch. 《~ *at* something》 ¶*He grabbed me by the collar.*① | *He grabbed at her purse.* **2.** take possession of (something) by unlawful methods. **—*n.*** [C] **1.** the act of seizing suddenly. **2.** something grabbed. **3.** a machine used for lifting or moving heavy articles.

—[他][自] 1.[…을] 움켜쥐다 ¶①그는 내 멱살을 움켜잡았다 2.가로채다, 약탈하다 —[名] 1.움켜쥐기 2.움켜쥔 것 3.[흙 따위를 치우는] 그랩

1) ***have the grab on,*** (*colloq.*) be in a better position than someone else.
2) ***make a grab at,*** suddenly seize (something).

[熟] 1)…보다 유리한 지위를 차지하다 2)…을 잡아채다

** **grace** [greis] *n.* [U] **1.** beauty of action or manner; delicacy; elegance. ¶*the ~ of action.* **2.** good will; kindness. ¶*an act of ~ | by special ~.*① **3.** the kindness of God. ¶*the ~ of God.* **4.** a period of time given beyond the fixed date. ¶*give someone two days' ~.*② **5.** 《sometimes *a* ~》 a short prayer of thanks at table. ¶*say ~.* **6.** 《*pl.*》 good points; charms. ¶*a girl full of pleasant graces.*

—[名] 1.[성질·태도의] 기품; 우아; 예의, 예절 2.호의; 친절 ¶①특별한 호의로 3.신의 은총; 하늘의 은혜 4.기한의 유예 ¶②이틀간의 유예를 주다 5.[식전·식후의] 감사 기도 6.장점; 매력

1) ***fall from grace,*** do wrong; commit a sin.
2) ***have the grace to do,*** be so kind as to do.
3) ***in the bad graces of*** (=*disfavored or disliked by*) *someone.*
4) ***in the good graces of*** (=*favored or liked by*) *someone.*
5) ***with*** [*a*] ***bad grace,*** unpleasantly; unwillingly.
6) ***with good grace,*** pleasantly; willingly.
—*vt.* give favor or honor to (someone or something). ¶*She graced the party with her presence.*③

[熟] 1)못된 짓을 하다; 종교상의 죄를 짓다 2)기특(친절)하게도 …하는 아량이 있다 3)…의 미움을 사서 4)…에게 호감을 사서 5)마지 못해, 울며 겨자먹기로 6)기꺼이, 자진하여
—[他]…에게 명예를 주다; 영광을 주다 ¶③그녀는 그 모임의 명예를 위해 참석했다

* **grace·ful** [gréisf(u)l] *adj.* having or showing grace; elegant. ▷**grace·ful·ness** [-nis] *n.*

—[形] 우아한, 얌전한

grace·ful·ly [gréisfuli] *adv.* in a graceful manner.

—[副] 우아하게, 얌전하게

* **gra·cious** [gréiʃəs] *adj.* **1.** graceful; courteous. **2.** merciful; kindly. ¶*a ~ king.* **—*interj.*** an exclamation of surprise.

—[形] 1.우아한, 정중한 2.인정 있는; 친절한 —[感] 놀람의 소리

gra·cious·ly [gréiʃəsli] *adv.* in a gracious manner.

—[副] 정중하게; 은혜 깊게

gra·cious·ness [gréiʃəsnis] *n.* [U] elegance; mercy; kindness.

—[名] 우아; 자비; 친절

gra·da·tion [grədéiʃ(ə)n] *n.* [C] [U] **1.** a gradual change from one thing to another. ¶*the ~ of color in the rainbow.*① **2.** 《usu. *pl.*》 steps, stages, or degrees in a series. ¶*~ between right and wrong.*② **3.** the act of arranging into a series.

—[名] 1.서서히 변화하기 ¶①무지개 빛의 변화 2.순서; 단계 ¶②선과 악 사이의 단계 3.순서를 매기기

* **grade** [greid] *n.* [C] **1.** a class or year in school. ¶*the first ~.* **2.** a step or stage in a course or process. **3.** a degree in rank, quality, order, etc. **4.** a class of persons or things of the same degree. **5.** 《*the ~s*》 (*U.S.*) an elementary school. **6.** (*U.S.*) a number or letter showing a pupil's skill in school work. (cf. *Brit.* mark) **7.** a slope of a road, railroad track, etc.

—[名] 1.학년; 학급 2.단계 3.등급 4.같은 계급의 사람(것) 5.《美》 국민학교 6.《美》 성적, 시험점수 7.구배(句配), 비탈

1) ***at grade,*** on the same level.
2) ***on the down*** (***up***) ***grade,*** ⓐ going down (up). ⓑ getting worse (better).
3) ***make the grade,*** ⓐ ascend a slope. ⓑ overcome difficulties; succeed.
—*vt.* **1.** classify. **2.** make (grounds, etc.) even or more level. **—*vi.*** take an indicated rank or position.

[熟] 1)동일 평면에서 2)ⓐ내리받이(치받이)에서 ⓑ쇠잔(번영)하여 3)ⓐ비탈을 오르다 ⓑ곤란을 극복하다, 잘 돼가다
—[他] 1.…을 유별하다 2.…을 평평하게 하다 —[自] 등급이 매겨져 있다

grade crossing [∠ ∠–] *n.* a place where two roads or tracks cross on the same level.

—[名] 수평 교차점

grad·er [gréidər] *n.* [C] **1.** a person or thing that grades. **2.** (*U.S.*) a person who is in a certain grade at school.

—[名] 1.등급 매기는 사람; 땅 고르는 기계 2.《美》 …학년생

gra·di·ent [gréidiənt] *n.* [C] **1.** a slope; the rate of inclination. **2.** (*Physics*) the rate at which temperature, pressure, etc. changes.

—[名] 1.경사; 구배 2.《理》 [온도·기압 따위의] 변화율(도)

gradual

* **grad·u·al** [grǽdʒu(ə)l] *adj.* moving by degrees; gentle and slow.
  — ⓐ 차츰…하는; 점진적인
* **grad·u·al·ly** [grǽdʒu(ə)li] *adv.* little by little.
  — ⓓ 차츰차츰
* **grad·u·ate** *v.* [grǽdʒuèit, *Brit.* -dju- ‖ → *n., adj.*] *vt.* **1.** permit (someone) to leave school after completing a course of study. ⇒N.B. ¶*Tokyo University graduated 2,000 students.* **2.** mark (a flask, tube, etc.) with regular divisions. **3.** classify (things) into grades according to size, quality, etc. —*vi.* **1.** complete a course of study. (*~ from* university, etc.) ¶*He graduated from Yale.* **2.** receive a degree.
  —*n.* [grǽdʒuit, -dʒuèit] *n.* ⓒ a person who has graduated.
  —*adj.* [grǽdʒuit] **1.** having received a diploma. **2.** for a graduate. ¶*a ~ school.*①
  — ⓑ 1. …을 졸업시키다 N.B. 영국에서는 대학에, 미국에서는 모든 학교에 씀 2. …에 눈금을 매기다 3. …에 등급을 매기다 — ⓐ 1. 졸업하다 2. 자격을 따다

  — ⓒ 졸업생
  — ⓐ 1. 졸업한 2. 졸업생을 위한 ¶① 대학원
* **grad·u·a·tion** [grædʒuéiʃ(ə)n, +*Brit.* -dju-] *n.* ⓤ **1.** the act of completing a course of study. **2.** a ceremony at which diplomas are received. ¶*~ exercises.*① **3.** (*pl.*) a mark or marks to show degrees for measuring.
  — ⓒ 1. 졸업 2. 졸업식 ¶①졸업식 3. 눈금

graft¹ [græft / gra:ft] *vt.* **1.** insert (a shoot, bud, etc.) into another tree so that it will grow there. **2.** (*Medicine*) move (a piece of skin, bone, etc.) from one part of the body to another so that it will grow there.
  — ⓑ 1. …에 접목(接木)하다 2. [피부·뼈 따위]를 이식하다
  —*n.* ⓒ **1.** the act of grafting. **2.** the part that is grafted. ▷**graft·er** [-ər] *n.*
  — ⓒ 1. 접목; 식피(植皮), 조직 이식 2. 접목한 부분

graft² [græft / gra:ft] *n.* ⓒⓤ (*U.S.*) **1.** the act of gaining money, etc. through the wrong use of one's position. **2.** the money, property, etc. thus acquired. —*vi., vt.* obtain (money, property, etc.) by graft. ▷**graft·er** [-ər] *n.*
  — ⓒ 1. 독직(瀆職), 수회 2. 부정 소득, 뇌물 — ⓐⓑ 수뢰하다

grail [greil] *n.* ⓒ a cup; a dish.
  — ⓒ 술잔; 접시

: **grain** [grein] *n.* ⓒ **1.** ⓤ (*collectively*) the seed of wheat, corn, oats, or rice. **2.** a very small and hard piece, such as sand, salt and sugar. **3.** the smallest possible amount. ¶*There is not a ~ of truth in what he says.*① **4.** the small unit of weight; 0.0648 grams. **5.** ⓤ natural character. ¶*a man of coarse ~ / against the ~.*②
  —*vt.* form (something) into grain.
  — ⓒ 1. 낟알; 곡물, 곡식 2. 알갱이, 입자(粒子) 3. 극소량; 아주 조금 ¶①그의 말에는 진실이라곤 눈물만큼도 없다 4. 1그레인(미량 단위) 5. 기질; 성질; 성벽 ¶②성미에 맞지 않게
  — ⓑ …을 알갱이 [모양]으로 하다

* **gram**, *Brit.* **gramme** [græm] *n.* ⓒ a unit of weight in the metric system.
  — ⓒ 그램
* **gram·mar** [grǽmər] *n.* ⓤ **1.** the study of forms of words and the structure of sentences. **2.** ⓒ a book on this subject. **3.** ⓤ statements about the use of words.
  — ⓒ 1. 문법 2. 문법책 3. 어법

gram·mar·i·an [grəméəriən] *n.* ⓒ a person who specializes in grammar.
  — ⓒ 문법학자

grammar school [⌞-⌝ ⌞⌝] *n.* **1.** (*U.S.*) an elementary school. **2.** (*Brit.*) a secondary school preparing for college. ⇒N.B.
  — ⓒ 1. (美) 국민학교 2. (英) 중학교 N.B. 옛날은 라틴어가 중요 학과, 지금은 public school에 해당하는 중학교

gram·mat·i·cal [grəmǽtik(ə)l] *adj.* **1.** according to the rules of grammar. **2.** of grammar. ¶*a ~ mistake.*①
  — ⓐ 1. 문법적으로 옳은 2. 문법의 ¶①문법상의 잘못

gramme [græm] *n.* (*Brit.*) =gram.

gram·o·phone [grǽməfòun] *n.* ⓒ (*Brit.*) a machine for reproducing sounds from records. (cf. *U.S.* phonograph)
  — ⓒ (英) 축음기

gran·a·ry [grǽnəri] *n.* ⓒ (pl. **-ries**) a place or building for storing grain.
  — ⓒ 곡물 창고, 곡창

* **grand** [grænd] *adj.* **1.** large and fine; splendid; magnificent. ¶*a ~ spectacle / a ~ house.* **2.** great; important. ¶*a ~ total.*② **3.** main; principal. ¶*the ~ staircase*② */ the grandstand.*③ **4.** dignified; noble; showing high social standing. ¶*the ~ style*④ */ a ~ manner.*④ **5.** (*colloq.*) very satisfactory. ¶*We had a ~ time yesterday.* **6.** complete; full. ¶*a ~ total.*⑥
  — ⓐ 1. 장려한; 당당한 2. 커다란; 중대한 ¶①대실패 3. 주요한 ¶②정면 계단/③특별 관람석 4. 위엄있는; 고귀한; 젠체하는 ¶④장중한 작품/⑤젠체하는 태도 5. 말할 나위 없는 6 전부의 ¶⑥총계

grand·aunt [grǽndæ̀nt / -à:nt] *n.* ⓒ the aunt of one's father or mother.
  — ⓒ 종조모, 대고모

: **grand·child** [grǽn(d)tʃàild] *n.* ⓒ (pl. **-chil·dren** [-tʃìldr(ə)n]) the child of one's son or daughter. ¶*a great-grand-*
  — ⓒ 손자 ¶①증손/②현손

*child*① / *a great-great-grandchild.*②

grand·dad [grǽn(d)dæ̀d] *n.* [C] (*child's word*) a grandfather. —[명] 할아버지

:grand·daugh·ter [grǽn(d)dɔ̀:tər] *n.* [C] the daughter of one's son or daughter. —[명] 손녀

gran·dee [grændí:] *n.* [C] a Spanish or Portuguese nobleman of the highest rank; a person of high rank. —[명] 대공(大公)(스페인 · 포르투갈의 최고 귀족); 고관

gran·deur [grǽndʒər, +*U.S.* -dʒuər] *n.* [U][C] splendor; magnificence; greatness; dignity; nobility. ¶*the ~ of Niagara Falls*① / *the ~ of his character*② / *the ~ of Mt. Fuji.* —[명] 장대(壯大); 장려; 위대; 위엄; 숭고 ¶①나이아가라 폭포의 장관/②그의 인격의 위대함

:grand·fa·ther [grǽn(d)fà:ðər] *n.* [C] the father of one's father or mother. ¶*a great-grandfather.*① —[명] 조부, 할아버지 ¶①증조부

gran·dil·o·quence [grændíləkwəns] *n.* [U] the use of lofty or big words. —[명] 호언장담

gran·dil·o·quent [grændíləkwənt] *adj.* using lofty or big words; speaking boastfully; exaggerated. —[형] 호언장담하는, 과장된

gran·di·ose [grǽndiòus] *adj.* grand; seeming grand but not really so. —[형] 장대한, 웅장한; 허세부리는

gran·di·os·i·ty [grændiásiti / -ɔ́s-] *n.* [U] the state of being grandiose. —[명] 장대; 과장; 허세

grand·ly [grǽndli] *adv.* in a grand manner. —[부] 장대하게; 장려하게; 숭고하게

:grand·ma [grǽn(d)mà:] *n.* [C] (*child's word*) a grandmother. —[명] 《小兒》 할머니

grand·ma·ma, -mam·ma [grǽn(d)mà:mə / -məmà:] *n.* =grandma. —[명] 할머니

:grand·moth·er [grǽn(d)mʌ̀ðər] *n.* [C] the mother of one's father or mother. —[명] 조모

grand·moth·er·ly [grǽn(d)mʌ̀ðərli] *adj.* of or like a grandmother. —[형] 조모의; 할머니 같은

grand·neph·ew [grǽn(d)nèfju:, +*Brit.* -nèvju:] *n.* [C] the son of one's nephew or niece. —[명] 조카[딸]의 아들, 종손

grand·niece [grǽn(d)nì:s] *n.* [C] the daughter of one's nephew or niece. —[명] 조카(딸)의 딸, 종손녀

:grand·pa [grǽn(d)pà:, grǽm-] *n.* [C] (*child's word*) a grandfather. —[명] 《小兒》 할아버지

grand·pa·pa [grǽnpà:pə / -pəpà:] *n.* =grandpa.

:grand·par·ent [grǽn(d)pɛ̀ər(ə)nt] *n.* [C] a grandfather or grandmother. —[명] 조부모

:grand·son [grǽn(d)sʌ̀n] *n.* [C] the son of one's son or daughter. —[명] 손자

grand·un·cle [grǽndʌ̀ŋkl] *n.* [C] the uncle of one's father or mother. —[명] 종조부

grange [greindʒ] *n.* [C] **1.** a farm with its buildings; a farmer's house. **2.** 《*G*》 (*U.S.*) an organization of farmers for mutual welfare and advancement. —[명] 1. 부속 건물이 있는 농장;농가의 저택 2. 농민 공제조합

·gran·ite [grǽnit] *n.* [U] a hard rock used for buildings and monuments. ¶*as hard as ~.*① —[명] 화강암 ¶①돌처럼 굳은

bite on granite, make a vain effort. [숙] 헛수고를 하다

·gran·ny, gran·nie [grǽni] *n.* [C] (pl. **-nies**) (*colloq.*) a grandmother; an old woman. —[명] 《口》 할머니(애칭)

:grant [grænt / gra:nt] *vt.* **1.** give one's consent to (something); allow. ¶*~ someone a favor.*① **2.** admit; agree. —[타] 1. …을 승락하다; 허가하다 ¶①…의 부탁을 들어 주다 2. …을 인정하다

take for granted, suppose to be true. ¶*I take it for granted that man is mortal.* [숙] 당연하게 여기다

—*n.* **1.** [U] the act of granting. **2.** [C] something granted; a sum of money given by the authorities. —[명] 1. 승락; 허가; 인가; 수여 2 하사물; 보조금

gran·u·lar [grǽnjulər] *adj.* of, like or containing grains or granules. ▷**gran·u·lar·ly** [-li] *adv.* —[형] 낟알의, 입상(粒狀)의; 과립상(顆粒狀)의

gran·u·late [grǽnjulèit] *vt.* **1.** form (something) into small grains. **2.** make the surface of (something) rough. **—*vi.*** become grains. —[타] 1 알갱이로 만들다 2. …의 표면을 도톨도톨하게 하다 —[자] 알갱이처럼 되다

gran·ule [grǽnju:l] *n.* [C] a small grain; a small bit or spot like a grain. —[명] 작은 알갱이; 미립(微粒)

:grape [greip] *n.* [C] a juicy fruit growing in clusters on a vine; a grapevine. —[명] 포도; 포도나무

grape·fruit [gréipfrù:t] *n.* [C] a pale-yellow, round fruit like an orange. —[명] 귤 비슷한 과실

grape sugar [ˊ ˊ-] *n.* the form of sugar found in ripe grapes; glucose. —[명] 포도당

grape·vine [gréipvàin] *n.* [C] **1.** a vine which bears —[명] 1. 포도 덩굴; 포도나무 2. (美口)

grapes. **2.** (*U.S. colloq.*) a network of rumor; a baseless report. 소문이 퍼지는 경로; 헛소문, 유언비어

graph [græf, +*Brit.* grɑːf] *n.* [C] a drawing that shows the relation between two quantities, the course of change in a thing, etc. —[名] 그라프, 도식(圖式), 도표

graph·ic [grǽfik], **-i·cal** [-ik(ə)l] *adj.* **1.** of drawing or painting. ¶*the ~ arts.*① **2.** vivid; lifelike. ¶*~ accounts of the scene.* **3.** of or about graphs; shown by a graph. ¶*a ~ formula*② / *a ~ curve.*③ —[形] **1.** 그림의, 도형의 ¶①필사(筆寫) 예술 **2.** 생생한 **3.** 도식의; 그라프의, 도시(圖示)된 ¶②구조식/③그라프 곡선

graph·i·cal·ly [grǽfikəli] *adv.* by graphs or pictures; vividly. —[副] 그라프로, 도식으로; 생생하게

graph·ite [grǽfait] *n.* [U] a kind of soft black carbon used in lead pencils. —[名] 석묵(石墨), 흑연(黑鉛)

grap·nel [grǽpn(ə)l] *n.* [C] a small anchor with several hooks; an instrument with a hook or hooks for seizing and holding things. ⇒fig. —[名] 네 갈고리 닻, 걸어 잡는 기구

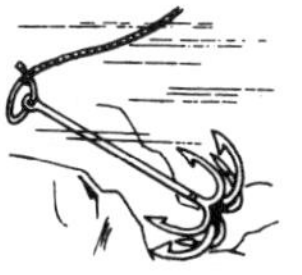

〔grapnel〕

grap·ple [grǽpl] *vt., vi.* **1.** grip firmly; seize. **2.** fight; struggle. ⟪~ *with* something⟫ ¶*~ with a task*① / *The two boys grappled with each other.*② **3.** use a grapnel. —[他][自] **1.** [···을] 잡다, 쥐다; 붙잡다 **2.** [···와] 맞붙어 싸우다 ¶①일에 달려들다/②두 소년은 맞붙어 싸웠다 **3.** 쇠갈고리로 걸어 잡다

—*n.* [C] **1.** the act of grappling. ¶*come to grapples with someone.* **2.** a grapnel. —[名] **1.** 붙잡기; 격투 **2.** 쇠갈고리 닻

⁑**grasp** [græsp / grɑːsp] *vt.* **1.** hold firmly; seize. ¶*He grasped my hand.* **2.** understand. ¶*I cannot ~ your meaning.* —*vi.* try to seize. ⟪~ *at* something⟫ ¶(*proverb*) *A drowning man grasps at a straw.*① —[他] **1.** ···을 꽉 쥐다, 잡다 **2.** ···을 이해하다 —[自] 붙잡으려고 하다 ¶①⟪俚⟫물에 빠진 사람은 지푸라기라도 잡는다

—*n.* [C] ⟪usu. *sing.*⟫ **1.** the act of grasping. **2.** [U] ⟪often *a* ~⟫ understanding. ¶*a mind of wide ~*② / *a problem beyond our ~.*③ **3.** control; power. —[名] **1.** 파악 **2.** 이해 ¶②이해력이 넓은 마음/③우리가 이해할 수 없는 문제 **3.** 지배; 권력

grasp·ing [grǽspiŋ / gɑ́ːsp-] *adj.* greedy; eager to get all one can. —[形] 욕심 많은, 탐욕스러운

⁑**grass** [græs / grɑːs] *n.* **1.** [U] ⟪*collectively*⟫ green plants growing on lawns and in pastures. ¶*a leaf of ~.*① **2.** [C] ⟪usu. *the* ~⟫ ground covered with grass; a pasture; a lawn. ¶*cut the ~*② / *Keep off the ~.*③ **3.** [C] any plant that has jointed stems and narrow pointed leaves, such as corn and bamboo. —[名] **1.** 풀, 목초 ¶①풀 잎 하나 **2.** 풀밭; 목초지, 잔디 ¶②풀밭을 깎다/③잔디에 들어가지 마시오 **3.** 포아풀과의 초본

—*vt.* **1.** cover (land) with grass. **2.** graze. —[他] **1.** ···을 풀로 덮다 **2.** ···에게 목초를 먹이다

***grass·hop·per** [grǽshɑ̀pər / grɑ́ːshɔ̀pə] *n.* [C] a kind of insect with wings and long, powerful hind legs for jumping. —[名] 메뚜기, 방아깨비, 여치

grass·land [grǽslæ̀nd / grɑ́ːs-] *n.* [U] land on which grass grows richly, used for pasture. —[名] 목초지, 목장

grass·y [grǽsi / grɑ́ːsi] *adj.* (**grass·i·er, grass·i·est**) of or like grass; covered with grass. —[形] 풀의; 풀 같은; 풀로 덮인

***grate**[1] [greit] *n.* [C] a framework of iron bars for holding coal or wood by a fireplace. —[名] 쇠창살로 만든 석탄 그릇 —*vt.* furnish (something) with iron bars. —[他] ···에 쇠창살을 대다

***grate**[2] [greit] *vt.* **1.** make (something) into bits by rubbing on a rough surface. ¶*~ cheese.* **2.** rub (something) with an unpleasant sound. **3.** irritate; annoy. —*vi.* **1.** make a rubbing sound. **2.** cause an annoyance. ⟪~ *on* (or *upon, against*) someone or something⟫ ¶*His manner grates on us all.*① —[他] **1.** ···을 비벼서 바수다, 채치다 **2.** 삐걱거리게 하다 **3.** ···을 짜증나게 하다 —[自] **1.** 삐걱거리다 **2.** 불쾌한 느낌을 주다 ¶①그의 태도는 모두에게 불쾌감을 준다

⁑**grate·ful** [gréitf(u)l] *adj.* **1.** thankful. ¶*I am very ~ to you for your help.* **2.** pleasant; agreeable. ¶*~ warmth.* —[形] **1.** 고맙게 여기는 **2.** 기분 좋은; 즐거운

grate·ful·ly [gréitfuli] *adv.* in a grateful manner. —[副] 고마와서, 기쁘게

grat·er [gréitər] *n.* [C] an instrument with a rough surface on it to grate vegetables, etc. —[名] 채치는 기구, 강판

grat·i·fi·ca·tion [græ̀tifikéiʃ(ə)n] *n.* **1.** [U] the act of gratifying; the state of being gratified. **2.** [C] something that gratifies. —[名] **1.** 만족; 기쁨 **2.** 만족시키는 것

***grat·i·fy** [grǽtifài] *vt.* (**-fied**) satisfy; please. ¶*~ one's* —[他] ···을 만족시키다; 기쁘게 하다

G

desire / *be gratified with the result.*①
¶①결과에 만족하다

grat·i·fy·ing [grǽtifàiiŋ] *adj.* satisfying; pleasing.
—[형] 만족시키는; 만족스러운

grat·ing[1] [gréitiŋ] *n.* [C] a framework of bars over a window or opening.
—[명] 창살, 격자(格子)

grat·ing[2] [gréitiŋ] *adj.* harsh; irritating.
—[형] 삐걱거리는, 신경에 거슬리는

grat·is [gréitis] *adv., adj.* for nothing; without charge; free. ¶*The sample is sent* ~.① / *Entrance is* ~.②
—[부][형] 무료로(의) ¶①견본은 무료로 보내드립니다/②입장 무료

* **grat·i·tude** [grǽtit(j)ù:d / -tjù:d] *n.* [U] thankfulness. ¶ *out of* ~① / *with* ~.②
—[명] 감사, 사의(謝意) ¶①감사하는 마음에서/②감사하여

gra·tu·i·tous [grət(j)ú(:)itəs / -tjú(:)-] *adj.* **1.** given or obtained free. **2.** without reason; unnecessary.
—[형] **1.** 무료의, 공짜로 준 **2.** 까닭없는; 불필요한

gra·tu·i·ty [grət(j)ú(:)iti / -tjú(:)-] *n.* [C] (pl. **-ties**) **1.** a payment for service; a tip. **2.** money paid to a soldier when he retires.
—[명] **1.** 팁, 행하(行下) **2.** [제대] 급여금

‡ **grave**[1] [greiv] *n.* [C] **1.** a hole in the ground where a dead body is placed; the mound or monument over it; a place of burial. ¶*find one's* ~ *in the sea*① / *from the cradle to the* ~② / *on this side of the* ~.③ **2.** 《*the* ~》 death. ¶*dread the* ~④ / *to one's* ~.⑤
have one foot in the grave, be near death; be very old or sick.
—[명] **1.** 무덤, 묘; 묘석, 묘비; 매장지 ¶①바다에서 죽다/②평생 동안/③이 세상에서 **2.** 죽음 ¶④죽음을 두려워하다/⑤죽을 때까지
[숙] 죽어 가고 있다; 아주 나이가 들었다, 병이 위중하다

‡ **grave**[2] [greiv] *adj.* **1.** important; momentous; serious. ¶*the* ~ *problem of the day.* **2.** sober; solemn. ¶*a* ~, *quiet man.* **3.** (of color) not gay; dull. **4.** (*Phonetics*) low in pitch. —*n.* [C] the grave accent(ˋ).
—[형] **1.** 중요한; 중대한; 심상치 않은 **2.** 진지한; 엄숙한 **3.** [빛깔이] 수수한 **4.** 《音聲》 억음(抑音)의 —[명] 억음

grave·dig·ger [gréivdìgər] *n.* [C] a person whose work is digging graves.
—[명] 무덤 파는 인부

* **grav·el** [grǽv(ə)l] *n.* [U] a mixture of small stones and pebbles. —*vt.* (**-eled, -el·ing** or *Brit.* **-elled, -el·ling**) **1.** cover (a road) with gravel. **2.** perplex.
—[명] 자갈 —[타] **1.** [도로]에 자갈을 깔다 **2.** …을 당황하게 하다

* **grave·ly** [gréivli] *adv.* in a grave manner.
—[부] 중대하게; 진지하게

grav·er [gréivər] *n.* [C] a person or thing that engraves.
—[명] 조각사(도)

grave·stone [gréivstòun] *n.* [C] a stone that marks a grave; a tombstone.
—[명] 묘비; 묘석

grave·yard [gréivjɑ̀:rd] *n.* [C] a place for burying the dead.
—[명] 묘지

grav·i·tate [grǽvitèit] *vi.* **1.** be drawn by gravity; sink. ¶~ *to the bottom*① / *The earth gravitates toward the sun.* **2.** be attracted. 《~ *to* or *toward* something》
—[자] **1.** 인력에 끌리다; 가라앉다 ¶①바닥에 가라앉다 **2.** 끌리다, 매혹되다

grav·i·ta·tion [grӕ̀vitéiʃ(ə)n] *n.* [U] **1.** the act of gravitating; the force of gravity. ¶*the law of* ~① / *universal* ~.② **2.** tendency to move. ¶*the* ~ *of population toward cities.*
—[명] **1.** 인력[작용] ¶①인력의 법칙/②만유인력 **2.** 경향 ¶③인구의 도시 집중 경향

* **grav·i·ty** [grǽviti] *n.* [U] **1.** the force which draws all bodies on the earth towards the center of the earth. **2.** the state of being grave; importance; seriousness. **3.** heaviness; weight. ¶*the center of* ~① / *specific* ~.② **4.** (*Phonetics*) lowness of pitch.
—[명] **1.** 중력(重力), 지구 인력 **2.** 중대; 진지함; 엄숙 **3.** 무게, 중량 ¶①중심(重心)/②비중 **4.** 《音聲》 저음, 억음(抑音)

gra·vy [gréivi] *n.* [U] the juice that comes out of meat in cooking; a sauce made from this juice.
—[명] 고기 즙; 고기즙으로 만든 소오스

‡ **gray,** *Brit.* **grey** [grei] *adj.* **1.** having a color between black and white. **2.** dark; cloudy. ¶*a* ~ *dawn.*① **3.** groomy; dismal. ¶*The future looks* ~. **4.** having gray hair. **5.** old; ancient. ¶~ *experience*② / *the* ~ *past.*③ —*n.* [U] **1.** gray color. **2.** gray cloth or clothing. —*vt., vi.* make or become gray.
—[형] **1.** 회색의, 쥐빛의 **2.** 어두운, 흐린 ¶①어둑어둑한 새벽 **3.** 음침한 **4.** 흰머리가 섞인 **5.** 낡은; 옛날의 ¶②노련/③태고, 고대 —[명] **1.** 회색 **2.** 회색의 천(옷) —[타][자] 회색이 되[게 하]다

gray·beard [gréibìərd] *n.* [C] an old man.
—[명] 노인

gray-head·ed [gréihédid] *adj.* having gray hair; old.
—[형] 흰머리가 섞인; 낡은 천

gray·hound [gréihàund] *n.* =greyhound.

gray·ish [gréiiʃ] *adj.* somewhat gray.
—[형] 잿빛이 도는

* **graze**[1] [greiz] *vi.* (of cattle, etc.) feed on growing grass. —*vt.* put (cattle, etc.) to feed on growing grass.
—[자] 생풀을 먹다 —[타] [가축]에게 생풀(목초)을 먹이다

graze[2] [greiz] *vt.* touch (something) lightly in passing; scratch (the skin, etc.). —*vi.* touch lightly against (something) in passing. —*n.* [C] the act of grazing; a slight wound made by grazing.
—[타] …을 가볍게 스치며 지나가다; [살갗]을 벗기다 —[자] 가볍게 스쳐 지나가다 —[명] 가볍게 스치기; 생채기, 찰상(擦傷)

G

gra·zier [gréiʒər, +*Brit.* -ziə] *n.* [C] a person who grazes cattle for sale.
—[名] 목축업자

graz·ing [gréiziŋ] *n.* [U] land for cattle, etc. to graze on; a pasture.
—[名] 목초(牧草)[지(地)]

* **grease** *n.* [gri:s → *v.*] [U] **1.** melted animal fat. **2.** any thick oily substance. ¶ *wool in the* ~.① —*vt.* [gri:s, gri:z] **1.** smear (something) with grease; put grease on or in (something). ¶ ~ *the wheels.* **2.** (*colloq.*) bribe or tip.
grease the palm of (=*offer bribe to*) *someone.*
—[名] **1.** 지방(脂肪), 수지(獸脂) **2.** 반고체의 유성 물질, 그리이스 ¶①기름을 빼지 않은 양털 —[他] **1.** …을 기름으로 더럽히다; …에 기름을 바르다 **2.** …에게 뇌물을 쓰다
[熟] …에게 뇌물을 주다

greas·y *adj.* (**greas·i·er, greas·i·est**) **1.** [grí:si → 2.] covered with grease; full of grease. **2.** [grí:zi] smooth; slippery. ¶ *a* ~ *road.*
—[形] **1.** 기름으로 더러워진; 기름투성이의 **2.** 미끌미끌한, 매끄러운

⁑ **great** [greit] *adj.* **1.** big; large. ¶ *a* ~ *river.* **2.** large in number, quantity, or degree; (of time) long. ¶ *a* ~ *crowd* / *a* ~ *while ago*① / *a* ~ *danger.* **3.** remarkable; eminent; famous. ¶ *a* ~ *writer.* **4.** important. ¶ *a* ~ *decision.* **5.** noble; generous. **6.** very good; fine; splendid. ¶ *I had a* ~ *time at the party.* **7.** much in use; favorite. ¶ *This is a* ~ *word among school girls.*
1) ***be great*** (=*be skillful*) ***at*** *something.*
2) ***be great on*** (=*be much interested in*) *something.*
—[形] **1.** 큰; 거대한 **2.** 다수의, 다량의; 장시간의 ¶①훨씬 이전에 **3.** 아주 뛰어난, 위대한; 유명한 **4.** 중대한 **5.** 고귀한; 관대한 **6.** 멋진, 아주 좋은 **7.** 많이 쓰이는; 즐겨 쓰는
[熟] 1)…에 능숙하다 2)…에 크게 흥미를 갖다

Great Britain [⌐ ⌐⌐] *n.* England, Wales, and Scotland.
—[名] 영국

great·coat [gréitkòut] *n.* [C] (esp. *Brit.*) a heavy overcoat.
—[名] 《英》 [두꺼운] 외투

great-grand·child [grèitgrǽn(d)tʃàild] *n.* (pl. **-chil·dren** [-tʃildr(ə)n]) [C] the grandchild of one's son or daughter.
—[名] 증손(曾孫)

great-grand·daugh·ter [grèitgrǽn(d)dɔ̀:tər] *n.* [C] the granddaughter of one's son or daughter.
—[名] 증손녀

great-grand·fa·ther [grèitgrǽn(d)fà:ðər] *n.* [C] the grandfather of one's father or mother.
—[名] 증조부

great-grand·moth·er [grèitgrǽn(d)mʌ̀ðər] *n.* [C] the grandmother of one's father or mother.
—[名] 증조모

great-grand·son [grèitgrǽn(d)sʌn] *n.* [C] the grandson of one's son or daughter.
—[名] 증손자

great-heart·ed [gréithá:rtid] *adj.* **1.** brave. **2.** noble; generous.
—[形] **1.** 용기 있는 **2.** 고결한, 관대한

⁑ **great·ly** [gréitli] *adv.* **1.** very much; highly. **2.** nobly; generously.
—[副] **1.** 대단히, 몹시 **2.** 위대하게, 관대하게

⁑ **great·ness** [gréitnis] *n.* [U] the quality of being great.
—[名] 거대; 탁월; 고귀; 관대

grebe [gri:b] *n.* [C] a large diving bird; a loon.
—[名] 농병아리

Gre·cian [grí:ʃ(ə)n] *adj.* Greek. ⇨[usage] ¶ ~ *architecture* / *a* ~ *nose.* —*n.* [C] **1.** a Greek. **2.** a scholar of Greek.
—[形] 그리이스의 [usage] 건축·사람의 용모에 씀 —[名] **1.** 그리이스 사람 **2.** 그리이스어 학자

* **Greece** [gri:s] *n.* a country in southeastern Europe. ⇨[N.B.]
—[名] 그리이스 [N.B.] 수도 Athens

greed [gri:d] *n.* [U] strong and selfish desire.
—[名] 탐욕, 욕심

greed·i·ly [grí:dili] *adv.* in a greedy manner.
—[副] 욕심내어; 게걸스럽게

greed·i·ness [grí:dinis] *n.* [U] the quality of being greedy.
—[名] 탐욕스러움; 욕심을 냄

⁑ **greed·y** [grí:di] *adj.* (**greed·i·er, greed·i·est**) **1.** wanting to eat and drink too much; wanting more than a fair share. **2.** wanting strongly; eager. ¶ *be* ~ *of* (or *for*) *praise*① / *be* ~ *to get a prize.*
—[形] **1.** 게걸스럽게 먹는; 탐욕한 **2.** 갈망(열망)하는 ¶①칭찬받기를 몹시 바라다

⁑ **Greek** [gri:k] *adj.* of Greece, its people, or their language. —*n.* [U] **1.** a person of ancient or modern Greece. **2.** [U] the Greek language.
be Greek (=*be not understandable*) ***to*** *someone.*
—[形] 그리이스의; 그리이스 사람(말)의 —[名] **1.** 그리이스 사람 **2.** 그리이스 말
[熟] 전혀 알 수 없다

⁑ **green** [gri:n] *adj.* **1.** having the color of growing grass. **2.** covered with growing grass. ¶ ~ *fields.* **3.** snowless; mild. ↔white ¶ *a* ~ *Christmas.* **4.** unripe. ¶ ~ *fruit.* **5.** raw; undried. ¶ ~ *timber*① / ~ *hide.*② **6.** unexperienced; untrained. ¶ *a* ~ *hand*③ / *He is still* ~ *at his job.* **7.** pale; jealous. **8.** fresh; new. ¶ ~ *memories.*
—*n.* [U] **1.** green color. **2.** green cloth or clothing. **3.** [C] a lawn; land covered with grass. **4.** 《*pl.*》 green
—[形] **1.** 초록빛의 **2.** 푸른 풀로 뒤덮인 **3.** 눈이 없는; 온화한 **4.** 익지 않은 **5.** 생(生)의 ¶①생나무/②생가죽 **6.** 경험 없는, 미숙한 ¶③미숙한 사람, 풋나기 **7.** 창백한; 질투심 많은 **8.** 신선한; 새로운
—[名] **1.** 초록빛 **2.** 초록빛의 천(옷) **3.** 잔디; 풀밭 **4.** 푸른 잎(가지) **5.** 채소,

leaves and branches used for decoration. **5.** ((*pl.*)) leaves and stems of plants used for food. **6.** [U] vigor; freshness; youth. ¶*in the ~.*④
야채 6. 생기; 신선한 맛; 젊음 ¶④기운차게

green·back [grí:nbæ̀k] *n.* [C] a piece of paper money of the United States printed in green.
—[名] 미국의 달러 지폐

green·er·y [grí:nəri] *n.* (pl. **-er·ies**) **1.** [U] ((*collectively*)) green leaves; green plants ¶*the ~ of the woods in May.* **2.** [C] a greenhouse.
—[名] 1. 푸른 잎; 푸른 나무 2. 온실

green·gro·cer [grí:ngròusər] *n.* [C] (*Brit.*) a person who sells fresh vegetables and fruit.
—[名] ((英)) 채소(청과물) 장수

green·gro·cer·y [grí:ngròus(ə)ri] *n.* (pl. **-cer·ies**) (*Brit.*) **1.** [C] the business of a greengrocer; a store that sells fresh vegetables and fruit. **2.** [U] ((*collectively*)) things sold by a greengrocer.
—[名] 1. 채소 가게, 청과물상 2. 채소, 청과물

green·horn [grí:nhɔ̀:rn] *n.* [C] (*colloq.*) a person who has no experience; a person easily fooled.
—[名] 미숙한 사람, 풋나기, 초심자; 얼간이

green·house [grí:nhàus] *n.* [C] (pl. **-hous·es** [-hàuziz]) a heated building for growing plants.
—[名] 온실

green·ish [grí:niʃ] *adj.* somewhat green.
—[形] 초록빛을 띤

Green·land [grí:nlənd] *n.* the largest island in the world, northeast of North America. ⇨[N.B.]
—[名] 그리인랜드 [N.B.] 덴마아크령

green·stuff [grí:nstʌ̀f] *n.* [U] vegetables.
—[名] 채소, 야채류; 초목

green·sward [grí:nsɔ̀:rd] *n.* [U] ground covered thickly with short grass.
—[名] 잔디

Green·wich [grínidʒ, grén-] *n.* a town in London.
—[名] 영국 런던 근처의 마을

Greenwich Time [ˊ- ˊ] *n.* the time measured at Greenwich, used as a basis for the standard time around the world. ⇨[N.B.]
—[名] 그리니지 표준시 [N.B.] Greenwich Mean Time 이라고도 하며 G. M.T.로 줄임

green·wood [grí:nwùd] *n.* [C] a forest when the trees are fully covered with leaves.
—[名] 푸른 숲

: **greet** [gri:t] *vt.* **1.** welcome; salute; receive. ¶*He greeted me with a smile.* **2.** be seen by (someone's eyes); be heard by (someone's ears). ¶*The mountain greeted my eyes.*① | *The music of Chopin greeted my ear.*
—[他] 1. …을 환영하다; …에게 인사하다; 마중하다 2. [눈]에 들어오다; [귀]에 들리다 ¶①산이 우리 눈에 보였다

· **greet·ing** [grí:tiŋ] **1.** [C] words of good will; a welcome. **2.** ((*pl.*)) a friendly message on a special occasion. ¶*send greetings* | *with the season's greetings.*①
—[名] 1. 인사 2. 인사의 말 ¶①계절의 문안과 함께

gre·nade [grinéid] *n.* [C] a small bomb thrown by hand.
—[名] 수류탄

: **grew** [gru:] *v.* pt. of **grow**.

: **grey** [grei] *adj.* (*Brit.*) =gray.

grey·beard [gréibìərd] *n.* (*Brit.*) =graybeard.

grey-head·ed [gréihédid] *adj.* (*Brit.*) =gray-headed.

grey·hound [gréihàund] *n.* [C] a tall, slender, swift dog, used for hunting and racing.
—[名] 그레이하운드(사냥개의 일종)

grey·ish [gréiiʃ] *adj.* (*Brit.*) =grayish.

grid [grid] *n.* [C] **1.** a framework of iron bars. **2.** a wire net that controls the flow of electrons in a vacuum tube.
—[名] 1. 쇠창살 2. [진공관 속의] 그릿

grid·i·ron [grídàiərn] *n.* [C] **1.** a framework of metal bars used for broiling meat or fish. **2.** (*U.S.*) a football field.
—[名] 1. [고기 굽는] 석쇠, 적쇠 2. ((美)) 미식축구 경기장

: **grief** [gri:f] *n.* (pl. **griefs**) [U] deep sorrow; [C] a cause of grief. ¶*in ~*① | *He is a great ~ to his parents.*
1) ***bring someone to grief,*** cause someone to meet with misfortune, injury, or ruin.
2) ***come to grief,*** meet with disaster; fail.
—[名] 깊은 슬픔; 비탄의 원인 ¶①비탄에 잠겨
[熟] 1)…을 불행에 빠뜨리다; 상처 입히다; 파멸시키다 2)재난을 만나다; 실패하다

griev·ance [grí:v(ə)ns] *n.* [C] a cause or reason for dissatisfaction or protest. ¶*nurse a ~.*①
—[名] 불평거리; 불평의 원인 ¶①불평을 품다

: **grieve** [gri:v] *vt.* cause (someone) to feel grief; make (someone) very sad. —*vi.* feel grief. ((*~ for* someone or something; *~ at* (or *about, over*) something; *~ to do*; *~ that* ...))
—[他] …을 깊이 슬퍼하게 하다; 비탄시키다 —[自] 깊은 슬픔을 맛보다

griev·ous [grí:vəs] *adj.* **1.** causing grief; showing grief. **2.** causing great pain or suffering; severe. ▷**griev·ous·ly** [-li] *adv.* —**griev·ous·ness** [-nis] *n.*
—[形] 1. 슬퍼하게 하는; 슬픈 2. 고통을 주는; 심한

grif·fin [grífin] *n.* ⓒ an imaginary animal with the head and wings of an eagle and the body of a lion.
grill [gril] *n.* ⓒ **1.** a gridiron, **2.** a dish of meat or fish cooked on a gridiron. **3.** a grillroom.
―*vt.* **1.** cook (meat or fish) on a gridiron. **2.** (*U.S.*) put severe questions to (someone). ―*vi.* **1.** be cooked on a gridiron. **2.** expose oneself to great heat.
grille [gril] *n.* ⓒ a screen of parallel bars used as a gate, door, or window.
grill·room [grílru(ː)m] *n.* ⓒ a restaurant or dining room, esp. one where broiled meat or fish is served.
* **grim** [grim] *adj.* (**grim·mer, grim·mest**) **1.** stern; severe. **2.** without mercy; cruel. **3.** horrible; ghastly.
hold on to something like grim death, hold on to something very firmly.
▷ **grim·ly** [grímli] *adv.* ―**grim·ness** [grímnis] *n.*
gri·mace [griméis] *n.* ⓒ the act of twisting the face; an ugly expression of the face. ―*vi.* make grimaces.
grime [graim] *n.* Ⓤ dirt that is hard to take off. ―*vt.* make (something) dirty with grime; soil.
* **grin** [grin] *v.* (**grinned, grin·ning**) *vi.* **1.** smile broadly. (*~ at someone*) **2.** show the teeth in pain, scorn, anger, etc. ―*vt.* express (something) by grinning. ¶*He grinned his pleasure.*①
grin and bear it, endure pain, disappointment, etc., with a broad smile or without complaint.
―*n.* ⓒ a broad smile.
⁝ grind [graind] *v.* (**ground**) *vt.* **1.** crush (something) into powder or small pieces. ¶*~ corn.* **2.** sharpen. ¶*~ an ax.* **3.** rub together; dash against (something). ¶*~ one's teeth in anger.*① **4.** cause (something) to work by turning a crank. ―*vi.* **1.** do the act of grinding something. **2.** can be ground. ¶*This wheat grinds well.*② **3.** study hard. ¶*~ for an examination* / *I ground [away] at my studies.*
1) *grind down,* ⓐ make (something) into powder by grinding. ⓑ wear away; oppress. ¶*~ down the poor*③ / *People are ground down by heavy taxes.*④
2) *grind out,* ⓐ produce (a tune) by playing musical instruments. ⓑ produce (something) with a long effort.
3) *grind the faces of* (=*oppress*) *the poor.*
4) *grind up,* make (something) into small pieces by grinding.
―*n.* ⓒ **1.** the act of grinding. **2.** a long, hard, monotonous task. **3.** (*colloq.*) a student who studies hard.
grind·er [gráindər] *n.* ⓒ a person or thing that grinds.
grind·stone [gráin(d)stòun] *n.* ⓒ a flat, round stone which axis on an axle, used for sharpening tools.
⁝ grip [grip] *n.* ⓒ **1.** a firm hold. ¶*lose one's ~*① / *take a ~ on a branch.*② **2.** the power of understanding. ¶*He has a good ~ of* (or *on*) *the problem.*③ **3.** a handle. **4.** (*U.S.*) a traveler's handbag.
1) *be at grips with,* be attacking (something) in earnest.
2) *come to grips* (=*struggle seriously*) *with a problem, etc.*
―*v.* (**gripped, grip·ping**) *vt.* grasp firmly; seize. ―*vi.* take a fast hold.
gripe [graip] *vt.* **1.** grasp; seize; grip. **2.** cause (someone) to have pain in the mind; distress. **3.** cause (someone) to have pain in the bowels. ―*vi.* **1.** feel sharp pains in the bowels. **2.** (*U.S. colloq.*) complain.
―*n.* ⓒ **1.** a firm hold. **2.** distress. **3.** (*pl.*) sharp pains in the bowels. **4.** (*U.S. colloq.*) a complaint.

―❷ 그리핀(독수리의 머리·날개에 사자의 몸을 한 전설상의 괴물)
―❷ 1. 석쇠 2. 불고기, 구운 생선 3. 그릴
―⑪ 1. [고기·생선]을 석쇠로 굽다 2. …에게 힐문하다 ―㉠ 1. 구워지다 2. 폭염에 노출되다
―❷ 창살, 격자창

―❷ 그릴(식당)

―⑪ 1. 엄격한; 엄한 2. 잔인한; 냉혹한 3. 무서운
熟 …에 결사적으로 달라붙다

―❷ 얼굴을 찡그리기; 찡그린 얼굴
―㉠ 얼굴을 찡그리다
―❷ 때; 더럼; 검댕 ―⑪ [때·검댕으로] …을 더럽히다
―㉠ 1. 싱글싱글 웃다 2. 이를 악물다
―❸ 싱글싱글하며 …을 나타내다 ¶①그는 기뻐서 싱글거렸다

熟 웃으면서 참다

―❷ 싱글거리는 웃음
―⑪ 1. …을 타다(바수다); 분쇄하다 2. …을 갈다 3. …을 갈다; …에 부딪치다 ¶①화가 나서 이를 갈다 4. …을 돌리다 ―㉠ 1. 바수다 2. 갈리다 ¶②이 밀은 잘 갈린다 3. 열심히 공부하다

熟 1)ⓐ…을 가루로 만들다 ⓑ…을 닳려 없애다; 학대하다 ⓒ③빈민을 괴롭히다/④사람들은 과도한 세금에 시달리고 있다 2)ⓐ악기를 타서 [곡을] 연주하다 ⓑ애써 만들어 내다 3)빈민을 학대하다 4)…을 갈아 바수다

―❷ 1. 갈기, 타기 2. 단조롭고 힘든 일 3.《口》부지런히 공부하는 학생
―❷ 가는(빻는) 사람; 숫돌
―❷ 회전 숫돌; 연마기(研磨機)

―❷ 1. 쥐기, 잡기, ¶①놓치다/②가지를 잡다 2. 이해력 ¶③그는 그 문제를 잘 파악하고 있다 3. 손잡이 4.《美》여행 가방
熟 1)…와 씨름하고 있다 2)열심히 [문제 따위]와 씨름하다

―⑪ …을 단단히 잡다; 이해하다 ―㉠ 쥐다, 잡다
―⑪ 1. …을 꼭 쥐다 2. …을 괴롭히다 3. …을 배앓이로 괴롭히다 ―㉠ 1. 배가 아프다 2.《美口》불평하다

―❷ 1. 쥐기, 잡기 2. 피로움; 고민 3. 복통 4.《美口》불평

gris·ly [grízli] *adj.* (**-li·er, -li·est**) horrible; ghastly; grim.
—[形] 무서운; 오싹하는

grist [grist] *n.* [U] grain to be ground; grain that has been ground; flour or meal made by grinding. ¶(*proverb*) *All is ~ that comes to his mill.*①
—[名] 제분용의 곡물; 빻은 곡식 ¶①《俚》무엇이든지 이용한다, 넘어져도 그냥은 안 일어난다

grit [grit] *n.* [U] **1.** 《*collectively*》 very tiny pebbles; sand. **2.** (*U.S. colloq.*) courage. —*v.* (**grit·ted, grit·ting**) *vt.* make a noise by rubbing (something). ¶*~ the teeth.*① —*vi.* make a noise by rubbing.
—[名] 1. 자갈;모래 2.《美口》 용기 —[他] …을 삐걱거리게 하다 ¶①이를 갈다 —[自] 삐걱거리다

grit·ty [gríti] *adj.* (**-ti·er, -ti·est**) **1.** of, like, or containing grit. **2.** (*U.S.*) brave.
—[形] 1. 모래의(같은), 모래가 있는 2. 《美》 용감한

griz·zled [grízld] *adj.* gray; gray-haired.
—[形] 회색의; 백발의

griz·zly [grízli] *adj.* (**-zli·er, -zli·est**) gray. —*n.* [C] (pl. **-zlies**) a bear found in the Rocky Mountains.
—[形] 회색의 —[名] 회색의 큰 곰

⁑**groan** [groun] *n.* [C] a deep sound of pain or sorrow. —*vi.* **1.** make a groan. **2.** make a sound like a groan. ¶*The old house groaned during the storm.* **3.** suffer deeply. ¶*~ under heavy taxes.* **4.** be overburdened. ¶*a shelf groaning with books.* —*vt.* express (something) by groaning.
—[名] 신음소리
—[自] 1. 신음하다; 낑낑거리다 2. 신음하는 듯한 소리를 내다 3. 신음하며 괴로와하다 4. 너무 쌓여 있다 —[他]…을 신음소리로 말하다

***gro·cer** [gróusər] *n.* [C] a person who sells food and household supplies.
—[名] 식료 잡화상

***gro·cer·y** [gróus(ə)ri] *n.* (pl. **-cer·ies**) **1.** [U] the trade of a grocer. **2.** (*U.S.*) [C] a grocer's store. **3.** 《*pl.*》 things sold by a grocer.
—[名] 1. 식료 잡화상 2. 식료 잡화점 3. 식료 잡화류

grog [grɑg / grɔg] *n.* [U] (esp. *Brit.*) a drink of rum or whisky mixed with water.
—[名] 《英》 물을 탄 럼술(위스키)

grog·gy [grági / grɔ́gi] *adj.* (**-gi·er, -gi·est**) **1.** unsteady; shaky. **2.** drunk.
—[形] 1. 흔들흔들하는 2. 술에 취한

groin [grɔin] *n.* [C] **1.** the part where the thigh joins the body. **2.** (*Architecture*) the curved line where two arched roofs cross. —*vt.* form or build (something) with groins.
—[名] 1. 서혜(鼠蹊), 사타구니 2.《建》 궁륭(穹窿) —[他] …을 궁륭으로 만들다

***groom** [gru(ː)m] *n.* [C] **1.** a man or boy who takes care of horses. **2.** a bridegroom. **3.** an officer of the English royal household. —*vt.* **1.** feed and take care of (horses). **2.** 《*chiefly in passive*》 make (someone) neat. ¶*He is well groomed.*①
—[名] 1. 바부 2. 신랑 3. 궁내관(宮內官) —[他] 1. [말]의 솔질을 하다 2. …을 단정히 몸차림하게 하다 ¶①그는 몸차림이 단정하다

groove [gruːv] *n.* [C] **1.** a narrow channel, esp. one cut by a tool. **2.** a habitual way of living. ¶*deviate from the social ~*① / *get* (or *fall*) *into a ~.*② —*vt.* make a groove or grooves in (something).
—[名] 1. 홈 2. 관례;상도(常道) ¶①사회 관습에서 벗어나다/②틀에 박히다 —[他] …에 홈을 파다

grope [group] *vi., vt.* search for (something) with the hands; search blindly. ¶*~ for the switch in the dark room* / *~ one's way.*①
—[自][他] 더듬어 찾다 ¶①손으로 더듬으며 나아가다

***gross** [grous] *adj.* **1.** thick; fat. ¶*a ~ body.* **2.** very bad. ¶*a ~ mistake.*① **3.** full of leaves; dense. ¶*the ~ vegetation of the tropical jungles.* **4.** whole; total. ↔ net ¶*the ~ amount.*②
—*n.* **1.** [U] 《usu. *the ~*》 the total amount. **2.** [C] (pl. **gross**) twelve dozen; 144. ¶*a great ~*③ / *a small ~.*④
1) ***by the gross,*** ⓐ by large amounts. ⓑ wholesale.
2) ***in the gross,*** ⓐ as a whole; in large amounts. ⓑ wholesale.
▷**gross·ly** [-li] *adv.* —**gross·ness** [-nis] *n.*
—[形] 1. 뚱뚱한 2. 심한, 형편없는 ¶①큰 잘못 3. 무성한, 우거진 4. 전체의 ¶②총액
—[名] 1. 총체, 총계 2. 그로스(12다스, 144개) ¶③12 그로스/④4 다스
[熟] 1)ⓐ전체로, 통틀어 ⓑ도매로 2)ⓐ대체로, 전체로 ⓑ도매로

gro·tesque [groutésk] *adj.* **1.** strange; odd; queer. ¶*a ~ appearance.* **2.** foolish; absurd. ¶*a ~ mistake.* —*n.* **1.** [C] a grotesque person, animal, figure, or design. **2.** 《*the ~*》 painting, carving, etc., produced in a grotesque style. ▷**gro·tesque·ly** [-li] *adv.*
—[形] 1. 그로테스크풍의; 괴기한, 이상한, 기괴한 2. 어리석은
—[名] 1. 기괴한 사람(것) 2. 그로테스크풍

grot·to [grátou / grɔ́t-] *n.* [C] (pl. **-toes** or **-tos**) a natural or man-made cave.
—[名] 작은 동굴, 석굴

grouch [grautʃ] *n.* [C] (*U.S. colloq.*) **1.** a habitually bad-tempered person; a person who is apt to complain. **2.** a fit of bad temper; a discontented feeling. —*vi.* be in a bad temper; complain.
—[名] 《美口》 1. 잘 토라지는 사람; 불평꾼 2. 시무룩함;불만 —[自] 시무룩해 있다; 불평하다

grouch·y [gráutʃi] *adj.* (**grouch·i·er, grouch·i·est**) (*U.S. colloq.*) bad-tempered; discontented.
—[形] 《美口》 토라진; 투덜거리는

⁝ground[1] [graund] *n.* **1.** Ⓤ ⟪often *the* ~⟫ the surface of the earth; soil; land. **2.** Ⓒ a piece of land for a special use. ¶*a football* ~. **3.** Ⓤ the bottom of the sea, lake, river, etc. **4.** ⟪*pl.*⟫ the gardens around a large house. **5.** ⟪usu. *pl.*⟫ cause; reason; foundation. **6.** Ⓤ position. ¶*common* ~.① **7.** Ⓒ a background.
1) ***above ground,*** alive.
2) ***below ground,*** dead and buried.
3) ***break fresh*** (or ***new***) ***ground,*** ⓐ cultivate new land. ⓑ do something that has not been attempted before.
4) ***cover ground,*** ⓐ travel. ⓑ deal with a variety of subjects.
5) ***down to the ground,*** thoroughly; in all respects.
6) ***fall to the ground,*** fail.
7) ***from the ground up,*** completely; thoroughly.
8) ***gain ground,*** move forward; make progress; win success or an advantage.
9) ***give*** (or ***lose***) ***ground,*** retreat; fail to keep one's position or advantage.
10) ***hold*** (or ***keep, stand***) ***one's ground,*** stand firm; do not yield; do not retreat.
11) ***on one's own ground,*** in a familiar situation; on a subject that one knows well; at home.
12) ***on the ground of,*** because of.
—*vt.* **1.** establish; base. ¶~ *one's arguments on experience* / *The novel is grounded on fact.* **2.** cause (a ship) to run aground. **3.** connect (an electric wire) with the ground. —*vi.* run aground.

—[名] 1. 지면, 땅; 흙; 토지 2. [어떤 목적을 위한] 장소; 운동장 3. 해저, 물밑바닥 4. 뜰, 정원; 부지(敷地), 대지 5. 원인; 이유; 기초 6. 입장 ¶①공통된 입장 7. 배경, 바탕

[熟] 1)살아 있는 2)죽은, 매장된 3)ⓐ처녀지를 개간하다 ⓑ신천지를 개척하다 4)ⓐ여행하다 ⓑ여러가지 분야를 다루다 5)철저하게; 모든 점에서 6)실패로 끝나다 7)완전히, 철저하게 8)전진하다; 진보하다; 우세하게 되다 9)퇴각하다; 불리한 입장에 서다 10)자신의 입장을 고수하다; 양보하지 않다 11)익숙한 입장에서; 잘 알고 있는 문제에서; 마음 편히 12)…의 이유로

—[他] 1. …을 수립하다; …의 기초를 두다 2. …을 좌초시키다 3. …을 접지(接地)시키다 —[自] 좌초하다

ground[2] [graund] *v.* pt. and pp. of **grind**.

ground floor [ˊ ˋ] *n.* **1.** the first floor. **2.** (*U.S.*) the beginning.
—[名] 1. 1층 2. ⟪美⟫ 시초

ground·less [gráundlis] *adj.* without foundation or reason.
—[形] 근거없는

ground·nut [gráun(d)nʌ̀t] *n.* Ⓒ a peanut.
—[名] 땅콩, 낙화생

ground plan [ˊ ˋ] *n.* **1.** the plan of a floor of a building. **2.** any first or essential plan.
—[名] 1. 1층 평면도 2. 기본 계획

ground·work [gráundwə̀:rk] *n.* Ⓤ foundation; basis.
—[名] 토대; 기초

⁝group [gru:p] *n.* Ⓒ **1.** a number of persons or things together. ¶*a* ~ *of persons* / *a* ~ *of stars* / *in a* ~ (or *groups*). **2.** a number of persons or things belonging or classed together. **3.** (*Art*) two or more objects forming a complete design. —*vt.* form (persons or things) into a group or groups. —*vi.* gather in a group.
—[名] 1. 떼, 무리, 그루우프 2. [예술·주의·신앙 따위의] 파; [분류학상의] 군(群) 3. [그림 따위에서 구도(構圖)상의] 군상(群像) —[他] …을 떼짓게 하다; 분류하다 —[自] 떼짓다; 한 무리가 되다

grouse [graus] *n.* Ⓒ (pl. **grouse** or **grous·es**) a game bird with plump body and feathered legs.
—[名] 뇌조(雷鳥)

⁎grove [grouv] *n.* Ⓒ a group of trees; a small wood.
—[名] 나무 숲, 작은 숲

grov·el [grʌ́vl, grávl / grɔ́vl, grʌ́vl] *vi.* (**-eled, -el·ing** or *Brit.* **-elled, -el·ling**) crawl on the ground; humble oneself. ¶~ *before a king* / ~ *in the dust.*①
—[自] 기다; 엎드리다; 자신을 낮추다 ¶①땅에 머리를 대다; 굽실거리다

⁝grow [grou] *v.* (**grew, grown**) *vi.* **1.** live and become bigger. ¶*She has grown into a pretty girl.* / *Your hair has grown.*① **2.** increase; develop. ¶*His debts are growing.* **3.** come out; spring up; sprout. ¶*Moss grows on the rock.*② **4.** become; get. ⟪~ *to do*⟫ ¶*He grew angry.* / *He grew to know her better.* —*vt.* cause (an animal or a plant) to grow; raise; cultivate.
1) ***grow on*** (or ***upon***), become gradually more attractive or effective to (someone). ¶*This book will soon* ~ *upon you.*③
2) ***grow out of,*** ⓐ be a result of (something). ¶*Invention grows out of necessity.* ⓑ become too big for (clothes, etc.). ⓒ abandon; give up usu, as a result of becoming older. ¶*He has grown out of his bad habits.*
3) ***grow up,*** become fully grown; become an adult.

—[自] 1. 성장하다; 자라다 ¶①머리가 자랐다 2. 발달하다; 늘다 3. 나오다, 싹트다 ¶②바위에는 이끼가 난다 4. …으로 되다; 변하다 —[他] …을 기르다; 재배하다

[熟] 1)차츰 좋아지게 되다; 더 효과 있게 되다 ¶③너는 곧 이 책이 좋아질 것이다 2)ⓐ…의 결과이다 ⓑ너무 커지다 ⓒ…에서 탈피하다 3)성인(어른)이 되다

grow·er [gróuər] *n.* Ⓒ **1.** a person who grows agricul-
—[名] 1. [화초·야채류의] 재배자 2. …

G

tural products; a cultivator. **2.** a plant that grows in a certain way. ¶*a slow* ~① / *a quick* ~.②
하게 자라는 식물 ¶①느리게(빠르게) 자라는 식물

* **growl** [graul] *vi.* **1.** make a low, angry sound. 《~ *at* someone》 ¶*The dog growled at him.* **2.** complain angrily. —*vt.* express (something) by growling. 《~ *out* something》 ¶~ *out an answer.*① —*n.* [C] **1.** a low, angry sound. **2.** an angry complaint.
—[自] 1. 으르렁거리다 2. 불평하다 —[他] …을 으르렁거리며 말하다 ¶①투덜투덜 대답하다 —[名] 1. 으르렁소리 2. 불평

⁑ **grown** [groun] *v.* pp. of **grow**.
—*adj.* arrived at full growth. ¶*a* ~ *man.*①
—[形] 성장한 ¶①성인

* **grown-up** [gróunʌ̀p] *adj.* adult; suitable for an adult. —*n.* [C] an adult.
—[形] 성인이 된; 어른에 맞는 —[名] 어른

* **growth** [grouθ] *n.* **1.** [U] the act of growing or developing. **2.** [U] increase. **3.** [U] cultivation. ¶*of foreign* ~.① **4.** [C] something growing or that has grown. **5.** [C] a tumor, cancer, etc.
—[名] 1. 성장, 발육, 발달 2. 증가 3. 재배 ¶①외국산의 4. 성장물, 초목 5. 종양(腫瘍)

grub [grʌb] *n.* [C] **1.** a soft, fat insect larva. **2.** a person who works hard at some long, uninteresting work. **3.** [U] (*colloq*) food.
—[名] 1. [곤충의] 유충, 구더기 2. 지루하고 하찮은 일을 부지런히 하는 사람 3. 《口》 먹을것, 음식

—*v.* (**grubbed, grub·bing**) *vt.* **1.** dig up; dig (roots) out of the ground. 《~ *up* or *out* something》 **2.** (*colloq.*) feed. —*vi.* **1.** dig in the ground. **2.** work hard; drudge. 《~ *on* something》
—[他] 1. …을 파다; [나무 뿌리]를 파내다 2. …을 먹이다 —[自] 1. 땅을 파다 2. 악착같이 일하다

grub·by [grʌ́bi] *adj.* (**-bi·er, -bi·est**) **1.** having grubs. **2.** dirty.
—[形] 1. 구더기가 생긴 2. 더러운

* **grudge** [grʌdʒ] *vt.* **1.** be unwilling to give or allow (someone or something). ¶~ *him money;* ~ *money to him.* **2.** envy. ¶~ *him his success.* —*n.* [C] a feeling of envy or ill-will. ¶*have* (or *bear*) *a* ~ *against someone*① / *work off a* ~.②
—[他] 1. …을 주기를 아까와하다 2. …을 샘내다 —[名] 원한, 악의 ¶①…에 원한을 품다/②원한을 풀다

grudg·ing [grʌ́dʒiŋ] *adj.* unwilling. ▷**grudg·ing·ly** [-li] *adv.*
—[形] 마지못해 하는

gru·el [grú:əl / grúəl] *n.* [U] a thin liquid food made by boiling grain in water or milk.
—[名] 묽은 죽

grue·some [grú:səm] *adj.* horrible; frightful.
—[形] 오싹하는; 무시무시한

gruff [grʌf] *adj.* **1.** harsh; hoarse. ¶*a* ~ *voice.* **2.** rough; rude. ¶*a* ~ *manner.* ▷**gruff·ly** [-li] *adv.*
—[形] 1. 목이 쉰, 거친 목소리의 2. 퉁명스러운; 무뚝뚝한

* **grum·ble** [grʌ́mbl] *vi.* **1.** murmur discontentedly. 《~ *at* (or *about, over*) something》 **2.** rumble. —*vt.* express (something) by grumbling. ¶~ *over one's food.* —*n.* [C] **1.** complaint. **2.** a rumbling sound.
—[自] 1. 투덜투덜 말하다 2. [우뢰가] 우르르 울리다 —[他] …을 불평스러운 말투로 말하다 —[名] 1. 불평 2. 우르르(천둥소리)

grum·bler [grʌ́mblər] *n.* [C] a person who grumbles.
—[名] 투덜거리는 사람

grump·y [grʌ́mpi] *adj.* (**grump·i·er, grump·i·est**) ill-tempered; surly. ¶*a* ~ *old woman.*
—[形] 기분나쁜, 까다로운

* **grunt** [grʌnt] *vi.* make a noise like a pig; grumble. —*vt.* express (something) by grunting. 《~ *out* something》 ¶~ *out an answer.* —*n.* [C] a low, deep, rough sound.
—[自] [돼지가] 꿀꿀거리다; 불평을 말하다 —[他] …을 불평스럽게 말하다 —[名] 꿀꿀소리

* **guar·an·tee** [gæ̀rəntí:] *n.* [C] **1.** a promise to cover another's loss. **2.** a person who gives such a promise. **3.** a person to whom such a promise is given. ↔guarantor
—[名] 1. 보증; 담보 2. 보증인 3. 피(被)보증인

stand guarantee (=*promise to pay*) ***for someone.***
[熟] …의 보증이 되다

—*vt.* **1.** give a guarantee for (someone). ¶~ *someone against* (or *from*) *loss*① / *This watch is guaranteed for one year.*② **2.** promise; affirm.
—[他] 1. …을 보증하다 ¶①…에 손해입히지 않을 것을 보증하다/②이 시계는 1년간 보증이 돼 있다 2. …을 약속하다; 장담하다

guar·an·tor [gǽrəntər, -tɔ̀:r / gæ̀rəntɔ́:] *n.* [C] a person who gives a guarantee.
—[名] 보증인

guar·an·ty [gǽrənti] *n.* [U][C] (pl. **-ties**) a guarantee.
—[名] 보증; 담보

⁑ **guard** [gɑ:rd] *vt.* watch over; defend; protect. —*vi.* be cautious. ¶~ *against disease.*
—[他] …을 망보다; 지키다; 보호하다 —[自] 조심하다

—*n.* **1.** [U] careful watch; caution. **2.** [C] a person or group that guards; a soldier or group of soldiers keeping guard. ¶*a* ~ *of honor*① / *relieve the* ~.② **3.** 《*pl.*》 (*Brit.*) troops employed to protect the sovereign. ¶*the Guards*③ / *the Dragoon Guards*④ / *the Grenadier Guards.*⑤ **4.** [C] (*Brit.*) a person in charge of a railway train.
—[名] 1. 망보기, 감시; 경계; 주의 2. 파수, 감시원; 수위; 경비병; 호위병(대) ¶①의장병/②보초를 교대하다 3. 근위병(대) ¶③근위 연대/④근위 기병 제1연대/⑤근위 보병 제1연대 4. 차장 5. 《英》 차장 6. 방호물(防護物) 7. [축

guarded [513] **guidepost**

(cf. *U.S. conductor*) **5.** ⓒ Ⓤ a position of defense, as in fencing, boxing etc. ¶*at open ~*. **6.** ⓒ a device for protection. **7.** ⓒ (*Football*) either of two players in the line; (*Basketball*) either of two players defending the goal.
1) *keep guard,* watch over.
2) *mount guard,* go on duty as a guard. (→ *n.* 2.)
3) *off one's guard,* unprepared against attack or danger.
4) *on one's guard,* prepared against attack or danger;
5) *stand guard,* act as a guard. (→ *n.* 2.) watchful.

구·농구 따위의] 가아드

🅺 1)파수보다 2)보초 서다 3)방심하여 4)경계하여 5)보초 서다

guard·ed [gáːrdid] *adj.* **1.** defended; protected. **2.** careful; cautious.
—⦿ 1. 방비가 된, 방어된 2. 조심성있는

guard·house [gáːrdhàus] *n.* ⓒ **1.** a building used by soldiers on guard. **2.** a building used as a jail for soldiers.
—⦿ 1. 위병소, 경비 초소 2. 구치소, 영창

* **guard·i·an** [gáːrdiən] *n.* ⓒ **1.** a person who guards. **2.** (*Law*) a person who has the care of other person or his property. ↔ward —*adj.* protecting. ¶*a ~ angel.*①
—⦿ 1. 보호자; 수호자 2. (法) 후견인
—⦿ 수호하는 ¶①수호 천사

guard·i·an·ship [gáːrdiənʃìp] *n.* Ⓤ the state of being a guardian; the position or office of a guardian.
—⦿ 후견인[의 직책·권한]; 보호, 수호

guard·rail [gáːrdrèil] *n.* ⓒ a rail for protection.
—⦿ 난간; 바퀴 보호용 레일

guard·room [gáːrdrù(ː)m] *n.* ⓒ **1.** a room used by soldiers on guard. **2.** a room used as a jail for soldiers.
—⦿ 1. 위병소, 위병 대기실 2. 영창

Gua·te·ma·la [gwæ̀timáːlə] *n.* a country in Central America, south and east of Mexico. ⇒N.B.
—⦿ 중미의 공화국 N.B. 수도 Guatemala

gu·ber·na·to·ri·al [gjùːbərnətɔ́ːriəl] *adj.* (usu. *U. S.*) of a governor.
—⦿ (美) 주지사의

gud·geon [gʌ́dʒ(ə)n] *n.* ⓒ **1.** a small fresh-water fish that is easy to catch and is used for bait. **2.** a person who is easily deceived.
—⦿ 1. 잉어과의 민물고기 2. 잘 속는 사람

guer·don [gáːrd(ə)n] *n.* ⓒ (*poetic*) a reward. —*vt.* reward.
—⦿ (詩) [포]상 —⦿ 상을 주다

gue·ril·la [gərílə] *n.* ⓒ a person engaged in an irregular war carried on by small, independent group of fighters; an irregular war so carried on. ⇒N.B.
—⦿ 게릴라 병, 비(非)정규병; 유격전 N.B. guerrilla 로도 씀

: **guess** [ges] *vt.* **1.** form an opinion or idea about (something) without certain reason. (*~ that ...; ~ to do; ~ what ...; ~ something at*) ¶*I'm not sure, but I ~ this book is hers.*① | *I ~ his age at fifty.*; *I ~ his age to be fifty.*; *I ~ that his age is fifty.* | *Can you ~ what I have in my pocket?*② **2.** (*U.S.*) think; suppose. (*~ that ...*) ¶*I ~ I'll come home by six.* —*vi.* form an opinion without certain reason. (*~ at* or *about something*)
—*n.* ⓒ **1.** an opinion formed without certain reason. **2.** an estimate.

at a guess; by guess, without certain reason.

—⦿ 1. …을 추측하다, 짐작으로 말하다, 알아(생각해) 맞히다 ¶①자신은 없지만 이 책은 그녀의 것이라 생각한다/②주머니에 뭣이 들었는지 알아 맞혀 봐라 2. …이라고 생각하다 —⦿ 추측하다, 짐작하다

—⦿ 1. 추측 2. 평가, 견적

🅺 어림짐작으로, 넘겨짚어서

guess·work [géswə̀ːrk] *n.* Ⓤ the act of guessing; the result of guessing.
—⦿ 추측, 억측; 어림짐작

: **guest** [gest] *n.* ⓒ **1.** a person who is entertained at the house or table of another; a visitor. ¶*a ~ of honor.*① **2.** a person staying at a hotel. ¶*a paying ~.*②
—⦿ 1. [초대 받은] 손님 ¶①주빈 2. 숙박인 ¶②하숙인

guf·faw [gʌfɔ́ː, gə-] *n.* ⓒ a loud, coarse burst of laughter. —*vi.* laugh in this way. [America. ⇒N.B.]
—⦿ 너털웃음 —⦿ 너털웃음을 웃다

Gui·a·na [giǽnə / giáːnə] *n.* a region in northern South
—⦿ 남미의 지방 N.B. 영국·프랑스

guid·ance [gáid(ə)ns] *n.* Ⓤ the act of guiding; the state of being guided; leadership; direction. ¶*under someone's ~*① | *vocational ~*.②
—⦿ 안내; 지휘; 지도 ¶①…의 지도 아래 /②직업 보도(輔導)

: **guide** [gaid] *vt.* **1.** show the way; lead; conduct. **2.** direct; instruct. **3.** manage; control. —*n.* ⓒ **1.** a person who shows the way. **2.** a person who gives help and advice; an advisor. **3.** a thing that shows the position or direction; a directing principle; a book of information. ¶*a ~ to English studies.*
—⦿ 1. …을 [길] 안내하다; 인도하다 2. …을 지도하다 3. …을 지배하다; 관리하다 —⦿ 1. 길로 안내하는 사람; [여행] 안내원 2. 지도자 3. 도표(道標); 지침; 안내서; 입문서

guide·book [gáidbùk] *n.* ⓒ a book of information for travelers.
—⦿ 여행 안내서

guide·post [gáidpòust] *n.* ⓒ a post at crossroads that
—⦿ 도표, 이정표

directs one to places; a sign-post.

guild [gild] *n.* [C] **1.** (*History*) a union of men in the same trade to protect their interests. **2.** an association for the mutual aid and protection of people in a common trade.
—[名] 1. [중세의] 동업조합, 길드 2. 동업조합

guild·hall [gíldhɔ́ːl] *n.* [C] **1.** a hall where members of a guild in the Middle Ages met. **2.** (*Brit.*) a town hall.
—[名] 1. 중세 길드의 집회소 2. 《英》 시청

guile [gail] *n.* [U] cunning; deceit; treachery.
—[名] 교활; 기만

guile·ful [gáilf(u)l] *adj.* full of guile; deceitful; crafty. ▷**guile·ful·ly** [-fuli] *adv.* —**guile·ful·ness** [-nis] *n.*
—[形] 교활한; 거만적인; 음험한

guile·less [gáillis] *adj.* without guile; honest; frank; innocent. ▷**guile·less·ly** [-li] *adv.*
—[形] 교활하지 않은; 정직한; 명랑한; 순진한

guil·lo·tine [gìlətíːn, ˊ--ˋ] *n.* [C] **1.** a machine for cutting off a person's head by means of a heavy knife sliding down between two posts. **2.** a machine for cutting paper, metal, etc. **—*vt.*** cut off the head of (someone) with a guillotine.
—[名] 1. 단두대, 길로틴 2. [종이·금속 따위의] 재단기 —[他] 길로틴으로 …의 목을 자르다

***guilt** [gilt] *n.* [U] crime; sin.
—[名] 죄; 범죄

guilt·i·ly [gíltili] *adv.* in a guilty manner.
—[副] 유죄로; 죄진 것처럼

guilt·i·ness [gíltinis] *n.* [U] the quality or state of being guilty.
—[名] 죄가 있음; 유죄

guilt·less [gíltlis] *adj.* **1.** not guilty; innocent. **2.** having no knowledge or experience. ¶*be ~ of deceit.*
—[形] 1. 죄 없는; 결백한 2. 알지 못하는; 경험 없는

⁑**guilt·y** [gílti] *adj.* (**guilt·i·er, guilt·i·est**) **1.** having done wrong; having committed a crime or a sin. ¶*a ~ deed*① / *a ~ mind*② / *be ~ of murder* / *be declared ~.*③ **2.** showing guilt; of guilt. ¶*a ~ conscience*④ / *a ~ look.*
—[形] 1. 유죄의; 죄를 저지른 ¶①범행 /②고의(故意)/③유죄로 선고되다 2. 죄지은 것 같은; 죄에 관한 ¶④가책되는 양심

guin·ea [gíni] *n.* [C] **1.** a gold coin, once used in England and worth 21 shillings. **2.** the amount of 21 shillings.
—[名] 1. 기니 금화 2. 21 실링

Guin·ea [gíni] *n.* **1.** a region along the western coast of Africa. **2.** 《*the Republic of ~*》 a country in this region. ⇒[N.B.]
—[名] 1. 기니아 지방 2. 기니아 공화국 [N.B.] 수도 Conakry

guinea fowl [ˊ-ˋ] *n.* a domestic fowl of the pheasant family, with a rounded body and dark feathers spotted with white.
—[名] [아프리카 원산] 꿩과의 가금(家禽)

guise [gaiz] *n.* [C] **1.** external appearance; an aspect. **2.** pretense. ¶*in* (or *under*) *the ~ of friendship.*①
—[名] 1. 외관; 용모; 겉치레 2. 구실; 가장 ¶①우정을 가장하여

gui·tar [gitáːr] *n.* [C] a six-stringed musical instrument, played with the fingers.
—[名] 기타아

gulch [gʌltʃ] *n.* [C] (*U.S.*) a deep, narrow, long valley with steep sides.
—[名] 《美》 골짜기, 협곡

⁑**gulf** [gʌlf] *n.* [C] **1.** a large bay. ¶*the Gulf of Mexico.* **2.** a deep hollow in the earth; an abyss. **3.** a wide separation. ¶*the ~ between rich and poor*① / *The quarrel left a ~ between the two families.*
—[名] 1. 만(灣) 2. 갈라진 깊은 틈; 심연 3. 커다란 격차 ¶①빈부의 차이

gull[1] [gʌl] *n.* [C] a graceful gray-white sea-bird with long wings.
—[名] 갈매기

gull[2] [gʌl] *n.* [C] a person who is easily deceived or cheated. **—*vt.*** deceive; cheat. ¶*They gulled him into going there.*① / *~ someone out of money.*
—[名] 잘 속는 사람 —[他] …을 속이다 ¶①그를 속여서 거기로 보냈다

gul·let [gʌ́lit] *n.* [C] **1.** the tube from the mouth to the stomach; the throat. **2.** a water channel.
—[名] 1. 식도, 목구멍 2. 수로(水路), 도랑

gul·li·ble [gʌ́libl] *adj.* easily deceived or cheated.
—[形] 속기 쉬운

gul·ly [gʌ́li] *n.* [C] a channel for water; a small valley. **—*vt.*** make gullies in (something).
—[名] 도랑; 협곡
—[他] …에 도랑을 만들다

gulp [gʌlp] *vt.* **1.** swallow quickly and greedily. ¶*~ down a glass of water.* **2.** check; hold back. ¶*~ down a sob.* **—*vi.*** make a gulping motion. **—*n.*** [C] the act of gulping; the amount swallowed at one time. ¶*at one* (or *a*) *~.*①
—[他] 1. …을 꿀꺽꿀꺽 마시다, 쭉 들이키다 2. …을 억누르다; 참다 —[自] 쭉 들이키다 —[名] 쭉 들이키기; 쭉 들이키는 분량 ¶①한 모금에

***gum**[1] [gʌm] *n.* [U] **1.** a sticky substance obtained from certain trees. **2.** chewing gum. **3.** a sticky substance used to fasten papers, etc. together. **4.** rubber; 《*pl.*》 rubber overshoes. **5.** [C] a gum tree.
—[名] 1. 수지(樹脂), 점성(粘性)고무 2. [씹는] 껌 3. 고무풀 4. 고무; 고무신 5. 고무나무

—*v.* (**gummed, gum·ming**) *vt.* stick (things) together with gum; spread gum on the surface of (something). **—*vi.*** give off gum; become sticky.
—[他] …을 고무풀로 접착하다; …의 표면에 수지를 바르다 —[自] 고무를 분비하다; 고무 모양이 되다

gum[2] [gʌm] *n.* [C] 《usu. *pl.*》 the flesh around the teeth.
—[名] 잇몸, 치은(齒齦)

G

gum·my [gʌ́mi] *adj.* (**-mi·er, -mi·est**) sticky; covered with gum; giving off gum.
—[形] 고무 같은; 고무로 덮인; 고무를 분비하는

gum tree [ˊ ˋ] *n.* a tree from which gum is got.
—[名] 고무나무

gun [gʌn] *n.* [C] **1.** a weapon that fires a shot, such as a cannon, rifle, pistol, or revolver. **2.** the shooting of a gun as a signal or salute. ¶*a salute of twenty-one guns.*①
—[名] 1. 총, 대포 2. 대포의 발사(신호포·예포·축포 따위) ¶①21 발의 예포

1) [*as*] ***sure as a gun,*** without doubt; certainly.
2) ***stick*** (or ***stand***) ***to one's guns,*** be firm; do not yield or retreat.
[熟] 1)틀림없이 2)입장을 고수하다; 굴복하지 않다

—*v.* (**gunned, gun·ning**) *vi.* shoot or hunt with a gun; go shooting or hunting. —*vt.* shoot (someone).
—[自] 총을 쏘다; 사냥 가다
—[他] …을 총으로 쏘다

gun for, hunt (animals) with a gun; look for (animals) in order to shoot them.
[熟] 총으로 …사냥을 가다; …을 쏘기 위해 찾다

gun·boat [gʌ́nbòut] *n.* [C] a small warship carrying heavy guns.
—[名] 포함(砲艦)

gun·fire [gʌ́nfàiər] *n.* [U] the act of shooting with a gun.
—[名] 포격; 발포; 포화

gun·man [gʌ́nmən, -mæ̀n] *n.* [C] (pl. **-men** [-mən, -mèn]) **1.** (*U.S. colloq.*) a man who uses a gun to rob or kill people. **2.** a person who makes guns.
—[名] 1. 총을 휴대한 악한 2. 총포공(工)

gun metal [ˊ ˋ-] *n.* **1.** a dark-gray mixture of metal; a variety of bronze. **2.** dark gray.
—[名] 1. 포금(砲金); 청동 2. 짙은 회색

gun·ner [gʌ́nər] *n.* [C] **1.** a person who works a gun. **2.** (in the navy) an officer in charge of a ship's guns. **3.** a person who hunts animals with a gun.
—[名] 1. 포수(砲手); 포병 2. 장포장(掌砲長) 3. 총 사냥꾼

gun·ner·y [gʌ́nəri] *n.* [U] **1.** the art and science of making and using heavy guns. **2.** the act of firing heavy guns. **3.** 《*collectively*》 heavy guns.
—[名] 1. 포술; 사격법 2. 포격; 발포 3. 포, 총포

gun·ny [gʌ́ni] *n.* (pl. **-nies**) **1.** [U] a strong, coarse cloth used for sacks and bags. **2.** [C] a sack or bag made of this cloth. ¶*a ~ sack* (or *bag*).
—[名] 1. 굵은 삼베, 즈크 2. 즈크로 만든 부대

gun·pow·der [gʌ́npàudər] *n.* [U] an bursting powder used in guns, fireworks, etc.
—[名] 화약

gun·shot [gʌ́nʃɑ̀t / -ʃɔ̀t] *n.* **1.** [C] a bullet or other shot fired from a gun. **2.** [C] the shooting of a gun. **3.** [U] the distance that a gun will shoot. ¶*within* (*out of*) *~.*①
—[名] 1. 발사된 탄환 2. 사격, 발포 3. 착탄(着彈) 거리 ¶①사정(射程) 안(밖)에

gun·wale [gʌ́nl] *n.* [C] the top edge of the side of a boat. ⇒[N.B.]
—[名] 배의 위 가장자리 [N.B.] gunnel로도 씀

gur·gle [gə́ːrgl] *vi.* **1.** flow with a bubbling sound. **2.** make a bubbling sound. —*vt.* express (something) with a gurgling sound. —*n.* [C] the act of gurgling; a gurgling sound.
—[自] 1. 물이 콸콸 흐르다 2. 꼴록꼴록 [목구멍 따위로] 소리내다 —[他] …을 꼴록꼴록 소리내며 말하다 —[名] 꼴록꼴록(꼴깍꼴깍·콸콸)소리

gush [gʌʃ] *vi.* **1.** flow out suddenly with force; pour out. 《~ *out* or *forth*》 **2.** (*colloq.*) talk with too much eagerness or admiration. —*vt.* cause (something) to pour out —*n.* [C] **1.** a sudden outflow of water or other liquid. **2.** (*colloq.*) silly, emotional talk.
—[自] 1. 흘러나오다, 뿜어 나오다 2. 《口》 지껄여대다 —[他] …을 유출시키다 —[名] 1. 유출, 분출 2. 《口》 과장된 감정적인 이야기

gush·er [gʌ́ʃər] *n.* [C] an oil well with a large natural flow.
—[名] 분유정(噴油井)

gush·ing [gʌ́ʃiŋ] *adj.* pouring out; flowing out abundantly.
—[形] 뿜어 나오는; [감정 따위] 용솟음치는

gus·set [gʌ́sit] *n.* [C] a triangular piece of cloth let into garment to enlarge or strengthen it.
—[名] 삼각천, 무, 섶

gust [gʌst] *n.* [C] **1.** a sudden rush of wind. ¶*a violent ~ of wind.*① **2.** an outburst of anger or other feeling.
—[名] 1. 돌풍 ¶①한 줄기의 강풍 2. [감정의] 폭발

gus·to [gʌ́stou] *n.* [U][C] (pl. **-tos**) **1.** taste; liking. **2.** keen enjoyment. ¶*with ~.*①
—[名] 1. 취미; 기호 2. 큰 즐거움 ¶①아주 즐겁게

gust·y [gʌ́sti] *adj.* (**gust·i·er, gust·i·est**) **1.** windy; stormy. **2.** marked by outbursts of emotion, sound, etc. ¶*~ anger.*
—[形] 1. 돌풍의 2. [감정·소리 따위] 돌발적인

gut [gʌt] *n.* **1.** 《*pl.*》 the bowels; intestines. ¶*the large* (*small*) *~*① / *the blind ~.*② **2.** 《*pl.*》 contents. ¶*have no guts.* **3.** 《*pl.*》 courage; endurance. ¶*a man with plenty of guts.*③ **4.** [U] a strong cord made from the intestines of animals, used for violin strings and tennis rackets. **5.** [C] a narrow channel.
—[名] 1. 장(腸), 내장 ¶①대(소)장/②맹장 2. 내용, 속 3. 용기; 내구력 ¶③배짱있는 사람 4. 장선(腸線), 거트 5. 좁은 수로(水路); 해협

—*vt.* (**gut·ted, gut·ting**) **1.** take the intestines out of (a fish). **2.** plunder; destroy the inside of (a building).
—[他] **1.** …의 창자를 뽑다 **2.** …의 속을 빼 버리다; …의 내부를 파괴하다

gut·ta·per·cha [gʌ́təpə́:rtʃə] *n.* [U] a rubberlike substance made from the juice of certain trees in Malaya.
—[名] 구타페르카

gut·ter [gʌ́tər] *n.* [C] **1.** a channel under the eaves of a building to carry off rain water. **2.** a channel or ditch along the side of a street to carry off water. **3.** 《*the* ～》 a low, poor place. ¶*rise from the* ～.①
—[名] **1.** [지붕의] 낙수 홈통 **2.** 도랑, 하수 **3.** 빈민굴 ¶①천한 신분에서 출세하다

—*vt.* furnish (something) with gutters; make gutters in (something). —*vi.* become channeled; (of a candle) melt in streams.
—[他] …에 홈통을 달다; 도랑을 내다
—[自] 도랑이 생기다; [양초의] 촛농이 흐르다

gut·tur·al [gʌ́t(ə)r(ə)l] *adj.* **1.** of the throat. **2.** produced in the throat. ¶*a* ～ *sound.*① —*n.* [C] (*Phonetics*) a sound produced in this way, such as [k] and [g].
—[形] **1.** 목구멍의 **2.** 목구멍에서 나오는 ¶①후음(喉音) —[名] 후음

***guy**[1] [gai] *n.* [C] a supporting rope, wire, or chain. ¶*the guys of a tent.* —*vt.* steady (something) with a guy.
—[名] 받침줄, 당김줄 —[他] 받침줄로 안정시키다

***guy**[2] [gai] *n.* [C] **1.** (*U.S. colloq.*) a fellow. **2.** a person of queer appearance or dress. —*vt.* make fun of (someone); tease.
—[名] **1.**《美口》 녀석, 놈, 친구 **2.** 이상한 복장(용모)의 사람, 별난 사람 —[他] …을 놀리다

guz·zle [gʌ́zl] *vi., vt.* eat or drink greedily.
—[自][他] 폭음하다, 게걸스럽게 먹다

***gym** [dʒim] *n.* (*colloq.*) [U] gymnastics; [C] a gymnasium.
—[名] 체조; 체육관

gym·na·si·a [dʒimnéiziə] *n.* pl. of **gymnasium**.

gym·na·si·um [dʒimnéiziəm] *n.* [C] (pl. **-ums** or **-si·a**) a large room or building for athletic practice.
—[名] 체육관

gym·nast [dʒímnæst] *n.* [C] an expert in gymnastics.
—[名] 체육교사, 체육가

gym·nas·tic [dʒimnǽstik] *adj.* of physical exercises or activities.
—[形] 체조의, 체육의

gym·nas·tics [dʒimnǽstiks] *n. pl.* 《used as *sing.*》 physical exercises for developing the body.
—[名] 체조; 훈련

gyp·sum [dʒípsəm] *n.* [U] a chalk-like substance used for making plaster of Paris.
—[名] 석고, 깁스

gyp·sy [dʒípsi] *n.* (pl. **-sies**) **1.** 《often *G-*》 [C] a member of a dark-skinned race of people who originally came from India. **2.** [U] the language of the Gypsies. —*adj.* of or like a gypsy. ⇒[N.B.]
—[名] **1.** 집시 **2.** 집시 말 —[形] 집시의, 집시 같은 [N.B.] 영국에서는 **gipsy**로도 씀

gy·rate [dʒái(ə)reit / ⌐⌐] *vi.* move in a circle; whirl.
—[自] 선회하다; 소용돌이치다

gy·ra·tion [dʒai(ə)réiʃ(ə)n] *n.* [U] the act of gyrating; [C] a revolution.
—[名] 선회

gy·ro·scope [dʒái(ə)rəskòup, +*Brit.* gáiə-] *n.* [C] a machine with a heavy spinning wheel which helps to keep ships and airplanes balanced. ⇒fig.
—[名] 자이로스코우프, 회전의(回轉儀)

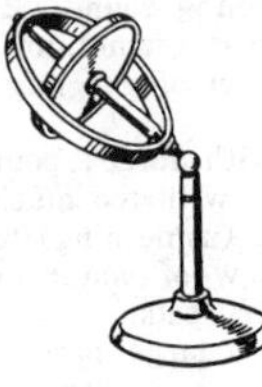

〔gyroscope〕

gyve [dʒaiv] *n.* 《usu. *pl.*》 a chain for the feet; a fetter; a shackle. —*vt.* fasten (the leg) with gyves; fetter.
—[名] 족쇄, 차꼬; 수갑
—[他] 족쇄(수갑)를 채우다

H

H, h [eitʃ] *n.* [C] (pl. **H's, Hs, h's, hs** [éitʃiz]) the eighth letter of the English alphabet.
—[名] 영어 자모의 여덟째 글자

h., H. 1. harbor **2.** height **3.** hit **4.** hundred.

***ha** [hɑ:] *interj.* **1.** an exclamation of wonder, surprise, joy, victory, doubt, etc. **2.** the sound of laughing.
—[感] **1.** 허어, 야아, 저런 **2.** 하하(웃음소리)

hab·er·dash·er [hǽbərdæ̀ʃər] *n.* [C] **1.** (*U.S.*) a dealer who sells men's furnishings, such as hats, ties, and shirts. **2.** (*Brit.*) a merchant who sells small good, such
—[名] **1.**《美》 남자용 장신구상[인] **2.**《英》 잡화 상인

as buttons, needles, and pins.

hab·er·dash·er·y [hǽbərdæ̀ʃəri] *n.* (pl. **-er·ies**) **1.** [U] (*U.S.*) men's furnishings, such as hats and shirts. **2.** [C] a haberdasher's shop.
—[名] 1.《美》 신사용 장신구류 2. 신사용 장신구점

ha·bil·i·ments [həbílimənts] *n. pl.* items of clothing.
—[名] 복장[예복·직복(職服) 따위]

‡**hab·it** [hǽbit] *n.* **1.** [U] [C] the tendency to do a certain thing without thought or need for it; a usual way of acting. ¶*be in the ~ of sitting up late*① | *form a good ~*② | *give up a bad ~*③ | *the ~ of smoking*④ | *Habit is* [*a*] *second nature.*⑤ | *He does it merely out of ~.*⑥ **2.** [U] [C] the condition of the body or mind. ¶*a cheerful ~.* **3.** [C] a special character of an animal or a plant. **4.** [C] the unique clothing of some religious group; a woman's riding dress. ¶*a monk's ~.*⑦
—[名] 1. 습관, 버릇 ¶①밤늦게까지 안 자는 버릇이 있다/②좋은 습관을 붙이다/③나쁜 습관을 버리다/④담배 피우는 버릇/⑤습관은 제 2의 천성이다/⑥그는 버릇으로 그렇게 할 뿐이다 2. 기질, 체질 3. 습성 4. [어떤 계급의] 복장, 부인용 승마복 ¶⑦법의(法衣)

1) ***break** oneself **of a habit,*** become free from one's own habit.
2) ***break** someone **of a habit,*** cause someone to give up his habit.
[熟] 1)[자기]의 버릇을 고치다 2)…의 버릇을 고쳐 주다

—*vt.* put a dress on (someone); clothe.
—[他] …을 입다; …에게 입히다

hab·it·a·ble [hǽbitəbl] *adj.* fit to live in.
—[形] 살기에 알맞은

hab·i·tat [hǽbitæ̀t] *n.* [C] **1.** the natural home of an animal or a plant. **2.** a living place.
—[名] 1. [동식물의] 산지, 서식지 2. 주소, 사는 곳

hab·i·ta·tion [hæ̀bitéiʃ(ə)n] *n.* **1.** [C] a place to live in; a home. **2.** [U] the act of inhabiting.
—[名] 1. 주소, 주택 2. 거주(居住)

***ha·bit·u·al** [həbítʃuəl, +*Brit.* -bítju-] *adj.* **1.** acting by habit. ¶*one's ~ seat.*① **2.** doing something by habit. ¶*a~ criminal.*②
—[形] 1. 습관적인, 평소의 ¶①늘 앉는 자리 2. 상습적인 ¶②상습범

ha·bit·u·al·ly [həbítʃuəli, +*Brit.* -bítju-] *adv.* as a habit; regularly.
—[副] 항상, 습관적으로

ha·bit·u·ate [həbítʃuèit, +*Brit.* -bítju-] *vt.* **1.** cause (someone) to form a habit; accustom. 《~ someone *to*》 ¶*~ oneself to a cold climate* | *He was habituated to hard work.*① **2.** visit (the same place) very often. ▷**ha·bit·u·a·tion** [həbìtʃuéiʃ(ə)n, +*Brit.* -bìtju-] *n.*
—[他] 1. …을 익숙하게 하다, …에 길들이다 ¶①그는 중노동에 길이 들었다 2. …에 자주 가다

ha·bit·u·é [həbítʃuèi / -bítju-] *n.* [C] a person who is in the habit of going to a place regularly. ¶*a ~ of a variety-hall.*①
—[名] 단골손님, 고객 ¶①연예관(演藝館)의 단골들

hack[1] [hæk] *vt.* cut roughly; cut (something) to pieces. ¶*Don't ~ your pencil.* —*vi.* give short, dry coughs. ¶*a hacking cough.* —*n.* [C] **1.** a rough cut. **2.** a tool for cutting. **3.** a short dry cough.
—[他] [난폭하게] …을 마구 자르다, 난도질하다 —[自] 마른기침을 하다 —[名] 1. 마구 자르기, 난도질 2. 도끼, 곡괭이 3. 마른기침

hack[2] [hæk] *n.* [C] **1.** (*U.S.*) a coach or carriage for hire. **2.** (*colloq.*) a taxi. **3.** (*Brit.*) a horse for hire. **4.** an old, worn-out horse. **5.** a horse for riding. **6.** a person employed to do uninteresting work,.
—[名] 1.《美》 세놓는 마차 2.《口》 택시 3.《英》 세놓는 말 4. 늙은 말 5. 승마용 말 6. 하청을 맡아 일하는 사람

—*vi.* **1.** ride a horse. **2.** work as a hack (*n.* 6.). —*vt.* hire out (a horse.) **2.** employ (someone) as a hack (*n.* 6.).
—[自] 1. [말]을 타다 2. 남의 밑에서 일하다 —[他] 1. [말]을 세놓다 2. …을 필경(筆耕)으로 고용하다

—*adj.* working merely for money; hired. ¶***a ~ writer.***
—[形] 고용된, 돈 때문에 일하는

hack·ney [hǽkni] *n.* [C] **1.** a horse used chiefly for riding. **2.** a carriage for hire. —*adj.* hired; ordinary; not new. —*vt.* use (a horse, etc.) too often.
—[名] 1. 승마용의 말 2. 세놓는 마차(말) —[形] 세놓는; 흔해빠진 —[他] …을 부려 먹다

hack·neyed [hǽknid] *adj.* well-worn; used too often; made common. ¶*a ~ phrase.*①
—[形] 써서 낡은, 평범한, 진부한 ¶①진부한 어구

***hack·saw** [hǽksɔ̀ː] *n.* [C] a narrow, toothed blade with a frame for cutting metal.
—[名] [금속을 자르는] 활톱, 쇠톱

‡**had** [hæd, həd, əd, d] *v.* pt. and pp. of **have**.
—[動] have의 과거·과거분사

1) ***had as good** do,* would prefer to do.
2) (*You*) ***had better** do,* (You) would be wiser to do.
3) (*You*) ***had better have** done,* (You) would have been wiser to do, but (you) didn't.
4) (I) ***had rather** do,* (I) would prefer to do.
[熟] 1)…하는 편이 낫다 2)…하는 편이 낫다 3)…하는 편이 좋았다 4)오히려 …하는 것이 좋다

had·dock [hǽdək] *n.* [C] (pl. **-docks** or *collectively* **-dock**) a small food fish of the North Atlantic.
—[名] 대구류

Ha·des [héidiːz] *n.* **1.** (in Greek mythology) the resting place of the dead, below the earth; Pluto, the king of this place **2.** [C] 《*h-*》 (*colloq.*) a hell.
—[名] 1. 저승, 황천, 명부(冥府) 2. 지옥

hadn't [hædnt] had not.
hadst [hædst, hədst, ədst] *v. (archaic)* =had. ⇒USAGE
— USAGE 주어 thou 에 씀

haft [hæft / haːft] *n.* ⓒ the handle of a knife, sword, etc.
—*vt.* furnish (a knife, etc.) with a handle.
— [주머니칼 따위의] 자루, 손잡이
— …에 자루(손잡이)를 달다

hag [hæg] *n.* ⓒ **1.** a very ugly old woman. **2.** a witch.
— 1. 추한 노파 2. 마녀

hag·gard [hǽgərd] *adj.* worn-out and anxious in appearance from tiredness, worry, etc. ▷ **hag·gard·ly** [-li] *adv.* —**hag·gard·ness** [-nis] *n.*
— [피로·근심 따위로] 여윈, 말라빠진

hag·gle [hǽgl] *vi.* talk to someone about a price. 《~ about or over a price, etc.》 ¶ ~ over pennies.
— [값·조건 따위로] 입씨름하다, 흥정하다

Hague [heig], The *n.* the political capital of the Holland. ⇒N.B.
— 네덜란드의 정치 수도 N.B. 헌법상의 수도는 Amsterdam

hah [haː] *interj.* =ha.

ha-ha [hɑ́ːhɑ́ː] *interj.* the sound of laughing.
— 하하, 아하하(웃음소리)

hail[1] [heil] *vt.* **1.** shout a welcome to (someone); greet. ¶They hailed him as king. **2.** call loudly; shout; summon. ¶ ~ a taxi. —*vi.* come. 《~ from a place, etc.》 ¶He hails from London.
—*n.* ⓤ **1.** the act of greeting; a shout of welcome. **2.** a loud call.
within (out of) hail, near enough (too far) to be hailed.
—*interj.* an exclamation of greeting. ¶All ~!; Hail to you!
— 1. …에게 인사하다, …을 환영하다 2. …을 큰 소리로 부르다 — …에서 오다, …의 출신이다
— 1. 인사, 환영 2. 외침, 부르는 소리
▣ 소리가 미치는(미치지 않는) 곳에
— 만세 ¶만세!, 반갑습니다!

hail[2] [heil] *n.* **1.** ⓤ small, round bits of ice that fall in a shower. **2.** ⓒ anything that falls like hail. ¶a ~ of questions.
—*vi.* come down in hail. ¶It hails. ⇒USAGE —*vt.* pour (something) in a shower like hail. 《~ something on or upon》 ¶They hailed blows upon him.
— 1. 싸락눈, 우박 2. 우박같이 쏟아지는 것 ¶①빗발 같은 질문
— 우박이 내리다 USAGE 비인칭의 it 가 주어 — …을 우박처럼 퍼붓다

hail·stone [héilstòun] *n.* ⓒ a small, round ball of ice coming down from thunder clouds.
— 우박, 싸락눈

hail·storm [héilstɔ̀ːrm] *n.* ⓒ a storm with hail.
— 마구 퍼붓는 우박(싸락눈)

hair [hɛər] *n.* **1.** ⓤ threadlike outgrowths from the skin of man and animals; the growth covering the human head; anything like this. ⇒USAGE ¶the ~ of the head / dress one's ~ / lose one's ~. **2.** ⓒ an extremely small space, distance, degree, etc. ¶He missed the target by a ~.
 1) *against the hair*, against the grain; contrary to its nature.
 2) *be not worth a hair*, be of no value.
 3) *do not turn a hair*, give no sign of being troubled.
 4) *get in someone's hair*, annoy; make (someone) angry.
 5) *a hair's breadth*, a very small distance.
 6) *let down one's hair*, ⓐ (of a woman) allow the hair to fall over the shoulders. ⓑ show the real state of one's affairs; speak frankly.
 7) *make someone's hair stand on end*, fill (someone) with great fear.
 8) *split hairs*, talk or argue over unimportant points.
 9) *tear the hair*, show signs of much pain, grief, or anger.
 10) *to [the turn of] a hair*, exactly.
— 1. 털; 머리카락; 털 모양의 것 USAGE 집합적으로 「머리카락」을 가리킬 때에는 불계수 명사. 「한 가락, 두 가락」의 털을 가리킬 때는 a hair, hairs 가 됨 ¶①조발하다/②머리가 벗겨지다 2. 극소, 사소 ¶③그는 과녁을 약간 벗어났다
▣ 1)성미에 거슬러, 본의 아니게 2)전혀 가치가 없다 3)조금도 곤란한 기색이 없다 4)…을 괴롭히다 5)위기일발 6)ⓐ머리를 풀어 어깨까지 늘이다 ⓑ터놓고 대하다 7)…을 오싹하게 하다 8)사소한 일을 꼬치꼬치 따지다 9)[고민·슬픔·노여움으로] 머리털을 쥐어뜯다 10)정확히, 꼬박

hair·breadth [hɛ́ərbrèdθ] *adj.* very narrow; very near. ¶a ~ escape. —*n.* ⓒ a very narrow space; a very small distance. ¶by a ~ / within a ~.
— 털끝만치의, 아슬아슬한 ¶①구사일생 — 털끝만치의 틈(폭), 위기일발 ¶②위기일발로

hair·brush [hɛ́ərbrʌ̀ʃ] *n.* ⓒ a brush for hair.
— 머리 빗는 솔

hair·cloth [hɛ́ərklɔ̀ːθ / -klɔ̀(ː)θ] *n.* ⓤ cloth woven with horsehair, etc.
— 마소직(馬巢織) (말총으로 짠 양복의 심감)

hair·cut [hɛ́ərkʌ̀t] *n.* ⓒ the act or style of cutting the hair.
— 이발, 머리 깎는 모양

hair·do [hɛ́ərdùː] *n.* ⓒ (pl. -dos) a way of arranging the hair.
— 머리치장, 머리 모양

hair·dress·er [hɛ́ərdrèsər] *n.* ⓒ a person who takes care of the hair.
— 이발사, 미용사

hair·less [hɛ́ərlis] *adj.* without hair; bald.
— 머리털이 없는, 대머리의

hair net [´ ´] *n.* a net worn to hold the hair in place.
— 머리에 쓰는 그물

hair·pin [hέərpìn] *n.* [C] a small, bent pin of wire, shell, etc., to hold the hair in place. **—***adj.* U-shaped. ¶*a ~ bend* (or *turn*).①
—[名] 머리핀 —[形] U자형의 ¶①U자형으로 꼬부라진 길

hair's-breadth, hairs·breadth [hέərzbrèdθ] *n., adj.* [=hairbreadth.]

hair·split·ter [hέərsplìtər] *n.* [C] a person who makes too fine or unnecessary differences.
—[名] 사소한 일을 꼬치꼬치 따지는 사람, 궤변가

hair·spring [hέərsprìng] *n.* [C] a delicate, hairlike coil spring that controls the balance wheel in a watch.
—[名] [회중시계의] 유사

hair·y [hέəri] *adj.* (**hair·i·er, hair·i·est**) **1.** covered with hair. **2.** of or like hair. ▷**hair·i·ness** [-nis] *n.*
—[形] 1. 털이 많은, 털투성이의 2. 털의, 털 같은

Hai·ti [héiti] *n.* a country in the West Indies.
—[名] 서인도 제도의 공화국

ha·la·tion [heiléiʃ(ə)n, hæ- / hə-] *n.* [U] (*Photography*) the excessive spread of light in a negative print.
—[名] 《寫》 [광선에 의한] 흐림

hal·berd [hǽlbə(:)rd] *n.* [C] a weapon formed of a spear and an axe, used in the 15th and 16th centuries. ⇒fig.
—[名] 미늘창(창·도끼 겸용의 중세의 무기)

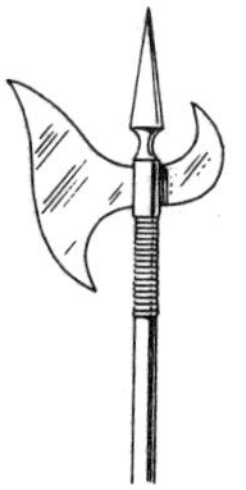
[halberd]

hal·bert [hǽlbə(:)rt] *n.* =halberd.

hal·cy·on [hǽlsiən] *adj.* (of the weather) calm; peaceful. ¶*~ days.*
—[形] 평온한, 온화한

hale [heil] *adj.* healthy; strong and well. ¶*~ and hearty.*①
—[形] 건강한, 탈 없는 ¶①[특히 노인이] 정정한

⁑**half** [hæf / hɑ:f] *n.* [C] (pl. **halves**) **1.** one of two equal parts, or a quantity equal to such a part. ¶*~ an hour* / *~ [of] the boys.* ⇒[usage] **2.** either of the two equal periods of a game.
1) ***by half,*** considerably; very much.
2) ***by halves,*** imperfectly; incompletely.
3) ***go halves with someone in,*** share (something) equally with someone.
4) ***have half a mind to do,*** feel like doing.
5) ***to*** (or ***for, at, on***) ***halves,*** ⓐ incompletely. ⓑ for half the crop or profits.
—*adj.* **1.** being one of two equal parts of a thing. ¶*the first ~ hour*① / *~ truth.* **2.** partial; incomplete. ¶*a ~ knowledge.*② **—***adv.* to the degree or extent of a half; partially; almost. ¶*~ asleep* / *He was ~ dead from hunger.*③
not half bad, fairly good; actually quite good.
—[名] 1. 반, 2분의 1 [usage] 관사 앞에 둠, 뒤에 명사가 올 때는 of를 생략하는 일이 많음. 대명사인 경우는 half of it로 함 2. 전반전, 후반전
[熟] 1)상당히; 대단히 2)불완전하게, 엉거주춤하게 3)[둘이서] 절반씩 나누다 4) …하고 싶은 생각이 들다 5)ⓐ불완전하게 ⓑ[이익을] 절반씩 갖기로 하고
—[形] 1. 반의 ¶①처음의 30분 2. 불완전한 ¶②얼치기 지식 —[副] 반[쯤]; 불충분하게 ¶③그는 굶어죽기 직전이었다
[熟] 꽤 좋은

half-a-crown [hǽfəkráun / há:f-] *n.* [C] a British silver coin worth 2s. 6d.; [U] the amount of 2s. 6d.
—[名] 반 크라운의 은화; 2실링 6펜스의 금액

half-and-half [hǽf(ə)nhǽf / há:f(ə)n(d)há:f] *adj.* **1.** half one thing and half another; composed of two parts. **2.** not clearly one thing or the other. **—***adv.* in two equal parts; equally.
—*n.* [U] **1.** (*U.S.*) a mixture of milk and cream. **2.** (*Brit.*) a mixture of ale and porter.
—[形] 1. 반반의, 두 개의 부분으로 이루어지는 2. 하다 만, 얼치기의 —[副] 반반으로
—[名] 1.《美》 우유와 크리임의 혼합 음료 2.《英》 [ale과 porter의] 혼성주

half·back [hǽfbæ̀k / há:f-] *n.* [C] (of football, hockey, etc.) a player whose position is behind the forward line.
—[名] [축구·하키의] 중위(中衛), 하아프백

half-baked [hǽfbéikt / há:f-] *adj.* **1.** not completely cooked. **2.** (*colloq.*) not complete. **3.** (*colloq.*) not experienced; foolish.
—[形] 1. 설 구워진 2. 미숙한, 불완전한 3. 경험 없는; 어리석은

half-blood [hǽfblʌ̀d / há:f-] *n.* [C] **1.** a half-breed. **2.** a person related to another by having one common parent.
—[名] 1. 잡종, 혼혈아 2. 배다른 형제자매

half blood [´ `] *n.* the relation between persons who are related through having one common parent.
—[名] 배다른 형제자매 관계

half-boiled [hǽfbɔ́ild / há:f-] *adj.* not completely boiled. ¶*a ~ egg.*
—[形] 설 익은, 반숙의

half boot [´ `] *n.* a boot extending about halfway to the knee.
—[名] 반장화

half-bred [hǽfbrèd / há:f-] *adj.* **1.** having parents of different races. **2.** ill-bred; rude.
—[形] 1. 잡종의 2. 버릇없는, 교양없는

half-breed [hǽfbrì:d / há:f-] *n.* [C] a person whose parents are of different races. **—***adj.* of mixed breed,
—[名] 혼혈아, 잡종 —[形] 혼혈의, 잡종의

race, etc.

half brother [ˊ ˊ–] *n.* a brother related through one parent only.
—[名] 아버지(어머니)가 다른 형제

half-caste [hǽfkæ̀st / há:fkà:st] *n.* [C] **1.** a child of mixed race, esp. of one European parent and one Hindu or Mohammedan parent. **2.** a half-breed person.
—[名] 1. 백인과 인도인·회교도 사이의 혼혈아 2. 혼혈아

half-cooked [hǽfkúkt / há:f-] *adj.* half-done; not well-cooked.
—[形] 설익은, 설구운, 반숙의; 미숙한

half-heart·ed [hǽfhá:rtid / há:fhá:t-] *adj.* with little interest, eagerness, etc. ▷**half-heart·ed·ly** [-li] *adv.*
—[形] 마음내키지 않는, 열심이 아닌, 냉담한

half-hour [hǽfàuər / há:fàuə] *n.* [C] thirty minutes. —*adj.* of or lasting a half-hour. ▷**half·hour·ly** [-li] *adv.*
—[名] 반시간, 30 분 —[形] 반시간의

half-length [hǽflèŋ(k)θ] *adj.* (of a portrait) showing only the upper part of the body. —*n.* [C] a portrait showing only the upper part of the body.
—[形] 반신(半身)의, 반신상의 —[名] 반신상

half-mast [hǽfmǽst / há:fmá:st] *n.* [U] (of a flag) the position half-way from the top of a pole, etc. ¶*a flag at* ~.①
—[名] 반기(半旗)의 위치 ¶①반기

half·pence [héip(ə)ns] *n.* pl. of **halfpenny.**

half·pen·ny [héip(ə)ni] *n.* [C] (pl. **-pen·nies** or **-pence**) a British bronze coin worth half a penny. ¶*receive more kicks than halfpence.*① —*adj.* **1.** worth only a halfpenny. **2.** having little value.
—[名] 반 페니 동화; 반 페니[의 가치] ¶①칭찬은커녕 호되게 야단맞다 —[形] 1. 반 페니의 2. 싸구려의

half·pen·ny·worth [héip(ə)niwə̀:rθ, *slang* héipəθ] *n.* [U] **1.** 《*collectively*》 things worth a halfpenny. **2.** a trifling value; only a little bit.
—[名] 1. 반 페니 값어치의 물건 2. 얼마 안 되는 가치; 극소량

half-price [hǽfpráis / há:f-] *adv.* at half the usual price.
—[副] 반액으로

half sole [ˊ ˊ] *n.* a sole of a shoe, from the toe to the instep.
—[名] [구두의] 앞창

half sovereign [ˊ ˊ––] *n.* a British gold coin with the value of ten shillings. ⇒[N.B.]
—[名] 반 파운드의 금화 [N.B.] 현재는 발행되지 않음

half tone [ˊ ˊ] *n.* **1.** a printing process in which a picture reproducing light and dark shades is obtained by means of a screen placed in the camera just in front of the sensitized plate. **2.** semitone.
—[名] 1. 망판(網版); 망판 인쇄 2. 반음

* **half·way** [hǽfwéi / há:f-] *adv.* half the way; in the middle. ***meet someone halfway,*** be ready to be friendly with someone. —*adj.* midway; not complete.
—[副] 중간(중도)에서; 불완전하게 [熟] [남과] 서로 타협하다 —[形] 중도의; 불완전한

half-wit·ted [hǽfwítid / há:f-] *adj.* weak in the mind; very stupid; foolish.
—[形] 바보의, 얼간이의

half-year·ly [hǽfjərli / há:fjə́:-] *adj.* happening every six months. —*adv.* at six-month intervals.
—[形] 반년마다의 —[副] 반년마다

hal·i·but [hǽlibət, +*U.S.* hál-] *n.* [C] (pl. **-buts** or *collectively* **-but**) a large, flat sea fish used for food.
—[名] 넙치류

⁑ **hall** [hɔ:l] *n.* [C] **1.** (*U.S.*) a passageway in a building. **2.** a room at the entrance of a building. **3.** a large room for public meetings, parties, etc. **4.** a public building. ¶*a music* ~ / *a town* ~.① **5.** a building of a school, college, or university. ¶*the Student's Hall.*② **6.** the house of an English landowner; a manor house.
—[名] 1.《美》복도 2. [현관의] 큰 호올, 대청 3. [모임·파아티를 위한] 큰 마루방, 호올 4. 공공건물, 회관, 공회당 ¶①읍사무소 5. 독립 교사(校舍), 학원, [대학의] 강당 ¶②학생 회관 6. [지주의] 저택

hal·le·lu·jah, -lu·iah [hæ̀lilú:jə] *interj., n.* an expression in praise of God; a song of praise to God.
—[感][名] 할렐루야(신을 찬미하는 말); 할렐루야 성가

hall·mark [hɔ́:lmà:rk] *n.* [C] **1.** a mark showing the standard of gold and silver in articles. **2.** a mark or sign of good quality. —*vt.* put a hallmark on (something or someone).
—[名] 1. [금은의] 순분 검증인(純分檢證印) 2. 품질 증명, 보증 —[他] …에 품질 증명의 각인(刻印)을 찍다; 보증하다

hal·lo [həlóu, hælóu] *interj.* **1.** a shout to get attention. **2.** a call of greeting or surprise; hello. —*n.* [C] (pl. **-los**) **1.** a shout to get attention. **2.** a call of greeting or surprise; hello. **3.** a shout. —*vi.* shout.
—[感] 1. 이봐, 여보세요 2. 저런, 어머나 (인사·놀람의 소리) —[名] 1. 여보세요 2. 저런, 어머나 3. 외침 —[自] 외치다

hal·loo [həlú:] *interj.* **1.** a call to make hunting dogs run faster. **2.** a shout to get attention. —*n.* [C] (pl. **-loos**) **1.** a call to make hunting dogs run faster. **2.** a shout to get attention. **3.** [U] the act of calling in a loud voice. ¶*cry* ~. —*vi., vt.* shout or call.
—[感] 1. 쉭! 2. 어어이, 여보세요 —[名] 1. 사냥개를 부추기는 소리 2. 남의 주의를 끌기 위한 외침소리 3. 큰 소리로 외치다 —[自][他] [사냥개를] 부추기다; 외치다, 고함치다

hal·low [hǽlou] *vt.* make (something) holy; honor (something) as holy.
—[他] …을 신성하게 하다, 숭상하다

Hal·low·een, -e'en [hæ̀louíːn, +*U.S.* hɑ́l-] *n.* the evening of October 31; the eve of All Saints' Day.
—[名] 만성제(萬聖祭)의 전날 밤(10월 31일)

hall·stand [hɔ́ːlstæ̀nd] *n.* [C] a piece of furniture with a mirror, for hanging coats, hats, etc.
—[名] 거울 달린 옷장

hal·lu·ci·na·tion [həlùːsinéiʃ(ə)n] *h.* [U] [C] the act of seeing or hearing things that are not really present; something thus seen or heard; an illusion.
—[名] 환각, 망상, 환상

hall·way [hɔ́ːlwèi] *n.* [C] **1.** (*U.S.*) a passageway in a building. **2.** a room at the entrance of a building.
—[名] 1.《美》낭하, 복도 2. 현관 방

ha·lo [héilou] *n.* [C] (pl. **-los** or **-loes**) **1.** a ring of light around the sun or the moon. **2.** a bright ring or disk of light drawn or painted around the head of a saint in pictures. —*vt.* surround (something) with a halo. —*vi.* form a halo.
—[名] 1. [해·달의] 무리, 훈륜(暈輪) 2. [성상(聖像)의] 후광, 광륜(光輪) —[他] …에 후광을 띠게 하다 —[自] 후광이 되다

‡halt [hɔːlt] *vi., vt.* stop for a time; cause (something) to stop. ¶ *The car halted at the crossroads.* —*n.* [C] a stop for a time. ¶ *bring one's horse to a* ~① / *call a* ~② / *come to* (or *make*) *a* ~.③
—[自][他] 멈추[게 하]다, 서[게 하]다, 휴지(休止)하다(시키다) —[名] 휴지, 정지, 휴식 ¶①말을 세우다/②정지를 명하다/③멈추다, 쉬다

hal·ter [hɔ́ːltər] *n.* [C] **1.** a rope or strap for leading or fastening an animal. ⇒fig. **2.** a rope used for hanging criminals. **3.** death by hanging. **4.** a backless blouse for women which ties around the neck.
come to the halter, be hanged.
—*vt.* tie (something) with a halter; hang.
—[名] 1. [마소의] 굴레 2. 교수용 밧줄 3. 교수[형] 4. [팔과 등을 드러나게 한] 부인용 운동복
[熟] 교수형을 받다
—[他] …에 굴레를 씌우다; …을 교수형에 처하다

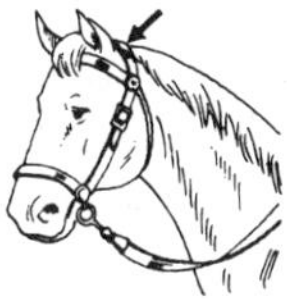
[halter 1.]

halve [hæv / hɑːv] *vt.* **1.** divide (something) into two equal parts. ¶ ~ *the profit with a person.*① **2.** lessen (something) to half. ¶ ~ *the cost.*
—[他] 1. …을 2등분하다, 절반씩 나누다 ¶①남과 이익을 반씩 나누다 2. …을 반으로 줄이다

halves [hævz / hɑːvz] *n.* pl. of **half.**

***ham** [hæm] *n.* **1.** [U] the upper part of the leg of a pig, smoked and salted for food. **2.** [C] (*slang*) a poor actor. **3.** [C] (*slang*) an amateur radio operator.
—[名] 1. 햄, 소금에 절인(훈제(燻製)한) 돼지고기 2. 서투른 배우 3. 아마튜어 무전사, 햄

ham·burg·er [hǽmbəːrgər] *n.* [C] ground beef, usu. shaped into a small mass and fried.
—[名] 햄버어그 스테이크

ham·let [hǽmlit] *n.* [C] a very small village.
—[名] 작은 마을, 한촌(寒村)

Ham·let [hǽmlit] *n.* a famous tragedy by Shakespeare; the main character in this play.
—[名] Shakespeare 작의 비극; 그 극의 주인공

‡ham·mer [hǽmər] *n.* [C] **1.** a tool with a heavy metal head, used to drive nails, break things, etc. ¶ *the* ~ *and sickle*① / *a knight of the* ~② / *throwing the* ~.③ **2.** a thing like a hammer in shape or use.
1) ***bring*** (or ***send***) *something* ***to the hammer,*** sell something by public sale. ⇒[N.B.]
2) ***come under the hammer; go to the hammer,*** be sold by public sale.
3) ***go*** (or ***be***) ***at it hammer and tongs,*** work with all one's force and strength.
4) ***up to the hammer,*** first-class; excellent; perfect.
—*vt., vi.* **1.** hit (something) with a hammer; work with a hammer; make (a piece of metal) flat with a hammer. **2.** force (an idea, etc.) into one's head. 《~ something *into*》 **3.** work hard. 《~ *at* a task, etc.》
1) ***hammer*** (=*work hard*) ***at*** *something.*
2) ***hammer away,*** ⓐ hit (something) again and again. ⓑ keep working hard at (a task).
3) ***hammer out,*** work out (an idea, etc.) with much effort.
—[名] 1. 해머, 망치 ¶①소련의 국기/②대장장이/③해머 던지기 2. 해머 모양의 것
[熟] 1)…을 경매에 붙이다 [N.B.] 경매 때에 hammer를 두드리는 데서 2)경매에 붙여지다 3)…에게 맹렬히 달려들다 4)말할 나위 없는, 멋있는
—[他][自] 1. […을] 망치로 두드리다; …을 두드려 펴다 2. [생각 따위]를 억지로 머리에 넣다 3. 열심히 일하다
[熟] 1)…을 열심히 일하다 2)ⓐ…을 연거푸 두드리다 ⓑ열심히 일하다 3)…을 궁리해 내다, 궁리하여 해결하다

ham·mock [hǽmək] *n.* [C] a hanging bed or couch made of canvas, net, etc. suspended by ropes at both ends.
—[名] 해먹, 달아매는 그물 침대

Ham·mond organ [hǽməndɔ́ːrgən] *n.* a musical instrument resembling a piano in shape.
—[名] 해먼드 오르간

ham·per[1] [hǽmpər] *vt.* prevent; hinder. ¶ *He is ham-*
—[他] …을 방해하다, 애먹이다 ¶①그

*pered by poor health.*①

ham·per² [hǽmpər] *n.* [C] a large basket with a cover.

hand [hænd] *n.* [C] **1.** the end of the human arm, including the palm, fingers, and thumb. ¶*on one's hands and knees.*① **2.** something like a hand in appearance or use. ¶*the hour* (*or short*) ~② / *the minute* (or *long*) ~.③ **3.** ⦅usu. *pl.*⦆ possession; control. ¶*fall into enemy's hands*④ / *The work is in my hands.*⑤ **4.** side; direction. ¶*At his right ~ sat the president.* **5.** skill; ability. ¶*The painting showed the ~ of a master.*⑥ **6.** a style of writing; handwriting. ¶*readable ~*⑦ / *write a good ~.* **7.** aid; assistance. ¶*lend a ~.*⑧ **8.** a laborer who uses his hands. ¶*factory hands*⑨ / *farm hands.*⑩ **9.** a person, as the performer of some action or task. ¶*a book written by various hands.* **10.** a person who has skill or ability enough to do something. ¶*He was a quite ~ with the violin.*⑪

1) ***ask for** someone's **hand,*** propose marriage.
2) ***at first hand,*** directly; from the original source.
3) ***at hand,*** within reach; nearby; ready for use.
4) ***at second hand,*** ⓐ indirectly. ⓑ not new; previously used.
5) ***at the hand*[*s*]** (=*through the action*) ***of** something.*
6) ***be hand in*** (or ***and***) ***glove*** (=*be very friendly*) ***with** someone.*
7) ***bear*** (or ***lend***) ***a hand*** (=*take part*) ***in** something.*
8) ***bear*** (or ***lend***) ***a hand with,*** help.
9) ***by hand,*** with the hands; not by machine.
10) ***change hands,*** pass from one owner to another.
11) ***come to hand,*** come into one's possession; come within reach.
12) ***feed out of** one's **hand,*** be willing and ready to obey.
13) ***fight hand to hand,*** fight at close quarters.
14) ***from hand to hand,*** from one person's possession to another's.
15) ***get** one's **hand in*** something, start something; begin something.
16) ***get the upper hand of*** (=*get an advantage over*) *someone.*
17) ***give** one's **hand on a bargain,*** shake hands as a sign that one will keep one's promise.
18) ***hand and foot,*** so that the hands and feet cannot move.
19) ***hand in hand with,*** ⓐ holding hands with one another. ⓑ together; in co-operation.
20) ***hand over hand*** (or ***fist***), easily; quickly and in large amounts.
21) ***hands down,*** easily; without effort.
22) ***Hands off!*** Don't touch!
23) ***Hands up!*** Hold up your hands!
24) ***have** one's **hand in*** (=*be related to; be connected with*) *someone* or *something.*
25) ***have** one's **hands full,*** have more than one can do; be too busy.
26) ***have** something* [***heavy***] ***on** one's **hands,*** don't know what to do with something.
27) ***in hand,*** ⓐ in possession. ⓑ in control or order. ⓒ being worked on. ⓓ under consideration.
28) ***keep** one's **hand in,*** continue practice in order to keep one's skill.
29) ***keep** one's **hand on; keep a firm hand on,*** control.
30) ***live from hand to hand,*** have nothing saved for the future.
31) ***off hand,*** at once.
32) ***off** one's **hands,*** out of one's care or control.
33) ***on hand,*** ⓐ in one's present possession. ⓑ be going to happen.
34) ***on*** (or ***upon***) ***one's hands,*** under one's care; as one's responsibility.
35) ***on the one hand,*** from one point of view.

는 건강이 나빠 애먹고 있다
—[名] 큰 광주리
—[名] 1. [주로 사람의] 손 ¶①네 발로 기어 2. 손의 모양(구실)을 가진 것 ¶②시침(時針)/③초침 3. 소유, 관리 ¶④적의 수중에 떨어지다/⑤그 일은 내 관리하에 있다 4. 쪽, 편; 방향 5. 솜씨, 수완 ¶⑥그 그림은 대가의 솜씨를 보이고 있다 6. 필체, 필적 ¶⑦읽기 쉬운 필체 7. 조력, 원조 ¶⑧거들다 8. 직공, 일손 ¶⑨직공/⑩농업 노동자 9. [어떤 일에] 종사하고 있는 사람 10. [기술·능력을 가진] 사람 ¶⑪그는 바이올린의 명수였다

[熟] 1)구혼하다 2)직접 3)가까이에; 가까운 장래에; 이용할 수 있는 상태로 4)ⓐ간접으로 ⓑ중고의 5)…의 손으로, …의 손에서 6)…와 아주 친하다 7)…에 관계하다 8)…을 거들다, 돕다 9)손으로, 수제(手製)의 10)소유주가 바뀌다 11)손에 들어오다 12)온순하다, 다루기 쉽다 13)접전하다 14)이 사람 손에서 저 사람 손으로 15)…에 착수하다 16)…보다 우세해지다 17)굳게 계약을 맺다 18)손발을 함께 [묶다] 19)ⓐ손을 마주잡고 ⓑ공동으로 20)쉽게 21)쉽게 22)만지지 마시오 23)손 들엇! 24)…에 관계하고 있다 25)몹시 바쁘다 26)주체 못하다; 어찌할 바를 모르다 27)ⓐ입수하여 ⓑ제어(制御)하여 ⓒ착수하여 ⓓ고려 중인 28)솜씨가 떨어지지 않도록 늘 연습하다 29)…을 지배하고 있다 30)그날 벌어 그날 먹고 살다 31)즉석에서 32)…의 손을 떠나서; 책임(소임)이 끝나서 33)ⓐ가지고 있어 ⓑ발생할 듯하여 34)…의 책임(부담)으로 35)한편에서는 36)이에 반하여 37)ⓐ걷잡을 수 없게 되어 ⓑ곧 ⓒ끝나서, 일단락되어 38)자신의 이익을 위해서 행동하다 39)서로의 이익이 되도록 행동하다 40)악수하다 41)…에 관계(가담)하다 42)ⓐ착수하다 ⓑ처리하다 43)단념하다 44)시도하다, 해보다 45)…에 손대다, 착수하다 46)…와 관계를 끊다 47)강압적으로

H

36) ***on the other hand,*** from another point of view.
37) ***out of hand,*** ⓐ out of control. ⓑ immediately; at once. ⓒ finished.
38) ***play for one's own hand,*** act so as to benefit oneself.
39) ***play into one another's hands,*** act for the advantage of one another.
40) ***shake hands,*** clasp each other's hands as a greeting, agreement, etc.
41) ***take a hand at*** (or ***in***), join [in]; take part in (something).
42) ***take in hand,*** ⓐ try; attempt. ⓑ handle; treat.
43) ***throw up one's hands,*** give up hopelessly.
44) ***try one's hand,*** make a trial.
45) ***turn*** (or ***put, set***) ***one's hand to,*** work at; undertake.
46) ***wash one's hands of*** (=*take no further responsibility in* or *for*) *something.*
47) ***with a high*** (or ***bold***) ***hand,*** with too much pride; not according to rules but according to one's own ideas.

—*vt.* **1.** pass (something) with the hand; give. ¶*Please ~ me the book. / I handed the letter to him.* **2.** lead or help (someone) with the hand. ¶*~ the lady out of the car.*

—[他] 1. …을 집어 주다, 넘겨주다; 주다 2. …의 손을 잡고 부축하다

1) ***hand down,*** ⓐ pass on to his heir; transmit. ⓑ announce (the decision of a court).
2) ***hand in,*** give; offer; submit.
3) ***hand it to,*** (*U. S. slang*) admit the abilities, success, etc. of.
4) ***hand on,*** pass along; transmit.
5) ***hand out,*** give out among a number of persons; deal out.
6) ***hand over,*** give up possession of (something); deliver.

[熟] 1)ⓐ[유산]을 남기다 ⓑ[판결]을 언도하다 2)…을 넘겨주다; 제출하다 3)《美俗》…의 능력(성공·승리)을 인정하다 4)…을 다음으로 돌리다 5)…에게 몫(배당)을 주다 6) …을 넘겨주다, 양도하다

hand·bag [hǽn(d)bæ̀g] *n.* Ⓒ **1.** a woman's small bag for money, keys, make-up, etc. **2.** a small traveling bag.

—[名] 1. [여자용] 핸드백 2. [여행용] 손가방

hand·bill [hǽn(d)bìl] *n.* Ⓒ a small printed advertisement to be distributed by hand.

—[名] 삐라, 광고 쪽지

hand·book [hǽn(d)bùk] *n.* Ⓒ **1.** a small book of reference on a special subject; a manual. ¶*a ~ on foreign literature.* **2.** a guidebook for tourists.

—[名] 1. 안내서, 편람 2. 여행(관광) 안내서

hand·cart [hǽn(d)kɑ̀:rt] *n.* Ⓒ a small cart moved by hand.

—[名] 손수레

hand·clap [hǽn(d)klæ̀p] *n.* Ⓒ the act of striking the palms of one's hands together, usu. to show approval.

—[名] 박수

hand·clasp [hǽn(d)klæ̀sp] *n.* Ⓒ the act of clasping hands by two or more people. ↔handshake

—[名] 악수

hand·cuff [hǽn(d)kʌ̀f] *n.* Ⓒ 《usu. *pl.*》 one of a pair of metal bracelets, joined by a short chain, locked around a prisoner's wrist to prevent his escape. —*vt.* hold back (someone) with handcuffs.

—[名] 수갑 —[他] …에 수갑을 채우다

***hand·ful** [hǽn(d)fùl] *n.* Ⓒ **1.** the amount one hand can hold. **2.** a very small number or quantity. ¶*Only a ~ of girls came.*① **3.** (*colloq.*) a person or thing that is hard to control.

—[名] 1. 손에 가득, 한 줌, 한 웅큼 2. 소량, 소수 ¶①아주 소수의 소녀가 왔다 3.《口》 다루기 힘든 사람(것), 골칫거리

hand glass [ˊ ˋ] *n.* a small mirror with a handle; a magnifying glass to be held in the hand.

—[名] 손거울; 확대경

hand·grip [hǽn(d)grìp] *n.* Ⓒ **1.** a handshake, as in greeting. **2.** 《usu. *pl.*》 a handle.

—[名] 1. 악수 2. 자루, 손잡이

hand·hold [hǽndhòuld] *n.* Ⓒ a place to put the hands.

—[名] 붙잡는 곳, 손잡이

***hand·i·cap** [hǽndikæ̀p] *n.* Ⓒ **1.** a disadvantage given to a superior contestant, or an advantage given to an inferior contestant, in order to give both a fair chance of winning in a game, contest, race, etc. **2.** something which keeps back, such as a difficulty; a disadvantage. **3.** a game or contest in which handicaps are given.

—[名] 1. 핸디캡(경기에서 우열을 고르게 하기 위해 우세한 사람에게 지우는 불리한 조건) 2. 장해, 불리한 조건 3. 핸디캡이 붙은 경주(경마)

—*vt.* (**-capped, -cap·ping**) **1.** give a handicap to (a racer, contestant, etc.). **2.** hinder.

—[他] 1. …에 핸디캡을 붙이다 2. …을 방해하다

hand·i·craft [hǽndikræ̀ft / -krɑ̀:ft] *n.* **1.** Ⓤ skillful use

—[名] 1. 손재주, 익숙한 솜씨 2. 수세공

H

of the hands. **2.** [C] any art needing skill with the hands.
(手細工), 수예, 수공, 수공업

hand·i·crafts·man [hǽndikræ̀ftsmən / -krɑ̀:fts] *n.* (pl. **-men** [-mən]) a person skilled with his hands in a trade or craft.
—[名] 수세공인(手細工人), 수공업자

hand·i·ly [hǽndili] *adv.* **1.** expertly. **2.** suitably.
—[副] 1. 솜씨있게 2. 편리하게

hand·i·ness [hǽndinis] *n.* [U] the state of being handy; convenience.
—[名] 솜씨있음, 능숙; 편리, 알맞음

hand·i·work [hǽndiwə̀:rk] *n.* **1.** [U] work done by the hands. **2.** [C] one's personal work.
—[名] 1. 수세공(手細工), 세공품 2. 제작물

⁑**hand·ker·chief** [hǽŋkərtʃif, -tʃì:f] *n.* [C] (pl. **-chiefs**) **1.** a square piece of cloth for wiping the nose, face, eyes, etc. **2.** a piece of cloth worn around the neck.
—[名] 1. 손수건 2. 목도리

⁑**han·dle** [hǽndl] *n.* [C] **1.** a part of a tool, vessel, etc., grasped by the hand. **2.** a chance; an opportunity. ¶*give a ~ to someone.*
—[名] 1. 핸들, 자루, 손잡이 2. 틈탈 기회, 구실

1) ***fly off the handle,*** (*colloq.*) get angry.
2) ***a handle to one's name,*** (*colloq.*) a title.
[熟] 1)(口)발끈하다 2)직함

—*vt.* **1.** touch (something) with the hand. **2.** manage; control. ¶*She was clever enough to ~ her pupils well.*① **3.** deal with (something or someone); treat. ¶*Don't ~ the animals so roughly.*② **4.** deal in (something); buy and sell. ¶*They ~ tobacco in that store.*③
—[他] 1. …에 손을 대다 2. 통제하다, 지휘하다 ¶①그녀는 영리해서 학생들을 잘 다룬다 3. …을 다루다, 처리하다 ¶②동물을 그렇게 거칠게 다루지 말아라 4. …을 매매(거래)하다 ¶③저 가게에서는 담배를 판다

handle bar [´-\`] *n.* ⦅often *pl.*⦆ a curved bar by which a bicycle, motorcycle, etc., is guided.
—[名] [자전거 따위의] 핸들

hand·less [hǽndlis] *adj.* having no hands; not skillful; awkward; unhandy.
—[形] 손이 없는; 솜씨없는

hand·made [hǽn(d)méid] *adj.* made by hand.
—[形] 수세공(手細工)의, 손으로 만든

hand·maid [hǽn(d)mèid] *n.* [C] a female servant or personal attendant.
—[名] 하녀, 시녀

hand·maid·en [hǽn(d)mèidn] *n.* =handmaid.

hand organ [´-\`] *n.* a portable barrel organ that is made to play tunes when a crank is turned.
—[名] 손으로 돌리는 풍금

hand·saw [hǽn(d)sɔ̀:] *n.* [C] a saw used with one hand.
—[名] [한 손으로 켜는] 작은 톱

hand·shake [hǽndʃèik] *n.* [C] an act of grasping and shaking another's hand in greeting.
—[名] 악수

:**hand·some** [hǽnsəm] *adj.* (**-som·er, -som·est**) **1.** good-looking; of pleasing appearance. ⇨[N.B.] **2.** fairly large; considerable. ¶*a ~ fortune.*① **3.** generous. ¶*~ treatment.*② ▷**hand·some·ness** [-nis] *n.*
—[形] 1. 아름다운, 잘생긴 [N.B.] 흔히 남자에게 씀 2. 상당한, 꽤 큰 ¶①꽤 많은 재산 3. 관대한, 통이 큰 ¶②우대

hand·some·ly [hǽnsəmli] *adv.* in a handsome manner.
—[副] 훌륭하게, 후하게

hand-to-hand [hǽn(d)təhǽnd] *adj.* close together. ¶*~ fighting.*
—[形] 접전(接戰)의

hand-to-mouth [hǽn(d)təmáuθ] *adj.* not providing for the future; unsettled.
—[形] 하루 벌어 하루 먹고 사는, 임시변통의

hand·work [hǽndwə̀:rk] *n.* [U] work done by hand.
—[名] 수세공(手細工), 세공

hand·writ·ing [hǽndràitiŋ] *n.* [U] **1.** the act of writing by hand. **2.** a person's way of writing.
—[名] 1. 손으로 쓰기 2. 필적, 필체

•**hand·y** [hǽndi] *adj.* (**hand·i·er, hand·i·est**) **1.** easy to use; convenient. **2.** skillful with the hands. **3.** easy to handle.
—[形] 1. 편리한 2. 솜씨있는, 능숙한 3. [도구 따위가] 다루기 쉬운

handy man [´-\`] *n.* a man who does various small jobs.
—[名] 무슨 일이나 휘뚜루 하는 사람

⁑**hang** [hæŋ] *v.* (**hung** →*vt.* 5., *vi.* 3.) *vt.* **1.** fasten or attach (something) to something above; suspend. ¶*~ a lamp from the ceiling.* **2.** suspend (something) from a nail, hook, etc. ¶*~ pictures on the wall* / *Hang your cap on the hook.* **3.** fasten or attach (something) by a hinge. ¶*~ a door.* **4.** bend down. ¶*~ one's head.* **5.** (**hanged**) put (someone) to death by hanging. ¶*He hanged himself.*① / *I'm* (or *I'll be*) *hanged if I know...*②. **6.** ornament, cover, or furnish (walls) by something suspended. ¶*~ wallpaper*③ / *~ the wall with pictures.*
—[他] 1. …을 위에 걸다, 매달다, 드리우다 2. [못·고리 따위에] …을 걸다 3. [경첩 따위로] …을 고정시키다 4. …을 숙이다, 내리다 5. …의 목을 매다; 목졸라 죽이다 ¶①그는 목을 매고 자살했다/②…을 알고 있다면 목을 매겠다(절대로 모른다) 6. [족자 따위로] …을 장식하다 ¶③벽지를 바르다

—*vi.* **1.** be suspended; be fastened to something above. **2.** be fastened by a hinge. **3.** (**hanged**) die by hanging. **4.** be doubtful or undecided; hesitate.
—[自] 1. 매달리다 2. 경첩으로 고정되다 3. 교수형을 받다 4. 망설이고 있다; 결정을 짓지 못하다

H

1) ***hang about*** (or ***around***), (*colloq.*) ⓐ spend time walking slowly or idly in a certain place. ⓑ group around.
2) ***hang back,*** be unwilling to do something.
3) ***hang by a*** [***single***] ***hair*** (or ***a thread***), be in a very dangerous position.
4) ***hang in the balance*** (or ***the wind***), be in doubt or uneasiness.
5) ***hang on,*** ⓐ grasp or hold firmly. ⓑ depend on.
6) ***hang out,*** ⓐ lean toward. ⓑ suspend out (something) in the open.
7) ***hang over,*** ⓐ project over (something). ⓑ threaten.
8) ***hang together,*** ⓐ stay together. ⓑ be coherent; remain united.
9) ***hang up,*** ⓐ place (something) on hooks or hangers. ⓑ place a telephone receiver on the hook, to break off communication.

[熟] 1)《口》ⓐ어슬렁거리다, 빈둥빈둥 돌아다니다 ⓑ떼지어 붙어다니다 2)주춤하다, 주저하다 3)아주 위험한 상태에 있다 4)미정 상태이다 5)ⓐ붙들고 늘어지다 ⓑ…에 달려 있다 6)ⓐ몸을 내밀다 ⓑ…을 위로 내걸다 7)ⓐ…의 위로 돌출하다 ⓑ… 위에 닥치다, 임박하다 8)ⓐ단결하다 ⓑ앞뒤가 들어맞다; 합동하다 9)ⓐ…을 걸다 ⓑ전화를 끊다

—*n.* [C] 《usu. *the*~》 **1.** the way something hangs. ¶*the ~ of an overcoat.* **2.** (*U.S. colloq.*) familiar knowledge or meaning; knack. ¶*get the~of…*

—[名] 1. 늘어진(매달린) 모양, 걸림새 2. 《美口》 의미, 취지; 요령

hang·ar [hǽŋ(g)ər, hǽŋgɑːr] *n.* [C] a shed for airplanes and other aircraft.

—[名] 격납고

hang·er [hǽŋər] *n.* [C] **1.** a person who hangs something. **2.** a tool or machine that hangs things. **3.** a kind of short sword.

—[名] 1. 거는 사람 2. 매다는 기구(갈고리·걸고리·옷걸이·휘장·커어튼 따위) 3. 단검

hang·er-on [hǽŋərɑ́n, / -ɔ́n] *n.* [C] (pl. **hang·ers-on**) **1.** a follower. **2.** an undesirable follower.

—[名] 1. 항상 따라다니는 사람, 부하 2. 식객(食客)

hang·ing** [hǽŋiŋ] *n.* [U] **1.** death by hanging. **2.** 《often *pl.*》 a thing that hangs from a wall, bed, etc., such as curtains and draperies. **—*adj. **1.** deserving punishment by hanging. **2.** fastened to something above.

—[名] 1. 교수형, 교살(絞殺) 2. 거는 물건(천), 휘장, 벽지 —[形] 1. 교수형에 처할 2. 걸린, 매달린

hang·man [hǽŋmən] *n.* [C] (pl. **-men** [-mən]) a public officer who puts criminals to death by hanging them.

—[名] 교수형 집행인

hang·nail [hǽŋnèil] *n.* [C] a small piece of loose skin near a fingernail.

—[名] [손가락의] 거스러미

hank [hæŋk] *n.* [C] a circular coil of yarn containing a definite number of yards.

—[名] [실의] 타래

han·ker [hǽŋkər] *vi.* long for; wish.

—[自] 동경하다, 갈망하다

han·som [hǽnsəm] *n.* [C] a two-wheeled covered cab for two passengers, drawn by one horse and with the driver at the back.

—[名] 한 필이 끄는 2인승 2륜마차 [NB] 발명자 J. A. Hansom (1803–82).

hap·haz·ard [hæ̀phǽzərd] *n.* [U] chance. ¶*at* (or *by*) ~.① **—*adj.*** accidental; not planned. **—*adv.*** by chance; at random. ▷**hap·haz·ard·ly** [-li] *adv.*

—[名] 우연 ¶①우연히, 아무렇게나 —[形] 우연의; 되는 대로의 —[副] 되는 대로, 아무렇게나

hap·less [hǽplis] *adj.* unlucky; unfortunate.

—[形] 불운한, 박복한

⁑**hap·pen** [hǽp(ə)n] *vi.* **1.** take place; occur. 《~ *to do*》 ¶~ *what* (or *whatever*) *may* ~ / *I don't know how it happened.* **2.** be or take place by chance. ¶*Accidents will ~.*
1) ***as it happens,*** by chance.
2) ***happen in,*** (*U.S.*) drop in.
3) ***happen on*** (or ***upon***), ⓐ meet (someone) by chance. ⓑ find (something) by chance.

—[自] 1. [사건이] 일어나다 2. 우연히 …하다, 뜻밖에 …하다

[熟] 1)우연히 2)《美》들르다 3)ⓐ우연히 만나다 ⓑ우연히 발견하다

hap·pen·ing [hǽp(ə)niŋ] *n.* [C] 《often *pl.*》 something that occurs quite unexpectedly; an event.

—[名] 우연히 일어난 일, 사건

⁑**hap·pi·ly** [hǽpili] *adv.* in a happy manner; with pleasure or joy.

—[副] 행복하게, 즐겁게

⁑**hap·pi·ness** [hǽpinis] *n.* [U] the state of being happy or glad; good fortune.

—[名] 행복, 행운

⁑**hap·py** [hǽpi] *adj.* (**-pi·er, -pi·est**) **1.** lucky; fortunate. ¶*a ~ home* / *Happy are those who are contented.* **2.** enjoying, giving or expressing pleasure; joyous. ¶*~ laughter.*① **3.** suitable and clever; fitting; apt. ¶*a ~ suggestion* / *a ~ way of expression.*②
1) ***as happy as the day is long; as happy as a king; as happy as happy can be,*** happier than anything else; as happy as possible.
2) ***hit*** (or ***strike***) ***the happy mean,*** be or remain moderate.

—[形] 1. 행복한, 기쁜 2. 즐거운; 유쾌한 ¶①즐거운 웃음 3. 적절한; 잘하는 ¶②그럴 듯한 표현

[熟] 1)더할나위 없이 행복한 2)중용을 지키다

hap·py-go-luck·y [hǽpigoulʌ̀ki] *adj.* taking things easy; easy-going; thoughtless.
—[形] 태평한, 될 대로 되라는 식의, 낙천적인

ha·rangue [hərǽŋ] *n.* [C] a long, noisy speech, esp toward a crowd. —*vi., vt.* make a harangue.
—[名] 열변, 연설 —[自][他] 열변을 토하다

har·ass [hǽrəs, +*U.S.* hərǽs] *vt.* annoy (someone) by repeated attacks; trouble; worry. ¶*Pirates used to ~ the villages along the coast.*
—[他] …을 끊임없는 공격으로 괴롭히다; 괴롭히다, 속썩이다

har·bin·ger [há:*r*bindʒə*r*] *n.* [C] a person or thing that goes ahead to announce another's coming; a forerunner. ¶*The cock is a ~ of day.* —*vt.* announce beforehand.
—[名] 선구자; 전조(前兆) —[他] …을 미리 알리다

⁑**har·bor,** *Brit.* **-bour** [há:*r*bə*r*] *n.* [C] **1.** a protected part of a sea, lake, etc., which serves as a shelter for ships and boats. ¶*in ~*①. **2.** any place of shelter or safety. —*vt.* **1.** give shelter to (a ship, etc.); protect. **2.** keep (unkind thoughts, etc.) in one's mind; cherish. ¶*Don't ~ suspicion.* —*vi.* (of ships) take shelter in a harbor.
—[名] 1. 항구 ¶①입항중인 2. 피난처, 잠복처
—[他] 1. …에 피난처를 주다, …을 비호(庇護)하다 2. [나쁜 마음 따위]를 품다 —[自] 항구에 정박하다

⁑**hard** [hɑ:rd] *adj.* **1.** solid and compact; firm. ↔soft ¶*~ and dry*① / *~ ground.* **2.** tight; firmly formed. **3.** difficult; not easy. ¶*a ~ problem.* **4.** severe; painful; troublesome. ¶*a ~ winter / a ~ illness / have a ~ time.*② **5.** stern; harsh; cruel. ¶*a ~ teacher / ~ treatment.* **6.** strong; forceful; vigorous. ¶*a ~ storm.* **7.** acting with energy; diligent. ¶*a ~ worker / ~ study.*
—[形] 1. 굳은, 딱딱한 ¶①딱딱하게 마른 2. 단단한 3. 곤란한, 어려운, 힘드는 4. 엄한, 모진; 쓰라린; 고통스러운 ¶②고통을 겪다 5. 엄격한; 가혹한 6. 강력한, 격렬한; 거친, 험악한 7. 부지런한

1) ***be hard on,*** ⓐ treat (someone) severely. ⓑ be difficult, unpleasant, or painful for (someone).
2) ***be hard up for,*** (*colloq.*) be in great need of (money, etc.).
3) ***hard and fast,*** (of rules, etc.) invariable; strict.

[熟] 1) ⓐ…을 구박하다 ⓑ…에게 견디기 힘들다 2)《口》[돈 따위에] 쪼들리다 3)[규칙 따위가] 엄한, 바꿀 수 없는

—*adv.* **1.** firmly; tightly. ¶*hold on ~ / It was frozen ~.* **2.** with great energy or force; earnestly; lively. ¶*work ~.* **3.** with effort or difficulty. ¶*The cork draws ~.*③ **4.** with vigor, strength or violence. ¶*hit ~.* **5.** 《often with *after, by* or *upon*》 close; near. ¶*He followed ~ after me.*④
—[副] 1. 굳게; 단단히 2. 열심히, 애써서 3. 간신히, 겨우 ¶③코르크 마개가 잘 뽑아지지 않는다 4. 맹렬히, 힘차게 5. 접근하여 ¶④그는 바로 내 뒤로 왔다

1) ***be hard put to it,*** be in great difficulty or trouble.
2) ***go hard with,*** treat or punish (someone) severely.
3) ***hard by,*** close by; not far away.

[熟] 1)곤란을 받고 있다 2)…을 혼내주다 3)바로 가까이에

hard-bit·ten [há:rdbítn] *adj.* stubborn; unyielding.
—[形] 고집 센, 만만치 않은

hard-boiled [há:rdbɔ́ild] *adj.* **1.** (of an egg) boiled until hard. **2.** (*colloq.*) unfeeling; tough. **3.** (*colloq.*) hard; stiff.
—[形] 1. [달걀을] 단단하게 삶은 2. 무감각한, 무정한 3. 완고한

hard cash [´ ´] *n.* **1.** metal coins. **2.** cash.
—[名] 1. 경화(硬貨) 2. 현금

***hard·en** [há:rdn] *vt., vi.* **1.** make or become hard. **2.** make or become firm. **3.** make or become unfeeling or harsh.
—[他][自] 1. 단단하게 하다(되다) 2. 세게(튼튼하게) 하다(되다) 3. 무감각(무자비)하게 하다

hard-head·ed [há:rdhédid] *adj.* **1.** not easily deceived; practical; shrewd. **2.** stubborn; obstinate.
—[形] 1. 냉정한; 실제적인; 빈틈없는 2. 완고한

hard-heart·ed [há:rdhá:rtid] *adj.* without pity or sympathy; unfeeling.
—[形] 몰인정한, 잔인한; 매정한

har·di·hood [há:rdihùd] *n.* [U] boldness; daring; impudence.
—[名] 대담, 배짱이 셈, 뻔뻔스러움

har·di·ly [há:rdili] *adv.* in a hardy manner; boldly.
—[副] 대담하게, 뻔뻔스럽게

har·di·ness [há:rdinis] *n.* [U] the quality of being hardy; strength; boldness; hardihood.
—[名] 튼튼함, 견고; 대담, 용기, 뻔뻔스러움

⁑**hard·ly** [há:rdli] *adv.* **1.** only just; barely. ¶*She ~ had time for breakfast. / We had ~ got to the station when* (or *before*) *it began to rain.*① **2.** probably not; scarcely. ¶*I can ~ believe it. / He ~ ever gets up before seven in the morning.* **3.** with difficulty or effort. ¶*money ~ earned.* **4.** harshly; severely. ¶*He was ~ treated.*
—[副] 1. 간신히, 겨우 ¶①우리가 역에 도착하자마자 비가 내리기 시작했다 2. 거의 …아니다(않다) 3. 고생하여, 애써서, 가까스로 4. 엄하게, 가혹하게, 몹시

hard·ness [há:rdnis] *n.* [U] the quality of being hard; hardship.
—[名] 견고, 곤란, 난해(難解)

***hard·ship** [há:rdʃìp] *n.* [U][C] something hard to endure, such as hunger, cold, or sickness.
—[名] 고난, 신고(辛苦), 곤궁, 압제

hard·ware [há:rdwɛ̀ər] *n.* [U] articles made from metal,
—[名] 쇠붙이, 철물

such as pots, pans, and knives.

hard·wood [há:rdwùd] *n.* [U] any hard, closely packed wood, such as oak, cherry, or maple.
—[名] 굳은 나무

* **har·dy** [há:rdi] *adj.* (**-di·er, -di·est**) **1.** able to bear hardship, fatigue, etc.; vigorous. **2.** (of plants) able to survive the cold of winter. ¶ ~ *plants.*① **3.** bold; daring.
—[形] 1. 고생(고통)에 견딜 수 있는, 튼튼한, 건장한 2. 내한성(耐寒性)의 ¶ ①내한성의 식물 3. 대담한, 용감한

* **hare** [hɛər] *n.* [C] (pl. **hares** or *collectively* **hare**) an animal like a large rabbit. ¶ (*proverb*) *First catch your ~* [, *then cook him*].①
1) ***as mad as a March hare,*** very wild or mad.
2) ***as timid as a hare,*** very shy.
3) ***hold*** (or ***run***) ***with the hare and run*** (or ***hunt***) ***with the hounds,*** try to serve both sides.
4) ***make a hare*** (=*make a fool*) ***of someone.***
5) ***start a hare,*** turn aside from the main subject in discussion.
—[名] 산토끼 ¶①《俚》토끼를 우선 잡고 나서 요리하라; 우선 사실(상대)을 확인하라
[熟] 1)(3월의 교미기의 토끼처럼) 미친 듯한 2)수줍어하고 소심한 3)양다리 걸치다 4)[토론에서] 지엽(枝葉)에 흐르다

hare·lip [hɛ́ərlìp] *n.* [C] a deformed lip, usu. the upper one.
—[名] 언청이

har·em [hɛ́ərəm] *n.* [C] **1.** the part of a Mohammedan house in which the women live. **2.** 《*collectively*》 the wives, female servants, etc., living in this part of the house.
—[名] 1. [회교국의] 부인 방 2. 하렘에 사는 처첩(妻妾)들

har·i·cot [hǽrikòu] *n.* [C] a kind of bean.
—[名] 강남콩

* **hark** [ha:rk] *vi.* 《chiefly in *imperative*》 listen.
—[自] 듣다, 귀를 기울이다

har·le·quin [há:rlikwin] *n.* [C] 《often *H-*》 a character in a dumb show, usu. masked and with clothing of varied colors and a wooden sword. —*adj.* varied in color; many-colored.
—[名] [무언극의] 광대, 익살꾼 —[形] 얼룩빛의, 잡색의

‡ **harm** [ha:rm] *n.* [U] injury; damage; evil; wrong-doing.
1) ***come to harm,*** get hurt.
2) ***do*** *someone* ***harm,*** hurt.
—*vt.* damage; hurt; injure.
—[名] 해(害), 손해, 손상; 해악, 위해
[熟] 1)혼나다 2)[남]에게 해를 끼치다
—[他] …을 해치다, 손상하다

* **harm·ful** [há:rmf(u)l] *adj.* causing damage; injurious; hurtful. ▷**harm·ful·ness** [-nis] *n.*
—[形] 해로운

harm·ful·ly [há:rmfuli] *adv.* in a harmful manner.
—[副] 해롭게

* **harm·less** [há:rmlis] *adj.* causing no harm; having no power to harm anyone or anything.
—[形] 해가 없는, 악의 없는, 천진난만한

har·mon·ic [ha:rmánik / ha:mɔ́n-] *adj.* having harmony; harmonious; musical. —*n.* [C] (*Music*) a fainter and higher tone heard along with the main tone.; an overtone.
—[形] 조화된; 화성의
—[名] 《樂》 배음(倍音)

har·mon·i·ca [ha:rmánikə / ha:mɔ́n-] *n.* [C] a small, musical wind instrument with metal reeds, played by the mouth; a mouth organ.
—[名] 하아모니카

har·mon·ics [ha:rmániks / ha:mɔ́n-] *n. pl.* 《used as *sing.*》 the science of musical sounds.
—[名] 화성학(和聲學)

* **har·mo·ni·ous** [ha:rmóuniəs] *adj.* **1.** agreeing in feeling, ideas, or actions. ¶ *a*[*n*] ~ *family.* **2.** sweet-sounding; melodious.
—[形] 1. 잘 조화된, 균형이 잡힌 2. 화음의, 가락이 맞는

har·mo·ni·ous·ly [ha:rmóuniəsli] *adv.* in a harmonious manner.
—[副] 조화하여, 화목하게

har·mo·ni·um [ha:rmóuniəm] *n.* [C] a small organ with metal reeds.
—[名] 작은 오르간

har·mo·nize [há:rmənàiz] *vt., vi.* **1.** bring into accord or agreement; be in harmony or agreement. 《~ *something with*》 ¶ *These colors ~ well with the walls.* **2.** add harmony to (a melody).
—[他][自] 1. [···을] 조화시키다(하다), ···의 균형을 잡다 2. ···에 화음을 붙이다

* **har·mo·ny** [há:rm(ə)ni] *n.* [U][C] (pl. **-nies**) **1.** agreement; accord. **2.** a pleasing combination or arrangement of related things. **3.** (*Music*) a pleasing combination of notes sounding together in a chord; sweet or pleasing sound; music. ↔discord
—[名] 1. 조화, 화합, 일치 2. [색채 따위의] 조화 3. 《樂》 화성, [협]화음; 음악

‡ **har·ness** [há:rnis] *n.* [U] **1.** 《*collectively*》 leather straps, bands, etc., used to attach a horse to a carriage, wagon, plow, etc. ⇒p. 528 fig. **2.** armor for a soldier or horse.
—[名] 1. [마차 끄는 말의] 마구(馬具) 2. [말·사람의] 갑옷, 장갑(裝甲)

Harold — harvest

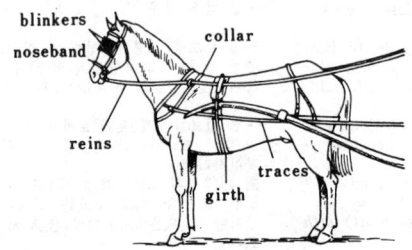

[harness 1.]

1) *die in harness,* work until death.
2) *in harness,* doing one's daily work.
3) *work* (or *run*) *in double harness,* work with a partner; earn a livelihood with one's wife.
— *vt.* **1.** put harness on (a horse, etc.) **2.** cause (water, wind, etc.) to produce power. **3.** (*archaic*) put armor on a soldier, etc.

Har·old [hǽr(ə)ld] *n.* a man's name.

• **harp** [ha:rp] *n.* ⓒ a stringed musical instrument set in a triangular frame, played with the fingers. — *vi.* **1.** play on a harp. **2.** keep on talking or writing about; refer constantly to. (*~on* or *upon* something) ¶*always ~ on the same string.*① ▷**harp·er** [-ər] *n.*

harp·ist [há:rpist] *n.* ⓒ a person who plays the harp.

har·poon [ha:rpú:n] *n.* ⓒ a barbed spear with a rope attached to it, used to catch whales and large fish. — *vt.* strike or kill (whales, etc.) with a harpoon.

harp·si·chord [há:rpsikɔ̀:rd] *n.* ⓒ a musical instrument like a piano, used before the piano.

Har·py [há:rpi] *n.* (pl. **-pies**) **1.** (in Greek mythology) a dirty, greedy monster with a woman's head and a bird's body. **2.** ⓒ (*h-*) a very greedy person.

Har·ri·et [hǽriət] *n.* a woman's name.

har·row [hǽrou] *n.* ⓒ an implement with iron teeth or disks which is drawn over plowed land to break up the soil. ¶*under the ~.*① ⇒fig. — *vt.* **1.** draw a harrow over (land, etc.) **2.** hurt the feelings of (someone); wound; distress.

[harrow]

Har·row [hǽrou] *n.* an old and famous boys' boarding school near London. ⇒N.B. [**2.** torment; worry.

har·ry [hǽri] *vt.* (**-ried**) **1.** attack (a place) and rob.

Har·ry [hǽri] *n.* a man's name; sometimes a nickname of Henry.

• **harsh** [ha:rʃ] *adj.* **1.** rough to the touch, taste, or hearing; sharp and unpleasant. ↔smooth ¶*a ~ sound / a ~ climate.*① **2.** unkind; cruel; severe. ¶*~ treat- ment.*

harsh·ly [há:rʃli] *adv.* in a harsh manner.

harsh·ness [há:rʃnis] *n.* Ⓤ the quality or state of being harsh; severeness.

hart [ha:rt] *n.* ⓒ (pl. **harts** or *collectively* **hart**) a male [of the red deer; a stag.

Har·vard [há:rvərd] *n.* the oldest university in the United States. ⇒N.B.

‡ **har·vest** [há:rvist] *n.* ⓒ **1.** the act of gathering in crops. **2.** the time or season for gathering in crops. **3.** gathered crops. ¶*The rice ~ was small this year.*① **4.** result; reward. ¶*reap the ~ of one's labors.*② — *vt., vi.* gather in (a crop of grain, etc.).

har·vest·er [há:rvistər] *n.* [C] **1.** a person who works to gather crops; a reaper. **2.** a machine for gathering crops.
—[名] 1. 수확자 2. 베어 들이는 기계

harvest festival [ˊ- ˊ--] *n.* a festival held in Christian churches for thanksgiving after the harvest has been gathered.
—[名] [교회에서 지내는] 추수 감사제

harvest home [ˊ- ˊ] *n.* **1.** the end of harvest. **2.** a festival celebrated at the end of harvest; a harvest song sung at this festival.
—[名] 1. 추수의 마지막 거두기 2. 추수를 끝낸 축하 잔치; 추수 완료의 축가

harvest moon [ˊ- ˊ] *n.* the full moon at harvest time or in late September.
—[名] 중추의 만월

⁑**has** [hæz, həz, əz, z] *v.* third person singular present indicative of **have.**

has-been [hǽzbìn, +*Brit.* -bì:n] *n.* [C] (*colloq.*) a person or thing that is no longer successful or popular.
—[名] 《口》 능력 · 명성이 한물 간 사람(것)

hash [hæʃ] *n.* **1.** [U] a dish of meat, mixed with potatoes, etc. and cut into small pieces. ¶~ *and rice.*① **2.** [C] a mixture of things used before; a mixture.
1) ***make*** [*a*] ***hash of,*** defeat or destroy (an opponent, an argument, etc.); do (something) badly.
2) ***settle someone's hash,*** (*colloq.*) silence or defeat someone completely; put an end to someone.
—*vt.* **1.** chop or cut (meat and vegetables) into small pieces. **2.** make a mess of (someone or something).
—[名] 1. 잘게 썬 고기 요리 ¶①해시라이스 2. 잡동사니, 중고품더미
[熟] 1)[상대]를 해치우다; …을 엉망으로 만들다 2)《口》[남]을 해치우다, …의 끝장을 내다
—[他] 1. [고기 · 야채]를 잘게 썰다 2. …을 망쳐 놓다

hash·er [hǽʃər] *n.* [C] a person who waits on others sitting at a table.
—[名] [식당의] 급사

∗**has·n't** [hǽznt] =has not.

hasp [hæsp / hɑ:sp] *n.* [C] a clasp, esp. a hinged metal clasp, used to fasten a door, lid, etc. ⇒fig.
—[名] 잠그는 고리, 빗장

[hasp]

has·sock [hǽsək] *n.* [C] **1.** a thick heavy cushion or mat to sit, or kneel on. **2.** a tuft of coarse grass.
—[名] 1. 무릎방석 2. 풀숲

∗**hast** [hæst, həst, əst, st] *v.* (*archaic*) =have. ⇒[usage]
—[助] [usage] 주어 thou에 씀

⁑**haste** [heist] *n.* [U] the act of hurrying; quickness of action or movement; rashness. ¶(*proverb*) *Haste makes waste.*①
1) ***in haste,*** in a hurry; rashly.
2) ***make haste,*** hurry.
—*vt., vi.* (rare) hasten.
—[名] 급속, 신속, 서두름, 경솔 ¶①《俚》 성급히 굴면 일을 그르친다
[熟] 1)서둘러서; 허겁지겁 2)서두르다
—[他][自] …을 재촉하다, 서두르다

⁑**has·ten** [héisn] *vt.* cause (someone) to hurry; speed up.
—*vi.* be quick; move with speed. ¶~ *away* (*back, down, out, home*) / *I* ~ *to explain.*
—[他] …을 서두르게 하다; [일 · 속도 따위]를 더 빨리 하다 —[自] 서두르다, 급히 …하다

∗**hast·i·ly** [héistili] *adv.* in a hasty manner.
—[副] 급히, 너무 서둘러서

hast·i·ness [héistinis] *n.* [U] the quality or state of being hasty.
—[名] 서두름, 성급함, 경솔

∗**hast·y** [héisti] *adj.* (**hast·i·er, hast·i·est**) **1.** hurried; quick. ¶*a* ~ *departure.* **2.** carelessly said or done; rash. ¶*His* ~ *remarks caused many misunderstandings.* **3.** quick-tempered.
—[形] 1. 서두르는, 신속한 2. 경솔한, 황급한 3. 성미 급한

⁑**hat** [hæt] *n.* [C] a covering for the head, usu. with a brim. ¶*a top* (or *high*) ~① / *have a* ~ *on*② / *Hats off!*③
1) ***hang up one's hat,*** pay a long visit (in a house); settle down.
2) ***hat in hand,*** respectfully; humbly.
3) ***pass*** (or ***send***) ***round the hat,*** (*colloq.*) ask for contributions of money at a meeting, etc.
4) ***take one's hat off*** (or ***raise one's hat***) ***to,*** express admiration or regard for the ability of (someone); praise.
5) ***talk through one's hat,*** (*colloq.*) talk nonsense.
6) ***throw*** (or ***toss***) ***one's hat into the ring,*** (*U.S. colloq.*) enter a competition, esp. an election.
7) ***under one's hat,*** secret; told or written in private.
— *vt.* (**hat·ted, hat·ting**) cover or provide (someone)
—[名] 모자 ¶①실크햇/②모자를 쓰고 있다/③탈모!
[熟] 1)남의 집에 너무 오래 머무르다 2)모자를 손에 들고, 공손히, 굽실거리며 3)《口》모자를 돌려 기부를 청하다 4)…에게 [감탄 · 경의 · 인사를 하기 위해] 모자를 벗다 5)《口》무책임한(어리석은) 말을 하다 6)《美》경기(선거)에 참가하다 7)비밀로, 몰래
—[他] …에게 모자를 씌우다

with a hat.

hat·band [hǽtbæ̀nd] *n.* [C] a band around a hat, just above the brim.
—[名] 모자의 리본

• **hatch¹** [hætʃ] *vt.* **1.** bring forth (young) from eggs. ¶~ *eggs* (*chickens*)① / (*proverb*) *Don't count your chickens before they are hatched.*② **2.** plot; plan. ¶~ *a rebellion.* —*vi.* bring forth young; come forth from the egg. —*n.* [C] the act of hatching; all the chickens, etc. hatched at one time.
—[他] 1. [알]을 부화(孵化)하다, [알·병아리]를 까다 ¶①알(병아리)을 까다/②《俚》까지도 않은 병아리를 세지 말라 2. …을 꾸미다, 계획하다 —[自] 부화하다, 알에서 나오다 —[名] 부화; 한 배[의 병아리]

• **hatch²** [hætʃ] *n.* [C] **1.** an opening in a deck. **2.** an opening in the floor or roof of a building, etc. **3.** a cover for such an opening. **4.** the lower half of a divided door.
—[名] 1. [갑판의] 승강구, 해치 2. [마루·지붕 따위에 낸] 들어서 여는 창 3. 해치의 뚜껑 4. [문의 일부에 마련한] 쪽문

hatch³ [hætʃ] *vt.* draw, cut or carve (something) on stone with parallel lines. —*n.* [C] one of such a set of lines.
—[他] …에 평행선을 긋다, 새기다, 음영(陰影)을 나타내다 —[名] 음영, 명암

hatch·er·y [hǽtʃəri] *n.* [C] (pl. **-er·ies**) a place where eggs, esp. those of fish or poultry, are hatched.
—[名] [물고기·새 알의] 인공 부화장

hatch·et [hǽtʃit] *n.* [C] a small ax with a short handle.
—[名] 손도끼
1) ***bury the hatchet,*** make peace; agree to end a quarrel.
2) ***take*** (or ***dig***) ***up the hatchet,*** start fighting; make war.
3) ***throw the hatchet,*** talk big; exaggerate.
[熟] 1)강화(講和)하다 2)전쟁을 시작하다 3)허풍떨다; 과장하다

hatch·way [hǽtʃwèi] *n.* [C] an opening in the deck of a ship for going below. ⇒fig.
—[名] 창구(艙口)

[hatchway]

:hate [heit] *vt.* dislike very strongly; detest. ↔love, like 《~ *to do*; ~ someone or something *to do*; ~ *doing*; ~ *that...*》 ¶*I ~ dogs.* / *I ~ troubling* (or *to trouble*) *you.*① / *I ~ to have you say such a thing.*② / *I ~ that you should think so.*③ —*vi.* feel a strong dislike.
—[他] …을 미워하다, 몹시 싫어하다, 유감으로 생각하다 ¶①폐를 끼쳐서 죄송합니다/②당신이 그런 말을 하는 것은 유감입니다/③당신이 그렇게 생각하는 것이 싫다 —[自] 싫어하다, 미워하다

hate out, (*U.S.*) drive out (someone) by a strong dislike.
[熟] 《美》 미워서 …을 추방하다

—*n.* [U] very strong dislike.
—[名] 미움, 증오

• **hate·ful** [héitf(u)l] *adj.* **1.** causing hate; deserving hate. **2.** full of hate; showing hate. ¶*a ~ glance.* ▷**hate·ful·ly** [-fuli] *adv.* —**hate·ful·ness** [-nis] *n.*
—[形] 1. 밉살(가증)스러운, 지긋지긋한 2. 증오에 찬, 증오심을 나타내는

• **hath** [hæθ, həθ, əθ] *v.* (*archaic*)=has.

hat·less [hǽtlis] *adj.* wearing no hat.
—[形] 모자를 쓰지 않은

hat·rack [hǽtræ̀k] *n.* [C] a rack, shelf, hooks, etc., to put hats on.
—[名] 모자걸이

• **ha·tred** [héitrid] *n.* [U] 《sometimes *a* ~》 very strong dislike; ill will; hate. ¶*have a ~ for* (or *of*) *someone*① / *in ~ of someone; out of the ~ for someone.*②
—[名] 증오, 원한, 앙심 ¶①…을 미워하다/②…을 미워하여

hat·ter [hǽtər] *n.* [C] a person who makes or sells hats.
—[名] 모자 제조자, 모자 장수
as mad as a hatter, (*colloq.*) very mad or angry.
[熟] 《口》 아주 미쳐서, 격분하여

haugh·ti·ly [hɔ́:tili] *adv.* in a haughty manner.
—[副] 거만하게, 건방지게

haugh·ti·ness [hɔ́:tinis] *n.* [U] the state of being haughty.
—[名] 거만함, 건방짐

• **haugh·ty** [hɔ́:ti] *adj.* (**-ti·er, -ti·est**) very proud and arrogant. ¶*a ~ gesture.*
—[形] 거만한, 건방진

• **haul** [hɔ:l] *vt.* **1.** pull or draw (something) with force; tug; drag. **2.** transport (something) by a truck, etc.; move. ⇒[usage] ¶~ *baggage.* —*vi.* **1.** pull; tug. ¶~ *at* (or *upon*) *a rope.* **2.** change the course of a ship; change direction; change one's course of action or opinion.
—[他] 1. …을 세게 끌다, 잡아당기다 2. …을 수송하다 [usage] 미국에서는 단순히 「수송하다」의 뜻이나 영국에서는 「애써서 끌다」의 뜻 —[自] 1. 끌어 당기다 2. 배가 방향을 바꾸다; 방향 전환하다; [행동·의견 따위]를 전향하다

1) ***haul down one's flag*** (or ***colors***), give in; surrender
2) ***haul off,*** ⓐ turn a ship away from a destination. ⓑ go back; withdraw. ⓒ (*colloq.*) draw one's arm back before hitting.
3) ***haul someone over the coals,*** scold; criticize; take someone to task.
4) ***haul to*** (or ***on, onto***) ***the wind,*** (*Nautical*) head
[熟] 1)항복하다 2)ⓐ진로를 바꾸다 ⓑ물러서다, 퇴각하다 ⓒ《口》[때리려고] 팔을 뒤로 빼다 3)꾸짖다, 벌주다 4)《海》뱃머리를 바람 불어오는 쪽으로 돌리다 5)ⓐ뱃머리를 바람 부는 쪽으로 돌리다 ⓑ정지하다 6)…을 나무라서 못하게 하다

haulage

the bow of a ship closer into the wind.
5) ***haul up,*** ⓐ turn a ship nearer to the direction of the wind ; change the course of (a ship). ⓑ stop.
6) ***haul someone up,*** stop someone from doing wrong.
—*n.* ⓒ **1.** the act of hauling ; a strong pull or tug. **2.** the distance over which a thing is pulled or drawn. **3.** a single pulling of a net ; the quantity of fish caught at one time ; loot ; booty. ¶*get* (or *make*) *a good* (or *a big, a fine*) *~.*① ▷**haul·er** [-*ər*] *n.*
haul·age [hɔ́:lidʒ] *n.* Ⓤ **1.** the act of hauling. **2.** the force used in hauling. **3.** the charge made for hauling.
haunch [hɔ:ntʃ, +*U.S.* hɑ:ntʃ] *n.* ⓒ **1.** ((usu. *pl.*)) the parts of an animal's or a man's body round the hips ; the hips. ¶*A cat sits on his haunches.* **2.** the leg and loin of an animal, used for food.
・**haunt** [hɔ:nt, +*U.S.* hɑ:nt] *vt.* **1.** visit (a place) often or repeatedly ; visit (someone) frequently. **2.** trouble or bother (someone) by constantly returning to his mind or memory. ¶*be haunted by fear.* —*n.* ⓒ **1.** ((often *pl.*)) a place often visited. ¶*a ~ of robbers.* **2.** (*colloq.*) a ghost. 　　　　　　　　[by ghosts.]
haunt·ed [hɔ́:ntid, +*U.S.* hɑ́:ntid] *adj.* visited or lived in
Ha·van·a [həvǽnə] *n.* **1.** the capital of Cuba. **2.** ⓒ a cigar made from Cuban tobacco.
‡**have** [hæv, həv, əv, v] *vt.* (**had**) **1.** hold as a possession ; own ; contain. ¶*I ~ a book. / She had a doll in her hand. / He doesn't ~* (or *hasn't*) *any money.*① ⇒ USAGE / *Has the house a good garage? / A week has seven days.* **2.** possess (something) as a mental or physical characteristic. ¶*I ~ a poor memory. / He has only one leg.* **3.** experience ; undergo. ¶*I had a nice time last night.* **4.** engage in ; carry on ; do ; perform.
⇒USAGE ¶*~ a dance / ~ a look / ~ a smoke / ~ a talk / ~ a try.* **5.** be affected with (a disease). ¶*~ a cold / The children ~ measles.*② **6.** receive ; get ; take ; eat ; drink. ¶*~ a bath / ~ a lesson / ~ a seat / He is having breakfast. / Will you ~ some cake?*③ **7.** cause (something) to be done ; bring (something) into a certain condition. ((*~ something done*)) ¶*I must ~ this bag repaired.*④ */ He had his purse stolen.*⑤ **8.** leave ; let ; keep. ¶*~ a baby sleeping / I can't ~ you idle.*⑥ **9.** cause (someone) to do or to be. ((*~ someone do*)) ⇒USAGE
¶*Have the maid sweep the room.*⑦ */ She had her son die.*⑧ */ We had the boys steal our dog.*⑨ **10.** ((in *negative*)) permit ; admit. ¶*I won't ~ this nonsense. / I will ~ no interference.* **11.** understand ; have knowledge or use of (something). ¶*My cook has no English.*
 1) ***have and hold,*** possess (something) by law ; have permanent possession of (something).
 2) ***have at,*** attack.
 3) ***Have done !,*** Stop ! ; Finish !
 4) ***have done with,*** have finished ; have (something) become unnecessary ; make oneself free from (someone). 　　　　　　　　　　　　　　　　[⇒N.B.]
 5) ***Have everything your own way.,*** Do as you like.
 6) ***have [got] to do,*** be obliged to do ; must.
 7) ***have someone in,*** have someone in one's room, house, etc. ; have someone visit one.
 8) ***have it,*** ⓐ declare ; believe ; tell. ⓑ (*colloq.*) beat ; defeat. ⓒ (*colloq.*) be hopeless.
 9) ***have it in for,*** wish harm to come to (someone) ; hold ill-will against (someone).
 10) ***have it out of someone,*** return ; repay.
 11) ***have it out with someone,*** get a final agreement

have

—ⓣ 1. 세게 당기기 2. 끌어당긴 거리 3. 한 그물[의 어획량] ; 벌이, 수확 ¶①고기를 많이 잡다, 큰 벌이를 하다

—ⓣ 1. [잡아]당기기 2. 끄는 힘 3. 운반비, 운임
—ⓣ 1. 엉덩이, 둔부 2. [식용으로서의] 동물의 다리와 허리 부분

—ⓗ 1. …에 자주 가다 ; …붙어 다니다 2. [기억・생각 따위가 사라지지 않고] …을 괴롭히다 —ⓣ 1. [사람・동물이] 자주 다니는 곳, 출몰 장소 ; 소굴 2. 유령

—ⓣ 유령이 잘 나오는
—ⓣ 1. 쿠바의 수도 2. 하바나 엽궐련

—ⓗ 1. …을 가지고 있다 ; …이 있다 ¶①그는 돈을 갖고 있지 않다 USAGE do not have는 미국 용법, have not 는 영국 용법 2. [정신적・신체적 특성이] 있다 3. …을 경험하다 ; 겪다 4. …을 하다 USAGE 동작을 나타내는 명사와 함께 동사의 의미를 나타냄 5. [병따위]에 걸리다 ¶②아이들은 홍역을 앓고 있다 6. 받다 ; 먹다 ; 마시다 ¶③케이크를 들겠어요 ? 7. …을 어떤 상태로 만들다 ; 당하다 ; …하여 받다 ¶④이 가방을 수리시켜야 한다/⑤그는 지갑을 도둑 맞았다 8. …을 그대로의 상태로 두다 ¶⑥너를 놀려 둘 수는 없다 9. …에게 어떤 행동을 시키다 ; 하여 받다, 당하다 USAGE 목적어로 「사람」이 옴 ¶⑦하녀에게 방을 쓸라고 해라 /⑧그녀는 아들이 죽었다/⑨우리는 아이들에게 개를 도둑맞았다 10. 허락하다, 용서하다 11. 이해하다

圏 1) [법률에 따라] …을 보유하다 2) …을 공격하다 3) 그만둬 ! 4) …이 끝났다 ; 불필요하게 되었다 ; …와 인연을 끊다 5) 네 멋대로 해라 N.B. 토론을 끝맺을 때에 씀 6) …하여야 한다 7) …을 초청해 들이다 8) ⓐ말하다 ⓑ(口) 패배시키다 ⓒ(口) 가망이 없다 9) …의 불행을 바라다 ; …에 원한을 품다 10) …에 보복하다 11) …이해할 때까지 …와 토론하다 12) 입고 있다 ; 쓰고 있다 13) …하기만 하면 되다 14) …와 관계(관련)가 있다 15) …을 고소하다

with someone through fights or discussions.
12) ***have something on,*** be dressed in something; wear.
13) ***have only to do,*** need not do anything but ....
14) ***have to do with*** (=*be related to; be connected with; be associated with*) *someone* or *something.*
15) ***have someone up,*** ⟪usu. in *passive*⟫ cause someone to appear before a court of law, etc.
—*auxil. v.* ⟪with *pp.* of *v.* forming *perfects,* expressing *completion, experience, continuance,* or *result*⟫ ¶*I've just finished it.*⑩ | *He has kept it.*⑪ | *When she awoke, the train had already started.*⑫ | *The train will ~ arrived there by ten.* | *It will ~ been raining a week by tomorrow.*⑬
—[助]「과거분사와 함께 완료시제를 만들어 완료·경험·계속·결과를 나타냄」 ¶⑩지금 막 끝났다/⑪그는 그것을 유지해 왔다/⑫그녀가 눈을 떴을 때 기차는 이미 떠나고 있었다/⑬내일로 일주일 동안 계속 비가 오는 것이 된다
—*n.* [C] ⟪usu. *pl.*⟫ a person or country that has much wealth or rich material.
—[名] 부자, 부국(富國)
haves and have-nots, the rich and the poor; the employers and the employees.
[熟] 유산자와 무산자; 경영주와 고용인

ha·ven [héiv(ə)n] *n.* [C] **1.** a sheltered harbor or port for ships. **2.** any place of shelter or safety. —*vt.* put (a ship) into a port.
—[名] 1. 항구, 정박소 2. 피난처 —[他] [배]를 피난시키다

‡ **have·n't** [hǽvn(ə)t] =have not.

hav·er·sack [hǽvərsæ̀k] *n.* [C] a bag used by soldiers and hikers for carrying provisions, etc.
—[名] [군인·여행자의] 잡낭(雜囊)

hav·oc [hǽvək] *n.* [U] very great damage or injury; ruin.
—[名] 대파괴, 황폐
1) ***cry havoc,*** (*U.S.*) warn of disaster or danger; (*Brit.*) give the sign to start destroying.
2) ***make havoc of; play havoc among,*** ⓐ destroy; ruin. ⓑ create disorder or confusion.
[熟] 1)⟪美⟫재난·위험을 예고하다; ⟪口⟫ 파괴의 구령을 내리다 2)ⓐ…을 때려 부수다, 파괴하다 ⓑ혼란을 일으키다

haw[1] [hɔː] *n.* [C] [the red berry of] a hawthorn.
—[名] 산사나무[의 열매]

haw[2] [hɔː] *interj., n.* [C] a stammering sound between words. —*vi.* hesitate in speaking.
—[感][名]「아아」「에에」하는 소리 —[自]「아아」「에에」하고 말하다

haw[3] [hɔː] *interj., n.* [C] a word of command to horses or oxen, directing them to turn to the left or near side. —*vt.* turn (horses or oxen) to the left. —*vi.* (of horses or oxen) turn to the left.
—[感][名] 말·소를 왼편으로 돌게 할 때의 소리 —[他] [말·소 따위]를 왼편으로 돌게 하다 —[自] [말·소]가 왼편으로 돌다

Ha·wai·i [həwáiiː, həwáijə, -wáːjə / hɑːwá(i)iː] *n.* the 50th State of the United States. ⇒[N.B.]
—[名] 하와이 주 [N.B.] 수도 Honolulu

Ha·wai·ian[həwáiən, həwáːjən / hɑːwáiiən] *adj.* of Hawaii, its people, or their language. —*n.* **1.** [C] a person of Hawaii. **2.** [U] the language of Hawaii.
—[形] 하와이의, 하와이 사람(말)의
—[名] 1. 하와이 사람 2. 하와이 말

* **hawk**[1] [hɔːk] *n.* [C] any of several fierce birds with a strong hooked beak and sharp curved claws. ¶*know a ~ from a handsaw.*① —*vi.* hunt with hawks. —*vt.* attack (someone or something) as a hawk does.
—[名] 매 ¶①판단력이 있다 —[自] 매사냥을 하다 —[他] [매처럼] …에 덤벼들다

hawk[2] [hɔːk] *vt., vi.* try to sell (goods) on the streets by crying out.
—[他][自] [물건을] 행상하다, 소리치며 팔다

hawk[3] [hɔːk] *vi.* clear the throat noisily. —*vt.* bring up (phlegm) by coughing. —*n.* [C] a noisy effort to clear the throat.
—[自] 헛기침을 하다 —[他] [가래침]을 뱉다 —[名] 헛기침

hawk·er[1] [hɔ́ːkər] *n.* [C] a person who carries about goods for sale and advertizes them by shouting; a peddler.
—[名] 행상인

hawk·er[2] [hɔ́ːkər] *n.* [C] a person who hunts with a trained hawk.
—[名] 매 부리는 사람

hawk·ing [hɔ́ːkiŋ] *n.* [U] the act of hunting with hawks.
—[名] 매사냥

haw·ser [hɔ́ːzər] *n.* [C] a strong rope or small cable used for mooring or towing ships.
—[名] 굵은 밧줄, 배 매는(끄는) 밧줄

haw·thorn [hɔ́ːθɔːrn] *n.* [C] a thorny shrub or tree of the rose family with white flowers and small red berries. ⇒[N.B.]
—[名] 산사나무 [N.B.] 흰 꽃은 may, 붉은 열매는 haw라 불림

Haw·thorne [hɔ́ːθɔːrn], **Nathaniel** *n.* (1804–1864) an American writer.
—[名] 미국의 소설가

‡ **hay** [hei] *n.* [U] grass, clover, etc., cut and dried for use as food for cattle, horses, etc. ¶(*proverb*) *Make ~ while the sun shines.*①
—[名] 건초 ¶①⟪俚⟫해가 났을 때 풀을 말려라, 물실호기
1) ***hit the hay,*** (*colloq.*) go to bed.
2) ***make hay of,*** ruin; throw (something) into disorder.
[熟] 1)⟪口⟫잠자리에 들다 2)…을 혼란시키다, 엉망진창을 만들다
—[自] 건초를 만들다 —[他] …에 건초를

—*vi.* make hay. —*vt.* supply (horses, etc.) with hay; make (grass, etc.) into hay.
주다; …을 건초로 만들다

hay·cock [héikɑ̀k / -kɔ̀k] *n.* [C] a small pile of hay shaped like a dome in a field.
—[名] 건초더미

hay fever [´ ˋ-] *n.* a disease like a cold affecting the nose, eyes, and throat, caused by the pollen of certain plants.
—[名] 건초열(열병의 일종)

hay·field [héifì:ld] *n.* [C] a field where grass, clover, etc., is grown for hay.
—[名] 건초밭, 목초장

hay·fork [héifɔ̀:rk] *n.* [C] a fork with a long handle, used to turn or lift hay.
—[名] 건초용 쇠스랑

hay·loft [héilɔ̀(:)ft] *n.* [C] a place in a barn where hay is stored.
—[名] 건초 쌓는 다락

hay·mak·er [héimèikər] *n.* [C] a person who throws and spreads hay to dry after it has been cut.
—[名] 건초 만드는 사람

hay·rick [héirìk] *n.* =haystack.
—[名] 건초더미

hay·stack [héistæ̀k] *n.* [C] a large heap of hay piled up in the open air.
—[名] 1.[옛날의] 주사위 도박; 운수 2. 위험, 모험

* **haz·ard** [hǽzərd] *n.* **1.** [U] an old gambling game using dice; [C] a chance. **2.** [C] a risk; a danger. ¶*run a ~ / It is a ~ to drive fast on a rainy day.*
1) ***at all hazards,*** in spite of great danger or peril.
2) ***at*** (or ***by***) ***hazard,*** hazardously; at random.
3) ***at the hazard*** (=*at the risk*) ***of*** *one's life.*
—*vt.* risk (one's life, fortune, etc.); leave (something) to danger; chance; venture on (a guess, an opinion, etc.)
[熟] 1)온갖 위험을 무릅쓰고 2)위험하게; 되는 대로, 아무렇게나 3)[목숨]을 걸고
—[他] [생명·재산 따위]를 걸다, …을 위험에 빠뜨리다, 운에 맡기고 …을 하다; [억측·의견 따위]를 대담하게 시도하다

haz·ard·ous [hǽzərdəs] *adj.* dangerous; risky.
—[形] 모험적인, 위험한

haze [heiz] *n.* [U][C] **1.** a slight mist, smoke, dust, etc., in the air. ¶*Hills came in sight through a thin ~.* **2.** vagueness of the mind; confusion of thought.
—[名] 1. 아지랭이, 안개 2.[정신상태의] 흐릿함, 몽롱; [지식·시력 따위의] 애매함

ha·zel [héizl] *n.* **1.** [C] a bushy shrub or small tree whose small rounded nuts are good to eat. **2.** [U] a light brown. —*adj.* light-brown.
—[名] 1. 개암나무; 개암 2. 엷은 갈색
—[形] 엷는 갈색의

ha·zel·nut [héizlnʌ̀t, +*U.S.* -nət] *n.* [C] a nut of a hazel.
—[名] 개암

ha·zy [héizi] *adj.* (**-zi·er, -zi·est**) **1.** misty; smoky. **2.** confused; vague; dim. ¶*a ~ memory.* ▷**ha·zi·ly** [-li] *adv.*
—[形] 1. 안개가 낀 2. 흐릿한, 몽롱한

H-bomb [éitʃbɑ̀m / -bɔ̀m] *n.* [C] a hydrogen bomb.
—[名] 수소폭탄

‡ **he** [hi:, i:, hi, i] *pron.* (pl. **they**) **1.** one particular boy, man, or male animal that has been named just before. **2.** the one who…; anyone. ¶*He who works hard will certainly succeed.*① —*n.* [C] (pl. **hes** [hi:z]) a boy; a man; a male animal. ¶*Is it a ~ or a she?*
—[代] 1. 그는(가) 2.[…하는 바의] 사람 ¶①노력하는 자는 반드시 성공한다 —[名] 남자, 수컷

he- [hi:] a word element meaning *male.*: *he-goat.*
—「남성, 수컷」이라는 뜻의 연결형

‡ **head** [hed] *n.* [C] **1.** the part of the body of an animal that contains the brain. ¶*cut off the ~ / from ~ to foot / lower one's ~*① */ He struck me on the ~.*② **2.** mind; intelligence; mental ability. ¶*have a good ~ for mathematics / He used his ~. / He is weak in the ~.*③ **3.** a leader; a chief; a director; the position or rank of a leader. ¶*the ~ of the section*④ */ He is the ~ of the class.*⑤ **4.** a person; the head as a symbol for a person. ¶*learned heads*⑥ */ crowned heads.*⑦ **5.** the top or uppermost part of anything. ¶*the ~ of a pin (a table, a hammer).* **6.** the front end; the foremost part. ¶*the ~ of a column of troops.*⑧ **7.** (pl. **head**) a person or an animal, as one of a number. ¶*one thousand dollars a ~*⑨ */ three ~ of cattle.* **8.** the front part of a ship. **9.** the source of a river. **10.** the foam that rises to the surface of some liquid. **11.** the heading of a book, composition, chapter, etc.; the title. **12.** a main division of a subject, theme, or topic. ¶*a speech arranged under five heads.*⑩ **13.** a crisis; a climax. **14.** the front surface of a coin.
1) ***be above*** *someone's* ***head,*** be too difficult for (someone).
2) ***beat*** *someone's* ***head off,*** (*U.S.*) beat someone mercilessly.
3) ***by the head and ears; by head and shoulders,*** forcibly.
—[名] 1. 머리 ¶①머리를 숙이다/②그는 내 머리를 두드렸다 2. 두뇌 작용; 지력(知力) ¶③그는 두뇌가 모자란다 3. 지도자; 우두머리; 지휘자 ¶④과장/⑤그는 학급에서 수석이다 4. 사람 ¶⑥학자들/⑦고귀한 사람들 5. 윗부분; [물건의] 머리, 꼭대기 6. 선두 ¶⑧군대 행렬의 선두 7. 머릿수, 마리 ¶⑨한 마리에 천 달러 8. 선수(船首) 9. [강의] 수원(水源) 10. [맥주 표면에 일어난] 거품 11. 표제 12. 항목 ¶⑩5항목으로 정리된 연설 13. 위기; 극치 14. 화폐의 표면
[熟] 1)…에게는 너무 어렵다 2)(美)[남을] 형편없이 지게 하다 3)거칠게, 우격다짐으로

4) ***come*** (or ***draw, gather***) ***to a head,*** ⓐ reach a crisis; reach the highest point. ⓑ be about to form pus.
5) ***give*** *someone* ***his head,*** let someone do as he likes.
6) ***go to the*** (or *someone's*) ***head,*** ⓐ confuse or excite someone; make someone drunk. ⓑ make someone vain or overconfident.
7) ***have a head*** (=*be gifted with talent*) ***for*** *something.*
8) ***have a head on*** *one's* ***shoulders,*** have common sense; be very clever.
9) ***head and ears,*** completely; perfectly.
10) ***head and shoulders above,*** considerably higher than (something); better than (something).
11) ***head first*** (or ***foremost***), headlong.
12) ***head on,*** facing frontward.
13) ***head over heels; heels over head,*** ⓐ completely; very eagerly. ⓑ upside-down.
14) ***hold*** *one's* ***head high,*** look very proud; give oneself airs.
15) ***keep*** *one's* ***head,*** maintain one's self-control; remain calm.
16) ***keep*** *one's* ***head above water,*** manage to be out of trouble, esp. debt.
17) ***lay heads together,*** consult or plan together.
18) ***lose*** *one's* ***head,*** lose one's self-control; get excited.
19) ***make head,*** go forward; advance.
20) ***make head against,*** resist; oppose.
21) ***off*** (or ***out of***) *one's* ***head,*** ⓐ excited. ⓑ mad; crazy.
22) ***over*** *someone's* ***head,*** ⓐ too difficult for someone to understand. ⓑ without consulting someone.
23) ***over the head of,*** in spite of someone's prior or more important claim.
24) ***put*** *something* ***into*** (***out of***) *someone's* ***head,*** cause someone to remember (forget) something.
25) ***take it into*** *one's* ***head,*** form an idea, plan, or intention in one's mind. ¶*I took it into my head to respect him.*
26) ***take the head,*** take the lead.
27) ***turn*** *someone's* ***head,*** cause someone to become conceited or to feel superior.

4)ⓐ위기에 빠지다; 기회가 무르익다 ⓑ[종기 따위가] 곪아 터지게 되다 5)…을 마음대로 하게 하다 6)ⓐ흥분시키다; [술 따위가] 취하게 하다 ⓑ자만심을 갖게 하다 7)…에 대한 재능이 있다 8)상식이 있다 9)온통 10)…보다 훨씬 큰; …보다 뛰어난 11)곤두박이로 12)정면으로 13)ⓐ완전히, 열심히 ⓑ곤두박이로 14)젠체하다 15)태연(침착)하다 16)빚지지 않고 있다 17)함께 의논(계획)하다 18)당황하다 19)전진하다 20)저항하다 21) ⓐ흥분하여 ⓑ미친 22)ⓐ너무 어려워 이해할 수 없는 ⓑ의논하지 않고 23)[승진 따위에서] …을 앞질러서 24)[…에게 어떤 일을] 상기시키다(잊게 하다) 25)…이 생각나다; …할 생각이 들다 26)앞장서다, 선도(先導)하다 27)…을 우쭐대게 하다

—*vt.* **1.** be first on (something). ¶*Tom's name headed the list.*⑪ **2.** be chief or leader of (a group). ¶*a cabinet headed by him.*⑫ **3.** strike or touch (someone or something) with the head. **4.** cut off the head or top of (something). ¶*~ a plant.*⑬ **5.** turn or direct the course of (a ship, etc.). ¶*~ the vessel toward shore.*⑭ **—*vi.*** **1.** travel; start. ¶*They were heading north.* **2.** grow or come to a head.
1) ***head along,*** go forward.
2) ***head back,*** ⓐ interfere; interrupt. ⓑ go in the opposite direction.
3) ***head off,*** interrupt the course of (something) in the middle; get ahead of and cause (something) to stop or turn away.

—[他] **1.** …의 선두에 서다 ¶⑪톰의 이름이 표의 제일 앞에 있었다 **2.** …의 책임자(우두머리)가 되다 ¶⑫그를 수반으로 하는 내각 **3.** …을 머리로 치다(받다) **4.** …의 머리를 자르다 ¶⑬초목의 순을 자르다 **5.** …의 진로를 바꾸다 ¶⑭항로를 해안으로 돌리다 —[自] **1.** 나아가다, 향하다 **2.** [양배추·상치 따위] 알이 들다
[熟] 1)전진하다 2)ⓐ…을 방해하다 ⓑ거꾸로 가다 3)…을 방해하다; …의 침로(針路)를 바꾸게 하다

∗**head·ache** [hédèik] *n.* **1.** [C][U] pain in the head. **2.** [C] (*U.S. colloq.*) a cause of worry, annoyance, or trouble.
—[名] **1.** 두통 **2.** 《美口》 고민거리

head·band [hédbæ̀nd] *n.* [C] a band worn around the head.
—[名] 머리띠

head·dress [héddrès] *n.* [C] **1.** a covering, often ornamental, for the head. **2.** the style of wearing or arranging the hair.
—[名] **1.** [여자의] 머리 장식 **2.** 머리 모양

head·ed [hédid] *adj.* **1.** with a head. **2.** shaped like a head.
—[形] **1.** 머리가 있는 **2.** 머리 모양의

head·er [hédər] *n.* [C] **1.** (*colloq.*) a fall or plunge headfirst. ¶*take a ~ off a ladder.*① **2.** a machine for cutting off the tops of grain, etc. **3.** a brick or stone laid with its length across the thickness of a wall.
—[名] **1.** 《口》 곤두박이로 떨어지기(뛰어들기) ¶①사닥다리에서 거꾸로 떨어지다 **2.** 이삭 잘라내는 기계 **3.** [쌓아올린] 벽돌의 마구리

head·first [hédfə́ːrst] *adv.* **1.** with the head in front. **2.** rashly; thoughtlessly; in haste.
—[副] **1.** 곤두박이로 **2.** 무모하게, 황급히

head·gear [hédgìər] *n.* Ⓤ **1.** a covering for the head, such as a hat or cap. **2.** the harness for the head of a horse, mule, etc.
— 图 1. 모자, 머리 장식 2. [말의] 굴레

head·i·ness [hédinis] *n.* Ⓤ stubbornness; obstinacy.
— 图 고집이 셈, 완고함

head·ing [hédiŋ] *n.* Ⓒ **1.** something that serves as a head, top, or front. **2.** a title or topic at the top of a paragraph, page, chapter, etc. ¶ *under the ~ of*.① **3.** Ⓤ (*Football*) the act of striking the ball with the head.
— 图 1. 끝(머리)의 구실을 하는 것 2. [절(節)·페이지·장(章) 따위의] 표제 ¶①…이라는 표제로, …이라는 항목으로 3. 〔蹴球〕 헤딩

head·land [hédlənd] *n.* Ⓒ a point of land projecting into water, etc.; a cliff.
— 图 [바다·호수 따위의] 갑(岬), 곶

head·less [hédlis] *adj.* **1.** having no head. **2.** without a leader. **3.** foolish; stupid.
— 图 1. 머리(목)가 없는 2. 지도자가 없는 3. 어리석은

head·light [hédlàit] *n.* Ⓒ **1.** a bright light on the front of an automobile, a streetcar, etc. **2.** a white light at a masthead.
— 图 1. [자동차의] 전조등(前照燈), 헤드라이트 2. [앞 돛대의] 백색등

head·line [hédlàin] *n.* Ⓒ **1.** words printed in large type at the top of an article in a newspaper. ¶ *go into headlines*.① **2.** a line at the top of a page which gives the title, page number, etc. —*vt.* furnish (a news article) with a headline.
— 图 1. [신문 따위의] 표제 ¶①신문에 커다랗게 나다 2. 책 페이지의 상단[난외(欄外)표제·페이지 따위가 적혀 있는 곳] — 他 [신문 기사에] 표제를 달다

• **head·long** [hédlɔ̀(ː)ŋ / -lɔ̀ŋ] *adv.* **1.** head first. ¶ *fall ~.*① **2.** without thinking; rashly; thoughtlessly. —*adj.* **1.** having the head first. **2.** rash; violent; reckless.
— 團 1. 곤두박이로 2. 무모하게 — 團 1. 거꾸로의 2. 무모한

head·man [hédmæn] *n.* Ⓒ (*pl.* -**men** [-mèn]) a leader; a chief.
— 图 수령, 우두머리

head·mas·ter [hédmǽstər / -máːstə] *n.* Ⓒ the principal teacher, esp. of a private school; a principal.
— 图 교장

head-on [hédán / -ɔ́n] *adj.* (of two things) meeting front to front; head to head. ¶ *a ~ collision*.①
— 團 정면[충돌]의 ¶①정면충돌

head·phone [hédfòun] *n.* Ⓒ (often *pl.*) a telephone or radio receiver held over the ears.
— 图 [머리에 쓰는] 수화기, 이어폰

head·piece [hédpìːs] *n.* Ⓒ **1.** a piece of armor for the head; a helmet. **2.** a covering for the head, such as a hat or cap. **3.** the head; intellect.
— 图 1. 투구 2. 두건 3. 머리, 지능, 지력(知力)

• **head·quar·ters** [hédkwɔ̀ːrtərz] *n. pl.* (used often as *sing.*) **1.** the place from which orders are sent out; the main office; any center of activity or authority. ¶ *the general ~.*① ⇒ⓊⓈⒶⒼⒺ **2.** (usu. *collectively*) all the people working at such a place.
— 图 1. 본부, 사령부; 본서(本署); 활동의 중심; 본거지 ¶①총사령부 ⓊⓈⒶⒼⒺ 본부·사령부의 의미로는 흔히 단수 취급 2. 본부원, 사령부원

heads·man [hédzmən] *n.* Ⓒ (*pl.* -**men** [-mən]) a man who puts criminals to death; a public executioner.
— 图 참수인(斬首人), 망나니

head·stone [hédstòun] *n.* Ⓒ **1.** a stone set up at the head of a grave. **2.** a cornerstone or keystone.
— 图 1. [묘지의] 삿갓돌, 묘석 2. 주춧돌, 귀돌

head·strong [hédstrɔ̀(ː)ŋ / -strɔ̀ŋ] *adj.* determined to have one's own way; obstinate; stubborn; selfish
— 團 고집이 센, 제멋대로의

head·wa·ters [hédwɔ̀ːtərz, +*U.S.* -wàt-] *n. pl.* sources or upper parts of a stream.
— 图 [강의] 원류(源流), 상류

head·way [hédwèi] *n.* Ⓤ **1.** forward motion, as of a ship. **2.** a clear space overhead permitting passage under a bridge, arch, etc.
— 图 1. [배 따위의] 전진, 진행 2. [다리·아치 따위의 아래에서 위까지의] 높이

head wind [´ ˋ] *n.* a wind that blows exactly against the front of a ship, an airplane, etc.
— 图 맞바람

head word [´ ˋ] *n.* a word used as a heading, esp. the first word of a dictionary entry.
— 图 표제어

head·work [hédwə̀ːrk] *n.* Ⓤ mental work or effort; the act of thinking; thought.
— 图 머리를 쓰는 일, 정신노동

head·y [hédi] *adj.* (**head·i·er, head·i·est**) **1.** willful; hasty; rash. **2.** (of liquor) apt to affect or go to one's head; exciting.
— 團 1. 완고한, 고집이 센, 무모한 2. [술이] 머리에 오르는, 판단력을 잃게 하는

• **heal** [hiːl] *vt.* **1.** bring back (the sick) to good health; get rid of (a disease); cure. (~ *someone of*) ¶ ~ *the sick* / *be healed of one's wound*. **2.** remedy (grief, trouble, etc.). —*vi.* become sound and well; get well. *heal up* (or *over*), (of a wound) become quite healthy.
— 他 1. [환자]를 회복시키다; [병]을 고치다, 낫게 하다 2. [슬픔·피로움 따위]를 없애다 — 圓 회복하다, 낫다

圓 [상처가] 낫다

heal·er [híːlər] *n.* ⓒ a person or thing that heals. ¶ *Time is a great ~ of everything.*
—ⓝ [병을] 고치는 사람(것), 치료자, 약

heal·ing [híːliŋ] *adj.* that heals; getting well; curing.
—*n.* ⓤ cure.
—ⓐ 치료의; 나아 가는
—ⓝ 치료법

health [helθ] *n.* ⓤ **1.** the state of being well; freedom from sickness. ¶ *[the] public ~*① / *a bill of ~*② / *out of ~*③. **2.** condition of body or mind. ⇒[usage] ¶ *be in good (bad, ill, poor) ~.* **3.** in honor of someone's health and happiness. ¶ *drink to the ~ of someone; drink to someone's ~ / To your ~!; Your ~!*④
—ⓝ **1.** [신체·정신의] 건강, 건전 ①공중 위생/②건강 진단서/③건강이 나빠져 **2.** 건강 상태, 몸의 형편 [usage] bad, good 따위의 단어와 함께 씀 **3.** [건강을 축원하는] 축배 ¶④건강을 축원합니다

health·ful [hélθf(u)l] *adj.* giving health; good for the health; wholesome; salutary. ¶ *~ exercise.*① ▷ **health·ful·ly** [-fuli] *adv.* —**health·ful·ness** [-nis] *n.*
—ⓐ 건강에 알맞은(좋은); 건전한 ¶①건강에 좋은 운동

health·y [hélθi] *adj.* (**health·i·er, health·i·est**) **1.** having good health. ¶ *a ~ child.* **2.** showing good health. ¶ *a ~ look.* **3.** healthful. ▷ **health·i·ness** [-nis] *n.*
—ⓐ **1.** 건강한 **2.** 건강해 보이는 **3.** 건강에 도움이 되는, 위생적인

heap [hiːp] *n.* ⓒ **1.** a number of things lying together; a pile. ¶ *a ~ of rocks.* **2.** (*colloq.*) (often *pl.*) a large quantity; a great deal. ¶ *heaps better.*①
1) *all of a heap,* ⓐ overwhelmed with great surprise; amazed. ⓑ quite suddenly.
2) *heaps of times,* often.
3) *in a heap,* in a pile. 「whelmed; overcome.」
4) *struck* (or *knocked*) *all of a heap,* (*colloq.*) over-
—*vt.* **1.** gather (something) in heaps; pile. 《*~ up* or *together* something》 ¶ *~ up stones.* **2.** fill (a plate, etc.) with a heap of something. ¶ *~ a basket with apples.* **3.** give (something) in large amounts to. ¶ *~ gifts upon someone / ~ favors upon someone; ~ someone with favors.*②
—ⓝ **1.** 쌓아올린 것, 더미 **2.** 《口》 다량, 다수 ¶①훨씬 좋은

🔳 1) ⓐ 깜짝 놀란 ⓑ 갑작스러운 2) 몇 번이고, 여러 번 3) 덩어리가 되어 4) 《口》 어리둥절한, 압도당한

—ⓥ **1.** …을 쌓아 올리다, 퇴적(堆積)하다 **2.** [접시 따위에] …을 수북하게 담다 **3.** …을 자꾸(수북하게) 주다 ¶②…에게 많은 은혜를 베풀다

hear [hiər] *v.* (**heard**) *vt.* **1.** catch (sound) through the ears. ¶ *~ a sound / I can't ~ you.* **2.** know the action of (someone or something) by sound. 《*~ someone do* or *doing*》 ⇒[usage] ¶ *~ Tom walking / I ~ a bird sing.* **3.** listen to; pay attention to (something). ¶ *~ a lecture / We had better ~ what he has to say.*① **4.** listen to (something) officially; give a chance to be heard to (something). ¶ *The judge heard the case in court.*② **5.** be informed of (something); get news of (something). ¶ *I have heard nothing of him since. / I ~ you are leaving town.* **6.** agree to (something); grant. ¶ *~ a prayer / He heard my entreaty.* —*vi.* **1.** catch or be able to catch sound through the ears. ¶ *The deaf don't ~.* **2.** be told; be informed.
1) *hear* (=get a letter) *from someone.*
2) *hear of,* ⓐ get news of (someone or something). ¶ *I have not heard of him lately.*② ⓑ (usu. in *negative*) approve of (something); admit. ¶ *I won't ~ of your request.*②
3) *hear someone out,* listen to someone until the end.
4) *I hear,* It is said that …
—ⓥ **1.** …이 들리다 **2.** [사람이 …하는] 것을 듣다 [usage] hear는 「들리다」, listen to는 「주의하여 듣다」 **3.** …에 귀를 기울이다 ¶①그의 말을 잘 듣는 편이 좋다 **4.** …을 청취하다; [사건]을 심리하다 ¶②재판관은 사건을 심리했다 **5.** [소문 따위를] 전해 듣다 **6.** [소원]을 들어 주다 —ⓥ **1.** 듣다, 들리다 **2.** [소문으로] 듣다; 소식을 받다

🔳 1) …으로부터 소식을 받다 2) ⓐ …을 소문으로 듣다 ¶③근래 그의 소식은 못 들었다 ⓑ …을 승낙하다 ¶④네 요구는 들어 줄 수 없다 3) [남의 말을] 마지막까지 듣다 4) …이라는 이야기도 있더라

heard [həːrd] *v.* pt. and pp. of **hear.**

hear·er [híərər] *n.* ⓒ a person who hears; a listener.
—ⓝ 듣는 사람, 방청인

hear·ing [híəriŋ] *n.* **1.** ⓤ the sense by which sound is perceived. ¶ *hard of ~*① / *My grandmother's ~ is poor.* **2.** ⓒ the act of perceiving sound. **3.** ⓒ a chance to be heard; a judicial trial; audience. ¶ *a preliminary ~*② / *a public ~*③ / *gain a ~*④ / *give someone a fair ~*⑤ / *The judge gave them a ~.* **4.** ⓤ the distance over which sound can be heard. ¶ *in someone's ~*⑥ / *out of* (*within*) *~.*⑦
—ⓝ **1.** 청각 ¶①귀가 먼 **2.** 듣기, 청취 **3.** 들어 주기; 심문 ¶②예심/③공청회/④발언의 기회를 얻다/⑤공명하게 들어 주다 **4.** 들리는 거리 ¶⑥남이 듣고 있는 곳에서/⑦들리지 않는(들리는) 곳에서

hear·say [híərsèi] *n.* ⓤ rumor; gossip. ¶ *~ evidence*① / *by* (or *from, on*) *~.*② 「the grave.」
—ⓝ 풍문, 소문 ¶①전문(傳聞)증거/②소문으로

hearse [həːrs] *n.* ⓒ a car for carrying dead bodies to
—ⓝ 영구차, 장의차

⁝heart [hɑːrt] *n.* [C] **1.** a muscular organ that pumps the blood throughout the body. **2.** feelings; mind; soul. ¶*She has a kind ~.* **3.** emotions of love. ¶*give one's ~.*① **4.** sympathy; kindness; tenderness. ¶*Her ~ was moved at the sight.*② **5.** courage; spirit. ¶*I haven't the ~ to tell her about the news.*③ **6.** the center; the core. ¶*the ~ of the town / the ~ of a tree.* **7.** something shaped like the human heart. **8.** a playing card marked with a red figure like a heart.

—[名] 1. 심장 2. 마음, 정 3. 애정, 사랑 ¶①사랑을 바치다 4. 동정심 ¶②그 광경을 보고 그녀는 동정했다 5. 용기, 기력 ¶③그녀에게 그 소식을 알릴 용기가 없다 6. 중심, 본질 7. 하아트 모양의 것 8. [카아드의] 하아트의 패

1) ***after one's own heart,*** just as one likes it; that suits or pleases one perfectly.
2) ***at heart,*** in one's mind; really.
3) ***break someone's heart,*** crush someone with sorrow or grief.
4) ***by heart,*** ⓐ by memory. ¶*learn by ~.*④ ⓑ perfectly.
5) ***eat one's heart out,*** feel deep sorrow.
6) ***from [the bottom of] one's heart,*** sincerely; cordially.
7) ***have (or bring) one's heart in one's mouth,*** be very frightened.
8) ***have one's heart in the right place,*** have a kind heart.
9) ***heart and soul (or hand),*** with all one's effort, affections, etc.
10) ***in one's heart [of hearts],*** in one's deepest feelings.
11) ***near someone's heart,*** of great value or importance to someone.
12) ***take heart,*** cheer up; grow braver.
13) ***take something to heart,*** think seriously about something; be troubled or grieved by something.
14) ***wear one's heart on one's sleeve,*** show one's feelings or affections plainly.
15) ***with all one's heart,*** ⓐ sincerely. ⓑ gladly; willingly.

[熟] 1)마음에 드는, 마음대로[의] 2)마음에; 실제는 3)…을 비탄에 잠기게 하다 4)ⓐ기억하여, 외어서 ¶④암기하다 ⓑ완전히 5)슬픔에 잠기다 6)마음[속]으로부터 7)몹시 놀라다 8)인정이 있다 9)열심히, 전력을 다하여 10)마음속으로는 11)…에게 아주 소중(중요)한 12)기운이 나다, 용기를 내다 13)…을 심각하게 생각하다; …을 슬퍼하다 14)생각(애정)을 노골적으로 드러내다 15)ⓐ충심으로 ⓑ기꺼이, 성심껏

heart·ache [háːrtèik] *n.* [U][C] sorrow; grief. —[名] 마음의 고통, 비탄

heart·beat [háːrtbìːt] *n.* [C] the movement of the heart; throb. —[名] 심장의 고동, 동계(動悸)

heart·break [háːrtbrèik] *n.* [C] deep sorrow or grief; bitter disappointment. —[名] 비탄, 실망

heart·break·ing [háːrtbrèikiŋ] *adj.* causing deep sorrow, grief or disappointment. —[形] 가슴이 찢어질 듯한, 애끓게 하는

heart·brok·en [háːrtbròuk(ə)n] *adj.* suffering from deep sorrow or grief. ▷**heart·bro·ken·ly** [-li] *adv.* —[形] 비탄에 잠긴

heart·burn [háːrtbəːrn] *n.* [C] discomfort in the stomach after a meal. —[名] 가슴앓이

heart·ed [háːrtid] *adj.* having a specified kind of heart. ¶*sad-hearted / faint-hearted.* —[形] …한 마음을 가진, 마음이 …한

heart·en [háːrtn] *vt.* give courage to (someone); cheer up; encourage. ¶*be heartened by good news.* —[他] …을 격려하다, 기운나게 하다

heart failure [ˊ ˊ–] *n.* a fatal disease of the heart. —[名] 심장마비

heart·felt [háːrtfèlt] *adj.* with true, warm and deep feelings; sincere. —[形] 진심에서의, 마음 깊이 느낀

***hearth** [hɑːrθ] *n.* [C] **1.** the floor of a fireplace. **2.** [U] the fireside; the home. —[名] 1. 벽로(壁爐)바닥 2. 난롯가; 가정

hearth·rug [háːrθrʌ̀g] *n.* [C] a carpet for the hearth. —[名] 벽로 앞에 까는 양탄자

***heart·i·ly** [háːrtili] *adv.* **1.** sincerely; in a warm, friendly manner. **2.** lively. ¶*eat ~.*① —[副] 1. 진심으로, 열심히 2. 힘차게, 실컷 ¶①마음껏 먹다

heart·i·ness [háːrtinis] *n.* [U] the state of being hearty. —[名] 친절; 원기

heart·less [háːrtlis] *adj.* without feeling or affection; cruel; pitiless. ▷**heart·less·ly** [-li] *adv.* —**heart·less·ness** [-nis] *n.* —[形] 무정한, 잔인한

heart-rend·ing [háːrtrèndiŋ] *adj.* causing much sorrow or intense distress. ▷**heart-rend·ing·ly** [-li] *adv.* —[形] 가슴이 미어질 듯한

heart·sick [háːrt-sìk] *adj.* very unhappy. —[形] 가슴아픈, 비통한

heart·strings [háːrt-strìŋz] *n. pl.* deepest feelings of love. —[名] 심금(心琴), 정서

heart wood [ˊ ˊ] *n.* the hard, central wood of a tree trunk. —[名] [목재의] 심재(心材)

***heart·y** [háːrti] *adj.* (**heart·i·er, heart·i·est**) **1.** friendly; warm-hearted. ¶*a ~ welcome.* **2.** high-spirited; healthy; cheerful. ¶*He is still hale and ~ at 80.*① **3.** —[形] 1. 충심에서의, 친절한 2. 기운찬 ¶①그는 여든 살인데도 정정하다 3. 풍부한, 푸짐한 ¶②왕성한 식욕

H

heat [hi:t] *n.* ⓤ **1.** the state of being hot. ↔cold ¶*the ~ of the sun / the ~ of a fire.* **2.** fierce feeling; excitement. ¶*the ~ of an attack / with some ~.*① **3.** hot weather. **4.** ⓒ one trial in a race. ¶*trial heats.*② **5.** (*slang*) pressure.
at a heat, at a breath.
—*vt.* **1.** make (something) hot or warm. **2.** excite.
—*vi.* **1.** become hot or warm. **2.** become excited.

heat·ed·ly [híːtidli] *adv.* in an angry, lively, or excited manner.

heat·er [híːtər] *n.* ⓒ a thing that gives heat, such as a stove, furnace, or radiator.

heath [hi:θ] *n.* **1.** ⓒ (*Brit.*) a stretch of waste land covered with heather and low shrubs. **2.** ⓤⓒ an evergreen shrub; heather.

• **hea·then** [híːð(ə)n] *n.* ⓒ a person who is not a Christian, Jew, or Mohammedan; a very uncivilized person. —*adj.* not Christian, Jewish, or Mohammedan.

hea·then·dom [híːð(ə)ndəm] *n.* ⓒ heathen lands or people. ↔Christendom

hea·then·ish [híːð(ə)niʃ] *adj.* of the heathen; like the heathen; barbarous.

hea·then·ism [híːðəniz(ə)m] *n.* ⓤ **1.** heathen worship or ways. **2.** lack of religion; barbarism.

heath·er [héðər] *n.* ⓤ a rough wild plant with very small red-blue flowers, found on waste land.

heath·y [híːθi] *adj.* (**heath·i·er, heath·i·est**) **1.** of or like a heath. **2.** covered with heath.

heat·ing [híːtiŋ] *adj.* that heats. ¶*a ~ apparatus.*①
—*n.* ⓤ the act of making (something) hot. ¶*steam~.*②

heat·stroke [híːt-stròuk] *n.* ⓤⓒ sudden illness caused by too much heat; sunstroke.

• **heave** [hi:v] *v.* (**heaved** or *nautical* **hove**) *vt.* **1.** raise (something heavy) with effort; lift. ¶*~ the anchor.* **2.** lift and throw (something), esp. with effort. ¶*~ the shot 10 meters.*① **3.** pull (a rope, etc.) with force or effort. **4.** cause (something) to swell or rise. ¶*~ one's chest.*② **5.** force out (a sigh, etc.) with effort or pain. ¶*~ a sigh.* **6.** cause (something) to rise and fall repeatedly. ¶*The waves heaved the ship up and down.* **7.** (*Nautical*) move (a ship) into a certain position. ¶*~ a ship backward.*③ —*vi.* **1.** rise. **2.** swell up. **3.** (*Nautical*) rise and fall repeatedly. **4.** give a sigh; breathe with effort.
1) *Heave away* [*ho*]*!,* (*Nautical*) Pull (or Push) hard together!
2) *heave in* (or *into*) *sight,* come in sight, as a ship
3) *heave out,* lift up (a flag, etc.). at sea.
—*n.* ⓒ **1.** an effort to lift or raise. **2.** a swell; a stretch, as of sea waves. **3.** the distance something is thrown.

‡ **heav·en** [hév(ə)n] *n.* ⓤⓒ **1.** (often *pl.*) the sky; the place where God and the angels live. ¶*the starry heavens*① */ Italy has a brighter ~ than ours.*② **2.** (-*H*) God. ¶*Thank Heaven!*③ */ Good Heaven*[*s*]*!*④ */ By Heaven*[*s*]*!*⑤ */ Heaven helps those who help themselves.*⑥ **3.** the place of greatest happiness. ↔hell
1) *go to heaven,* die.
2) *move heaven and earth,* do everything possible; make every effort.

• **heav·en·ly** [hév(ə)nli] *adj.* **1.** of or in heaven. ¶*the ~ bodies.*① **2.** like heaven; very beautiful. **3.** (*colloq.*) very happy; very delightful; excellent.

heav·en·ward [hév(ə)nwərd] *adj., adv.* toward heaven.
heav·en·wards [hév(ə)nwərdz] *adv.* =heavenward.

‡ **heav·i·ly** [hévili] *adv.* **1.** with a heavy weight. **2.**

severely, intensely.

heav·i·ness [hévinis] *n.* [U] the state or quality of being heavy. —[名] 무거움; 답답함

‡heav·y [hévi] *adj.* (**heav·i·er, heav·i·est**) **1.** weighty; hard to lift or carry. ↔light ¶*The box is too ~ for you to carry.* / *Gold is heavier than iron.* **2.** great in quantity or amount; rich ¶*a ~ crop*① / *a ~ drinker.*② **3.** grave; severe; hard to do or finish; hard to bear or suffer. ¶*~ work*③ / *~ taxes* / *~ sorrow* / *a ~ wound.*④ **4.** not easily digested. ¶*~ food.* **5.** forceful; powerful. ¶*a ~ blow.* **6.** loud and intense. ¶*~ applause.*⑤ **7.** cloudy; gloomy. ¶*a ~ sky.* **8.** thick; dense; full of. ¶*~ fog* / *air ~ with moisture.*⑥ **9.** violent. ¶*a ~ sea* / *a ~ storm.* **10.** muddy. ¶*a ~ road.* **11.** slow in action or in understanding; dull. ¶*a ~ fellow.*⑦ **12.** slow and troublesome. ¶*a ~ step.* **13.** feeling sorrow or grief. ¶*a ~ heart* / *~ news.*
—[形] 1. 무거운 2. 다량의 ¶①풍작/②술고래 3. 중대한, 심한; 쓰라린; 슬픈 ¶③힘드는 일/④중상 4. 소화가 잘 안 되는 5. 맹렬한 6. 격렬한 ¶⑤대갈채 7. 흐린, 음산한 8. 짙은; …으로 가득찬 ¶⑥습기찬 공기 9. 거친, 험악한 10. [땅·흙이] 차진; 질척질척한 11. 우둔한, 어리석은; 서투른, 솜씨없는 ¶⑦느림보, 굼벵이 12. 느릿느릿한 13. 슬픈

1) ***hang heavy on one's hands,*** (of time) pass slowly and dully.
2) ***have a heavy hand,*** ⓐ be unskillful; be left-handed. ⓑ be cruel; be overbearing.
3) ***heavy in*** (or ***on***) ***hand,*** ⓐ (of a horse) hard to drive. ⓑ tiresome; dull.
4) ***lie*** (or ***sit, weigh***) ***heavy on,*** ⓐ lean on (something). ⓑ cause great pain or trouble to (someone).
[熟] 1)[시간이] 지루하게 지나가다 2) ⓐ손재주가 없다 ⓑ잔인하다; 강압적이다 3)ⓐ[말 따위가] 부리기 어려운 ⓑ지루한, 단조로운 4)ⓐ…에 기대다 ⓑ…을 괴롭히다

heav·y-heart·ed [hévihá:rtid] *adj.* sorrowful; sad; gloomy. —[形] 슬픈, 우울한

heav·y·weight [héviwèit] *n.* [C] **1.** a person of much more than average weight. **2.** a heavyweight boxer or wrestler. —[名] 1. [경마 기수 등이] 평균 체중 이상의 사람 2. [권투·레슬링의] 헤비급 선수

He·bra·ic [hi(:)bréiik] *adj.* of or having to do with the Hebrews or their language. —[形] 헤브라이 사람(말)의

He·brew [hí:bru:] *n.* **1.** [C] a Jew. **2.** [U] the ancient language of the Jews; the present-day language of Israel. —*adj.* Jewish. —[名] 1. 헤브라이 사람, 유대 사람 2. 고대 헤브라이어; 현대 이스라엘어 —[形] 헤브라이 사람의

heck·le [hékl] *vt.* trouble (a public speaker) by asking many questions or by making fun of. —[他] [연사·강연자에게] 질문을 연발하여 애먹이다; 힐문하다

hec·tare [héktɛər, +*Brit.* -tɑ:] *n.* [C] a unit of area in the metric system; 100 acres. —[名] 헥타아르(면적의 단위)

hec·tic [héktik] *adj.* **1.** showing signs of a slow wasting disease; feverish. ¶*a ~ fever.*① **2.** (*colloq.*) very excited. —[形] 1. 소모열의(에 걸린), 열이 있는 ¶①소모열 2. 흥분한, 열광적인

hec·to- [héktou-] a word element meaning *one hundred.*: *hectogram.* —「백(百)」을 뜻하는 연결형

Hec·tor [héktər] *n.* a Trojan hero, son of King Priam, killed by Achilles in Homer's "*Iliad.*" —[名] 헥터(Homer 작 *Iliad*에 나오는 Troy의 용사)

hec·tor [héktər] *vt., vi.* talk to (someone) noisily in order to get out of a difficulty. —*n.* [C] a person who hectors. —[他][自] [곤경을 벗어나기 위해] 쓸데없이 고함치다 —[名] 고함치는 사람

·he'd [hi:d] **1.** he had. **2.** he would.

‡hedge [hedʒ] *n.* [C] **1.** a row of bushes forming a fence or dividing line. ¶*a quickset ~.*① **2.** a barrier. —[名] 산울타리, 생울타리 ¶①산울타리 2. 장벽, 경계

1) ***come down on the wrong side of the hedge,*** make a wrong decision.
2) ***take hedge,*** leave; go away.
[熟] 1)결정을 잘못하다 2)가 버리다, 떠나다

—*vt.* **1.** put a hedge around (something). **2.** protect (something) with a hedge, etc.; shelter. —[他] 1. […에] 산울타리를 두르다 2. [장벽으로] …을 지키다, 막다

1) ***hedge in,*** ⓐ surround. 《*~ in* a house, etc. *with*》 ⓑ give a limit to (someone). 《*~ in* someone *with* rules, etc.》
2) ***hedge out,*** shut out; lock out.
[熟] 1)ⓐ[집 따위를] …으로 둘러싸다 ⓑ[규칙으로써 남을] 속박(제한)하다 2)쫓아내다, 제외하다

hedge·hog [hédʒhɑ̀g, -hɔ̀:g / -(h)ɔg] *n.* [C] **1.** a kind of rat partly covered with a needle-like skin. **2.** an animal like a rat, covered with something like needles; a porcupine. —[名] 1. 고슴도치 2. 호저(豪猪)

hedge·row [hédʒròu] *n.* [C] a row of bushes or small trees forming a hedge. —[名] [산울타리를 이루는] 관목의 열

he·don·ism [hí:dounìz(ə)m] *n.* [U] a belief that regards pleasure or happiness as the highest good. —[名] 쾌락주의

he·don·ist [hí:dounist] *n.* [C] a person who believes in hedonism.
—[名] 쾌락주의자

‡heed [hi:d] *vt., vi.* pay attention to (something); take notice of (something). ¶*He heeded his mother's advice.*
—*n.* [U] careful attention.
1) ***give*** (or ***pay***) ***heed to,*** pay attention to (something).
2) ***take heed to*** (or ***of***)***,*** take notice of (something).
—[他][自] …에 주의하다; …을 유의하다 ¶①그는 어머니의 충고에 유의했다
—[名]주의, 조심
[熟] 1)…에 주의하다 2)…에 조심하다

heed·ful [hí:df(u)l] *adj.* careful; attentive. ↔neglectful
—[形] 주의 깊은, 조심성 있는

heed·less [hí:dlis] *adj.* careless; thoughtless. ▷**heed·less·ly** [-li] *adv.*
—[形] 부주의한, 조심성 없는

heed·less·ness [hí:dlisnis] *n.* [U] carelessness; thoughtlessness.
—[名] 부주의, 사려 없음

hee·haw [hí:hɔ̀:] *n.* [C] **1.** the sound made by a donkey. **2.** a loud, rough laugh. —*vi.* make such a sound.
—[名] **1.** 당나귀 울음소리 **2.** 바보 웃음
—[自] [당나귀가] 울다, 바보처럼 웃다

‡heel[1] [hi:l] *n.* [C] **1.** the back part of the foot of a man or an animal. **2.** 《usu. *pl.*》 the hind feet of an animal. **3.** the part of a stocking, sock, etc. which covers the heel; the back part attached to the sole of a shoe, supporting the heel. ¶*high heels.*
1) ***at heel,*** just behind.
2) ***be at*** (or ***on, upon***) *someone's* ***heels,*** follow someone closely.
3) ***come to heel,*** obey.
4) ***cool*** (or ***kick***) *one's* ***heels,*** (*colloq.*) wait or be kept waiting for a long time.
5) ***down at the heel,*** poorly dressed.
6) ***have*** (or ***get***) ***the heels*** (=*get ahead*) ***of*** *someone.*
7) ***heels over head; head over heels,*** upside down; in jumping, turning the body completely; passionately.
8) ***kick up*** *one's* ***heels,*** ⓐ be lively or merry. ⓑ have fun.
9) ***kick up*** *someone's* ***heels,*** ⓐ knock down. ⓑ defeat; beat.
10) ***lay*** *someone* ***by the heels,*** ⓐ put someone in jail. ⓑ overcome.
11) ***out at heel***[***s***]***,*** ⓐ having holes in the heels of one's shoes or socks. ⓑ poor; badly dressed.
12) ***raise*** (or ***lift***) ***the heel against,*** kick; give a kick to (someone).
13) ***show*** *one's* ***heels; show a clean pair of heels; take to*** *one's* ***heels,*** run away.
14) ***to heel,*** ⓐ close to one's heels; just behind. ⓑ under control.
15) ***turn on*** *one's* ***heels,*** turn sharply around.
16) ***turn*** (or ***lay, tip, topple***) ***up*** *one's* ***heels,*** die.
17) ***turn*** (or ***tumble***) ***up*** *someone's* ***heels,*** ⓐ kick down. ⓑ kill.
18) ***under the heel of*** (=*crushed by*) *someone* or *something.*
—*vt.* **1.** attach the heel to (shoes). **2.** follow (someone) closely. —*vi.* **1.** follow after someone. **2.** touch the ground with the heels.
—[名] **1.** 뒤꿈치 **2.** [동물의] 뒷발 **3.** 양말(구두)의 뒤꿈치
[熟] 1)바로 뒤에서 2)[남]의 뒤를 바싹 쫓아가다 3)복종하다 4)《口》오랫동안 기다리다 5)초라하게 입은 6)…을 앞지르다 7)곤두박이로; 열정적으로 8)ⓐ기뻐하다 ⓑ장난치다 9)ⓐ…을 넘어뜨리다 ⓑ해치우다 10)ⓐ…을 투옥하다 ⓑ…을 패배시키다 11)ⓐ신(양말) 뒤축에 구멍이 난 ⓑ옷차림이 초라한 12)…을 차다, …에게 발길질하다 13)도망치다 14)ⓐ뒤따라서; 바로 뒤에 ⓑ훈련되어 15)홱 뒤로 돌아서다 16)죽다 17)ⓐ넘어뜨리다 ⓑ죽이다 18)…에게 짓밟혀, …에게 학대받아
—[他] **1.** …에 뒤꿈치(뒤축)를 대다 **2.** …의 바로 뒤를 쫓다 —[自] **1.** 미행하다 **2.** 뒤꿈치를 땅에 대다

heel[2] [hi:l] *vi., vt.* (of a ship) lean to one side. 《~ *over* something》 —*n.* [C] a heeling movement.
—[自][他] [배가] 기울다, …을 기울이다
—[名] [배의] 기울기

heft [heft] *n.* [U] [C] **1.** weight. **2.** importance. —*vt.* judge the weight by lifting.
—[名] **1.** 무게 **2.** 중요성 —[他] …을 들어올려 무게를 재다

heft·y [héfti] *adj.* (**heft·i·er, heft·i·est**) **1.** heavy. **2.** big and strong.
—[形] **1.** 무거운 **2.** 힘센

he·gem·o·ny [hi(:)dʒéməni, hédʒimòuni / hi(:)gémə-] *n.* [U] leadership among a group of nations.
—[名] 주도권, 지배권, 패권

Heg·i·ra [hédʒirə, hidʒáiərə] *n.* **1.** the flight of Mohammed from Mecca to Medina in 622 A. D. **2.** [U] the Moslem era. **3.** [C] 《*h-*》 escape; flight.
—[名] **1.** 마호멧의 도피(622년) **2.** 회교기원, 헤지라 기원 **3.** 도피행, 도주

heif·er [héfər] *n.* [C] a young cow.
—[名] 어린 암소

heigh [hei] *interj.* an expression to call attention or to show surprise, questioning, pleasure, etc.
—[感] 에에(주의·놀람·질문·환희 따위를 나타냄)

heigh-ho [héihóu, +*U.S.* hái-] *interj.* an expression of sadness or tiredness.
—[感] 아아, 아이고(지루함·낙심 따위를 나타냄)

:height [hait] *n.* **1.** [U][C] the state of being high; the distance from the top to the base. **2.** [C] ((often *pl.*)) a high point or place. **3.** ((*the* ~)) the highest point; the utmost degree. ¶*the ~ of folly*① | *the ~ of a storm.*②
1) ***at the height of; at its height,*** ⓐ in the middle of something. ⓑ at the top of something.
2) ***in*** (or ***at***) ***the height of summer,*** in the middle of summer. ⇒[N.B.]

—[名] 1. 높이 2. 고지(高地) 3. 절정; 고귀함 ¶①어리석기 짝이 없음/②폭풍의 가장 심한 때
[熟] 1)ⓐ…이 한창인 때에 ⓑ…의 꼭대기에서 2)한여름에 [N.B.] in the depth of winter 는 한겨울에

height·en [háitn] *vt.* **1.** make (something) higher; increase the height of (something). **2.** make (something) stronger or greater. **—*vi.*** become higher; increase.
—[他] 1. …을 높이다, 높게 하다 2. …을 세게 하다 —[自] 높아지다, 증가하다

hei·nous [héinəs] *adj.* (of a crime) very bad.
—[形] [범죄 따위가] 극악한

:heir [ɛər] *n.* [C] a person who will get someone's property, rank or right when the latter dies. ¶*a male ~*① | *an ~ apparent.*②
—[名] 상속인, 법정(法定)상속인 ¶①남계(男系)상속인/②추정 상속인

heir·ess [ɛ́əris] *n.* [C] a woman heir.
—[名] 여자 상속인

heir·loom [ɛ́ərlù:m] *n.* [C] any valuable thing which is passed on to heirs for generations.
—[名] 상전동산(相傳動產), 조상 전래의 가보(家寶)

:held [held] *v.* pt. or pp. of **hold**[1].

Hel·en [hélin] *n.* **1.** (in Greek mythology) the very beautiful wife of King Menelaus of Sparta and the cause of the Trojan War. **2.** a woman's name.
—[名] 1. 헬레네(스파르타의 Menelau 왕의 아내로 트로이 전쟁의 원인이 되었음) 2. 여자 이름

hel·i·cop·ter [hélikὰptər / -kɔ̀ptə] *n.* [C] a kind of airplane that is able to go straight up into air by means of horizontal propellers.
—[名] 헬리콥터

he·li·o·graph [hí:liougræ̀f / -grὰ:f] *n.* [C] **1.** an instrument used for photographing the sun. **2.** an instrument used for sending messages by means of sunlight. **3.** an instrument used for measuring the strength of sunlight. **—*vt., vi.*** signal by heliograph; take a photograph with a heliograph.
—[名] 1. 태양 촬영용 사진기 2. 일광반사 신호기 3. 일조계(日照計) —[他][自] heliograph 로 송신하다(촬영하다)

he·li·o·trope [hí:liətróup / hél-] *n.* [C] **1.** a plant with purple flowers. **2.** [U] light red-blue color.
—[名] 1. ((植)) 헬리오트로우프 2. 엷은 자줏빛

he·li·port [hélipɔ̀:rt] *n.* [C] a landing place for helicopters.
—[名] 헬리콥터 발착장

he·li·um [hí:liəm] *n.* [U] a very light gas which is easily set on fire. ⇒[N.B.]
—[名] 헬륨 [N.B.] 화학 기호는 He

•hell [hel] *n.* [U][C] the place where bad persons are punished after death. ¶*a ~ on earth* | *Go to ~!*① | *What the ~ did you buy?*②
1) ***catch*** (or ***get***) ***hell,*** (*slang*) receive a severe scolding.
2) ***give someone hell,*** treat someone severely.
3) ***like hell,*** (*colloq.*) very much; very violently.

—[名] 지옥; 명부(冥府) ¶①뒈져라!, 빌어먹을!/②도대체 무엇을 샀느냐?
[熟] 1)((俗)) 호되게 야단맞다 2)[남]을 혼내 주다 3)((口))맹렬히, 지독하게

•he'll [hi:l] **1.** he will. **2.** he shall.

Hel·len·ic [helí:nik, +*U.S.* helén-] *adj.* **1.** Greek. **2.** of the Greek people or language.
—[名] 1. 그리이스의 2. 그리이스 사람(말)의

Hel·len·ism [hélinìz(ə)m] *n.* [U] **1.** the ancient culture, ideals, and nationality of Greece. **2.** the adoption or imitation of Greek culture.
—[名] 1. 그리이스 문화(정신·국민성) 2. 그리이스화(化), 그리이스 모방

Hel·len·is·tic [hèlinístik] *adj.* of Greek culture, language and history.
—[形] 그리이스 문화(어·역사)의

hell·fire [hélfàiər] *n.* [U] the fire of hell.
—[名] 지옥의 불

hell·ish [héliʃ] *adj.* **1.** of hell. **2.** devilish; very bad; horrible. ¶*It was ~ to see the scene of murder.* ▷**hell·ish·ly** [-li] *adv.* —**hell·ish·ness** [-nis] *n.*
—[形] 1 지옥의(같은) 2. 가증할; 소름끼치는

•hel·lo [helóu, ´-, hə-] *interj.* an expression of greeting, as in meeting or calling someone on the telephone; an expression of surprise.
—[感] 이봐, 여보 (부르는 말·인사말); [전화에서] 여보세요; 어머나

•helm [helm] *n.* [C] **1.** the handle of a rudder. **2.** a post of control, leadership or guidance. ▷**helm·less** [-lis] *adj.*
—[名] 1. 키의 손잡이 2. 지도

•hel·met [hélmit] *n.* [C] an iron covering worn to protect the head when fighting.
—[名] 투구, 철모, 헬멧

helms·man [hélmzmən] *n.* [C] (*pl.* **-men** [-mən]) a man who steers a ship or boat.
—[名] 키잡이, 조타수

Hel·ot [hélət] *n.* [C] **1.** a slave in ancient Sparta. **2.** ((*h-*)) a slave.
—[名] 1. 고대 스파르타의 노예 2. 노예

H

:help [help] *vt.* **1.** aid; assist; assist (someone) and cause him to do. 《~ someone *in* or *with* his work; ~ someone [*to*] *do*》 ¶*~ a boy with his homework*① | *I helped Mother in her needlework.* | *He helped her on with her overcoat.*② | *I helped him back to an honest trade.*③ | *Help me* [*to*] *find it.*④ **2.** get (someone) out of difficulties, etc. ¶*~ a wounded person* | (*proverb*) *Heaven helps those who help themselves.*⑤ **3.** give (someone) what he needs. 《~ someone *with* money, food, etc.》 **4.** make (something) easier to do; promote. ¶*The accident helped his ruin.*⑥ **5.** make better; cure; relieve. ¶*~ the toothache* | *~ a cough.* **6.** serve (someone) as a waiter. ¶*May I ~ you to some more vegetables?*⑦ | *Help yourself to the cake, please.*⑧ **7.** 《with *can, could*》 avoid; refrain from (something). ¶*I can't ~ it.; It can't be helped.*⑨ | *I could not ~ crying.*⑩

—[他] 1. …을 돕다, 거들다; 거들어서 …시키다 ¶①소년의 숙제를 도와 주다 /②그녀를 거들어 외투를 입혀 주었다 /③나는 그를 도와서 올바른 생업으로 돌아가게 해 주었다/④그것을 찾는 데 도와 주시오 2. [곤란 따위에서] …을 구하다 ¶⑤《俚》하늘은 스스로 돕는 자를 돕는다 3. [필요한 것을 주어] …을 구제하다 4. …을 하기 쉽게 하다; 조장하다 ¶⑥그 사고가 그의 파멸을 재촉했다 5. …을 고치다 6. …에게 시중들다 ¶⑦야채를 더 드시겠읍니까? /⑧케이크를 드시오 7. …을 피하다 ¶⑨할 수 없다/⑩울지 않을 수 없다

—*vi.* **1.** give assistance; be useful. **2.** act as a waiter.

—[自] 1. 돕다; 거들다 2. 시중들다

1) ***cannot help but do,*** cannot fail to do.
2) ***help someone out,*** help someone in getting or doing something.
3) ***help someone out of,*** help someone [to] get rid of (difficulty, etc.).
4) ***So help me God!*** I swear.

[熟] 1)…하지 않을 수 없다 2)[남]을 거들어 …을 완성시키다 3)[남]을 거들어 곤란 따위에서 구해 주다 4)맹세코

—*n.* **1.** [U] assistance; aid. **2.** [C] a remedy; relief; an escape. ¶*There is no ~ for it but to do so.*⑪ **3.** [C] a person or a thing that helps. ¶*It is a great ~ to me.*⑫ **4.** [C] 《often *collectively*》 (*U.S.*) a hired servant. ¶a domestic ~.

—[名] 1. 조력, 도움 2. 치료; 피하는 길 ¶⑪그렇게 하는 수밖에 도리가 없다 3. 쓸모가 있는 사람(것) ¶⑫그것은 큰 도움이 되겠다 4. 《美》하인

be of help, be helpful; be useful.

[熟] 도움이 되다

•help·er [hélpər] *n.* [C] a person who helps someone; an assistant.

—[名] 조력자, 조수

•help·ful [hélpf(u)l] *adj.* giving help; useful. ▷**help·ful·ly** [-fuli] *adv.* —**help·ful·ness** [-nis] *n.*

—[形] 도움이 되는, 유용한

help·ing [hélpiŋ] *adj.* assisting. ¶*a ~ hand.* **—*n.*** [C] a portion of the food served at a meal. ¶*a second ~*①.

—[形] 도움이 되는 —[名] [음식의] 한 그릇 ¶①두 그릇째

:help·less [hélplis] *adj.* not able to help oneself; weak; powerless.

—[形] 도움이 없는, 의지할 사람(곳)이 없는, 무력한

help·less·ly [hélplisli] *adv.* in a helpless manner.

—[副] 무력하게, 어찌할 수 없이

help·less·ness [hélplisnis] *n.* [U] the state of being helpless.

—[名] 도움이 없음

help·mate [hélpmèit] *n.* [C] a helpful partner, esp. a wife or husband.

—[名] 협력자, 아내, 남편

help·meet [hélpmì:t] *n.* =helpmate.

hel·ter-skel·ter [héltərskéltər] *adv.* in a hurry; in disorder. **—*adj.*** hurried and confused; disorderly.

—[副] 허둥지둥하여 —[形] 당황하는

helve [helv] *n.* [C] a handle of an ax, a hammer, etc.

—[名] [연장 · 무기 따위의] 자루

•hem¹ [hem] *n.* [C] a fastened edge of cloth.

—[名] [천 · 옷의] 가장자리, 감침질

—*vt.* (**hemmed, hem·ming**) fold over the edge of cloth and fasten it down with needle and thread.

—[他] …의 가장자리를 감치다

hem in, surround on all sides. ¶*be hemmed in by enemies.*

[熟] 둘러싸다

hem² [h(e)m, +*Brit.* mm] *interj., n.* [C] a sound like clearing the throat, used to attract attention or express doubt or hesitation.

—[感][名] 에헴! (망설이거나 주의를 환기시킬 때의 소리)

hem·i·sphere [hémisfìər] *n.* [C] a half of a ball or globe; a half of the earth's surface. ¶*the Eastern* (*Western*) *hemisphere.*①

—[名] 반구체(半球體); [하늘 · 지구의] 반구 ¶①동(서)반구

hem·lock [hémlɑk / -lɔk] *n.* **1.** [C] (*Brit.*) a poisonous plant; [U] a poisonous drink got from this plant. **2.** [C] an evergreen tree of the pine family.

—[名] 1. 《英》미나리과의 독초; 그 독약 2. 미국솔송나무

he·mo·glo·bin [hì:mouglóubin, hèmou-] *n.* [U] the red coloring matter in the blood, serving to carry oxygen to every part of the body.

—[名] 헤모글로빈, 혈색소(血色素)

hem·or·rhage [héməridʒ] *n.* [U][C] sudden and serious loss of blood; bleeding. ¶*cerebral ~.*①

—[名] 출혈 ¶①뇌출혈

hemp [hemp] *n.* [U] a plant grown in Asia, used for making a rope and heavy cloth.

—[名] 대마(大麻)

hemp·en [hémpən] *adj.* made of hemp.

—[形] 대마로 만든

hemstitch [543] hereabout

hem·stitch [hémstìtʃ] *n.* Ⓤ an ornament done with needle and thread, usu. at the edge of cloth. ⇒fig. —*vt.* finish (a tablecloth, etc.) with hemstitch.
—⑬ 천의 가장자리 장식 —⑭ [테이블보 따위]에 장식 뜨개질을 하다

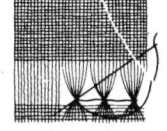
[hemstitch]

: hen [hen] *n.* Ⓒ **1.** a female domestic bird esp. a chicken. ↔cock **2.** any female bird. ¶*a ~ sparrow*①／*like a ~ with one chicken.*②
—⑬ 1. 암탉 2. 새의 암컷 ¶①참새의 암컷／②안절부절 못하여

: hence [hens] *adv.* **1.** from here. **2.** from this time. ¶*a year ~.*① **3.** therefore ; for this reason.
—⑭ 1. 여기서부터 2. 지금부터 ¶①지금부터 1년 후에 3. 그런 까닭에

* **hence·forth** [hénsfɔ́:rθ] *adv.* from this time on.
—⑭ 금후, 이후

hence·for·ward [hénsfɔ́:rwərd] *adv.* =henceforth.

hench·man [héntʃmən] *n.* Ⓒ (pl. **-men** [-mən]) a faithful follower ; a political supporter who blindly follows his leader.
—⑬ 충실한 추종자 ; 정치상의 후원자

hen·coop [hénkù:p] *n.* Ⓒ a cage for hens.
—⑬ [닭의] 어리, 둥우리

hen·house [hénhàus] *n.* Ⓒ a house for domestic birds.
—⑬ 닭장

hen·na [hénə] *n.* Ⓒ a small tree growing in Asia and Africa ; Ⓤ a red dye got from the leaves of this plant.
—⑬ 헤나 ; [그 잎사귀에서 얻는] 헤나 물감

hen·pecked [hénpèkt] *adj.* ruled by one's wife. ¶*a ~ husband.*①
—⑭ 엄처시하의 ¶①공처가

* **Hen·ry** [hénri] *n.* a man's name.
—⑬ 남자 이름

hep·ta·gon [héptəgàn / -gɔ̀n] *n.* Ⓒ a plane figure having seven sides and seven angles. ⌜seven persons.⌝
—⑬ 7 각(변)형

hep·tar·chy [héptɑ̀:rki] *n.* Ⓒ (pl. **-chies**) government by
—⑬ 칠두(七頭) 정치

her [hər, -ər / hə:, hə, ə(:)] *pron.* the possessive form of **she** ; the objective form of **she**.
—⑭ 그녀의 ; 그녀를(에게)

He·ra [híərə] *n.* a Greek goddess, wife of Zeus.
—⑬ Zeus신의 아내 (로마신화의 Juno)

: her·ald [hér(ə)ld] *n.* Ⓒ **1.** an officer who announces important news to the public. **2.** a person who carries news ; a messenger. ¶*The cuckoo is a ~ of spring.*①
—*vt.* announce.
—⑬ 1. 전령관(傳令官) 2. 보도자 ; 사자 (使者) ; 전조 ¶①뻐꾸기는 봄의 전조이다
—⑭ …을 [미리] 알리다

he·ral·dic [heræ̀ldik] *adj.* of heralds.
—⑭ 전령관의

her·ald·ry [hér(ə)ldri] *n.* Ⓤ science of the special designs used by families as marks of position, history, etc.
—⑬ 문장학(紋章學)

* **herb** [(h)ə:rb / hə:b] *n.* Ⓒ a plant used for making medicine. ¶*a[n] ~ garden.*①
—⑬ 약용 식물 ¶①약초원

her·ba·ceous [(h)ə(:)rbéiʃəs / hə:-] *adj.* **1.** of an herb.
—⑭ 풀의, 초본의

herb·age [(h)ə́:rbidʒ / hə́:rb-] *n.* Ⓤ (*collectively*) green grasses or herbs. ⌜about herbs.⌝
—⑬ 풀

herb·al [(h)ə́:rb(ə)l / hə́:b-] *adj.* of herbs. —*n.* Ⓒ a book
—⑭ 풀의 —⑬ 초본서(草本書)

herb·al·ist [(h)ə́:rb(ə)list / hə́:b-] *n.* Ⓒ **1.** originally, a botanist. **2.** now, a person who deals in herbs.
—⑬ 1. [옛날의] 식물학자 2. 약초 장수

Her·bert [hɑ́:rbərt] *n.* a man's name.
—⑬ 남자 이름

her·biv·o·rous [(h)ə:rbívərəs / hə:r-] *adj.* feeding on plants. ↔carnivorous
—⑭ 초식(草食)의

her·cu·le·an, Her- [hə̀:rkjulí(:)ən, hə:rkjú:liən] *adj.* of or like Hercules ; very powerful.
—⑭ 헤르쿨레스의(같은) ; 초인적 힘이 있는

Her·cu·les [hɑ́:rkjuli:z] *n.* (in Greek mythology) a hero famous for his great strength.
—⑬ 헤르쿨레스(Jupiter신의 아들)

: herd [hə:rd] *n.* Ⓒ **1.** a group of animals, esp. of cows, horses, and elephants. **2.** a large crowd of people. ¶*the common ~.*① / *the ~ instinct.*② —*vi.* flock together. 《*~ together with*》 —*vt.* form (cattle, etc.) into a group.
—⑬ 1. 짐승떼 2. 군중 ¶①일반 대중／②군중심리 —⑭ 떼짓다, 무리를 이루다 —⑭ …을 모으다

herds·man [hɑ́:rdzmən] *n.* Ⓒ (pl. **-men** [-mən]) a man who looks after a herd.
—⑬ 목동, 목자, 가축지기

: here [hiər] *adv.* **1.** in this place. ¶*this man ~* / *I live ~.* **2.** at this point. ¶*Here he is wrong.* **3.** to this place. ¶*Come ~.* / *Here he comes.* / *Here goes!*① / *Here we are.*② / *Here it is.*③ / *Here you are.*④
1) **Here!**, Yes! ; Present!
2) **Here's something for you**, I'll give you this.
—⑭ 1. 여기에[서] 2. 이 점에서 3. 이리로 ¶①자아!; 시작한다!／②자 도착했다／③자 여기 있다／④자 여기 있다

圈 1)예(호명에 대한 대답) 2)이것을 네게 주마

here·a·bout [híərəbàut] *adv.* about this place.
—⑭ 이 근방에

hereabouts [544] herself

here·a·bouts [híərəbàuts] *adv.* =hereabout. —❶ 금후
here·af·ter [hiəræftər / -áːftə] *adv.* after this time. —❷ 1. 미래 2. 내세
 —*n.* Ⓤ (*the* ~) 1. the future. 2. life after death.
here·by [hìərbái] *adv.* by this means. —❶ 이렇게 해서
he·red·i·tar·y [hirédìtèri / -t(ə)ri] *adj.* passed down from parents to children. —❷ 세습의, 부모로부터 물려받은
he·red·i·ty [hiréditi] *n.* Ⓤ the nature or character passed down from parents to children; the process of doing so. —❷ 유전
here·in [hìərín] *adv.* in this; in this place. —❶ 이 속에
here·in·af·ter [hìərinæftər / -áːftə] *adv.* afterward in this statement. —❶ [서류에서] 다음부터는
here·of [hìəráv / -ɔ́v] *adv.* of this; about this. —❶ 이것의, 이것에 관하여
here's [hiərz] here is.
her·e·sy [hérəsi] *n.* ⓊⒸ (pl. **-sies**) belief different from the accepted belief of a religion. —❷ [특히 그리스도교가 배척하는] 이교
her·e·tic [hérətik] *n.* Ⓒ a person whose belief is different because of heresy. —❷ 이교도
he·ret·i·cal [hirétik(ə)l] *adj.* of heresy; of a heretic. —❷ 이교의
 ▷**he·ret·i·cal·ly** [-kəli] *adv.* ⌈now.⌉
here·to·fore [híərtəfɔ́ːr] *adv.* before this time; until⌋ —❶ 지금까지, 이전에
here·up·on [hìərəpán, -pɔ́ːn / -pɔ́n] *adv.* at this point. —❶ 여기에 있어서
here·with [hìərwíθ, -wíð] *adv.* with this. —❶ 이것과 함께
her·it·a·ble [hérìtəbl] *adj.* that can be passed down from parents to children. ⌈to a child by his parents.⌉ —❷ 상속할 수 있는
her·it·age [héritidʒ] *n.* Ⓒ that which is passed down⌋ —❷ 세습 재산
Her·mes [hə́ːrmiːz] *n.* (in Greek mythology) the messenger for Zeus and other gods. —❷ 헤르메스(신들의 사자(使者)로서 학예 · 변론의 신)
her·met·ic [həːrmétik] *adj.* 1. closed so tight as to keep out all air or gas. 2. of the study aiming to change other materials into gold; of alchemy. ¶*the* ~ *art* (or *science*).① ▷**her·met·i·cal·ly** [-(ə)li] *adv.* —❶ 1. 밀봉(밀폐)한 2. 연금술의 ¶①연금술
· **her·mit** [hə́ːrmit] *n.* Ⓒ a person who lives by himself, shut off from other people. ▷**her·mit·like** [-làik] *adj.* —❷ 은둔자(隱遁者), 속세를 버린 사람
her·mit·age [hə́ːrmitidʒ] *n.* Ⓒ the home of a hermit. —❷ 은자가 사는 집
her·ni·a [hə́ːrniə] *n.* ⓊⒸ (pl. **-ni·as** or **-ni·ae**) the abnormal state of the pushing out of a part of the bowel through a break in the muscle wall of the abdomen. —❷ 헤르니아, 탈장(脫腸)
her·ni·ae [hə́ːrniːi] *n.* pl. of **hernia**.
⁑ **he·ro** [híərou] *n.* Ⓒ (pl. **-roes**) 1. a man admired for his bravery or noble deeds. ¶*one of my heroes*.① 2. the chief male person in a story, play, etc. —❷ 1. 영웅, 위인 ¶①내가 숭배하는 인물 2. [소설·극 따위의 남자] 주인공
· **he·ro·ic** [hiróuik] *adj.* 1. of a hero; like or fit for a hero. 2. courageous. —❶ 1. 영웅의 ; 영웅적인, 영웅에 어울리는 2. 모험적인
heroic age [-- -], **the** *n.* the time when the heroes of ancient Greece are supposed to have lived. —❷ 고대 그리이스의 영웅시대
he·ro·i·cal·ly [hiróuikəli] *adv.* in a heroic manner. —❶ 영웅적으로, 씩씩하게
· **her·o·in** [hérouin] *n.* Ⓤ medicine which stops the feeling of pain and causes someone to sleep. —❷ 헤로인(모르핀에서 추출하는 일종의 마취제)
her·o·ine [hérouin] *n.* Ⓒ 1. a woman admired for her bravery or noble deeds. 2. the chief female person in a story, play, etc. —❷ 1. 여걸, 여장부 2. [소설 따위의] 여자 주인공
her·o·ism [hérouìz(ə)m] *n.* 1. Ⓤ great bravery. 2. Ⓒ a very brave act. ⌈and neck.⌉ —❷ 1. 장렬, 용맹 2. 용맹스러운 행위
her·on [hérən] *n.* Ⓒ a large bird with very long legs⌋ —❷ 왜가리
· **her·ring** [hériŋ] *n.* Ⓒ (pl. **-rings** or *collectively* **-ring**) small fish used for food, found in North Atlantic waters. —❷ 청어
her·ring·bone [hériŋbòun] *n.* Ⓒ an ornamental design shaped like the backbone of a fish. ⇒fig. —❷ 오늬무늬

[herringbone]

⁑ **hers** [həːrz] *pron.* the possesive form of **she**; the one or ones belonging to her. —❷ 그녀의 것
⁑ **her·self** [hə(ː)rsélf] *pron.* (pl. **them·selves**) ⇒oneself. 1. a reflexive and emphatic form of **she** or **her**. ¶*She* ~ *will do it*.① / —❷ 1. she, her 의 재귀 용법 및 강조용법 ¶①그녀 자신이 그것을 할 것이다/②그녀는 자신을 비웃었다 2. 칠

he's [545] **hierarchy**

She laughed at ~. 2. her normal condition of body or of mind. ¶*She is now ~ again.*
착한 상태 ¶③다시 그녀는 침착을 찾았다
he's [(h)i:z / hi(:)z, iz] he is; he has.
hes·i·tan·cy [hézit(ə)nsi] *n.* Ⓤ hesitation; doubt. —ⓝ 주저, 망설임
hes·i·tant [hézit(ə)nt] *adj.* hesitating; doubtful. ▷**hes·i·tant·ly** [-li] *adv.* —ⓐ 주저하는, 망설이는
hes·i·tate [hézitèit] *vi.* pause or stop because one is undecided. 《~ to do》 ¶ *I ~ to affirm.* —ⓥ 주저하다 ¶①단언하고 싶지는 않다
hes·i·tat·ing·ly [hézitèitiŋli] *adv.* with hesitation. —ⓐⓓ 주저하여
hes·i·ta·tion [hèzitéiʃ(ə)n] *n.* ⓊⒸ the act of hesitating; doubt. ¶ *After some ~, she bought the red sweater.* —ⓝ 주저, 망설임
Hes·per·us [héspərəs] *n.* the evening star. —ⓝ 금성(金星), 개밥바라기
het·er·o·dox [hét(ə)roudàks / -dɔ̀ks] *adj.* different from the regularly accepted beliefs or doctrines. ↔orthodox —ⓐ 이설(異說)의, 이단(異端)의,
het·er·o·dox·y [hét(ə)rədàksi / -dɔ̀ksi] *n.* ⓊⒸ (pl. **-dox·ies**) a belief, doctrine, etc. different from the commonly accepted. —ⓝ 이단; 이설
het·er·o·ge·ne·ous [hèt(ə)rədʒí:niəs / hètərou-] *adj.* different in kind; unlike; varied. ↔homogeneous ▷**het·er·o·ge·ne·ous·ly** [-li] *adv.* —ⓐ 이종(異種)의, 잡다한
hew [hju:] *vt., vi.* (**hewed, hewn** or **hewed**) 1. cut (something) with an ax, etc. ¶ *~ to pieces.* 2. make (something) with cutting blows. —ⓐⓥ 1. [도끼 따위로] 자르다 ¶① 잘게 썰다 2. 잘라서 …을 만들다
hew·er [hjú:ər] *n.* Ⓒ a person or thing that hews. ¶ (in the Bible) *hewers of wood and drawers of water.* —ⓝ 자르는 사람; 채탄부(採炭夫) ¶①천한 일을 하는 사람, 하급 노동자
hewn [hju:n] *v.* pp. of **hew**.
hex·a·gon [héksəgɑ̀n / -gən] *n.* Ⓒ a plane figure having six angles and six sides. —ⓝ 6 각(변)형
hey [hei] *interj.* sound used to express surprise or a question. —ⓘ 야아, 이봐, 이키
hey·day [héidèi] *n.* Ⓒ 《sing. only》 the time of greatest strength or high spirits. —ⓝ 전성시대
hi [hai] *interj.* sound made to attract attention, usu. used on meeting. —ⓘ 이봐, 여어(주의를 환기하는 소리)
hi·ber·nate [háibə(:)rnèit] *vi.* (of some animals) spend the winter in a sleeping or an inactive state. —ⓥ [동물이] 동면하다; [사람이] 피한(避寒)하다
hi·ber·na·tion [hàibə(:)rnéiʃ(ə)n] *n.* Ⓤ the state or act of hibernating. —ⓝ 동면
hi·bis·cus [hibískəs, +*U.S.* hai-] *n.* Ⓒ a plant, shrub, or tree with large, colorful flowers. —ⓝ 무궁화
hic·cough [híkʌp] *n., v.* =hiccup.
hic·cup [híkʌp] *n.* Ⓒ (often *pl.*) a sudden catching of the breath with a short, sharp sound. ¶ *have the hiccups.* —*vi., vt.* make a noise of hiccups. —ⓝ 딸꾹질 ¶①딸꾹질하다 —ⓐⓥ 딸꾹질하다
hick·o·ry [híkəri] *n.* Ⓒ (pl. **-ries**) a nut-bearing American tree with hard wood; Ⓤ its wood. —ⓝ 히코리(북미산 호도과의 나무)
hid [hid] *v.* pt. and pp. of **hide**¹.
hid·den [hídn] *v.* pp. of **hide**¹.
hide¹ [haid] *v.* (**hid, hid·den** or **hid**) *vt.* keep (something) out of sight; keep (something) secret; cover (something) up; conceal. ¶ *~ oneself* / *~ a fact from someone.* —*vi.* hide oneself. —ⓥ …을 감추다, 숨기다 —ⓐ 숨다
hide² [haid] *n.* Ⓒ the skin of an animal. —ⓝ 짐승 가죽; 피혁
hide-and-seek [háidən(d)sí:k] *n.* Ⓤ a children's game in which one child hides and others try to find him. —ⓝ 술래잡기
hide·a·way [háidəwèi] *n.* Ⓒ a place where one can go to hide. —ⓝ 은신처, 피난처
hide·bound [háidbàund] *adj.* 1. with the skin sticking close to the bones. 2. very narrow-minded. —ⓐ 1. [영양부족으로] 말라빠진 2. 옹졸한, 도량이 좁은
hid·e·ous [hídiəs] *adj.* very ugly; very unpleasant; frightful; horrible. ▷**hid·e·ous·ly** [-li] *adv.* —ⓐ 흉한, 추악한; 무서운, 오싹하는
hid·e·ous·ness [hídiəsnis] *n.* the state of being hideous. —ⓝ 무시무시함, 무서움
hid·ing [háidiŋ] *n.* Ⓒ 《colloq.》 an act of beating. —ⓝ 채찍질, 매질
hiding place [-́ -̀] *n.* a place to hide. —ⓝ 은신처, 은닉처
hie [hai] *vi., vt.* (**hie·ing** or **hy·ing**) 《*poetic*》 go quickly; hasten. —ⓐⓥ 《詩》서두르다; …을 서두르게 하다
hi·er·ar·chy [háiərɑ̀:rki] *n.* Ⓒ (pl. **-chies**) 1. an or- —ⓝ 1. 계급 조직 2. 성자(聖者)의 지

ganization (of persons or things) with ranks of authority from lowest to highest. **2.** government by priests.

배, 성직자 정치

hi·er·o·glyph [háiərouglìf,] *n.* =hieroglyphic.

hi·er·o·glyph·ic [hàiərouglífik] *n.* [C] 《usu. *pl.*》 a picture or symbol standing for a word, an idea, or a sound. **—***adj.* **1.** of or written in hieroglyphics. **2.** symbolic. **3.** hard to read. ▷**hi·er·o·glyph·i·cal·ly** [-kəli] *adv.*

—[名] 상형(象形)문자 —[形] 1. 상형문자(풍)의 2. 상징적인 3. 읽기(알아보기) 힘든

hi-fi [háifái] (*colloq.*) =high-fidelity.

hig·gle·dy-pig·gle·dy [hígldipígldi] *adv.* in great disorder. **—***adj.* mixed up; confused. **—***n.* [U] disorder; confusion.

—[副] 뒤죽박죽으로 —[形] 뒤죽박죽이 된 —[名] 난잡, 뒤죽박죽

‡**high** [hai] *adj.* **1.** tall; lofty. ↔low ¶*a ~ tree (mountain, hill) / The wall is six feet ~.* **2.** far above the ground or sea level. ¶*~ up in the sky.* **3.** chief; important; noble. ¶*a ~ government official*① */ a man in ~ position / a man of ~ descent.*② **4.** expensive; costly. ¶*a ~ price / Rent is ~.* **5.** greater in size, amount, degree, power, etc. than usual. ¶*~ temperature / higher education / ~ speed.* **6.** luxurious. ¶*~ living.* **7.** too proud. **8.** fully advanced. ¶*~ noon*③ */ ~ summer.* **9.** (*Geography*) far from the equator.

1) ***high and dry,*** ⓐ (of a ship) on the shore. ⓑ alone and helpless; abandoned.
2) ***high and mighty,*** (*colloq.*) showing too much pride.
3) ***high seas,*** the open sea not belonging to any country.
4) ***high time,*** a good chance to begin an action.
5) ***high words,*** an excited argument.
6) ***in high spirits,*** happy; merry; lively.
7) ***in high terms,*** in words of praise.

—[形] 1. 높은 2. 지면(해면)에서 멀리 떨어진; 하늘 높은 3. 중요한; 고귀한 ¶ ①정부의 고급 관리/②명문 출신의 사람 4. 값비싼 5. 고도의, 강력한, 다량의 6. 호사스러운 7. 거만한 8. 한창인, 무르익은 ¶③한낮 9. 《地理》 위도(緯度)가 높은

[熟] 1)ⓐ[배가] 뭍에 올려진 ⓑ버림받은 2. 《口》 거만한 3)공해(公海) 4)무르익을 때, 호기(好機) 5)격론 6)즐거운, 명랑한 7)몹시 칭찬하여

—*n.* **1.** [C] [U] something that is of a high level or position. **2.** [C] an area of high atmospheric pressure. **3.** [U] an arrangement of gears giving the greatest speed.

—[名] 1. 높은 것 2. 고기압권 3. [자동차의] 고속 기어

on high, high above; in heaven.

[熟] 높은 곳에; 하늘에

—*adv.* **1.** to or at a high level, position, degree, etc. **2.** in a high manner. **3.** at a high pitch.

1) ***high and low,*** everywhere.
2) ***hold one's head high,*** act too proudly.
3) ***live high,*** live in a very expensive way.
4) ***rise high,*** succeed in life.
5) ***stand high in popular esteem,*** be estimated (respected) highly by everybody.

—[副] 1. 높게; 높은 지위에 2. 강하게, 심하게 3. 목소리를 높여

[熟] 1)도처에 2)거만하게 굴다 3)사치스러운 생활을 하다 4)출세하다 5)사람들에게 높이 평가(존경)받다

high·ball [háibɔ̀:l] *n.* [U] [C] (*U.S.*) whiskey, brandy, etc., mixed with soda water.

—[名] 하이보올(위스키에 소오다수 따위를 탄 음료)

high·born [háibɔ̀:rn] *adj.* of noble birth.

—[形] 고귀한 태생의

high·bred [háibréd] *adj.* **1.** born of a good family and well trained. **2.** very elegant.

—[形] 1. 명문 태생의 2. 교양있는

high·brow [háibràu] *n.* [C] **1.** a person who is interested in intellectual things. **2.** (*slang*) a person who puts on an appearance of great learning.

—[名] 1. 학식있는 사람 2. 인텔리인 체하는 사람

high-fi·del·i·ty [háifidéliti, -fai-] *n.* [U] the reproduction of sound by a phonograph or radio so that it sounds like the original.

—[名] 하이파이, 고충실도(高忠實度)

high-flown [háiflòun] *adj.* (of ideas, etc.) sounding important, but with little sense.

—[形] [사상 따위가] 과장된

high-grade [háigréid] *adj.* of fine quality; superior.

—[形] 우수한, 고급의

high-hand·ed [háihǽndid] *adj.* acting not according to rules but to one's own idea; overbearing. ▷**high-hand·ed·ly** [-li] *adv.* —**high-hand·ed·ness** [-nis] *n.*

—[形] 고압적인, 횡포한

high hat [´ ´] *n.* a top hat.

—[名] 실크햇

•**high·land** [háilənd] *n.* **1.** [C] high or mountainous land **2.** 《*the H-s*》 mountainous land in northern and western Scotland. 「the Highlands of Scotland.」

—[名] 1. 고지 2. 스코틀랜드 북부의 고지

High·land·er [háiləndər] *n.* [C] a person who lives in

—[名] 스코틀랜드 고지에서 사는 사람

high light [ˊ ˋ] *n.* **1.** a part of a photograph, etc, in which light is represented as falling with full force. **2.** the most interesting scene in a story, etc.
—[名] 1. [그림·사진 따위의] 강한 광선을 받은 부분 2. [이야기 따위의] 최고조에 이른 장면, 가장 중요한 점(사건)

high·light [háilàit] *vt.* emphasize; make (something) prominent.
—[他] …을 강조하다; 두드러지게 하다

⁑ **high·ly** [háili] *adv.* **1.** in a high degree; very much. ¶ ~ *amusing.*① **2.** favorably; with much approval.
1) ***speak highly*** (=*speak very well*) ***of someone.***
2) ***think highly of,*** respect greatly.
—[副] 1. 높게; 대단히 ¶①아주 재미있다 2. 칭찬하여, 존경하여
[熟] 1)격찬하다 2)매우 존경하다

high-mind·ed [háimàindid] *adj.* **1.** having noble character. **2.** proud. ▷**high-mind·ed·ly** [-li] *adv.* —**high·mind·ed·ness** [-nis] *n.*
—[形] 1. 고상한, 고결한 2. 거만한

∗ **high·ness** [háinis] *n.* [U] **1.** the state of being high. ¶*the ~ of prices*① **2.** 《*H-*》 a title given to people of royal families. ⇒[N.B.]
—[名] 1. 높음 ¶①물가고 2. 전하(殿下) [N.B.] 보통 His, Her, Your를 앞에 붙임

high-pitched [háipítʃt] *adj.* **1.** of high tone or sound. **2.** having a steep slope.
—[形] 1. 가락이 높은; 감도(感度)가 높은 2. 경사가 급한

high-pow·ered [háipáuərd] *adj.* having great power.
—[形] 고성능의

high-pres·sure [háipréʃər] *adj.* having more than the usual pressure.
—[形] 고압의

high-priced [háipráist] *adj.* expensive.
—[形] 값비싼

high-rank·ing [háirǽŋkiŋ] *adj.* high in position.
—[形] 높은 계급의

high-road [háiròud] *n.* [C] **1.** a main road; a highway. **2.** a direct way; an easy method. ¶*the ~ to success.*①
—[名] 1. 큰길, 간선도로 2. 편한 길 ¶①성공에의 지름길

high school [ˊ ˋ] *n.* a school attended after the elementary school. ¶*a junior*~① / *a senior* ~.②
—[名] 고등학교 ¶①중학교/②고등학교

high-sound·ing [háisáundiŋ] *adj.* (of writing style) written with too much expression.
—[形] 과장된, 어마어마한

high-spir·it·ed [háispíritid] *adj.* **1.** courageous. **2.** with great liveliness.
—[形] 1. 용감한 2. 혈기왕성한

high-strung [háistrʌ́ŋ] *adj.* very sensitive; nervous.
—[形] 극도로 긴장한; 민감한

high tea [ˊ ˊ] *n.* (*Brit.*) a meal, usu. in the evening, at which meat is served.
—[名] 《英》 오후에 먹는 고기 요리가 따르는 차

high-ten·sion [háiténʃ(ə)n] *adj.* (*Electricity*) that can be operated with a high voltage. ¶~ *currents.*①
—[形] 《電》 고압의 ¶①고압 전류

high tide [ˊ ˊ] *n.* the time when the tide is highest.
—[名] 만조, 한사리[때]

⁑ **high·way** [háiwèi] *n.* [C] a public road; a main road. ¶*highways and byways*① / *the king's* ~.②
—[名] 공로(公路), 큰길, 간선도로 ¶①큰 길과 작은 길/②천하의 공도(公道)

high·way·man [háiwèimən] *n.* [C] (pl. **-men** [-mən]) a man who robs travelers on a highway.
—[名] 노상강도

∗ **hike** [haik] *n.* [C] (*colloq.*) a long walk in the country for recreation or exercise. ¶*go on a* ~.① —*vi.* (*colloq.*) take a long walk.
—[名] [시골의] 도보 여행 ¶①도보 여행을 가다 —[自] 도보 여행하다

hik·er [háikər] *n.* [C] a person who hikes.
—[名] 도보 여행하는 사람

∗ **hik·ing** [háikiŋ] *n.* [C] a hike.
—[名] 도보 여행, 하이킹

hi·lar·i·ous [hiléəriəs] *adj.* very merry; cheerful. ▷**hi·lar·i·ous·ly** [-li] *adv.*
—[形] 명랑한

hi·lar·i·ty [hilǽriti] *n.* [U] merriness; cheerfulness.
—[名] 환희, 유쾌한 일

⁑ **hill** [hil] *n.* [C] **1.** a small and low mountain. **2.** a heap of earth. ¶*an ant* ~.①
—[名] 1. 작은 산, 언덕, 구릉 2. 쌓아 올린 흙 ¶①개미둑

hill·bil·ly [hílbili] *n.* [C] (pl. **-lies**) (*U.S. colloq.*) a person from the mountains of the southern United States.
—[名] 《美口》 [남부의] 산사람

hill·ock [hílək] *n.* [C] a small hill.
—[名] 작은 산, 작은 언덕

∗ **hill·side** [hílsàid] *n.* [C] the side of a hill.
—[名] 산허리

hill·top [híltàp / -tɔ̀p] *n.* [C] the top of a hill.
—[名] 언덕의 꼭대기

hill·y [híli] *adj.* (**hill·i·er, hill·i·est**) full of hills; having many hills. ¶*a ~ country.*① ▷**hill·i·ness** [-nis] *n.*
—[形] 작은 산이 많은, 구릉성의 ¶①산간 지역

hilt [hilt] *n.* [C] the handle of a sword, dagger, etc.
up to the hilt, completely; thoroughly.
—[名] [칼·단검 따위의] 손잡이, 자루
[熟] 완전히; 철두철미하게

⁑ **him** [him, im] *pron.* the objective case of **he**.
—[代] 그를, 그에게

Him·a·la·yan [hìməlé(i)ən, himá:l(ə)jən] *adj.* of the Himalayas.
—[形] 히말라야 산맥의

Him·a·la·yas [himəlé(i)əz], **the** *n. pl.* a mountain range extending along the north border of India.
—[名] 히말라야 산맥

H

⁝ him·self [(h)imsélf] *pron.* (pl. **them·selves**) ⇒oneself **1.** a reflexive and emphatic form of **he** or **him.** ¶*He ~ will do it.* / *He hurt ~ with a knife.* **2.** his normal physical or mental condition. ¶*He was not ~ then.*① / *He stumbled, but soon recovered ~.*②
—[代] 1. 그 자신, 그 스스로 2. 그의 [심신의] 정상적인 상태 ¶①당시의 그는 여느때의 그와는 달랐다/②그는 비틀거렸지만 곧 제대로 섰다

· hind¹ [haind] *adj.* (**hind·er, hind·most** or **hind·er·most**) back; rear. ↔fore
—[形] 뒤[쪽]의, 후부의

hind² [haind] *n.* [C] (pl. **hinds** or *collectively* **hind**) a female red deer. ↔stag
—[名] 붉은 암사슴

· hin·der [híndər] *vt.* prevent; keep. 《~ someone *from doing*》 ¶*be hindered in one's work*① / *The storm hindered us from starting.*②
—[他] …을 방해하다; 훼방놓다 ¶①일을 방해받다/②폭풍으로 출발할 수 없었다

hind·er·most [háindərmòust] *adj.* =hindmost.

Hin·di [híndiː, ⌐⌐] *n.* [U] a language of northern India.
—[名] [북부 인도의] 힌디 말

hind·most [háin(d)mòust] *adj.* furthest behind; last.
—[形] 맨 뒤의; 최후의

Hin·doo [híndu:, ⌐⌐] *n., adj.* =Hindu.

hin·drance [híndr(ə)ns] *n.* [U] the act of hindering; [C] a person or thing that hinders; an obstacle.
—[名] 방해; 방해자; 장해물

Hin·du [híndu:, ⌐⌐] *n.* [C] **1.** a member of a native race in India. **2.** a person who believes in Hinduism. ***—adj.*** of the Hindus, their language or religion.
—[名] 1. 힌두 사람 2. 힌두교 신봉자
—[形] 힌두 사람(말·교)의

Hin·du·sta·ni [hìndustáːni, -stǽni] *n.* [U] a language spoken in most parts of India.
—[名] 힌두스탄 말

· hinge [hindʒ] *n.* [C] a tool for joining two parts so that one of them can move, as on a door, gate, or lid. ¶*off the hinges.*① ***—vt.*** furnish (something) with hinges.
hinge *(=depend)* ***on something.***
—[名] 경첩 ¶①정상적인 상태가 아닌
—[他] …에 경첩을 달다
[熟] …에 달려 있다

· hint [hint] *n.* [C] a slight sign; an indirect suggestion. ¶*a delicate (broad) ~*① / *give* (or *drop*) *a ~*② / *take a ~.*③ ***—vt., vi.*** give a slight sign of (something); suggest indirectly. 《~ *at* something; ~ *that* …》 ▷**hint·er** [-ər] *n.*
—[名] 암시, 힌트, 시사 ¶①은근한(노골적인) 풍자/②암시하다/③암시를 알아채다 —[他][自] 암시하다

hin·ter·land [híntərlæ̀nd] *n.* [C] the land or district lying behind a coast.
—[名] [강기슭·해안에서 떨어진] 내륙, 오지(奧地)

· hip¹ [hip] *n.* [C] the part of the human body below the waist. ¶*a ~ pocket.*①
—[名] 엉덩이, 허리 ¶①뒷주머니

hip² [hip] *n.* [C] a pod containing the ripe seed of a rose bush.
—[名] 들장미의 열매

hippo [hípou] *n.* *(colloq.)* =hippopotamus.

hip·po·drome [hípədròum] *n.* [C] **1.** a place for horse races and chariot races in ancient Greece and Rome. **2.** an area for a circus, games, etc.
—[名] 1. [고대 그리이스·로마의] 전차 경주장 2. 서어커스장, 경기장

hip·po·pot·a·mi [hìpəpátəmài / -pɔ́t-] *n.* pl. of **hippopotamus**

hip·po·pot·a·mus [hìpəpátəməs / -pɔ́t-] *n.* [C] (pl. **-mus·es** or **-mi**) a very large wild animal with a thick hairless body and short legs, found in African rivers.
—[名] 하마

⁝ hire [háiər] *vt.* employ (someone) for a fixed payment; pay for the use of (something).
hire out, give one's work or lend (something) in return for payment.
—n. [U] the act of hiring.
for (or ***on***) ***hire,*** for use or work in return for payment. ¶*a car on ~.*①
—[他] …을 고용하다, …을 전세내다, 대절하다
[熟] 고용하다; …을 세 주다
—[名] 세 내고 빌리기, 고용
[熟] 세를 받고 빌려주는 ¶①전세 자동차

hire·ling [háiərliŋ] *n.* [C] a person who works only for money.
—[名] 고용인; 돈만 주면 일하는 사람

⁝ his [hiz, iz] *pron.* the possessive form of **he.** ¶*a friend of ~*① / *This is mine; that is ~.*
—[代] 그의 ¶①그의 친구

· hiss [his] *vi., vt.* **1.** make a sound like the [s]. **2.** show dislike by hissing. 《~ *away* or *down* someone or something》 ***—n.*** [C] a sound like the [s]
—[自][他] 1. 쉿하고 말하다 2. 쉿하고 제지하다 —[名] 쉿하는 목소리(소리)

· his·to·ri·an [histɔ́ːriən] *n.* [C] a person who writes about history.
—[名] 역사가

· his·tor·ic [histárik, -tɔ́ːr- / -tɔ́r-] *adj.* famous or important in history. ¶*a[n] ~ event*① / *~ scenes.*②
—[形] 역사상의; 역사상 유명한 ¶①역사적 사건/②사적, 유적

· his·tor·i·cal [histɔ́ːrik(ə)l / -tɔ́r-] *adj.* of history. ¶*~ evidence*① / *a[n] ~ method*② / *a[n] ~ novel.*③ ▷**his·tor·i·cal·ly** [-i] *adv.*
—[形] 역사적인; 사실(史實)의 ¶①사실/②역사적 방법/③역사 소설

his·to·ry [híst(ə)ri] *n.* (pl. **-ries**) **1.** [U] the study or story of past facts and events. ¶*ancient (medieval, modern)* ~ ① / *the* ~ *of England.*② **2.** [C] the past story of a man, nation, or thing. ¶*This sword has a* ~.③
—[名] 1. 역사 ¶①고대(중세 · 근세)사/②영국사 2. [한 개인 · 한 국가의] 경력 ¶③이 칼에는 유래가 있다

make history, do such important things as will live long in history.
[熟] 역사에 남을 큰 일을 하다

his·tri·on·ic [hìstriάnik / -ɔ́n-] *adj.* **1.** of actors or acting. **2.** artificial; not natural.
—[形] 1. 배우의; 연극의 2. 일부러 꾸미는, 연극조의

hit [hit] *v.* (**hit, hit·ting**) *vt.* **1.** give a blow to (someone); strike; knock. ¶*She* ~ *him too hard.* / *He* ~ *the robber on the head.*① ⇨[usage] / *I* ~ *him a blow.* / *Hit the ball over the wall.* / *We fired and* ~ *the tiger.* / *She* ~ *her head against the door.* **2.** come against (something). ¶*The car* ~ *the mailbox.* **3.** agree with (something); suit. ¶*The idea* ~ *his fancy.*② **4.** arrive at (a place); reach (a certain level). ¶*Prices* ~ *a new high yesterday.*③ **5.** have a serious influence upon (someone or something); affect. ¶*They were hard* ~ *by bankruptcy.*④ **6.** (of storms, revolution, etc.) attack. ¶*A heavy storm* ~ *the city.* **7.** find (something) by accident or as the result of searching. ¶~ *the right answer* / *We* ~ *the right path.* **8.** (*Baseball*) make (a base hit). ¶~ *a single*⑤ / ~ *a double.*⑥ —*vi.* **1.** deliver a blow. **2.** strike; bump. 《~ *against* something or someone》 ¶*I* ~ *against a wall.* **3.** find or come upon something by accident or after searching. 《~ *upon* something》 ¶~ *upon a good plan.*
—[他] 1. …을 치다, 부딪치다, 맞히다 ¶①그는 도둑의 머리를 때렸다 [usage] hit the robber's head 라 하지 않음 2. …에 부딪치다 3. …에 적합하다, 맞다 ¶②그 생각은 그의 마음에 꼭 들었다 4. …에 도착하다, 달하다 ¶③물가는 어제 최고를 기록했다 5. …에게 타격을 주다 ¶④그들은 파산으로 큰 타격을 받았다 6. …을 습격하다 7. [우연히 또는 용하게] 마주치다, 발견하다, …을 알아맞히다 8. 《野球》 안타를 치다 ¶⑤단타(單打)를 치다/⑥2루타를 치다 —[自] 1. 치다 2. 부딪치다 3. 생각나다, 마주치다

1) *hit at,* ⓐ aim a blow at (something). ⓑ attack (someone) in words.
2) *hit below the belt,* strike or treat unfairly.
3) *hit hard* (=*put emphasis*) *on something.*
4) *hit it,* guess rightly.
5) *hit it off,* (*U.S. colloq.*) get along well together.
6) *hit off,* follow the example of (someone); write down (something) briefly but well.
7) *hit or miss,* without definite direction or plan; aimless.
8) *hit out,* strike forcefully.
9) *hit the ceiling,* become very angry.
[熟] 1)ⓐ…을 겨냥하고 치다 ⓑ…을 비난하다 2)반칙을 범하다, 비겁한 짓을 하다 3)…을 역설하다 4)용케 알아맞히다 5)《美口》사이좋게 지내다 6)[남의] 흉내를 내다, 요령있게 잘 묘사하다 7)홍망(성패)을 운에 맡기고 8)세게 치다 9)몹시 성내다

—*n.* [C] **1.** a stroke; a blow. **2.** a stroke of good fortune; a successful and popular song, book, play, etc. **3.** an effectively witty or sarcastic remark. **4.** (*Baseball*) a base hit. **5.** a collision.
—[名] 1. 타격, 명중 2. 성공, 히트[곡·작] 3. 급소를 찌르는 말(풍자) 4. 《野球》 히트, 안타 5. 충돌

hitch [hitʃ] *vt.* move or lift suddenly; fasten or tie (something) with a hook. 《~ *up* something》 —*vi.* move abruptly; become fastened. —*n.* [C] a sudden pull; a sudden stop. ¶*without a* ~.①
—[他] …을 확 움직이다; 고리로 걸다(고정하다) —[自] 확 움직이다; 걸리다 —[名] 확 당기기; 급정지 ¶①막힘 없이

hitch·hike [hítʃhàik] *vi.* (*colloq.*) travel by walking and sometimes getting free rides from passing cars.
—[自] [여행 도중에 남의 차에] 편승하여 여행하다

hitch·hik·er [hítʃhàikər] *n.* [C] a person who hitchhikes.
—[名] 자동차 편승 여행자

• **hith·er** [híðər] *adv.* to this place; here. ¶~ *and thither.*① —*adj.* on this side. ¶*on the* ~ *side of the bank.*
—[副] 이리로, 이쪽으로 ¶①여기저기에 —[形] 이쪽의

• **hith·er·to** [híðərtú:] *adv.* up to this time; until now.
—[副] 지금까지

Hit·ler [hítlər], **Adolf** *n.* (1889–1945) a German dictator.
—[名] 독일의 독재자

• **hive** [haiv] *n.* [C] **1.** a house or box for bees to live in. **2.** a large number of bees living together in this place. **3.** a very busy place. —*vt.* put (bees) in a hive. —*vi.* (of bees) enter a hive.
—[名] 1. 벌통, 벌집 2. 벌떼 3. 붐비는(시끄러운) 장소 —[他] [벌]을 벌통에 넣다 —[自] [벌이] 벌통에 들어가다

hives [haivz] *n. pl.* 《used as *sing.* and *pl.*》 a skin disease.
—[名] 발진(發疹), 두드러기

h'm [hm] hem²; hum (*n.* 2.).

H.M. His (or Her) Majesty.

• **ho, hoa** [hou] *interj.* a call to get attention. ¶*Ho! ho! / Ho, there.*
—[感] 여어, 어어이, 이봐(주의 · 환기 · 놀람 · 만족 따위)

hoar [hɔ:r] *adj.* = hoary.

hoard [hɔ:rd] *n.* [C] a store of hidden money; a collection of things, esp. those kept secretly for one's own use
—[名] 숨겨둔 돈, 저장품

—*vt., vi.* gather and keep (something) secretly. 《~ *up* something》 ▷**hoard·er** [-ər] *n.*
—[他][自] [물건을] 몰래 저장하다

hoar·frost [hɔ́ːrfrɔ̀st] *n.* [U] white frost.
—[名] 서리, 흰 서리

hoarse [hɔːrs] *adj.* sounding rough and deep; having a rough voice; husky.
▷**hoarse·ly** [-li] *adv.* —**hoarse·ness** [-nis] *n.*
—[形] [목소리가] 쉰; 귀에 거슬리는

hoar·y [hɔ́ːri] *adj.* (**hoar·i·er, hoar·i·est**) **1.** white or gray, esp. with age; grayish-white; white-haired. **2.** very old; honorable. ▷**hoar·i·ness** [-nis] *n.*
—[形] 1. [특히 늙어서 머리 따위가] 회백색의, 백발의 2. 오래 묵은; 거룩한

hoax [houks] *n.* [C] the act of playing a trick; a practical joke. **—*vt.*** play a trick on (someone); deceive.
—[名] 남을 속이기, 짓궂은 장난 —[他] …을 감쪽같이 속이다; …을 골탕먹이다

hob [hab / hɔb] *n.* [C] **1.** a metal shelf at the side of a fireplace on which pots are kept warm. **2.** a peg used as a target.
—[名] 1. [주전자 따위를 올려놓는] 난로 양옆의 대(臺) 2. [고리 던지기의] 표적 기둥

hob·ble [hábl / hɔ́bl] *vi.* walk with difficulty; limp. 《~ *along* or *about* a place》 **—*vt.*** **1.** tie the legs of a horse together. **2.** cause (someone) to limp. **3.** prevent; stop. **—*n.*** [C] **1.** a limping walk. **2.** a rope or fetter for hobbling horses.
—[自] 절름거리다 —[他] 1. [말의] 두 다리를 한데 묶다 2. …에게 절름거리게 하다 3. …을 방해하다 —[名] 1. 절름거리며 걷기 2. [말의] 다리를 묶는 새끼

* **hob·by** [hábi / hɔ́bi] *n.* [C] (pl. **-bies**) a subject which a person studies for pleasure.
—[名] 취미, 도락

ride a hobby, be too much devoted to one's hobby.
[熟] 자기 취미에만 너무 열중하다

hob·by·horse [hábihɔ̀ːrs / hɔ́bihɔ̀ːs] *n.* [C] a stick with a horse's head or a rocking horse, used as a toy by children.
—[名] 목마, 흔들리는 장난감 말

hob·nail [hábnèil / hɔ́b-] *n.* [C] a short nail with a large head fixed in the bottoms of shoes.
—[名] [구두 바닥에 박는] 징

hob·nob [hábnàb / hɔ́bnɔ̀b] *vi.* be friendly with someone; talk and drink together.
—[自] 친하게 사귀다, 사이좋게 술 마시다

ho·bo [hóubou] *n.* [C] (pl. **-bos** or **-boes**) (*U.S. colloq.*) a tramp; a vagabond.
—[名] 《美口》 방랑자

hock [hak / hɔk] *n.* [C] a joint in the hind leg of a cow, horse, pig, etc.
—[名] [소·말·돼지 뒷발의] 무릎

hock·ey [háki / hɔ́ki] *n.* [U] a game played by two teams on grass or ice, using curved sticks and a ball. ¶*ice ~.*
—[名] 하키

ho·cus [hóukəs] *vt.* play a trick on (someone); cheat.
—[他] …을 속이다

hod [had / hɔd] *n.* [C] a wooden container for carrying bricks or mortar. ⇒fig.
—[名] 벽돌·회반죽을 나르는 나무통

[hod]

hodge·podge [hádʒpàdʒ / hɔ́dʒpɔ̀dʒ] *n.* [C] 《*sing.* only》 a thick stew of meat and vegetables; a disorderly mixture.
—[名] [고기와 야채의] 잡탕; 뒤범벅

hoe [hou] *n.* [C] a long-handled tool used for loosening the soil or removing weeds. **—*vt., vi.*** dig (the soil) or clear (weeds) with a hoe; work with a hoe.
—[名] 괭이; 제초기 —[他][自] 괭이로 일구다, 제초하다

* **hog** [hag, hɔːg / hɔg] *n.* [C] (pl. **hogs** or *collectively* **hog**) **1.** a pig. **2.** a greedy or dirty person. ¶*eat like a ~.*①
—[名] 1. 돼지 2. 탐욕스러운(버릇없는) 사내 ¶①돼지처럼 게걸스럽게 먹다

go the whole hog, (*slang*) do something thoroughly.
[熟] 《俗》 철저하게 하다

hog·gish [hágiʃ, hɔ́ːg- / hɔ́g-] *adj.* like a hog; selfish; greedy; dirty. ▷**hog·gish·ly** [-li] *adv.*
—[形] 돼지 같은, 이기적인, 상스러운

hogs·head [hágzhèd, hɔ́ːg- / hɔ́g-] *n.* [C] **1.** a large round wooden container for wine or strong drink. **2.** a liquid measure equal to $52\frac{1}{2}$ imperial gallons.
—[名] 1. 큰 술통 2. 영국의 액량(液量) 단위(52.5 갈론)

hoist [hɔist] *vt.* raise aloft; lift up (a flag, etc.) by means of ropes and pulleys. **—*n.*** [C] **1.** the act of lifting. **2.** an elevator or other apparatus for raising things. ⇒fig.
—[他] [돛·깃발을] 끌어올리다, 높이 달다 —[名] 1. 끌어올리기 2. 승강기; 권양기(捲揚機)

[hoist 2.]

‡ **hold**[1] [hould] *v.* (**held**) ***vt.*** **1.** take and keep (something) in the hand. ¶*He held me tight.* / *I ~ a writing brush in my hand.* / *She tried to ~ me by the hand.* **2.** prevent the movement or escape of (something); support. ¶*He held her so that she couldn't move.* / *These pillars ~ the stage.* **3.** restrain (someone or
—[他] 1. …을 손에 들다 2. [움직이거나 도망가지 않도록] …을 붙잡다; 버티다 3. …을 억제하다 ¶①입 다물어! /② [그대로 잠깐] 기다려라! 4. [어떤 위치·장소·상태에] …을 유지하다 ¶ ③그는 머리를 숙이고 있었다 5. [그릇이] …만큼 들다 6. …을 마음에 간직하

something) from acting or speaking. ¶*Hold your tongue!*① | *Hold it!*② **4.** keep (something) in a specified state. ¶*He held his head down.*③ | *Hold your head upright.* **5.** contain ; have space for (a specified number of people, etc.). ¶*This hall can ~ about 500 people.* | *This can holds about 4 gallons.* **6.** keep (something) in mind ; consider ; believe ; decide. ¶*~ the same view as him*④ | *~ the opinion that...* | *I ~ him [to be] guilty.* | *I ~ that he is honest.* **7.** occupy. ¶*~ the chair* | *He holds an important position.* | *He has held the office of mayor for four years.* **8.** retain possession or control of (something), as against an enemy. ¶*They held the town against the enemy.* **9.** have or carry on (a meeting conversation, etc.) ¶*~ a garden party* | *~ a conversation with friends* | *~ classes in the open air* | *~ [a] court.* **10.** require (someone) to fulfil ; obligate. ¶*We must ~ him to his word.*⑤

다; …이라고 생각하다; 결정하다 ¶④그와 같은 견해를 갖다 **7.** …을 차지하다 **8.** [적으로부터] …을 유지하다, 지키다 **9.** [모임]을 개최하다; [대화]를 하다 **10.** [의무·약속 따위를 남]에게 지키게 하다 ¶⑤그에게 약속을 지키게 해야 한다

—*vi.* **1.** maintain a grip or grasp. 《~ *on* or *to* something》 ¶*Hold tight!* **2.** remain or continue unchanged. ¶*Please ~ still.*⑥ | *The breeze holds all day.* | *This weather will not ~ long.* | *The wind held from the south.* **3.** be relevant ; remain true, correct, etc. ¶*This decision holds in all such cases.*⑦ **4.** have right. 《~ *from* or *of* something》

—[自] **1.** 붙들고 있다 **2.** 지속하다, 계속하다 ¶⑥가만히 있어 주시오 **3.** 적응하다 ¶⑦이 결정은 그러한 모든 경우에 적용할 수 있다 **4.** …의 권리를 가지다

1) ***hold back,*** ⓐ restrain ; check. ⓑ refrain from (some activity). ⓒ retain possession of (something).
2) ***hold back on,*** restrain oneself from (doing something).
3) ***hold by,*** stick to (something) ; maintain.
4) ***hold down,*** ⓐ keep (something) under control. ⓑ (*colloq.*) have and keep (a job, etc.).
5) ***hold forth,*** ⓐ speak at some length ; preach. ⓑ propose (a view, etc.).
6) ***hold good,*** remain legal or effective.
7) ***hold one's hand,*** be patient ; forgive.
8) ***hold in,*** ⓐ keep (someone or something) in or back. ⓑ control oneself or one's impulses.
9) ***hold off,*** ⓐ resist (the enemy's attack, etc.) ; push back ; prevent ; restrain. ⓑ delay (any action). ⓒ keep or restrain oneself from (doing something).
10) ***hold on,*** ⓐ continue, esp. on the telephone. ¶*Hold on a moment, please.*⑧ ⓑ (*colloq.*) Stop! Wait!
11) ***hold out,*** ⓐ offer (a hand, hope, promise, etc.) ⓑ continue. ⓒ endure.
12) ***hold over,*** ⓐ put off consideration of (a matter). ⓑ stay for an additional period or time.
13) ***hold still,*** remain motionless.
14) ***hold together,*** unite.
15) ***hold up,*** ⓐ support ; endure. ⓑ show ; exhibit. ⓒ delay (any action). ⓓ stop (someone) forcibly and rob ; obtain money from (someone) by threats.
16) ***hold water,*** be consistent or logical.
17) ***hold with,*** ⓐ agree with (someone). ⓑ approve of (doing something). ⓒ side with (someone).

[熟] 1)ⓐ…을 제지하다 ⓑ망설이다 ⓒ…을 보유하다 2)…을 자제하다 3)…을 고집하다;지지하다 4)ⓐ…을 억누르다 ⓑ《口》…을 유지하다 5)ⓐ[의견 따위]를 장황하게 말하다 ⓑ…제시하다, 제의하다 6)유효하다 7)참다, 용서하다 8)ⓐ…을 억누르다 ⓑ참다 9)ⓐ…을 저지하다, 가까이하지 않다 ⓑ…을 늦추다 ⓒ…을 삼가다 10)ⓐ계속하다 ¶⑧[전화에서] 끊지 말고 기다리세요 ⓑ《口》서라!, 기다려라! 11)ⓐ[손]을 내밀다, [희망·약속 따위를] 제시하다 ⓑ계속하다 ⓒ끝까지 견디다 12)ⓐ…을 연기하다 ⓑ예정된 이상으로 머무르다 13)끔짝않고 있다 14)단결하다 15)ⓐ…을 지지하다;지탱하다 ⓑ…을 보이다 ⓒ…을 연기하다 ⓓ…을 정지시키고 강탈하다, 위협하여 돈을 빼앗다 16)앞뒤가 맞다, 조리가 서 있다 17)ⓐ…와 의견이 일치하다 ⓑ…을 인정하다 ⓒ…에게 편들다

—*n.* **1.** [C] [U] the act of holding, as with the hands ; grasp. **2.** [C] [U] a controlling force ; strong influence. 《~ *on* or *over*》 **3.** [C] anything to hold by ; a thing with which to grasp something ; a place of grasp ; a place of security. ¶*The rock gave no ~ for one's foot.*⑨

—[名] **1.** 쥠, 파악, 붙들기 **2.** 지배력; 위력 **3.** 쥐는(붙잡는) 곳, 손잡이, 발걸이; 버팀 ¶⑨그 바위에는 발을 디딜 데가 없었다

1) ***catch*** (or ***get, lay, take***) ***hold of,*** take ; grasp.
2) ***keep hold on*** (=*hold* or *hang on to*) *something.*
3) ***lay*** (or ***take***) ***hold on,*** seize ; grasp.
4) ***let go one's hold,*** take one's hands off.
5) ***lose hold of,*** lose a clue or key to (something) ;

[熟] 1)…을 붙잡다, 쥐다 2)…을 붙잡고 있다 3)…을 장악하다, 붙들다 4)손을 놓다 5)…의 단서(실마리)를 잃다

H

lose all trace of (something).

hold[2] [hould] *n.* [C] a place below deck in which cargo is stored.
—[名] 선창(船倉)

hold·back [hóuldbæ̀k] *n.* [C] a thing that holds back; check; restraint; hindrance.
—[名] 견제물, 속박, 장해

* **hold·er** [hóuldər] *n.* [C] a person or thing that holds something. ¶*a pen-holder*① / *a record* ~.②
—[名] 소지인; 받치는 물건 ¶①펜대/②기록 보유자

hold·fast [hóuldfæ̀st / -fɑ̀:st] *n.* [C] a thing used to hold something together.
—[名] 꽉 누르는(죄는) 물건(못·찝쇠·다짐쇠·거멀못·꺾쇠 따위)

hold·ing [hóuldiŋ] *n.* [U][C] the act of a person who holds; something owned; property; a piece of land; stocks.
—[名] 붙잡음, 쥠; 보유; 소유물; 보유지; 소유주(株)

hold·up [hóuldʌ̀p] *n.* [C] (*U.S. colloq.*) the act of stopping (someone, trains, etc.) by force for the purpose of robbery. ¶*a ~ man.*①
—[名] [열차·자동차 승객의] 불법 억류, 강탈, 강도질 ¶①강탈자, 노상 강도

‡ **hole** [houl] *n.* [C] **1.** an open place. ¶*like a rat in a* ~.① **2.** a break in something solid.
1) ***be in a hole,*** be in a difficulty.
2) ***burn a hole in someone's pocket,*** (of money) make someone eager to spend money.
3) ***make a hole in*** (=*use up a large part of*) *something.*
4) ***pick holes in*** (=*find fault with*) *someone.*
5) ***a square peg in a round hole,*** a person unfit for the position he is in.
—[名] 1. 구멍 ¶①독 안에 든 쥐 꼴이 되어 2. 갈라진 틈
[熟] 1)곤경에 처해 있다 2)[돈이] 몸에 붙지 않다 3)…을 대량으로 소비하다 4)[남]의 흠을 찾다 5)부적임자(不適任者)

—*vt., vi.* make holes in (something).
1) ***hole out,*** (*Golf*) hit the ball into a hole. ¶*~ out in one.*②
2) ***hole up,*** spend the winter in sleep; shut oneself in a place; shut up (something or someone).
—[他][自] 구멍을 뚫다
[熟] 1)《골프》 공을 구멍에 넣다 ¶②한 번 쳐서 공을 구멍에 넣다 2)동면하다; 굴에 들어가 겨울을 나다; 꼭 틀어박히다; 가둬 놓다

‡ **hol·i·day** [hálidèi / hɔ́l-] *n.* [C] **1.** any day of rest; a day of rest from work. ¶*Sunday is a* ~. **2.** a day, appointed by law or custom, on which general business is stopped, usu. in celebration of some event. ¶*a national* ~.① **3.** 《often *pl.*》 (chiefly *Brit.*) a period of leisure or recreation; vacation. ¶*spend the holidays at home.*② **4.** a religious festival; a holy day.
—[名] 1. 휴일, 공일 2. 축일 ¶①국경일 3. 휴가[기간] ¶②휴가를 집에서 보내다 4. [종교상의] 축제일

1) ***make a holiday,*** rest from work.
2) ***on holiday,*** having a holiday.
3) ***take*** (or ***have***) ***a holiday,*** have a day free from work.
[熟] 1)휴업하다 2)휴가로 3)휴가를 얻다

—*adj.* **1.** fit for a holiday. **2.** joyous; gay. ¶*~ mood.*③
—[形] 1. 휴일의; 휴가중의 2. 즐거운 ¶③축제 기분

hol·i·day-mak·er [hálideimèikər / hɔ́lideimèikə] *n.* [C] a person spending a holiday at an amusement place.
—[名] 소풍객

ho·li·ness [hóulinis] *n.* [U] **1.** the state of being holy. **2.** 《*His H-*》 the title of the Pope.
—[名] 1. 신성(神聖) 2. 로마 교황의 존칭

hol·la [hálə, həlá: / hɔ́lə] *interj., n., v.* =hollo.

‡ **Hol·land** [hálənd / hɔ́l-] *n.* the Netherlands.
—[名] 네덜란드

Hol·land·er [háləndər / hɔ́ləndə] *n.* [C] a person of Holland; a Dutchman.
—[名] 네덜란드 사람

hol·lo [hálou / hɔ́l-] *interj., n.* a shout to attract attention; a cry of greeting or surprise. —*vt., vi.* call or shout to attract the attention of (someone).
—[感][名] 어어이 !, 이봐 !(인사·주의·환희의 소리) —[他][自] [···에게] 어어이 하고 외치다

hol·loa [hálou / hɔ́-] *interj., n., v.* =hollo.

‡ **hol·low** [hálou / hɔ́l-] *n.* [C] **1.** a hole that is wide but not deep. ¶*the ~ of the hand.*① **2.** a valley; a basin.
—[名] 1. 움푹한 데; 구멍; 공동(空洞) ¶①손바닥 2. 골짜기; 분지(盆地)

—*adj.* **1.** having an empty space inside; having nothing inside except air. ↔solid ¶*a ~ tree.* **2.** fallen; sunken. ¶*~ cheeks* / *~ eyes.* **3.** empty; worthless; false. ¶*a ~ promise*② / *~ words of praise.*③ **4.** (of a sound) dull and deep-toned, as if resounding from something empty. ¶*hear ~ sounds from a cave.* **5.** (*colloq.*) complete.
—[形] 1. 텅빈, 속이 빈 2. 움푹한, 쏙 들어간 3. 공허한; 거짓의 ¶②말뿐인 약속/③마음에도 없는 칭찬의 말 4. [소리가] 공허하게 울리는 5. 《口》 완전한

—*adv.* (*colloq.*) completely; thoroughly. ¶*beat someone* [*all*] *~.*④
—[副] 완전히 ¶④…을 완전히 해치우다

—*vt., vi.* make or become hollow. 《~ *out* something》 ¶*~ out a watermelon.*
—[他][自] 구멍을 뚫다, 우벼내다; 속이 비어지다

hol·low·ness [hálounis / hɔ́l-] *n.* [U] **1.** the state of being hollow; emptiness. **2.** lack of sincerity.
—[名] 1. 움푹함 2. 불성실, 허위

hol·ly [háli / hɔ́li] *n.* [U][C] (pl. **-lies**) an evergreen shrub or a small tree with hard shiny, prickly leaves and red berries.
—[名] 서양 감탕나무; 붉은 열매가 달린 그 가지(크리스마스 장식용)

hol·ly·hock [hálihàk, -hɔ̀:k / hɔ́lihɔ̀k] *n.* [C] a very tall plant with large flowers of various colors.
—[名] 접시꽃

Hol·ly·wood [háliwùd / hɔ́li-] *n.* a section of Los Angeles where many movies are made.
—[名] 헐리웃(미국 로스앤젤리스의 영화 제작지)

hol·o·caust [háləkɔ̀:st / hɔ́l-] *n.* [C] **1.** an offering all of which is burned. **2.** a great murder or destruction, esp. by fire.
—[名] 1. 통째로 구워 신전에 바치는 제물 2. 큰 화재; 대학살; 대파괴

Hol·stein [hóulstain, -sti:n / hɔ́lstain] *n.* [C] a kind of large black-and-white dairy cattle.
—[名] 홀스타인종의 소

hol·ster [hóulstər] *n.* [C] a leather pistol case, carried at the belt.
—[名] [허리에 차는] 가죽 권총집

‡ho·ly [hóuli] *adj.* (**-li·er, -li·est**) belonging to or having to do with God; sacred. ¶*the Holy Bible*① / *the Holy Land*② / *Holy Office*③ / ~ *orders*④ / *a* ~ *terror.*⑤
—[名] 신성한, 깨끗한; 거룩한 ¶①성서/②성지/③종교 재판소/④성직/⑤정말 무서운 사람, 골칫거리인 사람

***hom·age** [(h)ámidʒ / hɔ́m-] *n.* [U] an act of respect; an act of declaring oneself to be the loyal servant of one's lord. ¶*do* (or *render*) ~ *to* (*someone*)① / *pay* (or *do*) ~ *to* (*someone*)② / *in* ~ *to* (*someone*).
—[名] 존경; (봉건 시대의) 충성의 맹세, 신하의 예(禮) ¶①…에게 충성을 맹세하고 신하가 되다/②…에게 경의를 표하다

‡home [houm] *n.* **1.** [C][U] the house where one's family lives. ¶*I don't like my new* ~. **2.** [C] a family circle; household. ¶*keep a happy* ~.① **3.** [C][U] one's native place or country. ¶*leave* ~ *for America.* **4.** [C] the place of origin. ¶*the* ~ *of jazz.* **5.** [C] the place where an animal, a plant, etc. naturally lives or grows; a habitat. ¶*the* ~ *of the crane.* **6.** [C] an establishment for the shelter and care of the needy or infirm. ¶*a* ~ *for orphans*② / *a* ~ *for the aged.* **7.** [C] (*Sports*) the goal, esp. the home plate in baseball.
—[名] 1. 사는 집, 자택 2. 가정; 가정생활 ¶①행복한 가정생활을 하다 3. 본국; 고국 4. 본고장 5. [동·식물의] 서식지 6. 수용시설 ¶②고아 수용소 7. 결승점; [야구의] 본루(本壘)

1) ***at home,*** ⓐ in one's own house, city, or country. ¶*I stay at* ~ *today.*③ ⇒[N.B.] / *leave something at* ~. ⓑ as if in one's home; comfortable. ¶*Make yourself at* ~.④ ⓒ well-informed; familiar. ¶*He feels at* ~ *in several European languages.* ⓓ prepared to receive visitors. ¶*Mr. Gain will be at* ~ *every morning from 10 to 12.*
2) ***one's long*** (or ***last***) ***home,*** one's grave; one's tomb.
[熟] 1)ⓐ집에 있는; 자기 마을에; 자기 나라에 ¶③오늘은 집에 있다 [N.B.] 미국에서는 stay home이라 함 ⓑ마음 편하게, 편히 ¶④편히 하십시오 ⓒ잘하는, 능숙한 ⓓ면회할 수 있는 2)묘지(墓地)

—*adj.* **1.** of the family. ¶~ *life.* **2.** of one's country; domestic. ↔foreign ⇒[usage] ¶~ *industry* / *the* ~ *market* / ~ *consumption*⑤ / ~ *waters.*⑥ **3.** at the place thought of as the base of operation. ¶*the* ~ *office.*⑦ **4.** effective; to the point. ¶*a* ~ *question.*
—[形] 1. 가정의 2. 고향의, 본국의; 국내의 [usage] 「고향」을 미국에서는 보통 one's home town, 영국에서는 one's native town이라 함. 간단히 home이라 해도 좋음 ¶⑤국내 소비/⑥근해(近海) 3. 본부의 ¶⑦본부 4. 효과적인; 급소를 찌르는

—*adv.* **1.** to or at home. ¶*come* (or *go*) ~ / *be ordered* ~⑧ / *on one's way* ~ *from school* / *He is* ~ *from Cambridge for the holidays.* **2.** to the place or point intended. ¶*thrust the dagger* ~. **3.** to the heart of a matter; deeply. ¶*His words struck* ~.⑨
—[副] 1. 집에(으로); 고국에(으로) ¶⑧귀국하도록 명령받다 2. 겨냥한 곳에 3. 푹, 깊이, 급소를 찔러 ¶⑨그의 말은 핵심을 찔렀다

1) ***bring something home to,*** ⓐ make (someone) understand clearly. ¶*The scene brought* ~ *to him what misery really means.* ⓑ prove a charge against (someone).
2) ***come home,*** return, as to one's home.
3) ***come home to,*** reach (someone's) heart; become completely understood or realized by (someone).
4) ***see someone home,*** escort someone to his home.
5) ***write home about*** (=*boast* or *be proud of*) *something.* (*colloq.*)
[熟] 1)ⓐ절실히(분명히) 느끼게 (깨닫게) 하다 ⓑ…의 죄상을 입증하다 2)귀가하다 3)…이 가슴에 사무치다 4)[남]을 집까지 바래다 주다 5)…을 자랑하다

—*vi.* go to a home; fly home. —*vt.* furnish (someone) with a home.
—[自] 집으로 돌아오다; 둥지로 도로 날아오다 —[他] …에게 집을 마련해 주다

home-bound [hóumbáund] *adj.* going in the direction of one's home or country.
—[形] 본국(집)으로 돌아가는

home-brewed [hóumbrú:d] *adj.* prepared by mixing at home; homemade. ¶~ *beer.*
—[形] 집에서 만든, 자가 양조의

home·com·ing [hóumkʌ̀miŋ] *n.* **1.** [U] the act of coming
—[名] 1. 귀가 2. 1년에 한 번 여는 대

to one's home. **2.** [C] an event held at a college or university for its graduates every year. — 학동창회

home-grown [hóumgróun] *adj.* (of fruits or vegetables) grown at home; domestic; grown or produced for local use. — [形] 집에서 재배한, 본국산의; 지방용으로 재배(생산)된

home·land [hóumlæ̀nd] *n.* [C] one's native land. — [名] 본국, 고국

home·less [hóumlis] *adj.* having no home; without a home. — [形] 집 없는

home·like [hóumlàik] *adj.* like home; comfortable; friendly. — [形] 제 집 같은, 마음편한, 친밀해질 수 있는

home·li·ness [hóumlinis] *n.* [U] **1.** the state of being simple or plain. **2.** the quality of being common. **3.** the state of being ugly. — [名] 1. 소박함, 꾸밈없음 2. 평범, 통속 3. 추함, 못생김

* **home·ly** [hóumli] *adj.* (**-li·er, -li·est**) **1.** like home. **2.** plain; simple. ¶ *~ but hospitable manners*① / *You'll find him a ~ person.* **3.** (*U.S.*) not good-looking; ugly. — [形] 1. 제 집 같은 2. 검소한, 소박한 ¶①소박하면서 후한 태도 3. 《美》 못생긴, 보기 흉한

home·made [hóumméid] *adj.* made at home. — [形] 제 집에서(손으로) 만든; 국산의

home·mak·er [hóummèikər] *n.* [C] a housewife. — [名] 주부

hom·er [hóumər] *n.* [C] **1.** a home run in baseball. **2.** a homing pigeon. — [名] 1. 홈런, 본루타 2. 전서구(傳書鳩)

* **Ho·mer** [hóumər] *n.* a great Greek poet who lived about the ninth century B.C. — [名] 기원전 9세기의 그리이스의 시인

Ho·mer·ic [houmérik] *adj.* of Homer; like the style of Homer. ¶ *~ laughter.*① — [形] 호오머의, 호오머풍의 ¶①껄껄 웃음

home run [⌐ ⌐] *n.* a hit in baseball that lets the batter run round the bases without a stop. — [名] 홈런, 본루타

home·sick [hóumsìk] *adj.* sad because one is away from home; desiring to go home very much. ¶ *be* (or *feel, get, grow*) *~*① / *She got ~.* — [形] 망향병의, 향수의 ¶①집(고향)을 몹시 그리워하다

home·sick·ness [hóumsìknis] *n.* [U] the state of being homesick. — [名] 망향병, 향수

home·spun [hóumspʌn] *adj.* **1.** spun at home. **2.** plain; simple. **—*n.*** [U] cloth made of yarn spun at home; a strong, loosely woven cloth. — [形] 1. 손으로 짠 2. 소박한, 평범한 —[名] 수직물(手織物), 호움스펀

home·stead [hóumstèd] *n.* [C] a house including the land and other buildings. — [名] [토지·부속건물을 포함한] 주택

home·stretch [hóumstrétʃ] *n.* [C] **1.** the last part of a race before the goal. **2.** the last part of a journey, etc. — [名] 1. 최후의 직선 코오스 2. [여행 따위의] 최종 부분(일정)

* **home·ward** [hóumwərd] *adj., adv.* toward home. ¶ *We started ~.* / *Our ~ journey was a hard one.*① — [形][副] 귀로의; 집으로 향하여 ¶①귀로 여행은 고되었다

home·ward-bound [hóumwərdbáund]] *adj.* bound for home; sailing back toward home. — [形] 본국행의, 귀항 중의

home·wards [hóumwərdz] *adv.* =homeward.

: **home·work** [hóumwə̀:rk] *n.* [U] work, esp. a school lesson, which is to be done at home. — [名] 가정에서 하는 일(주로 숙제)

home·y [hóumi] *adj.* (**hom·i·er, hom·i·est**) (*colloq.*) like home; comfortable. ¶ *a ~ letter.* — [形] 《口》 가정적인; 가정 같은, 마음편한

hom·i·ci·dal [hàmisáidl / hɔ̀m-] *adj.* of homicide. — [形] 살인[범]의

hom·i·cide [hámisàid / hɔ́m-] *n.* **1.** [U] the act of killing someone. **2.** [C] a person who kills someone. — [名] 1. 살인 2. 살인자(범)

hom·i·ly [hámili / hɔ́m-] *n.* [C] (pl. **-lies**) **1.** a talk on a part of the Bible or a religious subject; a sermon. **2.** a serious, dull, moral talk or writing. — [名] 1. 설교 2. 장황한 훈계

hom·i·nes [hóuminì:z] *n.* pl. of **homo**.

hom·i·ny [hámini / hɔ́m-] *n.* [U] (*U.S.*) dry Indian corn, coarsely ground or broken and boiled as food. — [名] 《美》 간 옥수수

ho·mo [hóumou] *n.* [C] (pl. **hom·i·nes**) man. — [名] [학명으로서] 인간

ho·mo·ge·ne·i·ty [hòumədʒəní:iti, hàm- / hɔ̀moudʒe-] *n.* [U] the state of being homogeneous. — [名] 동종(同種), 동질[성]

ho·mo·ge·ne·ous [hòumoudʒí:niəs, + *U.S.* hàm-, + *Brit.* hɔ̀mou-] *adj.* of the same kind; made up of similar elements or parts. ↔heterogeneous ▷**ho·mo·ge·ne·ous·ly** [-li] *adv.* — [形] 동종의, 동질의

ho·mog·e·nize [houmádʒənàiz / -mɔ́dʒ-] *vt.* make (something) homogeneous. ¶ *homogenized milk.*① — [他] …을 균질(均質)이 되게 하다 ¶ ①균질(강화)우유

hom·o·nym [hámounìm / hɔ́m-] *n.* [C] a word that has the same pronunciation as another, but a different spelling and meaning. ⇒[N.B.] — [名] 동음 이의어 [N.B.] see와 sea, air와 heir, dear와 deer 따위

H

Ho·mo sa·pi·ens [hóumouséipiənz, +*U.S.* -sǽp-] *n.* man ; a human being.
—[名] 인류

hom·y [hóumi] *adj.* (**hom·i·er, hom·i·est**) (*colloq.*) like home ; comfortable.
—[形] (口) 내 집 같은, [마음] 편안한

Hon. Honorable ; Honorary.

Hon·du·ras [hɑnd(j)úərəs / hɔndjúə-] *n.* a country in Central America. ⇒[N.B.] ▷**Hon·du·ran** [-rən] *adj., n.*
—[名] 중미의 공화국 [N.B.] 수도 Tegucigalpa

hone [houn] *n.* [C] a smooth stone on which to sharpen tools, esp. razors. —*vt.* sharpen (something) on a hone.
—[名] 숫돌, 면도 숫돌 —[他] …을 숫돌로 갈다

⁑hon·est [ɑ́nist / ɔ́n-] *adj.* **1.** not telling lies ; not deceiving or stealing ; trustworthy. ¶*an ~ act / an ~ man / He was quite ~ in telling me the story.*① **2.** frank ; open ; sincere. ¶*an ~ face / ~ advice.* **3.** fair ; right. ¶*an ~ business / an ~ profit.*② **4.** pure ; real ; being what it seems. ¶*~ milk / an ~ price / ~ weight.*③
be honest (=*be sincere in one's relationship*) ***with someone.***
—[形] 1. 정직한, 신용할 수 있는 ¶①그는 아주 정직하게 그 일을 이야기해 주었다 2. 솔직한; 성실한 3. 공정한, 정당한 ¶②정당한 이익 4. 순수한, 진짜의, 본 그대로의 ¶③넘지도 모자라지도 않는 무게
[熟] …와 성실하게 사귀다

⁑hon·est·ly [ɑ́nistli / ɔ́n-] *adv.* in an honest manner.
—[副] 정직하게; 정말로

⁑hon·es·ty [ɑ́nisti / ɔ́n-] *n.* [U] the quality of being honest ; truthfulness ; sincerity. ¶*~ of purpose*① / *with ~*② / (*proverb*) *Honesty is the best policy.*③
—[名] 정직, 성실 ¶①착실, 성실/②정직하게 말하여/③(俚)정직은 최상책

⁑hon·ey [hʌ́ni] *n.* **1.** [U] a thick, sweet liquid made by bees from the drops which they collect from flowers. ¶*as sweet as ~.* **2.** [U] sweetness. **3.** [C] a sweetheart. ⇒[N.B.] ¶*my ~.*① —*adj.* of or like honey ; sweet. —*v.* (**-eyed** or **-ied**) *vt.* make (something) sweet with honey. —*vi.* talk sweetly. ▷**hon·ey·like** [-làik] *adj.*
—[名] 1. 꿀 2. 감미로운 것 3. 연인, 애인 [N.B.] 아내·애인 등에 대한 호칭 ¶①여보 —[形] 꿀 같은, 감미로운 —[他] …을 달게 하다 —[自] 달콤하게 이야기하다

hon·ey·bee [hʌ́nibì:] *n.* [C] a bee that makes honey.
—[名] 꿀벌

hon·ey·comb [hʌ́nikòum] *n.* [C] **1.** a wax structure containing rows of six-sided cells made by bees to store honey and their eggs. **2.** anything like a honeycomb. —*adj.* of or like a honeycomb. —*vt.* fill (something) with holes.
—[名] 1. 벌집 2. 벌집 같은 것 —[形] 벌집 같은 —[他] …을 벌집처럼 만들다

hon·ey·dew [hʌ́nid(j)ù:, / -djù:] *n.* **1.** [U] a sweet substance formed on the leaves and stems of certain plants in hot weather. **2.** [C] a kind of melon with a sweet taste.
—[名] 1. 감로(甘露)(식물의 잎에서 나오는 달콤한 즙) 2. 감로멜론

hon·eyed [hʌ́nid] *adj.* **1.** made sweet with honey ; filled or covered with honey. **2.** sweet as honey. ¶*~ words.*
—[形] 1. 꿀투성이의, 꿀로 달게 한 2. 꿀처럼 단

hon·ey·moon [hʌ́nimù:n] *n.* [C] **1.** a holiday spent together by a newly-married couple. **2.** the first month of marriage. **3.** a wedding trip. ¶*They went on a ~.*① —*vi.* have a honeymoon. (*~in* or *at* a place)
—[名] 1. 밀월(蜜月) 2. 신혼의 첫달 3. 신혼여행 ¶①그들은 신혼여행을 갔다 —[自] 신혼여행을 하다

hon·ey·suck·le [hʌ́nisʌ̀kl] *n.* [C] a climbing plant with sweet-smelling white, yellow, or red flowers shaped like trumpets.
—[名] 인동덩굴

Hong Kong, Hong·kong [hɑ́ŋkɑ́ŋ / hɔŋkɔ́ŋ] *n.* a British colony in southeast China.
—[名] 홍콩

hon·ied [hʌ́nid] *adj.* =honeyed.

honk [hɔ:ŋk, hɑŋk / hɔŋk] *n.* [C] **1.** the cry of a wild goose. **2.** any sound like this, as of an automobile horn. —*vi.* make such a sound. ¶*Geese ~.*
—[名] 1. 기러기 울음소리 2. [자동차 따위의] 경적 소리 —[自] 기러기가 울다; 경적을 울리다

Hon·o·lu·lu [hɑ̀nəlú:lu(:) / hɔ̀n-] *n.* the capital of Hawaii on Oahu.
—[名] 호놀룰루

⁑hon·or, *Brit.* **-our** [ɑ́nər / ɔ́nə] *n.* **1.** [U][C] glory ; the source of pride and joy. ¶*the guest of ~*① / *I feel it a great ~ to be invited to this party.*② **2.** [U] credit ; fame ; good reputation. ¶*a matter of ~.*③ **3.** [U] a keen sense of what is right. ¶*a man of ~ / a sense of ~ / conduct oneself with ~.*④ **4.** [U][C] a cause of respect ; a thing to which respect should be paid. ¶*pay* (or *give, show*) *~ to.*⑤ **5.** [U] a high rank or position ; (*H-*) a title of respect given to certain officials, as judges, mayors, etc., with a possessive pronoun before. ⇒[N.B.] ¶*His Honor the Mayor.*⑥ **6.** [C] (usu. *pl.*) a badge ; a sign of
—[名] 1. 명예; 영광 ¶①주빈/②이 파아티에 초대되어 큰 영광으로 생각합니다 2. 체면; 명성 ¶③체면에 관한 문제 3. 도의심 ¶④올바르게 처신하다 4. 존경, 경의 ¶⑤…에 경의를 표하다 5. 고위(高位); 각하 [N.B.] 영국에서는 주로 지방 판사, 미국에서는 거의 모든 재판관에 대한 경칭으로서 Your, His와 함께 씀 ¶⑥시장 각하 6. 훈장; 표창; 의식 7. 우등

H

respect given to a person; ⟪*pl.*⟫ ceremonies of respect. **7.** ⟪*pl.*⟫ special rank given to students who graduate or pass examinations with high marks. ¶*graduate with honors.*

1) ***do** someone **honor; do honor to** someone,* ⓐ show great respect for someone. ⓑ bring or cause honor to someone.
2) ***in honor*** (=*in order to keep the good memory of someone.*)
3) ***on*** (or ***upon***) *one's* [***word of***] ***honor,*** risking one's good name; sincerely.

[熟] 1)ⓐ[남]을 존경하다 ⓑ[남]의 명예가 되다 2)…의 기념으로 3)맹세코, 명예를 걸고

—*vt.* **1.** give an honor to (someone). ⟪~ someone *with*⟫ ¶*He was honored with doctor's degrees.*⑦ / *Will you ~ me with a visit?*⑧ **2.** respect; worship.

—[他] 1. …에게 명예를 주다 ¶⑦그는 박사학위를 받았다/⑧한 번 방문해 주십시오 2. …을 존경하다

⁑hon·or·a·ble, *Brit.* **-our-** [ɑ́n(ə)rəbl / ɔ́n-] *adj.* **1.** honest; upright; noble. ¶*~ conduct.*① **2.** worthy of honor; to be respected. **3.** having a title, rank, or position of honor. **4.** ⟪*H-*⟫ a title of respect before a name. ⇒[N.B.] ¶*the Honorable Mr. Justice King.*② ▷**hon·or·a·ble·ness** [-nis] *n.*

—[形] 1. 훌륭한, 고결한 ¶①훌륭한 행위 2. 존경할 만한 3. 명예가 있는 4. 각하(사람에게 붙이는 경칭) [N.B.] Hon. 으로 줄임 ¶②킹 판사 각하

hon·or·a·bly, *Brit.* **-our-** [ɑ́n(ə)rəbli / ɔ́n-] *adv.* honestly; as to be worthy of respect.

—[副] 훌륭하게, 창피하지 않도록

hon·or·ar·y [ɑ́nərəri / ɔ́n(ə)r-] *adj.* **1.** given or done as a mark of respect. ¶*an ~ degree.*① **2.** having a title or position without receiving pay and often without responsibility. ¶*an ~ member of a club.*②

—[形] 1. 명예[상]의 ¶①명예 학위 2. 명예직의, 무급의 ¶②클럽의 명예 회원

***hood** [hud] *n.* [C] **1.** a soft covering for the head, sometimes part of a cloak. **2.** anything like a hood in shape or use. **3.** a covering over an automobile engine.

—[名] 1. [외투 따위의] 두건 2. 두건 모양의 것 3. [자동차 엔진의] 덮개, 보닛

—*vt.* cover (something) with a hood. ▷**hood·less** [-lis] *adj.* —**hood·like** [-làik] *adj.*

—[他] …을 두건으로 덮다

hood·ed [húdid] *adj.* **1.** wearing a hood. **2.** shaped like a hood.

—[形] 1. 두건을 쓴 2. 두건 모양의

hood·lum [hú:dləm] *n.* [C] (*U.S. colloq.*) a rough, lawless fellow; a rough young person on the street.

—[名] ⟪美口⟫ 불량배, 건달, 깡패

hoo·doo [hú:du:] *n.* (*U.S. colloq.*) **1.** [U] Negro magic. **2.** [C] a person or thing that brings bad luck. **3.** [U] bad luck. **—*vt.*** (*colloq.*) bring bad luck to (someone).

—[名] ⟪美口⟫ 1. 북미 토인의 미신 2. 불행을 가져오는 사람(것) 3. 불운 —[他] ⟪口⟫ …에게 불행을 가져오다

hood·wink [húdwìŋk] *vt.* **1.** mislead (someone) by a trick; deceive. **2.** cover the eyes of (a horse, etc.).

—[他] 1. …을 속이다, …의 눈을 현혹시키다 2. …의 눈을 가리다

H

***hoof** [hu:f, +*U.S.* huf] *n.* [C] (pl. **hoofs** or *rarely* **hooves** [hu:vz]) **1.** a hard covering for the feet of a horse, cattle, sheep, etc. **2.** (*slang*) a man's foot.

—[名] 1. [동물의] 발굽 2. 인간의 발

on the hoof, alive.

[熟] 살아 있는

—*vi.* (*colloq.*) walk; dance. ¶*~ it.*① **—*vt.*** kick (something) with the hoofs. ▷**hoof·er** [-ər] *n.* —**hoof·less** [-lis] *adj.* —**hoof·like** [-làik] *adj.*

—[自] 걷다, 춤추다 ¶①걷다 —[他] …을 발굽으로 차다

hoofed [hu:ft, +*U.S.* huft] *adj.* having hoofs. ¶*~ animals.*①

—[形] 발굽이 있는 ¶①유제(有蹄)동물

⁑hook [huk] *n.* [C] **1.** a curved or bent piece of stiff material serving to catch, hold, or hang something. ¶*a ~ and eye.*① **2.** a trick; a curved piece of wire for catching fish. ¶*a fish ~ / bait a ~.*② **3.** a tool shaped like a hook, esp. a sickle. **4.** (*Boxing*) a short and swinging blow.

—[名] 1. 갈고리; 훅 ¶①옷의 훅 단추 2. 함정, 덫; 낚시바늘 ¶②낚시바늘에 미끼를 달다 3. 갈고리 모양의 도구, 특히 작은 낫 4. ⟪권투⟫ 훅

1) ***above one's hook,*** beyond one's power.
2) ***by hook or by crook,*** in one way or another; somehow.
3) ***get the hook,*** (*slang*) be discharged or dismissed.
4) ***go on the hook,*** neglect one's duty.
5) ***on one's own hook,*** (*colloq.*) by oneself; without the help or advice of others.

[熟] 1)역량 이상으로 2)무슨 수를 쓰든간에 3)⟪俗⟫해고당하다 4)꾀부리다 5)혼자의 힘으로

—*vt.* **1.** fasten or attach (something) with a hook. ¶*~ a door.* **2.** trick. ¶*I've been hooked.* **3.** make or bend (something) in the shape of a hook. **4.** catch (fish, animals, etc.) on or with a hook. ¶*~ a fish.* **5.** (*slang*) steal. **—*vi.*** **1.** curve like a hook. **2.** be fastened with a hook. ¶*The door hooks on the inside.*

—[他] 1. 갈고리(훅)로 …을 걸다 2. …을 계략에 빠뜨리다 3. …을 갈고리 모양으로 구부리다 4. [물고기 따위]를 낚시바늘에 걸다 5. 훔치다
—[自] 1. 갈고리처럼 구부러지다 2. 갈고리가 걸리다

hooked

1) *hook it,* (*slang*) run away.
2) *hook up,* ⓐ connect (something) with a hook or hooks. ⓑ arrange and connect the parts of (a radio, etc.). 2. supplied with hooks.
hooked [hukt] *adj.* 1. curved like a hook. ¶ *a ~ nose.*①
hook·nosed [húknòuzd] *adj.* having a hook-shaped nose.
hook-up [húkʌ̀p] *n.* ⓒ a connection of radio and television stations to send out the same program.
hook·worm [húkwə̀ːrm] *n.* ⓒ a small worm that gets into the bowels and causes a disease. ¶ *~ disease.*①
hoo·li·gan [húːligən] *n.* ⓒ (*slang*) a rough, lawless fellow; a rough young person. ¶ *a ~ gang.*①
hoo·li·gan·ism [húːligənìz(ə)m] *n.* Ⓤ rough, lawless acts.
hoop [huːp, +*U.S.* hup] *n.* ⓒ 1. a ring to hold the strips of wood forming the sides of a tub, barrel or the like. 2. a large circle to be rolled along the ground by a child. 3. (*pl.*) a wire ring used to hold out a woman's skirt. 4. an iron arch in the game of croquet. 5. anything shaped like a hoop.
—*vt.* fasten (something) with hoops. ▷**hoop·like** [-làik] *adj.*
hoop·er [húːpər, +*U.S.* húːp-] *n.* ⓒ a person who makes hoops or puts them on tubs, barrels, etc.
hoo·ray [huréi, +*U.S.* huː-] *interj., n., v.* =hurrah.
hoot [huːt] *n.* ⓒ 1. the cry of an owl. 2. a shout showing an unfavorable feeling. 3. a very small bit. ¶ *be not worth a ~.*①
—*vi.* 1. make the sound of an owl. 2. shout to show an unfavorable feeling or scorn. ((*~ at someone*)) —*vt.* scorn (someone) by hooting; drive (someone) away by hooting. ¶ *The audience hooted the actor off the stage.*
1) *hoot down,* make (someone) silent by hooting.
2) *hoot off* (or *away, out*), drive (someone) away by hooting.
hoot·er [húːtər] *n.* ⓒ 1. an owl. 2. a person who hoots. 3. a siren; a horn.
Hoo·ver Dam [húːvərdǽm] *n.* a dam on the Colorado River between Arizona and Colorado in the United States.
hooves [huːvz, +*U.S.* huvz] *n.* pl. of **hoof**.

‡**hop**¹ [hɑp / hɔp] *v.* (**hopped, hop·ping**) *vi.* move in short jumps with all the feet; jump about on one foot. ¶ *Frogs* (*Birds*) *~.* —*vt.* jump over (a fence, etc.).
—*n.* ⓒ 1. the act of hopping; a short jump. 2. (*colloq.*) a dance or dancing party. 3. (*colloq.*) a flight or short trip in an airplane.
hop off, (*colloq.*) (of an airplane) leave the ground; take off.
hop² [hɑp / hɔp] *n.* ⓒ 1. a vine with green flowers shaped like cones. 2. (*pl.*) the dried flowers of this vine, used to flavor beer, ale, etc. —*v.* (**hopped, hop·ping**) *vi.* pick hops. —*vt.* flavor (beer, etc.) with hops.

‡**hope** [houp] *n.* 1. Ⓤⓒ a desire that what one wishes may be gained; expectation; wish. ↔despair ¶ *lose all ~* / *cherish high hopes of...*① / *I have high hopes that he will succeed.*② / *There is no ~ of success.* 2. ⓒ a person or thing that gives hope to someone. ¶ *He is the ~ of our school.*
1) *be in great hopes that,* desire greatly that....
2) *be past* (or *beyond*) *all hope,* be in a hopelessly bad situation.
3) *in hopes of; in the hope that* (or *of*), in expectation of; having hope of.
—*vt.* desire with a feeling that one's desire may be gained; wish; want. ((*~ to do; ~ that...*)) ¶ *I ~ to see*

hope

圖 1)(俗)뺑소니치다 2)ⓐ훅으로 채우다(채워지다) ⓑ[라디오 따위의] 부분품을 조립하다
—៉ 1. 갈고리 모양의 ¶①매부리코
—៉ 매부리코의 2. 갈고리가 있는
—名 [방송국 사이의] 중계

—名 십이지장충 ¶①십이지장충병

—名 (俗) 난폭자, 불량배, 깡패 ¶①불량단, 폭력단
—名 망나니 행동, 횡포
—名 1. 테, 쇠테 2. [아이들이 굴리며 노는] 굴렁쇠 3. [스커어트 따위를 부풀리는] 버팀 살 4. [크로케의] 활 모양의 작은 문 5. 고리(테) 모양의 것

—他 …에 테를 두르다, …에 친친 감다

—名 테를 메우는 사람, 통장이

—名 1. 부엉(올빼미의 울음소리) 2. 야유, 야단치는 소리 3. 하찮은 것 ¶①조금도 값어치가 없다
—自 1. [올빼미가] 부엉부엉 울다 2. 야유하다, 북새 놓다 …을 조롱하다, …을 야유하여 쫓아 버리다

圖 1)…을 야유하여 침묵시키다 2)…을 야유하여 쫓아버리다

—名 1. 올빼미 2. 야유하는 사람 3. 사이렌, 기적
—名 미국 콜로라도강의 댐

—自 [두 발로] 훌쩍(깡충) 뛰다; [한 발로] 뛰어다니다 —他 [울타리 따위]를 뛰어넘다
—名 1. 깡충 뛰기, 한 발로 뛰기 2. (口) 댄스 [파아티] 3. (口) [비행기의] 1 항정(航程); 짧은 비행기 여행
圖 이륙하다

—名 1. (植) 홉 2. 홉의 말린 꽃 —他 홉의 열매를 따다 —他 [맥주 따위]에 홉으로 맛을 들이다

—名 1. 희망; 기대 ¶①…의 높은 희망을 품다/②그가 성공할 것을 크게 기대하고 있다 2. 희망을 주는 사람(것)

圖 1)…을 크게 기대하고 있다 2)희망이 전혀 없다 3)…을 희망(기대)하여

—他 …을 희망(기대)하다; 바라다, 원하다; 생각하다 —自 바라다; 대망하다

hope chest

you soon. / I ~ that we shall meet here again. —*vi.* have desire or expectation. (*~ for* something) ¶*I ~ for success.* / *I ~ so.*

hope chest [⌒ ⌒] *n.* a box used by a young woman to store things that will be useful after she marries. —명 [처녀의 결혼 준비용] 혼수 상자

• **hope·ful** [hóupf(u)l] *adj.* ↔hopeless **1.** feeling or showing hope; full of expectation. (*~ of* or *about* something; *~ that*...) ¶*He is ~ that he will succeed.* **2.** causing hope; promising. ¶*~ news.*

be hopeful of (or *about*), hope; expect.
—*n.* ⓒ a promising young person; a person with a bright future. ¶*a young ~.*

—형 1. 희망을 거는, 기대하는 ¶①그는 성공할 것을 기대하고 있다 2. 유망한

熟 …을 기대하다
—명 전도 유망한 사람 ¶②앞날이 기대되는 청년

hope·ful·ly [hóupfuli] *adv.* with hope; in a hopeful manner.
hope·ful·ness [hóupf(u)lnis] *n.* Ⓤ the state of being hopeful; hope.

—부 유망하게, 희망을 걸고
—명 유망

• **hope·less** [hóuplis] *adj.* ↔hopeful **1.** feeling no hope. (*~ of doing*) ¶*I am ~ of ever meeting her.* **2.** giving no hope. ¶*a ~ situation.*

be hopeless of (=*do not expect; give up all hope or expectation of*) *something.*

—형 1. 절망적인, 희망을 잃은 ¶①그녀를 만난다는 것은 도저히 생각도 못 한다 2. 가망이 없는
熟 …의 희망을 잃고 있다

hope·less·ly [hóuplisli] *adv.* without hope.
hop·per [hápər / hɔ́pər] *n.* ⓒ **1.** a person or thing that hops. **2.** an insect that hops, such as a grasshopper. **3.** a box with a wide opening in the top and a small hole in the bottom through which something is carried into a machine.
hop·ping [hápiŋ / hɔ́p-] *adj.* moving in short leaps; jumping about; limping.
hop·scotch [hápskàtʃ / hɔ́pskɔ̀tʃ] *n.* Ⓤ a children's game in which the players hop about in a design drawn on the ground.

—부 절망적으로, 희망 없이
—명 1. 한 발로 뛰는 사람(것) 2. [귀뚜라미처럼] 깡충깡충 뛰는 벌레 3. 깔때기 모양의 그릇

—형 깡충깡충 뛰는; 절름발이의
—명 돌차기놀이

Hor·ace [hɔ́:ris, hár- / hɔ́r-] *n.* a man's name.
horde [hɔ:rd] *n.* ⓒ **1.** a crowd. ¶*a ~ of wolves.* **2.** a wandering group of people. ¶*a gypsy ~.*

• **ho·ri·zon** [həráizn] *n.* ⓒ **1.** the line where the earth and sky seem to meet. **2.** the limit of one's thinking, experience, etc. ¶*Science gives us a new ~.*

• **hor·i·zon·tal** [hɔ̀:rizánt(ə)l, hàri- / hɔ̀rizɔ́n-] *adj.* ↔vertical **1.** running straight and parallel to the horizon. **2.** flat; level. —*n.* ⓒ a horizontal line.
hor·i·zon·tal·ly [hɔ̀:rizántəli, hàr- / hɔ̀r-] *adv.* like a horizontal line.

—명 남자 이름
—명 1. 큰 떼 2. 유목민의 무리 ¶① 집시의 무리
—명 1. 지(수)평선 2. [생각 따위의] 범위, 한계; 시야(視野)

—형 1. 지평의, 수평의 2. 평면의
—명 수평선, 지평선

—부 수평으로, 가로로

hor·mone [hɔ́:rmoun] *n.* ⓒ a chemical material formed in certain parts of the body and carried by the blood, influencing growth, the action of organs, etc.

—명 호르몬

‡ **horn** [hɔ:rn] *n.* ⓒ **1.** a hard bone-like material on the heads of cattle, goats, sheep, etc. **2.** the long, pointed, but not hard objects on the heads of some animals. ¶*a snail's ~.* **3.** a thing or container made of horn. ¶*a drinking ~.* **4.** a musical instrument played by blowing. **5.** an instrument that makes a loud sound as a warning signal. ¶*blow an automobile ~ / a fog ~.* **6.** anything shaped like a horn, as a new moon.

1) *blow one's own horn,* boast.
2) *draw* (or *pull*) *in one's horns,* become less active.
3) *on the horns of a dilemma,* forced to chose between two painful situations.
4) *show one's horns,* show one's real character.

—*adj.* made of horn. ¶*~* (something). ¶*~ in.*
—*vt.* hit (something) with horns; provide horns for.
horned [hɔ́:rnd, +*Brit.* hɔ́:nid] *adj.* having a horn or horns; like a horn. ¶*a ~ owl.*
hor·net [hɔ́:rnit] *n.* ⓒ **1.** a large bee-like insect whose sting is very severe. ¶*bring a hornets' nest about one's ears; stir up a hornets' nest.* **2.** an annoying person.

—명 1. 뿔 2. [동물의] 촉각 ¶①달팽이의 촉각 3. 뿔로 만든 기구 ¶②뿔 술잔 4. 각적(角笛), 호른 5. 경적 ¶③ 차의 경적을 울리다 / ④무적(霧笛) 6. 뿔 모양의 것(특히 초승달의 첨단 따위)

熟 1)자화자찬하다 2)[으스대던 사람이] 풀이 죽게 되다 3)딜레머에 빠져, 진퇴유곡에 빠져 4)본성을 드러내다

—형 뿔로 만든
—타 …뿔로 받다; …에 뿔을 달다
¶⑤주제넘게 나서다
—형 뿔이 있는, 뿔 모양의 ¶①수리부엉이
—명 1. 말벌 ¶①시끄러운 사태를 야기하다; 적을 많이 만들다 2. 골칫거리

hornless [hɔ́:rnlis] *adj.* having no horns. —֎ 뿔이 없는

horn·pipe [hɔ́:rnpàip] *n.* ⓒ **1.** a lively dance formerly popular among sailors. **2.** the music for it. **3.** an old musical instrument played by blowing. —֎ 1. [선원 사이에서 유행하던] 활발한 춤 2. 그 춤곡 3. 나무 피리의 일종

horn·y [hɔ́:rni] *adj.* (**horn·i·er, horn·i·est**) **1.** made of horn. **2.** hard like a horn. ¶*My hands got ~ from hard work.*① **3.** with horns. —֎ 1. 뿔로 만든 2. 뿔처럼 굳은 ¶①두 손 끝이 거친 일을 하여 굳어진 3. 뿔이 있는

horn·y-hand·ed [hɔ́:rnihǽndid] *adj.* with hands that are hard like horns. —֎ [막일을 하여] 손이 굳어진

hor·o·scope [hɔ́:rəskòup, hár- / hɔ́r-] *n.* ⓒ **1.** the position of the stars at the hour of someone's birth, as influencing his life. ¶*cast (read) a ~.*① **2.** an observation of the sky at a certain time, used in telling fortunes by the stars. —֎ 1. 천궁도(天宮圖), 십이궁도 ¶① [천궁도를 써서] 별점을 치다 2. 별점

* **hor·ri·ble** [hɔ́:ribl, hár- / hɔ́r-] *adj.* **1.** causing horror; terrible; dreadful. ¶*a ~ sight.* **2.** (*colloq.*) very unpleasant. ¶*a ~ headache / ~ weather.* ▷ **hor·ri·ble·ness** [-nis] *n.* —֎ 1. 무서운 2. 불쾌한

hor·ri·bly [hɔ́:ribli, hár- / hɔ́r-] *adv.* **1.** in a horrible manner; terribly; dreadfully. **2.** (*colloq.*) very; extremely. —֎ 1. 무섭게, 소름이끼칠 만큼 2. 《口》 몹시, 극단적으로

* **hor·rid** [hɔ́:rid, hár- / hɔ́r-] *adj.* **1.** terrible; frightful. **2.** (*colloq.*) very unpleasant. —֎ 1. 무서운, 오싹하는 2. 《口》 지독한, 아주 싫은

hor·ri·fy [hɔ́:rifài, hár- / hɔ́r-] *vt.* (**-fied**) **1.** fill (someone) with horror. ¶*I was horrified to see the scene.*① **2.** (*colloq.*) give a shock to (someone). —֎ 1. …을 무서워하게 하다 ¶①그 광경을 보고 오싹했다 2. …을 분개시키다

‡ **hor·ror** [hɔ́:rər, hár- / hɔ́rə] *n.* **1.** Ⓤ a strong fear or dread. ¶*in ~*① */ much to one's ~*② */ The story filled her with ~.* **2.** Ⓤ ⓒ a strong dislike or disgust. **3.** ⓒ a thing or person that causes horror. ¶*the horrors*③ */ the ~ of war.*④ **4.** ⓒ (*colloq.*) something very bad or unpleasant. —֎ 1. 공포, 전율 ¶①공포에 싸여/②오싹한 것은 2. 몸서리칠 만큼 싫음 3. 지긋지긋하게 싫은 사람(것) ¶③[중독의] 발작/④전쟁의 참화 4. 우울, 공포

have a horror of, dislike (something) very much. 熟 …을 몹시 싫어하다

hor·ror-strick·en [hɔ́:rərstrìk(ə)n, hár- / hɔ́rə-] *adj.* stricken with horror; horrified. —֎ 공포에 사로잡힌, 전율하는

hor·ror-struck [hɔ́:rərstrʌ̀k, hár- / hɔ́r-] *adj.* = horror-| stricken.|

hors d'oeu·vre [ɔ:rdə́:v / ɔ:də́:vr] *n.* (pl. ~ **d'oeuvres**) 《usu. *pl.*》 light food served before the main courses of a meal. —֎ 오르되브르, 전채(前菜)

‡ **horse** [hɔ:rs] ⓒ **1.** a large, strong animal with four legs, used for carrying loads, riding, etc. **2.** Ⓤ (*collectively*) soldiers on horses; cavalry. ¶*light ~*① */ There were one hundred ~.* **3.** (*Gymnastics*) a padded block on legs, used for jumping over. **4.** a frame with legs to support something. —֎ 1. 말 2. 기병[대] ¶①경기병 3. 목마 4. [체조용] 목마; 톱질 모탕; 물건을 거는 대(臺)

1) *back the wrong horse,* ⓐ bet on a horse that loses the race. ⓑ give support to the losing side.
2) *eat like a horse,* eat very much.
3) *flog* (or *mount on*) *a dead horse,* waste one's energies. |different matter.|
4) *a horse of another* (or *a different*) *color,* quite a|
5) *mount* (or *ride*) *the high horse; be on* one's *high horse,* behave in a very proud manner.
6) *play horse with,* treat (someone) rudely.
7) *put* (or *set*) *the cart before the horse,* do or put something in the wrong order; take the effect for|
8) *To horse!,* Get on your horse! |the cause.|

熟 1)ⓐ[경마에서] 지는 말에 걸다 ⓑ약자 편을 들다 2)대식(大食)하다 3)헛수고를 하다 4)전혀 다른 [성질의] 일 5)거만하게 굴다 6)버릇없이 대하다 7)본말(本末)을 전도하다 8)[구령으로] 승마!

—*vt.* **1.** supply (a carriage) with a horse or horses; put (something) on horseback. **2.** beat (someone) with a whip. —*vi.* ride on a horse; go on horseback. —֎ 1. [마차]에 말을 매다; …을 말에 태우다 2. …을 매질하다 —֍ 말에 타다; 말 타고 가다

* **horse·back** [hɔ́:rsbæ̀k] *n.* Ⓤ the back of a horse. ¶*go on ~.*① —*adv.* on the back of a horse. —֎ 말 등 ¶①말을 타고 가다 —֍ 말을 타고

horse·break·er [hɔ́:rsbrèikər] *n.* ⓒ a person who gives training to horses. —֎ 조마사(調馬師)

horse chestnut [ˊ ˋ] *n.* 1. a spreading shade tree with large leaves, white flowers, and reddish-brown seeds. 2. the seed of this tree. 「horses.」
— ⓝ 1. 마로니에 2. 그 열매

horse dealer [ˊ ˋ] *n.* a person who buys and sells
— ⓝ 말장수

horse·flesh [hɔ́:rsflèʃ] *n.* ⓤ 1. ((collectively)) horses. 2. the flesh of horses. 「horses and cattle.」
— ⓝ 1. 말 2. 말고기

horse·fly [hɔ́:rsflài] *n.* ⓒ (pl. -**flies**) a large fly that bites
— ⓝ 말파리, 등에

horse·hair [hɔ́:rshɛ̀ər] *n.* ⓤ 1. the long hair growing on the neck or tail of a horse. 2. a hard cloth made of this hair; haircloth.
— ⓝ 1. [갈기와 꼬리의] 말총, 말털 2. 말총으로 짠 직물

horse laugh [ˊ ˋ] *n.* a loud, rude laugh.
— ⓝ 너털웃음

・**horse·man** [hɔ́:rsmən] *n.* ⓒ (pl. -**men** [-mən]) 1. a man who rides on horseback. 2. a man skilled in managing or riding horses.
— ⓝ 1. 기수(騎手) 2. 승마의 명수

horse·man·ship [hɔ́:rsmənʃìp] *n.* ⓤ the art or skill of riding or managing horses. ¶ *feasts of ~*.①
— ⓝ 승마술 ¶①말의 곡예

horse·play [hɔ́:rsplèi] *n.* ⓤ rough, noisy fun.
— ⓝ 북새통, 난장판

horse·pow·er [hɔ́:rspàuər] *n.* ⓒ (pl. -**pow·er**) a unit of the power of engines, motors. etc. ⇒ N.B.
— ⓝ 마력(馬力) N.B. hp., h.p., Hp, H.P. 따위로 줄임

horse race [ˊ ˋ] *n.* a race by horses as a sport.
— ⓝ [1회의] 경마

horse·rad·ish [hɔ́:rsrædiʃ] *n.* 1. ⓒ a tall plant with a white, hot-tasting root. 2. ⓤ the flavor made of this root. 「sense.」
— ⓝ 1. 서양 고추냉이(식물) 2. 서양 고추냉이(양념)

horse sense [ˊ ˋ] *n.* (colloq.) plain, practical common
— ⓝ (口) 주먹구구식 상식, 속된 상식

horse·shoe [hɔ́:rsʃùː, hɔ́:rʃʃùː] *n.* ⓒ 1. a flat, U-shaped metal shoe to protect a horse's hoof. 2. anything shaped like a horseshoe. ¶ *a ~ magnet*.② 3. (*pl.* used as *sing.*) a game in which the players throw horseshoes at a post 40 feet away.
— *vt.* put horseshoes on (a horse's hoof).
— ⓝ 1. 편자, 제철(蹄鐵) 2. U자형의 것 ¶①U자형 자석 3. 편자 던지기 놀이
— ⓥ [말에] 편자를 박다

horse·tail [hɔ́:rstèil] *n.* ⓒ 1. a horse's tail. 2. a flowerless plant with hollow, jointed stems.
— ⓝ 1. 말꼬리 2. 속새속(屬)의 식물

horse·whip [hɔ́:rs(h)wìp] *n.* ⓒ a leather whip for driving or controlling horses. — *vt.* (-**whipped**, -**whip·ping**) beat (a horse, man, etc.) with a horsewhip.
— ⓝ 말 채찍 — ⓥ [말・사람 따위]를 채찍으로 때리다, 징벌하다

horse·wom·an [hɔ́:rswùmən] *n.* ⓒ (pl. -**wom·en** [-wìmin]) 1. a woman who rides on horseback. 2. a woman skilled in managing or riding horses.
— ⓝ 1. 여자 기수(騎手) 2. 여자 승마 명수

hors·y [hɔ́:rsi] *adj.* (**hors·i·er, hors·i·est**) 1. of or having to do with horses; like horses. 2. fond of horses or horse racing. 「gardening.」
— ⓐ 1. 말의, 말 같은 2. 말을 좋아하는, 경마광의

hor·ti·cul·tur·al [hɔ̀:rtikʌ́ltʃ(u)rəl] *adj.* of the art of
— ⓐ 원예[술]의

hor·ti·cul·ture [hɔ́:rtikʌ̀ltʃər] *n.* ⓤ the art or science of growing flowers, fruits, vegetables, etc.
— ⓝ 원예[술・학]

hor·ti·cul·tur·ist [hɔ̀:rtikʌ́ltʃ(u)rist] *n.* ⓒ a person skilled in gardening. 「God.」
— ⓝ 원예가

ho·san·na [houzǽnə] *interj., n.* ⓒ a shout of praise to
— ⓝⓘ 신을 찬미하는 말

hose [houz] *n.* ⓒⓤ 1. (pl. **hose**) ((pl.)) stockings. 2. (pl. **hoses** [hóuziz] or **hose**) a tube of rubber, used to carry water, etc., for a short distance. ¶ *by means of a ~*① / *a fire ~*.②
— *vt.* put water on (something) with a hose.
— ⓝ 1. 긴 양말 2. [소방・살수용의] 호오스 ¶①호오스로/②소방 호오스
— ⓥ [호오스로] …에 물을 뿌리다

ho·sier [hóuʒər] *n.* ⓒ a person who makes or sells men's socks, underwear, etc.
— ⓝ 양품상

ho·sier·y [hóuʒəri] *n.* ⓤ 1. ((collectively)) articles sold by a hosier. 2. business of a hosier.
— ⓝ 1. 양말 2. 양말(메리야스) 장수

hos·pice [háspis / hɔ́s-] *n.* ⓒ 1. a place of shelter for travelers, esp. one kept by a religious order. 2. a home for the poor, the sick, etc.
— ⓝ 1. [순례자가 묵는] 숙박소, 접대소 2. [병자・극빈자 등의] 수용소, 양육원

hos·pi·ta·ble [háspitəbl / hɔ́s-] *adj.* 1. giving a kind and generous welcome to guests or strangers. ¶ *~ entertainment*.① 2. favorably receptive or open. ¶ *He is ~ to new ideas.*② 「ously ; in a hospitable manner.」
— ⓐ 1. [손님・남을] 환대하는 ¶①후대 2. 쾌히 받아들이는 ¶②그는 새로운 생각을 잘 받아들인다

hos·pi·ta·bly [háspitəbli / hɔ́s-] *adv.* kindly and gener-
— ⓓ 친절하게, 환대하여

‡**hos·pi·tal** [háspit(ə)l / hɔ́s-] *n.* [C] **1.** a place for the treatment and care of the sick or the injured. ¶*a general* ~① / *a mental* ~② / *enter* (*leave*) [*the*] ~.③ / *He is in* (*out of*) [*the*] ~.④ ⇒[usage] **2.** a similar place for animals. **3.** (*Brit.*) a charitable institution for the poor, the aged, etc.
—[名] 1. 병원 ¶①종합병원/②정신병원/③입원(퇴원)하다/④그는 입원(퇴원)하고 있다 [usage] 미국에서는 입원·퇴원에 the를 붙이는 일이 많음 2. 가축병원 3. 양육원, 구호원

***hos·pi·tal·i·ty** [hàspitǽliti / hɔ̀s-] *n.* [U] the state of being hospitable; warm, friendly treatment given to guests.
—[名] 환대, 대접

hos·pi·tal·ize [háspitəlàiz / hɔ́s-] *vt.* put (someone) in a hospital.
—[他] …을 입원시키다

***host**[1] [houst] *n.* [C] **1.** a person who entertains guests warmly at his own house. ↔guest ¶*act as* ~.① **2.** a keeper of an inn or a hotel. **3.** a plant or an animal in or on which another lives.
—[名] 1. [손님을 접대하는] 주인 ¶①주인 노릇을 하다 2. [여관의] 주인 3. [기생 동·식물의] 숙주(宿主)

reckon (or ***count***) ***without one's host,*** forget to consider the effect of an important thing.
[熟] 중요한 점을 빠뜨리고 결론을 내리다

***host**[2] [houst] *n.* [C] a great number. ¶*a* ~ *of friends*① / *the heavenly* ~② / *the Lord of Hosts.*③
—[名] 무리, 다수 ¶①많은 친구들/②천사군(群); 천체(天體)/③천신(天神)

hos·tage [hástidʒ / hɔ́s-] *n.* [C] **1.** a person held by an enemy as an assurance that certain things will be carried out. ¶*be held as* ~① / *hostages to fortune.*② **2.** pledge; security.
—[名] 1. 인질 ¶①인질로 잡혀 있다/②운명의 인질(처자·재산 따위 잃을지도 모를 허무한 것) 2. 저당 담보

hos·tel [hást(ə)l / hɔ́s-] *n.* [C] a lodging place, esp. for young people on trips, hikes, etc.; an inn. ¶*a youth* ~.
—[名] [청년 남녀용] 숙박소, 합숙소; 기숙사

hos·tel·ry [hást(ə)lri / hɔ́s-] *n.* [C] (pl. **-ries**) (*archaic*) an inn; a hotel.
—[名] 여관, 여인숙

***host·ess** [hóustis] *n.* [C] **1.** a woman who receives and entertains guests. **2.** a woman who keeps an inn, etc. **3.** a woman employed to entertain or dance with guests.
—[名] 1. 여주인 2. 여관의 안주인 3. 접대부, 호스테스

***hos·tile** [hást(i)l / hɔ́stail] *adj.* of or like an enemy; opposed; unfriendly. ¶*a man* ~ *to reform*① / *He was* ~ *to our plan.*② ▷**hos·tile·ly** [-i] *adv.*
—[形] 적(敵)의; 적의를 품은, 반대하는 ¶①개혁에 반대하는 사람/②그는 우리 계획에 적의를 품었다

hos·til·i·ty [hastíliti / hɔs-] *n.* [U][C] (pl. **-ties**) **1.** a feeling as an enemy; opposition; unfriendliness. ¶*a personal* ~ *to the system.*① **2.** (usu. *pl.*) the state of being at war; warfare. ¶*cease* (*open*) *hostilities.*②
—[名] 1. 적의, 적개심; 반대 ¶①제도에 대한 개인적인 적개심 2. 적대 3. 교전 ¶②정전(개전)하다

hos·tler [(h)áslər, ás- / ɔ́slə] *n.* [C] a person who takes care of horses at an inn.
—[名] [여관의] 마굿간지기, 마부

‡**hot** [hat / hɔt] *adj.* (**hot·ter, hot·test**) **1.** having or giving heat; of a high temperature. ↔cold ¶*a cup of* ~ *tea* / *a* ~ *day* / *a spell of* ~ *weather.*① **2.** (*colloq.*) new; fresh; recent. ¶~ *news* / ~ *from the front.*② **3.** producing a burning sensation in the mouth, throat, etc. ¶~ *pepper.* **4.** excitable; passionate; angry. ¶*get* ~③/ *a* ~ *struggle.*④ **5.** (*slang*) excellent; good.
—[形] 1. 더운; 뜨거운 ¶①오랜 더위 2. 《口》 새로운; 최근의 ¶②전선에서 갓 돌아온 3. 매운, 얼얼한 4. 흥분하기 쉬운, [성미가] 격렬한, 성난 ¶③흥분하다/④격전 5. 《口》 아주 좋은, 멋진

1) ***be in hot water,*** be in trouble; have difficulties.
2) ***get it hot,*** (*colloq.*) be scolded severely.
3) ***hot and heavy; hot and strong,*** violently; severely.
4) ***make it*** [***too***] ***hot*** (=*make the situation extremely uncomfortable*) ***for someone.***

[熟] 1)고생하고 있다 2)《口》호되게 꾸지람듣다 3)맹렬히 4)남을 견디지 못하게 하다

—*adv.* in a hot manner.
—[副] 덥게, 뜨겁게; 맹렬히

hot·bed [hátbèd / hɔ́t-] *n.* [C] **1.** a bed of earth usu. covered with glass and kept warm for growing plants out of season. **2.** any place suitable for the rapid growth of something evil. ¶*a* ~ *of juvenile delinquency.*①
—[名] 1. 온상 2. [범죄·악습 따위의] 온상 ¶①소년 범죄의 온상

hot-blood·ed [hátblʌ́did / hɔ́t-] *adj.* easily excited or made angry; passionate.
—[形] 성미 급한, 화 잘 내는, 열렬한, 정열적인

hot cake [ˊ ˋ] *n.* a pancake; a griddlecake.
—[名] 호트케이크

hotch·potch [hátʃpàtʃ / hɔ́tʃpɔ̀tʃ] *n.* =hodgepodge.

hot dog [ˊ ˋ] *n.* (*colloq.*) sandwich made of a hot sausage in a split roll.
—[名] 뜨거운 소시지를 넣은 길쭉한 식빵

‡**ho·tel** [houtél / (h)outél] *n.* [C] a house or large building providing lodging, food, etc. ¶*run a* ~① / *put up at a* ~ / *stay at a* ~ / *The group of foreign sight-seers*
—[名] 호텔 ¶①호텔을 경영하다

H

is staying in the lake-side ~.

ho·tel·keep·er [houtélkì:pər / (h)outélkì:pə] *n.* [C] a person who keeps a hotel.
—[名] 호텔 경영자

hot·head [háthéd / hɔ́t-] *n.* [C] a quick-tempered person.
—[名] 성급한 사람

hot·head·ed [háthèdid / hɔ́t-] *adj.* quick-tempered; easily excited. ▷**hot·head·ed·ly** [-li] *adv.*
—[形] 성급한, 흥분 잘 하는

hot·house [háthàus / hɔ́t-] *n.* [C] a building covered with glass, kept warm for growing plants; a greenhouse.
—[名] 온실

hot·ly [hátli / hɔ́t-] *adv.* in a hot manner; with heat.
—[副] 덥게, 뜨겁게, 격렬하게

hot·ness [hátnis / hɔ́t-] *n.* [U] the quality of being hot; heat.
—[名] 뜨거움, 더위, 열렬, 격분

hot spring [⌐ ⌐] *n.* a natural spring having waters warmer than 98°F.
—[名] 온천

hot·spur [hátspə̀:r / hɔ́tspə̀:] *n.* [C] a thoughtless or reckless person; a hothead.
—[名] 성미 급한 사람, 무모한 사람

hot war [⌐ ⌐] *n.* a war characterized by actual fighting. ↔cold war
—[名] 열전(熱戰), 본격적인 전쟁

hot water [⌐ ⌐-] *n.* (*colloq.*) trouble.
—[名] 《口》 [스스로 초래한] 곤란

***hound** [haund] *n.* [C] **1.** a hunting dog of several breeds, most of which hunt by scent. ¶*follow hounds; ride to hounds.*① **2.** a scornful person. —*vt.* **1.** hunt (an animal, etc.) with hounds; chase. **2.** urge. 《~ someone *on*》 ¶*~ someone on his work.* **3.** incite (a hound, etc.) to pursuit or attack. ¶*~ a dog at someone.*
—[名] 1. 사냥개 ¶①[말을 타고] 사냥개를 앞세워 사냥을 하다 2. 비열한 놈 —[他] 1. …을 사냥개로 사냥하다; …을 추적하다 2. …을 격려하다 3. …에게 …을 부추기다

‡**hour** [auər] *n.* [C] **1.** sixty minutes. ¶*an hour's walk (work) / half an ~ / every two hours.*① **2.** the time of day expressed in hours [and minutes]. ¶*at an early (a late) ~*② */ The ~ is 5 : 30. / The clock has struck the ~.*③ **3.** an appointed or particular time of day. ¶*the ~ of his death.*④ **4.** one's customary and usual time of doing something. ¶*the dinner ~.* **5.** 《*pl.*》 a fixed period of time for work, study, etc. ¶*business (school) hours.*⑤ **6.** a short or limited period of time; a class period. ¶*The ~ lasted 50 minutes.*⑥ **7.** 《usu. *pl.*》 a period in one's lifetime. ¶*The happiest hours of my life were spent in Paris.* **8.** an hour's journey or ride. ¶*The town is an ~ from here.*⑦ **9.** the time of death. ¶*His ~ has come.*⑧
1) ***after hours,*** after the regular hours for school, business, etc.
2) ***at the eleventh hour,*** at the last moment.
3) ***hour by hour,*** each hour; momentarily.
4) ***in a good*** (or ***happy***) ***hour,*** fortunately.
5) ***keep bad*** (or ***late***) ***hours,*** rise and go to bed late.
6) ***keep good early hours,*** rise and go to bed early.
7) ***on the hour,*** just at a certain o'clock; sharp.
8) ***the small hours,*** the early hours of the morning between one and three o'clock.

—[名] 1. 한 시간, 60 분 ¶①두 시간마다 2. 시간, 시각 ¶②이른(늦은) 시각에/ ③시계가 시각을 쳤다 3. 특정의 시간 ¶④그의 죽음의 시각 4. 습관적으로 어떤 일을 하는 시각 5. [업무 따위의] 시간 ¶⑤영업(수업) 시간 6. 짧은 시간; 수업[의 한 시간] ¶⑥수업은 50 분 계속됐다 7. 인생의 한 시기 8. 한 시간의 노정(路程) ⑦마을까지는 여기에서 1 시간이 걸린다 9. 죽을 때, 임종시 ¶⑧그가 죽을 때가 왔다

[熟] 1)수업(근무)시간이 끝나고 2)마지막 순간에 3)시간마다 4)운좋게 5)밤늦게 자고 늦잠 자다 6)일찍 자고 일찍 일어나다 7)정각에, 여김없이 8)오전 한 시에서 세 시까지의 새벽

hour·glass [áuərglæ̀s / áuəglɑ̀:s] *n.* [C] a glass instrument containing water, sand, etc., used for measuring time.
—[名] 물시계, 모래시계

hour hand [⌐ ⌐] *n.* the short hand on a clock or watch to show the hour. ⇒[N.B.]
—[名] [시계의] 시침, 단침 [N.B.] 분침은 minute hand

hour·ly [áuərli] *adj.* **1.** happening every hour. **2.** frequent. —*adv.* **1.** every hour; hour by hour; once an hour. **2.** very often.
—[形] 1. 시간마다의, 매시간의 2. 끊임없는 —[副] 1. 한 시간마다 2. 끊임없이

‡**house** *n.* [haus →*v.*] [C] (pl. **hous·es** [háuziz]) **1.** a building for people to live in. ⇒[N.B.] ¶*a large ~ / a ~ for rent* (or *to let*) / A *man's ~ is his castle.* **2.** an inn; a theater. ¶*an opera ~.*① **3.** 《*collectively*》 audience. ¶*There was a full (poor) ~ for the show.*② */ He spoke to a full ~.* **4.** people living in a house; household; family. **5.** a line of ancestors and descendants. ¶*the ~ of Tudor.*③ **6.** 《*H-*》 a law-making body or group. ¶*the House of Representatives.*④ **7.** a place of business; a business company.
1) ***bring down the house,*** (*colloq.*) receive loud praise from the audience.
2) ***clean house,*** do away with undesirable conditions.
3) ***keep house,*** ⓐ take care of the affairs of a home.

—[名] 1. 집 [N.B.] house 는 건물로서의 집. home 은 「가정」의 뜻. 미국에서는 양쪽을 자유로 쓰는 경향이 있음 2. 여관, 극장 ¶①오페라 극장 3. 관객 ¶②쇼우에는 관객이 많았다(적었다) 4. 가정; 가족 5. 가계(家系) ¶③튜우더가(家) 6. 의회 ¶④하원 7. 상사(商社); 회사

[熟] 1)관중에게서 큰 갈채를 받다 2)질서있게 정돈하다 3)ⓐ살림을 꾸려나가다 ⓑ가정을 가지다 4)오는 사람

ⓑ start housekeeping.
4) ***keep open house,*** entertain as guests all those who come at any time.
5) ***keep the*** (or *one's*) ***house,*** always stay at home.
6) ***like a house on fire*** (or ***afire***), with great speed or energy.
7) ***on the house,*** free to the customers; let the customers eat for nothing at a restaurant, etc.
8) ***set***(or ***put***) *one's* ***house in order,*** =clean house.

은 누구나 환영하다 5)집에 틀어박혀 있다 6)자꾸자꾸; 왕성하게 7)공짜로; [음식 따위] 가게에서 거저 주는 8)질서를 회복하다

—*vt.* [hauz] **1.** furnish (someone) with a house. **2.** receive (someone) in a house. ¶*I housed him for a night.* **3.** store in a house. —*vi.* take shelter; live; dwell.

—[他] 1. …에 집을 주다 2. …을 수용하다; 재워 주다 3. [물건]을 저장하다; 간수해 두다 —[自] 묵다; 살다

house·boat [háusbòut] *n.* [C] a boat that can be used as a dwelling.
—[名] 주거용의 집같이 생긴 배

house·break·er [háusbrèikər] *n.* [C] a person who breaks into a house to steal. ⇒[N.B.]
—[名] 대낮의 강도, 낮도둑 [N.B.] 밤도둑은 burglar

house builder [⌐ ⌐–] *n.* a person whose business is to build houses.
—[名] 건축업자, 목수

house duty [⌐ ⌐–] *n.* tax which a person must pay for his own house.
—[名] 가옥세

house·fly [háusflài] *n.* [C] (pl. **-flies**) a common fly that lives around and in houses.
—[名] 집파리

• **house·hold** [háus(h)òuld] *n.* [C] **1.** all the persons living in a house; family; family and servants. **2.** ⟪*the H-*⟫ such a family or group of royal blood. —*adj.* of a household; domestic. ¶~ *affairs*① / *a* ~ *word.*②
—[名] 1. 가족, 집안 사람들 2. 황실, 왕실 —[形] 가족의, 집안의 ¶①집안일/②일상 흔히 쓰는 말

house·hold·er [háus(h)òuldər] *n.* [C] a person who owns a house; the head of a family.
—[名] 호주, 세대주, 가장

⁑ **house·keep·er** [háuskì:pər] *n.* [C] **1.** a woman who takes care of a home and its affairs. **2.** an upper-class servant who directs the housework servants.
—[名] 1. 주부 2. 하녀 우두머리

house·keep·ing [háuskì:piŋ] *n.* [U] the act of taking care of a household; the act of doing the housework.
—[名] 가정(家政), 가사

⁑ **house·maid** [háusmèid] *n.* [C] a woman servant employed for housework.
—[名] 하녀, 가정부

house·mast·er [háusmæ̀stər / -mà:stə] *n.* [C] the master of a house; the head of a family.
—[名] 호주, 가장

house·moth·er [háusmʌ̀ðər] *n.* [C] a woman who takes care of a group of people living together.
—[名] 여자 사감(舍監)

house party [⌐ ⌐–] *n.* **1.** an entertainment of guests staying overnight or longer. **2.** the guests at such a party.
—[名] 1. [별장 따위의] 머무르는 손님을 위한 연회 2. [그러한] 손님의 일단

house-to-house [háustəháus] *adj.* conducted from one house to the next. ¶~ *visits.*①
—[形] 집집마다의 ¶①호별 방문

house·top [háustàp / -tɔ̀p] *n.* [C] the top or roof of a house. ¶*cry* (or *proclaim*) *from the housetops.*①
—[名] 지붕 ¶①세상에 퍼뜨리다

house·warm·ing [háuswɔ̀:rmiŋ] *n.* [C] a party given on moving into a new house.
—[名] 집들이[잔치]

• **house·wife** *n.* [C] **1.** [háuswàif →2.] (pl. **-wives**) a woman who takes care of a home and its affairs. **2.** [hʌ́zif] (pl. **-wifes** or **-wives**) a small case for needles, thread, etc.
—[名] 1. 주부 2. 반짇고리

house·wife·ly [háuswàifli] *adj.* of or like a housewife.
—[形] 주부의, 주부다운

house·wives [háuswàivz] *n.* pl. of **housewife**.

house·work [háuswə̀:rk] *n.* [U] the work of housekeeping, such as washing, cleaning, and cooking.
—[名] 가사

hous·ing [háuziŋ] *n.* [U] **1.** the act of providing houses as homes; the act of giving homes to people. **2.** ⟪*collectively*⟫ houses. ¶*the* ~ *problem.*① **3.** a cover or shelter. **4.** a protective cover or container of a machine.
—[名] 1. 주택 공급 2. 집, 주택 ¶①주택 문제 3. 덮개 4. [기계의] 틀, 가구(架構)

hove [houv] *v.* pt. and pp. of **heave**.

hov·el [hʌ́v(ə)l, háv(ə)l / hɔ́v(ə)l, hʌ́v(ə)l] *n.* [C] **1.** a small, dirty house; a hut. **2.** a shed for cattle, tools, etc.
—[名] 1. 오두막집 2. [가축의] 우리; [연장을 넣어 두는] 헛간, 광

• **hov·er** [hʌ́vər, hávər / hɔ́və, hʌ́və] *vi.* **1.** stay or fly in the air near one place. ⟪~ *about* or *over* a place⟫ ¶*The bird hovered over its nest.*① **2.** stay or wait nearby. ⟪~ *about* (or *around, near*) someone or a place⟫ **3.** be in
—[自] 1. [새 따위가] 일정한 장소를 중심으로 날다 ¶①새가 둥지 위를 날아다니다 2. 배회하다 3. 불확실한 상태에 있다; 망설이다, ¶②생사의 경계를 헤

an uncertain condition; hesitate. 《~ *between* two things》 ¶~ *between life and death.*②

매다

⁑how [hau] *adv.* **1.** in what way or manner; by what means. ¶*How shall we begin it?*① | *How do you say this in English?* | *I don't know ~ to solve the problem.* | *Be careful ~ you act.*② **2.** in what state or condition. ¶*How are you getting along?*③ | *Tell me ~ Mr. Clark is.* **3.** 《with *adj.* or *adv.*》 to what degree, extent, or amount; at what rate. ¶*How long will it take you to do this?* | *How damaged is the car?* **4.** 《in *exclamations*》 very; greatly; surprisingly. ¶*How beautiful this flower is!* | *How she talks!*④ **5.** for what reason or purpose; why. ¶*I can't see ~ he came to do it.*⑤ | *How is it that they are late in coming?*⑥ **6.** to what effect; with what meaning. ¶*How do you mean?*⑦ **7.** by what name. ¶*We know ~ he is called among them.* **8.** for what price; at what sum. ¶*I inquired ~ the stock sold.* **9.** (*colloq.*) What?; I beg your pardon? ¶*How?*⑧ **10.** however; in whatever manner. ⇒[usage] ¶*Run ~ fast he will ....*⑨ | *Work ~ hard you may....*

—[副] 1. 어떻게 [하여] ¶①어떻게 시작하면 되겠느냐?/②행동(어떻게 처신할지)을 조심하다 2. 어떤 상황에서 ¶③어떻게 지내십니까? 3. 어느 정도, 얼마나 4. 야!, 거참 ¶④거 참 그 여자 잘도 지껄인다! 5. 무슨 까닭(목적)으로 ¶⑤그가 왜 그런 짓을 하게 됐는지 모르겠다/⑥그들이 늦는 이유는 뭘까? 6. 어떻게, 무슨 ¶⑦무슨 뜻입니까? 7. 어떤 이름으로 8. 얼마의 값으로 9. 뭐라고요?, 다시 말해 주시오 ¶⑧다시 말씀해 주시오 10. 아무리 …하더라도 [usage] 이 경우 동사+how+형용사(부사)+주어+may(will)의 문형을 흔히 취함 ¶⑨아무리 그가 빨리 달리더라도

1) ***How about...?*** What is your opinion about...?
2) ***How come?*** Why?; How does it happen that...?
3) ***How comes it that...?*** How does it happen that...?
4) ***How do you like...?*** What is your impression of...?
5) ***How goes it?*** How are you and your affairs in general progressing?
6) ***How now?*** What does this mean?
7) ***How say you?*** What do you think about it?
8) ***How so?*** Why is it so?
9) ***How then?*** What is the meaning of this?
10) ***No matter how...may,*** in whatever way or degree; however...may. ¶*No matter ~ hard you may work, you will not succeed.*

[熟] 1)…에 대해 어떻게 생각하느냐? 2)왜, 어째서 3)어째서 그러냐? 4)…에 대한 인상은 어떠냐? 5)어떤가?, 재미 좋은가? 6)이건 어찌 된 일이냐? 7)당신의 의견은? 8)무슨 까닭에 9)이것은 어찌된 일이냐? 10)아무리 …하더라도

—*n.* [C] 《usu. *the* ~》 a manner; means. ¶*Tell me the ~ and why of it.*⑩

—[名] 방식, 방법 ¶⑩그 방법과 이유를 말하시오

How·ard [háuərd] *n.* a man's name.

—[名] 남자 이름

how·e'er [hauέər] *conj., adv.* =however.

⁑how·ev·er [hauévər] *conj.* nevertheless; though; yet. ⇒[usage] ¶*Later, ~, he decided to go.* | *It is mine, ~ you may use it.* | *Our vacation is not very long; ~, we plan to go on a trip.* —*adv.* **1.** in whatever manner or degree; no matter how. ¶*The work, ~ difficult [it may be], must be finished by the time fixed.* **2.** in what manner; how. ¶*However could you do it?*

—[接] 그러나, …일지라도 [usage] 접속사로서의 however는 문장의 도중이나 끝에 흔히 쓰이며 커머로 구분됨 —[副] 1. 아무리 …이라도(하더라도) 2. 도대체 어찌하여

how·itz·er [háuitsər] *n.* [C] a short cannon for firing shells in a high curve.

—[名] 곡사포

⁑howl [haul] *vi.* **1.** give a long, loud, sad cry, as a dog, a wolf, etc. ¶*Wolves were howling in the distance.* **2.** give a long, loud cry of pain, anger or contempt. **3.** yell; shout. **4.** give a long cry like a strong wind. —*vt.* **1.** say (words) in a crying tone. **2.** make (someone) silent by howling.

—[自] 1. [개 따위]가 목을 길게 뽑으며 짖어대다 2. [사람이] 울부짖다 3. 호탕하게 웃다, 아우성치다 —[他] 1. 고함치며 말하다 2. 고함쳐서 …을 침묵시키다

howl down, stop (someone) from speaking by howling or otherwise showing contempt.

[熟] 고함쳐서 …을 침묵시키다

—*n.* [C] **1.** a long, loud, sorrowful cry. ¶*the ~ of a dog.* **2.** a loud cry of pain, etc. ¶*a ~ of pain.* **3.** a yell; a shout.

—[名] 1. 길게 짖는 소리 2. 울부짖음, 아우성 3. 호탕한 웃음, 외침소리

howl·er [háulər] *n.* [C] **1.** a person or thing that howls. **2.** (*colloq.*) an unreasonable mistake; a foolish mistake.

—[名] 1. 짖는 사람(것) 2. 《口》 큰 실수, 실책

howl·ing [háuliŋ] *adj.* **1.** producing or uttering a howl. **2.** lonely; lonesome. **3.** (*colloq.*) enormous.

—[形] 1. 짖는, 고함치는 2. 쓸쓸한 3. 《口》 어마어마한

how·so·ev·er [hàusouévər] *adv.* (*archaic*) in whatever manner or degree.

—[副] 《古》 아무리 …일지라도

hoy·den [hɔ́idn] *n.* [C] a rude, rough-mannered girl; a noisy, active girl.

—[名] 말괄량이

HP, H.P., hp., h.p. horsepower.

hr. hour; hours.
H.R.H. His (or Her) Royal Highness.
hrs. hours.
hub [hʌb] *n.* ⓒ **1.** the central part of a wheel. **2.** a center of interest, activity, etc. ¶*His office is at the ~ of the city.*①
hub·bub [hʌ́bʌb] *n.* ⓤ a loud, confused noise; an uproar.
Hu·bert [hjúːbə(ː)rt] *n.* a man's name.
huck·a·back [hʌ́kəbæk] *n.* ⓤ a heavy, coarse linen or cotton cloth, used for towels.
huck·le·ber·ry [hʌ́klbèri, +*Brit.* -b(ə)ri] *n.* ⓒ (*pl.* **-ries**) **1.** a small blue-black berry like a blueberry. **2.** the shrub that huckleberries grow on.
huck·ster [hʌ́kstər] *n.* ⓒ **1.** a walking merchant, esp. one who deals in fruits and vegetables. **2.** (*U. S. colloq.*) a person who is in the advertising business. —*vt., vi.* carry round (goods) for sale; deal in small articles.
∗**hud·dle** [hʌ́dl] *vi.* **1.** crowd together in a confused way. (*~ together*) ¶*~ together around the fire.* **2.** (*Football*) gather to get signals. **3.** hunch oneself up in a heap. —*vt.* **1.** cause (things or persons) to move in a heap or quickly and without order. ¶*~ the boys into a bus.* **2.** put on clothes hastily. (*~ on clothes*) **3.** do a task, etc. hurriedly or carelessly. (*~ a task through or over*) —*n.* ⓒ **1.** a confused crowd or group of things or persons. ¶*all in a ~.*① **2.** ⓤ disorder; confusion. **3.** a grouping of football players before a play to get signals. ***go into a huddle,*** (*slang*) have a secret discussion. ¶*The professors went into a ~.*
∗**hue**¹ [hju:] *n.* ⓒ a particular shade of color; a color; a tint. ¶*a dark ~* / *flowers of every ~*①/ *The ~ of death stole over his features.*②
hue² [hju:] *n.* ⓒ a cry, as in war or pursuit. ⇒usage
hue and cry, a loud cry of pursuit, alarm, or protest. ¶*raise a ~ and cry.*
huff [hʌf] *n.* ⓒ a burst of anger. ¶*get into a ~*① / *in a ~.*② —*vt.* **1.** make (someone) angry; offend. ¶*~ someone to pieces.* **2.** bully. (*~ someone into; ~ doing; ~ someone out of*) —*vi.* get angry.
huff·ish [hʌ́fiʃ] *adj.* rather angry; irritable.
huff·y [hʌ́fi] *adj.* (**huff·i·er, huff·i·est**) **1.** offended; keeping silent. **2.** easily made angry. ▷**huff·i·ly** [-li] *adv.* —**huff·i·ness** [-nis] *n.*
∗**hug** [hʌg] *vt.* (**hugged, hug·ging**) **1.** hold (someone) tight in the arms, esp. as a sign of affection. ¶*The girl hugged her doll.* **2.** cling to (an idea, etc.). ¶*~ a prejudice.*① **3.** (of a ship) keep close to a shore.
hug oneself on (or *for, over*), be pleased with (something). [*someone a ~.*②] —*n.* ⓒ a tight hold, esp. with the arms. ¶*give*
:**huge** [hju:dʒ] *adj.* (**hug·er, hug·est**) very large; enormous. ¶*~ profits.*① ▷**huge·ness** [-nis] *n*
huge·ly [hjúːdʒli] *adv.* to a great extent; very much.
hulk [hʌlk] *n.* ⓒ **1.** the body of an old, wrecked ship. **2.** a big, badly-made ship. **3.** a big, awkward person or thing. ¶*a ~ of a man.*①
hulk·ing [hʌ́lkiŋ] *adj.* bulky; clumsy.
hull¹ [hʌl] *n.* ⓒ **1.** the outer covering of a seed, fruit, and vegetable. **2.** any outer covering. —*vt.* remove the hull from (something). ¶*~ peas.* ▷**hull·er** [-ər] *n.*
hull² [hʌl] *n.* ⓒ the body or frame of a ship or an airship. | horizon.|
hull down, so far away that the hull is below the| —*vt.* strike or pierce the hull of (a ship).

──⊛ 1. [수레바퀴의] 바퀴통 2. [흥미·활동 따위의] 중심, 중추 ¶①그의 사무실은 도시의 중심지에 있다
──⊛ 왁자지껄함, 소동
──⊛ 남자 이름
──⊛ 거친 린네르로 짠 타월천

──⊛ 1. 월귤 비슷한 열매 2. 월귤나무 비슷한 관목

──⊛ 1. 행상인 2. 광고업자 ──⊕ ⊜ […을] 행상하다, 소리치며 팔다

──⊜ 1. 질서 없이 떼지어 모이다, 분잡하게 모이다 2. [축구 선수가] 신호를 받기 위해 모이다 ──⊕ 1. …을 마구 처넣다(밀어넣다) 2. [옷]을 급히 입다 3. [일]을 급히 아무렇게나 하다

──⊛ 1. 어중이떠중이의 집단 ¶①온통 뒤죽박죽이 되어 2. 혼란, 난잡 3. [축구 선수들의] 집합
⊛ 〈俗〉비밀 회담을 하다

──⊛ 색조, 색 ¶①여러가지 빛깔의 꽃들/②죽음의 빛깔이 어느새 그의 얼굴에 나타나 있었다
──⊛ 고함소리 usage 오늘날에는 다음 구에만 씀
⊛ [추적·놀램·항의의] 고함소리
──⊛ 골냄, 분노 ¶①화내어/②불끈하여 ──⊕ 1. …을 화나게 하다 2. …을 위협하다, …을 위협하여 …시키다
──⊕ 성내다
──⊛ 시무룩한, 골난, 거만한
──⊛ 1. 시무룩한 2. 성 잘 내는

──⊕ 1. …을 껴안다 2. …에게(을) 고집하다 ¶①편견을 고집하다 3. [배가 기슭 가까이를] 항행하다

⊛ …을 몹시 기뻐하다
──⊛ 껴안기, 포옹 ¶②…을 껴안다

──⊛ 거대한, 터무니없이 큰 ¶①막대한 이익
──⊕ 몹시, 대단히
──⊛ 1. 폐선(廢船) 2. 크고 다루기 힘든 배 3. 덩치가 큰 사람, 부피가 큰 것 ¶①덩치 큰 사내
──⊛ 부피가 큰, 모양 없는
──⊛ 1. 외피, 겉껍질, 꼬투리, [딸기의] 열매 받침 2. 덮개 ──⊕ …의 껍질을 벗기다
──⊛ 선체, 비행기의 동체

⊛ 돛대만 보여, 아주 멀리에
──⊕ [포탄으로] 배의 옆구리를 꿰뚫다

hul·lo [həlóu / hʌ́lóu] *interj.* hollo; hello. —[感] 어어이, 여어, 여보세요

*** hum** [hʌm] *v.* (**hummed, hum·ming**) *vi.* **1.** make a continuous sound like that of a bee. ¶ *The sewing machine is humming.*① **2.** make a low [m] sound in thought, hesitation, etc. **3.** sing without opening the lips. —*vt.* **1.** sing (a song) without opening the lips. **2.** put or bring (someone to do) by humming. ¶ *The mother hummed the baby to sleep.*②
—[自] 1. [벌 따위가] 윙윙거리다 ¶① 재봉틀이 윙윙 소리낸다 2. 우물우물 말하다, 웅얼거리다 3. [입을 다물고] 노래하다, 콧노래를 부르다 —[他] 1. [입을 다물고] …을 노래하다 2. …에 콧노래를 불러 …시키다 ¶② 어머니는 자장가를 불러 아기를 재웠다

—*n.* **1.** [C] a continuous buzzing sound like that of a bee. **2.** a low [m] sound uttered in thought, hesitation, etc. **3.** the sound of singing without opening the lips. —*interj.* a low [m] sound showing surprise, disagreement, doubt, hesitation, etc. ▷**hum·mer** [-ər] *n.*
—[名] 1. [벌 따위의] 윙윙 소리 2. 흐음 [하는 망설임 소리] 3. 콧노래 —[感] 흐음(놀람·불찬성·의심 따위를 나타냄)

: hu·man [hjú:mən] *adj.* **1.** of or characteristic of man or mankind. ¶ *a ~ being*① / *~ nature*② / *~ progress* / *I can't do everything; I'm only ~.* **2.** possessed by or suitable for man. ¶ *~ frailties*③ / *To err is ~, to forgive divine.*④ ⇒[N.B.]
—*n.* [C] (*colloq.*) a person; a human being. ¶ *humans and animals.*
—[形] 1. 사람의; 인간의 ¶① 인간/② 인간성 2. 사람에게 있기 쉬운, 인간다운; 인간에 어울리는 ¶③ 인간의 약점/④ 죄를 짓는 것은 사람이요, 용서하는 것은 신이니라 [N.B.] Pope의 말
—[名] 《口》 인간

*** hu·mane** [hju(:)méin] *adj.* **1.** kind; merciful. **2.** tending to be refined; polished. ¶ *~ learning.*① ⇒[N.B.] ▷**hu·mane·ness** [-nis] *n.*
—[形] 1. 인정있는, 자비심 깊은 2. 고상한, 우아한 ¶① 고전문학 [N.B.] human의 변형

hu·mane·ly [hju(:)méinli] *adv.* kindly; mercifully. —[副] 인정 있게, 자비심 깊게

*** hu·man·ism** [hjú:mənìz(ə)m] *n.* [U] **1.** human nature. **2.** system of thought or action concerned with human interests. **3.** literary culture based on Latin and Greek culture.
—[名] 1. 인간성 2. 인본(人本)주의 3. 인문학, 고전문학 연구

*** hu·man·ist** [hjú:mənist] *n.* [C] **1.** a person who studies human interests and values. **2.** a person who studies Latin and Greek culture.
—[名] 1. 인간성 연구가, 인본주의자 2. 고전문학 연구가

hu·man·is·tic [hjù:mənístik] *adj.* of humanism or humanists.
—[形] 인간 연구의, 인문학의, 인문주의적인, 고전적인

hu·man·i·tar·i·an [hju(:)mæ̀nitέəriən] *n.* [C] a person who is devoted to the health, good condition, happiness, etc. of human beings. —*adj.* devoted to the health, good condition, happiness, etc. of human beings.
—[名] 인도(박애)주의자 —[形] 인도주의의

hu·man·i·tar·i·an·ism [hju(:)mæ̀nitέəriənìz(ə)m] *n.* [U] humanitarian principles.
—[名] 인도(박애)주의

*** hu·man·i·ty** [hju(:)mǽniti] *n.* (pl. **-ties**) **1.** [U] 《*collectively*》 human beings; mankind. **2.** [U] the fact of being human; human nature. **3.** [U] the quality of being humane; kindness; mercy. **4.** 《*the -ties*》 ⓐ the Latin and Greek languages and literatures. ⓑ branches of learning concerned with language, literature, philosophy, art, etc.
—[名] 1. 인류 2. 인성(人性), 인간성 3. 자애, 자비, 인정 4. ⓐ 문학; [특히 그리이스·라틴의] 고전문학 ⓑ 인문과학(사회과학이나 자연과학에 대하여 문학·철학·예술 따위)

H

hu·man·ize [hjú:mənàiz] *vt.* **1.** give a human nature to (something). **2.** make (someone) kind or merciful. —*vi.* become human or humane.
—[他] 1. …에게 인간성을 주다 2. …을 다정하게 만들다 —[自] 인간다와지다, 다정해지다

hu·man·kind [hjú:mənkáind] *n.* [U] 《*collectively*》 human beings; mankind. —[名] 인류, 인간

hu·man·ly [hjú:mənli] *adv.* **1.** in a human way. **2.** in a kind manner.
—[副] 1. 인간적으로 2. 인정에서, 인간답게

: hum·ble [hʌ́mbl] *adj.* **1.** low in position or condition. ¶ *a ~ cottage.*① **2.** not thinking of one's own power; not proud. ¶ *He became very famous, but remained ~.*② —*vt.* make (someone) humble; make (someone) lower in position or pride. ¶ *The failure humbled him.*
—[形] 1. 천한, 보잘것 없는 ¶① 오막살이 2. 겸손한, 겸양하는 ¶② 그는 유명해졌지만 여전히 겸손했다 —[他] …을 천하게 하다, …의 품위를 떨어뜨리다

hum·ble·ness [hʌ́mblnis] *n.* [U] the state of being humble. —[名] 겸손, 겸양

hum·bly [hʌ́mbli] *adv.* in a humble manner. —[副] 겸손하게, 황송하여

hum·bug [hʌ́mbʌ̀g] *n.* **1.** [C] a dishonest person; a deceiver. **2.** [U][C] dishonest behavior or talk; the state of being deceitful. —*vt., vi.* deceive (someone) with dishonest behavior or talk. 《~ someone *into*; ~ someone *out of*》 —*interj.* Nonsense!
—[名] 1. 사기꾼, 협잡꾼 2. 허위, 협잡, 사기 —[他][自] 속이다, 기만하다, 사기를 하다 —[感] 엉터리다!

hum·drum [hʌ́mdrʌ̀m] *adj.* continuing without change; dull. —*n.* **1.** [C] a dull person. **2.** [U] the state of
—[形] 단조로운, 지루한 —[名] 1. 보잘것 없는 사람 2. 단조로움

being humdrum. ⌐▷**hu·mid·ness** [-nis] *n.*

hu·mid [hjúːmid] *adj.* wet; damp. ¶*a ~ climate.*
—[形] 습기가 있는, 축축한

hu·mid·i·ty [hju(ː)míditi] *n.* [U] **1.** the state of being humid; dampness. **2.** amount of water vapor in the air.
—[名] 1. 습기 2. 습도

hu·mil·i·ate [hju(ː)mílièit] *vt.* lower the pride of (someone); bring shame to (someone). ¶*He was humiliated.; He humiliated himself*① ▷**hu·mili·at·ing·ly** [-iŋli] *adv.*
—[他] …의 면목을 잃게 하다, …에게 창피를 주다 ¶①그는 창피를 당했다

hu·mil·i·a·tion [hju(ː)mìliéiʃ(ə)n] *n.* [U][C] **1.** the act of humiliating. **2.** the state or feeling of being humiliated.
—[名] 1. 창피를 주기, 욕을 보이기 2. 창피, 치욕, 굴욕

* **hu·mil·i·ty** [hju(ː)míliti] *n.* [U] the state of being humble; modesty.
—[名] 겸손, 스스로 낮추기

hum·ming [hʌ́miŋ] *adj.* **1.** making an unchanging buzzing sound; singing a song without opening the lips. **2.** quickly active; energetic. —*n.* [U] a buzzing sound made by a bee; the act of singing with a hum.
—[形] 1. 윙윙거리는; 콧노래를 부르는 2. 재빠른; 기운찬, 정력적인 —[名] 윙윙 소리; 콧노래[를 부르기]

hum·ming·bird [hʌ́miŋbəːrd] *n.* [C] a very small, brightly colored American bird that moves so rapidly as to make a humming sound.
—[名] [미국산] 벌새

hum·mock [hʌ́mək] *n.* [C] **1.** a very small, rounded hill or mound. **2.** a high part of an ice field.
—[名] 1. 작은 언덕 2. [빙원(氷原)의] 얼음 언덕

‡ **hu·mor,** *Brit.* **-mour** [hjúːmər] [U] **1.** a funny or amusing quality; the ability to see or express what is funny, amusing, etc. ¶*He has no sense of ~.*① / *The story is full of ~.* **2.** ((often *a ~*)) a mood; a state of mind. ¶*be in the ~ for…*② / *be in no ~ for…*③ / *He was in a good (bad) ~.*④ **3.** a person's natural way of feeling and acting; temperament. ¶(*proverb*) *Every man has his ~*⑤. **4.** [C] (*archaic*) any fluid or juice once considered to characterize the nature of an animal or a plant.
—[名] 1. 익살, 해학, 우스꽝스러움; 유우머에 대한 이해력 ¶①그는 유우머를 모른다 2. [일시적인] 기질, 기분 ¶②…할 생각이 있다/③…할 생각이 전혀 없다/④그는 기분이 좋았다(나빴다) 3. 성미, 성질 ¶⑤《俚》사람의 성품은 가지각색이다 4. 《古》[동물의] 체액(體液); [식물의] 수액(樹液)

out of humor, angry; irritated; in a bad mood.
[熟] 기분이 언짢아서

—*vt.* **1.** fit oneself to the mood or wishes of (someone); indulge. ¶*A sick child has to be humored.* **2.** act in agreement with the nature of (someone).
—[他] 1. …의 비위를 맞추다; [기질·취미 따위]를 만족시키다 2. …의 성질에 잘 맞추어 나가다

hu·mor·esque [(h)jùːmərésk] *n.* [C] a light, humorous piece of music.
—[名] 표일곡(飄逸曲), 유우머레스크

hu·mor·ist [(h)júːmərist] *n.* [C] a person who writes or says something with a sense of humor.
—[名] 해학자, 유우머 작가(배우)

hu·mor·ous [(h)júːmərəs] *adj.* full of humor; funny; amusing. ▷**hu·mor·ous·ness** [-nis] *n.*
—[形] 익살맞은; 우스꽝스러운; 재미있는

hu·mor·ous·ly [(h)júːmərəsli] *adv.* in a humorous manner.
—[副] 우스꽝스럽게, 익살맞게

hu·mour [(h)júːmər] *n., v.* (*Brit.*) =humor.

hump [hʌmp] *n.* [C] **1.** a rounded, raised-up part like that on the back of a camel **2.** a mound; a small, round hill. —*vt.* raise or bend (the back) into a hump. ¶*The cat humped its back.*①
—[名] 1. [등의] 혹, [낙타의] 육봉(肉峰) 2. 둥근 언덕 —[他] [등]을 구부리다, 둥글게 하다 ¶①고양이는 등을 둥글게 한다

hump·back [hʌ́mpbæ̀k] *n.* [C] **1.** a rounded, raised-up back; a crooked back. **2.** a person with a crooked back. **3.** a large whale that has a humplike fin.
—[名] 1. 굽은 등 2. 곱사등이, 꼽추 3. 혹고래

hump·backed [hʌ́mpbæ̀kt] *adj.* having a humpback.
—[形] 곱사등이의, 꼽추의

humph [hʌmf] *interj.* exclamation uttered in doubt, contempt, etc. —*n.* [C] this kind of exclamation. —*vi.* utter this kind of exclamation.
—[感] 흥(의심·경멸 따위를 나타냄) —[名] 흥하는 소리

Hum·phrey [hʌ́mfri] *n.* a man's name.
—[名] 남자 이름

hu·mus [hjúːməs] *n.* [U] rich soil made from decayed leaves and other vegetable matter.
—[名] 부식토(腐植土)

Hun [hʌn] *n.* [C] a member of a warlike, brutal Asiatic people who attacked Europe in the 5th century.
—[名] 흉노(아시아의 유목민)

hunch [hʌntʃ] *vt.* draw or bend (the back) to form a hump. ¶*He hunched his back to get into the hole.*
—[他] [등]을 활처럼 구부리다

—*n.* [C] **1.** a rounded, raised-up part; a hump. **2.** (*U.S. colloq.*) a feeling that something will happen. ¶*I have a ~ that something good will happen today.* **3.** a thick slice or piece.
—[名] 1. [등의] 혹, 육봉(肉峰) 2. 《美口》 직감, 예감 3. 두꺼운 조각

hunch·back [hʌ́ntʃbæ̀k] *n.* [C] **1.** a person with a hump-
—[名] 1. 꼽추 2. 곱사등이

ed back; a humpback. **2.** a rounded, raised-up back.

hunch·backed [hʌ́ntʃbæ̀kt] *adj.* having a crooked back; humpbacked.
—[形] 꼽추의, 곱사등이의

‡**hun·dred** [hʌ́ndrid, hʌ́ndrəd] *n.* [C] (pl. **-dreds** or *after a numeral* **-dred**) **1.** ten times ten; 100. ⇒[usage] **2.** division of an English county.
—*adj.* being ten times ten.
—[名] 1. 100 [개] [usage] 1백이면 a를 붙이고, 수사(數詞) 뒤에서 -s를 붙이지 않음 2. [영국의] 촌락 —[形] 100의, 100 개(명)의

hun·dred·fold [hʌ́ndridfòuld, -drəd-] *adj., adv., n.* a hundred times as much or as many.
—[形][副][名] 100배(의)(로)

‡**hun·dredth** [hʌ́ndridθ, -drədθ] *adj., n.* **1.** next after the 99th. **2.** one of 100 equal parts.
—[形][名] 1. 백 번째[의] 2. 100분의 1[의]

hun·dred·weight [hʌ́ndridwèit, -drəd-] *n.* [C] (pl. **-weights** or *after a numeral* **-weight**) a unit of weight equal to 100 pounds in the United States or 112 pounds in England. ⇒[N.B.]
—[名] 중량의 단위 [N.B.] cwt.로 줄임

‡**hung** [hʌŋ] *v.* pt. and pp. of **hang**.

Hun·gar·i·an [hʌŋgέəriən] *adj.* of Hungary, its people, or their language. **—*n.*** **1.** [C] a person of Hungary. **2.** [U] the language of Hungary. ⇒[N.B.]
—[形] 항가리[사람·말]의 —[名] 1. 항가리 사람 2. 항가리 말

Hun·ga·ry [hʌ́ŋgəri] *n.* a country in central Europe.
—[名] 항가리 [N.B.] 수도 Budapest

‡**hun·ger** [hʌ́ŋgər] *n.* **1.** [U] the weak condition caused by lack of food. **2.** the strong desire for food. **3.** ((usu. *a* ~)) a strong desire. ¶*He had a ~ for knowledge.*① **—*vi.*** **1.** feel hunger; be hungry. **2.** have a strong desire for something. ((~ *for* or *after* something)) **—*vt.*** make (someone) feel hunger; make (someone) do something because of hunger.
—[名] 1. 굶주림 2. 공복, 배고픔 3. 열망, 갈망 ¶①그는 지식에 굶주리고 있었다 —[自] 1. 굶주리다; 배가 고파지다 2. 열망하다 —[他] …을 굶주리게 하다; 굶겨서 …에게 …시키다

hun·gri·ly [hʌ́ŋgrili] *adv.* **1.** in hunger; in a hungry manner. **2.** with a strong desire.
—[副] 1. 굶주려서, 게걸스럽게 2. 열망하여, 갈망하여

‡**hun·gry** [hʌ́ŋgri] *adj.* (**-gri·er, -gri·est**) **1.** feeling hunger. ¶*He was ~ after the hard work.* **2.** showing hunger. ¶*a ~ look.* **3.** causing hunger. ¶*~ work.* **4.** having a strong desire; eager. ¶*He is ~ for information.*① **5.** not rich. ¶*~ soil.*
as hungry as a hunter, very hungry.
▷**hun·gri·ness** [-nis] *n.*
—[形] 1. 굶은, 배고픈 2. 배고픈 듯한 3. 배가 고파지는 4. 갈망하는, 동경하는 ¶①그는 지식을 갈망하고 있다 5. [토지가] 메마른
[熟] 몹시 배고픈

hunk [hʌŋk] *n.* [C] (*colloq.*) a big mass or piece.
—[名] ((口)) 큰 덩어리, 두꺼운 조각

‡**hunt** [hʌnt] *vt.* **1.** run after (wild animals, game birds, etc.) for the purpose of killing or catching them. ¶*~ a deer / go out hunting.*① **2.** search through (a region) looking for wild animals, etc. ¶*~ a woods.* **3.** chase; drive away; pursue; hound; pursue all the time; harry. ¶*~ a fox out of its earth.*② **4.** search (a place) carefully; look for (something); try to find. ¶*~ bargains.* **5.** use (dogs or horses) in hunting. ¶*~ a pack of hounds.* **—*vi.*** **1.** run after wild animals. ¶*go hunting.* **2.** seek. ((~ *for* or *after* something)) ¶*~ for a lost book.*
—[他] 1. …을 사냥하다 ¶①사냥하러 가다 2. [사냥감 있는 데를] 몰이하다 3. [사냥감]을 몰아내다; 추적하여 잡다; …을 부추기다; …을 박해하다; 괴롭히다 ¶②여우를 굴에서 몰아내다 4. [장소]를 뒤지다; …을 찾다 5. [개·말]을 사냥에 쓰다 —[自] 1. 사냥하다 2. 찾다

1) ***hunt down,*** run after (a wild animal, etc.) until successful in killing or catching it.
2) ***hunt out,*** find (something or someone) by searching.
3) ***hunt up,*** ⓐ search for. ⓑ find (someone) by searching.
[熟] 1)…을 좇아가서 잡다(죽이다) 2)…을 찾아내다 3)ⓐ…을 찾다 ⓑ…을 찾아내다

—*n.* [C] **1.** the act of hunting; a district covered in hunting; a group of people, with dogs and usu. horses, engaged in hunting. **2.** the act of running after in order to catch something or someone.
—[名] 1. 사냥; 수렵지구; 수렵대(隊), 수렵회 2. 탐색; 추적

‡**hunt·er** [hʌ́ntər] *n.* [C] **1.** a person who hunts. **2.** a horse or dog trained for hunting. **3.** a person who looks for something.
—[名] 1. 사냥꾼 2. 사냥말(개) 3. 탐구하는 사람

‡**hunt·ing** [hʌ́ntiŋ] *n.* [U] the act of a person or an animal that hunts.
—[名] 사냥; 탐구

hunt·ress [hʌ́ntris] *n.* [C] a woman who hunts.
—[名] 여자 사냥꾼

hunts·man [hʌ́ntsmən] *n.* [C] (pl. **-men** [-mən]) (*Brit.*) **1.** a hunter. **2.** a man who takes charge of hunting
—[名] ((英)) 1. 사냥꾼 2. [여우 사냥의] 사냥개 담당자

dogs during a hunt.

hur·dle [hə́:rdl] *n.* [C] **1.** a kind of fence to be jumped over in a race. **2.** ⟪*pl.*⟫ a race in which the runners jump over hurdles. **3.** something that prevents or hinders the action of a person; a difficulty. **4.** a frame made of sticks and used as a fence. **5.** in England, a frame on which criminals used to be dragged. —*vt.* **1.** jump over. ¶*He hurdled the last ditch.*① **2.** overcome. ¶*~ a difficulty.* **3.** enclose (a garden, land, etc.) with a frame of sticks. —*vi.* jump over a hurdle.

—[名] 1. [경기의] 장애물, 허어들 2. 장애물 경주 3. 장애, 곤란 4. [임시의] 나뭇가지로 엮어 만든 울타리 5. ⟪英史⟫ 죄인을 형장으로 싣고 가던 썰매 비슷한 수레 —[他] 1. …을 뛰어넘다 ¶①그는 마지막 도랑을 뛰어넘었다 2. …을 극복하다 3. …에 나뭇가지로 엮어 울타리를 만들다 —[自] 장애물(허어들)을 뛰어넘다

hur·dler [hə́:rdlər] *n.* [C] a person who jumps over hurdles in a race.

—[名] 장애물 경주자

hur·dy-gur·dy [hə́:rdigə́:rdi] *n.* [C] (pl. **-dies**) a barrel organ played by turning a handle, often pulled through the streets on wheels.

—[名] [노상에서 쓰는] 손풍금

***hurl** [hə:rl] *vt.* **1.** throw (something) with force. ¶*The soldiers hurled their spears.* **2.** utter (hard words, etc.) violently. —*vi.* (*colloq.*) (*Baseball*) pitch a ball. —*n.* [C] a violent throw. ▷**hurl·er** [-ər] *n.*

—[他] 1. …을 [힘껏] 던지다 2. [욕설 따위]를 퍼붓다 —[自] ⟪野球⟫ 투구하다 —[名] 힘껏 던지기

hurl·y-burl·y [hə́:rlibə̀:rli] *n.* [C] (pl. **-burl·ies**) confusion and noise; a disorder.

—[名] 야단법석, 소동; 혼란

Hu·ron [hjúərən], **Lake** *n.* the second largest of the five Great Lakes, between the United States and Canada.

—[名] 미국과 캐나다 사이의 5대호 중에서 둘째로 큰 호수

***hur·rah** [hərɑ́:, hur- / hurɑ́:] *interj., n.* [C] a shout of joy, praise, etc. —*vi.* shout hurrahs; cheer. —*vt.* meet or encourage (someone) by shouting hurrahs.

—[感][名] 만세 —[自] 만세를 부르다, 환성을 올리다 —[他] …을 환호로 맞이하다(응원하다)

hur·ray [həréi / huréi] *interj., n., v.* =hurrah.

hur·ri·cane [hə́:rikèin / hʌ́rikən, -kèin] *n.* [C] **1.** a storm with a violent wind and, usu. very heavy rain. **2.** a sudden, violent out burst (of praise, emotion, etc.).

—[名] 1. 폭풍, 태풍 2. [감정 · 갈채의] 폭발, 폭풍

***hur·ried** [hə́:rid / hʌ́rid] *adj.* forced to hurry; done or made in haste.

—[形] 서두르는; 황급한, 아무렇게나 하는

hur·ried·ly [hə́:ridli / hʌ́rid-] *adv.* in a hurried manner.

—[副] 황급히, 허둥지둥

⁑**hur·ry** [hə́:ri / hʌ́ri] *n.* (**hur·ries**) [U] **1.** haste; rush; eagerness. ¶*Everything is ~ and confusion.*① **2.** ⟪often *a* ~⟫ ⟪in *negative* or *interrogative*⟫ need for hurry. ¶*There is no ~. / What's the ~?*②

—[名] 1. 서두름; 열심 ¶①야단법석이었다 2. 서두를 필요 ¶②왜 그렇게 서둘러야 하느냐?

in a hurry, ⓐ anxious to act; quickly. ¶*They were in a ~ to set out.*③ / *I am in no ~ for your answer.*④ ⓑ (*colloq.*) willingly; readily. ⓒ ⟪in *negative*⟫ easily.

[熟] ⓐ서둘러서 ¶③그들은 한 시라도 빨리 떠나려고 했다/④네 대답은 급하지 않다 ⓑ⟪口⟫기꺼이; 자진하여 ⓒ쉽게 …[않다]

—*vt.* cause (someone) to act or move too hastily; hasten. ↔ delay. ¶*Don't ~ me. / ~ a decision.* —*vi.* act or move rapidly. ¶*Don't ~. / He hurried away.*

—[他] …을 서두르게 하다; 재촉하다 —[自] 서두르다

1) ***hurry on with,*** make haste with (something).
2) ***Hurry up.,*** Act or move rapidly.

[熟] 1)…을 진척시키다; 서두르게 하다 2)빨리 해라

hur·ry-scur·ry, hur·ry-skur·ry [hə́:riskə́:ri / hʌ́riskʌ́ri] *n.* [C] (pl. **-ries**) hurry and confusion. —*adj.* hurried and confused. —*adv.* with hurry and confusion.

—[名] 허둥지둥함 —[形] 황급한 —[副] 허둥지둥

⁑**hurt** [hə:rt] *vt.* (**hurt**) **1.** cause pain to (someone); give a wound to (someone); injure. **2.** offend; grieve (the feelings of a person) **3.** do damage or harm to (something). —*n.* [U] **1.** pain; injury; wound. **2.** a bad effect; damage; harm. ▷**hurt·er** [-ər] *n.*

—[他] 1. 아프게 하다, 다치게 하다 2. [남]의 감정을 해치다 3. …을 해치다, …에게 손실을 주다 —[名] 1. 고통, 상처, 다침 2. 해, 손해

hurt·ful [hə́:rtf(u)l] *adj.* causing hurt; harmful; injurious. ▷**hurt·ful·ly** [-fuli] *adv.*

—[形] 상처입히는, 해로운, 해가 되는

hur·tle [hə́:rtl] *vi.* **1.** dash or drive violently; rush suddenly. ⟪~ *against* something⟫ ¶*Spears hurtled against shields.*① **2.** move with a confused noise; rush noisily. ¶*The jet plane hurtled through the air.* —*vt.* dash or drive violently; dash against (something); make (something) meet and strike. —*n.* [C] the act or fact of hurtling; a loud, confused noise; clatter.

—[自] 1. 소리를 내며 부딪치다, 충돌하다 ¶①창이 [소리를 내며] 방패에 부딪쳤다 2. 소리를 내며 날다 —[他] …을 던지다, 부딪치다, 충돌시키다 —[名] 부딪치기, 부딪치는 소리, 충돌

⁑**hus·band** [hʌ́zbənd] *n.* [C] a man who has a wife. —*vt.* **1.** manage (money, etc.) with care and economy. ¶*He*

—[名] 남편 —[他] 1. …을 절약하다 2. [여성]과 결혼하다

husbandman

must ~ his money. **2.** marry (a woman). —명 농부

hus·band·man [hʌ́zbəndmən] *n.* ⓒ (pl. **-men** [-mən]) a farmer.

hus·band·ry [hʌ́zbəndri] *n.* ⓤ **1.** farming. **2.** domestic management; economical management. —명 **1.** 농업, 경작 **2.** 가정(家政), 절약

* **hush** [hʌʃ] *vt.* **1.** make (someone) silent or quiet. **2.** soothe; calm. —*vi.* become or keep silent. *hush up,* ⓐ stop discussion of. ⓑ cover up a love affair. 「Keep quiet!」 —*n.* ⓤⓒ silence; stillness. —*interj.* Be silent!; —(타) **1.** …을 조용하게 하다 **2.** …을 가라앉히다 —(자) 조용히 하다 熟 ⓐ…을 침묵시키다 ⓑ[사건 따위를] 쉬쉬해 버리다 —명 침묵, 정적 —감 쉿!, 조용히!

hush-hush [hʌ́ʃhʌ̀ʃ] *adj.* (*slang*) highly secret. —형 (俗) 극비의

hush money [´ `] *n.* money paid to keep someone from telling something. —명 입 막는 돈, 무마비

husk [hʌsk] *n.* ⓒ ((*usu. pl.*)) **1.** the dry outer covering of certain seeds or fruits. **2.** the worthless outer covering of anything. —*vt.* remove the husk from (something). ▷**husk·er** [-ər] *n.* —명 **1.** 껍질, 깍지 **2.** 찌끼 —(타) …의 껍질(깍지)을 벗기다

husk·i·ly [hʌ́skili] *adv.* in a husky voice. 「voice.」
husk·i·ness [hʌ́skinis] *n.* ⓤ a low, dry quality of the —(부) 목쉰 소리로 —명 목청이 쉼

husk·ing bee [hʌ́skiŋbìː] *n.* (*U.S.*) a gathering or a party of farm families to husk corn. —명 (美) 옥수수 껍질을 벗기는 이웃의 모임

husk·y [hʌ́ski] *adj.* (**husk·i·er, husk·i·est**) **1.** dry in the throat; hoarse. ¶*a ~ voice.*① **2.** of or like husks. **3.** (*U.S. colloq.*) big and strong. —*n.* ⓒ (pl. **husk·ies**) (*U.S. colloq.*) a big, strong person. —형 **1.** 목쉰 ¶①목쉰 소리 **2.** 껍질의, 깍지 같은 **3.** (口) 튼튼한, 건장한 —명 (美口) 건장한 사람

hus·sy [hʌ́zi, hʌ́si] *n.* ⓒ (pl. **-sies**) **1.** a bad-mannered girl; an ill-behaved girl. **2.** a worthless woman. —명 **1.** 말괄량이, 왈패 **2.** 시시한 여자

hus·tings [hʌ́stiŋz] *n. pl.* ((used as *sing.* and *pl.*)) **1.** a platform from which candidates for Parliament are nominated and address the voters. **2.** (*chiefly Brit.*) a platform from which speeches are made in a political campaign. **3.** legal actions in an election. —명 **1.** 영국 국회의원 선거의 연설단 **2.** (英) 선거운동의 연설단 **3.** 선거 절차

hus·tle [hʌ́sl] *vt.* **1.** force (someone) to do something hurriedly or roughly. (*~ someone into doing*) ¶*He hustled the customer into buying more.*① **2.** push or crowd roughly. (*~ someone into*; *~ someone out of*) ¶*The other boys hustled him out of the room.*① **3.** (*colloq.*) cause (something) to be done quickly. —*vi* ⓤ **1.** push; crowd. (*~ against*) **2.** (*colloq.*) work with tireless energy. —*n.* ⓤ ((often *a ~*)) **1.** rough push. **2.** (*colloq.*) energetic activity. ▷**hus·tler** [-ər] *n.* 「cabin.」 —(타) **1.** …에게 무리를 시키다, 강요하다 ¶①그는 그 손님에게 물건을 억지로 더 사게 했다 **2.** …을 난폭하게 밀다 ¶②다른 소년들은 그를 거칠게 방에서 밀어냈다 **3.** (口) …을 척척 해내다 —(자) **1.** 밀고 당기다, 붐비다 **2.** 척척 해치우다 —명 **1.** 거칠게 밀기 **2.** (口) 정력적 활동

‡ **hut** [hʌt] *n.* ⓒ a small, roughly built house; a small —명 오두막, 오막살이

hutch [hʌtʃ] *n.* ⓒ a box or chest to keep things, esp. one used as a home for small animals. —명 상자; [작은 짐승을 기르는] 통, 우리

huz·za [həzáː / huz-] *interj., n., v.* =hurrah.

hy·a·cinth [háiəsinθ] *n.* ⓒ **1.** a plant of the lily family grown from a bulb. **2.** ⓤ a reddish-orange gem. —명 **1.** 히아신드(식물) **2.** 풍신자석(風信子石)(보석)

hy·ae·na [ha(i)íːnə] *n.* =hyena.

hy·brid [háibrid] *n.* ⓒ **1.** a plant or an animal produced by parents of different species. **2.** anything made of parts of different origin. —*adj.* **1.** produced from two different species. **2.** of mixed origin. —명 **1.** 잡종 **2.** 혼성물 —형 **1.** 잡종의 **2.** 혼성의

Hyde Park [háidpáːrk] *n.* a park in London, England. —명 영국 런던의 공원

hy·dra [háidrə] *n.* ⓒ (pl. **-dras** or **-drae**) **1.** ((*H-*)) (in Greek mythology) a monstrous snake having nine heads. ⇒fig. **2.** any evil difficult to destroy. **3.** a kind of fresh water snake. —명 **1.** [그리이스 신화에서] 머리가 아홉인 뱀 **2.** 근절하기 힘든 것(재앙) **3.** 히드라(강장(腔腸)동물의 일종)

hy·drae [háidriː] *n.* pl. of **hydra**.

hy·dran·gea [haidréindʒə, +U.S. -drǽndʒiə] *n.* ⓒ a shrub with large gatherings of small white, pink, or blue flowers. —명 수국(水菊)

[Hydra 1.]

hy·drant [háidrənt] *n.* ⓒ a large pipe for drawing water directly in order to put out fires. — 图 [가로(街路)의] 소화전(消火栓)

hy·drate [háidreit] *n.* ⓒ a kind of material produced when certain substances combine with water. —*vi.* become a hydrate; combine with water to form a hydrate. —*vt.* cause (something) to become a hydrate. — 图 수산화물(水酸化物) — 自 수산화하다 — 他 …을 수산화시키다

hy·drau·lic [haidrɔ́:lik] *adj.* **1.** having to do with water in motion. **2.** worked by the pressure of water in motion. ¶ *a ~ elevator.*① **3.** hardened with water. ¶ *~ cement.*② — 形 1. 수력의 2. 수압의 ¶①수압식 엘리베이터 3. 물로 경화(硬化)하는, 수경(水硬)의 ¶②수경 시멘트

hy·drau·lics [haidrɔ́:liks] *n. pl.* (used as *sing.*) ⓤ the science of water and other liquids in motion. — 图 동수학(動水學), 수리학(水理學)

hy·dro [háidrou] *n.* ⓒ (pl. **-dros**) (*Chemistry*) (*colloq.*) a hydropathic establishment; a house or resting place for people taking mineral-water baths to cure illness. — 图 《化》《口》 수치료원(水治療院)

hy·dro- [háidrou-, -drə-] a word element meaning *water* or *hydrogen*. — 「물」「수소」를 뜻하는 연결형

hy·dro·car·bon [háidrouká:rbən] *n.* ⓒ any of a class of compounds containing only hydrogen and carbon. — 图 탄화수소

hy·dro·chlo·ric [háidroukló(:)rik] *adj.* of hydrochloric acid. — 形 염화수소의

hy·dro·e·lec·tric [hàidrouiléktrik] *adj.* of or related to the production of electricity by water power. — 形 수력전기의

* **hy·dro·gen** [háidrədʒ(ə)n] *n.* ⓤ a very light, tasteless, colorless gas that burns easily. ⇒N.B. ¶ *a ~ bomb.*① — 图 수소 N.B. 화학기호 H ¶①수소폭탄

hy·drom·e·ter [haidrámitər / -drɔ́mitə] *n.* ⓒ an instrument for determining the specific weight of water or other liquids. — 图 액체 비중계, 부칭(浮秤)

hy·dro·path·ic [hàidroupǽθik] *adj.* of or using hydropathy. —*n.* ⓒ a sanatorium that specializes in hydropathy. — 形 수치료법(水治療法) — 图 수치료원

hy·drop·a·thy [haidrápəθi / -drɔ́p-] *n.* ⓤ treatment of disease by using water. — 图 수치료법(水治療法)

hy·dro·pho·bi·a [hàidroufóubiə] *n.* ⓤ a dreadful disease that a mad dog brings to a man when it bites him; rabies. — 图 광견병, 공수병

hy·dro·plane [háidrouplèin] *n.* ⓒ **1.** a light motorboat that glides on the surface of water. **2.** an airplane that lands on and takes off from water; a seaplane. — 图 1. 수상 활주정(滑走艇) 2. 수상비행기

hy·dro·pon·ics [hàidroupániks / -pɔ́n-] *n. pl.* (used as *sing.*) the growing of plants by only water without any soil. — 图 수경법(水耕法)

hy·e·na [ha(i)í:nə] *n.* ⓒ a wolflike, flesh-eating wild animal of Africa and Asia. — 图 [아시아・아프리카산] 하이에나

hy·giene [háidʒi:n, +*U. S.* -dʒìi:n] *n.* ⓤ **1.** the science of keeping well. **2.** rules for keeping good health. — 图 1. 위생학 2. 건강법

hy·gi·en·ic [hàidʒiénik, -dʒí:n- / -dʒí:n-] *adj.* **1.** healthful; concerning heath. **2.** related to the science of health. — 形 1. 건강에 관한 2. 위생의

hy·gi·en·ics [hàidʒiéniks, -dʒí:n- / -dʒí:n-] *n. pl.* (used as *sing.*) ⓤ the science of health. — 图 위생학, 위생법

hy·gien·ist [haidʒí:nist, háidʒi:-] *n.* ⓒ a person who is expert in hygiene. — 图 위생학자

hy·grom·e·ter [haigrámitər / -grɔ́mitə] *n.* ⓒ an instrument for measuring the amount of water vapor in the air. — 图 온도계

Hy·men [háimən / -men] *n.* (in Greek mythology) the god of marriage. — 图 [그리이스 신화의] 결혼의 신

* **hymn** [him] *n.* ⓒ **1.** a song in praise of God. **2.** any song of praise. —*vt.* praise (God) with a hymn. —*vi.* sing a hymn. ▷ **hymn·like** [-làik] *adj.* — 图 1. 찬미가, 성가 2. 찬가 — 他 [찬미가로 신을] 찬미하다 — 自 찬미가를 부르다

* **hym·nal** [hímnəl] *n.* ⓒ a book of hymns. — 图 찬미가집(集)

hy·per·bo·la [haipə́:rbələ] *n.* ⓒ (*Geometry*) a curve formed when a cone is cut by a plane at a larger angle with the base than the side of the cone makes. — 图 《幾何》 쌍곡선

hy·per·bo·le [haipə́:rbəli] *n.* ⓤ extreme way of expression for more effective writing or speaking. — 图 과장법

hy·per·bol·ic [hàipə(:)rbálik / -pə(:)bɔ́l-] *adj.* **1.** of or like — 形 1. 과장된, 과대한 2. 쌍곡선의

hyperbole; exaggeratedly expressed. **2.** of or having to do with hyperbolas.

hy·per·crit·i·cal [hàipə(:)rkrítik(ə)l] *adj.* too fault-finding; too severe in finding fault with. ▷**hy·per·crit·i·cal·ly** [-kəli] *adv.* —[형] 혹평하는, 흠을 찾는

‡hy·phen [háif(ə)n] *n.* [C] a mark (-) used to join the parts of a compound word. —*vt.* join (words) with a hyphen; hyphenate. —[명] 하이픈, 연자부(連字符) —[타] [단어]를 하이픈으로 연결하다

hy·phen·ate [háifənèit] *vt.* join (words) with a hyphen. —[타] …을 하이픈으로 연결하다

hy·phen·at·ed [háifənèitid] *adj.* (*U.S. colloq.*) joined with a hyphen. —[형] 《美口》 하이픈으로 연결한, 하이픈이 있는

hy·phen·a·tion [hàifənéiʃ(ə)n] *n.* [U] the act of hyphenating words. —[명] 하이픈으로 잇기

hyp·no·ses [hipnóusi:z] *n.* pl. of **hypnosis.**

hyp·no·sis [hipnóusis] *n.* [U][C] (pl. **-ses**) the state like sleep in which a person has little feeling and acts by the suggestions of some special person. ¶*He was under* ~.① —[명] 최면, 최면 상태 ¶①그는 최면 상태에 있었다

hyp·not·ic [hipnátik / -nɔ́t-] *adj.* **1.** of hypnosis. **2.** easily put into hypnosis. —*n.* [C] **1.** a person who is in the state of hypnosis. **2.** a drug or other means of causing sleep. —[형] 1. 최면[술]의 2. 최면술에 걸리기 쉬운 —[명] 1. 최면 상태에 있는 사람 2. 최면약, 수면제

hyp·no·tism [hípnətìz(ə)m] *n.* [U] **1.** the act or process of hypnotizing. **2.** the science dealing with hypnosis. —[명] 1. 최면술을 걸기 2. 최면술

hyp·no·tist [hípnətist] *n.* [C] a person who hypnotizes. —[명] 최면술사

hyp·no·tize [hípnətàiz] *vt.* **1.** put (someone) into a hypnotic state. **2.** (*colloq.*) rule or control the will of (someone). ▷**hyp·no·tiz·a·ble** [-əbl] *adj.* —**hyp·no·tiz·er** [-ər] *n.* —[타] 1. …에 최면술을 걸다 2. …을 매혹하다

hy·po [háipou] *n.* [U] **1.** a colorless salt as clear as crystal, used in photography. **2.** =hypodermic. —[명] 1. 하이포, 현상정착제(現像定着劑)

hy·po·chon·dri·a [hàipoukándriə / -kɔ́n-, hìp-] *n.* [U] abnormal anxiety about one's health; low spirits without any real reason. —[명] 우울증

hy·po·chon·dri·ac [hàipoukándriæ̀k / -kɔ́n-, hì-] *n.* [C] a person suffering from hypochondria. —*adj.* of hypochondria; suffering from hypochondria. —[명] 우울증 환자 —[형] 우울증의

hy·poc·ri·sy [hipákrisi / -pɔ́k-] *n.* [U][C] (pl. **-sies**) the act of pretending to have more goodness than one really has. —[명] 위선

hyp·o·crite [hípəkrit] *n.* [C] a person who pretends to have goodness which he does not really have. —[명] 위선자

hyp·o·crit·i·cal [hìpoukrítik(ə)l] *adj.* of hypocrisy; like a hypocrite; dishonest. ▷**hyp·o·crit·i·cal·ly** [-kəli] *adv.* —[형] 위선의, 위선자 같은

hy·po·der·mic [hàipoudə́:rmik] *adj.* **1.** of the parts under the skin. **2.** injected under the skin through a needle. ¶*a ~ injection.*① —*n.* [C] **1.** an act of putting medicine under the skin. **2.** a medicine that is put under the skin through a needle. —[형] 1. 피하(皮下)의, 피하에 있는 2. 피하에 주입되는 ¶①피하주사 —[명] 1. 피하주사 2. 피하주사 약

hy·poth·e·ses [haipáθisi:z / -pɔ́θ-] *n.* pl. of **hypothesis.**

hy·poth·e·sis [haipáθisis / -pɔ́θ-] *n.* [C] (pl. **-ses**) something assumed to be true though it is not proved; an unproved theory. —[명] 가설

hy·po·thet·ic [hàipouθétik], **-i·cal** [-ik(ə)l] *adj.* of a hypothesis; not true. ▷**hy·po·thet·i·cal·ly** [-kəlili] *adv.* —[형] 가설의, 가상의

hys·te·ri·a [histíəriə] *n.* [U] a nervous disorder with violent fits of laughing and crying; senseless and uncontrolled excitement. —[명] 히스테리; 병적 흥분

hys·ter·ic [histérik] *n.* [C] 《usu. *pl.*》 a sudden and violent burst of uncontrolled crying or laughing; hysteria; a person suffering from hysteria. ¶*go off* (or *fall*) *into hysterics.*① —*adj.* =hysterical. —[명] 히스테리의 발작; 히스테리 환자 ¶①히스테리를 일으키다

hys·ter·i·cal [histérik(ə)l] *adj.* of or like hysteria; abnormally excited; violently uncontrolled. —[형] 히스테리의, 히스테리 같은

hys·ter·i·cal·ly [histérikəli] *adv.* in a hysterical manner. —[부] 히스테리처럼

I

I¹, i [ai] *n.* ⓒ (pl. **I's, Is, i's, is** [aiz]) **1.** the ninth letter of the English alphabet. **2.** the Roman number 1. —⑧ 1. 알파벳의 아홉째 글자 2. 로마 숫자의 I

‡ I² [ai] *pron.* (pl. **we**) the person who is speaking or writing. —⑭ 나는, 내가

-i·ble [-ibl] *suf.* able to: *visible* (=able to see). —(接尾) …할 수 있는

-ic [-ik] *suf.* **1.** of : *atomic* (=of an atom). **2.** having the nature of : *heroic* (=having the nature of a hero). —(接尾) 1. …의 2. …의 성질을 가진

-i·cal [-ik(ə)l] *suf.* =-ic: *hysterical* (=having the nature of hysteria).

‡ ice [ais] *n.* **1.** Ⓤ frozen water. **2.** ⓒ something like ice. **3.** ⓒ (*U.S.*) a frozen dessert made with fruit juice instead of cream ; (*Brit.*) an ice cream. —⑧ 1. 얼음 2. 얼음 모양의 것 3. (美) 과즙을 섞은 빙수; (英) 아이스크리임

 1) *break the ice,* ⓐ begin ; start something difficult or dangerous. ⓑ start being friendly. 熟 1) ⓐ …을 시작하다 ⓑ 친하게 되다
 2) *on thin ice,* in a dangerous or difficult position. 2) 위험한, 불안한
 —*adj.* of ice ; made of ice. —⑭ …을 얼음으로 만든
 —*vt.* **1.** cool (something) with ice ; put ice in (something) ; cover (something) with ice. **2.** freeze. —⑭ 1. …을 얼음으로 식히다; …에 얼음을 채우다; …을 얼음으로 덮다 2. …을 얼리다

ice age [⌣⌣] *n.* the period when ice covered a large area of the earth. —⑧ 빙하시대

ice ax (axe) [⌣⌣] *n.* an ax which is used to break ice when climbing a mountain. →fig. —⑧ 얼음 깨는 도끼, 피켈

[ice ax]

ice·berg [áisbəːrg] *n.* ⓒ a large mass of ice floating in the sea. —⑧ 빙산, 유빙(流氷)

ice·boat [áisbòut] *n.* ⓒ **1.** a boat used to break a channel in the frozen sea, etc. ; an icebreaker. **2.** a boat built for rapid movement on ice. —⑧ 1. 쇄빙선 2. 빙산 요트

ice·bound [áisbàund] *adj.* completely frozen ; shut in by ice. —⑭ 얼음이 언; 얼음에 갇힌

ice·box [áisbɑ̀ks / -bɔ̀ks] *n.* ⓒ (*U.S.*) a box for keeping food cool ; a refrigerator. —⑧ (美) 냉장고

ice·break·er [áisbrèikər] *n.* ⓒ (*U.S.*) a strong boat used to break a channel in frozen waters. —⑧ (美) 쇄빙선

ice cap [⌣⌣] *n.* a permanent layer of ice over an area. —⑧ [높은 산·극지의] 만년설(빙)

ice cream [⌣⌣ / ⌣⌣] *n.* a frozen dessert made of cream, sugar, eggs, etc. —⑧ 아이스크리임

iced [aist] *adj.* **1.** cooled with ice. **2.** covered with ice. —⑭ 1. 얼음으로 식힌 2. 얼음으로 덮인

ice field [⌣⌣] *n.* a large sheet or mass of floating ice. —⑧ [북극·남극의] 빙원(氷原)

ice-free [áisfríː] *adj.* (of a sea, a port, etc.) free of ice. —⑭ [항만 따위가] 얼지 않는

ice hockey [⌣⌣⌣] *n.* a game of hockey played on ice. —⑧ 아이스하키

ice·house [áishàus] *n.* ⓒ a building for storing ice. —⑧ 얼음 창고, 빙실(氷室)

Ice·land [áislænd, +*Brit.* -lənd] *n.* a country and large island in the North Atlantic. —⑧ 북대서양의 큰 섬(공화국) Iceland.

Ice·land·er [áislændər, +*Brit.* -ləndə] *n.* ⓒ a person of —⑧ 아이슬란드 사람

Ice·lan·dic [aislǽndik] *adj.* of Iceland, its people, or their language. —*n.* Ⓤ the language of Iceland. —⑭ 아이슬란드[사람·말]의 —⑧ 아이슬란드 말

ice·man [áismæn, -mən] *n.* ⓒ (pl. **-men** [-mèn, -mən]) (*U.S.*) a man who sells or delivers ice. —⑧ (美) 얼음 장수(배달부)

ice pack [⌣⌣] *n.* **1.** masses of ice floating in the sea. **2.** a bag containing ice used to cool the head, etc. —⑧ 1. 부빙군(浮氷群) 2. 얼음 주머니

ice skate [⌣⌣] *n.* (usu. *pl.*) a shoe with a metal blade used for sksting on ice. —⑧ 스케이트 구두

ice water [⌣⌣⌣] *n.* **1.** (*U.S.*) water cooled with ice. (cf. chiefly *Brit.* iced water). **2.** water formed by melted ice. —⑧ 1. (美) 얼음으로 차게 한 물 2. 얼음이 녹은 물

i·ci·cle [áisikl] *n.* ⓒ a pointed, hanging piece of ice formed by the freezing of dropping water. —⑧ 고드름

i·ci·ly [áisili] *adv.* in very cold manner. cold. —⑭ 얼음처럼, 차게

i·ci·ness [áisinis] *n.* Ⓤ the state of being icy or very —⑧ 얼음 같은 차가움

ic·ing [áisiŋ] n. ⓤⓒ a covering of sugar used to cover cakes. —ⓢ 과자에 입힌 설탕

i·con [áikɑn / -kɔn] n. ⓒ (pl. **i·cons** or **i·co·nes** [áikɔni:z]) a picture or image of a sacred person. —ⓢ [그리스 교회의] 성상(聖像), 성화

i·con·o·clast [aikánəklæst / -kɔ́n-] n. ⓒ 1. a person who is opposed to worshiping images of sacred persons. 2. a person who attacks traditional beliefs or customs. —ⓢ 1. 성상(聖像) 파괴자; 우상 파괴자 2. 인습 타파를 외치는 사람

* **i·cy** [áisi] adj. (**i·ci·er, i·ci·est**) 1. of ice; covered with ice. 2. very cold like ice. 3. cold and unfriendly. —ⓟ 1. 얼음의; 얼음으로 덮인 2. 얼음같이 찬 3. 냉담한

I'd [aid] I should; I would; I had.

I·da·ho [áidəhòu] n. a western State of the United States. ⇒NB. —ⓢ 아이다호우 주 NB Id.또는 Ida. 로 줄임. 수도 Baise

‡ **i·dea** [aidí:ə / -díə] n. ⓒ 1. a mental image; a thought; an opinion or mental impression; a concept; knowledge. ¶*the Greek ~ of man*① / *Many do not have a clear-cut ~ of what a university is.*② / *Have you any ~ of the time?* 2. a plan, a design; purpose. ¶*He is full of new ideas.*③ / *Put your main ideas into words.* 3. a fancy; a feeling that something is probable. ¶*I have the ~ that he never got undressed for bed.* / *The ~ of such a thing!*④
get ideas into one's **head,** hope for more than will be fulfilled. —ⓢ 1. 생각, 의견, 견해; 개념; 지식 ¶①그리스 사람의 인간관/②대학이 무엇이냐 하는데 대해 분명한 견해를 가진 사람은 적다 2. 착상; 계획; 의도 ¶③그는 새 아이디어가 많다 3. 상상, 있을 수 있다고 생각되는 것 ¶④설마 그럴라구!

熟 [실현되지 않을] 망상을 품다

: **i·de·al** [aidí:əl / -díəl] adj. 1. just as or equal to one's best wish; perfect. ¶*an ~ society.*① 2. existing only in imagination. —n. ⓒ something looked on as perfect; a perfect type. —ⓟ 1. 이상의, 이상적인 ¶①이상 사회 2. 공상상의 —ⓢ 이상; 전형

i·de·al·ism [aidí:əlìz(ə)m / -díəl-] n. ⓤ 1. the practice or opinion to live according to one's ideas. 2. (in art, etc.) representing beauty and perfection rather than fact. 3. (in philosophy) the theory that reality exists only in the form of ideas. —ⓢ 1. 이상주의 2. [예술·문학의] 이상주의 3. 유심론(唯心論), 관념론

i·de·al·ist [aidí:əlist / -díəl-] n. ⓒ 1. a person who practices or follows his ideals, often neglecting the practical matters. 2. (in art, philosophy, etc.) a person who believes in idealism. —ⓢ 1. 이상주의자, 이상가 2. [문예의] 이상주의자; [철학의] 관념론자

i·de·al·is·tic [aidì:əlístik / -dìəl-] adj. 1. acting according to ideals. 2. of idealism or idealists. —ⓟ 1. 이상의 2. 이상주의(자)의, 관념론(자)의

i·de·al·i·za·tion [aidì:əlizéiʃ(ə)n / -dìəlai-] n. 1. ⓤ the act of idealizing. 2. ⓒ a thing idealized; a result of being idealized. —ⓢ 1. 이상화 2. 이상화된 것

i·de·al·ize [aidí:əlàiz / -díəlaiz] vt. make (something or someone) ideal; look upon (something or someone) as perfect. —vi. imagine or form an ideal. —ⓥ …을 이상화하다, 이상적인 것으로 생각하다 —ⓥ 이상을 그리다, 이상을 좇다

i·de·al·ly [aidí:əli / -díəl-] adv. 1. according to an ideal; perfectly. 2. in idea or theory; not practically. —ⓟ 1. 이상적으로 2. 관념적으로

* **i·den·ti·cal** [aidéntik(ə)l] adj. 1. the same. ¶*The events happened at the ~ spot.* 2. exactly alike. ¶*No two faces are ~.*① ▷**i·den·ti·cal·ness** [-nis] n. —ⓟ 1. 동일한 2. 아주 비슷한 ¶①아주 똑같은 얼굴은 없다

i·den·ti·cal·ly [aidéntikəli] adv. in an identical manner. —ⓢ 동일하게, 한결같이

i·den·ti·fi·a·ble [aidéntifaiəbl] adj. that can be identified. —ⓟ 동일함을 증명할 수 있는

i·den·ti·fi·ca·tion [aidèntifikéiʃ(ə)n] n. 1. ⓤ the act of identifying or being identified. 2. ⓤⓒ anything by which a person or thing is identified. —ⓢ 1. 동일하다는 증명, 감정(鑑定); 신원조사 2. 신분증명

‡ **i·den·ti·fy** [aidéntifài] vt. (**-fied**) 1. show or recognize (someone or something) to be the same. 2. treat or consider (something) as the same. (*~ A with B*; *~ A and B*) ¶*He identified his interests with ours.* 3. (*reflexively*) associate; unite. (*~ oneself with*) ¶*She identified herself with the peace movement.* —ⓥ 1. …이 동일함을 확인(감정)하다 2. …을 동일하다고 간주하다, 동일시하다 3. …와 제휴하다, …와 함께 움직이다

i·den·ti·ty [aidéntiti] n. (pl. **-ties**) 1. ⓒⓤ the state of being a certain specific person or thing; individuality. ¶*He did not like the others to know his ~.*① 2. ⓤ the state of being the same one; exact likeness; sameness. —ⓢ 1. 개성, 정체, 신원 ¶①그는 남에게 신원이 알려지는 것을 좋아하지 않았다 2. 동일[상태], 일치

¶*He noticed the ~ of the two papers.*

id·e·o·gram [ídiougræ̀m, áid-] *n.* [C] an ideograph. —[名] 표의(表意)문자

id·e·o·graph [ídiougræ̀f, áid-, +*Brit.* -grɑ̀:f] *n.* [C] a written character that symbolizes a thing or an idea directly. —[名] 표의문자

i·de·o·log·i·cal [àidiəlάdʒikl / -lɔ́dʒ-] *adj.* of or concerned with ideology. —[形] 이데올로기의, 이데올로기에 관한

i·de·ol·o·gy [àidiάlədʒi, ìd- / -ɔ́l-] *n.* (pl. **-gies**) **1.** [C] a way of thinking; a set of doctrines or ideas. **2.** [U] abstract thinking, esp. of a not practical nature. —[名] 1. 관념 형태 2. 공리공론

id·i·o·cy [ídiəsi] *n.* (pl. **-cies**) **1.** [U] the state of being an idiot. **2.** [C] an act like an idiot's. —[名] 1. 백치 2. 백치 같은 행위

***id·i·om** [ídiəm] *n.* [C] **1.** a phrase having a particular meaning as a whole. **2.** the language of a certain people or region. **3.** a particular or individual way of expression. ¶*Goethe's ~.*① —[名] 1. 관용어법, 이디엄 2. 사투리, 방언 3. 특유한 표현, 특색 ¶①괴에테에 특유한 표현

id·i·o·mat·ic [ìdioumǽtik] *adj.* **1.** in accordance with idioms. **2.** using many idioms. **3.** of an idiom. —[形] 1. 관용 어법에 맞는 2. 관용어법을 쓴 3. 관용적인

id·i·o·syn·cra·sy [ìdiousíŋkrəsi] *n.* [C] (pl. **-sies**) a way of thinking or doing peculiar to one person. —[名] [각자의] 특질, 특징

***id·i·ot** [ídiət] *n.* [C] **1.** a person born with little mental power. **2.** a very stupid person. —[名] 1. 백치 2. 바보, 얼간이

id·i·ot·ic [ìdiάtik / -ɔ́t-] *adj.* of or like an idiot; very foolish. —[形] 백치의, 아주 바보의

id·i·ot·i·cal·ly [ìdiάtikəli / -ɔ́t-] *adv.* in an idiotic manner; very stupidly. —[副] 백치처럼

:i·dle [áidl] *adj.* (**i·dler, i·dlest**) **1.** not willing to work; lazy. ¶*an ~ fellow.*① **2.** not working; not being used; not active. ¶*an ~ workman / in my ~ moments / ~ funds / stand ~.*② **3.** useless; worthless; empty. ¶*an ~ attempt*③ */ ~ talk.* **4.** without any good reason or foundation. ¶*~ fears.* —[形] 1. 게으른, 나태한 ¶①게으름뱅이 2. 일하지 않는, 움직이지 않는 ¶②멍하니 서 있다 3. 쓸모 없는, 가치 없는 ¶③헛된 시도 4. 근거없는

—*vi.* **1.** spend time doing nothing; waste time. ¶*~ while others work.* **2.** (of a machine) running, but not engaged in useful work. —[自] 1. 게으름 피우고 있다, 빈둥빈둥 지내다 2. [기계가] 헛돌다

idle away, let (time) pass without working. ¶*~ away the afternoon.* [熟] 빈둥빈둥 [시간을] 보내다

***i·dle·ness** [áidlnis] *n.* [U] the state of being idle or useless. —[名] 태만, 게으름; 놀고 있음

i·dler [áidlər] *n.* [C] a lazy person; a person who wastes time in doing nothing. —[名] 게으름뱅이; [일을 하지 않고] 놀고 있는 사람

i·dly [áidli] *adv.* in an idle manner; without any particular purpose. —[副] 태만하게, 하는 일 없이

***i·dol** [áidl] *n.* [C] **1.** an image worshipped as a god; a false god. **2.** a person or thing very much loved or admired. —[名] 1. 우상, 신상(神像); 사신(邪神) 2. 숭배받는 사람(것)

i·dol·a·ter [aidάlətər / -dɔ́lətə] *n.* [C] **1.** a person who worships idols. **2.** an admirer. —[名] 1. 우상 숭배자 2. 숭배자

i·dol·a·trous [aidάlətrəs / -dɔ́l-] *adj.* **1.** worshipping idols. **2.** blindly admiring. ▷**i·dol·a·trous·ly** [-li] *adv.* —[形] 1. 우상 숭배의 2. 맹목적으로 숭배하는

i·dol·a·try [aidάlətri / -dɔ́l-] *n.* worship of idols; much love or admiration for a person or thing. —[名] 우상 숭배; 숭배

i·dol·ize [áidoulàiz] *vt.* **1.** worship (someone or something) as an idol. **2.** love or admire extremely. —[他] 1. …을 우상화(시)하다 2. …을 극도로 숭배하다

i·dyll, i·dyl [áidil, +*Brit.* í-] *n.* [C] **1.** a short poem describing a scene or event in the country. **2.** a scene or event suitable for this. —[名] 1. 전원시 2. 전원 풍경, 낭만적인 이야기

i·dyl·lic [aidílik, +*Brit.* i-] *adj.* suitable for an idyll; simple and pleasant like an idyll. —[形] 전원시의, 목가적인

-ie [-i] *suf.* little, darling: *doggie* (=little dog). —《接尾》 [애칭적으로] 소(小)…

i.e. [áií:, ðætíz] that is; that is to say. —《略》 즉

-ier [-iər] *suf.* (of an occupation) a person concerned with: *clothier* (=a person concerned with clothes). —《接尾》 …에 종사하는 사람

:if [if] *conj.* **1.** on condition that; in case that; supposing that. ¶*If you hit the center of the target, you win a prize. / If she were here, you would notice her.*① ⇨[usage] */ If she was here, you would have noticed her. / If you wash your hands, I'll give you a piece of cake. / What shall* (or *should*) *I do ~ [I should] fail again.*② */ If it* —[接] 1. 만일 …이면 ¶①그녀가 만일 여기 있다면 당신은 그녀를 알아볼 것이다 [usage] 현재의 사실에 반대되는 가정. be 동사는 모두 were가 되지만 대화체에서는 주어에 따라 was도 씀/ ②만일 또 실패하면 어쩔까 2. …[인

had been fine yesterday, we could have reached the summit. 2. whether. ¶*I wonder ~ he will come.*⑨ / *I wanted to see ~ the coat was big enough for me.* 3. even though; granting that. ¶*Even ~ she is tired, she must keep on working.*⑨ 4. (expressing a wish or surprise) ⇒[usage] ¶*If I only knew!*⑨ / *If he were here with me!* 5. whenever. ¶*If I don't understand, I ask questions.*
as if, as it would be if. ¶*He speaks English as ~ he were a native speaker.*

ig·loo [íglu:] *n.* ⓒ (*pl.* **-loos**) a dome-shaped Eskimo hut of snow. ⇒fig.

ig·ne·ous [ígniəs] *adj* 1. of fire. 2. produced by fire or volcanic action. ¶*an ~ rock.*⑰

ig·nite [ignáit] *vt.* 1. set fire to (something). 2. make (something) very hot. —*vi.* catch fire.

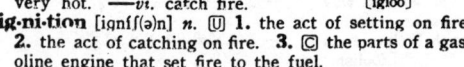
[igloo]

ig·ni·tion [igníʃ(ə)n] *n.* Ⓤ 1. the act of setting on fire. 2. the act of catching on fire. 3. ⓒ the parts of a gasoline engine that set fire to the fuel.

ig·no·ble [ignóubl] *adj.* ↔noble 1. mean; of low character. 2. of low birth. ¶*He comes from an ~ family.*

ig·no·bly [ignóubli] *adv.* in an ignoble manner. [able.]

ig·no·min·i·ous [ìgnoumíniəs] *adj.* shameful; dishonor-]

ig·no·min·y [ígnəmìni] *n.* (*pl.* **-min·ies**) 1. Ⓤ public shame or dishonor. 2. ⓒ a shameful act.

ig·no·ra·mus [ìgnəréiməs] *n.* ⓒ an ignorant person.

• **ig·no·rance** [íɡn(ə)r(ə)ns] *n.* Ⓤ lack of knowledge.

• **ig·no·rant** [íɡn(ə)r(ə)nt] *adj.* 1. knowing little; without knowledge. ¶*He may be ~, but he's not stupid.* 2. not aware. ¶*He was ~ of the rule.* 3. caused by lack of knowledge; showing ignorance.

ig·no·rant·ly [íɡn(ə)r(ə)ntli] *adv.* because of ignorance; showing ignorance. [refuse to notice.]

• **ig·nore** [ignɔ́ːr] *vt.* pay no attention to (something);]

i·gua·na [igwáːnə] *n.* ⓒ a large, tree-climbing, lizardlike animal in tropical America.

Il·i·ad [íliəd], **the** *n.* a long Greek narrative poem probably written by Homer.

‡ **ill** [il] *adj.* (**worse, worst**) 1. (chiefly as *predicative*) in bad health; sick; not well; having a disease. ↔well ⇒[usage] ¶*He is ~. / She fell ~. / Our cat looks ~.* 2. bad; evil; harmful; unfortunate. ¶*~ habit / ~ company / a sign of ~ omen / bear someone ~ will / (proverb). Ill weeds grow apace.* 3. poor; imperfect. ¶*~ management / ~ success.* [*me.*]
—*adv.* badly. ¶*speak ~ of someone / It goes ~ with*]
—*n.* 1. Ⓤ evil; harm. ¶*do ~.*⑰ 2. ⓒ (usu. *pl.*) a misfortune; a trouble; a sickness. ¶*the ills of life.*

Ill. Illinois.

‡ **I'll** [ail] I shall; I will.

ill-ad·vised [íladváizd] *adj.* acting or done without proper consideration. [ner.]

ill-ad·vis·ed·ly [íladváizidli] *adv.* in an ill-advised man-]

ill-bred [ílbréd] *adj.* badly brought up; not polite.

ill-con·di·tioned [ílkəndíʃ(ə)nd] *adj.* bad-natured; in a bad condition

ill-dis·posed [íldispóuzd] *adj.* unfriendly; unfavorable.

il·le·gal [ilí:g(ə)l] *adj.* not lawful; against the law. ↔legal

il·le·gal·i·ty [ìli(:)gǽliti] *n.* (*pl.* **-ties**) 1. Ⓤ the state of being illegal. 2. ⓒ an act against the law.

il·le·gal·ly [ilí:gəli] *adv.* in an unlawful manner.

il·leg·i·ble [iléd3ibl] *adj.* difficult or impossible to read.

지] 어떤지 ¶③그는 올까 3. 비록 … 일지라도 ¶④비록 피곤하더라도 그녀는 계속 일을 해야 한다 4. [usage] 주절을 생략한 조건절만의 형태로 쓰임 ¶⑤알기만 했더라면 5. …일 때는 언제나

霑 마치 …인 듯이
—ⓝ 에스키모 사람의 집

—ⓐ 1. 불의 2. 화성(火成)의 ¶①화성암

—ⓥ 1. …에 불을 붙이다, …을 태우다 2. …을 고도로 가열하다 —ⓥ 불이 붙다
—ⓝ 1. 점화 2. 인화, 발화 3. 점화장치

—ⓐ 1. 상스러운, 비열한 2. [태생이] 천한
—ⓐ 천하게, 상스럽게
—ⓐ 수치스러운, 불명예의
—ⓝ 1. 치욕, 창피, 불명예 2. 수치스러운 짓
—ⓝ 무식(무지)한 사람
—ⓝ 무식, 무학(無學)
—ⓐ 1. 무식한, 무학의 2. 모르는, 알아채지 못한 3. 무식에서 오는; 무식한 것 같은

—ⓐ 무식하게, 모르고

—ⓥ …을 무시하다, …을 모르는 체하다
—ⓝ 이구아나 (큰도마뱀)

—ⓝ 일리아드(Troy전쟁을 읊은 서사시)

—ⓐ 1. 병든, 편찮은, 아픈 [usage] 미국에서는 ill의 뜻에 sick도 쓰지만, 영국에서는 메스껍다는 뜻이 되어 상스러운 표현이 됨 2. 나쁜, 사악한; 불길한, 불운한 3. 빈약한, 불충분한

—ⓐ 나쁘게, 옳지 못하게
—ⓝ 1. 악, 죄악 ¶①못된 짓을 하다 2. 불행, 불운; 병, 고통

—ⓐ 무분별한

—ⓐ 무분별하게
—ⓐ 본데 없이 자란, 버릇없는
—ⓐ 성질이 못된, 짓궂은, 건강상태가 나쁜
—ⓐ 악의를 품은, 심술궂은
—ⓐ 비합법의, 불법의, 위법의
—ⓝ 1. 불법, 위법 2. 불법(위법)행위

—ⓐ 불법적으로
—ⓐ 읽기 힘든, 판독하기 어려운

il·le·git·i·ma·cy [ìlidʒítiməsi] *n.* [U] the fact or condition of being illegitimate.
—[名] 불법; 사생(私生); 불합리

il·le·git·i·mate [ìlidʒítimit] *adj.* **1.** against the law; illegal. **2.** born of unmarried parents. **3.** not logical.
—[形] 1. 불법의 2. 사생아의 3. 부조리한, 불합리한

ill-fat·ed [ílféitid] *adj.* destined to have a bad fate.
—[形] 운수 나쁜

ill-fa·vored, *Brit.* **-voured** [ílféivərd] *adj.* not pleasant in appearance; having an unpleasant look; ugly.
—[形] 못생긴, 보기 흉한

ill-got·ten [ílgátn / -gɔ́tn] *adj.* obtained by dishonest means.
—[形] 부정 수단으로 얻은

ill-hu·mored, *Brit.* **-moured** [íl(h)jú:mərd / -hjú:məd] *adj.* bad-tempered; cross; in a bad humor.
—[形] 기분이 언짢은

il·lib·er·al [ilíb(ə)r(ə)l] *adj.* **1.** not liberal; narrow-minded. **2.** not generous; stingy.
—[形] 1. 도량이 좁은 2. 인색한, 욕심 많은

il·lic·it [ilísit] *adj.* not allowed by law, etc.; illegal; improper.
—[形] 불법의, 부정한

il·lim·it·a·ble [ilímitəbl] *adj.* without limit; immeasurable; endless; vast.
—[形] 무한의, 헤아릴 수 없는

Il·li·nois [ìlinɔ́i, +*U.S.* -nɔ́iz] *n.* a middle-western State in the United States. ⇒[N.B.]
—[名] 일리노이 주 [N.B.] Ill.로 줄임. 수도 Springfield

il·lit·er·a·cy [ilít(ə)rəsi] *n.* [U] the state of being illiterate.
—[名] 무학, 무식; 문맹

il·lit·er·ate [ilít(ə)rit] *adj.* **1.** unable to read or write. **2.** not cultured; uneducated. **—*n.*** [C] an illiterate person.
—[形] 1. 읽고 쓸 수 없는, 문맹의 2. 교양 없는, 교육받지 못한 —[名] 문맹자, 교양 없는 사람

ill-na·tured [ílnéitʃərd] *adj.* of an ill nature; disagreeable; cross.
—[形] 성미가 못된, 심술궂은

* **ill·ness** [ílnis] *n.* [U][C] the state of being sick; sickness.
—[名] 병, 건강하지 못함

il·log·i·cal [iládʒik(ə)l / -lɔ́dʒ-] *adj.* not logical; not well reasoned. ▷**il·log·i·cal·ly** [-i] *adv.*
—[形] 비(非)이론적인, 불합리한

ill-starred [ílstá:rd] *adj.* born under an unlucky star; unfortunate.
—[形] 액운을 타고난, 운수가 나쁜

ill-tem·pered [íltémpərd] *adj.* having or showing bad temper; cross; quarrelsome.
—[形] 기분이 언짢은, 화를 잘 내는, 성미 급한

ill-timed [íltáimd] *adj.* coming or done at a bad time.
—[形] 때를 못 만난, 기회를 놓친

ill-treat [íltrí:t] *vt.* treat cruelly or unfairly.
—[他] …을 학대(냉대)하다

ill-treat·ment [íltrí:tmənt] *n.* [U] cruel, unfair or unkind treatment.
—[名] 학대, 혹사

* **il·lu·mi·nate** [ilú:minèit, +*Brit.* iljú:-] *vt.* **1.** give light to (something); light up. **2.** decorate (something) with lights. **3.** make (something difficult) clear; explain. **4.** decorate (an initial letter, a word or the border of a page) with colors, pictures, designs, etc.
—[他] 1. …을 비추다, 조명하다 2. …을 등불로 장식하다 3. …을 분명히 하다, 설명하다 4. …을 색무늬(금박)로 꾸미다

il·lu·mi·na·tion [ilù:minéiʃ(ə)n, +*Brit.* iljù:-] *n.* **1.** [U] the act of illuminating or lighting up. **2.** [U] the act of making clear; explanation. **3.** [C] ⟪usu. *pl.*⟫ decoration with lights. **4.** [C] ⟪usu. *pl.*⟫ decoration of initial letters, the borders of pages, etc. with gold and designs. **5.** [U] enlightenment.
—[名] 1. 조명, 비추기 2. 명시, 설명 3. 일루미네이션, 전등 장식 4. [사본의] 채식(彩飾) 5. 계몽

il·lu·mine [iljú:min] *vt.* make (something) bright; illuminate; light up.
—[他] …을 비추다, 밝게 하다

ill-us·age [íljú:sidʒ, -zidʒ / -zidʒ] *n.* [U] unfair or cruel treatment.
—[名] 학대, 혹사

ill-use *vt.* [íljú:z → *n.*] treat badly or cruelly. **—*n.*** [íljú:s] [U] bad or cruel treatment.
—[他] …을 학대하다, 악용하다
—[名] 학대, 혹사, 악용

* **il·lu·sion** [ilú:ʒ(ə)n] *n.* [U][C] **1.** something which gives a false or misleading appearance or impression. **2.** a false or mistaken idea, conception or belief; a delusion.
—[名] 1. 환상, 착각을 일으키게 하는 것, 환영(幻影) 2. 환상, 환각, 착각; 망상

il·lu·sive [ilú:siv] *adj.* of or producing illusion; unreal.
—[形] 착각의, 착각을 일으키게 하는

il·lu·so·ry [ilú:s(ə)ri] *adj.* illusive; unreal.
—[形] 착각의, 가공(架空)의

⁑ **il·lus·trate** [íləstrèit, +*U.S.* ilʌ́streit] *vt.* **1.** give (a book, etc.) pictures, diagrams, maps, etc. to help to explain or decorate it. ¶*The book is well illustrated.* **2.** make (something) clear by stories, examples, etc.
—[他] 1. …을 도해하다, …에 삽화를 넣다 2. …을 설명하다, 실례·비교 따위를 들어 해설하다

il·lus·trat·ed [íləstrèitid, +*U.S.* ilʌ́streit-] *adj.* explained, or ornamented by pictures, diagrams, etc.
—[形] 예해(例解)된, 도해된; 삽화를 넣은

⁑ **il·lus·tra·tion** [ìləstréiʃ(ə)n] *n.* **1.** [C] a picture, diagram, map, etc. used to explain or decorate. **2.** [C] a story, an example, etc. used to explain. **3.** [U] the act of explaining or decorating by the use of pictures or examples.
—[名] 1. 삽화, 설명도 2. [설명에 쓰는] 실례(實例), 이야기 [따위], 3. 설명, 예해(例解), 도해

il·lus·tra·tive [íləstrèitiv, +*U.S.* ilʌ́strətiv] *adj.* of or used for illustration. ¶*The example was ~ of the new idea.*
—[形] 예증(例證)이 되는, 설명적인

il·lus·tra·tor [íləstrèitər, +*U.S.* ilʌ́s-] *n.* [C] **1.** a person who makes pictures illustrating books, magazines, etc. **2.** a person or thing that explains.
—[名] 1. 삽화가 2. 설명자, 해설자; 설명이 되는 것(사람)

il·lus·tri·ous [ilʌ́striəs] *adj.* very famous; distinguished.
—[形] 유명한, 저명한

ill will [´ ´] *n.* unfriendly feeling; unfriendliness.
—[名] 악의; 적의(敵意); 원한

ill-wish·er [ílwíʃər] *n.* [C] a person who wishes misfortune to another.
—[名] 남의 불행을 바라는 사람

‡ **I'm** [aim] I am.

im- [im] *pref.* =in-, used before p, b, and m: *impossible*; *imbalance*; *immoral.*

‡ **im·age** [ímidʒ] *n.* [C] **1.** a thing drawn, painted, sculptured, etc. in the likeness of a person, an animal, etc. **2.** a person or thing closely like another; a counterpart. **3.** an impression seen in a mirror, through a lens, etc. **4.** a symbol. **5.** a picture in the mind; a mental conception.
—[名] 1. 상(像), 화상, 조상(彫像) 2. 아주 비슷한 사람(것) 3. 영상(映像) 4. 상징 5. 심상(心像)

—*vt.* **1.** make a picture or sculpture of (someone or something). **2.** reflect. **3.** make a picture of (something) in the mind; imagine. **4.** describe (something) vividly in words.
—[他] 1. …의 화상(조상)을 그리다(만들다) 2. …의 상(像)을 비추다 3. …을 마음에 그리다, 상상하다 4. 생생하게 묘사하다

im·age·ry [ímidʒ(ə)ri] *n.* [U] ⟪*collectively*⟫ **1.** pictures in the mind. **2.** figures of speech used to form pictures in the mind. **3.** images; statues.
—[名] 1. 심상(心像)(마음에 그리는 상) 2. 비유적 표현 3. 상, 초상, 조상(彫像)

im·ag·i·na·ble [imǽdʒ(i)nəbl] *adj.* that can be pictured in the mind; possible. ¶*the greatest joy ~*① / *every ~ method.*
—[形] 상상할 수 있는, 상상이 미치는 한의 ¶①상상도 못할 큰 기쁨

• **im·ag·i·nar·y** [imǽdʒinèri / -n(ə)ri] *adj.* existing only in the imagination; not real. ¶*an ~ number*① / *Fairies are ~.*②
—[形] 상상의, 실재하지 않는 ¶①허수(虛數)/②요정은 상상상의 존재다

‡ **im·ag·i·na·tion** [imæ̀dʒinéiʃ(ə)n] *n.* [U] **1.** the act or power of forming pictures of what is not actually present. **2.** the ability to create new things or ideas in the mind. **3.** [C][U] something imagined in the mind.
—[名] 1. 상상, 상상력 2. 창작력 3. 상상의 소산; 공상

im·ag·i·na·tive [imǽdʒinətiv, +*U.S.* -nèit-] *adj.* **1.** of, having or showing imagination. ¶*an ~ tale.* **2.** able to imagine well; creative. ¶*an ~ artist.*
—[形] 1. 상상상(想像上)의, 상상적인 2. 상상력이 풍부한

‡ **im·ag·ine** [imǽdʒin] *vt.* **1.** form a picture of (something) in one's mind. **2.** guess; suppose; think. ¶*I couldn't ~ what would be the result.*① —*vi.* use the imagination.
—[他] 1. …을 상상하다, 마음에 그리다 2. …을 추측(짐작)하다 ¶①결과가 어떻게 될지 짐작도 못하겠다 —[自] 상상력을 발동시키다

im·be·cile [ímbisil, -sì:l] *n.* [C] a person with a very weak mind; a very stupid person. —*adj.* very weak in mind; stupid.
—[名] 저능한 사람, 바보 —[形] 저능한, 어리석은

im·be·cil·i·ty [ìmbisíliti] *n.* (pl. **-ties**) **1.** [U] the state of being imbecile. **2.** [C] a foolish action, speech, etc.
—[名] 1. 저능, 치매(痴呆) 2. 어리석은 언동

im·bibe [imbáib] *vt.* **1.** drink; drink to excess. **2.** absorb. ¶*Sponge imbibes water.* **3.** receive (something) into one's mind.
—[他] 1. …을 [지나치게] 마시다 2. …을 흡수하다 3. …을 받아들이다; 섭취하다

im·bro·glio [imbróuliou] *n.* [C] (pl. **-glios**) **1.** a difficult or complicated situation. **2.** a confused or complicated misunderstanding or disagreement.
—[名] 1. 분규, 말썽 2. 뒤엉킨 사정, 복잡한 사정(오해)

im·brue [imbrú:] *vt.* make (something) wet, esp. with blood; stain. ¶*His hands were imbrued with blood.*①
—[他] …을 [피로] 물들이다, 더럽히다 ¶①그는 살인죄를 범했다

im·bue [imbjú:] *vt.* **1.** impress deeply; inspire. ¶*The soldiers were imbued with patriotism.*① **2.** cause (something) to be full of moisture or color. ⟪~ something *into* or *with*⟫ ¶*~ a fabric with blue.*②
—[他] 1. …을 불어 넣다, 고취하다 ¶①병사들은 애국심에 고취되었다 2. …에 스며들게 하다, 물들이다 ¶②천을 푸르게 물들이다

• **im·i·tate** [ímitèit] *vt.* **1.** do or try to do the same as; follow the example of (someone or something). **2.** make a likeness of (something).
—[他] 1. …을 흉내내다, 모방하다, 보고 배우다 2. …을 모조하다; …와 비슷하게 만들다

• **im·i·ta·tion** [ìmitéiʃ(ə)n] *n.* **1.** [U] the act of imitating. ¶*We learn by ~.* **2.** [C] a copy. —*adj.* made to
—[名] 1. 흉내내기, 모방 2. 모사(模寫)한 것, 모조품 —[形] 모조의, 인조의 ¶①모

resemble something real or superior; not real. ¶~ *pearls.*①
조 진주

im·i·ta·tive [ímitèitiv, +*Brit.* -tətiv] *adj.* of imitation; not original or real; imitating. ¶~ *words*① / ~ *art.*②
—[名] 모방의, 모조의 ¶①의성어(擬聲語)/②모조 미술

im·i·ta·tor [ímitèitər] *n.* [C] a person who imitates.
—[名] 흉내내는 사람, 모방자

im·mac·u·late [imǽkjulit] *adj.* **1.** without a spot or stain; spotless; clean. **2.** without fault or sin; pure.
—[形] 1. 더럽혀지지 않은, 오점 없는 2. 완벽한, 깨끗한

im·ma·nence [ímənəns], **-nen·cy** [-nənsi] *n.* [U] the state of being immanent.
—[名] 내재(內在)[성]

im·ma·nent [ímənənt] *adj.* **1.** living or remaining within. **2.** (of God) present throughout the universe.
—[形] 1. 내재의, 내재적인 2. [신이] 우주에 편재(遍在)하는

im·ma·te·ri·al [ìmətíəriəl] *adj.* **1.** not material; not consisting of matter. **2.** not important.
—[形] 1. 비(非)물질적인, 실체가 없는 2. 중요하지 않은; 보잘 것 없는

im·ma·ture [ìmət(j)úər / -tjúə] *adj.* not fully grown; not mature; not ripe.
—[形] 미숙한; 미완성의

im·ma·tu·ri·ty [ìmət(j)úəriti / -tjúə-] *n.* [U] the state of being immature.
—[名] 미숙[한 상태]; 미완성[상태]

im·meas·ur·a·ble [iméʒ(ə)rəbl] *adj.* too big to be measured; boundless; vast.
—[形] 잴 수 없는, 한없는, 광대한

im·meas·ur·a·bly [iméʒ(ə)rəbli] *adv.* to an immeasurable extent or degree; vastly.
—[副] 헤아릴 수 없을 만큼, 한없이, 광대하게

im·me·di·a·cy [imí:diəsi] *n.* [U] the state or quality of being immediate.
—[名] 직접, 밀접; 즉시[성]

‡**im·me·di·ate** [imí:diit] *adj.* **1.** happening or coming at once; without delay. ¶*an* ~ *reply.*① **2.** with nothing coming between; direct. ¶*an* ~ *result.*② **3.** closest; nearest. ¶*my* ~ *neighborhood.*③ **4.** of the present time; urgent.
—[形] 1. 조속한, 즉석의 ¶①즉답 2. 직접적인 ¶②직접적 결과 3. 바로 이웃의, 인접한 ¶③이웃 사람들 4. 당면한, 현하의

‡**im·me·di·ate·ly** [imí:diitli] *adv.* in an immediate manner; at once; directly. —*conj.* (chiefly *Brit.*) as soon as. ¶*Immediately he got home, he went to bed.*①
—[副] 즉석에서; 직접적으로 —[接] 《英》 …하자마자 곧 ¶①그는 집으로 오자 곧 잤다

im·me·mo·ri·al [ìmimɔ́:riəl] *adj.* extending beyond reach of memory; very old.
—[形] 기억을 초월한, 먼 옛날의; 태고의

‡**im·mense** [iméns] *adj.* **1.** very big; huge; vast. **2.** (*colloq.*) very good; splendid; excellent.
—[形] 1. 거대한, 광대한 2. 《口》 멋진, 훌륭한

im·mense·ly [iménsli] *adv.* **1.** to an immense degree; enormously. **2.** very much. ¶*I enjoyed the party* ~.
—[副] 1. 무한하게, 광대하게 2. 대단히, 엄청나게

im·men·si·ty [iménsiti] *n.* [U] **1.** very great extent or size; vastness. **2.** infinite space.
—[名] 1. 광대, 막대 2. 무한의 공간(퍼짐)

im·merse [imə́:rs] *vt.* **1.** dip (something) into a liquid. **2.** baptize (someone) by dipping him under water. **3.** involve or absorb deeply. ¶*be immersed in one's work.*
—[他] 1. …을 [액체 속에] 담그다, 잠그다 2. …에 침례(浸禮)를 베풀다 3. …을 열중(몰두)시키다

im·mer·sion [imə́:rʒ(ə)n, -ʃ(ə)n / -mə́:ʃ(ə)n] *n.* [U] **1.** the act of immersing; the state of being immersed. **2.** the state of being deeply engaged or absorbed.
—[名] 1. 침입(浸入, 沈入) 2. 전렴, 몰두

*****im·mi·grant** [ímigrənt] *n.* [C] a person who comes into a foreign country to live there permanently.
—[名] 이민, 이주자

im·mi·grate [ímigrèit] *vi.* come into a foreign country to live there permanently. —*vt.* bring in or send (someone) as an immigrant. ⇒[N.B.]
—[自] 이주해 오다 —[他] …을 이주시키다 [N.B.] 「이주하기 위해 나라를 떠나다」는 emigrate

im·mi·gra·tion [ìmigréiʃ(ə)n] *n.* **1.** [U] the act of coming into a foreign country to live there permanently. **2.** [C] the number of immigrants during a certain period.
—[名] 1. 이주, 이민 2. 이주민 수

im·mi·nence [íminəns] *n.* **1.** [U] the state of being imminent. **2.** [C] something, esp. something evil or dangerous, which is likely to happen soon.
—[名] 1. 절박(긴박)[한 상태] 2. 절박한 위험

im·mi·nent [íminənt] *adj.* likely to occur soon; threatening.
—[形] 절박한, 급박한

im·mo·bile [imóubil, -bi:l, +*Brit.* -bail] *adj.* **1.** not able to move or be moved; firmly fixed. **2.** not moving; motionless.
—[形] 1. 움직이기 어려운, 움직이지 않는; 고정한 2. 정지(靜止)의

im·mo·bil·i·ty [ìmoubíliti] *n.* [U] the state of being immobile.
—[名] 부동; 고정; 정지

im·mo·bi·lize [imóubilàiz] *vt.* make (something) immobile.
—[他] …을 고정시키다, 움직일 수 없게 하다

im·mod·er·ate [imɑ́d(ə)rit / -mɔ́d-] *adj.* not moderate; extreme; excessive.
—[形] 중용(中庸)을 잃은, 극단의, 과도한

im·mod·est [imádist / -mɔ́d-] *adj.* not modest.
—[형] 버릇없는, 근신하지 않는

im·mod·es·ty [imádisti / imɔ́d-] *n.* (pl. **-ties**) [U] the state of being immodest; lack of modesty; [C] an immodest act or remark.
—[명] 불근신, 뻔뻔스러움, 버릇없음; 버릇없는 짓(말)

im·mo·late [íməulèit] *vt.* kill or offer (something) as a sacrifice.
—[타] …을 [신에게 바치기 위해] 죽이다, 희생으로 바치다

im·mor·al [imɔ́:r(ə)l / -mɔ́r(ə)l] *adj.* not moral; wicked.
—[형] 부도덕한, 품행이 나쁜

im·mor·al·i·ty [ìmərǽliti] *n.* (pl. **-ties**) [U] the state of being immoral; wickedness; [C] an immoral act.
—[명] 부도덕, 패륜; 부도덕한 행위

im·mor·tal** [imɔ́:rtl] *adj.* **1.** living or lasting forever; never dying. **2.** never to be forgotten; remembered forever. **—*n. [C] **1.** a person who never dies. **2.** a person whose fame is remembered forever.
—[형] 1. 죽지 않는, 불사신의, 불멸의 2. 불후(不朽)의, 불후의 명성이 있는 —[명] 1. 죽지 않는 사람 2. 명성이 사라지지 않는 사람

im·mor·tal·i·ty [ìmɔ:rtǽliti] *n.* [U] **1.** a life which continues forever; the state of living forever. **2.** everlasting fame.
—[명] 1. 죽지 않음, 불멸 2. 불후의 명성

im·mor·tal·ize [imɔ́:rtəlàiz] *vt.* **1.** make (someone) immortal. **2.** give everlasting fame to (someone).
—[타] 1. …을 죽지 않게 하다, 영원성을 주다 2. …에게 불후의 명성을 주다

im·mov·a·ble [imú:vəbl] *adj.* **1.** not able to move or be moved. **2.** firm; unchanging. **—*n.*** [C] (*pl.*) immovable property, such as land, buildings, etc.
—[형] 1. 움직일 수 없는, 고정한 2. 확고한, 부동의 —[명] 부동산

im·mune [imjú:n] *adj.* **1.** protected from a particular disease. (~ *from* (or *against, to*) some disease) **2.** safe; free. ¶*He is ~ from punishment.*①
—[형] 1. 면역[성]의 2. 면제된 ¶①그는 처벌이 면제되어 있다

im·mu·ni·ty [imjú:niti] *n.* [U] **1.** the state of not being affected by a particular disease, poison, etc. ¶*The injection will give you ~ to the disease.*① **2.** freedom; exemption.
—[명] 1. 면역[성] ¶①이 주사로 너는 그 병에 대한 면역성이 생긴다 2. 면제, 면하기

im·mu·nize [ímju(:)nàiz] *vt.* protect (someone) from a particular disease; give immunity to (someone). (~ someone *against*)
—[타] …에게 면역성을 주다

im·mure [imjúər] *vt.* shut (someone) up in prison; imprison.
—[타] …을 유폐하다, 감금하다

im·mu·ta·bil·i·ty [imjù:təbíliti] *n.* [U] the state of being immutable.
—[명] 불변[성], 불역성(不易性)

im·mu·ta·ble [imjú:təbl] *adj.* never changing; unchangeable.
—[형] 불변의, 불역(不易)의

imp [imp] *n.* [C] **1.** a little devil or demon. **2.** a mischievous child.
—[명] 1. 작은 도깨비 2. 장난꾸러기

im·pact [ímpækt] *n.* [C][U] the act of striking against another; collision.
—[명] 충돌

im·pair [impέər] *vt.* lessen the value of (something); make (something) worse; injure.
—[타] …을 손상시키다, 줄이다, 해치다

im·pair·ment [impέərmənt] *n.* [U] the act of impairing; the state of being impaired; injury.
—[명] 손상, 감손(減損)

im·pale [impéil] *vt.* **1.** pierce through (something) with anything sharp. (~ something *upon* or *with*) **2.** kill (something) by thrusting upon a sharp stake.
—[타] 1. …을 꿰뚫다, 찔러 꽂다 2. …을 찔러 죽이다

im·pal·pa·ble [impǽlpəbl] *adj.* **1.** that cannot be perceived by the sense of touch. **2.** not easily grasped by the mind.
—[형] 1. 만져보아도 알 수 없는 2. 이해하기 어려운; 미묘한

im·part [impá:rt] *vt.* **1.** give a portion of (something); give. **2.** tell; disclose.
—[타] 1. …을 나누어 주다 2. …을 전하다, 알리다; 폭로하다

im·par·tial [impá:rʃ(ə)l] *adj.* not favoring one side or the other; fair; just.
—[형] 치우치지 않는, 공평한

im·par·ti·al·i·ty [ímpà:rʃiǽliti] *n.* [U] the state or quality of being impartial; fairness; justice.
—[명] 공평[무사], 공명정대

im·pass·a·bil·i·ty [impæ̀səbíliti / -pà:s-] *n.* [U] the state of being impassable.
—[명] 통행 불능

im·pass·a·ble [impǽsəbl / -pá:s-] *adj.* that cannot be passed through; not passable.
—[형] 통과(통행)할 수 없는

im·passe [ímpæs, -´ / æmpá:s] *n.* [C] **1.** a position or place from which no escape can be made; a deadlock. **2.** a road open only at one end.
—[명] 1. 막다른 골목, 난국, 곤경 2. 막힌 골목

im·pas·sioned [impǽʃ(ə)nd] *adj.* full of strong emotion; showing deep feeling; passionate.
—[형] 감격한, 열렬한

im·pas·sive [impǽsiv] *adj.* without showing or feeling emotion, pain, etc.; unmoved; insensible.
—[형] 무감각한; 무감동의; 고통을 느끼지 않는

im·pa·tience [impéiʃ(ə)ns] *n.* [U] **1.** the state or quality of being impatient; lack of patience. **2.** restless eagerness. —[名] 1. 참을 수 없음, 초조, 조바심 2. 갈망, 열망

* **im·pa·tient** [impéiʃ(ə)nt] *adj.* **1.** not patient; not willing to wait. **2.** restless; eager. ¶*They were ~ to start.* **3.** showing lack of patience. ¶*an ~ reply.* —[形] 1. 참을성 없는, 안절부절 못하는 2. 침착하지 못한 3. 성급한, 성마른

im·pa·tient·ly [impéiʃ(ə)ntli] *adv.* in an impatient manner. —[副] 성급하게, 조바심하여

im·peach [impíːtʃ] *vt.* **1.** bring (something) in question. **2.** accuse (someone) of wrongdoing. —[他] 1. …을 의심하다, 문제삼다 2. …을 비난하다; 고발하다

im·peach·ment [impíːtʃmənt] *n.* [U][C] the act of impeaching; the state of being impeached. —[名] 비난, 탄핵, 고소; 의혹

im·pec·ca·ble [impékəbl] *adj.* **1.** faultless. **2.** not doing wrong. ▷**im·pec·ca·bly** [-i] *adv.* —[形] 1. 결점 없는 2. 죄를 범하지 않은

im·pe·cu·ni·ous [ìmpikjúːniəs] *adj.* having little money; poor. —[形] 돈이 없는, 가난한

im·pede [impíːd] *vt.* obstruct; hinder. —[他] …을 방해하다, 훼방놓다

im·ped·i·ment [impédimənt] *n.* [C] **1.** a thing which hinders; an obstacle. **2.** a defect in speech. —[名] 1. 방해, 장해 2. 언어 장해

im·pel [impél] *vt.* (**-pelled, -pel·ling**) **1.** drive; force; compel. 《~ someone *to do*》 ¶*The rain impelled him to give up the plan.*① **2.** drive forward; push along. 《~ something *to do*》 ¶*The current impelled the boat to shore.* —[他] 1. …을 강요하다, 억지로… 시키다 ¶①비 때문에 그는 그 계획을 포기하지 않을 수 없었다 2. …을 밀고 나아가다, 추진시키다

im·pend [impénd] *vi.* **1.** be about to happen soon; be at hand; threaten. ¶*War seemed to ~.* **2.** hang over. —[自] 1. …이 일어나려 하고 있다; 임박하다 2. 위에 드리워지다

im·pend·ing [impéndiŋ] *adj.* **1.** about to happen soon; threatening. **2.** overhanging. —[形] 1. 지금이라도 일어날 듯한, 절박한 2. 머리 위에 걸린

im·pen·e·tra·ble [impénitrəbl] *adj.* **1.** that cannot be penetrated or passed through. ¶*an ~ wall.* **2.** not open to reason, sympathy, etc. **3.** that cannot be understood. —[形] 1. 꿰뚫을 수 없는, 지나갈 수 없는 2. [사상·감정에] 완고한, 둔한 3. 이해할 수 없는

im·pen·i·tence [impénit(ə)ns] *n.* [U] the state or quality of being impenitent. —[名] 뉘우치지 않음; 완고함

im·pen·i·tent [impénit(ə)nt] *adj.* not penitent; feeling no regret for wrongdoing. ▷**im·pen·i·tent·ly** [-li] *adv.* —[形] 완고한, 뉘우치지 않는

im·per·a·tive [impérətiv] *adj.* **1.** that cannot be avoided; necessary. ¶*It is ~ that he* [*should*] *stay in bed.*① **2.** commanding with authority. ¶*an ~ gesture.* —[形] 1. 피할 수 없는; 절대 필요한 ¶①그는 절대로 자리에 누워 있어야 한다 2. 명령적인, 권위 있는
—*n.* **1.** [C] a command; an order. **2.** [U] (*Grammar*) 《*the* ~》 the mood expressing command; [C] a form of a verb in this mood. —[名] 1. 명령 2.《文法》 명령법; 명령형

im·per·a·tive·ly [impérətivli] *adv.* in an imperative manner. —[副] 명령적으로

im·per·cep·ti·ble [ìmpərséptibl] *adj.* too small, slight, slow, etc. to be seen, heard or felt. —[形] 미세한, 희미한, 아주 느린, 지각(知覺)할 수 없는

* **im·per·fect** [impə́ːrfikt] *adj.* **1.** not perfect; with some faults. **2.** not complete. —[形] 1. 불완전한, 결점이 있는 2. 미완성의

im·per·fec·tion [ìmpə(ː)rfékʃ(ə)n] *n.* [U] **1.** the state or quality of being imperfect; incompleteness. **2.** [C] fault; defect. —[名] 1. 불완전, 미완성 2. 결점, 단점

im·per·fect·ly [impə́ːrfiktli] *adv.* in an imperfect manner. —[副] 불완전하게

* **im·pe·ri·al** [impíəriəl] *adj.* **1.** of an empire or emperor. **2.** of the rule or authority of a country over its dependents. **3.** majestic; magnificent. **4.** of a special (usu. large) size or quality. —[形] 1. 제국의; 황제의; 황실의 2. 지배하는, 지배자적인 3. 장엄한, 위엄 있는 4. 우수한, 특대의
—*n.* [C] a small beard beneath the lower lip. ⇒fig. ▷**im·pe·ri·al·ly** [-i] *adv.* —[名] 황제 수염

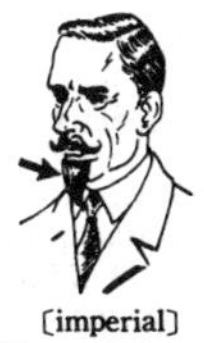
[imperial]

im·pe·ri·al·ism [impíəriəlìz(ə)m] *n.* [U] **1.** policy of a country of extending its rule over other countries. **2.** imperial power or government. —[名] 1. 제국주의, 영토확장 주의 2. 제정(帝政)

im·pe·ri·al·ist [impíəriəlist] *n.* [C] a person who supports imperialism. —[名] 제국주의자, 제정주의자

im·pe·ri·al·is·tic [impìəriəlístik] *adj.* of or supporting imperialism or imperialists. —[形] 제국주의의

im·per·il [impéril] *vt.* (**-iled, -il·ing** or *Brit.* **-illed, -il·ling**) put (someone or something) in danger. —[他] …을 위태롭게 하다, 위험에 빠뜨리다

im·pe·ri·ous [impíəriəs] *adj.* **1.** haughty; arrogant; overbearing. **2.** necessary; urgent. ▷**im·pe·ri·ous·ly** [-li] *adv.* —**im·pe·ri·ous·ness** [-nis] *n.*
—[形] 1. 제왕 같은, 거만한, 전제적인 2. 긴급한, 중대한

im·per·ish·a·ble [impériʃəbl] *adj.* not perishable; everlasting.
—[形] 불멸의, 죽지 않는, 불후의

im·per·ma·nent [impə́:rmənənt] *adj.* not permanent; temporary.
—[形] 영속적이 아닌, 일시적인

im·per·me·a·ble [impə́:rmiəbl] *adj.* not permitting fluid to pass through; impassable.
—[形] 스며들지 않는, 불침투성(不浸透性)의

im·per·son·al [impə́:rsn(ə)l] *adj.* **1.** relating not to any particular person but to all persons or to any person. **2.** not existing as a person.
—[形] 1. 개안에 속하지 않는, 비개인적인; 특정인을 가리키지 않는 2. 인격을 갖지 않은

im·per·son·ate [impə́:rsənèit] *vt.* **1.** play (a part) on the stage. **2.** pretend to be (someone or something); imitate. **3.** represent something in the form of a person.
—[他] 1. …으로 분장하다, …의 역을 맡아하다 2. …을 가장하다, …을 흉내내다 3. …을 의인화(擬人化)하다

im·per·son·a·tion [impə̀:rsənéiʃ(ə)n] *n.* **1.** [U] the act of impersonating. **2.** [C] an impersonated person or thing. **3.** [U] personification.
—[名] 1. 분장; 남의 모습으로의 가장 2. 구상화(具象化)된 사람(것) 3. 인격화, 의인화

im·per·ti·nence [impə́:rtinəns] *n.* [U] **1.** the state or quality of being impertinent; impudence. **2.** [C] an impertinent person, act or speech. **3.** [U] unsuitability; inappropriateness.
—[名] 1. 버릇없음, 무례 2. 버릇없는 사람(언행) 3. 부적당; 엉뚱함

im·per·ti·nent [impə́:rtinənt] *adj.* **1.** impudent; rude. **2.** not to the point; out of place.
—[形] 1. 주제넘은, 버릇없는 2. 엉뚱한, 부적절한

im·per·turb·a·ble [ìmpərtə́:rbəbl] *adj.* not easily excited; calm.
—[形] 침착한, 냉정한

im·per·vi·ous [impə́:rviəs] *adj.* **1.** not allowing entrance or passage. ¶*This cloth is ~ to rain.*① **2.** that cannot be affected or influenced. ¶*He was ~ to the argument.*② ▷**im·per·vi·ous·ness** [-nis] *n.*
—[形] 1. 소통하지 않는, 스며들지 않는 ¶①이 천은 비가 스미지 않는다 2. 둔감한, 잘 이해 못하는 ¶②그에게는 그 주장이 통하지 않는다

im·pet·u·os·i·ty [impètʃuásiti / -tjuɔ́s-] *n.* (pl. **-ties**) **1.** [U] impetuous quality. **2.** [C] an impetuous action.
—[名] 1. 맹렬, 성급함 2. 격렬한 행동

im·pet·u·ous [impétʃuəs / -tju-] *adj.* **1.** moving with great force and violence. ¶*an ~ wind.*① **2.** acting with sudden feeling and energy.
—[形] 1 맹렬한, 격렬한 ¶①강풍 2. 충동적인

im·pet·u·ous·ly [impétʃuəsli / -tju-] *adv.* in an impetuous manner.
—[副] 맹렬하게, 성급하게, 충동적으로

im·pe·tus [ímpitəs] *n.* **1.** [U] the force with which a body tends to move on. **2.** [C] a forward push; a stimulus.
—[名] 1. 운동량 2. 충동, 탄성; 자극

im·pi·e·ty [impáiəti] *n.* (pl. **-ties**) **1.** [U] lack of respect for God. **2.** [U] lack of respect for any usu. honored person, institution, or thing. **3.** [C] an impious act.
—[名] 1. 불신앙 2. [손위 사람·제도 따위에 대한] 불경(不敬), 버릇없음 3. 신앙심 없는 언행

im·pinge [impíndʒ] *vi.* **1.** hit; strike. **2.** infringe. ⟪~ *upon* something⟫
—[自] 1. 치다, 부딪치다 2. 범하다, 침해하다

im·pi·ous [ímpiəs] *adj.* not pious; not worshiping God.
—[形] 신앙심이 없는, 신을 공경하지 않는

imp·ish [ímpiʃ] *adj.* of or like an imp; mischievous.
—[形] 작은 악마 같은, 장난꾸러기의

im·plac·a·ble [implǽkəbl, -pléi-] *adj.* that cannot be pacified or soothed; relentless.
—[形] 달래기 어려운, 용서할 수 없는, 냉혹한

im·plant [implǽnt / -plá:nt] *vt.* **1.** instill; fix. ¶~ *the idea in the student.* **2.** insert; plant.
—[他] 1. …을 가르치다, 주입하다 2. …을 끼워 넣다, 심다

***im·ple·ment** *n.* [ímplimənt → *v.*] [C] a tool or an instrument, such as a plow, an ax or a shovel. —*vt.* [ímplimènt] put (something) into effect; carry out.
—[名] 도구, 용구(用具) —[他] …을 수행하다, 완성하다

im·ple·men·ta·tion [ìmplimentéiʃ(ə)n] *n.* [U] the act of implementing; the state of being implemented.
—[名] 이행, 실행; 성취

im·pli·cate [ímplikèit] *vt.* **1.** involve (something or someone); make (someone) concerned. ¶*He was implicated in the accusation.* **2.** imply. **3.** twist together; entangle.
—[他] 1. …을 연루(連累)(관련)시키다 2. …을 함축하다 3. …을 얽히게 하다

im·pli·ca·tion [ìmplikéiʃ(ə)n] *n.* **1.** [U] the act of implying; the state of being implied. **2.** [C] a thing which is implied; a hint. **3.** [U] the act of implicating; the state of being; implicated.
—[名] 1. 함축, 포함 2. 암시, 내포된 뜻 3. 연루, 관련

im·plic·it [implísit] *adj.* **1.** without doubt; absolute. ¶~ *faith.*① **2.** understood though not clearly expressed; implied. ↔explicit ¶~ *consent.*②
—[形] 1. 절대의, 맹목적인 ¶①맹신(盲信) 2. 암암리의, 은연중의, 함축적인 ¶②은연중의 동의

im·plic·it·ly [implísitli] *adv.* in an implicit manner.
—[副] 암암리에; 절대적으로

I

* **im·plore** [implɔ́ːr] *vt.* **1.** ask for (something) earnestly. **2.** ask (someone) to do something. ¶~ *him to go out.*
—[他] 1. …을 열심히 빌다, 열망하다 2. …에게 탄원(간청)하다

im·plor·ing·ly [implɔ́ːriŋli] *adv.* in an imploring manner.
—[副] 애원(탄원)하듯이

* **im·ply** [implái] *vt.* (**-plied, -ply·ing**) mean (something) without expressing it clearly; suggest indirectly. ¶*Silence implies consent.*①
—[他] …을 넌지시 말하다, 암시하다 ¶①침묵은 동의를 의미한다

im·po·lite [ìmpouláit] *adj.* not polite; showing bad manners; rude. ▷**im·po·lite·ness** [-nis] *n.*
—[形] 무례한, 버릇없는

im·po·lite·ly [ìmpouláitli] *adv.* in an impolite manner.
—[副] 무례하게, 버릇없이

im·pol·i·tic [impálitik / -pɔ́l-] *adj.* not politic; unwise.
—[形] 지각없는, 현명하지 못한

im·pon·der·a·ble [impánd(ə)rəbl / -pɔ́n-] *adj.* that cannot be precisely determined or measured.
—[形] 저울질할 수 없는; 미량(微量)의

‡ **im·port** *v.* [impɔ́ːrt → *n.*] *vt.* **1.** bring in (goods) from another country. ⟪~ something *from*⟫ ↔export ¶*imported goods* / *Most of our coffee is imported from Brazil.*① **2.** mean. ¶*What does this note ~?* **3.** be important to (someone). ¶*It is a problem that imports us closely.* **4.** introduce (ideas, etc.).
—[他] 1. …을 수입하다 ¶①우리나라의 코오피는 대개 브라질에서 수입된다 2. …을 의미하다 3. …에게 중대한 관계가 있다 4. [생각 따위]를 전하다

—*n.* [ˊ-] **1.** [U] the act of importing goods; [C] ⟪usu. *pl.*⟫ something imported. ↔export ¶~ *duties*② / *Our imports are made up largely of raw materials.*③ **2.** [U] meaning. ¶*the ~ of his message.*④ **3.** [U] importance. ¶*a matter of great ~.*⑤
—[名] 1. 수입; 수입품 ¶②수입세/③우리나라의 수입품의 대부분은 원료가 차지하고 있다 2. 의미 ¶④그의 메시지의 의미 3. 중요성 ¶⑤중대한 일

‡ **im·por·tance** [impɔ́ːrt(ə)ns] *n.* [U] the state of being important; significance. ¶*a person of ~*① / *a matter of great ~.*②
—[名] 중요성, 중대함; [사회적인] 무게, 관록, 유력 ¶①유력 인사/②중대한 일

‡ **im·por·tant** [impɔ́ːrt(ə)nt] *adj.* **1.** filled with meaning; worth noticing or considering; serious; valuable. **2.** having power or authority. **3.** acting as if important. ¶*He looks ~.*① ▷**im·por·tant·ly** [-li] *adv.*
—[形] 1. 중대한, 중요한 2. 유력한 3. 거만한, 젠체하는 ¶①그는 잘난 체한다

im·por·ta·tion [ìmpɔːrtéiʃ(ə)n] *n.* **1.** [U] the act of importing. **2.** [C] a thing which is imported.
—[名] 1. 수입 2. 수입품, 외래품

im·port·er [impɔ́ːrtər] *n.* [C] a person or company that is engaged in the business of importing.
—[名] 수입 업자

im·por·tu·nate [impɔ́ːrtʃunit / -tju-] *adj.* asking repeatedly; persistent; urgent.
—[形] 귀찮게 조르는, 추근추근한

im·por·tune [ìmpɔːrt(j)úːn / -pɔ́ːtjuːn] *vt.* ask repeatedly or urgently.
—[他] …을 추근추근 조르다(청하다)

im·por·tu·ni·ty [ìmpɔːrt(j)úːniti / -pɔːtjúː-] *n.* [U][C] (pl. **-ties**) the act of asking repeatedly.
—[名] 성가시게 조르기

* **im·pose** [impóuz] *vt.* **1.** put (a burden, a tax, a punishment, etc.) on (someone). ¶*Duties are imposed on wines and spirits.*① **2.** force (something) on another. ¶~ *one's opinion on others.*② ***impose on*** (or ***upon***), ⓐ take advantage of (someone). ⓑ deceive; trick.
—[他] 1. …에게 …을 부과하다 ¶①주류에는 세금이 부과되어 있다 2. …을 강요하다 ¶②남에게 자기의 의견을 억지로 받아들이게 하다
[熟] ⓐ…을 이용하다 ⓑ속이다

im·pos·ing [impóuziŋ] *adj.* very impressive; making a strong impression by means of great size, appearance, dignity, etc. ¶*He talked with an ~ attitude.*①
—[形] 인상적인, 이목을 끄는; 당당한 ¶① 그는 당당한 태도로 이야기했다

im·po·si·tion [ìmpəzíʃ(ə)n] *n.* **1.** [U] the act of imposing. **2.** [C] a tax, task, burden, etc. imposed on someone. **3.** [C] deception; fraud.
—[名] 1. 부과, 과세; 강요; 강제 2. 세금, 부담 3. 기만, 사기

im·pos·si·bil·i·ty [impàsibíliti / -pɔ̀s-] *n.* (pl. **-ties**) **1.** [U] the state of being impossible. **2.** [C] a thing which is impossible.
—[名] 1. 불가능[성] 2. 불가능한 일

‡ **im·pos·si·ble** [impásibl / -pɔ́s-] *adj.* **1.** that cannot be done; that cannot happen. ¶*It is ~ to live without water.* **2.** not easy or convenient. **3.** that cannot be true. ¶*an ~ rumor*① **4.** (*colloq.*) hard to endure; very objectionable. ¶*an ~ person.*②
—[形] 1. 불가능의, 할 수 없는 2. …하기 힘든, 형편이 나쁜 3. 있을 수 없는 ¶①정말일 수가 없는 소문 4. ⟪口⟫ 참을 수 없는, 몹시 싫은 ¶②싫은 녀석

im·post [ímpoust] *n.* [C] a tax, esp. one imposed on goods which are imported.
—[名] 세금, 수입세, 관세

im·pos·tor [impástər / -pɔ́stə] *n.* [C] a person who deceives others by assuming a false name or character; a swindler.
—[名] 성명·신분을 사칭하는 사람; 사기꾼, 협잡꾼

im·pos·ture [impástʃər / -pɔ́stʃə] *n.* [C][U] deception; fraud.
—[名] 사기, 협잡

im·po·tence [ímpət(ə)ns] *n.* [U] the state of being impotent; lack of power; helplessness.
—[名] 무력; 무기력; 허약; 불능

im·po·ten·cy [ímpət(ə)nsi] *n.* =impotence.

im·po·tent [ímpət(ə)nt] *adj.* not having physical, mental, or moral power; helpless.
—[形] 무기력한, 허약한; 옴짝달싹 못하는

im·pound [impáund] *vt.* **1.** shut up (cattle) in a pen. **2.** take (someone or something) into an enclosure. **3.** imprison. ▷**im·pound·ment** [-mənt] *n.*
—[他] 1. [가축]을 우리에 가두다 2. …을 가두다, 챙겨 넣다 3. …을 구류하다

im·pov·er·ish [impáv(ə)riʃ / -pɔ́v-] *vt.* **1.** make (someone) poor. **2.** use up the strength, richness, or resources of (land, etc.).
—[他] 1. …을 가난하게 하다 2. …을 허약하게 하다; 피폐시키다, [토지]를 메마르게 하다

im·prac·ti·ca·ble [impræ̃ktikəbl] *adj.* unsuitable for practical use; that cannot be done. ¶*This is an ~ plan.*①
—[形] 실천이 불가능한 ¶①이것은 실행 불가능한 계획이다

im·prac·ti·cal [impræ̃ktik(ə)l] *adj.* not practical.
—[形] 실행될 수 없는, 실제적이 아닌

im·pre·cate [ímprikèit] *vt.* call down (evil, misfortune, etc.) upon someone. ▷**im·pre·ca·tor** [-tər] *n.*
—[他] [남에게 불운·재앙을 내려 달라고] 빌다, 저주하다

im·pre·ca·tion [ìmprikéiʃ(ə)n] *n.* **1.** [U] the act of imprecating. **2.** [C] a curse.
—[名] 1. 저주하기 2. 저주

im·preg·na·ble [imprégnəbl] *adj.* that cannot be overcome by force; strong enough to resist the attack. ¶*hold an ~ belief.*①
—[形] 난공불락의, 확고한 ¶①확고한 신념을 갖다

im·preg·nate [imprégneit] *vt.* **1.** make pregnant. **2.** cause (something) to be filled with (something). **3.** inspire; imbue. 《~ someone *with*》 —*adj.* impregnated; pregnant.
—[他] 1. …에게 임신(수태)시키다 2. …에 충만하게 하다 3. …을 불어넣다, 스며들게 하다 —[形] 임신하고 있는, 스며든, 포화(飽和)한

:im·press¹ *vt.* [imprés → *n.*] **1.** produce a strong effect on the mind or emotion of (someone). ¶*The speaker impressed the audience.*① **2.** fix (something) deeply in the mind or memory. ¶*The scene was strongly impressed on my memory.*② **3.** produce (a mark, etc.) on (something) by pressing or stamping. ¶*~ a mark on the surface; ~ the surface with a mark.*
—[他] 1. …에게 생생한 인상을 주다; …을 감명시키다 ¶①그의 연설은 청중을 감동시켰다 2. …을 명기(銘記)하다; 인상지우다, 통감시키다 ¶②그 광경은 내게 강한 인상을 주었다 3. …을 누르다, …에 [자국]을 내다

—*n.* [´-] [C] **1.** a mark made by pressure. **2.** the act of impressing.
—[名] 1. 각인(刻印) 2. 인상을 주기; 날인

im·press² [imprés] *vt.* **1.** seize (something) by force for public use. **2.** force (someone) to serve in the navy or army. **3.** introduce.
—[他] 1. …을 징용(징발)하다 2. …을 강제로 군무에 복무시키다 3. …을 인용(이용)하다

im·press·i·ble [imprésibl] *adj.* impressionable.
—[形] 느끼기 쉬운, 감수성이 강한

:im·pres·sion [impréʃ(ə)n] *n.* [C] **1.** [C][U] an effect produced on the mind. ¶*He left a good ~ on me.*① **2.** a vague notion or feeling. ¶*I have an ~ that the plan will never be carried out.* **3.** a mark made by pressing. ¶*He found an ~ of someone's foot in the ground.*② **4.** the act of impressing; the state of being impressed.
—[名] 1. 인상, 감명 ¶①그는 내게 좋은 인상을 남겼다 2. 막연한 생각, 기분 3. 각인(刻印), 흔적 ¶②그는 운동장에서 누군가의 발자국을 발견했다 4. 인상을 주기(받기)

im·pres·sion·a·ble [impréʃ(ə)nəbl] *adj.* easily impressed or influenced; sensitive; impressible.
—[形] 느끼기 쉬운, 감수성 강한

im·pres·sion·ism [impréʃ(ə)nìz(ə)m] *n.* [U] the style of painting or writing which expresses general impressions without much attention to details.
—[名] 인상파, 인상주의

im·pres·sion·ist [impréʃ(ə)nist] *n.* [C] an artist, writer, or composer who practices impressionism.
—[名] 인상파 화가(조각가·작가)

·im·pres·sive [imprésiv] *adj.* strongly impressing the mind or feelings. ▷**im·pres·sive·ness** [-nis] *n.*
—[形] 강한 인상을 주는, 감동적인

im·print *n.* [ímprint → *v.*] [C] **1.** a mark made by pressing; a print. ¶*the ~ of a dirty foot on a floor.* **2.** an impression on the mind; a mark. ¶*an ~ of anxiety on her face.*① **3.** a listing of the printer's or publisher's name and address and the date and place of publication printed in a book.
—[名] 1. 새겨진 자국, 흔적 2. 모습, 인상 ¶①그녀 얼굴의 근심의 빛 3. [책 따위의] 간기(刊記)(인쇄인·발행자 등의 주소·성명과 발행 날짜 따위)

—*vt.* [imprínt] **1.** make a mark on or of (something) by pressing. ¶*~ the postmark on the envelope.*② **2.** press; impress.
—[他] 1. …을 누르다, 찍다 ¶②봉투에 소인을 찍다 2. 누르다, 꽉 누르다

·im·pris·on [imprízn] *vt.* **1.** put or keep (someone) in prison. **2.** confine.
—[他] 1. …을 투옥하다, 수감하다 2. …을 감금하다

im·pris·on·ment [impríznmənt] *n.* [U] **1.** the act of putting or keeping in prison; the state of being put or kept in prison. **2.** confinement; restraint.
—[名] 1. 투옥; 금고; 투옥당하기 2. 감금, 구속

im·prob·a·bil·i·ty [imprɑ̀bəbíliti / -prɔ̀b-] *n.* (pl. **-ties**) **1.** [U] the state of being improbable. **2.** [C] a thing which is improbable.
—[名] 1. 있을 듯싶지 않은 일(상태), 정말 같지 않음 2. 있을 듯싶지 않은 것(사물)

im·prob·a·ble [imprɑ́bəbl / -prɔ́b-] *adj.* not likely to happen or to be true; not probable.
—[形] 있을 듯싶지 않은, 일어날 것 같지 않은, 정말 같지 않은

im·promp·tu [imprɑ́m(p)t(j)u: / -prɔ́m(p)tju:] *adv., adj.* without preparation. ¶*a speech made ~.*① —*n.* [C] a thing which is made or done without preparation.
—[副][形] 즉석에서[의], 당장[의], 즉흥의 ¶①즉석 연설 —[名] 즉흥적으로 만든 것(한 일)

im·prop·er [imprɑ́pər / -prɔ́pə] *adj.* **1.** not proper; not suitable. **2.** wrong; incorrect. **3.** not decent.
—[形] 1. 부적당한 2. 틀린 3. 꼴사나운, 버릇없는

im·pro·pri·e·ty [ìmprəpráiəti] *n.* (pl. **-ties**) **1.** [U] the state or quality of being improper; lack of propriety. **2.** [C] an improper act, expression, etc.
—[名] 1. 부적당, 부정, 꼴사나움 2. 잘못, 틀림, 부적당한 표현

:im·prove [imprú:v] *vt.* **1.** make better. ¶*He has been improving his English.* **2.** make good use of (something); use well. ¶*~ one's opportunity.*① —*vi.* become better. ¶*His health is improving.*
improve on, make better; do better than in an earlier attempt.
—[他] 1. …을 개선(개량)하다, 증진하다 2. …을 이용하다 ¶①기회를 이용하다 —[自] 좋아지다, 개선되다
[熟] …보다 더 좋게 하다, …을 개량하다

:im·prove·ment [imprú:vmənt] *n.* [U] **1.** the act of making or becoming better. **2.** [C] a change or addition which makes something better.
—[名] 1. 개량, 개선, 진보, 향상 2. 개량공사, 개량점, 증축

im·prov·i·dence [imprɑ́vid(ə)ns / -prɔ́v-] *n.* [U] the state of being improvident.
—[名] 선견지명이 없음, 무분별한 행위, 낭비

im·prov·i·dent [imprɑ́vid(ə)nt / -prɔ́v-] *adj.* **1.** careless in providing for the future; not provident. **2.** not thrifty.
—[形] 1. 선견지명이 없는, 준비성이 없는 2. 절약심이 없는

im·pro·vi·sa·tion [imprɑ̀vizéiʃ(ə)n / ìmprəvai-] *n.* **1.** [U] the act of improvising. **2.** [C] a thing which is improvised.
—[名] 1. 즉석에서(즉흥적으로) 만들기 2. 즉석에서 만든 것(즉흥시·즉흥곡 따위)

im·pro·vise [ímprəvàiz] *vt.* **1.** make (verse, music, etc.) without preparation or plan. **2.** provide (something) roughly for an immediate need. ¶*~ a bed out of the leaves and branches.*①
—[他] 1. [시·음악]을 즉석에서 짓다 2. …을 임시변통으로 만들다, 급히 만들다 ¶①나뭇잎과 나뭇가지로 즉석 침대를 만들다

im·pru·dence [imprú:d(ə)ns] *n.* **1.** [U] the state of being imprudent. **2.** [C] an imprudent behavior.
—[名] 1. 경솔, 무분별 2. 경솔한 행위

·im·pru·dent [imprú:d(ə)nt] *adj.* not prudent; lacking caution; not careful.
—[形] 경솔한, 무분별한

im·pu·dence [ímpjud(ə)ns] *n.* **1.** [U] the state or quality of being impudent; lack of shame or modesty. **2.** [C] an impudent act or speech.
—[名] 뻔뻔스러움, 염치없음, 건방진 수작(언행)

im·pu·dent [ímpjud(ə)nt] *adj.* without shame or modesty; disrespectful; rude. ▷**im·pu·dent·ly** [-li] *adv.*
—[形] 뻔뻔스러운, 염치없는, 버릇없는, 무례한

im·pugn [impjú:n] *vt.* attack (someone) by words or arguments; call (something) in question; oppose or challenge as false.
—[他] …을 논란하다; 공격하다; 문제삼다

·im·pulse [ímpʌls] *n.* **1.** [C] a sudden driving force; the motion or effect caused by such a force. **2.** [U][C] a sudden desire or inclination to act. ¶*He did so under an ~ of pity.*① / *Many people are guided more by ~ than by reason.*②
—[名] 1. 충격, 추진력; 충동 2. [마음의] 충동, 자극 ¶①그는 동정심에서 그렇게 했다/②이성보다도 충동에 지배되는 사람이 많다

im·pul·sion [impʌ́lʃ(ə)n] *n.* **1.** [U] the act of impelling; the state of being impelled. **2.** [C] an impelling force; the effect or motion caused by this force.
—[名] 1. 추진 2. 추진력; 충격, 충동

im·pul·sive [impʌ́lsiv] *adj.* **1.** acting on or moved by sudden feeling. **2.** driving forward; pushing onward.
—[形] 1. 충동적인, 일시적 감정에 의한 2. 추진적인

im·pu·ni·ty [impjú:niti] *n.* [U] freedom from punishment, injury, harm, etc. ¶*You cannot do this with ~.*①
—[名] 형벌을 모면함, 무사함 ¶①이것을 하면 반드시 벌을 받는다

im·pure [impjúər] *adj.* mixed with another substance; not pure; dirty. ¶*~ air*① / *~ motives.*
—[形] 불순물이 섞인, 불순의; 불결한 ¶①불결한 공기

im·pu·ri·ty [impjúəriti] *n.* (pl. **-ties**) **1.** [U] the state of being impure; lack of purity. **2.** [C] ⟪often *pl.*⟫ a thing which is or which makes something else impure.
—[名] 1. 불순, 불결 2. 불순물; 혼합물, 불결한 것; 불순한 사물

im·pu·ta·tion [ìmpju(:)téiʃ(ə)n] *n.* **1.** [U] the act of imputing; the state of being imputed. **2.** [C] a fault or crime imputed.
—[名] 1. [죄·책임을] 돌리기, 전가(轉嫁) 2. 비난, 견책, 책망; 오명

im·pute [impjú:t] *vt.* charge (a crime, a fault, etc.) to (someone). ¶*~ the accident to the driver's carelessness* | *~ one's failure to another.*①
—[他] …에 [결점·죄 따위를] …의 탓으로 돌리다, 전가하다 ¶①자기의 실패를 남의 탓으로 돌리다

:in [in] *prep.* **1.** (of place or position) inside; within; at. ¶*live ~ Tokyo* | *~ school*① | *a wound ~ the head* | *sit ~ the shade*② | *I found it ~ the car.* **2.** (of action or motion) into. ¶*break ~ two*③ | *Put it ~ your pocket.* | *He just went ~ the room.* **3.** within a condition, situation, etc. ¶*~ despair*④ | *be ~ trouble* | *go out ~ the rain* | *be ~ business* | *be engaged ~ reading*⑤ | *~ a search for truth*⑥ | *We are ~ good health.* **4.** wearing; clothed by. ¶*a lady ~ white*⑦ | *a man ~ sandals.* **5.** (of time) during; when; within a period of time. ¶*~ the morning*⑧ | *~ [the] future* | *~ the past* | *~ 1970* | *~ spring* | *~ crossing the street.*⑨ **6.** at the end of a period of time; after. ¶*I will come ~ a few minutes.*⑩ **7.** within the scope of. ¶*~ one's sight* | *~ my experience* | *~ my opinion.*⑪ **8.** by means of; using. ¶*write ~ pencil*⑫ | *~ many colors* | *speaking ~ French.* **9.** made of; of. ¶*~ oak* | *a dress ~ silk.* **10.** because of; as a result of; for. ¶*jump ~ surprise* | *delight ~ praise* | *do this ~ my defense.* **11.** out of; from among. ¶*one ~ a hundred* | *the tallest girl ~ the class.* **12.** so as to form. ¶*stand ~ line*⑬ | *school boys ~ a row* | *arranged ~ curls.* **13.** with regard to; as to. ¶*weak ~ faith* | *They differ ~ height.*⑭ **14.** (of direction) toward. ¶*It flew ~ an easterly direction.* **15.** within the capacity of. ¶*She didn't have it ~ her.*⑮
—[前] 1. …의 안(속)에[서]; …에 있어서 ¶①학교에, 재학중/②그늘에 앉다 2. …의 속으로 ¶③둘로 갈라지다 3. [상태·상황을 나타내어] …에, …에서 ¶④절망하여/⑤독서하고 있다/⑥진리를 찾아 4. …을 입고, …을 신고 ¶⑦흰옷을 입은 부인 5. …중에, …의 사이; …이내에서 ¶⑧오전 중에/⑨도로를 건널 때 6. …의 뒤에, …이 지나서 ¶⑩몇 분내로 오겠다 7. …의 범위 안에서, …의 가운데서 ¶⑪나의 의견으로는 8. …을 사용하여 ¶⑫연필로 쓰다 9. …을 재료로 하여 10. …으로, …의 결과로서; …을 위해서 11. …에 대해, …의 사이에서 12. …을 이루어, …으로 ¶⑬줄을 지어 서다 13. …에 있어서 ¶⑭높이가 다르다 14…의 쪽으로 15. [능력을 나타내어] …에게 ¶⑮그녀에게는 그것을 할 수 없었다

—*adv.* **1.** from the outside to the inside; into a place. ¶*go ~* | *Please come ~.* **2.** at home, at the office, etc. ¶*Is your father ~?* **3.** in fashion; in season; arrived. ¶*Summer is ~.* | *Watermelons are ~.* | *The train is ~.*⑯
—[副] 1. 안에, 안으로 2. 집에 있어서, 출근하여 3. 유행하여, 도착하여 ¶⑯기차가 닿았다

—*adj.* **1.** inside; having power, office, etc. ¶*the ~ party.*⑰ **2.** coming in or turning in. ¶*an ~ train.*
—[形] 1. 가운데의, 세력을 갖고 있는 ¶⑰여당 2. 들어오는

—*n.* ((usu. *the ~s*)) the political party in power.
—[名] 여당

1) ***be in for*** (=*be competing in*) *a competition.*
2) ***be in for it,*** be sure to be punished.
3) ***be in*** (=*be familiar; be on good terms*) ***with*** *someone.*
4) ***in and out,*** alternately; first in, then out.
5) ***ins and outs,*** all the details.
6) ***in that,*** because.

[熟] 1)[경기에] 참가하여 2)벌을 받기로 되어 있다 3)…와 친하다 4)나타났다사라졌다, 번갈아 5)상세, 자초지종 6)…이기 때문에

in-[1] [in] *pref.* no; not; without; the opposite of: *incapable* (=not capable).
—((接頭)) 무(無)…, 불(不)…, 비(非)…

in-[2] [in] *pref.* in; into; within; toward: *inhabit* (=live in).
—((接頭)) …의 속에(의·으로)

in. inch; inches.

in·a·bil·i·ty [ìnəbíliti] *n.* [U] the state of being unable; lack of ability.
—[名] 할 수 없음, 불가능, 무능

in·ac·ces·si·ble [ìnæksésibl] *adj.* that cannot be reached or entered; hard to get to.
—[形] 가까이하기 어려운; 도달하기 어려운

in·ac·cu·ra·cy [inǽkjurəsi] *n.* (pl. **-cies**) **1.** [U] the state of being inaccurate. **2.** [C] an inaccurate thing; an error; a mistake.
—[名] 1. 부정확, 정밀하지 못함 2. 잘못, 오류

in·ac·cu·rate [inǽkjurit] *adj.* not accurate; not exact.
—[形] 부정확한

in·ac·tion [inǽkʃ(ə)n] *n.* [U] absence of action or motion; idleness.
—[名] 활동하지 않음, 휴지(休止); 게으름

in·ac·tive [inǽktiv] *adj.* that cannot act or move; not active; idle.
—[形] 불활발한; 게으른

in·ac·tiv·i·ty [ìnæktíviti] *n.* [U] absence of activity; idleness.
—[名] 활동하지 않음; 게으름

in·ad·e·qua·cy [inǽdikwəsi] *n.* [U] the state of being inadequate.
—[名] 불충분; 부적당

in·ad·e·quate [inǽdikwit] *adj.* not equal to the requirements; not sufficient; not enough; not suitable; not adequate. ▷**in·ad·e·quate·ly** [-li] *adv.*
—[形] 불충분한; 부적당한

in·ad·mis·si·ble [ìnədmísibl] *adj.* that cannot be admitted or allowed; not admissible.
—[形] 허용할 수 없는; 승인할 수 없는

in·ad·vert·ence [ìnədvə́:rt(ə)ns] *n.* **1.** [U] the state of being inadvertent; lack of attention; carelessness. **2.**
—[名] 1. 부주의 2. 잘못, 실수, 과오

[C] an inadvertent act; a mistake; an oversight.

in·ad·ver·ten·cy [inədvə́ːrt(ə)nsi] *n.* (pl. **-cies**) =inadvertence.

in·ad·vert·ent [ìnədvə́ːrt(ə)nt] *adj.* not attentive; thoughtless. ▷**in·ad·vert·ent·ly** [-li] *adv.* —[형] 부주의한

in·ad·vis·a·ble [ìnədváizəbl] *adj.* not wise or prudent; not advisable. —[형] 현명하지 못한, 어리석은; 권할 수 없는

in·al·ien·a·ble [inéiliənəbl] *adj.* that cannot be given away or taken away. ¶*Liberty is an ~ right.* —[형] 양도할 수 없는, 빼앗을 수 없는

in·ane [inéin] *adj.* **1.** silly; foolish. **2.** empty. —[형] 1. 어리석은 2. 공허한

in·an·i·mate [inǽnimit] *adj.* **1.** without life; lifeless. ¶*~ matter.*① **2.** spiritless; dull. —[형] 1. 생명이 없는; 죽은 ¶①무생물 2. 활기 없는

in·a·ni·tion [ìnəníʃ(ə)n] *n.* [U] **1.** lack of mental or moral vigor; emptiness. **2.** weakness from lack of food. —[명] 1. 공허 2. 영양실조

in·an·i·ty [inǽniti] *n.* [U] the state or quality of being inane. —[명] 공허; 어리석음

in·ap·pli·ca·ble [inǽplikəbl] *adj.* that cannot be applied; not suitable. —[형] 적용(응용)할 수 없는, 부적당한

in·ap·pre·ci·a·ble [ìnəpríːʃ(i)əbl, +*U.S.* -ʃiə-] *adj.* too small to be noticed or to have any value. —[형] 보잘것 없는; 아주 적은

in·ap·pro·pri·ate [ìnəpróupriit] *adj.* not suitable; not appropriate. —[형] 부적당한; 어울리지 않는

in·apt [inǽpt] *adj.* **1.** not suitable; not apt; unfit. **2.** lacking skill; awkward. ▷**in·apt·ly** [-li] *adv.* —[형] 1. 부적당한 2. 솜씨 없는; 서투른

in·ap·ti·tude [inǽptit(j)ùːd, / -tjùːd] *n.* [U] **1.** lack of suitability; unfitness. **2.** lack of skill; unskillfulness. —[명] 1. 어울리지 않음; 부적당 2. 서투름; 솜씨 없음

in·ar·tic·u·late [ìnaːrtíkjulit] *adj.* **1.** not able to speak understandably; not distinct. **2.** unable to speak; dumb. —[형] 1. 발음이 똑똑하지 않은 2. 말을 못하는, 벙어리의

in·ar·tis·tic [ìnaːrtístik] *adj.* lacking good taste; not artistic. —[형] 비예술적인; 몰취미한

in·as·much [ìnəzmʌ́tʃ] *adv.* ((used like a *conj.*, followed by *as*)) because; since. ¶*She is absent ~ as her mother is ill.*① —[부] …이므로, …인 까닭에 ¶①어머니가 아파서 나오지 않았다

in·at·ten·tion [ìnəténʃ(ə)n] *n.* [U] lack of attention; carelessness. —[명] 부주의

in·at·ten·tive [ìnəténtiv] *adj.* not attentive; careless. —[형] 부주의한

in·au·di·ble [inɔ́ːdibl] *adj.* that cannot be heard. —[형] 알아들을 수 없는

in·au·gu·ral [inɔ́ːgjur(ə)l] *adj.* of an inauguration. **—*n.*** [C] a speech made at an inauguration. —[형] 임관(任官)의, 취임식[의] —[명] 취임 연설

in·au·gu·rate [inɔ́ːgjurèit] *vt.* **1.** place (an official) in an important office with a ceremony. **2.** make a formal beginning of (something). **3.** open (something new) for public use with a celebration. —[타] 1. …을 취임시키다, …의 취임식을 거행하다 2. …을 정식으로 개시하다 3. …을 새로이 열다

in·au·gu·ra·tion [inɔ̀ːgjuréiʃ(ə)n] *n.* [C] **1.** an act or ceremony of inaugurating. **2.** a formal beginning. —[명] 1. 취임[식] 2. 개시

in·aus·pi·cious [ìnɔːspíʃəs] *adj.* unlucky; unfavorable. —[형] 불운한; 불행한; 불길한

in·board [ínbɔːrd] *adj., adv.* within the ship; towards the center of a ship. —[형][부] 배 안의(에); 배의 중심에

in·born [ínbɔ́ːrn] *adj.* born with or in a person; natural. —[형] 타고난, 선천적인

in·bred [ínbréd] *adj.* **1.** inborn; natural. **2.** bred from parents that are closely related. —[형] 1. 타고난 2. 동계교배(同系交配)(번식)에 의해 태어난

Inc. incorporated.

In·ca [íŋkə] *n.* [C] **1.** a member of the group of South American Indians who ruled Peru until the Spanish conquest. **2.** the ruler of this tribe. —[명] 1. 잉카 사람 2. 잉카 국왕

in·cal·cu·la·ble [inkǽlkjuləbl] *adj.* **1.** so great in number that it cannot easily be counted. **2.** that cannot be forecast. **3.** that cannot be relied on; uncertain; unsure. —[형] 1. 셀 수 없는, 무수한 2. 예상할 수 없는 3. 믿을 수 없는, 확실치 않은

in·can·des·cence [ìnkəndésns, +*Brit.* -kæn-] *n.* [U] the state of being incandescent. —[명] 백열(白熱)

in·can·des·cent [ìnkəndésnt, +*Brit.* -kæn-] *adj.* **1.** glowing with heat. ¶*an ~ lamp.*① **2.** bright; brilliant. —[형] 1. 백열의 ¶①백열 전등 2. 빛나는, 찬란한

in·can·ta·tion [ìnkæntéiʃ(ə)n] *n.* [C] a set of words sung or spoken to produce a magic effect. —[명] 주문(呪文)

in·ca·pa·bil·i·ty [inkèipəbíliti] *n.* [U] the state of being incapable; incapacity; unfitness. —[명] 무능; 부적당, 무자격

***in·ca·pa·ble** [inkéipəbl] *adj.* lacking ordinary ability; not able; helpless. —[형] …을 할 수 없는; 무능한; 무력한

incapacitate [588] incisive

in·ca·pac·i·tate [ìnkəpǽsitèit] *vt.* make (someone) powerless, unfit or unable to act. 《~ someone *for*》
— 他 …을 …할 수 없게 하다; 무능력하게 하다

in·ca·pac·i·ty [ìnkəpǽsiti] *n.* Ⓤ lack of ability, ordinary power or fitness.
— 名 무능

in·car·cer·ate [inkɑ́ːrsərèit] *vt.* shut up (someone) in a prison; imprison; confine.
— 他 …을 투옥하다; 감금하다

in·car·nate *adj.* [inkɑ́ːrnit / -neit → *v.*] appearing in physical form, esp. in human form. —*vt.* [inkɑ́ːrneit] **1.** provide (something) with flesh or a body; embody. **2.** be the type of (something). **3.** put (something) into an actual form; make real.
— 形 인간의 모습을 한, 화신(化身)의
— 他 1. …에게 육체를 주다 2. …의 화신이 되다 3. …을 구체화하다

in·car·na·tion [ìnkɑːrnéiʃ(ə)n] *n.* **1.** Ⓤ the act of taking on human form by a divine being. **2.** (*the I-*) the act by Jesus Christ of taking human form. **3.** Ⓒ any person or thing which represents a principle, a quality, an idea, etc.
— 名 1. 육체화, 인간화 2. 신의 그리스도로서의 현현(顯現) 3. 화신, 권화(權化)

in·case [inkéis] *vt.* put (something) into a case; enclose; encase.
— 他 …을 상자에 넣다; …을 싸다

in·cau·tious [inkɔ́ːʃ(ə)s] *adj.* not cautious; careless.
— 形 신중하지 않은, 부주의한

in·cen·di·a·rism [inséndiərìz(ə)m] *n.* Ⓤ **1.** the act of willfully setting fire to property. **2.** agitation.
— 名 1. 방화(放火) 2. 선동

in·cen·di·ar·y [inséndiəri] *adj.* **1.** of an incendiary (*n.* 1) **2.** causing a fire. ¶*an ~ bomb.*① **3.** stirring up passion; of agitation.
— 形 1. 방화의 2. 화재를 일으키는 ¶ ①소이탄 3. 선동하는; 부추기는
—*n.* Ⓒ (pl. **-ar·ies**) **1.** a person who sets fire to property. **2.** a person who stirs up passions; an agitator.
— 名 1. 방화 범인 2. 선동자

＊**in·cense¹** [ínsens] *n.* Ⓤ **1.** material burned to make a sweet smell. **2.** the smoke or odor given off by such material. **3.** any pleasant odor.
— 名 1. 향료, 향(香) 2. 향내, 향연(香煙) 3. 좋은 냄새, 방향

in·cense² [inséns] *vt.* make (someone) very angry.
— 他 …을 성나게 하다

in·cen·tive [inséntiv] *adj.* giving a desire to act or work; encouraging. —*n.* Ⓒ Ⓤ something which arouses someone to action or effort; a motive.
— 形 자극적인 — 名 자극, 유인(誘因), 동기

in·cep·tion [insépʃ(ə)n] *n.* Ⓒ beginning; start.
— 名 시초, 개시, 발단(發端)

in·cer·ti·tude [insəːrtit(j)ùːd / insə́ːtitjùːd] *n.* Ⓤ uncertainty; doubt. 〔▷**in·ces·sant·ly** [-li] *adv.*〕
— 名 불확실한 [한 상태]; 의혹

in·ces·sant [insésnt] *adj* not stopping; continuous.
— 形 그칠 새 없는, 끊임없는

in·cest [ínsest] *n.* Ⓤ sexual intercourse or marriage between persons very closely related.
— 名 근친 상간(相姦); 근친 결혼

‡**inch** [intʃ] *n.* Ⓒ **1.** a unit of length, equal to ¹/₁₂ of a foot. **2.** a very small amount, distance, etc.
 1) *by inches*, little by little; slowly.
 2) *every inch*, in all respects; completely.
 3) *to an inch*, precisely.
 4) *within an inch of*, very near to; not far from.
—*vt., vi.* move slowly.
— 名 1. 인치 2. 소량, 단거리, 소액
圈 1)서서히 2)전혀 3)정밀하게, 상세히 4)…에 근접하여; 거의 …할 뻔하여
— 他 自 조금씩 움직이다

in·cho·ate [inkóuit / ínkouèit] *adj.* just begun; undeveloped.
— 形 방금 시작된, ▯ 발달의

in·ci·dence [ínsid(ə)ns] *n.* Ⓤ **1.** the degree or range of occurrence or influence; extent of influence. **2.** the act of falling upon or influencing.
— 名 1. 사건(영향)의 정도, 범위; 영향이 미치는 범위 2. 낙하(落下), 영향을 미치기

‡**in·ci·dent** [ínsid(ə)nt] *n.* Ⓒ **1.** a happening; an event. **2.** an event unimportant in relation to a large one.
—*adj.* **1.** apt to happen. **2.** of incidence.
— 名 1. 사건 2. 부수적인 일; 삽화(揷話) 〔(投射)의〕
— 形 1. 일어나기 쉬운 2. 낙하의, 투사(投射)의

in·ci·den·tal [ìnsidéntl] *adj.* **1.** happening with something more important. **2.** occurring by chance.
—*n.* Ⓒ an incidental thing.
— 形 1. 부수적인 2. 우연의; 우발적인
— 名 부수적(우발적) 사건

in·ci·den·tal·ly [ìnsidént(ə)li] *adv.* in an incidental manner; by chance; by the way.
— 形 우연히; 우발적으로, 부수적으로; 하는 김에

in·cin·er·ate [insínərèit] *vt.* burn (something) to ashes.
— 他 …을 소각하다

in·cin·er·a·tor [insínərèitər] *n.* Ⓒ a furnace for burning waste.
— 名 쓰레기 소각로

in·cip·i·ent [insípiənt] *adj.* just beginning.
— 形 시초의, 초기의, 발단의

in·cise [insáiz] *vt.* cut into.
— 他 …을 자르다(째다), …을 절개(切開)하다

in·ci·sion [insíʒ(ə)n] *n.* **1.** Ⓤ the act of cutting into. **2.** Ⓒ a cut made in something.
— 名 1. 베기, 쩨기 2. 벤 자리

in·ci·sive [insáisiv] *adj.* sharp; keen.
— 形 날카로운

in·ci·sor [insáizər] *n.* [C] a cutting tooth.
—[名] 앞니

in·cite [insáit] *vt.* stir up; rouse.
—[他] …을 자극하다, 선동하다

in·cite·ment [insáitmənt] *n.* **1.** [U] the act of inciting. **2.** [C] a thing which stirs up or rouses.
—[名] 1. 격려; 자극; 선동 2. 자극·선동하는 것

in·ci·vil·i·ty [ìnsivíliti] *n.* [U][C] (pl. **-ties**) lack of good manners; rudeness; impoliteness.
—[名] 무례; 버릇없음

in·clem·en·cy [inklémənsi] *n.* [U] (of weather) the state or quality of being inclement.
—[名] [날씨의] 험악함, 매서움

in·clem·ent [inklémənt] *adj.* (of weather) rough; stormy.
—[形] 험악한; 사나운, 혹심한

* **in·cli·na·tion** [ìnklinéiʃ(ə)n] *n.* [C][U] **1.** the act of bending, leaning or sloping towards something. **2.** the difference in direction between two things as measured by the angle between them. **3.** a particular tendency of the mind; a liking; a preference.
—[名] 1. 기울기, 기대기 2. 경사, 물매 3. 경향, 성향(性向), 기호(嗜好)

‡ **in·cline** *v.* [inkláin → *n.*] *vt.* **1.** bow; bend; nod; lean. ¶*an inclined plane*① / *The fair lady graciously inclined her head.* **2.** ((usu. in *passive*)) turn (one's mind, etc.) in a certain direction; dispose; favor. ((~ someone *to do*)) ¶*I was not inclined to believe the man.* / *He is inclined to be idle.* / *This inclined her to leave.* —*vi.* **1.** lean; slope; bend. **2.** tend; have a liking. ((~ *to* something; ~ *to do*)) ¶*I ~ to his opinion.* / *The flowers ~ toward red.*②
—[他] 1. [머리 따위]를 숙이다, …을 기울이다 ¶①사면(斜面) 2. [마음]을 쏟다; …하고 싶다고 여기다; …하는 경향이 있다 —[自] 1. 기울다, 경사하다 2. …하고 싶다고 생각하다; …하기 쉽다; …하는 경향이 있다 ¶②그 꽃은 빨강에 가깝다

—*n.* [´–, –´] [C] a slope; an inclined surface. ¶*The car went slowly down the ~.*
—[名] 경사; 사면

* **in·close** [inklóuz] *vt.* =enclose.

in·clo·sure [inklóuʒər] *n.* =enclosure.

‡ **in·clude** [inklú:d] *vt.* put or enclose (something) within limits; contain (something) as a part of the whole; shut up; enclose.
—[他] …을 포함하다, 포괄하다; [일부분으로서] 포함시키다

in·clu·sion [inklú:ʒ(ə)n] *n.* **1.** [U] the act of including; the state of being included. **2.** [C] a thing which is included.
—[名] 1. 포함, 포괄 2. 함유물

in·clu·sive [inklú:siv] *adj.* **1.** including a great deal; taking everything into account. **2.** including the mentioned limits. ¶*from Monday to Friday ~.*
—[形] 1. 모든 것을 포함한, 포괄적인 2. …을 포함한

in·cog [inkág / -kɔ́g] *adj., adv., n.* (*colloq.*) =incognito.

in·cog·ni·ti [inkágniti / -kɔ́g-] *n.* pl. of **incognito.**

in·cog·ni·to [inkágnitou / -kɔ́g-] *adj., adv.* using a different name so as to escape notice. —*n.* [C] (pl. **-tos** or **-ti**) a person who is incognito.
—[形][副] 익명의(으로), 암행의(으로)
—[名] 익명자

in·co·her·ence [ìnkouhíər(ə)ns] *n.* [U] the state of being incoherent; lack of logical connection.
—[名] 지리멸렬, 모순된 말(생각)

in·co·her·ent [ìnkouhíər(ə)nt] *adj.* connected loosely; in bad order; lacking logical connection.
—[形] 지리멸렬의, 조리가 서지 않는

in·com·bus·ti·ble [ìnkəmbʌ́stibl] *adj.* that cannot be burned; fireproof.
—[形] 불타지 않는

‡ **in·come** [ínkʌm] *n.* [C][U] the amount of money coming in as payments, interest, profits, etc. ↔outgo
—[名] 수입, 소득

in·com·ing [ínkʌ̀miŋ] *adj.* coming in. ¶~ *profits.*①
—[形] 들어오는 ¶①수익(收益)

—*n.* [U][C] ((usu. *pl.*)) the act of coming in; arrival.
—[名] 도래(到來), 도착

in·com·men·su·rate [ìnkəménʃurit] *adj.* **1.** not adequate; not enough. **2.** having no common measure.
—[形] 1. 부적당한, 불충분한 2. 같은 표준으로 잴 수 없는

in·com·mode [ìnkəmóud] *vt.* bring discomfort to (someone); inconvenience; trouble.
—[他] …에게 불편을 주다; …에게 폐를 끼치다

in·com·mo·di·ous [ìnkəmóudiəs] *adj.* **1.** inconvenient; uncomfortable. **2.** inconveniently narrow.
—[形] 1. 불편한; 불쾌한 2. 비좁은, 옹색한

in·com·mu·ni·ca·ble [ìnkəmjú:nikəbl] *adj.* that cannot be communicated.
—[形] 전달할 수 없는, 연락이 없는

in·com·pa·ra·ble [inkámp(ə)rəbl / -kɔ́m-] *adj.* that cannot be compared; without equal.
—[形] 비교할 수 없는; 비교가 되지 않는, 비길 데 없는

in·com·pat·i·bil·i·ty [ìnkəmpæ̀tibíliti] *n.* [U] the state or quality of being incompatible; lack of harmony.
—[名] 양립하기 어려움, 상반(相反); 부조화

in·com·pat·i·ble [ìnkəmpǽtibl] *adj.* not able to live or act together in harmony; inconsistent. ¶*Excessive drinking is ~ with good health.*①
—[形] 양립하기 힘든, 조화되지 않는 ¶①과음은 건강과 양립할 수 없다

in·com·pe·tence [inkámpit(ə)ns / -kɔ́m-] *n.* [U] the state of being incompetent. —[名] 무능, 무자격

in·com·pe·ten·cy [inkámpit(ə)nsi / -kɔ́m-] *n.* =incompetence.

in·com·pe·tent [inkámpit(ə)nt / -kɔ́m-] *adj.* lacking ability, power or fitness; not competent. —[形] 무능한

in·com·plete [ìnkəmplí:t] *adj.* not complete; unfinished; imperfect. —[形] 불완전한; 미완성의

in·com·pre·hen·si·ble [inkàmprihénsibl / -kɔ̀m-] *adj.* that cannot be understood; beyond understanding. —[形] 이해할 수 없는

in·com·press·i·ble [ìnkəmprésibl] *adj.* that cannot be compressed. —[形] 압축할 수 없는

in·con·ceiv·a·ble [ìnkənsí:vəbl] *adj.* that cannot be imagined or believed. —[形] 상상도 못하는, 믿기도 어려운

in·con·ceiv·a·bly [ìnkənsí:vəbli] *adv.* in an inconceivable manner; to an inconceivable degree. —[副] 상상도 못하게, 믿기 어렵게

in·con·clu·sive [ìnkənklú:siv] *adj.* not conclusive; not decisive. —[形] 결정적이 아닌, 요령부득의

in·con·gru·i·ty [ìnkɑŋgrú:iti / -kɔŋgrú(:)i-] *n.* (pl. **-ties**) **1.** [U] the state or quality of being incongruous. **2.** [C] an incongruous thing. —[名] 1. 부조화, 불일치 2. 조화되지 않는 사람

in·con·gru·ous [inkáŋgruəs / -kɔ́ŋ] *adj.* **1.** not appropriate; out of place. **2.** lacking in agreement or harmony; not consistent. —[形] 1. 적합하지 않은, 어울리지 않는 2. 일치(조화)하지 않는

in·con·se·quent [inkánsikwènt / -kɔ́nsikwənt] *adj.* not logical; not logically connected; not to the point. —[形] 논리적이 아닌; 조리가 서지 않는; 엉뚱한

in·con·se·quen·tial [inkànsikwénʃ(ə)l / -kɔ̀n-] *adj.* **1.** inconsequent; illogical. **2.** not important. —[形] 1. 앞뒤가 안 맞는, 비논리적인 2. 중요하지 않은

in·con·sid·er·a·ble [ìnkənsíd(ə)rəbl] *adj.* not worth consideration; not important. —[形] 중요하지 않은, 시시한, 하찮은

in·con·sid·er·ate [ìnkənsíd(ə)rit] *adj.* thoughtless of the feelings, wishes or rights of others; careless. —[形] 인정머리 없는; 부주의한

in·con·sist·en·cy [ìnkənsíst(ə)nsi] *n.* (pl. **-cies**) **1.** [U] the state or quality of being inconsistent. **2.** [C] an inconsistent thing. —[名] 1. 불일치, 모순 2. 일치하지 않는 것

in·con·sist·ent [ìnkənsíst(ə)nt] *adj.* **1.** lacking in agreement or harmony. **2.** not holding together; having contradictions within itself. **3.** not keeping the same principles, etc.; changeable. —[形] 1. 일치하지 않는, 조화하지 않는 2. 모순되는, 양립할 수 없는 3. 변덕스러운, 일관성 없는

in·con·sol·a·ble [ìnkənsóuləbl] *adj.* that cannot be consoled; broken-hearted. —[形] [사람·슬픔이] 위로할 길 없는

in·con·spic·u·ous [ìnkənspíkjuəs] *adj.* not easily noticed. —[形] 눈에 띄지 않는, 주의를 끌지 않는

in·con·stan·cy [inkánst(ə)nsi / -kɔ́n-] *n.* [U] [C] (pl. **-cies**) the state of being inconstant; changeableness. —[名] 변하기 쉬움

in·con·stant [inkánst(ə)nt / -kɔ́n-] *adj.* not constant; likely to change. —[形] 변하기 쉬운, 변덕스러운

in·con·test·a·ble [ìnkəntéstəbl] *adj.* that cannot or should not be contested; unquestionable. —[形] 논의의 여지가 없는, 의심없는, 명백한

in·con·ti·nence [inkántinəns / -kɔ́n-] *n.* [U] the state or quality of being incontinent. —[名] 자제(自制)할 수 없음

in·con·ti·nent [inkántinənt / -kɔ́n-] *adj.* without self-restraint. —[形] 자제할 수 없는

in·con·tro·vert·i·ble [ìnkɑntrəvə́:rtibl / -kɔntrəvə́:t] *adj.* that cannot be disputed; unquestionable. —[形] 논의의 여지가 없는; 명백한

***in·con·ven·ience** [ìnkənví:niəns] *n.* **1.** [U] the state or quality of being not convenient. **2.** [C] something which is inconvenient. —*vt.* put (someone) to trouble or bother. —[名] 1. 불편, 부자유 2. 골칫거리 —[他] …을 불편하게 하다, …에게 폐를 끼치다

***in·con·ven·ient** [ìnkənví:niənt] *adj.* not convenient; causing difficulty or discomfort. —[形] 불편한; 부자유한; 불쾌한; 골치아픈; 성가신

in·con·vert·i·ble [ìnkənvə́:rtibl] *adj.* that cannot be converted or exchanged. —[形] 바꿀 수 없는

in·cor·po·rate *v.* [inkɔ́:rpərèit → *adj.*] *vt.* **1.** join or combine (something) into a whole; make (something) a part of something else. ¶ ~ *another's ideas into one's story.* **2.** form (individuals or units) into a legal corporation. **3.** give a material or physical form to (something). —[他] 1. …을 합동(합병)하다, 편입하다, 결합하다 2. …을 법인 조직으로 하다 3. …을 구체화하다
—*vi.* become combined; form a legal corporation. —[自] 법인 조직을 만들다, 법인이 되다
—*adj.* [inkɔ́:rp(ə)rit] combined into one body. —[形] 합동(합병)한

in·cor·po·rat·ed [inkɔ́:rpərèitid] *adj.* **1.** combined in one body. **2.** formed or organized as a corporation.
— ⓐ **1.** 결합한; 합체(合體)한 **2.** 법인 조직의

in·cor·po·ra·tion [inkɔ̀:rpəréiʃ(ə)n] *n.* Ⓤ Ⓒ the act of incorporating; the state of being incorporated.
— ⓝ 합체, 합동, 결합, 법인 조직

in·cor·po·re·al [ìnkɔ:rpɔ́:riəl] *adj.* not composed of matter.
— ⓐ 실체(實體)가 없는, 무형의

in·cor·rect [ìnkərékt] *adj.* not according to fact or truth; not right; wrong.
— ⓐ 옳지 않은, 틀린

in·cor·ri·gi·ble [inkɔ́ridʒəbl, -kɔ́:r- / -kɔ́r-] *adj.* (of a person, a bad habit, etc.) that cannot be made better; hopelessly bad.
— ⓐ 교정(矯正)할 수 없는, 고칠 수 없는

in·cor·rupt·i·ble [ìnkərʌ́ptəbl] *adj.* **1.** impossible to be made to do wrong, even by the offer of money. **2.** that cannot decay.
— ⓐ **1.** 매수할 수 없는 **2.** 썩지 않는

:**in·crease** *v.* [inkrí:s → *n.*] ↔decrease — *vi.* become greater in number, size, value, etc. — *vt.* make (something) greater in number, size, value, etc.; enlarge. ¶ ~ *one's wealth.*①
— ⓥ 늘다 — ⓥ …을 늘리다 ¶①재산을 늘리다

— *n.* [≁] **1.** Ⓒ Ⓤ a growth in number, size, value, etc. ¶*an ~ in population.*② **2.** Ⓒ the amount that is added.
— ⓝ **1.** 증가 ¶②인구의 증가 **2.** 증대량, 증가액

in·creas·ing·ly [inkrí:siŋli] *adv.* more and more.
— ⓐ 점점

in·cred·i·bil·i·ty [inkrèdibíliti] *n.* Ⓤ the state or quality of being incredible. [belief.]
— ⓝ 믿을 수 없음

•**in·cred·i·ble** [inkrédibl] *adj.* hard to believe; beyond
— ⓐ 믿을 수 없는

in·cred·i·bly [inkrédibli] *adv.* in an incredible manner; to an incredible degree.
— ⓐ 믿을 수 없을 만큼; 대단히

in·cre·du·li·ty [inkrid(j)ú:liti / -djú:-] *n.* Ⓤ the state or quality of being incredulous.
— ⓝ 의심 깊음; 불신

in·cred·u·lous [inkrédʒuləs / -krédju-] *adj.* not willing to or not able to believe; doubting.
— ⓐ 쉽게 믿지 않는; 의심 많은

in·cre·ment [ínkrimənt] *n.* **1.** Ⓤ increase; growth. **2.** Ⓒ the amount of increase. ▷ **in·cre·ment·al** [-əl] *adj.*
— ⓝ **1.** 증가, 증대 **2.** 증가량(액), 증가수

in·crim·i·nate [inkríminèit] *vt.* accuse (someone) of a crime. ¶ ~ *oneself.*①
— ⓥ …에게 죄를 씌우다 ¶①복죄(服罪)하다

in·crust [inkrʌ́st] *vt.* cover the surface of (something) with a thin, hard, outer covering.
— ⓥ …을 껍데기(외피)로 덮다

in·cu·bate [ínkjubèit, íŋk-] *vt.* bring the young out of (eggs) by keeping them warm; hatch.
— ⓥ [알]을 까다, 부화시키다

in·cu·ba·tion [ìnkjubéiʃ(ə)n, ìŋk-] *n.* Ⓤ Ⓒ the act of incubating; the state of being incubated. ¶*artificial* ~.①
— ⓝ 부화 ¶①인공 부화

in·cu·ba·tor [ínkjubèitər, íŋk-] *n.* Ⓒ a heated box for hatching eggs.
— ⓝ 부화기, 부란기(孵卵器)

in·cu·bi [ínkjubài] *n.* pl. of **incubus**.

in·cu·bus [íŋkjubəs, ínk-] *n.* Ⓒ (pl. **-bus·es** or **-bi**) **1.** a nightmare. **2.** an oppressive thing; a great worry.
— ⓝ **1.** 몽마(夢魔), 악몽 **2.** 압박하는 것, 무거운 짐

in·cul·cate [inkʌ́lkeit, +*U.S.* ←⊥←] *vt.* fix (something) firmly in the mind of someone by much repeating. ((~ something *on* or *upon*)) ¶ ~ *good manners on a child.*①
— ⓥ …을 […에게] 되풀이 가르치다, 차근차근 타이르다 ¶①아이에게 예법을 차근차근 가르치다

in·cum·bent [inkʌ́mbənt] *adj.* **1.** lying or resting with its weight on something else. **2.** pressing as a duty. ((~ *on, upon*)) ¶*It is ~ on you to warn them.*①
— ⓐ **1.** 기대는 **2.** 의무로서 지워지는 ¶①그들에게 경고하는 것이 네 의무다

•**in·cur** [inkɔ́:r] *vt.* (**-curred, -cur·ring**) get or fall into (something unpleasant); bring (something unpleasant) upon oneself. ¶*I incurred her anger.*①
— ⓥ [손해·불운]을 초래하다, 입다 ¶①그녀를 성나게 하고 말았다

in·cur·a·ble [inkjúərəbl] *adj.* that cannot be cured. ¶*an ~ disease.*①
— ⓐ 불치의 ¶①불치의 병

in·cur·sion [inkɔ́:rʒ(ə)n, -ʃ(ə)n / -ʃ(ə)n] *n.* Ⓒ **1.** a sudden attack. **2.** the act of running or flowing in.
— ⓝ **1.** 습격 **2.** 침입, 유입(流入)

Ind. 1. Indiana. **2.** India; Indian.

in·debt·ed [indétid] *adj.* owing money or gratitude. ¶*I am ~ to you for your kindness.*①
— ⓐ 빚(부채)이 있는 ¶①친절히 해 주셔서 고맙습니다

in·de·cen·cy [indí:snsi] *n.* (pl. **-cies**) **1.** Ⓤ the state of being indecent. **2.** Ⓒ an indecent act or speech.
— ⓝ **1.** 버릇없음, 꼴사나움 **2.** 버릇없는 언행

in·de·cent [indí:snt] *adj.* **1.** in very bad taste; not suitable. **2.** not fit to be seen or heard.
— ⓐ **1.** 꼴사나운, 보기 흉한 **2.** 상스러운, 음란한

in·de·ci·sion [ìndisíʒ(ə)n] *n.* Ⓤ the state or quality of being not able to make up one's mind; lack of decision. —[名] 우유부단, 결단성이 없음

in·de·ci·sive [ìndisáisiv] *adj.* not settling or deciding the matter; indefinite; hesitant. ¶*an ~ battle.*① —[形] 결정적이 아닌; 우유부단한 ¶① 승부가 안 나는 싸움

in·dec·o·rous [ìndékərəs, +*U.S.* -dikɔ́:-] *adj.* not suitable; against good manners. —[形] 버릇없는, 보기 흉한

in·de·co·rum [ìndikɔ́:rəm] *n.* **1.** Ⓤ the state or quality of being indecorous. **2.** Ⓒ an indecorous act or speech. —[名] 1. 무례, 버릇없음 2. 버릇없는 언동

‡**in·deed** [indí:d] *adv.* in fact; really; truly. ¶*He was ~ a remarkable man.* —*interj.* an expression of surprise, disbelief, interest, etc. —[副] 실제로; 정말로, 참으로 —[感] [놀람 따위를 나타내어] 설마!, 아니 저런!

in·de·fat·i·ga·ble [ìndifǽtigəbl] *adj.* never getting tired; tireless. —[形] 지치지 않는, 끈기 있는

in·de·fea·si·ble [ìndifí:zibl] *adj.* (of one's rights, etc.) that cannot be taken away or made void. —[形] 파기(취소)할 수 없는

in·de·fen·si·ble [ìndifénsibl] *adj.* **1.** that cannot be defended. **2.** (of behavior) that cannot be excused. —[形] 1. 지킬 수 없는 2. 변호할 수 없는; 구실이 안 서는

in·de·fin·a·ble [ìndifáinəbl] *adj.* that cannot be defined or described. —[形] 정의를 내릴 수 없는, 막연한

in·def·i·nite [indéfinit] *adj.* not exact; not clearly limited. ¶*an ~ answer.* —[形] 명확하지 않은; 한계가 없는

in·def·i·nite·ly [indéfinitli] *adv.* in an indefinite manner. —[副] 한없이; 애매하게

in·del·i·ble [indélibl] *adj.* that cannot be rubbed out or cleaned. ¶*an ~ pencil.*① —[形] 지울(씻을) 수 없는 ¶① 지워지지 않는 연필

in·del·i·ca·cy [indélikəsi] *n.* (pl. **-cies**) **1.** Ⓤ the state of being indelicate. **2.** Ⓒ an indelicate act or speech. —[名] 1. 상스러움, 야비함, 버릇없음 2. 천한 짓(말)

in·del·i·cate [indélikit] *adj.* not delicate; shameless. —[形] 상스러운, 버릇없는

in·dem·ni·fy [indémnifài] *vt.* (**-fied**) **1.** repay (someone) for loss or damage. 《~ someone *for*》 **2.** give security against (future damage or loss). —[他] 1. …에 [손해 따위의] 배상을 하다 2. …을 보장하다

in·dem·ni·ty [indémniti] *n.* (pl. **-ties**) **1.** Ⓤ protection or insurance against loss or damage. **2.** Ⓒ payment for loss or damage. —[名] 1. 보상, 보장 2. 손해배상

in·dent [indént] *vt.* **1.** give a toothlike line to (an edge, etc.). **2.** (in writing or printing) begin (a line) with one or more blank spaces. —[他] 1. …의 가장자리를 톱니 모양으로 만들다 2. [인쇄에서 첫행]을 약간 안으로 넣고 짜다

in·den·ta·tion [ìndentéiʃ(ə)n] *n.* **1.** Ⓤ the act of giving a toothlike edge to something. **2.** Ⓒ a toothlike line. —[名] 1. 들쭉날쭉하게 하기 2. 톱니 모양의 자국

in·den·tion [indénʃ(ə)n] *n.* **1.** Ⓤ the act of beginning a line with a blank space. **2.** ⓊⒸ indentation. —[名] 1. [새로운 행을] 들여 짜기 2. 톱니 모양[을 만들기]

in·den·ture [indéntʃər] *n.* Ⓒ **1.** 《usu. *pl.*》 a written agreement between a learner of a trade and his master. **2.** the act of making a toothlike line. —*vt.* bind (someone) by an indenture. —[名] 1. 도제살이 문서, 증서, 계약서 2. 톱니자국을 내기 —[他] [남의] 고용을 계약서로 약정하다

‡**in·de·pend·ence** [ìndipéndəns] *n.* Ⓤ the state of being free from the control, influence or support of others. —[名] 독립, 자립

‡**in·de·pend·ent** [ìndipéndənt] *adj.* **1.** not under another's control; free from another's influence; not willing to accept help from others. ¶*an ~ country* | *a man of ~ mind.* **2.** not dependent on others for one's living. ¶*He is ~ of his parents.*① **3.** not needing to work for a living. **4.** voting according to one's own ideas. ¶*an ~ voter.* **5.** not in connection with any other or each other; separate. ¶*~ research.*② —[形] 1. 남의 지배를 받지 않는; 독립의; 독립심이 강한 2. 자활하는; 남의 신세를 지지 않는 ¶① 그는 양친에게서 독립해 있다 3. 일하지 않고 살 수 있는 4. 무소속의 5. 관계 없는; 별개의 ¶② 독자적인 연구

—*n.* Ⓒ a person who exercises his own will or judgment, esp. in political matters. —[名] 독립한 사람; 정치적으로 무소속인 사람

in·de·pend·ent·ly [ìndipéndəntli] *adv.* in an independent manner. —[副] 독립하여

in·de·scrib·a·ble [ìndiskráibəbl] *adj.* that cannot be described; beyond description. —[形] 형언하기 힘든, 필설로 다할 수 없는

in·de·struct·i·ble [ìndistrʌ́ktibl] *adj.* that cannot be destroyed or broken up. —[形] 파괴할 수 없는; 불멸의

in·de·ter·mi·nate [ìnditə́:rm(i)nit] *adj.* not determined; indefinite; vague. —[形] 불확정의, 애매한

***in·dex** [índeks] *n.* Ⓒ (pl. **-es** or **-di·ces**) **1.** a thing which points out or indicates; a sign. **2.** an alphabetical list of names or subjects dealt with in a book. —*vt.* make an index for (a book). —[名] 1. 지시하는 것, 지표 2. 색인 —[他] [책]에 색인을 달다

In·di·a [índiə] *n.* a country in southern Asia. ⇒[N.B.]
—[名] 인도 [N.B.] 수도 New Delhi

In·di·an [índiən] *n.* **1.** [C] a person living in America before the Europeans came; an American Indian. **2.** [C] a person of India or the East Indies. **3.** [U] the language of the American Indians. —*adj.* of India or Indians.
—[名] 1. 북미 토인 2. 인도인 3. 북미 토인어 —[形] 인도의; 인도인의; 북미 토인의; 북미 토인어의

In·di·an·a [ìndiǽnə] *n.* a north central State of the United States. ⇒[N.B.]
—[名] 인디애너 주 [N.B.] Ind.로 줄임 수도 Indianapolis

Indian corn [ˊ- ˊ] *n.* a kind of grain that grows on large ears; maize.
—[名] 옥수수

Indian summer [ˊ- ˊ-] *n.* a period of pleasant, warm days in autumn.
—[名] 늦가을의 따뜻한 날씨

India paper [ˊ- ˋ-] *n.* a thin, tough paper for printing.
—[名] 인디언지(紙)

India (india) rubber [ˊ- ˊ-] *n.* rubber, esp. in a small piece used for rubbing out pencil marks.
—[名] 탄성 고무; 지우개

* **in·di·cate** [índikèit] *vt.* **1.** make known; point out; show. ¶*The arrow indicates the way to the station.* **2.** be a sign of (something). ¶*Fever indicates illness.*②
—[他] 1. …을 가리키다; 지시하다 2. …의 징조(징후)이다 ¶①열은 병의 징후이다

in·di·ca·tion [ìndikéiʃ(ə)n] *n.* **1.** [U] the act of indicating. **2.** [C] a thing which indicates; a sign.
—[名] 1. 지시, 지적 2. 지시하는 것; 징후

in·dic·a·tive [indíkətiv] *adj.* **1.** pointing out; showing; suggesting. **2.** (*Grammar*) expressing an act, state, or occurrence as actual.
—[形] 1. 나타내는, 표시하는 2. 직설법의; 서술법의

in·di·ca·tor [índikèitər] *n.* [C] **1.** a person or thing that indicates. **2.** a needle on the dial of an instrument that measures something; a measuring instrument.
—[名] 1. 지시자, 지시하는 것 2. 지침; 표시기(表示器)

in·di·ces [índisìːz] *n.* pl. of **index**.

in·dict [indáit] *vt.* charge (someone) with an offence or crime.
—[他] …을 고발하다

in·dict·ment [indáitmənt] *n.* **1.** [U] the act of indicting; the state of being indicted; accusation. **2.** [C] (*Law*) a formal written statement indicting a person.
—[名] 1. 기소, 고발 2. 기소장

* **in·dif·fer·ence** [indíf(ə)rəns] *n.* [U] **1.** lack of interest or attention. **2.** lack of importance. ¶*It is a matter of ~.*
—[名] 1. 무관심, 냉담 2. 중요하지 않음

* **in·dif·fer·ent** [indíf(ə)rənt] *adj.* **1.** having or showing no interest or concern. ¶*be ~ to one's clothes.* **2.** not partial; fair; neutral. **3.** of no importance. **4.** not very good and not very bad; rather bad. ¶*He is an ~ pianist.*①
—[形] 1. 무관심한 2. 공평한, 중립의 3. 그다지 중요하지 않은 4. 좋지도 나쁘지도 않은; 평범한, 하잘 것 없는 ¶①그는 대단한 피아니스트는 아니다

in·di·gence [índidʒ(ə)ns] *n.* [U] poverty.
—[名] 빈곤

in·dig·e·nous [indídʒinəs] *adj.* born or produced in a certain region or country; native.
—[形] 그 토지에 고유한, 토착(土着)의; 타고난

in·di·gent [índidʒ(ə)nt] *adj.* very poor; living in want.
—[形] 가난한, 빈곤한

in·di·gest·i·ble [ìndidʒéstibl, +*U.S.* -dai-] *adj.* cannot be digested; hard to digest.
—[形] 소화가 잘 안 되는, 소화하기 힘든

in·di·ges·tion [ìndidʒéstʃ(ə)n, +*U.S.* -dai-] *n.* [U] the state of being indigestible; difficulty in digesting; pain in the stomach caused by such a difficulty.
—[名] 소화가 안 됨, 소화불량

in·dig·nant [indígnənt] *adj.* angry at something unfair, unjust or mean.
—[形] 성난, 분개한

* **in·dig·na·tion** [ìndignéiʃ(ə)n] *n.* anger at something unfair, unjust or mean.
—[名] 의분, 분노

in·dig·ni·ty [indígniti] *n.* [U][C] (pl. **-ties**) behavior or remark to a person damaging his pride; an insult.
—[名] 모욕; 경멸

in·di·go [índigòu] *n.* (pl. **-gos** or **-goes**) **1.** [U] deep blue color. **2.** [C] a plant from which a blue coloring-matter is obtained.
—[名] 1. 남색, 쪽빛 2. 양람(洋藍)[물감]

* **in·di·rect** [ìndirékt, -dai-] *adj.* **1.** not in a direct line; not straight. ¶*make an ~ reference to someone.*① **2.** not directly connected. ¶*an ~ effect.*
—[形] 1. 똑바르지 않은; 완곡한 ¶①남에게 완곡하게 언급하다 2. 간접적인

in·di·rect·ly [ìndiréktli, -dai-] *adv.* in an indirect manner.
—[副] 간접적으로; 완곡하게

in·dis·creet [ìndiskríːt] *adj.* not wise or cautious.
—[形] 무분별한; 경솔한

in·dis·creet·ly [ìndiskríːtli] *adv.* in an indiscreet manner.
—[副] 무분별하게; 경솔하게

in·dis·cre·tion [ìndiskréʃ(ə)n] *n.* **1.** [U] the state or quality of being indiscreet. **2.** [C] an indiscreet or imprudent act.
—[名] 1. 무분별 2. 무분별한 짓

in·dis·crim·i·nate [ìndiskríminit] *adj.* not carefully choosing; without distinction; confused.
—[形] 무차별의; 난잡한, 어지러워진

I

* **in·dis·pen·sa·ble** [ìndispénsəbl] *adj.* absolutely necessary; essential. ¶*Water is ~ to life.*① —[形] 없어서는 안 될, 절대로 필요한 ¶①물은 생활에 없어서는 안 된다

in·dis·pose [ìndispóuz] *vt.* **1.** make (someone) unwilling. 《~ someone *for* or *to do*》 **2.** make (someone) slightly ill. **3.** make (someone) unfit or unable. 《~ someone *for* or *to do*》 —[他] 1. …을 싫증나게 하다, …할 마음을 잃게 하다 2. …을 가벼운 병에 걸리게 하다 3. …을 부적당(불가능)하게 하다

in·dis·posed [ìndispóuzd] *adj.* **1.** slightly ill. **2.** unwilling. ¶*He is ~ to help us.* —[形] 1. 찌뿌드드한 2. 마음이 내키지 않는, …할 생각이 없는

in·dis·po·si·tion [ìndispəzíʃ(ə)n] *n.* **1.** [C] a slight illness. **2.** [U] unwillingness. —[名] 1. 가벼운 병, 편찮은 2. 싫증

in·dis·put·a·ble [ìndispjú:təbl] *adj.* that cannot be disputed or doubted; unquestionable. —[形] 논의(의문)의 여지가 없는; 명백한

in·dis·sol·u·ble [ìndisáljubl / -sɔ́l-] *adj.* that cannot be dissolved or destroyed; firm. ¶*an ~ friendship.* —[形] 분해(파괴)할 수 없는; 확고한; 영속하는

in·dis·tinct [ìndistíŋ(k)t] *adj.* not clear; obscure; vague. —[形] 뚜렷하지 않은, 애매한

in·dis·tinct·ly [ìndistíŋ(k)tli] *adv.* in an indistinct manner. —[副] 애매하게, 희미하게

in·dis·tin·guish·a·ble [ìndistíŋgwiʃəbl] *adj.* that cannot be distinguished. —[形] 구분(분간)할 수 없는,

in·dite [indáit] *vt.* put (something) in words; compose. —[他] [시·글 따위]를 짓다, 쓰다

⁑ **in·di·vid·u·al** [ìndivídʒuəl, +*Brit.* -vídju-] *n.* [C] **1.** a person. ¶*an agreeable ~.*① **2.** a single person, animal or thing. —*adj.* **1.** particular; separate; single. ↔general ¶*each ~ person.*② **2.** of or belonging to one person or thing. **3.** peculiar to one person or thing; characteristic. —[名] 1. 사람 ¶①상냥한 사람 2. 개인; 개체 —[形] 1. 개개의, 단일의 ¶②각개인 2. 개인의; 개인적인 3. 고유의, 독특한

in·di·vid·u·al·ism [ìndivídʒuəlìz(ə)m, +*Brit.* -vídju-] *n.* [U] the doctrine that the right or welfare of an individual is more important than that of the group; absence of cooperation; egoism. —[名] 개인주의; 이기주의

in·di·vid·u·al·ist [ìndivídʒuəlist, +*Brit.* -vídju-] *n.* [C] a person who believes in or practices individualism. —[名] 개인주의자, 이기주의자

in·di·vid·u·al·is·tic [ìndivìdʒuəlístik] *adj.* of individualism or an individualist. —[形] 개인주의[자]의; 이기주의[자]의

in·di·vid·u·al·i·ty [ìndivìdʒuǽliti, +*Brit.* -vidju-] *n.* (pl. -ties) **1.** [U] [C] all the characteristics of a person or thing which makes him or it different from others. **2.** [U] the state or quality of being different or apart from others. —[名] 1. 개성 2. [개인적인] 특성, 특징

in·di·vid·u·al·ize [ìndivídʒuəlàiz, +*Brit.* -vídju-] *vt.* **1.** make (people or things) different from others. **2.** consider (someone or something) one by one. —[他] 1. …에게 개성을 주다 2. …을 개별화하다

in·di·vid·u·al·ly [ìndivídʒuəli, +*Brit.* -vídju-] *adv.* one by one; separately. —[副] 하나하나 별도로, 개인으로서

in·di·vis·i·bil·i·ty [índivìzibíliti] *n.* [U] the state of being indivisible. —[名] 분할할 수 없음

in·di·vis·i·ble [ìndivízibl] *adj.* that cannot be divided. —[形] 분할할 수 없는, 불가분의

in·doc·tri·nate [indáktrinèit / -dɔ́k-] *vt.* teach particular ideas or beliefs to (someone); teach. —[他] …에게 가르치다, 교훈하다

in·do·lence [índələns] *n.* [U] the state or quality of being indolent; laziness; idleness. —[名] 게으름, 나태

in·do·lent [índələnt] *adj.* not fond of work; lazy. —[形] 게으른, 나태한

in·do·lent·ly [índələntli] *adv.* in an indolent manner. —[副] 게으르게

in·dom·i·ta·ble [indámitəbl / -dɔ́m-] *adj.* that cannot be overcome; unconquerable. —[形] 굴복하지 않는, 불굴의

In·do·ne·sia [ìndouní:ʒə, -ʃə, +*Brit.* -zjə] *n.* a country composed of several islands in the East Indies. ⇒[N.B.] —[名] 인도네시아 [N.B.] 수도 Jakarta

In·do·ne·sian [ìndouní:ʒən, -ʃən, +*Brit.* -zjən] *n.* **1.** [C] a person of Indonesia. **2.** [U] the language of Indonesia. —*adj.* of Indonesia or Indonesians. —[名] 1. 인도네시아 사람 2. 인도네시아 말 —[形] 인도네시아의, 인도네시아 사람(말)의

in·door [índɔ̀:r] *adj.* of or done inside a building. ↔outdoor. ¶*~ games*① / *~ service.*② —[形] 실내의, 옥내의 ¶①실내 유희/②내근

* **in·doors** [índɔ́:rz] *adv.* in or into a house or building. ↔outdoors ¶*keep ~.*① —[副] 실내에, 옥내에 ¶①외출하지 않다

in·dorse [indɔ́:rs] *vt.* =endorse.

in·dorse·ment [indɔ́:rsmənt] *n.* =endorsement.

in·du·bi·ta·ble [ind(j)ú:bitəbl / -djú:-] *adj.* that cannot be doubted; unquestionable. ▷**in·du·bi·ta·bly** [-i] *adv.* —[形] 의심없는, 명백한

induce   [595]   inept

- **in·duce** [ind(j)ú:s / -djú:s] *vt.* **1.** lead on; persuade. (*~ someone to do*) ¶*I induced father to take me to the theater.* **2.** bring about; cause. ¶*Overwork induces illness.*① **3.** draw (a general conclusion or principle) from particular facts. **4.** produce (an electric or magnetic effect) by induction.
—⑪ 1. …을 타일러서 (권하여) …시키다 2. …을 일으키다, 유발하다 ¶①과로는 병을 유발한다 3. …을 귀납(歸納)하다 4. [전기·자기(磁氣)]를 유도하다

in·duce·ment [ind(j)ú:smənt / -djú:s-] *n.* **1.** ⓤ the act of inducing. **2.** ⓒ a thing which influences or persuades; a motive.
—⑬ 1. 유도, 권유 2. 유인(誘因), 동기

in·duct [indʌ́kt] *vt.* **1.** bring in; introduce. **2.** place (someone) in an office, etc. **3.** make (someone) a member of the army; enlist.
—⑪ 1. [자리 따위에] …을 이끌다, 끌어 들이다 2. …을 취임시키다 3. …을 병적에 넣다

in·duc·tion [indʌ́kʃən] *n.* ⓤⓒ **1.** the act or ceremony of inaugurating someone into an office. **2.** way of reasoning from many particular facts to one general law ; a conclusion reached in this way. **3.** (*Electricity*) the process by which an object having electrical or magnetic property produces similar properties in a nearby object without direct contact.
—⑬ 1. 취임[식] 2. 귀납법, 귀납법에 의한 결론 3. 전기(자기)유도

in·duc·tive [indʌ́ktiv] *adj.* of or using induction.
—⑬ 귀납의, 귀납적인; 유도(誘導)의

- **in·dulge** [indʌ́ldʒ] *vt.* **1.** give way to the wishes of (someone); yield to. ¶*The parents ~ their child too much.* **2.** give oneself up to (pleasures, desires, etc.). —*vi.* give way to one's pleasures; please oneself. (*~ in something*)
—⑪ 1. …을 제멋대로 하게 하다, …을 응석받다 2. …에 빠지다
—⑪ 쾌락에 빠지다

in·dul·gence [indʌ́ldʒ(ə)ns] *n.* **1.** ⓤ the act of indulging. **2.** ⓒ a thing indulged in. **3.** ⓤⓒ (*Catholic*) freedom given by a priest from punishment for sin.
—⑬ 1. 제멋대로 하게 하기, 너그러이 대함; 빠지기, 탐닉 2. 도락(道樂); 악습 3. (가톨릭) 면죄(免罪)

in·dul·gent [indʌ́ldʒ(ə)nt] *adj.* too kind; not critical.
—⑬ 응석 받는, 관대한

: **in·dus·tri·al** [indʌ́striəl] *adj.* of industry.
—⑬ 산업의, 공업의

in·dus·tri·al·ism [indʌ́striəliz(ə)m] *n.* ⓤ the system or principle of social and economic organization characterized by large industries.
—⑬ 산업(공업)제도; 산업주의

in·dus·tri·al·ist [indʌ́striəlist] *n.* ⓒ a person who owns or has an important position in an industrial enterprise.
—⑬ 실업가

in·dus·tri·al·ize [indʌ́striəlàiz] *vt.* make (something) industrial.
—⑪ …을 산업화하다

- **in·dus·tri·ous** [indʌ́striəs] *adj.* hard-working; diligent.
—⑬ 부지런한

: **in·dus·try** [índəstri] *n.* (pl. **-tries**) **1.** ⓤ steady effort; hard work; diligence. **2.** ⓒ any form of business, trade, or manufacture. **3.** ⓤ the act of manufacturing goods.
—⑬ 1. 근면 2. 산업 3. 공업

in·e·bri·ate [iní:brièit → *adj., n.*] *vt.* make (someone) drunk; intoxicate. —*adj.* [iní:briit] drunk; intoxicated. —*n.* [iní:briit] ⓒ a habitual drunkard.
—⑪ …을 취하게 하다 —⑬ 술취한
—⑬ 술주정뱅이; 술고래

in·e·bri·e·try [ìni(:)bráiətri] *n.* ⓤ the state of being drunken; drunkenness.
—⑬ 술취함

in·ed·i·ble [inédibl] *adj.* not fit to be eaten.
—⑬ 먹을 수 없는

in·ef·fa·ble [inéfəbl] *adj.* that cannot be expressed in words; beyond description.
—⑬ 말로 표현할 수 없는

in·ef·fec·tive [ìniféktiv] *adj.* of little use; not effective.
—⑬ 무효의; 무익한

in·ef·fec·tu·al [ìniféktʃuəl] *adj.* without the wanted effect; unsuccessful; useless. ⌈inefficient; inability.⌋
—⑬ 효과 없는, 헛된; 실패의; 쓸모없는

in·ef·fi·cien·cy [ìnifíʃ(ə)nsi] *n.* ⓤ the state of being
—⑬ 무능; 무력

in·ef·fi·cient [ìnifíʃ(ə)nt] *adj.* **1.** not able to get things done well. **2.** requiring unnecessary time, energy, etc.; not efficient. ¶*an ~ method of production.*①
—⑬ 1. 효과 없는, 쓸모없는 2. 비능률적인; 효율이 낮은 ¶①비능률적 생산방식

in·el·e·gance [inéligəns] *n.* **1.** ⓤ the state or quality of being not elegant. **2.** ⓒ an inelegant thing.
—⑬ 1. 우아하지 않음, 풍류를 모름, 아취가 없음 2. 아취 없는 짓(말)

in·el·e·gant [inéligənt] *adj.* not in good taste; not elegant; vulgar; crude.
—⑬ 우아하지 않은; 풍류를 모르는; 아취 없는

in·el·i·gi·ble [inélidʒibl] *adj.* unsuitable; unfit.
—⑬ 자격 없는; 부적당한

in·ept [inépt] *adj.* **1.** not suitable; out of place. **2.** absurd; foolish.
—⑬ 1. 부적당한 2. 터무니없는

in·ept·i·tude [inéptit(j)ùːd / -tjùːd] n. 1. Ⓤ foolishness. 2. Ⓒ a foolish act or speech.
─몡 1. 어리석음 2. 바보 같은 짓(말)

in·e·qual·i·ty [ìni(ː)kwáliti / -kwɔ́l-] n. (pl. **-ties**) 1. Ⓒ Ⓤ the state of being not equal. 2. Ⓤ the state or quality of not being even, regular or uniform. 3. Ⓒ an example of not being equal, even, etc.
─몡 1. 같지 않음 2. 불균형, 불명등 3. 불평등한 예(일)

in·eq·ui·ta·ble [inékwitəbl] adj. unfair; unjust.
─몡 불공정한; 불공평한

in·eq·ui·ty [inékwiti] n. Ⓤ Ⓒ (pl. **-ties**) the state or quality of being inequitable; unfairness; injustice.
─몡 불공평; 불공정

in·ert [inə́ːrt] adj. 1. having no power to act or move; lifeless. 2. inactive. 3. having no active chemical powers.
─몡 1. 자동력이 없는 2. 둔한, 완만한 3. 활성(活性)이 없는, 화학작용을 일으키지 않는

in·er·tia [inəːrʃə, +Brit. -nə́ːʃjə] n. Ⓤ 1. the state of not being willing to move or change. 2. the force which prevents a thing from being moved when it is still, and keeps it moving when it is moving.　[or avoided.]
─몡 1. 게으름, 굼뜸 2. 관성(慣性), 타성

in·es·cap·a·ble [ìnəskéipəbl] adj. that cannot be escaped
─몡 도망(모면)할 수 없는

in·es·ti·ma·ble [inéstəməbl] adj. too great, valuable, etc. to be measured. ¶of ~ value.
─몡 헤아릴 수 없는; 평가할 수 없는

* **in·ev·i·ta·ble** [inévitəbl] adj. not avoidable; certain. ¶the ~① / Death is ~.
─몡 피할 수 없는, 필연적이 ¶①필연적인 일

* **in·ev·i·ta·bly** [inévitəbli] adv. in an inevitable manner.
─몡 피할 수 없게, 필연적으로

in·ex·act [ìnigzǽkt] adj. not exact; not accurate.
─몡 부정확한

in·ex·cus·a·ble [ìnekskjúːzəbl] adj. that cannot be excused or justified; unjustifiable.
─몡 변명할 도리가 없는; 용서할 수 없는

in·ex·haust·i·ble [ìnegzɔ́ːstibl, -igz-] adj. 1. that cannot be used up; very abundant. 2. tireless.
─몡 1. 무진장의 2. 지칠 줄 모르는

in·ex·o·ra·ble [inéks(ə)rəbl] adj. that cannot be moved or influenced by prayers or entreaties; relentless; inflexible.
─몡 무정한, 냉혹한; 용서없는

in·ex·o·ra·bly [inéksərəbli] adv. in an inexorable manner.
─몡 무정하게, 냉혹하게

in·ex·pe·di·ent [ìnekspíːdiənt, -iks-] adj. not suitable or wise; not expedient.　[not expensive; cheap.]
─몡 부적당한; 형편이 나쁜, 현책(賢策)이 못되는

in·ex·pen·sive [ìnekspénsiv, -iks-] adj. costing little;
─몡 값싼, 비용이 들지 않는

in·ex·pe·ri·ence [ìnekspíəriəns, -iks-] n. Ⓤ the state of being not experienced; lack of experience or practice.
─몡 무경험; 미숙

in·ex·pe·ri·enced [ìnekspíəriənst, -iks-] adj. lacking in knowledge or skill gained from experience or practice; not experienced.
─몡 경험이 없는; 미숙한

in·ex·pert [ìnekspə́ːrt] adj. not expert; unskilled.
─몡 미숙한

in·ex·pi·a·ble [inékspiəbl] adj. (of a wrong act) that cannot be paid for. ¶an ~ sin.①
─몡 속죄할 수 없는; 죄 많은 ¶①속죄 못할 죄

in·ex·pli·ca·ble [ìnéksplikəbl] adj. that cannot be explained or understood; beyond understanding.
─몡 이해(설명)될 수 없는; 불가해한

in·ex·press·i·ble [ìneksprésibl, -iks-] adj. that cannot be put into words; beyond expression.
─몡 말로 표현할 수 없는, 이루 말할 수 없는

in·ex·pres·sive [ìneksprésiv] adj. lacking in expression; not expressive.
─몡 무감동의, 무표정한

in·ex·tin·guish·a·ble [ìnekstíŋgwiʃəbl, -iks-] adj. that cannot be put out or stopped.
─몡 지울 수 없는, 억누를 수 없는

in·ex·tri·ca·ble [inékstrikəbl] adj. that cannot be gotten free from; that cannot be solved.
─몡 탈출할 수 없는; 풀리지 않는

in·fal·li·bil·i·ty [infæləbíliti] n. Ⓤ the state or quality of being infallible.　[from error.]
─몡 절대 확실; 오류가 있을 수 없음

in·fal·li·ble [infǽlibl] adj. that cannot be mistaken; free
─몡 전혀 오류가 없는; 확실한

in·fa·mous [ínfəməs] adj. 1. having a bad reputation. 2. shameful; very evil. ¶an ~ crime.①
─몡 1. 악명 높은 2. 불명예스러운, 파렴치한 ¶①파렴치죄

in·fa·my [ínfəmi] n. (pl. **-mies**) 1. Ⓤ bad reputation; dishonor. 2. Ⓤ wickedness. 3. Ⓒ an infamous act.
─몡 1. 악명; 불명예 2. 사악(邪惡), 부도덕 3. 파렴치한 행위

* **in·fan·cy** [ínfənsi] n. Ⓤ 1. the state or time of being an infant; early childhood; babyhood. 2. the early, stage of development.
─몡 1. 유소(幼少), 유년[시대] 2. 초기; 초보

* **in·fant** [ínfənt] n. Ⓒ 1. a very young child; a baby. 2. (Law) a person who is under the age of 21; a minor.
─몡 1. 유아, 갓난아이 2. (法) 미성년자

—*adj.* **1.** of or for a child; very small or young. **2.** in an early stage.
—[形] 1. 유아의 2. 초기의; 초보의

in·fan·ti·cide [infǽntisàid] *n.* **1.** [U] the act of killing a baby. **2.** [C] a person who kills a baby.
—[名] 1. 영아(嬰兒) 살해 2. 영아 살해범

in·fan·tile [ínfəntàil, +*U.S.* -til] *adj.* **1.** of an infant or infants. **2.** like an infant; babyish. **3.** in an early stage.
—[形] 1. 유아의 2. 어린애 같은, 유치한 3. 초기의, 초보의

in·fan·tine [ínfəntàin, +*U.S.* -tì:n] *adj.* infantile; childish.
—[形] 유아의; 어린애 같은

in·fan·try [ínfəntri] *n.* 《*collectively*》 foot-soldiers.
—[名] 보병

in·fan·try·man [ínfəntrimən] *n.* [C] (pl. **-men** [-mən]) a soldier who fights on foot.
—[名] 보병

in·fat·u·at·ed [infǽtʃuèitid, +*Brit.* -fǽtju-] *adj.* showing a foolish fondness.
—[形] 얼빠진, 홀딱 반한

in·fat·u·a·tion [infæ̀tʃuéiʃ(ə)n, +*Brit.* -fæ̀tju-] *n.* [U] the state of being infatuated.
—[名] 열중, 홀림, 반함

* **in·fect** [infékt] *vt.* **1.** pass on a disease to (someone). ¶*an infected area.* **2.** affect; influence.
—[他] 1. …에게 병을 옮기다 2. …을 감화하다

in·fec·tion [infékʃ(ə)n] *n.* [U] **1.** the act of causing disease by the introduction of germs. **2.** influence spreading from one person to another. **3.** [C] a disease caused by germs.
—[名] 1. 전염, 감염 2. 영향, 감화 3. 전염병

in·fec·tious [infékʃəs] *adj.* **1.** caused or spread by infection. ¶*an ~ disease.* **2.** tending to spread to others.
—[形] 1. 전염하는, 전염병의 2. 감화하기 쉬운

in·fe·lic·i·tous [ìnfilísitəs] *adj.* **1.** unhappy. **2.** unsuitable.
—[形] 1. 불행한 2. 부적당한

in·fer [infə́:r] *vt.* (**-ferred, -fer·ring**) **1.** reach (a conclusion) by reasoning. **2.** conclude (something) from what has been known.
—[他] 1. [결론]에 도달하다 2. …을 추론(推論)하다

in·fer·a·ble [ìnfə́:rəbl] *adj.* that can be inferred.
—[形] 추론할 수 있는

in·fer·ence [ínf(ə)rəns] *n.* **1.** [U] the act or process of inferring. **2.** [C] a thing which is inferred; a deduction.
—[名] 1. 추론, 추측하기 2. 결론

* **in·fe·ri·or** [infíəriər] *adj.* ↔superior **1.** lower in rank, importance, value, place, etc. **2.** lower or poor in quality; second-rate. **—***n.* [C] a person who is lower in rank.
—[形] 1. 하등의, 열등한 2. 이류품의, 조악(粗惡)한 —[名] 손아랫사람, 하급자

in·fe·ri·or·i·ty [infìəriɔ́:riti, -ár- / -ɔ́r-] *n.* [U] the state or quality of being below others in rank, quality, importance, etc. ↔superiority
—[名] 하급, 하위, 열등

inferiority complex [-ˌ-ˊ-- ˊ-] *n.* an abnormal feeling of being inferior to others.
—[名] 열등감

in·fer·nal [infə́:rn(ə)l] *adj.* of or like hell.
—[形] 지옥의(같은)

in·fer·no [infə́:rnou] *n.* [C] (pl. **-nos**) **1.** hell. **2.** a hell-like place or thing.
—[名] 1. 지옥 2. 지옥같이 무서운 곳(것)

in·fest [infést] *vt.* (of something harmful) be numerous in (some place).
—[他] …에 만연하다

in·fi·del [ínfid(ə)l] *n.* [C] **1.** a person who does not believe in any religion. **2.** (of a certain religion) a person who does not believe in the religion. **—***adj.* of an infidel.
—[名] 1. 신앙심이 없는 사람, 무신론자 2. 이교도 —[形] 신앙심이 없는, 무신론자의, 이교도의

in·fi·del·i·ty [ìnfidéliti] *n.* [U] [C] (pl. **-ties**) **1.** disbelief in religion, esp. in the Christian religion. **2.** unfaithful or disloyal action; unfaithfulness.
—[名] 1. 신앙심이 없음; 그리스도교를 믿지 않음 2. 불신, 불신 행위, 불성실

in·field [ínfì:ld] *n.* [C] **1.** a baseball diamond. **2.** 《*collectively*》 (in baseball) the infield players. **3.** the part of a farm nearest the farmhouse.
—[名] 1. 내야(內野) 2. 내야수 3. 농가 주변의 농지

in·fil·trate [infíltrèit] *vt., vi.* pass or cause (water, etc.) to pass through or into the earth, etc.
—[他][自] …을 배어들게 하다, 배어들다

in·fil·tra·tion [ìnfiltréiʃ(ə)n] *n.* **1.** [U] the act of infiltrating; the state of being infiltrated. **2.** [C] a thing which infiltrates.
—[名] 1. 침투 2. 침투물

* **in·fi·nite** [ínfinit] *adj.* **1.** without limits; endless. **2.** extremely great; vast.
—[形] 1. 무한의 2. 막대한, 무수한

in·fi·nite·ly [ínfinitli] *adv.* to an infinite degree.
—[副] 무한하게

in·fi·ni·tes·i·mal [ìnfinitésim(ə)l] *adj.* too small to be measured.
—[形] 미소(微小)한, 극미(極微)의

‡ **in·fin·i·tive** [infínitiv] *n.* [C] a form of a verb not limited by person, number or time.
—[名] 부정사(不定詞)

in·fin·i·tude [infínit(j)ù:d / -tjù:d] *n.* **1.** [U] the state of being infinite. **2.** [C] an infinite number or extent.
—[名] 1. 무한 2. 무한한 수량

in·fin·i·ty [infíniti *n.*] (pl. **-ties**) **1.** [U] the state of being
—[名] 1. 무한 2. 무한한 수량(범위)

I

infirm [598] influenza

infinite; beyond measure in time, number, space or distance. **2.** ⓒ an infinite extent, number, amount, quantity, etc.

in·firm [infə́:*r*m] *adj.* **1.** not strong; weak. **2.** weak in mind or will. — ⓐ 1. 허약한 2. 의지가 약한

in·fir·ma·ry [infə́:*r*məri] *n.* ⓒ (pl. **-ries**) a place or room for sick or injured people; a hospital in a school, etc. — ⓐ 진료소

in·fir·mi·ty [infə́:*r*miti] *n.* ⓤⓒ (pl. **-ties**) the state or quality of being weak. — ⓐ 허약

* **in·flame** [infléim] *vt.* **1.** set (something) on fire. **2.** arouse passion, desire, etc. in (someone). **3.** stir up (passion, desire, etc.). **4.** make (someone) hot, red or swollen. —*vi.* **1.** catch fire. **2.** become excited. **3.** become hot, red or swollen. — ⓐ 1. …에 불을 붙이다 2. …을 흥분시키다 3. [감정 따위]를 부채질하다 4. …을 달아 오르게 하다, 충혈시키다 — ⓐ 1. 불이 붙다 2. 흥분하다 3. 달아 오르다, 충혈하다

in·flam·ma·ble [inflǽməbl] *adj.* **1.** easily set on fire. **2.** easily aroused or excited. — ⓐ 1. 불타기 쉬운 2. 격(흥분)하기 쉬운

in·flam·ma·tion [infləméiʃ(ə)n] *n.* **1.** ⓤ the act of inflaming; the state of being inflamed. **2.** ⓤⓒ the condition of any part of the body marked by heat, redness, swelling or pain; such a part. — ⓐ 1. 점화, 연소 2. 염증(을 일으킨 곳)

in·flam·ma·to·ry [inflǽmətɔ̀:ri / -t(ə)ri] *adj.* **1.** tending to excite or anger. ¶*an ~ speech.* **2.** (*Medicine*) of or causing inflammation. — ⓐ 1. 선동적인, 자극적인 2. 염증의 (을 일으키는)

in·flate [infléit] *vt.* **1.** swell (a balloon or tire) with gas or air. **2.** cause (someone) to be proud. **3.** (*Economics*) increase (prices or the currency) beyond the normal amount or level. — ⓐ 1. …을 [공기나 가스로] 부풀게 하다 2. …을 의기양양하게 하다 3. (經) [물가]를 울리다; [통화]를 팽창시키다

in·fla·tion [infléiʃ(ə)n] *n.* ⓤ **1.** the act of swelling; the state of being swollen. **2.** (*Economics*) the increase in the currency of a country caused by issuing too much paper money or by a sudden increase in prices. — ⓐ 1. 부풀게 하기; 팽창 2. (經) 통화 팽창, 인플레이션

in·flect [inflékt] *vt.* **1.** change the pitch or tone of (the voice). **2.** (*Grammar*) vary the form of (a word) to show case, number, person, tense, mood, etc. **3.** bend. — ⓐ 1. [목소리]의 음조를 바꾸다, …에 억양을 붙이다 2. (文法) [단어]를 변화시키다 3. …을 구부리다

in·flec·tion [inflékʃ(ə)n] *n.* **1.** ⓤ change in the pitch or tone of the voice; intonation. **2.** ⓤ (*Grammar*) a variation in the form of a word. **3.** ⓒ an inflected form of a word. — ⓐ 1. 음성의 억양 2. (文法) 어형 변화, 활용 3. 변화형, 활용형

in·flex·i·ble [infléksibl] *adj.* ↔flexible **1.** that cannot be bent; stiff. **2.** that cannot be changed; unyielding. — ⓐ 1. 구부릴 수 없는; 경직(硬直)한 2. 변경이 안 되는; 불굴의

in·flex·i·bly [infléksibli] *adv.* in an inflexible manner. — ⓐ 굴하지 않고

in·flex·ion [infléksʃ(ə)n] *n.* (*Brit.*) =inflection.

* **in·flict** [inflíkt] *vt.* **1.** give or cause (a wound, pain, etc.). **2.** put on or impose (a punishment or anything unwelcome) on someone. ¶*The teacher inflicts punishment upon lazy pupils.* / *He inflicts himself on his parents.*① — ⓐ 1. [상처·고통 따위]를 가하다, 입히다 2. [벌금·벌 따위]를 과하다, 주다 ¶①그는 부모의 신세를 지고 있다

in·flic·tion [inflíkʃ(ə)n] *n.* **1.** ⓤ the act of inflicting. **2.** ⓒ a thing which is inflicted; suffering; a punishment. ¶*~ from God.*① — ⓐ 1. [벌 따위를] 가하기, 과하기; [고통 따위를] 주기 2. 고통; 형벌, 폐, 신세 ¶①천벌

in·flow [ínflòu] *n.* ↔outflow **1.** ⓤ the act of flowing in. **2.** ⓒ something which flows in. — ⓐ 1. 유입(流入) 2. 유입물

: **in·flu·ence** [ínfluəns] *n.* **1.** ⓤⓒ an effect or the result of the use of power or an action towards a person or thing. ¶*the Eastern ~ on the West* / *under the ~ of alcohol.*① **2.** ⓤ the power that comes from wealth, social position, force of character, etc. ¶*a man of ~*② / *He exercised his ~ to settle the matter.*③ / *The teacher has no ~ over his pupils.*④ **3.** ⓒ a person or thing that has such power. ¶*He is an ~ for good.*⑤ —*vt.* have an influence on (someone or something); affect. ¶*He was influenced by what he had read.* — ⓐ 1. 영향; 감화[력] ¶①술김에 2. 영향력; [사람의] 세력; 설득력 ¶②유력자/③그는 일을 수습하는 데에 영향력을 행사했다/④그 교사는 학생들에게 위신이 안 선다 3. 유력자; 유력한 것 ¶⑤그는 선행을 촉진하는 사람이다 — ⓐ …에 영향(감화)을 미치다

in·flu·en·tial [ìnfluénʃ(ə)l] *adj.* having much influence. — ⓐ 영향력 미치다

in·flu·en·za [ìnfluénzə] *n.* ⓤ an illness like a very bad cold. →USAGE — ⓐ 인플루엔자, 독감 USAGE 대로 flu로 줄여서 쓰임

in·flux [ínflʌks] *n.* ⓤ ⓒ the act of flowing or coming in. ↔efflux ¶*an ~ of customers.*①

in·fold [infóuld] *vt.* **1.** wrap up. ¶*He was infolded in an overcoat.* **2.** embrace. ⇒N.B.

‡**in·form** [infɔ́:rm] *vt.* **1.** give knowledge of something to (someone); make something known to (someone). ⟨~ someone *of* (or *that, what, what to do*)⟩ ¶*He informed me of the news.* / *Please ~ me when you arrive.*① **2.** inspire; fill. ¶*I was informed with courage.*② —*vi.* make an accusation. ⟨~ *against* someone⟩ ¶*They informed against Tom.*③

in·for·mal [infɔ́:rm(ə)l] *adj.* ↔formal **1.** conducted without ceremony or formality. **2.** (of speech, etc.) suited for everyday, common use; colloquial.

in·for·mal·i·ty [ìnfɔːrmǽliti] *n.* (pl. **-ties**) ↔formality **1.** ⓤ the state of being informal; the absence of ceremony. **2.** ⓒ an informal act.

in·for·mal·ly [infɔ́:rməli] *adv.* in an informal manner.

in·form·ant [infɔ́:rmənt] *n.* ⓒ a person who gives information.

‡**in·for·ma·tion** [ìnfərméiʃ(ə)n] *n.* ⓤ **1.** the act of informing; the state of being informed. ¶*for your ~*① / *ask for ~.*② **2.** knowledge given or acquired; facts learnt; news. ¶*a man of ~*③ / *get a useful piece of ~.* **3.** (*Law*) accusation. ¶*lay ~ against someone.*④

in·for·ma·tion·al [ìnfərméiʃ(ə)n(ə)l] *adj.* giving information. ⌜edge. ¶*a well-~ man.*⌝

in·formed [infɔ́:rmd] *adj.* having information or knowl-⌟

in·form·er [infɔ́:rmər] *n.* ⓒ **1.** a person who informs against others. **2.** a person who informs; informant.

in·frac·tion [infrǽkʃ(ə)n] *n.* ⓤⓒ the act of breaking a law or rule.

in·fra·red [ìnfrəréd / ⌞⌞] *adj.* (*Physics*) of the invisible rays lying beyond the red end of the visible spectrum. ↔ultraviolet ¶*~ rays*① / *~ photography.*②

in·fre·quent [infrí:kwənt] *adj.* seldom happening or occurring; rare. ↔frequent ¶*an ~ visitor.*①

in·fre·quent·ly [infrí:kwəntli] *adv.* in an infrequent manner; not often; rarely.

in·fringe [infríndʒ] *vt.* break. ⟨~ *a law, a rule,* etc.⟩ —*vi.* trespass. ⟨~ *on* or *upon* something⟩ ¶*~ upon another person's privacy.*① ⌜fringing.⌝

in·fringe·ment [infríndʒmənt] *n.* ⓤⓒ the act of in-⌟

in·fu·ri·ate *vt.* [infjúərièit → *adj.*] make (someone) very angry; enrage. —*adj.* [infjúəriit] very angry.

in·fuse [infjú:z] *vt.* **1.** inspire. ⟨~ something *into*; ~ someone *with*⟩ ¶*The teacher infused confidence into Betty; The teacher infused Betty with confidence.*① **2.** put in; pour in. **3.** soak (something) in hot water.

in·fu·sion [infjú:ʒ(ə)n] *n.* **1.** ⓤ the act of infusing. **2.** ⓒ liquid obtained by soaking.

・**in·gen·ious** [indʒí:njəs] *adj.* **1.** clever; skillful; inventive. **2.** cleverly made or thought out. ¶*an ~ device.*

in·gen·ious·ly [indʒí:njəsli] *adv.* in an ingenious manner; cleverly; skillfully.

in·ge·nu·i·ty [ìndʒin(j)ú(:)iti / -njú(:)] *n.* ⓤ cleverness in planning, inventing, etc.; creativeness; cleverness.

in·gen·u·ous [indʒénjuəs] *adj.* frank; open; simple; innocent.

in·gen·u·ous·ly [indʒénjuəsli] *adv.* in an ingenuous manner; frankly; innocently. ⌜nocence.⌝

in·gen·u·ous·ness [indʒénjuəsnis] *n.* ⓤ frankness; in-⌟

in·glo·ri·ous [inglɔ́:riəs] *adj.* **1.** without fame or glory; shameful; disgraceful. **2.** not famous; unknown.

—몡 유입; 쇄도 ¶①손님들의 쇄도

—통 1. …을 싸다 2. …을 포옹하다 N.B. enfold로도 씀

—통 1. …에게 …을 알리다, 통지하다 ¶①언제 도착하시는지 알려 주십시오 2. …을 불어 넣다, 채우다 ¶②나는 용기를 얻었다 —자 고발(고소)하다 ¶③그들은 톰을 고소했다

—혱 1. 격식을 차리지 않는, 비공식의 2. 흉금을 터놓은, 회화체의

—몡 1. 비공식, 약식 2. 격식을 차리지 않는 행위

—튀 약식으로, 비공식으로, 회화체로
—몡 통지자, 통보자, 정보 제공자

—몡 1. 전달, 통보 ¶①귀하에게 참고 삼아/②문의하다 2. 지식; 견문; 정보; 알림 ¶③박식한 사람 3. 고발, 고소 ④남을 고소하다

—혱 정보(지식)를 제공하는

—혱 지식이 있는, 많이 알고 있는
—몡 1. 고발자, 밀고자 2. 통보자, 통지자

—몡 [법률·규칙의] 위반; 위반 행위

—혱 적외선의 ¶①적외선/②적외선 사진술

—혱 이따금의; 좀처럼 없는 ¶①이따금 오는 손님
—튀 이따금, 드물게

—타 [법률·규칙 따위를] 어기다 —자 침해하다 ¶①남의 사생활을 침범하다
—몡 위반; 침해; 위반 행위
—타 …을 격분시키다 —혱 격분한
—타 1. …을 불어 넣다, 고취하다 ¶①선생은 베티에게 자신을 불어 넣었다 2. …을 붓다, 부어 넣다 3. …을 달이다, 우려내다

—몡 1. 주입; 불어넣기 2. 달인 액체, 침출액(浸出液)
—혱 1. 영리한; 솜씨 좋은; 발명의 재간이 있는 2. 잘 만든, 착상이 좋은
—튀 영리하게, 솜씨있게, 교묘하게

—몡 발명의 재간; 독창성; 솜씨 좋음; 현명
—혱 솔직한; 숨기지 않는; 순진한

—튀 솔직하게; 순진하게

—몡 솔직; 순진함
—혱 1. 불명예스러운, 창피한 2. 유명하지 않은; 무명의

in·grain vt. [ingréin / ⌐⌐ ∥ → adj., n.] dye in the fiber before manufacture. —adj. [⌐⌐] dyed before manufacture. —n. [⌐⌐] ⓤ yarn, wool, etc. dyed before manufacture.
— 倒 [실·섬유]를 천으로 짜기 전에 염색하다 — 倒 실(섬유)에 물을 들인 — 名 만들기 전에 물들인 실

in·grained [ingréind, ⌐⌐ / ⌐⌐] adj. deeply fixed in; deepseated. ¶~ *prejudice.*①
— 倒 깊이 배어든; 뿌리 깊은 ¶①뿌리 깊은 편견

in·gra·ti·ate [ingréiʃièit] vt. bring (oneself) into favor.
— 倒 …에게 환심을 사려고 하다

in·grat·i·tude [ingrǽtit(j)ù:d / -tjù:d] n. ⓤ the state of not being thankful; lack of gratitude.
— 名 은혜를 모름, 배은망덕

in·gre·di·ent [ingrí:diənt] n. ⓒ a part of a mixture; element. ¶*the ingredients of candy.*①
— 名 혼합물의 성분; 요소 ¶①과자의 원료

in·gress [íngres] n. ↔egress 1. ⓤ the act of going in. 2. ⓒ a place for entering; entrance. 3. ⓤ the right to enter.
— 名 1. 들어가기 2. 입구 3. 입장권

• **in·hab·it** [inhǽbit] vt. live in (a place, a house, etc.); occupy. ¶*Tigers ~ the jungle. / Thoughts ~ the mind.*
— 倒 …에 살다; 깃들다; …을 차지하다

: **in·hab·it·ant** [inhǽbit(ə)nt] n. ⓒ a person or animal that lives in a place. 〔in.〕
— 名 거주자; [어떤 장소의] 서식 동물

in·hab·it·ed [inhǽbitid] adj. having inhabitants; lived〕
— 倒 사람이 살고 있는

in·ha·la·tion [ìnhəléiʃ(ə)n / -(h)əl-] n. 1. ⓤ the act of inhaling. 2. ⓒ medicine to be inhaled.
— 名 1. 흡입 2. 흡입약

in·hale [inhéil] vt. draw (air, smoke, etc.) into the lungs. ↔exhale —vi. breathe something into the lungs.
— 倒 …을 폐로 들이쉬다 —倒 숨을 들이쉬다

in·har·mo·ni·ous [ìnhɑ:rmóuniəs] adj. not harmonious; unmusical; conflicting. ↔harmonious ¶~ *sounds.*
— 形 [음·빛깔 따위가] 조화가 안 되는; 일치하지 않는

• **in·her·ent** [inhíər(ə)nt] adj. belonging to someone or something as a natural part; inborn. ¶*Modesty is a virtue ~ in his nature.*①
— 形 고유의, 본래의, 타고난 ¶①겸양은 그의 타고난 덕이다

• **in·her·it** [inhérit] vt. 1. receive (property, etc.) at the death of a former owner. ¶*Tom inherited his father's farm.* 2. get (something) from one's ancestors.
— 倒 1.[재산 따위]를 상속하다 2.[성질 따위]를 조상에게서 이어받다

• **in·her·it·ance** [inhérit(ə)ns] n. ⓤ 1. the act of inheriting. 2. the right of inheriting. 3. ⓤⓒ property or qualities inherited. 〔heir.〕
— 名 1.상속 2.상속권 3.유산, 상속 재산; 이어받은 것(성질)

in·her·i·tor [inhéritər] n. ⓒ a person who inherits; an〕
— 名 상속인

in·hib·it [inhíbit] vt. restrain; forbid. (~ someone *from doing*) ¶*a selfish desire.*
— 倒 …[하기]를 억제하다; 금하다

in·hi·bi·tion [ìn(h)ibíʃ(ə)n] n. ⓤⓒ 1. the act of inhibiting; the state of being inhibited. 2. an inner force that restrains or suppresses actions, emotions or thoughts.
— 名 1.억제; 억압; 금지 2.억제력

in·hos·pi·ta·ble [inhɑ́spitəbl, ⌐⌐⌐⌐ / -hɔ́s-] adj. 1. not friendly no visitors. ¶*an ~ host.* 2. (of a place, etc.) giving no shelter; barren. ¶*an ~ region.*①
— 形 1. 손님 대접이 나쁜, 푸대접의 2. 머무를 곳이 없는; 황량한 ¶①황야

in·hos·pi·tal·i·ty [ìnhɑ̀spitǽliti / ìnhɔ̀s-] n. ⓤ the state of being inhospitable.
— 名 무뚝뚝함

in·hu·man [inhjú:mən, +*U.S.* injú:-] adj. not like a human being; unfeeling; cruel; brutal. ¶~ *treatment.*
— 形 인간답지 않은; 무정한; 잔인한; 야만의

in·hu·mane [ìnhju:méin] adj. cruel; unkind.
— 形 무정한, 인정머리 없는

in·hu·man·i·ty [ìnhju(:)mǽniti, +*U.S.* ìnju(:)-] n. (pl. **-ties**) 1. ⓤ the state or quality of being inhuman. 2. ⓒ an inhuman or cruel act.
— 名 1.무정; 잔인 2.무정(잔인)한 행위

in·im·i·cal [inímik(ə)l] adj. 1. like an enemy; unfriendly; hostile. ¶*nations ~ to one another.*① 2. unfavorable; harmful. ¶*Smoking is ~ to* [*the*] *health.*
— 形 1.적의를 품은; 비우호적인 ¶① 서로 적대하는 국가 2.불리한; 해가 되는

in·im·i·ta·ble [inímitəbl] adj. that cannot be imitated; matchless. ¶*a man of ~ eloquence.*①
— 形 흉내낼 수 없는; 비길 데 없는 ¶①비할 데 없는 웅변가

in·iq·ui·tous [iníkwitəs] adj. unjust; wicked.
— 形 부정한; 사악한

in·iq·ui·ty [iníkwiti] n. (pl. **-ties**) 1. ⓤ the state or quality of being iniquitous; injustice; wickedness. 2. ⓒ an iniquitous act.
— 名 1.부정; 사악 2.부정행위; 무도한 짓

• **i·ni·tial** [iníʃ(ə)l] adj. at the beginning; first; earliest. ¶*an ~ letter*① */ one's ~ visit to Kyoto.*
—n. ⓒ the first letter of a word or name.
—vt. (**-tialed, -tial·ing** or esp. *Brit.* **-tialled, -tial·ling**) mark or sign (something) with one's initial or initials.
— 形 첫머리의; 최초의; 초기의 ¶①머리글자
— 名 머리글자
— 倒 …에 머리글자로 서명하다

i·ni·ti·ate vt. [iníʃièit → n.] **1.** begin ; start. ¶ ~ *a reform.*① **2.** admit or introduce (someone) into a club, society, etc. **3.** show (someone) how to do something new. ¶ *He was initiated into the study of Russian.*
— n. [-ʃiit, -èit] Ⓒ a person who is initiated.

— 他 **1.** …을 시작하다, …을 착수하다 ¶①개혁에 착수하다 **2.** …을 가입시키다; 입회(가입)시키다 **3.** …에게 첫 걸음(초보)을 가르치다, 기초를 지도하다 — 名 [신(新)]입회자; 입문자

i·ni·ti·a·tion [iniʃiéiʃ(ə)n] n. **1.** Ⓤ the act of initiating ; the state of being initiated. **2.** Ⓒ the ceremonies by which someone is admitted to a club, a group, etc.

— 名 **1.** 개시; 입회, 가입; 초보 지도 **2.** 입회식

· **i·ni·ti·a·tive** [iníʃiətiv, -ʃə-] n. **1.** Ⓤ (usu. *the* ~) the first step ; the lead. **2.** Ⓤ the ability to foresee and undertake what ought to be done. ¶ *A leader must have* ~.① **3.** (*the* ~) the right (of citizens, etc.) to introduce new laws. ⌈to do something.
 1) ***have the initiative,*** have the right to be the first⌋
 2) ***on one's own initiative,*** without any orders or suggestions from others.

— 名 **1.** 첫걸음, 초보; 솔선 **2.** 사물을 시작하는 능력; 진취의 기상 ¶①지도자에게는 선도력(先導權)이 있어야 한다 **3.** [국민의] 발의권(發議權)

🖫 1)주도권을 가지다 2)자발적으로

in·ject [indʒékt] vt. **1.** force (something) into some part of the body. ¶ ~ *a drug into the arm.* **2.** throw in.

— 他 **1.** …을 주입하다; 주사하다 **2.** …을 끼워 넣다

in·jec·tion [indʒékʃ(ə)n] n. **1.** Ⓤ Ⓒ the act of injecting. **2.** Ⓒ liquid which is injected.

— 名 **1.** 주입; 주사 **2.** 주사액

in·ju·di·cious [indʒu(ː)díʃəs] adj. lacking in judgment ; ⌈unwise.

— 형 지각없는; 무분별한

in·junc·tion [indʒʌ́ŋkʃ(ə)n] n. Ⓒ a command or order, esp. one from a law court ordering someone to do or not to do something. ⌈*other's feeling.*

— 名 명령; 지령; [법원의] 명령

‡ **in·jure** [índʒər] vt. harm ; hurt. ¶ ~ *one's hand* / ~ *an-*⌋

— 他 …을 해치다; 상처 입히다

in·ju·ri·ous [indʒúəriəs] adj. **1.** harmful ; hurtful. ¶ *a habit* ~ *to* [*the*] *health.* **2.** unfair ; unjust ; insulting

— 형 **1.** 해로운; 유해한 **2.** 불공명한; 불법의; 무례한

· **in·ju·ry** [índʒ(ə)ri] n. (pl. **-ries**) **1.** Ⓤ harm ; damage. ¶ *suffer an* ~ *to the head.*① **2.** Ⓒ a place that is hurt or wounded. **3.** Ⓒ an act of hurting, or damaging.

— 名 **1.** 해; 손해; 부상 ¶①머리에 부상을 입다 **2.** 상처; 손상 **3.** 상처를 입히기, 해치기

· **in·jus·tice** [indʒʌ́stis] n. **1.** Ⓤ the state of being unjust. **2.** Ⓒ an unjust act.
 do someone* [*an*] *injustice, judge (someone) unfairly.

— 名 **1.** 부정; 불공명 **2.** 불법(부정)행위

🖫 …을 오해하다

‡ **ink** [iŋk] n. Ⓤ a colored liquid used for writing or printing. ¶ *write with pen and* ~.
— vt. mark or stain (something) with ink.

— 名 잉크

— 他 …을 잉크로 표하다(더럽히다)

ink bottle [⌐ ⌐⌐] n. a bottle for holding ink.

— 名 잉크병

ink·ling [íŋkliŋ] n. Ⓒ a hint ; a vague noticing. ¶ *have an* ~ *of what is going on.*

— 名 암시; 어렴풋이 알아차리기

ink·pot [íŋkpàt / -pɔ̀t] n. Ⓒ a pot for holding ink.

— 名 잉크그릇(병)

ink·stand [íŋkstænd] n. Ⓒ a stand for holding ink and pens. ⌈*table.*

— 名 잉크스탠드

ink·well [íŋkwèl] n. Ⓒ an inkpot fitted into a desk or⌋

— 名 잉크병

ink·y [íŋki] adj. (**ink·i·er, ink·i·est**) **1.** dark or black like ink. **2.** covered or stained with ink.

— 형 **1.** 잉크처럼 검은 **2.** 잉크로 더러워진

in·laid [ínléid] adj. **1.** set in the surface as a decoration. **2.** decorated with a design set in the surface.
— v. pt. and pp. of **inlay**.

— 형 **1.** 상감(象嵌)한 **2.** 상감 무늬가 있는

· **in·land** adj. [ínlənd → adv., n.] **1.** situated in the interior of a country ; away from the sea. **2.** within a country ; domestic. ↔foreign ¶ ~ *trade.*①
— n. [ínlənd, -lænd] Ⓒ the interior of a country. —adv. [inlǽnd / ⌐⌐, -lənd] toward the interior. ⌈*marriage.*

— 형 **1.** 바다에서 먼; 내륙의 **2.** 국내의; 내지의 ¶①내국 무역

— 名 국내, 내지 — 부 국내에; 내지로

in·law [ínlɔ̀ː] n. (*colloq.*) Ⓒ (often *pl.*) a relative by⌋

— 名 인척

in·lay vt. [ínléi → n.] (-**laid, -lay·ing**) set (pieces of gold, silver, etc.) in the surface as a decoration ; decorate (the surface) with something set in.
— n. [⌐⌐] Ⓤ Ⓒ a design or pattern made by setting a decoration into a surface. ⇒fig.

— 他 …을 상감(象嵌)하다; …에 상감하다

— 名 상감(象嵌)세공, 상감 무늬

[inlay]

in·let [ínlet, +*Brit.* -lit] n. Ⓒ **1.** an arm of the sea reaching inland. **2.** an entrance. ↔outlet

— 名 **1.** 후미, 작은 만 **2.** 입구

in·mate [ínmèit] *n.* [C] **1.** a person kept in a prison, a hospital, etc. **2.** a member of a family or other group living under the same roof.
—[名] 1. 재감자(在監者); 입원자 2. 식구, 집안 사람; 동거인

in·most [ínmòust] *adj.* deepest within; most secret. ¶ *the ~ part of the jungle / my ~ desire.*①
—[形] 가장 안쪽의; 깊이 감춘 ¶①내 가슴속의 소망

∗**inn** [in] *n.* [C] a small hotel where travelers may get food and lodging; a public house; a tavern. ¶*put up* (or *stay*) *at an ~.*①
—[名] 여관; 여인숙; 선술집 ¶①여관에 묵다

in·nate [inéit, ⌐⌐, +*Brit.* ⌐⌐] *adj.* inborn; natural. ↔acquired ¶*an ~ gift.*①
—[形] 타고난, 생래(生來)의, 천부의 ¶①천부의 재능

∗**in·ner** [ínər] *adj.* **1.** inside; interior. ↔outer ¶*an ~ pocket.* **2.** private; secret. ¶*one's ~ feelings.* **3.** of the mind or soul. ¶*man's ~ life.*①
—[形] 1. 내부의; 안쪽의 2. 은밀한; 비밀의 3. 마음의; 정신의 ¶①인간의 정신생활

the inner man, ⓐ man's mind or soul. ⓑ the stomach.
[熟] ⓐ마음; 영혼 ⓑ위, 밥통

in·ner·most [ínərmòust] *adj.* deepest within; inmost.
—[形] 가장 안쪽의; 가장 내부의

in·ning [íniŋ] *n.* [C] **1.** a period in a baseball game during which each team is at bat in turn; a chance to play. **2.** the period when a person or a political party is in power. ¶*The Conservatives now have their ~.* ⇨[usage]
—[名] 1. 회(回); 타순(打順) 2. 활동기; 전성시대 [usage] 영국에서는 단·복수 모두 innings로 쓰며 동사는 모두 단수형으로 호응함

inn·keep·er [ínkì:pər] *n.* [C] a person who runs an inn.
—[名] 여관 주인

∗**in·no·cence** [ínousns] *n.* [U] **1.** the state of being innocent; freedom from sin or guilt. **2.** simplicity of heart.
—[名] 1. 무죄, 결백; 깨끗함 2. 순진, 천진난만

⁑**in·no·cent** [ínousnt] *adj.* **1.** free from guilt; doing no wrong. ↔guilty ¶*He is ~ of the crime.*① **2.** knowing no evil; pure in heart and life. ¶*She is as ~ as a baby.* **3.** harmless in meaning and effect. ↔harmful ¶*~ amusements / an ~ joke.* **4.** simple; foolish. **5.** (*colloq.*) lacking. ¶*hair ~ of pomade.*
—[形] 1. 무죄의; 결백한 ¶①그는 그 죄를 범하지 않았다 2. 천진난만한; 순진한 3. 해가 없는; 악의 없는 4. [머리가] 단순한; 어리석은 5. …이 없는

—*n.* [C] **1.** an innocent person or child. **2.** a fool.
—[名] 1. 죄없는 사람; 순진한 아이 2. 바보

in·no·cent·ly [ínousntli] *adv.* guiltlessly; harmlessly.
—[副] 죄없이; 순진하게

in·noc·u·ous [inákjuəs / inɔ́k-] *adj.* harmless.
—[形] 해(독) 없는

in·no·vate [ínouvèit] *vi.* introduce something new; make changes. ¶*~ on* (or *upon*) *an old custom.*①
—[自] 새로운 것을 도입하다; 쇄신하다 ¶①구습을 쇄신하다

in·no·va·tion [ìnouvéiʃ(ə)n] *n.* **1.** [U][C] the act of innovating; the introduction of something new. ¶*the ~ of an electronic computer.*① **2.** [C] a thing which is new; a change made in custom or method of doing.
—[名] 1. 쇄신; 새로운 것의 도입 ¶①전자 계산기의 도입 2. 새로운 사물

in·no·va·tor [ínouvèitər] *n.* [C] a person who makes changes or brings in a new method.
—[名] 개혁자; 혁신자; 선구자

in·nu·en·do [ìnju(:)éndou] *n.* [C] (pl. **-dos** or **-does**) an indirect remark or reference critical of somebody.
—[名] 빗대어 말하기, 풍자

∗**in·nu·mer·a·ble** [in(j)ú:m(ə)rəbl / -njú:-] *adj.* too many to be counted; countless.
—[形] 셀 수 없는; 무수한

in·oc·u·late [inákjulèit / -ɔ́k-] *vt.* **1.** inject vaccine, etc. into (a person or animal) to prevent a disease. ¶*~ a child against typhoid.*① **2.** fill someone's mind with (something) ¶*~ youth with dangerous ideas.*②
—[他] 1. …에 예방주사를 놓다 ¶①아이에게 티푸스의 예방주사를 놓다 2. …을 남의 마음에 불어 넣다 ¶②청년에게 위험한 사상을 불어 넣다

in·oc·u·la·tion [inàkjuléiʃ(ə)n / -ɔ̀k-] *n.* [U][C] the act of inoculating. ¶*an ~ against cholera.*①
—[名] 예방주사 ¶①콜레라의 예방주사

in·of·fen·sive [ìnəfénsiv] *adj.* not unpleasant; harmless.
—[形] 해가 되지 않는; 악의 없는

in·op·er·a·tive [inάp(ə)rətiv, -rèi- / -ɔ́p(ə)rə-] *adj.* (of laws, etc.) having no effect; not working.
—[形] 효력이 없는; 움직이고 있지 않는

in·op·por·tune [ìnɑpərt(j)ú:n / inɔ́pətjù:n] *adj.* coming or happening at a bad time; unsuitable. ¶*an ~ remark.*①
—[形] 계제가 나쁜; 시기를 놓친 ¶①엉뚱한 말

in·or·di·nate [inɔ́:rdinit] *adj.* too much; too great; excessive. ¶*~ demands*① / *~ pride.*②
—[形] 과도한; 터무니 없는 ¶①터무니 없는 요구/②엄청난 자존심

in·or·gan·ic [ìnɔ:rgǽnik] *adj.* not made up of plant or animal material. ¶*~ chemistry.*①
—[形] 무기(無機)의 ¶①무기화학

in·pa·tient [ínpèiʃ(ə)nt] *n.* [C] a person who stays in a hospital and receives medical treatment. ↔outpatient
—[名] 입원 환자

in·quest [ínkwest] *n.* **1.** [C] (*Law*) a legal examination with the aid of a jury, esp. one to determine the cause of a sudden death. **2.** (*collectively*) the jury appointed to make such an examination.
—[名] 1. 〔法〕 심리; 검시(檢屍) 2. 검시 배심원

I

in·qui·e·tude [inkwáiit(j)ù:d / -tjù:d] *n.* [U] uneasiness; anxiety.
—[名] 불안; 근심

⁑in·quire, en- [inkwáiər] *vt.* seek (information) by asking. ¶~ *the way to the station* / *He inquired how to get there.* —*vi.* ask questions. ¶~ *at the front desk.*①
1) ***inquire after*** (=*ask about the health or welfare of*) *someone.*
2) ***inquire for,*** ⓐ try to obtain (something). ⓑ ask to see (someone).
3) ***inquire into a matter,*** examine.
—[他] …을 묻다, 문의하다 —[自] 물어보다; 문의하다 ¶①안내계에 물어보다
[熟] 1)남의 건강(안부)을 묻다 2)ⓐ[가게에서 물건]을 찾다 ⓑ…에게 면회를 요청하다 3)…을 조사하다

in·quir·er [inkwáiərər] *n.* [C] a person who inquires.
—[名] 문의자, 조회자; 조사자

in·quir·ing [inkwáiəriŋ] *adj.* seeking information; expressing a desire to learn. ▷**in·quir·ing·ly** [-li] *adv.*
—[形] 알고 싶어하는; 미심쩍은 듯한

***in·quir·y, en-** [inkwáiəri] *n.* (pl. **-quir·ies**) **1.** [U] the act of inquiring. ¶*find out by* ~ / *Details will be given on* ~.① **2.** [C] a question. ¶*inquiries about the subject.* **3.** [C] an examination; an investigation. ¶*an* ~ *into the truth of a report.*
—[名] 1. 문의, 조회 ¶①세부 내용은 문의하시오 2. 질문 3. 조사, 취조, 심리

inquiry office [-́- -́-] *n.* a place where information is given.
—[名] 안내소; 접수구

in·qui·si·tion [ìnkwizíʃ(ə)n] *n.* **1.** [U] thorough examination. **2.** [C] (*Law*) an official inquiry before a jury. **3.** 《*the I-*》 (*History*) a Roman Catholic court to discover and punish those whose beliefs were thought to be wrong.
—[名] 1. 엄중한 조사 2. 심리 3. 종교 재판소

in·quis·i·tive [inkwízitiv] *adj* **1.** eager to learn; curious. **2.** fond of learning about other people's affairs.
—[形] 1. 알고 싶어하는; 호기심이 강한 2. 꼬치꼬치 캐는

in·quis·i·tor [inkwízitər] *n.* [C] **1.** a person who makes an inquisition. **2.** 《*I-*》 (*History*) a member of the Inquisition.
—[名] 1. 조사자; 심리자 2. 종교 재판관

in·quis·i·to·ri·al [ìnkwizitɔ́:riəl] *adj.* of or like an inquisitor.
—[形] 심리자(종교 재판관) 같은

in·road [ínròud] *n.* [C] a sudden attack. ¶*an* ~ *into the neighboring country.*①
make inroads (=*move, encroach*) into. ¶*The city is making inroads into the countryside.*
—[名] 내습, 침입 ¶①이웃나라를 급습하다
[熟] 잠식(蠶食)하다, 차츰 먹어 들어가다

in·rush [ínrʌʃ] *n.* [C] the act of rushing in.
—[名] 침입, 내습, 쇄도

in·sane [inséin] *adj.* **1.** mentally disordered; not sane; mad; crazy. **2.** for mad people. ¶*an* ~ *asylum.* **3.** very foolish; without common sense.
—[形] 1. 미친; 제 정신이 아닌 2. 광인을 위한 3. 아주 터무니없는, 상식에서 벗어난

in·san·i·tar·y [insǽnitèri / -t(ə)ri] *adj.* so dirty as to help the spread of disease.
—[形] 건강에 맞지 않는; 비위생적인

in·san·i·ty [insǽniti] *n.* (pl. **-ties**) **1.** [U] the state of being insane; madness; mental disease. **2.** [C] a mad or foolish act.
—[名] 1. 정신이상; 정신병 2. 미친 짓, 어리석기 짝이 없는 짓

in·sa·tia·ble [inséiʃ(i)əbl, +*Brit.* -ʃjə-] *adj.* that cannot be satisfied; very greedy. ¶*an* ~ *appetite.*①
—[形] 물릴 줄 모르는; 아주 탐욕스러운 ¶①맹렬한 식욕

in·sa·ti·ate [inséiʃiit] *adj.* insatiable.
—[形] 물리지 않는

in·scribe [inskráib] *vt.* **1.** write or engrave. 《~ letters, etc. *in* (or *on*); ~ something *with*》 ¶~ *a name in a book.* **2.** impress deeply. ¶*His words are inscribed in my memory.*① **3.** address (a book, etc.) to a friend, etc. as a mark of thanks. **4.** put (a name) on a list.
—[他] 1. …을 쓰다; 새기다 2. …을 명심하다 ¶①그의 말은 기억 속에 깊이 새겨져 있다 3. [책 따위]를 헌정하다 4. [성명]을 등록하다

***in·scrip·tion** [inskrípʃ(ə)n] *n.* **1.** [U] the act of inscribing. **2.** [C] something inscribed esp. words written in a book, etc. or engraved on a monument, a coin, a ring, etc.
—[名] 1. 명각(銘刻); 기입 2. 비문; 명(銘), 제명(題銘)

in·scru·ta·ble [inskrú:təbl] *adj.* that cannot be understood; hard to understand; mysterious. ¶*an* ~ *smile.*①
—[形] 이해하기 어려운, 불가해한 ¶①수수께끼 같은 미소

⁑in·sect [ínsekt] *n.* [C] **1.** a small animal with three pairs of legs and, usu., two pairs of wings. **2.** (*colloq.*) any small creeping or flying animal, such as a spider or a centipede.
—[名] 1. 곤충 2. 벌레

in·sec·ti·cide [inséktisàid] *n.* [C] a medicine for killing insects.
—[名] 살충제

in·se·cure [ìnsikjúər] (**-cur·er, -cur·est**) *adj.* not safe; not firm. ¶*an* ~ *lock.*
—[形] 안전하지 않은; 불확실한; 위태로운

in·se·cu·ri·ty [ìnsikjúəriti] *n.* (pl. **-ties**) **1.** [U] the state of not being secure. **2.** [C] a thing which is insecure.
—[名] 1. 불안전; 위험 2. 위태로운 것

in·sen·sate [insénseit] *adj.* **1.** without sensation. **2.**
—[形] 1. 감각이 없는 2. 무정한; 잔인

without regard or feeling; cold; cruel. **3.** senseless.
한 3. 무분별한; 어리석은

in·sen·si·bil·i·ty [insènsibíliti] *n.* Ⓤ **1.** the state or quality of being insensible; lack of feeling. **2.** lack of consciousness. ¶~ *to pain* / *in a state of* ~.①
—[名] 1. 무감각 2. 무의식 ¶①인사불성으로

in·sen·si·ble [insénsibl] *adj.* **1.** not able to feel. ¶*A blind man is* ~ *to colors.* **2.** unconscious. ¶*She fell to the ground* ~.① **3.** not aware; indifferent. ¶~ *of the danger.* **4.** hardly noticeable. ¶*by* ~ *degrees.*② ▷**in·sen·si·bly** [-bli] *adj.*
—[形] 1. 무감각한 2. 의식이 없는 ¶①그녀는 의식을 잃고 쓰러졌다 3. 알아채지 못한; 무관심한 4. 눈에 보이지 않을 정도의 ¶②아주 서서히

in·sen·si·tive [insénsitiv] *adj.* that cannot be impressed or influenced; slow to feel or notice. ¶~ *to beauty.*①
—[形] 둔감한; 감수성이 없는 ¶①미적(美的) 감각이 없는

in·sep·a·ra·ble [insép(ə)rəbl] *adj.* that cannot be separated. ¶~ *friends.*①
—[形] 분리할 수 없는; 떨어질 수 없는 ¶①친구

***in·sert** *vt.* [insə́:rt → *n.*] put in. (~ something *in* or *into*) ¶~ *a key in a lock.*① —*n.* [ˊ-] Ⓒ a thing put in, esp. an extra page put in a newspaper, etc.
—[他] …을 끼워 넣다 ¶①잠을쇠에 열쇠를 끼우다 —[名] 삽입물; 접어넣은 책장

in·ser·tion [insə́:rʃ(ə)n] *n.* **1.** Ⓤ the act of inserting. **2.** Ⓒ a thing inserted, esp. an advertisement in a newspaper.
—[名] 1. 삽입 2. 삽입물; 접어넣은 광고

in·set *vt.* [insét → *n.*] (**-set, -set·ting**) put in; insert. —*n.* [ˊ-] Ⓒ a thing set in, esp. a smaller map or picture set in the border of a larger one. ⇒fig.
—[他] …을 끼워 넣다; 삽입하다 —[名] 삽입물; 삽입한 그림(지도・사진)

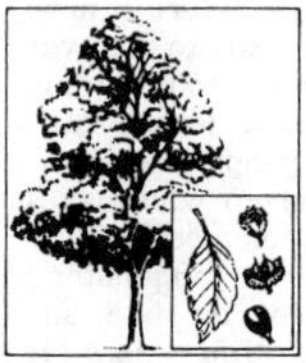

[inset]

in·shore [ínʃɔ́:r] *adj.* near the shore; moving toward the shore. ¶~ *fisheries* / *an* ~ *current.*① —*adv.* toward the shore. ¶*head* ~.②
—[形] 해안에 가까운; 해안으로 향하는 ¶①해안으로 밀리는 조수 —[副] 해안으로 향하는

‡**in·side** [ínsáid] *n.* **1.** Ⓒ (usu. *the* ~) the inner side or part of something. ¶*turn* ~ *out*① / *the* ~ *of a house.* **2.** (usu. *one's inside*[*s*]) (*colloq.*) the stomach and the area near it. ¶*I have a pain in my insides.*
—[名] 1. 내부, 안쪽 ¶①뒤집다 2. (口) 배, 위(胃)

—*adj.* **1.** inner. ¶*Put the money in the* ~ *pocket of your coat.* **2.** working indoors. ¶*an* ~ *man.*② **3.** private; secret. ¶~ *information*③ / ~ *affairs.*④
—[形] 1. 내부의 2. 실내에서 일하는 ¶②내근자 3. 개인적인; 비밀의 ¶③내부의 정보/④내부 사정

—*adv.* **1.** on or to the inside; within. ¶*Go* ~. **2.** indoors.
—[副] 1. 내부에; 안으로 2. 실내에

—*prep.* within. ¶*go* ~ *the gate.*
—[前] …의 내부에

in·sid·er [ínsáidər] *n.* Ⓒ **1.** a person who belongs to some circle, society, etc. ↔outsider **2.** (*colloq.*) a person who is in a position to obtain special information.
—[名] 1. 내부 인사; 회원; 부원 2. 내막을 알고 있는 사람; 소식통

in·sid·i·ous [insídiəs] *adj.* **1.** cunning; sly; treacherous. ¶~ *gossip.* **2.** advancing secretly. ¶*an* ~ *disease.*
—[形] 1. 교활한; 음흉한; 방심할 수 없는 2. [병 따위] 잠행성(潛行性)의

in·sight [ínsàit] *n.* Ⓤ (sometimes *an* ~) ability to see into the inside or inner parts of something; clear understanding. ¶*a man of* ~① / *He has an* ~ *into character.*②
—[名] 사물의 본질을 간파하는 힘; 통찰력 ¶①통찰력을 갖춘 사람/②그는 사람을 꿰뚫어 본다

in·sig·ne [insígni:] *n.* sing. of **insignia.**

in·sig·ni·a [insígniə] *n., pl.* (sing. **-sig·ne**) symbols of authority; badges of office or rank. ¶*army* ~.①
—[名] 기장(記章); 훈장 ¶①육군의 기장

in·sig·nif·i·cance [ìnsignífikəns] *n.* Ⓤ the state of being insignificant; unimportance; meaninglessness.
—[名] 하찮음, 사소함; 의미 없음

***in·sig·nif·i·cant** [ìnsignífikənt] *adj.* having little or no importance; meaningless. ¶*an* ~ *sum.*①
—[形] 하잘것 없는; 무의미한 ¶①근소한 액수

in·sin·cere [ìnsinsíər] *adj.* not sincere; that cannot be trusted; false.
—[形] 본심이 아닌; 위선적인; 불성실한

in·sin·cer·i·ty [ìnsinsériti] *n.* Ⓤ the state or quality of being insincere; Ⓒ an insencere act.
—[名] 불성실; 위선

in·sin·u·ate [insínjuèit] *vt.* **1.** hint or suggest indirectly. (~ *that* …) ¶*She insinuated that he was wrong.* **2.** (*reflexively*) put in or introduce (oneself) by clever, indirect means. ¶*A cat insinuated itself into the kitchen.*① / *He insinuated himself into the king's favor.*②
—[他] 1. …을 넌지시 암시하다 2. …에 몰래 들어가다; 교묘히 …의 환심을 사다 ¶①고양이가 몰래 부엌에 들어왔다/②그는 교묘하게 왕의 환심을 샀다

in·sin·u·a·tion [insìnjuéiʃ(ə)n] *n.* **1.** Ⓤ the act of insinuating. **2.** Ⓒ an indirect suggestion critical of someone.
—[名] 1. 차츰차츰 들어가기(환심을 사기) 2. 빗대기, 넌지시 알리기

in·sip·id [insípid] *adj.* **1.** without taste or flavor. ¶ *~ food / an ~ drink.* **2.** dull; uninteresting. ¶ *an ~ speech.*
— ⓐ 1. 맛없는; 김 빠진 2. 지루한; 재미없는

in·si·pid·i·ty [ìnsipíditi] *n.* (pl. **-ties**) **1.** Ⓤ the state or quality of being insipid. **2.** Ⓒ a thing which is insipid.
— ⓐ 1. 맛없음, 재미없음 2. 평범한 일 (것)

: **in·sist** [insíst] *vi., vt.* **1.** declare with force; express one's opinion earnestly; emphasize. ⟪*~ on or upon something; ~ that ...*⟫ ¶ *~ on the importance of being honest.*① / *I ~ on his innocence; I ~ that he is innocent.*② **2.** demand strongly. ⟪*~ on or upon something; ~ that ...*⟫ ¶ *Mother insists that we [should] wash our hands before eating.*③
— ⓐⓑ 1. 주장하다; 강조하다 ¶①정의의 중요성을 역설하다/②나는 그가 무죄임을 주장한다 2. 강력히 요구하다 ¶③어머니는 식사 전 손을 씻으라고 단단히 이르신다

in·sist·ence [insíst(ə)ns] *n.* Ⓤ the act of insisting; the state or quality of being insistent.
— ⓐ 강조; 주장; 강요; 무리한 권고, 강제되는 일

in·sis·tent [insíst(ə)nt] *adj.* **1.** continuing to make a demand or statement. ¶ *Though it was raining, he was ~ on going out.* **2.** calling attention strongly. ¶ *an ~ knocking on the door.*①
— ⓐ 1. 강요하는; 주장하는 2. 끈덕지게 졸라대는 ¶①재촉하는 듯한 노크 소리

in·sole [ínsòul] *n.* Ⓒ **1.** the inner bottom of a shoe. **2.** a removable thin, inner bottom of a shoe used for comfort, etc.
— ⓐ 1. 구두의 안창 2. [구두 속의] 깔개

in·so·lence [íns(ə)ləns] *n.* **1.** Ⓤ the state or quality of being insolent; rudeness. **2.** Ⓒ an insolent act or speech.
— ⓐ 1. 오만, 건방짐 2. 건방진 태도 (말)

in·so·lent [íns(ə)lənt] *adj.* very rude to others; insulting. ▷ **in·so·lent·ly** [-li] *adv.*
— ⓐ 무례한; 건방진; 거만한

in·sol·u·ble [insáljubl / -sɔ́l-] *adj.* **1.** that cannot be melted. **2.** that cannot be solved or explained.
— ⓐ 1. 용해(溶解)하지 않는 2. [문제 따위] 해결할(풀) 수 없는

in·sol·ven·cy [insálv(ə)nsi / -sɔ́l-] *n.* Ⓤ the state of being insolvent.
— ⓐ 지불 불능; 파산

in·sol·vent [insálv(ə)nt / -sɔ́l-] *adj.* not able to pay one's debts; bankrupt. — *n.* Ⓒ an insolvent person.
— ⓐ 지불 불능의; 파산한 — ⓐ 지불불능자; 파산자

in·som·ni·a [insámniə / -sɔ́m-] *n.* Ⓤ the state of being unable to sleep; sleeplessness.
— ⓐ 불면(증)

in·so·much [ìnsoumʌ́tʃ] *adv.* to such an extent or degree. ¶ *The snow fell heavily, ~ that all the traffic was interrupted.*①
— ⓐ …의 정도까지 ¶①폭설이 내려서 교통이 모두 마비됐다

• **in·spect** [inspékt] *vt.* **1.** examine carefully and critically. ¶ *The pupils' teeth are inspected twice a year.*① **2.** view or examine officially (troops, etc.). ¶ *~ a factory.*
— ⓐ 1. …을 공들여 조사하다 ¶①학생들은 1년에 두 번 이 검사를 받는다 2.[군대 따위]를 시찰하다

in·spec·tion [inspékʃ(ə)n] *n.* ⓊⒸ **1.** the act of inspecting; careful examination. ¶ *undergo a medical ~.*① **2.** an official examination or review.
— ⓐ 1. 조사; 검사 ¶①신체검사를 받다 2. 시찰

• **in·spec·tor** [inspéktər] *n.* Ⓒ a person who inspects; an officer appointed to inspect.
— ⓐ 조사자; 검사관; 감독관

• **in·spi·ra·tion** [ìnspiréiʃ(ə)n] *n.* **1.** Ⓤ the influence of thought and feelings on good actions; any influence arousing the creative power of the mind. **2.** Ⓒ a person or thing that gives such an influence. **3.** Ⓒ (*colloq.*) a bright idea. ¶ *have a sudden ~.*① **4.** Ⓤ the act of drawing air into the lungs. ↔ **expiration**
— ⓐ 1. 감화, 격려; 영감(靈感), 인스퍼레이션 2. 감화(영감)를 주는 사람(것) 3. 영묘한 착상 ¶①갑자기 좋은 생각이 떠오르다 4. 숨을 들이쉬기

: **in·spire** [inspáiər] *vt.* **1.** affect or encourage (someone) with a noble thought or feeling; produce or arouse (a feeling, a thought, etc.). ¶ *I inspired him to make greater efforts.*① / *His success inspired us with new courage.*② **2.** give inspiration to (someone); cause, guide or communicate with (someone or something) by divine influence. **3.** draw (air) into the lungs. ↔ **expire**
— ⓑ 1. …을 감동시키다; 감격시키다; [사상·감정]을 일어나게 하다 ¶①나는 그에게 더욱 노력하도록 격려했다/②그의 성공은 우리에게 새로운 용기를 주었다 2. …에 영감을 주다 3. [숨]을 들이쉬다

in·spir·it [inspírit] *vt.* encourage; hearten.
— ⓑ …의 기운을 북돋우다; 격려하다

inst. instant.

in·sta·bil·i·ty [ìnstəbíliti] *n.* Ⓤ lack of steadiness.
— ⓐ 불안정

• **in·stall** [instɔ́ːl] *vt.* **1.** put (someone) into office with ceremony. **2.** put (something) into a position or place where it can be used. ¶ *~ a sink.* **3.** (*reflexibly*) seat;
— ⓑ 1. [남]을 직위에 앉히다, 취임시키다 2. …을 설치하다 3. …을 앉게 하다, 착석시키다

settle. ¶*He installed himself in the easy chair.*

in·stal·la·tion [ìnstəléiʃ(ə)n] *n.* **1.** [U] the act of installing; the state of being installed. **2.** [C] a system of machinery placed in position for use.

—[名] 1. 임명, 취임; 시설, 설치 2. 설비, 장치

in·stall·ment¹, *Brit.* **-stal-** [instɔ́:lmənt] *n.* [C] **1.** a part of a debt that is to be paid at a certain time. ¶*buy a car on monthly installments.*① **2.** any of several parts supplied at successive times.

—[名] 1. 분할 불입금 ¶①월부로 차를 사다 2. 1회분

in·stall·ment² [instɔ́:lmənt] *n.* (*archaic*) =installation.

:in·stance [ínstəns] *n.* [C] **1.** a thing offered as an illustration; an example. ¶*give an ~.*① **2.** a case; an occasion. ¶*in this ~.*② **3.** a request; a suggestion. ¶*She sang at our ~.*③
1) ***for instance,*** as an example.
2) ***in the first*** (***last***) ***instance,*** firstly (lastly).
—*vt.* give or quote (something) as an example.

—[名] 1. 보기, 예, 실례 ¶①예를 들다 2. 경우 ¶②이 경우 3. 부탁, 의뢰; 권고 ¶③그녀는 우리의 청으로 노래를 불렀다
[熟] 1)예를 들면 2)첫째로(마지막으로)
—[他] …을 예로 들다

:in·stant [ínstənt] *n.* [C] **1.** a particular moment. ¶*Stop talking this ~!*① **2.** a short period of time. ¶*I shall have finished in an ~.*②
the instant [*that*], just as soon as.
—*adj.* **1.** immediate; urgent. ¶*an ~ death / There is an ~ need for action.*③ **2.** (*Commercial*) of this month. ⇒[N.B.] ¶*the 18th ~.* **3.** (of soup, etc.) ready to be prepared by adding a liquid. ¶*~ coffee.*

—[名] 1. 즉각 ¶①즉각 이야기를 그치시오 2. 순간 ¶②곧 끝납니다
[熟] …되자마자
—[形] 1. 즉석의; 긴급한 ¶③즉각 행동할 필요가 있다 2. 이 달의 [N.B.] inst.로 줄임 3. 즉석에서 쓸 수 있는

in·stan·ta·ne·ous [ìnst(ə)ntéiniəs] *adj.* occurring or made in an instant or at once. ¶*an ~ photograph*① / *an ~ reply.*②

—[形] 즉시의, 동시에 일어나는 ¶①스냅 사진/②즉답

in·stan·ta·ne·ous·ly [ìnst(ə)ntéiniəsli] *adv.* immediately; at once.

—[副] 즉시, 곧; 당장에

:in·stant·ly [ínstəntli] *adv.* at once; immediately. —*conj.* as soon as. ¶*I sent a telegram ~ I arrived there.*

—[副] 곧, 즉석에서 —[接] …하자마자

:in·stead [instéd] *adv.* in one's or its place. ¶*If you cannot go, let Tom go ~.*①
instead of, in place of.

—[副] 그 대신에 ¶①네가 갈 수 없으면 그 대신 톰을 보내라
[熟] …의 대신에

in·step [ínstèp] *n.* [C] **1.** the upper side of the human foot between the toes and the ankle. **2.** the part of a shoe, a stocking, etc. which covers this area.

—[名] 1. 발등 2. 양말(구두)의 등

in·sti·gate [ínstigèit] *vt.* urge on; stir up. ⦅*~ someone to do*⦆ ¶*~ a quarrel / The workers were instigated to go on* [*a*] *strike.*①

—[他] [남]을 충동(선동)하다, 부추기다 ¶①노동자들은 선동되어 파업을 일으켰다

in·sti·ga·tion [ìnstigéiʃ(ə)n] *n.* [U] the act of instigating.
at the instigation of (=*instigated by*) *someone.*

—[名] 충동질; 선동
[熟] …에 선동되어

in·sti·ga·tor [ínstigèitər] *n.* [C] a person who instigates.

—[名] 선동자

in·still, or **-stil** [instíl] *vt.* (**-stilled, -stil·ling**) **1.** introduce (ideas, etc.) little by little. ⦅*~something into*⦆ ¶*~a sense of honor into a child.*① **2.** put in (liquid) drop by drop.

—[他] 1. …을 서서히 가르쳐 주다 ¶①아이에게 명예심을 가르치다 2. …을 한 방울씩 넣다(떨어뜨리다)

:in·stinct¹ [ínstiŋ(k)t] *n.* **1.** [U] [C] a natural feeling or knowledge that one should do a necessary thing without taking conscious thought. ¶*act on ~*① / *It is the ~ of all animals to fear fire.*② **2.** [C] a natural ability; a talent. ¶*He has an ~ for art.*③

—[名] 1. 본능 ¶①본능에 따라 행동하다/②불을 무서워하는 것은 모든 동물의 본능이다 2. 천성; 소질 ¶③그는 예술에 소질이 있다

in·stinct² [instíŋ(k)t] *adj.* filled with. ¶*a picture ~ with life and beauty.*

—[形] …으로 가득찬, 넘치는

in·stinc·tive [instíŋ(k)tiv] *adj.* caused or done by instinct; not learned; natural. ¶*Eating is ~ in any animal.*

—[形] 본능적인; 천성의

in·stinc·tive·ly [instíŋ(k)tivli] *adv.* by instinct.

—[副] 본능적으로

***in·sti·tute** [ínstit(j)ù:t / -tjù:t] *vt.* **1.** set up; establish; organize. ¶*~ new rules / ~ a society.* **2.** begin; start. ¶*They instituted a search for the missing man.*①
—*n.* [C] **1.** a thing which is established; an established principle, law, custom, etc. **2.** a society or organization for some special, esp. public purpose. ¶*an art ~.*② **3.** a building used by such a society or organization. ¶*an ~ of music*③ / *the Pasteur Institute.*④

—[他] 1. …을 설립하다; 제정하다 2. …을 시작하다; 개시하다 ¶①행방불명자에 대한 수색을 시작했다
—[名] 1. 제도, 관례 2. 협회; 학회 ¶②미술 협회 3. 회관; 연구소 ¶③음악 학원/④파스퇴에르 연구소

:in·sti·tu·tion [ìnstit(j)ú:ʃ(ə)n / -tjú:-] *n.* [C] **1.** a society or organization for some, esp. public, purpose ¶*an educational ~.*① **2.** a building used by such a society or

—[名] 1. 회(會); 협회; 기관 ¶①교육 기관 2. 공공 시설, 회관, 연구소 3. 관례; 제도 4. 설립; 제정

organization. **3.** an established law, custom, etc. **4.** [U] the act of establishing or beginning. ¶*the ~ of new rules.* ⌈institution.⌉

in·sti·tu·tion·al [ìnstit(j)ú:ʃ(ə)n(ə)l / -tú:-] *adj.* of or like an institution.
—[形] 제도상의; 공공기관의; 협회의

⁑ in·struct [instrʌ́kt] *vt.* **1.** furnish (someone) with knowledge; teach; educate. 《~ someone *in*》 ¶*He instructs five classes in English.*① **2.** give orders or directions to (someone). 《~ someone *to do*》 ¶*I instructed him to come early.*② **3.** give information to (someone); inform; tell. 《~ *that* ...》 ¶*Our agent instructed us that we still owed Mr. Smith 500 dollars.*
—[他] 1. …을 가르치다 ¶①그는 다섯 학급에 영어를 가르친다 2. …에게 명령하다; 지시하다 ¶②나는 그에게 일찍 오도록 지시했다 3. …에게 통고하다; 알리다

⁑ in·struc·tion [instrʌ́kʃ(ə)n] *n.* **1.** [U] the act of teaching; education. **2.** 《*pl.*》 directions; orders.
1) ***give instruction in,*** teach.
2) ***give instructions to,*** order.
3) ***receive instruction in,*** learn.
—[名] 1. 가르치기; 교육 2. 지시; 명령
[熟] 1)…을 가르치다 2)…에게 명령하다 3)…을 배우다

*** in·struc·tive** [instrʌ́ktiv] *adj.* giving information or knowledge. ¶*This book is not only interesting but also ~.*①
—[形] 교육적인; 유익한 ¶①이 책은 재미있기도 하지만 유익하기도 하다

in·struc·tor [instrʌ́ktər] *n.* [C] **1.** a person who instructs; a teacher; a trainer. **2.** (*U.S.*) a lecturer in a universitiy.
—[名] 1. 교사; 지도자 2. 대학 강사

*** in·stru·ment** [ínstrumənt] *n.* [C] **1.** a person or thing used by someone to accomplish something; a means. ¶*use a person as an ~*① / *The army was the dictator's ~*② **2.** a tool used for delicate or scientific work. ¶*medical instruments*③ / *optical instruments.*④ **3.** a device for producing musical sounds. ¶*wind instruments.*⑤ **4.** (*Law*) a piece of formal writing.
—[名] 1. [남의] 앞잡이; 도구, 수단 ¶①남을 앞잡이로 쓰다/②군대는 독재자의 도구였다 2. 정밀(학술)기계 ¶③의료기계/④광학기계 3. 악기 ¶⑤관악기 4. 증서

in·stru·men·tal [ìnstruméntl] *adj.* **1.** serving as a means; helpful. **2.** of or for musical instruments. ↔vocal ¶~ *music.*① **3.** of an instrument.
—[形] 1. 수단이 되는; 도움이 되는 2. 악기의(를 위한) ¶①악곡 3. 기계의

in·stru·men·tal·ist [ìnstrumént(ə)list] *n.* [C] a person who plays on a musical instrument.
—[名] 기악가

in·stru·men·tal·i·ty [ìnstrumentǽliti] *n.* [U] help; means.
by (or ***through***) ***the instrumentality of,*** by means of.
—[名] 도움; 수단
[熟] …의 수단으로

in·sub·or·di·nate [ìnsəbɔ́:rd(i)nit] *adj.* resisting authority; disobedient.
—[形] 권위(권력)에 반항하는, 순종하지 않는

in·sub·or·di·na·tion [ínsəbɔ̀:rd(i)néiʃ(ə)n] *n.* [U] resistance to authority; disobedience.
—[名] 권위(권력)에 대한 반항; 불순종

in·sub·stan·tial [ìnsəbstǽnʃ(ə)l] *adj.* **1.** weak; not firm. **2.** unreal; imaginary.
—[形] 1. 약한; 튼튼하지 못한 2. 실재하지 않는; 비현실적인

in·suf·fer·a·bie [insʌ́f(ə)rəbl] *adj.* very hard to endure.
—[形] 참을 수 없는

in·suf·fi·cien·cy [ìnsəfíʃ(ə)nsi] *n.* [U] too small an amount; lack.
—[名] 불충분; 부족

in·suf·fi·cient [ìnsəfíʃ(ə)nt] *adj.* not enough.
—[形] 불충분한; 만족스럽지 못한

in·su·lar [ínsjulər] *adj.* **1.** of islands or islanders. **2.** narrow-minded. ¶~ *prejudices.*①
—[形] 1. 섬의; 섬 사람의 2. 도량이 좁은 ¶①섬나라 근성

in·su·lar·i·ty [ìnsjulǽriti] *n.* [U] **1.** the state of being an island. **2.** narrow-mindedness.
—[名] 1. 섬[나라]임 2. 섬나라 근성

in·su·late [ínsjulèit] *vt.* **1.** set (someone or something) apart; isolate. ¶~ *patients with infectious diseases.*① **2.** separate (something) by a material which will not conduct electricity, heat, or sound. ¶~ *an electric wire.*②
—[他] 1. …을 격리하다; 고립시키다 ¶①전염병 환자를 격리하다 2. [전기·열·음]을 절연(絶緣)하다 ¶②전선을 절연하다

in·su·la·tion [ìnsjuléiʃ(ə)n] *n.* [U] **1.** the act of insulating; the state of being insulated. **2.** materials used in insulating.
—[名] 1. 격리; 고립; 절연; 단열(斷熱); 방음 2. 절연(단열)재(材)

in·su·la·tor [ínsjulèitər] *n.* [C] a material or device which does not conduct electricity, heat or sound. ⇒fig.
—[名] 절연물, 절연체

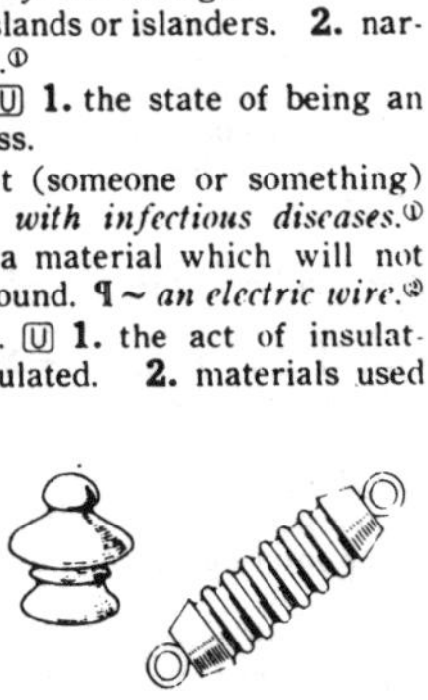
[electric insulator]

*** in·sult** *vt.* [insʌ́lt → *n.*] treat (someone or something) with rudeness or contempt.
—[他] …을 모욕하다 ¶①그녀는 그를 겁장이라고 모욕했다

¶*She insulted him by calling him a coward.*①
—*n.* [ˊ—] [C] [U] a rude or scornful action or speech.
—[名] 모욕[적인 언동]

in·sult·ing·ly [insʌ́ltiŋli] *adv.* in an insulting manner.
—[副] 무례하게도; 모욕적으로

in·su·per·a·ble [insúːp(ə)rəbl / -s(j)úːp-] *adj.* that cannot be overcome. ¶~ *difficulties.*
—[形] 극복할 수 없는

in·sup·port·a·ble [ìnsəpɔ́ːrtəbl] *adj.* unbearable; unendurable.
—[形] 견딜(참을) 수 없는

: in·sur·ance [inʃúərəns] *n.* **1.** [U] a system of guarding against financial loss from fire, accident, death, etc. **2.** [C] a contract insuring property, life, etc. **3.** [U] the amount of money paid for such a system; a premium. **4.** [U] the amount of money paid by an insurance company.
—[名] 1. 보험 2. 보험 계약; 보험 증서 3. 보험료 4. 보험금

*** in·sure** [inʃúər] *vt.* **1.** arrange for a money payment in case of accident, damage, injury, to (someone or something) or in case of someone's death. ¶~ *one's house against fire* / ~ *one's life for five million yen.* **2.** make sure; make safe; ensure. ⇒[N.B.]
—[他] 1. …에 보험을 걸다; …을 보험에 넣다 2. …을 확실히 하다; 안전하게 하다 [N.B.] 이 의미로는 ensure를 흔히 씀

in·sur·er [inʃúərər] *n.* [C] a person or company that insures.
—[名] 보험업자; 보험회사

in·sur·gent [insə́ːrdʒ(ə)nt] *n.* [C] a person who rises in revolt; a rebel. —*adj.* rising in revolt.
—[名] 폭도 —[形] 폭동을 일으키는

in·sur·mount·a·ble [ìnsə(ː)rmáuntəbl] *adj.* that cannot be overcome.
—[形] 이겨낼 수 없는; 넘을 수 없는

in·sur·rec·tion [ìnsərékʃ(ə)n] *n.* [U] [C] the act of rising against authority; rebellion.
—[名] 반란; 폭동

in·tact [intǽkt] *adj.* untouched; uninjured; whole. ¶*The town was ~ after the earthquake.*
—[形] 손대지 않은; 손상되지 않은; 완전한

in·take [íntèik] *n.* **1.** [C] a place through which water, air, gas, etc., is brought in. ↔outlet **2.** [U] the act of taking in. **3.** [C] the amount taken in.
—[名] 1. [물·공기의] 흡입구 2. 끌어(빨아)들이기 3. 흡입량; 섭취량

in·tan·gi·ble [intǽndʒibl] *adj.* **1.** that cannot be touched. **2.** not easily grasped by the mind; vague. —*n.* [C] a thing which is intangible.
—[形] 1. 만질 수 없는 2. 파악하기 어려운; 막연한 —[名] 막연한 일(것)

in·te·ger [íntidʒər] *n.* [C] (*Mathematics*) a whole number.
—[名] 《數》 정수(整數)

in·te·gral [íntigr(ə)l] *adj.* **1.** necessary for completeness; essential. **2.** entire; complete. **3.** (*Mathematics*) of whole numbers. ↔fractional
—[形] 1. 완전하기 위해서 필요한; 필수(必須)의 2. 완전한 3. 《數》 정수(整數)의

in·te·grate [íntigrèit] *vt.* **1.** bring together (parts) into a whole; make (something) into a whole; complete. **2.** (*U.S.*) make (schools, housing, etc.) open to all races on an equal basis.
—[他] 1. …[부분]을 전체에 통합하다; …을 완전히 하다 2. …의 인종차별을 폐지하다

in·te·gra·tion [ìntigréiʃ(ə)n] *n.* [U] the act of integrating.
—[名] 통합; 완성; 인종차별 폐지

in·teg·ri·ty [intégriti] *n.* [U] **1.** honesty; sincerity. **2.** wholeness; completeness.
—[名] 1. 정직; 성실 2. 완전; 무결

in·teg·u·ment [intégjumənt] *n.* [C] an outer covering, such as skin or a shell.
—[名] 외피(外皮)

in·tel·lect [íntilèkt] *n.* **1.** [U] the power of knowing; understanding. ¶*a man of high ~.* **2.** [C] a person who has much mental ability. ⇒[usage]
—[名] 1. 지성; 지력(知力) 2. 지식인 [usage] 「지식계급」의 의미로 집합명사로 쓰이는 일도 있음

*** in·tel·lec·tu·al** [ìntiléktʃuəl, +*Brit.* -tju-] *adj.* **1.** of the intellect or mind. ¶~ *faculties.*① **2.** needing intelligence. ¶*an ~ occupation.*② **3.** having or showing a high degree of intellect. ¶*an ~ face.* —*n.* [C] a person who is well informed and intelligent; a person who is interested in things of the mind instead of practical things.
—[形] 1. 지성의; 지력(知力)의 ¶①지적 능력 2. 지력을 필요로 하는 ¶②지적 직업 3. 지력이 있는; 이지적인 —[名] 지식인, 인텔리

in·tel·lec·tu·al·i·ty [ìntilèktʃuǽliti, +*Brit.* -tju-] *n.* [U] the state of being intellectual; intellectual power.
—[名] 지력, 지성, 총명

in·tel·lec·tu·al·ly [ìntiléktʃuəli, +*Brit.* -tju-] *adv.* **1.** in an intellectual manner. **2.** so far as intellect is concerned.
—[副] 1. 지적으로 2. 지성에 관하여는; 지력상(知力上)

: in·tel·li·gence [intélidʒ(ə)ns] *n.* [U] **1.** the ability to learn or understand and use what one has learned. ¶*The boy has high ~ for his age.*① **2.** news or information, esp. secret information.
—[名] 1. 이해력; 지력 ¶①그 소년은 나이에 비해 지능이 높다 2. 뉴우스; 정보; 비밀 정보

*** in·tel·li·gent** [intélidʒ(ə)nt] *adj.* **1.** showing intelligence. **2.** able to learn and to use what one has learned and understood.
—[形] 1. 이지적인, 머리가 좋은 2. 이해력이 있는

in·tel·li·gent·ly [intélidʒ(ə)ntli] *adv.* in an intelligent manner.
—⦿ 총명하게; 이해심 있게

in·tel·li·gent·si·a [intèlidʒéntsiə, -gén-] *n.* ((the ~)) ((collectively)) persons who are highly educated and enlightened; the intellectuals.
—⦾ 지식계급, 인텔리

in·tel·li·gi·bil·i·ty [intèlidʒibíliti] *n.* Ⓤ the quality of being intelligible.
—⦾ 이해할 수 있음; 명료함

in·tel·li·gi·ble [intélidʒibl] *adj.* that can be understood; clear. ¶*an ~ explanation.*① ▷**in·tel·li·gi·bly** [-bli] *adv.*
—⦿ 이해할 수 있는, 명료한 ¶①알기 쉬운 설명

in·tem·per·ance [intémp(ə)r(ə)ns] *n.* Ⓤ **1.** the state of being intemperate; lack of moderation; excess. **2.** excessive drinking.
—⦾ 1. 절제(절도)가 없음; 과도함 2. 과음, 폭음

in·tem·per·ate [intémp(ə)rit] *adj.* **1.** not moderate; lacking in self-control. ¶*~ conduct.* **2.** drinking too much.
—⦿ 1. 절제 없는; 과도한; 과격한 2. 과음(폭음)하는

: in·tend [inténd] *vt.* **1.** have (something) in mind as a purpose or aim; plan. ((~ *to do*; ~ *doing*; ~ *that* ...)) ¶*He intended no harm.*① / *I ~ to go myself; I ~ going myself.* **2.** design (someone or something) for a particular purpose. ((~ *someone for*; ~ *to do*; ~ *that*)) ¶*His father intends him for a lawyer; His father intends him to be a lawyer; His father intends that he* [*shall*] *be a lawyer.*② / *The gift was intended for you.*③ **3.** mean. ¶*What do you ~ by these words?*
—⦿ 1. …할 작정이다; …을 의도하다 ¶①그에게 악의는 없었다 2. [남]에게 …시키려고 하다; [물건]을 [어떤 목적]에 돌리려고 하다 ¶②그의 아버지는 그를 변호사로 만들 셈이었다/③그 선물은 네게 주는 것이었다 3. …을 의미하다

in·tend·ed [inténdid] *adj.* **1.** meant. **2.** prospective.
—*n.* Ⓒ (*colloq.*) ((*one's ~*)) a prospective husband or wife.
—⦿ 1. 의도된 2. 미래의 —⦾ 약혼자

·in·tense [inténs] *adj.* **1.** very great or strong; violent. ¶*~ cold*① / *an ~ pain.*② **2.** earnest; passionate. ¶*an ~ face*③ / *an ~ love.*④
—⦿ 1. 격렬한, 강렬한 ¶①혹한/②격통(激痛) 2. 열렬한; 진심으로의 ¶③진지한 얼굴/④열렬한 사랑

in·tense·ly [inténsli] *adv.* in an intense manner.
—⦿ 심하게; 열렬하게, 진지하게

in·ten·si·fi·ca·tion [intèns(i)fikéiʃ(ə)n] *n.* Ⓤ the act of intensifying; the state of being intensified.
—⦾ 강화, 증대

in·ten·si·fy [inténsifài] *vt.* make (something) more intense; increase. ¶*He intensified his efforts.*① —*vi.* become more intense. ¶*The pain intensified.*②
—⦿ …을 강화하다; 증대하다 ¶①그는 한층 더 노력했다 —⦿ 강화되다 ¶②아픔이 더해졌다

in·ten·sion [inténʃ(ə)n] *n.* **1.** Ⓤ a degree (of a quality, etc.). **2.** vigorous effort (of mind, etc.).
—⦾ 1: 세기, 강도 2. 긴장; [정신적] 노력

·in·ten·si·ty [inténsiti] *n.* Ⓤ **1.** the state or quality of being intense. ¶*the ~ of his anger.* **2.** strength or degree (of heat, sound, etc.).
—⦾ 1. 격렬[함]; 강렬[함]; 열렬[함] 2. [열·음 따위의] 세기, 강도(強度)

in·ten·sive [inténsiv] *adj.* **1.** thorough; concentrated. ↔extensive ¶*an ~ course in English.*① **2.** (*Grammar*) giving force or emphasis.
—⦿ 1. 철저한; 집중적인 ¶①영어 집중 강좌 2. 강의(強意)의

·in·tent¹ [intént] *n.* Ⓤ Ⓒ purpose; intention. ¶*with good* (*evil*) *~.*① **to all intents and purposes,** in almost every point; practically.
—⦾ 목적; 의지 ¶①선(악)의로
熟 모든 점에서; 사실상

·in·tent² [intént] *adj.* earnestly engaged or observed; concentrated. ¶*I was so ~ on my work that I heard nothing.*
—⦿ 전력하는, 열중하는, 몰두한

·in·ten·tion [inténʃ(ə)n] *n.* Ⓤ Ⓒ a thing which is intended or planned. ¶*act with good intentions.*①
1) **by intention,** on purpose.
2) **with the intention of** (= *for the purpose of*) *doing* something.
—⦾ 목적; 의도; 계획 ¶①선의를 가지고 행동하다
熟 1) 고의로, 일부러 2) …할 작정으로

in·ten·tion·al [inténʃən(ə)l] *adj.* done on purpose. ↔accidental
—⦿ 고의의

in·ten·tion·al·ly [inténʃən(ə)li] *adv.* on purpose.
—⦿ 일부러, 고의로

in·ter [intə́ːr] *vt.* (**-terred, -ter·ring**) put (a dead body) into the ground or a tomb; bury.
—⦿ [시체]를 매장하다

in·ter- [íntər] *pref.* **1.** one with the other: *intercommunicate* (=communicate with each other). **2.** between; among: *interpose* (=put between).
—《接頭》 1. 상호의 2. 중간의, 사이의

in·ter·act [ìntərǽkt] *vi.* act on each other.
—⦿ 서로 작용하다

in·ter·ac·tion [ìntərǽkʃ(ə)n] *n.* Ⓤ action on each other.
—⦾ 상호작용

in·ter·bred [ìntə(ː)rbréd] *v.* pt. and pp. of **interbreed.**

in·ter·breed [ìntə(ː)rbríːd] *vt., vi.* (**-bred**) breed by using different varieties of animals or plants.
—⦿⦿ 교배(交配)시키다(하다)

in·ter·cede [ìntə(:)rsí:d] *vi.* plead for another; act as peacemaker. 《~ *for* someone *with*》 ¶*I interceded for John with his father.*①
—[自] 중재하다; 사이에서 조정하다 ¶①나는 존을 그의 아버지에게 잘 말해 주었다

in·ter·cept [ìntər(:)sépt] *vt.* **1.** seize or stop (something or someone) on the way. ¶~ *a messenger* / *Can we ~ the enemy's attack?*① **2.** cut off (light, water, etc.).
—[他] 1. …을 도중에서 잡다 ¶①우리는 적의 공격을 도중에서 저지할 수 있을까? 2. …을 차단하다

in·ter·cep·tion [ìntə(:)rsépʃ(ə)n] *n.* [U][C] the act of intercepting.
—[名] 도중에서 잡기; 차단; 방해

in·ter·ces·sion [ìntərséʃ(ə)n] *n.* [U][C] the act of interceding. ¶*through someone's ~.*①
—[名] 중재; 조정 ¶①…의 조정을 통해

in·ter·change *vt.* [ìntə(:)rtʃéindʒ → *n.*] **1.** put (two or more things or persons) in the place of each other. ¶*The parts of these machines may be interchanged.*① **2.** exchange. 《~ something *with*》 ¶~ *letters* / *You'd better ~ study with play.*②
—[他] 1. …을 바꾸어 놓다, 바꾸다 ¶①이들 기계의 부속품은 바꿀 수 있다 2. …을 주고받다, 교환하다, 교대시키다 ¶②공부와 놀이는 번갈아 해라

—*n.* [íntə:rtʃèindʒ, +*Brit.* ´-´] **1.** [U][C] the act of interchanging. ¶*an ~ of calling cards.*③ **2.** [C] a junction of two or more highways, usu. express highways, by a system of separate road level.
—[名] 1. 바꾸어 놓기; 교환; 교대 ¶③명함의 교환 2. 고속도로의 입체 교차점, 인터체인지

in·ter·change·a·ble [ìntə(:)rtʃéindʒəbl] *adj.* that can be interchanged.
—[形] 바꾸어 놓을 수 있는; 교환(교대)할 수 있는

in·ter·col·le·gi·ate [ìntə(:)rkəlí:dʒiit] *adj.* between colleges or universities. ¶~ [*baseball*] *games.*①
—[形] 대학 사이의 ¶①대학 대항 [야구]시합

in·ter·co·lo·ni·al [ìntə(:)rkəlóuniəl] *adj.* between colonies. ¶~ *trade.*①
—[形] 식민지 사이의 ¶①식민지간 무역

in·ter·com·mu·ni·cate [ìntə(:)rkəmjú:nikèit] *vi.* **1.** communicate witn each other. **2.** lead from one room to the other.
—[自] 1. 서로 사귀다; 서로 연락하다 2. [방이] 서로 통하다

in·ter·com·mu·ni·ca·tion [ìntə(:)rkəmjù:nikéiʃ(ə)n] *n.* [U] communication with each other.
—[名] 서로 사귀기; 교제; 상호 연락

in·ter·con·ti·nen·tal [ìntə(:)rkàntinént(ə)l / -təkɔ́n-] *adj.* that can travel from one continent to another. ¶*an ~ ballistic missile.*① ⇒[N.B.]
—[形] 대륙간의 ¶①대륙간 탄도 미사일 [N.B.] I.C.B.M. 으로 줄임

***in·ter·course** [íntə:rkɔ̀:rs] *n.* [U] connection or communication between individuals, nations, etc. ¶*commercial ~*① / *social ~.*②
—[名] 관계; 교제; 교섭 ¶①통상/②사교

in·ter·de·pend [ìntə(:)rdipénd] *vi.* depend upon each other.
—[自] 서로 의존하다

in·ter·de·pend·ence [ìntə(:)rdipéndəns] *n.* [U] dependence upon each other.
—[名] 상호 의존

in·ter·de·pend·ent [ìntə(:)rdipéndənt] *adj.* dependent upon each other.
—[形] 서로 의존하는

in·ter·dict *vt.* [ìntə(:)rdíkt → *n.*] **1.** prohibit. **2.** restrain. —*n.* [´-`] [C] a formal prohibition, esp. of certain church privileges.
—[他] 1. …을 금지하다 2. …을 제지(억지)하다 —[名] 금지[명령]; 파문(破門)

in·ter·dic·tion [ìntə(:)rdíkʃ(ə)n] *n.* [U][C] the act of interdicting; the state of being interdicted.
—[名] 금지; 제지; 파문(破門)

:in·ter·est [ínt(ə)rèst / -rist] *n.* [U] **1.** [U][C] the feeling of wanting to know or to do; concern; curiosity. ¶*I have no ~ in music.* **2.** the power to arouse such a feeling. ¶*Local color adds ~ to a story.*① **3.** [C] something in which one has an interest; a hobby; an attraction. ¶*Volleyball is her chief ~.*② **4.** importance. ¶*a matter of primary ~.*③ **5.** [C] 《often *pl.*》 advantage; benefit; profit. ¶*common interests*④ / *for one's own ~.* **6.** the money paid by a borrower for the use of borrowed money. ¶*He lent her the money at 4 per cent ~.*⑤ **7.** [C] a share or part; a right or claim to something. ¶*Father owns an ~ in the farm.*⑥ **8.** 《often *pl.*》 a group of people concerned with some particular kind of work or business. ¶*steel interests*⑦ / *the farming interests.* **9.** something added in making a return. ¶*He returned the blow with ~.*⑧
—[名] 1. 흥미, 관심 2. 흥미를 일으키는 힘, 재미 ¶①지방색은 이야기의 재미를 더해 준다 3. 관심사, 취미 ¶②그녀의 중요한 관심사는 배구이다 4. 중요성 ¶③가장 중요한 일 5. 이익, 이해관계 ¶④공통의 이해 6. 이자, 이식 ¶⑤그는 그녀에게 4푼의 이자로 돈을 꾸어 주었다 7. 주(株); 이권, 요구권 ¶⑥아버지는 농장에 이권을 갖고 있다 8. 동업자 ¶⑦철강업자 9. 대가(代價)(보답)로 덧붙여 주는 것 ¶⑧그는 [맞은 것보다] 더 세게 때려 주었다

in the interest[*s*] *of,* on behalf of; for. ¶*in the ~ of humanity.*⑨
[熟] …을 위하여 ¶⑨인류를 위하여

—*vt.* **1.** cause or arouse the attention or curiosity of
—[他] 1. …에게 흥미(관심)를 일으키게

(someone). ¶ *Which course interests you most?*⑩ | *The story interests most boys; Most boys are interested in the story.* **2.** cause (someone) to take part in something; concern. ¶ *try to ~ him in the plan* | *He is not interested in the enterprise.*⑪

하다 ¶⑩어떤 코오스가 가장 흥미있느냐? 2. …을 관계시키다 ¶⑪그는 기업에는 관계하고 있지 않다

• **in·ter·est·ed** [ínt(ə)rèstid] *adj.* **1.** feeling or showing interest or curiosity. ↔uninterested ¶ *an ~ look.*① **2.** having a share or part; connected or concerned. ↔uninterested ¶ *the ~ parties.*② **3.** influenced by personal interests or considerations. ↔disinterested

—[形] 1. 흥미를 가진; 흥미있어 보이는 ¶①흥미를 느낀 듯한 표정 2. [이해] 관계가 있는 ¶②이해관계자 3. 사심이(私心)이 있는

‡ **in·ter·est·ing** [ínt(ə)rèstiŋ / -rist-] *adj.* arousing interest; holding one's attention. ¶ *an ~ book* | *~ conversation* | *an ~ person.* ▷**in·ter·est·ing·ly** [-li] *adv.*

—[形] 흥미있는; 주의를 끄는; 재미있는

• **in·ter·fere** [ìntərfíər] *vi.* **1.** (of things) come into opposition; obstruct; clash. ⟪~ *with* something⟫ ¶ *if nothing interferes*① | *Their plan interfered with ours.*② **2.** (of persons) take part in the affairs of others. ⟪~ *in* or *with* something⟫ ¶ *Don't ~ in other people's affairs.* | *He is always interfering with my work.*

—[自] 1. 방해가 되다; 충돌하다, 서로 용납하지 않다 ¶①지장이 없으면/②그들의 계획과 우리 것은 양립할 수 없었다 2. 간섭하다

• **in·ter·fer·ence** [ìntərfíər(ə)ns] *n.* [U] [C] **1.** the act of interfering. **2.** (*Physics*) the mutual action of two waves or streams of light, sound, etc. which reinforce or neutralize one another. **3.** (of radio) the confusion of sounds caused by unwanted signals.

—[名] 1. 방해; 간섭; 충돌 2. 간섭 3. 혼신(混信)

in·ter·fuse [ìntə(ː)rfjúːz] *vt.* cause (things) to mix together. **—*vi.*** mix together.

—[他] …을 혼합시키다 —[自] 혼합되다

in·ter·im [íntərim] *n.* ⟪*the* ~⟫ the time or period between; the meantime. **—*adj.*** of or for the interim; temporary. ¶ *an ~ report.*①

—[名] 짬, 사이; 잠시; 그 사이 —[形] 당분간의; 임시의; 일시적인 ¶①중간보고

‡ **in·te·ri·or** [intíəriər] *n.* [C] ⟪usu. *the* ~⟫ **1.** the inside. ¶ *the ~ of a building.* **2.** the part of a country away from the sea; inland. **3.** the home affairs of a nation. **—*adj.*** **1.** of the inside of something. ↔exterior ¶ *~ decoration.*① **2.** away from the sea. **3.** of the affairs within a nation; home; domestic. ↔foreign ¶ *~ trade.*

—[名] 1. 내부 2. 내지(內地); 벽지(僻地) 3. 내정(內政); 내무

—[形] 1. 내부의 ¶①실내 장식 2. 내지(內地)의, 벽지(僻地)의 3. 국내의

in·ter·ject [ìntə(ː)rdʒékt] *vt.* throw or put in (a remark, etc.) suddenly; insert.

—[他] 불쑥 말참견하다, 말난 김에 말하다

in·ter·jec·tion [ìntə(ː)rdʒékʃ(ə)n] *n.* **1.** [U] the act of interjecting. **2.** [C] (*Grammar*) a word used as an exclamation.

—[名] 1. 불쑥 지르는 소리; 감탄 2. ⟪文法⟫ 감탄사, 간투사

in·ter·lace [ìntə(ː)rléis] *vi.* cross over and under each other. **—*vt.*** unite (threads, strips, etc.) by lacing or weaving together.

—[自] 교차하다; 섞어 짜여지다 —[他] …을 교차시키다; 섞어 짜다; 합쳐 꼬다

in·ter·line[1] [ìntə(ː)rláin] *vt.* put a lining between the outer fabric and the ordinary lining of (a garment).

—[他] [옷의 거죽과 안 사이]에 심을 넣다

in·ter·line[2] [ìntə(ː)rláin] *vt.* write (words, etc.) between lines of writing or print. ¶ *~ a translation in an text.*

—[他] …을 행간에 써 넣다

in·ter·lin·e·ar [ìntə(ː)rlíniər] *adj.* written between the lines.

—[形] 행간에 기입된

in·ter·lock [ìntə(ː)rlák / -təlɔ́k] *vi., vt.* join with one another.

—[自][他] 맞물리[게 하]다

in·ter·lo·cu·tion [ìntə(ː)rloukjúːʃ(ə)n] *n.* [U] [C] interchange of speech; conversation.

—[名] 말을 주고받기; 대화, 문답

in·ter·lop·er [ìntə(ː)rlóupər, +*Brit.* íntə(ː)lòupə] *n.* [C] a person who interferes.

—[名] 주제넘은 사람; 훼방꾼

in·ter·lude [íntə(ː)rlùːd] *n.* [C] **1.** a pause between the acts of a play. **2.** an entertainment given during this period. **3.** a piece of music played between the parts of a song, etc. **4.** any event or period of time coming between.

—[名] 1. 막간 2. 막간의 연예 3. 간주곡 4. 사이[에 일어난 사건]

in·ter·mar·riage [ìntə(ː)rmǽridʒ] *n.* [U] [C] **1.** marriage between different tribes, races, religions, etc. **2.** marriage between closely-related persons.

—[名] 1. [다른 민족·인종·종교 사이의] 혼인 2. 근친 결혼

in·ter·mar·ry [ìntə(ː)rmǽri] *vi.* **1.** (of people of different tribes, races, religions, etc.) become connected by marriage. **2.** marry within one's family.

—[自] 1. [다른 민족·인종·종교 사이에서] 혼인관계를 맺다 2. 근친 결혼을 하다

in·ter·med·dle [ìntə(:)rmédl] *vi.* take part in a matter which really concerns only others; interfere; meddle.
—[自] 간섭하다; 참견하다

in·ter·me·di·ar·y [ìntə(:)rmí:dièri / -diəri] *n.* [C] (pl. **-ar·ies**) a person who acts between two persons; a go-between. —*adj.* **1.** acting between two persons. ¶ ~ *business.*① **2.** being between; intermediate.
—[名] 중개자; 매개인; 중재자 —[形] 1. 중개의, 매개의; 중재의 ¶①중개업 2. 중간의

in·ter·me·di·a·te [ìntə(:)rmí:diit] *adj.* being or coming between. —*n.* [C] **1.** something which lies between. **2.** a person who acts between others.
—[形] 중간에 있는; 중간에 위치한 —[名] 1. 중간물 2. 중개자; 조정자

in·ter·ment [intə́:rmənt] *n.* [U][C] the act of interring; burial.
—[名] 매장(埋葬)

in·ter·mi·na·ble [intə́:rminəbl] *adj.* very long; endless. ¶*an ~ speech.*
—[形] 끝없는, 무한한

in·ter·min·gle [ìntə(:)rmíŋgl] *vt., vi.* mix together.
—[他][自] 섞다, 혼합하다; 섞이다

in·ter·mis·sion [ìntə(:)rmíʃ(ə)n] *n.* **1.** [C] an interval of time between periods of activity; a break. **2.** [U] the act of stopping for a time.
—[名] 1. 끊긴 사이; 휴게시간; 중간 휴식 2. 휴지(休止), 중단

in·ter·mit [ìntə(:)rmít] *vt., vi.* (**-mit·ted, -mit·ting**) stop for a time.
—[他][自] 일시 중단(중지)시키다(하다)

in·ter·mit·tent [ìntə(:)rmít(ə)nt] *adj.* stopping and beginning again; repeated at intervals. ¶*an ~ rain*① / *an ~ spring.*②
—[形] 때때로 끊기는; 간헐성(間歇性)의 ¶①오다가 말다가 하는 비/②간헐천(泉)

in·ter·mit·tent·ly [ìntə(:)rmít(ə)ntli] *adv.* in an intermittent manner.
—[副] 단속적으로

in·ter·mix [ìntə(:)rmíks] *vt., vi.* mix together.
—[他][自] 섞다; 섞이다

in·ter·mix·ture [ìntə(:)rmíkstʃər] *n.* **1.** [U] the act of intermixing; the state of being intermixed. **2.** [C] a thing made by mixing things together.
—[名] 1. 혼합 2. 혼합물

in·tern¹ [intə́:rn] *vt.* force (someone) to stay within a country or definite area.
—[他] [일정 구역내에] …을 억류하다

in·tern² [íntə:rn] *n.* [C] (*U.S.*) a young doctor acting as an assistant in a hospital.
—[名] 수련의(修練醫), 인턴

* **in·ter·nal** [intə́:rnl] *adj.* ↔external **1.** of or on the inside. ¶*an ~ organ.*① **2.** coming from within the thing itself. ¶ ~ *evidence.*② **3.** within a country; domestic. ↔foreign ¶ ~ *products.*③
—[形] 1. 안의; 내부의 ¶①내장 2. 내면적인; 본질적인 ¶②내재적(內在的) 증거 3. 국내의; 내정(內政)의 ¶③국내 생산물

in·ter·nal·ly [intə́:rnəli] *adv.* in or on the inside.
—[副] 내부에, 내면적으로

‡ **in·ter·na·tion·al** [ìntə(:)rnǽʃ(ə)n(ə)l] *adj.* between or among nations; concerning several nations. ¶*an ~ conference*① / *an ~ exposition.*② —*n.* [C] (*I* ~) one of several international socialist or communist organizations.
—[形] 국제간의; 만국의; 국제적인 ¶①국제 회의/②만국 박람회 —[名] 국제 노동자 동맹

in·ter·na·tion·al·ism [ìntə(:)rnǽʃ(ə)nəlìz(ə)m] *n.* [U] **1.** the principle of co-operation among nations for their common good. **2.** international sympathies, ideas, etc.
—[名] 1. 국제주의 2. 국제성

in·ter·na·tion·al·i·za·tion [ìntə(:)rnæ̀ʃən(ə)lizéiʃ(ə)n, +*Brit.* -nǽʃən(ə)lai-] *n.* [U] the act of internationalizing; the state of being internationalized.
—[名] 국제화; 국제 관리[화]

in·ter·na·tion·al·ize [ìntə(:)rnǽʃ(ə)n(ə)làiz] *vt.* **1.** make (something) international. **2.** bring (land, area, etc.) under international control.
—[他] 1. …을 국제화하다 2. …을 국제 관리하에 두다

in·ter·na·tion·al·ly [ìntə(:)rnǽʃ(ə)nəli] *adv.* in an international manner.
—[副] 국제적으로

in·ter·ne·cine [ìntə(:)rní:si(:)n / -sain] *adj.* **1.** deadly; destructive. **2.** deadly or destructive to both sides.
—[形] 1. 치명적인, 살인적인, 파괴적인 2. 서로 파괴하는; 너 죽고 나 죽자는 식의

in·tern·ee [ìntə:rní:] *n.* [C] a person interned.
—[名] 피(被)억류자

in·tern·ment [intə́:rnmənt] *n.* [U] the act of interning; the state of being interned.
—[名] 유치, 억류; 수용

in·ter·pel·late [intə́(:)rpéleit, intə́:rpəlèit / intə́:pelèit] *vt.* ask (a government Minister, etc.) formally for an explanation of government policy, etc.
—[他] [장관]에게 정책에 관하여 설명을 요구하다

in·ter·pel·la·tion [ìntə:rpəléiʃ(ə)n / intə̀:peléi-] *n.* [C][U] a formal request for an explanation of government policy, etc.
—[名] 장관에 대한 정책 질의

in·ter·play [íntə(:)rplèi] *n.* [U] action or influence on each other.
—[名] 상호 작용

in·ter·po·late [intə́(:)rpoulèit] *vt.* **1.** alter (a text, etc.) by putting in a new word or group of words. **2.** put in (new words, etc.).
—[他] 1. [교과서 따위]를 개정(改訂)하다 2. [다른 어구]를 써 넣다

in·ter·po·la·tion [intə̀:rpouléiʃ(ə)n] *n.* **1.** [U] the act of interpolating; the state of being interpolate. **2.** [C] a word, etc. which is interpolated.
—[名] 1. 개정 2. 써 넣은 어구

in·ter·pose [ìntə(:)rpóuz] *vt.* **1.** put in or between. **2.** insert (a remark or an opinion) into a conversation. ¶~ *an objection at this point.*① **3.** interrup. —*vi.* come between parties in a quarrel.
—[他] 1 …을 사이에 두다 2. …을 끼워 넣다 ¶①이 점에서 이의를 제기하다 3. …의 방해를 하다 —[自] 중재하다

in·ter·po·si·tion [ìntərpəzíʃ(ə)n / intə̀:pəzíʃ(ə)n] *n.* **1.** [U] the act of interposing. **2.** [C] a thing which is interposed.
—[名] 1. 삽입; 중재 2. 삽입물

* **in·ter·pret** [intə́:rprit] *vt.* **1.** explain the meaning of (something). ¶*I can't ~ the passage.* **2.** (in acting or performing) bring out the meaning of (something). **3.** consider or understand the meaning of (something). 《~ something *as*》 ¶~ *her silence as consent.*①
—*vi.* act as an interpreter. 《~ *for* someone》
—[他] 1. …을 설명(해석)하다 2. …을 연출(연주)하다 3. …을 이해(양해)하다 ¶①그녀의 침묵을 동의로 알다
—[自] 통역하다; 해설하다

* **in·ter·pre·ta·tion** [intə̀:rpritéiʃ(ə)n] *n.* [U][C] **1.** the act of interpreting; explanation; translation. **2.** the act of bringing out the meaning of a dramatic part, music, etc.
—[名] 1. 해석; 설명; 통역 2. 연출, 연주

in·ter·pre·ta·tive [intə́:rpritèitiv, +*Brit.* -tətiv] *adj.* used for interpretation; explaining.
—[形] 해석의; 설명적인; 통역의

in·ter·pret·er [intə́:rpritər] *n.* [C] **1.** a person who translates a conversation or speech into another language. **2.** a person who explains.
—[名] 1. 통역[자] 2. 설명하는 사람; 해설자

in·ter·pre·tive [intə́:rpritiv] *adj.* interpretative.
—[形] 해석의; 설명적인; 통역의

in·ter·reg·na [ìntərégnə] *n.* pl. of **interregnum**.

in·ter·reg·num [ìntərégnəm] *n.* [C] (pl. **-nums** or **-na**) a period without any ruler between an old ruler and his successor.
—[名] [새 임금이 즉위할 때까지의] 궐위(闕位) 기간

in·ter·re·lat·ed [ìntəriléitid] *adj.* having a close connection with each other.
—[形] 상호관계가 있는

in·ter·re·la·tion [ìntə(:)riléiʃ(ə)n] *n.* [U][C] close connection with each other; mutual relation.
—[名] 상호관계

in·ter·ro·gate [intérəgèit] *vt.* ask questions of (someone); examine by questioning. —*vi.* ask questions.
—[他] …에 질문하다; …을 심문하다 —[自] 질문하다

in·ter·ro·ga·tion [intèrəgéiʃ(ə)n] *n.* **1.** [U] the act of asking questions. **2.** [C] a question.
—[名] 1. 질문(심문)[하기] 2. 물음, 질문

interrogation mark [-⌣-⌣-⌣ ⌣] *n.* (*Grammar*) a question mark.
—[名] 《文法》 의문부호(?)

in·ter·rog·a·tive [ìntərágətiv / -rɔ́g-] *adj.* **1.** having the form of a question. ¶*an ~ sentence.*① **2.** questioning; inquiring. ¶*an ~ look.*② —*n.* [C] (*Grammar*) a word used to make an interrogative sentence.
—[形] 1. 의문의 ¶①의문문 2. 미심쩍은 듯한 ¶②미심쩍은 듯한 표정
—[名] 《文法》 의문사

in·ter·ro·ga·tor [intérəgèitər] *n.* [C] a person who asks questions.
—[名] 심문자, 질문자

in·ter·rog·a·tory [ìntərágətɔ̀:ri / -rɔ́gət(ə)ri] *adj.* by questioning; expressing a question. ¶*an ~ method.*① —*n.* [C] (pl. **-ries**) a question; an inquiry.
—[形] 의문의, 의문을 나타내는 ¶①문답식 —[名] 질문, 심문

‡ **in·ter·rupt** [ìntərʌ́pt] *vt.* stop; cut off; hinder. ¶~ *him while he is speaking* / *That building interrupts the view.*① —*vi.* cut off; break in.
—[他] …을 막다, 방해하다 ¶①건물에 막혀 경치가 안 보인다 —[自] 방해하다

in·ter·rupt·er [ìntərʌ́ptər] *n.* [C] **1.** a person or thing that interrupts. **2.** (*Electricity*) a device for interrupting an electric current.
—[名] 1. 막는 사람(것) 2. [전류] 단속기(斷續器)

in·ter·rup·tion [ìntərʌ́pʃ(ə)n] *n.* **1.** [U] the act of interrupting; the state of being interrupted. **2.** [C] a thing that interrupts.
—[名] 1. 차단, 저지, 방해 2. 차단하는 것

without interruption, continually.
[熟] 간단없이

in·ter·sect [ìntə(:)rsékt] *vt.* cut across. ¶*The road intersects the railroad.* —*vi.* cross each other.
—[他] …을 가로지르다 —[自] 교차하다

in·ter·sec·tion [ìntə(:)rsékʃ(ə)n] *n.* **1.** [U] the act of intersecting; the state of being intersected. **2.** [C] a point or line where two things cross ⇒fig.; a place where two streets cross.
—[名] 1. 횡단, 교차 2. 교점(交點), 교선(交線); 교차점

[intersection 2.]

in·ter·sperse [ìntə(:)rspə́:rs] *vt.* **1.** put (something) here and there; scatter.
—[他] 1. …을 흩뿌리다; 점점이 박다; 산재시키다 2. …에 변화를 주다 ¶①

《~ something *between* or *among*》 ¶*cherry trees interspersed among the pine trees.* **2.** give variety to (something) 《~ something *with*》 ¶*~ a book with pictures.*①
책에 그림을 넣어 변화를 주다

in·ter·state [ìntə(:)rstèit] *adj.* (*U.S.*) between states.
—[形] 《美》 각 주(州) 사이의

in·ter·stice [intə́:rstis] *n.* [C] a very small opening; a crack.
—[名] 빈틈, 갈라진 금

in·ter·trib·al [ìntə(:)rtráib(ə)l] *adj.* between or among tribes.
—[形] [다른] 종족간의

in·ter·twine [ìntə(:)rtwáin] *vt., vi.* twine together.
—[他][自] 서로 얽히[게 하]다

:in·ter·val [íntərv(ə)l] *n.* [C] **1.** a space between objects. ¶*at intervals of ten feet.*① **2.** a period of time between events. ¶*after an ~ of fifty years / at long (short) intervals*② */ at regular intervals*③ */ in the ~.*④
at intervals, ⓐ here and there. ⓑ now and then.
—[名] 1. [위치의] 간격 ¶①10 피이트의 간격으로 2. [시간의] 사이 ¶②가끔(자주)/③일정한 시간을 두고/④그 사이에
[熟] ⓐ군데군데 ⓑ때때로

·in·ter·vene [ìntə(:)rví:n] *vi.* **1.** come or take place between two events. ¶*Years intervened between the two incidents.* **2.** step in; interfere. 《~ *between* persons; ~ *in* something》 ¶*~ in the internal affairs of another country.*①
—[自] 1. 사이에 들다(일어나다) 2. 중재하다, 간섭하다 ¶①다른 나라의 내정에 간섭하다

in·ter·ven·tion [ìntə(:)rvénʃ(ə)n] *n.* [U][C] the act of intervening; interference.
—[名] 개재; 중재; 간섭

·in·ter·view [íntərvjù:] *n.* [C] **1.** a meeting to talk something over. **2.** a meeting to give information to the press. **3.** an article giving such information. —*vt.* have an interview with (someone).
—[名] 1. 회견; 대담, 회담 2. 기자 회견 3. 방문기, 회견담 —[他] …와 회견하다

in·ter·view·er [íntərvjù:ər] *n.* [C] a person who interviews; a newspaper reporter, etc. who asks a famous person etc. questions
—[名] 회견자, 방문 기자

in·ter·weave [ìntə(:)rwí:v] *vt., vi.* (**-wove** or **-weaved, -woven** or **-weaved**) **1.** weave together. **2.** mix together.
—[他][自] 1. 섞어 짜다 2. 혼합하다

in·ter·wove [ìntə(:)rwóuv] v. pt. of **interweave.**

in·ter·woven [ìntə(:)rwóuvn] *v.* pp. of **interweave.**

in·tes·tate [intésteit, -tit] *adj.* having made no will. ¶*die ~.*① —*n.* [C] a person who has died intestate.
—[形] 유언을 남기지 않은 ¶①유언을 남기지 않고 죽다 —[名] 유언 없는 사망자

in·tes·ti·nal [intéstinl] *adj.* of or in the intestines.
—[形] 창자의, 장의

in·tes·tine [intéstin] *n.* [C] 《usu. *pl.*》 the long coiled tube below the stomach through which food passes; the bowels.
—[名] 장, 창자; 내장

in·ti·ma·cy [íntiməsi] *n.* [U] the state of being intimate; close friendship.
—[名] 친밀, 친교

·in·ti·mate¹ [íntimit] *adj.* **1.** very familiar; close. ¶*be on ~ terms with someone.*① **2.** coming from close study; deep. ¶*an ~ knowledge of Korea* **3.** private; personal. ¶*one's ~ affairs.*② —*n.* [C] an intimate friend. ▷**in·ti·mate·ly** [-li] *adv.*
—[形] 1. 친한 ¶①…와 친한 사이다 2. 자세한; 깊은 3. 일신상의, 개인적인 ¶②사사로운 일 —[名] 친구

in·ti·mate² [íntimèit] *vt.* **1.** suggest; hint. **2.** announce.
—[他] 1. …을 암시하다 2. …을 공표하다

in·ti·ma·tion [ìntiméiʃ(ə)n] *n.* **1.** [U] the act of intimating. **2.** [C] an announcement. **3.** [C] a hint.
—[名] 1. 암시하기, 공표하기 2. 공표, 고시 3. 암시

in·tim·i·date [intímidèit] *vt.* **1.** make (someone) afraid; frighten. **2.** force (someone) to do something by means of threats. 《~ someone *into*》
—[他] 1. …을 위협하다 2. …을 위협하여 …시키다

in·tim·i·da·tion [intìmidéiʃ(ə)n] *n.* [U] the act of intimidating; the state of being intimidated.
—[名] 위협, 협박

:in·to [íntu:, íntu, íntə ⇒[N.B.]] *prep.* **1.** to the inside of. ¶*put ~ the soup / Look ~ this report.*① */ She followed him ~ the room.* **2.** toward the middle of [a period of time]. ¶*He had to work far ~ the night.* **3.** to the state or condition of. ¶*turn water ~ ice / translate French ~ Korean / Winter passed ~ spring.*
—[前] [N.B.] [íntu]는 모음 앞, [íntu:]는 문장 끝, [íntə]는 자음 앞에 쓰임 1. 《場所》 …의 속(안)으로 ¶①이 보고를 보아라 2. 《時間》 …으로, …까지 3. 《狀態》 …에, …으로

in·tol·er·a·ble [intál(ə)rəbl / -tɔ́l-] *adj.* that cannot be endured; not tolerable; unbearable.
—[形] 견딜 수 없는, 참을 수 없는

in·tol·er·ance [intálər(ə)ns / -tɔ́l-] *n.* [U] **1.** unwillingness to allow others' opinions, religious beliefs, etc.; narrow-mindedness. **2.** lack of endurance.
—[名] 1. 도량이 좁음 2. 참을 수 없음

in·tol·er·ant [intálər(ə)nt / -tɔ́l-] *adj.* **1.** narrow-minded. **2.** unable or unwilling to endure or allow. 《~ *of*》
—[形] 1. 도량이 좁은 2. 참을 수 없는

in·to·na·tion [ìntounéiʃ(ə)n] *n.* **1.** [U] [C] the rise and fall of the voice. **2.** [U] the act of reciting in a singing voice.
—[名] 1. 억양, 인토네이션 2. 읊조리기, 영창(詠唱)

in·tone [intóun] *vt., vi.* **1.** recite in a singing voice. **2.** give a particular intonation to (something).
—[他][自] 1. [⋯을] 음창(吟唱)하다, 영창하다 2. [⋯에] 억양을 붙이다

in·tox·i·cant [intáksikənt / -tɔ́k-] *n.* [C] a thing that intoxicates; a strong liquor. —*adj.* intoxicating.
—[名] 취하게 하는 것, 마취제, 술
—[形] 취하게 하는

in·tox·i·cate [intáksikèit / -tɔ́k-] *vt.* **1.** make (someone) drunk. **2.** excite greatly. 《~ someone *with* or *by*》
—[他] 1. ⋯을 취하게 하다 2. ⋯을 흥분시키다, 열중하게 하다

in·tox·i·cat·ing [intáksikèitiŋ / -tɔ́k-] *adj.* causing intoxication; very exciting.
—[形] 취하게 하는, 열중하게 하는

in·tox·i·ca·tion [intàksikéiʃ(ə)n / -tɔ̀k-] *n.* [U] **1.** the state of being drunk; drunkenness. **2.** great excitement.
—[名] 1. 술취함 2. 흥분

in·trac·ta·bil·i·ty [intræ̀ktəbíliti] *n.* [U] the state of being intractable.
—[名] 다루기 힘듦

in·trac·ta·ble [intræ̀ktəbl] *adj.* hard to manage; difficult to treat.
—[形] 다루기 힘든, 힘에 겨운

in·tra·mu·ral [ìntrəmjúər(ə)l] *adj.* within a city, a college, a building, etc. ↔extramural
—[形] 도시 내의, 학교 내의; 건물 내의

in·tran·si·tive [intræ̀ns(i)tiv] *adj.* (of verbs) not taking a direct object. ↔transitive
—[形] 자동[사]의

in·trench [intréntʃ] *v.* =entrench.

in·trep·id [intrépid] *adj.* bold; brave; fearless.
—[形] 대담한; 용맹한

in·tre·pid·i·ty [ìntrepíditi] *n.* **1.** [U] the state or quality of being intrepid. **2.** [C] an intrepid act.
—[名] 1. 대담 2. 대담한 사물

in·tri·ca·cy [íntrikəsi] *n.* (pl. **-cies**) **1.** [U] the state of being intricate. **2.** 《*pl.*》 intricate things, events, etc.
—[名] 1. 복잡[성] 2. 복잡한 행위

in·tri·cate [íntrikit] *adj.* difficult to understand; complicated. ↔simple ▷**in·tri·cate·ly** [-li] *adv.*
—[形] 1. 복잡한, 난해한; 뒤얽힌

in·trigue [intrí:g] *vi.* **1.** carry on a secret plot. 《~ *with* someone》 **2.** have a secret love affair. —*vt.* excite the curiosity or interest of (someone). —*n.* **1.** [C] a secret plot. **2.** a secret love affair.
—[自] 1. 음모를 꾸미다 2. 간통하다
—[他] ⋯의 호기심(흥미)을 돋구다
—[名] 1. 음모 2. 간통

in·trin·sic [intrínsik] *adj.* belonging to a person or thing naturally; essential. ↔extrinsic
—[形] 본래 갖추어진; 본질적인

in·trin·si·cal·ly [intrínsikəli] *adv.* naturally; essentially.
—[副] 본래; 본질적으로

:in·tro·duce [ìntrəd(j)ú:s / -djú:s] *vt.* **1.** make (someone) known by name. 《~ someone *to*》 ¶~ *her into society*① / *Mrs. Brown, may I* ~ *Mr. Smith to you?* / *Let me* ~ *myself.* **2.** bring (something) into practice, use, notice, etc; offer (a new product) for sale. ¶~ *a new fashion*② / ~ *slang into a novel.* **3.** give (someone) experience or knowledge of something; lead. ¶*We introduced her to city life.*③ / *The teacher introduced the new pupils into their classroom.* **4.** bring (a subject, etc.) into conversation, etc.; bring forward. ¶~ *a bill into the Diet*④ / *A new subject was introduced for discussion.* **5.** put in; insert. ¶~ *a tube into her windpipe.* **6.** begin; open; start. ¶*He introduced his speech with an anecdote.*
—[他] 1. [남]을 [⋯에게] 소개하다 ¶①그녀를 사교계에 소개하다 2. ⋯을 도입하다, 들여 오다, 전하다; [새 제품]을 내 놓다 ¶②새 유행을 전하다 3. ⋯에게 경험시키다; ⋯을 이끌다, 알려주다 ¶③우리들은 그녀에게 도시 생활을 말해 주었다 4. [화제 따위]를 꺼내다; ⋯을 제출하다 ¶④국회에 의안을 제출하다 5. ⋯을 [⋯에] 끼워넣다, 넣다 6. ⋯을 시작하다

:in·tro·duc·tion [ìntrədʌ́kʃ(ə)n] *n.* **1.** [U] the act of introducing; the state of being introduced. **2.** [C] the first part of a book, speech, etc. leading up to the main part. **3.** [C] an elementary textbook. ¶*an* ~ *to science.*①
—[名] 1. 소개; 도입 2. 서문, 머리말 3. 입문[서] ¶①과학 입문

in·tro·duc·to·ry [ìntrədʌ́kt(ə)ri] *adj.* serving to introduce; beginning. ¶~ *remarks*① / *an* ~ *chapter.*②
—[形] 소개의, 머리말의, 준비의 ¶①서언, 머리말/②서설(序說)

in·tro·spec·tion [ìntrouspékʃ(ə)n] *n.* [U] the act of observing one's own mental processes.
—[名] 내성(內省), 자기 관찰

in·tro·spec·tive [ìntrouspéktiv] *adj.* of or inclined toward introspection.
—[形] 내성적인; 자기 관찰의

in·tro·vert *vt.* [ìntrouvə́:rt → *n.*] direct (one's own mind, thoughts, etc.) inward. —*n.* [íntrouvə̀:rt] [C] a person who introverts. ↔extrovert
—[他] [마음·생각 따위]를 안으로 향하게 하다 —[名] 내성적인 사람

·in·trude [intrú:d] *vt.* **1.** thrust. 《~ oneself *into*》 **2.** force. 《~ something or oneself *upon*》 —*vi.* force or thrust oneself. 《~ *into* something; ~ *upon* someone or something》
—[他] 1. ⋯을 밀어 넣다 2. ⋯을 억지로 강요하다 —[自] 밀고 들어가다; 침입하다; 훼방놓다

in·trud·er [intrú:dər] *n.* [C] a person who intrudes. —[名] 침입자, 주제넘은 사람

in·tru·sion [intrú:ʒ(ə)n] *n.* [U][C] the act of intruding. —[名] 강요; 침입

in·tru·sive [intrú:siv] *adj.* tending to intrude; intruding. —[形] 침입하는, 주제넘은

in·trust [intrʌ́st] *vt.* =entrust.

in·tu·i·tion [ìnt(j)u(:)íʃ(ə)n / -tju(:)-] *n.* **1.** [U] the power to perceive something immediately and without conscious thought. **2.** [C] something perceived or learned by this power. —[名] 1. 직각(直覺)[력], 직관[력] 2. 직관적 지식

in·tu·i·tive [int(j)ú(:)itiv / -tjú(:)-] *adj.* of intuition; having intuition; perceived by instinct. ▷**in·tu·i·tive·ly** [-li] *adv.* —[形] 직각(直覺)의, 직각적인; 직각력이 풍부한, 직관에 의한

in·un·date [ínʌndèit] *vt.* flood; cover (a place) as with a flood. —[他] …을 물에 잠기게 하다; …에 범람하다

in·un·da·tion [ìnʌndéiʃ(ə)n] *n.* [U][C] the act of inundating; a flood. —[名] 범람; 홍수

in·ure [in(j)úər / -njúə] *vt.* accustom; make (something) tough. 《~ someone or oneself *to*》 ¶*be inured to hardship.* —*vi.* be useful. ▷**in·ure·ment** [-mənt] *n.* —[他] …을 익숙하게 하다; …을 단련하다 ¶①고생에 익숙해 있다 —[自] 쓸모가 있다

‡in·vade [invéid] *vt.* **1.** enter (a country, etc.) to attack it. **2.** violate. ¶*~ the rights of others.* —[他] 1. …을 침략하다, 습격하다 2. …을 침해하다

in·vad·er [invéidər] *n.* [C] a person or thing that invades. —[名] 침략자, 침입자(물)

***in·va·lid**[1] [ínvəlid / -lì(:)d → *v.*] *adj.* **1.** not strong or healthy; weak. **2.** of or for a sick person. —*n.* [C] a sick or weak person. —[形] 1. 병약한 2. 환자용의 —[名] 환자, 병자

—*v.* [*Brit.* ìnvəlí:d] *vt.* **1.** make (someone) an invalid. **2.** treat (someone) as a sick person. —*vi.* become an invalid. —[他] 1. …을 병약하게 하다 2. …을 환자로 취급하다 —[自] 병약해지다

in·val·id[2] [invǽlid] *adj.* not valid; having no value or force. —[形] 가치 없는; 효력이 없는

in·val·i·date [invǽlidèit] *vt.* make (something) valueless or ineffective. —[他] …을 무효로 하다

in·va·lid·i·ty [ìnvəlíditi] *n.* [U] lack of validity. —[名] 무효

in·val·u·a·ble [invǽljuəbl] *adj.* very valuable; very precious; priceless. ↔valueless —[形] 아주 귀중한

***in·var·i·a·ble** [invέəriəbl] *adj.* never changing. —[形] 불변의

***in·var·i·a·bly** [invέəriəbli] *adv.* in an invariable manner; without change; always. —[副] 변함없이, 늘, 반드시

***in·va·sion** [invéiʒ(ə)n] *n.* [U][C] the act of invading; the state of being invaded. —[名] 침략; 침해

in·vec·tive [invéktiv] *n.* **1.** [U] the act of attacking violently in words. **2.** [C] 《often *pl.*》 violent words; curses. —[名] 1. 욕설, 악담 2. 욕설의 말

in·veigh [invéi] *vi.* attack violently in words. 《~ *against* someone or something》 —[自] 욕설을 퍼붓다, 통렬히 비난하다

in·vei·gle [inví:gl, -véi-] *vt.* trick; deceive; allure. 《~ someone *into* or *out of*》 —[他] …을 속이다, 유혹하다, 꾀다

‡in·vent [invént] *vt.* **1.** think out; find out; devise. ¶*Marconi invented the radio.* **2.** make up. ¶*~ an excuse.*① —[他] 1. …을 발명하다 2. …을 날조하다 ¶①구실을 꾸미다

‡in·ven·tion [invénʃ(ə)n] *n.* **1.** [U] the act of inventing. ¶*the ~ of the steam engine.* **2.** [U] the power of inventing. ¶(*proverb*) *Necessity is the mother of ~.*① **3.** [C] something invented. ¶*Television is a wonderful ~.* **4.** [C] something made up; a false statement; a lie. ¶*an ~ of a weekly magazine.*② —[名] 1. 발명 2. 발명의 재능 ¶①필요는 발명의 어머니 3. 발명품 4. 꾸며낸 이야기 ¶②주간지의 날조 기사

in·ven·tive [invéntiv] *adj.* of invention; that can invent; creative. —[形] 발명의; 발명력이 있는

‡in·ven·tor [invéntər] *n.* [C] a person who invents. —[名] 발명가(자)

in·ven·to·ry [ínvəntɔ̀:ri / -tri] *n.* [C] (pl. **-ries**) a detailed list of goods, furniture, etc.; the goods on such a list. —*vt.* make an inventory of (things). —[名] [상품·가재도구 따위의] 명세목록; 목록 속의 물품 —[他] [물품]을 목록으로 만들다

in·verse [invə́:rs] *adj.* opposite. —*n.* [U] the direct opposite. —[形] 반대의; 거꾸로의 —[名] 반대[의 것]

in·verse·ly [invə́:rsli] *adv.* in an inverse manner. —[副] 반대로, 거꾸로

in·ver·sion [invə́:rʒ(ə)n, -ʃ(ə)n / invə́:ʃ(ə)n] *n.* **1.** [U] the act of inverting; the state of being inverted. **2.** [C] something inverted. —[名] 1. 반대, 전도(轉倒) 2. 반대의(전도한) 것

in·vert [invə́:rt] *vt.* change (something) to its direct opposite; turn upside down. —[他] …을 전도시키다; 반대로 하다

in·ver·te·brate [invə́:rtibrit, -brèit] *adj.* **1.** (of animals) having no backbone. **2.** weak-willed. —*n.* [C] an invertebrate animal. —[形] 1. 척추가 없는 2. 우유부단한 —[名] 무척추 동물

* **in·vest** [invést] *vt.* **1.** put (money) into a business for profit. **2.** clothe; cover; surround; envelop. **3.** install (someone) in office with a ceremony. **4.** furnish (someone) with power, privilege or authority. —*vi.* invest money. 《~ *in* something》 ¶~ *heavily in a business.*
—[他] 1. [금전]을 투자하다 2. …에게 입히다, …을 싸다, 둘러싸다, 덮다 3. …을 임명하다 4. …에게 권리(특권·권위)를 주다 —[自] 투자하다

* **in·ves·ti·gate** [invéstigèit] *vt., vi.* examine carefully.
—[他][自] 조사하다, 연구하다

* **in·ves·ti·ga·tion** [invèstigéiʃ(ə)n] *n.* [U][C] the act of investigating; careful examination. ¶*on* ~① / *under* ~.②
—[名] 조사, 연구 ¶①조사의 결과/②조사중

in·ves·ti·ga·tive [invéstigeitiv] *adj.* of investigation; inclined to investigate.
—[形] 조사의, 취조의, 꼬치꼬치 캐기 좋아하는

in·ves·ti·ga·tor [invéstigèitər] *n.* [C] a person who investigates.
—[名] 조사자, 연구자

in·ves·ti·ture [invéstitʃər] *n.* **1.** [U] the act or ceremony of investing a person with an office, a title, etc. **2.** [C] a thing that covers, clothes, etc.
—[名] 1. 서임(敍任); 임명; 임명식 2. 덮는 것, 싸는 것

* **in·vest·ment** [invés(t)mənt] *n.* **1.** [U] the act of investing money. **2.** [C] a sum of money invested. **3.** [C] something in which money is invested.
—[名] 1. 투자 2. 투하 자본, 투자금 3. 투자 대상

in·ves·tor [invéstər] *n.* [C] a person who invests money.
—[名] 투자자

in·vet·er·ate [invét(ə)rit] *adj.* deep-rooted; habitual.
—[形] 뿌리 깊은; 상습적인

in·vid·i·ous [invídiəs] *adj.* likely to arouse ill-will or envy.
—[形] 불쾌한, 남의 시기를 받게 되는

in·vig·or·ate [invígərèit] *vt.* give vigor or strength to (someone); animate.
—[他] …을 기운내게 하다, …을 격려하다

in·vin·ci·bil·i·ty [invìnsibíliti] *n.* [U] the state of being invincible.
—[名] 이길 수 없음; 무적(無敵)

in·vin·ci·ble [invínsibl] *adj.* that cannot be conquered or overcome; unconquerable.
—[形] 이길 수 없는, 정복할 수 없는; 무적의

in·vi·o·la·bil·i·ty [invàiələbíliti] *n.* [U] the state of being inviolable.
—[名] 불가침[성]

in·vi·o·la·ble [inváiələbl] *adj.* that cannot be injured, violated or broken; sacred.
—[形] 불가침의; 신성한; 깨뜨릴 수 없는

in·vi·o·late [inváiəlit] *adj.* uninjured; not violated or broken; kept sacred.
—[形] 침범당하지 않은; 신성한, 모독당하지 않은

in·vis·i·bil·i·ty [invìzibíliti] *n.* [U] the state of being invisible.
—[名] 보이지 않음

* **in·vis·i·ble** [invízibl] *adj.* that cannot be seen; out of sight. ¶~ *to the naked eye.*① —*n.* 《*the* ~》 **1.** that which cannot be seen. **2.** the unseen or spiritual world.
—[形] 눈에 보이지(띄지) 않는 ¶①육안으로 보이지 않는 —[名] 1. 보이지 않는 것 2. 영계(靈界)

in·vis·i·bly [invízibli] *adv.* in an invisible manner; without being seen.
—[副] 눈에 보이지 않게

‡ **in·vi·ta·tion** [ìnvitéiʃ(ə)n] *n.* **1.** [U][C] the act of inviting. **2.** [C] a written letter, etc. inviting someone to a party, etc. **3.** [U][C] attraction; temptation.
—[名] 1. 초대, 안내 2. 초대장, 안내장 3. 사람의 마음을 끌기; 유혹, 권유

‡ **in·vite** [inváit] *vt.* **1.** ask (someone) politely to do something or to come somewhere. **2.** ask for; request. 《~ someone *to do*》 **3.** bring on. ¶*That invited the unhappy war.*① **4.** attract. ¶*The sea invites us to swim.* —*vi.* give an invitation.
—[他] 1. [남]을 부르다, 초대하다 2. [남]에게 …하도록 부탁하다 3. …을 유발(야기)하다 ¶①그것이 불행한 전쟁을 야기했다 4. 매혹하다 —[自] 초래하다

in·vit·ing [inváitiŋ] *adj.* of an agreeable nature; attractive.
—[形] 사람을 끄는, 유혹적인

in·vo·ca·tion [ìnvoukéiʃ(ə)n] *n.* [U][C] **1.** the act of calling upon God, a spirit, etc. in a prayer. **2.** the act of calling forth an evil spirit.
—[名] 1. [신·성령에게 구원을 비는] 기도 2. 악령을 부르는 기도

in·voice [ínvɔis] *n.* [C] a list of goods sent to a purchaser with details of prices, quantity, charges, etc. —*vt.* make an invoice of (goods).
—[名] 송장(送狀) —[他] [상품]의 송장을 만들다

* **in·voke** [invóuk] *vt.* **1.** call for (help, protection, etc.) in prayer. ¶~ *God's blessing.*① **2.** ask for (something) earnestly. ¶~ *the protection of the law.*② **3.** call forth (evil spirits, etc.) by magic.
—[他] 1. [신의 도움을] 빌다 ¶①신의 축복을 기구하다 2. …을 간청하다 ¶②법률의 보호를 간구하다 3. …을 주문(呪文)으로 불러내다

in·vol·un·tar·i·ly [inváləntèrili / -vɔ́lənt(ə)ri-] *adv.* in an involuntary manner; without a deliberate exercise of the will.
—[副] 무의식적으로; 자기도 모르게

in·vol·un·tar·y [inválәntèri / -vɔ́lənt(ə)-] *adj.* **1.** done without meaning to do so; unintentional. ¶*an ~ action.*① **2.** against one's will. ¶~ *consent.*②
—[形] 1. 무의식중의, 부지불식간의 ¶①무의식적인 행위 2. 본의 아닌 ¶②마지못해 하는 동의

* **in·volve** [inválv / -vɔ́lv] *vt.* **1.** cause (someone) to be unpleasantly concerned with; bring (someone or some-
—[他] 1. …을 [재난·위협 따위]에 끌어 넣다 ¶①그는 빚으로 꼼짝 못한다

thing) into difficulty, danger, etc. ¶*He is involved in debts.*① **2.** include (something) as a necessary condition or consequence; imply. ¶*Success always involves effort.*② **3.** ⟪chiefly in *passive*⟫ take up the attention of (someone); engage completely. ¶*be involved in working out a crossword puzzle.*③ **4.** wrap up; enfold; envelop. **5.** bring (something) into a complicated form or condition. ¶*an involved expression.*④
2. …을 [필연적으로] 포함하다 ¶②성공에는 노력이 필요하다 3. …을 열중시키다 ¶③크로스워어드 퍼즐을 푸는데에 열중하고 있다 4. …을 싸다, 감다 5. …을 복잡하게 하다 ¶④복잡한 표현

in·volve·ment [inválvmənt / -vɔ́l-] *n.* [U][C] the act of involving; the state of being involved.
—[名] 끌어넣기, 끌려 들어가기; 연루(連累); 개입; 연좌; 성가심

in·vul·ner·a·ble [invʌ́ln(ə)rəbl] *adj.* **1.** that cannot be injured; unconquerable. **2.** that cannot be answered or refuted. ¶*an ~ opinion.*①
—[形] 1. 상처를 입힐 수 없는, 이길 수 없는 2. 설파(說破)할 수 없는 ¶①반박 못하는 의견

***in·ward** [ínwərd] *adj.* ↔outward **1.** placed within; internal. ¶*~ organs.*① **2.** directed toward the inside or center. ¶*an ~ voyage.*② **3.** of the inner self; spiritual. ¶*~ happiness.*③ **4.** low; muffled. ¶*an ~ voice.*④
—[形] 1. 내부의 ¶①내장 2. 안으로 향하는 ¶②귀항(歸航) 3. 내적(內的)인, 정신적인 ¶③마음의 평화 4. [목소리 따위가] 낮은 ¶④낮은 목소리
—*adv.* **1.** toward the inside. **2.** into the spirit or mind.
—[副] 1. 안쪽으로 2. 마음 속에서

in·ward·ly [ínwərdli] *adv.* **1.** on or toward the inside. **2.** in the mind. **3.** secretly. **4.** in low tones.
—[副] 1. 내부(안쪽)로 2. 마음속에서 3. 몰래 4. 낮은 소리로

in·wards [ínwərdz] *adv.* =inward.

i·o·dine [áioudàin, -din, +*Brit.* -di:n] *n.* [U] a nonmetallic element found in seaweed.
—[名] 옥소(沃素), 옥도

I·on·ic [aiánik / aiɔ́nik] *adj.* **1.** of Ionia or its people. **2.** (*Architecture*) one of the classical orders of Greek architecture. —*n.* [U] the Ionian language.
—[形] 1. 이오니아의, 이오니아 사람의 2. 이오니아식의 —[名] 이오니아 말

I.O.U., IOU [áiòujú] *n.* [C] (pl. **IOUs, IOU's, I.O.U.s, I.O.U.'s**) a note showing a debt, esp. an informal one.
—[名] 차용증(I owe you.의 발음을 딴 약자)

I·o·wa [áiəwə, +*Brit.* áiouə] *n.* a state in the central United States.
—[名] [미국의] 아이오와 주

ir- [i, ir] *pref.* a form of in- before *r.*: *irresistable; irradiate.*

I·ran [irǽn, irá:n / irá:n] *n.* a country in southwest Asia; Persia.
—[名] 이란(서남 아시아의 왕국)

i·ras·ci·bil·i·ty [iræ̀sibíliti, aiəræ̀s-] *n.* [U] the quality or state of being irascible; quickness of temper.
—[名] 성 잘 내는 기질, 성미 급한

i·ras·ci·ble [irǽsibl, aiərǽs-] *adj.* easily angered; quick-tempered.
—[形] 성 잘 내는, 성미 급한

i·rate [áireit ⸗ˊ / ⸗ˊ] *adj.* angry; furious.
—[形] 성난

ire [éiər] *n.* [U] (*poetic*) anger.
—[名] 노여움, 화

***Ire·land** [áiərlənd] *n.* **1.** the large western island of the British Isles. **2.** **,the Republic of** a country in central and southern Ireland. ⇒[N.B.]
—[名] 1. 아일란드 2. 아일란드 공화국 [N.B.] Irish Republic, Eire로도 씀. 수도 Dublin

ir·i·des·cence [iridésns] *n.* [U] the state or quality of being iridescent; a many-colored appearance.
—[名] 무지개빛, 진주빛

i·ri·des [áiəridi:z] *n.* pl. of **iris**.

ir·i·des·cent [iridésnt] *adj.* showing rainbowlike colors as an opal; changing in color when light comes from different angles.
—[形] 무지개빛의, 진주 광택의

i·rid·i·um [irídiəm, airíd-] *n.* [U] a precious metalic element resembling platinum.
—[名] 이리듐

i·ris [áiəris] *n.* [C] (pl. **i·ris·es** or **i·ri·des**) **1.** the colored part of the eye around the pupil. **2.** a plant with large flowers and sword-shaped leaves. ⇒fig. **3.** a rainbow.
—[名] 1. [안구(眼球)의] 홍채(虹彩) 2. 붓꽃 3. 무지개

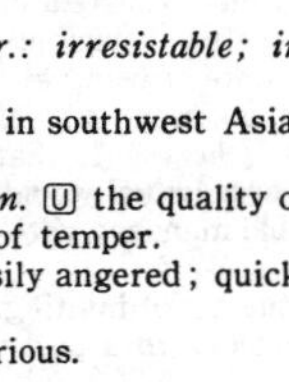
[iris 2.]

***I·rish** [áiəriʃ] *n.* [U] **1.** ⟪*the ~*⟫ the people of Ireland. **2.** the language spoken in Ireland. —*adj.* of Ireland or the Irish.
—[名] 1. 아일란드 사람 2. 아일란드 말 —[形] 아일란드[사람·말]의

I·rish·man [áiəriʃmən] *n.* [C] (pl. **-men** [-mən]) a person of Ireland; a man born in Ireland or of Irish descent.
—[名] 아일란드 사람

Irish potato [⸗ˊ⸗ˊ⸗] *n.* the common potato.
—[名] 감자

I·rish·wom·an [áiəriʃwùmən] *n.* ⓒ (pl. **-wom·en** [-wìːmin]) a woman born in Ireland or of Irish descent. — ㊁ 아일란드의 여성

irk [əːrk] *vt.* irritate; annoy. ¶*It irked him to wait.* — ㊀ …을 지루하게 하다

irk·some [ə́ːrksəm] *adj.* so dull as to cause weariness; tedious. — ㊁ 싫증나는, 지루한

:i·ron [áiərn] *n.* **1.** ⓤ a very common hard metal, from which tools, machines, etc. are made. ¶*cast ~*① / *sheet ~*. **2.** ⓒ a tool, an instrument or a weapon made from this metal. ¶*a soldering ~.*② **3.** ⓒ an instrument made of iron or steel for smoothing or pressing clothes. ¶*an electric ~*. **4.** ⓒ a golf club with a metal head. **5.** (*pl.*) bands and chains for a prisoner's hands and feet. ¶*The prisoners were put in irons.*③ **6.** ⓤ strength; hardness. ¶*a man of ~*④
— ㊁ 1. 쇠, 철 ¶①주철(鑄鐵) 2. 철제 기구 ¶②땜질 인두 3. 다리미 4. 쇠머리 골프채 5. 족쇄, 수갑 ¶③죄수들은 족쇄를 차고 있었다 6. 강력, 단단함 ¶④의지가 강한 사람

1) ***have* [*too*] *many irons in the fire*,** be trying to do [too] many things at once.
2) ***rule with a rod of iron,*** (*Bible*) control very firmly.
3) ***Strike while the iron is hot.,*** (*proverb*) do something at exactly the right moment.
圜 1)한꺼번에 여러가지 일에 손대다 2)《聖》압제를 펴다 3)《俚》좋은 기회는 놓치지 말라

— *adj.* **1.** of or made of iron. ¶*an ~ gate.* **2.** like iron; strong; firm. ¶*~ muscles* / *an ~ will.* **3.** cruel; severe. ¶*the ~ hand of war.*⑤
— ㊁ 1. 쇠의,철제의 2.쇠 같은, 불굴의 3. 냉혹한,엄한 ¶⑤전쟁의 냉혹한 손 길

— *vt.* **1.** press (clothes, etc.) with a hot iron. ¶*Mother irons the clothes.* **2.** cover or furnish (something) with *iron out,* smooth away; remove. ⌊iron.⌋
— ㊁ 1. …에 다리미질을 하다 2. …에 쇠를 씌우다
圜 …을 없애다,해결하다

i·ron·clad [áiərnklæ̀d] *adj.* **1.** (of warships, etc.) covered or protected with iron plates. **2.** (*U.S.*) unbreakable. ¶*an ~ agreement.* — *n.* ⓒ a warship protected with iron plates. ⇒[NB].⌊of freshly-broken-iron.⌋
— ㊁ 1. 장갑(裝甲)의 2.《美》논파할 수 없는; 엄한 — ㊁ 장갑함 [NB] 19세기의 용어

i·ron-gray, *Brit.* **-grey** [áiərngréi] *adj.* having the color
— ㊁ 철회색(鐵灰色)의

i·ron·ic [airánik / -rɔ́n-], **-i·cal** [-k(ə)l] *adj.* **1.** expressing the opposite of what one really means; of irony. ¶*an ~ person.*① **2.** contrary to what was, or might be, expected. ¶*by an ~ chance.*②
— ㊁ 1. 비꼬는, 빈정대는; 반어적인 ¶①비꼬는 사람 2. 엉뚱한 ¶②엉뚱하게도

i·ron·i·cal·ly [airánikəli / -rɔ́n-] *adv.* in an ironical manner. ⌈with a heated iron.⌋
— ㊁ 빈정대어; 반어적으로

i·ron·ing [áiərniŋ] *n.* ⓤ the act of pressing (clothes, etc.)
— ㊁ 다리미질

iron lung [⌴ ⌴] *n.* a device by which artificial respiration is given to a patient. ⇒fig.
— ㊁ 철폐(鐵肺)

i·ron·mon·ger [áiərnmʌ̀ŋgər] *n.* ⓒ (chiefly *Brit.*) a dealer in hardware.
— ㊁ 철물상

i·ron·ware [áiərnwɛ̀ər] *n.* ⓤ articles made of iron; hardware.
— ㊁ 철물, 철기

i·ron·work [áiərnwə̀ːrk] *n.* ⓤ things or parts of a thing made of iron. [iron lung]
— ㊁ 철제품, 철제부분

i·ron·works [áiərnwə̀ːrks] *n. pl.* (used as *sing.* and *pl.*) a place where iron is made or worked into iron articles.
— ㊁ 제철소, 철공소

i·ro·ny [áiərəni] *n.* ⓤⓒ (pl. **-nies**) **1.** a way of expressing the direct opposite of the thought in the speaker's mind. **2.** an event or a situation contrary to what was intended or expected. ¶*an ~ of fate*① / *life's ironies.*②
— ㊁ 1. 반어(反語), 비꼬기 2. [사건·운명의] 뜻밖의 결과 ¶①운명의 장난 /②인생의 장난

ir·ra·di·ate [iréidièit] *vt.* **1.** direct light upon (something); illuminate. **2.** brighten (something) as if with light. ¶*a face irradiated by a smile.*① **3.** treat (something) by exposing it to X-rays, ultraviolet rays, etc.
— ㊁ 1. …을 비추다 2. …을 밝히다; [기쁨으로] …을 환하게 하다 ¶①미소를 함빡 담은 얼굴 3. …을 X선(자외선)으로 조사(照射)하다

ir·ra·di·a·tion [irèidiéiʃ(ə)n] *n.* ⓤⓒ **1.** the act of irradiating; the state of being irradiated. **2.** a ray of light.
— ㊁ 1. 비추기 2. 광선

ir·ra·tion·al [irǽʃən(ə)l] *adj.* **1.** contrary to reason; unreasonable; absurd. ¶*an ~ fear.*① **2.** without reasoning powers. ¶*an ~ animal.*
— ㊁ 1. 불합리한, 어리석은 ¶①까닭없는 공포 2. 이성(理性)이 없는

ir·ra·tion·al·ly [irǽʃənəli] *adv.* in an irrational manner.
— ㊁ 불합리하게, 이성을 잃고

ir·re·claim·a·ble [irikléiməbl] *adj.* that cannot be reclaimed or reformed.
— ㊁ 돌이킬 수 없는

ir·rec·on·cil·a·ble [irékənsàiləbl] *adj.* that cannot be brought into harmony; opposed. —*n.* [C] a person who remains opposed to agreement. —[형] 조화하지 않는, 모순된 —[명] 비타협파의 사람

ir·re·cov·er·a·ble [ìrikʌ́v(ə)rəbl] *adj.* that cannot be recovered or remedied. —[형] 돌이킬 수 없는; 불치의, 고칠 수 없는

ir·re·deem·a·ble [ìridí:məbl] *adj.* **1.** that cannot be bought back. **2.** that cannot be exchanged for coins. ¶~ *paper money.*① **3.** hopeless; having no remedy. ▷**ir·re·deem·a·bly** [-i] *adv.* —[형] 1. 다시 살 수 없는 2. 태환(兌換)할 수 없는 ¶①불환 지폐 3. 가망 없는; 고칠 수 없는

ir·re·du·ci·ble [ìrid(j)ú:sibl / -djú:-] *adj.* that cannot be reduced. —[형] 삭감할 수 없는

ir·ref·ra·ga·ble [iréfrəgəbl] *adj.* that cannot be denied or disproved. —[형] 논박할 수 없는; 부정할 수 없는

ir·ref·u·ta·ble [iréfjutəbl / ìrifú:t-] *adj.* that cannot be refuted or disproved. —[형] 논박(반박)할 수 없는

***ir·reg·u·lar** [irégjulər] *adj.* **1.** not following rules; out of the proper order. ¶*at ~ intervals*① / *~ attendance.*② **2.** uneven; not symmetrical. ¶*an ~ group of trees.*③ —[형] 1. 불규칙한 ¶①불규칙한 간격을 두고서/②불규칙한 출석 2. 고르지 못한 ¶③난립한 나무숲

ir·reg·u·lar·i·ty [irègjulǽriti] *n.* (pl. **-ties**) **1.** [U] the state of being irregular. **2.** [C] an irregular act or thing. —[명] 1. 불규칙; 고르지 못함 2. 불규칙한(고르지 못한) 것(행위)

ir·rel·e·vant [irélivənt] *adj.* having no connection with the subject at hand; not to the point. —[형] 대중이 틀리는, 엉뚱한

ir·re·li·gious [ìrilídʒəs] *adj.* not religious; without respect for religion. —[형] 종교 없는; 무신앙의; 불경(不敬)한

ir·re·me·di·a·ble [ìrimí:diəbl] *adj.* that cannot be cured or repaired. —[형] 불치의, 고칠 수 없는

ir·rep·a·ra·ble [irép(ə)rəbl] *adj.* that cannot be repaired or restored. —[형] 고칠 수 없는; 불치의

ir·re·pres·si·ble [ìriprésibl] *adj.* that cannot be repressed or held back. —[형] 누를 수 없는, 힘에 겨운

ir·re·proach·a·ble [ìripróutʃəbl] *adj.* free from blame or fault; blameless; faultless. —[형] 결점이 없는, 말할 나위 없는

ir·re·sist·i·ble [ìrizístibl] *adj.* too great or strong to be resisted; overwhelming; very convincing. —[형] 저항할 수 없는, 억누를 수 없는, 아주 그럴 듯한

ir·res·o·lute [irézəlù:t] *adj.* not resolute; undecided. —[형] 결단력이 없는

ir·res·o·lu·tion [irèzəlú:ʃ(ə)n] *n.* [U] the state of being irresolute or undecided. —[명] 우유부단

ir·re·spec·tive [ìrispéktiv] *adj.* regardless. ⦅~ *of*⦆ ¶~ *of sex or age.*① —[형] …와 관계 없는 ¶①남녀노소를 불문하고

ir·re·spon·si·bil·i·ty [ìrispɑ̀nsibíliti / -pɔ̀n-] *n.* [U] the state of being irresponsible. —[명] 무책임

ir·re·spon·si·ble [ìrispɑ́nsibl / -pɔ́n-] *adj.* **1.** not responsible. **2.** that cannot be depended on. —[형] 1. 책임감이 없는 2. 믿을 수 없는

ir·re·triev·a·ble [ìritrí:vəbl] *adj.* that cannot be recovered; irreparable. —[형] 돌이킬 수 없는

ir·rev·er·ence [irév(ə)rəns] *n.* **1.** [U] the state of being irreverent. **2.** [C] an act or speech showing lack of respect. —[명] 1. 불경(不敬) 2. 불손한 언행

ir·rev·er·ent [irév(ə)rənt] *adj.* showing no respect; disrespectful. —[형] 불경한, 불손한

ir·re·vers·i·ble [ìrivə́:rsibl] *adj.* that cannot be reversed or turned inside out. —[형] 거꾸로 할 수 없는; 뒤집을 수 없는

ir·rev·o·ca·ble [irévəkəbl] *adj.* that cannot be recalled or undone; not alterable. —[형] 되불러 올 수 없는, 취소(변경)할 수 없는

ir·ri·gate [írigèit] *vt.* **1.** supply (land) with water for crops from artificial ditches. **2.** (*Medicine*) wash out (a wound, etc.) with a flow of some liquid. —[타] 1. [토지]를 관개(灌漑)하다 2. [상처]를 씻다, 세척하다

ir·ri·ga·tion [ìrigéiʃ(ə)n] *n.* [U][C] the act of irrigating; the state of being irrigated. —[명] 관개; 세척

ir·ri·ta·bil·i·ty [ìritəbíliti] *n.* [U] **1.** the quality or state of being irritable. **2.** the quality of being excitable by some stimulus. —[명] 1. 성마름, 성급함 2. 감수성, 흥분성

ir·ri·ta·ble [íritəbl] *adj.* **1.** easily excited to anger. **2.** extremely sensitive. —[형] 1. 성 잘 내는 2. 감각이 예민한

ir·ri·tant [írit(ə)nt] *adj.* causing irritation. —*n.* [C] something that irritates or excites. —[형] 자극하는, 자극적인 —[명] 자극물, 자극제

***ir·ri·tate** [íritèit] *vt.* **1.** make impatient or angry. ¶*be irritated to be kept waiting long.* **2.** cause (a part of the body) to be sore. —[타] 1. …을 짜증나게 하다 2. …을 열열하게 하다, …에 염증을 일으키다

ir·ri·ta·tion [ìritéiʃ(ə)n] *n.* [U][C] the act of irritating; the state of being irritated. —[명] 짜증나게 하기, 성내게 하기; 자극; 초조; 흥분

ir·rup·tion [irʌ́pʃ(ə)n] *n.* [U][C] the act of breaking or rushing in. —[名] 돌입, 침입

Ir·ving [ə́:rviŋ], **Washington** *n.* (1783–1859) an American story writer. —[名] 미국의 소설가

⁑**is** [iz] *vi.* third person, singular, present indicative of **be**.

-ish [-iʃ] *suf.* **1.** somewhat; rather: *oldish* (=somewhat old) / *reddish* (=somewhat red) **2.** having the nature of; like: *boyish* (=having the nature of a boy) —《接尾》 1. … 기미의 2. … 같은

Is·lam [ísləm, íz-, +*Brit.* ízlɑ:m] *n.* [U] **1.** the religion of the Moslems; Mohammedanism. **2.** 《*collectively*》 Mohammedans as a group. **3.** the Mohammedan countries or region. —[名] 1 회교, 마호멧교 2. 회교도 3 회교국; 회교권

⁑**is·land** [áilənd] *n.* [C] **1.** a piece of land surrounded by water. **2.** something like an island. ¶*safety islands in the street.*① —[名] 1. 섬 2. 섬 비슷한 것 ¶①[거리의] 안전 지대

is·land·er [áiləndər] *n.* [C] a person who is living on an island. —[名] 섬사람, 도민

⁑**isle** [ail] *n.* [C] a small island; an island. —[名] 작은 섬; 섬

is·let [áilet, -lit] *n.* [C] a small island. —[名] 작은 섬

ism [íz(ə)m] *n.* [C] a distinctive doctrine; a theory. —[名] 주의(主義)

-ism [-ìz(ə)m] *suf.* **1.** doctrine; principle: *socialism* (=socialist doctrine). **2.** action; practice. —《接尾》 1. …주의, …설 2. 행위, 상태

⁑**is·n't** [íznt] is not.

i·so·bar [áisoubɑ̀:r] *n.* [C] (of a weather map) a line that connects places having the same air pressure. —[名] [기상도의] 등압선

***i·so·late** [áisoulèit] *vt.* put apart or alone; separate (something or someone) from others. —[他] …을 격리(분리)하다, 고립시키다

i·so·lat·ed [áisoulèitid] *adj.* alone; separated. —[形] 고립한, 격리된

i·so·la·tion [àisouléiʃ(ə)n] *n.* [U] the act of putting apart; the state of being put apart; loneliness. —[名] 격리, 분리

i·so·la·tion·ism [àisouléiʃ(ə)nìz(ə)m] *n.* [U] (of politics, etc.) the principle of keeping out of the affairs of other countries. —[名] [정치적인] 고립주의

i·so·la·tion·ist [àisouléiʃ(ə)nist] *n.* [C] a supporter of the principle of keeping out of the affairs of other countries. —[名] 고립주의자

i·so·therm [áisouθə̀:rm] *n.* [C] (of a weather map) a line that connects places having the same average temperature. —[名] 등온선(等溫線)

i·so·ther·mal [àisouθə́:rm(ə)l] *adj.* of equality of temperatures. —[形] 등온[선]의

i·so·tope [áisoutòup] *n.* [C] an atom which is of the same chemical element as another, but has a different form. —[名] 동위 원소

Is·ra·el [ízriəl, -reiəl] *n.* **1.** 《*collectively*》 the Jews; the Jewish people. **2.** a modern country in theMiddle East; the Republic of Israel. ⇒[N.B.] —[名] 1. 이스라엘 민족, 유대 사람 2. 이스라엘 공화국 [N.B.] 수도 Jerusalem

***is·sue** [íʃu: / ísju:, íʃu:] *n.* **1.** [U][C] the act of passing or flowing out. ¶*the ~ of blood from a wound.*① **2.** [C] a thing comes, flows, or is sent out. ¶*be buried under the ~ from the volcano.*② **3.** [C] exit; the mouth of a river. **4.** [U][C] the act of publishing or distributing. ¶*the ~ of money / on the day of ~.*③ **5.** [C] that which is published or printed, usu. as a part of a series. ¶*the October ~ of Reader's Digest / the next ~ of a newspaper.*④ **6.** [C] a point or subject of argument, discussion, etc.; an important problem. ¶*raise a new ~.* **7.** [C] a result; a conclusion; an end. ¶*the ~ of a fight.*⑤ **8.** [U][C] profits of an enterprise, etc. ¶*the ~ of an estate.* **9.** [U] children.
—[名] 1. 유출 ¶①상처에서의 출혈 2. 유출물 ¶②화산의 분출물로 덮뒤이다 3. 출구; 강 어귀 4. 발행; 발포(發布) ¶③발행일에 5. 발행물; 인쇄물 ¶④신문의 다음 호 6. 쟁점; 문제 7. 결과, 결말 ¶⑤싸움의 결말 8. [사업·재산 따위에서 생기는] 이익 9. 자식, 자손

1) ***at issue,*** under discussion. ¶*the point at ~.*⑥
2) ***bring*** (or ***put***) ***a matter to an issue,*** cause a matter to reach the point where a decision can and must be made.
3) ***join issue*** (=*enter into an argument*) ***with*** *someone.*
4) ***take issue*** (=*disagree*) ***with*** *someone.*

[熟] 1)논쟁중인 ¶⑥쟁점(爭點) 2)[일]의 결말을 짓다 3)…와 논쟁하다 4) …에 반대하다

—*vi.* **1.** go or come out; flow out. 《~ *from* something》 ¶*The smoke issued from the chimney in rolling*
—[自] 1. 나오다, 유출하다 ¶⑦연기가 굴뚝에서 뭉게뭉게 나왔다 2. 발행되

*clouds.*⑦ **2.** be published. ¶*a magazine which is issued once a month.* **3.** come to an end; result. 《~ *in* something》 ¶*The game issued in a tie.*⑧ **—*vt.*** **1.** give (something) to the public; publish; send out; put forth. ¶~*a newspaper* / ~ *money and stamps.*⑨ **2.** supply (clothing, food, etc.) ¶~ *clothing to recruits.*

다 **3.** 결과가 …이 되다 ¶⑧시합은 무승부로 끝났다 —[他] **1.** …을 발행하다; …을 유포하다 ¶⑨화폐와 우표를 발행하다 **2.** [의류 따위]를 지급하다

-ist [-ist] *suf.* **1.** a person who does something. **2.** a person who is skilled in or knows well about some subject. **3.** a person who is occupied with something.

—《接尾》 **1.** …을 하는 사람 **2.** …가(家) **3.** …주의자

Is·tan·bul [ìstænbú:l] *n.* a city of Turkey.

—[名] 터어키의 도시

isth·mi [ísmai] *n.* pl. of **isthmus**.

* **isth·mus** [ísməs] *n.* [C] (pl. **-muses** [-məsiz] or **-mi**) a narrow neck of land joining two large bodies of land.

—[名] 지협(地峽)

⁑ **it** [it] *pron.* (pl. **they**) **1.** anything, except a person, already spoken about. ¶*I wrote a letter and sent it.* / *What is this?—It is a book.* / *She is beautiful, and she knows* ~.① **2.** a baby; a person whose sex is not known. ¶*The baby cried for its bottle.* / *Go and see who* ~ *is.*② / "*Who is that?*" "*It's a friend of mine.*" **3.** 《as the *subject* of an *impersonal verb* ⇒[usage]》 ¶*It snowed.* / *It grew dark.* / *It is four in the morning.* / *It is fifty feet to the filling station.* **4.** 《as a *formal subject* or a *formal object.* ⇒[usage]》 ¶*It is certain that he will succeed.* / *I found* ~ *impossible to sleep.* **5.** 《*It is* (or *It was*) … *that* (or *who, whom, which*) ⇒[usage]》 *It is you that are responsible.*③ / *It was yesterday that he broke the window.* **6.** 《*idiomatically*》 ¶*Cut* ~ *out.*④ / *Stick to* ~.⑤ / *lord* ~ *over*⑥ / *brave* ~ *out.*⑦

—[代] **1.** 그것은(이); 그것을(에게) ¶①그녀는 아름답고 또 그녀는 그것을 알고 있다 **2.** 어린애; 성별(性別)을 모르는 것 ¶②누군지 가 보아라 **3.** [usage] 비인칭 동사의 주어로서 날씨·때·거리 그밖의 사태를 막연히 가리킴 **4.** [usage] 형식상의 주어·목적어로서 문장의 첫머리 또는 가운데 둠 **5.** [usage] 중간에 있는 문장의 주어·목적어·부사어구를 강조함 ¶③책임이 있는 것은 너다 **6.** ¶④집어치워, 그만 둬/⑤단념하지 말아라/⑥군림하다/⑦용감히 해내다

⁑ **I·tal·ian** [itǽljən] *adj.* of Italy, its people or their language. **—*n.*** [C] a person of Italy; [U] the language of Italy.

—[形] 이탈리아의; 이탈리아 사람(말)의
—[名] 이탈리아 사람(말)

⁑ **i·tal·ic** [itǽlik] *adj.* of or in the kind of type in which letters slope to the right. **—*n.*** 《*pl.*》 a sloping kind of letter or printing.

—[形] 이탤릭체의 —[名] [활자의] 이탤릭체

i·tal·i·cize [itǽlisàiz] *vt.* print (words, etc.) in a sloping style.

—[他] …을 이탤릭체로 인쇄하다

⁑ **It·a·ly** [ítəli] *n.* a country in southen Europe on the Mediterranean.

—[名] 이탈리아

itch [itʃ] *n.* [U][C] **1.** a feeling on the skin giving a person a desire to scratch. **2.** a restless and strong desire. **—*vi.*** have an itch.

—[名] **1.** 가려움 **2.** 열망, 갈망
—[自] 가렵다

itch·y [ítʃi] *adj.* (**itch·i·er, itch·i·est**) itching; like an itch.

—[形] 가려운

* **i·tem** [áitem, -təm] *n.* [C] **1.** (of a list, etc.) a single and separate thing. **2.** a piece of news. ¶*Here's an interesting* ~ *from today's newspaper.*①

—[名] **1.** 항목, 종목 **2.** [신문 기사의] 항목, 한 기사 ¶①오늘 신문에 재미있는 기사가 하나 있다

i·tem·ize [áitemàiz, -təm-] *vt.* give the particulars of (something); state (something) by item.

—[他] …을 조목(항목)별로 쓰다, …을 항목으로 나누다

it·er·ate [ítərèit] *vt.* say again; repeat.

—[他] …을 되풀이하여 말하다

it·er·a·tion [ìtəréiʃ(ə)n] *n.* [U][C] the act of saying again; repetition.

—[名] 반향, 반복, 되풀이

it·er·a·tive [ítərèitiv, -ərə-] *adj.* repeating; repeated.

—[形] 되풀이하는, 반복의

i·tin·er·an·cy [aitín(ə)r(ə)nsi, itín-] *n.* [U][C] the act of traveling from place to place.

—[名] 순회; 순력(巡歷), 편력

i·tin·er·ant [aitín(ə)r(ə)nt, ití-] *adj.* traveling from place to place. ¶*an* ~ *library.*① ▷**i·tin·er·ant·ly** [-li] *adv.*

—[形] 순회하는; 순회의 ¶①순회 도서관

i·tin·er·ar·y [aitín(ə)rèri / -rəri] *n.* [C] (pl. **-ar·ies**) **1.** the route of a trip. **2.** the record of a trip. **3.** a guidebook for travelers. **—*adj.*** of traveling or routes of travel.

—[名] **1.** 여정(旅程), 여행 일정 **2.** 여행기 **3.** 여행 안내 —[形] 순회하는; 여로의

i·tin·er·ate [aitínərèit, itín-] *vi.* travel from place to place.

—[自] 순회하다

it'll [ítl] =it will.

⁑ **its** [its] *pron.* the possessive form of **it**; the one or ones belonging to one.

—[代] 그것의

⁑ **it's** [its] =it is; it has.

⁑ **it·self** [itsélf] *pron.* (pl. **them·selves**) **1.** a reflexive or emphatic form of **it**. ¶*Even the well* ~ *was empty.*① / *The bird hid* ~.② **2.** its normal physical or mental condition.

—[代] **1.** 그 자신, 그것(강조형); 그것 자신을(재귀형) ¶①우물조차도 비어 있었다/②그 새는 숨었다 **2.** 그것 자신

I've [aiv] =I have.
i·vied [áivid] *adj.* covered with ivy. —형 담쟁이로 덮인
i·vo·ry [áiv(ə)ri] *n.* (**-ries**) Ⓤ **1.** a white bonelike substance forming the long teeth of an elephant, etc. **2.** the color of ivory; creamy white. **3.** (*pl.*) things made of ivory. —명 1. 상아; [하마 따위의] 어금니 2. 상아빛 3. 상아 세공
Ivory Coast [⌐--⌐] *n.* a republic in West Africa. —명 상아해안(공화국)
ivory tower [⌐-- ⌐-] *n.* the condition of being distant from the actual world; the world of ideas and dreams. —명 상아탑
i·vy [áivi] *n.* Ⓤ Ⓒ (**-vies**) a climbing plant with large, evergreen leaves. —명 담쟁이
-ize [-aiz] *suf.* **1.** to make or cause to be: *dramatize* (= make into a drama). **2.** to become: *crystallize* (=become a solid mass). —(接尾) 1. …화(化)하다, …으로 하다 2. …이 되다

J

J, j [dʒei] *n.* Ⓒ (pl. **J's, Js, j's, js** [dʒeiz]) **1.** the tenth letter of the English alphabet. **2.** something that has the shape of J. —명 1. 알파벳의 열째 글자 2. J자형의 것
jab [dʒæb] *vt., vi.* (**jabbed, jab·bing**) **1.** stab (something) with sudden force. **2.** (in boxing) give a short, straight blow. —*n.* Ⓒ a sharp thrust or blow. —타자 1. […을] 찌르다, 쩨 찌르다 2. 날쌔게 쥐어 박다 [권투에서] 재브하다 —명 찌르기, 재브
jab·ber [dʒǽbər] *vt., vi.* talk very fast and indistinctly; chatter. —*n.* Ⓤ very fast, indistinct talk. —타자 […을] 재잘재잘 지껄이다 —명 재잘거림
ja·bot [ʒæbóu, +*Brit.* ⌐--] *n.* Ⓒ a frill of lace on the front of a woman's dress. —명 [부인복 앞가슴의] 주름 장식
jack [dʒæk] *n.* Ⓒ **1.** a man; a fellow. **2.** (*colloq.*) a sailor. **3.** a male of certain animals. **4.** a small national flag flown on a ship. **5.** a playing card with a picture of a young man. **6.** (*slang*) money. **7.** a tool for lifting heavy things. **8.** a jackknife. —*vt.* **1.** lift (something) with a jack. (*~ up* something) **2.** (*colloq.*) abandon; give up (something). —명 1. 사내 2. [口] 선원 3. 동물의 수컷 4. 배에 단 작은 국기 5. [카아드의] 잭 6. 《俗》 돈, 금전 7. [무거운 것을 드는] 잭 8. 잭나이프 —타 1. …을 잭으로 들어 올리다 2. …을 포기하다
Jack [dʒæk] *n.* a nickname for **John**. —명 John 의 애칭
jack·al [dʒǽkɔːl, +*U.S.* -əl] *n.* Ⓒ a wild, dog-like animal living in Asia and Africa. —명 재칼(여우와 늑대의 중간형)
jack·a·napes [dʒǽkəneips] *n.* Ⓒ a conceited fellow; a mischievous boy. —명 멋장이; 개구장이
jack·ass [dʒǽkæs] *n.* Ⓒ **1.** a male donkey or ass. **2.** a stupid person. —명 1. 나귀의 수컷 2. 얼간이
jack·daw [dʒǽkdɔː] *n.* Ⓒ a black European bird like a crow. —명 갈가마귀
jack·et [dʒǽkit] *n.* Ⓒ **1.** a short coat. **2.** a paper cover for a book, etc. ¶*a book ~* —명 1. 자켓, 짧은 웃옷 2. 책가위, 커버
jack-in-the-box [dʒǽkinðəbàks / -bɔ̀ks] *n.* Ⓒ a toy that springs out of a box when it is opened. —명 뚜껑을 열면 괴상한 인형이 나오는 장난감
jack·knife [dʒǽknàif] *n.* Ⓒ (pl. **-knives**) (*U.S.*) a large, strong, folding pocketknife. —명 《美》 잭나이프(대형의 휴대용 나이프)
jack-o'-lan·tern [dʒǽkəlæ̀ntərn] *n.* Ⓒ **1.** a pumpkin hollowed out and cut to look like a human face, used as a lantern. **2.** a will-o'-the-wisp. —명 1. 호박의 속을 우벼내어 만든 초롱 2. 도깨비불
Ja·cob [dʒéikəb] *n.* (in the Bible) the son of Isaac and father of the twelve tribes of Israel. ⇒N.B. —명 야곱 N.B. 유대인의 시조 Gen. 25-34
Jac·o·be·an [dʒæ̀kəbí(ː)ən] *adj.* of or belonging to the period of King James I of England, from 1603 to 1625. —형 영국왕 James 1세 시대의
jade¹ [dʒeid] *n.* Ⓤ a green stone used for jewels and ornaments. —명 비취(翡翠), 옥
jade² [dʒeid] *n.* Ⓒ **1.** an inferior or overworked horse. **2.** a disreputable woman; (*ironically*) any woman. —명 1. 야윈 말, 늙은 말 2. 말괄량이; 여자
jad·ed [dʒéidid] *adj.* worn out; exhausted. ¶*a ~ face.* —형 지쳐빠진, 야윈
jag [dʒæg] *n.* Ⓒ a sharp projection. or torn unevenly. —명 깔쭉깔쭉한, 뾰족한 너설
jag·ged [dʒǽgid] *adj.* with sharp projecting points; cut —형 톱니 모양의, 깔쭉한

jag·uar [dʒǽgwɑ:r / -gjuə, -gwə] *n.* [C] a fierce animal like a leopard, living in the warmer parts of South America. —[名] 아메리카 표범

* **jail** [dʒeil] *n.* [C] a prison. ¶*break* ~① / *in* ~② / *He escaped from* ~. —*vt.* put (someone) in [a] jail; imprison. ⇒[N.B.] —[名] 교도소, 형무소 ¶①탈옥하다/②수감되어 —[他] …을 투옥하다 [N.B.] 영국에서는 **gail**로도 씀

jail·bird [dʒéilbə̀:rd] *n.* [C] **1.** a prisoner in jail. **2.** a habitual criminal. —[名] **1.** 죄수 **2.** 상습범

jail·er, jail·or [dʒéilər] *n.* [C] a person in charge of a jail. ⇒[N.B.] —[名] [교도소의] 간수, 교도관 [N.B.] 영국에서는 **gailer**로도 씀

* **jam**[1] [dʒæm] *v.* (**jammed, jam·ming**) *vt.* **1.** press or squeeze (something) tightly. 《~ something *into* a suitcase, etc.》 **2.** crush; bruise. ¶~ *one's finger in a door.* **3.** (of a crowd) fill; block. ¶~ *a passage.* **4.** fix or fasten (a part of a machine) so that it cannot be operated. **5.** interfere with radio signals by sending other signals of the same wave length. —*vi.* **1.** become unworkable or wedged. **2.** push against something violently. —[他] **1.** …을 억지로 쑤셔넣다, 채우다 **2.** …을 누르다 **3.** …을 막다 **4.** [기계 따위의 일부]를 움직이지 않게 하다 **5.** …을 [같은 파장의 전파를 보내어] 방해하다 —[自] **1.** [막혀서] 움직이지 않게 되다, 막히다 **2.** 억지로 끼어들다

—*n.* [C] the act of jamming; the state of being jammed; a dense crowd; (*colloq.*) a difficult situation. —[名] 고장; 으깨기; 꽉 들어참; 군중; 《口》 궁지, 곤경

⁑ **jam**[2] [dʒæm] *n.* [U] a food made by boiling fruit with sugar. —[名] 잼

Ja·mai·ca [dʒəméikə] *n.* the largest island in the West Indies, south of Cuba. ⇒[N.B.] —[名] 자마이카 [N.B.] 수도 Kingston

jamb, jambe [dʒæm] *n.* [C] one of the side posts of a doorway, a window, etc.; 《*pl.*》 stone or brick sides of a fireplace. —[名] [문·창문의] 곁기둥; 벽로 양쪽에 쌓은 돌

jam·bo·ree [dʒæ̀mbərí:] *n.* [C] **1.** a noisy, lively party. **2.** an international meeting of Boy Scouts. —[名] **1.** 떠들썩한 잔치 **2.** 보이스카우트의 대회

⁑ **James** [dʒeimz] *n.* **1.** a man's name. ⇒[N.B.] **2.** (in the Bible) the name of one of Christ's disciples; one of the books of the New Testament. —[名] **1.** 남자 이름 [N.B.] 애칭은 Jamie, Jim, Jimmy **2.** 야곱[형제]; 야고보서(書)

jam-packed [dʒǽmpǽkt] *adj.* (*U.S. colloq.*) filled to the greatest possible extent. —[形] 《美口》 빽빽이 들어찬

⁑ **Jan.** January.

Jane [dʒein] *n.* a woman's name. —[名] 여자 이름

jan·gle [dʒǽŋgl] *vi., vt.* **1.** make a harsh noise; cause (something) to sound harshly. ¶~ *a fire bell.* **2.** talk noisily; dispute. —*n.* [C] a harsh sound; a dispute. —[自][他] **1.** 땡그랑땡그랑 울리다 **2.** 와글와글 떠들다; 말다툼하다 —[名] 귀에 거슬리는 소리; 말다툼

jan·i·tor [dʒǽnitər] *n.* [C] **1.** a person employed to take care of and clean a building, an office, etc. **2.** a doorkeeper. —[名] **1.** [가옥 따위의] 관리인 **2.** 문지기, 현관지기

⁑ **Jan·u·ar·y** [dʒǽnjuèri / -əri] *n.* the first month of the year. ⇒[N.B.] —[名] 1월 [N.B.] Jan.으로 줄임

Jap [dʒæp] *adj., n.* [C] (*colloq.*) =Japanese.

Jap. Japan; Japanese.

ja·pan [dʒəpǽn] *n.* [U] a hard, shining lacquer used on wood or metal; articles lacquered in the Japanese manner. —*vt.* (**-panned, -pan·ning**) put japan on (something). —[名] 옻; 칠기(漆器) —[他] …에 옻을 칠하다, 검정 와니스를 칠하다

⁑ **Ja·pan** [dʒəpǽn] *n.* a country off the eastern coast of Asia. —[名] 일본

⁑ **Jap·a·nese** [dʒæ̀pəní:z] *adj.* of Japan, its people, or their language. —*n.* [C] (pl. **Jap·a·nese**) **1.** a person of Japan; 《*collectively*》 the people of Japan. **2.** [U] the language of Japan. —[形] 일본의, 일본 사람(말)의 —[名] **1.** 일본인 **2.** 일본어

* **jar**[1] [dʒɑ:r] *n.* [C] **1.** a wide-mouthed container of glass, earthenware, etc. **2.** the amount that a jar can hold. —[名] **1.** 단지, 항아리, 병 **2.** 한 병(단지)의 분량

⁑ **jar**[2] [dʒɑ:r] *v.* (**jarred, jar·ring**) *vi.* **1.** shake harshly; make a harsh, unpleasant noise. **2.** have an unpleasant effect. 《~ *on* something or someone》 ¶*The sound jars on my ears.* **3.** disagree; quarrel. 《~ *with* someone or something》 —*vt.* **1.** cause (something) to shake; cause (something) to give a harsh, unpleasant noise. **2.** shock. —[自] **1.** 진동하다; 삐걱거리다 **2.** [신경에] 거슬리다 **3.** [의견 따위가] 일치하지 않다; 다투다 —[他] **1.** …을 진동시키게 하다; 삐걱거리게 하다 **2.** …을 깜짝 놀라게 하다

—*n.* [C] **1.** a harsh, unpleasant noise. **2.** a shock. **3.** a dispute; a quarrel. —[名] **1.** 귀에 거슬리는 잡음; 삐걱거리는 소리 **2.** 충격 **3.** 불화, 다툼

jar·gon [dʒɑ́:rgən, +*U.S.* -gɑn] *n.* [U] **1.** meaningless or unintelligible talk. **2.** special or technical words used —[名] **1.** 뜻을 알 수 없는 말, 횡설수설 **2.** 전문어 —[自] 뜻 모를 소리를 지껄이

jarring — **jeopardize**

within a certain profession. —*vi.* talk jargon.
jar·ring [dʒáːriŋ] *adj.* sounding harshly and unpleasantly. —형 귀에 거슬리는, 삐걱거리는
jas·mine, -min [dʒǽsmin, dʒǽz-] *n.* ⓒ a shrub with fragrant red, white or yellow flowers; ⓤ a perfume made from this flowers. ⇒[N.B.] —명 재스민(식물); 재스민 향수 [N.B.] jessamine 으로도 씀
jas·per [dʒǽspər] *n.* ⓤ a stone, usu. red, brown or yellow, used for ornamentation. —명 벽옥(碧玉)
jaun·dice [dʒɔ́ːndis, +*U.S.* dʒɑ́ːn-] *n.* ⓤ a disease that makes the skin, the eyes, etc. yellow. —명 황달(黃疸)
jaunt [dʒɔːnt, +*U.S.* dʒɑːnt] *n.* ⓒ a short pleasure trip; an excursion for pleasure. —*vi.* take such a trip. —명 소풍, 들놀이 —자 소풍가다
jaun·ty [dʒɔ́ːnti, +*U.S.* dʒɑ́ːn-] *adj.* (**-ti·er, -ti·est**) **1.** gay; pleasant. ¶*a ~ smile.* **2.** stylish. ¶*a ~ hat.* —형 1. 명랑한; 쾌활한 2. 멋을 부린, 젠체하는
jav·e·lin [dʒǽvlin] *n.* ⓒ a light spear thrown by hand, once used as a weapon. —명 투창
* **jaw** [dʒɔː] *n.* ⓒ **1.** either of the two bones of the mouth. **2.** (*pl.*) a mouth. ¶*escape the jaws of death.*① **3.** (*pl.*) a narrow entrance to a valley. **4.** either of the parts in a machine that hold something. —명 1. 턱 2. 입 ¶①사지(死地)를 벗어나다 3. [골짜기 따위의] 좁은 입구 4. [집게 따위의] 집는 부분
jaw·bone [dʒɔ́ːbòun] *n.* ⓒ the bone of the upper or lower jaw. —명 턱뼈
jaw·break·er [dʒɔ́ːbrèikər] *n.* ⓒ (*colloq.*) a word or sentence which is hard to pronounce. —명 《口》 발음하기 곤란한 말
* **jay** [dʒei] *n.* ⓒ **1.** a noisy American and European bird of the crow family. **2.** (*colloq.*) a person who talks too much; a stupid person. —명 1. 어치·견조(樫鳥)류 2.《口》수다장이; 바보
jay·walk·er [dʒéiwɔ̀ːkər] *n.* (*U.S. colloq.*) ⓒ a person who crosses a street disregarding traffic and traffic lights. —명 《美口》[교통 규칙을 무시한] 차도 무단 횡단자
jazz [dʒæz] *n.* ⓤ lively dance music, originally American Negroes'. —*adj.* of or like jazz. —*vt., vi.* play jazz; arrange (music) as jazz; dance to jazz. —명 재즈 음악 —형 재즈의 —타자 재즈를 연주하다(춤추다), …을 재즈풍으로 편곡하다
* **jeal·ous** [dʒéləs] *adj.* **1.** full of suspicion or envy. 《*~ of*》 ¶*be ~ of someone's success.*① **2.** (in the Bible) (of God) demanding complete faithfulness or worship. **3.** careful; watchful. ¶*keep a ~ eye on someone.* —형 1. 질투심 많은, 시샘하는 ¶①…의 성공을 시기하다 2. [신이] 다른 신을 믿기를 용서하지 않는 3. 조심성 깊은; 빈틈없는
jeal·ous·ly [dʒéləsli] *adv.* in a jealous manner. —부 시샘하여; 방심 않고
* **jeal·ous·y** [dʒéləsi] *n.* ⓤⓒ (*pl.* **-ous·ies**) the state of being jealous; jealous feeling. —명 질투, 시샘; 경계심
jean [dʒiːn, +*Brit.* dʒein] *n.* **1.** ⓤ a strong cotton cloth. **2.** (*pl.*) trousers of this cloth. —명 1. 능직(綾織) 무명 2. 즈봉, 작업복 바지
jeep [dʒiːp] *n.* ⓒ a small but powerful automobile originally made for military use. —명 지이프(자동차)
jeer [dʒiər] *vt., vi.* make fun of (someone); sneer at (someone); laugh rudely. 《*~ at* someone》 —*n.* ⓒ a rude or jeering remark. —타자 […을] 놀리다, 비웃다, 조소하다 —명 놀림, 비웃음, 조소
* **Jef·fer·son** [dʒéfərsn], **Thomas** *n.* (1743-1826) the third president of the United States, from 1801 to 1809. —명 미국의 제3대 대통령
Je·ho·vah [dʒihóuvə] *n.* the name of God in the Old Testament. —명 여호와
je·june [dʒidʒúːn] *adj.* **1.** poor; barren. **2.** dull; dry; uninteresting. —형 1. 빈약한, 결핍된; 불모의 2. 무미건조한
* **jel·ly** [dʒéli] *n.* ⓤⓒ (*pl.* **-lies**) **1.** a soft, half-solid food made by boiling down fruit juice, meat juice, etc. with sugar. **2.** a substance like jelly.
  beat someone to a jelly, knock someone down; defeat someone severely.
  —*vi., vt.* (**-lied**) become jelly; turn (something) into jelly. —명 1. 젤리 2. 젤리 모양의 것
  술 …을 늘씬하게 패 주다
  —자타 젤리로 되다(만들다)
jel·ly·fish [dʒélifìʃ] *n.* ⓒ (*pl.* **-fish·es** or *collectively* **-fish**) a sea animal with a boneless, umbrella-shaped, partly transparent body like jelly. —명 해파리
jen·ny [dʒéni] *n.* ⓒ (*pl.* **-nies**) **1.** a locomotive crane; a machine for spinning several threads at the same time. **2.** a female of some animals. ¶*the ~ ass.* —명 1. 이동 기중기; 방적기 2. [동물의] 암컷
jeop·ard·ize [dʒépərdàiz] *vt.* put (someone or something) in danger; risk. ¶*~ one's life.* —타 …을 위험에 빠뜨리다, 위태롭게 하다

jeop·ard·y [dʒépərdi] *n.* [U] danger; risk. ¶*All at once his life was in ~.*①
—[名] 위험 ¶①갑자기 그의 생명이 위험해졌다

Jer·e·mi·ah [dʒèrimáiə] *n.* (in the Bible) **1.** a great Hebrew prophet. **2.** the book of the Old Testament which contains his prophesies.
—[名] 1. 예레미아 2. 예레미아서(書)

* **jerk**¹ [dʒə:rk] *n.* [C] **1.** a sharp, sudden pull, twist, or other movement. ¶*give the rope a ~ / pull with a ~.*① **2.** a sudden and quick movement of a muscle which cannot be controlled. **—vt.** move or twist (something) suddenly. **—vi.** move or twist suddenly.
—[名] 1. 갑자기 잡아당기기(비틀기·움직이기) ¶①홱 당기다 2. 근육의 경련
—[他] …을 홱 움직이다(비틀다)
—[自] 홱 움직이다(비틀리다)

jerk² [dʒə:rk] *vt.* cut (meat, etc.) into long thin slices and dry it in the sun.
—[他] …을 얇게 썰어 햇볕에 말리다

jer·kin [dʒə́:rkin] *n.* [C] a short, close-fitting, sleeveless coat or jacket often made of leather, worn by men in olden times. ⇒fig.
—[名] 옛날의 남자용 자켓

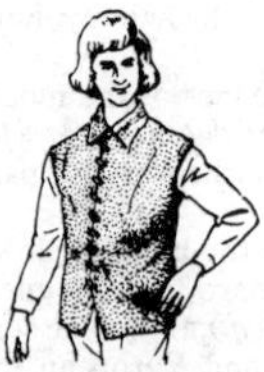
〔jerkin〕

jerk·y [dʒə́:rki] *adj.* (**jerk·i·er, jerk·i·est**) moving along with sudden starts and stops; full of jerks.
—[形] 홱 움직이는, 경련적인

jer·ry-build·ing [dʒéribìldiŋ] *n.* [U] building of poor quality with cheap materials.
—[名] 날림공사

jer·ry-built [dʒéribìlt] *adj.* built cheaply with bad materials.
—[形] 날림으로 지은

jer·sey [dʒə́:rzi] *n.* [C] **1.** a close-fitting woolen sweater, worn esp. in athletic exercises. **2.** a woman's close fitting knitted jacket.
—[名] 1. [운동용] 스웨터 2. 부인용 자켓

Jer·sey [dʒə́:rzi] *n.* **1.** one of a group of British islands near the coast of France. **2.** [C] a kind of cow originating here.
—[名] 1. 프랑스 해안에 가까운 영국령의 섬 2. 그 섬에서 나는 젖소

Je·ru·sa·lem [dʒərú:s(ə)ləm] *n.* the capital of Israel and ancient Palestine, considered a holy city by Jews, Christians, and Moslems. ⇒[N.B.]
—[名] 예루살렘 [N.B.] 이스라엘 공화국의 수도

jes·sa·mine [dʒésəmin] *n.* =jasmine.

⁑ **jest** [dʒest] *n.* **1.** [C] a joke. **2.** [U] the act of joking; fun.
1) ***be a standing jest,*** be always laughed at.
2) ***in jest,*** as a joke; not seriously.
—vi. **1.** joke. **2.** make fun.
—[名] 1. 농담 2. 비웃음; 놀림
[熟] 1)언제나 웃음가마리가 되다 2)농담으로
—[自] 1. 농담을 하다 2. 까불다

jest·er [dʒéstər] *n.* [C] a person who jests; (in medieval times) a fool or clown employed by a person of high rank to amuse him.
—[名] 농담하는 사람; 광대

Jes·u·it [dʒézjuit] *n.* [C] a member of the Society of Jesus. ⇒[N.B.]
—[名] 예수회 회원(수도사)

* **Je·sus** [dʒí:zəs] *n.* the founder of the Christian religion, called Jesus Christ or Jesus of Nazareth.
—[名] 예수

* **jet**¹ [dʒet] *n.* [C] **1.** a stream of water, gas, etc. gushing from an opening. **2.** a small opening sending out a jet. **3.** a jet plane. **—vi., vt.** (**jet·ted, jet·ting**) gush out; send out (water, gas, etc.).
—[名] 1. [물줄기 따위의] 분출, 분사(噴射) 2. 분출구, 내뿜는 구멍 3. 제트기
—[自][他] 분출하다(시키다)

jet² [dʒet] *n.* **1.** [U] a hard black mineral, used for making ornaments, buttons, etc. **2.** [U] a deep, shining black. **—adj.** **1.** made of jet. **2.** of deep, shining black.
—[名] 1. 흑옥(黑玉) 2. 흑옥색 —[形] 1. 흑옥[제]의 2. 흑옥색의, 새까만

jet·sam [dʒétsəm] *n.* [U] goods thrown overboard to lighten a ship in danger, esp. such goods when washed ashore. ⇒[N.B.]
—[名] 투하(投荷) [N.B.] 난파 때에 배를 가볍게 하려고 바닷속에 버리는 화물

jet·ty [dʒéti] *n.* [C] (pl. **-ties**) **1.** a structure built out into the water to break the force of the waves and to protect a harbor. **2.** a landing place; a pier.
—[名] 1. 방파제 2. 부두, 잔교, 선창

* **Jew** [dʒu:] *n.* [C] a person whose religion is Judaism; a Hebrew.
as rich as a Jew, very rich.
—[名] 유대인
[熟] [유대인같이] 큰 부자의

⁑ **jew·el** [dʒú(:)əl] *n.* [C] **1.** a precious stone; a gem. **2.** a valuable ornament set with gems. **3.** a person or thing of great value. **4.** a gem used as a bearing in a watch. **—vt.** (**-eled, -el·ing** or esp. *Brit.* **-elled, -el·ling**) adorn or set (someone or something) with jewels.
—[名] 1. 보석 2. 보석을 박은 장신구 3. 귀중한 사람 4. [회중 시계용의] 보석
—[他] …을 보석으로 장식하다, …에 보석을 박다

jew·el·er, *Brit.* **-el·ler** [dʒú(:)ələr] *n.* ⓒ a person who sells, repairs or makes jewelry. —名 보석상, 보석공

* **jew·el·ry**, *Brit.* **-el·ler·y** [dʒú(:)əlri] *n.* ⓤ ((*collectively*)) jewels and ornaments containing jewels. —名 보석[류]

* **Jew·ish** [dʒú(:)iʃ] *adj.* of or like the Jews. —形 유대인의; 유대풍의

jew's-harp, jews'- [dʒú:zhà:rp] *n.* ⓒ a musical instrument held in the mouth and struck by the finger. ⇒fig. —名 구금(口琴), 비파적(琵琶笛)

jib[1] [dʒib] *n.* ⓒ a three-cornered sail in front of the foremast. —名 이물의 삼각돛
the cut of one's jib, (*colloq.*) one's appearance. 熟 《口》풍채, 몸차림, 용모

jib[2] [dʒib] *vi.* (**jibbed, jib·bing**) (of a horse, etc.) move sideways or backward instead of ahead. ((~ *at* something)) —自 [말 따위가] 나아가려 하지 않다, 뒷걸음질치다

[jew's-harp]

jibe [dʒaib] *n.* =gibe.

jif·fy [dʒífi] *n.* (pl. **-fies**) =jiff.

jig[1] [dʒig] *n.* ⓒ a quick lively dance; the music for it. —*vi., vt.* (**jigged, jig·ging**) **1.** dance a jig. **2.** move quickly up and down or back and forth.
—名 지그(경쾌한 춤·춤곡) —自他 1. 지그를 추다 2. 격렬하게 뛰 흔들다(올리다)

jig[2] [dʒig] *n.* ⓒ **1.** a kind of fishing hook. **2.** any of various mechanical devices for guiding a drill, a file, etc.
—名 1. 추가 달린 낚시 바늘 2. 지그 (송곳 따위를 제자리에 갖다 대주는 공작 기계)

jig·gle [dʒígl] *vt.* shake slightly. —*n.* ⓒ a slight shake. —他 …을 가볍게 흔들다 —名 가볍 게 흔들기

jig·saw [dʒígsɔ̀:] *n.* ⓒ a thin-bladed saw used for cutting curves or irregular lines. —名 [곡선으로 켜는] 실톱

jigsaw puzzle [`-`] *n.* a puzzle in which a picture has been cut up into many small, irregular pieces. —名 조각그림 맞추기 놀이

Jill [dʒil] *n.* a woman's name. —名 여자 이름

jilt [dʒilt] *vt.* reject or cast off (a lover). —*n.* ⓒ a woman who rejects a previously accepted lover. —他 [여자가 남자]를 차 버리다 —名 남자를 차 버리는 여자

Jim [dʒim] *n.* a nickname of James. —名 James의 애칭

jim·my [dʒími] *n.* ⓒ (pl. **-mies**) a short crowbar used by burglars to break windows. —名 쇠지레

jin·gle [dʒíŋgl] *n.* ⓒ **1.** a sharp, tinkling sound, as of bells, etc. **2.** a verse that has a pleasing succession of rhymes. —*vi.* **1.** make a jingling sound. **2.** (of verse) have a series of simple, pleasing rhymes. —*vt.* cause (something) to jingle.
—名 1. 딸랑딸랑, 짤랑짤랑 2. 같은(비 슷한) 음을 반복하는 시구(詩句) —自 1. 딸랑딸랑 울리다 2. 듣기 좋게 울리 다, [시의] 운을 맞추다 —他 …을 딸 랑딸랑 울리다

jin·go [dʒíŋgou] *n.* ⓒ (pl. **-goes**) a person who supports his own country's warlike policy. —名 강경 외교 정책론자; 주전론자

jin·go·ism [dʒíŋgouìz(ə)m] *n.* ⓤ the spirit, policy, or practices of jingoes; aggressive patriotism. —名 강경 외교 정책; 맹목적 애국주의

jin·go·ist [dʒíŋgouist] *n.* ⓒ a person who believes in jingoism. 'goism. —名 강경 외교 정책론자; 맹목적 애국 자 '의의

jin·go·is·tic [dʒìŋgouístik] *adj.* of or like jingoes or jin- —形 대외 강경론의; 맹목적 애국주의

jinx [dʒiŋks] *n.* ⓒ (*colloq.*) a person or thing that is supposed to bring bad luck. —*vt.* bring bad luck to (someone). —名 《口》 재수가 없는 것, 징크스 —他 …에게 불운을 가져오다

jit·ney [dʒítni] *n.* ⓒ (*U.S. colloq.*) an automobile carrying passengers for a small fare, originally five cents. —名 《미口》 차삯이 싼 합승차

jit·ter·y [dʒítəri] *adj.* (*U.S. colloq.*) nervous. —形 《미口》 신경질의

Jo [dʒou] *n.* a nickname for Joseph or Josephine. —名 Joseph, Josephine의 애칭

Joan [dʒoun] *n.* a woman's name. —名 여자 이름

‡**job** [dʒɑb / dʒɔb] *n.* ⓒ **1.** a piece of work; anything a person must do for pay. **2.** (*U.S. colloq.*) a position; an employment. ¶ *out of a ~*. **3.** (*colloq.*) an affair; a matter. **4.** a piece of public work done so as to produce private profit.
1) *by the job*, [be paid] by contract for each piece of work done. | (someone) to be ruined.|
2) *do someone's job* [*for him*]; *do the job for*, cause

—名 1. 일, 삯일 2. 《미口》 지위; 직장 ¶ ①실직하여 3. 《口》 사건, 일, 사정 4. [공직을 이용한] 오직(汚職)

熟 1)도급으로, 청부로 2)…을 해치우 다, 파멸시키다 3)전력을 다하지 않다, 노력을 아끼다; 일에 실패하다 4)잘해

Job [628] **joint**

3) *lie down on the job,* be lazy; fail to do one's work well. 내다; 이익을 보다 5)*(俗)*일하여; 부지런히 일하여
4) *make a good job of it,* do (something) well; make a profit.
5) *on the job,* (*slang*) working; diligent at work.
—*vi., vt.* (**jobbed, job·bing**) 1. act as [a] broker. 2. turn a public job to private gain. 3. do a piece of work. —自他 1. [증권의] 중매(仲買)를 하다 2. [공직을 이용하여] 사리(私利)를 꾀하다 3. 품팔이 일(삯일)을 하다

Job [dʒoub] *n.* (in the Bible) a very patient man in the Old Testament; the book telling of Job in the Old Testament. —名 욥(히브리의 족장); 욥기(記)

job·ber [dʒábər / dʒɔ́bə] *n.* ⓒ 1. a wholesaler; a stockbroker. 2. a person who manages public business for his own profit. 3. a person who does odd jobs. —名 1. 도매상, 증권 매매상 2. 공직을 이용하여 사리를 꾀하는 사람 3. 품팔이꾼, 삯일

job·less [dʒáblis / dʒɔ́b-] *adj.* having no job; out of job. —形 실업의

jock·ey [dʒáki / dʒɔ́ki] *n.* ⓒ a man whose occupation is riding race horses. —*vi., vt.* 1. ride (a horse) in a race. 2. trick; cheat. —名 경마 기수 —自他 1. 기수가 되다 2. 속이다, 기만하다

jo·cose [dʒoukóus] *adj.* jesting; playful. —形 우스꽝스러운, 익살맞은

jo·cos·i·ty [dʒoukásiti / -kɔ́s-] *n.* Ⓤ Ⓒ (pl. **-ties**) the state of being jocose; a joke. —名 우스꽝스러움, 익살

joc·u·lar [dʒákjulər / dʒɔ́kjulə] *adj.* funny; joking. —形 우스꽝스러운, 익살맞은

joc·u·lar·i·ty [dʒàkjulǽriti / dʒɔ̀k-] *n.* Ⓤ Ⓒ (pl. **-ties**) the state of being jocular; a jocular act or remark. —名 우스꽝스러움, 익살[맞은 언동]

joc·und [dʒákənd / dʒɔ́k-, dʒóuk-] *adj.* cheerful; gay. —形 명랑한, 쾌활한, 즐거운 듯한

jo·cun·di·ty [dʒoukʌ́nditi] *n.* Ⓤ Ⓒ (pl. **-ties**) the state of being jocund; cheerfulness; gaiety. —名 명랑, 쾌활, 유쾌

Joe [dʒou] *n.* a nickname of Joseph. —名 Joseph 의 애칭; 놈, 녀석

jog¹ [dʒag / dʒɔg] *v.* (**jogged, jog·ging**)*vt.* 1. push (something) slightly; shake with a jerk. 2. rouse (one's memory). —*vi.* go slowly and laboriously. —自他 1. …을 살짝 밀다; 찌르다 2. [기억]을 환기하다 —自 터벅터벅 걷다, 서서히 나아가다
—*n.* ⓒ 1. a slight push or shake. 2. a hint to awaken attention, etc. 3. a slow and laborious way of walking. —名 1. 살짝 찌르기, [가벼운] 동요 2. 힌트 3. 서행

jog² [dʒag / dʒɔg] *n.* ⓒ (chiefly *U. S. colloq.*) an unevenness or sudden bend in a line or on a surface. —名 《美口》 울퉁불퉁함, 고르지 않음

jog·gle [dʒágl / dʒɔ́gl] *vi., vt.* shake or jerk slightly. —*n.* ⓒ a sudden shake. —自他 흔들[리]다; 진동하다 —名 흔들기, 진동

• **John** [dʒan / dʒɔn] *n.* 1. a man's name. 2. the Apostle John, one of Christ's disciples and supposed to be the author of the Gospel of Saint John, etc.; the Gospel of Saint John. —名 1. 남자 이름 2. 사도 요한; 요한 복음

John·ny [dʒáni / dʒɔ́ni] *n.* a nickname of John. —名 John 의 애칭

• **John·son** [dʒánsn / dʒɔ́n-], **Samuel** *n.* (1709-1784) an English author and dictionary-maker. —名 영국의 저작가·사전 편찬가

‡ **join** [dʒɔin] *vt.* 1. put (things) together; unite; be close to (something). ¶ ~ *two things together* | ~ *one thing to another.* 2. become a member of (a party); associate oneself with (something). ¶ ~ *the army.*① 3. enter the company of (someone); do something with (someone). ¶ *Will you ~ us for a walk?*② 4. return to (some place). ¶ ~ *one's ship.* —*vi.* 1. come together; connect. ¶ *The rivers ~ here.* 2. take part in something. —他 1. …을 맺다, 연결하다; …에 접합하다 2. …에 가입하다, …의 패에 끼다 ¶①군대에 가다 ¶③…에 동행하다, …와 동행하다 ¶②같이 산책 안 하겠음니까? 4. …으로 돌아가다; 귀속하다 —自 1. 합치다; 연결하다 2. 함께하다, 참가하다

join·er [dʒɔ́inər] *n.* ⓒ 1. a person or thing that joins. 2. a workman skilled in making the inside woodwork for houses. —名 1. 결합자, 연합자, 접합물(기) 2. 가구사(家具師), 소목장이

‡ **joint** [dʒɔint] *n.* ⓒ 1. the place where two things join. 2. the way in which parts are joined. 3. (*Anatomy*) a part of the body where two bones are joined together. 4. (*Botany*) the part of a stem from which a branch or leaf grows. 5. a large piece of meat with the bone. *out of joint,* ⓐ (of bones, etc.) dislocated. ⓑ out of order; disordered. —*vt.* 1. join (something) together. 2. divide (something) at the joints; separate (something) into joints; cut (meat) into joints. 3. plane the joints of (a board). —名 1. 접합점, 이은 곳, 이음매 2. 접합법 3. (解) 관절 4. (植) [가지·잎이 나오는] 마디 5. [요리용의] 뼈 붙은 고기 關 ⓐ관절이 삐어 ⓑ고장나서, 뒤죽박죽이 되어 —他 1. …을 접합하다 2. …을 이음매 (마디)로 나누다; [고기]를 큰 덩이로 베어 내다 3. [판자]의 이음매를 대패질하다

—*adj.* owned or done by two or more persons. ¶ ~ *ownership*① / ~ *authors*② / *a* ~ *convention.*③
—[形] 공동의, 합동의, 연합의 ¶①공유권/②공저자/③합동회의

joint·ed [dʒɔ́intid] *adj.* provided with joints.
—[形] 이음매(관절)가 있는

joint·less [dʒɔ́intlis] *adj.* having no joints.
—[形] 이음매(관절)가 없는

joint·ly [dʒɔ́intli] *adv.* in a joint manner; together; in common.
—[副] 공동으로, 연대적으로

joist [dʒɔist] *n.* [C] a piece of timber to which the boards of a floor or ceiling are fastened and by which they are supported.
—[名] [건물의] 장선, 들보

⁑ **joke** [dʒouk] *n.* [C] **1.** something said or done to make someone laugh. **2.** a person or thing which is the object of laughter.
—[名] **1.** 농담, 익살 **2.** 웃음거리

1) ***for joke,*** with the intention of causing someone to laugh.
2) ***in joke,*** not in earnest.
3) ***play a joke on,*** cause (someone) to be the victim of laughter.
[熟] 1)농담삼아, 장난으로 2)농담으로 3)…을 놀리다

—*vi., vt.* **1.** say or do (something) as a joke; jest. **2.** make fun of (someone).
—[自][他] **1.** 농담을 하다 **2.** …을 놀리다, 희롱하다

jok·er [dʒóukər] *n.* [C] **1.** a person who jokes. **2.** (*U.S.*) a hidden clause in a law, a contract, etc. which actually changes the apparent purpose of the whole. **3.** an extra playing card used in some games.
—[名] **1.** 농담하는 사람 **2.**《美》 눈가림 조항 **3.** [카아드의] 조우커

jok·ing·ly [dʒóukiŋli] *adv.* as a joke.
—[副] 농담으로, 장난삼아

jol·li·fy [dʒálifài / dʒɔ́l-] *vt., vi.* make (someone) jolly or merry; become gay.
—[他][自] …을 유쾌하게 하다, 명랑하게 하다

jol·li·ty [dʒáliti / dʒɔ́l-] *n.* [U][C] (pl. **-ties**) fun; merry-making.
—[名] 명랑, 즐거움; 떠들썩한 놀이

⁑ **jol·ly** [dʒáli / dʒɔ́li] *adj.* (**-li·er, -li·est**) **1.** full of life and fun; merry. **2.** (*Brit. colloq.*) pleasant; delightful.
—[形] **1.** 즐거운, 유쾌한, 명랑한 **2.**《英口》 멋진, 아주 재미있는

—*adv.* (*Brit. colloq.*) extremely; very; uncommonly. —*vt.* (**-lied**) (*colloq.*) make (someone) cheerful; flatter 《~ *up*》. ▷**jol·li·ly** [-li] *adv.* —**jol·li·ness** [-nis] *n.*
—[副]《英口》 아주, 대단히 —[他]《口》 …을 추어 올리다, 기쁘게 하다

jolt [dʒoult] *vi., vt.* move or shake with a jerk; give (something) a sudden jerk. —*n.* [C] a sudden or violent jerk.
—[自][他] 덜커덕거리[게 하]다, 흔들[리]다, 동요하다(시키다) —[名] 급격한 동요; 충격

jolt·y [dʒóulti] *adj.* moving or shaking with a jerk.
—[形] 덜커덕거리는, 동요하는

jon·quil [dʒáŋkwil, dʒán- / dʒɔ́ŋ-] *n.* [C] a plant of the narcissus family with yellow or white flowers and sword-shaped leaves.
—[名] 장수화(長壽花)

Jo·seph [dʒóuzif] *n.* **1.** a man's name. ⇨[N.B.] **2.** (in the Bible) Jacob's favorite son, who was sold by his jealous brothers into slavery in Egypt.
—[名] **1.** 남자 이름 [N.B.] 애칭 Jo, Joe **2.** 요셉(야곱의 아들)

Jo·se·phine [dʒóuzifì:n] *n.* a woman's name.
—[名] 여자 이름

jos·tle [dʒásl / dʒɔ́sl] *vt., vi.* push against (something); elbow roughly; push one another; make (one's way) through a crowd. —*n.* [C] push; knock.
—[他][自] 밀다, 찌르다, 밀치며 나아가다 —[名] 밀치기, 혼잡; 부딪치기

jot [dʒat / dʒɔt] *n.* [C] a little bit; a very small quantity. ¶*I do not know a* ~. —*vt.* write down briefly or quickly. 《~ *down*》 ▷**jot·ter** [-ər] *n.*
—[名] 조금; 소량 —[他] …을 간단히 적어두다

⁑ **jour·nal** [dʒə́:rnl] *n.* [C] **1.** a daily record of news or events. **2.** a daily newspaper; a magazine. **3.** a book in which daily business transactions are written down in a systematic form. **4.** a shaft or axle which rests on bearings.
—[名] **1.** 일기, 일지 **2.** 일간 신문; 잡지 **3.** 분개장(分介帳) **4.** 저어널(굴대의 목 부분)

jour·nal·ese [dʒə̀:rn(ə)lí:z, +*U.S.* -lí:s] *n.* [U] the style of writing such as is used in second-rate newspapers.
—[名] [이류 신문에서 틀에 박힌 것처럼 쓰는] 신문 용어[의 문체]

* **jour·nal·ism** [dʒə́:rn(ə)lìz(ə)m] *n.* [U] **1.** the work of writing for, editing, or producing a newspaper or periodical. **2.** 《*collectively*》 newspapers and magazines.
—[名] **1.** 신문・잡지업(기자), 문필업 **2.** 신문・잡지

jour·nal·ist [dʒə́:rn(ə)list] *n.* [C] a person who is engaged in journalism.
—[名] 신문・잡지업에 종사하는 사람, 언론인

jour·nal·is·tic [dʒə̀:rn(ə)lístik] *adj.* of or like journalism or journalists.
—[形] 문필업계의, 언론계의, 신문・잡지 기자의

⁑ **jour·ney** [dʒə́:rni] *n.* [C] a trip, esp. a trip taking a long time or going to a distant place. ¶*go on a* ~① / *take a* ~.②
—[名] 여행 ¶①여행을 가다/②여행하다

J

journeyman [630] **judge**

1) *be on a journey,* be away from home because of traveling.
2) *break one's journey,* get off the train, plane. etc. before arriving at one's destination.
—*vi.* make a journey; travel.

jour·ney·man [dʒə́ːrnimən] *n.* ⓒ (pl. **-men** [-mən]) **1.** a person who has mastered his trade or skill and who works for another. **2.** in olden times, a man who was hired to work for another, usu. by the day.

joust [dʒaust, +*U.S.* dʒʌst] *n.* ⓒ **1.** a combat with lances between two knights on horseback. **2.** ((*pl.*)) a ceremonial contest featuring such a combat.

Jove [dʒouv] *n.* **1.** Jupiter, the chief god in Roman mythology. **2.** (*poetic*) the planet Jupiter.
by Jove!, an exclamation of surprise, emphasis, etc.

jo·vi·al [dʒóuviəl] *adj.* gay; jolly; merry; good-humored.

Jo·vi·an [dʒóuviən] *adj.* **1.** of or like the god Jove. **2.** of the planet Jupiter.

jowl [dʒaul, +*U.S.* dʒoul] *n.* ⓒ **1.** the jaw, esp. the lower jaw. **2.** the cheek.

joy [dʒɔi] *n.* **1.** Ⓤ a feeling of great pleasure; happiness. ¶*He sobbed in his ~.* ① / *She jumped for ~ to hear the good news.* **2.** ⓒ something that causes such a feeling. ¶*His clever child is a ~ to him.* —*vi., vt.* rejoice.

joy·ful [dʒɔ́if(u)l] *adj.* **1.** full of happiness or joy. ¶*a ~ day.* **2.** causing joy. ¶*~ news.* **3.** showing joy. ¶*a ~ look.* ▷ **joy·ful·ness** [-nis] *n.*

joy·ful·ly [dʒɔ́ifuli] *adv.* with joy; in a joyful manner.

joy·less [dʒɔ́ilis] *adj.* without joy; dull; dismal.

joy·ous [dʒɔ́iəs] *adj.* joyful; glad; happy.

joy·ous·ly [dʒɔ́iəsli] *adv.* in a joyous manner.

joy·rid·den [dʒɔ́iridn] *v.* pp. of **joyride.**

joy ride [´-´] *n.* (*colloq.*) a pleasure ride in a motor car, esp. when the car is driven recklessly or used without the owner's permission. [joy ride.]

joy·ride [dʒɔ́iràid] *vi.* (**-rode, -rid·den**) (*colloq.*) take a

joy·rode [dʒɔ́iròud] *v.* pt. of **joyride.**

J.P. Justice of the Peace.

Jr., jr. Junior. [bi·lant·ly [-li] *adv.*]

ju·bi·lant [dʒúːbilənt] *adj.* expressing great joy. ▷ **ju-**

ju·bi·la·tion [dʒùːbiléiʃ(ə)n] *n.* ⓊⒸ a feeling of joy; a joyful celebration of something.

ju·bi·lee [dʒúːbiliː] *n.* ⓒ **1.** any occasion of exceptional celebration. **2.** a 25th or 50th anniversary. **3.** (in the Roman Catholic Church) a year in which punishment for sin is remitted.
1) *the diamond jubilee,* a 60th anniversary, esp. that in 1897 of Queen Victoria's coming to the throne.
2) *the silver jubilee,* a 25th anniversary of some event.

Ju·dae·a [dʒuːdíː(ː)ə] *n.* =Judea.

Ju·dah [dʒúːdə] *n.* **1.** (in the Bible) the fourth son of Jacob and Leah. **2.** the powerful tribes of Israel which are composed of his descendants. **3.** an ancient Hebrew kingdom in south Palestine.

Ju·da·ism [dʒúːdəìz(ə)m / -dei-] *n.* Ⓤ **1.** the religion of the Jews. **2.** the observance of Jewish rules, customs, etc.

Ju·das [dʒúːdəs] *n.* **1.** (in the Bible) Judas Iscariot, the disciple who betrayed Christ. **2.** ⓒ a treacherous person like Judas Iscariot; a traitor.

judge [dʒʌdʒ] *n.* ⓒ a person who decides right or wrong, good or bad, win or loss, etc. in a law suit or contest; an umpire. —*vt., vi.* **1.** decide or give an opinion on (something) as a judge. **2.** think; consider. ((*~ someone or something to be*)) ¶*We ~ her story to be false.* **3.** criticize; estimate. ¶*Don't ~ by appearances.* ①

──熟 1)여행중이다 2)도중하차하다

──自 여행하다
──名 1.[한 사람 몫의] 직공 2. 날품팔이꾼

──名 1.마상(馬上) 창시합 2. 마상 창시합 대회

──名 1.[로마 신화의] 조우브신 2.《詩》 목성(木星)
熟 맹세코!, 천만에!
──形 명랑한,쾌활한,유쾌한,즐거운
──形 1. 조우브 신의(같은) 2. 목성의

──名 1.턱;아래턱 2.볼,뺨
──名 1.기쁨,환희 ¶①그는 기쁨 나머지 흐느껴 울었다 2.기쁨의 원인,즐거움 ──自他 기뻐하다; …을 기쁘게 하다
──形 1.[사람·마음이]기쁨에찬, 기쁜 2. 반가운 3.기쁜 듯한,즐거운 듯한
──副 기쁜 듯이,즐겁게
──形 기쁘지 않은, 우울한
──形 기쁜,즐거운 듯한
──副 즐겁게,기뻐서

──名《口》[남의 차로 또는 맹렬한 속도로] 재미삼아 하는 드라이브

──自 재미삼아 드라이브하다

──形 환성을 올리는, 환희에 찬
──名 환희; 축하

──名 1.명절, 축제 2.25(50)년제 3.[로마 교황이 특사를 내리는] 성년(聖年)

熟 1)60년제 2)25년제

──名 1.유다(야곱의 네째 아들) 2. 유대 종족 3. Palestine 의 옛 왕국

──名 1. 유대교 2. 유대주의

──名 1.유다(그리스도를 배반한 제자) 2.모반자, 배신자

──名 재판관;판사;재정자(裁定者); 심사원;심판원 ──他 1.판결하다;재판하다;심판하다 2.생각하다 3.비판하다; 평가하다 ¶①외양만으로 판단하지 말라

‡ **judg·ment,** *Brit.* **judge-** [dʒʌ́dʒmənt] *n.* **1.** [U] the act of judging; the state of being judged. **2.** [U] [C] a decision or sentence given by a judge. **3.** [C] an opinion. **4.** [C] misfortune regarded as a punishment from God for a sin.
1) ***in my judgment,*** in my opinion.
2) ***Judgment Day,*** the day of the Last Judgment.
3) ***the* [*Last*] *Judgment,*** the final trial of all men by God.
4) ***pass judgment on,*** give a decision on (a case, etc.)
5) ***sit in judgment,*** judge; criticize.

—[名] **1.** 판단, 감별(鑑別), 재판, 심판 **2.** 판결[서] **3.** 의견, 견해 **4.** 천벌, 재앙
[熟] 1)나의 의견으로는 2)최후의 심판일 3)최후의 심판 4)…에 판결을 내리다 5)재판(비판)하다

ju·di·ca·ture [dʒúːdikətʃər, +*U.S.* -tʃùər] *n.* **1.** [U] duties or authority of a judge. **2.** [C] 《*collectively*》 a body of judges. **3.** [C] a court of justice.
—[名] **1.** 사법(재판)[권] **2.** 사법관, 재판관 **3.** 재판소

ju·di·cial [dʒu(ː)díʃ(ə)l] *adj.* **1.** of or by courts, judges, etc. **2.** ordered or inflicted by a court of justice. ¶*a ~ decision* / *a ~ murder*① / *~ process.* **3.** suitable for a judge; fair.
—[形] **1.** 재판관의, 재판상의 **2.** 재판에 의한 ¶①법의 살인(부당한 사형선고) **3.** 재판관다운, 공평한

ju·di·cial·ly [dʒu(ː)díʃəli] *adv.* done by a court of justice; legally; like a judge.
—[副] 재판상, 공정하게; 법관답게

ju·di·ci·ar·y [dʒu(ː)díʃièri, / -ʃiəri] *n.* [C] (pl. **-ar·ies**) **1.** the judicial part of the government; the system of law courts in a country. **2.** 《*collectively*》 the judges. —*adj.* of law courts or judges. ¶*~ proceedings.*①
—[名] **1.** 사법부;사법 제도 **2.** 사법관
—[形] 법원의, 법관의 ¶①재판 절차

ju·di·cious [dʒu(ː)díʃəs] *adj.* showing good judgment; wise. ¶*~ advice* / *a ~ step.* ▷**ju·di·cious·ly** [-li] *adv.*
—[形] 사려 분별이 있는, 현명한

jug [dʒʌg] *n.* [C] **1.** a vessel for liquids, usu. with a spout or a short neck and a handle. **2.** (*colloq.*) a jail. —*vt.* (**jugged, jug·ging**) **1.** (*colloq.*) put (someone) into jail. **2.** boil or stew (something) in a jug.
—[名] **1.** 물병, 물주전자, [맥주] 조끼 **2.** 《口》 감옥 —[他] **1.** 《口》 …을 감옥에 넣다 **2.** …을 단지에 넣어 삶다

jug·gle [dʒʌ́gl] *vi., vt.* **1.** perform tricks with (something). **2.** change (something) by means of a trick; cheat. ¶*~ a stick into a handkerchief.*
juggle with, ⓐ perform tricks with (something). ⓑ cheat (someone); falsify (facts).
—*n.* [C] **1.** the act of juggling. **2.** a deception; a trick.
—[自][他] **1.** 요술을 부리다 **2.** …을 속이다, 속여서 빼앗다
[熟] ⓐ…으로 요술을 부리다 ⓑ…을 속이다, [사실]을 의곡하다
—[名] **1.** 요술 **2.** 사기, 협잡

jug·gler [dʒʌ́glər] *n.* [C] **1.** a person who performs tricks. **2.** a person who deceives.
—[名] **1.** 요술장이, 마술사 **2.** 사기꾼, 궤변가

‡ **juice** [dʒuːs] *n.* [U] **1.** the liquid in fruit, vegetables, meat, etc. ¶*tomato ~* / *apple ~.* **2.** 《*the pl.*》 the liquid in the body. **3.** the essence ofanything.
—[名] **1.** [식물·과실의] 즙(汁)액. **2.** [동물질의] 육즙, 체액(體液) **3.** 정수(精髓), 본질

juic·y [dʒúːsi] *adj.* (**juic·i·er, juic·i·est**) **1.** full of juice. ¶*a ~ orange.* **2.** interesting; lively. ▷**juic·i·ly** [-li] *adv.*
—[形] **1.** 수분(즙)이 많은 **2.** 흥미진진한

juke·box [dʒúːkbɑ̀x -bɑ̀ks / -bɔ̀ks] *n.* [C] (*U.S. colloq.*) an automatic phonograph that plays after the required coin is put in the slot.
—[名] 《美口》 주우크복스; 자동 전축

Jul·ian [dʒúːljən] *adj.* of Julius Caesar.
—[形] 줄리어스 시이저의

‡ **Ju·ly** [dʒu(ː)lái] *n.* the seventh month of the year. ⇒[N.B.]
—[名] 7월 [N.B.] Jul., Jy.로 줄임

jum·ble [dʒʌ́mbl] *vi., vt.* mix together; confuse. 《*~ up* or *together* something》 —*n.* [C] a confused mixture.
—[自][他] 난잡하게 하다(되다), 뒤섞[이]다 —[名] 뒤범벅

‡ **jump** [dʒʌmp] *vi.* **1.** spring from the ground; spring upward or forward; leap. ¶*~ over the fence.* **2.** be surprised; be shocked. ¶*The news made me ~.* **3.** rise suddenly. ¶*The price of meat has jumped.* / *The temperature jumped by five degrees.*① **4.** pass from one thing to another; skip. ¶*He always jumps from one topic to another.* —*vt.* **1.** cause (something) to spring, leap, or bound. ¶*~ a horse over a hurdle.* **2.** leap over.
1) ***jump at,*** accept (an offer) willingly and hastily.
2) ***jump on,*** punish; scold.
—*n.* [C] **1.** a leap; a bound. ¶*a high ~.*① **2.** a surprise; a shock. **3.** a sudden rise.
—[自] **1.** 뛰다, 도약하다 **2.** 움찔 놀라다; [마음이] 설레다 **3.** 갑자기 오르다 ¶①기온이 단번에 5도나 올랐다 **4.** [화제 따위가] 비약하다 —[他] **1.** …을 뛰어오르게 하다 **2.** …을 뛰어넘다
[熟] 1) [제의]에 기꺼이 응하다 2)…을 처벌하다, 꾸짖다
—[名] **1.** 도약 ¶①높이뛰기 **2.** 놀람 **3.** 급등(急騰)

jump·er[1] [dʒʌ́mpər] *n.* [C] a person or thing that jumps.
—[名] 도약하는 사람(것)

jump·er[2] [dʒʌ́mpər] *n.* [C] **1.** a loose outer jacket worn by workmen, sailors, etc. **2.** a woman's sleeveless dress worn over a blouse. **3.** 《*pl.*》 rompers.
—[名] **1.** 잠바(웃옷) **2.** [부인용의] 헐거운 옷 **3.** 어린이의 막옷

J

jump·y [dʒʌmpi] *adj.* (**jump·i·er, jump·i·est**) **1.** moving by sudden, sharp jumps or jerks. **2.** nervous.
— ⓐ **1.** 갑작스레 움직이는, 도약의 **2.** 겁 많은, 잘 놀라는

junc·tion [dʒʌŋ(k)ʃ(ə)n] *n.* **1.** Ⓤ the act of joining; the state of being joined. **2.** Ⓒ a place where things join; a place where railroad lines, roads, etc. meet.
— ⓝ **1.** 접합, 연결(連接) **2.** 접합(연락)점; [강의] 합류점; 연락역

junc·ture [dʒʌŋ(k)tʃər] *n.* **1.** Ⓤ the act of joining; the state of being joined. **2.** Ⓒ a place where two things join or meet. **3.** Ⓒ a point of time; a crisis; a state of affairs. ¶*at this ~.*①
— ⓝ **1.** 결합, 연결 **2.** 이음매, 접합점 **3.** 시기; 위기; 사태 ¶①이 [중대한] 시기에

‡**June** [dʒuːn] *n.* the sixth month of the year.
— ⓝ 6월

jun·gle [dʒʌŋgl] *n.* Ⓒ any area thickly covered with trees, bushes, vines, etc. ¶*a ~ gym.*①
— ⓝ 밀림, 정글 ¶①[아동용의] 철골 운동 시설

‡**jun·ior** [dʒúːnjər] *adj.* ↔senior **1.** younger. ⇒N.B. ¶*John Smith, Jr.*① */ Smith Jr.*② **2.** of lower standing or position. **3.** youthful.
be junior to, younger than.
— *n.* Ⓒ **1.** the younger person of two. **2.** one of lower standing or position. **3.** (*U.S.*) a student in the third year of a four-year course in high school or college.
— ⓐ **1.** 손아래의, 연소한 N.B. Jr., jr. 로 줄임 ¶①존 스미드 2세/②젊은 쪽의 스미드 **2.** 하급의; 후진의 **3.** 젊은
— ⓝ **1.** 연소자 **2.** 하급자, 후진, 후배 **3.** 4년제 고교·대학의 3년생

ju·ni·per [dʒúːnipər] *n.* Ⓒ an evergreen shrub or tree of the pine family. ⌈tom and three masts.⌉
— ⓝ 노간주나무

junk¹ [dʒʌŋk] *n.* Ⓒ a Chinese sailing ship with a flat bot-
— ⓝ 정크(중국의 배)

junk² [dʒʌŋk] *n.* Ⓤ objects of no value; things discarded because they are useless.
— ⓝ 쓰레기; 폐물

jun·ket [dʒʌŋkit] *n.* **1.** ⓊⒸ a kind of food made from milk, such as cream, cheese. **2.** Ⓒ a feast. **3.** Ⓒ a picnic. — *vi.* **1.** feast. **2.** picnic.
— ⓝ **1.** 유제품(乳製品) **2.** 연회 **3.** 피크닉, 소풍 — ⓥ **1.** 잔치에 초대하다 **2.** 소풍가다

Ju·no [dʒúːnou] *n.* (pl. **-nos**) **1.** (in Roman mythology) the goddess of marriage and the wife of Jupiter. ⇒N.B. **2.** Ⓒ a stately and noble woman.
— ⓝ **1.** 주우노 여신 N.B. 그리이스 신화의 Hera에 해당 **2.** 기품 있는 미인

·**Ju·pi·ter** [dʒúːpitər] *n.* **1.** (in Roman mythology) the ruler of all the other gods. ⇒N.B. **2.** the largest planet in the solar system. ⌈of justice.⌉
— ⓝ **1.** 주피터 신 N.B. 그리스 신화의 Zeus에 해당 **2.** 목성(木星)

ju·rid·i·cal [dʒuərídik(ə)l] *adj.* of the administration
— ⓐ 재판상의, 법률상의

ju·ris·dic·tion [dʒùərisdík(ʃ)ə)n] *n.* Ⓤ **1.** the right of administering laws; the authority of a sovereign power. **2.** an extent of authority. **3.** Ⓒ the district over which a court has power. ▷ **ju·ris·dic·tion·al** [-ʃən(ə)l] *adj.*
— ⓝ **1.** 재판 사법권 **2.** 권한이 미치는 범위 **3.** 재판 관할구, 관할구역

ju·ris·pru·dence [dʒùərisprúːd(ə)ns] *n.* Ⓤ **1.** the science or philosophy of law. ¶*medical ~.*① **2.** the state of being well acquainted with laws. **3.** the system of
— ⓝ **1.** 법[률]학, 법리학 ¶①법의학(法醫學) **2.** 법률에 정통함 **3.** 법률 체계

ju·rist [dʒúərist] *n.* Ⓒ an expert in law. ⌈laws.⌉
— ⓝ 법률학자(학생)

ju·ror [dʒúərər] *n.* Ⓒ a member of a jury.
— ⓝ 배심원

·**ju·ry** [dʒúəri] *n.* Ⓒ (pl. **ju·ries**) **1.** A group of persons, usu. twelve in number, selected to decide whether or not an accused person is guilty in a court of law. **2.** a group of persons chosen to give a judgment on public matters. ⌈of a jury.⌉
— ⓝ **1.** 배심 **2.** [박람회 따위의] 심사 원단

ju·ry·man [dʒúərimən] *n.* Ⓒ (pl. **-men** [-mən]) a member
— ⓝ 배심원

‡**just** [dʒʌst] *adj.* **1.** right; fair. ¶*~ conduct | a ~ decision.* **2.** having a right reason or cause; due; proper. ¶*a ~ claim (reward) | ~ anger.* **3.** exact; correct.
— *adv.* **1.** exactly; precisely. ¶*at ~ five.* ⇒USAGE **2.** barely. ¶*He was ~ in time.*① **3.** (in the *perfect* tense) a moment ago; not long ago. ¶*He has ~ come.* **4.** (*colloq.*) quite; very. **5.** (*colloq.*) only; merely. ¶*Just a moment.*②
— ⓐ **1.** 바른; 공정한 **2.** 무리가 없는; 그럴 듯한; 정당한 **3.** 정확한, 옳은
— ⓥ **1.** 정확하게 USAGE 위치에 주의할 것 **2.** 겨우, 간신히 ¶①그는 겨우 시간에 댔다 **3.** 이제 방금, 막 **4.** (口) 전혀, 매우 **5.** (口) 단지, 조금 ¶②잠깐 기다려라

‡**jus·tice** [dʒʌstis] *n.* Ⓤ **1.** fair dealing; just conduct. ↔injustice ¶*treat a man with ~.* **2.** the state of being right or lawful. ¶*the ~ of our opinion.* **3.** trial and judgment by process of law. ¶*a court of ~.*① **4.** Ⓒ a judge. ¶*a ~ of the peace.*②
— ⓝ **1.** 공평, 정의 **2.** 정당, 타당, 적법(適法), 합법 **3.** 재판 ¶①법원 **4.** 법관, 재판관 ¶②치안 판사

1) *bring someone to justice,* legally punish an accused person for his crime.
圖 1) …을 법에 비추어 처벌하다 2) …을 공정하게 다루다 3)능력을 충분

justifiable [633] keel

2) ***do someone*** or ***something justice; do justice to*** someone or something, treat fairly.
3) ***do oneself justice***, show one's ability to the full.

jus·ti·fi·a·ble [dʒʌ́stifàiəbl] *adj.* that can be justified. ▷ **jus·ti·fi·a·bly** [-i] *adv.* —⑱ 정당하다고 인정되는, 이치에 맞는

jus·ti·fi·ca·tion [dʒʌ̀stifikéiʃ(ə)n] *n.* **1.** Ⓤ the act of justifying; the state of being justified. **2.** a good reason. —⑳ 1. 정당화; 변명 2. 정당한 이유

: jus·ti·fy [dʒʌ́stifài] *vt.* (**-fied**) **1.** show or prove (something) to be right. ¶*Can you ~ your absence?* **2.** declare (something done) to have been guiltless. —⑯ 1. …을 정당화하다, 정당하다고 인정하다 2. [정당하다고] …을 변명하다

just·ly [dʒʌ́stli] *adv.* in a just manner. —⑭ 올바르게, 정당하게

just·ness [dʒʌ́stnis] *n.* Ⓤ the state of being just. —⑳ 올바름, 공정, 정당

jut [dʒʌt] *vi.* (**jut·ted, jut·ting**) stick out; project. 《*~ out* or *forth*》¶*The tree branch juts out over the house.* —*n.* Ⓒ the part which projects; a projection. —⑯ 튀어나오다, 돌출하다 —⑳ 돌출[부]

jute [dʒuːt] *n.* Ⓤ a strong fiber obtained from tropical plants and used for making burlap, rope, etc. —⑳ 황마(黃麻) 섬유

ju·ve·nile [dʒúːvinàil, +*U.S.* -n(i)l] *adj.* **1.** young; youthful. **2.** suitable for young people. ¶*~ literature.* —*n.* Ⓒ **1.** a young person. **2.** a book, a magazine, etc. for young people. **3.** an actor who plays youthful parts. —⑱ 1. 젊은, 연소한 2. 소년다운, 소년 소녀용의 —⑳ 1. 소년, 소녀 2. 아동 도서 3. 아역(兒役)

jux·ta·pose [dʒʌ̀kstəpóuz, ´--́] *vt.* place (things) side by side. —⑯ …을 늘어놓다, 병렬(竝列)하다

jux·ta·po·si·tion [dʒʌ̀kstəpəzíʃ(ə)n] *n.* ⓊⒸ the act of placing side by side; the state of being placed in such a way. —⑳ 병렬, 병치(竝置)

K

K, k [kei] *n.* Ⓒ (pl. **K's, Ks, k's, ks** [keiz]) **1.** the eleventh letter of the English alphabet. **2.** anything shaped like the letter K. —⑳ 1. 영어 알파벳의 열 한째 글자 2. K자형의 것

kale [keil] *n.* Ⓤ a kind of cabbage with curly or wrinkled leaves. —⑳ 양배추의 일종

ka·lei·do·scope [kəláidəskòup] *n.* Ⓒ a tube with mirrors and small, loose pieces of colored glass inside. —⑳ 만화경(萬華鏡)

ka·lei·do·scop·ic [kəlàidəskápik / -skɔ́p-] *adj.* of or like a kaleidoscope; continually changing. —⑱ 만화경 같은, 변화무쌍한

: kan·ga·roo [kæ̀ŋɡərúː] *n.* Ⓒ (pl. **-roos** or *collectively* **-roo**) an Australian animal with powerful hind legs for leaping. —⑳ 캥거루우

· Kan·sas [kǽnzəs, -səs] *n.* a central State in the United States. ⇨N.B. ⌈losopher.⌉ —⑳ 캔자스 주 N.B. Kaṇs., Kan.으로 줄임

Kant [kænt], **Immanuel** *n.* (1724-1804) a German phi- —⑳ 독일의 철학자

ka·o·lin, -line [kéi(ə)lin] *n.* Ⓤ a white clay used in making fine china. —⑳ 고령토(高嶺土); 도토(陶土)

ka·pok [kéipɑk, kǽp- / -pɔk] *n.* Ⓤ the silky fibers obtained from the seeds of a tropical tree. ⇨N.B. —⑳ 판야솜 N.B. 이불·베개 따위의 속으로 씀 ⌈애칭⌉

Kate [keit] *n.* a nickname of Katherine or Catherine. —⑳ Katherine 또는 Catherine의

kay·ak [káiæk] *n.* Ⓒ an Eskimo boat for one person, made of sealskins stretched over a light frame of wood. —⑳ 카이액(에스키모인의 가죽 배)

Keats [kiːts], **John** *n.* (1795-1821) an English poet. —⑳ 영국의 시인

keel [kiːl] *n.* Ⓒ **1.** the lowest timber in the framework of a boat or ship. ⇨fig. **2.** a part in an airplane or airship which looks like a ship's keel. —*vt.* turn (a ship) upside down; upset. —*vi.* (of a ship) upset. —⑳ 1. 배의 용골(龍骨) 2. 비행선 따위의 용골

[keel 1.]

—⑯ [배]를 전복시키다 —⑯ [배가] 전복하다

keel over, ⓐ turn over; upset. ⓑ (*colloq.*) suddenly lose all feeling because of shock.

[熟] ⓐ뒤집히다 ⓑ(口)기절(실신)하다

:keen [ki:n] *adj.* **1.** sharp. ¶*a ~ edge*① / *a ~ sword.*② **2.** eager. ¶*He is ~ to go.* **3.** piercing. ¶*a ~ wind.* **4.** bitter. ¶*a ~ remark.* **5.** acute; sensitive. ¶*a ~ sense of smell.* **6.** quick; clever.

—[形] 1. 날카로운 ¶①예리한 날/②예리한 칼 2. 열심인 3. 살을 에는 듯한 4. 신랄한 5. 예민한 6. 기민한; 영리한

be keen on doing, be eager to do.

[熟] …하고 싶어하다

keen·ly [kí:nli] *adv.* sharply.

—[副] 날카롭게, 예민하게

keen·ness [kí:nnis] *n.* [U] sharpness.

—[名] 날카로움, 예민

:keep [ki:p] *v.* (**kept**) *vt.* **1.** continue (some action or state). 《~ *doing*》 ¶~ *silent* / *I kept thinking about it.*① **2.** make (someone or something) continue in a certain state. 《~ someone or something *warm, doing, etc.*》 ¶~ *the window open* / ~ *one's car in good condition* / *I kept him waiting for two hours.*② **3.** have (something) for a time in good condition; preserve. ¶~ *meat* / ~ *old diaries.* **4.** have (something) for sale; deal with (something). ¶*He keeps provisions at his store.*③ **5.** have and care for (something). ¶~ *a family* / ~ *a dog* / ~ *a car.* **6.** prevent; restrain. 《~ someone or something *from doing*》 ¶~ *children from going out.* **7.** write down regularly; record. ¶~ *a diary.* **8.** obey; follow; fulfill; carry out. ¶~ *the law* / ~ *a promise.* **9.** leave (something) unknown to others; conceal. ¶~ *a secret.* **10.** carry on; manage. ¶~ *a business.* **11.** save; hold; process. **12.** detain. **13.** continue to stay in (a place). ¶~ *one's bed* (*room*).

—[他] 1. [어떤 동작·상태]를 지속하다 ¶①나는 그 일을 계속 생각했다 2. …을 어떤 상태인 채로 두다 ¶②나는 그를 두 시간 기다리게 했다 3. …을 보존하다; 저장하다 4. [상품으로서] …을 갖고 있다, 장사하다 ¶③그의 가게에서는 식료품을 팔고 있다 5. …을 유지하며 돌보다; 부양하다 6. …을 방해하다; …시키지 않다 7. …을 적다; 기록하다 8. …을 지키다; …에 따르다; …을 다하다; 실행하다 9. …을 비밀로 해두다 10. …을 경영하다; …에 종사하다 11. …을 소유(보유)하다 12. …을 감금하다 13. …에 계속 머무르다

—*vi.* **1.** remain in some state. ¶~ *well*④ / ~ *smiling* / ~ *on smiling.* **2.** remain good. ¶*The meat will ~ for two days.*⑤ **3.** (chiefly *Brit.*) live; lodge.

—[自] 1. 어떤 상태에 있다 ¶④건강하다 2. 좋은 상태를 유지하다 ¶⑤그 고기는 이틀은 간다 3. 살다; 하숙하다

1) ***keep away,*** avoid coming; prevent (someone) from coming.
2) ***keep back,*** stay or make (someone) stay at a distance; hinder; restrain; conceal; reserve.
3) ***keep down,*** overcome and control (someone).
4) ***keep from*** (=*avoid*) *someone* or *something.*
5) ***keep*** *something* ***in,*** ⓐ restrain (a feeling). ⓑ order (a pupil) to stay in. ⓒ keep (a fire) burning.
6) ***keep in*** (=*remain on good terms*) ***with*** *someone,* remain on good terms with (someone).
7) ***keep it up,*** continue; not make slower; not loosen.
8) ***keep off,*** refrain from; repel.
9) ***keep on*** *doing,* continue; do repeatedly; not cease doing.
10) ***keep on with,*** continue doing.
11) ***keep out,*** not let (someone) enter.
12) ***keep to,*** obey; follow.
13) ***keep to*** *oneself,* be alone; be unsociable.
14) ***keep*** *something* ***to*** *oneself,* not share or reveal something.
15) ***keept to the left*** (***right***), follow the left (right) course.
16) ***keep under,*** hold (something) in subjection.
17) ***keep up,*** ⓐ keep and continue (an effort, an activity, etc.). ⓑ keep (something) in an efficient state. ¶~ *up a car.*
18) ***keep up*** *one's* ***end,*** finish one's part in a common effort.
19) ***keep up with,*** not give way to (grief, etc.); successfully compete with (something).
20) ***keep watch,*** be alert.

[熟] 1)…을 가까이 못 오게 하다; 가까이 하지 않다 2)…을 멀리하다; …에 접근하지 않다; 방해하다, 감추다; 넣어두다 3)…을 진압하다 4)…을 피하다; 삼가다 5)ⓐ[감정]을 억누르다 ⓑ[학생]을 [벌로서] 남게 하다 ⓒ[불]을 피워 두다 6)…와 사이좋게 지내다 7) 쉬지 않고 하다 8)…을 삼가다; 가까이 하지 않다 9)…을 계속하다; 계속되다 10)되풀이하다; 계속 …하다 11) …을 들이지 않다 12)…을 지키다; …에 따르다 13)남과 사귀지 않다 14)나누어 주지 않다; 알려주지 않다 15)좌측(우측)통행을 하다 16)…을 억누르다, 복종시키다 17)ⓐ…을 지속하다 ⓑ…을 [언제라도] 쓸 수 있게 해두다 18)자기가 할 몫은 다하다 19)…에 굽히지 않다, 뒤지지 않다 20)경계하다

—*n.* [U] **1.** maintenance. **2.** food. ¶*earn one's ~*① **3.** [C] (*History*) a tower; a stronghold; a citadel.

—[名] 1. 유지, 보전 2. 음식; 생계 ¶①생활비를 벌다 3. 탑, 요새

·keep·er [kí:pər] *n.* [C] **1.** a person who keeps. ¶*the ~ of the dog.* **2.** a guard; a watchman. **3.** a guardian.

—[名] 1. 지키는 사람; 소유주 2. 파수; 감시인 3. 보호자

keep·ing [kí:piŋ] *n.* [U] **1.** care; charge. **2.** observance; celebration. **3.** harmony.

—[名] 1. 돌봄; 관리 2. [축제 따위를] 지키기; 축하 3. 조화

1) ***in keeping with,*** in harmony with (something).

[熟] 1)…와 조화하여 2)[안전히] 보관

K

keepsake

2) *in someone's [safe] keeping,* be kept safely by someone.
되어
keep·sake [kí:psèik] *n.* Ⓒ something kept in memory of someone or of some event. ⌈10 gallons.⌉
—名 기념품
keg [keg] *n.* Ⓒ a small barrel, usu. holding less than
—名 작은 통
kelp [kelp] *n.* Ⓤ **1.** any of several kinds of large brown seaweed. **2.** ashes of seaweed, from which iodine is made.
—名 1. 해초 2. 해초를 태운 재(옥도의 원료)
ken [ken] *n.* Ⓤ **1.** range of sight. **2.** range of knowledge. ⌈known or not understood.⌉
1) *beyond* (or *outside*) *one's ken,* out of sight; not
2) *in* (or *within*) *one's ken,* in sight.
—名 1. 시계(視界) 2. 지력(知力) 범위
熟 1)눈이 미치지 않는 곳에 2)시야에
ken·nel [kénl] *n.* Ⓒ **1.** a house for a dog. **2.** (often *pl.*) a place where dogs are bred. —*vt., vi.* (**-neled, -nel·ing** or esp. *Brit.* **-nelled, -nel·ling**) put (a dog) into a kennel; keep (a dog) in a kennel; take shelter in a kennel. ¶ ~ *a dog.*
—名 1. 개집 2. 개우리 —他自 [개를] 개집에 넣다(가르다); 개집에서 살다
Kent [kent] *n.* a county in southeastern England.
—名 영국 서남부의 주
Ken·tuck·y [kəntʌ́ki / ken-] *n.* a State in the south central part of the United States. ⇒N.B.
—名 켄터키 주 N.B. Ky., Ken.으로 줄임. 수도 Frankfort
:kept [kept] *v.* pt. and pp. of **keep.**
kerb [kə:rb] *n.* (*Brit.*) =kerbstone.
kerb·stone [kə́:rbstòun] *n.* Ⓒ (*Brit.*) a stone edge of a street; a curbstone.
—名 〔英〕 가로(街路)의 가장자리 돌
ker·chief [kə́:rtʃif] *n.* Ⓒ **1.** a piece of cloth worn by women over the head or around the neck. **2.** a handkerchief.
—名 1. [부인의] 두건; 목도리 2. 손수건
ker·nel [kə́:rn(ə)l] *n.* Ⓒ **1.** the soft inner part of a nut or fruit. **2.** a grain of wheat, corn, etc. **3.** the central or important part of anything. ⌈or stoves.⌉
—名 1. [과일 따위의] 인(仁), 심 2. [밀 따위의] 낟알 3. [사물의] 중심부; 욧점
ker·o·sene [kérəsì:n, ⌐⌐] *n.* Ⓤ a thin oil used in lamps
—名 등유
ketch [ketʃ] *n.* Ⓒ a small sailing ship with two masts.
—名 쌍돛대의 돛배
ketch·up [kétʃəp] *n.* Ⓤ a sauce made from tomatoes, mushrooms, etc. ⇒N.B. ⌈spout for boiling water.⌉
—名 케첩 N.B. catchup, catsup으로도 씀
*****ket·tle** [kétl] *n.* Ⓒ a metal pot with a handle and a
—名 솥; 탕관; 주전자
ket·tle·drum [kétldrʌ̀m] *n.* Ⓒ a bowl-shaped drum.
—名 케틀드럼 (타악기의 일종)
:key [ki:] *n.* Ⓒ **1.** a metal instrument for opening and fastening a lock; anything like this in shape or use. ¶ *a* ~ *to a door* | *a* ~ *of a clock.* **2.** (*the* ~) the place or position controlling an entrance or commanding some area. ¶ *The Suez Canal is the* ~ *to the Mediterranean.*① **3.** a guide to solve problems; a clue. ¶ *a* ~ *to a puzzle* | *the golden* (or *silver*) ~.② **4.** the parts of a piano, a typewriter, etc. which the fingers press. **5.** a tone or mode of thought or expression. ¶ *speak in a high* ~.③
—*vt.* **1.** lock (something) with a key. **2.** regulate the tone of (a piano, etc.).
key someone up, bring someone into a state of nervous tension; excite; encourage.
—*adj.* basic; fundamental; essential.
—名 1. 열쇠; 열쇠 모양의 것 2. 관문; [관문과 같이 중요한] 요소(要所), 요처 ¶①수에즈 운하는 지중해의 관문이다 3. 해결책; 실마리, 단서 ¶②뇌물 4. [피아노 따위의] 건, 건반 5. [사상·표현의] 기조(基調); 어조 ¶③높은 어조로 말하다

—他 1. …에 쇠를 채우다 2. …의 음조를 맞추다
熟 …을 긴장시키다, 자극하다; 기운나게 하다
—形 중요한, 불가결의, 기간(基幹)의
key·board [kí:bɔ̀:rd] *n.* Ⓒ the row of keys on a piano, an organ, a typewriter, etc.
—名 건반
key·hole [kí:hòul] *n.* Ⓒ a small opening through which a key is inserted to turn a lock.
—名 열쇠 구멍
key·note [kí:nòut, ⌐⌐] *n.* Ⓒ **1.** (*Music*) the first note on which a series of tones is based. **2.** the main idea. ¶ *the* ~ *of his speech* | *a* ~ *address* (or *speech*).①
—名 1. 주음(主音); 기음(基音) 2. 요지 (要旨), 주안(主眼) ¶①[정당의] 기조 연설

key·stone [kí:stòun] *n.* Ⓒ **1.** (*Architecture*) the central stone at the top of an arch. ⇒fig. **2.** the fundamental principle or element.

⌈keystone 1.⌉

—名 1. (建) [아아치의] 종석(宗石); 쐐기돌 2. 주안, 요지; 근본 원리

kg. kilogram; kilograms.

kha·ki [kɑ́ːki, kǽki] *adj.* yellowish brown. —*n.* **1.** [U] a yellowish brown color. **2.** ⟪usu. *pl.*⟫ a military uniform or cloth of this color.

—[形] 카아키색의 —[名] 1. 카아키색 2. 카아키색의 군복(옷감)

***kick**[1] [kik] *vt.* **1.** strike (something) with the foot. **2.** (*Football*) score (a goal) by kicking the ball. —*vi.* **1.** strike out with the foot. **2.** (*Football*) make a kick. **3.** (*colloq.*) resist; object. **4.** (of a gun) push or spring back when fired.

—[他] 1. …을 차다 2. 공을 차서 득점하다 —[自] 1. 차다 2.⟪蹴球⟫ 킥하다 3. 반항하다; 반대하다 4. [총이] 반동(反動)하다

1) ***kick against*** (or ***at***), resist.
2) ***kick around,*** ⓐ treat (someone) unkindly. ⓑ (*slang*) examine (something) from various angles.
3) ***kick downstairs,*** make (someone) go out of a house.
4) ***kick one's heels,*** be kept waiting.
5) ***kick off,*** ⓐ start play in football. ⓑ take off (a shoe) by kicking one's leg.
6) ***kick out,*** (*slang*) send (someone) away; send (someone) away from his position.

[熟] 1)반항하다 2)ⓐ…을 불친절하게 대하다 ⓑ⟪俗⟫여러가지 각도에서 검토하다 3)…을 집에서 쫓아내다 4)기다리게 되다 5)ⓐ축구시합을 시작하다 ⓑ구두를 차서 벗다 6)…을 쫓아내다; 퇴학(퇴직)시키다

—*n.* [C] **1.** a blow with the foot. **2.** a backward push of a gun. **3.** (*Football*) an instance of kicking the ball.

—[名] 1. 차기 2. 총의 반동 3. [공의] 킥

kick·off [kíkɔ̀(ː)f / ⌐⌐] *n.* [C] (*Football*) the act of kicking off to start the game; the beginning.

—[名] ⟪蹴球⟫ 킥오프; 시합 개시

***kid** [kid] *n.* **1.** [C] a young goat. **2.** [U] flesh of a young goat. **3.** [U] leather made from the skin of young goats. **4.** ⟪*pl.*⟫ gloves or shoes made of this leather. **5.** [C] (*colloq.*) a child.

—[名] 1. 새끼 염소 2. 새끼 염소 고기 3. 새끼 염소 가죽 4. 염소가죽 장갑(구두) 5.⟪口⟫ 어린애

kid·dy, -die [kídi] *n.* [C] (pl. **-dies**) (*colloq.*) a child.

—[名] ⟪口⟫ 어린애

kid·nap [kídnæp] *vt.* (**-naped, -nap·ing** or esp. *Brit.* **-napped, -nap·ping**) carry off (someone) by force; steal (a baby).

—[他] …을 납치(유괴)하다

kid·nap·er, *Brit.* **-nap·per** [kídnæ̀pər] *n.* [C] a person who kidnaps.

—[名] 유괴자, 납치자

kid·ney [kídni] *n.* [C] either of the two bean-shaped organs of the body which take away waste water from the blood.

—[名] 신장(腎臟), 콩팥

kidney bean [⌐⌐ ⌐] *n.* a kind of bean like a kidney in shape.

—[名] 강남콩

***kill** [kil] *vt.* **1.** cause (a person or an animal) to die. **2.** put an end to (something); make useless; destroy. **3.** spend (time) idly. —*vi.* **1.** destroy life. **2.** be killed.
kill off, destroy all of (something) by killing.

—[他] 1. …을 죽이다 2. …을 끝나게 하다; 무효로(파괴)하다 3. …을 낭비하다 —[自] 1. 살인하다 2. 죽다
[熟] …을 멸종시키다

kill·er [kílər] *n.* [C] a person or a thing that kills.

—[名] 살인자; 죽이는 것

kiln [kil(n)] *n.* [C] a furnace or oven for burning or drying something, such as bricks and tiles.

—[名] 가마; 노(爐)

ki·lo [kíːlo, kílou] *n.* [C] (pl. **ki·los**) **1.** =kilogram. **2.** =kilometer.

kil·o- [kílou] *pref.* thousand.

—⟪接頭⟫「천」

kil·o·cy·cle [kílousàikl] *n.* [C] (*Electricity*) a unit equal to 1,000 cycles. ⇒[N.B.]

—[名] 킬로사이클 [N.B.] KC로 줄임

kil·o·gram, *Brit.* **-gramme** [kíləgræ̀m] *n.* [C] a unit of weight equal to 1,000 grams. ⇒[N.B.]

—[名] 킬로그램 [N.B.] kg, kg.로 줄임

kil·o·li·ter, *Brit.* **-tre** [kíloulìtər] *n.* [C] a unit of capacity equal to 1,000 liters. ⇒[N.B.]

—[名] 킬로리터 [N.B.] kl, kl. 로 줄임

kil·o·me·ter, *Brit.* **-tre** [kíloumìːtər] *n.* [C] a unit of length equal to 1,000 meters. ⇒[N.B.]

—[名] 킬로미터 [N.B.] km, km.으로 줄임

kil·o·watt [kíləwɑ̀t / -wɔ̀t] *n.* [C] a unit of electrical power equal to 1,000 watts. ⇒[N.B.]

—[名] 킬로와트 [N.B.] kw.로 줄임

kilt [kilt] *n.* [C] a short, pleated skirt worn by men in the Scottish Highlands. —*vt.* tuck up; form (a skirt, etc.) into pleats.

—[名] 킬트 —[他] [자락 따위]를 걷어 올리다; …의 주름을 잡다

***kin** [kin] *n.* [U] **1.** ⟪*collectively*⟫ one's family or relatives. ¶*My ~ live in Tokyo.* **2.** family relationship. ¶*What ~ is he to you?* **3.** someone or something of the same kind.

—[名] 1. 가족; 친족 2. 친족관계 같은 종족(종류)

1) ***near of kin*** [***to***], closely related to (someone).
2) ***next of kin*** [***to***], most closely related to (someone).
3) ***of kin,*** related; of the same family.

[熟] 1)「…의」 근친인 2)[…의] 가장 가까운 친척인 3)친척의; 같은 종류의

K

kind

—*adj.* related; of the same kind. ¶*be ~ to him.*

: kind¹ [kaind] *adj.* thoughtful of others and their feelings; friendly; gentle. ¶*How ~ you are!*
  1) *Be so kind as to do; Be kind enough to do,* Will you kindly do ...? 「*invite me.*」
  2) *It is kind of you,* Thank you. ¶*It is ~ of you to*

: kind² [kaind] *n.* **1.** ⓒ a race or natural group of animals, plants, etc. with the same general characteristics; a sort; a variety; a class. ¶*the human ~ | the cat ~ | All kinds of food are sold in the shop. | What ~ of house do you live in?* **2.** Ⓤ natural characteristic. **3.** Ⓤ (*archaic*) nature. **4.** ⓒ (*archaic*) manner.
  1) *in kind,* ⓐ in essential character. ⓑ in goods instead of money. ⓒ with something of the same sort.
  2) *a kind of,* something more or less like; vaguely similar.
  3) *kind of,* (*colloq.*) somewhat; rather. 「*like ...*」
  4) *nothing of the kind,* never; nothing at all; never
  5) *of a kind,* ⓐ of the same kind. ⓑ of poor quality.
  6) *something of the kind,* something like that.

kin·der·gar·ten [kíndərgàːrtn] *n.* ⓒ a school that prepares young children for an elementary school.

kind-heart·ed [káindháːrtid] *adj.* having or showing a kind heart; gentle.

* **kin·dle** [kíndl] *vt.* **1.** set (something) on fire; set fire to (something). ¶*~ straw.* **2.** make (something) bright; light up. **3.** excite; stir up. ¶*His speech kindled their anger.* —*vi.* **1.** catch fire; begin to burn. **2.** become bright. ¶*His eyes kindled with anger.* **3.** become excited. 《*~ at something*》 「*a kindly act.*」

kind·li·ness [káindlinis] *n.* **1.** Ⓤ kindly feeling. **2.** ⓒ

kin·dling [kíndliŋ] *n.* Ⓤ material for starting a fire, esp. small pieces of dry wood.

: kind·ly [káindli] *adj.* (**-li·er, -li·est**) **1.** kind; friendly; gentle. ¶*a ~ heart | a ~ woman.* **2.** pleasant; agreeable; mild. ¶*a ~ season.* —*adv.* **1.** in a kind manner. ¶*speak ~ | Would you ~ tell me the name of the book?* **2.** pleasantly; agreeably.
  take kindly to, ⓐ be naturally attracted to (something). ⓑ adapt oneself to (one's surroundings, etc.).

: kind·ness [káindnis] *n.* **1.** Ⓤ the state or quality of being good to others. ¶*He showed ~ by helping her.* **2.** ⓒ a kind act. ¶*He has done me many kindnesses.*
  1) *have a kindness for,* be friendly to (someone).
  2) *have the kindness to do,* be so kind as to do.
  3) *out of kindness,* because of being thoughtful of others.

* **kin·dred** [kíndrid] *n.* **1.** 《*collectively*, used as *pl.*》 relatives; relationship by birth or marriage. **2.** Ⓤ likeness; resemblance. —*adj.* **1.** related by birth or marriage. **2.** of the same kind; like; similar. ¶*Pity and love are ~ feelings.*

kin·e·ma [kínimə] *n.* (*Brit.*) =cinema.

kin·e·mat·o·graph [kìnimǽtəgræf / kàinimǽtəgràːf, kìn-] *n.* =cinematograph. 「↔static」

ki·net·ic [kinétik, kai-] *adj.* of or caused by motion.

ki·net·ics [kinétiks, kai-] *n. pl.* 《used as *sing.*》the science that deals with the motion of masses when force acts on them. ↔statics

: king [kiŋ] *n.* ⓒ **1.** the male chief ruler of some countries. ↔queen ¶*the ~ of England | King George V | (proverb) The ~ never dies.* **2.** (*colloq.*) a person who is thought to be very powerful. ¶*a baseball ~ | He is the ~ in all kinds of sports.* **3.** a plant, an animal, etc.

*king

—⒩ 친척인; 같은 종류인
—⒫ 친절한; 인정이 있는

🅐 1)부디 …해 주시오 2)정말 친절합 시다; 고맙습니다

—⒩ 1. [특히 동·식물의] 종류 2. 성질 3. 자연, 천성 4. 방법, 방식

🅐 1)ⓐ본질적으로 ⓑ[돈 대신] 물건으로 ⓒ같은 종류의 것으로 2)일종의 …, …에 가까운 3)(口)다소 …한 4)결코 … 않는; 전혀 다른 5)ⓐ같은 종류의 ⓑ빈약한, 엉터리의 6)그런 것

—⒩ 유치원

—⒫ 친절한; 다정한

—⒫ 1. …을 태우다; …에 불붙이다 2. …을 밝히 하다; …을 비추다 3. …을 부추기다; 선동하다 —⒤ 1. 불이 붙다; 타오르다 2. 빛나다; 반짝이다 3. 흥분하다

—⒩ 1. 친절심 2. 친절한 행위
—⒩ 불쏘시개

—⒫ 1. 친절한; 다정한 2. 기분 좋은; 온화한 —⒜ 1. 친절하게; 다정하게; 부디 […하여 주십시오] 2. 기꺼이, 기분 좋게

🅐 ⓐ …을 자연히 좋아하게 되다 ⓑ … 에 적응하다
—⒩ 1. 친절; 다정함 2. 친절한 행위

🅐 1)…에 호감을 품다 2)친절하게도 …하다 3)친절심에서

—⒩ 1. 친척; 친척관계 2. 유사(類似)
—⒫ 1. 친척의, 혈연의 2. 같은 종류의; 유사한 ¶①동정과 애정은 같은 감정이다

—⒫ 운동의
—⒩ 동력학(動力學)

—⒩ 1. 왕; 군주 ¶①왕은 죽지 않는다; 왕정은 망하지 않는다 2.(口)제1인자, 세력가 ¶②무는 운동에서나 는는 일인자다 3. 가장 좋은 품종; 왕에 비길 수 있는 것 ¶③백수(百獸)의 왕(사자)

that is supreme in its class. ¶*the ~ of beasts*③ | *the ~ of birds.*④ | *the ~ of the forest*⑤ | *the ~ of the jungle*⑥ | *the king of Heaven.*⑦ **4.** a playing card with a picture of a king. **5.** (*Chess*) the principal piece; (*Checkers*) a piece that has moved across the board to the opponent's base and can now move in either direction.
/④백조(百鳥)의 왕(독수리)/⑤떡갈나무/⑥호랑이/⑦신(神) **4.** [카아드의] 킹 **5.** [체스·체커의] 왕, 장군

:king·dom [kíŋdəm] *n.* [C] **1.** a country ruled by a king or queen. **2.** a territory where a person has control. ¶*the ~ of thought.*① **3.** one of the three classes into which all natural things are divided. ¶*the animal (mineral, vegetable) ~.*②
—[名] **1.** 왕국 **2.** 영역 ¶①사고의 영역 **3.** …계(界) ¶②동(광·식)물계

king·fish·er [kíŋfìʃər] *n.* [C] a bright-colored river bird which feeds on fish and insects.
—[名] 쇠새

king·like [kíŋlàik] *adj.* like a king; grand.
—[形] 국왕 같은; 당당한

king·ly [kíŋli] *adj.* (**-li·er, -li·est**) **1.** of or like a king; royal. **2.** suitable for a king. ▷**king·li·ness** [-nis] *n.*
—[形] **1.** 왕의; 왕다운 **2.** 왕에 어울리는, 위엄있는

King of Kings [ˊ- -ˊ] *n.* Jesus Christ; God.
—[名] 그리스도; 신(神)

king·ship [kíŋʃip] *n.* [U] the position, rank, or right of a king.
—[名] 왕위; 왕권

kink [kiŋk] *n.* [C] **1.** a twist or curl in rope, wire, thread, etc. **2.** a muscular stiffness or pain in some part of the body. **3.** (*colloq.*) a mental twist; a strange idea. —*vi., vt.* form a kink; cause (something) to form a kink.
—[名] **1.** 꼬임, 비틀림 **2.** [근육의] 경직(硬直) **3.** 마음의 뒤틀림; 별난 생각 —[自][他] 엉키다; …을 꼬이게 하다

kink·y [kíŋki] *adj.* (**kink·i·er, kink·i·est**) full of kinks; tightly-curled; twisted.
—[形] 배배 꼬인; 비틀린

kins·folk [kínzfòuk] *n. pl.* ((*collectively*)) relatives.
—[名] 친척

kin·ship [kínʃip] *n.* [U] **1.** relationship by birth or by marriage. **2.** the state of being similar in qualities.
—[名] **1.** 친척관계 **2.** 유사(類似)

kins·man [kínzmən] *n.* [C] (pl. **-men** [-mən]) a male relative.
—[名] 친척 남자

kins·wom·an [kínzwùmən] *n.* [C] (pl. **-wom·en** [-wìmin]) a female relative.
—[名] 친척 여자

ki·osk [kiɑ́sk / -ɔ́sk] *n.* [C] **1.** a small building for selling newspapers, tobacco, etc., or used as a telephone box. **2.** a summerhouse in Turkey, etc.
—[名] **1.** 정자식의 매점; 전화실 **2.** [터어키 등지의] 정자

kirk [kəːrk] *n.* [C] (*Scot.*) a church.
—[名] 교회

:kiss [kis] *n.* [C] **1.** a touch with the lips as a sign of love, respect, etc. **2.** a slight touch.
—[名] **1.** 입맞춤 **2.** 가볍게 스침

—*vt.* **1.** touch (something or someone) with the lips. **2.** touch (something) gently or lightly. —*vi.* **1.** give a kiss to someone. **2.** come in gentle contact.
—[他] **1.** …에 입맞추다 **2.** 가볍게 스치다 —[自] **1.** 키스하다 **2.** 가볍게 스치다

1) ***kiss away,*** remove (something) with kisses.
2) ***kiss one's hand to,*** wave a kiss to (someone).
3) ***kiss the dust*** (or ***ground***), ⓐ yield. ⓑ be killed.
4) ***kiss the rod,*** accept punishment without resistance.

[熟] 1) [눈물 따위] 키스로 닦아내다 2) …에게 키스를 던지다 3) ⓐ굴욕을 맛보다 ⓑ살해되다 4) 순순히 벌을 받다

kit¹ [kit] *n.* [C] **1.** a set of tools, materials, etc. for a particular job or purpose. ¶*a soldier's ~* | *a shoemaker's ~.* **2.** the case or bag for carrying or storing these tools. **3.** a circular wooden tub.
—[名] **1.** 도구 한 벌 **2.** 도구 상자, 가방 **3.** [나무]통

kit² [kit] *n.* =kitten.

kit-bag [kítbæ̀g] *n.* [C] a knapsack for a soldier; a traveling case.
—[名] [군인의] 잡낭; 여행 가방

:kitch·en [kítʃin] *n.* [C] a room where food is cooked.
—[名] 부엌, 취사장

kitch·en·ette, -et [kìtʃinét] *n.* [C] a small, compact kitchen.
—[名] 간이 취사장

kitchen garden [ˊ- ˊ-] *n.* a garden where vegetables and fruit are grown for a family's own use.
—[名] 채소밭

kitch·en·maid [kítʃinmèid] *n.* [C] a female servant who helps a cook.
—[名] 식모, 부엌 하녀

kitch·en·ware [kítʃinwɛ̀ər] *n.* [U] instruments used in a kitchen for cooking, such as pots, pans, and kettles.
—[名] 부엌 용품

•kite [kait] *n.* [C] **1.** a light frame of wood covered with paper or cloth, designed to be flown in the air on the end of a string. ¶*fly a ~.* **2.** a bird of the hawk family with long narrow wings. **3.** someone who plays a trick on another.
—[名] **1.** 연 **2.** 솔개 **3.** 사기꾼

kite-flying [káitflàiiŋ] *n.* [U] the act of flying a kite.
—[名] 연날리기

kith [kiθ] *n.* [U] (*archaic*) ⟪*collectively*⟫ friends; acquaintances.
—[名] 아는 사람; 친지
kith and kin, friends and relatives.
[熟] 친지와 친척

‡kit·ten [kítn] *n.* [C] a young cat.
—[名] 새끼 고양이

kit·ten·ish [kítniʃ] *adj.* **1.** like a kitten. **2.** playful.
—[形] 1. 새끼 고양이 같은 2. 까부는

kit·ty [kíti] *n.* [C] (pl. **-ties**) a pet name for a cat or kitten.
—[名] [새끼] 고양이의 애칭

km. **1.** kilometer; kilometers. **2.** kingdom.

knack [næk] *n.* [C] a special skill or ability needed to do something. ¶*get the ~ of serving in tennis.*①
—[名] 기교, 비결, 요령 ¶①테니스에서 서어브의 요령을 배우다

knap·sack [nǽpsæ̀k] *n.* [C] a leather or canvas bag for carrying food, clothes, etc. on the back.
—[名] 배낭, 란도셀

***knave** [neiv] *n.* [C] **1.** a tricky, dishonest person; a rogue. **2.** a playing card with a picture of a soldier or servant on it; a jack.
—[名] 1. 불한당; 악한 2. [카아드의] 잭

knav·er·y [néivəri] *n.* (pl. **-er·ies**) **1.** [U] behavior characteristic of a knave. **2.** [C] a dishonest act.
—[名] 1. 불한당 같은 짓 2. 부정행위

knav·ish [néiviʃ] *adj.* dishonest; like a knave.
—[形] 부정한; 악한 같은

knead [ni:d] *vt.* **1.** mix (dough, clay, etc.) and make into a mass. **2.** massage.
—[他] 1. 반죽하여 [빵·도자기 따위]를 만들다 2. [근육]을 주무르다, 안마하다

‡knee [ni:] *n.* [C] the joint between the thigh and the lower leg. ¶*at one's mother's ~*① / *rise on the knees.*②
—[名] 무릎; 무릎 관절 ¶①어머니 슬하에서/②무릎으로 서다
1) ***bend the knee to,*** kneel down to (someone) to beg; yield.
2) ***bring someone to his knees,*** force (someone) to yield.
3) ***give*** (or ***offer***) ***a knee to,*** help (someone).
4) ***on the knees of the gods,*** beyond human ability or control.
[熟] 1)…에 탄원하다, 굴복하다 2)…을 굴복시키다 3)…을 돕다 4)사람의 힘이 미치지 않는

knee breeches [∸ ∸–] *n. pl.* breeches reaching to the knees.
—[名] 반즈봉

knee·cap [ní:kæ̀p] *n.* [C] **1.** the flat, movable bone that covers the front of the knee. **2.** a covering to protect the knee.
—[名] 1. 무릎뼈, 슬개골(膝蓋骨) 2. 무릎받이

knee-deep [ní:dì:p] *adj.* as deep as the knees.
—[形] 무릎 깊이의

knee-high [ní:hái] *adj.* as high as the knees.
—[形] 무릎 높이의

***kneel** [ni:l] *vi.* (**knelt** or **kneeled**) rest on the bended knees. ⟪~ *over* someone or something⟫ ¶~ *in prayer.*①
—[自] 무릎꿇다 ¶①무릎꿇고 빌다

knell [nel] *n.* [C] ⟪*a* ~ or *the* ~⟫ **1.** the sound of a bell, esp. after a death or at a funeral. **2.** a sign of misfortune. **3.** a mournful sound.
—[名] 1. 애도의 종소리 2. 흉조 3. 애도의 소리

knelt [nelt] *v.* pt. and pp. of **kneel**.

‡knew [n(j)u: / nju:] *v.* pt. of **know**.

knick·er·bock·ers [níkərbὰkərz / níkəbɔ̀kəz] *n. pl.* short, wide breeches fastened at the knee.
—[名] [무릎에서 졸라매는] 헐거운 반즈봉

knick·ers [níkərz] *n. pl.* =knickerbockers.

knick·knack [níknæ̀k] *n.* [C] **1.** a trifle; a toy. **2.** a small ornamental article.
—[名] 1. 시시한 것; 장난감 2. 작은 장식품

‡knife [naif] *n.* [C] (pl. **knives**) a cutting instrument with a sharp-edged blade and handle. ¶*a table ~* / *a pocket-knife.*
—[名] 나이프; 작은 칼, 식칼
—*vt.* cut or kill (something or someone) with a knife.
—[他] …을 나이프로 자르다(찌르다)

‡knight [nait] *n.* [C] **1.** a mounted soldier of noble birth who served his king or lord in the Middle Ages. **2.** (*Brit.*) a man who has been raised to an honorable rank next below a baronet. ⇨[N.B.] **3.** (*Chess*) the piece with a horse's head.
—[名] 1. 기사(騎士); 무사 2. ⟪英⟫ 나이트작(爵) [N.B.] Baronet 다음의 최하위의 작위, 칭호는 Sir 3. [장기의] 나이트

knight-er·rant [náitérənt] *n.* [C] (pl. **knights-**) a knight traveling in search of adventure in the Middle Ages.
—[名] 무술 수행자(武術修行者)

knight-er·rant·ry [náitérəntri] *n.* [U] the actions of a knight-errant.
—[名] 무술 수행

knight·hood [náithùd] *n.* [U] **1.** the rank, character, or dignity of a knight. **2.** ⟪*collectively*⟫ a body of knights; the class of knights.
—[名] 1. 기사의 신분·기질·위신 2. 훈작사단(勳爵士團)

knight·ly [náitli] *adj.* of or like a knight; brave.
—[形] 기사의; 용감한; 의협적인

‡knit [nit] *v.* (**knit·ted** or **knit, knit·ting**) *vt.* **1.** make
—[他] 1. …을 뜨다, 짜다 2. …을 밀착시

K

knitted [640] **knothole**

(something) by looping a thread or yarn on needles. ¶~ *a sweater.* **2.** unite (something) closely; join. **3.** join together; wrinkle. ¶*She knits her forehead.* — *vi.* **1.** make something by looping thread or yarn together. ¶*She knitted all day long.* **2.** become united closely. ¶*A broken bone soon knits.*①
knit up, ⓐ repair (something) by knitting. ⓑ conclude.
knit·ted [nítid] *adj.* made by knitting.
knit·ting [nítiŋ] *n.* Ⓤ knitted work.
knitting needle [ㅡㅡㅡ] *n.* a long needle used for knitting.
⁑**knives** [naivz] *n.* pl. of **knife.**
knob [nɑb / nɔb] *n.* Ⓒ **1.** a small round lump on a surface; a knot. **2.** the rounded handle of a door.
knob·by [nábi / nɔ́bi] *adj.* (**-bi·er, -bi·est**) covered with knobs; like a knob.
⁑**knock** [nɑk / nɔk] *vt.* **1.** give a blow to (someone or something). **2.** hit or strike sharply against (something). **3.** (*colloq.*) find fault with (something). —*vi.* **1.** strike a blow with something hard. **2.** make a continuous noise by hitting heavily. **3.** find fault.
1) *knock about,* ⓐ damage (someone or something) with blows or falls. ⓑ lead an unsettled life. ⓒ wander over.
2) *knock against,* ⓐ dash and strike against (something). ⓑ come across; happen to meet (someone).
3) *knock at* (=*rap*) *something.*
4) *knock down,* ⓐ strike (someone) to the ground. ⓑ sell (something) at an auction sale.
5) *knock out,* strike (an opponent) in boxing unconscious so that he can no longer fight.
6) *knock together,* make up or build (a house, etc.) hurriedly.
7) *knock under,* submit; yield.
8) *knock up,* ⓐ rouse (someone) from sleep by knocking. ⓑ make (someone) very tired. ⓒ =knock together.
—*n.* Ⓒ **1.** (esp. at the door) a blow; a rap. **2.** a severe misfortune or hardship.
knock·a·bout [nákəbàut / nɔ́k-] *n.* Ⓒ **1.** a small sailing yacht. **2.** a foolish comedy; a comedian. —*adj.* **1.** noisy; rough. **2.** (of a garment, etc.) fit for rough use.
knock·down [nákdàun / nɔ́k-] *n.* Ⓒ **1.** the act of knocking down. **2.** something that overwhelms. —*adj.* **1.** that can knock down; overwhelming. **2.** that can be taken apart.
knock·er [nákər / nɔ́kə] *n.* Ⓒ a person or a thing that knocks; a small metal striker, etc. fixed to a door.
knock·out [nákàut / nɔ́k-] *n.* Ⓒ the act of knocking out; (*Boxing*) the final and decisive blow which makes one boxer lose consciousness. ⇒NB.
knoll [noul] *n.* Ⓒ a rounded small hill.
·**knot** [nɑt / nɔt] *n.* Ⓒ **1.** the place where two strings, ropes, etc. are tied. ¶*a ~ in a rope.* **2.** an ornamental bow of ribbon, etc. **3.** a hard, round lump in a piece of wood, etc. **4.** a group. ¶*a ~ of people.* **5.** a difficult or complicated problem. **6.** a tie; a bond. **7.** a unit for measuring the speed of ships at sea.
1) *cut the knot,* solve a problem, etc. quickly by force.
2) *in knots,* by twos or threes.
—*vt., vi.* (**knot·ted, knot·ting**) tie (something) in a knot; tie together (two strings); make or form a knot; tie together.
knot·hole [náthòul / nɔ́t-] *n.* Ⓒ a round hole in a board where a knot has fallen out.

키다; 결합하다 **3.** …에 이맛살을 찌푸리다 —㉮ **1.** 뜨개질을 하다 **2.** 결합하다 ¶①부러진 뼈는 붙는다

🖳 ⓐ짜깁다 ⓑ[토론 따위를] 끝맺다

—㉮ 뜨개질의
—㉭ 뜨개질
—㉭ 뜨개 바늘

—㉭ **1.** 혹, 마디 **2.** 문의 손잡이

—㉮ 마디(혹)가 많은; 혹 같은

—㉮ **1.** …을 때리다;치다 **2.** …에 부딪치다 **3.**(口)…의 흠을 찾다 —㉯ **1.** 두드리다 **2.** 연달아 치다 **3.** 헐뜯다

🖳 1)ⓐ[타격 따위로] …을 해치다 ⓑ불안정하게 살다 ⓒ…을 방랑하다. 2) ⓐ…에 부딪치다 ⓑ…을 우연히 만나다 3)…을 톡톡 두드리다 4)ⓐ…을 때려 눕히다 ⓑ…을 경매로 팔다 5)…을 녹아우트시키다 6)급히 만들다(짓다) 7)항복하다 8)ⓐ…을 두들겨 깨우다 ⓑ지쳐 빠지게 하다

—㉭ **1.**[문을] 두드리기; 치는 소리 **2.** 큰 타격
—㉭ **1.** 소형 요트 **2.** 왁자지껄한 희극[의 배우] —㉮ **1.** 시끄러운; 거친 **2.** [옷따위] 막일을 할 때 입는
—㉭ **1.** 구타; 타도 **2.** 압도적인 것 —㉮ **1.** 타도할 수 있는, 압도적인 **2.** 조립식의

—㉭ 두드리는 사람(것);노커, 노크 장치; 두드리는 쇠
—㉭ 타도; 녹아우트 NB k.o., K.O.로 줄임

—㉭ 작은 산, 언덕
—㉭ **1.** 매듭 **2.** 리본 따위의 장식 매듭 **3.** [초목 따위의] 옹이, 마디, 혹 **4.** 집단 **5.** 어려운 일, 복잡한 일 **6.** 인연;유대, 기반(羈絆) **7.** 노트 NB 한 시간 1해리(약 1,852미터)의 속도 단위

🖳 1)단호하게 난국을 처리하다 2)삼삼오오 [떼를 지어]
—㉮㉯ 매듭을 매다; 맺어놓다; 매듭이 생기다; 맺어지다

—㉭ [재목의] 옹이 구멍

knot·less [nátlis / nɔ́t-] *adj.* without a knot.
—[形] 매듭(옹이·혹)이 없는

knot·ted [nátid / nɔ́t-] *adj.* having a knot or knots.
—[形] 매듭(옹이·혹)이 있는

knot·ti·ness [nátinis / nɔ́t-] *n.* [U] **1.** the state of being full of knots. **2.** difficulty.
—[名] 1. 마디가 많음 2. 곤란

knot·ty [náti / nɔ́t-] *adj.* (**-ti·er, -ti·est**) **1.** full of knots. **2.** difficult to solve. ¶*a ~ problem.*
—[形] 1. 마디투성이의 2. 해결이 곤란한

knout [naut] *n.* [C] a whip formerly used in Russia to inflict punishment upon criminals. —*vt.* whip (criminals, etc.) with a knout.
—[名] 형벌용의 채찍 —[他] …을 채찍으로 때리다

⁑know [nou] *v.* (**knew, known**) *vt.* **1.** be aware, sure, or informed of (something); have knowledge of (something) by experience or study. ⟪~ *that, whether, what, how, etc.* …; ~ someone or something *to do*; ~ *how* (or *what, where, etc.*) *to do*⟫ ¶*I ~ nothing about it.* | *Do you ~ whether she will come or not?*① | *I ~ him to be honest.* | *Every boy knows one and one make two.* | *I don't ~ how to spell the word.* **2.** be acquainted with (someone). ¶*Do you ~ Mr. Johnson?* **3.** be familiar with; be versed in (something). ¶*I ~ the road.*② | *Do you ~ French?* **4.** be able to distinguish (something); recognize. ⟪~ something *from*⟫ ¶*I wouldn't ~ him in a crowd.*③ | *He knows good poems when he reads them.*④ | *It is hard to ~ an Englishman from an American.*⑤
—[他] 1. …을 알다; 알고 있다 ¶①그녀가 올지 안 올지 알고 있느냐? 2. …와 아는 사이다; 교제하고 있다 3. …에 익숙하다, 잘 알다 ¶②이 길은 알고 있다 4. …을 구별할 줄 알다; 식별할 수 있다 ¶③군중 속에서는 그를 식별하지 못할 게다/④그는 시를 읽으면 좋은 시가 어떤 것인지 안다/⑤영국인과 미국인을 구별하기는 힘든다

—*vi.* be informed.
—[自] 알고 있다

make oneself known, introduce oneself.
[熟] 자기 소개를 하다

know·a·ble [nóuəbl] *adj.* that can be known.
—[形] 알 수 있는

know-how [nóuhàu] *n.* [U] (*U.S. colloq.*) the knowledge, the ability, the technique, etc. of how to do something.
—[名] 〔美口〕 지식, 능력, 기술

•know·ing [nóuiŋ] *adj.* **1.** having knowledge; well-informed. **2.** clever; intelligent; shrewd; showing special knowledge. ¶*a ~ look.*
—[形] 1. 지식이 있는; 정통(精通)한 2. 영리한; 아는 체하는

know·ing·ly [nóuiŋli] *adv.* **1.** in a knowing manner. **2.** on purpose.
—[副] 1. 아는 체하여 2. 일부러

⁑knowl·edge [nálidʒ / nɔ́l-] *n.* [U] **1.** ⟪sometimes *a* ~⟫ what someone knows or acquires through study, experience, etc. ¶*He has a lot of ~.* **2.** learning. ¶*the branches of ~.* **3.** familiarity; the state or act of knowing; understanding. ¶*The ~ of his success caused great joy.*
—[名] 1. 지식, 아는 바 2. 학문 3. 잘 알고 있음, 통달; 알기; 이해, 인식

1) ***come to someone's knowledge,*** come to be known.
2) ***to*** [***the best of***] ***one's knowledge,*** as far as one knows.
3) ***without the knowledge of*** (=*not being known to*) *someone.*
[熟] 1)…에게 알려지다 2)아는 바에 의하면 3)…에게 알려지지 않게

⁑known [noun] *v.* pp. of **know**.
—*adj.* familiar.
—[形] 알려진

know-noth·ing [nóunʌθiŋ] *n.* [C] an ignorant person. —*adj.* completely ignorant.
—[名] 아무것도 모르는 사람 —[形] 무식한

knuck·le [nʌ́kl] *n.* [C] **1.** a finger joint, esp. at the root of a finger of the hand. **2.** the knee joint of a calf or pig, used as food.
—[名] 1. 손가락 관절 2. [소·돼지의] 무릎 관절

—*vt., vi.* strike or press with the knuckles; strike with a fist; shoot (a marble, etc.) with the fingers.
—[他][自] 손가락 마디(주먹)로 치다(누르다); [공깃돌 따위]를 퉁기다

1) ***knuckle down,*** ⓐ submit; surrender. ⓑ work hard.
2) ***knuckle under,*** submit; yield; surrender. ⟪~ *to*⟫
[熟] 1)ⓐ굴복하다; 항복하다 ⓑ열심히 일하다 2)굴복하다

knurl [nə:rl] *n.* [C] **1.** a knot on an old tree, etc. **2.** a small ridge on the edge of a coin, etc.
—[名] 1. 마디; 혹 2. [화폐 가장자리 따위의] 깔쭉깔쭉함

knurl·y [nə́:rli] *adj.* (**knurl·i·er, knurl·i·est**) full of knurls.
—[形] 마디(혹)투성이의

K.O., k.o. [kéióu] *n.* [C] (pl. **K.O.'s** or **k.o.'s**) knockout.
—[名] 녹아우트

Ko·ran [kourá:n / kɔ:-] *n.* ⟪usu. *the* ~⟫ the holy book of the Mohammedans.
—[名] 코오란(회교의 경전)

⁑Ko·re·a [kourí:ə / kəríə] *n.* a country on a peninsula in east Asia.
—[名] 한국

⁑Ko·re·an [kourí:ən / kəríən] *adj.* of Korea; of its people or their language. —*n.* **1.** [C] a person of Korea. **2.** [U] the language of Korea.
—[形] 한국의; 한국인(어)의 —[名] 1. 한국인 2. 한국어

kw. kilowatt.

Ky. Kentucky.

K

L

L, l [el] *n.* ⓒ (pl. **L's, Ls, l's, ls** [elz]) **1.** the twelfth letter of the English alphabet. **2.** anything shaped like the letter L. **3.** the Roman numeral for 50. ¶*LVIII.*①
L. £. =pound.
la [lɑ:] *n.* (*Music*) the sixth tone of the scale.
La. Louisiana.
***la·bel** [léibl] *n.* ⓒ **1.** a small piece of paper or other material attached to an article and giving information about it. **2.** a short phrase or catchword applied to persons, a theory, etc.
—*vt.* (**-beled, -bel·ing** or *Brit.* **-belled, -bel·ling**) **1.** put a label on (something). **2.** put (something) in a class; call (someone) as...; name. ¶~ *someone a miser.*
la·bi·al [léibiəl] *adj.* **1.** of the lips. **2.** (*Phonetics*) produced by nearly closing, or rounding the lips. —*n.* ⓒ (*Phonetics*) a sound produced in this way, such as p, b, and m.
:**la·bor,** *Brit.* **-bour** [léibər] *n.* **1.** Ⓤ work; toil. ¶*hard ~.* **2.** ⓒ a piece of work; a task. **3.** Ⓤ persons who work with their own hands; (*collectively*) all wage-earning workers. ¶*~ and capital.*① **4.** (*pl.*) ordinary affairs of life. ¶*His labors are over.*② **5.** Ⓤ the pains and efforts of childbirth; the period of these. ¶*easy* (*hard*) *~.* —*vi.* **1.** work hard. ¶*~ after wealth* / *~ to finish a piece of work.* **2.** move slowly and with difficulty; pitch and roll heavily. ¶*The old car labored up the hill.* **3.** have the pains of childbirth. —*vt.* work out (something) in too much detail.
***lab·o·ra·to·ry** [lǽbərətɔ̀:ri / ləbɔ́rət(ə)ri] *n.* ⓒ (pl. **-ries**) **1.** a place used for scientific work. **2.** a place where drugs, chemicals, etc. are made.
Labor Day [ˊ- ˋ] *n.* (*U.S.*) a legal holiday in honor of labor, in most States of the United States on the first Monday in September.
la·bored, *Brit.* **-boured** [léibərd] *adj.* **1.** showing signs of great care or effort. **2.** not natural; forced. ¶*a ~ smile.* **3.** hard; painful.
***la·bor·er,** *Brit.* **-bour·er** [léibərər] *n.* ⓒ a worker, esp. one who works with his hands.
la·bor·ing, *Brit.* **-bour·ing** [léibəriŋ] *adj.* habitually engaged in labor. ¶*a ~ man*① / *the ~ classes.*②
la·bo·ri·ous [ləbɔ́:riəs] *adj.* **1.** requiring hard work; difficult. ¶*a ~ enterprise.* **2.** hard-working; industrious; diligent. **3.** showing signs of effort; labored.
la·bo·ri·ous·ly [ləbɔ́:riəsli] *adv.* with great effort.
la·bor-sav·ing, *Brit.* **-bour-** [léibərsèiviŋ] *adj.* designed to reduce the amount of work required. ¶*a ~ appliance.*
labor union [ˊ- ˋˋ] *n.* (*U.S.*) an association of workers to protect and promote the welfare, interests, and rights of its members. (cf. *Brit.* trade union)
:**la·bour** [léibər] *n., v.* (*Brit.*)=labor.
la·boured [léibərd] *adj.* (*Brit.*)=labored.
la·bour·er [léibərər] *n.* (*Brit.*)=laborer.
la·bour·ing [léibəriŋ] *adj.* (*Brit.*)=laboring.
La·bour·ite [léibəràit] *n.* ⓒ (*Brit.*) a member of the British Labour Party.
la·bur·num [ləbə́:rnəm] *n.* ⓒ a small tree of the pea

—名 1. 영어 자모의 열 두째 글자 2. L 자형의 것 3. 로마 숫자의 50 ¶①58

—名 (樂) 장음계의 제 6음

—名 1. 찌지, 부전(附箋), 레테르, 라벨, 꼬리표 2. 부호, 표지(標識)

—他 1. …에 찌지를 붙이다, 라벨(레테르)을 붙이다 2. …으로 분류하다; …이라고 일컫다(칭하다)

—形 1. 입술의 2. (音聲) 순음(脣音)의
—名 (音聲) 순음

—名 1. 노동; 노력, 노고, 노역 2. [하나의] 일, 과업 3. 노동 계급; 근육 노동자 ¶①노동자와 자본가, 노자(勞資) 4. 속세의 일 ¶②그의 일생은 끝났다 5. 진통; 해산의 고통, 산고; 진통 시기
—自 1. 일하다, 노동하다; 힘쓰다, 노력하다 2. 애써 나아가다 3. 해산의 고통을 겪다 —他 …을 자세히 설명하다; 상론(詳論)하다

—名 1. 실험실, 시험소, 연구소 2. 제약소

—名 (美) 노동절(9월의 첫 월요일)

—形 1. 애쓴 흔적이 있는 2. 부자연한; 억지의; 일부러 짓는; 무리한 3. 곤란한; 괴로운

—名 노동자

—形 노동에 종사하는 ¶①노동자/② 노동 계급

—形 1. 힘드는; 곤란한 2. 부지런한, 근면한 3. 애쓴 흔적이 엿보이는

—副 힘들여, 애써서, 고생하여
—形 노력을 절약하는, 노동력 절약의

—名 (美) 노동조합

—名 (英) 노동당원

—名 노란등(콩과의 식물)

family with hanging clusters of yellow flowers.

lab·y·rinth [lǽbirinθ] *n.* [C] a complex network of winding paths through which it is hard to find one's way; a maze.
—[名] 미궁, 미로(迷路)

lab·y·rin·thine [læ̀birínθi(ː)n / -θain] *adj.* of or like a labyrinth; confusing; complicated.
—[形] 미궁의(같은); 뒤얽힌, 복잡한

⁑lace [leis] *n.* **1.** [U] an ornamental fabric of fine threads made in various designs. **2.** [C] a string or cord passed through holes for fastening shoes, etc. ¶*shoe laces.*① **3.** [U] an ornamental braid of gold or silver. ¶*gold (silver) ~.*② **—*vt.*** **1.** fasten (something) with a lace. ¶*~ [up] one's shoes.* **2.** decorate (something) with lace. **3.** weave (something) together. **4.** put (a cord) through a hole. **5.** add liquor to some drink. ¶*a cup of tea laced with brandy.* **6.** (*colloq.*) lash; beat. **—*vi.*** be fastened with a lace.
—[名] 1. 레이스(각종의 장식 천) 2. 끈, 줄, 끈 끈 ¶①구두 끈 3. 모오르 ¶②금(은)모오르 —[他] 1. …을 끈으로 묶다 2. …을 레이스로 장식하다 3. …을 섞어 짜다 4. [끈]을 꿰다 5. [홍차 따위에] 알코올 음료를 타다 6. 《口》 …을 매질하다, 치다, 때리다 —[自] 끈으로 매어지다

lace into (*colloq.*) ⓐ attack physically. ⓑ criticize sharply.
[熟] 《口》 …을 치다(때리다) ⓐ…을 맹렬히 비난하다

lace boots [ˊˋ] *n. pl.* boots fastened with laces.
—[名] 편상화(編上靴)

lac·er·ate [lǽsərèit] *vt.* **1.** tear (something) roughly. **2.** hurt (the feelings, etc.).
—[他] 1. …을 잡아찢다, 찢어발기다 2. [감정 따위]를 해치다, 괴롭히다

lac·er·a·tion [læ̀səréiʃ(ə)n] *n.* **1.** [U] the act of lacerating. **2.** [C] a tear; a wound.
—[名] 1. 찢기 2. 찢어진(찢긴) 자리; 찢어진 상처

lace·work [léiswə̀ːrk] *n.* [U] **1.** lace. **2.** any openwork like lace.
—[名] 1. 레이스 2. 레이스처럼 내 비치게 한 세공

lach·ry·mal [lǽkrim(ə)l] *adj.* of or for tears. ¶*the ~ gland.*① **—*n.*** 《*pl.*》 the glands that produce tears.
—[形] 눈물의 ¶①누선(淚腺) —[名] 누선

⁑lack [læk] *vt.* do not have enough of (something); need. ¶*He lacks common sense.* **—*vi.*** be wanting or missing; be short; be in need. ¶*He is lacking in courage. / Money is lacking.* **—*n.*** [U] want; shortage; need; [C] that which is wanted. ¶*The plants died for ~ of water.*①
—[他] …이 없다; …이 결핍되다 —[自] 결핍되다; 모자라다, 부족하다 —[名] 결핍; 부족; 부족한 것 ¶①그 식물은 수분 부족으로 말라죽었다

no lack of, enough.
[熟] 모자라지 않은, 충분한

lack·ey, lac·quey [lǽki] *n.* [C] **1.** a male servant; a footman. **2.** a follower who does not have his own will. **—*vt., vi.*** serve (someone) as a lackey.
—[名] 1. 하인, 머슴; 마부 2. 추종자 —[他][自] 하인(머슴) 노릇을 하다

lack·ing [lǽkiŋ] *prep.* without. ¶*Lacking water, we can't live.*
—[前] …이 없는, 부족한, …이 없이는

lack·lus·ter, *Brit.* **-tre** [lǽklʌ̀stər] *adj.* lusterless; dull.
—[形] 윤기 없는; 활기가 없는

la·con·ic [ləkánik / -kɔ́n-] *adj.* using few words; concise.
—[形] 말 수가 적은; 간결한

la·con·i·cal·ly [ləkánikəli / -kɔ́n-] *adv.* in a laconic manner; concisely.
—[副] 말 수가 적게; 간결하게

lac·quer [lǽkər] *n.* [U] **1.** a hard, bright, smooth varnish shellac made from sap of the sumac tree, etc. used for covering wood, etc. **2.** 《*collectively*》 wooden articles covered with lacquer. **—*vt.*** cover (something) with lacquer.
—[名] 1. 래커; 칠(漆), 옻 2. 칠기 —[他] …에 래커를 칠하다; 옻칠을 하다

lac·quey [lǽki] *n., v.* =lackey.

la·crosse [ləkrɔ́ːs / -krɔ́s] *n.* [U] an outdoor game, played by two teams of twelve, in which the ball is shot into the opposite goal with a racket called a crosse. ⇒[N.B.]
—[名] 러크로스 [N.B.] 캐나다의 국기(國技)인 구기(球技)의 일종

lac·tic [lǽktik] *adj.* of or obtained from milk. ¶*~ acid (bacteria).*①
—[形] 젖의; 젖에서 얻는 ¶①유산(乳酸)(유산균)

lac·y [léisi] *adj.* (**lac·i·er, lac·i·est**) of or like lace.
—[形] 레이스의(같은)

⁑lad [læd] *n.* [C] **1.** a boy; a young man. ↔lass **2.** (*colloq.*) a man. ¶*my lads.*①
—[名] 1. 소년; 젊은이 2. 《口》 남자 ¶①제군(諸君)

•lad·der [lǽdər] *n.* [C] **1.** a device for climbing up or down consisting of two long sidepieces and many crosspieces. **2.** a means by which a person achieves a purpose. ¶*the ~ of success.* **3.** (*Brit.*) a long vertical tear in a woman's stocking. (cf. *U.S.* run)
—[名] 1. 사닥다리 2. [목적 달성을 위한] 방법, 수단 3. 《英》 [양말 올이] 사닥다리 모양으로 풀리기

kick down the ladder, despise the persons or means by which someone has achieved a purpose.
[熟] 출세에 도움이 된 것(친구)을 버리다

lad·die [lǽdi] *n.* [C] (*Scot.*) a young boy; a lad.
—[名] 《스코》 젊은이, 소년

lade [leid] *vt.* (**lad·ed, lad·en** or **lad·ed**) put a cargo aboard (a ship). ¶*~ a ship with cargo.*①
—[他] [배]에 짐을 싣다 ¶①하물을 선적하다

•lad·en [léidn] *adj.* loaded; burdened. ¶*trees heavily ~ with apples / a mind ~ with grief.*①
—[形] 짐을 실은; 괴로와하는, 고민하는 ¶①슬픔에 가득찬 마음

L

lad·ing [léidiŋ] *n.* [U] cargo; freight. ¶*a bill of* ~.①
—[名] 뱃짐, 화물 ¶①선하증권

la·dle [léidl] *n.* [C] a cuplike spoon with a long handle, used for dipping out liquids. ⇒fig. —*vt.* dip out (water, etc.) with a ladle.
—[名] 국자 —[他] …을 국자로 푸다

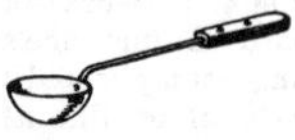
[ladle]

⁑la·dy [léidi] *n.* (pl. **-dies**) [C] **1.** a well-bred woman; a woman of high social position. ↔gentleman **2.** any woman. **3.** ⦅*L-*⦆ (*Brit.*) a title given to wives or daughters of men with certain high ranks. **4.** a wife.
—[名] **1.** 귀부인, 숙녀 **2.** 부인, 여사 **3.** ⦅英⦆ …부인, …영애(令愛) **4.** 아내, 주부

la·dy·bird [léidibə:rd] *n.* [C] a ladybug.
—[名] 무당벌레

la·dy·bug [léidibʌg] *n.* [C] a small round beetle with black spots on its back. ⇒[N.B.]
—[名] 무당벌레 [N.B.] lady bird, lady beetle이라고도 함

Lady Day [⌐-⌐] *n.* a festival on March 25 in honor of the day when the angel Gabriel told Mary that she would be the mother of Jesus; Annunciation Day.
—[名] 성모 마리아의 축일(3월 25일)

lady-in-waiting [léidiinwéitiŋ] *n.* [C] (pl. **la·dies-**) a lady who is attending on a queen or princess.
—[名] [여왕·왕녀의] 여관(女官), 시녀

la·dy·like [léidilàik] *adj.* like or suitable for a lady; refined.
—[形] 귀부인다운, 품위있는, 우아한

la·dy·ship [léidiʃìp] *n.* [U] **1.** the rank of Lady. **2.** ⦅*L-*⦆ (*Brit.*) a title used in speaking to or of a woman who has the title Lady. ¶*Your* (*Her*) *Ladyship.*①
—[名] **1.** 귀부인의 신분 **2.** ⦅英⦆ Lady의 칭호를 가진 부인의 경칭 ¶①영부인, 영양

lag [læg] *vi.* (**lagged, lag·ging**) move too slowly; delay. ¶~ *behind in promotion* / *She lagged because she was tired.* —*n.* [U] [C] the act of lagging; the amount by which a person or thing falls behind.
—[自] 느릿느릿 걷다; 늦어지다
—[名] 지연; 뒤짐, 뒤진 분량

la·ger [lá:gər] *n.* [U] a beer which is stored for several months before being drunk.
—[名] 저장 맥주

lag·gard [lǽgərd] *n.* [C] a person who moves too slowly or who falls behind. —*adj.* falling behind; backward; slow.
—[名] 느림보, 굼뜬 사람
—[形] 뒤진; 늦은, 뒤떨어진

la·goon [ləgú:n] *n.* [C] a small lake or pond, usu. one connected with a larger body of water or the sea; the shallow water inside an atoll, or a ring-shaped coral island.
—[名] 개펄; 늪, 못; 초호(礁湖)(환초)에 둘러싸인 해면(海面)

⁑laid [leid] *v.* pt. and pp. of **lay**.

laid paper [⌐ ⌐-] *n.* paper with close parallel lines of the watermark.
—[名] 투명 무늬가 있는 종이

⁑lain [lein] *v.* pp. of **lie**.

lair [lɛər] *n.* [C] a bed or resting place for a wild animal. —*vi.* (of wild animals) go to or rest in a lair.
—[名] 들짐승의 굴 —[自] [들짐승이] 굴로 가다, 굴에서 자다

lais·sez faire, lais·ser faire [lèseifέər / léiseifέə] *n.* [U] the policy of non-interference, esp. in matters of business and economics; the principle of non-interference in the individual matters of others.
—[名] 무간섭주의(정책), 자유 방임주의

la·i·ty [léiiti] *n.* (pl. **-ties**) [U] ⦅usu. *the* ~, *collectively*⦆ **1.** laymen of a church. ↔clergy **2.** those outside any particular profession.
—[名] **1.** 평신도, 속인들 **2.** 문외한, 아마튜어

⁑lake [leik] *n.* [C] a large area of water, nearly or entirely surrounded by land. ¶*the Great Lakes*① / *the Lake Country* (or *District*).②
—[名] 호수 ¶①[미국과 캐나다의 국경에 있는] 5대호/②[영국 서북부의] 호수 지방

la·ma [lá:mə] *n.* [C] a Buddhist priest in Tibet or Mongolia.
—[名] 라마교의 승려, 라마승

⁑lamb [læm] *n.* **1.** [C] a young sheep. **2.** [U] the meat from young sheep, served as food. **3.** [C] a gentle, innocent person, esp. a child.
the Lamb [*of God*], Christ.
—*vi.* (of female sheep) give birth to a lamb or lambs.
—[名] **1.** 새끼 양 **2.** 새끼 양 고기 **3.** 순진한(유순한) 사람
[熟] 하나님의 어린 양, 그리스도
—[自] [새끼 양을] 낳다

lam·bent [lǽmbənt] *adj.* **1.** (of a flame or light) moving lightly over a surface. **2.** (of the stars or eyes) shining softly and brightly. **3.** (of humor, etc.) gentle and bright.
—[形] **1.** [불꽃·빛이] 어른어른하는 **2.** [눈빛·별빛이] 부드럽게 빛나는 **3.** [기지(機知) 따위가] 경묘(輕妙)한

lamb·kin [lǽmkin] *n.* [C] **1.** a little lamb. **2.** a young and dear person.
—[名] **1.** 새끼 양 **2.** 귀여운(예쁜) 아기

lamb·skin [lǽmskìn] *n.* **1.** [U] the skin of a lamb with the wool still on it. **2.** [C] leather made from the skin of a lamb.
—[名] **1.** 새끼 양 가죽 **2.** 새끼 양의 유혁(鞣革)

⁑lame [leim] *adj.* **1.** not able to walk properly as a result
—[形] **1.** 절름발이의 ¶①[한쪽 다리가]

L

lament [645] land

of an injury in leg or foot, etc.; crippled. ¶*be* ~ *or in a leg*① / *go* ~. **2.** unsatisfactory. ¶*a* ~ *excuse.*② —*vt.* make (someone) lame.

절름발이다 2. 불충분한;서투른 ¶②서투른 핑계
—他 …을 절름발이로 만들다

- **la·ment** [ləmént] *n.* ⓒ **1.** an expression of grief. **2.** a poem or song that expresses grief; an elegy. —*vt.* feel or express grief for (something); mourn. —*vi.* feel or express grief; mourn. ↔rejoice ¶~ *for* (or *over*) *someone's death.*①

—名 1. 비탄, 한탄 2. 비가, 애도의 시
—他 …을 슬퍼하다, 애도하다
—自 슬퍼하다, 한탄하다 ¶①남의 죽음을 애도하다

lam·en·ta·ble [læmənt∂bl] *adj.* sorrowful; mournful.
lam·en·ta·bly [læmənt∂bli] *adv.* in a lamentable manner; sorrowfully.

—形 슬퍼해야 할; 슬픈
—副 구슬프게, 슬픈 듯이

lam·en·ta·tion [læ̀mentéiʃ(∂)n / -men-] *n.* **1.** Ⓤ the act of lamenting. **2.** ⓒ a lament; an expression of grief.

—名 1. 비탄, 애도 2. 슬퍼하는 목소리, 애가(哀歌)

lam·i·nate *v.* [læ̀mineit → *adj.*] *vt.* **1.** beat or roll (metal) into thin plates. **2.** cover (something) with a thin sheet of metal, wood, etc. —*vi.* split into thin layers. —*adj.* [læ̀minit] of or consisting of thin plates or layers.

—他 1. [금속 따위]를 얇은 판으로 두드려 펴다 2. …에 얇은 판을 씌우다
—自 얇은 조각으로 쪼개지다 —形 얇은 판의(으로 된)

‡ **lamp** [læmp] *n.* ⓒ **1.** something that gives light from electricity, oil, etc. ¶*an electric* ~① / *an oil* ~.② **2.** (*archaic*) the sun, the moon, a star, etc.

—名 1. 램프, 등, 등불 ¶①전등/②석유남포 2. 태양, 달, 별

lamp·black [lǽmpblæ̀k] *n.* Ⓤ **1.** fine soot produced by burning oil incompletely. **2.** a coloring matter made from this.

—名 1. 그을음, 유연(油煙) 2. 검정 그림물감

lamp·light [lǽmplàit] *n.* ⓒ the light from a lamp.
lamp·light·er [lǽmplàitər] *n.* ⓒ a person who went around the streets and lighted street lamps.

—名 램프의 빛, 등화(燈火)
—名 [가스등 시대의] 점등부(點燈夫)

lam·poon [læmpúːn] *n.* ⓒ a piece of writing that attacks and laughs at someone. —*vt.* attack (something or someone) by such a piece of writing.

—名 풍자문(시) —他 …을 풍자하다, 비방하다

lamp·post [lǽmppòust] *n.* ⓒ a post or pillar used to support a street lamp.

—名 가로등 기둥

lam·prey [lǽmpri] *n.* ⓒ a sea animal with gills and an eel-like body.
lamp·shade [lǽmpʃèid] *n.* ⓒ a shade of glass made of cloth, paper, etc. which is placed around a lamp.

—名 칠성장어
—名 램프의 갓

Lan·ca·shire [lǽŋkəʃiər, -ʃər] *n.* a county in northwestern England.

—名 영국 서북부의 주

- **lance** [læns / lɑːns] *n.* ⓒ **1.** a long wooden weapon like a spear with a pointed steel head. ⇒fig. **2.** (*pl.*) soldiers armed with lances; lancers. **3.** a lancet.
—*vt.* **1.** pierce (something) with a lance. **2.** cut (a part of body) open with a lancet.

—名 1. 창 2. 창기병(槍騎兵) 3. 란셋, 피침(披針)

—他 1. …을 창으로 찌르다 2. …을 란셋으로 절개하다

Lance·lot [lǽnslət/lɑ́ːn-] *n.* the bravest of King Arthur's Knights of the Round Table.

[lance 1.]

—名 랜슬럿(아아더왕의 원탁기사 중 가장 용감한 기사)

lanc·er [lǽnsər / lɑ́ːnsə] *n.* ⓒ a cavalry soldier armed with a lance.
lan·cet [lǽnsit / lɑ́ːn-] *n.* ⓒ a pointed, two-edged knife used by surgeons.

—名 창기병(槍騎兵)
—名 란셋, 피침(披針)

‡ **land** [lænd] *n.* **1.** Ⓤ the solid part of the earth's surface. ↔sea, water. ¶*travel by* ~. **2.** Ⓤ ground; soil. ¶*rich* ~ / *corn* ~. **3.** ⓒ a country; a nation; a region. ¶*one's native* ~. **4.** (*pl.*) the piece of ground considered as property. ¶*own lands.*①
—*vt.* **1.** cause (a plane or ship) to reach the land; bring (things or persons) to the land from a ship, etc. ¶~ *a plane* / ~ *the cargo* / *be landed at a station.*② **2.** bring (someone) to a certain place. ¶*This fight landed them both in jail.*③ / *This train will* ~ *you in Seoul.*④ **3.** (*colloq.*) win; get; secure. ¶~ *a job.*
—*vi.* **1.** leave a ship and come on shore; get off from train, etc. ¶~ *in* / ~ *from a train.* **2.** arrive. ¶~ *at an inn.*⑤ **3.** be in a bad state.

—名 1. 땅;육지 2. 토지;지면(地面) 3. 나라, 국가; 국토; 지역 4. 영토;소유지 ¶①토지를 소유하다

—他 1. …을 상륙시키다; 착륙시키다; [적하(積荷) 따위를] 부리다 ¶②정거장에서 내려지다 2. …을 어떤 특수한 장소로 보내다 ¶③이 싸움으로 두 사람이 다 형무소로 보내졌다/④이 열차는 서울행이다 3. (口) …을 획득하다, 얻다, 차지하다 —自 1. 상륙하다, 착륙하다 2. 도착하다 ¶⑤여관에 도착하다 3. [나쁜 상태에] 빠지다

lan·dau [lǽndɔː, +U.S. -dau] *n.* ⓒ **1.** a four-wheeled carriage with two seats and a top made to be folded in two sections. ⇒fig. **2.** an automobile with a similar top.

[landau.]

— 图 1. 랜도오 마차 2. 랜도오 자동차

land·ed [lǽndid] *adj.* **1.** owning land. **2.** of or consisting of land. ⌈or rents land.⌉
— 图 1. 토지를 소유하는 2. 토지의(로 된) ⌈지인⌉

land·hold·er [lǽndhòuldər] *n.* ⓒ a person who owns⌉
— 图 토지 소유자; 지주; 차지인(借

land·ing [lǽndiŋ] *n.* ⓒ **1.** a place where persons or goods are landed from a ship; landing place. **2.** a platform between two flights of stairs.
— 图 1. 상륙장; 양륙장 2. [계단의] 층계참

landing craft [ɔ́ー⌐] *n.* (*Navy*) a ship whose bows can be opened up to allow troops and military vehicles to go ashore. ⌈and take off.⌉
— 图 (海軍) 상륙용 주정(舟艇)

landing field [ɔ́ー⌐] *n.* a field where airplanes can land⌉
— 图 비행장; 이착륙장

landing net [ɔ́ー⌐] *n.* a small net with a handle for scooping fish up from the water.
— 图 [낚은 물고기를 떠내는] 뜰·채

landing place [ɔ́ー⌐] *n.* a place where people or goods are landed. ⌈ing people and goods.⌉
— 图 상륙장, 양륙장

landing stage [ɔ́ー⌐] *n.* a floating platform used for land-⌉
— 图 부잔교(浮棧橋), 선창

land·la·dy [lǽn(d)lèidi] *n.* ⓒ (pl. **-dies**) ↔landlord **1.** a woman who rents her houses or land to others. **2.** the mistress of a boarding house, inn or lodging house.
— 图 1. 여자 집주인; 여지주 2. 여주인, 안주인

land·locked [lǽndlɔ̀kt / -lɔ̀kt] *adj.* (of a bay, harbor, etc.) surrounded or nearly surrounded by land.
— 图 [만(灣)·항구 따위가] 육지로 둘러싸인

• **land·lord** [lǽn(d)lɔ̀ːrd] *n.* ↔landlady **1.** a person who rents his houses or land to others. **2.** the male keeper of a boarding house, inn, or lodging house.
— 图 1. 집주인; 지주 2. 주인, 가장

land·mark [lǽn(d)mὰːrk] *n.* ⓒ **1.** an object that marks the limits of land. **2.** an easily-seen and well-known mark which serves as a guide to travelers and sailors. **3.** an important fact or event.
— 图 1. [토지의] 경계표; 이정표 2. [항해의 안내가 되는] 육표(陸標) 3. 현저한 (획기적인) 사건

land·own·er [lǽndòunər] *n.* ⓒ a person who owns land.
— 图 토지 소유자, 지주

• **land·scape** [lǽn(d)skèip] *n.* ⓒ a piece of inland scenery; a picture showing such a piece of scenery.
— 图 경치, 풍경; 풍경화

land·slide [lǽn(d)slàid] *n.* ⓒ (*U.S.*) **1.** a fall of a mass of earth or rock from the slope of a cliff or a mountain. (cf. *Brit.* landslip) **2.** a decisive, overwhelming victory in an election.
— 图 (美) 1. 산사태, 토사의 사태 2. [선거의] 압도적 대승리

land·slip [lǽn(d)slìp] *n.* (*Brit.*) =landslide 1.

lands·man [lǽn(d)zmən] *n.* (pl. **-men** [-mən]) ⓒ **1.** a person who lives or works on land. ↔seaman **2.** (*Nautical*) an inexperienced sailor. ⌈seaward⌉
— 图 1. 육상 생활자 2. (海) 풋나기 선원

land·ward [lǽndwərd] *adj., adv.* toward the land. ↔⌉
land·wards [lǽndwərdz] *adv.* =landward.
— 图剛 육지쪽의; 육지쪽으로

‡ **lane** [lein] *n.* ⓒ **1.** a narrow way between hedges, houses, buildings, etc.; a little, narrow road or street. ¶*a blind ~*① / (*proverb*) *It is a long ~ that has no turning.*② **2.** a course or route used by ships or airplanes.
— 图 1. 좁은 길; 골목길; 열길 ¶①막다른 골목/②(俚)구부러지지 않은 길은 없다; 사물에는 반드시 변화가 있는 법 2. 항로

‡ **lan·guage** [lǽŋgwidʒ] *n.* **1.** Ⓤ human speech in general; a method of human communication in words. ¶*spoken ~*① */ written ~*② **2.** ⓒ the speech of one nation or race. ¶*the English ~*③ */ a foreign ~*. **3.** Ⓤ the manner of expression or using words. ¶*bad ~*④ */ strong ~ / literary ~*⑤. **4.** ⓒ terms and expressions for a special field. **5.** ⓒ a method of expression by symbols or gestures. ¶*the finger ~*⑥ */ the ~ of flowers.*⑦
— 图 1. 언어, 말 ¶①구어/②문어 2. 국어 ¶③영어 3. 어법, 말씨 ¶④천한 말씨/⑤문어 4. 술어, 전문어 5. [음성·문자를 사용하지 않는] 말 ¶⑥지화(指話)/⑦꽃말

lan·guid [lǽŋgwid] *adj.* **1.** weak; without energy. **2.** without interest; dull; not lively.
— 图 1. 힘 없는; 맥없는; 곤한한 2. 무관심한; 활발치 못한; 활기(원기) 없는

• **lan·guish** [lǽŋgwiʃ] *vi.* **1.** become weak; lose energy; droop. ¶*The flowers languished in the summer heat.*
— 自 1. 쇠약해지다; 생기가 없어지다; 노곤해지다; 시들다 2. 고달픈 생활을

2. live under unfavorable conditions. **3.** long; pine. 《~ *for* someone or something》. 하다 3. 그리워하다, 동경하다; 갈망하다

lan·guor [lǽŋgər] *n.* [U] physical or mental weakness; lack of energy, interest, activity, etc.; sluggishness. —[名] 무기력; 무관심; 활발치 못함, 맥빠짐; 권태, 노곤함

lan·guor·ous [lǽŋgərəs] *adj.* bringing about languor; languid. —[形] 나른한, 노곤한; 울적한; 지루한

lan·guor·ous·ly [lǽŋgərəsli] *adv.* in a languorous manner; dully. —[副] 노곤하게, 나른하게; 울적하게

lank [læŋk] *adj.* **1.** tall and thin; lean; slender. **2.** (of hair) straight and flat; not curled. ¶*a girl with ~ blonde hair.* —[形] 1. 마른, 호리호리한 2. [머리털이] 길고 부드러운; 곱슬곱슬하지 않은

lank·y [lǽŋki] *adj.* (**lank·i·er, lank·i·est**) awkwardly tall and thin. —[形] 호리호리한

∗**lan·tern** [lǽntərn] *n.* [C] **1.** a portable case to protect a light from rain, wind, etc. ¶*a paper ~.*① **2.** the top room of a lighthouse where, the light is kept. —[名] 1. 초롱, 각등(角燈), 등롱(燈籠) ¶①초롱 2. [등대의] 등실(燈室)

⁑**lap**[1] [læp] *n.* [C] **1.** the part of the body from the waist to the knees when a person is sitting; the part of the clothing covering this. ¶*sit on one's Mother's ~.*① **2.** a loosely hanging edge of clothing; a flap. **3.** an overlapping part. **4.** a complete circuit of racing. —[名] 1. 무릎(앉았을 때의 허리에서 무릎까지); 옷의 무릎을 덮는 부분 ¶①어머니 무릎 위에 앉다 2. [옷의] 늘어진 자락; 앞자락 3. 겹쳐진 부분 4. [경주에서] 한 바퀴, 일주(一周)

—*v.* (**lapped, lap·ping**) *vt.* **1.** fold. **2.** put (something) partly over another; overlap. **3.** wrap; enfold; surround. ¶*He lapped himself in a soft blanket.* / *Sorrow lapped her over.*① —*vi.* overlap. ¶*Her reign lapped over into the twentieth century.*② —[他] 1. …을 접다 2. …을 겹치게 하다 3. …을 싸다, 포장하다; 둘러싸다 ¶①슬픔이 그녀를 휩쌌다 —[自] 겹쳐지다 포개지다 ¶②그녀의 치세(治世)는 20세기까지 미쳤다

∗**lap**[2] [læp] *v.* (**lapped, lap·ping**) *vt.* **1.** drink (something) by the tongue, as a cat or dog does; lick. ¶*The dog lapped* [*up*] *all the milk.* **2.** (of water) wash against or beat upon (something) with a light, splashing sound. ¶*Waves lapped the shore.* —*vi.* **1.** wash or move in small waves with a light sound. ¶*Waves lapped on the beach.* **2.** lick up liquid with the tongue. —[他] 1. …을 핥다 2. [파도 따위가 기슭을] 씻다; 물결치다; …에 찰싹찰싹 쳐 밀려오다 —[自] 1. 파도가 기슭을 씻다; 밀려오다 2. 핥다

—*n.* [C] **1.** an act of lapping. **2.** the sound of lapping. —[名] 1. 핥기 2. [기슭을 씻는] 물결 소리; 핥는 소리

la·pel [ləpél] *n.* [C] 《usu. *pl.*》 the front part of a coat that is folded back on the chest ⇒fig. —[名] [상의의] 접은 깃

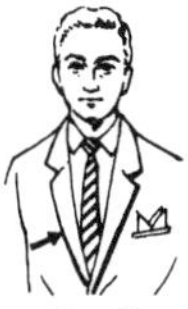
[lapel]

lap·i·dar·y [lǽpidèri / -dər-] *n.* [C] (pl. **-dar·ies**) a person whose job is to cut, polish, or engrave precious stones. —*adj.* **1.** of the art of cutting or engraving precious stones. **2.** engraved on the stone. —[名] 보석 세공인 —[形] 1. 보석 세공의 2. 돌에 새긴 [판]

Lap·land [lǽplæ̀nd] *n.* a region stretching across northern Norway, Sweden, Finland, and northwestern Russia. —[名] 랩랜드(유럽 최북부의 지역)

Lap·land·er [lǽplæ̀ndər] *n.* [C] a person of Lapland; a Lapp. —[名] 랩랜드 사람

Lapp [læp] *n.* **1.** [C] a member of a Mongoloid race living in Lapland. **2.** [U] the language of the Lapps. —[名] 1. 랩랜드 사람 2. 랩랜드 말

∗**lapse** [læps] *n.* [C] **1.** (of time) the act of passing away slowly. ¶*the ~ of time.* **2.** a slight mistake or error. ¶*a ~ of memory.*① **3.** the act of falling away from moral standards. ¶*a ~ from virtue*② / *a ~ into crime.*③ **4.** (*Law*) the loss of a right because it was not used or renewed. —[名] 1. [시간의] 경과 2. 잘못, 과실 ¶①착각, 기억 착오 3. 타락 ¶②타락/③죄를 범함 4. 《法》 [권리·특권의] 상실, 소멸

—*vi.* **1.** (of time) glide or slip slowly away; pass away. 《~ *away*》 **2.** make a slight mistake or error. **3.** fall or slip from moral standards. 《~ *into* idleness, etc.; ~ *from* good behavior, etc.》 ¶*He lapsed into bad habits.*④ **4.** (*Law*) (of a right or privilege) end; pass from one person to another, or become void because it has not been used or renewed. —[自] 1. [시간이] 경과하다 2. 죄를 범하다 3. 타락하다 ¶④그는 나쁜 습관에 빠져 들었다 4. 《法》 [권리·특권이] 소멸하다; [남의 손에] 넘어가다

lap·wing [lǽpwìŋ] *n.* [C] a European bird with a slow irregular flight and a peculiar wailing cry. —[名] 푸른도요

lar·board [lɑ́ːrbɔ̀ːrd / lɑ́ːbəd] *n.* [C] the left side of a ship as one faces the bow. ↔starboard ⇒[usage] —[名] 좌현(左舷) [usage] 현재는 보통 port

lar·ce·ny [lɑ́ːrsni] *n.* [U][C] (pl. **-nies**) (*Law*) the act —[名] 《法》 절도죄; 절도, 도둑질

L

larch [la:rtʃ] *n.* ⓒ a tree of the pine family with small cones and needlelike leaves which drop in the fall; Ⓤ the wood of this tree. ― 图 낙엽송; 낙엽송 재목

lard [la:rd] *n.* Ⓤ the refined, white fat of pigs, used in cooking. ― 图 라아드(돼지의 흰 비계로 정제 「한 반고체의 기름」)

lar·der [lá:rdər] *n.* ⓒ a small room in a house where food is stored; a pantry. ― 图 식품 저장실

lar·es and pe·na·tes [léəri:zəndpinéiti:z] *n.* (*pl.*) **1.** the gods of the household in ancient Rome. **2.** the cherished possessions of a family. ― 图 1. 가정의 수호신 2. 가보(家寶), 가재(家財)

‡ **large** [la:rdʒ] *adj.* **1.** occupying much space; that can hold a great amount; big. ¶*a ~ book / a ~ lake / a ~ box.* **2.** great in number. ¶*a ~ amount of money.* **3.** not little; not confined; generous. ¶*a ~ idea.*
at large, ⓐ free; not in prison. ¶*The murderer is at ~ in this city.*① ⓑ as a whole; representing the whole of a certain district. ― *adv.* largely.
― 图 1. 큰; 넓고 대규모의 2. 수량이 많은 3. 원대한; 한정되어 있지 않은; 관대한
图 ⓐ자유로운; 갇혀(붙잡혀) 있지 않은 ¶①살인범은 시내에 있다 ⓑ전체로서; 전체를 대표하는, 전지역에서
― 图 크게, 대체적으로 ㄴ선출된
― 图 크게; 주로; 후하게, 통이 크게, 관대하게

‡ **large·ly** [lá:rdʒli] *adv.* in great amounts; to a great extent; abundantly; mainly; generously.

large·ness [lá:rdʒnis] *n.* Ⓤ the state of being large; great size; generosity. ― 图 큼; 관대; 위대함 「scale; extensive.

large-scale [lá:rdʒskéil] *adj.* made or drawn on a large ― 图 대규모의; 확대한

lar·gess, -gesse [lá:rdʒes] *n.* Ⓤ the act of giving (something) generously; money or other gifts generously given. ― 图 아낌없이 금품(선물)을 주기; 부조, 축의금

lar·go [lá:rgou] *adj., adv.* (*Music*) slow and stately. ― *n.* ⓒ (pl. -gos) a passage or piece of music played in a slow and stately manner.
― 图图 《樂》 느리고 장엄한(하게)
― 图 라르고조의 악장(곡)

lar·i·at [læriət] *n., vt.* =lasso.

• **lark**¹ [la:rk] *n.* ⓒ a small bird with a sweet, clear note; a skylark. ― 图 종달새
1) *as happy as a lark,* very pleasant.
2) *rise with the lark,* get up early.
图 1)매우 즐거운 2)일찍 일어나다

lark² [la:rk] *n.* ⓒ a bit of fun; a frolic. ― 图 장난, 희롱
1) *for a lark,* in joke. ¶*He only said it for a ~.*
2) *have a lark,* do mischief.
3) *What a lark!* How funny this is! what fun!
图 1)농담으로 2)장난하다 3)이것 참 재미있군!
― *vi.* have fun; play pranks. ―自 장난치다, 희롱하다
lark about, do mischief and make noise. 图 장난치며 떠들다

lark·spur [lá:rkspər] *n.* ⓒ a tall garden plant with blue, white, or pink flowers. ― 图 참제비고깔(키가 큰 정원수의 일종)

lar·va [lá:rvə] *n.* ⓒ (pl. -vae [-vi:]) the early form of an insect, the stage between the egg and the pupa. ― 图 애벌레, 유충

lar·val [lá:rv(ə)l] *adj.* of larvae; in the form of a larva. ― 图 유충의

la·ryn·ges [ləríndʒi:z] *n.* pl. of larynx.

lar·ynx [læriŋks] *n.* ⓒ (pl. **-ynx·es** or **la·ryn·ges**) (*Anatomy*) the upper part of the windpipe, containing the vocal cords. ― 图 《解》 후두(喉頭) 「ing lust; lustful.

las·civ·i·ous [ləsíviəs] *adj.* causing, feeling, or show― ― 图 음란한, 호색적인; 도발적인

• **lash** [læʃ] *n.* ⓒ **1.** a whip, esp. the string part of it; a stroke or blow with this. **2.** a sudden, swift movement; the act of .violent beating. ¶*the ~ of waves against the rock.* **3.** a sharp remark. **4.** an eyelash.
― *vt.* **1.** strike (something) with a lash; strike violently. ¶*He lashed her across the face.*① / *The rain lashed the trees.* **2.** attack (someone) severely with words. ¶*~ someone to (or into) fury.*② **3.** wave or beat (something) back and forth; fling quickly. ¶*The dog lashed its tail.* **4.** fasten (things) with a cord or rope; bind. ¶*~ two pieces together / ~ one piece to another.* ― *vi.* move quickly or violently; strike with a whip; strike violently.
lash out, ⓐ (of a horse) hit; kick; strike. ⓑ speak bitterly.
― 图 1. 채찍; 채찍으로 한 번 치기, 채찍질 2. 홱(급격히) 움직이기; 격렬한 타격 3. 통렬한 비난 4. 속눈썹
― 图 1. …을 채찍으로 치다; 몹시 때리다 ¶①그는 그녀의 얼굴을 채찍으로 갈겼다 2. …을 심하게 꾸짖다; 비난하다 ¶②…을 욕하여 격분케 하다 3. [채찍 · 꼬리 따위]를 몹시 휘두르다 4. [밧줄 따위로] …을 묶다; 매다
―自 급격히 움직이다; 채찍질하다, 매질하다; 맹렬히 치다 「을 퍼붓다
图 ⓐ[말이] 차다, 발길질하다 ⓑ욕언

lash·ing [læʃiŋ] *n.* **1.** Ⓤ a cord, rope, etc. used for ― 图 1. 묶는 밧줄, 포승, 끈, 노끈 2. 다

lass

binding. **2.** ((*pl.*)) (*colloq.*) abundance; plenty. ((*~ of*))
* **lass** [læs] *n.* ⓒ **1.** a young woman; a girl. ↔lad **2.** a sweetheart.
las·sie [lǽsi] *n.* ⓒ **1.** a girl. **2.** a sweetheart.
las·si·tude [lǽsitj(ù):d / -tjù:d] *n.* ⓤ the state of being weary; lack of energy; weariness.
‡ **last**¹ [læst / lɑːst] *adj.* **1.** coming after all others; final. ↔first ¶*the ~ page of this book* | *~ but one* (*two*).① **2.** the last remaining. ¶*the ~ chance* | *I spent my ~ dollar.* **3.** most recent; latest; newest. ¶*~ night* | *~ year* | *the ~ news I heard* | *the ~ things in hats.*② **4.** most unlikely; most unsuitable. ¶*He is the ~ man we want to see.*③ | *He is the ~ man to accept a bribe.*④ **5.** lowest; the most inferior. ¶*the ~ boy in the class.*
—*adv.* **1.** finally; after all others. ¶*He arrived ~ at the party.* **2.** most lately. ¶*When did you see her ~ ?*
—*n.* ((the ~, usu. *sing.*)) **1.** a person or thing that comes last. ¶*the day before ~.*⑤ **2.** the end; the last moment; one's death. ¶*from first to ~.*
at [*long*] *last,* finally.
‡ **last**² [læst / lɑːst] *vi.* **1.** go on; continue in time. ¶*The fine weather lasted eight days.* **2.** be enough; continue unspent. ¶*while our money lasts.*① **3.** continue in use or alive; endure. ¶*He will not ~* [*out*] *till tomorrow.*
—*vt.* continue for (someone). ¶*The money lasted me* [*for*] *two months.*
* **last·ing** [lǽstiŋ / lɑ́ːst-] *adj.* lasting for a long period or forever; permanent. ↔temporary ▷**last·ing·ly** [-li] *adv.*
last·ly [lǽstli / lɑ́ːst-] *adv.* in the end; in conclusion; finally. ¶*~ first*; firstly
latch [lætʃ] *n.* ⓒ a device for fastening a door, a gate, etc. ⇒fig. ¶*be on* (*off*) *the ~.*① —*vt., vi.* close or fasten (a door, etc.) with a latch.
latch·key [lǽtʃkìː] *n.* ⓒ a key for drawing back or unfastening the latch of a door.
‡ **late** [leit] *adj.* (**lat·er, lat·est** or **lat·ter, last**) **1.** being after the usual or right time. ↔early ¶*~ dinner* | *~ spring* | *keep ~ hours*① | *a ~ marriage* | *be ~ for school.*② **2.** toward the end of a certain time; far advanced in a period. ¶*the ~ Middle Ages.* **3.** recent. ¶*of ~ years* | *the ~ fire.* **4.** no longer living; recently dead; former.
—*adv.* (**later, latest** or **last**) **1.** after the usual or proper time. ¶*come ~* | *Ten minutes later he came back.* **2.** until an advanced hour, esp. of the night; till late. ¶*We sat up ~ last night.*③ **3.** recently; lately.
* **late·ly** [léitli] *adv.* ((in *negative* or *interrogative*)) not long ago; recently. ¶*Have you seen her ~ ?*
late·ness [léitnis] *n.* ⓤ the state of being late.
la·tent [léit(ə)nt] *adj.* existing but not active; concealed; hidden. ¶*~ ability* | *~ heat*① | *the ~ period.*②
‡ **lat·er** [léitər] *adj.* compar. of **late**.
—*adv.* at a later time; after some time. ↔earlier, sooner ¶*five days ~.*①
　1) *later on,* afterward; subsequently.
　2) *sooner or later,* at some time; in time.
lat·er·al [lǽt(ə)r(ə)l] *adj.* of, at, toward, or coming from the side. ¶*a ~ branch of a family*① | *a ~ consonant.*② —*n.* ⓒ **1.** a lateral part, growth, branch, etc. **2.** (*Phonetics*) a lateral sound.
lat·est [léitist] *adj., adv.* superl. of **late**; most recent; newest; last.
la·tex [léiteks] *n.* ⓤⓒ (pl. **lat·i·ces** or **-tex·es** [-teksìz])

latex

량, 대량
—ⓝ 1. 소녀; 젊은 여자, 아가씨 2. 애인
—ⓝ 1. 소녀 2. 애인
—ⓝ 피로, 노곤함; 권태

—ⓐ 1. 최후의, 마지막의 ¶①마지막에 서 두(세) 번째의 ¶②최후에 남은 3. 최근의, 최신의 ¶②최신 유행의 모자 4. 절대로(가장) …할 것 같지 않은(어울리지 않는) ¶③우리는 그이만은 절대로 만나고 싶지 않다/④그는 절대로 뇌물을 받을 만한 사람은 아니다 5. 최저의; 최하급의
—ⓐ 1. 최후에, 맨 마지막으로 2. 요전, 전번에, 최근에
—ⓝ 1. 최후의 사람(것) ¶⑤그저께 2. 최종; 끝, 종말; 죽음

熟 드디어, 마침내, 결국
—ⓐ 1. 계속되다; 지속하다 2. 넉넉하다, 충분하다; 없어지지 않고 지탱해 나가다 ¶①돈이 있는 한 3. 오래 가다 (쓸 수 있다); 지탱하다; 오래 견디다
—ⓣ …에 지속하기에 충분하다; 견디다, 지탱해 나가다

—ⓐ 영속하는; 내구력이 있는; 영구(불변)의
—ⓐ 최후에; 끝으로, 마지막으로

—ⓝ 걸쇠, 빗장 ¶①걸쇠가 걸려(벗겨져) 있다 —ⓣⓐ 걸쇠를 걸다, 빗장을 잠그다

—ⓝ 걸쇠의 열쇠

—ⓐ 1. [때가] 늦은; 뒤늦은, 지각한 ¶①밤늦게까지 자지 않고 있다/②학교에 지각하다 2. 마지막에 가까운; 후기의; 만년의 3. 근래의; 최근의 4. 최근 죽은; 고(故)…; 먼저의, 앞서의

—ⓐ 1. 너무 늦어서; 늦어서 2. 늦게까지 ¶③우리는 어젯밤 늦게까지 자지 않고 있었다 3. 요사이; 최근

—ⓐ 요즈음, 요사이, 최근

—ⓝ 늦음, 지각
—ⓐ 잠복성의; 숨어 있는, 잠재적인 ¶①잠열(潛熱)/②잠복기
—ⓐ 나중의; 후에 ¶①닷새(5일) 후에

熟 1) 나중에, 추후 2) 언젠가는, 조만간

—ⓐ 옆의, 측면의 ¶①분가(分家)/②측음(側音)
—ⓝ 1. 옆쪽, 옆부분; 측면에서 생기는 것 2. (音聲) 측음

—ⓐⓐ 최근(의), 최신의; 최후의(에)
—ⓝ 유수지(乳樹脂), 수액(樹液)

a milky liquid found in certain plants and trees, such as the rubber tree, the poppy, etc.

lath [læθ / lɑːθ] *n.* [C] (pl. **laths** [læðz, læθs / lɑːθs, lɑːðz]) a thin, narrow strip of wood fastened to the framework of a house to support the plaster.
as thin as a lath, very skinny.

—[名] 욋가지, 외(椳)
[熟] 몹시 마른

lathe [leið] *n.* [C] a machine on which articles of wood, metal, etc. are turned to be shaped or polished.

—[名] 선반(旋盤)

lath·er [lǽðər / lɑ́ːðə] *n.* [U] ⟪sometimes *a* ~⟫ **1.** the foam or froth produced by soap and water. **2.** foamy sweat, as on a race horse. ¶*be* [*all*] *in a* ~.① —*vt.* cover (something) with lather (*n.* 1.). —*vi.* **1.** (of soap) form lather. **2.** (of horse) be soaked with sweat.

—[名] 1. 비누거품 2. [말의] 거품 같은 땀 ¶①땀에 흠뻑 젖어 있다 —[他] …에 비누거품을 칠하다 —[自] 1. [비누가] 거품이 일다 2. [말이] 땀투성이가 되다

lat·i·ces [lǽtisìːz] *n.* pl. of **latex**.

‡ **Lat·in** [lǽt(i)n] *adj.* **1.** of ancient Rome, its people, or their language. **2.** of the languages descended from that of ancient Rome; the people who speak these languages. —*n.* **1.** [U] the language of ancient Rome. **2.** [C] a member of one of the Latin races.

—[形] 1. 라틴[사람·말]의 2. 라틴어계(語系)의, 라틴계의 —[名] 1. 라틴 말 2. 라틴 사람

• **lat·i·tude** [lǽtit(j)ùːd / -tjùːd] *n.* [U] **1.** the distance of a place north or south of the equator as measured in degrees. ↔longitude ¶*at* ~ *40°N.*① **2.** ⟪*pl.*⟫ regions; districts. ¶*cold* (*calm*) *latitudes*② | *high* (*low*) *latitudes.*③ **3.** freedom of thought or action. **4.** extent; scope.

—[名] 1. 위도(緯度) ¶①북위 40도 2. 지역, 지방 ¶②한대(무풍 지대)/③고(저)위도 지방 3. [판단·사상·행동의] 자유 4. 범위

lat·i·tu·di·nar·i·an [læ̀tit(j)uːdinɛ́əriən / -tjuː-] *adj.* of liberal views, esp. in religious matters; tolerant; broad-minded. —*n.* [C] a person who is very liberal, esp. in his religious views.

—[形] 교리(신조)에 얽매이지 않는; 광교파(廣敎派)의 —[名] 광교파의 사람

‡ **lat·ter** [lǽtər] *adj.* compar. of **late** **1.** later; nearer to the end. ¶*the* ~ *part of the month.*① **2.** recent. ¶*in these* ~ *days.*② **3.** ⟪*the* ~⟫ the second of two persons or things mentioned. ↔the former ⇒[N.B.]

—[形] 1. 뒤쪽의, 마지막에 가까운 ¶① 그 달의 후반(하순) 2. 요즈음의, 작금의 ¶②요즈음은 3. 후자(後者) [N.B.] 형용사의 대명사적 용법

lat·ter·ly [lǽtərli] *adv.* of late; recently.

—[副] 요즈음에, 근래, 최근

lat·tice [lǽtis] *n.* [C] **1.** a frame of crossed wooden lathes, or iron bars. **2.** a window, a gate, etc. made of a lattice. —*vt.* form (a window, etc.) into a lattice; furnish (a gate, etc.) with a lattice.

—[名] 1. 창살 2. 격자창(格子窓), 창살문 —[他] [창 따위]를 격자무늬로 만들다; [문 따위]에 창살을 붙이다

lat·ticed [lǽtist] *adj.* made in the form of a lattice; furnished with a lattice. ¶*a* ~ *gate.*

—[形] 격자무늬로 만든; 창살을 붙인

lat·tice·work [lǽtiswə̀ːrk] *n.* **1.** [U] ⟪*collectively*⟫ lattices. **2.** [C] a lattice.

—[名] 1. 격자 세공 2. 격자

laud [lɔːd] *vt.* praise; glorify.
laud someone to the skies, speak very highly of someone; praise someone very much.
—*n.* **1.** [U] praise. **2.** [C] any songs or hymns of praise.

—[他] 칭찬하다, 찬양하다; 찬미하다
[熟] 남을 극구 칭찬하다
—[名] 1. 칭찬, 찬미 2. 찬가, 찬미가

laud·a·ble [lɔ́ːdəbl] *adj.* deserving praise; praiseworthy.

—[形] 칭찬할 만한

lau·da·num [lɔ́ːd(ə)nəm / lɔ́d-] *n.* [U] a solution of opium in alcohol used as a medicine.

—[名] 아편정기(阿片丁幾), 아편제(劑)

lau·da·tion [lɔːdéiʃ(ə)n] *n.* [U] the act of lauding; the state of being lauded; praise.

—[名] 칭찬, 찬미

laud·a·to·ry [lɔ́ːdətɔ̀ːri / -təri] *adj.* expressing praise.

—[形] 칭찬의, 찬미하는

‡ **laugh** [læf / lɑːf] *vi.* make sounds of the voice showing pleasure or amusement. —*vt.* **1.** express or say (something) with laughter. ¶*He laughed his consent.* **2.** influence (someone or something) by laughing. ¶*We laughed our fears away.* | *She laughed her tears away.* | *I tried to* ~ *him out of the foolish belief.*①
1) ***laugh at,*** ⓐ show disrespect to; make fun of (someone). ¶*Don't* ~ *at someone in trouble.*② ⓑ be amused by (something). ¶~ *at a joke.*
2) ***laugh away,*** get rid of (something unpleasant) by laughter.
3) ***laugh down,*** cause (a speech, etc.) to stop by laughing at it.
4) ***laugh in*** (or ***up***) ***one's sleeve,*** laugh secretly or in-

—[自] [소리내어] 웃다 —[他] 1. 웃으며 …을 말하다; 웃는 얼굴로 …을 나타내다; …처럼 웃다 2. 웃어서 …을 어떤 상태가 되게 하다 ¶①나는 웃어서 그가 그의 어리석은 생각을 버리게 하려 하였다
[熟] 1)ⓐ…을 비웃다(조소하다); 경멸하다 ¶②곤경에 처해 있는 사람을 비웃지 마라 ⓑ…을 보고(듣고) 웃다 2)…을 일소에 붙이다; 웃으며 시간을 보내다 3)…을 웃어서 말 못하게(연설을 중단하게) 하다 4)속으로(몰래) 웃다; 몰래 조소하다(고소해 하다) 5)웃으며

laughable [651] **lavishly**

wardly. ⌈at it.⌉
5) *laugh off*, avoid or reject (something) by laughing⌋
—*n.* ⓒ an act or a sound of laughing; laughter. ¶*burst into a ~*①/ *have a hearty ~* / *give a ~*.
have the last laugh on, succeed in (something) after overcoming many difficulties; surprise (someone) by succeeding in doing something he said one couldn't do, etc.

laugh·a·ble [lǽfəbl / láː f-] *adj.* causing laughter; amusing. ▷**laugh·a·ble·ness** [-nis] *n.* —**laugh·a·bly** [-i] *adv.*

laugh·ing [lǽfiŋ / láː f-] *adj.* 1. that laughs or seems to be merry. 2. causing laughter. ¶*It is no ~ matter.*①
—*n.* Ⓤ laughter. ¶*hold one's ~.*②

laughing gas [ː ː] *n.* Ⓤ (*Chemistry*) a colorless gas of nitrous oxide which makes people laugh.

laugh·ing·ly [lǽfiŋli / láː f-] *adv.* with laughter.

laugh·ing·stock [lǽfiŋstɑ̀k / láː fiŋstɔ̀k] *n.* ⓒ a person or thing that is laughed at.

:**laugh·ter** [lǽftər / láː ftə] *n.* Ⓤ the act or sound of laughing. ¶*burst* (or *break out*) *into ~*①/ *roars of ~*.②

***launch** [lɔːntʃ, lɑːntʃ] *vt.* 1. cause (a ship) to slide into the water. ¶*A new ship was launched from its supports.* 2. send forth (something) with some force. ¶*~ a rocket.* 3. start; begin. ¶*~ a new enterprise.*
launch out; *launch* [*out*] *into*, ⓐ put to sea. ¶*~ out on a voyage of discovery.* ⓑ start on some new enterprise. ⌈boat driven by an engine.⌉
—*n.* 1. Ⓤ the act of launching. 2. ⓒ a small open⌋

laun·der [lɔ́ːndər, láː n-] *vt.* wash and iron. ¶*beautifully-laundered sheets.* —*vi.* be able to be washed.

laun·dress [lɔ́ːndris, láː n-] *n.* ⓒ a woman whose work is washing and ironing clothes.

***laun·dry** [lɔ́ːndri, láː n-] *n.* (pl. **-dries**) 1. ⓒ a place where clothes, etc. are washed and ironed. 2. Ⓤ (*the ~*, *collectively*) something esp. clothes to be laundered.

laun·dry·man [lɔ́ːndrimæ̀n, láː n- / lɔ́ːndrimən] *n.* ⓒ (pl. **-men** [-mèn / -mən]) a man who works in a laundry; a man who collects and delivers laundry.

lau·re·ate [lɔ́ːriit] *adj.* crowned with a laurel wreath; honored. —*n.* ⓒ a poet who has been honored.

***lau·rel** [lɔ́ːrəl, lɑ́r- / lɔ́r-] *n.* ⓒ 1. a small evergreen tree with smooth, shiny leaves, used as a symbol of fame and honor. 2. a crown of laurel given as a prize or symbol of honor by the ancient Greeks and Romans. 3. (often *pl.*) honor; fame; victory. ¶*gain* (or *win*) *laurels.*①
1) *look to one's laurels*, be careful about one's reputation. ⌈that one has already gained.⌉
2) *rest on one's laurels*, be contented with the honors⌋

lau·reled, *Brit.* **-relled** [lɔ́ːrəld, lɑ́r- / lɔ́r(ə)ld] *adj.* crowned with laurel; honored.

***la·va** [láː və, lǽvə / láː -] *n.* Ⓤ the liquid rock flowing from a volcano; such rock when it has hardened.

lav·a·to·ry [lǽvətɔ̀ːri / -təri] *n.* ⓒ (pl. **-ries**) 1. a room for washing the hands and the face. 2. a fixed bowl or basin to wash in. 3. a toilet.

lav·en·der [lǽvindər] *n.* 1. ⓒ a small plant with pale purple flowers that have a sweet smell. 2. Ⓤ the color of pale purple.

lav·ish [lǽviʃ] *adj.* 1. very liberal; almost too generous in giving or spending. ¶*He is ~ of* (or *with*) *money*①. 2. very abundant; excessive. ¶*a ~ supply of food.* —*vt.* give or spend generously.

lav·ish·ly [lǽviʃli] *adv.* in a lavish manner.

―…을 물리치다; 일소에 붙이다

―名 웃음; 웃음소리 ¶③웃음을 터뜨리다. 폭소하다
熟 고생 끝에 …에 성공하다; 못하리라고 남이 생각했던 일을 해내어 남을 놀라게 하다

―形 우스운; 재미있는

―形 1. 웃[고 있]는, 쾌활한 2. 우스운 ¶①웃을 일이 아니다
―名 웃음 ¶②웃음을 참다

―名 〔化〕 웃음 가스, 일산화 질소

―副 웃으며, 조소하듯이
―名 웃음거리

―名 웃음; 웃음소리 ¶①웃음을 터뜨리다, 폭소하다/②왁자한 웃음소리

―他 1. [배]를 진수(進水)시키다 2. …을 내보내다; 진출시키다 3. …을 시작하다, 일으키다; 착수하다

熟 ⓐ[배가 바다로] 나가다 ⓑ[사업 따위]를 착수하다; 시작하다
―名 1. [배의] 진수 2. 런치; 똑딱선

―他 …을 세탁하다 ―自 세탁이 잘 되다, 잘 빨아지다
―名 세탁부(婦)

―名 1. 세탁소; 클리닝집 2. 세탁물, 빨래[감]

―名 세탁업자; 세탁물 수집원

―形 월계관을 쓴; 영광스러운, 영예의
―名 계관(桂冠) 시인
―名 1. 월계수 2. 월계관 3. 영예; 명성; 승리 ¶①영예를 차지하다

熟 1) 명성을 잃지 않도록 조심하다 2) 이미 얻은 명예에 만족하다; 조그마한 성공에 만족하다
―形 월계관을 쓴; 영예를 차지한

―名 용암(熔岩); 화산암

―名 1. 세면소; 화장실 2. 세면대 3. 변소

―名 1. 라벤더(향기로운 꿀풀과의 식물) 2. 라벤더 빛, 연보랏빛

―形 1. 아끼지 않는, 마음이 후한; 통이 큰 ¶①그는 돈을 아낌없이 잘 쓴다 2. 풍부한, 남아돌아가는 ―他 …을 아낌없이(선뜻) 주다; 낭비하다[허투루]
―副 아낌없이, 후하게; 함부로, 마구,

‡ **law** [lɔː] *n.* **1.** [C][U] a rule made by a government or a ruler. ¶*the civil* ~① | *keep* (*break*) *the* ~② | *There is a* ~ *against spitting in streetcars.* **2.** [U] ((often *the* ~)) the profession of lawyers or judges. ¶*follow the* ~③ | *practice* ~.④ **3.** [U][C] a rule of a game, trade etc.; a principle. ¶*the laws of tennis* | *the Law of Moses*⑤ | *Mendel's* ~⑥ | *the laws of God.*
1) ***be a law to oneself,*** follow one's own opinion.
2) ***go to law,*** take a problem to a law court.
3) ***lay down the law,*** speak as if one's opinions were absolutely right.

—[名] 1. 법, 법률 ¶①민법/②법률을 지키다(어기다) 2. 법률적 직업, 사법직(司法職) ¶③변호사가 되다/④변호사를 개업하다 3. 규칙, 법칙, 율법, 계율 ¶⑤모세의 율법/⑥멘델의 법칙
[熟] 1)자기 생각대로 하다 2)문제를 법정에 제기하다, 고소하다 3)독단적으로 말하다

law·break·ing [lɔ́ːbrèikiŋ] *n.* [U] the act of breaking the law. —*adj.* violating the law.
—[名] 위법 —[形] 위법의

law court [⌐ ⌐] *n.* a court of justice; a place where legal cases are judged.
—[名] 법정, 법원, 재판소

* **law·ful** [lɔ́ːf(u)l] *adj.* **1.** according to law; allowed by law; rightful. **2.** as decided by law. ¶~ *age.*①
—[形] 1. 합법적인; 정당한 2. 법정(法定)의 ¶①법정 연령

law·ful·ly [lɔ́ːfuli] *adv.* in a lawful manner; rightly.
—[副] 합법적으로; 정당하게

law·giv·er [lɔ́ːgìvər] *n.* [C] a man who forms or writes a system of laws; a lawmaker.
—[名] 입법자

law·less [lɔ́ːlis] *adj.* **1.** uncontrolled by the law; breaking the law; unruly. **2.** without laws. ¶*a* ~ *country.*
—[形] 1. 법률을 지키지 않는; 불법의, 비합법적인 2. 법률이 없는

law·less·ly [lɔ́ːlisli] *adv.* in a lawless manner.
—[副] 불법으로; 법률을 지키지 않고

law·mak·er [lɔ́ːmèikər] *n.* [C] a person who makes or helps to make laws; a legislator.
—[名] 입법자

‡ **lawn**[1] [lɔːn] *n.* [C] an area of grass kept closely cut. ¶*a tennis* ~.①
—[名] 잔디, 잔디밭 ¶①잔디를 깐 정구 코오트

lawn[2] [lɔːn] *n.* [U] a thin cloth of linen or cotton.
—[名] 로온, 한랭사(寒冷紗)

lawn mower [⌐ ⌐-] *n.* a machine used to cut grass on lawns.
—[名] 잔디 깎는 기계

lawn tennis [⌐ ⌐-] *n.* a kind of tennis, usu. played on a lawn.
—[名] 로온 테니스, 정구

law·suit [lɔ́ːsùːt / -s(j)ùːt] *n.* [C] a case in a law court. ¶*enter* (or *bring in*) *a* ~ *against someone.*①
—[名] 소송 ¶①남에게 대하여 소송을 제기하다

‡ **law·yer** [lɔ́ːjər] *n.* [C] a person who advises other persons about matters of law or acts, in a law court.
—[名] 변호사; 법률가

lax [læks] *adj.* **1.** not firm or strict; loose; careless. **2.** (of the bowels) loose; having lax bowels.
—[形] 1. 모호한, 미지근한 2. [창자가] 이완(弛緩)한, 설사하는

lax·a·tive [lǽksətiv] *adj.* making the bowels move or empty. —*n.* [C] a medicine that does this.
—[形] 대변을 통하게 하는; 설사나게 하는 성질이 있는 —[名] 하제(下劑),

lax·i·ty [lǽksiti] *n.* [U] lack of firmness or exactness.
—[名] 단정치 못함, 방종; 부정확함

‡ **lay**[1] [lei] *v.* (**laid**) *vt.* **1.** cause (something) to lie; place; put. ¶~ *oneself down*① | *She laid her hand on my shoulder.* **2.** place (something) in a certain place. ¶~ *a cable* | ~ *a pavement.* **3.** knock down; beat down. ¶*The wind has laid all the crops low.* **4.** cover. ¶~ *a floor with a carpet.* **5.** say or think that (something) belongs to another; ascribe; attribute. ¶~ *a fault to someone's charge.*② **6.** produce (eggs). ¶*The hens are laying well.*③ **7.** cause (something) to be quiet; settle. ¶~ *someone's fears* | *The rain has laid the dust.*④ **8.** make (something) ready; prepare. ¶~ *a table for dinner* | ~ *a snare* (or *trap*) *for foxes.*⑤ **9.** bet. ((~ *that* ...)) ¶*I* ~ *5 dollars that she will come.* **10.** ((usu. in *passive*)) locate; situate. ¶*The scene of the story is laid in Paris in 1927.*⑥ **11.** cause (someone or something) to be in a certain state. ¶~ *one's chest bare.*⑦ —*vi.* **1.** lay eggs. **2.** bet. **3.** lie.
1) ***lay about,*** (*Brit.*) hit out at (persons) on all sides.
2) ***lay aside*** (or ***away, by, in***), put (something) away for future use; save.
3) ***lay down,*** declare; state clearly and definitely.
4) ***lay for*** (=*lie in wait for; wait to attack*) *someone.*
5) ***lay into someone,*** (*Slang*) ⓐ beat. ⓑ scold; attack by words.

—[他] 1. …을 눕히다; 놓다, 두다 ¶①드러눕다 2. …을 깔다; 늘어놓다 3. …을 때려눕히다; 밀어 넘어뜨리다 4. …을 덮다; 씌우다 5. …을 남에게 돌리다(뒤집어씌우다); 남의 탓으로 하다 ¶②실패를 남의 탓으로 돌리다 6. [알]을 낳다 ¶③암탉들은 알을 잘 낳는다 7. …을 가라앉히다, 진정시키다, 침착하게 하다 ¶④비가 와서 먼지가 잤다 8. …의 준비를 하다; 준비하다 ¶⑤여우를 잡으려고 덫을 놓다 9. …을 걸다, 내기하다 10. …에 위치를 정하다 ¶⑥그 소설은 1927년의 파리를 무대로 하였다 11. …을 어떤 상태로 하다 ¶⑦흉금을 터놓다, 모조리 자백하다 —[自] 1. 알을 낳다 2. 내기를 하다 3. 드러눕다
[熟] 1)((英))전후좌우로 후려치다(공격하다) 2)치워 두다, 간직해 두다; 비축하다 3)단언하다; 분명히 말하다 4)…을 숨어서 기다리다 5)((俗))ⓐ…을 치다, 때리다 ⓑ…을 꾸짖다; 비난하다 6)ⓐ…을 추방하다; 해고하다 ⓑ…을 그만두다; 중지하다 7)…을 공격하다 8)

L

lay

6) ***lay off***, ⓐ send (someone) away from work; discharge. ⓑ stop doing (something) [for a time].
7) ***lay on***, attack (someone) with force.
8) ***lay open***, expose oneself to attack, blame, etc.
9) ***lay oneself out***, (colloq.) try very hard.
10) ***lay open***, cut open; expose.
11) ***lay out***, ⓐ spread out. ⓑ arrange; plan. ⓒ spend.
12) ***lay over***, ⓐ delay; postpone. ⓑ stay over.
13) ***lay up***, ⓐ put away (something) for future use. ⓑ cause (someone) to stay in bed because of illness. ⓒ put (a ship) in dock.

lay² [lei] *vi.* pt. of **lie**.

lay³ [lei] *adj.* **1.** of an ordinary person; of a person who is not a clergyman. ↔clerical **2.** nonprofessional.

lay⁴ [lei] *n.* ⓒ a short poem or song; a short narrative poem.

• **lay·er** [léiər] *n.* ⓒ **1.** a person who lays. ¶*a bricklayer.*① **2.** one thickness or fold of a material. **3.** a shoot that is grown into a root by bending it over and covering it with earth. ⇒fig.

lay·ette [leiét] *n.* ⓒ a collection of clothes, bedding, and other necessary things for a new-born baby.

lay figure [´-´-] *n.* **1.** a figure of the human body in clay or wax; a plastic model of the human body used for displaying clothes. **2.** a useless person.

[layer 3.]

lay·man [léimən] *n.* (pl. **-men** [-mən]) ⓒ **1.** a person who is not a priest but who belongs to a church. ↔ clergyman **2.** a person who is not skilled in some special professions. ↔expert

lay·out [léiàut] *n.* **1.** Ⓤ the act of planning or arranging land, streets, etc. **2.** ⓒ a plan or arrangement, etc. **3.** ⓒ a plan or design of a book, a newspaper, an advertisement.

la·zi·ly [léizili] *adv.* in a lazy manner.

la·zi·ness [léizinis] *n.* Ⓤ the state of being lazy.

‡**la·zy** [léizi] *adj.* (**la·zi·er**, **la·zi·est**) **1.** not willing to work; idle. ↔diligent **2.** not active; slow. ¶*a ~ correspondent*① / *a ~ river* / *a ~ day.*②

la·zy·bones [léizibòunz] *n. pl.* (usu. used as *sing.*) (colloq.) a lazy person or fellow.

lea [li:] *n.* ⓒ (poetic) a piece of grass land; a meadow.

leach [li:tʃ] *vt.* **1.** cause (water) to flow through a filter. **2.** wash (ashes, etc.) to extract some dissolved material. —*vi.* (of ashes, etc.) wash to extract some dissolved material.

‡**lead**¹ [li:d] *v.* (**led** [led]) *vt.* **1.** go before (someone) to show the way. **2.** guide (someone or something) by the hand, etc. ¶*~ the horse by the reins* / *~ someone out (in).*① **3.** direct; command. ¶*~ troops* / *~ an orchestra.* **4.** be at the head of or hold first place in (a parade, a race, etc.). ¶*He leads the class.* **5.** (of a road, etc.) take (someone) to a place. (*~ someone to*) ¶*This road will ~ you to the station.* **6.** cause (someone) to be in a certain state. ¶*Drink led him to destruction.* **7.** persuade (someone) to do or believe something. (*~ someone to do*) ¶*Poverty led him to steal.* / *I was led to believe that* ... **8.** spend; live (a certain kind of life, etc.); cause (someone) to live. ¶*~ a happy life* / *~ someone a dog's life.*②

—*vi.* **1.** act as guide or conductor; manage. ¶*~ in prayer.*③ **2.** act as head; be first; excel. ¶*She leads in French and English.* **3.** (of a road, etc.) extend; go;

lead

공격 따위에 몸을 드러내놓다 9)(口) 노력하다, …하려고 애쓰다 10)…을 절 개(切開)하다; 폭로하다 11)ⓐ…을 펼 치다 ⓑ…을 설계하다 ⓒ…을 쓰다, 소 비하다 12)ⓐ…을 지체시키다, 연기하 다 ⓑ도중에서 머물다 13)ⓐ…을 비축 해 두다 ⓑ…을 병실에 처박혀 있게 하 다 ⓒ(배)를 부두에 매다, 계선(繫船) 하다

—⊛ 1.(성직자에 대하여) 속인의 2. (전문가에 대하여) 비직업적인, 본업이

—⊛ 노래, 시; 이야기체로 된 시(아닌

—⊛ 1. 놓는(두는, 쌓는, 까는) 사람 ¶ ①벽돌 직공 2. 켜, 층(層), 겹 3. (원예 의) 취목(取木)

—⊛ 갓난아기 용품 한 벌

—⊛ 1. 인체 모형, 모델 인형, 마네킨 2. 아무 구실도 못하는 사람, 허수아비

—⊛ 1.(성직자에 대하여) 평신도, 속 인 2. 비전문가, 문외한

—⊛ 1.(정원·도로 따위의) 설계법 2. 설계 3.(서적·광고 따위의) 편집, 지면 배열, 레이아웃

—⊛ 게으르게, 나태하게, 빈들빈들
—⊛ 게으름, 나태
—⊛ 1. 게으른, 나태한 2. 굼뜬 ¶①글 을 쓰기 싫어하는 사람/②빈들빈들 지 낸 하루

—⊛ (口) 게으름뱅이, 나태한 사람

—⊛ (詩) 풀밭, 초원, 목장
—⊕ 1.(여과기에) …을 거르다 2.(재 따위로) 액체를 거르다 —⊜ 용해하다

—⊕ 1. …을 이끌다, (남)을 안내하다 2.(소·말 따위)를 끌고 가다 ¶①남 을 밖으로 데리고 나오다(데리고 들어 가다). 3. …을 지휘하다, 인솔하다, 지도 하다 4. …의 수위를 차지하다, 선두에 서다, 리이드하다 5. (도로가 사람)을 인도하다, 데리고 가다 6. (원인이 어떤 결과)로 이끌고 가다, 결과로 되다 7. …을 유인하다, 유혹하다, …할 마음이 나게 하다, 끌어들이다 8. (생활)을 보내 다, 지내다, 보내다, 살다; 살게(지내게) 하다 ¶②남을 비참한 생활을 하게 하 다

—⊜ 1. 안내하다, 앞장서다, 인도하다, 지휘하다 ¶③기도를 인도하다 2. 선두 에 서다, 수위를 차지하다, 리이드하다 3. (도로 따위가 …에) 이르다, (…으로

lead

run. 《~ to a certain place》 ¶*This road leads to the beach.* **4.** bring as a result. ¶*~ to a good result.*
1) ***lead off,*** begin; start. ⌈mislead.⌉
2) ***lead on,*** cause (someone) to continue a vain action;⌋
3) ***lead out,*** begin; take a partner to begin a dance.
4) ***lead up to*** (=*prepare the way for*) something.
—*n.* © **1.** 《*sing.* only》 the act of leading or conducting. ¶*under the ~ of ...*④ **2.** 《*the ~*》 the first place or position. ¶*gain the ~ in a race.* **3.** 《*sing.* only》 the amount by which one is in front of others. ¶*have a ~ of ten feet.* **4.** 《*sing.* only》 example; guidance. ¶*follow someone's ~.* **5.** (of a newspaper, etc.) a short introduction to an article. **6.** a hint; a suggestion. **7.** a chief part in a play; a chief actor.
take the lead, go into the first or head position; command.

:lead² [led] *n.* © **1.** Ⓤ a soft, heavy, easily-melted gray metal. ¶*heavy as ~*① / *dull as ~.*② **2.** a lump of lead used to measure the depth of water. ¶*cast* (or *heave*) *the ~.*② **3.** a long, thin piece of black lead as used in pencils. **4.** (*Printing*) a strip of lead used to separate lines of type. **5.** a ball of lead or other metal fired from a gun. **6.** 《*pl., collectively*》 strips of lead used to cover a roof, or to frame window glass.
—*vt.* **1.** cover (something) with lead. **2.** (*Printing*) separate (lines of type) with leads.

lead·en [lédn] *adj.* **1.** made of lead; of the color of lead. **2.** heavy as lead; oppressive. **3.** not active; dull.

:lead·er [líːdər] *n.* © **1.** a person who leads; a chief; a guide. **2.** (*Music, U.S.*) a conductor or director. **3.** a leading article in a newspaper. **4.** a piece of transparent material used to attach a fishhook to a fish line. **5.** a thing sold at a low price to attract customers. **6.** (*Printing*) a row of dots or hyphens.

• **lead·er·ship** [líːdərʃip] *n.* Ⓤ **1.** the post or duty of a leader. ¶*assume the ~ of*① / *under the ~ of.*② **2.** skill in leading; the power to lead. ¶*able (poor) ~.*

:lead·ing [líːdiŋ] *n.* Ⓤ the act of guiding; the power or authority to direct. ¶*men of light and ~.*①
—*adj.* **1.** conducting; at the head. **2.** high in rank; important. ¶*a ~ singer*② / *a ~ article.*③

:leaf [liːf] *n.* (pl. **leaves**) **1.** ©Ⓤ one of the flat green parts of a plant. ¶*be in ~*① / *the fall of the ~.*② **2.** ©Ⓤ a flower petal. **3.** a piece of paper forming, back to back, two printed pages of a book. **4.** a thin sheet of metal. ¶*gold ~.* **5.** a movable board used to extend the top of a desk, a table, etc.
1) ***come into leaf,*** have the leaf buds open.
2) ***take a leaf out of someone's book,*** follow someone's example; take a hint from another person.
3) ***turn over a new leaf,*** make a new start in life; give up bad ways and habits. ⌈etc.)⌋
—*vi.* form leaves. —*vt.* turn the pages of (a book,⌋

leaf bud [′ ′] *n.* a bud which grows into a leaf.

leaf·less [líːflis] *adj.* having no leaves; without leaves.

leaf·let [líːflet] *n.* © **1.** a young leaf; a division of a compound leaf. **2.** a small printed sheet, single or folded; a pamphlet. ¶*advertising leaflets.*①

leaf·y [líːfi] *adj.* (**leaf·i·er, leaf·i·est**) **1.** covered with many leaves; having many leaves. ¶*a ~ shade.*① **2.** like a leaf or leaves in shape. ¶*a ~ design.*②

:league¹ [liːg] *n.* © **1.** an agreement between two or more nations or persons for a mutual purpose; the union so formed. ¶*the League [of Nations].*① **2.** an associa-

league

통하다 4. [결과가 …이] 되다

熟 1)개시하다, [앞장서서] 시작하다 2)[남]을 유인하다, 끌어들이다, …하게 하다 3)시작하다, [남]을 [댄스의] 상대로 청해내다 4)…의 준비를 하다

—图 1. 선도, 솔선, 지휘, 지도 ¶④…의 지도 밑에 2. 선두; [경기의] 리드, 앞섬, 우세 3. 솔선(리이드한) 거리(시간) 4. 본, 본보기, 모범 5. [신문 기사의] 머리 글, 톱 기사 6. 단서, 실마리, 힌트 7. 주역[배우]; 주역

熟 솔선하다, 앞장서다, 솔선하여 모범을 보이다

—图 1. 납, 연(鉛) ¶①납처럼 무거운 /②납처럼 칙칙한 빛깔의 2. 측연(測鉛) ¶③측연을 던져서`수심을 재다 3. 연필심 4. 《印刷》인테르(행간에 끼우는 납조각) 5. 탄알, 납총알 6. [지붕이는 데 쓰는] 함석, 연판(鉛板) ; 납 창틀

—他 1. …에 납을 씌우다(메우다) 2. 《印刷》…에 인테르를 끼우다

—形 1. 납의; 납빛깔의 2. 무거운; 우중충한, 답답한 3. 무기력한, 둔한

—图 1. 지도자; 선도자; 지휘자; 리이더 2. 《美》《樂》오케스트라의 지휘자 3. [신문의] 사설, 논설 4. [낚시바늘을 매다는] 목줄 5. 손님을 끌기 위한 특가품 6. 《印刷》 점선(點線)

—图 1. 지휘자의 지위(임무) ¶①…을 지휘(통솔)하다/②…의 지휘하에 2. 통솔력, 영도력

—图 지도, 지휘, 통솔; 통솔력 ¶①대 지도자, 대가

—形 1. 이끄는, 선도하는 2. 일류의, 으뜸가는 ¶②일류 가수/③사설

—图 1. 잎, 나뭇잎 ¶①잎이 나와 있다 /②낙엽기; 가을 2. 꽃잎 3. [책의] 한 장, 2 페이지분 4. [금속의] 박(箔) 5. [접게 된 책상의] 자재판(自在板)

熟 1)잎이 나다(피기 시작하다) 2)[남의] 모범에 따르다 3)새 생활을 시작하다, 새출발하다; 마음을 고쳐먹다

—自 잎이 나다 —他 [책 따위]의 페이지를 넘기다, 책장을 넘기다

—图 잎눈, 잎의 싹

—形 잎이 없는

—图 1. 작은 잎; 엽편(葉片) 《複葉》의 한 조각》 2. 낱장으로 된 인쇄물 ¶①광고 삐라

—形 1. 잎이 우거진; 잎이 많은 ¶① 녹음(綠陰) 2. 나뭇잎 같은 ¶②나뭇잎 디자인

—图 1. 동맹; 맹약 ¶①국제 연맹 2. [야구 따위의] 경기 연맹

league

tion of baseball clubs, etc.
—*vi., vt.* unite or combine; join in a league.

league² [li:g] *n.* ⓒ an old measure of distance, about three miles.

lea·guer [lí:gər] *n.* ⓒ a member of a league.

leak [li:k] *n.* ⓒ **1.** a small hole or opening that water, gas, etc. passes through. ¶*a ~ in a roof.* **2.** the act of leaking. ¶*spring (or start) a ~.*① —*vi* **1.** (of a liquid, gas, etc.) enter or escape through a small hole. (《*~ in or out* something》) **2.** (of a secret, etc.) become known by chance. (《*~ out*》) ¶*The secret has leaked out.* —*vt.* make (something) pass in or out.

leak·age [lí:kidʒ] *n.* Ⓤ **1.** the act or process of leaking; a leak. **2.** that which leaks in or out. **3.** ⓒ the amount leaking in or out. ¶*leaking out a secret.*

leak·y [lí:ki] *adj.* (**leak·i·er, leak·i·est**) having a leak;

‡lean¹ [li:n] *v.* (**leaned** [li:nd, +*Brit.* lent] or **leant**) *vi.* **1.** be not quite upright; incline or bend from a vertical position. **2.** bend over; rest on something for support. (《*~ on, upon, against*》) ¶*~ against the wall* / *She leaned upon my arm.* / *~ on someone for support.* **3.** depend; rely on. (《*~ on* someone》) ¶*You must not ~ too much on* (or *upon*) *others.* **4.** incline in feeling, opinion, action, etc. ¶*~ toward socialism.* **5.** bend the upper part of the body. —*vt.* **1.** cause (something) to lean. **2.** place (something) for support. —*n.* Ⓤ the act of leaning; slope; bend.

‡lean² [li:n] *adj.* **1.** (of a person or animal) thin. ↔*fat*; (of meat) having little or no fat. ¶*~ meat.*① **2.** not productive; poor in quality. ¶*~ years* / *~ crops.* —*n.* Ⓤ meat without fat. [*~ towards pacifism.*]

lean·ing [lí:niŋ] *n.* ⓒ a trend; a fondness. ¶*He has a*

leant [lent] *v.* pt. and pp. of **lean.**¹

lean-to [lí:ntù:] *n.* (pl. **-tos**) ⓒ a small building built against a main house having a roof with only one slope; a rough shelter attached to trees, rocks, etc. ⇨fig. —*adj.* having supports fixed against a building. ¶*a ~ roof.*①

[lean-to]

‡leap [li:p] *n.* **1.** ⓒ a jump. **2.** a thing jumped over. **3.** the height or distance jumped.
 1) ***by leaps and bounds***, very quickly.
 2) ***a leap in the dark***, an effort to do something recklessly; a rash act; a guess.
 3) ***with*** (or ***at***) ***a leap***, at a bound; suddenly.
—*v.* (**leaped** or **leapt**) *vt.* **1.** pass over (something) by a jump or a bound. ¶*~ a ditch.* **2.** cause (a horse, etc.) to jump or bound. —*vi.* spring or jump; make a bound; move suddenly, as if with a jump.
 1) ***leap at***, seize. ¶*He leaped at the proposal.*①
 2) ***leap for*** (or ***with***) (*jump for* (or *with*)) ***joy***.
 3) ***leap out of one's skin***, jump suddenly with joy, surprize, fright, etc.
 4) ***Look before you leap***, (*proverb*) Think before acting.

leap·frog [lí:prɔ̀g, -frɑ̀g / -frɔ̀g] *n.* Ⓤ a game in which children jump over each other's backs. ⇨fig. ¶*play ~.*

leapt [li:pt / lept] *v.* pt. and pp. of **leap.**

leap year [⌣ ⌣] *n.* a year in which February has 29 days.

‡learn [lə:rn] *v.* (**learned** [lə:rnd, lə:rnt] or **learnt**) *vt.* **1.** get knowledge of (something) by study, instruction, or experience. (《*~ to do*; *~ how* (or *what*, *etc.*) *to*

[leapfrog]

learn

—自⑪ 동맹하다(시키다)
—名 리그(약 3마일의 거리 단위)

—名 동맹자, 연맹국

—名 1. 새는 곳(구멍) 2. 새기 ¶①새기 시작하다 —自 1. [액체 따위가] 새다, 새어나오다 2. [비밀 따위가] 점점 알려지다, 누설되다

—⑪ [비밀 따위]를 누설하다
—名 1. 새기, 새어나옴, 누출(漏出) 2. [비밀 따위의] 누설 3. 새는 양, 누출량

—形 새는, [비밀 따위를] 누설하기 쉬운

—自 1. 기울다, 경사지다, 굽다 2. [사람이] 기대다, 비스듬히 기대다 3. 의지하다, 매달리다 4. [마음이] 기울다, 동하다 5. 상체를 구부리다, 몸을 굽히다 —⑪ 1. …을 기울게 하다, 굽히다 2. …을 기대어 세우다, 기대어 놓다 —名 기울기, 경사, 치우침, 굽음

—形 1. [사람·동물이] 야윈, 마른, 홀쭉한; [고기가] 비계가 없는, 살코기의 ¶①살코기 2. 흉작의, 불모(不毛)의
—名 [비계가 없는] 살코기
—名 경향; 기호(嗜好)

—名 [원채에] 달아 지은 집(지붕)
—形 [원채에] 달아 지은 ¶①내려 이은 지붕

—名 1. 뛰기, 도약 2. 뛰어넘는 것 3. 한번 뛰는 높이(거리)
熟 1)껑충껑충, 급속도로 2)앞뒤를 가리지 않는 행동, 무모한 행동 3)한번 껑충 뛰어서, 단번에, 갑자스레

—⑪ 1. …을 뛰어넘다 2. …을 뛰어넘게 하다 —自 뛰다, 날뛰다, 약동하다

熟 1)…에 뛰어들다(달려들다) ¶①그는 그 제의에 달려들 듯이(기꺼이) 응했다 2)날뛰면서 좋아하다 3)[좋아서] 날뛰다 4)[俚]실행하기 전에 잘 살펴라

—名 등넘기(구부린 사람의 등을 짚고 뛰어넘는 놀이)

—名 윤년

—⑪ 1. …을 배우다, 익히다, 가르침을 받다, 공부하다, 연습하다, …할 수 있게 되다 ¶①그녀는 수영할 수 있게 되었다 2. …을 알다, 듣다, 확인하다, 탐지하

do》 ¶~ *French* | *She has learned to swim.*① | ~ *how to solve the problem.* **2.** find out; be aware of (something). 《~ *that* ...; ~ *how* ...》 ¶*I learned it from her that he had died.* | *I learnt that he had been in* [*the*] *hospital.* | *I learned how they had escaped.* | *I was sorry to* ~ [*from her*] *that he had died.* **3.** memorize. ¶~ *a poem by heart.* —*vi.* **1.** get knowledge or skill. ¶*The boy learns very fast.* **2.** hear; be told or informed. 《~ *of* something》 ¶~ *of the results of the examination.*

다 3. …을 외다, 기억하다, 암기하다 —[自] 1. 배우다, 익히다, 외다 2. 듣다, 알다

***learn·ed** [lə́:rnid] *adj.* having much knowledge or learning. ¶*a* ~ *man*① | *be* ~ *in the law*② | *the* ~ *professions.* ▷**learn·ed·ly** [-li] *adv.*

—[形] 학식이 있는;학문적인 ¶①학자/②법률에 정통하다

learn·er [lə́:rnər] *n.* [C] a person who is learning; a beginner.

—[名] 배우는 사람, 학습자

⁑learn·ing [lə́:rniŋ] *n.* [U] the knowledge or skill got by study. ¶*a man of* ~.

—[名] 학문, 학식, 지식, 배움

learnt [lə:rnt] *v.* pt. and p.p. of **learn.**

***lease** [li:s] *n.* [U] **1.** a written agreement for the renting of land or buildings for a certain time in exchange for rent paid; the rights given under such a contract. ¶*take on* ~① | *We signed a two-year*~ *for this house.*② **2.** [C] the length of time for which such agreement lasts. ¶*How long is your* ~ *on that land?*

—[名] 1. 차지(借地) 계약; 차가(借家) 계약; 차지권(借地權) ¶①…을 임차(賃借)하다/②이 집의 2년간 임대계약에 서명했다 2. 차지(임대차) 기간

1) ***by*** (or ***on***) ***lease,*** by rent. ¶*hold the land by* (or *on*) ~.
2) ***take*** (or ***get***) ***a new*** (or ***a fresh***) ***lease on life,*** get a chance to live better or more happily because of recovering one's health, position, money, etc.

[熟] 1)임대(賃貸)로 2)[병이 완쾌하여] 수명이 연장되다; 운이 좋아 더 좋은 여건에서 살 수 있게 되다

—*vt.* give or take ownership of (land, a building, etc.), for a certain time, by a contract.

—[他] [토지·건물]을 임대(임차)하다

lease·hold [lí:shòuld] *n.* [U] **1.** the right of holding land by lease. **2.** lands, buildings, etc. held by lease. —*adj.* held by lease.

—[名] 1. 차지(借地) 보유권 2. 차지, 조차지(租借地)
—[形] 임차의, 조차의

lease·hold·er [lí:shòuldər] *n.* [C] a person who holds a lease.

—[名] 차지인(借地人), 임차인, 조차인

leash [li:ʃ] *n.* [C] a chain or strap for holding a dog.

—[名] [사냥개를 매는] 가죽 끈, 쇠사슬

1) ***keep on a leash,*** control strictly. ¶*My father kept us children on a* ~.
2) ***strain at the leash,*** wait eagerly for permission to do something.

[熟] 1)지배하다, 제어하다 2)[사냥개가] 조급하게 가죽 끈을 잡아당기다; 자유를 갈망하다

—*vt.* fasten or hold (something) with a leash.

—[他] [사냥개]를 가죽 끈으로 매다

⁑least [li:st] *adj.* (superl. of **little**) smallest in size, degree, extent, importance, etc; slightest; shortest. ¶*the* ~ *movement* | *You haven't the* ~ *chance of success.* —*adv.* in the smallest or lowest degree. ¶*He is* ~ *wanted here.* —*n.* [U] 《usu. *the* ~》 the smallest in size, amount, importance, etc.

—[形] 가장 작은, 가장 적은, 가장 가치가 적은 —[副] 가장 적게, 제일 적게
—[名] 가장 작음(적음), 최소, 최소량

1) ***at*** [***the***] ***least,*** at the lowest estimate; at any rate; in any case.
2) ***least of all,*** less than any other.
3) ***not in the least,*** not at all.
4) ***to say the least of it,*** at least.

[熟] 1)적어도, 하다못해, 어쨌든 2)가장 …이 아니다, 절대로 …않다(…이 아니다) 3)조금도 …않다(…이 없다) 4)줄잡아 말해도, 적어도

⁑leath·er [léðər] *n.* [U] **1.** the skin of an animal prepared for human use. ¶*Morocco* ~① | *patent* [pǽtent] ~.② **2.** any of various articles made of this material. **3.** [C] 《*pl.*》 leather riding breeches. —*vt.* cover (something) with leather; strike (someone) with a leather strap.

—[名] 1. [무두질한] 가죽 ¶①모로코 가죽(양가죽으로 만듦)/②에나멜 가죽 2. 가죽 제품 3. 승마용 가죽 바지 —[他] …에 가죽을 대다(붙이다, 씌우다); …을 [가죽 끈 따위로] 때리다

leath·ern [léðərn] *adj.* **1.** made of leather. **2.** like leather.

—[形] 1. 가죽으로 만든, 혁제의 2. 가죽 같은

leath·er·y [lèðəri] *adj.* like leather; tough; not easily broken. ¶~ *meat.*① ▷**leath·er·i·ness** [-nis] *n.*

—[形] 가죽 같은; 가죽처럼 질긴 ¶①질긴 고기

⁑leave[1] [li:v] *v.* (**left** [left]) *vt.* **1.** go away or start from (a certain place). ¶~ *the house* | ~ *Japan for Europe.* **2.** stop living in (a certain place), attending (a school), or belonging to (a club), etc. ¶~ *a job* | ~ *a political party* | ~ *school before graduating.* **3.** forget; fail to take or bring; abandon. ¶~ *the book on the desk* | ~ *one's wife and family.* **4.** let (something or someone)

—[他] 1. …을 떠나다, 출발하다 2. …을 떠나다, [소속 단체에서] 물러나다, 나가다, 그만두다, 탈퇴하다, 사직하다, [학교]를 졸업(퇴학)하다 3. …을 버리다, 저버리다, 남겨놓다, 두고 가다, 둔 채 잊고 가다 4. …의 상태로 놔두다, …하는 대로 내버려두다, …하게 하다 5. …을

be in a certain state or condition; allow (someone, etc.) alone to do something. 《~ something *doing*; ~ something or someone *to do, doing* or *done*》 ¶~ *the door open* | *~someone alone* | *~ something unsaid.* **5.** keep (something) unused; remain; yield as a remainder. 《~ something *doing*; ~ something *for*》 ¶*There was little money left.* | *Leave some milk for the dog.* | *Three from eight leaves five.* **6.** give (money, etc.) at someone's death; give money, etc. to (someone) at one's death. ¶*The father left his son a large fortune.* **7.** cause or allow (something) to be in someone's care or trust. ¶*Leave it to me.* | *~ a matter to someone.* **8.** deliver; hand over. ¶*~ a message* | *The postman left two letters for me.* **9.** pass; go beyond. ¶*~ the village on the right.* ——*vi.* go away; depart. ¶*~ for America* | *We are leaving tomorrow morning.*

1) *leave* something *behind,* ⓐ forget; go away without something. ⓑ pass by.
2) *leave go* (or *hold*) *of,* relax one's hold; cease to hold.
3) *leave off,* stop; not wear.
4) *leave out,* omit; pass over; neglect.
5) *leave over,* (*Brit.*) be dealt with another time; let stand over for the time being.

leave² [líːv] *n.* **1.** Ⓤ permission; consent. ¶*He gave me ~ to go.* | *ask for ~* | *ask* (*get, refuse*) *~ to do.*① **2.** ⓊⒸ permission to be absent from work or duty. ¶*have ~.*② **3.** Ⓒ the period for which such permission lasts. ¶*a three-week ~* [*of absence*].

1) *by your leave,* with your permission.
2) *on leave,* absent from duty with permission.
3) *take French leave,* go without asking to be allowed to go. 「go; depart.」
4) *take one's leave of,* say good-bye to (*someone*) and
5) *take leave of one's senses,* go mad.

leav·en [lévn] *n.* Ⓤ yeast or similar substance used in making bread, beer, etc.
——*vt.* **1.** make (dough) light. **2.** transform (something) with some lightening element.
leaves [líːvz] *n.* pl. of **leaf**. 「or saying good-by.」
leave-tak·ing [líːvtèikiŋ] *n.* Ⓤ the act of taking leave,
leav·ings [líːviŋz] *n. pl.* what is left as worthless. ¶*Give the ~ to the dog.*① [Bible is read in church.」
lec·tern [léktərn] *n.* Ⓒ a reading desk from which the
: **lec·ture** [léktʃər] *n.* Ⓒ **1.** a speech full of knowledge given to an audience, a class, etc. ¶*give* (or *deliver*) *a ~ on.*① **2.** a scolding; a spoken criticism.
——*vi.* give a lecture. 《~ *on some subject*》 ¶*~ on chemistry to a class.* ——*vt.* **1.** instruct (someone) by a lecture. **2.** scold.
lec·tur·er [léktʃərər] *n.* a person who gives a lecture.
led [led] *v.* pt. and pp. of **lead**¹.
· **ledge** [ledʒ] *n.* Ⓒ **1.** a narrow shelf projecting out from a wall as under the window. ¶*a ~ for chalk at the bottom of a blackboard.* **2.** a flat area of rock under the sea. **3.** a layer of rock containing metal.
ledg·er [lédʒər] *n.* Ⓒ a book in which accounts of money are recorded.
· **lee** [líː] *n.* Ⓒ 《usu. *the ~*》 the side protected from the wind; the sheltered side; the direction toward which the wind is blowing.
1) *under* (or *on*) *the lee,* of the direction toward which the wind is blowing.
2) *under* (or *in*) *the lee of,* in the shelter of.
——*adj.* sheltered from the wind; of the part away from

남기다. [쓰거나 가지거나 하지 않고] …을 남겨놓다. 수(數)를 남게 하다 6. [뒤에 재산·처자 따위]를 남겨놓고 죽다. …을 유언으로 남기다.유언에 의해 물려주다 7. …을 맡기다.위임하다, 위탁하다,부탁하다 8. …을 배달하다, 인도하다,두고 가다 9. …을 지나가다, 통과하다 ——自 떠나다, 출발하다

熟 1)ⓐ …을 두고(남겨놓고) 가다 ⓑ …을 지나가다 2)…을 놓아주다 3)그만두다;…을 벗다 4)…을 생략하다, 고려하지 않다, 무시하다 5)《英》뒤로 미루다,연기하다,남기다

——名 1. 허가, 허락 ¶①…할 허가를 청하다(얻다, 거부하다) 2. 휴가 ¶②휴가를 얻다 3. 휴가 기간

熟 1)실례지만, 미안하지만 2)휴가로 3)아'나 없이 나가다, 무단히 자리를 뜨다 4)…에게 작별 인사를 하다,작별을 고하다 5)미치다, 실성하다

——名 효모(酵母), 발효소

——他 1. …을 발효시키다 2. …에 영향(변화)을 미치다

——名 작별 인사를 하기, 고별
——名 나머지, 찌꺼기 ¶①밥찌꺼기를 개에게 주어라
——名 [교회의] 성서대, 독경대
——名 1. 강의,강연 ¶①…의 강의를 하다 2. 설교, 훈계

——自 강의(강연)하다 ——他 1. …에게 강의하여 가르치다 2. …을 꾸짖다,설교하다
——名 강의자, 강사

——名 1. 선반 2. 선반처럼 튀어나온 바위 3. 광맥

——名 원장(元帳), 원부; 장부

——名 바람을 막아 주는 쪽; 응달; 바람이 불어 가는 쪽

熟 1)바람 불어 가는 쪽에 2)…의 그늘에

——他 바람 불어 가는 쪽의; 바람막이의

the wind. ↔windward ¶*the ~ side.*①
leech [li:tʃ] *n.* ⓒ **1.** a worm living in ponds and streams that sucks the blood of animals. **2.** a person who sucks as much profit as possible out of others. ¶*stick like a ~.*
leek [li:k] *n.* ⓒ a vegetable with a white stem which
leer [liər] *n.* ⓒ a cunning, mean, sideways look. —*vi.* look with a leer. ▷**leer·ing·ly** [líəriŋli] *adv.*
leer·y [líəri] *adj.* (*colloq.*) suspicious; cautious. ¶*be ~ of.*①
lees [li:z] *n. pl.* the things in a liquid which settle to
lee·ward [lí:wərd] *adj., adv.* in the direction toward which the wind blows; opposed to windward. ¶*It will be warmer on the ~ side of the deck.* —*n.* ⓤ the direction toward which the wind blows. ↔windward
lee·way [lí:wèi] *n.* ⓤ **1.** the sideward drift of a boat caused by the wind. **2.** (*colloq.*) extra space, time, money, etc.
make up leeway, make up time or distance lost.
‡**left**¹ [left] *adj.* the opposite of right. ↔right ⇒usage ¶*the ~ hand | the ~ fielder | on the ~ hand of.*
marry with the left hand, take a wife of a rank lower than one's own. 「*Left turn!*」
—*adv.* on or toward the left hand or side. ¶*turn ~ |* —*n.* ⓒ **1.** (usu. *the ~*) the part on the left side. ¶*to the ~ of*① */ turn to the ~ / keep to the ~.* **2.** (usu. *the L-*) (in politics) the socialist and labor parties and their supporters. **3.** (*Baseball*) a left fielder.
‡**left**² [left] *v.* pt. and pp. of **leave**.
left-hand [léfthǽnd] *adj.* on the left; of the left hand. ¶*a house on the ~ side of the street.*
left-hand·ed [léfthǽndid] *adj.* **1.** using the left hand more easily or skillfully than the right. **2.** done or made with or for the left hand. **3.** going around from right to left. **4.** awkward. **5.** doubtful; questionable.
left·o·ver [léftòuvər] *n.* ⓒ something left over, as from a meal. —*adj.* remaining unused, uneaten, etc.
‡**leg** [leg] *n.* ⓒ **1.** one of the parts of the body used for walking. ⇒N.B. ¶*sit with someone's legs crossed.* **2.** the part of a garment covering a leg. ¶*the ~ of a stocking | the legs of trousers.* **3.** something like a leg in shape or use; a bar or pole used as a support; one of the branches of a forked or jointed object. ¶*the legs of a chair (bed).* **4.** one section or stage of a journey, etc.
 1) *feel* (or *find*) *one's legs,* (of a baby) get the ability to stand or walk.
 2) *get* (or *be*) *on one's [hind] legs,* (*colloq.*) ⓐ stand up, esp. to speak. ⓑ (after an illness) be well enough to walk about again.
 3) *give* (*someone*) *a leg up,* ⓐ help (someone) to mount a horse or to climb up something. ⓑ help (someone) in time of need.
 4) *have not a leg to stand on,* (*colloq.*) have no facts or evidence to support an argument. 「worn out.」
 5) *on one's* (or *its*) *last legs,* (*colloq.*) near one's death;
 6) *pull someone's leg,* make fun of or fool (someone).
 7) *run someone off his legs,* tire (someone) by keeping him constantly busy.
 8) *shake a leg,* (*colloq.*) ⓐ hurry. ⓑ dance.
 9) *stand on one's own legs,* be independent.
 10) *stretch one's legs,* go for a walk, esp. after sitting
 11) *take to one's legs,* run away. 「a long time.」
leg·a·cy [légəsi] *n.* (pl. *-cies*) ⓒ **1.** money or pro-

¶① 바람 불어 가는 쪽
—名 1. 거머리 2. 남의 돈을 착취하는 사람

—名 부추 종류
—名 곁눈질, 심술궂은 눈초리 —自 곁눈질하다, 흘겨보다
—形 (口) 의심 많은; 교활한 ¶①…을 [의심하여] 조심하다
—名 재강, 찌꺼기
—形副 바람 불어 가는 쪽의(으로)
—名 바람 불어 가는 쪽

—名 1. 풍압(風壓); 항행 중인 배가 바람에 밀려 떠내려가기 2. 여유; 여지

熟 뒤떨어진 것을 만회하다
—形 왼편의; 왼쪽의 usage 한정용법에만 쓰임
熟 신분이 낮은(천한) 여자와 결혼하다

—副 왼편에, 왼쪽으로
—名 1. 왼편, 왼쪽, 좌측 ¶①…의 왼쪽으로 2. 급진당(急進黨); 좌익 3.《野球》 좌익[수]

—形 왼쪽편의; 왼손의

—形 1. 왼손잡이의 2. 왼손으로 한(든); 왼손용(用)의 3. 왼쪽으로 도는 4. 서투른, 어색한 5. 의심스러운·불성실한
—名 나머지, 남은 것, 먹다 남은 것, 잔반(殘飯) —形 나머지의, 잔반의
—名 1. 다리, 정강이 N.B. 다리는 leg, 발은 foot 2. 옷의 다리 부분, 바짓가랑이 3. [의자·책상·기계 따위의] 다리, 지지부, 지주(支柱), 버팀대 4. [여정(旅程) 따위의] 한 단락; [장거리 여행의] 한 여정

熟 1) [아기가] 걸을 수 있게 되다 2) 《口》ⓐ [연설하기 위하여] 기립하다, 일어서다 ⓑ [건강을 회복하여] 걸을 수 있게 되다 3) ⓐ [남]을 부축하면서 [말에] 태우다 ⓑ [남]을 도와 곤경에서 헤어나게 해주다 4) 《口》말발이 서지 않다, 의론이 성립되지 않다 5) 《口》가 죽어가서, 빈사상태에 놓여; 기진맥진하여 6) [남]을 우롱하다, 속이다 7) [일 따위가 사람을] 지치게 하다 8)《口》ⓐ 서두르다 ⓑ 춤추다 9) 독립하다, 혼자 힘으로 하다 10) [오래 앉아 있다가] 산책하다 11) 도망치다, 달아나다

—名 1. 유산(遺産) 2. 조상의 유물

perty left to another by someone's will. **2.** something handed down from an ancestor. ¶*a ~ of hatred* (or *ill will*).

* **le·gal** [lí:g(ə)l] *adj.* **1.** of law. ¶*~ affairs.* **2.** of lawyers. ¶*a ~ adviser.* **3.** lawful; according to law; admitted by law. ¶*a ~ fare.*
—[形] 1. 법률의 2. 변호사의 3. 합법적인, 적법의; 법률로 인정(허용)된

le·gal·i·ty [li(:)gǽliti] *n.* (pl. **-ties**) [U] the state of being according to the law; the state of being allowed by the law.
—[名] 적법, 합법[성]

le·gal·ize [lí:gəlàiz] *vt.* make (something) legal; authorize (something) by law.
—[他] …을 적법으로 하다; …을 합법적이라고 인정하다

le·gal·ly [lí:gəli] *adv.* **1.** in a legal manner. **2.** according to law.
—[副] 1. 법률적으로 2. 합법적으로

leg·a·tee [lègətí:] *n.* [C] a person who receives a legacy.
—[名] 유산 수령인

le·ga·tion [ligéiʃ(ə)n] *n.* **1.** [U] ((*collectively*)) a diplomatic minister and his staff. **2.** [C] the official residence of a minister; the position or office of a minister.
—[名] 1. 공사관원 전부 2. 공사관; 공사의 직(지위)

* **leg·end** [lédʒ(ə)nd] *n.* **1.** [C] a story handed down from the past. **2.** a story of the life of a saint. **3.** the words on a coin or medal. **4.** a short title or article under a picture, etc.
—[名] 1. 전설 2. 성도(聖徒) 이야기 3. [메달·화폐 따위의] 명(銘) 4. 범례(凡例); [삽화의] 제어(題語)

leg·end·ar·y [lédʒ(ə)ndèri / -d(ə)ri] *adj.* **1.** of or like legends. **2.** famous; celebrated. ¶*His deeds became ~ throughout the country.* —*n.* [C] a collection of saints' lives.
—[形] 1. 전설의(같은) 2. 유명한, 이름높은 —[名] 전설집

legged [lég(i)d] *adj.* ((often used in *compounds*)) having legs. ¶*thick-legged.*
—[形] 다리가 있는, 다리가 …한

leg·gings [léginz] *n. pl.* a pair of long, heavy coverings to protect legs from mud, cold, etc.
—[名] 각반, 정강이받이

leg·gy [légi] *adj.* (**-gi·er, -gi·est**) having long legs.
—[形] 다리가 호리호리한

leg·horn [léghɔ:rn →2.] *n.* [C] **1.** a hat made of Italian straw. **2.** [C] [léghɔ:rn / legɔ́:n] (sometimes L-) a kind of chicken
—[名] 1. 밀짚모자의 일종 2. 레그호온(닭의 한 품종)

leg·i·bil·i·ty [lèdʒibíliti] *n.* [U] the state of being easy to read.
—[名] 읽기 쉬움

leg·i·ble [lédʒibl] *adj.* (of handwriting, print, etc.) can easily be read. ↔illegible
—[形] [필적·인쇄가] 읽기 쉬운

* **le·gion** [lí:dʒ(ə)n] *n.* **1.** [C] ((*collectively*)) (in ancient Rome) a body of from 3,000 to 6,000 soldiers. **2.** [U] an army. **3.** [U] a great number of persons or things.
—[名] 1. 고대 로마의 군단(軍團)(3, 000 ~6, 000 명의 군사로 이루어짐) 2. 군대 3. 다수; 군중

leg·is·late [lédʒislèit] *vi.* make laws. —*vt.* cause (something) to happen by making laws.
—[自] 법률을 제정하다 —[他] 법률을 만들어 …하게 하다

* **leg·is·la·tion** [lèdʒisléiʃ(ə)n] *n.* **1.** [U] the act of making laws. ¶*the power of ~.* **2.** ((*collectively*)) the laws that are made. ¶*a bill of ~.*①
—[名] 1. 입법 2. 법률(laws) ¶①법률안

* **leg·is·la·tive** [lédʒislèitiv / -slə-] *adj.* having the power of making laws; of legislation. ¶*the ~ Assembly* (or *Council*)① / a *~ body*②
—[形] 입법의, 법제(法制)의 ¶①입법원 /②입법부

leg·is·la·tor [lédʒislèitər] *n.* [C] a maker of laws; a member of a legislature
—[名] 법률 제정자, 입법자

* **leg·is·la·ture** [lédʒislèitʃər] *n.* [C] the body of persons in a state or country having the power to make or alter laws.
—[名] 입법부; 주(州)의회

le·git·i·ma·cy [lidʒítiməsi] *n.* [U] the state of being legitimate.
—[名] 합법, 적법; 적출(嫡出), 정통(正統)

* **le·git·i·mate** *adj.* [lidʒítimit →*vt.*] **1.** recognized by the law as rightful; lawful. **2.** reasonable; right. ¶*a ~ reason.*① **3.** born of parents who are married. —*vt.* [lidʒítimèit] recognize (something) as lawful; justify. ▷**le·git·i·mate·ly** [-li] *adv.*
—[形] 1. 법률상 정당한, 합법적인 2. 합리적인, 정당한 ¶①정당한 이유 3. 적출(嫡出)의
—[他] …을 합법으로 인정하다; 정당화하다

le·gu·mi·nous [ligjú:minəs] *adj.* **1.** having seeds. **2.** of the group of plants which includes peas and beans.
—[形] 1. 꼬투리가 여는 2. 콩과의

** **lei·sure** [lí:ʒər / léʒə] *n.* [U] the time free from work or duties; the time when one may rest. ¶*have no ~ for reading.*
—[名] 한가한 시간, 여가

1) ***at leisure,*** not working or busy.
2) ***at one's leisure,*** when one has free time; at one's ease.
[熟] 1)한가하여, 틈이 나서 2)한가한 때에, 형편이 좋을 때에

—*adj.* free from work; not busy.
—[形] 한가한, 틈이 있는, 바쁘지 않은

lei·sured [lí:ʒərd / léʒəd] *adj.* **1.** having plenty of leisure. ¶*the ~ classes.*① **2.** slow and easy.
—[形] 1. 여가가 있는, 한가한 ¶①유한계급 2. 천천한, 여유가 있는

L

lei·sure·ly [lí:ʒərli / léʒəli] *adv.* without hurrying; slowly. ¶*work ~ / We strolled ~ through the park.*① — *adj.* not hurried; slow. ¶*~ moments.*
—[副] 유유히, 천천히 ¶①우리는 공원 안을 천천히 산책하였다 —[形] 유유한, 여유있는, 천천한

⁑ lem·on [lémən] *n.* [C] **1.** a small, yellow fruit with a sour juice, related to the orange. **2.** the tree bearing this fruit. **3.** [U] the color of lemons.
—[名] 1. 레몬[열매] 2. 레몬나무 3. 레몬빛

lem·on·ade [lèmənéid] *n.* [U] a drink made of lemon juice, water, and sugar.
—[名] 레모네이드, 레몬수

lemon squash [´- ´] *n.* a drink made of lemon juice and soda water.
—[名] 레몬 스콰시(레몬즙에 소오다수를 탄 음료)

le·mur [lí:mər] *n.* [C] a kind of monkey with a face like a fox. ⇒fig.
—[名] 여우 원숭이(마다가스카르 섬에서 사는 야행성 원숭이의 일종)

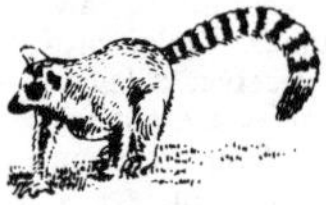
(lemur)

⁑ lend [lend] *vt.* (**lent**) **1.** allow (someone) to have or use something on the condition that it be returned. ↔borrow ¶*Please ~ me your book. / Lend some money to me.* **2.** give or provide (assistance, etc.); contribute; give for a time; add. ⟪~ something *to*⟫ ¶*Distance lends enchantment to the view.*
—[他] 1. …에게 […을] 빌려주다, 대여하다 2. [손·힘·귀·조력을] …에게 빌려주다, 제공하다, 첨가하다, 보태다, 주다

1) ***lend a*** [***helping***] ***hand,*** assist; help.
2) ***lend ear*** (or ***an ear, one's ear***), listen.
3) ***lend itself to*** (*=be suitable for; be useful for*) something.
4) ***lend oneself to,*** allow oneself to support.

[熟] 1)…을 거들어 주다, 원조하다 2)…에 귀를 기울이다 3)[물건이] …에 도움이 되다; 알맞다 4)…에 진력하다, 전렴(專念)하다

lend·er [léndər] *n.* [C] a person who lends.
—[名] 빌려주는 사람, 대주(貸主); 고리대금업자

⁑ length [leŋθ] *n.* [C] **1.** the distance of a thing from end to end. ¶*thirty meters in ~① / be of the same ~.* **2.** the state and quality of being long. **3.** extent in space, degree, or time. ¶*the ~ of a visit / He did not go to that ~.* **4.** a certain measure. ¶*a ~ of pipe.* **5.** (of a boat or horse race) its own length. ¶*The boat won by two length.*
—[名] 1. 길이; 세로; 키 ¶①길이 30미터 2. 긴 것 3. [시간적으로 계속되는] 길이, 기간, 동안; 범위, 정도 4. 어떤 길이, 일정한 길이의 것 5. [보우트의] 정신(艇身), [경마의] 마신(馬身)

1) ***at full length,*** ⓐ with the body fully stretched out. ⓑ in full.
2) ***at great length,*** over a very long period. ¶*He explained it at great ~.*
3) ***at length,*** ⓐ at last; for a long time. ⓑ with details.
4) ***at some length,*** with details.
5) ***go all lengths; go to great*** (or ***any***) ***lengths,*** do anything or everything possible.
6) ***go the length of,*** go so far as to do. ⟪~ *doing*⟫ ¶*I will not go the length of saying such things.*②
7) ***know*** (or ***get, have***) ***the length of*** *someone's* ***foot,*** perceive someone's weak point; have a key to someone's character.
8) ***over the length and breadth of,*** everywhere; all over; throughout.
9) ***keep*** *someone* ***at arm's length,*** avoid being friendly with someone.

[熟] 1)ⓐ큰 대(大)자로 [누워] ⓑ상세히, 자세히 2)기다랗게, 장황하게 3)ⓐ드디어, 마침내 ⓑ상세히 4)[상당히] 자상하게 5)어떤 짓이든 하다 6)…까지도 하다 ¶②그런 소리까지 할 생각은 없다 7)[남]의 약점을 알다; [남]의 성격을 파악하다 8)…을 남김없이, 샅샅이 9)남을 가까이하지 않다, 쌀쌀하게 대하다

• length·en [léŋ(k)θ(ə)n] *vt.* make (something) long or longer. ¶*Ask the tailor to ~ the skirt.* —*vi.* grow longer. ¶*The days ~ in March.*
—[他] …을 길게 하다, 늘이다
—[自] 길어지다, 늘어나다

length·wise [léŋ(k)θwàiz] *adj., adv.* in the direction from end to end.
—[形][副] 세로의(로)

length·y [léŋ(k)θi] *adj.* (**length·i·er, length·i·est**) very long; too long and dull. ¶*a ~ sermon.*①
—[形] 장시간의; 기다란, 장황한 ¶①장황한 설교

le·ni·ence [lí:niəns] *n.* [U] =leniency.

le·ni·en·cy [lí:niənsi] *n.* [U] the state of being mild and gentle.
—[名] 관대함, 온화함, 인자함

le·ni·ent [lí:niənt] *adj.* mild merciful; not severe. ¶*a ~ punishment.*①
—[形] 관대한, 너그러운; 무른, 가벼운 ¶①가벼운 형벌

len·i·ty [léniti] *n.* [U] the state or quality of being lenient.
—[名] 자비심 많음, 관대함

• lens [lenz] *n.* (pl. **lens·es**) [C] **1.** a piece of glass with curved sides used in cameras, etc. ¶*Lenses are used in cameras, telescopes and other instruments.* **2.** the part of the eye which focuses light.
—[名] 1. 렌즈 2. [눈의] 수정체(水晶體)

⁑ lent [lent] *v.* pt. and pp. of **lend**.

L

Lent [lent] *n.* (in the Christian Church) the 40 days before Easter Sunday, kept in some Christian churches with fasting and regretting for wrongdoing.
—[名] 사순절(四旬節)(Easter eve 전의 40 일간]

len·til [lént(i)l] *n.* [C] **1.** a kind of bean bearing edible seeds shaped like lenses **2.** the seed of this plant.
—[名] **1.** 렌즈콩 [나무] **2.** 렌즈콩 [열매]

le·o·nine [lí(:)ənàin] *adj.* of or like a lion.
—[形] 사자의(같은); 용맹스러운

leop·ard [lépərd] *n.* [C] a fierce animal of the cat family with black spots, found in Asia and Africa. ↔leopardess ¶(*Bible*) *Can the ~ change his spots?*①
—[名] 표범 ¶①《聖》 본성은 바뀌지 않는다, 개 꼬리 삼년 묵어도 황모 안 된다

leop·ard·ess [lépərdis] *n.* [C] a female leopard.
—[名] 암표범

lep·er [lépər] *n.* [C] a person suffering from leprosy.
—[名] 문둥이, 나병환자

lep·ro·sy [léprəsi] *n.* [U] a disease which slowly eats the body like acid.
—[名] 문둥병, 나병

lep·rous [léprəs] *adj.* having leprosy; of or like leprosy.
—[形] 문둥병에 걸린; 문둥병(나병)의

⁑ **less** [les] *adj.* (compar. of **little.** cf. lesser.) smaller in size, amount, or degree; not so large, great, or much. ↔more ⇒[usage] ¶*of ~ value* (*importance*) / *~ butter* / *~ people* / *Eat ~ meat and more vegetables.*
1) ***nothing less*** [***than***], 《used to emphasize a following adjective or noun》 the same thing as. ¶*It is nothing ~ than an invasion.*
2) ***something*** (or ***somewhat***) ***less than,*** far from being.
—[形] [수량·크기·정도가] …보다 적은, 더 작은, 열등한 [usage] 수의 경우는 less보다 fewer를 쓰는 것이 보통
[熟] 1)꼭 같은, 다를 바 없는; 바로 2)…와는 거리가 먼 것, 절대로 …이 아닌 것

—*adv.* to a smaller extent; in a lower degree. ¶*He is ~ fat than he was.* / *It is ~ important.* / *He is ~ known.*
1) ***little less than,*** almost the same as.
2) ***more or less,*** about; rather.
3) ***no less than,*** ⓐ as much (*or* many) as …; as ~ as. ¶*She has no ~ than 100 dollars.* / *No ~ than ten people offered to help us.* / *She is no ~ beautiful than her sister.*① ⓑ no other than; just as. ¶*He is no ~ a person than the prince.*
4) ***none the less,*** nevertheless.
—[副] 보다 적게, 보다 이하로, …만큼은 아니고
[熟] 1)…와 거의 같은 정도로 2)대략…만큼, 얼마간, 다소 3)ⓐ…와 같게, …에 못지 않게 ¶①그녀는 언니 못지 않게 아름답다 ⓑ다름아닌…의; 바로 4)그래도, 오히려, 그럼에도 불구하고

—*n.* [U] a smaller amount, quantity, a time. ¶*in ~ than a month* / *He is ~ of a fool than he looks.* / *Less than 30 of them remained.*
in less than no time, very quickly; at once; soon.
—[名] 보다 더욱 적은 양(수·액수)
[熟] 곧, 당장에

—*prep.* minus. ¶*a year ~ six days.*①
—[前] …만큼 적은; …을 뺀(감한) ¶① 6일 모자라는 1년

-less [-lis] *suf.* **1.** without; lacking. ¶*valueless.* (=*without value*) **2.** not be able to do; not become. ¶*countless* (=*cannot be counted*).
—[接尾] **1.** …이 없는 **2.** …할 수 없는

les·see [lesí:] *n.* [C] a person who rents land or a house under a lease. ↔lessor
—[名] 임차인(賃借人), 차지인(借地人), 차가인(借家人)

* **less·en** [lésn] *vt.* make (something) smaller or less; reduce. ¶*~ the danger.* —*vi.* become or grow less.
—[他] …을 적게 하다, 줄이다
—[自] 적어지다, 줄다

less·er [lésər] *adj.* (compar. of **little**) of a smaller amount; less; smaller; fewer. ↔greater
—[形] 보다 작은 쪽의, 적은 편의

⁑ **les·son** [lésn] *n.* [C] **1.** something learned by a pupil or student. **2.** a unit of study taught at one time. ¶*Lesson 3.*① ⇒[N.B.] **3.** 《*pl.*》 instruction in some subject. ¶*give* (or *teach*) *lessons in music*② / *take* (or *have*) *lesson in Latin from a teacher.*③ **4.** a part of the Bible read as part of a church service. **5.** something learned from experience; a warning example. ¶*This failure served as a ~ to him.*
—[名] **1.** 학과 **2.** [교과서 안의] 과(課) ¶①제 3 과 [N.B.] 이 경우 3은 three로 읽음 **3.** 수업, 교습 ¶②음악을 가르치다/③선생에게서 라틴어를 배우다 **4.** [교회에서 읽는 성서의] 일과 **5.** 교훈, 훈계, 본보기

les·sor [lésɔ:r, lesɔ́:r / lesɔ́:, lésɔ́:] *n.* [C] a person who gives a lease.
—[名] 임대인(賃貸人), 대지인(貸地人)

⁑ **lest** [lest] *conj.* **1.** in order that … not; for fear that. ¶*You must work hard ~ you* [*should*] *fail.* **2.** 《used after words expressing *fear*》 that. ¶*for fear ~ she should die* / *I am afraid ~ he should fail.*
—[接] **1.** …하지 않게; …하면 안 되니까 **2.** …하지나 않을까 하고

⁑ **let**[1] [let] *v.* (**let, let·ting**) *vt.* **1.** permit; allow. 《~ someone or something *do*》 ¶*Will you ~ me smoke?* / *She ~ no one enter the room.* **2.** 《used in the *imperative* with *1st* and *3rd persons* to express a request, a com-
—[他] **1.** …에게 […을] 하게 하다, …하도록 허락하다 **2.** [1인칭·3인칭의 명령법으로 써서 간청·명령·경고 따위를 나타내어] …하자, 시키자 ¶①가만

L

let [662] **letter-card**

mand, a warning, etc.). ¶ *Let me go home.* / *Let me see.*① / *Let her do her best.* **3.** allow (someone or something) to pass, go or come. ¶ *Let the blinds down; Let down the blinds.*② →N.B. **4.** allow (blood, etc.) to flow out or run out. ¶ ~ *someone blood* / *I was ~ blood.*③ **5.** (chiefly *Brit.*) rent; hire out. ¶ *This house is to ~.* / *~ a boat by the hour* / *Rooms to ~.* —*vi.* (chiefly *Brit.*) be rented.
1) *let alone*, ⓐ not to mention. ⓑ refrain from disturbing; not interfere with.
2) *let be*, cease to bother; let alone.
3) *let down*, ⓐ disappoint; fail. ⓑ lower.
4) *let drive* (=*strike a powerful blow*) *at someone.*
5) *let fall* (or *drop*), ⓐ drop. ⓑ say purposely; reveal.
6) *let go*, ⓐ set (someone or something) free or allow (someone) to go. ⓑ dismiss; fire.
7) *let go of* (=*stop holding*) something, such *as a rope.*
8) *let in*, allow (fresh air, etc.) to enter; admit.
9) *let someone in for*, involve someone in (hard work, difficulty, etc.)
10) *let someone into*, ⓐ admit someone to. ⓑ make someone acquainted with (a secret, etc.)
11) *let loose*, ⓐ free (someone or something) from restraint; release. ⓑ indulge in; do as one wishes.
12) *let off*, ⓐ set (someone) free. ⓑ set off; fire (a gun, etc.)
13) *let on*, (*colloq.*) ⓐ reveal ⓑ (*U.S.*) pretend.
14) *let out*, ⓐ permit (someone) to go out. ⓑ reveal (a secret) by accident. ⓒ make (a garment, etc.) looser.
15) *let up*, cease; stop; become less.

let² [let] *n.* ⓒ **1.** a hindrance; an obstacle. **2.** Ⓤ (*Tennis*) a served ball which touches the net before falling on the other side.
without let or hindrance, in perfect freedom.

-let [-lit] *suf.* little; small : *a booklet* (=a small book); *a wavelet* (=a small wave); *a ringlet* (=a small ring).

let-down [létdàun / létdáun] *n.* ⓒ **1.** a reduction in value, energy, etc. **2.** (*colloq.*) a disappointment; a disillusionment. ¶ *His lecture was a ~.*①

le-thal [líːθ(ə)l] *adj.* likely to cause death; fatal. ¶ *a ~ weapon.*①

leth·ar·gy [léθərdʒi] *n.* Ⓤ **1.** the state of being unnaturally sleepy; abnormal sleep. **2.** the state of being slow, lazy or not active; dullness. ▷ **le·thar·gic** [-ʒik] *adj.*

Le·the [líːθi(ː)] *n.* **1.** (in Greek mythology) a river in Hades, a drink of the water of which causes the dead to forget the past. ⇒N.B. **2.** Ⓤ forgetfulness.

: let's [lets] let us.

: let·ter [létər] *n.* ⓒ **1.** a [written or printed] mark or sign representing a sound of speech; an alphabetical symbol. ¶ *a capital* (*a small*) *~.*① **2.** written or printed words, usu. sent by mail. ¶ *a ~ of introduction* (*thanks*)② / *write a ~ to a person.*② **3.** (often *pl.*) an official document giving proof, conferring a privilege, etc. ¶ *a ~ of attorney.*③ **4.** (*the ~*) Ⓤ the outward, literal meaning of words. **5.** ⓒ (*pl.*) literature; learning. ¶ *a man of letters.*⑤ ⇒usage / *the republic* (or *commonwealth*) *of letters*⑤ / *be quick at one's letters.*⑦ **6.** (*collectively*) a style of printing type.
to the letter, according to the literal sense; exactly; precisely.
—*vt.* write or engrave letters on (something).

letter box [⌐ ⌐] *n.* a box in which letters are mailed or delivered.

letter-card [létərkɑ̀ːrd] *n.* ⓒ (*Brit.*) a postal card that

---

있자, 글쎄 **3.** …을 가게(오게) 하다, 통과시키다, ¶②그녀를 나의 서재로 안내했다 N.B. 목적어 다음에 come이나 go가 생략되어 있음 **4.** …을 새게 하다; [액체·기체를] 나오게 하다 ¶③나는 피를 뽑혔다 **5.** 《英》[집·토지 따위]를 빌려주다 —自 《英》[집·토지 따위]를 빌려주다 —自 《英》 빌려주다, 세놓아지다

🅗 1) 말할 것도 없이, …은 고사하고 ⓑ 내버려두다, 방임하다 2) …을 내버려 두다, 상관하지 않다 3) ⓐ …을 낙심시키다, 실망시키다 ⓑ …을 낮추다, 내리다 4) …에게 맹렬히 치고 덤비다 5) ⓐ …을 떨어뜨리다 ⓑ …을 무심코 지껄이다; 누설하다 6) ⓐ …을 해방(방면) 하다, 놓아주다 ⓑ …을 해고하다 7) [쥐고 있던 것]을 놓다 8) [빛·공기 따위]를 들이다, 통과시키다 9) [남을 곤란따위]에 빠뜨리다, 말려들게 하다 10) ⓐ …으로 들이다, 들여보내다 ⓑ [남에게 비밀 따위를] 알리다 11) ⓐ …을 놓아(풀어)주다, 해방하다 ⓑ 제멋대로 하다 12) ⓐ [남을] 방면하다 ⓑ [총 따위]를 발포하다 13) (口) ⓐ [비밀 따위]를 누설하다 ⓑ 《美》…인 체하다 14) ⓐ [남]을 내보내 주다 ⓑ [비밀]을 무심코 입밖에 내다 ⓒ [옷 따위]를 늦추다, 느슨하게 하다 15) 중지하다, 그만두다, [비바람 따위가] 누그러지다, 자다

—옙 1. 방해, 훼방; 장애 2. (庭球) 레트 (네트를 스치고 들어간 서어브공)

🅗 아무런 장애 없이

—(接尾) 작은 …, 소(小)…

—옙 1. 감소, 감퇴 2. (口) 실망, 환멸 ¶ 그의 강연에는 실망했다

—옝 목숨을 빼앗는, 치명적인

—옙 1. 혼수[상태] 2. 무기력

—옙 1. [그리이스 신화의] 망각의 강 N.B. 그 물을 마시면 이승의 괴로움을 잊는다는 저승의 강 2. 망각

—옙 1. 글자, 문자 ¶①대(소)문자 2. 편지 ¶②소개(감사)장/③남에게 편지를 쓰다 3. 증서, 면허장, …장(狀), …증(證) ¶④위임장 4. 문자 그대로의 뜻, 자의(字義) 5. 문학, 학문 ¶⑤학자, 문인 Usage 복수형은 men of letters /⑥문단, 문인 사회/⑦학문의 습득이 빠르다 6. 글씨체, 자체(字體)

🅗 문자 그대로; 정확히, 엄밀히
—⑨ …에 글씨를 쓰다(새기다), 글자를 써 넣다

—옙 우체통, 포우스트; [개인용의] 우편함(函)

—옙 《英》 봉함 엽서

letter carrier can be folded and sealed by a gummed edge.
letter carrier [⌣ ⌣–] *n.* a postman; a mail carrier. —图 우체부, 우편물 집배원
let·tered [létərd] *adj.* **1.** able to read and write; educated; learned. **2.** having literary attainments. **3.** having letters printed on it; inscribed with letters. —图 1. 읽고 쓸 수 있는; 교육을 받은; 교양이 있는 2. 문학적 소질이 있는 3. 글자를 넣은, 글씨를 새긴
let·ter·head [létərhèd] *n.* ⓒ **1.** the name and address printed at the top of a sheet of writing paper. **2.** a sheet of writing paper so printed. —图 1. 편지지 위쪽에 인쇄된 주소 성명(회사명·전화 번호 따위), 레터헤드 2. [주소·성명이 인쇄된] 편지지
let·ter·ing [létəriŋ] *n.* ⓤ **1.** the act of drawing or inscribing letters. **2.** the letters so drawn. —图 1. 글자를 써넣기(찍기, 새기기) 2. 쓴 글자
let·ter·press [létərprès] *n.* ⓒ the words on a printed page as distinguished from the illustrations. —图 [삽화에 대하여] 문자 인쇄면, 본문
let·tuce [létis] *n.* ⓒ ⓤ a garden plant with tender, crisp leaves which are much used in salads. —图 상치, 양상치.
lev·ee¹ [lévi] *n.* ⓒ **1.** (*U.S.*) a large bank built along a river to prevent overflowing. **2.** a place for landing passengers and goods from a ship. —图 1. 《美》제방, 강둑 2. 방파제
lev·ee² [lévi] *n.* ⓒ a morning reception held by a king or other ruler for men only; (*U.S.*) a reception held by the President or another high official. —图 [군주 따위의] 알현(謁見); 《美》 [대통령 등의] 접견, 초대회
:lev·el [lévl] *adj.* **1.** having no part higher than any other; perfectly flat and even; smooth; parallel to the surface of still water. ¶ *a* ~ *floor.* **2.** equal; of equal height, importance, degree, etc. 《~ *to* or *with*》 ¶ *a* ~ *race* / *The river is now* ~ *with its banks.* **3.** well-balanced in quality, style, temper, judgment, etc. ¶ *a* ~ *mind* / *have a* ~ *head.*① —图 1. 수평의, 평평한, 평탄한, [수평선에 대하여] 경사가 지지 않은 2. 같은 높이(수준·정도·중요성)의, 동등한, 3. 균형이 잡힌, 평온한, 온건한, 공평한, 정당한 ¶①분별이 있다
—*n.* ⓒ **1.** an instrument for showing whether a surface is level or not. ¶ *use a* ~.② **2.** something that is level; a flat and even area of land or other surface. **3.** a height; a horizontal position. ¶ *The water rose to a* ~ *of 20 meters.* / *3800 meters above sea* ~. **4.** social, moral, or intellectual standard; degree; rank, esp. an equal rank. ¶ *rise to higher intellectual levels.* —图 1. 수준기(水準器) ¶②수준기를 사용하다, 수준을 잡다 2. 수평[면]; 평지, 평면, 평원 3. 고도, 같은 높이의 면 4. [사회적·도덕적·지적] 수준, 표준; 동등; 동위(同位)
1) *do one's level best*, (*colloq.*) do all that one can do.
2) *find one's* (or *its*) *level*, reach one's (or its) proper or natural place according to one's abilities, etc.
3) *on the level* (*colloq.*) honestly; truthfully.
霽 1)전력(최선)을 다하다 2)자기 분수에 맞는 지위에 앉다 3)《口》곧이곧대로, 정직하게 ; 공평하게, 공명정대하게
—*v.* *(-eled, -el·ing or Brit. -elled, -el·ling) vt.* **1.** make (something) even, flat or uniform. ¶ ~ *ground* / ~ *a road up* (or *down*). **2.** aim; direct. ¶ ~ *a satire at* (or *against*) *a person* / ~ *a gun at a lion.* **3.** bring (something) to the level of the ground; knock down. 《~ *someone or something to* or *with*》 ¶ ~ *the tree* / *The first blow leveled him to the ground.* —*vi.* **1.** take aim; direct a gun, etc. **2.** become level. 《~ *at*》 —他 1. …을 고르게 하다, 평평하게 하다, 평등하게 하다, 한결같게 하다, 고르다, 수평으로 놓다 2. […에게 총을] 겨냥하다 ; [풍자·비난]을 퍼붓다 3. [건물 따위]를 쓰러뜨리다, 넘어뜨리다 ; 타도하다 —自 1. 겨냥하다, 조준하다 2. […와] 같은 높이가 되게 올리다(내리다)
lev·el·head·ed [lévlhédid] *adj.* possessing good common sense and sound judgment; sensible; calm. —图 분별이 있는, 온건한
lev·er [lévər, +*U.S.* lí:vər / lí:və] *n.* ⓒ a bar used to move a heavy thing. ⇒fig. —*vt.* move or lift (something) with a lever. 《~ *out* or *up* something》 —*vi.* use a lever. —图 지렛대 —他 …을 지렛대로 움직이다 —自 지렛대를 사용하다

[lever]

lev·er·age [lévəridʒ, lí:v-(ə)ridʒ] *n.* ⓤ the action of a lever. —图 지렛대의 작용
le·vi·a·than [liváiəθ(ə)n] *n.* ⓒ **1.** (in the Bible) a sea animal of a huge size; a water monster. **2.** anything enormous, esp. a huge ship. —图 1.《聖》바다에 사는 거대한 짐승 2. 거대한 것; [특히] 거선(巨船)
lev·i·ty [léviti] *n.* ⓤ lack of seriousness, proper behavior, or earnestness. —图 경솔, 경망; 들뜬 기분
lev·y [lévi] *v.* (**lev·ied**) *vt.* **1.** collect (something) by order or force; impose (a tax). **2.** call up (a man) for —他 1. …을 징수하다; 부과하다 2. [군대]를 소집하다 —自 과세하다

military service. —*vi.* impose a tax; get money by authority or force.

levy war on (or ***upon, against***), start a war against (a country, etc.).

[熟] [나라 따위]에 대하여 전쟁을 일으키다; …와 전쟁하다

—*n.* (**lev·ies**) **1.** [U] [C] the act of collecting money, a tax, etc. by order or force; the amount so collected. ¶*a capital* ~.① **2.** [U] the act of calling up men for military service; [C] the number of men so called up. ¶~ *in mass.*②

—[名] 1. 부과; [세금 따위의] 징수액 ¶①자본 과세 2. 소집; 소집 군대 ¶②국가 총동원, 충원(充員) 소집

lewd [lu:d / l(j)u:d] *adj.* full of low desire; indecent; immodest. ▷**lewd·ly** [-li] *adv.*

—[形] 음탕한; 상스러운; 야비한

lex·i·ca [léksikə] *n.* pl. of **lexicon**.

lex·i·cog·ra·pher [lèksikágrəfər / -kɔ́grəfə] *n.* [C] a person who makes dictionaries.

—[名] 사전 편집자

lex·i·cog·ra·phy [lèksikágrəfi / -kɔ́g-] *n.* [U] the act or art of making dictionaries.

—[名] 사전 편집[법]

lex·i·con [léksikən] *n.* [C] (pl. **-i·ca** [-kə] or **-cons**) a dictionary, esp. of an ancient language, such as Greek, Hebrew, and Latin.

—[名] 사전, 사서(辭書); 고전어 사전

li·a·bil·i·ty [làiəbíliti] *n.* (pl. **-ties**) **1.** [U] the state of being liable or under obligation; responsibility. ¶~ *for debt*① | *limited* (*unlimited*) ~.② **2.** ((*pl.*)) a sum of money that must be paid; a debt. ¶*assets and liabilities.*③ **3.** [U] the state of being apt to do; tendency. **4.** [C] a thing that works to one's disadvantage.

—[名] 1. 책임; 의무 ¶①채무(債務)/②유한(무한) 책임 2. 부채(負債) ¶③자산과 부채 3. …하기(빠지기) 쉬움; 경향 4. 불리한 일

* **li·a·ble** [láiəbl] *adj.* **1.** apt or likely to do. ((~ *to do*)) ¶*Glass is* ~ *to break.* | *We are all* ~ *to make a mistake.* **2.** obliged to take the responsibility for (something); be responsible legally. ((~ *for* or *to do*)) ¶*He is* ~ *for damages.*① | *He is* ~ *to pay his wife's debts.*②

—[形] 1. …하기 쉬운; [좋지 않은 일에] 걸리기(빠지기) 쉬운 2. 책임을 져야 할 ¶①그는 손해 배상의 책임이 있다/②그는 아내의 빚을 갚아야 한다

li·ai·son [lí:əzàn / li(:)éizɔn] *n.* **1.** [U] a connection or communication between units of a military force. ¶*a* ~ *officer.*① **2.** [C] (*Phonetics*) (in spoken French) the linking of a silent final consonant to a following word that begins with a vowel or mute *h*.

—[名] 1. [부대 간의] 연락 ¶①연락장교 2. ((音聲)) 연결 발음, 연성(連聲)[프랑스어에서 어미의 자음을 다음 말의 두모음(頭母音)에 붙여서 발음하는 일]

* **li·ar** [láiər] *n.* [C] a person who tells lies.

—[名] 거짓말장이

li·ba·tion [laibéiʃ(ə)n] *n.* [C] the wine offered to a god.

—[名] 헌주(獻酒), 신주(神酒)

li·bel [láib(ə)l] *n.* [C] **1.** a written or printed statement which injures someone's reputation; [U] the act or crime of publishing such a statement. **2.** anything that speaks ill of or defames a person's character.

—[名] 1. 중상문(中傷文); 모욕[죄], 문서명예훼손[죄] 2. [일반적으로] 불명예[가 되는 것]

—*vt.* (**-beled, -bel·ing** or *Brit.* **-belled, bel·ling**) publish a libel about (someone); make a false statement and defame (someone).

—[他] …의 중상 문서(中傷文書)를 공개하다; 거짓 표현을 하여 [남]의 명예를 훼손하다

li·bel·lous [láib(ə)ləs] *adj.* (*Brit.*) = libelous.

li·bel·ous [láib(ə)ləs] *adj.* containing that which defames a person; intended to injure a person's reputation.

—[形] 중상적인; 남을 중상하기 좋아하는

* **lib·er·al** [líb(ə)rəl] *adj.* **1.** generous; not sparing. ¶*a* ~ *giver* | *be* ~ *of* (or *with*) *one's money.*① **2.** plentiful; abundant; ample. ¶*a* ~ *reward* | *a* ~ *amount.* **3.** broad-minded; free from prejudice; not narrow in one's ideas. ¶*a* ~ *thinker.* **4.** free from literal meaning; not literal. ¶*a* ~ *interpretation* (*translation*). **5.** (of an education) fit for a gentleman; of a general and literary kind rather than technical. ¶~ *arts*② | ~ *education.*③ **6.** favoring progress and reforms; liberalistic. ↔conservative

—[形] 1. 마음이 후한, 통이 큰, 아끼지 않는 ¶①돈을 아낌없이 쓰다 2. 많은, 풍부한 3. 관대한, 도량이 큰, 공평한 4. 글자 뜻에 구애받지 않는, 자유로운 5. [교육이] 신사가 되는 데 적당한; 일반교양의 ¶②[대학의] 교양과목(전공과목에 대하여 이르는 말)/③일반(교양)교육(직업교육에 대하여 이르는 말) 6. 자유주의의

—*n.* **1.** [C] a person who has liberal political views. **2.** ((usu. *L-*)) a member of the Liberal Party.

—[名] 1. 자유주의자 2. 자유당원

lib·er·al·ism [líb(ə)rəlìz(ə)m] *n.* [U] the [belief in] liberal principles.

—[名] 자유주의

lib·er·al·i·ty [libərǽliti] *n.* (pl. **-ties**) **1.** [U] the quality of being generous; willingness in giving; large-heartedness. **2.** [C] ((*pl.*)) a gift, esp. one showing generosity.

—[名] 1. 마음이 후함, 아끼지 않음: 도량이 큼; 관대 2. 선사, 선물

lib·er·al·ly [líb(ə)rəli] *adv.* in a liberal manner; generously; abundantly.

—[副] 관대히; 아낌없이; 충분히, 풍부하게; 공평히

Liberal Party [⌐-- ⌐-] *n.* a political party in Great

—[名] ((英)) 자유당

L

Britain that promotes democratic reforms, etc.

lib·er·ate [líbərèit] *vt.* set (a prisoner, etc.) free; release. ¶~ *slaves*① | ~ *the mind from prejudice.*②

lib·er·a·tion [lìbəréiʃ(ə)n] *n.* [U] the act of liberating; the state of being liberated.

lib·er·a·tor [líbərèitər] *n.* [C] a person who sets a person or persons free.

Li·be·ri·a [laibíəriə] *n.* a republic on the western coast of Africa. ⇒[N.B.]

lib·er·tine [líbərtì:n / líbə(:)tàin, -tì(:)n] *n.* [C] a person who leads an immoral life or does shameful conduct.

‡ **lib·er·ty** [líbərti] *n.* (pl. **-ties**) **1.** [U] the state of being free; freedom. ¶*Prisoners long for* ~.① **2.** [U] the right to do something without restraint; the freedom of choice. ¶~ *of speech* (*the press*).② **3.** ((usu. *pl*)) the rights and privileges granted by authority. **4.** [C] an improper, excessive freedom or familiarity.

1) ***at liberty,*** ⓐ (of a person) free; not busy. ⓑ (of things) not in use. ⓒ out of employment.
2) ***set someone at liberty,*** set someone free; release.
3) ***take liberties with*** (=be too familiar with) *someone.*
4) ***take the liberty of doing*** (or ***to do***), do (something) without asking someone's permission.

li·brar·i·an [laibrέəriən] *n.* [C] a person in charge of a library.

‡ **li·brar·y** [láibrèri / -brəri] *n.* [C] (pl. **-brar·ies**) **1.** a building or room in which a collection of books is kept for reading. ¶*a traveling* ~.① **2.** ((collectively)) a collection of books belonging to an individual. ¶*He has a fine* ~.② **3.** a series of books of the same kind issued by the same publishing company. ¶*The Home University Library.*③ **4.** a room containing books and used for private study, reading, etc.; a study.

a walking library, a very well-informed person; a walking dictionary.

Lib·y·a [líbiə] *n.* a country in northern Africa. ⇒[N.B.]

Lib·y·an [líbiən] *adj.* of Libya or its people. **—*n.*** [C] a person of Libya.

lice [lais] *n.* pl. of **louse**.

li·cence [láis(ə)ns] *n.* =license.

* **li·cense** [láis(ə)ns] *n.* **1.** [C][U] a formal statement of per mis- sion to do something granted by law or authority. ¶*under* ~.① **2.** [C] a written certificate of legal permission. ¶*a* ~ *to fish*② | *a* ~ *to practise medicine.*③ **3.** [U] excessive freedom of action; willful, unruly conduct. ¶*Little* ~ *was shown by the occupation forces.*④ **4.** [U] freedom from rules in art, etc. ¶*poetic* ~.⑤
—*vt.* give (someone) permission to do something.

li·cen·see [làis(ə)nsí:] *n.* [C] a person with a license.

li·cen·tious [laisénʃəs] *adj.* ignoring the common rules or principles; sexually immoral; lustful.

li·chen [láikən] *n.* [C][U] a mosslike plant without flowers and leaves which grows on rocks, tree trunks, etc.

* **lick** [lik] *vt.* **1.** pass the tongue over (something). ¶*Dogs* ~ *their wounds.* | *The little boy licked his fingers clean.* **2.** (of flames, waves, etc.) move or pass over (something). ¶*The flames were licking the roof of my house.* **3.** (*colloq.*) defeat. ¶*Our baseball team can* ~ *yours.* **4.** (*colloq.*) beat; hit. **—*vi.* 1.** (of flames, etc.) move lightly and quickly. ¶*The waves licked about his feet.* **2.** hasten. ¶*as hard as one can* ~.①

1) ***lick one's chops*** (or ***lips***), show a desire, esp. for food.
2) ***lick something*** or ***someone into shape,*** make someone or something complete or suitable by training.
3) ***lick off*** (or ***up***), take off (something) by licking.
4) ***lick someone's shoes,*** lower oneself before someone.
5) ***lick the dust,*** be completely overcome; die, usu.

—[他] …을 해방하다, 석방하다 ¶①노예를 해방하다/②편견을 품지 않다

—[名] 자유롭게 해주기; 석방, 해방

—[名] 해방자

—[名] 리베리아(아프리카 서해안의 공화국) [N.B.] 수도는 Monrovia

—[名] 품행이 나쁜 사람; 방탕아, 난봉꾼

—[名] **1.** 자유 ¶①죄수는 자유를 갈망한다 **2.** 자유권(權) ¶②언론(출판)의 자유 **3.** 특권(자치권 · 참정권 따위) **4.** 방자함, 제멋대로 함, 방종

[熟] 1)ⓐ자유로; 한가하여 ⓑ[물건이] 사용되고 있지 않은, 쓰고 있지 않은 ⓒ실직하여 2)[남]을 해방하다 3)[남]에게 버릇없이 치근거리다 4)염치없이(제멋대로) …하다

—[名] 도서관원

—[名] **1.** 도서관, 도서실 ¶①순회 도서관 **2.** 장서(藏書) ¶②그는 훌륭한 장서를 갖고 있다 **3.** 총서(叢書), 문고 ¶③가정 대학 총서 **4.** 서재

[熟] 박식한 사람; 살아 있는 사전

—[名] 리비아(북아프리카의 나라) [N.B.] 수도는 Tripoli와 Benghazi

—[形] 리비아[사람]의 —[名] 리비아 사람

—[名] **1.** 면허, 인가, 허가 ¶①허가를 받고 **2.** 면허장, 인가서 ¶②어업 감찰(鑑札)/③의사 개업 면허장 **3.** 제멋대로임, 방종, 방자 ¶④점령군들은 방자한 태도가 조금도 없었다 **4.** 파격(破格) ¶⑤시적(詩的) 파격(시가 문법 · 사실 따위에 어긋나도 허용되는 일)

—[他] …을 면허(인가)하다

—[名] 면허(인가 · 허가)를 얻은 사람

—[形] 품행이 좋지 않은, 부도덕한; 방종한; 방탕한; 음란한

—[名] 지의(地衣)[류]

—[他] **1.** …을 핥다 **2.** [물결 · 불꽃 따위가] …을 스치다, 널름거리다, 쓸고 지나가다, 가볍게 건드리다 **3.** ((口)) …을 지우다, …에 이기다 **4.** ((口)) …을 때리다, 치다

—[自] **1.** [불꽃 따위가] 너울거리다, 핥듯이 움직이다 **2.** 서두르다 ¶①전속력으로

[熟] 1)…에 입맛을 다시다 2)…을 상당한 것으로 만들다, 제구실을 하게 하다 3)…을 핥아 없애다, 말끔히 핥다 4)[남]에게 굴복하다, 아첨하다, 알랑거리다 5)굴복하다

L

violently
—*n.* **1.** [U] [C] the act of licking with the tongue or an instance of this. **2.** [C] a small amount; a bit. **3.** (*colloq.*) a sharp blow; an example of great speed; a fast pace. **4.** (*U.S.*) a place where salt is found on the surface and where animals come to lick it up.
a lick and a promise, a quick, rough washing, sweeping, piece of work, etc.

—[名] 1. 핥기, 한 번 핥기 2. 한 번 핥을 만한 분량, 적은 분량, 소량 3.《口》 강타; 빠른 속도, 스피이드 4.《美》 동물들이 소금을 핥으러 가는 곳, 함염지(含鹽地)
[熟] 아무렇게나 대강 하는 청소

* **lid** [lid] *n.* **1.** [C] a movable cover for an opening. ¶*the ~ of a box*① **2.** an eyelid. **3.** (*slang*) a hat; a cap.

—[名] 1. 뚜껑, 덮개 ¶①상자 뚜껑 2. 눈까풀 3. 모자

‡ **lie**[1] [lai] *vi.* (**lay, lain, ly·ing**) **1.** be in a flat or horizontal position. ¶*a book lying on the table.* **2.** be or put oneself in a flat or resting position. ¶*~ down on the bed.* **3.** be situated. ¶*The island lies east of Japan.* **4.** be kept or remain in a specified state. ¶*~ ill in bed / ~ in prison / ~ sleeping / ~ hidden / The corn lies wasting in the granary.* **5.** be; exist. ¶*The fault lies here.* **6.** be spread out to view. ¶*The valley lies at our feet.* **7.** be in the grave. ¶*His body lies in Boston.*
1) ***as far as in me lies,*** as well as I can.
2) ***lie back,*** get into or be in a resting position.
3) ***lie by,*** ⓐ stop; pause for rest. ⓑ remain unused.
4) ***lie down under** something,* accept something without protest or resistance.
5) ***lie in,*** ⓐ remain in bed because of childbirth. ⓑ consist in(something).
6) ***lie** (=**depend**) **on** something.*
7) ***lie over,*** (of an action) be postponed until some future time.

—[自] 1. [물건이] 놓여 있다, 있다 2. [동작을 나타내어] 눕다, 드러눕다 3. [토지 따위가] 위치하다 4. [보어와 함께] …의 상태에 있다, [어떤 상태에] 놓여 있다, 5. […에] 존재하다, 있다 6. […이] 펼쳐져 있다 7. […이] 묻혀 있다, 지하에 누워 있다
[熟] 1)나의 힘이 미치는 한 2)뒤로 비스듬히 기대다 3)ⓐ잠시 쉬다, 가만히(꼼짝 않고) 있다 ⓑ사용되지 않고 있다 4)[모욕 따위]를 달게 받다 5)ⓐ산욕(産褥)에 눕다 ⓑ…에 존재하다 6)…에 달려 있다, …에 의하여 결정되다 7)연기되다

‡ **lie**[2] [lai] *v.* (**lied, ly·ing**) *vi.* speak falsely with intent to deceive; (of things) convey a false impression to a person. ¶*Don't ~ about it.* —*vt.* bring, put, etc. (someone or something) by lying. ¶*~ someone out of something*① */ ~ someone into doing.*② —*n.* [C] a false statement made in order to deceive. ¶*act a ~ / tell a ~.*
give the lie to, ⓐ openly accuse (someone) of lying. ⓑ prove (something) to be false.

—[自] 거짓말하다; [물건이] 사람을 현혹시키다(속이다) —[他] …을 속이다, 거짓말하여 현혹시키다 ¶①[남]을 속여서 …을 빼앗다/②[남]을 부추겨서 …하게 하다
—[名] 거짓말, 허위, 허언
[熟] ⓐ[남]을 거짓말하였다고 비난하다 ⓑ…이 거짓임을 밝히다(증명하다)

lied [li:d] *n.* [C] (pl. **~er** [-ər]) a German song or lyric.

—[名] 단시(短詩), 리이드, 가곡, 가요곡

lief [li:f] *adv.* willingly; gladly.
would as lief ~ as ...; would liefer ~ than ..., would rather or more willingly ~ than ... ¶*I would as lief go there as stay.*

—[副] 기꺼이, 쾌히
[熟] …하느니 차라리 …하는 편이 낫다

liege [li:dʒ] *n.* [C] **1.** a lord having a right to receive service and devotion from his subject. **2.** a person who has been given land from a lord, and therefore must help or give service to him. —*adj.* **1.** having the right to receive service and devotion from one's subject. ¶*a ~ lord.*① **2.** having the duty of giving service and devotion to a lord. ¶*a ~ man.*②

—[名] 1. 군주, 왕후(王侯) 2. 신하, 가신(家臣) —[形] 1. 군주[로서]의 ¶①영주 2. 신하[로서]의 ¶②가신

liege·man [lí:dʒmən / -mæn] *n.* [C] (pl. **-men** [-mən / mèn]) [C] a subject; a faithful dependent; a liege.

—[名] 신하, 부하

lien [lí:(ə)n] *n.* [C] (*Law*) a claim on possessions or property until the owner's debt to one is paid.

—[名] 선취득권(先取得權)

lieu [lu: / l(j)u:] *n.* [U] (*archaic*) place.
in lieu of, instead of or in place of.

—[名]《古》 장소, 곳
[熟] …의 대신에

* **lieu·ten·ant** [lu:ténənt / *Brit. Army* leftén- or *Navy* letén-] *n.* [C] **1.** an officer who assists a commanding officer. **2.** an officer below a captain in the army. ¶*a first* (*a second*) *~.*① **3.** a junior officer below a lieutenant commander in the navy. ¶*a ~ junior grade.*②

—[名] 1. 부관, 상관 대리자 2. 육군 중위 ¶①육군 중위(소위) 3. 해군 대위 ¶②해군 중위

lieutenant colonel [-´- ´-] *n.* an army officer below the rank of colonel.

—[名] 육군 중령

lieutenant commander [-´- -´-] *n.* a naval officer in rank next above lieutenant.

—[名] 해군 소령

lieutenant governor [-´- ´--] *n.* **1.** (*U.S.*) a vice-governor of a state. **2.** (*Brit.*) an official under a governor general of a colony, etc.

—[名] 1.《美》 [주(州)의] 부지사 2.《英》 [식민지 따위의] 부총독

life [laif] *n.* (pl. **lives** [laivz]) **1.** [U] the quality that human being, animals, and plants have and that rocks and metals have not; the state of being alive; existence. ¶*the struggle for* ~ | *have no regard for human* ~.① **2.** [C] the period during which a person or thing is alive or useful. ¶*through* ~ | *a machine's* ~. **3.** [U] 《*collectively*》 living things. ¶*animal* ~ | *vegetable* ~.② **4.** [U][C] a way or manner of living. ¶*single* (*married*) ~ | *city* ~ | *a* ~ *of poverty.* **5.** [U] human social activity and relationships; human existence; human experience. ¶*real* ~ | *this* ~ | *get on in* ~.③ **6.** [C] a biography. ¶*a* ~ *of Churchill.* **7.** [U] spirit; energy; vitality; cheering influence. ¶*full of* ~ | *the* ~ *of the party* | *Put more* ~ *into your work.* **8.** [U] living form; life-size figure. ¶*a portrait* (*picture*) *drawn from* [*the*] ~.

—[名] 1. 생명, 생존 ¶①사람 목숨을 소중히 여기지 않다 2. 한평생, 생애, 수명, 계속 기간 3. 살아 있는 것, 생물 ¶②식물 4. 살림살이, 생활[상태] 5. 이 세상, 이승, 세상살이, 인간사, 실생활 ¶③입신 출세하다 6. 전기(傳記), 일대기 7. 생기, 활기, 원기, 정력; 중심력 8. 실물, 진짜, 실물대(大), 원형

1) ***bring*** *someone* or *something* ***to life,*** ⓐ bring someone back to consciousness. ⓑ cause something to be lively.
2) ***come to life,*** recover from a faint; become lively after a dull period.
3) ***for dear*** (or *one's*) ***life,*** with desperate energy, as if to save one's own life.
4) ***for life,*** during one's life.
5) ***for the life of me,*** (*colloq.*) 《in *negative*》 by any means.
6) ***not on your life,*** (*colloq.*) certainly not.
7) ***see*** (or ***learn***) ***life,*** have a wide variety of social experiences.
8) ***take life,*** kill.
9) ***take one's own life,*** commit suicide.
10) ***to the life,*** exactly like the living original.
11) ***true to life,*** true to reality; as in real life.

[熟] 1)ⓐ…의 의식을 회복시키다, 소생시키다, ⓑ활기띠게 하다 2)생기를 되찾다, 활기띠다, 소생하다 3)필사적으로, 간신히 [목숨만 건져] 4)일생(한평생)의 5)《口》[보통 부정 구문] 아무래도 […아니다] 6)《口》결코 …이 아니다, 확실히 …은 아니다 7)세상을 내다보다(알다), 폭넓은 경험을 하다 8)…을 죽이다 9)자살하다 10)실물 그대로 11)실물(실제)대로, 현실적으로

life belt [´ ˌ] *n.* a belt filled with cork, etc., used for making a person float in the water. ⇨fig. —[名] 구명대(救命帶), 구명 부대(浮帶)

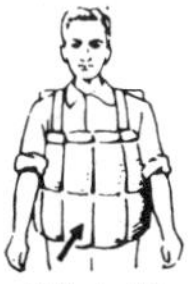
〔life belt〕

life·blood [láifblʌ̀d] *n.* [U] **1.** the blood required to live. **2.** something that gives energy or strength. —[名] 1. 생(生)피 2. 원기의 근원, 활력원(源)

life·boat [láifbòut] *n.* [C] a strong boat for saving persons after an accident at sea. —[名] 구명정(救命艇)

life buoy [´ ˌ] *n.* a ring which keeps a person afloat in the water, and so saves his life. —[名] 구명 부표(浮標)(부륜(浮輪))

life-giv·ing [láifgìviŋ] *adj.* that gives or can give life, vitality, or strength; inspiring. —[形] 생명(활력)을 주는, 원기를 북돋우는

life·guard [láifgɑ̀:rd] *n.* [C] a swimmer employed to help drowning persons at a swimming pool, a beach, etc. —[名] 수영장의 감시원(구조원)

life insurance [´ ˌ--] *n.* the system by which a certain sum of money is paid to a person's family at his death by an insurance company. —[名] 생명보험

life jacket [´ ˌ-] *n.* a jacket made of material that is able to float a person in the water. —[名] 구명 자켓

life·less [láiflis] *adj.* **1.** not living; dead. ¶*a* ~ *body.*① **2.** not lively; not active. ▷**life·less·ness** [-nis] *n.* —[形] 1. 생명이 없는; 죽은 ¶①시체 2. 활기 없는

life·less·ly [láiflisli] *adv.* in a lifeless manner. —[副] 죽은 듯이, 생기 없이

life·like [láiflàik] *adj.* looking like a living thing; resembling. ¶*a* ~ *portrait.*① ▷**life·like·ness** [-nis] *n.* —[形] 살아 있는 것 같은, 생생한 ¶①꼭 닮은(실물 같은) 초상화

life line [´ ˌ] *n.* a rope used for saving the life of someone who has fallen into deep water, etc. —[名] 구명 밧줄

life·long [láiflɔ̀:ŋ / -lɔ̀ŋ] *adj.* lasting or continuing through a person's life. —[形] 한평생의, 일생의, 종신(終身)의

life net [´ ˌ] *n.* a strong net used to catch persons jumping from a high, burning building. —[名] [소방용의] 구명망(網)

life-size [láifsáiz] *adj.* (of pictures, statues, etc.) having the same size as the living model. —[形] 실물 크기의, 실물대의, 등신대(等身大)의

life·time [láiftàim] *n.* [C] the whole time during which a person lives. —*adj.* of the whole time during a person's life; for life. —[名] 일생; 생애 —[形] 일생의

life·work [láifwə́:rk] *n.* ⓒ a work to which a person's lifetime is devoted; a work taking the whole life of a person.

⁑**lift** [lift] *vt.* **1.** move (something or someone) into a higher position; raise; hold up; take up. ¶~ *a chair* / ~ *a baby*① **2.** raise (something or someone) in rank, level, etc. ¶~ *someone from obscurity.*② **3.** take (a crop) from the ground; dig up. ¶~ *potatoes.* **4.** remove. ¶~ *a tent* / ~ *a worry from one's heart.* **5.** use (another's writings) as if they were one's own; steal. ¶~ *a passage from someone's writing* / ~ *goods things from a store.* —*vi.* **1.** move upward; rise; be raised. **2.** (of clouds, fog, etc.) become less thick; pass away. ¶*The fog lifted.* / *The gloom lifts.*
1) *lift a hand* (or *finger*) (=*make a slight effort*) *to do.*
2) *lift a* (or *one's*) *hand against* (=*almost strike*) *someone.*
3) *lift* [*up*] *one's eyes,* look up.
—*n.* ⓒ **1.** the act of lifting; an instance of this; a lifting power or influence on the mind. ¶*give a stone a* ~. **2.** a piece of help; assistance, esp. by taking someone somewhere by car. ¶*give someone a* ~① / *Give me a* ~ *with this job.* **3.** a rise to a higher position or rank. ¶*a* ~ *in one's career.* **4.** (chiefly *Brit.*) an elevator. (cf. *U.S.* elevator) **5.** a piece of leather raising the heel of a shoe.

lift·man [líftmən / -mæn, -mèn] *n.* ⓒ (chiefly *Brit.*) an operator of an elevator.

lig·a·ment [lígəmənt] *n.* ⓒ **1.** (*Anatomy*) a band of muscle that joins bones together or that holds an organ of the body in place. **2.** a tie; a band.

lig·a·ture [lígətʃər / -tʃuə] *n.* ⓒ **1.** a thing used for binding up. **2.** (in surgery) a piece of thread used to tie up a bleeding vein. **3.** the act of binding. **4.** (*Printing*) a type of two or three letters joined together. **5.** (*Music*) a slur.

⁑**light**¹ [lait] *n.* **1.** ⓤ that which makes it possible to see ↔darkness; brightness; radiance. ¶~ *and shade* / *the* ~ *of the candle.* **2.** ⓤ daylight; daytime; dawn. ¶*get up before* ~. **3.** ⓒ anything that gives light or start-something burning; a source of light like a candle, a lamp, a star, or a lighthouse. ¶*strike a* ~ / *Please give me a* ~. **4.** ⓤ the state of being visible; public view or knowledge. ¶*bring a matter to* ~① / *come to* ~.② **5.** ⓤⓒ illumination of the mind; knowledge or information that helps to explain things. ¶*shed* (or *throw*) [*a*] *new* ~ *on a question.*③ **6.** ⓤ knowledge. **7.** ⓒ the aspect in which something is viewed; an appearance from a particular point of view. **8.** ⓒ a prominent or famous person. **9.** ⓒ a window or other means of letting in light; a skylight. [ciples, ability, etc.]
1) *according to one's lights,* according to one's principles.
2) *between the lights,* at dusk or evening.
3) *between two lights,* at night; in the dark.
4) *by the light of nature,* without the aid of teaching.
5) *in the light of,* with knowledge of; considering.
6) *see the light* [*of day*], ⓐ be born; come into existence. ⓑ understand exactly.
7) *stand in one's own light,* harm oneself or one's reputation by acting foolishly or thoughtlessly.
—*v.* (**light·ed** or **lit** ⇨NB). *vt.* **1.** set fire to (a candle, a lamp, etc.); cause (a fire) to give off light or burn. ¶~ *a fire* / ~ *a lamp.* **2.** give light to (something); illuminate; brighten. ¶~ *the streets.* **3.** show the way to

—名 일생(평생)의 사업

—他 1. …을 올리다, 끌어올리다, 들어 올리다, 안아 올리다 ¶①아기를 들어 올리다 2.[지위·처지·정신 따위]를 향상시키다, 양양하다, 높이다, 고상하게 하다 ¶②무명의 [사람]을 출세시키다 3.[농작물]을 캐내다 4. …을 제거하다 치우다 5.[남의 문장]을 도용(표절)하 다; …을 훔치다 —自 1. 올라가다 2. [구름·안개 따위가] 걷히다, 개다

熟 1)…하는 데 약간의 수고를 하다 2)…을 때리려고 하다, 칠 듯이 덤비다 3)쳐다보다, 우러러보다

—名 1. 들어올리기, 들기, 올리기; [정신]의 앙양; 향상 2. 돕기, 거들기; [남을] 차에 태워 주기 ¶③[남]을 차에 태워 주다; [남]을 거들어 주다 3. 입신출세, 승진, 승급 4.《英》 엘리베이터, 승강기 5.[구두의] 뒤축 가죽의 한 장

—名 《英》 엘리베이터 운전수

—名 1.《解》 인대(靭帶) 2. 끈, 띠; 기반 (羈絆)

—名 1. 끈, 띠 2.《外科》 봉합사(縫合絲) 3. 묶기, 동이기, 잡아매기 4.《印刷》 연자 (連字), 합자(合字), 포자(抱字)[Æ,Œ, fi 따위] 5. 연결선

—名 1. 빛, 광선, 광휘, 광명, 밝음, 빛남 2. 햇빛; 낮; 새벽, 여명 3. 발광체(發光體), 천체, 광원(光源), 점화구(성냥불 따위); 등대, 등화(燈火) 4. 명백, 드러남 ¶①일을 세상에 밝히다(폭로하다) /②나타나다, 탄로나다 5. [정신적] 광명; [문제의 설명에] 단서가 되는 사실 ¶③문제에 광명을 던지다(분명하게 하다) 6. 지식 7. 양상, 견해 8. 빛나는 인물, 권위자 9. 채광창, 들창

熟 1)각자의 주의(견해·능력)에 따라 2)해질 무렵에, 저녁때에 3)[낮과 낮 사이인] 밤에, 어둠을 타고 4)직감으로, 배우지 않고 5)…에 비추어, …으로서 6)ⓐ태어나다, 세상에 나오다 ⓑ을바로 이해하다 7)[어리석은 짓이나 실책을 하여] 스스로 자기의 불리를 초래하다

—動 NB 형용사적 용법의 과거분사 는 lighted 가 보통 —他 1. …에 불을 붙이다, [불]을 때다 2. …에 등불을 달다, …을 비추다, 빛나게 하다, 환하게

light

(someone) by or as by giving light. ¶ ~ *someone through the dark street* / *The girl lighted me downstairs.* —*vi.* **1.** take fire; begin burning. **2.** be lighted; brighten. 《~ *up*》 ¶*His face lit up with hope.*
—*adj.* **1.** bright; having light; not dark. ↔dark ¶*a ~ room.* **2.** not dark or deep in color; pale; whitish. ¶*~ green* / *~ hair.*

light² [lait] *adj.* **1.** having little weight; of less than usual weight. ↔heavy ¶*a ~ pair of shoes* / *a ~ coin.* **2.** easy to do; not very difficult to bear. ¶*~ punishment* / *~ work.* **3.** aiming to entertain; not serious; amusing. ¶*a ~ comedy.* **4.** (of wine, etc.) containing little alcohol. ¶*~ wine.* **5.** active in motion; not moving slowly. ¶*~ footsteps.* **6.** slight; not important. ¶*a ~ mistake* / *~ losses.* **7.** happy; cheerful; gay. ¶*with a ~ heart* / *~ spirits.* **8.** lightly armed. ¶*~ cavalry.* **9.** less than usual in amount, force, etc. ¶*a ~ sleep (frost, snow, wind).* **10.** thoughtless; lacking proper seriousness; loose in morals. ¶*a ~ woman* / *a ~ opinion.* **11.** (of food) easy to digest. ¶*~ food.*
—*adv.* lightly. ¶(*proverb*) *Light come, ~ go.*①
1) *light in the head,* ⓐdizzy. ⓑsilly; foolish. ⓒ crazy.
2) *make light of,* treat (someone or something) as of little importance; pay little or no attention to (someone or something).

light³ [lait] *vi.* (**lit** or **light·ed**) (of a bird) come to 'rest; land; get down (from a horse, etc.)

* **light·en**¹ [láitn] *vt.* make (something) bright or clear. —*vi.* **1.** become bright. **2.** give out flashes of lightning. ¶*It thundered and lightened all night.*
* **light·en**² [láitn] *vt.* **1.** reduce (something) in weight. **2.** make (someone) more cheerful. —*vi.* become lighter or more cheerful.
light·er¹ [láitər] *n.* Ⓒ a person or thing that lights to 「set a fire.」
light·er² [láitər] *n.* Ⓒ a flat boat for carrying goods in a harbour or a river. —*vt.* carry (goods) in a lighter.
light-fin·gered [láitfiŋgərd] *adj.* skillful in using the fingers; skillful at stealing.
light-hand·ed [láithǽndid] *adj.* **1.** skillful in using the hands or in managing something. **2.** having little in the hands to carry. **3.** not harring as many men to help as necessary.
light-head·ed [láithédid] *adj.* **1.** confused in one's mind. **2.** wandering or changeable in one's mind.
light-heart·ed [láithá:rtid] *adj.* free from care; merry; cheerful. ▷**light-heart·ed·ness** [-nis] *n.*
light-heart·ed·ly [láithá:rtidli] *adv.* cheerfully.
light·house [láitháus] *n.* Ⓒ a tower with a bright brilliant light at the top to guide ships at night.
light·ing [láitiŋ] *n.* Ⓤ **1.** the way of using lights [on the stage, etc.]; illumination. **2.** the act of giving light.
: **light·ly** [láitli] *adv.* **1.** with little force; softly. **2.** easily. ¶(*proverb*) *Lightly come, ~ go.*① 「seriousness.」
light-mind·ed [láitmáindid] *adj.* thoughtless; lacking 」
light·ness¹ [láitnis] *n.* Ⓤ **1.** the state or quality of being light in color; brightness. **2.** pale in color.
light·ness² [láitnis] *n.* Ⓤ **1.** the state of not being heavy. **2.** skillfulness. **3.** delicacy; gracefulness. **4.** cheerfulness. **5.** lack of seriousness.
: **light·ning** [láitniŋ] *n.* Ⓤ a flash of light made by electricity in the sky. —*vi.* make a flash of light.
lightning conductor [⸺ ⸺⸺] *n.* a thin metal bar placed above the top of a building and connected with the earth to prevent a thunderbolt from doing damage.

lightning conductor

(횔가며게)하다 3. 등불을 밝혀 …의 길을 안내하다 —自 1. 불이 붙다, 불 타오르다 2. 밝아지다, 빛나다, [얼굴이] 환해지다

—形 1. 밝은, 환한 2. [빛깔이] 연한, 옅은 빛깔의, 희읍스름한

—形 1. 가벼운, 무겁지 않은; [규정된 것보다] 가벼운 2. 쉬운, 용이한; [벌·부담이] 엄하지 않은, 너그러운, 관대한 3. 딱딱하지 않은, 오락적인 4. 알코올 성분이 적은 5. 가뿐가뿐한, 경쾌한 6. 사소한, 하찮은 7. 즐거운, 쾌활해 보이는 8. 경장(輕裝)의 9. [정도·분량이] 적은, 경미(輕微)한 10. 경솔한, 경망스러운, 마음이 들뜬, 바람난, 품행이 좋지 않은 11. 소화가 잘 되는

「쉽게 얻은 것은 잃기도 쉽다」
—副 가볍게, 쉽게, 경쾌하게 ¶①(俚) 1)ⓐ어지러운, 현기증나는 ⓑ어리석은 ⓒ정신이 이상한, 미친 2)…을 얕보다, 경시하다

—自 [새가] 내려 앉다, [말 따위에서] 내리다
—他 …을 밝게 하다; 명백히 하다, 밝히다 —自 1. 밝아지다, 환해지다; 맑아지다, 개다 2. 번갯불이 번쩍이다
—他 1. …을 가볍게 하다, 완화(경감)하다, 덜다 2. …을 즐겁게 하다, 쾌활하게 하다 —自 가벼워지다; 쾌활해지다
—名 불을 붙이는 사람; 라이터
—名 거룻배 —他 [짐을] 거룻배로 운반하다

—形 손재주 있는; 손버릇이 나쁜

—形 1. 솜씨가 좋은, 손재주 있는 2. 손에 든 것이 별로 없는, 빈손의 3. 일손이 모자라는

—形 1. 머리가 이상한 2. 변덕스러운

—形 아무 근심이 없는, 속 편한; 쾌활한, 명랑한
—副 마음 편히, 쾌활하게
—名 등대

—名 1. 조명, 조명법 2. 점화(點火)

—副 1. 가볍게 2. 손쉽게, 용이하게 ¶ ①(俚)쉽게 얻은 것은 잃기도 쉽다
—形 경솔한, 경박한, 방정맞은
—名 1. 밝음, 밝기 2. [색깔이] 옅음, 희읍스름함
—名 1. 가벼움, 가볍기 2. 솜씨좋음 3. 우아(우미)함 4. 쾌활함 5. 경솔, 경박

—名 번갯불 —自 번개가 치다

—名 피뢰침

light·ship [láitʃìp] *n.* ⓒ a ship with a bright light that anchors in a dangerous place to warn other ships. ⇨fig.

light·some [láitsəm] *adj.* **1.** light and quick [in movement]. **2.** merry. **3.** lacking seriousness.

light·weight [láitwèit] *n.* ⓒ a boxer or wrestler between a feather weight and a welterweight; esp., a boxer who weighs less than 135 pounds. ⇨N.B.

[lightship]

lig·nite [lígnait] *n.* ⓤ soft, dark-brown coal.

lik·a·ble [láikəbl] *adj.* liked by most people; that can be liked.

‡**like**[1] [laik] *adj.* (usu. **more like, most like**) **1.** almost the or exactly the same in amount, character, form, etc. **2.** similar; equal. ¶*a ~ sum / in ~ manner.*
  1) ***nothing like,*** not nearly; not at all like.
  2) ***something like,*** almost like; about.
  —*adv.* (colloq.) probably. ¶*Like enough it will rain.*
  —*prep.* **1.** similar to; resembling. ¶*She is ~ a bird. / He has eyes ~ stars.* **2.** in the same way as. ¶*speak ~ a fool / work ~ mad / She sings ~ a bird.* **3.** characteristic of; suitable for. ¶*Such behavior is ~ him.* **4.** in the proper mood for; inclined to do something. ¶*It looks ~ snow.*
  1) ***feel like,*** be in the mood for doing. ¶*I feel ~ sleeping.*
  2) ***like anything,*** (colloq.) to an extreme degree.
  3) ***like enough*** (or ***very like***), probably. ¶*~ he said.*
  —*conj.* (colloq.) as; in the same way as. ¶*It was just*
  —*n.* ⓒ a person or thing that is like another; something of a similar nature each other. ¶*I have never seen the ~ of it.*[1]
  1) ***and the like,*** and others of the same kind.
  2) ***the likes of me*** (or ***you, him, etc.***), people of the same class, rank, etc. as me, you, etc.

‡**like**[2] [laik] *vt.* **1.** be pleased with or be fond of (something or someone); enjoy. ¶*I ~ fruit. / He likes sports. / I ~ swimming.* **2.** wish; wish for; have a preference for (someone or something). (*~ to do; ~ someone or something to do* or *doing*) ¶*I ~ to swim in the river. / I don't ~ to be poor. / I ~ them to tell the truth. / I ~ my tea hot. / I ~ my eggs boiled.* ⇨USAGE **3.** suit the health of (someone). ¶*I ~ fish but it doesn't ~ me.*[1] —*vi.* be pleased; choose. ¶*do as you ~.*
  I should (or ***would***) ***like,*** ⇨USAGE ⓐ want to have. ¶*He would ~ a cup of tea.* ⓑ wish. (*~ to do; ~ something or someone to do*) ¶*I should* (or *would*) *~ to go. / I should ~ you to know it.*
  —*n.* (usu. *pl.*) preferences; tastes; affections.

-like [làik] *suf.* like: suitable for; characteristic of; suitable for: *boylike* (=like or characteristic of a boy) / *godlike* (=like or suitable for a god) / *childlike* (=characteristic of a child) / *businesslike* (=fit for business).

like·li·hood [láiklihùd] *n.* ⓤ probability; something which appears to be probable. ¶*In all ~, he will fail.*

‡**like·ly** [láikli] *adj.* (*-li·er, -li·est*) **1.** probable, believable. ¶*a ~ story*[1] */ I called at every ~ place.*[2] **2.** to be expected. (*~ to do* or *that …*) ¶*It is ~ to rain. / It is ~ that he will succeed.* **3.** fitting; proper.
  —*adv.* (*often* used with *very* or *most*) probably. ¶*I very ~ go out.* ⌈*shall about it as ~ as not.*
  1) ***as likely as not,*** very probably. ¶*He'll forget all*

―名 등대선(등대 구실을 하는 배)

―形 1. 민활한, 경쾌한 2. 쾌활한, 명랑한 3. 경솔한, 경박한

―名 라이트급 선수 N.B. 권투에서는 체중 59~62kg, 레슬링에서는 63~67kg, 역도에서는 61~67.5kg

―名 아탄(亞炭), 갈탄(褐炭)
―形 마음에 드는, 호감을 가질 수 있는
―形 1. 같은, 동등한; 같은 액수의, 같은 양의 2. 같은 모양의, 비슷한

熟 1)결코 있을 성싶지 않은 2)다소 …와 같은; 대략, 약
―副 아마도, 필시
―前 1. …와 같은, …와 비슷한 2. …처럼, …와 마찬가지로 3. …에 어울리는, …다운 4. …할 성싶은, …할 것 같은

熟 1)…할 것같이 느껴지다 2)(口)몹시, 대단히, 맹렬히 3)아마 …일 것이다

―接 (口) …와 같이, …하듯이
―名 비슷한 것, 닮은 것; 동류의(동등한) 사람 ¶①그런 것은 본 일이 없다

熟 1)그밖의 같은 종류의 것, … 따위, … 등 2)… 같은 사람들

―他 1. …을 좋아하다, 좋다; 즐기다 2. …하고 싶다, 바라다, 원하다; …이었으면 하다 USAGE 부정사(不定詞)를 목적어로 할 때에는 특정한 행위를, 동명사를 목적어로 할 때에는 일반적인 행위를 서술하는 일이 많음 3. …에 맞다, 적합하다 ¶①나는 생선을 좋아하지만 그것은 내 몸에 맞지 않는다
―自 USAGE 바라다
熟 USAGE 미국어나 영국어의 구어에서는 1인칭에는 would를 씀 ⓐ좋아하다 ⓑ…하고 싶다

―名 좋아하는 것, 기호(嗜好)
―(接尾) …와 같은, …다운, …의 특징을 지닌, …에 알맞은

―名 있을 법함, 가망

―形 1. 있을 법한, 정말 같은, 그럴 듯한 ¶①(때로 반어적으로) 설마/②있을 법한 곳은 모조리 가 보았다 2. …할 것 같은, …일(할) 듯한 3. 적당한, 안성맞춤의 ―副 아마, 필시

熟 1)혹시 …일지도 모르는, 아마, 모르

2) ***likely enough,*** perhaps.
면 모르되 2)아마 [···일 것이다]

like-mind·ed [láikmáindid] *adj.* with the same opinions, purposes, tastes, etc.
—[形] 같은 마음의(의견의, 목적의, 취미의)

lik·en [láik(ə)n] *vt.* represent as like; compare. ⟪~ something *to*⟫ ¶*Life is often likened to a voyage.*①
—[他] ···에 비기다, 비유하다 ¶①인생은 흔히 항해에 비유된다

* **like·ness** [láiknis] *n.* **1.** [U] the state of being like; similarity; [C] a point of resemblance; something that is like. ¶*I can find no ~ between you and your father.* **2.** [C] a picture; a portrait. ¶*I had my ~ painted.*① **3.** [U] appearance; form.
—[名] 1. 비슷함, 닮음; 유사; 유사점(물) 2. 사진; 초상 ¶①나는 나의 초상화를 그리게 했다 3. 외관; 겉보기

‡ **like·wise** [láikwàiz] *adv.* in the same manner; in addition; also. ¶*I want to see it ~. / He is ~ my classmate.*
—[副] 똑 같게, 마찬가지로; 또, 게다가, 그 위에

* **lik·ing** [láikiŋ] *n.* [C] a fondness; a taste.
1) ***have a liking for*** (=*be fond of*) *something.*
2) ***take a liking to*** (=*be pleased with*) *something.*
3) ***to one's liking,*** appealing to one's taste.
—[名] 좋아함; 취미
[熟] 1)···을 좋아하다; 사랑하다 2)···이 마음에 들다 3)마음에 들어, 취미에 맞아서

li·lac [láilək] *n.* **1.** [C] a small tree with hanging bunches of fragrant white or pale violet flowers. **2.** [U] a pale violet color. **—*adj.*** of or having a pale violet color.
—[名] 1. 라일락, 자정향(紫丁香) 2. 라일락색, 엷은 보라색 —[形] 라일락색의, 엷은 보라색의

Lil·li·pu·tian [lìlipjú:ʃən / -ʃjən] *adj.* **1.** of Lilliput. **2.** very small. **—*n.*** [C] **1.** a person of Lilliput. **2.** a very small person; a midget.
—[形] 1. 소인국(小人國)의, 릴리퍼트의 2. 매우 작은 —[名] 1. 소인국의 주민 2. 꼬마 사람

lilt [lilt] *vt., vi.* sing or play (a tune) with a gay, light rhythm. **—*n.*** [C] **1.** a lively rhythm or movement. **2.** a gay song.
—[他][自] [곡조를] 명랑(경쾌)하게 노래하다(연주하다) —[名] 1. 경쾌한 리듬(동작) 2. 경쾌한 노래

‡ **lil·y** [líli] *n.* [C] (pl. **lil·ies**) a plant with beautiful bell-shaped flowers. ¶*the ~ of the valley*① / *a tiger ~.*② **—*adj.*** [white, pure] like a lily.
—[名] 나리, 백합 ¶①은방울꽃/②참나리 —[形] 백합 같은, 백합같이 흰(순결한)

lily-white [líli(h)wáit] *adj.* white as a lily.
—[形] 백합처럼 흰

‡ **limb** [lim] *n.* [C] **1.** (of a man or an animal) a leg or an arm; (of a bird) a wing. **2.** a main or large branch of a tree; a bough. **3.** a person or thing regarded as a part, a branch, a wing, etc. ¶*a ~ of Satan.*① **4.** (*colloq.*) a mischievous child.
—[名] 1. [사람·동물의] 손발, 수족; [새의] 날개 2. 나무의 큰 가지 3. 앞잡이; [손발·날개 같은] 부분 ¶①악마의 앞잡이 4. 장난꾸러기, 개구장이

limb from limb, completely separated.
[熟] 갈래갈래로, 갈기갈기

—*vt.* cut off a limb from (a body).
—[他] 사지(날개·가지)를 자르다

lim·ber [límbər] *adj.* flexible that can easily bend. **—*vi.*** become flexible. **—*vt.*** make (something) flexible.
—[形] 휘기 쉬운, 휘청휘청한 —[自] 유연해지다 —[他] ···을 유연하게 하다

lim·bo [límbou] *n.* [C] (pl. **-bos**) **1.** ⟪often *L-*⟫ (*Roman Catholicism*) a supposed place between hell and heaven where line the souls of unbaptized infants and those of good people who died before Christ's coming. **2.** [U] forgetfulness; oblivion. **3.** [C] a prison.
—[名] 1. 지옥의 변방(邊方)(천국과 지옥 사이에 있는 가공의 지역); 림보(세례를 받지 않은 유아와 그리스도 강림 이전의 사람들의 영혼이 삶) 2. 망각 3. 감옥, 유치장, 교도소

* **lime**[1] [laim] *n.* [U] **1.** a white powder made by burning limestone, sea shells, bones, etc. ¶*caustic* (or *quick*) *~.*① / *slaked ~.*② **2.** a sticky material used for catching birds; birdlime. **—*vt.*** **1.** put lime on (a field, etc.). **2.** cover (a twig, a branch, etc.) with birdlime; catch (a bird) with birdlime.
—[名] 1. 석회 ¶①생석회/②소(消)석회 2. 새 잡는 끈끈이 —[他] 1. ···에 석회를 뿌리다 2. [나뭇가지 따위]에 새 잡는 끈끈이를 바르다; [새]를 끈끈이로 잡다

lime[2] [laim] *n.* [C] a fruit much like a lemon, but smaller and sourer; its tree.
—[名] 라임 열매; 그 나무

lime[3] [laim] *n.* [C] a well-known European tree with small, sweet-smelling flowers; the linden.
—[名] 참피나무; 보리수

lime·light [láimlàit] *n.* [U] **1.** a strong light produced by heating lime in a hot flame. **2.** ⟪*the ~*⟫ the center of public attention and interest. ¶*in the ~.*①
—[名] 1. [옛날의 무대 조명용] 석회등(燈) 2. 주목의 대상 ¶①사람 눈을 끄는 곳에; 세상의 이목을 끌어, 각광을 받고

* **lime·stone** [láimstòun] *n.* [U] a rock composed chiefly of calcium carbonate, used for road construction, etc.
—[名] 석회석

lime tree [ˊ ˋ] *n.* a linden.
—[名] 참피나무

lime·wa·ter [láimwɔ̀:tər] *n.* [U] a solution of lime in water, used to counteract an acid.
—[名] 석회수

‡ **lim·it** [límit] *n.* **1.** [C] the farthest edge or the point where something ends or must end; the greatest amount; boundary. ¶*the ~ of human knowledge* (*endurance*).① **2.** ⟪*pl.*⟫ bounds; boundary lines.
—[名] 1. 한도; 한계 ¶①인지(人知)(인내)의 한계 2. 경계; 범위

1) ***off limits,*** (*U.S.*) outside the limits of the area that one is allowed to enter; out of bounds.
2) ***within limits,*** in moderation.
3) ***without limit,*** to any extent or degree.
—*vt.* keep (something) shut within bounds; restrict. ¶ *~ the speed of a car to 50 miles an hour.*②

[熟] 1)〔美〕출입금지[지역] 2)적당하게, 알맞게 3)한없이, 무한히
—[他] …을 한정하다; 제한하다 ¶②자동차의 속도를 시속 50 마일로 제한하다

* **lim·i·ta·tion** [lìmitéiʃ(ə)n] *n.* [U] the act of limiting; the state of being limited; [C] a limit of capability.
—[名] 제한, 한정; [능력·지력 따위의] 한도, 한계, 범위

lim·it·ed [límitid] *adj.* **1.** kept within certain limits; restricted; narrow. **2.** (*U.S.*) (of a train, a bus, etc.) making only a few stops
—[形] 1. 제한된, 한정된; 유한(有限)의; 좁은 2.〔美〕급행의

lim·it·less [límitlis] *adj.* without limit; boundless.
—[形] 무한한; 광대한

lim·ou·sine [líməzìːn, ---- / límu(:)zìːn] *n.* [C] a motorcar with a compartment for from three to five persons, and a separate driver's seat.
—[名] 리무진 자동차(3~5 인승 간막이 자동차)

* **limp**¹ [limp] *n.* [C] a lame way of walking. —*vi.* walk lamely.
—[名] 절름발이 —[自] 절름거리다

limp² [limp] *adj.* not stiff; weak.
—[形] 유연한, 부드러운; 약한, 가냘픈

lim·pet [límpit] *n.* [C] a small shellfish that clings tightly to rocks.
—[名] 소라, 삿갓조개

lim·pid [límpid] *adj.* clear; transparent.
—[形] 투명한, 맑은; 명쾌한

lim·pid·i·ty [limpíditi] *n.* [U] the state of being limpid; clearness.
—[名] 맑음; 투명

limp·ly [límpli] *adv.* in a limp manner; flexibly; weakly.
—[副] 유연하게, 나긋나긋하게; 힘없이, 가냘프게

linch·pin [líntʃpìn] *n.* [C] a pin that is passed through a hole in the end of an axle to keep the wheel in place. ⇒fig.
—[名] 바퀴를 축(軸)에서 빠지지 않게 하기 위한 핀

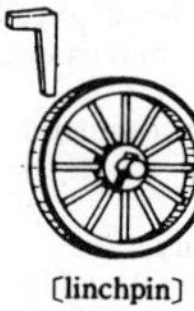
[linchpin]

: Lin·coln [líŋkən], **Abraham** *n.* (1809–1865), the 16th president of the United States.
—[名] 미국의 제 16 대 대통령

lin·den [líndən] *n.* [C] a large tree with heart-shaped leaves and scented yellow flowers.
—[名] 보리수; 참피나무

: line¹ [lain] *n.* [C] **1.** a string; a cord; a rope; a wire. ¶ *a telephone ~ / a fishing ~.*① **2.** a very thin, thread-like mark. ¶ *a straight ~.* **3.** a wrinkle. ¶ *deep lines in his face.* **4.** a row of words on a page or in a column; a short letter. ¶ *the first ~ of the page / Drop me a ~.*② **5.** a row of things or persons. **6.** (*pl.*) outline. ¶ *a ship's lines / He has good lines in his face.*③ **7.** a series of persons in a family; lineage. ¶ *of noble ~ / one's family ~.* **8.** a regular course or service of ships, planes, trains, etc. ¶ *an airline*④ */ Japan Air Lines*⑤ */ the Tokaido Line / There are many bus lines in this city.*⑥ **9.** (often *pl.*) plan; principle. ¶ *on these lines*⑦ */ take a strong ~.*⑧ **10.** a boundary; a border. ¶ *the state ~.* **11.** business; profession. ¶ *What is your ~? / That's not in my ~.*⑨ **12.** (*pl.*) fate. ¶ *hard lines.*
—[名] 1. 끈, 노끈; 밧줄; 전선(電線) ¶①낚싯줄 2. 선 3. 주름 4. [책 따위의] 행(行); 짧은 편지 ¶②몇 자 적어 보내 주시오 5. 열(列) 6. 윤곽 ¶③그는 얼굴 윤곽이 잘 생겼다 7. 가계(家系) 8. 항로; 노선 ¶④공로(空路)/⑤대한항공/⑥이 도시에는 버스 노선이 많다 9. 계획; 방침 ¶⑦이 방침들로/⑧단순한 방침을 취하다 10. 경계선 11. 사업; 직업 ¶⑨그것은 내 소관사가 아니다 12. 운명

1) ***all along the line,*** everywhere; at every point.
2) ***bring something into line,*** cause something to agree.
3) ***come into line with*** (=*agree to*) *something.*
4) ***draw the*** (or ***a***) ***line,*** set a limit; refuse to go beyond.
5) ***get*** (or ***have***) ***a line on*** (=*get information about*) *something.*
6) ***hit the line,*** try boldly or firmly to do something.
7) ***hold the line,*** stand firmly; permit no retreat.
8) ***on a line,*** on the same plane; level.
9) ***on the line,*** not clearly one thing nor the other.
10) ***out of line,*** not in agreement.
11) ***read between the lines,*** find a hidden meaning or purpose in something written, said, or done.
12) ***toe the line,*** do exactly what has been commanded.

[熟] 1)도처에서, 전선(全線)에 걸쳐서; 모든 점에서 2)…을 일치(협력)시키다 3)…와 일치(협력)하다 4)한계를 정하다; 경계를 짓다; …이상은 하지 않다 5)…의 정보(새 지식)를 얻다 6)과감하게 해보다 7)고수하다; 일보도 후퇴하지 않다 8)동등한, 평균하여 9)이도 저도 아닌 10)일치하지 않은; 흩어져서 11)글 속의 숨은 뜻을 알아내다 12)명령대로 행하다

—*vt.* **1.** draw lines on (paper, etc.); cover (something) with lines. ¶ *~ the paper / a face lined with pain.*⑩ **2.** form a line along (a place). ¶ *a street lined with trees*⑪ */ Cars lined the road for two miles.*⑫ —*vi.* form a line.
—[名] 1. …에 줄(선)을 긋다; …을 선으로 덮다 ¶⑩고생으로 주름진 얼굴 2. …에 한 줄로 서다(늘어서다) ¶⑪가로수 길/⑫그 길에는 자동차가 2 마일이나 늘어서 있었다 —[自] 한 줄이 되다

line up, ⓐ form a line. ⓑ bring into a line. — [熟] ⓐ한 줄을 이루다 ⓑ로 (늘어서다)

line² [lain] *vt.* **1.** cover the inside of (something). ¶*My coat is lined with fur.* **2.** fill. 《~ something *with*》 — [他] 1. …의 안을 대다 2. …을 채우다

lin·e·age [líniidʒ] *n.* [U] the line of ancestors; ancestry. — [名] 혈통; 계통

lin·e·al [líniəl] *adj.* **1.** descending in the direct line of ancestors; ancestral. **2.** of a line or lines; linear. — [形] 1. 직계의; 조상으로부터의 2. 줄(선)의

lin·e·ar [líniə*r*] *adj.* of a line; like a line; made of lines. ¶*a ~ measure.*① — [形] 줄의, 선의; 선상(線狀)의 ¶①척도(尺度)

line·man [láinmən] *n.* [C] (pl. **-men** [-mən]) **1.** a person who repairs telephone, telegraph or other wires. **2.** (*U.S.*) (of football) a player who plays on the forward line. ⇒[N.B.] — [名] 1. 보선공(保線工), 선로반원 2. 《美》《蹴球》 전위(前衛) [N.B.] linesman으로도 씀

⁑lin·en [línən] *n.* **1.** [U] cloth made from flax. **2.** 《*collectively*》 articles, such as clothing and sheets made of linen cloth. — [名] 1. 린네르, 아마포(亞麻布) 2. 린네르 제품(이불잇·샤쓰 따위)

***wash one's dirty linen in public* (*at home*),** (do not) let people know about one's unpleasant private affairs. — [熟] 내부의 창피스러운 일을 외부에 드러내다(드러내지 않다)

—*adj.* made of linen. — [形] 린네르의

lin·er [láinər] *n.* [C] **1.** a ship or airplane of a commercial line. **2.** a person who makes lines. **3.** (*Baseball*) a straight hit; a line drive. — [名] 1. 정기선(定期船); 정기 항공기 2. 줄치는(선을 긋는) 사람 3. 《野球》 라이너

lines·man [láinzmən] *n.* [C] (pl. **-men** [-mən]) **1.** a lineman. **2.** (*Sports*) a person assisting the referee who watches the lines and sees if the ball crosses the line. — [名] 1. 보선공(保線工) 2. 《스포오츠》 선심(線審)

line-up [láinʌp] *n.* [C] an arrangement of the players in certain games; a formation of people into a line; all the members of a group, etc. ¶*the starting ~.*① — [名] [구기(球技)의] 라인업, 정렬, 진용 ¶①[시합] 개시 때의 진용

lin·ger** [líŋgər] *vi.* stay on; loiter 《~ ***around or ***about*** a place》; delay. 《~ ***on*** (or ***upon, over***) something》 ¶*~ over the work.* **—*vt.*** pass (time) idly. ¶*~ out one's life*① — [自] 우물쭈물하다, 꾸물거리다, 질질 끌다; 서성대다 —[他]…을 질질 끌[어 시간을 보내]다 ¶①허송세월하며 살아가다

lin·ge·rie [lɑ̀:nʒəréi, lǽnʒərì: / lǽnʒərì:] *n.* [U] women's underwear. — [名] 여자용 속옷류, 랑제리

lin·ger·ing [líŋg(ə)riŋ] *adj.* prolonging in time; slow. — [形] 질질 끄는; 꾸물거리는, 우물쭈물하는

lin·go [líŋgou] *n.* [C] (pl. **-goes**) language, esp. strange, technical or foreign, that one is not familiar with. — [名] 알아들을 수 없는 말(전문어·외국어 따위)

lin·gual [líŋgwəl] *adj.* **1.** of the tongue. **2.** (*Phonetics*) pronounced with the aid of the tongue. ⇒[N.B.] — [形] 1. 혀의 2. 《音聲》 설음(舌音)의 [N.B.] d, l, n 따위

lin·guist [líŋgwist] *n.* [C] **1.** a person who is skilled in foreign languages. **2.** a person who studies language. — [名] 1. 외국어에 능통한 사람 2. 언어학자

lin·guis·tic [liŋgwístik] *adj.* of language or the study of languages. — [形] 언어의, 말의

lin·guis·tics [liŋgwístiks] *n. pl.* 《used as *sing.*》 the science of languages. — [名] 언어학, 어학

lin·i·ment [línimənt] *n.* [C][U] a liquid to be rubbed on the skin for easing aches, pains, etc. — [名] 도포약(塗布藥)

***lin·ing** [láiniŋ] *n.* **1.** [U] the act of covering the inner surface of something; any material used for this purpose. ¶(*proverb*) *Every cloud has a silver ~.*① / *the ~ of a pocket.* **2.** [C] the contents of something. — [名] 1. 안을 대기(붙이기); 안감(안을 대는 자료) ¶①《俚》고생 끝에 낙이 온다 2. 알맹이, 내용

link¹** [liŋk] *n.* [C] **1.** a ring of a chain. **2.** anything that connects two parts, persons, objects, etc. ¶*a ~ with the past.*① **3.** a unit of length. ⇒[N.B.] **4.** one of a pair of buttons connected by a chain and used to fasten shirtcuffs. **—*vt. connect. 《~ things ***together***; ~ something ***to***》 **—*vi.*** join; be connected. 《~ ***up*** something》 ¶*Our plane links up with that of America in Los Angeles.* — [名] 1. 사슬의 고리 2. 연결하는 것 ¶①과거에 연결되는 것 3. 링크 [N.B.] 길이의 단위로서 100분의 1체인(chain), 약 20 cm 4. [한 개의] 커프스 단추, 암수 단추 —[他] …을 연결하다 —[自] 이어지다, 연결되다

link² [liŋk] *n.* [C] a torch. — [名] 횃불

links [liŋks] *n. pl.* 《often used as *sing.*》 a golf course; a sandy ground by the seashore. — [名] 골프장; 해변가의 풀밭

lin·net [línit] *n.* [C] a small, brown, singing bird. — [名] 홍방울새류의 명금(鳴禽)

li·no·le·um [linóuliəm / lai-] *n.* [U] a floor covering made of cork and linseed oil. — [名] 리놀륨(마루에 까는 것)

lin·seed [línsi:d] *n.* [U] the seed of flax. — [名] 아마(亞麻)씨

L

linseed oil [∠- ∠] *n.* a kind of oil made by pressing linseed, used in paints.
—[名] 아마씨 기름(도료용)

lint [lint] *n.* [U] **1.** a soft cloth made by scraping linen, used for covering wounds. **2.** bits of thread.
—[名] 1. 린트천(상처를 덮는 데 씀) 2. 실오라기

lin·tel [líntl] *n.* [C] a piece of stone or wood placed above a door or window to support the wall above it. ⇒fig.
—[名] 상인방(上引枋)(문이나 창 위에 댄 가로장)

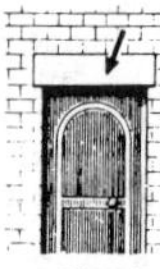
[lintel]

⁑ li·on [láiən] *n.* [C] **1.** a large, powerful, flesh-eating animal living in Africa. **2.** a brave man. **3.** a famous man; a star; ⟪*pl.*⟫ (*Brit.*) noted sights. ¶*see the lions.*① **4.** ⟪*L-*⟫ the national symbol of Great Britain. ¶*the British Lion.*②
1) ***beard the lion in his den,*** meet and challenge someone in his own home, etc.
2) ***a lion in the path*** (or ***way***)***,*** an obstacle in the way.
3) ***make a lion of*** (=*praise*) *someone.*
4) ***put*** *one's* ***head into a lion's mouth,*** take a great risk.
5) ***take the lion's share,*** take the largest share. ¶*He took the lion's share of the profits.*
6) ***twist the lion's tail,*** speak ill of Great Britain.
—[名] 1. 사자, 라이온 2. 용맹스러운 사람 3. 인기인, 유행아; ⟪英⟫ 명승지, 명소(名所) ¶①명승지(명소)를 구경하다(안내하다) 4. 사자문(紋), 영국의 상징 ¶②영국 국민
[熟] 1)자기 영토 내에서(유리한 환경에서) 적과 맞서다 2)앞길에 가로놓인 장애 3)…을 몹시 추어 주다 4)위험을 무릅쓰다, 대모험을 하다 5)제일 좋은 부분을 갖다, 단물을 빨다 6)영국의 욕을 하다

li·on·ess [láiənis] *n.* [C] a female lion.
—[名] 암사자

li·on·heart·ed [láiənhɑ̀ːrtid] *adj.* brave as a lion.
—[形] [사자처럼] 용감한, 용맹스러운

li·on-hunt·er [láiənhʌ̀ntər] *n.* [C] **1.** a person who hunts lions. **2.** a person who wants to make the acquaintance of many famous people.
—[名] 1. 사자 사냥꾼 2. 명사를 좇아다니는 사람

li·on·ize [láiənàiz] *vt.* **1.** treat (someone) as a famous or distinguished person. **2.** (*Brit.*) see the sights of (a place).
—[他] 1. …을 추어올리다; 명사 취급을 하다 2. ⟪英⟫ …의 명승지(명소)를 구경하다

⁑ lip [lip] *n.* [C] **1.** one of the two edges of the mouth; ⟪*pl.*⟫ the mouth. **2.** an edge of an open container that has a hole inside. ¶*the ~ of a bottle.*
1) ***bite*** *one's* ***lips,*** hide one's feelings of anger, laughter, etc.
2) ***carry*** (or ***keep***) ***a stiff upper lip,*** do not become discouraged; do not show discouragement.
3) ***curl*** *one's* ***lips,*** laugh scornfully.
4) ***hang*** *one's* ***lips,*** be about to cry; almost cry.
5) ***hang on*** *someone's* ***lips,*** listen attentively.
6) ***make up a lip,*** push out the lips as a sign of displeasure.
7) ***smack*** (or ***lick***) *one's* ***lips,*** show pleasure in food.
—*adj.* not sincere; only on the surface.
—[名] 1. 입술; 입 2. [밥그릇 따위 용기의] 가장자리
[熟] 1)감정을 억누르다 2)낙담하지 않다 3)[경멸하여] 입을 삐쭉거리다 4)[울 듯이] 입을 삐쭉거리다 5)주의하여 듣다, 경청하다 6)[불평을 나타내어] 입을 삐쭉거리다 7)[맛이 있어] 입맛을 다시다
—[形] 입으로만의, 말로만 발라맞추는

lipped [lipt] *adj.* having [something like] a lip or lips.
—[形] 입술(따르는 주둥이)이 있는

lip·stick [lípstìk] *n.* [U][C] a stick used for coloring the lips.
—[名] [막대 모양의] 입술 연지, 루우즈

liq·ue·fac·tion [lìkwifǽkʃ(ə)n] *n.* [U] the state or process of changing into a liquid.
—[名] 액화(液化); 용해(溶解)

liq·ue·fy [líkwifài] *v.* (**-fied**) *vi.* become liquid; melt. —*vt.* change (something) into a liquid.
—[自] 액화하다; 용해하다 —[他] …을 액화시키다, 용해시키다

li·queur [likə́ːr / -kjúə] *n.* [U] a kind of strong and sweet alcoholic drink.
—[名] 리큐르 술

⁑ liq·uid [líkwid] *n.* **1.** [U][C] a substance which can flow freely, like water. **2.** [C] the sound of [l] or [r]. —*adj.* **1.** in the form of a liquid; freely flowing. **2.** clear and bright. **3.** (of a sound) smoothly flowing or pure. **4.** (of currency) easy to change into cash.
—[名] 1. 액체 2. 유음(流音)(l과 r의 음)
—[形] 1. 액체의; 유동적인 2. 투명한, 맑은 3. 유음의 4. 현금으로 바꾸기 쉬운

liq·ui·date [líkwidèit] *vt.* **1.** pay (a debt). **2.** change (something) into cash. **3.** get rid of (something or someone). **4.** put an end to (something). —*vi.* fail in business and go bankrupt.
—[他] 1. …의 부채(빚)를 갚다, 2. …을 현금으로 바꾸다 3. …을 제거(일소)하다, 해치우다, 없애다 4. …을 끝마치다
—[自] [사업에 실패하여] 파산하다

liq·ui·da·tion [lìkwidéiʃ(ə)n] *n.* [U] the state of having one's debts paid off.
go into liquidation, go bankrupt.
—[名] 빚을 갚기, 청산, 변제
[熟] 파산하다

⁑ liq·uor [líkər] *n.* [U][C] **1.** an alcoholic drink. **2.** [U] a liquid.
—[名] 1. 알코홀 음료 2. 액체

have (or *enjoy*) *a liquor,* have a drink.

li·ra [líərə] *n.* [C] (pl. **li·re** or **li·ras**) the unit of money in Italy.

li·re [líəri] *n.* pl. of **lira**.

Li·sa [lí:zə, láizə] *n.* a girl's name, short for Elizabeth.

Lis·bon [lízbən] *n.* the capital of Portugal.

lisp [lisp] *vi.* **1.** pronounce the sound of [s] or [z] like that of [th]. **2.** speak like a baby. 《~ *out* some word》 —*vt.* speak (a word, etc.) imperfectly, like a baby. —*n.* [C] an act of lisping in speaking. ▷**lisp·er** [-ər] *n.*

lis·some, lis·som [lísəm] *adj.* flexible; soft; quick in manner; active.

⁑ **list**[1] [list] *n.* [C] a record of names, numbers, words, etc. ¶*a free* ~① / *a price*~② / *make a* ~ *of* (*something*).
be on the sick list, be sick usu. in bed.
—*vt.* make a list of (something); enlist. —*vi.* be recorded.

list[2] [list] *n.* [C] the edge of cloth. —*vt.* put a border around the edge of (something).

list[3] [list] *n.* [C] a state of leaning to one side. —*vi.* lean to one side.

⁑ **lis·ten** [lísn] *vi.* **1.** try to hear; pay attention so as to hear. 《~ *to* something》 ¶~ *to the radio* / *Listen to me carefully.* ⇒[N.B.] **2.** obey; follow advice. 《~ *to* something》 ¶*listen to reason*① / *Don't* ~ *to him.*
listen in, ⓐ listen to radio programs. ⓑ listen to another's telephone conversation usu. without his knowledge.

lis·ten·er [lísnər] *n.* [C] a person who listens.

lis·ten·er-in [lísnərín] *n.* [C] (pl. **-ers-in**) a person who listens to the radio.

list·less [lístlis] *adj.* seeming inactive; absent-minded; indifferent.

list price [∠ ∠] *n.* the price given in a list; the official price.

* **lit** [lit] *v.* pt. and pp. of **light**.

li·ter, *Brit.* **-tre** [lí:tər] *n.* [C] the unit of measure for liquids in the metric system. ⇒[N.B.]

lit·er·a·cy [lít(ə)rəsi] *n.* [U] the ability to read and write. ↔illiteracy

lit·er·al [lít(ə)rəl] *adj.* **1.** of the letters of the alphabet. **2.** following the given words or the original exactly; word for word. ¶*a* ~ *translation* / *in the* ~ *sense of the word.*① **3.** apt to understand words without imagination or exaggeration. ¶*a* ~ *mind.*

* **lit·er·al·ly** [lít(ə)rəli] *adv.* word for word; exactly.

⁑ **lit·er·ar·y** [lítərèri / lít(ə)rə-] *adj.* **1.** of literature. ¶~ *works.*① **2.** acquainted with literature.

lit·er·ate [lítərit] *adj.* **1.** able to read and write. ↔illiterate **2.** acquainted with literature. —*n.* [C] a person who can read and write; a learned person.

⁑ **lit·er·a·ture** [lít(ə)rətʃər, -tʃùər / -ritʃə] *n.* [U] **1.** imaginative writings such as poems, novels, plays, and essays. **2.** the occupation of authors. **3.** 《*collectively*》 the writings on a certain subject. ¶*the* ~ *of music.* **4.** 《*collectively*》 (*colloq.*) any printed material.

lithe [laið] *adj.* bending or twisting easily; flexible.

lith·o·graph·ic [lìθəgrǽfik] *adj.* of a lithograph; made by lithography.

lith·o·gra·phy [liθágrəfi / -θɔ́g-] *n.* [U] the process or art of printing from designs on a prepared stone or metal surface.

lit·i·gate [lítigèit] *vt.* go to law with (someone); engage in a law case with (someone); contest with (someone) in a law court. —*vi.* go to law.

lit·i·ga·tion [lìtigéiʃ(ə)n] *n.* [U] the act of litigating; [C] a lawsuit.

lit·mus [lítməs] *n.* [U] a substance that turns red in acid and blue in alkali.

litmus paper [∠- ∠-] *n.* a strip of paper treated with litmus and used to show whether something is acid or alkali.

li·tre [lí:tər] *n.* (*Brit.*)=liter.

[熟] 한잔하다
—[名] 리라(이탈리아의 화폐 단위)

—[名] 여자 이름(Elizabeth의 애칭)
—[名] 포르투갈의 수도
—[自] 1. 부정확하게 발음하다([s, ʒ]를 [θ, ð]로 발음하다) 2. 혀 짧은 소리로 말하다, —[他]…을 혀짤배기 소리로 말하다 —[名] 혀가 잘 돌지 않는 발음
—[形] 나긋나긋한; 민첩한, 쾌활한

—[名] 표, 일람표, 목록; 명부 ¶①무료 입장자 명부; 면세품 목록/②가격표
[熟] 앓고 있다, 와병중이다
—[他] …을 표에 기입하다 —[自] 기록에 오르다
—[名] 피륙의 가장자리 —[他] …에 가장자리천을 대다
—[名] 한쪽으로의 경사 —[自] 한쪽으로 기울다
—[自] 1. [주의를 기울여] 듣다, 경청하다 [N.B.] hear는 귀에 들려와서 듣다 2. 귀를 빌려주다; 들어 주다 ¶①도리를 알[아 듣]다
[熟] ⓐ[라디오를] 청취하다 ⓑ[전화를] 도청하다
—[名] 듣는 사람, 경청자; 청취자
—[名] 라디오 청취자

—[形] 노곤한, 나른한; 마음이 내키지 않는, 무관심한
—[名] 표기(表記) 가격

—[名] 리터 [N.B.] l., lit.로 줄여 씀

—[名] 읽고 쓸 줄 아는 능력
—[形] 1. 문자의 2. 문자대로의; 축어적(逐語的)인 ¶①문자 그대로의 뜻으로 3. 자구(字句)에 구애된, 상상력이 없는; 과장이 없는

—[副] 축어적으로; 정확히, 정말로
—[形] 1. 문학[상]의 ¶①문학 작품 2. 문학에 정통한
—[形] 1. 읽고 쓸 줄 아는 2. 문학을 잘 아는 —[名] 읽고 쓸 줄 아는 사람; 학식이 있는(배운) 사람
—[名] 1. 문학; 문예 2. 문필업; 저술업 3. [어떤 제목에 관한] 저작; 문헌 4. 인쇄물

—[形] 나긋나긋한, 유연한, 잘 휘는
—[形] 석판화(石版畫)의; 석판인쇄의

—[形] 석판인쇄; 석판술

—[他] …에 대하여 소송을 제기하다; …와 법정에서 싸우다 —[自] 소송하다

—[名] 소송; 기소

—[名] 리트머스 (산에서는 붉게, 알칼리에서는 푸르게 변함)
—[名] 리트머스 시험지

L

* **lit·ter** [lítər] *n.* **1.** [U] rubbish scattered about; things left in disorder. **2.** [C] 《*a* ~》 a condition of disorder. ¶*in a* ~.① **3.** [C] (of some animals) all the young borne at a single birth. ¶*a* ~ *of kittens.* **4.** [U] straw, hay, etc. used as bedding for animals. **5.** [C] a frame for carrying a sick or wounded person; a stretcher. **6.** [C] a bed enclosed with curtains and carried on men's shoulders or by animals in old times.

—[名] 1. 쓰레기, 잡동사니; 어질러져 있는 것 2. 난잡함 ¶①너절하게 어질러져서 3. [동물의] 한 배 새끼 4. [동물의] 잠자리에 까는 짚 5. 들것, 담가 6. 가마(옛날의 탈것)

—*vt.* **1.** make (something) untidy; scatter (things) about. 《~ *up* a place; ~ a place *with*》 **2.** scatter straw, hay, etc. to make a bed for(an animal). 《~ *down* an animal》 **3.** (of some animals) give birth to (a number of young). —*vi.* (of some animals) give birth to a number of young at one time.

—[他] 1. …을 난잡하게 하다; 흩뜨려(어질러) 놓다 2. [동물]을 위하여 짚을 깔아 주다 3. [동물의 새끼]를 낳다 —[自] [동물이] 새끼를 낳다

⁝ **lit·tle** [lítl] *adj.* (**less** or **les·ser, least**; or *colloq.* **lit·tler, lit·tlest**) **1.** small in size; not great or big; young and small. ¶*a* ~ *town* / *a* ~ *boy.* **2.** small in amount, degree, or number. ⇒[usage] ¶*a* ~ *sugar and a* ~ *butter* / *have a* ~ *money.* **3.** short in time or distance; not long. ¶*a* ~ *while* (*distance*).① **4.** not important; small in value; trivial. ¶*a* ~ *matter.* **5.** narrow-minded; not generous. ¶*a* ~ *mind* / ~ *thoughts.*

1) ***but little,*** almost no. ¶*There is but* ~ *chance.*
2) ***no little; not a little,*** very much.
3) ***only a little,*** a very small amount of.

—[形] 1. 작은, 조그마한, 젊고(어리고) 작은 2. 적은; 얼마 안 되는 [usage] little은 「조금밖에 없는」, a little은 「조금은 있는」의 뜻 3. [시간·거리가] 짧은 ¶①짧은 동안(거리) 4. 하찮은; 사소한 5. 도량이 좁은, 마음이 옹졸한

[熟] 1)거의 없는 2)상당히; 적지않이 3)아주 적은(조금마한)

—*adv.* (**less, least**) in a small degree; not at all. ⇒ [usage] ¶*I felt a* ~ *tired.* / *Little did I dream that he would succeed.*② / *He opened the window only a* ~.

—[副] 조금; 근소하게; 조금도(전혀) …않다(없다); 거의 …않다(없다) [usage] little 은 「거의 …않다(없다)」, a little 은 「조금은 …이다(있다)」 ¶②그가 성공하리라고는 꿈에도 생각지 못했다

—*n.* [U] **1.** a small amount, quantity, or degree. ¶*I have seen* ~ *of life.*③ / *He knows a* ~ *of everything.*④ / *I will do the* ~ *I can.*⑤ **2.** 《*a* ~》 a short time or distance. ¶*after a* ~ / *Please wait a* ~.

1) ***in little,*** on a small scale.
2) ***little by little,*** gradually; by degrees.
3) ***little or nothing; little if anything,*** hardly anything. ¶*I know* ~ *or nothing about it.*
4) ***make little of,*** treat (something) as unimportant.
5) ***not a little,*** much.

—[名] 1. 조금, 소량; 소액 ¶③나는 아직 세상사를 거의 모른다/④그는 무슨 일이든 조금씩은 다 알고 있다/⑤적으나마 할 수 있는 데까지는 하겠다 2. 짧은 시간; 짧은 거리

[熟] 1)소규모로 2)조금씩 조금씩, 점점 3)거의 …않다(없다) 4)…을 대수롭지 않게 여기다 5)적지않이; 매우

lit·to·ral [lítərəl] *adj.* of or on a shore. —*n.* [C] a region along a shore.

—[形] 해안의, 연안의 —[名] 연해지

lit·ur·gy [lítə(:)rdʒi] *n.* [C] (pl. **-gies**) **1.** a form of public worship in a Christian church. **2.** 《*the L-*》 the Book of Common Prayer used in the Anglican Church.

—[名] 1. 예배식 2. [영국 교회의] 기도서

liv·a·ble [lívəbl] *adj.* **1.** (of a house, a climate, etc.) fit to live in. **2.** (of a person) easy to live with; companionable. **3.** (of life) worth living; endurable.

—[形] 1. 살기 좋은(알맞은) 2. 같이 살 수 있는, 사귀기 쉬운 3. [인생이] 살 보람이 있는; 견딜 수 있는

⁝ **live**[1] [liv] *vi.* **1.** dwell; inhabit. ¶*I have lived here for the last ten years.* / *He lives in Osaka.* **2.** be alive; be living. ¶~ *in water* / *He still lives.* **3.** continue or remain alive. 《~ *to do*》 ¶~ *to be old*① / ~ *to the age of 85* / ~ *to see one's grandchild.*② **4.** pass one's life in a certain way. ¶~ *happily* / ~ *high*③ / ~ *in comfort.* **5.** enjoy a full and varied life. ¶*At 38 she was just beginning to* ~.④ / *I lived in those days.* **6.** survive; remain in the memory. ¶*Their good deeds* ~ *after them.* —*vt.* practice or carry out (something) in one's life; spend or pass (a certain life). ¶~ *a lie.*⑤

—[自] 1. 살다 2. 살아 있다 3. 오래 살다, 살아 남다 ¶①늙을 때까지 살다/②오래 살아서 손자까지 보다 4. …한 생활을 하다 ¶③호화로운 생활을 하다 5. 재미있게 살다; 충실한 인생을 즐기다 ¶④38세에 이르러 그녀는 비로소 진정한 인생살이를 시작하고 있었다 6. 존속하다; [그대로] 남다 —[他] …한 생활을 하다 ¶⑤거짓 인생을 보내다

1) ***live down,*** live so as to have others forget one's past mistakes. ¶*She lived down the scandal.*
2) ***live off*** (=*live at the expense of*) ***someone.***
3) ***live out*** (=*live until the end of*) ***something.***
4) ***live through,*** experience and survive; endure.
5) ***live up to,*** act according to (one's ideals, reputation, etc.); fulfill (something expected).
6) ***live well,*** live in luxury; lead a virtuous life.

[熟] 1)그 후의 행위로 불명예 따위를 씻다 2)…에 기식하다; …의 신세를 지다 3)[끝까지] 살아 남다; 생명을 부지하다, 고비를 넘기다 4)…을 헤어나가다 5)…에 따라 [알맞게] 살아가다; [주의 따위에] 따라 행동하다 6)유복하게(호화롭게) 살다

live² [laiv] *adj.* ⟪used only as *an attributive*⟫ **1.** alive; living. ¶~ *fish.* **2.** full of life, energy, or activity; energetic. **3.** up-to-date; of present interest. ¶*a ~ topic / a ~ issue.* **4.** burning; glowing; ardent. ¶~ *coals / a ~ hatred.* **5.** carrying an electric current. ¶*a ~ wire.* **6.** fresh; pure. ¶~ *air.*
—[形] **1.** 살아 있는, 산 **2.** 활기 있는, 활발한 **3.** 당면한; 목하 관심거리가 되고 있는 **4.** [불이] 타고 있는; 불타는 듯한 **5.** 전류가 통하고 있는 **6.** 생방송의; 실연(實演)의

*__live·li·hood__ [láivlihùd] *n.* [C] ⟪usu. *sing.*⟫ a means of supporting life.
—[名] 생계; 살림

live·li·ly [láivlili] *adv.* in a lively manner; cheerfully.
—[副] 힘차게, 활발하게, 팔팔하게, 명랑하게

live·li·ness [láivlinis] *n.* [U] the state of being lively; brightness; cheerfulness; gaiety.
—[名] 활발함, 명랑함

live·long [lívlɔ̀:ŋ / -lɔ̀ŋ] *adj.* (*poetic*) long in passing; whole.
—[形] ⟪詩⟫ 오랜, 지루하고 긴

‡**live·ly** [láivli] *adj.* (**-li·er, -li·est**) **1.** full of life; vigorous; active. ¶*a ~ discussion.* **2.** (of a color, a light, etc.) bright; vivid. ¶~ *colors of neon signs.* **3.** (of the mind) alive; alert; acute. ¶*a ~ imagination.* **4.** cheerful; gay. ¶~ *jazz.* **5.** (of a portrait, a description, etc.) lifelike. **6.** (*colloq.*) excitingly or thrillingly dangerous.
—[形] **1.** 기운찬, 활발한 **2.** 선명한, 강렬한 **3.** 예민한 **4.** 명랑한, 신나는 **5.** 박력있는, 실물 같은, 생생한 **6.** ⟪口⟫ 아슬아슬한, 위험한, 활극 같은

liv·en [láivn] *vi.* become cheerful or lively. ⟪~ *up*⟫ —*vt.* make (someone or something) cheerful or lively; brighten.
—[自] 명랑해지다, 쾌활해지다
—[他] …을 명랑(쾌활)하게 하다

*__liv·er__¹ [lívər] *n.* [C] a large organ in the body which produces a liquid which is called bile.
—[名] 간장(肝臟)

liv·er² [lívər] *n.* [C] a person who lives in a certain manner. ¶*a fast* (or *a loose*) ~.① / *a free* ~.②
—[名] 생활하는 사람 ¶①방탕아, 난봉꾼/②사치스러운 사람; 미식가(美食家)

liv·er·ied [lívərid] *adj.* dressed in a livery. ¶~ *waiters.*
—[形] 제복(정복)을 입은

liv·er·y [lívəri] *n.* (pl. **-er·ies**) **1.** [U] ⟪*collectively*⟫ a uniform for male servants or for the members of any group or profession. ¶*in* (*out of*) ~.① **2.** [U] ⟪*collectively*⟫ characteristic dress; outward appearance. ¶*trees in the ~ of spring.*② **3.** [C] the act of keeping horses, vehicles, etc. for pay; the act of hiring out horses, vehicles, etc. **4.** [C] (*U.S.*) a livery stable.
—[名] **1.** [하인·종업원 등의] 제복, 정복 ¶①제복(평복)을 입고 **2.** 특수한 의상; 옷차림, 겉치레 ¶②봄의 옷을 입은 나무들 **3.** 말(마차)을 세놓기(빌리기) **4.** ⟪美⟫ 마차 세놓는 집

livery stable [ˊ-- ˋ] *n.* a place where horses and vehicles are kept or let out for pay.
—[名] 마차 세놓는 집; 사육료를 받고 말을 맡아 두는 집

live·stock [láivstɑ̀k / -stɔ̀k] *n.* [U] ⟪*collectively*⟫ farm animals.
—[名] 가축

liv·id [lívid] *adj.* of a leaden color; black and blue; pale.
—[形] 납빛의, 잿빛의; 검푸른; 창백한

‡**liv·ing** [líviŋ] *adj.* **1.** having life; alive. ¶*all ~ things.* **2.** still in use; still existing. ¶*a ~ language / the greatest ~ writer.*① **3.** of or for life. ¶~ *conditions / the ~ standard / ~ expenses.* **4.** enough to live on. ¶*a ~ wage.* **5.** strong; active. ¶*a ~ faith / a ~ discussion.* **6.** lifelike; true to life; real. ¶*He is the ~ image of his father.*② —*n.* **1.** [U] the state of being alive. **2.** [C] ⟪usu. *sing.*⟫ money or things necessary for life; livelihood. ¶*make* (or *earn*) *one's* ~ / *I must work for a* ~. **3.** [U] manner of life. ¶*plain ~ and high thinking.*③
—[形] **1.** 살아 있는 **2.** 현재 사용되고 있는; 현존하는; 현대의 ¶①현존하는 일류 작가 **3.** 생활의 **4.** 생활하기에 충분한 **5.** 강한; 활발한 **6.** 실물 같은, 꼭 닮은; 생생한 ¶②그는 아버지의 모습을 고대로 닮았다
—[名] **1.** 살아 있기; 생존 **2.** 생활비; 생활 필수품; 생계 **3.** 생활 방식; 생활양식 ¶③검소하면서도 철학적인 생활

living room [ˊ-- ˋ] *n.* a room designed for general family use; a sitting room.
—[名] 거실(居室)

lla·ma [lɑ́:mə] *n.* [C] (pl. **-mas** or *collectively* **-ma**) an animal like a camel but without a hump, living in South America. ⇒fig.
—[名] 라마, 아메리카 낙타

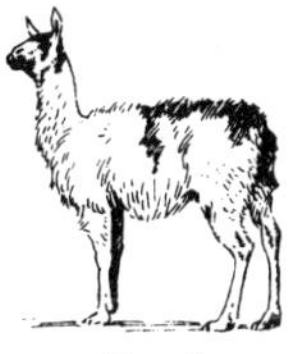

[llama]

lo [lou] *interj.* (*archaic*) look!; see!
—[感] ⟪古⟫ 보라!

‡**load** [loud] *n.* [C] **1.** a heavy burden. ¶*bear a ~ on one's shoulders.* **2.** something that makes one's mind heavy; a worry. ¶*a ~ of debt.* **3.** a bundle of goods to be carried; a piece of cargo. **4.** a quantity of goods carried at one time. ¶*sell by the* ~① / *three truck loads of vegetables.*② **5.** the act of putting powder and bullet in a gun; a charge. **6.** (in electricity) the amount of electric current given by a dynamo.
—[名] **1.** 짐; 무거운 짐 **2.** [정신상의] 부담, 무거운 짐, 걱정거리 **3.** 하물; 화물 **4.** 한 차(배)분의 짐, 한 짐, 한 바리 ¶①한 짐(바리)에 얼마로 팔다/②트럭 3대분의 야채 **5.** [화약 따위의] 장전; 장탄(裝彈) **6.** ⟪電⟫ 부하(負荷)

L

loadstar [678] **localism**

loads of, (*colloq.*) a lot of; much; many.
— *vt.* **1.** fill up (a ship, a cart, etc.) with goods; put (goods) on a ship, cart, etc. ¶ ~ *a truck with coal;* ~ *coal in a truck.* **2.** pile or heap heavily; fill. ¶ *a table loaded with dishes*② / *a tree loaded with fruit* / ~ *one's stomach with food.* **3.** give too much. ¶ *He loaded her with compliments.*④ **4.** put powder and bullet in (a gun); put film in (a camera). — *vi.* put on a load; take on a load; become loaded.
1) ***get a load of,*** (*slang*) listen to; look at (something)
2) ***have a load on,*** (*slang*) be drunk. [or someone).
3) ***take a load off someone's mind,*** set someone's heart at ease; relieve someone of anxiety.
load·star [lóudstə:*r*] *n.* =lodestar.
load·stone, lode- [lóudstòun] *n.* **1.** ⓒ ⓤ a kind of stone that attracts iron as a magnet; a natural magnet. **2.** ⓒ something that attracts.
• **loaf**¹ [louf] *n.* ⓒ (pl. **loaves**) **1.** bread shaped as one piece. ¶ *a* ~ *of bread* / *loaves and fishes*① / (*proverb*) *Half a* ~ *is better than none.*② **2.** a mass of sugar shaped like a cone.
loaf² [louf] *vi.* live lazily; walk slowly; loiter. 《~ *about*》 — *vt.* waste (time). 《~ *away* time》
loaf·er [lóufə*r*] *n.* ⓒ **1.** a person who loafs; a lazy or idle person. **2.** a kind of sport shoe.
loam [loum] *n.* ⓤ a mixture of clay, sand, etc. used for plastering. [loam.]
loam·y [lóumi] *adj.* (**loam·i·er, loam·i·est**) of loam; like]
‡ **loan** [loun] *n.* **1.** ⓒ something lent; a sum of money lent at interest. **2.** ⓤ the act of lending. ¶ *ask someone for the* ~① / *have the* ~ *of something.*②
on loan, lent. [money.]
— *vt., vi.* (chiefly *U.S.*) lend. ¶ *He loaned me some*]
loan word [´ ´] *n.* a word adopted into one language from another and naturalized.
loath [louθ, +*U.S.* louð] *adj.* (only as *predicative*) unwilling; reluctant. 《~ *to* do; *for* someone *to* do; ~ *that ...*》 ¶ *She was* ~ *to leave her native village.*
nothing loath, with pleasure; willingly.
loathe [louð] *vt.* feel extreme dislike for (someone or something); hate; detest. ¶ *She loathes him.*
loath·ing [lóuðiŋ] *n.* ⓤ strong dislike or hatred.
loath·some [lóuðsəm] *adj.* hateful; detestable; disgust-]
loaves [louvz] *n.* pl. of **loaf**¹. [ing.]
lob [lɑb / lɔb] *n.* ⓒ (of tennis) a ball hit high in the air.
— *vi., vt.* (**lobbed, lob·bing**) hit (a ball) high in the air.
lob·by [lɑ́bi / lɔ́bi] *n.* ⓒ (pl. -**bies**) **1.** an entrance hall; a waiting room. **2.** (*the L-*) (of the House of Commons (*Brit.*) or the Senate (*U.S.*)) a large hall where members interview visitors. **3.** (chiefly *U.S.*) a group of persons who try to exercise influence over law-makers.
— *vi., vt.* (**lob·bied**) (chiefly *U.S.*) try to exercise influence over law-makers.
lobe [loub] *n.* ⓒ **1.** the lowest, rounded part of the ear. **2.** any rounded, projecting part.
lob·ster [lɑ́bstə*r* / lɔ́bstə] *n.* ⓒ a shellfish with two large claws and eight legs, used for food.
‡ **lo·cal** [lóuk(ə)l] *adj.* **1.** of a place or places. **2.** limited to a particular place. ¶ ~ *news*① / ~ *self-government.*② **3.** of a certain part of the body. ¶ *a* ~ *disease.*③ **4.** (of a train) stopping at all stations. ¶ *a* ~ *train.* — *n.* ⓒ **1.** a local train. **2.** news of a certain district.
lo·cal·ism [lóukəlìz(ə)m] *n.* **1.** ⓒ a pronunciation, usage or custom peculiar to a particular district. **2.** ⓤ affection

驪 〔口〕 많은, 다량의
—⑪ 1. …에 짐을 싣다; [배 따위에] …을 적재하다 2. …에 잔뜩 쌓다(틀어넣다,채우다) ¶③음식이 잔뜩 차려진 식탁 3. …을 함부로 주다 ¶④그는 그녀에게 찬사를 잔뜩 늘어 놓았다 4. [총]에 탄알을 재다; [카메라]에 필름을 끼우다 —⾃ 짐을 싣다; 짐을 지다

驪 1)〔俗〕…을 듣다;보다 2)취해 있다
3)마음의 무거운 부담을 없애다; 시름을 놓다(놓게 하다)

—⑬ 1. 천연 자석(天然磁石) 2. 흡인력 (吸引力)이 있는 물건

—⑬ 1. 빵 한 덩이 ¶①현세의 이득/ ②〔俚〕반 덩어리라도 없는 것보다는 낫다 2. 덩어리 설탕

—⾃ 편둥편둥 놀며 지내다; 빈들빈들 거닐다 —⑪ [시간]을 낭비하다
—⑬ 1. 게으름뱅이, 건달 2. 운동화의 일종
—⑬ 로움(진흙·모래 따위의 혼합물로서 회반죽용)
—㉟ 로움의; 로움질(質)의
—⑬ 1. 빌린 것; 대부금 2. 대부 ¶① …에게 돈을 빌려달라고 부탁하다/② …을 차용하다
驪 대부하여, 차입하여
—⑪⾃〔美〕[…을] 대부하다, 빌려주다
—⑬ 외래어

—㉟ 싫은, 지긋지긋한

驪 싫기는커녕, 기꺼이
—⑪ …을 몹시 싫어하다; 미워하다

—⑬ 싫음, 혐오
—㉟ 싫은, 지긋지긋한, 염증나는

—⑬ 《庭球》 고완구(高緩球), 로브
—⾃⑪ [공]을 높이 치다
—⑬ 1. 현관; 대합실, 로비 2.〔英〕하원 의사당의 회견실 3.《美》 원외단(院外團)

—⾃⑪〔美〕[의원에게] 원외에서 [의 안통과] 운동을 하게 하다
—⑬ 1. 귓불 2. 둥근 돌출부

—⑬ 대하(大蝦), 왕새우

—㉟ 1. 장소의 2. 지방 [특유]의 ¶① 지방 소식/②지방 자치제 3. 국부의; 부분적인 ¶③국부적 병증(病症) 4. [직행에 대해] 역마다 정거하는 —⑬ 1. 구간(보통)열차 2. [신문의] 지방기사
—㉟ 1.지방 사투리; 지방의 습관 2. 지방(향토)주의, 향토 편애(偏愛)

lo·cal·i·ty [loukǽliti] *n.* (pl. **-ties**) ⓒ a place; a spot where something occurs; Ⓤ the peculiar condition of a place. ¶*a sense of* ~.①
— 명 장소; [사전의] 현장; [어떤 장소에] 자리잡기, 위치 ¶①장소(방향)의 감각

lo·cal·ize [lóukəlàiz] *vt.* **1.** limit (something) to a particular place. **2.** make (something) local in character. **3.** attach (an army, etc.) to a particular district.
— 타 1. …을 한 장소에 국한(제한)하다 2. …을 지방화(化)하다 3. [군대 따위]를 한 지방에 배치하다

lo·cal·ly [lóukəli] *adv.* in a local manner; in a particular place.
— 부 지방적으로; 위치상

‡ **lo·cate** [lóukeit, -́- / loukéit] *vt.* **1.** find out or show the place of (someone or something) **2.** establish (a building, etc.) in a particular place. ¶*I located my new store in Ginza.* **3.** (often used as *reflexive* or *passive*) take up one's residence in (a place); settle. ¶*be located in Tokyo.*① —*vi.* settle down in a place.
— 타 1. …의 장소를 찾아내다(나타내다) 2. [건물 따위를] 어떤 장소에 설립하다 3. [어떤 장소]에 거주하다, 정착하다 ¶①서울에 거주하다 — 자 거주하다, 거처를 정하다

* **lo·ca·tion** [loukéiʃ(ə)n] *n.* **1.** ⓒ a place; a position. **2.** Ⓤ the act of locating; the state of being located. **3.** Ⓤⓒ a place outside of a film studio where a motion picture is filmed. ⌈the sea.⌋
— 명 1. 장소, 위치 2. 장소에 두기, 위치 선정 3. 야외 촬영[지], 로케[이션]

loch [lɑk, lɔx / lɔk, lɔx] *n.* ⓒ (*Scot.*) a lake; an arm of⌉
— 명 호수; 작은 만, 후미

lo·ci [lóusai] *n.* pl. of **locus**. ⌈a tuft of wool, silk, etc.⌉
  ⌈리 2. [실 따위의] 한 타래⌋
lock¹ [lɑk / lɔk] *n.* ⓒ **1.** a curl of hair; (*pl.*) **2.**⌋
— 명 1. [머리의] 타래; 말린 머리; 머

‡ **lock**² [lɑk / lɔk] *n.* ⓒ **1.** an instrument for fastening a door, a window, a lid, etc. by using a key. ¶*on (off) the* ~.① **2.** a part of a canal enclosed by gates at each end so that boats can move up or down from one level to another. **3.** the part of a gun by which it is fired. **4.** a device to keep a wheel from turning.
— 명 자물쇠 ¶①자물쇠를 잠그고 (잠그지 않고). 2.[운하의] 수문, 갑문(閘門) 3.[총포의] 발사 장치 4.제륜(制輪) 장치

—*vt.* **1.** fasten (a door, etc.) with a lock; shut. ¶~ *a suitcase.* **2.** keep (someone) shut in; confine; imprison. ¶~ *someone* [*up*] *in a room* / ~ *up a prisoner*. **3.** hold (something) fast; embrace tightly; link. ¶~ *a child in one's arms* / *The ship was locked in ice.* —*vi.* **1.** become locked. ¶*This door doesn't* ~. **2.** become fastened or fixed.
— 타 1. …에 자물쇠를 잠그다; …을 닫다 2. …을 가두어 넣다; 거두어 (챙겨) 넣다; 감금하다 3. …을 움직이지 못하게 하다; 끌어 안다 — 자 1. 자물쇠가 잠기다 2. 고착하다, 꼭 끼다, 들어 박히다

1) ***lock away,*** store (something) in a locked box, etc.
2) ***lock out,*** shut (something) out by locking the door, etc. ⌈tirely.⌋
3) ***lock, stock, and barrel,*** (*colloq.*) completely; en-⌋
4) ***lock up,*** ⓐ imprison (someone) for a crime. ⓑ fasten the doors of (a building, etc.) by locking them.
5) ***under lock and key,*** in a safe place.
— 숙 1)자물쇠를 잠가 …을 챙겨 넣다 2)…을 내쫓다; 폐쇄하다 3)(口)아주, 완전히; 모조리, 전부 4)ⓐ감금하다, 폐쇄하다 ⓑ자물쇠를 잠그다 5)안전한 장소에

lock·er [lɑ́kər / lɔ́kə] *n.* ⓒ **1.** a person who locks. **2.** a cupboard or chest that can be locked.
— 명 1. 자물쇠를 채우는 사람 2. 로커 (자물쇠로 잠그게 된 찻장·장롱 따위)

lock·et [lɑ́kit / lɔ́kit] *n.* ⓒ a small case for holding a lock of hair or a picture, usu. worn on a necklace. ⇒fig.
— 명 작은 금합(金盒)(목걸이 따위에 매다는 작은 케이스)

[locket]

lock·out [lɑ́kaut / lɔ́k-] *n.* ⓒ the act of an employer's shutting down a business until the workers accept terms.
— 명 공장 폐쇄, 록아웃

lock·smith [lɑ́ksmiθ / lɔ́k-] *n.* ⓒ a person who makes or repairs locks and keys.
— 명 자물쇠 제조업자(수선공)

lock·up [lɑ́kʌp / lɔ́k-] *n.* ⓒ **1.** the act of locking up; the state of being locked up; a jail. **2.** the time for locking up a store, etc.
— 명 1. 감금, 구류; 유치장, 구치소 2. 폐문 시간

lo·co·mo·tion [lòukəmóuʃ(ə)n] *n.* Ⓤ **1.** the act of moving; the ability to move from place to place. **2.** means of traveling.
— 명 1. 운동, 이동; 운동력 2. 교통기관

* **lo·co·mo·tive** [lòukəmóutiv / lóukəmòutiv] *n.* ⓒ a railroad engine that pulls trains. —*adj.* of locomotion; moving from place to place; movable.
— 명 기관차 — 형 이동의, 이동하는(할 수 있는)

lo·cus [lóukəs] *n.* ⓒ (pl. **lo·ci**) **1.** a place. **2.** (*Mathematics*) a curve, surface, or other figure which satisfies
— 명 1. 장소 2. (幾) 궤적(軌跡)

lo·cust [lóukəst] *n.* Ⓒ **1.** a kind of grasshopper which feeds on crops and destroys them. **2.** (*U.S.*) a cicada.
—图 1. 메뚜기, 누리 2.《美》매미

lo·cu·tion [loukjúːʃ(ə)n] *n.* **1.** Ⓤ a style of speech. **2.** Ⓒ an idiom.
—图 1. 말씨; 말투 2. 관용어법

lode [loud] *n.* Ⓒ a vein of metal in a rock.
—图 광맥

lode·star, load- [lóudstàːr] *n* Ⓒ **1.** a star that shows the way; (*the ~*) the North Star. **2.** a guiding principle.
—图 1. 길잡이 별; 북극성 2. 지도 원리, 지표(指標)

lode·stone [lóudstòun] *n.* =loadstone.

: lodge [ladʒ / lɔdʒ] *n.* Ⓒ **1.** a small house, esp. for hunters, mountaineers, etc.; a hut; a cabin. ¶*a hunting ~*. **2.** a small house used by the gatekeepers or other servants of a great house. **3.** a branch of a certain society.
—图 1. 오두막집, 오막살이 2. 파수집, 문지기 집, 수위실 3. [조합 따위의] 지부(支部)

—*vi.* **1.** live in a certain place for a time; live in another house as a paying guest. ¶~ *at a hotel* (*in a home, with a family*). **2.** come to be placed and fixed firmly. ¶*The bullet lodged in his arm.*① / *The snow lodged on the wall.* —*vt.* **1.** provide (someone) with a house or room to live in for a time; take (someone) into one's house as a paying guest. ¶*Can you ~ us for the night?* **2.** put (something) into a certain place or position by shooting. ¶~ *a bullet in the wall.* **3.** bring (an accusation, etc.) legally before a judge or other government official. ¶~ *a complaint against* (*with, at*) *someone.*② **4.** confer; deposit. 《~ *something in or with*》¶~ *power in* (*with, in the hands of*) *someone.*
—自 1. 하숙하다; 투숙하다, 묵다 2. 정착하다; [내려] 앉다, 얹히다; 박히다, 꽂히다 ¶①탄알이 그의 팔에 박혔다 —他 1. ⋯을 숙박시키다, 묵게 하다; 숙식시키다; 숙소를 제공하다 2. [탄알 따위]를 쏘아 박다 3. [불평 따위]를 제기하다; 법정에 제소하다 ¶②⋯에 대한 불평을 제기하다 4. ⋯을 맡기다, 위임하다, 위탁하다

lodge·ment [ládʒmənt / lɔ́dʒ-] *n.* (*Brit.*) =lodgment.

lodg·er [ládʒər / lɔ́dʒ-] *n.* Ⓒ a person living in a rented room; a roomer. ¶*take in a ~* ①
—图 하숙인, 숙박인 ¶①하숙인을 두다

· lodg·ing [ládʒiŋ / lɔ́dʒ-] *n.* **1.** Ⓒ a place to sleep or live in temporarilly. **2.** Ⓤ the act of putting someone up in a room for rent. **3.** (*pl.*) a room or rooms for rent in a private house. ¶*board and ~.*①   「rent.」
—图 1. 임시 거처; 숙소. 2. 하숙 3. 셋방, 하숙집 ¶①식사도 나오는 하숙

lodging house [ˊ-ˋ] *n.* a house which has rooms for
—图 하숙집

lodg·ment, *Brit.* **lodge-** [ládʒmənt / lɔ́dʒ-] *n.* **1.** Ⓤ the act of lodging; the state of being lodged. **2.** Ⓒ something accumulated or deposited. **3.** Ⓒ a foothold gained in a certain place; (*Military*) a position gained from an enemy.
—图 1. 숙박, 하숙 2. 퇴적물; 침전물 3. 발판; 거점(據點)

effect (or *make*) *a lodgment*, gain a foothold.
熟 발판을 얻다, 거점을 차지하다

lo·ess [lóues / lóuis] *n.* Ⓤ a yellowish-brown clay or loam, usu. formed by the wind. ⇒N.B.
—图 황토, 로우에스 N.B. 중국 북부나 라인강 유역 같은 데 있음

loft [lɔːft / lɔft] *n.* Ⓒ **1.** a room directly under the roof of a house; an attic. **2.** (*U.S.*) an upper floor of a warehouse, a business building, etc. **3.** (*Golf*) the act of hitting a ball high in the air. —*vt.* **1.** keep (something) in an attic. **2.** (*Golf*) hit (a ball) high in the air.   「grandly; haughtily.」
—图 1. 고미다락방 2.《美》[창고·상화 따위의] 최상층 3. [골프] [공]을 높이 치기 —他 1. ⋯을 고미다락방에 저장하다 2.《골프》[공]을 높이 쳐올리다

loft·i·ly [lɔ́ːftili / lɔ́ft-] *adv.* in a lofty manner; highly;
—副 높이, 웅장하게; 거만하게

loft·i·ness [lɔ́ːftinis / lɔ́ft-] *n.* Ⓤ the state of being lofty; height; grandness; haughtiness.
—图 높음, 고상함, 웅장함; 거만

· loft·y [lɔ́ːfti / lɔ́fti] *adj.* (**loft·i·er, loft·i·est**) **1.** (of a hill, a tower, etc.) very high. **2.** (of principles, aims, etc.) noble; dignified; grand; (of manners) haughty; proud. ¶*in a ~ manner.*①
—形 1. [언덕·탑 따위가] 매우 높은, 우뚝 솟은 2. [주의·목적 따위가] 숭고한, 고상한; [태도가] 거만한 ¶①거만한 태도로

: log [lɔːg, lag / lɔg] *n.* Ⓒ **1.** a round piece of a tree, usu. in its natural state. ¶*a ~ bridge.* **2.** an instrument for measuring the speed of a ship. **3.** a diary aboard a ship's voyage. ⇒N.B.
—图 1. 통나무 2. [배의 속도를 재는] 측정기 3. 항해일지 N.B. logbook 라고도 함

1) *be as easy as rolling off a log,* (*U.S.*) be very easy.
2) *roll logs for* (=*endeavor to help*) *someone.*
熟 1)《美》아주 쉽다, 식은 죽 먹기다 2) ⋯을 위하여 애쓰다

—*vt.* (**logged, log·ging**) **1.** cut (a tree) into logs. **2.** cut down trees on (land). **3.** enter (something) in a
—他 1. [원목]을 통나무로 자르다 2. [토지에서] 나무를 베어 쓰러뜨리다, 벌

ship's record book.
목하다 3. …을 항해일지에 기입하다

log·a·rithm [lɔ́:gərìθ(ə)m, lág- / lɔ́g-] *n.* [C] (*Mathematics*) a figure showing how many times a number called "the base" must be multiplied by itself to produce a given number.
—[名]《數》대수(對數)

log·book [lɔ́:gbùk, lág- / lɔ́g-] *n.* [C] a book in which the events of a ship's voyage are written down every day.
—[名] 항해일지, 항정표(航程表)

log·ger·head [lɔ́:gərhèd, lág- / lɔ́gəhèd] *n.* [C] **1.** a stupid person; a blockhead. **2.** a kind of sea turtle chiefly living in the tropical Atlantic.
—[名] 1. 얼간이, 바보 2. 왕바다거북

log·gia [ládʒə, lɔ́:dʒ- / lɔ́dʒiə] *n.* [C] (pl. **-gias** or **-gie** [-dʒei]) a roofed, but not enclosed, gallery or arcade projecting from the side of a building. ⇨fig., [N.B.]
—[名] 로지아 [N.B.] 이탈리아 특유의 건축으로서 여름철에 거실 따위로 사용함

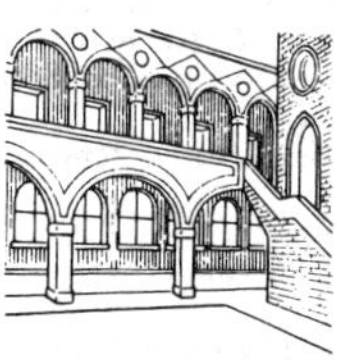
〔loggia〕

log·ging [lɔ́:giŋ, lág- / lɔ́g-] *n.* [U] the work of cutting down trees, making them into logs, and moving them from the forest.
—[名] 통나무로 베어내기, 벌목

***log·ic** [ládʒik / lɔ́dʒ-] *n.* [U] **1.** the science of reasoning. ¶*deductive* (*inductive*) *~.*① **2.** sound and clear thinking or reasoning; a mode of reasoning. ¶*the ~ of facts.*②
—[名] 1. 논리학 ¶①연역(演繹)(귀납) 논리학 2. 정확하고 명석한 사고(思考), 논리; 논법 ¶②어쩔 수 없는 논리의 (필연의) 사태

***log·i·cal** [ládʒik(ə)l / lɔ́dʒ-] *adj.* **1.** logic; according to the rules of logic. **2.** reasonable. ¶*a ~ argument.*
—[形] 1. 논리학[상]의 2. 이치에 맞는, 합리적인; 당연한

log·i·cal·ly [ládʒikəli / lɔ́dʒ-] *adv.* in a logical manner.
—[副] 논리상, 합리적으로

lo·gi·cian [loudʒíʃ(ə)n] *n.* [C] a person who is skilled in logic.
—[名] 논리가, 논법가; 논리학자

loin [lɔin] *n.* **1.** (*pl.*) the part of the back between the hipbones and the lowest rib. **2.** [U] a piece of meat from this part of an animal.
—[名] 1. 허리 2. 동물의 허릿살

loi·ter [lɔ́itər] *vi., vt.* waste time in moving from place to place; pass (time) idly; linger. 《*~ away*》 ¶*~ on the way to school*① / *He loitered away his time.*
—[自][他] 어정거리다, 빈들빈들 거닐다; 늑장부리다; [시간]을 헛되이 보내다 ¶①등교길에 딴전을 피우다

loi·ter·er [lɔ́itərər] *n.* [C] a person who loiters.
—[名] 어정버정 거니는 사람; 펀둥거리는 사람

loll [lal / lɔl] *vi.* **1.** lean lazily. ¶*~ in a chair.* **2.** (of the tongue, etc.) hang out loosely. —*vt.* allow [the tongue] to hang out loosely.
—[自] 1. 축 늘어져 기대다 2. [혀 따위가] 축 늘어지다
—[他] [혀]를 축 늘어뜨리다

lol·li·pop [lálipàp / lɔ́lipɔ̀p] *n.* [C] a kind of hard candy on the end of a small stick.
—[名] 막대 끝에 붙인 사탕과자, 막대사탕

⁑**Lon·don** [lʌ́ndən] *n.* the capital of England.
—[名] 영국의 수도

Lon·don·er [lʌ́ndənər] *n.* [C] a person of London.
—[名] 런던 사람, 런던내기

***lone** [loun] *adj.* (used as *attributive*) alone; lonely; solitary. ¶*a ~ house.*
—[形] 혼자의; 외로운, 쓸쓸한; 인적이 드문, 외딴

lone·li·ness [lóunlinis] *n.* [U] the state of being or feeling lonely.
—[名] 고독, 외로움

⁑**lone·ly** [lóunli] *adj.* (**-li·er, -li·est**) feeling alone; without companions; solitary.
—[形] 고독한, 외로운, 쓸쓸한; 외딴, 인적이 드문

***lone·some** [lóunsəm] *adj.* feeling lonely; solitary.
—[形] 외로운, 쓸쓸한; 외딴, 인적이 드문

⁑**long** [lɔ:ŋ / lɔŋ] *adj.* **1.** great in distance or time from end to end. ↔short ¶*a ~ distance* / *~ hair* / *a ~ war* / *have a ~ wait* / *a ~ spell of rainy weather*① / *make a ~ visit.* **2.** far-reaching; extending to a great distance. ¶*a ~ memory* / *have ~ sight.*② **3.** of greater than usual or standard length. **4.** slow; tedious. ¶*a ~, boring speech.* **5.** in length. ¶*thirty feet ~* / *six hours ~.* **6.** tall. ¶*a ~ tree* / *a ~ man.*
—[形] 1. [시간·거리가] 긴, 오랜 ¶①장마 2. 멀리까지 미치는 ¶②멀리까지 보이다 3. 더 긴; 보통보다 긴 4. 기나긴, 오랜; 지루한 5. 길이가 …한(의), …의 길이의 6. 키가 큰, 키다리의

1) ***be long*** [*in*] ***doing,*** take a long time in doing.
2) ***have a long arm,*** can make one's power felt over a wide area.
3) ***have a long face,*** look cheerless or sad.
4) ***have a long head,*** be clever and sensible.
5) ***have a long wind,*** be able to run far without stopping.
6) ***in the long run,*** in the end; as the last result.
7) ***the long and*** [***the***] ***short of,*** all that can be said

[熟] 1)…하는 데 시간이 걸리다 2)널리(멀리까지) 세력을 미칠 수가 있다 3)침울한(슬픈) 얼굴을 하고 있다 4)약빠른, 빈틈없는; 민감한 5)단숨에 멀리까지 달릴 수 있다 6)결국; 마침내 7)…에 대해 말할 수 있는 것 전부 8)팔을 쭉 뻗다

L

about; in brief.　「as possible.」
8) *make a long arm*, stretch one's arm as far as possible.
—*adv.* **1.** for a long time. ¶*I have ~ been intending to do it.* **2.** throughout a certain period of time. ¶*He lay awake all night ~.* **3.** far distant from a certain point in time. ¶*~ before (ago, since).*
1) *no longer*, not now or from now on as in the past.
2) *So long!*, (*colloq.*) Good-by!　「that ...」
3) *so* (or *as*) *long as*, on condition that ... ; provided
—*n.* ⓤ a long time. ¶*before ~ | for ~② | It will not take ~.*　—*vi.* wish very much; have a strong desire. 《*~ to do*; *~ for* something》¶*He longed to see her.*

long-dis·tance [lɔ́ːŋdístəns / lɔ́ŋ-] *adj.* (*U.S.*) located a long way away. ¶*a ~ telephone call | a ~ flight.*

long-drawn [lɔ́ːŋdrɔ́ːn / lɔ́ŋ-] *adj.* lasting for a long time; prolonged.

lon·gev·i·ty [lɑndʒévəti / lɔn-] *n.* ⓤ long life.

long·hand [lɔ́ːŋhǽnd / lɔ́ŋ-] *n.* ⓤ the usual kind of writing. ↔shorthand

long-head·ed [lɔ́ːŋhédid / lɔ́ŋ-] *adj.* **1.** having a long head. **2.** clever; foresighted.

long·ing [lɔ́ːŋiŋ / lɔ́ŋ-] *n.* ⓒⓤ an earnest desire. 《*~ for*》—*adj.* having or showing strong desire.

lon·gi·tude [lándʒit(j)ùːd / lɔ́ndʒitjùːd] *n.* ⓤ the distance east or west, measured in degrees, from a line running from the North to the South Pole through Greenwich, near London. ⇒ N.B.

lon·gi·tu·di·nal [làndʒit(j)úːdin(ə)l / lɔ̀ndʒitjúː-] *adj.* **1.** of longitude. **2.** of or in length. **3.** running lengthwise.

long-lived [lɔ́ːŋlívd, -láivd / lɔ́ŋ-] *adj.* living long; old.

long·shore·man [lɔ́ːŋʃɔ́ːrmən / lɔ́ŋʃɔ́ː-] *n.* ⓒ (pl. **-men** [-mən]) a man whose work is to load or unload ships.

long-sight·ed [lɔ́ːŋsáitid / lɔ́ŋ-] *adj.* **1.** able to see farther than a normal person; far-sighted. **2.** foreseeing; wise.　「for a long time.」

long-stand·ing [lɔ́ːŋstǽndiŋ / lɔ́ŋ-] *adj.* having lasted

long-suf·fer·ing [lɔ́ːŋsʌ́fəriŋ / lɔ́ŋ-] *adj.* enduring hardships patiently for a long time.　—*n.* ⓤ patient endurance of hardships.

long·ways [lɔ́ːŋwèiz / lɔ́ŋ-] *adv.* in the direction of the length; along the length; lengthwise.

long-wind·ed [lɔ́ːŋwíndid / lɔ́ŋ-] *adj.* **1.** able to exist for a long time without breathing. **2.** (of a speech, writing, etc.) tiresome; writing or talking tediously.

long·wise [lɔ́ːŋwàiz / lɔ́ŋ-] *adv.* =longways; lengthwise.

‡look [luk] *vi.* **1.** try to see; direct one's eyes. 《*~ at* something》¶*I looked, but saw nothing.*① | *Look up at the bright stars in the sky.* | *Look this way.* **2.** be careful; pay attention. 《*~* [*to it*] *that ...*》¶*Look* [*to it*] *that nothing worse happens.* **3.** appear; seem. ¶*You ~ pale.* | *She never looks her age.*② **4.** face. ¶*Our house looks upon a garden (on the road, toward the south).* **5.** examine; search.　—*vt.* **1.** direct one's eyes on (someone). ¶*~ him in the face.*③ **2.** try to find; seek; search. ¶*Look where you are.* | *Look how it rains.* **3.** express (one's mind) by one's looks or appearance. ¶*She looked her thanks.*
1) *look about*, glance around; search about for (something) 《*~ about for* something》
2) *look after* (=*take care of*) someone or something.
3) *look alive*, (*colloq.*) 《usu. as *imperative*》hurry up; be alert. ¶*Look alive!*
4) *look at*, ⓐ observe (something) with attention; pay attention to (something). ⓑ examine.

5) ***look away,*** turn one's face aside.
6) ***look back,*** recall; recollect. ⟪~ back *on* (or *upon, in, into*)⟫
7) ***look down on*** (=*feel superior to*) *someone.*
8) ***look for,*** ⓐ try to find; search for. ⓑ expect.
9) ***look forward to*** (=*expect*) [*something pleasant*].
10) ***look in,*** make a short visit. ⟪~ in *on* someone; ~ in *at* a place⟫
11) ***look into*** (=*examine*) *something.*
12) ***look on*** (or ***upon***), ⓐ regard; consider. ⟪~ on someone or something *as*⟫ ⓑ watch; look at. ⓒ face to.
13) ***look out,*** ⓐ pay attention to; take care of. ⟪~ out *for* something⟫ ⓑ (*Brit.*) search for (something).
14) ***look over,*** ⓐ examine; inspect. ⓑ overlook.
15) ***look to,*** ⓐ be careful of. ⓑ rely on. ⓒ face to. ⓓ expect.
16) ***look up,*** ⓐ search for (the meaning of a word, etc.) in a dictionary, etc. ⓑ pay a visit to (someone).
17) ***look up to*** (=*respect* or *admire*) *someone.*

다 9)…을 [희망을 걸고] 기대하다 10)…에 들르다 11)…을 조사하다 12)ⓐ…이라고 간주하다 ⓑ…을 [유심히] 바라보다 ⓒ…으로 면하다, …을 향하다 13)ⓐ…에 주의하다 ⓑ⟪英⟫…을 찾아내다 14)ⓐ…을 조사하다 ⓑ…을 눈감아 주다 15)ⓐ…에 유의하다 ⓑ…에 의지하다 ⓒ…에 면하다 ⓓ…을 기대하다 16)ⓐ…을 사전 따위에서 찾아보다 ⓑ…을 방문하다 17)…을 우러러보다, 존경하다

—*n.* Ⓒ **1.** an act of looking; a glance. ¶*have* (or *get, take, give*) *a ~ at someone / steal* (*cast, shoot*) *a ~ at someone.* **2.** ⟪often *pl.*⟫ personal appearance, esp. of a pleasing nature. ¶*good looks / She has looks and youth.*④ **3.** ⟪often *pl.*⟫ appearance; aspect. ¶*the ~ of the sky / an ugly ~ in the eye.*⑤

—[名] **1.** 보기; 일견(一見), 일별(一瞥) **2.** 얼굴 생김새, 용모, 표정; 미모 ¶④그녀는 젊음과 미모를 지니고 있다 **3.** 모습, 외관; 눈초리 ¶⑤성난 눈초리

look·er-on [lúkərán, -ɔ́:n / lúkərɔ́n] *n.* Ⓒ (pl. **look·ers-**) a person who watches a game, etc. without joining in; an onlooker.

—[名] 구경꾼; 방관자

look-in [lúkìn] *n.* Ⓒ a glance; a short visit.
have a look-in, stand or have a good chance; get a share.

—[名] 한 번 흘끗 보기, 일별; 짧은 방문
[熟] 승산이 있다; 몫을 받다

look·ing [lúkiŋ] *adj.* having a certain appearance. ⇒[usage] ¶*angry-looking / a good-looking girl.*

—[形] …처럼 보이는 [usage] 형용사에 붙어 합성어를 만듦

look·ing-glass [lúkiŋglæ̀s / -glɑ̀:s] *n.* Ⓒ a mirror.

—[名] 거울, 면경

look·out [lúkàut] *n.* Ⓒ **1.** a careful watch. **2.** a person who keeps a careful watch. **3.** a place from which to watch. **4.** (chiefly *Brit.*) prospect; view. **5.** (*colloq.*) business.
1) ***be on the lookout for,*** watch for (something) carefully; await eagerly.
2) ***keep a sharp*** (or ***good***) ***lookout for,*** keep a careful watch for (something).

—[名] **1.** 망보기; 경계 **2.** 망보는 사람 **3.** 망보는 곳, 망대(望臺) **4.**⟪英⟫ 가망, 전도, 전망 **5.**⟪口⟫ 일, 임무
[熟] 1)…을 경계하다 2)…을 엄중히 지켜보다(경계하다)

* **loom**[1] [lu:m] *n.* Ⓒ a machine for making cloth.

—[名] 직조기, 베틀

loom[2] [lu:m] *vi.* appear dimly and in a larger form than in reality. ¶*~ through the mist.*
loom large, seem large and threatening.

—[自] 어렴풋이 나타나다, 흐릿하게 보이다
[熟] 크고 무시무시하게 보이다; 불안스럽게 다가오다

loon[1] [lu:n] *n.* Ⓒ a large water bird with a short neck and a pointed bill.

—[名] 되강오리

loon[2] [lu:n] *n.* Ⓒ a silly person.

—[名] 바보, 얼간이

* **loop** [lu:p] *n.* Ⓒ **1.** a curved line that crosses itself at both ends. **2.** anything shaped like this. **3.** a curve or bend in a river, a road, etc. ¶*the ~ of a river.*
—*vt.* **1.** make a loop of (string, etc.). **2.** fasten (something) with a loop or loops. **3.** encircle (something) with a loop. **—*vi.*** form into a loop.
loop the loop, (of an airplane, etc.) make a vertical loop in the air.

—[名] **1.** [끈 따위의 양끝을 엇걸어서 만든] 고리, 올가미 **2.** 고리 모양의 것; 고리 **3.** 만곡(彎曲)[부]
—[他] **1.** …을 고리로 만들다 **2.** …을 고리로 매다(묶다) **3.** …을 고리로 두르다(둘러싸다) —[自] 고리로 되다
[熟] [비행기 따위가] 재주넘기를 하다, 공중회전하다

loop·hole [lú:phòul] *n.* Ⓒ **1.** a narrow hole in a wall through which a gun is fired. ⇒fig. **2.** a way of escape.

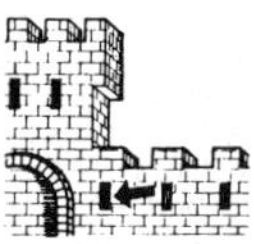
[loophole 1.]

—[名] **1.** 총안(銃眼) **2.** 도망하는 길, 도피로; 빠져나가는 구멍

** **loose** [lu:s] *adj.* **1.** not tight. ¶*a ~ collar / a ~ coat.* **2.** not fastened; not bound together; not tied up. ¶*~ hair / a ~ window / the ~ end of a rope.*① **3.** not packed. ¶*~ coffee / ~ wool.* **4.** not controlled; free. ¶*let the dog ~.* **5.** not strict or exact. ¶*a ~ translation / ~ thinking.* **6.** careless about morals or conduct.
—*adv.* in a loose manner; loosely.

—[形] **1.** 헐거운, 헐렁헐렁한 **2.** 고정되어 있지 않은; 철하지 않은; 매지(묶지) 않은 ¶①매지 않은 밧줄의 한 끝 **3.** 포장하지 않은; 흐트러진 **4.** 통제되어 있지 않은, 자유로운 **5.** 해이한; 부정확한; 산만한 **6.** 절제 없는; 품행이 방정치 못한
—[副] 느슨하게, 헐렁하게; 단정치 못하게

L

loosen

1) **at a loose end,** (*colloq.*) having nothing to do; without any definite occupation. ⌈uncertain condition.⌉
2) **at loose ends,** (*colloq.*) ⓐ in disorder. ⓑ in an
3) **break loose,** free oneself by force; escape.
4) **cast loose,** become or make loose; untie; unfasten.
5) **cut loose,** make oneself free from a relation or
6) **get loose,** escape. ⌊control; become free.
—*vt.* 1. make (something) free or loose; untie; unbind; loosen. ¶ ~ *a knot* / ~ *one's hold of a rope* / ~ *a boat from its moorings.*② **2.** shoot. ¶ ~ *an arrow.*

loos·en [lúːsn] *vt.* **1.** make (something) loose or less tight; unfasten. **2.** make (something) less dense. —*vi.* become loose.

loot [luːt] *n.* Ⓤ (*collectively*) things stolen or taken from the enemy. —*vt.* rob (something) by force.

lop¹ [lɔp / lɔp] *vt., vi.* (**lopped, lop·ping**) cut away (branches, etc.). ¶ ~ [*off or away*] *branches.*

lop² [lɔp / lɔp] *vi.* (**lopped, lop·ping**) hang down loosely.

lope [loup] *vi.* run or walk with easy and long steps.

lo·quat [lóukwɔt, -kwæt / -kwɔt] *n.* Ⓒ an evergreen tree in Japan, China, etc.; its yellow, edible fruit.

‡**lord** [lɔːrd] *n.* Ⓒ **1.** a ruler; an owner; a master. ¶ *feudal lords*① / *Man is the* ~ *of creation.*② **2.** (usu. *the L-*) God; the Savior; (often *Our L-*) Christ. ¶ *the Lord's Prayer*③ / *Jesus Our Lord* / *Lord bless us (me)!*④ **3.** (*Brit.*) a nobleman; a member of the House of Lords; a title used in speaking to noblemen of certain ranks. ¶ *Lord Chamberlain*⑤ / *Lord Bishop.*⑥
—*vi.* act like a lord; rule. (~ *it over someone*) ¶ *He lords it over his inferiors.*⑦ ⌈lord.⌉

lord·ling [lɔ́ːrdliŋ] *n.* Ⓒ a young lord; a petty or minor⌋

lord·ly [lɔ́ːrdli] *adj.* (**-li·er, -li·est**) **1.** suitable for a lord; noble and magnificent. **2.** proud; haughty.

Lord Mayor [⌞ ⌝] *n.* the title of the mayor of London or of any of several other English cities.

Lord's day [⌞ ⌝], **the** *n.* Sunday.

lord·ship [lɔ́ːrdʃip] *n.* Ⓤ **1.** the state or dignity of a lord; rule. ¶ *have* ~ *over land and sea.*① **2.** (*His or Your L-*) a term of respect used when speaking to or speaking of a nobleman or a judge.

lore [lɔːr] *n.* Ⓤ **1.** traditional facts or stories about a certain subject; knowledge of such facts or stories. ¶ *ghost* ~.① **2.** learning.

lor·gnette [lɔːrnjét] *n.* Ⓒ **1.** a pair of eyeglasses with a handle attached. ⇨fig. **2.** a pair of opera glasses.

lorn [lɔːrn] *adj.* (*poetic*) having no person who cares for one; forlorn.

lor·ry [lɔ́ːri, lári / lɔ́ri] *n.* (pl. **lor·ries**) Ⓒ **1.** (*Brit.*) a motor truck; [lorgnette 1.] a motor lorry. (cf. *U.S.* truck) **2.** a railway car used for carrying goods.

Los An·ge·les [lɔːsǽndʒələs, -lːz, -ǽŋgələs] *n.* a large city in California in the United States.

‡**lose** [luːz] *v.* (**lost**) *vt.* **1.** have no longer; become unable to find. ¶ ~ *a key* / ~ *one's way.* **2.** get rid of (something); get over. ¶ ~ *all pain (one's fears).* **3.** fail to see, hear, or understand. ¶ *She did not* ~ *a word of his speech.*① **4.** fail to have, get, or catch; be too late for (something); miss. ↔catch ¶ ~ *one's train.* **5.** fail to win or gain. ¶ ~ *a game (a prize).* **6.** cause (someone) the loss of something; cause someone the loss of (something); cost. ¶ *The failure lost him all his fortune.*② / *The delay lost the battle for them.*③ **7.**

《often in *passive*》 destroy. ¶*The ship was lost with all its crew.* **8.** fail to keep; waste. ↔gain ¶*~ money / We shall ~ no time in beginning work.* **—*vi.*** **1.** fail to win; be defeated in an election. ¶*Our team has lost. / He lost by 30 votes.* **2.** suffer loss. ¶*I don't care whether I gain or ~.* **3.** (of a watch or clock) become slow. ¶*My watch loses three minutes a day.*
체하였기 때문에 그들은 싸움에 패하였다 7. …을 멸망시키다, 파괴하다 8. …을 낭비하다 —[自] 1. 지다, 패배하다; 실패하다 2. 손해를 입다, 손해보다 3. 시계가 늦게 가다

be lost (=*be absorbed or interested*) ***in something.***
[熟] …에 열중(몰두)해 있다

los·er [lúːzər] *n.* [C] a person who loses or fails; a person who is defeated in an election; a person who has failed, lost a game, etc. ¶*a good (bad) ~.*①
—[名] 손실자; 유실자; 실패자; 패자; 손실물(액) ¶①지면 깨끗이 지는(미련을 갖는) 사람

los·ing [lúːziŋ] *adj.* likely to lose in the end.
—[形] 성공할 것 같지 않은, 승산이 없는

⁑**loss** [lɔːs / lɔs] *n.* **1.** [U] the act of losing; state of being lost. ¶*the ~ of one's parents.* **2.** [C] the damage; a thing or amount lost. ↔profit ¶*His death is a serious ~ for the country.*① **3.** [C] waste; decrease. ¶*~ of blood / ~ in* [or *of*] *weight.* **4.** [C] failure to win, get or keep; defeat. **5.** 《*pl.*》 the number of soldiers lost in battle.
—[名] 1. 분실; 유실; 상실 2. 손실; 손실물(액) ¶①그의 죽음은 그 나라에 있어서 큰 손실이다 3. 낭비; 감소, 감손 4. 실패; 패배 5. 병력의 손실; 사상자

be at a loss, not know what to do or say.
[熟] 어찌할 바를 모르다; 당황하다

⁑**lost** [lɔːst / lɔst] *v.* pt. and pp. of **lose**.
—*adj.* **1.** no longer present; departed. ¶*a ~ friend.* **2.** missing; no longer possessed. ¶*a ~ article.*① **3.** having gone astray. ¶*a ~ child.* **4.** not won or gained. ¶*a ~ battle / a ~ cause.*② **5.** wasted; useless. ¶*~ labor*③ */ ~ time.* **6.** destroyed; ruined. **7.** hopeless. ¶*~ souls.*④
—[形] 1. 사라진; 가 버린; 없어진 2. 잃어버린, 유실한 ¶①유실물 3. 길 잃은 4. 진, 패배한; 놓쳐 버린 ¶②실패로 돌아간 주장 5. 허비한, 낭비의; 소용없는 ¶③헛수고, 도로(徒勞) 6. 파멸한; 망한 7. 가망없는, 절망적인 ¶④구제받을 수 없는(지옥에 떨어진) 영혼

1) ***be lost in,*** be absorbed in (something). ¶*He was ~ in thought.*
2) ***be lost on*** (or ***upon***)***,*** be wasted on (someone); have no influence on. ¶*Your kindness was not ~ on me.*
3) ***be lost to,*** ⓐ no longer have (any sense of shame, pity, etc.) ⓑ (of good luck, happiness, etc.) be no longer approachable to (someone). ¶*Hope is ~ to him.*⑤ ⓒ do not belong to (someone) any longer.
[熟] 1)…에 잠기다, 몰두하다 2)…에 소용이 없다, 효험이 없다 3)ⓐ…을 느끼지 않다, …한 줄 모르다 ⓑ…에게는 더 이상 얻을 수 없다 ¶⑤그에게는 인제 희망이 없다 ⓒ더 이상 …의 것은 아니다

⁑**lot** [lɑt / lɔt] *n.* **1.** [C] a thing used to decide something by chance. ¶*draw lots.* **2.** [U] such a method for deciding. ¶*The committee chose the chairman by ~.* **3.** [C] a share; a portion. **4.** [C] fate; destiny; fortune. ¶*a hard ~ / be contented with one's ~.*① **5.** [C] a piece of ground. ¶*a parking ~ / a building ~.* **6.** [C] the whole number or quantity; a group; a collection. ¶*the ~ of us*② */ They are an interesting ~.* **7.** [C] (*colloq.*) a person of a certain kind. ¶*He is a bad ~.*
—[名] 1. 제비 2. 제비뽑기; 추첨 3. 몫 4. 운명; 운 ¶①운명에 만족하다 5. 지소(地所); 부지(敷地), 지구 6. 한 무더기, 한 벌; 떼, 집단 ¶②우리들 전부 7. 《口》 놈; 작자

1) ***a lot,*** very much. ¶*Thanks a ~. / It is a ~ better.*
2) ***a lot of; lots of,*** many; much. ¶*a ~ of books.*
[熟] 1)대단히, 매우; 훨씬 2)많은, 숱한

loth [louθ] *adj.* =loath.

lo·tion [lóuʃ(ə)n] *n.* [U][C] a liquid used for soothing or cleaning the skin, the eyes, etc.
—[名] 로우션, 화장수; 씻는 약, 세제(洗劑)

lot·ter·y [lɑ́təri/lɔ́t-] *n.* [C] (pl. **-ter·ies**) a game of drawing lots in which prizes are given to the lucky numbers.
—[名] 복권(福券)

lo·tus [lóutəs] *n.* [C] **1.** a water lily. **2.** (in Greek legend) a plant whose fruit was supposed to make a person dreamy and forgetful of everything.
—[名] 1. 연(蓮) 2. 《그리이스 신화》 그 열매를 먹으면 황홀경에 들어가 만사를 잊는다는 식물

lo·tus-eat·er [lóutəsìːtər] *n.* [C] a person living an easy, idle life.
—[名] 안일한 생활을 영위하는 사람

⁑**loud** [laud] *adj.* **1.** (of a sound) strong; not quiet or soft. ¶*a ~ bell*① */ in a ~ voice.* **2.** insistent. ¶*He was ~ in denying it.* **3.** (*colloq.*) (of colors, clothes, etc.) too bright; showy; flashy. ¶*a ~ suit.*② **4.** (*colloq.*) (of behavior) noisy and rude; unrefined; vulgar.
—[形] 1. 큰 소리의; 소란한, 시끄러운 ¶①소리가 큰 벨 2. 끈덕진, 성가신 3. 《口》 화려한, 야단스러운, 야한 ¶②야한 옷 4. 《口》 야비한, 천한; 버릇없는

—*adv.* in a loud manner.
—[副] 큰 소리로

⁑**loud·ly** [láudli] *adv.* **1.** in a loud voice. **2.** in a showy manner.
—[副] 1. 큰 소리로, 시끄럽게 2. 야하게, 난하게

loud-speak·er [láudspìːkər / ⌐⌐–] *n.* [C] an electrical device for making sounds loud enough to be heard.
—[名] 확성기

loud-spo·ken [láudspóukn] *adj.* with a loud voice when
—[形] 목소리가 큰

L

Lou·is [lú(:)i] *n.* a man's name. ¶*Louis XIV.*①
lounge [laundʒ] *vi.* **1.** walk unhurriedly (《~ *along streets*》; spend time idly. **2.** stand or rest leaning against something in a lazy way. —*vt.* spend (time) in idleness. 《~ *away* or *out* time》
—*n.* ⓒ **1.** the act of lounging. **2.** a place with comfortable chairs for lounging. **3.** a couch.
lounge suit [´ ´] *n.* (chiefly *Brit.*) a man's suit usually worn during the day. (cf. *U.S.* business suit)
lour [láuər] *vi., n.* =lower.²
lour·ing·ly [láuəriŋli] *adv.* =loweringly.
louse [laus] *n.* ⓒ (pl. **lice**) a small insect that lives in dirty hair on dirty skin.
lous·y [láuzi] *adj.* (**lous·i·er, lous·i·est**) **1.** having lice. **2.** (*slang*) dirty; disagreeable. **3.** (*slang*) well-supplied.
lout [laut] *n.* ⓒ a dull and clumsy person.
lout·ish [láutiʃ] *adj.* unskillful.
Lou·vre [lú:vr, -vər], **the** *n.* a museum in Paris, formerly a royal palace of France. ⌈*child.*①
lov·a·ble [lʌ́vəbl] *adj.* worthy of love; amiable. ¶*a ~*
‡**love** [lʌv] *n.* **1.** Ⓤ strong affection. ¶*~ for children | ~ of country | ~ toward one's neighbors.* **2.** Ⓤ (often *a ~*) strong liking. ¶*a ~ of learning*① *| a ~ for music.* **3.** Ⓤ strong and passionate affection between man and woman. **4.** ⓒ a person or thing that one loves; a sweetheart. ⇨N.B. ¶*my ~ | What a ~ of a cat!*② **5.** Ⓤ (in tennis) no score. ¶*~ all*① *| ~ game.*④
1) *fall in love with* (=*come to feel love for*) someone.
2) *for love,* ⓐ without pay. ¶*The rich man takes care of a poor boy for love.* ⓑ for pleasure; out of liking.
3) *for love or money,* (in *negative*) by any means. ¶*We can't get it for ~ or money.*
4) *for the love* (=*for the sake*) *of something.*
—*vt.* **1.** have, feel, or show love for (someone). **2.** like very much. 《~ *doing*; ~ [someone] *to do*》 ¶*I should ~ to go with you. | I ~ reading (skating).*
love·less [lʌ́vlis] *adj.* **1.** not loving; feeling no love. **2.** receiving no love. ⌈love for someone.
love letter [´ ´ ´] *n.* ⓒ a letter written to express one's
love·li·ness [lʌ́vlinis] *n.* Ⓤ beauty; charm.
love·lorn [lʌ́vlɔ̀:rn] *adj.* broken-hearted; suffering from a loss of love, etc.
‡**love·ly** [lʌ́vli] *adj.* (**-li·er, -li·est**) **1.** beautiful; attractive. **2.** (*colloq.*) very enjoyable; delightful.
•**lov·er** [lʌ́vər] *n.* ⓒ **1.** a person who loves someone; a man who is in love; a woman's sweetheart. **2.** (*pl.*) a man and woman in love with each other. **3.** a person who is very fond of something. ¶*a ~ of music.*
love·sick [lʌ́vsìk] *adj.* wasting away or lacking vitality because one is in love.
•**lov·ing** [lʌ́viŋ] *adj.* feeling or showing love; affectionate.
‡**low**¹ [lou] *adj.* **1.** not high or tall; near the ground or other base. ¶*a ~ hill (roof, ceiling).* **2.** below the usual level. ¶*The water is ~.*① **3.** small in amount or degree. ¶*a ~ price | ~ speed.* **4.** not loud; soft. ¶*in a ~ voice.* **5.** humble; mean; vulgar (↔*noble*); poor. ¶*~ of birth | ~ life | ~ tastes | ~ spirits | a ~ diet.* **6.** feeble; weak. ¶*~ health.*
—*adv.* **1.** in, to, or toward a low position. ¶*fly ~.* **2.** quietly; softly; in a low voice. ¶*speak ~.* **3.** cheaply; humbly; meanly; poorly.
1) *lay low,* overthrow.
2) *lie low,* keep quiet or hidden; be inactive.

—⒜ 남자 이름 ¶①루이 14세
—ⓥ 1.어슬렁어슬렁 걷다 2.축 늘어져 기대다 —ⓦ ···을 펀둥펀둥 보내다

—⒜ 1.어정버정 거닐기 2.휴게실,라운지 3.[드러누울 수 있게 된] 긴 의자
—⒜ 《英》 신사복

—⒜ 이

—⒜ 1.이가 들끓는 2.《俗》 더러운,불결한 3.《俗》 듬뿍 있는,많은
—⒜ 버릇없는 놈,시골뜨기
—⒜ 버릇없는; 서투른
—⒜ 루우브르 박물관(파리에 있는 미술 박물관) ⌈「아이」
—⒜ 사랑스러운,귀여운 ¶①귀여운
—⒜ 1.사람,애정 2.좋아함,취미; 기호(嗜好),취미 ¶①향학심 3.연애; 연정 4.사랑하는 것; 연인,애인 N.B. love 는 남자측에서 본 애인, lover 는 여자측에서 본 애인 ¶②고양이 참 귀엽기도 하지! 5.영점,무득점 ¶③0 대 0 /④제로 게임; 영패의 승부
熟 1)···에게 반하다,···와 사랑하게 되다 2)ⓐ무보수로, 무료로 ⓑ[부정으로 써서] 어떻게 하여도 3)···을 위하여, ···때문에

—ⓥ 1.···을 사랑하다 2.···을 몹시 좋아하다; ···을 찬미(찬양)하다

—⒜ 1.애정이 없는,매정한 2.사랑을 받지 못하는
—⒜ 연애편지, 러브레터
—⒜ 아름다움; 사랑스러움; 매력
—⒜ 애인에게 버림받은,실연한

—⒜ 1.아름다운, 귀여운, 사랑스러운 2.《口》 아주 즐거운,유쾌한
—⒜ 1.애인,연인 2.애인들,연인끼리 3.애호자

—⒜ 사랑에 번민하는, 상사병에 걸린

—⒜ 애정이 깊은,사랑하는
—⒜ 1.낮은 2.보통 수준보다 낮은 ¶①수면이 낮다 3.[양·정도가] 적은 4.[소리·음성이] 낮은,저음의 5.천한, 비천한; 저속한; 가난한 6.약한, 가냘픈

—⒜ 1.낮게 2.조용히; 낮은 목소리(가락)로; 목소리를 낮추어서 3.싸게; 초라하게; 비열하게,천하게; 가난하게
熟 1)타도하다; 멸망시키다 2)가만히 때가 오기를 기다리다; 꼼짝 않고 숨어 있다

low [687] **lucid**

—*n.* ⓒ that which is low; a low place; the lowest point. ─❷ 낮은 것; 저지(低地); 최하점, 최저수준
low² [lou] *vi.* make the sound of a cow. —*n.* ⓒ the ┌sound made by a cow.┐ ─㉠ [소가] 음매하고 울다 ─❷ 음「매하고 우는 소리」
low-born [lóubɔ́ːrn] *adj.* born of humble parents. ─❷ 천한 태생의
low-bred [lóubréd] *adj.* ill-mannered; vulgar. ─❷ 버릇없는; 천한
low-brow [lóubràu] (*colloq.*) *n.* a person without intellectual interests or culture. ↔highbrow —*adj.* of a low-brow. ─❷ (口) 교양이 낮은 사람 ─❷ 교양이 낮은
low-down [lóudàun] *adj.* (*colloq.*) not honest; mean. —*n.* ⓒ (*the* ~) (*slang*) secret information. ─❷ (口) 천한, 비열(야비)한 ─❷ (俗) 실정, 내막
:low·er¹ [lóuər] *vt.* 1. let or put (something) down. ↔ heighten 2. make (a price, a degree, etc.) lower. ¶*~ the prices.* 3. weaken or lessen. 4. make (something) humble. —*vi.* become lower; sink; fall. ─❷ 1. …을 낮추다 2. …을 내리다 3. [목소리 따위]를 약하게 하다 4. …을 억누르다, 꺾다 ─㉠ 낮아지다, 내려가다; 가라앉다, 꺼지다
low·er² [láuər] *vi.* 1. frown. (*~ at, upon* or *on*) 2. (of a sky, clouds, etc.) appear dark and threatening. ¶*a lowering sky.* —*n.* ⓒ 1. a frowning look; a frown. 2. a threatening look. ─㉠ 1. 얼굴을 찡그리다 2. [하늘이 흐려서] 어두워지다, [날씨가] 험악해지다 ─❷ 1. 찌푸린 얼굴 2. 험악한 날씨
low·er·most [lóuərmòust] *adj.* lowest. ─❷ 가장 낮은, 최저의, 최하의
low·land [lóulənd, +*U.S.* -lænd] *n.* ⓒ 1. (usu. *pl.*) land lower than the level of the surrounding land. 2. (*the L~s*) the southern and eastern regions of Scotland. ↔ the Highlands —*adj.* of, in or from the lowlands. ─❷ 1. 저지(低地) 2. 스코틀랜드 저지 지방 ─❷ 저지[로부터]의
low·land·er [lóuləndər] *n.* ⓒ a person who lives in a lowland or the Lowlands. ─❷ 저지(低地) 사람
low·ly [lóuli] *adj.* (-li·er, -li·est) 1. of a low position or rank. 2. (of manners, etc.) modest; humble. —*adv.* in a low manner; humbly. ─❷ 1. 지위가 낮은, 신분이 천한 2. 겸손한 ─❷ 천하게, 초라하게; 겸손하게
low-necked [lóunékt] *adj.* (of a dress, etc.) cut low so as to lay the neck, shoulders or back bare. ─❷ [부인복이] 목·어깨·등을 드러낸, 깃을 크게 판
low-pitched [lóupítʃt] *adj.* 1. having a low tone. ¶*a ~ voice.* 2. (of a roof) having little slope; gentle in slope. ─❷ 1. 저조(低調)의 2. [지붕 따위의] 물매가 뜬
low-spir·it·ed [lóuspíritid] *adj.* depressed; spiritless; cheerless. ─❷ 우울한, 의기소침한; 기운 없는
***loy·al** [lɔ́i(ə)l] *adj.* 1. faithful to one's king or country. ↔disloyal ¶*a ~ subject.* 2. faithful to one's promise, duty or ideals; upright. ─❷ 1. 충성스러운 ¶①충신 2. 충실한; 고결한
loy·al·ist [lɔ́iəlist] *n.* ⓒ a person who remains faithful to his king or his country's government, esp. in times of revolt or disturbance. ┌truly.┐ ─❷ 충신; 왕당파(王黨派)
loy·al·ly [lɔ́i(ə)li] *adv.* in a loyal manner; faithfully;」 ─❷ 충성, 충성스럽게; 충실하게, 성실히
***loy·al·ty** [lɔ́i(ə)lti] *n.* Ⓤ the state or quality of being loyal; faithfulness. ─❷ 충절(忠節); 충실
loz·enge [lázindʒ / lɔ́zi-] *n.* ⓒ 1. a diamond-shaped figure. 2. a small tablet, usu. sweetened and diamond-shaped. ─❷ 1. 마름모꼴 2. 마름모꼴의 정제(錠劑)
LP [élpí:] *n.* ⓒ (pl. **LPs** or **LP's**) (*Trademark*) a phonograph record to be played at 33 ⅓ revolutions per minute; short for 'Long Playing.' ┌Sons Ltd.┐ ─❷ 엘피 음반, 장시간 레코드[1분간 33⅓ 회전]
Ltd., ltd. [límitid] (*Brit.*) limited. ¶*Hiram Walker &*」
lub·ber [lʌ́bər] *n.* ⓒ 1. a big, slow, careless and rough person. 2. an inexperienced and unskilled seaman. ─❷ 1. 투미한 사람, 얼간이 2. 풋나기 선원
lub·ber·ly [lʌ́bərli] *adj.* clumsy; stupid. —*adv.* in a lubberly manner. ─❷ 볼품없는, 어색한 ─❷ 어색하게, 서투르게
lu·bri·cant [lú:brikənt, -brə-] *n.* ⓒ oil for making the parts of machines work smoothly. ─❷ 윤활유, 기계유
lu·bri·cate [lú:brikèit, -brə-] *vt.* make (a machine, etc.) run smoothly by adding oil. —*vi.* act as a lubricant. ─❷ …에 기름을 쳐서 매끄럽게 하다 ─㉠ 윤활제 구실을 하다
lu·bri·ca·tion [lù:brikéiʃ(ə)n, -brə-] *n.* Ⓤ the act of lubricating; oiling. ┌transparent; clear.┐ ─❷ 매끄럽게 하기, 윤활; 주유(注油), 급유
lu·cent [lú:snt] *adj.* 1. bright; luminous; shining. 2.」 ─❷ 1. 빛나는, 번쩍이는 2. 투명한
lu·cerne, -cern [lu:sə́:rn] *n.* Ⓤ (chiefly *Brit.*) a cloverlike plant, grown as feed for cattle; alfalfa. ─❷ (英) 자주개자리
lu·cid [lú:sid] *adj.* 1. easily understood. 2. clearheaded. 3. clear; transparent. 4. mentally sound; rational; sane. ─❷ 1. 명쾌한, 알기 쉬운 2. 두뇌가 명석한 3. 맑은, 투명한 4. 지각이 정상적

5. (*poetic*) bright; shining.
인, 제정신의 5.《詩》빛나는, 밝은

lu·cid·i·ty [lu:síditi] *n.* [U] the state or quality of being lucid.
—[名] 명쾌; 명석; 밝음; 제정신임

Lu·ci·fer [lú:sifər, -sə-] *n.* **1.** (*poetic*) the planet Venus as the morning star. **2.** Satan. **3.** 《*l*-》 [C] an early type of match.
—[名] 1.《詩》샛별, 금성(金星) 2. 마왕(魔王), 사탄 3. [초기의] 황린(黃燐)성냥

:luck [lʌk] *n.* [U] **1.** the force that brings good or bad to someone; fortune; chance. ¶*Good ~ [to you]!*① **2.** good fortune. ¶*have no ~.*②
1) ***be down on one's luck,*** have no luck.
2) ***in luck,*** lucky.
3) ***out of luck,*** unlucky.
4) ***try one's luck,*** try to do something just to see what one can do.
5) ***worse luck,*** unluckily. ¶*And then, worse ~, he came into the room.*
—[名] 1. 운, 운수, 기연(機緣) ¶①행운을 빕니다! 2. 행운 ¶②운수가 나쁘다, 운이 없다
[熟] 1)운이 나쁘다 2)운 좋게 3)운 나쁘게 4)운수를 시험해 보다, 운수에 맡기고 해보다 5)불행히도, 운수 사납게

:luck·i·ly [lʌ́kili] *adv.* by or with good luck; fortunately.
—[副] 운 좋게, 다행히도

luck·less [lʌ́klis] *adj.* having no good luck.
—[形] 불행한, 불운한

:luck·y [lʌ́ki] *adj.* (**luck·i·er, luck·i·est**) **1.** having good luck; fortunate. ¶*a ~ guess* (or *hit, shot*).① **2.** bringing good luck. ¶*a ~ day*② */ the ~ seventh.*③
—[形] 1. 운 좋은, 행운의 ¶①요행수 2. 행운을 가져오는 ¶②길일(吉日)/③[야구의] 러키 세븐, 행운의 제 7 회

lu·cra·tive [lú:krətiv] *adj.* producing wealth or profit; profitable.
—[形] 유리한, 이익이 나는

lu·cre [lú:kər] *n.* [U] profit; money.
—[名] 이익, 벌이; 금전

Lu·cy [lú:si] *n.* a girl's name.
—[名] 여자 이름

lu·di·crous [lú:dikrəs] *adj.* so amusingly silly as to make one laugh; laughable.
—[形] 익살스러운, 우스꽝스러운

lug [lʌg] *v.* (**lugged, lug·ging**) *vt.* pull (something heavy) with an effort. 《~ something *along* or *about*》 ¶*~ a heavy cart along the streets.* **—*vi.*** pull hard. 《~ *at* something》 **—*n.*** [C] the act of lugging; hard pulling.
—[他] …을 힘껏 끌다 —[自] 억지로(세게) 끌다 —[名] 세게 끌기

:lug·gage [lʌ́gidʒ] *n.* [U] 《*collectively*》 (*Brit.*) suitcases, bags, etc. of a traveller. ¶*a piece of ~.*①
—[名]《英》여행자의 수하물 ¶①수하물 한 개

lug·ger [lʌ́gər] *n.* [C] a small boat. ⇒fig., [N.B.]
—[名] 러거 [N.B.] 4각의 종범(縱帆)을 단 작은 돛배

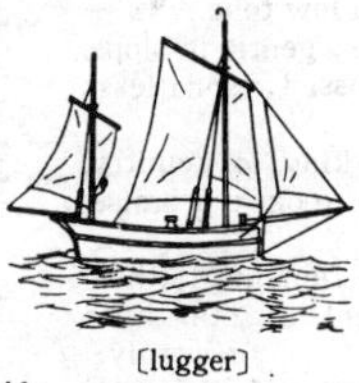
[lugger]

lu·gu·bri·ous [lu(:)g(j)ú:briəs] *adj.* very sad; gloomy.
—[形] 슬픈 듯한, 애처로운; 우울한

Luke [lu:k, +*Brit.* lju:k] *n.* (in the Bible) **1. Saint,** one of the early Christian disciples and the author of the Gospel of St. Luke. **2.** the Gospel of St. Luke, which is the third book of the New Testament and which tells the story of Jesus' life.
—[名] 1.《聖》성(聖)누가 2. [신약의] 누가복음

luke·warm [lú:kwɔ̀:rm] *adj.* **1.** (of a liquid) slightly warm. **2.** not eager; indifferent. ¶*He was ~ in his support of the bill.*①
—[形] 1. 미지근한 2. 미온적인, 마지못해 하는, 열성이 없는 ¶①그는 그 법안을 지지하는 데 별로 열의가 없었다

lull** [lʌl] *vt.* **1.** lead (a child) to fall asleep, esp. by singing and rocking it. ¶*~ a baby to sleep.* **2.** 《usu. as *passive*》 make (a storm, a wind, etc.) quiet. ¶*The wind was lulled.* **3.** make (suspicions, fears, pain, etc.) less intense; soothe. **—*vi. become calm. **—*n.*** [C] a short period of quietness.
—[他] 1. [어린애]를 재우다, 달래다, 어르다 2. [비바람 따위]를 가라앉히다, 누그러지게 하다 3. [의심·고통]을 완화시키다 —[自] 잠잠해지다, 가라앉다 —[名] [폭풍우 따위의] 자기, 잠잠함; 뜸함, 소강(小康)

lull·a·by [lʌ́ləbài] *n.* [C] (pl. **-bies**) a song for leading a child to sleep; a cradlesong.
—[名] 자장가

lum·ba·go [lʌmbéigou] *n.* [U] rheumatic pain in the lower back and in the loins; backache.
—[名] 요부(腰部) 신경통, 요통(腰痛)

:lum·ber [lʌ́mbər] *n.* [U] **1.** useless things that are stored away; unused furniture; rubbish. **2.** (*U.S.*) wood sawn into planks, boards, etc. **—*vt.* 1.** fill or obstruct (a place) with useless things. 《~ a place *with*》 ¶*a room lumbered up with old furniture.*① **2.** (*U.S.*) cut.
—[名] 1. 잡동사니, 쓰레기 2.《美》재목, 제재목 —[他] 1. …을 잡동사니로 채우다(막다), 방해하다 ¶①낡은 가구로 가득 찬 방 2.《美》[재목]을 베어내다

lum·ber·jack [lʌ́mbərdʒæ̀k] *n.* [C] (*U.S.*) a man who cuts down trees and prepares them for selling; a lumberman.
—[名]《美》벌목 인부; 재목상

lum·ber·man [lʌ́mbərmən] *n.* [C] (pl. **-men** [-mən]) (*U.S.*) **1.** a lumberjack. **2.** a man whose business is to buy and sell lumber.
—[名]《美》1. 벌목 인부 2. 재목상

L

lum·ber·mill [lʌ́mbərmìl] *n.* [C] (*U.S.*) a building in which wood is sawn into planks, boards, etc.
—[名] 《美》 제재소

lum·ber·yard [lʌ́mbərjɑ̀:rd] *n.* [C] (*U.S.*) a place where lumber is kept for sale.
—[名] 《美》 재목 두는 장소

lu·mi·nar·y [lú:minèri / -nəri] *n.* [C] (pl. **-nar·ies**) **1.** a heavenly body, such as the sun or the moon. **2.** a body or an object that gives light. **3.** a learned person with high morals.
—[名] 1. [태양·달 따위] 하나의 천체(天體) 2. 발광체(發光體) 3. 계몽자, 대(大)지도자·

lu·mi·nos·i·ty [lù:minɑ́siti / -nɔ́s-] *n.* (pl. **-ties**) **1.** [U] the quality of being luminous; brightness. **2.** [C] a body or an object that gives light.
—[名] 1. 광도(光度), 휘도(輝度) 2. 발광체(發光體)(물)

* **lu·mi·nous** [lú:minəs] *adj.* **1.** giving light; bright. ¶*a ~ paint.*① **2.** full of light. **3.** easy to understand; clear. ¶*a ~ discourse.*② ▷**lu·mi·nous·ly** [-li] *adv.*
—[形] 1. 빛을 발하는, 빛나는, 번쩍이는 ¶①발광 도료(塗料) 2. 밝은 3. 명백한 ¶②명료한 논술(論述)

⁑ **lump** [lʌmp] *n.* [C] **1.** a solid mass often with an irregular shape. ¶*a ~ of sugar*① / *a ~ of clay.*② **2.** a swelling on a body. ¶*a ~ on the forehead.* **3.** (*colloq.*) a fool.
1) ***all of a lump,*** in the mass; all together.
2) ***in the lump,*** as a whole.
3) ***lump sum,*** a sum of money to pay for various things at one time.
—[名] 1. 덩어리 ¶①각설탕 한 개/②한 덩어리(줌)의 흙; 《聖》 인간 2. 혹, 부스럼 3. 《口》 바보, 얼간이
[熟] 1)한 덩어리가 되어, 통틀어 2)전체로, 통틀어 3)총액, 일시불(一時拂)

—*vt.* make (something) into a lump; put (things) together; deal with (things) in the mass. 《~ things *together* or *with*》 —*vi.* **1.** form a lump. **2.** move heavily. 《~ *along* the street》
—[他] …을 덩어리가 되게 하다, 총괄하다; 한결같이 다루다 —[自] 1. 덩어리지다, 한 덩어리가 되다 2. 뒤룩뒤룩(육중하게) 걷다

lump·ish [lʌ́mpiʃ] *adj.* **1.** like a lump. **2.** dull; stupid.
—[形] 1. 덩어리 같은 2. 얼뜬, 둔한; 어리석은

lump·y [lʌ́mpi] *adj.* (**lump·i·er, lump·i·est**) **1.** full of lumps; clumsy. **2.** choppy; rough. ¶*~ water.*
—[形] 1. 혹(덩어리)투성이, 모양 없는 2. 물결이 이는, 거칠게 파도치는

lu·na·cy [lú:nəsi] *n.* (pl. **-cies**) [U] madness; great foolishness; 《sometimes *pl.*》 a very foolish act.
—[名] 정신 이상, 광기(狂氣); 매우 우매함; 어리석은(미친) 짓, 우매한 행동

lu·nar [lú:nər] *adj.* of or like the moon. ↔solar ¶*~ calendar*① / *~ eclipse*② / *a ~ module.*③
—[形] 달의, 달 같은 ¶①[태]음력/②월식/③달 착륙선

lu·na·tic [lú:nətik] *n.* [C] **1.** a madman. **2.** a foolish person. —*adj.* **1.** mad; crazy. ¶*a ~ asylum.*① **2.** foolish.
—[名] 1. 미치광이, 광인(狂人) 2. 바보 —[形] 1. 미친, 정신이상의 ¶①정신병원 2. 어리석은

⁑ **lunch** [lʌntʃ] *n.* [U][C] the light midday meal; a light meal. —*vi.* eat lunch. —*vt.* entertain (someone) with lunch.
—[名] 점심[식사], 런치; 경식사 —[自] 점심을 먹다 —[他] …에게 점심을 대접하다

* **lunch·eon** [lʌ́ntʃ(ə)n] *n.* [U][C] a lunch, esp. a formal lunch. ¶*a ~ party.*
—[名] 점심[식사], [특히 정식의] 오찬

* **lung** [lʌŋ] *n.* [C] a breathing organ (of which there are usu. two) in any airbreathing animal.
1) ***at the top of one's lungs,*** at the top of one's voice; very loudly.
2) ***have good lungs,*** have a loud voice.
3) ***try one's lungs,*** cry at the top of one's voice; cry loudly.
—[名] 폐(肺), 폐장
[熟] 1)목청껏 2)목소리가 크다 3)목청껏 소리치다

lunge [lʌndʒ] *n.* [C] a sudden thrust. —*vi.* plunge. 《~ *at*》 ¶*~ at one's opponent.*①
—[名] [국] 찌르기 —[自] 찌르다; 돌진하다 ¶①적을 향해 돌진하다

lurch[1] [lə:rtʃ] *n.* [C] a sudden leaning to one side. —*vi.* lean or sway suddenly to one side; stagger.
—[名] [갑작스러운] 경사; 동요, 비틀거림 —[自] [갑자기] 기울다; 비틀거리다

lurch[2] [lə:rtʃ] *n.* [C] (*archaic*) a crushing defeat. ⇒[usage]
leave someone in the lurch, leave someone in a helpless condition.
—[名] 《古》 참패, 대패 [usage] 다음 숙어로만 씀
[熟] 궁지에 빠져 있는 …을 저버리다(버려 두다)

* **lure** [luər / ljuə, luə] *n.* [C] **1.** a trained bird or other animal used to attract others. **2.** an artificial bait. **3.** an attraction; a charm. —*vt.* attract; tempt. 《~ something *away*; ~ someone or something *into*》 ¶*~ a fox into a trap*① / *~ someone away from his duty.*②
—[名] 1. 미끼새 2. 가짜 미끼 3. 매혹(유인)물 —[他] …을 꾀어들이다, 유혹하다 ¶①여우를 꾀어들여 함정에 빠뜨리다(덫에 걸리게 하다)/②…을 유혹하여 임무를 게을리하게 하다

lu·rid [lúərid / l(j)úərid] *adj.* **1.** glaring in color. ¶*the sky ~ with flames.* **2.** terrible; surprising; sensational.
—[形] 1. 무시무시하게 번쩍이는, 2. 무서운, 깜짝 놀랄 만한, 떠들썩하게 하는

* **lurk** [lə:rk] *vi.* lie or wait in hide. —*n.* [C] the act of lurking. ¶*on the ~.*①
—[自] 매복하다, 잠복하다 —[名] 몰래 감 ¶①살금살금 냄새를 맡고 다니며

lus·cious [lʌ́ʃəs] *adj.* sweet in taste; delicious. ¶*a ~ pear.*
—[形] 감미로운; 맛좋은

lush [lʌʃ] *adj.* **1.** fresh and green; growing abundantly. **2.** abundant. ¶*fields ~ with clover.*
—[形] 1. 푸릇푸릇한, 싱싱하게 우거진, 무성한 2. 풍부한

* **lust** [lʌst] *n.* [U][C] a strong desire; a sexual desire. —*vi.* have a strong desire, esp. a strong sexual desire.
—[名] 욕망, 갈망; 색정, —[自] 열망(갈망)하다; [특히] 색욕을 일으키다

L

lus·ter, *Brit.* **lus·tre** [lʌ́stər] *n.* ⓤ **1.** brightness and smoothness of the surface; shine; gloss. ¶*the ~ of silk / add ~ to the skin.*① **2.** fame; glory. ¶*throw ~ on one's name.*②
— 图 1. 광택, 윤; 광채, 빛 ¶①가죽에 광택이 더 나게 하다 2. 영광, 영예 ¶②이름을 빛나게 하다

lust·ful [lʌ́stful] *adj.* moved by sexual desire; sensual.
— 匣 호색의, 음탕한

lust·i·ly [lʌ́stili] *adv.* in a lusty manner; vigorously.
— 匣 기운 좋게, 활발히

lus·trous [lʌ́strəs] *adj.* bright; glossy; shining.
— 匣 광택이 있는, 번들거리는; 번쩍번쩍하는

lust·y [lʌ́sti] *adj.* (**lust·i·er, lust·i·est**) healthy; vigorous.
— 匣 튼튼한, 기운 좋은

lute [lu:t / l(j)u:t] *n.* ⓒ stringed musical instrument of olden times. ⇒ fig. N.B.
— 图 류우트 N.B. mandolin 비슷한 14-17세기경의 현악기

[lute]

Lu·ther [lú:θər / l(j)ú:-], **Martin** *n.* (1483-1546) the German leader of the Protestant Reformation.
— 图 독일의 종교 개혁자

Lu·ther·an [lú:θərən / l(j)ú:-] *adj.* of Martin Luther; belonging to the Protestant church named for Martin Luther. —*n.* ⓒ a member of the Lutheran Church; a follower of Martin Luther.
— 匣 루터의, 루터교(파)의 — 图 루터교도

lux·u·ri·ance [lʌgzúəriəns, lʌkʃ- / lʌgzjúəri-] *n.* ⓤ the state or quality of being luxuriant; abundant growth; richness.
— 图 우거짐, 무성, 다산(多産), 풍부; [문장 따위의] 화려함

lux·u·ri·ant [lʌgzúəriənt, lʌkʃ- / lʌgzjúəri-] *adj.* growing thick; very productive; rich in decoration. ¶*~ foliage*① */ a ~ style.*②
— 匣 우거진, 무성한; 풍요로운; 다산의; 화려한 ¶①무성한 나뭇잎/②화려한 문체

lux·u·ri·ate [lʌgzúərièit, lʌkʃ- / lʌgzjúəri-] *vi.* **1.** grow more than enough. **2.** take great delight in (something). (*~ in*) ¶*~ in sunshine.*①
— 圓 1. 우거지다, 무성하다 2. 즐기다 ¶①일광욕을 즐기다

lux·u·ri·ous [lʌgzú(:)riəs, lʌkʃú(:)- / lʌgzjúə-] *adj.* fond of luxuries; splendid and comfortable; extravagant. ▷**lux·u·ri·ous·ly** [-li] *adv.*
— 匣 사치스러운, 화사한, 호화로운

lux·u·ry [lʌ́kʃ(ə)ri] *n.* (pl. **-ries**) **1.** ⓤ the state or way of life in which one can enjoy or use expensive things; extravagance. ¶*live in ~.*① **2.** ⓒ something pleasant but not necessary. ¶*necessaries before luxuries.*②
— 图 1. 사치, 호사, 호화 ¶①사치스럽게 살다 2. 사치품 ¶②사치품보다 우선 필수품

ly·cée [li:séi / lí:sei] *n.* ⓒ a government-supported secondary school in France.
— 图 [프랑스의] 국립 고등학교, 대학 예비 학교

ly·ce·um [laisí(:)əm] *n.* ⓒ **1.** (*L-*) the small lecture hall in Athens where Aristotle taught. **2.** a lecture hall. **3.** (*U.S.*) [a building of] an association providing public lectures, concerts, etc.
— 图 1. 아리스토텔레스가 철학을 가르친 아테네의 학원 2. 학원(學院), 학회 3.《美》문화 운동 단체, 문화회(관), 강연회, 토론회, 음악회

ly·ing¹ [láiiŋ] *v.* ppr. of **lie**¹. —*n.* ⓤ the act of telling a lie. —*adj.* false; untruthful.
— 图 거짓말하기 — 匣 거짓말하는, 거짓의

ly·ing² [láiiŋ] *v.* ppr. of **lie**².

lymph [limf] *n.* ⓤ a colorless fluid in an animal body.
— 图 임파액(淋巴液)

lym·phat·ic [limfǽtik] *adj.* **1.** of or containing lymph. **2.** lacking energy; lazy. —*n.* ⓒ a tube which carries lymph. 「death without a legal trial.」
— 匣 1. 임파의, 임파를 함유한 2. 둔한, 굼뜬, 지둔(遲鈍)한 — 图 임파선(관)

lynch [lintʃ] *vt.* punish (someone) by hanging him to
— 他 …을 린치[사형(死刑)]에 처하다

lynx [liŋks] *n.* ⓒⓤ (pl. **lynx·es** or *collectively* **lynx**) any of several large wildcats. 「sighted.」
— 图 스라소니, 살쾡이

lynx-eyed [líŋksàid] *adj.* having very sharp eyes; keen-
— 匣 눈이 날카로운

lyre [láiər] *n.* ⓒ a harplike stringed musical instrument in ancient Greece. ⇒fig.
— 图 [고대 그리이스의] 수금(竪琴)

lyr·ic [lírik] *n.* ⓒ a short, musical poem expressing personal emotions. ↔epic —*adj.* =lyrical.
— 图 서정시

lyr·i·cal [lírik(ə)l] *adj.* (of poetry) expressing very personal feelings, like a song; emotional.
— 匣 서정시적인, 서정시조(調)의; 감정을 과장한

[lyre]

Ly·sol [láisɔ:l, -soul] *n.* ⓤ (*Trademark*) a brown liquid, used to prevent the disease germs.
— 图 《商標》 리조올 [소독제]

M

M, m [em] *n.* ⓒ (pl. **M's, Ms, m's, ms** [emz]) **1.** the 13th letter of the English alphabet. **2.** the Roman number for 1,000.
M. [məsjá:r] Monsieur.
m. 1. male. **2.** mark; marks. **3.** married. **4.** masculine. **5.** mass. **6.** meter; meters. **7.** mile; miles. **8.** minute; minutes. **9.** month. **10.** moon. **11.** mountain.
* **ma** [ma:] *n.* ⓒ (*colloq.*) mamma; mother.
M.A. Master of Arts. ⇒N.B.
* **ma'am** [mæm, ma:m, məm] *n.* ⓒ (*colloq.*) madam.
ma·ca·bre [məká:brə, -bər/-br] *adj.* **1.** horrible; ghastly. **2.** of death.
mac·a·ro·ni [mækəróuni] *n.* (pl. **-nis** or **-nies**) **1.** ⓤ dried flour paste made into long, thin, hollow tubes. **2.** ⓒ a dandy.
mac·a·roon [mækərú:n] *n.* ⓒ a small, sweet cookie made of egg white, sugar, and crushed almonds or coconut.
Mac·beth [məkbéθ, mæk-] *n.* **1.** a play by Shakespeare. **2.** the main character of this play.
mace [meis] *n.* ⓒ **1.** a large club used as a weapon in the Middle Ages. ⇒fig. **2.** a staff carried before a mayor, etc. as a symbol of authority.
Mac·e·don [mǽsidàn / -d(ə)n] *n.* =Macedonia.
Mac·e·do·ni·a [mæ̀sidóuniə] *n.* an ancient kingdom in Europe, in the north of Greece. ▷ **Mac·e·do·ni·an** [-n] *adj., n.*
Mach, mach [ma:k] *n.* ⓒ Mach number.
Mach·i·a·vel·li [mækiəvéli] *n.* [mace 1.] (1469-1527) an Italian statesman and writer. ⇒N.B.
Mach·i·a·vel·li·an, -vel·i·an [mækiəvéliən] *adj.* **1.** of Machiavelli or his political opinion that rulers should use craftiness to keep their authority. **2.** cunning; crafty. ——*n.* ⓒ a follower of Machiavelli's principles.
: **ma·chine** [məʃí:n] *n.* ⓒ **1.** an instrument for doing work consisting of a number of fixed and moving parts. ¶*a mowing ~*① / *a printing ~*② / *a sewing ~*③ / *a vending ~*④ / *the ~ age*⑤ / *a ~ shop.*⑥ **2.** a mechanism. **3.** an automobile; an airplane. **4.** leaders of a political party. **5.** a person or group that acts like a machine, without thinking at all.
——*vt.* make or shape (something) with a machine.
machine gun [- ´ ˋ] *n.* a gun that fires bullets continuously.
ma·chine-made [məʃí:nmèid] *adj.* made by machinery. ↔man-made
: **ma·chin·er·y** [məʃí:nəri] *n.* ⓤ **1.** (*collectively*) machines as a group or whole. ¶*a lot of ~*① **2.** the working parts of a machine. **3.** the organization by which something is kept in action. ¶*the ~ of government.*②
ma·chin·ist [məʃí:nist] *n.* ⓒ a person who controls, makes, and repairs machinery; a person who is skillful at using machine tools.
mack·er·el [mǽk(ə)rəl] *n.* ⓒ (pl. **-els** or *collectively* **-el**) an oily seafish with a blue-striped back.
mack·in·tosh [mǽkintɑ̀ʃ / -tɔ̀ʃ] *n.* **1.** ⓒ a waterproof

——名 1. 영어 알파벳의 열 세째 글자 2. 로마 숫자의 1,000
——[略] 프랑스어로 Mr.의 뜻

——名 〈口〉 엄마
——[略] 문학 석사 N.B. A.M.이라고
——名 마님, 부인 [도함
——名 1. 무시무시한; 오싹하는 2. 죽음의
——名 1. 마카로니 2. 멋쟁이

——名 매커루운(과자)

——名 1. 세익스피어작의 비극 2. 그 주인공
——名 1. 철퇴(옛 무기) 2. 직장(職杖)

——名 마케도니아(그리이스 북부의 옛 왕국)

——名 마하
——名 이탈리아의 작가·정치가 N.B. 권모술수 정치의 창도자
——形 1. 마키아벨리[주의]의 2. 권모술수의 ——名 마키아벨리 주의자, 권모술수가

——名 1. 기계 ¶①풀 베는 기계/②인쇄기/③재봉틀/④자동 판매기/⑤기계 시대/⑥기계 공장 2. 기구(機構), 장치 3. 자동차, 비행기 4. [정당의] 지도 기관 5. 기계적으로 일하는 사람

——他 …을 기계로 만들다
——名 기관총

——形 기계로 만든

——名 1. 기계류 ¶①많은 기계 2. 기계 장치 3. 조직, 기구 ¶②정치기구

——名 기계공(수리공); 기계 기사

——名 고등어

——名 1. 고무를 씌운 방수포 외투 2. 그

overcoat. **2.** [U] waterproof cloth used for this overcoat. ⇒[N.B.]
방수포 [N.B.] 발명자 Charles Macintosh의 이름에서

mac·ro·cosm [mǽkrəkὰz(ə)m / -kɔ̀zəm] *n.* [C] the universe. ↔microcosm
—[名] 대우주

⁑ mad [mæd] *adj.* (**mad·der, mad·dest**) **1.** out of one's mind; crazy; insane. **2.** greatly excited; wild. ¶*He is ~ with joy.* **3.** very foolish. **4.** filled with great eagerness or desire; very fond. ¶*She is ~ about him.* **5.** (*colloq.*) very angry. ¶*She was ~ at* (or *with*) *me for saying so.*① **6.** wildly gay or merry. ¶*in ~ spirits.*② **7.** (of animals) having rabies. ¶*a ~ dog.*
—[形] 1. 미친 2. 미친 듯이 흥분한 3. 어리석은 4. 열광한, 열중한 5. 성난 ¶①그녀는 내가 그렇게 말해서 몹시 화내고 있었다 6. 들떠서 흥청거리는 ¶②들뜬 기분으로 7. 공수병에 걸린

1) ***drive someone mad,*** cause someone to become mad.
2) ***go*** (or ***run***) ***mad,*** become mad.
[熟] 1)…을 미치게 하다 2)미치다

Mad·a·gas·car [mæ̀dəgǽskər] *n.* a republican island in the Indian Ocean, off the southeastern coast of Africa.
—[名] 아프리카 동남 해안 앞바다에 있는 공화국

*** mad·am** [mǽdəm] *n.* [C] (pl. **-ams** or **mes·dames**) **1.** a polite word used in speaking or writing to a lady. **2.** (*colloq.*) the mistress of a household.
—[名] 1. 마님, 부인(부인에 대한 경칭) 2. 주부, 안주인

mad·ame [mǽdəm] *n.* [C] (pl. **mes·dames**) a French form, not British or American, used in speaking or writing to a married woman. ⇒[N.B.] ¶*Madame Curie.*①
—[名] 부인, 마님 [N.B.] Mdme.으로 줄임 ¶①퀴우리 부인

mad·cap [mǽdkæ̀p] *n.* [C] a wild and thoughtless person, esp. a girl. —*adj.* thinking nothing of the possible results; mad-brained.
—[名] 무모한 사람, [특히] 더퍼리 처녀

mad·den [mǽdn] *vt.* **1.** make (someone) mad. **2.** make (someone) very angry.
—[他] 1. …을 미치게 하다 2. …을 격분시키다

mad·den·ing [mǽdniŋ] *adj.* **1.** causing to become mad. **2.** driving into great anger.
—[形] 1. 미칠 듯한 2. 격분하게 하는

mad·ding [mǽdiŋ] *adj.* **1.** mad, or acting madly; furious. ¶*the ~ crowd.* **2.** maddening.
—[形] 1. 미친; 미친 듯한 2. 미치게 하는

⁑ made [meid] *v.* pt. and pp. of **make**.
—*adj.* **1.** produced by men. ¶*a ~ dish*① / *~ ground*② / *American-made articles* / *home-made goods*③ / *a ~ word*④ / *ready-made clothes.* **2.** built. ¶*a well-made man*⑤ **3.** successful. ¶*a ~ man*⑥ / *a selfmade man.*
—[形] 1. [인공적으로] 만든; 지은; 요리한 ¶①모듬 요리/②매립지(埋立地)/③국산품/④조어(造語) 2. 몸집이 …한 ¶⑤건장한 체격의 사람 3. 성공한 ¶⑥성공한 사람

ma·de·moi·selle [mæ̀dəməzél] *n.* [C] (pl. **mes·de·moi·selles**) a French form used in speaking or writing to an unmarried woman. ⇒[N.B.]
—[名] 아가씨, 영양 [N.B.] 프랑스어로 영어의 Miss에 해당

made-to-or·der [méidtuɔ́:rdər] *adj.* made according to the customer's wishes. ↔ready-made
—[形] 주문하여 만든, 마춘

made-up [méidʌ́p] *adj.* **1.** arranged. **2.** not true. ¶*a ~ story.* **3.** man-made.
—[形] 1. 각색한, 편곡된 2. 꾸며낸 3. 인공의

mad·house [mǽdhaus] *n.* [C] a hospital or home for insane people.
—[名] 정신병원

mad·ly [mǽdli] *adv.* **1.** in a mad manner. ¶*be ~ in love with him.* **2.** wildly; without self-control.
—[副] 1. 미친 듯이, 열렬하게 2. 광폭하게

mad·man [mǽdmən] *n.* [C] (pl. **-men** [-mən]) a crazy person; a lunatic. ¶*become wild like a ~.*①
—[名] 미치광이, 광인 ¶①미치광이처럼 날뛰다

⁑ mad·ness [mǽdnis] *n.* [U] **1.** the state of being mad. ¶*love to ~*① / *in one's ~.*② **2.** great anger. **3.** a foolish act. ¶*It is ~ to swim in such weather.*
—[名] 1. 정신착란 ¶①미칠 듯이 사랑하다/②광란하여 2. 격분 3. 미친 짓, 지랄

Ma·don·na [mədɑ́nə / -dɔ́n-] *n.* **1.** the Virgin Mary (the mother of Jesus Christ). **2.** [C] a picture or statue of Mary.
—[名] 1. 성모 마리아 2. 마리아의 초상

Ma·drid [mədríd] *n.* the capital of Spain.
—[名] 스페인의 수도

mad·ri·gal [mǽdrig(ə)l] *n.* [C] **1.** a sentimental love poem set to music. **2.** a type of song sung in five or six voices without any musical accompaniment.
—[名] 1. 짤막한 연가(戀歌) 2. 마드리갈곡

mael·strom [méilstrəm / -strɔ̀um] *n.* **1.** ⟪*the M-*⟫ a great sea current turning around rapidly off the northwestern coast of Norway. **2.** [C] a great sea current turning around rapidly. **3.** [C] a violently confused state of feelings or mind.
—[名] 1. 노르웨이 서북 해안의 큰 소용돌이 2. 큰 소용돌이 3. [감정·정신의] 큰 혼란

⁑ mag·a·zine [mæ̀gəzí:n, +*U.S.* mǽgəzì:n] *n.* [C] **1.** a collection of various kinds of reading matter regularly published. ¶*edit a ~*① / *take a ~.*② **2.** a place for
—[名] 1. 잡지 ¶①잡지를 편집하다/②잡지를 보다 2. 탄약고, 두기고 3. [총의] 탄창 4. [카메라의] 필름 감는 틀

M

keeping guns and gunpowder. **3.** a space in a gun to hold the cartridges. **4.** a place in a camera for rolls of film.

mag·got [mǽɡət] *n.* ⓒ a worm-like larva of a fly living in decaying flesh, food, etc. —图 구더기

Ma·gi [méidʒai], **the** *n. pl.* (sing. **Magus**) (in the Bible) the Three Wise Men from the East who came to celebrate the birth of Jesus. —图 동방의 세 박사

‡ **mag·ic** [mǽdʒik] *n.* ⓤ **1.** the art which makes wonderful things happen by using supernatural power. ¶*black* ~.① **2.** a mysterious power. ¶*the ~ of music*.② **3.** mysterious effects made by tricks. —*adj.* ((usu. as *attributive*)) **1.** having magic. ¶*a ~ carpet* / *a ~ hand* / *a ~ lantern*③ / *~ words*.④ **2.** mysterious. ¶*~ beauty*. —图 1. 마술 ¶①악마의 마술 2. 불가사의한 힘, 마력 ¶②음악의 매력 3. 요술, 기술(奇術) —图 1. 마법의 ¶③환등/④마법의 주문(呪文) 2. 불가사의한

mag·i·cal [mǽdʒik(ə)l] *adj.* **1.** done by magic. **2.** having magic power. ¶*in a ~ way* / *The effect was ~*. —图 1. 마술의 2. 불가사의한

mag·i·cal·ly [mǽdʒikəli] *adv.* **1.** by means of magic. **2.** in a magic manner. ⌈in magic. —图 1. 마술로 2. 불가사의하게

* **ma·gi·cian** [mədʒíʃ(ə)n] *n.* ⓒ a person who is skilled —图 마법사, 요술장이

mag·is·te·ri·al [mædʒistíəriəl] *adj.* **1.** of a magistrate. **2.** showing authority. **3.** having a masterful manner or aspect. ▷ **mag·is·te·ri·al·ly** [-li] *adv.* —图 1. 행정 장관의 2. 엄연한 3. 거만한

mag·is·tra·cy [mǽdʒistrəsi] *n.* ⓤⓒ (pl. **-cies**) **1.** the position of a magistrate. **2.** ((*collectively*)) a body of magistrates. —图 1. 행정 장관의 직 2. 행정 장관

* **mag·is·trate** [mǽdʒistrèit, -trit] *n.* ⓒ **1.** a chief officer of the government who has power to apply the law. **2.** a local judge who judges minor law cases. —图 1. [사법권이 있는] 행정 장관 2. 지방 판사

Mag·na Char·ta, Mag·na Car·ta [mǽɡnə káːrtə] *n.* the great charter of liberties of the English people which King John was forced to accept in 1215. —图 마그나 카르타, 대헌장

mag·na·nim·i·ty [mæɡnəníməti] *n.* (pl. **-ties**) **1.** ⓤ the quality or nature of being magnanimous. **2.** ⓒ a magnanimous act. ⌈generous. —图 1. 도량이 큼, 통이 큼 2. 고매한 (관대한) 행위

mag·nan·i·mous [mæɡnǽniməs] *adj.* noble-minded; —图 고결한; 관대한

mag·nate [mǽɡneit] *n.* ⓒ **1.** a person of high rank. **2.** a rich and powerful person in an industry. ¶*a financial ~*① / *an oil ~*.② —图 1. 고관 2. 거물, …왕 ¶①재계의 거물/②석유왕

mag·ne·si·um [mæɡníːziəm, -ʃiəm] *n.* ⓤ a light silvery metal element which burns with a bright white light. —图 마그네슘

* **mag·net** [mǽɡnit] *n.* ⓒ **1.** a piece of iron that draws other pieces of iron toward it, or which points north and south. **2.** a thing or a person that attracts. —图 1. 자석 2. 사람을 끄는 것(사람)

mag·net·ic [mæɡnétik] *adj.* **1.** having the qualities of a magnet. ¶*the ~ field*① / *a ~ needle*② / *the ~ pole*.③ **2.** attractive. ¶*a ~ personality* / *His speech was really ~*. —图 1. 자기(磁氣)를 띤 ¶①자장(磁場)/②자침/③자극(磁極) 2. 매력적인

mag·net·ism [mǽɡnitìz(ə)m] *n.* ⓤ **1.** the qualities of a magnet. **2.** the science of magnets. **3.** attractive power. ⌈strong magnetic power. —图 1. 자력 2. 자기학 3. 매력

mag·net·ite [mǽɡnitàit] *n.* ⓤ an iron ore having —图 자철광(磁鐵鑛)

mag·net·ize [mǽɡnitàiz] *vt.* **1.** make (iron or steel) magnetic. ¶*become magnetized*.① **2.** attract. ▷ **mag·net·i·za·tion** [mæ̀ɡnitizéiʃ(ə)n / -tai-] *n.* —图 1. [금속]을 자화(磁化)하다 ¶①자기를 띠다 2. …을 매혹하다

mag·ne·to [mæɡníːtou] *n.* ⓒ (pl. **-tos**) a small electric generator with permanent magnets. —图 자석 발전기

mag·ni·fi·ca·tion [mæ̀ɡnifikéiʃ(ə)n] *n.* ⓤ **1.** the act of magnifying. **2.** the power of magnifying. —图 1. 확대 2. 배율(倍率)

mag·nif·i·cence [mæɡnífisns] *n.* ⓤ the quality of being magnificent; splendor. —图 웅대, 장려(壯麗)

‡ **mag·nif·i·cent** [mæɡnífisnt] *adj.* **1.** very fine; splendid; grand. **2.** excellent; very good. ⌈manner. —图 1. 멋들어진; 장려한 2. 우수한; 아주 좋은

mag·nif·i·cent·ly [mæɡnífisntli] *adv.* in a magnificent —图 장려하게

* **mag·ni·fy** [mǽɡnifài] *vt.* **(-fied) 1.** make (something) look larger than its real size. ¶*a magnifying glass*① / —图 1. …을 확대하다 ¶①확대경/②이 현미경은 물체를 5백 배로 확대한

*This microscope magnifies objects five hundred times.*② **2.** think or speak of (something) as being much greater than it really is. ¶~ *difficulties.*③

다 2. …을 과장하다 ¶③곤란을 너무 크게 생각하다

mag·nil·o·quence [mægníloukwəns] *n.* **1.** [U] the state of being too proud of oneself; the act of talking big. **2.** [C] speech or writing made up of big words.

—[名] 1. 호언장담 2. 과장(문체 따위)

mag·nil·o·quent [mægníloukwənt] *adj.* **1.** boastful; talking big. **2.** using big words.

—[形] 1. 호언장담하는 2. 과장된

mag·ni·tude [mǽgnit(j)ù:d / -tjù:d] *n.* [U] **1.** largeness; size. **2.** importance. ¶*a matter of* ~.① **3.** the degree of brightness of a star; the strength of an earthquake.

—[名] 1. 크기 2. 중요성 ¶①중요한 일 3. [별의] 광도(光度), 등급; [지진의] 강도(强度)

mag·no·li·a [mægnóuliə] *n.* [C] a tree with large white or pink blossoms and darkgreen leaves.

—[名] 태산목(泰山木)

mag·pie [mǽgpài] *n.* [C] **1.** a black-and-white bird of the crow family, famous for its noisy chattering. **2.** a person who talks continuously.

—[名] 1. 까치 2. 수다장이

Ma·gus [méigəs] *n.* sing. of **Magi**.

ma·ha·ra·ja, -jah [mà:hərá:dʒə] *n.* [C] the title of a ruling prince in India.

—[名] 대군(大君)[인도의 군후(君侯)의 존칭]

ma·hat·ma [məhǽtmə, -há:t-] *n.* [C] a holy person in India who is respected highly for his wisdom, selfishlessness and extraordinary powers.

—[名] [인도의] 대성(大聖)

mah·jongg, mah·jong [má:dʒɔ́:ŋ / -dʒɔ́ŋ] *n.* [U] a Chinese game played by four persons with 136 pieces until one of the players forms winning combinations.

—[名] 마작(麻雀)

ma·hog·a·ny [məhágəni / -hɔ́g-] *n.* **1.** a hard reddish-brown wood of a tropical American tree, used to make furniture which can be polished highly. **2.** [U] dark reddish-brown.

—[名] 1. 마호가니 재목 2. 마호가니색, 적갈색

Ma·hom·e·dan [məhámidən / -hɔ́m-] *n., a.* =Mohammedan.

Ma·hom·et [məhámit / -hɔ́m-] *n.* =Mohammed.

Ma·hom·e·tan [məhámit(ə)n / -hɔ́mi-] *n., a.* =Mohammedan.

‡**maid** [meid] *n.* [C] **1.** a young girl. **2.** an unmarried woman. ¶*an old* ~.① **3.** a woman servant. ¶*a lady's* ~② / *a* ~ *of all work.*③

—[名] 1. 소녀 2. 미혼 여성 ¶①노처녀 3. 하녀 ¶②시녀/③잡역부

‡**maid·en** [méidn] *n.* [C] a girl; a young, unmarried woman. —*adj.* **1.** unmarried. ¶*a* ~ *aunt* / *a* ~ *name.*① **2.** first; new. ¶*a* ~ *voyage*② / *a* ~ *speech* / ~ *work.*

—[名] 소녀, 처녀 —[形] 1. 미혼의 ¶① 여자의 결혼 전의 성(姓) 2. 처음의; 첫번의 ¶②처녀 항해

maid·en·hood [méidnhùd] *n.* [U] the state or time of being a maiden.

—[名] 처녀성, 처녀시절

maid·en-like [méidnlàik] *adj.* =maidenly.

maid·en·ly [méidnli] *adj.* **1.** of a maiden. **2.** like a maiden; suitable to a maiden. ▷**maid·en·li·ness** [-nis] *n.*

—[形] 1. 처녀다운 2. 얌전한, 수줍은

maid·ser·vant [méidsə:rvənt] *n.* [C] a woman servant.

—[名] 하녀

‡**mail**¹ [meil] *n.* (esp. *U.S.*) **1.** [U] 《*collectively*》 letters, papers, parcels, etc., sent through the post office. ¶*deliver* ~.① **2.** [C] the government system which carries and delivers such mail. ¶*by* ~② / *by air* ~③ / ~ *matter.*④ —*vt.* (*U.S.*) send (letters, etc.) by mail. (cf. *Brit.* post)

—[名] 《주로 美》 1. 우편 ¶①우편을 배달하다 2. 우편제도 ¶②우편으로/③항공우편으로/④우편물 —[他] [편지]를 우편으로 부치다

mail² [meil] *n.* [U] a body armor made of steel rings linked together.

—[名] 사슬 갑옷

mail·bag [méilbæ̀g] *n.* [C] **1.** a mailman's shoulder bag for carrying mail. **2.** a bag for carrying mail.

—[名] 1. 우편가방 2. 우편대(袋)

mail·box [méilbàks / -bɔ̀ks] *n.* [C] (*U.S.*) **1.** a public box into which mail is put for collection. **2.** a private box into which delivered mail is put. (cf. *Brit.* letter box)

—[名] 《美》 1. 우편함, 우체통 2. [개인의] 우편함

mail·man [méilmæ̀n] *n.* [C] (pl. **-men** [-mèn]) (*U.S.*) a person who collects and carries mail. (cf. *Brit.* postman)

—[名] 《美》 우체부, 우편 집배원

maim [meim] *vt.* cause (someone) to lose the use of a part of the body. ¶*be seriously maimed by an accident.*①

—[他] …을 불구로 만들다 ¶①사고로 심한 불구가 되다

‡**main** [mein] *adj.* **1.** chief; principal; most important. ¶*the* ~ *street.* **2.** largest; of the highest degree. ¶*by* ~ *force* (or *strength*).① —*n.* [C] **1.** a principal pipe for

—[形] 1. 주요한 2. 최고도의 ¶①전력을 다하여 —[名] 1. [수도 · 가스 따위의] 본관(本管) 2. 《美》 큰 바다, 대해

M

carrying water, gas, etc. **2.** (*poetic*) the wide sea.
1) ***in the main,*** for the most part; on the whole.
2) ***with might and main,*** with all one's strength.

[熟] 1)대부분은, 대체로 2)전력을 다하여

main·land [méinlæ̀nd] *n.* [C] a large and principal part of a country or broad land, not a small island or peninsula. ¶*the U.S.* ~.①

—[名] 본토; [부근의 섬이나 반도와 구별하여] 대륙 ¶①미국 본토

* **main·ly** [méinli] *adv.* for the most part; chiefly.

—[副] 주로

main·mast [méinmæ̀st / -mɑ̀:st, *nautical* -məst] *n.* [C] the chief mast of a ship.

—[名] 큰 돛대, 대장(大檣)

main·sail [méinsèil, méinsl] *n.* [C] the largest sail set from the mainmast.

—[名] 큰 돛대의 큰 돛, 주범(主帆)

main·spring [méinsprìŋ] *n.* [C] **1.** the principal spring in a mechanism such as a clock or watch which keeps it going. **2.** the chief cause.

—[名] 1. [시계의] 큰 태엽 2. 주요원인

main·stay [méinstèi] *n.* [C] **1.** the strong rope which supports the mainmast of a ship. **2.** the main support.

—[名] 1. 대장지색(大檣支索) 2. 의지할 곳, 큰 기둥

* **main·tain** [meintéin, mən-] *vt.* **1.** go on; keep on. ¶~ *peace and order.*① **2.** support. ¶~ *one's family* / ~ *life* / ~ *oneself*② / ~ *a cause* (or *an argument*). **3.** insist as a belief. 《~ *that* ...》 ¶~ *one's opinion.*

—[他] 1. …을 유지하다; 계속(지속)하다 ¶①평화와 질서를 유지하다 2. …을 부양하다; 관리하다; 지지하다 ¶②자활하다 3. …을 주장하다

* **main·te·nance** [méintənəns] *n.* [U] **1.** the act of maintaining; the state of being maintained. ¶*the cost of* ~① / ~ *of peace.*② **2.** the act of defending. **3.** a means of supporting life.

—[名] 1. 유지; 지속 ¶①유지비/②평화유지 2. 옹호, 주장 3. 부양, 생계

maize [meiz] *n.* [C] a plant that bears grain on large ears; Indian corn. ⇒[N.B.]

—[名] 옥수수 [N.B.] 미국·캐나다 등지에서는 corn이라 함

Maj. Major.

* **ma·jes·tic** [mədʒéstik] *adj.* having a noble and dignified character or appearance.

—[形] 위엄있는

ma·jes·ti·cal [mədʒéstikəl] *adj.* =majestic.

ma·jes·ti·cal·ly [mədʒéstikəli] *adv.* in a majestic manner.

—[副] 위엄있게, 당당하게

⁑ **maj·es·ty** [mǽdʒisti] *n.* [U] **1.** dignity; nobility. **2.** royal power or authority. **3.** 《*M-*》 a form in speaking or writing to a king, queen, emperor, or empress. ⇒[usage] ¶*Your* ~① / *His Majesty.*②

—[名] 1. 위엄 2. 왕자(王者)의 주권 3. 폐하 [usage] 받는 동사는 3인칭 ¶①[직접적인 호칭으로] 폐하/②국왕 폐하

⁑ **ma·jor** [méidʒər] *adj.* **1.** greater or large of two things in number, extent, or quality; important. ↔minor ¶*the* ~ *part of* ...① / ~ *industries*② / *a* ~ *poet*③ / *the* ~ *premise.*④ **2.** (*Brit.*) senior. ¶*Brown* ~.⑤ **3.** (*Music*) of a musical scale which has half-tones between the third and fourth, and seventh and eighth notes. ¶*a sonata in C* ~.⑥ **4.** (*U.S.*) of the main subject of study.

—[形] 1. 더 큰, 주요한 ¶①…의 대부분/②주요 산업/③일류 시인/④[논리의] 대전제 2. 《英》 손위의, 형의 ¶⑤큰 쪽의(형인) 브라운 3. 《樂》 장조의 ¶⑥다장조 소나타 4. 《美》 주요 과목의, 전공의

—*n.* [C] **1.** (*Law*) a person of legal age. ↔minor **2.** (*U.S.*) the main subject that a student studies; a student of a special subject. **3.** an army officer ranking above a captain.

—[名] 1. 《法》 성년자 2. 《美》 전공과목; 전공 학생 3. 육군(공군) 소령

—*vi.* (*U.S.*) study a major subject. ¶~ *in English literature*

—[自] 《美》 전공하다

major gen·er·al [⏑– ⏑–⏑] *n.* an army officer ranking below a lieutenant general.

—[名] 육군 소장

* **ma·jor·i·ty** [mədʒɔ́:riti, -dʒár- / -dʒɔ́r-] *n.* (pl. **-ties**) **1.** [C] 《*collectively,* usu. used as *pl.*》 the greater number. ↔minority ¶*an absolute* ~① / *a* ~ *party*② / *a* ~ *proposal*③ / *The* [*great*] ~ *of people wish for peace.*④ / *The* ~ *is for him*⑤ / *be selected by a* ~ *of 30 to 3.* **2.** [C] the number of votes by which one side is larger than another. ¶*win by a* ~ *of 50*⑥ / *by a large* ~.⑦ **3.** [U] the legal age. ¶*He will attain* (or *reach*) *his* ~ *next year.*⑧

—[名] 1. 대다수 ¶①절대 다수/②다수당/③다수안(案)/④대다수의 사람들은 평화를 바라고 있다/⑤대다수는 그에게 찬성이다 2. 득표 차이 ¶⑥50표의 차이로 이기다/⑦큰 차이로 3. 성년 ¶⑧그는 내년에 성인이 된다

⁑ **make** [meik] *v.* (**made**) *vt.* **1.** put things together so as to produce (a new object); build; form. ¶~ *a dress* / ~ *a poem* / *This box is made of wood.* / *Wine is made from grapes.*① ⇒[usage] / *Wheat is made into flour.* **2.** produce something for (someone); produce (something) for someone's use. ¶~ *her a new dress;* ~ *a new dress for her.* **3.** cause (something) to develop. ¶~ *oneself*② / ~ *one's character* / ~ *one's own life.*③ **4.** prepare

—[他] 1. …을 만들다; 조립하다 ¶①포도주는 포도로 만든다 [usage] make of (*or* out of)는 제조 후에도 재료가원형을 보존하는 경우, make…from은 제조 후 그 원료의 질이 변질되는 경우에 씀 2. [남]에게 …을 만들어 주다 3. …을 만들어 내다; 발달시키다 ¶②독학하다; 자기를 형성하다/③생활방침

M

(something) for use; arrange. ¶~ *a bed* / ~ *tea* / ~ *a fire.* **5.** get; earn; win. ¶~ *money* / ~ *one's living* / *How much does he* ~ *a week?*④ **6.** bring about; give rise to; be the cause of (something). ¶~ *a noise* / ~ *trouble.* **7.** do; execute; perform; engage in. ¶~ *a speech* / ~ *an answer* / ~ *one's appearance* / ~ *a decision* / ~ *a discovery* / ~ *a promise* / ~ *a suggestion.* **8.** equal; amount to (a certain quantity). ¶*Two and three make[s] five.* / *Twelve inches* ~ *a foot.*⑤ **9.** become; develop into (a kind of person). ¶*He will* ~ *a good doctor.* / *He will* ~ *her a good husband.*⑥ **10.** reach; arrive at (a place). ¶*He made London on the way to Rome.*⑦ **11.** go; travel; cover the distance of (20 miles, etc.). ¶~ *one's way* / *This car can* ~ *80 miles an hour.* **12.** (of quantity or quality) judge (something) to be; guess. ¶*How large do you* ~ *the party?*⑧ / *I* ~ *it 80.* **13.** form (some idea, etc.) in the mind. ¶~ *a plan* / *What do you* ~ *of this?* **14.** cause (someone or something) to become or to be. ¶*The news made us happy.* / *His father made him a doctor.*; *His father made a doctor of him.* / *I could not* ~ *myself understood in French.*⑨ **15.** cause; force. ⟪~ someone *do*⟫ ⇒[usage] *What made you do such a thing?*⑩

—*vi.* **1.** start; begin an action. ⟪~ *to do*⟫ ¶*She made to go, but I called to her.* **2.** go; proceed. ⟪~ *for* a place⟫ ¶~ *for home.* **3.** (of tides, etc.) flow; rise. ¶*The tide is making fast.*

1) ***make after*** (=*follow; run after*) *something.*
2) ***make against*** (=*be contrary, unfavorable, harmful to*) *something.*
3) ***make away with,*** steal (something) and go away; get rid of, kill, or destroy (something).
4) ***make believe,*** pretend.
5) ***make** something **do; make do with** something,* manage with something though it is not really good nor what is wanted.
6) ***make good*** (=*pay or compensate for*) *a loss.*
7) ***make it,*** succeed.
8) ***make it up*** (=*become friends again*) ***with** someone* [after quarrel].
9) ***make little (much) of,*** treat (something) as of little (much) importance.
10) ***make off,*** hurry away; run away.
11) ***make out,*** ⓐ write out (a list, a check, etc.). ⓑ understand. ⓒ see (something) with difficulty. ⓓ manage; succeed. ⓔ suggest. ⟪~ out *that*...⟫; try to prove. ⟪~ someone or something *to be*⟫
12) ***make** something **over,*** make something different; hand over (one's property, etc.).
13) ***make the best of,*** use (something) in the best way.
14) ***make the most of,*** use (something) to the greatest advantage.
15) ***make up,*** ⓐ put together or form (something). ⓑ invent (a story, an excuse, etc.). ⓒ become friends again. ⓓ put powder, paint, etc. on the face.
16) ***make up*** (=*pay or compensate*) ***for*** a loss.
17) ***make up** one's **mind,*** decide; make a resolution.
18) ***make up to** someone,* flatter.

—*n.* [C] **1.** the way in which something is made; style; build. ¶*a hat of a new* ~. **2.** nature; character. ¶*one's mental* ~. **3.** physical build. ¶*a man of slender* ~. **4.** a sort; a brand. ¶*cars of* ~ / *What* ~ *of car is hers?*⑪ **5.** the amount made. **6.** the act of making. ¶*be in the* ~.⑫

on the make, (*colloq.*) concerned with making a profit.

을 정하다 **4.** …을 준비하다;정비하다 **5.** …을 얻다; 벌다 ¶④그는 1주일에 얼마나 버느냐? **6.** …을 야기하다; …의 원인이 되다 **7.** …을 하다 **8.** …와 같다; 구성하다 ¶⑤12인치는 1피이트가 된다 **9.** …이 되다 ¶⑥그는 그녀에게 좋은 남편이 될 것이다 **10.** …에 도착하다 ¶⑦로마로 가는 도중 런던에 들렀다 **11.** …을 가다; 나아가다 **12.** …을 …으로 간주하다; 판단하다 ¶⑧파아티는 어느 정도의 규모가 될 것 같습니까? **13.** …을 마음에 품다; [생각 따위]를 갖다 **14.** …을 …으로 하다; …으로 되게 하다 ¶⑨프랑스말을 썼더니 알아듣지를 못했다 **15.** …에게…시키다; 억지로 …시키다 [usage] 수동태일 경우는 to do로 됨 ¶⑩왜 그런 짓을 했느냐?

—[自] **1.** …하려고 하다 **2.** 나아가다 **3.** [조수 따위가] 밀려 들다; 늘다

[熟] 1)…을 뒤쫓다 2)…에게 불리해지다; …을 방해하다 3)…을 갖고 도망치다; 없애다, 죽이다 4)…인 체하다 5)…으로 임시변통하다 6)[손실을] 벌충하다, 메우다 7)잘 해내다 8)…와 사화(화해)하다 9)…을 얕보다(중시하다) 10)급히 가 버리다; 도망치다 11)ⓐ[표·어음 따위]를 쓰다 ⓑ이해하다 ⓒ간신히 분간하다 ⓓ이럭저럭 해나가다; 잘 해내다 ⓔ…이라고 하다;증명하다 12)…을 양도하다 13)…을 최대로 이용하다 14)…을 최대로 이용하다 15)ⓐ만들다, 성립시키다 ⓑ[구실 따위]를 꾸며대다 ⓒ화해하다 ⓓ화장(분장)하다 16)…을 메우다, 벌충하다 17)결심하다 18)…의 비위를 맞추다

—[名] **1.** 만듦새; 양식; 지음새 **2.** 성격; 기질 **3.** 체격 **4.** 종류 ¶⑪그녀의 차는 무슨 형입니까? **5.** 생산고 **6.** 제조 ¶⑫제작중이다

[熟] ⟪口⟫성공(승진)을 추구하는

make-be·lieve [méikbilì:v] *n.* **1.** [U] the act of pretending. **2.** [C] a person who pretends. **—***adj.* pretended. ¶~ *sleep.*① —[名] 1. 겉치레; 핑계 2. [···인] 체하는 사람 —[形] 거짓의 ¶①꾀잠

mak·er [méikər] *n.* **1.** [C] a person who makes something. **2.** [U] (*the M-*) God. —[名] 1. 만드는 사람 2. 신(神)

make·shift [méikʃìft] *n.* [C] a thing used for a time instead of the right thing. ¶*use a candle as a* ~.① **—***adj.* temporary. —[名] 임시변통 ¶①양초를 일시적 방편으로 쓰다 —[形] 임시변통의

make-up [méikʌ̀p] *n.* [C] **1.** the way in which a thing is composed; structure. ¶*the mental ~ of a man.*① **2.** nature. ¶*He is of a nervous ~.*② **3.** the way in which an actor paints and powders his face to look his part. **4.** paint and powder put on the face. —[名] 1. 조립;구조 ¶①사람의 정신적 구조 2. 성질 ¶②그는 신경질적인 사람이다 3. [배우의] 화장 4. 화장품

mak·ing [méikiŋ] *n.* [U] **1.** the act or process of making. **2.** structure; make-up. **3.** cause of success; means of advancement. **4.** (usu. *pl.*) capacity; talent. **5.** (*pl.*) material needed for making something. **6.** [C] something made. —[名] 1. 만들기, 발전의 과정 2. 조립;구조 3. [성공·발전의] 원인 4. 소질, 자질(資質) 5. 원료, 재료 6. 제조품, 만들어진 것

in the making, in the process of being made; not yet completed. [熟] 제작중의; 미완성의

mal- [mæl-] *pref.* **1.** bad; badly: *maltreat* (=treat badly). **2.** not; un-: *malcontent.* **3.** imperfect: *malformation.* —(接頭) 1. 나쁜, 나쁘게 2. 불(不)··· 3. 불완전한

mal·ad·just·ed [mæ̀lədʒʌ́stid] *adj.* **1.** poorly adjusted. **2.** not well fit for one's circumstances. ¶*a ~ child.* —[形] 1. 조절이 잘 안 된 2. 환경에 적응하지 못하는

mal·ad·just·ment [mæ̀lədʒʌ́stmənt] *n.* [U][C] the state of being maladjusted. —[名] 조절 불량; 부적응

mal·a·droit [mæ̀lədrɔ́it] *adj.* **1.** not skillful. **2.** not clever; not smart. —[形] 1. 서투른 2. 꾀(재치) 없는

mal·a·dy [mǽlədi] *n.* [C] (pl. **-dies**) a disease; a sickness; an illness. —[名] 질병; 병폐, 폐해

ma·lar·i·a [məlέəriə] *n.* [U] a tropical illness with a high fever, chills, and sweating caused by the bite of a certain kind of mosquito. —[名] 말라리아

ma·lar·i·al [məlέəriəl] *adj.* of malaria. ¶~ *fever.* —[形] 말라리아의

Ma·lay [məléi, +*U.S.* méilei] *n.* **1.** [C] a group of brown-skinned people living on the Malay Peninsula and nearby islands. **2.** [U] their language. **—***adj.* of Malay; of the language and people of Malay. —[名] 1. 말레이 사람 2. 말레이 말 —[形] 말레이의, 말레이 사람(말)의

Ma·lay·a [məléiə] *n.* the Malay Peninsula. —[名] 말레이 반도

Ma·lay·an [məléiən] *n., adj.* =Malay.

Ma·lay·sia [məléiʒə, -ʃə / -ziə] *n.* an independent federation of southeast Asia; the Malay Archipelago. —[名] 말레이지아; 말레이 제도

Ma·lay·sian [məléiʒən, -ʃən/-ziən] *n.* [C] a person of Malaysia. **—***adj.* of Malaysia, its people and their language. —[名] 말레이지아 사람 —[形] 말레이 제도[사람·말]의

mal·con·tent [mǽlkəntènt] *adj.* not contented. **—***n.* [C] a person who is not contented. —[形] 불만의 —[名] 불만을 품은 사람

* **male** [meil] *adj.* **1.** of the sex such as men, boys, and he-animals. ↔female ¶*a ~ animal.* **2.** of a plant that does not produce fruit. **—***n.* [C] **1.** a person or an animal of this sex. **2.** a male plant. ↔female —[形] 1. 남자의, 수컷의 2. 수술만 있는, 웅성(雄性)의 —[名] 1. 남자; 수컷 2. 웅성 식물

mal·e·dic·tion [mæ̀lidíkʃ(ə)n] *n.* [C] the act or fact of speaking evil of someone; a curse. ↔benediction —[名] 악담; 저주

mal·e·fac·tion [mæ̀lifǽkʃ(ə)n] *n.* [U][C] an evil act. ↔benefaction —[名] 못된 짓, 죄악

mal·e·fac·tor [mǽlifæ̀ktər] *n.* [C] **1.** a person who does an evil act. **2.** a person who commits a crime. ↔benefactor —[名] 1. 악인 2. 범인

ma·lef·i·cent [məléfisnt] *adj.* **1.** hurtful; harmful. **2.** causing evil. —[形] 1. 유해한 2. 못된 짓을 하는

ma·lev·o·lence [məlévələns] *n.* [U] the wish that something bad or harmful may happen to others; ill will. ↔benevolence —[名] 악의, 남의 불행을 바라는 마음

ma·lev·o·lent [məlévələnt] *adj.* showing malevolence; full of ill-feeling. —[形] 악의를 품은

mal·fea·sance [mælfí:z(ə)ns] *n.* [U][C] (*Law*) an evil deed by an official in relation to public affairs. —[名] (法) [공무원의] 부정행위, 비행

mal·for·ma·tion [mæ̀lfɔ:rméiʃ(ə)n] *n.* [U] the wrong and abnormal structure of a body or a part of it. —[名] 기형, 불구

* **mal·ice** [mǽlis] *n.* [U] the evil desire to hurt others; —[名] 적의(敵意); 악의

M

ill-will. ¶*She didn't do it out of ~.*

bear malice to (or ***toward***), have an evil will toward (someone).

[熟] …에 적의를 품다

ma·li·cious [məlíʃəs] *adj.* showing the desire to hurt others; having ill-will.

—[形] 심술궂은; 악의를 품은

ma·li·cious·ly [məlíʃəsli] *adv.* with the desire to hurt others.

—[副] 악의를 품고

ma·lign [məláin] *adj.* filled with harm; having a desire to hurt others; malignant. ↔benign ¶*have a ~ influence.*① —*vt.* speak evil of (someone); curse.

—[形] 유해한; 악성의; 적의를 품은 ¶①나쁜 영향이 있다 —[他] …을 비방(중상)하다; 저주하다

ma·lig·nan·cy [məlígnənsi], **-nance** [-nəns] *n.* [U] **1.** the state of being malignant. **2.** (*Medicine*) the tendency to cause death.

—[名] 1. 악의, 적의 2. [병의] 악성, 불치증(不治症)

ma·lig·nant [məlígnənt] *adj.* **1.** showing the desire to hurt others. **2.** (*Medicine*) dangerous; causing death. ↔benignant ¶*a ~ disease.* ▷**ma·lig·nant·ly** [-li] *adv.*

—[形] 1. 악의의 2. 악성의; 생명에 관계되는

ma·lig·ni·ty [məlígniti] *n.* (pl. **-ties**) [U] **1.** the state of being malign. **2.** (*Medicine*) the quality of being malignant.

—[名] 1. 악의 2. [병의] 악성

mal·lard [mǽlərd] *n.* [C] (pl. **-lards** or *collectively* **-lard**) a male wild duck; any common wild duck.

—[名] 물오리의 수컷

mal·le·a·bil·i·ty [mæ̀liəbíliti] *n.* [U] the quality or state of being malleable.

—[名] [금속의] 가단성(可鍛性), 유연성, 순응성

mal·le·a·ble [mǽliəbl] *adj.* **1.** that can be struck or pressed into various shapes by a hammer without being broken. **2.** that can fit oneself to new conditions.

—[形] 1. 가단성[전성(展性)]이 있는 2. 순응성이 있는

mal·low [mǽlou] *n.* [C] a plant with pink and white flowers and hairy leaves and stems.

—[名] 아욱속(屬)

mal·nu·tri·tion [mæ̀ln(j)u(:)tríʃ(ə)n / -nju(:)-] *n.* [U] lack of nourishment caused by poor food or wrong diet.

—[名] 영양불량(실조)

mal·o·dor·ous [mælóudərəs] *adj.* smelling bad.

—[形] 악취가 나는

mal·prac·tice [mælprǽktis] *n.* [C] **1.** (*Medicine*) a doctor's unlawful and injurious treatment of a patient. **2.** (*Law*) an official's wrong act or practice.

—[名] 1. [의사의] 부정 요법 2. [공무원의] 배임행위

malt [mɔ:lt] *n.* [U] **1.** barley or other grain which has begun to grow in water, then dried and used in making strong drinks. **2.** (*colloq.*) beer or ale. —***adj.*** made with malt. ¶*~ liquor*① / *~ sugar.*② —***vt.*** **1.** change (grain) into malt. **2.** make (liquor) with malt. —***vi.*** change into malt.

—[名] 1. 맥아(麥芽), 엿기름 2. 《口》 맥주 —[形] 엿기름으로 만든 ¶①맥아주(ale, beer, stout)/②맥아당(糖) —[他] 1. …을 맥아로 만들다 2. …에 맥아를 넣다 —[自] 맥아로 되다

mal·treat [mæltrí:t] *vt.* treat or use in a wrong manner.

—[他] …을 학대하다, 혹사하다

mal·treat·ment [mæltrí:tmənt] *n.* [U] rough and unkind treatment.

—[名] 학대, 혹사

* **ma·ma** [má:mə / məmá:] *n.* [C] a mother; a mamma.

—[名] 엄마

‡ **mam·ma** [má:mə / məmá:] *n.* [C] (chiefly a *child's word*) a mother. ↔papa

—[名] 《주로 小兒》 엄마

mam·mal [mǽməl] *n.* [C] an animal that has a backbone and feeds its young with its milk, such as human beings, dogs, bats, or whales.

—[名] 포유동물

mam·moth [mǽməθ] *n.* [C] a very large, hairy elephant with long curved tusks which disappeared from the earth in prehistoric ages. —***adj.*** very large; gigantic. ¶*a ~ enterprise*① / *a ~ ship.*②

—[名] 매머드 —[形] 거대한, 매머드 같은 ¶①거대(매머드) 기업/②초대형선

* **mam·my** [mǽmi] *n.* (pl. **-mies**) [C] **1.** (*a child's word*) a mother. ↔daddy. **2.** a Negro woman who looks after white children in the southern States of the United States.

—[名] 1. 《小兒》 엄마 2. [미국 남부의 백인에게 고용된] 흑인 할멈(아줌마)

‡ **man** [mæn] *n.* (pl. **men**) [C] **1.** a grown male person. ↔woman; boy **2.** a human being; a person. ¶*Any ~ can do it.* / *What can a ~ do in such a case?* **3.** 《*sing.* only, without an *article*》 the human race. ¶*Man is mortal.*① **4.** a male employee; a manservant or a workman; 《usu. *pl.*》 soldiers, esp. common soldiers. ¶*officers and men.*② **5.** a husband. ¶*~ and wife.* **6.** a person with manly qualities. ¶*play the ~*③ / *He was*

—[名] 1. [남자] 어른 2. 사람 3. 인간, 인류 ¶①인간은 죽는다 4. 사용인, 머슴, 노동자; 군인, 병사 ¶②장교와 병졸 5. 남편 6. 사내다운 사람; 대장부 ¶③사내답게 굴다/④그는 철두철미 사내다왔다 7. [체스·체커의] 말, 졸

manacle [699] **mane**

every inch a ~. 7. one of the pieces used in playing chess or checkers. ⌈in chorus.⌉
1) *as one man,* in complete agreement; with one voice;
2) *be one's own man,* be free to do as one pleases.
3) *make a man of,* make (someone) honorable.
4) *man and boy,* (as *adv. phrase*) from boyhood on.
5) *to a man,* all; without exception.
—*vt.* (**manned, man·ning**) **1.** supply (a ship, a fort, etc.) with men. ¶*~ the ship with 50 sailors.* **2.** take (one's place) for work. ¶*a ship manned by sailors.* **3.** make (someone) strong or manly. ¶*~ oneself.*③

man·a·cle [mǽnəkl] *n.* ⓒ **1.** (usu. *pl.*) rings or chains to lock about the wrist of a prisoner; a handcuff. **2.** restriction. —*vt.* **1.** put manacles on (someone). **2.** place restrictions on (someone).

‡**man·age** [mǽnidʒ] *vt.* **1.** control; direct; handle. ¶*~ a boat / ~ one's husband / ~ a business.* **2.** succeed somehow in doing (something). 《*~ to do*》 ¶*I think I can ~ it.*① / *She managed to get what she wanted.*② **3.** (*colloq.*) (often with *can*) eat. ¶*Can you ~ another piece of cake?* —*vi.* **1.** deal with affairs; do business. ¶*I won't be able to ~ without help.* **2.** get along. ¶*Does he ~ on his monthly income?*

man·age·a·ble [mǽnidʒəbl] *adj.* that can be managed; easily controlled or managed.

‡**man·age·ment** [mǽnidʒmənt] *n.* Ⓤ **1.** the act of managing. ¶*The firm is under foreign ~.*① **2.** the managing ability. ¶*The business failed because of poor ~.*② **3.** Ⓤ Ⓒ (*collectively*) persons who are in charge of a business. ¶*~ and labor.*③

‡**man·ag·er** [mǽnidʒər] *n.* ⓒ **1.** a person who is in charge of management. ¶*a stage ~.*① **2.** a person who looks after a household skillfully. ¶*His wife is a poor ~.*

man·ag·ing [mǽnidʒiŋ] *adj.* **1.** having a power of controlling. ¶*a ~ director.*① **2.** skillful in managing. **3.** too careful and economical about money. **4.** wishing to control others.

man-at-arms [mǽnətáːrmz] *n.* ⓒ (pl. **men-** [mén-]) a soldier, esp. a heavily armed soldier on horseback in the Middle Ages.

Man·ches·ter [mǽntʃestər] *n.* a town in Lancashire, the center of cotton manufacturing in western England. ¶*~ goods.*①

man·da·rin [mǽndərin] *n.* **1.** ⓒ a Chinese official of high rank in the old Chinese Empire. **2.** Ⓤ (*M-*) one of the Chinese dialects spoken by educated Chinese. **3.** ⓒ a kind of small, sweet orange; a tangerine. ¶*a ~ orange.* **4.** Ⓤ deep orange-colored dye.

man·da·tar·y [mǽndətèri / -t(ə)ri] *n.* (pl. **-taries**) (*Law*) ⓒ a person or a country that carries out a mandate over another person or country.

man·date [mǽndeit] *n.* ⓒ **1.** an official command. **2.** orders from people to those chosen (usu. shown by election.) —*vt.* put (a country or a land) under the rule of another country.

man·da·to·ry [mǽndətɔ̀ːri / -t(ə)ri] *adj.* **1.** having a nature of command. **2.** having control over another country or person. ¶*~ administration*① / *a ~ power.*② —*n.* ⓒ a mandatary.

man·do·lin [mǽnd(ə)lin] *n.* ⓒ a musical instrument with a round sound box and wire strings.

mane [mein] *n.* ⓒ **1.** the long hair growing on the back of or about the neck of a horse, lion, etc. **2.** a person's long and thick hair like mane.

熟 1)만장일치로; 일제히; 이구 동성으로 2)남의 지배를 받지 않다 3)…을 장성한(능력있는) 사나이로 만들다 4) 소년시절부터 5)한 사람 남김 없이; 예외 없이
—他 1. [배 따위]에 인원을 배치하다 2. …에 착수하다; 자기 부서에 임하다 3. …을 기운내게 하다 ¶⑤분기하다

—名 1. 수갑 2. 구속 —他 1. …에 수갑을 채우다 2. …을 속박하다

—他 1. …을 제어하다;다루다;경영(관리)하다 2. 잘(용케) …하다 ¶①어떻게 든 그것을 할 수 있으리라 생각한다 /②그녀는 바라던 것을 용케 입수했다 3. (口) …을 먹다 —自 1. 사무를 처리하다;사업을 경영하다 2. 이럭저럭 살아가다(해나가다)

—形 다룰 수 있는; 관리하기 쉬운, 처리하기 쉬운

—名 1. 다루기, 통어(統御) ¶①회사는 외국인이 관리하고 있다 2. 경영[의 재능], 지배[력] ¶②사업은 경영이 서툴러서 실패했다 3. 경영자측 ¶③노사(勞使) 양측

—名 경영자, 지배인, 감독 ¶①무대 감독 2. [집안 일 따위의] 꾸려나가는 사람

—形 1. 지배하는, 관리하는 ¶①전무이사 2. 경영을 잘하는 3. 인색한 4. 참견하기 좋아하는

—名 [중세의] 장갑(기마)병

—名 영국 서부의 면업(綿業) 중심지 ¶①맨체스터제(製) 면포류

—名 1. [중국 청나라 따위의] 관리 2. [중국의] 관화(官話), 표준어 3. 귤 4. 등황색(橙黃色)의 염료

—名 《法》 수탁자(受託者), 위임 통치국

—名 1. 명령, 훈령 2. [선거구민이 위임한] 권한 —他 …의 통치를 위임하다

—形 1. 명령의 2. 위임의 ¶①위임 통치/②위임 통치국 —名 위임을 받은 사람(나라)

—名 만돌린

—名 1. [말의] 갈기 2. 갈기 같은 머리털

man-eat·er [mænìːtər] *n.* ⓒ **1.** a person eating human flesh; a cannibal. **2.** an animal that eats human flesh, esp. a shark, lion, or tiger.
—图 1.식인종 2.식인 상어(사자·호랑이)

ma·neu·ver, *Brit.* **-noeu·vre** [mənúːvər] *n.* ⓒ **1.** a well-planned movement or change of position of troops or ships. **2.** (*pl.*) a series of military exercises done under conditions like a real war. **3.** a skillful movement or plan. ¶ *a political* ~.①
—*vi.* (of troops, ships, etc.) move according to a plan.
—*vt.* **1.** cause (troops, ships, etc.) to move or change their position according to a plan. **2.** handle skillfully.
—图 1.[군대·함대의] 전략적 이동, 작전 행동 2.[군대의] 연습 3.교묘한 행동, 책략 ¶①정치 공작
—图 [군대·함대가] [기동]연습하다
—他 1.[군대·함대]를 기동연습시키다 2.책략으로 …시키다

man·ful [mænf(u)l] *adj.* showing bravery and determination like a man. ↔*cowardly*　[*r.* man.)
man·ful·ly [mænfuli] *adv.* resolutely and bravely like)
—图 사내다운, 씩씩한
—图 사내답게

man·ga·nese [mæŋɡənìːz, ⌐⌐] *n.* ⓤ a hard and gray metal element that is easily broken, used in making glass, paint, and medicine.
—图 망간

man·ger [méindʒər] *n.* ⓒ a box to place hay in for feeding cattle and horses.
—图 여물통, 구유

man·gle¹ [mæŋɡl] *vt.* **1.** cut (flesh, etc.) into pieces. **2.** spoil (something) by mistakes.
—他 1.…을 갈기갈기 썰다, 난도질하다 2.[잘못하여] …을 망쳐 놓다

man·gle² [mæŋɡl] *n.* ⓒ a machine for pressing wet clothes to dry them. ⇒fig. —*vt.* press (wet clothes, etc.) with a mangle.
—图 [빨래 마무리용의] 압착 로울러
—他 …을 압착 로울러에 걸다

man·go [mæŋɡou] *n.* ⓒ (pl. **-goes** or **-gos**) a pear-shaped, juicy, yellowish-red fruit grown in the tropical zone; a tree bearing this fruit.　[mangle²]
—图 망고 열매; 망고 나무

man·go·steen [mæŋɡoustìːn] *n.* ⓒ a juicy, reddish-brown fruit grown in the East Indies; a tree bearing this fruit.
—图 망고스틴의 열매; 그 나무

man·han·dle [mænhændl] *vt.* **1.** move (something) by human strength. **2.** treat roughly.
—他 1.…을 인력으로 움직이다 2.…을 거칠게 다루다

Man·hat·tan [mænhǽt(ə)n] *n.* the island which contains the main business section of New York City.
—图 맨해턴 섬(뉴욕시의 주요 상가)

man·hole [mænhòul] *n.* ⓒ a hole through which a man enters an underground pipe or channel to inspect or repair it.
—图 맨호울

* **man·hood** [mænhùd] *n.* ⓤ **1.** the state or quality of being a man. **2.** the time of being a man. ¶ *be in early* ~① / *grow to* ~.② **3.** a manly quality. ¶ *be in the prime of* ~.③ **4.** ((*collectively*)) men. [The adult.)
—图 1.인간다움 2.성인 ¶①성인이 된 지 얼마 안 되다/②어른이 되다 3.남자다움 ¶③남자로서 한창때이다 4.남자

man·hood suf·frage [⌐⌐ ⌐⌐] *n.* ⓒ the right to vote for)
—图 보통 선거권

man·hour [mænáuər] *n.* ⓒ a time-unit of work equal to an hour of work done by one man.
—图 연(延)시간(한 사람 한 시간의 노동량)

ma·ni·a [méiniə] *n.* **1.** ⓤ a kind of violent madness and wild excitement. **2.** ⓒ a strong liking; unusual enthusiasm. ¶ *a* ~ *for dancing.*① 　[man; a lunatic.)
—图 1.[정신병의] 조병(躁病) 2.열광, …광(狂) ¶①댄스광

ma·ni·ac [méiniæk] *adj.* mad; insane. —*n.* ⓒ a mad-)
—图 광인의, 미친 —图 광인

ma·ni·a·cal [mənáiək(ə)l] *adj.* insane; mad; crazy.
—图 미친

ma·ni·a·cal·ly [mənáiək(ə)li] *adv.* in a wild and mad way.
—图 미친 듯이

man·i·cure [mænikjùər] *n.* ⓤ the act of polishing and cleaning the fingernails. —*vt.* give a manicure to (the fingernails). ¶ *have one's fingernails manicured.*
—图 매니큐어 —他 [손톱]에 매니큐어를 하다

man·i·cur·ist [mænikjùərist] *n.* ⓒ a person who manicures others as a profession.
—图 매니큐어사(師)

* **man·i·fest** [mænifèst] *adj.* clear to be seen. —*vt.* **1.** show clearly. **2.** make (something) clear to be true; prove. ¶ ~ *the truth.* **3.** show (one's feelings). ¶ ~ *dissatisfaction.* —*vi.* (of a ghost, etc.) appear.
—图 분명한 —他 1.…을 뚜렷이 나타내다 2.…을 증명하다 3.[감정 따위]를 나타내다 —图 [유령 따위가] 나타나다

man·i·fes·ta·tion [mænifestéiʃ(ə)n] *n.* ⓒⓤ **1.** the act of manifesting. **2.** something that manifests; a dis-
—图 I.명시 2.나타남; 표시; 입증 3.[정부·정당의] 정견 발표

manifesto [701] **man-of-war**

play; a proof. **3.** a public announcement of policy, etc.
man·i·fes·to [mæ̀niféstou] *n.* ⓒ (pl. **-tos** or **-toes**) a public declaration of thoughts, plans, etc. by a government or an important person or group. ¶*a political ~.* —ⓝ [정책 따위의] 선언[서]; 성명[서]

* **man·i·fold** [mǽnifòuld] *adj.* **1.** of many kinds; various. **2.** having many parts or forms. —*n.* ⓒ **1.** a pipe with several openings used for connecting with other pipes. **2.** one of many copies. —*vt.* make many copies of (something) by means of a duplicating machine. —ⓗ 1. 여러가지의, 많은 종류의 2. 다방면의 —ⓝ 1. 분기관(分岐管) 2. [1통의] 사본 —ⓥ [복사기로] …의 사본을 많이 뜨다

man·i·kin [mǽnikin] *n.* ⓒ **1.** a small man; a dwarf. **2.** an anatomical model of the human body, used by artists, tailors, etc. **3.** a mannequin. —ⓝ 1. 난장이 2. 인체 해부 모형 3. 모델 인형, 마네킨

Ma·nil·a [mənílə] *n.* **1.** a city in the Philippines. →N.B. **2.** (often *m-*) Ⓤ Manila hemp; Manila rope; Manila paper. —ⓝ 1. 마닐라 N.B. 필리핀의 수도 2. 마닐라 삼; 마닐라 로우프; 마닐라 종이

ma·nip·u·late [mənípjulèit] *vt.* **1.** handle (machines) skillfully with the hands. **2.** manage (someone) cleverly by using unfair means. **3.** treat (an account, etc.) dishonestly for one's own advantage. —ⓥ 1. …을 손으로 교묘하게 다루다 2. …을 부정수단으로 조종하다 3. [장부]를 조작하다, 농간부리다

ma·nip·u·la·tion [mənìpjuléiʃ(ə)n] *n.* ⓊⒸ the act of manipulating or handling skillfully; good use of the hands. —ⓝ 교묘하게 다루기; 교묘한 손재주

ma·nip·u·la·tor [mənípjulèitər] *n.* ⓒ a person who manipulates. —ⓝ 손으로 교묘하게 다루는 사람; 조종자

‡ **man·kind** *n.* Ⓤ **1.** [mænkáind →2.] the human race. ¶*the welfare of ~.* **2.** [ˋˋ] the male sex; men. ↔**womankind** —ⓝ 1. 인류, 사람 2. 남자

man·like [mǽnlàik] *adj.* like a man in nature. —ⓗ 남자다운; 남성적인

man·li·ness [mǽnlinis] *n.* Ⓤ the state of being manly. —ⓝ 남자다움

* **man·ly** [mǽnli] *adj.* (**-li·er, -li·est**) manlike (frank, brave, honorable, strong, etc.). ↔**womanly** ¶*a ~ man*① / *in a ~ way.*② —ⓗ 사나이다운, 씩씩한 ¶①남성적인 남자/②사내답게

man-made [mǽnméid] *adj.* **1.** made by man. **2.** made up chemically and not by a natural means. —ⓗ 1. 인공의 2. 합성의

man·na [mǽnə] *n.* ⓒ 1. Ⓤ (in the Bible) the food supplied to the Israelites in the wilderness. **2.** holy food. **3.** something good unexpectedly given. —ⓝ 1. 이스라엘 사람이 광야에서 신에게서 받은 음식물 2. 하늘이 베푸는 물건 3. 뜻밖에 얻은 것

man·ne·quin [mǽnikin] *n.* ⓒ **1.** a woman who puts on new clothes and shows them to the customers in a shop. **2.** =manikin (3.) —ⓝ 마네킨

‡ **man·ner** [mǽnər] *n.* ⓒ **1.** the way in which something happens or is done. ¶*after this ~*① / *in such a ~.*② **2.** the way of acting or behaving. ¶*a kind (an awkward) ~.*③ **3.** (*pl.*) personal behavior in public; polite ways of behaving. ¶*good (bad) manners* / *She has no manners.*④ **4.** (*pl.*) customs; ways of living. ¶*manners and customs.*⑤ **5.** a style in literature or art. ¶*a picture in the ~ of Picasso.*⑥ **6.** (pl. **man·ner**) a kind or sort. ¶*all ~ of things.*
1) *by all manner of means*, most certainly.
2) *by no manner of means*, by no means; not at all.
3) *in a manner*, to some degree or extent. —ⓝ 1. 방법, 방식 ¶①,②이런 식으로 2. 태도, 모양, 거동 ¶③친절한(어색한) 태도 3. 예절, 예법 ¶④그녀에게는 예절을 모른다 4. 습관; 풍습 ¶⑤풍속 습관 5. [예술상의] 양식, …류(流), 작풍(作風) ¶⑥피카소풍의 그림 6. 종류

圖 1)확실히, 어떻게 해서든 2)결코 … 않다 3)다소; 어느 의미에서는

man·nered [mǽnərd] *adj.* **1.** having manners of a certain kind. ¶*well-mannered.* **2.** affected; having mannerism. —ⓗ 1. 예절이 …한 2. 틀에 박힌

man·ner·ism [mǽnərìz(ə)m] *n.* Ⓤ too much use of the same style in speaking, writing, behaving, etc. **2.** a strange habit. [manners.] —ⓝ 1. 매너리즘(문체 따위가 틀에 박히는 일) 2. [언어·동작의] 버릇

man·ner·less [mǽnərlis] *adj.* impolite; lacking good —ⓗ 예절을 모르는

man·ner·ly [mǽnərli] *adj.* polite; having good manners. —ⓗ 예의바른

man·ni·kin [mǽnikin] *n.* ⓒ =manikin.

man·nish [mǽniʃ] *adj.* **1.** like a man. **2.** trying to be like a grown-up man. ▷**man·nish·ly** [-li] *adv.* —ⓗ 1. 남자 같은 2. 어른 티를 내는

ma·noeu·vre [mənúːvər] *n., v.* (*Brit.*) =maneuver.

man-of-war [mǽnəvwɔ́ːr] *n.* (pl. **men-** [mén-]) ⓒ a warship. —ⓝ 군함

manor — manuscript

man·or [mǽnər] *n.* ⓒ a piece of land part of which is used by the owner and the rest is farmed by his peasants. —图 장원(莊園)

ma·no·ri·al [mənɔ́ːriəl] *adj.* of a manor. —형 장원의

man power [´ ² ´] *n.* **1.** man's physical power. **2.** (*Machinery*) 1/10 horsepower. —图 1. 인력 2. 1/10 마력

man·pow·er [mǽnpàuər] *n.* Ⓤ the total amount of labor force needed for a piece of work; the number of workers needed for such a force. —图 인력; 유효(소요) 총인원

man·sard [mǽnsɑːrd] *n.* ⓒ **1.** a roof having two slopes on each side. ⇒fig. **2.** a room just below the roof; an attic. —图 1. 2 단으로 경사진 지붕 2. [그러한 지붕의] 다락방

man·serv·ant [mǽnsə̀ːrvənt] *n.* ⓒ (pl. **men·serv·ants**) a male servant. —图 하인, 머슴

man·sion [mǽnʃ(ə)n] *n.* ⓒ a very large house; a grand residence. —图 대저택

[mansard 1.]

man·slaugh·ter [mǽnslɔ̀ːtər] *n.* Ⓤ **1.** the act of killing a person. **2.** (*Law*) the act of killing a person unlawfully but without planning to do so. ⇒N.B. —图 1. 살인 2. (法) 과실 치사 N.B. murder 보다 가벼운 죄

man·tel [mǽntl] *n.* =mantelpiece.

man·tel·piece [mǽntlpìːs] *n.* ⓒ **1.** a decorated frame above and around a fireplace. ⇒N.B., fig. **2.** (*U.S.*) the shelf above a fireplace. (cf. *Brit.* mantelshelf) —图 1. 벽난로 장식 N.B. 미국에서는 보통 mantel 2. 벽난로 선반

man·tel·shelf [mǽntlʃèlf] *n.* (pl. **-shelves**) =mantelpiece.

man·tel·shelves [mǽntlʃelvz] *n.* pl. of mantelshelf.

man·tes [mǽntiːz] *n.* pl. of mantis.

man·tis [mǽntis] *n.* ⓒ (pl. **-tis·es** or **-tes**) an insect that folds its front legs as if praying and attacks and eats other insects. —图 사마귀(곤충)

[mantelpiece 1.]

man·tle [mǽntl] *n.* ⓒ **1.** a loose cape or cloak. **2.** a cover. ¶*a soft ~ of snow.* —*vt.* **1.** cover (something) with a mantle. ¶*peaks mantled with snow.* **2.** conceal —*vi.* **1.** (of the face) become red; blush. **2.** spread the wings over the legs. **3.** form a coating on a surface. —图 1. 망토; 외투 2. 덮개; 뚜껑 —他 1. …을 망토로 싸다 2. [물건]을 감추다 —他 1. [얼굴이] 붉어지다 2. 날개를 펴다 3. 더껑이가 앉다

man·u·al [mǽnjuəl] *adj.* done or worked by hand. ¶*~ crafts*① / *~ training* / *~ work* (or *labor*)② / *a sign ~.*③ —*n.* **1.** a small guide book; a handbook. ¶*a reference ~ for students* / *a teacher's ~.* **2.** (*Military*) the drill in handling weapons. **3.** an organ keyboard. ▷**man·u·al·ly** [-i] *adv.* —图 손의; 손으로 하는 ¶①수공업/②공작/③자서(自署) —图 1. 편람; 입문서; 소책자; 안내서 2. (軍) 집총훈련 3. [오르간의] 건반

man·u·fac·to·ry [mæ̀njufǽkt(ə)ri] *n.* ⓒ (pl. **-ries**) a factory; a workshop. ⇒N.B. [making of articles.] —图 제조소, 공장 N.B. 현재는 factory 를 많이 씀

man·u·fac·tur·al [mæ̀njufǽktʃərəl] *adj.* relating to the

: **man·u·fac·ture** [mæ̀njufǽktʃər] *vt.* **1.** make (things) from raw materials by hand or by machine in a factory. ¶*toys manufactured in Korea* **2.** write (novels, etc.) too much or too easily. **3.** make up (a story). —*n.* **1.** Ⓤ the making of something in a factory, usu. on a large scale. ¶*cotton ~* / *home ~* / *iron ~.* **2.** ⓒ articles; anything made. ¶*a Korean ~.* —图 제조[업]의 —他 1. …을 제조하다 2. [소설 따위를] 남작(濫作)하다 3. [이야기]를 꾸며내다, 날조하다 —图 1. [대량의] 제조; 제조 공업 2. 제품

: **man·u·fac·tur·er** [mæ̀njufǽktʃərər] *n.* ⓒ a person who manufactures, esp. an owner of a workshop. —图 [대규모의] 제조업; 제조 업자, [특히] 공장주

man·u·fac·tur·ing [mæ̀njufǽktʃəriŋ] *adj.* engaged in manufacture. ¶*a ~ industry.*① —图 제조[업]에 종사하는 ¶①제조공업

ma·nure [mən(j)úər / -njúə] *n.* Ⓤ material added to or spread over the soil to make it richer. ¶*artificial ~*① / *farmyard ~.*② —*vt.* put manure on or in (a place). —图 비료; 거름 ¶①인조 비료/②퇴비 —他 …에 비료를 주다

· **man·u·script** [mǽnjuskrìpt] *n.* ⓒ **1.** a book or paper written by hand or on the typewriter, not printed. **2.** —图 1. 사본(寫本) 2. 원고 N.B. MS. 로 줄임. 복수는 MSS. —图 사본의,

an author's copy written by hand. ⇒[N.B.] —*adj.* written by hand or with a typewriter.
원고의

‡ **man·y** [méni] *adj.* (**more, most**) a large number of; a lot of. ↔few ⇒[usage] ¶*Did you see ~ children there?*
1) ***a good*** (or ***great***) ***many,*** a large number of.
2) ***as*** (or ***so***) ***many,*** the same in number as. ¶*He made five mistakes in as ~ lines.*① / *Those ten days in the town were like so ~ years to me.*②
3) ***as many as,*** of the same number as.
4) ***many a,*** many.
5) ***many times,*** often.
6) ***one too many for,*** more than a match for; cleverer than.
—*n.* (*collectively,* used as *pl.*) **1.** a great number; many people or things. ¶*Many of them are poor.* **2.** (*the ~*) most people; the public.

—[形] [수가] 많은, 다수의 [usage] 주어를 수식하는 경우 이외는 보통 a large number of, a lot of 따위를 씀
[熟] 1)다수의 2)…와 같은 수의 ¶①그는 5행 속에 다섯 군데가 틀렸다/②이 도시에서의 열흘간은 나에게 10년간처럼 느껴졌다 3)…와 동수의, …의 수만큼 4)많은 5)몇 번이고 6)하나가 더 많은, …보다 영리한
—[名] 1. 다수; 다수의 사람(것) 2. 대다수의 사람들, 민중

man·y-sid·ed [ménisáidid] *adj.* **1.** having many sides or aspects. **2.** having many interests or abilities.
—[形] 1. 다방면의 2. 다재다능한

‡ **map** [mæp] *n.* [C] a drawing or model of the surface of the earth or part of it, showing countries, rivers, mountains, etc.
—*vt.* (**mapped, map·ping**) draw or make a map of (a place).
map out, plan; arrange. ¶*~ out a new city.*
—[名] [한 장의] 지도
—[他] …의 지도를 만들다
[熟] …의 계획을 세우다; 만반의 조치를 해두다

* **ma·ple** [méipl] *n.* [U] **1.** [C] a kind of tree found in the northern zone with star-shaped leaves and winged seeds. **2.** the wood of this tree. **3.** the sap of certain kinds of maples, used in making sugar and syrup.
—[名] 1. 단풍나무 2. 단풍나무 재목 3. 단풍 당밀

* **mar** [ma:*r*] *vt.* (**marred, mar·ring**) damage; spoil. ¶*~ the beauty of the streets.*①
—[他] …에 흠을 내다, 못쓰게 만들다 ¶①거리의 미관을 해치다

Mar. March.

mar·a·thon [mǽrəθàn / -θ(ə)n] *n.* **1.** (*M-*) an old battlefield near Athens, in Greece. **2.** [C] a long distance foot race of 42.195 kilometers. **3.** [C] any long contest or race.
—[名] 1. 그리이스의 옛싸움터 2. 마라톤 경주 3. [일반적으로] 장거리 경주

ma·raud [mərɔ́:d] *vi.* (as in war) wander about in search of something valuable. ¶*~ on a town.*① —*vt.* take (something) by force.
—[自] 약탈하다 ¶①약탈하기 위해 도시를 습격하다 —[他] …을 약탈하다

ma·raud·er [mərɔ́:də*r*] *n.* [C] a person or an animal that marauds.
—[名] 약탈자, 약탈하며 다니는 짐승

‡ **mar·ble** [má:*r*bl] *n.* [U] **1.** a white or colored hard limestone used in making statues and buildings. **2.** (*pl.*) a group of sculptures made of marble. **3.** [C] a small round piece, esp. of marble or other hard stone used as a child's plaything.
—*adj.* **1.** like marble; white. **2.** heartless.
—[名] 1. 대리석 2. 대리석 조각품 3. 공깃돌
—[形] 1. 대리석의; 흰 2. 무정한

mar·bled [má:*r*bld] *adj.* colored to look like marble.
—[形] 대리석 무늬의

mar·ble-heart·ed [má:*r*blhá:*r*tid] *adj.* heartless like a stone; having no feeling.
—[形] [돌처럼] 무정한, 감각 없는

‡ **march** [ma:*r*tʃ] *vi.* **1.** walk with a regular step like soldiers. ¶*The army marched into the town.*① **2.** progress regularly. ¶*Science has marched forward tremendously these past few decades.*② —*vt.* cause (someone) to move on. ¶*They marched him off to prison.*
—*n.* **1.** [U][C] the act of marching. **2.** [C] progress. ¶*the ~ of time.* **3.** [U] pace. ¶*double ~*③ / *quick ~.* **4.** [C] a musical composition for marching.
1) ***be on*** (or ***in***) ***the march,*** be marching.
2) ***march past,*** a march of troops which passes in front of an official who looks at it.
3) ***steal a march*** (or ***upon***), get a better position over (someone) without being noticed.
—[自] 1. 행진하다, 진군하다 ¶①군대가 도시로 행진해 들어왔다 2. 진전하다 ¶②과학은 지난 10년 동안 장족의 진보를 했다 —[他] …을 끌고가다; 줄지어 가게 하다
—[名] 1. 행진 2. 진전, 발전 3. 보조 ¶③구보 4. 행진곡
[熟] 1)진행중이다 2)분열 행진 3)…의 선수를 치다

‡ **March** *n.* the third month of the year. ⇒[N.B.]
—[名] 3월 [N.B.] Mar.로 줄임

mar·chion·ess [má:*r*ʃ(ə)nis, +*U.S.* mà:*r*ʃənés] *n.* [C] (*Brit.*) the wife or widow of a marquis.
—[名] 《英》 후작 부인

* **mare** [mɛə*r*] *n.* [C] a female horse.
—[名] 암말

Mar·ga·ret [má:*r*gərit] *n.* a woman's name.
—[名] 여자 이름

mar·ga·rine [má:*r*dʒəri(:)n / mà:dʒərí:n] *n.* [U] imitation butter made from vegetable oils and animal fats.
—[名] 인조 버터, 마아가린

M

* **mar·gin** [má:rdʒin] *n.* [C] **1.** a border; an edge. ¶*the ~ of the lake.* **2.** the space around the printing or writing on a page. ¶*a note on* (or *in*) *the ~.*① **3.** a borderline. ¶*be on the ~ of bare subsistence.*② **4.** an extra amount (of money, time). **5.** (*Commerce*) the difference between the cost and the selling price. ¶*a narrow ~ of profit.*③
—*vt.* provide with a border; furnish (something) with a margin.

—[名] 1. 가장자리, 가, 변두리 2. [페이지의] 난외(欄外), 여백 ¶①난외의 주(註) 3. 한계 ¶②겨우 입에 풀칠만 하고 있다 4. [시간·돈의] 여유 5.《商》판매수익, 이문 ¶③얼마 안 되는 이문
—[他] …에 가장자리를 대다

mar·gin·al [má:rdʒin(ə)l] *adj.* **1.** written on the margin of a page. **2.** at the limit. **3.** of a very narrow margin of profits.

—[形] 1. [페이지의] 난외에 쓴 2. 가장자리(끝)의 3. 겨우 수지만 맞출 정도의

mar·gue·rite [mà:rgəri:t] *n.* [C] a kind of daisy with white flowers.

—[名] 데이지꽃의 일종

mar·i·gold [mǽrigòuld] *n.* [C] a garden plant with bright yellow or orange flowers.

—[名] 금잔화

* **mar·ine** [məri:n] *adj.* **1.** of the sea; formed by the sea. ¶*~ cable.* **2.** living in the sea. **3.** of sea-trade; nautical.
—*n.* [C] **1.** a sailor serving on land and in the air as well. **2.** 《*collectively*》 the navy of a country; all the merchant ships of a country. **3.** a picture of the sea.

—[形] 1. 바다의; 바다에서 나는 2. 바다에 사는 3. 선박의; 항해의
—[名] 1. 해병대원 2. [한 나라의] 해군, 선박 3. 바다 그림

mar·i·ner [mǽrinər] *n.* [C] (*poetic*) a sailor.

—[名] 《詩》 선원, 수부

mar·i·o·nette [mæ̀riənét] *n.* [C] a doll moved by strings or by the hands.

—[名] 꼭두각시, 망석중이

mar·i·time [mǽritàim] *adj.* **1.** connected with the sea. ¶*a ~ nation.* **2.** near the sea. **3.** of sailing.

—[形] 1. 바다의; 해사(海事)의 2. 해안가까이의, 연해의 3. 항해의

⁝ **mark**[1] [ma:rk] *n.* [C] **1.** a printed or written symbol. ¶*punctuation marks*① / *a trademark.* **2.** a spot, cut, etc., made on a surface. ¶*a ~ of a wound.* / *Who has made dirty marks on this hat?* **3.** a sign of some quality, characteristic, etc. ¶*a ~ of age.* **4.** influence; impression. ¶*The doctor left his ~ on the thought of his time.*② **5.** a target; a goal. **6.** [U] importance; fame. ¶*a man of ~.* **7.** a number or letter to show the score. ¶*50 marks* / *I got full marks* (or *a full ~*) *in mathematics.*③ **8.** 《*sing.* only》 what is usual or expected. ¶*up to the ~.*④ **9.** a line, a dot, etc. to show position; a line to show the starting point. ¶*On your marks.*⑤

—[名] 1. 표; 기호; 부호 ¶①구둣점 2. 반점(斑點), 얼룩, 상처자국 3. 특징; 징후 4. 영향; 감명 ¶②박사는 시대사조에 영향을 남겼다 5. 표적; 목표 6. 저명함; 유명 7. 점수 ¶③수학에서 만점을 땄다 8. 표준 ¶④표준에 달하여; 말할 나위없는 9. 경계선; 출발점 ¶⑤[육상 경기 따위에서] 위치에 서서

1) ***beyond the mark,*** too much.
2) ***get off the mark,*** start.
3) ***hit (miss) the mark,*** succeed (fail).
4) ***make one's mark,*** become famous.
5) ***Save the mark!,*** Pardon me for having said such a horrible thing.
6) ***toe the mark,*** follow a rule; do exactly as told.
7) ***wide of the mark,*** not hitting the thing aimed at; off the point.

[熟] 1)과도하게 2)출발하다; 시작하다 3)과녁을 맞히다(빗나가다); 성공(실패)하다 4)유명해지다 5)심한 말을 해서 미안합니다 6)관례에 따르다; 규칙을 지키다 7)과녁을 빗나가서; 얼토당토않게

—*vt.* **1.** put or make a mark on (something). ¶*~ a river on a map.*⑥ **2.** record (the score, etc.); give marks to (examination papers, etc.). **3.** give a character to (something); be a sign of (something); make (someone) distinct. ¶*A lot of scientific discoveries marked the century.*⑦ / *His abilities ~ him for a leader.*⑧ **4.** show or form (something) by marks. ¶*He marked his pleasure by smiling.*; *His smile marked his pleasure.*⑨ **5.** pay attention to (something); notice. ¶*Mark my words, boys.*⑩

—[他] 1. …에 표를 하다 ¶⑥지도에 강을 기입하다 2. …을 기록하다; 채점하다 3. …을 특징지우다; 두드러지게 하다 ¶⑦많은 과학상의 발견이 금세기의 특징이다/⑧그의 능력이 지도자로서 그를 두드러지게 한다 4. …을 표로 나타내다; 정하다 ¶⑨미소가 그의 만족함을 나타낸다 5. …에 주의하다; …을 주의하여 듣다(보다) ¶⑩내 말을 잘 들어! 얘들아.

1) ***mark off*** (or ***out***)***,*** show the position of (something) by lines; separate.
2) ***mark time,*** ⓐ move the feet as if marching but without moving forward. ⓑ make no further progress.

[熟] 1)…에 경계를 긋다; …을 구별하다 2)ⓐ제자리걸음을 하다 ⓑ꾸물거리다

mark[2] [ma:rk] *n.* [C] the unit of money of the former German Empire and of West Germany.

—[名] 마르크(서독의 화폐 단위)

marked [ma:rkt] *adj.* **1.** having a mark. ¶*a ~ tree.*

—[形] 1. 표가 있는 2. 현저한; 두드러진,

M

markedly

2. clear, remarkable. ¶ *a ~ difference*① / *show a ~ increase.*②

mark·ed·ly [máːrkidli] *adv.* in a marked manner; remarkably.

mark·er [máːrkər] *n.* ⓒ **1.** a person or a thing that marks. **2.** a person keeping the score in the game. **3.** a bookmark. **4.** a sign.

‡**mar·ket** [máːrkit] *n.* ⓒ **1.** a place where goods are bought and sold. ¶ *a cattle ~.* **2.** the trade in particular articles. **3.** demand. ¶ *There is no ~ for the goods.*① **4.** the state of trade as shown by prices.
 1) *at the market,* at market price.
 2) *be in* (or *on*) *the market,* be on sale.
 3) *bring one's eggs* (or *hogs, goods*) *to a bad* (or *the wrong*) *market,* miscalculate; fail in one's plan.
 4) *find a market,* be in demand.
 5) *make a* (or *one's*) *market* (=*make good use*) *of* something. ¶ *make a ~ of war.*
 6) *play the market,* (*U.S.*) gamble in (stocks etc.).
 7) *put* (or *place*) *something on the market,* try to sell something.
 —*vi., vt.* **1.** buy or sell (something) in a market. **2.** send (something) to market. ¶ *being marketable.*

mar·ket·a·bil·i·ty [mùːrkitibíliti] *n.* Ⓤ the state of

mar·ket·a·ble [máːrkitəbl] *adj.* fit for sale.

mar·ket·er [máːrkitər] *n.* ⓒ a person who sells or buys in a market.

mar·ket·ing [máːrkitiŋ] *n.* Ⓤ **1.** the trade at a market. **2.** the shopping at a market. ¶ *do one's ~.*①

market place [⌐ ⌐] *n.* a place where a market is held.

market price [⌐ ⌐] *n.* **1.** the price of articles when sold in a market. **2.** the present price.

market town [⌐ ⌐] *n.* the town where a market is held.

mark·ing [máːrkiŋ] *n.* **1.** ⓒ a mark. **2.** Ⓤ the act of making a mark. **3.** Ⓤ the act of giving marks. **4.** ⓒ a spot; a dot.

marks·man [máːrksmən] *n.* ⓒ (pl. **-men** [-mən]) a person who shoots a rifle, etc. well.

mar·ma·lade [máːrməlèid] *n.* Ⓤ jam made of oranges or lemons boiled with their outer skins.

ma·roon¹ [mərúːn] *n.* Ⓤ a dark-red color. —*adj.* colored dark-red.

ma·roon² [mərúːn] *vt.* **1.** leave (someone) on a desert island. **2.** isolate (someone) in a place. —*n.* ⓒ **1.** a person whose ancestor was an escaped Negro slave. **2.** a person left on a desert island.

mar·quee [maːrkíː] *n.* ⓒ **1.** (esp. *Brit.*) a large tent used for garden parties. **2.** a rooflike shelter projecting over an entrance to a theater, hotel, etc. ⇒fig.

mar·quess [máːrkwis] *n.* ⓒ (esp. *Brit.*) =marquis.

mar·que·try [máːrkitri] *n.* Ⓤ (pl. **-tries**) thin decorative pieces of wood, ivory, metal, etc. fitted together to form a design, used in furniture or flooring.

[marquee 2.]

mar·quis [máːrkwis] *n.* ⓒ a nobleman below a duke and above an earl. ⇒N.B. ↔marchioness

mar·riage [mǽridʒ] *n.* Ⓤ ⓒ **1.** the act of marrying; the state of being married. **2.** ⓒ a wedding ceremony. ¶ *a ~ service.*① **3.** the married life of two persons as husband and wife; the relation between husband and wife. ¶ *break up a ~.* **4.** ⓒ an intimate union.

[705]

marriage

눈에 띄는 ¶①현저한 차이/②두드러진 증가를 보이다
—⚑ 두드러지게; 현저하게; 뚜렷이

—图 1. 표를 하는 사람(것) 2. [게임 따위의] 채점 기록자 3. 서표(書標) 4. 표지(標識), 표적

—图 1. 시장, 장 2. [일정 상품의] 거래 3. 수요(需要) ¶①이 상품은 안 나간다 4. 시황(市況); 시세

🖳 1)시장 가격으로 2)팔려고 내놓고 있다 3)예상 착오를 하다, 오산하다 4)살 작자가 나서다 5)…을 이용하다 6)(美)[주식 따위의] 투기를 하다 7)[물건]을 시장에 내놓다

—自他 1. 시장에서 팔다(사다) 2. 시장에 내놓다
—图 시장성
—⚑ 매매할 수 있는; 시장성이 있는
—图 시장에서 파는(사는) 사람

—图 1. 시장에서 매매하기 2. [시장에서의] 장보기, 구매 ¶①장을 보다
—图 장이 서는 광장
—图 1. 시장가격 2. 시세

—图 장이 서는 고장
—图 1. 표, 점 2. 표를 하기 3. 채점 4. 반점, 무늬

—图 사격의 명수; 사수(射手)

—图 마아멀레이드(오렌지·레몬으로 만든 잼)
—图 적갈색 —⚑ 적갈색의

—⚑ 1. …을 무인도에 버리다 2. …을 고립시키다 —图 1. 탈주한 흑인의 자손 2. 무인도에 버림받은 사람

—图 1. [옥외 행사용의] 큰 천막 2. [영화관·호텔 따위의] 입구의 차양

—图 [가구 장식용의] 조각나무[상감(象嵌)] 세공

—图 후작 N.B. 영국 이외에서는 duke와 count의 중간 작위
—图 1. 결혼 2. 결혼식 ¶①[교회의] 결혼식 3. 결혼생활, 부부관계 4. 밀접한 결합

M

mar·riage·a·ble [mǽridʒəbl] *adj.* fit for marriage; old enough to marry. ¶~ *age*① / *a ~ girl.*②
—֎ 결혼할 수 있는; 혼기에 달한 ¶①혼기/②결혼 적령기의 처녀

* **mar·ried** [mǽrid] *adj.* **1.** joined in marriage; having a husband or wife. ↔single ¶*a ~ man (woman)* / *Their ~ life was happy.* **2.** closely united.
—֎ 1. 결혼한; 남편(아내)이 있는 2. 밀접하게 결합한

mar·row [mǽrou] *n.* Ⓤ **1.** the soft substance filling the hollow part of a bone. **2.** the essential part.
—֍ 1. 골수(骨髓) 2. 정수(精髓)

⁑ **mar·ry** [mǽri] (**-ried**) *vt.* **1.** take (a husband or wife) in marriage. ¶~ *a fortune.*① / *He married a pretty girl.*② **2.** (of a priest, etc.) unite (a man and woman) as husband and wife. ¶*The priest married them.* **3.** (of parents, etc.) give (a son or daughter) in marriage. ¶*He married his daughter to a young lawyer.*③ **4.** unite closely. —*vi.* enter into a marriage; be married; get married. ¶~ *for money*④ / *When did he get married? marry off,* succeed in arranging a marriage for one's child.
—֎ 1. …와 결혼하다 ¶①부자와 결혼하다/②그는 미인과 결혼했다 2. [목사 등이] …을 결혼시키다 3. [부모가] …을 시집(장가)보내다 ¶③그는 딸을 젊은 변호사에게 시집보냈다 4. …을 밀착시키다 —֍ 결혼하다 ¶④돈 때문에 결혼하다

֎ 시집보내다

* **Mars** [ma:rz] *n.* **1.** (in Roman mythology) the Roman god of war. **2.** the planet nearest to the earth.
—֍ 1. 군신(軍神) 2. 화성(火星)

Mar·seil·laise [mà:rsəléiz, -seiéiz] *n.* the French national song, written in 1792, during the French Revolution.
—֍ 프랑스 국가

* **marsh** [ma:rʃ] *n.* Ⓒ a piece of low and wet land.
—֍ 늪, 소택지, 습지

* **mar·shal** [má:rʃ(ə)l] *n.* Ⓒ **1.** the highest rank in some armies, esp. of France. **2.** (*Brit.*) a general of the Air Force. **3.** (*Brit.*) an official who looks after ceremonies, etc. **4.** (*U.S.*) a national officer having police duty; the head of a fire or police department.
—*vt.* (**-shaled, -shal·ing** or *Brit.* **-shalled, -shal·ling**) **1.** make (persons) get into a line. **2.** put (things) in order. **3.** guide (someone) into a place. —*vi.* **1.** stand in a line. **2.** meet together.
—֍ 1. [특히 프랑스의] 육군 원수 2. 《英》공군 장성 3.《英》[왕실의] 의전관(儀典官) 4.《美》연방 재판소의 집행관; 경찰서장; 소방대장

—֎ 1. …을 정렬시키다 2. …을 정리하다 3. …을 안내하다 —֍ 1. 정렬하다 2. 집합하다

Marshall Islands [⌐ ⌐–], **the** *n.* a group of islands in the North Pacific.
—֍ 북태평양의 제도(諸島)

marsh·mal·low [má:rʃmælou, +*U.S.* -mèl-] *n.* Ⓤ a soft, spongy candy with a flavor made from the root of the marsh mallow. ⌊which grows in marshes.⌋
—֍ 마시맬로우 (marsh mallow 의 뿌리로 만든 전분 과자)

marsh mallow [⌐ ⌐–] *n.* a plant with large pink flowers
—֍ 양아욱

marsh·y [má:rʃi] *adj.* (**marsh·i·er, marsh·i·est**) **1.** like a marsh. **2.** having many marshes. ▷**marsh·i·ness**[-nis]*n.*
—֎ 1. 늪 같은 2. 늪이 많은

mar·su·pi·al [ma:rsú:piəl / ma:s(j)ú:-] *n.* Ⓒ an animal that carries its young in a bag-like part of its body.
—֍ 유대(有袋) 동물

mart [ma:rt] *n.* Ⓒ (*poetic*) a market; a trading center.
—֍ 시장; 상업 중심지

mar·ten [má:rtin] *n.* (pl. **-tens** or collectively **-ten**) **1.** Ⓒ a small brown animal like a weasel. **2.** Ⓤ the fur of this animal.
—֍ 1. 담비 2. 담비의 모피

mar·tial [má:rʃ(ə)l] *adj.* **1.** of war. **2.** eager to fight. **3.** military. ↔civil ¶~ *law.*① ▷**mar·tial·ly** [-i] *adv.*
—֎ 1. 전쟁의 2. 호전적인 3. 군사의 ¶①계엄령

Mar·ti·an [má:rʃən / má:ʃiən] *adj.* of Mars. —*n.* Ⓒ an imaginary person living on Mars.
—֎ 화성의 —֍ 화성인

mar·tin [má:rt(ə)n / má:tin] *n.* Ⓒ a small bird of the swallow family.
—֍ 흰털발제비

mar·ti·net [mà:rtinét] *n.* Ⓒ a person who is very strict in training, esp. in the army.
—֍ 규율에 엄격한 사람

* **mar·tyr** [má:rtər] *n.* Ⓒ **1.** a person who dies or suffers pain for his religion, principles, etc. ¶*die a ~ to principle*① / *make a ~ of someone.*② **2.** a person who suffers pain for a long time. ¶*a ~ to gout.*③ —*vt.* kill or give great pain to (someone) because of his religion, etc.
—֍ 1. 순교자, 신념을 위해 목숨을 바치는 사람/②…을 희생시키다 2. 항상 고통받는 사람 ¶①통풍으로 고통받는 사람 —֎ …을 박해하다, 죽이다

mar·tyr·dom [má:rtərdəm] *n.* Ⓤ death or suffering for the sake of a faith or principle.
—֍ 순교, 순사(殉死); 고난

* **mar·vel** [má:rv(ə)l] *n.* Ⓒ a wonderful thing or person. ¶*do marvels*① / *a ~ of beauty.*② —*vi.* (**-veled, -vel·ing** or *Brit.* **-velled, -vel·ling**) be struck with wonder. 《~ *at* something》 —*vt.* wonder. 《~ *why* (or *how, that,*
—֍ 놀랄 만한 일(사람) ¶①놀라운 일을 해내다/②절세의 미인 —֎ 놀라다 —֎ …을 이상하게 여기다

etc.)...》

mar·vel·lous [má:rviləs] *adj.* (*Brit.*) =marvelous.

‡ mar·vel·ous [má:rviləs] *adj.* **1.** extraordinary; astonishing. ¶*a ~ view.*① **2.** hard to believe.
—[形] 1. 놀랄 만한 ¶①멋있는 경치 2. 믿어지지 않는

mar·vel·ous·ly [má:rviləsli] *adv.* in a marvelous manner.
—[副] 놀랍게, 놀랍도록

Marx [mɑ:rks], **Karl.** *n.* (1818–83) a German socialist and political economist.
—[名] 마르크스(독일의 사회주의자·정치 경제학자)

Marx·i·an [má:rksiən] *adj.* of Marx or his principles. —*n.* [C] a Marxist.
—[形] 마르크스[주의]의 —[名] 마르크스주의자

Marx·ism [má:rksiz(ə)m] *n.* [U] the principles of Marx.
—[名] 마르크스주의

Marx·ist [má:rksist] *n.* [C] a follower of the principles of Marx.
—[名] 마르크스주의자

Mar·y¹ [méəri] *n.* a woman's name.
—[名] 여자 이름

Mar·y² [méəri] *n.* **1.** the mother of Jesus; the Virgin Mary or Saint Mary. **2.** either of two queens of England, Mary I (1516–58) and Mary II (1662–94).
—[名] 1. 성모 마리아 2. 영국 여왕의 이름

Mar·y·land [mériland] *n.* an eastern State of the United States. ⇒[N.B.] ▷**Mar·y·land·er** [-ər] *n.*
—[名] 미국 동부의 주 [N.B.] Md.로 줄임. 수도 Annapolis

mas·cot [mǽskət] *n.* [C] any person, animal, or thing that is supposed to bring good luck; one's pet.
—[名] 행운을 가져다 준다고 믿는 사람(동물·물건), 마스코트

• mas·cu·line [mǽskjulin, +*Brit.* má:s-] *adj.* ↔feminine **1.** (*Grammar*) of the gender of a male. **2.** of a male; manly. —*n.* [U] (*Grammar*) the gender of a male.
—[形] 1. 남성의 2. 남자의; 남자다운 —[名] 남성

mash [mæʃ] *n.* **1.** [U] a crushed malt or grain mixed in hot water and used for making beer. **2.** any soft mixture. **3.** a mixture of the skins of wheat or meal and warm water and used for feeding horses. —*vt.* crush (something) into a soft mass. ▷**mash·er** [-ər] *n.*
—[名] 1. 엿기름 물(맥주의 원료); [감자 따위의] 짓이겨 만든 즙 2. [밀기울 따위를 넣은 마소의] 사료 —[他] …을 짓이기다

• mask [mæsk / mɑ:sk] *n.* [C] **1.** a covering to hide or protect the face. ¶*a flu ~*① / *a gas ~* **2.** a false face worn by an actor, etc. **3.** a clay model of some-one's face. ¶*a death ~.* **4.** pretense; an excuse. ¶*under the ~ of charity.*② **5.** a person who wears a mask. **6.** a dancing party at which masks are worn.
—[名] 1. 마스크, 복면 ¶①감기 마스크 2. [극 따위에서 쓰는] 가면 3. 데드마스크 4. 핑계, 구실 ¶②자선을 빙자하여 5. 가장한 사람 6. 가면 무도회

1) ***put on a mask,*** hide one's real feelings.
2) ***throw off one's mask,*** show one's real character.
[熟] 1)본심을 숨기다 2)…의 정체를 나타내다

—*vt.* cover (a face) with a mask; conceal. —*vi.* put on a mask. ▷**mask·er** [-ər] *n.*
—[他] …을 가장시키다, 감추다 —[自] 가장하다

masked [mæskt / mɑ:skt] *adj.* **1.** putting on a mask; disguised. ¶*a ~ ball.* **2.** hidden; covered.
—[形] 1. 가면을 쓴; 변장한 2. 숨겨진, 숨은

• ma·son [méisn] *n.* [C] a builder in stone or brick.
—[名] 석공; 벽돌 직공

ma·son·ic, Ma- [məsánik / -sɔ́n-] *adj.* of Freemasons.
—[形] 비밀 공제 조합[원]의

ma·son·ry [méisnri] *n.* [U] (pl. **-ries**) **1.** the job or skill of a mason. **2.** something built by a mason.
—[名] 1. 석공의 직(기술) 2. 석조 건축물

masque [mæsk / mɑ:sk] *n.* [C] **1.** a short play with songs, dances, and a little speaking. **2.** a masked ball.
—[名] 1. 무용 가극 2. 가장 무도회

mas·quer·ade [mæ̀skəréid] *n.* **1.** [C] a dance or party in which people wear masks and fancy dresses. **2.** [U] change in one's appearance; pretense. —*vi.* **1.** attend a masquerade party. **2.** pretend; change one's appearance. 《~ *as* something》
—[名] 1. 가면(가장) 무도회 2. 가장; 구실(口實) —[自] 1. 가면(가장) 무도회에 나가다 2. …인 체하다; 가장하다

mas·quer·ad·er [mæ̀skəréidər] *n.* [C] a person who masquerades.
—[名] 가면 무도자

‡ mass¹ [mæs] *n.* [C] **1.** a solid body of matter without regular shape; a lump. **2.** a large number or quantity. ¶*a ~ of people.* **3.** the greater part. **4.** 《*the -es*》 people in general; the lower classes.
—[名] 1. 덩어리 2. 집단, 군중, 다수, 다량 3. 대부분 4. 일반, 대중; 하층민

1) ***in a mass,*** altogether.
2) ***in the mass,*** as a whole.
[熟] 1)모두 합쳐서 2)통틀어서

—*adj.* on a large scale; for a mass of people or things. ¶*~ communication / ~ production.*
—[形] 대규모의; 대중을 위한; 다수의

—*vt., vi.* gather into a mass.
—[他][自] 한 덩어리로 만들다; 모이다

Mass, mass² [mæs, +*Brit.* mɑ:s] *n.* **1.** [U] special services and prayers offered in the Roman Catholic Church. ¶*attend ~*① / *read ~.*② **2.** [C] music to be used for Mass.
—[名] 1. 미사 ¶①미사에 나가다/②미사를 올리다 2. 미사곡

Mass. Massachusetts.

Mas·sa·chu·setts [mæ̀sətʃú:sets] *n.* a northeastern State
—[名] 미국 동북부의 주 [N.B.] Mass.로

M

massacre [708] **masterpiece**

of the United States, on the Atlantic Coast. ⇒N.B.
mas·sa·cre [mǽsəkər] *n.* ⓒ the cruel and violent killing of many people or animals. —*vt.* kill (people or animals) cruelly and in large numbers.
—名 대학살 —動 [사람이나 동물]을 학살하다

mas·sage [məsá:ʒ / mǽsɑ:ʒ] *n.* ⓤ ⓒ the act of rubbing the body to lessen pain. —*vt.* rub (the body) with the hands. ¶~ *someone on the shoulders.*①
—名 마사지 —動 …을 마사지하다 ¶①남의 어깨를 마사지하다

• **mas·sive** [mǽsiv] *adj.* **1.** huge and heavy. ¶*a ~ style.* **2.** strong; impressive. ¶*He is a man of ~ character.*
—形 1. 크고 무거운, 육중한 2. [정신이] 굳센, 착실한

mass media [´ ´-] *n. pl.* the means of communication used to reach great numbers of people.
—名 대중 매체(媒體), 매스미디어

mass meeting [´ ´-] *n.* a large public meeting of people to hear or discuss public affairs, etc.
—名 [특히 정치적인] 국민(민중)대회

mass production [´ -´-] *n.* the production of goods in large quantities by machinery.
—名 대량 생산

mass·y [mǽsi] *adj.* (**mass·i·er, mass·i·est**) massive; heavy.
—形 육중한; 무거운

• **mast**¹ [mæst / mɑ:st] *n.* ⓒ **1.** a tall pole to support the sails of a ship. ⇒fig. **2.** any upright pole. ¶*radio masts.*①
sail before the mast, be a common sailor.
—名 1. 돛대 2. 높은 기둥 ¶①무전탑

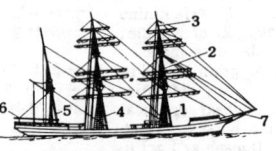
[mast¹ 1.]
1. foremast 2. fore-topmast 3. foretopgallant mast 4. mainmast 5. mizzenmast 6. boom 7. bowsprit

▩ 평(平)선원이다

mast² [mæst / mɑ:st] *n.* ⓤ the nuts of the chestnut, oak, beech, etc., when used as food for pigs.
—名 떡갈나무·밤나무 따위의 열매(돼지의 사료)

: **mas·ter** [mǽstər / mɑ́:stə] *n.* ⓒ **1.** a person who rules or commands; an employer; an owner. ¶*a stationmaster / a ~ of a factory.* **2.** the man at the head of a household. **3.** the captain of a merchant ship. **4.** (esp. *Brit.*) a male teacher; a schoolmaster. **5.** a great artist. **6.** a work by a great artist. **7.** a person who has some special skill or ability. ¶*a ~ of the piano.* **8.** 《with *a boy's name*》 young Mr. ¶*Master Tom.*① **9.** 《*the M-*》 Christ. **10.** 《*M-*》 a degree given at a college or a university. ¶*Master of Arts.*② ⇒N.B.
1) *be master of,* know (a situation) thoroughly; have (a situation) under control.
2) *be master of oneself,* have one's feelings and actions perfectly under the control of one's reason.
3) *be one's own master,* be free to do as one pleases.
4) *make oneself master of,* learn thoroughly the facts about (something) or the way to use (it).
5) *the Master of Ceremonies,* a person in charge of a ceremony or an entertainment. ⇒N.B.
—*adj.* eminently skilled; chief; of a master. ¶*a ~ carpenter.*③
—*vt.* **1.** become master of (someone or something); control. **2.** become skillful at (something); learn thoroughly.
—名 1. 주인; 고용주; 소유주 2. 가장(家長), 세대주 3. 선장 4. (英) 남자 선생 5. 대예술가; 거장(巨匠) 6. 거장의 작품 7. 명장(名匠), 명공, 명인 8. 도련님, 군(君) ¶①톰 도련님 9. 그리스도 10. 석사 ¶②문학 석사 N.B. M.A. 또는 A.M.으로 줄임

▩ 1)…에 통달하고 있다; …을 자유로 할 수 있다 2)자제력이 강하다 3)마음대로 [행동]할 수 있다 4)…에 숙달하다; …을 자유로 하다 5)사회자 N.B. M.C.로 줄임

—形 뛰어난; 으뜸가는; 우두머리의 ¶③목수의 우두머리
—動 1. …의 주인이 되다, 지배하다; …을 억누르다 2. …에 숙달하다; …을 완전히 배우다

mas·ter·ful [mǽstərf(u)l / mɑ́:stə-] *adj.* **1.** fond of gaining control over others. **2.** skillful. ¶*a ~ speech.*①
—形 1. 건방진 2. 교묘한, 뛰어난 ¶①명연설

mas·ter·ful·ly [mǽstərfuli / mɑ́:stə-] *adv.* too proudly; skillfully.
—副 거만하게

master key [´- ´] *n.* a key for opening different sets of locks.
—名 [여러가지 자물쇠에 맞는] 열쇠, 곁쇠

mas·ter·ly [mǽstərli / mɑ́:stə-] *adj.* very clever; skillful.
—*adv.* in a masterly manner. ▷ **mas·ter·li·ness** [-nis] *n.*
—形 교묘한, 능숙한 —副 교묘하게, 훌륭하게

• **mas·ter·piece** [mǽstərpì:s / mɑ́:stə-] *n.* ⓒ anything made
—名 명작, 걸작

or done in a masterly way; the best piece of work of a writer, painter, etc.

mas·ter·ship [mǽstərʃìp / mɑ́:stə-] *n.* **1.** [U] the state of being a master. **2.** [C] the position of a master, esp. of a schoolmaster. **3.** [U] control; skill.
—[名] 1. 주인임 2. [특히 학교의] 교사의 직 3. 지배; 교묘함

mas·ter·y [mǽst(ə)ri / mɑ́:s-] *n.* [U] **1.** control. ¶*gain the ~ of a town*① **2.** skill and complete knowledge. ¶*acquire a ~ of Russian.*②
—[名] 1. 지배 ¶①마을을 지배하다 2. 숙달 ¶②러시아어에 숙달하다

mast·head [mǽsthèd / mɑ́:st-] *n.* [C] **1.** the top of a ship's mast. **2.** a sailor who looks out from near the masthead.
—[名] 1. 돛대의 꼭대기 2. [돛대 꼭대기의] 감시인

mas·ti·cate [mǽstikèit] *vt.* chew.
—[他] …을 씹다

mas·ti·cation [mæ̀stikéiʃ(ə)n] *n.* [U] the act of chewing.
—[名] 씹기, 저작(咀嚼)

mas·tiff [mǽstif, +*Brit.* mɑ́:s-] *n.* [C] a large powerful dog with a broad mouth and hanging lips.
—[名] 마스티프 개(맹견의 일종)

mas·to·don [mǽstədàn / -dɔ̀n] *n.* [C] a huge, extinct animal much like an elephant.
—[名] 마스토돈(코끼리 비슷한 태고의 거대한 동물)

‡mat[1] [mæt] *n.* [C] **1.** a small floor covering. ¶*a door ~.*① **2.** a flat piece of cloth, etc. for use under a vase, etc. **3.** an entangled or disorderly mass of hair or grass.
leave someone ***on the mat,*** do not allow someone to come into a house.
—[名] 1. 매트, 돛자리, 거적 ¶①[현관의] 신발 닦는 매트 2. [꽃병 따위의] 깔개 3. [털・풀의] 헝클어짐
[熟] …을 문간에서 깝살리다

—*v.* (**-mat·ted, -mat·ting**) *vt.* **1.** cover (something) with a mat. **2.** cause (something) to tangle or become disorderly. ¶*become matted.*② —*vi.* become tangled.
—[他] 1. …을 매트로 덮다 2. …을 헝클어지게 하다 ¶②헝클어지다 —[自] 헝클어지다

mat[2] [mæt] *adj.* not polished. ¶*~ silver.*① —*vt.* make a surface of (metal, etc.) dull.
—[形] 윤을 없애는 ¶①윤을 없앤 은
—[他] …의 윤을 없애다

mat·a·dor [mǽtədɔ̀:r] *n.* [C] a man who kills a bull with a sword in a bull-fight; a professional bull-fighter.
—[名] 투우사

‡match[1] [mætʃ] *n.* [C] **1.** a game; a contest. ¶*a golf ~.* **2.** a person or a thing having equal power to another in a contest; a rival. ¶*You are no ~ for me.*① **3.** a person or a thing exactly like another; one of a pair. **4.** a person or a thing that is suitable for another. ¶*The hat is a very good ~ for your coat.* **5.** a person who is suitable as a marriage partner. ¶*The girl is a suitable ~ for our son.* **6.** a marriage. ¶*make a ~*② / *At last they made a ~ of it.*③
—[名] 1. 시합, 경기 2. 호적수, 경기 상대 ¶①너는 내게 어림도 없다 3. 한 쌍, 짝을 이룬 것의 한쪽 4. 잘 어울리는 것 5. [결혼의] 어울리는 상대 6. 결혼 ¶②중매를 서다/③결국 그들은 결혼했다

—*vt.* **1.** cause (someone or something) to fight against another. **2.** be equal to; be a match for (someone or something). ¶*No one can ~ him in mathematics.*④ **3.** fit; suit. ¶*His necktie does not ~ his coat.* **4.** find something suitable for (another). ¶*Can you ~ [me] this cloth?*⑤ **5.** cause (someone) to be married. ¶*He matched his daughter with* (or *to*) *the young man.* —*vi.* **1.** be equal or suitable. **2.** go well together. ¶*The colors ~ well.*⑥
—[他] 1. …에게 시합시키다 2. …에 필적(匹敵)하다 ¶④수학에서는 아무도 그에게 못 당한다 3. …와 어울리다, 조화하다 4. …에 어울리는 것을 찾다 ¶⑤이 천에 맞는 것을 찾아 주시겠어요? 5. …을 결혼시키다 —[自] 1. 어울리다, 맞다 2. 조화하다 ¶⑥이 색은 잘 어울린다

‡match[2] [mætʃ] *n.* [C] a short piece of wood with a head that catches fire when rubbed. ¶*light* (or *strike*) *a~.*
—[名] 성냥

match·box [mǽtʃbàks / -bɔ̀ks] *n.* [C] a small box for matches.
—[名] 성냥갑

matched [mætʃt] *adj.* having a match or a rival.
—[形] 잘 어울리는

match·less [mǽtʃlis] *adj.* having no equal; unrivaled. ▷**match·less·ly** [-li] *adv.* —**match·less·ness** [-nis] *n.*
—[形] 비길 데 없는

match·lock [mǽtʃlàk / -lɔ̀k] *n.* [C] an old gun with a cord to light the powder.
—[名] 화승총

match·mak·er [mǽtʃmèikər] *n.* [C] **1.** a person who arranges marriages for others. **2.** a person who arranges matches for prize fights, races, etc.
—[名] 1. 중매장이 2. 경기의 대전 계획을 짜는 사람

match·mak·ing [mǽtʃmèikiŋ] *n.* [U] **1.** the act of arranging marriages. **2.** an arranging of prize fights.
—[名] 1. 중매[를 서기] 2. [권투]시합을 짜기

match·wood [mǽtʃwùd] *n.* [U] small pieces of wood, esp. for making matches.
—[名] 성냥개비용 나무

‡mate[1] [meit] *n.* [C] **1.** a companion. **2.** one of a pair; a husband or wife. **3.** a ship's officer below the rank of
—[名] 1. 동료 2. 한 쌍의 한쪽; 배우자의 한쪽 3. 항해사 ¶①1 등 항해사

captain. ¶*a chief* ~.① **4.** an assistant. ¶*a cook's* ~. **—*vt., vi.*** join as a pair or couple.
—[他][自] 부부가 되[게 하]다; 짝짓[게 하]다

mate² [meit] ***n., v., interj.*** =checkmate.

ma·ter [méitər] ***n.*** [C] (*Brit. colloq.*) a mother. ↔pater.
—[名] 《英口》 어머니

‡ **ma·te·ri·al** [mətíəriəl] ***n.*** **1.** [U][C] the substance of which anything is made. ¶*raw* ~.① **2.** [U] subject matter; facts. ¶*the ~ for a novel.* **3.** ⦅*pl.*⦆ tools or articles. ¶*writing materials.*② **4.** [U] cloth.
—*adj.* **1.** of matter or substance. ↔spiritual ¶*a ~ being*③ / *~ evidence.*④ **2.** of the body or bodily needs. **3.** essential; important. ¶*be ~ to ….*⑤
—[名] 1. 원료, 재료 ¶①원료 2. 소재, 제재(題材) 3. 도구 ¶②필기도구 4. 천, 감
—[形] 1. 물질의, 물질적인 ¶③유형물/④물적 증거 2. 육체상의; 관능적인 3. 본질적인; 중요한 ¶⑤…에게 중하다

ma·te·ri·al·ism [mətíəriəlìz(ə)m] ***n.*** [U] **1.** the theory that nothing exists except matter. ↔idealism **2.** the tendency to think more highly of material things than of spiritual things.
—[名] 1. 유물론, 유물주의 2. 물질주의

ma·te·ri·al·ist [mətíəriəlist] ***n.*** [C] **1.** a person who believes in materialism. **2.** a person who values material things more than spiritual things.
—[名] 1. 유물론자 2. 물질주의자

ma·te·ri·al·is·tic [mətìəriəlístik] ***adj.*** of materialism or materialists.
—[形] 유물론[자]의

ma·te·ri·al·i·za·tion [mətìəriəlizéiʃ(ə)n / -lai-] ***n.*** [U] the act of materializing; the state of being materialized.
—[名] 구체화, 물질화

ma·te·ri·al·ize [mətíəriəlàiz] ***vt.*** **1.** give material or concrete form to (something). ¶~ *one's ideas.*① **2.** make (something) appear in material form. **3.** make (something) materialistic. **—*vi.*** **1.** become fact. **2.** appear in material form.
—[他] 1. …에게 형체를 주다 ¶①자기의 생각을 구체화하다 2. [영혼]을 형체로 나타내다 3. …을 물질(실질)적으로 하다 —[自] 1. 실현하다 2. 형체로 나타나다

ma·te·ri·al·ly [mətíəriəli] ***adv.*** **1.** in a material manner. ↔spiritually **2.** in matter or substance. ↔formally **3.** considerably.
—[副] 1. 물질적으로 2. 실질적으로 3. 크게

ma·ter·nal [mətə́:rn(ə)l] ***adj.*** **1.** of or like a mother. ↔paternal ¶~ *love.*① **2.** on the mother's side of the family. ¶~ *relatives.*②
—[形] 1. 어머니의(같은) ¶①모성애 2. 어머니쪽의 ¶②외가 친척

ma·ter·nal·ly [mətə́:rnəli] ***adv.*** in a maternal way.
—[副] 어머니답게

ma·ter·ni·ty [mətə́:rniti] ***n.*** [U] **1.** the state of being a mother. **2.** the qualities of a mother. **—*adj.*** for a woman having a baby. ¶*a ~ hospital.*①
—[名] 1. 어머니임 2. 어머니다움 —[形] 임부(姙婦)를 위한 ¶①산부인과 병원

math·e·mat·i·cal [mæ̀θimǽtik(ə)l], **-mat·ic** [-mǽtik] ***adj.*** **1.** of the nature of mathematics. **2.** very exact.
—[形] 1. 수학적인 2. 정확한

math·e·mat·i·cal·ly [mæ̀θimǽtikəli] ***adv.*** **1.** in a mathematical way. **2.** with accuracy; exactly.
—[副] 1. 수학적으로 2. 정확히

math·e·ma·ti·cian [mæ̀θimətíʃ(ə)n] ***n.*** [C] a person who is skillful in mathematics.
—[名] 수학자

• **math·e·mat·ics** [mæ̀θimǽtiks] ***n. pl.*** ⦅used as *sing.*⦆ [U] the science of space and numbers. ⇨[N.B.]
—[名] 수학 [N.B.] math.로 줄임. 회화체에서는 maths 또는 math

mat·i·née, -nee [mæ̀tinéi / mǽtinèi] ***n.*** [C] a daytime show in a theater.
—[名] 낮흥행, 주간 공연

ma·tri·ces [méitrisi:z] ***n.*** pl. of **matrix.**

ma·tri·cide [méitrisàid] ***n.*** **1.** [U][C] the act of killing one's own mother. **2.** [C] a person who kills his own mother.↔patricide
—[名] 1. 모친 살해 2. 모친 살해범

ma·tric·u·late [mətríkjulèit] ***vt.*** admit (someone) as a student at a university, etc. **—*vi.*** be admitted to a college or university.
—[他] [학생]에게 대학 입학을 허락하다 —[自] 대학 입학을 허락받다

ma·tric·u·la·tion [mətrìkjuléiʃ(ə)n] ***n.*** [U] the act of matriculating; the state of being matriculated.
—[名] 입학 허가

mat·ri·mo·ni·al [mæ̀trimóuniəl] ***adj.*** of marriage.
▷**mat·ri·mo·ni·al·ly** [-li] ***adv.***
—[形] 결혼의

mat·ri·mo·ny [mǽtrimòuni / -məni] ***n.*** [U] **1.** marriage. **2.** married life.
—[名] 1. 결혼 2. 결혼생활

ma·trix [méitriks] ***n.*** [C] (pl. **-tri·ces** or **-trix·es**) **1.** something from which a thing grows. **2.** a rock in which a gem, fossil, etc. is enclosed. **3.** a shape into which hot metal is poured.
—[名] 1. 모체 2. [보석 · 화석 따위의] 모암(母岩) 3. 주형(鑄型)

ma·tron [méitrən] ***n.*** [C] **1.** an elderly married woman. **2.** a woman in charge of household affairs in a hospital,
—[名] 1. [나이 지긋한] 기혼 부인 2. 가정부; 간호부장; 여자 사감(감독)

M

school, etc.

ma·tron·ly [méitrənli] *adj.* **1.** like a matron. **2.** noble and calm.

Matt [mæt] *n.* a nickname of Matthew.

mat·ted [mǽtid] *adj.* **1.** covered with a mat. **2.** entangled closely.

‡ **mat·ter** [mǽtər] *n.* **1.** [U] substance; material. ↔mind, spirit ¶*solid (liquid, gaseous) ~.*① **2.** [U] stuff; any particular thing. ¶*coloring ~*② */ printed ~ / postal ~.*③ **3.** ⟪*the ~*⟫ the content of thought or expression. ↔manner, style ¶*the ~ of the lecture.*④ **4.** [C] an affair; a subject for discussion; a cause. ¶*a serious ~ / money matters*⑤ */ a ~ of* (or *for*) *regret*⑥ */ It's no laughing ~.*⑦ */ Matters are quite different here.*⑧ **5.** [U] ⟪used with *no* or *what*⟫ importance. ¶*It's* [*of*] *no ~. / [Of] What ~ is it?*⑨ **6.** ⟪*the ~*⟫ difficulty; trouble. ¶*What is the ~ with him?*⑩ **7.** [U] the yellow liquid which comes out of a wound, etc.; pus.

1) ***as a matter of fact,*** in fact; really.
2) ***as the matter stands,*** in the present state of things.
3) ***for that matter,*** so far as that is concerned.
4) ***in the matter of*** (=*as regards*) *something.*
5) ***a matter of,*** about. ¶*a ~ of three days.*
6) ***no matter how*** (***when, which, who, what,*** etc.), however (whenever, whichever, etc). ¶*No ~ what you may say, I will never believe you.*
7) ***to make matters worse,*** to mention a fact which is worse.

—*vi.* **1.** be important. ¶*It matters little to me.* **2.** (of a wound, etc.) form or give out matter (*n.* 7.).

Mat·ter·horn [mǽtərhɔ̀:rn] *n.* a mountain of the Alps.

mat·ter-of-fact [mǽtərə(v)fǽkt] *adj.* **1.** concerned with facts. **2.** practical. **3.** lacking imagination.

mat·ting [mǽtiŋ] *n.* [U] ⟪*collectively*⟫ a piece of rough woven fabric used for covering floors, for wrapping things, etc.

mat·tock [mǽtək] *n.* [C] a tool with a flat or pointed blade on either side, used for digging, etc. ⇨fig.

(mattock)

mat·tress [mǽtris] *n.* [C] a cloth-covered pad filled with straw, hair, cotton, etc., used as a bed.

• **ma·ture** [mət(j)úər / -tjúə] *adj.* **1.** ripe; fully grown. ¶*a ~ age.*① **2.** thought out carefully. **3.** reached the limit of time for payment.

—*vt.* **1.** bring (something) to a fully-grown state. ¶*wine natured by age.*② **2.** work out (something) carefully; develop (something) fully. **—*vi.*** **1.** come to a fully-grown state. **2.** reach the limit of time for payment. ▷**ma·ture·ly** [-li] *adv.*

• **ma·tu·ri·ty** [mət(j)úəriti / -tjúə-] *n.* [U] **1.** the state or process of ripening or growing fully. ¶*come to ~.*① **2.** the state of being completed. **3.** the time a debt, note, etc. ought to be paid. ¶*pay at ~.*②

maud·lin [mɔ́:dlin] *adj.* **1.** easily moved to tears. **2.** stupid and sentimental.

maul [mɔ:l] *n.* [C] a large, heavy hammer of wood. **—*vt.*** **1.** do harm to (someone) by beating. **2.** handle (someone) in a rough way.

maun·der [mɔ́:ndər] *vi.* **1.** talk in a foolish and aimless way. **2.** move or act in an aimless way. ⟪*~ along* or *about* something⟫

mau·so·le·a [mɔ̀:səlí:ə / -líə] *n.* pl. of **mausoleum**.

mau·so·le·um [mɔ̀:səlí(:)əm] *n.* [C] (pl. **-le·ums** or **-le·a**) a large, imposing tomb.

mauve [mouv] *n.* [U] a light purple color. **—*adj.*** of a light purple color.

maw [mɔ:] *n.* [C] the stomach of an animal.

—[形] 1. 기혼 부인다운 2. 침착한
—[名] Matthew의 애칭
—[形] 1. 돗자리(거적)를 깐 2. 헝클어진
—[名] 1. 물질; 물체[의 구성 요소] ¶① 고(액·기)체 2. …체(體), …물(物) ¶②색소/③우편물 3. 내용, 주지(主旨) ¶④강의의 내용 4. 일, 사정; 문제; 원인 ¶⑤금전문제/⑥유감스러운 일/⑦웃을 일이 아니다/⑧여기서는 사정이 전혀 다르다 5. 중대한 일 ¶⑨그게 뭐가 대단하냐? 6. 곤란, 고장, 지장 ¶⑩그가 어찌 됐읍니까? 7. 고름
[熟] 1)실제로는; 사실상 2)현재의 상태로는 3)그 일이라면 4)…에 관하여는 5)대략, 약 6)비록 어떻게(언제, 어느것이, 누가, 무엇이) …일지라도 7)더욱 나쁜 것은
—[自] 1. 중대하다 2. 곪다; 고름이 나오다
—[名] 알프스 산맥의 높은 봉우리
—[形] 1. 사실의 2. 실제적인 3. 무미건조한
—[名] 돗자리, 거적
—[名] 곡괭이의 일종
—[名] [솜·털·짚 따위를 넣은 침대용의] 요, 매트리스
—[形] 1. 익은 ¶①철이 든 나이 2. 신중한 3. [어음 따위] 만기의
—[他] 1. …을 성숙시키다, 무르익게 하다 ¶②오랫동안 묵힌 포도주 2. …을 완성시키다 —[自] 1. 성숙하다 2. [어음이] 만기가 되다
—[名] 1. 무르익음, 성숙 ¶①무르익다 2. 완성 3. [어음의] 만기일 ¶②만기일에 지불하다
—[形] 1. 눈물을 잘 흘리는 2. 마음이 약한, 감상적인
—[名] 큰 나무 망치(메) —[他] 1. …을 때려 상처를 내다 2. …을 거칠게 다루다
—[自] 1. 종잡을 수 없는 말을 오래 지껄이다 2. 어슬렁어슬렁 거닐다, 헤매다
—[名] 영묘(靈廟), 능
—[名] 연한 자줏빛 —[形] 연한 자줏빛의
—[名] [동물의] 위

M

mawk·ish [mɔ́:kiʃ] *adj.* **1.** causing (someone) to feel sick. **2.** sentimental in a silly way.
—[形] 1. [냄새·맛이] 메스꺼운, 구역질 나는 2. 아주 감상적인

*** max·im** [mǽksim] *n.* [C] **1.** a short expression of a general truth. **2.** a briefly-expressed rule to guide people.
—[名] 1. 격언 2. 처세술

max·i·ma [mǽksimə] *n.* pl. of **maximum.**

*** max·i·mum** [mǽksiməm] *n.* [C] (pl. **-mums** or **-ma**) the greatest possible number, amount, quantity, degree or point. ↔minimum ¶*The confusion was at its ~.*① —*adj.* greatest; highest.
—[名] 최대한, 최대량, 극대(極大) ¶① 혼란은 그 극에 달했다
—[形] …최고(최대)의, 극한의

⁑ may [mei] *auxil. v.* (**might**) **1.** be allowed to; be free to. ↔must not ¶*"May I come in?" "Yes, you ~ (No, you ~ not)." | I ~ sit down, mayn't* [meint] *I?*① **2.** be able to; can. ↔can not ¶*It ~ safely be said that … | Work hard while you ~.*② **3.** will possibly. ¶*It ~ or ~ not be true. | He ~ come, but I'm not sure. | He ~ have called on her.*③ ⇒[usage] **4.** ⦅used after *ask, wonder,* etc.; expressing *some doubt*⦆ ¶*I wonder who he ~ be.* **5.** ⦅expressing *wishes*⦆ ¶*May he live long!* **6.** ⦅expressing *a request*⦆ ¶*You ~ stand up, Tom.* **7.** ⦅in *adv. clause* expressing *purpose*⦆ ¶*He works hard* [*so*] *that he ~ succeed.* **8.** ⦅in *adv. clause* expressing *concession*⦆. ¶*However* (or *No matter how*) *tired you ~ be, you must do the work.*④
1) ***as best one may,*** as well as possible.
2) ***be that as it may,*** although some [contrasting fact] may be true.
3) ***come what may,*** whatever may happen.
4) ***may as well do,*** have no special reason not to do.
5) ***may well do,*** have good reason to do.
—[助] 1. …해도 좋다 ¶①앉아도 좋겠지요? 2. …할 수 있다 ¶②일할 수 있을 때에 열심히 일해라 3. …인지도 모르다 ¶③그는 그녀를 방문했을지도 모른다 [usage] 과거의 일을 말할 때는 may+have+*pp*.로 됨 4. …일까? 5. 하여 주소서 6. [가벼운 명령으로] …해라 7. …하기를 8. 비록 …일지라도 ¶④아무리 피곤할지라도 이 일은 해야 한다
[熟] 1)될 수 있는 대로 잘 2)그것은 그렇다치고 3)어떤 일이 있을지라도 4)…하는 편이 좋다 5)하는 것이 당연하다(무리가 아니다)

⁑ May [mei] *n.* the fifth month of the year.
—[名] 5월

⁑ may·be [méibi(:)] *adv.* perhaps; possibly.
—[副] 아마

May Day [´ ˋ] *n.* the first day of May, celebrated as a spring festival; nowadays labor parades and meetings are held.
—[名] 5월제; 메이데이, 노동절

may·on·naise [mèiənéiz] *n.* [U] a cream-like salad dressing or sauce.
—[名] 마요네에즈[소오스]

⁑ may·or [méiər, mɛ́ər] *n.* [C] the chief officier of a city.
—[名] 시장

may·or·al·ty [méiərəlti, mɛ́ərəl-] *n.* [U] the position or term of office of mayor.
—[名] 시장의 직(임기)

may·or·ess [méiəris, mɛ́ə-] *n.* [C] the wife of a mayor.
—[名] 시장 부인

May·pole, may- [méipòul] *n.* [C] a tall pole decorated with ribbons, flowers, etc., around which people dance on May Day. ⇒fig.
—[名] 5월제의 기둥(5월제에 꽃 따위로 장식한 기둥)

[maypole]

May queen [´ ˋ] *n.* a girl, chosen as the queen on May Day.
—[名] 5월의 여왕(5월제에 뽑혀 화관을 씀)

maze [meiz] *n.* [C] **1.** a complicated path from which it is hard to find a way out. ¶*a ~ of streets.*① **2.** a confused state of mind. ¶*He is lost in a ~.*② —*vt.* ⦅in *passive*⦆ puzzle; confuse.
—[名] 1. 미로(迷路) ¶①아주 복잡한 길 2. 혼란 ¶②그는 어찌할 바를 모르고 있다 —[他] …을 어리둥절하게 하다

ma·zur·ka, ma·zour·ka [məzə́:rkə] *n.* **1.** [C] a lively Polish dance. **2.** [U] the music for this dance.
—[名] 1. 마주르카 2. 마주르카 춤곡

ma·zy [méizi] *adj.* (**-zi·er, -zi·est**) **1.** like a maze. **2.** bewildering; puzzling. ▷**maz·i·ness** [-nis] *n.*
—[形] 1. 미로 같은 2. 혼란된

M. D. Doctor of Medicine.

⁑ me [mi:, mi] *pron.* the objective case of **I.**
—[代] 나를(에게)

Me. Maine.

⁑ mead·ow [médou] *n.* [U] a field covered with grass which animals eat for food.
—[名] 목초지

mead·ow·land [médoulæ̀nd] *n.* [U] meadow.
—[名] 목초지

mead·ow·lark [médoulɑ̀:rk] *n.* [C] a little American
—[名] [미국산] 종다리의 일종

mea·ger, *Brit.* **mea·gre** [míːɡər] *adj.* (**-ger·er, -ger·est** or *Brit.* **-grer, -grest**) **1.** poor. ¶*a ~ income.* **2.** lacking in flesh; thin.
mea·ger·ly, *Brit.* **-gre-** [míːɡərli] *adv.* in a meager manner.
mea·ger·ness, *Brit.* **-gre-** [míːɡərnis] *n.* ⓤ the state or quality of being thin or poor.
‡**meal**¹ [miːl] *n.* ⓒ all the food that is eaten at one time. ¶*daily meals / a square ~*① */ have* (or *eat, take*) *a ~*② */ make a hearty ~* (or *good*) *~ of* (*something*).③ */ To be taken two hours after meals.*④ **2.** ⓤ mealtime.
meal² [miːl] *n.* **1.** ⓤ any eatable grain that is roughly ground, esp. corn meal. **2.** grain ground to rough flour.
meal·time [míːltàim] *n.* ⓤ the usual time for eating a meal.
meal·y [míːli] *adj.* (**meal·i·er, meal·i·est**) **1.** like meal. **2.** covered with meal. **3.** (of potatoes) dry and powdery. **4.** pale.
meal·y-mouth·ed [míːlimáuðd] *adj.* not willing to tell the truth frankly.
‡**mean**¹ [miːn] *v.* (**meant**) *vt.* **1.** have (an idea) in mind; intend to do (something); purpose; design. (*~ to do*) ¶*They ~ you no harm.* / *They ~ no harm to you.*① */ She means mischief.*② */ Do you ~ to stay long? / I meant to have helped her.*③ */ I meant it for your good.* **2.** intend to cause (someone) to do. (*~ someone to do*) ¶*I ~ you to marry him.*④ **3.** intend to express (something). (*~ that* ...) ¶*What do you ~ by the word?*⑤ */ I ~ that you are a coward.* **4.** be a sign of (something); signify. ¶*What does the word ~?* **5.** cause (something) to happen; result in (something). ¶*This means the ruin of me.* **6.** have a value equal to (something). (*~ something to*) ¶*His mother means the world to him.* ——*vi.* have a certain kind of feeling.
1) **be meant for,** ⓐ have been decided or destined to become (a doctor, etc.). ¶*She is meant for his wife.* / *They are meant for each other.*⑥ ⓑ have been decided to belong to (someone). ¶*This doll is meant* 2) *I mean what I say.*, I say it seriously. [*for her.*⑦
3) **mean business,** be serious.
4) **mean well by** (or **to, toward**) *someone,* have good intentions toward (someone).
‡**mean**² [miːn] *adj.* **1.** low in quality, grade, or rank; humble. ¶*a man of ~ birth.* **2.** of poor appearance. ¶*a ~ house.* **3.** morally low; base; small-minded. ¶*~ thoughts.*① **4.** giving or spending very little; not generous; selfish. ¶*He is ~ about* (or *over*) *money.*② **5.** of small importance. ¶*the meanest flower.*③
1) **have a mean opinion of** (=*make light of*) someone.
2) **no mean,** not bad; good. ¶*no ~ scholar.*
∗**mean**³ [miːn] *adj.* **1.** just halfway; middle; average. ¶*the ~ annual temperature*① */ 5 is the ~ number between 3 and 7.* **2.** ordinary; not too much or too little. ¶*take a ~ course.* **3.** (of the time) between two events. ¶*for the meantime*② */ in the meantime.*③ ——*n.* ⓤ something that is halfway; the average.
me·an·der [miændər] *n.* ⓒ **1.** (often *pl.*) the winding course of a stream. **2.** a wandering without any special aim. ——*vi.* **1.** follow a winding course. ¶*~ through hills and fields.*① **2.** walk about idly or without any special goal. (*~ along* a river)
∗**mean·ing** [míːniŋ] *n.* ⓒⓤ something meant or intended; significance; sense. ¶*a hidden ~* / *grasp* (or *catch*) *the ~ of something*① */ This word has a double ~.*
——*adj.* full of meaning or significance. ¶*a ~ glance.*

——ⓝ 1. 빈약한 ¶①얼마 안 되는 수입 2. 야윈

——ⓐ 빈약하게; 야위어
——ⓝ 빈약, 야윔

——ⓝ 1. [1회분의]식사 ¶①충분한 식사/②식사를 하다/③배불리 먹다/④식후 두 시간 후에 복용할 것 2. 식사 시간

——ⓝ 1. 거칠게 간 옥수수 2. 체로 치지 않은 굵은 가루
——ⓝ 식사 시간

——ⓐ 1. 가루 모양의 2. 가루를 뿌린 3. [감자 따위] 말라서 가루처럼 된 4. 창백한

——ⓐ 솔직히 사실을 말하지 않는
——ⓥ 1. …을 뜻(의도)하다; …할 작정이다 ¶①그들이 너에게 해를 끼치려는 것은 아니다/②그녀는 장난을 꾸미고 있다/③나는 그녀를 도와줄 작정이었는데 2. …에게 …시킬 작정이다 ¶④너를 그와 결혼시킬 작정이다 3. …의 뜻으로 말하다 ¶⑤무슨 뜻으로 그런 말을 하느냐? 4. …을 의미하다 5. …을 초래(야기)하다 6. …만큼 중요하다 ——ⓘ […에 대하여 …한] 기분을 갖고 있다

🔲 1)ⓐ…으로 될 예정(운명)이다 ¶⑥그들은 결혼하기로 되어 있다 ⓑ…용(…의 몫)이다 ¶⑦이 인형은 그녀에게 줄 것이다 2)내 말은 진담이다 3)[농담이 아니고] 진담이다 4)…에게 호감을 품다

——ⓐ 1. 열등한, 저급한; 천한 2. 초라한 3. 상스러운, 비열한 ¶①비열한 생각 4. 인색한; 이기적인 ¶②그는 돈에 인색하다 5. 보잘것 없는 ¶③이름도 없는 꽃

🔲 1)…을 멸시하다 2)꽤 좋은

——ⓐ 1. [분량·위치가] 중간의 ;평균의 ¶①연간 평균 온도 2. 보통의, 중용의 3. [시간의] 사이의, 중간의 ¶②잠깐 동안, 일시적으로/③그 동안에, 그러는 사이에 ——ⓝ 중간, 중도, 중용

——ⓝ 1. [강의] 굽이, 굴곡 2. 어슬렁거리기, 배회 ——ⓘ 1. 굽이쳐 흐르다 ¶①언덕과 들판 사이를 꾸불꾸불 흐르다 2. 정처없이 거닐다

——ⓝ 의미, 의의 ¶①…의 의미를 파악하다

——ⓐ 의미심장한

mean·ing·ful [mí:niŋf(u)l] *adj.* full of significance. ▷**mean·ing·ful·ness** [-nis] *n.*
—[形] 의미심장한

mean·ing·ful·ly [mí:niŋfuli] *adv.* in a significant manner.
—[副] 의미심장하게

mean·ing·less [mí:niŋlis] *adj.* without meaning.
—[形] 무의미한

mean·ing·ly [mí:niŋli] *adv.* in a meaning manner; with meaning or significance.
—[副] 의미심장하게

mean·ly [mí:nli] *adv.* **1.** in a poor or humble manner; poorly; humbly. **2.** in a base or vulgar manner. **3.** in a stingy, miserly manner.
—[副] 1. 빈약하게; 초라하게 2. 상스럽게, 비열하게 3. 인색하게

think meanly of (=*despise*) *someone.*
[熟] …을 경멸하다

mean·ness [mí:nnis] *n.* [U] the state or quality of being mean.
—[名] 비천(卑賤); 빈약; 비열; 인색

‡**means** [mi:nz] *n. pl.* **1.** 《used as *sing.* or *pl.*》 a way in which something is done. ¶*a ~ to an end*① / *the ~ of communication and transportation.*② **2.** 《used as *pl.*》 property; wealth; income. ¶*a man of ~*③
—[名] 1. 수단, 방법 ¶①목적 달성의 수단 / ②통신·교통기관 2. 재산; 수입 ¶③재산가

1) ***by all means,*** without fail; certainly
2) ***by any means,*** somehow; in any way possible.
3) ***by fair means or foul,*** by any method.
4) ***by means of,*** through; by using (something). ¶*We express our thought by ~ of words.*④
5) ***by no means,*** in no way; certainly not. ¶*He is by no ~ equal to the task.*⑤

[熟] 1)반드시 2)어떻게든지 3)수단을 가리지 않고 4)…에 의하여 ¶④사상은 말로 나타낸다 5)결코 …않다 ¶⑤그는 그런 일은 결코 해낼 수 없다

‡**meant** [ment] *v.* pt. and pp. of **mean.**

‡**mean·time** [mí:ntàim] *n., adv.* [in] the time between two occasions. ¶*in the ~*① / *Father will be home in the ~.* / *Meantime, Mother baked bread in an oven.*
—[名] 그 사이[에] ¶①그러는 사이에

‡**mean·while** [mí:n(h)wàil] *n., adv.* =meantime.

mea·sles [mí:zlz] *n. pl.* 《used as *sing.*》 an infectious disease which children commonly have, with fever and small red spots on the skin.
—[名] 홍역

mea·sly [mí:zli] *adj.* (**-sli·er, -sli·est**) **1.** of measles; having measles. **2.** (*colloq.*) meager; worthless.
—[形] 1. 홍역의, 홍역에 걸린 2. 《口》 비열한; 하찮은

meas·ur·a·ble [méʒ(ə)rəbl] *adj.* can be measured.
—[形] 잴 수 있는

meas·ur·a·bly [méʒ(ə)rəbli] *adv.* to a measurable amount or degree.
—[副] 잴 수 있게; 눈에 보이게

‡**meas·ure** [méʒər] *vt.* **1.** find out the size, weight, volume, etc. of (something or someone). ¶*The tailor measured her for a new dress.* **2.** judge the value of (someone); estimate. ¶*We can not ~ a person at a glance.*① **3.** compare. 《~ someone or something *with*》 ¶*~ one's strength with someone.*② —*vi.* **1.** have a certain size, weight, volume, etc. ¶*The cloth measures ten yards.*③ **2.** find out sizes or amounts. ¶*Can you ~ correctly?*
—[他] 1. …을 재다 2. …을 판단하다; 평가하다 ¶①흘깃 보고 사람을 판단할 수는 없다 3. …을 비교하다;겨루게 하다 ¶②…와 힘을 겨루다 —[自] 1. [길이·크기 따위] …이다 ¶③그 천은 10 야아드이다 2. 재다

1) ***measure one's length,*** fall at full length.
2) ***measure off,*** mark off (ground) by measuring.
3) ***measure out,*** ⓐ take a part of (something) by measuring. ⓑ give (something) to each by measuring. ¶*~ out food to the people.*
4) ***measure swords*** (=*fight*) ***with someone.***

[熟] 1)벌렁 자빠지다 2)[땅]을 재어서 구분하다 3)ⓐ[분량]을 재어서 갖다 ⓑ[재어서] 분배하다 4) …와 싸우다

—*n.* **1.** [U] the extent, size, volume, etc. of anything. **2.** [C] a tool for measuring. ¶*a tape ~*④ / *a yard ~.*⑤ **3.** [U] a method or system of measuring. ¶*metric ~.*⑥ **4.** 《*the ~*》 any standard for measuring. **5.** 《often *pl.*》 a limit. ¶*above* (or *beyond, out of*) *~*⑦ / *keep measures*⑧ / *You should set ~ to your desire.*⑨ **6.** [U] quantity; degree. ¶*a great ~ of truth*⑩ / *in a* (or *some*) *~.*⑪ **7.** 《often *pl.*》 a course of action. ¶*foolish measures*⑫ / *take measures.*⑬ **8.** [C] a plan or law. **9.** [U] rhythm in poetry or music.
—[名] 1. 크기; 치수;부피 2. [자·되 따위의] 계량기구 ¶④줄자/⑤야아드 자 3. 계량법 ¶⑥미터 도량법 4. 척도;표준 5. 한도;적당한 정도 ¶⑦몹시; 과도하게/⑧중용을 지키다/⑨너는 욕망을 억제해야 한다 6. 양(量); 정량;정도 ¶⑩상당한 진실성/⑪어느 정도까지 7. 조치; 수단; 방법 ¶⑫어리석은 조치/⑬수단을 강구하다 8. 법안 9. 운율(韻律); 박자

1) ***give full*** (***short***) ***measure,*** give the right (less than the right) amount.
2) ***tread a measure,*** dance.

[熟] 1)되(분량)가 후하다(박하다) 2)댄스를 하다

meas·ured [méʒərd] *adj.* **1.** determined by some stand-
—[形] 1. 정확히 잰, 표준에 맞는; 한결

measureless — **median**

ard; regular. **2.** (of speech) careful and considered. **3.** rhythmical. ¶*walk with ~ tread* (or *steps*).
meas·ure·less [méʒərlis] *adj.* immeasurable; endless; boundless.
* **meas·ure·ment** [méʒərmənt] *n.* Ⓤ **1.** the act of measuring. **2.** (usu. *pl.*) the size, volume, weight, etc., found by measuring. ¶*inside* (*outside*) *~*① / *The measurements of this room are 10 by 15 feet.*② **3.** the system of measuring.
‡ **meat** [miːt] *n.* Ⓤ **1.** animal flesh used as food; the part that can be eaten, as of shellfish, egg, and fruit. ¶*crab ~* / *fat ~*① / *lean ~*.② **2.** the most important part. ¶*the ~ of 'a story.*③ **3.** (*colloq.*) something that one is good at. ¶*Tennis is my ~.* [*to someone.*] *be meat and drink* (=*be very important* or *pleasant*)
meat·y [míːti] *adj.* (**meat·i·er**, **meat·i·est**) **1.** of or like meat. **2.** full of meat. **3.** substantial.
Mec·ca [mékə] *n.* **1.** the capital of Saudi Arabia, where Mohammed was born. ⇒N.B. **2.** Ⓒ (*m-*) a place which many people desire to visit. ¶*a tourist ~*.
* **me·chan·ic** [mikǽnik] *n.* Ⓒ a worker who is skillful at using or repairing machinery. ¶*an auto ~* / *a farm ~* / *an aviation* (or *aircraft*) *~*.
* **me·chan·i·cal** [mikǽnik(ə)l] *adj.* **1.** of or made by a machine. ¶*~ power* / *~ products*① / *~ engineering.*② **2.** acting without thinking, like a machine. ¶*a ~ smile.*③
me·chan·i·cal·ly [mikǽnikəli] *adv.* in a mechanical manner. ¶*make one's notes ~.*①
mech·a·ni·cian [mèkəníʃ(ə)n] *n.* Ⓒ a worker who is skillful at making or repairing machinery.
me·chan·ics [mikǽniks] *n. pl.* (used as *sing.*) **1.** the science of machinery. **2.** the science of forces and motion.
* **mech·a·nism** [mékənìz(ə)m] *n.* **1.** Ⓒ a machine; the working parts of any machine. ¶*the ~ of a watch.*① **2.** Ⓒ any structure or system of parts working together. ¶*the ~ of government.*② **3.** Ⓤ technique. **4.** Ⓤ the theory that everything in this universe can be explained by the laws of physics and chemistry,
mech·a·ni·za·tion [mèkənizéiʃ(ə)n / -nai-] *n.* Ⓤ the act of mechanizing; the state of being mechanized. (esp. of an army).
mech·a·nize [mékənàiz] *vt.* have (work) done by machines; perform (work) by means of machines.
* **med·al** [médl] *n.* Ⓒ a coinlike piece of metal, marked with a design or words, given as a reward or honor, or for celebrating a great event. ¶*award a ~.*①
me·dal·li·on [midǽljən] *n.* Ⓒ **1.** a large medal. **2.** any round ornament with a design or raised figure on it.
med·al·ist, *Brit.* **-al·list** [médlist] *n.* Ⓒ **1.** a person who makes medals. **2.** a person who has been given a medal. ¶*a gold ~.*①
* **med·dle** [médl] *vi.* **1.** take part in others' affairs unnecessarily. (*~ in* or *with something*) ¶*~ in other people's affairs.*① **2.** touch or handle others' things without permission. (*~ with something*) ¶*Don't ~ with my gun.*②
med·dler [médlər] *n.* Ⓒ a person who meddles.
med·dle·some [médlsəm] *adj.* apt to meddle in others' affairs.
me·di·a [míːdiə] *n. pl.* of **medium**.
me·di·ae·val [mèdìːvəl, mìː-] *adj.* =medieval.
* **me·di·al** [míːdiəl] *adj.* **1.** situated in the middle. **2.** of an average.
* **me·di·an** [míːdiən] *adj.* in the middle. ¶*a ~ line* (*num-*

ber, point). —*n.* [C] (*Mathematics*) **1.** the middle number of a series. **2.** a line or point in the middle.
점(中點), 중선(中線)

me·di·ate [mí:dièit→*adj.*] *vt.* **1.** settle (something) as a go-between. ¶~ *a dispute.*① **2.** carry (a gift, etc.) from one person to another; communicate (knowledge, etc.). —*vi.* act as a peacemaker between people who quarrel. 《~ *between* two countries》 —*adj.* [mí:diit] indirect. ↔immediate
—[타] 1.[협정 따위]를 조정하다 ¶①분쟁을 조정하다 2.[선물]을 전하여 주다; [사상]을 전달하다 —[자] 조정(중재)하다 —[형] 간접의

me·di·a·tion [mì:diéiʃ(ə)n] *n.* [U] the act of mediating; the state of being mediated.
—[명] 중재

me·di·a·tor [mí:dièitər] *n.* **1.** [C] a person who mediates. **2.** 《*the M-*》 Christ.
—[명] 1.중재자 2.그리스도

me·di·a·to·ry [mí:diətɔ̀:ri / -èit(ə)ri] *adj.* of or directed toward mediation.
—[형] 중재의

⁑**med·i·cal** [médik(ə)l] *adj.* **1.** of medicine. ¶~ *attendance*① / ~ *science*② / ~ *treatment.*③ **2.** of the treatment of disease by drugs. ↔surgical ¶~ *ward.*④
—[형] 1.의학의 ¶①진료/②의학/③의료 2.냇과의 ¶④냇과 병원

medi·cal·ly [médikəli] *adv.* **1.** by medicine. **2.** from the medical point of view.
—[부] 1.의학에 의하여 2.의학적으로

med·i·cat·ed [médikèitid] *adj.* having some medical power or properties. ¶~ *soap*① / *a* ~ *bath.*②
—[형] 약물(藥物)을 가한 ¶①약용 비누/②약탕(藥湯)

me·dic·i·nal [medísin(ə)l] *adj.* **1.** of medicine. **2.** useful as medicine. ¶*a* ~ *herb.*① ▷**me·dic·i·nal·ly** [-li] *adv.*
—[형] 1.약의 2.약효가 있는 ¶①약초

⁑**med·i·cine** [méd(i)s(i)n] *n.* [U] **1.** [U][C] any drug used to prevent or cure disease. ¶*a patent* ~① / *a dose of* ~② / *take medicine[s]*③ / (*proverb*) *A good* ~ *tastes bitter.*④ **2.** the science of preventing, treating, and curing disease. ¶*preventive* ~.⑤ **3.** a branch of this science making use of treatment by drugs, diet, etc. ↔surgery **4.** magical power believed to cure disease among North American Indians, etc.
—[명] 1.약 ¶①[특허] 매약(賣藥)/②약 한 첩/③약을 먹다/④《俚》양약은 입에 쓰다 2.의학 ¶⑤예방 의학 3.냇과적 치료 4.[북미 토인 등의] 주문, 마법의 힘

*__me·di·e·val__ [mèdií:vəl, mì:-] *adj.* of the Middle Ages. ⇒[N.B.]
—[형] 중세의 [N.B.] A.D. 500–1450 년경

me·di·o·cre [mí:diòukər] *adj.* only average; neither very good nor very bad; commonplace.
—[형] 보통의; 평범한

me·di·oc·ri·ty [mì:diákriti / -ɔ́k-] *n.* (pl. **-ties**) **1.** [U] the state or quality of being mediocre. **2.** [C] a person of mediocre ability.
—[명] 1.평범 2.평범한 사람

*__med·i·tate__ [méditèit] *vi.* think deeply and seriously. 《~ *on* or *upon* something》 —*vt.* plan (something) in the mind. ¶~ *revenge.*①
—[자] 숙고하다 —[타] …을 기도(企圖)하다 ¶ ①복수를 꾀하다

med·i·ta·tion [mèditéiʃ(ə)n] *n.* [U] the act of meditating; deep thought or reflection.
—[명] 명상(瞑想); 숙려(熟慮)

med·i·ta·tive [méditèitiv, +*Brit.* -tətiv] *adj.* of meditation; deep in thought; apt to meditate.
—[형] 명상의; 명상에 잠기는; 명상적인

med·i·ta·tive·ly [méditèitivli, +*Brit.* -tətiv-] *adv.* in a meditative manner; with deep and serious thought.
—[부] 명상에 잠겨서

med·i·ta·tor [méditèitər] *n.* [C] a person who meditates.
—[명] 명상자

*__Med·i·ter·ra·ne·an__ [mèditəréiniən], **the** *n.* a large inland sea between Africa and Europe. —*adj.* of the Mediterranean Sea or the region around it.
—[명] 지중해 —[형] 지중해[지방]의

*__me·di·um__ [mí:diəm] *n.* (pl. **-ums** or **-di·a**) **1.** [U] the state or condition of being in the middle; moderateness. **2.** [C] a means by which something is accomplished. ¶*an advertising* ~① / *mass media*② **3.** [C] a substance through which something exists, acts, or is carried. **4.** [C] a person who is supposed to receive messages from the spirit world.
—[명] 1.중용(中庸) 2.수단 ¶①광고 매체/②대중 매체 3.매체, 매질(媒質) 4.영매(靈媒)

by the medium of, through.
[熟] …을 통하여

—*adj.* moderate in position, condition, or degree. ¶~ *quality*③ / *a medium-range ballistic missile.*④
—[형] 중간의 ¶③중간 품질/④중거리 탄도탄

me·di·um-sized [mí:diəmsáizd] *adj.* of a moderate size; neither too large nor too small.
—[형] 중형의

med·lar [médlər] *n.* [C] a tree of the rose family or its apple-like fruit.
—[명] 서양모과나무[의 열매]

med·ley [médli] *n.* [C] **1.** a mixture of things of different kinds. **2.** a musical piece made up of different parts slected from several pieces. —*adj.* made up of dif-
—[명] 1.[이것저것] 주워모은 것 2.혼성곡 —[형] 주워모은 ¶①혼합 경주[경영(競泳)]/②혼합 계주(繼走)

M

meek [mi:k] *adj.* mild and gentle.
[*as*] **meek as a lamb,** very mild and gentle.
[mí:kli] *adv.* in a mild and gentle manner.
—웹 온순한, 부드러운
圈 아주 온순한
—웹 온순하게

meek·ness [mí:knis] *n.* Ⓤ the state or quality of being meek; mildness; gentleness.
—명 온순

meer·schaum [míərʃəm, +U.S. -ʃɔ:m] *n.* **1.** Ⓤ a soft, white clay-like stone used to make tobacco pipes. **2.** Ⓒ a tobacco pipe made of this material.
—명 1. 해포석(海泡石) 2. 해포석 파이프

‡ **meet** [mi:t] *v.* (**met**) —*vt.* **1.** come face to face with (someone); come upon (someone). ¶*I met Mr. Smith in the park.* **2.** be present at the arrival of (someone). ¶*They met the doctor at the airport.* **3.** be introduced to (someone); become acquainted with (someone). ¶*When did you first ~ my sister? / I am glad to ~ you.*① ⇒N.B. **4.** fight; experience (a difficulty, etc.). ¶*~ objections*② */ ~ one's father's death.* **5.** satisfy (a demand, etc.); pay (a bill, etc.). ¶*~ debts / I will do my best to ~ your wishes.* **6.** touch; join; reach. ¶*Her hand met mine. / This road meets the highway. / The sound of the sea met the ear.*③ —*vi.* **1.** come face to face; come together; get acquainted with each other. **2.** be long enough to touch or join; touch; join. ¶*This belt won't ~ around my waist.*④ */ make the two ends ~.*⑤
1) **meet someone halfway,** give up one's own opinion, etc. to some extent in order to agree with another person.
2) **meet trouble halfway,** be too much afraid of what may happen. ⌈chance.⌋
3) **meet with,** come across (someone or something) by —*n.* Ⓒ a meeting. ¶*a track-and-field ~.*⑥
—타 1. …를 만나다; 마주치다 2. …을 마중하다 3. …에게 소개되다 4. …에 대항하다(곤란 따위에) 직면하다 ¶②반대에 직면하다 5. …을 충족(만족)시키다; 지불하다 6. …에 접촉하다; 교차하다; 닿다 ¶③파도 소리가 들렸다 —자 1. 만나다; 회합하다; 알게 되다 2. 접촉하다; 합치다; [두 끝 따위가] 닿다 ¶④이 허리띠는 동여매기에 짧다/⑤수지를 맞추다; 수입 범위 안에서 생활하다

圈 1)…와 타협(절충)하다 2)쓸데없는 걱정을 하다 3)우연히 만나다

—명 모임; 대회 ¶⑥육상 경기 대회

‡ **meet·ing** [mí:tiŋ] *n.* Ⓒ **1.** ⓊⒸ the act or state of coming together, esp. for a special purpose; an assembly. ¶*an athletic ~ / a farewell ~ / a welcome ~ / break up* (or *dissolve*) *a ~*① */ call* (*hold*) *a ~.*② **2.** a point where things come together. **3.** a duel. **4.** an encounter.
—명 1. 집합, 모임, 집회 ¶①폐회하다/②모임을 소집(개최)하다 2. 합류점 3. 결투 4. 만남, 마주침

meeting house [´- -´] *n.* a building used for public worship, esp. by Protestants. ⇒N.B.
—명 교회당, 예배당 N.B. 영국에서는 비국교도의 예배당을 이름

meg·a·cy·cle [mégəsàikl] *n.* Ⓒ one million cycles.
—명 100만 사이클

meg·a·lo·ma·ni·a [mègəloumèiniə] *n.* Ⓤ an insane enthusiasm for greatness, power, wealth, etc.
—명 과대망상증

meg·a·phone [mégəfòun] *n.* Ⓒ a large funnel-shaped horn used to make the voice louder.
—명 메가폰, 확성기

meg·a·ton [mégətàn] *n.* Ⓒ a unit of explosive power equal to that of a million tons of T.N.T. ⇒N.B.
—명 메가톤 N.B. 원자폭탄의 폭발력에 쓰는 단위

mel·an·cho·li·a [mèlaŋkóuliə] *n.* Ⓒ a disordered mental condition marked by extreme depression of spirits and gloomy feelings.
—명 우울병

mel·an·chol·ic [mèlaŋkálik / -kɔ́l-] *adj.* **1.** (*rare*) melancholy. **2.** of melancholia.
—웹 1. 우울한 2. 우울병의

* **mel·an·chol·y** [méləŋkòli / -kəl-] *n.* Ⓤ **1.** a sad and gloomy state of mind. **2.** melancholia. —*adj.* **1.** sad and low in spirits; gloomy. **2.** causing sadness and depression. ¶*a ~ scene.*
—명 1. 우울 2. 우울병 —웹 1. 우울한 2. [풍경 따위가] 쓸쓸한

Mel·a·ne·sia [mèləní:ʒə / -ziə] *n.* a group of islands in the South Pacific, northwest of Australia.
—명 멜라네시아(대양주 중부의 여러 섬의 총칭)

me·lee, -lée [méilei / mélei, ´-´] *n.* Ⓒ a confused hand-to-hand fight.
—명 난투

* **mel·low** [mélou] *adj.* **1.** (of fruit) mature; soft, sweet, and juicy because of ripeness. ¶*~ apple / a ~ peach.* **2.** (of wine, etc.) having a rich smell. ¶*~ port.* **3.** (of personality) grown wise and gentle by age and experience. ¶*~ character / ~ wisdom.* **4.** (of color, sound, etc.) soft, full, and rich. ¶*~ light / ~ tones.*
—웹 1. [과일 이] 익은, 달콤한, 감미로운 2. [포도주 따위가] 향기로운 3. [인품이] 원만한, 원숙한 4. [빛깔·음 따위가] 부드러운; 풍부하고 아름다운 5. 명랑한; 거나하게 취한 —자타 익게 하다, 익다; 원숙하게 하다(되다); 부

5. (*colloq.*) pleasant; cheerful; merrily drunk. **—*vt., vi.*** make (someone or something) become mature, gentle or soft. ¶*Age mellowed her.*
드럽게 하다(되다)

mel·low·ly [mélouli] *adv.* in a mellow way.
—[副] 익어서; 달콤하게

mel·low·ness [mélounis] *n.* [U] the state or quality of being mellow.
—[名] 원숙; 감미로움

me·lo·di·ous [melóudiəs] *adj.* **1.** sounding agreeable to the ear. **2.** producing sweet melody. ¶*a ~ voice.*① ▷**me·lo·di·ous·ly** [-li] *adv.*
—[形] 1. 듣기 좋은 2. 선율적인 ¶①아름다운 목소리

mel·o·dist [mélədist] *n.* [C] a person who sings or composes melodies.
—[名] 선율이 아름다운 작곡가(성악가)

mel·o·dra·ma [méloudrὰ:mə, +*U.S.* -drӕ̀mə] *n.* **1.** [C] a sensational romantic drama. **2.** [C] an event similar to this kind of drama. **3.** [U] any sensational writing, speech, or behavior.
—[名] 1. 멜로드라마(낭만적이고 감상적인 통속극) 2. 사건 3. 연극조의 언동

mel·o·dra·mat·ic [mèloudrəmǽtik] *adj.* like a melodrama; sensational and exaggerated.
—[形] 멜로드라마적인; 연극조의

∗ **mel·o·dy** [mélədi] *n.* (pl. **-dies**) **1.** [U] sweet music. **2.** [C] a chief part in music. **3.** [C] the leading part in a song or other composition.
—[名] 1. 아름다운 곡조 2. 선율 3. 가곡, 곡조, 가락

mel·on [mélən] *n.* [C] any of the varieties of the muskmelon; a watermelon. ▷**mel·on·like** [-laik] *adj.*
—[名] 멜론(참외류)의 총칭; 수박

‡ **melt** [melt] *v.* (**melt·ed, melt·ed** or **mol·ten**) *vi.* **1.** become a liquid from a solid. ¶*Ice melts at 0°C.*① | *I'm simply melting.*② | *Sugar melts in the mouth.* | *The snow has melted away in the sun.* **2.** become mixed or disappear gradually. ¶*One color melts into another.*③ **3.** (of feelings, heart, etc.) become soft or tender. ¶*Her anger melts under kindness.* **—*vt.*** **1.** change (something) from a solid into a liquid state. ¶*Heat melts butter.* **2.** make (someone) tender or gentle. ¶*kindness that melts the heart.*
—[自] 1. 녹다 ¶①얼음은 섭씨 영도에서 녹는다/②더워서 죽을 지경이다 2. 차츰 섞이다(사라지다) ¶③빛깔이 다른 빛깔과 융합되어 있다 3. [감정 따위가] 누그러지다 —[他] 1. …을 녹이다 2. …을 부드럽게 하다

melt·ing [méltiŋ] *adj.* sentimental.
—[形] 감상적인; 감미로운

melting point [⌐– ⌐] *n.* the degree of temperature at which a solid melts into a liquid.
—[名] 융점(融點)

mel·ton [mélt(ə)n] *n.* [U] a smooth, heavy woolen cloth used for overcoats.
—[名] 외투용 옷감의 일종

‡ **mem·ber** [mémbər] *n.* [C] **1.** a person who belongs to a group, a team, or a society. ¶*a ~ of a club* | *a class ~.* | *Member of Parliament.*① ⇒[N.B.] | *a ~ of Congress.*② ⇒[N.B.] **2.** a part or an element of a whole. **3.** a part of a person, an animal, or a plant, esp. a leg or arm.
—[名] 1. 일원, 회원 ¶①[영국의] 국회의원 [N.B.] M.P.로 줄임/②[미국의] 국회의원 [N.B.] M.C.로 줄임 2. 부분 3. [사람·동식물 따위의] 일부, [특히] 손발

∗ **mem·ber·ship** [mémbərʃìp] *n.* **1.** [U] the state of being a member; the position as a member. ¶*a ~ card.*① | *a ~ fee.*② **2.** [C] the whole group of persons who belong to an organization. ¶*have a large ~.*③
—[名] 1. 회원임; 그 지위 ¶①회원증/②회비 2. 전(全)회원 ¶③회원이 많다

mem·brane [mémbrein] *n.* **1.** [C] a thin, sheet-like layer in animals or plants. **2.** [U] a writing material made from the skin of an animal; parchment.
—[名] 1. 엷은 막(膜) 2. 양피지

me·men·to [meméntou] *n.* (pl. **-toes** or **-tos**) a thing to remember (something or someone) by; a souvenir; a token.
—[名] 기념품, 유품, 추억이 되는 것

mem·o [mémou] *n.* (pl. **-os**) (*colloq.*) =memorandum. ¶*make a ~.*①
—[名] 《口》 메모 ¶①메모를 하다

mem·oir [mémwɑ:r] *n.* **1.** [C] a biography. **2.** 《*pl.*》 a written record of events closely connected with one's own experiences. **3.** [C] a record of scientific or academic study. **4.** 《*pl.*》 a collection of the studies by a learned society.
—[名] 1. 전기(傳記) 2. [사건 따위의] 회고록; 체험담; 자서전 3. 연구논문; 보고서 4. 학회지(學會誌)

mem·o·ra·ble [mémərəbl] *adj.* worthy of being remembered; not easily forgotten; very remarkable.
—[形] 기억할 만한; 잊을 수 없는; 현저한

mem·o·ran·da [mèmərǽndə] *n.* pl. of **memorandum.**

mem·o·ran·dum [mèmərǽndəm] *n.* [C] (pl. **-dums** or **-da**) **1.** a short note to remember something by. **2.** a short informal message from one country to other countries.
—[名] 1. 메모 2. [외교상의] 각서

M

· **me·mo·ri·al** [memɔ́:riəl] *adj.* in memory of some person or event. ¶*a ~ festival*① | *a ~ service*② | *a ~ address.*③
—[形] 기념의 ¶①기념제/②추도회/③기념 연설

—*n.* **1.** [C] something that makes people remember some person or event. **2.** ⦅usu. *pl.*⦆ a record.
—[名] 1. 기념물 2. 각서; 기록

Memorial Day [-ˊ-- ˋ] *n.* (*U.S.*) a day for honoring dead soldiers, May 30; Decoration Day. ⇨[N.B.]
—[名] 전몰 장병 기념일; 현충일 [N.B.] 대다수의 주에서 5월 30일

me·mo·ri·al·ize [mimɔ́:riəlaiz] *vt.* keep the memory of (someone) by a memorial; commemorate.
—[他] …을 기념하다

* **mem·o·rize** [meməràiz] *vt.* **1.** (chiefly. *U.S.*) learn (something) by heart. **2.** note (something) down.
—[他] 1. ⦅美⦆ …을 암기하다 2. …을 기록하다

▷**mem·o·ri·za·tion** [mèməraizéiʃ(ə)n] *n.*

‡ **mem·o·ry** [méməri] *n.* (pl. **-ries**) [U] **1.** the act of remembering; the ability to remember. ¶*be fresh in one's* ~① | *commit to* ~② | *bear in* ~③ | *have a long* ~④ | *have a bad* ~⑤ | *keep one's* ~ *alive*⑥ | *to the best of my* ~⑦ | *His* ~ *declined.* **2.** [C] things or persons remembered. ¶*memories of childhood.* **3.** the length of time during which things are remembered. ¶*beyond the* ~ *of man.*⑧ **4.** reputation after death. ¶*love someone's* ~⑨ | *honor the* ~ *of the deceased.*⑩
—[名] 1. 기억[력] ¶①기억에 새롭다/②기억하다/③잘 기억해 두다/④기억력이 좋다/⑤기억력이 나쁘다/⑥기억을 생생하게 해두다/⑦내가 기억하고 있는 한 2. 기념이 되는 것(사람) 3. 기억의 범위 ¶⑧인류의 기억에도 없는 4. [죽은 후의] 명성/⑨고인의 기억을 그리워하다/⑩죽은 사람의 추억을 되새기다

in memory (=*in honor or remembrance*) ***of*** someone.
[熟] …을 기념하여

‡ **men** [men] *n.* pl. of **man**.

* **men·ace** [ménəs] *n.* **1.** [C] anything that makes a threat. ¶*a public* ~.① **2.** [U] the act of threatening; the condition of being threatened. —*vt.* threaten. ¶~ *someone with death.*
—[名] 1. 위협 ¶①공해 2. 협박 —[他] …에 위협을 주다

men·ac·ing [ménəsiŋ] *adj.* making a menace.
—[形] 위협적인

men·ac·ing·ly [ménəsiŋli] *adv.* in a menacing way.
—[副] 위협적으로

me·nag·er·ie [minǽdʒəri] *n.* [C] a collection of wild animals kept for exhibition; a place where such animals are kept.
—[名] 야성 동물의 전시; 순회 동물원

‡ **mend** [mend] *vt.* **1.** bring back (something) to a good condition; repair. ¶~ *a broken window* (*doll, stocking,* etc.) | ~ *a road* | *I had my coat mended.*① **2.** make (something) better; reform; correct. ¶~ *a fault* | ~ *one's ways*② | (*proverb*) *Least said, soonest mended.*③ | *Regrets will not* ~ *matters.*④ **3.** increase; improve; quicken. ¶~ *one's pace* | ~ *the fire.*⑤ —*vi.* become better; improve. ¶*The patient is mending.*
—[他] 1. …을 고치다; 수선하다 ¶①코우트를 고치게 했다 2. …을 고치다, 개선(개혁)하다 ¶②행실을 고치다/③말수가 적으면 고치기도 쉽다/④후회한다고 일이 호전되지 않는다 3. …을 늘리다; 재촉하다 ¶⑤불을 더 잘 타게 하다 —[自] [건강·사태가] 나아지다

—*n.* **1.** [C] a mended place. **2.** [U] (of a person, his health, etc.) the act or state of improving.
—[名] 1. 고친 장소 2. 고치기, 나아지기, 개량

be on the mend, be getting better in health or condition.
[熟] 나아지는 방향으로 가고 있다

men·da·cious [mendéiʃəs] *adj.* false; not true.
—[形] 허위의

men·dac·i·ty [mendǽsiti] *n.* (pl. **-ties**) **1.** [U] the state of being mendacious. **2.** [C] a lie.
—[名] 1. 거짓[말장이]임 2. 거짓, 허위

mend·er [méndər] *n.* [C] a person who mends something.
—[名] 수선(개량)자

men·di·cant [méndikənt] *adj.* begging; living by charity. ¶*a* ~ *tramp* | *a* ~ *order.*① —*n.* [C] **1.** a beggar. **2.** a begging friar.
—[形] 구걸하는, 탁발(托鉢)의 ¶①[가톨릭교의] 탁발 수도회 —[名] 1. 거지 2. 탁발승

men·folk [ménfòuk] *n.* ⦅usu. *pl.*⦆ (*colloq.*) men, esp. those in a family or community. ↔womenfolks
—[名] ⦅口⦆ [어떤 가족·지역 내의] 남자들

me·ni·al [mí:niəl] *adj.* suitable for or belonging to a servant; mean; lowly. ¶*a* ~ *task* | ~ *labor.* —*n.* [C] a servant who does the most lowly tasks.
—[形] 천한 [일을 하는]; 하인의 —[名] 하인, 머슴

men·ses [ménsi:z] *n. pl.* the monthly flow of bloody fluid in women.
—[名] 월경

men·sur·a·ble [ménʃurəbl] *adj.* measurable.
—[形] 잴 수 있는

men·su·ra·tion [mènʃuréiʃ(ə)n] *n.* [U] **1.** the act of measuring. **2.** a branch of mathematics dealing with finding size, area, volume, etc.
—[名] 1. 측정 2. 구적법(求積法), 측정법

‡ **men·tal** [méntl] *adj.* **1.** of the mind. ↔physical ¶~ *age*① | *a* ~ *blow*② | *a* ~ *disease*③ | ~ *faculties*④ | *a* ~ *test*⑤ | ~ *work.* **2.** done by the mind. ¶~ *arithmetic.*⑥ **3.** of mental disease. ¶*a* ~ *institution* (or *hospital*).
—[形] 1. 정신의 ¶①정신 연령/②정신적 타격/③정신병/④지력(知力)/⑤지능검사 2. 머리 속으로 하는 ¶⑥암산 3. 정신병의

men·tal·i·ty [mentǽliti] *n.* (pl. **-ties**) **1.** [U] mental ability or power. ¶*a man of average* ~. **2.** [C] a state of mind; a mental attitude.
—[名] 1. 지력 2. 정신 상태, 사고 방식

men·tal·ly [méntəli] *adv.* in or with the mind.
—♣ 마음으로; 정신적으로

men·thol [ménθoul, -θəl / -θɔl] *n.* ⓤ a white, waxy substance obtained from the oil of peppermint and used in medicine.
—명 멘토올, 박하뇌(薄荷腦)

‡men·tion [ménʃ(ə)n] *vt.* speak or write of (someone or something) briefly. 《~ *that* ...》 ¶*as mentioned above*① / *to* ~ *a single example*② / *Don't* ~ *it.*③
not to mention, to say nothing of (something or someone); besides. ¶*He can speak French, not to* ~ *English.*④
—*n.* ⓤ the act of mentioning; ⓒ a brief statement about something. ¶*There was no* ~ *of it in the papers.*
make mention (=*speak briefly about*) *of* someone or something.
—타 …에 대하여 말하다(쓰다); 언급하다; [이름]을 들다 ¶①위에서 말한 바와 같이 ②한 가지 예를 들면/③천만에요
熟 …은 말할 것도 없이 ¶④그는 영어는 말할 것도 없이 프랑스말도 한다

—명 언급, 진술
熟 …을 들어 말하다

*men·u [ménju:, méi- / ménju:] *n.* **1.** ⓒ a list of dishes served at a meal. **2.** ⓤ the dishes served in a meal.
—명 1. 메뉴, 식단표 2. 요리; 식사

me·ow [miáu / mju:] *n.* ⓒ the sound a cat or kitten makes. —*vi.* make this sound.
—명 고양이 울음소리 —자 고양이가 [야웅하고] 울다

mer·can·tile [mə́:rkəntil, -tàil / mə́:kəntail] *adj.* **1.** of merchants or trade. ¶*a* ~ *firm*① / *the* ~ *marine*② / ~ *law*③ / *a* ~ *paper.*④ **2.** (*Economics*) of mercantilism.
—형 1. 상업의 ¶①상사(商社)/②[한 나라의] 상선③상법/④상업 어음 2. 중상(重商)주의의

mer·ce·nar·y [mə́:rsinèri / -sin(ə)ri] *adj.* **1.** working or done for money or reward only; influenced by a desire for gain or reward. ¶~ *motives.*① **2.** hired in a foreign army. —*n.* ⓒ (*pl.* **-nar·ies**) a hired soldier in a foreign army.
—형 1. 돈(보수)을 바라고 하는; 욕심이 앞서는 ¶①돈이 목적인 동기 2. [외국 군대에] 돈으로 고용된 —명 [외국군의] 용병(傭兵)

mer·cer [mə́:rsər] *n.* ⓒ (*Brit.*) a dealer in cloth, esp. silks.
—명 (英) 피륙 상인; [특히] 비단 장수

*mer·chan·dise [mə́:rtʃəndàiz] *n.* ⓤ 《*collectively*》 articles for sale. ¶*No* ~ *can be returned.*① / *general* ~.②
—*vt., vi.* buy and sell; trade. ▷**mer·chan·dis·er** [-ər] *n.*
—명 상품 ¶①반품 사절/②잡화
—타자 매매하다, 거래하다

‡mer·chant [mə́:rtʃənt] *n.* ⓒ **1.** a person who buys and sells goods. **2.** (*Brit.*) a person who trades on a large scale with foreign countries. **3.** (*U.S.*) a storekeeper; *a retailer.* —*adj.* of trade. ·¶~ *ships.*①
—명 1. 상인 2. 무역상 3. 소매 상인
—형 상업의 ¶①상선

mer·chant·a·ble [mə́:rtʃəntəbl] *adj.* marketable; that can be sold. ¶*a merchant ship.*
—형 장사에 알맞은, 팔리는

mer·chant·man [mə́:rtʃəntmən] *n.* ⓒ (*pl.* **-men** [-mən])
—명 상선

merchant prince [⌴⌴] *n.* a very rich merchant.
—명 호상(豪商)

merchant service [⌴⌴] *n.* the merchant navy, which is occupied in trade by sea.
—명 상선대(商船隊)

*mer·ci·ful [mə́:rsif(u)l] *adj.* having or showing mercy; tender-hearted. ▷**mer·ci·ful·ly** [-fuli] *adv.*
—형 자비로운, 인정 많은; 관대한

mer·ci·less [mə́:rsilis] *adj.* without mercy; cruel.
▷**mer·ci·less·ly** [-li] *adv.* —**mer·ci·less·ness** [-nis] *n.*
—형 무자비한, 잔인한

mer·cu·ri·al [mə:rkjúəriəl] *adj.* **1.** of, like, or having mercury. ¶~ *column*① / ~ *poisoning.*② **2.** 《*M-*》 of the god Mercury or the planet Mercury. **3.** lively or active; apt to change. —*n.* ⓒ a drug containing mercury.
—형 1. 수은의 ¶①수은주/②수은 중독 2. 수성(水星)의; 머어큐리신(神)의 3. 활기 있는; 변덕스러운 —명 수은제(水銀劑)

*mer·cu·ry [mə́:rkjuri] *n.* (*pl.* **-ries**) **1.** ⓤ a heavy silvery metal element, liquid at ordinary temperatures; quicksilver. **2.** ⓒ the column of mercury in a thermometer or barometer. ¶*a* ~ *thermometer*① / *The* ~ *is rising.*② **3.** 《*M-*》 the Roman god of commerce. **4.** 《*M-*》 the planet nearest to the sun. **5.** ⓒ A messenger; a guide.
—명 1. 수은 2. 수은주 ¶①수은 온도계/②온도가 올라가고 있다. 경기(기분)가 나아지고 있다 3. 머어큐리신 4. 수성(水星) 5. 사자(使者); 안내인

‡mer·cy [mə́:rsi] *n.* (*pl.* **-cies**) **1.** ⓤ kindness, pity, or forgiveness shown to the weaker; ⓒ an act of kindness. ¶*an angel of* ~① / *without* ~② / *for mercy's sake*③ / *have* (or *take*) ~ *on someone.*④ / *Mercy on me!*⑤ / *throw oneself on an enemy's* ~.⑥ **2.** ⓒ something to be grateful for; a blessing. ¶*It's a* ~ *that I've met you.*
at the mercy (=*completely in the power*) *of* a god, etc.
—명 1. 자비, 연민, 인정; 친절한 행위 ¶①자비의 천사/②인정사정 없이/③제발, 부디/④…을 불쌍히 여기다/⑤이런!, 어머나!/⑥적의 자비심에 매달리다 2. 행운; 고마운 것

熟 …의 처분대로

‡mere [míər] *adj.* (*superl.* **mer·est**) nothing more than; only; simply. ¶*a* ~ *folly*① / *by* ~ *accident*② / *a* ~ *child*③/ *The* ~ *sight of a snake makes him shudder.*④
—형 단순한, 단지 …의 ¶①어리석기 짝이 없음/②아주 우연히/③그는 뱀을 보기만 해도 떤다

mere·ly [míərli] *adv.* simply ; purely.
 not merely...but [**also**]**...**, not only...but also....
mer·e·tri·cious [mèritríʃəs] *adj.* attractive in a false or showy way; vulgar.
merge [məːrdʒ] *vt.* **1.** cause (something) to be absorbed. **2.** join together ; combine. —*vi.* become absorbed or combined. ¶*Two small banks merged with a large one.*
merg·er [məːrdʒər] *n.* Ⓤ Ⓒ the act of combining several companies to make a large one.
me·rid·i·an [mərídiən] *n.* Ⓒ **1.** an imaginary line on the earth's surface passing through the North and South Poles. **2.** noon. **3.** the highest point; a period of great success, happiness, health, etc., in one's life. ¶*the ~ of life.*① **4.** the highest point reached by the sun or a star. —*adj.* **1.** of a meridian (*n.* 1.). **2.** of noon. **3.** of a period of success, happiness, health, etc. in life.
me·rid·i·o·nal [mərídiən(ə)l] *adj.* **1.** of a meridian (*n.* 1, 3). **2.** of southern Europe, esp. of southern France. **3.** southern. —*n.* (often *M-*) the people of southern Europe, esp. those of France.
me·ri·no [mərí:nou] *n.* (pl. **-nos**) **1.** Ⓒ a kind of sheep with long silky wool. **2.** Ⓤ the wool of this sheep; a soft cloth made from this wool.
mer·it [mérit] *n.* **1.** Ⓤ Ⓒ good points. ¶*a man of ~*① / *the merits of a book.* **2.** Ⓒ something that is worthy of reward. **3.** Ⓒ a reward or punishment. **4.** (*pl.*) a quality that is worthy of reward or punishment.
 make a merit of (=*take merit to oneself for*) *something.* ⌈*who merited respect.*⌉
 —*vt.* be worthy of (something) ; deserve. ¶*a man*
mer·i·to·ri·ous [mèritɔ́:riəs] *adj.* worthy of reward or praise. ¶*have ~ features.*①
mer·maid [məːrmèid] *n.* Ⓒ **1.** an imaginary girl in the sea who is like a fish from the waist down. **2.** a very good woman swimmer.
mer·man [məːrmæn] *n.* Ⓒ **1.** an imaginary man in the sea who is like a fish from the waist down. **2.** a very good swimmer.
mer·ri·ly [mérili] *adv.* in a merry manner.
mer·ri·ment [mérimənt] *n.* Ⓤ fun and joy.
mer·ry [méri] *adj.* (**-ri·er**, **-ri·est**) full of joy and laughter; cheerful; jolly. ¶*I wish you a ~ Christmas; Merry Christmas to you.*① / *~ laughter* / *Merry England.*①
 1) *make merry,* be filled with laughter and gaiety.
 2) *make merry over* (=*make fun of* or *enjoy*) *someone* or *something.*
mer·ry-go-round [mérigouràund] *n.* Ⓒ a large round platform with wooden animal-shaped seats, and which goes round to music by machinery.
mer·ry·mak·er [mérimèikər] *n.* Ⓒ a person who shares in merriment and gaiety.
mer·ry·mak·ing [mérimèikiŋ] *n.* Ⓤ gaiety ; gay entertainment ; gay festivities. —*adj.* jolly, festive.
mes·dames [mèidɑ́:m / méidæm] *n.* pl. of **madame.**
mes·de·moi·selles [mèidəmɔzél] *n.* pl. of **mademoiselle.**
mesh [meʃ] *n.* **1.** Ⓒ one of the open spaces of a network or wire screen. ¶*a net of coarse ~*① / *wire ~*① **2.** (*pl.*) **3.** the threads or cords of a net. **3.** a net or network. **4.** (usu. *pl.*) a snare. **5.** Ⓤ the uniting of the teeth of two gear wheels to fit each other.
 in mesh, fitted together ; in gear.
 —*vi, vt.* **1.** catch (something) in a net ; be caught in a net. **2.** (of gears) fit together. ⌈*mesmerism.*⌉
mes·mer·ic [mezmérik, +*U.S.* mes-] *adj.* of or caused by

—⓿ 단지, 단순히
⓿ 단지 ···뿐 아니라 ···도
—⓿ 저속한, 야한, 겉보기뿐의

—他 1. ···을 흡수시키다 2. ···을 합동(병합)시키다 —自 흡수되다; 합동(합병)하다
—名 합병

—名 1. 자오선 2. 정오 3. 전성기 ¶①장년(壯年) 4. [하늘에서의 태양·별의] 최고점

—形 1. 자오선의 2. 정오의 3. 전성기의, 혈기왕성한
—形 1. 자오선의; 전성기의 2. 남유럽의;[특히] 남프랑스의 3. 남쪽의 —名 남유럽의 주민, [특히] 남프랑스 사람

—名 1. 메리노 양(羊) 2. 메리노 나사(羅紗)

—名 1. 장점 ¶①우수한 사람 2. 칭찬할 만한 것 3. 상벌(賞罰) 4. 공과(功過)

⓿ ···을 자랑하다

—他 ···할 가치가 있다
—形 칭찬할 만한 ¶①여러가지 가치가 있는 특색이 있다
—名 1. [여자] 인어(人魚) 2. 여자 수영 선수

—名 1. [남자] 인어 2. 남자 수영 선수

—⓿ 즐겁게
—名 유쾌, 환락
—形 명랑한 ¶①크리스마스를 축하합니다 / ②즐거운 영국(옛날부터의 호칭)

⓿ 1) 흥겹게 놀다 2) ···을 놀리다

—名 회전목마

—名 흥겹게 노는 사람

—名 흥겹게 놀기 —形 명랑한, 흥겹게 노는

—名 1. 그물코 ¶①코가 거친 그물 / ② 철망의 그물코 2. 그물코를 이룬 실(철사) 3. 그물; 그물 세공 4. 올가미 5. 톱니바퀴의 맞물림

⓿ [톱니바퀴가] 맞물려서
—自 1. ···을 그물로 잡다;그물에 걸리다 2. [톱니바퀴가] 맞물다
—形 최면술의

mes·mer·ism [mézm(ə)rìz(ə)m, més-] *n.* ⓤ the art of causing someone to sleep. ⌈mesmerizes.⌉
mes·mer·ist [mézm(ə)rist, més-] *n.* ⓒ a person who
mes·mer·ize [mézməràiz, -més-] *vt.* exercise mesmerism on (someone). ▷ **mes·mer·iz·er** [-ər] *n.*
Mes·o·po·ta·mi·a [mès(ə)pətéimiə] *n.* a region in Asia between the Tigris and Euphrates rivers. ▷ **Mes·o·po·ta·mi·an** [-ən] *n., adj.* ⌈tiles. —*adj.* of this era.⌉
Mes·o·zo·ic [mèsouzóuik] *n.* the geological era of rep-
* **mess** [mes] *n.* ⓒ **1.** the state of being dirty or confused; a mass of things. **2.** a state of difficulty or trouble. ¶*get into a ~*① / *make a ~ of*② **3.** a group of people, esp. soldiers or sailors, taking their meals together; the meals of such a group. ¶*be at ~ / go to ~.*
in a mess, in confusion.
—*vt.* **1.** supply (someone) with meals. **2.** make (something) dirty; spoil. —*vi.* eat together in a group.
1) *mess about* (or *around*), be busy without doing any real work.
2) *mess up,* make (something) dirty or untidy; spoil.
: **mes·sage** [mésidʒ] *n.* ⓒ **1.** words or news, etc., sent from one person to another. ¶*I'll give him your ~.*① / *leave a ~ with someone*② / *a ~ form.*③ **2.** (*U.S.*) a formal, official speech or writing. ¶*the President's ~.*④
go on a message, go on an errand.
: **mes·sen·ger** [mésindʒər] *n.* ⓒ a person who carries a message or does an errand.
Mes·si·ah [misáiə] *n.* **1.** the savior who is expected to set the Jewish people free. **2.** Jesus the Christ. **3.** ⓒ (often *m-*) a person who saves a people or a nation.
mes·sieurs [mésərz] *n. pl.* of *monsieur.*
mess·mate [mésmèit] *n.* ⓒ a person who regularly eats together with others in the army or navy.
Messrs. [mésərz] *n.* =messieurs. ⌈mess; dirty.⌉
mess·y [mési] *adj.* (**mess·i·er, mess·i·est**) in or like a
: **met** [met] *v.* pt. and pp. of **meet.** ⌈bolism.⌉
met·a·bol·ic [mètəbálik / -ból-] *adj.* (*Biology*) of meta-
me·tab·o·lism [metǽbəlìz(ə)m] *n.* ⓤ (*Biology*) the process of changing food into living matter, and then into waste matter, in a living body.
: **met·al** [métl] *n.* ⓤ **1.** any chemical element, such as iron, gold, tin, silver, etc.; a mixture of such elements. ¶*base metals*① / *light (heavy) metals*② / *noble metals*③ / *sheet metals.*④ **2.** (*Brit.*) broken stones used for roads and road beds. ¶*road ~.* **3.** (*pl.*) (*Brit.*) the railway. ¶*leave* (or *run off*) *the metals.*⑤ **4.** something made of metal. **5.** material; stuff.
—*vt.* (**-al·ed, -a·ling** or *Brit.* **-alled, -al·ling**) cover (something) with metal.
me·tal·lic [metǽlik] *adj.* of or like metal; made of metal.
met·al·lur·gy [métələ̀:rdʒi] *n.* ⓤ the science or art of getting metal from ore.
met·al·work [métlwə̀:rk] *n.* ⓤ **1.** things made of metal. **2.** the making of such things.
met·al·work·er [métlwə̀:rkər] *n.* ⓒ a person who works at or in metalworking.
met·al·work·ing [métlwə̀:rkiŋ] *n.* ⓤ the act or process of making things out of metal.
met·a·mor·phose [mètəmɔ́:rfouz] *vt., vi.* change (something) in form or character; transform. (*~ to* or *into* something) ⌈**phosis.**⌉
met·a·mor·pho·ses [mètəmɔ́:rfəsi:z] *n. pl.* of **metamor-**
met·a·mor·pho·sis [mètəmɔ́:rfəsis] *n.* ⓤⓒ (*pl.* **-ses**) a striking change in form or character by natural growth,

— 名 최면술
— 名 최면술사
— 他 …에게 최면술을 걸다

— 名 메소포타미아

— 名 중생대(中生代) — 形 중생대의
— 名 **1.** 혼란 상태; 불결; 뒤범벅 **2.** 난처함; 곤란 ¶①난처하게 되다/②…을 망쳐놓다 **3.** [군대 따위에서의] 식사 동료; 식사

熟 혼란(당황)하여
— 他 **1.** …에게 급식하다 **2.** …을 엉망으로 만들다; 더럽히다 — 自 회식하다

熟 1)꾸물거리다 2)…을 더럽히다, 망쳐놓다
— 名 **1.** 메시지; 전갈, 전언 ¶①그에게 말을 전하겠다/② …에게 전갈을 부탁하다/③메모지 **2.** 교서 ¶④대통령 교서
熟 심부름가다
— 名 사자, 심부름꾼

— 名 **1.** [유대인의] 구세주 **2.** 그리스도 **3.** [민족·국가의] 구제자, 해방자

— 名 [군대 따위에서] 같이 식사하는 친구

— 形 더러운

— 形 《生》 신진대사의
— 名 《生》 신진대사

— 名 **1.** 금속; 합금 ¶①[구리·납 따위의] 비금속/②경(중)금속/③귀금속/④판금(板金) **2.** (英) [도로에 까는] 자갈 **3.** 《英》 [철도의] 궤도, 선로 ¶⑤[열차가] 탈선하다 **4.** 금속제품 **5.** 재료, 물질

— 他 …에 금속을 입히다(씌우다)

— 形 금속의, 금속성의, 금속제의
— 名 야금학(冶金學), 야금술

— 名 **1.** 금속 세공품 **2.** 금속 세공

— 名 금속 세공사

— 名 금속 세공

— 他 自 변형(변질)시키다(하다), 변태시키다(하다)

— 名 변형, 변태

development, etc.

met·a·phor [métəfər] *n.* [U][C] a way of using a word or phrase to express an idea different from its usual meaning. — [名] 은유(隱喩)

met·a·phys·i·cal [mètəfízik(ə)l] *adj.* **1.** of metaphysics. **2.** very abstract and difficult to understand. ▷**met·a·phy·si·cal·ly** [-li] *adv.* — [形] 1. 형이상학의 2. 추상적인

met·a·phy·si·cian [mètəfizíʃ(ə)n] *n.* [C] a specialist in metaphysics. — [名] 형이상학 학자

met·a·phys·ics [mètəfíziks] *n. pl.* ⟪used as *sing.*⟫ **1.** a branch of philosophy that deals with the nature of being, the universe, and the theory of knowledge. **2.** (*colloq.*) abstract talk. — [名] 1. 형이상학, 순정(純正)철학 2. 추상적 논의

mete [mi:t] *vt.* **1.** divide (something) among several persons. ⟪~ *out* something *to*⟫ **2.** measure. — [他] 1. …을 할당하다 2. …을 재다

* **me·te·or** [mí:tiər] *n.* [C] a falling star; a piece of matter coming from outer space into the earth's atmosphere at a great speed and burning with a bright glow. — [名] 유성, 운석(隕石)

me·te·or·ic [mì:tiɔ́:rik, -árik / -ɔ́rik] *adj.* **1.** of a meteor ¶*a ~ stone.*① **2.** brilliant for a short time like a meteor. **3.** of the atmosphere. — [形] 1. 유성의 ¶①운석 2. 유성 같은, 일시적으로 화려한 3. 기상(氣象)의

me·te·or·ite [mí:tiəràit], **-or·o·lite** [-ərəlàit] *n.* [C] a body of stone or metal that falls to the earth from outer space; a fallen meteor. — [名] 운석, 유성

me·te·or·o·log·i·cal [mì:tiərəládʒik(ə)l / -lɔ́dʒi-] *adj.* of meteorology. ¶*~ observation*① / *The Central Meteorological Observatory*② / *a ~ station.*③ — [形] 기상[학상]의 ¶①기상 관측/②중앙 관상대/③측후소

me·te·or·ol·o·gist [mì:tiərálədʒist / -rɔ́l-] *n.* [C] a person who specializes in meteorology. — [名] 기상학자

me·te·or·ol·o·gy [mì:tiərálədʒi / -rɔ́l-] *n.* [U] the science of the atmosphere, weather, and climate. — [名] 기상학

me·ter[1], *Brit.* **me·tre** [mí:tər] **1.** *n.* [C] a unit of length in the metric system. **2.** [U] any poetic rhythm; (*Music*) a form of rhythm and time. — [名] 1. 미터(길이의 단위) 2. 운율; 박자

* **me·ter**[2] [mí:tər] *n.* [C] an instrument for measuring. ¶*an electric ~ / a gas ~* — [名] 계량기, 미터

meth·ane [méθein] *n.* [U] a colorless, odorless gas which burns well, produced by the decay of living things. — [名] 메탄

⁑ **meth·od** [méθəd] *n.* **1.** [C] a way of doing something. ¶*a teaching ~ / a deductive ~.*① **2.** [U] an orderly arrangement of ideas. ¶*a man of ~.*② — [名] 1. 방법 ¶①연역법(演繹法) 2. 질서 ¶②꼼꼼한 사람

me·thod·i·cal [meθádik(ə)l / -θɔ́d-] *adj.* **1.** arranged or done in an orderly way; systematic. **2.** having a habit of doing things in an orderly way. — [形] 1. 질서가 있는 2. 꼼꼼한

me·thod·i·cal·ly [meθádikəli / -θɔ́d-] *adv.* in a methodical manner. — [副] [질서] 정연하게

Meth·od·ism [méθədìz(ə)m] *n.* [U] the organizations, beliefs, and teachings of the Methodists. — [名] 메더디스트[교]파

Meth·od·ist [méθədist] *n.* [C] a member of one of several Protestant religious bodies originally developed from the teachings and work of John Wesley in the 18th century. —*adj.* of the Methodists or Methodism. — [名] 메더디스트 교도(교파) —[形] 메더디스트 교도(교파)의

meth·od·ize [méθədàiz] *vt.* arrange (work, etc.) in a methodical way. — [他] [일 따위]에 순서를 매기다

meth·yl [méθil, +*Brit.* mí:θail] *n.* [U] a kind of alcohol that is poisonous if drunk. ¶*~ alcohol.* — [名] 메틸

me·tic·u·lous [mitíkjuləs] *adj.* extremely careful about small matters. — [形] 하찮은 일에 마음을 쓰는, 소심한

me·tic·u·lous·ly [metíkjuləsli] *adv.* in a meticulous manner. — [副] 소심하게, 좀스럽게

me·ton·y·my [metánimi / -tɔ́n-] *n.* [U] the use of the name of one thing for another with which it is associated, as "crown" for "king." — [名] 환유(換喩)

me·tre [mí:tər] *n.* (*Brit.*) =meter.

met·ric [métrik] *adj.* of the measuring system based on the meter. ¶*the ~ system.*① — [形] 미터[법]의 ¶①미터법

met·ri·cal [métrik(ə)l] *adj.* **1.** of or in a rhythm of a poem. ¶*a ~ composition.*① **2.** of or for measurement. — [形] 1. 운율의 ¶①운문 2. 측량[용]의

M

〔metronome〕

met·ro·nome [métrənòum] *n.* [C] an instrument to beat time, used esp. in practicing music. ⇒fig. —[名] 메트로놈

* **me·trop·o·lis** [metrápəlis / -tróp-] *n.* [C] **1.** the capital of a country. ¶*the Governor of the Seoul ~ / Seoul is the ~ of Korea* **2.** any large city; a principal center of business and culture. ¶*Pusan is a ~ of Korea* ⇒[usage] —[名] 1. 수도 2. 주요도시 [usage] capital(수도)과 대조하는 경우는 주요 도시의 뜻으로 씀. 미국에서는 New York는 metropolis이고 Washington D C.는 capital임

* **met·ro·pol·i·tan** [mètrəpálitən / -pól-] *adj.* of a large city or metropolis. ¶*the Seoul Metropolitan Government.*① **—*n.*** [C] **1.** a person living in a capital **2.** an archbishop. —[形] 수도의 ¶①서울시청 —[名] 1. 수도의 주민 2. 대사교, 대주교

met·tle [métl] *n.* [U] **1.** a state of mind; disposition. **2.** courage; spirit ¶*a man of ~.*①
1) ***be on*** (or ***upon***) ***one's mettle,*** prepare to do one's best.
2) ***put someone on his mettle,*** encourage someone.
—[名] 1. 기질 2. 용기, 원기 ¶①기개 있는 사람 [熟] 1)분발하다 2)…을 분기시키다

met·tle·some [métlsəm] *adj.* full of mettle; high-spirited; courageous. —[名] 원기 있는, 기운찬, 용기 있는

mew[1] [mju:] *n.* [C] the cry of a cat. **—*vi.*** make this sound. —[名] 고양이 울음소리 —[自] 야옹하고 울다

mew[2] [mju:] *n.* [C] a gull. —[名] 갈매기

* **Mex·i·can** [méksikən] *adj.* of Mexico or its people. **—*n.*** [C] a person of Mexico. —[形] 멕시코[사람]의 —[名] 멕시코[사람]의 —[名] 멕시코 사람

* **Mex·i·co** [méksikòu] *n.* a country in North America, just south of the United States. ¶*the Gulf of ~.*① —[名] 멕시코 ¶①멕시코 만

mez·za·nine [mézənì:n, ⌣⌣ˊ, +*Brit.* métsə-] *n.* [C] **1.** a low story between two main stories of a building, often in the form of a balcony. **2.** (*Brit.*) the floor below the stage of a theater. —[名] 1. 중이층(中二層) 2. 《英》 무대 밑, 무대 밑의 지하실

mez·zo [médzou, métsou] *adj.* (*Music*) moderate; middle. —[副] 적절하게

mez·zo-so·pran·o [métsousəprǽnou, -prá:nou / médzousəprá:nou] *n.* (*Music*) [C] **1.** a voice between soprano and contralto. **2.** a singer having such a voice. —[名] 《樂》 1. 메조소프라노, 중고음(中高音) 2. 메조소프라노 가수

mg. milligram; milligrams.

mi [mi:] *n.* [C] (*Music*) the third tone of the scale. —[名] 《樂》 미(전음계의 세째 음)

mi. mile; miles

Mi·am·i [maiǽmi, -á:mi] *n.* a city in southeastern Florida. —[名] 미국 Florida 주의 도시

mi·aow, mi·aou [mi(:)áu] *n.* =meow; mew.

mi·ca [máikə] *n.* [U] a mineral that can be easily separated into thin, partly transparent sheets. —[名] 운모(雲母)

⁑ **mice** [mais] *n.* pl. of **mouse.**

Mich. 1. Michigan **2.** Michaelmas.

Mi·chael [máikl], **Saint** *n.* (in the Bible) an archangel who, with the loyal angels, won the war with revolting angels. —[名] 천사장(天使長) 미카엘

Mi·chael [máikl] *n.* a man's name. ⇒[N.B.] —[名] 남자 이름 [N.B.] 애칭 Mike

Mich·ael·mas [míklməs] *n.* (*Brit.*) the festival of the archangel Michael, held on September 29. ⇒[N.B.] —[名] 《英》 미카엘 제(祭) [N.B.] quarterdays(사계 지불일)의 하나

Mi·chel·an·ge·lo [màikəlǽndʒilou], **Buonarroti** *n.* (1475–1564) an Italian sculptor, painter, architect and poet. —[名] 이탈리아의 조각가·미술가·건축가·시인

* **Mich·i·gan** [míʃigən] *n.* a north central State of the United States. ⇒[N.B.] —[名] 미시간 주 [N.B.] Mich.로 줄임. 수도 Lansing

mi·cra [máikrə] *n.* pl. of **micron.**

mi·cro- [máikrə-, máikrou-] a word element meaning "small" or "little". —「소(小)」「미(微)」를 뜻하는 연결형

mi·crobe [máikroub] *n.* [C] **1.** a very small living thing which can be seen only through a microscope. **2.** a disease germ. ¶*a ~ bomb*① / *a ~ hunter.*② —[名] 1. 미생물 2. 세균 ¶①세균탄/②세균과 싸우는 사람(학자)

mi·cro·cosm [máikroukàzəm / -kòz(ə)m] *n.* [C] **1.** a miniature universe. **2.** a man or society thought of as a miniature of the universe. —[名] 1. 소우주 2. [우주의 축도로서의] 인간[사회]

mi·cro·film [máikroufìlm] *n.* [C] a film containing photographs of books, pictures etc. on a very small scale. —[名] 마이크로 필름

mi·crom·e·ter [maikrámitrə / -krómitə] *n.* [C] an instru- —[名] 측미계(測微計)

M

micron [725] **midrib**

ment for measuring exactly small distances, angles, etc.
mi·cron [máikrɑn / -krɔn] *n.* ⓒ (pl. **-cra** or **-crons**) one millionth of a meter. ⇒(N.B.) —名 미크론 [N.B.] μ로 나타냄
mi·cro·or·gan·ism [màikrouɔːrgənìz(ə)m] *n.* Ⓤ any living thing which can be seen only through a microscope. —名 미생물
* **mi·cro·phone** [máikrəfòun] *n.* ⓒ an instrument which changes sounds into electric currents to be strengthened and sent out. ⇒(N.B.) —名 마이크로폰 [N.B.] mike로 줄임
* **mi·cro·scope** [máikrəskòup] *n.* ⓒ an instrument with several lenses for making very small objects large enough to be seen. ¶*an electron* ~① / *under a* ~.② —名 현미경 ¶①전자 현미경/②현미경으로
mi·cro·scop·ic [màikrəskápik / -skɔ́p-], **-i·cal** [-ik(ə)l] *adj.* **1.** of a microscope. **2.** so small as to be seen only through a microscope. ¶*a* ~ *organism*.① —形 1. 현미경의 2. 현미경으로만 보이는; 미세한 ¶①미생물
mi·cro·scop·i·cal·ly [màikrəskápikəli / -skɔ́p-] *adv.* **1.** with the help of a microscope. **2.** in a minute and careful manner. —副 1. 현미경으로 2. 현미경적으로, 미세하게
mi·cro·wave [máikrouwèiv] *n.* ⓒ a very short electromagnetic wave. —名 초단파
* **mid**¹ [mid] *adj.* middle. ¶*in midsummer.* —形 중간의
mid, 'mid² [mid] *prep.* (*poetic*) =amid.
mid·air [midέər] *n.* Ⓤ any point in the air which does not touch the earth or any other thing. ¶*in* ~.① —名 공중 ¶①공중에서
* **mid·day** [míddèi] *n.* Ⓤ the middle of the day. —名 정오
‡ **mid·dle** [mídl] *adj.* halfway between two ends, sides, limits, etc.; in the center. ¶*a* ~ *finger* / *in one's* ~ *twenties.*① —形 한가운데의 ¶① 20대 중간
—*n.* ⓒ **1.** (usu. *the* ~) a point between two ends, sides, limits, etc.; the center. ¶*the* ~ *of the road* / *in the* ~ *of a hot day.* **2.** the middle of a body; the waist. —名 1. 중앙, 한가운데, 한복판 2. [인체의] 허리
—*vt.* put (something) in the middle. —他 …을 한가운데에 놓다
middle age [⌐ ⌐] *n.* the period of life between youth and old age ⇒(N.B.) —名 중년 [N.B.] 약 40세에서 60세까지
mid·dle-aged [mídléidʒd] *adj.* of middle age —形 중년의
Middle Ages [⌐ ⌐], **the**, *n. pl.* the medieval period in the history of Europe, from about 500 A.D. to about 1450 A.D. —名 중세
middle class [⌐ ⌐] *n.* the social class between the very rich class and the working class. ⇒(N.B.) —名 중산 계급
Middle East [⌐ ⌐] *n.* the lands from the eastern Mediterranean to India. ⇒(N.B.) —名 중동 [N.B.] Far East(극동), Near East(근동)
mid·dle·man [mídlmæ̀n] *n.* ⓒ (pl. **-men** [-mèn]) a trader who buys goods from the producer and sells them to other merchants or to consumers. —名 중매인(仲買人)
mid·dle·most [mídlmòust] *adj.* =midmost.
Middle West [⌐ ⌐] *n.* the part of the United States between the Appalachian and Rocky Mountains, bounded on the south by Kansas, Missouri, and the Ohio River. —名 미국 중서부
mid·dling [mídliŋ] *adj.* middle or moderate in size, quality, or degree. —*adv.* (*colloq.*) moderately; fairly. —*n.* (*pl.*) products of medium size, quality, or price. —形 중치의, 가운데쯤의 —副 상당히, 꽤 —名 중치, 중등품
* **mid·dy** [mídi] *n.* (pl. **-dies**) (*colloq.*) =midshipman.
middy blouse [⌐ ⌐] *n.* a loose blouse with a sailor collar, worn esp. by children and young girls. ⇒(N.B.) —名 미디 블라우스, 세일러 복 [N.B.] 단지 middy라고도 함
midge [midʒ] *n.* ⓒ **1.** a very small fly, gnat, or similar flying insect. **2.** a very small person. —名 1. [등에·각다귀 따위] 작은 곤충 2. 난장이
midg·et [mídʒit] *n.* ⓒ **1.** a very small person; a dwarf. **2.** anything very small. —名 1. 몹시 작은 사람; 난장이 2. 초소형의 것
mid·land [mídlənd] *adj., n.* [of] the central part of a country. —形名 내륙(內陸)[의]
mid·most [mídmòust] *adj.* being in the middle or nearest the middle; middlemost. —形 한복판의
‡ **mid·night** [mídnàit] *n.* Ⓤ twelve o'clock at night; the middle of the night. ¶*at* ~① / *dark as* ~.② —名 한밤중 ¶①한밤중에/②캄캄한
burn the midnight oil, study till late at night 熟 밤늦게까지 공부하다
mid·rib [mídrìb] *n.* ⓒ the central vein of a leaf. —名 [잎사귀의]. 중륵(中肋)

mid·riff [mídrif] *n.* [C] a muscular wall between the chest cavity and the abdomen; the diaphragm.
—[名] 횡격막(横隔膜)

mid·ship [mídʃìp] *adj., n.* [in *or* of] the middle part of a ship.
—[形][名] [선체의] 중앙부[의]

mid·ship·man [mídʃìpmən] *n.* [C] (pl. **-men** [-mən]) **1.** (*U.S.*) a student at the United States Naval Academy. **2.** (*Brit.*) a graduate from a government naval school.
—[名] 1.《美》해군 사관학교 생도 2.《英》해군 소위 후보생

‡ **midst**[1] [midst] *n.* [C] 《*the* ~》 middle.
—[名] 한복판, 한가운데

midst, 'midst[2] [midst] *prep.* (*poetic*) =amidst.

mid·stream [mídstríːm] *n.* [C] the middle part of a stream.
—[名] 중류

mid·sum·mer [mídsʌ́mər, -sʌ̀m- / -sʌ̀mə] *n.* [U] **1.** the middle of the summer. ¶*Midsummer Day.*① **2.** the time about June 21st, the longest day of the year.
—[名] 1. 한여름 ¶①세례 요한의 축제일(6월 24일, 사계 지불일의 하나) 2. 하지(夏至)

mid·way [mídwéi → *n.*] *adj., adv.* halfway. —*n.* [⏊⏊ / ⏊⏊] [C] **1.** a half-way point. **2.** (*U.S.*) the place at a fair for side shows.
—[形][副] 중도(中途)의(에서) —[名] 1. 중도 2. 박람회 따위의 여흥장

mid·wife [mídwàif] *n.* [C] (pl. **-wives**) a woman whose profession is to help women in childbirth.
—[名] 조산원

mid·wife·ry [mídwàif(ə)ri / -wif(ə)ri] *n.* [U] the work of helping women in childbirth.
—[名] 조산술

mid·win·ter [mídwíntər] *n.* [U] **1.** the middle of winter. **2.** the time about December 21st, the shortest day of winter.
—[名] 1. 한겨울 2. 동지

mid·wives [mídwàivz] n. pl. of **midwife.**

mien [miːn] *n.* [U] a person's appearance or manner.
—[名] 모습, 용모; 태도

‡ **might**[1] [mait] *auxil. v.* pt. of **may. 1.** 《in the *subjunctive*》 ¶*Anyone ~ do the same, if he had the opportunity.*① / *If he had been there, he ~ have done it.* **2.** 《in *requests*》 ¶*You ~ mail this letter for me.* **3.** 《in *mild blame*》 ¶*You ~ tell (have told) the truth.*② **4.** 《in expressing *possibility* or *probability*》 ¶*You ~ get into trouble.* **5.** 《in *permission*》 ¶*Might I ask you a question?*
—[助] 1. …일 것이다; …인지도 모른다 ¶①기회만 있으면 누구나 그렇게 했을 것이다 2. …하여 주시겠읍니까 3. …해도 좋을 텐데 ¶②사실을 말해 주는 것이 좋을(좋았을) 텐데 4. …일지도 모르다 5. …해도 좋다

1) ***might as well*** *do this* ***as*** *do that,* do this is just as good as to do that.
2) ***might well*** *do something,* there is good reason for doing something.
[熟] 1)…하느니 …하는 편이 낫다 2)…하는 것도 당연하다

‡ **might**[2] [mait] *n.* [U] great strength of body or mind; power to carry out one's will. ¶*Might is right.*①
—[名] 힘; 능력 ¶①힘은 정의다

with might and main, with all one's strength.
[熟] 전력을 다하여

might·i·ly [máitili] *adv.* **1.** in a mighty manner; powerfully. **2.** (*colloq.*) very much; extremely.
—[副] 1. 세게, 힘차게 2.《口》몹시, 대단히

might·i·ness [máitinis] *n.* [U] the state or quality of being mighty.
—[名] 힘셈, 힘참

‡ **might·y** [máiti] *adj.* (**might·i·er, might·i·est**) **1.** showing power; powerful. ¶*The pen is mightier than the sword.*① **2.** (*colloq.*) very great. —*adv.* (*colloq.*) very much; extremely. ¶*He is ~ pleased.*②
—[形] 1. 힘센, 힘찬 ¶①붓은 칼보다 강하다 2. 큰 —[副]《口》몹시 ¶②그는 굉장히 좋아하고 있다

mi·gnon·ette [mìnjənét] *n.* **1.** [C] a plant with small, sweet-smelling, greenish-white flowers. **2.** [U] grayish green.
—[名] 1. 목서초(木犀草) 2. 회록색(灰綠色)

mi·graine [máigrein, +*Brit.* míː-] *n.* [U] a periodical headache on one side only.
—[名] 편두통

mi·grant [máigrənt] *n.* [C] a person, bird, or an animal that migrates as the seasons change. —*adj.* moving from place to place; migratory. ¶*a ~ worker.*①
—[名] 이주자; 철새; 이주 동물 —[形] 이동하는 ¶①떠돌이 노동자

* **mi·grate** [máigreit, +*Brit.* -⏊] *vi.* (of a person) move from one place to another to settle there; (of birds) travel from one region to another as the seasonal changes.
—[自] [특히 해외로] 이주하다; [새 따위가 정기적으로] 이동하다

mi·gra·tion [maigréiʃ(ə)n] *n.* [U] the act of migrating; [C] a group of persons, animals, or birds migrating together.
—[名] 이주, 이동; 이주하는 떼

mi·gra·to·ry [máigrətɔ̀ːri / -t(ə)ri] *adj.* migrating; of migration. ¶*a ~ bird.*①
—[形] 이주하는; 아동의 ¶①철새

* **mike** [maik] *n.* (*colloq.*) =microphone.

milch [miltʃ] *adj.* kept to provide milk; giving milk. ¶*a ~ cow.*①
—[形] 젖이 나는 ¶①젖소; 《비유》 돈줄

‡ **mild** [maild] *adj.* **1.** gentle; kind. ¶*be ~ in disposition*① / *be ~ of manner.*② **2.** not severe or violent. ¶*~ weath-*
—[形] 1. 온환한, 온순한 ¶①성질이 온순하다/②태도가 온화하다 2. 따뜻한,

er / *in ~ climates.*⑤ **3.** having a pleasant taste; not bitter. ↔strong, bitter ¶*a ~ medicine.*
화창한 ¶③기후가 온화한 토지에서 **3.** [맛이] 독하지 않은, 순한

mil·dew [míld(j)u: / -dju:] *n.* [U] any small plant that appears on paper, clothes, leather, etc. in warm and damp weather. **—*vt., vi.*** affect or become covered with mildew.
—[名] 곰팡이 —[他][自] 곰팡이가 나[게 하]다

mil·dew·y [míld(j)ù:i / -dju:i] *adj.* **1.** covered with mildew. **2.** of mildew. **3.** like mildew.
—[形] **1.** 곰팡이가 생긴 **2.** 곰팡이의 **3.** 곰팡이 같은

mild·ly [máildli] *adv.* in a mild manner; gently.
—[副] 온화하게, 부드럽게

mild·ness [máildnis] *n.* [U] the state or quality of being mild.
—[名] 온화; 따뜻함

‡**mile** [mail] *n.* [C] a unit of length or distance equal to 5,280 feet.
—[名] 마일(약 1.6킬로)

mile·age [máilidʒ] *n.* [U] the total distance in miles; the total number of miles covered in a certain time.
—[名] 총마일 수(數), [일정기간의 진행] 마일 수

mile·stone [máilstòun] *n.* [C] **1.** a roadside stone showing the distance to a certain place. **2.** an important event in history, one's life, etc.
—[名] **1.** 마일 도표, 이정표 **2.** 획기적 사건

mil·i·tan·cy [mílit(ə)nsi] *n.* [U] the state or quality of being aggressive; fighting spirit.
—[名] 교전 상태; 호전성, 투지

mil·i·tant [mílit(ə)nt] *adj.* fighting; anxious to fight. **—*n.*** [C] a person who is anxious to fight.
—[形] 교전하고 있는; 호전적인 —[名] 투사; 호전적인 사람

mil·i·ta·rism [mílitərìz(ə)m] *n.* [U] the theory that a nation's safety depends on armed forces; military spirit.
—[名] 군국주의; 군국적 정신

mil·i·ta·rist [mílitərist] *n.* [C] a supporter of militarism.
—[名] 군국주의자

‡**mil·i·tar·y** [mílitèri / -t(ə)ri] *adj.* **1.** of war or soldiers; fit for war. ↔civil ¶*the Military Academy.*① / *~ affairs.*② **2.** of the army. ↔naval **—*n.*** 《*the ~*》 《*collectively*》 the armed forces; soldiers; the army.
—[形] **1.** 군대의, 군사의, 군인의 ¶①육군 사관학교/②군사 **2.** 육군의 —[名] 군인, 군대

mi·li·tia [milíʃə] *n.* [C] 《usu. *the ~*》 a group of citizens trained for defense of their country in war.
—[名] 예비군, 민병, 의용군

mi·li·tia·man [milíʃəmən] *n.* [C] (pl. **-men** [-mən]) a member of the militia.
—[名] 민병, 국민병, 재향군인

‡**milk** [milk] *n.* [U] **1.** the white liquid produced by female animals, esp. cows, for feeding their young. ¶*a land of ~ and honey.*① / *~ of human kindness*② / *mother's ~*③ / (*proverb*) *It is no use crying over spilt ~.*④ **2.** the white juice of some plants; any liquid like milk.
1) ***as white as milk,*** pure white.
2) ***in*** [***the***] ***milk,*** yield milk.
—*vt.* draw milk from (a cow, etc.) ¶*the milking machine.*⑤ **—*vi.*** yield milk. ¶*The cow milks well.*
—[名] **1.** 젖; 우유, 밀크 ¶①풍요한 땅/②따뜻한 인정/③모유(母乳)/④엎지른 물은 다시 담을 수 없다 **2.** [식물의] 수액(樹液); 유액(乳液); 젖 모양의 것
[熟] 1)새하얀, 순백의 2)젖이 나는
—[他] …의 젖을 짜다 ¶⑤자동 착유기(搾乳器) —[自] 젖이 나다

milk·maid [mílkmèid] *n.* [C] a woman who milks cows.
—[名] 젖 짜는 여자

milk·man [mílkmæ̀n / -mən] *n.* [C] (pl. **-men** [-men]) a man selling or delivering milk; a man who milks cows.
—[名] 우유 장수(배달부); 젖 짜는 사람

milk·sop [mílksàp / -sɔ̀p] *n.* [C] a weak, timid boy or man.
—[名] 뱅충맞이, 소심한 사람, 겁보

milk tooth [⌐ ⌐] *n.* one of the first set of teeth of a young child or animal.
—[名] 젖니

milk-white [mílk(h)wáit] *adj.* white as milk.
—[形] 유백색(乳白色)의

milk·y [mílki] *adj.* (**milk·i·er, milk·i·est**) of or like milk; yielding milk. ¶*the Milky Way.*①
—[形] 젖 같은, 유백색의; 젖을 내는 ¶①은하수

‡**mill** [mil] *n.* [C] **1.** a machine for grinding grain into flour; any machine for crushing or grinding. ¶*a hand ~*① / *a coffee ~* / (*proverb*) *No ~, no meal.*② **2.** a building with such machines. ¶*a water ~*③ / *a windmill* / *a flour ~.* **3.** a machine used in making goods. ¶*a rolling ~.*④ **4.** a factory. ¶*a cotton (steel) ~.*⑤
1) ***draw water to one's mill,*** look out for one's own interests.
2) ***go through the mill,*** have hard training or experience.
—*vt.* **1.** grind or form (something) by or in a mill. **2.** cut regular markings on the edge of (a coin). ¶*a milled coin.* **—*vi.*** **1.** use a mill. **2.** (of cattle, crowds of people, etc.) move about in confusion. 《*~ about* or
—[名] **1.** 제분기; 분쇄기; 맷돌 ¶①손으로 돌리는 맷돌/②《俚》부뚜막의 소금도 넣어야 짜다 **2.** 제분소 ¶③물방아[간] **3.** 제조기 ¶④압연기(壓延機) **4.** 공장 ¶⑤방적(紡績)(제철)소
[熟] 1)아전인수(我田引水)하다; 깍정이 짓을 하다 2)고생(시련)을 겪다
—[他] **1.** …을 맷돌로 갈다; 가루로 만들다 **2.** [화폐의 가장자리를] 깔쭉깔쭉하게 하다 —[自] **1.** 맷돌(제분기)을 사용하다 **2.** [가축 떼가] 빙빙 돌아다니다

M

around a place, etc.》

mill·dam [míldæ̀m] *n.* [C] the dam of a mill-pond. —[名] 물방아용의 연못

mil·len·ni·a [miléniə] *n.* pl. of **millennium.**

mil·len·ni·um [miléniəm] *n.* [C] (pl. **-ni·ums** or **-ni·a**) **1.** a period of a thousand years. **2.** 《*the* ~》 the period when Christ is to rule on earth. —[名] 1. 천년[간] 2. [그리스도가 재림하여 천년간 지상을 다스린다는] 지복천년(至福千年)

⁝ mill·er [mílər] *n.* [C] a person who owns or works a mill. ¶(*proverb*) *Every ~ draws water to his own mill.*① —[名] 물방앗간(제분소) 주인 ¶①《俚》 아전인수(我田引水)

mil·let [mílit] *n.* [C] a grain-bearing grass grown for its seeds which are used as food. —[名] 수수, 조

mill·hand [mílhæ̀nd] *n.* [C] a workman working in a mill. —[名] 제분공, 직공

mil·li·gram, *Brit.* **-gramme** [míligræ̀m] *n.* [C] one thousandth part of a gram. ⇨[N.B.] —[名] 밀리그램 [N.B.] mg.으로 줄임

mil·li·me·ter, *Brit.* **-tre** [mílimìːtər] *n.* [C] one thousandth part of a meter. ⇨[N.B.] —[名] 밀리미터 [N.B.] mm.로 줄임

mil·li·ner [mílinər] *n* [C] a person who makes and sells women's hats, etc. —[名] 부인 모자 장수(장신구상)

mil·li·ner·y [mílinèri / -n(ə)ri] *n.* [U] **1.** 《*collectively*》 women's hats or headdresses. **2.** the business of making and selling women's hats. —[名] 1. 부인 모자류 2. 부인 모자 제조 판매업

⁝ mil·lion [míljən] *n.* [C] **1.** one thousand thousand; a large number. ¶*hundreds of millions of ...*① / *millions* [*and millions*] *of people.*② **2.** 《*the* ~》 the masses. **—*adj.*** one thousand thousand; very many. —[名] 1. 100 만; 다수 ¶①몇 억씩이나 되는 …/②무수한 사람들 2. 민중 —[形] 100 만의; 다수의

· mil·lion·aire [mìljənɛ́ər] *n.* [C] a person having at least a million dollars, etc.; a very rich person. —[名] 백만장자, 부호

mil·lionth [míljənθ] *adj.* coming last in a series of a million. **—*n.*** [C] one of a million parts. —[形] 100 만 번째의 —[名] 100 만분의 1

mil·li·pede [mílipìːd], **-ped** [-pèd] *n.* [C] a small worm with many legs. —[名] 《動》 노래기

mill·pond [mílpɑ̀nd / -pɔ̀nd] *n.* [C] a pond from which water flows to drive a mill wheel. —[名] 물방아용 저수지

mill·race [mílrèis] *n.* [C] the stream of water flowing to a mill-wheel. —[名] 물방아용 물줄기(도랑)

mill·stone [mílstòun] *n.* [C] **1.** one of a pair of round stones for grinding grain. **2.** a heavy burden. —[名] 1. 맷돌의 돌 2. 무거운 짐

mill wheel [⌐ ⌐] *n.* the wheel supplying power for a mill. —[名] 물방아[의 바퀴]

mill·wright [mílràit] *n.* [C] a person building or repairing water mills. —[名] 수레 목수

Mil·ton [mílt(ə)n], **John** *n.* (1608–74) an English poet. —[名] 영국의 시인

mim·e·o·graph [mímiougræ̀f / -grɑ̀ːf] *n.* [C] a machine for making copies of written material. **—*vt.*** make (copies) with this machine. —[名] 복사기 —[他] …을 복사기로 복사하다

mi·met·ic [mimétik] *adj.* of imitation; not real; mimic. —[形] 흉내내는; 가짜의

mim·ic [mímik] *adj.* inclined to imitate; not real. ¶~ *coloration.*① **—*n.*** [C] a person who imitates. **—*vt.*** (**-icked, -ick·ing**) imitate (something) to make fun of it; copy (something) closely. ¶~ *another's voice.* —[形] 흉내내는; 가짜의 ¶①보호색 —[名] 흉내내는 사람(특히 광대) —[他] …의 흉내를 내다; …와 비슷하게 시늉하다

mim·icked [mímikt] *v.* pt. and pp. of **mimic.**

mim·ick·ing [mímikiŋ] *v.* ppr. of **mimic.**

mim·ic·ry [mímikri] *n.* (pl. **-ries**) [U] the act of mimicking; [C] a mimic play or drama. —[名] 흉내; 광대극, 희극

mi·mo·sa [mimóuzə, +*U.S.* -sə] *n.* [C] a low tree with heads of white or pink flowers. —[名] 함수초(含羞草)

min·a·ret [mínərèt] *n.* [C] a tall, slender tower of a Mohammedan temple. ⇨fig. —[名] [회교 사원의] 뾰족탑, 첨탑

mince [mins] *vt.* **1.** cut (meat, etc.) into small pieces. **2.** speak with assumed delicacy. ¶*do not ~ matters* (or *one's words*).① **—*vi.*** speak or walk in an unnatural manner. **—*n.*** [U] meat which has been minced. —[他] 1. [고기 따위]를 잘게 저미다(다지다) 2. …을 에둘러(완곡하게) 말하다 —[自] 젠체하면서 걷다(말하다) —[名] 잘게 저민 고기

mince·meat [mínsmìːt] *n.* [U] a mixture of apples, raisins, etc., sometimes with meat, used as a filling for pies. —[名] 파이의 재료

minc·ing [mínsiŋ] *adj.* pretending; too polite. —[形] 점잔빼는, 젠체하는

[minaret]

minc·ing·ly [mínsiŋli] *adv.* in a mincing manner.
—[副] 젠체하며

⁝ **mind** [maind] *n.* **1.** [C] the part of a person that thinks, feels, etc. ↔body ¶*in the back of one's ~*① | (*proverb*) *A sound ~ in a sound body.*② **2.** [C] the way or process of thinking, feeling, etc. ¶*the English mind*③ | *a frame of ~*④ | *a turn of ~*⑤ | (*proverb*) *So many men, so many minds.*⑥ **3.** [U] the mental ability; intellect. ↔heart ¶*a strong* (*weak*) *~* | *have a logical ~.* **4.** [U] memory. ¶*Out of sight, out of ~.*⑦ **5.** [C] a person who has a mind of a certain kind. ¶*the greatest minds of the world.* **6.** [C] what a person thinks, feels, etc.; opinion. ¶*speak one's ~* | *in my ~*⑧ | *change one's ~* | *open one's ~ to someone* | *meeting of minds.*⑨ **7.** [U] reason; health of mind. ¶*be* (*go*) *out of one's ~*⑩ | *Is he in his right ~?*⑪
—[名] 1. 마음; 정신 ¶①마음 속에서/②《俚》건전한 마음은 건전한 몸에 깃든다 2. 정신 상태; 사고 방식 ¶③영국 정신/④기분/⑤마음씨/⑥《俚》십인십색(十人十色) 3. 지력;지성 4. 기억[력] ¶⑦멀리 떨어지면 정도 멀어진다, (지척이 천리면 마음도 천리) 5. [마음의 소유주로서의] 사람 6. 생각; 느낌 ¶⑧내 생각으로는/⑨의견의 일치 7. 제정신; 이성(理性) ¶⑩제 정신이 아니다(미치다)/⑪그는 제 정신인가?

1) ***apply*** (or ***bend***) ***the mind to*** (=*work hard at*) *something.*
2) ***be of a*** (or ***one***) ***mind,*** agree.
3) ***bear*** (or ***have, keep***) *something* ***in mind,*** remember something.
4) ***give*** *one's* ***mind*** (=*direct one's attention* or *one's effort*) ***to*** *something.*
5) ***have a good mind to*** *do,* be very willing to; be almost resolved to do.
6) ***have a mind to*** *do,* intend to do or think of doing.
7) ***have*** *something* ***upon*** *one's* ***mind,*** be troubled about something.
8) ***make up*** *one's* ***mind*** (=*decide*) ***to*** *do.*
9) ***put*** *someone* ***in mind of,*** remind someone of (something).
10) ***take*** *one's* ***mind off,*** turn one's attention away from (something).
11) ***turn*** *one's* ***mind*** (=*direct one's attention or thoughts*) ***to*** *something.*

[熟] 1)…에 마음을 쏟다 2)같은 의견이다 3)…을 기억하고 있다 4)…에 마음을 기울이다 5)…할 생각이 많다 6)…할 생각이 있다 7)…을 걱정하고 있다 8)…하기로 결심하다 9) …에게 …을 생각나게 하다 10)…에서 주의를 딴 데로 돌리다 11)…으로 주의를 돌리다

—*vt.* **1.** attend to (something); be careful of (something). 《~ *what* (or *how, where,* etc.) ...》 ¶*~ rules*⑫ | *Mind what I tell you.* | *Mind your step.* | *Mind the dog.*⑬ | *Mind your own business.*⑭ **2.** take care of or look after (someone or something). ¶*~ the baby* | *~ the house.*⑮ **3.** 《chiefly in *negative* or *interrogative*》 be troubled by or feel an objection to (something). 《~ *doing*》 ¶"*Do you ~ opening the window?*" "*No, not at all.*"⑯ ⇒[N.B.] —*vi.* **1.** be careful. ¶*If you don't ~, you will fall down.* | *Mind and write to me.*⑰ | *Mind out!*⑱ **2.** feel dislike; care; object. ¶*Never ~* (*about that*). | *Do you ~ if I open the window?; Would you ~ if I opened the window?* ⇒[N.B.] | *Come to the party if you don't ~.*
—[他] 1. …에 주의하다; 조심하다 ¶⑫규칙에 따르다/⑬개 조심/⑭네 일이나 걱정해라(쓸데없는 참견 말라) 2. …을 보살피다 ¶⑮집안 일을 보다 3. …에 마음을 쓰다, 꺼리다 ¶⑯「창을 열어도 괜찮겠읍니까?」「예, 좋습니다」 [N.B.] 승낙한다는 답은 No(=I don't mind)가 되므로 주의 —[自] 1. 주의하다; 조심하다 ¶⑰잊지 말고 편지해 주시오/⑱정신 차려!, 비켜! 2. 걱정하다, 염려하다, 마음쓰다 [N.B.] 가정법을 쓰는 것이 공손한 말씨

mind you, please note, observe, listen, etc.
[熟] 이것봐!, 잘 들어[봐]

mind·ed [máindid] *adj.* **1.** having a mind. **2.** inclined.
—[形] 1. 마음이 …한 2. …할 생각이 있는

mind·er [máindər] *n.* [C] a person who takes care.
—[名] 돌보는(지키는) 사람

mind·ful [máin(d)f(u)l] *adj.* attentive; careful.
—[形] 잊지 않는, 주의하는

mind·less [máindlis] *adj.* careless; foolish; stupid.
—[形] 부주의한; 어리석은

⁝ **mine**[1] [main] *pron.* a possessive form of **I**; the one or ones belonging to me. ¶*a friend of ~.* —*adj.* 《before *a vowel* or *h-*》 (*poetic, archaic*) my. ¶*~ eyes.*
—[代] 나의 것 —[形] 나의

* **mine**[2] [main] *n.* [C] **1.** a tunnel or deep hole for taking metals, coal, etc., from the earth. ¶*a coal ~* | *the mines.*① **2.** a rich source. ¶*a ~ of information.*② **3.** a bomb buried under the ground or in the sea. **4.** a secret plot. —*vt.* **1.** make a hole below (the earth); dig (coal, etc.) from the earth. **2.** lay bombs on land or in the sea. **3.** destroy (something) by a secret means.
—[名] 1. 광갱(鑛坑); 광산 ¶①광업 2. 보고(寶庫), 부원(富源) ¶②지식의 보고 3. 지뢰, 수뢰, 기뢰 4. 비밀 계략(모의) —[他] 1. …에 갱도를 파다; …을 채굴하다 2. …에 지뢰(수뢰)를 부설하다 3. …을 비밀수단으로 뒤엎다

mine field [∸ ∸] *n.* [C] **1.** a land where mines are kept. **2.** a land or sea where there are explosive mines.
—[名] 1. 광석 매장지 2. 지뢰(기뢰) 부설지

* **min·er** [máinər] *n.* [C] a person working in a mine.
—[名] 갱부, 광부

⁝ **min·er·al** [mín(ə)r(ə)l] *n.* [C] **1.** a substance having a constant chemical composition; a substance obtained by
—[名] 1. 광물, 광석 2. 광천(鑛泉); 탄산수 —[形] 광물의, 광물을 함유하는; 무기

mineralogist [730] **Minos**

mining. **2.** ((usu. *pl.*)) a mineral spring; (*Brit.*) mineral water. —*adj.* of or containing minerals; not organic.
min·er·al·o·gist [mìnərǽlədʒist] *n.* ⓒ a student of mineralogy.
min·er·al·o·gy [mìnərǽlədʒi] *n.* Ⓤ the science of minerals.
Mi·ner·va [miné:rvə] *n.* the Roman goddess of wisdom, defensive of war and arts. ⇒N.B. [sea, etc.
mine sweeper [⌞⌞-] *n.* a ship for removing mines at
* **min·gle** [míŋgl] *vt.*, *vi.* **1.** mix; become mixed. ((~something *with*)) **2.** join. ((~ *in* or *with* something))
* **min·i·a·ture** [mín(i)ətʃər] *n.* ⓒ a very small painting; a small model.
in miniature, on a small scale.
—*adj.* done on a small scale. ¶*a ~ edition*① / *a ~ garden.*② —*vt.* copy (something) on a small scale.
min·i·ma [mínəmə] *n.* pl. of **minimum**.
min·i·mize [mínimàiz] *vt.* make (something) as small as possible; estimate (something) at the smallest degree; hold (someone) cheap.
* **min·i·mum** [mínimam] *n.* ⓒ (pl. **-mums** or **-ma**) the smallest amount possible; the least. ↔maximum ¶*with a ~ of effort*. —*adj.* smallest possible; lowest. ¶*~ wages.*①
* **min·ing** [máiniŋ] *n.* Ⓤ the work of getting coal, etc. from the ground.
min·ion [mínjən] *n.* ⓒ **1.** a favorite; a servant who obeys a master without question. ¶*a ~ of fortune.*① **2.** a follower. ¶*a ~ of the law.*②
: **min·is·ter** [mínistər] *n.* ⓒ **1.** the head of a government department. ¶*the Prime Minister*① / *the Ministers.*② **2.** a person representing his own government in a foreign country. **3.** a clergyman. **4.** a servant. —*vi., vt.* give help to (someone); contribute. ((~ *to* someone or something)) ¶*a ministering angel.*③
min·is·te·ri·al [mìnistíəriəl] *adj.* **1.** of a minister; executive. ¶*a ~ change*① / *the ~ party.*② **2.** serving as a minister or an agent; subordinate.
min·is·trant [mínistrənt] *adj.* ministering. —*n.* ⓒ a person who helps or supports. [as a clergyman.
min·is·tra·tion [mìnistréiʃ(ə)n] *n.* Ⓤ the act of serving
* **min·is·try** [mínistri] *n.* ⓒ (pl. **-tries**) **1.** the office, function, or service of a minister or clergyman. **2.** (often *M*-) ((collectively)) all the ministers of a state; the Cabinet; the department under a minister of government.
mink [miŋk] *n.* **1.** ⓒ an animal like a weasel living on land and in water. **2.** Ⓤ its valuable fur.
Minn. Minnesota.
Min·ne·so·ta [mìnisóutə] *n.* a middle northern State of the United States. ⇒N.B.
Min·ne·so·tan [mìnisout(ə)n] *n.* ⓒ a person of Minnesota. —*adj.* of Minnesota.
min·now [mínou] *n.* ⓒ (pl. **-nows** or collectively **-now**) a small fresh-water fish; (*U.S.*) any very small fish. ¶*throw out a ~ to catch a whale.*①
* **mi·nor** [máinər] *adj.* ↔major **1.** less; smaller; not important; inferior. ¶*~ poets.*① / *of ~ importance.*② **2.** (*Music*) less by half a tone than the major interval. ¶*the ~ scale.*③ —*n.* ⓒ **1.** a person below the age of 21. **2.** (*Music*) the minor scale. ¶*Violin concerto in E ~*.
* **mi·nor·i·ty** [mainɔ́:riti, minár- / mainɔ́r-, mi-] *n.* (pl. **-ties**) **1.** ⓒ the smaller number; the smaller of two totals of votes. ↔majority **2.** Ⓤ the state of being under full legal age.
Mi·nos [máinəs, -nɑs / -nɔs] *n.* (in Greek mythology) a

(無機)의

—ⓢ 광물학자

—ⓢ 광물학

—ⓢ 로마 신화의 지혜·예술·전쟁의 여신 N.B. 그리이스 신화의 Athena
—ⓢ 소해정(掃海艇)
—他自 1. 섞다, 섞이다 2. 함께 하다(되다); 참가하다

—ⓢ 작은 화상(畫像), 세밀화; 작은 모형
圖·소규모로; 소형의; 세밀화로
—ⓢ 소형의 ¶①축쇄판(縮刷版)/②작은 뜰 —他 …을 축사(縮寫)하다

—他 …을 최소한으로 하다; 최소로 어림하다; …을 깔보다

—ⓢ 최소한; 극소 —形 최소의; 최저의 ¶①최저 임금

—ⓢ 채광, 채광업

—ⓢ 1. 마음에 드는 사람 ¶①행운아 2. 노예; 앞잡이 ¶②경관, 간수

—ⓢ 1. 장관, 대신 ¶①국무총리/②각료 2. 공사, 사절 3. 목사 4. 하인, 머슴
—自他 […을] 섬기다, …을 돕다; 공헌하다 ¶③구원의 천사

—形 1. 장관의, 내각의; 행정상의, 정부의 ¶①내각의 경질/②여당 2. 대리의, 보좌의
—形 섬기는, 봉사의 —ⓢ 봉사자, 거드는(보좌하는) 사람
—ⓢ [목사의] 직무, 봉사, 조력
—ⓢ 1. 장관의 직, 목사의 직 2. 장관; 내각; 부(部), 성(省)

—ⓢ 1. 밍크(족제비류) 2. 밍크 모피

—ⓢ 미국 중북부의 주 N.B. Minn.으로 줄임. 수도 St. Paul
—ⓢ 미네소타 사람 —形 미네소타의

—ⓢ (魚) 연준모치; (美) [일반적으로] 작은 물고기 ¶①새우로 잉어를 낚다, 작은 밑천으로 큰 이익을 얻다
—形 1. 작은 쪽의, 중요하지 않은, 이류의 ¶①이류 시인/②별로 중요하지 않은 2. (樂) 단음(短音)의, 단조의 ¶③단음계 —ⓢ 1. 미성년자 2. 단음계

—ⓢ 1. 소수, 소수당; 소수 민족; 적은 투표수 2. 미성년

—ⓢ 미노스(크레타의 왕)

king and lawgiver of Crete.

Min·o·taur [mínətɔ̀:r / máinətɔ:] *n.* (in Greek mythology) a monster with the body of a man and the head of a bull.
—[名] 미노타우루스(몸은 사람이고 머리는 소인 괴물)

min·strel [mínstr(ə)l] *n.* [C] **1.** a wandering singer, musician, or poet of the Middle Ages. **2.** ⦅*pl.*⦆ a group of black-face performers who sing Negro songs.
—[名] 1. [중세의] 음유(吟遊) 시인; 시인 2. 흑인으로 분장하여 흑인의 노래 따위를 부르는 순회 극단

min·strel·sy [mínstr(ə)lsi] *n.* [U] **1.** ⦅*collectively*⦆ minstrels. **2.** the art or songs of minstrels. **3.** the singing and poetry of minstrels.
—[名] 1. 음유 시인 2. 음유 시인의 연예(시) 3. 시가(詩歌)

* **mint**[1] [mint] *n.* [C] a sweet-smelling plant whose leaves are used for flavoring.
—[名] 박하(薄荷)

mint[2] [mint] *n.* [C] **1.** a place where coins are made under government authority. **2.** a large sum. **3.** the source of supply or invention. —*adj.* new, as if freshly coined. ¶*in ~ state.*① —*vt.* coin (money); invent (new words, idea, etc.).
—[名] 1. 조폐국(局) 2. 거액, 다량 3. 근원; 재원(財源) —[形] [화폐 따위] 발행된 지 얼마 안 되는 ¶①[화폐 따위] 새것의 —[他] [화폐]를 주조하다; …을 만들어 내다

mint·age [míntidʒ] *n.* [U] the act or process of minting.
—[名] 화폐 주조

min·u·et [mìnjuét] *n.* [C] a slow and graceful dance in triple time; the music for this.
—[名] 메누엣; [박자가 느린] 춤곡

⁑ **mi·nus** [máinəs] *adj.* less; showing subtraction; negative. ↔plus —*prep.* less; wanting; without. ¶*7 ~ 3 is 4.* / *He came back ~ an arm.* —*n.* [C] a minus sign; a negative quantity. ¶*a grade of A- ~.*①
—[形] 마이너스의; 부(負)의 —[前] …을 뺀, …이 없는 —[名] 마이너스의 부호(—); 부수(負數) ¶①A—의 등급

⁑ **min·ute**[1] [mínit] *n.* [C] **1.** sixty seconds; the sixtieth part of an hour or of a degree. ¶*a ~ hand*① / *in a few minutes*② / *ten minutes later.*③ **2.** a moment. ¶*in a ~*④ / *Wait a ~.*⑤ **3.** a short note or memo. **4.** ⦅*pl.*⦆ an official record of a meeting.
—[名] 1. [시간·각도의] 분(分) ¶①[시계의] 분침, 긴 바늘/②몇 분 안에/③10분 뒤에 2. 잠깐, 순간 ¶④곧/⑤잠깐 기다려라 3. 각서, 비망록, 메모 4. 의사록

1) ***the minute*** [***that***], as soon as. ¶*The ~* [*that*] *I saw him, he ran away.*
2) ***to the minute,*** at the exact time; punctually.
3) ***up to the minute,*** up to date.
[熟] 1)…하자마자 2)정각에 3)최신의

* **mi·nute**[2] [main(j)ú:t, mi- / -njú:t] *adj.* **1.** very small; not important. **2.** exact; precise. ¶*a ~ inquiry.*
—[形] 1. 아주 작은; 사소한 2. 자세한, 정밀한

min·ute·ly[1] [mínitli] *adv.* every minute; often.
—[副] 1분마다, 자주

mi·nute·ly[2] [main(j)ú:tli, mi- / -njú:t-] *adv.* in a minute manner or in great detail; precisely.
—[副] 상세히, 세밀하게; 정밀하게

mi·nute·ness [main(j)ú:tnis, mi- / -njú:t-] *n.* [U] the quality of being very small; precise attention; exactness.
—[名] 미세함, 극히 작음, 상세

minx [miŋks] *n.* [C] an impolite or wild girl or woman.
—[名] 말괄량이, 왈가닥

* **mir·a·cle** [mírəkl] *n.* [C] a very marvelous event; any wonderful happening; a remarkable thing. ¶*escape by a ~*① / *work* (or *do, perform*) *miracles* / *to a ~.*②
—[名] 기적, 불가사의한 사물; [그리스도의] 기적 ¶①기적적으로 도망치다/②기적적으로

miracle play [´-‐´] *n.* a kind of drama popular in the Middle Ages, based on the life of Christ or the saints.
—[名] [중세의] 기적극(奇跡劇)

mi·rac·u·lous [mirǽkjuləs] *adj.* like a miracle; wonderful; supernatural.
—[形] 기적적인, 이상한, 놀랄 만한

mi·rac·u·lous·ly [mirǽkjuləsli] *adv.* in a miraculous manner; by a miracle.
—[副] 기적적으로, 이상하게, 초자연의 힘으로

mi·rage [mirá:ʒ, +*Brit.* ´-] *n.* [C] **1.** an image of a distant object, often upside down, seen as if it were near, esp. in the desert. **2.** an illusion.
—[名] 1. 신기루(蜃氣樓) 2. 몽상; 공상; 망상

mire [máiər] *n.* [U] the wet ground; the mud.
—[名] 진창, 수렁

1) ***drag through the mire,*** put (someone) to shame.
2) ***find*** (or ***stick***) ***oneself in the mire,*** be in a dilemma.
[熟] 1)…에게 창피를 주다 2)궁지에 처하다, 수렁에 빠지다

—*vt., vi.* cover (something) with mud; cause (someone) to be stuck in mud; sink in mud.
—[他][自] 진흙으로 더럽히다; …을 곤경에 빠뜨리다; 진창에 빠지다

⁑ **mir·ror** [mírər] *n.* [C] **1.** a looking glass; a surface reflecting an image. ¶*a rear-view ~*① / *look at oneself in the ~*② **2.** anything which gives a true likeness; a model; an example. ¶*a ~ of what a man ought to be.*③ —*vt.* reflect (something) in a mirror.
—[名] 1. 거울 ¶①백미러/②자신을 거울에 비춰보다 2. 모범, 귀감 ¶③사람이 살아가는 본보기 —[他] …을 거울에 비추다

* **mirth** [mə:rθ] *n.* [U] joyfulness; merriment; gladness.
—[名] 명랑함; 환희; 유쾌

mirth·ful [mə́:rθf(u)l] *adj.* merry; full of mirth.
—[形] 유쾌한, 즐거운

mirth·ful·ly [mə́:rθfuli] *adv.* in a mirthful manner.
—[副] 즐겁게, 유쾌하게, 명랑하게

miry　　　　　　　　　　[732]　　　　　　　　　　mischief

mir·y [máiəri] *adj.* (**mir·i·er, mir·i·est**) muddy; swampy. ─ 形 진흙투성이의, 진창의
mis- [mis-] *pref.* bad[ly]; wrong[ly]: *misprint* (=a mistake in printing); *misread* (=read incorrectly); *misuse* (=use badly). ─ 〔接頭〕 틀린; 나쁜; 불리한
mis·ad·ven·ture [mìsədvéntʃər] *n.* Ⓤ Ⓒ bad luck; a misfortune. ¶*by ~.*① 「esp. in marriage.」 ─ 名 불행; 재난 ¶①운수 나쁘게, 잘못하여
mis·al·li·ance [mìsəláiəns] *n.* Ⓒ an improper alliance, ─ 名 신분이 틀리는 결혼
mis·an·thrope [mísənθròup, míz-] *n.* Ⓒ a person who hates or distrusts human beings. ─ 名 인간을 싫어하는 사람, 염세가
mis·an·throp·ic [mìs(ə)nθrápik, miz- / mìz(ə)nθróp-] *adj.* hating or distrusting mankind or human society. ─ 形 인간을 싫어하는, 염세적인
mis·an·thro·py [misǽnθrəpi, miz- / miz-] *n.* Ⓤ hatred or distrust of human beings or human society. ─ 名 인간을 싫어함, 염세
mis·ap·pli·ca·tion [mìsæplikéiʃ(ə)n] *n.* Ⓤ the act of misapplying; the state of being misapplied. ─ 名 오용(誤用), 악용
mis·ap·ply [mìsəplái] *vt.* use badly or wrongly; apply dishonestly. ─ 他 …을 오용하다, 악용하다, 남용하다
mis·ap·pre·hend [mìsæprihénd] *vt.* misunderstand. ─ 他 …을 오해하다, 잘못 생각하다
mis·ap·pre·hen·sion [mìsæprihénʃ(ə)n] *n.* Ⓤ the act of misapprehending; Ⓒ a mistaken idea. ─ 名 오해; 잘못 알기
mis·ap·pro·pri·ate [misəpróuprièit] *vt.* take and use (something) wrongly; use (another person's money) as one's own. 「of misappropriating.」 ─ 他 〔남의 것〕을 자기 것으로 하다, 〔남의 돈〕을 횡령하다
mis·ap·pro·pri·a·tion [mìsəpròupriéiʃ(ə)n] *n.* Ⓤ the act ─ 名 횡령, 착복; 악용
mis·ar·range [mìsəréindʒ] *vt.* arrange (things) improperly. 「oneself.」 ─ 他 …의 배열을 잘못하다
mis·be·have [mìsbihéiv] *vi., vt.* behave badly. ¶*~* ─ 自 他 나쁜 짓을 하다, 못되게 굴다
mis·be·haved [mìsbihéivd] *adj.* rough; impolite; rude. ─ 形 버릇없는, 품행이 나쁜
mis·be·hav·ior, *Brit.* -iour [mìsbihéivjər] *n.* Ⓤ wrong or improper behavior. ─ 名 버릇없음; 못된 행실; 부정행위
mis·be·lief [mìsbilíːf] *n.* Ⓤ a wrong, false belief or opinion, esp. in religion. ─ 名 이교(異敎) 신앙, 그릇된 신앙
mis·be·liev·er [mìsbilíːvər] *n.* Ⓒ a person who has a wrong belief, esp. in religion. ─ 名 오신자(誤信者), 이교도
mis·cal·cu·late [miskǽlkjulèit] *vt., vi.* calculate (amounts, etc.) incorrectly; miscount. ¶*~ a distance.* ─ 他自 계산을 잘못하다; 잘못 판단하다
mis·cal·cu·la·tion [mìskælkjuléiʃ(ə)n] *n.* Ⓤ the act of miscalculating. ─ 名 오산
mis·call [miskɔ́ːl] *vt.* call (someone) by a wrong name. ─ 他 …을 잘못 부르다, 잘못 호칭하다
mis·car·riage [miskǽridʒ] *n.* 1. Ⓤ the state of failure or error; Ⓒ an error; a failure. ¶*a ~ of justice.*① 2. Ⓤ failure in sending mail, etc. 3. Ⓤ Ⓒ the birth of a baby before it has grown enough to live. ─ 名 1. 실패, 실책 ¶①오심(誤審) 2. 〔편지의〕 배달 착오, 불착(不着) 3. 유산(流産)
mis·car·ry [miskǽri] *vi.* (**-ried**) 1. (of a plan, etc.) fail. 2. (of a letter, etc.) fail to reach the destination. 3. give birth to a child before the proper time. ─ 自 1. 〔계획 따위가〕 실패하다 2. 〔편지가〕 배달되지 않다 3. 유산하다
mis·cast [miskǽst / -káːst] *vt.* (**-cast**) give (an actor) a part or role not fit for him. ─ 他 〔배우〕에게 부적당한 배역을 맡기다
mis·cel·la·ne·ous [mìsiléiniəs] *adj.* 1. formed of various kinds. ¶*~ goods.*① 2. having various qualities; many-sided. ▷ **mis·cel·la·ne·ous·ly** [-li] *adv.* ─ 形 1. 여러가지 잡다한 ¶①잡화 2. 다방면의
mis·cel·la·ny [mísəlèini / miséləni] *n.* (*pl.* **-nies**) 1. Ⓒ a mixture of various kinds of things. 2. (often *pl.*) a book that consists of various authors' writings. ─ 名 1. 혼합물 2. 잡록(雜錄); 논집(論集)
mis·chance [mistʃǽns / -tʃɑ́ːns] *n.* 1. Ⓤ bad or hard luck. 2. Ⓒ a piece of bad luck.
by mischance, by mistake; unhappily. ─ 名 1. 불행 2. 한 가지 불행한 일
圜 운 나쁘게; 불행하게
• **mis·chief** [místʃif] *n.* (*pl.* **-chiefs**) 1. Ⓤ the act of doing thoughtless tricks. ¶*keep children out of ~.*① 2. Ⓒ (*slang*) a person making mischief. 3. Ⓤ harm; damage.
1) *go* (*or get*) *into mischief,* begin to do mischief.
2) *make mischief between,* cause people to quarrel.
3) *out of mischief,* half in fun.
4) *play the mischief with,* put into disorder; injure. ─ 名 1. 장난 ¶①아이들이 장난을 못하게 해두다 2.(俗) 장난꾸러기 3. 해독, 재해
圜 1)장난을 시작하다 2)…사이를 이간질하다 3)장난삼아 4)엉망진창을 만들다; 고장을 일으키다; 〔건강 따위〕를 해치다

mis·chie·vous [místʃivəs] *adj.* **1.** causing injury; harmful. **2.** playful in an annoying way; teasing.
—[形] 1. 해로운, 유해한 2. 장난을 좋아하는

mis·chie·vous·ly [místʃivəsli] *adv.* in a mischievous manner.
—[副] 해롭게; 장난으로

mis·con·ceive [mìskənsí:v] *vt., vi.* misunderstand; judge incorrectly.
—[他][自] 오해하다, 잘못 생각하다

mis·con·cep·tion [mìskənsépʃ(ə)n] *n.* [U][C] a wrong interpretation; a misunderstanding.
—[名] 오해, 잘못된 생각, 오인(誤認)

mis·con·duct [miskándʌkt / -kɔ́n- ∥ →*v.*] *n.* [U] **1.** wrong behavior. **2.** dishonest management.
—[名] 1. 간통, 불의(不義) 2. 부정(위법)행위
—*vt.* [mìskəndʌ́kt] **1.** behave badly; behave (oneself) improperly. **2.** manage badly. ¶~ *a business.*
—[他] 1. 잘못 처신하다 2. …을 실수하다; …의 처리를 잘못하다

mis·con·struc·tion [mìskənstrʌ́kʃ(ə)n] *n.* [U][C] the state or act of misunderstanding.
—[名] 잘못된 구성; 오해; 그릇된 해석

mis·con·strue [mìskənstrú] *vt.* understand (someone's words, acts, etc.) wrongly.
—[他] …의 뜻을 잘못 해석하다

mis·count [miskáunt →*n.*] *vt., vi.* count incorrectly.
—[他][自] 오산하다
—*n.* [+*U.S.* ´-] [C] an incorrect count.
—[名] 오산

mis·cre·ant [mískriənt] *adj.* having no conscience.
—[形] 사악한, 무도한
—*n.* [C] a very wicked person.
—[名] 악한

mis·deed [misdí:d] *n.* [C] a bad deed; a crime.
—[名] 나쁜 짓, 범죄, 부정행위

mis·de·mean·or [mìsdimí:nər], *Brit.* **-our** *n.* [C] **1.** (*Law*) an unlawful but not very serious act. **2.** (*rare*) bad behavior.
—[名] 1.⟪法⟫ 경범죄 2. 행실이 나쁨

mis·di·rect [mìsdirékt] *vt.* **1.** direct badly. **2.** aim badly. ¶*a misdirected arrow.* **3.** put a wrong address on (a letter, etc.). ¶~ *a letter.*
—[他] 1. …을 잘못 지도하다 2. …을 잘못 겨냥하다 3. [편지]의 겉봉을 잘못 쓰다

mis·do·ing [misdú:iŋ / ´´-] *n.* [C] a misdeed.
—[名] 나쁜 짓, 비행

* **mi·ser** [máizər] *n.* [C] a person who loves money too much.
—[名] 구두쇠, 수전노

* **mis·er·a·ble** [míz(ə)r(ə)bl] *adj.* **1.** wretched; unhappy. ¶~ *weather.* **2.** shameful; mean. ¶*a* ~ *liar.* **3.** poor; worthless. ¶*a* ~ *dinner.*① ▷**mis·er·a·ble·ness** [-nis] *n.*
—[形] 1. 불쌍한, 비참한 2. 파렴치한, 구두쇠의 3. 빈약한, 볼품없는 ¶①보잘것 없는 식사

mis·er·a·bly [míz(ə)r(ə)bli] *adv.* **1.** in a miserable manner. **2.** (*colloq.*) very.
—[副] 1. 불쌍하게 2.⟪口⟫ 심하게, 몹시

mi·ser·ly [máizərli] *adj.* loving money too much; greedy; stingy.
—[形] 구두쇠의; 욕심 많은

* **mis·er·y** [míz(ə)ri] *n.* [U] (pl. **-er·ies**) **1.** the state of great unhappiness. ¶*the* ~ *of human life.*① **2.** extreme pain.
—[名] 1. 불행, 비참 ¶①인생의 비참한 일 2. 괴로움, 고통

mis·fire [misfáiər / ´´] *vi.* **1.** (of a gun, etc.) fail to fire. **2.** (of an internal combustion engine) fail to start action. —*n.* [C] a failure to fire, start action, etc.
—[自] 1. [총이] 불발이 되다 2. [내연기관이] 점화되지 않다 —[名] 불발; 점화되지 않음

mis·fit [misfít, ´-] *n.* **1.** [C] something that does not fit well. **2.** a person in a position for which he is unfitted. —*vt., vi.* (**-fit·ted, -fit·ting**) be too large, or too small for (someone or something).
—[名] 1. 맞지 않는 것 2. 비적임자(非適任者) —[他][自] 잘 맞지 않다

* **mis·for·tune** [misfɔ́:rtʃ(ə)n] *n.* [U][C] ill fortune; bad luck. ¶*Misfortunes never come singly* (or *single*).①
—[名] 불행, 불운; 재난 ¶①화불단행(禍不單行)

mis·gave [misgéiv] *v.* pt. of **misgive**.

mis·give [misgív] *vt.* (**-gave, -giv·en**) cause (someone) to have doubt, fear, etc. ⟪~ someone *that*...⟫ ¶*Her heart misgave her that she might fail.*①
—[他] …에게 의혹을 품게 하다 ¶①그녀는 실패하지 않을까 하는 생각이 들었다

mis·giv·en [misgívn] *v.* pp. of **misgive**.

mis·giv·ing [misgíviŋ] *n.* [C] a feeling of suspicion; [U] doubt.
—[名] 불안

mis·guide [misgáid] *vt.* ⟪chiefly in *passive*⟫ lead (someone) in the wrong way; mislead.
—[他] …의 지도를 그르치다

mis·guid·ed [misgáidid] *adj.* wrongly led; led in the wrong way by error or misconduct. ¶*a* ~ *opinion.*
—[形] 잘못 인도된(안)

mis·hap [míshæp, -´] *n.* [U] the state of bad luck; [C] an unlucky accident. ¶*without* ~.①
—[名] 불행, 재난; 불행한 사건 ¶①별일없이

mis·in·form [mìsinfɔ́:rm] *vt.* give incorrect information to (someone).
—[他] …에게 오보(誤報)를 전하다

mis·in·for·ma·tion [mìsinfərméiʃ(ə)n / mísinfəméi-] *n.* [U] false information or news.
—[名] 오보; 오전(誤傳)

mis·in·ter·pret [mìsintə́:rprit] *vt.* understand or explain wrongly.
—[他] …을 오해하다; …에 틀린 해석을 하다

mis·in·ter·pre·ta·tion [mìsintə̀:rpritéiʃ(ə)n] *n.* [U][C] a wrong interpretation.
—[名] 오역; 오해

M

mis·judge [misdʒʌ́dʒ] *vt., vi.* judge wrongly.
—[他][自] 잘못 판단하다;오심(오진)하다

mis·laid [misléid] *vt.* pt. and pp. of **mislay**.

mis·lay [misléi] *vt.* (**-laid**) put (something) in a place and then forget where it is; put (something) in the wrong place.
—[他] …을 두고 잊어버리다; 잘못 두다

•**mis·lead** [mislí:d] *vt.* (**-led**) **1.** lead (someone) in the wrong way. ¶*The guide misled them in the woods.* **2.** give (someone) a wrong idea.
—[他] **1.** …을 잘못 인도하다 **2.** …에게 오해하게 하다

•**mis·lead·ing** [mislí:diŋ] *adj.* giving a wrong impression; deceiving.
—[形] 잘못 인도하는;오해(현혹)시키는

mis·led [misléd] *vt.* pt. and pp. of **mislead.**

mis·man·age [mismǽnidʒ / ˊˊ-] *vt.* manage wrongly.
—[他] …을 잘못 처리(관리)하다

mis·name [misnéim] *vt.* call (someone or something) by a wrong name.
—[他] …의 이름을 잘못 부르다

mis·no·mer [misnóumər] *n.* [C] a wrong name; an incorrect use of a name.
—[名] **1.** …틀린 명칭; 명칭의 오용

mis·place [mispléis / ˊˊ] *vt.* **1.** put (something) in a wrong place. **2.** (*colloq.*) mislay. **3.** give (one's love, trust, etc.) to an improper person.
—[他] **1.** …을 잘못 두다 **2.** 《口》 …을 두고 잊어버리다 **3.** [애정·신용 따위]를 부당한 사람(것)에게 주다

mis·place·ment [mispléismənt / ˊˊ-] *n.* [U] the state of misplacing.
—[名] 잘못 두기

mis·print [mísprint, ˊˊ / ˊˊ ‖ →*v.*] *n.* [C] a mistake in printing. **—*vt.*** [misprínt] make a mistake in printing of (something).
—[名] 인쇄의 잘못, 오식 —[他] …을 오식하다; 잘못 인쇄하다

mis·pro·nounce [mìsprənáuns] *vt., vi.* pronounce (a word) incorrectly.
—[他][自] 잘못 발음하다

mis·pro·nun·ci·a·tion [mìsprənʌ̀nsiéiʃ(ə)n] *n.* **1.** [U] the state of pronouncing incorrectly. **2.** [C] a mispronounced word.
—[名] **1.** 잘못 발음하기 **2.** 틀린 발음

mis·read [misrí:d / ˊˊ] *vt.* (**-read** [-réd]) **1.** read or understand incorrectly. **2.** interpret wrongly.
—[他] **1.** …을 잘못 읽다; …의 뜻을 잘못 알다 **2.** …을 오해하다

mis·rep·re·sent [mìsreprizént / ˊˊ-ˊ] *vt.* represent wrongly; give a wrong account or impression of (something).
—[他] …을 잘못 전하다, …을 틀리게 설명하다

mis·rule [misrú:l / ˊˊ] *n.* [U] **1.** bad government. **2.** disorder. **—*vt.*** rule or govern (people) unjustly.
—[名] **1.** 악정(惡政), 실정(失政) **2.** 무질서 —[他] …의 정치를 잘못하다

⁝**miss**[1] [mis] *n.* **1.** [C] a word used in speaking to a girl or a young unmarried woman; a young lady. **2.** 《*M-*》 a title used before the name of a girl or an unmarried woman. ⇒[N.B.] ¶*Good morning, Miss! / Miss Brown / Miss Marie Brown.*
—[名] **1.** 소녀, 처녀; 아가씨 **2.** 양(孃) [N.B.] 자매가 둘 이상일 경우는 언니에게는 성만을 붙이고 동생에게는 이름까지 붙임

⁝**miss**[2] [mis] *vt.* **1.** fail to hit (something). ¶*~ one's aim / He fired at the bird, but missed it.* **2.** fail to get, catch, meet or reach (something). ¶*~ a prize / ~ a train / He missed the bank and fell in the water.*① **3.** fail to see, find, hear, or understand (something). ¶*~ the point of the joke*② */ No one will ~ the notice.*③ */ I looked for the word in the dictionary, but missed it.* **4.** be absent from (a party, etc.) ¶*I missed Mr. Smith's class.*④ **5.** leave out. ¶*Never ~ a word in your reading.* **6.** escape; avoid. 《*~ doing*》 ¶*He barely missed being run over.*⑤ **7.** become aware of the absence of (something). ¶*I suddenly missed my bag.* **8.** feel sad at the absence or loss of (someone). ¶*I will ~ you very much.* **—*vi.*** **1.** fail to hit. ¶*His shot missed.* **2.** fail to be successful. ¶*~ in one's attempt.*
—[他] **1.** …을 맞히지 못하다 **2.** …을 얻지 못하다;…에 도달하지 못하다 ¶①그는 둑에 닿지 못하고 물에 빠졌다 **3.** …이 눈(귀)에 들어오지 않다; …을 이해할 수 없다 ¶②농담의 참뜻을 이해 못하다/③그 게시를 못 보는 사람은 아무도 없을 것이다 **4.** …에 결석하다 ¶④스미드 선생의 수업에 나가지 못했다 **5.** …을 빠뜨리다, 빼다 **6.** …을 피하다; 도망치다 ¶⑤하마터면 차에 치일 뻔했다 **7.** …이 없는 것을 깨닫다 **8.** …이 없어서 쓸쓸하게 여기다 —[自] **1.** 과녁에 빗나가다 **2.** 실패하다

1) ***miss fire,*** (of a gun) fail to go off.
2) ***miss one's footing,*** slip, as in climbing.
3) ***miss the mark,*** fail to succeed.

[熟] 1)[총이] 불발로 끝나다 2)발을 헛디디다 3)과녁에 빗나가다; 실패하다

—*n.* [C] **1.** a failure to hit, meet, obtain, see, etc. **2.** an escape. ¶*a lucky ~.*
—[名] **1.** 실패, 과녁에 빗나감 **2.** 모면, 도망

Miss. =Mississippi.

mis·shap·en [misʃéip(ə)n / ˊˊ-] *adj.* poorly shaped; deformed.
—[形] 잘못 만든, 기형의; 모양이 흉한

•**mis·sile** [mís(i)l / mísail] *n.* [C] a weapon or object that is shot or thrown, such as a stone, an arrow, a bullet, or a rocket. ¶*guided missiles*① */ an intercontinental (an intermediate-range) ballistic ~.*②
—[名] 날아가는 무기, 미사일;탄도탄 ¶①유도탄/②대륙간(중거리) 탄도탄

‡ miss·ing [mísiŋ] *adj.* **1.** not to be found. ¶*The girl is still ~.* **2.** lacking; lost; absent ¶*a ~ page.*①
—[形] 1. 행방불명의, 보이지 않는 2. 결여된, 없어진 ¶①낙장(落張)

missing link [⌐-⌐] *n.* something necessary for filling a gap or blank in a series.
—[名] 계열상 빠진 요소; 유인원과 사람의 중간에 있었다고 가상되는 생물

*** mis·sion** [míʃ(ə)n] *n.* [C] **1.** a group of persons sent to another country for a special purpose; (*U.S.*) the diplomatic delegation; the embassy. ¶*a commercial~.*① / **2.** business or duty on which one is sent; any errand; one's life work; a calling ¶*have a ~ in life.* **3.** 《*pl.*》 an organized missionary effort to spread the Christian religion; the district assigned to a priest.
—[名] 1. 외교 사절[단]; 해외 공사(공관) ¶①무역 사절단 2. [파견되는] 특수 임무; [사람이 생애를 거는] 사명, 천직 3. [그리스도교의] 전도, 전도 활동; 전도 지구, 선교지

*** mis·sion·ar·y** [míʃ(ə)nèri / -nəri] *n.* [C] (pl. **-ar·ies**) a person who works to spread his religious ideas by trying to convert other people. ¶*a foreign~.*① —*adj.* of missions, esp. religious missions.
—[名] 선교사, 전도사 ¶①외인 선교사
—[形] 포교의, 전도의

*** Mis·sis·sip·pi** [mìsisípi] *n.* **1.** 《*the-*》 the large river in North America. **2.** a southern State of the United States. ⇒[N.B.]
—[名] 1. 미시시피강(미국 중부의 긴 강) 2. 미시시피 주 [N.B.] Miss.로 줄임

Mis·sis·sip·pi·an [mìsəsípiən / -sis-] *adj.* **1.** of the Mississippi River. **2.** of the State of Mississippi. —*n.* a person of the state of Mississippi.
—[形] 1. 미시시피강의 2. 미시시피 주의
—[名] 미시시피 주의 주민

mis·sive [mísiv] *n.* [C] a letter; a written note.
—[名] 신서(信書), 서한

Mis·sour·i [mizúəri] *n.* **1.** a middle western State of the United States. ⇒[N.B.] **2.** 《*the ~*》 a river flowing southwestward from Montana to the Mississippi.
—[名] 1. 미주우리 주 [N.B.] Mo.로 줄임 2. 미주우리강

mis·spell [misspél / ⌐⌐] *vt.* (**-spelled** or **-spelt**) spell (a word) wrongly.
—[他] …의 철자를 틀리다

mis·spelt [misspélt / ⌐⌐] *v.* pt. and pp. of **misspell**. —*adj.* misspelled.
—[形] 철자가 틀린

mis·spend [misspénd / mís-] *vt.* (**-spent**) spend wrongly; waste.
—[他] …을 낭비하다, 잘못 쓰다

mis·spent [misspént / ⌐⌐] *v.* pt. and pp. of **misspend**. —*adj.* used wrongly.
—[形] 낭비된

‡ mist [mist] *n.* **1.** [C][U] a thin fog or vapor in the air. ¶*The mist cleared.* **2.** [C] something that makes the eye not clear; something that darkens the mind. ¶*a ~ of tears.*
in a mist, in a puzzle; confused.
—*vi.* come down in the form of mist; be covered with mist; become dim. —*vt.* cover or dim (something) with mist; make (something) not clear.
—[名] 1. 안개, 운애 2. [눈·유리의] 흐림; [이해 따위를] 흐리게 하는 것
[熟] 당황하여, 갈피를 못 잡아
—[自] 안개가 끼다, 흐려지다 —[他]…을 안개로 덮다, 흐리게 하다, 희미하게 하다

mis·tak·a·ble [mistéikəbl] *adj.* that can be mistaken or misunderstood.
—[形] 틀리기 쉬운, 오해받기 쉬운

‡ mis·take [mistéik] *vt.* (**-took, -tak·en**) **1.** understand wrongly. ¶*~ the road / There's no mistaking it.*① **2.** take (someone or something) for another. ¶*I mistook you for your brother.*② —*vi.* be wrong.
—*n.* [U][C] a misunderstanding; an error; a fault.
1) ***and no mistake,*** (*colloq.*) without doubt; surely.
2) ***beyond mistake,*** certainly.
3) ***by mistake,*** mistakenly.
4) ***make a mistake,*** commit an error.
—[他] 1. …을 틀리다, 오해하다 ¶①틀릴 리가 없다 2. …을 잘못 생각하다 ¶②나는 당신을 당신 동생인 줄 알았다 —[自] 틀리다, 잘못하다
—[名] 잘못, 틀림, 오해; 실수
[熟] 1)《口》 틀림없이 2)확실히 3)잘못하여 4)잘못을 저지르다

‡ mis·tak·en [mistéik(ə)n] *v.* pp. of **mistake**. —*adj.* wrong; having a wrong opinion; judging wrongly. ¶*~ kindness*① / *You are ~.*②
—[形] 틀린, 오해한 ¶①달갑지 않은 친절/②너는 잘못 생각하고 있다

mis·tak·en·ly [mistéik(ə)nli] *adv.* by mistake.
—[副] 잘못되어

mis·ter [místər] *n.* **1.** 《usu. *Mr.*》 a title used before a man's name or the name of his office. ¶*Mr. Brown / Mr. President / Mr. Officer*①. **2.** (*colloq.*) sir.
—[名] 1. Mr.로 줄여 성명·관직명 앞에 붙임 ¶①순경 양반 2. [호칭으로서] 선생

mist·i·ly [místili] *adv.* not clearly; in a misty manner.
—[副] 안개가 자욱하여, 희미하게

mis·tle·toe [mísltòu] *n.* [C] a plant growing on the branches and trunks of other trees, often used as a Christmas decoration.
—[名] 겨우살이(크리스마스의 장식으로 쓰는 기생 식물)

‡ mis·took [mistúk] *vt.* pt. of **mistake**.

mis·trans·late [mìstrænsléit] *vt.* translate incorrectly.
—[他] …을 오역하다

mis·trans·la·tion [mìstrænsléiʃ(ə)n] *n.* [C][U] an incorrect
—[名] 오역

M

mis·treat [mistríːt / ⌣⌢] vt. (chiefly U.S.) treat wrongly; make a bad use of (something). —⊕ …을 학대하다, 혹사하다

mis·treat·ment [mistríːtmənt / ⌣⌢⌣] n. ⓤ ill treatment. —⊛ 학대, 혹사

‡ **mis·tress** [místris] n. ⓒ **1.** a woman who is at the head of a family. ¶ *the ~ of a house.*① **2.** (often *M-*) someone or something regarded as like a female ruler. ↔master ¶ *the ~ of the night.*② **3.** (chiefly Brit.) a woman teacher in a school; a woman having much knowledge. **4.** a woman supported by a man but not married to him. ¶ *keep a ~.*③ **5.** (*M-*) a title once used before the name of any woman. ⇒N.B.
1) *be one's own mistress,* be free to do as one pleases.
2) *the Mistress of the Adriatic,* another name for Venice.
3) *the Mistress of the Seas,* another name for England.

—⊛ **1.** [하인의] 안주인, 주부, 마님 ¶①한 집안의 주부 **2.** [여자의] 지배자, …의 여왕 ¶②밤의 여왕(달) **3.** 여자 교사; 박식한 여자 **4.** 첩, 정부 ¶③첩을 두다 **5.** 보통 여자에 대한 경칭 N.B. 지금은 Mrs., Miss를 씀

註·1)자유의 몸이다 2)베니스의 별명 3)영국의 별명

mis·trust [mistrʌ́st / ⌣⌢] vt. doubt; suspect. —⊕ …을 신용하지 않다, 의심하다
—n. ⓤ lack of trust; suspicion. ⌈suspicious.⌉ —⊛ 불신, 의심

mis·trust·ful [mistrʌ́stf(u)l / ⌣⌣⌢] adj. lacking confidence; —⊕ 의심 많은; 신용하지 않는

mist·y [místi] adj. (**mist·i·er, mist·i·est**) **1.** covered with mist; tearful. ¶ *~ weather.*① **2.** not clearly seen; vague. ▷**mist·i·ly** [-li] adv. —**mist·i·ness** [-nis] n.
—⊕ **1.** 안개 깊은, 눈물로 희미한 ¶①안개낀 날씨 **2.** 희미한, 똑똑히 안 보이는

* **mis·un·der·stand** [mìsʌndərstǽnd] vt. (-**stood**) understand (words or actions) wrongly; gather the wrong meaning from (a remark, etc.). —⊕ [말·행위를] 오해하다; …에 틀린 해석을 하다

mis·un·der·stand·ing [mìsʌndərstǽndiŋ] n. ⓤⓒ **1.** a mistake as to meaning or motive. **2.** disagreement; a quarrel caused by a misunderstanding.
—⊛ **1.** 오해 **2.** 의견의 상이; [오해로 인한] 불화

mis·un·der·stood [mìsʌndərstúd] v. pt. and pp. of **misunderstand.**
—adj. incorrectly understood.
—⊕ 오해된, 의미를 잘못 안

mis·us·age [misjúːsidʒ, -úːz- / -júːzidʒ] n. ⓤⓒ an incorrect usage; ill treatment.
—⊛ [말 따위의] 오용; 학대; 혹사

mis·use [misjúːz / ⌣⌢ / →n.] vt. use (someone or something) for a wrong purpose; treat badly. —n. [misjúːs / ⌣⌢] ⓒ a wrong use.
—⊕ …을 오용하다; 학대하다, 혹사하다 —⊛ 오용, 악용

mite¹ [mait] n. ⓒ a very small insect like a spider. —⊛ 진드기

mite² [mait] n. ⓒ **1.** a very small coin or sum of money. **2.** (colloq.) any small thing, such as a small child.
not a mite, not in the least; not at all.
—⊛ **1.** 잔돈, 약간의 돈 **2.** (口) 아주 작은 것, 꼬마
註 조금도 …않다

mi·ter, Brit. **mi·tre** [máitər] n. **1.** ⓒ a kind of crown worn by archbishops and bishops. **2.** ⓤ the rank or position of a bishop.
—⊛ **1.** [가톨릭 교회의 bishop이 쓰는] 사교관(司敎冠) **2.** 사교의 신분·지위

mit·i·gate [mítigèit] vt. soften (anger, pain, etc.); make less severe or painful. ¶ *~ a punishment.*①
—⊕ …을 누그러뜨리다, 경감하다, 달래다 ¶①벌을 가볍게 하다

mit·i·ga·tion [mìtigéiʃ(ə)n] n. ⓤ the act of mitigating; ⓒ anything that mitigates.
—⊛ 완화, 경감; 누그러뜨리는 것

mi·tre [máitər] (Brit.) =miter.
mi·tred [máitərd] adj. Brit. =mitered.

mitt [mit] n. ⓒ **1.** a kind of glove without fingers. **2.** (slang) the hand. **3.** (pl.) boxing gloves. **4.** a baseball glove with a thick pad over the palm.
—⊛ **1.** 벙어리장갑 **2.** 손, 주먹 **3.** 전투용 글러브 **4.** [야구의] 미트

mit·ten [mítn] n. ⓒ a glove that covers the four fingers together and the thumb separately; a lady's glove that covers the arm and the hand. ⌈dismissed.⌉
1) *get the mitten,* (colloq.) be refused as a lover; be
2) *give the mitten to,* reject (someone) as a lover; dismiss. ⌈mercilessly.⌉
3) *handle someone without mittens,* deal with someone
—⊛ 벙어리장갑, [부인용의] 긴 장갑

註 1)(口)퇴짜를 맞다; 해고당하다 2)…에 퇴짜를 놓다; …을 해고하다 3)…을 사정없이 다루다

‡ **mix** [miks] v. (**mixed** or **mixt**) vt. **1.** put (things) together into a single mass or compound; combine; confuse. ¶ *~ water with wine* / *~ facts.* **2.** make (something) by blending different things. ¶ *~ a salad dressing* / *~ a poison.* —vi. **1.** be mixed; mingle. ¶ *Oil and*
—⊕ **1.** …을 섞다, 혼합하다; 결합하다 **2.** [혼합하여] …을 만들다 —⊛ **1.** 섞이다 **2.** 교제하다; 사이좋게 지내다 ¶①사교계에 출입하다

water will not ~. **2.** keep company; associate; get along in a friendly way. ¶*~ in society*① / *~ with others at a party.*

mix up, ⓐ mix thoroughly. ⓑ confuse. ⓒ involve; concern. [熟] ⓐ잘 섞다 ⓑ혼동하다 ⓒ관련(관계)시키다

—*n.* [C] **1.** mixture. **2.** (*colloq.*) a mixed condition; a mess. —[名] 1. 혼합 2.《口》 혼란

mixed [mikst] *adj.* **1.** made up of different kinds. ¶*a ~ brigade*① / *a ~ train.*② **2.** having both boys and girls; of both women and men. ¶*a ~ chorus*③ / *a ~ school.* **3.** mentally confused. ¶*~ emotions.* —[形] 1. 섞인, 잡다한 ¶①혼성 여단/②혼합 열차 2. [남녀]공학의; 남녀 혼합의 ¶③혼성 합창 3. 머리가 혼란한

mixed number [⌐ ⌐–] *n.* a number consisting of a whole number and a fraction. —[名] 대분수(帶分數)

mix·er [míksər] *n.* [C] **1.** a mixing machine. ¶*a concrete ~.*① **2.** (*U.S. colloq.*) a person keeping company with others in society. ¶*a good ~.*② —[名] 1. 혼합기, 믹서 ¶①콘크리이트 믹서 2. 교제가 ¶②교제를 잘하는 사람

mixt [mikst] *v.* pt. and pp. of **mix**.

⁑mix·ture [míkstʃər] *n.* [C] **1.** something that is mixed. **2.** [U] the state of being mixed. ¶*speak in a ~ of French and Italian.*① **3.** two or more substances mixed together but not chemically united. —[名] 1. 혼합물 2. 혼합 ¶①프랑스어와 이탈리아어가 섞인 말을 쓰다 3. [화합물과 구별하여] 혼합물

mix-up [míksʌ̀p] *n.* [C] **1.** confusion. **2.** a fight or quarrel. —[名] 1. 혼란 2. 싸움, 다툼

miz·zen [mízn] *n.* [C] a fore-and-aft sail set on the mizzenmast. —[名] 뒷돛대의 세로돛

miz·zen·mast [míznmæ̀st / -mὰ:st] *n.* [C] the rear mast in a two-masted or three-masted ship. —[名] [세 돛대 배의] 뒷돛대

Mme. (pl. **Mmes.** [meidɑ́:m]) Madame.

Mo. **1.** molybdenum. **2.** Monday. **3.** Missouri.

***moan** [moun] *n.* [C] a long, low sound of sorrow or pain; any similar sound. —[名] [슬픔·고통의] [신음]소리, 끙끙 소리; [바람 따위의] 구슬픈 소리

moan·ful [móunf(u)l] *adj.* showing sorrow or pain. —[形] 신음하는, 슬픈 듯한

moat [mout] *n.* [C] a deep, wide ditch, usu. water-filled, dug around a castle, etc. as a defense. **—*vt.*** surround (a place) with a moat. —[名] [성벽 따위의 주위에 둘러 판] 도랑, 해자(垓字) —[他] …에 해자를 두르다

mob** [mɑb / mɔb] *n.* [C] **1.** (*collectively*) a large number of disorderly, rude people. **2.** (*the ~*) the common mass of people. **—*vt. (**mobbed, mob·bing**) attack (someone or some place) in a disorderly crowd. —[名] 1. 폭도, 난민(亂民), 오합지졸 2. 하층민, 민중 —[他] 떼를 지어 …을 습격하다

mo·bile [móub(ə)l / -bail] *adj.* **1.** movable; easy to move. **2.** moving or changing easily. —[形] 1. 가동(可動)의, 이동성의 2. 움직이기 쉬운, 변하기 쉬운

mo·bil·i·ty [moubíləti] [U] *n.* the state of being mobile. —[名] 가동성, 이동성, 변덕

mo·bi·li·za·tion [mòubiləzéiʃ(ə)n / -lai-] *n.* [U] **1.** the act of mobilizing. ¶*industrial ~*① / *national ~.*② **2.** the state of being mobilized. —[名] 1. 동원 ¶①산업 동원/②국가 총동원 2. 운용(運用), 유통

mo·bi·lize [móubilàiz] *vt.* **1.** call (troops, etc.) into active use. **2.** put (wealth, etc.) into motion or active use. **—*vi.*** become organized and ready for war, etc. —[他] 1. [군대 따위]를 동원하다 2. [재화 따위]를 유통시키다 —[自] 동원되다, 전시체제로 되다

moc·ca·sin [mɑ́kəsin / mɔ́k-] *n.* [C] **1.** a deerskin or other soft leather shoe or sandal. **2.** a poisonous snake of the southern United States. —[名] 1. 사슴가죽 신 2. [미국산] 독사

⁑mock [mɑk / mɔk] *vt.* **1.** make fun of (someone) by acting in the same way as he; imitate. **2.** laugh at; scoff at (someone). **3.** make light of (someone); despise. **4.** deceive. **—*adj.*** not real; false; imitation. ¶*a ~ trial.*① **—*n.*** [U] an action or a speech that mocks; a thing scorned. ¶*make a ~ of someone.* —[他] 1. …을 흉내내어 조롱하다 2. …을 조롱하다, 놀리다 3. …을 업신여기다 4. …을 속이다 —[形] 모조의, 가짜의 ¶①모의 재판 —[名] 조롱, 경멸

mock·er [mɑ́kər / mɔ́kə] *n.* [C] a person who mocks. —[名] 조롱하는 사람, 흉내내는 사람

mock·er·y [mɑ́kəri / mɔ́k-] *n.* (pl. **-er·ies**) **1.** [U] the act of mocking; ridicule; **2.** [C] someone or something to be mocked. **3.** [C] an imitation of another's action. —[名] 1. 조소, 조롱 2. 웃음거리, 조소의 대상 3. 흉내

mock·ing·bird [mɑ́kiŋbə̀:rd / mɔ́kiŋbə̀:d] *n.* [C] a small songbird of the southern United States. —[名] 앵무새의 일종

mock·ing·ly [mɑ́kiŋli / mɔ́k-] *adv.* in a mocking manner. —[副] 넘보고, 조롱하여

mo·dal [móudl] *adj.* **1.** of mode, manner, or form. **2.** (*Grammar*) of the mood of a verb. —[形] 1. 양식(樣式)의, 모양의, 형식의 2.《文法》 법(法)의

mode [738] **modify**

* **mode** [moud] *n.* ⓒ **1.** a manner; a fashion; a way; a method; a style. **2.** (*Grammar*) mood. **3.** (*Music*) a form of scale; one of the two classes of keys in music.
: **mod·el** [mádl / mɔ́dl] *n.* ⓒ **1.** a small copy. ¶*a ~ of a plane*① / *a wax ~ for a statue.*② **2.** a style or design. ¶*the latest ~.*③ **3.** a thing or person to be imitated. ¶*the ~ of beauty.*④ **4.** a person who poses for painters, etc. **5.** a person, esp. a woman, who wears newly-designed clothes to show people.
—*vt.* (**-eled, el·ing** or *Brit.* **-elled, -el·ling**) **1.** make a plan or model of (someone or something); shape; mold; form. ¶*~ a horse out of clay.* **2.** follow as a model. (*~* oneself *on* (or *upon, after*)) ¶*~ oneself on* (or *upon*) *one's father.*⑤ —*vi.* be a model.
—*adj.* serving as a model; worthy of being imitated.
mod·el·er, *Brit.* **-el·ler** [mádlər / mɔ́dlə] *n.* ⓒ a person who models.
: **mod·er·ate** [mád(ə)rit / mɔ́d- ‖ →*v.*] *adj.* **1.** not extreme; reasonable; calm. ↔immoderate **2.** medium; average.
—*n.* ⓒ a person holding moderate opinions.
—*v.* [mádərèit / mɔ́d-] *vt.* make (something) less violent, extreme, etc.; cause (something) to become moderate. —*vi.* become less violent, extreme, etc.; become moderate.
mod·er·ate·ly [mád(ə)ritli / mɔ́d-] *adv.* in a moderate manner. ¶*a ~ hot day.*① (of being moderate.)
mod·er·ate·ness [mád(ə)ritnis / mɔ́d-] *n.* Ⓤ the state
mod·er·a·tion [màdəréiʃ(ə)n / mɔ̀d-] *n.* Ⓤ temperance; calmness; lack of violence. ¶*in ~.*①
mod·e·ra·to [màdərá:tou / mɔ̀d-] *adj., adv.* (*Music*) in moderate time.
mod·er·a·tor [mádərèitər / mɔ́dərèitə] *n.* ⓒ **1.** a chairman. **2.** a person acting as judge to settle a quarrel. **3.** a regulator.
: **mod·ern** [mádərn / mɔ́dən] *adj.* of the present time; up-to-date; not old-fashioned. ↔ancient —*n.* ⓒ (usu. *pl.*) a person of modern times; a person who has modern tastes.
mod·ern·ism [mádərnìz(ə)m / mɔ́dən-] *n.* **1.** Ⓤ a modern view or method. **2.** ⓒ a modern thought or practice. **3.** ⓒ a modern word or phrase.
mod·ern·ist [mádərnist / mɔ́dən-] *n.* ⓒ a person who holds modern views, uses modern methods, etc.
mod·ern·is·tic [màdərnístik / mɔ̀dən-] *adj.* modern; of modernism or modernists.
mo·der·ni·ty [madə́:rniti / mɔdə́:-] *n.* Ⓤ the state of being modern; ⓒ something modern.
mod·ern·ize [mádərnàiz / mɔ́dən-] *vt.* make (something) modern. —*vi.* become modern. ▷**mod·ern·i·za·tion** [màdərnizéiʃ(ə)n / mɔ̀dənaiz-] *n.* —**mod·ern·iz·er** [-ər] *n.*
: **mod·est** [mádist / mɔ́d-] *adj.* **1.** not boastful or proud. **2.** able to feel shame; shy. **3.** not too great; moderate; humble.
mod·est·ly [mádistli / mɔ́d-] *adv.* in a modest manner.
* **mod·es·ty** [mádisti / mɔ́d-] *n.* Ⓤ the state of being modest; humility; moderation. [amount.]
mod·i·cum [mádikəm / mɔ́di-] *n.* ⓒ (*sing.* only) a small
mod·i·fi·ca·tion [màdifikéiʃ(ə)n / mɔ̀di-] *n.* Ⓤ the act of modifying or being modified; ⓒ a change or changing made by modifying.
mod·i·fi·er [mádifàiər / mɔ́di-] *n.* ⓒ **1.** (*Grammar*) a word or group of words that modifies, such as an adjective, adverb, etc. **2.** a person or thing that modifies.
* **mod·i·fy** [mádifài / mɔ́di-] *vt.* **1.** change (something)

—ⓢ **1.** 방법, 양식, 유행, 형식 **2.** (文法) [동사의] 법, 서법(叙法) **3.** (樂) 음계, 선법(旋法)

—ⓢ **1.** 모형, 축소형, 원형 ¶①비행기의 모형 ②조상(彫像)의 왁스 원형 **2.** 형(型), 양식 ¶③최신형 **3.** 모범, 전형, 표본 ¶④미(美)의 전형 **4.** [화가 등의] 모델 **5.** [양장점의] 마네킹

—ⓣ **1.** …의 모형(본)을 만들다; …을 모델로 하여 제작하다; 본뜨다 **2.** …을 본보기로 삼다 ¶⑤아버지를 본받다
—自 모델이 되다

—形 모범의, 전형적인
—名 모형 제작자

—形 **1.** 극단에 흐르지 않는, 적당한, 온건한 **2.** 보통의
—名 온화한 사람, 온건파의 사람
—他 …을 완화하다, 적당하게 하다
—自 누그러지다, 온화해지다; 적당하게 되다

—副 적당하게, 알맞게 ¶①알맞게 더운 날씨
—名 적당, 온건
—名 적당, 중용(中庸); 절제, 온화; 온건 ¶①적당하게, 알맞게
—形副 (樂) 중간 속도의(로)

—名 **1.** 의장, 사회 **2.** 중재자, 조정자 **3.** 조절기, 조정기

—形 현대의, 근래의, 신식의, 현대식의
—名 현대인, 새 사상을 가진 사람

—名 **1.** 현대(근대)풍, 근대적 방법 **2.** 근대(현대)사조, 현대주의 **3.** 현대어

—名 현대(근대)주의자

—形 근대(현대)적인, 근대(현대)주의[자]의
—名 근대(현대)성, 근대(현대)적임; 근대(현대)적인 것
—他 …을 근대(현대)화하다 —自 근대(현대)적으로 하다

—形 **1.** 겸손한, 조심성 있는 **2.** 정숙한, 수줍어하는, 품위 있는 **3.** 적당한; 온당한; 검소한
—副 겸손하게, 품위있게
—名 겸손, 사양, 정숙함, 수줍음, 수수함, 알맞음
—名 소량, 소액
—名 가감, 제한, 조절, 변경, 수정; 변경(수정)된 것

—名 **1.** (文法) 수식어 **2.** 변경(수정)하는 사람(것)

—他 **1.** …을 [일부] 변경하다 ¶①

slightly. ¶~ *the terms of a contract.*① **2.** reduce; limit (the meanings of words, etc.); moderate. ¶~ *one's demands.*② **3.** (*Grammar*) qualify. ¶*Adjectives ~ nouns.* ▷**mod·i·fi·a·ble** [-əbl] *adj.*
약조건을 변경하다 2. …을 경감하다, 한정(제한)하다, 가감하다 ¶②요구를 가감하다 3.《文法》수식하다

mod·ish [móudiʃ] *adj.* fashionable; stylish.
—[形] 현대풍의, 유행을 따르는

mod·u·late [mádʒulèit / mɔ́dju-] *vt.* **1.** regulate; adjust; vary; soften. **2.** change (the voice, etc.). **3.** change the frequency of (electrical waves). —*vi.* (*Music*) pass from one key to another.
—[他] 1. …을 조절하다, 조정하다 2. [목소리 따위]를 바꾸다 3. [주파수]를 변조하다 —[自]《樂》조바꿈하다

mod·u·la·tion [màdʒuléiʃ(ə)n / mɔ̀dju-] *n.* [U][C] the act of modulating or the state of being modulated.
—[名] 변조, 조바꿈, 조절

mo·hair [móuhɛ̀ər] *n.* [U] **1.** cloth made from the hair of the Angora goat. **2.** an imitation of such a material.
—[名] 1. 모헤어[천] 2. 모헤어의 모조품

Mo·ham·med [mouhǽmed] *n.* (570?–632 A.D.) an Arabian prophet of Islam. ⇒[N.B.]
—[名] 마호멧 [N.B.] Mahomet, Muhammad로도 씀

Mo·ham·med·an [mouhǽmid(ə)n] *adj.* of Mohammed or the Moslem religion. —*n.* [C] a follower of Mohammed. ⇒[N.B.]
—[形] 마호멧[교]의, 회교의 —[名] 마호멧 교도, 회교도 [N.B.] Mahometan으로도 씀

Mo·ham·med·an·ism [mouhǽmid(ə)nìz(ə)m] *n.* [U] the Moslem religion.
—[名] 마호멧교, 회교

moil [mɔil] *vi.* work hard. ¶*toil and ~.*① —*n.* [C] hard work.
—[自] 부지런히 일하다, 뼈빠지게 일하다 —[名] 고된 일, 중노동

* **moist** [mɔist] *adj.* slightly wet; damp; watery; rainy.
—[形] 습기가 있는, 축축한, 비가 많이 오는

moist·en [mɔ́isn] *vt.* make (something) moist. ¶~ *one's lips* (or *throat*).① —*vi.* become moist. ¶~ *at one's eyes.*②
—[他] …을 축축하게 하다, 적시다 ¶①술을 마시다 —[自] 축축해지다, 젖다 ¶②눈물짓다

* **mois·ture** [mɔ́istʃər] *n.* [U] slight wetness; water vapor in the air or on a surface.
—[名] 습기, 물기, 수증기

mo·lar [móulər] *n.* [C] a back tooth used to grind one's food. —*adj.* **1.** used for grinding. **2.** of the molar teeth.
—[名] 어금니, 구치(臼齒) —[形] 1. 갈아(씹어) 부수는 2. 어금니의

mo·las·ses [məlǽsiz] *n. pl.* 《used as *sing.*》 a sweet syrup obtained from sugar during the process of manufacture.
—[名] 당밀

* **mold**[1], *Brit.* **mould** [mould] *n.* [C] **1.** a hollow shape in which anything is cast or formed. ¶*Hot metal was poured into the ~.* **2.** something formed in a mold. ¶*a ~ of jelly.*① **3.** a pattern; a model. **4.** a shape; a form. ¶*He is manly in ~ and bearing.*② **5.** [U][C] character; nature. ¶*a man of gentle ~ / He was cast in a heroic ~.*③ */ The brothers were cast in the same ~.*④
—[名] 1. 거푸집, 주형(鑄型) 2. 주형으로 만든 것(주물 따위) ¶①젤리 한 개 3. 형, 틀, 모형 4. 모양, 모습 ¶②그는 모습이나 태도가 사내답다 5. 성격; 성질 ¶③그는 영웅기질이었다/④형제는 같은 성격이었다

—*vt.* **1.** form or make (something) in a mold; give a shape to (something). ¶~ *a statue in* (or *out of*) *clay*⑤ */ ~ clay into a statue.*⑥ **2.** shape the character of (someone); train; develop. ¶~ *one's character.*⑦
—[他] 1. …을 틀에 넣어 만들다, 주조하다 ¶⑤⑥점토로 상(像)을 만들다 2. 의 성격을 형성하다; (인격을) 도야하다 ¶⑦성격을 형성하다

mold[2], *Brit.* **mould** [mould] *n.* [U] soft, fine, rich soil. —*vt.* cover (something) over with mold. 《~ *up* something》 ¶~ *up potatoes.*①
—[名] 부식토(腐植土); 양토(壤土) —[他] …을 양토로 덮다 ¶①감자에 흙을 덮다

mold[3], *Brit.* **mould** [mould] *n.* [U] a wool-like or fur-like tiny plant which grows on wet cloth, old bread, etc. ¶*blue ~*① */ a smell of ~.*② —*vi.* become covered with mold. —*vt.* cover (something) with mold.
—[名] 곰팡이 ¶①푸른 곰팡이/②곰팡내 —[自] 곰팡이로 덮이다; 곰팡이가 슬다 —[他] …을 곰팡이가 슬게 하다

mold·er[1], *Brit.* **mould·er** [móuldər] *vi.* turn into dust; decay; waste away. —*vt.* cause (something) to decay.
—[自] 썩어 무너지다, 붕괴하다 —[他] …을 썩게 하다

mold·er[2], *Brit.* **mould·er** [móuldər] *n.* [C] a person or thing that molds or shapes.
—[名] 조형자(造型者), 주형공(鑄型工)

mold·ing, *Brit.* **mould·ing** [móuldiŋ] *n.* **1.** [U] the act of shaping. **2.** [C] something molded. **3.** 《often *pl.*》 an ornamental strip used around the upper part of the wall of a room or of a picture frame, etc.
—[名] 1. 틀을 만들기, 주조, 소조(塑造) 2. 주조물, 소조물 3. [벽 위의] 쇠시리

mold·y, *Brit.* **mould·y** [móuldi] *adj.* (**mold·i·er, mold·i·est** or *Brit.* **mould·i·er, mould·i·est**) **1.** covered with mold. **2.** musty; damp; old-fashioned. ▷**mold·i·ness** [-nis] *n.*
—[形] 1. 곰팡이 슨 2. 곰팡내나는, 축축한, 케케묵은, 진부한

* **mole**[1] [moul] *n.* [C] a small, dark, slightly raised spot on the skin.
—[名] 사마귀, 검은 점

M

mole² [moul] *n.* [C] a small animal that lives chiefly underground. ¶*blind as a* ~.① ▷**mole like** [-làik] *adj.*
—[名] 두더지 ¶①아주 눈이 먼

mo·lec·u·lar [moulékjulər] *adj.* of or consisting of molecules. ¶*a* ~ *formula*① / ~ *weight*.②
—[形] 분자(分子)의, 분자로 이루어지는 ¶①분자식/②분자량

mol·e·cule [málikjù:l / mɔ́l-] *n.* [C] (*Chemistry, Physics*) the smallest particle of an element; a very small particle.
—[名] 《化·理》 분자, 미분자

mole·hill [móulhìl] *n.* [C] a small mound of earth raised up by moles. ***make a mountain out of a molehill,*** exaggerate; make (something) too important.
—[名] 두더지가 파 놓은 흙무더기 [熟] 침소봉대하여(과장하여) 말하다

mo·lest [moulést] *vt.* 《usu. in *negative*》 annoy; trouble; disturb. ¶*She should not be molested in any way.* ▷**mo·lest·er** [-ər] *n.*
—[他] …을 괴롭히다, …의 훼방을 놓다

mo·les·ta·tion [mòulestéiʃ(ə)n] *n.* [U] the act of molesting; disturbance.
—[名] 훼방, 방해

mol·li·fi·ca·tion [màlifikéiʃ(ə)n / mɔ̀l-] *n.* [U] the act of mollifying; the state of being mollified.
—[名] 누그러뜨리기, 진정(鎭靜), 완화, 경감, 달래기

mol·li·fy [málifai / mɔ́l-] *vt.* (**-fied**) calm; soften; make (someone or something) quiet.
—[他] …을 누그러뜨리다, 진정시키다, 가라앉히다, 경감하다

mol·lusc [máləsk / mɔ́l-] *n.* (*Brit.*) =mollusk.

mol·lusk [máləsk / mɔ́l-] *n.* [C] any of a large group of animals with soft bodies, usu. covered by a hard shell.
—[名] 연체(軟體) 동물

molt, *Brit.* **moult** [moult] *vt., vi.* (of animals) cast off one's feathers, skin, etc. before a new growth; shed (feathers, etc.). —*n.* [C] the act or season of molting.
—[他][自] [털을] 갈게 하다(갈다); [동물이] 허물을 벗다 —[名] 털갈이, 허물벗기[시기]

mol·ten [móult(ə)n] *v.* pp. of **melt**.
—*adj.* **1.** melted by heat. **2.** made by melting and casting. ¶~ *gold.*
—[形] **1.** 녹은 **2.** 주조(鑄造)한

mo·lyb·de·num [moulíbdinəm] *n.* [U] a hard, silver-white metallic element.
—[名] 몰리브덴

mom [mɑm / mɔm] *n.* [C] (*U.S. colloq.*) mother; mamma.
—[名] 《美口》 엄마

⁑**mo·ment** [móumənt] *n.* **1.** [C] a very short time; an instant. ¶*in a* ~① / *for a* ~② / *Wait a* ~.; *Just a* ~.; *One* ~, *please.* **2.** [U] a special point of time. ¶*at the* ~③ / *for the* ~④ / *to the very* ~⑤ / *He fell down at the last* ~.⑥ **3.** [C] the present time. ¶*the question of the* ~.⑦ **4.** [U] importance. ¶*The business is of great* ~.
—[名] **1.** 순간; 한때 ¶①곧/②잠깐 사이 **2.** 때; 시기 ¶③바로 지금(그때)/④당분간/⑤꼭 정각에/⑥그는 중요한 순간에 쓰러졌다 **3.** 현재 ¶⑦현하의 문제 **4.** 중요성

mo·men·tar·i·ly [móuməntèrili / -t(ə)ri-] *adv.* for a moment; at every moment; at any moment.
—[副] 잠깐, 잠시; 시시각각으로, 당장

***mo·men·tar·y** [móuməntèri / -t(ə)ri] *adj.* lasting for a moment; temporary. ▷**mo·men·tar·i·ness** [-nis] *n.*
—[形] 순간의; 일시적인

mo·men·tous [mouméntəs] *adj.* very important; serious. ▷**mo·men·tous·ness** [-nis] *n.*
—[形] 중요한, 중대한

mo·men·tum [məméntəm] *n.* [U] (*Machinery*) **1.** the force of motion of a moving object. **2.** an object's tendency to continue moving forward.
—[名] 《機》 **1.** 운동량 **2.** 반동력, 타성

Mon. Monday.

Mon·a·co [mánəkòu / mɔ́n-] *n.* a very small country on the Mediterranean coast ⇒[N.B.]
—[名] 모나코 [N.B.] 지중해 북안의 세계 최소의 독립 공국

***mon·arch** [mánərk / mɔ́nək] *n.* [C] **1.** a supreme ruler; a sovereign. **2.** a person or thing like a monarch.
—[名] **1.** 군주, 왕 **2.** 왕자(王者), 왕자에 비길 만한 사람(것)

mo·nar·chic [məná:rkik / mɔná:kik], **-chi·cal** [-kik(ə)l] *adj.* of or like a monarch or monarchy.
—[形] 군주[국]의, 군주 정체의

mon·ar·chism [mánərkìz(ə)m / mɔ́nəkìz(ə)m] *n.* [U] the principles of monarchy.
—[名] 군주주의

mon·ar·chist [mánərkist / mɔ́nəkist] *n.* [C] a person who supports or believes in government by a monarch.
—[名] 군주주의자

mon·ar·chy [mánərki / mɔ́nəki] *n.* [U] government by a monarch; [C] a nation governed by a monarch. ¶*an absolute* ~.①
—[名] 군주정치, 군주정체, 군주국 ¶①전제 군주국

mon·as·ter·y [mánəstèri / mɔ́nəst(ə)ri] *n.* [C] (pl. **-ter·ies**) a building for monks to live in.
—[名] [남자] 수도원

mo·nas·tic [mənǽstik] *adj.* of or like monks or nuns or their way of life; self-denying. ¶*lead a* ~ *life.*
—[形] 수도사의(같은), 금욕적인, 은둔적인

mo·nas·ti·cism [mənǽstisìz(ə)m] *n.* [U] the system or
—[名] 수도원 제도, 수도(금욕) 생활

M

condition of life according to monastic rules.

⁝ **Mon·day** [mʌ́ndi, -dei] *n.* the second day of the week. ⇒[N.B.]
—[名] 월요일 [N.B.] Mon.으로 줄임

mon·e·tar·y [máiətèri, mʌ́n- / mʌ́nit(ə)ri] *adj.* of money or currency. ¶*a ~ unit*① / *in ~ difficulties.*②
—[形] 화폐의, 금전상의 ¶①화폐 단위 /②재정 곤란으로

⁝ **mon·ey** [mʌ́ni] *n.* [U] **1.** coins ; bank notes. ¶*paper ~* / *change ~*① / *~ out of hand.*② **2.** anything used to pay for things, such as precious metals and checks. **3.** wealth ; property.
—[名] **1.** 금전(경화 · 지폐 따위) ¶①환전하다/②현금 **2.** 통화 **3.** 부(富);재산

1) ***get one's money's worth,*** get full value for what one has spent.
2) ***make money,*** get money ; become rich.
3) ***marry money,*** marry a rich person.
[熟] 1) 쓴 돈만큼의 값어치를 얻다 2) 돈을 벌다, 재산을 모으다 3)부자와 결혼하다

mon·ey·bag [mʌ́nibæ̀g] *n.* **1.** [C] a bag for money. **2.** ⟪*pl.*, used as *sing.*⟫ (*colloq.*) wealth ; riches ; a wealthy person.
—[名] **1.** 지갑, 돈주머니 **2.**⟪口⟫ 부(富), 재산; 부자

mon·ey-chang·er [mʌ́nitʃèindʒər] *n.* [C] a person whose business is to exchange money ; a machine to exchange money quickly at fixed rates.
—[名] 환전상(換錢商); 환전기(換錢機)

mon·eyed [mʌ́nid] *adj.* **1.** wealthy; rich. **2.** of money. ¶*~ assistance.*①
—[形] **1.** 부자의 **2.** 금전상의 ¶①금전적 원조

mon·ey·grub·ber [mʌ́nigrʌ̀bər] *n.* [C] a person whose only interest in life is to make money.
—[名] 탐욕한 사람

mon·ey·lend·er [mʌ́nilèndər] *n.* [C] a person whose business is to lend money at interest.
—[名] 대금(貸金)업자

mon·ey·lend·ing [mʌ́nilèndiŋ] *n.* [U] the act of lending money at interest.
—[名] 돈을 빌려주기, 대금

mon·ey-mak·er [mʌ́nimèikər] *n.* [C] **1.** a person successful at getting money. **2.** something that produces gain of money.
—[名] **1.** 축재가 **2.** 돈벌이가 되는 일(것)

mon·ey-mak·ing [mʌ́nimèikiŋ] *n.* [U] the making of money. —*adj.* profitable.
—[名] 돈벌이 —[形] 돈벌이가 되는, 돈벌이의

money market [⌐-- ⌐-] *n.* the financial center which decides the rate of interest on borrowed capital.
—[名] 금융시장

money order [⌐-- ⌐-] *n.* an order for the payment of money. ¶*a bank ~* / *a telegraphic ~.*
—[名] 환(換), 우편환

mon·ger [mʌ́ŋgər] *n.* [C] (*Brit.*) a dealer or trader in some article. ⇒[usage] ¶*a fishmonger.*
—[名]⟪英⟫ 상인, …장수 [N.B.] 보통 합성어로 씀

Mon·gol [máŋgəl, -gɑl / mɔ́ŋgɔl, -gəl] *n.* **1.** [C] a member of the Asiatic race living in Mongolia between China and Siberia. **2.** [U] the language of the Mongolians. —*adj.* of the Mongolian people or thier language.
—[名] **1.** 몽고 인종 **2.** 몽고 말 —[形] 몽고 사람(말)의

Mon·go·li·a [maŋgóuliə / mɔŋ-] *n.* a vast region in Asia between China and Siberia.
—[名] 몽고

Mon·go·li·an [maŋgóuliən / mɔŋ-] *n.* **1.** [C] a person of Mongolia. **2.** [U] the Mongolian language. —*adj.* of Mongolia, its people, or their language.
—[名] **1.** 몽고인 **2.** 몽고 말 —[形] 몽고[인종]의, 몽고 말의

mon·grel [mʌ̀ŋgr(ə)l, +*U.S.* máŋ-] *n.* [C] an animal, esp. a dog or a plant of mixed breed ; a person of mixed birth. —*adj.* of mixed breed, race, etc.
—[名] 잡종[의 개]; 혼혈아 —[形] 잡종의, 혼혈의

mon·ism [mániz(ə)m / mɔ́n-] *n.* [U] (*Philosophy*) the doctrine that the universe can be explained in terms of only one basic substance or principle. ¶*idealistic ~.*①
—[名]⟪哲⟫ 일원론(一元論), 일원설 ¶①유심(유물) 일원론

mo·ni·tion [mouníʃ(ə)n] *n.* [C][U] **1.** warning ; caution. **2.** an official or legal notice.
—[名] **1.** 경고, 권고, 주의 **2.** [공식]통고[장], 경고[장]

* **mon·i·tor** [mánitər / mɔ́n-] *n.* [C] **1.** a senior pupil of a school who is given special duties by the teacher. **2.** a person who advises or warns. **3.** a receiver used for checking radio or TV programs.
—[名] **1.** 급장, [교사의 보좌를 하는] 감독생(監督生) **2.** 훈계(경고, 권고)자, 모니터 **3.** 감시기

—*vt.* check (radio or TV programs) by listening in or watching.
—[他] [라디오 · 텔레비전 방송]을 청취하다, 모니터하다

mon·i·to·ri·al [mànitɔ́:riəl / mɔ̀n-] *adj.* of a monitor ; serving to warn ; using monitors.
—[形] 급장의, 감독생(監督生)의, 권고[자]의; 모니터를 쓰는

mon·i·to·ry [mánitɔ̀:ri / mɔ́nit(ə)ri] *adj.* warning. ¶*a ~ letter.*① —*n.* [C] a letter containing a warning.
—[形] 권고의, 경고의 ¶①권고서 —[名] 계고장(戒告狀)

M

* **monk** [mʌŋk] *n.* [C] one of a group of men who give up everything else for religion.
—[名] 수도사, 승려

⁑ **mon·key** [mʌ́ŋki] *n.* [C] **1.** the animal nearest to man. **2.** a mischievous person, esp. a child; an imitating child.
1) ***get*** (or ***have***) ***one's monkey up,*** become angry.
2) ***put*** (or ***get***) ***someone's monkey up,*** (*Brit.*) make (someone) angry.
—*vi.* play the fool; act as a monkey does. ¶ ~ [*about, around*] *with a gun.*①
—[名] **1.** 원숭이 **2.** 장난꾸러기; 흉내 잘 내는 아이
[熟] 1)성내다 2)《英》성나게 하다
—[自] 장난치다, 가지고 놀다 ¶①총으로 장난을 하다

monkey business [ˊ-- ˋ-] *n.* (*U.S. slang*) **1.** unfair and secret action. **2.** mischievous behavior.
—[名] 《俗》 **1.** 속임수, 협잡 **2.** 짓궂은 장난

mon·key·ish [mʌ́ŋkiiʃ] *adj.* like a monkey; mischievous.
—[形] 원숭이 같은; 장난을 잘 치는

monkey wrench [ˊ- ˋ] *n.* a spanner used for turning nuts, bolts, etc. ⇒[N.B.]
—[名] 자재(自在) 스패너 [N.B.] monkey spanner 라고도 씀

monk·ish [mʌ́ŋkiʃ] *adj.* of or like a monk; like monks for their way of life.
—[形] 승려의, 승려 같은

mon·o- [mánou- / mɔ́nou-] *pref.* one; single: *monorail* (=a railway with a single rail). ⇒[usage] ↔poly-
—《接頭》 하나의, 단독의 [usage] 모음 앞에서는 mon-

mon·o·chro·mat·ic [mànoukrəmǽtik / mɔ̀n-] *adj.* of one color; of or producing light of one wave length.
—[形] 단색의

mon·o·chrome [mánəkròum / mɔ́n-] *n.* [C] a painting or drawing in a single color.
—[名] 단색

mon·o·cle [mánəkl / mɔ́nɔkl] *n.* [C] an eyeglass to be worn over one eye.
—[名] 외알 안경

mon·o·cot·y·le·don [mànoukàtilí:d(ə)n / mɔ́noukɔ̀tilí:-] *n.* [C] a plant with only one leaf growing at first from the seed.
—[名] 단자엽(單子葉) 식물

mon·o·dy [mánədi / mɔ́n-] *n.* [C] (pl. **-dies**) **1.** a sad, mourn ful song. **2.** a poem in which a person feels sorrow for another's death.
—[名] **1.** 애가(哀歌) **2.** 애도시(哀悼詩)

mo·nog·a·mist [mənágəmist / mɔnɔ́g-] *n.* [C] a person who practices or believes in monogamy. ↔polygamist
—[名] 일부일처(一夫一妻)주의자

mo·nog·a·mous [mənágəməs / mɔnɔ́g-] *adj.* practicing or believing in monogamy; of monogamy.
—[形] 일부일처(주의)의

mo·nog·a·my [mənágəmi / mɔnɔ́g-] *n.* [U] the act or state of having only one wife or husband at a time. ↔polygamy
—[名] 일부일처제《주의》

mon·o·gram [mánəgræ̀m / mɔ́n-] *n.* [C] a design composed decorative letters, esp. the initials of a name. ⇒[N.B.]
—[名] 짜맞춘 글자(기호) [N.B.] 성명의 첫글자를 도안화한 것

mon·o·graph [mánəgræ̀f / mɔ́nəgrà:f] *n.* [C] a book or article on one particular subject.
—[名] 전공 논문

mon·o·log, -logue [mánəlɔ̀:g, -làg / mɔ́nəlɔ̀g] *n.* [C] **1.** a long speech by one person in a play, etc. **2.** a dramatic scene for one performer only. **3.** a part of a play in which only one person speaks.
—[名] **1.** [한 사람만의] 장황한 이야기 **2.** 1인극 **3.** 독백

mon·o·ma·ni·a [mànouméiniə / mɔ́n-] *n.* [U] the state of mind in which a person is abnormally interested in one subject or idea only.
—[名] 편집광(偏執狂)

mon·o·ma·ni·ac [mànouméiniæ̀k / mɔ́n-] *n.* [C] a person who is a victim of monomania.
—[名] 편집광(偏執狂)의 사람, 한 가지 일에 열중하는 사람

mon·o·plane [mánouplèin / mɔ́n-] *n.* [C] an airplane with a single wing on its body.
—[名] 단엽 비행기

mo·nop·o·list [mənápəlist / -nɔ́p-] *n.* [C] a person who has a monopoly or who believes in monopolies.
—[名] 전매자, 독점자, 전매론자

mo·nop·o·li·za·tion [mənàpəlizéiʃ(ə)n / -nɔ̀pəlai-] *n.* [U] the act or the process of monopolizing; the state of being monopolized.
—[名] 전매, 독점[판매]

mo·nop·o·lize [mənápəlàiz / -nɔ́p-] *vt.* **1.** have or get power strong enough to possess or control (something) while shutting out all others. **2.** occupy the whole of (something or someone). ¶ ~ *the conversation.*①
—[他] **1.** …의 전매권을 갖다(획득하다) **2.** …을 독점하다 ¶①회화를 독점하다

* **mo·nop·o·ly** [mənápəli / -nɔ́p-] *n.* [C] (pl. **-lies**) **1.** the shutting out of all others; the control of the entire supply of something. ¶*a* ~ *on* (or *of*) *tobacco.* **2.** a commercial product or service that is so controlled. **3.** a person or company that has a monopoly of something.
—[名] **1.** [상품 따위의] 전매[권], 독점[권], **2.** 전매품, 독점품 **3.** 전매권을 가진 사람(회사), 전매(독점)회사

mon·o·rail [mánourèil / mɔ́n-] *n.* [C] a railway with a single rail. —[名] 단궤(單軌) [철도]

mon·o·syl·lab·ic [mɔ́nousilǽbik / mɔ́n-] *adj.* having only one syllable; made up of a word or words of one syllable. —[形] 단음절(單音節)의; 단음절[어]로 된

mon·o·syl·la·ble [mánəsìləbl / mɔ́n-] *n.* [C] a word of one syllable. —[名] 단음절어
speak in monosyllables, speak plainly. [熟] 무뚝뚝하게 말하다

mon·o·the·ism [mánouθi:ìz(ə)m / mɔ́n-] *n.* [U] the doctrine or belief that there is only one God. —[名] 일신교(一神敎)

mon·o·the·ist [mánouθi:ìst / mɔ́n-] *n.* [C] a person who believes that there is only one God. —[名] 일신교 신봉자(론자)

mon·o·tone [mánətòun / mɔ́n-] *n.* [C] sameness of tone, style, color, etc. ¶*read in a* ~.① —[名] 단조로움 ¶①책을 단조롭게 읽다

* **mo·not·o·nous** [mənátənəs / -nɔ́t-] *adj.* **1.** continuing in the same tone; without change. **2.** tiresome; dull. ▷**mo·not·o·nous·ly** [-li] *adv.* —[形] 1. 단조로운; 변화가 없는 2. 지루한

mo·not·o·ny [mənátəni / -nɔ́t-] *n.* [U] the state of being monotonous; sameness; dullness. —[名] 단조로움; 변화가 없음; 지루함

mon·sieur [məsjə́:*r*] *n.* [C] (pl. **mes·sieurs** [mesjə́:*r*]) Mr.; sir. ⇒[N.B.] —[名] …씨, 님 [N.B.] 프랑스어의 경칭

mon·soon [mansú:n / mɔn-] *n.* [C] **1.** a seasonal wind in the Indian Ocean and in southern Asia. **2.** a rainy season that comes with the southwest monsoon. —[名] 1. 계절풍 2. 장마철

* **mon·ster** [mánstə*r* / mɔ́nstə] *n.* [C] **1.** any animal or plant that is unnatural. **2.** a very big creature or thing; a giant. **3.** a very wicked or cruel person. ¶*a* ~ *of cruelty.*① —*adj.* very big. —[名] 1. 괴물, 도깨비 2. 거인, 거물 3. 극악무도한 사람 ¶①아주 잔인한 사람 —[形] 거대한

mon·stros·i·ty [manstrásiti / mɔnstrɔ́s-] *n.* (pl. **-ties**) **1.** [C] a monster. **2.** [U] the state of being monstrous. —[名] 1. 거대한 것, 기형물, 극악무도한 행위 2. 기형, 괴이함

* **mon·strous** [mánstrəs / mɔ́n-] *adj.* **1.** very big; not normal; like a monster. **2.** shocking; horrible; dreadful. —*adv.* very; extremely. —[形] 1. 거대한; 기괴한; 괴물 같은 2. 무시무시한, 오싹하는 —[副] 몹시, 대단히

mon·tage [mantá:ʒ / mɔn-] *n.* [U][C] **1.** the act of making a new picture by arranging several pictures; a picture so made. **2.** (in motion pictures) the use of a rapid succession of very short scenes. —[名] 1. 몽타아즈(사진) 2. [영화의] 몽타아즈

Mon·tan·a [mantǽnə / mɔn-] *n.* a western State of the United States. ⇒[N.B.] —[名] 몬타나 주 [N.B.] Mont.로 줄임. 수도 Helena

Mon·tan·an [mantǽnən / mɔn-] *n.* [C] a person of Montana. —*adj.* of Montana. —[名] 몬타나 사람 —[形] 몬타나의

‡ **month** [mʌnθ] *n.* [C] **1.** one of the twelve parts into which the year is divided. ¶*last* ~① / *next* ~② / ~ *by* (or *after*) ~; ~ *in,* ~ *out*③ / *the* ~ *before last*④ / *this day* ~⑤ / *this* ~.⑥ **2.** the period of time from a day of one month to the same day of the next month. ¶*a* ~ *of Sundays*⑦ / *the past* ~.⑧ —[名] 1. [1년중의] 달, 월 ¶①지난 달/②내월/③다달이, 매월/④전전달/⑤내달(전달)의 오늘/⑥이 달 2. 한 달, 1개월 ¶⑦매우 오랫동안, 결코 …않다/⑧지난 한 달

* **month·ly** [mʌ́nθli] *adj.* **1.** of a month; for a month; lasting a month. **2.** done, happening, etc. once a month. —*adv.* once a month; every month. —*n.* [C] a magazine published each month. —[形] 1. 1개월의; 1개월간의; 한 달 동안 계속하는 2. 월 1회의, 매월의, 매달의 —[副] 한 달에 한 번, 매달 —[名] 월간잡지

Mont·re·al [màntriɔ́:l / mɔ̀nt-] *n.* a seaport in Quebec, Canada, on the St. Lawrence River. ⇒[N.B.] —[名] 캐나다의 항구도시 [N.B.] 상공업의 중심지

‡ **mon·u·ment** [mánjumənt / mɔ́n-] *n.* [C] **1.** a building, statue, tomb, etc. set up to keep a person or an event from being forgotten. ¶*build a* ~ *to a person's memory.*① **2.** anything that is of special historic interest. ¶*an ancient* ~② / *a natural* ~.③ **3.** an achievement or work worth remembering. ¶*a* ~ *of scientific research.*④ —[名] 1. 기념관(비), 묘비 ¶①남의 추억을 위해 기념비를 세우다 2. [역사적] 기념물, 기념 건축물; 유적 ¶②역사적 기념물/③천연 기념물 3. 불후의 업적 ¶④과학 연구상의 불후의 업적

mon·u·men·tal [mànjuméntl / mɔ̀n-] *adj.* **1.** of a monument. **2.** lasting a long time; important. ¶*a* ~ *event.* **3.** very great. —[形] 1. 기념비의 2. 불멸의; 기념이 되는 3. 터무니없는

moo [mu:] *n.* [C] (pl. **moos**) the sound made by a cow. —*vi.* make the sound of a cow. —[名] 소의 울음소리 —[自] [소가] 울다

* **mood**[1] [mu:d] *n.* **1.** [C] a state of mind or feeling; a humor. ¶*in a merry* ~ / *I was in the* ~ *for study.*① —[名] 1. 기분, 심사 ¶①공부하고 싶은 생각이 들었다 2. 언짢은 기분, 변덕 ¶

M

mood [744] **mope**

2. ((often *pl.*)) fits of bad temper. ¶*a man of moods.*②   ②변덕장이
*****mood**² [muːd] *n.* ⓒ (*Grammar*) one of the forms of a verb that serves to show the speaker's manner. ¶*imperative* ~ ① / *subjunctive* ~.②   —图 〈文法〉법, 서법(敍法) ¶①명령법/②가정법
mood·i·ly [múːdili] *adv.* in a moody manner.   —則 시무룩하여, 성미 까다롭게
mood·i·ness [múːdinis] *n.* ⓤ the state of being moody.   —图 시무룩함, 성미 까다로움
mood·y [múːdi] *adj.* (**mood·i·er**, **mood·i·est**) 1. having changes of mood. 2. often having gloomy moods; gloomy; sad; melancholy.   —形 1. 변덕스러운, 마음이 잘 바뀌는 2. 시무룩한, 기분이 언짢은; 우울한; 음산한

‡**moon** [muːn] *n.* ⓒ 1. ((usu. *the* ~)) the heavenly body which moves around the earth. 2. the moon at a certain period of time; an appearance of the moon. ¶*a full* ~① / *a half-moon*② / *a new* ~.③ 3. the moon as an object that can be seen. ¶*Is there a* ~ *tonight?*④ 4. the time between one new moon and the next; (*poetic*) a month. 5. ⓤ (*the* ~)) moonlight. ¶*I walked in the* ~. 6. something which looks like the moon. 7. any heavenly body which moves around a planet. 1) *beyond the moon,* far beyond one's reach. 2) *once in a blue moon,* rarely; seldom. —*vi.* move about or look around idly. —*vt.* spend (time) idly. ¶~ *away the holidays.*⁵⁾   —图 1. 달 2. [어떤 시기의] 달 ¶①보름달 ②반달 ③초승달 3. [하늘에 떠 있는] 달 ¶④오늘밤은 달이 떴다 4. 태음월(太陰月); 한 달 5. 달빛 6. 달 모양의 것 7. 위성

熟 1)손이 닿지 않는 곳에; 엄청나게 2)아주 드물게   —自 한 일 없이 돌아다니다, 멍하니 바라보다 —他 [시간을] 헛되게 보내다 ¶⑤휴일을 빈들빈들 보내다

moon·beam [múːnbìːm] *n.* ⓒ a ray of moonlight.   —图 달빛, 월광
moon·calf [múːnkæf / -kɑ̀ːf] *n.* ⓒ (pl. **-calves**) a born fool.   —图 타고난 바보, 천치
moon·calves [múːnkæ̀vz / -kɑ̀ːvz] *n.* pl. of **mooncalf**.
moon·less [múːnlis] *adj.* without the moon; lacking the light of the moon.   —形 달 없는; 달빛이 비추지 않는
‡**moon·light** [múːnlàit] *n.* ⓤ the light of the moon.   —图 달빛
moon·lit [múːnlìt] *adj.* lighted by the moon.   —形 달빛이 비추는, 달밤의
moon·shine [múːnʃàin] *n.* ⓤ 1. moonlight. 2. foolish or idle talk; nonsense.   —图 1. 달빛 2. 지어낸 이야기, 허튼 소리
moon·struck [múːnstrÀk] *adj.* crazy; mad.   —形 머리가 돈, 미친
moon·y [múːni] *adj.* (**moon·i·er**, **moon·i·est**) 1. of or like the moon. 2. dreamy.   —形 1. 달의, 달 같은 2. 꿈 같은

moor¹ [múər] *vt.* fasten (a ship, etc.) with ropes or an anchor; anchor. ¶~ *a ship at the pier.* —*vi.* moor a ship; be made secure by ropes, anchors, etc.   —他 [배 따위]를 매다, 정박시키다, 투묘(投錨)하다 —自 투묘하다, 정박하다
*****moor**² [múər] *n.* ⓤⓒ (*Brit.*) a wild piece of land covered with grass and heather.   —图 〈英〉황야, 황무지
moor·age [múərìdʒ] *n.* ⓤⓒ the act of mooring; the state of being moored; the money charged for mooring a ship; ⓒ a place for mooring.   —图 [배 따위의] 계류(繫留), 정박; 정박소 사용료; 정박지(소)
moor·ings [múəriŋz] *n. pl.* 1. the ropes, cables, etc., by which a ship is fastened. 2. the place where a ship is moored. 「moors.」   —图 1. 계선구(繫船具); 계류 장치 2. 정박소, 계선소
moor·ish [múəriʃ] *adj.* of or like a moor; abounding in   —形 황야의, 황야에 나는(사는)
moor·land [múərlənd] *n.* ⓤ a wild piece of land covered with heather; a moor.   —图 황야, 원야(原野)
moose [muːs] *n.* ⓒ (pl. **moose**) a big deer living in the northern part of the United States or in Canada.   —图 [미국·캐나다산의] 큰 사슴
moot [muːt] *adj.* needing discussion. —*vt.* 1. discuss; talk about (a question). 2. propose (a subject, etc.) for discussion. —*n.* ⓒ a discussion.   —形 의론의 여지가 있는 —他 1. …을 논하다 2. [문제 따위]를 제출하다 —图 토론, 토의
mop [mɑp / mɔp] *n.* ⓒ 1. a bundle of many pieces of cloth fastened to the end of a long stick, used for washing floors, etc. 2. a thick head of hair like a mop. ¶*a* ~ *of hair.*① —*vt.* (**mopped, mop·ping**) 1. wash or clean with a mop. 2. wipe.   —图 1. 긴 자루가 달린 걸레, 몹 2. 머리카락의 뭉치 ¶①헝클어진 머리 —他 1. [걸레로] …을 소제하다 2. …을 훔치다, 닦다

mop up, ⓐ clean up (spilt water) by mopping. ⓑ finish (work, etc.).   熟 ⓐ …을 닦아내다 ⓑ …을 치우다

mope [móup] *vi.* be low-spirited; be sad.   —自 풀이 죽다, 우울해지다
mope away one's time, spend one's time in feeling sad or in feeling sorry for oneself.   熟 우울하게 날을 보내다

—*n.* [C] a person who mopes. ▷**mop·er** [-ər] *n.*
—[名] 침울해 있는 사람

mop·ish [móupiʃ] *adj.* gloomy.
—[形] 침울한, 의기소침한

‡mor·al [mɔ́:rəl, mɑ́r- / mɔ́r-] *adj.* **1.** good in manner or character; right. ↔immoral ¶*a ~ man / live a ~ life.* **2.** able to understand right and wrong. ¶*Man is a ~ being.*① **3.** of the difference between right and wrong; ethical. ¶*a ~ question / ~ character*② */ ~ laws.*③ **4.** showing examples of right behavior. ¶*a ~ book.* **5.** of the mind and feelings; spiritual. ¶*~ support*④ */ a ~ victory.*⑤ **6.** probable. ¶*a ~ certainty.*⑥
—[形] 1. 도덕적으로 올바른 2. 도덕 관념이 있는 ¶①인간은 도덕적 존재이다 3. 도덕의; 도의상의; 윤리적인 ¶②품성(品性)/③도덕률 4. 교훈적인 5. 정신적인 ¶④정신적 원조/⑤정신적 승리 6. 있을 듯 싶은 ¶⑥십중팔구 틀림없는 일

—*n.* **1.** [C] a moral lesson taught by a fable, an event, etc. **2.** ⟪*pl.*, used as *sing.*⟫ principles of right and wrong; ethics. **3.** ⟪*pl.*⟫ social standards of right and wrong; a manner judged from a moral point of view.
—[名] 1. [우화·사건 따위의] 교훈; 우의(寓意) 2. 도덕; 윤리학 3. [사회의] 풍기, 기강; [개인의] 품행, 행실

moral certainty [⌐– ⌐––] *n.* something so probable that there is little room for doubt.
—[名] 십중팔구 틀림없는 일, 확실성

mo·rale [mərǽl / mɔrɑ́:l] *n.* [U] the state of mind as regards hope, courage, good spirits, etc.
—[名] [군대 따위의] 사기, 풍기

mor·al·ist [mɔ́:rəlist, mɑ́r- / mɔ́r-] *n.* [C] a person who lives a moral life; a teacher of or writer on morals.
—[名] 도덕가, 도덕주의자; 도학자

mor·al·is·tic [mɔ̀:rəlístik, mɑ̀r- / mɔ̀r-] *adj.* moralizing; concerned with morals.
—[形] 도학적인; 교훈이 되는; 도덕주의의

mo·ral·i·ty [mərǽliti, +*U.S.* mɔ:-] *n.* **1.** [U] the rightness or wrongness of an action. **2.** [C] good morals; virtue. ¶*a woman of easy ~.*① **3.** [C] a moral teaching or lesson. **4.** [C] a kind of religious play popular in the 16th century in England.
—[名] 1. 도덕, 윤리(학) 2. 도덕적 탁월; 덕성, 품행 ¶①행실이 나쁜 여자 3. 도덕적 교훈, 우의(寓意) 4. 권선징악극(勸善懲惡劇)

mor·al·i·za·tion [mɔ̀:rəlizéiʃ(ə)n, mɑ̀r- / mɔ̀rəlai-] *n.* [U] the act of moralizing; the state of being moralized.
—[名] 훈계; 설교; 교화; 도덕적 해석

mor·al·ize [mɔ́:rəlàiz, mɑ́r- / mɔ́r-] *vt.* **1.** explain (something) in terms of right and wrong. **2.** talk about morality to (someone); improve the morals of (someone). —*vi.* think, talk, or write about questions of right and wrong. ⟪*~ on* or *upon* something⟫
—[他] 1. 선악으로 …을 설명하다 2. …에게 설교하다, 도리를 가르치다 —[自] 도리를 가르치다, 교훈이 되다, 설교하다

mor·al·ly [mɔ́:rəli, mɑ́r- / mɔ́r-] *adv.* in a moral manner; ethically; virtually; practically.
—[副] 도덕상, 도덕적으로; 윤리적으로; 실질상; 실제로

mo·rass [mərǽs] *n.* [C] **1.** a piece of soft, wet ground; a swamp. **2.** a difficult situation.
—[名] 1. 소택지, 늪지대 2. 난국

mor·a·to·ri·a [mɔ́:rətɔ́:riə / mɔ̀r-] *n.* pl. of **moratorium**.

mor·a·to·ri·um [mɔ́:rətɔ́:riəm / mɔ̀r-] *n.* [C] (pl. **-ri·ums** or **-ri·a**) a government order by which payments of money need not be made for the period during which the order is in effect.
—[名] 지불 유예 명령, 지불 연기

mor·bid [mɔ́:*r*bid] *adj.* **1.** unhealthy; gloomy, sad and unpleasant. ¶*a ~ liking for horrors.*① **2.** caused by disease; ill. ¶*Cancer is a ~ growth.*
—[形] 1. 불건전한, 음산한 ¶①불건전한 공포 취미 2. 병에 의한, 질병의

mor·bid·i·ty [mɔ:*r*bíditi] *n.* [U] **1.** an abnormal or unhealthy state of mind. **2.** the rate of disease in a locality.
—[名] 1. 정신적으로 병적인 상태, 불건전 2. [한 지방 전체의] 질병 유행률

mor·bid·ly [mɔ́:*r*bidli] *adv.* in a morbid manner.
—[副] 병적으로, 불건전하게

mor·bid·ness [mɔ́:*r*bidnis] *n.* [U] the quality of being morbid.
—[名] 병적 상태, 불건전

mor·dant [mɔ́:*r*d(ə)nt] *adj.* **1.** (of a word) biting; cutting; severe. ¶*a ~ tongue.*① **2.** (of a liquid) destroying metal, such as an acid.
—[形] 1. 신랄한, 심한, 격렬한 ¶①독설 2. 부식성의

‡more [mɔ:*r*] *adj.* compar. of **many** or **much**. **1.** greater in amount or degree. ↔less ¶*I have ~ money than you. / He has much ~ ability than I.* **2.** greater in number. ↔fewer ¶*You shouldn't buy ~ books than you can read. / More than ten persons are (More than one person is) needed.* ⇒[usage] **3.** further; other. ¶*for there ~ days / a little ~ butter / How many ~ boys are there in the garden? / There is no ~ ink in the bottle.*
—[形] 1. 더 다량의 2. 더 다수의 [usage] 영어의 more than 10은 「11 이상」. 우리나라 말의 「10 이상」은 엄밀히 번역하면 10 and more임. 또 more than one은 의미상으로는 복수이나 동사는 단수로 받음 3. 또 그 밖의

—*n.* [U][C] **1.** a greater amount or degree. ↔less ¶*He*
—[名] 1. 더 많은 양 2. 더 많은 수(사람

moreover [746] **morsel**

ate much, but I ate ~. | There is more in him than you imagine. **2.** ((used as *pl.*)) a greater number; a greater number of people. ↔fewer ¶*Yesterday half the members were present, but ~ of them are expected today.* **3.** something in addition; some other things or persons. ¶*More can be said.*② *| I should like a little ~ of that meat. | Did any ~ happen to be there?*③
—*adv.* compar. of *much.* **1.** in or to a greater degree or extent. ↔less ¶*You should walk ~. | I love you ~ than any other person does. | He is ~ clever than honest.*④ ⇨USAGE **2.** ((forming the *compar.* of an *adj.* or *adv.*)) ¶*~ careful (interesting, just) | ~ carefully (easily, justly).* **3.** in addition. ¶*I could not run any ~. | Do it once ~.*
1) *all the more,* in that degree; by that amount.
2) *be no more,* be dead.
3) *more and more,* to an increasing extent or degree.
4) *more or less,* somewhat; about; nearly.
5) *more than all,* above all.
6) *never more,* never again.
7) *no* (or *not any*) *more than,* only.
8) *no more ...* (or *not ... any more*) *than,* not ..., nor ... ¶*He is no ~ diligent than you are.*⑤
9) *not more than,* at most.
10) *not more ... than,* not so ... as ... ¶*He is not ~ diligent than you are.*⑥
11) *what is more,* moreover.
- **more·o·ver** [mɔːróuvər] *adv.* also; besides; in addition.
Mor·mon [mɔ́ːrmən] *n.* ⓒ a member of a religious organization founded in the United States in 1830 by Joseph Smith (1805-1844). [tem of the Mormons.]
Mor·mon·ism [mɔ́ːrmənìz(ə)m] *n.* ⓤ the religious sys-
- **morn** [mɔːrn] *n.* ⓒ (*poetic*) morning.
‡ **morn·ing** [mɔ́ːrniŋ] *n.* ⓒ **1.** the early part of the day; the part of the day not later than noon. ¶*from ~ till night*① *| in the ~*② *| this ~*③ *| on the ~ of Monday.*④ ⇨USAGE **2.** the first or early part of something; ⓤ dawn. ¶*the ~ of life.* [in a park of a ~.] *of a morning,* often in the morning. ¶*I take a walk*
morn·ing-glo·ry [mɔ́ːrniŋglɔ̀ːri] *n.* ⓒ (pl. **-ries**) a climbing plant with trumpet-shaped flowers of various colors.
mo·roc·co [mərákou / -rɔ́k-] *n.* ⓤ a fine leather made from goatskin. [Africa.]
Mo·roc·co [mərákou / -rɔ́k-] *n.* a country in northwest
mo·ron [mɔ́ːran / -rɔn] *n.* ⓒ a person whose mental ability stopped developing when he was young. ⇨N.B.
mo·rose [mərous] *adj.* gloomy; ill-humored. ↔amiable; pleasant ▷**mo·rose·ly** [-li] *adv.* —**mo·rose·ness** [-nis] *n.*
Mor·phe·us [mɔ́ːrfiəs, mɔ́ːfjuːs] *n.* (in Greek mythology) the god of dreams. ⇨N.B.
mor·phi·a [mɔ́ːrfiə] *n.* ⓤ =morphine.
mor·phine [mɔ́ːrfiːn] *n.* ⓤ a drug made from the seed of the white poppy and used to lessen pain.
mor·phin·ism [mɔ́ːrfinìz(ə)m] *n.* ⓤ an unhealthy state caused by the habitual use of morphine; the morphine habit.
mor·phol·o·gy [mɔːrfálədʒi / mɔːrfɔ́l-] *n.* ⓤ **1.** a science dealing with the forms and structures of animals and plants. **2.** a science dealing with the forms of words.
mor·row [mɔ́ːrou, már- / mɔ́r-] *n.* ⓒ **1.** (*poetic*) the next day or time. **2.** (*archaic*) morning.
Morse [mɔːrs], **Samuel F. B.** *n.* (1791-1872) an American inventor. ⇨N.B.
mor·sel [mɔ́ːrs(ə)l] *n.* ⓒ a small piece or bite.

들) 3. 그밖에 다른 것(사람들) ¶②이밖에도 여러 가지 말을 할 수 있다/③또 그밖에도 누가 있었는가?

—튀 1. 더 많이; 더 크게 ¶④그는 정직하다기보다 영리하다 USAGE 두 개의 형용사 A, B를 비교하여 「오히려 B보다 A다」라고 할 때에는 어미를 변화시키지 않고 more를 씀 2. 보다 …, 더욱 … 3. 게다가, 그 위에

熟 1) 그만큼 더, 점점 더 2) 이제는 없다; 죽었다 3) 더욱 더, 점점 4) 다소; 약; 거의 5) 특히; 그중에서도 6) 다시는 …않다 7) 단지 8) …이 아닌 것과 마찬가지로 …이 아니다 ¶⑤네가 부지런하지 않은 것처럼 그도 부지런하지 않다 9) 많아야, 기껏해야 10) … 이상으로 …이 아니다 ¶⑥그도 부지런하기는 하지만 너만은 못하다 11) 더우기, 게다가

—튀 그 위에 또, 게다가, 더구나
—영 모르몬 교도

—영 모르몬교[의 교리]

—영 아침
—영 1. 아침; 오전 ¶①아침부터 밤까지/②아침 중에, 오전에/③오늘 아침/월요일 아침에 USAGE 특정의 날은 in the morning of라 하지는 않음 2. 초기; 새벽
熟 아침에 흔히
—영 나팔꽃

—영 모로코 가죽

—영 모로코
—영 노둔(魯鈍) N.B. 지능이 8세 정도의 어른
—형 시무룩한, 침울한; 성미 까다로운

—영 모르페우스 신 N.B. 잠의 신 Hypnos의 아들로서 꿈의 신

—영 모르핀

—영 모르핀 상용(常用); 모르핀 중독

—영 1. 형태학 2. 언어 형태학

—영 1. (詩) 내일 2. (古) 아침

—영 미국의 발명가 N.B. 모르스식 전신기의 발명가
—영 한 조각, 한 입

: mor·tal [mɔ́ːrtl] *adj.* **1.** be fated to die sometime. ↔immortal ¶*Man is ~.*① **2.** causing the death; fatal. ¶*a ~wound.* **3.** causing the death of the soul. ¶*~ sins.* **4.** of death. ¶*the ~ hour*② / *~ agony.*③ **5.** lasting until death. ¶*a ~ enemy.*④ **6.** of man; human. ¶*~ power.* **7.** (*colloq.*) very great; extreme; long and tiresome. ¶*two ~ hours.*
—*n.* [C] anything that is to die; a human being.
—[形] 1. 죽어야 할 운명에 있는 ¶①인간은 죽음을 면할 수 없다 2. 치명적인 3. 영원한 죽음을 초래하는 4. 죽음의 ¶②임종/③죽음의 고통 5. 죽을 때까지 계속되는 ¶④꼭 죽여야만 하는 원수 6. 인간의 7. 《口》 대단한; 기다란, 지루한
—[名] 죽어야 하는 것; 인간

mor·tal·i·ty [mɔːrtǽliti] *n.* [C] **1.** [U] the state of being mortal or subject to death. **2.** death on a large scale. ¶*the ~ from airplane accidents.* **3.** the death rate.
—[名] 1. 죽어야 할 운명(상태) 2. 대량의 죽음 3. 사망률

mor·tal·ly [mɔ́ːrtəli] *adv.* **1.** as causing death; fatally. **2.** very greatly; bitterly.
—[副] 1. 치명적으로 2. 몹시, 대단히, 도저히

mor·tar¹ [mɔ́ːrtər] *n.* [U] a mixture of lime, sand, and water used to hold bricks or stones together. —*vt.* fasten (bricks, etc.) with mortar; fix (stones, etc.) with mortar.
—[名] 회반죽, 모르타르 —[他] [벽돌·돌 따위]를 모르타르로 접합하다

mor·tar² [mɔ́ːrtər] *n.* [C] **1.** a bowl for pressing something to make a powder of it. ⇨fig. **2.** a very short cannon.
—[名] 1. 맷돌, 약연(藥碾) 2. 박격포

〔mortar² 1.〕

mor·tar·board [mɔ́ːrtərbɔ̀ːrd] *n.* [C] **1.** a board used to hold mortar. **2.** a cap with a flat and square top, worn by teachers and students at school ceremonies.
—[名] 1. [회반죽의] 흙받기 2. [대학의] 각모(角帽)

*** mort·gage** [mɔ́ːrgidʒ] *n.* [C] **1.** the right to get another's house, land, etc. as one's own property if a debt is not paid. ¶*lend money on a ~.*① **2.** a document that gives such a right. —*vt.* give (someone) a mortgage.
—[名] 1. 저당[권], 담보 ¶①저당잡고 돈을 빌려 주다 2. 저당 증서 —[他] …을 저당에 넣다

mor·ti·cian [mɔːrtíʃ(ə)n] *n.* [C] (*U.S.*) an undertaker.
—[名] 《美》 장의사 주인

mor·ti·fi·ca·tion [mɔ̀ːrtifikéiʃ(ə)n] *n.* [U] **1.** the feeling of anger and shame. ¶*shed tears* [*in one's*] *~.*① **2.** [C] a cause of such a feeling. **3.** the act of mortifying; the state of being mortified. **4.** (*Medicine*) the death of one part of the body while the rest is still alive.
—[名] 1. 분함, 굴욕 ¶①분해서 눈물을 흘리다 2. 억울한(분한) 일 3. 고행(苦行), 금욕 4. 회저(壞疽), 탈저(脫疽)

mor·ti·fy [mɔ́ːrtifài] *vt.* (**-fied**) **1.** overcome (one's physical desires, etc.) by training. ¶*~ the flesh.*① **2.** cause (someone) to feel ashamed; hurt the feelings of (someone) ¶*be mortified by* (or *at*) *one's mistake.*② **3.** cause (a part of the body) to decay.
—*vi.* (*Medicine*) (of a part of the body) decay or die.
—[他] 1. [정욕 따위]를 억제하다 ¶①육욕을 억누르다 2. …에 굴욕을 느끼게 하다; …의 마음을 아프게 하다 ¶②실수를 저지르고 분해하다 3. 탈저(脫疽)에 걸리게 하다
—[自] 탈저에 걸리다

mor·tise [mɔ́ːrtis] *n.* [C] a hole cut in a piece of wood, etc. into which another piece, called a *tenon,* fits so as to form a joint. —*vt.* cut a mortise in (something); fasten (something) securely with a mortise and tenon.
—[名] 장붓구멍 —[他] …에 장붓구멍을 파다; 장부촉 이음으로 하다

mor·tu·ar·y [mɔ́ːrtʃuèri / mɔ́ːtjuəri] *n.* [C] (pl. **-ar·ies**) a place where dead bodies may be kept for a short time until burial. —*adj.* of death or burial.
—[名] [매장·화장 전의] 시체 임시 안치소 —[形] 죽음의; 매장의

mo·sa·ic [mouzéiik / məzéiik, mo(u)-] *n.* [U][C] a design or picture made by fitting together small pieces of differently colored stone, marble, glass, etc; anything like mosaic; [C] a piece of such work. —*adj.* made of or like mosaic.
—[名] 모자이크, 조각나무 세공, 모자이크 무늬; 모자이크식의 것; 주워 모아 만든 작품 —[形] 모자이크의; 주워 모은

Mo·sa·ic [mouzéiik] *adj.* of Moses. ¶*the ~ law.*①
—[形] 모세의 ¶①모세의 율법

Mos·cow [máskou / mɔ́s-] *n.* the capital of the Union of Soviet Socialist Republics. ⇨[N.B.]
—[名] 소련의 수도 [N.B.] 소련 이름은 Moskva

Mo·ses [móuziz, +*U.S.* -zis] *n.* **1.** (in the Bible) the great leader of the Israelites who led them out of Egypt and gave them laws. **2.** [C] a lawgiver; a leader.
—[名] 1. 《聖》 모세(유대의 입법자·건국자) 2. 입법자; 지도자

Mos·lem [mázləm / mɔ́zlem] *n.* [C] (pl. **-lems** or *collectively* **-lem**) a Mohammedan. —*adj.* of Mohammedans and their religion.
—[名] 마호멧 교도, 회교도 —[形] 마호멧교[도]의

mosque [mɑsk / mɔsk] n. ⓒ a Moslem temple.

* **mos·qui·to** [məskíːtou] n. ⓒ (pl. **-toes** or **-tos**) a small flying insect whose female stings the skin of people and animals to suck their blood. ¶*Mosquitoes hummed.*①

mosquito boat [-́-- -́] n. a speedy, unarmored motorboat equipped with torpedoes and small guns. ⇒N.B.

mosquito craft [-́-- -́] n. a small armed ship capable of moving quickly and making sudden attacks on big ships.

mosquito curtain [-́-- -́--] n. =mosquito net.

mosquito net [-́-- -́] n. a net for keeping out mosquitos.

* **moss** [mɔːs / mɔs] n. Ⓤ a small plant with tiny leaves which grows like a thick mat on damp ground, trees, rocks, etc. ¶(*proverb*) *A rolling stone gathers no ~.*①

moss-grown [mɔ́ːsgròun / mɔ́s-] adj. **1.** covered with moss. **2.** old-fashioned.

moss·y [mɔ́ːsi, / mɔ́si] adj. (**moss·i·er, moss·i·est**) covered with moss; like moss. ▷ **moss·i·ness** [-nis] n.

‡ **most** [moust] adj. superl. of **much** and **many**. **1.** greatest in amount or degree. ↔least ¶*He has* [*the*] *~ money of the three.* **2.** greatest in number. ↔fewest ¶*Who has* [*the*] *~ books?* **3.** 《usu. without *definite article*》 almost all. ¶*Most people think so.*
for the most part, mainly; usually.
—n. **1.** 《*the ~*》 the greatest amount or degree. ¶*This is the ~* [*that*] *I can do for you.*① **2.** 《*the ~*》 the greatest number. **3.** 《usu. without *definite article*》 almost all; nearly all people. ¶*Most of the work was done during the day.* / *Most like it.*
1) *at* [*the*] *most,* not more than.
2) *make the most of something,* make the best use of something; use something fully.
—adv. superl. of **much**. **1.** in or to the greatest extent or degree. ↔least ¶*The play which pleased me* [*the*] *~ was "Hamlet."* **2.** 《forming the *superl.*》 ¶*~ careful* (*interesting, etc.*) / *~ carefully.* **3.** very. ¶*a ~ beautiful girl.* **4.** (*U. S. colloq.*) almost. ¶*~ all.*②

‡ **most·ly** [móus(t)li] adv. chiefly; usually; generally.

mote [mout] n. ⓒ a very small particle of dust in the air, a small fault.

mo·tel [moutél] n. ⓒ (*U. S.*) a roadside hotel for motorists; a group of cottages for people traveling by car.

* **moth** [mɔːθ / mɔθ] n. ⓒ (pl. **moths** [-ðz, -θs]) **1.** a small, four-winged insect very much like a butterfly, usu. most active at night. **2.** an insect of this kind, whose larva feeds on wool, fur, etc.

moth ball [-́ -́] n. a small ball of camphor used to keep moths away from clothing.

moth-eat·en [mɔ́ːθiːtn / mɔ́θ-] adj. eaten by clothesmoths; worn-out; out-of-date.

‡ **moth·er** [mʌ́ðər] n. ⓒ **1.** a woman parent; 《often *M-*》 one's own mother. **2.** a woman like a mother. ¶*She was a ~ to the poor.* **3.** the head of a convent; Mother Superior. **4.** an old woman. ¶*Mother Adams.* **5.** the cause or source of something. ¶*Necessity is the ~ of invention.*① **6.** 《usu. *the ~*》 a mother's love.
every mother's son, (*colloq.*) everybody.
—adj. **1.** that is a mother. ¶*a ~ bird.* **2.** of or like a mother. ¶*~ love* / *a ~ship.*② **3.** native. ¶*~ wit* / *one's ~ tongue.*
—vt. take care of (someone) as a mother does.

moth·er·hood [mʌ́ðərhùd] n. Ⓤ **1.** the state of being a mother. **2.** the character or spirit of a mother. **3.** 《*collectively*》 mothers.

moth·er-in-law [mʌ́ðərinlɔ̀ː] n. ⓒ (pl. **moth·ers-**) the

—명 마호멧교 사원

—명 모기 ¶①모기가 앵앵거렸다

—명 쾌속 어뢰정 NB 현재는 PT boat라 함

—명 쾌속 소형 함정

—명 모기장

—명 이끼 ¶①(俚)구르는 돌에는 이끼가 끼지 않는다

—형 1.이끼 낀 2.고풍의

—형 이끼 낀; 이끼와 같은

—형 1.[분량·정도가] 가장 많은 2.숫자가 제일 많은 3.거의 모든

黑 대개는

—명 1.최대량; 최대한 ¶①이것이 네게 해줄 수 있는 최대의 것이다 2.최다수 3.대부분,대개의 사람들

黑 1)기껏해야; 많아야 2)…을 최대로 이용하다

—부 1.가장;가장 많이 2.[형용사·부사의 최상급을 만들어] 가장,제일 3.대단히,몹시 4.《美口》거의 ¶②거의 모두

—부 대개; 대체로

—명 먼지,더럼; 결점

—명 《美》자동차 여행자를 위한 간이 숙박소

—명 1.나방 2.[모직물 따위를 해치는] 좀

—명 [나프탈린 따위의] 좀약

—형 좀먹은; 써서 낡은; 시대에 뒤진

—명 1.모친;[자신의] 어머니 2.어머니 같은 사람 3.수녀원장 4.노부인; 아주머니 5.근원, 근본 ¶①필요는 발명의 어머니다 6.모성애

黑 《口》누구나 모두

—형 1.모친의 2.모친의;어머니 같은, 어머니다운 ¶②모선(母船) 3.모국의; 타고난

—타 …을 돌보다, 보살피다

—명 1.어머니임 2.모성,어머니의 특성 3.어머니

—명 장모,시어머니

motherland

mother of one's husband or wife. ↔father-in-law

moth·er·land [mʌ́ðərlænd] *n.* ⓒ **1.** the country of one's birth. **2.** the country where one's parents or ancestors were born.

moth·er·like [mʌ́ðərlàik] *adj.* =motherly.

moth·er·ly [mʌ́ðərli] *adj.* of or like a mother; showing the affection or concern of a mother.

moth·er-of-pearl [mʌ́ð(ə)rə(v)pə́:rl] *n.* Ⓤ the hard, rainbow-colored lining of some shells, esp. the pearl-oyster. ⇨N.B.

mo·tif [moutí:f] *n.* ⓒ **1.** a subject or main idea in a work of literature or music. **2.** a feature in a decoration or design.

: mo·tion [móuʃ(ə)n] *n.* **1.** Ⓤ the act of changing from one place or position to another; movement; action; ↔rest ¶*law of ~*① / *the motions of the planets* / *It seemed to be in slow motion.* **2.** (usu. *pl.*) the act of moving the parts of the body, esp. the hand; a gesture. ¶*Her motions were graceful.* **3.** Ⓤ a combination of parts in a mechanism; the mechanism. **4.** ⓒ a proposal or suggestion, esp. one made at a meeting; (*Law*) an application to a court for a ruling, an order, etc. ¶*second the ~*② / *on the ~ of....*③

1) *go through the motions of,* show (something) by gestures; pretend to do (something).
2) *in motion,* moving; traveling; in operation.
3) *make a motion,* propose in a committee meeting or legislative group that a certain action be taken.
4) *of one's own motion,* of one's own will.
5) *put* (or *set*) *in motion,* start or cause to move.

—*vi.* make a gesture expressing a wish, meaning, etc. (《 ~ *to do*》 ¶*He motioned for her to be seated.* —*vt.* show (someone) what to do by a gesture. (《~ [to] someone *to do* something》 ¶*~ the group to go on.*

* **mo·tion·less** [móuʃ(ə)nlis] *adj.* not moving; still. ¶*lie ~*① ▷ **mo·tion·less·ly** [-li] *adv.* [a movie[s].]

motion picture [⌐ ⌐] *n.* ⓒ (*U. S.*) a moving picture;

mo·ti·vate [móutivèit] *vt.* provide (something or someone) with a reason; influence or give a motive to do (something).

mo·ti·va·tion [mòutivéiʃ(ə)n] *n.* Ⓤ the act of motivating; the state of being motivated.

* **mo·tive** [móutiv] *n.* Ⓤ **1.** the inner reason or feeling which makes a person do something. ¶*the ~ for which they act* / *perform an act for a ~.* **2.** the main idea or theme in art, literature, and music; a motif.

of (or *from*) *one's own motive,* of one's own will.
—*adj.* causing motion. ¶*~ power.* —*vt.* =motivate.

mot·ley [mátli / mɔ́t-] *n.* ⓒ a garment of various colors, once worn by clowns; a cloth of mixed colors. —*adj.* of various colors; of various mixed kinds or parts; of varied character.

wear [the] motley, play the part of a clown or fool.

: mo·tor [móutər] *n.* ⓒ **1.** an engine that causes something to move or work; a dynamo; an internal-combustion engine. **2.** an automobile. **3.** a person or thing that produces motion.

—*adj.* producing or causing motion. ¶*a ~ ship.*①
—*vi.* ride in a motor vehicle; travel by automobile.
—*vt.* carry (something or someone) by automobile.

motor bicycle [⌐ ⌐⌐] *n.* a bicycle propelled by a motor; a motorcycle.

mo·tor·bike [móutərbàik] *n.* (*colloq.*) **1.** =motor bicycle. **2.** motorcycle.

—名 1. 모국 2. 조국, 선조의 나라

—形 어머니의, 어머니 같은; 다정한

—名 [조가비의 안쪽의] 진주층, 자개
  N.B. 단추·자개 세공 따위로 쓰임

—名 1. [문학·예술 작품의] 주제, 테에마; [악곡의] 동기 2. 의장(意匠)의 주지(主旨)(주요소)

—名 1. 운동, 이동, 운행 ¶①운동의 법칙 2. [신체의 일부 특히 손을] 움직이기, 몸짓 3. 기계 장치; 기구(機構) 4. [회의의] 발의(發議), 동의; [원고 또는 피고의] 신청, 신립 ¶②동의에 찬성하다/③…의 동의로

熟 1) …의 시늉을 하다, 몸짓을 하다
2) 움직이고 있는, 운전 중인 3) [회의 따위에서] 어떤 동의를 제출하다 4) 자진하여 5) …을 움직이다, 운전(운전)시키다

—自 손짓으로 신호하다 —他 …에 [몸짓·손짓]으로 지시하다, 신호하다

—形 움직이지 않는, 정지(靜止)한 ¶①가만히 움직이지 않고 있다
—名 《美》영화
—他 …에 동기를 부여하다; …을 움직이다, 선동하다

—名 동기를 주기; 자극, 유도

—名 1. [행동의] 동기, 목적; 유인(誘因), 자극 2. [문학·예술 작품의] 주제

熟 자진하여
—形 원동력이 되는; 동기의 ¶①원동력, 기동력(起動力)
—名 얼룩덜룩한 옷; 얼룩덜룩한 천
—形 잡색의, 여러 종류의, 얼룩덜룩한; [사람이] 잡다한
熟 광대(바보) 노릇을 하다

—名 1. 원동기, 발전기, 모우터, 내연기관 2. 자동차 3. 움직이는 사람(것)

—形 움직이게 하는, 원동력의, 발동의 ¶①발동선
—自 자동차에 타다(로 가다)
—他 …을 자동차로 나르다
—名 모우터 달린 자전거

mo·tor·boat [móutərbòut] *n.* [C] a boat run by a motor. —[名] 모우터 보우트

mo·tor·bus [móutərbʌ̀s] *n.* [C] a bus run by a motor. —[名] 버스, 합승 자동차

mo·tor·car [móutərkɑ̀:r] *n.* [C] an automobile. —[名] 자동차

* **mo·tor·cy·cle** [móutərsàikl] *n.* [C] a two-wheeled vehicle propelled by an internal-combustion engine, resembling a bicycle but usu. larger and heavier. —*vi.* ride a motorcycle. —[名] 오오토바이 —[自] 오오토바이에 타다

mo·tor·cy·clist [móutərsàiklist] *n.* [C] a person who rides a motorcycle. —[名] 오오토바이 타는 사람

mo·tor·drome [móutərdròum] *n.* [C] a rounded track for automobile or motorcycle racing or testing. —[名] 오오토바이(자동차) 경주장

mo·tor·ing [móutəriŋ] *n.* [U] the act of driving an automobile. —[名] 자동차 운전, 드라이브

mo·tor·ist [móutərist] *n.* [C] a person who drives an automobile or who usu. travels by automobile. —[名] 자동차 여행자, 자동차 상용자

mo·tor·ize [móutəràiz] *vt.* equip (vehicles) with motors; supply (troops, etc.) with motor vehicles. —[他] [차]에 모우터를 달다; [군대 따위]를 자동차화하다

motor lorry [ˊ-- ˊ--] *n.* (chiefly *Brit.*) a motor truck. —[名] 《英》 화물 자동차

mo·tor·man [móutərmən] *n.* [C] (pl. **-men** [-mən]) (*U.S.*) **1.** a man who operates a motor, esp. on an electric trolley or train. **2.** a man who runs a motor. —[名] 《美》 1. 전차(전기 기관차)의 운전수 2. 모우터 계원

motor truck [ˊ-- ˊ] *n.* (*U.S.*) a motor-driven truck. —[名] 《美》 화물 자동차, 트럭

mot·tle [mátl / mɔ́tl] *n.* [U][C] a large, irregular spot; a spotted pattern or coloring, as of marble. —*vt.* 《usu. in *passive*》 mark (something) with spots of different colors or shades. —[名] [대리석 따위의] 얼룩, 반문(斑紋) —[他] …을 잡색으로 하다, 얼룩덜룩하게 하다

* **mot·to** [mátou / mɔ́t-] *n.* [C] (pl. **-toes** or **-tos**) **1.** a short sentence or phrase used as a rule of conduct. **2.** a short sentence, word or phrase written or cut on an object. —[名] 1. 모토, 좌우명; 명언, 금언 2. [책 따위의] 제구(題句); 명(銘)

* **mould** [mould] *n., v.* (*Brit.*) =mold.

mould·er [móuldər] *n., v.* (*Brit.*) =molder.

mould·ing [móuldiŋ] *n.* (*Brit.*) =molding.

mould·y [móuldi] *adj.* (*Brit.*) (**mould·i·er, mould·i·est**) =moldy.

moult [moult] *n., v.* (*Brit.*) =molt.

* **mound** [maund] *n.* [C] **1.** a bank or heap of earth, stones or sand made by man to mark a grave or to use as a fort. **2.** a small hill. **3.** (*Baseball*) the pitcher's plate. —[名] 1. 둑, 제방; 둔덕, 토루(土壘) 2. 작은 산, 언덕 3. 《野球》 투수판
—*vt.* surround (something) with a mound; heap up (something) in a mound. —[他] …에 둔덕을 만들다; 둑으로 막다; 쌓아 올리다

‡ **mount**¹ [maunt] *vt.* **1.** go up; climb. ¶~ *a hill* / ~ *a ladder.* **2.** get up on (a platform, a horse, etc.). **3.** put (someone or something) on a horse; furnish (someone) with a horse. ¶*He is well mounted.*① **4.** put (something) in a proper position for use; fix; set. ¶~ *a specimen on a slide*② / ~ *a jewel in gold* / ~ *a picture on cardboard.* **5.** have; carry (guns); furnish (a fortress, a ship, etc.) with guns. ¶*a battleship mounting twenty guns*③ / *a tank mounted with four guns.*④ —*vi.* **1.** go up; rise; increase. ¶*Prices will* ~.⑤ **2.** get on horseback. ¶~ *on a horse* / *The man mounted and rode away.* —[他] 1. …으로 오르다; 올라가다 2. …의 위에 타다 3. …을 말에 태우다 ¶①그는 좋은 말을 타고 있다 4. …을 설치(장치)하다; …에 받침[대지(臺紙)]을 끼우다 ¶②검경물(檢鏡物)을 슬라이드 유리 위에 얹다 5. [대포]를 장비하다 ¶③포 20문을 장비한 전함/④포 4문을 갖춘 전차 —[自] 1. 올라가다; 오르다; 멀다 ¶⑤제반 물가가 오를 것이다 2. 말을 타다

1) ***mount guard,*** act as a guard.
2) ***mount guard over,*** guard; protect.
[熟] 1)보초를 서다; 지키다 2)…을 감시하다; …을 지키다

—*n.* [C] **1.** a thing on which anything is mounted. **2.** a horse or other animal for riding. —[名] 1. 물건을 얹는 대(臺) 2. [사람을 태우는] 말

mount² [maunt] *n.* [C] (chiefly *poetic* except in *proper names*) a mountain; a high hill. ⇒[N.B.] ¶*Mount Everest* / *the Sermon on the Mount.*① —[名] …산; 언덕 [N.B.] 고유명사로서 현재도 쓰임; Mt.로 줄임 ¶①산상 수훈(垂訓)

‡ **moun·tain** [máunt(i)n] *n.* [C] **1.** a very high hill. **2.** 《*pl.*》 a chain or group of such hills. ¶*the Rocky Mountains.*① **3.** anything of great size or amount. ¶*a* ~ *of mail.* —[名] 1. 산 2. 산맥, 산지(山地) ¶①로키 산맥 3. 산더미 [같은 것], 다량, 다수

moun·tain·eer [màuntiníər] *n.* [C] a person who lives in the mountains; a mountain climber. —*vi.* climb mountains for sport. —[名] 등산가, 산의 주민 —[自] 등산하다

* **moun·tain·ous** [máuntinəs] *adj.* having many mountains; extremely large; huge. ¶~ *regions*① / ~ *waves.*② —[形] 산이 많은; 거대한 ¶①산이 많은 지역/②산더미 같은 파도

mountain range [ˊ-- ˊ] *n.* a series of connected moun- —[名] 산맥

M

tains considered as a single group.

mountain sickness [ˊ-- ˋ-] *n.* illness caused by insufficient oxygen in the air at high altitudes.
—[名] 산악병(山岳病)

moun·tain·side [máuntinsàid] *n.* [C] a slope of a mountain.
—[名] 산허리

moun·tain·top [máuntintɑ̀p / -tɔ̀p] *n.* [C] the top of a mountain; the summit.
—[名] 산꼭대기

moun·te·bank [máuntibæ̀ŋk] *n.* [C] **1.** a person selling worthless medicines, esp. in a public place. **2.** a person who deceives people.
—[名] 1. 엉터리 약장수 2. 투기사, 협잡꾼

mount·ed [máuntid] *adj.* **1.** seated on horseback. ¶~ *police.*① **2.** set up and ready for use; fixed. **3.** set or framed in (something). ¶*a gold-mounted sword.*
—[形] 1. 말에 탄 ¶①기만 순경 2. 대(臺)를 붙인; 장치(조립)한, 설치한 3. 상감(象嵌)한

‡mourn [mɔːrn] *vi., vt.* feel or express sorrow; grieve at someone's death; lament. 《~ *over* or *for* someone's death, etc.》 ¶~ *over his tragic fate.*①
—[自][他] 슬퍼하다, 비탄해 하다; 애도하다; 몽상(蒙喪)하다 ¶①그의 비극적인 운명을 슬퍼하다

mourn·er [mɔ́ːrnər] *n.* [C] **1.** a person who mourns. **2.** a person who attends a funeral as a friend or relative of the dead person.
—[名] 1. 슬퍼하는 사람, 애도자 2. 문상객

***mourn·ful** [mɔ́ːrnful] *adj.* sorrowful; sad.
—[形] 슬픔에 잠긴; 슬픈

mourn·ful·ly [mɔ́ːrnfuli] *adv.* in a mournful manner.
—[副] 슬픔에 잠겨, 슬픈 듯이

mourn·ing [mɔ́ːrniŋ] *n.* [U] **1.** grief; sorrow. **2.** an outward expression of sorrow, such as black clothes. **3.** the period during which a person mourns for a dead person.
—[名] 1. 슬픔, 애도 2. 상복, 상장(喪章), 상 3. 기중(忌中)

1) ***go into*** (or ***put on, take to***) ***mourning,*** observe mourning; wear mourning for someone's death.
2) ***in mourning,*** in mourning clothes; in the period of mouring (*n.* 3).
3) ***leave off*** (or ***go out of***) ***mourning,*** stop wearing observing.
[熟] 1)몽상하다; 상복을 입다 2)상복을 입고, 상중인 3)탈상하다

mourning band [ˊ-- ˋ] *n.* a black cloth, usu. worn around the arm, to show mourning. ⇒[N.B.]
—[名] 상장(喪章) [N.B.] mourning badge라고도 함

‡mouse *n.* [maus →*v.*] [C] (pl. **mice**) **1.** a tiny, soft-furred animal with a long tail something like, but smaller than a rat. ⇒[N.B.] ¶*a house* (*a field, a wood*) ~.① **2.** a timid or spiritless person.
—[名] 1. 새앙쥐 [N.B.] 보통 집안에 있는 쥐 ¶①집(들)쥐 2. 겁장이

1) ***like a drowned mouse,*** be poor-looking; be wet to the skin.
2) ***play like a cat with a mouse,*** make sport of and tease (something or someone).
[熟] 1)초라한 모습으로; 기가 죽어서 2)…을 못 살게 굴다

—*vi.* [mauz, +*Brit.* maus] (of a cat) hunt for; seek about or search for (something) busily and stealthily.
—[自] 쥐를 잡다; 살금살금 찾아다니다

mouse about, search for (something).
[熟] …을 찾아다니다

mouse·trap [máustræ̀p] *n.* [C] a trap for catching mice.
—[名] 쥐틀

mous·tache [mʌ́stæʃ, məstǽʃ / məstɑ́ːʃ, mus-] *n.* (*Brit.*) =mustache.

‡mouth *n.* [mauθ →*v.*] [C] (pl. **mouths** [mauðz]) **1.** an opening through which an animal takes in food. **2.** an opening like a mouth in shape or position. ¶*the ~ of a river.* **3.** 《usu. *pl.*》 persons to be fed. ¶*useless, hungry mouths*① / *He has ten mouths to feed.*② **4.** a twisted look of the face. ¶*make mouths at someone.*③
—[名] 1. 입 2. 입 모양의 것 3. [부양해야 할] 입, 식구 ¶①밥벌레/②그는 열 명을 먹여 살려야 한다 4. 찡그린 얼굴 ¶③ …에게 얼굴을 찡그리다

1) ***down in the mouth,*** in low spirits.
2) ***give mouth to*** (=*speak out*) *something.*
3) ***put words into someone's mouth,*** tell someone what to say.
4) ***with one mouth,*** in chorus.
[熟] 1)낙심하여 2)…을 입밖에 내다; 말하다 3)…에게 뭐라고 말할지를 가르쳐 주다 4)이구동성으로, 일제히

—*vt.* [mauð] **1.** take (food) into the mouth. **2.** say (something) in a pretended or unnatural way. ¶~ *one's words.* **—*vi.*** **1.** speak in a pretended or unnatural manner. **2.** make a twisted look of the face. ¶*He mouthed at me.*
—[他] 1. …을 입에 넣다, 먹다 2. …을 젠체하며 말하다 —[自] 1. 젠체하며 말하다 2. 상을 찡그리다

mouth·ful [máuθfùl] *n.* [C] as much as the mouth can hold at one time; a small amount of food. ¶*take a ~ of dinner*① / *at a ~*② / *make a ~ of* (*something*).③
—[名] 입 가득, 한 입; 소량[의 음식] ¶①음식을 한 입 먹다/②한 입에/③…을 한 입에 삼키다

mouth or·gan [ˊ-ˋ-] *n.* a harmonica.
—[名] 하아모니카

mouth·piece [máuθpìːs] *n.* [C] **1.** the part of a pipe, a
—[名] 1. [담뱃대의] 입에 대는 부분;

musical instrument, etc. that is placed against the lips or in the mouth. **2.** a person, newspaper, etc. expressing the opinions of others; a spokesman.

[악기의] 부는 구멍; 구금(口金); [수도관 따위의] 주둥이, [전화의] 송화구 **2.** 대변자, 시대를 대변하는 신문

mov·a·ble [mú:vəbl] *adj.* that can be carried from one place to another; changing from one state to another; unfixed. ↔immovable ¶*~ prefabricated hospitals*① | *a ~ feast*② | *~ property.*③ —*n.* ⟪*pl.*⟫ personal property that can be moved. ↔immovables

—[形] 움직일 수 있는, 이동하는; 부정(不定)의 ¶①조립식 이동병원/②해마다 날짜가 달라지는 축제/③동산(動産) —[名] 가재(家財), 동산

⁑**move** [mu:v] *vt.* **1.** change the position of (something). ¶*He moved his chair nearer to the window.* **2.** set or keep (something) in motion; cause (something) to act. ¶*The wind moved the leaves.* | *The machine is moved by a spring.*① **3.** stir or arouse the feelings of (someone). ¶*The story moved her to tears.*② **4.** cause; persuade. ⟪~ someone *to do*⟫ ¶*Nothing could ~ him to do the work.* | *No argument will ~ him from his opinion.* **5.** propose (one's opinion, etc.) formally, as in a meeting. ¶*~ a resolution*③ | *I ~ that the meeting be adjourned.*④ —*vi.* **1.** change position; change one's place of living. ¶*We moved into a new house.* | *She moved from her seat to the fire.* **2.** be in motion; be active; act; take part. ¶*~ with grace* | *You should ~ in this matter.*⑤ | *A piston moves by steam pressure.* | *Miss Garner moves in society.*⑥ **3.** make progress. ¶*The work moves slowly.* **4.** make a formal request. ⟪~ *for* something⟫ **5.** (of goods) be sold.

—[他] **1.** …을 움직이다;이동시키다 **2.** …을 발동시키다; 활동시키다 ¶①시계는 태엽으로 움직인다 **3.** …을 감동시키다; …의 마음을 움직여 …시키다 ¶②그 이야기를 듣자 그녀는 감동하여 눈물을 흘렸다 **4.** …에게 …할 마음이 나게 하다 **5.** [동의]를 제출하다; 제안하다 ¶③결의안의 동의를 제출하다/④모임의 연기를 제의합니다 —[自] **1.** 움직이다;이사하다 **2.** 활동하다;행동하다;관여하다 ¶⑤이 일을 처리해야 한다/⑥가아너 양은 사교계에 드나들고 있다 **3.** 나아가다, 발전하다 **4.** 신청하다;제의하다 **5.** 팔리다

1) ***feel moved*** (=*be willing* or *want*) ***to do.***
2) ***move heaven and earth,*** try every possible way.

[熟] 1)…할 마음이 생기다 2)온갖 수단을 다 써 보다

—*n.* [C] **1.** the act of moving; a change of position; the changing of one's place of living. **2.** an action taken for a certain purpose.

—[名] **1.** 움직임; 이동; 이사 **2.** 수단; 조치

1) ***make a move,*** go; change one's place; begin to act.
2) ***on the move,*** moving about from place to place.

[熟] 1)나아가다;움직이다; 수단을 취하다 2)움직여; 이동중; 진행중

⁑**move·ment** [mú:vmənt] *n.* **1.** [C] the act of moving; action or activity. **2.** ⟪*pl.*⟫ a particular manner of moving. ¶*His movements are always awkward.* **3.** [U] the moving parts of a watch, a machine, etc. **4.** [C] a series of organized activities by people for a special purpose. ¶*a temperance ~.*① **5.** [C] the act of changing the location; a racial migration. **6.** [C] the growth of a plant; the act of removing unnecessary matter from the bowels **7.** [U] a change in the price of stocks or commodities. **8.** [U] the progress of events in a literary. work. **9.** [U] (*Music*) tempo; rhythm; any of the principal divisions of a symphony.

—[名] **1.** 동작;움직임; 운동;행동 **2.** 태도 **3.** [시계 따위의] 진동;기계 장치 **4.** [정치적] 운동 ¶①금주 운동 **5.** 이사; [군대의] 기동; [동물·민족 등의] 이동 **6.** [식물의] 발육, 성장; 변통(便通) **7.** [시장의] 변동 **8.** [소설 따위] 줄거리의 진행, 파란 **9.** ⟪樂⟫ 악장; 속도

mov·er [mú:vər] *n.* [C] **1.** a person or thing that moves or causes (something) to move; a person whose work is moving furniture, etc. for those changing residences. **2.** the motive power; a motor. **3.** a person proposing a motion; a projector; an originator.

—[名] **1.** 움직이는 사람(것); 이전자;이삿짐 나르는 업자 **2.** 원동력, 발동기 **3.** 발기인; 동의(動議) 제출자

⁑**mov·ie** [mú:vi] *n.* (*U.S. colloq.*) [C] ⟪usu. *pl.*⟫ a moving picture; a motion-picture theater. ¶*an 8mm. ~ camera*① | *a movie-goer*② | *a ~ house*③ | *go to the movies.*④

—[名] 영화;영화관 ¶①8밀리 영화 촬영기/②영화 팬/③영화관/④영화를 보러 가다

mov·ing [mú:viŋ] *adj.* **1.** that moves. ¶*~ assembly* | *a ~ stairway.* **2.** causing motion; stirring the emotions.

—[形] **1.** 움직이는 **2.** 움직이게 하는; 감동시키는

mov·ing·ly [mú:viŋli] *adv.* in a moving manner.

—[副] 감동시키게시리, 불쌍하게

mow¹ [mou] *vt., vi.* (**mowed, mowed** or **mown**) cut down (grass, grain, etc.) with a scythe or a machine.

—[他][自] [풀 따위]를 베다

mow down, kill or shoot (the enemy) in great numbers.

[熟] …을 베어 쓰러뜨리다, 소사(掃射)하다

mow² [mou] *n.* [C] **1.** a heap of hay, straw etc. **2.** the part of a barn where hay or grain is stored.

—[名] **1.** 건초더미 **2.** 건초 두는 곳

mow·er [móuər] *n.* [C] a person or machine that mows.

—[名] 풀 베는 사람(기계)

mow·ing [móuiŋ] *n.* [U] the quantity of hay mowed in

—[名] 일정 시간에 풀을 베는 분량

M

a single specified period.

mown [moun] *v.* pp. of **mow**.

Mo·zart [móuza:rt / móutsa:t], **Wolfgang Amadeus** *n.* (1756–91) an Austrian composer. —[名] 오스트리아의 작곡가

M. P., MP. [émpí:] **1.** Member of Parliament. **2.** Military Police. **3.** melting point. **4.** Metropolitan Police. **5.** Mounted Police.

mph, m. p. h miles per hour. —《略》 시속 …마일

‡ **Mr., Mr** [místər] (pl. **Messrs.**) Mister, used before the name; the title of a man. ¶ ~ *Brown* / ~ *President.* —《略》 …씨, 님, 군, 선생

‡ **Mrs., Mrs** [mísiz] (pl. **Mmes.** [meidá:m]) Mistress, now used as a title before the name of a married woman. ⇒[N.B.] ¶ ~ *[Alfred L.] Harris* / ~ *Kitty Evans.* —《略》 …부인 [N.B.] 미국에서는 Mrs. 의 뒤에 부인의 이름을 보통 씀

Mss., MSS., mss. [émesés] *pl.* manuscripts.

‡ **Mt.** [maunt] (pl. **Mts.**) Mount. ¶ ~ *Everest.*

‡ **much** [mʌtʃ] *adj.* (**more, most**) great in quantity, amount, or degree; a lot of. ↔little ⇒[usage] ¶ *Much time is necessary for me to do it.* / *There was (was not) ~ truth in her speech.* / *She takes too ~ pride in her beauty.* —[形] [분량·정도 따위가] 많은, 다량의 [usage] 긍정문에서는 보통 a lot [of], a great quantity [of], a good deal [of] 따위를 씀. 그러나 주어를 수식하거나 too, how, as, so 따위와 함께 쓰일 때는 긍정문에서도 much를 보통 씀

—*n.* [U] **1.** a great quantity, amount, or degree. ↔little ¶ *Have you learned ~ from that book?* / *Much has been said about this.* / *Too ~ is as bad as none at all.*① / *So ~ for this story.* **2.** (《usu. in *negative sense*》) something great, important, etc. ¶ *His picture is not ~ to look at.*② / *He is not ~ of a scholar.*③ —[名] **1.** 다량; 다대 ¶①지나친 것은 미치지 못한 것과 같다 **2.** 중요한 일; 뛰어난 것 ¶②그의 그림은 볼품이 없다 /③그는 대단한 학자는 아니다

1) ***make*** (or ***think***) ***much of,*** treat or consider (something or someone) as important.
2) ***this*** (***that***) ***much,*** the amount indicated; so much.
3) ***too much for,*** superior to (someone) in skill, ability, etc. ¶ *He is too ~ for me in mathematics.*

[熟] 1)…을 중히 여기다 2)이것(그것)만[은] 3)…의 힘에 겨운

—*adv.* **1.** to a great extent or degree. ↔little ⇒[usage] ¶ *I like it very ~.* / *I am ~ interested in science.* / *I arrived ~ too soon.* / *You can swim ~ better than I.* / *He is ~ the greatest poet.* **2.** nearly; about. ¶ ~ *the same way*/ *They are pretty ~ alike.*④ / *They are ~ of a size.* —[副] **1.** 크게, 몹시; 훨씬 [usage] much는 과거분사를 수식함. 또 형용사의 비교급·최상급을 수식하지만 원급은 수식하지 않음 **2.** 거의 ¶④그들은 아주 비슷하다

1) ***as much again as*** (=*twice as much as*) *something.*
2) ***as much as to say,*** as if to say.
3) ***much less,*** (《preceded by a *negative clause*》) then it is needless to say that the following does not apply. ¶ *She does not know English ~ less French.*
4) ***much more,*** (《preceded by an *affirmative clause*》) then it is needless to say that the following case applies. ¶ *A child can do it well, ~ more I.*
5) ***not so much A as B,*** *B* rather than *A.*
6) ***not so much as*** *do something,* not even do something.

[熟] 1)…의 2배 2)마치 …이라고 말할 듯이 3)하물며(더구나) …의 경우는 더욱 …이 아니다 4)하물며(더구나) …의 경우는 더욱 그렇다 5)…이라기보다는 오히려 …이라는 편이 낫다 6)…조차 않다(없다)

mu·ci·lage [mjú:silidʒ] *n.* [U] a sticky, gummy substance used to stick things together, taken from certain plants. —[名] 점액(粘液) [N.B.] 영국에서는 gum 이라 함

muck [mʌk] *n.* [U] **1.** dirt; moist farmyard manure; a fertilizer. **2.** (*Brit. colloq.*) anything that is unpleasant or untidy. —[名] **1.** 오물; [마소의] 똥; 거름 **2.** 《英口》 쓰레기, 폐물; 싫은 것

make a muck of, make (something) dirty or untidy; spoil. [熟] …을 더럽히다; 엉망진창으로 만들다

—*vt., vi.* fertilize (the earth) with muck; make (something) dirty; spoil. —[他][自] 거름을 주다; 더럽히다

1) ***muck about,*** (*colloq.*) idle away; loaf about.
2) ***muck up,*** disarrange (a room); spoil (something).

[熟] 1)《口》빈들빈들 지내다;일 없이 돌아다니다 2)…을 어지럽히다, 더럽히다

mu·cous [mjú:kəs] *adj.* of, like or producing mucus. ¶ *the ~ membrane.*① —[形] 점액질의(같은); 점액을 분비하는 ¶①점막(粘膜)

mu·cus [mjú:kəs] *n.* [U] the sticky, slimy substance coming from the mucous membrane of the nose, throat, etc. —[名] [동식물의] 점액

‡ **mud** [mʌd] *n.* [U] soft, wet earth. ¶ *His name was ~.*① —[名] 진흙; 진창 ¶①그의 명성(신용)은 떨어졌다

1) ***fling*** (or ***throw***) ***mud at,*** speak evil of (someone); try to damage someone's reputation.
2) ***mud in your eye,*** drink to your health and remember me. ¶ *Here's ~ in your eye.*②

[熟] 1)…의 명성을 해치다, …을 헐뜯다 2)건강을 위해서(축배의 말) ¶②그럼 축배를 듭시다 3)진창에 빠지다;

M

3) ***stick in the mud,*** fall in deep mud; reach the end of the road; be very conservative. 오도가도 못하게 되다; 보수적이다

mud·di·ness [mʌ́dinis] *n.* [U] the state of being muddy. —[名] 진흙투성이임

mud·dle [mʌ́dl] *vt.* **1.** confuse (the brain, etc.); bring (someone) into a state of confusion and disorder. **2.** mix up (a drink, etc.). **3.** make a mess of (something). ¶~ *a plan.* **4.** waste. 《~ *away* one's money, etc.》 —*vi.* act or think in a confused way. 《~ *with* one's work, etc.》
—[他] 1. …을 혼란케 하다; 어리둥절케 하다; [술 따위로 머리를] 멍하게 하다 2. [음식 따위]를 뒤섞다 3. …을 엉망진창을 만들다 4. …을 낭비하다 —[自] 위태로운 짓(생각)을 하다

1) ***muddle about,*** walk about; work carelessly.
2) ***muddle on*** (or ***along***)**,** struggle on somehow.
3) ***muddle through,*** succeed in spite of confusion.

[熟] 1)어정거리다; 되는 대로 일을 해치우다 2)그럭저럭 해나가다 3)간신히 해치우다

—*n.* [C] 《usu. *sing.* only》 **1.** a state of disorder and confusion. **2.** mental confusion. —[名] 1. 혼란 2. 어리둥절함, 멍함

1) ***in a muddle,*** in a puzzle; in disorder.
2) ***make a muddle,*** make a big mistake.

[熟] 1)어리둥절하여; 멍하니; 지리멸렬하게 2)실수를 하다

⁑mud·dy [mʌ́di] *adj.* **(-di·er, -di·est) 1.** full of mud; covered with mud; filthy. **2.** not clear; confused. ¶~ *brains.* **3.** dark-colored; dull. ¶*a ~ complexion.* —*v.* **(-died)** *vt.* make (something) dirty with mud; confuse. —*vi.* become dirty.
—[形] 1. 진창의, 진흙투성이의; 더러운 2. 흐리멍덩한, 혼란된 3. 흐린, 탁한, 둔한 —[他] …을 진흙으로 더럽히다; 혼란시키다 —[自] 진흙투성이가 되다

mud·guard [mʌ́dgɑ̀:rd] *n.* [C] a cover or shield over the wheel of a bicycle, an automobile, etc. to protect against mud flying up from below. ⇒[N.B.] —[名] [차의] 진흙받이 [N.B.] 자전거의 진흙받이는 wing 또는 fender라고 함

mu·ez·zin [mju(:)ézin] *n.* [C] a Mohammedan official whose job is to announce the hour of prayer. —[名] [회교국의] 기도 시간을 큰 소리로 알리는 사람

muff [mʌf] *n.* [C] **1.** a warm, soft cover, usu. of fur, for ladies to put their hands into for warmth. **2.** any failure; an unskillful fellow; a fool. **3.** (*Sports*) a failure to hold a ball when catching it. —[名] 1. 안에 털을 댄 부인용 토시(보온용) 2. 실수, 그르침; 서투른 사람; 바보 3. 공을 받지 못하기(놓치기)

make a muff of, (=*make a mistake in*) *something.* [熟] …을 실수하다

—*vt.* make an unskillful mistake in (something); miss (a catch). —[他] …에 실수를 하다; [공]을 놓치다

muf·fin [mʌ́fin] *n.* [C] a small, light, round cake, usu. served hot with butter. —[名] 살짝 구운 둥근 빵

muf·fle [mʌ́fl] *vt.* **1.** wrap or cover (something) up for warmth. ¶~*one's head.* **2.** wrap up (something) so as to lessen the sound; lessen or dull (a sound). —[他] 1. …을 싸다, 뒤덮다 2. 소리를 작게 하기 위해 …을 싸다; 소리를 죽이다

muf·fler [mʌ́flər] *n.* [C] a scarf worn about the neck for warmth; a hood; a device for silencing noises of an automobile, etc. —[名] 목도리, 머플러; 두건; [자동차 따위의] 소음기(消音器)

muf·ti [mʌ́fti] *n.* [C] the civilian clothes worn by a soldier, sailor, etc. who normally wears a uniform. ↔uniform —[名] 평복, 사복

mug [mʌg] *n.* [C] **1.** a large, heavy cup with a handle. **2.** the amount a mug holds. ¶*a ~ of beer.* —[名] 1. 원통형의 찻잔 2. 한 잔

mug·gy [mʌ́gi] *adj.* **(-gi·er, -gi·est)** (of the weather) hot, wet, and close. ¶~ *weather.*① —[形] 무더운, 후텁지근한 ¶①후텁지근한 날씨

mu·lat·to [mju(:)lǽtou, +*U.S.* mə-] *n.* [C] (pl. **-toes**) a person who has one white and one Negro parent; any person of mixed white and Negro blood. —[名] 흑백 혼혈아

mul·ber·ry [mʌ́lbèri / -b(ə)ri] *n.* (pl. **-ries**) **1.** [C] a tree with broad, dark-green leaves on which silkworms feed; a sweet, dark-purple, berrylike fruit of this tree. **2.** [U] a dark, purplish-red color. —[名] 1. 뽕나무; 오디 2. 짙은 자줏빛

mulch [mʌltʃ / mʌl(t)ʃ] *n.* [C] a layer of dead leaves, straw, etc. spread over the ground to protect the roots of newly-planted trees. —*vt.* cover (roots, etc.) with mulch. —[名] [이식한 식물의] 뿌리덮개 —[他] …에 뿌리덮개를 하다

mulct [mʌlkt] *n.* [C] the money taken from someone as punishment. —*vt.* **1.** punish (someone) by means of a mulct. **2.** rob or deprive. 《someone *of*》 ¶*be mulcted of £20.* —[名] 벌금 —[他] 1. …에게 벌금을 부과하다 2. …에서 …을 빼앗다

•mule[1] [mju:l] *n.* [C] **1.** a strong work animal whose father is a donkey and whose mother is a mare. **2.** (*colloq.*) —[名] 1. 노새 2.《口》고집통이 ¶①아주 고집이 세다, 완고하다 3. 뮤울 정방

mule [755] **mumps**

a person having very firm ideas or opinions. ¶*be as stubborn (obstinate) as a ~*.① **3.** a kind of spinning machine.
mule² [mjuːl] *n.* ⓒ a heelless slipper.
mu·le·teer [mjùːlitíər] *n.* ⓒ a driver of mules.
mul·ish [mjúːliʃ] *adj.* **1.** like a mule. **2.** fixed in idea or opinion; stubborn; obstinate. ▷ **múl·ish·ly** [-li] *adv.* — **múl·ish·ness** [-nis] *n.* ¶*~ over an idea.*
mull¹ [mʌl] *vt., vi.* (*U.S. colloq.*) think about for a long time.
mull² [mʌl] *vt.* heat (wine, etc.) with sugar, spices, etc.
mull³ [mʌl] *n.* Ⓤ a thin, soft muslin.
mul·lion [mʌ́liən] *n.* ⓒ an upright bar or column between two parts of a window.
mul·ti- [mʌ́lti-] *pref.* many.
mul·ti-col·ored, *Brit.* **-loured** [mʌ̀ltikʌ́lərd] *adj.* having many colors.
mul·ti·far·i·ous [mʌ̀ltiféəriəs] *adj.* many and various. ¶*~ activities (expenses).*① 「or shapes.」
mul·ti·form [mʌ́ltifɔ̀ːrm] *adj.* having many forms
mul·ti·lat·er·al [mʌ̀ltilǽt(ə)rəl] *adj.* many-sided.
mul·ti·mil·lion·aire [mʌ̀ltimìljənέər] *n.* ⓒ a person whose wealth reaches several millions of dollars, pounds, francs, etc.
mul·ti·ple [mʌ́ltipl] *adj.* **1.** having, or made up of, many parts or elements. **2.** (*Mathematics*) repeated many times. —*n.* ⓒ (*Mathematics*) a number that can be divided by another number without a remainder. ¶*16 is a ~ of 4.*
mul·ti·plex [mʌ́ltiplèks] *adj.* multiple; manifold.
mul·ti·pli·ca·tion [mʌ̀ltiplikéiʃ(ə)n] *n.* **1.** Ⓤ the act of multiplying; the state of being multiplied; an increase; an abnormal increase of parts. **2.** ⓤⓒ (*Arithmetic*) the way of finding the answer when a number is multiplied. 「great number or variety.」
mul·ti·plic·i·ty [mʌ̀ltiplísiti] *n.* Ⓤ ((sometimes *a ~*)) a
mul·ti·pli·er [mʌ́ltiplàiər] *n.* ⓒ (*Mathematics*) the number by which another number is multiplied.
* **mul·ti·ply** [mʌ́ltiplài] *vt.* (**-plied**) cause (a quantity or number) to increase a certain number of times. ↔divide ¶*~ three by two*① / *Five multiplied by three is fifteen.*② —*vi.* increase in number or extent.
* **mul·ti·tude** [mʌ́ltitjùːd, +*U.S.* -tùːd] *n.* **1.** Ⓤ a great number; a great crowd. ¶*multitudes of admirers.*①
2. (*the ~*) the people.
a multitude of, a great number of.
mum [mʌm] *adj.* saying nothing; silent. 「at all.」
  1) *as mum as a mouse* (or *mice*), speaking nothing
  2) *sit mum,* not joining in a conversation.
—*n.* Ⓤ silence.
Mum's the word, Be silent.; Say nothing.
—*interj.* silence!; hush! sh! —*vi.* (**mummed, mumming**) become silent.
mum·ble [mʌ́mbl] *vi., vt.* speak unclearly. ¶*~ some objection to working hard.* —*n.* ⓒ an indistinct way of speaking; a mumbled sound.
mum·mer·y [mʌ́məri] *n.* ⓒ (*pl.* **-mer·ies**) **1.** a sort of dumb show. **2.** a useless or ridiculous ceremony.
mum·mi·fy [mʌ́mifài] *vt.* (**-fied**) make (a dead body) into or like a mummy. —*vi.* dry up.
mum·my¹ [mʌ́mi] *n.* ⓒ (*pl.* **-mies**) (esp. in ancient Egypt) a dead body kept from decay by chemicals or by being dried. —*vt.* (**-mied**) mummify (a dead body).
mum·my² [mʌ́mi] *n.* ⓒ a child's word for its mother; a mamma.
mumps [mʌmps] *n. pl.* ((used as *sing.*)) a disease that

기(精紡機)
——名 뒤축 없는 슬리퍼
——名 노새 모는 사람
——形 1. 노새 같은 2. 고집이 센;완고한

「생각하다」
——他自〔美口〕 머리를 짜다, …을 잘
——他 …에 향료를 넣고 데우다
——名 얇은 무명 모슬린
——名 세로창찰

——'接頭」많은
——形 여러 빛깔의

——形 여러가지의;다방면의 ¶①다방면의 활동(지출)
——形 여러 가지[모양]의
——形 다변(多邊)의
——名 백만장자

——形 1.복식의, 다수의, 다양한, 많은 부분으로 이루어지는 2.〔數〕배수(倍數)의 ——名〔數〕배수

——形 복합의; 다양한; 다중(多重)의
——名 1. 증가;증식, 번식 2.〔數〕곱셈, 승법(乘法)

——名 다수; 중복; 다양성
——名 승수(乘數)

——他 …을 곱하다, 곱셈을 하다 ¶①3에 2를 곱하다/②5곱하기 3은 15
——自 번식하다

——名 1.다수;군중 ¶①많은 찬미자들 2. 대중, 민중

形 많은, 다수의
——形 말없는, 침묵의
形 1)전혀 말을 하지 않는 2)대화에 끼지 않다
——名 침묵

形 입 다물어라; 아무 말도 하지 말라
——感 조용해!, 쉿! —自 조용해지다

——自他〔입 속에서〕우물우물 말하다
——名 똑똑치 않은 말; 중얼거림

——名 1. 무언극 2. 허례(虛禮)

——他 …을 미이라로 만들다 —自 마르다
——名 미이라 —他 …을 미이라로 만들다

——名 엄마

——名 유행성 이하선염(耳下腺炎), 항아

causes swelling under the ear and difficulty in swallowing.
리손님

munch [mʌntʃ] *vt., vi.* eat (something) noisily and with much movement of the mouth. ¶~ *popcorn* / ~ *at an apple.*
—[他][自] 우적우적 먹다(씹다)

mun·dane [mʌ́ndein, -ˊ] *adj.* of this world; worldly; earthly. ¶*the ~ world.*①
—[形] 현재의; 세속적인 ¶①뜬세상

Mu·nich [mjú:nik] *n.* a city in West Germany.
—[名] 서독의 도시

* **mu·nic·i·pal** [mju(:)nísip(ə)l] *adj.* of a town or city or its government. ¶*the ~ council*① / *a ~ office.*
—[形] 시(市)의 ¶①시의회

mu·nic·i·pal·i·ty [mju(:)nìsipǽliti] *n.* [U] a town, city, or other district that has local self-government; the governing body of such a town, etc.
—[名] 지방 자치단체

mu·nif·i·cence [mju(:)nífisns] *n.* [U] great generosity.
—[名] 아낌없이 주기

mu·nif·i·cent [mju(:)nífisnt] *adj.* extremely generous. ▷**mu·nif·i·cent·ly** [-li] *adv.*
—[形] 아낌없이 주는, 인심이 좋은

mu·ni·tion [mju(:)níʃ(ə)n] *n.* 《usu. *pl.*》 materials used in war, such as guns, bombs, and other things.
—[名] 군용품; 무기, 탄약

—*vt.* provide (someone) with munitions.
—[他] …에 군수물자를 공급하다

mu·ral [mjúərəl] *adj.* of or like a wall; on a wall. ¶*a ~ painting.*① —*n.* [C] a painting on a wall; (*U.S.*) the decoration of a wall.
—[形] 벽의, 벽 위의 ¶①벽화 —[名] 벽화; 《美》 벽장식

‡ **mur·der** [mə́:rdər] *n.* [U][C] the unlawful killing of a person that is planned beforehand. ¶*commit ~.*①
—[名] 살인[사건] ¶①살인을 하다

—*vt.* **1.** kill (someone) on purpose and unlawfully. **2.** spoil (something) because of poor skill or knowledge. ¶~ *music.*②
—[他] 1. …을 살해하다; 모살(謀殺)하다 2. …을 망쳐놓다 ¶②음악을 망쳐놓다

* **mur·der·er** [mə́:rdərər] *n.* [C] a person who is guilty of murder.
—[名] 살인범

mur·der·ess [mə́:rdəris] *n.* [C] a woman murderer.
—[名] 여자 살인범

mur·der·ous [mə́:rdəris] *adj.* **1.** of or like murder; that can murder. ¶*a ~ weapon.*① **2.** brutal.
—[形] 1. 살인[용]의, 살인적인 ¶①흉기 2. 잔인한

mur·der·ous·ly [mə́:rdərisli] *adv.* in a murderous or cruel manner.
—[副] 살인적으로; 흉악하게

murk·y [mə́:rki] *adj.* (**murk·i·er, murk·i·est**) dark; gloomy; heavy and gloomy with mist, etc.
—[形] 어두운, 음침한; [안개 따위가] 짙은

‡ **mur·mur** [mə́:rmər] *n.* [C] **1.** a low, continuous, indistinct sound of a running stream. **2.** a whisper. **3.** a complaint in a low tone. ¶*without a ~.*
—[名] 1. 살랑살랑(졸졸) 소리 2. 속삭임, 중얼거림 3. 불평소리

—*vi., vt.* **1.** make a low, continuous, indistinct sound. **2.** speak in a low voice; whisper. **3.** complain. 《~ *at* or *against* something》 ¶~ *at ill treatment.*
—[自][他] 1. 졸졸(살랑살랑) 소리내다 2. 속삭이다, 중얼거리다 3. 투덜거리다, 불평하다

mur·rain [mə́:rin / mʌ́rin] *n.* [U] a disease spreading from one animal to another, esp. of cattle.
—[名] 가축(특히 소)의 전염병

‡ **mus·cle** [mʌ́sl] *n.* **1.** [C][U] a part of the body that can be tightened or loosened to produce movement. ¶*an involuntary (a voluntary) ~*① / *He has strong muscles.* **2.** [U] 《*collectively*》 bodily strength. ¶*a man of ~.*②
—[名] 1. 근육 ¶①불수의근(不隨意筋)(수의근) 2. 체력, 완력 ¶②완력이 있는 사람

not move a muscle, be perfectly still.
[熟] 꿈쩍도 않다

—*vi.* use or appeal to force.
—[自] 완력을 휘두르다

muscle in, break into another's sphere of influence.
[熟] 남의 영역을 침범하다

Mus·co·vy [mʌ́skəvi] *n.* an old name for Russia.
—[名] 러시아의 옛이름

mus·cu·lar [mʌ́skjulər] *adj.* of the muscles; having well-developed muscles; strong. ¶~ *strength*① / *the ~ system.*②
—[形] 근육의; 근육이 억센; 강한 ¶①완력/②근육 조직

mus·cu·lar·i·ty [mʌ̀skjulǽriti] *n.* [U] the state or quality of being muscular; energy.
—[名] 근골(筋骨)이 건장함; 강건

* **muse** [mju:z] *vi.* **1.** think deeply; meditate. 《~ *on* (or *upon, over*) something》 ¶~ *over past memories.*① **2.** gaze earnestly or wonderingly (on someone or something). ▷**mus·er** [-ər] *n.*
—[自] 1. 숙고하다; 곰곰이 생각하다 ¶①과거의 추억에 잠기다 2. 유심히 바라보다

Muse [mju:z] *n.* **1.** (in Greek mythology) any one of the nine sister-goddesses who protected and encouraged the fine arts, poetry, music, etc. **2.** 《*the m-*》 poetic inspiration or genius; the goddess who inspires a poet. **3.** 《*m-*》 [C] a poet.
—[名] 1. 뮤우즈 신 2. 시상(詩想), 시흥, 시재(詩才); 시신(詩神) 3. 시인

‡mu·se·um [mju:zí:əm / -zíəm] *n.* [C] a building in which objects of all kinds are collected and displayed; (*U.S.*) an art gallery. ¶*a ~ piece.*①
—[名] 박물관; 《美》 미술관 ¶①중요 미술품, 일품(逸品)

mush [mʌʃ] *n.* [U] **1.** any soft, thick mixture or soft mass; (*U.S.*) corn meal boiled in water. **2.** (*colloq.*) silly talk; sentimentality.
make a mush of (=*spoil*) something.
—[名] 1. 흐물흐물한 것;《美》 옥수수 죽 2.《口》 허튼소리, 감상(感傷)
[熟] …을 엉망진창으로 만들다

mush·room [mʌ́ʃrum, +*U.S.* -ru:m] *n.* [C] a kind of eatable and fast-growing plant with no green leaves and shaped like an umbrella. —*adj.* of or like a mushroom, either in shape or in its rapid growth. ¶*a ~ cloud.*① —*vi.* **1.** gather mushrooms. ¶*go mushrooming.*② **2.** grow or spread very fast.
—[名] [특히 식용의] 버섯 —[形] 버섯의(같은); 버섯 모양의, 갑자기 발생하는 ¶①버섯구름
—[自] 1. 버섯을 따다 ¶②버섯 따러 가다 2. 급속히 성장하다(퍼지다)

mush·y [mʌ́ʃi] *adj.* (**mush·i·er, mush·i·est**) **1.** like mush. **2.** (*colloq.*) sentimental; emotional.
—[形] 1. 죽 같은 2.《口》 감상적인; 눈물을 잘 흘리는

‡mu·sic [mjú:zik] *n.* [U] **1.** the art of combining and arranging pleasing sounds. ¶*a ~ band*① / *~ paper*② / *the Music of the Spheres*③ / *dance to the ~.*④ **2.** a musical score; a musical piece. **3.** any pleasing sound; harmony; melody. ¶*the ~ of the distant breakers.*⑤
1) ***set*** (*a poem*) ***to music,*** provide (a poem) with music.
2) ***face the music,*** face one's critics; face a difficult situation boldly.
3) ***have no ear for music,*** have no sense of music.
—[名] 1. 음악 ¶①악대/②악보용지, 오선지/③천체가 움직일 때 생긴다고 옛사람이 생각한 음악/④음악에 맞춰 춤추다 2. 악보; 악곡 3. 듣기 좋은 소리; 가락 ¶⑤멀리서 부서지는 파도 소리
[熟] 1)[시]에 가락을 붙이다 2)태연하게 난국에 대처하다 3)음악을 모르다

‡mu·si·cal [mjú:zik(ə)l] *adj.* of music; melodious; fond of music; skillful in music. ¶*a ~ entertainment*① / *a ~ composer*② / *a ~ director*③ / *a ~ instrument* / *~ scales* / *a ~ score.* —*n.* [C] a musical play or comedy.
—[形] 음악의; 아름다운 가락(음)의; 음악을 좋아하는(잘하는) ¶①음악 연주/②작곡가/③지휘자 —[名] 희가극; 음악극

musical box [´-- ´] *n.* (*Brit.*) =music box.

mu·si·cale [mjù:zikǽl] *n.* [C] (*U.S.*) a social musical entertainment, usu. held privately.
—[名] 《美》 사교 음악회, [비공개의] 음악 연주회

music box [´- ´] *n.* a case or box which produces music mechanically.
—[名] 자동 주악기(奏樂器)

music hall [´- ´] *n.* **1.** a hall in which musical performances are held. **2.** (*Brit.*) a theater for variety shows.
—[名] 1. 음악회장 2.《英》 연예관

‡mu·si·cian [mju(:)zíʃ(ə)n] *n.* [C] a person skilled in music, esp. one who plays music for pay; a composer of music.
—[名] 음악가; 악사; 작곡가

mus·ing [mjú:ziŋ] *adj.* meditative; reflective. —*n.* [U] the act of meditating; meditation.
—[形] 생각에 잠긴 —[名] 심사숙고

mus·ing·ly [mjú:ziŋli] *adv.* in a musing manner.
—[副] 생각에 잠겨, 묵상하여

musk [mʌsk] *n.* **1.** [U] a strong-smelling substance obtained from the male musk deer and used in perfumes. **2.** [C] =musk deer.
—[名] 1. 사향(麝香)의 향기 2. 사향노루

musk deer [´ ´] *n.* a small hornless deer living in central Asia.
—[名] 사향노루

mus·ket [mʌ́skit] *n.* [C] an old style of gun formerly used by foot-soldiers, now replaced by the rifle.
—[名] 구식 소총

mus·ket·eer [mʌ̀skitíər] *n.* [C] in old days, a foot-soldier armed with a musket.
—[名] [옛날의] 머스킷 총병(銃兵)

mus·ket·ry [mʌ́skitri] *n.* [U] **1.** 《*collectively*》 muskets; the soldiers armed with muskets. **2.** the art of firing or the use of small arms.
—[名] 1. 소총; 소총대 2. 소총 사격[술]

musk·mel·on [mʌ́skmèlən] *n.* [C] any of several sweet, juicy fruits of a trailing plant. ⇒[N.B.]
—[名] 사향참외 [N.B.] 참외의 일종, 별명 Cantaloupe

musk·rat [mʌ́skræ̀t] *n.* [C] a rat-like water animal living in North America; its valuable fur which is used for coats, etc.
—[名] 사향쥐; 그 모피

Mus·lem, -lim [mʌ́zlim, múslim] *n., adj.* =Moslem.

mus·lin [mʌ́zlin] *n.* [U] soft cotton cloth used for dresses, fine curtains, etc.; (*U.S.*) calico.
—[名] 무명 모슬린; 《美》 캘리코우

mus·sel [mʌ́sl] *n.* [C] an eatable fresh-water shellfish whose dark-blue shells are used in making buttons.
—[名] 섭조개

‡must[1] [mʌst, məst] *auxil. v.* (**must**) ⇒[usage] **1.** 《expressing *necessity* or *obligation*》 have to; need [to]; be
—[助] [usage] 1, 2, 3의 과거형은 had to. 단 간접화법의 종속절 속에서는 must를

M

obliged to. ↔need not; do not have to ¶*One ~ eat to live.* | *You ~ earn money to support your family.* | *We ~ obey the laws of the country.* **2.** ⟪expressing *a command* or *a strong request*⟫ should; ought to; have to. ↔must not ¶*You ~ do it at once.* | *You ~ come and see us sometimes.* **3.** ⟪expressing *insistence*⟫ insist that one will. ¶*She ~ have rings everywhere.*① | *I ~ know your reason.* **4.** ⟪expressing *certainty* or *strong probability*⟫ be sure to; be certain to. ↔cannot ¶*He ~ be a good man.* | *He ~ be mad to do such a thing.* | *She ~ have been beautiful when young.* | *All men ~ die.* **5.** unfortunately or unluckily happened to. ¶*As soon as he had recovered from his illness, he ~ break his leg.*②

써도 좋음. 미래는 will *or* shall have to. 4의 과거는 must have+과거분사를 씀 **1.** …하여야 하다, …하지 않으면 안되다 **2.** [명령·요구] …해야 한다, …해라 **3.** [주장] 꼭 …해야 한다 ¶①그녀는 어디를 가나 반지를 끼고 가야 한다 **4.** [당연한 추정] …임에 틀림없다, 반드시 …하다 **5.** [과거에] 불행히도 …했다 ¶②병에서 회복하자마자 그는 불행히도 다리를 분질렀다

must needs do; needs must do, must surely do; cannot help or avoid doing.

[熟] …하지 않을 수 없다

—n. [C] something that must be done, had, etc. ¶*This book is a ~.*

—[名] 절대 필요한 것

must[2] [mʌst] *n.* [U] the juice pressed from grapes before it can cause a slow chemical change; new wine.

—[名] 포도액(즙); 새 포도주

must[3] [mʌst] *n.* [U] something produced upon decaying organic matter; mold. ¶*~ on a cake.*

—[名] 곰팡이

mus·tache, *Brit.* **mous-** [mʌ́stæʃ, məstǽʃ / məstɑ́:ʃ, mus-] *n.* [C] the hair growing near a man's upper lip; the short, stiff hairs growing near the mouth of an animal.

—[名] 입수염; 동물의 수염

mus·ta·chio [məstɑ́:ʃou] *n.* (pl. **-chios**) =mustache.

mus·tang [mʌ́stæŋ] *n.* [C] a small but strong, half-wild horse living on the North American plains.

—[名] 야생마, 들말

mus·tard [mʌ́stərd] *n.* [U] **1.** a plant with yellow flowers and long pods containing seeds. **2.** the yellow powder made from the seeds of this plant used in cooking because it has a hot taste. ¶ *ground ~*① | *~ oil.*②

—[名] **1.** 겨자(식물) **2.** 겨자(양념) ¶①겨자 가루/②겨자 기름

mus·ter [mʌ́stər] *n.* [U] **1.** the act of gathering. **2.** an assembly of persons to see if all are present or not.

—[名] **1.** [사람·동물 따위의] 집합, 모임 **2.** 소집, 점호, 검열

pass muster, be thought to be satisfactory; be fit for the purpose required.

[熟] 검열에 통과되다, 합격되다

—vi., vt. 1. come together; gather or summon, esp. soldiers, to see if all are present or not. ¶*~ the forces for a struggle.*① **2.** collect; show. ⟪*~ up* courage, etc.⟫ ¶*~ up strength.*②

—[自][他] **1.** 모이다; [검열·점호]에 소집하다 ¶①싸움을 위해 힘을 내다(군대를 모으다) **2.** [용기 따위]를 불러 일으키다 ¶②힘을 떨쳐 일으키다

1) ***muster in,*** (*U.S.*) accept (*someone*) into military service.
2) ***muster out,*** (*U.S.*) discharge (someone) from military service.

[熟] 1)…을 입영시키다 2)…을 제대시키다

·must·n't [mʌ́snt] =must not.

mu·ta·tion [mju(:)téiʃ(ə)n] *n.* [U][C] **1.** a change. **2.** in plants and animals, the sudden appearance of new, well-marked characteristics which are different from those of the parents.

—[名] **1.** 변경; 변화 **2.** 돌연변이

·mute [mju:t] *adj.* **1.** not making a sound; silent. ¶*stand ~.*① **2.** without the power of speech; dumb. **3.** not sounded or pronounced such as the *b* in *dumb.* **—n.** [C] **1.** a dumb person. **2.** a letter that is not sounded. **—vt.** make the sound of (a musical instrument) less loud.

—[形] **1.** 소리 없는; 무언의 ¶①[죄상을 부인하여] 묵비권을 행사하다 **2.** 벙어리의 **3.** 묵자(默字)의 —[名] **1.** 벙어리 **2.** 묵자 —[他] [천 따위를 씌워] …의 소리가 나지 않게 하다

mu·ti·late [mjú:tilèit] *vt.* **1.** cut off (a limb, etc.). ¶*a man mutilated in hands and feet.* **2.** make (a story, etc.) imperfect by removing a necessary part.

—[他] **1.** …을 절단하다 **2.** [이야기 따위의 일부]를 삭제하여 불완전하게 하다

mu·ti·la·tion [mjù:tiléiʃ(ə)n] *n.* [U][C] the act of mutilating; the state of being mutilated.

—[名] [손발의] 절단; 훼손

mu·ti·neer [mjù:tiníər] *n.* [C] a person who takes part in a mutiny.

—[名] 폭로, 반항자

mu·ti·nous [mjú:tinəs] *adj.* bold and disobedient; showing a spirit of opposition. ▷**mu·ti·nous·ly** [-li] *adv.*

—[形] 반항적인; 모반한

mu·ti·ny [mjú:tini] *n.* [U][C] (pl. **-nies**) resistance by force against someone in authority, esp. that of soldiers or sailors against their officers. ¶*the Caine ~.*① **—vi.** (**-nied**) rise against or resist authority by force.

—[名] 폭로; 반항 ¶①케인호의 반란 —[自] 폭동을 일으키다; 반항하다

M

***mut·ter** [mʌ́tər] *vi., vt.* speak (something) in a low, indistinct voice; murmur; complain. 《~ *at* or *against* something》 ¶~ *curses*.① —— *n.* [C] a muttered sound; a murmur.
—[自][他] 투덜투덜하다; 중얼거리다; 불평하다 ¶①투덜투덜 저주의 말을 뱉다 —[名] 중얼거림; 속삭임

***mut·ton** [mʌ́tn] *n.* [U] the meat of a sheep. ¶~ *chop*.
—[名] 양고기

***mu·tu·al** [mjú:tʃuəl] *adj.* **1.** done or felt by each of two toward the other. ¶~ *assistance* (or *aid*).① **2.** common to two or more persons. ¶*our* ~ *friend*.②
by mutual consent (or *agreement*), by common consent.
—[形] **1.** 상호간의 ¶①상호 부조 **2.** 공동의, 공통의 ¶②우리들 공통의 친구
[熟] 합의로

mu·tu·al·i·ty [mjù:tʃuǽliti / -tju-] *n.* [U] the state of being mutual.
—[名] 상호관계, 상관

mu·tu·al·ly [mjú:tʃuəli] *adv.* each other; one another.
—[副] 서로

muz·zle [mʌ́zl] *n.* [C] **1.** the nose and mouth of a four-footed animal, such as a dog, horse, etc. **2.** the open end of a pistol. **3.** a guard or cover for the mouth of an animal to prevent its biting.
—*vt.* put a muzzle (*n.* 3.) on (an animal); prevent (someone) from telling or writing of something.
—[名] **1.** [개·말 따위의] 주둥이, 코·입부분 **2.** 총구, 포구 **3.** [동물의] 입마개
—[他] …에 입마개를 씌우다; …을 입막음하다

⁑my [mai, mi, mə] *pron.* belonging to me. ¶~ *pen* / ~ *father*. —*interj.* an exclamation of surprise, dismay, etc. ¶*Oh,* ~ *friend!*① / *My goodness!*②
—[代] 나의 —[感] 호칭에 붙여서 친밀감을 나타냄 ¶①여어, 자네/②어머나!, 저런!

my·o·pi·a [maióupiə] *n.* [U] short-sightedness; nearsightedness.
—[名] 근시안

my·op·ic [maiápik / -ɔ́p-] *adj.* short-sighted.
—[形] 근시안의

myr·i·ad [míriəd] *n.* [C] ten thousand; a very great number. —*adj.* innumerable; countless.
—[名] 1만; 무수 —[形] 무수한

myrrh [mə:r] *n.* [U] the substance obtained from a tree in Arabia and East Africa, used in medicine or perfumes because of its sweet smell.
—[名] 몰약(沒藥)(향료·약제용)

myr·tle [mə́:rtl] *n.* [C] **1.** an evergreen tree with shiny leaves, white sweet-smelling flowers, and black berries. **2.** a blue-flowered creeping vine.
—[名] **1.** 도금양(桃金孃)(지중해산의 상록 관목) **2.** 빙카(덩굴 식물)

⁑my·self [maisélf] *pron.* (pl. **our·selves**) ⇒oneself. **1.** a reflexive and emphatic form of **I** or **me**. ¶*I did it* ~① / *I laid* ~ *on the grass*.② **2.** one's own normal physical or mental condition. ¶*I was not* ~ *yesterday*.③
1) [*all*] *by myself*, without any help.
2) *for myself*, by my own effort.
—[代] **1.** 나 자신; 자기자신 ¶①자신이 그것을 했다/②풀 위에 누웠다 **2.** 자신의 상태(常態) ¶③어제는 여느때의 내가 아니었다
[熟] 1)독력으로, 자기 혼자서 2)독립하여; 혼자서

⁑mys·te·ri·ous [mistíəriəs] *adj.* full of mystery; difficult to understand or explain. ¶*a* ~ *enemy*① / *a* ~ *fire*.②
▷**mys·te·ri·ous·ly** [-li] *adv.* —**my·ste·ri·ous·ness** [-nis] *n.*
—[形] 신비한, 불가사의한; 수상한 ¶①알 수 없는 적/②괴화(怪火)

⁑mys·ter·y [míst(ə)ri] *n.* [C] (pl. **-ter·ies**) **1.** [U][C] something strange or secret. ¶*a clue to the* ~.① **2.** 《*pl.*》 secret religious ceremonies performed in ancient times. **3.** a secret principle. **4.** a novel designed to excite curiosity by keeping some facts secret until the end.
make a mystery of, keep (something) secret.
—[名] **1.** 신비; 수상함 ¶①수수께끼의 단서 **2.** 성찬식 **3** [그리스도교의] 인지(人知)를 초월한 교리 **4.** 추리 소설
[熟] …을 비밀로 하다

mystery play [⌐–– ⌐] *n.* a form of drama in the Middle Ages in which scenes from the Bible were shown and performed.
—[名] 신비극

mys·tic [místik] *adj.* having a spiritual meaning not understood by everybody.
—[形] 신비[주의]의, 비법(秘法)의

mys·ti·cal [místik(ə)l] *adj.* =mystic.

mys·ti·cal·ly [místik(ə)li] *adv.* in a mysterious manner.
—[副] 불가사의하게, 신비하게

mys·ti·cism [místisìz(ə)m] *n.* [U] the beliefs of mystics; the belief that knowledge of real truth and of God may be obtained through personal insight and inspiration.
—[名] 신비주의; 신비교(神秘教)

mys·ti·fi·ca·tion [mìstifikéiʃ(ə)n] *n.* [U] the act of mystifying or being mystified; [C] something that mystifies.
—[名] 신비화, 어리둥절하게 하기; 신비한 것

mys·ti·fy [místifài] *vt.* (**-fied**) **1.** make (something) mysterious. **2.** confuse very much; puzzle.
—[他] **1.** …을 신비화하다 **2.** …을 어리둥절케 하다, 헛갈리게 하다

***myth** [miθ] *n.* [C] **1.** an old story told about persons and events in early history existing only in imagination;
—[名] **1.** 신화 ¶①그리이스·로마 신화 **2.** 가공의(신비한) 사람(것)

M

mythical [760] **naked**

⑪ (*collectively*) such stories. ¶ *the myths of Greece and Rome.*① **2.** a person, thing, story or event that is imaginary or invented.
myth·i·cal [míθik(ə)l] *adj.* **1.** of myths ; existing only in myths. ¶ *the ~ age.*① **2.** unreal ; imaginary.
myth·o·log·i·cal [mìθəládʒik(ə)l / -lɔ́dʒ-] *adj.* of mythology or myths ; unreal ; imaginary.
my·thol·o·gist [miθálədʒist / -θɔ́l-] *n.* ⓒ a student or writer of mythology.
my·thol·o·gy [miθálədʒi / -θɔ́l-] *n.* (pl. **-gies**) **1.** ⑪ the study of myths. **2.** ⑪ (*collectively*) myths ; ⓒ a collection of myths.

—形 1. 신화의 ¶①신화시대 2. 공상의
—形 신화[학]의, 신화 같은; 실재하지 않는; 상상적인
—名 신화학자(작가)

—名 1. 신화학 2. 신화; 신화집

N

N, n [en] *n.* ⓒ (pl. **N's, Ns, n's, ns** [enz]) **1.** the 14th letter of the English alphabet. **2.** anything shaped like the letter N.
n. 1. neuter. **2.** new. **3.** nominative. **4.** noon. **5.** north. **6.** northern. **7.** noun. **8.** number.
nab [næb] *vt.* (**nabbed, nab·bing**) **1.** catch suddenly. **2.** arrest.
na·dir [néidər, -diər] *n.* ⓒ **1.** the point in the heavens directly beneath the observer. ↔zenith **2.** the lowest point ; a time of great difficulty. ¶ *the ~ of one's career.*①
nag¹ [næg] *vi., vt.* (**nagged, nag·ging**) constantly find fault with (someone) about little things ; trouble (someone) by never-ending complaints. —*n.* ⓒ **1.** an act of nagging. **2.** (*colloq.*) a person, esp. a woman, who nags.
nag² [næg] *n.* ⓒ **1.** a small horse ; a pony. **2.** (*colloq.*) a horse ; a poor or inferior horse.
nai·ad, Nai- [náiæd, +U.S. néi-] *n.* ⓒ (pl. **-ads** or **-a·des** [-ədiːz]) **1.** (in Greek mythology) a fairy girl living in a stream, fountain, etc. **2.** a girl swimmer.
:nail [neil] *n.* ⓒ **1.** a metal pin pointed at one end, used to hold separate pieces of wood, etc. together. **2.** a thin, hard plate on the end of a finger or a toe.
  1) *hit the nail on the head*, say or do the right thing ; be correct in guessing or understanding.
  2) *on the nail*, at once ; on the spot.
  —*vt.* **1.** fasten (something) with a nail or nails. ¶ *~ a notice on* (or *to*) *the door.*① **2.** hold (something) fast ; keep (something) fixed. ¶ *The fire nailed him to the spot.*② **3.** (*colloq.*) catch. **4.** make (a bargain, etc.) certain. ⌈nailing.⌉
  1) *nail down*, make (something) secure by or as by
  2) *nail up*, fasten (a window, etc.) with nails.
nail·brush [néilbrʌʃ] *n.* ⓒ a small brush for cleaning fingernails.
nail scissors [⌄ ⌃⌃] *n.* a pair of small scissors used to cut and shape fingernails ; a nail clipper.
na·ive, -ïve [nɑːíːv, +Brit. naíːv] *adj.* simple like a child ; innocent. ⌈manner ; innocently.⌉
na·ive·ly, -ïve- [nɑːíːvli, +Brit. naíːv-] *adv.* in a naive⌉
na·ive·té, -ïve- [nɑːːvtéi / nɑːíːvtei] *n.* **1.** ⑪ the quality or state of being naive. **2.** ⓒ a natural action or⌉
na·ive·ty, -ïve- [nɑːːfːvti] *n.* =naïveté. ⌊saying.⌋
:na·ked [néikid] *adj.* **1.** completely undressed ; nude. ¶ *~ feet* / *go ~.*① **2.** without any covering ; bare. ¶ *a*

—名 1. 알파벳의 열 네째 글자 2. N자형의 것

—他 1. …을 불시에 잡다 2. …을 체포하다
—名 1. 천저(天底)[관측자의 바로 밑에 있는 천구(天球)의 점] 2. 최하점 ; 구렁텅이 ¶①가장 고생하던 시절

—自他 잔소리를 하다 —名 1. 시끄러운 잔소리 2. 잔소리꾼(특히 여자)

—名 1. 망아지 2. (口) 말, 쓸모없는 말

—名 1. 물의 요정(妖精) 2. 젊은 여자 수영자

—名 1. 못, 징 2. 손톱, 발톱
圈 1) 핵심을 찌르다, 알아 맞히다 2) 곧, 당장, 그 자리에서

—他 1. 못박아 붙이다 ¶①문에 게시문을 못박다 2. …을 고정시키다 ; (사람·주의)를 끌다, 음짝달싹 못하게 하다 ¶②화재로 그는 그 자리에서 옴쭉도 못했다 3. (口) …을 붙잡다 4. (계약 따위)를 결정짓다

圈 1) 못박아 붙이다 2) (창 따위)를 못박아 달다
—名 [매니큐어용] 손톱솔

—名 손톱 깎는 가위

—形 천진난만한, 순진한

—副 천진난만하게
—名 1. 천진난만 2. 순진한 언동

—形 1. 벌거벗은 ¶①벌거벗고 살다 2. 노출된 3. 적나라한, 명백한 ¶②육안

tree ~ *of leaves.* **3.** without any addition; plain. ¶*the* ~ *eye.*②
(肉眼)

na·ked·ly [néikidli] *adv.* in a naked manner.
—[副] 적나라하게

na·ked·ness [néikidnis] *n.* [U] the state of being naked; plainness; bareness.
—[名] 벌거숭이, 적나라[한 상태]; 있는 그대로임

‡name [neim] *n.* [C] **1.** a word by which a person or thing is called; a title. ¶*a family* ~; *a surname*① / *a middle* ~② / *a first* (or *a given, a Christian*) ~.③ ⇒ [N.B.] / *He is Bob by* ~. / *I know the man by* ~.④ / *What* ~ *shall I say?*⑤ **2.** fame; reputation; a well-known person. ¶*a good* (*a bad*) ~ / *He has a* ~ *for honesty.*⑥ / *make* (or *win*) *a* ~ *for oneself*⑦ / *Faulkner is a great* ~ *in American literature.* **3.** a group of persons that has one name; a family, a race, etc. ¶*the last of his* ~.⑧
1) ***call** someone **names**,* hurt the feelings of someone by using bad names.
2) ***Give it a name.**,* Say what you wish [to have].
3) ***in the name*** (=*with the authority*) ***of*** *someone, God. etc.*
4) ***have not** a **penny to** one's **name**,* do not have any money.
5) ***put** one's **name down*** (=*apply*) ***for*** *something.*
—*vt.* **1.** give a name to (someone or something). ¶*We named the dog Ricky.* / *The baby was named after* (or *for*) *his grandfather.*⑨ **2.** call (someone or something) by name. ¶*Can you* ~ *this fish?* / *Three pupils were named in the teacher's remarks.*⑩ **3.** appoint. ¶~ *someone as chairman* / *He was named president.*⑪
1) ***name the day**,* (of a woman) fix the day for her wedding.
2) ***Name your price.**,* Say what price you want.

—[名] 1. 이름; 명칭 ¶①성(姓)/②중간이름/③세례명 [N.B.] Christina Georgina Rossetti 의 경우 Christina 가 ③, Georgina 가 ②, Rossetti 가 ①. ②는 initial 로 쓰는 일이 많음/④그 남자의 이름을 알고 있다/⑤실례지만 성함이 어떻게 되십니까? 2. 명성; 평판; 유명인 ¶⑥그는 정직하다는 평판이 있다/⑦이름을 떨치다 3. 씨족; 가계(家系) ¶⑧그의 일문(一門) 중의 마지막 사람

[熟] 1)…을 욕하다 2)[한턱 낼 때] 무엇을 낼까? 3)…의 이름을 걸고 4)자기의 돈이라고는 일전 한푼 없다 5)…에 신청하다

—[他] 1. …에 이름을 붙이다 ¶⑨갓난애는 할아버지의 이름을 따서 명명되었다 2. …의 이름을 부르다 ¶⑩선생의 말 속에서 세 학생의 이름이 거론되었다 3. …을 …으로 지명(임명)하다 ¶⑪그는 회장으로 지명되었다

[熟] 1)결혼 날짜를 정하다 2)값을 불러 보시오

name·less [néimlis] *adj.* **1.** having no name; unknown. ¶*a* ~ *writer.* **2.** impossible to describe clearly. ¶*a* ~ *melancholy.* ▷**name·less·ness** [-nis] *n.*
—[形] 1. 이름없는; 무명의; 익명의 2. 형언할 수 없는; 언어도단의

•name·ly [néimli] *adv.* that is to say; in other words. ⇒[usage] ¶*two girls,* ~, *Mary and Susie.*
—[副] 즉 [usage] 접속사의 구실을 함

name·sake [néimsèik] *n.* [C] a person who has the same name as another; a person named after another.
—[名] 같은 이름의 사람

Nan·cy [nǽnsi] *n.* a woman's name.
—[名] 여자 이름

nan·ny goat [nǽnigòut] *n.* (*colloq.*) a female goat. ↔billygoat
—[名] 《口》 암 염소

•nap¹ [næp] *n.* [C] a short, light sleep, esp. in the daytime. ¶*take a* ~.① —*vi.* (**napped, nap·ping**) **1.** sleep for a short time; be half asleep. **2.** be careless; be off one's guard.
—[名] 1. 낮잠 ¶①낮잠자다 —[自] 낮잠자다, 졸다 2. 방심하다

nap² [næp] *n.* [U] the short hairs on the surface of cloth. —*vt.* put a nap on (cloth, etc.) by brushing.
—[名] 보풀 —[他] [천 따위에] 보풀이 일게 하다

nape [neip, +*U.S.* næp] *n.* [C] the back of the neck.
—[名] 목덜미

naph·tha [nǽpθə, nǽfθə] *n.* [U] a clear liquid got from petroleum, coal tar, etc., used in cleaning and lighting.
—[名] 나프타, 휘발유

‡nap·kin [nǽpkin] *n.* [C] **1.** a piece of cloth or paper used while eating. **2.** (*Brit.*) a piece of cloth used as a baby's underclothing.
—[名] 1. 냅킨 2.《英》 기저귀

napkin ring [∸-∸] *n.* a broad ring of metal, ivory, etc., used to hold a folded table napkin.
—[名] [고리 모양의] 냅킨 꽂이

Na·ples [néiplz] *n.* a city in Italy, famous for its beautiful bay. ¶(*proverb*) *See* ~ *and die.*①
—[名] 나폴리 ¶①《俚》금강산이나 보고 뭘 봤다고 해라

•Na·po·le·on [nəpóuliən], **Bonaparte** *n.* (1769–1821) a French general and Emperor.
—[名] 프랑스의 장군·황제

Na·po·le·on·ic [nəpòuliánik / -ɔ́n-] *adj.* of or like Napoleon. ¶~ *ambition.*①
—[形] 나폴레옹의(같은) ¶①큰 야심

nar·cis·si [nɑːrsísai] *n.* pl. of **narcissus.**

nar·cis·sus [nɑːrsísəs] *n.* (pl. **-cis·sus·es** or **-cis·si**) **1.** [C] a spring plant with yellow or white flowers and thin leaves; the flower of this plant. **2.** 《*N-*》 (in Greek mythology) a beautiful youth who fell in love with his
—[名] 1. 수선화 2. 나르시수스

N

own image in a spring and changed into the flower of the narcissus.

nar·cot·ic [nɑːrkátik / naːkɔ́t-] *n.* ⓒ a drug used to produce sleep or to lessen pain. —*adj.* having the power or effect of a narcotic.
— 名 마취제, 수면제 — 形 마취성의

nar·rate [næréit, +U.S. ´-] *vt.* tell the story of (something); relate. ¶ ~ *one's experiences in a war.* —*vi.* tell stories in speech or writing.
— 他 …을 이야기하다, 말하다
— 自 이야기를 말하다(쓰다)

*• **nar·ra·tion** [næréiʃ(ə)n, +Brit. nə-] *n.* 1. Ⓤ the act or manner of narrating. ¶ *direct (indirect)* ~.① 2. ⓒ a story.
— 名 1. 서술; 화법 ¶ ① 직접(간접) 화법 2. 이야기

*• **nar·ra·tive** [nǽrətiv] *n.* 1. ⓒ a story. 2. Ⓤ the art of telling a story; narration. —*adj.* of story-telling; narrating.
— 名 1. 이야기 2. 화술, 화법
— 形 이야기[체]의

nar·rat·or [næréitər, +U.S. ´--] *n.* ⓒ a person who narrates; a person who reads some passages between the speeches or scenes of a play in a theater, on radio or television.
— 名 이야기하는 사람

‡ **nar·row** [nǽrou] *adj.* (~·er, ~·est) 1. not broad or wide; less wide than usual for its kind. ↔ broad, wide 2. limited; small. ¶ *a* ~ *circle of friends*① / ~ *views*② / *in the narrowest sense*. 3. with little space, time, etc. to spare; close; near. ¶ *He had a* ~ *escape from drowning*.③ 4. unwilling to spend or give much money; not liberal. ↔ generous ¶ *He is* ~ *with his money.*④ 5. careful; thorough. ¶ *make a* ~ *inquiry.*⑤ —*n.* (usu. *pl.*) the narrow part of a river, a strait, a valley, etc. —*vt.* make (something) narrower; limit. ¶ ~ *an argument.* —*vi.* become narrower.
— 形 1. 가는, 폭이 좁은 2. 제한된, 좁은 ¶ ① 좁은 교우(交友) 범위 / ② 옹졸한 견해 3. 가까스로의 ¶ ③ 가까스로 물에 빠지지 않았다 4. 인색한 ¶ ④ 그는 돈에 인색하다 5. 주의깊은; 정밀한 ¶ ⑤ 자세히 조사하다 — 名 [강 따위의] 폭이 좁은 곳; 해협; 계곡; 좁은 길 — 他 …을 좁히다; 제한하다 — 自 좁아지다

nar·row·ly [nǽrouli] *adv.* 1. in a narrow or limited manner. 2. with difficulty; barely. ¶ *He* ~ *escaped death*.① 3. carefully; closely.
— 副 1. 편협하게 2. 가까스로 ¶ ① 그는 하마터면 죽을 뻔했다 3. 면밀하게

nar·row-mind·ed [nǽroumáindid] *adj.* not having an open mind. ▷ **nar·row-mind·ed·ly** [-li] *adv.* —**nar·row-mind·ed·ness** [-nis] *n.* [row.
— 形 옹졸한, 도량이 좁은

nar·row·ness [nǽrounis] *n.* Ⓤ the state of being narrow.
— 名 좁음, 편협

na·sal [néiz(ə)l] *adj.* 1. of the nose. ¶ ~ *inflammation*.① 2. coming through the nose. ¶ *a* ~ *discharge*② 3. (*Phonetics*) spoken or pronounced through the nose. —*n.* ⓒ (*Phonetics*) a nasal sound such as [m] and [n] etc.
— 形 1. 코의 ¶ ① 콧물 2. 코에서 나오는 ¶ ② 비염(鼻炎) 3. 《音聲》 비음(鼻音)의
— 名 《音聲》 비음

na·sal·ize [néizəlàiz] *vt.* pronounce (a word) through the nose. —*vi.* talk with a nasal sound.
— 他 [낱말]을 콧소리로 발음하다, 비음화하다 — 自 비음으로 말하다

nas·cent [nǽsnt] *adj.* 1. coming into existence. 2. beginning to grow or develop. ¶ *a* ~ *revolutionary tendency.*①
— 形 1. 발생하려고 하는 2. [사상·문화 따위] 초기의 ¶ ① 혁명 초기의 경향

nas·ti·ly [nǽstili / náː-] *adv.* in a nasty manner.
— 副 불결하게

nas·ti·ness [nǽstinis / náːs-] *n.* Ⓤ the state of being nasty.
— 名 불결; 더러운 것

na·stur·tium [nəstə́ːrʃəm] *n.* ⓒ a plant with shield-shaped leaves and yellow, orange or red flowers.
— 名 한련(旱蓮)

*• **nas·ty** [nǽsti / náːs-] *adj.* (-ti·er, -ti·est) 1. very dirty and disagreeable; bad in taste. ¶ *a* ~ *food*① / *a* ~ *medicine.* 2. immoral. ¶ ~ *language*② / *a* ~ *book.* 3. very unpleasant. ¶ ~ *weather.*③ 4. ill-natured; troublesome. ¶ *make a* ~ *remark.* ⌜ ~ *day* / *one's* ~ *place.*⌝
— 形 1. 더러운; 메스꺼워지는 ¶ ① 욕지기나는 음식, 추잡한, 상스러운 ¶ ② 상소리, 험악한, 사나운; 위험한 ¶ ③ 사나운 날씨 4. 심술궂은, 성가신

na·tal [néitl] *adj.* of one's birth; (*poetic*) native. ¶ *one's*
— 形 출생의; 고향의

‡ **na·tion** [néiʃ(ə)n] *n.* ⓒ 1. the people of a country; an independent country. ¶ *the French* ~① / *Western nations.*② 2. a race of people of the same religion, customs, and language. ¶ *the Jewish* ~.③
— 名 1. 국민; 국가 ¶ ① 프랑스 국민 / ② 서방 제국 2. 민족 ¶ ③ 유대 민족

‡ **na·tion·al** [nǽʃ(ə)n(ə)l] *adj.* 1. of a nation. ¶ *a* ~ *language*① / *a* ~ *flag.*② 2. belonging to a nation. ¶ *a* ~ *bank*③ / *a* ~ *park.* —*n.* ⓒ 1. a citizen of a nation. 2. (usu. *pl.*) citizens of a nation living in foreign countries.
— 形 1. 국민의, 국가의 ¶ ① 국어 / ② 국기 2. 국유의 ¶ ③ 국립 은행 — 名 1. 국민의 한 사람 2. [해외] 동포

na·tion·al·ism [nǽʃ(ə)nəlìz(ə)m] *n.* [U] **1.** a strong love for one's country. **2.** a desire for national independence in a country ruled by another.
—[名] 1. 국가(민족)주의 2. 독립주의

na·tion·al·ist [nǽʃ(ə)nəlist] *n.* [C] a person who supports and fights for nationalism. —*adj.* =nationalistic.
—[名] 국가주의자

na·tion·al·is·tic [næ̀ʃ(ə)nəlístik] *adj.* of nationalism or nationalists.
—[形] 국가주의[자]의

* **na·tion·al·i·ty** [næ̀ʃ(ə)nǽliti] *n.* (pl. **-ties**) **1.** [U][C] the state of belonging to one nation. ¶*the ~ of a ship*① / *What is her ~?*② **2.** [U] independence as a nation. ¶*Many African states are obtaining ~.*③
—[名] 1. 국적 ¶①선적(船籍)/②그녀의 국적은 어디냐? 2. 국가 ¶③아프리카의 여러 주가 독립을 얻고 있다

na·tion·al·i·za·tion [næ̀ʃ(ə)nəlizéiʃ(ə)n / -lai-] *n.* [U] the act of nationalizing; the state of being nationalized.
—[名] 국가화, 국유화

na·tion·al·ize [nǽʃ(ə)nəlàiz] *vt.* **1.** make (a nation); change (a dependent country, etc.) into a nation. **2.** bring (railways, land, industries, etc.) under the control of a nation.
—[他] 1. …을 독립국가로 만들다 2. [철도·토지·산업 따위를] 국유화하다

na·tion-wide [néiʃ(ə)nwàid] *adj.* stretching throughout the whole nation.
—[形] 전국적인

⁑ **na·tive** [néitiv] *n.* [C] **1.** a person who is born in a certain place or country. ¶*a ~ of Cheju* ① **2.** a person who lives originally in an uncivilized country. **3.** an animal or a plant found in a particular place.
—[名] 1. …태생의 사람 ¶①제주 출신의 사람 2. 원주민 3. 토착의 동식물

—*adj.* **1.** of one's birthplace. ¶*one's ~ town*② / *one's ~ language.*③ **2.** inborn. ¶*~ aptitude*④ / *~ talent.*⑤ **3.** of the original people in any country, usu. uncivilized. ¶*a ~ costume.*⑥ **4.** (of minerals) found in a natural state. ¶*~ salt.*⑦ **5.** (of animals or plants) originally found in a certain place.
—[形] 1. 출생지의; 자국(自國)의 ¶②태어난 고장/③모국어 2. 타고난 ¶④타고난 소질/⑤타고난 재능 3. [백인이 보아] 토착민의 ¶⑥민속 의상 4. 천연의 ¶⑦천연염(鹽) 5. [동식물 따위] 토착의

na·tive-born [néitivbɔ́:rn] *adj.* born in a particular place or country.
—[形] 본토박이의

na·tiv·i·ty [nətíviti] *n.* (pl. **-ties**) **1.** [U][C] birth. **2.** ⟪*the N-*⟫ the birth of Christ. **3.** ⟪*the N-*⟫ a picture of the birth of Christ.
—[名] 1. 탄생 2. 그리스도 탄생 3. 그리스도 탄생의 그림

nat·ty [nǽti] *adj.* (**-ti·er, -ti·est**) neat and smart in clothes or general appearance. ¶*a ~ naval officer*① / *in a ~ business suit.*② ▷**nat·ti·ly** [-li] *adv.*
—[形] 말쑥한, 깨끗한 ¶①말쑥한 해군장교/②깨끗한 작업복을 입고

⁑ **nat·u·ral** [nǽtʃ(u)rəl] *adj.* **1.** of nature. ¶*~ phenomena* / *~ science* / *~ history.*① **2.** produced or provided by nature; not man-made. ¶*~ gas* / *~ resources.*② **3.** belonging to a person by nature; not acquired. ¶*a ~ gift*③ / *a ~ poet.*④ **4.** true to nature. ¶*The portrait looks ~.* **5.** to be expected; normal; ordinary. ¶*a ~ death*⑤ / *It is only ~.*⑥ / *It is quite ~ that he should fail.*⑦ **6.** not pretending; simple; honest. ¶*a ~ manner.* **7.** (*Music*) without sharps or flats. ¶*a ~ sign.*⑧
—[形] 1. 자연의 ¶①박물학 2. 천연의 ¶②천연 자원 3. 타고난, 날 때부터의 ¶③천부의 재능/④태어나면서부터의 시인 4. 그대로 꼭 닮은 5. 자연스러운; 보통의; 당연한 ¶⑤자연사/⑥아주 당연하다/⑦그가 실패할 것은 틀림없다 6. 꾸미지 않은, 본래의 7. ⟪樂⟫ 본위(本位)의 ¶⑧제자리표

come natural to (=*be easy for*) *someone.*
[熟] …에게는 문제가 아니다(쉽다)

—*n.* [C] **1.** (*colloq.*) a fool by birth. **2.** (*Music*) a white key on the piano; a musical melody which is not sharp or flat; the sign for this (♮). **3.** (*colloq.*) a person or thing sure to be successful.
—[名] 1. [선천적인] 천치 2. [피아노의] 흰 건(鍵); 제자리 음; 제자리표 3. 성공이 틀림없는 사람(것)

nat·u·ral·ism [nǽtʃ(u)rəlìz(ə)m] *n.* [U] **1.** an action or a thought based on natural desire. **2.** a theory in literature that wants to show things as they really are. **3.** (*Philosophy*) the belief that there are no supernatural things or events in this world.
—[名] 1. 자연주의 2. 자연(사실)주의 3. 자연(실증)주의

nat·u·ral·ist [nǽtʃ(u)rəlist] *n.* [C] **1.** a person who studies the things of nature, such as plants, minerals and animals. **2.** a realist.
—[名] 1. 박물학자 2. [문예 따위의] 자연주의자

nat·u·ral·is·tic [næ̀tʃ(u)rəlístik] *adj.* **1.** having the characteristics of naturalism in art or literature. **2.** of natural history or naturalists. **3.** like nature; realistic.
—[形] 1. 자연주의의 2. 박물학적인 3. 사실적인

nat·u·ral·i·za·tion [næ̀tʃ(u)rəlizéiʃ(ə)n / -lai-] *n.* [U] the act of naturalizing; the state of being naturalized.
—[名] 자연화, 귀화(歸化)

nat·u·ral·ize [nǽtʃ(u)rəlàiz] *vt.* **1.** give (a foreigner) cit-
—[他] 1. [외국인]을 귀화시키다 ¶①귀

izenship. ¶*a naturalized Korean* ① / *become naturalized.*② **2.** accept (a foreign word, custom, etc.). ¶*a naturalized word.*③ **3.** bring in (a plant or an animal) from another country. ¶*The cherry has been naturalized in parts of Washington.*④ **4.** make (something) natural. —*vi.* **1.** become naturalized. **2.** study natural history.
화한 한국인/②귀화하다 **2.** …을 받아들이다, 도입하다 ¶③외래어 **3.** [다른 나라의] …을 이식하다 ¶④벚나무는 워싱턴 지방에도 이식되었다 **4.** …을 자연적으로 하다 —[自] **1.** 귀화하다; 풍토에 순화(馴化)하다 **2.** 박물학을 연구하다

⁝ nat·u·ral·ly [nǽtʃ(u)rəli] *adv.* **1.** in a natural manner. **2.** by nature. ¶~ *curly* / ~ *clever.*① **3.** of course. ¶*Yes, ~.*②
—[副] **1.** 자연히 **2.** 본래, 나면서부터 ¶①본래가 영리한 **3.** 당연히 ¶②예, 물론입니다

⁝ na·ture [néitʃər] *n.* **1.** [U] the whole material world that is not the work of man. ¶*a lover of ~.*① **2.** [U] ⦅sometimes *N-*⦆ the powers, forces, etc. that control this material world; the Creator; God. ¶*the laws of ~ / Nature's engineering.*② **3.** [U] the state of man in the earliest times. ¶*go back to ~ / live in a state of ~.*③ **4.** [U][C] the essential quality of a thing; the most important point. ¶*by the ~ of things.*④ **5.** [U][C] the mental and spiritual character of a man; a person with a certain character. ¶*[a] good ~ / a generous ~*⑤ / *It is against ~ to kill oneself.*⑥ **6.** [C] a sort; a kind; a type. ¶*pictures of this ~.*⑦
1) ***by nature,*** because of the essential qualities; naturally.
2) ***in the nature of,*** having the character of; of the same kind as; like.
3) ***pay the debt of nature,*** die.
—[名] **1.** 자연; 자연계 ¶①자연을 사랑하는 사람 **2.** 자연의 힘; 조물주 ¶②조화의 오묘함 **3.** 자연 그대로임; 원시상태 ¶③야생 그대로 살다; 나체로 생활하다 **4.** 특질; 본질; 성질 ¶④사물의 본질상; 필연적으로 **5.** 성격; 본성; 인간성; 어떤 성질을 가진 사람 ¶⑤너그러운 사람(마음)/⑥자살은 인간의 본성에 어긋난다 **6.** 종류; 타이프 ¶⑦이런 종류의 그림
[熟] 1)나면서부터; 본질상; 원래 2)…의 성질을 가진; …와 같은 종류의; 비슷한 3)죽다

• naught [nɔːt] *n.* [U] (*archaic*) nothing. ¶*bring to ~*① / *come to ~.*②
1) ***all for naught,*** in vain; uselessly.
2) ***set something at naught,*** make light of something; disregard; ignore.
—*adj.* (*archaic*) useless.
—[名] ⦅古⦆ 무(無) ¶①무효로 하다/②쓸모없게 되다
[熟] 1)헛되이 2)…을 무시하다
—[形] ⦅古⦆ 가치없는

naugh·ti·ly [nɔ́ːtili] *adv.* in a naughty manner.
—[副] 장난으로

naugh·ti·ness [nɔ́ːtinis] *n.* [U] the state of being naughty. ⇒[N.B.]
—[名] 장난 [N.B.] 어린이에게 쓰는 말

• naugh·ty [nɔ́ːti] *adj.* (**-ti·er, -ti·est**) causing mischief; behaving badly; harmful.
—[形] 장난꾸러기의; 버릇없는; 못된

nau·sea [nɔ́ːʒə, -siə / nɔ́ːsiə, -ʃiə] *n.* [U] **1.** a feeling that one is going to throw up food through the mouth. **2.** seasickness. **3.** a strong dislike.
—[名] **1.** 욕지기, 구역질 **2.** 뱃멀미 **3.** 몹시 싫음

nau·se·ate [nɔ́ːʒièit, -si- / -sièit] *vi., vt.* cause (someone) to feel nausea. ⦅~ *at* something⦆ ¶*He was nauseated by the sight of blood.*①
—[自][他] 구역질 나[게 하]다 ¶①그는 피를 보자 구역질이 났다

nau·seous [nɔ́ːʃəs, -ziəs / -siəs] *adj.* causing nausea or dislike. ▷**nau·seous·ly** [-li] *adv.*
—[形] 구역질이 나는; 싫은

nau·ti·cal [nɔ́ːtik(ə)l] *adj.* of ships, sailors or navigation. ¶*a ~ almanac*① / *a ~ term.*② ▷**nau·ti·cal·ly** [-i] *adv.*
—[形] 항해의, 배의 ¶①항해력(曆)/②선원 용어

nautical mile [ˊ-- ˋ] *n.* a unit of linear measure for ships.
—[名] 해리(海里) (1,852 미터)

nau·ti·li [nɔ́ːtilài] *n.* pl. of **nautilus**.

nau·ti·lus [nɔ́ːtiləs] *n.* [C] (pl. **-lus·es** or **-li**) any of several tropical shellfish with a spiral shell.
—[名] 앵무조개

• na·val [néiv(ə)l] *adj.* of a navy, warships or ships. ¶*a ~ battle*① / *a ~ port.*②
—[形] 해군의, 군함의, 배의 ¶①해전/②군함

nave[1] [neiv] *n.* [C] the central part of a church or cathedral between the side aisles where people sit.
—[名] [교회의] 본당

nave[2] [neiv] *n.* [C] the central part of a wheel.
—[名] [수레의] 바퀴통

na·vel [néiv(ə)l] *n.* [C] **1.** the round, small pit in the surface of the belly. **2.** the middle; the center.
—[名] **1.** 배꼽 **2.** 한복판, 중심

navel orange [ˊ- ˋ-] *n.* a seedless orange with a pit like a navel on the surface.
—[名] 네이블(오렌지)

nav·i·ga·ble [nǽvigəbl] *adj.* **1.** able to navigate. **2.** fitted for a ship or airplane to navigate. ¶*The river is ~ only by great skill.*①
—[形] **1.** 항행할 수 있는 **2.** 항행에 알맞은 ¶①그 강의 운항에는 큰 기술이 필요하다

nav·i·gate [nǽvigèit] *vi.* **1.** travel by ship or plane. **2.** operate a ship or an aircraft. —*vt.* **1.** direct (a ship or an aircraft). **2.** travel over, through or on (a river, the sea, etc.). ¶~ *the sea*① / ~ *the air.*②
—[自] **1.** 항행하다 **2.** 조종하다 —[他] **1.** [배·비행기 따위]를 조종하다 **2.** [강·바다 따위]를 항행하다 ¶①항해하다/②항공하다

• nav·i·ga·tion [næ̀vigéiʃ(ə)n] *n.* [U] **1.** the act of navi-
—[名] **1.** 항해, 항공, 항행 **2.** 항해술, 항공

gating. **2.** the science of finding out the course or position for ships, airplanes, etc. **3.** ⟪*collectively*⟫ ships.
술 **3.** 선박

nav·i·ga·tor [nǽvigèitər] *n.* [C] **1.** a person who sails on the seas. **2.** a person who decides the course of a ship or an airplane. **3.** a person in charge of navigating. **4.** a person who explores an island, etc. by ship.
—[名] **1.** 항행자 **2.** 조종자 **3.** 항해장(航海長) **4.** 해양 탐험가

nav·vy [nǽvi] *n.* [C] (pl. **-vies**) (*Brit. colloq.*) an unskilled laborer who is employed to dig in making roads, railways or canals.
—[名] 《英口》 토역꾼, 인부

⁑**na·vy** [néivi] *n.* [C] (pl. **-vies**) **1.** ⟪*collectively*⟫ all the warships of a nation; the whole sea force of a nation including ships, officers, men, shipyards, etc. ¶*the Royal Navy*① / *the ~ yard.*② **2.** ⟪*collectively*⟫ officers and men of the navy; persons engaged in naval work.
—[名] **1.** 해군; 해군력 ¶①영국 해군/②미국 해군 조선소 **2.** 해군 군인

navy blue [⌐–⌐] *n.* very dark blue.
—[名] 감색(紺色)

***nay** [nei] *adv.* **1.** (*archaic*) no. ↔yea **2.** (*literary*) not only that, but also. ¶*It's difficult, ~ impossible.*① —*n.* [C] a refusal. ¶*the yeas and nays*
—[副] **1.** 《古》 아니 **2.** 《文學》 …이라기보다는 오히려 ¶①곤란이라기보다는 불가능이다 —[名] 거절

Naz·a·rene [næ̀zəríːn] *n.* [C] **1.** a person born or living in Nazareth; ⟪*the ~*⟫ Jesus Christ. **2.** a Christian. —*adj.* of Nazarenes or Nazareth.
—[名] **1.** 나사렛 사람; 그리스도 **2.** 나사렛[사람]의
—[形] 나사렛 사람의

Naz·a·reth [nǽzəriθ] *n.* an ancient town in Palestine where Jesus Chirist spent his early life.
—[名] 나사렛

Na·zi [náːtsi] *n.* [C] a member of the German fascist political party, found in 1919 by Adolf Hitler; ⟪*the ~s*⟫ the party. —*adj.* of a Nazi or the Nazis.
—[名] 나찌스 당원; 나찌스당 —[形] 나찌스당[원]의

N. B. *nota bene* ⇒[N.B.]; note well.
—《略》 주의하라 [N.B.] 라틴어

neap [niːp] *adj.* of a very low tide. ¶*a ~ tide.* ↔spring tide
—[形] 소조(小潮)의

Ne·a·pol·i·tan [ni(ː)əpálit(ə)n / -pɔ́l-] *adj.* of Naples or its people. —*n.* [C] a person of Naples.
—[形] 나폴리[사람]의 —[名] 나폴리 사람

⁑**near** [niər] *adv.* **1.** at a short distance in space or time; not far; almost; nearly. ¶*Spring is drawing ~.*① / **2.** closely; intimately. ¶*They are ~ related.*②
—[副] **1.** 가까이에; 이웃하여; 거의 ¶①봄이 다가오고 있다 **2.** 친하게; 밀접하게 ¶②그들은 친척간이다

1) ***come near*** [*to*] ***doing,*** almost do.
2) ***come near to do,*** almost do.
3) ***far and near,*** in every direction; everywhere.
4) ***near at hand,*** in the near future; within easy reach.
5) ***near by,*** not far off; near at hand.

[熟] 1)2) 하마터면 …할 뻔하다 3)도처에 4)멀지 않아; 가까이에 5)바로 가까이에

—*adj.* **1.** close in distance or time. ¶*the ~ future* / *the nearest way to the station* / *The park is quite ~.* **2.** closely related in blood. ¶*a ~ relative.* **3.** close in friendship; intimate. **4.** close in degree; resembling closely. ¶*a ~ resemblance*③ / *a ~ translation*④ / *a ~ guess*⑤ / *a ~ escape* (or *thing*)⑥ **5.** on the left side. ↔off, right. ¶*the ~ side* / *the ~ wheels of a car.*⑦ **6.** unwilling to spend or give money. ¶*He is very ~ with money.*
—[形] **1.** 가까운; 접근한 **2.** 근친의 **3.** 친밀한 **4.** 가까운 관계의; 아주 가까운; 모조의 ¶③혹사(酷似)/④축어역(逐語譯)/⑤별로 빗나가지 않은 추측/⑥구사일생 **5.** 왼쪽의 ¶⑦자동차의 왼쪽 바퀴 **6.** 인색한

a near race, a race in which the two sides are equally matched.
[熟] 우열을 가리기 어려운 승부

—*prep.* close to in space, time, degree, etc. ¶*~ the river* / *He is ~ seventy years of age.*⑧
—[前] …의 가까이에; 옆에 ¶⑧그는 일흔 살에 가깝다

—*vt., vi.* come or draw near to (something). ¶*~* [*to*] *one's end.*⑨
—[他][自] 다가가다, 접근하다 ¶⑨임종이 가까와지다

***near·by** [níərbái / ⌐⌐] *adj., adv.* close at hand; near. ⇒[N.B.] ¶*a ~ house* / *A plane lands ~.*
—[形][副] 가까이의(에) [N.B.] 부사 용법일 경우 영국에서는 near by로 씀

Near East [⌐⌐], **the** *n.* the territory including the Balkans, Egypt and the countries of southwestern Asia.
—[名] 근동

⁑**near·ly** [níərli] *adv.* **1.** almost. ¶*It's ~ ten o'clock.* / *He was ~ run over by a car.* **2.** closely; intimately. ¶*It concerns you ~.*
—[副] **1.** 거의; 간신히; 이럭저럭 **2.** 친밀하게

not nearly, nothing like. ¶*It's not ~ enough.*①
[熟] 도저히 … 아니다(약한 의미의 강조) ¶①도저히 모자란다

near·ness [níərnis] *n.* [U] the state or quality of being near in time, distance, relation, etc.
—[名] 가까움; 근사; 근친; 친함

near-sight·ed [níərsáitid] *adj.* able to see things clearly at short distances only; short-sighted. ▷**near-sight·ed·ly** [-li] *adv.* —**near-sight·ed·ness** [-nis] *n.*
—[形] 근시안의

N

neat [ni:t] *adj.* **1.** clean; tidy. ¶*a ~ room* | *~ in one's habits* | *as ~ as a pin.*① **2.** simple and well-arranged. ¶*He is ~ in his person.*② **3.** brief and clever; skillful. ¶*a ~ reply* | *a ~ explanation.* **4.** unmixed with anything; pure. ¶*~ weight* | *take a drink of whisky ~.*
—[형] 1. 정돈된, 깨끗한 ¶①아주 깨끗한 2. [외관이] 산뜻한, 말쑥한 ¶②그는 몸차림이 산뜻하다 3. [말이] 적절한; [행동이] 세련된 4. 순수한

neath, 'neath [ni:θ, +*U.S.* ni:ð] *prep.* (*poetic*) =beneath.

neat·ly [ní:tli] *adv.* in a neat manner.
—[부] 산뜻하게, 깨끗하게

neat·ness [ní:tnis] *n.* [U] the state of being neat.
—[명] 청초; 정돈; 솜씨좋은

Ne·bras·ka [nibrǽskə] *n.* a State in the middle west of the United States. ⇒[N.B.]
—[명] 네브라스카 주 [N.B.] Nebr.로 줄임. 수도 Lincoln

neb·u·la [nébjulə] *n.* [C] (pl. **-lae** or **-las**) (*Astronomy*) a bright, cloud-like heavenly body composed of a group of stars or burning gas.
—[명] 성운(星雲)

neb·u·lae [nébjuli] *n.* pl. of **nebula.**

neb·u·lous [nébjuləs] *adj.* **1.** of or like a nebula. **2.** misty; unclear. ¶*a ~ memory*① | *~ fears.*
—[형] 1. 성운[모양]의 2. 막연한 ¶①막연한 기억

nec·es·sar·i·ly [nèsisérili, ⌐—⌐— / nésis(ə)rili] *adv.* as a necessary and sure result; inevitably. ¶*War ~ causes misery.*① | *It's not ~ interesting.*②
—[부] 필연적으로, 물론 ¶①전쟁은 반드시 재난을 초래한다/②반드시 재미있다고는 할 수 없다

nec·es·sar·y [nésisèri / nésis(ə)ri] *adj.* **1.** needed; required; indispensable; essential. ¶*Food is ~ for life.* | *It is ~ that everybody should obey the law.* **2.** certain to happen; inevitable. ¶*a ~ conclusion* | *a ~ evil.*①
—[형] 1. 필요한; 없어서는 안 되는; 필수의 2. 필연의; 피할 수 없는 ¶①필요악

—*n.* [C] (pl. **-sar·ies**) a necessary or very important thing. ¶*daily necessaries*② | *household necessaries.*
—[명] 필요한 것 ¶②일용품

ne·ces·si·tate [nisésitèit] *vt.* **1.** make (something) necessary. ¶*~ an operation.*① **2.** ⟪usu. in *passive*⟫ force; compel. ¶*We are necessitated to do so.*
—[타] 1. …을 필요로 하다 ¶①수술할 필요가 있다 2. 부득이 …하게 하다

ne·ces·si·tous [nisésitəs] *adj.* very poor; in great need. ¶*~ members of the community.*①
—[형] 가난한 ¶①사회(부락)의 빈곤한 사람들

ne·ces·si·ty [nisésiti] *n.* (pl. **-ties**) **1.** [U] the state of being necessary. ¶*There is no ~ to do so.*① | (*proverb*) *Necessity is the mother of invention.*② **2.** [C] that which comes about or happens as a result of natural law. ¶*Death is a ~ to life.*③ | *Cause is a ~ to change.*④ **3.** [C] ⟪often *pl.*⟫ something which is greatly necessary for our life. ¶*daily necessities.*⑤ **4.** [U] the state of being very poor; need. ¶*In case of ~, you can call on me.*⑥
—[명] 1. 필요[성] ¶①그렇게 할 필요는 없다/②⟪俚⟫필요는 발명의 어머니 2. 필연[성] ¶③생명에는 죽음이 따르는 법/④변경하려면 이유가 필요하다 3. 필요[물], 필수품 ¶⑤일용품 4. 빈곤, 곤궁 ¶⑥돈에 쪼들리면 찾아오너라

1) ***as a necessity,*** inevitably.
2) ***be under the necessity of doing,*** be forced to do.
3) ***bow to necessity,*** do what one is compelled to do.
4) ***make a virtue of necessity,*** accept without any protest what one is forced to do; take honor for doing what one has to do.

[熟] 1)필연적으로 2)부득이 …하지 않을 수 없다 3)운명으로서 체념하다 4)마지못해 하면서도 자진해서 하는 체하다; 해야 할 일을 하고도 공을 세운 체하다

neck [nek] *n.* [C] **1.** the part of the body between the head and the shoulders. **2.** the part of the clothes that fits the neck. ¶*the ~ of a shirt.* **3.** anything like a neck in shape or position. ¶*the ~ of a bottle.* **4.** a narrow way or passage of water; a narrow strip of land.
—[명] 1. 목 2. [의복의] 목 부분, 옷깃 3. 목 모양의 것 4. 해협; 지협(地峽)

1) ***a stiff neck,*** a person who is hard to control; a stubborn person.
2) ***break the neck*** (=*do the hardest part*) ***of a piece of work.***
3) ***get it in the neck,*** (*slang*) suffer a heavy blow.
4) ***save one's neck,*** escape hanging; escape death.
5) ***win by a neck,*** (in a horse race) win by the length of a horse's head and neck.
6) ***neck and crop,*** altogether; completely.
7) ***neck and neck,*** running side by side; just even in a contest.
8) ***neck or nothing,*** taking all possible chances; in a desperate way.

[熟] 1)고집통이 2)[일의] 가장 힘든 고비를 넘기다 3)큰 타격을 입다 4)교수형을 모면하다; [과실에 대한] 처벌을 모면하다 5)[경마에서] 목 하나의 차이로 이기다 6)몽땅 그대로; 전혀 7)[경마 따위에서] 나란히; 비등비등하게 8)망하느냐 흥하느냐; 필사적으로

—*vi., vt.* (*U.S. slang*) clasp one another around the neck; embrace and kiss.
—[자][타] 목을 서로 껴안다, 껴안고 키스하다

neck·band [nékbæ̀nd] *n.* [C] **1.** a band worn around the neck. **2.** a part of a shirt to which the collar is fastened.
—[명] 1. 목끈 2. 샤쓰의 깃

neck·er·chief [nékərtʃif] *n.* [C] (pl. **-chiefs**) a long piece of cloth worn around the neck.
—[名] 목도리

neck·lace [néklis] *n.* [C] a decorative string of jewels, gold, beads, etc., worn around the neck.
—[名] 목걸이

neck·tie [néktài] *n.* [C] a narrow band of cloth worn around the neck and tied in front.
—[名] 넥타이

neck·wear [nékwɛ̀ər] *n.* [U] articles worn around the neck, such as neck collars, ties, scarfs, etc.
—[名] 목도리류(넥타이 · 칼라 · 목도리류)

nec·ro·man·cer [nékroumæ̀nsər] *n.* [C] **1.** a person who is believed to foretell the future. **2.** a magician.
—[名] 1. 점장이 2. 마술사

ne·cro·ses [nekróusi:z] *n.* pl. of **necrosis**.

ne·cro·sis [nekróusis] *n.* [U][C] (pl. **-ses**) (*Medicine*) the death or decay of a part of the living body.
—[名] [醫] 회저(壞疽); 탈저(脫疽)

nec·tar [néktər] *n.* [U] **1.** (in Greek mythology) the drink of the gods. **2.** any sweet drink. **3.** the sweet liquid found in flowers.
—[名] 1. 신주(神酒) 2. 감미로운 음료 3. 꿀

nec·tar·ine [nèktəríːn / nékt(ə)rin] *n.* [C] a kind of peach that has a smooth, thin skin.
—[名] 승도복숭아

née, nee [nei] *adj.* by birth; born. ⇒[N.B.] ¶*Mrs. Lang, ~ Jones.*
—[形] 구성(舊姓)은 … [N.B.] 기혼 부인의 결혼 전의 성을 나타낼 때 씀

⁑need [ni:d] *n.* [U] **1.** 《sometimes *a* ~》 the lack of something necessary. ¶*His novel showed ~ of humor.*① **2.** [C] something wanted or necessary. ¶*our daily needs*② / *Water was our greatest ~.*③ **3.** necessity. ¶*There is no ~ to hurry.*④ / *He is in ~ of help.*⑤ **4.** a situation or time when help is required. ¶(*proverb*) *A friend in ~ is a friend indeed.*⑥ / *They failed me in my ~.*⑦ **5.** the state of being very poor.
—[名] 1. 결핍; 부족 ¶①그의 소설에는 유우머가 별로 없다 2. 부족한 것; 필요품 ¶②일용 필수품/③물이 가장 필요한 것이었다 3. 필요 ¶④서두를 필요가 없다/⑤그에게는 도움이 필요하다 4. 위급한 경우, 난국 ¶⑥어려울 때의 친구가 참된 친구다/⑦그들은 내가 곤경에 빠졌을 때 나를 버렸다 5. 궁핍, 가난

1) ***had need do*** (or ***to do***), (*literary*) ought to do.
2) ***have need to do,*** must; have to; ought to.
3) ***if need be*** (or ***were***), if it is (or were) necessary.
[熟] 1)…하여야 하다 2)…하지 않으면 안 되다 3)필요하면

—*vt.* **1.** have need of (something); require. 《~ *doing;* ~ *to do*》 ¶*This work will ~ a lot of time.* / *Does she ~ any help?* / *My shoes ~ mending* (or ~ *to be mended*).⑧ **2.** be obliged. 《~ *to do*》 (→*auxil. v.*) ¶*He needs to be more careful.* / *He doesn't ~ to see her.*
—[他] 1. …을 필요로 하다 ¶⑧내 구두는 수선할 필요가 있다 2. …하지 않으면 안 되다

—*auxil. v.* 《in *negative* or *interrogative*》 must; have to; should; need to. ¶*Need she come?* / *He ~ not see her.* / *You ~ not have done it.*⑨ / *You hardly ~ help him.*
—[助] 《의문문에서》 …하지 않으면 안 되는가; 《부정문에서》 …할 필요는 없다 ¶⑨너는 그것을 할 필요가 없었다

need·ful [ní:df(u)l] *adj.* **1.** needed; necessary. ¶*all ~ regulations.*① **2.** 《*the* ~》 ⓐ (*slang*) money; cash in hand. ⓑ something needed. ▷**need·ful·ly** [-fuli] *adv.*
—[形] 1. 필요한 ¶①필요한 모든 규칙 2. ⓐ돈, 자금 ⓑ필요한 것

⁑nee·dle [ní:dl] *n.* [C] **1.** a thin, sharp-pointed tool for sewing. **2.** anything like a needle. ¶*a knitting ~* / *a phonograph ~.* **3.** a needle-shaped leaf of some trees.
—[名] 1. 바늘 2. 바늘 모양의 것 3. 침엽수의 잎

1) ***as sharp as a needle,*** very intelligent.
2) ***look for a needle in a haystack,*** try to look for something which is almost impossible to find.
[熟] 1)영리하기 짝이 없는 2)도저히 불가능한 일을 시도하다; 헛수고를 하다

***need·less** [ní:dlis] *adj.* unnecessary. ¶~ *work.*①
—[形] 쓸데없는 ¶①쓸데없는 일

needless to say, it is not necessary to say.
[熟] 말할 필요도 없이

need·less·ly [ní:dlisli] *adv.* unnecessarily.
—[副] 불필요하게

nee·dle·wom·an [ní:dlwùmən] *n.* [C] (pl. **-wom·en** [-wìmin]) a woman who does sewing, esp. to earn money.
—[名] 침모, 재봉부(婦)

nee·dle·work [ní:dlwə̀:rk] *n.* [U] the work done with a needle, as sewing, embroidery, etc.
—[名] 바느질

need·n't [ní:dnt] =need not.

needs [ni:dz] *adv.* necessarily. ⇒[usage]
—[副] 반드시, 꼭 [usage] must의 앞뒤에 함께 씀

needs must do, be compelled to do. ¶*He ~ must do so.* / *He ~ must come.* / (*proverb*) *Needs must* [*go*] *when the devil drives.*①
[熟] …하지 않을 수 없다 ¶①《俚》필요에 쫓기면 꼭 하게 된다

need·y [ní:di] *adj.* (**need·i·er, need·i·est**) very poor; in want.
—[形] 가난한

ne'er [nɛər] *adv.* (*poetic*) =never.

ne'er-do-well [nɛ́ərdu(:)wèl] *n.* [C] a person who never does anything useful. **—*adj.*** worthless.
—[名] 쓸모없는 사람 —[形] 쓸모없는

ne·far·i·ous [niféəriəs] *adj.* very evil; unlawful. ▷**ne·far·i·ous·ly** [-li] *adv.* — ⓐ 사악한; 불법의

ne·gate [nigéit, +*U.S.* ní:geit] *vt.* deny the existence of (something); say "no." — ⓑ …을 부정하다

ne·ga·tion [nigéiʃ(ə)n] *n.* Ⓤ **1.** the act of denying. ↔ affirmation. ¶*double ~.*① **2.** the state of lacking or denying something real or positive. ¶*Sameness is the very ~ of liberty.*② — ⓑ 1. 부정 ¶①이중 부정 2. 무(無) 결여; 반대 ¶②획일성은 자유의 정반대이다

· **neg·a·tive** [négətiv] *adj.* **1.** expressing refusal or denial. ↔affirmative ¶*a ~ answer.*① **2.** not positive; not active; not forceful. ↔positive ¶*~ virtue*② / *a colorless, ~ character.*③ **3.** (*Mathematics*) less than zero; minus. ¶*the ~ sign.*④ **4.** of the kind of electricity made in silk etc. by rubbing it on glass. ↔positive ¶*the ~ pole.*⑤ **5.** (*Photography*) of the film or plate in which the lights and shadows are shown in reverse. ¶*a ~ plate* (or *film*).⑥ — ⓐ 1. 부정의, 부인하는 ¶①부정적 회답 2. 소극적인 ¶②[나쁜 덕은 가지 않는다는 정도의] 소극적 덕성(德性)/③특징 없는 소극적 인물 3.(數) 부(負)의 ¶④부호(負號) 4. 음전기의 ¶⑤음극 5. 음화(陰畫)의 ¶⑥음화

—*n.* Ⓒ **1.** a word showing denial. ⇒N.B. **2.** the side that stands against something. **3.** (*Mathematics*) a minus quality. **4.** negative electricity. **5.** (*Photography*) a negative film or plate. — ⓑ 1. 부정어 N.B. not, never, no more 따위 2. [의론·투표 따위의] 반대측 3. 부수(負數) 4. 음전기 5. 음화

in the negative, on the side of denying a plan, suggestion, etc.; with a negative or denial answer. 图 부정적으로, 거부적으로

—*vt.* **1.** deny. **2.** make (something) useless; prove (something) false. — ⓗ 1. …을 부정하다 2. …을 무효로 하다; [이론 따위]를 부정하다

neg·a·tive·ly [négətivli] *adv.* in a negative manner. ↔positively — ⓗ 부정적으로

: **ne·glect** [niglékt] *vt.* **1.** give no attention to (something); ignore; disregard. ¶*He neglects his family.* **2.** fail to do (something); take no care of (something). 《*~ to do*; *~ doing*》 ¶*~ writing an answer* / *~ to wind up a clock.* —*n.* Ⓤ the act of neglecting; the state of being neglected. — ⓗ 1. …을 무시하다 2. 태만하여 …하지 않다 —ⓑ 게을리하기, 태만; 무시, 무시

ne·glect·er, -or [nigléktər] *n.* Ⓒ a person who neglects. — ⓑ 태만한 사람

ne·glect·ful [nigléktf(u)l] *adj.* **1.** careless; heedless. 《*~ of*》 ¶*He is ~ of his duties.*① **2.** failing to do things habitually. ¶*He was not ~ and would write to me.*② — ⓐ 1. 태만한 ¶①그는 직무를 게을리한다 2. 무관심한, 냉담한 ¶②그는 관심을 갖고 나에게 편지를 자주 썼다

ne·glect·ful·ly [nigléktfuli] *adv.* in a neglectful manner. — ⓗ 태만하게; 부주의하게

neg·li·gee [nèɡliʒéi / néɡli(:)ʒèi] *n.* Ⓒ **1.** a loose house gown worn by women. **2.** any informal dress. — ⓑ 1. [부인용의] 실내복, 네글리제 2. 평상복

neg·li·gence [néɡlidʒ(ə)ns] *n.* Ⓤ the state or quality of being negligent. ¶*His ~ cost him his job.*① — ⓑ 태만; 단정하지 못함 ¶①그는 직무태만으로 해고당했다

neg·li·gent [néɡlidʒ(ə)nt] *adj.* lacking care or attention; neglecting one's duty; neglectful; careless. 《*~ of* or *in*》 ¶*be ~ in dress.*① / *be ~ of one's duty.* — ⓐ 무관심한; 게으른; 부주의한 ¶① 옷차림에 무관심하다

neg·li·gent·ly [néɡlidʒ(ə)ntli] *adv.* in a negligent manner. — ⓗ 게으르게, 무관심하게

neg·li·gi·ble [néɡlidʒibl] *adj.* that can be easily neglected; of less importance. ¶*a ~ personality.*① — ⓐ 무시해도 좋은; 하찮은 ¶①보잘것 없는 사람

ne·go·tia·ble [niɡóuʃ(i)əbl] *adj.* **1.** that can be negotiated. **2.** that can be passed from one person to another in return for money or its equivalent. ¶*a ~ bill.*① **3.** (of roads etc.) that can be passed through or over. ¶*a road ~ by bus.*② — ⓐ 1. 협정할 수 있는 2. 양도할 수 있는 ¶①유통 어음의 3. 통행할 수 있는 ¶②버스가 다닐 수 있는 길

ne·go·ti·ate [niɡóuʃièit] *vi.* discuss and make an agreement with others in political affairs or business deals. 《*~ with someone*》 ¶*~ with them on a peace treaty.*① —*vt.* **1.** make arrangements for (something). ¶*~ a treaty.*② **2.** give or get money for (bonds, stocks, etc.). ¶*~ a check.* **3.** (*colloq.*) pass over or through (something). ¶*The old car can hardly ~ the hill.* — ⓘ 정치적 교섭(협상)을 하다 ¶①그들과 평화조약을 협정하다 —ⓗ 1. [협약·거래 따위]를 협정하다 ¶②조약을 협정하다 2. [어음·증권 따위]를 유통(양도)하다, 돈으로 바꾸다 3. (口) [장애물·곤란 따위]를 빠져나가다, 헤쳐나가

· **ne·go·ti·a·tion** [niɡòuʃiéiʃ(ə)n] *n.* ⒸⓊ (often *pl.*) the act of negotiating. ¶*diplomatic negotiations*① / *The negotiations came to an end.*② — ⓑ 교섭; 양도; 거래 ¶①외교 교섭 /②그 교섭은 종료되었다

ne·go·ti·a·tor [niɡóuʃièitər] *n.* Ⓒ a person who negotiates. — ⓑ 교섭자; 협상자

Ne·gress, ne- [níːɡris] *n.* Ⓒ a Negro woman or girl. — ⓑ 흑인 여자

: **Ne·gro, ne-** [níːɡrou] *n.* Ⓒ (pl. **-groes**) a person who — ⓑ 흑인 —ⓐ 흑인[계]의

belongs to the dark African race, with black skin and curly hair. —*adj.* of Negroes.

Ne·groid, ne- [ní:grɔid] *adj.* of or like the Negro race. —*n.* [C] a person of the Negroid race.
—[形] 흑인의(같은) —[名] 흑인계의 사람

neigh [nei] *n.* [C] a gentle cry of a horse. —*vi.* (of a horse) utter a gentle cry.
—[名] 말의 울음 소리 —[自] [말이] 울다

⁑neigh·bor, *Brit.* **-bour** [néibər] *n.* [C] **1.** a person who lives next to another. ¶*a good ~.*① **2.** a fellow human being. ¶(in the Bible) *Love thy neighbor as thyself.*② **3.** a person, country, or thing that is near another. ¶*a mountain towering above its neighbors.*
—*vt.* live or be situated next to (something or someone). —*vi.* **1.** live or be situated near-by. **2.** be friendly. 《~ *with* someone》 ▷**neigh·bor·less** [-lis] *adj.*
—[名] 1. 이웃[사람] ¶①이웃간에 의가 좋은 사람 2. 동포 ¶②그대를 사랑하듯 그대의 이웃을 사랑하라 3. 인접해 있는 사람(나라・것)
—[他] …에 인접하다 —[自] 1. 가까이에 살다(있다) 2. 친하게 지내다

⁑neigh·bor·hood, *Brit.* **-bour-** [néibərhùd] *n.* **1.** [U] the state of being neighbors; nearness in position. **2.** [C] the district near a place or thing. ¶*Our ~ has a new supermarket.*① / *I'm a stranger in this ~.*② **3.** 《*collectively*》 people living near one another. **4.** [C] the part of a country where one lives.
—[名] 1. 근접해 있음; 이웃 2. 근처 ¶①근처에 새 수우퍼 마아킷이 있다/②이 근처는 낯이 설다 3. 이웃 사람들 4. [자기가 사는] 지방

in the neighborhood of, ⓐ not far from. ⓑ nearly; about.
[熟] ⓐ…의 근처에 ⓑ대략, …만큼

⁑neigh·bor·ing, *Brit.* **-bour-** [néib(ə)riŋ] *adj.* living or being near; very near.
—[形] 이웃의; 인접한

neigh·bor·li·ness, *Brit.* **-bour-** [néibərlinis] *n.* [U] the state or quality of being neighborly.
—[名] 이웃 같음; 친절함

neigh·bor·ly, *Brit.* **-bour-** [néibərli] *adj.* like a neighbor; kind and friendly.
—[形] 이웃 같은; 친절한

⁑neigh·bour [néibər] *n.* (*Brit.*) =neighbor.

⁑nei·ther [ní:ðər / náiðə] *conj.* **1.** 《followed by *nor*》 not either; not one and not another. ¶*I saw ~ him nor her.* / *I could ~ move nor utter a word.* / *Neither he nor I am* (or *Neither I nor he is*) *in the wrong.*① ⇒ [usage] **2.** 《preceded by *a negative clause*》 nor; and not. ¶*If you do not go, ~ shall I.* / *I am not rich, ~ do I wish to be.*② / *"I am not going." "Neither am I."*③
—[接] 1. …도 아니고 …도 아니다 ¶①그도 너도 틀리지 않았다 [usage] 주어에 쓰는 경우 동사는 nor 뒤의 단어에 일치시킴 2. …도 또한 …않다 ¶②나는 부자도 아니고 또 되고 싶지도 않다/③「나는 안 가겠다」「나도 안 가겠다」

—*adj.* not either. ¶*Neither story is interesting.* / *I will take ~ side in the dispute.*④ / *I can go in ~ case.*
—[形] 어느 쪽의 …도 …않다 ¶④나는 그 분쟁의 어느 편에도 들지 않겠다

—*pron.* 《usu. used as *sing.*》 none of the two; not either. ⇒[N.B.] ¶*I know ~ of them.* / *Neither of them is drunk.*⑤ / *He gave me two books, and ~ was satisfactory.*
—[代] 어느 쪽도 …않다 [N.B.] 부분 부정은 not both ¶⑤그들 두 사람 모두 취하지 않았다

Nell [nel] *n.* a woman's name.
—[名] 여자 이름

Nel·lie, Nel·ly [néli] *n.* a woman's name.
—[名] 여자 이름

Nel·son [nélsn], **Viscount Horatio** *n.* (1758-1805) an English admiral famous for his victory in the battle of Trafalgar.
—[名] 넬슨(영국의 제독, Trafalgar 해전에서 큰 승리를 얻었음)

Nem·e·ses [némisì:z] *n.* pl. of **Nemesis**.

Nem·e·sis [némisis] *n.* (pl. **-ses**) **1.** a Greek goddess of punishment and revenge. **2.** [C] 《*n-*》 a person who decides or gives punishment; [U] just punishment; inevitable result.
—[名] 1. 응보・복수의 여신 2. 벌을 주는 사람; 천벌; 응보

ne·o- [ní:ou-, ní:ə-] a word element meaning *new* or *recent*.
— 「새로운」「근대의」를 의미하는 연결형

ne·o·lith·ic [nì:oulíθik] *adj.* of the later part of the Stone Age; of the period when man used polished stone weapons and tools. ↔paleolithic ¶*the Neolithic Age.*①
—[形] 신석기 시대의 ¶①신석기 시대

ne·on [ní:ɑn / -ən] *n.* [U] a rare gas with no color or smell that gives a glow when electricity passes through it. ¶*a ~ sign.*①
—[名] 네온 ¶①네온사인

ne·o·phyte [ní:oufàit] *n.* [C] **1.** a person who has recently been admitted to a religion. **2.** a beginner in art, business, etc.
—[名] 1. 새로운 신자 2. 초심자

ne·pen·the [nipénθi] *n.* [C] **1.** (*poetic*) a medicine believed by ancient Greeks to make a person forget sorrow or trouble. **2.** a pitcher plant.
—[名] 1.《詩》 슬픔・시름을 잊게 하는 약 2. 저롱초속(猪籠草屬)

neph·ew [néfju(:), +*Brit.* névju(:)] *n.* ⓒ the son of one's brother or sister. ↔niece

Nep·tune [népt∫u:n / -tju:n] *n.* **1.** (in Roman mythology) the god of the sea. **2.** the third largest planet.

Ne·re·id, ne- [níəriid] *n.* ⓒ (in Greek mythology) a fairy girl living in the sea; a sea nymph.

Ne·ro [níərou] *n.* a Roman emperor (37-68 A.D.), famous for his cruelty and tyranny. ⇒N.B.

nerve [nə:rv] *n.* **1.** ⓒ a cordlike part of an animal's body that carries feelings and impulses between the brain and other parts of the body. **2.** ⓒ a strong cordlike part of the body which joins a muscle to a bone. **3.** Ⓤ mental strength; courage. ¶*a man of ~* ① / *lose one's ~.*② **4.** Ⓤ strength; energy. **5.** (*pl.*) an unhealthy state of mind when a person is easily excited or frightened. ¶*have a fit of nerves*③ / *She is all nerves.*④ **6.** Ⓤ (*colloq.*) rude boldness. ¶*You've got some nerve.*⑤ **7.** ⓒ a vein of a leaf.
 1) ***get on someone's nerves***, worry or irritate someone.
 2) ***have the nerve*** (=*be brave or bold enough*) ***to do***.
 3) ***strain every nerve***, make a great effort.
 —*vt.* give strength or courage to (someone). ¶*They nerved themselves for danger.*⑥

nerve·less [nə́:rvlis] *adj.* **1.** having no vigor or courage; having no firmness. **2.** (*Anatomy, Botany*) without a nerve or nerves. **3.** cool.

nerve·less·ly [nə́:rvlisli] *adv.* in a nerveless manner.

nerv·ous [nə́:rvəs] *adj.* **1.** of the nerve. ¶*the ~ system* / *~ breakdown.*① **2.** having delicate nerves; easily excited; restless and uneasy. **3.** lively in style of writing.
 feel nervous (=*worry much*) *about something*.

nerv·ous·ly [nə́:rvəsli] *adv.* in a nervous manner.

nerv·ous·ness [nə́:rvəsnis] *n.* Ⓤ the state or quality of being nervous.

nerv·y [nə́:rvi] *adj.* (**nerv·i·er, nerv·i·est**) **1.** (*rare*) strong; vigorous. **2.** (*U.S. colloq.*) rude and bold. **3.** (*Brit.*) nervous; easily excited or angry.

nest [nest] *n.* ⓒ **1.** a place where birds or other animals lay eggs and care for their young. ¶*a ~ of eggs*① / *leave a ~.*② **2.** a warm or comfortable place. **3.** a secret place where people gather. ¶*a ~ of brigands.*③ **4.** birds or animals living in a nest.
 —*vi.* build or live in a nest. —*vt.* put (a bird) in a nest; make a nest for (a bird, etc.).

nest egg [⸗ ⸗] *n.* **1.** a real or false egg left in a nest to encourage a hen to go on laying eggs there. **2.** money that is put aside for future use; money saved as the beginning of a fund.

nes·tle [nésl] *vi.* lie or settle down closely and comfortably. ¶*a temple nestling among the hills.*① —*vt.* press (one's head, face, etc.) closely in affection; cuddle. ¶*The little girl nestles her doll at her breast.*

nest·ling [néslin] *n.* ⓒ **1.** a young new-hatched bird unable to leave the nest. **2.** a young child.

net¹ [net] *n.* ⓒ **1.** woven material of string, cord, thread, wire, etc. with small holes arranged regularly. **2.** anything made of this material. ¶*a mosquito ~* ① / *cast a ~*② / *lay a ~.*③ **3.** a trap. ¶*He was caught in the ~ of lies.*④
 —*vt., vi.* **1.** make (something) into a net. **2.** catch (something) with a net. **3.** get (something) with effort. **4.** use a net in (something) to catch or protect. ¶*~ a river.*

—名 조카

—名 1. 해신(海神) 2. 해왕성

—名 바다의 요정

—名 폭군 네로 N.B. 그리스도 교도를 박해한 잔인한 폭군

—名 1. 신경 2. 건(腱) 3. 기력; 용기 ¶①배짱 있는 사내/②용기(침착성)를 잃다 4. 체력; 정력; 활력 5. 신경과민 ¶③신경과민이 되다(발작을 일으키다)/④심한 신경과민증에 걸려 있다 6. (口) 뻔뻔스러움 ¶⑤너는 좀 뻔뻔스럽군 7. (식물의) 엽맥(葉脈)

熟 1) 남의 신경을 건드리다 2) …할 용기가 있다; 뻔뻔스럽게도 …하다 3) 전력을 다하다

—他 …에 힘을 주다; …의 용기를 북돋우다 ¶⑥그들은 용기를 내어 위험에 맞섰다

—形 1. 용기가 없는; (문제가) 짜임새가 없는 2. (解) 신경이 없는; (植) 엽맥이 없는 3. 냉정한

—副 무기력하게, 배짱 없게

—形 1. 신경의 ¶①신경쇠약 2. 신경질의; 흥분을 잘하는; 안달하는 3. (문체가) 힘찬

熟 …을 근심하다

—副 신경질적으로; 힘차게; 억세게
—名 신경과민; 겁 많음

—形 1. 기골이 장대한; 원기 있는 2. (美口) 뻔뻔스러운, 대담한 3. (英) 신경과민의; 흥분하기 쉬운

—名 1. 둥우리 ¶①한 둥우리의 알/②둥지를 떠나다 2. 보금자리, 안식처 3. (도둑 따위의) 소굴 ¶③산적의 소굴 4. (둥우리 속의 새·벌레의) 떼; 한 배의 새 새끼 —自 둥우리를 틀다; 둥지에 앉다 —他 (새)를 둥우리에 넣다; (새 따위)에 둥우리를 만들어 주다

—名 1. 밑알 2. 비상금; 밑천, 밑돈

—自 기분좋게 드러눕다; 바싹 다가붙다 ¶①산기슭에 자리잡은 절 —他 (머리·얼굴 따위)를 비벼대다

—名 1. 아직 날지 못하는 새 새끼 2. 젖먹이

—名 1. 그물 2. 그물 모양의 것 ¶①모기장/②그물을 던지다/③그물을 치다 3. 덫, 함정 ¶④그는 거짓말에 속아 넘어갔다

—他自 1. 그물을 만들다 2. 그물로 잡다 3. 노력하여 얻다 4. 그물로 덮다; 그물을 치다

net² [net] *adj.* left over after taking away all necessary expenses. ↔gross ¶ ~ *weight*① / ~ *price*② / *a* ~ *profit.*③ —*vt.* (**net·ted, net·ting**) gain (a certain amount) as a net profit. ¶ ~ *£10,000 a year.*④
—[形] 에누리없는; 정미(正味)의 ¶①정미 중량/②정가(正價)/③순이익 —[他] …의 순이익을 올리다 ¶④ 1년에 1만 파운드의 순이익을 올리다

neth·er [néðər] *adj.* (*archaic*) lower. ↔upper ¶*one's* ~ *lip*① / *the* ~ *world.*②
—[形] 아래의 ¶①아랫입술/②지옥

Neth·er·land·er [néðərlændər] *n.* [C] a person of the Netherlands.
—[名] 네덜란드 사람

Neth·er·lands [néðərləndz], **the** *n.* a country in western Europe, also called Holland.
—[名] 네덜란드

net·ting [nétiŋ] *n.* [U] **1.** the act of making nets. **2.** a netted material.
—[名] 1. 그물 뜨기 2. 그물 세공; 그물

net·tle [nétl] *n.* [C] (*Botany*) any wild plant having leaves with stinging hairs. —*vt.* **1.** sting (someone) with a nettle. **2.** make (someone) angry; irritate; annoy.
—[名] 쐐기풀 —[他] 1. …을 쐐기풀로 찌르다 2. …을 안달나게 하다

* **net·work** [nétwə:rk] *n.* **1.** [U] net; netting. ¶*a fine piece of* ~.① **2.** [C] any net-like system of lines, roads, railways, etc. **3.** [C] a group of radio or television stations connected together as a unit. ¶*a radio* ~.
—[名] 1. 그물 세공 ¶①훌륭한 망직물(網織物) 2. 망상(網狀)조직 3. [텔레비전·라디오의] 방송망

neu·ral [n(j)úər(ə)l / njúə-] *adj.* of nerves or the nerve organ.
—[形] 신경[계]의

neu·ral·gia [n(j)u(ə)rældʒə / nju(ə)-] *n.* [U] a sharp pain in the nerves along the course of a nerve.
—[名] 신경증

neu·ro·ses [njuróusi:z / njuə-] *n.* pl. of **neurosis.**

neu·ro·sis [n(j)u(ə)róusis / nju(ə)-] *n.* [C] [U] (pl. **-ses**) (*Medicine*) a mental or nervous disorder or disease.
—[名] 《醫》 신경증, 노이로오제

neu·rot·ic [n(j)u(ə)rátik / njuərɔ́t-] *adj.* of neurosis. —*n.* [C] a person suffering from neurosis.
—[形] 신경[계]의 —[名] 신경병 환자

neu·ter [n(j)ú:tər / njú:tə] *adj.* **1.** (*Grammar*) neither masculine nor feminine. **2.** (*Botany, Zoology*) without a sexual organ. —*n.* [C] **1.** (*Grammar*) a neuter word or gender. **2.** an animal or a plant without sex.
—[形] 1. 《文法》 중성의 2. 《植·動》 무성(無性)의 —[名] 1. 《文法》 중성 2. 무성 동식물

* **neu·tral** [n(j)ú:trəl / njú:-] *adj.* **1.** taking neither side in a war or quarrel. ¶*a* ~ *state*① / *a* ~ *zone.*② **2.** not belonging to any of the two sides. ¶*a* ~ *opinion.*③ **3.** having no clear and exact quality. ¶*a* ~ *tint.*④ **4.** (*Chemistry*) neither acid nor alkaline; (*Electricity*) neither negative nor positive; (*Zoology*) neuter. —*n.* [C] a country or person that does not take part in a war or quarrel.
—[形] 1. 중립의 ¶①중립국/②중립 지대 2. 중립적인 ¶③불편부당의 의견 3. 분명하지 않은 ¶④엷은 햇빛 4. 《化》 중성의; [전기의] 중성의; 《動》 무성의 —[名] 중립국(자)

neu·tral·i·ty [n(j)u:trǽliti / nju:-] *n.* [U] **1.** a country's policy of not taking part in any war between other nations. ¶*strict* ~.① **2.** (*Chemistry*) the state or quality of being neutral.
—[名] 1. 국외(局外) 중립 ¶①엄정 중립 2. 《化》 중성

neu·tral·i·za·tion [n(j)ù:trəlizéiʃ(ə)n / njù:trəlai-] *n.* [U] the act of neutralizing; the state of being neutralized.
—[名] 중립; 중화

neu·tral·ize [n(j)ú:trəlàiz / njú:-] *vt.* **1.** make (a country, etc.) neutral. **2.** (*Chemistry*) destroy the active or clear nature of (something). ¶ ~ *an acid with a base.*① **3.** make (something) inactive. ▷**neu·tral·iz·er** [-ər] *n.*
—[他] 1. [나라 따위]를 중립화하다 2. …을 중화하다 ¶①산(酸)을 알칼리로 중화하다 3. …을 무효로 하다

neu·tron [n(j)ú:trɑn / njù:trɔn] *n.* [C] (*Physics*) one of the basic particles in an atom, having the same mass as a proton.
—[名] 《理》 뉴우트론, 중성자(中性子)

Nev. Nevada.

Ne·va·da [nevǽdə, -vɑ́:-] *n.* a western State of the United States. ⇒[N.B.]
—[名] 네바다주 [N.B.] Nev.로 줄임. 수도 Carson City

Ne·va·dan [nevǽdən, -vɑ́:-] *n.* [C] a person of Nevada.
—[名] 네바다 사람

⁑ **nev·er** [névər] *adv.* **1.** not ever; not at any time. ¶*I have* ~ *heard such a thing.* / *I shall* ~ *forget his kindness.* **2.** not at all. ¶ ~ *say a word* / *Better late than* ~. / *It is* ~ *too late to mend.* / *Never mind.*①
1) ***never so,*** no matter how.
2) ***Well, I never!,*** I'm surprised!
—[副] 1. 일찌기 …없다; 어떤 때에도 …없다 2. 어떤 경우에도 …없다; 조금도(결코) …없다 ¶①괜찮습니다
[熟] 1)가령 …일지라도 2)설마; 정말 놀랐다!

nev·er-end·ing [névəréndiŋ] *adj.* lasting all the time; endless.
—[形] 끝없는

nev·er-fail·ing [névərféiliŋ] *adj.* lasting all the time; that never changes.
—[形] 끝없는; [친절 따위] 변함 없는

N

nev·er·more [nèvərmɔ́:r] *adv.* never again. —働 두 번 다시 …하지 않다

‡**nev·er·the·less** [nèvərðəlés] *adv., conj.* however; in spite of that. ¶ *It was raining;* ~, *we went out.* —働❽ 그럼에도 불구하고

‡**new** [n(j)u: / nju:] *adj.* **1.** not known before; discovered or produced for the first time. ↔old ¶ *a* ~ *invention* / *This information is* ~ *to me.*① **2.** recently made or acquired; fresh. ¶ ~ *milk.* **3.** not used before; not worn out. ¶ ~ *furniture* / *This is as good as* ~.② **4.** beginning again; following that which has gone before. ¶ *lead a* ~ *life*③ / *a* ~ *year* / *a* ~ *moon.*④ **5.** different; changed. ¶ *I feel like a* ~ *man.*⑤ **6.** not familiar; not yet accustomed. ¶ *I am* ~ *to the work.* **7.** modern; recent. ¶ *the* ~ *mode* / *the* ~ *woman.*⑥ ⌈cently.⌉
—*adv.* **1.** again. **2.** (usu. in *compounds*) newly; re-
—® 1. 새로운, 처음 듣는(보는) ¶① 이 이야기는 나로서는 처음이다 2. 새로 생긴; 신선한 3. 새로 만든; 낡지 않은 ¶② 이것은 신품이나 마찬가지다 4. 새로와진; 갱생한; 처음으로 되돌아 간 ¶③ 새 생활로 들어가다 / ④ 초승달 5 이전과 달라진 ¶⑤ 나는 다른 사람 이 된 기분이다 6. 익숙하지 않은 7. 근대적인; 현대풍의 ¶⑥ 신여성
—働 1. 다시 2. 새로이

new·born [n(j)ú:bɔ́:rn / njú:bɔ́:n] *adj.* **1.** recently or just born. ¶ *a* ~ *baby.*① **2.** born again. ¶ ~ *courage.* —® 1. 갓태어난 ¶① 신생아 2. 새로 생긴

new·com·er [n(j)ú:kʌ̀mər / njú:kʌ̀mə] *n.* © a person who has just arrived. ⌈ern United States.⌉ —® 새로 온 사람

New England [⌐ ∠-] *n.* the six States in the northeast- —® 미국 동북부의 6개주

New Eng·land·er [n(j)ù:íŋgləndər / njù:íŋgləndə] *n.* a person of New England. —® 뉴우잉글란드 사람

new·fan·gled [n(j)ú:fǽŋgld / njú:-] *adj.* **1.** of a new fashion; new but somewhat strange. ¶ *a* ~ *idea.*① **2.** fond of newness and strangeness. —® 1. 신기한, 신유행의 ¶① 신기한 생각 2. 신기한 것을 좋아하는

new·fash·ioned [n(j)ú:fǽʃ(ə)nd / njú:-] *adj.* of a new fashion; made in a new style. —® 신유행의

New·found·land [n(j)ú:f(ə)ndlǽnd →2.] *n.* **1.** a large island just off the eastern coast of Canada. **2.** [n(j)u(:)-fáundlənd / nju:-] © a large, long-haired, intelligent dog raised originally in Newfoundland. —® 1. 뉴우펀들란드 섬 2. 뉴우펀들란 드 개(그 섬 원산이며 헤엄을 잘 치는 큰 개)

New Guin·ea [n(j)ù:gíni / njú:-] *n.* a large island, north of Australia, now also called Papua. —® 뉴우기니아 섬

New Jersey [⌐ ∠-] *n.* an eastern State of the United States. ⇒N.B. —® 뉴우저어지 주 N.B. N.J.로 줌임. 수도 Trenton

***new·ly** [n(j)ú:li / njú:-] *adv.* recently; in a new manner or form. ¶ *a newly-built house*① / *a thought* ~ *expressed.*② —働 최근; 새로이 ¶① 신축한 집 / ② 새로운 사상

New Mexico [⌐ ∠--] *n.* a southwestern State of the United States. ⇒N.B. —® 뉴우멕시코 주 N.B. N. Mex., N.M.로 줌임

‡**news** [n(j)u:z / nju:z] *n.* ⓤ **1.** new or recent information. ¶ *a piece of good* ~① / *a* ~ *broadcast.*② **2.** some new or fresh information about something. ¶ *Is there any* ~?③ / *That's quite* ~ *to me.*④ / (*proverb*) *No* ~ *is good* ~.⑤ **3.** (*N-*) a newspaper.
break the news to someone, tell someone bad news.
—® 1. 보도, 뉴우스 ¶① 길보 / ② 뉴우 스 방송 2. 별다른 일; 소식 ¶③ 뭐 별 다른 일이라도 있나? / ④ 이건 처음 듣 는 이야기다 / ⑤ (俚) 무소식이 희소식이 다 3. 신문
熟 …에게 흉보를 전하다

news agency [⌐ ∠--] *n.* a business organization that gathers and supplies news to newspaper offices or publishing houses. ⌈papers or magazines.⌉ —® 통신사

news agent [⌐ ∠-] *n.* (*Brit.*) A person who sells news- —® (英) 신문·잡지 판매인

news·boy [n(j)ú:zbɔ̀i / njú:z-] *n.* © a boy who delivers or sells newspapers. —® 신문팔이, 신문 배달원

news·cast [n(j)ú:zkæ̀st / njú:zkà:st] *vt., vi.* (*U.S.*) broadcast (news) on radio or television. —*n.* © a radio or television program of news reports. —他自 (美) 텔레비전·라디오로 [뉴 우스를] 방송하다 —® 뉴우스 방송

news·man [n(j)ú:zmən / njú:z-] *n.* © (pl. **-men** [-mən]) **1.** a newsboy. **2.** a reporter on a newspaper. —® 1. 신문 배달원(팔이) 2. 신문기자

‡**news·pa·per** [n(j)ú:zpèipər / njú:spèipə] *n.* © a paper which contains daily news, advertisements, and other pieces of information. ¶ *a daily* ~① / *take a* ~.② —® 신문[지] ¶① 일간 신문 / ② 신문 을 구독하다

news·print [n(j)ú:zprìnt / njú:z-] *n.* ⓤ a kind of paper used for newspapers. ⌈showing recent events.⌉ —® 신문용지

news·reel [n(j)ú:zrì:l / njú:z-] *n.* © a motion picture —® 뉴우스 영화

news room [⌐ ∠] *n.* a room where the news is edited or prepared to be broadcast; (*Brit.*) a room where newspapers or magazines can be read. —® (英) 뉴우스 편집실; 신문·잡지 열람실

news·stand [n(j)ú:zstæ̀nd / njú:z-] *n.* [C] (*U.S.*) a stand where newspapers and magazines are sold.
—[名] 《美》 신문·잡지 매점

news·ven·dor [n(j)ú:zvèndər / njú:zvèndə] *n.* [C] a newspaper seller, esp. on the street.
—[名] 거리의 신문팔이

news·y [n(j)ú:zi / njú:zi] *adj.* (**news·i·er, news·i·est**) having much news or gossip. —*n.* [C] (pl. **news·ies**) (*colloq.*) a newsboy.
—[形] 뉴우스가 많은; 화제가 풍부한 —[名] 신문팔이

newt [n(j)u:t / nju:t] *n.* [C] a small animal like a lizard which lives both on land and in water.
—[名] 영원(蠑螈)

∗ **New·ton** [n(j)ú:t(ə)n / njú:-], **Isaac** *n.* (1642–1727) an English scientist and mathematician.
—[名] 영국의 과학자·수학자

New World [∠ ∠], **the** *n.* North and South America. ↔The Old World
—[名] 신세계; 미대륙

⁑ **New York** [∸ ∠] *n.* **1.** an eastern State of the United States. **2.** the largest city in the United States.
—[名] 1. 뉴욕 주 2. 뉴욕 시

New Zea·land [n(j)ù:zí:lənd / njù:-] *n.* a country in the South Pacific. ⇒[N.B.]
—[名] 뉴우지일란드 [N.B.] 수도 Wellington

⁑ **next** [nekst] *adj.* **1.** coming immediately after in time, order, etc. ↔last ¶*~ week* (*month, year*)① / *the ~ week* (*month, year*)② ⇒[usage] / *~ Saturday; on Saturday ~*③ / *on Saturday ~ week*④ / *Who is the ~ man to see me?* **2.** nearest in place or position. ¶*the ~ room* / *a house ~ to ours.* **3.** following immediately in rank, importance, etc.; nearest in relation. ¶*the ~ prize*⑤ / *the person ~ to him in rank.*⑥
1) ***be*** (or ***get***) ***next to,*** (*U.S. colloq.*) be (or get) acquainted with (someone).
2) ***in the next place,*** secondly, thirdly, etc.
3) ***next door,*** [in] the next house.
4) ***next time,*** 《as *conj.*》 at the next time when ....
—*n.* 《usu. *the ~* or *one's ~*》 the next person[s] or thing[s]. ¶*in my ~* [*letter*] / *the ~ of kin.*⑦ —*adv.* in the nearest time, place, etc.; on the next occasion. ¶*the ~ best thing*⑧ / *the largest city ~ to Seoul*⑨ / *Who came ~?*
1) ***next to,*** ⓐ almost. ¶*The flight is ~ to impossible.*⑩ ⓑ beside. ¶*She sat ~ to me.*
2) ***What next!,*** I wonder what will happen next!
—*prep.* beside; nearest to. ¶*the seat ~ mine.*

—[形] 1. 다음의; 이번의 ¶①내주(내월, 내년)/②그 다음 주(달·해) [usage] 현재를 기준으로 한 경우에는 the를 붙이지 않고 과거를 기준으로 한 경우에는 붙임 ¶③다음 토요일/④내주의 토요일 2. 이웃의 3. [가치 따위가] 다음가는; [관계가] 가장 가까운 ¶⑤다음 상(賞)/⑥그에게 다음가는 지위의 사람
[熟] 1)…와 친해지다 2)다음에 3)이웃집[에] 4)다음 번에; 이번에; 다음에 …할 때
—[名] 다음의 사람(것) ¶⑦가장 가까운 친척 —[副] 다음에; 이웃에; 이번은 ¶⑧차선(次善)의 것/⑨서울에 다음가는 도시
[熟] 1)ⓐ거의 ¶⑩비행은 거의 불가능하다 ⓑ…의 다음(이웃)에 2)다음에는 무슨 일이 일어날지
—[前] …의 다음(이웃)에

next-door [nékstdɔ̀:r] *adj.* in the next house. ¶*a ~ neighbor.*①
—[形] 이웃집의 ¶①이웃집 사람

nex·us [néksəs] *n.* [C] (pl. **nex·us** or **~·es**) **1.** a connection; a link. **2.** a connected series or group. **3.** (*Grammar*) a word connected; the relation between a predicate and a subject.
—[名] 1. 유대, 연결; 관계 2. [관념·사물 따위의] 연쇄적 집단 3. 《文法》 넥서스, 서술적 관계[표현]

Ni·ag·a·ra Falls [naiǽg(ə)rəfɔ́:lz] *n.* the falls on the Niagara River, which flows from Lake Erie into Lake Ontario.
—[名] 나이애가라 폭포

nib [nib] *n.* [C] (chiefly. *Brit.*) a pen-point.
—[名] 펜촉

nib·ble [níbl] *vi., vt.* **1.** bite (food, etc.) away a little at a time. **2.** (of fish, etc.) continue to eat (food) by biting off small pieces. 《*~ at* food, etc.》 —*n.* [C] a small bite; the act of nibbling.
—[自][他] 1. [음식 따위를] 조금씩 씹다 2. [물고기가 미끼 따위를] 쪼다 —[名] 조금씩 씹기; [물고기가] 쪼기

⁑ **nice** [nais] *adj.* **1.** pleasing; agreeable; good. ¶*a ~ room* / *~ weather.* **2.** kind; thoughtful. ¶*He is ~ to girls.* / *It is very ~ of you to say so.*① **3.** difficult to explain; minute; delicate. ¶*~ shades of meaning.*② **4.** keen; precise; accurate. ¶*a ~ observer* / *a ~ sense of color* / *He has a ~ ear for music.*③ **5.** (in choice or taste) hard to please; not easily satisfied. ¶*He is ~ in his food.*④ / *She is ~ about the choice of words.* **6.** requiring care or skill. ¶*a ~ problem.* **7.** refined as to manners, language, etc.; well-bred. ¶*Nice people would not say such a thing.* **8.** (*ironical*) difficult; bad; nasty. ¶*a ~ state of affairs*⑤ / *You are a ~ fellow, I must say.*⑥
—[形] 1. 좋은; 기분좋은; 맛있는 2. 친절한 ¶①친절하게 잘 말씀해 주셨읍니다 3. 미세한; 미묘한 ¶②미묘한 의미의 차이 4. 예민한; 치밀한 ¶③그는 음악을 잘 안다 5. [기호(嗜好)가] 까다로운 6. 세심한 주의(기술)를 요하는 7. 고상한, 세련된; 점잖은 8. 《反語》 곤란한; 난처한, 나쁜 ¶④난처한 사태/⑤정말 너는 난처한 녀석이구나

nice-looking [774] **night club**

nice and ..., quite; satisfactorily. ¶ *~ and warm.*
nice-looking [náislúkiŋ] *adj.* having a pretty appearance; agreeable and attractive.
nice·ly [náisli] *adv.* **1.** in a nice manner. **2.** (*colloq.*) satisfactorily; very well. ¶ *The dress will suit her ~.*
ni·ce·ty [náisiti] *n.* (pl. **-ties**) **1.** Ⓤ accuracy. ¶ *the ~ of observation.*① **2.** Ⓒ a very delicate point. ¶ *a ~ of argument.*② **3.** (*pl.*) something refined or elegant.
 1) *to a nicety,* exactly; precisely.
 2) *with great nicety,* very exactly
niche [nitʃ] *n.* Ⓒ **1.** a hollow in a wall to place a statue, vase, etc. in. ⇨fig. **2.** a place suitable for a man or thing. ¶ *He found his ~ in teaching.*①
Nich·o·las [ník(ə)ləs] *n.* **1.** a patron saint of Russians, young people, sailors, etc. **2.** Santa Claus. **3.** a man's name. ⇨N.B.
nick [nik] *n.* Ⓒ a small cut in an edge or surface; a notch. ¶ *a ~ in the rim of a glass*① / *a ~ in a ruler.*② [niche 1.]
 in the nick of time, just in time.
 —*vt.* make a small cut or break in (something). ¶ *~ the tree trunk.* [보통 Old Nick]
Nick [nik] *n.* **1.** a nickname of Nicholas. **2.** the Devil.
• **nick·el** [níkl] *n.* **1.** Ⓤ (*Chemistry*) a hard, silvery-white metallic element. ⇨N.B. ¶ *~ plate*① / *~ silver.*② **2.** Ⓒ (*U.S.*) a coin made of nickel worth 5 cents. ¶ *Would you lend me a ~?* —*vt.* (**-eled, -el·ing** or *Brit.* **-elled, -el·ling**) coat (something) with nickel.
 not worth a nickel, quite worthless.
• **nick·name** [níknèim] *n.* Ⓒ a familiar name given to a person or thing in place of a real name. —*vt.* give a nickname to (someone). [leaves.]
nic·o·tine [níkəti:n] *n.* Ⓤ a poison, found in tobacco
: **niece** [ni:s] *n.* Ⓒ the daughter of one's brother or sister. ↔nephew
Ni·ge·ri·a [naidʒíəriə] *n.* a country in West Africa.
nig·gard [nígərd] *n.* Ⓒ a person who is mean in money matters; a person who does not want to spend money for any purpose; a miser. —*adj.* mean in money matters; miserly.
nig·ger [nígər] *n.* Ⓒ (*colloq.*) **1.** a Negro. ⇨N.B. **2.** a member of the black-skinned race. ¶ *a ~ melody*
• **nigh** [nai] *adj., adv.* (**nigh·er** or *archaic* **near, nigh·est** or *archaic* **next**) (*archaic, poetic*) near; nearly.
: **night** [nait] *n.* Ⓒ **1.** the time between evening and morning, or sunset and sunrise. ↔day ¶ *a dirty ~*① / *at nights*② / *by ~*③ / *in the ~* / *last ~.* **2.** Ⓤ the darkness of night; the dark. ¶ *under cover of ~*④ / *She went out into the ~.* **3.** a state or time somewhat like night. ¶ *the long ~ of the Middle Ages.*⑤
 1) *all night* [*long*]; *all the night,* throughout the whole
 2) *have a good night,* sleep well. [night.]
 3) *make a night of it,* spend the night in enjoyment.
 4) *night after night; night by night,* every night.
 5) *night and day,* always; continuously.
 6) *o'night,* (*slang*) at night; during the night.
 7) *turn night into day,* do at night what is usu. done during the day. [worn in bed.]
night clothes [⌐⌐] *n. pl.* any kind of clothes to be
night club [⌐⌐] *n.* a place where people can drink, eat, and enjoy dancing or watching a floor show till late

🈺 충분히, 말할 나위 없이
—🈺 예쁜; 애교 있는

—🈺 1. 기분좋게; 훌륭하게 2. (口) 꼭, 정확히; 잘
—🈺 1. 정확한 ¶①관찰의 정밀한 2. 미세한 점 ¶②미묘한 논점 3. 품위있는(·우아한) 것
🈺 1)정확히 2)아주 정확하게

—🈺 1. 벽의 움푹한 데 2. 알맞은 자리, 적소 ¶①그는 교직이라는 알맞은 직업을 찾았다

—🈺 1. 성(聖) 니콜라스 2. 산타 클로오스 3. 남자 이름 N.B. 애칭 Nick

—🈺 새긴(벤) 금; [그릇의] 이 빠진 곳 ¶①잔 가장자리의 이 빠진 곳/② 자의 새김눈
🈺 아슬아슬한 때에
—🈺 …에 새김눈을 내다
—🈺 1. Nicholas의 애칭 2. 악마 N.B.
—🈺 1. (化) 니켈 N.B. 기호 Ni ¶①니켈 도금(鍍金)/②양은 2. (美) 5센트백통전 —🈺 …을 니켈로 도금하다

🈺 한푼의 가치도 없다
—🈺 별명; 애칭 —🈺 …에 별명을 붙이다

—🈺 니코틴
—🈺 조카딸

—🈺 나이지리아 연방

—🈺 구두쇠 —🈺 인색한

—🈺 (口) 1. 흑인 N.B. 경멸적으로 쓰임 2. 흑색 토인 ¶ *a ~ melody*

—🈺🈺 가까이의(에)

—🈺 1. 밤, 저녁 ¶①비오는 밤/②밤이면 밤마다/③밤에는 2. 어둠, 야음 ¶④야음을 틈타다 3. 암흑의 시대(상태)(침체·무지·불행·죽음 따위) ¶⑤중세의 긴 암흑시대

🈺 1)밤새도록 2)잘 자다 3)늦게까지 떠들다; 술 마시며 밤새우다 4)매일밤 5)밤이고, 낮이고, 언제나 6)밤에 7)낮에 해야 할 일을 밤에 하다

—🈺 잠옷
—🈺 나이트 클럽

at night.

night·dress [náitdrès] *n.* [C][U] a kind of night clothes.
—[名] 잠옷

night·fall [náitfɔ̀:l] *n.* [U] the coming of evening. ↔daybreak.
—[名] 땅거미, 저녁때

night·gown [náitgàun] *n.* [C] a long, loose dress for women or children, usu. worn in bed.
—[名] [부인·아동용의] 잠옷

night·hawk [náithɔ̀:k] *n.* [C] **1.** a kind of American bird that flies and feeds at night. **2.** (*colloq.*) a person who works, studies, or goes about till late at night.
—[名] 1. 북미산의 쏙독새의 일종 2. 밤에 일하는 사람; 밤에 나다니는 사람

night·in·gale [náitiŋgèil, +*U.S.* -t(ə)n-] *n.* [C] (*Brit.*) a small, reddish-brown bird, the males of which sing sweetly.
—[名] 《英》 지빠귀과의 작은 철새

night·long [náitlɔ̀:ŋ / -lɔ̀ŋ] *adj.* lasting through the night. ¶*a ~ festivity.*① —*adv.* throughout the night.
—[形] 철야의 ¶①철야의 축제 —[副] 철야로

night·ly [náitli] *adj.* of the night; happening or done every night. —*adv.* every night. ¶*We gathered ~ to talk over the matter.*①
—[形] 밤의; 밤마다의 —[副] 밤마다 ¶①그 문제를 의논하러 밤마다 모였다

night·mare [náitmɛ̀ər] *n.* [C] **1.** a terrible dream. ¶*have a ~.*① **2.** a terrible fear; a terrible experience.
—[名] 1. 악몽 ¶①악몽을 꾸다 2. 공포; 악몽 같은 경험

night school [⌐ ⌐] *n.* an evening school for persons who work during the day. ↔day school
—[名] 야간 학교

night shift [⌐ ⌐] *n.* the night-work hours in a factory; (*collectively*) the laborers who work at night. ¶*work on the ~.*
—[名] [주야 교대의] 야근; 야근자

night·shirt [náitʃə:rt] *n.* [C] a long, loose dress like a shirt worn by men or boys in bed.
—[名] [남자용의] 잠옷

night·time [náittàim] *n.* [U] the period of darkness between sunset and sunrise.
—[名] 야간

night train [⌐ ⌐] *n.* a train that runs at night.
—[名] 야간 열차

night·walk·er [náitwɔ̀:kər] *n.* [C] **1.** a person who moves around asleep at night. **2.** a person who walks about at night, such as a thief or someone with other bad purposes.
—[名] 1. 몽유병자 2. [매춘부·도둑 등] 밤에 나다니는 사람

night watch [⌐ ⌐] *n.* **1.** the act of guarding during the night.; a person who is on guard at night. **2.** the period when such a guard is kept.
—[名] 1. 야간 경계; 야경꾼 2. 야경의 근무시간

night watchman [⌐ ⌐-] *n.* a watchman who is on duty during the night.
—[名] 야경꾼, 야간 감시인

ni·hil·ism [náiəlìz(ə)m, níhə- / nái(h)il-] *n.* [U] **1.** the complete denial of the meaning of existence. **2.** the belief of certain Russian revolutionaries, which was against all authority; violent revolutionary beliefs.
—[名] 1. 허무주의 2. [일반적으로] 폭력 혁명 주의

ni·hil·ist [náiəlist, níhə- / nái(h)il-] *n.* [C] **1.** a person who believes in nihilism. **2.** a person who believes in violent revolution; a terrorist.
—[名] 1. 허무주의자 2. 폭력 혁명 주의자

ni·hil·is·tic [nàiəlístik, nìhə- / nài(h)ilís-] *adj.* of nihilism or a nihilist.
—[形] 허무주의[자]의; 혁명주의[자]의

nil [nil] *n.* [U] zero; a score of nothing; none at all. ⇒[N.B.] ¶*four goals to ~.*①
—[名] 영(零), 무 [N.B.] 경기의 득점에 쓰임 ¶①4 대 0

Nile [nail], **the** *n.* a great river in eastern Africa flowing through Egypt into the Mediterranean.
—[名] 나일강

nim·bi [nímbai] *n.* pl. of **nimbus**.

nim·ble [nímbl] *adj.* **1.** quick and swift in movement. ¶*He is ~ on his feet.*① / *She is ~ in her service.*② **2.** quick in understanding. ¶*a ~ mind.*③
—[形] 1. 날랜, 빠른 ¶①그는 발이 빠르다/②그녀는 재치있게 일한다 2. 이해가 빠른 ¶③예민한 마음

nim·bus [nímbəs] *n.* [C] (pl. **-bus·es** or **-bi**) **1.** a ring of light around the head of a saint or god in a picture; a halo. **2.** a rain cloud.
—[名] 1. [그리스도·불상(佛像) 따위의] 후광(後光), 광륜(光輪) 2. 비구름

‡**nine** [nain] *n.* **1.** [U] the number between eight and ten; 9. **2.** [C] any group or set of nine persons or things, esp. a baseball team.
—[名] 1. 아홉, 9 2. 아홉 개(사람) 한 벌(일조); 야구 티임

dressed* [*up*] *to the nines, (*colloq.*) dressed very smartly and gorgeously.
[熟] 《口》 성장(盛裝)하여

—*adj.* of 9. ¶*a ~ days' wonder*① / *~ times out of ten.*②
—[形] 9의 ¶①한때의 소문/②십중팔구

nine·fold [náinfòuld] *adj., adv.* **1.** nine times as much or as many. **2.** having nine parts.
—[形][副] 1. 9배의(로) 2. 아홉 겹의(으로)

nine·pins [náinpìnz] *n. pl.* ((used as *sing.*)) a game played with nine bottle-shaped wooden pins and a ball. ⇨fig. ¶*fall over like a lot of ~*.[1]

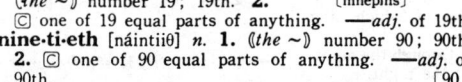
[ninepins]

: nine·teen [náintí:n] *n.* Ⓤ the number between eighteen and twenty; 19. ——*adj.* of 19.

: nine·teenth [náintí:nθ] *n.* **1.** ((*the ~*)) number 19; 19th. **2.** Ⓒ one of 19 equal parts of anything. ——*adj.* of 19th.

: nine·ti·eth [náintiiθ] *n.* **1.** ((*the ~*)) number 90; 90th. **2.** Ⓒ one of 90 equal parts of anything. ——*adj.* of 90th.

: nine·ty [náinti] *n.* Ⓒ nine times of ten; 90. ——*adj.* of

: ninth [nainθ] *n.* **1.** ((*the ~*)) number 9; 9th. **2.** Ⓒ one of 9 equal parts of anything. ——*adj.* of 9th.

Ni·o·be [náiəbi(:) / -bi] *n.* **1.** (in Greek mythology) a mother whose fourteen children were killed and herself was turned into a stone from which tears flow forever. **2.** Ⓒ a woman who weeps for her lost children.

nip[1] [nip] *v.* (**nipped, nip·ping**) *vt.* **1.** press or pinch (something) tight with the fingers; bite. **2.** (of frost, wind, etc.) hurt; injure. ¶*~ buds on a plant*.[1] **3.** cut off the end of (something) by biting. **4.** stop the growth of (something). **5.** (*colloq.*) catch suddenly and rudely. ——*vi.* **1.** pinch by the fingers; bite. **2.** (of wind) cause pain on the skin. **3.** (*Brit.*) move off
1) *nip along*, go hurriedly.⌐quickly.⌐
2) *nip in*, ⓐ enter hurriedly. ⓑ press oneself into (something) by force. ⌐ginning.⌐
3) *nip in the bud*, stop (something) in the very be-⌐
4) *nip and tuck*, (*U.S. colloq.*) even or close in a contest or race. ⌐cold.⌐
——*n.* Ⓒ **1.** a tight pinch; a sudden bite. **2.** a sharp

nip[2] [nip] *n.* Ⓒ a small amount of liquor. ——*vi., vt.* drink a little (liquor). ⌐breaking wire; pincers.⌐

nip·pers [nípərz] *n. pl.* a tool for nipping, bending, and

nip·ple [nípl] *n.* Ⓒ **1.** the pointed part of a breast through which milk is given. **2.** the rubber mouthpiece of a baby's milk bottle.

Nip·pon [nipán, ⌐- / nípɔn] *n.* =Japan.

Nip·pon·ese [nìpəní:z] *adj., n.* =Japanese.

nir·va·na, Nir- [niərvá:nə, +*U.S.* nərvǽnə] *n.* Ⓤ (*Buddhism*) a state of perfect happiness gained by devoting oneself to the supreme spirit.

Ni·sei [ní:séi] *n.* Ⓒ ((used as *pl.* and *sing.*)) a native American citizen whose parents are or were Japanese.

ni·ter, *Brit.* **-tre** [náitər] *n.* Ⓤ a white crystalline salt used in making gunpowder. ▷**ni·tric** [-trik] *adj.*

ni·trate [náitreit] *n.* ⒸⓊ a salt of nitric acid.

• **ni·tro·gen** [náitrədʒ(ə)n] *n.* Ⓤ a gas without color and smell which forms four-fifths of the air. ⌐nitrogen.⌐

ni·trog·e·nous [naitrádʒinəs / -trɔ́dʒ-] *adj.* of or having

ni·tro·glyc·er·in, -ine [nàitrouglís(ə)ri(:)n] *n.* Ⓤ a thick, oily explosive used in dynamite.

: no [nou] *adj.* **1.** not a; not any. ¶*There is ~ ink in the bottle.* / *He has ~ brother(s).* / *No stars can be seen tonight.* / *I saw ~ children in the park.* / *No other boy could do it.* **2.** not at all; far from being. ¶*It was ~ small loss.*[1] / *He is ~ scholar.*[2] **3.** ((as a prohibition)) ¶*No smoking.* / *No credit.*[3] / *No admission.*
There is no doing., It is impossible to do.
——*adv.* **1.** ((expressing denial, refusal, disagreement))

——⊛ 구주희(九柱戲) ¶①차례로 모조리 쓰러지다

——⊛ 19 ——㉠ 19의

——⊛ 1. 제 19 2.19분의 1 ——㉠ 제 19의; 19분의 1의

——⊛ 1.제 90 2.90분의 1 ——㉠ 제 90의; 90분의 1의

——⊛ 90 ——㉠ 90의
——⊛ 1.아홉째의 2.9분의 1 ——㉠ 아홉째의; 9분의 1의
——⊛ 1.니오베 2.자식을 잃고 비탄에 잠기는 여자

——㉠ 1.…을 꼬집다; 깨물다 2.[바람·서리가 싹 따위]를 시들게 하다; 얼게 하다 ¶①나무의 싹을 말라 죽이다 2.…을 따다 4.…의 성장을 저해하다 5.(口) …을 잡아채다 ——㉡ 1.꼬집다; 깨물다 2.[바람 따위가] 살을 에다 3.(英) 서두르다
図 1)급히 가다 2)ⓐ급히 들어가다 ⓑ…에 억지로 끼어들다 3)…을 미연에 막다 4)(美口)막상막하[의], 백중지세[로]

——⊛ 1. 꼬집기; 깨물기 2. [바람·추위 따위] 살을 에는 듯함
——⊛ [술의] 한 잔; 소량 ——自他 [술을] 조금씩 마시다
——⊛ 못뽑이,집게,뻰찌
——⊛ 1.젖꼭지 2.[우윳병의] 고무 꼭지

——⊛ [불교의] 열반(涅槃); 더할 나위 없는 행복

——⊛ [일본계의] 이세(二世)

——⊛ 질산 칼슘; 칠레 초석(硝石)

——⊛ 질산염; 질산 소오다(비료용)
——⊛ 질소

——㉠ 질소의
——⊛ 니트로글리세린

——㉠ 1.[사람·물건]이 없는; 한 사람 (하나,조금)도 없는 2.결코 …아닌 ¶①결코 작은 손실이 아니었다/②그는 결코 학자는 아니다 3.…금지 ¶③以上 사절

※ …하기는 도저히 불가능하다
——㉰ 1.아니오 usage 물음에 관계없이

No. [777] **nod**

not so. ⇒Usage ¶"*Can you swim?*" "*No [, I can't].*" / "*Can't you swim?*" "*No [, I can't].*" / "*Get out of the room.*" "*No, I'll never go out.*" **2.** (used with comparative) not any. ¶*He is ~ better than a beggar.*④
1) *no less than*, as much as. ⌈*his.*⑤
2) *no less...than*, as...as. ¶*He is ~ less careful than*
3) *no sooner...than*, as soon as.... ¶*No sooner had he arrived than he fell ill.*⑥
4) *whether or no*, in either case.
—*n.* ⓒ (pl. **noes** or **nos**) **1.** a word used to deny, refuse, or disagree. **2.** a negative vote or voter. ↔aye; yea **3.** a denial; a refusal.

No. 1. north; northern. **2.** number.

No·ah [nóuə] *n.* (in the Bible) the man who survived the Flood with his family and a pair of each animal by means of a big box-like ship.

nob [nɑb / nɔb] *n.* ⓒ (*colloq.*) **1.** a head. **2.** a person of wealth or high rank in society.

No·bel [noubél], **Alfred Bernhard** *n.* (1833–1896) a Swedish inventor of dynamite and the founder of the Nobel prizes.

Nobel prizes [´- ´-] *n. pl.* the five prizes given every year by the Nobel Foundation to those who have done great work in physics, chemistry, literature, medicine and the advancement of peace.

****no·bil·i·ty** [noubíliti] *n.* Ⓤ **1.** the state of being noble in character or mind. **2.** the high rank of a person. ¶*a man of ~ / the ~ of gold.*① **3.** (*the ~, collectively*) people of high rank and noble birth; the whole body of noblemen. ⇒N.B.

:no·ble [nóubl] *adj.* **1.** great and pure in mind or character. ¶*a man of ~ character.*① **2.** high in social rank or title by birth. ¶*a ~ family.*② **3.** very splendid; grand. ¶*a ~ cathedral.* **4.** (of metal) precious. ↔base ¶*~ metals.*③ —*n.* ⓒ a person of high rank by birth; a peer. ⌈pearance.⌉

no·ble-look·ing [nóubllúkiŋ] *adj.* having a noble ap-

no·ble·man [nóublmən] *n.* ⓒ (pl. **-men** [-mən]) a man of noble rank, title or birth. ⌈mind.⌉

no·ble-mind·ed [nóublmáindid] *adj.* great and noble in

no·ble-mind·ed·ness [nóublmáindidnis] *n.* Ⓤ the state of being great and noble in mind.

no·ble·ness [nóublnis] *n.* Ⓤ the state of being noble.

no·blesse [noublés] *n.* Ⓤ **1.** noble birth. **2.** (*collectively*) the nobility.

no·ble·wom·an [nóublwùmən] *n.* ⓒ (pl. **-wom·en** [-wìmin]) a woman of the nobility. ⌈like a noble.⌉

no·bly [nóubli] *adv.* in a noble way; with a noble mind;

:no·bod·y [nóubɑ̀di, -bʌ̀di, bədi / -bədi, -bɔ̀di] *pron.* no one.
—*n.* ⓒ (pl. **-bod·ies**) (often *sing.* without *an article*) a man of no importance. ¶*I felt ~ in the presence of him.*①

noc·tur·nal [nɑktə́:rnl / nɔk-] *adj.* **1.** of the night. ¶*a ~ journey.*① **2.** active or busy at night. ¶*~ birds.*② **3.** (of flowers) open at night.

noc·tur·nal·ly [nɑktə́:rnəli / nɔk-] *adv.* at night.

noc·turne [nɑ́ktə:rn / nɔ́k-] *n.* ⓒ **1.** a dreamy piece music fit for night. **2.** a painting of a night scene.

:nod [nɑd / nɔd] *v.* (**nod·ded, nod·ding**) *vi.* **1.** bend the head forward slightly and quickly, as in agreement, greeting, etc. **2.** allow the head to bend forward sometimes from sleepiness. ¶*sit nodding.*① **3.** become careless and dull; make a careless mistake. ¶*Even Homer sometimes nods.*② **4.** swing or move quickly. ¶*Trees ~ in the wind.*③ —*vt.* **1.** bend (the head) forward

이 대답의 내용이 부정이면 no, 긍정이면 yes를 씀 **2.** 조금도 ···이 아니다 ¶④거지보다 조금도 나을 게 없다

熟 1) ···만큼이나 2) ···에 못지않게 ··· ¶⑤그는 형에 못지않게 조심성이 있다 3) ···하자마자 곧 ¶⑥그는 도착하자마자 곧 병에 걸렸다 4) 어느 쪽이라도

—名 1. 부정(거부)하는 말 2. 반대표; 반대 투표자 3. 부정; 거부

—名 노아

—名 ⌈口⌋ 1. 머리 2. 고관, 부자, 귀인

—名 스웨덴의 발명가·노오벨상의 창설자

—名 노오벨상

—名 1. 고결함 2. 고귀한 신분 ¶①금의 고귀성 3. 귀족계급; 귀족 N.B. 영국에서 쓰이는 칭호는 duke, marquis, earl, viscount, baron

—形 1. 고귀한 ¶①고결한 품성의 사람 2. 신분이 높은 ¶②귀족 3. 웅대한; 장엄한 4. 귀중한 ¶③귀금속
—名 귀족

—形 풍채가 있는
—名 귀족

—形 마음이 고결한
—名 고결함

—名 고결, 고귀
—名 1. 귀족 2. 귀족계급

—名 귀족 부인

—副 고귀하게
—代 아무도 ···않다 —名 보잘것 없는 사람 ¶①나는 그의 앞에서는 위축됐다

—形 1. 밤의 ¶①밤 여행 2. 밤에 활동하는 ¶②야행성(夜行性)의 조류 3. [꽃이] 밤에 피는
—副 밤에
—名 1. 야상곡(夜想曲) 2. 야경화(夜景畫)

—自 1. 머리를 숙이다; 끄덕이다; 묵례하다 2. [꾸벅거려서] 구벅거리다 ¶①앉은 채 졸다 3. 깜박 잊다; 실수하다 ¶②원숭이도 나무에서 떨어질 때가 있다 4. [나무 따위가] 흔들리다. 끄떡이다 ¶③나무들이 바람에 흔들린다 —他 1. [머리]를 끄덕이게 하다 2. 끄덕여서

node

slightly and quickly. ¶ ~ *the head.* **2.** express (agreement, etc.) by nodding. ¶ ~ *thanks*① / *He nodded a greeting to me.*
have a nodding acquaintance with, know (someone) slightly but not as a friend.
—*n.* ⓒ an act of nodding the head. ¶ *answer with a* ~ / *the land of Nod*② / *He gave me a* ~ *when he came in.*
···을 나타내다 ¶①끄덕여서 고마움을 나타내다

🌑 묵례를 주고받는 사이다
—名 끄덕임; 묵례; 졸음 ¶⑤졸음

node [noud] *n.* ⓒ **1.** (*Botany*) the part of a stem from which leaves come out. **2.** a knot; a round mass.
—名 1. 〔植〕〔줄기가 나는〕마디 2. 매듭; 옹이, 혹

nod·ule [nádʒu:l / nɔ́dju:l] *n.* ⓒ **1.** a small round mass, knot or swelling. **2.** (*Botany*) a small knot on a stem or root.
—名 1. 작은 마디; 작은 혹 2. 〔植〕 결절(結節)

no·ël [nouél] *n.* **1.** ⓒ a Christmas carol. **2.** (*N-*) Christmas.
—名 1. 크리스마스 축가 2. 크리스마스

‡noise [nɔiz] *n.* ⓤⓒ **1.** a confused and unpleasant sound. ¶ *far from the city* ~.① **2.** a sound.
—名 1. 소음 ¶①도시의 소음에서 떠나서 2. 소리

1) **make a noise,** make a sound; complain about something.
2) **make a noise in the world,** become famous.
—*vt.* (*rare*) spread a rumor about (someone or something).
🌑 1) 떠들다, 불평하다 2) 평판이 나다

—他 ···의 평판(소문)을 내다

It is noised abroad that..., The rumor says...; It is said that...
🌑 ···이라는 소문이 자자하다

* **noise·less** [nɔ́izlis] *adj.* making no noise; quiet; silent. ¶ *a* ~ *typewriter*① / *a* ~ *revolver.*②
—形 소리가 나지 않는 ¶①소리가 나지 않는 타자기 / ②소음(消音) 권총

noise·less·ly [nɔ́izlisli] *adv.* silently; quietly.
—副 조용히

noise·less·ness [nɔ́izlisnis] *n.* ⓤ the state of being silent or quiet.
—名 소리가 나지 않음

nois·i·ly [nɔ́izili] *adv.* in a noisy manner.
—副 시끄럽게

nois·i·ness [nɔ́izinis] *n.* ⓤ the state of being noisy.
—名 시끄러움

‡nois·y [nɔ́izi] *adj.* (**nois·i·er, nois·i·est**) **1.** making much noise. **2.** full of confused and unpleasant sound. ¶ ~ *children*① / *a* ~ *street.*②
—形 1. 시끄러운 2. 떠들썩한 ¶①시끄러운 아이들 / ②떠들썩한 거리

no·mad [nóumæd / -məd] *n.* ⓒ **1.** a member of a tribe that moves about from one place to another, such as the Arabs or gypsies. **2.** a wanderer. —*adj.* **1.** moving about from place to place. **2.** wandering in search of pasture.
—名 1. 유랑민 2. 방랑자 —形 1. 방랑의 2. 유목(遊牧)의

no·mad·ic [noumædik] *adj.* =nomad.

no·men·cla·ture [nóumənklèitʃər, nouménklətʃər] *n.* ⓒ **1.** a system of names or words, esp. in the classification of the sciences. **2.** the special words and phrases used to explain things in the various sciences; terminology.
—名 1. [여러가지 과학 분류학상의] 명명법 2. 학술 용어

nom·i·nal [námɪnl / nɔ́m-] *adj.* **1.** not real; existing only in name. ↔real ¶ *a* ~ *king.*① **2.** of name. ¶ *a* ~ *list.*② **3.** very small in number, etc.; hardly worth counting. ¶ *a bird of* ~ *species.*③ **4.** (*Grammar*) of a noun; noun-like.
—形 1. 이름만의 ¶①유명무실한 왕 2. 명칭상의 ¶②명부 3. 아주 적은 ¶③아주 드문 새 4. 〔文法〕 명사[명-법]의

nom·i·nal·ly [námɪnəli / nɔ́m-] *adv.* in name only; by name.
—副 이름뿐으로; 명의상

* **nom·i·nate** [námɪnèit / nɔ́m-] *vt.* **1.** name (someone) as a candidate for election, etc. **2.** appoint (someone) to an office. 《 someone *for* a mayor, presidency, etc.》
—他 1. [후보자에] ···을 추천하다 2. [관직에] ···을 지명하다

* **nom·i·na·tion** [nàmɪnéiʃ(ə)n / nɔ̀m-] *n.* ⓤⓒ the act of nominating. ¶ ~ *for President.*①
—名 추천(지명) ¶①대통령의 지명

nom·i·na·tive [námɪnətiv / nɔ́m-] *adj.* **1.** (*Grammar*) showing the subject of a verb. ¶ *the* ~ *case.*① **2.** named or appointed for election or a position. —*n.* ⓒ (*Grammar*) a nominative case.
—形 1. 주격의 ¶①주격 2. 지명(추천)된 —名 주격

nom·i·nee [nàmɪníː / nɔ̀m-] *n.* ⓒ a person who is nominated.
—他 피(被)추천자

non- [nan- / nɔn-] *pref.* ⇨usage **1.** no; not: *nonprofessional* (=not professional). **2.** nothing; without: *nonsense* (=talk without sense). **3.** lacking; before: *nonage* (=before the legal age)
—(接頭) usage 명사·형용사·부사와 함께 쓰임 1. 무(無); 비(非) 2. 결여

nonce [nans / nɔns] *n.* 《*the* ~》 the present occasion.
for the nonce, for the time being.
—名 방금, 당분간
🌑 당분간

non·cha·lance [nánʃəl(ə)ns / nɔ́n-] *n.* ⓤ the state of being nonchalant.
—名 무관심; 냉정

non·cha·lant [nánʃ(ə)lənt / nɔ́n-] *adj.* **1.** showing lack
—形 1. 무관심한 2. 냉정한 ¶①아무렇

of interest; indifferent. **2.** unexcited; without eagerness. ¶*with a ~ air.*① [lant manner.]
non·cha·lant·ly [nánʃ(ə)ləntli / nɔ́n-] *adv.* in a noncha-
non·com·bat·ant [nɑnkámbət(ə)nt / nɔnkɔ́m-] *n.* ⓒ a person in a war or an army who does not actually fight in battle, such as a surgeon or nurse. ——*adj.* of noncombatants.
non·com·mis·sioned [nɑ̀nkəmíʃ(ə)nd / nɔ̀n-] *adj.* not yet appointed to the rank of second lieutenant. ¶*a ~ officer.*①
non·com·mit·tal [nɑ̀nkəmítl / nɔ̀n-] *adj.* giving no clear opinions or purposes. ¶*a ~ reply.*①
non·con·duc·tor [nɑ̀nkəndʌ́ktər / nɔ̀nkəndʌ́ktə] *n.* ⓒ (*Physics*) anything that does not let heat, electricity, etc. pass easily through.
non·con·form·ist [nɑ̀nkənfɔ́:rmist / nɔ̀n-] *n.* ⓒ **1.** a person who does not agree with accepted church belief. **2.** (*N-*) a Protestant who does not belong to the Church of England.
non·de·script [nándiskrìpt / nɔ́n-] *adj.* hard to describe; not clear. ¶*a row of ~ humble houses.*① ——*n.* ⓒ a nondescript person or thing.
⁞ none [nʌn] *pron.* **1.** ⦅used as *pl.* and *sing.*⦆ no one. ¶*There were* (or *was*) *~ present.*① / *None of them has* (or *have*) *come.* **2.** not any; nothing. ¶*He has much money, but I have ~.* / *There is ~ of the water left.* ——*adv.* not at all; never. ¶*He is ~ the better for the medicine.*② / *The price is ~ too high.*③ / *I slept ~ last* ⌐
none the less, nevertheless.   ⌊*night.*⌐
non·en·ti·ty [nɑnéntiti / nɔn-] *n.* ⓒ (pl. *-ties*) **1.** a person or thing of no importance. **2.** a thing that does not exist.
non·es·sen·tial [nɑ̀nesénʃ(ə)l / nɔ̀n-] *adj.* not necessary; not very important. ——*n.* ⓒ a person or thing that is not essential.
none·the·less [nʌ̀nðəlés] *adv.* however; nevertheless.
non·ex·ist·ence [nɑ̀nigzíst(ə)ns / nɔ̀n-] *n.* Ⓤ **1.** the state of not existing. **2.** a thing that does not exist.
non·ex·ist·ent [nɑ̀nigzíst(ə)nt / nɔ̀n-] *adj.* not present; not living in the world.
non·in·flam·ma·ble [nɑ̀ninflǽməbl / nɔ̀n-] *adj.* not easily set on fire; very hard to burn.
non·in·ter·fer·ence [nɑ̀nintərfíər(ə)ns / nɔ̀nintəfíər-] *n.* Ⓤ the act of not taking part in other countries' affairs.
non·in·ter·ven·tion [nɑ̀nintərvénʃ(ə)n / nɔ̀nintə(:)-] *n.* Ⓤ a policy of a country holding back from interference in the affairs of other countries.
non·me·tal·lic [nɑ̀nmetǽlik / nɔ́n-] *adj.* not metallic.
non·pay·ment [nɑnpéimənt / nɔ́npéi-] *n.* Ⓤ neglect to pay; the condition of being unpaid.
non·plus [nɑ́nplʌ́s, ╌ / nɔ́nplʌ́s, ╌] *vt.* (**-plused, -plus·ing** or *Brit.* **-plussed, -plus·sing**) cause (someone) to be completely puzzled or perplexed. ——*n.* ⓒ a state of being nonplus. ¶*be* (or *stand*) *at a ~.*①
put someone to a nonplus, perplex someone completely.
non·res·i·dent [nɑnrézid(ə)nt / nɔ́n-] *adj.* not living in a particular place; living away from one's place of work. ——*n.* ⓒ a nonresident person.
non·re·sist·ant [nɑ̀nrizíst(ə)nt / nɔ̀n-] *adj.* making no resistance; not opposing. ——*n.* ⓒ a person who never opposes constituted authority or force.
• **non·sense** [nɑ́nsens / nɔ́ns(ə)ns] *n.* Ⓤ **1.** foolish or meaningless words or actions. ¶*sheer ~*① / *talk ~.* **2.** acts or things of little worth.

지도 않게

—働 무관심하게
—图 비전투원 —働 비전투원의

—働 [장교로] 임명되지 않은 ¶①[육군의] 하사관

—働 언질을 주지 않는; 애매한 ¶① 분명치 않은 대답
—图 [열·전기의] 절연체

—图 1. 준봉(遵奉)하지 않는 사람 2. [영국의] 비국교도

—働 정체를 모를 ¶①정체 모를 초라한 집들 —图 정체 모를 사람(것)

—代 1. 아무도 …않다 ¶①아무도 없었다 2. 조금도 …않다 —働 조금도 …않다 ¶②그는 약 쓴 것치고는 조금도 특히 좋아지지 않았다/③그 값은 결코 비싸지 않다

熟 그럼에도 불구하고
—图 1. 보잘것 없는 사람(것) 2. 실재(在實)하지 않는 것

—働 반드시 필요하지는 않은; 비본질적인 —图 중요하지 않는 것(사람)

—働 그럼에도 불구하고
—图 1. 무(無) 2. 존재하지 않는 것

—働 존재하지 않는

—働 불가연성(不可燃性)의

—图 [외교상의] 불간섭

—图 [외교상의] 불간섭

—働 비금속의
—图 지불하지 않음

—働 …을 당황하게 하다 —图 당황 ¶①당황하고 있다

熟 …을 어찌할 바를 모르게 하다
—働 […에] 살지 않는; 임지(任地)에 없는 —图 비거주자; 임지에 없는 사람
—働 무저항의 —图 무저항 주의자

—图 1. 어리석은(무의미한) 말(행동) ¶①터무니없는 소리 2. 하찮을 없는 행위(것)

non·sen·si·cal [nɑnsénsik(ə)l / nɔn-] *adj.* foolish; full of nonsense. ▷**non·sen·si·cal·ly** [-kəli] *adv.*
—[形] 얼토당토않은; 무의미한

non·stop [nάnstάp / nɔ́nstɔ́p] *adj., adv.* without a stop.
—[形][副] 도중에서 멎지 않는(않고)

non·un·ion [nɑnjú:niən / nɔn-] *adj.* **1.** not belonging to a labor union. **2.** not recognizing a labor union.
—[形] 1. 노동조합에 가입하지 않은 2. 노동조합을 인정하지 않는

noo·dle[1] [nú:dl] *n.* 《usu. *pl.*》 a food like macaroni used in soup, etc.
—[名] 국수(수우프에 넣어 먹음)

noo·dle[2] [nú:dl] *n.* Ⓒ **1.** (*colloq.*) a fool. **2.** (*slang*) the head.
—[名] 1.《口》 바보 2.《俗》 머리

nook [nuk] *n.* Ⓒ **1.** an inside angle or corner. **2.** a sheltered place.
—[名] 1. 구석 2. 구석진 곳

look in every nook and corner, look everywhere.
[熟] 샅샅이 뒤지다

⁑**noon** [nu:n] *n.* Ⓤ **1.** twelve o'clock in the daytime; the middle of the day. ¶*at ~.*① **2.** 《usu. *the ~*》 the highest point. ¶*at the ~ of life.*②
—[名] 1. 정오, 한낮 ¶①정오에 2. 전성기 ¶②장년기에

noon·day [nú:ndèi] *n.* Ⓤ, *adj.* noon, midday. ¶*the ~ sun.*①
—[名][形] 정오[의] ¶①대낮의 태양

noon·tide [nú:ntàid] *n.* =noon.
—[名] 정오

noose [nu:s, +*Brit.* nu:z] *n.* Ⓒ **1.** a loop with a slip knot, which becomes tight when one end is pulled. ⇒fig. **2.** a trap; a bond.
—[名] 1. [한 끝을 당기면 죄어지는] 올가미 2. 덫; 유대(紐帶)

(noose 1.)

put one's neck (or ***head***) ***into a noose,*** allow oneself to be caught in a dangerous position.
[熟] 자승자박하다

—*vt.* catch (something) with a noose; form a noose in or of (a rope, etc.).
—[他] …을 올가미로 잡다; …으로 올가미를 만들다

⁑**nor** [nɔ:*r*, nə*r*] *conj.* **1.** 《preceded by *neither* or *not*》 and not; and not either. ¶*It is neither hot ~ cold.* / *Neither she ~ I am* (or *Neither I ~ she is*) *happy.* ⇒[usage] / *She can neither read ~ write.* **2.** 《preceded by a *negative clause*》 and not. ¶*I said that I had not bought it, ~ had I.*① / *I don't know, ~ can I guess.* / *You don't like him, ~ do I.* / *His speech was long, ~ did they listen.*② **3.** 《at the beginning of a sentence》 and not. ¶*Nor will I deny the fact.*
—[接] 1. …도 역시…않다 [usage] 동사는 가장 가까운 주어에 호응함 2. 또 …않다 ¶①나는 그것을 사지 않았다고 말했는데 사실 사지는 않았다/②그의 연설은 길었거니와 그들은 듣지도 않았다 3. 또한 …않다

Nor. **1.** Norway. **2.** North.

Nor·dic [nɔ́:*r*dik] *adj.* of or belonging to the blond-races of northwestern Europe. —*n.* Ⓒ a member of the Nordic races.
—[形] 북유럽 사람의(특히 스칸디나비아의 금발의 인종) —[名] 북유럽 사람

Nor·folk [nɔ́:*r*fək] *n.* **1.** a seaport in southeastern Virginia. **2.** a county in eastern England.
—[名] 1. 미국 동해안에 있는 Virginia 주의 도시 2. 영국 동해안의 주

norm [nɔ:*r*m] *n.* Ⓒ a standard, model or pattern for a group.
—[名] 표준, 규준, 노르마

⁑**nor·mal** [nɔ́:*r*m(ə)l] *adj.* of the ordinary standard; regular; natural; usual; not mad. ↔abnormal ¶*a ~ condition.*① —*n.* **1.** Ⓤ anything normal; the ordinary state, condition, quantity, etc. **2.** Ⓒ (*Mathematics*) a line that is at an angle of 90 degrees.
—[形] 표준의, 보통의; 자연의, 정상적인 ¶①정상 상태 —[名] 1. 표준(규준)적인 것; 정상 상태; 정상 2.《數》 수직선

nor·mal·cy [nɔ́:*r*m(ə)lsi] *n.* =normality.

nor·mal·i·ty [nɔ:*r*mǽliti] *n.* Ⓤ the state of being normal.
—[名] 정상 상태, 정상

nor·mal·ize [nɔ́:*r*məlàiz] *vt.* **1.** make (something) normal. **2.** bring (something) into agreement with a standard, pattern, rule, etc. ▷**nor·mal·i·za·tion** [nɔ̀:*r*məlizéiʃ(ə)n / -nɔ:məlai-] *n.* —**nor·mal·iz·er** [-ə*r*] *n.*
—[他] 1. …을 정상 상태로 하다 2. …을 표준에 일치시키다

nor·mal·ly [nɔ́:*r*məli] *adv.* in a normal manner; ordinarily. ¶*a ~ educated person.*①
—[副] 보통으로; 온당하게 ¶①보통의 교육을 받은 사람

normal school [´– ´] *n.* a school where high-school graduates are trained to become teachers.
—[名] 사범학교

Nor·man [nɔ́:*r*mən] *n.* **1.** Ⓒ a person of Normandy, in France. **2.** Ⓤ the language of the Normans. —*adj.* of Normandy or the Normans. ¶*~ architecture.*①
—[名] 1. 노르만 사람 2. 노르만 말 —[形] 노르만[사람·말]의 ¶①노르만 건축

Norman Conquest [´– ´–] *n.* the conquest of England by the Normans in 1066.
—[名] 노르만 사람의 영국 정복

Norman French [´– ´] *n.* French spoken by the Normans in England after the Conquest.
—[名] 노르만 프랑스 말

Nor·man·dy [nɔ́:*r*məndi] *n.* a district on the English Channel in northern France.
—[名] 노르만디(프랑스 북부 영불해협에 면한 지방)

Norse [nɔːrs] *adj.* of ancient Scandinavia, esp. of Norway, its people or their language. —*n.* **1.** 《*the N-*》 《used as *pl.*》 the people of ancient Scandinavia. **2.** [U] the Norwegian language.
—[形] 고대 스칸디나비아[사람·말]의; 노르웨이[사람·말]의 —[名] 1. 고대 스칸디나비아 사람 2. 노르웨이 말

Norse·man [nɔ́ːrsmən] *n.* [C] (pl. **-men** [-mən]) a person of ancient Scandinavia or Norway; a Northman.
—[名] 고대 스칸디나비아 사람; 노르웨이 사람

‡**north** [nɔːrθ] *n.* 《usu. *the* ~》 **1.** one of the four main points of the compass, opposite to the south. ¶*in the ~ of.*① **2.** 《*N-*》 any part of the earth toward north; the northern part of the United States. —*adj.* being in the north; coming from the north; toward the north. ¶*a ~ wind.* —*adv.* to the north. ¶*northbound traffic.*②
—[名] 1. 북쪽, 북부, 북방 ¶①…의 북부에 2. 북반구; 북극 지방; 미국 북부 제주(諸州) —[形] 북쪽에 있는; 북쪽에서의; 북향의 —[副] 북쪽으로 ¶②북으로 가는 차

North Carolina [ˊ ˋ–ˊ–] *n.* a southeastern State of the United States, on the Atlantic coast. ⇒[N.B.]
—[名] 노오드 캐롤라이나 주 [N.B.] N.C.로 줄임. 수도 Raleigh

North Da·ko·ta [nɔ́ːrθdəkóutə] *n.* a north central State of the United States. ⇒[N.B.]
—[名] 노오드 다코우타 주 [N.B.] N.Dak.으로 줄임. 수도 Bismarck

‡**north·east** [nɔ̀ːrθíːst, *nautical* nɔːríːst] *adj.* **1.** halfway between north and east. **2.** directed toward, facing or coming from the northeast. —*n.* [U] 《usu. *the* ~》 a northeast direction; a part or place that lies in this direction. —*adv.* to or toward the northeast.
—[形] 1. 동북의 2. 동북에 면한, 동북에서의 —[名] 동북, 동북부(지방) —[副] 동북에(으로)

north·east·er [nɔ̀ːrθíːstər, *nautical* nɔːríːstər] *n.* [C] a strong wind or storm from the northeast.
—[名] 북동풍

north·east·er·ly [nɔ̀ːrθíːstərli, *nautical* nɔːríːst-] *adj.* moving toward or in the northeast; coming from the northeast. —*adv.* toward the northeast.
—[形] 동북의; 동북으로부터의 —[副] 동북에(으로)

north·east·ern [nɔ̀ːrθíːstərn, *nautical* nɔːríːst-] *adj.* **1.** of the northeast. **2.** at, in, from, or toward the northeast.
—[形] 1. 동북의 2. 동북에 있는(에서의, 으로의)

north·east·ward [nɔ̀ːrθíːstwərd, *nautical* nɔːríːst-] *adv., adj.* =northeasterly.

north·er [nɔ́ːrðər] *n.* [C] a cold, strong wind or storm from the north, esp. in Texas and on the Gulf of Mexico.
—[名] 강한 북풍(가을·겨울에 Texas 나 Mexico 만에서 붊)

north·er·ly [nɔ́ːrðərli] *adj.* moving toward the north; coming from the north; of the north. ¶*a ~ breeze.*① —*adv.* toward or from the north. ¶*The wind blew ~.*②
—[形] 북으로의; 북에서의 ¶①북풍 —[副] 북으로; 북에서 ¶②바람은 북쪽에서 불어 왔다

‡**north·ern** [nɔ́ːrðərn] *adj.* **1.** of the north. **2.** at, in, or toward the north; from the north. **3.** 《*N-*》 (*U.S.*) of or in the North of the United States. —*n.* [C] a person who lives in a northern area; a northerner.
—[形] 1. 북[쪽]의 2. 북쪽에 있는(으로 향하는, 에서) 3. 북부 지방의 —[名] 북부 지방의 사람

north·ern·er [nɔ́ːrðərnər] *n.* [C] **1.** a person living in the north. **2.** 《usu. *N-*》 (*U.S.*) a person living in or coming from the northern part of the United States. ↔southerner
—[名] 1. 북국(北國) 사람 2. 미국 북부의 사람(출신자)

north·ern·most [nɔ́ːrðərnmòust] *adj.* farthest north.
—[形] 가장 북쪽의

north·land [nɔ́ːrθlənd] *n.* [C] the northern part of a country or an area; the land in the north.
—[名] 북부 지방, 북쪽에 있는 나라, 북국

North·man [nɔ́ːrθmən] *n.* [C] (pl. **-men** [-mən]) **1.** one of the ancient Scandinavians. **2.** a person or people of northern Europe.
—[名] 1. 고대 스칸디나비아 사람 2. 북유럽 사람

North Pole [ˊ ˊ] *n.* the northern end of the earth's axis.
—[名] 북극

North Star [ˊ ˊ] *n.* the star just above the North Pole.
—[名] 북극성

north·ward [nɔ́ːrθwərd] *adv.* to or toward the north. —*adj.* moving to or toward the north. —*n.* [U] the north.
—[副] 북쪽으로 —[形] 북쪽으로의 —[名] 북향

north·wards [nɔ́ːrθwərdz] *adv.* northward.
—[副] 북쪽으로

***north·west** [nɔ̀ːrθwést, *nautical* nɔ̀ːrwést] *n.* 《usu. *the* ~》 the point or direction halfway between north and west; an area that lies in this direction.
—[名] 서북
—*adj.* being in the northwest; moving toward the northwest; coming from the northwest.
—[形] 서북의, 서북으로의, 서북에서의
—*adv.* to the northwest.
—[副] 서북으로(에)

north·west·er [nɔ̀ːrθwéstər, *nautical* nɔ̀ːrwést-] *n.* [C] a strong wind or storm from the northwest.
—[名] 서북풍

north·west·er·ly [nɔ̀ːrθwéstərli, *nautical* nɔːrwést-] *adj.* moving toward or in the northwest; coming from the
—[形] 서북의, 서북에서의 —[副] 서북으로(에)

N

northwest. —*abv.* toward the northwest.

north·west·ern [nɔ̀:rθwéstərn, *nautical* nɔ̀:rwést-] *adj.* **1.** of the northwest. **2.** at or in the northwestern; coming from the northwest; moving toward the northwest.
—[形] 1. 서북의 2. 서북으로의(에서의)

* **Nor·way** [nɔ́:rwei] *n.* a country in northern Europe.
—[名] 노르웨이

Nor·we·gian [nɔ:rwí:dʒ(ə)n] *adj.* of Norway, its people or their language. —*n.* [C] **1.** a person of Norway. **2.** [U] the language of Norway.
—[形] 노르웨이[사람 · 말] —[名] 1. 노르웨이 사람 2. 노르웨이 말

Nos. numbers.

⁝ **nose** [nouz] *n.* **1.** [C] an organ on the face with which people and animals smell. ¶*an aquiline* ~① | *blow one's* ~② | *hold one's* ~③ | *pick one's* ~.④ **2.** [C] anything like a nose in shape or position. ¶*a* ~ *of an airplane.*⑤ **3.** 《usu. *a* ~》 the sense of smell. ¶*have a good* ~.⑥
1) ***as plain as the nose in one's face,*** very clear; obvious.
2) ***bite someone's nose off,*** speak sharply to someone.
3) ***by a nose,*** by a very narrow margin.
4) ***count*** (or ***tell***) ***noses,*** count the number [esp. of votes].
5) ***follow one's nose,*** go straight ahead.
6) ***lead by the nose,*** have complete control over.
7) ***nose to nose,*** face to face.
8) ***on the nose,*** precisely; exactly.
9) ***put someone's nose out of joint,*** spoil or ruin someone's plan or hopes, etc.
10) ***put*** (or ***poke***) ***one's nose into,*** interfere with (something) esp. when it is not one's business.
11) ***turn up one's nose at,*** treat (someone or something) with contempt.
12) ***under someone's*** [***very***] ***nose,*** directly in front of someone; plainly visible.
—*vt.* **1.** discover (something) by smell; search for (something). ¶*The dog nosed out a rat.* **2.** press the nose against (something); touch (something) with the nose. —*vi.* **1.** smell at or about an object. **2.** pry. ¶~ *into another's affairs.*⑦ **3.** push one's way.
1) ***nose down*** (***up***), (of an airplane) turn down (up) the nose.
2) ***nose one's way,*** (of a ship, etc.) move or push forward slowly.

—[名] 1. 코 ¶①매부리코/②[때로 눈물을 감추기 위해] 코를 풀다/③코를 쥐다/④콧구멍을 쑤시다 2. [코와 같은] 돌출부 ¶⑤기수(機首) 3. 후각(嗅覺) ¶⑥냄새를 잘 맡다
[熟] 1)아주 명백한 2)퉁명스럽게 대답하다 3)근소한 차이로 4)찬성자의 수를 세다 5)똑바로 나아가다 6)…을 자기 멋대로 부리다 7)얼굴을 맞대고 8)바로, 정확히 9)…의 계획을 뒤엎다; …보다 한수 더 뜨다 10)…에 간섭하다; …을 방해하다 11)…을 코웃음치다 12)…의 면전에서
—[他] 1. …을 냄새맡다; 찾아내다 2. …에 코를 비벼대다
—[自] 1. 냄새맡다; 냄새를 맡으며 다니다 2. 간섭하다; 꼬치꼬치 캐다 ¶①남의 일에 참견하다 3. 전진하다
[熟] 1)기수(機首)를 내리다(올리다) 2)나아가다

nose bag [ˊ ˋ] *n.* a bag with food to be hung over a horse's head.
—[名] [말의 머리에 매다는] 여물 자루

nose·bleed [nóuzblì:d] *n.* [U] bleeding from the nose.
—[名] 코피, 코의 출혈

nose dive [ˊ ˋ] *n.* **1.** a head-on dive of an airplane. **2.** any sudden and sharp drop.
—[名] 1. 급강하 2. [가격 따위의] 폭락

nose-dive [nóuzdàiv] *vi.* (of an airplane, etc.) make a nose dive.
—[自] [비행기가] 급강하하다; 폭락하다

nose·gay [nóuzgèi] *n.* [C] a beautifully-arranged bunch of sweet-smelling flowers.
—[名] [향기 있는] 꽃다발

nose ring [ˊ ˋ] *n.* **1.** a ring passed through the nose of an animal for leading it. **2.** a ring worn in the nose as an ornament.
—[名] 1. [소 따위의] 코뚜레 2. [야만인의] 코고리

nos·tal·gia [nɑstǽldʒ(i)ə / nɔs-] *n.* [U] **1.** homesickness. **2.** a strong desire for something in the past.
—[名] 1. 향수[병] 2. [과거에 대한] 동경, 그리움

nos·tal·gic [nɑstǽldʒik / nɔs-] *adj.* of nostalgia.
—[形] 향수에 잠긴, 과거를 그리워하는

* **nos·tril** [nɑ́stril / nɔ́s-] *n.* [C] one of the two outer openings in the nose.
—[名] 콧구멍

nos·trum [nɑ́strəm / nɔ́s-] *n.* [C] a medicine sold at a drug store. etc., the effect of which is doubtful; a quack medicine.
—[名] [엉터리] 비방약, 만병 통치약

nos·y, nos·ey [nóuzi] *adj.* (**nos·i·er, nos·i·est**) (*colloq.*) very curious; eager to know other people's affairs.
—[形] 참견하기 잘하는; 꼬치꼬치 캐는

⁝ **not** [nɑt, nt, n / nɔt, nt, n] *adv.* 《used to make meaning *negative*》 ¶*I'm* ~ *a child.* | *I haven't* (or *U. S.* usu. *I don't have*) *a watch.* | *Won't you join the party?* | *Don't come nearer.* | *It's mine,* ~ *yours.*① | *Not a cloud was seen in the sky.*② | *I told her* ~ *to go.*③ | *He is* ~
—[副] …이 아니다 ¶①그것은 내것이다, 네것이 아니다/②하늘에는 구름 한 점 없었다/③나는 그녀에게 말하지 말라고 했다/④그는 내 아들이 아니라 동생이다

*my son, but my brother.*④
***not that** ...,* [though] it is not suggested that ...
[熟] …이라는 것은 아니다

no·ta·bil·i·ty [nòutəbíliti] *n.* (pl. **-ties**) **1.** [U] the state of being notable. **2.** [C] an important or distinguished person.
—[名] 1. 저명 2. 저명 인사

N

* **no·ta·ble** [nóutəbl] *adj.* worthy of notice; remarkable. ¶*a ~ increase of population*① | *His deed was very ~.*② —*n.* [C] a notable person. ¶*the home of a ~.*
—[形] 주목할 만한 ¶①인구의 뚜렷한 증가/②그의 공적은 주목할 만하다
—[名] 명사(名士)

no·tably [nóutəbli] *adv.* in a notable way; remarkably; strikingly. ¶*Sugar consumption was ~ higher.*①
—[副] 현저하게; 명백히 ¶①설탕의 소비는 현저하게 올라갔다

no·ta·ry [nóutəri] *n.* [C] (pl. **-ries**) a public official who makes certain the truthfulness of documents.
—[名] 공증인

no·ta·tion [noutéiʃ(ə)n] *n.* [C] [U] **1.** a set of signs, symbols or letters used to represent numbers, quantities, etc. **2.** the act of recording by such symbols or signs. ¶*musical ~*① | *the Roman ~.*② **3.** [C] a written record.
—[名] 1. 표기 2. 표시법 ¶①음악 기호법/②로마 숫자법(Ⅰ, Ⅱ, Ⅲ, Ⅳ…) 3. 기록

* **notch** [nɑtʃ / nɔtʃ] *n.* [C] **1.** a V-shaped cut in an edge or on a surface. **2.** a deep, narrow pass between mountains. **3.** (*colloq.*) a step; a grade; a degree. ¶*top notch*① | *He is a ~ above the others.*② —*vt.* make a notch on (something).
—[名] 1. [V자 모양의] 새김눈 2. 협곡 3. [口] 단(段); 급 ¶①일류, 일급/②그는 다른 사람들보다 한 수 높다
—[他] …에 새김눈을 내다

⁑ **note** [nout] *n.* [C] **1.** a memo; a memorandum. ¶*notes for a speech.*① **2.** a comment; an explanation. ¶*a ~ on* (or *to*) *the text.*② **3.** a short letter. ¶*a ~ of invitation*③ | *a diplomatic ~.*④ **4.** paper money; a bank note; a check. ¶*a ~ of hand.*⑤ **5.** [U] greatness; fame. ¶*a person of ~.*⑥ **6.** [U] notice; attention. ¶*be worthy of ~.* **7.** any sign or mark. ¶*a ~ of exclamation*⑦ | *a ~ of interrogation.*⑧ **8.** (*Music*) a musical sound or tone; a sign to show the pitch and length of a sound; a key of a piano, etc. **9.** the way of speaking. ¶*change one's ~.*⑨
—[名] 1. 메모, 비망록 ¶①연설의 초고 2. 주석 ¶②원본에 단 주 3. 짧은 편지; [외교상의] 통첩 ¶③초대장/④외교 각서 4. 지폐; 어음 ¶⑤약속 어음 5. 저명; 명성 ¶⑥유명한 사람 6. 주의; 주목 7. 표, 기호, 부호 ¶⑦감탄부호(!)/⑧물음표(?) 8. [樂] 악음; 음표; [피아노 따위의] 건(鍵) 9. 어조, 말씨 ¶⑨어조를 바꾸다

1) ***compare notes,*** exchange ideas or opinions.
2) ***make*** (or ***take***) ***a note*** (or ***notes***) ***of,*** write down (things) to be remembered.
3) ***take note of,*** take notice of; give attention to.
[熟] 1)의견을 주고 받다 2)메모를 하다, 기록하다 3)…을 주의하다; …에 주목하다

—*vt.* **1.** make a note of (something). **2.** give attention to (something); notice; observe.
—[他] 1. …의 메모를 하다 2. …을 주의하다; …에 주목하다

note down, write down (something) as a memo.
[熟] …의 메모를 하다

⁑ **note·book** [nóutbùk] *n.* [C] a book for taking notes or opinions.
—[名] 수첩, 필기장, 공책

* **not·ed** [nóutid] *adj.* well-known; distinguished; famous. ¶*a ~ poet*① | *He was ~ for his bravery.*②
—[形] 유명한 ¶①저명한 시인/②그는 용감한 것으로 유명하다

note·paper [nóutpèipər] *n.* [U] paper for writing letters; writing paper.
—[名] 편지지

note-taking [nóuttèikiŋ] *n.* [U] the act of taking notes.
—[名] 메모를 하기

note·wor·thy [nóutwə̀:rði] *adj.* worthy of note; remarkable. ¶*make a ~ contribution to the state.*①
—[形] 주목할 만한 ¶①나라를 위해 주목할 만한 공헌을 하다

⁑ **noth·ing** [nʌ́θiŋ] *pron.* not anything. ⇒[usage] ¶*There is ~ new in his story.* | *There's ~ like home.*① | *Nothing could be more strange.* | *I can give you ~ but this.*②
—[代] 아무것도 없는; 아무 일도 …않는 [usage] 형용사는 뒤에 옴 ¶①제 집[가정]같이 [좋은] 곳은 아무데도 없다/②네게 줄 수 있는 것은 이것밖에 없다

—*n.* **1.** [U] a thing that does not exist; zero. ¶*Now that he is dead, he is ~.* | *He is six feet ~.*③ | *Twice ~ is ~.*④ | *Of ~, comes ~.*⑤ **2.** [C] ⦅sometimes *pl.* or *a ~*⦆ a thing or person that is not important. ¶*the little nothings of life* | *He is ~ without his money.*⑥
—[名] 1. 무(無); 영 ¶③ 꼭 6피이트다/④영의 2배는 영/⑤무에서 유는 생기지 않는다 2. 시시한 사람(것) ¶⑥그는 돈이 없으면 보잘것 없는 사내다

1) ***all to nothing,*** by far; completely.
2) ***come to nothing,*** fail; turn out useless.
3) ***for nothing,*** ⓐ without payment; free. ⓑ in vain; uselessly. ⓒ without reason.
4) ***have nothing to do with,*** have no connection with something; avoid dealing with something.
5) ***make nothing of,*** ⓐ treat or regard (something) as unimportant. ⓑ ⦅preceded by *can*⦆ can not understand (a question, etc.). ⓒ ⦅preceded by *can*⦆ fail
[熟] 1)훨씬, 충분히 2)실패하다; 헛수고로 끝나다 3)ⓐ공짜로 ⓑ무익하게 ⓒ까닭없이 4)…와 관계가 없다; …와 교제하지 않다 5)ⓐ…을 아무렇지도 않게 여기다; 예사로 알다 ⓑ…을 이해할 수 없다 ⓒ…을 이용할 수 없다; …을 해낼 수 없다 6)단지 7)…이나 다

to use (one's talents, etc.); fail to do (a job, etc.).
6) ***nothing but***, only.
7) ***nothing less than*** (or ***short of***), just the same as (something).
8) ***think nothing of,*** consider or treat (someone or something) as unimportant.
9) ***to say nothing*** (=*not to speak*) ***of something.***
—*adv.* not at all; in no manner or degree. ¶*It helps me ~.* | *He cared ~ how he looked.* | *She is ~ wiser than before.*[7] | *This poem is ~ like so good as that one.*[8]

름없는 8)…을 경시하다 9)…은 말할 것도 없이
—[副] 조금도 …않다 ¶⑦그녀는 조금도 철이 나지 않았다 ⑧이 시는 저 시에 비하면 훨씬 못하다

noth·ing·ness [nʌ́θiŋnis] *n.* [U] **1.** the state of being nothing; non-existence. **2.** the state of no value. **3.** unconsciousness.

—[名] 1. 무 2. 무가치 3. 인사불성

⁑**no·tice** [nóutis] *n.* **1.** [U] attention; heed. ¶*attract ~* | *escape one's ~.*[1] **2.** [C] an announcement; an information. ¶*issue a ~*[2] | *till further ~.*[3] **3.** [U] warning; caution beforehand. ¶*at a moment's ~*[4] | *give a month's ~*[5] | *without ~.*[6] **4.** [C] a short article that gives some news. ¶*The play got a favorable ~.*[7]
1) ***give notice,*** warn; inform; tell.
2) ***have notice*** (=*be told*) ***of something.***
3) ***serve notice,*** give warning; inform.
4) ***take notice of,*** become aware of (something); give attention to (something); observe.
—*vt.* **1.** become aware of (something); find. ¶*I noticed my purse was missing.* **2.** pay attention to (something). **3.** speak or write about (something). ¶*~ a book in a newspaper.*

—[名] 1. 주의 ¶①남의 주의를 못 끌다 2. 토지; 정보 ¶②통지를 내다/③추후 통지가 있을 때까지 3. 경고; 예고; 통고 ¶④즉석에서/⑤1개월 후에 계약을 해제할 것을 통고하다/⑥예고 없이;무단히 4. [신문 따위의] 짤막한 기사; 공고; 게시 ¶⑦그 극은 호평을 받았다
[熟] 1)…을 알리다; 통고하다 2)통지를 받다 3)예고하다; 알리다 4)알아채다; 주의(주목)하다
—[他] 1. …을 알아채다 2. …에 주의(주목)하다 3. …에 언급하다

no·tice·a·ble [nóutisəbl] *adj.* **1.** easily observed or noticed. **2.** worthy of attention. ¶*The torn place wasn't ~.*[1]

—[形] 1. 눈에 띄는 2. 이목을 끄는 ¶①찢어진 곳이 눈에 띄지 않았다

no·tice·a·bly [nóutisəbli] *adv.* to a noticeable degree; remarkably.

—[副] 눈에 띄게

notice board [ˊ- -ˋ] *n.* a board on which notices are shown.

—[名] 게시판

no·ti·fi·ca·tion [nòutifikéiʃ(ə)n] *n.* **1.** [U] the act of making something known. **2.** [C] a notice.

—[名] 1. 통지; 고시 2. 통지서; 공고문; 신고서

⁑**no·ti·fy** [nóutifài] *vt.* (**-fied**) **1.** make (something) known. ⟪~ someone *of*; ~ someone *that* …⟫ ¶*~ the post office of one's change of address.*[1] **2.** report; announce. ⟪~ something *to* someone⟫

—[他] 1. …을 통지하다 ¶①우체국에 거주 변경을 계출하다 2. …을 발표하다

⁑**no·tion** [nóuʃ(ə)n] *n.* [C] **1.** a general idea. ¶*I've no ~ of the new word.*[1] **2.** an opinion; a belief. ¶*Such is the common ~.*[2] **3.** a natural tendency toward some course of action; an intention. ¶*I got a sudden ~ to go out to the country.*[3] **4.** ⟪*pl.*⟫ (*U. S.*) small, useful articles, such as pins, needles and thread.

—[名] 1. 개념; 관념 ¶①새 단어의 의미를 모르겠다 2. 의견; 견해 ¶②그러한 것이 일반의 생각이다 3. 의향, 의사 ¶③갑자기 시골에 갈 생각이 났다 4. ⟪美⟫ 잡화, 자질구레한 실용품

no·tion·al [nóuʃən(ə)l] *adj.* **1.** of a notion. **2.** abstract. **3.** imaginary; fanciful.

—[形] 1. 개념상의 2. 추상적인 3. 공상적인; 변덕스러운

no·to·ri·e·ty [nòutəráiəti] *n.* (pl. **-ties**) **1.** [U] the state of being widely known for something bad. **2.** [C] a person having ill fame.

—[名] 1. [나쁜 의미의] 평판 2. 악명 높은 사람

no·to·ri·ous [noutɔ́:riəs] *adj.* widely known in a bad sense. ¶*a ~ liar* | *This district is ~ for smog.*[1]

—[形] 악명 높은 ¶①이 지구는 스모그로 유명하다

No·tre Dame [nòutrədɑ́:m] *n.* **1.** Our Lady; the Virgin Mary, mother of Jesus. **2.** a famous cathedral in Paris.

—[名] 1. 성모 마리아 2. 노트르담 사원

⁎**not·with·stand·ing** [nàtwiθstǽndiŋ / nɔ̀t-] *prep.* in spite of. ¶*He failed ~ my advice.* —*conj.* (*archaic*) in spite of the fact that … —*adv.* however; nevertheless.

—[前] …에도 불구하고 —[接] ⟨古⟩ 그럼에도 불구하고 —[副] …이라고 하나

nou·gat [nú:gɑ:, +*U.S.* nú:gət] *n.* [C] a sweet candy made of sugar, nuts, etc.

—[名] 누가(사탕 과자)

nought [nɔ:t] *n.* =naught.

⁎**noun** [naun] *n.* [C] (*Grammar*) a word used as the name of a person, place, condition, etc. ¶*an abstract ~*[1] | *a collective ~.*[2] —*adj.* used as a noun. ¶*a ~ clause (phrase).*[3]

—[名] ⟪文法⟫ 명사 ¶①추상명사/②집합명사 —[形] 명사 용법의 ¶③명사절(구)

* **nour·ish** [nə́:riʃ / nʌ́r-] *vt.* **1.** give food to (an animal, etc.) to make it grow. ¶ *~ a baby with milk.*① **2.** have (a hope, an ill feeling, etc.) in mind. ¶ *~ a hope* / *It has nourished the dream in us.*②
—[他] 1. [동물 따위]를 기르다 ¶①우유로 갓난애를 기르다 2. [희망·원한 따위]를 품다 ¶②그것은 우리에게 꿈을 갖게 했다

nour·ish·ment [nə́:riʃmənt / nʌ́r-] *n.* [U] **1.** food; something which helps to improve quality or help growth. ¶ *intellectual ~.*① **2.** the act of nourishing; the state of being nourished. ¶ *devote oneself to the ~ of education.*②
—[名] 1. 음식; 자양물 ¶①지식의 양식 2. 영양을 주기; 영양이 되기(되는 것) ¶①교육의 발전에 헌신하다

Nov. November.

* **nov·el**[1] [nάv(ə)l / nɔ́v-] *adj.* **1.** new; recent. **2.** strange; unusual.
—[形] 1. 새로운 2. 보통이 아닌, 희한한

⁑ **nov·el**[2] [nάv(ə)l / nɔ́v-] *n.* [C] a long story presenting imaginary characters and events as if they were real.
—[名] 소설

nov·el·ette [nὰv(ə)lét / nɔ̀v-] *n.* [C] a short novel.
—[名] 단편소설

nov·el·ist [nάv(ə)list / nɔ́v-] *n.* [C] a person who writes novels.
—[名] 소설가

* **nov·el·ty** [nάv(ə)lti / nɔ́v-] *n.* (pl. **-ties**) **1.** [U] the state of being strange; newness; unusualness. **2.** [C] something new or unusual. **3.** ⦅chiefly *pl.*⦆ small, cheap, but cleverly-made articles such as toys and paper hats.
—[名] 1. 진기함 2. 새로운 것 3. 진기한 것

⁂ **No·vem·ber** [nouvémbər] *n.* the eleventh month of the year.
—[名] 11월

nov·ice [nάvis / nɔ́v-] *n.* [C] **1.** an inexperienced person; a beginner. **2.** a person who begins a life given to God; a person who is to become a monk or a nun.
—[名] 1. 초심자 2. 견습 수도사(수녀)

no·vi·ti·ate, no·vi·ci·ate [nouvíʃiit, -èit] *n.* [C][U] the state or the period of being a novice.
—[名] 초심자임, 견습 기간

⁂ **now** [nau] *adv.* **1.** at the present time. ↔then ¶ *Where is your mother ~?* / *Tom must be a man ~.*① **2.** at once. ¶ *Do it ~.* **3.** under these conditions. ¶ *I would do anything ~.*② **4.** since; because. ¶ *Let's go for a walk, ~ the rain has stopped.*③ **5.** (in a story) and then; after this; next. **6.** ⦅used to *begin* or *emphasize* a sentence⦆ ¶ *Now what do you mean?* / *Now let's go.*
—[副] 1. 지금, 벌써, 목하 ¶①톰은 이제 어른임에 틀림없다 2. 곧 3. 현재의 사정으로는 ¶②이렇게 됐으니 이제는 무엇이나 하겠다 4. …이니까 ¶③비가 그쳤으니까 산책이나 가자 5. 그리고 나서 6. 그런데; 자아, 여봐; 이런, 저런

1) [*every*] ***now and then*** (or ***again***), sometimes.
2) ***just now,*** only a few moments ago.
3) ***now*** … ***now*** (or ***then***) …, sometimes …, and sometimes ….
4) ***now now,*** ⦅expressing a *mild warning*⦆ now then.
5) ***now or never,*** at this moment or not at all.

[熟] 1)때때로 2)방금 3)때로는 … 또 때로는 … 4)이봐 이봐 5)지금이야말로 좋은 기회다

—*conj.* ⦅often followed by *that*⦆ as a result of the fact; since. ¶ *Now* [*that*] *you are grown up, you must work harder.*
—[接] …이니까; …인 이상은

—*n.* [U] the present; this time. ¶ *by ~*④ / *for ~*⑤ / *from ~ on*⑥ / *until* (or *up to*) *~*⑦ / *Now is the time.*⑧
—[名] 지금 ¶④지금쯤은 이미/⑤당분간/⑥금후/⑦지금까지/⑧지금이 바로 그 때이다

* **now·a·days** [náuədèiz] *adv.* at the present time; in these days. —*n.* [U] the present time.
—[副] 요즈음은 —[名] 요즈음, 현대

no·way [nóuwèi] *adv.* =noways.

no·ways [nóuwèiz] *adv.* not at all; by no means.
—[副] 결코 … 않다

⁑ **no·where** [nóu(h)wὲər] *adv.* not anywhere; not in, at, to, or from any place. ¶ *My pen is ~ to be found.*①
—[副] 아무데도 … 없다 ¶①펜은 아무데도 보이지 않는다

1) ***be*** (or ***come in***) ***nowhere,*** (in a contest) fail completely to win.
2) ***nowhere near,*** far from.

[熟] 1)참패하다 2)좀처럼 … 아니다

no·wise [nóuwàiz] *adv.* not at all.
—[副] 결코 … 아니다

nox·ious [nάkʃəs / nɔ́k-] *adj.* poisonous; harmful. ¶ *~ weeds*① / *a ~ T.V. program.*② ▷**nox·ious·ly** [-li] *adv.*
—[形] 유해(유독)한 ¶①독초/②불건전한 텔레비 프로

N.T. New Testament. ↔ O. T.

nu·ance [n(j)ú:ɑ:ns, -ˊ / njú:-, -ˊ] *n.* [C] a delicate difference in tone, color, feeling, expression, meaning, etc.
—[名] 뉘앙스, [빛깔·음·의미·감정 따위의] 미묘한 차이

nu·cle·ar [n(j)ú:kliər / njú:kliə] *adj.* of a nucleus. ¶ *a ~ bomb*① / *~ energy.*②
—[形] [세포, 원자] 핵의 ¶①핵 폭탄/②원자력

nu·cle·i [n(j)ú:kliài / njú:-] *n.* pl. of **nucleus**.

nu·cle·us [n(j)ú:kliəs / njú:-] *n.* [C] (pl. **-cle·i** or **-cleus·es**) **1.** a central part around which other matter is collected
—[名] 1. 핵, 중심 ¶①학생들의 중핵(中核) 2. [세포]핵 3. 원자핵

or grows. ¶*the ~ of the students.*① **2.** (*Biology*) the central part of a cell of an animal or a plant. **3.** (*Physics*) the central part of an atom.

N

nude [n(j)u:d, / nju:d] *adj.* **1.** naked; bare; without clothes. **2.** not hidden; plain. **—*n.*** **1.** [C] (*Art*) a naked human figure. **2.** 《*the* ~》 the state of being naked. ▷**nude·ness** [-nis] *n.*
—[形] 1. 나체의, 벌거벗은 2. 있는 그대로의 —[名] 1. 나체화 2. 나체의 상태

nudge [nʌdʒ] *vt.* touch or push (someone) slightly with the elbow to attract attention. ¶*He nudged me to go ahead.*① **—*n.*** [C] a slight touch or push with the elbow.
—[他] …을 팔꿈치로 슬쩍 찌르다 ¶①그는 먼저 가라고 나를 찔렀다 —[名] 팔꿈치로 슬쩍 찌르기

nu·di·ty [n(j)ú:diti / njú:-] *n.* (pl. **-ties**) **1.** [U] the state of being naked. **2.** [C] something naked.
—[名] 1. 벌거숭이[임] 2. 벌거벗은 것

nug·get [nʌ́git] *n.* [C] **1.** a lump of gold found in a rock or the earth. **2.** anything precious or valuable.
—[名] 1. [천연의] 금괴 2. 가치 있는 것

* **nui·sance** [n(j)ú:sns / njú:-] *n.* [C] a disagreeable thing person or act that troubles people. ¶*No Nuisances.*① / *What a ~!*②
—[名] 폐, 성가심; 폐가 되는 것; 귀찮은 사람(것) ¶①소변 금지(게시문)/②에이 귀찮다!
make a nuisance of; make oneself a nuisance, annoy.
[熟] 폐를 끼치다

null [nʌl] *adj.* **1.** having no legal force; useless in law. **2.** having no value or importance. ¶*as ~ as nothing.*① **3.** (*Mathematics*) amounting to zero.
—[形] 1. [법률상] 무효의 2. 가치없는 ¶①무(無)나 다름없는 3. 영(零)의
null and void, having no legal force.
[熟] 무효의

nul·li·fy [nʌ́lifài] *vt.* (**-fied**) make (something) of no value or effect; declare that something is legally useless; cancel. ▷**nul·li·fi·er** [-ər] *n.*
—[他] [법률상] …을 무효로 하다; 취소하다

nul·li·ty [nʌ́liti] *n.* (pl. **-ties**) **1.** [U] the state of being null. **2.** [C] something or someone null. **3.** [C] something with no legal force.
—[名] 1. 무효 2. 보잘것 없는 것(사람) 3. [법률상] 무효인 것

numb [nʌm] *adj.* having lost the sense of feeling or moving. **—*vt.*** make (something) numb. ¶*The icy cold numbed our fingers.*①
—[形] 곱은; 감각을 잃은 —[他] …의 감각을 없애다 ¶①어는 듯한 추위로 손가락이 곱아졌다

*** **num·ber** [nʌ́mbər] *n.* [C] **1.** [C] [U] a quantity; an amount; the sum. ¶*a whole ~*① / *an odd* (*an even*) *~*② / *a positive* (or *a plus*) *~*③ / *a negative* (or *a minus*) *~*④ / *cardinal* (*ordinal*) *numbers*⑤ / *the ~ of books in this library* / *They are twenty in ~.*⑥ **2.** [C] [U] a sign or word that shows how many; a figure; a numeral. **3.** the grade, rank, turn, position, etc. in a series. ¶*a house ~*⑦ / *Room No. 312.* / *No. 10, Downing Street.*⑧ **4.** a copy of a newspaper, magazine, etc. ¶*the April ~.* **5.** 《*pl.*》 a large quantity; a lot; many people; several people; fellows. ¶*There are numbers who believe so.*⑨ / *A small ~ are of this opinion.*⑩ / *He is not of our ~.*⑪ **6.** 《*pl.*》 arithmetic.
—[名] 1. 수; 총수 ¶①정수(整數)/②기수(우수)/③정소(正數)/④부수(負數)/⑤기수(基數)(서수)/⑥그들은 수가 20명이다 2. 숫자 3. 번호; …번 ¶⑦집의 번지/⑧다우닝가 10번지(영국 수상의 관저) 4. [신문·잡지 따위의] …호 5. 다수; 많은 사람들; 얼마간의 사람들; 동료 ¶⑨그렇게 믿고 있는 사람들도 많다/⑩소수의 사람들이 이 같은 의견이다/⑪그는 우리들의 한패가 아니다(여기에는 들어 있지 않다) 6. 산술

1) ***a back number,*** an old copy of a magazine, etc.; an old-fashioned person or thing.
2) ***a number of,*** many; several.
3) ***in numbers,*** in separate forms; in the forms of poetry.
4) ***to the number of,*** amounting to.
5) ***without*** (or ***out of***) ***number,*** too many to be counted.

[熟] 1)[잡지 따위의 과월호(過月號); 시대에 뒤진 사람(것) 2)다수의[것]; 얼마간의[것] 3)여러 권으로 나누어; 시의 형태로 4)…에 달하는 5)헤아릴 수 없는; 무수한

—*vt.* **1.** give a number to (something). **2.** amount to (a certain number). ¶*The visitors numbered fifty.* **3.** limit the length of (something, esp. one's life). ¶*His days are numbered.*⑫
—[他] 1. …에 번호를 붙이다 2. …에 달하다 3. …을 세다 ¶⑫목숨이 얼마 안 남았다

num·ber·less [nʌ́mbərlis] *adj.* **1.** very numerous; that not be counted. ¶*the ~ sands on the seashore.* **2.** without a number. ¶*a ~ page.*
—[形] 1. 무수한 2. 번호가 없는

numb·ness [nʌ́mnis] *n.* [U] the state of being numb.
—[名] 마비; 무감각

nu·mer·al [n(j)ú:m(ə)r(ə)l / njú:-] *n.* [C] a word, letter, or figure expressing a number. ¶*Arabic* (*Roman*) *numerals.*① **—*adj.*** of number; expressing numbers.
—[名] 숫자 ¶①아라비아 숫자[1, 2…](로마 숫자[Ⅰ, Ⅱ…]) —[形] 수의; 수를 나타내는

nu·mer·ate [n(j)ú:mərèit / njú:-] *vt.* **1.** count (something). **2.** read (a numerical expression).
—[他] 1. …을 세다 2. [숫자]를 읽다

nu·mer·a·tor [n(j)ú:mərèitər / njú:-] *n.* [C] **1.** (*Mathemat-*
—[名] 1. 《數》 분자 [N.B.] fraction 분

numerical [787] **nut**

ics) the number above the line in a fraction. ⇒N.B. **2.** a person who counts by numbers. — 수, denominator 분모 2. 계산자(者)

nu·mer·i·cal [n(j)uːmérik(ə)l / -njuː-] *adj.* of numbers. ¶*a ~ equation*① / *~ order*② / *a ~ statement.*③ —形 수의; 숫자로 나타낸 ¶①수식/②번호순/③통계

nu·mer·i·cal·ly [n(j)uːmérik(ə)li / njuː-] *adv.* in a numerical manner; by numbers. —副 수(數)로; 숫자로으로

‡**nu·mer·ous** [n(j)úːm(ə)rəs, / njúː-] *adj.* great in number; very many. ¶*a ~ family*① / *make ~ telephone calls.*② —形 다수의 ¶①많은 가족/②빈번하게 전화를 걸다

Nu·mid·i·a [n(j)uːmídiə / njuː-] *n.* a very old kingdom in North Africa. ⇒N.B. —名 북아프리카의 옛 왕국 N.B. 현대의 Algeria

nu·mis·mat·ic [n(j)ùːmizmǽtik, -mis- / njùː-] *adj.* of coins or medals; of numismatics. —形 화폐의; 화폐[고전(古錢)]학의

nu·mis·mat·ics [n(j)ùːmizmǽtiks, -mis- / njuː(ː)-] *n. pl.* (used as *sing.*) the study of coins or medals. —名 화폐학, 고전(古錢)학

nu·mis·ma·tist [nju(ː)mízmətist, -mís-, njuː-] *n.* Ⓒ a person who collects coins and medals; a expert in numismatics. —名 고전(古錢) 수집가; 화폐(고전)학자

num·skull [nʌ́mskʌl] *n.* Ⓒ (*colloq.*) a stupid fellow; a fool. —名 바보

* **nun** [nʌn] *n.* Ⓒ a woman in a convent who leads a religious life in the service of God. ↔monk —名 수녀

nun·ci·o [nʌ́nʃiou] *n.* Ⓒ a diplomatic representative of the Pope to a foreign country. —名 로마교황 사절

nun·ner·y [nʌ́nəri] *n.* Ⓒ (pl. **-ner·ies**) a place where nuns live; a convent. —名 수녀원

nup·tial [nʌ́p/(ə)l] *n.* (usu. *pl.*) a wedding. ⌈marriage or wedding.⌉ —*adj.* of —名 결혼식 —形 결혼[식]의

‡**nurse** [nəːrs] *n.* Ⓒ **1.** a person who takes care of the sick, the injured, etc. **2.** a woman who takes care of children. ⇒N.B. **3.** a person who feeds and protects. **4.** a place where something is protected or grows. ¶*Ancient Greece was the ~ of learning.*① —*vt.* **1.** take care of (the sick, the injured, etc.). **2.** take care of (a baby); give milk to (a baby) at one's breast. **3.** hold (a baby, a pet, etc.) closely. **4.** make (a baby, a plant, etc.) grow with special care. —*vi.* **1.** be a nurse; act as a nurse. **2.** give milk to a baby at one's breast. **3.** (of a baby) be given milk from a mother or a nurse at her breast. —名 1. 간호인, 간호부 2. 유모 N.B. a wet nurse 라고 함; 보모; 아이 보는 여자 N.B. a dry nurse 라고 함 3. 보호자, 보육자 4. 양성소, 발상지 ¶①고대 그리스는 학문의 온상이었다 —他 1. …을 간호하다 2. [갓난애]를 돌보다; …에 젖을 먹이다 3. …을 품에 안다 4. …을 기르다 —自 1. 돌보다; 간호하다 2. 젖을 먹이다 3. [갓난애가] 젖을 빨다

nurse·ling [nə́ːrsliŋ] *n.* =nursling. ⌈children.⌉
nurse·maid [nə́ːrsmèid] *n.* Ⓒ a maid hired to look after —名 아이 보는 여자

* **nurs·er·y** [nə́ːrs(ə)ri] *n.* Ⓒ (pl. **-er·ies**) **1.** a room for young children or babies. ¶*a ~ governess.*① **2.** a place where young plants are grown. **3.** a place that helps something to nourish, grow and develop. —名 1. 육아실 ¶①보모 겸 가정교사 2. 못자리, 모판 3. 양성소; 온상

nurs·er·y·man [nə́ːrs(ə)rimən] *n.* Ⓒ (pl. **-men** [-mən]) a man who owns a nursery for growing plants to sell. —名 묘목업자, 묘포 경영자

nursery rhyme [⌐ ⌐ ⌐] *n.* a short, traditional poem or song for small children. ⌈the ages of 2~5.⌉ —名 동요; 자장가

nursery school [⌐ ⌐ ⌐] *n.* a school for children under —名 보육학교

nurs·ling [nə́ːrsliŋ] *n.* Ⓒ **1.** any baby or infant that is taken care of by a nurse. **2.** any person or thing that is tenderly cared for. —名 1. 젖먹이 2. 소중히 길러낸 사람(것)

nur·ture [nə́ːrtʃər] *n.* Ⓤ **1.** anything that gives nourishment. **2.** the act of bringing up; training; education. ¶*the ~ of chicks.*① —*vt.* **1.** feed; nourish. **2.** train and teach. ▷**nur·tur·er** [-tʃərər] *n.* —名 1. 자양물 2. 양육; 교육 ¶①병아리의 사육 —他 1. …에게 자양물을 주다 2. …을 양육하다

‡**nut** [nʌt] *n.* Ⓒ **1.** a dry fruit with a hard shell and seeds inside it that may be eaten. **2.** (*Machinery*) a small block with a hole to be screwed on to the end of a bolt. **3.** (*colloq.*) the head. **4.** a crazy or eccentric person. **5.** (*colloq.*) a dandy; a fop. —名 1. 나무 열매 2.(機) 너트 3.(口) 머리 4. 미치광이 5.(口) 멋장이

1) *be nuts on,* ⓐ be crazy about (something). ⓑ be good at (something).
2) *be nuts to* (or *for*), be very charming to (someone).
3) *don't care a nut,* don't mind at all.
4) *for nuts,* at all. ⇒usage ¶*She can't sing for nuts.*①

熟 1)ⓐ…에 열중하고 있다 ⓑ…을 아주 잘 하다 2)…이 아주 좋아하는 것이다 3)조금도 마음에 두지 않다 4)전혀, 도저히 N.B. 부정어를 수반한 ¶①그녀는 노래는 전혀 못한다 5)(口)난문제

5) ***a hard nut to crack,*** (*colloq.*) a very hard problem.
6) ***off** one's **nut,*** (*colloq.*) ⓐ mad. ⓑ drunken.
—*vi.* (**nut·ted, nut·ting**) gather nuts. ¶*go nutting.*②

6)ⓐ《口》미친 ⓑ술 취한
—[自] 나무 열매를 줍다 ¶②나무 열매를 주우러 가다

nut·crack·er [nʌ́tkrӕkər] *n.* [C] **1.** 《often *pl.*》 a tool for cracking nuts. **2.** a bird of the crow family that feeds on nuts.

—[名] 1. 호도 까는 집게 2. 산갈가마귀

nut·meg [nʌ́tmeg] *n.* [C] a hard, nutlike seed of an East Indian tree, used a as spice or as medicine; its tree.

—[名] 육두구(肉荳蔻); 그 나무

nu·tri·ent [n(j)ú:triənt / njú:-] *n.* [U] anything that gives nourishment. **—*adj.*** nutritious.

—[名] 영양물 —[形] 영양이 풍부한

nu·tri·ment [n(j)ú:trimənt / njú:-] *n.* [U] anything that gives nourishment; food. ¶*Wheat contains a great amount of ~.*①

—[名] 자양물; 음식 ¶①밀에는 많은 자양분이 있다

nu·tri·tion [n(j)ù:tríʃ(ə)n / njù:-] *n.* [U] **1.** the act of nourishing; the state of being nourished. **2.** nourishment; food.

—[名] 1. 영양[작용·섭취·상태] 2. 영양물; 음식

nu·tri·tious [n(j)u:tríʃəs / nju:-] *adj.* having or supplying much nourishment. ¶*a ~ diet.*①

—[形] 자양분이 많은 ¶①영양이 많은 식사

nu·tri·tive [n(j)ú:tritiv / njú:-] *adj.* **1.** of nutrition. **2.** promoting the process of nourishing; nutritious.

—[形] 1. 영양의 2. 영양이 풍부한, 영양이 되는

nut·shell [nʌ́tʃèl] *n.* [C] the hard shell of a nut.
in a nutshell, very clearly and briefly.

—[名] [호도·밤 따위의] 껍데기
[熟] 아주 간결하게

nut·ty [nʌ́ti] *adj.* (**-ti·er, -ti·est**) **1.** having many nuts. **2.** having a taste like nuts. **3.** (*colloq.*) excessively fond of (something); crazy; mad. ¶*be ~ about sports cars.* **4.** (*colloq.*) smart; showy.

—[形] 1. 나무 열매가 많은 2. 나무 열매의 맛이 나는 3.《口》열중한; 미친 4.《口》멋진; 화려한

nuz·zle [nʌ́zl] *vt., vi.* **1.** (of hogs, etc.) root up land with the nose. **2.** push the nose against (something). **3.** lie or sleep close together; hold lovingly. ¶*~ oneself against (into, up to, etc.) something.*①

—[他][自] 1. [돼지 따위가] 주둥이로 구멍을 파다 2. 코를 비벼대다 3. 붙어자다; 끌어안다 ¶①…에 바싹 다가붙다

N. Y. New York State.
N. Y. C. New York City.

•**ny·lon** [náilɑn / -lɔn] *n.* [U] **1.** a very strong chemical substance used to make clothes and stockings. **2.** 《*pl.*》 stockings made of this material.

—[名] 1. 나일론 2. 나일론 양말

•**nymph** [nimf] *n.* [C] **1.** (in Greek and Roman mythology) a goddess living in rivers, seas, springs, trees, hills, etc. **2.** (*poetic*) a beautiful girl.

—[名] 1. 님프 2. 미소녀

O

O¹, o [ou] *n.* [C] (pl. **O's, Os, o's, os**) **1.** the 15th letter of the English alphabet. **2.** anything shaped like the letter O. **3.** a zero.

—[名] 1. 영어 알파벳의 열 다섯째 글자 2. O자형[의 것] 3. 영(零)

⁝**O², oh** [ou] *interj.* an exclamation that shows surprise, terror, wish, joy, etc. ¶*O dear me!*① / *Oh, I miss you!* [⇒usage]

—[感] 오오!, 아아!, 어머나, ¶①어머나! [N.B.] O에는 코머를 안 붙이나 oh에는 붙임

o' [ə] *prep.* =of; on. ¶*3 o'clock.*

⁝**oak** [ouk] *n.* [C] **1.** a tree with hard, tough wood and nuts called acorns. **2.** a leaf of this tree. **3.** the wood of this tree. **—*adj.*** [made] of oak.

—[名] 1. 오우크나무 2. 오우크나무 잎사귀 3. 오우크 재목 —[形] 오우크 나무의; 오우크 재목의

oak·en [óuk(ə)n] *adj.* made of oak.

—[形] 오우크나무의, 오우크나무로 만든

oa·kum [óukəm] *n.* [U] the loose fiber of old hemp used for filling up the cracks of a ship.

—[名] 뱃밥(배의 판자 틈을 메우는 것)

•**oar** [ɔ:r] *n.* [C] **1.** a long pole with a flat end, used for rowing a boat. **2.** a person who uses an oar; an oarsman.
1) ***be chained to the oar,*** be forced to do hard work.
2) ***have an oar in every man's boat,*** put a word in about everything.
3) ***lie*** (or ***rest***) ***on one's oar,*** stop work for a time and rest.
4) ***pull a good oar,*** row skillfully.

—[名] 1. 노(櫓) 2. 노젓는 사람
[熟] 1)중노동을 강요당하다 2)누구의 일에고 참견하다 3)잠시 쉬다 4)능란하게 젓다

oar·lock [ɔ́:rlɑ̀k / ɔ́:lɔ̀k] *n.* ⓒ a U-shaped metal support on the side of a boat on which an oar is rested; a rowlock. ⇒fig. —名 노받이

oars·man [ɔ́:rzmən] *n.* ⓒ (pl. **-men** [-mən]) a person who uses an oar. —名 노젓는 사람

o·a·ses [ouéisi:z] *n.* pl. of **oasis**.

o·a·sis [ouéisis, +U.S. óuə-] *n.* ⓒ (pl. **-ses**) a place in a desert where there are trees and water. —名 오아시스(사막 가운데의 녹지대)

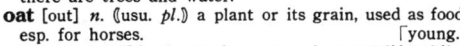
[oarlock]

• **oat** [out] *n.* ((usu. *pl.*)) a plant or its grain, used as food, esp. for horses. —名 귀리, 연맥(燕麥)
「young.」
sow one's wild oats, lead a gay or immoral life while 熟 젊었을 때에 방탕하다

oat·en [óutn] *adj.* of or made of oats or an oat straw. —形 귀리[제(製)]의 ¶①보리피리
¶*an ~ pipe* (or *flute*).①

• **oath** [ouθ] *n.* ⓒ (pl. **oaths** [ouðz, ouθs]) **1.** a solemn statement or promise to God, expressing that something is true. ¶*a false ~*① / *an ~ of office; an official ~*①/ *on* (or *upon*) *my* [*Bible*] *~*③ / *make* (or *swear, take*) *an ~.*④ **2.** a curse; a swear-word. ¶*He threw a stone at the dog with an ~.*⑤
—名 1. 맹세; [법정에 있어서의] 선서 ¶①거짓 맹세/②취임 선서/③맹세코/④서약하다; 선서하다 2.저주; 욕설 ¶⑤그는 욕을 하며 개에게 돌을 던졌다

take one's oath that ... (or *on something*), promise or declare something by making an oath; swear solemnly. ¶*I'll take my ~ that I was there.*
熟 …은 확실하다고 맹세하다;…을 선서하다

oat·meal [óutmì:l] *n.* Ⓤ the meal made from oats. —名 오우트미일 죽

ob·du·ra·cy [ábd(j)urəsi / ɔ́bdju-] *n.* Ⓤ the quality or state of being obdurate. —名 고집, 완고, 냉혹

ob·du·rate [ábd(j)urit / ɔ́bdju-] *adj.* hard-hearted; stubborn; obstinate. ¶*an ~ old man.* ▷**ob·du·rate·ly** [-li] *adv.* —**ob·du·rate·ness** [-nis] *n.*
—形 완고한; 고집 센; 냉혹한

• **o·be·di·ence** [əbí:diəns] *n.* Ⓤ the act of obeying what is told or ordered; the state of being obedient; submission; faithfulness. ¶*blind ~*① / *in ~ to something*② / *reduce to ~.*③
—名 복종; 순종; 충실 ¶①맹종/②…에 복종하여, …에 따라서/③복종시키다

‡ **o·be·di·ent** [əbí:diənt] *adj.* willing to obey; eager to do what is told or ordered. ¶*~ to one's parents.*①
—形 순종하는, 유순한 ¶①부모에게 효성스러운

o·be·di·ent·ly [əbí:diəntli] *adv.* in an obedient manner; faithfully. —副 순종하여

o·bei·sance [oubéis(ə)ns, +U.S. oubí:-] *n.* **1.** ⓒ a low bow that expresses respect. ¶*make an ~ to someone.*① **2.** Ⓤ homage; obedience; submission. ¶*do* (or *make, pay*) *~ to someone.*②
—名 1. 절, 인사 ¶①…에게 절하다 2. 존경; 복종 ¶②…에게 경의를 표하다

ob·e·lisk [ábilisk / ɔ́b-] *n.* ⓒ a high, four-sided stone pillar, pointed at the top, set up as a monument. —名 방첨탑(方尖塔), 오벨리스크

o·bese [oubí:s] *adj.* very fat; stout. 「being obese.」 —形 뚱뚱한
o·bes·i·ty [oubésiti / -bí:s-] *n.* Ⓤ the quality or state of —名 비만, 비대

‡ **o·bey** [oubéi] *vt., vi.* **1.** do what is told or ordered; follow the rules. **2.** act according to (an instinct, etc.). ¶*Animals ~ their instincts.*
—他自 1. [명령 따위에] 복종하다; [법령 따위를] 지키다 2. [양심·본능 따위]에 따라서 행동하다

o·bit·u·ar·y [oubítʃuèri / -tju(ə)ri] *n.* ⓒ a notice of someone's death in a newspaper, often with a short account of his life; a register of dead persons. —*adj.* of death. ¶*an ~ notice.*
—名 사망 공고; 사망자 명부 —形 사망의, 죽은 사람의

‡ **ob·ject** *n.* [ábdʒikt / ɔ́b- → *v.*] ⓒ **1.** anything that can be seen or touched; a material thing. **2.** a person or thing to which people direct their feeling, thought, or action. ¶*an ~ of love.* **3.** (*colloq.*) a pitiful or funny person or thing. ¶*What a funny-looking ~ he is!* **4.** an aim; a purpose; a goal; an end. ¶*I came here with the sole ~ of making money.*① **5.** (*Grammar*) a word or group of words to which the action of the verb is directed or to which a preposition expresses some relation.
—名 1. 사물; 물체 2. [감정·사상·동작의] 대상 3. (口) 우스운 것, 불쌍한 녀석 4. 목표; 목적 ¶①단지 돈을 벌기 위해 여기 왔다 5. 《文法》 목적어

—*v.* [əbdʒékt] *vi.* protest; be opposed; feel dislike. ((~ *to something*)) ¶*She objected to being treated like a*
—自 항의하다; 이의를 신립하다; 싫어하다 ¶②그녀는 어린애 취급을 받는

objection — obnoxious

child. / *I don't ~ to a good glass of whisky.* —*vt.* give a reason against (something); oppose. (*~ that ...*) ¶*They ~ that he was dishonest.* / *He objected two facts against* (or *to*) *the theory.*

ob·jec·tion [əbdʒékʃ(ə)n] *n.* **1.** ⒸⓊ the act of objecting; opposition; disapproval; dislike. ¶*I feel an ~ to going* / *I have no ~ to going there.* **2.** Ⓒ something objected to; an obstacle; a defect. ¶*the chief ~ to the novel.*
make (or *take*) *objection to* (or *against*), oppose.
¶*He made an ~ to what I said.*

것을 싫어했다 ③위스키 한 잔을 달게 먹겠읍니다 —他 반대 이유로서 …을 꺼내다(말하다)

—名 1. 반대; 이의(異議); 불만 ¶①가고 싶지 않다/②나는 거기 가는 데에 반대하지 않겠다 2. 난점(難點); 결함; 지장(支障) ¶③그 소설의 주요한 난점
熟 …에 반대하다

ob·jec·tion·a·ble [əbdʒékʃ(ə)nəbl] *adj.* **1.** tending to cause objection. **2.** unpleasant; undesirable.

—形 1. 반대할 만한, 불쾌한, 불만인 2. 마음에 들지 않는; 불쾌한

ob·jec·tive [əbdʒéktiv] *n.* Ⓒ **1.** (*Grammar*) the objective case. **2.** the object or purpose which is aimed at.
—*adj.* **1.** of the outward things. **2.** (*Philosophy*) really existing outside the mind; real. ↔subjective ¶*an ~ method.* **3.** of the object or purpose of an action or thought. **4.** (*Grammar*) of the object of a verb or preposition. ¶*~ genitive* (or *possessive*).

—名 1. 〔문법〕목적격 2. 목표, 목적
—形 1. 외계의 2. 〔哲〕실재(實在)의, 객관적인 ¶①객관적 방법 3. 목적의 4. 〔文法〕목적격의 ¶②목적 소유격

ob·jec·tive·ly [əbdʒéktivli] *adv.* in an objective manner.
ob·jec·tiv·i·ty [ὰbdʒektíviti / ɔ̀b-] *n.* Ⓤ the state of being objective; impersonal or impartial judgement.

—副 객관적으로, 객관적 견지에서
—名 객관성, 객관적 타당성

ob·jec·tor [əbdʒéktər] *n.* Ⓒ a person who objects or protests.

—名 반대자

ob·jur·gate [ábdʒə(ː)rgéit, əbdʒə́ːrgeit / ɔ́bdʒəːgèit] *vt.* scold; abuse; blame.
ob·jur·ga·tion [ὰbdʒə(ː)rgéiʃ(ə)n / ɔ̀bdʒə-] *n.* Ⓤ the act of objurgating; abuse.

—他 …을 구짖다, 질책하다; 비난하다
—名 꾸지람; 비난

ob·li·ga·tion [ὰbligéiʃ(ə)n / ɔ̀b-] *n.* **1.** ⓊⒸ a duty. **2.** Ⓤ a sum which one must pay; a debt.
1) *be under an obligation to* (=*must do something*)
2) *of obligation,* required. [*for*) *someone.*
3) *repay an obligation,* return another's kindness.

—名 1. 의무; 의리 2. 채무
熟 1) …에 의리(의무)가 있다 2) 의무적인 3) 은혜에 보답하다

o·blige [əbláidʒ] *vt.* **1.** force; compel. (*~ someone to do*) ¶*I won't ~ you to stay here any longer.* **2.** do a kindness to (someone); satisfy a desire of (someone). ¶*Oblige me by shutting the door.* / *Will any gentleman ~ a lady?* / *She obliged me with a song.* / *I am much obliged to you.* —*vi.* (*colloq.*) be kind enough to do something. ¶*Can you ~ a song?*

—他 1. …을 어쩔 수 없이 …하게 하다, 강제하다 2. …에게 친절히 하다; 은혜를 베풀다; …의 소원을 들어주다 ¶①어느 분이시든 숙녀에게 자리를 양보하시지 않겠읍니까?/②그녀는 고맙게도 노래를 해 주었다 —自 《口》 호의를 보이다, 소원을 들어 주다

o·blig·ing [əbláidʒiŋ] *adj.* willing to do favors; kind.
▷**o·blig·ing·ly** [-li] *adv.*

—形 친절한

ob·lique [əblíːk] *adj.* **1.** slanting; (*Mathematics*) neither vertical nor horizontal. ¶*~ lines.* **2.** not frank; indirect. ¶*~ praise.* —*vi.* slant; turn aside; change the original direction.

—形 1. 비스듬한, 기운; 사선(斜線)의 ¶①사선 2. 간접적인, 완곡한 ¶②넌지시 하는 칭찬 —自 〔비스듬히〕기울다; 구부러지다; 빗나가다

ob·liq·ui·ty [əblíkwiti] *n.* ⓊⒸ the state of being oblique; indirectness; dishonesty.

—名 비스듬함, 사각(斜角); 완곡함; 부정(不正)

ob·lit·er·ate [əblítərèit] *vt.* rub out or blot out (something); remove all traces of (something); destroy. ¶*The earthquake obliterated an entire city.*

—他 …을 말살하다; 흔적을 없애다 ¶①지진으로 온 도시가 흔적도 없이 사라졌다

ob·liv·i·on [əblíviən] *n.* Ⓤ the state of being forgotten; the act of forgetting. ¶*in utter ~ of something.*
fall (or *sink*) *into oblivion,* become forgotten; die from the memory of the world.

—名 망각 ¶①…을 완전히 잊고서
熟 세상에서 잊혀지다

ob·liv·i·ous [əblíviəs] *adj.* forgetful; not mindful. ¶*be ~ of something.* ▷**ob·liv·i·ous·ly** [-li] *adv.* —**ob·liv·i·ous·ness** [-nis] *n.*

—形 잊기 쉬운; 부주의한, 희미한 ¶①…을 잊다

ob·long [áblɔːŋ / ɔ́blɔŋ] *adj.* greater in length than in breadth. —*n.* Ⓒ a figure longer than it is broad; a rectangle.

—形 장방형의, 타원형의 —名 장방형, 타원형

ob·lo·quy [áblokwi / ɔ́b-] *n.* Ⓤ bad words spoken of a person or thing; ill repute; disgrace.

—名 욕설; 오명; 불명예, 창피

ob·nox·ious [əbnάkʃəs / -nɔ́k-] *adj.* very unpleasant; disagreeable; hateful. ¶*an ~ odor.* ▷**ob·nox·ious·ly**

—形 기분 나쁜, 불쾌한; 싫은, 미음에 산 ¶①역겨운 냄새

[-li] *adv.* —**ob·nox·ious·ness** [-nis] *n.*

o·boe [óubou] *n.* [C] a wind musical instrument made of wood.
—[名] 오보에(고음 목관 악기)

ob·scene [əbsí:n] *adj.* (**-scen·er, -scen·est**) filthy; not decent; impure.
—[形] 외설스러운, 음탕한

ob·scen·i·ty [əbséniti, -sí:n-] *n.* [U] the state of being obscene in language or action.
—[名] 외설

***ob·scure** [əbskjúər] *adj.* **1.** not easily understood; not clear in meaning; vague. ¶*an ~ meaning (answer, argument, explanation).* **2.** not well known; not famous; hidden. ¶*an ~ scholar / of ~ origin (birth).*① **3.** dim; dark; gloomy. ¶*an ~ corner of the back room.* —*vt.* **1.** darken; hide. ¶*The sun was obscured by clouds.* **2.** make (something) less clear; make (something) difficult to be understood.
—[形] **1.** 알기 어려운; 뚜렷하지 않은; 애매한 **2.** 잘 알려져 있지 않은, 무명의; 숨겨진 ¶①기원(태생)이 분명치 않은 **3.** 어두컴컴한
—[他] **1.** …을 어둡게 하다; 흐리게 하다; 덮어 가리다 **2.** …을 희미하게 하다; 애매하게 하다

ob·scure·ly [əbskjúərli] *adv.* in an obscure manner.
—[副] 어둡게; 희미하게; 이름 없이

ob·scu·ri·ty [əbskjúəriti] *n.* (pl. **-ties**) **1.** [U] the state of being obscure; darkness; dimness. **2.** [C] an obscure or indistinct thing. **3.** [C] an unknown person or place.
—[名] **1.** 불명료; 어둠; 몽롱함 **2.** 불분명[한 곳] **3.** 무명의 사람[장소]

sink into obscurity, be buried without ever having become famous.
[熟] 세상에 파묻히다

ob·se·quies [ábsikwiz / 5b-] *n. pl.* the funeral ceremonies.
—[名] 장례식

ob·se·qui·ous [əbsí:kwiəs] *adj.* eager to obey and serve, esp. in expectation of reward. ▷**ob·se·qui·ous·ly** [-li] *adv.* —**ob·se·qui·ous·ness** [-nis] *n.*
—[形] 비위를 맞추는, 알랑거리는

ob·serv·a·ble [əbzə́:rvəbl] *adj.* **1.** that can be seen or noticed. **2.** remarkable; noticeable. **3.** deserving to be kept.
—[形] **1.** 관찰할 수 있는 **2.** 주목할 만한, 눈에 띄는 **3.** 지켜야 할

***ob·serv·ance** [əbzə́:rv(ə)ns] *n.* **1.** [U] the act of observing or keeping a law, custom, etc. **2.** [C] a customary ceremony; a custom. ¶*Church services are religious observances.*①
—[名] **1.** [법률·습관 따위의] 준수 **2.** [특히 종교상의] 의식; 관례 ¶①교회의 예배는 종교상의 의식이다

ob·serv·ant [əbzə́:rv(ə)nt] *adj.* quick to pay attention; watchful; attentive. ▷**ob·serv·ant·ly** [-li] *adv.*
—[形] 주의 깊은; 관찰력이 날카로운

‡**ob·ser·va·tion** [àbzə(:)rvéiʃ(ə)n / ɔ̀bzə(:)v-] *n.* **1.** [U] the act of observing; careful notice; the state of being observed. ¶*escape ~.*① **2.** the power of noticing. ¶*a man of no ~.*② **3.** [C] a result or fact obtained by observing; something noticed; 《*pl.*》 the notes, remarks, or records of what is observed. **4.** [C] a remark or comment based on observing. ¶*make an ~ about something.*③
—[名] **1.** 관찰; 관측; 주목 ¶①눈에 띄지 않다 **2.** 관찰력 ¶②관찰력이 없는 사내 **3.** [관찰에 의해 얻은] 지식; 관측기록 **4.** 관찰에 입각한 소견; 강평, 소견 ¶③…에 대해 소견을 말하다(발언하다)

come (or ***fall***) ***under*** *someone's* ***observation,*** catch someone's attention. ¶*An unlawful act has come under the policeman's ~.*④
[熟] …의 눈에 띄다 ¶④어떤 부정행위가 경관의 눈에 띄었다

ob·serv·a·to·ry [əbzə́:rvətɔ̀:ri / -zə́:vət(ə)ri] *n.* [C] (pl. **-ries**) a building for observing and studying the sun, stars, etc.; a place for observing the weather, etc.
—[名] 천문대; 관측소

‡**ob·serve** [əbzə́:rv] *vt.* **1.** watch carefully. 《~ *how* or *what* …》 ¶*~ the stars / Observe how to do that.*① **2.** be aware of (something); notice. 《~ someone *do* or *doing*; ~ *that*…》 ¶*I observed something queer in his behavior.*② */ I observed him open* (or *opening*) *the door. / Then I observed that she had turned pale.* **3.** keep; follow; obey. ¶*~ a rule.* **4.** celebrate. ¶*~ Christmas (someone's birthday).* **5.** remark; say. 《~ *that* …》 ¶*She observed that we might have rain soon. / He observed nothing on the subject.* —*vi.* **1.** take notice; act as an observer. ¶*He observed keenly but said nothing.* **2.** say; remark. 《~ *on* or *upon* something》 ¶*No one observed on that subject.*
—[他] **1.** …을 관찰하다; 잘 보다 ¶①그것을 하는 방법을 잘 봐 둬라 **2.** …을 알아채다; [관찰에 의하여] …을 알게 되다 ¶②그의 처신에서 어딘가 이상한 점을 알게 됐다 **3.** [법률 따위]를 지키다 **4.** [식]을 거행하다; [축제]를 축하하다 **5.** …을 [의견으로서] 말하다; …이라고 말하다 —[自] **1.** 알아채다; 관찰하다 **2.** 의견을 말하다

***ob·serv·er** [əbzə́:rvər] *n.* [C] **1.** a person who watches. **2.** a person who follows certain rules or customs. **3.** a person who attends a meeting, etc. but has no part in it.
—[名] **1.** 관찰자 **2.** 준수자 **3.** 어브저어버(표결권 없이 회의에 참석하는 사람)

ob·serv·ing [əbzə́:rviŋ] *adj.* observant; quick to notice.
—[形] 관찰력이 날카로운; 주의 깊은

ob·sess [əbsés] *vt.* 《usu. *in passive*》 fill the mind with
—[他] [근심·망상 따위가] 들다, 붙다

(a fear, a wild fancy, etc.) completely. ¶*She is always obsessed by* (or *with*) *the idea of her own inferiority.*①
¶①그녀는 언제나 열등감에 사로잡혀 있다

ob·ses·sion [əbséʃ(ə)n] *n.* **1.** [U] the state of being ruled by a fixed idea. **2.** [C] a fixed idea which takes possession of one's mind.
—[名] 1. [귀신 따위에] 들리기, 사로잡혀 있기 2. 강박관념

ob·so·les·cent [àbsoulésnt / ɔ̀b-] *adj.* going out of use; becoming obsolete.
—[形] 없어져(스러져) 가는

ob·so·lete [ábsəlìːt / ɔ́b-] *adj.* out of date; no longer used or in fashion.
—[形] 스러진, 안 쓰이는

* **ob·sta·cle** [ábstəkl / ɔ́b-] *n.* [C] something that stands in the way and stops progress; hindrance. ¶*an ~ race* / *High tariffs are the chief obstacles to free trade.*①
—[名] 방해물; 장애; 지장(支障) ¶①높은 관세가 자유 무역의 주요 장애이다

ob·stet·ric [əbstétrik / ɔb-] *adj.* of the care of women in childbirth.
—[形] 산과(産科)의; 산파의

ob·sti·na·cy [ábstinəsi / ɔ́b-] *n.* (pl. **-cies**) [U] the state of being obstinate; stubbornness; [C] an obstinate act or attitude.
—[名] 완고, 고집; 완고한 행위(태도)

* **ob·sti·nate** [ábstinit / ɔ́b-] *adj.* **1.** not giving up one's opinion; unwilling to obey; stubborn. ¶*an ~ person.* **2.** (of disease) hard to recover from. ¶*an ~ cough.*①
—[形] 1. 완고한; 외고집의; 끈덕진 2. [병이] 난치의 ¶①잘 멎지 않는 기침

ob·sti·nate·ly [ábstinitli / ɔ́b-] *adv.* in an obstinate manner.
—[副] 완고하게, 고집 세게

ob·struct [əbstrʌ́kt] *vt., vi.* make (progress, development, etc.) difficult; disturb; hinder.
—[他][自] [진보 따위를] 방해(저해)하다

ob·struc·tion [əbstrʌ́kʃ(ə)n] *n.* [U] the act of obstructing. [C] something that obstructs.
—[名] 방해; 장애; 방해물

ob·struc·tive [əbstrʌ́ktiv] *adj.* causing or likely to cause obstruction. ¶*The noises from the streets are ~ to his study.*① —*n.* [C] a person or thing that obstructs.
—[形] 방해하는, 방해가 되는 ¶①거리의 소음이 그의 공부의 방해가 된다 —[名] 방해자(물)

⁑ **ob·tain** [əbtéin] *vt.* **1.** get or gain (something) through effort. ¶*~ a reward* / *~ a livelihood.* **2.** accomplish; fulfill. —*vi.* be established; be in fashion; prevail. ¶*The custom still obtains in some districts.*①
—[他] 1. …을 얻다 2. …을 해내다 —[自] 행하여지다; 유행(통용)되다 ¶①그 습관은 어떤 지역에 아직 남아 있다

ob·tain·a·ble [əbtéinəbl] *adj.* that can be obtained.
—[形] 얻을 수 있는, 수행할 수 있는

ob·trude [əbtrúːd] *vt., vi.* push (oneself, one's opinions, etc.) forward against other's will; force oneself upon others. ¶*Don't ~ your opinions upon others.*①
—[他][自] [의견 따위를] 강요하다, 강제하다; 주제넘게 나서다 ¶①자기의 의견을 남에게 강요하지 말라

ob·tru·sive [əbtrúːsiv] *adj.* inclined to obtrude.
—[形] 주제넘은

ob·tuse [əbt(j)úːs / -tjúːs] *adj.* **1.** (of a knife, etc.) not sharp or pointed; blunt. ↔sharp **2.** (of an angle) having between 90° and 180°. ↔acute **3.** slow to understand; dull. ▷**ob·tuse·ly** [-li] *adv.*
—[形] 1. 무딘; 잘 들지 않는 2. 둔각(鈍角)의 3. 둔감한, 바보의

ob·verse *n.* [ábvəːrs → *adj.* / ɔ́bvəːs] [C] ((*usu. the ~*)) **1.** the side of a coin or medal which has the main design. **2.** the counterpart of a fact. ↔reverse —*adj.* [+*U.S.* abvə́ːrs] **1.** facing the obverse. **2.** being the counterpart of a fact.
—[名] 1. [메달 따위의] 표면 2. [사실 따위의] 이면, 내막 —[形] 1. 표면의 2. 이면의

ob·vi·ate [ábvièit / ɔ́b-] *vt.* remove; clear away; prevent (an disease, etc.)
—[他] [곤란 따위]를 제거하다, 방지하다

* **ob·vi·ous** [ábviəs / ɔ́b-] *adj.* easy to see; evident at a glance; clear. ¶*It is ~ that you are in the wrong.*①
—[形] 분명한, 명백한 ¶①네가 틀렸다는 것은 분명하다

⁑ **ob·vi·ous·ly** [ábviəsli / ɔ́b-] *adv.* clearly; evidently.
—[副] 분명히, 명백히

⁑ **oc·ca·sion** [əkéiʒ(ə)n] *n.* **1.** [C] a particular time; an event. ¶*on this ~* / *on one ~*① / *on several occasions* / *on the ~ of his death.* **2.** [C] a chance; an opportunity. ¶*improve the ~*② / *on the first ~*③ / *This is not an ~ for laughter.*④ **3.** [U] reason; cause; need. ¶*have no ~ to do* / *There is no ~ for you to get excited.*⑤
—[名] 1. [어떤 일이 일어난] 때; 사건 ¶①일찌기, 한 때 2. 기회; 좋은 기회, [···에 알맞은] 경우 ¶②기회를 이용하다/③기회가 있는 대로/④웃을 일이 아니다 3. 근거, 이유; 필요 ¶⑤흥분할 필요는 없다

1) ***on*** (or ***upon***) ***occasion,*** sometimes; now and then.
2) ***rise to the occasion,*** do whatever suddenly becomes necessary.
3) ***take*** (or ***seize***) ***occasion,*** use an opportunity.

[熟] 1)가끔, 때때로 2)임기응변의 조치를 취하다 3)기회를 이용하다

—*vt.* cause. ((*~ someone to do*)) ¶*Her behavior occasioned her parents much anxiety.*
—[他] …의 원인이 되다; …을 야기하다

* **oc·ca·sion·al** [əkéiʒ(ə)n(ə)l] *adj.* **1.** happening sometimes; coming now and then. ¶*an ~ earthquake.* **2.** used
—[形] 1. 이따끔의 2. 임시의

or suitable to a special event or time.

:oc·ca·sion·al·ly [əkéiʒ(ə)nəli] *adv.* now and then; sometimes.

—[副] 때때로, 가끔

Oc·ci·dent [ɑ́ksid(ə)nt / ɔ́k-] *n.* **1.** ⦅*the* ~⦆ the West; Europe and America. ↔Orient **2.** ⦅*the o-*⦆ the west.

—[名] 1. 서양; 구미(歐美) 2. 서방

Oc·ci·den·tal [ɑ̀ksidéntl / ɔ̀k-] *adj.* **1.** of the Occident. ↔Oriental **2.** ⦅*o-*⦆ western. **—*n.*** [C] a person of Occidental countries.

—[形] 1. 서양의 2. 서쪽의 —[名] 서양인

oc·cult [əkʌ́lt, +*U.S.* ɑ́kʌlt] *adj.* **1.** concealed; hidden; secret. **2.** supernatural; magical; mysterious. ¶*Alchemy is one of the ~ sciences.* **—*vt., vi.*** hide or become hidden from view.

—[形] 1. 숨은; 비밀의 2. 초자연적인; 마법적인; 불가사의한 —[他][自] …을 덮어 가리다; 숨다

oc·cu·pan·cy [ɑ́kjupənsi / ɔ́k-] *n.* [U] the act of occupying; the period during which a house, etc. is occupied.

—[名] 점유; 점유 기간

oc·cu·pant [ɑ́kjupənt / ɔ́k-] *n.* [C] a person who makes use of a building, house, or room.

—[名] 점유자; 거주자

:oc·cu·pa·tion [ɑ̀kjupéiʃ(ə)n / ɔ̀k-] *n.* **1.** [C] a business; a profession; [U] employment. ¶*a man out of ~.*① **2.** [U] the act of occupying; the state of being occupied. ¶*an ~ army.* **3.** [U] the period during which a land, a house, etc. is occupied.

—[名] 1. 일; 업무; 직업; 고용 ¶①실업자 2. 점유, 점령; 거주 3. 점유 기간

oc·cu·pa·tion·al [ɑ̀kjupéiʃ(ə)n(ə)l / ɔ̀k-] *adj.* of an occupation. ¶*an ~ disease.*①

—[形] 직업의 ¶①직업병

:oc·cu·py [ɑ́kjupài / ɔ́k-] *vt.* (**-pied**) **1.** take possession of (land, etc.); live in (some place). ¶*~ the enemy's territory*① / *~ a house.* **2.** take up or fill (a certain amount of space, time, position, etc.). ¶*Mr. Jones occupies an important position in this company.*② / *His speech occupied more than one hour.*

—[他] 1. …을 점유(점령)하다; …에 거주하다 ¶①적의 영토를 점령하다 2. [장소·시간 따위]를 차지하다 ¶②조운즈씨는 이 회사에서 중요한 지위를 차지하고 있다

occupy onself in (or ***about, with***)***; be occupied in,*** engage in (something). ¶*He occupied himself with solving the problem.*③ / *We were occupied in building a new bridge.*④

[熟] …에 종사하다 ¶③그는 그 문제의 해결에 몰두했다/④우리들은 새 다리의 건설에 종사했다

:oc·cur [əkə́:r] *vi.* (**-curred, -cur·ring**) **1.** happen; take place. **2.** exist; be found. ¶*Several misprints ~ on the last page.* **3.** come into one's mind. ⦅*~ to* someone⦆ ¶*It occurred to me that I should call on him.*①

—[自] 1. [사물이] 일어나다, 발생하다 2. 있다; 나타나다 3. 마음에 떠오르다 ¶①그를 찾아가 보았으면 하는 생각이 들었다

·oc·cur·rence [əkə́:r(ə)ns / əkʌ́r-] *n.* **1.** [U] the act or fact of occurring. **2.** [C] a happening; an event; an incident. ¶*an everyday ~.*①

—[名] 1. [사건 따위의] 발생 2. 일어난 일; 사건 ¶①일상의 일

be of frequent (***rare***) ***occurence,*** occur frequently (rarely).

[熟] 자주(드물게) 일어나다

:o·cean [óuʃ(ə)n] *n.* [C] **1.** the sea. ¶*the Pacific Ocean.* **2.** a vast expanse of something. ¶*an ~ of light.*① **3.** ⦅usu. *pl.*⦆ (*colloq.*) great quantity. ¶*oceans of money.*

—[名] 1. 대양; 해양; …양(洋) 2. 널따랗게 퍼진 것(곳) 3.⦅口⦆ 많음, 다량

o·ce·an·ic [òuʃiǽnik] *adj.* **1.** of or like the ocean. **2.** living in or produced by the ocean. **3.** vast.

—[形] 1. 해양의; 바다 같은 2. 바다에서 나는; 해산(海産)의 3. 광대한

o·cher, o·chre [óukər] *n.* [U] **1.** a yellowish clay, used for making yellow-brown paint. **2.** a yellow-brown color.

—[名] 1. 황토(그림물감의 원료) 2. 오우커(황갈색)

:o'clock [əklɑ́k / -lɔ́k] *adv.* of the clock; according to the clock. ¶*at three ~.*

—[副] …시(時)

Oct. October.

oc·ta·gon [ɑ́ktəgɑ̀n, -gən / ɔ́ktəgən] *n.* [C] a plane figure with eight sides and eight angles.

—[名] 8 변(각)형, 8 각형의 것

oc·tag·o·nal [ɑktǽgənl / ɔk-] *adj.* of an octagon.

—[形] 8 변(각)형의

oc·tave [ɑ́ktiv, -teiv / ɔ́k-] *n.* [C] **1.** (*Music*) the eighth note in the musical scale; a distance of eight notes on a scale; all the notes within this distance. **2.** (*Poetry*) the first eight lines of a sonnet.

—[名] 1. 제 8 음; 제 8 도; 1 음계 2. 14 행시(sonnet)의 첫 8 행

:Oc·to·ber [ɑktóubər / ɔktóubə] *n.* the tenth month of the year. ⇨[N.B.]

—[名] 10 월

oc·to·pi [ɑ́ktəpai / ɔ́k-] *n.* pl. of **octopus.**

oc·to·pus [ɑ́ktəpəs / ɔ́k-] *n.* [C] (pl. **-pus·es** or **-to·pi** [-pai]) a sea animal with a soft body and eight long arms.

—[名] 문어

oc·u·lar [ɑ́kjulər / ɔ́kjulə] *adj.* of the eyes or sight. ¶*an ~ witness.*①

—[形] 눈의; 시력의 ¶①목격자

:odd [ɑd / ɔd] *adj.* **1.** a little more [than what is needed]; left over. ¶*three hundred* [*and*] *~ pupils*① / *the ~ mon-*

—[形] 1. 여분의, 나머지의 ¶①300 명 남짓한 학생/②6 달러 남짓 2. [두 개 한

O

*ey / Six dollars ~.*② **2.** not paired; missing a part of a set. ¶*an ~ stocking (glove, shoe) / ~ volumes.* **3.** extra; for a short time; occasional. ¶*~ jobs / an ~ hand* (or *man, lad*).③ **4.** (of numbers) not even; not able to be divided by two. ¶*One, three, five, and seven are ~ numbers.* **5.** strange; queer; peculiar. ¶*It is ~ that you did not know it.*

벌로 된 것의] 한 짝의; 짝짝이의; 자투리의 **3.** 임시의; 단기의; 이따금의 ¶③임시 고용원 **4.** 기수(奇數)의 **5.** 별난, 이상한, 기묘한

at odd times (or ***moments***), in spare moments.

熟 때때로, 이따금

odd·i·ty [áditi / ɔ́d-] *n.* (pl. **-ties**) [U] the state of being odd; strangeness; [C] a queer person, thing or act.

—[名] 기묘함, 기이함; 기묘한 것(사람), 괴짜

odd·ly [ádli / ɔ́d-] *adv.* in an odd manner.

—[副] 기묘하게, 이상하게, 기이하게

odd·ment [ádmənt / ɔ́d-] *n.* [C] ⟪usu. *pl.*⟫ something left over; an odd piece.

—[名] 나머지 물건, 동강난 것; 허섭쓰레기

odds [adz / ɔdz] *n. pl.* ⟪sometimes used as *sing.*⟫ **1.** things which are not equal; inequalities. **2.** advantages; chances in favour of one side and against another. ¶*The ~ are in our favor.*①

—[名] **1.** 불평등[한 것]; 차이 **2.** 승산; 유리한 조건 ¶①우리에게 승산이 있다

1) ***be at odds*** (=*quarrel*) ***with*** *someone.*
2) ***by long*** (or ***all***) ***odds,*** by far. ¶*This is by all ~ the easier way.*②
3) ***make no odds,*** keep balanced.
4) ***make odds even,*** make equal.
5) ***odds and ends,*** useless things left over.
6) ***set at odds,*** make (someone) quarrel.

熟 1)…와 다투고 있다 2)훨씬 ¶②이 편이 훨씬 쉽다 3)균형이 잡혀 있다 4)비등비등하게 만들다 5)허섭쓰레기 6)…을 다투게 하다

ode [oud] *n.* [C] a poem which expresses noble feelings in a solemn style, usu. in honor of a person or event.

—[名] 송시(頌詩), 부(賦)

o·di·ous [óudiəs] *adj.* hateful; unpleasant; ugly. ▷**o·di·ous·ly** [-li] *adv.* —**o·di·ous·ness** [-nis] *n.*

—[形] 미운, 밉살스러운; 불쾌한; 추악한

o·di·um [óudiəm] *n.* [U] hatred; ill feeling.

—[名] 증오, 반감

• **o·dor,** *Brit.* **-dour** [óudər] *n.* **1.** [C] smell; scent; fragrance. **2.** [U] reputation.

—[名] **1.** 냄새; 향기, 방향(芳香) **2.** 평판, 인기

o·dor·ous [óudərəs] *adj.* having an odor; sweet-smelling; fragrant.

—[形] 향기 있는, 방향(芳香)을 내는

O·dys·se·us [oudísjuːs, -siəs] *n.* =Ulysses.

Od·ys·sey [ádisi / ɔ́d-] *n.* an epic poem about Odysseus, a Greek hero, written by Homer.

—[名] Homer가 쓴 대서사시

• **o'er** [ouər / ɔːr] *prep., adv.* (*poetic*) =over.

⁝ **of** [ʌv, əv, v, +*U.S.* ɑv, +*Brit.* ɔv] *prep.* **1.** belonging to. ¶*the men ~ that time / a leg ~ a table / a friend ~ mine.* **2.** parted from; cut from. **3.** containing. ¶*a cup ~ tea.* **4.** made of or from; using as the material. ¶*a house ~ wood / made ~ brick / a piece ~ paper.* **5.** about; concerning. ¶*be hard ~ hearing / be sixty years ~ age*① */ tell someone ~ an accident / be quick ~ eye*② */ be afraid ~ dying.*③ **6.** that is [the same as]; named. ¶*the city ~ New York / [the] three ~ us*④ */ an angel ~ a girl*⑤ */ the fact ~ my having done it.*⑥ **7.** away from. ¶*three miles west ~ the river / rob him ~ a purse*⑦ */ borrow money ~ one's brother.* **8.** caused by. ¶*die ~ heart failure*⑧ */ die ~ sorrow.* **9.** having; being. ⇒[N.B.] ¶*a man ~ ability*⑨ */ a girl ~ twelve*⑩ */ a look ~ pity.* **10.** by. ¶*the works ~ Shakespeare.* **11.** toward; directed to. ¶*the love ~ God / the fear ~ God.* **12.** (of time) on; during. ¶*~ recent years*⑪ */ ~ late years / ~ a Sunday.* **13.** (of time) (*U.S. colloq.*) before; to. ↔after ¶*at ten minutes ~ six.*⑫

—[前] **1.** …의; …에 속하는 **2.** …의 일부의; …의 가운데의 **3.** …이 들어간 **4.** …으로 만든; …을 재료로 한 **5.** …에 대해서[는], 관해서[는] ¶①나이는 60이다/②눈이 빠르다/③죽음을 두려워하다 **6.** …이라고 하는; …인 바의 ¶④우리들 세 사람/⑤천사 같은 소녀/⑥내가 그것을 했다는 사실 **7.** …에서 [떠나서] ¶⑦그에게서 지갑을 빼앗다 **8.** …에 의한; …의 원인으로 ¶⑧심장마비로 죽다 **9.** …을 가진; …인 [N.B.] of+명사로 형사구를 만듦 ¶⑨재능이 있는 사람/⑩12세의 소녀 **10.** …의 손으로 된 **11.** …으로의; …에 대한 **12.** …의 때; …의 사이 ¶⑪근래 몇 년 동안 **13.** …전 ¶⑫ 6시 10분 전

⁝ **off** [ɔːf / ɔ(ː)f] *prep.* **1.** not on; away from. ¶*three miles ~ the road / A button is ~ your coat.*① */ She took the ring ~ her third finger.* **2.** seaward from. ¶*~ the coast of / ~ the harbor.* **3.** less than. ¶*It was sold at ten percent ~ the usual price.*②

—[前] **1.** …에서 [떨어져서, 벗어나서] ¶①웃옷의 단추가 벗겨져 있다 **2.** 앞바다로 **3.** …에서 빼고, …보다 적게 ¶②그것은 가격보다 1할 싸게 팔렸다

—adv. **1.** away. ¶*take ~ one's hat / work with one's coat ~*③ */ go ~ on a journey.*④ **2.** distant in time or space. ¶*three years ~ / far ~ / three miles ~.* **3.** so as to stop or make less. ¶*turn the water ~*⑤ */ leave ~ work.*⑥ **4.** in full; wholly; completely. ¶*drink*

—[副] **1.** 떠나서; 떨어져; 벗어져 ¶③웃옷을 벗고 일하다/④여행을 떠나다 **2.** [시간・거리가] 떨어져서 **3.** 멈춰서; 줄어서 ¶⑤물을 막다/⑥일을 끝마치다 **4.** 완전히, 끝까지 **5.** 일을 쉬어; 한

~ / *clear ~ the table.* **5.** without work. ¶*We were ~ for the afternoon.* / *We get two days ~ at Christmas.*

가하여

—*adj.* **1.** farther; far. ¶*on the ~ side of the wall.* **2.** away from work; not busy; not active. ¶*during ~ hours* / *an ~ day* / *an ~ season for fishing.* **3.** wrong; in error; not normal. ¶*You are ~ on that point.* / *He is a little ~, but he's really harmless.*⑦ **4.** on the way; beginning; starting. ¶*The train started and we were ~ on our trip.*⑧

—[形] 1. 먼쪽의, 저쪽의 2. 쉬는; 임무에서 떠난; 불활발한 3. 틀려서; 머리가 돌아서; 정상이 아닌 ¶⑦그는 좀 머리가 돌았지만 위험은 전혀 없다 4. 떠나는, 출발하는 ¶⑧기차가 발차하여 우리는 여행 길에 오르게 되었다

1) ***be off,*** go away; leave quickly.
2) ***Keep off!,*** Don't come near!
3) ***off and on; on and off,*** now and then.
4) ***Off with you!,*** Go away!; Depart!

[熟] 1)떠나다; 도망하다 2)가까이 오지 말라! 3)때때로 4)꺼져라!, 없어져라

of·fal [ɔ́ːf(ə)l, ɑ́f- / ɔ́f-] *n.* [U] the useless parts of fish or other animals killed for food; waste and worthless matter.

—[名] 찌꺼기 고기; 쓰레기, 폐물

‡of·fence [əféns] *n.* (*Brit.*) =offense.

•of·fend [əfénd] *vt.* **1.** hurt the feelings of (someone); make (someone) angry or displeased. ¶*I am sorry if I've offended you.*① / *She was offended at* (or *by*) *his rude manners.* **2.** cause (someone) to sin. —*vi.* commit a crime; break a law, custom, religious code, etc.

—[他] 1. …의 감정을 해치다; …을 성나게 하다 ¶①네 기분을 해쳤다면 미안하다 2. …에게 죄를 저지르게 하다 —[自] 죄를 저지르다; [법률 따위를] 어기다

offend the ear (***the eye***), be a displeasing sound (sight).

[熟] 귀(눈)에 거슬리는

of·fend·er [əféndər] *n.* [C] a person who breaks a law or rule. ¶*a first ~*① / *an old* (or *a repeated*) *~.*②

—[名] 범죄자; 위반자 ¶①초범자/②상습범

‡of·fense, *Brit.* **-fence** [əféns] *n.* **1.** [C] the act of breaking a law or rule; sin; crime. ¶*an ~ against good manners.* **2.** [U] attack. **3.** [C] something that hurts a person's mind; insult; displeasure.

—[名] 1. 위반; 반칙; 죄; 범죄 2. 공격 3. 불쾌한 일; 모욕

1) ***give offense to,*** make (someone) displeased; insult.
2) ***take offense*** (=*become displeased*) ***at*** *something.*

[熟] 1)…을 불쾌하게 하다; 모욕하다 2)…에 불쾌해지다

•of·fen·sive [əfénsiv] *adj.* **1.** unpleasant; disgusting. ¶*~ to the eye*① / *That smell is ~.*② **2.** insulting; not respectful. ¶*~ language.*③ **3.** attacking; aggressive. ↔defensive —*n.* [C] (*often the ~*) an attack; an aggression.

—[形] 1. 싫은 ¶①눈에 거슬리는/②저 냄새는 역겹다 2. 무례한, 괘씸한 ¶③욕설 3. 공격적인 —[名] 공격, 공세

take the offensive, be aggressive.

[熟] 공세로 나가다

‡of·fer [ɔ́ːfər, ɑ́f- / ɔ́fə] *vt.* **1.** give (someone) a chance to get; present. (*~to do*) ¶*~ to help someone*① / *~ one's hand*② / *She offered me her help.* **2.** present (something) to God. ¶*~ a prayer* [*to God*] / *~ up sacrifices.* **3.** propose; suggest. ¶*Everyone offered his own solution.* **4.** try; attempt. (*~ to do*) ¶*He offered to strike me.* **5.** show (something) for sale; bid (an amount of money) as a price. ¶*He offered* [*me*] *forty dollars for the goods.*

—[他] 1. …에 제의하다; …을 제공하다; 내밀다 ¶①원조를 제의하다/②손을 내밀다 2. …을 [신에게] 바치다, 드리다 3. …을 제의(제안)하다 4. …하려고 하다; 기도하다, 시도하다 5. …을 팔려고 내놓다; …의 값을 부르다

—*vi.* **1.** occur; be proposed. ¶*I shall seize the first opportunity that offers.* **2.** sacrifice in worship.

—[自] 1. 일어나다; 나타나다; 제공되다 2. [제물로서] 바치다

—*n.* [C] **1.** the act of offering; something offered. ¶*an ~ of help.* **2.** a price offered. ¶*an ~ of $35,000 for a house.*

—[名] 1. 신청; 제공; 제의 2. 매긴 값; 산 값

goods on offer, goods for sale at a certain price.

[熟] 팔 것

•of·fer·ing [ɔ́ːfəriŋ, ɑ́f- / ɔ́f-] *n.* **1.** [U] the act of making a proposal. **2.** [C] a gift esp. to the church.

—[名] 1. 신청, 신입 2. 봉납[물], 제물; [교회에 대한] 헌금

off·hand [ɔ́ːfhǽnd / ɔ́(ː)f-] *adj.* made or done without preparation; careless. —*adv.* in an offhand manner; without preparation.

—[形] 즉석의; 되는 대로의 —[副] 즉석에서; 아무렇게나

off·hand·ed [ɔ́ːfhǽndid] *adj.* =offhand.

‡of·fice [ɔ́ːfis, ɑ́f- / ɔ́f-] *n.* [C] **1.** a building or room used as a business place. ¶*a lawyer's ~* / *a dentist's ~* / *a branch ~.*① **2.** [C][U] a public position; a post. ¶*The President holds the highest public ~ in the United States.*② **3.** a government department. ¶*the Foreign Office.*③ **4.** a duty; a task; a job. ¶*A teacher's ~ is teaching.* **5.** (*the ~*) all the people working in an office. ¶*The whole ~ was at the wedding.*④ **6.** (usu. *pl.*) act; kind or unkind services. ¶*by her good offices.*⑤ **7.** a religious ceremony or prayer. ¶*the last offices.*⑥

—[名] 1. 사무소; 사무실; 영업소 ¶①지사(支社) 2. 공직; 지위 ¶②미국에서는 대통령이 최고위의 공직이다 3. 부, 성 ¶③외무부 4. 근무, 직무; 일 5. 사무실 직원 전체 ¶④그의 결혼식에는 직원 전체가 참석했다 6. 친절(불친절)한 행위; 서어비스 ¶⑤그녀의 호의에 의해서 7. [종교상의] 의식; 기도 ¶⑥장례식 8. 집안 일을 보는 곳(부엌·헛간·목욕실·지하실 따위)

O

office boy [796] **oil**

8. (*pl.*) rooms in a house used for household work, such as the kitchen, cellar, or bathroom.

of·fice boy [´-△] *n.* a boy employed in an office to do small jobs. —명 급사, 보이

of·fice·hold·er [ɔ́:fiʃhòuldər, áf- / ɔ́fiʃhòuldə] *n.* ⓒ a person holding an office, esp. a public office; a public servant. —명 공무원

‡ **of·fi·cer** [ɔ́:fisər, áf- / ɔ́fisə] *n.* ⓒ **1.** a person whose business is to perform a public duty. **2.** a person who is appointed to manage the affairs of an organization. **3.** (*Military*) a person who is appointed to command others; (*Nautical*) the captain; a person below the rank of captain. ¶*a commanding* ~① / *a first* (*a second, a third*) ~.② —명 1. 관리, 관원, 공무원 2. 역원, 직원 3. 장교; 선장, 고급 선원 ¶①사령관/②1등(2등·3등) 항해사

‡ **of·fi·cial** [əfíʃ(ə)l] *adj.* **1.** of an office or a position of authority. ¶~ *responsibilities*① / *an* ~ *report*.② ↔unofficial, private **2.** approved by authority; authorized; formal. ¶*The news is not* ~.③ — *n.* ⓒ a person who works in a public office; an officer. ¶*a government* (*a public*) ~.④ —형 1. 관(官)의, 직무상의, 공무상의 ¶①직무상의 책임/②공보(公報) 2. 공인의; 공식의 ¶③그 뉴우스는 공식적인 것이 아니다 —명 관공리; 역원, 직원 ¶④관공리

* **of·fi·cial·ly** [əfíʃəli] *adv.* in an official manner. —부 관공리로서, 공식으로

of·fi·ci·ate [əfíʃièit] *vi.* carry out the duties of an office; carry out the duties in a religious service. —자 직무를 집행하다; 사회를 보다, 예배를 집전(執典)하다

of·fi·cious [əfíʃəs] *adj.* very fond of giving unwelcome services or advice. ▷**of·fi·cious·ly** [-li] *adv.* —형 참견 잘하는, 남의 일에 잘 나서는

off·ing [ɔ́:fiŋ / ɔ́(:)f-] *n.* ⓒ (usu. *the* ~) the distant part of the sea as far as can be seen from the land. —명 앞바다, 난바다

off·print [ɔ́:fprìnt] *n.* ⓒ a reprint of an article from a magazine, etc. —명 [잡지 기사 따위의] 발췌 인쇄

off·set *n.* [ɔ́:fsèt → *v.* / ɔ́(:)f-] ⓒ **1.** something which makes a balance between loss and gain; compensation. **2.** Ⓤ (*Printing*) a kind of printing process. **3.** something developed or set off from something else; (*Botany*) a side shoot from a main stem or root; a branch; an offshoot. **4.** the beginning; the start. —명 1. 상쇄(벌충)가 되는 것, 차감(差減) 계정 2. [印刷] 오프셋 판 3. 갈림, 분파; [식물의] 분지(分枝); 측복지(側匐枝) 4. 시초, 출발

— *vt.* [*U.S.* ɔ̀:fsét] (**-set, -set·ting**) make up for (something); balance. —타 …을 메우다, 보충하다, 차감계정을 하다

off·shoot [ɔ́:fʃùːt / ɔ́(:)f-] *n.* ⓒ anything of secondary development from a main part or source; a shoot from a main stem; a branch; a separate family. —명 갈림; 분지; 지파(支派); 지류; 분파; 분가

off·shore [ɔ́:fʃɔ́:r / ɔ́(:)fʃɔ́:] *adv.* away from the shore. — *adj.* coming from the shore; moving towards the sea. ¶*an* ~ *wind*.① —부 앞바다에(를 향하여) —형 앞바다의; 앞바다로 향하는 ¶①앞바다 쪽으로 부는 바람

* **off·spring** [ɔ́:fspriŋ / ɔ́(:)f-] *n.* ⓒ (pl. **off·spring**) **1.** a child or children; decendants. **2.** the result; something created. —명 1. 자식; 자손 2. 결과, 소산

* **oft** [ɔ:ft / ɔ(:)ft] *adv.* (*poetic*) =often.

‡ **of·ten** [ɔ́:f(ə)n / ɔ́(:)fn] *adv.* many times; frequently. ¶*once too* ~① / *as* ~ *as*② / ~ *and* ~.③
as often as not; more often than not, frequently. ¶*More* ~ *than not, he visited the village.* —부 종종, 자주 ¶①보통보다 한 번 많이/②…할 때마다/③몇 번이고 몇 번이고
熟 자주, 종종

of·ten·times [ɔ́:f(ə)ntàimz / ɔ́(:)fn-] *adv.* (*poetic*) =often.
oft·times [ɔ́:f(t)tàimz] *adv.* (*poetic*) =often.

o·gle [óugl] *vi., vt.* look at (someone) meaningly. —자타 […에] 추파를 던지다

o·gre [óugər] *n.* ⓒ (in fairy tales) a monster or giant who eats people; a cruel, ugly man. —명 [동화의] 사람을 잡아먹는 도깨비; 무섭고 추악한 사람

o·gre·ish [óugəriʃ] *adj.* like an ogre. —형 도깨비 같은

‡ **oh, Oh** [ou] *interj.* =O².

O·hi·o [ouháiou] *n.* a northeastern State of the United States. ⇒N.B. —명 오하이오 주 N.B. O.로 줄임. 수도 Columbus

ohm [oum] *n.* ⓒ a unit of resistance to an electric current. —명 오옴(전기 저항의 단위)

o·ho [ouhóu] *interj.* an exclamation of surprise, etc. —감 호오!, 하하아!, 이런

‡ **oil** [ɔil] *n.* **1.** ⓤⓒ a thick, greasy liquid used for fuel, cooking, driving machinery, etc. ¶*machine* ~.① **2.** (*pl.*) an oil painting; an oil color. —명 1. 기름; 기름 모양의 것 ¶①기계유 2. 유화(油畫); 유화의 그림물감

oil cake

1) ***burn*** (or ***consume***) ***the midnight oil,*** sit up late at night working or studying.
2) ***pour*** (or ***throw***) ***oil on the flame,*** make a quarrel worse; agitate.
3) ***pour*** (or ***throw***) ***oil on*** [***troubled***] ***waters,*** put down a quarrel, etc.
4) ***strike oil,*** gain profit; suddenly become rich.
—*vt.* **1.** put oil in or on (a machine, etc.); supply (something) with oil. **2.** bribe (someone). —*vi.* (of butter, etc.) become oil by melting.
1) ***have a well-oiled tongue,*** be very talkative.
2) ***oil someone's hand*** (or ***palm***), give (someone) a bribe.
3) ***oil one's*** (or ***the***) ***tongue,*** flatter.
4) ***oil the wheels,*** make things go smoothly [by bribes].

熟 1)밤 늦게까지 공부하다(일하다) 2)불에 기름을 붓다;선동하다 3)[싸움따위를 가라앉히다 4)노다지를 만나다; 투기사업이 들어맞다, 벼락부자가 되다

—他 1.[기계 따위]에 기름을 칠하다; 기름을 붓다 2. …에게 뇌물을 주다
—自 [버터 따위가 녹아서] 액체처럼 되다
熟 1)잘도 재잘거리다 2)…에게 뇌물을 쓰다 3)아첨하다 4)[뇌물로] 일을 원만히 진행시키다

oil cake [⌒ ⌒] *n.* cattle food made from crushed oil seeds.
—名 [기름을 짜고 난] 깻묵

oil·can [ɔ́ilkæn] *n.* ⓒ a can with a long narrow projecting tube, used for pouring oil into machines. ⇒fig.
—名 기름통, 기름치는 기구

oil·cloth [ɔ́ilklɔ(ː)θ] *n.* Ⓤ cotton cloth waterproofed with oil paint.
—名 유포(油布)

oil·er [ɔ́ilər] *n.* ⓒ **1.** a person who pours oil on machinery. **2.** an oilcan. **3.** a ship built for carrying oil; a tanker.
—名 1.급유자; 주유자 2.기름치는 기구 3.유조선

oil field [⌒ ⌒] *n.* an area where mineral oil is found.
—名 유전

[oilcan]

oil painting [⌒ ⌒⌒] *n.* **1.** the art of painting in oilcolors. **2.** a picture painted in oil-colors.
—名 1. 유화법 2. 유화

oil·skin [ɔ́ilskìn] *n.* **1.** Ⓤ cloth waterproofed with oil. **2.** ((*pl.*)) a coat or pair of trousers made of oilskin.
—名 1. 유포(油布), 방수포 2. 유포로 만든 옷

oil well [⌒ ⌒] *n.* a well yielding oil.
—名 유정(油井)

oil·y [ɔ́ili] *adj.* (**oil·i·er, oil·i·est**) **1.** of or like oil; covered with oil. **2.** (of manner or speech) smooth-tongued; flattering.
—形 1.기름의; 기름진; 기름을 칠한 2. 말주변이 있는, 아첨을 잘하는

oint·ment [ɔ́intmənt] *n.* Ⓤ ⓒ a greasy substance often used as skin medicine.
—名 연고(軟膏), 고약

OK, O. K. [óukéi] *adj., adv.* all right; correct [ly]; approved. ⇒N.B. —*n.* ⓒ (*pl.* **OK's** or **O.K.'s**) (originally *U.S. informal*) an approval. —*vt.* (**OK'd** or **O.K.'d, OK'ing** or **O.K.'ing**) approve.
—形副 좋다;틀림없다;검사필의 N.B. okay, okeh, okey 로도 씀 —名 동의, 인가; 승인 —他 …을 승인하다

o·kay [óukéi] *adj., adv., vt., n.* =O.K.

Ok·la·ho·ma [òukləhóumə] *n.* a southwestern State of the United States. ⇒N.B.
—名 오오클라호우마 주 N.B. Okla. 로 줄임. 수도 Oklahoma City

‡**old** [ould] *adj.* **1.** having lived or existed for a long time; aged. ↔young ¶*grow* (or *get*) ~ / *He looks* ~ *for his age.* **2.** of age; in age. ¶*How* ~ *is he?* / *a girl* [*of*] *twelve years* ~ / *He is three years older than I.* **3.** not new; made long ago; much used. ¶~ *clothes* / *an* ~ *school.* **4.** former; past. ¶*the* ~ *year* / *an* ~ *pupil of his* / *an* ~ *boy.*① **5.** ancient; of a time long past. ¶~ *Japanese Literature* / ~ *civilizations* / *Old English.* **6.** experienced. ¶*He is an* ~ *hand at this work.*② **7.** familiar; long known or in use. ¶~ *friends* / ~ *familiar faces.* **8.** (*colloq.*) dear. ¶~ *boy* / *my dear* ~ *fellow.* —*n.* Ⓤ former times; the past. ⇒usage ¶*days of* ~.
—形 1. 나이 많은, 늙은 2. …살의 3. 낡은,해묵은; 써서 낡은 4.이전의;원래의; 과거의 ¶①[이전의] 졸업생; OB. 5.옛날의; 고대의 6.노련한 ¶②그는 이 일에 있어서는 노련한 일꾼이다 7.옛날부터의;예(例)의; 옛친구의; 오래 전부터의 8.《口》친애하는

—名 옛날 usage 전치사 뒤에 씀

old·en [óuld(ə)n] *adj.* old; ancient. ¶*in the* ~ *days; in* ~ *times.*①
—形 옛날의 ¶①옛날은

• **old-fash·ioned** [óuldfǽʃ(ə)nd] *adj.* keeping to old ways, customs, ideas, etc.; out of date. ¶*an* ~ *dress.*①
—形 예스러운,구식의,유행에 뒤진 ¶ ①시대에 뒤진 드레스

old·ish [óuldiʃ] *adj.* somewhat old.
—形 좀 늙은, 고풍의

old maid [⌒ ⌒] *n.* an elderly woman who has never married.
—名 노처녀

old·maid·ish [óuldméidiʃ] *adj.* like an old maid.
—形 노처녀 같은

old-time [óuldtàim] *adj.* of past times.
—[形] 옛날의, 옛날부터의

old-tim·er [óuldtáimər] *n.* [C] (*colloq.*) a person who has been a member, worker, etc. for a long time; a veteran; an old-fashioned person.
—[名] 〔口〕 고참, 선임자; 구식 사람

old-wom·an·ish [óuldwúməniʃ] *adj.* of or like an old woman; fussy.
—[形] 노파의; 잔소리 심한

old-world [óuldwə́:rld] *adj.* **1.** of or belonging to the ancient world. **2.** 《often *O- W-*》 of the Old World. ¶ *~ customs.*
—[形] 1. 고대의; 고풍의 2. 구세계의

* **Old World** [⌐ ⌐], **the** *n.* Europe, Asia, and Africa; the Eastern Hemisphere. ↔the New World
—[名] 구세계, 동반구

Old Year's Day [⌐ ⌐ ⌐], **the** *n.* New Year's Eve; the last day of the year.
—[名] 섣달 그믐날

o·le·an·der [òuliǽndər] *n.* [C] a poisonous evergreen shrub with rose-colored or white flowers.
—[名] 서양유도화

ol·fac·to·ry [ɑlfǽktəri / ɔl-] *adj.* of the sense or organ of smell. ¶*the ~ nerve*① / *the ~ organ.*② **—*n.*** [C] (pl. **-ries**) 《usu. *pl.*》 an olfactory organ; the sense of smell.
—[形] 후각(嗅覺)의, 후관(嗅官)의 ¶①후신경/②후관(嗅官) —[名] 후관; 코; 후각

ol·i·garch [áligɑ:rk / ɔ́ligɑ:k] *n.* [C] one of the rulers of an oligarchy.
—[名] 과두(寡頭)정치의 집정자

ol·i·gar·chy [áligɑ:rki / ɔ́ligɑ:ki] *n.* (pl. **-chies**) [U] the form of government ruled by a few powerful persons; [C] a country governed in this way.
—[名] 과두정치[국]

‡ **ol·ive** [áliv / ɔ́l-] *n.* **1.** [C] an evergreen tree that grows near the Mediterranean Sea; the fruit of this tree; the tree itself. **2.** [U] the wood of this tree. **3.** [U] a dull yellowgreen color. **—*adj.*** of an olive; of a dull yellowishgreen.
—[名] 1. 올리브; 올리브의 열매(나무) 2. 올리브 재목 3. 올리브 빛, 엷은 초록빛 —[形] 올리브의; 올리브 빛의

O·lym·pi·a [oulímpiə] *n.* a plain in Greece where the ancient Olympic Games were held.
—[名] 올림피아

O·lym·pi·ad, o·lym- [oulímpiæ̀d] *n.* [C] **1.** a period of four years between celebrations of the Olympic games in ancient Greece. **2.** the modern Olympic games.
—[名] 1. 다음 올림픽 대회까지의 4년간 2. 국제 올림픽 대회

O·lym·pi·an [oulímpiən] *adj.* **1.** of Olympia or Mt. Olympus. **2.** like an Olympian god; godlike; magnificent. **3.** of the Olympic games of ancient Greece. **—*n.*** [C] **1.** one of the twelve major Greek gods who were supposed to live on Mt. Olympus. **2.** a player taking part in the ancient or modern Olympic games.
—[形] 1. 올림피아의; 올림퍼스 산의 2. 올림퍼스의 신 같은; 거룩한; 위풍당당한 3. 고대 올림픽 경기의 —[名] 1. 올림퍼스의 신 2. 올림픽 경기 출전 선수

* **O·lym·pic** [oulímpik] *adj.* of Olympia. **—*n.*** 《*the O-s*》 Olympic Games.
—[形] 올림피아의 —[名] 올림픽 경기

Olympic Games [⌐⌐ ⌐], **the** *n. pl.* **1.** the festival with contests in athletics, music, poetry, etc. held every four years at Olympia in ancient Greece. **2.** the international sports contest of modern times held every four years in a different country.
—[名] 1. 올림피아 경기 2. 국제 올림픽 대회

O·lym·pus [oulímpəs] *n.* the mountain in Greece where the gods were supposed to live.
—[名] 올림퍼스 산

o·meg·a [oumí:gə, -méigə, óumegə / óumigə] *n.* [C] **1.** the last letter of the Greek alphabet (Ω or ω). **2.** the last; the end. ¶*alpha and ~.*①
—[名] 1. 그리이스 자모의 마지막 글자 2. 최후; 끝; 죽음 ¶①처음과 끝, 전체

om·e·let, -lette [ám(ə)lit / ɔ́mlet] *n.* [C] a dish made of eggs, milk, and other materials, cooked and folded in a pan. ¶(*proverb*) *You cannot make an ~ without breaking eggs.*①
—[名] 오믈렛 ¶①《俚》잠을 자야 꿈을 꾸지

o·men [óumən, +*Brit.* -men] *n.* [C][U] a sign that something good or bad is going to happen. ¶*an ~ of misfortune* / *be of good* (*bad*) *~.*①
—[名] 전조, 징조, 조짐 ¶①징조가 좋다(나쁘다)

om·i·nous [ámінəs / ɔ́m-] *adj.* of an evil omen; unlucky. ▷**om·i·nous·ly** [-li] *adv.* —**om·i·nous·ness** [-nis] *n.*
—[形] 흉조의, 불길한, 재수가 나쁜

o·mis·sion [oumíʃ(ə)n] *n.* **1.** [U] the act of omitting; the state of being omitted. ¶*sins of ~.*① **2.** [C] something which is omitted or neglected.
—[名] 1. 태만, 소홀; 탈락, 누락 ¶①태만죄 2. 생략된 것

* **o·mit** [oumít] *vt.* (**-mit·ted, -mit·ting**) **1.** fail to do; neglect. 《*~ doing* or *to do*》 ¶*I omitted to lock the window.*①
—[他] 1. …할 것을 잊다; …을 게을리하다 ¶①창문에 잠을쇠를 잠그는 것을

2. fail to include (something); leave out. ⦅~ something *from*⦆ ¶*~ a word from a sentence.*②
잊었다 2. …을 빠뜨리다; 생략하다, 빼다 ¶②문장에 한 단어를 빠뜨리다

om·ni·bus [ámnibʌs / ɔ́m-] *n.* [C] a large vehicle which carries many passengers; a bus. **—***adj.* including many different items; used for several purposes. ¶*an ~ bill.*①
—[名] 합승 마차; 합승 자동차, 버스
—[形] 많은 항목을 포함하는; 총괄적인 ¶①총괄적 의안

om·nip·o·tence [amnípət(ə)ns / ɔm-] *n.* [U] infinite power; unlimited power. ¶*the ~ of God.*
—[名] 전능

om·nip·o·tent [amnípət(ə)nt / ɔm-] *adj.* having infinite or unlimited power; all-powerful. ¶*the Omnipotent.*①
—[形] 전능의, 무한의 힘이 있는 ¶①신

om·ni·pres·ence [àmniprέz(ə)ns / ɔ̀m-] *n.* [U] the state of being present everywhere at the same time. ¶*God's ~.*①
—[名] 편재(遍在), 보편 ¶①신의 편재

om·ni·pres·ent [àmniprέz(ə)nt / ɔ̀m-] *adj.* present everywhere at the same time.
—[形] 편재하는, 보편의

om·nis·cience [amníʃ(ə)ns / ɔmnísiəns] *n.* [U] complete or unlimited knowledge; ⦅*the O-*⦆ God.
—[名] 전지(全知), 박식; 신

om·nis·cient [amníʃ(ə)nt / ɔmnísiənt] *adj.* knowing all; having complete or infinite knowledge.
—[形] 전지의; 박식한

om·niv·o·rous [amnívərəs / ɔm-] *adj.* **1.** eating both animal and vegetable food; eating any kind of food. ¶*an ~ animal.*① **2.** taking in everything; reading at random. ¶*He is an ~ reader.*
—[形] 1. 잡식(雜食)의; 아무거나 먹는 ¶①잡식 동물 2. 닥치는 대로의; 남독(濫讀)의

‡**on** [ɔn, ən, n, +*U.S.* an] *prep.* **1.** in the state of touching the surface of; upon. ¶*a book ~ the table / flies ~ the ceiling*① */ She put the ring ~ her finger.* **2.** close to; near; along. ¶*a house ~ the river / a farm ~ the road.* **3.** to the surface of; onto. ¶*drop a fork ~ one's lap.*② **4.** toward; (*U.S.*) against. ¶*have pity ~ the poor*③ */ call ~ someone / march ~ Paris / The feeling stole ~ me.*④ **5.** about; concerning. ¶*a lecture ~ Shakespeare.* **6.** upon the basis of. ¶*act ~ someone's advice / a story based ~ fact / rely ~ something.* **7.** at the time of; during; after [thinking, etc.]. ¶*~ examination*⑤ */ ~ Christmas Eve / ~ arriving at the station.*⑥ **8.** in a condition or state of. ¶*~ sale*⑦ */ ~ fire*⑧ */ He is always ~ the move.*⑨ */ The workers are ~ strike.*⑩ **9.** by means of; by the use of. ¶*go ~ foot*⑪ */ wipe one's hands ~ a towel / play a waltz ~ the piano.*⑫ **10.** added to. ¶*errors ~ errors*⑬ */ loss ~ loss.* **11.** for the purpose of. ¶*go to New York ~ urgent business.*
—[前] 1. …의 표면 위에; …에 접하여 ¶①천장에 앉은 파리 2. …에 근접하여 3. 따라서 3. …의 위로 향하여 ¶②무릎 위에 포오크를 떨어뜨리다 4. …을 향하여; ⦅美⦆ 대하여 ¶③가난한 사람들에게 동정하다/④어느 사이에 그런 기분이 나에게 들었다 5. …에 대한; 관한 6. …에 입각하여; …에 의한 7. …의 때에; …의 사이; …의 위에서 ¶⑤시험에서/⑥역에 도착했을 때에(도착하자마자) 8. …의 상태에서; …으로 ¶⑦판매되어/⑧불이 붙어/⑨그는 언제나 가만히 있지 못한다/⑩노동자들은 파업중이다 9. …에 의하여; …을 써서 ¶⑪도보로 가다/⑫피아노로 왈츠를 치다 10. …에 더하여 ¶⑬이중 삼중의 잘못 11. …의 목적으로

—*adv.* **1.** forward; ahead. ¶*further ~ / march ~ / move ~.* **2.** lastingly; continuously; in progress. ¶*sleep ~ / Go ~ with the story.* **3.** in the state of touching, covering, or being supported. ¶*Put your shoes ~. / He had nothing ~.* **4.** in use or action. ¶*The radio was ~. / Switch ~ the light. / The movie was already ~ when we arrived.*⑭
—[副] 1. 앞쪽에 2. 계속하여; 진전하여 3. 접하여; 덮어서; 받혀져서 4. 사용(행동) 중; 가동 중 ¶⑭우리가 도착했을 때는 영화는 이미 시작되어 있었다

1) ***and so on,*** and more of the same; and so forth.
2) ***on and on,*** without stopping; continuously.
3) ***on and off; off and on,*** not continuously; intermittently.

[熟] 1)그밖에 여러가지, …따위 2)자꾸; 계속하여 3)때때로, 단속적(斷續的)으로

‡**once** [wʌns] *adv.* **1.** one time; one time only. ¶*~ a week / He comes ~ every day.* **2.** ⦅usu. in *negative*⦆ ever; at all. ¶*I haven't seen her ~.* **3.** even one time; at any time. ¶*When ~ he understands, he will never make a mistake.*① **4.** formerly; some time ago. ¶*I have seen him ~. / a once-powerful nation / He ~ lived in Paris.*
—[副] 1. 한 번, 1회[만] 2. 한 번도 [… 않다] 3. 한 번이라도; 일단 […하기만 하면]; 언제라도 ¶①그는 일단 이해하기만 하면 결코 틀리지 않는다 4. 전에; 이전에; 옛날에

1) ***once and again,*** repeatedly; time after time.
2) ***once*** [***and***] ***for all,*** finally; decisively; conclusively.
3) ***once in a while,*** now and then.
4) ***once or twice,*** not often; a few times.
5) ***once upon a time,*** long ago; once.
6) ***once more; once again,*** again; another time.

[熟] 1)재삼; 몇 번이고 2)이번만; 단연코; 요번만 3)이따금 4)한두 번; 드물게 5)옛날 6)다시 한 번; 한 번 더

—*conj.* if ever; whenever; as soon as; if once; when
—[接] 한 번 …하기만 하면; …하자마자

oncoming

once. ¶*Once you cross the river, you are safe.*
—*n.* ⓤ one time; a single occasion. ¶*Once is enough for you.*①
1) *all at once,* suddenly.
2) *at once,* immediately; at the same time.
3) *for once,* for one time at least.
—*adj.* former. ¶*my ~ friend | his ~ master.*

on·com·ing [ánkʌmiŋ, ɔ́ːn- / ɔ́n-] *adj.* coming nearer; approaching. —*n.* ⓤ approach.

one [wʌn] *adj.* 1. a single; the only. ¶*~ dollar | with ~ voice*① *| This is the ~ way to learn foreign languages.* 2. a certain; some. ¶*~ day | ~ Brown*② *| from ~ side to the other.* 3. same; unchanging; united; undivided. ¶*~ and the same thing | of ~ height.*
—*n.* 1. ⓤ the first and smallest number. 2. (*~,* or *the ~*) a single person or thing. ¶*~ of these days | He gave me the ~ I wanted.* 3. (*the O-*) ⓤ God. ¶*the Holy One; the One above | the Evil One.*
1) *all one,* united or agreed; all the same.
2) *at one* (=*in agreement*) *with someone.*
3) *one and all,* everybody.
4) *one by one,* one after another.
5) *one with another,* on the average.
6) *all in one,* combined.
—*pron.* some person or thing; any person or thing; the same person or thing. ¶*One must do one's (or his) best.*① *| I'll choose this ~.*② *| " Would you like an apple (some apples)?"   " Yes, I'd like ~ (some)."*

one-eyed [wʌ́náid] *adj.* having only one eye.

one-legged [wʌ́nlég(i)d] *adj.* having only one leg; leaning to one side. ¶*a ~ job.*

one-man [wʌ́nmǽn] *adj.* of one man; done by one man.

one-ness [wʌ́nnis] *n.* ⓤ the state of being one or single; unity; agreement; sameness.

on·er·ous [ánərəs / ɔ́n-] *adj.* making many troubles; burdensome.

• **one·self** [wʌnsélf] *pron.* 1. a reflexive and emphatic form of **one.** ¶*amuse ~ | kill ~ | speak to ~*① *| teach ~*② *| It is important to do it ~. | write a letter ~.*② 2. one's normal physical or mental condition.
1) *be oneself,* ⓐ be normal in mind or body. ⓑ have full control of one's mind or body. ⓒ act naturally.
2) *beside oneself,* mad; lost in something.
3) *by oneself,* alone.
4) *come to oneself,* recover one's senses.
5) *for oneself,* without help from others.
6) *in spite of oneself,* without consciousness.
7) *of oneself,* of its own accord; automatically.

one-sid·ed [wʌ́nsáidid] *adj.* 1. having only one side. 2. seeing only one side of something; unfair; prejudiced. 3. not even; not equal. ¶*a ~ game.*

one-time [wʌ́ntàim] *adj.* of the past; former.

one-way [wʌ́nwéi] *adj.* moving or proceeding in only one direction. ¶*~ traffic.*① —*n.* ⓒ a single ticket.

• **on·ion** [ʌ́njən] *n.* ⓒ a plant of the lily family, the bulb-like root of which is eaten. ▷**on·ion·like** [-làik] *adj.*

on·look·er [ánlùkər, ɔ́ːn- / ɔ́nlùkə] *n.* ⓒ a person who looks on at something happening without taking part in it; a watcher; a spectator.

‡ **on·ly** [óunli] *adj.* 1. sole; single. ¶*an ~ daughter (child, son) | my one and ~ friend.* 2. best. ¶*He is the ~ man for the position.*
—*adv.* merely; solely; and no one or nothing more. ¶*Only I can do it. | She was ~ doing it to please him.*
1) *if only,* I wish that ... ¶*If ~ it would stop snowing!*①
2) *not only A but* (*also*) *B,* B as well as A.

only

—⓺ 한 번; 1회 ¶②너는 한 번으로 족하다
뜻 1)벼란간 2)곧, 당장; 동시에 3)적어도 한번은
—⓽ 이전의
—⓽ 접근한 —⓺ 접근

—⓽ 1. [단지] 하나의 ¶①일제히; 이 구동성으로 2.어떤 [하나의] ¶②브라운이라는 사람 3.동일한; 불변의; 한몸의; 불가분의

—⓺ 1.하나, 1 2.한 개; 한 사람 3.신

뜻 1)일치하여, 매한가지 2)…와 일치하여; 동의하여; 협력하여 3)모두 4)하나씩; 차례로 5)평균하여 6)결합하여

—⓺ 어떤 사람(것); [일반적으로] 사람, 것; 세상 사람; 동일한 사람(것) ¶③사람은 최선을 다해야 한다/④나는 이것을 택하겠다
—⓽ 애꾸눈의, 외눈의
—⓽ 외다리의; 한쪽으로 치우친
¶*a ~ job.*
—⓽ 혼자의; 혼자서 다루는
—⓺ 혼자임; 단일성; 일치, 동의; 동일성
—⓽ 골치아픈, 성가신, 귀찮은

—⓺ 1. 자기 자신, 스스로 ¶①혼잣말을 하다/②독학하다/③스스로 편지를 쓰다 2. [심신의] 정상 상태

뜻 1)ⓐ[정신·몸에] 이상이 없다 ⓑ 자제하다 ⓒ자연스럽게 처신하다 2)미쳐서; 제정신을 잃고 3)혼자서 4)제정신이 들다 5)혼자의 힘으로 6)나도 모르게 7)저절로

—⓽ 1. 한쪽만의, 한쪽의 2. 한쪽에 치우친 3. 불균등한, 일방적인

—⓽ 기왕의; 이전의
—⓽ 한쪽만의; 편도(片道)의 ¶①일 방통행 —⓺ 편도 차표
—⓺ 양파

—⓺ 방관자; 목격자; 구경꾼

—⓽ 1. 단 혼자(하나)의; …뿐의 2. 가장 좋은, 비실데 없는

—⓳ 단지, 다만 …뿐

뜻 1)…하기만 하면 좋겠는데 ¶①는이 그쳤으면 좋겠는데 2)A뿐만 아니

onrush [801] **open**

3) *only too,* very. ¶*I'm ~ too glad to see you.*
—*conj.* but then; except that. ¶*I would do that with pleasure, ~ [that] I am too busy.*
only for, but for.   [forward.]
on·rush [ánrʌʃ, ɔ́:n- / ɔ́n-] *n.* Ⓒ a strong or violent rush
on·set [ánsèt, ɔ́:n- / ɔ́n-] *n.* Ⓒ **1.** an attack. **2.** a first step forward; a start; a beginning. ¶*at the first ~*① / *at the ~ of the journey.*②
on·shore [ánʃɔ̀:r, ɔ́:n- / ɔ́nʃɔ̀:] *adj., adv.* moving toward the shore; situated on the land; toward the shore.
on·slaught [ánslɔ̀:t, ɔ́:n- / ɔ́n-] *n.* Ⓒ a furious or violent attack. ¶*The natives made an ~ on the settlers.*①
* **on·to** [ántu:, ɔ́:n-, -tə / ɔ́n-] *prep.* on; upon; to a place.
o·nus [óunəs] *n.* Ⓒ a burden; a task; duty; responsibility.
* **on·ward** [ánwərd, ɔ́:n- / ɔ́nwəd] *adv.* forward; to the front. —*adj.* moving toward the front; going forward; advancing.
* **on·wards** [ánwərdz, ɔ́:n- / ɔ́nwədz] *adv.* =onward.
on·yx [ániks / ɔ́n-] *n.* Ⓤ a kind of stone in layers of various colors.
oo·long [ú:lɔ:ŋ, -laŋ / ú:lɔŋ] *n.* Ⓤ a Chinese black tea.
ooze [u:z] *vi.* **1.** flow gently; leak out gradually. ¶*Blood oozed out of the wound.* **2.** (of secrets, etc.) be disclosed or revealed. —*vt.* **1.** give off (water, etc.) slowly. **2.** disclose; reveal.
—*n.* Ⓒ Ⓤ **1.** a soft mud, esp. at the bottom of a river. **2.** a slow flow; something that flows.
oo·zy [ú:zi] *adj.* (**-zi·er, -zi·est**) flowing or leaking out gently; muddy. ▷**oo·zi·ly** [-li] *adv.*
o·pac·i·ty [oupǽsiti] *n.* Ⓤ Ⓒ (pl. **-ties**) the state of being opaque; something opaque.
o·pal [óup(ə)l] *n.* Ⓒ a precious stone which shows beautiful changes of color.
o·pal·es·cent [òupəlésnt] *adj.* of or like an opal.
o·paque [oupéik] *adj.* **1.** not allowing light to pass through; not transparent. **2.** dark; dull; stupid. —*n.* ((*the ~*)) something opaque. ↔transparent ▷**o·paque·ness** [-nis] *n.* —**o·paque·ly** [-li] *adv.*
‡ **o·pen** [óup(ə)n] *adj.* (**~·er, ~·est**) **1.** not closed; not shut. ¶*an ~ book | leave the door ~.* **2.** not enclosed; free for (people, traffic, etc.) to go in or out. ¶*an ~ field / a street ~ to traffic.*① **3.** not decided. ¶*an ~ question.* **4.** unfilled; vacant. ¶*The position is still ~.*② **5.** public; free to all. ¶*an ~ meeting (lecture, library).* **6.** not protected. **7.** not prohibited. ¶*an ~ season for hunting.* **8.** frank; liberal. ¶*an ~ manner / an ~ mind.* **9.** known to all; not secret. ¶*an ~ secret.*③
1) *be open to,* ⓐ willingly receive. ¶*He is ~ to persuasion.*④ ⓑ be not protected against (something). ¶*be ~ to temptation.*⑤
2) *be open with* (=*speak frankly to*) someone.
3) *in the open air,* outdoors.
—*vt.* **1.** cause (something) to be open. ¶*~ a book / a letter / Open the box for me.* **2.** unfold; spread out. ¶*~ an umbrella.* **3.** make (something) known or public; reveal. ¶*He opened his heart to his mother.* **4.** begin; start; begin to use. ¶*~ a new store / ~ fire on the enemy.*⑥ —*vi.* **1.** become open. ¶*The door opened easily.* **2.** begin. ¶*School opens at eight.* **3.** unfold; bloom. ¶*The flowers in the garden are opening.*⑦ **4.** lead into; face to. ((*~ to* or *into* some place)) ¶*The window opens to the road.* ⌜opening; the open sea.⌝
—*n.* ((*the ~*)) Ⓤ the outdoors; open or clear space;
come out into the open, come into public view; make

라 B도 3)몹시, 매우
—㉗ 그러나, …만 아니라면(없다면)

熟 …이 없으면
—名 돌진, 돌격

—名 1. 습격, 공격 2. 시작; 시초; 착수
¶①개시로/②여행 초에

—形副 육지의(로); 육상의(으로)

—名 맹공격 ¶①원주민들은 정착자들에게 맹공격을 가했다
—前 …의 위에; …에 향하여
—名 무거운 짐; 부담; 의무; 책임
—形 앞으로, 나아가서, 먼저 —形 전진하는; 향상적인

—名 줄마노(瑪瑙)

—名 〔중국의〕 우을롱 차(茶)
—自 1. 줄줄 흘러나오다; 스며 나오다 2. [비밀 따위가] 새다 —他 1. [물 따위]를 찔끔찔끔 내다 2. [비밀 따위]를 누설하다
—名 1. 말랑말랑한 진흙, 2. 분비[물]

—形 줄줄 흘러나오는, 새는; 부드러운 진흙의(이 있는)
—名 불투명; 어둠; 우둔; 불투명체

—名 단백석(蛋白石)

—形 단백석의, 젖빛의
—形 1. 불투명한 2. 어두운; 충충한; 우둔한 —名 불투명체; 암흑

—形 1. 열린 2. 개방된; 출입이 자유로운 ¶①통행이 자유로운 거리 3. 미결의 4. 빈 ¶②그 지위는 아직 비었다 5. 공개의; 자유로 참가할 수 있는 6. [위험 따위에] 노출된, 드러난 7. 금지되지 않은 8. 솔직한, 관대한 9. 널리 알려진; 공공연한 ¶③공공연한 비밀

熟 1)ⓐ쾌히 받아들이다 ¶④그는 남의 말을 고분고분 잘 듣는다 ⓑ…에 대한 방비가 없다; …당하기 쉽다 ¶⑤유혹에 약하다 2)…에 솔직하게 말하다 3)옥외에서
—他 1. …을 열다 2. …을 펼치다 3. …을 공개하다; 털놓다 4. …을 시작하다; 이용하기 시작하다 ¶⑥적에게 사격을 개시하다
—自 1. 열리다 2. 시작되다 3. 펴지다; 꽃피다 ¶⑦마당의 꽃이 피기 시작했다 4. 통해 있다; 면하다; 향해 있다

—名 옥외; 빈터, 광장; 해양(海洋)
熟 세상에 밝혀지다; …을 공표하다

open-air [802] **opine**

one's ideas or plans known. 「~ *school*.①
o·pen-air [óup(ə)nèər] *adj.* outdoor. ¶*an ~ theater / an* ─형 옥외의; 야외의 ¶①임간학교
open-armed [óup(ə)ná:rmd] *adj.* extending one's hands; hearty; sincere. ─형 두 손을 벌린; 충심에서의
open door [⸺ ⸺] *n.* the policy of trading with any country freely and on equal terms; a policy of admission without any limit. ─명 기회 균등; 문호 개방
o·pen·er [óup(ə)nər] ⓒ *n.* a person who opens; a thing that opens, such as a can opener, a bottle opener, etc. ─명 여는 사람, 개시자; 여는 연장(깡통 따개 따위)
o·pen-eyed [óup(ə)náid] *adj.* **1.** having the eyes wide open, as in surprise. **2.** watchful. ─형 1. 눈을 둥그렇게 뜬, 놀란 2. 빈틈없는, 방심 않는
open-faced [óup(ə)nféist] *adj.* **1.** having a gentle, honest look. **2.** with the face uncovered. ─형 1. 온화한 얼굴의 2. 맨얼굴의
o·pen-hand·ed [óup(ə)nhǽndid] *adj.* willing to give; generous. 「erous.」 ─형 선뜻선뜻 잘 주는, 손큰; 관대한
o·pen-heart·ed [óup(ə)nhá:rtid / -hà:t-] *adj.* frank; gen- ─형 솔직한; 관대한
‡ **o·pen·ing** [óup(ə)niŋ] *n.* ⓒ **1.** a gap; a hole; an open space; an open piece of land in the forest. ¶*an ~ in a fence.* **2.** a beginning; a start. **3.** a chance; an opportunity; a vacant position. ¶*an ~ for trade.* ─명 1. 구멍, 빈틈, 광장; 숲 사이의 빈터 2. 개시, 최초 3. 좋은 기회; 취직자리
* **open·ly** [óup(ə)nli] *adv.* frankly; publicly. ─부 솔직하게, 터놓고, 공공연하게
o·pen-mind·ed [óup(ə)nmáindid] *adj.* willing to listen to new ideas or arguments; unprejudiced. ─형 마음이 넓은, 허심탄회한
o·pen·ness [óup(ə)nnis] *n.* Ⓤ **1.** the state of being open. **2.** frankness; willingness to listen to new ideas or arguments. ─명 1. 개방 상태 2. 솔직; 마음이 넓음
open shop [⸺ ⸺] *n.* (*U.S.*) a factory or shop which employs both members and nonmembers of labor unions. ─명 개방적 공장(노동조합의 비조합원도 채용함)
‡ **op·er·a**¹ [áp(ə)rə / ɔ́p-] *n.* **1.** ⓒⓊ a play in which actors sing their parts to the accompaniment of an orchestra. **2.** ⓒ a theater where operas are played. ─명 1. 오페라, 가극 2. 오페라 극장
op·er·a² [áp(ə)rə / ɔ́p-] *n.* pl. of **opus**.
op·er·a·ble [áp(ə)rəbl / ɔ́p-] *adj.* admitting of a surgical operation; practicable. 「eyes used in theaters.」 ─형 수술이 가능한; 실시할 수 있는
opera glasses [⸺ ⸺⸺] *n. pl.* small glasses for both ─명 관극용 쌍안경
opera hat [⸺ ⸺] *n.* a man's tall, black silk hat which may be folded flat. 「played.」 ─명 접는 식의 실크햇
opera house [⸺ ⸺] *n.* a theater where operas are ─명 가극장
‡ **op·er·ate** [ápərèit / ɔ́p-] *vt.* **1.** cause (a machine, etc.) to work; run. ¶*~ the machine.* **2.** (*U.S.*) manage. **3.** bring about (an effect). ─*vi.* **1.** (of a machine, etc.) work; act. **2.** (of medicines, etc.) produce a certain effect. ¶*Some drugs ~ harmfully on the human body.* **3.** perform a surgical operation to cure disease. ─타 1. [기계 따위]를 움직이다, 조작하다 2. 〈美〉…을 경영하다, 관리하다 3. [효과 따위]를 나타내다 ─자 1. [기계 따위가] 움직이다, 가동하다, [일이] 작용하다 2. [약이] 듣다 3. 수술하다
op·er·at·ic [àpərǽtik / ɔ̀p-] *adj.* of or like an opera. ─형 가극[풍]의
‡ **op·er·a·tion** [àpəréiʃ(ə)n / ɔ̀p-] *n.* **1.** Ⓤ action; working. **2.** ⓒ the act, method, or way of operating; management. **3.** ⓒ (*often pl.*) a series of movements of an army or a fleet; a plan of action. **4.** ⓒ A surgical treatment. 1) *come* (or *go*) *into operation*, begin to be operated. 2) *get into operation*, cause (a machine, etc.) to work. 3) *in operation*, working; in effect or use. 4) *put into operation*, execute; start. ─명 1. 작업, 일, 작용, 작업(공작)과정 2. 운전, 운용[법], 시행, 경영 3. 군사행동; 작전 4. 수술
熟 1) 실시(개시)되다 2) …을 활동시키다 3) 작업중, 운전중, 시행중 4) [법령 따위]를 실시하다, 개시하다
op·er·a·tive [ápərèitiv, áp(ə)rə- / ɔ́p-] *adj.* **1.** operating; working; in effect. ¶*Such a law will not be ~ any more.* **2.** of surgical operations. ¶*~ surgery.* ─형 1. 일을 하는, 활동하는; 효력이 있는 2. 수술의
* **op·er·a·tor** [ápərèitər / ɔ́pərèitə] *n.* ⓒ a person who operates a machine. ─명 조종자, 기사, 기계 운전수, 교환수; 경영자, 수술자
op·er·et·ta [àpərétə / ɔ̀p-] *n.* ⓒ a short opera. ─명 오페레타, 소희가극
o·pi·ate [óupiit, -èit] *n.* ⓒ **1.** a drug containing opium that brings sleep or rest. **2.** anything that brings sleep or rest. ─*adj.* **1.** containing opium. **2.** tending to bring sleep. 「an opinion.」 ─명 1. 아편제(劑) 2. [일반적으로] 마취시키는 것 ─형 1. 아편을 함유하는 2. 졸음이 오게 하는
o·pine [oupáin] *vt., vi.* think; suppose; have or express ─자타 [의견을] 말하다, …이라고 생 「각하다」

opinion — oppression

o·pin·ion [əpínjən] *n.* **1.** ⓒⓊ what one thinks about a subject. **2.** ⓒ a judgment about someone or something. **3.** ⓒ a formal statement by an expert.
— 名 1. 의견, 견해 2. 평가, 평판 3. [의사·법률가 등의] 전문적인 의견, 감정 (鑑定)
熟 1) 소신대로 하다 2) …이라는 의견이다 3) …을 높이(낮게, 나쁘게) 평가하다, …에 탄복하다(을 경시하다) 4) …을 좋게 안 보다 5) …의 의견에 따르면

1) *act up to one's opinions*, act according to what one thinks right.
2) *be of [the] opinion* (=*believe* or *consider*) *that* …
3) *have a high (low, bad) opinion of*, make much (light, little) of (someone).
4) *have no opinion of*, make little of (something); disregard. 「*one.*」
5) *in the opinion* (=*according to the opinion*) *of* some-

o·pin·ion·at·ed [əpínjənèitid] *adj.* obstinate.
— 形 자기 주장을 굽히지 않는, 완고한

o·pi·um [óupiəm] *n.* Ⓤ a powerful drug made from a certain kind of poppy and used to cause sleep and make less pain.
— 名 아편

o·pos·sum [əpásəm / əpós-] *n.* ⓒ a small American tree animal which pretends to be dead when captured.
— 名 [미국산] 유대류(有袋類)의 쥐
熟 죽은 체하다; 꾀병부리다; 모른 채하다
 play opossum, pretend to be dead, ill, ignorant, etc.

op·po·nent [əpóunənt] *n.* ⓒ a person who takes the other side in a game, discussion, or fight. —*adj.* acting against each other; opposing.
— 名 [시합·의논 따위의] 상대자, 적수 —形 반대의, 적대하는

op·por·tune [àpərt(j)ú:n ⌐ / ɔ́pətjù:n] *adj.* (of time) good; right for the purpose; (of an event or action) happening or done at the right time; timely. ▷*op·por·tune·ly* [-li] *adv.* —*op·por·tune·ness* [-nis] *n.*
— 形 시기(형편)가 좋은, 알맞은; [사건·행위 따위] 시기에 알맞은

op·por·tun·ism [àpərt(j)ú:niz(ə)m / ɔ́pətjù:n-] *n.* Ⓤ the policy or manner of making decisions on the basis of the circumstances of each particular time.
— 名 기회주의

op·por·tun·ist [àpərt(j)ú:nist / ɔ́pətjú:n-] *n.* ⓒ a person who practices opportunism.
— 名 기회주의자

op·por·tu·ni·ty [àpərt(j)ú:niti / ɔ́pətjú:-] *n.* ⓒⓊ (pl. **-ties**) a good chance; time and circumstance that are good for a purpose. ¶*equality of* ~① / *afford* (or *give*) *an* ~② / *at* (or *on*) *the first* ~③ / *find* (*miss*) *an* ~.④
 take (or *seize*) *the opportunity*, make use of a particular moment.
— 名 […하기에 좋은] 기회, 초기 ¶① 기회 균등/② 기회를 주다/③ 기회가 있는 대로 /④ 기회를 찾다(잃다)
熟 기회를 잡다

op·pos·a·ble [əpóuzəbl] *adj.* **1.** that may be opposed. **2.** that may be put opposite to something else.
— 形 1. 반대(대항)할 수 있는 2. 마주 보게 할 수 있는

op·pose [əpóuz] *vt.* **1.** stand or fight against somebody or something; resist. **2.** contrast; set against. 《~ something *with*》 ¶~ *anger with good nature* / ~ *force with reason*.
— 他 1. …에 반대하다; 저항하다 2. …와 대립시키다; 마주보게 하다

op·po·site [ápəzit / ɔ́p-] *adj.* **1.** facing; front to front or back to back. ¶*the* ~ *side of the road* / *the tree* ~ *my house.*① **2.** just contrary. ¶*in the* ~ *direction.*
—*prep.* in front of. ¶*a storehouse* ~ *the post-office.*
—*n.* ⓒ 《often *the* ~》 a thing or person that is opposite. ¶*White is the* ~ *of black.* / *Long and short are opposites.*
— 形 1. …에 면해 있는; 마주보는; 등을 맞댄 ¶① 우리집 앞의 나무 2. 정반대의; 거꾸로의
— 前 …의 맞은편에
— 名 정반대의 사람(사물)

op·po·site·ly [ápəzitli / ɔ́p-] *adv.* in an opposite manner; face to face with.
— 副 반대로; 마주보고

op·po·si·tion [àpəzíʃ(ə)n / ɔ̀pə-] *n.* Ⓤⓒ **1.** the act of opposing; resistance; hostility. ¶*The police met with fierce* ~.① **2.** contrast. **3.** ⓒ an opposing political party.
1) *have an opposition to* (=*stand against* or *oppose*) someone or something.
2) *in opposition to*, against.
3) *offer opposition to* (=*oppose*) someone or something.
— 名 1. 반대, 대립, 저항 ¶① 경찰은 치열한 저항을 만났다 2. 대조 3. 반대당, 야당
熟 1) …에 반대이다 2) …에 반대하여 3) …에 반대(저항)하다

op·press [əprés] *vt.* **1.** treat (someone) harshly; rule (a nation) unjustly or cruelly. ¶*The tyrant oppressed his poor subjects.* **2.** weigh heavily on the mind of (someone); distress. **3.** make (someone) weary.
— 他 1. …을 압박하다, 학대하다 2. …에 압박감(중압감)을 주다, 피롭히다 3. …의 기운을 없애다

op·pres·sion [əpréʃ(ə)n] *n.* Ⓤⓒ **1.** the act of oppressing; cruel or severe treatment; a burdening. **2.** a heavy
— 名 1. 압제, 압박, 포학, 억압 2. 중압감, 침울, 노곤함

feeling; a feeling of discomfort; weariness.

op·pres·sive [əprésiv] *adj.* **1.** tyrannical; unjust; severe. **2.** (of weather) heavy; sultry. ▷**op·pres·sive·ly** [-li] *adv.* —**op·pres·sive·ness** [-nis] *n.*
—[形] 1. 압박하는, 압제적인, 포학한, 엄한 2. 무더운; 후텁지근한

op·pres·sor [əprésər] *n.* [C] a person who is cruel or severe to his inferiors.
—[名] 압제자, 압박자, 학대자

op·pro·bri·ous [əpróubriəs] *adj.* showing scorn or reproach; insulting; disgraceful.
—[形] 욕설하는; 모욕적인; 상스러운; 불명예의

op·pro·bri·um [əpróubriəm] *n.* [U] reproach or disgrace because of shameful conduct; scorn; dishonor.
—[名] 비난, 욕설; 불명예

op·tic [áptik / ɔ́p-] *adj.* of the eye or the sense of sight. ¶*the ~ angle*① / *the ~ nerve.*②
—[形] 눈의, 시각(시력)의 ¶①시각/②시신경(視神經)

op·ti·cal [áptik(ə)l / ɔ́p-] *adj.* **1.** of the eye; of [the sense of] sight. ¶*an ~ defect.*① **2.** made to help eyesight. ¶*an ~ instrument.*② ▷**op·ti·cal·ly** [-kəli] *adv.*
—[形] 1. 눈의, 시력(시각)의 ¶①시각장애 2. 시력을 돕는; 광학의 ¶②광학기계

op·ti·cian [ɑptíʃ(ə)n / ɔp-] *n.* [C] a maker or seller of spectacles, telescopes, and other optical instruments.
—[名] 안경 장수; 광학 기구상

op·tics [áptiks / ɔ́p-] *n. pl.* 《used as *sing.*》 the science of light and vision.
—[名] 광학

op·ti·mism [áptimìz(ə)m / ɔ́p-] *n.* [U] **1.** a habitual state of mind of looking on the bright side of things. **2.** the belief that everything in life will end happily. ↔pessimism
—[名] 1. 낙관주의; 낙관설 2. 낙천적임, 낙관, 태평

op·ti·mist [áptimist / ɔ́p-] *n.* [C] a person who always looks on the bright side of things; a believer in optimism. ↔pessimist
—[名] 낙천가, 낙관주의자

op·ti·mis·tic [àptimístik / ɔ̀p-] *adj.* disposed to look on the bright side of things; of optimism. ↔pessimistic ▷**op·ti·mis·ti·cal·ly** [-kəli] *adv.*
—[形] 낙천(낙관)적인, 낙관주의의

op·tion [ápʃ(ə)n / ɔ́p-] *n.* [U][C] the right or power of choice; the act of choosing; choice. ¶*Leave it to her ~.* / *We had no ~ but to obey him.*①
1) ***at one's option,*** as one pleases; at will; freely.
2) ***make one's option,*** choose.
—[名] 선택의 자유, 선택권, 선택 ¶①우리는 그에게 복종할 수밖에 없었다
[熟] 1)임의로 2)선택하다

op·tion·al [ápʃən(ə)l / ɔ́p-] *adj.* left to one's choice; free [to be chosen]. ¶*an ~ subject*① / *Attendance is ~.*② ▷**op·tion·al·ly** [-əli] *adv.*
—[形] 임의의, 마음대로의 ¶①선택 과목/②출석은 마음대로이다

op·u·lence [ápjuləns / ɔ́p-] *n.* [U] wealth; riches; abundance.
—[名] 부유; 풍부

op·u·lent [ápjulənt / ɔ́p-] *adj.* wealthy; rich; abundant.
—[形] 부유한; 풍부한

o·pus [óupəs] *n.* [C] (pl. **o·pe·ra** or **o·pus·es**) a work; a composition; a musical composition. ⇒[N.B.] ¶*Beethoven op. 15.*①
—[名] 저작, 작품 [N.B.] op.로 줄임 ¶①베에토벤 작품 15번

‡**or** [ɔ:r, ər] *conj.* **1.** a word used to express a choice or difference. ⇒[usage] ¶*You can go ~ stay.* / *You ~ I am to go.* **2.** that is; in other words. ¶*botany, ~ the science of plants.* **3.** and if not; otherwise. ¶*Work hard, ~ you'll fail.* / *Ask him whether he wants it ~ not.*
—[接] 1. 또는; …이든가 …이든가; 혹은 [usage] or로 주어가 연결된 경우 동사는 가까운 쪽의 인칭·수에 일치시킴 2. 즉; 바꿔 말하면 3. 그렇지 않으면

or·a·cle [ɔ́:rəkl / ɔ́r-] *n.* [C] **1.** (in ancient Greece) the answer of a god given to a question about future. **2.** a place where a god gives answers; 《*pl.*》 the Scriptures. **3.** a person who gives a god's answers; a prophet; a very wise person.
—[名] 1. 신탁(神託), 탁선(託宣) 2. 신탁소; 성서 3. 신탁을 말하는 사람; 예언자; 현인(賢人)

o·rac·u·lar [ɔ:rǽkjulər / ɔrǽkjulə] *adj.* **1.** of or like an oracle. **2.** mysterious; obscure. **3.** solemn; dogmatic; wise.
—[形] 1. 신탁의(같은) 2. 수수께끼 같은 3. 엄연한, 독단적인; 현명한

o·ral [ɔ́:rəl] *adj.* **1.** spoken; not written; using speech. ¶*an ~ examination*① / *~ instruction.*② **2.** (*Anatomy*) of the mouth. ¶*~ hygiene*③ / *the ~ cavity.*④
—[形] 1. 구두(口頭)의, 구술(口述)의 ¶①구두시험/②구두 지시 2. 입의, 입 부분의 ¶③입 부분의 위생/④구강(口腔)

o·ral·ly [ɔ́:rəli] *adv.* by spoken words.
—[副] 구두(口頭)로

‡**or·ange** [ɔ́:rindʒ / ɔ́r-] *n.* **1.** [C] a reddish-yellow, round, juicy fruit; an evergreen tree that bears this fruit. ¶*the bitter ~*① / *the mandarin ~.*② **2.** [U] a reddish-yellow color.
—*adj.* of oranges; reddish-yellow.
—[名] 1. 오렌지; 귤나무 ¶①등자나무/②밀감 2. 오렌지빛, 등황색
—[形] 오렌지[색]의

or·ange·ade [ɔ́:rindʒéid / ɔ́r-] *n.* [U] sweet drink made by mixing sugar, orange juice, and water.
—[名] 오렌지 수(水)

or·ange·ry [ɔ́:rindʒri / ɔ́rindʒəri] *n.* ⓒ an orchard or glass-house where orange trees are grown and cultivated.
—⨂ 오렌지 밭(온실)

o·rang·ou·tang, -u·tang [ɔ:ræŋutǽn / ɔ:ræŋútæn] *n.* ⓒ a large, long-armed ape living in Borneo and Sumatra.
—⨂ 성성(猩猩)이, 오랑우탄

o·ra·tion [ɔ:réiʃ(ə)n] *n.* ⓒ a formal public speech, usu. one given on a special occasion. ¶ *a funeral ~.*①
—⨂ 연설; 식사(式辭) ¶①조사, 추도사

or·a·tor [ɔ́:rətər / ɔ́rətər] *n.* ⓒ a person who speaks very fluently in public; a skillful public speaker.
—⨂ 연설자, 변사, 웅변가

or·a·tor·i·cal [ɔ:rətɔ́:rik(ə)l / ɔ̀rə-] *adj.* of or like oratory or an orator; rhetorical.
—働 연설의, 연설자의; 웅변가다운; 수사(修辭)적인

or·a·to·ri·o [ɔ:rətɔ́:riou / ɔ̀rə-] *n.* ⓒ (pl. **-os**) a musical composition, usu. on a sacred, religious theme, sung with orchestral accompaniment.
—⨂ 오라토리오, 성담곡(聖譚曲)

or·a·to·ry¹ [ɔ́:rətɔ̀:ri / ɔ́rət(ə)ri] *n.* Ⓤ the art of public speaking; eloquence; rhetoric.
—⨂ 웅변술; 웅변; 수사(修辭)

or·a·to·ry² [ɔ́:rətɔ̀:ri / ɔ́rət(ə)ri] *n.* ⓒ (pl. **-ries**) a small chapel in a church or a private house.
—⨂ 기도소, 작은 예배당

orb [ɔ:rb] *n.* ⓒ a sphere; a round body such as the sun or the moon.
—⨂ 구(球); 천체(태양·달 따위)

* **or·bit** [ɔ́:rbit] *n.* ⓒ **1.** the path of a star or other heavenly body moving round another. **2.** the regular course of life; the extent or sphere of activity, experience, or influence. **3.** (*Anatomy*) the eye socket.
—⨂ 1. [천체의] 궤도; 2. 생활의 궤도, 활동(경험·세력) 범위 3.(解) 눈구멍

or·bit·al [ɔ́:rbitl] *adj.* of an orbit.
—働 궤도의; 눈구멍의

* **or·chard** [ɔ́:rtʃərd] *n.* ⓒ a field where fruit trees are grown and cultivated; ((*collectively*)) fruit trees.
—⨂ 과수원; 과수

* **or·ches·tra** [ɔ́:rkistrə] *n.* ⓒ **1.** a group of musicians who play together on their instruments, esp. stringed instruments. **2.** the place in front of the stage where these musicians play together.
—⨂ 1. 오오케스트라, 관현악[단]; 관현악 부원 2. [극장의] 오오케스트라 석

or·ches·tral [ɔ:rkéstrəl] *adj.* of an orchestra.
—働 오오케스트라[용]의

or·ches·tra·tion [ɔ̀:rkistréiʃ(ə)n] *n.* Ⓤ the act of arranging music for an orchestra.
—⨂ 관현악 작곡(편곡)[법]

or·chid [ɔ́:rkid] *n.* ⓒ **1.** a plant with beautiful, colorful flowers having three petals. **2.** a light purple color.
—*adj.* light purple.
—⨂ 1. 난초, 엷은 자줏빛
—働 엷은 자줏빛의

* **or·dain** [ɔ:rdéin] *vt.* **1.** give orders to (someone); (of God, destiny a law, etc.) decide; appoint; regulate. **2.** appoint (someone) a minister in a Christian church. ¶ *be ordained priest.*①
—働 1. …에게 명하다, [신·운명·법률 따위가] …이라고 정하다, …을 제정하다 2. …을 목사로 임명하다 ¶①목사가 되다

or·deal [ɔ:rdí:l, -dí(:)əl] *n.* **1.** Ⓤ (in former times) a method to decide whether someone is guilty or not by having him pass through fire, take poison, etc. **2.** ⓒ a severe test; a difficult or painful experience.
—⨂ 1. 고대의 범죄 유무 판별법 2. 엄한 시련; 쓰라린 체험

‡ **or·der** [ɔ́:rdər] *n.* **1.** Ⓤ regular arrangement; the way one thing comes after another. ¶ *names arranged in alphabetical ~.*① **2.** ⓒ a social rank, grade, or class. ¶ *the lower orders / the ~ of knights.* **3.** Ⓤ rightly arranged conditions. ¶ *put* (or *set*) *things in ~.* **4.** Ⓤ the way or condition in which things happen according to law or rule. ¶ *peace and ~ / the ~ of nature.* **5.** ⓒ ((often *pl.*)) a command. ¶ *give strict orders.* **6.** ⓒ a request for goods or services; causing demand. ¶ *mail an ~ / That book is on ~.*② *He gave an ~ for 15 tons of coal.*③ **7.** ⓒ a written or printed paper directing someone to pay money. ¶ *a money ~.* **8.** Ⓤ condition; state. ¶ *The machine is in good ~.* **9.** ⓒ a kind; a sort. ¶ *talents of a high ~*④ */ This is a matter of quite another ~.*⑤ **10.** ((*pl.*)) a group in the plant or animal world between family and class. **11.** ⓒ a badge worn by persons of high rank. ¶ *the Order of the Garter.*
1) *by order of* (= *according to an order given by*) *someone.*
2) *in order,* ⓐ in the right position. ⓑ in good con-⌐ dition; suitable. ⌐

—⨂ 1. 순서 ¶①알파벳 순으로 늘어놓은 이름 2. 계급; 석차 3. 정돈 4. 질서 5. 명령 6. 주문[품] ¶②그 책은 주문중이다/③그는 석탄을 15톤 주문했다 7. 환(換) 8. 정상적인(건강한) 상태 9. 종류 ¶④뛰어난 재능/⑤이것은 전혀 별문제이다 10. [생물 분류상의] 목(目) 11. 훈장

麗 1)…의 명예에 따라서 2)ⓐ순서 바르게 ⓑ건강한 상태로; 적절한 3)…의 차례로 4)…할 수 있도록 5)…하기

orderliness [806] **organism**

3) *in order of* (=*arranged according to*) *something.*
4) *in order that one may...*, so that one may...
5) *in order to do,* for the purpose of doing.
6) *in short order,* quickly ; in a short time.
7) *on the order of,* like ; similar to ; belonging to the
8) *out of order,* not in order.　　　class or kind of.
9) *to order,* according to the buyer's wishes.
　—*vt.* **1.** command ; bid ; tell. ((someone *to do* ; ~ *that* ;
~ *something* [*to be*] *done*) ¶*He ordered me back* (*home,
away*).① / *She ordered the book* [*to be*] *brought to her*.② /
He ordered that the windows [*should*] *be locked*.③ / *He
ordered silence.* / *The doctor ordered absolute quiet.* **2.**
request (something) to be supplied, made, or furnished.
((~ *something from*) ¶~ *a new book from America*④ /
*She ordered her daughter a new dress.*⑤ **3.** keep or
put (something) in order ; manage ; arrange. ¶~ *one's
life for greater leisure.* —*vi.* give an order. ¶*He
wanted to ~, but the waiter was busy.*
　order about (or *around*), send (someone) here and
there ; often give orders to (someone).　　　　［order.
or·der·li·ness [ɔ́:rdərlinis] *n.* Ⓤ the state of being in
・**or·der·ly** [ɔ́:rdərli] *adj.* **1.** tidy ; well arranged ; in order.
2. keeping order ; obedient and quiet ; well behaved. **3.**
being on duty. —*n.* Ⓒ (pl. **-lies**) **1.** a soldier who attends on an officer to carry out his orders. **2.** a military hospital attendant who works to keep things clean
and in order. ▷**or·der·li·ness** [-nis] *n.*

or·di·nal [ɔ́:rd(i)nl] *adj.* showing order in a series.
↔cardinal ¶~ *numbers.*① —*n.* Ⓒ an ordinal number.
or·di·nance [ɔ́:rd(i)nəns] *n.* Ⓒ a rule or law made by the
authorities of a town or city.　　　　　［ally ; commonly.
or·di·nar·i·ly [ɔ̀:rdinérili, ＿＿＿ / ɔ́:rd(i)n(ə)ri-] *adv.* usu-
:**or·di·nar·y** [ɔ́:rdinèri / ɔ́:d(i)n(ə)ri] *adj.* usual ; normal ;
customary. ¶*an* ~ *meeting*① / *in an* [*the*] ~ *way*.②
　1) *out of the ordinary,* unusual ; not regular or cus-
　2) *in ordinary,* in regular service.　　　　　　［tomary.
　3) *above the ordinary,* better than usual.
　4) *by ordinary,* ordinarily.
or·di·na·tion [ɔ̀:rdinéiʃ(ə)n] *n.* Ⓤ the ceremony of admitting a person as a Christian priest or minister.
ord·nance [ɔ́:rdnəns] *n.* Ⓤ (*collectively*) the cannon ;
the heavy guns ; the military weapons.　　　［obtained.
・**ore** [ɔ:r] *n.* ⓊⒸ the rock or earth from which metal is
Or·e·gon [ɔ́:rigən, -gàn, ár- / ɔ́rig(ə)n, -gɔ̀n] *n.* a northwestern State of the United States, on the Pacific coast.
:**or·gan** [ɔ́:rgən] *n.* Ⓒ **1.** a musical wind instrument
played by touching keys and pressing pedals. ⇨Ⓝ.Ⓑ.
2. the part of an animal or plant that has a special
function and duty, such as an eye or a stomach. ¶*digestive organs.* **3.** a means of expressing or communicating public opinion, thoughts, etc ; a newspaper or
magazine that makes known what people think. ¶*the*
~ *of the government.*①

or·gan·ic [ɔ:rgǽnik] *adj.* **1.** (*Medicine*) of some organs
of the body. ¶~ *disease*.① **2.** having an organized
structure, such as plants or animals. **3.** of a chemical
compound which contains carbon. ↔inorganic **4.** made
up of related parts ; systematic ; essential.
or·gan·i·cal·ly [ɔ:rgǽnikəli] *adv.* by or through organization ; in an organic manner.
・**or·gan·ism** [ɔ́:rgənìz(ə)m] *n.* Ⓒ **1.** a living thing with
organs or an organized structure ; an animal or a plant.
2. an organized body or system which has many parts
dependent upon each other.

위해서 6)조속히; 곧 7)…에 비슷한;
…같은;…의 종류에 속하는 8)어지럽
혀져서; 고장(탈)이 나서 9)주문에 따
라

—他 **1.** …을 명령하다 ; 지시하다 ¶①
그는 나에게 돌아가라(집으로 가라, 떠
나라)고 명했다/②그녀는 그 책을 가
져오도록 명했다/③그는 창문에 잠을
쇠를 잠그도록 명했다 **2.** …을 주문하
다, 마추다 ¶④미국에 신간서를 주문
하다/⑤그녀는 딸에게 새옷을 마쳐 주
었다 **3.** …을 정리(처리, 배열)하다 ; 가
지런히 하다 —自 명령을 내리다 ; 주문
하다

屬 …을 사방으로 심부름을 보내다 ; 마
구 부리다
—名 질서정연
—形 **1.** 질서 바른 ; 정돈된 **2.** 규칙 바른,
유순한 ; 정숙(靜肅)한 **3.** 당번의 —名
1. 전령[하사관] **2.** [군 병원의] 간호병

—形 순서의 ¶①서수(序數) (first,
second, third 따위) —名 서수
—名 조령, 법령, 포고

—副 보통, 대개
—形 보통의 ; 평범한 ; 통상의 ¶①정
기적 모임/②여느때같이(같으면)

屬 1)보통을 벗어난 ; 드문 2)상임의, 상
무의 3)뛰어난, 비범한 4)통례

—名 서품(叙品)[식]

—名 대포, 무기, 병기

—名 광석, 조광(粗鑛)
—名 오레곤 주
—名 **1.** 오르간 Ⓝ.Ⓑ. 미국에서는 보통
교회에 있는 pipe organ을 이름 **2.** [생
물의] 기관(器官) **3.** [의견 발표의] 기
관(機關) ; 기관지(신문·잡지 따위) ¶
①정부의 기관지

—形 **1.** (醫) 기관(器官)의 ¶①기질성
(器質性) 질환 **2.** 유기체(물)의 **3.** [화학
에서] 유기(有機)의 **4.** 조직적인, 계통
적인 ; 본질적인

—副 기관에 의해 ; 유기적으로

—名 **1.** 유기체(물) ; 동(식)물, 생물 **2.**
유기적 조직체(사회 따위)

or·gan·ist [ɔ́:rgənist] *n.* ⓒ a person who plays an organ.
: or·gan·i·za·tion [ɔ̀:rgənizéiʃ(ə)n / -nai-] *n.* **1.** ⓤ the act of organizing; the state of being organized. **2.** ⓒ a group of persons united for some purpose or work, such as a club or a church. **3.** ⓒ an organized body or system. ¶*The ~ of the human body is very complex.*①
: or·gan·ize [ɔ́:rgənàiz] *vt.* **1.** get together and arrange (things) in order; establish. ¶*~ a baseball team.* **2.** 《esp. used in *pp.*》 furnish (something) with organs; give organic structure to (something). ¶*an organized body.*① —*vi.* become organized.
or·gan·iz·er [ɔ́:rgənàizər] *n.* ⓒ a person who organizes things, such as a party, a factory, or a company.
or·gy [ɔ́:rgi] *n.* (pl. **-gies**) **1.** ⓒ party with wild merry-making; a drunken revel. **2.** (*pl.*) (in ancient Greece and Rome) secret ceremonies in honor of the gods, esp. of wine.
o·ri·el [ɔ́:riəl] *n.* ⓒ a window projecting from an upper story. ⇨fig.
• o·ri·ent [ɔ́:riənt → *v.*] *n.* **1.** (*the O-*) the East, the countries of Asia. ↔Occident **2.** ⓤ (*poetic*) the east. —*adj.* **1.** (*O-*) (*poetic*) eastern; of the countries of Asia. **2.** bright or shining like pearls. **3.** rising; dawning. —*vt.* [ɔ́:riènt] (usu. *reflexively*) **1.** find the true position of (oneself). **2.** make (oneself) fit for one's surroundings.

[oriel]

• o·ri·en·tal [ɔ̀:riéntl] *adj.* **1.** (*O-*) of the Orient. ↔Occidental ¶*Oriental civilization.* **2.** eastern. —*n.* ⓒ 《*O-*》 a person of the Orient, esp. a Japanese or a Chinese.
O·ri·en·tal·ist, o- [ɔ̀:riéntəlist] *n.* ⓒ a person who studies or knows Oriental languages, literature, art, etc.
o·ri·en·tate [ɔ́:rientèit] *vt.* =orient.
o·ri·en·ta·tion [ɔ̀:rientéiʃ(ə)n] *n.* ⓤ the act of orientating; the state of being orientated.
or·i·fice [ɔ́:rifis, ár- / ɔ́r-] *n.* ⓒ a mouth of a cave, pipe, tube, etc; an opening.
orig. original; originally.
: or·i·gin [ɔ́:ridʒin, ári- / ɔ́ri-] *n.* ⓤⓒ **1.** the source from which anything comes; the beginning. ¶*the ~ of a word* / *of ancient ~*① / *the ~ of the rumor.*② **2.** birth; family; background. ¶*a man of noble ~*① / *by ~.*②
: o·rig·i·nal [ərídʒin(ə)l] *adj.* **1.** of the beginning; first; not copied; newly-created. ¶*the ~ plan* / *the ~ settlers of America*① / *the ~ edition of a book.*② **2.** able to create; new and fresh. ¶*an ~ writer* / *an ~ idea.* —*n.* ⓒ the first model from which another is copied or translated. ¶*read in the ~.*②
• o·rig·i·nal·i·ty [ərìdʒinǽliti] *n.* (pl. **-ties**) **1.** ⓤ the ability to create something new. **2.** ⓤ freshness; novelty. **3.** ⓒ a queer person; a curious thing.
• o·rig·i·nal·ly [ərídʒinəli] *adv.* by origin; at first.
• o·rig·i·nate [ərídʒinèit] *vt.* bring (something) into being; create; invent. —*vi.* start; begin; begin to exist. (*~ from someone or something*; *~ in something*; *~ with someone*) ¶*The fire originated in the bathroom.*①
o·rig·i·na·tion [ərìdʒinéiʃ(ə)n] *n.* ⓤⓒ the act of originating; the state of being originated; origin.
o·ri·ole [ɔ́:riòul] *n.* ⓒ an American songbird with yellow and black feathers.
O·ri·on [ouráiən / ərái-] *n.* **1.** (in Greek mythology) a handsome hunter with a belt around his waist and a

—名 오르간 연주자
—名 1. 조직, 편성; 기구(機構) 2. 조합, 협회, 단체 3. 유기체 ¶①인체의 조직은 아주 복잡하다

—他 1. …을 편성하다, 조직하다;[클럽 따위]를 창립하다 2. …에 기관(器官)을 주다; 유기적으로 하다 ¶①유기체
—自 조직적으로 하다

—名 조직자, 편성자, 창립자

—名 1. 북새통; 진탕 마시며 떠드는 술잔치 2. [고대 그리이스·로마의] 비밀 주신제(酒神祭)

—名 벽에서 내민 창

—名 1. 동양 2. 동쪽 —形 1. 동방의; 동양의 2. [보석이] 최고급의, 찬란하게 빛나는 3. [태양이] 뜨는, 돋는 —他 1. …의 올바른 위치를 알다 2. …을 적응시키다

—形 1. 동양의 2. 동쪽의, 동방의 —名 동양인

—名 동양학자, 동양통(通)

—名 방위[측정]; 입장 결정; 적응

—名 [동굴·관 따위의] 구멍, 아가리

—名 1. 기원(起源); 출처 ¶①기원이 오래된/②그 소문의 출처 2. 태생, 혈통 ¶③태생이 고귀한 사람/④태생은

—形 1. 원래의; 처음의; 원작의, 원문의 ¶①미국에의 최초의 이주자/②초판본 2. 독창적인; 참신한

—名 원형; 원본, 원서, 원문 ¶③원문으로 읽다
—名 1. 독창력 2. 참신함; 신기함, 기발함 3. 괴짜; 진품(珍品)

—副 원래, 처음에는
—他 …을 일으키다, 시작하다; 창작(창설)하다; 발명하다 —自 시작되다; 생겨나다 ¶①불은 욕실에서 났다

—名 개시, 시초; 창작, 발명; 기인(起因)

—名 꾀꼬리과의 새의 일종

—名 1. 오리온 2. 오리온좌(座)

orison [808] **ostler**

sword by his side. **2.** a group of bright stars near the equator of the heavens named for this hunter.
or·i·son [ɔ́:riz(ə)n / ɔ́ri-] *n.* ⓒ ((usu. *pl.*)) a prayer. —图 기도
or·na·ment *n.* [ɔ́:rnəmənt→ *v.*] **1.** Ⓤ adornment; decoration. **2.** ⓒ something to add beauty, such as furniture, vases, or pieces of china. **3.** ⓒ a person or his act that adds honor or grace to his society. **4.** ((*pl.*)) things used in church services, such as vestments, plates, bells, etc. —*vt.* [ɔ́:rnəmènt] make (something) beautiful; decorate. ((~ something *with*)) —图 1. 장식 2. 장식품 3. [사회 따위에] 빛을 더해 주는 사람, 자랑이 되는 행위 4. 교회의 예배용품
—他 …을 장식하다
or·na·men·tal [ɔ̀:rnəméntl] *adj.* of ornament; decorative. —形 장식적인, 장식이 많이 있는
or·na·men·ta·tion [ɔ̀:rnəmentéiʃ(ə)n] *n.* Ⓤ **1.** the act of ornamenting; the state of being ornamented. **2.** ((*collectively*)) decorations; ornaments. —图 1. 장식, 수식 2. 장식품
or·nate [ɔ:rnéit] *adj.* adorned or decorated too much. —形 야단스럽게 꾸민, 지나치게 화려한
or·ni·thol·o·gist [ɔ̀:rniθálədʒist / ɔ̀:niθɔ́l-] *n.* ⓒ a person who studies birds. —图 조류 학자
or·ni·thol·o·gy [ɔ̀:rniθálədʒi / ɔ̀:niθɔ́l-] *n.* Ⓤ the study of birds. —图 조류학
or·phan [ɔ́:rf(ə)n] *n.* ⓒ a child who has lost both or one of his parents by death. —*adj.* of or for orphans; being without one or both parents. —*vt.* deprive (a child) of one or both parents. —图 양친 (또는 한쪽 부모)이 없는 아이, 고아 —形 고아의, 양친(또는 한쪽 부모)이 없는 —他 …을 고아가 되게 하다
or·phan·age [ɔ́:rf(ə)nidʒ] *n.* **1.** Ⓤ the state of being an orphan. **2.** ⓒ a home for orphans. —图 1. 고아임 2. 고아원, 육아원
Or·phe·us [ɔ́:rfiəs, -fju:s / ɔ́:fju:s] *n.* (in Greek mythology) a musician who charmed even birds and beasts by playing his lyre sweetly. —图 오르페우스
or·tho·dox [ɔ́:rθədɑ̀ks / ɔ́:θədɔ̀ks] *adj.* **1.** generally accepted, esp. in religion. ↔heterodox **2.** approved; usual; customary.
the Orthodox Church, the group of Eastern or Greek Catholic churches that recognizes a head other than the Pope in Rome. —形 1. [종교상] 정설(正說)의, 정통파의 2. 옳다고 인정된; 아주 보통의; 전통적인
熏 그리이스 정교회
or·tho·dox·y [ɔ́:rθədɑ̀ksi / ɔ́:θədɔ̀k-] *n.* Ⓤⓒ (pl. **-dox·ies**) the state of being orthodox; orthodox belief; orthodox practice. ↔heterodoxy —图 정설, 정교(正敎); 정설 신봉, 정통파; 일반적인 설에 따르기
or·thog·ra·phy [ɔ:rθágrəfi / ɔ:θɔ́g-] *n.* Ⓤ **1.** the art of writing words with the right letters; correct spelling. **2.** the science which treats of spelling and letters. —图 1. 철자법; 정자법(正字法) 2. 문자론, 철자론
os·cil·late [ásəlèit / ɔ́s-] *vi.* **1.** swing to and fro like a pendulum. **2.** be very changeable in one's states, opinions or purposes. —*vt.* cause (someone or something) to oscillate. —自 1. 진동하다, 흔들리다 2. [의견 따위가] 자주 바뀌다 —他 …을 진동(동요)시키다
os·cil·la·tion [àsəléiʃ(ə)n / ɔ̀s-] *n.* Ⓤⓒ **1.** the act of oscillating; a single swing of a pendulum, etc. **2.** the state of being changeable in one's states, etc. —图 1. 진동; [진자(振子) 따위의] 흔들림 2. [의견 따위의] 동요
os·prey [áspri / ɔ́s-] *n.* ⓒ a large fish-eating bird of the hawk family. —图 물수리
os·si·fi·ca·tion [àsifikéiʃ(ə)n / ɔ̀s-] *n.* Ⓤ the process of ossifying; the state of being ossified; ⓒ the part that is ossified; bone structure. —图 골화(骨化); 골화된 부분; 골격
os·si·fy [ásifài / ɔ́s-] *vi., vt.* **1.** change into bone. **2.** become hard or fixed like bone; make (something) hard. —自他 1. …을 골화하다; 뼈로 되다 2. 굳어지다, 고정하다; 경화(硬化)하다
os·ten·si·ble [əsténsibl / ɔs-] *adj.* on the surface only; apparent; pretended. ↔real; actual ¶ ~ *purpose*. —形 표면상의; 외양만의; 겉치레의
os·ten·si·bly [əsténsibli / ɔs-] *adv.* in an ostensible manner; apparently. —副 표면상으로
os·ten·ta·tion [àstentéiʃ(ə)n / ɔ̀s-] *n.* Ⓤ vain or unnecessary display of wealth, knowledge, etc. to attract others; boastful exhibition. —图 허세[를 부리기]; 과시
os·ten·ta·tious [àstentéiʃəs / ɔ̀s-] *adj.* done for unnecessary display to attract notice. —形 허세를 부리는, 허식의
os·ten·ta·tious·ly [àstentéiʃəsli / ɔ̀s-] *adv.* in an ostentatious manner. —副 허세를 부려
ost·ler [áslər / ɔ́slə] *n.* =hostler.

os·tra·cism [ástrəsìz(ə)m / ɔ́s-] *n.* ⓤ the act of ostracizing; the state of being ostracized.
—名 [옛 그리스의] 패각(貝殼) 추방; 배척; 추방

os·tra·cize [ástrəsàiz / ɔ́s-] *vt.* 1. (among the ancient Greeks) banish a marked citizen for a time by popular vote. 2. banish (someone) from society; shut (someone) out from privileges.
—他 1. [옛 그리스에서] …을 패각 추방으로 하다 2. …을 추방하다; 배척하다

os·trich [ɔ́:stritʃ, ás- / ɔ́s-] *n.* ⓒ a very large, fast-running African bird which cannot fly. 「food.
1) *have the digestion of an ostrich,* can digest any
2) *ostrich belief* (or *policy*), belief or policy that is founded on self-delusion or a refusal to accept facts.
—名 타조
熟 1)식욕이 왕성하다 2)[머리를 감추고 꽁지를 안 감추는 타조의 습성과 같은] 눈 가리고 아웅하기

O·thel·lo [ouθélou] *n.* 1. a play by Shakespeare. 2. the hero of this play.
—名 1. 셰익스피어 작의 비극 2. 그 극의 주인공

‡**oth·er** [ʌ́ðər] *adj.* 1. different. ¶*any ~ girl* / *any person ~ than yourself.* 2. more; further. ¶*Have you any ~ questions?* 3. 《with *the* or *one's*》of the rest; remaining; another. ¶*the ~ hand*① / *the ~ girls.* 4. opposite; reverse. ¶*the ~ side of the road.* 5. former. ¶*people of ~ days.*
—*pron.* 1. 《*the ~*》 the other one; the second of two. ¶*Each loved the ~.* 2. 《*pl.*》 other persons or things;
1) *every other,* every second; alternate.   [the rest.
2) *of all others,* above all others.
3) *the other day,* a few days ago; recently.
—*adv.* differently; otherwise.   「*her.*②
other than, except for. ¶*I could not do ~ than love*
—形 1. 다른, 틀리는 2. 그 밖의; 그 위에 3. 나머지의, 또하나의   ¶①또 한쪽의 손 4. 거꾸로의, 반대의 5. 이전의

—代 1. 다른 것; 다른 한쪽 2. 다른 사람(물건)
熟 1)하나 걸러의 2)특히, 그 중에서도 3)전날
—副 다른 방법으로
熟 …외에는 ¶②그녀를 사랑하지 않을 수 없었다

‡**oth·er·wise** [ʌ́ðərwàiz] *adv.* 1. in another manner; differently. ¶*or ~*① / *You should have done ~.*② 2. in other respects. ¶*They are noisy, but ~ very nice boys.* 3. or else; or; if not. ¶*Work hard, ~ you shall not eat.* / *I went at once, ~ I would have missed her.*
—*adj.* different; in another condition; of another nature. *and otherwise,* and others.
—副 1. 다른 방법으로; 달리 ¶①또는 그 반대로/②너는 다른 방법으로 해야 했다 2. 그 밖의 점에서는 3. 그렇지 않으면; 만일 그렇게 하지 않으면

—形 다른; 다른 종류의
熟 기타

o·ti·ose [óuʃious, +*U.S.* óuti-] *adj.* serving no practical use; not effective; unnecessary.
—形 무효의; 불필요한

Ot·ta·wa [átəwə / ɔ́t-] *n.* the capital of Canada.
—名 오타와

ot·ter [átər / ɔ́t-] *n.* ⓒ (pl. **-ters** or *collectively* **-ter**) a fish-eating animal that lives in and near the water and is valued for its fur.
—名 수달의 일종

Ot·to [átou / ɔ́t-] *n.* a man's name.
—名 남자 이름

Ot·to·man [átəmən / ɔ́tə-] *n.* ⓒ a Turk. —*adj.* Turkish.
—名 터어키 사람 —形 터어키의

ot·to·man [átəmən / ɔ́tə-] *n.* ⓒ a cushioned seat like a sofa or chair without back or arms.   「pain.
—名 [등과 팔걸이가 없는] 쿠션 의자

ouch [autʃ] *interj.* an exclamation expressing sudden
—間 아야!

‡**ought** [ɔːt] *auxil. v.* 《used with *to do*》 1. have a duty to; should. ¶*You ~ to pay your debts.* / *I ~ to have told you.* 2. need; had better. ¶*You ~ to start before it rains.* 3. be almost sure; be expected. ¶*I ~ to be through with it by Sunday.*
—助 1. …하여야 한다; …하지 않으면 안 되다 2. 바람직하다; …하는 편이 좋다 3. 아마 …일 것이다; 아마 …할 것이다

•**ounce** [auns] *n.* ⓒ 1. a unit of weight equal to 1/16 of a pound. ⇒NB. 2. a very small amount; a little bit.
—名 1. 온스 NB oz.로 줄임 2. 소량

‡**our** [auər] *pron.* the possessive form of *we.*
—代 우리들의

‡**ours** [auərz] *pron.* anything that belongs to us. ¶*this house of ~* / *Ours is a big school.*
—代 우리들의 것

our·self [àuərsélf] *pron.* myself.
—代 나 스스로

‡**our·selves** [àuərsélvz] *pron.* a reflexive and emphatic form of *we* or *us.* ¶[*all*] *by ~*① / *We had better do it ~.* / *We dressed ~.*
—代 우리를 스스로; 우리 자신을(에게) ¶①혼자의 힘으로, 우리들만으로

oust [aust] *vt.* 1. drive out (someone), esp. by unfair means. 《*~ someone from*》 ¶*He was ousted from this country.* 2. dispossess. 《*~ someone of*》 ¶*The Government ousted him of his passport.*①
—他 1. [부정수단으로] …을 쫓아내다 2. …을 빼앗다 ¶①정부는 그의 여권을 빼앗았다

‡**out** [aut] *adv.* 1. not present; not at home; not at a place. ¶*He is ~.* / *She is ~ shopping.* 2. outdoors;
—副 1. 부재(不在)로, 외출하여 2. 옥외에서 3. 발표되어, 알려져 ¶①그 비밀

outside. ¶*go ~ for a walk / They are ~ in the garden.* **3.** in public. ¶*The secret is ~ at last.*① / *His new book is ~.* **4.** completely; to an end. ¶*be tired ~*② / *argue it ~.*③ **5.** aloud. ¶*sing (shout, cry) ~.* **6.** into sight. ¶*The moon came ~.* **7.** to a state of no longer existing. ¶*The fire is ~.* / *blow ~ the light*④ / *die ~* / *The wine has run ~.* **8.** no longer in fashion or use. ¶*Long skirts have gone ~.* **9.** off the coast. **10.** (of a flower) in bloom. ¶*The flowers will soon be ~.*⑤ **11.** in the state of being excluded. ¶*lock ~*⑥ / *The batter is ~.* **12.** to others. ¶*give ~ the books.*⑦ **13.** from among others. ¶*pick ~* / *find ~.* **14.** (of a girl) into society. ¶*This girl has just come ~.*

은 드디어 탄로났다 **4.** 완전히; 최후까지 ¶②지쳐빠지다/③결론이 날 때까지 논하다 **5.** 큰 소리로 **6.** 보여서; 나타나서 **7.** 다하여; 없어져 ¶④불을 불어서 끄다 **8.** 스러져; 쓰이지 않게 되어 **9.** 가운데에 **10.** 피어서 ¶⑤꽃은 머지않아 핀다 **11.** 제외되어; 아우트가 되어 ¶⑥문을 잠그고 들이지 않다 **12.** 남에게 ¶⑦책을 나눠주다 **13.** 많은 것 중에서 **14.** 사교계에 나와

1) ***be out for*** (or ***to do***), make efforts to get or to do (something).
2) ***out and away,*** by far; without comparison.
3) ***out and out,*** completely; thoroughly.
4) ***out from under,*** (*colloq.*) away from difficulty or danger.
5) ***out of,*** ⓐ away from inside. ¶*go ~ of the house / look ~ of the window.* ⓑ beyond. ¶*~ of control*⑧ / *~ of patience*⑨ / *He went ~ of the yard.* ⓒ lacking. ¶*~ of money / ~ of breath.*⑩ ⓓ because of. ¶*cry ~ of joy.*
6) ***Out with him!,*** Turn him out!

[熟] 1)…을 얻으려고(하려고) 노력하다 2)훨씬 3)완전히, 철저하게 4)궁지(위험)에서 벗어나 5)ⓐ밖으로 ⓑ…을 넘어서 ¶⑧다루기 어려운/⑨참을 수 없는 ⓒ…이 없는, 결여된 ¶⑩숨이 차서 ⓓ… 때문에 6)쫓아내라!

—*prep.* (*U.S.*) out of. ¶*throw something ~ the window / come ~ the door.* —[前] 《美》 …의 밖으로

—*adj.* outer; on the outside. ¶*an ~ island.* —[形] 밖의, 바깥의

—*vi.* become known; go or come out. ¶*Truth will ~ soon.* —[自] 알려지다, [놀러] 나가다

out-and-out [áut(ə)n(d)áut] *adj.* complete; thorough. —[形] 완전한, 철저한

out·bal·ance [àutbǽləns] *vt.* =outweigh.

out·bid [àutbíd] *vt.* (**-bid, -bid·den** or **-bid, -bid·ding**) offer to pay more than someone else. ¶*~ each other.*① —[他] …보다 비싼 값을 부르다 ¶①서로 값을 경합하다

out·bid·den [àutbídn] *v.* pp. of **outbid**.

out·bound [áutbàund] *adj.* outward bound; not homeward bound. ¶*a ship ~ for Africa.* —[形] 외국(외지)으로 가는

out·brave [autbréiv] *vt.* challenge bravely; excel in bravery. —[他] …에 용감히 맞서다; 용기로 압도하다

* **out·break** [áutbrèik] *n.* [C] **1.** the act of breaking out; outburst. ¶*an ~ of sorrow.* **2.** a riot; a revolt; a rebellion. —[名] **1.** [전쟁·유행병 따위의] 발발; [감정의] 격발 **2.** 반란, 폭동

out·build·ing [áutbìldiŋ] *n.* [C] a building separate from a main building. —[名] 딴채(헛간 따위)

out·burst [áutbə̀:rst] *n.* [C] the act of bursting forth; an eruption; a sudden intense expression of feelings. ¶*the ~ of Mt. Asama / an ~ of anger.* —[名] [화산의] 폭발, [감정의] 폭발

out·cast [áutkæ̀st / -kɑ̀:st] *adj.* exiled; driven out; homeless; friendless. **—*n.*** [C] a person or animal driven away from home or from his country. —[形] 추방된; 집 없는; 배척된 —[名] 추방인; 집 없는 사람, 부랑인

out·class [àutklǽs / -klɑ́:s] *vt.* excel in skill, quality, class, etc.; be much superior to (someone or something). —[他] …을 능가하다, …보다 상급에 속하다

* **out·come** [áutkʌ̀m] *n.* [C] the result; the consequence. —[名] 결과, 성과

out·crop [áutkràp / -krɔ̀p] *n.* [C] (of a layer or vein) the part of a mineral vein that appears on the surface of the ground. ¶*the ~ of a vein of gold.* **—*vi.*** (**-cropped, -crop·ping**) appear; crop out. —[名] [광맥의] 노출, 노두(露頭) —[自] [지층 따위가] 노출하다, 나타나다

out·cry [áutkrài] *n.* [C] (pl. **-cries**) **1.** a loud cry or shout; a sudden cry or uproar; a confused noise. **2.** an auction. —[名] **1.** 외침 소리, 큰 소동 **2.** 경매, 외치며 팔기

out·did [àutdíd] *v.* pt. of **outdo**.

out·dis·tance [àutdístəns] *vt.* leave (something or someone) behind by going or running faster. —[他] …을 훨씬 앞서다

out·do [àutdú:] *vt.* (**-did, -done**) do better than someone else; surpass; excel. ¶*~ oneself.*① —[他] …을 능가하다, …보다 뛰어나다 ¶①전에 없이 썩 잘하다

out·done [àutdʌ́n] *v.* pp. of **outdo**.

* **out·door** [áutdɔ̀:r] *adj.* **1.** in the open air; open-air. ¶*~ games.* **2.** (*Brit.*) outside of a poorhouse, hospital etc. ¶*~ relief.*① —[形] **1.** 옥외의, 야외의 **2.** 《英》 원외(院外)의 ¶①[수용되어 있지 않은 빈민에 대한] 원외 구호

outdoors [811] outline

* **out·doors** [àutdɔ́:rz] *adv.* in the open air; outside a building. —*n.* ((*the* ~)) the world outside of houses; the open air. ―副 옥외에서, 야외에서(로) ―名 옥외, 야외
* **out·er** [áutər] *adj.* near the outside; exterior. ¶*the* ~ *man*① / ~ *space*. ―形 바깥쪽의, 외부의 ¶①풍채 좋은 「사람」
out·er·most [áutərmòust] *adj.* farthest outside. ―形 가장 밖의; 가장 바깥쪽의
out·face [àutféis] *vt.* stare at (someone) boldly; face up to (someone) without fear. ―他 …을 노려보다, …에 태연히 맞서다
out·field [áutfì:ld] *n.* © ((*the* ~)) (*Baseball*) the part of the field beyond the infield or diamond; ((*collectively*)) the outfielders. ↔infield ―名 《野球》 외야; 외야수
out·field·er [áutfì:ldər] *n.* © (*Baseball*) a player who is stationed in the outfield. ↔infielder ―名 《野球》 외야수
* **out·fit** [áutfìt] *n.* © 1. ((*collectively*)) all the articles necessary for a special purpose; a set of clothes; equipment. ¶*a baseball* ~ / *a carpentry* ~.① 2. (*U.S.*) a group of people associated for a certain purpose.
—*vt.* (**-fit·ted, -fit·ting**) furnish (something) with an outfit; equip. ¶~ *an expedition to the Antarctic zone*.② ―名 1.도구 한 벌;채비;복장; ¶①목수 도구 한 벌 2.《美》부대,여행단;직공의 무리
―他 …을 채비하다, …에게 공급하다 ¶②남극 탐험의 장비를 갖추다
out·fit·ter [áutfìtər] *n.* © a shopkeeper dealing in an outfit. ¶*a sporting* ~.① 「*of water.*」 ―名 장신구상,여행용품 장수 ¶①운동구점
out·flow [áutflòu] *n.* © the act of flowing out. ¶*the* ~ ―名 유출,분출(噴出)
out·go [áutgòu] *n.* © (pl. **-goes**) the amount of money that is spent or paid out; expenditure. ↔income ―名 비용; 지출
out·go·ing [áutgòuiŋ] *adj.* going out; departing; retiring.
—*n.* 1. ⓤ© the act of going out; departure. 2. ((*pl.*)) expenditure; expenses. ↔incoming ―形 나가는, 떠나가는 ―名 1. 출발 2. 비용, 경비
out·grew [àutgrú:] *v.* pt. of **outgrow**.
out·grow [àutgróu] *vt.* (**-grew, -grown**) 1. become too big for (something). ¶~ *one's clothes*. 2. grow away from (something). ¶*She outgrew her impudent nature*.① 3. become taller or bigger than (someone). ¶*My sister has outgrown me*. ―他 1. …보다 커지다 2.[성장하여] …을 벗다(잃다), 못 입게 되다 ¶①그녀는 성장하여 뻔뻔스러움이 없어졌다 3. …보다 크게 성장하다
out·grown [àutgróun] *v.* pp. of **outgrow**.
out·growth [áutgròuθ] *n.* ©ⓤ 1. a natural development or result. ¶*The present success is the* ~ *of his diligence for years*. 2. something that has grown out of something else; an offshoot. 3. the act of growing forth. ¶*the* ~ *of a tree* (*new leaves*). ―名 1.자연의 발전,결과 2.파생물;결가지,분지(分枝) 3.성장; 싹틈
out·house [áuthàus] *n.* © a building belonging to a main building; a detached shed. 「*excursion.*」 ―名 딴채; 헛간
out·ing [áutiŋ] *n.* © a pleasure trip; a walk; a hike; an ―名 유람여행; 산책,소풍
out·laid [àutléid] *v.* pt. and pp. of **outlay**.
out·land·ish [autlǽndiʃ] *adj.* 1. strange; queer; unfamiliar. 2. looking like something foreign. ―形 1.기이한, 눈에 선 2.이국풍의
out·last [àutlǽst / -lá:st] *vt.* last longer than (something); outlive (someone). ―他 …보다 오래 계속하다, 오래 살다(가다)
out·law [áutlɔ̀:] *n.* © 1. a person deprived of the protection of the law. 2. a lawless wanderer; a habitual criminal. —*vt.* 1. take legal protection away from (someone). 2. take legal force away from (something). 3. expel (someone) from society. 4. make (something) unlawful; prohibit. 「*of being outlawed.*」 ―名 1.법률상의 보호를 박탈당한 사람 2.부랑인; 상습법 ―他 1. …에서 법률의 보호를 박탈하다 2. …에서 법률의 효력을 잃게 하다 3. …을 추방하다 4. …을 비합법화(금지)하다
out·law·ry [áutlɔ̀:ri] *n.* ⓤ the act of outlawing; the state ―名 보호 박탈;사회적 추방;비합법화
out·lay *n.* [áutlèi →*v.*] © expense; expenditure. —*vt.* [àutléi] (**-laid**) spend (money). ―名 비용;지출 ―他 …을 소비하다
* **out·let** [áutlet] *n.* © 1. a way out; a passage; a means of expression. ¶*an* ~ *for the youth's energy*. 2. a market for goods. ―名 1. 출구; 배출구 2. 판로(販路)
* **out·line** [áutlàin] *n.* © 1. a line that forms or traces the outer limits of an object. 2. a brief sketch or draft. 3. a short summary; a general plan. ¶*in* ~① / *an* ~ *of world history*. 「*terms.*」 ―名 1. 윤곽[선], 외형 2.약도; 초벌 밑그림 3.개요, 요강(要綱); 대강의 계획 ¶①윤곽의,대강의
give an outline of, describe (something) in general 熟 …의 개요를 말하다
—*vt.* 1. draw or trace the outer line of (something or ―他 1. …의 윤곽을 그리다, 초벌그림

someone); sketch. **2.** describe or state (something) in a few words. — (약도, 밑그림)을 그리다 2. …의 개요를 말하다, …을 약술(略述)하다

out·live [àutlív] *vt.* live or last longer than (someone or something); survive; outlast. — [他] …보다 오래 살다, 살아 남다, 오래 살아 …을 잃다

out·look [áutlùk] *n.* [C] [U] **1.** view. **2.** prospect for the future. ¶*a hopeful* ~. **3.** a point of view. ¶*a cheerful* ~ *on life.* — [名] 1. 전망, 조망(眺望), 경치 2. 형세, 앞날의 가망 3. …관(觀), 견지

out·ly·ing [áutlàiiŋ] *adj.* far from the center; distant; remote. — [形] 중심에서 멀리 떨어진, 외딴

out·ma·neu·ver [àutmənú:vər] *vt.* surpass (the enemy) in maneuvering; get an advantage over (the enemy) by maneuvering. — [他] …을 책략으로 이기다, …의 계략을 뒤엎다

0

out·ma·noeu·vre [àutmənú:vər] *vt.* (*Brit.*) =outmaneuver.

out·match [àutmǽtʃ] *vt.* be superior to (someone or something); excel. — [他] …을 능가하다, …보다 낫다

out·mod·ed [àutmóudid] *adj.* out-of-date. — [形] 유행에 뒤진

out·most [áutmòust] *adj.* outermost; farthest out. — [形] 가장 바깥의, 가장 먼

out·num·ber [àutnʌ́mbər] *vt.* be greater in number than (someone or something). — [他] …보다 수효에 있어서 우세하다

out-of-date [áutəvdéit] *adj.* old-fashioned; not up-to-date. — [形] 시대에 뒤진, 구식의

out-of-door [áutəvdɔ́:r] *adj.* =outdoor.

out-of-doors [àutəvdɔ́:rz] *adj.* outdoor. —*n., adv.* outdoors. — [形] 옥외의 —[名][副] 옥외(에서)

out-of-the-way [áutə(v)ðəwéi] *adj.* **1.** remote; hidden. **2.** unusual; strange. ¶*an* ~ *proposal.* — [形] 1. 외딴, 구석진 2. 이상한, 별난

out·pa·tient [áutpèiʃ(ə)nt] *n.* [C] a person who comes to a hospital to receive treatment. ↔inpatient — [名] [병원의] 외래 환자

out·play [àutpléi] *vt.* play better than (someone); beat. — [他] [경기에서] …을 지게 하다

out·post [áutpòust] *n.* [C] **1.** a military guard stationed at a distance from the main body of soldiers. **2.** the place so occupied. — [名] 1. 전초, 전초 중대 2. 전초 지점

out·pour *n.* [áutpɔ̀:r →*v.*] [C] that which is poured out. —*vi., vt.* [ˋˊ] pour out. — [名] 유출[물] —[自][他] 흘러나오[게 하]다

out·pour·ing [áutpɔ̀:riŋ] *n.* **1.** [C] anything that is poured out. **2.** 《usu. *pl.*》 outflow of thoughts or feelings. — [名] 1. 유실; 유실물 2. [감정의] 발로, 쏟아져 나옴

∗**out·put** [áutpùt] *n.* [C] [U] **1.** the amount produced or able to be produced, usu. in a certain time; production. **2.** power or energy that can be produced. — [名] 1. 생산고; 생산 2. [기계 따위의] 출력, 마력

∗**out·rage** [áutreidʒ] *n.* [C] [U] **1.** a violent or cruel act; an act against law or morality. **2.** insult. —*vt.* **1.** do violence to (someone or something), break (the law, etc.); harm. **2.** insult. — [名] 1. 난폭, 폭행, 불법, 무도(無道) 2. 모욕 —[他] 1. …에 폭행하다, …을 학대하다, [법률 따위]를 어기다, …을 해치다 2. …을 모욕하다

out·ra·geous [autréidʒəs] *adj.* violent; immoral; cruel; extremely offensive; insulting. — [形] 난폭한, 괘씸한, 잔인한, 불법의, 언어도단의

out·ra·geous·ly [autréidʒəsli] *adv.* in an outrageous manner. — [副] 난폭하게, 잔인하게, 불법으로

out·ran [àutrǽn] *v.* pt. of **outrun**.

out·range [àutréindʒ] *vt.* have a greater or longer range than (something). — [他] 착탄(着彈) 거리에 있어서 …보다 능가하다

out·rid·den [àutrídn] *v.* pp. of **outride**.

out·ride [àutráid] *vt.* (**-rode, -rid·den**) ride faster or farther than (something or someone); reach faster than (something or someone); ride past. — [他] …보다 빨리(멀리) 타고 가다; (타고서) …보다 빨리 닿다; …을 앞질러 타고 지나가다

out·rid·er [áutràidər] *n.* [C] a servant who rides on a horse before or beside a carriage. — [名] 말을 타고 마차를 수행하는 사람

out·rig·ger [áutrìgər] *n.* [C] **1.** a projecting device fastened at the side of a boat. ⇒fig. **2.** a boat with such a device. **3.** a projecting board or beam attached for temporary or special use. — [名] 1. [보우트 현외(舷外)의] 노걸이 받침쇠 2. 그것이 있는 보우트 3. [돛자락을 펴는] 현외부재(舷外浮材)

〔outrigger 1.〕

out·right *adv.* [áutráit / ˋˊ ‖ →*adj.*] **1.** completely; entirely; utterly. **2.** openly; frankly. **3.** at once; immediately; at one time. —*adj.* [ˊˋ] **1.** frank; straightforward; direct. **2.** complete; thorough. — [副] 1. 완전히, 몽땅, 마음껏, 철저히 2. 숨김없이, 공공연히 3. 당장에, 즉석에서 —[形] 1. 노골적인, 솔직한 2. 충분한, 철저한

out·ri·val [àutráiv(ə)l] *vt.* (**-valed, -val·ing** or *Brit.* **-valled, -val·ling**) beat (others) in a race; defeat; excel. ——他 …을 이기다, …을 능가하다

out·rode [àutróud] *v.* pt. of **outride**.

out·run [àutrʌ́n] *vt.* (**-ran, -run, -run·ning**) **1.** go or run faster than (something or someone). **2.** go beyond; exceed. ——他 1. …보다 빨리 달리다(가다), …을 추월하다 2. …을 초과하다

out·set [áutsèt] *n.* (*the* ~) the beginning; the start.
1) *at* (or *in*) *the outset*, firstly; in or at the beginning.
2) *from the outset*, from the beginning.
——名 최초; 착수, 발단
熙 1)시초에 2)처음부터

out·shine [àut·ʃáin] *vt.* (**-shone**) shine more brightly than; excel. ——他 …보다 더욱 빛나다, 보다 빛이 강하다; …보다 뛰어나다

out·shone [àut·ʃóun] *v.* pt and pp. of **outshine**.

out·shoot [àut·ʃúːt →*n.*] *vt.* (**-shot**) **1.** shoot faster or better than (someone). **2.** shoot out or send forth (something). ——*n.* [´‿] ⓒ projection; offshoot; (*Baseball*) a pitched ball that curves away from the batter.
——他 1. …보다 빨리(잘) 쏘다 2. [이삭이나 가지]를 돋게 하다 ——名 뚫고(뻗어) 나옴, 돌출; [野球] 아웃커어브

out·shot [àut·ʃát / -ʃɔ́t] *v.* pt. and pp. of **outshoot**.

‡**out·side** [áut·sáid ´‿, ‿´] *n.* Ⓤ **1.** outer side or part.
¶*the ~ of a box* / *open the door from ~*. **2.** appearance. ¶*He has a rough ~ but a good heart.* **3.** the farthest limit.
at the outside, at most.
—*adj.* **1.** on or of the outside. ¶*~ repairs.*① **2.** coming from the outside. ¶*You should not expect ~ help.*② **3.** not main; not regular. ¶*an ~ job.* **4.** extreme; greatest possible. ¶*an ~ estimate.*
—*adv.* **1.** outdoors; in the open air. **2.** to or on the outside.
—*prep.* **1.** on the outside of. **2.** beyond; except. ¶*No one knew it ~ us.*③

——名 1. 바깥쪽; 외부 2. 겉보기, 외관 3. 극한
熙 기껏, 많아야
——形 1. 외부의 ¶①바깥쪽의 수리 2. 외래의; 밖에서의 ¶②남의 원조를 기대해서는 안 된다 3. 부(副)의 4. 극한(極限)의; 가까스로의
——副 1. 옥외에서 2. 밖으로(에)
——前 1. …의 밖에서 2. …을 넘어서(제외하고) ¶③우리들 이외에는 아무도 모른다

out·sid·er [àut·sáidər] *n.* ⓒ a person who does not belong to a special group or class; a stranger. ——名 국외자, 문외한, 조합(당) 외의 사람

out·skirts [áut·skə̀ːrts] *n. pl.* the outer edge of a town or place. ¶*the ~ of the town.* ——名 [시의] 변두리, 교외

out·spo·ken [àut·spóuk(ə)n] *adj.* speaking or spoken openly; frank. ▷**out·spo·ken·ly** [-li] *adv.* ——形 숨김없이 말하는, 솔직한

out·spread *vi., vt.* [àut·spréd →*adj.*] (**-spread**) spread out; extend. —*adj.* [´‿] spread out; extended. ——自他 퍼지다, 펼치다; 퍼지다, 퍼뜨리다 ——形 펼쳐진, 퍼진

***out·stand·ing** [àut·stǽndiŋ] *adj.* **1.** standing out. **2.** distinguished; well-known. **3.** unpaid; unsettled; undone.
¶*He had a lot of work ~.* ▷**out·stand·ing·ly** [-li] *adv.*
——形 1. 돌출한 2. 눈에 띄는, 현저한 3. 미불(未拂)의; 미해결의

out·stay [àut·stéi] *vt.* stay longer than (someone). ¶*~ the other guests.*
outstay one's welcome, stay longer than one is wanted.
——他 [다른 손님보다] 오래 머물다, 오래 체재하다
熙 오래 머물러 미움을 사다

out·stretched [àut·strétʃt] *adj.* stretched out or spread. ¶*~ arms.* ——形 펼친, 뻗친

out·strip [àut·stríp] *vt.* (**-stripped, -strip·ping**) **1.** go or run faster than (others) as in a race. **2.** do something better than (someone else); excel. ——他 1. …을 앞지르다, 추월하다 2. …을 능가하다

out·vote [àutvóut] *vt.* defeat (someone) in voting. ——他 투표 수로 …을 이기다

***out·ward** [áutwərd] *adj.* **1.** going toward the outside; going away from one place. **2.** of or on the outside. ↔*inward* ¶*the ~ appearance of the building.*① **3.** obvious; apparent.
to outward seeming, apparently.
——形 1. 밖으로 향하는 2. 외부(바깥쪽)의 ¶① 그 건물의 외관 3. 명백한
熙 외관상

out·ward·ly [áutwərdli] *adv.* on the outside; in appearance. ——副 외부(외면)에; 외관상

***out·wards** [áutwərdz] *adv.* toward the outside; away from the port; on the outside; in appearance. ——副 밖으로(에); 국외(해외)에; 바깥쪽에; 외견상은

out·wear [àutwɛ́ər] *vt.* (**-wore, -worn**) **1.** last or wear (something) longer than another. **2.** wear out (something); use up (something). ——他 1. …보다 오래 가다 2. …을 입어서(써서) 낡게 하다

out·weigh [àutwéi] *vt.* be greater than (something or someone) in weight, value, importance, etc. ——他 …보다 무겁다; [가치·중요성 따위에] 있어서] …을 능가하다

out·wit [àutwít] *vt.* (**-wit·ted, -wit·ting**) excel (someone) in wit; beat (someone) by cunning. ——他 기지(機知)에 있어서 …을 능가하다; 속이다, …보다 꾀가 있다

out·wore [àutwɔ́:r] *v.* pt. of **outwear.**

out·work *n.* [áutwə̀:rk → *v.*] [C] (*Military*) a defensive wall or ditch built away from the center of the defences. —*vt.* [⏝⏝] work harder or faster than (another).
—[名] 외루(外壘), 외보(外堡) —[他] …보다 열심히(빨리) 일을 하다

out·worn *adj.* [áutwɔ́:rn → *v.*] **1.** that is worn out. **2.** out-of-date. ¶*an ~ fashion.* —*v.* [⏝⏝] pp. of **outwear.**
—[形] 1. 입어서 낡은, 해진 2. 시대에 뒤진

o·val [óuv(ə)l] *adj.* egg-shaped. —*n.* [C] something egg-shaped.
—[形] 달걀 모양의 —[名] 달걀 모양의 것

o·va·ry [óuvəri] *n.* [C] (pl. **-ries**) **1.** the organ of the female body in which eggs are produced. **2.** the part of a plant in which seeds are produced.
—[名] 1. 난소(卵巢) 2. 자방(子房)

o·va·tion [ouvéiʃ(ə)n] *n.* [C] an enthusiastic applause; a hearty public welcome.
—[名] 대갈채; 열렬한 환영

***ov·en** [ʌ́vn] *n.* [C] an enclosed space in a stove for baking food.
—[名] 솥, 가마, 화덕

‡**o·ver** [óuvər] *prep.* ↔under **1.** above; higher than. ¶*the sky ~ our heads.* **2.** so as to cover; on; upon. ¶*put one's hands ~ one's face | a blanket lying ~ a bed.* **3.** across; from one side to the other side of; on the other side of. ¶*fly ~ the lake | lands ~ the sea.*① **4.** here and there in; through all parts of. ¶*travel all ~ the country | spread butter ~ bread.* **5.** more than. ¶*~ 30 miles.* **6.** above in authority, power, position, etc. ¶*reign ~ a country.* **7.** during; through; until after. ¶*stay ~ the night.* **8.** concerning; about. ¶*talk ~ the matter | quarrel ~ a matter.* **9.** while doing or engaged in. ¶*fall asleep ~ work*② *| Let us discuss the matter ~ dinner.*③ **10.** by means of. ¶*She told me ~ the phone.* **11.** along. ¶*drive ~ a highway.*
—[前] 1. …의 [바로 위에]; …보다 높게 2. …을 덮어; …에 덮여서 3. …을 넘어서 저쪽으로; …의 저쪽에 ¶①바다 건너의 땅 4. 전면(全面)에; …의 여기저기를; …의 도처에 5. …이상 6. …을 능가하여; …을 지배하여 7. …에 걸쳐서 …이 끝날 때까지; …의 사이, …중 8. …에 대하여, …에 관하여 9. …하면서; …에 종사하여 ¶②일하면서 졸다/③그 일은 식사를 하면서 논의하자 10. …에 의하여 11. …을 따라서

—*adv.* **1.** above. ¶*hang ~.* **2.** completely; all through; covering the entire area. ¶*be covered ~ with paint.* **3.** across; to or on the other side; at some distance. ¶*~ here*④ *| go ~ to America | hand the money ~.*⑤ **4.** down from a standing position; upside down; into an opposite position. ¶*roll ~ and ~*⑥ *| turn ~ the pages*⑦ *| knock something ~.* **5.** finished; at an end. ¶*All is ~. | The game is ~.* **6.** through; from start to finish. ¶*all the year ~ | He took out his money and counted it ~.* **7.** again; once more; another time. ¶*Try it ~. | six times ~.* **8.** more; too. ¶*I have six dollars and ~.*
—[副] 1. 위쪽(머리 위)에 2. 전면에; 도처에 3. …을 넘어서; …저편에; 떨어진 곳에 ¶④이쪽에, 이쪽에서/⑤돈을 건네다 4. 쓰러져서; 뒤집혀서 ¶⑥데굴데굴 구르다/⑦페이지를 넘기다 5. 끝나서 6. 처음부터 끝까지; 완전히 7. 되풀이하여; 다시; 다시 한번 8. 여분으로; 너무

1) ***all over,*** ⓐ on or in every part; throughout. ⓑ finished.
2) ***all the world over,*** all over the world.
3) ***over again,*** again; once more.
4) ***over against,*** opposite to or in contrast with.
5) ***over all,*** from end to end; as a whole.
6) ***over and above,*** in addition to; more than; besides.

[熟] 1)ⓐ전면에; 도처에 ⓑ끝나서 2)전세계에 3)다시 한 번 4)…의 정면에; …와 대조하여 5)끝에서 끝까지; 전체로서 6)… 이상, …에 더하여

o·ver·act [òuvərǽkt] *vt., vi.* act to excess; act (one's part) in an exaggerated way.
—[他][自] 지나치게 하다; [극의 역할을] 과장하여 연기하다

o·ver·ac·tive [òuvərǽktiv] *adj.* too active.
—[形] 너무 활동적인

o·ver·all [óuvərɔ̀:l] *adj.* including all; whole. —*adv.* throughout; entirely.
—[形] 전체에 걸친; 전부터의
—[副] 완전히, 전체로

o·ver·anx·ious [óuvərǽŋkʃəs] *adj.* too anxious.
—[形] 너무 근심하는

o·ver·ate [òuvəréit / òuvərét] *v.* pt. of **overeat.**

o·ver·awe [òuvərɔ́:] *vt.* overcome (someone) with awe.
—[他] …을 위압하다, 위협하다

o·ver·bal·ance [òuvərbǽləns] *vt.* **1.** be greater than (something) in weight, value, influence, etc. **2.** cause (someone or something) to lose balance.
—[他] 1. 중량(가치)에 있어서 …을 능가하다 2. …에 평균(평형)을 잃게 하다

o·ver·bear [òuvərbέər] *vt.* (**-bore, -borne**) overcome; bear down.
—[他] …을 압도하다, 위압하다

o·ver·bear·ing [òuvərbέəriŋ] *adj.* haughty; self-important.
—[形] 건방진, 거만한; 자존심이 있는

o·ver·blown [òuvərblóun] *adj.* **1.** blown off. **2.** more than full-blown. ¶*an ~ flower.*
—[形] 1. 날려가 버린 2. [꽃이] 활짝 필 때가 지난

o·ver·board [óuvərbɔ̀:rd] *adv.* from a ship into the water.
—[副] 배 밖에, [배에서] 물 속으로

o·ver·bold [óuvərbóuld] *adj.* too bold; reckless.
—[形] 무모한, 앞뒤를 헤아리지 않는

o·ver·bore [òuvərbɔ́:r] *v.* pt. of **overbear**.
o·ver·borne [òuvərbɔ́:rn] *v.* pp. of **overbear**.
o·ver·bur·den [òuvərbə́:rdn] *vt.* load (someone or something) with too great a burden; overload. —他 …에 짐을 너무 지우다(싣다); …을 과로하게 하다
* **o·ver·came** [òuvərkéim] *v.* pt. of **overcome**.
o·ver·care·ful [òuvərkɛ́ərf(u)l] *adj.* too careful. —형 지나치게 조심하는
o·ver·cast *adj.* [óuvərkæ̀st / -kɑ̀:st ∥ →*v.* 2] cloudy; dark. ¶ *an ~ sky.* — *vt.* **1.** [-́-́] cover (the sky) with clouds; make (the sky) dark. **2.** [-́-́] sew over (the edges of a seam) to prevent the cloth from separating into threads. —형 흐린, 음산한 —他 1. …을 구름으로 가리다; 어둡게 하다 2. [가장자리]를 감치다
o·ver·charge *vt., vi.* [òuvərtʃɑ́:rdʒ →*n.*] **1.** load (something) too heavily. **2.** ask (someone) for too much money as payment for something. —*n.* [-́-́] ⓤⓒ **1.** too heavy a load. **2.** too great a request of money for something. —他国 1. 짐을 너무 싣다 2. 부당하게 비싼 값을 요구하다 —명 1. 적하(積荷) 과중 2. 부당한 가격 청구
o·ver·cloud [òuvərkláud] *vt.* **1.** cover (the sky) with clouds. **2.** make (someone) gloomy. —他 1. …을 구름으로 가리다 2. …을 음산하게 하다
* **o·ver·coat** [óuvərkòut] *n.* ⓒ a heavy coat worn over ordinary clothes in cold weather. —명 외투
‡ **o·ver·come** [òuvərkʌ́m] *vt.* (**-came, -come**) **1.** defeat; conquer. ¶ *~ a difficulty*. **2.** (usu. in *passive*) make (someone) weak or exhausted. ¶ *He was ~ by* (or *with*) *hunger*.① —他 1. …을 이겨내다, 압도하다; 정복하다 2. …을 지쳐빠지게 하다 ¶①그는 굶주림으로 지쳤다
   ┌ too much self-reliance. ┐
o·ver·con·fi·dence [òuvərkɑ́nfid(ə)ns / óuvəkɔ́n-] *n.* ⓤ —명 과신(過信); 자부
o·ver·con·fi·dent [òuvərkɑ́nfid(ə)nt / óuvəkɔ́n-] *adj.* too confident. —형 과신하는, 자부심이 강한
   ┌ 하게 하다 ┐
o·ver·crowd [òuvərkráud] *vt.* crowd (a hall, bus, etc.) —他 …에 너무 많이 들여보내다, 혼잡
o·ver·de·vel·op [òuvərdivéləp] *vt.* (*Photography*) develop (film) too long. ¶ *~ a photograph*. —他 《寫》 …을 과도하게 현상하다
o·ver·did [òuvərdíd] *v.* pt. of **overdo**.
o·ver·do [òuvərdú:] *vt.* (**-did, -done**) **1.** do (something) too much. **2.** exaggerate. **3.** cook (food, etc.) too much; exhaust. —他 1. …을 지나치게 하다 2. …을 과장하다 3. …을 너무 익히다(굽다); [몸]을 과로하게 하다
o·ver·done [òuvərdʌ́n] *v.* pp. of **overdo**.
o·ver·dose *vt.* [òuvərdóus → *n.*] cause (someone) to take too much medicine. —*n.* [-́-́] ⓒ too big a dose. —他 약을 너무 많이 복용시키다 —명 [약의] 정량 초과
o·ver·draw [òuvərdrɔ́:] *vt.* draw more money from (a bank account) than one has in the bank. —他 [어음]을 지나치게 발행하다;[예금]을 초과 인출하다
o·ver·dress *vt., vi.* [òuvərdrés → *n.*] dress too richly or extravagantly. —*n.* [-́-́] ⓒ a woman's dress worn over the main dress. —他国 지나치게 옷치장하다 —명 [얇은 천의] 부인용 웃옷
o·ver·due [òuvərd(j)ú: / òuvədjú:] *adj.* unpaid at the time expected for payment; behind time. —형 지불 기한이 지난; [기차·기선이] 연착한
o·ver·eat [òuvərí:t] *vi.* (**-ate, -eat·en**) eat too much. —자 과식하다
o·ver·eat·en [òuvərí:tn] *v.* pp. of **overeat**.
o·ver·es·ti·mate *vt.* [òuvəréstimèit → *n.*] estimate at too high (a number, value, amount, etc.); overvalue. —*n.* [óuvəréstimit] ⓒ an estimate that is too high. ▷ **o·ver·es·ti·ma·tion** [óuvərèstiméiʃ(ə)n] *n.* —他 …을 과대평가하다, 지나치게 어림잡다, 과신하다 —명 과대 평가, 과대 견적
o·ver·ex·pose [òuvərekspóuz] *vt.* (*Photography*) expose (film) too much or for too long. —他 《寫》 [건판]을 광선에 과도하게 노출하다
o·ver·ex·po·sure [óuvərekspóuʒər] *n.* ⓤ too much or too long an exposure (of photographic film). —명 노출 과도
o·ver·fed [òuvərféd] *v.* pt. and pp. of **overfeed**.
o·ver·feed [òuvərfí:d] *vt., vi.* (**-fed**) feed (someone) to excess; eat too much. ¶ *~ oneself*.① —他国 과식하[게 하]다 ¶①과식하다
* **o·ver·flow** *v.* [òuvərflóu → *n.*] *vt.* **1.** flow over or beyond the proper limits; flood. ¶ *The river often overflowed its banks.* **2.** flow over the top of (something). —*vi.* flow over; abound. 《*~ with* something》 —*n.* [-́-́] ⓒ **1.** the act of flowing over; an excessive amount. **2.** an outlet for overflowing liquid. —他 1. …을 넘치게 하다 2. …에서 넘치다 —자 넘치다; 충만하다 —명 1. 홍수; 범람; 충만, 과잉 2. 배수구(로)
o·ver·grew [òuvərgrú:] *v.* pt. of **overgrow**.
o·ver·grow [òuvərgróu, -́-́] *vi., vt.* (**-grew, -grown**) **1.** grow over. ¶ *a garden overgrown with weeds*. **2.** outgrow. —자他 1. 만연하다(시키다) 2. … 이상으로 성장하다

o·ver·grown [òuvərgróun, ∸–∸] *v.* pp. of **overgrow**. **—***adj.* grown too big; covered with grass, leaves, etc.
—[形] 너무 자란; [식물이] 사면에 우거진

o·ver·growth [óuvərgròuθ] *n.* **1.** [U] too great growth. **2.** [C] something that has grown or spread too much.
—[名] 1. 과도 성장; 우거짐, 무성; 만연 2. 사면에 자란 것, 부착물

o·ver·hand [óuvərhæ̀nd] *adj., adv.* (*Sports*) [played] with the hand raised above the shoulder; down from above. ¶*an ~ service*① / *an ~ stroke*.
—[形][副] 팔을 어깨 위로 올린(올리고), [공을] 아래를 향해 치는; 팔을 교대로 물 위로 내미는 ¶①내려치는 서어브

o·ver·hang *vt.* [òuvərhǽŋ → *n.*] (**-hung**) **1.** hang or project over (something). ¶*The trees ~ the street to give good shade in summer.* **2.** threaten; impend. **—***n.* [∸–∸] [C] something that is projecting over.
—[他] 1. …으로 내밀다(돌출하다) 2. …을 위협하다 —[名] 불쑥 내밈, 돌출

o·ver·haul [òuvərhɔ́:l → *n.*] *vt.* **1.** examine (something) thoroughly in order to repair and improve it. **2.** (of a ship, etc.) catch up with (something); overtake. **—***n.* [∸–∸] [C] a thorough examination.
—[他] 1. …을 분해 검사하다 2. [배 따위가] …을 앞지르다; …에 따라잡다 —[名] 철저한 조사

o·ver·head** *adv.* [óuvərhéd → *adj.*] in the sky; above one's head. ¶*the stars ~*. **—adj.* [∸–∸] being or passing overhead; placed overhead.
—[副] 위로 높이, 머리 위로 —[形] 머리 위의(를 지나는); 고가(高架)의

o·ver·hear [òuvərhíər] *vt.* (**-heard**) hear (something) by accident or when one does not mean to hear it; hear (something) without the speaker's notice.
—[他] …을 무심코 듣다, 엿듣다

o·ver·heat [òuvərhí:t] *vt.* heat (something) to excess. **—***vi.* become overheated.
—[他] …을 과열시키다 —[自] 과열하다

o·ver·hung *v.* [òuvərhʌ́ŋ → *adj.*] pt. and pp. of **overhang**. **—***adj.* [∸–∸] hung from above.
—[形] 위에 걸린

o·ver·in·dulge [òuvərindʌ́ldʒ] *vt.* indulge (someone) to excess.
—[他] …을 지나치게 응석받다

o·ver·joyed [òuvərdʒɔ́id] *adj.* very pleased. ⦅~ *at*⦆
—[形] 크게 기뻐하는

o·ver·lad·en [òuvərléidn] *adj.* overburdened; overloaded; excessively covered [with ornament].
—[形] [짐을] 너무 실은; 지나치게 장식한

o·ver·laid [òuvərléid] *v.* pt. and pp. of **overlay**.

o·ver·land [óuvərlæ̀nd] *adv., adj.* on land; by land.
—[副][形] 육상에서(의), 육로에서(의)

o·ver·lap [òuvərlǽp] *vi., vt.* (**-lapped, -lap·ping**) lap or project over (something); lie so as to cover a part.
—[自][他] 겹치[게 하]다; 겹쳐지다

o·ver·lay *vt.* [òuvərléi → *n.*] (**-laid**) **1.** place (something) over another thing. **2.** make (something) dark or gloomy. **3.** weigh down. **—***n.* [∸–∸] [C] something laid over something else.
—[他] 1. [···에] ···을 씌우다, 깔다, 칠하다 2. ···을 흐리게(어둡게) 하다 3. ···을 압도하다 —[名] 거죽에 까는(걸치는) 것

o·ver·leap [òuvərlí:p] *vt.* leap over (something); jump too far; disregard.
—[他] …을 뛰어넘다, 너무 멀리 뛰다; 무시하다

o·ver·load *vt.* [òuvərlóud → *n.*] put too much load on (something). **—***n.* [∸–∸] [C] too great a load.
—[他] …에 지나치게 싣다 —[名] 초과 적재

***o·ver·look** [òuvərlúk] *vt.* **1.** (of a place or building) look down on (something) from above. **2.** fail to see; pass over; miss. ¶*~ the mistake.* **3.** look over; watch. ¶*be overlooked by one's manager.*
—[他] 1. …을 내려다보다 2. …을 못 보고 넘어가다; 관대히 보아 주다 3. …을 감독하다, 시찰하다

o·ver·mas·ter [òuvərmǽstər / òuvəmá:stə] *vt.* overcome; conquer; overpower.
—[他] …을 압도하다, 정복하다, …을 이겨내다

o·ver·much [óuvərmʌ́tʃ] *adj., adv.* too much.
—[形][副] 과다한(하게), 지나친, 지나치게

o·ver·night** *adv.* [óuvərnáit → *adj.*] during or through the night. ¶*stay ~*. **—adj.* [*U.S.* ∸–∸] **1.** of only one night; lasting through a night. **2.** of a short journey.
—[副] 철야로, 밤새 —[形] 1. 하룻밤 자는, 철야의 2. 단기 여행용의

o·ver·pass *vt.* [òuvərpǽs → *n.* / òuvəpá:s] (**-passed** or **-past**) **1.** pass over (a river, bounds, etc.). **2.** overlook; miss. **3.** exceed; surpass. **—***n.* [*U.S.* ∸–∸] [C] a bridge over a road, railroad, etc.
—[他] 1. [강 따위]를 건너다, 넘다, 통과하다 2. …을 못 보고 넘어가다 3. …을 능가하다, …을 초월하다 —[名] 고가도로(철도)

o·ver·past [òuvərpǽst / òuvəpá:st] *v.* pt. and pp. of **overpass**.

o·ver·pop·u·la·tion [óuvərpὰpjuléiʃ(ə)n / óuvəpɔ̀p-] *n.* [U] too much population.
—[名] 인구 과잉

o·ver·pow·er [òuvərpáuər] *vt.* **1.** overcome; defeat; conquer. ¶*~ an enemy.* **2.** affect greatly. ¶*be overpowered by* (or *with*) *grief.*
—[他] 1. …을 이겨 내다, …을 압도하다 2. [정신적으로] …을 압도하다

o·ver·pro·duc·tion [óuvərprədʌ́kʃ(ə)n] *n.* [U] too much production.
—[名] 생산 과잉, 제조 과다

o·ver·ran [òuvərǽn] *v.* pt. of **overrun**.

o·ver·rate [òuvəréit] *vt.* estimate (something) too highly.
—[他] …을 과대평가(견적)하다

o·ver·reach [òuvərí:tʃ] *vt.* **1.** reach or extend over
—[他] 1. …을 지나쳐 가다, …을 너무 뻗

overridden [817] **overt**

(something); reach too far. ¶~ *oneself*.⓪ **2.** cheat (someone) by cunning. 다 ¶①무리를 하여 실패하다 2. …을 속여 넘기다, …보다 한수 더 뜨다

o·ver·rid·den [òuvərídn] *v.* pp. of **override**.

o·ver·ride [òuvəráid] *vt.* (**-rode, -rid·den**) **1.** ride over (something); trample on (something). **2.** refuse; disregard. ¶~ *all the previous rules.* **3.** tire out (a horse) by riding it too much. —⓺ 1. …을 짓밟다 2. …을 거절하다, 무시하다 3. [말]을 너무 타서 쓰러지게(지치게) 하다

o·ver·rode [òuvəróud] *v.* pt. of **override**.

o·ver·rule [òuvərú:l] *vt.* **1.** decide against (someone's idea, etc.); set aside. ¶*He overruled their suggestion.* **2.** rule over (someone); govern; defeat. —⓺ 1. …을 각하하다, 폐기하다 2. …을 지배하다, …을 이겨내다

o·ver·run [òuvərʌ́n] *vt.* (**-ran, -run, -run·ning**) **1.** spread over in great numbers. ¶*Weeds overran his garden.* **2.** run over so as to harm; invade. **3.** run beyond (something). ¶~ *it first base* / ~ *oneself*.⓪ —⓺ 1. [잡초 따위가] …에 우거지다 2. …을 약탈하고 다니다; 침략하다 3. …을 넘다; 도망치다 ¶①너무 달려 지치다

o·ver·saw [òuvərsɔ́:] *v.* pt. of **oversee**.

o·ver·sea [óuvərsí:] *adv., adj.* =overseas.

o·ver·seas *adv.* [òuvərsí:z → *adj.*] across the sea; abroad. —*adj.* [‴‴] of countries across the sea; foreign. —⓹ 해외로(에), 외국에 —⓺ 해외[에서]의, 외국의

o·ver·see [òuvərsí:] *vt.* (**-saw, -seen**) keep watch over and direct (someone); manage. —⓺ …을 감독하다, 단속하다

o·ver·seen [òuvərsí:n] *v.* pp. of **oversee**.

o·ver·se·er [óuvərsì:ər] *n.* Ⓒ a person who keeps watch over the work of others.　「throw; overturn.」 —⓷ 감독, 직공장, 단속자, 관리자

o·ver·set [òuvərsét] *vt., vi.* (**-set, -set·ting**) upset; over-」 —⓺⓷ 뒤집어 엎다; 뒤집히다

o·ver·shad·ow [òuvərʃǽdou] *vt.* **1.** cast a shadow on (something); darken; make (someone) gloomy. ¶*The father's honor was overshadowed by his son's shameful conduct.* **2.** become more important than (something). —⓺ 1. …의 위에 그림자를 던지다; …을 흐리게 하다; 어둡게 하다; 우울하게 하다 2. …을 무색하게 하다

o·ver·shoe [óuvərʃù:] *n.* Ⓒ (usu. *pl.*) a waterproof rubber shoe worn over another shoe for protection against getting wet. —⓷ 방수용 덧신

o·ver·shoot [òuvərʃú:t] *vt.* (**-shot**) **1.** shoot over or beyond (something). **2.** go over or beyond (something); go too far.　「much; exaggerate.」
overshoot oneself (or *the mark*), do something too」 —⓺ 1. …을 너무 멀리 쏘다 2. …을 지나쳐 가다, 너무 멀리 가다

⓹ 지나치게 하다; 과장하다

o·ver·shot [òuvərʃɑ́t / òuvəʃɔ́t] *v.* pt. and pp. of **overshoot**. —*adj.* driven by water passing over from above. —⓷ 위에서 물을 받는

o·ver·sight [óuvərsàit] *n.* ⓤⓒ **1.** failure to notice because of carelessness or idleness. **2.** supervision; watchful care. —⓷ 1. 못 보고 넘기기, 간과 2. 감독, 감시

by (or *through*) *an oversight*, carelessly; by mistake. ⓹ 잘못하여; 깜짝 실수하여

o·ver·sleep [òuvərslí:p] *vt., vi.* (**-slept**) sleep beyond the time set for rising. ¶~ *oneself*.⓪ —⓺⓷ 너무 자다 ¶①너무 자다

o·ver·slept [òuvərslépt] *v.* pt. and pp. of **oversleep**.

o·ver·spread [òuvərspréd] *vt.* (**-spread**) spread over; cover. ¶*Black clouds soon ~ the whole sky.* —⓺ …을 가득히 펴다

o·ver·state [òuvərstéit] *vt.* state or express too strongly; exaggerate. ↔understate　「statement; exaggeration.」 —⓺ …을 과장하여 말하다, 과장하다

o·ver·state·ment [óuvərstéitmənt] *n.* ⓤⓒ extravagant」 —⓷ 과장

o·ver·stay [òuvərstéi] *vt.* stay beyond the expected time. *overstay one's welcome*, stay longer than one is wanted. —⓺ …에 너무 오래 머물러 있다
⓹ 오래 머물러 미움을 사다

o·ver·step [òuvərstép] *vt.* (**-stepped, -step·ping**) step over or beyond; exceed. ¶~ *one's authority.* —⓺ …을 밟고 넘다, 넘어가다; …을 지나치게 하다

o·ver·stock [òuvərstɑ́k / òuvəstɔ́k ∥ → *n.*] stock too much or too many of (something). —*n.* [‴‴ / ‴‴] ⓤⓒ too great a supply. —⓺ …을 너무 많이 사들이다; 지나치게 공급하다 —⓷ 공급과다, 재고과잉

o·ver·strain [òuvərstréin] *vt.* stretch too tightly; overwork. ¶~ *one's eyes.* —*n.* ⓤ too excessive a tension; overwork. —⓺ …을 너무 팽팽하게 하다, 무리(과도)하게 쓰다 —⓷ 지나친 긴장(공부), 과로

o·ver·sup·ply [òuvərsəplái → *n.*] (**-plied**) supply too much. [‴‴] ⓤⓒ (pl. **-plies**) an excessive supply. —⓺ …을 너무 공급하다 —⓷ 공급과다

o·vert [ouvə́:rt, ‴] *adj.* open; public. ↔covert ¶*market* ~.⓪ ▷**o·vert·ly** [-li] *adv.* —⓺ 명백한, 공공연한 ¶①공개 시장

overtake [818] **overwork**

* **o·ver·take** [òuvərtéik] *vt.* (**-took, -tak·en**) **1.** come up or catch up with (something or someone). **2.** (of trouble, storms, etc.) come upon (someone) suddenly or unexpectedly.
be overtaken in (or *with*) *drink,* be drunk.
— 他 1. [사람·뒤진 일 따위]를 쫓아가다, 도달하다 2. [폭풍우·재난 따위가] ⋯을 갑자기 덮치다, ⋯을 불시에 치다

熟 술 취해 있다

o·ver·tak·en [òuvərtéik(ə)n] *v.* pp. of **overtake**.

o·ver·task [òuvərtǽsk / óuvətá:sk] *vt.* give too great or too heavy tasks to (someone).
— 他 ⋯에게 무리한 일을 시키다, ⋯을 혹사하다

o·ver·tax [òuvərtǽks] *vt.* **1.** tax too much. **2.** lay too heavy a burden on (someone or something).
— 他 1. ⋯에게 과중한 세금을 부과하다 2. ⋯에 무리한 짓을 강요하다

o·ver·threw [òuvərθrú:] *v.* pt. of **overthrow**.

* **o·ver·throw** *vt.* [òuvərθróu → *n.*] (**-threw, -thrown**) **1.** overturn; upset. **2.** overcome the power of (someone or something); defeat. ¶*The people overthrew the king.* **3.** (*Baseball*) throw above and beyond (where the player is aiming).
— 他 1. ⋯을 뒤엎다, 쓰러뜨리다 2. [국가·정부 따위]를 와해시키다; 패배시키다 3. [野球] ⋯을 폭투(暴投)하다

—*n.* [⌣⌢] ⓒ **1.** the act of overthrowing or the state of being overthrown; ruin; defeat. **2.** (*Baseball*) a throw above and beyond where it is aimed.
— 名 1. 전복; 멸망; 패배 2. [야구의] 폭투(暴投)

give (or *have*) *the overthrow,* overturn; be overturned; ruin; be ruined.
熟 전복시키다(하다), 멸망시키다(하다)

o·ver·thrown [òuvərθróun] *v.* pp. of **overthrow**.

o·ver·time [óuvərtàim → *v.*] *n.* ⓤ **1.** extra time; time worked beyond the regular hours. **2.** extra work done after regular working hours are over; very much work.
— 名 1. 규정외 노동시간; 초과 근무시간 2. 시간외 노동; 초과 근무

—*adv., adj.* beyond the regular working hours.
— 副形 규정외 시간에(의)

—*vt.* [⌣⌢] give too much time to (something).
— 他 ⋯에 시간을 너무 들이다

o·ver·tone [óuvərtòun] *n.* **1.** ⓒ a fainter and higher tone than the main tone. **2.** ((usu. *pl.*)) an additional meaning; a hint.
— 名 1. 배음(倍音) 2. 암시, 함축

o·ver·took [òuvərtúk] *v.* pt. of **overtake**.

o·ver·top [óuvərtáp / òuvətɔ́p] *vt.* (**-topped, -top·ping**) rise over or above the top of (something or someone); surpass; excel.
— 他 ⋯보다 높다, ⋯의 위에 솟다, ⋯을 능가하다

o·ver·ture [óuvərtʃər, -tʃùr, +*Brit.* óuvətjùə] *n.* ⓒ ((often *pl.*)) **1.** a proposal; an offer. ¶*overtures of peace.* **2.** music played as an introduction to an opera, oratorio, etc.
— 名 1. 교섭 개시, 제안, 제의 2. 서곡, 전주곡

make overtures to, ⓐ make an offer to (someone). ⓑ begin to deal with (someone) in the hope of reaching an agreement.
熟 ⓐ ⋯에 제안하다 ⓑ ⋯와 교섭을 개시하다

* **o·ver·turn** *vt.* [òuvərtə́:rn → *n.*] **1.** turn over; upset. ¶*The boat was overturned.* **2.** cause (someone or something) to fall down; destroy. ¶*The government was overturned.* —*n.* [⌣⌢] ⓒ the act of overturning; the state of being overturned.
— 他 1. ⋯을 뒤엎다, 전복시키다(하다) 2. ⋯을 타도하다, 멸망시키다 — 名 전복, 와해, 멸망

o·ver·ween·ing [òuvərwí:niŋ / òuvə-] *adj.* haughty; arrogant; conceited; self-confident.
— 形 거만한, 자부심이 강한

o·ver·weigh [òuvərwéi] *vt.* **1.** be heavier than (something or someone); overbalance. **2.** oppress.
— 他 1. ⋯보다 무겁다, 중요하다 2. ⋯을 압박하다

o·ver·weight *n.* [óuvərwèit → *adj.*] ⓤ too much weight; extra weight. ¶*pay for the ~ of a letter.* —*adj.* weighing more than is normal, necessary, or allowed.
— 名 중량 초과, 과중 — 形 중량을 초과한

* **o·ver·whelm** [òuvər(h)wélm] *vt.* **1.** overcome completely; crush or destroy utterly; overpower. ¶*be overwhelmed with grief.* **2.** (of a flood, waves, etc.) cover completely and swallow up (something). ¶*The boat was overwhelmed by the high waves.*
— 他 1. ⋯을 산산이 부수다; [감정 따위가] 압도하다 2. [홍수 따위] ⋯에 범람하다, ⋯을 물속에 가라앉히다

o·ver·whelm·ing [òuvər(h)wélmiŋ] *adj.* too powerful or too much to be resisted; overpowering. ¶*~ majority / ~ grief.* ▷ **o·ver·whelm·ing·ly** [-li] *adv.*
— 形 압도적인, 저항할 수 없는

* **o·ver·work** *vt., vi.* [òuvərwə́:rk → *n.*] (**-worked** or **-wrought**) work or cause (someone or something) to work too much or too hard. —*n.* [⌣⌢] ⓤ **1.** too much or too hard work. **2.** extra work.
— 他自 ⋯을 과로시키다, 과도하게 일 시키다; 너무 일을 하다 — 名 1. 지나치게 일하기; 과로 2. 초과 노동

overwrought

o·ver·wrought [òuvərɔ́:t] *v.* pt. and pp. of **overwork**.
— *adj.* **1.** very excited; overworked. ¶ ~ *nerves*. **2.** decorated to excess.
— 형 1. 너무 긴장(흥분)한; 과로의 2. 지나치게 장식한

* **owe** [ou] *vt.* **1.** must pay; be in debt to (someone). ¶ *I ~ ten dollars to the baker.; I ~ the baker ten dollars.* **2.** be obliged or indebted for (something). ⟪~ something to⟫ ¶ *I ~ my success to you. / We ~ a great deal to our parents.* — *vi.* be in debt. ¶ *She still owes for what she bought last summer.*
— 타 1. …에 빚이 있다, 지불할 의무가 있다 2. …에게 신세지고(은혜를 입고) 있다 — 자 빚이 있다; 빚지다

‡ **ow·ing** [óuiŋ] *adj.* due as a debt; owed; not paid. ¶ *This will pay what is ~.*
— 형 빚이 있는, 미불(未拂)의
owing to, ⓐ because of; on account of. ⓑ as a result of.
熟 ⓐ …때문에, …의 원인으로 ⓑ …의 결과로

‡ **owl** [aul] *n.* © **1.** a bird with great, round eyes which eats small animals and which is active at night. **2.** a wise-looking stupid person.
— 명 1. 올빼미 2. 약아 보이지만 어리석은 사람

as blind (*stupid*) *as an owl,* very blind (stupid).
熟 아주 장님(바보)의

owl·et [áulit] *n.* © a small owl; a young owl.
— 명 올빼미 새끼

owl·ish [áuliʃ] *adj.* like an owl; trying to look wise.
— 형 올빼미 비슷한; 점잔빼는

‡ **own** [oun] *adj.* belonging to oneself; peculiar to oneself.
¶ *my ~ children / He has his ~ troubles. / He did it in his ~ way. / I am my ~ master.② / He is his ~ man.②*
— *n.* ⟪one's ~⟫ that which belongs to oneself. ¶ *He claims it as his ~.③*
— 형 자기 자신의; 특유한 ¶①나는 속박받고 있지 않다/②자유의 몸이다 (자기 멋대로 행동하다)
— 명 내 것; 독특한 것 ¶③그는 그것이 자기 것이라 주장했다

1) *come into one's own,* receive what properly belongs to one; get the credit, fame, etc. that one deserves.
2) *hold one's own,* keep one's position against an attack; be not forced back.
3) *of one's own,* belonging to oneself.
4) *on one's own,* (*colloq.*) by one's own efforts; by oneself.
熟 1)정당한 명예·신용 따위를 얻다 2)자기의 입장을 지키다; 굽히지 않다 3)자기 자신의 4)스스로, 혼자의 힘으로

— *vt.* **1.** have; possess. ¶ *He owns much land.* **2.** recognize (something) as one's own. ¶ *He refused to ~ her.④* **3.** admit; acknowledge; confess; recognize. ⟪~ something *to be*; *~ that* …⟫ ¶ *At last he owned his guilt. / ~ oneself in the wrong / Do you ~ the story to be a lie? / He owned that I was in the right.* — *vi.* confess. ⟪~ *to* something; *~ to doing*⟫ ¶ *He owned to many faults. / The boy owned to having stolen the book.*
— 타 1. …을 갖고 있다; 소유하다 2. …을 자기 것으로 인정하다; 인지(認知)하다 ¶④그는 그녀를 자기 자식으로 인정하지 않았다 3. …을 인정하다; 승인하다; 고백하다 — 자 고백(자백)하다

‡ **own·er** [óunər] *n.* © a person who owns or possesses.
— 명 임자, 소유자

own·er·less [óunərlis] *adj.* without an owner; not belonging to anybody.
— 형 임자 없는

own·er·ship [óunərʃip] *n.* Ⓤ the state or condition of being an owner; the right of possession.
— 명 임자임; 소유권

‡ **ox** [aks / ɔks] *n.* © (pl. **ox·en**) a full-grown male of cattle. ⇒N.B.
— 명 소, 수소 N.B. 특히 거세한 소

ox·cart [ákskà:rt / ɔ́kskà:t] *n.* © a cart drawn by oxen.
— 명 우차

ox·en [áks(ə)n / ɔ́ks(ə)n] *n.* pl. of **ox**.

ox·ford [áksfərd / ɔ́ksfəd] *n.* (usu. *pl.*) a kind of low shoe.
— 명 단화의 일종

* **Ox·ford** [áksfərd / ɔ́ksfəd] *n.* **1.** a city in soutern England. **2.** the famous university located in Oxford.
— 명 1. 옥스퍼드 2. 옥스퍼드 대학

ox·i·da·tion [àksidéiʃ(ə)n / ɔ̀ks-] *n.* Ⓤ the act of oxidizing; the state of being oxidized.
— 명 산화(酸化)

ox·ide [áksaid / ɔ́ks-] *n.* ©Ⓤ a compound of oxygen with some other element.
— 명 산화물

ox·i·dize [áksidàiz / ɔ́ks-] *vt.* **1.** combine (something) with oxygen. **2.** rust. — *vi.* be combined with oxygen; become rusty.
— 타 1. …을 산화시키다 2. …을 녹슬게 하다 — 자 산화하다; 녹슬다

* **ox·y·gen** [áksidʒ(ə)n / ɔ́ks-] *n.* Ⓤ a gas without color, smell, or taste, which is essential to life and to burning.
— 명 산소

* **oys·ter** [ɔ́istər] *n.* © an edible shellfish living in shallow sea water and which has a rough shell.
— 명 굴

oz. ounce; ounces.

o·zone [óuzoun, -́-] *n.* Ⓤ a form of oxygen which is produced in the air after thunderstorms.
— 명 오존

P

P, p [piː] *n.* ⓒ (pl. **P's, Ps, p's, ps** [píːz]) **1.** the 16th letter of the English alphabet. **2.** anything shaped like the letter P. ⌈says.⌉ *mind one's P's and Q's*, be careful what one does or
— 图 1. 영어 자모의 열 여섯째 글자 2. P자 모양의 것
— 熟 언행을 삼가다

pa [paː] *n.* ⓒ (*child's word*) papa ; father.
— 图 〈小兒〉아빠

:pace [peis] *n.* ⓒ **1.** a single step ; the length of a single step. **2.** the rate of speed. ¶ *go at a good ~*①/*a ~ of three miles an hour.*② **3.** a way of stepping. ¶ *an alderman's ~.*③ ⌈freely.⌉
1) *go the pace,* ⓐ go at great speed. ⓑ spend money
2) *keep pace* (=*get into step*) *with someone.*
3) *put someone through his paces,* test someone's knowledge, ability, etc.
4) *set* (or *make*) *the pace,* ⓐ set an example of speed for others to keep up with. ⓑ be an example or a model for others to follow.
— *vi., vt.* **1.** walk with slow or regular steps. **2.** measure (something) by paces. ¶ *~ off a plot of ground.*④
— 图 1. 한 걸음, 일보(一步); 보폭(步幅) 2. 보조, 속도 ¶①상당한 속도로 가다/②시속 3마일의 속도 3. 걸음걸이 ¶③당당한 걸음걸이
— 熟 1) ⓐ종종걸음으로 걷다 ⓑ호화롭게 살다 2)…와 보조를 맞추다 3)[…의] 역량을 시험해 보다 4)ⓐ보조를 정하다, 정조(整調)하다 ⓑ본보기를 보이다
— 自他 1. 천천히(고른 보조로) 걷다 2. […을] 보측(步測)하다 ¶④지면(地面)을 보측하다

:pa·cif·ic [pəsífik] *adj* **1.** peaceful ; making peace ; loving peace. **2.** ((P-)) of, on, or near the Pacific Ocean. ¶ *the Pacific* [*Ocean*].①
— 图 1. 평화적인 ; 평화를 사랑하는 2. 태평양[연안]의 ¶①태평양

pac·i·fi·ca·tion [pæ̀səfikéiʃ(ə)n] *n.* ⓤ the act of pacifying ; the state of being pacified.
— 图 강화, 화해

pac·i·fism [pǽsifìz(ə)m] *n.* ⓤ the principle that military force should never be used.
— 图 평화주의, 부전(不戰)주의

pac·i·fist [pǽsifist] *n.* ⓒ a believer in pacifism.
— 图 평화(부전)주의자

pac·i·fy [pǽsifài] *vt.* (**-fied**) make (someone) peaceful or calm ; bring peace to (a country, etc.).
— 他 …을 진정시키다, 달래다 ; …에 평화를 가져오다

:pack [pæk] *n.* ⓒ **1.** a set of things tied together to be carried. **2.** a lot ; a group. ¶ *a ~ of thieves*①/*He often tells a ~ of lies.*② **3.** a set of playing cards. **4.** (*U.S.*) a small package or container. ¶ *a ~ of cigarettes.* **5.** a group of dogs hunting together ; a group of wild animals living together. ¶ *a ~ of hounds.*③ **6.** a soft mixture used by a woman to make her face beautiful. **7.** a wet cloth used for a sick or injured person.
— *vt.* **1.** put (things) into a bag, box, etc. ; put things into (a bag, box, etc.). ¶ *~ a suitcase*/*He packed* [*up*] *his clothes for the trip.*④ **2.** make (something) into a wrapped parcel. ¶ *~ a lunch.* **3.** fill tightly. ¶ *The theater was packed with a large audience.* **4.** put (something) into tins, etc. for shipping or marketing. ¶ *be packed in cans.* — *vi.* **1.** become packed. **2.** be filled ; become firmly pressed. **3.** leave in haste.
1) *pack someone off,* send someone away.
2) *send someone packing,* send someone away at once.
— 图 1. 다발 ; 꾸러미, 보따리 ; 짐 2. 다수, 다량 ; 한 떼(무리) ¶①군도(群盜)/②그는 가끔 거짓말을 한 보따리씩 늘어 놓는다 3. [카아드] 한 벌 4. 〈美〉 한 상자, 한 곽 5. 사냥개의 한 떼 ; 군거(群居)하는 동물의 떼 ¶③사냥개 떼 6. 여자가 얼굴에 바르는 미용 도포제(塗布劑) 7. [찜질용의] 습포(濕布)
— 他 1. …을 꾸리다, 싸다 ; …에 채워넣다 ¶④그는 여행용 옷가지를 꾸려 않다 2. …을 포장하다 3. [사람을] 꽉(가득히) 채우다 4. [시장 따위에 보내기 위해] …을 통조림 따위로 만들다 — 自 1. 짐을 꾸리다 ; 포장하다 2. 가득히(꽉) 차다 3. 황급히(허둥지둥) 떠나다
— 熟 1)…을 해고하다 2)…을 당장 내쫓다, 해고하다

:pack·age [pǽkidʒ] *n.* ⓒ a bundle of things packed together ; a parcel ; ⓤ the act of packing.
— 图 꾸러미, 소포 ; 포장, 짐꾸리기

pack animal [⸺ ⸺] *n.* an animal used to carry goods, such as a horse and camel.
— 图 짐 운반용 짐승

pack·er [pǽkər] *n.* ⓒ **1.** a person or machine that packs. **2.** a person who packs meat, fruit, etc. for sale.
— 图 1. 짐꾸리는 사람, 포장업자 ; 포장 기계 2. 통조림 업자 ; 출하(出荷) 업자

pack·et [pǽkit] *n.* ⓒ **1.** a small bundle ; a parcel. **2.** a small ship used to carry mail, message, etc.
— 图 1. 다발, 묶음 ; 소포 2. 우편선(船)

pack·ing [pǽkiŋ] *n.* ⓤ any material used in packing.
— 图 포장용품, 포장 재료 ; 메워넣는 것

pack·man [pǽkmən] *n.* ⓒ (pl. **-men** [-mən]) a person who goes from place to place selling goods ; a peddler.
— 图 행상인, 도부장수 ⌊물건, 패킹

pact [pækt] *n.* [C] an agreement between persons or nations. ¶*a peace ~.*①
—[名] 협정, 협약, 조약; 계약 ¶①강화 조약

* **pad** [pæd] *n.* [C] **1.** a soft mass used for comfort, protection, or filling out. **2.** the soft underpart of the foot of some animals; the foot of a fox, hare, etc. **3.** a number of sheets of writing or blotting paper fastened together along one edge. ¶*a writing ~.*①
—[名] 1. 덧대는 물건;메워넣는 물건;가슴받이 2. [동물의] 육지(肉趾); [여우·토끼 따위의] 발 3. 떼어 쓰게 된 종이철 ¶①편지지철

—*vt.* (**pad·ded, pad·ding**) **1.** fill or stuff (something) with something soft. **2.** expand (a speech, a piece of writing, etc.) by using unnecessary words.
—[他] 1. …에 덧대는 물건을 대다, 속을 메워넣다 2. [강연·문장 따위]에 군말을 넣어 늘이다

pad·ding [pǽdiŋ] *n.* [U] any soft material used to pad.
—[名] 속에 메워넣는 물건

* **pad·dle** [pǽdl] *n.* [C] **1.** a short broad oar used without a rowlock to propel a small boat, etc. **2.** a flat instrument used to mix, stir, or beat. **3.** one of the broad boards fixed around a waterwheel or a paddle-wheel.
—[名] 1. 짧고 넓적한 노 2. [뒤섞거나 휘저을 때 쓰는] 주걱 3. [기선 외륜(外輪)의] 물 젓는 판

—*vt., vi.* move (a boat or canoe) with a paddle or paddles; stir (something) with a paddle.
—[他][自] [···을] 노로 젓다;주걱으로 휘젓다

paddle one's own canoe, do (something) without depending on others.
[熟] 혼자 힘으로 세상을 살아나가다

paddle steamer [´-- ´--] *n.* a steamer propelled by paddle wheels.
—[名] 외륜선(外輪船), 외륜 기선

paddle wheel [´-- ´] *n.* a wheel with paddles fixed around it, used to propel a boat.
—[名] 기선의 외륜(外輪)

pad·dock [pǽdək] *n.* [C] **1.** a small grass field used for exercising or keeping horses. **2.** an enclosed place near a race track where horses are assembled before a race.
—[名] 1. [마굿간 근처의] 목장; 조마용(調馬用)의 울타리 두른 잔디밭 2. [경마 전에 말들이] 집합하는 장소

pad·dy [pǽdi] *n.* (pl. **pad·dies**) **1.** [U] rice, esp. in the husk. **2.** [C] a rice field.
—[名] 1. 쌀; 벼 2. 논

pad·lock [pǽdlὰk / -lɔ̀k] *n.* [C] a lock that can be put on and taken off. —*vt.* fasten (something) with a padlock.
—[名] 맹꽁이자물쇠 —[他] …에 맹꽁이자물쇠를 잠그다

pae·an, pe·an [píːən] *n.* [C] a song of joy, praise or thanksgiving for victory.
—[名] 기쁨의 노래; 승리·감사의 노래

pa·gan [péigən] *n.* [C] **1.** a person who is not a Christian, a Moslem, or a Jew. **2.** a person without any religion.
—[名] 1. 이교도, 사교도 2. 신앙이 없는 사람

—*adj.* of pagans or paganism; not religious.
—[形] 이교도의; 신앙이 없는

pa·gan·ism [péigənìz(ə)m] *n.* [U] the state of being pagan; pagan beliefs, attitudes and customs.
—[名] 이교 [신봉]

‡ **page**[1] [peidʒ] *n.* [C] **1.** one side of a leaf of paper in a book. ¶*open a book at* (or *to*) *~ 15*① */ turn over the ~.*② **2.** 《often *pl.*》 a record; an episode. ¶*in the pages of history.*③
—[名] 1. 페이지, 면(面) ¶①책의 15 페이지를 펼치다/②책장을 넘기다 2. 기록; 삽화(插話) ¶③역사상에

—*vt.* number the pages of (a book, etc.).
—[他] …에 페이지 수를 매기다

page[2] [peidʒ] *n.* [C] **1.** a boy who does errands in a hotel, club, etc. **2.** a boy attending on a person of high rank.
—[名] 1. 급사, 보이 2. 아이 종, 방자

—*vt.* attend (someone) as a page.
—[他] …에 급사로서 일하다

pag·eant [pǽdʒ(ə)nt] *n.* **1.** [C] a splendid colorful show or public performance, esp. a procession of magnificently dressed people on horseback. **2.** [C] an outdoor play made up of scenes from the history of a place, etc.
—[名] 1. 화려한 행렬;장관(壯觀) 2. [역사에서 취재한] 야외극

pag·eant·ry [pǽdʒ(ə)ntri] *n.* [U] 《*collectively*》 pageants; splendid, colorful display.
—[名] 구경거리; 장관

pa·go·da [pəgóudə] *n.* [C] an Oriental towering temple with many stories. ⇒fig.
—[名] [동양의 불교 사찰에 있는] 탑

〔pagoda〕

* **paid** [peid] *v.* pt. and pp. of **pay**.
—*adj.* **1.** receiving money for work; hired. **2.** settled.
—[形] 1. 유급(有給)의;고용된 2. 지불을 필한, 이미 지불한

* **pail** [peil] *n.* [C] **1.** a round, deep vessel of wood, metal, etc. with an arched handle used for carrying liquids; a bucket. **2.** a pailful.
—[名] 1. 양동이, 바께쓰 2. 바께쓰 하나 가득한 분량

pail·ful [péilful] *n.* [C] as much as a pail holds.
—[名] 바께쓰 하나 가득[한 분량]

‡ **pain** [pein] *n.* [U] **1.** very unpleasant feeling of body or mind; trouble. ¶*the ~ of parting.* **2.** [C] an ache. ¶*a ~ in the head.*① **3.** 《*pl.*, used as *sing.* and *pl.*》 care; efforts. ¶(*proverb*) *No pains, no gains.*②
—[名] 1. [심신의] 고통, 고뇌 2. [부분적인] 아픔 ¶①두통 3. 수고, 고생;노력 ¶②《俚》수고 없이 소득 없다

painful [822] palate

1) **be at the pain[s] of doing**, take the trouble to do.
2) **for someone's pains**, as thanks or in return for someone's service.
3) **in pain**, feeling pain.
4) **on** (or **under**) **pain of death**, on condition that someone will be put to death if he breaks his promise, etc. ¶*great pains with his work.*
5) **take pains**, do one's best; make efforts. ¶*He takes*
6) **with pain**, because of pain.
—vt. cause (someone) to feel pain; hurt. ¶*It pains me to walk.* —vi. have a feeling of pain.
- **pain·ful** [péinf(u)l] *adj.* 1. feeling or causing pain; full of pain. 2. requiring effort; difficult.
pain·ful·ly [péinfuli] *adv.* in a painful manner.
pain·ful·ness [péinf(u)lnis] *n.* Ⓤ the state of being painful.
pain·less [péinlis] *adj.* causing no physical pain; without pain. ¶*very industrious.*
pains·tak·ing [péinztèikiŋ] *adj.* taking pain; careful;
: **paint** [peint] *n.* Ⓤ coloring matter mixed with oil or water that gives color to a surface; ((often *pl.*)) coloring materials in tubes or cakes. ¶*Wet* (or *Damp, Fresh*) *Paint.*①
—vt. 1. cover or coat (something) with paint, lotion, medicine, etc. 2. picture (something) in colors. ¶*John painted a picture of his mother.* 3. describe vividly. ¶*He painted his experience in glowing colors.*② —vi. practice painting. ¶~ *in water colors.*③
paint out something, cover up something with paint.
paint box [⌣⌣] *n.* a box with cakes or tubes of paint.
paint·brush [péintbrʌʃ] *n.* Ⓒ a brush used for painting.
- **paint·er** [péintər] *n.* Ⓒ a person who paints pictures; a workman who paints houses, walls, etc.
: **paint·ing** [péintiŋ] *n.* Ⓒ a painted picture.
: **pair** [pεər] *n.* Ⓒ (pl. **pairs** or ((sometimes after *a numeral*)) **pair**) 1. a set of two things of the same kind. ¶*a ~ of stockings.* 2. a thing with two parts, each of which cannot be used without the other. ¶*a ~ of glasses*① / *a ~ of pants.*② 3. a couple of animals; a married or engaged couple. ¶*a ~ of rascals.*③ 4. the other part of a pair. ¶*I cannot find out the ~ to this* *another pair of shoes*, another matter.
—vt. join or unite (persons or things) in couples.
—vi. 1. be joined in couples. 2. become man and *pair off*, make up couples. wife; mate.
pa·ja·mas, Brit. **py·ja·mas** [pədʒɑ́:məz, +*U.S.* -dʒǽməz] *n. pl.* a sleeping suit consisting of a loose-fitting jacket and trousers.
- **pal** [pæl] *n.* Ⓒ (colloq.) a close friend. ¶*a pen ~.*
: **pal·ace** [pǽlis] *n.* Ⓒ 1. a large, grand house such as that of a king, a nobleman, or a bishop. 2. a very large, fine house.

pal·an·quin, pal·an·keen [pæ̀ləŋkíːn, -ləŋk-] *n.* Ⓒ a covered seat carried on the shoulders of men, usu. used in India, China, etc. ⇒fig.

[palanquin]

pal·at·a·ble [pǽlətəbl] *adj.* having a pleasant taste; delicious; pleasing.
pal·a·tal [pǽlətl] *adj.* of the palate; (*Phonetics*) made by placing the tongue near the hard palate. —*n.* Ⓒ (*Phonetics*) a palatal sound.
pal·ate [pǽlit] *n.* 1. Ⓒ the roof of the mouth. ¶*the hard* (*soft*) ~.① 2. Ⓤ the sense of taste; liking. ¶*suit one's ~.*②

圀 1)…하는 수고를 하다 2)수고한 보답(값)으로 3)고통스러워하는,피로와 하는 4)[약속을 어기면] 사형에 처한다 는 조건으로 5)수고하다 6)고통(고뇌) 때문에

—他 …을 괴롭게 굴다, 고통을 주다; 아프게 하다 ¶③걸으면 발이 아프다
—自 괴로워하다; 아프다
—形 1. 아픈,피로운 2. 힘든, 곤란한

—副 아픈 듯이; 괴롭게
—名 아픔,피로움, 신고(辛苦)
—形 아프지 않은, 고통이 없는;피로 하지 않은 「성질 하는
—形 수고를 아끼지 않는; 공들인,정
—名 뺑끼,페인트;도료(塗料); 그림물 감 ¶①칠 주의!〔게시 문구〕
—他 1. …에 뺑끼칠을 하다; 화장하다 2. [그림물감으로] …을 그리다 3. …을 생생하게 묘사하다 ¶②그는 자기의 경험을 화려한 필치로 묘사하였다

—自 그림을 그리다 ¶③수채화를 그리다
圀 …을 뺑끼칠하여 지우다
—名 그림물감 상자
—名 화필(畫筆),그림붓
—名 화가;뺑끼칠장이, 도장공(塗裝工)

—名 그림, 유화(油畫),수채화
—名 1. 한 쌍(켤레·짝·벌) 2. (따로따로는 쓸 수 없는) 한쌍의 물건 ¶①안경/②바지 한 벌 3. (동물의) 암수 한 쌍; 부부;2인조 ¶③2인조의 악한 4. [쌍을 이루는 것의] 한 짝 ¶④이 구두의 한 짝을 찾을 수가 없다

圀 별문제, 딴 문제
—他 …을 짝짓다 —自 한 쌍이 되다

圀 두 개씩 분리하다, 둘씩 짝짓다
—名 파자마, 잠옷

—名 (口) 동료;친구
—名 1. 궁전;[대주교·고관의] 관저 2. 호화로운 대저택

—名 [인도·중국 등의] 가마; 탈것

—形 맛 좋은, 입에 맞는;유쾌한

—形 구개(口蓋)의; 《音聲》 구개음의
—名 《音聲》 구개음

—名 1. 구개 ¶①경(연)구개 2. 미각; 좋아하는 것

pa·la·tial [pəléiʃ(ə)l] *adj.* like a palace; magnificent.
—[形] 궁전 같은; 웅장한, 호화로운

pa·lav·er [pəlǽvər / -lάːvə] *n.* **1.** [C] a conference, esp. with African natives. **2.** [U] idle talk. —*vi., vt.* talk idly.
—[名] 1. 협상; 교섭 2. 잡담, 한담 —[自][他] 잡담(한담)하다

:pale[1] [peil] *adj.* **1.** having very little color; whitish. ¶*You look ~.* **2.** not bright or brilliant; dim. ¶*a ~ pink.* —*vi., vt.* become or make (something) pale.
—[形] 1. 창백한, 파랗게 질린 2. 희미한, 어둠침침한 —[自][他] 창백해지다(하게 하다); 어둠침침해지다(하게 하다)

pale[2] [peil] *n.* [C] **1.** a long, narrow, pointed board used for fences. **2.** a fence; a boundary. ¶*within* (*out of, beyond*) *the ~ of the law.*①
—[名] 1. 말뚝(울타리를 만드는 데 씀) 2. 경계, 한계 ¶①법률의 범위 안(밖)에

pale·face [péilfèis] *n.* [C] a white person.
—[名] 백인

pale·ness [péilnis] *n.* [U] the state or quality of being pale.
—[名] 창백함

Pal·es·tine [pǽlistàin] *n.* a former country in southwest Asia, on the Mediterranean Sea.
—[名] 팔레스티나(원래 지중해 동해안의 한 나라)

pal·ette [pǽlit, +*Brit.* -et] *n.* [C] a board for mixing colors.
—[名] [회화용] 팔레트, 조색판(調色板)

pal·ing [péiliŋ] *n.* [C] a fence made of pales.
—[名] 말뚝을 둘러 박은 울타리

pal·i·sade [pæ̀liséid] *n.* **1.** [C] a long, strong, pointed wooden stake. **2.** a fence of such stakes. **3.** 《*pl.*》 a line of high, steep cliffs, usu. along a river. —*vt.* surround or fortify (something) with a palisade.
—[名] 1. 말뚝 2. 말뚝울타리, 방책(防柵) 3. [강가의] 벼랑 —[他] … 둘레에 말뚝울타리를 두르다

pal·ish [péiliʃ] *adj.* somewhat pale.
—[形] 좀 창백한, 해쓱한

pall[1] [pɔːl] *n.* [C] **1.** a heavy cloth used to cover a coffin, tomb, etc. **2.** something which covers, darkens, etc.
—[名] 1. 관(棺)에 씌우는 묵직한 천(우단) 2. [어둠 따위의] 장막

pall[2] [pɔːl] *vi.* become uninteresting; become dull.
—[自] 김이 빠지다; 흥미가 없어지다

pal·let [pǽlit] *n.* [C] a bed of straw; a poor bed.
—[名] 짚자리; 빈약한 잠자리

pal·li·ate [pǽlièit] *vt.* **1.** make (pain or a disease) somewhat better without curing it. **2.** excuse.
—[他] 1. [고통·병을] 일시 완화시키다 2. 변명하다, 발라맞추다

pal·li·a·tion [pæ̀liéiʃ(ə)n] *n.* [U][C] **1.** the act of palliating; the state of being palliated. **2.** an excuse.
—[名] 1. [고통·병의] 일시적 억제(완화) 2. 핑계, 변명

pal·li·a·tive [pǽliətiv, +*U.S.* -lièitiv] *adj.* serving to palliate; excusing. —*n.* [C] a thing that palliates.
—[形] 경감(완화)하는; 일시 억제하는; 변명하는 —[名] 완화제(劑); 변명, 핑계

pal·lid [pǽlid] *adj.* (**-lid·er, -lid·est**) pale.
—[形] 창백한, 파랗게 질린

pal·lor [pǽlər] *n.* [U] paleness, esp. of the face.
—[名] [얼굴의] 창백

:palm[1] [pɑːm] *n.* [C] **1.** the inner surface of the hand between the wrist and the fingers. **2.** any broad, flat part at the end of an arm, a handle, etc.
—[名] 1. 손바닥 2. 넓죽한 부분, 편평부(偏平部); 손바닥 모양의 물건

1) ***grease*** (or ***gild, tickle***) someone's ***palm,*** pay someone money to do wrong; bribe.
2) ***have an itching palm,*** be greedy for money.
3) ***have*** (or ***hold***) *someone* ***in the palm of*** one's ***hand,*** control completely.

[熟] 1) 뇌물을 주다 2) 욕심이 사납다 3) …을 완전히 지배하다, 손아귀에 넣다

—*vt.* **1.** hide (something) in the palm. **2.** touch (something) with the palm.
—[他] 1. …을 손바닥에 감추다 2. …을 손바닥으로 어루만지다

palm off *something* ***on*** *someone,* give, sell or pass something worthless to someone by a trick or by lies.
[熟] 남을 속여서 …을 떠맡기다

palm[2] [pɑːm] *n.* [C] **1.** a tall tree growing in warm climates, with large leaves at the top. **2.** a palm leaf, shown as a symbol of victory. **3.** 《*the ~*》 victory; triumph. ¶*bear* (or *carry off*) *the ~.*①
—[名] 1. 종려나무; 야자수 2. 종려나무의 잎(승리의 표상) 3. 승리 ¶①이기다; 우승하다

palm·er [pάːmər] *n.* [C] a pilgrim who had traveled to the Holy Land and brought back a palm leaf as a sign of this.
—[名] 성지 순례자

palm·ist [pάːmist] *n.* [C] a person who tells fortunes by examining the palm of the hand.
—[名] 손금장이, 수상가(手相家)

palm oil [´ ˊ] *n.* the oil obtained from the fruit of the palm tree.
—[名] 야자유(油)

palm·y [pάːmi] *adj.* (**palm·i·er, palm·i·est**) **1.** abounding in or shaded with palms. **2.** successful; prosperous. ¶*one's ~ days.*①
—[形] 1. 종려나무가 많은; 종려나무로 뒤덮인 2. 번영(번창)하는 ¶①전성 시대

pal·pa·ble [pǽlpəbl] *adj.* that can be felt or touched; obvious; evident.
—[形] 감촉할 수 있는; 명료한, 명백한

pal·pa·bly [pǽlpəbli] *adv.* in a palpable manner; obviously.
—[副] 감촉할 수 있게; 명백히

pal·pi·tate [pǽlpitèit] *vi.* **1.** (of the heart) beat rapidly. **2.** quiver; tremble.
—[自] 1. [가슴이] 두근거리다, 고동하다 2. 떨리다

pal·pi·ta·tion [pæ̀lpitéiʃ(ə)n] *n.* [U][C] irregular, quickened beating of the heart.
—[名] 가슴의 두근거림, 고동

pal·sied [pɔ́ːlzid] *adj.* having palsy; paralyzed; trembling.
—[形] 중풍의(에 걸린); 마비된; 떨리는

pal·sy [pɔ́ːlzi] *n.* [U][C] a disease which causes trembling
—[名] 중풍; 마비

P

pal-ter [pɔ́:ltər] *vi.* 1. talk or act insincerely; trifle deceitfully. 《~ *with* someone》 2. treat or decide lightly or carelessly. 3. bargain; haggle. 《~ *with* someone》 ¶ ~ *with* someone *about the* (or *a*) *price*.① 「worthless.」
—㉠ 1. 속이다 2. 얼렁뚱땅 얼버무리다 3. 흥정하다; 값을 깎다 ¶①값을 흥정하다

pal-try [pɔ́:ltri] *adj.* (**-tri-er, -tri-est**) unimportant; mean;
—㉭ 보잘것 없는, 하찮은; 무가치한

pam-pa [pǽmpə] *n.* 《usu. *pl.*》 a wide treeless plain of South America, esp. in Argentina. 「much.」
—㉠ 팸퍼스(남미, 특히 Argentina 의 나무 없는 대초원)

pam-per [pǽmpər] *vt.* treat too kindly; indulge too
—㉣ …을 응석받다, 지나치게 귀여워

• **pam-phlet** [pǽmflit] *n.* ⓒ a small book with a paper cover.
—㉠ 팜플렛, 소책자

pam-phlet-eer [pæ̀mflitíər] *n.* ⓒ a writer of pamphlets. —*vi.* write or publish pamphlets.
—㉠ 팜플렛의 필자 —㉣ 팜플렛을 쓰다(발행하다)

: **pan** [pæn] *n.* ⓒ 1. a broad, shallow dish for cooking. ¶*pots and pans*① / *a frying* ~.② 2. anything like a pan in shape; either of the dishes on a pair of scales. —*vt.* (**panned, pan-ning**) cook (something) in a pan.
—㉠ 1. 바닥이 판판한 냄비 ¶①취사 도구/②프라이팬 2. 접시 모양의 기물; 천칭(天秤) 접시
—㉣ …을 냄비로 끓이다

Pan [pæn] *n.* (in Greek mythology) the god of woods and fields.
—㉠ [그리스 신화의] 판신(神), 목신(牧神)

pan- [pæn-] *pref.* all: *Pan-American* (=of all the countries and peoples of North, Central and South America).
—《接頭》전(全)…, 범(汎)…

pan-a-ce-a [pæ̀nəsí(:)ə] *n.* ⓒ a remedy for all diseases or ills; a cure-all.
—㉠ 만병 통치약

• **Pan-a-ma** [pǽnəmá:, ⌐⌐] *n.* 1. a country in central America; its capital. 2. 《sometimes *p-*》 a Panama hat.
—㉠ 1. 중미의 공화국 2. 파나마 모자

Pan-A-mer-i-can [pæ̀nəmérikən] *adj.* 1. of all the countries and peoples of North, Central and South America. 2. of all Americans. 「batter and fried in a pan.」
—㉭ 1. 범미(汎美)의 2. 전미(全美)의

pan-cake [pǽnkèik] *n.* ⓒ a thin, flat cake made of
—㉠ 팬케이크(일종의 핫케이크)

pan-cre-as [pǽŋkriəs] *n.* ⓒ a part of the body near the stomach producing a digestive juice.
—㉠ 췌장(膵臟)

pan-de-mo-ni-um [pæ̀ndimóuniəm] *n.* 1. ⓒ 《*P-*》 the abode of all the demons; the hell. 2. Ⓤ wild disorder or confusion.
—㉠ 1. 복마전(伏魔殿); 지옥 2. 대혼란, 수라장

Pan-do-ra [pændɔ́:rə] *n.* (in Greek mythology) a woman sent to the earth to punish mankind for Prometheus having stolen the fire from Heaven.
—㉠ [그리스 신화의] 판도라(하늘의 불을 훔쳤기 때문에 인류를 벌하려고 하계로 내려보낸 인류 최초의 여자)

• **pane** [pein] *n.* ⓒ a single sheet of glass in a window.
—㉠ [한 장의] 창 유리

pan-e-gyr-ic [pæ̀nidʒírik] *n.* ⓒ a speech or piece of writing to praise a person or thing.
—㉠ 칭찬[의 말]

• **pan-el** [pǽn(ə)l] *n.* ⓒ 1. a flat piece of wood or other material set into a door, wall, etc. that is distinct from the surrounding areas. 2. a thin board used for oil painting; a picture on such a board. 3. a list of persons called as a jury; the jury as a whole. 4. a group formed for discussion. ¶*a five-man* ~① / *a* ~ *of experts*② / *a* ~ *discussion.*③
—*vt.* (**-eled, -el-ing** or *Brit.* **-elled, -el-ling**) cover or decorate (something) with panels.
—㉠ 1. 판벽널, 장식 판자 2. 화판(畫板); 패널화(畫) 3. [한 장의] 배심원 명부; 배심원 총원 4. [토론회·좌담회 따위의] 위원회 ¶①5인 위원회/②전문가의 위원회/③패널 토론회
—㉣ …에 장식 판자를 대다

pan-el-ing, *Brit.* **-el-ling** [pǽn(ə)liŋ] *n.* Ⓤ 《*collectively*》 panels. 「*the pangs of death.*①」
—㉠ 판벽널, 장식 판자

• **pang** [pæŋ] *n.* ⓒ a sharp, sudden pain or feeling. ¶
—㉠ 격통(激痛), 쑤시는 듯 아픔/아픔 「음 아픔 ¶①죽음의 괴로움」

• **pan-ic** [pǽnik] *n.* Ⓤⓒ 1. a sudden, unreasoning fear spreading among many people. ¶*The fire caused a* ~ *among the crowd.*① 2. a sudden financial fear which leads to mistrust. —*vt.* (**-icked, -ick-ing**) affect (someone) with panic.
—㉠ 1. 공포; 겁먹음; 당황 ¶①화재로 군중은 몹시 당황하였다 2. [경제] 공황
—㉣ …에 공황을 일으키다

pan-icked [pǽnikt] *v.* pt. and pp. of **panic**.
pan-ick-ing [pǽnkiŋ] *v.* ppr. of **panic**.
pan-ick-y [pǽniki] *adj.* in a panic. 「madly frightened.」
—㉭ 공황[상태]의

pan-ic-strick-en [pǽnikstrìk(ə)n] *adj.* filled with panic;
—㉭ 공포에 질린

pan-ni-er [pǽniər] *n.* ⓒ 1. one of a pair of baskets for carrying on the shoulder of a person or on the back of a horse. 2. a frame used for stretching out the skirt
—㉠ 1. [길마에 없는] 웅구; 등에 지는 바구니·패니어(스커어트를 퍼지게 하기 위한 테)

at the hip.

pan·o·ply [pǽnəpli] *n.* [C] (pl. **-plies**) a complete suit of armor.

pan·o·ram·a [pæ̀nərǽmə / -rɑ́:mə] *n.* [C] **1.** a wide, unbroken view. **2.** a scene which is constantly changing. **3.** a continuous series of pictures that is unrolled so that it seems as if a person were looking at it from a central point.

pan·o·ram·ic [pæ̀nərǽmik] *adj.* of or like a panorama. ¶*a ~ view.*①

* **pan·sy** [pǽnzi] *n.* [C] (pl. **pan·sies**) a small plant with flowers of several colors.

* **pant** [pænt] *vi.* **1.** breathe rapidly or violently. **2.** long eagerly. ⦅~ *for, after* something⦆ **—***vt.* utter words in short gasps. **—***n.* [C] a short, rapid breath.

pan·ta·loon [pæ̀ntəlú:n] *n.* **1.** [C] ⦅*P*-⦆ a character in Italian comedy, usu. a thin, foolish old man wearing pantaloons. **2.** ⦅*pl.*⦆ (*U.S.*) a kind of trousers.

pan·the·ism [pǽnθi(:)ìz(ə)m] *n.* [U] **1.** the doctrine that God is the universe and the universe is God. **2.** the worship of all the gods.

pan·the·ist [pǽnθi(:)ist] *n.* [C] a person who believes in pantheism.

Pan·the·on [pǽnθi:ɑ́n / -θiən] *n.* **1.** ⦅*the* ~⦆ a Roman temple for all the gods, built in 27 B.C. **2.** ⦅*the* ~⦆ a building for the burial or commemoration of the famous men of a nation. **3.** ⦅*p*-⦆ all the gods of a people.

pan·ther [pǽnθər] *n.* [C] (pl. **-thers,** *collectively* **-ther**) **1.** a leopard. **2.** a mountain lion; a puma; a cougar.

pan·to·graph [pǽntougræ̀f, +*Brit.* -grɑ̀:f] *n.* [C] **1.** an instrument for copying a map, drawing, etc. on any scale desired. ⇒fig. **2.** anything like it in shape.

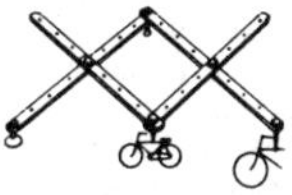

〔pantograph 1.〕

pan·to·mime [pǽntəmàim] *n.* [C] **1.** a play without words, in which the actors express themselves by gestures. **2.** (*Brit.*) a play based on a fairy tale. **3.** [U] gestures without words. **—***vt., vi.* express (thought, feeling, etc.) or act in pantomime.

* **pan·try** [pǽntri] *n.* [C] (pl. **-tries**) a room in which food or tableware is kept.

pants [pænts] *n. pl.* (*U.S. colloq.*) trousers; drawers.

pap [pæp] *n.* [U] soft food for infants or sick persons such as bread soaked in milk.

‡ **pa·pa** [pɑ́:pə / pəpɑ́:] *n.* [C] (*child's word*) father; daddy.

pa·pa·cy [péipəsi] *n.* (pl. **-cies**) [U][C] ⦅usu. *the* ~⦆ **1.** the position, rank, or authority of the Pope. **2.** the period during which a pope rules.

pa·pal [péip(ə)l] *adj.* **1.** of the Pope or the papacy. **2.** of the Roman Catholic Church.

pa·pa·ya [pəpɑ́:jə / -páiə] *n.* [C] a tropical tree with large leaves and melonlike fruit at the top; its fruit.

‡ **pa·per** [péipər] *n.* **1.** [U] a thin material made of wood pulp, etc. used for writing, printing, wrapping, etc. ¶*a sheet of ~*① / *a piece of ~*② / *wrapping ~.*③ **2.** [C] a newspaper. ¶*Bring me today's ~.*④ **3.** ⦅*pl.*⦆ documents carried to prove who or what one is. **4.** ⦅often *pl.*⦆ an official document; a written matter. ¶*state papers*⑤ / *valuable papers.*⑥ **5.** [C] a set of questions for an examination; a student's written answers to the questions. ¶*collect the papers.*⑦ **6.** [C] an essay on a particular topic; (*U.S.*) an essay which a student is required to write. ¶*write a ~.*⑧ **7.** [U] a written promise to pay money; a bank note; paper money.

on paper, ⓐ in writing. ⓑ in theory.

—*adj.* **1.** made of paper. ¶*a ~ screen.* **2.** existing only on paper; little more than a mere name.

—[名] 갑옷·투구의 한 벌

—[名] 1. 전경(全景) 2. 연속적으로 바뀌는 광경 3. 파노라마, 회전화(回轉畫)

—[形] 파노라마[식]의 ¶①전경(全景)

—[名] 팬지(여러 가지 색깔의 꽃이 피는 작은 초본)

—[自] 1. 헐떡거리다 2. 열망하다, 동경하다 —[他] …을 헐떡거리며 말하다 —[名] 헐떡거림, 숨참

—[名] 1. [이탈리아 희극의] 말라깽이 노인역, 늙다리 광대역 2. ⦅美⦆ 바지

—[名] 1. 범신론(汎神論), 만유신교(萬有神敎) 2. 다신교(多神敎)

—[名] 범신론자

—[名] 1. 판테온, 만신전(萬神殿) 2. 한 나라의 위인을 함께 모신 신전 3. [한 나라 국민의] 모든 신들

—[名] 1. 표범 2. 아메리카 사자, 퓨우마

—[名] 1. 사도기(寫圖器), 축도기(縮圖器) 2. 팬터그래프

—[名] 1. 무언극 2. ⦅英⦆ 팬터마임, 동화극 3. 몸짓, 손짓

—[他][自] 몸짓(손짓)으로 표현하다

—[名] 식료품 저장실, 식기실(食器室)

—[名] ⦅美口⦆ 양복바지; 팬츠; 드로우어스

—[名] 빵죽

—[名] ⦅小兒⦆ 아빠

—[名] 1. 로마 교황의 직(지위), 교황권(權) 2. 교황의 임기

—[形] 1. 로마 교황[권]의 2. 가톨릭교의

—[名] 파파야[의 열매]

—[名] 1. 종이 ¶①종이 한 장/②한 장의 종이쪽지/③포장지 2. 신문 ¶④오늘 신문을 갖다 다오 3. 신분증명서 4. 서류, 문서 ¶⑤공문서/⑥중요 서류 5. 시험 문제; 답안 ¶⑦답안지를 모으다 6. 논문; ⦅美⦆ [학생에게 할당된] 논문 ¶⑧논문을 쓰다 7. 어음; 지폐

[熟] ⓐ씌어져, 필기하여 ⓑ이론상으로는

—[形] 1. 종이로 만든 2. 지상(紙上)의; 가치가 없는

P

—*vt.* **1.** cover (something) with paper; put paper on (a wall, etc.). **2.** write (something) on paper.
—[他] 1. …을 종이로 싸다; …에 종이를 바르다 2. …을 종이에 쓰다

pa·per·back [péipərbæ̀k] *n.* [C] **1.** a book bound in a paper cover. **2.** a low-priced edition of a book.
—[名] 1. 종이 표지 책, 문고본 2. 염가본

paper money [⁄-- ⁄--] *n.* money made of paper.
—[名] 지폐

pa·py·ri [pəpáiərai, -ri:] *n.* pl. of **papyrus.**

pa·py·rus [pəpáiərəs] *n.* (pl. **-rus·es** or **-ri**) [U] **1.** a tall water plant. **2.** a kind of paper made from this plant by the ancient Egyptians, etc. **3.** ⦅*pl.*⦆ an ancient document or manuscript on papyrus.
—[名] 1. 파피루스, 지초(紙草) 2. 파피루스 종이 3. [파피루스 종이에 쓴] 고문서(古文書)

par [pɑ:r] *n.* [U] **1.** ⦅sometimes *a* ~⦆ equal value, level, etc.; equality. **2.** the average or normal amount, degree, or state. ¶*I feel below* ~.① **3.** (*Commercial*) the value of stocks, bonds, etc. that is printed on them; the face value. **4.** the normal value of the money of one country established in terms of that of another country. **5.** (in golf) the number of strokes set as the standard of any given hole or course.
—[名] 1. 동등, 등가(等價) 2. 기준, 정상 상태 ¶①몸이 언짢다 3. 액면대로의 가치, 액면 가격 4. 환평가(換平價), 환평준(換平準) 5. ⦅골프⦆ 기준 타수(打數)

on a par with (=*equal to*) *something.*
[熟] …와 같은, …와 동등하여

—*adj.* **1.** average; normal. **2.** of or at par. ¶~ *value.*②
—[形] 1. 기준의, 표준의 2. 평가(平價)의; 액면의(으로) ¶②액면 가격

par·a·ble [pǽrəbl] *n.* [C] a short story told to illustrate moral teaching. ¶*take up one's* ~.①
—[名] 우화(寓話), 비유담 ¶①설교를 시작하다

pa·rab·o·la [pərǽbələ] *n.* [C] a curve formed by cutting a cone with a plane parallel to its side.
—[名] 포물선(抛物線)

par·a·bol·ic [pæ̀rəbɑ́lik / -bɔ́l-] *adj.* of or like a parabola.
—[形] 포물선의

par·a·chute [pǽrəʃù:t] *n.* [C] an umbrellalike apparatus used for descending from a great height. —*vi.* descend by a parachute. —*vt.* drop or convey (something) by a parachute.
—[名] 낙하산, 파라슈 —[自] 낙하산으로 강하하다 —[他] …을 낙하산으로 떨어뜨리다

par·a·chut·ist [pǽrəʃù:tist] *n.* [C] a person who uses a parachute.
—[名] 낙하산 강하자, 낙하산병

* **pa·rade** [pəréid] *n.* [C] **1.** a march for display; a procession. **2.** a review of troops; a place where soldiers drill. **3.** a display; a great show. ¶*make a* ~ *of.*① **4.** a group of people walking for display or pleasure. **5.** a public promenade, square, etc.
—[名] 1. 행진 2. 관병(열병)식; 열병장, 연병장 3. 과시; 자랑해 보이기; 시위 행진 ¶①…을 자랑해 보이다, 과시하다 4. 행렬; 행진하는 사람들 5. 산책장, 유보장(遊步場); 광장, 운동장

—*vt.* **1.** assemble (troops) for review. **2.** march through (some place) with display. **3.** make a display of (something). —*vi.* **1.** march in a parade. **2.** assemble in military order for review.
—[他] 1. [군대]를 정렬시키다, 열병하다 2. 줄지어 행진하다, 분열 행진하다 3. …을 과시하다 —[自] 1. 행진하다, 줄지어 행진하다 2. 정렬하다

par·a·digm [pǽrədàim, +*U.S.* -dim] *n.* [C] **1.** a pattern; an example. **2.** (*Grammar*) an example of a noun, verb, pronoun, etc. in all its inflections.
—[名] 1. 범례; 모범 2. ⦅文法⦆ 어형 변화표; 활용례

⁑ **par·a·dise** [pǽrədàis] *n.* **1.** ⦅*the P-*⦆ the garden of Eden. **2.** [U] heaven.
—[名] 1. 에덴 동산 2. 천국, 극락, 낙원

* **par·a·dox** [pǽrədɑ̀ks / -dɔ̀ks] *n.* [C] **1.** a statement which seems absurd, but which may be true. **2.** a statement which says two opposite things.
—[名] 1. 역설, 패러독스 2. 모순된 말, 조리에 맞지 않는 말

par·a·dox·i·cal [pæ̀rədɑ́ksik(ə)l / -dɔ́ks-] *adj.* of paradoxes; expressing a paradox; fond of using paradoxes.
—[形] 역설의, 역설적인; 역설(궤변)을 부리기 좋아하는

par·af·fin, -fine [pǽrəfin] *n.* [U] a white, tasteless substance like wax, used for making candles, etc.
—[名] 파라핀, 파라핀유(油)

par·a·gon [pǽrəgən, +*U.S.* -gɑ̀n] *n.* [C] a model of perfection or excellence. ¶*a* ~ *of beauty*① / *a* ~ *of virtue.*
—[名] 모범, 본보기 ¶①미(美)의 전형, 절세의 미인

⁑ **par·a·graph** [pǽrəgræ̀f, +*Brit.* -grɑ̀:f] *n.* [C] **1.** a distinct section of a piece of writing. **2.** a brief article, item, etc. in a newspaper or magazine. **3.** a sign used to show where a paragraph begins.
—[名] 1. 절(節), 항(項), 단락(段落) 2. [신문·잡지 따위의] 짤막한 기사, 짤막한 논설 3. 단락표, 단락 기호(¶)

—*vt.* **1.** separate or arrange (a sentence) in paragraphs. **2.** write paragraphs about (something).
—[他] 1. [문장]을 절(節)로 나누다 2. …에 관해 짤막한 기사를 쓰다

Par·a·guay [pǽrəgwài, -gwèi] *n.* a country in central South America. ⇒[N.B.]
—[名] 파라과이 [N.B.] 수도는 Asuncion

par·a·keet [pǽrəki:t] *n.* [C] any of several kinds of small, long-tailed parrots.
—[名] 작은 잉꼬

* **par·al·lel** [pǽrəlèl] *adj.* **1.** never meeting because always
—[形] 1. 평행의 ¶①평행선/②[체조용

parallelism [827] **parchment**

at the same distance from each other. ¶~ *lines*① / ~ *bars*.② **2.** like; similar.
—*n.* ⓒ **1.** a parallel line or surface. **2.** a person or thing like or similar to another; similarity; resemblance. ¶*bear a close ~ to*③ / *without ~.*④ **3.** comparison. ¶*draw a ~ between.*⑤ **4.** one of the parallel circles marking the degrees of latitude on a globe. **5.** an arrangement in an electrical system. ↔series
—*vt.* (**-leled, -lel·ing** or *Brit.* **-lelled, -lel·ling**) **1.** be parallel with (something). ¶*The road parallels the river.*⑥ **2.** compare. **3.** correspond to (something).
par·al·lel·ism [pǽrəlèliz(ə)m] *n.* Ⓤ **1.** the state of being parallel. **2.** similarity; resemblance.
par·al·lel·o·gram [pæ̀rəléləugræm] *n.* ⓒ a four-sided figure whose opposite sides are parallel and equal.
par·a·lyse [pǽrəlàiz] *vt.* (*Brit.*) =paralyze.
pa·ral·y·sis [pərǽlisis] *n.* (*pl.* **-ses** [-sìːz]) **1.** Ⓤ loss of the power of motion or sensation in any part of the body. ¶*cerebral ~.*① **2.** Ⓤⓒ the loss of energy, willpower, etc. ¶*a ~ of trade.*②
par·a·lyt·ic [pæ̀rəlítik] *adj.* of paralysis; having paralysis. —*n.* ⓒ a person who has paralysis.
par·a·lyze, *Brit.* **-lyse** [pǽrəlàiz] *vt.* **1.** affect (someone) with paralysis. **2.** make (someone) powerless.
par·a·mount [pǽrəmàunt] *adj.* supreme; chief; superior. (~ *to*) —*n.* ⓒ a person who has supreme power.
par·a·pet [pǽrəpit, -pèt] *n.* ⓒ **1.** a low wall or railing at the edge of a roof, bridge, balcony, etc. **2.** a low wall of stone, earth, etc. to protect soldiers. ⇒fig.
par·a·pet·ed [pǽrəpitid, -pètid] *adj.* having a parapet or parapets.
par·a·pher·nal·ia [pæ̀rəfərnéiliə] *n. pl.* **1.** personal belongings. **2.** ((sometimes used as *sing.*)) equipment; apparatus.   〔parapet 2.〕
par·a·phrase [pǽrəfrèiz] *n.* ⓒ an expression of the meaning of a passage in other words. —*vt., vi.* express (a passage) in a paraphrase.
par·a·site [pǽrəsàit] *n.* ⓒ **1.** an animal or a plant which lives on another. **2.** a person who lives at another's expense.
par·a·sit·ic [pæ̀rəsítik], **-i·cal** [-k(ə)l] *adj.* of or like a parasite; living at another's expense.
par·a·sol [pǽrəsɔ̀ːl, -sɔ̀l / pǽrəsɔ̀l, pæ̀rəsɔ̀l] *n.* ⓒ a light umbrella used by women as a sunshade.
par·a·troop·er [pǽrətrùːpər] *n.* ⓒ a soldier in the paratroops. 「onto a battlefield by parachute.」
par·a·troops [pǽrətrùːps] *n. pl.* troops trained to drop」
par·a·ty·phoid [pæ̀rətáifɔid] *n.* Ⓤ a kind of fever like typhoid. —*adj.* of paratyphoid. 「roasting, etc.」
par·boil [páːrbɔ̀il] *vt.* boil (food) for a short time before」
par·cel [páːrsl] *n.* ⓒ **1.** a small, wrapped bundle; a package. ¶*~ delivery*① / *send away* (or *off*) *a ~.*② **2.** (*archaic*) a portion; a part. ¶*a ~ of land*③ / *part and ~.*④ —*vt.* (**-celed, -cel·ing** or *Brit.* **-celled, -cel·ling**) divide (something) into portions.
parcel post [`́`-`̀`] *n.* a branch of the post office which collects and delivers parcels.
parch [paːrtʃ] *vt.* **1.** roast (something) over a fire. ¶*~ some peanuts.* **2.** make (something or someone) dry or thirsty by heating. —*vi.* become dry or thirsty.
parch·ment [páːrtʃmənt] *n.* **1.** Ⓤ a writing material prepared from the skin of sheep, goats, etc. **2.** ⓒ a

—名 평행봉 **2.** 서로 같은, 상사(相似)의

—名 **1.** 평행선(면) **2.** 상사[물], 동등[물], 필적[자] ¶③…와 아주 흡사하다/④유례없이, 무비(無比)의 **3.** 비교 ¶⑤…을 비교하다 **4.** 위선(緯線), 위도선 **5.** (電) 병렬(竝列)

—他 **1.** …와 평행하다 ¶⑥그 길은 강과 평행을 이루고 있다 **2.** …와 비교하다 **3.** …에 적합하다

—名 **1.** 평행; 평행 상태 **2.** 유사(類似)

—名 평행 4 변형

—名 평행시키다

—名 **1.** 마비, 중풍 ¶①졸도 **2.** 무력, 무기력; 무능; 침체(沈滯) ¶②무역의 침체

—形 마비성의, 중풍에 걸린
—名 중풍 환자

—他 **1.** …을 마비시키다; 저리게 하다 **2.** …을 무력하게 하다

—形 최고의; 주요한; 가장 뛰어난, 탁월한 —名 최고의 사람; 수령

—名 **1.** [지붕·다리·발코니 따위의] 난간, 나지막한 담장 **2.** 흉벽(胸壁), 흉장(胸墻)

—形 난간(흉벽)이 있는

—名 **1.** [개인의] 잔 세간 **2.** 설비, 장비

—名 [알기 쉽게] 바꾸어 말하기, 의역(意譯) —他自 의역하다, 바꾸어 말하다

—名 **1.** 기생 동물; 기생 식물; 기생충(균); 겨우살이 **2.** 기식자, 식객

—形 기생 동물(식물)의 (같은); 기식하는, 식객으로 있는

—名 [여자용] 양산, 파라솔

—名 낙하산병, 공수단원

—名 낙하산 부대, 공수 부대

—名 파라티푸스 —形 파라티푸스의

—他 …을 슬쩍 데치다, 반숙하다
—名 **1.** 꾸러미, 소포, 소하물 ¶①소포배달/②소하물을 부치다 **2.** (古) 일부분 ¶③한 구획의 토지/④중요부 —他 …을 부분으로 나누다, 분배하다

—名 소포 우편

—他 **1.** …을 볶다; 굽다 **2.** …을 건조시키다, 바싹 말리다 —自 바짝 마르다; [목이] 마르다

—名 **1.** 양피지(羊皮紙) **2.** 양피지에 쓴 사본(문서) **3.** 양피지 같은 종이

manuscript or document written on parchment. **3.** Ⓤ paper that looks like parchment.

: par·don [páːrdn] *n.* Ⓤ Ⓒ **1.** forgiveness. **2.** the act of setting someone free from punishment; a document confirming this act.
I beg your pardon, ⓐ Please excuse me. ⓑ I did (or could) not hear what you said.
—*vt.* set (someone) free from punishment; forgive; excuse. ¶*Pardon me, but....*① / *There is nothing to ~.*②

par·don·a·ble [páːrdnəbl] *adj.* that can be pardoned.

pare [pɛər] *vt.* **1.** cut away the outer part of (something). **2.** cut away (something) little by little.

: par·ent [pέərənt] *n.* Ⓒ **1.** a father or mother. **2.** an animal or a plant that produces offspring. **3.** an origin; a source. ¶*the ~ of vice.*①

par·ent·age [pέər(ə)ntidʒ] *n.* Ⓤ **1.** descent from parents or ancestors; family line; birth. **2.** fatherhood or motherhood.

pa·ren·tal [pəréntl] *adj.* of a parent.

pa·ren·the·ses [pərénθisi:z] *n.* pl. of **parenthesis**.

pa·ren·the·sis [pərénθisis] *n.* Ⓒ (pl. **-ses**) **1.** an explanatory word, phrase, sentence, etc. put into an already complete sentence. **2.** (usu. *pl.*) either or both of the curved lines ( ) used to mark off a parenthesis. ¶*the words in parentheses.*① **3.** an episode.

par·en·thet·ic [pὲər(ə)nθétik], **-cal** [-k(ə)l] *adj.* **1.** placed in parentheses. **2.** using parentheses; explaining.

par·fait [paːrféi] *n.* Ⓤ Ⓒ a dessert made of ice cream, eggs, syrup, etc. frozen together.

par·i·ah [pǽriə, +*U.S.* pəráiə, páːriə] *n.* Ⓒ a member of a low caste in South India and Burma; a social outcast.

par·ing [pέəriŋ] *n.* Ⓤ The part pared off.

＊Par·is [pǽris] *n.* **1.** the capital of France. **2.** (in Greek mythology) the son of Priam, King of Troy.

＊par·ish [pǽriʃ] *n.* Ⓒ (*Brit.*) a part of a country with one church and one clergyman; the people of a parish.
go on the parish, receive financial help from a parish.

pa·rish·ion·er [pəríʃ(ə)nər] *n.* Ⓒ a member of a certain parish.

Pa·ri·sian [pəríʒən, +*Brit.* -rízjən] *adj.* of or like Paris or its people. —*n.* Ⓒ a person of Paris.

par·i·ty [pǽriti] *n.* Ⓤ (sometimes *a.~*) equality in rank, quality, etc; resemblance. ¶*~ of treatment.*①

: park [paːrk] *n.* Ⓒ **1.** a large, open space of ground for public recreation. ¶*a national ~.*① **2.** a large area of woods and fields around a country house. **3.** a place where a motorcar may be left for a time. ¶*a car ~.*②
—*vt.* leave (a motorcar, etc.) in a certain place; put (arms, etc.) in a park.

par·ka [páːrkə] *n.* Ⓒ a fur jacket with a hood, worn in [Alaska, etc.

park·way [páːrkwèi] *n.* Ⓒ a broad road bordered with grass and trees. [*paper ~*① / *in common ~.*]

par·lance [páːrləns] *n.* Ⓤ a way of speaking. ¶*news-*

par·ley [páːrli] *n.* Ⓒ Ⓤ a discussion, esp. with an enemy.
—*vi.* have a discussion, esp. with an enemy.

: par·lia·ment [páːrləmənt] *n.* Ⓤ Ⓒ a meeting or a group of elected persons that makes the laws of a country; (*P-*) the legislating body of Great Britain. ¶*the Houses of Parliament*① / *enter* (or *go into*) *Parliament*② / *a Member of Parliament.*③

par·lia·men·tar·i·an [pὰːrləmentέəriən] *n.* Ⓒ **1.** a person who has much knowledge about a parliament and its procedures. **2.** (*P-*) a person who supported Parliament against Charles I.

par·lia·men·ta·ry [pὰːrlémént(ə)ri] *adj.* **1.** of parliament;

[828]

parliamentary

—⻝ 1. 용서 2. 사면, 특사; 면죄(免罪) [부(符)]
—ⓐ ⓐ미안(죄송)합니다 ⓑ죄송하지만 다시 한 번 말씀해 주시오
—⻬ …을 용서하다; 관대히 봐주다; 사면하다 ¶①미안(죄송)하지만/②천만의 말씀입니다
—⻬ 용서할 수 있는
—⻬ 1. …을 깎[아 다듬]다; …의 껍질을 벗기다 2. …을 조금씩 줄이다
—⻝ 1. 어버이[, 부모 2. [동·식물의] 어미 3. 원천 ¶①악덕의 원천

—⻝ 1. 혈통, 가문, 태생 2. 어버이임, 부모임; 어버이의 지위
—⻬ 어버이의; 어버이다운, 어버이로서의
—⻝ 1. 삽입어(구·문) 2. 괄호 ¶①괄호 속의 말 3. 삽화(揷話)

—⻬ 1. 괄호로 싼 2. 삽입구를 쓰는, 설명적인, 삽입구적인
—⻝ 파페이(아이스크림·계란·시럽 따위를 섞은 디저어트)
—⻝ 파아리아(남부 인도·버마의 최하층민); 사회에서 추방당한 사람
—⻝ 벗긴 (깎은) 껍질 (부스러기)
—⻝ 1. 프랑스의 수도 2. [그리이스 신화의] 파리스(Troy왕 Priam의 아들)
—⻝ (英) 교구(敎區); 교구민

 교구의 구호를 받다
—⻝ 교구민

—⻝ 파리(식)의, 파리 사람의
—⻝ 파리 사람
—⻝ 동격, 동등; 유사(類似) ¶①동등 (균등)대우
—⻝ 1. 공원 ¶①국립 공원 2. [지방의 대저택 주위의] 대정원(大庭園) 3. 주차장 ¶②주차장

—⻬ [자동차를] 주차하다; [포차(砲車) 따위를] 한곳에 정렬시켜 두다
—⻝ 두건 달린 모피 자켓
—⻝ 공원 도로, 자동차 전용 도로

—⻝ 말씨, 말투, 어조 ¶①신문 용어
—⻝ 담판; 회담 —⻬ 담판하다

—⻝ 의회, 국회; 영국 의회 ¶①영국 국회 양원; 영국 국회 의사당/②하원의원이 되다/③하원 의원

—⻝ 1. 의회법 학자, 의회 법규에 정통한 사람, 의회인 2. (英史) 의회당원

—⻬ 1. 의회의; 의회에서 제정한 2. 정

passed by a parliament **2.** polite. ¶~ *language.*①
중한 ¶①의회 용어, 정중한 말

‡par·lor, *Brit.* **-lour** [pάːrlər] *n.* [C] **1.** (originally) a room for receiving guests; (now) a living room. **2.** a semi-private room in a hotel, an inn, etc. **3.** (*U.S.*) a decorated room for business; a shop. ¶*a beauty* ~① / *a tea* ~.②
—[名] 1. 개인 집의 응접실; 거실(居室) 2. [호텔·여관 따위의] 담화실, 휴게실 3. 《美》 영업실; 가게, 상점 ¶①미장원/②다방

parlor car [´-ˋ] *n.* (*U.S.*) a very fine railroad car for day travel.
—[名] 《美》 특별 객차

pa·ro·chi·al [pəróukiəl] *adj.* **1.** of or in a parish. **2.** narrow in thought.
—[形] 1. 교구(敎區)의 2. 좁은, 편협한

parochial school [-´--ˋ] *n.* a school established by a church.
—[名] 교구[부속]학교

par·o·dist [pǽrədist] *n.* [C] a writer of parodies.
—[名] 풍자적 개작시(改作詩) 작자

par·o·dy [pǽrədi] *n.* [C][U] (pl. **-dies**) a comic imitation of a serious writing; [C] a poor imitation. **—*vt.*** write a parody of; imitate poorly.
—[名] 풍자적 개작 시문; 서투른 모방 —[他] …을 풍자적으로 개작하다; 서투르게 모방하다

pa·role [pəróul] *n.* [U] **1.** a promise by a military prisoner not to try to escape. **2.** (*U.S.*) the act of making a prisoner free before his time is up.
—[名] 1. [포로가 도망하지 않겠다는] 약속, 서언(誓言) 2. 《美》 가석방, 가출옥 허가

par·ox·ysm [pǽrəksìz(ə)m] *n.* [C] a sudden attack or outburst of pain, laughter, anger, etc. ¶*a* ~ *of disease.*①
—[名] 발작; 격발(激發) ¶①병의 발작

par·quet [pɑːrkéi / ´-] *n.* [C] a floor of parquetry. ⇨fig.
—[名] 조각 나무 세공을 한 마루

par·quet·ry [pάːrkitri] *n.* [U] wood-work fitted together to make an ornamental pattern.
—[名] 조각 나무 세공

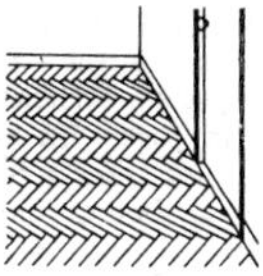
〔parquet〕

‡par·rot [pǽrət] *n.* [C] **1.** a bird that can repeat a person's words. **2.** a person who merely repeats others' words.
—[名] 1. 앵무새 2. [뜻도 모르고] 남의 말을 되풀이하는 사람

par·ry [pǽri] *vt., vi.* (**-ried**) turn (a blow) aside; avoid (a question). **—*n.*** [C] (pl. **-ries**) the act of parrying, esp. in fencing.
—[他][自] [공격을] 받아 넘기다; [질문을] 회피하다 —[名] 받아 넘기기; [특히 펜싱에서] 슬쩍 몸을 피하기

parse [pɑːrs / pɑːz] *vt.* (*Grammar*) explain (a word) grammatically, pointing out its part of speech, case, etc.; explain (a sentence) showing the relationship of the parts.
—[他] [말의] 품사 및 문법적 관계를 설명하다; [문장을] 해부하다

par·si·mo·ni·ous [pὰːrsimóuniəs] *adj.* too economical.
—[形] 지극히 검소한, 인색한, 쩨쩨한

par·si·mo·ny [pάːrsimòuni / -məni] *n.* [U] extreme economy.
—[名] 극도의 절약, 인색

pars·ley [pάːrsli] *n.* [U] a vegetable with green leaves, used with meat or in salad.
—[名] 파아슬리(서양요리에 곁들여 놓음)

pars·nip [pάːrsnip] *n.* [C] a vegetable with a long, white root.
—[名] 양방풍나물

***par·son** [pάːrsn] *n.* [C] 《*the* ~》 a clergyman in a parish; (*colloq.*) any clergyman.
—[名] 교구(敎區)의 목사; 목사

par·son·age [pάːrsnidʒ] *n.* [C] a house for a clergyman.
—[名] 목사관(館)

‡part [pɑːrt] *n.* [C] **1.** that which is less than the whole; one of the pieces which something is made up of. ¶*He ran* ~ *of the way.*① / *It is pretty cold here for a great* ~ *of the year.*② **2.** each of a number of equal portions composing a whole. ¶*a third* ~③ / *I have finished two of the three parts of the work.*④ **3.** an organ of the body; a piece of a machine. ¶*the inward parts of the body*⑤ / *spare parts for a machine.*⑥ **4.** a section to which a number is given in a book. ¶*a story in three parts.* **5.** a person's duty, share, or concern; a share in some job. ¶*Everyone must do his* ~.⑦ **6.** a role of an actor or actress. ¶*play the* ~ *of Ophelia.*⑧ **7.** one of the sides in a contest, dispute, or transaction. ¶*He always takes his brother's* ~ *in a quarrel.*⑨ **8.** 《usu. *pl.*》 ability; talent. ¶*a man of parts.*⑩ **9.** 《usu. *pl.*》 a region or district. ¶*in foreign parts.*⑪ **10.** a melody sung by one of a group of singers. ¶*sing the bass* ~.

1) ***for my part,*** as far as I am concerned.
2) ***for the most part,*** mostly.
3) ***in part,*** partly; to some extent.
4) ***on one's part; on the part of,*** ⓐ on one's side. ⓑ as far as one is concerned.

—[名] 1. 부분, 일부 ¶①그는 길 가던 도중에 좀 뛰었다/②이곳은 1년중 태반은 춥다 2. 비율; …분의 1 ¶③3분의 1/④일의 3분의 2를 마쳤다 3. 신체의 기관(器官); [기계의] 부품 ¶⑤내장/⑥기계의 예비 부품 4. [서적 따위의] 부(部), 편(編) 5. [그 사람이] 해야할 일, 임무, 역할 ¶⑦사람은 누구든지 자기의 본분을 다하지 않으면 안 된다 6. [연극의] 역할, 배역 ¶⑧오필리아의 역할을 연기하다 7. [다툼·논쟁·거래 따위의] …측, 쪽, 자기 편 ¶⑨그는 말다툼이 났을 때는 항상 그의 동생 편을 든다 8. 재능 ¶⑩유능한 사람 9. 지방 ¶⑪외국에서 10. 악곡의 부, 음부(音部)

[熟] 1)나로서는 2)대부분은, 대개는 3)부분적으로, 일부분, 얼마간 4)ⓐ…의 쪽에 ⓑ…에 관한 한 5)중요 부분 6)품사 7)…의 역할을 하다 8)…을 선의로 해석하다 9)…에 참가하다, 참여하다,

P

5) ***part and parcel,*** an essential element.
6) ***part of speech,*** one of the various grammatical classes into which words are grouped.
7) ***play a part*** (=*have a role*) ***in*** something.
8) ***take something in good part,*** accept something with a good spirit.
9) ***take part in,*** join; help in.

거들다

—*adv.* partly. ¶*Your opinion is ~ right.*

—[副] 일부분은, 얼마간, 어느 정도

—*vt.* 1. divide (something) into two or more pieces; divide (the hair) in opposite directions. ¶*~ the crowd*⑫ / *~ one's hair in the middle.* **2.** separate; break or tear. ¶*~ the fighting dogs.* **—*vi.* 1.** go away; separate. ¶*I parted with him on bad terms.* **2.** come to pieces; break.
1) ***part company,*** bring a friendship, an association, etc. to an end.
2) ***part from,*** leave.
3) ***part with,*** ⓐ part from. ⓑ give up; let (something) go.

—[他] 1. …을 부분으로 나누다; 가리마 타다 ¶⑫군중을 헤치다 ¶⑬머리 가운데에서 가리마를 타다 2. …을 분리시키다; …을 잡아찢다 —[自] 1. 헤어지다, 떠나다 2. 나뉘다; 찢어지다, 쪼개지다
[熟] 1) …와 절교하다, 헤어지다 2) …와 떨어지다, …을 떠나다 3) ⓐ…와 헤어지다 ⓑ…을 포기하다, 손 떼다

* **par·take** [pɑːrtéik] *v.* (**-took, -tak·en**) *vi.* **1.** take part in an activity. 《~ *of* something》 ¶*~ of refreshments*① / *~ of wine.*② **2.** have some of the nature of. 《~ *of* something》 ¶*He partakes of the character of his mother.*③ **—*vt.*** take a part of (something).

—[自] 1. 함께 하다, 참여하다; 나누어 받다(먹다, 갖다) ¶①다과를 함께 들다 /②포도주를 조금 마시다 2. 다소 …한 성질이 있다 ¶③그는 다소 어머니의 성질을 닮았다 —[他] …을 함께 하다

par·tak·er [pɑːrtéikər] *n.* [C] a person who partakes.

—[名] 함께 하는 사람; 관계자, 분담자

Par·the·non [pɑ́ːrθinɑ̀n / pɑ́ːθinən] *n.* 《*the* ~》 the ancient Greek temple of Athena on the Acropolis in Athens.

—[名] 파르테논(아테네의 아크로폴리스 언덕에 있는 여신 Athena의 신전)

* **par·tial** [pɑ́ːrʃ(ə)l] *adj.* **1.** not complete; in part. ¶*a ~ eclipse.*① **2.** showing favor to only one side, not both. ¶*He is always ~ to his youngest son.*② **3.** being fond of. 《~ *to* some food》 ¶*be ~ to tomatoes.*

—[形] 1. 불완전한, 부분적인 ¶①부분식(蝕) 2. 편파적인, 불공평한 ¶②그는 항상 막아들을 편애한다 3. 특히 좋아하는

par·ti·al·i·ty [pɑ̀ːrʃ(i)ǽliti] *n.* (pl. **-ties**) **1.** [U] the state or quality of being not fair to both sides. ¶*without ~.*① **2.** [C][U] a particular liking. ¶*have a ~ for poetry.*②

—[名] 1. 편파적임, 치우침, 불공평 ¶①공평하게 2. 특별히 좋아하기 ¶②시를 특히 좋아한다

par·tial·ly [pɑ́ːrʃəli] *adv.* not completely; partly; in a partial manner.

—[副] 불완전하게; 부분적으로; 불공평하게

par·tic·i·pant [pɑːrtísipənt] *n.* [C] a person who participates.

—[名] 참가자, 참여자, 관계자

par·tic·i·pate [pɑːrtísipèit] *vi.* take part in something; have a share with other people. 《~ *in* something》 ¶*~ in a conversation.*①

—[自] 참여하다, 참가하다 ¶①이야기에 참여하다

par·tic·i·pa·tion [pɑːrtìsipéiʃ(ə)n] *n.* [U] the act of participating.

—[名] 참가, 참여, 관계

par·tic·i·pa·tor [pɑːrtísipèitər] *n.* [C] a person who participates.

—[名] 관계자, 참가자

par·ti·cip·i·al [pɑ̀ːrtisípiəl] *adj.* of a participle. ¶*~ construction*① / *~ phrase.*②

—[形] 분사(分詞)의 ¶①분사 구문/②분사구(句)

* **par·ti·ci·ple** [pɑ́ːrtisìpl] *n.* [C] a word derived from a verb and having the functions of both verb and adjective.

—[名] 분사

* **par·ti·cle** [pɑ́ːrtikl] *n.* [C] **1.** the smallest possible amount; a very small portion. **2.** (*Grammar*) a minor part of speech. ⇨[N.B.]

—[名] 1. 극소량; 작은 조각 2. 《文法》 불변화사 [N.B.] 관사·전치사·접속사·접두사·접미사 따위

par·ti·col·ored, *Brit.* **-oured** [pɑ́ːrtikʌ̀lərd] *adj.* having or showing many different colors.

—[形] 가지가지 색깔로 이루어진, 잡색의, 얼룩덜룩한; 다채로운

‡ **par·tic·u·lar** [pərtíkjulər] *adj.* **1.** different or distinct from others; special. ↔general ¶*on that ~ day*① / *I have nothing ~ to do now.* **2.** belonging to each single person or thing. ¶*my ~ interests.*② **3.** outstanding. ¶*There is no ~ news today.*③ **4.** hard to please; very careful. ¶*a teacher ~ about manners.*④ **5.** telling all without omitting any small thing. ¶*a ~ account.*
be particular about, be not easily satisfied with (something); be very careful about.

—[形] 1. 특수한, 특별한, 다른 것과는 틀리는 ¶①그날따라 2. 개개의, 독자적인, 각자의, 독특한 ¶②나 개인의 이익 3. 현저한, 두드러진, 각별한 ¶③오늘은 이렇다 할 새로운 소식이 없다 4. 괴까다로운, 괴팍한; 꼼꼼한 ¶④예의범절에 까다로운 선생 5. 상세한, 아주 자상한
[熟] 괴까다로운; 꼼꼼한

—*n.* 1. [C] a detail; an item. ¶*be complete in every ~.*⑤ **2.** 《*pl.*》 a full report. ¶*write the particulars of the case.*
in particular, especially. ↔in general

—[名] 1. 세목(細目), 항목, 사항 ¶⑤모든 점에서 완전하다 2. 명세서
[熟] 특히

par·tic·u·lar·i·ty [pərtìkjulǽriti] *n.* (pl. **-ties**) [U][C] the state or quality of being particular; 《*pl.*》 something particular.

—[名] 상세; 정밀, 면밀; 특별; 까다로움, 꼼꼼함; 상세한 사항

par·tic·u·lar·ize [pərtíkjulərài z] *vt., vi.* describe (some-

—[他][自] [···을] 상세히 말하다; 낱낱이

par·tic·u·lar·ly [pərtíkjulərli] *adv.* in a particular manner; especially; in detail; one by one.
 ― ⓐ 특히, 상세히, 낱낱이

part·ing [pá:rtiŋ] *n.* 1. ⓤ ⓒ the act of taking leave; departure. ¶*on* ~① / *at* ~.② 2. ⓤ ⓒ [a point of] separation; division. ¶*at the* ~ *of the ways.*③ ― *adj.* 1. departing. 2. dividing. ¶*a* ~ *line*. 3. given, spoken, done, etc. at parting. ¶*a* ~ *gift*④ / *a* ~ *request*.
 ― ⓝ 1. 작별, 이별; 출발 ¶①작별에 즈음하여 /② 헤어질 때에 2. 분리; 분기[점];분할, 구분 ¶③가로에 [서서]
 ― ⓐ 1. 떠나가는 2. 나누는, 분할(분리)하는 3. 이별(작별)의 ¶④이별의 선물

• **par·ti·san, -ti·zan** [pá:rtiz(ə)n / pà:tizǽn] *n.* ⓒ 1. a strong, eager supporter of a party, group, cause, etc. 2. a member of a group of irregular troops engaged in guerrilla fighting. ― *adj.* of or like a partisan.
 ― ⓝ 1. [당・당파・주의 따위의] 지지자 2. 게릴라 대원, 빨치산; 도당(徒黨)
 ― ⓐ 당파의; 당파심이 강한; 게릴라 대원의

par·ti·san·ship [pá:rtiz(ə)nʃip / pà:tizǽnʃip] *n.* ⓤ strong support; blind or strong loyalty.
 ― ⓝ 당파심, 당파 근성; 맹목적 충성

par·ti·tion [pɑ:rtíʃ(ə)n] *n.* 1. ⓤ the act of dividing. 2. ⓒ a part so formed; one of divided parts; a section; a thin wall between rooms, etc. ― *vt.* divide (something) into sections; distribute.
 ― ⓝ 1. 간막이하기, 분할 2. 간막이, 격벽(隔壁), 간막이한 방 ― ⓥ …을 간막이하다; 분할하다; 분배하다

par·ti·zan [pá:rtiz(ə)n / pà:tizǽn] *n., adj.* =partisan.

‡ **part·ly** [pá:rtli] *adv.* in part; to some extent.
 ― ⓐ 부분적으로; 조금은, 얼마간

‡ **part·ner** [pá:rtnər] *n.* ⓒ 1. a member of a company who owns stocks and carries on the business in co-operation with others. ¶*an acting* (or *active*) ~① / *a general* ~.② 2. a person who shares; an associate. 3. a husband or wife. 4. one of two persons who dance together; (in a game, a sport, etc.) a player on the same team; a companion.
 ― *vt.* join (others) together as partners.
 ― ⓝ 1. 공동 출자자; [출자] 조합원, 사원 ¶①업무 집행 사원, 근무 사원/②일반(무한책임) 사원 2. 동료, 짝패, 동류 3. 배우자, 배필 (남편 또는 아내) 4. 파아트너(댄스의 상대), [놀이 따위의] 짝
 ― ⓥ …을 제휴시키다

• **part·ner·ship** [pá:rtnərʃip] *n.* ⓤ the state of being a partner; ⓒ a joint business; an association. ¶*enter into* ~ *with one's friend*① / *in* ~ *with (others)*② / *take someone into* ~③ / *a limited* ~.④
 ― ⓝ 공동, 협력; 조합, 상사(商社) ¶①친구와 공동 경영을 시작하다/②…와 협력하여/③남을 공동 경영자로 삼다/④합자회사

par·took [pɑ:rtúk] *v.* pt. of **partake**.

• **par·tridge** [pá:rtridʒ] *n.* ⓒ (pl. **par·tridg·es** or *collectively* **par·tridge**) a game bird of several varieties, smaller than a pheasant; ⓤ its flesh as food.
 ― ⓝ 자고(鷓鴣)(꿩보다 작은 엽조); 그 고기

part song [＾＾] *n.* a harmonized song in which the parts are sung by different people, often unaccompanied.
 ― ⓝ 합창곡

part-time [pá:rttàim / pá:ttáim] *adj.* working less than the standard hours. ↔full-time ― *adv.* on a part-time basis.
 ― ⓐ 파아트타임의, 비상임(非常任)의
 ― ⓐ 파아트타임으로, 시간제로

part-tim·er [pá:rttàimər / pá:ttáimə] *n.* ⓒ a person who is employed to work part-time.
 ― ⓝ 시간제로 근무하는 사람, 비상임 근무자

‡ **par·ty** [pá:rti] *n.* ⓒ (pl. **par·ties**) 1. a group of people united for the same purpose or by the same interest. ¶*a search* ~.① 2. a company met together for pleasure or entertainment; a social gathering. ¶*a garden* ~② / *a birthday* ~. 3. a group of people who share the same political opinions, etc.; a political organization. ¶*the government* (*opposition*) ~③ / *the Democratic Party*. 4. a person interested in or concerned in some affair; one who takes part in something. ¶*all the parties concerned*④ / *He was a* ~ *to the crime.*⑤
 ― *adj.* 1. of a social gathering. ¶*a* ~ *dress*. 2. of political organizations. ¶*a* ~ *government.*⑥
 ― ⓝ 1. [목적・관심을 함께 하는] 사람들, 일행 ¶①수색대 2. [사교상의] 모임, 회합, 파아티 ¶②원유회, 가아든파아티 3. 당, 당파; 정당 ¶③여당(야당) 4. [소송・계약 따위의] 당사자, 상대, 관계자; 한 패, 공범 ¶④당사자(관계자) 일동/⑤그는 그 범죄에 가담하고 있었다
 ― ⓐ 1. 파아티의 2. 당파의, 정당의 ¶⑥정당 내각

par·ty-col·ored, *Brit.* **-oured** [pá:rtikʌ̀lərd] *adj.* =parti-colored.

pa·sha [pǽʃə, pá:ʃə, pəʃá: / pá:ʃə] *n.* ⓒ a former title of high-ranking officers or officials in Turkey.
 ― ⓝ 파샤(터어키의 옛 문무 고관의 존칭)

‡ **pass**¹ [pæs / pɑ:s] *vi.* 1. move from one place to another; go past; proceed. ¶~ *along a street* / *I saw a party of students* ~. 2. change from one state into another. ¶*The weather passed suddenly from hot to cold*. 3. (of time) go by; be spent. ¶*Five years have passed* 들다(열거하다)
 ― ⓥ 1. 통해서 가다; 지나가다; 통과하다; 나아가다 2. 옮아가다, 변화하다 3. [시간이] 지나가다, 경과하다 4. 꺼지다, 소멸하다; 죽다; 지나가 버리다; 끝나다 ¶①사라져 없어지다/②너의 걱정거리

since I last saw him. **4.** disappear; die; go away; come to an end. ¶*~ out of existence*① | *Your trouble will soon ~ away.*② **5.** happen; be done or said (between persons). ¶*Tell me all that passed.*③ **6.** be accepted or recognized. ⟪*~ as* or *for* something or someone⟫ ¶*~ as* (or *for*) *a first-rate artist.* **7.** go through an examination, etc. successfully; (of a bill or law) be approved by a majority. ¶*The bill passed.* | *He passed first in the examination.* **8.** be current; go or be sent about from person to person. ¶*The letter passed from hand to hand.* **9.** (of a court, etc.) express or pronounce the judgment; (of a judgment, etc.) be expressed or pronounced. ⟪*~ on* (or *upon, for, against*) someone or something⟫ ¶*The judgment passed against us.*④ | *The jury passed on the case.* **10.** (*Football, etc.*) throw or kick the ball to another player of one's own team. **11.** (*Cards*) refuse one's turn to play, bid, etc.

는 곧 없어질 것이다 5. [일이] 일어나다, 발생하다; [말 따위가] 입에서 나오다 ¶③자초지종을 모두 이야기해 봐라 6. …으로 통하다, 통용되다, 인정되다 7. [시험 따위에] 합격하다; [의안이] 통과되다, 제정되다 8. 통용되다; [손에서 손으로] 넘어가다 9. [법정 따위가] 판결을 내리다; [판결 따위가] 내려지다 ¶④우리에게 불리한 판결이 내려졌다 10. ⦅蹴球⦆ 공을 패스하다, 넘겨주다 11. ⦅카아드놀이⦆ 패스하다 (기권하여 다음 차례로 돌리다)

—*vt.* **1.** go by, beyond, over, across, through (something or someone); overtake. ¶*~ a house* | *~ a hill* | *~ an ocean.*⑤ **2.** allow (someone) to go past or enter; cause (someone) to move past. ¶*The soldier on guard passed him.* | *The general passed the troops in review.* **3.** cause (something) to go through; put (a rope, etc. through). ¶*~ air through a liquid* | *~ a rope around a log.* **4.** spend (time, etc.). ¶*~ a pleasant evening.* **5.** be successful in (an examination, etc.). ¶*~ an examination.* **6.** (of a committee, law-making body, etc.) approve (a motion, law, etc.). ¶*~ the bill* **7.** hand (something) from one to another. ¶*~ the wine* | *Please ~* [*me*] *the butter.* **8.** express or pronounce (an opinion or a judgment). ⟪*~* something *on* or *upon*⟫ ¶*~ sentence of death on the criminal.* **9.** be better than (something); go beyond the limit of (something). ¶*His behavior passes my understanding.*⑥ **10.** (*Football, etc.*) throw or kick (a ball) to another player of one's own team.

—[他] 1. …을 지나가다, 통과하다, 건너다; 앞지르다 ¶⑤바다를 건너다 2. …을 통과시키다, 들이다; 열병(閱兵)하다 3. …을 뚫고 지나가게 하다; [밧줄 따위]를 걸다 4. [시간]을 보내다, 경과시키다 5. [시험 따위]에 합격하다 6. [의회 따위가 동의·법안]을 통과시키다, 가결하다 7. …을 넘겨(건네)주다, 인도하다, [식탁 따위에서 음식을] 돌리다 8. [판결]을 내리다 9. …을 능가하다, 보다 더 낫다; …을 초월하다 ¶⑥그의 행동은 나로서는 이해할 수가 없다 10. [공]을 패스하다

1) ***pass away,*** die; come to an end.
2) ***pass off,*** ⓐ disappear gradually ⓑ come to an end. ⓒ put on a false appearance of (someone else); pretend; deceive someone by giving (a false thing). ¶*~ oneself off as an artist.*⑦ ⓓ ignore; treat (something) as unimportant.
3) ***pass on,*** ⓐ move forward. ⓑ repeat. ⓒ hand (something) from one to another. ⓓ die.
4) ***pass out,*** (*colloq.*) lose consciousness; die.
5) ***pass over,*** ignore; fail to notice.
6) ***pass the time of day,*** say "Good morning", "Good afternoon," etc. to someone on meeting him; greet; exchange simple, everyday remarks.
7) ***pass through,*** experience.
8) ***pass up,*** refuse; give up.

[熟] 1)죽다; 끝나다 2)ⓐ점점 사라져 없어지다 ⓑ끝나다 ⓒ거짓으로 …인 체하다; …을 속이다 ¶⑦예술가인 체하다 예술가로 통하다 ⓓ…을 무시하다; 얕보다, 경시하다 3)ⓐ나아가다 ⓑ되풀이하다 ⓒ…을 다음으로 넘기다 ⓓ죽다 4)기절하다; 죽다 5)…을 무시하다; 못 보고 넘어가다 6)인사를 하다 7)…을 경험하다 8)…을 거절하다; 포기하다

—*n.* [C] **1.** the act of passing; success in an examination. **2.** a ticket allowing one to go somewhere; a free ticket. ¶*a free ~ to a theater.*⑧ **3.** state; condition; crisis; difficult circumstances. ¶*a pretty ~* | *Things have come to a strange ~.*⑨ **4.** a trick played by moving the hands quickly and skillfully; a gesture. ¶*make passes.*⑩ **5.** (*Football, etc.*) an act of passing the ball from one player to another. **6.** (*Cards*) an act of not taking one's turn. **7.** (*Fencing*) a thrust with the sword.

—[名] 1. 통과; 합격, 급제 2. 입장권; 허가증; 무료승차(입장)권 ¶⑧극장의 무료 입장권 3. 상태, 사태; 위기, 궁지, 난관 ¶⑨일이 이상한 상태로 빠졌다 4. 요술, 속임수; 손짓, 몸짓 ¶⑩손을 놀려 최면술을 걸다 5. ⦅蹴球⦆ [공의] 패스, 송구(送球) 6. ⦅카아드놀이⦆ 패스(기권하고 다음 차례로 돌리기) 7. ⦅펜싱⦆ 찌르기

‡**pass²** [pæs / pɑːs] ***n.*** [C] a narrow way or course, esp. over or through a range of mountains. ¶*a teahouse on a ~.*①

—[名] 산길, 오솔길 ¶①고갯길의 찻집

pass·a·ble [pǽsəbl / pá:s-] *adj.* **1.** that can be passed through or over. **2.** fairly good; moderate. ¶*a ~ composition.* **3.** current. ¶*a ~ coin.*① **4.** (of a bill, etc.) that may be enacted.

—[形] 1. 통행할 수 있는 2. 쓸쓸한; 보통의, 어연간한 3. 통용(유통)되는 ¶① 유통 경화(硬貨) 4. [법안 따위가] 가결될 수 있는, 통과할 수 있는

pass·a·bly [pǽsəbli / pá:s-] *adv.* pretty; fairly; moderately.

—[副] 쓸쓸하게; 보통 정도로

˸pas·sage [pǽsidʒ] *n.* [U] **1.** the act of passing or proceeding; movement from one place to another; change from one condition to another. ¶*the ~ of time / the ~ of men and vehicles.*① **2.** [C] a voyage across the sea from one place to another; a journey. ¶*birds of ~*② / *have a smooth ~.*③ **3.** a passenger's accommodations on a ship; the payment for this. ¶*pay one's ~*④ / *book one's ~ on a steamer*⑤ / *work one's ~.*⑥ **4.** [C] a long and narrow way, esp. between rooms in a house; a hall; a lobby; the course of a river or sea. ¶*We walked through the ~.* **5.** the right or permission to pass through, over, or into. **6.** [C] a piece from a speech or writing. ¶*a ~ from Shakespeare.* **7.** approval of a bill, law, resolution, etc. ¶*the ~ of a bill through Congress.* **8.** [C] what is said or done between two persons. ¶*a ~ of* (or *at*) *arms.*⑦

—[名] 1. 통행, 통과; [시간 따위의] 경과, 추이(推移); 변천 ¶①사람과 차량의 통행 2. 항해, 도항(渡航); 여행 ¶②철새/③순탄한 항해를 하다 3. 배의 수용 설비; 뱃삯, 승선료 ¶④뱃삯을 치르다/⑤승선을 예약하다/⑥뱃삯 대신에 배에서 일하다 4. 통로, 복도; 호올; 대합실, 로비; 수로, 항로 5. 통행권(權); 통행의 허가 6. [연설·문장 따위의] 1절 7. [의안 따위의] 통과, 가결 8. [사람과 사람과의] 의견 교환; 논쟁, 싸움 ¶⑦입씨름, 논쟁

pas·sage·way [pǽsidʒwèi] *n.* [C] a corridor; a passage.

—[名] 복도, 통로

pas·sé [pæséi / pá:sei, pǽs-] *adj.* old-fashioned; out of date.

—[形] 과거의; 케케 묵은, 시대에 뒤떨어진

˸pas·sen·ger [pǽsindʒər] *n.* [C] **1.** a person who travels on a train, bus, boat, etc. **2.** a traveler, esp. on foot; a wayfarer.

—[名] 1. 승객, 여객; 선객(船客) 2. 도보 여행자

passenger boat [⌐-- ⌐] *n.* a boat for carrying passengers.

—[名] 객선(客船)

passenger car [⌐-- ⌐] *n.* a railroad car for carrying passengers; an automobile for carrying no more than nine passengers.

—[名] 객차; [승객 9명 이하의] 승용 자동차

passenger plane [⌐-- ⌐] *n.* an airplane for carrying passengers.

—[名] 여객기

passenger train [⌐-- ⌐] *n.* a train for carrying passengers.

—[名] 여객 열차, 객차

pass·er [pǽsər / pá:sə] *n.* [C] a person who passes; a passer-by.

—[名] 통행인, 나그네

pass·er-by [pǽsərbái / pá:sə-] *n.* [C] (pl. **pass·ers-by**) a person who passes by, usu. by walking.

—[名] 지나가는 사람, 통행인

pass·ing [pǽsiŋ / pá:s-] *adj.* **1.** transient; incidental. ¶*~ pleasure.*① **2.** current. ¶*during the ~ year.*
—*adv.* (*archaic*) very; surpassingly.
—*n.* [U] the act of passing.
in passing, by the way; incidentally.

—[形] 1. 한 때의, 잠시동안의; 우연의 ¶①잠시동안의 쾌락 2. 현재의, 당면한
—[副] 몹시, 굉장히
—[名] 통행, 통과, 경과
[熟] …하는 김에, 겸하여; 우연히

˸pas·sion [pǽʃ(ə)n] *n.* **1.** [U][C] very strong feeling, emotion or enthusiasm; deep love or affection. ¶*a leader lacking in ~*① / *one's ruling* (or *master*) *~.*② **2.** ⦅*a ~*⦆ an outburst of rage. ¶*fly* (or *get*) *into a ~*③ / *in a ~.*④ **3.** [C] a very strong liking. ⦅*~ for*⦆ **4.** [U] suffering; ⦅*the P-*⦆ the sufferings of Christ on the cross.

—[名] 1. 열정; 정열; 열심; 열중; 열애 ¶①열의 없는 지도자/②주정(主情), 지배적인 감정 2. 울화, 격분, 격앙, 홍분 ¶③버럭 성을 내다/④몹시 격분하여 3. 기호(嗜好), 굉장히 좋아하는 것 4. 수난; 그리스도의 수난

∗pas·sion·ate [pǽʃ(ə)nit] *adj.* easily moved or excited by passion; expressing or having strong feelings; easily get angry.

—[形] 열렬한, 정열적인; 다정다감한; 성잘 내는, 성미급한

pas·sion·less [pǽʃ(ə)nlis] *adj.* having no passion; calm.

—[形] 정열이 없는; 냉정한, 침착한

∗pas·sive [pǽsiv] *adj.* **1.** being acted upon but not acting. **2.** (*Grammar*) showing that the subject is acted upon by the verb. ↔active **3.** not resisting; submissive; inactive. ¶*a ~ nature / be ~ in an action.*①
—*n.* ⦅*the ~*⦆ (*Grammar*) the passive voice.

—[形] 1. 수동적인, 피동의 2. ⦅文法⦆ 수동태(態)의 3. 무저항의, 소극적인; 남이 시키는 대로 하는; 활기없는 ¶①행동이 소극적이다
—[名] ⦅文法⦆ 수동태

pas·siv·i·ty [pæsíviti] *n.* [U] the state or quality of being passive; passiveness; inaction.

—[名] 수동성; 비(非)활동; 복종; 무저항

pass·key [pǽskì: / pá:s-] *n.* **1.** [C] a key designed to open several locks; a master key. **2.** a private key.

—[名] 1. 결쇠 2. 개인용의 열쇠

Pass·o·ver [pǽsòuvər / pá:sòuvə] *n.* an annual Jewish holiday in memory of the sparing of the Jewish houses when God killed the first-born children in Egypt.

—[名] 유월절(逾越節) [N.B.] 유대 달력으로 1월 14일에 행하는 유대인의 축제

P

pass·port [pǽspɔ:rt / pá:spɔ:t] *n.* ⓒ **1.** an official document giving permission to travel abroad. **2.** something that enables someone to win or obtain something.

pass·word [pǽswə̀:rd / pá:swə̀:d] *n.* ⓒ a secret word that must be uttered by a person before he passes a guard; a watchword.

‡**past** [pæst / pɑ:st] *adj.* **1.** of an earlier time. ¶*This picture reminds me of my ~ days.*① **2.** (as *predicative*) gone by; over. ¶*Her sorrows are ~.*② **3.** just ended; ago. ¶*the ~ week*③ / *ten years ~* / *for some time ~.*④ **4.** no longer in office; former. ¶*a ~ chair man.* **5.** (*Grammar*) expressing what is gone by. ¶*the ~ tense.*
—*n.* **1.** (usu. *the ~*) time gone by. ¶*In the ~*① / *in the remote ~.* **2.** ⓒ a happening in past time; a past life, history, career, etc. ¶*The school has a glorious ~.* **3.** ⓒ (*a ~*) one's past life, esp. that which is kept concealed. ¶*a woman with a ~.*② **4.** (usu. *the ~*) (*Grammar*) the past tense.
—*prep.* **1.** beyond in time; after. ¶*~ noon* / *at a quarter ~ four.* **2.** beyond in place; going by or beyond. ¶*run ~ the post office* / *Bullets whistled ~ their ears.* **3.** beyond in number, amount or degree. ¶*It's ~ three pounds.* **4.** beyond the power, reach, scope, or influence of. ¶*~ endurance* / *~ belief.*
—*adv.* so as to pass by. ¶*walk ~* / *drive ~.*

*** paste** [peist] *n.* Ⓤ **1.** a mixture of flour, water, etc., used for sticking (paper, etc.) together. **2.** a soft mixture of flour and water with butter, etc. used in making pastry. **3.** a way of preparing foodstuffs by beating them up into a soft and moist mass. **4.** a soft jelly-like candy. **5.** the glassy substance used in making artificial precious stones.
—*vt.* stick (something) with paste; cover (a wall, etc.) by pasting things on it. (*~ up* (or *down, together*) something; *~* something *on* or *with*)

paste·board [péistbɔ̀:rd] *n.* Ⓤ a stiff, boardlike material made by pasting several sheets of paper together.

pas·tel [pǽstel, pæstél] *n.* **1.** Ⓤ a kind of crayon made of coloring matter mixed with gum, etc. used in drawing. **2.** ⓒ a drawing made with such crayons. **3.** Ⓤ a method of drawing with such crayons.

pas·tern [pǽstə:rn] *n.* ⓒ the part of a horse's foot between the hoof and the fetlock. →**fetlock** (fig.)

pas·teur·i·za·tion [pæ̀stərizéiʃ(ə)n / -tərai-, pù:stərai-] *n.* Ⓤ the method of pasteurizing.

pas·teur·ize [pǽstəràiz, +*Brit.* pá:s-] *vt.* heat and suddenly cool (milk, etc.) to destroy harmful bacteria.

*** pas·time** [pǽstàim / pá:s-] *n.* ⓒ anything done for amusement or recreation.

pas·tor [pǽstər / pá:stə] *n.* ⓒ a minister in charge of a church or parish; a clergyman; a priest.

pas·tor·al [pǽst(ə)r(ə)l / pá:s-] *adj.* **1.** of shepherds or rural life; rustic; (of land) used for pasture. ¶*a ~ life*① / *~ poetry* (*music*).② **2.** of a priest or his duties. ¶*a ~ staff.*③ —*n.* ⓒ a poem, play, picture, etc. on rural life.

*** pas·try** [péistri] *n.* (pl. **-tries**) Ⓤ paste mixed with flour, oil and water and baked in an oven; piecrust; Ⓤ (*collectively*) things made of pastry; ⓒ one of these things.

pas·tur·age [pǽstʃuridʒ / pá:s-] *n.* Ⓤ **1.** grass used as food for cattle. **2.** grassland for grazing; pasture.

‡**pas·ture** [pǽstʃər / pá:stʃə] *n.* **1.** Ⓤ land on which cattle can feed; ⓒ a piece of land of this kind. **2.** Ⓤ grass

—명 1. 여권, 통항증(通航證), 패스포오트 2. 수단

—명 암호, 군호(軍號)

—형 1. 지나간, 과거의, 옛날의 ¶①이 사진을 보니 옛날 일이 생각난다 2. 지나가 버린; 끝난 ¶②그녀의 슬픔은 끝났다 3. 방금 지난; 지금으로부터 … 전의 ¶③지난 주/④얼마 전부터 4. 전임(前任)의, 전… 5. 《文法》 과거의
—명 1. 과거 ¶⑤과거에, 이전에, 종래에 2. 지나간 일, 과거지사; 이력, 경력 3. [알려지지 않았거나 수상쩍은] 경력 ¶⑥과거가 불미한 여자 4. 《文法》 과거시제(時制)
—전 1. [시간]이 지나서, [몇 시] 지나 2. [장소]를 지나서(넘어서) 3. [수량이] …이상으로 4. [정도·범위 따위]를 넘어서; …이 미치지 못하는

—부 지나쳐서, 지나서

—명 1. 풀 2. [밀]가루 반죽 3. 반죽한 것 4. [젤리 모양의] 일종의 당과(糖菓) 5. 유리질의 혼합물(모조 보석의 원료)

—타 …을 풀로 붙이다(바르다); 풀로 붙여서 덮다

—명 두꺼운 종이, 판지, 마분지

—명 1. 파스텔 2. 파스텔화(畵) 3. 파스텔 화법

—명 발목(말 따위의 발굽과 복사뼈 사이)

—명 저온 살균법

—타 [우유 따위에] 저온 살균법을 실시하다
—명 오락; 유희; 기분 전환

—명 목사

—형 1. 양 치는 목동의; 전원생활의, 시골의; 목축에 알맞은 ¶①전원생활/②전원시(음악) 2. 목사의 ¶③목장(牧杖) —명 전원시; 목가; 전원화(畵)

—명 [밀]가루 반죽; 파이 따위의 껍질; 가루 반죽으로 만든 과자(파이·케이크 따위)

—명 1. 목초 2. 목장

—명 1. 목장, 목초지 2. 목초
—타 1. [가축을] 방목하다 2. [가축이]

used as food for cattle. —*vt.* **1.** put (cattle, sheep, etc.) out to feed in a pasture. **2.** (of cattle, etc.) feed on (grass, etc.). —*vi.* feed on growing grass.
목초]를 뜯어먹다 —[自] 풀을 뜯어먹다

past·y¹ [péisti] *adj.* (**past·i·er, past·i·est**) like paste; (of the complexion, etc.) pale.
—[形] 풀 같은;[안색 따위가] 창백한

past·y² [péisti / pǽsti, pá:sti] *n.* [U] a pie, esp. a meat pie.
—[名] 고기 파이

* **pat¹** [pǽt] *v.* (**pat·ted, pat·ting**) *vt.* strike (something) gently with something flat; tap (someone's shoulder, etc.) with the hand, often as a sign of sympathy or affection. ¶~ *someone on the back* (*head, shoulder*).
—[他] …을 가볍게 두드리다 —[自] 가벼운 발소리를 내며 걷다(뛰다)
—*vi.* walk or run with a patting sound.
—*n.* [C] **1.** a light, quick blow with the hand; the light sound of this. **2.** a small mass, esp. of butter.
—[名] **1.** 가볍게 두드리기; 가볍게 두드리는 소리 **2.** [버터 따위의] 작은 덩이

pat² [pæt] *adj.* suitable; apt; timely. ¶*a ~ arrival.*
—[形] 적절한, 알맞은; 꼭 맞는
—*adv.* aptly; exactly.
—[副] 적절하게, 알맞게; 꼭 맞게
1) ***have*** (or ***know***) *something* [***down***] ***pat,*** (*colloq.*) know thoroughly. 2) ***stand pat on,*** (*colloq.*) refuse to change (one's plans, purposes, etc.).
[熟] 1)《口》…을 모조리 알고 있다 2)《口》고수하다, [끝까지] 버티고 나가다

: patch [pætʃ] *n.* [C] **1.** a small piece of cloth, etc. put on to mend a hole. **2.** a piece of plaster put over a cut or wound; a pad worn to protect a hurt eye. **3.** a small plot of ground. **4.** a small, uneven spot.
—[名] **1.** [덧대어 깁는] 헝겊 조각 **2.** 반창고 한 조각; 안대(眼帶) **3.** 작은 땅뙈기, 한 구획 **4.** 반점
not a patch on, (*colloq.*) not equal to someone; very inferior to (someone).
[熟]《口》…와는 비교도 안 되는(안 될 만큼 뒤떨어지는)
—*vt.* put a patch or patches on (something); mend (something) with patches.
—[他] …에 헝겊 조각을 덧대다; …을 덧대어 고치다(수선하다)
patch up, ⓐ settle (a quarrel, etc.). ⓑ mend (something) hastily or roughly.
[熟] ⓐ[싸움 따위를] 가라앉히다 ⓑ임시미봉하다(고치다)

patch·work [pǽtʃwə̀:rk] *n.* [C] [U] **1.** a fancywork made of pieces of cloth of different colors. **2.** a rough and disorderly mixture; a jumble.
—[名] **1.** 덧대어 깁기 **2.** 주워 모은 것, 잡동사니

patch·y [pǽtʃi] *adj.* (**patch·i·er, patch·i·est**) made up of patches; not regular; uneven.
—[形] 누덕누덕 기운, 주워 모은; 불규칙한, 부조화의

pate [peit] *n.* [C] (*colloq.*) the head; brains.
—[名]《口》머리;두뇌

* **pat·ent** [pǽt(ə)nt, +*Brit.* péit-] *n.* [C] an official license giving the sole right to make or sell a new invention; an official document granting such a right; an invention that is patented. ¶*apply for a ~*① / *get* (or *take out, obtain*) *a ~ for* (or *on*) *an invention.*②
—[名] 특허[권]; 전매 특허증(證);특허품 ¶①특허를 신청하다/② 발명품의 특허를 얻다
—*vt.* get a patent for (a new invention).
—[他] …의 전매특허를 얻다
—*adj.* **1.** given or protected by a patent. **2.** evident; plain. **3.** open to the public.
—[形] **1.** 전매특허의 **2.** 명백한 **3.** 공개의

pat·ent·ee [pæ̀t(ə)ntí:, +*Brit.* pèi-] *n.* [C] a person who holds a patent.
—[名] [전매]특허권 소유자

patent leather [´- ´-] *n.* leather with a hard, smooth, glossy surface, usu. black.
—[名] [검정] 에나멜 가죽

patent medicine [´- ´--] *n.* medicine that is patented.
—[名] [특허] 매약

pa·ter [péitər] *n.* [C] (*Brit. colloq.*) father.
—[名]《英口》아버지

pa·ter·nal [pətə́:rn(ə)l] *adj.* **1.** of or like a father; fatherly. **2.** on the father's side of the family. ¶*a ~ grandmother.* **3.** received or inherited from a father.
—[形] **1.** 아버지의;아버지다운 **2.** 아버지 쪽의, 부계(父系)의 **3.** 부조 전래(父祖傳來)의

pa·ter·ni·ty [pətə́:rniti] *n.* [U] **1.** the state of being a father; fatherhood. **2.** paternal origin. **3.** origin.
—[名] **1.** 아버지임; 부성(父性) **2.** 부계(父系) **3.** 기원

pat·er·nos·ter [pèitərnástər, pæ̀t- / pǽtənɔ́stə] *n.* [C] the Lord's Prayer, esp. in Latin.
—[名] [특히 라틴어의] 주기도문

: path [pæθ / pɑ:θ] *n.* [C] (pl. **paths** [pæθs, pæðz / pɑ:ðz]) **1.** a way made by the footsteps of men or animals. **2.** a line along which a person or thing moves. ¶*the ~ of the moon.*① **3.** a course of conduct or action. ¶*a ~ to success.*②
—[名] **1.** 오솔길; [사람·동물이] 밟고 다녀서 난 길; 소로(小路) **2.** 통로; 진로 ¶①달의 궤도 **3.** 행로(行路); 방침 ¶②성공에의 길

* **pa·thet·ic** [pəθétik] *adj.* arousing sympathy and pity; pitiful.
—[形] 동정심(연민의 정)을 일으키는; 애처로운, 슬픈

pa·thet·i·cal·ly [pəθétikəli] *adv.* in a pathetic manner.
—[副] 애처롭게, 동정심을 일으킬 만큼

path·find·er [pǽθfàindər / pá:θfàində] *n.* [C] a person who finds or makes a path or way where none had existed; an explorer.
—[名] 길을 트는 사람; 개척자; 탐험자

path·less [pǽθlis / pá:θ-] *adj.* having no paths; untrodden.
—[形] 길 없는; 전인미답(前人未踏)의

path·o·log·i·cal [pæ̀θəlɑ́dʒik(ə)l / -lɔ́dʒ-] *adj.* **1.** of pathology. **2.** due to disease.
—[形] 1. 병리학의 2. 병에 의한

pa·thol·o·gy [pəθɑ́lədʒi / -θɔ́l-] *n.* [U] **1.** the science which deals with the causes and nature of diseases. **2.** all the conditions, processes, or results of a particular disease.
—[名] 1. 병리학 2. 병리;병상(病狀)

pa·thos [péiθɑs / -θɔs] *n.* [U] the quality in something spoken, written, etc. that arouses a feeling of pity or sadness.
—[名] 연민의 정을 자아내는 힘; 비애; 비통

path·way [pǽθwèi / pɑ́:θ-] *n.* [C] a path.
—[名] 오솔길, 소로

-pa·thy [-pəθi] a word element meaning *feeling, disease,* or *treatment of disease.*
—「감정 · 고통 · 요법」의 뜻을 나타내는 단어 요소

: **pa·tience** [péiʃ(ə)ns] *n.* [U] **1.** the state, ability, or fact of being patient. ↔impatience ¶*have ~ with / lose [one's] ~ with.* **2.** a card game played by one person.
1) ***be out of patience with,*** be no longer able to endure.
2) ***have no patience with,*** be unable to permit or bear.
3) ***patience of Job,*** patience without end.
—[名] 1. 인내, 참을성;견인(堅忍); 끈기 2.《카아드놀이》혼자서 놀기, 패떼기
[熟] 1)…에 더 이상 참을 수가 없다 2) …은 참을 수가 없다 3)[욥 같은] 비상한 인내

: **pa·tient** [péiʃ(ə)nt] *adj.* enduring pain, hardship, etc. without complaint. ↔impatient ¶*be ~ with* (or *toward, towards*) *others.*①
—[形] 참을성있는, 끈기있는, 끈덕진 ¶ ①남에게 대해 인내하다

—*n.* [C] a sick person receiving medical treatment.
—[名] 환자, 병자

pa·tient·ly [péiʃ(ə)ntli] *adv.* in a patient manner.
—[副] 참을성있게, 끈기있게, 꾸준히

pa·tri·arch [péitriɑ̀:rk] *n.* [C] **1.** a father and head of a family or tribe. **2.** an old and respected man. **3.** a bishop in the early Christian church.
—[名] 1. 가장(家長), 족장(族長) 2. 장로, 원로 3. [초기 그리스도 교회의] 주교

pa·tri·ar·chal [pèitriɑ́:rk(ə)l] *adj.* **1.** of a patriarch; worthy of respect. **2.** ruled by a patriarch.
—[形] 1. 가장의; 족장의; 존경할 만한 2. 가장(족장)이 지배하는

pa·tri·cian [pətríʃ(ə)n] *n.* [C] **1.** a nobleman of ancient Rome. ↔plebeian **2.** an aristocrat —*adj.* of the patricians; aristocratic.
—[名] 1. [고대 로마의]귀족 2. [일반적으로]귀족 —[形] 귀족의; 귀족적인

pat·ri·mo·ni·al [pæ̀trimóuniəl] *adj.* of a patrimony.
—[形] 조상 전래(傳來)의, 세습의

pat·ri·mo·ny [pǽtrimòuni / -məni] *n.* [C] (pl. **-nies**) **1.** property given by one's father or ancestors. **2.** church property.
—[名] 1. 부모(조상)에게서 물려받은 재산; 세습 재산 2. 교회의 재산

• **pa·tri·ot** [péitriət] *n.* [C] a person who shows great love for his country.
—[名] 애국자, 우국지사

• **pa·tri·ot·ic** [pèitriɑ́tik / pæ̀triɔ́tik] *adj.* having the qualities of a patriot.
—[形] 애국심이 강한, 애국적인

• **pa·tri·ot·ism** [péitriətìz(ə)m / pǽt-] *n.* [U] the feelings and qualities of a patriot.
—[名] 애국심

pa·trol [pətróul] *vi., vt.* (**-trolled, -trol·ling**) go to (a district or section) regularly and repeatedly for watching or guarding.
—[自][他] [···을] 순찰(순시)하다

—*n.* **1.** [U] the act of patrolling. **2.** [C] a person or persons who patrol. **3.** [C] a group of soldiers, ships, airplanes, etc. sent out for guarding and for getting information about the enemy. **4.** [C] a group of boy scouts.
—[名] 1. 순찰, 순시 2. 순시자, 순찰(정찰)병 3. 척후, 초계정, 정찰기 4. 보이스카우트의 분대

pa·trol·man [pətróulmən / -mæ̀n] *n.* [C] (pl. **-men** [-mən / -mèn]) a man, esp. a policeman, who patrols.
—[名] 순시자; 순찰 경관

• **pa·tron** [péitr(ə)n] *n.* [C] **1.** a person who gives support to someone. **2.** a regular customer. **3.** a guardian saint or god; a patron saint.
—[名] 1. 후원자, 지원자, 보호자 2. [상점 따위의] 단골손님, 고객 3. 수호성인(守護聖人), 수호신

pa·tron·age [péitrənidʒ / pǽt-] *n.* [U] **1.** support or encouragement given by a patron. ¶*under the ~ of.*① **2.** regular business given by customers.
—[名] 1. 후원; 보호 ¶①···의 보호 아래 2. [상점 따위의] 단골 거래, 애고(愛顧)

pa·tron·ess [péitrənis] *n.* [C] a woman patron.
—[名] patron의 여성형

pa·tron·ize [péitrənàiz / pǽt-] *vt.* **1.** act as a patron toward (someone); support; protect. **2.** be a regular customer of (a shop, etc.) **3.** treat (someone) as an inferior.
—[他] 1. ···을 후원하다;보호하다 2. ···을 단골로 삼다 3. ···을 아랫사람으로서 다루다

pat·ter¹ [pǽtər] *vi.* make sound with rapid taps of the feet. —*vt.* cause (something) to make a pattering sound. —*n.* [C] a series of rapid taps.
—[自] 후두둑후두둑 소리내다 —[他] 후두둑후두둑(찰박찰박) 소리나게 하다
—[名] 후두둑후두둑(타박타박) 소리

pat·ter² [pǽtər] *n.* **1.** [U] rapid and easy talk. **2.** [U] the particular dialect or slang of a class or group. —*vt., vi.* talk rapidly with little meaning.
—[名] 1. 잽싸게 지껄이는 말 2. 변말, 은어(隱語)
—[他][自] 잽싸게 지껄이다

‡ **pat·tern** [pǽtərn] *n.* [C] **1.** a fine example meant to be followed. **2.** an arrangement of forms, figures, colors, etc. used in decoration; a design.
—*vt.* **1.** decorate (something) with a pattern. **2.** make or do (something) in imitation of a model.
—[名] 1. 모범, 본보기 2. 도안, 무늬
—[他] 1. …에 무늬를 넣다(놓다) 2. 본떠서 만들다

pat·ty [pǽti] *n.* [C] [U] (pl. **-ties**) a small pie containing meat, etc.
—[名] 작은 [고기] 파이

pau·ci·ty [pɔ́ːsiti] *n.* [U] smallness of number or quantity; lack.
—[名] 소수; 소량; 부족

Paul [pɔːl] *n.* a man's name.
—[名] 남자 이름

Paul·ine [pɔ́ːlain] *n.* a woman's name.
—[名] 여자 이름

paunch [pɔːntʃ] *n.* [C] the belly; the stomach.
—[名] 배; 위(胃)

pau·per [pɔ́ːpər] *n.* [C] a person supported by charity; a very poor person.
—[名] [빈민 구제법의 적용을 받는] 빈곤자, 극빈자, 피구호자; 빈민

pau·per·ism [pɔ́ːpərìz(ə)m] *n.* [U] poverty; 《*collectively*》 paupers.
—[名] 빈곤; 빈민

pau·per·ize [pɔ́ːpəràiz] *vt.* bring (someone) to the state of being a pauper; make (someone) very poor.
—[他] …을 요구호 대상자가 되게 하다; 가난하게 하다

‡ **pause** [pɔːz] *n.* [C] **1.** a short period during which work is ceased; a stop; a rest. ¶*make a* ~. **2.** a temporary stop or break in speaking or reading to emphasize or clarify the meaning. **3.** hesitation; delay. **4.** (*Music*) a sign (𝄐 or 𝄑) over or under a note showing that the note is to be prolonged.
—*vi.* **1.** make a pause; stop for a time. **2.** hesitate; linger. 《~ *on* or *upon* something》
—[名] 1. 휴지(休止), 중지 ¶①멈추다, 휴지하다 2. 구두(句讀), 단락(段落) 3. 망설임, 주저 4. 《樂》 연성(延聲) 기호
—[自] 1. 멈추다, 휴지하다; 잠시 멈추다 2. 망설이다, 머뭇거리다

* **pave** [peiv] *vt.* cover (a road, street, etc.) with stones, asphalt, etc.
pave the way for, prepare for (*something*); make (*something*) smooth or easy.
—[他] [도로]를 포장하다
[熟] …의 길을 열다; …을 용이하게 하다

* **pave·ment** [péivmənt] *n.* **1.** [U] the paved surface. **2.** [U] material used in paving. **3.** [C] (*Brit.*) a paved path for foot-passengers. (cf. *U.S.* sidewalk)
—[名] 1. 포장한 면 2. 포장용 재료 3. 《英》 보도(步道)

〔pavilion 1.〕

* **pa·vil·ion** [pəvíliən] *n.* [C] **1.** a large tent. ⇨fig. **2.** a light and usu. open building used for shelter, performances, etc. **3.** a part of a building higher and more decorated than the rest.
—[名] 1. 대형 천막 2. [연예장 따위의] 임시 건물; 오락장, 여흥관 3. 누각(樓閣), 정자(亭子)

pav·ing [péiviŋ] *n.* [U] pavement; material for pavement.
—[名] 포장(鋪裝); 포장용 재료

‡ **paw** [pɔː] *n.* [C] a soft foot of a four-footed animal. —*vt.* **1.** (of animals) touch roughly or beat (something) with the forepaw. **2.** (of persons) (*colloq.*) handle wildly.
—[名] [개·고양이 따위 네발짐승의] 발
—[他] 1. …을 앞발로 긁다(치다) 2. 《口》 …을 난폭하게(거칠게) 다루다

pawl [pɔːl] *n.* [C] a short iron bar on the teeth of a wheel to prevent the wheel from turning back.
—[名] 톱니 멈추개

pawn[1] [pɔːn] *vt.* leave (something valuable) in return for the right to borrow money. —*n.* **1.** [C] something left with a lender of money. **2.** [U] the state of something being pawned. ¶*in* ~.①
—[他] …을 전당잡히다 —[名] 1. 저당(전당)물 2. 저당, 전당; 담보 ¶①전당잡혀

pawn[2] [pɔːn] *n.* [C] **1.** the least valuable piece in the game of chess. **2.** an unimportant person used by others for their own purposes.
—[名] 1. [서양 장기의] 졸 2. [남의] 앞잡이

pawn·bro·ker [pɔ́ːnbròukər] *n.* [C] a person whose business is to lend money on goods left with him.
—[名] 전당업자

pawn·shop [pɔ́ːnʃɑ̀p / -ʃɔ̀p] *n.* [C] a pawnbroker's shop.
—[名] 전당포

pawn ticket [´ ˘-] *n.* a ticket for goods in pawn.
—[名] 전당표

‡ **pay** [pei] *v.* (**paid**) *vt.* **1.** give (someone) money in return for goods or services; give (money) in return for goods or services. ¶~ *him money;* ~ *money to him* / ~ *one's servant* / *You must* ~ *fifty cents to ride the bus.* / *He paid a dime for the ice cream.* **2.** give (someone) money owed or due; give back (a debt). ¶~ *one's debts* / ~ *a tax.* **3.** give or offer (a service, a visit, etc.). ¶~ *a visit to* (or *on*) *someone;* ~ *someone a visit* / ~ *attention to what she says.* **4.** return (someone or something) for favors or hurts; suffer (a penalty, etc.). ¶*He paid her insults in kindness.*① **5.** be profitable to (some-
—[他] 1. …에게 돈을 지불하다; [돈]을 치르다 2. [빚 따위]를 갚다, 청산하다 3. [방문 따위]를 하다; [경의 따위]를 표하다 4. …에 보답하다, 갚다; [벌]을 받다 ¶①그는 그녀의 모욕에 대해 친절로 보답했다 5. [남에게] 이익을 주다; …의 보상이 되다 ¶②농업은 수지가 맞지 않는다/③그 증권은 작년에 5%의 수익이 났다 —[自] 1. 지불하다; [빚 따위를] 갚다 2. [일 따위가] 돈이 벌리다; 수지가 맞다 ¶④그 사업은

P

payable

one); give (profit, interest, etc.). ¶*Farming does not ~ me.*① / *That stock paid 5% last year.*③ —*vi.* **1.** give money in return for goods or services; give what is owed. ¶*~ for a book.* **2.** (of business, etc.) be profitable. ¶*The business will not ~.*④ **3.** suffer a penalty; make up. (*~ for something*) ¶*You must ~ for your rudeness.*
1) ***pay away***, spend.
2) ***pay back***, ⓐ return borrowed money. ⓑ give the same treatment as received.
3) ***pay in***, put (money, etc.) into a bank, etc.
4) ***pay off***, ⓐ pay (a debt) completely. ⓑ give (someone) his wages and discharge (him).
5) ***pay out***, punish (someone) for what he has done.
6) ***pay up***, pay (a debt) completely or on time.
7) ***pay one's way***, live without borrowing money.
—*n.* Ⓤ the act of paying; money given for things or work; salary or wages. ¶*What is the ~ ?*②
in the pay of (=*working for and paid by*) *a company, etc.*
pay·a·ble [péiəbl] *adj.* that must or can be paid.
pay·day [péidèi] *n.* Ⓤ Ⓒ the day on which a salary is paid.
pay·ee [peií:] *n.* Ⓒ a person to whom money is paid or is to be paid.
pay·er [péiər] *n.* Ⓒ a person who pays or is to pay money.
pay·mas·ter [péimæstər / -mà:stə] *n.* Ⓒ a person whose job is to pay out pay.
pay·ment [péimənt] *n.* Ⓤ Ⓒ **1.** the act of paying. ¶*~ by installment*① / *~ in advance*② / *~ in part*③ / *~ in full*④ / *~ in kind.*⑤ **2.** the money or the amount of money paid. **3.** reward; punishment.
pay roll [⸌⸍] *n.* (*U.S.*) a list of employees and the salary of each; the total amount of their salaries.
pea [pi:] *n.* Ⓒ (pl. **peas** or **pease** [pi:z]) a plant of the bean family; the seed of this plant, used as food. ¶*as like as two peas*, exactly alike. 「*green peas.*①
‡**peace** [pi:s] *n.* Ⓤ **1.** freedom from war. ↔war **2.** an agreement to end war. **3.** ((usu. *the ~*)) the public order for keeping a quiet and safe state. ¶*a breach of the ~.*① **4.** a quiet state; calmness. 「*quiet state.*
1) *at peace*, free from war; living in harmony; in a
2) *break the peace*, cause civil disorder, etc.
3) *hold* (or *keep*) *one's peace*, keep silent.
4) *keep the peace*, obey the laws and avoid civil disorder. 「*again after a quarrel.*
5) *make one's peace with*, be friendly with someone
6) *make peace*, stop fighting and come to an agreement.
peace·a·ble [pí:səbl] *adj.* loving peace. 「*ment.*
‡**peace·ful** [pí:sf(u)l] *adj.* **1.** calm; quiet. ¶*a ~ death.* **2.** loving peace; free from war. ¶*~ uses of atomic energy.*① ▷**peace·ful·ness** [-nis] *n.*
peace·ful·ly [pí:sfuli] *adv.* in a peaceful manner.
peace·mak·er [pí:smèikər] *n.* Ⓒ a person who stops a fight.
peace·time [pí:stàim] *n.* Ⓤ the period free from war. ↔wartime ¶*in ~.*① —*adj.* of peacetime.
‡**peach** [pi:tʃ] *n.* **1.** Ⓒ a sweet, juicy fruit with a white or yellowish pink skin; the tree bearing this fruit. **2.** Ⓤ the color of a peach, usu. a soft, yellowish pink. —*adj.* yellowish-pink.
•**pea·cock** [pí:kùk / -kɔ̀k] *n.* Ⓒ (pl. **-cocks** or *collectively* **-cock**) a large bird with beautiful green, blue, and gold feathers. ↔peahen ¶*proud as a ~*① / *play the ~.*②
pea·fowl [pí:fàul] *n.* Ⓒ a peacock or peahen.
pea green [⸌⸍] *n.* a bright, light-green color.

pea green

수지가 맞지 않을 것이다 **3.** 벌을 받다, 보상하다

熟 1)[돈]을 쓰다 2)ⓐ빚을 갚다 ⓑ보답하다 3)[돈]을 은행에 불입하다 4)ⓐ[빚]을 모두 갚다,청산하다 ⓑ…에게 급료를 주어 해고하다 5)…에게 앙갚음하다 6)[빚 따위]를 모두 지불하다;기한대로 지불하다 7)빚지지 않고 살다

—图 지불; 임금, 급료, 봉급, 보수 ¶⑤ 보수는 얼마인가?
熟 …에 고용되어

—阙 지불해야 할; 지불할 수 있는
—图 봉급날, 지불일
—图 피(被)지불인, 영수인

—图 지불인

—图 경리부장, 회계과장; 재정관

—图 1. 지불; 납부, 불입 ¶①분할 지불/②선불(先拂)/③일부 지불/④전액 지불/⑤현물 지불, 물납(物納) 2. 지불금[액] **3.** 보수; 징계, 처벌
—图 〔美〕 급료지불 명부; 지불 급료 총액

—图 완두[콩]
¶①청완두(요리용)
熟 꼭같이 닮다
—图 **1.** 평화 **2.** 강화(講和), 강화 조약 **3.** 치안, 질서 ¶①치안 방해 **4.** 평온, 편안

熟 1)평화롭게;사이좋게; 안심하여 2)분쟁을 일으키다; 치안을 문란케 하다 3)침묵을 지키다 4)치안을 유지하다; 평화를 지키다 5)…과 화해하다 6)화목하다, 강화하다

—阙 평화를 애호하는
—阙 **1.** 평온한, 온화한;조용한 **2.** 평화를 애호하는;전쟁에서 떠난 ¶①원자력 평화이용
—阙 평화적으로; 평온하게
—图 조정자, 중재인

—图 평화시 ¶①평[화]시에 —阙 평화시의
—图 **1.** 복숭아;복숭아나무 **2.** 복숭아빛(노르스름한 핑크색) —阙 복숭아빛의

—图 공작[의 수컷] ¶①몹시 뽐내는, 우쭐대는/②뽐내다, 허세부리다

—图 공작(암·수컷의 총칭)
—图 황록색

pea·hen [píːhèn] *n.* ⓒ a female peafowl. ──명 공작의 암컷

:peak¹ [piːk] *n.* ⓒ **1.** the top of a mountain or hill. **2.** the highest point of development, activity, etc. ¶*the ~ hour of traffic volume.*① **3.** a pointed end. ¶*the ~ of a knife.*② **4.** (of a cap) the front part over the eyes. ──명 **1.** 산꼭대기, 정상 **2.** 최고점 ¶① 교통량의 최고 시점(時點) **3.** [뾰족한] 끝, 첨단 ¶②나이프의 끝 **4.** [모자의] 챙

peak² [piːk] *vi.* (of a person or an animal) grow thin and weak. ──자 야위다, 수척해지다

peaked¹ [piːkt, +*U.S.* -kid] *adj.* having a peak. ──형 뾰족한; 챙이 있는

peak·ed² [píːkid / piːkt] *adj.* thin, pale and weak-looking. ──형 수척해진, 야윈

* **peal** [piːl] *n.* ⓒ **1.** a loud sound of gunfire, etc. ¶*a ~ of thunder.*① **2.** a set of tuned bells; the harmony of these bells. ¶*in ~.*② ──*vi.* ring loudly. ──*vt.* cause (a bell, etc.) to ring loudly. ──명 **1.** [대포 소리 따위의] 울림, 굉음 ¶①천둥소리, 뇌성 **2.** [음악적으로 배열한] 한 벌의 종; 그 화음 ¶②가락을 맞추어 ──자 울려 퍼지다 ──타 ⋯을 울려 퍼지게 하다

pean [píːən] *n.* =paean.

pea·nut [píːnʌt] *n.* ⓒ a nut-like seed in a hard shell. ──명 땅콩, 낙화생

* **pear** [pɛər] *n.* ⓒ a yellowish, juicy fruit, usu. narrower at the upper part; the tree bearing this fruit. ──명 서양배; 서양배나무

:pearl [pəːrl] *n.* ⓒ **1.** a round, bright, white jewel found in a certain shellfish. ¶*a cultured ~*① / *an artificial ~.*② **2.** something like a pearl, such as a tear. **3.** a valuable thing; a very fine example of a class. **4.** ⓤ the color of a pearl. **5.** ⓤ the shiny inside of a certain shellfish containing a pearl; a mother-of-pearl. ──*adj.* of, like, or having pearls. ──명 **1.** 진주 ¶①양식(養殖) 진주 ¶②인조(모조) 진주 **2.** 진주 모양의 것 **3.** 귀중한 것; 전형(典型), 정수(精粹) **4.** 진주빛 **5.** 진주층 ──형 진주[빛]의(같은)

pearl oyster [⌐ ⌐⌐] *n.* a kind of shellfish which produces pearls. ──명 진주조개

pearl·y [pə́ːrli] *adj.* (**pearl·i·er, pearl·i·est**) of or like a pearl; decorated with pearls. ──형 진주의(같은); 진주로 장식한

peas·ant [péz(ə)nt] *n.* ⓒ in Europe, a poor farmer or farm laborer. ──*adj.* of peasants. ⇒ N.B. ──명 농부, 소(小)자작농 ──형 소작농의 N.B. peasant 는 없음

peas·ant·ry [péz(ə)ntri] *n.* ⓤ (usu. *the ~*) (collectively, used as *pl.*) peasants. ──명 소작농·소작인 계급

pea·shoot·er [píːʃùːtər] *n.* ⓒ a toy consisting of a tube through which dried peas can be shot. ──명 장난감 콩알총

pea soup [⌐ ⌐] *n.* a thick soup made from dried peas. ──명 완두로 만든 진한 수우프

pea-soup·er [píːsùːpər] *n.* ⓒ (*colloq.*) a thick, yellow fog, esp. in London. ──명 [런던의] 노란 짙은 안개

peat [piːt] *n.* ⓤ a coal-like mass made of decayed plants used for burning. ──명 이탄(泥炭); 이탄 덩어리

peb·ble [pébl] *n.* ⓒ a small, round stone worn smooth by water. ──*vt.* cover (a path, etc.) with small stones. ──명 [물의 작용으로 동그스름해진] 조약돌, 자갈 ──타 ⋯에 자갈을 ⋯을 덮다

peb·bly [pébli] *adj.* having many pebbles; covered with pebbles. ──형 자갈이 많은, 자갈투성이의

pec·ca·ble [pékəbl] *adj.* tending to sin easily. ──형 죄를 범하기 쉬운

peck¹ [pek] *n.* ⓒ **1.** a measure for grain equal to 2 gallons. **2.** a lot. ¶*a ~ of worries.* ──명 **1.** 펙(약 9 리터) **2.** 다량, 많음

* **peck**² [pek] *vt.* **1.** (of a bird) strike or pick up (something) with the beak. **2.** make (a hole) with the beak or a pointed tool. **3.** (*colloq.*) eat bit by bit. ──*vi.* (of a bird) strike or pick up food with the beak. ──*n.* ⓒ **1.** an act of pecking. **2.** a hole or mark made by the act of pecking. ──타 **1.** ⋯을 부리로 쪼다, 쪼아먹다 **2.** ⋯을 쪼아 헤집다(파다) **3.** 조금씩 먹다 ──자 부리로 쪼다, 쪼아 먹다 ──명 **1.** 쪼기 **2.** 쪼아 파서 생긴 구멍

pec·to·ral [péktər(ə)l] *adj.* of or put on the breast or chest. ──형 가슴의; 가슴에 다는

:pe·cu·li·ar [pikjúːliər] *adj.* **1.** belonging to one special person, thing or place; individual; special. (*~ to*) ¶*There are expressions ~ to American English.*① **2.** strange; unusual. ¶*~ ways.*② ──*n.* ⓒ something belonging to one only. ──형 **1.** 독특한; 고유의; 특별한 ¶①미국식 영어에는 독특한 표현이 있다 %. 기묘한, 별난 ¶②별난 풍습 ──명 사유재산

pe·cu·li·ar·i·ty [pikjùːliǽriti] *n.* (pl. **-ties**) **1.** ⓤ the state of being special or strange. **2.** ⓒ a special qualtiy; an odd quality. ──명 **1.** 독특함, 기묘함, 특색, 특성 **2.** 버릇, 기이한 습관, 별남

pe·cu·li·ar·ly [pikjúːliərli] *adv.* personally; especially; oddly. ──부 개인적으로; 특히, 각별히; 기묘하게

pe·cu·ni·ar·y [pikjúːnièri / -niəri] *adj.* of or concerned with money. ──형 금전[상]의

ped·a·gog·ic [pèdəgádʒik / -gɔ́dʒ-], **-i·cal** [-ik(ə)l] *adj.* of teachers or teaching; of pedagogy. ──형 교육자의; 교수법의; 교육[학]의

ped·a·gogue [pédəgàg / -gɔ̀g] *n.* ⓒ a teacher. ──명 교사, 선생

ped·a·go·gy [pédəgòudʒi, -gà- / -gɔ̀dʒi, -gi] *n.* [U] the science or art of teaching.
—[名] 교육학; 교수법

ped·al [pédl → *adj.*] *n.* [C] (of a bicycle, an organ, etc.) a device operated by the foot. —*vt., vi.* (**-aled, -al·ing** or *Brit.* **-alled, -al·ling**) move or operate by a pedal or pedals; use the pedals of (something). —*adj.* [pédl, +*Brit.* pí:dl] **1.** of the foot or feet. **2.** of or operated by a pedal or pedals.
—[名] 페달, 발판 —[他][自] 페달을 밟아 움직이다; …의 페달을 밟다 —[形] 1. 발의 2. 페달의, 발판의

ped·ant [péd(ə)nt] *n.* [C] a person, esp. a teacher, who shows off his knowledge more than is necessary.
—[名] 학자 티를 내는 사람, 현학자(衒學者)

pe·dan·tic [pidǽntik] *adj.* showing off one's knowledge more than is necessary.
—[形] 학자 티를 내는; 아는 체하는

ped·ant·ry [péd(ə)ntri] *n.* [U][C] (pl. **-ries**) the act of showing off one's knowledge.
—[名] 학자 티를 내기, 현학(衒學)

ped·dle [pédl] *vi.* go from place to place selling small articles. —*vt.* **1.** carry (something) from place to place in order to sell them. **2.** sell (something) little by little.
—[自] 행상(行商)하다, 도부치다 —[他] 1. …을 행상하다(도부치다) 2. …을 소매하다, 산매하다

ped·dler, ped·lar [pédlər] *n.* [C] a person who peddles.
—[名] 행상인, 도부장수

ped·es·tal [pédistl] *n.* [C] **1.** a base on which a statue stands. **2.** a base or foundation for various things.
put (or ***set***) ***someone on a pedestal,*** think someone with great admiration.
—[名] 1. [흉상(胸像)의] 받침, 대좌(臺座); 주각(柱脚) 2. 기초, 근거
[熟] …을 존경하다

* **pe·des·tri·an** [pidéstriən] *n.* [C] a person who is walking. —*adj.* **1.** going on foot; walking. **2.** (of writing, etc.) without imagination; dull.
—[名] 보행자, 도보 여행자 —[形] 1. 도보의, 보행의 2. [문체 따위가] 평범한; 단조로운, 재미없는

pe·di·a·tri·cian [pì:diətríʃ(ə)n, +*U.S.* pèd-] *n.* [C] a doctor who specializes in pediatrics.
—[名] 소아과 의사

pe·di·at·rics [pì:diǽtriks, +*U.S.* pèd-] *n. pl.* ((used as *sing.*)) the branch of medicine dealing with children's diseases.
—[名] 소아과학

ped·i·gree [pédigrì:] *n.* [C] a list showing the line of a family; [C][U] the line of a family.
—[名] 족보, 계도(系圖); 가계(家系)

ped·i·greed [pédigrì:d] *adj.* having a good or famous pedigree.
—[形] 가문이 좋은, 혈통이 분명한

ped·i·ment [pédimənt] *n.* [C] a triangular part at the top of a house. ⇒fig.
—[名] 박공, 박공벽

[pediment]

ped·lar [pédiər] *n.* =peddler.

peek [pi:k] *vi.* look quickly and secretly. —*n.* [C] a quick, secret look.
—[自] [슬쩍] 엿보다 —[名] 엿보기

* **peel** [pi:l] *n.* [U] the outer skin of fruit. —*vt.* **1.** take the skin off (fruit, etc.). ¶~ *an orange.* **2.** strip off. ¶~ *the bark from trees.* —*vi.* come off; become bare. ¶*The wallpaper is peeling* [*off*].① / *He got sunburnt and his face peeled.*
—[名] 과일의 껍질 —[他] 1. [과일]의 껍질을 벗기다 2. [나무껍질 따위]를 벗기다 —[自] 벗겨져 떨어지다; 탈피하다 ¶①벽지가 벗겨져 떨어지고 있다

* **peep**¹ [pi:p] *vi.* **1.** look through a small or narrow opening; look secretly. ¶~ *at someone through the keyhole* / ~ *over a wall.*① **2.** come slowly or partly into view. ¶*The stars were beginning to* ~ [*out*].
—[自] 1. 엿보다; 몰래 보다, 훔쳐보다 ¶①담 위로 엿보다 2. 점점 보이다, 차차 나타나다

—*n.* [C] **1.** an act of peeping. ¶*take a* ~ *at something.*② **2.** the first appearance. ¶*at the* ~ *of day.*③ **3.** [C] a small hole to look through.
—[名] 1. 엿보기, 몰래 들여다보기 ¶②…을 슬쩍 보다 2. 나타나기 시작하기, 출현 ¶③새벽에 3. 들여다보는 구멍(틈)

peep² [pi:p] *n.* [C] a sound made by a young bird, a mouse, etc. —*vi.* **1.** make a peep. **2.** speak in a weak voice.
—[名] 짹짹, 삐악삐악; 찍찍
—[自] 1. 짹짹(찍찍) 울다 2. 작은 목소리로 말하다

peep·er [pí:pər] *n.* [C] a person who looks secretly.
—[名] 엿보는(들여다보는) 사람

peep·hole [pí:phòul] *n.* [C] a hole through which a person can peep.
—[名] 들여다보는 구멍

⁑ **peer**¹ [piər] *n.* [C] **1.** a person of the same rank; an equal. ¶*without a* ~.① **2.** (*Brit.*) a person who has a title, such as a duke, a marquis, etc.; a nobleman.
—[名] 1. 동료, 동배; 동등한 사람 ¶①비길 데 없는 2. ((英)) 귀족

⁑ **peer**² [piər] *vi.* **1.** look closely; peep. ¶~ *into a person's face.* **2.** appear slightly; come into sight.
—[自] 1. 응시하다; 자세히 들여다보다 2. 나타나다; 보이기 시작하다

peer·age [píəridʒ] *n.* **1.** ((*collectively*)) the whole body
—[名] 1. 귀족, 귀족 계급 2. 귀족의 지위

of peers. **2.** ⓒ the rank of a peer. **3.** ⓒ a book giving a list of the peers of a country.
peer·ess [píəris] *n.* ⓒ **1.** the wife of a peer. **2.** a woman having the rank of peer in her own right.
peer·less [píərlis] *adj.* without equal; matchless.
pee·vish [píːviʃ] *adj.* hard to please; irritable; complaining.
pee·vish·ly [píːviʃli] *adv.* in a peevish manner.
pee·vish·ness [píːviʃnis] *n.* Ⓤ the state of being peevish.
* **peg** [peg] *n.* ⓒ **1.** a short piece of wood, metal, etc. used to fasten something or to hang something on; a small bolt. ¶*hat pegs.*① **2.** a stick used to hold the ropes of a tent; a piece of wood used to fill a hole in a cask, etc. ¶*tent pegs.*② **3.** (*Brit.*) a clothes-pin. **4.** an excuse. ¶*a ~ to hung a claim on.*③
1) *a square peg in a round hole*; *a round peg in a square hole*, a person not fitted to his work or position.
2) *off the peg*, (of clothes) ready-made.
3) *take someone down a peg* [*or two*], make someone humble; humiliate.
— *v.* (**pegged, peg·ging**) *vt.* **1.** put a peg into (something); hold (something) with a peg. **2.** fix or maintain (prices, etc.) at a certain level. ¶*~ the price of beer at 180 yen.* —*vi.* work hard and diligently. (*~ away at a task, etc.*) ¶*~ away at English*
Peg·a·sus [pégəsəs] *n.* **1.** (in Greek mythology) the winged horse of the Muses. ⇒fig. **2.** Ⓤ poetic genius; poetic inspiration.
peg top [≤ ≤] *n.* **1.** a pear-shaped wooden top. **2.** (*pl.*) trousers wide at the hips and narrowing to the ankle; peg top trousers.
Pe·king [píːkíŋ] *n.* the capital of Communist China.

[Pegasus 1.]

pe·lag·ic [peláedʒik] *adj.* of the ocean or the open sea.
pelf [pelf] *n.* Ⓤ money; riches. ⇒USAGE
pel·i·can [pélikən] *n.* ⓒ a large waterbird with a baglike part under its huge bill.
pel·let [pélit] *n.* ⓒ **1.** a little ball of mud, paper, medicine, etc. **2.** a small lead bullet for a gun; a bullet.
pell-mell, pell mell [pélmél] *adv.* in a disorderly manner; quickly. —*adj.* disorderly; headlong. —*n.* ⓒ Ⓤ disorder; hurry and confusion.
pel·lu·cid [pelúːsid, +*Brit.* -ljúː-] *adj.* **1.** very clear, like water. **2.** easy to understand; expressed clearly.
pelt¹ [pelt] *vt.* throw (something) at (something or someone); throw (objects) continuously. ¶*~ a boy with snowballs.* —*vi.* beat or strike heavily. ¶*The rain is pelting.* —*n.* Ⓤ **1.** the act of pelting. **2.** speed. ¶*at full ~*
pelt² [pelt] *n.* Ⓤ the skin of a sheep, goat, etc. with the wool or hair left on; rawhide.
pel·ves [pélviːz] *n.* pl. of **pelvis**.
pel·vis [pélvis] *n.* ⓒ (pl. **-vis·es** or **-ves**) the basinshaped hollow made by the end of the backbone and the hip bone.
pem·mi·can, pem·i- [pémikən] *n.* Ⓤ dried meat beaten and mixed into cakes.
pen¹ [pen] *n.* ⓒ **1.** an instrument used for writing with ink. ¶*a fountain ~*① / *~ and ink.* **2.** style of writing; writing. ¶*He lives by the ~.*② / *The ~ is mightier than the sword.*③ —*vt.* (**penned, pen·ning**) write.
pen² [pen] *n.* ⓒ a small enclosed place, esp. for sheep,

3. 귀족 명감(名鑑)

—名 1 귀족 부인 2. 부인 귀족

—形 비길 데 없는, 무비의
—形 괴팍한; 성마른; 불평이 많은, 투정하는
—副 괴팍하게, 토라져서
—名 괴팍함, 성마름
—名 1. [나무·쇠 따위로 만든] 대못, 쐐기 ¶①모자걸이 못 2. [천막 따위의] 말뚝; [술통 따위의] 마개 ¶②천막 말뚝 3. (英) 빨래 집게 4. 구실, 핑계 ¶③요구를 내걸 계기

熟 1) [일·지위 따위에서] 부적임자(不適任者) 2) [양복 따위가] 기성품의 3)…을 마구 해대다, 창피를 주다

—他 1. …에 나무못을 박다; …을 나무못으로 죄다 2. [가격 따위]를 안정시키다, 시세를 고정시키다 —自 부지런히 일하다 ¶④부지런히 영어를 공부하다
—名 1. 시신(詩神) 뮤우즈가 타는 날개 돋친 말, 페가수스, 천마(天馬) 2. 시재(詩才); 시적 감흥

—名 1. 배 모양의 나무 팽이 2. 팽이 모양의 바지

—名 북경(중공의 수도)

—形 원양(遠洋)의
—名 금전 USAGE 경멸적으로 쓰는 말
—名 펠리칸
—名 1. [진흙·종이 따위를 둥글게 뭉친] 작은 공; 작은 알약 2. 작은 총알
—副 난잡하게, 뒤죽박죽으로
—形 혼란한, 뒤죽박죽의; 무모한
—名 난잡; 뒤범벅, 뒤새통
—形 1. 투명한; 맑은 2. 명백한; 명석한

—他 …에게 물건을 던지다; …을 연방 던지다 —自 [비가] 억수같이 퍼붓다 —名 1. 던지기, 타격; 억수같이 쏟아지기 2. 속도; 속력

—名 생가죽; 모피

—名 골반(骨盤)

「은 식품)
—名 페미칸(말린 고기를 케이크에 섞)
—名 1. 펜 ¶①만년필 2. 문체; 문필 ¶②그는 문필로 생계를 꾸려 나가고 있다/③문(文)은 무(武)보다 강하다
—他 …을 쓰다
—名 [가축 따위의] 울, 우리

penal [842] **penitently**

pigs, cows, etc. —*vt.* (**penned** or **pent, pen·ning**) shut up (cattle, etc.) in a pen; enclose. ―囲 [가축 따위]를 우리에 넣다; 가두다, 감금하다

pe·nal [pí:nəl] *adj.* of punishment or a punished person. ¶*the ~ code*① / *a ~ offense*② / *~ servitude.*③ ―형 형벌의,형의 ¶①형법/②형사범죄/③징역형

pe·nal·ize, -ise [pí:nəlàiz, +*U.S.* pénəl-] *vt.* 1. declare (an action, etc.) punishable by law or rule; punish. 2. give a penalty to (a player, etc.). ―타 1. …을 유죄라고 선고하다; 벌하다 2. …에게 벌을 주다

* **pen·al·ty** [pén(ə)lti] *n.* (pl. **-ties**) 1. ⓤⓒ a punishment. ¶*the death ~*① / *It is forbidden under ~ of death.*② / *pay the ~.*③ 2. ⓒ a fine. 3. ⓒ (in sport) a disadvantage to which a player or team must submit for breaking a rule. ―명 1. 형벌 ¶①사형/②그 금지를 어기면 사형된다/③벌을 받다 2. 벌금 3. 반칙에 대한 벌;벌점

pe·nance [pénəns] *n.* ⓤ punishment which one imposes upon oneself for sin, esp. at a priest's direction. ―명 죄갚음,고행(苦行)

pen-and-ink [pénən(d)íŋk] *adj.* drawn with pen and ink. ―형 펜으로 쓴

* **pence** [pens] *n.* (*Brit.*) pl. of **penny**.

‡ **pen·cil** [pénsl] *n.* ⓒ a pointed instrument for writing or drawing. —*vt.* (**-ciled, -cil·ing** or *Brit.* **-cilled, -cil·ling**) write or draw (something) with a pencil. ―명 연필 ―타 …을 연필로 쓰다

pencil case [⌢ ⌣] *n.* a case for pencils. ―명 필통

pend·ant [péndənt] *n.* ⓒ 1. an ornament hanging from a necklace or bracelet. 2. an ornament hanging down from a ceiling or roof. —*adj.* =pendent. ―명 1.[목걸이·귀고리 따위의] 늘어뜨린 장식 2.[천장·지붕에서] 늘어뜨린 장식

pend·ent [péndənt] *adj.* 1. hanging; overhanging. 2. undecided; pending. —*n.* =pendant. ―형 1. 드리운, 매달린; 튀어나온 2. 미결[정]의, 계류중인

pend·ing [péndiŋ] *adj.* not yet decided or settled. ¶*a ~ question.*① —*prep.* 1. during. ¶*~ investigation.*② 2. until. ¶*~ his arrival.*③ ―형 미결[정]의,계류중인 ¶①현안문제 의 1. …중에 ¶②조사중에 2. …까지 ¶③그가 도착할 때까지

pen·du·lous [péndʒuləs / -dju-] *adj.* hanging loosely; swinging. ―형 대롱대롱하는; 흔들리는

pen·du·lum [péndʒuləm /-dju-] *n.* ⓒ a body hung from a point, swinging to and fro. ing penetrable. ―명 [시계 따위의] 추,진자(振子)

pen·e·tra·bil·i·ty [pènitrəbíliti] *n.* ⓤ the quality of be- ―명 침투(관통)가능, 투철성

pen·e·tra·ble [pénitrəbl] *adj.* that can be penetrated. ―형 투입(관통) 가능한;간파할 수 있

* **pen·e·trate** [pénitrèit] *vt.* 1. enter into; pierce. ¶*Its sharp claws penetrated the skin.* 2. spread through; soak through. ¶*Her clothes are penetrated with a sweet smell.* 3. see through or into; understand. ¶*We soon penetrated his disguise.*① —*vi.* pierce; affect the feelings or mind deeply. (~ *into* or *through* something) ―타 1. …을 꿰뚫다;관통하다 2. …에 침투하다, 스며(배어)들다 3. …을 꿰뚫어보다;간파하다 ¶①우리는 금방 그의 변장을 간파하였다 ―자 통하다;침투하다;스며(배어)들다

pen·e·trat·ing [pénitrèitiŋ] *adj.* sharp; piercing; keen; understanding thoroughly. ―형 침투하는; 통찰력이 날카로운; 날카로운; 꿰뚫어 보는

pen·e·tra·tion [pènitréiʃ(ə)n] *n.* ⓤ 1. the act or power of penetrating. 2. sharpness of mind; insight. ―명 침투; 투입(透入); 투철력 2. 통찰력

pen·e·tra·tive [pénitrèitiv, +*Brit.* -trə-] *adj.* able to penetrate; piercing. South Pole. ―형 침투하는;예민한; 통찰력이 있는

pen·guin [péŋgwin] *n.* ⓒ a seabird found around the ―명 펭귄

pen·hold·er [pénhòuld(ə)r] *n.* ⓒ 1. a handle by which a pen point is held in writing. 2. a rack for pens. ―명 1. 펜대 2. 필가(筆架)

pen·i·cil·lin [pènisílin] *n.* ⓤ a very powerful drug for destroying bacteria. ―명 페니실린

* **pen·in·su·la** [pinínsjulə] *n.* ⓒ a long strip of land almost surrounded by water. ―명 반도

pen·in·su·lar [pinínsjulər] *adj.* of or like a peninsula. ―형 반도[모양]의

pen·i·tence [pénit(ə)ns] *n.* ⓤ regret for sin or wrongdoing; repentance. ―명 후회; 참회

pen·i·tent [pénitənt] *adj.* showing penitence. —*n.* ⓒ a person who is sorry for his sin or wrongdoing. ―형 후회하고 있는; 참회한 ―명 회개자,참회자.

pen·i·ten·tial [pènitén∫(ə)l] *adj.* of or showing penitence or penance. ―형 회개의,회오의;참회의; 징벌의

pen·i·ten·tia·ry [pènitén∫əri] *n.* ⓒ (pl. **-ries**) (*U.S.*)·a prison, esp. a state or federal prison. —*adj.* 1. of or for penance or punishment. 2. (*U.S.*) making a person liable to punishment. ―명 (美) 교도소,형무소 ―형 1. 후회의; 징벌의 2. [그것을 어기면] 징벌을 받는

pen·i·tent·ly [pénit(ə)ntli] *adv.* in a penitent manner. ―부 회개하여,회오하여

penknife [843] people

pen·knife [pénnàif] *n.* ⓒ (pl. **-knives**) a small pocket-knife.
pen·knives [pénnàivz] *n.* pl. of **penknife**.
—⒨ 주머니칼

pen·man [pénmən] *n.* ⓒ (pl. **-men** [-mən]) **1.** a writer; an author. **2.** a person skilled in handwriting.
—⒨ 1. 작가, 문인 2. 글씨를 잘 쓰는 사람, 서예가, 서가(書家)

pen·man·ship [pénmənʃìp] *n.* Ⓤ the art, style or practice of handwriting.
—⒨ 서도, 서법(書法), 습자

pen name [´ ´] *n.* a name used by an author instead of his real name.
—⒨ 필명, 아호(雅號), 펜네임

pen·nant [pénənt] *n.* ⓒ **1.** a long, narrow, triangular flag used on ships, etc. **2.** a flag given to a champion team in a sport, esp. baseball. ¶*win the* ~.①
—⒨ 1. [삼각형의] 장기(長旗) 2. 페넌트, 우승기 ¶①우승하다

pen·ni·less [pénilis] *adj.* without a penny; very poor.
—⒧ 무일푼의, 찢어지게 가난한

pen·non [pénən] *n.* ⓒ **1.** a long, triangular flag borne on a lance. **2.** a flag or banner.
—⒨ 1. 창기(槍旗) 2. 기

penn'orth [pénərθ] *n.* =pennyworth.

Penn·syl·va·ni·a [pènsilvéiniə] *n.* an eastern State of the United States. ⇒N.B.
—⒨ 미국 동부의 주 N.B. Pa., Penn., Penna.로 줄여 씀. 수도는 Harrisburg

‡**pen·ny** [péni] *n.* ⓒ (pl. **-nies** or collectively **pence**) **1.** a British bronze coin equal to one-twelfth of a shilling. ¶*There are four pennies.* | *It cost four pence.* | (*proverb*) *A ~ saved is a ~ gained.*① **2.** (U.S., Can.) a cent.
—⒨ 1. 페니(영국의 청동화로서 1/100 파운드. 예전에는 1/12실링, 1/240파운드) ¶①(俚)한 푼을 절약하면 한 푼을 번다 2. (美·캐나다) 센트

pen·ny-wise [péniwàiz] *adj.* economical over small sums. ¶(*proverb*) *Penny-wise and pound-foolish.*①
—⒧ 한 푼을 아끼는 ¶①(俚)한 푼을 아끼다가 천 냥을 잃기; 싼 게 비지떡

pen·ny·worth [péniwə̀:rθ / pénəθ, péniwə̀:θ] *n.* ⓒ the amount which can be bought for a penny; a small amount. ¶*a ~ of salt* | *a ~ of advice.*①
—⒨ 1페니로 살 수 있는 분량; 소액 ¶①자그마한 충고

*__pen·sion__¹ [pénʃ(ə)n] *n.* ⓒ a regular payment to a person who has ceased active work because of illness, injury, old age, etc. ¶*retire on a* ~① | *draw one's* ~.②
—*vt.* give a pension to (someone).
—⒨ 연금, 은급, 부조금, 양로 연금 ¶①연금을 받고 퇴직하다/②연금을 받다
—⒨ …에게 연금을 주다

pen·sion² [pá:nsiən / pá:ŋsjɔ:ŋ] *n.* ⓒ a boarding house or boarding school in France and other Continental countries. [pension.]
—⒨ 하숙; 기숙 학교

pen·sion·er [pénʃ(ə)nər] *n.* ⓒ a person who receives a pension.
—⒨ 연금(은급) 수령자

pen·sive [pénsiv] *adj.* engaged in serious thought; thoughtful; melancholy.
—⒧ 깊은 생각에 잠긴; 명상에 잠긴, 수심에 잠긴

pent [pent] *v.* pt. and pp. of **pen.**²
—*adj.* shut up; kept in.
—⒧ 갇힌, 유폐된

pen·ta·gon [péntəgàn / -gən] *n.* **1.** ⓒ a figure having five sides and five angles. **2.** (*the P-*) the building in Arlington, Virginia, in which the Department of Defense of the United States. [in English verse.]
—⒨ 1. 5변형; 5각형; 5능보(稜堡) 2. 미국 국방성의 건물

pen·tam·e·ter [pentǽmitər] *n.* ⓒ a line with five feet
—⒨ 5운각(韻脚), 5보격(步格)

pen·tath·lon [pentǽθlən / -lɔn] *n.* ⓒ an athletic contest in which each competitor participates in five events.
—⒨ 5종 경기

Pen·te·cost [péntikɔ̀:st, -kɑ̀st / -kɔ̀st] *n.* **1.** the Jewish harvest festival, the fiftieth day after the Passover. **2.** Whitsunday; the seventh Sunday after Easter.
—⒨ 1. 유월절 후 50일째에 행하는 유대인의 축제 2. 성령 강림절

pent·house [pénthàus] *n.* ⓒ **1.** a small house with a sloping roof projecting from a building; the projecting part of a sloping roof. **2.** an apartment or a small house built on the top of a building.
—⒨ 1. 다른 건물 벽 위에 비스듬히 걸쳐 이은 결채; 그렇게 이은 지붕 2. 옥상 가옥

pe·num·bra [pinʌ́mbrə] *n.* ⓒ (pl. **-brae** or **-bras**) (*Astronomy*) a partially shadowed area around the complete shadow during an eclipse.
—⒨ 《天文》 반음영(半陰影), 반영(半影)

pe·num·brae [pinʌ́mbri:] *n.* pl. of **penumbra**.

pe·nu·ri·ous [pin(j)úəriəs / -njúəri-] *adj.* poor; scanty.
—⒧ 가난한; 근소한; 인색한

pen·u·ry [pénjuri] *n.* Ⓤ extreme poverty; want. ⟪~ *of*⟫
—⒨ 가난; 궁핍; 결핍

pe·o·ny [pí:əni / píə-] *n.* ⓒ (pl. **-nies**) a garden plant bearing large, showy, many-petaled flowers; its flower. ¶*a tree* ~.①
—⒨ 작약(芍藥) ¶①모란

‡**peo·ple** [pí:pl] *n.* (pl. **peo·ple** or (for 1.) **-ples**) (used as *pl.*) **1.** ⓒ (chiefly *a* ~ or *peoples*, collectively) the members of a particular race or nation. ⇒USAGE ¶ *all the peoples of the world* | *The Japanese are a polite*
—⒨ 1. 국민, 민족 USAGE 단수 취급, 때로 구성원을 생각하여 복수 취급 2. 사람들; 세상 사람들 3. [한 지역·한 집단의] 사람들; 가족, 친척, 집안 사람들

~. 2. ⟪*collectively*⟫ persons; men, women, and children; persons in general. ¶*What will ~ say? / The streets were crowded with ~.* **3.** ⟪*collectively*⟫ persons living in a place or belonging to a group; ⟪*one's ~*⟫ one's family or relatives. ¶*village ~ / I want you to see my ~.* **4.** ⟪*the ~*⟫ persons of the lower classes. **5.** ⟪*one's ~* or *the ~*⟫ persons in relation to a ruler, etc.; one's subjects.
4. 평민; 인민 5. 종자(從者)들, 신하들, 부하들

—*vt.* fill (a place, etc.) with people; put people, animals, etc. in (a place, etc.). ¶*a thickly-peopled country.*
—[他] …을 사람들로 가득차게 하다; …에 사람·동물을 거주시키다

pep [pep] *n.* [U] (*U.S. colloq.*) spirit; energy.
—[名] ⟪美口⟫ 원기, 기력
—*vt.* (**pepped, pep·ping**) make (someone) energetic; encourage; stimulate. ⟪~ *up*⟫
—[他] …을 기운나게 하다, 기운을 북돋우다

• **pep·per** [pépər] *n.* **1.** [U] a seasoning with a hot taste, used for soup, meats, etc. **2.** [C] a plant bearing a somewhat hollow, spicy, green or red fruit; its fruit. ¶*green ~*① / *Chinese* (or *Japanese*) *~*② / *red ~.*③ —*vt.* **1.** season (food) with pepper. **2.** sprinkle thickly.
—[名] 1. 후추 2. 고추 ¶①사자 고추/②산초(山椒)/③고추 —[他] 1. [음식]을 후추로 양념하다 2. …을 흩뿌리다

pep·per-and-salt [pépər(ə)nsɔ́:lt] *adj.* having black and white finely mixed.
—[形] 희고 검은 점이 섞인

pepper castor (caster) [´-- ´-] *n.* a small container with holes, used for sprinkling pepper on food.
—[名] 후추병

pep·per·mint [pépərmìnt] *n.* [U] **1.** a strong-smelling plant. **2.** an oil made from this plant. **3.** [C] a candy flavored with this oil.
—[名] 1. 서양 박하 2. 박하유(油) 3. 박하사탕

pep·sin [pépsin] *n.* [U] a liquid produced in the stomach which helps to digest food; a medicine to help digestion.
—[名] 펩신, 위액소(胃液素); 소화제

⁝ **per** [pər, pə:r] *prep.* **1.** by means of; through. ¶*~ post.*① **2.** for each. ¶*interest ~ annum*② / *150 dollars ~ week.*③
—[前] 1. …에 의하여; …으로 ¶①우편으로 2. …에 대하여, …마다 ¶②연리(年利)/③주(週) 150 달러

per·ad·ven·ture [pə:rədvéntʃər] *adv.* (*archaic*) **1.** perhaps. **2.** by chance.
—[副] ⟪古⟫ 1. 아마 2. 우연히

per·am·bu·late [pərǽmbjulèit] *vt., vi.* walk through or about (a place, etc.); walk through and examine.
—[他][自] [··· 을] 배회하다; 순회하다; 답사하다

per·am·bu·la·tor [pərǽmbjulèitər] *n.* [C] **1.** a small, light carriage for a baby, pushed by hand. ⇒[N.B.] **2.** a person who perambulates.
—[名] 1. 유모차(乳母車) [N.B.] pram으로 줄여 씀 2. 순시자, 답사자

⁝ **per·ceive** [pərsí:v] *vt.* **1.** become aware of (someone or something) through the senses; notice. ⟪~ someone or something *do*; ~ someone or something *doing*⟫ ¶*~ a person approach.*① **2.** understand. ⟪~ *that...*⟫ ¶*I perceived that he would refuse.*②
—[他] 1. …을 지각(知覺)하다, 인지(認知)하다; …을 알아차리다 ¶①사람이 다가오는 것을 알아차리다 2. …을 이해하다 ¶②그가 거절하리라는 것을 알았다

⁝ **per·cent, per cent** [pərsént] *n.* [C] (pl. **-cent**) one of a hundred parts; percentage. ⇒[N.B.]
—[名] 퍼센트, 백분(百分) [N.B.] 기호 %; 약호 p.c., per.ct.

• **per·cent·age** [pərséntidʒ] *n.* [C] [U] the rate per hundred; a proportion.
—[名] 백분율, 퍼센트; 비율, 율

per·cep·ti·ble [pərséptibl] *adj.* that can be perceived through the senses.
—[形] 지각(인지)할 수 있는; 알아차릴 수 있는

per·cep·ti·bly [pərséptibli] *adv.* in a perceptible manner; to a perceptible degree.
—[副] 지각할 수 있을 만큼; 현저히

per·cep·tion [pərsépʃ(ə)n] *n.* [U] the act, faculty or power of perceiving. ¶*a man of keen ~.*①
—[名] 지각, 지각력 ¶①지각력이 예민한 사람

per·cep·tive [pərséptiv] *adj.* of perception; able to perceive.
—[形] 지각의; 감지(感知)할 수 있는

• **perch**[1] [pə:rtʃ] *n.* [C] **1.** a bar or branch on which a bird can rest. **2.** any high, secure place or position. **3.** a measure of length equal to 5 1/2 yards; a rod.
—[名] 1. 횃대 2. 높고 안전한 지위 3. 길이의 단위(5 야아드 반)

1) ***Come off your perch!,*** (*colloq.*) Don't be so proud!
2) ***hop the perch,*** die.
[熟] 1)⟪口⟫비싸게 굴지 마라 2)죽다

—*vi.* sit on a perch. —*vt.* place or set (something) on a perch.
—[自] [새가] 앉다, 횃대에 앉다 —[他] …을 앉히다; 놓다, 설치하다

perch[2] [pə:rtʃ] *n.* [C] (pl. **perch·es** or *collectively* **perch**) a kind of small fresh-water fish with sharp fins, used for food.
—[名] 농어류의 민물고기

per·chance [pərtʃǽns / pətʃɑ́:ns] *adv.* by chance; perhaps.
—[副] 우연히; 아마

per·co·late [pɔ́:rkəlèit] *vi.* pass through very small spaces; filter. —*vt.* cause (a liquid) to pass through small spaces; filter.
—[自] 거르다, 여과하다; 침투하다 —[他] …을 여과하다; 침투시키다

per·co·la·tor [pə́:rkəlèitər] *n.* ⓒ **1.** a thing that percolates. **2.** a coffee pot in which boiling water filters through ground coffee. ⇒fig.

per·cus·sion [pərkʌ́ʃ(ə)n] *n.* ⓤ the act of striking one thing against another violently. **2.** the shock, vibration or noise made by striking.

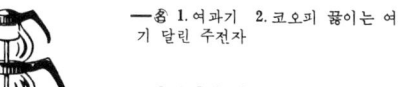

[percolator 2.]

Per·cy [pə́:rsi] *n.* a man's name.

per·di·tion [pə:rdíʃ(ə)n] *n.* ⓤ **1.** ruin; destruction. **2.** the loss of the soul or of hope for salvation; hell.

per·e·grine [périgrin, -grì:n], **-grin** [-grin] *adj.* foreign; (of birds) migratory. ——*n.* ⓒ a large, swift falcon.

per·emp·to·ry [pərém(p)tri] *adj.* **1.** allowing no denial or refusal. ¶*a ~ command.* **2.** (*Law*) final; absolute; decisive. **3.** dogmatic. ¶*a ~ attitude.*

per·en·ni·al [pəréniəl] *adj.* **1.** lasting throughout the whole year. **2.** lasting for a very long time. **3.** (of plants) living for a number of years.

per·en·ni·al·ly [pəréniəli] *adv.* in a perennial manner; [perpetually.]

‡ per·fect [pə́:rfikt] *adj.* **1.** complete; faultless. ¶*a ~ crime*① / *The set was ~.* / *His arithmetic paper was ~.* **2.** exact; accurate. ¶*a ~ square.* **3.** completely skilled; excellent. ¶*~ in the use of arms.*② **4.** entire; utter. ¶*a ~ fool / a ~ stranger.*③ **5.** (*Grammar*) of a tense showing an event or action completed at the time of the present, the past or the future. ¶*~ tenses.*
——*n.* ⓒ (*Grammar*) the perfect tense.
——*vt.* [pərfékt] make (something) perfect; improve (something) as far as possible. ¶*She worked to ~ her piano technique.* / *He perfected himself in English.*④

‡ per·fec·tion [pərfékʃ(ə)n] *n.* ⓤ **1.** the state of being perfect; completeness. **2.** the act of making something complete; completion. **3.** the highest excellence.

‡ per·fect·ly [pə́:rfiktli] *adv.* in a perfect manner; completely.

per·fid·i·ous [pə(:)rfídiəs] *adj.* faithless; treacherous.

per·fi·dy [pə́:rfidi] *n.* (pl. **-dies**) ⓤ the act of breaking faith; ⓒ a faithless or treacherous act.

per·fo·rate [pə́:rfərèit] *vt.* **1.** make a hole through (something). **2.** make a row of holes through (something) so that it can be torn off easily.

per·fo·ra·tion [pə̀:rfəréiʃ(ə)n] *n.* **1.** ⓤ the act of perforating; the state of being perforated. **2.** ⓒ a hole or a line of holes bored or punched through something.

per·force [pə(:)rfɔ́:rs] *adv.* by or through necessity; necessarily. ——*n.* ⓤ compulsion. ¶*by* (or *of*) *~.*①

‡ per·form [pərfɔ́:rm] *vt.* **1.** do; carry out. ¶*~ a duty / ~ a task.* **2.** act (a play, etc.); play (music). ——*vi.* act a part; exhibit skill in public.

‡ per·form·ance [pərfɔ́:rməns] *n.* **1.** ⓤ the act of performing. **2.** ⓒ a thing performed; an act; a deed. **3.** ⓒ a public exhibition; a play; a concert.

per·form·er [pərfɔ́:rmər] *n.* ⓒ a person who performs.

• per·fume *n.* [pə́:rfju:m, +*U.S.* -́- →*v.*] ⓤ **1.** a sweet smell. **2.** a liquid having the sweet smell of a flower. ——*vt.* [pə(:)rfjú:m, +*Brit.* pə́:fju:m] fill (something) with a pleasant smell; put a perfume on (something). ¶*~ oneself.*①

per·fum·er [pə(:)fjú:mər] *n.* ⓒ **1.** a person who makes or sells perfume. **2.** a person or thing that gives out a sweet smell.

per·fum·er·y [pə(:)rfjú:məri] *n.* (pl. **-er·ies**) **1.** ⓤ a perfume; (*collectively*) perfumes. **2.** ⓒ a place where

——名 1. 여과기 2. 커피 끓이는 여과기 달린 주전자

——名 1. 충격; 충돌 2. 진동; 격동; 음향

——名 남자 이름
——名 1. 파멸 2. 영원한 죽음; 지옥

——形 외국의; [새가] 이주하는 ——名 송골매

——形 1. 거절 못하게 하는, 이유를 불문하는, 단호한 2. 《法》 결정적인, 절대적인 3. 독단적인

——形 1. 사철 그치지 않는 2. 여러 해 계속되는 3. 《植》 다년생의

——副 다년간에 걸쳐; 끊임없이
——形 1. 완전한, 더할 나위 없는, 흠 없는 ¶①완전 범죄 2. 정확한 3. 아주 숙달한; 우수한 ¶②총기의 사용에 숙달한 4. 순전한, 순수한 ¶③전혀 생소한 사람 5. 《文法》 완료의

——名 《文法》 완료 시제(時制)
——他 …을 완성하다, 마무리하다; …을 숙달시키다 ¶④그는 영어에 숙달하였다

——名 1. 완전 2. 완성 3. 극치; 탁월

——副 완전히; 더할 나위 없이

——形 불성실한; 믿을 수 없는
——名 불실(不實), 불신; 불신 행위

——他 1. …에 구멍을 뚫다 2. …에 바늘구멍으로 점선을 내다

——名 1. 구멍 뚫기; 관통 2. 바늘 구멍(점선)

——副 어쩔 수 없이, 부득이 ——名 강제 ¶①강제로, 필연적으로
——他 1. …을 행하다; 실행하다; 다하다 2. …을 연기하다; 연주하다 ——名 [연극]을 공연하다

——名 1. 실행, 수행, 성취 2. 일; 행위 3. 공연; 연주; 흥행

——名 실행자; 배우; 연주자
——名 1. 방향, 향기 2. 향수
——他 …에 향기를 풍기다; 향수를 뿌리다(바르다) ¶향수를 뿌리다

——名 1. 향수 제조인; 향수 장수 2. 향기를 풍기는 사람(것)

——名 1. 향수; 향수류 2. 향수 제조소; 향수점(店)

perfumes are made or sold.

per·func·to·ri·ly [pə(:)fʌ́ŋkt(ə)rili] *adv.* in a perfunctory manner.
—[副] 형식대로, 기계적으로, 되는 대로

per·func·to·ry [pə(:)fʌ́ŋ(k)t(ə)ri] *adj.* done carelessly only as a form or routine; superficial; hasty.
—[形] 형식적인; 겉으로만의; 되는 대로의

per·go·la [pə́:rgələ] *n.* [C] a shady place formed by a trellis supported by posts.
—[名] 정자; 덩굴 시렁, 퍼골러

‡per·haps [pərhǽps, p(ə)rǽps] *adv.* possibly; maybe.
—[副] 아마, 혹시, 어쩌면

per·i·carp [périkɑ̀:rp] *n.* [C] the covering of fruit.
—[名] 과피(果皮)

***per·il** [péril] *n.* [U] very great danger; risk. ¶*at one's ~.*① —*vt.* (**-iled, -il·ing** or *Brit.* **-illed, -il·ling**) put (something) in danger.
—[名] 위험, 위난; 모험 ¶①위험을 무릅쓰고 —[他] …을 위험하게 하다

per·il·ous [périləs] *adj.* dangerous; risky. ▷**per·il·ous·ly** [-li] *adv.*
—[形] 위험한; 모험적인

pe·rim·e·ter [pərímitər] *n.* [C] **1.** the outer boundary of a figure. **2.** the length of this line.
—[名] 1. 둘레, 주위; 주변 2. 주위의 길이

‡pe·ri·od [píəriəd] *n.* [C] **1.** a certain length of time; the time after which the same things begin to happen again. ¶*the growing ~*① / *for a short ~ of time.*② **2.** a certain number of years in history, a civilization, etc.; an era. ¶*the Caesarian ~.* / *Men will enter a more brilliant ~ in the 21st century.*③ **3.** a mark (.) at the end of a sentence; a full stop. **4.** one of the parts of time into which a school day is divided. ¶*We have four periods on Saturday.*④ **5.** ((*the* ~)) the present day or time. ¶*young men of the ~.*⑤ **6.** end. ¶*put a ~ to.*⑥
—[名] 1. [일정한] 기간; 주기(周期) ¶①성장기/②잠시동안 2. 시대 ¶③인류는 21 세기에 한층 찬란한 시대로 접어들 것이다 3. 종지부(점) 4. 수업시간 ¶④토요일에는 네 시간이 들어있다 5. 현대 ¶⑤현대의 젊은이들 6. 종결, 종말 ¶⑥…을 끝마치다

pe·ri·od·ic [pìəriɑ́dik / -riɔ́d-] *adj.* **1.** occurring at regular intervals. ¶*a ~ wind.*① **2.** occurring occasionally. **3.** of a time in history.
—[形] 1. 주기적인, 정기의 ¶①계절풍 2. 단속적(斷續的)인, 간헐적인 3. 시대의

pe·ri·od·i·cal [pìəriɑ́dik(ə)l / -riɔ́di-] *adj.* **1.** occurring at intervals. **2.** published at regular intervals. —*n.* [C] a magazine published at regular intervals.
—[形] 1. 주기적인 2. 정기 간행의 —[名] 정기 간행물, 잡지

pe·ri·od·i·cal·ly [pìəriɑ́dikəli / -riɔ́di-] *adv.* at regular intervals; from time to time.
—[副] 정기적으로, 주기적으로; 단속적으로, 이따금

per·i·pa·tet·ic [pèripətétik] *adj.* **1.** moving from place to place. **2.** ((*P-*)) of the philosophy of Aristotle, who walked about while teaching. —*n.* [C] ((*P-*)) a follower of Aristotle.
—[形] 1. 걸어 돌아다니는; 순회의 2. 소요학파(逍遙學派)의 —[名] 소요학파의 학도

pe·riph·er·y [pərífəri] *n.* [C] (pl. **-er·ies**) a boundary line; an outside surface.
—[名] 주위; 외위(外圍); 바깥 면

pe·riph·ra·ses [pərífrəsì:z] *n.* pl. of **periphrasis.**

pe·riph·ra·sis [pərífrəsis] *n.* [U][C] (pl. **-ses**) a roundabout way of speaking; a periphrastic expression.
—[名] 우회적 표현법, 완곡법(婉曲法), 완곡한 말

per·i·phras·tic [pèrifrǽstik] *adj.* of or expressed in periphrasis.
—[形] 우회적인, 완곡한; 에둘러 말하는

per·i·scope [périskòup] *n.* [C] an instrument with mirrors and lenses by which the observer can see over an obstacle. ⇒fig.
—[名] 잠망경

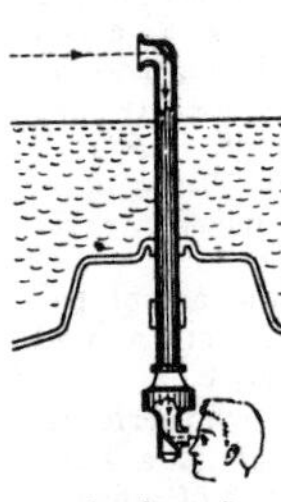
[periscope]

per·i·scop·ic [pèriskɑ́pik / -kɔ́p-] *adj.* **1.** giving distinct vision all around. **2.** of or by a periscope.
—[形] 1. 사방의 전망을 볼 수 있는 2. 잠망경의

‡per·ish [périʃ] *vi.* die; be destroyed. ¶*~ with hunger.*①
—[自] 죽다; 멸망하다; 썩다 ¶①굶어 죽다

Perish the thought!, Don't even consider such a possibility!
[熟] 집어치워라!, 당치도 않은 생각!

per·ish·a·ble [périʃəbl] *adj.* liable to spoil or decay. —*n.* ((*pl.*)) something perishable.
—[形] 썩기 쉬운; 사멸하기 쉬운 —[名] 썩기 쉬운 물건(식품)

per·i·to·ni·tis [pèritounáitis] *n.* [U] (*Medicine*) inflammation of the lining of the abdomen.
—[名] ((醫)) 복막염

per·i·wig [périwig] *n.* [C] a wig.
—[名] 가발(假髮)

per·i·win·kle¹ [périwìŋkl] *n.* [U] a creeping, evergreen plant with blue or white flowers.
—[名] ((植)) 빙카

per·i·win·kle² [périwìŋkl] *n.* [C] a seasnail with a spiral shell.
—[名] 경단고둥류의 식용 고둥

per·jure [pə́:rdʒər] *vt.* ((*reflexively*)) make (oneself) guilty
—[他] 위증(僞證)하다 ¶①그 목격자는

perjury [847] **perpetuation**

of swearing falsely that something is true. ¶*The witness perjured himself.*① ▷**per·jur·er** [-dʒ(ə)rər] *n*.
per·ju·ry [pə́:rdʒ(ə)ri] *n*. (pl. **-ju·ries**) **1.** ⓤ the act of perjuring oneself. **2.** ⓒ a willfully false statement.
perk [pə:rk] *vi*. **1.** lift up one's head brisky or spiritedly. **2.** become lively or active; recover from sickness. —*vt*. **1.** raise (the head, etc.) briskly or spiritedly. **2.** (*reflexively*) make (oneself) trim or smart in appearance.
perk·y [pə́:rki] *adj*. (**perk·i·er, perk·i·est**) lively; active; saucy. ▷**perk·i·ness** [-nis] *n*. ⌜permanent.⌝
per·ma·nence [pə́:rmənəns] *n*. ⓤ the state of being
per·ma·nen·cy [pə́:rmənənsi] *n*. (pl. **-cies**) **1.** =permanence. **2.** ⓒ a permanent person, thing, or position.
‡per·ma·nent, [pə́:rmənənt] *adj*. lasting; continuing in the same state. ¶*a ~ residence*①/*a ~ tooth*②/*a ~ wave*.③
per·ma·nent·ly [pə́:rmənəntli] *adv*. in a permanent manner.
per·me·a·bil·i·ty [pə̀:rmiəbíliti] *n*. ⓤ the state or quality of being permeable.
per·me·a·ble [pə́:rmiəbl] *adj*. that can be permeated.
per·me·ate [pə́:rmièit] *vt*. pass into (something) and fill every space of it. —*vi*. spread; diffuse.
per·me·a·tion [pə̀:rmiéiʃ(ə)n] *n*. ⓤ the act of permeating; the state of being permeated. ⌜allowable.⌝
per·mis·si·ble [pə:rmísibl] *adj*. able to be permitted;
• per·mis·sion [pə(:)rmíʃ(ə)n] *n*. ⓤ the act of allowing or permitting. ¶*ask for ~*①/*grant (or give) ~*.②
per·mis·sive [pə:rmísiv] *adj*. permitting; permitted.
‡per·mit *v*. [pə(:)rmít →*n*.] (**-mit·ted, -mit·ting**) *vt*. **1.** allow; give leave to (someone or something). (*~ someone or something to do; ~ doing*) ¶*Permit me to smoke.; Permit my smoking. | Permit me a few words.; Permit a few words to me.*① **2.** make (something) possible; admit; do not prevent. (*~ doing; ~ someone to do*) ¶*~ parking | The law does not ~ the sale of this book.*② —*vi*. **1.** afford opportunity; allow. ¶*I'll go, weather permitting.*③ */ Please drop in when time permits.* **2.** admit (*~ of something*) ¶*The situation permits of no delay.*④
—*n*. [pə́:rmit, +*U. S.* pərmít] ⓒ a written order allowing someone to do something. ¶*a ~ to hunt.*
per·mu·ta·tion [pə̀:rmju(:)téiʃ(ə)n] *n*. ⓒ **1.** (*Mathematics*) any one of the possible orders in which a number of things can be arranged. **2.** alteration.
per·ni·cious [pə(:)rníʃəs] *adj*. destructive; harmful; fatal.
per·ox·ide [pə(:)rɑ́ksaid / pə(:)rɔ́k-] *n*. ⓤⓒ an oxide containing a large amount of oxygen. ¶*hydrogen ~.*①
per·pen·dic·u·lar [pə̀:rp(ə)ndíkjulər] *adj*. **1.** upright; at right angles. ↔horizontal ¶*a ~ line.*① **2.** very steep. ¶*a ~ cliff.* —*n*. **1.** ⓒ a perpendicular line. **2.** ⓤ a perpendicular position. ¶*out of* [*the*] *~*.②
per·pen·dic·u·lar·ly [pə̀:rp(ə)ndíkjulərli] *adv*. in a perpendicular manner. ⌜(bad).⌝
per·pe·trate [pə́:rpitrèit] *vt*. do or commit (something)
per·pe·tra·tor [pə́:rpitrèitər] *n*. ⓒ a person who perpetrates (something).
• per·pet·u·al [pərpétʃuəl] *adj*. **1.** lasting forever; eternal. **2.** lasting throughout life. ¶*~ annuity.*① **3.** continuous. ¶*~ change.*
per·pet·u·al·ly [pərpétʃuəli] *adv*. forever; constantly.
per·pet·u·ate [pərpétʃuèit] *vt*. make (something) perpetual; cause (something) to be remembered forever.
per·pet·u·a·tion [pərpètʃuéiʃ(ə)n] *n*. ⓤ the act of per-

위증하였다

—⒩ 1. 위증; 위증죄 2. 허언(虛言)

—ⓥ 1. 으스대다, 젠체하다; 거만하게 굴다 2. 기운을 회복하다
—ⓥ 1. [머리]를 기운차게 쳐들다 2. 몸단장하다, 모양내다

—ⓐ 의기양양한; 모양을 낸; 건방진

—⒩ 영구(永久); 불변
—⒩ 1. 영구; 불변 2. 변함없는 사람; 영구물, 영속하는 지위
—ⓐ 영구적인; 영속적인 ¶①영구(永住)/②영구치(齒)/③퍼머머넌트
—ⓐⓓ 영구히, 영속적으로

—⒩ 투과성(透過性), 침투성

—ⓐ 침투할 수 있는, 투과성이 있는
—ⓥ …에 배어들다, 스며 퍼지다
—ⓥ 침투하다, 보급하다
—⒩ 침투; 투과(透過); 보급

—ⓐ 허용할 수 있는
—⒩ 허가; 허용 ¶①허가를 청하다/②허가를 주다; 허가하다
—ⓐ 허락하는; 허락받은
—ⓥ 1. …을 허락하다, 허가하다 ¶① 몇 마디 발언하게 해주시오 2. …을 가능하게 하다; …을 인정하다; …하게 내버려두다 ¶②법률은 이 책의 판매를 허용하지 않고 있다
—ⓥ 1. 허락하다 ¶③날씨가 좋으면 가겠다 2. 인정하다 ¶④사태는 지체를 허락하지 않는다(매우 긴박하다)

—⒩ 허가증, 면허장

—⒩ 1. (數) 순열(順列) 2. 변환(變換), 변경

—ⓐ 파괴적인; 유해한; 치명적인
—⒩ 과산화물(過酸化物) ¶①과산화수소

—ⓐ 1. 곧추 선, 직립의; 수직의 ¶①수선(垂線) 2. 몹시 가파른 —⒩ 1. 수선 2. 수직, 수직 위치 ¶②경사하여

—ⓐⓓ 수직으로; 몹시 가파르게

—ⓥ [못된 짓 따위]를 행하다, 저지르다, 범하다
—⒩ 못된 짓을 하는 사람, 가해자, 범인

—ⓐ 1. 영구의; 영원한 2. 종신(終身)의 ¶①종신 연금(年金) 3. 끊임없는

—ⓐⓓ 영구히; 끊임없이, 쉴새 없이
—ⓥ …을 영속(永續)케 하다; 불후(不朽)하게 하다

—⒩ 영구화(化); 불후

perpetuity [848] **personal**

petuating; the state of being perpetuated.

per·pe·tu·i·ty [pè:rpit(j)ú:iti] *n.* (pl. **-ties**) **1.** ⓤ the state of being perpetual. **2.** ⓒ something perpetual. **3.** ⓤ (*Law*) a perpetual possession. **4.** ⓒ a perpetual annuity. *in perpetuity*, forever.

—⑧ 1. 영속, 불멸 2. 영속물 3. (法) 영대(永代) 재산 4. 종신 연금(年金)
圞 영구히, 불후하게

· **per·plex** [pərpléks] *vt.* make difficult for (someone) to understand; puzzle; bewilder; confuse. 《*be perplexed at* (or *about, with*)》 ¶*He is perplexed with the problem.*① [fused.]

—⑩ …을 난처하게 하다, 당황케 하다, 어쩔 줄 모르게 하다 ¶①그는 그 문제로 어찌할 바를 모르고 있다

per·plexed [pərplékst] *adj.* puzzled; bewildered; con-
per·plex·ing [pərpléksiŋ] *adj.* puzzling; bewildering; confusing. ▷**per·plex·ing·ly** [-li] *adv.*

—⑱ 난처한, 당황한, 어찌할 바를 모「르는
—⑱ 난처하게 하는, 당황하게 하는, 까다로운

per·plex·i·ty [pərpléksiti] *n.* (pl. **-ties**) **1.** ⓤ the state of being perplexed; puzzlement; bewilderment; confusion. ¶*in one's ~.*① **2.** ⓒ something that perplexes. ¶*to one's ~.*②

—⑧ 1. 난처함, 당황, 혼란 ¶①당황하여, 난처하게 하는 것 ¶②난처한 일은, 난처하게도.

per·qui·site [pə́:rkwizit] *n.* ⓒ any profit or right added [to one's regular pay.]

—⑧ 임시 수당(수입)

· **per·se·cute** [pə́:rsikjù:t] *vt.* **1.** treat (someone) cruelly, esp. because of religious reasons. **2.** annoy. 《~ someone *with*》 ¶~ *someone with questions.*①

—⑩ 1. [이교도 등]을 학대하다 2. …을 괴롭히다 ¶①…을 질문으로 괴롭히다

per·se·cu·tion [pə̀:rsikjú:ʃ(ə)n] *n.* ⓤⓒ the act of persecuting; the state of being persecuted. ¶~ *mania.*①

—⑧ 박해; 학대; 졸라대기 ¶①피해망상

per·se·cu·tor [pə́:rsikjù:tər] *n.* ⓒ a person who persecutes. [the queen of the lower world.]

—⑧ 박해자, 학대자

Per·seph·o·ne [pə:rséfəni] *n.* (in Greek mythology) [그리이스 신화의] 지옥계의 여 |왕]

Per·seus [pə́:rsju:s, -sjəs] *n.* (in Greek mythology) the hero who killed Medusa.

—⑧ [그리이스 신화의] 메두사를 죽인 영웅

· **per·se·ver·ance** [pə̀:rsivíərəns] *n.* ⓤ the act of persevering; patience; refusal to give up.

—⑧ 인내(력); 불요불굴(不撓不屈), 견인불발(堅忍不拔)

per·se·vere [pə̀:rsivíər] *vi.* continue steadily in spite of hardship; persist. 《~ *in* or *with* something》 ¶~ *in one's studies*① / ~ *with one's task.*②

—⑨ 참다, 인내하다; 꾸준한 노력하다 ¶①연구에 꾸준한 노력을 하다/②일을 꾸준히 계속하다

per·se·ver·ing [pə̀:rsivíəriŋ] *adj.* refusing to give up; keeping on trying; patient. [Asia. ⇒N.B.]

—⑱ 참을성 있는, 끈기 있는 「개칭」

Per·sia [pə́:rʒə, -ʃə / -ʃə] *n.* a country in southwestern

—⑧ 페르샤 N.B. 1935년 Iran 이라

· **Per·sian** [pə́:rʒ(ə)n, -ʃ(ə)n / -ʃ(ə)n] *adj.* of Persia, its people, or their language. ——*n.* ⓒ **1.** a person of Persia. **2.** ⓤ the language of Persia. [light mockery.]

—⑱ 페르샤의, 페르샤 사람의; 페르샤 말의 —⑧ 1. 페르샤 사람 2. 페르샤 말

per·si·flage [pə̀:rsiflá:ʒ, +*Brit.* pɛ́əsi-] *n.* ⓤ joking talk;

—⑧ 농담, 농; 조롱

per·sim·mon [pə(:)rsímən] *n.* ⓒ a yellow, sweet fruit; the tree which produces this fruit.

—⑧ 감, 감나무

· **per·sist** [pə(:)rsíst, +*U.S.* -zíst] *vi.* **1.** continue steadily in spite of difficulty; insist. 《~ *in* something》 ¶~ *in one's opinion.*① **2.** last; stay.

—⑨ 1. 고집하다; 주장하다 ¶①자기의 의견을 고집하다 2. 살아 남다, 생존하다, 존속하다

per·sist·ence [pə(:)rsíst(ə)ns, -zíst-], **-en·cy** [-(ə)nsi] *n.* ⓤ the act of persisting; the state of being persistent.

—⑧ 고집; 줄기찬 인내; 영속

· **per·sist·ent** [pə(:)rsíst(ə)nt, -zíst-] *adj.* persisting; lasting; continuing. ¶~ *attacks*① / ~ *efforts.*②

—⑱ 고집하는; 영속적이 ¶①집요한 공격 /②부단한 노력

per·sist·ent·ly [pə(:)rsíst(ə)ntli, -zíst-] *adv.* in a persistent manner; insistently; steadily.

—⑨ 고집하여, 꾸준히, 굽히지 않고

‡ **per·son** [pə́:rsn] *n.* ⓒ **1.** a man, woman, or child; a human being. ¶*a young ~.*① **2.** one's body or bodily appearance. ¶*No symptom of disease was observed on her ~.*② **3.** a character in a play, etc. **4.** (*Grammar*) one of the three forms of pronouns to show the person speaking (first person), the person spoken to (second person), or the person or thing spoken of (third person). ¶*the first* (*the second, the third*) *~.*③ [in the flesh.]
1) *in person,* ⓐ in one's own person; by oneself. ⓑ
2) *in the person of,* named; under the name of.

—⑧ 1. 사람(남자·여자·아이들); 인간 ¶①젊은이(특히 여자에게 씀) 2. 신체; 풍채, 용모 ¶②그녀의 몸은 아무런 병의 징후는 없었다 3. [연극의] 역(役), 등장 인물 4. (文法) 인칭 ¶③제1(2, 3)인칭

圞 1)ⓐ스스로, 자신이 ⓑ[사진 따위가 아니고] 본인 자신이 2)…이라는 이름(명칭)의

per·son·a·ble [pə́:rs(ə)nəbl] *adj.* good-looking; handsome.

—⑱ 용모가 아름다운, 품위있는

per·son·age [pə́:rs(ə)nidʒ] *n.* ⓒ **1.** a person of importance. **2.** a person in a play, etc.

—⑧ 1. 명사, 중요 인물, 귀인 2. [연극 따위의] 역, 등장 인물

‡ **per·son·al** [pə́:rs(ə)nl] *adj.* **1.** individual; private. ↔*pub-*

—⑱ 1. 개인의, 사사로운 ¶①인사란

lic ¶*a ~ column*① / *~ abuse.* **2.** done in person or by oneself. ¶*a ~ interview.*② **3.** of a person's body or appearance. ¶*~ appearance*③ / *~ beauty.*④ **4.** (*Grammar*) expressing persons. ¶*~ pronoun.*
(人事欄) 2. 자신이 [스스로] 행하는 ¶②직접 면접 3. 신체의; 풍채의; 용모의 ¶③풍채/④용모의 아름다움 4.《文法》 인칭의

:per·son·al·i·ty [pə̀:rs(ə)nǽliti] *n.* (pl. **-ties**) **1.** [U] the state, quality, or fact of being a person; one's character. **2.** [U] one's existence as an individual, a person, or personage. **3.** [C] a person of importance. **4.** 《often *pl.*》 unpleasant remarks about a person.
—[名] 1 개성; 인격, 성격 2. 개인으로서의 존재; 사람 3. 명사, 중요 인물 4. 인물 비평, 인신공격

***per·son·al·ly** [pə́:rs(ə)n(ə)li] *adv.* **1.** without help from others; by oneself. **2.** as a person. **3.** as far as one is concerned; as regards oneself.
—[副] 1. 몸소, 친히 2. 한낱 인간으로서; 개인으로서 3. 자기로서는

per·son·ate [pə́:rs(ə)nèit] *vt., vi.* play a part in a drama, etc.; pretend to be (another person).
—[他][自] 역(役)을 맡아 하다; [남을] 가장하다, 남 행세를 하다; 이름을 사칭하다

per·son·a·tion [pə̀:rs(ə)néiʃ(ə)n] *n.* [U] the act of personating; the state of being personated.
—[名] 역을 맡아 하기; [신분의] 사칭

per·son·i·fi·ca·tion [pə:rsɑ̀nifikéiʃ(ə)n / pə:sɔ̀n-] *n.* **1.** [U] [C] the act of personifying; the state of being personified. **2.** [C] a person or thing imagined as a striking example of some quality. ¶*He is the ~ of selfishness.*①
—[名] 1. 인격화, 의인법(擬人法) 2. 구현(具現), 권화(權化), 화신(化身) ¶①그는 이기주의의 화신이다

per·son·i·fy [pə:rsɑ́nifài / pə:sɔ́n-] *vt.* (**-fied**) regard or imagine (something) as a person; stand for in one's person; represent. ¶*Satan personifies evil.*
—[他] …을 의인화하다, 인격화하다, …의 화신이 되다

per·son·nel [pə̀:rs(ə)nél] *n.* [U] 《*collectively*》 the persons employed in a company, etc.; a body of employees.
—[名] 전(全)직원, 사원

per·spec·tive [pə(:)rspéktiv] *n.* **1.** [U] the art of drawing to show depth and distance. **2.** [C] a picture so drawn. **3.** [U] the relationship of objects, scenes, or events. **4.** [C] a distant view; a view in front.
—[名] 1. 투시화법(透視畫法), 원근법 2. 투시화 3. 배경, 원근; [보았을 때의] 조화 관계 4. 원경(遠景), 전망, 조망

in perspective, ⓐ according to the rules of perspective. ⓑ in a true relationship.
[熟] ⓐ원근법에 의하여 ⓑ올바른 관계에 있어서

—*adj.* of or drawn in perspective.
—[形] 투시화법의, 원근법에 따른

per·spi·ca·cious [pə̀:rspikéiʃəs] *adj.* quick to understand or judge; acute.
—[形] 이해력이 빠른, 총명한

per·spi·cac·i·ty [pə̀:rspikǽsiti] *n.* [U] the state of being perspicacious; keen perception; acuteness.
—[名] 안식(眼識), 통찰력; 총명

per·spi·cu·i·ty [pə̀:rspikjú(:)iti] *n.* [U] the quality of being perspicuous; acuteness; clearness; plainness.
—[名] 총명; 명석, 명백

per·spic·u·ous [pə(:)rspíkjuəs] *adj.* easy to be understood; clearly expressed; clear. ¶*~ writing.*
—[形] 명쾌한, 명료한; [언어가] 똑똑한

per·spic·u·ous·ly [pə(:)rspíkjuəsli] *adv.* in a perspicuous manner; clearly.
—[副] 명료하게

per·spi·ra·tion [pə̀:rspəréiʃ(ə)n] *n.* [U] the act of perspiring; sweat. ¶*drops of ~.*①
—[名] 발한[작용], 땀 ¶①땀방울

per·spire [pərspáiər] *vi., vt.* sweat. ⇒[usage] ¶*She perspired heavily when she played volleyball.*
—[自][他] 땀이 나다 [usage] sweat 보다 다소 점잖은 말

:per·suade [pə(:)rswéid] *vt.* get (someone) to do as one wishes; cause (someone) to believe; convince. 《~ someone *to do* or *into doing*; ~ someone *of* or *that* …》 ¶*~ someone out of these ideas*① / *~ someone to come*② / *~ someone of the truth; ~ someone that it is true*③ / *be persuaded of someone's innocence; be persuaded that someone is innocent*④ / *~ oneself that …*⑤
—[他] …을 설득하여 …시키다; …을 납득시키다 ¶①…을 설득하여 이러한 생각들을 버리게 하다/②…을 오도록 설득하다/③…에게 그것이 진실임을 납득시키다/④…의 무죄를 믿다/⑤…이라고 믿다

per·sua·sion [pə(:)rswéiʒ(ə)n] *n.* [U] the act or power of persuading; the state of being persuaded; belief; conviction.
—[名] 설득[력]; 신념; 확신

per·sua·sive [pə(:)rswéisiv] *adj.* having the power to persuade; convincing.
—[形] 설득력 있는, 구변 좋은

per·sua·sive·ly [pə(:)rswéisivli] *adv.* in a persuasive manner.
—[副] 설득력 있게

pert [pə:rt] *adj.* rude in speech or manner; impudent. ↔modest ¶*a ~ girl.*
—[形] 건방진, 주제넘은

per·tain [pə(:)rtéin] *vi.* belong; refer; be suitable for or to. 《~ *to* something》 ¶*a disease which pertains to poverty.*①
—[自] 속하다, 관계하다, 적절하다 ¶①가난에 따르기 마련인 질병

per·ti·na·cious [pə̀:rtinéiʃəs] *adj.* holding firmly to an opinion, a purpose, an action, etc.; stubborn; persistent.
—[形] 굳게 결심한, 불굴의; 완고한, 고집하는

per·ti·nac·i·ty [pə̀:rtinǽsiti] *n.* ⓤ the state or quality of being pertinacious. — 名 집착, 집요, 끈덕짐, 완고

per·ti·nence [pə́:rtinəns], **-nen·cy** [-nənsi] *n.* ⓤ the state or quality of being pertinent; fitness. — 名 적절, 타당

per·ti·nent [pə́:rtinənt] *adj.* right and proper; to the point. (~ *to*) ¶*be* ~ *to the subject.*① — 形 적절한, 꼭 들어맞는 ¶①이 문제에 적절하다

per·turb [pə(:)rtə́:rb] *vt.* make anxious or afraid; disturb (someone), esp. in mind; agitate. — 他 …을 불안하게 하다, 당황하게 하다; 교란하다

per·tur·ba·tion [pə̀:rtə(:)rbéiʃ(ə)n] *n.* **1.** ⓤ the act of perturbing; the state of being perturbed; disturbance. **2.** ⓒ a thing or cause that perturbs. — 名 1. 동요, 당황, 불안 2. 불안하게 하는 것, 불안의 원인

Pe·ru [pərú:] *n.* a country on the west coast of South America. ⇒NB. — 名 페루(남미 서해안의 공화국)NB. 수도는 Lima

pe·ruke [pərú:k] *n.* ⓒ a wig. ⇒fig. — 名 가발(假髮)

pe·rus·al [pərú:z(ə)l] *n.* ⓤ the act of reading carefully. — 名 숙독(熟讀), 정독

pe·ruse [pərú:z] *vt.* read carefully. — 他 …을 숙독(정독)하다

Pe·ru·vi·an [pərú:viən] *adj.* of Peru or its people. —— *n.* ⓒ a person of Peru. — 形 페루[사람]의 — 名 페루 사람

per·vade [pə(:)rvéid] *vt.* spread throughout; penetrate. — 他 …에 고루 퍼지다, 보급하다

[peruke]

per·va·sion [pə(:)rvéiʒ(ə)n] *n.* ⓤ the act of pervading; the state of being pervaded. — 名 고루 퍼지기, 보급; 침투

per·va·sive [pə(:)rvéisiv] *adj.* tending to spread throughout. ▷**per·va·sive·ly** [-li] *adv.* —**per·va·sive·ness** [-nis] *n.* — 形 퍼지는; 보급하는; 골고루 퍼지는

per·verse [pə(:)rvə́:rs] *adj.* **1.** persisting in doing something undesired; contrary. **2.** persistent in wrong. **3.** ill-tempered; wicked. ▷**per·verse·ly** [-li] *adv.* — 形 1. 성미가 비꼬인, 심술궂은 2. 고집센, 완고한 3. 나쁜, 사악한

per·ver·sion [pə(:)rvə́:rʒ(ə)n / -ʃ(ə)n] *n.* ⓤ the act of perverting; the state of being perverted; ⓒ an abnormal or wrong form of something. — 名 곡해; 악용; 악화

per·ver·si·ty [pə(:)rvə́:rsiti] *n.* ⓤⓒ (pl. **-ties**) the state or quality of being perverse. — 名 사악; 제멋대로 함; 외고집

per·ver·sive [pə(:)rvə́:rsiv] *adj.* tending to pervert. — 形 나쁜 길로 이끄는

per·vert *vt.* [pə(:)rvə́:rt → *n.*] turn away from the right way or purpose; misuse; twist the meaning of (something). —— *n.* [pə́:rvə(:)rt] ⓒ a perverted person. — 他 …을 그릇되게 하다; 악용하다; 곡해하다 — 名 배교자(背敎者), 타락자

per·vi·ous [pə́:rviəs] *adj.* that can be penetrated; giving passage to something. (~ *to*) ¶*Glass is* ~ *to light.*① — 形 통하게 하는, 투과시키는, 받아들이는 ¶①유리는 빛을 통과시킨다

pe·so [péisou] *n.* ⓒ (pl. **-sos**) the unit of money and a silver coin used in Latin American countries or in the Philippines. — 名 페소(라틴아메리카 제국 및 필리핀의 화폐 단위, 또는 그 은화)

pes·si·mism [pésimìz(ə)m] *n.* ⓤ the tendency to think the worst of everything. ↔optimism — 名 비관[주의], 염세[주의]

pes·si·mist [pésimist] *n.* ⓒ a person who believes in pessimism. ↔optimist — 名 비관론자, 염세주의자

pes·si·mis·tic [pèsimístik] *adj.* taking the worst view ⌈of everything.⌉ — 形 염세적인, 비관적인

pest [pest] *n.* **1.** ⓒ a thing or person that causes trouble or harm. **2.** ⓤⓒ pestilence. — 名 1. 귀찮은 것(사람), 골칫거리 2. 역병(疫病), 페스트, 흑사병

pes·ter [péstər] *vt.* trouble; worry. — 他 …을 괴롭히다, 애먹이다

pest·house [pésthàus] *n.* ⓒ (pl. **-hous·es** [-hauziz]) a hospital for people with highly dangerous diseases. — 名 [특히 페스트 환자의] 격리 병원

pes·tif·er·ous [pestífərəs] *adj.* spreading diseases; harmful; troublesome. ⌈which spreads rapidly.⌉ — 形 전염성의; 해로운; 성가신, 귀찮은 ⌈[病]⌉

pes·ti·lence [péstiləns] *n.* ⓤⓒ any dangerous disease — 名 전염병, 유행병, 페스트, 역병(疫)

pes·ti·lent [péstilənt] *adj.* bad for health, peace, etc.; bringing death. — 形 역병을 일으키는; 해로운, 치명적인

pes·ti·len·tial [pèstilénʃ(ə)l] *adj.* carrying dangerous diseases; harmful; dangerous. ⌈powder in a mortar.⌉ — 形 역병을 일으키는, 해로운; 위험한 ⌈[이]⌉

pes·tle [pés(t)l] *n.* ⓒ a stick used for breaking things to — 名 유봉(乳棒), 약연(방아·절구)공

• **pet**¹ [pet] *n.* ⓒ **1.** a small animal, bird, etc. kept in the house. **2.** a darling; a favorite. ¶*make a ~ of a little girl.* —— *adj.* **1.** treated as a pet. **2.** favorite; especially liked. —— *vt.* (**pet·ted, pet·ting**) **1.** treat (an — 名 1. 애완동물 2. 총아, 귀염둥이, 예쁜이 — 形 1. 애완의, 총애하는 2. 귀여워하는, 특히 좋아하는

pet [851] **Pharisee**

animal, etc.) as a pet. **2.** touch (someone) in a loving way.
—타 1. …을 애완하다 2. …을 쓰다듬다, 어루만지다, 애무하다

pet² [pet] *n.* ⓒ an unsatisfied state of mind; a burst of ill humor. ¶*in a ~.*①
—명 기분 나쁨, 심술남, 토라짐 ¶①토라져서, 뿌루퉁하여

pet·al [pétl] *n.* ⓒ the colored part of a flower.
—명 꽃잎, 화판(花瓣)

Pe·ter [pí:tər] *n.* a man's name. ¶*Peter the Great.*① / *Saint* (or *St.*) *Peter.*②
—명 남자 이름 ¶①피이터 대제(大帝) /②성(聖)베드로

• **pe·ti·tion** [pitíʃ(ə)n] *n.* ⓒ an earnest request or prayer; a formal request from a lower to a higher officer; a letter containing such requests. ¶*a ~ to the mayor for cleaner streets.*①
[~ someone to do]
—*vt.* make a petition to (someone). 《~ someone *for*;》
—명 청원, 탄원; 기원(祈願); 신청; 청원서 ¶①거리를 더 깨끗이 해달라는 시장에의 탄원서

—타 …에게 청원(탄원)하다

pe·ti·tion·er [pitíʃ(ə)nər] *n.* ⓒ a person who petitions.
—명 청원자

pet·rel [pétr(ə)l] *n.* ⓒ a black and white sea bird.
—명 바다제비과의 작은 새

pet·ri·fac·tion [pètrifǽkʃ(ə)n] *n.* ⓤ the act of petrifying; the state of being petrified.
—명 석화(石化)[작용]; 어안이 벙벙함, 망연자실

pet·ri·fy [pétrifài] *v.* (**-fied**) *vt.* **1.** turn (something) into stone. **2.** make (someone or something) motionless with fear or surprise. ¶*be petrified with fear.*① —*vi.* **1.** become stone. **2.** be stony or motionless.
—타 1. …을 석화(石化)시키다 2. …을 움츠리게(움찔하게) 하다 ¶①무서워서 움츠리다 —자 1. 석화하다 2. 움츠리다

pet·rol [pétr(ə)l] *n.* ⓤ (*Brit.*) gasoline.
—명 《英》 가솔린

pe·tro·le·um [pitróuliəm] *n.* ⓤ a heavy, brown oil obtained from the earth.
—명 석유

pet·ti·coat [pétikòut] *n.* ⓒ **1.** a underskirt worn by girls and women. **2.** (*colloq.*) a woman; a girl. —*adj.* of or by a woman; feminine. ¶*~ government.*①
—명 1. 페티코우트(속치마) 2. 《口》 여자, 소녀 —형 여자의, 여성에 의한 ¶①여인 천하, 엄처시하, 부인정치

pet·tish [pétiʃ] *adj.* ill-tempered and complaining; easily angered; peevish.
—형 토라지기 잘 하는; 골 잘 내는

• **pet·ty** [péti] *adj.* (**-ti·er, -ti·est**) **1.** small; unimportant. ¶*~ cash.*① **2.** narrow-minded; mean. **3.** on a small scale. ¶*a ~ farmer.*② ▷**pet·ti·ly** [-li] *adv.* —**pet·ti·ness** [-nis] *n.* [of being petulant.]
—형 1. 작은, 사소한, 하찮은 ¶①소액의 현금, 용돈 2. 마음이 좁은, 옹졸한; 인색한 3. 소규모의 ¶②소농(小農)

pet·u·lance [pétʃuləns / -tju-] *n.* ⓤ the state or quality
—명 토라지기; 성마름, 발끈하기

pet·u·lant [pétʃulənt / -tju-] *adj.* impatient and ill-tempered.
—형 성 잘 내는; 성마른, 성미 급한

pe·tu·ni·a [pitjú:niə] *n.* ⓒ a garden plant with flowers shaped like a trumpet. ⇒*fig.*
—명 댕강나무메꽃, 피튜우니어

pew [pju:] *n.* ⓒ a fixed wooden bench in a church.
—명 교회의 좌석

pew·ter [pjú:tər] *n.* **1.** ⓤ mixture of tin and lead used for making pots, etc. **2.** ⓒ dishes, pots, etc. made of pewter.
—명 1. 백랍 2. 백랍으로 만든 기물

pha·lan·ges [fəlǽndʒi:z] *n.* pl. of **phalanx.**

pha·lanx [fǽlæŋks, féɪl- / fǽl-] *n.* ⓒ [petunia] (pl. **-lanx·es** →3.) **1.** a group of heavily-armed ancient Greek soldiers in close ranks. **2.** any tightly massed body of persons united for one purpose. **3.** (pl. **-lan·ges**) a bone of the fingers or toes. [2. a ghost.]
—명 1. 밀집진(密集陣), [고대 그리이스의] 방진(方陣) 2. 밀집대(隊) 3. 지골(指骨)

phan·tasm [fǽntæz(ə)m] *n.* ⓒ **1.** an imaginary vision.
—명 1. 허깨비, 환영(幻影) 2. 유령

phan·tas·mal [fæntǽzm(ə)l] *adj.* of a phantasm; imag-
—형 허깨비의, 유령의; 공상의

phan·ta·sy [fǽntəsi, -zi] *n.* =fantasy. [inary.]

phan·tom [fǽntəm] *n.* ⓒ **1.** a ghost. **2.** something imagined. —*adj.* **1.** of or like a ghost. **2.** imagined. ¶*a ~ ship.*① [cient Egypt.]
—명 1. 유령, 허깨비 2. 환영(幻影) —형 1. 유령의, 허깨비의 2. 환영의, 망상의 ¶①유령선(船)

Phar·aoh [féərou] *n.* ⓒ the title for the kings of an-
—명 파라오(고대 이집트왕의 칭호)

Phar·i·sa·ic [færiséiik], **-i·cal** [-ik(ə)l] *adj.* **1.** of the Pharisees. **2.** (*p-*) thinking a form to be the most important thing of all. **3.** (*p-*) pretending to be highly moral without the real spirit; hypocritical.
—형 1. 바리새 파(사람)의 2. 형식에 구애되는, 격식 차리는 3. 위선의

Phar·i·see [fǽrisì:] *n.* ⓒ **1.** a member of an ancient Jewish religion. **2.** (*p-*) a pharisaic person.
—명 1. 바리새 파의 사람 2. 형식주의자; 위선자

phar·ma·ceu·ti·cal [fɑ̀ːrməsúːtik(ə)l] *adj.* of pharmacy. —[形] [제]약학의; 약제(藥劑)의

phar·ma·cist [fáːrməsist] *n.* [C] a person who prepares medicines; a druggist. —[名] 약제사

phar·ma·col·o·gy [fɑ̀ːrməkálədʒi / fɑ̀ːməkɔ́l-] *n.* [U] the science of drugs, their preparation, etc. —[名] 약학, 약물학(藥物學)

phar·ma·co·poe·ia [fɑ̀ːrməkəpíːə] *n.* [C] **1.** an official list of medicines and their preparation and use. **2.** a stock of drugs. —[名] 1. 약전(藥典), 처방(處方), 조제서 2. 약물류

phar·ma·cy [fáːrməsi] *n.* (pl. **-cies**) **1.** [U] the science of making medicines. **2.** [C] a shop for selling medicines. —[名] 1. 조제술, 약학 2. 약국, 약방

pha·ryn·ges [fərínd ʒiːz] *n.* pl. of **pharynx.**

phar·ynx [fǽriŋks] *n.* [C] (pl. **-ynx·es** or **-ryn·ges**) the tube at the back of the mouth. —[名] 인두(咽頭)

* **phase** [feiz] *n.* [C] **1.** a stage or state in the development of events; one side or view of a subject. **2.** one appearance of the moon in its series of changes. —[名] 1. 단계; 국면 2. 달의 상(相), 위상(位相)(초승달·조각달·보름달 따위)

Ph. D. Doctor of Philosophy. —《略》 철학박사

pheas·ant [féznt] *n.* [C] (pl. **-ants** or *collectively* **-ant**) a large bird with a long tail and beautiful feathers. —[名] 꿩

Phe·ni·cia [finíʃ(i)ə] *n.* =Phoenicia.

phe·nix [fíːniks] *n.* =phoenix.

phe·nol [fíːnoul, -nɑl / fíːnɔl] *n.* [U] (*Chemistry*) a poisonous substance produced from coal tar; carbolic acid. —[名] 《化》 페놀, 석탄산

phe·nom·e·na [finámina / -nɔ́m-] *n.* pl. of **phenomenon.**

phe·nom·e·nal [finámінl / -nɔ́m-] *adj.* **1.** of a phenomenon or phenomena. **2.** unusual; wonderful. —[形] 1. 현상의 2. 현저한, 두드러진, 경이적인

* **phe·nom·e·non** [finámінàn / -nɔ́minən] *n.* [C] **1.** (pl. **-na**) a natural event, fact, etc. that can be seen. **2.** 《*pl.*》 something unusual or wonderful. ¶*an infant* ~.① —[名] 1. 현상 2. 비범한 사람, 희한한 것(사람) ¶①신동(神童)

phew [fjuː] *interj.* a sound spoken suddenly with a strong feeling of dislike. —[感] 체!, 피이! (초조·불쾌 따위를 나타냄)

phi·al [fái(ə)l] *n.* [C] a small glass bottle for medicine. —[名] 작은 유리병, 약병

phil. philology; philosophy.

Phil. Philippine.

phi·lan·der [filǽndər] *vi.* (of a man) make love without serious intentions. —[自] [여자에게] 치근거리다, 희롱하다

phil·an·throp·ic [filənθrápik / -θrɔ́p-] *adj.* of philanthropy; kindly. —[形] 박애의, 인애(仁愛)의, 인정 많은

phi·lan·thro·pist [filǽnθrəpist] *n.* [C] a person who loves mankind and does good for them. —[名] 박애주의자, 자선가

phi·lan·thro·py [filǽnθrəpi] *n.* **1.** [U] the love of mankind; the desire to help mankind. **2.** 《*pl.*》 an action that serves humanity. —[名] 1. 박애, 자선 2. 박애(자선)사업

phi·lat·e·list [filǽtəlist] *n.* [C] a person who collects postage stamps. —[名] 우표 수집가

phi·lat·e·ly [filǽtəli] *n.* [U] the act of collecting postage stamps. —[名] 우표 수집

phil·har·mon·ic [filhɑːrmánik, filər- / filɑːmɔ́nik] *adj.* loving music. —*n.* [C] a philharmonic society or concert. —[形] 음악 애호의 —[名] 음악협회; [음악협회가 개최하는] 음악회

Phil·ip [fílip] *n.* **1.** a man's name. **2.** (in the Bible) one of the twelve persons who served Jesus Christ. —[名] 1. 남자 이름 2. 빌립(그리스도 12 사도 중의 한 사람)

* **Phil·ip·pine** [fílipìːn] *adj.* of the Philippine Islands or their people. —[形] 필리핀 군도(사람)의

Philippine Islands [⌐–⌐ ⌐–], **the** *n.* =Philippines.

* **Phil·ip·pines** [fílipìːnz], **the** *n.* a group of islands in the western Pacific Ocean; a country consisting of these islands. ⇒[N.B.] —[名] 필리핀 군도, 필리핀 공화국 [N.B.] 수도는 Quezon City

phil·o·log·i·cal [filəládʒik(ə)l / -lɔ́dʒ-] *adj.* of philology. —[形] 언어학(문헌학)[상]의

phi·lol·o·gist [filálədʒist / -lɔ́l-] *n.* [C] a person expert in philology. ⇒[N.B.] —[名] 언어학자 [N.B.] 최근에는 linguist를 씀; 문헌학자

phi·lol·o·gy [filálədʒi / -lɔ́l-] *n.* [U] **1.** the study of the history of language; linguistics. **2.** the study of written records. —[名] 1. 언어학 2. 문헌학

* **phi·los·o·pher** [filásəfər / -lɔ́səfə] *n.* [C] **1.** a person who studies philosophy. **2.** a person who always faces all events calmly. —[名] 1. 철학자, 철인 2. 깨달은 사람, 현인(賢人)

phil·o·soph·ic [fìləsάfik / -sɔ́f-], **-i·cal** [-ik(ə)l] *adj.* **1.** of or like philosophy or a philosopher. **2.** devoted to philosophy. **3.** calm; reasonable.
—[形] 1. 철학의, 철학자 같은 2. 철학에 정통한 3. 냉정한, 이성적(理性的)인

phi·los·o·phize [filάsəfàiz / -lɔ́s-] *vi.* think or use one's reason like a philosopher.
—[自] 철학적인 사색을 하다; 사색하다

‡phi·los·o·phy [filάsəfi / -lɔ́s-] *n.* (pl. **-phies**) **1.** [U] a study of the general truth of the universe, life, morals, etc. **2.** [U][C] an explanation or a theory of the universe. **3.** [U] calmness; a calm manner of accepting things. **4.** [U][C] a system for guiding life.
—[名] 1. 철학 2. 철리(哲理), 원리 3. 냉정, 깨달음 4. 인생관

phlegm [flem] *n.* [U] **1.** a thick liquid which comes from the nose and throat. **2.** slowness; coolness; calmness.
—[名] 1. 가래, 담 2. 지둔(遲鈍); 냉담; 무기력

phleg·mat·ic [flegmǽtik] *adj.* **1.** of or producing phlegm. **2.** slow; cool; calm.
—[形] 1. 가래의(가 많은) 2. 굼뜬, 냉담한, 무기력한

Phoe·ni·cia [fi(ː)níʃ(i)ə] *n.* an ancient country on the coast of Syria.
—[名] 페니키아(시리아 해안에 있던 고대 국가)

Phoe·ni·cian [fi(ː)níʃən] *adj.* of Phoenicia, its people, or their language. **—***n.* **1.** [C] a person of Phoenicia. **2.** [U] the language of Phoenicia.
—[形] 페니키아[사람·말]의 —[名] 1. 페니키아 사람 2. 페니키아 말

phoe·nix [fíːniks] *n.* [C] a mythical Arabian bird which burns itself after a long life and rises fresh again from the ashes.
—[名] 불사조, 페닉스

***phone** [foun] *n.* =telephone.

pho·net·ic [founétik] *adj.* **1.** of or representing speech sounds. ¶~ *symbols* (or *signs*).① **2.** of phonetics.
—[形] 1. 음성(音聲)을 나타내는, 음성[상]의 ¶①발음기호 2. 음성학[상]의

pho·ne·ti·cian [fòunitíʃ(ə)n] *n.* [C] an expert in phonetics.
—[名] 음성학자

pho·net·ics [founétiks] *n. pl.* 《used as *sing.*》 [U] the study of speech sounds and the way of pronunciation.
—[名] 음성학

phon·ic [fάnik / fóun-, fɔ́n-] *adj.* of [speech] sounds.
—[形] 음의, 음성의

pho·no·graph [fóunəgræ̀f, +*Brit.* -grὰːf] *n.* [C] (*U.S.*) a machine that reproduces the sounds of a record; a record player. (cf. *Brit.* gramophone)
—[名] 축음기

pho·ny [fóuni] *adj.* (**-ni·er, -ni·est**) (*U.S. slang*) not real; not true. **—***n.* [C] (pl. **-nies**) a person or thing that is phony.
—[形] 가짜의, 속임수의 —[名] 가짜 [물건·사람]

phos·phate [fάsfeit / fɔ́s-] *n.* [U] **1.** a chemical compound containing phosphorus. **2.** the substance containing this compound that makes soil fertile.
—[名] 1. 인산염(燐酸鹽) 2. 인산 비료

phos·pho·res·cence [fὰsfərésns / fɔ̀s-] *n.* [U] **1.** the act or process of giving out light without heat. **2.** the light so produced.
—[名] 1. 인광(燐光)을 내기, 파란 빛 2. 인광(燐光)

phos·pho·res·cent [fὰsfərésnt / fɔ̀s-] *adj.* giving out phosphorescence.
—[形] 인광을 발하는, 파란 빛을 내는

phos·phor·ic [fasfɔ́ːrik / fɔs-] *adj.* of or like phosphorus. ¶~ *acid.*①
—[形] 인(燐)의(같은) ¶①인산

phos·pho·rus [fάsf(ə)rəs / fɔ́s-] *n.* [U] (*Chemistry*) a yellowish or red material that lights and burns easily, used in making matches, etc.
—[名] 인(燐)

‡pho·to [fóutou] *n.* [C] (pl. **-tos**) (*colloq.*) a photograph.
—[名] 《口》 사진

photo finish [⁄-- ⁄-] *n.* (in racing) a close finish that can be decided only from a photograph; any close finish of a game.
—[名] [경마에서] 사진 판정을 요하는 결승; [막상막하의] 접전(接戰)

pho·to·flash lamp [fóutəflæ̀ʃlǽmp] *n.* an electric bulb which gives a sudden bright light when one takes a photograph.
—[名] [사진용] 섬광 전구(閃光電球)

pho·to·gen·ic [fòutoudʒénik] *adj.* looking well in a photograph. ¶*a* ~ *face.*
—[形] 사진에 적합한; 사진이 잘 찍히는

‡pho·to·graph [fóutəgræ̀f, +*Brit.* -grὰːf] *n.* [C] a picture made with a camera. ¶*have* (or *get*) *one's* ~ *taken.*① **—***vt.* take a picture of (something) with a camera. **—***vi.* be photographed. ¶*She photographs well.*②
—[名] 사진 ¶①[남을 시켜] 사진을 찍다 —[他] …을 촬영하다 —[自] 사진에 찍히다 ¶②그녀는 사진이 잘 찍힌다

pho·tog·ra·pher [fətάgrəfər / -tɔ́grəfə] *n.* [C] a person who takes photographs.
—[名] 사진사

pho·to·graph·ic [fòutəgrǽfik] *adj.* of photography.
—[形] 사진[술]의

pho·tog·ra·phy [fətάgrəfi / -tɔ́g-] *n.* [U] the art of taking photographs.
—[名] 사진술

pho·to·play [fóutəplèi] *n.* [C] a motion-picture play.
—[名] 영화극

‡phrase [freiz] *n.* [C] **1.** (*Grammar*) a group of words
—[名] 1. 《文法》 구(句), 프레이즈 ¶①성

P

phraseology [854] **pick**

not containing a subject and a prdicate, used as a single word. ¶*a set ~.*① **2.** an expression often used as a unit. **3.** a short, striking expression. **4.** (*Music*) a short part of a music piece. —*vt.* express (something) in words.

phra·se·ol·o·gy [frèiziάlədʒi / -ɔ́l-] *n.* Ⓤ Ⓒ (pl. **-gies**) the manner of expression; a particular selection and arrangement of words. — 图 말씨, 어법, 문체, 표현법

phys·ic [fízik] *n.* Ⓤ **1.** medicine. **2.** the science of medicine. —*vt.* (**-icked, -ick·ing**) give medicine to (someone); cure. — 图 1. 약 2. 의술 —他 …에게 약을 먹이다; …을 치료하다

: phys·i·cal [fízik(ə)l] *adj.* **1.** of nature; of the laws of nature; natural. **2.** of material things; material. ↔spiritual ¶*the ~ evidence.*① **3.** of the body. ¶*~ training.*② **4.** the science of physics. — 形 1. 자연의, 자연 법칙의 2. 물질의 ¶①물적 증거 3. 육체의, 신체의 ¶②체조 4. 물리학의, 물리적인

phys·i·cal·ly [fízikəli] *adv.* **1.** concerning the body. ¶*~ and mentally.*① **2.** with reference to the natural world; materially. ⌈¶*consult a ~.* — 副 1. 육체적으로, 신체상 ¶①신체적·정신적으로, 심신이 다 2. 자연의 법칙에 따라; 물질적으로

: phy·si·cian [fizíʃ(ə)n] *n.* Ⓒ a doctor, esp. of medicine.⌉ — 图 의사; 내과 의사

phys·i·cist [fízisist] *n.* Ⓒ a person who studies physics. — 图 물리학자

phys·icked [fízikt] *v.* pt. and pp. of **physic**.

pys·ick·ing [fízikiŋ] *v.* ppr. of **physic**.

• **phys·ics** [fíziks] *n. pl.* (used as *sing.*) the science that studies matter and the forces of the natural world. — 图 물리학

phys·i·og·no·my [fiziágnəmi / -ɔ́nə-] *n.* (pl. **-mies**) **1.** Ⓤ the art of judging the character of a person by his face; **2.** Ⓒ the features of a face. **2.** Ⓒ (*colloq.*) the face. **3.** Ⓒ the general appearance (of a landscape). — 图 1. 관상(인상)술; 인상 2. 얼굴 3. 외관, 외형

phys·i·o·log·i·cal [fìziələdʒik(ə)l / lɔ́dʒ-] *adj.* of physiology. ⌈studies physiology.⌉ — 形 생리학[상]의

phys·i·ol·o·gist [fìziάlədʒist. / -ɔ́l-] *n.* Ⓒ a person who **phys·i·ol·o·gy** [fìziάlədʒi / -ɔ́l-] *n.* Ⓤ the science that studies the parts of a living body and their operation. — 图 생리학자 — 图 생리학

phy·sique [fizíːk] *n.* Ⓤ the form and development of the body; bodily structure. — 图 체격

pi·a·nis·si·mo [pìːəní́simòu / pjæní́simòu] *adj.* very soft. —*adv.* (*Music*) very softly. ↔fortissimo ⌈piano.⌉ — 形 아주 약한(부드러운) —副 (樂) 아주 약하게(부드럽게)

pi·an·ist [píːənist / píən-] *n.* Ⓒ a person who plays the⌉ — 图 피아니스트

• **pi·an·o**¹ [piǽnou] *n.* Ⓒ (pl. **-an·os**) a musical instrument with many wires sounded by hammers. — 图 피아노

pi·an·o² [piάːnou, +*Brit.* pjάː-] *adj.* soft. —*adv.* (*Music*) softly. ↔forte — 形 약하고 부드러운 —副 (樂)약하고 부드럽게

pi·an·o·for·te [piænoufɔ́ːrti / pjænoufɔ́ːti] *n.* =piano¹.

pic·co·lo [píkəlòu] *n.* Ⓒ (pl. **-los**) a small flute. — 图 피콜로(작은 플루우트)

: pick¹ [pik] *vt.* **1.** make a hole in (soil, rock, etc.) by striking with a pointed instrument; use a pointed instrument, such as the fingernail, on (something) in order to remove (something). ¶*~ [the] ground* / *~ one's teeth.*① **2.** remove feathers, etc. from (a cock, hen, etc.); take (flowers, fruit, etc.) from a tree or plant. ¶*~ a chicken*② / *She likes to ~ flowers.* **3.** choose or select carefully. ¶*~ the best one* / *~ a partner.* **4.** seek purposely an opportunity or occasion for (something); begin (a quarrel, fight, etc.). ¶*~ fault*③ / *He picked a fight with his brother.* **5.** take up (bits of food) with the bill or teeth; (of a person) eat in a small quantity. ¶*~ grains.* **6.** open (a lock) with a wire, etc. without using a key. ¶*The burglar picked the lock with a wire.* **7.** steal from (someone's pocket); rob. ¶*~ a pocket* / *~ someone's brain.*④ **8.** pluck (the guitar, etc.) with the fingers. ¶*~ a banjo.* —*vi.* **1.** use a pointed instrument on something; dig lightly. **2.** (of a cock, etc.) peck at the ground or take bits of food with the bill. **3.** choose carefully. — 他 1. …을 파다, 찍어파다; 쑤시다, 우비다 ¶①이를 쑤시다 2. …의 깃털을 뽑다(쥐어뜯다); 식물에서 [꽃이나 열매 따위]를 따다, 채집하다 ¶②닭의 깃털을 뽑다 3. [주의하여] …을 고르다 4. […의 기회 따위]를 잡다, 포착하다, [싸움 따위]를 걸다 ¶③흠을 찾다 5. [먹이를] 쪼다, 쪼아먹다; …을 조금씩 먹다 6. [자물쇠]를 비집어 열다 7. …을 훔치다, 훔치다 ¶④…의 생각(고안)을 훔치다(도용하다) 8. …을 손가락으로 퉁기다(타다) —自 1. 찌르다, 우비다 2. [닭 따위가] 쪼다, 쪼아 먹다 3. 정선(精選)하다

1) ***pick at,*** ⓐ eat (one's food) only a little at a time. ⓑ find fault with (someone); annoy (someone) by criticizing.
2) ***pick off,*** shoot or kill one by one.
3) ***pick on,*** choose or select (someone) as a victim; blame.
4) ***pick out,*** ⓐ choose. ¶*~out one's successor.* ⓑ distinguish (someone or something) from others.
5) ***pick up,*** ⓐ get or acquire unexpectedly. ¶*~ a watch up on the street.* ⓑ lift or raise (something) with the fingers. ¶*~ up the ashtray.* ⓒ learn or grasp. ¶*She picked up some English words from her music teacher.* ⓓ recover (one's health, etc.); cheer up. ⓔ continue. ⓕ give a ride to (someone); meet and take along. ¶*He picked up her on the way to school.* ⓖ happen to make friends with (someone).

[熟] 1)ⓐ…을 조금씩 먹다 ⓑ…의 흠을 찾다;…에게 잔소리하다 2)한 사람씩 겨누어 쏘다 3)희생으로 하여 …을 골라내다; …에게 잔소리하다 4)ⓐ…을 고르다 ⓑ…을 분간하다, 구별하다 5)ⓐ…을 우연히 손에 넣다 ⓑ…을 주워(집어)올리다 ⓒ…을 터득(파악)하다, 알게 되다 ⓓ[건강]을 회복하다, [기운]을 내다 ⓔ…을 계속하다 ⓕ[남]을 태우고 가다, [남]과 만나 동행하다 ⓖ[남]과 우연히 알게(사귀게) 되다

—n. 1. [U] the act or the right of selecting. ¶*Take your ~.*⑤ **2.** [C] a person or thing selected; the best part.
—[名] 1. 선택 ¶⑤고르시오 2. 골라 뽑은 사람(것), 정선한 것; 알짜

pick² [pik] *n.* [C] **1.** an iron tool with a sharp point, used for breaking up roads, etc. **2.** a small pointed instrument used for cleaning the teeth, the ears, etc.
—[名] 1. 곡괭이 2. 파는(우비는, 찍는) 연장(이쑤시개 따위)

pick·ax, -axe [píkæ̀ks] *n.* [C] a tool, having an pointed iron head at one end and the blade. ⇒fig.
—[名] 곡괭이

〔pickax〕

picked [pikt] *adj.* **1.** especially chosen or selected. **2.** gathered from plants.
—[形] 1. 정선한, 알짜의 2. 따 낸, 뜯어 낸

pick·er [píkər] *n.* [C] a person or tool that gathers, picks, etc.
—[名] 따는(뜯는) 사람; 따는(뜯는) 연장; 곡괭이

pick·et [píkit] *n.* [C] **1.** a post fixed in the ground to make a fence, to tie a horse, etc. **2.** a group of soldiers acting as a guard. **3.** ⦅*pl.*⦆ persons watching at a factory, shop, etc., during a strike.
—[名] 1. 뾰족한 말뚝 2. 경비대(警備隊), 초병(哨兵), 전초(前哨) 3. 피켓, 파업·파괴자 감시원

—*vt.* 1. enclose (a farm, etc.) with pickets; fence. **2.** tie (a horse, etc.) to a picket. **3.** watch or guard. **4.** place (someone) as a guard. **—*vi.*** serve as a picket.
—[他] 1. …에 말뚝 울타리를 두르다 2. …을 말뚝에 매다 3. …을 감시하다 4. …을 감시에 배치하다
—[自] 감시자가 되다, 감시원 노릇을 하다

pick·ing [píkiŋ] *n.* [C] **1.** a thing which is picked. **2.** ⦅*pl.*⦆ a thing left over.
—[名] 1. 채집품; 훔친 물건, 장물 2. 찌꺼기

pick·le** [píkl] *n.* [U] **1.** a solution of salt vinegar, etc. used to keep or give a taste to meat, fish, vegetable, etc. **2.** ⦅usu. *pl.*⦆ a vegetable, esp. cucumber, preserved in pickle. **3.** [C] a difficult situation. ¶*be in a ~.*① **—*vt. keep (a vegetable) in pickle.
—[名] 1. [채소·생선 따위를 절이는] 간국, 절이는 국물 2. 장아찌, 오이지 3. 난처한 입장, 곤경 ¶①곤경에 처해 있다
—[他] …을 간국(소금물)에 절이다

pick·pock·et [píkpɑ̀kit / -pɔ̀k-] *n.* [C] a person who steals from people's pockets.
—[名] 소매치기

pick·up [píkʌ̀p] *n.* [C][U] **1.** the part of a record player in which the needle is set. **2.** an informal acquaintance. **3.** [U] increase in speed; speeding up. **4.** (*colloq.*) the state of getting better in business, health, etc.; recovery. **5.** a small, often open truck.
—[名] 1. [전축·축음기의] 픽업 2. 우연히 알게 된 사람 3. 가속(加速) 4. ⦅口⦆ 개량; 나아지기, 회복 5. 소형 트럭

***pic·nic** [píknik] *n.* [C] **1.** a short trip on which someone carries food for an outdoor meal. ¶*go on a ~.*① **2.** a pleasant time, experience, etc. **—*vi.* (-nicked, -nicking)** go on a picnic.
—[名] 1. 피크닉, 소풍, 들놀이 ¶①피크닉(소풍) 가다 2. 즐거운 일 —[自] 피크닉(소풍) 가다

pic·nicked [píknikt] *v.* pt. and pp. of **picnic.**

pic·nick·ing [píknikiŋ] *v.* ppr. of **picnic.**

pic·to·ri·al [piktɔ́ːriəl] *adj.* of or like pictures; expressed in pictures. **—*n.*** [C] a magazine with many pictures.
—[形] 그림의(같은); 그림으로 나타낸
—[名] 그림 있는 잡지, 화보

‡pic·ture [píktʃər] *n.* [C] **1.** a painting, drawing, portrait, or photograph. ¶*take a ~*① / *have one's ~ taken*② / *sit for one's ~.*③ **2.** a very beautiful scene, person or thing like a picture. ¶*She is a perfect ~.* **3.** something or someone that resembles another; an image. ¶*You are the ~ of your cousin.* **4.** a type or symbol. ¶*She looks the ~ of health.* **5.** a very clear or color-
—[名] 1. 그림, 회화; 초상화; 사진 ¶①사진을 찍다/②[남을 시켜] 자기의 사진을 찍다/③[남을 시켜] 자기의 초상화를 그리게 하다 2. 그림처럼 아름다운 경치(사람·것) 3. 꼭 닮은 것 4. 상징, 전형(典型) 5. 그림 같은 묘사 6. 심상(心像), 상상 7. [텔레비전·영화의] 화

P

ful description. ¶*give realistic pictures of life in colonial days.* **6.** a mental image or idea. ¶*recall a ~ from the past.* **7.** an image on television or in a movie. **8.** a motion picture· (chiefly *Brit.*) ⟪*the ~s*⟫ movies. ¶*go to the pictures*④
—*vt.* **1.** paint or draw. ¶*~ a country scene.* **2.** see (something) in the mind; imagine. ¶*I could not ~ him as a cowboy.* / *Try to ~ yourself in his situation.*⑤

면 **8.** 〔英〕 영화;[흥행으로서 상영하는] 영화 ¶④영화구경 가다
—[他] **1.** …을 그리다;…을 묘사하다 **2.** …을 마음속에 그리다,상상하다 ¶⑤그의 입장이 되어 생각해 보게

picture gallery [´– ˋ––] *n.* a place for showing pictures.
—[名] 미술관,화랑

•**pic·tur·esque** [pìktʃərésk] *adj.* **1.** as beautiful as a picture; vivid. **2.** suitable for a picture.
—[形] **1.** 그림처럼 아름다운; 생생한 **2.** 그림으로 그리기 알맞은

•**pie** [pai] *n.* [U][C] a baked dish of fruit or meat enclosed in pastry.
have a finger in the pie, be concerned in the matter.
—[名] 파이(고기·과일 따위를 가루 반죽에 넣어 구운 음식)
[熟] 간섭하다

pie·bald [páibɔ̀:ld] *adj.* having markings in two colors, esp. white and black. —*n.* [C] a black and white horse.
—[形] [흑·백색] 얼룩의, 잡색의 —[名] [흑백의] 얼룩말

⁑**piece** [pi:s] *n.* [C] **1.** a part separated or broken off from a whole. ¶*a ~ of cake* / *The bottle broke in pieces.* **2.** a single thing of a set. ¶*a dinner service of 60 pieces.*① **3.** a unit of things of a kind; a limited part; a section; a quantity. ¶*a ~ of furniture*② / *a ~ of land* / *a ~ of cloth* / *a ~ of bread.* **4.** a single and separate instance or example. ¶*a ~ of advice* / *a ~ of information*③ / *a ~ of nonsense.* **5.** a coin. ¶*a five-cent ~.* **6.** a musical or literary work, esp. a short one. ¶*a Beethoven ~.*④ **7.** a definite size or amount in which various articles are sold; an amount of work forming a single job. ¶*a ~ of wallpaper*⑤ / *The workmen are paid by the ~.*⑥ **8.** a rifle or gun.
1) ***go to pieces,*** become very nervous; lose control.
2) ***of a piece,*** of the same kind; alike.
3) ***piece by piece,*** part by part; one piece at a time.
—*vt.* **1.** mend or patch (something) by adding a piece. ¶*~ a skirt.* **2.** make (something) by joining sections together.
1) ***piece out,*** complete (something) by joining parts or pieces.
2) ***piece together,*** join (things) so that they make a whole. ¶*~ together the fragments of a broken vase.*

—[名] **1.** 일부분,한 조각,파편,단편 **2.** [한 벌 중의] 한 개 ¶①60개 한 벌의 정찬용 식기 **3.** 한 개,한 장,한 덩어리,한 뙈기[의 땅] ¶②가구 한 개 **4.** 하나의 보기,일례 ¶③하나의 정보 **5.** 화폐 **6.** [예술상의] 작품 ¶④베에토오벤의 곡 **7.** 일정한 분량; 작업량 ¶⑤벽지(도배지) 한 뭉치(길이 12야아드의것)/⑥노무자들은 작업량에 따라 노임을 받는다 **8.** 총,포
[熟] 1)신경질이 되다; 자제심을 잃다 2)같은 종류의,한결 같은 3)하나하나,하나씩
—[他] **1.** …을 이어 깁다(수선하다) **2.** …을 결합(접합)하다
[熟] 1)…을 이어붙여서 완전하게 하다 2)…을 결합(접합)하다

piece·meal [pí:smì:l] *adv.* bit by bit; piece by piece.
—[副] 조금씩,차츰차츰;하나씩,하나하나

piece·work [pí:swə̀:rk] *n.* [U] work paid for according to the amount done. ↔time work
—[名] 작업량에 따라 임금을 받는 일,도급(청부)일

pied [paid] *adj.* having many colors; spotted.
—[形] 얼럭덜럭한,잡색의

•**pier** [piər] *n.* [C] **1.** a post for supporting an arch, a bridge, etc. ⇒fig. **2.** a roadway reaching out into the sea from the land. **3.** the part of a wall between windows, doors, etc.
—[名] **1.** 교각(橋脚),홍예다리 **2.** 선창,부두,잔교(棧橋) **3.** 창 사이 벽; 문 사이 벽

〔pier 1.〕

•**pierce** [piərs] *vt.* **1.** make a hole in or through (something). ¶*The rose thorn pierces the finger easily.*① **2.** go into; go through (something). **3.** understand; see through or into; move (the feelings, etc.). ¶*a heart pierced with pity.*② —*vi.* enter. ⟪*~ through* something⟫ ¶*The sun pierced through the clouds.*③
—[他] **1.** …을 꿰뚫다; 꿰찌르다,찌르다 ¶①장미꽃 가시는 손가락에 찔리기 쉽다 **2.** …에 뚫고 들어가다;…을 관통하다 **3.** …을 이해하다,통찰하다;…을 감동시키다 ¶②연민의 정으로 감동된 마음 —[自] 뚫고 지나가다,관통하다 ¶③태양이 구름을 뚫고 나왔다

pierc·ing [píərsiŋ] *adj.* sharp.
—[形] 날카로운

Pi·er·rot [pì(:)əróu / píərou] *n.* [C] (pl. **-rots** [-z]) an actor with a painted white face, amusing people by his foolish movements.
—[名] 피에로(얼굴에 분을 바르고 익살부리는 광대)

pi·e·ty [páiəti] *n.* [U][C] **1.** deep respect for God. **2.** deep love and respect for one's parents, ancestors, etc.
—[名] **1.** 경건,경신(敬神) **2.** 효도

⁑**pig** [pig] *n.* **1.** [C] a fat animal used for food; [U] its meat; pork. **2.** [C] a dirty person; a person having a great desire for food. **3.** [U] a small bar or mass of metal.
—[名] **1.** 돼지; 돼지고기 **2.** [돼지처럼] 추접한 사람; 게걸장이,욕심꾸러기 **3.** 금속 덩이,쇳덩이

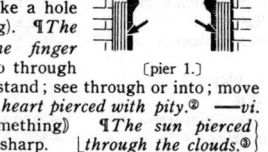

1) ***buy a pig in a poke,*** buy something which one does not properly know about.
2) ***make a pig of oneself,*** eat too much.
[熟] 1)잘 살펴보지도 않고 물건을 사다 2)[돼지처럼] 많이 먹다

⁑**pi·geon** [pídʒin] *n.* [C] a bird with the power of finding its way home. ¶*a carrier* (or *homing*) ~① / *a wood* ~.②
—[名] 비둘기 ¶①전서구(傳書鳩)/②산비둘기

pigeon breast [ˊ- ˋ] *n.* a swelling chest like that of a pigeon.
—[名] 새가슴

pi·geon·hole [pídʒinhòul] *n.* [C] **1.** a hole in which pigeons nest. **2.** one of a set of boxes where papers are put. —*vt.* place (a paper) in a pigeonhole.
—[名] 1. 비둘기장의 드나드는 구멍 2. 서류 정리함(분류함)의 한 간 —[他] [서류]를 분류함에 넣다

pig·gish [pígiʃ] *adj.* like a pig.
—[形] 돼지 같은

pig·gy [pígi] *n.* [C] (pl. **-gies**) a little pig.
—[名] 돼지새끼

pig·head·ed [píghédid] *adj.* unwilling to listen to reason; stubborn.
—[形] 고집 센, 옹고집의

pig iron [ˊ ˋ-] *n.* rough iron.
—[名] 무쇠, 선철

pig·ling [pígliŋ] *n.* [C] a young pig.
—[名] 돼지새끼

pig·ment [pígmənt] *n.* [U] coloring matter to make paints; [C] a paint.
—[名] 그림물감, 안료(顏料)

pig·my [pígmi] *n.* =pygmy.

pig·skin [pígskìn] *n.* [U] the skin of a pig; [C] leather goods made from it.
—[名] 돼지 가죽

pig·sty [pígstài] *n.* [C] (pl. **-sties**) an enclosed place for pigs.
—[名] 돼지 우리

pig·tail [pígtèil] *n.* [C] **1.** a twisted bunch of hair hanging from the back of the head. **2.** a tail of a pig.
—[名] 1. 변발(辮髮), 길게 땋아 늘어뜨린 머리 2. 돼지 꼬리

pig·wash [pígwàʃ / -wɔ̀ʃ] *n.* [U] waste food for pigs.
—[名] 꿀꿀이죽(돼지 먹이)

pike[1] [paik] *n.* [C] a weapon with a long stick and a pointed metal head.
—[名] [옛날 보병이 쓰던] 창

pike[2] [paik] *n.* =turnpike.

pike·staff [páikstæ̀f / -stɑ̀:f] *n.* [C] (pl. **-staves**) the stick of a pike.
—[名] 창의 자루

pike·staves [páikstéivz] *n.* pl. of **pikestaff.**

pi·las·ter [pilǽstər] *n.* [C] an ornamental column forming the part of a wall.
—[名] 벽기둥(벽의 일부에서 튀어나온 장식 기둥)

⁑**pile**[1] [pail] *n.* [C] **1.** a number of things lying one upon another; a heap; a mass. ¶*a ~ of sand / a ~ of hay.* **2.** (*colloq.*) a large amount. ¶*a ~ of things to do.*① **3.** a large building or group of buildings.
—[名] 1. [차곡차곡 쌓아 올린] 퇴적(堆積);…더미 2. 대량, 다수 ¶①많은 할 일 3. 대(大)건축물[의 떼]

—*vt.* **1.** place or throw (something) in a pile. ¶*~ books one on top of the other.* **2.** cover (something) with large amounts; fill. ¶*a wagon piled with hay.* —*vi.* **1.** form a pile. **2.** go confusedly in a group; crowd. ¶*They piled into the car.*②
—[他] 1. …을 쌓아 올리다 2. …에 산더미처럼 쌓다 —[自] 1. 더미를 이루다 2. 꾸역꾸역 밀려가다 ¶②그들은 우루루 차에 올라탔다

pile up, grow great in quantity. ¶*Don't let bills ~ up.*
[熟] 많이 쌓이다, 많이 모이다

pile[2] [pail] *n.* (usu. *pl.*) a post put into the earth for supporting a foundation. —*vt.* drive piles into (the ground).
—[名] 말뚝 —[他] …에 말뚝을 박다

pile[3] [pail] *n.* [U] soft, fine hair; short hair on thick cloth or a carpet.
—[名] 부드러운 털, 솜털; [천·융단 따위의] 보풀

pile driver [ˊ ˋ-] *n.* a machine for driving piles into the ground.
—[名] 말뚝 박는 기계

pil·fer [pílfər] *vt., vi.* steal (something) in small amounts.
—[他][自] 좀도둑질하다

***pil·grim** [pílgrim] *n.* [C] **1.** a person who travels on foot to a holy place. **2.** a traveler; a wanderer.
—[名] 1. 순례자 2. 나그네; 방랑자

pil·grim·age [pílgrimidʒ] *n.* [C] a journey to a holy place; a human lifetime. ¶*go on a ~.*①
—[名] 순례; 인생항로; 생애, 일생 ¶①순례(편력)의 길을 떠나다

Pilgrim Fathers [ˊ-- ˊ-], **the** *n. pl.* the Puritans who left England and landed at Massachusetts in 1620.
—[名] 1620년 Mayflower 호를 타고 미국으로 건너온 영국 청교도단

***pill** [pil] *n.* [C] **1.** a small ball of medicine to be swallowed whole. **2.** (*colloq.*) something unpleasant but unavoidable; an unpleasant person.
—[名] 1. 알약, 환약 2.《口》 싫은 것(사람)

pil·lage [pílidʒ] *n.* **1.** [U] the act of taking goods by force, esp. in war. **2.** [C] a thing stolen by force, esp. in war. —*vt., vi.* rob (something) violently; plunder.
—[名] 1. [특히 전시중의] 약탈 2. 약탈품 —[他][自] […을] 약탈하다, 강탈하다

***pil·lar** [pílər] *n.* [C] **1.** an upright, ornamental post to support a structure; a column. **2.** something shaped like a pillar. ¶*a ~ of smoke.*① **3.** a firm, important supporter. ¶*a ~ of the state.*②
—[名] 1. 기둥; 푯말; 받침다리 2. 기둥 모양의 물건 ¶①연기의 기둥 3. 거물; 중진, 중심 인물 ¶②국가의 기둥감 인물

pillar box [ˊ- ˋ] *n.* (*Brit.*) a letterbox in the street. (cf. *U.S.* mail box)
—[名] 《英》 우체통, 포스트

P

pillbox / pinch

pill·box [pílbɑks / -bɔks] *n.* ⓒ **1.** a small box for holding pills. **2.** a small, low, concrete and steel fortress with machine guns. — 名 1. 환약(알약) 그릇 2. 토오치카

pil·lo·ry [píləri] *n.* (pl. **-ries**) **1.** ⓒ a wooden framework with holes for the head and hands, used to punish criminals in olden days. ⇒fig. **2.** ((*the ~*)) public shame. ¶*be in the ~.*① —*vt.* (-ried) put (someone) in the pillory; expose (someone) to public shame. — 名 1. 칼(죄인의 머리와 손을 널빤지 사이에 끼워 거리에 내놓던 옛날 형틀) 2. 웃음거리 ¶웃음거리가 되다 —他 …을 칼을 쐬우다;웃음거리가 되게 하다

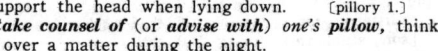
[pillory 1.]

:**pil·low** [pílou] *n.* ⓒ cushion used to support the head when lying down. ***take counsel of*** (or ***advise with***) *one's pillow,* think over a matter during the night. —*vt.* place (one's head) on a pillow, etc.; serve as a pillow for (someone). ¶*~ one's head upon one's arm.* — 名 베개

熟 하룻밤 동안 잘 생각해 보다

—他 베개를 베다; …의 베개 구실을 하다

pil·low·case [pílouhèis] *n.* ⓒ a removable covering for a pillow.
pil·low·slip [pílouslìp] *n.* =pillowcase. — 名 베갯잇

·**pi·lot** [páilət] *n.* ⓒ **1.** a person who guides a ship into or out of a harbor. **2.** a person who flies a plane. ¶*a test ~.* **3.** a guide; a leader. ¶*drop the ~.* —*vt.* act as the pilot of (a ship, an airplane etc.); guide; lead. — 名 1. 수로(水路) 안내인 2. 조종사 3. 안내인; 지도자 —他 …의 수로 안내를 하다; …을 조종하다; 안내하다

pi·lot·age [páilətidʒ] *n.* Ⓤ **1.** the act or art of piloting. **2.** the fee paid to a pilot. (=pimiento.) — 名 1. 수로 안내; 항공기 조종술 2. 수로 안내료(料)

pi·men·to [piméntou] *n.* (pl. **-tos**) **1.** =allspice. **2.**
pi·mien·to [pimjéntou] *n.* ⓒ (pl. **-tos**) a sweet pepper. — 名 피멘토우 고추

pim·per·nel [pímpərnèl] *n.* ⓒ a small annual plant with red, white, or blue flowers. — 名 나도개별꽃

pim·ple [pímpl] *n.* ⓒ a small, pointed, inflamed swelling (on the skin.) — 名 여드름, 뾰루지
pim·pled [pímpld] *adj.* having or covered with pimples. — 他 여드름투성이의
pim·ply [pímpli] *adj.* (**-pli·er, -pli·est**) =pimpled.

:**pin** [pin] *n.* ⓒ **1.** a short piece of wire with a point at one end and a head at the other. ¶*a safety ~ / a tie ~.* **2.** anything used to fasten things together; a nail; a bar used for fastening a door. **3.** ((chiefly in *negative*)) anything of small value; a bit. ¶*I don't care a ~.*① / *not worth a ~.*② **4.** ((usu. *pl.*)) ((*colloq.*)) legs. **5.** (*Bowling*) a wooden club used as a target.
1) *be on one's last pins,* be going to die. (walker.)
2) *be quick* (*slow*) *on one's pins,* be a good (bad)
3) *sit* (or *be*) *on pins and needles,* feel uneasy.
4) *stick pins into* (=*trouble*) someone.
—*vt.* (**pinned, pin·ning**) **1.** fasten (something) with a pin. ¶*~ up a notice on the wall.*② **2.** hold fast. ((~ *something against* a wall, etc.)) (thing.)
1) *pin someone down* (=*make someone stick*) *to* some-
2) *pin one's faith on someone,* believe someone absolutely. (of something on someone.)
3) *pin something on someone,* put the responsibility
— 名 1. 핀, 옷핀 2. 못;쐐기;빗장;마개 3. 하찮은 것;소량(少量) ¶①조금도 상관없다/②아무 값어치도 없다 4. (口) 다리 5. (보울링의) 핀(곤봉 모양의 막대)

熟 1)죽어 가고 있다 2)걸음이 빠르다(느리다) 3)안절부절 못하다 4)…을 괴롭히다

—他 1. …을 핀으로 고정시키다; …에 빗장을 지르다 ¶③고시를 핀으로 벽에 꽂다 2. …을 움직이지 않게 하다

熟 1)남에게 …을 강요하다, 속박하다 2)절대적으로 신용하다 3)…에게 …의 책임을 지우다

pin·ball [pínbɔ̀ːl] *n.* ⓒ Ⓤ (*U. S.*) a game played with small metal balls on an inclined table. — 名 (美) 핀보울, 회전 당구

pince-nez [pǽnsnèi] *n.* (pl. **pince·nez** [-neiz]) ((used as *sing.* and *pl.*)) a pair of eyeglasses with a spring clip which grips the nose. — 名 코안경

pin·cers [pínsərz] *n., pl.* **1.** a tool like scissors, used to grip or draw (something). ¶*a pair of ~.*① **2.** the large claws of a crab, a lobster, etc. — 名 1. 집게, 못뽑이, 족집게 ¶①펜찌 한 자루 2. (게·새우 따위의) 집게발

·**pinch** [pintʃ] *vt.* **1.** press (something) between the thumb and a finger or between two hard edges. ¶*~ one's nose / ~ out young buds.* **2.** press on and give pain to (someone or something). ¶*The shoe pinches me at the heel.*① **3.** ((usu. in *passive*)) cause (someone) to become thin or worn or to be in difficulties. ¶*be pinched with cold.*② / *be pinched for money.*③ —*vi.* **1.** press hard. **2.** be — 他 1. …을 꼬집다, 집다, 물다 2. …을 죄다 ¶①구두 뒤축이 꼭 낀다 3. …을 쇠약하게 하다, 곤란하게 하다 ¶②추위에 시달리다/③돈에 쪼들리다 — 自 1. 죄다 2. 절약하다; 째째하게 굴다 ¶④각정이 짓을 하여 돈을 모으다

pinch hitter [859] **pipe**

careful in spending; be mean. ¶ ~ *and save.*
 know where the shoe pinches, know the difficulty.
 —*n.* ⓒ **1.** the act of pinching. ¶*give someone a ~.* **2.** as much as one can take up with the thumb and a finger; a bit. ¶*a ~ of salt.* **3.** something difficult.
pinch hitter [⌣ ⌣–] *n.* (*Baseball*) a person who bats for another player at a critical moment.
pin·cush·ion [pínkuʃ(ə)n] *n.* ⓒ a small cushion to stick [pins in.
‡**pine**¹ [pain] *n.* ⓒ **1.** an evergreen tree with needle-shaped leaves and cones; Ⓤ the wood of this tree. ¶*a ~ cone / a ~ needle.* **2.** a pineapple.
pine² [pain] *vi.* **1.** become thin and weak from anxiety, distress, etc. ⟨~ *away something*⟩ ¶ ~ *away [one's health].* **2.** long eagerly. ⟨~ *for* (or *after, to do*) *something*⟩ ¶ ~ *for one's family.*
· **pine·ap·ple** [páinæpl] *n.* ⓒ a tropical plant which bears a large, cone-shaped fruit; the large, juicy fruit of this plant.
ping [piŋ] *n.* ⓒ a sharp sound, such as that of a rifle bullet whistling through the air. —*vi.* make this sound.
ping·pong [píŋpɔŋ / -pɔ̀ŋ] *n.* Ⓤ a game somewhat like tennis, played on a table with rackets and a light ball; table tennis. [tiny, worthless object.
pin·head [pínhéd] *n.* ⓒ **1.** the head of a pin. **2.** a]
pin·hole [pínhòul] *n.* ⓒ a hole made by a pin; a small hole in which a pin or peg fits.
pin·ion [pínjən] *n.* ⓒ **1.** the end joint of a bird's wing; a wing feather. **2.** (*poetic*) a wing. —*vt.* **1.** cut off a pinion of (a bird) to prevent flight. **2.** bind (someone's hand or arms) tightly to his side; make (someone) powerless by binding his arms.
‡**pink**¹ [piŋk] *n.* **1.** ⓒ a garden plant like the carnation with flowers of various colors. **2.** Ⓤ a very pale red color. **3.** Ⓤ the highest degree or condition. ¶*She is in the ~ of health.* —*adj.* of a very pale red color.
pink² [piŋk] *vt.* **1.** prick or pierce (something or someone) with a sword, a spear, etc. **2.** decorate (cloth, leather, etc.) with small holes or by cutting the edges.
pin money [⌣ ⌣–] *n.* the amount of money given to a wife for her own use; pocket money.
pin·nace [píniş] *n.* ⓒ **1.** a boat carried on board a larger ship. **2.** a small sailing ship with two masts.
pin·na·cle [pínəkl] *n.* ⓒ **1.** a slender, pointed tower. ⇨*fig.* **2.** a high, slender mountain peak. **3.** The highest point. ¶*be at the ~ of one's fame.* —*vt.* furnish (something) with pinnacles; place (something) on a pinnacle.
· **pint** [paint] *n.* ⓒ a measure of capacity equal to half a quart. ⇨N.B. [pinnacle 1.]
pin·up [pínʌp] *n.* ⓒ (*U.S. colloq.*) a picture of a very attractive girl, to be displayed on a wall; a very attractive girl. —*adj.* very attractive. ¶*a ~ girl.*
· **pi·o·neer** [pàiəníər] *n.* ⓒ a person who does something first to prepare the way for others; a settler in a frontier country; an explorer. ¶*pioneers in the teaching of English.* —*vi.* act as a pioneer. —*vt.* open up (a way, etc.); take the lead in (something). | ↔*impious*|
· **pi·ous** [páiəs] *adj.* showing respect for God; religious.|
pip¹ [pip] *n.* ⓒ a small seed, as of an orange or apple.
pip² [pip] *n.* (*the ~*) a disease of fowls characterized by scales in the mouth and throat.
‡**pipe** [paip] *n.* ⓒ **1.** a tube made of metal, wood, etc.

▒ 난점(문젯점)을 알다
—客 1. 꼬집기, 집기, 쥐기 ¶⑤…을 꼬집다 2. 한 번 집기; 조금, 소량 3. 곤란

—客 (野球) 핀치히터, 대타자(代打者)

—客 바늘겨레
—客 1. 소나무; 소나무 재목 ¶①솔방울/②솔잎 2. 파인애플

—自 1. [조심·고민 따위로] 수척해지다 ¶⑤슬픔의 나머지 건강을 해치다 2. 애틋하게 그리워하다, 간절히 바라다 ¶②가족을 간절히 만나고 싶어하다
—客 파인애플 나무; 파인애플 [열매]

—客 핑[하는 소리] —自 핑소리가 나다
—客 탁구, 핑퐁

—客 1. 핀의 대가리 2. 하찮은 것
—客 바늘 구멍; 작은 구멍

—客 1. 새의 날개의 끝부분; 날개의 깃털 2. 날개 —他 1. [날지 못하게] 날개의 끝을 자르다 2. [남의 팔]을 붙잡아 매다; 묶다

—客 1. 패랭이꽃, 석죽(石竹) 2. 분홍색, 핑크색 3. 최고도, 극치 ¶①그녀는 더할 나위 없이 건강하다 —形 분홍빛의, 핑크색의
—他 1. …을 찌르다, 꿰뚫다 2. [천·가죽 따위]에 장식 구멍을 뚫다; 가장자리를 갈쭉갈쭉하게 베다

—客 [아내에게 주는] 용돈

—客 1. 함재정(艦載艇) 2. 쌍돛대의 작은 범선
—客 1. 뾰족탑, 첨탑 2. 높은 봉우리, 꼭대기, 정상 3. 정점(頂點), 극점 ¶①명성의 절정에 있다 —他 …에 뾰족탑을 세우다; …을 높은 곳에 두다

—客 파인트 N.B. (英) 약 0.57 리터, (美) 약 0.47 리터
—客 (美口) [벽에 핀으로 꽂아 붙이는] 미인 사진; 미인 —形 벽에 핀으로 붙이기 알맞은, 매력있는

—客 개척자, 선구자; 주창자; 선봉 ¶①영어 교육의 선구자 —自 개척자가 되다 —他 …을 개척하다; 주창하다

—形 경건한, 신앙심 깊은
—客 [오렌지·사과 따위의 작은] 씨
—客 가금(家禽)의 입병(목병)
—客 1. 관(管), 통 2. 체내의 파이프 모

through which water, gas, etc. moves. ¶*a water ~*. **2.** a tube-like organ of the body; ⟪*pl.*⟫ such an organ used to breathe. **3.** an L-shaped tube used for smoking tobacco; the amount of tobacco such a tube can be filled with. ¶*He smoked a ~ of tobacco.*① **4.** a musical instrument played by blowing air into it; a flute; a whistle. **5.** a keen voice like that of a child or bird. ¶*the ~ of a cuckoo.* **6.** a large cask of wine.
양의 기관;기관(氣管) **3.** 파이프, 담뱃대;[담배] 한 대 ¶①그는 파이프 담배를 한 대 피웠다 **4.** 피리, 플루우트, 호각 **5.** 포도주의 큰 통

1) ***put** someone's **pipe out,*** try to keep someone from succeeding.
2) ***Put that in your pipe and smoke it,*** Think it over.
[熟] 1)…의 성공을 훼방놓다 2)잘 생각해 보게

—*vi.* **1.** play on a musical pipe; whistle. **2.** make a keen voice; (of birds) sing. **—*vt.*** **1.** supply (something) with a pipe. ¶*~ a boiler for water.* **2.** play (a note) on a musical pipe; call (someone or something) by a whistle. **3.** move or carry (something) by a pipe.
—[自] **1.** 피리를 불다; 휘파람을 불다 **2.** 큰 소리를 지르다; [새가] 지저귀다
—[他] **1.** …에 관(管)을 달다 **2.** …을 피리로 연주하다; …을 피리로 부르다 **3.** …을 관(管)으로 운반하다

1) ***pipe away,*** give a signal by a whistle for a boat to start.
2) ***pipe up,*** ⓐ speak up suddenly. ⓑ begin to sing or play.
[熟] 1)호각을 불어 보우트를 출발시키다 2)ⓐ갑자기 소리를 지르다 ⓑ노래부르기 시작하다; 연주하기 시작하다

pipe line [ˊ ˋ] *n.* **1.** a line of pipes for carrying oil, gas, water, etc., usu. underground. **2.** a source of information.
—[名] **1.** [석유·가스·물 따위의] 도관(導管), 송수(송유)관 **2.** [기밀]정보 루우트

pip·er [páipər] *n.* [C] a person who plays on a pipe, esp. a bagpipe.
—[名] 피리를 부는 사람, 풍적수(風笛手)

pi·pette [pipét] *n.* [C] a slender tube or pipe used to transfer or measure liquids.
—[名] 피펫(액체를 옮기거나 측정하는 데 쓰는 작은 관)

pip·ing [páipiŋ] *n.* [U] **1.** the sound produced by a pipe.; a shrill voice or call. **2.** ⟪*collectively*⟫ pipes. **—*adj.*** **1.** shrill; high-pitched. **2.** peaceful. ¶*the ~ times of peace.* **—*adv.*** so as to hiss.
—[名] **1.** 피릿소리;날카로운 소리 **2.** 관(管) —[形] **1.** 날카로운 소리를 내는 **2.** 평화로운 —[副] 숫숫 소리를 낼 만큼

pi·quan·cy [píːkənsi] *n.* [U] the state of being piquant.
—[名] 얼얼함, 매움;신랄

pi·quant [píːkənt] *adj.* **1.** agreeably sharp or biting to the taste. **2.** exciting interest.
—[形] **1.** 얼얼한, 매운 **2.** 흥미를 돋구는, 신나게 하는

pique [piːk] *n.* [U] slight anger or irritation; displeasure. **—*vt.*** **1.** wound the pride of (someone); irritate; excite. ¶*be piqued at someone.*③ **2.** pride (oneself). ⟪*~ oneself on something*⟫
—[名] 화, 불쾌, 기분 언짢음 —[他] **1.** …의 자존심을 손상하다; 자극하다 ¶①…에 화를 내다 **2.** …을 자랑하다

pi·que [piːkéi / ˊ ˋ] *n.* [U] a cotton material with raised stripes.
—[名] 피케(코르덴처럼 이랑지게 짠 면직물)

pi·ra·cy [páiərəsi] *n.* [U][C] (pl. **-cies**) **1.** robbery by pirates. **2.** the act of pirating another's literary work.
—[名] **1.** 해적 행위 **2.** 저작권 침해

•pi·rate [páiərit] *n.* [C] **1.** a sea robber; a ship used by pirates. **2.** a person who uses another's literary work, etc. without permission.
—[名] **1.** 해적;해적선 **2.** 저작권 침해자

—*vt., vi.* **1.** practice piracy (upon something). **2.** use (a literary work, etc.) without permission. ¶*a pirated edition.*①
—[他][自] **1.** 해적질하다 **2.** 저작권을 침해하다 ¶①해적판

pi·rat·i·cal [pai(ə)rǽtik(ə)l] *adj.* of or like a pirate; engaged in piracy.
—[形] 해적의; 저작권 침해의

pir·ou·ette [pìruét] *n.* [C] a rapid spinning around on one foot or on the toes in dancing. **—*vi.*** dance in this way.
—[名] [무용에서] 발끝으로 돌기 —[自] 발끝으로 돌다

pis·ci·cul·ture [písikʌ̀ltʃər] *n.* [U] the act or art of breeding and raising fish.
—[名] 어류 양식(養殖), 양어법(養魚法)

pish [piʃ, pʃ] *interj.* an exclamation of contempt or impatience. **—*vi.*** make this exclamation.
—[感] 피이!, 체! —[自] 「홍!」하다

pis·til [pístil] *n.* [C] the seed-bearing part of a flower. ↔stamen
—[名] 암술, 자예(雌蕊)

•pis·tol [pístl] *n.* [C] a small, short gun made to be held in one hand. **—*vt.*** (**-toled, -tol·ing** or *Brit.* **-tolled, -tol·ling**) shoot (someone or something) with a pistol.
—[名] 피스톨, 권총 —[他] …을 권총으로 쏘다

pis·ton [píst(ə)n] *n.* [C] (*Machinery*) a round piece or cylinder which moves to and fro in a cylinder.
—[名] ⟪機⟫ 피스톤

:pit¹ [pit] *n.* [C] **1.** a hole in the ground. **2.** a covered hole serving as a trap. **3.** a deep hole made in the earth to dig out coal or other minerals. **4.** ⟪*the ~*⟫ the ground floor of a theater. **5.** a hollow part of the body. **6.** a mark left by smallpox.
—[名] **1.** 구멍 **2.** 함정 **3.** 구덩이, 수갱(竪坑), 탄갱 **4.** 극장의 바닥자리 **5.** 신체의 오목한 부분 **6.** 마마 자국

—*vt.* (**pit·ted, pit·ting**) **1.** make a pit in (some place).
—[他] **1.** …에 구멍을 뚫다 **2.** [동물 따

2. set (one animal) to fight against another. ¶*I pitted my dog against the cat.* **3.** keep (something) in a pit.
위]를 싸움 붙이다 **3.** …을 굴 속에 저장하다

pit² [pit] *n.* [C] (*U.S.*) the hard seed of a cherry, peach, plum, etc.; a stone. —*vt.* (**pit·ted, pit·ting**) remove pits from (fruit).
—[名] 〔美〕 [버찌·복숭아·살구 따위의] 씨 —[他] …의 씨를 빼다

***pitch¹** [pitʃ] *n.* [U] **1.** a thick black material made from boiled tar and used to pave roads or to mend holes. **2.** the sap of a pine tree.
—[名] **1.** [타르 따위에서 채취하는] 피치, 역청(瀝靑) **2.** 송진

as dark as pitch, very black; very dark.
[熟] 피치같이 검은, 새까만, 캄캄한

—*vt.* cover (something) with pitch.
—[他] 피치를 칠하다

‡pitch² [pitʃ] *vt.* **1.** throw. ¶~ *a stone.* **2.** (*Music*) set (a tune, etc.) in a certain key or note. ¶~ *a tune in a higher key.*① **3.** lay out (something) for sale. **4.** fix (something) in the ground; set up. ¶~ *a tent.* / ~ *oneself.*② —*vi.* **1.** throw. ¶*He pitched for our team.* **2.** fall headfirst. **3.** set up a tent. **4.** (of a ship) move up and down. ↔roll **5.** choose or decide without thinking over. 《~ *on* or *upon* something or someone》
—[他] **1.** …을 던지다 **2.** [음조 따위]를 조절하다 ¶①음조를 높이다 **3.** [상품]을 진열하다 **4.** …을 땅에 장치하다(앉히다, 치다) ¶②[땅에] 앉다
—[自] **1.** 던지다 **2.** 거꾸로 떨어지다 **3.** 야영하다; 텐트를 치다 **4.** 아래위로 흔들리다 **5.** [잘 생각지 않고] 고르다, 결정하다

1) ***pitch in,*** (*colloq.*) begin to work hard.
2) ***pitch into,*** (*colloq.*) eat (something) as if one is very hungry; blame or scold (someone) in a severe tone.
3) ***pitch it strong,*** (*colloq.*) talk big; boast.
4) ***pitch on*** (or ***upon***), decide on; encounter.
[熟] 1)〔口〕열심히 하기 시작하다 2)〔口〕아귀같이 먹다; 악다구니를 들이대며 덤비다, 몹시 꾸짖다 3)허풍치다 4)결정하다; 우연히 마주치다

—*n.* [C] **1.** the act of pitching. **2.** [U] [C] a musical note. ¶*at a high* (*low*) ~.③ **3.** degree. **4.** height; top. ¶*at the ~ of one's voice.*④ **5.** [C] [U] slope.
—[名] **1.** 던지기; 배가 아래위로 흔들리기 **2.** 음의 고저, 음조 ¶③높은(낮은) 음조로 **3.** 도(度) **4.** 높이; 정점(頂點) ¶④목청껏 **5.** 경사, 물매

1) ***queer the pitch for,*** spoil (someone's) plans to nothing.
2) ***take up one's pitch,*** keep one's part.
[熟] 1)…의 계획을 좌절시키다 2)분수를 지키다

pitch·blende [pítʃblènd] *n.* [U] a black, shining mineral containing uranium, radium, etc.
—[名] 역청(瀝靑) 우란광(鑛)

pitch-dark [pítʃdá:rk] *adj.* very dark.
—[形] 새까만, 캄캄한, 칠흑 같은

***pitch·er¹** [pítʃər] *n.* [C] a large pot with a handle and lip for holding and pouring liquids. ¶(*proverb*) *Little pitchers have long* (or *big*) *ears.*①
—[名] 물주전자 ¶①〔俚〕아이들은 귀가 밝다

***pitch·er²** [pítʃər] *n.* [C] a person who pitches; the player who pitches the ball to the batter.
—[名] 던지는 사람; 〔野球〕 투수, 피처

pitch·fork [pítʃfɔ̀:rk] *n.* [C] a large fork with a long handle used for tossing hay or straw. —*vt.* toss (hay, straw, etc.) with a pitchfork.
—[名] 건초용 포오크, 쇠스랑
—[他] [건초 따위를] 쇠스랑으로 긁어올리다

pitch·y [pítʃi] *adj.* (**pitch·i·er, pitch·i·est**) **1.** full of pitch. **2.** like pitch; sticky; black.
—[形] **1.** 피치가 많은 **2.** 피치 같은; 끈득거리는; 검은

pit·e·ous [pítiəs] *adj.* arousing sorrow or pity. ▷**pit·e·ous·ness** [-nis] *n.*
—[形] 가련한, 측은한, 슬픈

pit·e·ous·ly [pítiəsli] *adv.* in a piteous manner.
—[副] 가련하게도, 비참하게

pit·fall [pítfɔ̀:l] *n.* [C] a hidden pit used to catch animals; a hidden danger or trap.
—[名] [동물을 잡기 위한] 함정, 덫; 생각지 않았던 위험, 함정

pith [piθ] *n.* [U] **1.** the soft, spongy material in the center of the stem of certain plants. **2.** a similar soft tissue. **3.** the main part of a thing. ¶*of great ~ and moment.*① **4.** strength; energy.
—[名] **1.** [나무의] 고갱이 **2.** 골수, 척수 **3.** 골자, 요점 ¶①매우 중요한 **4.** 체력; 정력

pith·y [píθi] *adj.* (**pith·i·er, pith·i·est**) **1.** having much pith; of or like pith. **2.** forceful; full of meaning.
—[形] **1.** 고갱이가 있는; 고갱이(골수) 같은 **2.** 힘있는, 힘찬; 함축성 있는

pit·i·a·ble [pítiəbl] *adj.* **1.** arousing pity. ¶*a ~ sight.* **2.** arousing contempt or scorn.
—[形] **1.** 가엾은, 불쌍한, 측은한 **2.** 경멸할 만한, 비열한

pit·i·a·bly [pítiəbli] *adv.* in a pitiable manner.
—[副] 불쌍하게도; 비열하게도

pit·i·ful [pítif(u)l] *adj.* **1.** arousing pity or sorrow. **2.** feeling or showing pity. **3.** arousing contempt. ▷**pit·i·ful·ly** [-fuli] *adv.*
—[形] **1.** 불쌍한, 가엾은 **2.** 인정(동정심) 많은 **3.** 경멸할 만한, 비열한

pit·i·less [pítilis] *adj.* without pity or mercy.
—[形] 무자비한, 무정한

pit·i·less·ly [pítilisli] *adv.* in a pitiless manner.
—[副] 무자비하게, 무정하게

pit·man [pítmən] *n.* [C] (pl. **-men** [-mən]) a person who works in a pit, esp. in a coal mine.
—[名] 갱부(坑夫); 탄갱부

pit·tance [pít(ə)ns] *n.* [C] **1.** a small allowance of money. **2.** a small amount.
—[名] **1.** 얼마 안 되는 수당 **2.** 소량, 소액

·**Pitts·burgh** [pítsbə:rg] *n.* a city in southwestern Pennsylvania.
—[名] 미국 Pennsylvania 주 서남부의 도시

P

:pit·y [píti] *n.* (pl. **pit·ies**) **1.** [U] the feeling of sorrow over the trouble of others; mercy. **2.** [C] a cause of regret or pity. ¶*The ~ is that he has failed.*

1) ***for pity's sake,*** an expression of annoyance.
2) ***have*** (or ***take***) ***pity on*** (=*show mercy to*) *someone.*
3) ***in pity of,*** feeling pity.

—*vt*: (**pit·ied**) feel pity for (someone or something).

—[名] 1. 동정; 연민 2. 애석한(불쌍한) 일, 유감스러운 일
[熟] 1)제발, 불쌍히 여기고 2)…을 불쌍해하다, …에게 동정하다 3)…을 불쌍히 여겨
—[他] …을 불쌍히 여기다, …에게 동정하다

piv·ot [pívət] *n.* [C] **1.** a shaft, pin or point on which a thing turns. **2.** a thing on which something important depends; the central point. ¶*the ~ of hope.*① **—*vt.*** place on or supply (something) with a pivot. **—*vi.*** turn on a pivot.

—[名] 1. 선회축, 피봇 2. 중심점, 요점 ¶①희망의 중심점 —[他] …을 축 위에 놓다; …에 축을 달다 —[自] 축 위에서 선회하다

piv·ot·al [pívətl] *adj.* of or serving as a pivot.

—[形] 추축(樞軸)의; 중추의, 중요한

pix·y, pix·ie [píksi] *n.* [C] (pl. **pix·ies**) a small elf or fairy.

—[名] 작은 요정(妖精)

pl. 1. place. **2.** plural.

plac·ard *n.* [plǽkɑːrd / -kərd] [C] a poster; a large printed notice. **—*vt.*** place placards on or in (some place); advertise (something) by means of placards.

—[名] 벽보, 게시(揭示), 포스터; 삐라; 플래카아드 —[他] …에 포스터를 붙이다; …을 삐라로 광고하다

pla·cate [pléikeit, plækéit / pləkéit, pléikeit] *vt.* take away the anger of (someone); calm.

—[他] …을 달래다; 위로하다

:place [pleis] *n.* [C] **1.** a part of space where someone or something exists; an area. ¶*a market ~*① / *This is no ~ for men.*② / *from ~ to ~.*③ **2.** a region; a district. ¶*It snows heavily in this ~.*④ **3.** a city; a town; a village. **4.** a special spot. ¶*a sore ~ on the arm.*⑤ **5.** a house and its grounds. ¶*Come round to my ~.*⑥ **6.** a building or space used for a special purpose. ¶*a ~ of business* / *a ~ of amusement.*⑦ **7.** [U] space; room. ¶*leave ~ for him.*⑧ **8.** [C] a seat. ¶*keep a ~ for someone* / *Go back to your ~.*⑨ **9.** a position; a job; another's state. ¶*If I were in your ~.* **10.** a duty or piece of business. ¶*It's my ~ to show you the way.*⑩ **11.** an order of a discussion, a race, etc. ¶*in the first ~*⑪ / *win the first ~.*⑫

1) ***a place in the sun,*** an advantage; success.
2) ***find a place,*** get a job.
3) ***give place to*** (=*make way for*) *someone.*
4) ***in someone's place,*** instead of someone.
5) ***in place,*** in the right place; properly.
6) ***in place of,*** instead of.
7) ***keep someone in his proper place,*** make someone do only his own duty.
8) ***know one's place,*** be humble enough.
9) ***out of place,*** not in the right or proper place or order.
10) ***take place,*** happen.
11) ***take the place*** (=*act instead*) ***of*** *someone.*

—*vt.* 1. put (something) in a place. ¶*Place them in order.*⑬ **2.** put (someone) in a post, position, etc. **3.** order (something) for or from a firm, etc. 《~ something *with*》; put (money) into a business. 《~ something *in*》 ¶*~ an order with a firm.* **4.** know; recognize; estimate. ¶*a person difficult to ~.*⑭ **5.** show the position or order in a race.

—[名] 1. 장소, 곳; 고장 ¶①장터, 시장/②여기는 남자들이 올 곳이 아니다/③여기저기에, 이곳저곳으로 2. 지방, 지역 ¶④이 지방은 눈이 몹시 내린다 3. 시, 읍, 면 4. 개소(個所), 국부 ¶⑤팔의 쑤시는 부분 5. 집, 처소, 저택 ¶⑥우리 집에도 와 주시오 6. 건물, 본부, …장(場), …소(所) ¶⑦오락장 7. 여지, 공간 ¶⑧그가 들어올 여지를 남겨놓다 8. 좌석, 자리 ¶⑨네 자리로 돌아가라 9. 지위, 직; [남의] 입장 10. 직무, 일 ¶⑩안내해 드리는 것이 저의 직무입니다 11. 순서, 단계, 순위 ¶⑪첫째로, 맨 처음에/⑫1위(1착)를 하다
[熟] 1)양지쪽, 유리한 지위, 우위 2)직업을 얻다, 취직하다 3)…에게 길(지위)을 양보하다 4)… 대신에 5)적절한 위치에, 적소에; 적절히 6)… 대신에 7)…에게 자기 분수를 지키게 하다 8)자기 분수를 알다 9)본래의 자리를 떠나서, 제 자리가 아닌; 부적당하게 10)일어나다, 발생하다 11)…의 대리를 하다
—[他] 1. …을 놓다, 두다, 배열하다 ¶⑬그것들을 가지런히 놓으시오 2. …을 [지위 따위]에 앉히다, 임명하다 3. [주문]을 내다, [돈]을 투자하다 4. 알다, 알아보다; 평가하다 ¶⑭정체를 모를 사람 5. 순위를 정하다

place·ment [pléismənt] *n.* [U] **1.** the act of placing; the state of being placed. **2.** the act of finding work or a job for a person.

—[名] 1. 두기, 놓기; 배치 2. 직업 소개

plac·er [pléisər] *n.* [C] a place where gold or other minerals can be obtained by washing sand, stones, etc.

—[名] 사금 채취소, 사광(砂鑛)

plac·id [plǽsid] *adj.* calm; peaceful. ▷**plac·id·ly** [-li] *adv.* —**plac·id·ness** [-nis] *n.*

—[形] 조용한, 평온한; 차분한

plac·id·i·ty [plæsíditi] *n.* [U] calmness; peace.

—[名] 평온; 평정(平靜)

plack·et [plǽkit] *n.* [C] an opening at the top of a skirt to make it easy to put on.

—[名] [스커어트의] 옆을 터놓은 부분, [스커어트의] 호주머니

pla·gi·a·rism [pléidʒiərìz(ə)m] *n.* **1.** [U] the act of plagiarizing. **2.** [C] a plagiarized idea, passage, etc.

—[名] 1. 표절; 표절 행위 2. 표절물

pla·gia·rist [pléidʒ(j)ərist] *n.* ⓒ a person who plagiarizes. —영 표절자

pla·gia·rize [pléidʒ(j)əràiz] *vt.* take and use (the ideas, works, etc. of another) as one's own. —영 [타인의 고안·문장 따위]를 표절하다

* **plague** [pleig] *n.* ⓤ **1.** a deadly disease which spreads rapidly; (*the* ~) a dangerous disease spread by rats and carried to man by fleas. **2.** a punishment thought to be given by God. **3.** ⓒ a person or thing that causes great trouble.
—*vt.* **1.** cause (someone) to suffer from a plague. **2.** trouble; worry. ¶~ *someone with questions.*①
—영 1. 역병(疫病), 페스트 2. 천벌 3. 성가신 일(사람); 끝칫거리 일(사람)

—태 1. …을 역병에 걸리게 하다 2. …을 성가시게 굴다; 피롭히다 ¶①…에게 성가시게 질문하다

pla·guy [pléigi] *adj.* (*colloq.*) annoying; troublesome. —형 〈口〉성가신, 귀찮은; 끝칫거리인

plaice [pleis] *n.* ⓒ (pl. **plaic·es** or *collectively* **plaice**) a flat sea-fish. —영 넙치·가자미류의 식용어

plaid [plæd] *n.* **1.** ⓤ woolen cloth with a square pattern of different colors. **2.** ⓒ a long piece of this cloth worn over the shoulder and breast by Scottish Highlanders. —영 1. 바둑판 무늬의 스코틀랜드 나사(羅紗) 2. 바둑판 무늬의 긴 어깨걸이

: **plain** [plein] *adj.* **1.** clear; easy to understand. ¶*The matter is quite* ~. **2.** simple; frank; common. ¶~ *living* / *in* ~ *clothes.*① **3.** not lovely or not pretty. ¶*a* ~ *girl.* **4.** flat. *be plain with you; in plain words,* frankly speaking. —*adv.* clearly. ¶*speak* ~.
—*n.* ⓒ a large field; a large area of open space.
—형 1. 명백한, 명료한, 알기 쉬운 2. 간소한, 검소한, 수수한; 꾸미지 않는, 솔직한; 보통의 ¶①평복으로 2. 예쁘지 않은, 수수하게 생긴 4. 평평한, 평탄한
熟 솔직이 말해서
—위 똑똑히, 분명히, 알기 쉽게
—영 평지, 평원

* **plain·ly** [pléinli] *adv.* in a plain manner. —위 평이(平易)하게, 명료하게, 솔직히

plain·ness [pléinnis] *n.* ⓤ the state of being plain. —영 평명함; 명백; 솔직; 검소, 간소

plains·man [pléinzmən] *n.* ⓒ (pl. **-men** [-mən]) a person who lives on the plains. —영 평원의 주민

plain-spo·ken [pléinspóuk(ə)n] *adj.* frank in speech. ¶*a*~ *opinion.*① —형 솔직한 ¶①솔직한 의견

plaint [pleint] *n.* ⓤⓒ **1.** (*poetic*) a lament; lamentation. **2.** complaint. —영 1.〈詩〉애가(哀歌); 비탄 2. 불평, 불만

plain·tiff [pléintif] *n.* ⓒ (*Law*) a person who brings a suit in a law court. ↔defendant —영〈法〉원고(原告)

plain·tive [pléintiv] *adj.* showing sorrow or melancholy; mournful. —형 구슬픈, 애처로운

plait [pleit / plæt] *n.* ⓒ **1.** a flat fold; a pleat. **2.** a strip of woven hair; a braid. ¶*She wore her hair in a* ~. —*vt.* make (something) into a braid or plait. ¶*a plaited skirt*① / *plaited straw.*② —영 1.〈천 따위의〉주름 2. 변발(辮髮); [밀짚] 노끈, 꼰 끈 —태 …에 주름을 잡다; …을 엮다, 짜다, 땋다, 꼬다 ¶①주름치마/②밀짚 노끈

: **plan** [plæn] *n.* ⓒ **1.** a map showing the arrangement of the parts of anything. ¶*a raised* ~① / *a floor* ~.② **2.** a way or scheme for making, doing or arranging something. ¶*Everything went according to* [*the*] ~.③
—*vt.* (**planned, plan·ning**) **1.** make a drawing of (a structure). **2.** think out a scheme for doing (something). **3.** (*U.S.*) intend; expect. ¶*I am planning to go to Africa.* —*vi.* make a plan.
—영 1. 설계도, 도면 ¶①밑그림/②평면도 2. 계획, 설계 ¶③만사가 계획대로 되어 갔다

—태 1. …의 설계도를 그리다, 작도(作圖)하다 2. …을 계획하다 3.〈美〉…할 생각(작정)이다
—자 계획을 세우다

: **plane**¹ [plein] *n.* ⓒ **1.** a surface that is smooth, flat and level. **2.** a grade of development; a level. **3.** an airplane. ¶*go by* ~.① **4.** the surface of the wings of an airplane.
—*adj.* flat; even. ¶~ *geometry.*②
—*vi.* make a surface flat; travel by plane.
—영 1. 평면; 면 2. [발달의] 정도; 단계; [지식 따위의] 수준 3. 비행기 ¶①비행기로 가다 4. [비행기의] 날개관
—형 평면의; 평평한, 평탄한 ¶②평면기하학
—자 비행기로 가다

plane² [plein] *n.* ⓒ a tool to make the surface smooth. ⇒fig. —*vt.* smooth (the surface) with a plane. —영 대패 —태 …을 대패로 깎다, …을 대패질하다

[plane²]

: **plan·et** [plænit] *n.* ⓒ one of the heavenly bodies which moves around the sun. ⇒N.B. —영 혹성(惑星) N.B. 항성은 fixed star

plan·e·tar·i·a [plæ̀nitɛ́əriə] *n.* pl. of **planetarium**.

plan·e·tar·i·um [plæ̀nitɛ́əriəm] *n.* ⓒ (pl. **-tar·i·a** or **-tar·i·ums**) a room with an apparatus for showing the movements of heavenly bodies. —영 천문관(天文館)

plan·e·tar·y [plǽniteri / -t(ə)ri] *adj.* **1.** of a planet or planets. ¶~ *system.*① **2.** of the earth or this world; terrestrial. **3.** moving like a planet. —형 1. 혹성의 ¶①태양계 2. 지상의, 이 세상의, 지구상의 3. 궤도를 운행하는

***plank** [plæŋk] *n.* [C] **1.** a broad, thick piece of timber. **2.** a thing which supports. **3.** an article of the statement of principles of a political party.
—[名] 1. 두꺼운 판자, 널빤지 2. 의지가 되는 것 3. [정당의] 강령의 한 조항

—*vt.* cover (something) with planks.
—[他] …에 널빤지를 대다

plank·ing [plǽŋkiŋ] *n.* [C] 《*collectively*》 planks in a floor.
—[名] 바닥에 깐 판자, 마루 판자

plank·ton [plǽŋktən / -tɔn] *n.* [U] very small animal and plant organisms floating in water.
—[名] 플랭크톤, 부유 생물

⁑**plant** [plænt / plɑːnt] *n.* [C] **1.** a living thing that grows usu. from the ground, having a stem, a root, and leaves. ¶*Birds are not plants.* **2.** such a small organism, in contrast with a tree or shrub. **3.** a young organism ready for putting into other soil. ¶*tomato plants.*① **4.** the building and equipment of a factory, business, etc.; an apparatus used for a mechanical process in a factory, etc. ¶*a water-power ~*② / *an automobile ~.*③
—[名] 1. 식물 2. 풀, 초목 3. 묘목 ¶① 토마토 묘목 4. 공장; 설비 ¶②수력발전소/③자동차 공장

—*vt.* **1.** put (young trees, seeds, etc.) in the ground to make them grow; sow. ¶*~ a tree.* **2.** provide (land) with plants. 《~ a place *with*》 ¶*~ a garden with roses.*④ **3.** fix (something) in position; put. ¶*She planted herself in front of the stove.* **4.** introduce (young fish) in a river, lake, etc. **5.** introduce (an idea, a feeling, etc.). ¶*~ a love for learning.* **6.** settle (people) in a colony; set up (a colony, a city, etc.).
—[他] 1. …을 심다, 씨를 뿌리다 2. [토지]에 심다 3. …에 장치하다; …을 세우다 4. [어린 물고기]를 강 따위에 놓아주다 5. [주의 따위]를 주입하다, 심어 넣다 6. [사람들]을 식민하다; [식민지]를 건설하다

plan·tain [plǽntin, +*Brit.* -plɑ́ːn-] *n.* [C] **1.** a common weed with broad leaves. ⇒fig. **2.** a kind of banana.
—[名] 1. 질경이 2. 바나나의 일종

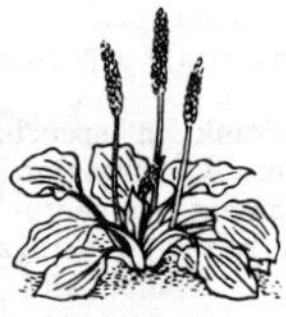
[plantain 1.]

***plan·ta·tion** [plæntéiʃ(ə)n, +*Brit.* plɑːn-] *n.* [C] **1.** a large farm in tropical countries where cotton, tobacco, sugar, rubber, etc. are grown. **2.** a large planting of trees. **3.** the act of settling colonists; 《*pl.*》 a colony.
—[名] 1. [특히 열대·아열대 지방의 대규모의] 농장, 농원, 재배장 2. 식림(植林) 3. 식민; 식민지

plant·er [plǽntər / plɑ́ːntə] *n.* [C] **1.** a person who owns or manages a plantation. **2.** a person who plants. **3.** a planting machine. **4.** a colonist.
—[名] 1. 농장주 2. 심는 사람, 재배자 3 파종기(播種器) 4. 식민자(植民者)

plant louse [⌐ ⌐] *n.* a harmful insect which sucks the sap of plants; an aphid.
—[名] 진디

plaque [plæk / plɑːk, plæk] *n.* [C] **1.** a thin piece of metal, clay, etc. used as an ornament on the wall. **2.** a platelike ornament or badge.
—[名] 1. [금속·도기(陶器) 따위로 만든] 액자; 장식판, 현판(懸板) 2. 배지

plash [plæʃ] *n.* [C] **1.** 《*sing.* only》 a splashing sound of water. **2.** a puddle. —*vi., vt.* splash.
—[名] 1. 철썩, 텀벙[하는 소리] 2. 웅덩이 —[自][他] 철썩(텀벙)소리나다(내다)

plash·y [plǽʃi] *adj.* (**plash·i·er, plash·i·est**) **1.** full of pools or puddles. **2.** making a sound like a splash of water; splashing.
—[形] 1. 물웅덩이가 많은 2. 철썩철썩하는

***plas·ter** [plǽstər / plɑ́ːstə] *n.* [U] **1.** a mixture of lime, sand, and water used for coating walls and ceilings. **2.** a white powder that becomes a thick paste when mixed with water and becomes hard as it dries; plaster of Paris. **3.** a substance applied to the body to relieve soreness, etc. ¶*an adhesive ~*① / *a mustard ~.*②
—[名] 1. 회반죽 2. 석고 3. 고약 ¶①반창고/②겨자 연고

—*vt.* **1.** cover (a wall, a ceiling, etc.) with plaster. **2.** apply a plaster to (a wound, etc.). **3.** cover (something) all over.
—[他] 1. …에 회반죽을 칠하다(바르다) 2. …에 고약을 붙이다 3. …에 온통 [더덕더덕] 바르다

plas·ter·er [plǽst(ə)rər / plɑ́ːst(ə)rə] *n.* [C] a person who plasters walls and ceilings.
—[名] 미장이

plas·tic [plǽstik] *adj.* **1.** molding or giving form to matter. **2.** that can be formed or molded easily. **3.** easily influenced.
—[形] 1. 조형적인 2. 소조(塑造)할 수 있는, 가소성(可塑性)의 3. 감화하기 쉬운, 감수성이 강한

—*n.* [U] 《often *pl.*》 a substance that is made into various shapes by heat, pressure, etc. ¶*a ~ toy.*①
—[名] 플래스틱, 합성수지 ¶①플래스틱제 장난감

plas·tic·i·ty [plæstísiti] *n.* [U] the quality of being plastic.
—[名] 가소성; 적응성

plastic surgery [⌐ ⌐ ⌐] *n.* a branch of surgery dealing with the repair of lost or deformed parts of the
—[名] 성형(成形)외과

plate [pleit] *n.* Ⓒ **1.** a flat, open dish for holding food. **2.** the amount of food a plate will hold. ¶ *a ~ of soup*① / *a fruit ~*② **3.** food served to one person at a meal. ¶ *two dollars a ~.*③ **4.** Ⓤ ((*collectively*)) dishes, knives, forks, etc. made of gold, silver, or other metals. ¶ *family ~.*④ **5.** a thin, flat piece or sheet of metal, glass, etc. ¶ *a tin ~.* **6.** a thin, flat piece of metal with a person's name, etc. ¶ *a doorplate.* **7.** a full-page picture in a book; a sheet of metal used for printing. **8.** (*Photography*) a thin sheet of glass on which a photograph is taken. **9.** the home base in baseball.
— *vt.* **1.** cover (esp. a ship) with metal plates for protection. **2.** coat (metal) with gold, silver, etc.

—⑧ 1. [얕은] 접시 2. 한 접시분(分); [접시에 담은] 요리 ¶①수우프 한 접시/②과일 코오스 3. 1인분의 식사 ¶③식사 1인분 2 달러 4. [금은제 따위의] 식기류 ¶④가문(家紋)을 새긴 가보인 식기 5. 판금(板金)·판유리 6. 금속제의 명찰 7. [책 속의] 1페이지 크기의 도판(圖版); 금속판(版) 8. [사진의] 감광판 9. [야구의] 호옴베이스, 본루

—⑩ 1. [배 따위]에 금속판을 씌우다, 장갑(裝甲)하다 2. [금속]에 도금하다

* **pla·teau** [plætóu, +*Brit.* ´−] *n.* (*pl.* **-teaus** or **-teaux**) Ⓒ an elevated, flat piece of land; a tableland.

—⑧ 고원(高原), 대지(臺地)

pla·teaux [plætóuz] *n. pl.* of **plateau**.
plat·en [plǽt(ə)n] *n.* Ⓤ **1.** a flat metal plate or cylinder of a printing press that presses the paper onto the inked type. **2.** the roller of a typewriter.

—⑧ 1. [인쇄기의] 인자판(印字版), 윤전기의 로울러 2. [타이프라이터의] 인자부

‡ **plat·form** [plǽtfɔ:rm] *n.* Ⓒ **1.** a raised floor or stage for speakers. **2.** a raised level surface beside the track at a railroad station. **3.** (*U.S.*) a statement of the main principles of a political party.

—⑧ 1. 연단, 교단, 강단 2. 플랫포옴, [역의] 승강장 3. [정당의] 강령

plat·ing [pléitiŋ] *n.* Ⓤ **1.** the art of coating with gold or silver. **2.** a thin coating of gold, silver or other metals.

—⑧ 1. 도금술 2. [금·은 따위의] 도금

plat·i·num [plǽtinəm] *n.* Ⓤ a silvery metal used for jewelry, etc.
plat·i·tude [plǽtitj(j)ù:d / -tjù:d] *n.* **1.** Ⓒ a dull or flat remark, esp. one uttered as if it were fresh. **2.** Ⓤ the quality of being dull and flat.

—⑧ 백금, 플래티나
—⑧ 1. 상투적인 문구 2. 단조로움, 평범; 진부함

Pla·to [pléitou] *n.* (427 ?-347 ? B. C.) a Greek philosopher.
Pla·ton·ic [plətánik / -tɔ́n-] *adj.* **1.** of Plato or his philosophy. **2.** idealistic or impractical. **3.** ((also *p-*)) not sensual but spiritual. ¶ ~ *love.*①

—⑧ 플라톤(그리이스의 철학자)
—⑩ 1. 플라톤[철학]의 2. 관념적인 3. 순(純)정신적인 ¶①정신적 연애, 플라토닉 러브

pla·toon [plətú:n] *n.* Ⓒ **1.** a small group of about 60 soldiers acting as a unit. **2.** (*U.S.*) a small unit of policemen. **3.** a small group.

—⑧ 1. 보병 소대 2. (美) 경찰대(警察隊) 3. 일단(一團), 한 떼

plat·ter [plǽtər] *n.* Ⓒ a large, flat dish for serving meat, fish, etc.
plau·dits [plɔ́:dits] *n. pl.* **1.** the act of clapping hands to show approval. **2.** the enthusiastic expression of public praise.

—⑧ 큰 접시
—⑧ 1. 박수갈채 2. 칭찬; 절찬

plau·si·bil·i·ty [plɔ̀:zibíliti] *n.* Ⓤ the state or quality of being plausible.

—⑧ 그럴 듯함, 정말 같음

* **plau·si·ble** [plɔ́:zibl] *adj.* appearing to be true or reasonable.

—⑩ 그럴 듯한, 정말 같은

‡ **play** [plei] *vt.* **1.** take part in (a game, a sport, etc.). ¶ ~ *baseball* / ~ *bridge.* **2.** take part in a game against (someone or something); fill (a position) or use (a player, etc.) in a game. ¶ ~ *another team* / *I played center forward.* **3.** act the part of (someone) in a play or in real life; perform (a drama, etc.) on the stage; perform in (a city, etc.). ¶ ~ [*the part of*] *Cinderella* / ~ *a tragedy* / ~ *the madman*① / *They played Tokyo for a month.* **4.** produce music or sound from (a musical instrument, tape recorder, etc.); perform (a piece of music) on an instrument. ¶ ~ *the piano* / ~ *a waltz* / ~ *a record.* **5.** do (a trick, joke, etc.) either in fun or to deceive; cause. ¶ ~ *havoc*② / ~ *someone a mean trick;* ~ *a trick on someone.*③ **6.** imitate or pretend to be (someone) or to do (something) in fun. ((~ *that* ...)) ¶ ~ *house*④ / *The children played that they were pirates.* **7.** cause (something) to move, act, or work; direct (a jet of water, a searchlight, etc.). ¶ ~ *a horse on a lawn* / ~ *one's stick freely.*

—⑩ 1. [유희 따위]를 하다; [시합·경기]에 참가하다 2. …을 상대로 시합(승부)하다; …을 선수로 기용하다; [포지션]을 차지하다 3. [연극·역(役)]을 연기하다; …으로 분장하다; …처럼 행동하다; [도시 따위]에서 흥행을 하다 ¶①미치광이처럼 행동하다 4. [악기 따위]를 연주하다; [악곡]을 연주하다 5. [장난·농담]을 걸다; [해로움 따위]를 주다 ②해를 주다/③…을 속이다 6. 흉내를 내며 놀다 ¶④소꿉질하다 7. …을 쓰다, 움직이다; [물·빛 따위]를 향하게 하다

—*vi.* **1.** spend time doing something pleasant, not working. ¶*She likes to ~ with her doll.* **2.** be not at work. ↔work **3.** toy; fool; trifle handle. 《*~ with* something》 ¶*~ with fire.* **4.** do something in sport; take part in a game; gamble. ¶*~ for money.*⑤ **5.** (of ground) be in a certain condition. ¶*The ground plays well.* **6.** act on the stage; (of a play, film, etc.) be performed or be showing. ¶*The actor plays well. | What's playing tonight?*⑥ **7.** perform music on an instrument; (of a musical instrument) sound in performance. ¶*~ on the piano | The strings played well.*⑦ **8.** behave or act in a certain way. ¶*~ false with a friend.*⑧ **9.** (of light, water, etc.) be moving with a dancing motion; (of a fountain, a jet of water, etc.) be in operation. ¶*Sunlight plays on the water.*

—[自] 1. 놀다, 장난치다 2. 동맹파업하다; 일하지 않고 놀다 3. 만지작거리다; 가지고 놀다 4. 유희를 하다; 시합(경기)하다; 노름하다, 내기하다 ¶⑤돈 걸고 내기하다 5. [토지의 상태가] 어떤 상태에 있다 6. 연극에 출연하다; 연기하다; [연극·영화 따위가] 상연(상영)되다 ¶⑥오늘 밤에는 무슨 영화가 상영됩니까? 7. [음악·악기가] 연주되다, 울리다; [악기를] 연주하다 ¶⑦현악기 연주가 좋았다 8. 행동하다, 처신하다 ¶⑧친구에게 부정수단을 쓰다 9. [빛·물 따위가] 흔들흔들하다, 어른거리다 [분수·물 따위가] 분출하다

1) ***be played out,*** be exhausted; be worn out.
2) ***play at,*** do for pleasure. 《*~ doing*》
3) ***play down,*** make light of (something).
4) ***play into** someone's **hands,*** give someone an advantage without intending to.
5) ***play off,*** ⓐ practise. ⓑ deceive.
6) ***play off** one person **against** another,* set one person against another for one's own advantage.
7) ***play on*** (or ***upon***)***,*** try to make use of (someone's feelings, honesty, etc.) for one's advantage.
8) ***play out,*** play to the end.
9) ***play up,*** ⓐ work hard or perform one's duty. ⓑ emphasize.
10) ***play up to** someone,* do or say in order to gain favor, etc.

[熟] 1)기진맥진하다, 녹초가 되다 2)…하며 놀다 3)…을 얕보다, 경시하다 4)…에게 뜻하지 않게 이익을 주다(이기게 하다) 5)ⓐ…을 행하다 ⓑ…을 속이다 6)갑과 을을 반목케 하여 어부지리를 얻다 7)[…의 감정]을 이용하다; …의 약점을 이용하다 8)…을 끝까지 연기(연주)하다 9)ⓐ일 따위를 열심히 하다 ⓑ강조하다 10)…에게 알랑거리다, 아양떨다

—*n.* **1.** [U] action or exercise for amusement. ¶(*proverb*) *All work and no ~ makes Jack a dull boy.*⑨ **2.** [C] a game; sport. **3.** [C] a turn to play in a game; a move or act in a game. ¶*a ~ in baseball | It's your ~ next.* **4.** [U] manner of playing; conduct; action. ¶*fair ~*⑩ *| foul ~.* **5.** [C] fun; amusement; joke. ¶*say something in ~ | a ~ on words.*⑪ **6.** [U] activity; use; operation; freedom or room for movement; scope. ¶*be in full ~ | give full ~ to one's imagination*⑫ *| This wheel has too much ~.* **7.** [C] a drama; the written text for this. ¶*act a ~ | a moral ~.*⑬ **8.** [U] light, quick, changeable movement. ¶*the ~ of light and shade on a wall | the ~ of expression in a face.*⑭

—[名] 1. 놀기, 놀이, 유희 ¶⑨《俚》공부만 하고 놀지 않는 아이는 머리가 둔해진다 2. 승부, 경기, 시합 3. 승부(경기)의 차례 4. 시합하는 솜씨; 태도, 행동 ¶⑩공명정대한 행위 5. 위안, 즐거움, 낙, 농담 ¶⑪말의 장난 6. 활동; 운용(運用); 작용; 자유로운 활동; 활동 범위 ¶⑫상상을 자유분방하게 구사하다 7. 극, 연극, 희곡, 각본 ¶⑬권선징악극(勸善懲惡劇) 8. [빛 따위의] 움직임, 번득임, ¶⑭얼굴 표정의 움직임

play·back [pléibæk] *n.* [C] **1.** the act of reproducing recorded sound. **2.** the device used for it.
—[名] 1. 녹음 재생 2. 재생 장치

play·bill [pléibìl] *n.* [C] **1.** a poster advertising the performance of a play. **2.** a program of a play.
—[名] 1. 연극의 광고(포스터) 2. [연극의] 프로그램

play·boy [pléibɔ̀i] *n.* [C] (*colloq.*) a fellow who is chiefly interested in seeking pleasure.
—[名] 난봉꾼, 한량

play·day [pléidèi] *n.* [C] a holiday.
—[名] 휴일

:play·er [pléiər] *n.* [C] **1.** a person who plays a game. **2.** a musician. **3.** an actor. **4.** a device for playing a musical instrument automatically. ¶*a ~ piano.*①
—[名] 1. 선수 2. 연주자 3. 배우 4. 자동 연주 장치 ¶①자동 피아노

play·fel·low [pléifèlou] *n.* [C] a playmate.
—[名] 놀이 친구

play·ful [pléif(u)l] *adj.* **1.** fond of playing or fun. **2.** humorous; not serious; joking.
—[形] 1. 놀기 좋아하는, 명랑한 2. 농담의

play·ful·ly [pléifuli] *adv.* gaily; humorously.
—[副] 명랑하게, 농담으로

play·ful·ness [pléif(u)lnis] *n.* [U] the state of being playful.
—[名] 농담, 장난

play·go·er [pléigòuər] *n.* [C] a person who goes often or habitually to the theater.
—[名] 연극 구경을 자주 하는 사람

:play·ground [pléigràund] *n.* [C] a ground for children's play; a place of amusement.
—[名] 운동장, 놀이터

play·house [pléihàus] *n.* [C] **1.** a theater. **2.** (*U.S.*) a small house for children to play in. **3.** a toy house.
—[名] 1. 극장 2. 《美》 어린이의 놀이집 3. [어린이의] 장난감집

playing cards [⌐-⌐] *n. pl.* cards used in playing games.
—[名] 트럼프, 화투

playing field [867] **plebeian**

playing field [⌐ ⌐] *n.* (chiefly *Brit.*) any official ground where various games are played. 「games.」
― 名 〔주로 英〕 [공식·공인의] 경기장, 구기장(球技場)

play·mate [pléimèit] *n.* ⓒ a companion in play or ― 名 놀이 친구

play·thing [pléiθiŋ] *n.* ⓒ a thing to play with; a toy.
― 名 장난감, 노리개

play·time [pléitàim] *n.* ⓤ a period for play or recreation. 「for the theater; a dramatist.」
― 名 노는 시간, 휴식 시간

play·wright [pléirait] *n.* ⓒ a person who writes plays〕
― 名 각본가, 극작가

pla·za [pláːzə, plǽzə] *n.* ⓒ a public square or open place in a city or town.
― 名 대광장

plea [pliː] *n.* ⓒ **1.** a request; an appeal. **2.** an excuse. **3.** (*Law*) an answer by a defendant to charges in a law court. ¶*He made a ~ of not guilty.*①
on the plea of (=*making an excuse of,* or *on the pretence of*) *something.*
― 名 1 청원 2 변명, 핑계 3. 항변(抗辯) ¶①그는 무죄임을 항변했다
熟 …을 핑계로

plead [pliːd] *vi.* **1.** argue or reason for or against something. **2.** make an earnest appeal; beg earnestly. **3.** make a plea in a law court. ― *vt.* **1.** defend (a case) by arguments in a law court. **2.** answer (something) to a charge. **3.** offer (something) as an excuse. ¶*She pleaded ignor ℎ 1ce of the fact.*①
plead guilty ₁. (=*admit oneself to be responsible for*) *something.* 「lawyer in a court.」
― 自 1. 변론하다 2. 탄원하다 3, 항변하다 ― 他 1. …을 변호하다 2. …을 실립하다 3. 핑계로서 …이라고 말하다 ¶①그녀는 사실을 알지 못했다고 변명했다
熟 …에 대해 책임이 있다고 말하다

plead·er [plíːdər] *n.* ⓒ **1.** a person who pleads. **2.** a〕
― 名 1. 변론자 2. 변호사

plead·ings [plíːdiŋz] *n. pl.* (*Law*) the statements by a plaintiff and a defendant in a court.
― 名 《法》소답(訴答) [서면]

‡**pleas·ant** [pléznt] *adj.* **1.** delightful; pleasing. ¶*a ~ voice*① / *a ~ evening.*② **2.** having an agreeable or charming manner; amiable.
― 形 1. 유쾌한 ¶①기분 좋은 목소리/②즐거운 밤 2. 상냥한

• **pleas·ant·ly** [pléznli] *adv.* in a pleasant manner.
― 副 유쾌하게

pleas·ant·ness [plézntnis] *n.* ⓤ the state or quality of being pleasant.
― 名 유쾌함, 즐거움

pleas·ant·ry [pléznri] *n.* (*pl.* **-ries**) **1.** ⓤ humor; merriment. **2.** ⓒ a humorous speech; a joke.
― 名 1. 우스꽝스러움 2. 농담

‡**please** [pliːz] *vt.* give pleasure or delight to (someone); satisfy. ⇒USAGE ¶*~ oneself*① / *This book will ~ you.* / *He is pleased at his son's success.* / *She was pleased with the news.* / *It pleased him to go.* ― *vi.* **1.** wish; desire; intend. ¶*I'll do as I ~.* / *Take as many as you ~.* **2.** be agreeable; win favor; make oneself pleasant. ¶*the desire to ~* / *He is anxious to ~.* **3.** (used only as a polite addition to requests or commands) if you like; if you please. ¶*Come in, ~.* / *Please take your seat.* 「pleased to do so.②」
1) *be pleased* (=*be glad* or *happy*) *to do.* ¶*I shall be*〕
2) *if you please,* ⓐ if you wish. ¶*Give me a cup of tea, if you ~.* ⓑ expressing surprise. ¶*The next moment, if you ~, the man was out of sight.*③
3) *please God,* if it is God's wish.
― 他 …을 기쁘게 하다, 만족시키다; …의 마음에 들다 at(with, in 따위)의 형으로 형용사처럼 쓰임 ¶멋대로 행동하다 ― 自 1. 바라다, 좋아하다 2. 남의 마음에 들다, 남을 기쁘게 하다;기분이 좋다 3. 부디, 제발
熟 1)기꺼이 …하다 ¶①기꺼이 그렇게 하겠읍니다 2)ⓐ원하신다면 ⓑ놀라운 일은 ¶③놀랍게도 다음 순간에 그 사내는 이미 모습을 감추었더라 3)신의 뜻이라면

• **pleas·ing** [plíːziŋ] *adj.* giving pleasure; agreeable.
▷ **pleas·ing·ly** [-li] *adv.* 「able.」
― 形 기분좋은

pleas·ur·a·ble [pléʒərəbl] *adj.* giving pleasure; enjoy-〕
― 形 즐거운; 유쾌한

‡**pleas·ure** [pléʒər] *n.* **1.** ⓤ a feeling of satisfaction; enjoyment. ¶*It gave me much ~ to hear the news.*① **2.** ⓒ a thing which gives joy or delight; a source of joy. ¶*It's a ~ to talk to her.*② **3.** ⓤ desire; choice.
1) *at one's pleasure,* as one likes.
2) *take* [*a*] *pleasure in,* enjoy.
3) *with pleasure,* willingly.
― 名 1. 만족, 즐거움 ¶①그 소식을 듣고 매우 기뻤다 2. 즐거움(기쁨)을 주는 것(일) ¶②그녀와 이야기하는 것은 즐겁다 3. 기호(嗜好); 희망
熟 1)멋대로, 좋을 대로 2)…을 즐기다 3)기꺼이

pleat [pliːt] *n.* ⓒ a fold made in cloth by doubling it and pressing it down. ― *vt.* make a pleat in (cloth). ¶*a pleated skirt.*①
― 名 주름, 플리이트 ― 他 …에 주름을 달다 ¶①주름 달린 스커어트

ple·be·ian [plibíː(ː)ən] *n.* ⓒ **1.** one of the ancient Roman common people. **2.** a common person. ― *adj.* **1.** of the plebeian. **2.** common.
― 名 1. [고대 로마의] 평민 2. 서민
― 形 1. 평민의, 서민의 2. 보통의

pleb·i·scite [plébisit, -sàit] *n.* ⓒ a direct vote by the people on some important issue. —명 국민 투표, 일반 투표

plebs [plebz] *n.* 《*collectively*, used as *pl.*》 **1.** the common people in ancient Rome. **2.** the common people. —명 1. [고대 로마의] 평민 2. 대중

plec·tra [pléktrə] *n.* pl. of **plectrum**.

plec·trum [pléktrəm] *n.* ⓒ (pl. **-trums** or **-tra**) a small, thin instrument of metal or ivory used for plucking certain stringed instruments. —명 플렉트럼, 픽 (만돌린·기타아 따 위의 줄을 튕기는 나무나 상아 조각)

* **pledge** [pledʒ] *n.* **1.** ⓒ something given as security or a guarantee; the state of being held as security. ¶*He took the watch out of ~.*① **2.** ⓒ something given to show love, friendship, etc. **3.** ⓒ the act of drinking to someone's health. **4.** ⓤ an agreement; a promise. ¶*under ~ of secrecy.*② —명 1. 담보물; 담보 ¶①그는 전당 잡 혔던 시계를 찾았다 2. 보증, 표시, 증거 3. 축배 4. 서약 ¶②비밀을 지킨다는 약속으로

—*vt.* **1.** give (something) as security; put (something) in pawn. **2.** drink a health to (someone). **3.** make a solemn promise to do (something). ¶*He pledged* [*himself*] *to stop drinking.*③ | *He pledged* [*his word*] *to do his best.*④ ▷ **pledg·er** [-ər] *n.* —타 1. …을 담보에 넣다; …을 전당 잡히다 2. …에 축배를 들다 3. …할 것 을 서약하다 ¶③그는 술을 끊는다고 맹세했다/④그는 최선을 다하겠다고 맹세했다

ple·na·ry [plí:nəri, +*U. S.* plén-] *adj.* **1.** complete; absolute. **2.** attended by all the members who are entitled to be present. ¶*a ~ session.*① —형 1. 완전한 2. 전원이 출석한 ¶① 본회의

plen·i·po·ten·ti·ar·y [plènipəténʃ(ə)ri] *n.* ⓒ (pl. **-ar·ies**) a person given full power or authority by his government. —*adj.* having full power and authority. —명 전권 대사; 전권 위원 —형 전권 을 가진

plen·i·tude [plénit(j)u:d | -tjù:d] *n.* ⓤ the state of being full or complete; abundance. ¶*in the ~ of his power.*① —명 충분; 충만; 절정; 풍부 ¶①권 력의 절정에서

plen·te·ous [pléntiəs] *adj.* 《*poetic*》 plentiful; fruitful. —형 《詩》 충분한, 열매를 많이 맺는

* **plen·ti·ful** [pléntif(u)l] *adj.* abundant; great in quantity. ¶*a ~ harvest.*① ↔scarce ▷**plen·ti·ful·ness** [-nis] *n.* —형 풍부한, 충분한 ¶①풍작

plen·ti·ful·ly [pléntifuli] *adv.* amply; abundantly. —부 풍부하게, 충분히

: plen·ty [plénti] *n.* ⓤ a full or sufficient supply; the state ⎫ *plenty of,* much. ⎭ ⎰of being plentiful.⎱ —명 풍부; 다량 蕪 많은

pleu·ra [plúərə] *n.* ⓒ (pl. **-rae**) the thin membrane covering the chest. —명 늑막(肋膜)

pleu·rae [plúəri:] *n.* pl. of **pleura**.

pleu·ri·sy [plúərisi] *n.* ⓤ inflammation of the pleura. —명 늑막염

pli·a·bil·i·ty [plàiəbíliti] *n.* ⓤ the quality of being pliable. ⎱ ⎰[ble.⎱ —명 유연(柔軟)[성]; 유순

pli·a·ble [pláiəbl] *adj.* **1.** that can be easily bent; flexi- ⎭ **2.** easily influenced or persuaded. —형 1. 구부리기 쉬운 2. 고분고분한

pli·an·cy [pláiənsi] *n.* =pliability. —명 유연[성]; 유순

pli·ant [pláiənt] *adj.* pliable. —형 구부리기 쉬운; 고분고분한, 유순한

pli·ers [pláiərz] *n. pl.* 《used as *sing.*》 a kind of small pincers with long jaws, used for bending wires, etc. —명 집게, 펜치

* **plight**¹ [plait] *n.* ⓒ a state or condition, usu. unfavorable or bad. ¶*He is in a sad ~ now.*① —명 [나쁜] 상태, 궁지, 곤경 ¶①그는 지금 슬픈 입장에 있다

plight² [plait] *vt.* pledge; promise. ¶*~ one's word.*① —타 맹세하다 ¶①서약하다

plinth [plinθ] *n.* ⓒ the square base of a column. —명 주각(柱脚); 대좌(臺座)

plod [plɑd | plɔd] *vi.* **1.** walk or move slowly and heavily. 《*~ on* or *along one's way*, etc.》 ¶*~ one's way.*① **2.** work slowly with great effort. ¶*~ through a task.*② —*vt.* walk slowly and heavily along or over (some place). —자 1. 터벅터벅 걷다 ¶①터벅터벅 걸어가다 2. 꾸준히 일하다 ¶②애써 서 일을 해내다 —타 …을 따라 터 벅터벅 걷다

plod·der [plάdər | plɔ́də] *n.* ⓒ a walker or worker who plods. ⎰way of walking or working.⎱ —명 터벅터벅 걷는 사람; 꾸준히 일하 는 사람

plod·ding [plάdiŋ | plɔ́d-] *adj.* slow and steady in one's ⎭ —형 터벅터벅 걷는; 꾸준히 일하는

plop [plɑp | plɔp] *n.* ⓒ a sound of or like something dropping into water without a splash. —*v.* (**plopped, plop·ping**) *vi.* **1.** drop with such a sound. **2.** make this sound. —*vt.* cause (something) to make or drop with this sound. —*adv.* with a plop. —명 첨벙 [소리] —자 1. 첨벙하고 떨 어지다 2. 첨벙하고 소리내다 —타 …을 첨벙하고 떨어뜨리다 —부 첨벙하고

: plot [plɑt | plɔt] *n.* ⓒ **1.** a secret plan, esp. to do something evil. **2.** the plan or main story of a play, novel, etc. **3.** a small piece of land. ¶*a ~ of potatoes.*① —*v.* (**plot·ted, plot·ting**) *vt.* **1.** make a secret plan for —명 1. 음모 2. [소설·각본 따위의] 구상; 줄거리 3. [구획정리를 한] 작은 지구 ¶①감자밭 —타 1. …을 꾀(뜻)하다 2. …도면으로

(something). **2.** make a map of (something). ¶~ *the course of the ship.*② **3.** divide (land) into plots. —*vi.* take part in a plot. ⟪~ *for* or *against* someone⟫
그리다 ¶②배의 항로를 그리다 **3.** [토지]를 구획하다 —[自] 음모를 꾸미다(에 가담하다)

plot·ter [plátər / plɔ́tə] *n.* [C] a person who plots; a conspirator.
—[名] 음모자

plotting paper [ˊ-ˋ-] *n.* [U] paper ruled into small squares of the same size.
—[名] 방안지(方眼紙)

plough [plau] *n.* (*Brit.*) =plow.

plov·er [plʌ́vər] *n.* [C] a shore bird with pointed wings and a short tail.
—[名] 물떼새

* **plow,** *Brit.* **plough** [plau] *n.* [C] **1.** a tool used for cutting and turning up the soil. **2.** any tool like a plow. **3.** ⟪*the P-*⟫ a group of seven stars shaped like a plow.
—[名] **1.** 쟁기 **2.** 쟁기 비슷한 도구 **3.** 북두칠성

1) ***be at the plow,*** work as a farmer.
2) ***be under the plow,*** be turned up by the plow.
3) ***follow the plow,*** be or become a farmer.
4) ***put one's hand to the plow,*** set to work.

[熟] 1)농사를 짓고 있다 2)경작되어 있다 3)농업에 종사하다 4)일에 착수하다

—*vt.* **1.** cut and turn up (the soil) with a plow. ¶~ *a field.* **2.** make a long deep cut in (the earth, one's face, etc.). ¶*Her face is plowed with wrinkles.*① **3.** cut or force a way through (something). ¶~ *the waves* / ~ *one's way through a crowd.*② —*vi.* **1.** work with a plow. **2.** cut a way. ⟪~ *through* water, snow, etc.⟫ ¶~ *through the mud.*
—[他] **1.** [토지를] 경작하다 **2.** [토지에] 밭이랑을 만들다; [얼굴에] 주름지게 하다 ¶①그녀의 얼굴에는 주름살이 져 있다 **3.** …을 헤치고 나아가다 ¶②군중을 헤치고 나아가다 —[自] **1.** 경작하다 **2.** 헤치고 나아가다

plow·boy, *Brit.* **plough-** [pláubɔ̀i] *n.* [C] a boy who leads the horses drawing a plow.
—[名] 쟁기를 단 말을 모는 소년

plow·man, *Brit.* **plough-** [pláumən] *n.* [C] (pl. **-men** [-mən]) a person who operates a plow; a farmer.
—[名] 경작자; 농부

plow·share, *Brit.* **plough-** [pláuʃὲər] *n.* [C] the sharp blade of a plow.
—[名] 쟁기의 날

⁑ **pluck** [plʌk] *vt.* **1.** pick off (flowers, fruit, feathers, etc.); pull out the feathers of (a fowl, etc.). ¶~ *feathers from a goose.*① **2.** pull at (something) sharply. ¶~ *a handkerchief from the pocket of a coat* / *The little boy plucked my shirt.*② **3.** make a musical sound by pulling at (the strings of a guitar, etc.). —*vi.* pull suddenly. ⟪~ *at* something⟫
—[他] **1.** …을 뜯다; …의 깃을 뜯다 ¶①거위의 털을 뽑다 **2.** …을 잡아채다, 잡아당기다 ¶②그 아이는 내 샤쓰를 잡아당겼다 **3.** [악기]를 퉁기다, 뜯다 —[自] 홱 당기다

—*n.* [U] **1.** courage; spirit. **2.** [C] an act of pulling sharply. **3.** (*Brit. colloq.*) a failure in an examination.
—[名] **1.** 용기 **2.** 홱 당기기 **3.** 낙제

pluck up courage, gain or collect courage.
[熟] 용기를 내다, 분발하다

pluck·y [plʌ́ki] *adj.* (**pluck·i·er, pluck·i·est**) courageous; brave.
—[形] 용기 있는

plug [plʌg] *n.* [C] **1.** a piece of some material to fit into a hole. **2.** a place where the hose is attached in a fire; a fireplug. **3.** an electrical device for connection.
—[名] **1.** 마개 **2.** 소화전(消火栓) **3.** [전기 연결용의] 플럭

—*vt.* (**plugged, plug·ging**) fill (something) with a plug.
—[他] …에 마개를 하다

⁑ **plum** [plʌm] *n.* [C] **1.** a small juicy fruit with a smooth red skin; its tree. **2.** a raisin used in cake.
—[名] **1.** 서양오얏[나무] **2.** 건포도

plum·age [plú:midʒ] *n.* [U] ⟪*collectively*⟫ a bird's feathers.
—[名] 깃털

plumb [plʌm] *n.* [C] **1.** a small weight at the end of a line, used to find the depth of water, the upright line of a wall, etc. **2.** the state of standing upright. —*adj.* standing upright. —*adv.* in a plumb state or manner; directly. —*vt.* test the depth of (water) or the upright line of (something) with a plumb line; see deeply into (something).
—[名] **1.** 추(錘), 측연(測鉛) **2.** 수직 —[形] 수직의 —[副] 수직으로 —[他] [수선(垂線) 또는 수심]을 재다; …을 재어서 알다

plumb·er [plʌ́mər] *n.* [C] a person who installs and repairs water or gas pipes in buildings.
—[名] [수도·가스 따위의] 배관공(配管工)

plumb·ing [plʌ́miŋ] *n.* [U] the water or gas pipes in a building.
—[名] 연관류(鉛管類)

* **plume** [plu:m] *n.* [C] **1.** a long, large feather. **2.** an ornamental feather worn on a hat. —*vt.* **1.** (of a bird) clean and smooth (feathers). **2.** decorate (something) with feathers.
—[名] **1.** 깃털 **2.** [모자의] 깃털 장식 —[他] **1.** [새가 깃털]을 가지런히 하다 **2.** …을 깃털로 장식하다

plume oneself on, be proud of (something).
[熟] …을 자랑하다

plum·met [plʌ́mit] *n.* =plumb.

* **plump**[1] [plʌmp] *adj.* fat. —*vt.* make (someone) fat.
—[形] 토실토실 살찐 —[他] …을 살찌게

plump —*vi.* become fat.

plump² [plʌmp] *vi.* fall or drop heavily; sit heavily or suddenly. 《~ *down* (or *into, upon*) something》 ¶*He plumped down on a chair.*① —*vt.* drop, place, or throw heavily or suddenly. ¶*The girl plumped a book on the floor.*②
—*adv.* **1.** heavily. **2.** suddenly. **3.** in plain words; directly.
—*adj.* direct.
—*n.* ⓒ (*colloq.*) a sudden, heavy fall.

plum·y [plúːmi] *adj.* (**plum·i·er, plum·i·est**) **1.** decorated with plumes. **2.** like a plume.

* **plun·der** [plʌ́ndər] *vt., vi.* steal (something) by force, esp. in war times. —*n.* Ⓤ the act of plundering; Ⓒ the things that are plundered.

‡ **plunge** [plʌndʒ] *vt.* **1.** throw or push (something) suddenly into something else. 《~ *something into*》 ¶*~ one's hand into hot water | ~ a knife into her heart.* **2.** put (something) into a certain condition. 《~ *something into*》 ¶*~ a room into darkness*① / *be plunged into the depths of grief.*② —*vi.* **1.** fall, dive, or sink into water, etc. **2.** rush. 《~ *into* (or *in, up, down*) something》 ¶*~ into a fight.*③ **3.** leap with the body forward and the legs up, as a horse does; pitch, as a ship. **4.** (*colloq.*) spend much money; bet very much money. ¶*~ into debt.*④
—*n.* ⓒ **1.** the act of plunging; a sudden fall; a dive. **2.** (*colloq.*) a heavy gamble.
take the plunge, ⓐ venture to do something difficult or new. ⓑ make a fresh start.

plung·er [plʌ́ndʒər] *n.* ⓒ **1.** a person or thing that plunges. **2.** a piston in a machine.

plu·per·fect [plúːpə́ːrfikt] *n., adj.* (*Grammar*) [the tense] of the past perfect.

‡ **plu·ral** [plúər(ə)l] *adj.* showing more than one. ↔singular ¶*the ~ number.*① —*n.* **1.** Ⓤ (*Grammar*) the plural number. **2.** ⓒ the form of a noun showing more than one.

plu·ral·i·ty [pluərǽliti] *n.* (pl. **-ties**) **1.** Ⓤ the state or fact of being plural. **2.** ⓒ a great number. **3.** ⓒ (*U.S.*) (of an election) the difference between the first and the second in the number of votes.

* **plus** [plʌs] *prep.* with the addition of. ¶*Three ~ seven equals ten.*① —*adj.* (*Mathematics*) **1.** showing addition. ¶*a ~ sign.*② **2.** (*Electricity*) showing positive.

plush [plʌʃ] *n.* Ⓤ a kind of cloth softer and thicker than velvet.

Plu·to [plúːtou] *n.* **1.** (in Greek and Roman mythology) the god of the underworld. **2.** (*Astronomy*) the planet farthest from the sun.

plu·toc·ra·cy [pluːtɑ́krəsi / -tɔ́k-] *n.* (pl. **-cies**) **1.** Ⓤ government by wealthy people. **2.** ⓒ a group of wealthy people.

plu·to·crat [plúːtəkræt] *n.* ⓒ **1.** a person who is powerful because of his wealth. **2.** (*colloq.*) a rich person.

* **ply**¹ [plai] *v.* (**plied**) *vt.* **1.** work hard at (something). **2.** use. ¶*The woman plied her needle.*① **3.** urge repeatedly. 《~ *someone with*》 ¶*They plied him with food and drink.* —*vi.* (of a bus, boat, etc.) run regularly between two places.

ply² [plai] *n.* ⓒ (pl. **plies**) **1.** a layer or thickness of cloth. **2.** a twist in a rope, cord, etc.

ply·wood [pláiwùd] *n.* Ⓤ a tough board made of thin layers of wood stuck together.

‡ **P. M., p. m.** afternoon. ⇒N.B. ¶*at 9 p. m.*

하다 —ⓐ 살찌다
—ⓐ 털썩 떨어지다; 털썩 앉았다 ¶그는 의자에 털썩 앉았다 —ⓗ …을 털썩 떨어뜨리다 ¶②소녀는 책을 마루에 털썩 떨어뜨렸다
—ⓟ 1. 털썩하고 2. 갑자기 3. 노골적
—ⓟ 노골적인 [으로]
—ⓝ 털썩 떨어지기
—ⓟ 1. 깃털로 장식한 2. 깃털 같은

—ⓗⓐ …을 약탈하다 —ⓝ 약탈[품]

—ⓗ 1. …을 던져 넣다, 찔러 넣다 2. …을 [어떤 상태로] 빠뜨리다 ¶①방을 갑자기 어둡게 하다 / ②갑자기 슬픔의 구렁텅이에 빠지다 —ⓐ 1. 빠져들다, 뛰어들다; 잠기다 2. 돌진하다, 돌입하다 ¶③전쟁에 뛰어들다 3. [말이] 뒷발을 들고 뛰어 오르다; [배가] 세로로 흔들리다 4. (口) 큰 돈을 쓰다; 큰 노름을 하다 ¶④큰 빚을 지게 되다

—ⓝ 1. 뛰어들기, 돌진, 낙하 2. 큰 노름
熟 ⓐ 과감하게 새로운(어려운) 일을 시작하다 ⓑ 새출발을 하다
—ⓝ 1. 뛰어드는 사람(것) 2. 막대 피스톤

—ⓝⓟ《文法》과거완료[의]

—ⓟ 복수의 ¶①복수 —ⓝ 1.《文法》복수[형] 2. 복수형의 단어

—ⓝ 1. 복수[임] 2. 다수 3. 《美》[선거에서의] 초과 득표 수

—ⓗ …을 보탠 ¶①3에 7을 보태면 10이 되다 —ⓟ 1. 《數》정(正)의 ¶②더하기표(＋) 2.《電》양(陽)의
—ⓝ 플러시 천(벨벳 비슷함)

—ⓝ 1. 명부(冥府)의 왕 2.《天文》명왕성(冥王星)

—ⓝ 1. 금권(金權)정치 2. 재벌

—ⓝ 1. 금권가(金權家) 2. (口) 부자

—ⓗ 1. …에 열성을 내다 2. [도구 따위]를 쓰다 ¶①부인은 열심히 바느질을 하고 있었다 3. …을 끈덕지게 권하다 ¶②그들에게 음식을 자꾸 권했다 —ⓐ 정기적으로 다니다
—ⓝ 1. 주름 2. [밧줄 따위의] 가닥

—ⓝ 합판, 베니어판

—ⓟ 오후 N.B. 라틴어의 post me- [ridiem에서]

pneu·mat·ic [n(j)u(:)mǽtik / nju(:)m-] *adj.* of air; filled with air. ¶*a ~ pillow*① / *a ~ tire.*② —[形] 공기의; 공기를 채운 ¶①공기베개/②공기를 넣은 타이어

pneu·mo·nia [n(j)u(:)móuniə / nju(:)m-] *n.* [U] a serious illness of one or both of the lungs. —[名] 폐렴

P. O. post office.

poach¹ [poutʃ] *vt., vi.* hunt or fish in a secret and illegal way. —[他][自] 몰래 사냥(고기잡이)하다

poach² [poutʃ] *vt.* cook (an egg) by breaking it into boiling water. ¶*poached eggs.*① —[他] [달걀]을 끓는 물에 삶다(반숙하다) ¶①수란(水卵)

P. O. Box, P. O. B. Post Office Box. —《略》 우편 사서함

pock [pak / pɔk] *n.* [C] a mark on the skin left by some diseases. —[名] 곰보자국, 마마자국

‡**pock·et** [pákit / pɔ́k-] *n.* [C] **1.** a small bag fixed on one's clothing to carry money or other small articles. **2.** any small bag fixed on something to hold small articles. ¶*A golf bag has a ~ for golf balls.*① **3.** a place in the air in which an airplane drops suddenly; an air pocket. —[名] 1. 옷의 호주머니, 포켓 2. 포켓, 작은 자루 ¶①골프 백에는 공을 넣는 포켓이 있다 3. 에어포켓

1) ***be in pocket,*** have or have obtained money.
2) ***be out of pocket,*** have not or have lost money.
3) ***deep pocket,*** wealth; riches.
4) ***empty pocket,*** lack of money.
5) ***have someone in one's pocket,*** have someone in one's power.
6) ***keep one's hands in one's pockets,*** be idle.
7) ***put one's hand in one's pocket,*** spend money; pay.
8) ***put one's pride in one's pocket,*** do not show one's pride.
9) ***suffer in one's pocket,*** lose.

[熟] 1)벌고 있다; 돈이 있다 2)손해를 보고 있다; 돈이 없다 3)재산, 부(富) 4)무일푼, 빈털터리 5)[남]을 좌우하다 6)수수방관하다, 게으름 피우다 7)돈을 쓰다; 지불하다 8)자존심을 누르다 9)손해를 보다

—*vt.* **1.** put (something) into a pocket. **2.** get or take (money, etc.) usu. without right. ¶*He pocketed our money.*② **3.** hide or not show (one's feelings, etc.). —[他] 1. …을 호주머니에 넣다 2. [권리 없이 돈 따위]를 벌다, 착복하다 ¶②그는 우리 돈을 착복했다 3. [감정 따위]를 나타내지 않다, 보이지 않다

—*adj.* that can be carried in a pocket; small. —[形] 호주머니에 들어가는, 작은

pock·et·book [pákitbùk / pɔ́k-] *n.* [C] **1.** a leather case for carrying money, papers, etc.; a woman's purse. **2.** (*Brit.*) a small notebook. —[名] 1. 지갑 2. 수첩

pock·et·ful [pákitf(u)l / pɔ́k-] *n.* [C] the amount a pocket can hold. —[名] 호주머니 가득

pock·et·knife [pákitnàif / pɔ́k-] *n.* [C] (pl. **-knives** [-nàivz]) a small knife with blades that fold into the handle. —[名] 주머니칼

pocket money [ˊ-- ˋ--] *n.* money for small expenses. —[名] 용돈, 잡비

pock-marked [pákmà:rkt / pɔ́kma:kt] *adj.* having pocks. —[形] 마마자국이 있는

pod [pad / pɔd] *n.* [C] a long seed container of peas, beans, etc. —*v.* (**pod·ded, pod·ding**) *vi.* form pods. 《~ *up*》 —*vt.* take off the pods of (peas, beans, etc.). —[名] [콩 따위의] 깍지, 꼬투리 —[自] 꼬투리가 되다 —[他] [콩 따위]의 꼬투리를 벗기다

podg·y [pádʒi / pɔ́dʒi] *adj.* (**podg·i·er, podg·i·est**) (*colloq.*) fat and short; dumpy. —[形] 땅딸막한

Poe [pou], **Edgar Allan** *n.* (1809–1849) an American poet, critic and writer. —[名] 미국의 시인·평론가·작가

‡**po·em** [póuem, -im] *n.* [C] a rhythmical composition of words, often expressing deep feeling and great beauty of language or thought. —[名] 시, 시가(詩歌), 시적인 문장

po·e·sy [póuezi] *n.* [U] (*archaic*) the art of writing poetry; 《*collectively*》 poetry; poems. —[名] 《古》 작시법(作詩法); 시

‡**po·et** [póuet, -it] *n.* [C] a person who writes verses or poems. —[名] 시인

po·et·as·ter [póuetæ̀stər / ˋ-ˊ-] *n.* [C] a writer of second-rate or poor verse. —[名] 엉터리 시인

po·et·ess [póuetes] *n.* [C] a female poet. —[名] 여류 시인

po·et·ic [pouétik], **-i·cal** [-k(ə)l] *adj.* **1.** of poets or poetry. **2.** showing the characteristics of good poetry. —[形] 1. 시[인]의 2. 시취(詩趣)가 있는

***po·et·ry** [póuitri] *n.* [U] **1.** 《*collectively*》 poems. ¶*epic ~.*① **2.** the art of writing poems. **3.** something poetic. —[名] 1. 시 ¶①서사시 2. 작시(作詩)[법] 3. 시적인 것

poign·an·cy [pɔ́inənsi] *n.* [U] the state or quality of being poignant. —[名] 통렬함

poign·ant [pɔ́inənt] *adj.* **1.** sharp or painful to the feelings. ¶*~ sorrow.* **2.** keen; bitter. ¶*~ sarcasm.* **3.** sharp or stinging to the taste or smell. —[形] 1. [슬픔·후회 따위가] 격렬한 2. 신랄한 3. 콕 쏘는, 매운, 자극적인

poin·set·ti·a [pɔinsétiə] *n.* [C] a plant with large, scarlet, petal-like leaves and tiny, greenish flowers. —[名] 포인세티아(크리스마스 장식용)

‡**point** [pɔint] *n.* [C] **1.** a sharp end of a stick, pin, weapon, etc. ¶*the ~ of a needle.* **2.** a place or spot. ¶*a* —[名] 1. 끝, 첨단 2. 점, 지점 3. 중대한 순간 ¶①죽는 순간에 4. 주안점, 요점,

weak ~. **3.** a moment when something important is going to happen. ¶*at the ~ of death.*① **4.** ⟪*the* ~⟫ a main idea or purpose in a story, joke, etc.; [U] aim. ¶*What is your ~ in saying so?*② **5.** a characteristic. ¶*Kindness is her good ~.*③ **6.** a full stop or period. **7.** a piece of land going out into the sea; a small cape. **8.** a degree of a thermometer; a score; a mark or grade. **9.** ⟪*pl.*⟫ short rails used to enable a train to pass from one track to another.

취지; 목적 ¶②그렇게 말하는 목적은 무엇인가? **5.** 특징, 특질 ¶③친절하다는 것이 그녀의 특징이다 **6.** 종지부, 구둣점 **7.** 갑(岬), 곶 **8.** [온도계 따위의] 도(度); 득점; 등급 **9.** 전철기(轉轍器)

1) ***at all points,*** in every respect; completely.
2) ***beside*** (or ***away from, off***) ***the point,*** not to the point.
3) ***come to the point,*** get to the essential part.
4) ***make a point of doing; make it a point to do*** (=*be sure to do*) *something.*
5) ***on the point of doing*** (=*just about to do*) *something.*
6) ***to the point,*** getting to the essential part; apt.

[熟] 1)모든 점에서; 완전히 2)엉뚱한, 빗나간 3)중요한 대목에 이르다 4)꼭 …하다; 으례(반드시) …하다 5)막 …하려고 하는 6)적절한, 요령있는

—*vt.* **1.** make (something) sharp. ¶*~ a knife.* **2.** emphasize. ¶*He pointed his remarks with illustrations.*④ **3.** direct or aim. ⟪~ something *at, to, toward*⟫ ¶*She pointed her finger at me.*⑤ **4.** mark (something) with points. —*vi.* direct the finger, eye, etc. ⟪~ *at* (or *to, toward*) something⟫ ¶*Don't ~ at others.*⑥
1) ***point off,*** divide a sentence by a comma.
2) ***point out,*** direct attention to (something).
3) ***point up,*** emphasize.

—[他] **1.** …을 뾰족하게 하다, 날카롭게 하다 **2.** …을 강조하다 ¶④그는 예를 들며 그의 주장을 강조했다 **3.** …을 돌리다, 겨냥하다 ¶⑤그녀는 나에게 손가락질했다 **4.** …에 점을 찍다 —[自] 손가락으로 가리키다; 눈을 돌리다 ¶⑥남에게 손가락질해서는 안 된다
[熟] 1)코머로 나누다 2)…을 지적하다 3)강조하다

point-blank [pɔ́intblǽŋk] *adj.* **1.** aimed directly at the mark. **2.** direct; plain. ¶*a ~ refusal.* —*adv.* **1.** straight. **2.** directly; without hesitation.

—[形] **1.** 직사(直射)의 **2.** 직접의, 노골적인 —[副] **1.** 직사로 **2.** 노골적으로, 단호하게

:point·ed [pɔ́intid] *adj.* **1.** having a sharp point like a needle. ¶*a ~ pencil.* **2.** sharp; direct; striking. ¶*a ~ reproof.*① ▷**point·ed·ly** [-li] *adv.*

—[形] **1.** 뾰족한 **2.** 날카로운; 눈에 띄는 ¶①호된 꾸지람

point·er [pɔ́intər] *n.* [C] **1.** a thing or person that points. **2.** a long, slender stick used for pointing out things on a map, etc. **3.** a short-haired dog trained to point out where hunted birds are hiding, etc. ⇒fig.

—[名] **1.** 가리키는 사람(것) **2.** 채찍, 교편 **3.** 포인터(사냥개)

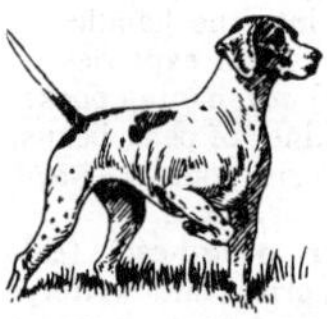
〔pointer 3.〕

point·less [pɔ́intlis] *adj.* **1.** having a dull edge. **2.** without meaning or sense. **3.** (in a game) without a point scored.

—[形] **1.** 끝이 무딘 **2.** 무의미한 **3.** 득점 없는

points·man [pɔ́intsmən] *n.* [C] (pl. **-men** [-mən]) (*Brit.*) **1.** a railway switchman. **2.** a policeman who directs traffic.

—[名] ⟪英⟫ **1.** 전철수(轉轍手) **2.** 교통순경

point switch [ˊ ˋ] *n.* a device of two movable rails to turn a train from one railroad track to another.

—[名] 전철기

***poise** [pɔiz] *n.* **1.** [U] mental or physical balance. **2.** [C] the manner in which a person moves.
—*vt.* keep (something) in the state of balance; carry or hold steadily. ¶*He poised himself on his hands.*①
—*vi.* **1.** be balanced; remain in balance. **2.** (of birds, etc.) remain in the air; hover.

—[名] **1.** 평형; [마음의] 평정(平靜); 균형 **2.** 몸가짐, 자세; 태도
—[他] …을 균형잡히게 하다; …의 균형을 잡다 ¶①그는 물구나무서기를 했다
—[自] **1.** 균형잡히다 **2.** [새 따위가] 하늘을 날다

:poi·son [pɔ́iz(ə)n] *n.* [U][C] **1.** any substance that is dangerous to life if taken into the body. **2.** anything dangerous. —*vt.* **1.** kill or injure (someone) by poison; put poison into or on (something). **2.** have an evil or harmful influence on (someone).

—[名] **1.** 독 **2.** 해로운 것 —[他] **1.** …을 독살하다; 독으로 해치다; …에 독을 넣다(바르다) **2.** …을 해치다, 나쁜 영향을 주다

poison gas [ˊ- ˊ] *n.* a gas which kills or injures, used in chemical warfare.

—[名] 독가스

poi·son·ous [pɔ́iz(ə)nəs] *adj.* **1.** having poison; dangerous to life if taken into the body. **2.** (*colloq.*) very unpleasant; disagreeable. ▷**poi·son·ous·ly** [-li] *adv.*

—[形] **1.** 독이 있는; 해로운 **2.** 불쾌한, 악취를 뿜는

* **poke** [pouk] *vt.* **1.** push (someone or something) with a finger, a stick, etc. ¶*He poked me in the ribs.*① **2.** stir up (a fire). ¶*~ the fire.* **3.** thrust or intrude (someone or something). ¶*Don't ~ your nose into my affairs.*② **—*vi.*** **1.** push with a stick, etc. 《*~ at* something》. **2.** look for something; search. ¶*~ into another's private affairs.*
 1) ***poke about,*** search; be eager to know another's private affairs.
 2) ***poke fun at,*** make fun of (something).
 —*n.* [C] a push or thrust. ¶*give a ~.*

—[他] **1.** [막대기·손가락으로] …을 찌르다 ¶①그는 내 옆구리를 쿡 찔렀다 **2.** [묻은 불]을 헤집어 일으키다 **3.** …을 찔러넣다 ¶②내 일에는 참견하지 말게 —[自] **1.** 막대기 따위로 찌르다 **2.** 찾다; 꼬치꼬치 캐다

[熟] 1)꼬치꼬치 캐다 2)…을 놀리다

—[名] 찌르기

pok·er[1] [póukər] *n.* [C] **1.** a person or thing that pokes. **2.** an iron bar for stirring a fire.
 as stiff as a poker, very cold and hard in behavior or manner.

—[名] **1.** 찌르는 사람(것) **2.** 부지깽이

[熟] [태도 따위가] 몹시 딱딱한 ¶①무표정한 얼굴

pok·er[2] [póukər] *n.* [U] a card game in which the players bet on the value of the cards they hold. ¶*a ~ face.*①

—[名] [트럼프의] 포우커 ¶①무표정한 얼굴

pok·y, pok·ey [póuki] *adj.* (**pok·i·er, pok·i·est**) **1.** slow; dull. **2.** uncomfortably small; shabby.

—[形] **1.** 둔한, 굼뜬 **2.** 비좁은, 초라한, 볼품없는

* **Po·land** [póulənd] *n.* a country in central Europe lying between Germany and Russia. ⇒[N.B.]

—[名] 폴란드 [N.B.] 수도 Warsaw

* **po·lar** [póulər] *adj.* **1.** of or near the North or South Pole. ¶*a ~ bear*① / *the ~ circle*② / *the ~ lights.*③ **2.** (*Electricity*) of a magnetic pole.

—[形] **1.** 남(북)극의; 극지의 ¶①북극곰, 흰곰/②극권(極圈)/③극광 **2.** 《電》 자극(磁極)의

Po·lar·is [poulǽris] *n.* the North Star.

—[名] 북극성

po·lar·i·ty [poulǽriti] *n.* [U] **1.** the magnetic power to point north and south. **2.** the state of showing two opposite qualities, principles, etc.

—[名] **1.** 자극성(磁極性) **2.** [성질·주의 따위의] 정반대; 대립

⁑ **pole**[1] [poul] *n.* [C] a long, slender piece of wood or other solid material. ¶*~ jump.*① **—*vt.*** push (a boat, etc.) with a pole.

—[名] 막대, 장대, 기둥 ¶①봉고도
—[他] [보우트 따위]를 막대로 밀다

* **pole**[2] [poul] *n.* [C] one of the two ends of the axis of the earth or other round bodies; one of two opposite forces or parts. ¶*the North Pole*① / *the South Pole.*②

—[名] [천체·지구의] 극(極); 자극(磁極); [정반대의] 극단 ¶①북극/②남극

Pole [poul] *n.* [C] a person of Poland.

—[名] 폴란드 사람

po·lem·ic [poulémik / pɔl-], **-i·cal** [-ik(ə)l] *adj.* apt to argue; fond of discussion. ¶*a ~ writer.*①

—[形] 논쟁을 좋아하는 ¶①논객(論客)

pole·star [póulstàːr] *n.* **1.** 《*the ~*》 the North Star; Polaris. **2.** [C] a guiding principle.

—[名] **1.** 북극성 **2.** 지도 원리

pole vault [ˊ ˋ] *n.* a field event in which a jump is performed over a high crossbar with the aid of a long bar; a polejump.

—[名] 봉고도

⁑ **po·lice** [pəlíːs] *n.* **1.** [U] the department of government organized to keep order and enforce law. **2.** 《*the ~, collectively*》 the member of this department; policemen. ⇒[usage] ¶*the harbor ~*① / *the Metropolitan Police*② / *a ~ station.*③ **—*vt.*** **1.** control or protect (a district, etc.) by means of police. **2.** provide (a district, etc.) with police.

—[名] **1.** 경찰 **2.** 경관 [usage] 항상 복수동사를 취함 ¶①수상 경찰/②수도경찰, 시경/③경찰서

—[他] **1.** …의 치안을 유지하다 **2.** …에 경찰을 두다

⁑ **po·lice·man** [pəlíːsmən] *n.* [C] (pl. **-men** [-mən]) a member of a police force.

—[名] 경관

po·lice·wom·an [pəlíːswùmən] *n.* [C] (pl. **-wom·en** [-wìmin]) a female member of a police force.

—[名] 여자 경관

* **pol·i·cy**[1] [pálisi / pɔ́l-] *n.* (pl. **-cies**) **1.** [C] [U] a way or principle of action by a person or group, esp. a government. ¶*foreign ~*① / *domestic ~.*② **2.** [U] practical wisdom. ¶(*proverb*) *Honesty is the best ~.*③

—[名] **1.** 방식; 정책; 정치 ¶①외교 정책/②국내 정책 **2.** 지혜 ¶③《俚》정직은 최상의 정책이다

pol·i·cy[2] [pálisi / pɔ́l-] *n.* [C] (pl. **-cies**) a written contract issued by an insurance company. ¶*a life insurance ~*① / *take out a ~ on one's life.*②

—[名] 보험 증권 ¶①생명보험 증권/②생명보험에 들다

po·li·o [póuliou] *n.* (*colloq.*) =poliomyelitis.

po·li·o·my·e·li·tis [pòulioumàiəláitis / pɔ̀ul-] *n.* [U] a disease of the nervous system esp. of children.

—[名] 소아마비, 척수 회백질염(灰白質炎)

⁑ **pol·ish** [páliʃ / pɔ́l-] *vt.* **1.** make (something) smooth and shiny by rubbing. 《*~ up* (or *away, out*) something》 **2.** make (someone) refined or elegant. ¶*a polished*

—[他] **1.** …을 닦다 **2.** …을 품위있게 하다 ¶①고상한 신사 —[自] **1.** 광이 나다 ¶②이 나무는 광이 잘 안 난다 **2.**

Polish

gentleman.① —vi. **1.** become smooth and bright. ¶*This wood won't ~.*② **2.** become refined or elegant.
polish off, (*colloq.*) finish or defeat quickly.
—*n.* ⓤ **1.** the act of polishing; a smooth, shiny surface; gloss. ¶*the brilliant ~ of silver.*③ **2.** a substance for polishing. **3.** elegance; culture.

- **Pol·ish** [póuliʃ] *adj.* of Poland, its people or their language. —*n.* ⓤ the language of the Poles.
pol·ish·er [páliʃər / póliʃə] *n.* **1.** ⓒ a person who polishes. **2.** ⓤ any substance used in polishing.
⁑ **po·lite** [pəláit] *adj.* (**-lit·er, -lit·est**) having good manners; refined; cultured. ¶*~ society.*①
- **po·lite·ly** [pəláitli] *adv.* in a polite manner; courteously.
- **po·lite·ness** [pəláitnis] *n.* ⓤ the state of being polite; ⓒ a polite act or statement.
pol·i·tic [pálitik / pól-] *adj.* **1.** cunning. **2.** prudent. **3.** useful. ¶*a ~ remark.* **4.** political.
- **po·lit·i·cal** [pəlítik(ə)l] *adj.* of politics, government or public affairs. ¶*~ circles*① / *a ~ party*② / *~ science*③ / *a ~ view.*④ 「from a political point of view.」
po·lit·i·cal·ly [pəlítikəli] *adv.* in a political manner;
- **pol·i·ti·cian** [pàlitíʃ(ə)n / pòli-] *n.* **1.** ⓒ a person who is active in political affairs. **2.** (*U.S.*) a person who is working for his political party, often as a means of personal gain.
⁑ **pol·i·tics** [pálitiks / pól-] *n. pl.* **1.** (used as *sing.*) the study of government; the management of political affairs. **2.** political plans, ideas, etc. ¶*party ~.*①
pol·i·ty [páliti / pól-] *n.* (pl. **-ties**) **1.** ⓤ the political condition of being organized as a state. **2.** ⓒ a state or community having a government.
pol·ka [póu(l)kə / póul-, pól-] *n.* ⓒ a lively dance for couples; the music for such a dance.
- **poll** [poul] *n.* ⓒ **1.** the total number of votes. ¶*a heavy ~*① / *at the head of the ~.*② **2.** (*pl.*) (*U.S.*) a place to vote. ¶*go to the polls.*③ **3.** a list of voters. **4.** the head of a body. **5.** an inquiry into the opinions, etc. of many people.
—*vt.* **1.** enter (someone) in a list. **2.** obtain (a vote); give (a vote) to (someone). **3.** cut off (the head of a tree) short. **4.** ask the opinions, etc. of others on (something). —*vi.* give one's vote. (*~ for someone*)
pol·len [pálin / pól-] *n.* ⓤ the powder in a flower carried by bees, etc. 「(other flowers).」
pol·li·nate [pálinèit / pól-] *vt.* (of bees) carry pollen to
poll tax [ˊˋ] *n.* a tax on every person.
pol·lute [pəlúːt, -ljúːt] *vt.* make (something) dirty; make (the mind, morals, etc.) impure.
pol·lu·tion [pəlúːʃən, +*Brit.* -ljúː-] *n.* ⓤ the act of polluting; the state of being polluted.
po·lo [póulou] *n.* ⓤ a game played on horseback with wooden sticks and one small wooden ball.
po·lo·naise [pòlənéiz, pòul- / pòlə-] *n.* ⓒ a slow, stately Polish dance; the music for this dance.
pol·troon [paltrúːn / pol-] *n.* ⓒ a coward.
poly- [pɑli- / pɔli-] a word element meaning *many, much* or *more than one.*
po·lyg·a·mist [pəlígəmist / pɔ-] *n.* ⓒ a man who has more than one wife. 「having more than one wife.」
po·lyg·a·my [pəlígəmi, +*Brit.* pɔ-] *n.* ⓤ the custom of
pol·y·glot [páliglàt / póliglòt] *adj.* knowing several languages; written in several languages. ¶*a ~ student.*
pol·y·gon [páligàn / póligən] *n.* ⓒ a plane figure with more than four angles. ¶*a regular ~.*①

polygon

품위가 생기다

熨 〔口〕재빨리 끝내다(해치우다)
—名 1. 광택, 윤; 닦기 ¶③은의 번쩍이는 광택 2. 윤내는 약 3. 우아함; 교양

—形 폴란드[사람·말]의 —名 폴란드 말

—名 1. 닦는 사람 2. 윤내는 약

—形 예의바른; 세련된; 교양있는 ¶①상류사회

—副 공손하게

—名 공손함; 은근한 태도(말)

—形 1. 교활한 2. 분별있는 3. 요령있는, 적절한 4. 정치상의

—形 정치[학]상의; 정치에 관한 ¶①정치계/②정당/③정치학/④정견

—副 정치상; 정략적으로

—名 1. 정치가 2.《美》당리당략에 움직이는 정치가, 정상배

—名 1. 정치학, 정치 2. 정책 ¶①정당정책

—名 1. 정치 형태 2. 국가, 정치적조직체

—名 폴카; 폴카곡

—名 1. 투표수 ¶①투표 다수/②최고 득표의 2.《美》투표소 ¶③투표소로 가다 3. 선거인 명부 4. 머리 5. 여론조사
—他 1. …을 등록하다 2. […를] 획득하다; …에 [표]를 던지다 3. [초목의 끝]을 자르다 4. …에 대하여 여론조사를 하다 —自 투표하다

—名 꽃가루, 화분

—他 …에 수분(授粉)하다
—名 인두세(人頭稅)
—他 …을 더럽히다; …을 불결하게 하다

—名 더럽히기; 오염

—名 포울로우

—名 폴로네에즈

—名 겁장이
—「다(多), 중(重), 복(複)」따위의 뜻을 나타내는 연결형
—名 일부다처 주의자

—名 일부다처제
—形 수개 국어를 말하는; 수개 국어로 써어진
—名 다각형 ¶①정(正)다각형

Pol·y·ne·sia [pàliníːʒə, -ʃə / pɔ̀l-, -zjə] *n.* a group of many small islands in the Pacific Ocean. —[名] 폴리네시아 제도

pol·y·syl·lab·ic [pàlisilǽbik / pɔ̀l-] *adj.* (of a word) having more than three syllables. ↔monosyllabic. —[形] 다음절(多音節)의

pol·y·syl·la·ble [pálisìləbl / pɔ́l-] *n.* [C] a word made up of more than three syllables. —[名] 다음절(名音節)

pol·y·tech·nic [pàlitéknik / pɔ̀l-] *adj.* dealing with various arts or sciences. —*n.* [C] a polytechnic school. —[形] 여러 공예(工藝)의 —[名] 공예 학교

pol·y·the·ism [páliθi(ː)ìz(ə)m / pɔ́l-] *n.* [U] the belief in many gods. —[名] 다신론(多神論); 다신교

pol·y·the·ist [páliθì(ː)ist / pɔ́l-] *n.* [C] a person who believes in polytheism. —[名] 다신론자; 다신교도

po·made [pouméid, -máːd / -máːd] *n.* [U] a substance containing oil and used for keeping the hair in place. —[名] 향유; 포마드

pome·gran·ate [pám(ə)grǽnit / pɔ́m-] *n.* [C] a fruit having many whitish seeds which are covered with red flesh; the tree bearing this fruit. —[名] 석류[나무]

pom·mel [pʌ́m(ə)l, +*U.S.* pam-] *n.* [C] **1.** a round knob on the handle of a sword, etc. ⇨fig. **2.** a round part at the front of a saddle. ⇨fig. —*vt.* (**-meled, -mel·ing** or *Brit.* **-melled, -mel·ling**) beat (something or someone) with the hands closed tight. ▷**pom·mel·er** [-ər] *n.* —[名] 1. 칼자루 끝 2. 안장머리 —[他] …을 주먹으로 치다

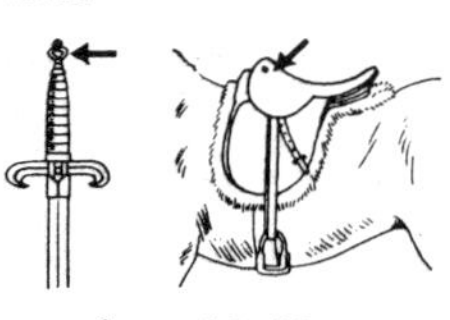

〔pommel 1., 2.〕

* **pomp** [pamp / pɔmp] *n.* [U] **1.** brilliant or splendid display; magnificence. **2.** ⦅often *pl.*⦆ a vain show. —[名] 1. 화려함 2. 과시, 자랑삼아 보이기

pom·pon [pámpan / pɔ́ːmpɔŋ] *n.* [C] **1.** an ornamental ball worn on hats, shoes, etc. **2.** a kind of dahlia or chrysanthemum bearing small, round flowers. —[名] 1. 모자의 술(리본) 2. 퐁퐁다알리아(국화)

pom·pous [pámpəs / pɔ́m-] *adj.* **1.** acting with self-importance. ¶*in a ~ manner.* **2.** full of splendor. ▷**pom·pous·ly** [-li] *adv.* —**pom·pous·ness** [-nis] *n.* —[形] 1. 거만한, 젠체하는 2. 화려한

pon·cho [pántʃou / pɔ́n-] *n.* [C] (pl. **-chos**) a piece of cloth with a hole in the center, worn in South America. —[名] [남미의] 외투의 일종

⁑ **pond** [pand / pɔnd] *n.* [C] a small pool of water. —[名] 연못

pon·der [pándər / pɔ́ndə] *vt.* think deeply about (something). —*vi.* consider something carefully. ⦅~ *on* or *over* something⦆ ¶*~ over a matter.*① —[他] …을 숙고하다 —[自] 숙고하다, 궁리하다 ¶①문제를 잘 생각하다

pon·der·ous [pándərəs / pɔ́n-] *adj.* **1.** very heavy and slow. **2.** dull in speech or writing. ¶*in a ~ way.*① —[形] 1. 무거운 2. 무겁고 답답한 ¶①무거운 말투로

pon·tiff [pántif / pɔ́n-] *n.* [C] **1.** the Roman Catholic Pope. **2.** a bishop. **3.** a high or chief priest. —[名] 1. 로마 교황 2. 사교(司教) 3. 제사장(祭司長)

pon·tif·i·cal [pantífik(ə)l / pɔn-] *adj.* of a pontiff. —*n.* ⦅*pl.*⦆ robes or special objects for bishops, etc. worn in ceremonies. ▷**pon·tif·i·cal·ly** [-kəli] *adv.* —[形] 교황의; 사교(司教)의 —[名] 사교의 제복; 기장(記章)

pon·tif·i·cate [pantífikit / pɔn-] *n.* [U] the position of a pontiff; the term of a pontiff. —[名] 교황(사교)의 직(지위, 임기)

pon·toon [pantúːn / pɔn-] *n.* [C] **1.** a flat-bottomed boat used to support a bridge. ¶*a ~ bridge.*① **2.** a flat-bottomed boat. **3.** a device attached to the bottom of an airplane for floating on water. —[名] 1. 주교(舟橋)용 보우트 ¶①주교, 배다리 2. 거룻배 3. 수상 비행기의 부주(浮舟)

⁑ **po·ny** [póuni] *n.* [C] (pl. **-ni·es**) a horse of a small breed; a small or young horse. —[名] 포우니종의 작은 말

poo·dle [púːdl] *n.* [C] a pet dog with long hair, usu. cut into some pattern. ⇨fig. —[名] 푸우들 개

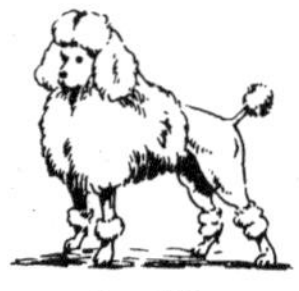

〔poodle〕

⁑ **pool¹** [puːl] *n.* [C] **1.** a small body of still water. ¶*a ~ of water.* **2.** a still, deep part in a river. **3.** a swimming pool. —[名] 1. 물웅덩이; 연못 2. 강의 깊은 곳 3. 수영장, 푸울

* **pool²** [puːl] *n.* **1.** [U] a kind of billiards. **2.** [C] the total amount of money gathered by —[名] 1. 당구의 일종 2. 합동 자금; 기업합동 —[他] …을 공동 출자하다 ¶①

some persons for a common purpose; a combination of corporations in business. —*vt.* put (money) into one common fund. ¶~ *money to buy a car.*① — 사동차를 사기 위해 돈을 추렴하다

poop [pu:p] *n.* [C] a raised deck in the back part of a ship. — [名] 선미루(船尾樓) 갑판; 선미

⁑ poor [puər] *adj.* **1.** having little or no money or goods. ↔rich ¶*become* ~ / *the* ~.① **2.** small in amount; lacking. ¶*a* ~ *crop*② / ~ *in natural resources.*③ **3.** not good; inferior. ¶*a* ~ *picture* / *I am a* ~ *hand at playing tennis.*④ **4.** badly made; mean. ¶~ *clothes.* **5.** needing sympathy or pity; unfortunate. **6.** having little value; worthless. ¶*in my* ~ *opinion.*⑤ — [形] 1. 가난한 ¶①빈민 2. 빈약한, 불충분한, 결핍된 ¶②얼마 안 되는 수확/③천연자원이 빈약한 3. 서투른; 하치의 ¶④나는 테니스가 서투르다 4. 초라한, 보잘것 없는 5. 가엾은, 불쌍한; 불행한 6. 시시한, 하찮은 ¶⑤어리석은 소견으로는

poor box [ˊ ˊ] *n.* a box into which people put money to help the poor. — [名] 자선함(函)

poor law [ˊ ˊ] *n.* [C] a law offering relief to the poor at public expense. — [名] 빈민 구제법

*** poor·ly** [púərli] *adv.* in a poor manner. ¶*People in this country are poorly off.*① —*adj.* sickly; in poor health. ¶*I feel* ~.② — [副] 가난하게 ¶①이 나라의 사람들은 가난하다 —[形] 병적인, 허약한 ¶②몸이 불편하다

poor·ness [púərnis] *n.* [U] the state or quality of being poor. — [名] 결핍; 열등; 허약

poor-spir·it·ed [púərspíritid] *adj.* having or showing a poor spirit; having no courage. — [形] 겁 많은; 마음 약한

poor white [ˊ ˊ] *n.* a poor and lazy white person in the southern United States. — [名] 가난한 백인

*** pop**[1] [pap / pɔp] *n.* [C] **1.** a short, sharp, quick sound. ¶*The cork came out with a* ~. **2.** a shot from a gun. **3.** [U] any kind of sweet drink made with soda water. — [名] 1. 펑(빵, 탕)하는 소리 2. [총의] 한 방 3. [탄산수 따위를 섞은] 달콤한 음료

—*v.* (**popped, pop·ping**) *vi.* **1.** make a short, sharp, quick sound; burst. ¶*A balloon pops when it is heated.* **2.** move, come, enter, or appear suddenly. ¶~ *in and out.* **3.** (of the eyes) stick out. —*vt.* **1.** cause (something) to make a short, sharp, quick sound; (*U.S.*) heat corn, etc. till it bursts open. ¶~ *corn.* **2.** place or thrust suddenly. ¶~ *a coin into one's pocket.* — [自] 1. 펑하고 소리내다; 빵하고 터지다; 파열하다 2. 갑자기 오다(들어오다, 나타나다) 3. [눈이] 튀어나오다 —[他] 1. …을 펑하고 울리다; 《美》 [옥수수 따위]를 볶아 튀기다 2. …을 갑자기 놓다; …을 갑자기 움직이다

pop the question, (*colloq.*) propose marriage. — 熟 《口》 구혼하다

—*adv.* with a pop; unexpectedly or suddenly. ¶*go* ~. — [副] 펑하고; 갑자기

pop[2] [pap / pɔp] *n.* [C] 《usu. *pl.*》 (*colloq.*) a popular concert; a popular song or piece of music. — [名] 《口》 통속 음악회

—*adj.* (*colloq.*) popular. ¶*a* ~ *concert.* — [形] 《口》 통속적인

pop·corn [pápkɔ̀:rn / pɔ́pkɔ:n] *n.* [U] a kind of corn which bursts open when heated. — [名] 팝코온, 튀긴 옥수수

*** Pope, pope** [poup], **the** *n.* [C] the head of the Roman Catholic Church. — [名] 로마 교황

pop·gun [pápgʌn / pɔ́p-] *n.* [C] a toy gun that shoots a pellet with a loud pop. — [名] 장난감 총

pop·in·jay [pápindʒèi / pɔ́p-] *n.* [C] a vain, chattering, thoughtless person. — [名] 수다스러운 맵시꾼

pop·ish [póupiʃ] *adj.* (unfriendly) of the Pope or the Roman Catholic Church. ▷**pop·ish·ly** [-li] *adv.* — [形] 로마 교황의; 가톨릭교의

pop·lar [páplər / pɔ́plə] *n.* [C] a tall tree with small heart-shaped leaves; [U] the wood of this tree. — [名] 포플라; 포플라 재목

pop·lin [páplin / pɔ́p-] *n.* [U] a silk and woolen cloth. — [名] 포플린 천

pop·py [pápi / pɔ́pi] *n.* **1.** [C] (pl. **-pies**) a plant with showy flowers of various colors and notched leaves. ¶*a field* (or *red*) *poppy.*① **2.** [U] poppy red; scarlet. — [名] 1. 양귀비 ¶①개양귀비 2. 양귀비빛; 주황빛, 진홍빛

pop·u·lace [pápjuləs / pɔ́p-] *n.* [U] 《usu. *the* ~, *collectively*》 the great mass of common people. — [名] 민중

⁑ pop·u·lar [pápjulər / pɔ́pjulə] *adj.* **1.** liked by many people. ¶*The singer is* ~ *with girls.* **2.** of, for or by the common people. **3.** widespread among people. ¶*a* ~ *song.* **4.** suitable for most people. ¶*a* ~ *novel.* — [形] 1. 인기있는 2. 민중의(을 위한, 에 의한) 3. 유행의(하고 있는) 4. 대중용의, 통속적인

*** pop·u·lar·i·ty** [pàpjulǽriti / pɔ̀p-] *n.* [U] the state of being liked by many people. ¶*enjoy general* ~.① — [名] 인기, 호평 ¶①인기를 얻다

pop·u·lar·i·za·tion [pàpjulərizéiʃ(ə)n / pɔ̀pjulərai-] *n.* [U] the act of making something popular; the state of being popular. — [名] 통속화; 보급

pop·u·lar·ize [pápjuləràiz / pɔ́p-] *vt.* make (something) popular. — [他] …을 통속(대중)화하다

pop·u·lar·ly [pápjulərli / pópjuləli] *adv.* **1.** in a popular manner. ¶*a popularly-written book.* **2.** by the people generally. ¶*That is ~ known.*
— ㉿ **1.** 통속적으로 ¶①통속적으로 씌어진 책 **2.** 일반적으로 ¶②그 일은 일반에 알려져 있다

pop·u·late [pápjuleit / póp-] *vt.* **1.** supply (a town, country, etc.) with people. **2.** live in (a country or town). ¶*Many Englishmen populated America.* / *Seoul is densely populated.*
— ㉿ **1.** [나라·지역]에 사람을 살게 하다;…에 식민하다 **2.** …에 거주하다 ¶①서울은 인구밀도가 높다

‡**pop·u·la·tion** [pàpjuléiʃ(ə)n / pòp-] *n.* **1.** Ⓤ Ⓒ the total number of people living in a country, city, etc. ¶*The area has a large (small) ~.* **2.** (*collectively*) the people or a group of people in a city, country, etc. ¶*the adult ~* / *the farm ~.* [thickly populated.]
— ㉿ **1.** 인구; 주민수; 인원 수 ¶①그 지역의 인구는 많다(적다) **2.** [일정 지역의] 주민 ¶②성년 주민/③농민, 농촌 인구

pop·u·lous [pápjuləs / póp-] *adj.* having many people;
— ㉿ 인구가 많은; 인구밀도가 높은

por·ce·lain [pɔ́:rslin / pɔ́:s-] *n.* Ⓤ **1.** fine, white earthenware. **2.** (*collectively*) dishes or ornaments made of the porcelain; china.
— ㉿ **1.** 자기(磁器) **2.** 자기 제품

:**porch** [pɔ:rtʃ] *n.* Ⓒ **1.** a covered entrance to a doorway or other building. **2.** (U.S.) a veranda.
— ㉿ **1.** [본 건물의] 현관 **2.** 《美》 베란다

por·cu·pine [pɔ́:rkjupàin / pɔ́:k-] *n.* Ⓒ an animal with sharp spines on its body to protect it from enemies.
— ㉿ 호저(豪猪)

pore¹ [pɔ:r] *vi.* **1.** gaze closely and steadily. **2.** think or read earnestly (*~ at* (or *on, over*) something).
— ㉿ **1.** 응시하다 **2.** 숙고하다; 몰두하다; 자세히 읽다

pore² [pɔ:r] *n.* Ⓒ a very small opening in the skin of animals or in the surface of leaves.
— ㉿ 털구멍; 기공(氣孔)

＊**pork** [pɔ:rk] *n.* Ⓤ the meat of pigs used for food.
— ㉿ 돼지고기

pork·er [pɔ́:rkər / pɔ́:kə] *n.* Ⓒ a pig fattened for food.
— ㉿ 식용 돼지

po·rous [pɔ́:rəs] *adj.* **1.** full of pores or very small holes. **2.** absorbing a liquid or air. ▷ **po·rous·ness** [-nis] *n.*
— ㉿ **1.** 구멍이 많은 **2.** [액체·공기가] 스며드는

por·poise [pɔ́:rpəs] *n.* Ⓒ (pl. **-pois·es** or *collectively* **-poise**) a sea animal of the whale family; a dolphin.
— ㉿ 돌고래

por·ridge [pɔ́:ridʒ / pɔ́r-] *n.* Ⓤ (*Brit.*) a soft food made of cereal or vegetables boiled in water or milk.
— ㉿ 《英》 오우트밀 죽

por·rin·ger [pɔ́rindʒər / pɔ́rindʒə] *n.* Ⓒ a small shallow dish for porridge, etc.
— ㉿ 죽 접시(대접)

‡**port**¹ [pɔ:rt] *n.* Ⓒ **1.** a place where ships take refuge from storms. **2.** a place where ships arrive and depart. **3.** a town with a harbor.
— ㉿ **1.** 피난항(港) **2.** 선착장(船着場); 항구 **3.** 항구도시

port² [pɔ:rt] *n.* Ⓒ the left side of a ship. ↔ starboard ¶*on the ~ bow.* —*adj.* on the left side of a ship. —*vt., vi.* turn to the left side of a ship; turn the helm to the left. [bearing.]
— ㉿ [배의] 좌현(左舷) ¶①좌현 선수에 — ㉿ 좌현의 — ㉿ 좌현으로 향하[게 하]다; 좌현으로 선회하다

port³ [pɔ:rt] *n.* Ⓤ the way in which a person behaves;
— ㉿ 태도; 외양, 풍채

port⁴ [pɔ:rt] *n.* Ⓤ a strong, sweet, dark red wine, originally from Portugal. ¶*a ~ typewriter.* [moved.]
— ㉿ [포르투갈 원산의] 포도주

＊**port·a·ble** [pɔ́:rtəbl] *adj.* that can be easily carried or
— ㉿ 들고 다닐 수 있는; 휴대용의

por·tage [pɔ́:rtidʒ] *n.* **1.** Ⓤ the act of carrying. **2.** Ⓤ the act of carrying boats, cargo, goods, etc. overland from one river to another. **3.** Ⓒ the place where this transportation is done.
— ㉿ **1.** 운반 **2.** 두 수로(水路) 사이의 육운(陸運) **3.** 두 수로 사이의 육로

por·tal [pɔ́:rtl] *n.* Ⓒ a large gateway or entrance.
— ㉿ [으리으리한] 정문, 입구

port·cul·lis [pɔ:rtkʌ́lis] *n.* Ⓒ a strong iron frame of bars that can be raised or lowered at the entrance of a castle or fort. [thing usu. bad) beforehand; foretell.]
— ㉿ [성문 따위의] 내리닫이 쇠창살문

por·tend [pɔ:rténd] *vt.* give warning or a sign of (something.
— ㉿ …의 전조(前兆)가 되다; …을

por·tent [pɔ́:rtənt] *n.* Ⓒ a sign of some evil to come.
— ㉿ [흉사의] 전조 [예시하다]

por·ten·tous [pɔ:rténtəs] *adj.* **1.** showing or giving a portent. **2.** extraordinary; marvelous.
— ㉿ **1.** 불길한, 흉조의 **2.** 경이적인

:**por·ter**¹ [pɔ́:rtər] *n.* Ⓒ **1.** a person who carries burdens or baggage, esp. at a station or hotel. **2.** (U.S.) a person who serves passengers in a railroad parlor car or sleeping car; a waiter.
— ㉿ **1.** 운반인; 포오터; [호텔에서 손님의 짐을 나르는] 보이 **2.** [침대차 따위의] 보이

por·ter² [pɔ́:rtər] *n.* Ⓒ a doorman; a gate keeper.
— ㉿ 문지기, 현관지기

por·ter·house [pɔ́:rtərhàus] *n.* Ⓒ a kind of large steak; a porterhouse steak.
— ㉿ 고급 비이프 스테이크

port·fo·li·o [pɔːrtfóuliou] *n.* [C] (pl. **-li·os**) **1.** a case for carrying papers, etc; a brief case. **2.** the position of a minister of state. ¶*hold the ~ of Finance.*①
—[名] 1. 손가방; 휴대용 서류가방 2. 장관의 직 ¶①재무장관의 자리에 있다

port·hole [pɔ́ːrthòul] *n.* [C] **1.** a small, round window in the side of a ship. **2.** an opening in a ship, fort, etc. through which to shoot.
—[名] 1. 현창(舷窓) 2. 총안(銃眼); 포문

por·ti·co [pɔ́ːrtikòu / pɔ́ː-] *n.* [C] (pl. **-coes** or **-cos**) a porch with a roof supported by columns.
—[名] 주랑(柱廊); 현관

:por·tion [pɔ́ːrʃ(ə)n] *n.* [C] **1.** a part of the whole. **2.** the quantity of food served to one person. **3.** the part of an estate given to an heir; a share.
—[名] 1. 부분 2. [식사의] 1인분 3. 상속재산; 배당, 몫
a portion of, *a small amount of* (*something*).
[熟] 약간의
—*vt.* divide (something) into shares.
—[他] …을 분배하다

port·ly [pɔ́ːrtli] *adj.* (**-li·er, -li·est**) **1.** fat; stout. **2.** dignified. ¶*a ~ man.* ▷**port·li·ness** [-nis] *n.*
—[形] 1. 뚱뚱한; 체격이 좋은 2. 위엄이 있는

P

port·man·teau [pɔːrtmǽntou] *n.* [C] (pl. **-teaus** or **-teaux**) (*Brit.*) a large traveling bag, that opens like a book.
—[名] 여행가방

port·man·teaux [pɔːrtmǽntouz] *n.* pl. of **portmanteau.**

·por·trait [pɔ́ːrtrit] *n.* [C] **1.** a picture of a person. **2.** a vivid description of a person's appearance or character.
—[名] 1. 초상[화]; 인물 사진 2. 생생한 묘사

por·trai·ture [pɔ́ːrtritʃər] *n.* **1.** [U] the act or art of portraying. **2.** [C] a portrait; ⦅*collectively*⦆ a collection of portraits. **3.** [U] vivid description of a person's appearance or character.
—[名] 1. 묘사[법]; 초상화법 2. 초상화; 초상화집(集) 3. [말에 의한] 인물 묘사

por·tray [pɔːrtréi] *vt.* **1.** make a portrait of (someone). **2.** describe clearly (someone or something) in words. **3.** play (a part) on the stage. ▷**por·tray·er** [-ər] *n.*
—[他] 1. …의 초상을 그리다 2. …을 생생하게 묘사하다 3. …의 역을 연기하다

por·tray·al [pɔːrtréiəl] *n.* **1.** [U] the act of portraying. **2.** [C] a portrait or description.
—[名] 1. [그림]그리기, 묘사 2. 초상화; 묘사물

Por·tu·gal [pɔ́ːrtʃug(ə)l, +*Brit.* pɔ́ːtju-] *n.* a small country in Europe, just west of Spain. ⇒[N.B.]
—[名] 포르투갈 [N.B.] 수도는 Lisbon

Por·tu·guese [pɔ̀ːrtʃugíːz, +*Brit.* pɔ̀ːtju-] *n.* **1.** [C] a person of Portugal. **2.** [U] the language of Portugal.
—[名] 1. 포르투갈 사람 2. 포르투갈 말
—*adj.* of Portugal or Portuguese.
—[形] 포르투갈[사람·말]의

pose [pouz] *n.* [C] **1.** a position of the body. **2.** a mental attitude assumed for effect; a pretense.
—[名] 1. 자세, 포우즈 2. 마음가짐, 일부러 짓는 태도; 겉치레
—*vi.* **1.** hold a certain position of the body. ¶*She posed for a picture.*① **2.** pretend to be what one really is not. ¶*The man poses as an actor.* —*vt.* **1.** put (someone) in a position suitable for a picture, photograph, etc. **2.** put (a question, etc.) for consideration.
—[自] 1. 포우즈를 취하다 2. 짐짓 …인 체하다 —[他] 1. …에 포우즈를 취하게 하다 2. [문제 따위]를 제출하다

Po·sei·don [pousáid(ə)n, +*Brit.* pɔ-] *n.* (in Greek mythology) the god of the sea and of horses. ⇒fig., [N.B.]
—[名] 해신(海神) [N.B.] 로마 신화에서 Neptune

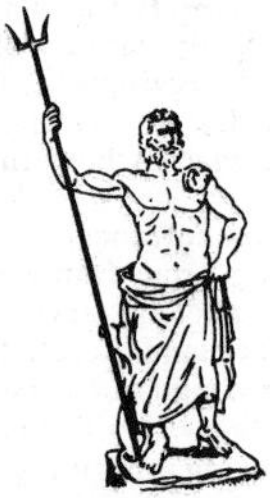
〔Poseidon〕

pos·er [póuzər] *n.* [C] **1.** a difficult question or problem. **2.** an affected person.
—[名] 1. 난문(難問) 2. 젠체하는 사람

:po·si·tion [pəzíʃ(ə)n] *n.* [C] **1.** the place where a thing or person is. ¶*The villa has a very good ~.*① **2.** [U] the proper place. ¶*He is in ~.*② **3.** the way in which a person or thing is placed or arranged; a posture. ¶*set in a comfortable ~.*③ **4.** social rank. **5.** a job. **6.** a way of thinking; a mental attitude. ¶*the conservative ~.*④
—[名] 1. 위치 ¶①별장은 대단히 좋은 위치에 있다 2. 적소(適所) ¶②그는 알맞은 자리에 있다 3. 자세; 상태 ¶③편한 자세로 앉다 4. 지위 5. 일자리 6. 견해 ¶④보수적인 견해

·pos·i·tive [pázitiv / pɔ́z-] *adj.* **1.** clearly expressed; sure; unquestionable; that can not be denied. ¶*a ~ fact.*① **2.** quite sure; certain. ¶*He is ~ about his success.* **3.** real; practical; constructive. ¶*a ~ mind.*② **4.** showing agreement; approving. ¶*a ~ answer.* **5.** (*Physics, Electricity*) not negative; plus. ¶*~ electricity.*③ **6.** (*col-*
—[形] 1. 명백한, 확실한, 의심할 여지 없는, 부정할 수 없는 ¶①확고한 사실 2. 확신한 3. 실제적인, 현실적인, 실증적인; 건설적인 ¶②실제적인 사람 4. 긍정적인 5. ⦅理·電⦆ 정(正)의, 플러스의 양(陽)의 ¶③양전기 6. ⦅口⦆ 완전한,

loq.) complete ; quite. ¶*a* ~ *fool.* **7.** (*Grammar*) in its simple form, as of an adjective or adverb. 순전한 **7.**〔文法〕 원급의

—*n.* [C] **1.** reality. **2.** (*Grammar*) a positive degree. **3.** a positive quantity. **4.** a positive photographic print. —[名] **1.** 실재(實在) **2.**〔文法〕 원급 **3.** 정량(正量) **4.** [사진의] 양화(陽畫)

pos·i·tive·ly [pázitivli / pɔ́z-] *adv.* in a positive manner; absolutely ; decidedly. —[副] 확실히 ; 단호하게

pos·i·tive·ness [pázitivnis / pɔ́z-] *n.* [U] the state of being positive. —[名] 결정적인 ; 적극성

pos·i·tiv·ism [pázitivìz(ə)m / pɔ́z-] *n.* [U] **1.** ((also *P-*)) the philosophical system of Auguste Comte, which rejects any abstract speculation. **2.** the state of being positive. —[名] **1.** 실증철학 **2.** 적극성 ; 명확성

⁑pos·sess [pəzés] *vt.* **1.** have (something) as one's own ; hold. **2.** ((usu. in *passive*)) occupy (something) by an evil spirit, etc. **3.** maintain or control (one's mind). —[他] **1.** …을 소유하다 **2.** [악령(惡靈) 따위가] …에 들러붙다 **3.** [마음]을 유지하다 ; 자제하다

1) ***be possessed by*** (=*have one's mind occupied by something evil.*)
2) ***be possessed of,*** own or hold.

[熟] 1)…에 사로잡혀 있다 2)…을 소유하고 있다

⁑pos·ses·sion [pəzéʃ(ə)n] *n.* **1.** [U] the act of possessing ; the state of being possessed ; ownership. **2.** [C] a thing possessed ; ((*pl., collectively*)) wealth. ¶*a national* ~① / *It was his most treasured* ~.② **3.** [C] a territory ruled by another country. **4.** [U] self-control. —[名] **1.** 소유 **2.** 소유물 ; 재산 ¶①국가 소유물/②그것이 그가 가장 소중히 간수하는 것이다 **3.** 영지(領地), 속국 **4.** 자제(自制)

1) ***hold possession of*** (=*take and keep*) *something.*
2) ***in*** [***the***] ***possession of,*** having as one's own.

[熟] 1)…을 갖고 있다 2)…을 소유하는

pos·ses·sive [pəzésiv] *adj.* **1.** of possession. **2.** (*Grammar*) showing possession. —[形] **1.** 소유의 **2.**〔文法〕 소유를 나타내는

—*n.* [C] (*Grammar*) **1.** the possessive case. **2.** a word in that case. —[名] 《文法》 **1.** 소유격 **2.** 소유격의 단어

pos·ses·sor [pəzésər] *n.* [C] a person who has something ; an owner. —[名] 임자, 소유자

⁑pos·si·bil·i·ty [pàsibíliti / pɔ̀s-] *n.* (pl. **-ties**) **1.** [U] the state of being possible. ¶*There is much* ~ *of his success.*① **2.** [C] something that may happen. —[名] **1.** 가능성 ¶①그가 성공할 가망이 다분히 있다 **2.** 있을(일어날) 수 있음

⁑pos·si·ble [pásibl / pɔ́s-] *adj.* **1.** that can be done; within the limit of one's ability or power. ¶*as … as* ~① /*if* ~.② **2.** that may be or happen. ¶*It was quite* ~ *that he should do so.* **3.** (*colloq.*) that can be considered ; that can be put up with. ¶*He is not a* ~ *person.*③ —[形] **1.** 할 수 있는, 가능한 ¶①될 수 있는 한 …하게/②가능하면 **2.** 있을(일어날) 수 있는 **3.** 상당한, 참을 수 있는 ¶③그는 못쓸 사람이다

—*n.* **1.** ((*the* ~, *one's*, or *pl.*)) something that can be done. ¶*I will do my* ~.④ **2.** the highest possible score in shooting, etc. ¶*score a* ~.⑤ —[名] **1.** 할 수 있음, 전력 ¶④전력을 다하겠다 **2.** [사격 따위의] 최고점 ¶⑤최고점을 따다

⁑pos·si·bly [pásibli / pɔ́s-] *adv.* **1.** perhaps ; maybe. ¶*He may* ~ *come.* **2.** by any means. ¶*I cannot* ~ *go.* —[副] **1.** 아마 **2.** 도저히…할 수 없는 ; 아무래도

pos·sum [pásəm / pɔ́s-] *n.* [C] (*U.S. colloq.*) an opossum. —[名] 《美口》 유대류(有袋類)의 쥐

play possum, pretend to take no notice ; pretend to be sick, ignorant, etc. [熟] 시치미떼다 ; 속이다

⁑post[1] [poust] *n.* [C] a piece of wood, metal, etc. set upright to hold something up ; a pole. ¶*a telegraph* ~.① —[名] 기둥, 푯말, 말뚝, 장대 ¶①전봇대

—*vt.* **1.** fix or put up a poster, etc. on (a wall, etc.) ¶*Don't* ~ *this wall.* **2.** put (a name etc.) in a list that is published ; bring (something) to public notice. ¶~ *someone for a robber.*② **3.** (*U.S.*) close (a place, etc.) to the public by means of signs or notices. —[他] **1.** [벽 따위에] …을 붙이다 **2.** …을 공고하다, 고시하다 ; 널리 알리다 ¶②…을 강도라고 공시하다 **3.** [토지]에 출입 금지의 게시를 하다

⁑post[2] [poust] *n.* [C] **1.** a situation ; an office ; a job. ¶*have a* ~ *in a company.*① **2.** a place where a soldier is on watch. ¶*Remain at your* ~.② **3.** a place where soldiers are stationed. **4.** a trading place in an uncivilized region. —[名] **1.** 지위 ; 직장 ¶①회사에 근무하고 있다 **2.** 감시소, 부서, 초소 ¶②네 부서를 지켜라 **3.** 주둔지 **4.** 교역지

—*vt.* station or assign (someone) at a post. ¶~ *guards at the Diet Building.*③ —[他] [사람]을 배치하다 ¶③국회 의사당에 경비병을 배치하다

⁑post[3] [poust] *n.* **1.** [U] ((usu. *the* ~)) (esp. *Brit.*) the system of carrying and delivering letters, cards, and parcels. ¶*send something by* ~① / *by return of* ~.② **2.** [C] (*Brit.*) letters (cf. *U.S.* mail). ¶*Today's* ~ *has not come yet.*③ **3.** [C] (*Brit.*) a post office ; a post box. **4.** [C] an express messenger ; a postman. —[名] **1.**《英》 우편, 우편 제도 ¶①…을 우송하다/②편지 받는 대로 곧 **2.**《英》 우편물 ¶③오늘 우편은 아직 안 왔다 **3.**《英》 우체국, 우편함 **4.** 보발(步撥) ; 우체부

—*vt.* **1.** send (a letter, etc.) by mail. ¶~ *a letter* / —[他] **1.** …을 우송하다 **2.** …을 우체통

~ a parcel. **2.** put (a letter, etc.) into the post; mail. **3.** (usu. in *passive*) inform (someone) of something. ¶*He is well posted in the latest event.*④ **4.** hasten. —*vi.* go or start in haste.

post- [poust-] a word element meaning *after* or *behind*. ―「…의 뒤」를 나타내는 연결형

· post·age [póustidʒ] *n.* Ⓤ the amount charged for sending anything by mail. ¶~ *due* (*free*).① ―명 우편 요금 ¶①우세(郵稅) 부족 (무료)

postage stamp [́́ ́ ́] *n.* Ⓒ a government stamp put on letters or parcels to show that postage has been paid. ―명 우표

· post·al [póust(ə)l] *adj.* of mail or post offices. ¶*the ~ charge*① / ~ *service.*② —*n.* Ⓒ (*U.S.*) a post card. ―형 우편[국]의 ¶①우편요금/②우편 ―명 《美》관제 엽서

post bag [́́ ́ ́] *n.* (*Brit.*) a mailbag. ―명 《英》우편 행낭

post-bel·lum [póustbéləm] *adj.* after the war. ↔ante-bellum ―형 전후(戰後)의

post·box [póustbɑks / -bɔks] *n.* Ⓒ (*Brit.*) a mailbox. ―명 《英》 우체통

: post card [́́ ́ ́] *n.* **1.** a card issued by a government on which a postage stamp is printed; a postal card. **2.** (*U.S.*) a private card to be sent by mail. ―명 1. 《美》 우편(관제)엽서 2. 《美》 사제(私製) 엽서

post·date [poustdéit / ́́ ́ ́] *vt.* **1.** give a later date than the actual date to (a letter, a check, etc.). **2.** follow (something) in time. ¶*His fame postdated his death.*① ―타 1. [편지·수표 따위의] 날짜를 늦추다 2. …의 뒤에 오다 ¶①그는 죽어서 유명해졌다

post·er [póustər] *n.* Ⓒ a large printed card or notice posted in a public place. ―명 포스터, 삐라

poste restante [pòustrestáːnt] *n.* **1.** a direction on a letter to show that it should be held at the post office until called for. **2.** (*Brit.*) the post office department in charge of such letters. ―명 1. 유치(留置) 우편 2. 《英》 유치 우편과

pos·te·ri·or [pɑstíəriər / pɔstíəriə] *adj.* **1.** behind. ↔anterior **2.** later in time or order. ↔prior —*n.* Ⓒ **1.** the hinder parts. **2.** (often *pl.*) the parts at the back of the hip, esp. of animals; the buttocks. ―형 1. 후부(後部)의 2. [시간적으로] 나중의; [순서가] 다음의 —명 1. 후부 2. 둔부, 엉덩이

· pos·ter·i·ty [pɑstériti / pɔs-] *n.* Ⓤ **1.** (*collectively*) those who come after in family line. **2.** all future generations. ―명 1. 자손 2. 후세(後世)

postal charges. **2.** (*Brit.*) postpaid. ―「불의」
post-free [póustfríː] *adj.* **1.** that can be sent free of ―명 1. 우편요금 무료의 2. 우편료 선

post·grad·u·ate [poustgrǽdʒuit / ́́ ́ ́-, -dʒuit] *adj.* of a course of study after graduation from a college or university. —*n.* Ⓒ a student who studies after graduation at a college or university. ―형 대학 졸업 후의; 대학원의 —명 연구생; 대학원생

post·haste [póusthéist] *adv.* (*archaic*) quickly; with great haste. ―「hire to travelers.」 ―부 《古》황급히

post horse [́́ ́ ́] *n.* a horse for post chaises or for ―명 역마(驛馬), 파발마

post·hu·mous [pástʃuməs / póstju-] *adj.* **1.** born after the death of the father. ¶*a ~ child.*① **2.** published after the death of the author. ¶*a ~ work.*② **3.** happening after one's death. ¶~ *fame.*③ ―형 1. 아버지가 죽은 후에 태어난 ¶①유복자 2.저자의 사후에 출판된 ¶②유고(遺稿) 3. 죽은 후의 ¶③사후의 명성

: post·man [póus(t)mən] *n.* Ⓒ (pl. **-men** [-mən]) a man who works at the post office to collect or deliver mail; a letter carrier. (cf. *U.S.* mailman) ―명 우편 집배인

post·mark [póus(t)mɑːrk] *n.* Ⓒ a post office mark stamped on letters, parcels, etc. giving the place and the date. —*vt.* stamp (a letter, etc.) with a postmark. ―명 우편의 소인(消印) —타 …에 소인을 찍다

post·mas·ter [póus(t)mæstər / -mɑːstə] *n.* Ⓒ the director of a post office. ―명 우체국장

postmaster general [́́ ́ ́ ́́ ́ ́-] *n.* (pl. **-ters ~**) **1.** (*Brit.*) the Minister in charge of the postal department. **2.** (*U.S.*) the head of a government's postal system. ―명 1. 《英》 우정(郵政)대신 2. 《美》 체신장관

post me·rid·i·em [pòus(t)mərídiəm / póust-] *adj.* of the afternoon. ↔ante meridiem ⇒N.B. ―명 오후 N.B. P.M. 또는 p.m.으로 줄임

post·mis·tress [póus(t)mìstris] *n.* Ⓒ a woman director of a post office. ―명 여자 우체국장

post·mor·tem [pòus(t)mɔ́ːrtəm] *adj.* after death. ¶*a ~ examination.*① —*n.* Ⓒ the examination of a dead body, esp. to find the cause of death. ―형 사후(死後)의 ¶①시체 해부, 검시 ―명 시체 해부, 검시

: post office [́́ ́ ́] *n.* **1.** the place where the collection, ―명 1. 우체국 2. 체신부

post·paid [póustpéid] *adj.* with the postage paid in advance. —形 우편요금 선불의

post·pone [pous(t)póun] *vt.* put off (something) till a later time; delay. 「postponing.」 —他 …을 연기하다

post·pone·ment [pous(t)póunmənt] *n.* —名 연기

post·script [póus(t)skript] *n.* ⓒ **1.** a note or message added after the signature of a letter. ⇒N.B. **2.** a supplementary part added to a book or an article. —名 1. 추신(追伸) N.B. P.S.로 줄임 2. 후기(後記)

pos·tu·late [pástʃuleit → *n.* / pástju-] *vt.* **1.** demand (something). **2.** assume (something) without proof as a basis of reasoning.
—*n.* [U.S. -lut] ⓒ something self-evident or assumed without proof as a basis of reasoning.
—他 1. …을 요구하다 2. …을 자명(自明)한 것이라 가정하다
—自 자명한 이치, 기초 조항, 공리(公理)

pos·ture [pástʃər / póstʃə] *n.* **1.** ⓒⓊ the way a person holds himself. ¶ *in a sitting* ~① / *take the* ~ *of defense.*② **2.** ⓒ a mental attitude. **3.** Ⓤ the state or condition of affairs.
—*vi.* take a certain position, esp. for effect. —*vt.* set (someone) in a particular position.
—名 1. 자세, 태도, 포우즈 ¶①앉은 자세로/②방어 자세를 취하다 2. 마음가짐 3. 상태
—自 포우즈를 취하다; …인 체하다
—他 …에 포우즈를 취하게 하다

post·war [póustwɔ́:r] *adj.* after the war. ↔prewar —形 전후(戰後)의

po·sy [póuzi] *n.* (pl. **sies**) a flower or bunch of flowers. —名 꽃; 꽃다발

pot [pɑt / pɔt] *n.* ⓒ **1.** a round vessel or container, such as a coffeepot or a teapot. ¶ *(proverb) A little ~ is soon hot.*① **2.** the amount such a vessel can hold. ¶ *a ~ of milk.* **3.** a vessel for holding plants; a flowerpot. **4.** (*colloq.*) a large sum of money. ¶ *pots of money.* **5.** a prize, esp. a silver cup. **6.** a shot aimed at a short distance.
1) *go to pot,* (*colloq.*) become useless; be ruined.
2) *keep the pot boiling,* make one's living; keep things going.
3) *make the pot boil,* earn enough money to live on.
4) *The pot calls the kettle black.,* Someone finds fault with another when both are equally to blame.
—*v.* (**pot·ted, pot·ting**) *vt.* **1.** put (something) into a pot. ¶ ~ *flowers.*② **2.** keep (something) in a pot. ¶ ~ *jam.* **3.** shoot. —*vi.* shoot. (~ *at* something)
—名 1. 단지, 병, 주발 ¶①(俚)소인은 금방 화를 낸다 2. 한 단지(병, 주발)의 분량 3. 화분 4. 큰 돈, 거액 5. 상(賞), 상품, 은상배(銀賞杯) 6. 가까운 거리에서 쏘기
(熟 1)(口)파멸하다, 못쓰게 되다 2)생계를 세워 나가다; 경기 좋게 일을 해 나가다 3)생계를 세우다 4)솥이 검정 나무란다
—他 1. …을 단지에 넣다 ¶②꽃을 화분에 심다 2. …을 단지에 넣어 보존하다 3. …을 겨냥하여 쏘다 —自 겨냥하여 쏘다

pot·ash [pátæʃ / pɔ́t-] *n.* Ⓤ any of several substances obtained from wood ashes and used in making soap, fertilizers, etc. —名 잿물; 가성(苛性)칼리

po·tas·si·um [pətǽsiəm] *n.* Ⓤ a soft, light, silver-white metal found only in compounds. —名 칼륨

po·ta·tion [poutéiʃ(ə)n] *n.* Ⓤ the act of drinking. —名 마시기

po·ta·to [pətéitou] *n.* ⓒ (pl. **-toes**) **1.** a plant with root-like bulbs, or tubers which can be eaten; one of these tubers. **2.** (*U.S.*) a sweet potato. 「and salted.」 —名 1. 감자 2. (美) 고구마

potato chip [-́-- -́] *n.* a thin slice of potato fried crisp —名 얇게 썬 감자 튀김

pot·boil·er [pátbɔilər / pɔ́tbɔ̀ilə] *n.* ⓒ (*colloq.*) a literary or artistic work produced only to make money. —名 (口) 돈 벌기 위한 작품

po·ten·cy [póut(ə)nsi] *n.* Ⓤ **1.** the state of being potent; power; strength. **2.** capacity of development. —名 1. 세력 2. 능력

po·tent [póut(ə)nt] *adj.* **1.** having great power; strong. **2.** having authority and influence. ¶ *a ~ reason.*
—形 1. 힘이 있는, 세력이 있는 2. 남을 신복(信服)시키는

po·ten·tate [póut(ə)ntèit] *n.* ⓒ a powerful person or ruler. —名 권력자; 군주

po·ten·tial [pouténʃ(ə)l] *adj.* that can come into existence, but not in existence at present; able to be developed. ↔actual ¶ *a ~ genius.*①
—*n.* Ⓤ something that is potential; a potentiality.
—形 가능한; 잠재하는 ¶①천재의 소질이 있는 사람
—名 가능; 잠재 세력

po·ten·ti·al·i·ty [poutènʃiǽliti] *n.* (pl. **-ties**) Ⓤ **1.** the state or quality of being potential; potential characteristic; hidden power; possibility of development. **2.** (*pl.*) something potential.
—名 1. 가능성; 잠재 능력; 발전의 가능성 2. 가능한 것

po·ten·tial·ly [pouténʃəli] *adv.* in a potential state; possibly, but not yet actually.
— 副 가능하도록·어쩌면

poth·er [pɑ́ðər / pɔ́ðə] *n.* ⓤⓒ **1.** a choking cloud of dust, smoke, etc. **2.** an uproar; a disturbance.
— 名 1. 자욱한 구름(모래, 연기) 2. 소요, 혼란

pot-herb [pɑ́t(h)ə:rb / pɔ́tha:b] *n.* ⓒ any herb that is boiled and eaten or used to flavor food.
— 名 [삶아서 먹는] 야채

pot·hook [pɑ́thùk / pɔ́t-] *n.* ⓒ a hook for hanging a pot or kettle over a fire.
— 名 남비[따위]를 거는 고리

po·tion [póuʃ(ə)n] *n.* ⓒ a dose of liquid medicine or poison.
— 名 [물약 또는 독약의] 한 첩

pot·luck [pɑ́tlʌ̀k / pɔ́tlʌ́k] *n.* ⓤ food which happens to be available for a meal.
— 名 있는 것으로 장만한 요리

pot·sherd [pɑ́tʃə:rd / pɔ́tʃə:d] *n.* ⓒ a piece of broken earthenware.
— 名 질그릇 깨진 조각

pot·tage [pɑ́tidʒ / pɔ́t-] *n.* ⓤ *(archaic)* soup thickened with vegetables and meat; broth.
— 名 진한 수우프

pot·ted [pɑ́tid / pɔ́t-] *adj.* **1.** planted in a pot. ¶ *a ~ plant.* **2.** cooked and kept in sealed pots or cans.
— 形 1. 화분에 심은 2. 단지에 넣은; 동조림의

pot·ter¹ [pɑ́tər / pɔ́tə] *n.* ⓒ a person who makes pots, dishes, vases, etc. ¶ *potter's clay*① / *a potter's wheel.*②
— 名 도공(陶工) ¶①도토(陶土)/②도공 녹로(轆轤)

pot·ter² [pɑ́tər / pɔ́tə] *vt., vi.* (chiefly *Brit.*) =putter.

pot·ter·y [pɑ́təri / pɔ́t-] *n.* (pl. **-ter·ies**) **1.** (*collectively*) things made from clay and hardened in ovens, such as pots and dishes. **2.** ⓤ the art of making earthenware. **3.** ⓒ a place where earthenware is made.
— 名 1. 도자기류 2. 도자기 제조법 3. 도자기 제조소

pouch [pautʃ] *n.* ⓒ **1.** a small bag or sack. **2.** a baglike or pocketlike part of some animals. ¶ *A kangaroo carries its young in a ~.*
—*vt.* **1.** put (something) into a pouch. **2.** make (something) into the form of a pouch. —*vi.* form a pouch.
— 名 1. 작은 자루 2. [동물의] 주머니 모양의 부분
— 他 1. …을 작은 자루에 넣다 2. 자루처럼 만들다 — 自 자루 모양이 되다

poul·ter·er [póult(ə)rər] *n.* ⓒ (chiefly *Brit.*) a person who deals in poultry.
— 名 (英) 새장수

poul·tice [póultis] *n.* ⓒ a soft, moist mass of herbs, mustard, etc. applied to the skin as a medicine. —*vt.* apply a poultice on a sore place.
— 名 습포(濕布) — 他 …에 습포를 붙이다

***poul·try** [póultri] *n.* ⓤ (*collectively*, used as *pl.*) domestic fowls such as chickens, turkeys and ducks.
— 名 가금류(家禽類)

pounce [pauns] *vi.* leap or dash suddenly to seize something. (~ *on* (or *upon, at*) *something*) —*n.* ⓒ a sudden leap or attack. ¶ *make a ~ upon a rat.*①
— 自 갑자기 달려들다; 느닷없이 덮치다 — 名 갑자기 덥비기 ¶①쥐를 덮치다

‡**pound**¹ [paund] *n.* ⓒ **1.** a unit of weight, equal to 16 ounces. ⇒N.B. **2.** a unit of money in Great Britain, equal to 20 shillings. ⇒N.B.
— 名 1. 파운드 N.B. 영국의 중량 단위. lb.로 줄임 2. 파운드 N.B. 영국의 화폐 단위. £ 또는 l.로 줄임

pound² [paund] *vt.* **1.** beat or crush (something) into small pieces or powder. **2.** beat (something) with force repeatedly. (~ *out* or *down something*) —*vi.* **1.** hit heavily or repeatedly. (~ *at* or *on something*) ¶ ~ *on the door* (*a drum*).① **2.** walk or run heavily or noisely.
— 他 1. 을 빻다 2. …을 연달아 치다 — 自 1. 연타하다, 세게 치다 ¶①문(북)을 쾅쾅(둥둥) 두드리다 2. 무거운 발걸음으로 [쿵쿵] 걷다(달리다)

pound³ [paund] *n.* ⓒ **1.** an enclosure for keeping stray animals. **2.** a prison.
— 名 1. 우리 2. 유치장

pound·age [páundidʒ] *n.* ⓤ a fee, rate or tax of so much per pound of money or weight.
— 名 1파운드에 대한 수수료(세금)

pound-fool·ish [páundfú:liʃ] *adj.* foolish or careless in handling large sums of money. ¶ (*proverb*) *Penny-wise and ~.*①
— 形 한 푼을 아끼다 천 냥을 잃는 ¶①(俚)한 푼을 아끼다 천 냥을 잃는다

‡**pour** [pɔ:r] *vt.* **1.** cause (a liquid, etc.) to flow or fall in a stream; shed. ¶ ~ *coffee into a cup from a pot* / ~ *someone a cup of tea*; ~ *a cup of tea for someone* / ~ *arrows.*① **2.** send forth (light, etc.). —*vi.* **1.** flow. ¶ *Tear poured from her eyes.* **2.** rain or fall heavily. ¶ (*proverb*) *It never rains but it pours.*² **3.** rush in a crowd. (~ *into some place*)
1) *pour cold water on,* discourage.
2) *pour in,* come one after another.
3) *pour oil on troubled waters,* settle trouble peacefully.
—*n.* ⓒ a heavy rain.
— 他 1. …을 붓다, 따르다, 흘리다, [비처럼] 퍼붓다 ¶①화살을 퍼붓다 2. [빛 따위]을 쏟다 — 自 1. 흐르다, 붓다 2. [비 따위가] 억수같이 쏟아지다 ¶②(俚)화불단행(禍不單行) 3. 쇄도하다
熟 1)…에 찬물을 끼얹다, 흥을 깨뜨리다 2)연달아 오다 3)분규를 원만히 해결하다
— 名 억수 같은 비

pout [paut] *vi.* push out the lips to show contempt, displeasure, etc. **—n.** [C] the act of pouting.
—[自] 입을 삐쭉 내밀다, 뿌루퉁하다 —[名] 입을 삐쭉 내밀기

*** **pov·er·ty** [pávərti / pɔ́vəti] *n.* [U] **1.** the state of being poor. ¶*be brought up in* ~① | *rise out of* ~.② **2.** lack of something essential or necessary. 《~ *of* or *in*》 ¶~ *of thought*③ | ~ *in vitamins.*④
—[名] 1. 가난 ¶①가난하게 자라다/②출세하여 가난을 벗어나다 2. 결핍 ¶③사상의 빈곤/④비타민의 결핍

pov·er·ty-strick·en [pávərtistrìk(ə)n / pɔ́vəti-] *adj.* very poor.
—[形] 아주 가난한

⁑ pow·der [páudər] *n.* [U] **1.** any dry, solid, dustlike substance; fine dust. ¶*soap* ~.① **2.** a drug in the form of powder. **3.** any special kind of powder applied to hair, teeth, face, etc. as a cosmetic. ¶*put* ~ *on one's cheeks.* **4.** gun powder.
—[名] 1. 가루 ¶①가루비누 2. 가루약 3. 치마분(齒磨粉); [화장용] 분; 머리분 4. 화약

1) ***keep one's powder dry,*** prepare for trouble.
2) ***not worth the powder and shot,*** not worth the trouble.
3) ***smell a powder,*** have the experience of war.
[熟] 1)만일에 대비하다 2)애쓴 보람이 없는 3)전쟁 경험이 있다

—vt. **1.** make (something) into powder. **2.** cover (something) with powder. ¶*The woman was thickly powdered.*② **—vi.** **1.** become powder. **2.** use powder on the face, hair, etc.
—[他] 1. …을 가루로 만들다 2. …에 가루를 뿌리다 ¶②그 부인은 짙은 화장을 하고 있다 —[自] 1. 가루가 되다 2. 화장하다

pow·dered [páudərd] *adj.* made into powder; covered with powder.
—[形] 가루 모양의; 분을 바른

powder mill [´-- ˋ] *n.* a factory where gunpowder is produced.
—[名] 화약 공장

powder puff [´-- ˋ] *n.* [U] a small, soft pad for applying cosmetic powder to the skin.
—[名] 분첩, 퍼프

pow·der·y [páudəri] *adj.* **1.** of or like powder. ¶~ *snow.*① **2.** covered with powder. **3.** that can be easily made into powder. ¶*a* ~ *rock.*②
—[名] 1. 가루의(같은) ¶①가루 눈 2. 가루투성이의 3. 푸석푸석한 ¶②잘 부서지는 바위

⁑ pow·er [páuər] *n.* **1.** [C] ability to do something. ¶*It is not in my* ~ *to do it.*① **2.** [U] strength; force; energy. ¶*obtain* ~ *from water*② | *More* ~ *to your elbow!*③ **3.** [U] authority; influence; control. ¶*the party in* ~.④ | *I have* ~ *over them*⑤ **4.** [C] a person of great authority or influence; 《usu. *pl.*》 a nation having authority or influence. ¶*the Great Powers*⑥ | *a sea* ~.⑦ **5.** [U] (*Mathematics*) the result gained by multiplying a number by itself. ¶*16 is the fourth* ~ *of 2.*⑧ **6.** [C] (*colloq.*) a large number or amount. ¶*a* ~ *of work.* **7.** [U] the magnifying capacity of a lens. **8.** [U] (*Physics*) energy used to do work; the rate at which work is done.
—[名] 1. 능력 ¶①그것을 하기에는 내 능력이 모자란다 2. 힘, 체력, 정력, 동력 ¶②물에서 동력을 얻다/③힘을 내라 3. 권력, 지배력 ¶④여당/⑤그들을 마음대로 할 수 있다 4. 유력자, 권력자; 강대국 ¶⑥열강(列强)/⑦해군국(력) 5. 《數》 자승, 제곱, 멱(冪) ¶⑧16은 2의 4승 6. 다수, 다량 7. 렌즈의 확대력 8. 동력, 효력

the powers that be, (*colloq.*) the authorities.
[熟] 《口》 관계 당국

—adj. **1.** producing or supplying power. ¶*a* ~ *plant.*⑨ **2.** operated by engines or motors. ¶~ *tools.*⑩
—[形] 1. 동력을 공급하는(내는) ¶⑨발전소 2. 동력으로 움직이는 ¶⑩전력으로 움직이는 기구

⁑ pow·er·ful [páuərf(u)l] *adj.* having great force, authority or influence; full of power; having considerable effects on other bodies. ¶*a* ~ *nation*① | *a* ~ *odor*② | *a* ~ *politician.*③
—[形] 강력한, 유력한; 효과가 있는 ¶①강국/②강한 냄새/③유력한 정치가

pow·er·ful·ly [páuərfuli] *adv.* in a powerful manner; with great power or strength; strongly.
—[副] 강하게; 유력하게

pow·er·house [páuərhàus] *n.* [C] a building where electric power is produced.
—[名] 발전소

pow·er·less [páuərlis] *adj.* having no power, authority or ability; helpless. ¶*I am* ~ *to do anything.*①
—[形] 무력한 ¶①나에게는 아무것도 할 힘이 없다

power shovel [´-- ˋ] *n.* a large digging machine operated by an electric motor. ⇒fig.
—[名] [흙을 파는] 동력 삽

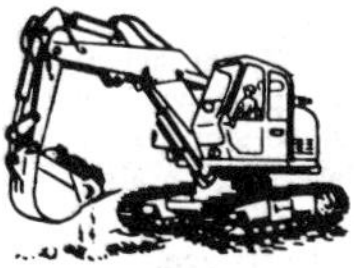
「power shovel」

power station [´-- ˋ-] *n.* a powerhouse.
—[名] 발전소

pox [paks / pɔks] *n.* [U] any disease that covers the skin with spots or sores.
—[名] 천연두, 두창(痘瘡)

pp. **1.** pages. **2.** past participle.

p. p. **1.** past participle. **2.** postpaid.

prac·ti·ca·bil·i·ty [præ̀ktikəbíliti] *n.* [U] the state or quality of being practicable.
—[名] 실행할 수 있음; 실용성

prac·ti·ca·ble [prǽktikəbl] *adj.* that can be done, prac-
—[形] 실행할 수 있는; 실용적인; 사용할

ticed or used. ¶*a ~ road.*①

수 있는 ¶①통행할 수 있는 도로

: prac·ti·cal [prǽktik(ə)l] *adj.* **1.** of action; obtained through practice rather than theory. ↔theoretical ¶*~ difficulty*① / *a ~ nurse.*② **2.** able; experienced. ¶*a ~ engineer.*③ **3.** useful; that can be used. ¶*~ knowledge*. **4.** having an inclination to action rather than thinking.

—[形] 1. 실지의, 실제의 ¶①실지의 곤란/②[면허 없는] 간호부 2. 유능한; 경험이 풍부한 ¶③노련한 기사 3. 쓸모 있는; 실용적인 4. 실행적인

: prac·ti·cal·ly [prǽktikəli →2.] *adv.* **1.** in a practical manner; in practice; really. ¶*Practically, it is impossible.*① **2.** [prǽktikli] (*colloq.*) almost. ¶*There was ~ nothing left in it.*②

—[副] 1. 실제로; 실용적으로; 사실상 ¶①실제로 그것은 불가능하다 2. 《口》 거의 ¶②거의 아무것도 남아 있지 않았다

: prac·tice [prǽktis] *n.* **1.** [U] the act of carrying out something; performance. ↔theory ¶*Theory is one thing and ~ is another.*① **2.** [C] a habit or custom. ¶*It's my ~ to get up early.* **3.** [U] the act of doing something over and over; exercise. ¶(*proverb*) *Practice makes perfect.*② **4.** [U] the business of a doctor or lawyer. ¶*The doctor has a large ~.*③

—[名] 1. 실지, 실행 ¶①이론과 실지는 다르다 2. 습관, 풍습, 관계 3. 연습, 실습 ¶②《俚》연습하면 안 될 일이 없다 4. [의사·변호사 등의] 업무 ¶③그 의사는 사업이 잘된다

1) ***in practice,*** ⓐ not as a mere theory but based on actual experience. ⓑ in the course of practice. ⓒ at work.
2) ***make a practice of,*** do (something) habitually.
3) ***out of practice,*** poor at or unable to do (something) because of lack of exercise or training.
4) ***put in*** (or ***into***) ***practice,*** carry out (something).

[熟] 1)ⓐ실지로, 실제상 ⓑ연습하여 ⓒ일하여, 개업하여 2)늘 …하다 3)연습 부족으로 미숙하여 4)…을 실행하다

—*vt.* **1.** do (something) habitually or repeatedly. ¶*~ early sleeping and early rising.* **2.** put (something) into actual use. ¶*Practice what you preach.*④ **3.** do exercise in (something). ¶*~ the piano; ~ playing the piano.* **4.** work at (something) as a profession, etc. —*vi.* **1.** exercise oneself. **2.** work at a profession.

—[他] 1. …을 늘(되풀이하여) 하다 2. …을 실행(실시)하다 ¶④자기의 말을 실행하라 3. …을 연습하다 4. …을 개업하다; …에 종사하다 —[自] 1. 연습하다 2. 개업하다

prac·ticed, *Brit.* **-tised** [prǽktist] *adj.* skilled through experience; learned through practice; expert.

—[形] 숙련된; 연습을 많이 한

: prac·tise [prǽktis] *v.* (*Brit.*) =practice.

prac·ti·tion·er [præktíʃ(ə)nər] *n.* [C] a person who is engaged in a profession, esp. medicine or law.

—[名] 종사자(從事者); [특히] 개업의사, 변호사

prae·tor [príːtər] *n.* [C] a public officer of ancient Rome who managed civil justice.

—[名] 집정관

prag·mat·ic, [prægmǽtik]**, -i·cal** [-ik(ə)l] *adj.* **1.** judging by practical value or results; of pragmatism. **2.** dogmatic. **3.** active in affairs; meddlesome.

—[形] 1. 실천적인, 실용주의의 2. 독단적인 3. 활동적인; 참견 잘하는

prag·ma·tism [prǽgmətìz(ə)m] *n.* [U] **1.** (*Philosophy*) the theory that the value of a conception depends upon its practical results or effects. **2.** dogmatism. **3.** the act of interfering in the matters of others.

—[名] 1. 《哲》 실용주의 2. 독단 3. 참견

prair·ie [prέəri] *n.* [C] a large, treeless grassland, esp. in the central area of the United States.

—[名] [특히 북미 중앙부의] 대초원

prairie schooner [⌐–⌐–] *n.* (*U.S.*) a large covered wagon used by pioneers to travel to the West. ⇒fig.

—[名] 《美》 포장마차

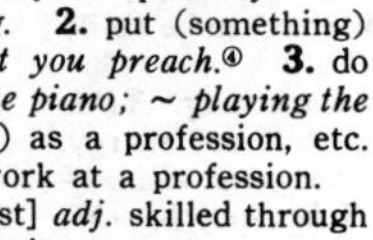

[prairie schooner]

: praise [preiz] *n.* [U] **1.** the act of speaking well of a thing or person; the expression of approval. ¶*deserve ~*① / *win high ~.*② **2.** the act or words of worshipping God. —*vt.* **1.** speak well of (someone or something). **2.** glorify and worship (God).

—[名] 1. 칭찬 ¶①칭찬할 만한/② 크게 칭찬받다 2. [신에 대한] 찬미 —[他] 1. …을 칭찬하다 2. [신]을 찬미하다

praise·wor·thy [préizwəːrði] *adj.* deserving praise; commendable.

—[形] 칭찬할 만한

pram [præm] *n.* [C] (*Brit. colloq.*) a baby carriage.

—[名] 《英口》 유모차

prance [præns / prɑːns] *vi.* **1.** (of horses) spring or bound forward on the hind legs. 《~ *along* a place, etc.》 **2.** (of persons) walk in a proud, arrogant manner; jump about gaily.

—[自] 1. [말이] 날뛰며 달리다 2. 뽐내며 걷다; 뛰어다니다

prank¹ [præŋk] *n.* [C] a mischievous or playful trick. ⌈¶*play pranks on someone.*⌉

—[名] 장난, 농담

prank [885] **precious**

prank[2] [præŋk] *vt.* adorn or dress (someone or something) in a gay or showy manner. —*vi.* dress oneself up ¶~ *with the best.*①
— 他 …을 장식하다 — 自 차려 입다
¶①제일 좋은 옷으로 차려 입다

prate [preit] *vi., vt.* talk much about (something) foolishly or idly. —*n.* Ⓤ foolish talk.
— 自他 지껄여대다 — 名 수다, 객담

prat·tle [prǽtl] *vt., vi.* **1.** prate. **2.** talk just like a child. —*n.* Ⓤ **1.** foolish talk. **2.** childish talk.
— 自他 1. 수다 떨다 2. 객담하다 — 名 1. 수다 2. 객담

prawn [prɔ:n] *n.* Ⓒ an edible shellfish like a shrimp.
— 名 수염이 긴 식용 새우

: pray [prei] *vt., vi.* **1.** offer praise or an earnest appeal, esp. to God. 《~ *for* something; ~ *that* …》 ¶*I prayed that I might be forgiven.*① **2.** ask or beg earnestly for (something). 《~ *for* something》 ¶~ *for pardon.*② **3.** please. ¶*Pray let me hear from you.*③
— 他自 1. […을] 빌다 ¶①용서를 빌었다 2. […을] 간청하다 ¶②용서를 빌다 3. 제발, 부디 ¶③부디 소식을 전해 주십시오

• **pray·er**[1] [préiər] *n.* Ⓒ a person who prays.
— 名 비는 사람

: prayer[2] [prɛər] *n.* Ⓒ **1.** the act of praying. ¶*kneel in* ~.① **2.** the words used in praying. **3.** an earnest request. **4.** 《often *pl.*》 a religious service consisting chiefly of prayers.
— 名 1. 기도 ¶①무릎 꿇고 기도하다 2. 기원문(祈願文) 3. 탄원 4. 기도식

prayer book [⌒ ⌒] *n.* **1.** a book of religious prayer. **2.** 《*P- B-*》 the Book of Common Prayer used in services of the Church of England.
— 名 1. 기도서 2. 영국 국교의 기도서

pre- [pri:-, pri-, prə-] *pref.* **1.** before in time: *prewar* (= before the war.). **2.** before in place: *prealtar* (=before the altar). **3.** before in rank or order: *prejudgement* (=judgment in advance).
—(接頭) 1. 이전 2. 장소로서 「앞」 3. 순서 따위의 「앞」

: preach [pri:tʃ] *vi.* speak to people about religion; give advice on a moral or religious subject. —*vt.* **1.** speak and teach (a sermon). **2.** make (something) known by preaching; urge (something) strongly. ¶~ *the Gospel*① / ~ *against smoking.*②
— 自 1. 전도(傳道)하다; 설교하다
— 他 …을 설교하다 2. 설유(說諭)하다; 타일러 가르치다 ¶①복음을 가르치다/②끽연의 해로움을 가르치다

• **preach·er** [prí:tʃər] *n.* Ⓒ a person who preaches; a [clergyman.]
— 名 설교자, 전도자

pre·am·ble [prí:æmbl / pri:ǽmbl] *n.* Ⓒ an introduction to a book or speech; an introducing statement in a legal document. [forehand.]
— 名 서문; 법률 따위의 전문(前文)

pre·ar·range [prì:əréindʒ] *vt.* arrange (something) be-]
— 他 …을 미리 정돈하다

pre·car·i·ous [prikέəriəs] *adj.* **1.** dependent on circumstances or the will of another; uncertain. ¶*a* ~ *livelihood*① / *a* ~ *argument.*② **2.** dangerous. ¶*a* ~ *life.*③
▷ **pre·car·i·ous·ly** [-li] *adv.*
— 形 1. 남의 마음대로 되는; 불안정한 ¶①불안정한 생계/②불확실한 주장 2. 위험한 ¶③위험한 생활

• **pre·cau·tion** [prikɔ́:ʃ(ə)n] *n.* **1.** Ⓤ the care taken beforehand to avoid danger or harm. **2.** Ⓒ something done beforehand to avoid possible danger. 《~ *against* danger etc.》 ¶*Precautions against fires.*①
— 名 1. 조심, 경계 2. 예방책 ¶①불조심

pre·cau·tion·ar·y [prikɔ́:ʃənèri / -ʃnəri] *adj.* for or using precaution. ¶~ *measures.*①
— 形 예방의 ¶①예방 수단

• **pre·cede** [pri(:)sí:d] *vt., vi.* **1.** go before (something) in place; happen or come before (something) in time. ¶*The regiment was preceded by its band.*① **2.** be higher than (someone or something) in rank, position, etc. ¶*Some people think money precedes everything else.*②
— 他自 1. …에 앞서다, 선행하다 ¶①군대의 선두에는 군악대가 있었다 2. …을 능가하다 ¶②돈이 무엇보다도 중요하다고 생각하는 사람도 있다

prec·e·dence [présid(ə)ns, pri(:)sí:d-], **-en·cy** [-(ə)nsi] *n.* Ⓤ the state or right of preceding in time, place, position, importance, etc. ¶*the order of* ~.①
take precedence of, be superior to.
— 名 앞섬; 상위; 우선권 ¶①석차
熟 …보다 우월하다

prec·e·dent [présid(ə)nt] *n.* Ⓒ something that serves as an example for the future.
— 名 선례(先例); 판결례

pre·cept [prí:sept] *n.* Ⓤ Ⓒ a rule of action as a guide or an example. ¶*Example is better than* ~.①
— 名 교훈; 격언 ¶①실례(實例)는 교훈보다 낫다

pre·cep·tor [priséptər] *n.* Ⓒ a teacher.
— 名 교사

pre·cinct [prí:siŋkt] *n.* Ⓒ **1.** a space enclosed by walls, esp. within a church. **2.** 《*pl.*》 a neighborhood. **3.** 《*U.S.*》 a small area in a town or city marked off for voting or police purposes. ¶*police precincts.*①
— 名 1. 경내(境內), 구내 2. 부근 3. 《美》선거구; 경찰 관할구 ¶①경찰 관할구

: pre·cious [préʃəs] *adj.* **1.** very valuable. ¶~ *metals*① /
— 形 1. 귀중한 ¶①귀금속/②보석 2.

~ *stones*.② **2.** very dear; highly valued. ¶*my ~ child*. **3.** too refined. ¶*a ~ style*.③ **4.** (*colloq.*) complete. ¶*a ~ liar*.
—*adv.* (*colloq.*) very. ¶*~ little money* / *It's ~ cold*.④

prec·i·pice [présipis] *n.* ⓒ **1.** a very steep surface of a cliff. **2.** a dangerous situation.

pre·cip·i·tate *vt.* [prisípitèit → *n., adj.*] **1.** throw (something) downward from a height. **2.** cause (something) to happen sooner than expected. **3.** (*Chemistry*) separate (a solid part) from a liquid and cause (it) to fall to the bottom; (*Physics*) condense (steam) into a liquid.
—*vi.* **1.** fall with the head first. **2.** hurry on. **3.** (*Chemistry*) be separated from a liquid and fall to the bottom, (*Physics*) (of steam) be condensed into a liquid.
—*n.* [prisípitit] ⓒ (*Chemistry*) a substance separated from a liquid; (*Physics*) a liquid condensed from steam.
—*adj.* [prisípitit] **1.** falling with the head first. **2.** sudden; hasty.

pre·cip·i·ta·tion [prisìpitéiʃ(ə)n] *n.* ⓤ the act of precipitating; the state of being precipitated.

pre·cip·i·tous [prisípitəs] *adj.* of or like a precipice; very steep.

pré·cis [préisi:] *n.* ⓒ (*pl.* **pré·cis** [-si:z]) (used as *sing.* and *pl.*) something that describes the point of a book, etc. within a limited number of words; a summary.

* **pre·cise** [prisáis] *adj.* **1.** exact. **2.** (of a person) strictly following rules; (of behavior) overcareful in details; (of speech) speaking clearly and definitely.

* **pre·cise·ly** [prisáisli] *adv.* **1.** in a precise manner. **2.** (as an answer) just so; quite true; exactly.

pre·ci·sian [prisíʒ(ə)n] *n.* ⓒ a person who strictly observes rules, esp. of religion. ⌜exactness.⌝
pre·ci·sion [prisíʒ(ə)n] *n.* ⓤ the quality of being precise;⌟
pre·clude [priklú:d] *vt.* **1.** eliminate. ¶*~ all doubts*. **2.** prevent; make (something) impossible in advance.

pre·clu·sion [priklú:ʒ(ə)n] *n.* ⓤ the act of precluding; the state of being precluded. ⌜ventive.⌝
pre·clu·sive [priklú:siv] *adj.* tending to preclude; pre-⌟
pre·co·cious [prikóuʃəs] *adj.* showing skill or development earlier than usual. ¶*a ~ child*.④

pre·coc·i·ty [prikásiti / -kɔ́s-] *n.* ⓤ the state or quality of being precocious; precociousness.

pre·con·ceive [prì:kənsí:v] *vt.* form an opinion of (something) beforehand. ¶*a preconceived notion*.④

pre·con·cep·tion [prì:kənsépʃ(ə)n] *n.* ⓒ an opinion formed beforehand. ⌜thing) beforehand.⌝
pre·con·cert [prì:kənsə́:rt] *vt.* settle or arrange (some-⌟
pre·da·cious [pridéiʃəs] *adj.* living by eating other animals; predatory.

pred·a·to·ry [prédətɔ̀:ri / -t(ə)ri] *adj.* **1.** living by plundering or robbing. **2.** =predacious.

pred·e·ces·sor [prédisèsər, prí:d- prèdisésər / prí:disèsə, prì:diséså] *n.* ⓒ **1.** an ancestor. **2.** a person who comes before another in the same position; a thing that comes before another. ↔successor

pre·des·ti·nate *vt.* [pri(:)déstinèit → *adj.*] **1.** destine (a man's fate) beforehand. **2.** determine beforehand; predestine. —*adj.* [pri(:)déstinit] **1.** determined by God's will. **2.** determined beforehand.

pre·des·ti·na·tion [pri(:)dèstinéiʃ(ə)n] *n.* ⓤ **1.** the act of God of deciding what shall happen. **2.** the act of predestinating; the state of being predestinated.

pre·des·tine [pri(:)déstin] *vt.* settle or determine (something) beforehand.

소중한, 귀여운 **3.** 진체하는, 까다로운 ¶⑤까다로운 문체 **4.** 〔口〕 지독한, 대단한
—⊕ 몹시 ¶④몹시 춥다
—⊛ **1.** 절벽 **2.** 위기

—⊕ **1.** …을 거꾸로 떨어뜨리다 **2.** …을 촉진시키다 **3.** 〔化〕 …을 침전시키다; 〔理〕 …을 응결(凝結)시키다 —⊜ **1.** 거꾸로 떨어지다 **2.** 허둥대다 **3.** 〔化〕 침전하다; 〔理〕 응결하다

—⊛ 침전[물]; 응결한 수분

—⊕ **1.** 거꾸로의 **2.** 몹시 서두르는

—⊛ 추락; 촉진; 침전; 응결

—⊕ 절벽의; 가파른

—⊛ 대의(大意)

—⊕ **1.** 정확한 **2.** 규칙대로의, 꼼꼼한; 명확한

—⊕ **1.** 정확하게 **2.** 〔대답으로〕 바로 그렇다
—⊛ 꼼꼼한 사람, 형식을 차리는 사람
—⊛ 정확; 정도(精度)
—⊕ **1.** …을 없애다 **2.** …을 방해하다; 불가능하게 하다

—⊛ 배제(排除); 방지

—⊕ 제외하는; 예방적인
—⊕ 조숙한, 숙성한 ¶①숙성한 아이

—⊛ 조숙

—⊕ …을 예상하다 ¶①선입관

—⊛ 예상; 선입관

—⊕ …을 미리 협정하다; 사전에 타⌝
—⊕ 식육(食肉)의 ⌞합하다⌟

—⊕ **1.** 약탈하는

—⊛ **1.** 선조 **2.** 선임자; 앞의 것

—⊕ **1.** 〔운명〕을 미리 정하다 **2.** …을 예정하다 —⊕ **1.** 운명에 의해 정해진 **2.** 예정된

—⊛ **1.** 신이 미리 정하기, 운명 **2.** 숙명

—⊕ …을 미리 운명지우다

predetermination

pre·de·ter·mi·na·tion [prì:ditə̀:rminéiʃ(ə)n] *n.* Ⓤ the act of predetermining; the state of being predetermined. ― 图 미리 결정하기; 예정

pre·de·ter·mine [prì:ditə́:rmin] *vt.* determine or settle (something) beforehand. ― 他 미리 결정하다; 예정(선결)하다

pre·dic·a·ment [pridíkəmənt] *n.* Ⓒ a dangerous or unpleasant condition; any condition. ― 图 곤경, 궁지, 난처한 처지

* **pred·i·cate** [prédikit → *v.*] *n.* Ⓒ (*Grammar*) the part of a sentence expressing something about the subject. ―*adj.* of the predicate. ―*vt.* [prédikèit] say (something) to be true with certainty; affirm.
― 图 《文法》 술부(述部) ―圈 술어의
― 他 …을 단정하다

pred·i·ca·tive [prédikèitiv / pridíkə-] *adj.* **1.** showing predication. **2.** (*Grammar*) serving as a predicate. ↔attributive
― 圈 1. 단정적인 2. 서술적인

* **pre·dict** [pridíkt] *vt., vi.* try to make (something) known before it happens; foretell. ¶ ~ *a bad crop.*① ▷ **pre·dict·a·ble** [-əbl] *adj.* ―**pre·dic·tor** [-ər] *n.*
― 圈自 예언하다; 예보하다 ¶① 흉작을 예언하다

pre·dic·tion [pridíkʃ(ə)n] *n.* **1.** Ⓤ the act of predicting. the state of being predicted. **2.** Ⓒ a thing predicted.
― 图 1. 예언; 예보 2. 예언된 것; 예보

pre·dic·tive [pridíktiv] *adj.* predicting.
― 圈 예언적인

pre·di·gest [prì:didʒést, -dai-] *vt.* make (food) more digestible by a special process before it is eaten.
― 他 …을 소화가 잘 되도록 요리하다

pre·di·lec·tion [prèdilékʃ(ə)n / prì:d-] *n.* Ⓒ a favor; a liking.
― 图 호의, 기호

pre·dis·pose [prì:dispóuz] *vt.* (of a disease) give influence on (someone) easily; cause (someone) to incline to something; cause someone to incline to (something). ¶ *A cold predisposes someone to other diseases.*①
― 他 …을 [병에] 걸리기 쉽게 하다; [남]을 …의 쪽으로 기울게 하다 ¶① 감기는 만병의 근원

pre·dis·po·si·tion [prì:dispəzíʃ(ə)n] *n.* Ⓒ the quality of being predisposed.
― 图 병에 걸리기 쉬운 체질

pre·dom·i·nance [pridɔ́mənəns / -dɔ́m-] *n.* Ⓤ the state or quality of being predominant.
― 图 우세; 지배

pre·dom·i·nant [pridɔ́mənənt / -dɔ́m-] *adj.* greater in power, number, etc. ▷ **pre·dom·i·nant·ly** [-li] *adv.*
― 圈 우세한; 뛰어난

pre·dom·i·nate [pridɔ́mənèit / -dɔ̀m-] *vi.* be greater in power, number, influence, etc.
― 自 우세하다; 뛰어나다

pre·em·i·nence [pri(:)émənəns] *n.* Ⓤ the state or quality of being pre-eminent; excellence.
― 图 우위(優位), 탁월

pre·em·i·nent [pri(:)émənənt] *adj.* superior to others. ¶ *a ~ position.*① ▷ **pre·em·i·nent·ly** [-li] *adv.*
― 圈 뛰어난, 빼어난 ¶① 우세한 입장

pre·emp·tion [pri(:)ém(p)ʃ(ə)n] *n.* Ⓤ the act or right of buying something before other people.
― 图 선매(先買)[권]

preen [pri:n] *vt.* **1.** (of a bird) smooth or clean (the feathers) with its bill. **2.** dress up (oneself).
― 他 1. [깃]을 부리로 가지런히 하다 2. [자신]의 몸차림을 하다

pre·ex·ist [prì:egzíst, -igz-] *vi.* exist before something else. ⌜the soul before birth.⌝
― 自 선재(先在)하다

pre·ex·ist·ence [prì:egzíst(ə)ns, -igz-] *n.* Ⓤ existence of ⌟
― 图 영혼의 선재(先在); 전세(前世)

pre·ex·ist·ent [prì:egzíst(ə)nt, -igz-] *adj.* existing before something else. ⌜―*adj.* prefabricated.⌝
― 圈 선재(先在)하는

pre·fab [prí:fæb] *n.* Ⓒ (*U.S.*) a prefabricated house.⌟
― 图 《美》 조립식 가옥 ―圈 조립식의

pre·fab·ri·cate [prì:fǽbrikèit] *vt.* **1.** make up (something) beforehand. **2.** make up the standard parts of (a house) in a factory. ¶ *a prefabricated house.*①
― 他 1. …을 미리 만들어 내다 2. [조립식 주택]의 부분품을 만들다 ¶① 조립식 주택

* **pref·ace** [préfis] *n.* Ⓒ an introduction at the beginning of a book or speech ↔conclusion. ―*vt.* introduce (a book or speech) with some statement. ⌜ductory.⌝
― 图 서문 ―他 …의 서문(서두)을 쓰다 (말하다)

pref·a·to·ry [préfətɔ̀:ri / -təri] *adj.* of a preface; intro-⌟
― 圈 서문의

pre·fect [prí:fekt] *n.* Ⓒ **1.** a high official of military and civil affairs in ancient Rome. **2.** a chief official of a department of France. **3.** (*Brit.*) a student with authority over others in a school. ⌜fecture.⌝
― 图 1. 고대 로마의 장관 2. 프랑스의 지사 3. 《英》 급장, 반장

pre·fec·tur·al [priféktʃurəl, +*Brit.* -tjur-] *adj.* of a pre-⌟
― 圈 현(縣)의, 시(市)의

* **pre·fec·ture** [prí:fektʃər, +*Brit.* -tjuə] *n.* **1.** Ⓒ an administrative area in certain countries. **2.** Ⓤ the office or the term of a prefect.
― 图 1. 현, 시 2. 지사·장관의 직(임기)

prefecture

pre·fer [prifə́:r] vt. (-ferred, -fer·ring) 1. like (something) better than other things. 《~ something *to*; ~ *to do*; ~ *doing*; ~ *that* ...》 ¶*Which do you ~? | I ~ autumn to spring.*① *| I should ~ not to do it.*② *| He preferred to wait here rather than to go at once.*③ 2. move (someone) up to a higher rank; promote. 3. offer (something) for consideration. ¶*He preferred a charge against me.*④
pref·er·a·ble [préf(ə)rəbl] *adj.* more liked; more desirable. ¶*English is ~ to geography.*①
pref·er·a·bly [préf(ə)rəbli] *adv.* by preference; rather.
· **pref·er·ence** [préf(ə)r(ə)ns] *n.* 1. ⓊⒸ the act of liking one thing over another. ¶*a matter of personal ~.*① 2. Ⓒ something preferred. ¶*Her ~ in reading is a fairy tale.*② 3. Ⓤ the right to choose something first.
  1) *have a preference for*, like (something).
  2) *in preference to*, rather than (something).
pref·er·en·tial [prèfərénʃ(ə)l] *adj.* showing, giving or receiving preference. ¶*a ~ right*① *| ~ treatment.*②
pre·fer·ment [prifə́:rmənt] *n.* Ⓤ 1. the act of moving up to a higher rank or position; promotion. 2. a higher position, esp. in the church.
pre·fig·ure [pri:fígjər / -gə] *vt.* 1. suggest a figure or type of (something) beforehand. 2. imagine (something) beforehand. ▷ **pre·fig·ure·ment** [-mənt] *n.*
pre·fix *n.* [prí:fiks →*v.*] Ⓒ (*Grammar*) a word or syllable put in front of a word. —*vt.* [pri:fíks] put at the beginning of (something); put (something) as a prefix.
preg·nan·cy [prégnənsi] *n.* Ⓤ 1. the state of being pregnant. 2. the state of being filled with meaning.
preg·nant [prégnənt] *adj.* 1. (of a woman) having a child growing in her body. 2. filled with meaning; full of ideas; significant. 3. abounding; filled. ¶*an event ~ with grave consequences.*①
pre·hen·sile [prihénsil / -sail] *adj.* (of an animal) adapted for holding or seizing. ¶*a monkey's ~ tail.*①
pre·his·tor·ic [prì:histɔ́:rik, -tár- / -tɔ́r-] *adj.* of the time before recorded history.
pre·judge [pri:dʒʌ́dʒ] *vt.* judge (someone or something) beforehand or without evidence.
· **prej·u·dice** [prédʒudis] *n.* 1. ⓊⒸ an opinion formed without any knowledge or fair judgement; an unreasonable opinion. 2. Ⓤ injury; damage.
  1) *in* (or *to the*) *prejudice of*, to injure 「rights.」
  2) *without prejudice*, without injuring any claims or
  —*vt.* 1. cause (someone) to have a prejudice. 《~ someone *against* or *in favor of*》 ¶*All of them are prejudiced on this subject.*① 2. injure or harm, esp. in a law case. 「harm or danger.」
prej·u·di·cial [prèdʒudíʃ(ə)l] *adj.* causing prejudice;
prel·ate [prélit] *n.* Ⓒ a high-ranking priest or clergyman.
pre·lim [prí:lim, prilím] *n.* Ⓒ (*colloq.*) =preliminary.
· **pre·lim·i·nar·y** [prilímineri / -nəri] *adj.* coming before the main thing; introductory; preparatory. ¶*a ~ examination*① *| a ~ hearing*② *| a ~ negotiation.*③
  —*n.* (*pl.* **-nar·ies**) 1. a preliminary examination. 2. (usu. *pl.*) introductory actions, steps, etc. ¶*an indispensable ~ to the plan*① *| without preliminaries.*②
prel·ude [prélju:d, prí:lu:d / préljuːd] *n.* Ⓒ 1. something that comes before and introduces a more important matter. 2. a piece of music that introduces another musical work.
  —*vt., vi.* serve or give as a prelude to (something).
pre·ma·ture [prì:mət(j)úər, -tʃúər / prèmətjúə] *adj.* happening or coming before the proper time; too early;

[888] **premature**

—他 1. 오히려 …의 쪽을 좋아하다 ¶
①봄보다 가을을 좋아한다/②오히려 그
것은 하고 싶지 않다/③그는 곧 떠나기
보다는 오히려 여기서 기다리기를 바
랐다 2. …을 승진시키다 3. …을 제출
(제기)하다 ¶④그는 나를 고소했다

—形 오히려 나은 ¶①영어가 지리보
다 오히려 낫다

—副 즐겨; 오히려

—名 1. 더 좋아함 ¶①기호의 문제 2.
좋아하는 것 ¶②그녀의 독서에 있어
서의 기호는 동화이다 3. 선택권; 우선
권

熟 1)…을 좋아하다 2)…보다 오히려

—形 우선(優先)의; 차별적인 ¶①우선
권/②우대

—名 1. 승진 2. 성직자의 고위(高位)

—他 1. …의 형상을 미리 나타내다, 예
시하다 2. …을 예상하다

—名 《文法》 접두사 —他 …의 앞에 두
다; …을 접두사로 달다

—名 1. 임신 2. 함축성이 있음

—形 1. 임신하고 있는 2. 함축성 있는
3. …으로 가득찬 ¶①중대한 결과를
안은 사건

—形 쥐기에 알맞은 ¶①쥐기에 알맞
은 꼬리

—形 유사 이전의

—他 …을 미리 판단하다; …을 충분히
심리하지 않고 판결하다

—名 1. 편견; 선입관 2. 침해; 불이익

熟 1)…의 손해가 되게 2)편견 없이;
권리를 침해하지 않고

—他 1. …에 편견(선입관)을 품게 하
다 ¶①누구나 이 문제에는 편견을 갖
고 있다 2. [권리 따위를] 침해하다

— 편견을 품게 하는; 손해를 입히는
—名 고위 성직자

—形 예비의; 서문의 ¶①예비 시험/②
예심/③예비 교섭

—名 1. 예비 시험 2. 예비 행위; 준비
¶①계획에 있어서 없어서는 안 될 준
비/②단도직입적으로

—名 1. 서두, 서문 2. 서곡

—他自 서두(서문)를 두다(가 되다)
—形 너무 이른; 조숙한 ¶①조산

untimely. ¶*a ~ birth.*①

pre·med·i·tate [pri(:)méditèit] *vt., vi.* think about, plan or consider beforehand.
—[他][自] 미리 숙고(계획)하다

pre·med·i·ta·tion [pri(:)mèditéiʃ(ə)n] *n.* [U] the act of premeditating.
—[名] 사전의 생각(계획)

* **pre·mier** [primíər / prémiə] *n.* [C] the prime minister. —*adj.* first in rank, importance, time, etc.
—[名] 수상 —[形] 수위(首位)의; 최초의

pre·mière [primíər / prémiɛə] *n.* [C] **1.** the first public performance of a play. **2.** (in a play, etc.) the leading actress.
—[名] 1. [연극의] 초연(初演) 2. 주연 여배우

pre·mier·ship [primíərʃìp / prémiə-] *n.* [U] the office or term of a prime minister.
—[名] 수상의 직(임기)

prem·ise *n.* [prémis → *v.*] [C] **1.** (*Logic*) a statement used as a foundation from which a conclusion is to be drawn. **2.** 《*pl.*》 (*Law*) a fact or thing mentioned beforehand. **3.** 《*pl.*》 a house or building with its grounds. —*v.* [+primáiz] *vt.* set forth (something) as a premise. —*vi.* give a premise.
—[名] 1. 《論》 전제 2. 《法》 기술(旣述) 사항(물건) 3. 가옥, 저택 —[他] …을 전제로 말하다; 전제하다 —[自] 전제를 두다

pre·mi·um [prí:mìəm] *n.* [C] **1.** a reward or prize. **2.** a sum of money above the ordinary amount paid or charged. ↔discount **3.** an amount of money paid for a contract of insurance.
—[名] 1. 상, 상금 2. 할증금(割增金), 프리미엄 3. 보험료

1) ***at a premium,*** ⓐ at a price higher than normal. ⓑ much in demand; very valuable.
2) ***put a premium on,*** give importance to (something); tempt others to prefer (something).
[熟] 1)ⓐ액면 이상으로, 프리미엄을 붙여 ⓑ수요가 큰; 진귀한 2)…을 중시하다; …의 유인(誘因)이 되다

pre·mo·ni·tion [prì:məníʃ(ə)n] *n.* [C] **1.** an act of warning in advance. **2.** a feeling that something is going to happen; foreboding.
—[名] 1. 예고; 전조 2. 예감

pre·mon·i·to·ry [primánitɔ̀:ri / -mɔ́nit(ə)ri] *adj.* giving warning in advance; acting as a premonition. ¶*a ~ symptom.*①
—[形] 예고의; 전조가 되는 ¶①징후

pre·na·tal [pri:néitl / ⁻⁻⁻] *adj.* occurring or existing before birth.
—[形] 태어나기 전의

pren·tice [préntis] *n.* [C] (*archaic*) =apprentice.

pre·oc·cu·pa·tion [prì(:)ɑkjupéiʃ(ə)n / -ɔk-] *n.* [U] the act of preoccupying; the state of being preoccupied.
—[名] 선취(先取); 몰두; 선입관

pre·oc·cu·py [pri(:)ákjupài / pri(:)ɔ́k-] *vt.* (**-pied**) **1.** hold all the attention of (someone). **2.** take possession of (land, etc.) before others.
—[他] 1. […의 마음]을 빼앗다; …에 사로잡히게 하다 2. [토지 따위]를 선취하다

pre·or·dain [prí:ɔ:rdéin] *vt.* decide (a fate, etc.) beforehand.
—[他] [운명]을 미리 정하다

prep [prep] *adj.* (*colloq.*) preparatory. —*n.* **1.** [C] (*U.S. colloq.*) a preparatory school. **2.** =preparation.
—[形] 《口》 예비의, 준비의 —[名] 《美口》 예과(豫科); 예비교

prep. **1.** preparation. **2.** preparatory. **3.** preposition.

pre·paid [pri:péid / ⁻⁻] *v.* pt. and pp. of **prepay**.

⁑ **prep·a·ra·tion** [prèpəréiʃ(ə)n] *n.* **1.** [U][C] the act of preparing; the state of being prepared. **2.** [C] things done to prepare for something; food, medicine, or other substances made for special use.
—[名] 1. 준비, 채비 2. 준비된 것; 요리된 음식, 조제된 약

pre·par·a·tive [pripǽrətiv] *adj.* preparatory. —*n.* [U] something that serves to prepare.
—[形] 준비의 —[名] 예비; 준비

pre·par·a·to·ry [pripǽrətɔ̀:ri / -t(ə)ri] *adj.* **1.** preparing. **2.** undergoing preparation for entering college.
—[形] 1. 예비의, 준비의 2. 입학 준비의

⁝ **pre·pare** [pripέər] *vt.* **1.** make (something) ready for a particular purpose or use; fit; train. 《~ something *for*》 ¶*~ a meal*① / *~ a house for habitation.* **2.** get ready for (a lesson, etc.) by study, work, practice, etc. ¶*~ one's lessons*② / *He prepared a speech he intended to make.* **3.** put (someone) in a desired state of mind; make (someone) ready. 《~ someone *for*; ~ someone *to do*》 ¶*~ a boy for college*③ / *I prepared him for the bad news.* / *He prepares himself to die.; He prepares himself for death.*④ **4.** make or form (chemical products, etc.). ¶*~ a drug.* **5.** supply (something) with what is needed. ¶*They prepared an expedition.* —*vi.* make things ready; make oneself ready in one's mind. 《~ *for* something; ~ *to do*》 ¶*~ for a journey* / *~ for*
—[他] 1. …을 준비하다, 채비하다 ¶①식사 준비를 하다 2. …을 예습하다 ¶②학과를 예습하다 3. …에게 마음의 준비를 시키다; 준비시키다 ¶③소년에게 대학에 갈 준비를 시키다/④그는 죽음에 대한 각오를 하고 있다 4. [약 따위]를 조제하다, 작성하다 5. …의 필요품을 갖추다 —[自] 준비하다, 채비하다; 마음의 준비를 하다 ¶⑤만일에 대비하다

preparedness [890] prescription

*an emergency.*① / *She prepares to go to school early.*
pre·par·ed·ness [pripéərdnis] *n.* ⓤ **1.** the state of being prepared. **2.** the possession of enough military forces. —名 1. 준비 2. 군비
pre·pay [pri:péi / ⌒⌒] *vt.* (**-paid**) pay for (something) in advance. ¶~ *a reply to a telegram.*① —他 …을 선불하다 ¶①전보의 반신료를 선납하다
pre·pay·ment [pri:péimənt / ⌒⌒-] *n.* ⓤⓒ payment in advance. 「state of being preponderant.」 —名 선불, 선납
pre·pon·der·ance [pripánd(ə)rəns / -pɔ́n-] *n.* ⓤ the 」—名 무게가 더 나감; 우세
pre·pon·der·ant [pripánd(ə)r(ə)nt / -pɔ́n-] *adj.* **1.** great in weight. **2.** superior in number, power, influence, etc. ▷**pre·pon·der·ant·ly** [-li] *adv.* —形 1. 무게가 더 나가는 2. 우세한
pre·pon·der·ate [pripándəreit / -pɔ́n-] *vi.* **1.** be heavier than something else. **2.** exceed in power, number, amount, influence, etc. —自 1. 무게가 더 나가다 2. 우세하다
:prep·o·si·tion [prèpəzíʃ(ə)n] *n.* ⓒ (*Grammar*) a word that connects a noun or pronoun with other words to show a relation between them. —名 《文法》 전치사
prep·o·si·tion·al [prèpəzíʃ(ə)n(ə)l] *adj.* of a preposition; serving as a preposition. ¶*a ~ phrase.*① —形 전치사의 ¶①전치사구
pre·pos·sess [pri:pəzés] *vt.* (usu. in *passive*) fill (someone) with a favorable feeling or opinion; prejudice. —他 …에 [호의·인상]을 미리 품게 하다
pre·pos·sess·ing [prì:pəzésiŋ] *adj.* making a favorable impression; attractive. —形 붙임성 있는; 호감을 사는
pre·pos·ses·sion [prì:pəzéʃ(ə)n] *n.* ⓒ an impression in a favorable sense formed beforehand; a favorable prejudice or a liking. —名 선입관; 편견; 편듦
pre·pos·ter·ous [pripást(ə)rəs / -pɔ́s-] *adj.* contrary to reason, common sense or common sense; ridiculous; absurd. —形 터무니없는; 어리석은
pre·req·ui·site [pri(:)rékwizit] *adj.* required beforehand. —*n.* ⓒ something required beforehand. (*~ for, to*) —形 사전에 필요한 —名 전제 조건
pre·rog·a·tive [prirágətiv / -rɔ́g-] *n.* ⓒ a right or privilege that belongs to a person, class, etc. according to rank or position. ¶*the ~ of mercy.*① —名 특권, 대권(大權), 특전 ¶①사면권
pre·sage *n.* [présidʒ → *v.*] ⓒ **1.** a sign foretelling that something is going to happen; an omen. **2.** a feeling that something is going to happen. —名 1. 전조 2. 예감
—*vt.* [+priséidʒ] **1.** have a presentiment of (something). **2.** give a sign of (something) to happen. **3.** foretell; predict. —他 1. …을 예감하다 2. …을 예시하다 3. …을 예고하다; 예언하다
pres·by·ter [prézbitər] *n.* ⓒ **1.** an elder in the early Christian Church. **2.** an elder in authority in the Presbyterian Church. **3.** a priest or minister in the Episcopal church. —名 1. [초기 교회의] 장로 2. [장로교회의] 장로 3. [영국 국교의] 목사
Pres·by·te·ri·an [prèzbitíəriən] *adj.* of the Presbyterian Church or its form of government. —*n.* ⓒ a member of the Presbyterian Church. —形 장로교회의; 장로제의 —名 장로교회 신도
pres·by·ter·y [prézbitèri / -t(ə)ri] *n.* ⓒ (pl. **-ter·ies**) (*Religion*) **1.** a court consisting of all the ministers and a few elders from a district. **2.** the district under the control of such a court. **3.** the house of the parish priest. —名 1. 장로회 2. 장로회 관할구 3. 사제관(司祭館)
pre·school [prí:skú:l] *adj.* before the age of entering an elementary school. —形 국민학교 입학 전의; 학령(學齡) 미달의
pre·sci·ence [prí:ʃ(i)əns, préʃ- / présiəns, -ʃiə-] *n.* ⓤ the knowledge of things before they happen; foreknowledge; foresight. —名 예지(豫知); 선견
pre·sci·ent [prí:ʃ(i)ənt, préʃ- / présiənt, -ʃiə-] *adj.* knowing or seeing ahead of time. —形 미리 아는, 선견지명이 있는
•**pre·scribe** [priskráib] *vt., vi.* **1.** set down (something) as a direction or rule. **2.** order (something) as a medical treatment. ¶*~ medicine for one's patient.*① —他自 1. …을 지시하다, 규정하다 2. [약·요법 따위]를 지시하다 ¶①환자의 약을 처방하다
pre·scrip·tion [priskrípʃ(ə)n] *n.* **1.** ⓤ a direction; an order. **2.** ⓒ a written order for making or using medicine. ¶*a ~ for medicine.*① **3.** ⓒ the medicine directed by a doctor. **4.** ⓤ a right or title gained by long use —名 1. 규정, 법규 2. 처방[전] ¶①약의 처방전 3. 처방약 4. [취득] 시효(時效) ¶②소멸 [취득] 시효

or possession. ¶*negative* (*positive*) *~*.②

pre·scrip·tive [priskríptiv] *adj.* **1.** directing; providing for a direction. **2.** based on a legal prescription.

—[形] 1. 규정하는 2. 시효(時效)에 의한

‡ **pres·ence** [préz(ə)ns] *n.* [U] **1.** the state of being present; attendance. ↔absence ¶*~ of a ghost.*① **2.** the place where a person is; the nearness of another person. ¶*saving your ~*② | *be admitted to someone's ~*③ | *be banished from someone's ~*④ | *in the ~ of others.*⑤ **3.** [U][C] the appearance. ¶*a man of dignified ~.*

—[名] 1. 존재;출석 ¶①유령의 존재 2. 남이 있는 자리;면전 ¶②당신의 면전이지만/③배알을 허락받다/④…의 면전에서 쫓겨나다/⑤…의 면전에서 3. 풍채, 태도

presence of mind, composure; coolness.

[熟] 침착; 평정(平靜)

‡ **pres·ent**[1] [préz(ə)nt] *adj.* **1.** being in a certain place. ¶*I am ~, sir.* | *the people ~ there.* ↔absent **2.** at this time; not of the past or future. ¶*the ~ fashion*① | *at the ~ day.* **3.** at hand or in sight; instant. ¶*a ~ wit.*② **4.** being discussed, written, read, etc. now. ¶*the ~ volume*③ | *the ~ writer.*④

—[形] 1.[어떤 장소에] 있는, 출석한 2. 현재의, 오늘날의 ¶①오늘날의 유행 3. 가까이 있는, 보이는, 즉석의 ¶②기지(機知) 4. 지금 논의되고(씌어지고, 읽혀지고) 있는 ¶③이 책/④필자

—*n.* [U] **1.** 《usu. *the ~*》 the present time. **2.** (*Grammar*) the present tense.

—[名] 1. 현재 2.《文法》 현재시제

‡ **pre·sent**[2] *v.* [prizént →*n.*] *vt.* **1.** make a gift to (someone); give (something) as a gift. 《*~* something *to*; *~* someone *with*》 ¶*~ a gold medal to a winner; ~ a winner with a gold medal.*① **2.** bring (something) before the public; show or exhibit. ¶*~ a new play* | *~ a poor appearance*② | *The situation presents great difficulties.*③ **3.** put (oneself) in another's presence; introduce. ¶*He presented his brother to the teacher.* | *He presented himself before the principal.*④ **4.** hand; deliver; offer. 《*~* something *to*》 ¶*~ a report* | *~ an argument*⑤ | *~ one's bill.* **5.** aim or point (one's face, arms, etc.) ¶*~ a pistol at someone.*

—[他] 1. …에게 선물하다; …을 보내다 ¶①승자에게 메달을 주다 2.[극]을 상연하다;…을 보이다, 나타내다 ¶②초라하게 보이다/③사태는 큰 곤란을 드러내고 있다 3. 출두하다; [남]을 소개하다 ¶④그는 교장 앞에 출두했다 4. …을 건네다; 제출하다; 꺼내다 ¶⑤문제를 제기하다 5.[얼굴·무기 따위]를 돌리다

—*n.* [préz(ə)nt] [C] something given; a gift. ¶*She received a ~ on her birthday.*

—[名] 선물

pre·sent·a·ble [prizéntəbl] *adj.* **1.** suitable to be seen. **2.** suitable to be introduced into society. **3.** fit to be presented or offered.

—[形] 1. 사람 앞에 내놓아도 부끄럽지 않은, 보기 흉하지 않은 2. 소개할 수 있는 3. 선물로 알맞은

pres·en·ta·tion [prèzentéiʃ(ə)n] *n.* **1.** [U] the act of presenting; the state of being presented. ¶*the ~ of a gift.*① **2.** [C] a gift. **3.** [U] a formal introduction; an audience. **4.** [U][C] a public performance; production. **5.** [U] the act of offering or bringing forward.

—[名] 1. 증정;수여 ¶①선물의 증정 2. 선물 3. 소개;배알 4. 상연, 연출 5. 제출, 표시

pres·ent-day [préz(ə)ntdéi] *adj.* of the present time; modern; current.

—[形] 현대의

pre·sent·er [prizéntər] *n.* [C] **1.** a giver. **2.** an introducer.

—[名] 1. 증여자 2. 소개자; 추천자

pre·sen·ti·ment [prizéntimənt] *n.* [C] a feeling that something, esp. of an evil nature, is going to happen.

—[名] [나쁜] 예감

‡ **pres·ent·ly** [préz(ə)ntli] *adv.* **1.** in a little while; before long; soon. **2.** at the present time.

—[副] 1. 멀지 않아, 곧 2. 현재

pre·sent·ment [prizéntmənt] *n.* **1.** [U][C] a statement; a description. **2.** [U] the act of showing or offering; a presentation. **3.** [U] the act of putting a play or other show on the stage; performance.

—[名] 1. 진술, 서술, 묘사 2. 제시, 제출; 신청;증정 3. 상연, 연출

pres·er·va·tion [prèzərvéiʃ(ə)n] *n.* [U] the act of preserving; the state of being preserved. ¶*books in good ~.*①

—[名] 보존; 유지; 저장; 보호 ¶①훌륭하게 보존된 책

pre·serv·a·tive [prizə́:rvətiv] *n.* [C] any substance that prevents (foods, etc.) from decay. —*adj.* that prevents; having the nature of preserving.

—[名] 방부제 —[形] 보존의, 보존력이 있는; 예방적인

‡ **pre·serve** [prizə́:rv] *vt.* **1.** keep (something) from harm, damage, or being forgotten; protect or save. ¶*~ eggs from damage* | *~ the wild animals from being killed* | *May God keep and ~ you.*① **2.** keep (foods) from being spoiled, as by canning, salting or smoking. ¶*~ fish in salt* | *~ oranges in sugar.* **3.** keep (something) alive; maintain. ¶*~ silence* | *~ health* | *~ the scene in a motion picture*② | *a well-preserved man.*③ **4.** keep (birds or animals) from being hunted. ¶*~ game.*④

—[他] 1. …을 보호하다; 지키다 ¶①신이 당신을 지켜 주시기를 2.[식품]을 부패에서 막다 3. …을 잃지 않도록 하다;…을 유지하다 ¶②그 광경을 영화로서 보존하다/③젊어 보이는 노인 4.[새·짐승]의 사냥을 금하다 ¶④사냥을 금하다

preserver

—n. ⓒ 1. (usu. *pl.*) fruit cooked with sugar; jam. ¶*apple preserves.*② 2. a place where wild animals or birds are protected.
—❀ 1. 설탕에 전 과일; 잼 ¶⑤사과잼 2. 금렵지(禁獵地)

pre·serv·er [prizə́:rvər] *n.* ⓒ a person or thing that saves, protects or defends.
—❀ 보존자, 보호자; 구조자

・**pre·side** [prizáid] *vi.* 1. act as chairman at a meeting. (*~ at* or *over* a ceremony, etc.) ¶*The conference was presided over by Mr. A.*① 2. have direction, authority or control. (*~ at* or *over* something) ¶*The manager presides over the business of a firm.*②
—自 1. 의장이 되다, 사회하다 ¶①그 회의는 A씨가 사회했다 2. 통할하다, 주재하다, 지배하다 ¶②지배인은 상사(商社)의 업무를 총괄한다

pres·i·den·cy [prézid(ə)nsi] *n.* (usu. *the ~*) the office or term of a president.
—❀ 대통령(장관·학장·사장 등)의 직(임기)

‡**pres·i·dent** [prézid(ə)nt] *n.* ⓒ 1. (*P-*) the highest executive officer of a modern republic. ¶*President Lincoln.*① 2. the chief officer of a company, college, club, etc. ¶*a party ~*② / *a steel company ~*.③
—❀ 1. 대통령 ¶①링컨 대통령 2. 총재, 장관, 의장, 총장, 학장, 사장, 회장, 은행장 ¶②당(黨)총재/③철강회사 사장

・**pres·i·den·tial** [prèzidénʃ(ə)l] *adj.* of a president. ¶*a ~ election* / *a ~ year* / *a ~ candidate*.
—🅟 대통령(장관·학장·사장 등)의

‡**press** [pres] *vt.* 1. push (something) with force and weight. ¶*~ clothes* / *~ flowers.*① 2. hold (something) tightly; take (someone or something) into one's arms; embrace. ¶*~ someone's hand.* 3. insist strongly; make (someone) do something by force. ¶*~ someone to come* / *~ someone for money.*② 4. insist; lay stress on (something). ¶*~ the point.* 5. (chiefly in *passive*) get (someone) to be troubled with or about something. ¶*She pressed me with questions.* / *be pressed for money.*③
—他 1. …을 누르다, 압착하다 ¶①[책갈피 따위에 끼워] 꽃을 납작하게 하다 2. …을 꽉 쥐다, 꼭 껴안다 3. …을 조르다, 강요하다, 몰아세우다 ¶②남에게 돈을 조르다 4. …을 주장하다; 강조하다 5. …을 곤란하게(시달리게) 하다 ¶③돈에 쪼들리다

—*vi.* 1. push with force. (*~ against* or *on* something). ¶*~ on the button.* 2. force one's way; hurry. (*~ on* or *forward* to some place). 3. be urgent. ¶*Time presses.*④ 4. crowd. (*~ up* or *round* some place).
—自 1. 누르다, 밀다, 압박을 가하다 2. 밀어젖히고 나아가다, 서두르다 3. 절박하다, 급박하다 ¶④시간이 절박하다 4. 몰려들다, 밀어닥치다

1) *hard pressed,* in difficulty; at a loss.
2) *press hard upon,* cause (someone) to be troubled with arguments, questions, etc.
3) *press on,* ⓐ go on with a stong will. ⓑ go in haste toward (some place).
4) *press on one's way,* go in haste.
熟 1)곤란하여, 곤궁에 처하여 2)[남]에게 육박하다; [남]을 추궁하다 3)ⓐ결의로써 나아가다 ⓑ… 방향으로 서둘러 가다 4)길을 재촉하다

—*n.* ⓒ 1. the act of pushing with force. 2. a machine used for pressing. 3. a printing machine. 4. Ⓤ (*the ~, collectively*) newspapers and magazines. ¶*the daily ~.*⑤ 5. a large number of people together; a crowd. 6. a closet.
1) *have a good press,* be highly spoken of in the newspapers.
2) *in the press,* being printed.
3) *out of press,* (of books, etc.) sold out and no copies remaining.
—❀ 1. 압박, 압착, 꽉 쥐기 2. 압착기, 압축기 3. 인쇄기 4. 신문·잡지 ¶⑤일간신문 5. 군중 6. 벽장, 찬장, 옷장, 책장
熟 1)신문에서 호평을 얻다 2)인쇄중인 3)절판(絶版)되어, 매진되어

・**press·ing** [présiŋ] *adj.* demanding immediate attention; urgent. ¶*a ~ necessity*① / *a ~ demand.*
—🅟 지급을 요하는, 긴급한, 급박한 ¶①급박한 필요

press·man [présmən] *n.* ⓒ (pl. **-men** [-mən]) 1. a person who operates a printing press. 2. a journalist; a reporter.
—❀ 1. 인쇄공 2. 신문 기자

‡**pres·sure** [préʃər] *n.* Ⓤ 1. a steady press by a force. ¶*the gentle ~ of her hand.*① 2. the force of air, gas, etc. against a unit area. ¶*the ~ of water*② / *high (low) blood ~.*③ 3. a burden on the mind; trouble; distress; (often *pl.*) hardships. ¶*financial pressures.*④ 4. the state of being compelled; oppression. ¶*~ of public opinion.*⑤ 5. urgent demand. ¶*the ~ of business.*⑥
1) *at high pressure,* as quickly as possible and with the utmost energy.
2) *bring pressure to bear* (or *put pressure*) *on* (or *upon*), oppress; force or try to force.
—❀ 1. 누르기; 밀기 ¶①부드럽게 누르는 그녀의 손 2. 압력 ¶②수압/③고(저)혈압 3. 고난, 곤란; 곤경, 곤궁 ¶④재정난 4. 억압, 강제, 압박 ¶⑤여론의 압박 5. 긴급한 필요, 다망 ¶⑥사무의 다망
熟 1)속력으로, 전력을 다하여 빠르게 2)[남]을 압박하다; [남]에게 강요(강제)하다

pres·tige [prestí:ʒ, +U.S. préstidʒ] *n.* Ⓤ the influence or reputation gained by one's achievement, abilities, position, etc. ¶*national ~.*①
—❀ 위신, 신망, 명성 ¶①국위(國威)

pres·to [préstou] *adj., adv.* (*Music*) quick[ly]. —*n.* [C] (pl. **-tos**) a passage to be played quickly. —[形][副] 《樂》 급속한(하게) —[名] 급속곡

pre·sum·a·ble [prizúːməbl / -z(j)úːm-] *adj.* that can be taken for granted or expected; probable. —[形] 당연한;가정할 수 있는, 있음직한

pre·sum·a·bly [prizúːməbli / -z(j)úːm-] *adv.* as may be presumed or taken for granted; probably. —[副] 생각컨대, 아마

***pre·sume** [prizúːm / -z(j)úːm] *vt.* **1.** take (something) for granted; suppose. 《~ *that*…; ~ something *to do*》 ¶*I ~ that they have seen him.*① / *I ~ this decision to be final.*② **2.** dare to do (something); venture. 《~ *to do*》 ¶*May I ~ to ask you where you are going?*③ —*vi.* **1.** make suppositions; guess. **2.** take liberties; act with unreasonable rudeness; take advantage of someone's weak point, etc. 《~ *on* or *upon* something》 ¶*presume upon someone's good nature* / *You ~.*④ —[他] **1.** …을 당연한 일로 생각하다;추정하다, …이라고 생각하다 ¶①그들은 그를 만났으리라 생각하는데/②아마 이것이 최종 결정일 것이다 **2.** 감히(대담하게도) …하다 ¶③실례지만 어디로 가십니까? —[自] 추측하다;생각하다; 주제넘게 나서다, 건방지게 참견하다 ¶④주제넘구나

pre·sum·ing [prizúːmiŋ / -z(j)úːm-] *adj.* impudent; arrogant; too forward. —[形] 주제넘은; 뻔뻔스러운, 건방진;촐싹거리는

pre·sump·tion [prizʌ́m(p)ʃ(ə)n] *n.* **1.** [U][C] the act of presuming; a reason for presuming; probability. ¶*~ of fact.*① **2.** [U] unpleasant arrogance or boldness. —[名] **1.** 가정, 추정[의 이유];가망 ¶①기지(旣知)의 사실에 입각한 추정 **2.** 주제넘음, 촐싹거림, 주착없음

pre·sump·tive [prizʌ́m(p)tiv] *adj.* based on presumption; without direct proof; taking for granted. ¶*~ evidence* (or *proof*).① —[形] 가정의, 추정의 ¶①추정 증거

pre·sump·tu·ous [prizʌ́m(p)tʃuəs, +*Brit.* -zʌ́m(p)tju-] *adj.* too self confident or bold; boasting too much. —[形] 건방진, 주제넘은; 외람된, 추착없는

pre·sup·pose [prìːsəpóuz] *vt.* **1.** assume or suppose beforehand. **2.** demand or require (something) as a prior condition. ¶*A healthy body presupposes healthful living.*① —[他] **1.** …을 미리 가정하다, 예상하다 **2.** …을 전제로 하다 ¶①건강체는 건전한 생활을 전제로 한다

pre·sup·po·si·tion [prìːsʌpəzíʃ(ə)n] *n.* [U] **1.** the act of presupposing. **2.** [C] that which is assumed beforehand; a guess. —[名] **1.** 가정, 예상 **2.** 예정, 전제

pret. preterit.

***pre·tence** [priténs] *n.* (*Brit.*) =pretense.

****pre·tend** [priténd] *vt.* **1.** make believe 《~ *to do*; ~ *that* …》 ¶*~ illness*① / *She pretended that she was asleep.* **2.** dare to do; attempt. ¶*I cannot ~ to ask him for money.* —*vi.* **1.** lay claim. 《~ *to* something》 ¶*~ to genius* / *~ to the throne* (or *the crown*)②. **2.** make believe; make a false show of something. —[他] **1.** …을 가장하다, …인 체하다, …에게 …처럼 보이게 하다 ¶①꾀병부리다 **2.** 감히 …하려고 하다;…을 꾀하다 —[自] **1.** 권리를 주장하다 ¶②왕위계승권을 주장하다 **2.** 가장하다, …인 체하다

pre·tend·ed [priténdid] *adj.* not real; false. —[形] 거짓으로 꾸민, 가짜의

pre·tend·er [priténdər] *n.* [C] **1.** a person who pretends. **2.** a person who makes a claim, esp. to a throne, without a right. —[名] **1.** 가장하는 사람, …인 체하는 사람; 사칭자 **2.** 요구자; 왕위 요구자

***pre·tense,** *Brit.* **-tence** [priténs, +*U.S.* príːtens] *n.* **1.** [U] the act of pretending; make-believe. ¶*~ of illness*① / *She made a ~ to faint.*② **2.** [C] a false allegation or claim; an excuse. ¶*make pretenses*③ / *under* (or *on*) *the ~ of illness.* **3.** [U] a false show or appearance. —[名] **1.** 가장, 가면, …체하기, 흉내, 허위 ¶①꾀병/②그는 기절한 체하였다 **2.** 구실, 핑계 ¶③이리저리 핑계를 꾸미다 **3.** 자랑하기, 뽐내기, 허세

pre·ten·sion [priténʃ(ə)n] *n.* **1.** [C] a claim; a right to claim. ¶*He had ~ to the throne.* **2.** [U] false show; outward appearance; display. ¶*without ~.*① **3.** [C] 《often *pl.*》 self-importance. **4.** [C] an excuse, a pretext. —[名] **1.** 주장, 요구, [요구할] 권리 **2.** 겉치레, 허식; 허세 ¶①허세부리지 않고 **3.** 자부, 자처 **4.** 구실, 핑계

pre·ten·tious [priténʃəs] *adj.* assuming an appearance of great importance, worth, etc.; showy. ¶*a ~ person.* —[形] 허세부리는; 젠체하는; 야단스러운, 야한

pret·er·it, -ite [prét(ə)rit] *n.* [C] (*Grammar*) the past tense. —*adj.* past. —[名] 《文法》 과거, 과거 시제 —[形] 과거의

pre·ter·nat·u·ral [prìːtərnǽtʃ(u)rəl] *adj.* beyond the regular course of nature; supernatural. —[形] 초자연적인; 불가사의한

pre·text [príːtekst] *n.* [C] an excuse. ¶*find a ~ for absence* / *on some ~ or other.*① —[名] 구실, 핑계; 변명 ¶①이 핑계 저 핑계로

pret·ti·ly [prítili] *adv.* in a pretty manner. —[副] 곱게, 예쁘게; 얌전하게

pret·ti·ness [prítinis] *n.* [U] the state of being pretty. —[名] 예쁨, 고움

****pret·ty** [príti] *adj.* (**-ti·er -ti·est**) **1.** charming; lovely. ¶*a ~ girl* / *A baby is ~ and innocent.* **2.** fine; good. —[形] **1.** 매력적인, 귀여운, 예쁜, 참한 **2.** 훌륭한, 좋은 ¶①훌륭한 태도 **3.** 어처구

¶~ *ways.*① **3.** awful; surprising. ¶*Here's a ~ mess!*② **4.** (*colloq.*) large. ¶*a ~ sum of money.*
—*n.* [C] 《used as *My pretty!*》 a pretty child.
—*adv.* (*colloq.*) **1.** to some extent; fairly. ¶*I feel ~ well now.*③ **2.** very; quite. ¶*I am ~ tired.*④
1) ***be pretty sick about*** (=be worried or concerned about) *something.*
2) ***pretty much the same thing,*** almost the same thing.

니없는; 지독한, 굉장한 ¶②이게 도대체 무슨 꼴인가 4.《口》 상당한, 큰, 꽤 많은
—[名] 예쁜이, [부르는 말] 아가
—[副] 《口》 1. 꽤, 상당히 ¶③인제 상당히 기분이 좋아졌다 2. 몹시, 매우, 아주 ¶④몹시 피토하다
[熟] 1)몹시 따분하다; 지긋지긋하다 2) 거의 같은 일

* **pre·vail** [privéil] *vi.* **1.** be widespread or prevalent; be in general use. ¶*Bad cold prevails throughout the country.*① **2.** be victorious; succeed; win. 《~ *against* or *over* someone》 ¶~ *over the enemy.* **3.** be effective. **4.** persuade. 《~ *on* (or *upon, with*) someone》 ¶*I finally prevailed on her to go.*②
—[自] 1. 유행하다, 보급되다, 퍼지다 ¶①악성 감기가 전국에 유행하고 있다 2. 우세하다; 잘 되어가다; 이기다 3. 효과가 있다 4. 설복시키다 ¶②나는 마침내 그녀를 설복시켜 가게 하였다

P

* **pre·vail·ing** [privéiliŋ] *adj.* having strong influence or superior force; widely and generally existing; common.
—[形] 유력한, 우세한; 일반적인, 보급되고 있는, 보통의

prev·a·lence [prév(ə)ləns] *n.* [U] the state of being prevalent. ¶*the ~ of television*① | *the ~ of cholera.*②
—[名] 유행, 우세, 탁월 ¶①텔레비전의 보급/②콜레라의 유행

* **prev·a·lent** [prév(ə)lənt] *adj.* widely existing; widespread; superior. ¶*Colds are ~ in winter.*①
—[形] 널리 행해지는, 유행하는, 우세한 ¶①감기는 겨울에 유행한다

pre·var·i·cate [privǽrikèit] *vi.* avoid telling the truth; make untrue statements; lie.
—[自] 말끝을 얼버무리다, 속이다

pre·var·i·ca·tion [privæ̀rikéiʃ(ə)n] *n.* [U] the act of prevaricating; [C] a statement or reply that turns aside from the truth.
—[名] 말끝을 얼버무림, 얼렁뚱땅해 넘김; 속임, 발뺌

pre·var·i·ca·tor [privǽrikèitər] *n.* [C] a person who prevaricates.
—[名] 얼렁뚱땅해 넘기는(속이는) 사람

‡ **pre·vent** [privént] *vt.* stop or keep (someone or something) from doing something or happening; hinder. ¶~ *disease* (*war*)① | *if nothing prevents you*② | *The heavy rain prevented me from going out.; The heavy rain prevented me* (or *my*) *going out.*
—[他] …을 막다, 방지하다; [남]을 방해하여 …못하게 하다, 훼방놓다 ¶①병(전쟁)을 방지하다/②만약 지장이 없으시다면

pre·vent·a·ble [privéntəbl] *adj.* that can be prevented.
—[形] 예방할 수 있는; 방해할 수 있는

pre·vent·i·ble [privéntibl] *adj.* =preventable.

* **pre·ven·tion** [privénʃ(ə)n] *n.* **1.** [U] the act of preventing; hindrance. ¶*the ~ of juvenile crimes*① | *the Society for the Prevention of Cruelty to Animals.*② ⇒[N.B.] | (*proverb*) *Prevention is better than cure.*③ **2.** [U][C] the means taken to guard against danger, disease, etc. ¶*by way of ~.*
—[名] 1. 방지; 방해; 훼방; 예방 ¶①소년 범죄의 방지/②동물 애호회 [N.B.] S.P.C.A.로 줄여 씀/③《俚》예방은 치료보다 낫다, 「소 잃기 전에 외양간을 고쳐라」 2. 예방법; 방지책

pre·ven·tive [privéntiv] *adj.* serving to prevent. ¶~ *medicine* (*measures*)① | *be ~ of accidents.*② —*n.* [C] anything that prevents; a means or medicine for keeping off disease, etc.
—[形] 예방의, 방지하는; 방해하는 ¶①예방약(책)/②사고를 방지하다 —[名] 예방(방지)하는 것, 방지법, 예방약

pre·view [prí:vjù:, +*Brit.* ´´] *n.* [C] **1.** a performance or showing in advance of the regular performance or showing of a motion picture, play, etc. **2.** a brief showing of scenes from a motion picture for advertisement.
—*vt.* look at (a motion picture, play, etc.) beforehand.
—[名] 1. 시사회(試寫會); 시연회(試演會) 2. [영화의] 예고편 —[他] 시사(시연)를 보다

‡ **pre·vi·ous** [prí:viəs] *adj.* occurring earlier in time; preceding; former. ¶*a ~ engagement*① | *a ~ illness*② | *on the ~ day*③ | ~ *to one's departure.*④
—[形] 먼저의, 이전의 ¶①선약(先約)/②기왕증(既往症)/③전날에/④ 출발에 앞서서

* **pre·vi·ous·ly** [prí:viəsli] *adv.* at an earlier time; beforehand.
—[副] 먼저, 미리

pre·vi·sion [pri(:)víʒ(ə)n] *n.* [U] foresight; forecast; foreknowledge.
—[名] 예지(豫知); 선견(先見)

pre·war [prí:wɔ́:r] *adj.* before the war. ↔postwar
—[形] 전쟁 전의, 전전(戰前)의

‡ **prey** [prei] *n.* [C] **1.** an animal caught or killed by another for food. **2.** [U] a habit of catching and killing animals for food. ¶*an animal* (or *a beast*) *of ~*① | *a bird of ~.*② **3.** a person or an animal sacrificed, injured, etc.; a victim. ¶*become a ~ to a lion* (*vanity*).③
—[名] 1. 먹이, 미끼 2. 잡아먹는 습성 ¶①맹수/②맹금(猛禽) 3. 희생[자] ¶③사자의 밥이 되다(허영에 사로잡히다)

—*vi.* **1.** hunt or kill animals, birds, etc. for food; plunder. 《~ *on* or *upon* a bird, etc.》 **2.** have an exhausting effect or influence. 《~ *on* something》 ¶*Care preyed on her health.*④
—[自] 1. 먹이로 하다, 잡아먹다; 약탈하다 2. 괴롭히다, 차츰 손상시키다 ¶④근심걱정으로 그녀는 건강을 해쳤다

:price [prais] *n.* [C] **1.** the amount of money for which a thing is bought, sold, etc; the cost. **2.** money offered for the capture of a person; reward. ¶*set a ~ on someone's head.*① **3.** something given or done for getting a thing. **4.** [U] value; worth.
1) ***above*** (or ***beyond, without***) ***price,*** priceless; invaluable.
2) ***at any price,*** no matter what the cost.
3) ***at the price of*** (=*at the sacrifice of*) *something.*

—[名] 1. 값, 가격, 시세 2. 상금, 현상금; 보수 ¶①…의 목에 상금을 걸다 3. 대상(代償); 희생 4. 가치, 값어치
[熟] 1)값을 매길 수 없을 만큼 비싼; 더할 나위 없이 귀중한 2)어떠한 희생(대가)을 치르더라도 3)…을 희생하고

price·less [práislis] *adj.* above price; of the greatest value.
—[形] 값으로 따질 수 없는, 매우 귀중한

***prick** [prik] *n.* [C] **1.** a sharp point. **2.** a small hole made by a sharp pointed thing. **3.** sharp pain. ¶*the pricks of conscience.*①
kick against the pricks, hurt oneself in opposing others.
—*vt.* **1.** make a hole in (something) with something pointed. **2.** cause (someone) to feel pain. **3.** erect; raise. **—*vi.*** **1.** feel a sharp pain. **2.** point upwards.
1) ***prick a bladder*** (or ***bubble***), discover a dishonest trick.
2) ***prick up*** [*one's*] ***ears,*** ⓐ raise the ears upwards. ⓑ listen closely.

—[名] 1. 찌르는 물건 2. 찔려서(쑤셔서) 생긴 작은 구멍 3. 격통(激痛) ¶①양심의 가책
[熟] 쓸데없는 저항을 하다
—[他] 1. …에 구멍을 내다 2. …에게 고통을 주다 3. …을 쫑긋이 세우다
—[自] 1. 고통(격통)을 느끼다, 따끔따끔 아프다 2. 쫑긋 서다
[熟] 1)거짓의 허울(가면)을 벗기다 2) ⓐ귀를 쫑긋이 세우다 ⓑ주의해 듣다

prick·er [príkər] *n.* [C] a person or thing that pricks.
—[名] 찌르는 사람, 찌르는 물건

prick·le [príkl] *n.* [C] **1.** a small, sharp point on a plant; a thorn. **2.** a feeling of sharp pain. **—*vt.*** **1.** prick (someone or something) with something sharp. **2.** give a pricking sensation to (something). **—*vi.*** feel a pain like pricking.
—[名] 1. 가시, 바늘 2. 쑤시는 듯한 아픔
—[他] 1. …을 찌르다 2. …에게 쑤시는 듯한 아픔을 주다 —[自] 따끔따끔 아프다

prick·ly [príkli] *adj.* (**-li·er, -li·est**) **1.** full of sharp points or thorns. **2.** having a sharp pain caused by a sting.
—[形] 1. [식물 따위가] 가시투성이의, 바늘이 있는 2. 따끔따끔 아픈(쑤시는)

:pride [praid] *n.* [U] **1.** 《sometimes *a* ~》 a high opinion of one's own ability or importance; conceit. ¶*Pride goes before a fall.*① **2.** a sense of one's own dignity or worth; self respect. **3.** a feeling of pleasure or satisfaction in one's accomplishments or possessions. **4.** something that gives someone pleasure or satisfaction. **5.** the best part; the most flourishing state or period.
—*vt.* 《*reflexively*》 take a pride in; claim credit for (something).
pride oneself on (or ***upon***) (=*be proud of; be pleased with*) *something.*

—[名] 1. 자랑, 거만, 오만; 교만심 ¶①교만한 자는 오래가지 못한다 2. 자부심, 자존심, 긍지 3. 만족 4. 자랑거리 5. 전성(全盛), 정화(精華), 화려
—[他] …을 자랑하다
[熟] …을 자랑하다

:priest [pri:st] *n.* [C] **1.** a person who serves gods to perform religious acts. **2.** a clergyman or minister of a Christian church.
—[名] 1. 성직자, 승려 2. 그리스도교의 목사, 사제(司祭)

priest·hood [prí:sthùd] *n.* [U] **1.** the position or duties of a priest. **2.** 《*collectively*》 all priests.
—[名] 1. 성직, 사제직 2. 성직자

priest·ly [prí:stli] *adj.* (**-li·er, -li·est**) of, for, or like a priest.
—[形] 사제의, 성직의; 성직자다운

prig [prig] *n.* [C] a narrow-minded person who is unusually strict about speech or conduct.
—[名] 딱딱한 사람, 잔소리꾼

prig·gish [prígiʃ] *adj.* like a prig.
—[形] 딱딱한

prim [prim] *adj.* (**prim·mer, prim·mest**) very stiff and not easy in appearance or conduct; extremely neat or precise.
—*vt., vi.* (**primmed, prim·ming**) put (the face, lips, etc.) into a prim expression.
prim out (or ***up***), decorate affectedly.

—[形] 꼼꼼한, 딱딱한; 단정한
—[他][自] 근엄한 얼굴을 하다, 입을 꾹 다물다, 점잔빼다
[熟] …을 점잔빼다, 꾸미다

pri·ma·cy [práiməsi] *n.* [U] **1.** the state of being at the top or first in time, order, importance, etc. **2.** the office, rank or dignity of a primate. **3.** the superior power of the Pope in the Roman Catholic Church.
—[名] 1. 제 1 위, 탁월 2. 대사교의 직(지위) 3. 교황의 수위권(首位權)

pri·ma don·na [prí(:)mədɑ́nə / -dɔ̀nə] *n.* (~ **don·nas** or **pri·me don·ne**) the leading woman singer in an opera.
—[名] 주역 여가수, 프리마돈나

pri·mae·val [praimí:v(ə)l] *adj.* =primeval.

pri·ma fa·ci·e [práiməféiʃi:, -ʃil:] *adv., adj.* at first sight; on the face of it.
—[副][形] 얼핏 보기에[는], 첫인상으로[는]

pri·mal [práim(ə)l] *adj.* **1.** of the first age of the world; very ancient; first. **2.** highest in rank or authority; at
—[形] 1. 최초의, 원시의 2. 제일의, 주요한; 근본의

the head ; basic.

pri·mar·i·ly [praimérili, práimərili / práimərili] *adv.* **1.** mainly ; principally ; chiefly. **2.** in the first instance ; originally.

—[副] 1. 주로 2. 최초로, 근본적으로, 원래

* **pri·ma·ry** [práiməri, +*U.S.* -meri] *adj.* **1.** first in time or order. **2.** first of the kind ; of the beginning ; existing from the first ; basic ; original. ¶~ *meaning of the word.*① **3.** of the first in importance ; chief. **4.** fundamental. ¶~ *education.*②

—[形] 1. 첫째의; 최초의 2. 원시의, 본래의, 근본의, 기본적인 ¶①단어의 원뜻 3. 가장 중요한; 주요한 4. 초보의; 기초적인 ¶②초등 교육

—*n.* [C] (pl. **-ries**) **1.** something which comes first in importance. **2.** one of the primary colors. **3.** (*U.S.*) an election to name the candidates for the main election.

—[名] 1. 주요한 사물 2. 원색 3. 《美》 예비 선거

pri·mate [práimeit, -mit] *n.* [C] **1.** an archbishop or chief bishop of a country. **2.** the highest rank of mammals, including human beings, apes and monkeys.

—[名] 1. 대감독, 대사교 2. 영장류(靈長類)의 동물

* **prime**[1] [praim] *adj.* **1.** highest in rank ; chief ; most important. ¶*of ~ importance.*① **2.** first in time ; original. **3.** first in quality ; best. ¶~ *pork.*② **4.** that can be divided evenly only by 1 or itself. ¶*a ~ number.*③

—[形] 1. 수위(首位)의, 가장 중요한 ¶①가장 중요한 2. 첫째의, 최초의, 근본의 3. 최상의 ¶②제일 좋은 돼지 고기 4. 소수(素數)의 ¶③소수

—*n.* [C] 《usu. *the ~, one's ~*》 **1.** the time of a person's life in which he is best in health, mind, beauty, etc. ¶*during* [*one's*] *~.*④ **2.** the best part of anything. **3.** the beginning ; youth. ¶*the ~ of the year.*⑤

—[名] 1. 전성기 ¶④전성기에 2. 가장 좋은 부분 3. 최초, 초기; 청춘 ¶⑤봄

prime[2] [praim] *vt.* **1.** get (a gun) ready for firing by putting in gunpowder. **2.** supply (someone) with information. ¶*primed with the latest news.*

—[他] 1. [총]에 화약을 재다 2. …에 미리 가르치다, 귀띔해 주다

prim·er [prímər, +*Brit.* práimə] *n.* [C] **1.** a book containing the first lessons in reading. **2.** the first training book in any subject.

—[名] 1. 초보 독본 2. 입문서

pri·me·val ,-mae- [praimí:v(ə)l] *adj.* of the earliest ages; very old. ¶*a ~ forest.*①

—[形] 원시시대의 ¶①원생림(原生林)

prim·ing [práimiŋ] *n.* [U] **1.** gunpowder or other material used for setting fire to an explosive. **2.** an undercoat or first coat of paint, etc.

—[名] 1. 기폭제(起爆劑), 점화약 2. 초벌칠

⁑ **prim·i·tive** [prímitiv] *adj.* **1.** of the earliest time. ¶*a ~ man.* **2.** simple ; rough. **3.** original. ¶~ *colors.*

—[形] 1. 원시의; 태고의 2. 단순한, 소박한 3. 원래의

—*n.* [C] **1.** a primitive person. **2.** a painter or sculptor, or his work, of a period before the Renaissance.

—[名] 1. 원시인 2. 문예부흥 전의 작가(그 작품)

pri·mo·gen·i·tor [pràimoudʒénitər] *n.* [C] **1.** an ancestor. **2.** the earliest ancestor of a family, a race, etc.

—[名] 1. 선조 2. 시조

pri·mo·gen·i·ture [pràimoudʒénitʃər] *n.* [U] **1.** the state of being the first-born child of the parents. **2.** (*Law*) the right of the eldest son to get all the property after his father dies.

—[名] 1. 장자임 2. 《法》 장자 상속권

prim·rose [prímròuz] *n.* **1.** [C] a plant, usu. with pale yellow flowers. ⇒fig. **2.** [U] the color of this flower.

—[名] 1·앵초(櫻草) 2. 담황색

—*adj.* **1.** pale yellow. **2.** like a primrose ; merry ; cheerful.

—[形] 1. 담황색의 2. 앵초 같은; 명랑한

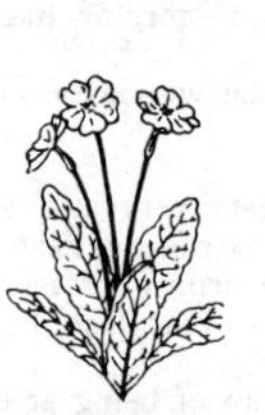
〔primrose 1.〕

⁑ **prince** [prins] *n.* [C] **1.** a son of a king or queen. **2.** the son of a royal family. **3.** the ruler of a small country. **4.** the greatest or the best person in a group.

—[名] 1. 왕자, 황자 2. 왕족의 남자 3. 작은 나라의 통치자 4. 제 1 인자

prince·ly [prínsli] *adj.* (**-li·er, -li·est**) **1.** worthy of a prince. **2.** of or like a prince ; noble.

—[形] 1. 왕후(王侯)(왕자)다운 2. 왕후 같은, 고귀한

⁑ **prin·cess** [prínses / prinsés, prínses] *n.* [C] **1.** the daughter of a king or queen. **2.** the wife or widow of a prince. **3.** the daughter of a royal family.

—[名] 1. 왕녀, 공주 2. 왕자비 3. 황족의 여자

⁑ **prin·ci·pal** [prínsip(ə)l] *adj.* most important ; main ; chief.

—[形] 주요한; 첫째의; 중요한

—*n.* [C] **1.** the principal person. **2.** a person who takes a leading part. **3.** the head or director of a school or college. **4.** a person actually responsible for a crime. **5.** [U] the sum on which interest is paid. **6.** [C] a per-

—[名] 1. 우두머리, 웃사람 2. 중심인물, 주역 3. 교장, 학장 4. 주범(主犯) 5. 원금, 기본 재산 6. [대리인에 대하여] 본인

principality   [897]   **privacy**

son who hires another to act for him.

prin·ci·pal·i·ty [prìnsipǽliti] *n.* ⓒ (pl. **-ties**) a country or territory ruled by a prince.
—名 왕후(王侯) 영토; 공국, 후국(侯國)

prin·ci·pal·ly [prínsipəli] *adv.* chiefly; mainly; for the most part.
—副 주로; 대개는

‡ prin·ci·ple [prínsipl] *n.* **1.** ⓒ a truth on which other truths are based. ¶*the principles of economics.*① **2.** Ⓤ settled rules of action or conduct. ¶*as a matter of ~.*② **3.** ⓒ a standard of honesty or righteousness. **4.** ⓒ a natural or scientific law by which something works.
 1) *in principle,* with reference to general truth; generally.
 2) *on principle,* ⓐ according to a principle. ⓑ by [principle.
—名 1. 원리, 원칙 ¶①경제 원리 2. 주의, 방침 ¶②주의로서 3. 지조(志操), 도의(道義) 4. 자연의 법칙

熟 1)원칙으로서; 대체로 2)ⓐ원칙에 따라서 ⓑ주의(主義)로서

‡ print [print] *n.* ⓒ **1.** a mark made on a surface of paper, sand, etc. by pressing something against it. ¶*the ~ of a foot on the floor.*① **2.** a mark left on a person's face by sorrow, etc.; an impression. **3.** Ⓤ the act of pressing letters or words; pressed things. **4.** (chiefly U.S.) a newspaper; special paper used for newspapers. **5.** a picture, design, etc. made of block or plate and used to press; a picture made from a photographic film. **6.** Ⓤ cotton cloth on which a picture, design, etc. is
 1) *in print,* published.   [pressed.
 2) *out of print,* no longer published; out of press.
—*vt.* **1.** mark (something) by pressure; impress. ¶*~ the mark of one's foot on the sand.* **2.** press or publish (books, etc.). ¶*~ a leaflet.*② **3.** impress (something) upon the mind. ¶*The scene is printed on my memory.*
—*vi.* make a print; publish books.
—名 1. [누른] 자국, 흔적 ¶①마루 위의 발자국 2. 인상, 모습 3. 인쇄; 인쇄물 4. 신문; 신문지 5. 판화(版畫); [사진의] 양화(陽畫) 6. 사라사

熟 1)인쇄되어, 출판되어 2)절판(絶版)의
—他 1. …의 자국을 내다 2. …을 인쇄하다, 출판하다 ¶②삐라를 인쇄하다 3. …을 마음에 새기다
—自 인쇄하다; 출판하다

print·er [príntər] *n.* ⓒ a person or thing that prints; an owner of a printing business.
—名 인쇄직공, 인쇄기; 인쇄업자

• print·ing [príntiŋ] *n.* Ⓤ **1.** printed letters, words, etc. **2.** all the copies (of a book, etc.) printed at one time. **3.** letters that resemble print; the style of printing.
—名 1. 인쇄된 문자(말) 2. 인쇄물 3. 활자체[의 문자]

• pri·or¹ [práiər] *adj.* **1.** earlier; previous. ¶*a ~ engagement.*① **2.** first in importance or order.
 prior to, before.
—形 1. 전의, 먼저의 ¶①선약 2. 가장 중요한
熟 …보다 먼저

pri·or² [práiər] *n.* ⓒ the head of a priory for men or monastery.   [women.
—名 작은 수도원의 원장

pri·or·ess [práiəris] *n.* ⓒ the head of a priory for]
—名 작은 수녀원의 원장

pri·or·i·ty [praiɔ́riti / -ɔ́ri-] *n.* Ⓤ **1.** the state of being or coming first in time, order, importance, etc. **2.** the right to precede.
—名 1. 먼저임, 우선 2. 우선권; 상위(上位)

pri·o·ry [práiəri] *n.* ⓒ (pl. **-ries**) a religious house ruled by a prior or prioress, usu. ranked under an abbey.
—名 작은 수도원

prism [príz(ə)m] *n.* ⓒ **1.** a block of regular shape with three or more flat sides and with two flat ends that are the same in size and shape. **2.** a glass body of this shape, usu. three-sided which breaks up a ray of sunlight into the colors of the rainbow. ¶*~ glasses.*①
—名 1. 각주(角柱) 2. 프리즘, 분광기 ¶①프리즘 쌍안경

pris·mat·ic [prizmǽtik] *adj.* **1.** of or like a prism. **2.** (of colors) formed or divided by a prism. **3.** of these colors.
—形 1. 각주의(같은) 2. 분광(分光)의 3. 무지개 빛의, 여러가지 빛깔의

‡ pris·on [prízn] *n.* **1.** ⓒ a building where law breakers are kept and punished. **2.** Ⓤ any place where a person is held against his will.
—名 1. 교도소, 감옥; 구치소, 유치장 2. 감금소, 유폐소

‡ pris·on·er [prízənər] *n.* ⓒ a person who is shut up against his will, such as a criminal or a soldier taken by the enemy.   [original; unspoiled and pure.
—名 잡힌 사람, 자유를 빼앗긴 사람; 죄수; 포로

pris·tine [prísti(ː)n, -tain / -tain] *adj.* of the earliest ages;]
—形 초기의, 원시시대의; 소박한

pri·va·cy [práivəsi] *n.* Ⓤ **1.** the state of being away from other people. **2.** the state of being secret.
 1) *in privacy,* secretly.   [the heart.
 2) *in the privacy of* [*one's*] *thoughts,* deep down in]
—名 1. 남의 눈을 피하기; 사생활; 은퇴, 은둔 2. 비밀, 은밀

熟 1)비밀히, 숨어서 2)마음 속에서

: pri·vate [práivit] *adj.* **1.** belonging to a single person; personal. ↔public ¶*on ~ business*① / *~ life* / *a ~ school.*② **2.** not official. ¶*as a ~ person*③ / *~ clothes.* **3.** not known to others; secret. ¶*a ~ letter.*④ **4.** holding the lowest rank as a soldier.
—*n.* [C] **1.** a common soldier. **2.** (*pl.*) the secret parts of the body.
in private, secretly.

—[形] 1. 개인의, 사유의 ¶①개인의 볼일로/②사립학교 2. 비공식의, 민간의, 사적(私的)인 ¶③개인으로서, 비공식으로 3. 비밀의 ¶④친전(親展) 4. 병졸의
—[名] 1. 병졸, 병사 2. 음부(陰部)
[熟] 비밀리, 몰래

pri·va·teer [pràivətíər] *n.* [C] **1.** an armed private ship allowed by the government to attack enemy ships. **2.** the captain or one of the crew of such a ship.

—[名] 1. 전시에 적선을 나포할 수 있는 면허를 받은 민간 무장선; 사략선(私掠船) 2. 그 선장(선원)

pri·va·tion [praivéiʃ(ə)n] *n.* [U][C] **1.** the lack of the needs of life, esp. food and clothing. **2.** the state of being taken away; loss; absence.
1) ***die of privation,*** die of poverty.
2) ***suffer many privations,*** have many difficulties.

—[名] 1. 결핍, 궁핍 2. 박탈, 상실
[熟] 1)가난으로 죽다 2)온갖 고생을 맛보다

priv·et [prívit] *n.* [C] a shrub with dark green leaves and small white flowers, much used for hedges.

—[名] 쥐똥나무 속(屬)

: priv·i·lege [prívilidʒ] *n.* [U] a special advantage, right or favor given to a person or a body of persons. ¶*the ~ of birth*① / *a writ of ~.*②
enjoy the privilege of one's friendship, have the honor of keeping company with someone.
—*vt.* give a special right to (someone).

—[名] 특권, 특전, 영광 ¶①타고날 때부터 갖고 있는 특권/②특사장(特赦狀)
[熟] …와 교제하는 영광을 맛보다
—[他] …에게 특권(특전)을 주다

priv·i·leged [prívilidʒd] *adj.* having or granted a special right or advantages. ¶*the ~ classes.*①

—[形] 특권이 있는, 특허의 ¶①특권계급

priv·i·ly [prívili] *adv.* not publicly; in a secret manner.

—[副] 비밀히, 몰래, 은밀히

priv·y [prívi] *adj.* (**priv·i·er, priv·i·est**) **1.** belonging to a single person. ¶*the ~ purse.*① **2.** having secret information. (*~ to*) —*n.* [C] (pl. **priv·ies**) an outdoor toilet.

—[形] 1. 개인의; 사유의; 사용(私用)의 ¶①내탕금(內帑金) 2. 비밀리에 관여하고 있는 —[名] 옥외 변소

⁝ prize[1] [praiz] *n.* [C] **1.** something given to honor a person who has won a race, etc. ¶*He won the first ~ in the marathon race.* **2.** anything worth making efforts to get. ¶*the prizes of life.*① **3.** something good or valuable. ¶*She picked up a ~ at a bargain sale.*②
—*adj.* **1.** given as a prize; got as a prize. ¶*a ~ novel.* **2.** worth getting a prize; fine.
—*vt.* value highly. ¶*~ honor above life.*

—[名] 1. 상, 상품, 상금 2. 노력하여 얻을 가치가 있는 것 ¶①인생의 목적물(재산·명예 따위) 3. 훌륭한 것, 귀중한 것 ¶②특매장에서 멋있는 것을 샀다
—[形] 1. 상품으로 탄 2. 상을 받을 만한
—[他] …을 존중하다

prize[2] [praiz] *n.* [C] something taken from the enemy in war, etc.
1) ***become the prize of*** (or ***to***) (=*be captured by*) *someone* or *something.*
2) ***make a prize of*** (=*capture*) *someone* or *something.*

—[名] 노획품, 전리품
[熟] 1)…에게 나포되다 2)나포하다

prize fight [⌐⌐] *n.* a boxing match for money.

—[名] 현상 권투 시합; 프로 복싱

prize ring [⌐⌐] *n.* the square space enclosed by ropes where a boxing match takes place.

—[名] 현상 권투장

prize winner [⌐⌐⌐] *n.* **1.** a person who wins a prize. **2.** a novel, etc. which is given a prize.

—[名] 1. 수상자 2 수상작품

pro[1] [prou] *adv.* in favor of; for. —*n.* [C] (pl. **pros**) an argument or a reason in favor of something. ↔con
pros and cons of (=*arguments for and against*) *a question.*

—[副] 찬성하여 —[名] 찬성 [의견]
[熟] 찬부[양론]

pro[2] [prou] *n.* [C] (pl. **pros**) (*colloq.*) a professional player of a sport, etc. —*adj.* (*colloq.*) professional.

—[名] 프로, 직업선수 —[形] 직업적인

pro-[1] [prou] *pref.* **1.** to the front; forward: *proceed* (=go forward). **2.** in favor of: *pro-slavery* (=in favor of slavery). **3.** instead of: *pronoun* (=a word used instead of a noun). **4.** publicly: *proclaim* (=announce publicly).

—(接頭) 1. 앞으로 2. 찬성의, 한편의 3. …의 대신에 4. 공적으로

pro-[2] [prou] *pref.* before; in front of: *prologue.* (=an introduction to something).

—(接頭) 전, …의 앞에

• prob·a·bil·i·ty [pràbəbíliti / prɔ̀b-] *n.* (pl. **-ties**) **1.** [U] the state or quality of being probable; likelihood. ¶*What are the probabilities?* **2.** [C] something likely to happen. ¶*The probability is that he will win.*
in all probability, most likely; probably.

—[名] 1. 있음직함, 그럴 듯함, 가망; 가능성 2. 있음직한 일
[熟] 아마, 십중팔구

prob·a·ble [prábəbl / prɔ́b-] *adj.* **1.** likely to happen. ¶*the ~ result* | *the ~ cost.*① **2.** likely to be true; giving reason for belief. ¶*~ evidence.*②
—形 1. 있음직한, 있을 듯싶은 ¶①추산 비용 2. 확실한 듯한 ¶②확실하다고 생각되는 증거

prob·a·bly [prábəbli / prɔ́b-] *adv.* very likely. ¶*It will ~ rain tomorrow.*
—副 아마, 십중팔구는

pro·ba·tion [proubéiʃ(ə)n] *n.* Ⓤ Ⓒ **1.** a trial or test of a person's conduct, ability, character, etc. ¶*take someone on ~*① / *pass ~.*② **2.** the period of such trying or testing. **3.** the legal system of permitting young law breakers to go free under police management. ¶*place* (or *put*) *an offender on ~.*③
—名 1. 시험, 검정 ¶①남을 시험삼아 채용하다/②시험에 통과하다, 정규로 채용되다 2. 견습 기간 3. 보호 관찰; 형의 집행유예 ¶③범죄자를 [집행유예 중] 보호 관찰을 받게 하다

pro·ba·tion·al [proubéiʃ(ə)n(ə)l] *adj.* =probationary.

pro·ba·tion·ar·y [proubéiʃ(ə)nèri / -ʃ(ə)n(ə)ri] *adj.* **1.** of probation. **2.** on probation.
—形 1. 시험의 2. 견습 중의; 집행유예 중의

pro·ba·tion·er [proubéiʃnər] *n.* Ⓒ a person who is on probation.
—名 수습생(修習生), 시보(試補), 가(假)채용자(입학자); 집행유예 중인

probe [proub] *n.* Ⓒ **1.** a long, thin instrument used by doctors in examining a wound. **2.** the careful examination.
—*vt.* **1.** examine (a wound) with a probe. **2.** search or examine closely. —*vi.* search or examine with a probe. 《*~ into something*》
—名 1. 탐침(探針) 2. 조사 [죄인]
—1. [상처]를 탐침으로 조사하다 2. …을 조사하다 —自 탐침으로 조사하다

pro·bi·ty [próubiti] *n.* Ⓤ honesty; righteousness; goodness; sincerity.
—名 청렴, 결백; 성실

prob·lem [práblǝm / prɔ́b-] *n.* Ⓒ **1.** a question hard to understand; a matter hard to settle or decide. ¶*the basic problems of our times.*① **2.** (in mathematics) something to be solved.
—*adj.* causing difficulty. ¶*a ~ child.*②
—名 1. 문제, 난문 ¶①현대의 기본적 문제 2. 문제, 과제
—形 문제의; 난제(難題)의 ¶②문제아

prob·lem·at·ic [pràblimǽtik / prɔ̀b-] *adj.* having problems; doubtful; questionable.
—形 문제의(가 있는), 의심스러운

prob·lem·at·i·cal [pràblimǽtik(ə)l / prɔ̀b-] *adj.* =problematic.

pro·bos·ci·des [prəbásidìːz / prəbɔ́s-] *n.* pl. of proboscis.

pro·bos·cis [proubásis / -bɔ́s-] *n.* Ⓒ (pl. **-cis·es** or **-ci·des**) **1.** an elephant's trunk. **2.** any long, easily bent nose of other animals. **3.** the stretched mouth part of certain insects used for sucking liquids, etc.
—名 1. 코끼리의 코 2. [무소 따위의] 코 3. [곤충의] 수등이

pro·ce·dure [prəsíːdʒər] *n.* Ⓤ Ⓒ **1.** the act or manner of proceeding in a course of action. **2.** a particular course of action. **3.** an established way of carrying on legal or parliamentary business.
—名 1. 진행, 진행 방법 2. [진행] 순서 3. [공식] 절차

pro·ceed [prəsíːd] *vi.* **1.** move or go on, esp. after stopping. ¶*~ on a journey.*① **2.** carry on or continue to do something. 《*~ with* or *in something*》 ¶*~ with work.*② **3.** begin. 《*~ to do something*》 ¶*~ to eat his dinner.*③ **4.** take place; go or come forth. 《*~ from* or *out of something*》 ¶*This proceeded from ignorance.*④ **5.** begin and carry on a legal action.
—自 1. 나아가다; 가다 ¶①여행을 떠나다 2. 계속(속행)하다 ¶②일을 계속하다 3. 시작하다 ¶③식사를 시작하다 4. 일어나다, 나타나다 ¶④이것은 무지에서 일어났다 5. 소송을 일으키다

pro·ceed·ing [prəsíːdiŋ] *n.* Ⓒ **1.** Ⓤ an action or a course of action. **2.** the mode of procedure. **3.** 《*pl.*》 a law process. **4.** 《*pl.*》 a record of things done at a meeting.
—名 1. 행동, 진행 2. 하는 방식, 절차 3. 소송 절차 4. 의사록

pro·ceeds [próusiːdz] *n.* pl. the amount of money gained from a business, etc.; the results from a business, etc.; the profit.
—名 매상고, 수익, 수입

proc·ess [práses / próus-] *n.* **1.** Ⓤ the course of being done. **2.** Ⓤ the course of time. **3.** Ⓤ a continuous action or series of actions which lead to some end. **4.** Ⓒ a special method of manufacturing or treatment. **5.** Ⓒ the part that grows out, esp. on bone. **6.** Ⓒ a written order or summons to appear in a law court.
1) *in process,* in the course of being done.
2) *in process of time,* in the course of time; soon.
—名 1. 과정, 진행 2. 경과 3. 순서, 방법 4. 공정(工程); 제법(製法) 5. 돌기(突起), 융기(隆起) 6. [법정에의] 소환장

熟 1)진행중; …중 2)시간이 감에 따라; 멀지 않아 3)…에 영장을 발행하다

procession [900] **produce**

3) *serve a process on,* issue a written order for someone's arrest.
—*vt.* **1.** start legal proceeding against (someone). **2.** treat (something) in a certain way.
—*adj.* treated in a special way.
- **pro·ces·sion** [prəséʃ(ə)n] *n.* **1.** ⓒ a formal parade. ¶*a funeral ~.*① **2.** ⓤ the act of going forward.
—ⓜ 1. 행렬, 행진 ¶①장례식 행렬 2. 진행; 전진

pro·ces·sion·al [prəséʃən(ə)l] *adj.* **1.** of a procession. **2.** used in a procession. ¶*a ~ cross.*① —*n.* ⓒ **1.** a piece of music suitable for a religious procession. **2.** a book containing hymns and prayers for religious processions.
—ⓜ 1. 행렬의, 행진의 2. 행렬용의 ¶①행렬용의 십자가 —ⓢ 1. 행렬 성가 2. 행렬식서(書)

: **pro·claim** [prəkléim] *vt.* **1.** announce formally and publicly. ¶*~ war against*① */ ~ him [to be] a traitor; ~ that he is a traitor.* **2.** make (something) known to the general public. ¶*~ one's opinion.* **3.** show; reveal. ¶*His accent proclaims him an American.*①
—ⓜ 1. …을 선언하다, 포고하다 ¶①…에 대하여 선전을 포고하다 2. …을 발표하다, 성명하다 3. …을 나타내다, 증명하다 ¶②그의 악센트로 미국인임을 알 수 있다

proc·la·ma·tion [pràkləméiʃ(ə)n / prɔ̀k-] *n.* ⓒ a formal announcement.
—ⓢ 성명

pro·cliv·i·ty [prouklíviti] *n.* ⓒ (pl. **-ties**) a tendency; a willingness.
—ⓢ 경향; 성벽(性癖)

pro·con·sul [proukánsəl / -kɔ́n-] *n.* ⓒ **1.** an ancient Roman provincial governor. **2.** a governing official in a colony.
—ⓢ 1. 고대 로마의 지방 총독 2. 식민지 총독

pro·cras·ti·nate [proukrǽstinèit] *vi.* put off action from day to day; go slowly; delay. —*vt.* put off; postpone.
—ⓐ 지연하다, 오래 끌다, 우물우물하다 —ⓜ …을 연기하다

pro·cras·ti·na·tion [proukrǽstinéiʃ(ə)n] *n.* ⓤ the act or habit of putting something off till later.
—ⓢ 지연, 연기

pro·cre·ate [próukrièit] *vt., vi.* become the father of (someone); beget. 「creating.」
—ⓜⓐ [아버지가 자식]을 낳다, 생기게 하다

pro·cre·a·tion [pròukriéiʃ(ə)n] *n.* ⓤ the act of pro-
—ⓢ 자식을 보기, 생식(生殖)

pro·cre·a·tive [próukrièitiv] *adj.* of or having the power of procreating or producing.
—ⓜ 생식의; 생산의; 생식력이 있는; 생산력이 있는

proc·tor [práktər / prɔ́ktə] *n.* ⓒ **1.** an official who keeps order in a university or school. **2.** a person who acts for another in a law court.
—ⓢ 1. 대학 학생감 2. 대리인; 대소인(代訴人)

pro·cur·a·ble [proukjúərəbl / prə-] *adj.* that can be obtained or acquired.
—ⓜ 입수(획득)할 수 있는

proc·u·ra·tion [pràkjuréiʃ(ə)n / prɔ̀kju-] *n.* ⓤ authority for acting for another.
—ⓢ 대리권

proc·u·ra·tor [prákjurèitər / prɔ́kurèitə] *n.* ⓒ a person who acts or has power to act for another.
—ⓢ 대소인(代訴人), 대리인

* **pro·cure** [proukjúər / prəkjúə] *vt.* **1.** get; obtain. **2.** cause (something) to happen.
—ⓜ 1. …을 획득하다, 입수하다, 얻다 2. …을 초래하다, 야기시키다

prod [prad / prɔd] *n.* ⓒ **1.** a pointed instrument used to prick or urge. **2.** a thrust; a poke. —*vt.* (**prod·ded, prod·ding**) **1.** punch or poke (cattle, etc.) with a pointed instrument. **2.** urge; rouse.
—ⓢ 1. 찌르는 막대 2. 찌르기, 쑤시기 —ⓜ 1. …을 뾰족한 것으로 찌르다 2. …을 재촉하다; 자극하다

prod·i·gal [prádigəl / prɔ́d-] *adj.* **1.** careless with money; wasteful. **2.** too free in giving or spending. 《*~ of*》 —*n.* ⓒ a person who wastes money.
—ⓜ 1. 낭비하는, 방탕의 2. 아낌없이 주는, 통이 큰
—ⓢ 낭비자, 난봉꾼

prod·i·gal·i·ty [pràdigǽliti / prɔ̀d-] *n.* ⓤ **1.** the act of spending money in a careless or too generous manner. **2.** plentifulness; richness.
—ⓢ 1. 낭비; 아낌없음 2. 풍부

pro·di·gious [prədídʒəs] *adj.* **1.** extremely large; very great. **2.** wonderful; beyond what is ordinary.
—ⓜ 1. 거대한; 막대한 2. 놀랄 만한, 이상한

prod·i·gy [prádidʒi / prɔ́d-] *n.* ⓒ (pl. **-gies**) **1.** a wonderful or surprising thing or event. **2.** a person, esp. a child, with wonderful talent or power.
—ⓢ 1. 경탄할 만한 사물(사건) 2. 천재; 신동

: **pro·duce** *v.* [prəd(j)úːs, -djúːs →*n.*] *vt.* **1.** bring (something) into existence; cause. ¶*~ a reaction*① */ ~ misery.* **2.** write (a novel, etc.); draw (a painting, etc.). ¶*~ a poem.* **3.** create. ¶*~ rice.*② **4.** bring forth; bear. ¶*The tree produces fruit.* **5.** provide, supply or yield. ¶*The mine produces fine gold.*③ **6.** bring (some-
—ⓜ 1. …을 생기게 하다, 일으키다 ¶①반작용을 일으키다 2. [소설 따위]를 쓰다; [그림 따위]를 그리다 3. …을 생산하다 ¶②쌀을 생산하다 4. …을 낳다, 결실하다 5. …을 공급하다, 산출하다 ¶③그 광산은 양질의 금을 산출

producer [901] **professorial**

thing) to view; exhibit. ¶*The driver produced his license for the policeman.* **7.** bring (a play, a movie, etc.) before the public. —*vi.* create or bring forth something.
—*n.* [prád(j)u:s / pródju:s] ((*collectively*)) that which is produced ; Ⓤ the amount of something produced.
다 6. …을 전시하다, [대중]에게 보이다 7. [극·영화 따위]를 상연하다 —⾃ 생산(산출)하다, 만들어내다 —⾃ 생산물 ; 생산고

* **pro·duc·er** [prəd(j)ú:sər / -djú:sə] *n.* Ⓒ **1.** a person who produces. **2.** a person who presents a drama, a motion picture, etc.
—⾃ 1. 생산자, 제작자 2. [극의] 연출자, 영화 제작자

: **prod·uct** [prádəkt / pród-] *n.* Ⓒ **1.** ((usu. *pl.*)) a thing that is produced. ¶*natural products*① / *factory products.*② **2.** the result of action. **3.** the result of multiplying two or more numbers.
—⾃ 1. 산출물, 생산품, 제작품 ¶①천연의 산물/②공장 제품 2. 성과, 결과 3. 《數》적(積)

: **pro·duc·tion** [prədʌ́kʃ(ə)n] *n.* **1.** Ⓤ the act of producing. ¶*efficient ~ method.*① **2.** Ⓒ a thing that is produced. ¶*a literary ~.*② **3.** Ⓤ the amount of what is produced. ¶*Production is up this week.*③
—⾃ 1. 생산, 제작 ¶①능률적 생산 방법 2. 생산물, 제작품, 작품 ¶②문예 작품 3. 생산고(량) ¶③금주는 생산량이 늘었다

* **pro·duc·tive** [prədʌ́ktiv] *adj.* **1.** producing; yielding. **2.** making something of value. **3.** producing much; rich; fruitful. ¶*a ~ writer.*
—⾃ 1. …을 생기게 하는, …을 낳는 2. 생산하는, 생산력이 있는 ; 생산적인 3. 다산의, 풍부한

pro·duc·tiv·i·ty [pròudʌktívəti / pròd-] *n.* Ⓤ **1.** the state of being productive. **2.** the power to bring forth.
—⾃ 1. 생산 ; 풍요(豊饒) 2. 생산력

pro·em [próuem] *n.* Ⓒ a preface or an introduction to some writing, a speech, etc.
prof. professor.
—⾃ 서문, 머리말

prof·a·na·tion [pròufənéiʃ(ə)n / pròf-] *n.* Ⓤ the act of profaning ; the state of being profaned ; talking about God without piety.
—⾃ 신성을 더럽힘, 신을 모독함

pro·fane [prəféin] *adj.* (**-fan·er, -fan·est**) **1.** not belonging to God ; of this world. ¶*a ~ person.*① **2.** relating to things not in the Bible. **3.** paying no respect to God or holy things.
—⾃ 1. 세속적인, 범속한 ¶①속인 2. 이단[異端]의 ; 이교의 3. 신성을 더럽히는, 모독적인

—*vt.* **1.** treat (something sacred) with abuse or contempt. **2.** put (something) to improper use.
—⾃ 1. [신성]을 더럽히다, 모독하다 2. …을 남용하다

pro·fan·i·ty [prəfǽniti] *n.* (*pl.* **-ties**) **1.** Ⓒ disrespectful conduct or speech ; impious talk about God ; an impious word or remark. **2.** Ⓤ want of respect.
—⾃ 1. 모독적인 행위(말) 2. 불경(不敬), 모독

* **pro·fess** [prəfés] *vt.* **1.** make a public declaration of (something). **2.** claim falsely ; pretend. **3.** declare one's belief in (something). **4.** have (something) as one's profession. —*vi.* make a public declaration.
—⾃ 1. …을 공언하다, 성명하다 2. …이라 자칭하다 ; 가장하다 3. …에 대한 신앙을 고백하다 4. …을 직업으로 하다 —⾃ 공언을 하다

pro·fessed [prəfést] *adj.* **1.** openly declared. **2.** pretended. **3.** having taken an oath and entered into a religious order.
—⾃ 1. 공언된 2. 거짓의 3. 서약하고 수도회에 들어간

pro·fess·ed·ly [prəfésidli] *adv.* **1.** by admission ; openly. **2.** so far as appearances go.
—⾃ 1. 허가(승인)되어 ; 공공연히 2. 「표면상」

: **pro·fes·sion** [prəféʃ(ə)n] *n.* Ⓒ **1.** an occupation requiring special education or training. ¶*adopt some ~*① / *He is a lawyer by ~.*② **2.** Ⓤ (*the ~*) the group of persons engaged in an occupation. ¶*the legal ~*③ / *the medical ~.*④ **3.** an open declaration ; a confession of faith.
—⾃ 1. 직업, 전문직 ¶①직업을 갖다/②그의 직업은 변호사다 2. 동업자들 ¶③법조계/④의학계 3. 공언 ; 고백

: **pro·fes·sion·al** [prəféʃən(ə)l] *adj.* **1.** of a profession ; suitable for a profession. ¶*~ knowledge.*① **2.** engaged in an occupation. **3.** making a trade of something which others practice for pleasure. ↔amateur
—⾃ 1. 직업의, 직업에 어울리는, 전문가의 ¶①전문 지식 2. 직업에 종사하고 있는 3. 직업적인, 프로의

—*n.* Ⓒ **1.** a person who is engaged in an occupation requiring special education. **2.** a person who plays sport as an occupation. ↔amateur
—⾃ 1. 직업인, 전문가 2. 직업선수

pro·fes·sion·al·ism [prəféʃənəlìz(ə)m] *n.* Ⓤ professional habits of mind, qualities, etc. 「manner.
—⾃ 전문가 기질, 직공 기질

pro·fes·sion·al·ly [prəféʃənəli] *adv.* in a professional
—⾃ 직업적으로, 전문적으로

: **pro·fes·sor** [prəfésər] *n.* Ⓒ **1.** a teacher of the highest rank in a college or university. **2.** a person who publicly declares a religious belief.
—⾃ 1. 대학 교수 2. 신앙 고백자

pro·fes·so·ri·al [pròufəsɔ́:riəl / pròfes-] *adj.* of or characteristic of
—⾃ 교수의, 교수다운, 학자티를 내는

professorship [902] **prognostic**

acteristic of a professor; or rank at a university. —名 교수의 직(지위)
pro·fes·sor·ship [prəfésərʃip] *n.* ⓒ a professor's post

prof·fer [práfər / prɔ́fə] *vt.* present (something) for acceptance; tender. —*n.* ⓒ an offer. —他 …을 제출(제공)하다 —名 제출; 제공[물]; 신청

pro·fi·cien·cy [prəfíʃənsi] *n.* ⓤ the state of being proficient; ability gained by practice. —名 숙달, 능숙

pro·fi·cient [prəfíʃənt] *adj.* skilled; having much knowledge. —*n.* ⓒ a person who has skill in some special thing; an expert. —形 숙달한, 능숙한 —名 능숙한 사람, 대가, 명인

pro·file [próufail / -fi:l] *n.* ⓒ 1. a side view of a human face. 2. an outline. 3. a short, vivid description of someone's life, abilities, etc. 4. a picture of a side view. *in profile*, sideward. —*vt.* draw a profile or an outline of (someone or something). —名 1. [사람의] 옆모습, 프로필 2. 윤곽 3. 인물 소개; 약전(略傳) 4. 측면도
熟 옆모습으로(의); 옆에서 보아
—他 …의 옆얼굴(윤곽)을 그리다

: **prof·it** [práfit / prɔ́f-] *n.* 1. ⓤ gain, advantage, or benefit to someone's character, etc. ¶*What's the ~ of doing so?*① 2. ⓒ (often *pl.*) money gained in business. ¶*a net ~*② / *gross profits.*③ 3. ⓒ (usu. *pl.*) interest.
1) *make a profit on,* earn much money by selling (something).
2) *small profits and quick returns,* sell large quantities in a short period at small profits.
—*vt.* bring profit to or serve (someone or something).
—*vi.* gain profit.
—名 1. [인격상의] 득, 이익 ¶①그렇게 해서 무슨 득이 있는가? 2. 이득, 이윤, 이익, 벌이 ¶②순이익/③총수익 3. 이자
熟 1) …으로 벌다 2) 박리다매
—他 …의 이익이 되다 —自 이익을 얻다

· **prof·it·a·ble** [práfitəbl] *adj.* bringing profit; giving advantage; useful. —形 유리한; 유익한; 이익이 있는 benefit.

prof·it·a·bly [práfitəbli / prɔ́f-] *adv.* with gain; with —副 유리하게, 유익하게

prof·it·eer [pràfitíər / prɔ̀fitíə] *vi.* make great profits unfairly. —*n.* ⓒ a person who makes big profits unfairly during a period of scarcity. —自 [특히 전시에] 부당한 이문을 남기다, 폭리를 보다 —名 모리배, 부당이득자

prof·it·less [práfitlis / prɔ́f-] *adj.* bringing no profit; of no advantage; useless. ¶*make ~ efforts.*① —形 이익이 없는, 무익한, 쓸데없는 ¶①헛수고하다

prof·li·ga·cy [práfligəsi / prɔ́f-] *n.* ⓤ the state of being profligate; careless extravagance. —名 방탕; 낭비

prof·li·gate [práfligit / prɔ́f-] *adj.* 1. living in an evil way; wicked. 2. carelessly spending much money. —*n.* ⓒ a profligate person. —形 1. 행실이 나쁜 2. 낭비하는 —名 행실이 나쁜 사람, 낭비자

· **pro·found** [prəfáund] *adj.* (**-found·er, -found·est**) 1. deep. ¶*a ~ sleep*① / *a ~ interest.*② 2. deep in meaning. 3. deeply felt. 4. having or marked by great knowledge or thoughts. ¶*~ knowledge.*③ 5. humble; bent low. sincerely. —形 1. 깊은 ¶①깊은 잠/②깊은 흥미 2. 심원한; 의미심장한 3. 충심에서의 4. 조예가 깊은, 학식이 많은 ¶③깊은 학식 5. 겸손한; 허리를 굽힌

pro·found·ly [prəfáundli] *adv.* in a profound manner; —副 깊게; 공손하게; 간절히

pro·fun·di·ty [prəfʌ́nditi] *n.* (pl. **-ties**) 1. ⓤ the state of being deep; depth. 2. ⓒ a thing or place that is very deep. —名 1. 깊음; 깊이; 심원 2. 깊은 곳, 심연

pro·fuse [prəfjúːs] *adj.* 1. very plentiful; abundant. ¶*He was ~ in his apologies.*① 2. spending freely; giving generously; wasteful. ¶*be ~ with* (or *of*) *money.*② —形 1. 풍부한 ¶①그는 백배 사죄했다 2. 아낌없는, 통이 큰 ¶②씀씀이가 헤프다

pro·fuse·ly [prəfjúːsli] *adv.* in a profuse manner; generously. —副 다량으로; 아낌없이

pro·fu·sion [prəfjúːʒ(ə)n] *n.* ⓤ 1. great plenty. ¶*in ~*① / *a ~ of.*② 2. the act of spending money in a careless or too generous manner; wastefulness. —名 1. 풍부 ¶①풍부하게/②많은 2. 사치, 낭비

pro·gen·i·tor [proudʒénitər] *n.* ⓒ an earlier member of the family; an ancestor; a forefather. —名 선조

prog·e·ny [prádʒini / prɔ́dʒ-] *n.* ⓒ (pl. **-nies**) children; descendants. —名 자손

prog·no·ses [pragnóusiːz / prɔg-] *n.* pl. of **prognosis**.

prog·no·sis [pragnóusis / prɔg-] *n.* (pl. **-ses**) ⓒ a forecast or an expectation, esp. of the probable course of a disease. —名 예측, 예지(豫知); 예후(豫後)

prog·nos·tic [pragnástik / prɔgnɔ́s-] *adj.* telling something of the future. —*n.* ⓒ 1. a sign or an indication of —形 전조의 —名 1. 전조 2. 예측; 예지

what will happen. **2.** a forecast.

prog·nos·ti·cate [pragnástikèit / prəg-] *vt.* show a sign of (something); declare (something) from facts beforehand; foretell; predict.
—[他] …의 징조를 보이다; …을 예언하다, 예지하다

prog·nos·ti·ca·tion [pragnàstikéiʃ(ə)n / prəgnɔ̀s-] *n.* **1.** [U] the act of foretelling or warning. **2.** [C] something which shows what is to come; an omen; a sign.
—[名] 1. 예언, 예지 2. 전조, 징후

⁑ pro·gram, *Brit.* **-gramme** [próugræm] *n.* [C] **1.** a list of events in a public show, etc. ¶*the first item on the ~.*① **2.** a group of things or events for a radio or television broadcast. ¶*appear on the T. V. ~*② / *What is the next ~?*③ **3.** a plan to be done. ¶*What is the ~ for next Sunday?*④
—[名] 1. 프로그램, 차례표 ¶①프로그램의 첫째 항목 2. 상연 종목, 연주 곡목 ¶②텔레비전 프로에 나가다/③다음 프로는 뭔니까? 3. 계획, 예정 ¶④다음 일요일의 예정은 무엇입니까?

—*vt.* (**-grammed, -gram·ming**) **1.** make a program of (something); plan for (something). **2.** enter (something) in a program.
—[他] 1. …의 프로그램을 짜다, 예정을 세우다 2. …을 계획에 짜넣다, 프로그램에 싣다

⁑ pro·gress *n.* [prágres / próu- ∥ → *v.*] [U] **1.** the act of moving or going forward; advance. ¶*in the ~ of time.*① **2.** growth; development. ¶*the ~ of science.*② **3.** course. ¶*the ~ of events.*③ **4.** [C] (*archaic*) a journey of a king, etc. ¶*a royal ~*④ / "*The Pilgrim's Progress.*"⑤
1) ***in progress,*** happening; going on.
2) ***make progress,*** ⓐ develop; improve. ⓑ go forward.
—[名] 1. 전진; 진행 ¶①시간이 지남에 따라 2. 진보, 발달, 숙달 ¶②과학의 진보 3. 진척, 경과 ¶③사건의 경과 4. 《古》 거둥, 순행(巡幸) ¶④임금의 거둥/⑤「천로역정」
[熟] 1)진행중인 2)ⓐ진보하다, 진척하다 ⓑ전진하다

—*vi.* [prougrés] **1.** move or go forward. ¶*Our work is progressing.*⑥ **2.** develop. 《*~ in* something》
—[自] 1. 전진하다 ¶⑥우리들의 일은 진척되어 있다 2. 진보하다

pro·gres·sion [prougréʃ(ə)n] *n.* [U] the act of progressing.
—[名] 전진; 진행

∗ pro·gres·sive [prougrésiv] *adj.* **1.** going forward; making better. **2.** ready to agree to new ideas. **3.** (*Grammar*) indicating an action which is going on. ¶*a ~ form.*① **4.** favoring progress in government. ¶*the Progressive Party.*② —*n.* [C] a person who favors political progress or reforms.
—[形] 1. 전진적인 2. 진보적인; 진취적인; 진보주의의 3. 《文法》 진행을 나타내는, 진행형의 ¶①진행형 4. 진보당의 ¶②진보당 —[名] 진보론자; 진보당원

∗ pro·hib·it [prouhíbit] *vt.* **1.** forbid (something) by law. ¶*Smoking is strictly prohibited.*① **2.** prevent someone from (doing something). ¶*Prohibit him from coming.; Prohibit his coming.*②
—[他] 1. …을 금하다 ¶①끽연 엄금 2. …을 방해하다 ¶②그를 오지 못하게 해라

⁑ pro·hi·bi·tion [pròu(h)ibíʃ(ə)n] *n.* **1.** [U] the act of prohibiting. **2.** [C] a law or an order which forbids. **3.** [U] the act of forbidding by law the making and selling of alcoholic drinks. ¶*the ~ law.*①
—[名] 1. 금지 2. 금지령 3. 법에 의한 주류의 제조·판매 금지 ¶①금주법

pro·hi·bi·tion·ist [pròu(h)ibíʃ(ə)nist] *n.* [C] a person who favors prohibiting by law the making and selling of alcoholic drinks.
—[名] 금주주의자

pro·hib·i·tive [prouhíbitiv] *adj.* tending to prohibit. ¶*a ~ price.*①
—[形] 금지의 ¶①금지된 가격

pro·hib·i·to·ry [prouhíbitɔ̀ːri / -t(ə)ri] *adj.* prohibitive.
—[形] 금지의

⁑ proj·ect *n.* [prádʒekt / prɔ́dʒ- ∥ → *v.*] [C] **1.** a plan; a design. **2.** an enterprise. —*v.* [proudʒékt] *vt.* **1.** plan. **2.** make (something) stand out. **3.** throw out. **4.** make (a beam of light) fall on a surface; make (a shadow) fall on a surface. ¶*~ a motion picture on the screen.*① —*vi.* stand out; stretch out.
—[名] 1. 계획, 기획; 설계 2. 사업 —[他] 1. …을 계획하다 2. …을 돌출시키다 3. …을 내던지다 4. [빛]을 투사(投射)하다; …을 투영(投影)하다 ¶①스크리인에 영화를 비추다 —[自] 돌출하다; 내밀다

pro·jec·tile *adj.* [proudʒéktil / -tail ∥ → *n.*] shooting forward. ¶*a ~ weapon.*① —*n.* [prádʒiktail] [C] an object thrown or shot; a cannon ball ; a bullet.
—[形] 발사하는 ¶①날아가는 무기
—[名] 발사물; 포탄, 탄환

pro·jec·tion [proudʒékʃ(ə)n] *n.* **1.** [C] a part that stands out; [U] the state of standing out. **2.** [U] the state of being shot. ¶*the ~ of a cannon ball.*① **3.** [U] the act of casting an image or a film on a screen.
—[名] 1. 돌출부; 돌기(突起) 2. 발사 ¶①포탄의 발사 3. 영사(映寫)

pro·jec·tor [proudʒéktər] *n.* [C] **1.** an instrument for throwing a picture on a screen. **2.** a person who makes plans.
—[名] 1. 영사기 2. 계획자

pro·le·tar·i·an [pròuletέəriən] *adj.* of or belonging to the proletariat. —*n.* [C] a member of the proletariat.
—[形] 프롤레타리아의, 노동계급의
—[名] 노동계급의 사람

pro·le·tar·i·at [pròuletέəriət] *n.* [C] (pl. **-at**) **1.** the very
—[名] 1. 프롤레타리아(무산) 계급 2. 노

P

poor; the lowest class of society. **2.** (in Europe) the working classes. ↔bourgeoisie
동자 계급

pro·lif·ic [proulífik] *adj.* **1.** producing many children. **2.** producing much. ¶*a ~ writer.*①
—[形] 1. 다산(多產)의 2. 풍부한 ¶①다작(多作)의 작가

be prolific in, be full of.
[熟] …이 풍부하다

pro·lix [proulíks, ⌐⌐] *adj.* using too many words; long and tiring.
—[形] 장황한, 지루한

pro·lix·i·ty [proulíksiti] *n.* [U] the state of being prolix.
—[名] 용장(冗長); 지루함

pro·logue, pro·log [próulɔ:g, -lɑg / -lɔg] *n.* [C] **1.** an introduction spoken by an actor at the beginning of a play. **2.** an introduction to a novel, a poem, etc. **3.** any event or act serving as an introduction.
—[名] 1. 서막사(序幕詞) 2. 머리말, 서언, 서사(序詞) 3. 서막적 사건

* **pro·long** [proulɔ́:ŋ, -lɔ́ŋ] *vt.* make (something) longer. ¶*~ a party.*①
—[他] …을 길게 끌다 ¶①파아티를 연장하다

pro·lon·ga·tion [pròulɔ:ŋgéiʃ(ə)n / -lɔŋ-] *n.* **1.** [U] the state of being prolonged in time. **2.** [C] the part added to make something longer.
—[名] 1. 연기 2. 연장한 부분

prom [prɑm / prɔm] *n.* **1.** [C] (*U.S. colloq.*) a ball or dance held by a college. **2.** (*Brit. colloq.*) a promenade concert.
—[名] 1. 〔美口〕 [대학의] 무도회 2. 〔英口〕 유보(遊步)음악회(연주 중에 청중이 걸어다녀도 괜찮음)

prom·e·nade [pràminéid / prɔ̀minɑ́:d] *n.* [C] **1.** a walk for joy or show. ¶*a ~ concert.*① **2.** a public place, esp. fit for walking. **3.** a ball or dance held by a college.
—[名] 1. 산책; 유보(遊步) ¶①유보 음악회 2. 산책장(길) 3. 대학의 무도회

—*vi.* walk for joy.
—[自] 산책하다

Pro·me·the·us [proumí:θiəs, -θju:s] *n.* (in Greek mythology) the god who stole fire from Mt. Olympus and taught men its use.
—[名] 프로메테우스

prom·i·nence [prɑ́minəns / prɔ́m-] *n.* **1.** [U] the state of being prominent. ¶*a man of ~.*① **2.** [C] something that stands out; a high place.
—[名] 1. 탁월, 현저, 명성 ¶①저명한 사람 2. 돌출부

* **prom·i·nent** [prɑ́minənt / prɔ́m-] *adj.* **1.** famous; important. **2.** clearly seen; noticeable. **3.** standing out beyond a surface. ¶*~ eyes.*① ▷**prom·i·nent·ly** [-li] *adv.*
—[形] 1. 저명한 2. 눈에 띄는 3. 튀어나온 ¶①퉁방울 눈

prom·is·cu·i·ty [pràmiskjú(:)iti / prɔ̀m-] *n.* [U] the state of being promiscuous.
—[名] 혼란, 뒤죽박죽

pro·mis·cu·ous [prəmískjuəs] *adj.* **1.** confused; mixed. **2.** making no distinction; not limited to any particular person or class.
—[形] 1. 난잡한, 뒤죽박죽의 2. 차별 없는, 한정되지 않은

‡ **prom·ise** [prɑ́mis / prɔ́mis] *n.* **1.** [C] an agreement given to another to do or not to do something; an informal contract. ¶*a false ~*① / *a breach of ~*② / *make a ~.* **2.** [C] something that a person agrees to do or not to do. ¶*Don't you forget your ~.*③ **3.** [U] something which shows hope of success in the future. ¶*a boy that shows ~.*④
—[名] 1. 약속; 계약 ¶①말뿐인 약속/②약속 불이행 2. 약속한 일 ¶③네가 약속한 일은 잊지 말아라 3. 장래의 가망, 촉망 ¶④전도유망한 소년

1) ***keep*** (***break***) ***one's promise,*** fulfil (do not fulfil) one's promise.
2) ***the Land of Promise,*** Canaan. ⇒[N.B.]
[熟] 1)약속을 지키다(깨뜨리다) 2)가나안의 땅 [N.B.] 신이 이스라엘 사람에게 약속한 땅

—*vt.* **1.** make a promise to (someone). 《*~ to do*; ~ someone *to do*; ~ someone *that* …; *~ that* …》 ¶*He promised us the money.; He promised the money to us.*⑤/ *I promised him to go.; I promised him that I would go.*⑥/ *He promised to tell the truth.* / *He promised that he would never come here.* **2.** give hope of (something); be likely to do (something). ¶*The weather promises heavy snow.*⑦ **—*vi.*** **1.** make a promise. **2.** 《often with *well* or *fair*》 give hope of something. ¶*The weather promises well.*⑧
—[他] 1. …에게 약속하다 ¶⑤그는 우리에게 그 돈을 주겠다고 약속했다/⑥나는 그에게 가겠다고 약속했다 2. …의 가망이 있다; …할 성싶다 ¶⑦이 날씨는 큰 눈이 올 것 같다 —[自] 1. 약속하다 2. …한 가망(전망)이다 ¶⑧날씨는 좋아질 것 같다

‡ **prom·is·ing** [prɑ́misiŋ / prɔ́m-] *adj.* giving hope of success; hopeful. ¶*a ~ student.*①
—[形] 유망한 ¶①유망한 학생

prom·is·so·ry [prɑ́misɔ̀:ri / prɔ́misəri] *adj.* containing a promise.
—[形] 약속의

promissory note [⌐⌐⌐ ⌐] *n.* a written promise to pay a certain sum of money at a fixed date.
—[名] 약속어음

prom·on·to·ry [prɑ́məntɔ̀:ri/prɔ́mənt(ə)ri] *n.* [C] (pl. **-ries**) a point of land which extends into the sea; a cape.
—[名] 갑(岬), 곶

* **pro·mote** [prəmóut] *vt.* **1.** give (someone) a higher posi-
—[他] 1. …을 진급시키다, 승진시키다

tion or rank. ¶*be promoted to.* **2.** help the growth or development of (something). ¶*~ digestion.*① **3.** start to organize (something). ¶*~ a business.*② **4.** help to sell (something) by advertising it.

2. …을 촉진하다 ¶①소화를 촉진하다 3. …을 조직화하다 ¶②사업을 시작하다 4. 선전으로 …의 판매를 촉진하다

pro·mot·er [prəmóutər] *n.* [C] **1.** a person or thing that promotes. **2.** a person who organizes a new company.

—[名] 1. 촉진자(물) 2. 발기인, 창립자

***pro·mo·tion** [prəmóuʃ(ə)n] *n.* **1.** [U][C] advance in rank or importance. **2.** [U] the act of helping the growth. ¶*the ~ of health.*① **3.** [C] the act of starting to organize a company, etc.

—[名] 1. 승진, 진급 2. 증진, 촉진, 조장 ¶①건강의 증진 3. 발기(發起), 창립

***prompt** [prampt / prɔm(p)t] *adj.* **1.** ready and quick in action. ¶*She gives a ~ reply.; She is ~ to reply.*① **2.** done at once or instantly. ¶*~ cash*② / *a ~ assistance.*
—*vt.* **1.** cause (someone) to do something; move (someone) to action. ¶*prompted by instinct / The weather prompted us to go out.*③ **2.** remind (someone) of something; suggest; inspire. **3.** help (an actor) by telling him words which he has forgotten.
—*n.* [C] an act or words for prompting an actor, etc.
—*adv.* (*colloq.*) just; sharp. ¶*at five ~.*

—[形] 1. 즉석의; 재빠른 ¶①그녀는 곧 대답한다 2. 지체없는 ¶②즉시불(即時拂)
—[他] 1. …을 자극하다, 촉진하다 ¶③날씨가 좋아서 외출했다 2. [사람에게] …을 생각나게 하다, [사상·감정을] 불어넣다 3. [배우]에게 잊어버린 대사를 뒤에서 가르쳐 주다
—[名] 무대 뒤에서 배우에게 대사를 일러주기
—[副] 《口》 꼬박, 정확히

prompt·er [prámptər / prɔ́m(p)tə] *n.* [C] a person who tells actors their speeches when they forget them on the stage.

—[名] 프롬프터; 격려자

promp·ti·tude [prámptit(j)ù:d / prɔ́m(p)titjù:d] *n.* [U] the state of being prompt.

—[名] 신속, 기민

⁑**prompt·ly** [prámptli / prɔ́m(p)t-] *adv.* in a prompt manner; readily; quickly; at once.

—[副] 신속하게; 당장

prom·ul·gate [práməlgèit, proumʌ́lgeit / prɔ́məl-] *vt.* **1.** make (something) known formally and officially. ¶*~ news*① / *~ a law.*② **2.** spread (something) widely; make (something) widely known.

—[他] 1. …을 발포(發布)(공포)하다 ¶①뉴우스를 공표하다/②법령을 공포하다 2. …을 퍼뜨리다, 보급하다

prom·ul·ga·tion [pràməlgéiʃ(ə)n, pròum- / prɔ̀məl-] *n.* [U] the act of promulgating; the state of being promulgated.

—[名] 발포, 발표, 보급

pron. **1.** pronoun; pronominal. **2.** pronunciation.

prone [proun] *adj.* **1.** having a tendency; likely. **2.** lying with the face downward. ¶*lie ~.*

—[形] 1. …의 경향이 있는, …하기 쉬운 2. 수그린, 엎드린

prong [prɔ:ŋ/prɔŋ] *n.* [C] one of the pointed parts of a fork.
—*vt.* stick (something) with a pointed instrument.

—[名] 포오크 따위의 뾰족한 끝 —[他] …을 찌르다, 꿰다

pronged [prɔ:ŋd / prɔŋd] *adj.* divided into branches.

—[形] 갈래(가랑이)가 있는

pro·nom·i·nal [prounámin(ə)l / -nɔ́m-] *adj.* of or having the nature or function of a pronoun.

—[形] 대명사의, 대명사적인

pro·nom·i·nal·ly [prounáminəli / -nɔ́m-] *adv.* as a pronoun.

—[副] 대명사로서

⁑**pro·noun** [próunàun] *n.* [C] a word used instead of a noun.

—[名] 대명사

⁑**pro·nounce** [prənáuns] *vt.* **1.** make the sounds of (words) clearly. ¶*~ every word clearly and correctly.* **2.** say (something) with a decision. ¶*~ judgment on.*① **3.** announce (something) formall . —*vi.* **1.** make sounds. **2.** give one's opinion. **3.** give a judgement. ¶*The committee will ~ upon the matter.*②
1) ***pronounce against,*** express an opposing opinion to (*something*).
2) ***pronounce for*** (=*speak in favor of*) *something.*

—[他] 1. …을 발음하다 2. …을 공언하다, 단언하다 ¶①…에 판단을 내리다 3. …을 선고하다 —[自] 1. 발음하다 2. 의견을 말하다 3. 판단을 내리다 ¶②위원회는 그 문제에 관해 판단을 내릴 것이다
[熟] 1)…에 반대 의견을 말하다 2)…에 찬성 의견을 말하다

***pro·nounced** [prənáunst] *adj.* exact; clear; strongly marked.

—[形] 단호한; 현저한, 눈에 띄는

pro·nounce·ment [prənáunsmənt] *n.* [C] **1.** a public statement; a declaration. **2.** an opinion; a judgment.

—[名] 1. 공고 2. 의견; 결정

***pro·nun·ci·a·tion** [prənʌ̀nsiéiʃ(ə)n] *n.* **1.** [U][C] the way of pronouncing sounds. **2.** [U] the act of pronouncing.

—[名] 1. 발음법 2. 발음

⁑**proof** [pru:f] *n.* (pl. **proofs**) **1.** [U] the act of showing that something is true or beyond doubt. ¶*in ~ of his innocence.*① **2.** [C] a fact that proves the truth of something; an evidence. ¶*produce a ~.*② **3.** [C] a test or an examination. ¶*The ~ of the pudding is in the eating.*③ **4.** [U] the tested strength of arms, etc.; the standard

—[名] 1. 증명, 입증 ¶①그의 무죄를 입증하기 위해서 2. 증거 ¶②증거를 제출하다 3. 시험, 음미(吟味) ¶③말보다 실증(實證) 4. [무기 따위의] 시험필의 강도(强度); [알코홀의] 표준 농도 5. 《法》 증거서류; 증언 6. 《印刷》 교정쇄

strength of alcohol. **5.** ⦅*pl.*⦆ (*Law*) documents used to prove something; testimony. **6.** [C] (*Printing*) an impression taken from type as a way to correct mistakes; (*Photography*) the first print taken from a negative.

(校正刷) 7. [사진의] 시험 인화(印畫)

—*adj.* **1.** strong or hard enough to resist something. ¶*This watch is ~ against water.* **2.** tested.

—[形] 1. …에 견디는, …을 통하지 못하게 하는 2. 검사필의, 보증된

-proof [-pru:f] a word element meaning *against*: *waterproof* (=that will not let water in or through).

—「…을 통하게 하지 않는, 내(耐)…, 방(防)…」의 뜻의 연결형

proof·read·er [prú:frì:dər] *n.* [C] a person who reads and corrects printed matter.

—[名] 교정원

prop [prɑp / prɔp] *vt.* (**propped** [prɑpt / prɔpt], **prop·ping**) **1.** support (something) by placing other thing against it. **2.** support; back up. **—*n.*** [C] a person or thing that supports another one. ¶*A good son is a ~ for one's old age.*①

—[他] 1. …을 버티다, 받치다 2. …을 지지하다 ¶①착한 아들은 늘그막에 의지가 된다

• **prop·a·gan·da** [prɑ̀pəgǽndə / prɔ̀p-] *n.* [U] **1.** plans or efforts to spread some opinion. **2.** an opinion or belief spread on purpose.

—[名] 1. 확장 운동, 선전 계획 2. 선전되는 주의(주장)

prop·a·gan·dist [prɑ̀pəgǽndist / prɔ̀p-] *n.* [C] a person who spreads some opinion or belief by means of a plan or method.

—[名] 선전자, 전도자

prop·a·gan·dize [prɑ̀pəgǽndaiz/prɔ̀pə-] *vt.* spread a principle, belief of (something). **—*vi.*** spread propaganda.

—[他] …을 선전하다, 포교하다 —[自] 포교하다

prop·a·gate [prɑ́pəgèit / prɔ́pə-] *vt.* **1.** increase the number of (plants or animals) naturally reproduce (a kind of animal or plant). **2.** spread (news, etc.). ¶*~ doctrines.*① **—*vi.*** **1.** reproduce one's species. **2.** (of news) go in all directions.

—[他] 1. …을 번식시키다; 증식시키다 2. …을 보급시키다 ¶①교리(教理)를 널리 알리다 —[自] 1. 번식(증식)하다 2. 보급하다

prop·a·ga·tion [prɑ̀pəgéiʃ(ə)n / prɔ̀p-] *n.* [U] **1.** the act of propagating; the state of being propagated. **2.** (of news) the act of spreading abroad. **3.** (of disease, heat, etc.) the state of being carried farther.

—[名] 1. 증식(增殖) 2. 보급 3. 전염

pro·pel [proupél] *vt.* (**-pelled, -pel·ling**) push forward; drive forward. ¶*~ a boat by rowing.*①

—[他] …을 밀다; 추진하다 ¶①저어서 보우트를 나아가게 하다

pro·pel·ler [proupélər] *n.* [C] **1.** a device with turning round blades for propelling an airplane. **2.** a person who propels.

—[名] 1. 프로펠러 2. 추진자(者)

pro·pen·si·ty [proupénsiti] *n.* [C] (pl. **-ties**) the way in which a person naturally feels and acts; a tendency. ¶*a ~ for gambling.*①

—[名] 경향; 성벽(性癖) ¶①도박벽

⁑ **prop·er** [prɑ́pər / prɔ́pə] *adj.* **1.** fit; suitable. ¶*Do it in the ~ way. / as you think ~.*① **2.** right; correct. ¶*a ~ way of making a sound.*② **3.** belonging to one thing and not to others; peculiar. ⦅*~ to* something⦆ ¶*a climate ~ to Korea*③ **4.** ⦅usu. placed after a ***noun***⦆ rightly so called; real. ¶ *England ~*④ / *literature ~ / in the ~ sense of the word.*⑤ **5.** modest; following etiquette. ¶*~ behavior.* **6.** (*colloq.*) complete.

—[形] 1. 적당한, 어울리는, 알맞은 ¶①적당히, 적절히 2. 올바른 ¶②소리를 내는 올바른 법 3. 독특한, 고유의 ¶③한국 고유의 기후 4. 엄밀한 의미에서의, 본래의, 진정한 ¶④영국 본토/⑤그 말의 엄밀한 의미에 있어서 5. 예의바른 6. ⦅口⦆ 순전한, 완전한

⁑ **prop·er·ly** [prɑ́pərli / prɔ́pəli] *adv.* **1.** in a proper manner; suitably. ¶*He ~ refused.*① **2.** correctly; fairly. ¶*behave ~ / ~ speaking; speaking ~; to speak ~.*②

—[副] 1. 적당히, 알맞게 ¶① 그가 거절한 것은 당연하다 2. 정확하게 ¶②정확히 말하면

prop·er·tied [prɑ́pərtid / prɔ́pət-] *adj.* possessing a great deal of money, land, etc. ¶*the ~ classes.*①

—[形] 재산이 있는 ¶①지주 계급

⁑ **prop·er·ty** [prɑ́pərti / prɔ́pəti] *n.* (pl. **-ties**) [U] ⦅*collectively*⦆ **1.** a thing or things possessed. ¶*own a large ~*① / *lose one's ~* ② **2.** the right of possession. ¶*literary ~.*③ **3.** property consisting of land and a house. ¶*a ~ owner.*④ **4.** a clear quality of a thing. ¶*a ~ of salt.*⑤ **5.** ⦅*pl.*⦆ a piece of furniture or an item of dress used on the stage. ¶*a ~ man.*⑥

—[名] 1. 소유물; 재산 ¶①재산이 있다/②재산을 없애다 2. 소유권 ¶③저작권 3. 소유지, 토지, 부동산 ¶④지주 4. 특성 ¶⑤소금의 특성 5. 소도구 ¶⑥소도구 계원

• **proph·e·cy** [prɑ́fisi / prɔ́f-] *n.* [C] (pl. **-cies**) the act of telling future events; something said about the future.

—[名] 예언하기; 예언

proph·e·sy [prɑ́fisài / prɔ́f-] *vt., vi.* (**-sied**) predict (something that will happen in the future); foretell (some-

—[他][自] 예언하다, 영감에 의하여 예언하다

thing) by means of help from God.

* **proph·et** [prɑ́fit / prɔ́f-] *n.* **1.** [C] a person who prophesies. **2.** ((*the P-*)) Mohammed. **3.** ((*the Prophets*)) the books in the Old Testament written by prophets.
—[名] 1. 예언자 2. 마호멧 3. 예언서

proph·et·ess [prɑ́fitis / prɔ́f-] *n.* [C] a woman prophet.
—[名] 여자 예언자

pro·phet·ic [proufétik] *adj.* **1.** of a prophet; containing a prophecy. **2.** telling something beforehand.
—[形] 1. 예언[자]의, 예언적인 2. 예언하는

pro·phy·lac·tic [pròufilǽktik] *adj.* serving to prevent disease. ¶ ~ *treatment.*① —*n.* [C] a medicine or treatment which prevents disease.
—[形] 질병 예방의 ¶①예방 조치 —[名] 예방약; 예방법, 예방 조치

pro·pin·qui·ty [proupíŋkwiti] *n.* [U] **1.** nearness in time and place. **2.** nearness of blood; likeness.
—[名] 1. 가까움 2. 근친; 유사(類似)

pro·pi·ti·ate [prəpíʃièit] *vt.* gain the good will of (someone); make (some angry person) quiet or calm.
—[他] …의 비위를 맞추다, …을 달래다

pro·pit·i·a·tion [prəpìʃiéiʃ(ə)n] *n.* [U] the act of propitiating.
—[名] 달래기, 비위 맞추기

pro·pi·ti·a·to·ry [prəpíʃiətɔ̀:ri / -ət(ə)ri] *adj.* serving to calm someone or make him friendly.
—[形] 비위를 맞추는, 화해의

pro·pi·tious [prəpíʃəs] *adj.* **1.** favorable. **2.** favorably inclined. ¶*a ~ sign.*①
—[形] 1. 호의를 갖고 있는 2. 상서로운, 행운의 ¶①길조(吉兆)

: pro·por·tion [prəpɔ́:rʃ(ə)n] *n.* **1.** [U] the amount of one thing measured in relation to another. ¶*a ~ of five to one*① / *the ~ of births to the population.*② **2.** [U] the well-balanced arrangement of parts. **3.** ((*pl.*)) the space that a thing occupies; length, width or thickness. **4.** [C] the part belonging to each one. ¶*The workmen receive a ~ of the profits.*③
—[名] 1. 비율 ¶①1 대 5의 비/②인구에 대한 출생률 2. 균형, 조화, 균정(均整) 3. 크기, 부피, 용적 4. 배당, 몫 ¶③노동자는 이익의 일부를 받는다

1) ***in proportion,*** well-balanced.
2) ***in proportion to*** (or ***as***), in proper relation to; in balance with.
3) ***out of proportion,*** unbalanced.

[熟] 1)균형잡힌 2)…에 비례하여 3)균형잡히지 않은

—*vt.* **1.** make (something) in proper proportion; set (something) just right. **2.** divide and give out (something) in fair shares.
—[他] 1. 균형잡히게 하다 2. …을 할당하다

pro·por·tion·al [prəpɔ́:rʃən(ə)l] *adj.* in proportion. ¶*be directly ~ to.*①
—[形] 균형잡힌 ¶①…에 정비례하다

pro·por·tion·ate [prəpɔ́:rʃ(ə)nit] *adj.* in proper proportion; proportional. —*vt.* make (something) proportional. ▷**pro·por·tion·ate·ly** [-li] *adv.*
—[形] 균형잡힌 —[他] …을 균형시키다

* **pro·pos·al** [prəpóuz(ə)l] *n.* **1.** [U][C] the act of offering something; a proposed method or scheme. ¶*a compromise ~.*① **2.** [C] an offer of marriage.
—[名] 1. 신청, 제의; 계획, 안(案) ¶①타협안 2. 결혼의 신청, 구혼

: pro·pose [prəpóuz] *vt.* **1.** offer (a plan) for consideration or acceptance. ¶*I ~ that we* [*should*] *go at once.*① **2.** name (someone) as a candidate for an office for membership in a club, etc. ¶~ *someone for membership.*② **3.** intend; plan. ¶~ *to dine out.* —*vi.* **1.** make an offer of marriage. **2.** suggest a plan. **3.** form a plan.
—[他] 1. …을 제안하다 ¶①곧 가는 것이 어떨까 2. …을 지명하다 ¶②남을 회원으로 추천하다 3. …을 꾀하다 —[自] 1. 결혼을 신청하다 2. 제안하다 3. 계획하다

* **prop·o·si·tion** [prɑ̀pəzíʃ(ə)n / prɔ̀p-] *n.* [C] **1.** something that is proposed. **2.** something stated. **3.** a rule that can be proved to be true. **4.** a problem to be solved. **5.** a task undertaken.
—[名] 1. 제안 2. 진술 3. 정리(定理) 4. 명제(命題) 5. 일

pro·pound [prəpáund] *vt.* offer (something) for consideration. ¶~ *a question.*
—[他] …을 제출하다, 제안하다

pro·pri·e·tar·y [prəpráiətèri / -t(ə)ri] *adj.* **1.** possessing. **2.** having much money, land, etc. ¶~ *class.*① **3.** possessed by a certain private person or company. ¶~ *rights.*② —*n.* **1.** [C] a person who owns; a group of such persons. **2.** [U] the right of possession.
—[形] 1. 소유의 2. 재산이 있는 ¶①유산계급 3. 독점의 ¶②소유권 —[名] 1. 소유자; 소유 단체 2. 소유권

* **pro·pri·e·tor** [prəpráiətər] *n.* [C] an owner; a person who possesses a shop, factory, etc. ¶*a landed ~.*①
—[名] 소유자; 경영자 ¶①지주

pro·pri·e·tress [prəpráiətris] *n.* [C] a woman proprietor.
—[名] 여자 소유자

pro·pri·e·ty [prəpráiəti] *n.* (pl. **-ties**) **1.** [U] the state or quality of being proper or fitting. **2.** ((*pl.*)) proper manners and customs kept by polite people. ¶*observe the proprieties.*①
—[名] 1. 적당, 타당 2. 예의바름; 예절 ¶①예의범절을 지키다

pro·pul·sion [prəpʌ́lʃ(ə)n] *n.* [U] **1.** the act of pushing forward. **2.** a pushing force.
—[名] 1. 추진 2. 추진력

propulsive [908] prostitute

pro·pul·sive [prəpʌ́lsiv] *adj.* pushing (something) more forward by force. ¶~ *force.*① ⌈roguing a meeting.⌉
—形 추진력이 있는 ¶①추진력

pro·ro·ga·tion [pròurəgéiʃ(ə)n] *n.* ⓊⒸ the act of pro-
—名 폐회, 정회(停會)

pro·rogue [prəróug] *vt., vi.* break off the meetings of (a lawmaking body, esp. the British Parliament) for a while. ⌈fanciful; dull; common.⌉
—他自 …을 폐회하다

pro·sa·ic [prouzéiik] *adj.* (of sentences) ordinary; not
—形 산문[체]의, 산문적인; 지루한,

pro·sa·ic·al·ly [prouzéiikəli] *adv.* in a prosaic manner.
—副 산문적으로, 평범하게 [평범한]

pro·sce·ni·a [prousí:niə] *n.* pl. of proscenium.

pro·sce·ni·um [prousí:niəm] *n.* Ⓒ (pl. -ums or -ni·a) the part of a stage in front of the curtain.
—名 앞무대

pro·scribe [prouskráib] *vt.* **1.** forbid (someone) to do something; forbid someone (to do something). **2.** put (someone) outside the protection of the law. **3.** force (someone) to go away.
—他 1. …에게 금지하다, …을 금하다 2. …을 법률의 보호 밖에 두다 3. …을 추방하다

prose [prouz] *n.* Ⓤ **1.** the usual style of spoken or written language. **2.** uninteresting talk. ——*adj.* **1.** belonging to prose; like prose. **2.** common; not fanciful. ——*vi., vt.* speak or write (something) in a long and tiring manner.
—名 1. 산문[체] 2. 시시한 이야기
—形 1. 산문의; 산문적인 2. 평범한
—自他 무미건조하게 이야기하다(쓰다)

pros·e·cute [prásikjù:t / prɔ́s-] *vt.* **1.** bring (someone) before a court of law. ¶~ *someone for theft.*① **2.** complete (a task). **3.** continue (a business, a task, etc.). ¶~ *one's studies.*②
——*vi.* blame someone for a crime.
—他 1. …을 기소하다, 고소하다 ¶① …을 절도죄로 기소하다 2. …을 수행하다 3. …을 속행하다 ¶②연구를 계속하다
—自 기소하다

pros·e·cu·tion [pràsikjú:ʃ(ə)n / prɔ̀s-] *n.* **1.** ⓊⒸ the act of prosecuting someone. **2.** Ⓤ Ⓒ (*the* ~) the group of persons that begins a legal prosecution against someone. **3.** Ⓤ the act of carrying on.
—名 1. 기소 2. 기소자측, 검찰 3. 수행

pros·e·cu·tor [p.ásikjù:tər / prósikjú:tə] *n.* Ⓒ **1.** a law official who works against a prosecuted person. **2.** a person who prosecutes someone.
—名 1. 검찰관 2. 기소자

pros·e·lyte [prásilait / prɔ́s-] *n.* Ⓒ a person who has changed from one belief or opinion to another. ——*vt., vi.* change or make (someone) change his opinions or belief. ⌈change from one belief to another.⌉
—名 개종자(改宗者), 전향자 —他自 개종시키다(하다)

pros·e·lyt·ize [prásilitàiz / prɔ́s-] *vt.* make (someone)
—他 …을 개종(전향)시키다

pros·o·dy [prásədi / prɔ́s-] *n.* Ⓤ the science or study of the style of poetry.
—名 작시법(作詩法)

: **pros·pect** [práspekt / prɔ́s-] *n.* **1.** ⓊⒸ something looked forward to or expected; the act of expecting. **2.** ⓊⒸ an outlook for the future. ¶*I see no ~ of his success.*① *The ~ is gloomy.*② **3.** Ⓒ a possible customer. **4.** Ⓒ a view or scene that is seen. ¶*The window has a southern ~.*③
——*vt., vi.* search or examine (a place) for minerals.
—名 1. 예상되는 일; 기대 2. 전망, 가망 ¶①그가 성공할 가망은 없다/②전망이 흐리다 3. 고객이 될 성싶은 손님 4. 조망(眺望), 경치 ¶③그 창은 남향이다
—他自 시굴(試掘)하다, 답사하다

pro·spec·tive [prəspéktiv] *adj.* likely to happen; expected; concerned with the future.
—形 예상되는; 미래의; 장래에 관한

pros·pec·tor [práspektər / prəspéktə] *n.* Ⓒ a person who searches or examines a place, for minerals.
—名 탐광자(探鑛者); 투기자

pro·spec·tus [prəspéktəs] *n.* Ⓒ a short printed account giving information about the activities of an enterprise, a school, etc.
—名 취지서; 사업계획 요강; [학교 따위의] 안내서

• **pros·per** [práspər / prɔ́spə] *vi.* succeed; flourish. ——*vt.* make (something) successful or prosperous.
—自 성공하다; 번영하다 —他 …을 성공시키다, 번영시키다

: **pros·per·i·ty** [prəspériti / prɔs-] *n.* Ⓤ the state of being prosperous; good luck; success. ↔adversity
—名 번영; 행운; 성공

• **pros·per·ous** [práspərəs / prɔ́s-] *adj.* successful; fortunate; flourishing; favorable; helpful. ¶*in a ~ hour.*
—形 성공한; 행운의; 번창하는; 형편이 좋은, 도움이 되는

pros·ti·tute [prástitjù:t / prɔ́s-] *n.* Ⓒ **1.** an immoral woman who offers her body for money. **2.** a person who does base things for money. ——*vt.* put (something) to wrong or base uses; sell (one's body, talent, etc.) for money.
—名 1. 매춘부 2. 금전에 좌우되는 사람 —他 …을 악용하다, [몸·재능을] 돈을 위해서 팔다

prostitution

pros·ti·tu·tion [prɑ̀stitjúːʃ(ə)n / prɔ̀s-] *n.* Ⓤ the act of prostituting; the state of being prostituted; a base or wrong use, as of one's abilities.
— 图 매춘; 지조를 팔기; [재능 따위의] 악용

pros·trate *vt.* [prǽstreit / prɔstréit → *adj.*] **1.** lay (something) flat on the ground. ¶*~ oneself*① / *trees prostrated by the gust.*② **2.** make (someone) tired; exhaust. ¶*He was prostrated by the heat.*③ —*adj.* [*Brit.* prɔ́streit] **1.** lying face down. **2.** lying flat on one's back. ¶*lie ~.* **3.** utterly exhausted; powerless; helpless.
— 卧 1. …을 넘어뜨리다 ¶①부복하다, 굴복하다/②돌풍에 쓰러진 나무 2. …을 지쳐빠지게 하다 ¶③그는 더위에 지쳐 버렸다 —卧 1. 부복한 2. 발딱 쓰러진 3. 지쳐빠진; 무력한

pros·tra·tion [prɑstréiʃ(ə)n / prɔs-] *n.* Ⓤ Ⓒ the act of prostrating; the state of being prostrated; Ⓤ great weariness.
— 图 부복, 굴복; 피로, 쇠약, 의기소침

pros·y [próuzi] *adj.* (**pros·i·er, pros·i·est**) of or like prose; not interesting or pleasant; long and dull.
— 卧 산문의(같은); 흥미없는; 평범한; 지루한, 장황한

pro·tag·o·nist [proutǽgənist] *n.* Ⓒ **1.** the most important character in a novel, play, etc. **2.** a person taking a leading part in any movement.
— 图 1. [극·소설 따위의] 주역, 주인공 2. 주창자

pro·te·an [próutiən, + *Brit.* proutíːən] *adj.* changeable like Proteus; able to assume many shapes and forms.
— 卧 [Proteus신처럼] 변화무쌍한

: pro·tect [prətékt] *vt.* defend (someone or something) from danger, injury, etc.; guard. 《*~ someone* or *something from* or *against*》 ¶*~ home industries*① / *~ one's friend from* (or *against*) *temptation.*②
— 卧 …을 [위험 따위에서] 보호하다, 지키다 ¶①국내 산업을 보호하다/② 친구를 유혹에서 지키다

: pro·tec·tion [prətékʃ(ə)n] *n.* **1.** Ⓤ the act of protecting; the state of being protected. ¶*put oneself under someone's ~*① / *take someone under one's ~*② / *She went there under the ~ of policemen.*③ **2.** Ⓤ the system of protecting home industries by laying taxes on imported goods. **3.** Ⓒ a person or thing that protects. 《*~ from* or *against*》 ¶*a ~ against the sun.*④
— 图 1. 보호, 방어, 방위 ¶①남의 비호(庇護)를 받다/②남을 비호하다/③그녀는 경관의 보호를 받으며 그곳으로 갔다 2. 보호무역 제도 3. 보호자(물) ¶④차양

pro·tec·tion·ism [prətékʃənlzəm] *n.* Ⓤ the economic principle of protection; the system protecting domestic industries by laying taxes on imported goods.
— 图 보호무역 주의; 보호무역 정책

pro·tec·tion·ist [prətékʃənist] *n.* Ⓒ a person who supports protectionism. —*adj.* of or favoring protectionism; of a protectionist.
— 图 보호무역 주의자 — 卧 보호무역 주의[자]의

pro·tec·tive [prətéktiv] *adj.* giving protection; guarding; defensive. ¶*~ custody*① / *~ trade.*②
— 卧 보호하는; 지키는 ¶①보호 감금/②보호 무역

• **pro·tec·tor** [prətéktər] *n.* Ⓒ **1.** a person or thing that protects; a guardian. **2.** (*Brit. History*) a person who rules the kingdom in place of a king or queen; a regent.
— 图 1. 보호자(물) 2.〈英史〉섭정(攝政)

pro·tec·tor·ate [prətéktərit] *n.* Ⓒ the country which is governed or controlled by a strong nation.
— 图 보호국, 보호령

pro·tec·tress [prətéktris] *n.* Ⓒ a woman who protects.
— 图 여자 보호자

pro·te·ge [próuteʒèi] *n.* Ⓒ a person who is under the protection of another. ⇒N.B.
— 图 피(被)보호자 N.B. 여성형은 protegee

pro·teid [próutiːd] *n.* = protein.

pro·tein [próutiː(i)n] *n.* Ⓒ Ⓤ an important compound essential to all living animals and plants, found in all foods.
— 图 단백질

: pro·test *v.* [prətést → *n.*] *vt.* **1.** express an objection against (something); object to. ¶*~ the heavy taxes.*① **2.** declare or affirm solemnly. 《*~ that…*》 ¶*~ someone's innocence; ~ that someone is innocent.*② —*vi.* **1.** express an objection. 《*~ against* something》 ¶*~ against a decision.*③ **2.** say positively; declare.
—*n.* [próutest] Ⓤ Ⓒ the act of protesting; an expression of objection. ¶*He made a ~ against the judgment.*④
— 卧 1. …에게 항의하다, …에 이의를 신립하다 ¶①무거운 세금에 항의하다 2. …을 단언하다, 주장하다 ¶②남의 무죄를 단언하다 —自 1. 항의하다 ¶③결정에 항의하다 2. 단언하다
— 图 항의; 단언 ¶④그는 그 판결에 이의를 신립했다

• **Prot·es·tant** [prɑ́tist(ə)nt / prɔ́t-] *n.* Ⓒ a member of any of the Christian churches divided from the Roman Catholic church in the 16th century.
—*adj.* of Protestants or Protestantism.
— 图 신교도
— 卧 신교[도]의

Prot·es·tant·ism [prɑ́tist(ə)ntìz(ə)m / prɔ́t-] *n.* Ⓤ the religion or principles of Protestants.
— 图 신교

prot·es·ta·tion [pròutestéiʃ(ə)n, + *U.S.* prɑ̀t-] *n.* Ⓤ Ⓒ
— 图 항의; 단언

the act of protesting; a formal expression of disagreement; a strong or solemn statement.

Pro·teus [próutiəs, -tju:s] *n.* (in Greek mythology) a sea god who can change his appearance very easily. —명 프로테우스

pro·to·col [próutəkàl / -kɔ̀l] *n.* **1.** ⓒ an original draft of a treaty, negotiation, etc. **2.** ⓤ the rules of etiquette, esp. in diplomacy. —명 1. 조약 원안; 의정서(議定書) 2. 의례(儀禮)

pro·ton [próutan] *n.* ⓒ the tiny positive unit of electricity forming a part of an atom. —명 양자(陽子)

pro·to·plasm [próutəplæz(ə)m] *n.* ⓤ the jelly-like, essential material of living animal and plant cells; the living substance in such cells. —명 원형질(原形質)

pro·to·type [próutoutàip] *n.* ⓒ the original form of anything; a fine example; a pattern; a model. —명 원형(原型), 모범, 견본

pro·to·zo·an [pròutəzóuən] *n.* ⓒ any of a number of animals composed of a single cell. —*adj.* of a protozoan. —명 원생(原生)동물 —형 원생동물의

pro·tract [proutrǽkt] *vt.* **1.** make (something) longer in time; prolong; lengthen. ¶ ~ *a discussion.* **2.** stretch or thrust out; extend. **3.** draw (something) with a scale and protractor. —타 1. …을 질질 끌다, 늘이다 2. …을 내밀다; 뻗다 3. [분도기로] …을 제도(製圖)하다

pro·trac·tion [proutrǽkʃ(ə)n] *n.* ⓤⓒ **1.** the act of protracting; the state of being protracted. **2.** the act of drawing a figure, plan, etc. with a scale and protractor. —명 1. 질질 끌기; 연장 2. 제도, 도면을 뜨기

pro·trac·tor [proutrǽktər] *n.* ⓒ **1.** a person or thing that protracts. **2.** an instrument for measuring angles. —명 1. 질질 끄는 사람(것) 2. 분도기

pro·trude [proutrú:d] *vt., vi.* stick out; thrust forth; extend forward; jut out. —타자 돌출[하게]하다. 비어져 나오[게 하]다

pro·tru·sion [proutrú:ʒ(ə)n] *n.* **1.** ⓤ the act of protruding; the state of being protruded. **2.** ⓒ a protruding part. —명 1. 돌출, 비어져나오기 2. 융기[부]

pro·tru·sive [proutrú:siv] *adj.* thrusting forward; projecting. —형 밀어내는; 내민, 튀어나온

pro·tu·ber·ance [prout(j)ú:b(ə)rəns / -tjú:-] *n.* **1.** ⓤ the state of being protuberant. **2.** ⓒ a thing which sticks out; a knob. —명 1. 융기, 돌기 2. 돌기부, 혹, 결절(結節)

pro·tu·ber·ant [prout(j)ú:b(ə)rənt / -tjú:-] *adj.* sticking out; swelling outward; projecting. —형 돌출한, 돌기가 있는; 불룩하게 올라온

‡ **proud** [praud] *adj.* **1.** feeling or showing proper pleasure or satisfaction; highly pleased. 《~ *of;* ~ *to do*》¶ *The father was* ~ *of his son's success.*① / *We are* ~ *to fight for our country.* **2.** thinking well or making much of oneself. ¶ ~ *ladies.* **3.** making much of one's honor; self-respecting. ¶ ~ *poverty*② / *be too* ~ *to beg.*③ **4.** giving reason to be praised. ¶ *the proudest moment of my life.*④ **5.** (of things) looking splendid or magnificent. ¶ *The* ~ *building towered over the huts.* —형 1. 자랑하는, 뽐내는; 영광(명예)으로 여기는 ¶①그 부친은 자식의 성공을 자랑으로 여기고 있었다 2. 거만한 3. 명예를 존중하는, 자존심이 있는 ¶②청빈(淸貧)/③비력질을 하기에는 자존심이 허락치 않다 4. 영광으로 여겨야 할 ¶④내 생애에서 가장 자랑으로 여기는 시기 5. 훌륭한, 당당한

do someone proud, (*colloq.*) do something which causes someone else to feel proud or honored. ¶ *You do me* ~.⑤ 國 (口) …을 기쁘게 하다, 만족시키다 ¶⑤더 없는 영광입니다

* **proud·ly** [práudli] *adv.* in a proud manner; with pride. —부 뽐내어, 자랑스러운 듯이, 당당[하게]

prov·a·ble [prú:vəbl] *adj.* that can be proved. —형 증명할 수 있는

‡ **prove** [pru:v] *v.* (**proved, proved** or **prov·en**) *vt.* **1.** show (something) to be true; make (something) sure. 《~ *that* …; ~ *someone* or *something to be*》¶ ~ *someone's innocence*① / *I can* ~ *that what he says is true.*② / *He has been proved* [*to be*] *wrong.*③ / *He proved himself* [*to be*] *worthy of confidence.*④ **2.** test (something) by experiment. —*vi.* turn out to be; be found to be. 《~ *to be*》 —타 1. …을 증명하다, 입증하다 ¶①남이 무죄임을 증명하다/② 그의 말이 진실임을 증명할 수 있다/③그가 틀렸음이 입증되었다/④그는 신뢰할 만함을 입증했다 2. …을 시험하다 —자 …이 되다, …임을 알게 되다

prov·en [prú:v(ə)n] *v.* (*archaic* or *U.S.*) pp. of **prove.**

prov·en·der [právindər / próvində] *n.* ⓤ coarse dried food, esp. for horses, cattle, etc. —명 여물

* **prov·erb** [právərb / próvəb] *n.* ⓒ **1.** a short, wise and usu. —명 1. 속담, 금언 ¶①[구약성경의] 잠

traditional saying that expresses a truth. ¶*the* [*Books of*] *Proverbs*① | *as the ~ says* (or *goes*).② **2.** a person or thing wellknown to be typical of a certain character; a byword. ¶*to a ~*③ | *His ignorance is a ~.*④

언(箴言)/②속담에 있듯이 **2.** 어떤 사람(것)으로 알려진 사람(것);웃음거리 ¶③소문이 날 만큼/④그의 무식은 소문났다

pro·ver·bi·al [prəvə́:rbiəl] *adj.* **1.** of or like a proverb. ¶*~ wisdom.*① **2.** widely or generally known.

—[形] 1. 속담의(같은) ¶①속담 2. 널리 알려진

pro·ver·bi·al·ly [prəvə́:rbiəli] *adv.* by means of a proverb; as known in a proverb; notoriously.

—[副] 속담대로; 널리 [알려져서]

: pro·vide [prəváid] *vt.* **1.** get ready or make preparations for (something); prepare. 《~ something *for*》 ¶*~ a meal*① | *~ food for a voyage.* **2.** give (food, etc. needed); supply. 《~ someone *with*; ~ something *for* or *to*》 ¶*~ one's child with clothes*② | *This house is not provided with a veranda.*③ **3.** (of a rule, etc.) declare (a matter) to be necessary. 《~ *that*》 ¶*The club's rules ~ that dues must be paid monthly.* **—*vi.*** **1.** make preparations. 《~ *for* or *against* something》 ¶*~ against danger*④ | *~ for old age.* **2.** give what is necessary. 《~ *for* someone》 ¶*~ for one's family.*

—[他] 1. …을 준비하다, 마련하다 ¶①식사 준비를 하다 2. [필요품]을 공급하다, 주다 ¶②아이에게 옷을 주다/③이 집에는 베란다가 없다 3. [규칙 따위가] …을 규정하다 —[自] 1. 준비하다; 대비하다 ¶④위험에 대비하다 2. 필요한 것을 주다, 부양하다

pro·vid·ed [prəváidid] *conj.* on the condition that …; if. 《~ *that* …》 ¶*Provided* [*that*] *it is true, you may go.*

—[接] …이라는 조건으로; 만일 …이라면

• prov·i·dence [prάvid(ə)ns / prɔ́v-] *n.* [U] **1.** 《often *P*-》 the care or guidance of God; God. **2.** prudent care or preparation for the future; foresight.

—[名] 1. 섭리, 신의(神意); 하늘의 도움; 신 2. 장래에 대한 배려; 선견지명

prov·i·dent [prάvid(ə)nt / prɔ́v-] *adj.* **1.** having foresight. **2.** cautious. **3.** economical; saving.

—[形] 1. 선견지명이 있는 2. 조심성 깊은 3. 검소한

prov·i·den·tial [prὰvidénʃ(ə)l / prɔ̀v-] *adj.* **1.** having good fortune; lucky; fortunate. **2.** of or by God's will.

—[形] 1. 행운의 2. 신의(神意)에 의한

pro·vid·ing [prəváidiŋ] *conj.* =provided.

: prov·ince [prάvins / prɔ́v-] *n.* [C] **1.** a large division of certain countries. **2.** 《*pl.*》 an area remote from the capital or largest cities. ¶*in the provinces.*① **3.** a sphere or field of action, knowledge, business, etc.; a section; a department. ¶*It is not* [*in, within*] *my ~.*②

—[名] 1. 주(州), 도(道), 성(省) 2. 지방, 시골 ¶①시골에서 3. 직분; 범위; 영역; 분야 ¶②그것은 내 분야가 아니다

pro·vin·cial [prəvínʃ(ə)l] *adj.* **1.** of or belonging to a province. ¶*a ~ tour.*① **2.** having or showing the manners, viewpoints, etc. of people living in the country; rustic. ¶*~ accents.*② **3.** not polished; rude; narrow. **—*n.*** [C] **1.** a person living in a province or the provinces. **2.** an uncultivated, rude person.

—[形] 1. 주(州)의, 나라의; 지방의, 시골의 ¶①지방 순회 2. 시골 같은 ¶②시골 사투리 3. 촌스러운, 편협한

—[名] 1. 지방민, 시골 사람 2. 촌스러운 사람

pro·vin·cial·ism [prəvínʃəlìz(ə)m] *n.* [C][U] **1.** the state of being provincial. **2.** a provincial manner, idea, way of speech, etc. **3.** an example of narrowness of viewpoint or outlook. **4.** a word, an accent, or a phrase, etc. peculiar to a certain province.

—[名] 1. 시골풍; 지방성 2. 시골풍의 일(것) 3. 편협 4. 시골 사투리, 방언

: pro·vi·sion [prəvíʒ(ə)n] *n.* **1.** [U][C] careful preparation; arrangement made, esp. for the future. 《~ *against* or *for*》 ¶*make ~ against* (or *for*) *a rainy day.*① **2.** [C] 《often *pl.*》 something prepared or provided; food. ¶*run out* (or *short*) *of provisions.*② **3.** [C] a condition or clause in a law. **—*vt.*** supply (someone) with food.

—[名] 1. 준비; 대비 ¶①만일의 경우에 대비하다 2. 저장품;식료품 ¶②식량이 없어지다 3. [법률의] 조항 —[他] …에 식량을 대주다

pro·vi·sion·al [prəvíʒən(ə)l] *adj.* of temporary arrangement; lasting for only a short time. ¶*a ~ agreement.*①

—[形] 일시적인, 임시의, 가(假)… ¶①가조약

pro·vi·so [prəváizou] *n.* (pl. **-sos** or **-soes**) [C] a sentence that states a condition in a legal document or other agreement; a condition. ¶*with* [*a*] *~.*①

—[名] 단서(但書), 조건 ¶①조건부로

prov·o·ca·tion [prὰvəkéiʃ(ə)n / prɔ̀v-] *n.* **1.** [U] the act of provoking. **2.** [C] something that stirs up anger, resentment, etc. ¶*feel ~*① | *give ~*② | *under ~.*③

—[名] 1. 성나게 하기, 도발 2. 화나게 하는 것 ¶①성내다/②성나게 하다/③도발당하여

pro·voc·a·tive [prouvάkətiv / -vɔ́k-] *adj.* exciting to anger; stirring up action, feeling, etc.; stimulating. ¶*be ~ of curiosity.* **—*n.*** [C] something that provokes.

—[形] [남을] 성나게 하는; 도발적인;자극하는 —[名] 성나게 하는(도발하는) 것

• pro·voke [prəvóuk] *vt.* make (someone) angry; stir up (someone's actions, feelings, etc.); irritate; excite. 《~

—[他] …을 화나게 하다;[행동·감정 따위]를 불러 일으키다; …을 약올리다;

P

someone *to do*; ~ someone *into doing*》 ¶~ *sorrow* (*laughter*) | ~ *someone to anger* | *His haughty manner provoked me into discharging him at once.*① — 흥분시키다 ¶①그의 거만한 태도에 화가 나서 당장 그를 해고했다

pro·vok·ing [prəvóukiŋ] *adj.* that provokes; exciting to anger; annoying; irritating. ¶~ *children* | ~ *words.* — —[形] 화나는, 약오르는, 지긋지긋한; 귀찮은

prov·ost [právəst, próuv- / prɔ́v-] *n.* [C] **1.** the head of certain colleges, universities or churches. **2.** the chief magistrate in certain towns of Scotland; a mayor. — —[名] 1. 대학 학장; 사제장(司祭長) 2. [스코틀랜드의] 시장(市長)

prow [prau] *n.* [C] **1.** the front part of a boat or ship; something like it. **2.** the forward part of an airplane. — —[名] 1. 이물, 뱃머리; 뱃머리 모양의 것 2. 기수(機首)

prow·ess [práuis] *n.* [U] **1.** courage; bravery; brave or valorous actions. **2.** great ability or skill. — —[名] 1. 무용(武勇); 용감[한 행위] 2. 훌륭한 솜씨

prowl [praul] *vi., vt.* walk about slowly or cautiously looking for something to eat or steal; wander; roam. 《~ *about* or *around* a place》 —*n.* [C] the act of prowling. ¶*take a* ~.① — —[自][他] 기웃거리다, 찾아 돌아다니다; 헤매다 —[名] 헤매기, 기웃거리기 ¶① 배회하다

prox. proximo.

prox·i·mate [práksimit / prɔ́k-] *adj.* **1.** nearest in time, place, etc. ¶*the house* ~ *to the river.*① **2.** almost the same; nearly correct; approximate. — —[形] 1. …에 가장 가까운 ¶①강에 가까운 집 2. 근사(近似)의

prox·im·i·ty [praksímiti / prɔk-] *n.* [U] closeness; nearness. — —[名] 근접

prox·i·mo [práksimòu / prɔ́k-] *adj.* of or in the next month. ⇒[N.B.] ¶*on the 6th* ~. — —[形] 내달에 [N.B.] prox.로 줄임

prox·y [práksi / prɔ́ksi] *n.* (pl. **prox·ies**) **1.** [U] the act or authority of taking the place of another. **2.** [C] a person or company that acts for another. **3.** [C] a document giving the authority to act or vote for another. — —[名] 1. 대리, 대리권 2. 대리인; 대리점 3. 위임장

prude [pru:d] *n.* [C] a person, esp. a woman, who is extremely modest or proper in manners, speech, etc. — —[名] 예의범절에 까다로운 사람, 얌전빼는 사람

pru·dence [prú:d(ə)ns] *n.* [U] **1.** knowledge and good judgment. **2.** wisdom in a keen, practical sense. — —[名] 1. 사려 분별[이 있음] 2. 빈틈없음

***pru·dent** [prú:d(ə)nt] *adj.* taking careful thought for the future; thoughtful; careful in speech and action. — —[形] 신중한, 사려 분별이 있는, 조심성 깊은; 빈틈없는

pru·den·tial [pru(:)dénʃ(ə)l] *adj.* careful in speech and action; cautious; thoughtful. — —[形] 신중한, 조심성 있는, 분별있는

pru·dent·ly [prú:d(ə)ntli] *adv.* in a prudent manner. — —[副] 조심성 있게; 빈틈없이

prud·er·y [prú:dəri] *n.* (pl. **-er·ies**) [U] the state of being extremely proper or modest; an example of this. — —[名] 얌전빼기; 예의범절에 까다로움

prud·ish [prú:diʃ] *adj.* extremely proper or modest. — —[形] 예의범절에 까다로운

***prune**[1] [pru:n] *n.* [C] a kind of dried plum. — —[名] 말린 오얏

prune[2] [pru:n] *vt.* **1.** cut away worthless parts from (something). **2.** cut unnecessary twigs or branches from (a tree, etc.). **3.** take away (something). — —[他] 1. …의 쓸데 없는 것을 베어내다 2. [나무]의 불필요한 가지를 치다 3. …을 베어내다

prun·ers [prú:nərz] *n. pl.* pruning scissors; a tool used for pruning. ⇒fig. — —[名] 전지(剪枝) 가위

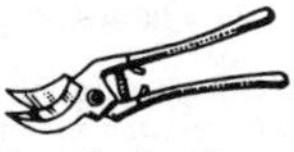

〔pruners〕

pruning hook [prú:niŋhùk] *n.* [C] an edged tool used for pruning twigs. — —[名] 전지용 낫

pru·ri·ent [prúəriənt] *adj.* full of lustful desire; not pure; indecent. — —[形] 호색적인, 외설스러운

Prus·sia [prʌ́ʃə] *n.* a former state of Germany, in the northern part. — —[名] 프러시아(구독일연방의 한 나라)

Prus·sian [prʌ́ʃ(ə)n] *n.* [C] a person of Prussia. —*adj.* of Prussia or Prussians. — —[名] 프러시아 사람 —[形] 프러시아[사람]의

prus·sic acid [prʌ́sikǽsid] *n.* a deadly poisonous acid. — —[名] 청산(青酸)

pry[1] [prai] *vi.* (**pried**) look closely or curiously. ¶~ *into other people's affairs.*① —*n.* [C] (pl. **pries**) a person who attempts to gain information by questions. — —[自] 들여다보다, 훔쳐보다, 꼬치꼬치 캐다 ¶①남의 일을 꼬치꼬치 캐다 —[名] 꼬치꼬치 캐는 사람

pry[2] [prai] *vt.* (**pried**) **1.** lift up (something) with a lever. **2.** gain (something) by making a hard try. —*n.* [C] (pl. **pries**) a lever. — —[他] 1. …을 지레로 들어 올리다 2. …을 간신히 입수하다 —[名] 지레

P.S., p.s. postscript.

***psalm** [sa:m] *n.* [C] **1.** a sacred song or hymn. **2.** 《*a P*~》 one of the sacred songs in the Old Testament. **3.** 《*the P*~*s*》 the book of the Old Testament consisting of 150 psalms. — —[名] 1. 찬미가, 성가 2. 시편(詩篇) 중의 한 편 3. 시편

psalm·ist [sá:mist] *n.* [C] **1.** a person who writes psalms — —[名] 1. 찬미가 작자 2. [시편 작자인]

2. 《*the P~*》 David, as the author of the Psalms. — 다윗왕

psal·mo·dy [sǽlmədi, sá:m-] *n.* (pl. **-dies**) **1.** [U] the act of singing psalms. **2.** 《*collectively*》 a book of psalms. —[名] 1. 성가 영창 2. 찬송가집

psal·ter [sɔ́:ltər] *n.* **1.** 《*the P-*》 the Book of Psalms. **2.** [C] a prayer book containing any special version of the Psalms. —[名] 1. 시편 2. [기도용의] 시편

pseu·do·nym [sú:dənim / (p)s(j)ú:d-] *n.* [C] a name used by a writer in place of his real name; a pen name. —[名] 필명, 아호(雅號)

Psy·che [sáiki(:)] *n.* **1.** (in Greek mythology) the soul, represented as a beautiful girl loved by Cupid. **2.** [C] 《*p-*》 the soul or mind of a human. —[名] 1. 사이키 2. 영혼, 정신

psy·chi·a·trist [saikáiətrist] *n.* [C] a doctor treating mental diseases. —[名] 정신과 의사, 정신병 학자

psy·chi·a·try [saikáiətri] *n.* [U] the treatment and healing of mental diseases. —[名] 정신병학, 정신병 치료법

psy·chic [sáikik] *adj.* **1.** of the soul or spirit. **2.** beyond recognized laws of physics. **3.** easily influenced by psychic effect. —*n.* [C] **1.** a person who is easily influenced by supernatural forces. **2.** a person able to receive messages from the spirits of the dead. —[形] 1. 영혼의; 정신의 2. 심령적(心靈的)인 3. 심령작용을 받기 쉬운 —[名] 1. 심령 현상을 잘 느끼는 사람 2. 영매(靈媒); 무녀(巫女)

psy·chi·cal [sáikik(ə)l] *adj.* psychic; mental. —[形] 영혼의; 심령의; 정신상의

psy·cho·a·nal·y·sis [sàikouənǽlisis] *n.* [U] a method for treating certain mental disorders; a branch of psychology which studies the unconscious. —[名] 정신분석[학]

psy·cho·an·a·lyst [sàikouǽnəlist] *n.* [C] a person who practices psychoanalysis. —[名] 정신분석가(학자)

psy·cho·log·i·cal [sàikəládʒik(ə)l / -lɔ́dʒ-] *adj.* of the mind; of psychology. —[形] 심리[학]의, 심리[학]적인

psy·chol·o·gist [saikálədʒist / -kɔ́l-] *n.* [C] a person who studies psychology. —[名] 심리학자

* **psy·chol·o·gy** [saikálədʒi / -kɔ́l-] *n.* [U] the science that studies the human mind and its activities. —[名] 심리학

psy·cho·ther·a·py [sàikouθérəpi] *n.* [U] the medical treatment of disease by psychological methods. —[名] 정신요법

P. T. A. Parent-Teacher Association.

P. T. O., p. t. o. please turn over. —《略》 뒷면으로 계속; 뒷면 참조

Ptol·e·ma·ic sys·tem [tàliméiiksístim/tɔ̀l-], **the** *n.* the system or theory taught by Ptolemy that the sun, moon, and planets moved around the earth. —[名] 천동설(天動說)

pub [pʌb] *n.* [C] (*Brit. slang*) a public house. —[名] 《口》 선술집

pu·ber·ty [pjú:bərti] *n.* [U] the physical beginning of manhood or womanhood. —[名] 사춘기

‡ **pub·lic** [pʌ́blik] *adj.* **1.** of or belonging to a nation and its people. ¶ *~ opinion*① / *a ~ holiday*② / *~ interests*③ / *~ health*.④ **2.** for the use of all people; open to all people. ¶*a ~ building*⑤ / *a ~ library*⑥ / *in a ~ place*.⑦ **3.** working for a nation and its people. ¶*a ~ servant*⑧ / *a ~ office*.⑨ **4.** known to people in general; open. ¶*a ~ scandal* / *make something ~*. ↔private, personal. —*n.* [U] 《*the ~*, used as *sing.* and *pl.*》 **1.** people in general. ¶*the ~ at large*.⑩ **2.** a special class of people. ¶*the reading ~*. —[形] 1. 공적(公的)인, 공공의; 사회의, 국민의 ¶①여론/②공휴일/③공익/④공중위생 2. 공중용의; 공개의 ¶⑤공공건물/⑥공립 도서관/⑦공개 장소에서 3. 국가 및 국민을 위해 일하다 ¶⑧공무원/⑨관공서 4. 널리 알려진, 공공연한 —[名] 1. 국민대중 ¶⑩일반대중 2. …계급, …사회, …계(界)

* **pub·li·ca·tion** [pʌ̀blikéiʃ(ə)n] *n.* **1.** [U] the act of making something known to the public. **2.** [U] the act of printing and offering books, newspapers, etc. to the public. **3.** [C] a thing which is published, as a newspaper, a magazine, a book, etc. ¶*a monthly ~*.① —[名] 1. 발표, 공포 2. 발행, 출판 3. 출판물 ¶①월간지

public house [∸ ∸] *n.* **1.** (*Brit.*) a small house where alcoholic drinks are sold to be drunk there. **2.** an inn. —[名] 1. 《英》 선술집 2. 여인숙

pub·li·cist [pʌ́blisist] *n.* [C] **1.** a specialist in internaional law. **2.** a writer on current public or political topics; a journalist who deals with political matters. —[名] 1. 국제법 학자 2. 정치 평론가; 정치 기자

* **pub·lic·i·ty** [pʌblísiti] *n.* [U] **1.** the state of being widely known. **2.** printed or spoken matter used to get public attention. —[名] 1. 널리 알려짐, 주지(周知) 2. 공포, 공고; 선전, 광고

pub·li·cize [pʌ́blisàiz] *vt.* (*U.S.*) make (something) known to the public. —[他] …을 공포(광고·선전)하다

pub·lic·ly [pʌ́blikli] *adv.* in a public manner; in the presence of people; openly.
—⓶ 공개적으로; 공적으로; 공공연히

pub·lic-mind·ed [pʌ́blikmáindid] *adj.* public-spirited.
—⓷ 공공심이 있는

public relations [⌞–⌟ ⌞–⌟] *n. pl.* ((used as *sing.*)) the activities of improving the relations of an organization with the public. ⇒N.B.
—⓷ 섭외[사무]; 홍보(弘報)[활동] N.B. P.R.로 줄임

public school [⌞– ⌟] *n.* **1.** (*Brit.*) a private boarding school. **2.** (*U.S.*) a free school supported by taxes.
—⓷ 1.《英》사립 중고등학교(기숙제) 2.《美》공립 국민·중학교

pub·lic-spir·it·ed [pʌ́blikspíritid] *adj.* having or showing a desire for the public welfare.
—⓷ 공공심이 있는

:pub·lish [pʌ́bliʃ] *vt.* **1.** make (something) known publicly. ¶~ *the news.* **2.** make (a law, etc.) known formally. **3.** print and offer (a book, a magazine, etc.) for sale.
—⓶ 1. …을 발표하다, 공표하다 2. [법률·명령 따위]를 발표(공포)하다 3. [서적]을 발행(간행)하다

·pub·lish·er [pʌ́bliʃər] *n.* ⓒ a person or company that publishes a book, a magazine, etc.
—⓷ 출판자(사), 발행자(소)

puck¹ [pʌk] *n.* ⓒ (often *P*-) the name of a mischievous elf in English folk tales.
—⓷ 장난꾸러기 요정(妖精)

puck² [pʌk] *n.* ⓒ a hard rubber disk used in playing ice hockey.
—⓷ [아이스하키의] 퍽

puck·er [pʌ́kər] *vt.* gather (the skin, lips, etc.) into small wrinkles. —*vi.* wrinkle. —*n.* ⓒ a wrinkle or a group of wrinkles.
—⓶ …에 주름을 잡다, 쭈글쭈글하게 하다 —⓸ 주름지다, 주름잡히다 —⓷ 주름, 주름살

·pud·ding [púdiŋ] *n.* ⓤ ⓒ **1.** a soft, boiled, sweet food. **2.** a kind of sausage.
—⓷ 1. 푸딩 2. 소시지의 일종

pud·dle [pʌ́dl] *n.* **1.** ⓒ a small pool of dirty water. **2.** a mixture of clay, sand, and water. —*vt.* **1.** make (something) muddy. **2.** work (clay) with water. **3.** turn (melted iron) into wrought iron by melting and stirring. —*vi.* poke about in muddy or dirty water.
—⓷ 1. 물웅덩이 2. 흙반죽
—⓶ 1. …을 더럽히다, 흙투성이가 되게 하다 2. 흙반죽을 만들다 3. [녹인 쇳물]을 교련(攪鍊)하다 —⓸ 물웅덩이 속을 걸어다니다

pu·er·ile [pjú(:)əril / pjúərail] *adj.* childish; silly.
—⓷ 어린애 같은, 철없는

pu·er·il·i·ty [pju(:)əríliti] *n.* ⓤ the state of being puerile; childishness; foolishness.
—⓷ 철없음, 유치함

Puer·to Ri·co [pwɜ́:rtourí:kou] *n.* an island of the West Indies, belonging to the United States.
—⓷ 푸에르토리코 섬

:puff [pʌf] *n.* ⓒ **1.** the act of sending out breath, smoke, etc. in a short, quick way; the sound of such an act; a bit of vapor, smoke, etc. sent out by this act; a sudden rush of wind. ¶*a ~ of smoke* / *a ~ of wind* / *the ~ of a locomotive.*① **2.** anything light, soft and round. ¶*a ~ of hair.*② **3.** a small pad used for putting powder on the skin. **4.** the act of giving exaggerated praise.
—⓷ 1. 훅 불기, 훅 부는 소리; 한 줄기의 바람 ¶①기관차의 치익하는 소리 2. 가볍고 부드럽고 둥근 것(의복의 부푼 부분·만두·슈우크리임·머리다발 따위) ¶②부풀게 한 머리 3. 퍼프, 분첩 4. 과장된 칭찬

—*vi.* **1.** send out air, steam, etc. in puffs or blasts. **2.** breathe quick and hard, esp. after extreme physical effort. ¶*pant and ~.*③ **3.** swell up with wind, pride, etc.; stick out. ((~ *up* or *out* something)) ¶~ *out one's cheeks.* **4.** move or go with puffs. ¶*The train puffed out of the station.* —*vt.* **1.** send out (smoke, etc.) in a short and quick way. **2.** smoke. ¶~ *a cigar.* **3.** make (someone) breathe quick and hard. **4.** swell (something) by puffing; swell (someone) with pride. ¶*be puffed up with pride.* **5.** praise too much.
—⓸ 1. 훅훅 불다 2. 헐떡거리다, 숨차하다 ¶③헐떡거리다 3. 부풀어 오르다 4. 훅훅하고 움직이다 —⓶ 1. [연기 따위]를 내뿜다 2. [담배 따위]를 뻐끔뻐끔 피우다 3. …을 숨차게 하다 4. …을 부풀어 오르게 하다; …을 으쓱거리게 하다 5. …을 마구 추어 올리다

puff·y [pʌ́fi] *adj.* (**puff·i·er, puff·i·est**) **1.** swollen; fat. ¶~ *eyelids.* **2.** blowing in puffs. **3.** breathing hard.
—⓷ 1. 불룩한, 피둥피둥 살찐 2. 획 부는 3. 헐떡거리는

pug [pʌg] *n.* ⓒ **1.** a small dog with an upturned nose and a curly tail. **2.** a short upturned nose.
—⓷ 1. 발바리의 일종 2. 들창코

pug-nosed [pʌ́gnóuzd] *adj.* having an upturned nose.
—⓷ 들창코의

:pull [pul] *vt.* **1.** cause (someone or something) to move toward oneself; draw. ¶~ *a door open* / ~ *someone by the sleeve* / *Pull the handle toward you in an emergency.*① **2.** draw (something) apart from another; extract (teeth). ¶~ *weeds* / *I have had my tooth pulled.*② **3.** remove (feathers) from the skin; pick up (flowers). **4.** row (a boat). ¶~ *a boat.* **5.** draw or take out (a knife, etc.). ¶*He pulled a dollar from his pocket.*③ /
—⓶ 1. …을 끌다 ¶①비상시에는 핸들을 앞으로 당기시오 2. …을 떼어 내다, [이 따위]를 뽑다 ¶②이를 뺐다 3. [것털]을 뜯다; [꽃]을 꺾다 4. [배]를 젓다 ¶[나이프 따위]를 꺼내다 ¶③그는 주머니에서 1달러를 꺼냈다 6. ㈜[계획 따위]를 해내다; …을 하다 ¶④장난을 치다 —⓸ 1. 끌다 ¶⑤밧

~ *a knife.* **6.** (*colloq.*) carry out or do (a plan, etc.). ¶~ *a trick.*④ **—*vi.*** **1.** draw. (~ *at* something) ¶~ *at a rope.*⑤ **2.** have a drink or smoke. ¶~ *at a jug.*⑥ **3.** row a boat; be rowed. **4.** manage to do something with difficulty. (~ *through* something)

줄을 당기다 **2.** 쭉 들이켜다; [담배를] 피우다 ¶⑥조끼로 쭉 들이켜다 **3.** 보우트를 젓다, [배가] 저어지다 **4.** 난국을 타개하다

1) ***pull a face,*** make the face look ugly; frown.
2) ***pull about,*** treat roughly.
3) ***pull down,*** ⓐ destroy (a house, etc.). ⓑ make (someone) weak. ⓒ humble.
4) ***pull in,*** ⓐ draw (one's head, etc.) in. ⓑ (of a train) arrive at a station. ⓒ save.
5) ***pull** someone's **leg,*** make fun of someone; make a fool of someone.
6) ***pull off,*** ⓐ take off (one's coat, etc.). ⓑ win (a prize, etc.); succeed in gaining something.
7) ***pull on,*** put on clothes.
8) ***pull out,*** ⓐ make (a story, etc.) longer. ⓑ draw out (a cork, a tooth, etc.). ⓒ (of a train) begin to leave a station.
9) ***pull round,*** cause (someone) to recover from illness.
10) ***pull together,*** work together.
11) ***pull** something **to pieces,*** tear something to pieces.
12) ***pull up,*** stop; make (something) stop.
13) ***pull up to*** (or ***with***)***,*** come up level with (someone) from behind; overtake.

[熟] 1)찡그린 상을 짓다 2)…을 거칠게 다루다 3)ⓐ…을 파괴하다 ⓑ[남]을 약하게 만들다 ⓒ[거만한] 콧대를 꺾다 4)ⓐ[목 따위]를 움츠리다 ⓑ[기차가] 역에 닿다 ⓒ절약하다 5)…을 놀리다, 조롱하다 6)ⓐ…을 벗다 ⓑ[상]을 타다, …을 잘 해내다 7)입다 8)ⓐ[이야기 따위]를 오래 끌다 ⓑ…을 뽑다 ⓒ[기차가] 역을 떠나다 9)[남]의 건강을 회복시키다 10)협력하여 일하다 11)…을 갈기갈기 찢다 12)멈추다, 세우다 13)…을 따라잡다

—*n.* [C] **1.** the act of pulling, drawing or rowing. **2.** an attraction; something attractive; an influence.

—[名] **1.** 끌기, 당기기; 젓기 **2.** 매력[이 있는 것]; 세력

pull·er [púlər] *n.* [C] **1.** a person or thing that pulls. **2.** an instrument or a machine for pulling. **3.** a person who rows a boat.

—[名] **1.** 끄는 것, 끄는 사람 **2.** 뽑는 도구 **3.** 젓는 사람

pul·ley [púli] *n.* [C] a wheel which is grooved to receive a rope, used for changing the direction of power. ⇒fig.

—[名] 도르래, 활차

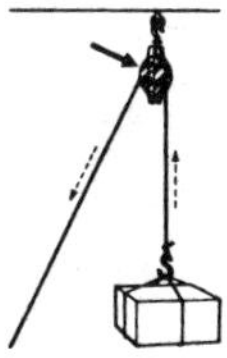

[pulley]

pull·o·ver [púlòuvər] *n.* [C] a sweater which is put on from the head.

—[名] 머리로부터 뒤집어써서 입는 스웨터

pul·mo·nar·y [pʌ́lmənèri / -nəri] *adj.* of the lungs.

—[形] 폐(肺)의

***pulp** [pʌlp] *n.* [U] **1.** the soft part of fruit. **2.** a soft, wet mass. ¶*wood* ~.①

—[名] **1.** 과육(果肉) **2.** 펄프, 흐물흐물한 것 ¶①목재 펄프

1) ***be reduced to*** [*a*] ***pulp,*** be completely melted; be tired out.
2) ***beat** someone **to a pulp,*** beat thoroughly.

[熟] 1)흐물흐물해지다; 녹초가 되다 2)…을 완전히 해치우다

—*vt.* reduce (something) to [a] pulp.

—[他] …을 펄프로 만들다, 흐물흐물하게 하다

pul·pit [púlpit, +*U.S.* pʌ́l-] *n.* [C] **1.** a raised desk for a preacher in a church. **2.** (*the* ~, *collectively*) the preachers; the work of preaching. ¶*occupy the* ~.①

—[名] **1.** 설교단 **2.** 설교자; 설교 ¶①설교하다

pulp·y [pʌ́lpi] *adj.* (**pulp·i·er, pulp·i·est**) **1.** of pulp; like the soft part of fruit. **2.** soft; juicy.

—[形] **1.** 펄프의, 과육[모양]의 **2.** 말랑말랑한; 즙(汁)이 많은

pul·sate [pʌ́lseit, +*Brit.* pʌlséit] *vi.* **1.** (of the heart) beat. **2.** (of a voice in singing) quiver.

—[自] **1.** [맥박이] 뛰다, 동계(動悸)하다 **2.** 목소리가 떨리다

pul·sa·tion [pʌlséiʃ(ə)n] *n.* **1.** [U][C] (of the heart) the beat. **2.** [C] (of a sound) the quiver.

—[名] **1.** 고동; 동계 **2.** [음의] 진동, 파동

***pulse**[1] [pʌls] *n.* [C] **1.** the beat of the heart; the beat felt in the wrist. **2.** the wave or quiver of sound or light. **3.** intentions; feelings.

—[名] **1.** 고동, 동계; 맥박 **2.** 파동, 진동 **3.** 의향, 기분, 경향

1) ***feel** someone's **pulse,*** ⓐ try to feel the pulse of someone in the wrist. ⓑ try to discover the intentions or feelings of someone.
2) ***stir** someone's **pulses,*** excite someone.

[熟] 1)ⓐ[남]의 맥을 짚어 보다 ⓑ[남]의 의향을 떠 보다 2)[남]을 흥분시키다

—*vi.* beat; throb.

—[自] 맥박치다, 고동하다

pulse[2] [pʌls] *n.* (*collectively*, often used as *pl.*) peas; beans.

—[名] 콩류, 콩

pul·ver·ize [pʌ́lvəràiz] *vt.* grind (something) into powder.

—[他] …을 가루로 만들다, 빻다, 찧다

—*vi.* become powder or dust.

—[自] 가루가 되다, 부서지다

pu·ma [pjúːmə] *n.* ⓒ a large American wildcat. —영 퓨우마, 아메리카 사자

pum·ice [pʌ́mis] *n.* ⓤ a light, spongy stone, used for cleaning or polishing. —영 경석(輕石)

pum·mel [pʌ́m(ə)l] *vt.* (-meled, -mel·ing or *Brit.*-melled, -mel·ling) strike (something) with the fists; pommel. —타 …을 주먹으로 치다

:pump¹ [pʌmp] *n.* ⓒ a machine used for raising water or for forcing air in and out. ¶*a bicycle ~*① / *a feed* (or *feeding*) *~*②
—영 펌프 ¶①자전거용 공기 펌프/②급수 펌프
—*vt.* **1.** raise (water, etc.) by means of a pump. 《*~ something up* or *out*》¶*~ water.* **2.** fill something with (air, etc.) by means of a pump. ¶*~ air into a tire.* **3.** ask (someone) closely; get (information, etc.) by asking closely. ¶*~ information out of someone* / *She pumped me about my mother.*③ **4.** cause (someone) to get tired or to be out of breath. 《*~ someone out*》
—타 1. [물 따위]를 펌프로 올리다 2. [공기 따위]를 펌프로 넣다 3. [남]에게 꼬치꼬치 질문하다; 꼬치꼬치 물어서 …을 알아내다 ¶③그녀는 우리 어머니에 대해 캐물었다 4. [남]을 지쳐 빠지게 하다, 휠떡거리게 하다 —자 1. 펌프를 사용하다, 펌프로 물을 푸다 2. 슬쩍 넘겨짚다
—*vi.* **1.** use a pump; raise water by means of a pump. **2.** get information by repeatedly asking questions.
1) *be pumped out,* be tired out.
2) *pump up,* raise water; fill with air.
圖 1)기진맥진하다 2)물을 푸다; 공기를 넣다

pump² [pʌmp] *n.* ⓒ (usu. *pl.*) light low shoes without laces. —영 뒤축이 낮은 슬리퍼식 신

・**pump·kin** [pʌ́m(p)kin, +*U.S.* pʌ́ŋkin] *n.* ⓒ a large, round, yellow fruit of a plant with heart-shaped leaves, used for pies, etc. —영 호박

pun [pʌn] *n.* ⓒ a witty use of one word in two senses; a play on words that have the same sound but different meanings. —*vi.* (**punned, pun·ning**) make a play on words. —영 말재롱, 곁말 —자 말재롱부리다, 재담하다

・**punch¹** [pʌntʃ] *n.* ⓒ **1.** a tool for making holes. **2.** a machine to stamp and cut sheet metal into pieces. **3.** a blow with the fists. ¶*get a ~ on the head.*
—영 1. 구멍 뚫는 기구, 천공기(穿孔器) 2. 타인기(打印器) 3. 주먹으로 때리기
—*vt.* **1.** make a hole in (a ticket, etc.). **2.** drive (a nail, etc.) in (or out) with a punch. **3.** strike (something) with the fist. **4.** press (a button, etc.).
—타 1. …에 구멍을 뚫다 2. [못 따위]를 때려박다 3. …을 주먹으로 때리다 4. …을 누르다

punch² [pʌntʃ] *n.* ⓤⓒ a drink made of wine or other liquor mixed with water, sugar, lemons, etc.
—영 펀치(포도주·레몬즙·설탕 따위의 혼합 술)

pun·cheon [pʌ́ntʃ(ə)n] *n.* ⓒ a large cask for holding liquor. —영 큰 술통

punch·er [pʌ́ntʃər] *n.* ⓒ a person or tool that makes holes. —영 구멍 뚫는 사람(도구)

・**punc·tu·al** [pʌ́ŋ(k)tʃu(ə)l, +*Brit.* -tjuəl] *adj.* arriving or appearing exactly at the fixed time; not late; on time.
—형 시간 엄수의, 늦지 않는
1) *as punctual as the clock,* keeping a schedule as exactly as the clock.
2) *punctual to the minute,* arriving exactly at the appointed time.
圖 1)시계처럼 시간이 정확한 2)1분도 틀리지 않는

punc·tu·al·i·ty [pʌ̀ŋ(k)tʃuǽliti, +*Brit.* -tju-] *n.* ⓤ the state of being punctual; the habit of being in good time. —영 시간 엄수; 꼼꼼함

punc·tu·al·ly [pʌ́ŋ(k)tʃuəli, +*Brit.* -tju-] *adv.* in a punctual manner. —부 시간대로; 꼼꼼하게

punc·tu·ate [pʌ́ŋ(k)tʃuèit, +*Brit.* -tju-] *vt.* **1.** mark (a sentence) with periods, commas, etc. **2.** interrupt (a speech, etc.). **3.** give point to (something); emphasize. ¶*He punctuated each word by a blow.*③ —*vi.* use punctuation marks.
—타 1. [문장]에 구둣점을 찍다 2. [박수·야유 따위로 연설]을 중단시키다 3. …을 강조하다 ¶①그는 테이블을 치며 한 마디 한 마디 강조했다 —자 구둣점을 쓰다

punc·tu·a·tion [pʌ̀ŋ(k)tʃuéiʃ(ə)n, +*Brit.* -tju-] *n.* ⓤ **1.** the use of certain marks, such as commas and periods, to make the sense clear in writing and printing. **2.** a punctuation mark.
—영 1. 구두(句讀)[법] 2. 구둣점

punctuation marks, marks such as colons, semicolons, commas and periods.
圖 구둣점

punc·ture [pʌ́ŋ(k)tʃər] *n.* ⓒ **1.** a small hole made by something pointed. **2.** the act of puncturing.
—영 1. 찌른 구멍 2. 찌르기, 구멍을 뚫기
—*vt.* **1.** make a small hole in (something) with a needle or something pointed. **2.** (*colloq.*) make (a tire) flat with a nail, etc. —*vi.* (of a tire) be punctured.
—타 1. …을 찌르다, …에 구멍을 뚫다 2. [타이어]를 빵꾸시키다
—자 [타이어가] 빵꾸나다

pun·gen·cy [pʌ́ndʒ(ə)nsi] *n.* Ⓤ **1.** the quality of having a sharp smell or taste. **2.** sharpness; severity.
pun·gent [pʌ́ndʒ(ə)nt] *adj.* **1.** exciting to the organs of taste and smell. **2.** sharp. ▷**pun·gent·ly** [-li] *adv.*
:**pun·ish** [pʌ́niʃ] *vt.* **1.** cause (someone) to suffer for a fault or crime; inflict a penalty for (an offense). ¶*He punished me for neglecting my work.*① **2.** (*colloq.*) handle severely. ▷**pun·ish·er** [-ər] *n.*
pun·ish·a·ble [pʌ́niʃəbl] *adj.* deserving to be punished.
:**pun·ish·ment** [pʌ́niʃmənt] *n.* Ⓤ Ⓒ **1.** the act of punishing; the state of being punished. **2.** a penalty imposed for an offence. ¶*inflict ~ upon*① / *capital ~*② / *corporal ~.*③ **3.** severe handling; pain or damage.
pu·ni·tive [pjú:nitiv] *adj.* of or inflicting punishment. ¶*a ~ expedition*① / *~ justice.*②
pun·ster [pʌ́nstər] *n.* Ⓒ a person who habitually makes puns.
punt [pʌnt] *n.* Ⓒ **1.** a flat-bottomed boat moved by pushing with a pole. ⇒fig. **2.** a kick at a football dropped from the hands before it touches the ground.
—*vt.* **1.** advance (a boat) with a pole. **2.** kick (a football) dropped from the hands before it touches the ground.
pu·ny [pjú:ni] *adj.* (**-ni·er, -ni·est**) **1.** smaller, weaker, etc., than usual; undersized. **2.** of no importance.
[punt 1.]
pup [pʌp] *n.* =puppy.
pu·pa [pjú:pə] *n.* Ⓒ (pl. **-pas** or **-pae**) a stage of an insect's life when it rests in a case; an insect in this stage.
pu·pae [pjú:pi:] *n.* pl. of **pupa**.
pu·pal [pjú:p(ə)l] *adj.* of or in a pupa.
:**pu·pil**¹ [pjú:p(i)l] *n.* Ⓒ a boy or girl who is taught by a teacher. 「through which light enters.」
pu·pil² [pjú:p(i)l] *n.* Ⓒ the black opening in the eye
pup·pet [pʌ́pit] *n.* Ⓒ **1.** a doll worked by wires, strings, or the hands. **2.** a person who obeys others blindly.
*•**pup·py** [pʌ́pi] *n.* Ⓒ (pl. **-pies**) **1.** a young dog. **2.** a vain, silly young man.
pur·blind [pə́:rblàind] *adj.* **1.** partly blind. **2.** stupid; dull. 「with money.」
pur·chas·a·ble [pə́:rtʃəsəbl] *adj.* that can be bought
:**pur·chase** [pə́:rtʃəs] *vt.* **1.** get (something) by paying money; buy. ¶*~ a car for 500,000 won* ① **2.** get (something) at the cost of labor, etc. ¶*~ victory with blood.*② **3.** move or raise (something) by means of some mechanical power. ¶*~ an anchor.*
—*n.* **1.** Ⓤ the act of purchasing. ¶*make a ~.*③ **2.** Ⓒ a thing purchased. **3.** Ⓤ a yearly income obtained from land as rent; value or worth. ¶*His life is not worth a day's ~.*④ **4.** Ⓤ Ⓒ a firm hold to help in moving or raising something. 「thing.」
pur·chas·er [pə́:rtʃəsər] *n.* Ⓒ a person who buys some-
:**pure** [pjuər] *adj.* **1.** not mixed with anything else; clean; clear. ¶*~ air* / *~ gold.* **2.** free from sins; innocent. **3.** mere; absolute. **4.** dealing simply with the theory of a subject. ↔applied ¶*~ physics.*①
pure and simple, and nothing else; nothing but.
pu·rée [pjúərei] *n.* Ⓤ Ⓒ **1.** any soft food boiled and pushed through a sieve. **2.** the thick soup made from this. 「wholly. **2.** merely.」
*•**pure·ly** [pjúərli] *adv.* **1.** in a pure manner; entirely;
pure·ness [pjúərnis] *n.* Ⓤ the state of being pure.

—⒨ 1. 자극성, 얼얼함 2. 신랄함, 날카로움
—⒨ 1. 얼얼한, 자극성의 2. 신랄한, 날카로운
—⒯ 1. [사람·죄]를 처벌하다 ¶①그는 일을 게을리했다고 나를 처벌했다 2.(口) …을 난폭하게 다루다, 혼내 주다
—⒨ 처벌할 만한
—⒨ 1. 처벌, 벌을 받기 2. 형벌 ¶①…을 처벌하다/②극형/③체형(體刑) 3. 징벌, 징계; 혼내 주기

—⒨ 형벌의 ¶①응징 원정(遠征)/②인과응보
—⒨ 재담 잘하는 사람
—⒨ 1. 바닥이 판판한 배 2. 공이 땅에 닿기 전에 차기

—⒯ 1. …을 삿대로 젓다 2. [공]을 펀트하다

—⒨ 1. 아주 작은; 미약한 2. 시시한, 보잘것 없는

—⒨ 번데기

—⒨ 번데기의
—⒨ 생도 ⓃⒷ student 와 구별하여 국민학교·중학교 학생을 이름
—⒨ 눈동자, 동공(瞳孔)
—⒨ 1. 꼭둑각시 2. 남의 앞잡이, 허수아비
—⒨ 1. 강아지 2. 건방진 애송이(풋나기)
—⒨ 1. 반소경의 2. 우둔한

—⒨ 돈으로 살 수 있는
—⒯ 1. …을 구입하다, 사다 ¶①자동차를 50만원으로 구입하다 2. [희생을 치르고] …을 획득하다 ¶②피를 흘려 승리를 얻다 3. [기계력으로] …을 움직이다, 올리다
—⒨ 1. 구입, 구매, 획득 ¶③물건을 사다 2. 구입품 3. [토지에서의] 연수(年收); 가격, 가치 ¶④그의 생명은 앞으로 하루 갈지말지다 4. 지레; 도르래

—⒨ 구매자
—⒨ 1. 깨끗한, 순수한, 섞인 것이 없는 2. 결백한, 죄 없는, 순결한 3. 단순한, 순전한 4. 순정(純正)의, 순리(純理)의 ¶①순물리학
⒨ 잡것이 섞이지 않은, 순전한
—⒨ 1. 퓨레(채소·고기를 삶아 체로 거른 것) 2. 퓨레 수우프

—⒨ 1. 순수하게, 청결하게; 순전히 2. 단지
—⒨ 순수, 결백, 순결

pur·ga·tion [pə:rgéiʃ(ə)n] *n.* [U] the act of purging.
—[名] 정화(淨化); 숙청; 변통(便通)

pur·ga·tive [pə́:rgətiv] *adj.* having the power of cleansing the bowels. —*n.* [C] a medicine used to empty the bowels.
—[形] 변을 통하게 하는; 하제(下劑)의 —[名] 하제

pur·ga·to·ry [pə́:rgətɔ̀:ri / pə́:gət(ə)ri] *n.* [C] (pl. **-ries**) **1.** (*Catholic*) a place where the souls of those who have died are purified from sin by temporary suffering. **2.** any place or state of temporary suffering.
—[名] 1.《가톨릭》 연옥(煉獄) 2. 일시적인 고난[의 장소]

* **purge** [pə:rdʒ] *vt.* **1.** make (something) free from impurities; cleanse. **2.** eliminate (an undesirable person) from a party, a government, etc. **3.** empty the bowels of (someone) with medicine. —*n.* [C] **1.** the act of purging. **2.** a medicine which empties the bowels.
—[他] 1. …을 깨끗이 하다, 순수하게 하다 2. …을 숙청하다, 추방하다 3. …에 하제를 쓰다 —[名] 1. 정화, 순화(醇化); 숙청 2. 하제

pu·ri·fi·ca·tion [pjùərifikéiʃ(ə)n] *n.* [U] the act of purifying or making someone clear of guilt or sin.
—[名] 깨끗이 하기, 세척(洗滌), 정화

pu·ri·fi·er [pjúərifàiər] *n.* [C] **1.** a person who purifies. **2.** a kind of instrument for purifying gas or water.
—[名] 1. 깨끗이 하는 사람 2. 청정기(淸淨器), 정화 장치

pu·ri·fy [pjúərifài] *v.* (**-fied**) *vt.* make (something) pure. —*vi.* become pure.
—[他] …을 깨끗이 하다, 정화하다 —[自] 깨끗해지다

pur·ism [pjúəriz(ə)m] *n.* [U] avoidance of foreign words or slang words in order to purify a language.
—[名] 언어 순화(醇化)

pur·ist [pjúərist] *n.* [C] a person who insists on purism.
—[名] 언어 순화 주의자

Pu·ri·tan [pjúərit(ə)n] *n.* [C] **1.** a member of a group of English Protestants who wanted a simpler form of worship and stricter morals. **2.** 《*p*-》 a person who is very strict in religion and morals.
—[名] 1. 청교도 2. 근엄한 사람

—*adj.* **1.** of the Puritans. **2.** 《*p*-》 of a puritan.
—[形] 1. 청교도의 2. 엄격한

pu·ri·tan·ic [pjùəritǽnik], **-i·cal** [-k(ə)l] *adj.* of or like a Puritan; very strict.
—[形] 청교도의(같은); 엄격한

Pu·ri·tan·ism [pjúəritənìz(ə)m] *n.* [U] the principles and beliefs of the Puritans.
—[名] 청교(淸敎), 청교주의

pu·ri·ty [pjúəriti] *n.* [U] **1.** the state of being pure; cleanness. **2.** moral cleanness; innocence; virtue. **3.** correctness.
—[名] 1. 청정(淸淨), 순수 2. 청렴, 결백 3. [문체·국어 따위의] 순정(純正)

purl[1] [pə:rl] *vi.* flow with a gentle sound, as a small stream among stones. —*n.* [C] the gentle murmur of a stream.
—[自] 졸졸 흐르다 —[名] 졸졸 흐르는 물소리

purl[2] [pə:rl] *n.* [U][C] **1.** a chain of small loops used to edge lace, ribbon, or the like. **2.** an inverted stitch in knitting. **3.** a cord of twisted gold or silver wire. —*vt.* **1.** edge (something) with small loops. **2.** invert (stitches) in knitting.
—[名] 1. 장식한 가장자리 2. [편물의] 안뜨기 3. [가장자리 장식·자수용의] 금실, 은실 —[他] 1. …에 장식 가장자리를 달다 2. …을 안뜨기로 하다

pur·loin [pər:lɔ́in] *vt.* steal.
—[他] …을 훔치다

⁑ **pur·ple** [pə́:rpl] *n.* [U] **1.** a color made by mixing red and blue. **2.** crimson. **3.** clothing worn by someone of imperial or royal rank. **4.** royal power or dignity. —*adj.* **1.** of the color of purple. **2.** of royal power or dignity; imperial; royal. —*vt., vi.* make or become purple.
—[名] 1. 자줏빛 2. 심홍색 3. 자줏빛 옷 4. 왕권
—[形] 1. 자줏빛의, 심홍색의 2. 왕권의, 제왕의 —[他][自] 자줏빛으로 하다(되다)

pur·plish [pə́:rpliʃ] *adj.* somewhat purple.
—[形] 엷은 자줏빛의(이 도는)

pur·port *n.* [pə́:rpɔ:rt, +*Brit.* pə́:pət → *v.*] [U] meaning; intended meaning.
—[名] [문서·연설 따위의] 의미, 취지, 요지(要旨)

—*vt.* [pərpɔ́rt, +*Brit.* pə́:pət] **1.** mean; imply. **2.** profess; give an impression of (something). 《~ *to do*》 ¶ *the law that purports to be in the interest of peace.*①
—[他] 1. …을 의미하다, …의 취지이다 2. …이라 일컫다, …을 뜻하다 ¶①치안을 위해 있다고 하는 법

⁑ **pur·pose** [pə́:rpəs] *n.* **1.** [C] something which a person eagerly wants to get; an object or intention. **2.** [U] will; resolution. ¶ *He is wanting in ~.*① **3.** [C] a matter under discussion.
—[名] 1. 목적, 의도 2. 의지, 결심 ¶①그는 의지가 약하다 3. 논점(論點)

1) ***on purpose,*** not by accident; intentionally.
2) ***to little purpose,*** almost uselessly or in vain.
3) ***to no purpose,*** not at all usefully.
4) ***to some purpose,*** with a rather good result.
5) ***to the purpose,*** serving one's purpose.

[熟] 1)고의로, 일부러 2)거의 헛되이 3)패, 상당히 잘 4)적절히

—*vt.* intend; plan. 《~ *to do*; ~ *doing*》 ¶ *I ~ finishing* (or *to finish*) *my work in a week.*
—[他] …하려고 생각하다, …을 뜻하다

pur·pose·ful [pə́:rpəsf(u)l] *adj.* **1.** having a purpose;
—[形] 1. 목적이 있는; 고의의 2. 의미

purposely

doing or done with an intention. **2.** full of meaning.
pur·pose·ly [pə́:rpəsli] *adv.* on purpose; intentionally.
purr [pə:r] *vi.* make a low murmuring sound, as a cat does when it is satisfied. —*n.* ⓒ a murmuring sound.
‡**purse** [pə:rs] *n.* ⓒ **1.** a small bag or case for carrying money. **2.** money; wealth. ¶*the public ~.*② **3.** a sum of money collected for a certain purpose or given as a prize. ¶*collect a ~ for the retiring teacher.*③
  1) ***have a common purse***, possess wealth in common.
  2) ***make up a purse for*** (=*collect money for*) *something* or *someone*.
  3) ***open*** *one's* ***purse***, give or spend one's money.
  4) ***put up a purse***, offer money as a prize.
—*vt.* draw together (the lips) in folds. —*vi.* become wrinkled.
purs·er [pə́:rsər] *n.* ⓒ an officer having charge of the accounts, tickets, etc. of a ship.
purse strings [´ ´] *n. pl.* the power or right to control the money.
  1) ***hold the purse strings***, control the spending of money.
  2) ***loosen*** (***tighten***) ***the*** (or ***one's***) ***purse strings***, be generous (economical) in spending money.
pur·su·ance [pərsú:əns / pəs(j)ú(:)-] *n.* ⓤ **1.** the act of pursuing. **2.** the act of carrying out.
  in pursuance of, ⓐ in accordance with. ⓑ in the carrying out of.
pur·su·ant [pərsú:ənt / pəs(j)ú(:)-] *adj.* in accordance with. ¶*~ to one's intentions.*① —*adv.* in a way that is pursuant; in accordance.
‡**pur·sue** [pərsú: / pəs(j)ú:] *vt.* **1.** follow to catch or kill (something). **2.** seek or aim at (something). ¶*~ pleasure.* **3.** continue or follow. ¶*~ one's studies.* **4.** follow (a path, a way, a course of action, etc.).
—*vi.* follow to catch: follow; continue.
pur·su·er [pərsú:ər / pəs(j)ú(:)ə] *n.* ⓒ **1.** a person who follows after something. **2.** a person who pursues some object or aim. **3.** a person who continues, follows, engages in, or studies something. **4.** (in English Civil Law) a prosecutor.
***pur·suit** [pərsú:t / pəs(j)ú:t] *n.* **1.** ⓤ the act of pursuing; the act of following to catch or kill something. **2.** ⓤ the act of following or engaging in something. **3.** ⓒ a profession; a business; recreation. ¶*agricultural* (*commercial*) *pursuits*① / *daily pursuits.*② **4.** ⓒ (*U.S.*) a pursuit plane.
  1) ***in hot pursuit***, pursuing in earnest.
  2) ***in pursuit of*** (=*following after or aiming at*) something.
pursuit plane [´ ´ ´] *n.* an airplane used for fighting.
pur·sy [pə́:rsi] *adj.* (**-si·er**, **-si·est**) **1.** easily becoming out of breath. **2.** fat.
pu·ru·lence [pjúəruləns] *n.* ⓤ **1.** the formation of yellowish-white matter in wounds. **2.** the yellowish-white matter produced by wounds.
pu·ru·lent [pjúərulənt] *adj.* full of or forming yellowish-white matter in wounds.
pur·vey [pə(:)rvéi] *vt.* provide; supply (esp. food).
pur·vey·ance [pə:rvéiəns] *n.* ⓤ **1.** the act of supplying food, etc. **2.** the food etc. supplied.
pur·vey·or [pə:rvéiər] *n.* ⓒ a person who supplies a large amount of food and other materials for an army, a city, etc.
pur·view [pə́:rvju:] *n.* ⓒ the extent or range of operation, authority, activity or concern.
pus [pʌs] *n.* ⓤ the yellowish-white matter formed in wounds.

—㉠ 고의로, 일부러
—㉠ [고양이 따위가] 목을 가랑거리다
—㉢ 목을 가랑거리는 소리
—㉢ 1. 지갑 2. 돈, 금전, 자재 ¶①국고 3. 현상금, 증여금 ¶②퇴직하는 선생을 위해 전별금을 모으다

圞 1)공통기금을 갖고 있다 2)…을 위해 모금하다 3)돈을 내다 4)상금을 주다

—㉠ [입]을 지갑처럼 굳게 다물다
—㉠ 주름지다
—㉢ [배의] 사무장

—㉢ 돈을 출납하는 권리

圞 1)금전 출납을 맡아 보다 2)돈 씀씀이가 헤프다(인색하다)

—㉢ 1. 추적, 추구 2. 수행, 이행

圞 ⓐ …에 따라, …에 의하여 ⓑ …을 이행하여
—㉠ 따르는, 따른, 준(準)한 ¶①뜻한 대로 —㉠ 따라서, 의거하여, 준하여

—㉠ 1. …을 추적하다, 추격하다 2. …을 추구하다 3. …을 속행하다 4. …을 따라가다, 쫓다 —㉠ 추적하다, 쫓다, 속행하다

—㉢ 1. 추적자 2. 추구자 3. 속행자, 종사(연구)자 4. 기소자, 고발자

—㉢ 1. 추적, 추격 2. 속행, 종사 3. 업무, 일, 오락 ¶①농업(상업)/②일상의 일 4. 《美》추격기

圞 1)맹렬히 추구하여 2)…을 추적하여; 추구하여
—㉢ 추격기, 전투기
—㉠ 1. 숨이 차는 2. 살찐
—㉢ 1. 화농(化膿) 2. 고름

—㉠ 고름의, 화농한, 화농성의
—㉠ …을 공급하다, 조달하다
—㉢ 1. [식료품위] 조달; 납입 2. 식료품
—㉢ 식료품 공급자; 조달인; [군대의] 조달업자

—㉢ 범위, 권한, 한계

—㉢ 고름

‡push [puʃ] *vt.* **1.** press (someone or something) to move. ↔pull ¶~ *a baby carriage* / *Push him outdoors.* **2.** put forth (buds, etc.); cause (something) to go forward. ¶*The tree pushes its roots deep into the soil.* **3.** press or urge (someone); emphasize. 《~ someone *to do*》 ¶~ *someone to make a speech*① / *The store is pushing dry goods.*② **4.** force (one's way, etc.). ¶~ *one's way through the crowd.* **5.** extend; expand. ¶*He pushes his business.* **—***vi.* **1.** press or thrust. **2.** go forward by force. ¶*The party pushed on through the jungle.*

—[他] 1. …을 밀다, 찌르다 2. [싹]을 내다; …을 내밀다 3. …에게 권하다, 조르다, 강요하다 ¶①…에게 연설하도록 조르다/②그 가게에서는 피륙 판매에 주력하고 있다 4. [길]을 밀어젖히며 나아가다 5. …을 확장하다, 증대하다 —[自] 1. 밀다, 찌르다 2. 밀고 나아가다

1) ***be pushed for time (money),*** be short of time (money).
2) ***push off,*** move off from the shore.
3) ***push on,*** hurry on.

[熟] 1)시간(돈)에 쪼들리다 2)배를 밀어내다 3)서둘러 나아가다

—*n.* **1.** [C] the act of pushing. ¶*He gave the car a ~ to see if he could start it.* **2.** [U] [C] energy; effort. **3.** [C] a situation which requires that one do something necessary without losing any time; an emergency.

—[名] 1. 찌르기, 밀기, 추진 2. 정력; 노력, 분발 3. 위기, 절박

push·cart [púʃkɑ̀ːrt] *n.* [C] a cart which is pushed by tne hand. ⇒fig.

—[名] 손수레

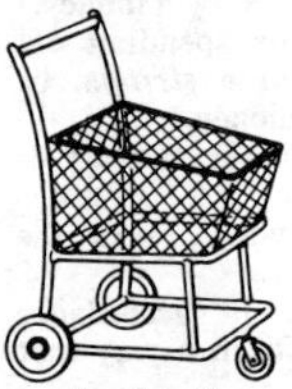
〔pushcart〕

push·ful [púʃf(u)l] *adj.* =pushing.

push·ing [púʃiŋ] *adj.* **1.** active. **2.** being busy with what is not one's concern.

—[形] 1. 활동적인, 활발한 2. 주제넘은, 뻔뻔스러운

pu·sil·la·nim·i·ty [pjùːsilənímiti] *n.* [U] the state of being pusillanimous.

—[名] 무기력, 비겁, 겁 많음

pu·sil·lan·i·mous [pjùːsilǽniməs] *adj.* lacking strength of mind or courage.

—[形] 무기력한, 겁 많은, 비겁한

puss [pus] *n.* [C] **1.** a cat. **2.** a girl.

—[名] 1. 고양이 2. 소녀

***puss·y** [púsi] *n.* [C] (pl. **puss·ies**) a cat.

—[名] 고양이

pus·tule [pʌ́stʃul / -tjuːl] *n.* [C] a spot on the skin containing pus.

—[名] 부스럼, 헌데

‡put¹ [put] *v.* (**put, put·ting**) *vt.* **1.** move (something or someone) into a certain place; set; place; lay; throw. ¶~ *a vase on the table* / ~ *some water in a jug* / ~ *someone in prison*① / *What ~ that into your head?*② **2.** cause (something or someone) to be in a certain state or relation. ¶~ *someone in rage* / ~ *someone at his ease*③ / ~ *someone out of temper* / ~ *someone out of countenance*④ / ~ *a room in order*⑤ / ~ *one's ideas into shape* / ~ *a watch right* / ~ *it to good use.* **3.** turn (something) in a certain direction; apply; attach. ¶~ *one's mind to a problem*⑥ / ~ *a glass to one's lips.* **4.** present or propose (something) for attention or consideration. ¶~ *a question before a committee.* **5.** state or express; translate; write. ¶~ *it in French* / ~ *one's name to a document*⑦ / ~ *ideas clearly.* **6.** force; drive; subject. ¶~ *someone to expense* / ~ *the enemy to flight*⑧ / ~ *someone to shame* / ~ *someone to death.* **7.** lay (blame, a duty, etc.); impose. 《~ something *on* or *upon*》 ¶~ *a tax on beer* / ~ *blame on others.* **8.** fix (a limit, etc.). ¶~ *an end* (or *a period*) *to something* / *He ~ a stop to that.* **9.** form an opinion or judgment about (value, price, size, etc.). ¶*I ~ the price at ten dollars.*⑨ **10.** lay out (money) to profitable use. **—***vi.* (of a ship) take a certain cource. ¶~ *out to sea.*

—[他] 1. [어떤 장소에] …을 두다, 놓다; 얹다, 넣다 ¶①…을 투옥하다/②어떻게 그런 생각이 들었느냐? 2. …을 [어떤 상태로] 하다, 가지런히 하다 ¶③…을 편안하게 하다/④…을 당황하게 하다/⑤방을 정돈하다 3. [어떤 방향으로] …을 돌리다, 쓰다; …에 붙이다 ¶⑥문제에 정신을 집중하다 4. [주의・고려를 위해] …을 내다, 제안하다 5. …을 말하다, 설명하다; 번역하다; 쓰다 ¶⑦문서에 서명하다 6. [남]에게 …하지 않을 수 없게 하다; …에 [고통 따위를] 받게 하다 ¶⑧적을 도주시키다 7. [벌 따위]를 과하다; …을 할당하다 8. [제한 따위]를 주다 9. [가치 따위]를 어림하다, 평가하다 ¶⑨나는 그 값을 10달러쯤으로 생각한다 10. …에 투자하다 —[自] [배가] 나아가다

1) ***put about,*** ⓐ change the course of (a boat). ⓑ spread (gossip, etc.).
2) ***put across,*** ⓐ take over (someone or something) in a boat. ⓑ express or explain effectively.
3) ***put aside,*** ⓐ place (something) to one side. ⓑ save (money, etc.) for later use.
4) ***put away,*** ⓐ put (something) in its proper place; lay aside. ⓑ save (money, etc.) for later use. ⓒ

[熟] 1)ⓐ[배]의 진로를 바꾸다 ⓑ[소문 따위]를 퍼뜨리다 2)ⓐ…을 배로 건네다 ⓑ…을 효과적으로 나타내다 3)ⓐ…을 옆으로 치우다 ⓑ[장래를 위해] …을 저축하다 4)ⓐ…을 해치우다 ⓑ…을 저축해 두다, 따로 두다 ⓒ《口》먹다, 마시다 5)ⓐ[배가] 기슭으로 돌아가다 ⓑ…을 다시 제자리에 두다 6)…을

(*colloq.*) eat or drink.
5) ***put back,*** ⓐ (of a boat) return to the shore. ⓑ put (something) where it was before.
6) ***put by,*** keep (something) in order to make use of it later.
7) ***put down,*** ⓐ place down (something). ⓑ record; write down. ⓒ stop (a riot, etc.) by force. ¶~ *down a rebellion.*
8) ***put forth,*** ⓐ grow (leaves, shoots, etc.). ⓑ propose; offer.
9) ***put forward,*** ⓐ suggest; propose. ⓑ cause (something) to go forward.
10) ***put in,*** ⓐ place in (something); insert. ⓑ name or choose (someone) for a position. ⓒ set forward (something); present. ⓓ enter a harbor; visit (some place). ⓔ spend (time) in a certain manner.
11) ***put in for,*** (*colloq.*) ask or apply for (something).
12) ***put off,*** ⓐ take off (a coat, etc.); remove. ⓑ postpone. ⓒ keep (someone) from doing something; stop. ⓓ start.
13) ***put on,*** ⓐ clothe oneself in (something). ⓑ assume the appearance of (something). ⓒ add to (something); gather (speed, etc.). ⓓ bring (a play) on the stage. ⓔ move forward (the hands of a clock, etc.).
14) ***put out,*** ⓐ hold out one's hand; put forth (something). ⓑ stop (fire from burning). ⓒ put money into (a business, etc.). ⓓ make (someone) angry.
15) ***put through,*** ⓐ carry out; accomplish. ⓑ connect (someone) by telephone with another.
16) ***put to it,*** worry.
17) ***put together,*** form (a whole) out of parts; construct.
18) ***put up,*** ⓐ hold up (a flag, etc.). ⓑ build (a house). ⓒ propose (someone) for election; offer (something) for sale. ⓓ put (something) back where it was before. ⓔ stay at a hotel, etc. ⓕ cause (a wild bird or animal) to drive out of its hiding place. ⓖ offer (a prayer).
19) ***put someone up to*** (=*talk someone into doing*) *something.*
20) ***put up with,*** bear or endure.

따로 두다 7)ⓐ…을 내려놓다 ⓑ…을 기록하다 ⓒ[폭동 따위]를 진압하다 8)ⓐ[싹 따위를] 내다 ⓑ…을 제출하다, 제안하다 9)ⓐ…을 제안하다, 제출하다 ⓑ…을 나아가게 하다 10)ⓐ…을 넣다 [말]을 끼우다 ⓑ…을 지명하다, 임명하다 ⓒ…을 제출하다 ⓓ입항하다;…에 들르다 ⓔ[시간]을 보내다, 쓰다 11)《口》…에 신청하다 12)ⓐ[옷]을 벗다;…을 제거하다 ⓑ…을 연기하다 ⓒ[남]에게 단념시키다; [남]을 방해하다 ⓓ출발하다, 출항하다 13)ⓐ[옷]을 입다 ⓑ…을 가장하다 ⓒ[속력 따위]를 늘리다 ⓓ[극]을 상연하다 ⓔ…을 나아가게 하다 14)ⓐ손을 내밀다; …을 제출하다 ⓑ[불]을 끄다 ⓒ…에 투자하다 ⓓ…을 성나게 하다 15)ⓐ…을 수행하다 ⓑ…에 전화를 잇다 16)…을 괴롭히다 17)…을 조립하다 18)ⓐ[깃발 따위]를 올리다 ⓑ[집]을 세우다 ⓒ…을 후보자로 세우다;…을 팔려고 내놓다 ⓓ…을 제자리에 돌려놓다 ⓔ숙박하다 ⓕ[사냥감]을 몰아대다 ⓖ[기도]를 바치다 19)…하도록 남을 설득하다 20)…을 참다

put² [pʌt] *vt.* =putt.

pu·tre·fac·tion [pjù:trifǽkʃ(ə)n] *n.* [U] (of food) the act or process of putrefying.
—[名] 음식의 부패

pu·tre·fy [pjú:trifài] *vt.* (**-fied**) make (some part in a living body, food, etc.) go bad. —*vi.* become bad or worse.
—[他] …을 화농시키다, 썩게 하다 —[自] 곪다, 썩다

pu·trid [pjú:trid] *adj.* being putrefied; dirty; producing a strong, bad smell.
—[形] 부패한, 더러운, 구린

putt [pʌt] *n.* [C] (*Golf*) a gentle stroke used to drive the ball into the hole. —*vt., vi.* (*Golf*) drive (the ball) into the hole with a gentle stroke. ▷**put·ter** [-ər] *n.*
—[名] 《골프》 경타(輕打), 퍼트 —[他][自] 경타하다, 구멍에 쳐 넣다

put·tee [pʌ́ti] *n.* [C] a long strip of cloth wound from the ankle to the knee.
—[名] 감는 각반(脚絆)

put·ter [pʌ́tər] *vi.* work in an idle way; walk without purpose.
—[自] 꾸물거리며 일하다, 어슬렁거리다

put·ty [pʌ́ti] *n.* [U] soft cement used for filling cracks or for fastening glass in a window frame. —*vi.* (**-tied**) fill with putty; fix glass with putty.
—[名] 퍼티(접합제) —[自] 퍼티로 메우다, 퍼티로 접합하다

:puz·zle [pʌ́zl] *n.* [C] **1.** a difficult problem; a very hard question. **2.** a state of being unable to answer or decide; a state of being confused. ¶*in a* ~.①
—[名] 1. 난문(難問) 2. 당황 ¶①당황하여

—*vt.* make (someone) unable to answer or understand; confuse. ¶*I'm puzzled what to do.*② —*vi.* be confused; be unable to answer or decide.
—[他] …을 당황케 하다 ¶②어찌할 바를 몰랐다 —[自] 당황하다

puzzle out, find the answer of (something) by thinking hard.
[熟] …을 풀다, …의 해답을 내다

puz·zle·ment [pʌ́zlmənt] *n.* [U] the state of being puzzled.
—[名] 당황

P.X. [pí:éks] (pl. **PXs** [-éksiz]) (in the Army of U.S.A.) post exchange.
—《略》 물품 판매점; 군대 매점

P

pyg·my [pígmi] *n.* [C] (pl. **-mies**) **1.** a very small person. **2.** ⟪*P-*⟫ a member of an African race of very small people. —*adj.* of a pygmy; very small.
—[名] 1. 난장이 2. 피그미족의 사람 —[形] 난장이의; 매우 작은

py·ja·mas [pədʒɑ́:məz, +*U.S.* -dʒǽm-] *n. pl.* (*Brit.*) =pajamas.

py·lon [páilɑn / -lən] *n.* [C] **1.** a gate of an Egyptian temple. ⇒fig. **2.** a tower marking the course for an airplane. **3.** one of a series of towers supporting electric wires.
—[名] 1. [옛 이집트의] 탑문(塔門) 2. [비행장의] 목표탑 3. [고압선용의] 철탑

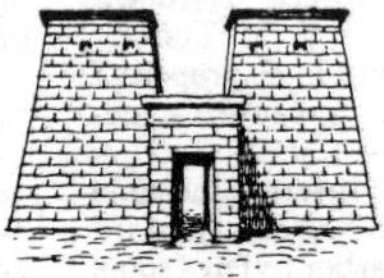

〔pylon 1.〕

∗ pyr·a·mid [pírəmid] [C] **1.** (*Geometry*) a solid body with a flat base and triangular sides meeting at the top; something shaped like such a body. **2.** ⟪often *P-*⟫ one of the ancient Egyptian royal tombs shaped like a pyramid.
—[名] 1. ⟪幾何⟫ 각추(角錐)[모양의 것] 2. 피라밋

py·ram·i·dal [pirǽmidl] *adj.* having the shape of a pyramid. ¶*a ~ roof.*①
—[形] 각추 모양의, 피라밋 모양의 ¶① 뾰족 지붕

pyre [páiər] *n.* [C] a heap of wood for burning a dead body.
—[名] 화장용 장작

py·ri·tes [pairáiti:z] *n.* [U] a mineral compound of sulfur, iron, copper, etc.
—[名] 황철광, 황동광

py·ro·tech·nic, **-ni·cal** [pàirouték nik], [-nik(ə)l] *adj.* of fireworks.
—[形] 꽃불의

py·ro·tech·nics [pàiroutékniks] *n. pl.* ⟪usu. as *sing.* and *pl.*⟫ the art of making fireworks; the showing of fireworks.
—[名] 꽃불 제조술; 꽃불을 쏘아 올리기

Py·thag·o·ras [piθǽgərəs / paiθǽgəræs] *n.* (582-507 B.C.) a Greek philosopher and mathematician.
—[名] 그리이스의 철학가·수학자

Py·thag·o·re·an [piθægərí(:)ən / pai-] *adj.* of Pythagoras. ¶*the ~ proposition* (or *theorem*).①
—[形] 피타고라스의 ¶①피타고라스의 정리

py·thon [páiθɑn, -θən / páiθ(ə)n] *n.* [C] a very large snake with no poison.
—[名] 비단뱀

Q

Q, q [kju:] *n.* [C] (pl. **Q's, Qs, q's, qs** [kju:z]) the 17th letter of the English alphabet.
—[名] 영어 알파벳의 열 일곱째 글자

∗ qt. **1.** quantity. **2.** quart[s].

quack[1] [kwæk] *n.* [C] the cry of a duck. —*vi.* make a sound like a duck's cry.
—[名] 오리 울음소리 —[自] 꽥꽥 울다

quack[2] [kwæk] *n.* [C] a person who pretends to be skilled in a particular field, esp. in medicine. —*adj.* false; sham. ¶*a ~ doctor.*①
—[名] 돌팔이 의사; 협잡꾼, 사기꾼 —[形] 엉터리의 ¶①돌팔이 의사

quack·er·y [kwǽkəri] *n.* [U] [C] (pl. **-er·ies**) the practice or method of a quack.
—[名] 엉터리 치료[법]

quad [kwɑd / kwɔd] *n.* (*colloq.*) =quadrangle

quad·ran·gle [kwɑ́dræŋgl / kwɔ́d-] *n.* [C] **1.** (*Mathematics*) a figure having four angles and four sides. **2.** the four-sided courtyard surrounded by buildings.
—[名] 1. ⟪數⟫ 사변형 2. 안뜰

quad·ran·gu·lar [kwɑdrǽŋgjulər / kwɔdrǽŋgjulə] *adj.* having four sides and four angles.
—[形] 사변(사각)형의

quad·rant [kwɑ́drənt / kwɔ́d-] *n.* [C] **1.** (*Mathematics*) one fourth of a circle. **2.** (*Astronomy, Nautical*) an instrument formerly used for measuring altitudes or angles.
—[名] 1. ⟪數⟫ 사분원(四分圓) 2. ⟪天文·海⟫ 사분의(四分儀), 상한의(象限儀)

quad·rat·ic [kwɑdrǽtik / kwəd-] *adj.* (*Mathematics*) involving the square of an unknown quantity but no higher powers. ¶*a ~ equation.*①
—[形] ⟪數⟫ 2차의 ¶①2차 방정식

qua·drille [kwədríl] *n.* [C] a square dance for four couples; music for this.
—[名] 카드리유[의 곡]

quad·ru·ped [kwɑ́drupèd / kwɔ́d-] *n.* [C] an animal that has four feet. —*adj.* having four feet.
—[名] 네발짐승 —[形] 네발짐승의

quad·ru·ple [kwɑdrúːpl, kwɑ́drupl / kwɔ́dru(ː)pl] *adj.* **1.** having or composed of four parts. **2.** four times as much or as many; fourfold. ¶*a size ~ to that of the moon.*① —*n.* (*the ~*) a number or quantity four times as much or as many. —*vt., vi.* make (something) or become four times as much or as many.
—[形] 1. 네 개의 부분으로 이루어지는 2. 4 배의; 네겹의 ¶①달의 4 배의 크기 —[名] 4 배수, 4 배량 —[他][自] …을 4 배로 하다; 4 배가 되다

quaff [kwɑːf, +*U.S.* kwæf, +*Brit.* kwɔf] *vi., vt.* drink in large quantities. (*~ off* or *up* a glass of whisky, etc.) —*n.* [C] the act of drinking deeply.
—[自][他] 벌컥벌컥 마시다 —[名] 경음(鯨飮)

quag·mire [kwǽgmàiər] *n.* [C] a soft, muddy piece of land; a marsh.
—[名] 수렁, 진창

quail[1] [kweil] *n.* [C] (pl. **quails** or *collectively* **quail**) a game bird like a partridge.
—[名] 메추라기

quail[2] [kweil] *vi.* shrink back from fear of pain; lose courage. (*~ at* or *before* something)
—[自] 움추리다; 풀이 죽다

* **quaint** [kweint] *adj.* odd but attractive; curious.
—[形] 별스러운; 기묘한

quaint·ly [kwéintli] *adv.* in a quaint manner.
—[副] 별나게

quake [kweik] *vi.* shake; tremble. (*~ with* or *for* something) ¶*He was quaking with fear.*① —*n.* [C] **1.** the act of shaking or trembling. **2.** (*colloq.*) an earthquake.
—[自] 흔들리다, 진동하다 ¶①그는 공포로 떨고 있었다 —[名] 1. 흔들림, 동요 2. 지진

Quak·er [kwéikər] *n.* [C] a member of a Christian sect formally called the Society of Friends.
—[名] 퀘이커 교도

Quak·er·ism [kwéikərìz(ə)m] *n.* [U] the principles, customs or ways of the Quakers.
—[名] 퀘이커주의(교리·관습)

qual·i·fi·ca·tion [kwɑ̀lifikéiʃ(ə)n / kwɔ̀l-] *n.* [U][C] **1.** the act of qualifying; the state of being qualified. ¶*have the qualifications of a teacher.*① **2.** a restriction; a modification; a limiting condition.
—[名] 1. 자격 부여; 자격 ¶①교사 자격이 있다 2. 제한; 수정; 조건

qual·i·fied [kwɑ́lifàid / kwɔ́l-] *adj.* **1.** having the required qualifications ¶*a ~ medical practitioner.* **2.** limited; modified. ¶*~ consent.*①
—[形] 1. 자격이 있는, 면허를 받은 2. 제한된; 조건부의 ¶①조건부 승낙

* **qual·i·fy** [kwɑ́lifài / kwɔ́l-] *v.* (**-fied**) *vt.* **1.** make (someone) fit for a job, an office, etc. ¶*The training qualified him for the job.*① **2.** give (someone) legal power or authorization. ¶*be qualified to teach.* **3.** call; name. (*~* someone or something *as* or *for*) ¶*He may be qualified as a villain.*② **4.** make (something) less strong, positive, etc. ¶*~ the whisky with water.* **5.** (*Grammar*) modify; limit. —*vi.* become fit or competent for something; get a license.
—[他] 1. …에 필요한 실력을 주다, 자격을 주다 ¶①그 훈련으로 그는 그 일에 대한 자격을 얻었다 2. …에게 권한(권능)을 주다 3. …을 [···이라고] 간주하다, …이라고 일컫다 ¶②그는 악당이라 해도 좋다 4. …을 완화하다 5. 《文法》 …을 수식(제한)하다 —[自] 자격을 얻다, 면허를 따다

qual·i·ta·tive [kwɑ́litèitiv, +*Brit.* kwɔ́litə-] *adj.* of or concerned with quality or qualities. ↔quantitative
—[形] 질(質)의, 질적인

qualitative analysis [∠--- -∠--] *n.* a chemical analysis of a substance in order to determine its nature or element.
—[名] 정성(定性) 분석

* **qual·i·ty** [kwɑ́liti / kwɔ́l-] *n.* [U][C] (pl. **-ties**) **1.** something which makes someone or something different from others; the essential nature; a characteristic. **2.** value; worth. ¶*Quality matters more than quantity.*① **3.** kinds of worth; excellence. ¶*goods of ~.*② **4.** [U] high social rank; (*the ~*) people of high rank.
—[名] 1. 특징, 특성; 질, 성질 ¶①양보다 질 2. 가치, 품질[의 좋고 나쁨] 3. 상질(上質), 우수성 ¶②고급품 4. 높은 신분; 상류사회의 사람

qualm [kwɑːm] *n.* [C][U] **1.** a sudden feeling of faintness or sickness. **2.** uneasiness or disturbance of conscience. **3.** a misgiving; a doubt; uneasiness.
—[名] 1. 현기증, 메스꺼움 2. 양심의 가책 3. 불안, 의심

quan·da·ry [kwɑ́ndəri / kwɔ́n-] *n.* [C] (pl. **-ries**) a state of uncertainty or being puzzled; a dilemma.
—[名] 난처한 처지, 곤경, 궁지

***be in a* [*great*] *quandary*,** be at one's wit's end; be very puzzled what to do.
[熟] 진퇴유곡에 빠져 있다

quan·ta [kwɑ́ntə / kwɔ́n-] *n.* pl. of **quantum.**

quan·ti·ta·tive [kwɑ́ntitèitiv, +*Brit.* kwɔ́ntitə-] *adj.* **1.** of or concerned with quantity. ↔qualitative **2.** that can be measured.
—[形] 1. 양(量)의, 정량(定量)의 2. 양적으로 잴 수 있는

quantitative analysis [∠--- -∠--] *n.* a chemical analysis of a substance to determine the amounts of its elements.
—[名] 정량 분석

Q

Q

‡ quan·ti·ty [kwántiti / kwɔ́n-] *n.* (pl. **-ties**) **1.** [U][C] an amount. ¶*a large ~ of milk.*① ↔quality **2.** ⦅often *pl.*⦆ a large amount; a large number. ¶*We've had quantities of rain this fall.*② **3.** [U] (*Music*) the length of a note or a sound. **4.** [C] (*Mathematics*) something that can be measured. ¶*a known ~.*③

—[名] 1. 양(量) ¶①대량의 우유 2. 다량, 다수 ¶②올 가을에는 비가 많이 왔다 3. ⦅樂⦆ 음절의 길이 4. ⦅數⦆ 수량으로 표시되는 것 ¶③기지수

quan·tum [kwántəm / kwɔ́n-] *n.* [C] (pl. **-ta**) an amount; a quantity.

—[名] 양(量)

quar·an·tine [kwɔ́:r(ə)nti:n, kwár- / kwɔ́r-] *n.* [U] **1.** the time during which incoming ships are kept in order to be examined for disease. **2.** the act of keeping a person who has a contagious disease away from others; the state of being kept away. ¶*be in ~.*① **3.** [C] a place where people or animals are kept away from others.
—*vt.* keep (a person or an animal) away from others.

—[名] 1. 검역 정선(停船) 기간 2. 격리, 고립 ¶①격리되어 있다 3. 격리소(병원)
—[他] …을 격리하다

‡ quar·rel [kwɔ́:r(ə)l, kwár- / kwɔ́r-] *n.* [C] **1.** an angry argument; a dispute. ¶*have a ~ with someone* / *take up another's ~*① / *fasten* (or *fix*) *a ~ on someone*② / *make up one's* (or *a*) *~*③ / *seek* (or *pick*) *a ~ with someone.*④ **2.** a cause of dispute; a complaint. ¶*fight in a good ~*⑤ / *find ~ in a straw*⑥ / *I have no ~ against* (or *with*) *you.* **3.** the lack of harmony or agreement; the act of breaking friendly relations.

—[名] 1. 싸움, 말다툼 ¶①남의 싸움을 떠맡다/②[남]에게 시비를 걸다/③사화하다/④[남]에게 싸움을 걸다 2. 싸움(말다툼)의 원인; 불평의 씨 ¶⑤이유가 정당한(정의의) 싸움을 하다/⑥사소한 일에도 시비를 걸다 3. 불화, 반목

—*vi.* (**-reled, -rel·ing** or *Brit.* **-relled, -rel·ling**) **1.** dispute. ¶*~ with someone about* (or *for, over*) *something* / *They always ~ over trifles.* **2.** find fault; complain. ⦅*~ with* something or someone⦆ ¶(*proverb*) *A bad workman quarrels with his tools.*⑦ **3.** break off friendly relations.

—[自] 1. 싸움(말다툼)하다 2. 나무라다, 불평(잔소리)을 하다 ¶⑦서투른 무당이 장구를 나무란다 3. 반목하다; 틀어지다

quarrel with one's bread and butter, give up or leave one's employment.

[熟] 자기의 생업을 버리다

quar·rel·some [kwɔ́:r(ə)lsəm, kwár- / kwɔ́r-] *adj.* fond of disputing or fighting.

—[形] 툭하면 싸우는

quar·ry[1] [kwɔ́:ri, kwári / kwɔ́ri] *n.* [C] (pl. **-ries**) a place where stone is obtained by cutting or blasting. **—*vt.*** get (stone) from the earth.

—[名] 채석장 —[他] [돌]을 떠내다

quar·ry[2] [kwɔ́:ri, kwár- / kwɔ́r-] *n.* [C] (pl. **-ries**) an animal that is hunted; game.

—[名] [사냥의] 불치, 사냥감; 목적물

*** quart** [kwɔ:rt] *n.* [C] **1.** a measure of liquids or small, dry goods. **2.** a container holding a quart.

—[名] 1. 쿼오트 2. 쿼오트들이의 용기

‡ quar·ter [kwɔ́:rtər] *n.* [C] **1.** one of four equal parts: one fourth part. ¶*a ~ of a mile* / *a mile and three quarters*① / *three less a ~*② / *divide an apple into quarters.* **2.** a fourth of a year or a school year; a three-month period for the payment of rent, etc. ¶*the first ~*③ / *pay one's rent at the end of each ~* / *The first ~ begins in September.* **3.** a fourth of an hour; 15 minutes. ¶*at a ~ past* (*to*) *two.* **4.** (*U.S.* or *Can.*) a fourth of a dollar; 25 cents; a silver coin having this value. **5.** one of four parts of an animal, including one leg. **6.** any one of four main directions of the compass. **7.** ⦅often *pl.*⦆ a region; a district; a particular section of a city or town. ¶*the Jewish ~*④ / *the business quarters* / *from all quarters.*⑤ **8.** a person or persons serving as a source of information. ¶*from a reliable ~* / *The news came in from several quarters.*⑥ **9.** ⦅often *pl.*⦆ a place, house or room to stay in or lodge at; lodgings. ¶*the servants' quarters.*⑦ **10.** [U] mercy granted to an enemy; permission to live. ¶*ask for* (or *cry*) *~*⑧ / *give ~ to someone.*⑨ **11.** a fourth of the moon's monthly revolution around the earth. ¶*the first* (*last*) *~.*⑩ **12.** (*Nautical*) the back part of a ship's side; the post or position appointed to a crew on a ship. ¶*on the ~*⑪ / *be at quarters.*⑫ **13.** one of four parts into which a shield is divided by lines.

—[名] 1. 4 분의 1 ¶①$1\frac{3}{4}$마일/②$2\frac{3}{4}$ 2. 4 분의 1 년; [4 학기제 학교의] 1 학기; [사계(四季) 지불기의] 1 기 ¶③제일 사분기 3. 1 시간의 4 분의 1; 15 분 4. 1/4 달러[화]; 25 센트 5. 짐승의 4 반절 6. [동서남북의] 방위(方位), 방향 7. 지방, 지역; 구역, 지구; …가(街) ¶④유대인가/⑤사방팔방에서 8. [정보 따위의] 출처 ¶⑥그 소식은 각 방면에서 들어왔다 9. [숙식하는] 방, 숙소; 거처, 주거; [군대의] 막사 ¶⑦하인방 10. [항복자 등에 대한] 관대, 자비, 용서 ¶⑧[포로 등이] 목숨을 빌다/⑨[남]의 목숨을 살려 주다 11. 달이 차고 이지러지는 주기의 4 분의 1, 현(弦) ¶⑩상(하)현 12. ⦅海⦆ [배의] 고물쪽; [함선 내의] 부서 ¶⑪고물에서/⑫부서에 자리잡고 있다 13. 방패의 4 분의 1

1) ***a bad quarter of an hour,*** a short, unpleasant experience.

[熟] 1)불쾌한 한때 2)접근하여

quarter day

2) *at close quarters,* near and in the small space.
—*vt.* 1. divide (something) into four equal parts. ¶ ~ *a cake* | *The traitor was condemned to be quartered.* 2. provide lodgings for (soldiers); place (troops) in lodgings. ¶*Soldiers were quartered in the houses on the hill.* —*vi.* lodge; stay. (~ *at* a place or *with* someone) 「on which quarterly payments are due.」
—⑩ 1. …을 4[등]분하다 2. [병사]를 숙박시키다, 막사에 들게 하다 —⑪ [병사가] 숙박하다

quarter day [´-´] *n.* one of the four days of the year
—⑫ 사계 지불일

quar·ter·deck [kwɔ́ːrtərdèk] *n.* ⓒ the part of the upper deck of a ship restricted to officers; (*the* ~, *collectively*) the officers of a ship.
—⑫ 뒷갑판; 고급 선원

quar·ter·ly [kwɔ́ːrtərli] *adj.* occurring four times a year. —*adv.* once every three months. —*n.* ⓒ (pl. **-lies**) a magazine issued every three months.
—⑩ 1년에 네 번의 —⑪ 1년에 네 번
—⑫ 계간지(季刊誌)

quar·ter·mas·ter [kwɔ́ːrtərmæ̀stər / kwɔ́ːtəmɑ̀ːstə] *n.* ⓒ 1. (*Nautical*) an officer on a ship having charge of steering, signals, etc. 2. (*Army*) an officer in charge of supplies for the soldiers. ⇒N.B.
—⑫ 1.(海)조타수(操舵手) 2.(軍) 보급부대 장교 N.B. Q.M.으로 줄임

quar·tet, *Brit.* '**-tette** [kwɔːrtét] *n.* ⓒ 1. (*Music*) a group of four musicians; a piece of music to be performed by such a group. 2. anything consisting of four parts; a group of four persons or things.
—⑫ 1. 4중주(창)단, 4중주(창)곡 2. 4인조, 네 개 한벌

quar·to [kwɔ́ːrtou] *n.* (pl. **-tos**) ⓒⓊ a book size, usu. about 9 by 12 inches; ⓒ a book of this size. ⇒N.B.
—⑫ 4절판(折判)[의 책] N.B. 4to 또는 4°로 줄임

• **quartz** [kwɔːrts] *n.* Ⓤ a hard, common mineral.
—⑫ 석영(石英)

quash [kwɑʃ / kwɔʃ] *vt.* 1. put down; crush; subdue. ¶~ *a rebellion.* 2. set aside; wipe out. 「most.」
—⑩ 1. …을 누르다, 진압하다 2. …을 무효로 하다, 취소하다

qua·si [kwéizai, -sai, kwɑ́ːzi] *adv., adj.* in a sense; al-
—⑩⑩ 어떤 의미에서(의); 거의

quat·rain [kwɑ́trein / kwɔ́t-] *n.* ⓒ a stanza of four lines.
—⑫ 4행시(行詩)

quat·re·foil [kǽtərfɔ̀il, kǽt(r)ə-] *n.* ⓒ 1. a leaf or flower with four leaflets or petals. 2. (*Architecture*) an ornament in this shape.
—⑫ 1. 네 잎, 꽃잎이 네 개인 꽃 2. (建) 네 잎 장식

qua·ver [kwéivər] *vi., vt.* tremble; speak or sing in a trembling voice. —*n.* ⓒ 1. a quivering sound. 2. (*Music*) an eighth note. 「unload; a wharf.」
—⑪⑩ 떨[리]다, 떨리는 목소리로 말(노래)하다 —⑫ 1. 떨리는 소리 2. 8분음표

quay [kiː] *n.* ⓒ a landing place for ships to load and
—⑫ 부두, 안벽(岸壁)

quea·sy [kwíːzi] *adj.* (**-si·er**; **-si·est**) 1. sick at the stomach. 2. hard to please; uncomfortable.
—⑩ 1. 메스꺼운, 구역질나는 2. 성미 까다로운; 불쾌한

‡ **queen** [kwiːn] *n.* ⓒ 1. the wife of a king. 2. a woman ruler. 3. a goddess. 4. a girl or woman who is very important, beautiful, etc. 5. the only female in a group of bees, ants, etc., that lays eggs. 6. a playing card bearing a picture of a queen. —*vt.* reign over (a country) as queen. ⇒N.B.
—⑫ 1. 왕비 2. 여왕 3. 여신 4. 여왕 같은 여자 5. 여왕벌(개미) 6. [카아드의] 퀴인 —⑩ …에 여왕으로 군림하다 N.B. queen it [over]처럼 의미없는 it를 쓰는 일이 많음

queen·ly [kwíːnli] *adj.* (**-li·er**; **-li·est**) like or proper to a queen. ¶*a* ~ *mother.* —*adv.* in a queenly manner.
—⑩ 여왕다운, 여왕인 체하는
—⑪ 여왕답게

‡ **queer** [kwiər] *adj.* 1. different from what is normal in some way; strange; odd. ¶*a* ~ *fish.* 2. not well; slightly; ill giddy. ¶*feel a little* ~. 3. probably bad; doubtful. 4. not genuine; counterfeit. ¶~ *money.*
—*vt.* spoil. ¶*Bad weather queered our plan.*
—⑩ 1. 별난, 기묘한, 보통과 다른 ¶① 괴짜 2. [몸이] 탈이 난, 현기증이 나는 3. 수상쩍은, 미심쩍은 4. 가짜의 —⑩ …을 망쳐 놓다

queer·ly [kwíərli] *adv.* in a queer manner.
—⑪ 기묘하게

queer·ness [kwíərnis] *n.* Ⓤ 1. the state of being queer; singularity; discomfort. 2. something strange or odd.
—⑫ 1. 기묘; 몸이 편치 않음 2. 기묘한 일 「를 억누르다」

quell [kwel] *vt.* put down; overcome.
—⑩ …을 가라앉히다; [공포 따위]

• **quench** [kwentʃ] *vt.* 1. put out. ¶~ *a fire.* 2. put an end to (something); cease. ¶~ *thirst.*① 3. cool suddenly. ¶~ *steel.*
—⑩ 1. …을 끄다 2. …을 잊게 하다 ¶①갈증을 풀다 3. …을 급히 냉각하다

• **quer·u·lous** [kwér(j)uləs] *adj.* complaining; fretful.
—⑩ 투덜거리는; 짜증내는

que·ry [kwíəri] *n.* ⓒ (pl. **-ries**) 1. a question. 2. a doubt. 3. the question mark (?).
—*vt.* (**-ried**) ask about; express doubt about (something). (~ someone *about*; ~ *whether* or *if...*) ¶*I* ~ *whether his word can be relied upon.*①
—⑫ 1. [의심을 품은] 질문 2. 의문 3. 물음표
—⑩ …에게 […인지 어떤지] 묻다, …을 의심하다 ¶①그의 말이 믿을 수 있을지 어떨지 의심스럽다

• **quest** [kwest] *n.* [C] **1.** a search; a hunt. ¶*the ~ of the Holy Grail.*① **2.** an adventurous expedition made by knights. —*vi.* (of a dog, etc.) make a search.
—[名] 1. 탐색, 추구 ¶①성배(聖杯)의 탐색 2. [중세 기사의] 원정 —[自] 뒤를 밟다, 찾다

⁑ **ques·tion** [kwéstʃ(ə)n] *n.* [C] **1.** the act of asking; an inquiry; something asked. ¶*May I ask a ~?* **2.** something doubtful or uncertain; a doubt. ¶*raise a ~ about the matter.*① **3.** a matter to be discussed or inquired into; a problem. ¶*a ~ of housing*②. **4.** a sentence in the interrogative form.
—[名] 1. 질문, 질의 2. 의심, 미심쩍은 일 ¶①어떤 일에 대해 질문을 하다 3. 문제, 논점(論點), 현안(懸案) ¶②주택 부족의 문제 4. 의문문

1) ***beyond question,*** undoubtedly; certainly.
2) ***in question,*** in dispute; in doubt.
3) ***make no question of,*** have no doubts in one's mind about (something).
4) ***out of question,*** not to be considered; impossible.

[熟] 1)의심할 여지 없이, 확실히 2)문제가 되어 있는, 심의중인 3)…을 의심하지 않다 4)생각조차 할 수 없는, 불가능한

—*vt.* **1.** ask; interrogate. 《~ someone *about* or *on*》 **2.** doubt. ¶*~ whether he will succeed.*
—[他] 1. …에 대하여 묻다 2. …을 의심하다

ques·tion·a·ble [kwéstʃ(ə)nəbl] *adj.* doubtful; uncertain.
—[形] 의심스러운; 애매한

question mark [⌐ ⌐ ´] *n.* a mark (?) placed at the end of a sentence asking a question.
—[名] 물음표

ques·tion·naire [kwèstʃənɛ́ər, +*Brit.* -tiənɛ́ə] *n.* [C] a list of questions with spaces to write answers in.
—[名] [기입식의] 질문표, 앙케이트

queue [kju:] *n.* [C] **1.** a braid of hair hanging down the back. **2.** a line of persons waiting their turn. ¶*form a ~ / in a ~.* —*vi.* form a line. 《*~ up*》 ¶*Queue here.*① / *~ up for a movie.*
—[名] 1. 변발(辮髮), 땋아늘인 머리 2. [차례를 기다리는 사람·차의] 열 —[自] 줄을 짓다 ¶①여기에 줄로 서시오

quib·ble [kwíbl] *n.* [C] **1.** the use of skillful but unfair words to avoid talking about the subject under discussion. **2.** a witty joke; a pun. —*vi.* use a quibble.
—[名] 1. 궤변, 발뺌, 핑계 2. 재담, 신소리 —[自] 재담을 하다; 얼버무려 넘기다

⁑ **quick** [kwik] *adj.* **1.** coming soon; immediate. ¶*a ~ answer.* **2.** fast; rapid. ¶*a ~ sports car / in ~ motion*① / *A gallop is the quickest gait of a horse.*② **3.** done in a short time. ¶*a ~ meal / a ~ note.*③ **4.** (of work, study, etc.) acting swiftly or rapidly. ¶*a ~ worker.* **5.** easily excited. ¶*a ~ temper.* **6.** (of the senses) keen and lively. ¶*a ~ sense of hearing / He is very ~ at smelling cookies.* **7.** understanding or learning rapidly; clever. ¶*He is a ~ learner.*
—[形] 1. 즉석의 2. 빠른, 급속한 ¶①재빨리/②갤럽은 말의 가장 빠른 보조이다 3. 짧은 시간에 한, 서두르는 ¶③급히 쓴 메모 4. 민첩한, 날랜 5. 성마른, 성급한 6. 민감한 7. 이해가 빠른

—*n.* [U] 《usu. *the ~*》 **1.** a very tender part of the body, esp. the skin under the fingernail. **2.** 《*the ~*》 living persons. ¶*the ~ and the dead.*④ **3.** the most important part.
—[名] 1. 육신, 생살, 손톱의 속살 2. 살아 있는 사람 ¶④산 자와 죽은 자 3. 급소, 아픈 곳

to the quick, very deeply. ¶*cut* (or *hurt, touch, wound*) *to the ~.*
[熟] 아주 깊은 곳까지, 철저하게

—*adv.* in a quick manner; rapidly; soon. ¶*Come as ~ as you can.*
—[副] 즉석에서; 빨리

• **quick·en** [kwík(ə)n] *vt.* **1.** hasten; hurry. **2.** bring (someone) to life; make (someone) live; arouse. —*vi.* become more alive or rapid.
—[他] 1. …을 서두르게 하다 2. …을 되살아나게 하다; 자극하다 —[自] 활기 띠다; 빨라지다

quick-freeze [kwíkfrí:z / ⌐ ´] *vt.* (**-froze, -fro·zen**) freeze (food) rapidly in order to store it.
—[他] [보존용 식품]을 급속히 냉동하다

quick-froze [kwíkfróuz / ⌐ ´] *v.* pt. of **quickfreeze.**

quick-fro·zen [kwíkfróuz(ə)n / ⌐ ´ ⌐] *v.* pp. of **quickfreeze.**

quick·lime [kwíklàim] *n.* [U] a white substance obtained by burning limestone and used for making mortar.
—[名] 생석회

⁑ **quick·ly** [kwíkli] *adv.* in a quick manner.
—[副] 재빨리; 성급하게

quick·ness [kwíknis] *n.* [U] the state or quality of being quick.
—[名] 기민, 날램; 성급, 성마름

quick·sand [kwíksæ̀nd] *n.* [U][C] a dangerous, deep mass of loose and wet sand which will not support a person's weight.
—[名] 유사(流砂)

quick·set [kwíksèt] *n.* [C] a hedge formed of living plants, esp. of hawthorn.
—[名] [산사나무 따위의] 생울타리

quick·sil·ver [kwíksìlvər] *n.* [U] mercury.
—[名] 수은

quick·step [kwíkstèp] *n.* [C] the rapid step used in marching; music in a march rhythm of quick time.
—[名] 속보(速步); 행진곡

quick-tem·pered [kwíktémpərd] *adj.* quick to lose one's temper; short-tempered; easily angered.
—[形] 화 잘 내는, 성미 급한

quick time — quit

quick time [ˊˋ] *n.* (*Military*) an ordinary rate of marching, 120 paces a minute. —名 〔軍〕 속보(速步)

quick-wit·ted [kwíkwítid] *adj.* alert or clever in action, speech, or mind. —형 꾀 많은, 약삭빠른

qui·es·cence [kwaiésns] *n.* Ⓤ the state of being quiescent. —名 정지(靜止); 침묵

qui·es·cent [kwaiésnt] *adj.* motionless; calm; still. —형 정지(靜止)한; 조용한

‡**qui·et** [kwáiət] *adj.* 1. still; moving very little. ¶*The sea was ~.* 2. with no or little noise; free from disturbance; silent. ¶*a ~ machine / Everybody, be ~ for a moment.*① 3. making no disturbance or trouble; gentle; mild. ¶*She is a ~ girl at school.* 4. with the usual or natural condition not disturbed by sudden happenings; peaceful; calm. ¶*a ~ place in the country.* 5. not showy or bright. ¶*Beige is a ~ color.*② 6. secret; private. ¶*I kept it ~.* 7. (of business); not busy or active. ¶*a ~ market.* —*n.* Ⓤ the state of being quiet; stillness; calmness; peace. —*vt.* make (someone or something) quiet. ¶*She quieted the crying baby. / The evening light has a quieting effect on us.*③ —*vi.* become quiet.
—형 1.고요한, 움직이지 않는 2.소음이 없는(적은), 조용한 ¶①여러분, 잠깐 조용해 주시오 3. 말썽을 일으키지 않는, 얌전한 4.평온한, 평화스러운 5. 수수한, 점잖은 ¶②베이지는 수수한 빛깔이다 6.비밀의, 은밀한 7.장사가 잘 안 되는, 한산한
—名 고요, 정적; 평화
—他 …을 조용하게 하다, 얌전하게 하다 ¶③저녁 햇살은 우리의 마음을 차분하게 만든다 —自 조용해지다, 얌전해지다

qui·et·ly [kwáiətli] *adv.* in a quiet manner; silently; peacefully; in a modest way. stillness; peacefulness. —부 조용하게; 평온하게; 수수하게

qui·et·ness [kwáiətnis] *n.* Ⓤ the state of being quiet;
qui·e·tude [kwáiət(j)ùːd / -tjùːd] *n.* Ⓤ the state of being quiet; stillness; calmness; repose.
—名 정온(靜穩); 평온
—名 정온(靜穩), 평온; 휴식

qui·e·tus [kwaiíːtəs] *n.* Ⓒ the final release of someone 1) *get one's quietus,* die. from debt, duty, or life. 2) *give someone his quietus,* kill.
—名 인생의 총결산; 죽음 熟 1)죽다 2)…을 죽이다

quill [kwil] *n.* Ⓒ 1. a long, strong feather. 2. a pen made from such a feather. ⇒fig.
—名 1.[날개·꽁지의] 큰 깃 2. 깃으로 만든 펜

quilt [kwilt] *n.* Ⓒ a soft bedcover made of two pieces of cloth with a layer of cotton or wool between and stitched in an ornamental pattern. —*vt.* make (a quilt); stitch (a piece of cloth, etc.) in an ornamental pattern or design. 〔quilt 2.〕
—名 누비이불; 덧이불 —他 [깃이불]을 만들다; …을 누비다

quilt·ing [kwíltiŋ] *n.* Ⓤ 1. something made by quilting. 2. material for making quilts. tree.
—名 1. 누비이불 제품 2. 누비이불 감

quince [kwins] *n.* Ⓒ a hard, yellow, pear-like fruit; its —名 마르멜로

qui·nine [kwáinain / kwiníːn], **quin·i·a** [kwíniə] *n.* Ⓤ a medicine used for preventing or curing malaria.
—名 키니네[제(劑)]

quin·sy [kwínzi] *n.* Ⓤ a disease of the throat with an abscess in the tonsils. —名 편도선염

quin·tal [kwíntl] *n.* Ⓒ a unit of weight; a hundredweight. —名 형량(衡量) 단위

quin·tes·sence [kwintésns] *n.* Ⓤ 1. the purest form of something. 2. the most typical example of something.
—名 1. 가장 순수한 본질, 정수(精髓) 2. 전형(典型)

quin·tet, -tette [kwintét] *n.* Ⓒ 1. a group of five musicians. 2. a piece of music for this group. 3. a group of five persons or things.
—名 1. 5중주(창)단 2. 5중주(창)곡 3. 5인조, 다섯 개 한 벌

quip [kwip] *n.* Ⓒ 1. a witty or ironic saying. 2. a quibble. 3. something queer. —*vi.* (**quipped, quipping**) make a quip. of paper.
—名 1. 경구(警句); 풍자, 비꼼 2. 구실, 핑계 3. 기묘한 것 —自 빈정거리다

quire¹ [kwáiər] *n.* Ⓒ a set of 24 or 25 uniform sheets —名 [종이] 한 첩

quire² [kwáiər] *n.* Ⓒ (*archaic*) a choir. —名 성가대

quirk [kwəːrk] *n.* Ⓒ 1. a peculiar manner; a quick turn of mind. 2. a clever or witty evasion of the truth in speaking. 3. a flourish in writing.
—名 1.괴상한 버릇, 변덕 2. 궤변, 핑계 3. [글씨·그림의] 멋부린 데

quis·ling [kwízliŋ] *n.* Ⓒ a traitor, esp. one who betrays his own country by helping an invading enemy.
—名 매국노; 배신자

‡**quit** [kwit] *v.* (**quit·ted** or **quit, quit·ting**) *vt.* 1. stop. (*~ doing*) ¶*Quit gambling. / Quit teasing me.* 2. leave; go away from (some place); give up. ¶*~ work /*
—他 1. …을 그만두다 2. …을 버리다; …와 헤어지다; …을 사직하다 3. …에 앙갚음하다; [빚]을 갚다 —自 1. 중지

~ *the army* / ~ *school* / *I've* ~ *the business.* **3.** pay back; pay off (a debt). ¶~ *love with hate.* —*vi.* **1.** stop doing something. **2.** go away; leave. ¶*We have received notice to* ~.① **3.** give up one's job. —*adj.* free. (~ *of*) ¶*He was* ~ *of his debts.*

: **quite** [kwait] *adv.* **1.** completely; entirely; absolutely. ¶*I'm* ~ *sure.* / *She is not* ~ *well.*① / *I was* ~ *pleased with it.* **2.** actually; really. ¶*It is* ~ *a picture.* / *He is* ~ *an artist.* **3.** to a considerable degree; rather. ¶*It's* ~ *cold.* **4.** (*Brit.*) (as *an answer* to a question) *quite a few*, many; a lot. ⌊true; yes.⌋

quit·tance [kwít(ə)ns] *n.* **1.** Ⓤ a discharge from a debt or an obligation; a document certifying this; Ⓒ a receipt. **2.** Ⓤ a repayment; a return.

* **quiv·er**¹ [kwívər] *vi.* tremble. ¶~ *with fear.*① —*n.* Ⓒ a shudder; a trembling movement or sound.

quiv·er² [kwívər] *n.* Ⓒ a case for carrying arrows. ⇨fig.

Qui·xo·te [kihóuti, kwíksət], **Don** *n.* the absurdly chivalrous title character of a famous Spanish novel.

quix·ot·ic [kwiksátik / -sɔ́t-] *adj.* **1.** like Don Quixote; absurdly chivalrous or romantic. **2.** not practical.

quiz [kwiz] *vt.* (**quizzed, quiz·zing**) **1.** (*U. S.*) examine (someone) by questions; give (a pupil) an informal examination. **2.** make fun of (someone). —*n.* Ⓒ (*pl.* **quiz·zes**) **1.** (*U. S.*) an informal test. **2.** an absurd or puzzling question. **3.** a person who makes fun of others; a practical joke.

[quiver²]

quiz·mas·ter [kwízmæstər / -mà:stə] *n.* Ⓒ a person who asks questions in a game of a radio or television program. ⌈fond of teasing.⌋

quiz·zi·cal [kwízik(ə)l] *adj.* **1.** odd; funny; comic. **2.**⌋

quoin [k(w)ɔin] *n.* Ⓒ **1.** an exterior angle or corner of a building; one of the stones forming such an angle or corner; a cornerstone. ⇨fig. **2.** a wedge-shaped stone or piece of metal.

quoit [kwɔit, +*Brit.* kɔit] *n.* **1.** (*pl.*) a flat iron ring meant to be thrown at a peg. **2.** (*pl.*, used as *sing.*) a kind of game played with such rings.

[quoin 1.]

quon·dam [kwándæm / kwɔ́n-] *adj.* former.

quo·rum [kwɔ́:rəm, +*U.S.* kwár-] *n.* Ⓤ the number of members of a society or body, generally more than half, needed at a legal meeting.

quo·ta [kwóutə] *n.* Ⓒ a share.

quot·a·ble [kwóutəbl] *adj.* that can be quoted; worth quoting.

: **quo·ta·tion** [kwoutéiʃ(ə)n] *n.* **1.** Ⓤ the act of quoting. **2.** Ⓒ words or a passage from a speech, a book, a poem, etc. of another. ¶*His speech was full of quotations from the Bible.*① **3.** Ⓒ the current market price.

quotation marks [-́ - -́] *n. pl.* a mark of punctuation ("" or '') used at the beginning or end of a quotation.

: **quote** [kwout] *vt.* **1.** repeat a passage from (a book, a poem, etc.); repeat (words, etc.). **2.** state the current market price of (something). —*n.* Ⓒ **1.** a quotation. **2.** (usu. *pl.*) quotation marks.

* **quoth** [kwouθ] *vt.* (*archaic, poetic*) said. ⇨Ⓝ.Ⓑ. ¶"*Very true,*" ~ *he.*

quo·tient [kwóuʃ(ə)nt] *n.* Ⓒ the result obtained when one number is divided by another.

하다 2. 떠나가다, 가 버리다 ¶①우리 는 나가라는 통지를 받았다 3. 사직하 다

—囮 자유로운; 면제된
—튀 1. 아주, 전혀, 절대적으로 ¶①그 녀는 아직 완전히 낫지 않았다 2. 사실 상, 정말로 3. 상당히, 꽤 4. (英) [대답 으로서] 예, 그대로입니다.

熨 상당수의
—囵 1. 면제, 사면; 영수증 2. 보상, 보 답

—圓 떨다 ¶①무서워서 떨다 —囵 떨 림; 떨리는 소리
—囵 화살통

—囵 돈 키호테(Cervantes 작의 소 설 및 그 주인공)

—囮 1. 돈 키호테 같은; 기사(騎士) 인 체하는 2. 환상적인

—囮 1. (美) …에게 질문하다, [교사 가] 시험삼아 질문하다 2. [남]을 놀리 다 —囵 1. [교사의] 간단한 질문, 시험 2. 퀴즈 3. 장난꾸러기; 짓궂은 장난

—囵 퀴즈 프로의 사회자

⌈하는⌋
—囮 1. 별난, 익살맞은 2. 짓궂게 장난
—囵 1. [건물의] 외각(外角); 귓돌 2. 쐐기

—囵 1. 쇠고리 2. 쇠고리 던지기

—囮 예전의, 이전의
—囵 정족수(定足數), 정원

—囵 몫; 배당; 할당량
—囮 인용할 수 있는, 인용할 만한

—囵 1. 인용 2. 인용문(구·어) ¶①그 의 연설에는 성서에서의 인용이 많았 다 3. 시세, 시가(時價)

—囵 인용부호

—囮 1. [남의 말·문장]을 (에서) 인용 하다 2. 시세(값)를 부르다 —囵 1. 인 용문 2. 인용부호

—囮 가로되, 왈 Ⓝ.Ⓑ. 제 1,3 인칭 서술 법 과거를 나타냄
—囵 나눗셈의 답, 상(商)

R

R, r [ɑːr] *n.* (pl. **R's, Rs, r's, rs** [ɑːrz]) *n.* [C] **1.** the eighteenth letter of the English alphabet. **2.** something shaped like the letter R.
—[名] 1. 알파벳의 열 여덟째 글자 2. R 형의 것

the three R's, reading, writing and arithmetic.
熟 읽기, 쓰기, 산수

‡rab·bit [rǽbit] *n.* [C] a small, short-tailed animal with long ears and soft fur.
—[名] 집토끼

rab·ble [rǽbl] *n.* [C] **1.** a disorderly crowd; a mob. **2.** ⟪*the* ~⟫ the lower class.
—[名] 1. 어중이떠중이 2. 하층 사회

rab·id [rǽbid] *adj.* **1.** furious; violent. **2.** affected with rabies; mad. ¶*a ~ dog.*① ▷**rab·id·ly** [-li] *adv.*
—[形] 1. 광포한, 격렬한 2. 광견병의; 미친 ¶①미친 개

ra·bies [réibiːz, -biìːz, rǽb-] *n.* [U] a disease of dogs and other animals causing madness.
—[名] 광견병, 공수병

rac·coon [rækúːn / rə-] *n.* [C] a small grayish animal with a ringed tail, which lives in trees. ⇒fig., [N.B.]
—[名] 너구리의 일종 [N.B.] racoon 으로도 씀

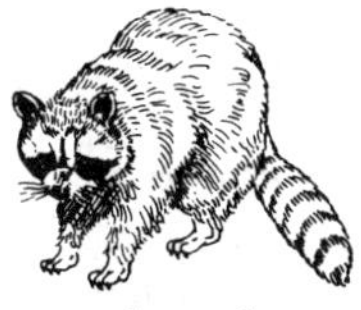
[raccoon]

‡race¹ [reis] *n.* [C] **1.** a contest of speed in running, skating, swimming, etc. ¶*a boat (horse, dog) ~ / run a ~*① */ He has won the ~.* **2.** ⟪*the ~s*⟫ a series of horse-racing events on a regular course. ¶*go to the races*② */ play the races.*③ **3.** a contest for a prize, an office, etc. ¶*a ~ for wealth.* **4.** a swift current of water; a channel for a current of water. **5.** the course of life. ¶*His ~ is nearly run.*④
—[名] 1. 경주 ¶①경주하다 2. 경마 ¶②경마에 가다/③경마에 걸다 3. [일반적으로] 경쟁 4. 급류; 수로(水路) 5. 인생 행로 ¶④그의 수명은 거의 다됐다

—*vi.* **1.** run a race. **2.** go swiftly; hurry. **3.** attend horse-racing regularly. **—*vt.*** **1.** compete against (someone or something) in speed. ¶*I'll ~ you to the corner.* **2.** cause (a horse, etc.) to compete in a race. ¶*~ a yacht* **3.** cause (something or someone) to go swiftly. ¶*~ the bill through the House.*⑤
—[自] 1. 경주(경쟁)하다 2. 질주하다; 서두르다 3. 경마에 열중하다 —[他] 1. …와 경주(경쟁)하다 2. …을 경주(경쟁)시키다 3. …을 서두르게 하다 ¶⑤급히 의안을 통과시키다

‡race² [reis] *n.* [C] **1.** a group of people having a common origin. ¶*a man of noble ~.*① **2.** a group of animals or plants belonging to the same kind. ¶*the winged ~*② */ the human ~.*③ **3.** a group of people with a common language, religion, culture and other background factors.
—[名] 1. 일족, 자손 ¶①명문 출신의 사람 2. 종족, 종류 ¶②조류/③인류 3. 인종, 민족

rac·er [réisər] *n.* [C] **1.** a person, horse, bicycle, car, etc. that takes part in races. **2.** a black American snake.
—[名] 1. 경주하는 사람, 경주에 쓰는 것 2. 미국산 검정뱀

race track [ˊ ˋ] *n.* a field or course for races.
—[名] 경주로(競走路), 경마장

ra·cial [réiʃ(ə)l] *adj.* of or about a race.
—[形] 민족의; 인종의; 종족의

ra·cial·ism [réiʃəlìz(ə)m] *n.* [U] ill feeling between different races; racial prejudice.
—[名] 인종적 편견

ra·cial·ly [réiʃəli] *adv.* in respect to a race.
—[副] 인종상

rac·ism [réisiz(ə)m] *n.* [U] the belief or doctrine that certain races are by nature superior or inferior to others; racial prejudice.
—[名] 인종적 편견; 인종차별

‡rack¹ [ræk] *n.* [C] **1.** ⟪usu. in *compounds*⟫ a framework of bars, pegs, shelves, etc. on or in which articles may be hung, held, or displayed. ¶*a hat ~*① */ a clothes ~ / a baggage~.*② **2.** a framework for holding hay and other food for cattle. ¶*a hay ~.* **3.** an old instrument of torture; torment; strain. ¶*put someone on* (or *to*) *the ~.*③ **4.** a bar with teeth into which the teeth on a wheel fit. ⇒fig.
—[名] 1. …걸이; 서류 선반; [기차의] 그물 선반 ¶①모자걸이/②[기차 따위의] 그물 선반 2. 꼴을 쌓아 두는 시렁 3. 고문대; 고문; 긴장 ¶③…을 고문하다 4. [톱니바퀴의] 톱니받침

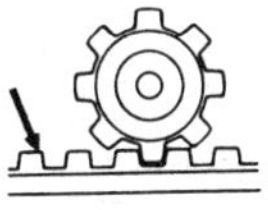
[rack¹ 4.]

be on the rack, be in a very painful situation. — [熟] 몹시 괴로와하고 있다

—*vt.* **1.** torture; hurt very much; strain. ¶*be racked with a cough.*④ **2.** put (something) on a rack. **3.** (of a landlord) oppress (a tenant) by demanding too much rent. — [他] 1. …을 고문하다; 괴롭히다 ¶④ 기침으로 괴로움 받다 2. …을 걸이(서류선반)에 얹다 3. …을 착취하다

rack one's brains, think very hard. — [熟] 머리를 짜다

rack[2] [ræk] *n.* [U] a flying mass of broken clouds driven by the wind. — [名] 조각구름

rack[3] [ræk] *n.* [U] destruction. — [名] 파괴

go to rack and ruin, become decayed. — [熟] 황폐해지다; 썩다

‡ **rack·et**[1] [rǽkit] *n.* **1.** [U][C] loud noise; [U] noisy talk and play. **2.** [C] (*U.S. colloq.*) a dishonest way of getting money from others. **3.** (*U.S. slang*) [C] a business. —*vi.* move about noisily; live gaily. — [名] 1. 시끄러운 소동; 소음; 떠들썩함 2.《美口》사기, 갈취 3.《美俗》장사, 직업 —[自] 떠들며 돌아다니다; 명랑하게 살다

rack·et[2] [rǽkit] *n.* [C] **1.** a light, wide bat with a network stretched in a frame, used in games such as tennis and badminton. **2.** a paddle with a handle, used in table tennis. ⇒[N.B.] — [名] 1. [정구 따위의] 라켓 2. [탁구의] 라켓 [N.B.] racquet 으로도 씀

rack·et·eer [rækitíər] *n.* [C] a person who gets money by threatening or by violence. — [名] 공갈꾼; 날강도

rack·e·ty [rǽkiti] *adj.* noisy. — [形] 시끄러운

ra·coon [rækúːn, rək-] *n.* =raccoon.

rac·y [réisi] *adj.* (**rac·i·er, rac·i·est**) **1.** vigorous; lively. **2.** with a peculiar taste. ▷**rac·i·ly** [-li] *adv.* — [形] 1. 팔팔한, 기운찬 2. 독특한 맛이 있는

* **ra·dar** [réidɑːr / -də] *n.* [C][U] an instrument for finding the direction and distance of unseen objects by the reflection of radio waves. — [名] 전파 탐지기, 레이다아

ra·di·al [réidiəl] *adj.* **1.** arranged like rays. **2.** of a ray. — [形] 1. 방사상(放射狀)의 2. 광선의

ra·di·ance [réidiəns] *n.* [U] **1.** brightness. **2.** radiation. — [名] 1. 빛남 2. 방사, 복사(輻射)

* **ra·di·ant** [réidiənt] *adj.* **1.** sending out rays of light or heat. **2.** shining; brilliant. **3.** full of joy, delight, etc. ¶*be ~ with hope.* — [形] 1. 빛(열)을 방사하는 2. 빛나는, 번쩍이는 3. [기쁨·즐거움 따위로] 밝은, 환한

ra·di·ant·ly [réidiəntli] *adv.* brightly. — [副] 번쩍번쩍, 빛나서

ra·di·ate *v.* [réidièit →*adj.*] *vi.* **1.** give out rays of light or heat. **2.** come out from a center. **3.** spread joy, happiness, etc. —*vt.* **1.** send out (light, heat, etc.) in rays. **2.** spread (happiness, etc.) in every direction. —*adj.* [réidiit] radiating from a center. — [自] 1. 빛·열을 방사하다 2. 중심에서 퍼지다 3. [기쁨·사랑 따위를] 널리 퍼뜨리다 —[他] 1. …을 방사하다 2. …을 발산하다 —[形] 방사하는, 방사상의

ra·di·a·tion [rèidiéiʃ(ə)n] *n.* **1.** [U] the act of giving out light or heat. **2.** [C] something radiated from a center. — [名] 1. 발광(發光), 방열(放熱) 2. 방사물

ra·di·a·tor [réidièitər] *n.* [C] **1.** a device for heating a room or building consisting of a set of pipes through which hot water or steam passes. **2.** a device for cooling a motor. — [名] 1. 방열기 2. 모우터 냉각장치

* **rad·i·cal** [rǽdik(ə)l] *adj.* **1.** of or from a root or roots; basic; fundamental. ¶*a ~ error.* **2.** ⟪often *R-*⟫ (of a political party or view) favoring an extreme change; extreme. ¶*a ~ program.* —*n.* [C] **1.** a person with an extreme opinion; a person belonging to a radical party. **2.** (*Mathematics*) a root. **3.** (*Chemistry*) an atom or a group of atoms acting as a unit. — [形] 1. 근본의, 뿌리로부터의, 기본적인 2. [정당 따위가] 급진적인, 과격한 —[名] 1. 과격론자; 급진당원 2.《數》근(根) 3.《化》기(基)

rad·i·cal·ism [rǽdikəlìz(ə)m] *n.* [U] the principles of radicals; radical views. — [名] 급진주의; 과격론

rad·i·cal·ly [rǽdikəli] *adv.* fundamentally; completely. — [副] 근본적으로, 완전히

rad·i·cle [rǽdikl] *n.* [C] **1.** a little root. **2.** the part of a seed that grows into the main root. — [名] 1. 작은 뿌리 2. 어린 뿌리

ra·di·i [réidiài] *n.* pl. of **radius**.

‡ **ra·di·o** [réidiòu] *n.* (pl. **-di·os**) **1.** [U] ⟪often *the ~*⟫ the way of sending or receiving messages, music, etc. by means of electric waves; broadcasting. ¶*over the ~.* **2.** [C] an instrument for receiving broadcasting. **3.** [C] a message sent by radio. ¶*listen to the ~.* —*adj.* on or of radio. ¶*a ~ set.* —*vt.* send (a message, etc.) by radio. —*vi.* send a message, music, etc. by radio. — [名] 1. 라디오 방송, 무선 전신 2. 라디오 수신기 3. 무선 통신[문] —[形] 라디오의 —[他] …을 무선 방송하다 —[自] 무선으로 방송하다

ra·di·o·ac·tive [rèidiouǽktiv / réi-] *adj.* (*Physics*) giving off rays of energy by breaking down atoms. — [形]《理》방사능의

ra·di·o·ac·tiv·i·ty [rèidiouæktíviti / réi-] *n.* [U] the condition of being radioactive.
—[名] 방사능(성)

radio frequency [´-- ´--] *n.* the frequency of electrical vibrations.
—[名] 무선 주파수

ra·di·o·gram [réidiougræm] *n.* [C] **1.** a telegram sent by radio. **2.** an x-ray photograph; a radiograph. **3.** a combined radio-receiver set and record player; a radiogramophone.
—[名] 1. 무선 전보 2. 방사선 사진 3. 라디오 겸용 전축

ra·di·o·graph [réidiougræf / -grà:f] *n.* [C] an X-ray photograph. —*vt.* make a radiograph of (something).
—[名] 방사선 사진 —[他] …을 방사선 사진으로 찍다

ra·di·og·ra·phy [rèidiágrəfi / -ɔ́g-] *n.* [U] the art of making radiographs.
—[名] 방사선 사진술

ra·di·o·i·so·tope [rèidiouáisətòup] *n.* [C] a radioactive isotope, used in medical or biological research.
—[名] 방사성 동위원소

ra·di·o·phone [réidioufòun] *n.* =radiotelephone.

ra·di·o·tel·e·graph [rèidioutéligræf / -grà:f] *n.* [C] a telegraph sent by radio.
—[名] 무선전신

ra·di·o·tel·e·phone [rèidioutélifòun] *n.* [C] a telephone in which sound is sent by radio waves.
—[名] 무선전화

ra·di·o·ther·a·py [rèidiouθérəpi] *n.* [U] the treatment of disease by means of radioactive substances or X-rays.
—[名] 방사선 치료법

radio tube [´-- ´] *n.* a vacuum tube for a radio set.
—[名] 라디오용 진공관

rad·ish [rǽdiʃ] *n.* [C] a garden plant whose red or white root is used in salads.
—[名] 무우

***ra·di·um** [réidiəm] *n.* [U] a metallic chemical element, which gives off rays which are used in treating cancer.
—[名] 라듐

ra·di·us [réidiəs] *n.* [C] (pl. **-di·i** or **-di·us·es**) **1.** a straight line from the center of a circle or sphere to its edge. **2.** the area bounded by a circle of a given radius. **3.** a range; a scope. ¶*within the ~ of one's capacity.*①
—[名] 1. 반경(半徑) 2. 반경의 범위 3. 범위 ¶①[사람의] 능력의 범위 내에서

RAF, R.A.F. Royal Air Force.
—《略》 영국 공군

raf·fle [rǽfl] *n.* [C] a sale in which people have chances to win a prize for a small sum of money. —*vt.* sell (something) by means of a raffle. 《~ *off* something》 ¶*~ off a watch.* —*vi.* take part in a raffle. 《~ *for* something》 ¶*~ for a color television set.*①
—[名] 추첨식 판매 —[他] …을 추첨식 판매로 팔다 —[自] 추첨식 판매에 한몫 끼다 ¶①천연색 텔레비전의 추첨식 판매에 가입하다

raft [ræft / ra:ft] *n.* [C] a number of logs tied together to make a flat boat. —*vt.* send (something) by raft; make (logs) into a raft. —*vi.* go on a raft; use a raft.
—[名] 뗏목 —[他] …을 뗏목으로 나르다; 뗏목을 만들다 —[自] 뗏목으로 건너다; 뗏목을 쓰다

raft·er[1] [rǽftər / rá:ftə] *n.* [C] a sloping beam to support a roof.
—[名] 서까래

from cellar to rafter, everywhere in a house.
[熟] 집안 구석구석까지

raft·er[2] [rǽftər / rá:ftə] *n.* [C] a person who is employed on a raft; a raftsman.
—[名] 뗏목 타는 사람

rafts·man [rǽftsmən / rá:fts-] *n.* (pl. **-men** [-mən]) =rafter[2].

***rag** [ræg] *n.* [C] **1.** a piece of old cloth torn from a larger piece. **2.** 《*pl.*》 worn-out, shabby clothes. ¶*a man in rags.*① **3.** anything that resembles a rag; a cheap, valueless newspaper or magazine. **4.** a small piece of anything; a small amount. ¶*a ~ of cloud.*②
—[名] 1. 넝마[천] 2. 누더기옷 ¶①누더기 입은 사내 3. 넝마 같은 것; 싸구려의 저속한 신문(잡지) 4. 작은 조각, 단편(斷片), 소량 ¶②조각 구름

not a rag of, no... at all. ¶*There is not a ~ of evidence.*③
[熟] 조금도 …않다 ¶③증거가 조금도 없다

—*vt.* (**ragged, rag·ging**) tease; scold.
—[他] …을 놀리다; 꾸짖다

rag·a·muf·fin [rǽgəmʌ̀fin] *n.* [C] a ragged, dirty child or fellow.
—[名] 누더기를 입은 아이(사람)

***rage** [reidʒ] *n.* **1.** [C][U] violent anger; fury. ¶*in a ~*① / *fly into a ~*② / *His arms quivered with ~.* **2.** [U] uncontrolled violence. ¶*the ~ of the wind.* **3.** [C] a strong desire. ¶*have a ~ for fishing.*③ **4.** [C] the fashion. ¶*Wrestling is [all] the ~ among our local boys.* **5.** [C] a fit of emotion. ¶*burst into a ~ of tears.*④
—[名] 1. 격분 ¶①발끈하여/②발끈 화내다 2. 격렬, 맹위 3. 열망 ¶③낚시에 열중하다 4. [일시적인] 대유행물 5. 감동, 격동 ¶④왈칵 울음을 터뜨리다

—*vi.* **1.** be violently angry. **2.** (of a storm, etc.) be violent. ¶*A storm is raging.*
—[自] 1. 격분하다 2. [폭풍우 따위가] 맹위를 떨치다

rage itself out, (of violence, etc.) come to an end. ¶*The storm raged itself out.*⑤
[熟] 제풀에 그치다 ¶⑤폭풍우가 그쳤다

* **rag·ged** [rǽgid] *adj.* **1.** torn into rags; dressed in worn-out clothing. **2.** uneven; rough; neglected. ¶*a sleeve ~ at the edge* / *a ~ garden* / *~ rocks.* **3.** harsh. ¶*a ~ sound.* ▷**rag·ged·ness** [-nis] *n.*
—[形] 1. 누더기의; 누더기 옷을 입은 2. 울퉁불퉁한; 손질을 하지 않은 3. 귀에 거슬리는

rag·ged·ly [rǽgidli] *adv.* in rags; unevenly; roughly; harshly.
—[副] 누더기를 입고; 오톨도톨하게; 귀에 거슬리게

rag·lan [rǽglən] *n.* [C] a kind of overcoat with sleeves continuing from the collar without shoulder seams. ⇒fig.
—[名] 라글란 외투

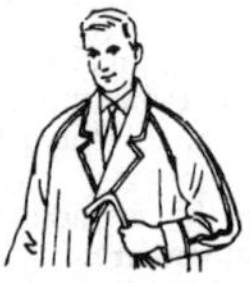
〔raglan〕

rag·man [rǽgmæ̀n, -mən] *n.* [C] (pl. **-men** [-mèn, -mən]) a person who deals in rags.
—[名] 넝마장수, 넝마주이

rag·time [rǽgtàim] *n.* [U] rhythm in which the accents fall at unusual places; jazz.
—[名] 랙타임[절분음(切分音)이 많은 음악]; [초기의] 재즈

raid [reid] *n.* [C] **1.** a sudden attack. ¶*an air ~*① / *make a ~ on* (or *upon*) *someone* or *something.*② **2.** an unexpected, sudden visit by the police to search for illegal goods or a suspect. 《*~ on, upon, into*》 **—*vt.*** attack suddenly. ¶*The police raided the gambling house.*③ **—*vi.*** engage in a raid.
—[名] 1. 급습 ¶①공습/②…을 습격하다 2. 경찰의 단속(수색) —[他] …을 습격하다 ¶③경찰이 그 도박장을 급습했다 —[自] 급습하다

raid·er [réidər] *n.* [C] a person or thing that makes a raid.
—[名] 습격자; 습격물(군함·비행기 따위)

⁑ **rail**[1] [reil] *n.* [C] **1.** any level bar of wood or metal. ¶*a ~ fence.* **2.** a railroad. **3.** one of the two metal lines on which trains run.
1) ***by rail,*** by train.
2) ***off the rails,*** (of trains, etc.) derailed.
—*vt.* **1.** enclose (something) with bars. **2.** lay rails on (something). **3.** send (a parcel, etc.) by railway.
—[名] 1. 가로장; 난간 2. 철도 3. 선로
[熟] 1)기차로 2)탈선하여
—[他] 1. …을 가로장으로 둘러막다 2. …에 레일을 깔다 3. …을 철도로 보내다

rail[2] [reil] *vi.* reproach or complain bitterly; speak angrily. 《*~ against* or *at* someone》
—[自] 욕설하다; 꾸짖다

rail[3] [reil] *n.* [C] any of several kinds of wading birds with a short tail and wings but long legs. ⇒fig.
—[名] 뜸부기

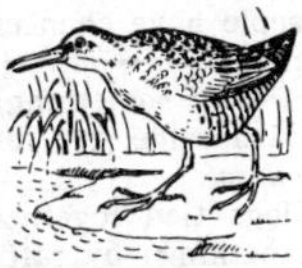
〔rail[3]〕

rail·ing[1] [réiliŋ] *n.* [C] **1.** 《often *pl.*》 a fence or barrier made of rails and supports. **2.** 《*collectively*》 material for making rails.
—[名] 1. 난간, 가로장, 울타리 2. 난간의 재료

rail·ing[2] [réiliŋ] *n.* [U] bitter reproach or complaint; abuse.
—[名] 욕지거리, 폭언

rail·ler·y [réiləri] *n.* (pl. **-ler·ies**) **1.** [U] good-natured satire or ridicule; banter. **2.** [C] a playful, teasing act or remark.
—[名] 1. 놀림, 조롱 2. 놀리는 행위(말)

⁑ **rail·road** [réilròud] *n.* [C] (chiefly *U.S.*) **1.** a track laid with two parallel rails on which trains run. **2.** a whole railroad system, including tracks, trains, etc.
—*vt.* **1.** send (something) by railroad; lay a railroad on (a place). ¶*~ a plain.*① **2.** (*colloq.*) put through quickly usu. without following the proper form. ¶*~ an urgent motion through the committee.*② **—*vi.*** work on a railroad; travel by train.
—[名] 《주로 美》 1. 철도 선로 2. 철도 [시설]
—[他] 1. …을 철도로 수송하다; …에 철도를 깔다 ¶①평원에 철도를 깔다 2. …을 단숨에 통과시키다 ¶②위원회에서 긴급동의를 일거에 통과시키다 —[自] 철도에서 일하다; 철도로 여행하다

⁑ **rail·way** [réilwèi] *n.* (*Brit.*) =railroad.

rai·ment [réimənt] *n.* [U] (*poetic*) clothing.
—[名] 의복

⁑ **rain** [rein] *n.* **1.** [U][C] the water falling to earth in small drops; the fall of such drops; [U] rainy weather. ⇒[usage] ¶*a heavy* (*light*) *~*① / *in the ~*② / *It look like ~* **2.** 《*the ~s*》 the rainy season in a tropical country. **3.** [U] 《*a ~*》 something falling rapidly or thickly like rain. ¶*a ~ of ashes* / *a ~ of tears* / *a ~ of kiss is*
rain or shine, in any event.
—*vi.* **1.** (of rain) fall. ⇒[usage] ¶*It has stopped raining.*③ / *It is raining cats and dogs.*④ **2.** fall like rain. ¶*Shells and bullets rained upon us.* / *Letters rained upon her.* **—*vt.*** pour down in rain or like rain. ¶*It rained blood.* / *I rained blows upon him.* / *It has rained itself out.*⑤ / *They rained presents on the bride and groom.*
—[名] 1. 비; 강우; 우천 [usage] 형용사를 수반할 때는 보통 부정관사를 붙임 ¶①큰 비(가랑비)/②비를 맞고 2. [열대 지방의] 장마철 3. 빗발치듯 하는 것
[熟] 비가 오든 볕이 나든
—[自] 1. 비가 오다 [usage] 보통 주어는 it ¶③비가 그쳤다/④비가 억수같이 쏟아지고 있다 2. [… 이] 비오듯 하다 —[他] [it를 주어로 하여] 비를 내리다, 빗발치듯 퍼붓다 ¶⑤비가 그쳤다

R

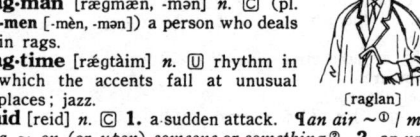

It never rains but it pours, (*proverb*) Troubles never come singly. 熟 (俚)비가 오기만 하면 억수로 쏟아진다; 화불단행(禍不單行).

* **rain·bow** [réinbòu] *n.* ⓒ an arch of light in seven colors which appears in the sky soon after rain. —名 무지개
  all the colors of the rainbow, many different colors. 熟 온갖 빛깔
* **rain·coat** [réinkòut] *n.* ⓒ a coat worn to protect oneself against the rain. —名 우비, 레인코우트
* **rain·drop** [réindràp / -drɔ̀p] *n.* ⓒ a drop of rain. —名 빗방울, 낙수물
* **rain·fall** [réinfɔ̀:l] *n.* ⓒ a shower of rain; ⓤ the amount of rain falling within a given time and area. —名 강우; 강우량
* **rain gauge** [⌣ ⌣] *n.* an instrument for measuring rainfall. —名 우량계
* **rain·less** [réinlis] *adj.* without rain. —形 비가 안 오는
* **rain·proof** [réinprù:f] *adj.* keeping from rain. ¶*a ~ coat.* —*vt.* keep (something) from being damaged or made wet by rain. —形 [옷이] 방수용의 —他 …에 비가 스미지 않게 하다
* **rain·storm** [réinstɔ̀:rm] *n.* ⓒ a storm with heavy rain. —名 폭풍우
* **rain water** [⌣ ⌣⌣] *n.* water coming down as rain. —名 빗물
‡ **rain·y** [réini] *adj.* (**rain·i·er, rain·i·est**) having much rain; wet with rain. ¶*the ~ season.* —形 비가 많이 오는, 비가 잘 오는; 비에 젖은
  rainy day [⌣ ⌣] *n.* **1.** a day with rain. **2.** a time in future when a person will need money. ¶*Save money for a ~.* —名 **1.** 비오는 날 **2.** 급할 때, 만약의 경우
‡ **raise** [reiz] *vt.* **1.** cause (someone or something) to rise; lift. ¶*~ a flag | ~ one's eyebrows | ~ a sunken ship | ~ one's glass to someone① | ~ one's hand to someone② | ~ one's hat to someone.* ⇒[N.B.] **2.** build; construct; set upright. ¶*~ a monument.* **3.** cause (the dust, etc.) to be or appear. ¶*~ a cloud of dust.* **4.** stir up (someone) to some action; incite. ¶*~ a rebellion | ~ the country against the enemy.* **5.** (often *reflexively*)'cause (someone) to rise in the world; promote. ¶*~ oneself③ | ~ a salesman to be a manager.* **6.** increase (something) in value, amount, degree, etc.; advance (fame, etc.). ¶*~ the rent | ~ a salary | ~ one's reputation.* **7.** bring back (someone) from death; rouse. ¶*~ old memories | ~ someone from the dead.* **8.** collect; gather. ¶*~ funds | ~ armies.* **9.** utter (a cry, etc.) loudly; bring up (an objection, etc.) for consideration; mention. ¶*~ a cheer | ~ a question.* **10.** grow; rear; bring up. ¶*~ cattle | ~ a family | ~ wheat.* **11.** make (dough) rise or lighten. ¶*~ bread.* **12.** end; give up (a siege, etc.).
  1) *raise a dust,* make a fuss.
  2) *raise Cain* (or *hell, the devil*), cause a disturbance.
  3) *raise one's voice against,* protest.
  —他 **1.** …을 일으키다, 세우다; 들어올리다 ¶①…을 위해 축배하다/②…을 향해 손을 올리다 [N.B.] 자동사는 rise **2.** [집 따위를] 짓다 **3.** [먼지 따위를] 일게 하다 **4.** …을 분발시키다, 기운나게 하다; [소동 따위를] 불러 일으키다 **5.** …을 출세(승진)시키다 ¶③출세하다 **6.** [가격·임금 따위를] 올리다; [명성 따위를] 높이다 **7.** [죽은 사람을] 되살아나게 하다, …을 불러 일으키다 **8.** [돈·군사 따위를] 모으다 **9.** [합성 따위를] 올리다; [이의 따위를] 제기하다 **10.** …을 기르다, 재배하다, 사육하다 **11.** [빵을] 부풀게 하다 **12.** [포위 따위를] 풀다

  熟 1) 소동을 일으키다 2) 소동을 일으키다 3) …에 항의하다
  —*n.* ⓤⓒ **1.** the act of raising. **2.** (*U.S.*) an increase in salary, etc. ¶*give someone a raise.* —名 **1.** 올리기 **2.** 《美》 승급, 봉급 인상; 증가
* **rais·er** [réizər] *n.* ⓒ a person who grows plants or animals. —名 키우는 사람; 재배자; 사육자
* **rai·sin** [réizn] *n.* (usu. *pl.*) a small dried grape. —名 건포도
* **rai·son d'ê·tre** [réizɔ:ndéitr] *n.* reason for existence. —名 존재 이유
* **ra·jah, ra·ja** [rá:dʒə] *n.* ⓒ (*India*) a king; a nobleman. —名 왕; 귀족
* **rake**¹ [reik] *n.* ⓒ a farm or garden tool having a bar with a row of teeth at the end of a long handle, used for smoothing the soil or gathering together leaves, hay, etc. ⇒fig. ¶*thin as a ~.* —*vt.* **1.** gather (leaves) with a rake. **2.** gather together. **3.** search carefully. —*vi.* **1.** use a rake. **2.** make a close search. —名 갈퀴, 쇠스랑 —他 **1.** …을 갈퀴로 긁다 **2.** …을 모으다 **3.** …을 수색하다 —自 **1.** 갈퀴를 쓰다 **2.** 샅샅이 뒤지다

[rake¹]

rake² [reik] *n.* ⓒ a slope. ¶*the ~ of a ship's funnel.*① —*vi.* incline; slant. —*vt.* cause (something) to incline. —名 경사 ¶①배의 굴뚝의 경사 —自 경사하다 —他 …을 경사시키다
rake³ [reik] *n.* ⓒ a man of bad character. —名 방탕한 사람

rak·ish¹ [réikiʃ] *adj.* smart; sporty.
—[形] 멋진; 날씬한

rak·ish² [réikiʃ] *adj.* like a rake; immoral.
—[形] 방탕한

* **ral·ly**¹ [rǽli] *v.* (**-lied**) *vt.* **1.** bring (men, troops, animals, etc.) together. **2.** revive; recover. —*vi.* **1.** come together for a purpose or an action. ¶ ~ *round the flag.*① **2.** come to help someone. **3.** recover strength. **4.** (in tennis) hit a ball rapidly back and forth.
—*n.* [C] (pl. **-lies**) **1.** the act of rallying; the state of being rallied; an assembly. **2.** a recovery from an illness. **3.** (in tennis) a series of action of hitting a ball rapidly back and forth.
—[他] 1. …을 다시 모으다 2. …을 회복하다 —[自] 1. 모이다; 집결하다 ¶①깃발 주위에 집결하다 2. 도우러 오다 3. 원기를 회복하다 4. 연거푸 공을 받아넘기다
—[名] 1. 재집합 2. 병후의 회복 3. [정구에서] 공을 연거푸 받아넘기기

ral·ly² [rǽli] *vt.* (**-lied**) laugh at; ridicule.
—[他] …을 놀리다, 조롱하다

Ralph [rælf / reif, rælf] *n.* a man's name.
—[名] 남자 이름

* **ram** [ræm] *n.* [C] **1.** a male sheep. **2.** a device used for battering the walls of forts. —*vt.* (**rammed, ram·ming**) **1.** strike against (something) violently. ¶ *A car rammed the pole.*① **2.** pack (something) roughly or forcibly; stuff. ¶ ~ *earth into a hole.*②
—[名] 1. 수 양(羊) 2. 파성퇴(破城槌) —[他] 1. …에 세게 부딪치다 ¶①자동차가 기둥에 부딪쳤다 2. …을 다져넣다 ¶②구멍에 흙을 다져넣어 굳히다

ram·ble [rǽmbl] *vi.* **1.** wander about without purpose. **2.** talk or write about first one thing and then another without useful connections. **3.** (of a plant) grow and spread in various directions. —*n.* [C] **1.** an aimless walk. **2.** aimless talking or writing.
—[自] 1. 어슬렁거리다 2. 두서없이 이야기하다(쓰다), 마음내키는 대로 이야기하다(쓰다) 3. 만연(蔓延)하다 —[名] 1. 어슬렁거림, 산보 2. 만담, 만필

ram·bler [rǽmblər] *n.* [C] **1.** a person who rambles. **2.** a climbing rose.
—[名] 1. 어슬렁거리는 사람; 만담하는 사람 2. 덩굴장미

ram·i·fi·ca·tion [ræ̀mifikéiʃ(ə)n] *n.* [U][C] **1.** the act of ramifying; the state of being ramified. **2.** a branch; a part.
—[名] 1. 분지(分枝) 2. 분파; 작은 구분

ram·i·fy [rǽmifài] *v.* (**-fied**) *vi.* spread out into branches. —*vt.* ((in *passive*)) divide (something) into branches.
—[自] 갈래지다 —[他] …을 갈래지게 하다; 작게 구분하다

ramp [ræmp] *n.* [C] a short, sloping way connecting two different levels of a building or road. —*vi.* **1.** stand or rise on the hind legs. **2.** move violently or excitedly.
—[名] 비탈길, 경사로 —[自] 1. 뒷발로 서다(일어서다) 2. 날뛰다

ram·page *n.* [rǽmpeidʒ → *v.* / ræmpéidʒ] [C] a violent and noisy behavior. —*vi.* [ræmpéidʒ] run about violently.
—[名] 날뛰기, 미쳐 날뛰기 —[自] 날뛰다

ramp·ant [rǽmpənt] *adj.* **1.** violent. **2.** growing widely. **3.** (*Heraldry*) standing on the hind legs.
—[形] 1. 광포한 2. 무성한 3. ((紋章)) 뒷발로 선

ram·part [rǽmpɑːrt, -pərt] *n.* [C] a wide wall of earth placed around a fort for protection. —*vt.* make a wall around (a fort, etc.).
—[名] 성벽, 누벽(壘壁) —[他] …에 성벽을 두르다

ram·rod [rǽmrɑ̀d / -rɔ̀d] *n.* [C] a rod for pushing gunpowders, etc. into firearms.
—[名] 총열에 화약을 다져넣는 꼬챙이

ram·shack·le [rǽmʃæ̀kl] *adj.* loosely made; shaky.
—[形] 흔들흔들하는; 덜컹거리는

⁑ **ran** [ræn] *v.* pt. of **run**.

* **ranch** [ræntʃ / rɑːntʃ] *n.* [C] **1.** (*U.S.*) a large farm for raising cattle. **2.** a farm for a special crop. ¶ *a fruit* ~.① **3.** ((*the* ~, *collectively*)) persons working on a ranch. —*vi.* manage a ranch; work on a ranch.
—[名] 1. ((美)) 큰 목장 2. 농장 ¶①과수원 3. 목장 경영자; 목장 노동자들 —[自] 목장을 경영하다; 목장에서 일하다

ranch·er [rǽntʃər / rɑ́ːntʃə] *n.* [C] a person who owns or works on a ranch.
—[名] 목장주; 목장 노동자

ranch·man [rǽntʃmən / rɑ́ːntʃ-] *n.* (pl. **-men** [-mən]) =rancher.

ran·cid [rǽnsid] *adj.* having an unpleasant, smell or taste, like stale fat or butter; not fresh.
—[形] [버터 따위] 썩은 냄새(맛)가 나는; 역한

ran·cor, *Brit.* **-cour** [rǽŋkər] *n.* [U] deep hatred; ill will.
—[名] 깊은 원한, 앙심

ran·cor·ous [rǽŋkərəs] *adj.* full of rancor; spiteful.
—[形] 원한이 있는, 악의를 품은

* **ran·dom** [rǽndəm] *adj.* occurring without definite aim or reason; guided by chance. ¶ *a* ~ *shot* / *a* ~ *guess.*①
at random, aimlessly; with no purpose.
—[形] 되는 대로의, 아무렇게나 한 ¶①어림짐작
[熟] 되는 대로, 엉터리

⁑ **rang** [ræŋ] *v.* pt. of **ring**.

⁑ **range** [reindʒ] *n.* [C] **1.** [U] the extent or scope; the area; the distance at which someone can see or hear. ¶ *within (out of) one's* ~① / *outside the* ~ *of human understanding* / *a wide* ~ *of meadows* / *It is in the* ~ *of my influence.* **2.** the distance between limits. ¶ *a wide* ~ *of prices.*② **3.** [C][U] the distance to which a gun will
—[名] 1. 범위; 지력의 범위; 퍼짐; 시계(視界); 음역 ¶①힘이 닿는(닿지 못하는) 2. 변동의 범위 ¶②상품의 넓은 가격 폭 3. 사정(射程), 착탄 거리 ¶③원(근)거리에서 4. 줄, 열; 연속; 산맥; 계급 5. ((美)) [가축의] 방목 구역 6. 취

shoot. ¶*within* (*out of*) ~ / *at long* (*short*) ~.③ **4.** [C][U] a row, line, or series; a chain of mountains; a rank. ¶*a ~ of mountains.* **5.** (*U.S.*) an unfenced land where cattle eat grass. **6.** a large cooking stove.

사용 가스 난로

—*vt.* **1.** arrange (someone or something) in order or in a row or rows; classify. ¶*~ books on a shelf.* **2.** travel or wander over. ¶*~ the woods.* **3.** (*U.S.*) pasture (cattle, etc.) on a range. **4.** ⟪*reflexively* or in *passive*⟫ take sides. ¶*be ranged against*④ / *be ranged among*⑤ / *be ranged with* (or *on the side of*); *~ oneself with.*⑥ **5.** aim or point (a gun, telescope, etc.) at someone or something. ¶*~ a pistol on someone.* **—*vi.*** **1.** stretch; extend; lie in a line. **2.** vary within limits. ¶*~ between A and B; ~ from A to B.*⑦ **3.** wander about; move freely. ¶*His studies ~ over many subjects.*

—[他] 1. …을 가지런히 놓다, 정렬시키다; 분류하다 2. …을 헤매다, 돌아다니다 3. [가축]을 방목 구역에 방목하다 4. …에 편들다 ¶④…의 반대쪽에 서다/⑤…의 속에 끼다/⑥…에 편들다 5. [총·망원경 따위]를 돌리다, 조준하다 —[自] 1. 연해 있다; 일직선이 되어 있다; […와] 평행하다 2. [일정한 범위 안에서] 변화하다 ¶⑦A와 B 사이에서 움직이다 3. 헤매다

range finder [ˊ ˋˋ] *n.* an instrument used for determining the distance from an observer to an object.

—[名] 거리 측정기, 거리계

rang·er [réindʒər] *n.* [C] **1.** a person employed to guard a tract of forest. **2.** a member of a body of mounted men patrolling a large area. **3.** a wanderer. **4.** ⟪*pl.*⟫ soldiers esp. trained for surprise attacks.

—[名] 1. 삼림 경비원 2. 기마 경찰대원 3. 걸어 돌아다니는 사람; 부랑자 4. 유격병, 특공대원

‡rank[1] [ræŋk] *n.* **1.** [C] a line or row. ¶*break* (*keep*) ~.① **2.** [C][U] a distinct grade in the army, navy, etc.; a social class or division. ¶*a man of high* (*no*) ~② / *men of all ranks and classes.*③ **3.** [U] high social position; eminence, honor, or dignity. ¶*a lady of* ~④ / *the ~ and fashion*⑤ / *a writer of the first ~.*⑥ **4.** [C] a row of soldiers ranged side by side. ↔file ¶*the front* (*rear*) ~.⑦ **5.** ⟪*the ranks*⟫ the common soldiers; the common people. ¶*rise* (or *come up*) *from the ranks.*⑧

—[名] 1. 열, 줄 ¶①열을 흩뜨리다(질서를 유지하다) 2. 지위, 등급; 계급 ¶②신분이 높은(낮은) 사람/③상하 귀천 3. 높은 지위, 고관 ¶④귀부인/⑤상류사회/⑥일류 작가 4. 횡렬(橫列) ¶⑦앞줄, 뒷줄 5. 병졸; 낮은 신분의 사람 ¶⑧졸병에서 장교가 되다, 낮은 신분에서 출세하다

—*vt.* **1.** place (someone or something) in a rank or ranks. ¶*~ books on a shelf.* **2.** assign a rank or class to (someone or something); classify; estimate. ¶*I ~ her abilities very high.* **3.** (*U.S.*) have a higher rank than (someone). ¶*Ambassadors ~ ministers.* **—*vi.*** hold a rank or position; equal.

—[他] 1. …을 나란히 세우다, 정렬시키다 2. …에 등급을 매기다; …을 분류하다; 평가하다 3. ⟪美⟫ …보다 높은 지위에 있다 —[自] 지위가 있다, 나란히 서다

rank[2] [ræŋk] *adj.* **1.** (of plants, grass, etc.) growing too thickly. **2.** bad-smelling; disagreeable to the taste or sense of smell. **3.** (in a bad sense) excessive. ¶*a ~ mistake.*

—[形] 1. 무성한, 우거진 2. 냄새가 역한, 맛이 고약한 3. 지독한, 어처구니 없는

rank and file [ˊ - ˊ] *n.* **1.** common soldiers. **2.** general membership of an organization; common people.

—[名] 1. 하사관, 병졸 2. 평사원, 보통 사람; 민중

rank·er [rǽŋkər] *n.* [C] an officer risen from the ranks.

—[名] 하사관 출신의 장교

rank·ing [rǽŋkiŋ] *n.* [U] relative position. **—*adj.*** of the first class. ¶*a ~ player.*

—[名] 순위, 서열 —[形] 일류의, 빼어난

ran·kle [rǽŋkl] *vi.* (*poetic*) **1.** continue to be painful. **2.** be the source of mental pain or irritation.

—[自] ⟪詩⟫ 1. 곪다, 쑤시다 2. 마음에 사무치다

ran·sack [rǽnsæk] *vt.* **1.** search thoroughly. **2.** take (something) by force; rob.

—[他] 1. …을 샅샅이 뒤지다 2. …을 약탈하다

∗ran·som [rǽnsəm] *n.* **1.** [C] a price paid or demanded for the release of a captive, etc. ¶*hold someone for ~.*① **2.** [U] freedom obtained through payment of a price. **—*vt.*** **1.** pay a price for (a captive) to be set free. **2.** set (a captive) free by obtaining a price.

—[名] 1. 보석금, 몸값 ¶①…을 억류하고 몸값을 요구하다 2. 보석, 속량 —[他] 1. …을 몸값을 주고 구해 내다 2. …을 몸값을 받고 석방하다

rant [rænt] *n.* [U] wild, loud and meaningless speech. **—*vi.*, *vt.*** speak in a wild, loud meaningless manner; utter (something) in a violent manner. ▷**rant·er** [-ər] *n.*

—[名] 호언장담 —[自][他] 호언장담하다; …을 열광적으로 떠벌리다

∗rap [ræp] *v.* (**rapped, rap·ping**) ***vt.*** **1.** strike (something) quickly or lightly; tap. **2.** say sharply. **—*vi.*** knock something smartly so as to make a noise. ⟪~ *at* or *on* something⟫ ¶*~ on a door.* **—*n.*** [C] a quick and light blow.

—[他] 1. …을 [똑똑] 두드리다 2. …을 혹평(비난)하다 —[名] 똑똑 두드리기

ra·pa·cious [rəpéiʃəs] *adj.* **1.** seizing by force or violence. **2.** greedy.

—[形] 1. 강탈하는 2. 탐욕스러운

rape[1] [reip] *n.* [U][C] **1.** the act of seizing or carrying off

—[名] 1. 강탈 2. [부녀] 강간, 폭행

R

rape — **raspberry**

by force. **2.** the act of forcing a woman to have sexual intercourse against her will. —*vt.* **1.** seize or take (something) by force. **2.** violate (a woman). —他 1. …을 강탈하다 2. …을 강간하다

rape² [reip] *n.* ⓤⓒ a plant used as food for sheep, etc. —图 평지

rape·seed [réipsi:d] *n.* ⓒⓤ **1.** the seed of the rape, from which oil is obtained. **2.** the plant itself. —图 1. 평지의 씨 2. 평지

:rap·id [rǽpid] *adj.* (sometimes ~·**er**, ~·**est**) occurring or happening in a short time; very quick; swift. —*n.* ((usu. *pl.*)) a part of a stream where the water runs very fast. ⌈succession.⌉ —形 빠른, 급한, 신속한 —图 여울, 급류

rap·id-fire [rǽpidfáiər] *adj.* firing or occurring in rapid⌋ —形 속사(速射)의, 재빠른

ra·pid·i·ty [rəpíditi] *n.* ⓤ quickness; swiftness; speed. —图 급속, 신속; 속도

:rap·id·ly [rǽpidli] *adv.* with great speed; swiftly. —副 신속하게, 민첩하게

rap·ine [rǽpin / rǽpain] *n.* ⓤ (*poetic*) the act of robbing by force; violent seizure. —图 강탈, 약탈

rap·port [rəpɔ́:rt] *n.* ⓤ harmonious relation or connec-⌋ ⌈tion.⌉ —图 관계, 친교

rap·proche·ment [rӕprouʃmάːŋ / rӕprɔ́ʃmɑːŋ] *n.* ⓤ establishment or re-establishment of friendly relations. —图 친선, 화해, 국교 회복

rapt [rӕpt] *adj.* deeply absorbed; lost in delight. —形 열중한, 여념이 없는, 넋을 잃은

·rap·ture [rǽptʃər] *n.* ⓒⓤ (often *pl.*) **1.** very great joy or delight. **2.** the expression of great joy. —图 1. 광희(狂喜), 환희 2. 기쁨의 표현

rap·tur·ous [rǽptʃərəs] *adj.* full of rapture or delight; delighted. ▷**rap·tur·ous·ly** [-li] *adv.* —形 기뻐 날뛰는, 열광적인

:rare¹ [rɛər] *adj.* **1.** scarce; not often found; unusual. ¶*a ~ book*① / *on ~ occasions.*② **2.** unusually great or excellent. **3.** thin; not dense; scattered. ¶*the ~ air*③ / *a few ~ houses here and there.*④ —形 1. 드문, 진귀한 ¶①진서(珍書) / ②드물게 2. 아주 훌륭한 3. 희박한, 드문드문 있는 ¶③희박한 공기/④드문드문 있는 집
  rare and ..., (*colloq.*) very. ¶*I'm ~ and happy.*⑤ ▷**rare·ness** [-nis] *n.* ⌈~ *steak.*⌉ 國 (口) 몹시 ¶⑤아주 행복하다

rare² [rɛər] *adj.* underdone; not thoroughly cooked. ¶*a*⌋ —形 설구워진; 덜 익힌

rar·e·fac·tion [rὲərifǽkʃ(ə)n] *n.* ⓤ the act of rarefying; the state of being rarefied. ↔condensation —图 희박하게 하기; 희박

rar·e·fy [rέərifài] *v.* (-**fied**) *vt.* **1.** make (air, gas, etc.) rarer or thinner. ¶*The air is rarefied at this great height.*① **2.** refine; purify. ¶*~ one's earthly desires.* —*vi.* become rarefied. ⌈*well.* ¶*He is ~ honest.*⌋ —他 1. (기체)를 희박하게 하다 ¶①이 정도의 높이에서는 공기가 희박하다 2. …을 정화(淨化)하다, 순화(純化)하다 —自 희박해지다

:rare·ly [rέərli] *adv.* **1.** seldom; not often. **2.** unusually⌋ *rarely,* (*ever if*), (*colloq.*) seldom. —副 1. 드물게 2. 희한하게도 國 (口) 좀처럼; 드물게

rar·i·ty [rέəriti] *n.* (pl. -**ties**) **1.** ⓤ the state or quality of being rare. ¶*the ~ of the air high in the mountains*① / *a thing of great ~.*② **2.** ⓒ something rare or uncommon. ¶*an expensive ~*③ / *Such a fine day is a ~ here.* —图 1. 진기, 좀처럼 없음, 희박 ¶①높은 산에서의 공기의 희박/②굉장한 진품 2. 진품 ¶③값비싼 진품

·ras·cal [rǽsk(ə)l / rάːs-] *n.* **1.** a bad or dishonest person. **2.** a mischievous or playful child. —图 1. 악당, 무뢰한 2. [어린이에게 다정하게] 녀석, 놈

ras·cal·i·ty [rӕskǽliti / rɑːs-] *n.* ⓒⓤ (pl. -**ties**) a bad, dishonest act, conduct or character. —图 못된 짓; 악당 근성

ras·cal·ly [rǽskəli / rάːs-] *adj.* mean; base; dishonest. —*adv.* in a rascally manner. —形 비열한, 천한, 악랄한 —副 교활하게; 악랄하게

rase [reiz] *vt.* =raze. ⌈spots.⌉

rash¹ [rӕʃ] *n.* ⓒ a skin eruption with many small red⌋ —图 뾰루지, 발진(發疹)

·rash² [rӕʃ] *adj.* hasty; careless. ▷**rash·ness** [-nis] *n.* —形 경솔한, 무모한

rash·er [rǽʃər] *n.* ⓒ a thin slice of bacon or ham for cooking; a group of such thin slices. ⌈tion; recklessly.⌉ —图 베이컨(햄)의 엷은 조각

rash·ly [rǽʃli] *adv.* too hastily; without due considera-⌋ —副 경솔하게, 무모하게

rasp [rӕsp / rɑːsp] *vt.* **1.** rub; scrape. ((~ *off* or *away* something)) ¶*The water rasps away the rocks.* **2.** irritate ¶*Her singing rasps my nerves.* **3.** utter (something) in a rasping voice. ¶*~ out an order.* —*vi.* **1.** grate roughly. **2.** make a grating, harsh voice. —他 1. …을 줄로 쓸다 2. …을 짜증나게 하다 3. …을 거친 목소리로 말하다 —自 1. 바각바각 쓸리다 2. 삐걱거리다
—*n.* ⓒ **1.** a metal tool for smoothing surfaces. **2.** a rough, grating sound. **3.** irritation of mind. —图 1. 줄 2. 줄질[하는 소리] 3. 짜증

rasp·ber·ry [rǽzbèri / rάːzb(ə)ri] *n.* ⓒ (pl. -**ries**) **1.** a small berry, usu. red or black, which grows on a bush. **2.** a plant which bears this berry. —图 1. 나무딸기 2. 나무딸기 나무

‡ rat [ræt] *n.* [C] **1.** a long-tailed animal like a mouse, usu. gray, brown or white. **2.** a mean person; a person who abandons his fellows esp. in trouble.
smell a rat, have suspicions about something.
—*vi.* **1.** hunt or catch rats. **2.** behave like a mean or disloyal person.

—[名] 1. 쥐 2. 비열한 놈, 배신자
[熟] 수상쩍게 여기다
—[自] 1. 쥐를 잡다 2. 비열한 짓을 하다, 배신하다

rat·a·ble [réitəbl] *adj.* **1.** that can be rated or appraised. **2.** (*Brit.*) liable to pay local taxes. **3.** proportional. ¶~ *share.*①

—[形] 1. 평가할 수 있는 2.《英》 지방세 납부의 의무가 있는 3. 비례상의 ¶① 비례 배분

ra·tan [rætǽn / rə-] *n.* =rattan.

ratch·et [rǽtʃit] *n.* [C] **1.** a hinged piece which stops a gearwheel from turning backward. **2.** a gearwheel which is controlled by a ratchet. **3.** a device consisting of a gearwheel and a ratchet. ⇒fig. **—*vt.*** fit (a wheel) with ratchets.

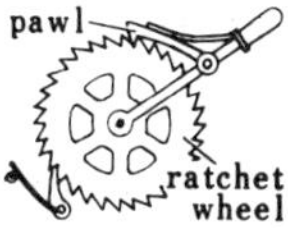

〔ratchet 3.〕

—[名] 1. 래칫(톱니바퀴의 역회전을 막는 장치) 2. 깔쭉 톱니바퀴 3. 후진(後進) 방지 장치 —[他] [차바퀴]에 후진 방지 장치를 달다

‡ rate¹ [reit] *n.* [C] **1.** the amount or degree of something in relation to something else. ¶*the birth* (*death*) ~① / *the* ~ *of interest*② / *at the* ~ *of.*③ **2.** speed. ¶*at a dangerous* ~④ / *at the* ~ *of 30 miles an hour.* **3.** a fixed relation between two things. ¶*the* ~ *of exchange.*⑤ **4.** a set price or wage; a charge. ¶*at a high* (*low*) ~ / *at any easy* ~⑥ / *buy at a cheap* ~ / *postal rates* / *railroad rates.* **5.** a class or grade. ¶*a ship of the first* ~. **6.** 《*pl.*》 (*Brit.*) a local property tax. ¶*rates and taxes.*⑦
1) **at any rate,** in any case; whatever happens.
2) **at that rate,** in that case; if what you say is true.
3) **at this rate,** in this way; if the present situation continues.
—*vt.* **1.** estimate or judge the value of (something); regard as; consider. ¶~ *someone's merit high*⑧ / *He is rated as one of the richest men of this city.* **2.** (*U.S.*) deserve. ¶*The essay rates a high grade.* **3.** (*Brit.*) fix the rate on (property) for local taxes. **—*vi.*** be ranked or valued. 《~ *as*》 ¶*England rates highest in the cotton industry.*

—[名] 1. 비율, 율 ¶①출생률(사망률) ②이자율/③…의 비율로 2. 속도 ¶④위험한 속력으로 3. 시세 ¶⑤환시세 4. 가격; 요금 ¶⑥싼 값으로, 용이하게 5. 등급 6.《英》 지방세 ¶⑦지방세와 국세
[熟] 1)어쨌든, 좌우간 2)그렇다면 3)이런 형편으로는, 이래가지고는
—[他] 1. …을 견적하다; …으로 간주하다 ¶⑧[남]의 공적을 높이 평가하다 2.《美》 …할 가치가 있다 3.《英》 …에 지방세를 부과하다 —[自] 평가받다; 등급이 …이다

rate² [reit] *vt., vi.* scold. ¶~ [*at*] *someone for his dishonesty.*①

—[他][自] […을] 꾸짖다 ¶①…의 부정을 꾸짖다

‡ rath·er [rǽðər / rá:ðə →5.] *adv.* **1.** more willingly; preferably; sooner. ¶*I will go to meet him* ~ *than wait for him.* / *I should* ~ *think so.*① **2.** more accurately. ¶*We got home late last night, or* ~, *early this morning.* ⇒[usage] **3.** somewhat; to some extent. ¶*That is a* ~ *clever book.* / *I feel* ~ *better today.* / *It is* ~ *cold today.* / *This book is* ~ *too easy for me.*② **4.** on the contrary. ¶*He is no worse;* ~, *he is better.* **5.** (*Brit. colloq.*) [rá:ðə́:] (in answering a question) certainly. ¶*Do you think so? Rather!*
had (or **would**) **rather,** would prefer. ¶*He had* ~ *drink tea than coffee.* / *I had* ~ *have never been born than have seen this day of shame.*③

—[副] 1. 오히려, 어느쪽인가 하면 ¶①그렇고 말고 2. 폐; 더 정확히 말하면 [usage] 관사의 위치는 대체로 영국에서는 rather a cold day, 미국에서는 a rather cold day로 씀 3. 좀, 다소, 약간 ¶②이 책은 나에게 다소 쉽다 4. 오히려, 반대로 5.《英》 그렇고 말고
[熟] 오히려 …하는 편이 낫다 ¶③이런 창피를 당하느니 차라리 태어나지 않았던 편이 낫다

rat·i·fi·ca·tion [rætifikéiʃ(ə)n] *n.* [U][C] the act of ratifying; the state of being ratified; confirmation.

—[名] 비준(批准), 승인

rat·i·fy [rǽtifài] *vt.* (**-fied**) make (a treaty, etc.) valid by signing; approve; confirm. ¶~ *the treaty.*①

—[他] [조약 따위]를 비준하다, 승인하다 ¶①조약을 비준하다

rat·ing [réitiŋ] *n.* **1.** [U] the act of valuing; the amount fixed as a rate. **2.** [U][C] classification according to relative value. **3.** 《*pl.*》 all the members of a ship's crew of the same rank.

—[名] 1. 평가; 할당 2. 등급, 등급을 매기기 3. 같은 계급의 선원 전원

• ra·ti·o [réiʃiòu] *n.* [U][C] (pl. **-tios**) **1.** the relation between two things in number, degree or quantity. ¶*the* ~ *of births to deaths.*① **2.** proportion. ¶*The audience contains a very high* ~ *of young people.*②

—[名] 1. 비(比), 비율 ¶①출생과 사망의 비율 2. 몫, 비율 ¶②청중은 젊은이가 차지하는 비율이 크다

ra·ti·oc·i·nate [ræʃiásinèit / rætiɔ́s-] *vi.* reason or deduce logically.

—[自] 추리하다, 추론(推論)하다

R

ra·tion [rǽʃ(ə)n, réi-] *n.* [U] **1.** a fixed allowance or portion of food or supplies. ¶*rations of sugar (coal).*① **2.** 《usu. *pl.*》 the daily allowance of food for a soldier or sailor. **—*vt.*** supply (someone) with rations; distribute (food, supplies, etc.) in limited amounts.
—[名] 1. 정량(定量), 배급[량] ¶①설탕(석탄)의 배급 2. 병사의 1일분 식량 —[他] …에게 정액(정량)을 주다, [식량 따위]를 제한하다

* **ra·tion·al** [rǽʃən(ə)l] *adj.* **1.** of reason; based on reasoning; able to reason clearly. ¶*Man is a ~ animal.*① **2.** reasonable; sensible; moderate. **3.** (*Mathematics*) expressible by finite terms. ¶*a ~ number.*②
—[形] 1. 이성(理性)의, 추리의; 이성적인 ¶①인간은 이성 있는 동물이다 2. 분별있는, 도리에 맞는 3. 《數》 유리(有理)의 ¶②유리수

ra·tion·ale [ræ̀ʃənǽl, -nɑ́:li / ræ̀ʃiənɑ́:l] *n.* [C] **1.** a reasoned explanation. **2.** the fundamental principle or reason.
—[名] 1. 이론적 해석 2. 근본적 이유

ra·tion·al·ism [rǽʃ(ə)nəlìz(ə)m] *n.* [U] the theory that reason is the supreme source of knowledge.
—[名] 이성론, 합리주의

ra·tion·al·ist [rǽʃ(ə)nəlist] *n.* [C] a person who believes in rationalism.
—[名] 이성론자, 합리주의자

ra·tion·al·is·tic [ræ̀ʃ(ə)nəlístik] *adj.* of rationalism.
—[形] 이성주의의, 합리주의의

ra·tion·al·i·ty [ræ̀ʃ(ə)nǽliti] *n.* [U] (pl. **-ties**) the quality of being rational; reasonableness; 《usu. *pl.*》 a reasonable practice, view or belief.
—[名] 합리성; 이성적 행동(견해·생각)

ra·tion·al·i·za·tion [ræ̀ʃ(ə)nəlizéiʃ(ə)n / -əlai-] *n.* [U] the act of rationalizing; the state of being rationalized.
—[名] 합리화

ra·tion·al·ize [rǽʃ(ə)nəlàiz] *vt.* **1.** make (something) rational or more efficient. ¶*~ an industry.*① **2.** treat or explain (something) entirely by reason. ¶*~ myths.*② **3.** justify (one's behavior, etc.) to oneself; find excuses for (a fault, etc.). ¶*She rationalized her prejudice.* **—*vi.*** think or act in a rational manner; practice rationalism.
—[他] 1. …을 합리화하다 ¶①산업을 합리화하다 2. …을 이론적으로 생각(설명)하다 ¶②신화를 합리적으로 설명하다 3. …에 이유를 달다, 구실을 찾다 —[自] 이론적으로 생각하다; 합리화하다

rat·line, -lin [rǽtlin] *n.* [C] 《usu. *pl.*》 any of the small ropes across the shrouds of a ship, used as a ladder. ⇒shroud (fig.)
—[名] [배의] 새끼사다리[의 디딤줄]

rats·bane [rǽtsbèin] *n.* [U] any poison to kill rats.
—[名] 쥐약

rat·tan [rætǽn / rə-] *n.* **1.** [U] a palm tree with long, tough stems. **2.** [C] a walking stick made of the wood of this tree.
—[名] 1. 등나무 2. 등나무 지팡이

rat·ter [rǽtər] *n.* [C] **1.** a person, an animal or a device that catches rats. ¶*Our cat is a good ~.*① **2.** a person who betrays his associates; a deserter.
—[名] 1. 쥐 잡는 사람(동물·기구) ¶①우리집 고양이는 쥐를 잘 잡는다 2. 변심한 사람, 탈당자

* **rat·tle** [rǽtl] *vi.* **1.** make short, sharp sounds in rapid succession. ¶*The window rattled in the wind. / Someone rattled at the door.*① **2.** go or move with such a sound. ¶*The old car rattled along the road.* **3.** talk rapidly and thoughtlessly. ¶*~ on (or away) for hours.* **—*vt.*** **1.** cause (something) to make a rattling noise. ¶*The wind rattled the window.* **2.** utter rapidly. 《*~ off* something》 ¶*The girl rattled off the poem.* **3.** perform some action rapidly. ¶*~ the bills through the House.* **4.** (*colloq.*) confuse; cause (someone) to be nervous.
—[自] 1. 달캉달캉(덜컥덜컥) 소리나다 ¶①누가 우리 문을 덜걱거렸다 2. [차 따위가] 덜컹덜컹 달리다 3. 재잘재잘 지껄이다 —[他] 1. …을 덜걱거리게 하다 2. …을 재잘재잘 지껄이다 3. …을 후딱후딱 해치우다 4. …을 혼란시키다, 당황하게 하다

—*n.* [C] **1.** a rattling sound. **2.** loud chatter; a person who rattles. **3.** a baby's toy which makes a rattling sound.
—[名] 1. 덜컹덜컹[소리] 2. 재잘재잘 지껄이기; 수다장이 3. 딸랑딸랑(장난감)

rat·tle·brain [rǽtlbrèin] *n.* [C] an empty-headed, noisy person.
—[名] 머리가 텅빈 수다장이

rat·tle·brained [rǽtlbrèind] *adj.* having an empty brain; thoughtless; careless.
—[形] 머리가 텅빈, 생각이 모자라는

rat·tler [rǽtlər] *n.* [C] **1.** anything that makes a clattering sound. **2.** a rattlesnake. **3.** a chatterer.
—[名] 1. 덜컹거리는 것 2. 방울뱀 3. 수다장이

rat·tle·snake [tǽtlsnèik] *n.* [C] a poisonous American snake whose tail rattles sharply when disturbed.
—[名] 방울뱀

rat·tling [rǽtliŋ] *adj.* **1.** making a rattling noise. ¶*a ~ window.* **2.** (*colloq.*) vigorous; brisk. ¶*at a ~ pace.*① **3.** (*colloq.*) splendid; excellent. ¶*have a ~ time (dinner).*
—[形] 1. 덜컹거리는 2. 《口》 기운찬, 활발한, 빠른 3. 《口》 멋진, 훌륭한

rau·cous [rɔ́:kəs] *adj.* harsh-sounding; hoarse.
—[形] 목쉰 소리의, 귀에 거슬리는

rav·age [rǽvidʒ] *vt.* rob (something) with violence; ruin; destroy. ¶*The enemy ravaged the city.*① **—*vi.***
—[他] …을 약탈하다, 노략질하다 ¶①적은 그 도시를 약탈했다 —[自] 약탈하

rave

do ruinous damage; commit ravages. —*n.* **1.** Ⓤ destruction by violence; ruin. **2.** (usu. *pl.*) destructive effects; havoc. ¶*the ravages of war.*①

rave [reiv] *vi., vt.* **1.** talk wildly or irrationally. **2.** (*colloq.*) talk in an extreme manner, usu. enthusiastically. (*~ about* or *of* something) ¶*He raves about his trip to Kyoto.* **3.** (of the sea, wind, etc.) howl; roar. ¶*The sea raves against the cliff.*①

rav·el [rǽv(ə)l] *v.* (**-eled, -el·ing** or *Brit.* **-elled, -el·ling**) *vt.* **1.** draw out the threads of (something); untwist. **2.** tangle; confuse. —*vi.* **1.** become unwoven. ¶*The sweater began to ~ at the elbow.*① **2.** become tangled or confused. —*n.* Ⓒ an unraveled thread; a confused condition.

ra·ven [réivn] *n.* Ⓒ a large, black bird like a crow. —*adj.* deep, shining black. ¶*~ hair.*

rav·en·ous [rǽvinəs] *adj.* very hungry; starving; greedy. ¶*~ for food.* ▷**rav·en·ous·ly** [-li] *adv.*

ra·vine [rəvíːn] *n.* Ⓒ a long, deep valley, usu. worn by running water; a gorge.

rav·ing [réiviŋ] *adj.* **1.** raging; frenzied. ¶*a ~ storm.* **2.** (*U.S. colloq.*) remarkable; notable. ¶*a ~ beauty.*① —*n.* (often *pl.*) wild, irrational talk. ¶*the ravings of a madman.*②

rav·ish [rǽviʃ] *vt.* **1.** fill (someone) with strong emotion or delight; enchant. **2.** (*archaic*) take away (something) by force; violate (a woman).

‡**raw** [rɔː] *adj.* **1.** not cooked. ¶*~ meat*① / *eat fish ~.* **2.** in the natural state; unprocessed; unrefined. ¶*~ cotton* / *~ material*② / *~ rubber.* **3.** not trained; not experienced. ¶*a ~ recruit*③ / *He is ~ to the work.* **4.** (of the weather) damp and cold. ¶*a ~ morning.* **5.** (of wounds) with the skin rubbed off; painful. ¶*a ~ cut.*④ **6.** (*U.S. colloq.*) harsh; unjust; indecent. ¶*a ~ deal.*⑤
—*n.* (*the ~*) an exposed sore spot on the body.
1) *in the raw,* (*U.S.*) in the natural state; naked.
2) *touch someone on the raw,* wound someone in a very sensitive spot.

raw·boned [rɔ́ːbòund] *adj.* having little flesh covering the bones; very thin; bony. ¶*a ~ horse.*①

‡**ray**¹ [rei] *n.* Ⓒ **1.** a line or beam of light; a line or stream of heat, electrons, etc. ¶*X rays*① / *the rays of the sun.* **2.** one of several parts coming out from a common center. ¶*the rays of a daisy* / *a starfish's rays.*② **3.** a beam of mental light. ¶*a ~ of truth*③ / *a ~ of hope.*④ —*vi.* issue in rays.

ray² [rei] *n.* Ⓒ a flat, fan-shaped fish with a thin, whip-like tail ⇒fig. ⌐mond.⌐

Ray [rei] *n.* a nickname for Ray-⌐

Ray·mond [réimənd] *n.* a man's name.

ray·on [réiɑn / -ɔn] Ⓤ a silklike fiber or fabric made from wood pulp; artificial silk.

raze [reiz] *vt.* **1.** scratch away; erase. [ray²] **2.** destroy utterly; bring (something) down to the ground. ¶*The whole town was razed by the earthquake.*① ⇒N.B.

∗**ra·zor** [réizər] *n.* Ⓒ a sharp-edged tool, used esp. for shaving hair off the skin. ¶*a safety ~.*①
as sharp as a razor, very sharp.

ra·zor·back [réizərbæk] *n.* Ⓒ **1.** a kind of whale. **2.** a half-wild hog with a sharp ridge-like back, living in

razorback

다, 파괴하다 —③ 1. 파괴, 황폐 2. 파피의 자국 ¶②전화(戰禍)

—⾃⽥ 1. 헛소리하다 2. 열광적으로(정신없이) 지껄이다 3. (바람·바다 따위가) 거칠다, 휘몰아치다 ¶①거친 바다[물결]가 벼락에 부딪친다

—⽥ 1. …의 얽힌 것을 풀다 2. …을 얽히게 하다; 분류시키다 —⾃ 1. 풀리다 ¶①스웨터의 팔꿈치가 풀리기 시작했다 2. 얽히다, 분규하다 —③ 실의 얽힘; 혼란

—③ 큰 까마귀
—⽥ 새까만
—⽥ 굶주린, 게걸스럽게 먹는

—③ 협곡, 산꼴짜기

—⽥ 1. 미쳐 날뛰는 2. 〔美口〕 대단한, 유명한 ¶①굉장한 미인
—③ 헛소리 ¶②미치광이의 헛소리

—⽥ 1. …을 기뻐 날뛰게 하다, 황홀하게 하다 2. …을 강탈하다; 〔여자〕를 강간하다

—⽥ 1. 날것의, 요리하지 않은 ¶①날고기 2. 원료 그대로의, 가공하지 않은 ¶②원료 3. 미숙한; 경험이 없는 ¶③신병 4. 으슬으슬한 5. 살갗이 벗겨진; 열열한 ¶④생살이 나온 상처 6. 〔美口〕심한; 불공평한; 상스러운 ¶⑤부당한 처사
—③ 살갗이 벗겨진 곳
图 1) 자연 그대로의; 나체의 2) …의 아픈 곳을 건드리다

—⽥ 말라빠진, 뼈가 앙상한 ¶①야윈 말

—③ 1. 광선, 사선(射線), 열선(熱線), 방사선 ¶①뢴트겐선 2. 〔별과 같은〕 사출형(射出形)의 것 ¶②불가사리의 팔 3. 광명, 한 가닥의 희망 ¶③진리의 번득임 / ④일루의 희망 —⾃ 〔빛 따위가〕 번득이다
—③ 가오리

—③ Raymond의 애칭
—③ 남자 이름

—③ 레용, 인조견사

—⽥ 1. …을 지우다, 없애다 2. …을 완전히 파괴하다, 무너뜨리다 ¶①마을 전체가 지진으로 무너졌다 N.B rase로도 씀
—③ 면도칼 ¶①안전 면도

图 빈틈없는; 기민한
—③ 1. 멸치고래 2. 등이 뾰족한 산돼지 3. 뾰족한 〔산〕등

the southern United States. **3.** a sharp, narrow back like a razor.

razor·edge [réizərèdʒ] *n.* [C] **1.** the sharp edge of a razor; a sharp ridge of a hill. **2.** a critical point.
be on a razoredge, be in extreme difficulty or danger.
—[名] 1. 면도날; 뾰족한 산등성이 2. 위기, 아슬아슬한 고비
[熟] 위기에 처해 있다

R.C. **1.** Red Cross. **2.** Reserve Corps. **3.** Roman Catholic.

Rd. Road.

re [riː] *prep.* (chiefly *Law, Commerce*) (*colloq.*) in the matter of; concerning. ¶*I'd like to have a talk with you ~ your plan.*①
—[前] (주로 法·商) (口)…에 관하여, …에 대하여 ¶①네 계획에 대하여 이야기하고 싶다

Re (*Chemistry*) rhenium.

re- [riː-, ri-, re-] *pref.* **1.** again; anew. : *rearrange* (=arrange again) / *rebuild* (=build again) **2.** back: *reclaim* (=*claim* back) / *repay* (=pay back)
—(接頭) 1.「다시」「되풀이하여」「새로이」 2.「되돌리다」

‡**reach** [riːtʃ] *vt.* **1.** arrive at; get or come to; attain to. ¶*~ Tokyo / ~ a conclusion / ~ a good age*① */ ~ one's destination / The letter did not ~ me.* **2.** extend to; amount to. ¶*The path reaches the sea. / The cost has reached millions.* **3.** communicate with. ¶*You can ~ them by cable.* **4.** stretch out (the hand, etc.). ¶*~ one's hand across a table.* **5.** touch or seize (something) by stretching out the hand; get and pass (something) to someone else. ¶*Please ~ me the salt.*② */ Can you ~ that book for me?* **6.** influence; affect. ¶*~ someone's conscience.* —*vi.* **1.** stretch out the hand, foot, etc. ¶*~ for a flower / ~ out for a pen.*③ **2.** try to obtain. ¶*~ after happiness.* **3.** extend in space, time, etc. ¶*The park reaches down to the sea.* **4.** (of the eye, voice, etc.) go as far as. ¶*as far as the eye can ~.*④
—[他] 1. …에 도착하다, 달하다, 닿다 ¶①늙다 2. …에 미치다, 퍼지다; [수량이] …에 이르다 3. …와 연락하다 4. [손 따위]를 뻗다 5. …을 팔을 뻗쳐 잡다 ¶②소금을 집어 주시오 6. [남의 마음]을 움직이다 —[自] 1. 손(발)을 뻗다 ¶③펜을 집으려고 손을 뻗다 2. 얻으려고 애쓰다 3. 퍼지다 4. [눈길·목소리가] 닿다, 도달하다 ¶④눈길이 닿는 데까지

—*n.* [C] ⦅usu. *a ~*⦆ **1.** the act of reaching or stretching out (the hand, etc.). ¶*get a book by a long ~ / make a ~ for a thing.*⑤ **2.** the distance someone or something can stretch; range; [U] the power of reaching. ¶*above* (or *beyond, out of*) *one's ~*⑥ */ within one's ~.* **3.** the power of grasping with the mind. ¶*This arithmetic problem is beyond my ~.* **4.** [C] a continuous stretch or extent; an expanse; a straight part of a river. ¶*a ~ of woodland. / the upper reaches of a river.*⑦
—[名] 1. 집으려고 손을 뻗기 ¶⑤물건을 집으려고 손을 뻗다 2. 도달하는 거리; 뻗는 능력 ¶⑥손이 닿지 않는 곳에 3. 이해력 4. 퍼진 넓이; [강이] 한눈에 바라보이는 구역 ¶⑦강의 상(하)류

reach-me-down [ríːtʃmidàun] *n.* ⦅usu. *pl.*⦆ a ready-made piece of clothes. —*adj.* (*Brit. colloq.*) hand-me-down; ready-made; cheap.
—[名] 기성복 —[形] 기성복의; 싸구려의

re·act [rí(ː)ǽkt] *vi.* **1.** act in return; have a reverse effect upon each other. ⦅~ *on* or *upon* something⦆ **2.** respond. ⦅~ *to* something⦆ ¶*~ to a mother's affection.*① **3.** act in opposition; return to a previous state. ¶*~ against a plan.*
—[自] 1. 거꾸로 작용하다, 반동하다 2. 감응하다, 반응을 보이다 ¶①어머니의 애정에 반응하다 3. 반발하다; 되돌아가다

re-act [riːǽkt] *vt.* act or perform again.
—[他] …을 다시 되풀이하다; 재연(再演)하다

***re·ac·tion** [ri(ː)ǽkʃ(ə)n] *n.* [U][C] **1.** an opposing action. **2.** a response to some force. **3.** a political movement back to a former condition. **4.** a chemical change.
—[名] 1. 반동, 반발 2. 반응 3. 복고(復古) 운동, 보수 운동 4. 화학반응

re·ac·tion·ar·y [ri(ː)ǽkʃ(ə)nèri / ri(ː)ǽkʃ(ə)nəri] *adj.* of political reaction. —*n.* [C] a person who opposes political progress.
—[形] 보수 반동의 —[名] 반동주의자, 보수주의자

re·ac·tor [ri(ː)ǽktər] *n.* [C] a large tank in which atomic energy is produced.
—[名] 원자로

‡**read**[1] [riːd] *v.* (**read** [red]) *vt.* **1.** get the meaning of (something written or printed). ¶*~ a book / ~ English / ~ a novel through* (or *over*).① **2.** learn the true meaning of (something); understand; solve. ¶*be read as …*② */ ~ someone's hand*③ */ ~ something in* (or *on*) *a face*④ */ ~ the signs of the times.*⑤ **3.** say aloud (something written or printed). ¶*~ out a letter to someone / Read me* [*off*] *the list.* **4.** show; point out; indicate. ¶*The thermometer reads 20°.* **5.** bring (someone) into a certain state by reading. ¶*~ a child to sleep*⑥ */ ~ oneself to sleep.* —*vi.* **1.** get the meaning of something written or printed; say aloud something written
—[他] 1. …을 읽다 ¶①소설을 끝까지 읽다 2. …을 해석하다; 이해하다 ¶②…이라고 해석되다/③…의 손금을 보다 /④안색으로 …을 판단하다/⑤세태를 간파하다 3. …을 음독(音讀)하다 4. [온도계 따위가] …을 나타내다 5. …에게 읽어 주어 …시키다 ¶⑥아이에게 책을 읽어 재우다 —[自] 1. 읽다; 음독하다, 낭독하다 ¶⑦책의 어떤 곳을 골라 낭독하다/⑧독서에 몰두하다 2. 읽어서 알다 3. 연구하다 ¶⑨학위를 따기 위해(변호사가 되기 위해) 연구하

or printed. ¶~ *aloud* / ~ *from* (or *out of*) *a book*① / ~ *in a book.*② **2.** learn by reading. ⟪~ *of* or *about* something⟫ **3.** study. ¶~ *for a degree* (*the Bar*).⑨ **4.** give a certain meaning. ¶*The passage reads as follows.* / *The sentence reads oddly.*⑩ — 다 4.…이라고 씌어 있다 ¶⑩그 문장은 내용이 묘하다

1) ***read between the lines,*** find a meaning which is not actually expressed.
2) ***read into*** (=*give a certain explanation to; find a certain meaning in*) *something.*
3) ***read to oneself,*** read silently.
4) ***read up*** (=*make a special study of*) *something.*

[熟] 1)언외(言外)의 의미를 알아 내다 2)…의 의미임을 알다 3)묵독(默讀)하다 4)[어떤 과목]을 전공하다

—*n.* [C] the act of reading; a period of time given to reading. ¶*I have no time for a long* ~. —[名] 독서; 1회의 독서 시간

read·a·ble [ríːdəbl] *adj.* easy to read; interesting to read. —[形] 읽기 쉬운, 재미있게 읽히는

re·ad·dress [rìːədrés] *vt.* **1.** write a new address on (a letter, etc.) **2.** speak to (someone) again. —[他] 1.[편지의] 겉봉을 고쳐 쓰다 2.…에게 다시 말을 걸다

⁑**read·er** [ríːdər] *n.* [C] **1.** a person who reads, esp. one who reads something ready for printing for a publisher. **2.** a text-book for reading. —[名] 1.독서가, 독자, 출판사의 고문, 교정원 2.독본

⁑**read·i·ly** [rédili] *adv.* **1.** quickly. **2.** easily. **3.** willingly; without hesitation. —[副] 1.재빨리 2.쉽사리 3.기꺼이, 주저하지 않고

***read·i·ness** [rédinis] *n.* [U] **1.** the state of being ready. **2.** quickness. **3.** ease. —[名] 1.준비 2.신속 3.용이함

1) ***in readiness,*** ready.
2) ***with readiness,*** willingly; easily.

[熟] 1)준비가 되어 2)자진하여, 쉽사리

⁑**read·ing** [ríːdiŋ] *n.* **1.** [U] the study of books. **2.** [U][C] a written or printed thing to be read. **3.** [C] a record of an instrument shown by letters, figures, or signs. **4.** [U] literary knowledge. —*adj.* fond of reading a book. —[名] 1.서적 연구 2.기사, 읽을거리 3.기록, 표시 도수 4.문학상의 지식 —[形] 책을 좋아하는

R

re·ad·just [rìːədʒʌ́st] *vt.* arrange or put (something) in order again. —[他] …을 새로이 정리하다

re·ad·just·ment [rìːədʒʌ́stmənt] *n.* [U][C] the act of readjusting; the state of being readjusted. —[名] 재정리

⁑**read·y** [rédi] *adj.* (**read·i·er, read·i·est**) **1.** ⟪as *predicative*⟫ prepared. ⟪~ *for*; ~ *to do*⟫ ¶*Dinner is* ~. / *Everything is* ~ *for work.* / *I am* ~ *to go.* / *Ready! Say! Go!*① **2.** ⟪as *predicative*⟫ willing. ⟪~ *for*; ~ *to do*⟫ ¶*I am* ~ *for death.*② / *I am* ~ *to forgive you.* **3.** ⟪as *predicative*⟫ about to; likely; apt. ⟪~ *to do*⟫ ¶*The ship was* ~ *to sink any time.* / *Don't be so* ~ *to find fault.*③ **4.** prompt; handy. ¶*a* ~ *answer*④ / *a* ~ *pen* (or *writer*)⑤ / ~ *wit*⑥ / *the readiest way to do something* / *be* ~ *at excuses*⑦ / *be* ~ *at* (or *to*) *hand*⑧ / *pay* ~ *money.*⑨ —[形] 1.준비를 갖춘 ¶①준비, 땅! 2.언제나(기꺼이) …하는 ¶②언제라도 죽을 각오가 되어 있다 3.막 …하려고 하는; …하기 쉬운 ¶③그렇게 남의 흠만 찾지 말라 4.재빠른, 즉석의; 가까이에 있는, 편리한 ¶④즉답(即答) / ⑤달필가 / ⑥기지(機知) / ⑦핑계를 잘 대다 / ⑧가까이에 있다 / ⑨맞돈으로 치르다

get (or ***make***) ***ready*** (=*prepare*) ***for*** *something.* [熟] …의 준비를 하다

—*adv.* **1.** in a state of preparation. ⇒[usage] ¶*The boxes are packed* ~ (or ~ *packed*). **2.** promptly. —[副] 1.준비하여 [usage] 주로 과거분사와 함께 쓰임 2.신속하게

***read·y-made** [rédiméid] *adj.* **1.** already made for immediate use or for general sale. ¶*a* ~ *suit.* ↔custom-made, made-to-order **2.** not original. —[形] 1.만들어 놓은, 기성품의 2.제것이 아닌, 빌려온

read·y-to-wear [réditəwέər] *adj.* (*U.S.*) (of clothes) ready-made. —[形] ⟪美⟫ 기성복의

read·y-wit·ted [rédiwítid] *adj.* quick in thought or understanding. —[形] 재치있는, 임기응변의

re·a·gent [riéidʒ(ə)nt] *n.* [C] a substance used to produce a chemical change. —[名] 시약(試藥)

⁑**re·al** [ríəl, ríː(ə)l] *adj.* (sometimes ~·**er**, ~·**est** **1.** existing in fact; true; not imagined. ↔imaginary, ideal ¶~ *image*① / ~ *life.*② **2.** genuine; not man-made. ↔artificial ¶~ *silk*③ / *a* ~ *friend* / *a* ~ *man*④ / *the* ~ *thing*⑤ / ~ *money*⑥ / *effect a* ~ *cure.*⑦ **3.** (*Law*) not movable. ↔personal ¶~ *estate* (or *property*).⑧ —[形] 1.실재(實在)의; 현실의 ¶①실상(實像) / ②실생활 2.진짜의, 진정(眞正)한 ¶③본견(本絹) / ④거짓이 없는 사람 / ⑤진짜; 극상품 / ⑥경화(硬貨) / ⑦근치(根治)하다 3.⟪法⟫ 부동산의 ¶⑧부동산

—*adv.* (*colloq.*) really. ¶*We have a* ~ *good time.* —[副] 정말로

—*n.* ⟪*the* ~⟫ something that actually exists; reality. —[名] 현실; 실체(實體)

re·al·ism [ríː(ː)əlìz(ə)m] *n.* [U] **1.** a tendency to be practical. **2.** (*Literature, Art*) the attempt to describe people and things as they really are. **3.** (*Philosophy*) the theory —[名] 1.현실주의 2.[문학·미술상의] 사실(寫實)주의 3.실재론(實在論), 실체론

that material objects exist in themselves, independent of the mind; consciousness of them. ↔idealism

re·al·ist [rí(:)əlist] *n.* ⓒ **1.** a person who is interested in practical matters. **2.** a writer or an artist who tries to describe or paint things exactly as they really are. **3.** a believer in realism.
—명 1. 현실주의자 2. 사실주의자 3. 실재론자

re·al·is·tic [rì(:)əlístik] *adj.* **1.** with a tendency to face facts; practical. **2.** (*Literature, Art*) describing life as it really is; true to life. **3.** of realism.
—형 1. 현실적인 2. 사실적인, 사실파의, 박진적(迫眞的)인 3. 실재론의

‡re·al·i·ty [ri(:)ǽliti] *n.* (pl. **-ties**) **1.** ⓊⒸ real existence. **2.** ⓒ a person or thing that is real. **3.** Ⓤ close resemblance to the original. *in reality,* really; in fact.
—명 1. 실재, 현실 2. 실재물(인) 3. 실물 그대로임, 박진성
熟 정말은, 실제로는

•**re·al·i·za·tion** [rì(:)əlizéiʃ(ə)n / -əlai-] *n.* Ⓤ **1.** the act of realizing; the state of being realized. **2.** the act of bringing something imagined into real existence. ¶*the ~ of one's hopes*① / *be brought to ~.*② **3.** change of property into money.
—명 1. 이해, 실감 ¶①희망의 실현/②실현되다 3. [재산을] 현금으로 바꾸기

‡re·al·ize [rí(:)əlàiz] *vt.* **1.** understand fully; become fully aware of (something). ¶*~ one's own danger.*① **2.** make (something) real; bring (something) into being. ¶*His plan was fully realized.*② **3.** change (property) into money. **4.** gain; get (something) as a profit.
—타 1. …을 충분히 이해하다, 실감하다 ¶①몸의 위험을 깨닫다 2. …을 실현하다 ¶②그의 계획은 완전히 실현됐다 3. [재산]을 돈으로 바꾸다 4. …을 벌다

‡re·al·ly [rí(:)əli] *adv.* in fact; actually; truly; indeed. ¶*Oh, ~?*① / *Do you ~ mean it?*
—부 실제로, 정말로, 전혀 ¶①정말입니까?

‡realm [relm] *n.* ⓒ **1.** a kingdom. **2.** a region; a sphere. ¶*the ~ of science.*①
—명 1. 왕국 2. 영역, 범위 ¶①과학의 분야

re·al·ty [rí(:)əlti] *n.* Ⓤ real estate; one's land or house.
—명 부동산

ream [ri:m] *n.* ⓒ 480 or 500 sheets of paper.
—명 연(連)(480~500매)

ream·er [rí:mər] *n.* ⓒ **1.** a tool for enlarging holes. ⇒fig. **2.** a device for making juice by squeezing lemons, oranges, etc.
—명 1. 구멍 넓히는 기구 2. 리이머(주스 만드는 기구)

[reamer 1.]

re·an·i·mate [rì:ǽnimèit] *vt.* restore (something or someone) to life; give (something or someone) fresh courage, strength, etc.
—타 …을 소생시키다, 활기띠게 하다, 격려하다

•**reap** [ri:p] *vt., vi.* **1.** cut and gather in a crop. ↔sow **2.** gain (something) as a reward.
1) *reap as* (or *what*) *one has sown; reap the fruits of one's action* (or *labor*[s]), receive the result of what one has done; suffer for what one has done.
2) *reap where one has not sown,* make a profit from what others have done.
—타자 1. […을] 베어들이다, 수확하다 2. [보답으로서 …을] 얻다

熟 1)자기가 뿌린 씨를 거둬들이다, 인과응보 2)남의 공을 가로채다

reap·er [rí:pər] *n.* ⓒ a person who reaps; a reaping machine.
—명 베어들이는 사람, 수확기

re·ap·pear [rì:əpíər] *vi.* appear again.
—자 다시 나타나다

re·ap·pear·ance [rì:əpíərəns] *n.* Ⓤ the act of appearing again.
—명 재현, 재발

re·ap·point [rì:əpɔ́int] *vt.* appoint (someone) again; place (someone) again in a former position.
—타 …을 다시 임명하다, 복직시키다

‡rear¹ [riər] *n.* ⓒ **1.** the back part of something. ↔front **2.** the back part of an army or a fleet.
1) *at* (or *in, on*) *the rear of,* behind.
2) *bring up the rear,* march last.
3) *take* (or *attack*) *the enemy, etc. in the rear,* attack the enemy, etc. from behind.
—*adj.* at or in the back.
—명 1. 뒤, 배후, 맨 뒤 2. [군대의] 후미, 후위
熟 1)뒤에, 후미에 2)후미를 맡아보다 3)[적 따위]를 배후에서 공격하다
—형 후부의, 후미의

rear² [riər] *vt.* **1.** make (someone or something) grow; bring up. ¶*~ a child* / *~ crops.* **2.** set up; build. ¶*~ a monument.* —*vi.* stand on the hind legs, as a horse. (*~ up*)
—타 1. …을 기르다, 사육하다, 재배하다 2. …을 일으키다, 세우다 —자 [말 따위가] 뒷발로 서다
[above a captain.]

rear admiral [⌣ ⌣—] *n.* a naval officer who ranks
—명 해군 소장

rear guard [⌣ ⌣] *n.* a group of soldiers guarding the rear of an army.
—명 [군대의] 후위, 후진(後陣)
[with new weapons.]

re·arm [rì:ɑ́:rm] *vt., vi.* arm again; supply (someone)
—타자 […에] 재군비시키다(하다)

re·ar·ma·ment [rì:ɑ́:rməmənt] *n.* Ⓤ the act of rearming;
—명 재군비, 재무장

the state of being rearmed.

rear·most [ríərmòust] *adj.* farthest back; coming last of all.
—[形] 맨 뒤의

re·ar·range [rí:əréindʒ] *vt.* arrange (something) in a different way; arrange again.
—[他] …을 다시 배열하다; 재정리하다

re·ar·range·ment [rí:əréindʒmənt] *n.* [U] the act of rearranging; the state of being rearranged.
—[名] 재배열, 재정리

rear·ward [ríərwərd] *adj.* at, in or toward the rear. —*adv.* =rearwards.
—[形] 후방에 있는, 후방의

rear·wards [ríərwərdz] *adv.* backward; toward the rear.
—[副] 배후에, 후방에

‡**rea·son** [rí:zn] *n.* **1.** [U] the ability to think, judge, etc.; sanity. ¶*Man has ~; animals do not.* | *lose one's ~*① | *come* (or *be restored*) *to ~.*② **2.** [U] what is right or generally agreed; common sense. ¶*disregard ~*③ | *bring someone to ~*④ | *There is ~ in what he says.*⑤ **3.** [U][C] a cause for action or thought; a motive. ¶*the woman's ~*⑥ | *The ~ for his absence was illness.* | *Give me your reasons for doing it.*⑦ | *He complains, and with* [*good*] *~.*⑧ | *There is every ~ why you should be displeased.*⑨
—[名] 1. 이성, 판단력; 제 정신 ¶①정신을 잃다/②제 정신이 들다 2. 도리; 상식 ¶③도리에 맞다/④…에게 도리를 깨닫게 하다/⑤그의 말에는 일리가 있다 3. 이유, 까닭; 동기 ¶⑥여자의 논리(이유)/⑦그것을 하는 이유를 말해 보라/⑧그가 불평을 하는 데에는 이유가 있다/⑨네가 기분이 나쁜 것도 충분한 이유가 있다

1) ***by reason of,*** because of.
2) ***hear*** (or ***listen to***) ***reason,*** pay attention to reasonable advice.
3) ***in reason,*** reasonable.
4) ***out of reason,*** unreasonable.
5) ***stand to reason,*** be reasonable.
6) ***without rhyme or reason; neither rhyme nor reason,*** lacking common sense; without meaning.

[熟] 1)…때문에 2)도리를 알아 듣다 3)도리에 맞는 4)도리에 맞지 않는 5)도리에 맞다 6)도무지 영문을 모르는

—*vi.* **1.** think logically; draw conclusions from data. ¶*~ from experience.*⑩ **2.** talk in a logical way. ¶*~ with someone on* (or *about*) *his folly.*⑪ —*vt.* **1.** think logically about (something); discuss. 《*~ that …; ~ what …; ~ whether …; ~ why …*》 ¶*They reasoned that he was guilty.*⑫ **2.** give one's reasons to (someone) and make him accept one's wishes, ideas, etc.; persuade. 《*~* someone *into* or *out of*》 ¶*~ oneself into a conviction* | *~ someone out of his fears.*⑬
—[自] 1. 추론(推論)하다; 결론을 내리다 ¶⑩경험으로 추론하다 2. 도리를 따져 설득하다 ¶⑪…에 도리를 따져 자신의 어리석음을 깨닫게 하다 —[他] 1. …을 논하다 ¶⑫그들은 그가 유죄라고 논단(論斷)했다 2. 도리를 가르쳐 …시키다 ⑬ ¶…을 설명하여 공포심을 없애다

rea·son·a·ble [rí:z(ə)nəbl] *adj.* **1.** having the power to think clearly or logically; sensible. ¶*a ~ excuse*① | *a ~ employer.* **2.** (of a price, etc.) not very high; not excessive; moderate; fair. ¶*a ~ price* | *on ~ terms.*②
—[形] 1. 도리에 맞는, 사려·분별이 있는 ¶①그럴 듯한 핑계 2. [값이] 알맞은; 온당한 ¶②온당한 조건으로

re·as·sem·ble [rì:əsémbl] *vt., vi.* gather (things) again; put (machines, etc.) together again; come together again.
—[他][自] 다시 모으다(모이다); [기계 따위를] 다시 조립하다

re·as·sert [rí:əsə́:rt] *vt.* say positively again.
—[他] …을 다시 단언하다

re·as·sume [rì:əsú:m / -s(j)ú:m] *vt.* take or seize (something) again.
—[他] …을 다시 가지다, 되찾다

re·as·sur·ance [rì:əʃúərəns] *n.* [U] the act of reassuring; the state of being reassured; new assurance.
—[名] 안심; 재보증, 새로운 자신; 재보험

re·as·sure [rì:əʃúər] *vt.* **1.** set (someone's mind) at ease; give fresh confidence to (someone). **2.** assure (someone or something) again.
—[他] 1. …을 안심시키다, …에게 자신을 갖게 하다 2. …을 재보증하다

re·as·sur·ing [rì:əʃúəriŋ] *adj.* setting someone's mind at ease; giving fresh confidence to; encouraging.
—[形] 안심시키는, 기운나게 하는

re·bate *n.* [rí:beit, ribéit → *v.*] [C] a return of part of a payment; a discount; a reduction. —*vt.* [ribéit] give a rebate to (someone); reduce; deduct.
—[名] 환불(還拂), 리베이트; 할인 —[他] …에게 환불하다, 할인하다

Re·bec·ca [ribékə] *n.* a girl's name.
—[名] 여자 이름

***reb·el** *n.* [rébl → *v.*] [C] a person who resists authority or government. —*adj.* resisting authority; rebellious.
—[名] 반역자, 반항자 —[形] 반역의

—*vi.* [ribél] (**-elled, -el·ling**) resist authority or government by force; revolt. 《*~ against* a ruler, etc.》 ¶*Such treatment would make anybody ~.*①
—[自] 반역하다, 배반하다 ¶①그렇게 취급하면 누구나 반항할 것이다

***re·bel·lion** [ribéljən] *n.* [U][C] the act of rebelling; armed resistance to authority or government. ¶*rise in ~.*①
—[名] 반란, 폭동; 반항 ¶①폭동을 일으키다

re·bel·lious [ribéljəs] *adj.* **1.** resisting government or control; acting like a rebel. **2.** hard to manage. ▷**re·bel·lious·ly** [-li] *adv.* —**re·bel·lious·ness** [-nis] *n.*
—[形] 1. 반항적인, 반역적인 2. 다루기 힘든, 완고한

re·birth [ríːbə́ːrθ] *n.* [U][C] new birth; revival. —[名] 신생(新生), 부활, 재생

re·born [ríːbɔ́ːrn] *adj.* born again; having a new life. —[形] 다시 태어난

re·bound *vi.* [ribáund →*n.*] spring back; bounce back. —*n.* [ríːbàund, ribáund] [C] the action of springing back. —[自] 되튀다 —[名] 되튀기

re·broad·cast [ríːbrɔ́ːdkæ̀st / -kɑ̀ːst] *vt., vi.* (**-cast** or **-cast·ed**) **1.** broadcast again. **2.** broadcast (a program, etc. received from another station); relay. —[他][自] **1.** 재방송하다 **2.** 중계방송하다
—*n.* [C] **1.** the act of rebroadcasting. **2.** a program that is rebroadcast. —[名] **1.** 중계방송 **2.** 중계 프로

re·buff [ribʌ́f] *n.* [C] a flat refusal of another's advice, help, etc. —*vt.* give a rebuff to (someone). —[名] 거절, 퇴짜 —[他] …을 퇴짜놓다, 저지하다

re·build [ríːbíld] *vt.* (**-built** [-bílt]) build (something) again or in a new way. —[他] …을 재건하다, 고쳐 짓다

* **re·buke** [ribjúːk] *vt.* find fault with (someone); blame; scold. —*n.* [C][U] a severe criticism. ¶*receive a* ~. —[他] …을 비난하다, 견책하다 —[名] 비난, 견책

re·bus [ríːbəs] *n.* [C] a riddle composed of pictures that suggest syllables or words. —[名] 수수께끼 그림

re·but [ribʌ́t] *vt.* (**-but·ted, -but·ting**) push back; prove (what has been said, etc.) to be wrong. —[他] …을 물리치다, 논박하다, 반증(反證)을 들다

re·but·tal [ribʌ́tl] *n.* [C] the act of rebutting. —[名] 반박, 반증

re·cal·ci·trance [rikǽlsitrəns] *n.* [U] refusal to obey authority, etc.; disobedience. —[名] 반항; 고집

re·cal·ci·trant [rikǽlsitrənt] *adj.* refusing to obey authority, etc.; disobedient. (~ *against, at*) —*n.* [C] a disobedient person. —[形] 반항하는, 고집 센 —[名] 고집통이

R

‡ **re·call** *vt.* [rikɔ́ːl →*n.*] **1.** call back; bid (someone) to return. ¶~ *the ambassador.*① **2.** take back; withdraw (an order, etc.) ¶~ *one's words.*② **3.** call (something) back to mind; remember. —[他] **1.** …을 도로 부르다, 소환하다 ¶①대사를 소환하다 **2.** …을 철회하다, 취소하다 ¶②자기 말을 취소하다 **3.** …을 상기하다
—*n.* [*U.S.* ríːkɔl] [U][C] **1.** the act of calling back. **2.** the right or procedure of removing an official by popular vote. **3.** [U] the act of remembering. —[名] **1.** 소환, 도로 부르기 **2.** [일반 투표에 의한 관공리의] 해임[권] **3.** 회상
beyond (or ***past***) ***recall,*** unable to be brought back or remembered; forgotten. [熟] 돌이킬 수 없는, 생각이 안 나는

re·cant [rikǽnt] *vt., vi.* take back (a statement, an opinion, etc.) publicly. —[他][自] [진술·의견 따위를] 취소하다, 철회하다

re·can·ta·tion [rìːkæntéiʃ(ə)n] *n.* [U][C] the act of recanting. —[名] 취소, 철회

re·ca·pit·u·late [rìːkəpítʃulèit / -tju-] *vt., vi.* sum up; tell (the contents, etc.) briefly or in outline; repeat the chief points of (arguments, etc.). —[他][自] […을] 요약하다, 요점을 되풀이하다

re·ca·pit·u·la·tion [ríːkəpìtʃuléiʃ(ə)n / -tju-] *n.* [C][U] **1.** repetition of main points. **2.** a summary. —[名] **1.** 요점의 되풀이 **2.** 요약

re·cap·ture [ríːkǽptʃər] *vt.* capture again. —*n.* [U] the act of taking again; [C] a thing which is recaptured. —[他] …을 도로 찾다 —[名] 탈환; 탈환물

re·cast *vt.* [ríːkǽst →*n.* / -kɑ́ːst] (**-cast**) **1.** cast or mold again. **2.** reconstruct; remodel. —*n.* [*U.S.* ríːkæ̀st] [C] the act of recasting; a thing which is recast. —[他] **1.** …을 개주(改鑄)하다, 고쳐 만들다 **2.** …을 개조하다 —[名] 개주[물]; 개작[물]

re·cede [risíːd] *vi.* **1.** go or move backward. (~ *from* something) **2.** incline backward. ¶*a receding chin.*① **3.** withdraw. (~ *from* something) ¶~ *from a contract.*② —[自] **1.** 물러나다 **2.** 뒤로 기울다 ¶①쑥 들어간 턱 **3.** 손을 떼다 ¶②계약에서 손을 떼다
recede into the background, lose influence; become less important. [熟] 세력을 잃다; 중요하지 않게 되다

* **re·ceipt** [risíːt] *n.* **1.** [C] a piece of paper showing that money or goods have been received. **2.** (*pl.*) money or goods received. **3.** [U] the act of receiving. —[名] **1.** 영수증 **2.** 수령액, 수익 **3.** 수령(受領)
1) ***be in*** [***the***] ***receipt of,*** receive.
2) ***on*** [***the***] ***receipt of,*** as soon as a person receives. [熟] 1)…을 받다 2)…을 받는 대로
—*vt.* mark or sign (a bill) as a receipt for money, goods, etc. —[他] [계산서]에 영수했다는 서명(표시)을 하다

re·ceiv·a·ble [risíːvəbl] *adj.* **1.** that can be received; suitable for acceptance. **2.** requiring payment. ¶*bills* ~.① —[形] **1.** 받을 수 있는 **2.** 지불을 요구하는 ¶①수취 어음

‡ **re·ceive** [risíːv] *vt.* **1.** take; get; be given. ¶~ *a letter* / ~ *a good education* / *I received a telegram from my mother.* **2.** undergo; suffer; experience. ¶~ *a mortal* —[他] **1.** …을 받다, 얻다 **2.** …을 입다, 겪다; 경험하다 **3.** …을 수리하다, 받아들이다 ¶①…의 고백을 듣다 **4.** …을

received [945] **recitative**

wound | ~ *a hearty welcome* | ~ *punishment.* **3.** accept. ¶~ *a proposal* | ~ *someone's confession.*① **4.** admit; entertain; welcome. ¶~ *a guest* / *I cannot ~ him this morning.* **5.** recognize (something) as true. —*vi.* **1.** get something. **2.** be at home to guests or visitors. ¶*She receives on Wednesday.*②

re·ceived [risíːvd] *adj.* generally accepted as correct.

re·ceiv·er [risíːvər] *n.* ⓒ **1.** a person who receives. **2.** the part of a telephone which is held to the ear. **3.** the part of a receiving set for a radio, etc. **4.** a person appointed by a court to take charge of another's property or money.

re·cent [ríːsnt] *adj.* not long past; done or made lately; modern; new. ¶*a* ~ *event* / *in* ~ *years.*①

re·cent·ly [ríːsntli] *adv.* not long ago; lately. ¶*until* ~ / *He has* ~ *been to Osaka.* ⇒ USAGE

re·cep·ta·cle [riséptəkl] *n.* ⓒ anything used to contain or hold something, such as a bag or a cup; a container

re·cep·tion [risépʃ(ə)n] *n.* **1.** ⓤ the act of receiving; the state of being received. **2.** ⓒ the way of receiving. ¶*a favorable* ~.① **3.** ⓒ a gathering to welcome or honor guests. ¶*A* ~ *was held in honor of the ambassador.*

re·cep·tion·ist [risépʃənist] *n.* ⓒ a person employed to receive visitors.

re·cep·tive [riséptiv] *adj.* able or quick to receive new ideas, impressions, etc. ¶*ness to receive.*

re·cep·tive·ness [riːséptivnis] *n.* ⓤ ability or willingness

re·cess [risés] *n.* **1.** ⓤ a brief stop of work, study, business, etc.; (*U.S.*) a vacation. **2.** ⓒ an alcove. **3.** (*usu. pl.*) an inner part. ¶*ing, etc.*) *take a recess.* —*vt.* make a recess in (something). —*vi.* (of a meet-

re·ces·sion [riséʃ(ə)n] *n.* **1.** ⓤ the act of going back; withdrawal. **2.** ⓒ a part which recedes. **3.** ⓒ a period of reduced economic activity.

re·ces·sion·al [riséʃ(ə)n(ə)l] *adj.* **1.** of the recession of the clergy and choir. ¶*a* ~ *hymn.*① **2.** (*Brit.*) of a parliamentary recess. —*n.* ⓒ a recessional hymn or music sung or played while the clergy and choir leave the chancel.

re·ces·sive [risésiv] *adj.* tending to go back.

rec·i·pe [résipi(ː)] *n.* ⓒ a list of directions for preparing or mixing medicine, foods, drinks, etc.; a prescription.

re·cip·i·ent [risípiənt] *n.* ⓒ a person or thing that receives. ¶*the* ~ *of the prize.*① —*adj.* receiving; ready to receive.

re·cip·ro·cal [risíprək(ə)l] *adj.* done or given in return; mutual. ¶~ *help*① / *a* ~ *treaty* / ~ *affection.*

re·cip·ro·cal·ly [risíprəkəli] *adv.* in a reciprocal manner; mutually.

re·cip·ro·cate [risíprəkèit] *vt.* **1.** give or get (something) in exchange; interchange; give (something) in return. **2.** make (something) move back and forth. —*vi.* **1.** interchange. **2.** move back and forth. ¶*ciprocating.*

re·cip·ro·ca·tion [risìprəkéiʃ(ə)n] *n.* ⓤ the act of re-

rec·i·proc·i·ty [rèsiprásiti / -prɔ́s-] *n.* ⓤ **1.** a reciprocal state; mutual action. **2.** mutual exchange of privileges.

re·cit·al [risáitl] *n.* ⓒ **1.** a program of music given by a single singer or player. **2.** the act of reciting; narration.

rec·i·ta·tion [rèsitéiʃ(ə)n] *n.* ⓤⓒ **1.** the act of reciting prose or poetry in public. **2.** (*U.S.*) the act of reciting a lesson prepared in advance by pupils in a classroom.

rec·i·ta·tive [rèsitətíːv] *n.* **1.** ⓤ a style of music half-way between speaking and singing, used in opera. **2.**

들이다; 맞이하다, 환영하다 **5.** …을 용인(容認)하다

—自 **1.** 받다 **2.** 방문을 받다 ¶②*그녀는 수요일을 면회일로 삼고 있다*

—形 용인된

—名 **1.** 수취인; 접대자 **2.** [전화의] 수화기 **3.** 수신기, 수상기 **4.** 재산 관리인

—形 최근의, 근래의, 근대의, 새로운 ¶①근년

—副 최근 USAGE lately 나 of late 와 마찬가지로 완료형·과거형에 모두 쓰임

—名 용기(容器), 그릇

—名 **1.** 받기; 수령 **2.** 대우, 평판 ¶①호평 **3.** 환영회, 리셉션

—名 접수계, 수부

—形 잘 받아들이는, 이해력이 있는, 감수성이 풍부한

—名 감수성, 수용성(受容性)

—名 **1.** 휴게[시간]; 《美》 휴가 **2.** 후미진 곳, 벽감(壁龕) **3.** 구석, 귀퉁이
—他 …을 우묵하게 하다 —自 휴회(휴교)하다

—名 **1.** 후퇴 **2.** 움푹한 곳 **3.** 경기후퇴[기]

—形 **1.** [목사·성가대의] 물러날 때의, 퇴장 때의 ¶①*목사가 퇴장할 때 부르는 찬미가* **2.** [의회의] 휴회의 —名 퇴장할 때 부르는 찬미가

—形 퇴행의, 역행의

—名 [의약의] 처방, 요리법

—名 수납자; 그릇, 용기 ¶①상금 수상자 —形 수령하는, 받아들이기 쉬운

—形 서로의, 상호간의; 보답으로 얻는, 보복의 ¶①호혜 조약
—副 서로, 상호, 호혜적으로

—他 **1.** …을 교환하다; 보답으로 …을 주다 **2.** …에 왕복운동을 시키다 —自 **1.** 교환하다 **2.** 왕복운동하다

—名 교환, 답례, 왕복운동
—名 **1.** 상호관계; 상호작용 **2.** 호혜(互惠), 상호 이익

—名 **1.** 독창(주)회, 리사이틀 **2.** 낭송, 음송(吟誦)

—名 **1.** 낭송 **2.** 《美》 암송, 복창

—名 **1.** 서창조(敍唱調) **2.** 서창조의 말

re·cite [risáit] *vt.* **1.** repeat (a poem, prose, etc.) from memory. **2.** give an account of (something) in detail. **3.** (*U.S.*) repeat (a lesson) in the classroom. —*vi.* repeat something learnt by heart.
— 他 1. [시 따위]를 낭송(암송)하다 2. …을 상세하게 보고하다 3. [학과]를 암송하다 —自 암송하다, 낭송하다, 상세히 말하다

:reck·less [réklis] *adj.* without care; careless about results; rash. ¶~ *driving* | *be* ~ *of danger*.
—形 부주의한, 무모한, 개의치 않는

reck·less·ly [réklisli] *adv.* in a reckless manner; carelessly.
—副 무모하게, 거리낌없이

re·ck·on [rék(ə)n] *vt.* **1.** count; calculate. ¶~ *up the bill.*① **2.** judge; consider; regard. ¶~ *someone an enemy* | *I* ~ *him as* (or *for, to be*) *a wise man.* | *We* ~ *him among our supporters.*② **3.** (*colloq.*) think; suppose. ((~ *that* …)) ¶*I* ~ *that it is going to rain.* | *He will come soon, I* ~.③ —*vi.* **1.** count. ¶~ *from 10 to 100.* **2.** rely; depend. ((~ *on* or *upon* something)) ¶~ *on someone's help.*
1) *reckon in* (=*include*) something.
2) *reckon with,* ⓐ settle accounts with (someone). ⓑ take (something) into account.
3) *reckon without one's host,* overlook some important factor
— 他 1. …을 세다, 계산하다; 총계하다 ¶①계산서의 합계를 내다 2. …을 평가하다, …으로 간주하다 ¶②우리는 그를 지지자의 한 사람으로 생각하고 있다 3. (口) …이라고 생각하다 ¶③그는 곧 올 것이라 생각한다 —自 1. 계산하다 2. 기대하다, 의지하다
熟 1)…을 계산에 넣다 2)ⓐ…와 청산하다 ⓑ…을 고려에 넣다 3)중요한 점을 빠뜨리다

reck·on·er [rék(ə)nər] *n.* ⓒ **1.** a person who reckons. **2.** a book of mathematical tables.
—名 1. 계산자(者) 2. 계산 속견표(速見表)

reck·on·ing [rék(ə)niŋ] *n.* ⓒ a bill for goods or services. *the day of reckoning,* ⓐ the day when accounts must be settled. ⓑ the Day of Judgment.
—名 계산서
熟 ⓐ계산일 ⓑ최후의 심판일

re·claim [rikléim] *vt.* **1.** lead (someone) into better ways; reform. **2.** bring (something) into use; bring (land) under cultivation. **3.** ask for the return of (something). —*n.* Ⓤ reformation; restoration.
— 他 1. …을 개심시키다, …을 교화(化)하다 2. …을 이용하다; …을 농지화 하다 3. …의 반환을 요구하다 —名 교화, 개심; 회복

rec·la·ma·tion [rèkləméiʃ(ə)n] *n.* ⓤⓒ the act of reclaiming; the state of being reclaimed.
—名 개심; 개간; 회복; 반환 요구

re·cline [rikláin] *vt.* cause (something) to lean back. ¶~ *one's head on*….④ —*vi.* lean back. ((~ *against* something)) ¶~ *against the wall.*
— 他 …에 기대게 하다 ¶①…에 머리를 기대다 —自 기대다

rec·luse [rí:klu:s, +*U.S.* réklu:s, → *adj.*] ⓒ a person who lives apart from the world; a hermit. —*adj.* [ríklú:s] withdrawn from the world.
—名 은둔자 —形 세상을 버린

*rec·og·ni·tion** [rèkəgníʃ(ə)n] *n.* Ⓤ **1.** the act of recognizing; the state of being recognized; notice; salutation. ¶*He gave no sign of* ~.① **2.** acknowledgement. ¶*the* ~ *of a new state.*② **3.** favorable notice; acceptance.
—名 1. 알아보기, 인사 ¶①그는 아는 체도 안했다 2. 승인, 인지(認知) ¶②신생국가의 승인 3. 인정(認定)

rec·og·niz·a·ble [rékəgnàizəbl] *adj.* that can be recognized.
—形 인식(승인)할 수 있는; 알아볼 만한

rec·og·niz·a·bly [rékəgnàiz(ə)bli] *adv.* **1.** in a recognizable manner. **2.** to a recognizable extent or degree.
—副 1. 뚜렷이 눈에 보이게 2. 꽤, 상당히

rec·og·ni·zance [rikágniz(ə)ns / -kɔ́g-] *n.* ⓒ recognition; (*Law*) the recorded promise to do some particular act.
—名 승인; 서약

:rec·og·nize [rékəgnàiz] *vt.* **1.** acknowledge; take notice of (something); accept; admit. ¶~ *the new government*① | ~ *a baby as one's son.*② **2.** realize to have seen (something) before; identify. ¶~ *an old friend.*
— 他 1. …을 인정하다; 승인하다; 인지 (認知)하다 ¶①신정부를 승인하다/② 갓난애를 자기의 아들로서 인지하다 2. …을 알아보다

re·coil [rikɔ́il] *vi.* **1.** spring back; come back. **2.** retreat. **3.** shrink back. ((~ *at* (or *before, from*) something)) —*n.* ⓒ sudden backward, esp. of a gun when it is fired.
—自 1. 되튀다, 뒤로 물러나다 2. 퇴각(패주)하다 3. 움찔하다 —名 되튀기; [총포의] 반동

*rec·ol·lect** [rèkəlékt] *vt.* call (something) back to mind; remember.
— 他 …을 회상하다, 상기하다

re·col·lect [rí:kəlékt] *vt.* **1.** gather or collect again. **2.** compose (one's thoughts, etc.); recover (oneself). ¶*be recollected* | ~ *oneself.*
— 他 1. …을 다시 모으다 2. [마음 따위]를 가라앉히다; [용기 따위]를 불러 일으키다

*rec·ol·lec·tion** [rèkəlékʃ(ə)n] *n.* **1.** Ⓤ the act or power of calling back to the mind. ¶*be in or* (*within*) *one's* ~① | *be past* (or *beyond*) ~② | *have no* ~ *of*….③ **2.** ⓒ (often *pl.*) a memory.
—名 1. 상기, 회상; 기억[력] ¶①기억에 남아 있다/②기억이 안 나다/③…의 기억이 없다 2. 추억

re·com·mence [rí:kəméns] *vt., vi.* start or begin again.
— 他自 다시 시작하다, 고쳐 하다

recommend

* **rec·om·mend** [rèkəménd] vt. 1. speak or write well of (someone or something). 2. advise. 3. make (someone) attractive. ¶*Her honesty recommends her.*
* **rec·om·men·da·tion** [rèkəmendéiʃ(ə)n] n. 1. Ⓤ the act of recommending. 2. Ⓒ a letter recommending someone to another.
* **rec·om·pense** [rékəmpèns] vt. pay back; reward; make amends. —n. Ⓤ Ⓒ a reward; amends.
* **rec·on·ci·la·ble** [rèkənsàiləbl] adj. that can be reconciled.
* **re·con·cile** [rékənsàil] vt. 1. make (persons) friends again after a quarrel. ¶~ *Tom and Jack with each other.* 2. settle (a quarrel, etc.) 3. harmonize. ¶~ *rights and duties*② / ~ *words with actions.*
  be reconciled to; reconcile oneself to, get used to.
* **rec·on·cil·i·a·tion** [rèkənsiliéiʃ(ə)n] n. Ⓤ Ⓒ 1. the act of reconciling; the state of being reconciled. 2. the act of settling a quarrel or dispute.
* **rec·on·dite** [rékəndàit, rikán- / rikɔ́n-] adj. 1. profound; difficult to understand. 2. little known; hidden.
* **re·con·di·tion** [rì:kəndíʃ(ə)n] vt. put (something) to a good condition again; repair.
* **re·con·nais·sance** [rikánis(ə)ns / -kɔ́n-] n. Ⓤ Ⓒ an investigation for military or scientific purposes.
* **rec·on·noi·ter**, *Brit.* **-tre** [rèkənɔ́itər] vt., vi. examine or explore for military or scientific purposes.
* **re·con·sid·er** [rì:kənsídər] vt. consider again.
▷ **re·con·sid·er·a·tion** [rì:kənsìdəréiʃ(ə)n] n. 「remodel.」
* **re·con·struct** [rì:kənstrʌ́kt] vt. construct again; rebuild;
* **re·con·struc·tion** [rì:kənstrʌ́kʃ(ə)n] n. Ⓤ the act of rebuilding, remodeling or restoring.
* **re·con·struc·tive** [rì:kənstrʌ́ktiv] adj. of reconstruction; tending to rebuild or restore.
‡ **re·cord** vt. [rikɔ́:rd →n.] 1. set down in writing to keep the memory of (something); register. ¶~ *events / I recorded his speech.* 2. put (sounds, etc.) on a phonograph disk, tape, etc. 3. (of an instrument) show; indicate. ¶*The thermometer records 20°C.*
—n. [rékərd / -kɔ:d] Ⓒ 1. the act of recording; Ⓤ the state or fact of being recorded. ¶*a matter of ~.*① 2. a written account of events, facts, etc.; an official document containing an account of events, etc. ¶*a court of ~*② / *a congressional ~ / keep to (travel out of) the ~.*③ 3. the facts known about one's career, conduct, etc. ¶*have a good (bad) ~ / His ~ is against him.*④ 4. The best achievement, esp. in sports. ¶*beat (or break, cut) the ~*⑤ / *set [up] a new ~ / hold the world's ~.*⑥ 5. a disk used on a phonograph.
1) *bear record to* (=*give proof of*) *something.*
2) *off the record,* not for publication.
—adj. making a record; quite different from others.
re·cord·er [rikɔ́:rdər] n. Ⓒ 1. a person who makes and keeps official records. 2. a machine which keeps records. 3. a musical instrument like a flute. ⇒fig.
record holder [´- ´-] n. a person who officially holds the best record.
re·cord·ing [rikɔ́:rdiŋ] n. Ⓤ the act of a person who records; Ⓒ the act of registering sound on a record.
—adj. that records.

[recorder 3.]

recording angel [-´- ´-] n. an angel who makes records of a man's good and evil deeds.
record player [´- ´-] n. an instrument for producing

record player

—他 1. …을 추천하다 2. …을 권하다 3. [행위·성질 따위가] …을 호감사게 하다
—名 1. 추천, 천거, 권고, 충고 2. 추천장

—他 …에 보답하다; 갚다; …의 보상을 하다 —名 보수, 보상
—形 화해할 수 있는; 조화할 수 있는
—他 1. …을 화해시키다 2. [싸움 따위]를 조정하다 3. …을 조화시키다 ¶ ①권리와 의무를 조화(양립)시키다

熟 …에 만족하다
—名 1. 화해, 사화 2. 조정

—形 1. 심원한; 난해한 2. 애매한; 숨겨진

—他 …을 수리(수선)하다

—名 정찰, 탐색

—他自 정찰하다

—他 …을 재고하다, 다시 생각하다

—他 …을 재건(개조)하다
—名 재건; 개조; 부흥

—形 재건의, 개조의, 부흥의

—他 1. …을 기록하다, 적어 두다 …을 등록하다 2. …을 녹음(녹화)하다 3. [온도계 따위가] …을 나타내다

—名 1. 기록, 적어두기, 등록 ¶①기록된 일 2. 기록한 것; 기록 문서; 공문서 ¶②등록 재판소 /③본론에서 벗어나지 않다(벗어나다) 3. 이력; 성적 ¶④그의 이력은 불리하다 4. [스포오츠 따위의] 최고 기록 ¶⑤기록을 깨뜨리다 /⑥세계기록을 보유하다 5. 축음기판, 레코오드

熟 1)…의 증언을 하다 2)공표하여서는 안 되는, 비공식의
—形 기록적인, 공전(空前)의
—名 1. 기록자; 등록계 2. 기록기; 녹음기 3. 옛날 피리의 일종

—名 최고 기록 보유자

—名 기록하기; 녹음 —形 기록(녹음)하는

—名 [사람의 행동에 대하여 선악을 기록하는] 기록 천사
—名 전축, 축음기

recount [rikáunt] *vt.* tell (something) in detail. —他 …을 자세히 말하다

re·count [rí:káunt] *vt.* count again. —他 …을 다시 세다

re·coup [rikú:p] *vt.* **1.** make up for (a loss, etc.); make good. ¶ *I recouped my loss.* **2.** (*Law*) deduct. —他 1. [손실 따위]를 메우다, 벌충하다 2. 《法》 공제하다

re·course [rí:kɔ:rs, rikɔ́:rs / rikɔ́:s] *n.* **1.** ⓤ an appeal for help or protection. **2.** ⓒ a person or thing turned to for help. —名 1. 의지, 의뢰 2. 의지가 되는 사람 (것)

: **re·cov·er** [rikʌ́vər] *vt.* **1.** get back; regain. ¶ ~ *one's health* / ~ *consciousness*① / ~ *a lost watch.* **2.** (*reflexively*) regain control, balance, etc. of (oneself). ¶ ~ *oneself.*② **3.** make up for (a loss). ¶ ~ *one's losses*③ / ~ *lost time.*④ **4.** obtain (payment for a loss or for damage) by a legal process. —*vi.* **1.** get well again; regain health, prosperity, etc. 《~ *from* something》 ¶ ~ *from a disaster* / ~ *from* (or *of*) *an illness* / *I have quite recovered from my cold.* **2.** obtain a favorable judgment in a suit. **3.** regain one's balance, etc. *recover one's feet* (or *legs*), get up after a fall. —他 1. …을 도로 찾다; 회복하다; 재발견하다 ¶①의식을 다시 찾다 ②[침착성·제정신으로] 돌아오다 ¶②[침착성·제정신·원기]를 회복하다; 소생하다 3. …을 메우다 ¶③손실을 메우다/④잃어버린 시간을 벌충하다 4. …의 배상을 받다 —自 1. 회복하다; 원상으로 회복하다 2. 소송에 이기다 3. 안정을 되찾다

圈 [넘어졌다가] 일어나다

re·cov·er [rí:kʌ́vər] *vt.* put a new cover on (something). —他 …을 다시 덮다

・**re·cov·er·y** [rikʌ́v(ə)ri] *n.* ⓤ **1.** the act of getting back. **2.** the state of being healthy or normal again. —名 1. 회수, 되찾기 2. 회복, 복구

rec·re·ant [rékriənt] *adj.* **1.** (*poetic*) cowardly. **2.** (*poetic*) faithless to one's duty or cause. —*n.* ⓒ a coward; an unfaithful person. —形 1.《詩》겁 많은 2.《詩》불성실한 —名 겁장이; 불성실한 사람

rec·re·ate [rékrièit] *vt.* refresh physically or mentally; relax. —*vi.* take relaxation. —他 …을 기운을 돋우다; 휴식(기분전환)시키다 —自 휴양하다

re·cre·ate [rí:krièit] *vt.* create (something) anew. —他 …을 고쳐 만들다

・**rec·re·a·tion** [rikriéiʃ(ə)n] *n.* ⓤⓒ refreshment of mind or body after work; any form of relaxation or amusement. —名 휴양, 기분전환, 리크리에이션

rec·re·a·tive [rékrièitiv] *adj.* serving as recreation; refreshing. —形 휴양(기분전환)이 되는, 기운을 —名 맞히난, 맞고소 [회복시키는

re·crim·i·na·tion [rikrìminéiʃ(ə)n] *n.* ⓤⓒ the act of expressing mutual reproach; accusation in return.

re·cru·des·cence [rì:kru:désns] *n.* ⓤ (of disease, evil, etc.) the act of breaking out anew. —名 [질병·범죄 따위의] 재발

・**re·cruit** [rikrú:t] *n.* ⓒ a man who has just entered military service; a person who has just joined a group, class etc.; a rookie. —*vt.* **1.** enlist (new soldiers, members); get (someone) to join the military forces, a club, etc.; enroll. ¶ ~ *men for the army.* **2.** restore (health or strength). ¶ ~ *oneself*① / ~ *one's health.*② —*vi.* **1.** get new men or fresh supplies. **2.** recover health or strength. —名 신병; 신회원; 신참자 —他 1. [신병·신회원]을 모집하다, …을 신병(신회원)으로 만들다 2. [원기·기운]을 회복시키다 ¶①보양(保養)(정양)하다/②건강을 회복하다 —自 1. 신병(신회원)을 모집하다(낳다); 보충하다 2. 건강을 회복하다

rec·ta [réktə] *n.* pl. of **rectum**.

rec·tan·gle [réktæŋgl] *n.* ⓒ a four-sided figure having four right angles. —名 장방형

rec·tan·gu·lar [rektǽŋgjulər] *adj.* shaped like a rectangle. —形 장방형의

rec·ti·fi·ca·tion [rèktifikéiʃ(ə)n] *n.* ⓤ the act of rectifying; the state of being rectified. —名 개정, 수정, 조정;《化》정류(精溜);《電》정류(整流)

rec·ti·fy [réktifài] *vt.* (**-fied**) **1.** amend; correct. **2.** (*Chemistry*) refine; purify. **3.** (*Electricity*) change (an alterating current) to a direct current. —他 1. …을 개정(수정)하다; 고치다 2.《化》…을 정류(精溜)하다 3.《電》 …을 정류(整流)하다

rec·ti·lin·e·al [rèktilíniəl] *adj.* =rectilinear. —形 직선의

rec·ti·lin·e·ar [rèktilíniər] *adj.* formed by straight lines; in a straight line. [rectness; honesty.

rec·ti·tude [réktit(j)ù:d / -tjù:d] *n.* ⓤ righteousness; cor- —名 공정; 정직

rec·tor [réktər] *n.* ⓒ **1.** a clergyman in charge of a parish in the Protestant Episcopal Church or the Church of England. **2.** the head of a university, school, etc. —名 1. [미국 성공회의] 교구 목사(신부); [영국 국교의] 교구장 2. [대학·학교 따위의] 총장, 학장, 교장

rec·to·ry [rékt(ə)ri] *n.* ⓒ (pl. **-ries**) a rector's house or income. ·end of the intestine. —名 rector의 주택(수입)

rec·tum [réktəm] *n.* ⓒ (pl. **-ta**) (*Anatomy*) the lower —名《解》직장(直腸)

re·cum·bent [rikʌ́mbənt] *adj.* leaning; reclining. —形 기댄, 드러누운

re·cu·per·ate [rik(j)ú:p(ə)rèit / -kjú:-] *vi., vt.* recover from —自他 [질병·손실 따위에서] 회복하

illness, losses, etc.; regain health.
다(시키다)

re·cu·per·a·tion [rik(j)ù:pəréiʃ(ə)n / -kjù:-] *n.* [U] the act of recuperating; recovery from illness, losses, etc.
—[名] [질병·손실 따위에서의] 회복

re·cu·per·a·tive [rik(j)ú:pərèitiv / -kjú:pərə-] *adj.* of recovery; helping or promoting recuperation.
—[形] 회복하는, 기운을 돋우는, 회복에 도움이 되는

re·cur [rikə́:r] *vi.* (**-curred, -cur·ring**) **1.** (of thoughts, memories, etc.) come back to mind; be remembered; (of subjects, etc.) go back; return. ¶ ~ *to* (or *in, on*) *one's mind* ~① / ~ *to the former subject.*② **2.** (of problems, etc.) come up or occur again; repeat.
—[自] 1. [생각·기억 따위가] 다시 마음에 떠오르다; [화제 따위가] 되돌아가다 ¶①마음에 떠오르다/②원래의 화제로 돌아가다 2. [문제 따위가] 재발하다; 되풀이되다

re·cur·rence [rikə́:rəns / -kʌ́rəns] *n.* [U] [C] the act of recurring; recollection.
—[名] 재기; 재발; 회상

re·cur·rent [rikə́:rənt / -kʌ́rənt] *adj.* coming back at intervals; occurring periodically.
—[形] 재발하는

‡**red** [red] *adj.* (**red·der, red·dest**) **1.** of the color of fresh blood. ¶*be* ~ *with anger.*① **2.** inflamed; bloodstained; fierce. ¶ ~ *eyes* / *a* ~ *hand* / *a* ~ *battle.*② **3.** ((often *R-*)) of the Soviet Union or Communism; politically radical. ¶ ~ *ideas* / *the Red Army*③ / *Red China* / *Red Square*④ / *become* ~.⑤
—[形] 1. 붉은, 빨간 ¶①화가 나서 빨개지다 2. 핏발 선; 피에 물든; 격렬한 ¶②혈전 3. 소련의; 공산주의의; [정치적으로] 붉은, 과격한 ¶③[소련의] 적군(赤軍)/④[모스크바의] 붉은 광장/⑤적화하다

—*n.* **1.** [U] [C] the color of red; a pigment producing this color. **2.** [U] red clothes. ¶*be dressed in* ~. **3.** [C] ((often *R-*)) a communist.
—[名] 1. 빨강; 적색; 빨강 그림물감 2. 빨간 옷 3. 공산당원(주의자)

1) ***in*** (***out of***) ***the red,*** (*colloq.*) in (not in) debt.
2) ***see red,*** (*colloq.*) become very angry.
[熟] 1)((口))적자의(적자가 아닌) 2)((口)) 발끈하다, 격분하다

red·breast [rédbrèst] *n.* [C] (*U.S.*) a robin.
—[名] ((美)) 방울새

red·cap [rédkæ̀p] *n.* [C] (*U.S.*) a porter who works at a railroad station.
—[名] ((美)) [철도 따위의] 수하물 운반인, 짐꾼

red·coat [rédkòut] *n.* [C] (*colloq.*) a British soldier of former days.
—[名] ((口)) [옛날의] 영국 병사

Red Cross [ˊ ˊ], **the** *n.* an international or a national society for helping those who have been sick and wounded in a war, in a flood, etc. ⇒[N.B.]
—[名] 적십자 [N.B.] 정식으로는 the Red Cross Society

red·den [rédn] *vt., vi.* make (something) red; become red; blush.
—[他][自] [···을] 붉게 하다(되다); 얼굴을 붉히다

red·dish [rédiʃ] *adj.* tinged with red; somewhat red.
—[形] 불그스름한, 불그레한

***re·deem** [ridí:m] *vt.* **1.** buy (something) back; regain (something) by paying a price. ¶ ~ *mortgaged property.*① **2.** restore; recover. ¶ ~ *one's right* (*position, honor*). **3.** fulfil; perform. ¶ ~ *a promise.* **4.** make up for (a fault, mistake, etc.). **5.** (*Religion*) free (someone) from sin.
—[他] 1. ···을 되사다, 도로 찾다 ¶①저당된 재산을 도로 찾다 2. ···을 [노력하여] 회복하다 3. ···을 이행하다 4. [결점·과실 따위]를 보충하다, 메우다 5. [신이] ···을 죄에서 구하다

re·deem·er [ridí:mər] *n.* **1.** [C] a person who redeems. **2.** ((*the R-*)) Jesus Christ.
—[名] 1. 되사는 사람; 신원 보증인; 저당물을 찾아내는 사람 2. 구세주

re·demp·tion [ridém(p)ʃ(ə)n] *n.* [U] the act of redeeming; the state of being redeemed; rescue; ransom; salvation.
beyond (or ***past***) ***redemption,*** impossible to save or recover.
—[名] 되사기; 저당물을 찾기; 속전(贖錢)을 치르고 구해내기; 구출; 보상, [그리스도교에 의한] 구원, 속죄
[熟] 구제할 길 없는

re·demp·tive [ridém(p)tiv] *adj.* of redemption; tending or serving to redeem.
—[形] 되사는; 상각(償却)의

red-hand·ed [rédhǽndid] *adj.* **1.** having hands red with blood. **2.** in the very act of committing a crime. ¶*He was caught* ~.① **3.** (of actions) bloody; violent.
—[形] 1. 손이 피투성이가 된 2. 현행범의 ¶①그는 현행범으로 잡혔다 3. 피비린내나는; 난폭한

red·head [rédhèd] *n.* [C] a person with red hair.
—[名] 머리칼이 빨간 사람

red-hot [rédhát / -hɔ́t] *adj.* **1.** red from high heat; very hot. **2.** greatly excited; furious. **3.** very fresh from the source. ¶ ~ *news.*①
—[形] 1. 적열(赤熱)의; 몹시 더운 2. 몹시 흥분한; 격렬한 3. 최신의 ¶①최신 뉴우스

Red Indian [ˊ ˊ-‐] *n.* a North American Indian.
—[名] 북미 토인

re·dis·cov·er [rì:diskʌ́vər] *vt.* discover (something) again.
—[他] ···을 재발견하다

re·dis·trib·ute [rì:distríbju(:)t] *vt.* distribute (something) again.
—[他] ···을 다시 분배(구분)하다

red·ness [rédnis] *n.* [U] the state of being red.
—[名] 붉음, 적색

red·o·lent [rédoulənt] *adj.* **1.** fragrant; scented; smelling ¶*be* ~ *of roses.* **2.** suggestive. ((~ *of*))
—[形] 1. 향기가 좋은; 냄새가 나는 2. 생각나게 하는, 암시하는

re·dou·ble [ri(:)dʌ́bl] *vt., vi.* **1.** double again. **2.** increase greatly. ¶ ~ *one's effort.* **3.** echo; resound.
—[他][自] 1. [···을] 배가(倍加)하다 2. [···을] 강하게 하다(되다) 3. 반향하다

re·doubt·a·ble [ridáutəbl] *adj.* awaking fear or respect.
—[形] 가공할; 공경해야 할

R

redound [ridáund] *vi.* **1.** have an effect; contribute. 《~ *to someone*》 ¶*The sins of the fathers do not ~ to the children.*① **2.** come back upon someone. 《~ *upon someone*》 ¶*His praises ~ upon himself.*② **3.** increase. 《~ *to something*》 ¶*~ to one's credit.*
—自 1. […에] 미치다 ¶①부친의 죄는 자식에게까지 미치지 않는다 2. […으로] 돌아가다 ¶②그의 칭찬은 자신에 대한 칭찬이 된다 3. 늘다

re·dress *vt.* [ridrés → n.] **1.** make (something wrong or out of order) right; repair; compensate. **2.** relieve.
—*n.* [rí:dres, ridrés / ridrés] Ⓤ the act of making right; compensation for a wrong or loss.
—他 1. …을 고치다, 교정(矯正)하다, 배상하다 2. …을 구제하다
—名 교정; 배상; 구제

red·skin [rédskìn] *n.* =Red Indian.

red tape [⌐ ⌐] *n.* **1.** a tape of a red color used for tying official documents. **2.** excessive or rigid formality.
—名 1. 공문서를 매는 붉은 끈 2. 관료적 형식주의, 관청식

:re·duce [rid(j)ú:s / -djú:-] *vt.* **1.** make (something) smaller or less in size, number, weight, price, etc. ¶*~ ~ the price | ~ the speed | ~ one's weight | ~ one's expenditure.* **2.** lower (someone) in rank or grade. 《~ *someone to*》 ¶*~ an officer in rank.* **3.** make (someone) weak physically. ¶*~ one's sight | greatly reduced by illness*③ | *be reduced to nothing* (or *a skeleton*).② **4.** change (something) into another form. 《~ *something to*》 ¶*~ wood to pulp | ~ one's ideas to writing | ~ dollars to cents*③ | *~ a rule to practice.*④ **5.** bring (someone) to a certain condition; bring (someone or something) under control; conquer. 《~ *someone to*》 ¶*~ an enemy | ~ someone to tears* (*silence*) | *~ someone to submission.*⑤ **6.** 《usu. used in *passive*》 compel by force of circumstances to do (something). ¶*be reduced to stealing.*⑥ **7.** bring (something) into order, groups, classes, etc. 《~ *something to*》 ¶*~ language to rules.* **8.** restore (a broken or displaced bone, etc.) to its the normal position. —*vi.* **1.** become reduced. **2.** (*colloq.*) become thinner by dieting.
—他 1. [모양・수량・가격 따위]를 줄이다 2. [지위 따위]를 끌어 내리다, 강등시키다 3. [체력]을 쇠퇴하게 하다, 약하게 하다 ¶①병으로 쇠약해져서/②말라서 뼈와 가죽만 남다 4. …을 바꾸다, 변형하다 ¶③달러를 센트로 바꾸다/④규칙을 실행으로 옮기다 5. …을 [억지로] …시키다; 복종시키다; 항복시키다 ¶⑤…을 굴복시키다 6. [환경 따위가] …이 되게 하다 ¶⑥몰락하여 도둑질까지 하게 되다 7. …을 가지런히 하다, 정돈하다, 분류하다 8. [탈구(脫臼) 따위]를 복원(復元)하다 —自 1. 줄다 2. 《口》 [식이요법으로] 체중을 줄이다

re·duc·i·ble [rid(j)ú:sibl / -djú:s-] *adj.* that can be reduced.
—他 변형(축소)할 수 있다

・re·duc·tion [ridʌ́kʃ(ə)n] *n.* Ⓤ Ⓒ **1.** the act of reducing; the state of being reduced. ¶*~ of armaments.*① **2.** the amount by which something is reduced. ¶*No ~ is*
—名 1. 변형; 축소, 감소 ¶①군비 축소 2. 할인액 ¶②에누리 없음

re·dun·dance [ridʌ́ndəns] *n.* =redundancy. | *made.*②

re·dun·dancy [ridʌ́ndənsi] *n.* (pl. **-cies**) **1.** Ⓤ the state of being more than enough. **2.** Ⓒ something or a part of something that is redundant.
—名 1. 과다(過多), 여분; 용장(冗長) 2. 여분의 것(부분)

re·dun·dant [ridʌ́ndənt] *adj.* **1.** more than enough; excessive. **2.** plentiful. **3.** using more words than are needed. ▷**re·dun·dant·ly** [-li] *adv.* ┌copy.┐
—他 1. 여분의, 과잉의 2. 풍부한 3. 산만한, 용장(冗長)한

re·du·pli·cate [rid(j)ú:plikèit / -djú:-] *vt.* double; repeat;
re·du·pli·ca·tion [rid(j)ù:pliké ́iʃ(ə)n / -djù:-] *n.* **1.** Ⓤ the act of reduplicating; repetition. **2.** Ⓒ a copy.
—他 …을 이중으로 하다; 되풀이하다
—名 1. 이중으로 하기, 반복 2. 사본

red·wood [rédwùd] *n.* Ⓒ a very large Californian tree.
—名 미국 삼나무

re·ech·o [ri(:)ékou] *vt., vi.* echo back; resound. —*n.* Ⓒ (pl. **-oes**) an echo; an echo of an echo.
—他自 되울리다, 울려 퍼지다 —名 반향; 이중 메아리

・reed [ri:d] *n.* Ⓒ **1.** a kind of tall grass growing near water. **2.** a musical pipe made of the stem of this grass. **3.** a thin, vibrating tongue in a musical instrument; 《usu. *pl.*》 such musical instruments.
a broken reed, a person too weak to be relied upon.
—名 1. 갈대 2. 갈대 피리 3. [악기의] 혀, 리이드
▤ 믿을 수 없는 사람

reed·y [rí:di] *adj.* (**reed·i·er, reed·i·est**) **1.** full of reeds. **2.** made of reeds. **3.** like a reed; long; weak. **4.** sounding like a reed instrument. ▷**reed·i·ness** [-nis] *n.*
—他 1. 갈대가 우거진 2. 갈대로 만든 3. 갈대 같은 4. 갈대 피리 소리 같은

reef¹ [ri:f] *n.* Ⓒ a sand bar or a shelf of rock or coral at or near the surface of the water.
—名 암초; 모래톱; 산호초

reef² [ri:f] *n.* Ⓒ a part of a sail which can be folded or rolled to shorten the sail. —*vt.* reduce (a sail) by folding or rolling up a part of it
—名 [돛의] 축범부(縮帆部) —他 [돛]을 감아 줄이다

reek [ri:k] *n.* Ⓤ steam; a disagreeable smell. —*vi.* send out vapor or a strong unpleasant smell.
—名 김, 증기; 악취 —自 연기 나다, 나다; 악취가 나다

•reel[1] [riːl] *n.* [C] **1.** a device with a frame turning on an axis, for winding thread, wire, rope, etc. ⇒fig. **2.** a spool. **3.** something held in a reel, esp. a strip of film. **—*vt.*** **1.** wind (thread, etc.) on or off a reel. **2.** draw in (a fish, etc.) by winding a line on a reel.
—[名] 1. 감는 틀, 리일 2. 실패 3. 감는 틀에 감은 것, 「필름의」 한 리일 —[他] 1. [실 따위]를 얼레(실패)에 감다; 실을 잣다 2. [물고기 따위]를 리일을 돌려 당기다

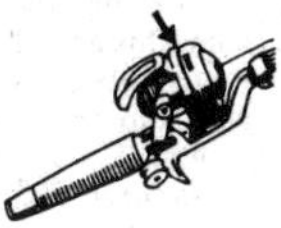

〔reel[1] 1.〕

reel off, tell a story in a rapid and easy manner.
[熟] 재잘재잘 지껄이다

reel[2] [riːl] *vi.* **1.** stagger from side to side in walking. ¶~ *along.* **2.** feel dizzy. ¶*My brain reels.*
—[自] 1. 비틀거리다, 갈짓자 걸음으로 걷다 2. 현기증 나다

reel[3] [riːl] *n.* [C] a lively Scottish dance; the music for this dance.
—[名] 리일 춤; 그 음악

re·e·lect [ríːilékt] *vt.* elect again.
—[他] …을 재선(再選)하다

re·em·bark [ríːimbáːrk] *vt., vi.* put (something) or go on board a ship again.
—[他][自] 다시 승선시키다(하다)

re·en·force [ríːinfɔ́ːrs] *vt.* =reinforce.

re·en·ter [ríːéntər] *vt., vi.* enter again.
—[他][自] 다시 들어가다, 다시 넣다

re·en·try [riːéntri] *n.* [C] (pl. **-tries**) **1.** the act of entering again. **2.** the act of coming back to the Earth's atmosphere.
—[名] 1. 다시 들어가기 2. [대기권으로의] 재돌입

re·es·tab·lish [ríːistǽbliʃ] *vt.* establish again.
—[他] …을 재건하다, 복구(부흥)하다

re·fec·tion [rifékʃ(ə)n] *n.* **1.** [U] the act of recovering one's vigor by eating or drinking. **2.** [C] a light meal.
—[名] 1. [음식에 의한] 원기 회복 2. [가벼운] 식사

re·fec·to·ry [rifékt(ə)ri] *n.* [C] (pl. **-ries**) a dining room in a monastery, school, etc.
—[名] [수도원·학교 따위의] 식당

‡re·fer [rifə́ːr] *v.* (**-ferred, -fer·ring**) *vt.* **1.** tell (someone) to ask or consult in order to know a certain fact. ⟪~ someone *to*⟫ ¶*I beg to ~ you to Mr. Smith for my character.*① | *I ~ you to the dictionary for the correct meaning.* **2.** cause (someone) to consult. ⟪~ someone *to*⟫ ¶*This mark refers readers to a footnote.*② **3.** leave (something) to others' decision. ⟪~ something *to*⟫ ¶*~ a bill to a committee*③ | *~ a dispute to the law court.* **4.** regard (something) as the cause. ⟪~ something *to*⟫ ¶*~ one's success to Providence*④ | *He referred his wealth to his own hard work.* **—*vi.*** **1.** seek information from something. ⟪~ *to* something⟫ ¶*~ to the Bible* | *~ to a former employer for someone's character.* **2.** speak of something; mention. ⟪~ *to* something⟫ ¶*He referred to his past experience.* **3.** apply to something; concern. ¶*The rule refers only to special cases.*⑤ **4.** pay attention to something.
—[他] 1. …을 조회시키다; 참조시키다 ¶①내 신상에 관해서는 스미드씨에게 문의해 주시오 2. …의 주의를 돌리게 하다 ¶②이 표는 각주(脚註)를 보라는 지시다 3. [문제 따위]를 맡기다 ¶③의안을 위원회에 회부하다 4. …을 …으로 돌리다 ¶④성공을 하늘의 도움으로 돌리다 —[自] 1. 참조(참고)하다; 조회하다 2. 언급하다, 인용하다 3. 들어맞다; 관련되어 있다 ¶⑤그 규칙은 특별한 경우에만 적용된다 4. 주목하다

re·fer·a·ble [réf(ə)rəbl / rifə́ːr-] *adj.* that can be considered as a result of something else. ⟪~ *to*⟫
—[形] [⋯의] 탓(덕)이라 할 수 있는

ref·er·ee [rèfəríː] *n.* [C] a judge or an umpire in a game.
—[名] 심판원, 레퍼리

•ref·er·ence [réf(ə)rəns] *n.* **1.** [U][C] the act of consulting something for information or help. ¶*a ~ to a dictionary for* …①. **2.** [U] the act of speaking of something; [C] a matter spoken of. **3.** [C] a letter or person that tells of another person's character or ability. ¶*an excellent ~*② | *Who is your ~?*③ **4.** [C] a book or note used for information; a source of information. ¶*a book of ~; a ~ book.*④ **5.** [U] relation. ⟪~ *to*⟫
—[名] 1. 참조하기, 참고로 하기 ¶①…을 사전을 보고 조사하기 2. 언급, 논급 3. 신원 조회처, 신원 증명서 ¶②훌륭한 증명서/③조회처는 누굽니까? 4. 인용문; 참고 재료 ¶④참고서 5. 관계

1) ***in*** (or ***with***) ***reference to,*** about; in regard to.
2) ***make reference to,*** refer to; mention; speak of.
3) ***without reference to,*** having no relation to.
[熟] 1)…에 관하여 2)…을 참조하다, …에 언급하다 3)…에 관계없이

ref·er·en·da [rèfərénda] *n.* pl. of **referendum**.

ref·er·en·dum [rèfəréndəm] *n.* [C] (pl. **-da** or **-dums**) the process of submitting a law to all the people of a country, state, etc. asking for their opinion of the law.
—[名] [의회를 통과한 정책 따위에 대해 그 가부를 선거민에게 묻는] 국민투표

re·fill *vt., vi.* [riːfíl / ríːfíl ‖ → *n.*] fill again; become filled again. **—*n.*** [ríːfìl] [C] **1.** a replacement. ¶*a ~ for a lipstick case.* **2.** a second serving of food or drink.
—[他][自] 다시 채우다 —[名] 1. 보충물, 다시 채운 것 2. [음식물의] 두 그릇째

refine [952] **reformation**

* **re·fine** [rifáin] *vt.* **1.** make (something) pure or fine. ¶*~ metal* / *~ one's thought.* **2.** make (something) polished or cultivated. ¶*~ one's taste.* —*vi.* **1.** become pure or fine. **2.** improve. ((*~ on* or *upon* something)) **3.** become more polished, as in language, etc.
— ⓣ 1. …을 순화(純化)하다, 정련(精鍊)하다 2. …을 품위있게 하다, [문장 따위]를 다듬다 —ⓙ 1. 순수해지다, 품위있게 되다 2. 개량하다 3. [말씨 따위가] 세련되다

re·fined [rifáind] *adj.* **1.** made pure. ¶*~ sugar.*① **2.** having good manners, taste, etc.
— ⓣ 1. 정제(精製)한 ¶① 정당(精糖) 2. 품위있는, 세련된

* **re·fine·ment** [rifáinmənt] *n.* Ⓤ **1.** the act of refining; the state of being refined. **2.** elegance; good manners and taste. ¶*a person of ~.*①
— ⓣ 1. 정제(精製), 정련(精鍊) 2. 세련, 고상 ¶① 고상한 사람

re·fin·er [rifáinər] *n.* Ⓒ a person or thing that makes something pure, polished or fine.
— ⓣ 정제(정련)하는 사람(기계), 고상하게 하는 사람(것)

re·fin·er·y [rifáinəri] *n.* Ⓒ (pl. **-er·ies**) a factory for making pure sugar, metal, etc.
— ⓣ 정제소(精製所), 정련소(精鍊所)

re·fit [rí:fít] *v.* (**-fit·ted, -fit·ting**) *vt.* prepare (something) for use again; repair. —*vi.* be made ready for use again. —*n.* Ⓤ the act of refitting.
— ⓣ …을 수리하다, [배 따위]를 개장(改裝)하다 —ⓙ [특히 배가] 수리를 받다 —ⓝ [특히 배의] 수리

‡ **re·flect** [riflékt] *vt.* **1.** throw back (light, heat, sound, etc.). ¶*A mirror reflects light.* **2.** give back an image of (something) as a mirror does. ¶*The calm water reflects the hills.* **3.** express. ¶*His face reflected his emotions.*① **4.** bring back (something) as a result. ((*~ something on* or *upon*)) ¶*His conduct reflected great credit on him.*② **5.** think carefully; consider. ((*~ that …* ; *~ how …* ; *~ what …*)) ¶*He reflected how to get out of the difficulty.* —*vi.* throw back light, sound, etc.; give back an image.
reflect on (or *upon*), ⓐ cast blame. ¶*~ upon someone's honesty.* ⓑ have a bad effect. ¶*This decision will ~ on his future career.* ⓒ think deeply. ¶*Reflect upon all I have said to you.*③
— ⓣ 1. …을 반사하다 2. …을 비추다 3. …을 나타내다; 반영하다 ¶① 그의 얼굴은 그의 감정을 나타내고 있다 4. …을 초래(야기)하다 ¶② 그의 행위가 그로 하여금 큰 신용을 얻게 했다 5. …을 곰곰이 생각하다, 숙고하다 —ⓙ 반사(반향)하다; 모습을 비추다

Ⓔ ⓐ …을 비난하다, 헐뜯다 ⓑ …에 나쁜 영향을 주다 ⓒ …을 숙고하다 ¶③ 내가 한 말을 잘 생각해 봐라

* **re·flec·tion** [riflékʃ(ə)n] *n.* **1.** Ⓤ the act of reflecting; the state of being reflected. **2.** Ⓤ Ⓒ a sound, light, etc. which is reflected. **3.** Ⓒ an image. ¶*We could see the ~ of the mountain in the lake.*① **4.** Ⓤ careful thinking; meditation. ((*~ on, upon*)) **5.** ((usu. *pl.*)) an idea, a remark or thought which is the result of careful thinking. ¶*Emerson's reflections on the universe.*② **6.** Ⓒ an unfavorable remark; blame.
— ⓣ 1. 반사, 반향 2. 반사광(열), 반향음 3. 영상(映像), 그림자 ¶① 호수에는 산 그림자가 비추어져 있었다 4. 숙고, 반성 5. 감상, 소견, 생각 ¶② 우주에 대한 에머슨의 소견 6. 잔소리, 비난

re·flec·tive [rifléktiv] *adj.* **1.** throwing back light, an image, etc. **2.** thoughtful. ¶*a ~ mind.*
— ⓣ 1. [빛·그림자를] 반사하는, 반영하는 2. 사려깊은

re·flec·tor [rifléktər] *n.* Ⓒ anything which sends back heat, light, sound, etc.
— ⓣ 반사물(기), 반사경

re·flex [rí:fleks] *adj.* **1.** showing an automatic or unconscious response. ¶*a ~ action.* **2.** likely to turn back upon the mind. —*n.* Ⓒ **1.** a reflection of light, sound, etc.; a mirrored image. **2.** a result. **3.** an unconscious movement.
— ⓣ 1. 반사적인, 반사 작용의 2. 반성적인, 내성적인 —ⓝ 1. [빛·음 따위의] 반사, 반영; 영상, 그림자 2. 결과 3. 반사 작용

re·flex·ion [riflékʃ(ə)n] *n.* =reflection.

re·flex·ive [rifléksiv] *adj.* (*Grammar*) (of a verb or pronoun) indicating an action that turns back on the subject. —*n.* Ⓒ a reflexive verb or pronoun. ⇒Ⓝ·Ⓑ· ▷**re·flex·ive·ly** [-li] *adv.*
— ⓣ 재귀(再歸)의 —ⓝ 재귀동사, 재귀 대명사 Ⓝ·Ⓑ· He killed himself.의 kill은 재귀동사, himself는 재귀대명사

re·flux [rí:flʌks] *n.* Ⓤ the act of flowing back; the ebb tide.
— ⓝ 역류; 썰물

re·for·est [rí:fɔ́:rist, -fɑ́r-/-fɔ́r-] *vt.* replant trees on (land). ▷**re·for·est·a·tion** [rí:fɔ:ristéiʃ(ə)n, -fɑr-/-fɔ́r-] *n.*
— ⓣ 다시 조림(造林)하다 —ⓝ 재조림

‡ **re·form** [rifɔ́:rm] *vt.* make or change (something) better by removing its faults; improve. ¶*~ the system of society* / *~ oneself.* —*vi.* become better. —*n.* Ⓤ Ⓒ **1.** a change for a better state. **2.** a change from a bad to a good character. ▷**re·form·a·ble** [-əbl] *adj.*
— ⓣ …을 개심시키다, 교정(矯正)하다; [제도·사태]를 개선(개량)하다, 개정(혁신)하다 —ⓙ 개심하다, 면목을 일신하다 —ⓝ 1. 개혁, 개량, 쇄신 2. 개심

re·form [rí:fɔ́:rm] *vt., vi.* make or form again.
— ⓣⓙ 고쳐 만들다, 다시 만들다

ref·or·ma·tion [rèfərméiʃ(ə)n] *n.* **1.** Ⓤ Ⓒ the act of reforming; the state of being reformed; a change for the better in social or political conditions. **2.** ((*the R-*))
— ⓝ 1. 개혁, 쇄신, 유신, 개량 2. 종교 개혁

the religious movement in Europe, begun by Martin Luther in the 16th century. —[名] ...

re·form·a·tive [rifɔ́ːrmətiv] *adj.* able to reform; tending to reform. —[形] 개혁할 수 있는, 개량하는

re·form·a·to·ry [rifɔ́ːrmətɔ̀ːri / -fɔ́ːmət(ə)ri] *adj.* tending to correct. —*n.* [C] (pl. **-ries**) a school for the special training of young offenders against the law. —[形] 감화하는 —[名] 감화원

re·form·er [rifɔ́ːrmər] *n.* [C] a person who carries out a change for the better. —[名] 개혁자

re·fract [rifrǽkt] *vt.* bend (a ray of light) from a straight line as it enters or leaves water. —[他] [광선]을 굴절시키다

re·frac·tion [rifrǽkʃ(ə)n] *n.* [U] the act of refracting; the state of being refracted. —[名] [광선·음파 따위의] 굴절[작용]

re·frac·tive [rifrǽktiv] *adj.* having the power of refraction. —[形] 굴절하는, 굴절력이 있는

re·frac·to·ry [rifrǽkt(ə)ri] *adj.* **1.** fixed in one's opinion; unmanageable. **2.** (of illness) hard to cure. **3.** (of metals) hard to melt. ▷**re·frac·to·ri·ly** [-li] *adv.* —[形] 1. 완고한, 다루기 힘든 · 2. [병 따위] 난치(難治)의 3. [금속이] 잘 용해되지 않는

*__re·frain__[1] [rifréin] *vi.* stop oneself from doing something; hold oneself back from doing something. 《~ *from*》 ¶~ *from one's tears*① / *She could not ~ from laughing.*② —[自] 그만두다, 참다, 삼가다 ¶①눈물을 참다/②그녀는 웃지 않을 수 없었다

re·frain[2] [rifréin] *n.* [C] a phrase or verse repeated in a poem or song. —[名] [노래의] 후렴

*__re·fresh__ [rifréʃ] *vt.* **1.** make (something or someone) fresh again; give (someone or something) new energy with food, drink or rest. ¶~ *oneself with a cup of coffee.* **2.** renew. ¶~ *one's memory by ...*① —*vi.* become fresh again; take refreshment. —[他] 1. …을 상쾌하게 하다; 활기띠게 하다 2. …을 새로이 하다 ¶①기억을 …으로 새로이 하다 —[自] 원기를 회복하다; 음식을 먹다

re·fresh·er [rifréʃər] *n.* [C] a person or thing that refreshes. —[名] 상쾌하게 하는 사람(것)

re·fresh·ing [rifréʃiŋ] *adj.* making fresh again; pleasant to the senses. ¶*a ~ breeze*① / *~drinks.*② —[形] 기분을 상쾌하게 하는 ¶①상쾌한 산들바람/②청량음료

*__re·fresh·ment__ [rifréʃmənt] *n.* **1.** [U] the act of refreshing; the state of being refreshed. **2.** 《often *pl.*》 something that refreshes; food and drink served to guests at a party, meeting, etc. —[名] 1. 기분을 상쾌하게 하기; 원기회복 2. 원기를 회복시키는 것; [파아티 따위의] 음식물; 다과(茶菓)

refreshment car [-ˊ- ˊ] *n.* (*Brit.*) a dining coach or car; a diner. —[名] 《英》 식당차

refreshment room [-ˊ- ˊ] *n.* (*Brit.*) a dining room at a station or on a train. —[名] [역·열차의] 식당

re·frig·er·ant [rifrídʒ(ə)rənt] *adj.* cooling; (*Medicine*) reducing fever. —*n.* [C] any substance that makes cool. —[形] 냉각하는; 《醫》 해열의 —[名] 냉각제; 해열제

re·frig·er·ate [rifrídʒərèit] *vt.* make or keep (something) cool; freeze. —[他] …을 식히다, 냉장하다, 냉동시키다

re·frig·er·a·tion [rifrìdʒəréiʃ(ə)n] *n.* [U] the act of refrigerating; the state of being refrigerated. —[名] 냉각, 냉장

*__re·frig·er·a·tor__ [rifrídʒərèitər] *n.* [C] a cabinet, box, room, etc. in which food, drink, etc. are kept cool. —[名] 냉장고, 빙실(氷室)

re·fu·el [riːfjúːəl] *v.* (**-eled, -el·ing** or *Brit.* **-elled, -el·ling**) *vt.* provide (something) with fuel again; —*vi.* take on a fresh supply of fuel. —[他] …에 연료를 보급하다 —[自] 연료를 보급하다

*__ref·uge__ [réfjuːdʒ] *n.* [C] **1.** a place of safety from danger or trouble; a shelter. **2.** a person or thing that protects or defends someone from dangers, difficulties, etc. **3.** [U] the act of keeping off from danger, distress, etc. ¶*a house of ~*① / *give ~ to someone*② / *seek ~ from a storm.*③ —[名] 1. 피난처, 은신처, 안전지대 2. 보호자; 위안물 3. 피난, 도피 ¶①양육원/②…을 숨기다/③폭풍을 피하다

ref·u·gee [rèfju(ː)dʒíː] *n.* [C] a person who flees for safety, esp. to another country for political reasons. —[名] 피난자; 망명자

re·ful·gent [rifʌ́ldʒ(ə)nt] *adj.* shining radiantly; splendid. —[形] 빛나는; 찬란한

re·fund *vt., vi.* [rifʌ́nd → *n.*] give or pay back (money). —*n.* [ríːfʌnd] =refundment. —[他][自] 갚다, 반환(반제)하다

re·fund·ment [rifʌ́ndmənt] *n.* [U] return of money paid; repayment. —[名] 반제(返濟); 환불

*__re·fus·al__ [rifjúːz(ə)l] *n.* **1.** [U][C] the act of refusing; rejection; denial. ¶*receive a ~.*① **2.** 《*the ~*》 the right to refuse or accept something. ¶*give the ~ of a proposal.* —[名] 1. 거절, 사퇴 ¶①거절당하다 2. 취사 선택권, 거부권

‡**re·fuse**[1] [rifjúːz] *vt., vi.* decline to accept (an invitation, a request, etc.); reject or deny (a demand, etc.). 《~ someone help, etc.; ~ help, etc. *to* someone; ~ *to do*》 —[他][自] 거절(거부)하다 ¶①입장을 거절하다/②그는 내 명령에 복종하기를 거부했다/③그는 그녀에게는 무슨 일

¶ *~ admittance*① / *He refused to obey my orders.*② / *He can ~ her nothing.*; *He can ~ nothing to her.*③ — 이고 거절을 못한다

ref·use² [réfju:s] *n.* [U] useless material; rubbish; garbage. **—*adj.*** useless; worthless. — —[名] 폐물; 쓰레기 —[形] 쓰레기의, 가치 없는

ref·u·ta·tion [rèfju(:)téiʃ(ə)n] *n.* [U] the act of refuting; [C] something that proves something else to be false. — —[名] 논박; 반박하는 의론(의견)

re·fute [rifjú:t] *vt.* prove (an opinion, etc.) to be false; defeat (an opinion, etc.) by argument. — —[他] …을 논박하다, 논파하다

***re·gain** [rigéin] *vt.* **1.** get back; recover. ¶ *~ health* / *~ consciousness.*① **2.** reach again; return to (a place, a state, etc.). ¶ *~ one's native country.* — —[他] 1. …을 되찾다; 회복하다 ¶①의식을 회복하다 2. …으로 복귀하다, 돌아가다

re·gal [rí:g(ə)l] *adj.* royal; fit for a king. — —[形] 제왕의; 왕자(王者)다운

re·gale¹ [rigéil] *vt.* delight; entertain. 《~ someone *with* or *on*》 ¶ *~ oneself with a glass of wine.*① **—*vi.*** feast; eat a rich meal. 《~ *on*》 ▷**re·gale·ment** [-mənt] *n.* — —[他] …을 크게 대접하다, 기쁘게 하다 ¶①술을 한잔 하다 —[自] 진수성찬을 먹다

re·ga·le² [rigéili:] *n.* sing. of **regalia**.

re·ga·li·a [rigéiliə / -ljə] *n. pl.* (sing. **-ga·le**) the symbol of royalty, such as the crown, scepters, etc. — —[名] 왕권의 상징

‡re·gard [rigá:rd] *vt.* **1.** look at (something) attentively. ¶*She regarded him with a strong stare.* / *He regards her with favor (dislike).*① **2.** think of (something); consider. 《~ someone or something *as*》 ¶ *~ the situation as serious*② / *They regarded him as a great artist.* **3.** pay attention to (something). ¶*None regarded her absence.*③ **4.** respect. ¶*She regards honesty highly.* **5.** concern. ¶*This does not ~ me at all.* — —[他] 1. …을 주시(응시)하다 ¶①그는 호의를 갖고(염오의 눈초리로) 그녀를 바라본다 2. …을 고려하다; 간주하다 ¶②사태를 중시하다 3. …에 주의하다 ¶③아무도 그녀가 자리에 없는 것을 유의하지 않았다 4. …을 존중(존정)하다 5. …와 관계하다

as regards (=*as to*; *concerning*) *something.* — [熟] …에 관하여는

—*n.* [U] **1.** care; attention; consideration. ¶*He has no ~ for the feelings of others.* / *He paid no ~ to his studies.*④ **2.** respect; esteem. ¶*a high ~ for courage*⑤ / *hold someone in high (low) ~.*⑥ **3.** 《*pl.*》 compliments; best wishes. ¶*Please give my kindest (or best, cordial) regards to your mother.*⑦ / *With kind regards.*⑧ **4.** relation; point. ¶*in this ~.* — —[名] 1. 주의, 관심, 고려 ¶④그는 공부에 관심을 전혀 두지 않았다 2. 존경, 존중 ¶⑤용기에 대한 깊은 존중/⑥…을 크게 존경(경멸)하다 3. 인사 ¶⑦어머님에게 안부 전해 주시오/⑧경구(敬具) 4. 관계, 사항

1) ***with*** (or ***in***) ***regard to,*** in relation to; concerning.
2) ***without regard to,*** not taking into account. — [熟] 1)…에 관하여 2)…에 상관없이

re·gard·ful [rigá:rdf(u)l] *adj.* mindful; showing respect. — —[形] 주의깊은; 경의를 표하는

***re·gard·ing** [rigá:rdiŋ] *prep.* concerning; about; in respect of. ¶*He knew nothing ~ the lost book.* — —[前] …에 관하여[는], …에 대하여서[는]

***re·gard·less** [rigá:rdlis] *adj.* careless; indifferent. 《*~of*》 ¶ *~ of expense.*① ▷**re·gard·less·ly** [-li] *adv.* — —[形] 부주의한; 무관심한 ¶①비용에 상관없이

re·gat·ta [rigǽtə] *n.* [C] a boat or yacht race. — —[名] 보우트(요트) 경조(競漕)

re·gen·cy [rí:dʒ(ə)nsi] *n.* [C][U] (pl. **-cies**) government by a regent; the office or position of a regent. — —[名] 섭정(攝政) 정치; 섭정의 직

re·gen·er·ate *v.* [ridʒénərèit → *adj.*] *vt.* **1.** produce (something) anew. **2.** improve or reform morally. **3.** cause (someone) to be reborn spiritually. **—*vi.*** **1.** be produced anew. **2.** be improved morally. **3.** be filled with new life or power. **—*adj.*** [ridʒénərit] spiritually reborn; reformed. ▷**re·gen·er·a·tor** [-ər] *n.* — —[他] 1. …을 재생시키다 2. …을 갱생시키다 3. …을 새로 태어나게 하다 —[自] 1. 재생하다 2. 갱생하다 3. 새로운 생명을 얻다 —[形] 새 생명을 얻은; 개량된

re·gen·er·a·tive [ridʒén(ə)rèitiv / -rətiv] *adj.* tending to regenerate. — —[形] 갱생(신생, 재생)시키는

re·gent [rí:dʒ(ə)nt] *n.* [C] a person who rules in the name and place of another. **—*adj.*** ruling in place of another. ⇒[usage] ¶*the Prince Regent.*① — —[名] 섭정 —[形] 섭정하는 [usage] 명사 뒤에 둠 ¶①섭정 황태자

reg·i·cide [rédʒisàid] *n.* [U] the act or crime of killing a king; [C] a murderer of a king. — —[名] 국왕 살해[범·범죄]

re·gime, ré·gime [riʒí:m / rei-] *n.* [C] **1.** a social or political system. **2.** =regimen. — —[名] 1. 사회제도; 정체(政體)

reg·i·men [rédʒimən / -mèn] *n.* [U] a system of diet, exercise, etc. to improve health. — —[名] 섭생(攝生), 식이요법(食餌療法)

reg·i·ment** *n.* [rédʒ(i)mənt → *v.*] [C] **1.** an organized body of soldiers. **2.** 《often *pl.*》 a large number. **—*vt. [rédʒimènt] organize. — —[名] 1. 연대(聯隊) 2. 다수, 큰 떼 —[他] …을 조직화하다

reg·i·men·tal [rèdʒiméntl] *adj.* of a regiment. **—*n.*** (*pl.*) a military uniform. ▷**reg·i·men·tal·ly** [-təli] *adv.*
—[形] 연대(聯隊)의 —[名] 군복

reg·i·men·ta·tion [rèdʒimentéiʃ(ə)n] *n.* [U] **1.** the act of forming into organized groups of soldiers. **2.** organization; systematization.
—[名] 1. 연대(聯隊)의 편성 2. 조직화

:re·gion [ríːdʒ(ə)n] *n.* [C] **1.** (often *pl.*) an area; a large part of a country; a district. ¶*forest regions.* **2.** a sphere; a realm. ¶*the lower* (*upper*) *regions*① / *the ~ of science.* **3.** a part of the body.
—[名] 1. 지방, 지역, 지대 2. 범위; 영역; 분야 ¶①지옥(천국) 3 [신체의] 부위(部位), 국부

re·gion·al [ríːdʒən(ə)l] *adj.* of an area, a country, etc.; local.
—[形] 지방의, 지역의

:reg·is·ter [rédʒistər] *n.* [C] **1.** a record, a list. **2.** a book in which such records or lists are written. ¶*a hotel ~*① / *a ship's ~.*② **3.** a machine for recording speed, numbers, etc. ¶*a cash ~.*③ **4.** (in a stove, furnace, etc.) a device for regulating the passage of air. **5.** the range of the human voice or of a musical instrument.
—[名] 1. 기록, 등록 2. 등록부, 등기부 ¶①숙박부/②선적(船籍) 증명서 3. 자동 기록기 ¶③금전 등록기 4. [스토우브 따위의] 통풍 장치 5. 성역(聲域), 음역

—*vt.* **1.** record officially. ¶*a registered trademark*④ / *My father was registered as a doctor.* **2.** protect (a letter or parcel) from loss or damage by payment of a special fee. ¶*registered mail*⑤ / *have* (or *get*) *a letter registered.*⑥ **3.** record in one's mind; remember. ¶*I registered the event in my memory.* **4.** (of instruments) indicate; record. ¶*The thermometer registers five degrees of frost.* **—*vi.*** write one's name in a register. ¶*~ at a hotel.*⑦
—[他] 1. …을 등기(등록)하다 ¶④등록 상표 2. …을 등기로 하다 ¶⑤등기우편/⑥편지를 등기로 하다 3. …을 마음에 새기다 4. [온도계 따위가] …을 나타내다 —[自] 숙박부에 기명하다 ¶⑦호텔에 투숙하다

reg·is·trar [rédʒistràːr / rèdʒistráː] *n.* [C] a person whose task is to keep records.
—[名] 기록계, 등기소 직원

reg·is·tra·tion [rèdʒistréiʃ(ə)n] *n.* **1.** [U] the act of registering; the state of being registered. **2.** [C] the total number of persons registered.
—[名] 1. 기록, 등록, 기장(記帳) 2. 등록자 총수

reg·is·try [rédʒistri] *n.* (pl. **-tries**) **1.** [U] the act of registering. ¶(*U.S.*) *the ~ fee.*① **2.** [C] a place where records are kept. ¶*a ~ office.*②
—[名] 1. 기재(記載), 등기, 등록 ¶①《美》 등기료 2. 등기소 ¶②호적 등기소

reg·nant [régnənt] *adj.* **1.** ruling; reigning. **2.** prevailing; having more power than others.
—[形] 1. 통치하는, 지배하는 2. 우세한, 유력한

re·gress *n.* [ríːgres → *v.*] [U] backward a movement. (~ *in* or *into*) **—*vi.*** [rigrés] go back; move backwards.
—[名] 역행, 후퇴; 퇴보 —[自] 되돌아가다, 역행하다

re·gres·sion [rigréʃ(ə)n] *n.* [U] the act of going back; a movement which is opposite to the usual direction.
—[名] 후퇴, 역행; 복귀; 퇴보

:re·gret [rigrét] *vt.* (**-gret·ted, -gret·ting**) **1.** feel sorrow for or grieve for (something); deplore. ¶*~ someone's death / I ~ to hear of his loss.* **2.** remember (something lost) with sorrow; miss. ¶*~ one's happy youth.*① **3.** feel sorry for (one's own act, word, etc.); repent of (something). (~ *to do*; ~ *doing*; ~ *that*) … ¶*~ the foolish behaviors of one's youth / I ~ being unable to help you.; I ~ that I cannot help you.*② */ I ~ to have done such a thing.; I ~ having done such a thing.*③
—[他] 1. …을 유감으로 생각하다; 애도하다 2. …이 없는 것을 쓸쓸하게 여기다; 서운해하다 ¶①행복했던 청춘시절을 그리워하다 3. …을 후회하다; 분하게 여기다 ¶②너를 도울 수 없는 것이 섭섭하다/③그런 짓을 한 것을 후회하고 있다

—*n.* [U][C] **1.** sorrow; grief; disappointment. ¶*hear with ~ of* (or *that* …). **2.** painful feeling for one's own wrong act; repentance; remorse. ¶*to one's ~*④ / *feel ~ for past misdeeds / It is a matter of ~ that I could not help him at that time.*⑤ **3.** (often *pl.*) a polite expression or letter of refusal. ¶*send regrets*⑥ / *refuse with many regrets / Please accept my regrets.*⑦
—[名] 1. 슬픔, 실망, 유감 2. 후회, 뉘우침, 회한; 섭섭함 ¶④섭섭하지만/⑤그때 그를 돕지 못한 것은 유감이다 3. 정중한 사절 [편지] ¶⑥초대에 대한 사절 편지를 내다/⑦섭섭하지만 받을 수 없읍니다

re·gret·ful [rigrétf(u)l] *adj.* feeling sorry for a loss; remembering with sorrow or disappointment.
—[形] 뉘우치는, 후회하는; 슬퍼하는; 서운해하는

re·gret·ful·ly [rigrétfuli] *adv.* in a regretful manner.
—[副] 서운한 듯이; 슬픈 듯이

re·gret·ta·ble [rigrétəbl] *adj.* causing a wish that it had been otherwise; to be regretted. ⇒[usage]
—[形] 분한, 유감스러운 [usage] I am regrettable 로는 쓰지 않음

:reg·u·lar [régjulər] *adj.* **1.** according to a rule, principle, etc.; orderly; systematic. ¶*~ work / ~ features*① / *lead a ~ life.* **2.** not changing; usual; habitual. ¶*a ~ customer / a ~ member.*② **3.** happening at fixed times or at the same interval of time; constant. ¶*a ~ beat-*
—[形] 1. 규칙적인; 질서정연한; 계통적인 ¶①균형잡힌 얼굴 2. 불변의; 평상시와 같은, 여느때의 ¶②정회원 3. 정기적인; 규칙바른 ¶③심장의 규칙적인 고동/④정례회 4. 면허를 얻은; 정

*ing of the heart*③ | ~ *meals* | *a* ~ *meeting.*④ **4.** formally admitted; recognized. ¶*a* ~ *doctor* | *a* ~ *cook*⑤ | *the* ~ *army*⑥ | ~ *soldiers.*⑦ **5.** (in grammar) having normal changes of the form. ¶*a* ~ *verb.* **6.** (*colloq.*) thorough; complete. ¶*a* ~ *hero* | *a* ~ *rascal.* **7.** (*U.S. colloq.*) pleasant; amiable. ¶*a* ~ *fellow.*
규의 ¶⑤전문적인 요리사/⑥정규군/⑦정규병 5. 규칙 변화의 6.《口》 완전한, 순전한 7.《美俗》 기분좋은

—*n.* [C] **1.** 《usu. *pl.*》 a regular soldier. **2.** (*colloq.*) a person who is regular; a regular customer.
—[名] 1. 정규병 2. 상시 고용인; 단골손님

reg·u·lar·ize [régjuləràiz] *vt.* make (something) regular.
—[他] …에 질서를 세우다

***reg·u·lar·ly** [régjulərli] *adv.* in a regular manner; at regular intervals.
—[副] 규칙바르게; 정기적으로

***reg·u·late** [régjulèit] *vt.* **1.** control (something) by a rule, an established custom, etc. **2.** keep (something) in proper order; put (something) in a desirable or proper condition. ¶*The clock is regulated every week.*①
—[他] 1. …을 [규칙 따위로] 단속하다 2. …을 규칙바르게 하다; 조정하다 ¶①시계는 매주 조정된다

***reg·u·la·tion** [règjuléiʃ(ə)n] *n.* **1.** [U] control or adjustment. **2.** [C] a rule or law. —*adj.* standard; ordinary. ¶*a* ~ *uniform*① | *of the* ~ *size.*②
—[名] 1. 단속, 규제; 조정 2. 규칙, 규정 —[形] 정규의, 표준의 ¶①제복/②표준 크기의

reg·u·la·tor [régjulèitər] *n.* [C] **1.** a person or thing that regulates. **2.** a device in a clock or watch to control its speed.
—[名] 1. 규정자, 단속자, 조정자; 조정기 2. [시계의] 시간 조정기

re·gur·gi·tate [rigə́:rdʒitèit] *vt.* pour or throw back.
—[他] …을 되뿜다; 게우다

re·ha·bil·i·tate [rì:(h)əbílitèit] *vt.* restore (someone or something) to a former state or to a good condition.
—[他] …을 원상으로 되돌리다; 복구(제대·복권·복직)시키다, 회복시키다

re·ha·bil·i·ta·tion [rí:(h)əbìlitéiʃ(ə)n] *n.* [U] the act of rehabilitating; the state of being rehabilitated.
—[名] 복구; 제대; 복권; 복직, 사회 복귀

re·hash [rí:hǽʃ / rí:hæʃ] *vt.* arrange (something already used) and use again in a new form. —*n.* [C] something old put in a new form.
—[他] [낡은 재료로] …을 고쳐 만들다, 개작하다 —[名] 재탕, 개작

re·hears·al [rihə́:rs(ə)l] *n.* **1.** [U] the act of rehearsing. **2.** [C] a practice in preparation for a public performance. ¶*a* [*full*] *dress* ~① | *a public* ~.
—[名] 1. 예행 연습을 하기 2. 예행 연습 ¶①[의상을 입고 하는] 연극의 무대 연습

re·hearse [rihə́:rs] *vt.* practice (a play, a ceremony, etc.) in preparation for a public performance. —*vi.* practice in a rehearsal.
—[他] …을 예행 연습하다 —[自] 시연(試演)하다, 예행 연습하다

Reich [raik, *G.* raiç] *n.* Germany.
—[名] 독일

:reign [rein] *n.* **1.** [U] sovereignty; supreme rule; royal power. **2.** [C] the period of a ruler. ¶*a long and splendid* ~. **3.** [U] prevailing influence. ¶*Night resumes her* ~.① —*vi.* rule; prevail. ¶*Silence reigned in the wood.* | *The Queen reigned over a vast dominion.*②
—[名] 1. [제왕 등의] 통치; 군림; 통치권 2. 치세(治世) 3. 지배력 ¶①다시 밤의 세계가 된다 —[自] 지배하다; 널리 퍼지다 ¶②여왕은 광대한 영토를 지배했다

re·im·burse [rì:imbə́:rs] *vt.* pay back; compensate.
—[他] …을 갚다, 변상(상환)하다

re·im·burse·ment [rì:imbə́:rsmənt] *n.* [U][C] the act of reimbursing; the state of being reimbursed.
—[名] 상환, 변상

***rein** [rein] *n.* [C] **1.** 《often *pl.*》 one of the two long straps used to control or guide a horse. ¶*adjust the reins.*① **2.** 《usu. *pl.*》 a means of control. ¶*assume the reins of government.*②
—[名] 1. 고삐 ¶①고삐를 다루다 2. 제어법; 억제법 ¶②정권을 장악하다

give rein to, allow to act without any control.
[熟] …에게 자유를 주다, 멋대로 하게 하다

—*vt.* guide; control; restrain.
—[他] …을 지배하다; 억제하다

re·in·car·nate *vt.* [rì:inkɑ́:rnèit → *adj.*] give a new body to (a soul). —*adj.* [rì:inkɑ́:rnit] taking a new body.
—[他] …을 다시 태어나게 하다; 다시 육신을 부여하다 —[形] 화신(化身)한

re·in·car·na·tion [rì:inkɑ:rnéiʃ(ə)n] *n.* [U][C] rebirth in a new bodily form; a new embodiment.
—[名] 다시 육신을 줌; 화신

rein·deer [réindìər] *n.* [C] (pl. **-deer**) a kind of deer with large horns, found in northern regions. ⇒fig.
—[名] 순록(馴鹿), 말사슴

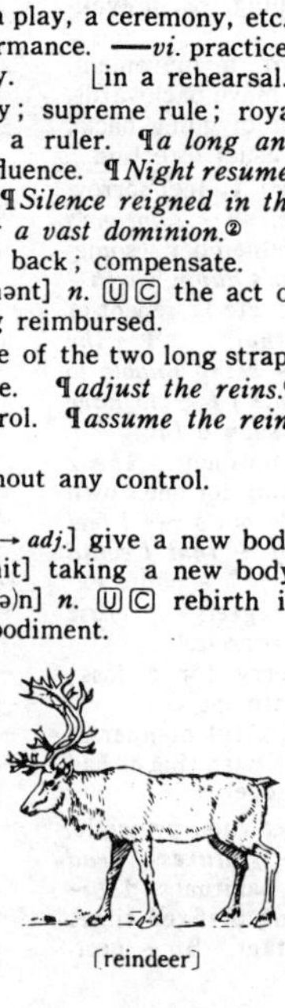
[reindeer]

re·in·force [rì:infɔ́:rs] *vt.* **1.** make (something) stronger with additional material or support. ¶*reinforced concrete.*① **2.** make (an army) stronger by adding new forces.
—[他] 1. …을 보강하다; 보충하다 ¶①철근 콘크리트 2. …에 원병을 보내다, 증원(증강)하다

re·in·force·ment [rì:infɔ́:rs-
—[名] 1. 증강; 증원 2. 증원군

mənt] *n.* **1.** Ⓤ the act of reinforcing; the state of being reinforced. **2.** Ⓒ (often *pl.*) additional troops or warships to reinforce an army or a fleet.

re·in·state [rìːinstéit] *vt.* put (someone) back into a former position or condition.
— 他 …을 원래의 지위·상태로 되돌아가게 하다, 복직시키다

re·in·state·ment [rìːinstéitmənt] *n.* Ⓤ the act of reinstating; the state of being reinstated.
— 名 복직; 회복

re·in·vig·or·ate [rìːinvígərèit] *vt.* give life or energy again to (someone or an animal); refresh; invigorate again.
— 他 …을 되살아나게 하다; 다시 활기띠게 하다

re·is·sue [rìːíʃuː] *vt.* publish again. —*n.* Ⓒ something issued again.
— 他 …을 재발행하다 — 名 재발행 「물, 재판」

re·it·er·ate [riːítərèit] *vt.* say or do again and again; repeat. ¶ several times; Ⓒ a repetition.
— 他 [말·행동을] 되풀이하다

re·it·er·a·tion [riːìtəréiʃ(ə)n] *n.* Ⓤ the act of repeating.
— 名 되풀이, 반복

∗**re·ject** *vt.* [ridʒékt] **1.** refuse to take, believe or use (something). ¶~ *an offer.* **2.** throw (something) away as worthless or useless. ↔accept ¶~ *a candidate.*① **3.** throw up (food); vomit. ▷**re·ject·er** [-ər] *n.*
— 他 1. …을 거절하다 2. …을 [쓸데없거나 가치없다고] 버리다, 퇴짜놓다 ¶①지원자를 퇴짜놓다 3. [음식]을 게우다

re·jec·tion [ridʒékʃ(ə)n] *n.* **1.** Ⓤ the act of rejecting; the state of being rejected. **2.** Ⓒ something rejected.
— 名 1. 거절, 각하, 구토 2. 거부된 것, 구토물

∗**re·joice** [ridʒɔ́is] *vi.* feel joy; be glad. ((~ *at* (or *in*, *over*) something; ~ *to do*; ~ *that* …)) ¶~ *at one's success.* —*vt.* **1.** give joy to (someone); make (someone) glad. ¶ *The news rejoiced him.* **2.** (in *passive*) be glad or happy. ((~ *to do*; ~ *at* or *by* something)) ¶ *I am rejoiced to hear* (or *at hearing, by hearing*) *the news.*
— 自 기뻐하다, 즐거워하다 — 他 1. …을 기쁘게 하다, 즐겁게 하다 2. …을 기뻐하다

re·joic·ing [ridʒɔ́isiŋ] *n.* Ⓤ **1.** gladness; happiness. **2.** (usu. *pl.*) celebration.
— 名 1. 기쁨 2. 축하, 놀이, 환호

re·join¹ [rìːdʒɔ́in] *vt.* **1.** meet (someone) again. **2.** unite to or with (someone) again. —*vi.* become joined together again.
— 他 1. …을 다시 만나다 2. …와 재결합하다 — 自 재결합하다

re·join² [ridʒɔ́in] *vi., vt.* answer; reply.
— 自他 대답하다

re·join·der [ridʒɔ́indər] *n.* Ⓒ an answer; a reply.
— 名 응답; 대답

in rejoinder, in reply.
關 대답으로, 응답하여

re·ju·ve·nate [ridʒúːvinèit] *vt., vi.* make or become young again. 「venating.」
— 他自 다시 젊어지(게 하)다

re·ju·ve·na·tion [ridʒùːvinéiʃ(ə)n] *n.* Ⓤ the act of rejuvenating.
— 名 젊어짐; 원기 회복; 갱신(更新)

re·kin·dle [rìːkíndl] *vt.* set (something) on fire again; excite (someone) again. —*vi.* catch fire again; become excited again.
— 他 …을 재연(再燃)시키다; 다시 흥분시키다 — 自 재연하다; 다시 흥분하다

re·lapse [riláeps] *vi.* become ill or worse again after a change for the better. ¶~ *into crime.* —*n.* Ⓒ the state of relapsing. ¶*have a* ~.
— 自 [잘 돼 가다가] 다시 악화되다, [병이] 도지다, 퇴보하다 — 名 역행; 재발; 악화; 타락

‡**re·late** [riléit] *vt.* **1.** tell; give an account of (something). **2.** bring (something) into connection with or association to another thing. ¶~ *A with* (or *to*) *B.*① **3.** (usu. in *passive*) be connected by birth or marriage. ((~ *to* some one)) —*vi.* have a connection; refer. ((~ *to* something))
— 他 1. …에 대하여 이야기하다, 말하다 2. …을 관계시키다 ¶①A를 B와 연관시키다 3. 혈연(인척) 관계가 있다
— 自 관계하다

∗**re·lat·ed** [riléitid] *adj.* **1.** connected. **2.** connected by origin, marriage, etc. of the same kind.
— 他 1. 관계가 있는 2. 인척의; 동류의

‡**re·la·tion** [riléiʃ(ə)n] *n.* **1.** Ⓤ connection in thought or meaning. ¶*the* ~ *between cause and effect.*① **2.** Ⓒ (often *pl.*) connection between persons, groups, states, etc. ¶*keep close relations with the neighboring countries.*② **3.** Ⓒ a member of the same family; a person connected by birth or marriage. ⇒N.B. **4.** Ⓤ consideration; the act of looking in a book, etc. for consideration.
1) *bear no relation to* (=*have nothing to do with*) something.
2) *in* (or *with*) *relation to,* as regards; in reference to.
3) *make relation to* (=*tell about*) something. 「to.」
— 名 1. [추상적인] 관계 ¶①원인과 결과의 관계 2. [단체·국민·국가 간의] 관계 ¶②이웃 나라와 긴밀한 관계를 유지하다 3. 가족; 친척 N.B. 나중의 의미로는 relative가 보통 4. 고려; 참조

關 1) …와 관계가 없다 2) …에 관하여 3) …에 언급하다

∗**re·la·tion·ship** [riléiʃ(ə)nʃìp] *n.* **1.** Ⓤ connection by birth or marriage. **2.** Ⓒ connection.
— 名 1. 친척(인척)[관계] 2. 관계

‡**rel·a·tive** [rélətiv] *adj.* **1.** relating to; considered in connection with something else. ((~ *to*)) ¶*a newspaper*
— 他 1. 관계가 있는, 관련되어 있는 2. 비교상의; 상대적인 ¶①우열(優劣)/

~ *to the matter* / '*Hot*' *and* '*cold*' *are* ~ *terms.* **2.** comparative; not absolute. ¶~ *merits*① / *the* ~ *advantages of gas and electricity.*② **3.** having proportion. 《~ *to*》 ¶*Supply is* ~ *to demand.* **4.** having mutual relations. ¶*the* ~ *responsibilities of a ruler and his people.* **5.** (*Grammar*) relating to a word which goes before in a sentence. ¶~ *adjectives*③ / *a* ~ *pronoun.*

②가스와 전기의 이점의 비교 **3.** 비례되는 **4.** 상호의 **5.** 《文法》 관계를 나타내는 ¶③관계 형용사

—*n.* [C] **1.** a person connected by blood or marriage; a family relation. **2.** (*Grammar*) a relative word, esp. a relative pronoun.

—[他] **1.** 친척, 집안 **2.** 《文法》 관계사(특히 관계 대명사)

* **rel·a·tive·ly** [rélətivli] *adv.* **1.** in relation to something else; compared with something else. **2.** in proportion to.

—[副] **1.** 상대적으로; 비교적으로 **2.** …에 비례하여

rel·a·tiv·i·ty [rèlətíviti] *n.* [U] **1.** the state of being relative. **2.** (*Physics*) Einstein's theory of the universe. ¶*the principle of* ~.

—[名] **1.** 상관적임; 관계가 있음 **2.** 《理》 아인시타인의 상대성 원리

* **re·lax** [rilǽks] *vt.* **1.** make (something) loose; stop the strain on (one's nerves). ¶~ *one's hold.* **2.** make (something) less strict. ¶*I hope this college will* ~ *its regulations.*① **3.** reduce; weaken. ¶~ *one's efforts.*

—[他] **1.** …을 늦추다; 힘을 빼다 **2.** …을 관대히 하다 ¶①이 대학은 학칙이 관대하면 좋겠다 **3.** …을 경감하다

—*vi.* **1.** become loose; become less strict. **2.** rest from effort or work.

—[自] **1.** 느슨해지다, 누그러지다 **2.** 쉬다, 긴장을 풀다

re·lax·a·tion [rì:lækséiʃ(ə)n] *n.* [U] **1.** the act of loosening or making less strict. **2.** rest from effort or work; [C] something providing amusement; recreation.

—[名] **1.** 늦추기; 경감; 완화 **2.** 긴장을 풀기; 휴양, 휴식; 위안, 오락

re·lay *n.* [rí:lei / riléi ∥ → 3., *v.*] [C] **1.** a fresh supply of men or horses to take over work from tired ones. **2.** a relay race. **3.** [rí:léi] an electric device to control a current. **4.** (of radio or television) a program or broadcast sent from another station and rebroadcasted to the listeners.

—[名] **1.** 교대자, 갈아 타는 말 **2.** 릴레이 경주 **3.** 계전기(繼電器)[장치] **4.** 중계방송

work in (or ***by***) ***relays,*** work in turns.

[熟] 교대로 일하다

—*vt.* [rí:lei / rí:léi] **1.** supply (new men, horses, etc.) **2.** receive and then pass on (something). **3.** rebroadcast.

—[他] **1.** …을 공급하다 **2.** …을 중계하다 **3.** 중계방송하다

re-lay [rí:léi] *vt.* (**-laid**) lay again.

—[他] …을 다시 놓다

relay race [⌐–⌐] *n.* a race between teams in which each member runs only one part of the course.

—[名] 계주(繼走), 릴레이 경주

⁑ **re·lease** [rilí:s] *vt.* **1.** set (someone) free; free (someone) from duties, suffering, a tax, etc. 《~ someone *from*》 ¶~ *someone from pain.*① **2.** let (someone or something) go; unfasten. ¶*The man released an arrow from his bow.*② **3.** allow (movies, books, news, etc.) to be shown, known, issued, etc. for the first time. **4.** (*Law*) give (a claim, right, estate, etc.) to someone.

—[他] **1.** …을 해방하다; 면제하다 ¶①…의 고통을 없애다 **2.** …을 놓다; 벗기다 ¶②그 사람은 활에서 화살을 놓았다(활을 쏘았다) **3.** …을 발표하다; 개봉(開封)하다 **4.** 《法》 [권리 따위를] 양도하다

—*n.* [U] **1.** [U][C] the act of setting free; an order to set free; relief. ¶*apply for* ~ *from duty.*③ **2.** the act of letting go. **3.** (of books, movies, news, etc.) the state of being released to the public; [C] a book, film, etc. which has been released. **4.** (*Law*) [U] the act of giving up (a claim or right); [C] a document by which this is done. **5.** [C] (*Machinery*) a device for holding or releasing a mechanism.

—[名] **1.** 해방[명령]; 면제 ¶③의무의 면제를 신청하다 **2.** 놓기, 투하 **3.** 발표; 개봉; 간행된 책; 개봉 영화 **4.** 《法》 기권; 양도[증서] **5.** 《機》 방기(放氣) 장치

rel·e·gate [réligèit] *vt.* **1.** send (someone) to a lower position or grade; send (someone) into exile. 《~ someone *to*》 **2.** hand over (a matter) for decision or carrying out. 《~ something *to*》

—[他] **1.** …을 좌천하다; 추방하다 **2.** [결정·처리를 위해] …을 이관하다, …을 위임하다

rel·e·ga·tion [rèligéiʃ(ə)n] *n.* [U] the act of relegating; the state of being relegated.

—[名] 추방; 좌천; 이관, 위임

re·lent·less [riléntlis] *adj.* without pity; cruel; harsh.

—[形] 무정한; 잔인한

re·lent·less·ly [riléntlisli] *adv.* cruelly; harshly.

—[副] 잔인하게; 용서없이

rel·e·vance [rélivəns] *n.* [U] the state of being relevant; relation; connection.

—[名] 관련성; 적절, 적당

rel·e·van·cy [rélivənsi] *n.* =relevance.

rel·e·vant [rélivənt] *adj.* related; connected; to the point;

—[形] 관련된; 적절한

rel·e·vant·ly [rélivəntli] *adv.* in a relevant manner. —⓶ 관련하여, 적절하게

re·li·a·bil·i·ty [rilàiəbíliti] *n.* ⓤ the state or quality of being reliable; trustworthiness. —⓷ 신뢰할 수 있음; 확실성

* **re·li·a·ble** [riláiəbl] *adj.* fit to be trusted or relied on; trustworthy; dependable. ¶*a ~ man* / *a ~ source of information.* ⌈liable degree.⌉ —⓶ 의지가 되는; 신뢰할 만한; 신용할 수 있는, 확실한

re·li·a·bly [riláiəbli] *adv.* in a reliable manner; to a re- —⓶ 신뢰할 수 있도록; 확실히

re·li·ance [riláiəns] *n.* 1. ⓤ trust; confidence; dependence. 2. ⓒ something or someone relied on. *in reliance on* (or *upon*), trusting. —⓷ 1.신뢰; 신용 2.의지로 삼는 것 (사람) 熟 …을 의지(기대)하여

re·li·ant [riláiənt] *adj.* having trust, confidence, or dependence. (*~ on* or *upon*) —⓶ 신뢰하는; 기대하는

* **rel·ic** [rélik] *n.* ⓒ 1. (*pl.*) a thing or a custom that remains from the past. 2. ruins remaining from the past. 3. (*Religion*) a part of the body or an object kept as a sacred memorial of a saint, etc. —⓷ 1. 유물; 유풍(遺風) 2. 유적 3. [성인 등의] 유골, 성해(聖骸), 성보(聖寶)

‡ **re·lief**¹ [rilí:f] *n.* ⓤ 1. freedom from previous pain, trouble, difficulty, etc. ¶*draw a breath of ~*① / *It was a ~ to know that the children had been rescued.*② 2. help given to poor, aged or handicapped people. ¶*a ~ fund.*③ 3. help given in time of need or danger. 4. release from work, duty, etc. 5. the exchange of persons on duty; ⓒ a person who replaces someone else in his work. —⓷ 1.[고통·곤란 따위의] 경감·안심 ¶①안도의 숨을 쉬다 / ②아이들이 무사하다는 것을 알고 안심했다 2.[빈민·불구자 등의] 구제 ¶③구제 기금 3. 구원, 구조 4. 휴식 5. 교대; 교대자

re·lief² [rilí:f] *n.* ⓤ (in sculpture) the projection of a figure from the flat surface; ⓒ a piece of work so made. ¶*a ~ map.*① —⓷ [조각에서] 배경보다 돋아 올라와 있음; 돋을새김, 양각(陽刻) ¶①모형지도

‡ **re·lieve** [rilí:v] *vt.* 1. remove or reduce (pain or trouble). ¶*A cup of coffee relieved my tiredness.*① 2. set (someone) free from a burden or duty. (*~ someone of* or *from*). ¶*~ someone from anxiety.*② 3. give help to (someone). 4. make (someone) free from duty; take the place of (someone on duty). ¶*~ a sentry.*③ 5. send (someone) away from his position; send (someone) out of his own country as a punishment. 6. make (something) sharply distinct (*~ something against*); make (something) less monotonous.
1) *relieve one's feelings,* express one's feelings.
2) *relieve someone of* (=*rob someone of*) *something.* —⓸ 1.[고통·근심]을 없애다, 누그러지게 하다 ¶①한 잔의 코오피가 피로를 풀어 주었다 2. …을 [무거운 짐·고통에서] 해방하다 ¶②…의 근심을 없애다 3. …을 구원하다 4. …와 교대하다 ¶③보초를 교대하다 5. …을 해임하다; 추방하다 6. …을 두드러지게 하다; 변화를 주다

熟 1)[실컷 울거나 화풀이하여] 울분 (감정)을 풀다 2)…의 …을 빼앗다

‡ **re·li·gion** [rilídʒ(ə)n] *n.* ⓤ 1. belief in and worship of some superhuman power as the creator or ruler of the universe. 2. ⓒ a particular system of worship, etc. ¶*the Buddhist ~.*① 3. ⓤ devotion to a religious faith; a way of life based on this. ¶*the life of ~.*②
1) *enter [into] religion,* become a monk, etc.
2) *make [a] religion of doing something,* do something very seriously and without fail. —⓷ 1. 종교 2. 종파, …교(敎) ¶①불교 3. 신앙; 신앙생활 ¶②신앙생활

熟 1)수도원에 들어가다; 신앙생활에 들어가다 2)반드시 …하다

‡ **re·li·gious** [rilídʒəs] *adj.* 1. of religion. ¶*a ~ ceremony.* 2. devoted to a religious faith. ⌈strictly.⌉ —⓶ 1. 종교의; 종교적인 2. 신앙심 깊은 「적으로」

re·li·gious·ly [rilídʒəsli] *adv.* in a religious manner; —⓶ 종교적으로; 신앙심 깊게; 양심

re·lin·quish [rilíŋkwiʃ] *vt.* 1. give up (a plan, policy, habit, etc.). 2. give (one's right, claim, etc.) to someone else. 3. stop holding or grasping (something). —⓶ 1.[계획 따위]를 버리다, 그만두다 2.[권리 따위]를 양도하다; 포기하다 3. …을 놓다

rel·ish [réliʃ] *n.* 1. ⓤ a good flavor; a pleasant taste. 2. ⓤ enjoyment; pleasure. ¶*He ate his meal with ~.*① 3. ⓒⓤ anything served with food to give a pleasant taste. ⌈enjoyable.⌉
1) *give relish to,* make (something) taste better or
2) *have no relish for,* do not like at all.
—*vt.* 1. enjoy; like. 2. give flavor to (something).
—*vi.* taste; have the flavor. (*~ of something*) —⓷ 1. 맛; 풍미 2. 기호(嗜好); 즐거움 ¶①그는 맛있게 식사를 했다 3. 조미료, 양념
⌈미가 없다⌉
熟 1)…에 맛이 나게 하다 2)…에 흥
—⓶ 1. …을 맛보다 2. …에 맛을 내다
—⓸ 맛이 나다; 맛이 있다

re·load [rí:lóud] *vt.* 1. put a load on (a cart, etc.) again. 2. charge (a gun) again. —⓶ 1. …에 짐을 다시 싣다 2.[총]에 다시 탄환을 재다

re·luc·tance [rilʌ́ktəns] *n.* [U] **1.** a feeling of not wanting to do something; unwillingness. **2.** (*Electricity*) magnetic resistance.
1) ***with reluctance,*** unwillingly.
2) ***without reluctance,*** willingly.

—[名] 1. 본의 아님; 마음내키지 않음 2. 《電》 자기(磁氣) 저항

[熟] 1)마지못해 2)기꺼이

***re·luc·tant** [rilʌ́ktənt] *adj.* unwilling; disinclined. ¶*She was ~ to marry.*

—[形] 마음내키지 않는; 마지못해 하는

re·luc·tant·ly [rilʌ́ktəntli] *adv.* unwillingly.

—[副] 마지못해

***re·ly** [rilái] *vi.* (**-lied**) depend; trust; have confidence. 《~ *on* or *upon* someone》 ¶*You can always ~ on me to do my best.*① | *He cannot be relied upon.*

—[自] 의지하다; 신뢰하다 ¶①내가 언제나 최선을 다하는 것으로 나를 믿어도 좋다

re·made [ri:méid] *v.* pt. and pp. of **remake**.

‡re·main [riméin] *vi.* **1.** stay; continue in the same place. ¶*~ abroad* | *~ at home.* **2.** be left after a part has been taken away. ¶*the years of life that remain*① | *If you take 2 from 6, 4 remains.* | *The victory remained with them.*② **3.** be left to be done, told, etc. 《~ *to do*》 ¶*Nothing remains but to wait for him.*③ | *Much remains to be done.* | *That remains to be seen.*④ **4.** continue to be. ¶*~ silent* | *The weather remained unsettled.* | *Let it ~ as it is.* | *I ~, yours truly* (or *sincerely*).⑤
—*n.* [C] 《usu. *pl.*》 **1.** what is left; a person who is left. **2.** a dead body. **3.** ancient ruins.

—[自] 1. [가지 않고] 남아 있다; 체재하다 2. 뒤에 남다; 잔존하다 ¶①여생/②승리는 결국 그들의 것이 되었다 3. […하(되)지 않고] 남다 ¶③이제는 그를 기다릴 수밖에 없다/④그것은 두고 봐야 한다 4. …인 채로 있다 ¶⑤[편지의 끝맺음말로서] 경구(敬具)

—[名] 1. 나머지[것]; 잔존자 2. 시체 3. 유적; 유물

***re·main·der** [riméindər] *n.* [C] **1.** 《usu. *the ~*》 the remaining people or things; the rest. ¶*He ate the ~ of the candy.*① **2.** a book sold at a reduced price after sales have slowed. **3.** (*Mathematics*) the number left after subtraction or division.

—[名] 1. 남아있는 사람들(것), 잔여물 ¶①그는 과자의 나머지를 먹었다 2. [잘 팔리지 않아] 싸게 파는 책 3. 《數》 나머지

re·make [rí:méik] *vt.* (**-made**) make again; make differently.

—[他] …을 다시 만들다; 개작하다

re·mand [rimǽnd / -má:nd] *vt.* **1.** send (something) back. **2.** (*Law*) send (a prisoner) back to jail. **—*n.*** **1.** [U] the act of remanding; the state of being remanded. **2.** [C] a person remanded.

—[他] 1. …을 되돌려 보내다 2. …을 다시 구류(구치)하다 —[名] 1. 반송; 재구류 2. 재구류자

‡re·mark [rimá:rk] *vt.* **1.** notice; perceive. ¶*We remarked his sad face.*① **2.** say or write (something) as a comment. 《~ *that* …》 ¶*He remarked that I had better see the doctor.*② **—*vi.*** make a comment. 《~ *on* or *upon* something…》 **—*n.*** **1.** [U] observation; notice. ¶*worthy of ~.*③ **2.** [C] a comment; what is said briefly.
1) ***pass a remark about*** (or ***on***) (=*say*) ***something.***
2) ***pass*** *something* ***without remark,*** admit something without saying anything about it.
3) ***the theme of general remark,*** the topic talked about by everybody.

—[他] 1. …을 알아채다; 주의(주목)하다 ¶①우리는 그의 슬픈 표정을 눈치챘다 2. [의견]을 말하다 ¶②의사에게 가 보라고 그는 말했다 —[自] 논평하다 —[名] 1. 주의; 관찰 ¶③주목할 만한 2. 논평; 촌평

[熟] 1)…에 대하여 소견을 말하다 2)묵과하다 3)항간의 화젯거리

‡re·mark·a·ble [rimá:rkəbl] *adj.* worthy of notice; unusual; uncommon.

—[形] 주목할 만한; 현저한; 비범한; 상당한

re·mark·a·bly [rimá:rkəbli] *adv.* in a remarkable way; to a remarkable degree.

—[副] 현저하게; 눈에 띄게; 상당히, 꽤

re·mar·riage [rí:mǽridʒ] *n.* [U][C] the act of marrying again.

—[名] 재혼

re·me·di·a·ble [rimí:diəbl] *adj.* that can be remedied; curable.

—[形] 치료할 수 있는

re·me·di·al [rimí:diəl] *adj.* intending or helping to cure; of a remedy.

—[形] 치료의(를 위한)

rem·e·di·less [rémidilis] *adj.* that can not be remedied; incurable.

—[形] 불치(不治)의

‡rem·e·dy [rémidi] *n.* [U][C] (pl. **-dies**) **1.** a medicine or a treatment that cures a disease. ¶*a ~ for a cold.* **2.** a method of removing any bad condition. ¶*There is no ~ but to….*① **—*vt.*** **1.** cure. **2.** repair; correct

—[名] 1. 의약; 의료 2. 교정법(矯正法); 구제책 ¶①…하는 외에 다른 방법이 없다 —[他] 1. …을 치료하다 2. …을 보수하다; 교정하다

‡re·mem·ber [rimémbər] *vt.* **1.** keep (someone or something) in the memory. 《~ *doing*; ~ *that*…; ~ *how* (or *what*, etc) *to do*; ~ *how* (or *what, etc.*)…; ~ someone or something *as* or *against*》 ↔forget ¶*~ what is told* | *I ~ seeing him once.*; *I ~ that I saw him once.* ⇒[usage] | *I don't ~ how to open the safe.* | *I ~ her as a girl.* **2.** be careful not to forget. 《~ *to do*》 ↔forget ¶*Remember to write to him.* ⇒[usage] **3.** call back (something or someone) to mind by an effort of will;

—[他] 1. …을 기억하고 있다 [usage] ~ having seen이 정확한 용법이나 ~ seeing을 보통 씀 2. 잊지 않고 …하다 [usage] ~to do는 미래의 경우, ~ doing은 과거의 경우에 쓰임 3. …을 상기하다, 회상하다 ¶①문득 생각나다 4. …에게 선물하다; …에게 유산을 주다 ¶②유언으로 유산을 주다 5. …으로부터 안부를 전하다 —[自] 1. 기억력

have (something) come into one's memory again. 《~ doing; ~ someone or something doing; ~ that...》 ¶~ oneself① / I just can't ~ him (or his) saying so. **4.** give (someone) a present or tip; leave (someone) some money or a piece of property. ¶~ someone in one's will.② **5.** mention (someone) to another as sending greetings. 《~ someone to another》 ¶Remember me [kindly] to Mr. A. / He wished to be remembered to you. —vi. **1.** possess the power of memory. ¶As a person gets older he does not ~ as he used to. **2.** have in mind; call back to mind. 《~ of something or someone》 ¶as I ~③ / She remembered of her aged mother.

- **re·mem·brance** [rimémbr(ə)ns] n. **1.** ⓤⓒ the act of remembering; the state of being remembered; memory. ¶a sad ~.① **2.** ⓤ the power to remember. **3.** ⓒ a thing which reminds someone of a person, an event, etc.; a souvenir; a memento. **4.** (pl.) (used in a letter) greetings. ¶Give my kind remembrances to your mother.②
  1) **bear** (or **have, keep**) **something in remembrance,** keep something in mind; remember.
  2) **bring something to remembrance,** cause someone to remember something.
  3) **come to remembrance,** come into one's mind.
  4) **escape one's remembrance,** cannot be remembered.
  5) **have no remembrance of,** do not remember (something) at all.
  6) **in remembrance of** (=in memory of) **something.**

: **re·mind** [rimáind] vt. make (someone) think of (something); cause (someone) to remember. 《~ someone of (or to do, that...)》 ¶You ~ me of your father.① / That reminds me.② 「minds.

re·mind·er [rimáindər] n. ⓒ a person or thing that re-
rem·i·nis·cence [rèminísns] n. **1.** ⓤ the act of recalling past experience; recollection. **2.** ⓒ something remembered; a memory. **3.** (pl.) a story of interesting events in one's life remembered. **4.** ⓒ a thing that suggests something else; a reminder.

rem·i·nis·cent [rèminísnt] adj. **1.** talking of or recalling past events. **2.** bringing to mind something else; suggestive. 《~ of》

re·miss [rimís] adj. (as predicative) careless in duty; neglectful; not energetic. 《~ in》 ¶be ~ in one's duty.①
re·miss·ness [rimísnis] n. ⓤ the state of being remiss.
re·mis·si·ble [rimísibl] adj. that can be remitted.
re·mis·sion [rimíʃ(ə)n] n. **1.** ⓤⓒ the act of remitting; discharge of debt, punishment, etc. **2.** ⓤⓒ forgiveness of sins or crimes; pardon. **3.** ⓤ the act of lessening pain or a disease.

re·mit [rimít] vt. (**-mit·ted, -mit·ting**) **1.** forgive (sins). **2.** cancel (a penalty, a tax, etc.) **3.** make (something) less; lessen; decrease. ¶~ one's anger (efforts). **4.** send (money). **5.** put off; postpone.

re·mit·tance [rimít(ə)ns] n. ⓤ the act of sending money; ⓒ the sum of money sent. ¶make [a] ~.①

- **rem·nant** [rémnənt] n. ⓒ (often the ~) what is left over; a remainder; a small remaining part.

re·mod·el [ri:mádl / -mɔ́dl] vt. (**-eled, -el·ing** or Brit. **-elled, -el·ling**) make (something) again; remold.
re·mold [ri:móuld] vt. make or shape again.
re·mon·strance [rimánstrəns / -mɔ́n-] n. ⓤⓒ protest; complaint; advice.
re·mon·strant [rimánstrənt / -mɔ́n-] adj. objecting; protesting. —n. ⓒ a person who remonstrates.
re·mon·strate [rimánstreit / -mɔ́n-] vi. urge reasons in

이 있다 2. 기억하다; 상기하다 ¶③내 기억으로는

—⊛ **1.** 기억; 추억 ¶①슬픈 추억 **2.** 기억력 **3.** 생각나게 하는 것; 기념품 **4.** 전갈; 안부; 인사 ¶②어머님에게 안부 전해 주시오

🈺 1)…을 기억하다 2)…을 생각나게 하다 3)…을 회상하다 4)…을 잊다 5)…을 조금도 기억하고 있지 않다 6)…의 기념으로

—⊕ …을 생각나게 하다 ¶①너를 보면 네 아버지 생각이 난다/②그것으로 생각이 났다

—⊛ 생각나게 하는 사람(것)
—⊛ **1.** 옛추억; 회상 **2.** 추억 **3.** 추억담; 회고담 **4.** 생각나게 하는 것

—⊛ **1.** 회상하는; 추억에 잠기는 **2.** 생각나게 하는; 암시하는

—⊛ 부주의한; 태만한; 기운 없는 ¶①직무태만이다
—⊛ 부주의; 태만
—⊛ 용서할 수 있는
—⊛ **1.** [빚·벌 따위의] 면제; 용서 **2.** [죄 따위의] 사면 **3.** [고통·질병 따위의] 경감

—⊕ **1.** [죄]를 용서하다 **2.** [벌·세금 따위]를 면제하다 **3.** …을 경감하다; 누그러뜨리다 **4.** [금전]을 보내다 **5.** …을 연기하다

—⊛ 송금; 송금액 ¶①송금하다

—⊛ 나머지; 찌끼, 나부랑이

—⊕ …을 다시 만들다; 개조하다, 개주(改鑄)하다
—⊕ …을 개조하다; …을 개주하다
—⊛ 항의; 충고

—⊛ 항의하는; 충고의 —⊛ 항변자, 충고자
—⊜ 항의하다; 충고하다

remorse [962] **rename**

opposition; protest; complain. ⟪~ *with* someone; ~ *against* or *on* something⟫ —*vt.* say in protest, objection, etc. ⟪~ *that*...⟫ 「wrong-doing; a sense of guilt.」
—惯 …에 항의하여 말하다

* **re·morse** [rimɔ́:rs] *n.* Ⓤ the deep regret for one's past *without remorse*, pitilessly. 「morse.」
—名 후회; 양심의 가책
熟 용서없이

re·morse·ful [rimɔ́:rsf(u)l] *adj.* feeling or showing re-
—形 뉘우치는

re·morse·less [rimɔ́:rslis] *adj.* having no pity; merciless; cruel. ▷**re·morse·less·ly** [-li] *adv.*
—形 무자비한; 무정한; 잔인한

* **re·mote** [rimóut] *adj.* (-**mot·er, -mot·est**) **1.** (of a place) distant; far away; set apart. ¶*a ~ place* / *a house ~ from the village* / *live ~ from the town.* **2.** (of time) far from the present. ¶*in the ~ past (future).*③ **3.** distant in relation, connection, etc. ¶*a ~ relative*② / *a ~ cause.*③ **4.** (of an intention, idea, etc.) slight; faint. ¶*a ~ possibility*② / *I haven't the remotest* (or *have only a ~*) *idea* [*of*] *what you mean.*⑤ 「indirectly; slightly.」
—形 1.[장소가] 먼; 외딴 2.[시간이] 현재에서 먼 ¶①먼 옛날(미래) 3. 관계가 먼; 간접적인; 몹시 틀리는 ¶②먼 친척/③원인(遠因) 4. 근소한, 희미한 ¶④희박한 가능성/⑤네가 무슨 말을 하는지 전혀 모르겠다

re·mote·ly [rimóutli] *adv.* in a remote manner; far off;
—副 멀리; 간접적으로; 희미하게

re·mote·ness [rimóutnis] *n.* Ⓤ the state of being re-
—名 멀리 떨어져 있음; 관계없음

re·mould [rimóuld] (*Brit.*) =remold. 「mote.」

re·mount *vt., vi.* [ri:máunt→*n.*] **1.** get on (a horse) again; go up (something) again. **2.** supply (someone or something) with fresh horses. **3.** put (a precious stone) in a new metal setting. —*n.* [rí:maunt, -́-] Ⓒ a fresh horse to replace another.
—他自 1.[말에] 다시 타다;[…에] 다시 올라가다 2. …에 새 말을 지급하다 3.[보석을] 바꿔 박다 —名 갈아 탈 말, 보충된 말

re·mov·a·ble [rimú:vəbl] *adj.* that can be removed.
—形 옮길 수 있는; 제거할 수 있는

* **re·mov·al** [rimú:v(ə)l] *n.* **1.** Ⓤ Ⓒ the act of removing; the state of being removed; change of place. **2.** Ⓤ dismissal.
—名 1.이동; 이전 2. 면직

: **re·move** [rimú:v] *vt.* **1.** move (something) from a place; take away; withdraw. ⟪~ something *from*⟫ ¶*~ oneself*① / *~ one's hand* / *~ the dishes from the table.* **2.** take off. ¶*Remove your hat.* **3.** wipe out; get rid of; kill. ¶*~ stains* / *~ a name from a list* / *~ the cause of a trouble* / *He was removed by poison.*② **4.** dismiss (someone) from an official position; transfer (someone) to another post. ⟪~ someone *from* or *for*⟫ ¶*~ a boy or girl from school* / *~ the mayor for failing to do his duty.* —*vi.* go from one place to another; change *remove mountains,* perform a miracle. 「residence.」
—他 1. …을 옮기다, 이전하다;치우다; [손 따위]를 치우다 ¶①물러가다 2. …을 벗다 3. …을 닦아내다; 없애다; …을 죽이다 ¶②그는 독살되었다 4. …을 쫓아내다, 면직(해고)하다 —自 이동하다; 이사하다

熟 기적을 행하다

—*n.* Ⓒ **1.** a degree of distance; one step in a scale of distances ~② / *a specified distance in relationship.* ¶*at a certain ~*② / *a cousin at first ~*④ / *Genius is only one ~ from insanity.* / *He is many removes from the wild days of his youth.*③ **2.** (*rare*) a move; a change of residence. ¶(*proverb*) *Three removes are as bad as a fire.*④ **3.** (*Brit.*) a promotion to a higher class.
—名 1.거리; [간격의] 한 단계; [혈족간의] 친등(親等), 촌수 ¶③조금 멀어져서 보면, 사촌의 아들/⑤그는 젊었을 때의 거친 생활로 보면 큰 차이가 있다 2.이전, 이동 ¶⑥(俚)이사 세 번은 집이 불난 것이나 다름없다 3.(英) 진급, 승진

re·moved [rimú:vd] *adj.* **1.** remote; distant; not connected. ⟪~ *from*⟫ **2.** separated by a specified number of degrees of relationship. ¶*a cousin once ~.*②
—形 1. 먼, 멀어진; 관계가 없는 2. …촌의, …친등의 ¶①재종(再從)

re·mov·er [rimú:vər] *n.* Ⓒ a person or thing that removes. ¶*a stain ~.*①
—名 제거하는 사람(것); 이전자 ¶①얼룩 빼는 약

re·mu·ner·ate [rimjú:nəreit] *vt.* pay (someone) for work, service, loss, etc.; make up for (something); reward.
—他 …에게 보수를 주다; 배상하다, 보답하다

re·mu·ner·a·tion [rimjù:nəréiʃ(ə)n] *n.* Ⓤ the act of remunerating; reward; pay; compensation.
—名 보수; 배상

re·mu·ner·a·tive [rimjú:nərèitiv / -n(ə)rə-] *adj.* rewarding; profitable.
—形 보수가 있는; 유리한

* **ren·ais·sance** [rènisá:ns, -zá:ns, rinéis(ə)ns / rənéis(ə)ns] *n.* **1.** Ⓒ cultural or artistic revival. **2.** ⟪*the R-*⟫ the great revival in art and literature in Europe in the 14th, 15th, and 16th centuries; the period when this revival occurred; the style of art, literature, etc. of this period.
—名 1.[문화·예술의] 부흥 2. 문예부흥[기]; 르네상스의 미술·문예의 양식

re·nal [rí:n(ə)l] *adj.* of the kidneys. 「something).」
—形 신장(腎臟)의

re·name [rí:néim] *vt.* give a new name to (someone or
—他 …의 이름을 바꾸다, 개명하다

re·nas·cence [rinǽsns] *n.* [C] **1.** a new birth; revival. **2.** ⦅*the R-*⦆ =the Renaissance.
—[名] 신생; 부활

re·nas·cent [rinǽsnt] *adj.* showing new life; reviving.
—[形] 재생한; 부활한

rend [rend] *v.* (**rent**) *vt.* **1.** break (cloth, etc.) by pulling apart violently. **2.** split (something) violently. **3.** take (something or someone) away violently. ⦅~ *from* (or *off, away*) something⦆ ¶~ *a child from his mother.*① **4.** disturb violently. —*vi.* tear or split apart.
—[他] 1. …을 찢다 2. …을 쪼개다; 분열시키다 3. …을 강탈하다 ¶①어머니에게서 아이를 빼앗다 4. …을 휘젓다; 괴롭히다 —[自] 찢어지다; 쪼개지다

‡ren·der [réndər] *vt.* **1.** give (something) in return; give (something due or owed); show (obedience, etc.). ⦅~ something *to* or *for*⦆ ¶~ *thanks to God* / ~ *good for evil*① /~ *honor to someone* / ~ *a present to a conqueror.* **2.** give; provide; do (a service, etc.) ¶~ *someone assistance;* ~ *assistance to someone* / ~ *help in time of need*② / *What service has he rendered?* **3.** present (an account for payment, a statement, etc.) ¶~ *a bill* / *The committee rendered a report.* **4.** make; cause (someone or something) to be or become. ¶*Running renders me tired.* / *My efforts were rendered useless.*③ **5.** hand over; deliver; give up; surrender. ¶~ *a message* / ~ [*up*] *a city to the enemy.* **6.** play; perform; express artistically. ¶*The piano sólo was well rendered.*④ **7.** translate. ⦅~ something *into*⦆ ¶~ *English into Japanese.*
—[他] 1. …을 보답으로 주다, 보복하다; …을 치르다, 바치다; [복종심 따위]를 나타내다 ¶①악을 선으로 갚다 2. [남에게 원조 따위]를 주다; …을 하다 ¶②필요한 때에 도와주다 3. [계산서·설명 따위]를 제출하다 4. …을 …으로 하다 ¶③내 노력은 헛되이 끝났다 5. …을 넘겨주다; 명도(明渡)하다, 포기하다 6. …을 연출(연주)하다; 예술적으로 표현하다 ¶④피아노 독주는 아주 훌륭했다 7. …을 번역하다

ren·dez·vous [rɑ́:ndivù: / rɔ́n-] *n.* [C] (pl. **-vous** [-vu:z]) **1.** a meeting by appointment. **2.** an appointed place for meeting; an assembling place for troops or ships. **3.** an appointment to meet at a certain time or place. —*vi., vt.* meet at a certain time or place.
—[名] 1. [약속에 의한] 회합 2. 예정된 회합 장소; [군대·함선의] 지정 집합지 3. [회합의] 약속
—[自][他] 회합하다

ren·di·tion [rendíʃ(ə)n] *n.* [C] **1.** performance of music; performance of a part in a drama, etc. **2.** translation.
—[名] 1. 연주; 출연 2. 번역

ren·e·gade [rénigèid] *n.* [C] a person who changes his religion or political beliefs; a deserter; a traitor.
—[名] 배교자(背教者); 변절자; 탈당자; 배신자

‡re·new [rin(j)ú:: / rinjú:] *vt.* **1.** make (something) new, fresh, or strong again. **2.** put back (an original spirit, freshness, etc.) as it was. **3.** begin (something) again; repeat. **4.** replace (something) by something new of the same kind; fill (something) again. **5.** extend (a contract, etc.) ¶~ *a magazine subscription.* —*vi.* become new again; start again.
—[他] 1. …을 다시 새롭게(젊게, 강하게) 하다 2. [원기·신선함 따위]를 되찾다; 부흥하다 3. …을 재개하다; 되풀이하다 4. …을 새것과 바꾸다; 다채우다 5. …을 갱신하다 —[自] 다시 새로와지다; 재개하다

re·new·a·ble [rin(j)ú(:)əbl / -njú(:)-] *adj.* that can be renewed.
—[形] 새로이 할 수 있는

re·new·al [rin(j)ú:əl / -njú:-] *n.* [U][C] the act of renewing; the state of being renewed; restoration; revival.
—[名] 쇄신, 갱신; 회복; 재개; 부활, 소생

re·nounce [rináuns] *vt.* **1.** give up (a claim, right, etc.) formally; abandon (a habit). **2.** refuse to recognize (something). ¶~ *friendship* (or *a friend*).①
—[他] 1. 공식적으로 …을 포기하다; [습관]을 끊다, 그만두다 2. …을 거절하다; 부인하다 ¶①절교하다

ren·o·vate [rénəvèit] *vt.* make (something) new again; put (something or someone) in good condition; refresh; repair; clean up.
—[他] …을 새롭게 하다; …에 원기를 회복시키다; …을 수선하다; 청결하게 하다

ren·o·va·tion [rènəvéiʃ(ə)n] *n.* [U][C] the act of renovating; the state of being renovated; renewal; refreshment; repair.
—[名] 혁신, 쇄신; 원기 회복; 수선

ren·o·va·tor [rénəvèitər] *n.* [C] a person who renovates.
—[名] 수선자; 혁신자

***re·nown** [rináun] *n.* [U] fame; reputation.
—[名] 명성

be of* [*great, high*] *renown, [very] famous.
[熟] [아주] 유명한

re·nowned [rináund] *adj.* famous. ¶*be* ~ *for*....①
—[形] 유명한 ¶①…으로 유명하다

***rent¹** [rent] *n.* [U][C] a sum of money for the use of a house, room, land, machinery, etc.
—[名] 집세; 방세; 지대(地代); 사용료

for rent, available to be rented. ¶*a house for* ~① / *For* ~.②
[熟] 빌려주는 ¶①셋집/②[광고로] 셋집(셋방) 있음

—*vt.* **1.** occupy (something) in return for paying rent. ¶*We* ~ *a house from Mr. Smith.* **2.** allow (someone) to occupy (a house, etc.) in return for paying rent. ¶*He rents the house cheaply.*③
—[他] 1. …을 임대하다 2. [집 따위]를 빌리다 ¶③그는 집을 싸게 빌려 준다

rent² [rent] *n.* [C] a split; a torn place.
—[名] 째진 틈; 해진 데; 협곡

R

rent³ [rend] *v.* pt. and pp. of **rend**.
rent·al [réntl] *n.* Ⓤ the amount paid or received as rent. —名 총(總)사용료
rent·er [réntər] *n.* Ⓒ a person who pays rent. —名 세든 사람, 소작인
rent-free [réntfríː] *adj.* without any rent-charge. —形 지대(집세)가 없는
re·nun·ci·a·tion [rinʌ̀nsiéiʃ(ə)n] *n.* Ⓤ the act of giving up a right, possession, etc. —名 [권리 따위의] 포기; 단념
re·o·pen [ríːóup(ə)n] *vt., vi.* open again. —他自 다시 열다
re·or·gan·i·za·tion [riːɔ̀ːrɡənizéiʃ(ə)n / -naiz-] *n.* Ⓤ the act of reorganizing; the state of being reorganized. —名 재편성
re·or·gan·ize [riːɔ́ːrɡənàiz] *vt., vi.* arrange (something) in a new way; form (something) into a new system. —他自 다시 편성하다
re·paid [ri(ː)péid] *v.* pt. and pp. of **repay**.
re·paint [ríːpéint] *vt.* paint again. —他 …에 뻬끼를 다시 칠하다
⁑ **re·pair**¹ [ripéər] *vt.* **1.** mend; put (something broken or wrong) in good condition again. ¶*She repaired her shoes.*① **2.** cure (a wound). **3.** correct (a mistake). —*n.* Ⓤ **1.** the act of repairing; ((usu. *pl.*)) an instance of repairing. ¶*Repairs will be done while you wait.*② **2.** the state of being repaired; the general state of needing repairs. ⎡lack of daily care.⎤ *out of repair; in bad repair,* needing repairs from⎦ —他 1. …을 수선하다 ¶①그녀는 구두를 수선했다 2. [상처]를 치료하다 3. …을 정정하다 —名 1. 수선, 수리; 수리 공사 ¶②기다리시는 동안 수선하겠읍니다 2. 수리된 상태; 수리를 해야 하는 상태 熟 손질이 잘 안 된
re·pair² [ripéər] *vi.* go; walk. —自 가다
re·pair·a·ble [ripéərəbl] *adj.* that can be repaired. —形 수선할 수 있는
re·pair·er [ripéərər] *n.* Ⓒ a person who repairs. —名 수리인
rep·a·ra·tion [rèpəréiʃ(ə)n] *n.* Ⓤ the act of putting a mistake right; the act of giving satisfaction to someone by repairing damage done at him; ((*pl.*)) money paid for damages. —名 배상; 배상금
rep·ar·tee [rèpərtíː / -ɑːt-] *n.* Ⓒ a quick, clever reply; conversation made up of such remarks. —名 재치있는 응답, 명답
re·pass [ríːpǽs / -pɑ́ːs] *vi., vt.* pass again. —自他 다시 통과하다
re·past [ripǽst / ripɑ́ːst] *n.* Ⓒ **1.** a meal. **2.** food. —名 1. 식사 2. 음식물
re·pa·tri·ate [riːpéitrièit / -pǽt-] *vt.* send (someone) back to his native country. —*n.* Ⓒ a person so sent back. —他 …을 본국으로 송환하다 —名송환되는 사람
re·pa·tri·a·tion [riːpèitriéiʃ(ə)n / -pæt-] *n.* Ⓤ the act of repatriating someone; the state of being repatriated. —名 본국 송환
∗ **re·pay** [ripéi] *vt.* (**-paid**) **1.** pay back (money). ¶*I'll ~ the money you lent.*① **2.** make return for (something). ¶*~ someone for his kindness.*② —他 1. [금전]을 갚다 ¶①빌린 돈을 갚겠다 2. …에 보답하다 ¶②…의 친절에 보답하다
re·pay·a·ble [ripéiəbl] *adj.* that can be repaid. —形 돌려줄 수 있는
re·pay·ment [ripéimənt] *n.* ⓊⒸ the act of repaying. —名 반환, 상환, 상각
re·peal [ripíːl] *vt.* cancel. —他 [법률 따위]를 무효로 하다
⁑ **re·peat** [ripíːt] *vt.* **1.** speak again. ¶*She repeated the question.* / *I repeated my words.* **2.** do again; make again. ¶*History repeats itself.*① / *He often repeats the same mistake.* **3.** say the same thing that some one else has already said; say the same words soon after another person. ¶*She said, "Repeat this sentence after me," to her pupils.*② **4.** say (a poem, etc.) over and over again to memorize it. —*vi.* happen again; say or do anything again. —*n.* Ⓒ **1.** an act of repeating. **2.** something repeated, esp. a part to be played once more in music. —他 1. …을 되풀이하여 말하다 2. …을 되풀이하여 행하다 ¶①역사는 되풀이된다 3. [남의 말]을 되풀이하다, …을 남의 뒤를 따라 말하다 ¶②그녀는 학생들에게 자기의 뒤를 따라 이 글을 읽으라고 말했다 4. [시 따위]를 암송하다 —自 다시 일어나다; 되풀이되다 —名 1. 되풀이, 반복 2. 되풀이되는 것; 반복 악절(樂節)
∗ **re·peat·ed** [ripíːtid] *adj.* done, said or made again. —形 되풀이되는; 빈번한
re·peat·ed·ly [ripíːtidli] *adv.* over and over again; frequently. —副 되풀이하여; 자주
re·pel [ripél] *vt.* (**-pelled, -pel·ling**) **1.** drive back; force away. ¶*We repelled the enemy.*① **2.** reject; refuse. ¶*~ the offer.* **3.** cause dislike; displease. —他 1. …을 쫓아버리다 ¶①적군을 격퇴했다 2. …을 거절하다 3. …을 불쾌하게 느끼게 하다
re·pel·lent [ripélənt] *adj.* causing dislike; disagreeable. —形 불쾌한, 호감이 안 가는
∗ **re·pent** [ripént] *vi.* feel sorry for one's own act, thought, etc. —*vt.* feel sorry for (something). ¶*You shall ~ [of] this.*① —自 회개하다, 후회하다 —他 …을 회개하다, 후회하다 ¶①언제고 후회할 게다
re·pent·ance [ripéntəns] *n.* Ⓤ the act of repenting. —名 후회

re·pent·ant [ripéntənt] *adj.* feeling regret or sorrow.
—[形] 후회하는; 후회의

re·per·cus·sion [rìːpərkʌ́ʃ(ə)n] *n.* [U] [C] **1.** an indirect result of something done or said. **2.** a rebound; the act of springing back.
—[名] 1. 반향, 영향 2. 되퉁기기

rep·er·toire [répərtwɑ̀ː, -wɔ̀ː] *n.* [C] the list of plays, operas, musical pieces or parts that a company, an actor, or a musician is ready to play or sing.
—[名] 레퍼터리, 상연 목록, 연주 곡목

rep·er·to·ry [répərtɔ̀ːri / -t(ə)ri] *n.* [C] (pl. **-ries**) **1.** =repertoire. **2.** a storehouse. **3.** a stock of things.
—[名] 2. 창고 3. 저장물

* **rep·e·ti·tion** [rèpitíʃ(ə)n] *n.* **1.** [U] [C] the act of repeating; something repeated. **2.** [C] a copy.
—[名] 1. 되풀이, 반복 2. 복사(複寫)

rep·e·ti·tious [rèpitíʃəs] *adj.* full of repetitions.
—[形] 되풀이하는, 지루한

re·pet·i·tive [ripétitiv] *adj.* =repetitious.

re·pine [ripáin] *vi.* complain; be discontented.
—[自] 불평을 말하다

⁑ **re·place** [ripléis] *vt.* **1.** put back. ¶*He replaced the book on the shelf.* **2.** fill or take the place of (something). ¶*~ coal fires by gas.*① ▷**re·place·a·ble** [-əbl] *adj.*
—[他] 1. …을 원래의 장소에 두다 2. …와 교대하다, …을 …으로 바꾸다 ¶①석탄을 가스로 바꾸다

re·place·ment [ripléismənt] *n.* **1.** [U] the act of replacing. **2.** [C] a person who takes the place of another.
—[名] 1. 제자리에 놓기 2. 교대 요원, 보충 요원

re·plant [riplǽnt / -plɑ́ːnt] *vt.* plant again.
—[他] …을 다시 심다

re·plen·ish [riplénìʃ] *vt.* fill up (something) again; make (something) complete again. ¶*~ the stock of goods.*①
—[他] …을 다시 채우다 ¶①물건의 재고(在庫)를 보충하다

re·plen·ish·ment [riplénìʃmənt] *n.* [U] the act of replenishing.
—[名] 보충

re·plete [riplíːt] *adj.* completely filled.
—[形] 충만한

re·ple·tion [riplíːʃ(ə)n] *n.* [U] fullness.
—[名] 충만

rep·li·ca [réplikə] *n.* [C] a copy of a picture or statue.
—[名] [그림·조각의] 모사(模寫), 모형

⁑ **re·ply** [ripláì] *v.* (**-plied**) *vi.* answer in words or by an action. 《~ *to* something》 ↔ask; inquire ¶*~ to a question* / *The enemy did not ~ to our fire.*① —*vt.* say or write (something) in answer. 《~ *that* …》
—[自] 대답하다; 응답하다, 응전하다 ¶①적은 우리의 포화에 응전하지 않았다 —[他] …이라고 대답하다

reply for, answer instead of another.
[熟] …에 대신하여 답변하다

—*n.* [C] (pl. **-plies**) the act of replying; an answer in words or by an action. ↔question; inquiry ¶*a ~ card*② / *~ paid*③ / *in ~ to a question*④ / *make a ~.*⑤
—[名] 대답; 응답; 응전 ¶②왕복 엽서 /③반신료 지불필/④질문에 대답하여 /⑤대답하다

⁑ **re·port** [ripɔ́ːrt] *vt.* **1.** give an account of (what one has seen, heard, learned, etc.); communicate. 《~ something *to*; ~ *that* …; ~ someone or something *to do*; ~ *doing*》 ¶*They reported having seen her.* / *It is reported that the war is over.*; *The war is reported to be over.*① **2.** announce officially; give an account of (something) regularly. ¶*The Treasury reports the total receipt and expenditure for the year.*② **3.** write an account of (an event, etc.) for publication. ¶*~ a speech.* **4.** complain about (someone) to the authorities. 《~ someone *to*》 ¶*~ a salesgirl to the manager.*③ **5.** 《*reflexively*》 present (oneself) to someone in authority. 《~ oneself *to*》 ¶*Report* [*yourself*] *to the manager between 1 and 3 o'clock.*④
—[他] 1. …을 보고하다; 보도하다; 전달하다 ¶①전쟁은 끝났다고 한다 2. …을 공표하다; 정기적으로 보고하다 ¶ 재무성은 총세입·세출액을 공표한다 3. …의 기사를 쓰다 4. [상사(上司) 등에게] …의 일을 일러바치다 ¶③판매원을 지배인에게 일러바치다 5. …의 곳에 출두시키다 ¶④한 시에서 세 시까지 지배인 앞으로 출두하시오

—*vi.* **1.** make a report. 《~ *on* something》 ¶*~ on the condition of the crops.* **2.** work as a reporter. 《~ *for* something》 ¶*~ for the Times.*⑤ **3.** present oneself at a given place or time. 《~ *to* or *for* a place》 ¶*~ to the police* / *~ for duty* / *~ at the office.*
—[自] 1. 보고하다, 보고서를 만들다 2. 기자 노릇을 하다 ¶⑤타임즈지(紙)의 기자 노릇을 하고 있다 3. 출두하다

—*n.* [C] **1.** a statement or an account of something seen, heard, done, etc. ¶*make a ~*⑥ / *make a ~ on the state of the roads.* **2.** an official statement; a statement as to a pupil's work and conduct issued by his teachers. ¶*The boy has had a bad ~ this term.* **3.** [U] [C] rumor; [U] reputation. ¶*be of good (ill) ~*⑦ / *through good and evil ~*⑧ / *as ~ has it*⑨ / *Report goes* (or *runs, has it*) *that ….* **4.** the sound of an explosion. ¶*the ~ of a gun.* **5.** 《usu. *pl.*》 books containing a record of court cases, etc.
—[名] 1. 보고[서], 보도, 기사 ¶⑥보고하다 2. 공보; [학교의] 성적표, 통신부 3. 소문; 평판 ¶⑦평이 좋다(나쁘다) /⑧평판이 좋든 나쁘든간에 /⑨소문에 의하면 4. 폭음, 포성, 총성 5. 판결록; 의사록

re·port·ed·ly [ripɔ́ːrtidli] *adv.* according to the report.
—[副] 전하는 바에 의하면, 기보한 바와 같이

* **re·port·er** [ripɔ́ːrtər] *n.* [C] **1.** a person who reports. **2.** a person who collects news for a newspaper.
—[名] 1. 보고자 2. 통신원, 기자

R

repose [ripóuz] *vi.* **1.** lie down to rest. ¶*Kate reposed on the bench.* **2.** be asleep; lie in a grave. ¶*He reposes at Arlington Cemetery.* —*n.* ⓤ **1.** rest; sleep. ¶*disturb one's* ~① **2.** calmness; quietness.
re·pose·ful [ripóuzf(u)l] *adj.* quiet.
re·pos·i·to·ry [ripázitɔ̀:ri / -pɔ́zit(ə)-] *n.* ⓒ (pl. **-ries**) a place or container in which things are stored.
re·pos·sess [rì:pəzés] *vt.* possess again.
rep·re·hend [rèprihénd] *vt.* blame; scold.
rep·re·hen·si·ble [rèprihénsibl] *adj.* blamable.
rep·re·hen·sion [rèprihénʃ(ə)n] *n.* ⓤ blame.
: **rep·re·sent** [rèprizént] *vt.* **1.** portray (something or someone) by pictures, language, or in some other way. ¶*What does this picture* ~?① **2.** describe; explain; point out. 《~ something or someone *as*; ~ something *to*; ~ someone *to do*; ~ *that* ...》 ¶*He represented the differences clearly.*② / *They represented him as stern.*③ **3.** mean; symbolize. ¶*Such excuses* ~ *nothing at all to me.*④ / *The dove represents peace.*⑤ **4.** correspond to. ¶*These bills* ~ *seven hours' work.* **5.** act or speak in place of or as agent for (someone or a body of persons); appear as a fair sample of (something). ¶~ *a client* / *He represents this city.* **6.** perform (a play); play the part of (someone). ¶~ *Hamlet.*
 represent to oneself, imagine.
• **rep·re·sen·ta·tion** [rèprizentéiʃ(ə)n] *n.* ⓤⓒ **1.** the act of representing; the state of being represented. **2.** ⓒ a picture portraying someone. **3.** a sign or symbol.
: **rep·re·sent·a·tive** [rèprizéntətiv] *n.* ⓒ **1.** a person who stands for a group of people. **2.** a characteristic example. 「Congress of the United States.」
 the House of Representatives, the lower house of
 —*adj.* **1.** typical; characteristic. **2.** having authority to stand for a group of people.
re·press [riprés] *vt.* keep (something or someone) under control; put down; suppress. ¶~ *the rebellion*① / *He repressed a sigh.*② / *The parents repressed their child.*
re·press·i·ble [riprésibl] *adj.* that can be repressed.
re·pres·sion [ripréʃ(ə)n] *n.* ⓤⓒ the act of repressing; the state of being repressed; suppression.
re·pres·sive [riprésiv] *adj.* tending to repress.
re·prieve [riprí:v] *vt.* **1.** delay the execution of (a prisoner sentenced to death). **2.** give (someone) relief for a while from pain, trouble, etc.
 —*n.* ⓒ **1.** temporary delay in carrying out the sentence of a judge. **2.** relief for a while.
rep·ri·mand *n.* [réprimæ̀nd / -mà:nd ∥ → *v.*] ⓤⓒ severe reproof. —*vt.* [+rèprimí:nd / -má:nd] give (someone) a severe scolding, esp. for a fault.
re·print *vt.* [rí:prínt → *n.*] print again. —*n.* [*U. S.* rí:prìnt] ⓒ a reprinted book.
re·pris·al [ripráiz(ə)l] *n.* ⓤ injury or revenge done in return for an injury, esp. by one country to another in a war.
• **re·proach** [ripróutʃ] *n.* ⓤ blame; ⓒ an expression of blame. —*vt.* blame; scold; disgrace.
re·proach·a·ble [ripróutʃəbl] *adj.* blamable.
re·proach·ful [ripróutʃf(u)l] *adj.* full of reproach; expressing reproach. 「manner.」
re·proach·ful·ly [ripróutʃfuli] *adv.* in a reproachful
rep·ro·bate [réproubèit] *n.* ⓒ a sinful or wicked person rejected by God. —*adj.* wicked; vicious. —*vt.* disapprove of (something) strongly. 「ing; disapproval.」
rep·ro·ba·tion [rèprəbéiʃ(ə)n] *n.* ⓤ the act of reprobat-

──自 1. 쉬다; 휴식하다 2. 자다; 영면하다 ─图 1. 휴식; 휴양; 안면 ¶① 안면방해를 하다 2. 침착, 안정(安靜)

─图 조용한, 평온한
─图 창고; 그릇, 용기

─他 …을 다시 소유하다, 되찾다
─他 …을 질책하다, 꾸짖다
─图 비난할 만한, 패씸한
─图 질책, 구지람
─他 1. …을 그리다, 표현하다 ¶①이 그림은 무엇을 그린 것이냐? 2. …이라고 말하다, 진술하다; …을 설명하다, 지적하다 ¶②그는 차잇점을 분명히 지적했다/③그들은 그가 엄하다고 말했다 3. …을 의미하다; 상징하다 ¶④그런 핑계는 나에게 전혀 의미가 없다/⑤비둘기는 평화를 상징한다 4. …에 상당하다 5. …의 대리 노릇을 하다; …을 대표(대변)하다; …의 일례(一例)이다 6. [극]을 상연하다; …의 역을 연기하다

慣 마음에 그리다
─图 1. 표현; 묘사; 대표; 대리; 상연 2. 초상화 3. 표, 기호; 상징

─图 1. 대표자, 대리인 2. 견본, 표본

慣 하원
─图 1. 대표적인, 전형적인 2. 대표하는, 대리의
─他 …을 제지하다; 억압하다, 진압하다 ¶①반란을 진압하다/②그는 한숨을 억제했다
─图 억누를 수 있는
─图 진압; 억압

─图 진압의, 억압적인
─他 1. …의 사형집행을 유예하다 2. […의 괴로움 따위]를 잠시 편하게 하다
─图 1. 사형집행 유예 2. 일시적 모면

─图 질책, 징계; 비난 ─他 …을 질책하다

─他 [책 따위]를 재판(再版)하다
─图 재판
─图 앙갚음, 보복

─图 비난 ─他 …을 나무라다; …의 체면을 손상하다
─图 꾸짖을 만한, 패씸한
─图 꾸짖는; 비난의

─副 꾸짖듯이, 나무라듯이
─图 타락자; 신에게서 버림받은 사람
─图 타락한 ─他 …을 비난하다; …에 불찬성이라고 하다
─图 비난

re·pro·duce [rì:prəd(j)ú:s / -djú:s] *vt.* **1.** produce again. ¶ ~ *a scene from a play.* **2.** make a copy of (something). **3.** bear (something) as offspring.
—㉠ 1. …을 재생하다, 재현하다 2. …을 복사하다, …의 복제(複製)를 만들다 3. …을 낳다

re·pro·duc·i·ble [rì:prəd(j)ú:sibl / -djú:s-] *adj.* that can be reproduced.
—㉠ 재생산할 수 있는

re·pro·duc·tion [rì:prədʌkʃ(ə)n] *n.* **1.** ⓤ the act of reproducing. **2.** ⓒ a copy.
—㉡ 1. 재생 2. 복사, 복제

re·pro·duc·tive [rì:prədʌ́ktiv] *adj.* of reproduction.
—㉡ 생식(生殖)의; 재생의

re·proof [riprú:f] *n.* ⓤ blame; ⓒ an expression or words of blame.
—㉡ 비난, 질책; 비난의 말

re·prove [riprú:v] *vt.* reproach; scold; blame. 《~ someone *for*》
—㉠ …을 꾸짖다; 비난하다

re·prov·ing·ly [riprú:viŋli] *adv.* in a blaming manner.
—㉡ 비난하듯이

rep·tile [réptil / -tail] *n.* ⓒ **1.** any cold-blooded animal that creeps, such as a snake. **2.** a mean person. —*adj.* **1.** of or like a reptile (*n.* 1.); creeping. **2.** low; mean.
—㉡ 1. 파충류(爬蟲類) 2. 비열한 인간 —㉡ 1. 파충류의; 기어다니는 2. 비열한

rep·til·i·an [reptíliən] *adj.* **1.** of reptiles. **2.** mean.
—㉡ 1. 파충류의 2. 비열한

: re·pub·lic [ripʌ́blik] *n.* ⓒ **1.** a nation ruled by elected representatives of the people. **2.** the form of such government.
—㉡ 1. 공화국 2. 공화 정체

· re·pub·li·can [ripʌ́blikən] *adj.* **1.** of a republic. **2.** 《R-》 (*U.S.*) of the Republican Party in the United States. —*n.* ⓒ **1.** a person who favors republican government. **2.** 《R-》 (*U.S.*) a member of the Republican Party.
—㉡ 1. 공화국의, 공화 정체의 2. 공화당의 —㉡ 1. 공화제 주의자 2. 공화당원

re·pub·li·can·ism [ripʌ́blikənìz(ə)m] *n.* ⓤ **1.** republican principles. **2.** 《*R* ~》 principles or policies of the Republican Party in the United States.
—㉡ 1. 공화주의 2. 공화당의 주의(정책)

Republican Party [-´-- -´-], **the** *n.* one of the two major political parties in the United States.
—㉡ 미국 공화당

re·pub·li·ca·tion [rì:pʌblikéiʃ(ə)n] *n.* ⓤ the act of publishing again; ⓒ a book published again.
—㉡ 재판(再版)[된 책]

re·pu·di·ate [ripjú:dièit] *vt.* **1.** refuse to accept (something); reject. **2.** refuse to have anything to do with (someone). **3.** refuse to pay (a debt, etc.).
—㉠ 1. …을 거부하다 2. …와 인연을 끊다 3. [부채 따위]의 지불을 거절하다

re·pu·di·a·tion [ripjù:diéiʃ(ə)n] *n.* ⓤ the act of repudiating; the state of being repudiated. 《*against*》
—㉡ 거부; 절연(絶緣)

re·pug·nance [ripʌ́gnəns] *n.* ⓤⓒ strong dislike. 《~ *to,*》
—㉡ [심한] 혐오

re·pug·nant [ripʌ́gnənt] *adj.* disagreeable; unpleasant. 《~ *to*》 ¶ *This work is ~ to lazy men.*②
—㉡ 비위에 안 맞는 ¶①이 일은 게으름뱅이에게는 괴롭다

re·pulse [ripʌ́ls] *vt.* **1.** repel; drive back. **2.** reject. ¶ *She coldly repulsed him.* —*n.* ⓤ **1.** an act of driving back. ¶ *meet with* (or *suffer*) [*a*] ~.② A refusal.
—㉠ 1. [적]을 격퇴하다 2. [제의 따위]를 물리치다, 퇴짜놓다 —㉡ 1. 격퇴 ¶①격퇴되다 2. 거부

re·pul·sion [ripʌ́lʃ(ə)n] *n.* ⓤ **1.** strong dislike. **2.** the act of driving back.
—㉡ 1. 혐오 2. 격퇴

re·pul·sive [ripʌ́lsiv] *adj.* causing strong dislike. ↔attractive ¶ *Snakes are ~ to some people.*
—㉡ 싫은, 불쾌한

rep·u·ta·ble [répjutəbl] *adj.* having a good reputation; honorable. ▷**rep·u·ta·bly** [-i] *adv.*
—㉡ 명판이 좋은; 존경할 만한

: rep·u·ta·tion [rèpjutéiʃ(ə)n] *n.* ⓤⓒ the general opinion of a person; good name; fame. ¶ *a man of ~*① / *He is in good* (*bad*) *~.*② / *He has the ~ of being bright.*③
—㉡ 평판; 명성 ¶①명망가/②그는 평판이 좋다(나쁘다)/③그는 머리가 좋다는 평판이다

re·pute [ripjú:t] *n.* ⓤ reputation; fame. ¶ *a man of good ~*① / *the author of ~.*② —*vt.* (usu. *passive*) think; suppose. ¶ *He is reputed to be stingy.*
—㉡ 평판; 호평 ¶①평판 높은 사람/②유명한 작가 —㉠ …이라고 생각하다; 간주하다

re·put·ed [ripjú:tid] *adj.* supposed; considered to be.
—㉡ …이라고 하는(생각되는)

re·put·ed·ly [ripjú:tidli] *adv.* by reputation.
—㉤ 소문에 의하면

: re·quest [rikwést] *n.* **1.** ⓤⓒ the act of asking for something. ¶ *yield to ~*① / *I did it at his ~.* / *I made a ~ for his help.* / *A catalog will be mailed free on* (or *upon*) *~.*② **2.** ⓒ that which is asked for. ¶ *What is your ~?* / *Your requests are granted.* **3.** ⓤ demand. ¶ *She is such a good dancer that she is in great ~.*③
  1) *by request*, in answer to a request.
  2) *in request*, asked for by many people; in demand.
—*vt.* ask for (something); ask (someone) to do something. 《~ something *from* (or *for, of*); ~ someone *for*;》
—㉡ 1. 부탁, 소원, 요구, 간청 ¶①요구에 따르다/②카탈로그는 바라시는 대로 무료로 보내드립니다 2. 부탁하는 일, 요구물 3. 수요 ¶③그녀는 댄스를 잘 하므로 크게 인기가 있다

圖 1)의뢰를 받고 2)수요가 많은

—㉠ …을 …에게 부탁하다, 간청하다 ¶④친구에게 돈을 구어 달라고 하다

~ someone *to do*; ~ *that* ...》 ¶ ~ *a loan from a friend*④ / *He requested his guests to sit down; He requested that his guests* [*should*] *sit down.* ⇒[usage] / *Your presence is requested immediately.*⑤

[usage] 미국영어에서는 that-clause의 should는 보통 생략됨/⑤곧 와 주시기 바랍니다

req·ui·em [rékwiəm, rí:k-] *n.* [C] (*Catholic*) a mass for the dead; music for this mass.

—[名] 《가톨릭》 진혼(鎭魂) 미사; 그 가곡

:re·quire [rikwáiər] *vt.* **1.** demand; order. 《~ something *of* someone; ~ someone *to do*; ~ *that* ...》 ¶ *The police required my appearance.* / *He did all that was required of him.* / *He required me to pay the money.; He required that I* [*should*] *pay the money.* ⇒[usage] **2.** need; want. 《~ *to do*; ~ *doing*; ~ *that* ...》 ¶ *We shall ~ more help.* / *We ~ to know it.* / *These girls ~ looking after.*① —*vi.* be necessary; demand. ¶ *if circumstances ~.*②

—[他] **1.** …을 요구하다; 명하다 [usage] 미국에서는 that-clause의 should는 대개 생략됨 **2.** …을 필요로 하다 ¶①이 소녀들은 돌봐 줘야 할 필요가 있다 —[自] 필요하다 ¶②부득이한 사정이 있으면

·re·quire·ment [rikwáiərmənt] *n.* [C] a need; something required. ¶ *the requirements for entrance to college.*①

—[名] 요구; 필요[물] ¶①대학에 입학하기 위한 필요한 조건

req·ui·site [rékwizit] *adj.* necessary; very much required. —*n.* [C] something required. ¶ ~ *for life.*①

—[形] 꼭 소용되는; 필요한 —[名] 필수품 ¶①살기 위한 필수품

req·ui·si·tion [rèkwizíʃ(ə)n] *n.* **1.** [U][C] the act of requiring. **2.** [C] a formal demand. **3.** [C] an essential condition. —*vt.* demand; order. 《~ something *for*》

—[名] **1.** 요구 **2.** 청구(요구)[서] **3.** 필요조건 —[他]…을 요구하다, 소집하다

re·quit·al [rikwáit(ə)l] *n.* [U] repayment; return.

—[名] 보수; 보복

re·quite [rikwáit] *vt.* pay back; reward.

—[他] …에 보복하다

re·read [rí:rí:d] *vt.* (**-read** [-red]) read again.

—[他] …을 다시 읽다

re·scind [risínd] *vt.* cancel; repeal; cut off by force.

—[他] …을 취소하다, 무효로 하다

re·scis·sion [risíʒ(ə)n] *n.* [U] the act of rescinding.

—[名] 취소, 무효

re·script [rí:skript] *n.* [C] an official announcement by a ruler, etc.

—[名] 칙령(勅令); 조칙(詔勅)

:res·cue [réskju:] *vt.* save. 《~ someone *from* danger or harm》 —*n.* [U][C] the act of saving from danger or harm. ¶ *He went to her ~.*①

—[他] …을 구하다 —[名] 구조, 구출 ¶①그는 그녀를 구조하러 갔다

res·cu·er [réskju(:)ər] *n.* [C] a person who rescues.

—[名] 구조자

·re·search [risə́:rtʃ] *n.* [U][C] careful study for accurate or new information; investigation. —*vi.* make researches; investigate; study.

—[名] 탐구; 연구; 조사 —[自] 연구하다, 조사하다

re·search·er [risə́:rtʃər] *n.* [C] a person who does research; an investigator.

—[名] 연구자; 조사자

re·seat [ri:sí:t / rí:sí:t] *vt.* **1.** seat again. **2.** supply (a theater, etc.) with new seats.

—[他] **1.** …을 다시 앉히다 **2.** …에 새 자리를 마련하다

re·sem·blance [rizémbləns] *n.* [U][C] the state of being similar; something which resembles; likeness; similarity. ¶ *He shows a great ~ to his mother.*①

—[名] 유사[점] ¶①그는 어머니를 꼭 닮았다

bear (or ***have***) ***a resemblance to*** (=*be very similar to*) *someone* or *something.*

[熟] …을 닮다

:re·sem·ble [rizémbl] *vt.* be like; be very similar to (someone). ¶ *She resembles her sister.*

—[他] …을 닮다

·re·sent [rizént] *vt.* feel angry at [doing] (something); be irritated by (someone or something).

—[他] …에 화내다, …을 불쾌하게 여기다

re·sent·ful [rizéntf(u)l] *adj.* feeling anger or displeasure; angry.

—[形] 분개한

·re·sent·ment [rizéntmənt] *n.* [U] anger; displeasure.

—[名] 원한; 분개

·res·er·va·tion [rèzərvéiʃ(ə)n] *n.* **1.** [U][C] the act of holding back; 《often *pl.*》 arrangement by which something is reserved for a person; something reserved. **2.** [U][C] limitation. **3.** [C] (*U.S.*) land set aside, esp. for American Indians.

—[名] **1.** 보류; 예약 **2.** 제한 **3.** [미국의 인디언을 위한] 유보지(留保地)

1) ***make reservations,*** reserve.
2) ***with reservations,*** conditionally.
3) ***without reservations,*** unconditionally.

[熟] 1)예약을 하다 2)조건부로 3)무조건으로

:re·serve [rizə́:rv] *vt.* **1.** keep back (something) for later use. ¶ ~ *money for emergencies* / *Reserve your strength* (or *yourself*) *for the climb.*① **2.** keep (something) for a special person. ¶ *All seats reserved.*② **3.** put off (something) till a later time; postpone; delay. ¶ *I'll ~ my decision until I hear from him.*③ **4.** keep (something) for oneself; retain. ¶ *He reserves all rights in his books.*

—[他] **1.** …을 따로 남겨 두다 ¶①등산에 대비하여 힘을 저축해 둬라 **2.** …을 예약해 두다 ¶②전좌석 지정제 **3.** …을 연기하다 ¶③그의 편지를 볼 때까지 결정을 연기하자 **4.** …을 보유하다 **5.** …을 운명지우다 ¶④이 소년은 전도가 양양하다

5. destine. ¶*A great future is reserved for this boy.*④ / *The invention was reserved for Edison.*

—n. 1. [U] the state of being reserved; [C] something reserved. ¶*a ~ of food* / *a gold ~*⑤ / *have* (or *keep*) *a little food in ~.* **2.** (often *pl.*) troops kept back for use when needed. ¶*call up the reserves.*⑥ **3.** [C] an area of land reserved for a special use. ¶*a game ~.*⑦ **4.** [U][C] limitation; exception; condition. ¶*We publish this with all ~.*⑧ **5.** [U] self-control in speech and behavior. ¶*break down* (or *throw off*) *~.*⑨

—[名] 1. 비축; 예비품, 적립금 ¶⑤금준비 2. 예비대 ¶⑥예비군을 소집하다 3. 특별 보류지 ¶⑦금렵구(禁獵區) 4. 제한; 제외, 조건 ¶⑧발표는 하나 진위(眞僞)는 보증하지 않는다 5. 자제(自制); 삼감; 사양 ¶⑨흉금을 터놓다

—adj. kept in reserve; forming a reserve. ¶*a ~ fund.*⑩

—[形] 예비의; 준비의 ¶⑩예비금

re·served [rizə́:rvd] *adj.* **1.** kept in reserve. ¶*a ~ car* / *a ~ seat.*① **2.** quiet in manner; self-restrained in action or speech. ¶*She is a very ~ girl.*

—[形] 1. 보류된; 전세낸 ¶①예약(지정)석 2. 서름서름한, 속을 터놓지 않는

re·serv·ist [rizə́:rvist] *n.* [C] a soldier or sailor not on active service.

—[名] 예비병

res·er·voir [rézə:rvwɑ̀:r] *n.* [C] a place where water is stored for future use. ¶*There are several reservoirs supplying water to the city.*①

—[名] 저장소, 저수지 ¶①그 도시에는 몇 개의 저수지가 있다

re·set [rí:sét] *vt.* (**-set, -set·ting**) set or place again. **—n.** [U] the act of resetting.

—[他] …을 다시 놓다 —[名] 다시 놓기

re·set·tle [rí:sétl] *vt.* settle again.

—[他] …을 다시 정주(定住)시키다

re·shape [rí:ʃéip] *vt.* form (something) into a new shape.

—[他] …을 다시 만들다

re·shuf·fle [rí:ʃʌ́fl] *vt.* mix (playing cards) again; organize or arrange again. ¶*~ the Cabinet.*

—[他] [트럼프의 패]를 다시 치다; 재편성하다

* **re·side** [rizáid] *vi.* **1.** live (*~ at* or *in* a particular place); dwell. ¶*He resides in New York, but is now staying in the country.*① **2.** (of rights, etc.) exist. (*~ in* someone or something) ¶*In a democracy it is with the people that the real power resides.*②

—[自] 1. 살다; 거주하다 ¶①그는 뉴욕에 살고 있지만 지금은 시골에 가 있다 2. 존재하다, 있다 ¶②민주주의에서는 참된 힘은 국민에게 있다

‡ **res·i·dence** [rézid(ə)ns] *n.* **1.** [C] a home; a large and fine house. **2.** [U] the act of living; the act of dwelling.

—[名] 1. 주거(住居), 주택 2. 거주

* **res·i·dent** [rézid(ə)nt] *n.* [C] a person who lives in a place. ¶*summer residents*① / *foreign residents*② / *He is a ~ of London.*③ **—adj.** staying; dwelling.

—[名] 거주자 ¶①피서객/②재류 외국인/③그는 런던의 주민이다 —[形] 거류하는

res·i·den·tial [rèzidénʃ(ə)l] *adj.* of or related to residence. ¶*He lived in a good ~ quarter.*①

—[形] 주택의 ¶①그는 좋은 주택 구역에 살고 있다

re·sid·u·a [rizídʒuə / -djuə] *n.* pl. of **residuum**.

re·sid·u·al [rizídʒuəl / -dju-] *adj.* left over.

—[形] 나머지의, 잔여의

re·sid·u·ar·y [rizídʒuèri / -djuəri] *adj.* remaining.

—[形] 나머지의

res·i·due [rézid(j)ù: / -djù:] *n.* [C] what remains after a part has been taken away.

—[名] 나머지, 여분

re·sid·u·um [rizídʒuəm / -dju-] *n.* [C] (pl. **-sid·u·a**) something that remains at the end of a process; a remainder.

—[名] 찌꺼기; 나머지

* **re·sign** [rizáin] *vt.* **1.** give up a position (of some organization). ¶*~ one's position on the school board.*① **2.** give up. **—vi.** give up a position or an office. (*~ from* or *as* chairman, etc.)

—[他] 1. …을 그만두다, 사직하다 ¶①교육위원의 직을 그만두다 2. …을 체념(단념)하다 —[自] 사직하다, 사임하다

resign* oneself *to, commit oneself to (something). ¶*He resigned himself to fate.*

[熟] …에 몸을 맡기다

re-sign [rí:sáin] *vt.* sign again.

—[他] …에 다시 서명하다

res·ig·na·tion [rèzignéiʃ(ə)n] *n.* **1.** [U] the act of giving up; the act of giving up a position. **2.** [C] a formal statement showing that one gives up a position. **3.** [U] the state of being resigned to something. ¶*She bore the pain with ~.*①

—[名] 1. 단념; 사직 2. 사표 3. 체념 ¶①그녀는 체념하고 고통을 꾹 참았다

re·signed [rizáind] *adj.* accepting calmly and with patience.

—[形] 체념한, 달게 참는

re·sign·ed·ly [rizáinidli] *adv.* in a resigned manner.

—[副] 체념하여

re·sil·i·ence [rizíliəns] *n.* [U] the ability to spring back.

—[名] 되튐, 반동

re·sil·i·ent [rizíliənt] *adj.* **1.** springing back. ¶*~ steel.* **2.** cheerful. ¶*a ~ nature.*①

—[形] 1. 되튀는, 탄력 있는 2. 쾌활한 ¶① 쾌활한 성질

res·in [rézin] *n.* [U][C] a sticky material found in certain trees, esp. the pine and the fir. ¶*~ soap.*①

—[名] 송진, 수지(樹脂) ¶①수지 비누

res·in·ous [rézinəs] *adj.* made of resin; containing resin.

—[形] 수지(樹脂)[질]의

‡ **re·sist** [rizíst] *vt.* **1.** fight back against (someone or something); oppose. ¶*The door resisted her efforts to open it.* **2.** try to prevent; keep from. (*~ doing*) ¶*I couldn't*

—[他] 1. …에 저항하다, 반대하다 2. …을 참다 ¶①웃지 않을 수 없었다

R

re·sist·ance [rizíst(ə)ns] *n.* Ⓤ **1.** the act of resisting or opposing. ¶*He made no ~ to the robber.*① **2.** power to resist. ¶*He has little ~ to germ.*
re·sist·ant [rizíst(ə)nt] *adj.* resisting.
re·sist·less [rizístlis] *adj.* that cannot be resisted.
re·sis·tor [rizístər] *n.* Ⓒ a conducting body used in an electric circuit.
re·sol·u·ble [rizáljubl / -zɔ́l-] *adj.* capable of being re-⎰solved.⎱
res·o·lute [rézəluːt] *adj.* firm; determined.
res·o·lu·tion [rèzəluːʃ(ə)n] *n.* **1.** Ⓤ Ⓒ fixed determination. ¶*a man of ~.*① **2.** Ⓒ a formal expression of opinion. **3.** Ⓤ Ⓒ the act of solving; solution.
re·solv·a·ble [rizálvəbl / -zɔ́l-] *adj.* that can be resolved.
⁑re·solve [rizálv / -zɔ́lv] *vt.* **1.** make up one's mind; determine. 《~ *to do*; ~ *that ...*》 ¶*I resolved to give up smoking.* | *He resolved that no one should prevent him from going to America.*① **2.** decide (something) by vote. **3.** find the answer to (a problem, etc.); solve; make (doubts, etc.) clear. ¶*All doubts were resolved.* **4.** separate (something) into parts; analyze; transform. 《~ *something into*》 ¶*~ a substance into its elements.* —*vi.* **1.** be resolved. 《~ *into* or *to*》 ↔combine **2.** determine. 《~ *on* or *upon something*》 ¶*He resolved on going up to Tokyo.*
be resolved (=have made up one's mind) **to do.**
—*n.* Ⓤ Ⓒ a fixed intention; something determined; a resolution; firmness of character or purpose. ¶*a man of ~*① / *keep one's ~.*②
re·solved [rizálvd / -zɔ́lvd] *adj.* firm; determined.
re·solv·ent [rizálvənt / -zɔ́l-] *adj.* resolving.
res·o·nance [réz(ə)nəns] *n.* Ⓤ resounding quality; echo.
res·o·nant [réz(ə)nənt] *adj.* resounding; vibrating.
⁑re·sort [rizɔ́ːrt] *vi.* **1.** go; visit; go often. 《~ *to a place*》 ¶*~ to the seaside.* **2.** use something as a help or means. 《~ *to something*》 ¶*~ to violence.*①
—*n.* **1.** Ⓤ the act of resorting to a place. ¶*a place of popular ~.*② **2.** Ⓒ a place to which people often go for health or recreation. ¶*a health ~* / *a holiday ~* / *a summer* (*winter*) *~.*③ **3.** Ⓒ Ⓤ help; means. ¶*have* (or *make*) *~ to force*④ / *as* (or *in*) *the last ~.*⑤
re·sound [rizáund] *vi.* echo; make a loud sound.
⁕re·source [rísɔːrs, +*U.S.* ⸺] *n.* **1.** (usu. *pl.*) any supply of anything useful. ¶*natural resources.* **2.** (usu. *pl.*) the wealth of a country; property. **3.** Ⓒ knowledge of what to do in a difficulty or an emergency.
re·source·ful [risɔ́ːrsf(u)l] *adj.* **1.** abounding in resources. **2.** good at finding a way of doing things. ▷**re·source·ful·ly** [-fuli] *adv.* —**re·source·ful·ness** [-nis] *n.*
re·source·less [risɔ́ːrslis] *adj.* lacking in resource or resources.
⁑re·spect [rispékt] *vt.* **1.** feel or show esteem for (someone). ¶*~ oneself*① / *I ~ him for his bravery.* **2.** pay attention to; take care of (something). ¶*We must ~ his opinion.* **3.** keep; obey. ¶*We should ~ the laws of our country.* / *I ~ his silence.*
—*n.* **1.** Ⓤ esteem; honor. ¶*with all ~ for your opinion*② / *They have great ~ for him.* **2.** (*pl.*) greetings. ¶*We paid our respects to the hostess.* | *Give* (or *Send*) *them our best respects.*③ **3.** Ⓤ attention; regard. ¶*I pay* (or *have*) *~ to.* **4.** Ⓤ relation. ¶*It has ~ to this event.* **5.** Ⓒ a point; a detail. ¶*in all* (*many, some*) *respects*④ / *I think you are wrong in this ~.*

1) *in respect of* (or *to*) (=*with regard to*) *something.*

―名 1. 저항; 반항; 방해 ¶①그는 도둑에게 저항하지 않았다 2. 저항력

―形 저항하는
―形 저항할 수 없는
―名 [전기의] 저항기

―形 분해할 수 있는
―形 결심이 굳은
―名 1. 결심, 결의(決意) ¶①성격이 단단한 사람 2. 결의(決議)[사항] 3. 해답, 해결
―形 해결할 수 있는
―他 1. …을 결심하다 ¶①그는 누가 뭐라고 해도 미국에 가기로 결심했다 2. …을 결의하다 3. [문제 따위]를 풀다; [의문 따위]를 풀다 4. …을 분해(용해, 분석)하다; [분해하여]변형시키다

―自 1. 분해하다, 바꾸다 2. 결심하다

熟 …할 결심으로 있다
―名 결심, 결의; 의결; 결단 ¶②과단성 있는 사람/③결심을 지속하다

―形 단호한
―形 분해하는
―名 반향
―形 [소리가] 울려퍼지는
―自 1. 가다; 자주 가다 2. 의지하다, 호소하다 ¶①폭력에 호소하다

―名 1. 가기 ¶②사람이 잘 가는 곳 2. 사람들이 모이는 곳; 휴양지, 유원지 ¶③피서(한)지 3. 의지; 수단 ¶④폭력에 호소하다/⑤최후의 수단으로

―自 울려퍼지다; 반향하다
―名 1. 재원(財源); 자재 2. [한 나라의] 물자 3. 임기응변, 방편, 기략(機略)

―形 1. 자력이 풍부한 2. 계략이 많은, 재치있는

―形 방책(자원)이 없는

―他 1. …을 존경하다 ¶①자존심이 있다 2. …에 주의하다; …을 고려하다; 존중하다 3. …을 어기지 않다; …에 따르다

―名 1. 존경; 존중 ¶②지당한 말씀이오나 2. 인사, 문안 ¶③여러분에게 안부 전해 주시오 3. 주의, 관심 4. 관계 5. 점, 세목(細目) ¶④모든(많은, 어떤) 점에서

熟 1) …의 점에서는 2) …을 생각하면,

2) ***in respect that ...,*** considering; because of the fact that ...
3) ***with respect to*** (=*concerning; as to*) *something.*
4) ***without respect*** (=*paying no attention*) ***to*** *something.*

…이므로 3)…에 대하여는 4)…을 고려하지 않고

re·spect·a·bil·i·ty [rispèktəbíliti] *n.* [U] the quality of being respectable; good character.

—[名] 존경할 만함

* **re·spect·a·ble** [rispéktəbl] *adj.* **1.** worthy of honor; considered right or good enough to be respected; of good character; having a good reputation. **2.** fairly large or good. ▷**re·spect·a·bly** [-i] *adv.*

—[形] 1. 존경할 만한 2. 상당한, 꽤 많은

re·spect·ful [rispéktf(u)l] *adj.* showing respect; polite. ▷**re·spect·ful·ly** [-fuli] *adv.* —**re·spect·ful·ness** [-nis] *n.*

—[形] 경의를 표하는; 예의바른

re·spect·ing [rispéktiŋ] *prep.* concerning; regarding; about.

—[前] …에 관하여

* **re·spec·tive** [rispéktiv] *adj.* belonging to each; individual. ¶*Go to your ~ rooms.*①

—[形] 각자의 ¶①각자의 방으로 가라

re·spec·tive·ly [rispéktivli] *adv.* as relating to each.

—[副] 제각기, 저마다, 각자

res·pi·ra·tion [rèspiréiʃ(ə)n] *n.* [U] the act or process of breathing. ¶*artificial ~.*①

—[名] 호흡; 한 번의 호흡 ¶①인공호흡

res·pi·ra·tor [réspirèitər] *n.* [C] a device used in giving artificial respiration.

—[名] 인공호흡 장치; 마스크

res·pi·ra·to·ry [réspirətɔ̀:ri, rispáiərət(ə)ri] *adj.* of breathing.

—[形] 호흡의

re·spire [rispáiər] *vt., vi.* breathe.

—[他][自] 호흡하다

res·pite [réspit / -pait] *n.* [C] **1.** a delay; the act of putting off. **2.** a rest from work.

—[名] 1. 연기(延期) 2. 휴식

re·splend·ence [rispléndəns] *n.* [U] the quality of being resplendent; brightness.

—[名] 빛남

re·splend·ent [rispléndənt] *adj.* brilliant; very bright; splendid.

—[形] 빛나는; 멋진

* **re·spond** [rispánd / -pɔ́nd] *vi.* **1.** answer; reply. 《~ *to* something》 ¶*~ to a question.* **2.** act as an answer to another person's deed. 《~ *to* something》

—[自] 1. 대답하다 2. 응하다, 응답하다

* **re·sponse** [rispáns / -spɔ́ns] *n.* **1.** [C] a reply; an answer. ¶*My letter to him brought no ~.*① **2.** [U] an action as an answer to another person's action.

—[名] 1. 대답; 응답 ¶①그에게 보낸 편지에 회답이 없었다 2. 반응

‡ **re·spon·si·bil·i·ty** [rispànsibíliti / -spɔ̀n-] *n.* (pl. **-ties**) **1.** [U] the state of being responsible. ¶*He does not feel much ~.*① **2.** [C] a matter for which a person must be responsible; a duty; a burden.

—[名] 1. 책임 ¶①그는 별로 책임을 느끼지 못하고 있다 2. 의무, 무거운 짐

‡ **re·spon·si·ble** [rispánsibl / -spɔ́n-] *adj.* **1.** expected to do something correctly; expected to make something go right; that can be trusted with important matters. ¶*a ~ job*① **2.** reliable; trustworthy. ¶*He is a ~ person.*② **3.** having the cause of something. ¶*He is ~ for it.*③

—[形] 1. 책임있는 ¶①책임이 있는 일 2. 신뢰할 수 있는 ¶②그는 믿을 수 있는 사람이다 3. …의 원인인 ¶③그는 그 일에 책임이 있다

re·spon·sive [rispánsiv / -spɔ́n-] *adj.* answering; easily moved. ▷**re·spon·sive·ly** [-li] *adv.* —**re·spon·sive·ness** [-nis] *n.*

—[形] 대답하는, 응하는; 감응하기 쉬운

‡ **rest**[1] [rest] *n.* **1.** [C][U] a period of free time from work, activity, etc. ¶*a long ~ / a temporary ~ / take a ~*① / *give a ~.*② **2.** [U] the condition of having free time. ¶*need ~.* **3.** [U] ease; quiet; peace. ¶*~ of mind (soul, conscience).*③ **4.** [U][C] sleep. ¶*I had eight hours of ~ last night.*④ **5.** [C] a resting or lodging place. ¶*a seamen's ~.*⑤ **6.** [U] death; grave. ¶*go to one's ~.*⑥ **7.** [C] that on which something rests; a support. ¶*a chin ~ for a violin.*⑦ **8.** [C] (*Music*) an interval of silence; a sign which marks this. ¶*an eighth (a half) ~.*⑧

—[名] 1. 휴식 시간; 휴게 ¶①쉬다/②쉬게 하다 2. 휴식 상태 3. 안락; 평안 ¶③마음(영혼·양심)의 평안 4. 잠, 수면 ¶④어젯밤은 여덟 시간 잤다 5. 휴식소; 숙박소 ¶⑤선원 숙박소 6. 영면(永眠); 무덤 ¶⑥영면하다 7. [물건을 올려놓는] 대 ¶⑦바이올린의 턱받침 8. 《樂》 휴지(休止), 쉼표 ¶⑧8분(2분) 쉼표

1) ***at rest,*** ⓐ still. ⓑ free from activity. ⓒ free from care. ⓓ dead.
2) ***come to rest,*** stop moving.
3) ***go*** (or ***retire***) ***to rest,*** go to bed.
4) ***lay to rest,*** bury.
5) ***set a question at rest,*** settle a question.
6) ***set someone's mind at rest,*** make someone free from anxiety.

[熟] 1)ⓐ정지(靜止)하여 ⓑ휴식하여 ⓒ안심하여 ⓓ영면하여 2)멈추다 3)자다 4)매장하다 5)문제를 해결하다 6)…의 마음을 안심시키다

—*vi.* **1.** stop working; be still. ¶*~ a while / ~ from toil.*⑨ **2.** sleep; be dead. ¶*~ in peace*⑩ / *~ in the grave.*⑪ **3.** be at peace or ease. **4.** believe; trust. 《~ *in* something》 ¶*~ in God.* **5.** lean; lie; sit. ¶~

—[自] 1. 쉬다; 정지하다 ¶⑨일손을 쉬다 2. 자다; 영면하다 ¶⑩고이 잠들다/⑪영면하다 3. 안심하다; 침착해 있다 4. 믿다 5. 기대다; 위치하다 ¶⑫팔베

R

against a tree | ~ *on a couch* | ~ *on one's arm.*⑫ **6.** be placed; be fixed. 《~ *on* something》 ¶*The responsibility rested upon him.*⑬ | *His eyes rested on the picture.* **7.** rely. 《~ *on* or *upon* someone or something》 ¶*Our hope rests on you.* | *I cannot ~ on your promise.* **8.** continue to be; remain. ¶~ *assured*⑭ | *The meaning rests unknown.* **9.** depend; have the base. 《~ *with* someone》 ¶*Government rests with the people.*⑮ —*vt.* **1.** give rest to (someone). ¶~ *oneself*⑯ | ~ *one's eyes* | *May God ~ his soul!* **2.** cause (something) to be supported; put; place. ¶~ *one's head on a pillow* | ~ *a stick against the wall.*⑰

개를 하다 **6.** 존재하다; [시선이 …으로] 돌려지다; …에게 지워지다 ¶⑬책임은 그에게 달려 있다 **7.** 의지하다, 신뢰하다 **8.** …으로 [남아] 있다 ¶⑭안심하고 있다 **9.** …에 달려 있다 ¶⑮정부는 그 국민에 달려 있다 —[他] **1.** …을 쉬게 하다 ¶⑯휴식하다 **2.** …을 놓다; 얹다 ¶⑰지팡이를 벽에 기대어 놓다

rest² [rest] *n.* 《*the* ~, *sing.* only》 **1.** what is left. ¶*You know the ~.* **2.** 《used as *pl.*》 the others.
1) ***and*** [***all***] ***the rest*** [***of it***]**,** and everything else.
2) [***as***] ***for the rest,*** as to other matters.

—[名] **1.** 나머지, 잔여물 **2.** 그 밖의 사람들
[熟] 1)그 밖의 모두 2)그 외는, 나머지는

re·state [ríːstéit] *vt.* state again or in a new way. —[他] …을 다시 말하다; 바꿔 말하다

re·state·ment [ríːstéitmənt] *n.* [U] statement made again or in a new way. —[名] 재진술; 환언(換言)

⁎**res·tau·rant** [réstərənt / -t(ə)rɔ̃ː(ŋ)] *n.* [C] a place where meals are served to customers; an eating house. —[名] 요리점, 레스토랑

rest·ful [réstf(u)l] *adj.* giving rest; quiet. ¶*a ~ life.*① —[形] 평안한, 고요한 ¶①평안한 생애

res·ti·tu·tion [rèstit(j)úːʃ(ə)n / -tjúː-] *n.* [U] **1.** the act of giving back what has been taken away to its owner. **2.** payment for damage done. —[名] **1.** 반환, 상환 **2.** 손해배상

res·tive [réstiv] *adj.* uneasy; rebellious; (of a horse) refusing to go ahead. ▷**res·tive·ly** [-li] *adv.* —[形] 고집 센; 다루기 힘든

⁎**rest·less** [réstlis] **1.** *adj.* always active; always moving. ¶*a man of ~ energy.*① **2.** uneasy. ¶*a ~ child.* **3.** without sleep. ¶*a ~ night.* —[形] **1.** 휴식 없는; 끊임없는 ¶①활동가 **2.** 침착하지 못한 **3.** 잠잘 수 없는

rest·less·ly [réstlisli] *adv.* without rest; continuously; uneasily. —[副] 쉬지 않고, 부단히; 침착하지 못하게

rest·less·ness [réstlisnis] *n.* [U] the state of being restless or uneasy. —[名] 침착하지 못함, 불안

re·stock [riːstɑ́k / -stɔ́k] *vt.* supply (some place) with a new stock again. —[他] …에 새로이 사들이다, 보충하다

⁎**res·to·ra·tion** [rèstəréiʃ(ə)n] *n.* **1.** [U] the act of putting back as it was. **2.** 《*the R-*》 [the period of] the English re-establishment of the monarchy in 1660. —[名] **1.** [건강의] 회복, 복구; 복고(復古), [그림·건조물 따위의] 복원(復元) **2.** [영국의] 왕정복고 [시대]

re·stor·a·tive [ristɔ́ːrətiv / -stɔ́r-] *adj.* having the power to bring back to a former condition. —[形] 회복시키는; 힘을 내게 하는

⁑**re·store** [ristɔ́ːr] *vt.* **1.** bring back; put (something or someone) back as it was or to a former condition. ¶~ *the book to the shelf.* **2.** reconstruct (something) as it was; repair. ¶~ *an old temple* | *be restored out of all recognition.*① **3.** give back. 《~ something *to*》 —[他] **1.** …을 제자리로 돌리다 **2.** …을 부흥(복원)하다 ¶①몰라 볼 정도로 복구되다 **3.** …을 상환(반환)하다

re·stor·er [ristɔ́ːrər] *n.* [C] a person or thing that restores. —[名] 원상으로 되돌리는 사람(것)

⁎**re·strain** [ristréin] *vt.* **1.** hold back; check. 《~ someone *from doing*》 ¶~ *oneself*① | *He could not ~ her from going.* **2.** keep (someone) in prison. ▷**re·stain·a·ble** [-əbl] *adj.* —**re·strain·er** [-ər] *n.* —[他] **1.** …을 억누르다 ¶①참다 **2.** …을 감금(구속)하다

⁎**re·straint** [ristréint] *n.* [U][C] **1.** the act of holding back; self-control. **2.** confinement. —[名] **1.** 억제; 제지 **2.** 구속

⁎**re·strict** [ristríkt] *vt.* keep (something) within limits. 《~ something *to* or *within*》 —[他] …을 제한하다

re·strict·ed [ristríktid] *adj.* limited; narrow. —[形] 한정된; 좁은

⁎**re·stric·tion** [ristríkʃ(ə)n] *n.* [U][C] the act of restricting; something that restricts. ¶*place restrictions on the use of the gymnasium.*① —[名] 제한[하는 것] ¶①체육관의 사용에 제한을 두다

re·stric·tive [ristríktiv] *adj.* limiting; restricting. ▷**re·stric·tive·ly** [-li] *adv.* —[形] 제한하는; 한정하는

rest room [ˊ ˋ] *n.* (*U.S.*) a lavatory. —[名] 《美》 변소

⁑**re·sult** [rizʌ́lt] *n.* [U][C] that which is produced by a cause; effect. ¶*a satisfactory ~*① | *as a ~ of*② | *in* [*the*] *~*③ | *with the ~ that …*④ | *I made every effort without ~.*⑤ —*vi.* **1.** follow as a consequence. 《~ *from* something》 ¶*Nothing has resulted from my efforts.*

—[名] 결과, 결말, 성과 ¶①만족할 만한 결과/②…의 결과로서/③결국/④그 결과 …이다/⑤내 노력은 모두 헛수고가 됐다 —[自] **1.** [결과로서] 일어나다; 생기다 **2.** 결국 …으로 끝나다 ¶⑥좋은

2. end; have as a consequence. 《~ *in* something》 ¶~ *in good.*® 결과가 되다

re·sult·ant [rizʌ́lt(ə)nt] *adj.* producing as a result; resulting. —*n.* [C] that which results; a consequence. —[形] 결과로서 생기는 —[名] 결과

* **re·sume** [rizú:m / -z(j)ú:m] *vt.* **1.** begin again; go on (doing something) after stopping. ¶~ *a story.* **2.** take (something) again after once leaving or losing. ¶*He resumed his health.*① —[他] 1. …을 다시 시작하다; 계속하다 2. …을 다시 차지하다, 되찾다 ¶①그는 건강을 회복했다

ré·su·mé [rèzuméi / -zju-] *n.* [C] a summary; an outline. —[名] 요약, 개요

re·sump·tion [rizʌ́m(p)ʃ(ə)n] *n.* [U] [C] the act of resuming. —[名] 재개시; 속행; 회복

re·sur·gence [risə́:rdʒ(ə)ns] *n.* [U] the act of rising again. —[名] 재기

re·sur·gent [risə́:rdʒ(ə)nt] *adj.* rising again. —[形] 재기하는, 재기의

res·ur·rect [rèzərékt] *vt.* bring (someone) back to life; bring (something) back into use. —[他] …을 부활시키다

res·ur·rec·tion [rèzərékʃ(ə)n] *n.* **1.** [U] [C] the act of resurrecting; revival. **2.** 《*the R-*》 Christ's rising from the grave. —[名] 1. 재기 2. 그리스도의 부활

re·sus·ci·tate [risʌ́sitèit] *vt.* bring (something) back to life. —*vi.* come back to life. —[他] …을 부활시키다 —[自] 부활하다

re·sus·ci·ta·tion [risʌ̀sitéiʃ(ə)n] *n.* [U] the act of resuscitating. —[名] 부활

* **re·tail** [rí:teil → *v.*] *n.* [U] the sale of goods in small quantities or amounts. ¶*a ~ dealer*① / *sell at* (or *by*) *~.*② —[名] 소매 ¶①소매 상인/②…을 소매하다
—*adv.* by the sale of goods in small quantities. —[副] 소매로
—*v.* [rí:teil →2. / ri(:)téil] *vt.* **1.** sell (goods) in small quantities directly to the consumer. **2.** [*U.S.* ritéil] tell (gossip, rumor) to others. —*vi.* be sold in small quantities directly to consumers. 《~ *at* or *for* a certain price》 ¶*The pencil retails at* (or *for*) *20 yen.* —[他] 1. …을 소매하다 2. …을 퍼뜨리다, 말을 전하다 —[自] [얼마로] 소매되다

re·tail·er [rí:teilər / ri(:)téilə] *n.* [C] a merchant who sells at retail. —[名] 소매인

⁑ **re·tain** [ritéin] *vt.* **1.** keep; preserve; continue to hold. ¶~ *an old custom.* **2.** keep (something) in mind; remember. **3.** employ (a lawer, etc.) by payment of advance fee. —[他] 1. …을 보유(유지)하다 2. …을 기억하고 있다 3. [변호사 등]을 고용해 두다, 의뢰해 두다

re·tain·er [ritéinər] *n.* [C] **1.** a fee paid to a lawyer **2.** a person who serves someone of high rank; a servant. —[名] 1. 변호료 2. 부하; 하인

re·take [rí:téik] *vt.* (**-took, -tak·en**) take again. —*n.* [C] a second or subsequent photographing of a scene in a movie, etc. —[他] …을 다시 갖다; 다시 촬영하다 —[名] 재촬영

re·tak·en [rí:téikn] *vt.* pp. of **retake**.

re·tal·i·ate [ritǽlièit] *vi., vt.* return blow for blow, wrong for wrong; pay back (wrong, injury) in the same way. —[自][他] [상대와 같은 수단으로] 보복하다

re·tal·i·a·tion [ritæ̀liéiʃ(ə)n] *n.* [U] the act of retaliating. —[名] 보복

re·tal·i·a·tive [ritǽlièitiv / -liətiv] *adj.* disposed to retaliate. —[形] 보복적인

re·tal·i·a·to·ry [ritǽliətɔ̀:ri / -ət(ə)ri] *adj.* returning evil for evil. —[形] 보복적인

re·tard [ritá:rd] *vt.* delay; keep back; hinder. —[他] …을 지연시키다

re·tar·da·tion [rì:ta:rdéiʃ(ə)n] *n.* [U] [C] delay; hindrance. —[名] 지연; 방해

retch [retʃ] *vi.* try to vomit. —[自] 토하려고 하다

re·tell [rí:tél] *vt.* (**-told**) tell again. —[他] …을 다시 이야기하다

re·ten·tion [riténʃ(ə)n] *n.* [U] **1.** the act of retaining. **2.** the ability to remember. —[名] 1. 보유; 보존 2. 기억

re·ten·tive [riténtiv] *adj.* **1.** able to keep. **2.** able to remember. 《~ *of*》 —[形] 1. 유지(보유)하는 2. 기억력이 좋은

ret·i·cence [rétis(ə)ns] *n.* [U] tendency to be silent. —[名] 침묵

ret·i·cent [rétis(ə)nt] *adj.* tending to be silent; reserved in speech. —[形] 침묵을 지키는; 말수 적은

re·tic·u·late [ritíkjulit] *adj.* netlike; covered with something like a network. —[形] 그물 모양의, 그물코가 있는

ret·i·na [rétinə] *n.* [C] (pl. **-nas** or **-nae**) the back of the eye which reacts to light. —[名] 눈의 망막(網膜)

ret·i·nae [rétini:] *n.* pl. of **retina.**

ret·i·nue [rétin(j)ù: / -njù:] *n.* [C] 《*collectively*》 the group of followers and servants of a prince or nobleman. —[名] 시종, 수행원

⁑ **re·tire** [ritáiər] *vi.* **1.** give up one's business, position, etc.; go away to a place kept apart from others. ¶~ *from business* / ~ *from the world*① / ~ *into oneself*② / ~ *into the country* / ~ *under the age clause.*③ **2.** go —[自] 1. 퇴직하다, 은퇴하다; 은거(隱居)하다 ¶①은퇴하다/②입을 다물다; 세상을 버리다/③정년으로 퇴직하다 2. 떠나다, 물러나다, 퇴각하다 3. 자리에

away; go back; withdraw. ¶~ *to one's room* / *The moon retired behind the mountains.* **3.** go to bed. ¶~ *at ten o'clock* / ~ *for rest.*④ —*vt.* **1.** cause (someone) to retire. **2.** take (bills, etc.) out of circulation.
—*n.* [C] a signal to troops to retire.

re·tired [ritáiərd] *adj.* **1.** withdrawn from activity. **2.** reserved; shy; hidden.

re·tir·ing [ritáiəriŋ] *adj.* shy; quiet; modest.

re·told [ri:tóuld] *v.* pt. and pp. of **retell**.

re·took [ri:túk] *v.* pt. of **retake**.

***re·tort**¹ [ritɔ́:rt] *vt.* answer back sharply or quickly; pay back. —*vi.* answer sharply or quickly. —*n.* [U][C] a sharp, angry, or ready reply.

re·tort² [ritɔ́:rt] *n.* [C] a container for turning liquids to vapor. ⇒fig.

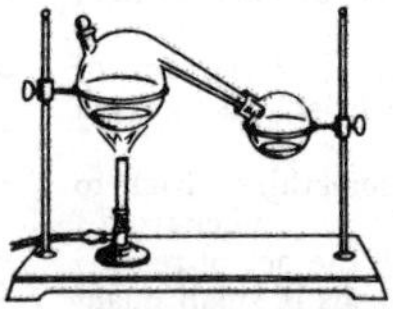
[retort²]

re·touch [rí:tʌ́tʃ] *vt.* touch up; improve (a painting, photograph, etc.) by adding a few touches.

re·trace [ritréis] *vt.* go back again; recollect.

re-trace [rí:tréis] *vt.* trace over again. ¶~ *the drawing.*

re·tract [ritrǽkt] *vt.* draw back; take back (one's opinion, promise, etc.)

re·trac·tion [ritrǽkʃ(ə)n] *n.* [U][C] the act of taking or drawing back.

: re·treat [ritrí:t] *vi.* go back; draw back from action. —*n.* **1.** [U][C] the act of going back or drawing back. **2.** [C] a safe, quiet place. ¶*a summer* ~.①
beat a retreat, go back.

re·trench [ritréntʃ] *vt.* cut down (payments, money used, etc.). —*vi.* cut down expenses.

re·tri·al [rí:trái(ə)l] *n.* [C] a second examination; a second trial.

ret·ri·bu·tion [rètribjú:ʃ(ə)n] *n.* [U] reward or punishment which comes to oneself. ¶*the day of* ~.①

re·trib·u·tive [ritríbjutiv] *adj.* paying back.

re·triev·al [ritrí:v(ə)l] *n.* [U] the act of retrieving.

re·trieve [ritrí:v] *vt.* **1.** get (something lost) back again; recover. ¶*He retrieved his spirits.*① **2.** bring back (something damaged) to a former condition. **3.** (of a hunting dog) find and bring back (a dead or wounded animal or bird) to a hunter. ▷**re·triev·a·ble** [-əbl] *adj.*

re·triev·er [ritrí:vər] *n.* [C] a trained dog which finds and brings back shot animals or birds to its master.

ret·ro·grade [rétrougrèid] *vi.* move backward; become worse. —*adj.* moving backward; becoming worse.

ret·ro·gress [rétrougrès] *vi.* move backward; become worse.

ret·ro·gres·sion [rètrougréʃ(ə)n] *n.* [U] backward movement; return to an inferior, worse state.

ret·ro·gres·sive [rètrougrésiv] *adj.* moving backward.

ret·ro·spect [rétrouspèkt] *n.* [U] the act of thinking about past events. ¶*in* ~.

ret·ro·spec·tion [rètrouspékʃ(ə)n] *n.* =retrospect.

ret·ro·spec·tive [rètrouspéktiv] *adj.* thinking about past events.

⁝ re·turn [ritə́:rn] *vi.* **1.** go or come back. ¶~ *home*① / ~ *from abroad* / ~ *to Tokyo.* **2.** go back again in thought or treatment. ⟪~ *to* something⟫ ¶*Let's* ~ *to the subject.*② / *To* ~.③ **3.** go back to a former state; happen or appear again. ⟪~ *to* something⟫ ¶~ *to one's work* / ~ *to oneself*④ / ~ *to dust*⑤ / ~ *to life*⑥ / *Consciousness has not returned yet.* / *The fine weather has returned.*⑦ —*vt.* **1.** bring or put back. ¶~ *a book to*

들다, 자다 ¶④쉬다 —[他] 1. …을 은퇴(퇴직)시키다 2. [지폐 따위]를 회수하다

—[名] 퇴각 나팔

—[形] 1. 은퇴한; 퇴직한 2. 수줍어하는; 시골 구석의

—[形] 수줍어하는

—[他] …에게 말대꾸하다; 보복하다
—[自] 말대꾸하다 —[名] 말대꾸

—[名] 레토르트; 증류기

—[他] [그림·사진 따위]에 손질을 하다, …을 수정하다

—[他] …을(에서) 되돌아오다; 회상하다

—[他] …위에 다시 투사(透寫)하다
—[他] [신체의 일부]를 쏙 들어가게 하다; [의견 따위]를 취소하다
—[名] 앞서 한 말의 취소; 철회
—[自] 물러나다; 은퇴하다
—[名] 1. 퇴각; 은퇴 2. 피난처 ¶①피서지
[熟] 퇴각하다
—[他] [비용 따위]를 바짝 줄이다
—[自] 절약하다
—[名] 재시험; [재판의] 재심
—[名] 천벌, 응보(應報) ¶①최후의 심판일
—[形] 응보의
—[名] 회복; 복구; 만회
—[他] 1. …을 되찾다 ¶①그는 기운을 되찾았다 2. …을 보상(벌충)하다 3. [사냥개가 잡은 짐승]을 찾아 가지고 오다

—[名] 리트리이버(잡은 짐승을 찾아오도록 훈련된 사냥개)
—[自] 후퇴하다; 악화하다 —[形] 후퇴의; 악화의
—[自] 되돌아가다; 악화하다

—[名] 후퇴; 퇴화, 악화

—[形] 후퇴하는, 퇴화하는
—[名] 회고, 추상

—[形] 회고하는, 추억의

—[自] 1. 돌아가다(오다) ¶①귀가하다 2. [화제 따위] …으로 돌아가다 ¶②본론으로 돌아가자/③본론으로 돌아가서 3. [원래의 상태로] 역행(복귀)하다; 재발하다 ¶④제정신으로 돌아 오다/⑤흙으로 돌아가다; 죽다/⑥되살아나다/⑦날씨가 회복되었다 —[他] 1. …을 되돌리다; 도로 주다 2. …에 보답(답례)

the case / Return my pen, please. **2.** give back (something) in the same manner. ¶*~ a visit*⑧ / *~ a blow*⑨ / *~ thanks / ~ good for evil.*⑩ **3.** reply; answer. **4.** report officially. **5.** elect. ⦅~ someone *to* Parliament⦆ ¶*He was returned [to Parliament] for Devonshire.*

하다 ¶⑧답례로서 방문하다/⑨되받아 때리다/⑩악에 은혜로 보답하다 3. …에 대답하다 4. …을 보고하다, 답신(答申)하다 5. …을 선출하다

—*n.* **1.** [U][C] the act of going or coming back. ¶*a ~ home / Await his ~ from a journey.* **2.** [U][C] the act of coming again; reappearance. ¶*a ~ of illness / Many happy returns [of the day]!*⑪ **3.** [U][C] something returned; repayment. ¶*the ~ of a salute*⑫ / *I asked him the ~ of the money. / make ~ for something.*⑬ **4.** [C] a reply. **5.** ⦅often *pl.*⦆ a profit. ¶*a poor ~ on one's investment / give a ~.*⑭ **6.** [C] an official report. ¶*official returns*⑮ / *make a ~ of the survey.*⑯ **7.** [U][C] an election. ¶*secure a ~ for California.*⑰ **8.** [C] a return ticket.

—[名] 1. 돌아가기; 귀환; 반환 2. 회귀(回歸), 재발 ¶⑪이 복된 날이 몇 번이고 되풀이되길(생일 축하의 말) 3. 반환, 반제; 답례 ¶⑫답례[포]/⑬ …에 보답하다 4. 대답 5. 수익, 보수 ¶⑭보수를 내다 6. 보고[서] ¶⑮공보/⑯조사의 보고(신고)를 하다 7. 선출 ¶⑰캘리포니아 주에서 선출되다 8. 왕복표

1) ***by return [of mail],*** by the next mail out.
2) ***in return,*** as a return.
3) ***in return for*** (or ***to***) (=*as repayment for*) something.

[熟] 1) 지급 회신으로 2) 답례로 3) …의 답례로; 보복으로

—*adj.* returning; returned; of a return. ¶*a ~ ticket*

—[形] 돌아가는; 답례의; 왕복의

re·un·ion [ríːjúːnjən] *n.* **1.** [U] the state of coming together again. ¶*the ~ of parted friends.*① **2.** [C] a happy meeting of friends who have not met for a long time.

—[名] 1. 재합동, 재결합; 재회 ¶①헤어진 친구의 재회 2. 친목회, 회합

re·u·nite [ríːju(ː)náit] *vt.* unite (persons) again after separation. **—*vi.*** become joined again.

—[他] …을 재회시키다 —[自] 다시 결합하다

Rev. Reverend.

re·val·u·a·tion [ríːvæljuéiʃ(ə)n] *n.* [U] value estimated or recognized again.

—[名] 재평가

re·val·ue [ríːvǽljuː] *vt.* estimate value of (something) again.

—[他] …을 재평가하다

re·vamp [ríːvǽmp] *vt.* mend; patch up.

—[他] …을 수선하다; …에 조각을 대다

‡re·veal [rivíːl] *vt.* expose to view (what has been hidden); show; make known. ¶*~ a secret / ~ oneself.*

—[他] …을 나타내다, …을 폭로하다; 알리다

rev·el [révl] *vi.* (**-eled, -el·ing** or *Brit.* **-elled, -el·ling**) be very gay and noisy; take great pleasure. ⦅~ *in* something⦆ ¶*They reveled all day long.*① **—*n.*** ⦅often *pl.*⦆ a gay and noisy celebration with drinks.

—[自] 흥청거리며 놀다; 마음껏 즐기다 ¶①그들은 온종일 즐겼다 —[名] 술잔치

rev·e·la·tion [rèviléiʃ(ə)n] *n.* **1.** [U] the act of making known something previously secret. **2.** [C] something that is made known; something unexpected. ¶*It was a ~ to me.*①

—[名] 1. 발각 2. 의외의 사실 ¶①나에게는 정말 의외의 이야기였다

rev·el·er, *Brit.* **-el·ler** [rév(ə)lər] *n.* [C] a person who enjoys revels.

—[名] 술잔치하는 사람

rev·el·ry [révlri] *n.* [U] a gay and noisy state, with much drinking.

—[名] 술마시며 떠들기, 환락

‡re·venge [rivéndʒ] *vt.* do harm to (someone) in return for a wrong. ¶*~ wrong with wrong*① / *~ one's deceased father.*② **—*n.*** **1.** [U] the act of paying back harm for harm. **2.** a desire to return evil for evil.

—[他] …에 복수하다 ¶①악에는 악으로써 대하다/②죽은 아버지의 원수를 갚다 —[名] 1. 복수 2. 복수심

re·venge·ful [rivéndʒf(u)l] *adj.* wanting to revenge always.

—[形] 집념 깊은

•rev·e·nue [révin(j)ùː / -njùː] *n.* [U] income.

—[名] 소득, 수입

revenue stamp [ˊ-- ˋ] *n.* a stamp to show that a person has paid a tax to the government.

—[名] 수입인지

re·ver·ber·ate [rivə́ːrbərèit] *vt., vi.* **1.** echo back; resound. ¶*The thunder reverberated throughout the house.*① **2.** reflect (light, etc.).

—[他][自] 1. [···을] 반향시키다(하다) ¶①우뢰가 집을 울렸다 2. [빛 따위]를 반사하다

re·ver·ber·a·tion [rivə̀ːrbəréiʃ(ə)n] *n.* [U] **1.** the act of echoing back; the state of being reverberated. **2.** reflection.

—[名] 1. 반향 2. 반사

re·vere [rivíər] *vt.* respect and love.

—[他] …을 존경하다

•rev·er·ence [rév(ə)r(ə)ns] *n.* [U] **1.** a feeling of respect mixed with wonder. **2.** [C] a deep bow.

—[名] 1. 존경 2. [정중한] 절, 인사

•rev·er·end [rév(ə)r(ə)nd] *adj.* **1.** worthy of deep respect. **2.** ⦅*the R-*⦆ used as a title for a clergyman.

—[形] 1. 존경할 만한 2. …사(師)(성직자의 경칭)

rev·er·ent [rév(ə)r(ə)nt] *adj.* feeling reverence.

—[形] 존경하는

rev·er·en·tial [rèvərénʃ(ə)l] *adj.* =reverent.

rev·er·ie [révəri] *n.* [U][C] dreamy thoughts.

—[名] 환상, 몽상

re·ver·sal [rivə́ːrs(ə)l] *n.* [U][C] a change to the opposite.

—[名] 역전

•re·verse [rivə́ːrs] *vt.* **1.** turn (something) inside out,

—[他] 1. …을 거꾸로 하다; 반대로 하

R

reversely [976] **revocation**

upside down, or backward. ¶~ *a cup.* **2.** put (things) in each other's place. ¶*Their positions are now reversed.* **3.** cause (something) to move backward. ¶~ *an engine.*① **4.** (*Law*) take away the value of (something); cancel. ¶~ *a sentence.*② —*vi.* move in the opposite direction. ¶*The dancers reversed.*
—*n.* ⓒ **1.** (*sing* only, *the* ~) the opposite or contrary of something. ¶*He did the* ~ *of what he was asked to do.*① **2.** ⓒ the back of a coin or medal. ↔obverse **3.** ⓒ a change from good to bad; a misfortune. ¶*the* ~ *of fortune* / *have a*~.② **4.** Ⓤ (of a machine) backward movement. ¶*He drove his car in* ~.③
—*adj.* opposite; contrary; upside-down; inside-out; inverted. ¶~ *circulation*⑥
re·verse·ly [rivə́ːrsli] *adv.* in an opposite direction; on the other hand.
re·vers·i·ble [rivə́ːrsibl] *adj.* that can be reversed.
re·ver·sion [rivə́ːrʒ(ə)n / rivə́ːrʃ(ə)n] *n.* Ⓤⓒ the act of going back to a former condition.
re·vert [rivə́ːrt] *vi.* go back to a former condition, opinion, etc. (~ *to* a wild state, etc.).
rev·er·y [révəri] *n.* (pl. **-ries**) =reverie.
: re·view [rivjúː] *vt.* **1.** pass over (past events, etc) again in one's mind; (*U.S.*) study (something previously learnt) again. ¶*She reviewed the day's happenings.*① / *He reviewed his lessons every day.* **2.** inspect (troops, etc.) formally or officially. ¶~ *soldiers.*② **3.** look at (something) again to examine it. **4.** write a criticism of (a new book, play, etc.) in a magazine or newspaper.
—*n.* **1.** Ⓤ the act of looking over, studying, considering, etc. again. **2.** ⓒⓊ the formal inspection of soldiers, etc. **3.** Ⓤ the second exact view or examination. **4.** ⓒⓊ a criticism of a new book, play, etc. printed in a magazine or newspaper.
re·view·er [rivjúːər] *n.* ⓒ a person who writes a criticism of a book, play, etc. in a magazine or newspaper.
re·vile [riváil] *vt., vi.* use bad words to (someone); call (someone) bad names.
re·vise [rivái̇z] *vt.* **1.** read again, esp. to discover and correct errors in (a text, etc.); correct. ¶*revised and enlarged.*① **2.** change. ¶~ *one's opinion.*② —*n.* Ⓤ ⓒ the process of revising.
re·vis·er [riváizər] *n.* ⓒ a person who revises.
Re·vised Version [riváizdvə́ːrʒ(ə)n,-ʃ(ə)n] *n.* the revised form of the Authorized Version of the Bible. ⇒N.B.
re·vi·sion [riviʒ(ə)n] *n.* Ⓤ the act of revising.
re·vis·it [ríːvízit] *vt.* visit again.
re·viv·al [riváiv(ə)l] *n.* ⓊⓒⒸ **1.** the state of being brought back to life. ¶*the* ~ *of a drowned man.*① **2.** the act of coming back to public use and attention, the state of being brought to public use and attention; restoration. ¶*the* ~ *of an old style*② / *the* ~ *of learning* (or *letters*)③ / *the* ~ *of old movies.* **3.** a meeting or series of meetings to arouse interest in religion.
• re·vive [riváiv] *vi.* **1.** come back to life or consciousness. **2.** return to a healthy and lively state. ¶*Flowers* ~ *in water.* **3.** come back to public use and attention. —*vt.* **1.** cause (someone) to come back to life or consciousness. **2.** refresh; give (someone) strength and energy again. ¶*Tea often revives a tired person.*① **3.** bring back (something) to public use and attention. ¶*Many old movies are being revived now.*
rev·o·ca·ble [révəkəbl] *adj.* that can be canceled.
rev·o·ca·tion [rèvəkéiʃ(ə)n] *n.* ⓊⒸ the act of canceling.

다; 뒤집다 2. …을 바꾸어 놓다; 교환하다 3. …을 역동(逆動)(역전)시키다 ¶①엔진을 역전하다 4.(法) …을 파기하다, 취소하다 ¶②판결을 파기하다 —自 연전하다, 거꾸로 돌다

—名 1. 역(逆), 반대 ¶③그는 하라고 하는 일을 거꾸로 했다 2. 뒤; 이면 3. 악화; 실패; 불운 ¶④실패(패배)하다 4. 역전 ¶⑤그는 자동차를 뒤로 몰았다

—形 반대의; 거꾸로의; 뒤집은; 역전하는 ¶⑥역류
—副 거꾸로; 이에 반하여

—形 거꾸로 할 수 있는
—名 되돌아가기, 역행

—自 되돌아가다, 복귀하다

—他 1. …을 회고하다; (美) [학과 위]를 복습하다 ¶①그녀는 그날 일어났던 일을 뒤돌아 보았다 2. …을 검열하다 ¶②열병(閱兵)하다 3. …을 재조사하다 4. [잡지 따위에서] …을 비평하다, 평론하다

—名 1. 회고 2. 검열 3. 재조사 4. [잡지 따위에 실은 신간서·연극 따위의] 비평, 평론

—名 평론가

—他自 […을] 욕하다

—他 1. …을 교정(校訂)하다, 개정하다, 정정하다 ¶①개정증보[판]의 2. [의견 따위]를 바꾸다 ¶②의견을 바꾸다
—名 교정, 개정
—名 교정자
—名 개정역(改訂譯) 성서 N.B. Authorized Version을 개역, R.V.로 줄임]
—名 교정, 개정
—他 …을 다시 방문하다
—名 1. 소생, 부활 ¶①물에 빠진 사람의 소생 2. 부흥, 재흥; [영화 따위의] 재상영 ¶②옛 스타일의 재흥/③문예부흥 3. [신앙 부흥을 위한] 전도집회

—自 1. 되살아나다; 의식을 회복하다 2. 기운이 나다 3. 부흥하다 —他 1. …을 되살아나게 하다; …의 의식을 되찾게 하다 2. …을 기운나게 하다 ¶①차는 피로한 사람을 회복시키는 일이 흔히 있다 3. …을 부흥시키다

—形 취소할 수 있는
—名 폐지, 취소

re·voke [rivóuk] *vt.* cancel; withdraw. ¶~ *a license.* —[他] …을 취소하다; 철회하다

*__re·volt__ [rivóult] *n.* [C] the people's act of rising up against authority. —*vi.* **1.** rise up against authority. 《~ *against* someone》 ¶*The people revolted against the dictator.*① **2.** be disgusted by something bad or unpleasant. 《~ *by* something》 —[名] 반란 —[自] **1.** 반란을 일으키다 ¶①사람들은 독재자에게 반란을 일으켰다 **2.** 메스꺼워지다

⁑**rev·o·lu·tion** [rèvəl(j)ú:ʃ(ə)n] *n.* [C][U] **1.** a complete change in the government or political system; any complete change in habits of thought, methods of labor, etc. ¶*the ~ in modern physics.*① **2.** one complete turn of a motor. **3.** [U] the act of turning of a heavenly body around a central point; the time it takes to complete one such revolution. ¶*the ~ of the seasons.*② —[名] **1.** 혁명, 변혁 ¶①근대 물리학의 대변혁 **2.** [기계의] 회전 **3.** [천체의] 공전(公轉); [세월·계절의] 주기, 순환 ¶②사철의 순환

*__rev·o·lu·tion·ar·y__ [rèvəlú:ʃ(ə)nèri / -ʃ(ə)nəri] *adj.* of or causing a revolution. —*n.* (pl. **-ar·ies**) =revolutionist. —[形] 혁명의; 대변혁을 가져오는

rev·o·lu·tion·ist [rèvəlú:ʃ(ə)nist] *n.* [C] a person who supports or takes part in a revolution. —[名] 혁명당원

rev·o·lu·tion·ize [rèvəlú:ʃ(ə)nàiz] *vt.* cause a complete change in (something). —[他] …에 혁명을 일으키다

*__re·volve__ [riválv / -vɔ́lv] *vi.* **1.** turn around on the central point of itself. ¶*The earth revolves once in 24 hours.*① / *The wheels of a train revolves when it runs.*② **2.** move in a curved path around a center. 《~ *around* something》 ¶*The moon revolves around the earth.*③ —*vt.* **1.** cause (something) to move around a center. **2.** consider (something) again and again from many points of view. ¶~ *a scheme in one's mind.* —[自] **1.** [지구·차바퀴 따위가] 자전(自轉)하다 ¶①지구는 24시간에 1회 자전한다/②기차의 바퀴는 달릴 때 회전한다 **2.** [다른 물체의 주위를] 회전하다 ¶③달은 지구의 주위를 회전한다 —[他] **1.** …을 회전시키다 **2.** …을 심사숙고하다

re·volv·er [riválvər / -vɔ́lvə] *n.* [C] a pistol with a revolving cylinder so that several shots may be fired at one loading. —[名] 연발 권총

re·vue [rivjú:] *n.* [C][U] an amusing musical play with several changes of scene and many songs and dances. —[名] 가벼운 음악극, 레뷰우

re·vul·sion [rivʌ́lʃ(ə)n] *n.* [U] a sudden and violent change of feeling. —[名] [감정·운명 따위의] 격변

⁑**re·ward** [riwɔ́:rd] *n.* **1.** [U] something given in return for service. **2.** [C] the money given for the return of something lost, for information or for the capture of a criminal. —*vt.* give a reward to (someone); give a reward for (a service, etc.). 《~ someone *for* or *with*》 —[名] **1.** 보수; 사례 **2.** [유실물·범죄인 발견의] 상금, 사례금 —[他] …에 보답하다; 보수(보상)를 주다

re·wire [rí:wáiər] *vt.* **1.** telegraph again. **2.** put new wires on or in (a house, etc.). —[他] **1.** …에 다시 전보를 치다 **2.** [집 따위]에 배선(配線)을 바꾸다

*__re·write__ [rí:ráit] *vt.* (**re·wrote, re·writ·ten**) write again. —[他] …을 다시 쓰다, 고쳐 쓰다

re·writ·ten [ri:rítn / ⌐⌐] *v.* pp. of **rewrite**.

re·wrote [ri:róut / rí:-] *v.* pt. of **rewrite**.

rhap·so·dize [rǽpsədàiz] *vi.* write or talk with great enthusiasm. —[自] 열광적으로 쓰다(이야기하다)

rhap·so·dy [rǽpsədi] *n.* [C] (pl. **-so·dies**) **1.** (*Music*) a very emotional instrumental composition irregular in form. **2.** an expression of very excited feeling. —[名] **1.** 《樂》 광상곡, 광시곡 **2.** 열광적 발언(문장)

rhe·a [rí:ə / riə] *n.* [C] a small South American three-toed ostrich. ⇒fig. —[名] 미국 타조

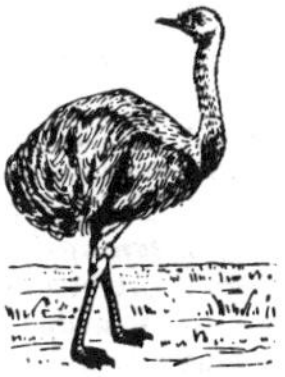
〔rhea〕

Rhen·ish [réniʃ / rí:niʃ] *adj.* of the river Rhine or the regions near it. —[形] 라인강의; 라인강 유역의

rhet·o·ric [rétərik] *n.* [U] the art of the correct, forceful and effective use of language. —[名] 수사법(修辭法), 작문법

rhe·tor·i·cal [ritɔ́:rik(ə)l, -tár- / -tɔ́ri-] *adj.* of or like rhetoric. —[形] 수사법의, 수사적인

rhetorical question [-⌐-- ⌐-] *n.* a question asked only for effect. —[名] 수사 의문, 반어(反語)

rhet·o·ri·cian [rètəríʃ(ə)n] *n.* [C] a person skilled in rhetoric. —[名] 수사학자

rheu·mat·ic [ru(:)mǽtik] *adj.* of or having rheumatism. ¶~ *fever.* —[形] 류우머티즘의(에 걸린) ¶①류우머티즘

—*n.* [C] a person suffering from rheumatism. —[名] 류우머티즘 환자

rheu·ma·tism [rú(:)mətìz(ə)m] *n.* [U] disease causing painful swelling of the muscles and joints. —[名] 류우머티즘

• **Rhine** [rain]**, the** *n.* a river flowing through Switzerland, Germany and the Netherlands into the North Sea. —[名] 라인강

Rhine·land [ráinlæ̀nd]**, the** *n.* the region along the Rhine. —[名] 라인 지방

rhi·no [ráinou] *n.* (pl. **-nos**) =rhinoceros.

rhi·noc·er·os [rainás(ə)rəs/-nɔ́s-] *n.* [C] (pl. **-os** or **-os·es**) a large, thick-skinned animal with one or two horns on its nose, found in Africa and south Asia. ⇒fig. —[名] 무소

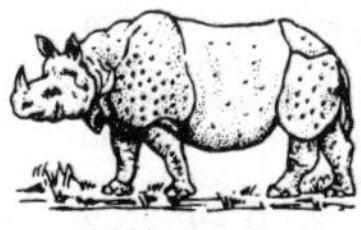

〔rhinoceros〕

rhi·zome [ráizoum] *n.* [C] a rootlike stem lying along or under the ground. —[名] 지하경(莖); 근경(根莖)

Rhode Island [roudáilənd] *n.* a State in the northeastern part of the United States, which is the smallest State in the United States. ⇒[N.B.] —[名] 로우드 아일런드 주 [N.B.] R.I.로 줄임. 수도 Providence

rho·do·den·dron [ròudədéndr(ə)n] *n.* [C] an evergreen treelike plant with large pink or white flowers. —[名] 만병초의 일종

rhu·barb [rú:bɑ:*r*b] *n.* [U] **1.** a plant with large leaves and thick red stalks. ⇒fig. **2.** the stem of this plant, used as food. **3.** the medicine made from the roots of a kind of rhubarb. —[名] 1. 대황(大黃) 2. 대황의 앞줄기 3. 대황 뿌리로 만든 약

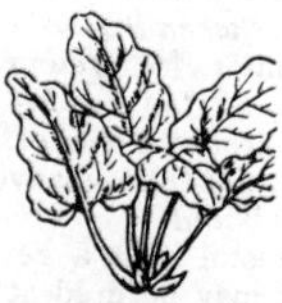

〔rhubarb 1.〕

• **rhyme** [raim] *n.* **1.** [C] a word ending with the same sound as another. **2.** [U] agreement or similarity in sound of a certain part, esp. the final part, of two or more words or lines of verse. **3.** 《usu. *pl.*》 verse or poetry with agreement in the final sounds of the lines. —[名] 1. 동운어(同韻語) 2. 운(韻), 각운 3. 운문, 시

—*vi.* **1.** sound alike in the final part. **2.** make verse. —*vt.* **1.** compose (verse, etc.) in metrical form and with rhyme. **2.** use (a word or words) to rhyme with another. —[自] 1. 운을 맞추다, 운이 맞다 2. 운문(시)을 짓다 —[他] 1. [운문·시]를 짓다 2. …에 운을 맞추게 하다

rhythm [ríð(ə)m] *n.* [U][C] **1.** a regular beat of poetry, music, or dancing. ¶*the ~ of speech.*① **2.** arrangement of beats in a line of poetry. —[名] 1. 리듬 ¶①말의 리듬 2. 운율(韻律)

rhyth·mic [ríðmik]**, -cal** [-k(ə)l] *adj.* of rhythm; having rhythm. ▷**rhyth·mi·cal·ly** [-kəli] *adv.* —[形] 리듬의; 리듬이 있는

⁑ **rib** [rib] *n.* [C] **1.** one of the curved bones of the breast. **2.** any narrow curved piece of material. —*vt.* (**ribbed, rib·bing**) furnish or strengthen (something) with ribs. —[名] 1. 늑골(肋骨) 2. 늑골 모양의 —[他] …에 늑골[늑재(肋材)]을 달다

rib·ald [ríb(ə)ld] *adj.* (of person, jokes, etc.) low; unpleasant; dirty. —*n.* [C] a ribald person. —[形] 말이 상스러운; 야비한 —[名] 비열한 사람, 입버릇 나쁜 사람

rib·ald·ry [ríb(ə)ldri] *n.* [U] ribald language. —[名] 상스러운 말

⁑ **rib·bon** [ríbən] *n.* **1.** [U][C] a long, narrow band or strip of silk, satin, etc. **2.** [C] anything like such a strip. —[名] 1. 리본 2. 끈 모양의 것

rib·boned [ríbənd] *adj.* with a ribbon or ribbons. —[形] 리본을 단

⁑ **rice** [rais] *n.* [U] **1.** a kind of grass grown for its seed. **2.** the seed of this plant boiled for food. —[名] 1. 벼 2. 쌀

⁑ **rich** [ritʃ] *adj.* **1.** having much money or property; wealthy. ↔poor ¶*a ~ man* / *He was born ~.*① / *The ~* (or *Rich people*) *are not always happy.* **2.** having much; abundant. ¶*words ~ in variety of meanings*② / *He is ~ in knowledge.* **3.** (of land, etc.) producing much; fertile. ¶*~ land* / *a ~ mine.* **4.** valuable; costly. ¶*~ silk* / *the richest jewel.* **5.** plentiful; ample. ¶*a ~ harvest* / *~ experience.* **6.** (of food) thick; nutritious; very tasty; very sweet. ¶*~ milk* / *a ~ dish.* **7.** (of sound, color, etc.) full; deep; vivid. ¶*~ red.* **8.** (*colloq.*) very amusing; absurd. ¶*a ~ joke* / *That's ~.* —[形] 1. 부유한, 부자의 ¶①그는 부자로 태어났다 2. 풍부한, 복받은 ¶②여러가지 의미를 가진 말 3. 기름진; 많이 산출하는 4. 귀중한; 값비싼 5. 풍성한, 풍요한 6. 영양이 많은; 맛이 좋은 7. [음이] 낭랑한; [빛깔이] 진한, 선명한 8. 《口》 아주 우스운; 어리석기 짝이 없는

Rich·ard [rítʃərd] *n.* a man's name.
—[名] 남자 이름

***rich·es** [rítʃiz] *n. pl.* wealth; abundance.
—[名] 부(富), 재화; 풍부

rich·ly [rítʃli] *adv.* in a rich manner; abundantly.
—[副] 풍부하게, 부유하게

Rich·mond [rítʃmənd] *n.* the capital of Virginia.
—[名] 미국 Virginia 주의 도시

rich·ness [rítʃnis] *n.* [U] the state of being rich.
—[名] 부유, 풍부

rick [rik] *n.* [C] a stack of hay, straw, etc. ⇒fig. —*vt.* make (hay, straw, etc.) into a rick.
—[名] [건초·밀짚 따위의] 더미, 가리, 퇴적 —[他] …을 짚가리로 쌓다

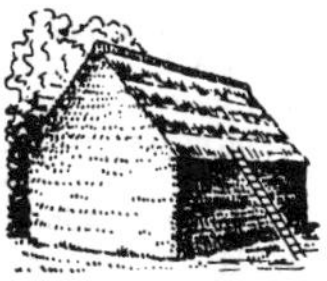
[rick]

rick·ets [ríkits] *n. pl.* ((used as *sing.*)) a disease of children caused by lack of vitamin D, calcium, or sunshine and marked by curving of the bones.
—[名] 구루병(佝僂病); 곱사병

rick·et·y [ríkiti] *adj.* **1.** suffering from rickets. **2.** feeble; shaky.
—[形] 1. 구루병에 걸린 2. 흔들흔들하는, 비틀거리는

ric·o·chet [rìkəʃéi / ríkəʃèi] *n.* [C] the jumping or skipping motion of an object as it goes along a flat surface; the motion of rebounding from one surface to another.
—[名] [물수제비 뜨듯이] 스쳐 날기
—*vi.* (**-cheted, -chet·ing** or *Brit.* **-chet·ted, -chet·ting**) move with such a motion.
—[自] 스쳐 날다

‡**rid** [rid] *vt.* (**rid** or **rid·ded, rid·ding**) make free. ((~ something *of*)) ¶ *~ the house of the rats*① / *~ oneself of debt.*②
—[他] …을 면하게 하다; 없애다 ¶①집에서 쥐를 잡아 없애다/②빚을 갚아 없애다
1) ***be rid of*** (=*be freed from or relieved of*) *something undesirable.*
2) ***get rid of*** (=*get free from; do away with*) *something undesirable.*
[熟] 1)…을 면하다, 벗어나다 2)…을 면하다; 없애다; 쫓아버리다

rid·dance [ríd(ə)ns] *n.* [U][C] the act of ridding; the state of being rid. ¶*make clean ~ of.*①
—[名] 모면; 제거 ¶①…을 일소하다

‡**rid·den** [rídn] *v.* pp. of **ride**.
—*adj.* pressed down; under the control of; obsessed. ⇒[usage] ¶*bed-ridden*① / *fear-ridden people* / *a country ~ by soldiers.*②
—[形] 괴로움을 받은 [usage] 주로 복합어로 쓰임 ¶①자리에 누워만 있는/②군인이 지배하는 나라

***rid·dle**¹ [rídl] *n.* [C] **1.** a puzzling question. **2.** a person or thing difficult to understand. ¶*read a ~.*①
—[名] 1. 수수께끼 2. 수수께끼 같은 사람, 난해한 사물 ¶①수수께끼를 풀다
speak in riddles, speak with a doubtful meaning.
[熟] 수수께끼 같은 소리를 하다
—*vi.* speak with a doubtful meaning. **—*vt.*** answer (a riddle).
—[自] 수수께끼 문제를 내다 —[他] [수수께끼를] 풀다

rid·dle² [rídl] *n.* [C] a coarse sieve. **—*vt.*** **1.** sift. ¶*~ sand.* **2.** make many holes in (something). ¶*~ the target with bullets.*
—[名] 체, 어레미 —[他] 1. …을 체질하다; 정밀히 조사하다 2. …을 구멍투성이로 만들다

‡**ride** [raid] *v.* (**rode, rid·den**) *vi.* **1.** be carried in a car, train, boat, etc. ((~ *in* or *on* a train, *etc.*)) ¶*~ on a bicycle* / *~ in a bus* / *~ 60 miles.*① **2.** sit on a horse or other animal and make it go. ¶*~ horseback*② / *~ bareback* / *~ behind*③ / *~ away* (or *off*)④ / *~ at full gallop*⑤ / *She likes to ~ for pleasure.* **3.** sit on as if on a horse, etc. ((*~ on* something)) ¶*~ on someone's back* (*shoulders*).⑥ **4.** (of a ship) lie at anchor; move or float on the water. ¶*The ship is riding at anchor.* **5.** (of the moon, the sun, etc.) seem to be floating through the sky. ¶*The moon is riding high* (*above the clouds*). / *The bird rides on the wind.* **6.** be in a specified condition for riding or being ridden. ¶*This horse rides easy* (*hard*).⑦ / *The ground rides soft.* **—*vt.*** **1.** sit on or in and cause (a horse, a vehicle, etc.) to move. ¶*~ a horse* / *~ a car* / *~ one's horse at a fence.* **2.** ride through or over. ¶*~ the country* (*deserts*). **3.** be carried on; float on. ¶*The ship rides the waves.* **4.** carry (someone) on something as if riding on horseback. ¶*~ a child on one's shoulders.*
—[自] 1. [자동차·기차 따위에] 타다 ¶①60 마일을 달리다 2. [말이나 그 밖의 동물에] 타다, 타고 가다 ¶②말에 타다/③[기수의] 뒤에 타다/④말을 타고 가 버리다/⑤전속력으로 말을 달리다 3. [말 타듯] 걸터 타다 ¶⑥…의 등에 걸터앉다(어깨 위에 걸터앉다) 4. [배가] 정박하다; 파도를 타고 나아가다 5. [달·해 따위가] 공중에 떠오르다 6. 탄 기분이 …하다 ¶⑦이 말은 탄 기분이 좋다(나쁘다) —[他] 1. [말·탈것 따위에] 타다, 타고 가다 2. …을 말을 타고 지나가다(건너다) 3. … 위에 뜨다; 버티어지다 4. …을 등에 업다, 어깨에 앉히다
1) ***ride down,*** ⓐ overtake (someone) by riding. ⓑ overcome. ⓒ exhaust (a horse) by riding it too hard. ⓓ allow one's horse or vehicle to hit and knock down
[熟] 1)ⓐ말로 …을 쫓아가다 ⓑ…을 압도하다 ⓒ[말 따위] 태워서 녹초가 되게 하다 ⓓ…에 말(탈것)을 부딪쳐 쓰

R

(someone or something).
2) ***ride for a fall,*** ⓐ ride recklessly. ⓑ act recklessly.
3) ***ride one's horse to death,*** kill one's horse by exhausting it.
4) ***ride out,*** ⓐ come through safely. ⓑ endure successfully.
5) ***ride*** [***roughshod***] ***over,*** treat (something) without sympathy.
6) ***ride to hounds,*** go fox-hunting.

러뜨리다 2)ⓐ난폭하게 말을 몰다 ⓑ 난폭한 짓을 하다 3)말을 너무 타서 지쳐 쓰러지게 하다 4)ⓐ…을 무사히 넘기다 ⓑ…을 잘 견디다 5)…을 짓밟다 6)[사냥개로] 여우 사냥을 하다

—*n.* [C] **1.** an act of riding; a journey on a horse, on or in a vehicle, etc. ¶*a ~ on a bicycle / give someone a ~ / The hotel is situated within ten minutes' ~ of the station.* **2.** a road for riding.

—[名] 1.[말·탈것 따위에] 타기, 태우기; 타고 가기 2.승마 도로

rid·er [ráidər] *n.* [C] **1.** a person who rides. **2.** an addition to a bill, a document, etc. ¶*by way of ~ to ….*①

—[名] 1.타는 사람, 기수(騎手) 2.추가 조항, 첨부 서류 ¶①…의 추가로서

⁑ **ridge** [ridʒ] *n.* [C] **1.** the backbone of an animal. ¶*the ~ of a whale.* **2.** a long and narrow range of hills or mountains. **3.** the long, narrow top of something. **4.** the raised part between furrows. ¶*the ~ of a wave.*① **5.** a line where two sloping surfaces meet. —*vt.* make (something) into ridges; cover (something) with ridges. —*vi.* be covered with ridges.

—[名] 1.[동물의] 등 2.산등;산맥 3.융기(隆起) 4.이랑, 두둑 ¶①파도의 물마루 5.지붕 마룻대; 능선(稜線) —[他] …을 이랑 모양으로 하다; …에 이랑을 세우다 —[自] 이랑지다, 물결이 일다

ridge·pole [rídʒpòul] *n.* [C] a horizontal timber along the top of a roof or tent.

—[名] [집의] 마룻대; [천막의] 들보

rid·i·cule [rídikjù:l] *n.* [U] mocking laughter. ¶*bring someone into ~; turn someone to* (or *into*) *~.*① —*vt.* laugh at; make fun of (someone).

—[名] 조소, 조롱; 놀림 ¶①조소하다; 놀리다 —[他] …을 비웃다; 놀리다

• **ri·dic·u·lous** [ridíkjuləs] *adj.* deserving or exciting ridicule; absurd.

—[形] 어이없는; 우스운

ri·dic·u·lous·ly [ridíkjuləsli] *adv.* in a ridiculous manner.

—[副] 우습게; 어리석게

rid·ing habit [ráidiŋhæbit] *n.* clothes esp. a woman's dress, for riding on horseback.

—[名] [주로 부인용의] 승마복

riding master [⌐– ⌐–] *n.* a person who teaches horseback riding.

—[名] 마술(馬術) 교사

rife [raif] *adj.* common; widespread; full of. ⟪*~ with*⟫ ¶*Reports became ~*①. / *a thesis ~ with errors.*

—[形] 유행하는; 많은, 수없는 ¶①소문이 퍼졌다

riff·raff [rífræf] *n.* ⟪*the ~, collectively*⟫ worthless people.

—[名] 하층민, 천민; 어중이떠중이

⁑ **ri·fle**[1] [ráifl] *n.* [C] **1.** a gun with spiral grooves inside its barrel. **2.** one of the spiral grooves inside such a gun. —*vt.* cut spiral grooves in (a gun barrel).

—[名] 1.라이플총, 소총 2.[총포의] 강선(腔綫)
—[他] [총포]에 강선을 내다

ri·fle[2] [ráifl] *vt.* plunder.

—[他] …을 약탈하다

ri·fle·man [ráiflmən] *n.* [C] (pl. **-men** [-mən]) a soldier armed with a rifle; a man skilled in using a rifle.

—[名] 라이플 총병; 라이플총의 명사수

rift [rift] *n.* [C] a cleft; a split; a crack. ¶*a ~ in the rock / a ~ in the mind.* —*vt., vi.* split; crack.

—[名] 끊어진 틈, 갈라진 틈
—[他][自] [···을] 찢다; 찢어지다

rig [rig] *vt.* (**rigged, rig·ging**) **1.** equip (a ship) with ropes, sails, masts, spars, etc. **2.** provide (someone) with clothing, etc; dress. **3.** fit out; set up; erect. ¶*~ a tent by a river.* **4.** deal with (something) dishonestly. ¶*~ the prices.* —*n.* **1.** [C] an arrangement of sails, masts, etc. on a ship. **2.** [U] (*colloq.*) clothes, esp. those designed for a particular purpose.

—[他] 1.[배]에 색구(索具) 따위를 준비하다 2.…에 의상을 준비하다, …을 차려 입게 하다 3.…을 임시로(급히) 짓다(만들다) 4.…을 부정하게 다루다
—[名] 1.의장(艤裝) 2.⟪口⟫ 의상

rig·ging [ríɡiŋ] *n.* [U] the ropes, chains, etc. used to support and work the masts, sails, etc. on a ship.

—[名] [배의] 색구(索具)

⁑ **right** [rait] *adj.* **1.** obeying the moral law; just; good. ↔wrong ¶*act a ~ part*① / *It was ~ to say so.* **2.** correct; true. ↔wrong ¶*the ~ answer / the ~ leather*② / *get it ~*③ / *the ~ way*④ / *~ or wrong.*⑤ **3.** fit; suitable; proper. ¶*the ~ man for the position*⑥ / *That's ~.* **4.** satisfactory; most convenient. ¶*All's ~* [*with the world*].⑦ / *Right you are.*⑧ / *Things will probably be all ~.* **5.** healthy; normal; sound. ¶*I feel all ~.* / *Is he in his ~ mind?*⑨ **6.** on or toward the side opposite to the left side. ↔left ¶*one's ~ hand / the ~ bank of a river*⑩ / *make a ~ turn at the corner.* **7.** front; upper; most finished or ornamental. ↔wrong ¶*the ~ side of the medal / the ~ side of cloth.* **8.** straight;

—[形] 1.[도덕적으로] 옳은, 올바른 ¶①올바른 행위를 하다 2.옳은, 정확한; 정말의 ¶②진짜 가죽/③옳게 이해시키다(하다)/④옳은 길, 정도(正道), 진상/⑤좋건 나쁘건 3.알맞은, 적당한; 당연한 ¶⑥적재적소 4.말할 나위 없는, 형편이 좋은 ¶⑦만사가 순조롭다/⑧네 말이 맞다; 좋다 5.건강한; 제정신의 ¶⑨그는 제정신입니까? 6.오른쪽의, 우편의 ¶⑩강의 오른쪽 기슭(하류를 향하여) 7.거죽의, 표면의 8.똑바른; 직각의 ¶⑪직선 9.[정치적으로] 우익의

R

of 90°. ¶*a ~ line*[11] / *a ~ angle.* **9.** ((often *the R-*)) (of political opinion, etc.) conservative.

1) ***get something right,*** ⓐ correct. ⓑ understand clearly.
2) ***on the right side of fifty,*** under.
3) ***put*** (or ***set***) ***someone*** or ***something right,*** put something in order; correct; restore.

[熟] 1)ⓐ…을 고치다 ⓑ…을 분명히 이해하다 2)…살 전(이하)에 3)…을 정리하다, 고치다; 다시 건강하게 하다

—*adv.* **1.** morally; justly. ¶*act ~ / guess ~.*[12] **2.** properly; in a satisfactory manner. ¶*turn out ~*[13] / *The dinner is served ~.* **3.** straight; directly; all the way. ¶*come ~ back / ~ at a target / sink ~ to the bottom.*[14] **4.** exactly; precisely. ¶*~ here.* **5.** completely. ¶*turn ~ round.* **6.** to the right hand or side. ¶*turn ~.* **7.** (in time or position) immediately. ¶*~ now / ~ after dinner / ~ by the hospital.*

—[副] 1. [도덕상] 옳게 ¶⑫알아맞히다 2. 순조롭게; 적당히 ¶⑬잘 돼 가다 3. 똑바로; 바로, 줄곧 ¶⑭바로 바닥에 가라앉다 4. 꼭, 정확히 5. 완전히, 아주 6. 오른쪽으로(에) 7. [시간·장소가] 바로, 곧

1) ***right and left,*** in all directions; freely.
2) ***right away*** (or ***off***), at once; immediately.

[熟] 1)사방에; 자유로 2)바로, 곧

—*n.* **1.** [U] that which is morally or legally right; justice; truth; correctness. ¶*be in the ~*[15] / *Might is ~.*[16] **2.** [U] [C] privilege; a just claim; [C] that to which a person has a just claim. ¶*the ~ to vote / defend one's ~ / civil rights / I have no ~ to say such a thing to him.* **3.** ((*the ~* or *one's ~*, *sing.* only)) the right side or direction. ↔left ¶*on one's ~ / on the ~ of*[17] / *go* (or *turn*) *to the ~*[18] / *keep on one's ~*[19] / *Keep to the ~.* **4.** ((*pl.*)) a true fact. ¶*the rights* [*and wrongs*] *of the matter.*[20] **5.** ((usu. *the R-*)) a conservative party; people who have conservative political ideas.

—[名] 1. [도덕·법률적으로] 옳음; 정의, 정당 ¶⑮사고방식이 올바르다, 도리에 맞다/⑯힘은 정의다 2. 권리 3. 오른쪽 ¶⑰…의 오른쪽에/⑱뒤로 돌다; 주의 따위를 바꾸다/⑲우측으로 나아가다; 정도를 나아가다 4. 진상 ¶⑳일의 진상 5. 보수당, 우파; 보수적인 사람들

1) ***by*** (or ***of***) ***right; by*** [***good***] ***rights,*** justly; properly.
2) ***by*** (or ***in***) ***right of,*** by virtue of; on account of.
3) ***in one's own right,*** through one's own ability, authority, etc.
4) ***put*** (or ***set***) ***something to rights,*** put something in order; correct; repair.

[熟] 1)바르게, 정말로 2)…의 권한으로; …의 이유로 3)자기의 능력(권위)으로 4)…을 정돈하다; 고치다

—*vt.* **1.** correct. ¶*~ a wrong / ~ errors.* **2.** put (something) in order; make (something) straight or upright. ¶*~ oneself*[21] / *~ the room / ~ a capsized boat.* **3.** do justice to (someone); secure rights for (someone); relieve. ¶*~ the oppressed.*[22] **—*vi.*** get into a correct or upright position.

—[他] 1. …을 바르게 하다, 고치다 2. …을 정리하다; 직립시키다, 세우다 ¶㉑명예(권리)를 회복하다 3. …에 정의를 부여하다; 당연한 권리를 얻게 하다; …을 구제하다 ¶㉒압박당하고 있는 자를 구하다 —[自] [기울어진 배가] 바로 서다

right·a·bout [ráitəbàut] *n.* ((*the ~*)) the direction directly opposite. **—*adj., adv.*** in the opposite direction.

—[名] 반대 방향 —[形][副] 반대 방향의(으로)

right angle [ˊ ˊ–] *n.* an angle of 90 degrees.

—[名] 직각의

right-down [ráitdàun] *adj.* thorough. **—*adv.*** thoroughly.

—[形] 철저한 —[副] 철저하게

right·eous [ráitʃəs] *adj.* **1.** doing what is right; just. ¶*a ~ act.* **2.** justifiable. ¶*~ anger over injustice.*

—[形] 1. 올바른, 정의의, 공평한 2. 정당한, 당연한

right·eous·ly [ráitʃəsli] *adv.* in a righteous manner.

—[副] 올바르게, 공정하게, 당연히

right·eous·ness [ráitʃəsnis] *n.* [U] the state of being right; justice.

—[名] 공정; 정의; 당연

right·ful [ráitf(u)l] *adj.* right; just; according to law; lawful. ¶*one's ~ property*[1] / *the ~ heir to the throne.*

—[形] 올바른; 합법의; 정당한 ¶①합법적인 재산

right·ful·ly [ráitf(u)li] *adv.* properly; according to law.

—[副] 올바르게; 합법적으로; 정당히

right-hand [ráithæ̀nd] *adj.* **1.** on or to the right; of, for, or with the right hand. **2.** most helpful or reliable.

—[形] 1. 오른쪽의, 우측의 2. 심복의, 믿을 만한

right-hand·ed [ráithǽndid] *adj.* **1.** using the right hand more skillfully than the left. ↔left-handed **2.** done with the right hand. **3.** made to be used with the right hand. **4.** turning from left to right.

—[形] 1. 오른손잡이의 2. 오른손으로 하는, 오른손을 쓰는 3. 오른손용의 4. 오른쪽으로 도는

right·ly [ráitli] *adv.* **1.** justly; properly. **2.** correctly.

—[副] 1. 올바르게, 정당하게 2. 정확하게

right-mind·ed [ráitmáindid] *adj.* having right opinions; honest.

—[形] 마음이 올바른; 정직한

right·ness [ráitnis] *n.* [U] the state or quality of being right.

—[名] 올바름, 정직, 공정

right of way [ˊ – ˊ] *n.* **1.** the right to pass over another's property. **2.** the right to go first.

—[名] 1. 통행권 2. 선행권(先行權)

right·ward [ráitwərd] *adj.* toward the right; directed to the right. **—*adv.*** toward the right; in the direc-

—[形] 오른쪽으로 향하는; 우측의 —[副] 오른쪽으로(에); 우측으로(에)

tion of the right.

right·wards [ráitwərdz] *adv.* =rightward.

right-wing [ráitwíŋ] *adj.* of the right wing. —[形] 우익의, 우파의

right wing [⌐ ⌐] *n.* **1.** a conservative or reactionary political party or a group of such parties; the people who have conservative or reactionary ideas. **2.** the more conservative or reactionary section of a party. —[名] **1.** 보수당; 반동 정당; 보수적인 사람들 **2.** 우익, 우파, 보수파

*** rig·id** [rídʒid] *adj.* **1.** not bending; hard; stiff. ¶*a ~ stick.* **2.** strict; severe. ¶*~ discipline*① / *~ rules.* **3.** firmly fixed; not easily bent. ¶*~ in one's views.* —[形] **1.** 곧은, 딱딱해진 **2.** 엄한, 엄격한 ¶①엄격한 규율 **3.** 완고한, 굳은

ri·gid·i·ty [ridʒíditi] *n.* [U] **1.** stiffness. **2.** strictness. —[名] **1.** 굳음, 경직(硬直) **2.** 엄격

rig·id·ly [rídʒidli] *adv.* in a rigid manner. —[副] 굳게, 엄격하게, 완고하게

rig·ma·role [rígmərὸul] *n.* [C] a foolish talk; nonsense. —[名] 시시한 장광설, 허튼소리

rig·or, *Brit.* **-our** [rígər] *n.* [U] **1.** strictness; severity. ¶*moral ~*① / *with ~.*② **2.** 《often *pl.*》 hardship; severity. ¶*experience the rigors of pioneer life / the rigors of a northern winter.*③ **3.** preciseness; exactness. —[名] **1.** 엄격 ¶①도덕상의 엄격/②엄격하게 **2.** 어려움, 곤궁; 매서움 ¶③북쪽 겨울의 매서운 추위 **3.** 엄밀, 정밀

rig·or·ous [rígərəs] *adj.* **1.** very severe; strict; harsh. **2.** exact; precise. —[形] **1.** 엄한; 엄격한 **2.** 정밀한, 정확한

rill [ril] *n.* [C] (*poetic*) a little brook. —[名] 《詩》 시내, 개천

*** rim** [rim] *n.* [C] an edge; a margin; a border. ¶*the ~ of an eyeglass*① / *the golden ~*② / *the ~ of a wheel.*③ —*vt.* (**rimmed, rim·ming**) put a rim around (something). —[名] 가장자리, 가두리 ¶①안경 테/②왕관/③바퀴 테 —[他] …에 가장자리를 달다

rime¹ [raim] *n., v.* =rhyme.

rime² [raim] *n.* [U] (*poetic*) white frost. —*vt.* cover (something) with rime. —[名] 흰 서리 —[他] …을 흰 서리로 덮다

rind [raind] *n.* [U][C] **1.** the firm outer covering of a nut, a piece of fruit, etc. **2.** the bark of a tree. —[名] **1.** [과실 따위의] 껍질 **2.** 나무 껍질

⁝ ring¹ [riŋ] *n.* [C] **1.** a circular band of metal, wood, etc. used for holding or fastening; a circular band, often of a precious metal set with gems, worn on a finger. ¶*a key ~ / a rubber ~ / a nose ~ / a wedding* (*an engagement*) *~.* **2.** a circle; anything circular. ¶*a ~ of smoke / rings in water*① / *form a ~*② / *sit in a ~ / dance in a ~.*③ **3.** an annual layer in the trunk of a tree. **4.** an enclosed place for contests, exhibitions, sports, etc. ¶*the ~ of a circus.* **5.** a group of persons working together, often for unlawful purposes. ¶*a black market ~.* **6.** 《*the ~*》 the sport of boxing. —[名] **1.** 고리; 반지 **2.** 원; 원형의 것 ¶①파문/②원을 이루다/③원을 이루어 춤추다 **3.** 나이테, 연륜 **4.** [원형의] 시합장, 경기장; 경마장; 권투장 **5.** 도당, 한패, 동맹 **6.** 권투

—*vt.* **1.** surround; encircle. ¶*~ [up] cattle*④ / *Indians ringed the camp.* **2.** provide (something) with a ring. ¶*~ a bull.* **3.** toss a ring over (a pin, etc.). —*vi.* **1.** form into a ring. **2.** move in a ring. **3.** (of a bird) fly in circles. —[他] **1.** …을 둥글게 둘러싸다, 에워싸다 ¶④주위를 돌며 가축을 모으다 **2.** …에 반지 따위를 끼우다 **3.** [놀이로서] 고리(말굽쇠)를 던지다 —[自] **1.** 원형이 되다 **2.** 빙글빙글 돌다 **3.** 원을 그리며 날아오르다

⁝ ring² [riŋ] *v.* (**rang, rung**) *vi.* **1.** (of a bell, a coin, etc.) sound musically or clearly when struck. ¶*The doorbell rang loudly. / A shot rang out.* **2.** produce a certain effect when heard; seem; appear to be. ¶*Her words rang true.*① **3.** signal by sounding a bell or buzzer. ¶*Did you ~? / We rang at the front door. / She rang for the servant.* **4.** sound loudly and clearly. ¶*Her voice rings through the house. / His words are still ringing in my ears.* **5.** (of a place) be filled with sound; be famous. 《*~ with* something》 ¶*The room rang with cheers. / The world rang with his fame.*② —*vt.* **1.** cause (a bell, etc.) to sound. ¶*~ the bell.* **2.** announce, summon, signal, warn, etc. (someone or something) by the sound of a bell. ¶*~ an alarm / ~ a maidservant in* (*down, up*).③ —[自] **1.** [벨 따위가] 울리다 **2.** …처럼 들리다 ¶①그녀의 말은 정말처럼 들렸다 **3.** 벨을 울리다; 울려서 부르다 **4.** [음·목소리가] 울려 퍼지다; [마음에] 울리다 **5.** [장소가] 울리다, 반향하다; 평판이 높다 ¶②온 세계에 그의 명성이 퍼졌다 —[他] **1.** [벨 따위]를 울리다 **2.** 벨을 울려 …을 부르다(신호하다) ¶③벨을 울려 하녀를 안(아래·위)으로 부르다

1) ***ring down*** (***up***) ***the curtain,*** lower (raise) a theater curtain; give a signal for lowering (raising) a theater curtain; end (begin).
2) ***ring off,*** end a phone call.
3) ***ring the bell,*** be successful.
4) ***ring up,*** make a phone call.

[熟] 1)[벨로 신호하여] 극장의 막을 내리다(올리다); 내리는(올리는) 신호를 하다; 끝나다(시작되다) 2)전화를 끊다 3)잘 돼 가다 4)전화를 걸다

—*n.* [C] **1.** the sound of or like a bell; an act of ring- —[名] **1.** 벨을 울리기; 울리는 소리 **2.**

ing a bell. ¶*There is a ~ at the door.* / *The coin has the true* (or *the right*) ~. **2.** ⟪*sing.* only⟫ any loud sound. ¶*the ~ of voices.* **3.** a telephone call. ¶*Give me a ~ tomorrow.* **4.** ⟪*sing.* only⟫ a sound or tone that suggests a particular quality. ¶*the ~ of truth.*④

울려퍼지는 소리; 소리, 울림 3. 전화를 걸기 4. 가락; 느낌 ¶④정말 같은 느낌

ringed [riŋd] *adj.* **1.** marked with, or formed like, a ring or rings. **2.** wearing a ring or rings; married or engaged.
—[形] 1. 고리가 있는; 고리 모양의 2. 반지를 낀; 결혼한; 약혼한

ring·er[1] [ríŋər] *n.* [C] a person or thing that rings or encircles.
—[名] 둘러싸는 사람(것)

ring·er[2] [ríŋər] *n.* [C] a person or thing that rings a bell, chime, etc; a person who greatly resembles someone else.
—[名] 종을 울리는 사람; 종치는(초인종) 장치; 남을 몹시 닮은 사람

ring finger [⸗ ⸗-] *n.* the third finger, esp. of the left hand.
—[名] [특히 왼손의] 약손가락, 무명지

ring·lead·er [ríŋlìːdər] *n.* [C] a person who leads others in a riot, a crime, etc.
—[名] [폭동 따위의] 장본인

ring·let [ríŋlit] *n.* [C] **1.** a little ring. **2.** a long curl of hair.
—[名] 1. 작은 고리 2. 곱슬머리

ring·side [ríŋsàid] *n.* [C] the place just outside the ring at a boxing match, etc.
—[名] [권투 따위의] 링 앞 좌석

rink [riŋk] *n.* [C] a sheet of artificial ice for skating; a smooth floor used for roller skating.
—[名] 스케이트장; 로울러 스케이트장

rinse [rins] *vt.* wash lightly; wash (something) in clean water. ⟪~ *away* (or *off, out*) something; ~ something *out of*⟫ ¶*~ the soap out of one's hair*① / *~ out the mouth.*② **—*n.*** [C] the act of rinsing.
—[他] …을 헹구다, 가시다; 씻어내다 ¶①머리에서 비누를 씻어내다/②입안을 가시다 —[名] 헹구기, 헹구어 빨기

ri·ot [ráiət] *n.* **1.** [C] a noisy, unlawful act by a crowd of people. ¶*raise a ~.*① **2.** [U] loose living; disorderly conduct. **3.** ⟪*a* ~⟫ luxuriance; a great quantity. ¶*The garden is a ~ of color.*②
—[名] 1. 폭동, 소동 ¶①폭동을 일으키다 2. 방탕; 난봉 3. 빛깔의 다채로움; 풍부 ¶②정원에는 꽃이 다채롭게 피어 있다

run riot, act without restraint; grow wildly.
[熟] 방탕하다; 다채롭게 피다

—*vi.* take part in a riot; live in a loose, wild manner; revel. **—*vt.*** waste (money, time, etc.) in loose, wild living. ⟪~ *away* something⟫
—[自] 폭동을 일으키다; 방탕하다; 술 마시며 떠들다 —[他] …을 방탕한 생활로 낭비하다

ri·ot·er [ráiətər] *n.* [C] a person who riots.
—[名] 폭도; 방탕자

ri·ot·ous [ráiətəs] *adj.* taking part in a riot; behaving lawlessly; disorderly.; running wild.
—[形] 폭동을 일으키는; 시끄러운; 방탕한

ri·ot·ous·ly [ráiətəsli] *adv.* in a riotous manner.
—[副] 시끄럽게, 방탕하게

***rip** [rip] *v.* (**ripped, rip·ping**) *vt.* **1.** cut or tear (something) with violence. ¶*~ a sack open*① / *~ one's coat on a nail*② / *~ off.*③ **2.** saw (wood) along the grain. **3.** (*colloq.*) speak with violence. ⟪~ *out* an oath, etc.⟫
—[他] 1. …을 찢다, 째다 ¶①자루를 잡아 째다/②못에 옷이 찢기다/③벗겨내다 2. [목재]를 세로 켜다 3. …을 거칠게 말하다

—*vi.* **1.** become torn apart. **2.** (*colloq.*) move with speed and violence.
—[自] 1. 찢어지다, 째지다 2. 돌진하다

—*n.* [C] a torn place; a long tear.
—[名] 찢어진 곳, 해진 데

ri·par·i·an [ripέəriən, raip- / raipέə-] *adj.* of or on the bank of a river, a lake, etc.
—[形] 강기슭의; 호반의

⁑**ripe** [raip] *adj.* **1.** (of fruit, etc.) ready to be gathered and used for food; full-grown. **2.** (of persons) fully developed; mature. ¶*a person of ~ years* / *~ beauty*① / *die at a ~ age.*② **3.** prepared; ready. ¶*~ for war.*③
—[形] 1. 익은; 먹을 만하게 된 2. 성숙한, 원숙한, 한창의 ¶①성숙한 아름다움/②노령으로 죽다 3. 준비가 된 ¶③전기(戰機)가 무르익다

rip·en** [ráipn] *vi.* become ripe. ¶*His thought ripened into action.* **—*vt. make (something) ripe.
—[自] 익다 —[他] …을 익게 하다

rip·ping [rípiŋ] *adj.* (*Brit. slang*) splendid.
—[形] ⟪英俗⟫ 멋들어진

rip·ple** [rípl] *n.* [C] **1.** a very little, gentle wave. **2.** a slight curling. **3.** a light, soft sound like that of rippling water. ¶*A ~ of laughter went through the audience.* **—*vt. form (something) into ripples. **—*vi.*** be formed into ripples; make a light, soft sound.
—[名] 1. 잔물결, 파문 2. [머리카락 따위의] 곱슬곱슬함 3. 잔물결 소리 —[他] …에 잔물결을 일으키다 —[自] 잔물결이 일다; 찰랑찰랑 소리를 내다

rip·plet [ríplit] *n.* [C] a little ripple.
—[名] 잔물결, 작은 파문

⁑**rise** [raiz] *v.* (**rose, ris·en**) *vi.* **1.** stand up. ⟪~ *from* or *to* something⟫ ¶*~ from the table*① / *~ to one's feet*② / *~ from one's knees.*③ **2.** get up from bed. ¶*~ early.* **3.** go or move up. ↔fall ¶*A balloon rises.* / *Smoke rises up* [*into*] *the air.* / *The curtain rises.* / *The mists ~.*④ / *Morning* (*Dawn*) *rises.*⑤ **4.** (of the sun, the moon, etc.) appear above the horizon. ↔set ¶*The sun rises in*
—[自] 1. 일어서다; 일어나다 ¶①[식사가 끝나고] 식탁에서 일어서다/②일어서다/③무릎꿇은 자세에서 일어서다 2. 기상하다 3. 올라가다; [하늘로] 오르다 ¶④안개가 개다/⑤아침(새벽)이 되다 4. [해·달 따위가] 솟다, 뜨다 5. 높아지다; 성장하다; 우뚝 솟다 6. 반

the east. **5.** grow taller or higher; be built up or erected. ¶*The ground rises gradually.* / *The tower rises high above the trees.* / *The new skyscraper rises higher each day.* **6.** revolt; rebel. 《~ *against* the government, etc.》 ¶*~ in arms*⑥ / *~ against a king.* **7.** come into view or existence; appear. ¶*Land rose on the right.* / *Thoughts ~ in the mind.* **8.** increase in degree, amount, price, etc. ¶*Prices are rising.* / *His spirit rises.* / *His temper rose.* / *His voice rose in excitement.* / *The wind often rises to a wild fury.*⑦ / *Her color rose.* **9.** go to a higher position in society; become famous, successful, etc. ¶*~ in the world*⑧ / *~ to fame*⑨ / *~ from the ranks.* **10.** begin; happen; occur; have a source or origin. ¶*A rumor rose.*⑩ / *A wind rose suddenly.* / *This river rises in the mountains.* **11.** end a meeting. ¶*The parliament will ~ next month.* **12.** increase in size; swell. ¶*The bread is rising.* / *The river is rising rapidly.* **—*vt.*** cause (birds) to fly up from the ground; cause (fish) to come to the surface of the water.

향하다; 반항하여 일어서다; 모반하다 ¶⑥무기를 들고 일어서다 7. 보이게 되다; 나타나다; [마음에] 떠오르다 8. [물가·정도·분량 따위가] 오르다, 늘다 ¶⑦바람은 가끔 미쳐 날뛴다 9. 입신출세하다, 승진하다, 유명해지다 ¶⑧출세하다/⑨명성을 얻다 10. 시작되다; 발생하다; 생겨나다; 근원이 있다 ¶⑩소문이 났다 11. 폐회되다, 산회하다 12. 부풀다 —[他] [새]를 날아오르게 하다; [물고기]를 수면에 떠오르게 하다

—*n.* [C] **1.** the act of rising or going up. ¶*the ~ of a balloon.* **2.** an increase in degree, amount, price, etc. ¶*a sudden ~ in food prices* / *The price is on the ~.*⑪ / *The ~ of the river was four meters.* **3.** advance in rank, power, position, etc. ¶*her ~ to fame* / *have* (or *make*) *a ~.*⑫ **4.** an upward slope; a small hill. ¶*a ~ in the road*⑬ / *the ~ of a roof.* **5.** an origin or a source. ¶*the ~ of the stream* / *The river takes* (or *has*) *its ~ in the mountains.* **6.** (*Brit.*) an increase in salary or wages. (cf. *U.S.* raise) **7.** the process of beginning or developing. ¶*the ~ and fall of Rome.*⑭

—[名] 1. 올라가기 2. 증가, 증대 ¶⑪물가는 오르고 있다 3. 입신 출세, 승진 ¶⑫출세(승진)하다 4. 오르막길, 비탈, 언덕, 높은 지대 ¶⑬비탈길 5. 기원(起源), 발생 6. 승급 7. 융성; 흥륭 ¶⑭로마의 성쇠

give rise to, cause; produce.

[熟] …을 낳다, 야기하다

:ris·en [rízn] *v.* pp. of **rise.**

ris·er [ráizər] *n.* [C] **1.** a person who rises. ¶*an early ~.*① **2.** the upright part of a step, a stair, etc. ⇒fig.

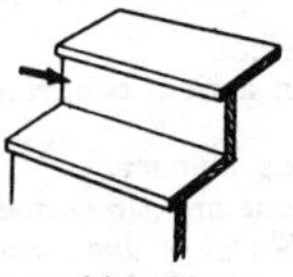
[riser 2.]

—[名] 1. 일어나는 사람 ¶①아침 일찍 일어나는 사람 2. [계단 따위의] 수직널

ris·ing [ráiziŋ] *n.* **1.** [U] upward movement. **2.** [U] resurrection. **3.** [C] a revolt; a rebellion. **—*adj.*** **1.** going up; advancing. ¶*the ~ sun* / *a ~ opera singer.* **2.** growing; maturing. ¶*the ~ generation.*

—[名] 1. 올라가기, 상승 2. 부활 3. 반란, 모반 —[形] 1. 올라가는; 승진하는; 신진의 2. 발달 중인

:risk [risk] *n.* [U][C] a chance of damage, harm, or loss; danger. ¶*at all risks; at any ~*① / *at one's own ~*② / *at the ~ of*③ / *run* (or *take*) *a ~.*④ **—*vt.*** **1.** expose (something) to risk. ¶*~ one's fortune.* **2.** take a chance of (something). ¶*~ a fight.*

—[名] 위험; 모험 ¶①어떤 위험을 무릅쓰고라도/②자신의 책임으로/③…의 위험을 무릅쓰고/④모험하다 —[他] 1. …을 위태롭게 하다 2. …을 모험하다

risk·y [ríski] *adj.* (**risk·i·er, risk·i·est**) having danger; dangerous.

—[形] 위험한; 아슬아슬한

rite [rait] *n.* [C] a solemn, formal ceremony. ¶*burial* (or *funeral*) *rites*① / *a ~ of baptism.*②

—[名] 의식, 의례(儀禮) ¶①장례식/②세례식

rit·u·al [rítʃuəl] *adj.* of a rite or rites; done as a rite. **—*n.*** [C] **1.** 《*collectively*》 a set form or system of rites. **2.** [C] a book of prescribed rites.

—[形] 의식의; 의례의 —[名] 1. 의식, 예식 2. 의식서(儀式書)

:ri·val [ráiv(ə)l] *n.* [C] a competitor; an equal. ¶*without a ~*① / *a ~ in love* (*trade*).② **—*adj.*** acting as a rival; competing. **—*vt.*** (**-valed, -val·ing** or *Brit.* **-valled, -val·ling**) try to equal or surpass; compete with (someone); be close (in some quality). ¶*She rivals her sister in beauty.*③

—[名] 경쟁자, 적수, 상대; 맞먹는 사람, 호적수 ¶①비길데 없이/②연적(戀敵)(장사 경쟁자) —[形] 경쟁하는 —[他] …을 경쟁하다, …에 대항하다 ¶③그녀는 언니에 못지않게 아름답다

ri·val·ry [ráiv(ə)lri] *n.* [U][C] (pl. **-ries**) the state of being rivals; competition.

—[名] 경쟁, 적대

rive [raiv] *vt., vi.* (**rived, riv·en,** or **rived**) split; tear apart; cleave.

—[他][自] 찢다, 찢어지다; 쪼개다, 쪼개지다

riv·en [rív(ə)n] *v.* pp. of **rive.** **—*adj.*** split; torn apart.

—[形] 쪼개진, 찢어진

:riv·er [rívər] *n.* [C] **1.** a large stream of water. **2.** any

—[名] 1. 강 2. 강물 같은 흐름 ¶①용암

great stream or flow. ¶*a ~ of lava.*①
(熔岩)의 흐름

river basin [´-- ˋ--] *n.* the area drained by a river.
—[名] [강의] 유역

riv·er·bed [rívərbèd] *n.* [C] the sandy bottom of a river.
—[名] 강바닥; 하상(河床)

riv·er·head [rívərhèd] *n.* [C] the source of a river.
—[名] [강의] 수원(水源)

riv·er·side [rívərsàid] *n.* [C] the bank of a river. —*adj.* on the bank of a river.
—[名] 강가, 강변 —[形] 강가의, 강변의

riv·et [rívit] *n.* [C] a short metal bolt with a head on one end, used to fasten together two or more pieces of wood, metal, etc. ⇒fig. —*vt.* **1.** fasten (plates, etc.) with a rivet or rivets. **2.** fasten firmly. **3.** fix (the eyes, the mind, etc.) firmly. ¶*~ one's attention on* (or *upon*) *something.*① ▷**riv·et·er** [-ər] *n.*
—[名] 리벳, 대갈못 —[他] 1. …을 리벳으로 고정시키다 2. …을 고정시키다 3. [눈·마음 따위]를 집중하다 ¶①…에 주의를 쏟다

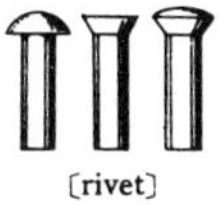
[rivet]

riv·u·let [rívjulit] *n.* [C] a very small stream.
—[名] 시내, 개울

R. N. **1.** registered nurse. **2.** Royal Navy.
—《略》 1. 공인 간호부 2. 영국 해군

roach [routʃ] *n.* [C] (pl. **roach·es** or *collectively* **roach**) a fresh-water fish of the carp family.
—[名] 잉어과의 민물고기

⁑**road** [roud] *n.* [C] **1.** a highway along which people can travel; a public way for travel. ¶*the beaten ~*① / *by ~*② / *make a ~*③ / *This ~ goes to London.* **2.** a way; a course; a means to approach. ¶(*proverb*) *There is no royal ~ to learning.*④ **3.** (*U.S.*) a railroad. **4.** (often *pl.*) a roadstead.
—[名] 1. 도로, 길, 가도 ¶①밟아다진 길; 상도(常道)/②육로로/③길을 내다 2. 방법, 길 ¶④《俚》학문에 왕도(王道)는 없다 3. 철도 4. [항구 밖의] 정박소

1) ***get in one's road,*** hinder.
2) ***get out of one's*** (or ***the***) ***road,*** move out of the way.
3) ***go on*** (or ***take to***) ***the road,*** ⓐstart traveling. ⓑ (*archaic*) become a highwayman.
4) ***on the road,*** traveling; on tour.

[熟] 1)방해하다 2)통행에 방해가 안 되도록 비키다 3)ⓐ여행을 떠나다 ⓑ《古》노상강도가 되다 4)여행 중, 지방 공연 중

road·bed [róudbèd] *n.* [C] the foundation or bed for a road or railroad.
—[名] 노상(路床); [철도의] 노반(路盤)

road·house [róudhàus] *n.* [C] a tavern, an inn, or a night club at the side of a road in the country.
—[名] 길가의 술집(여인숙·나이트클럽)

road·man [róudmən] *n.* [C] (pl. **-men** [-mən]) a man who is employed to keeps roads in repair.
—[名] 도로공사 인부

road show [´ ˋ] *n.* **1.** a show performed by a touring group of actors. **2.** a special show of a new motion picture, usu. at a special advanced price.
—[名] 1. 순회 흥행 2. 영화의 특별 흥행

road·side [róudsàid] *n.* [C] 《usu. *the ~*》 the side of a road. ¶*by* (*on*) *the ~.* —*adj.* on or at the side of a road.
—[名] 길가 —[形] 길가의

road·stead [róudstèd] *n.* [C] a stretch of water near the shore where ships can ride at anchor.
—[名] [항구 밖의] 정박소

road·ster [róudstər] *n.* [C] **1.** a horse used for driving or riding on the road. **2.** an open automobile with a single seat, usu. for two persons.
—[名] 1. [도로용의] 승용 말 2. [2~3인승의] 무개(無蓋) 자동차

road·way [róudwèi] *n.* [C] a road; the part of a road used by vehicles.
—[名] 도로; 차도

***roam** [roum] *vi., vt.* wander; go from place to place aimlessly. 《*~ about* a place, etc.》 ¶*~ about the forest* / *~ the countryside.* —*n.* [C] a walk with no special aim.
—[自][他] […을] 걸어다니다, 배회하다
—[名] 떠돌아다니기, 배회

roan [roun] *adj.* deep reddish-brown or yellowish, thickly sprinkled with gray or white. —*n.* [U] a roan color; [C] a roan horse.
—[形] 밤색에 흰 털이 섞인 —[名] 밤색에 흰 털이 섞인 말

⁑**roar** [rɔːr] *vi.* **1.** utter a loud, deep sound. ¶*A storm roars.* / *Cannons ~ far away.*① **2.** cry or laugh loudly. ¶*~ with laughter.*② —*vt.* shout loudly at (someone); utter (something) with a loud, deep sound. ¶*~ a speaker down*③ / *He roared out a song.* / *He roared himself hoarse.*④
—*n.* [C] a loud, deep sound; a loud cry or noise; a loud burst of laughter. ¶*a ~ of disapproval.*⑤
—[自] 1. 짖다, 포효하다; 요란하게 울리다 ¶①멀리서 대포 소리가 들린다 2. 고함치다; 큰 소리로 웃다 ¶②큰 소리로 웃다 —[他] …에게 고함치다; 외치다 ¶③[변사를] 고함질러 말 못하게 하다/④그는 너무 소리를 질러 목이 쉬었다 —[名] 으르렁거림, 포효; 왁자함; 큰 웃음 ¶⑤요란한 반대 소리

roar·ing [rɔ́ːriŋ] *n.* [U] the sound made by a person or thing that roars. —*adj.* **1.** noisy. **2.** brisk; active.
—[名] 으르렁 소리, 포효 —[形] 1. 짖는; 울리는 2. 활발한

⁑**roast** [roust] *vt.* cook (meat or other food) in an oven or before a fire. —*vi.* be cooked in an oven or before a fire. —*n.* [C] a piece of meat to be roasted.
—[他] …을 굽다, 볶다 —[自] 구워지다, 볶아지다 —[名] 불고기용의 고기

rule the roast, be a master.
[熟] 좌지우지하다, 주인 노릇을 하다

R

—*adj.* roasted. ¶~ *beef.*
—[形] 구워진

roast·er [róustər] *n.* [C] **1.** a pan for roasting. **2.** a young pig, chicken, etc. suitable to be roasted.
—[名] 1. 굽는 기구 2. 불고기용의 새끼 돼지·영계 따위

⁑**rob** [rɑb / rɔb] *v.* (**robbed, rob·bing**) *vt.* take something away from (someone) by force; deprive (someone) of his rights or property. 《~ someone *of*》 ¶~ *a lady of her handbag* / ~ *a bank.* —*vi.* commit an act of robbing.
—[他] …에서 빼앗다, 강탈하다, …을 훔치다 —[自] 강도질을 하다

Rob [rɑb / rɔb] *n.* a nickname of Robert.
—[名] Robert의 애칭

*__rob·ber__ [rɑ́bər / rɔ́bə] *n.* [C] a person who robs.
—[名] 강도, 도둑

rob·ber·y [rɑ́bəri / rɔ́bə-] *n.* [C][U] (pl. **-ber·ies**) the act of robbing.
—[名] 강도

⁑**robe** [roub] *n.* [C] **1.** a long, loose indoor garment. **2.** 《often *pl.*》 a ceremonial dress worn as a sign of rank, office, etc. ¶*the judge's* ~. **3.** (*U.S.*) a wrap. —*vt.* dress (someone) with a robe. —*vi.* put on a robe.
—[名] 1. 길고 헐거운 실내복 2. 예복 3. 무릎덮개 —[他] …에 예복을 입히다 —[自] 예복을 입다

Rob·ert [rɑ́bərt / rɔ́bət] *n.* a man's name.
—[名] 남자 이름

⁑**rob·in** [rɑ́bin / rɔ́b-] *n.* [C] **1.** a small bird with a red breast. **2.** (*U.S.*) a large American thrush with a red breast.
—[名] 1. 지빠귀과의 유리새 2. 〔美〕 미국 물새

Rob·in [rɑ́bin / rɔ́b-] *n.* a nickname of Robert.
—[名] Robert의 애칭

Rob·in·son Cru·soe [rɑ́binsnkrú:sou / rɔ́b-] *n.* a novel by Daniel Defoe; the hero of this novel.
—[名] Defoe 작의 소설; 그 주인공

ro·bot [róubɑt / -bɔt] *n.* [C] **1.** a machine that acts or looks like a man. **2.** a person who acts like a machine.
—[名] 1. 인조인간, 로봇 2. 감정이 없고 기계적인 인간

ro·bust [roubʌ́st] *adj.* (sometimes **~·er, ~·est**) strong; healthy. ¶*a ~ person.* ▷**ro·bust·ly** [-li] *adv.*
—[形] 강건한, 건전한

roc [rɑk / rɔk] *n.* [C] an enormous bird in old Arabian tales.
—[名] [아라비아 전설의] 큰 괴조(怪鳥)

⁑**rock**¹ [rɑk / rɔk] *n.* **1.** [U][C] a large mass of stone. **2.** [C] a piece of stone of any size. **3.** [C] the mass of mineral matter forming the earth's crust.
—[名] 1. 바위, 암석 2. 바윗덩이 3. 암상(岩床), 암반(岩盤)

on the rocks, ⓐ (of a ship) wrecked on rocks. ⓑ (of a person) bankrupt.
[熟] ⓐ[배가] 난파하여 ⓑ[사람이] 파산하여

⁑**rock**² [rɑk / rɔk] *vt.* move (something) backward and forward. —*vi.* move backward and forward. —*n.* [U] a rocking movement.
—[他] …을 앞뒤로 움직이다 —[自] 앞뒤로 움직이다 —[名] 흔들리기

rock candy [ˊ ˊ-] *n.* (*U.S.*) sugar in the form of rocks.
—[名] 〔美〕 얼음사탕

rock crystal [ˊ ˋ-] *n.* a colorless, transparent quartz.
—[名] 수정광(水晶鑛)

rock·er [rɑ́kər / rɔ́kə] *n.* [C] **1.** one of the curved pieces of wood on which a cradle or a rocking chair moves backward and forward. **2.** a rocking chair.
—[名] 1. [요람·흔들의자의 밑에 댄] 굽은 막대 2. 흔들의자

rock·er·y [rɑ́kəri / rɔ́k-] *n.* [C] (pl. **-er·ies**) a rock garden for growing plants.
—[名] [식물을 심기 위한 정원] 석가산(石假山)

*__rock·et__ [rɑ́kit / rɔ́k-] *n.* [C] **1.** a machine propelled by means of self-contained gases. **2.** a kind of firework shooting high into the air, used in displays or for signaling. —*vi.* go up high and fast.
—[名] 1. 로켓 2. 봉화, 화전(火箭) —[自] 곧추 날아오르다

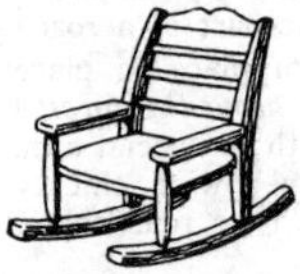
〔rocking chair〕

Rock·ies [rɑ́kiz / rɔ́k-], **the** *n. pl.* =the Rocky Mountains.

rock·ing chair [rɑ́kiŋtʃɛ̀ər / rɔ́kiŋtʃɛ̀ə] *n.* a chair set on rockers for rocking back and forth. ⇒fig.
—[名] 흔들의자

rocking horse [ˊ- ˋ] *n.* a toy horse on rockers for children. ⇒fig.
—[名] 흔들목마

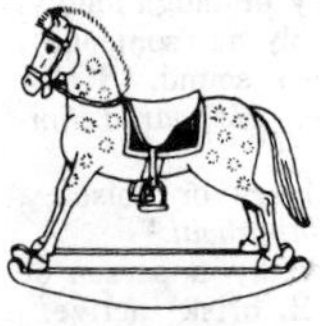
〔rocking horse〕

rock salt [ˊ ˋ] *n.* salt got from mines in solid form.
—[名] 암염(岩鹽)

*__rock·y__¹ [rɑ́ki / rɔ́ki] *adj.* (**rock·i·er, rock·i·est**) **1.** full of rocks; made of rocks; like rock. **2.** firm.
—[形] 1. 바위가 많은, 바위로 된, 바위 같은 2. 단단한, 굳은

*__rock·y__² [rɑ́ki / rɔ́ki] *adj.* (**rock·i·er, rock·i·est**) **1.** not firm; shaky. **2.** dizzy.
—[形] 1. 흔들흔들하는, 흔들리는 2. 현기증이 나는

Rocky Mountains [ˊ- ˊ-], **the** *n. pl.* the chief moun-
—[名] 록키 산맥

tain range in North America, extending from New Mexico to Alaska.

ro·co·co [rəkóukou] *n.* [U] a style of architecture or decoration with very much ornamentation. **—*adj.*** of or on this style.
—[名] 로코코식 —[形] 로코코식의

⁑rod [rɑd / rɔd] *n.* [C] **1.** a long, straight stick made of wood or metal. **2.** a stick or whip used to punish. ¶*kiss the ~*① | (*proverb*) *Spare the ~ and spoil the child.*② **3.** a fishing rod. **4.** a measure of length, equal to $5^1/_2$ yards. **5.** power; authority.
—[名] 1. 막대, 장대, 지팡이 2. 채찍 ¶①죄를 달게 받다/②《俚》매를 아끼면 자식을 망친다 3. 낚싯대 4. 길이의 척도로서 5야아드 반 5. 권력, 권위

make a rod for** one's **own back, get into trouble by oneself.
[熟] 스스로 화를 청하다

⁑rode [roud] *v.* pt. of **ride**.

ro·dent [róud(ə)nt] *n.* [C] any animal that gnaws with its front teeth, which are constantly growing. **—*adj.* 1.** of or like a rodent. **2.** gnawing; biting.
—[名] 설치류(齧齒類) 동물(토끼·쥐·다람쥐 따위) —[形] 1. 설치류의(같은) 2. 갉는; 무는

ro·de·o [róudiou / roudéiou] *n.* [C] (pl. **-de·os**) (*U.S.*) **1.** a contest in which cowboys show skills in roping cattle or riding horses. **2.** the act of driving cattle together; a round-up.
—[名] 《美》 1. 카우보이의 경기회 2. 목우(牧牛)를 모으기

roe¹ [rou] *n.* [U] fish eggs.
—[名] 어란(魚卵), 곤이, 이리

roe² [rou] *n.* [C][U] (pl. **roes** or *collectively* **roe**) a small kind of deer found in Europe and Asia.
—[名] 유럽·아시아산의 노루

roe·buck [róubʌk] *n.* [C] (pl. **-bucks** or *collectively* **-buck**) a male deer.
—[名] 노루의 수컷

Roent·gen rays [réntgənrèiz] *n.* X-rays.
—[名] 뢴트겐선

Rog·er [rɑ́dʒər / rɔ́dʒə] *n.* a man's name.
—[名] 남자 이름

***rogue** [roug] *n.* [C] **1.** a dishonest person; a rascal. **2.** a mischievous or playful person. **3.** an animal with a savage nature, living apart from the group.
—[名] 1. 부정직한 사람, 악한 2. 장난꾸러기 3. 무리를 떠나 떠도는 맹수

ro·guer·y [róugəri] *n.* (pl. **-guer·ies**) **1.** [C][U] a dishonest trick. **2.** [U] playful mischief.
—[名] 1. 못된 짓; 사기 2. 장난

ro·guish [róugiʃ] *adj.* **1.** dishonest. **2.** mischievous.
—[形] 1. 부정한, 못된 2. 장난의

roist·er [rɔ́istər] *vi.* talk noisily and loudly; feast merrily.
—[自] 시끄럽게 떠들다; 술 마시며 떠들다

roist·er·er [rɔ́istərər] *n.* [C] a person who roisters.
—[名] [술 마시며] 떠드는 사람

Ro·land [róulənd] *n.* a man's name.
—[名] 남자 이름

***role, rôle** [roul] *n.* [C] **1.** a part taken by an actor or an actress in a play. **2.** a part in real life. ¶*He played an important ~ in the conference.*①
—[名] 1. [연극의] 배역 2. 임무, 역할 ¶①그는 그 회의에서 중요한 역할을 했다

⁑roll [roul] *vi.* **1.** move along by turning over and over; move on wheels. ¶*~ down*① | *~ in bed*② | *The ball rolled into a hole.* **2.** (of time) pass. 《*~ on* or *by*》 ¶*Time rolls on.* | *Two years rolled by.* **3.** (of the eyes) move round. ¶*His eyes ~ strangely.* **4.** (of a ship, etc.) swing from side to side. ↔pitch ¶*During the storm, the ship rolled.* **5.** (of surfaces) have gentle rising and falling slopes; gently rise and fall. ¶*a rolling plain* | *The hills ~ down to the sea.*③ | *The sea rolls.* **6.** float gently. ¶*a rolling mist* | *Smoke rolls up.*④ **7.** make a loud and echoing sound. ¶*The thunder rolls in the distance.*⑤ **8.** travel about; wander. **—*vt.* 1.** cause (something) to move by turning over and over. ¶*~ a wheel* | *~ a ball.* **2.** wrap or wind (something) into the shape of a ball or cylinder. ¶*~ yarn into a ball*⑥ | *She rolled her child in a blanket.*⑦ **3.** turn (one's eyes) from side to side. ¶*He rolled his eyes on us.* **4.** make (something) flat, smooth, or thin by using a roller. ¶*~ sheet metal*⑧ | *~ the grass.* **5.** give a swinging motion to (a ship). **6.** move (something) in a rising and falling motion. ¶*The sea rolls its waves against the rock.*⑨
—[自] 1. 구르다; 회전하다 ¶①굴러 떨어지다/②돌아 눕다 2. [세월이] 흐르다 3. [눈알이] 돌다 4. [배 따위가] 흔들리다 5. 기복하다; 굽이치다 ¶③산은 기복을 이루며 바다까지 연해 있다 6. 떠돌다, 뭉게뭉게 오르다 ¶④연기가 뭉게뭉게 올라간다 7. 울리다 ¶⑤먼데서 우뢰가 울린다 8. 여행하다; 헤매다 —[他] 1. …을 굴리다; 회전시키다 2. …을 동그랗게 하다; 똘똘 뭉치다; 싸다 ¶⑥실을 똘똘 몽치다/⑦그녀는 아이를 담요로 쌌다 3. [눈알]을 굴리다 4. …을 로울러로 고르다(늘이다) ¶⑧금속판을 늘이다 5. [배]를 옆으로 흔들리게 하다 6. …을 굽이치게 하다 ¶⑨바다가 굽이쳐서 물결이 바위에 부딪치고 있다

1) ***be rolling in*** (=*have much*) ***money, etc.***
2) ***roll in,*** ⓐ come in large numbers. ⓑ go to bed.
3) ***roll up,*** ⓐ wrap up (something) by turning over and over. ⓑ increase; collect. ⓒ arrive.

[熟] 1)[돈 따위가] 엄청나게 많다 2)ⓐ 떼지어 오다 ⓑ자다 3)ⓐ…을 둘둘 말다(싸다) ⓑ[돈 따위] 모이다; 저축하다 ⓒ나타나다

—*n.* [C] **1.** the act of rolling; a rolling motion. **2.** a
—[名] 1. 구르기, 회전 2. 넘실거림; 기복

gentle rising and falling on the surface. ¶*the ~ of a plain (waves).* **3.** a loud and echoing sound. ¶*a distant ~ of thunder.*[10] **4.** a list of names. ¶*the ~ of honor*[11] */ call a ~*[12] */ put on the rolls.*[13] **5.** anything made into the shape of a pipe or cylinder by being rolled. ¶*a ~ of paper.* **6.** a small kind of bread.
3. 울리는 소리 ¶⑩먼 우렛소리 4. 명부; 목록 ¶⑪전사자 명부/⑫점호하다; 출석을 부르다/⑬명부에 싣다 5. 두루마리; 한 권 6. 로울 빵

roll call [ˊ ˋ] *n.* the act of calling a list of names to find out who are present.
—[名] 출석 조사; 점호

***roll·er** [róulər] *n.* [C] **1.** a heavy cylinder of stone, metal, or a wood for grinding, smoothing, crushing, etc. **2.** a large wave. **3.** a kind of canary.
—[名] 1. 로울러; 땅 고르는 기계; 압연기(壓延機), 녹로(轆轤), 고패 2. 큰 파도 3. 쇠새; 비둘기의 일종

roller coaster [ˊ- ˋ-] *n.* a railroad for amusement with a train that runs along high, winding, often descending tracks.
—[名] 오락용 활주차(滑走車)

roller skate [ˊ- ˋ] *n.* a skate with small wheels used on a floor etc.
—[名] 로울러 스케이트

roller-skate [róulərskèit] *vi.* skate on roller skates.
—[自] 로울러 스케이트를 타다

rol·lick [rálik / rɔ́l-] *vi.* act in a merry way. **—*n.*** [U] [C] the state of being merry; a frolic.
—[自] 까불며 뛰놀다 —[名] 좋아 날뛰기

rol·lick·ing [rálikiŋ / rɔ́l-] *adj.* merry; frolicking.
—[形] 쾌활한, 까부는

roll·ing mill [róuliŋmìl] *n.* **1.** a factory where metal is rolled into sheets and bars. **2.** a machine used for doing this.
—[名] 1. 압연(壓延)공장 2. 압연기

rolling pin [ˊ- ˋ] *n.* a cylinder for rolling out dough. ⇒fig.
—[名] 국수 방망이

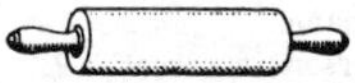
(rolling pin)

rolling stock [ˊ- ˊ] *n.* ⟪*collectively*⟫ the cars of a railroad.
—[名] [철도] 차량

roll-top desk [róultɔpdesk / -tɑp-] *n.* a desk with a flexible, sliding cover. ⇒fig.
—[名] 뚜껑을 접어넣게 된 책상

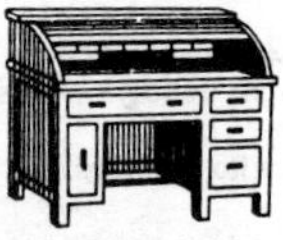
(roll-top desk)

ro·ly-po·ly [róulipóuli] *n.* [C] (pl. **-lies**) **1.** a pudding that is rolled up. **2.** a short and fat person. **—*adj.*** short and thick.
—[名] 1. 소용돌이처럼 생긴 푸딩의 일종 2. 땅딸막한 사람 —[形] 땅딸막한

‡**Ro·man** [róumən] *adj.* **1.** of Rome or its people. **2.** of the Roman Catholic Church. **3.** ⟪usu. *r-*⟫ of or in roman type. ¶*~ letters.* **—*n.*** [C] **1.** a citizen of Rome. **2.** a Roman Catholic. **3.** [C] ⟪usu. *r-*⟫ roman type used in printing.
—[形] 1. 로마[사람]의 2. 로마 가톨릭교의 3. 로마 자체(字體)의 —[名] 1. 로마 사람 2. 로마 가톨릭 교도 3. 로마 자체

Roman Catholic [ˊ- ˊ--] *n.* a member of the Church of Rome. **—*adj.*** of the Church of Rome.
—[名] 로마 가톨릭 교도 —[形] 로마 가톨릭교의

‡**ro·mance** [roumǽns / rə(u)-] *n.* **1.** [C] the unreal; the fanciful; that which is far away in time or space. **2.** [C] a fanciful story; a love story. **3.** [C] a real event that is like a story; a love affair. **4.** [U] ⟪*R-*⟫ a language which comes from Latin, such as French, Italian, and Spanish.
—*adj.* of Romance languages.
—*vi.* make up a fanciful story.
—[名] 1. 가공(架空)의 일; 지어낸 일 2. 공상적인 이야기; 연애 이야기 3. 소설 같은 사건; 정사(情事) 4. 로만스어(라틴어 계통의 프랑스어·이탈리아어 따위)
—[形] 로만스어의
—[自] 꾸며낸 이야기를 하다

ro·manc·er [roumǽnsər] *n.* [C] the writer of a romance; a person who makes up a fanciful story.
—[名] 전기(傳奇) 소설가; 지어낸 이야기를 하는 사람, 공상가

Ro·man·esque [ròumənésk] *n.* [U] a style of building using round arches, popular in Europe in the early Middle Ages. **—*adj.*** of this style.
—[名] 로마네스크식(중세 초기에 유행, 둥근 아아치를 썼음) —[形] 로마네스크식의

Ro·man·ic [roumǽnik] *adj.* **1.** of Romance languages. **2.** of Rome; of a person of Rome.
—[形] 1. 로만스어의 2. 로마[사람]의

Ro·man·ist [róumənist] *n.* [C] **1.** a member of the Roman Catholic Church. **2.** a student of Roman law.
—[名] 1. 로마 가톨릭 교도 2. 로마법 연구가

Ro·man·ize [róumənàiz] *vt., vi.* **1.** make (something) or become Roman in character. **2.** make (someone) or become Roman Catholic.
—[他][自] 1. 로마식으로 하다(되다) 2. 로마 가톨릭교로 하다(되다)

***ro·man·tic** [roumǽntik] *adj.* **1.** full of romance; fanciful. **2.** fanciful and imaginative rather than real and correct in art or literature. ¶*the ~ movement.*
—*n.* **1.** [C] a writer or an artist who believes in romanticism; a romantic person. **2.** ⟪*pl.*⟫ a romantic charac-
—[形] 1. 전기(傳奇)소설 같은; 공상적인 2. 낭만주의의
—[名] 1. 낭만파의 사람; 낭만적인 사람 2. 공상적인 표현, 정서(情緒)

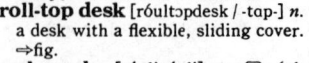

terestic, feeling etc. ▷**ro·man·ti·cal·ly** [-kəli] *adv.*

ro·man·ti·cism [roumǽntisìz(ə)m] *n.* [U] the romantic movement or spirit in art and literature.
—[名] 낭만주의(18세기말 유럽에서 일어났음)

ro·man·ti·cist [roumǽntisist] *n.* [C] a writer or an artist who believes in romanticism.
—[名] 낭만주의자

:Rome [roum] *n.* **1.** the capital of Italy. **2.** the ancient Roman Empire. ¶(*proverb*) *Do in ~ as the Romans do.*① / *~ was not built in a day.*
—[名] **1.** 로마(이탈리아의 수도) **2.** 고대 로마 제국 ¶①《俚》입향순속(入鄕循俗)

romp [rɑmp / rɔmp] *vi.* play in a lively and rough way; run quickly and without effort. —*n.* [C] a lively game or frolic; a child who likes to romp.
—[自] [어린아이가] 까불며 뛰놀다; 뛰어다니다 —[名] 까불며 뛰놀기; 장난치며 노는 아이

romp·ers [rámpərz / rɔ́mpəz] *n. pl.* a one-piece outer garment worn by small children at play.
—[名] 롬퍼스(아이들의 놀이옷)

Rom·u·lus [rámjuləs / rɔ́m-] *n.* (in Roman mythology) the founder and first king of Rome.
—[名] 고대 로마의 건설자, 초대의 왕

ron·do [rándou / rɔ́n-] *n.* [C] (pl. **-dos**) (*Music*) a work in which the theme is repeated in a certain way.
—[名] 《樂》 론도, 회선곡(回旋曲)

Rönt·gen rays [réntgənrèiz] *n. pl.* X-rays.
—[名] X선

rood [ru:d] *n.* [C] **1.** a cross with the figure of Christ on it. **2.** a quarter of an acre.
—[名] **1.** 그리스도의 상이 있는 십자가 **2.** 4분의 1에이커

by the rood, certainly.
[熟] 확실히

:roof [ru:f, +*U.S.* ruf] *n.* [C] (pl. **roofs**) **1.** the top covering of a building. **2.** something like a roof.
—[名] **1.** 지붕 **2.** 지붕 비슷한 것

under someone's roof, staying at someone's house.
[熟] …의 집에 묵고 있는

roof·less [rú:flis, +*U.S.* rúf-] *adj.* without a roof.
—[形] 지붕이 없는

roof·tree [rú:ftrì:, +*U.S.* rúf-] *n.* [C] the large timber or piece of wood along the top of the roof.
—[名] 들보

rook[1] [ruk] *n.* [C] **1.** a black bird like a crow. **2.** a person who gets money using a trick at dice, cards, etc. —*vt.* cheat (someone) to get money by using a trick at cards.
—[名] **1.** 땅까마귀 **2.** 도박자, 사기꾼
—[他] [카아드놀이에서] …을 속이다

rook[2] [ruk] *n.* [C] a chess piece, a castle.
—[名] [장기의] 성장(城將)

rook·er·y [rúkəri] *n.* [C] (pl. **-er·ies**) **1.** a colony of rooks or certain other birds such as penguins; a place where rooks, penguins, etc. breed. **2.** a group of dirty and poor houses.
—[名] **1.** 땅까마귀의 떼; 펭귄 따위의 떼; 그 번식 장소 **2.** 빈민굴

:room [ru(:)m] *n.* **1.** [C] a part of a house or other building enclosed by walls. ¶*a dining ~ / a living ~ / a ~ to let.*① **2.** [U] space. ¶*This desk takes up too much ~.*② / *There is ~ in the car for another person.*③ **3.** [U] the space within which something may happen; chance; opportunity. ¶*There is no ~ for doubt.* **4.** 《*collectively, the ~*》 the people in a room. ¶*The ~ became silent.* **5.** 《*pl.*》 a set of rooms; an apartment. ¶*Rooms for rent.*④
—[名] **1.** 방 ¶①셋방 **2.** 빈터; 장소; 여지 ¶②이 책상은 장소를 너무 차지한다/③차에는 한 사람 더 탈 수 있다 **3.** 가능성; 기회 **4.** 방에 있는 사람들 **5.** 한 벌의 방, 하숙방, 셋방 ¶④셋방 있음(게시문)

in the room of, in place of.
[熟] …의 대신에

—*vi.* (*U.S.*) live in a room or rooms of another's house; lodge. 《*~ at* a place, *~ with* someone》 ¶*He rooms at Mr. Smith's house.*
—[自] 《美》 하숙하다; 기숙(유숙)하다

room·ful [rú(:)mfùl] *n.* [C] enough in number or amount to fill a room; the people in a room.
—[名] 방 가득; 실내의 사람들

room·ing house [rú(:)miŋhàus] *n.* (*U.S.*) a house with rooms to rent; a boarding house.
—[名] 《美》 하숙집

room·mate [rú(:)mmèit] *n.* [C] (*U.S.*) a person who shares a room with one or more persons.
—[名] 《美》 동숙인(同宿人)

room·i·ness [rú(:)minis] *n.* [U] the state of being spacious.
—[名] 넓음

room·y [rú(:)mi] *adj.* (**room·i·er, room·i·est**) having plenty of space; spacious.
—[形] 널따란

roost [ru:st] *n.* [C] **1.** a branch or bar where a bird rests. **2.** a place to rest.
—[名] **1.** 새가 쉬는 나뭇가지, 홰; 잠자리, 숙소 **2.** 휴식소

1) *at roost,* on a perch; sleeping.
2) *rule the roost,* dominate; control.
[熟] 1)[새가] 보금자리에 든; [사람이] 잠든 2)…을 지배하다

—*vi.* sit on a perch; go to bed.
—[自] 홰에 앉다; 잠자리에 들다

roost·er [rú:stər] *n.* [C] a mail chicken; a cock.
—[名] 수탉

:root [ru:t] *n.* [C] **1.** a part of a plant usu. growing under the ground; 《*pl.*》 a plant with a root used as food;
—[名] **1.** 뿌리; 근채류(根菜類) **2.** 뿌리 모양의 것, 밑동; 기슭 ¶①혀 뿌리

root crop

root crops. **2.** a part of anything like a root. ¶*the ~ of the tongue*① / *at the ~ of a hill.*② **3.** the essential part; the cause; the source; the origin. ¶*go to* (or *get at*) *the ~ of a matter*③ / *The love of fame is the ~ of his ruin.* **4.** (*Mathematics*) a quantity that produces a given quantity when multiplied by itself. ¶*a cubic* (*a square*) *~.*④ **5.** the essential form of a word.
1) *root and branch*, entirely; thoroughly.
2) *take* (or *strike*) *root*, ⓐ send out roots. ⓑ become established.
—*vt.* **1.** cause (a plant) to take roots; plant. **2.** fix firmly. ¶*Fear rooted him to the ground.*⑤ **3.** be the cause, base, principle, etc. of (something); establish deeply. ¶*be rooted in the fact*⑥ / *The matter is rooted in his idleness.*⑦ **4.** remove completely. ¶*~ out superstition.* —*vi.* send out roots; become established.

root crop [⌐⌐] *n.* a crop grown for its root, which people eat, such as sweet potatoes.
root·er [rúːtər] *n.* Ⓒ (*U.S. slang*) a person who supports
root·let [rúːtlit, +*U.S.* rúːt-] *n.* Ⓒ a branch of a root.
root·stock [rúːtstɑ̀k / -stɔ̀k] *n.* Ⓒ a stem under the ground like a root.

‡**rope** [roup] *n.* **1.** ⒸⓊ a thick, strong cord. **2.** (*the ~*) a cord used in hanging; punishment by hanging. **3.** Ⓒ a number of things linked together in the form of a cord. ¶*a ~ of pearls.*①
1) *give someone* [*plenty of*] *rope*, give someone free-
2) *know the ropes*, know very well about the details of a business, etc.
3) *on the high ropes*, in high spirits.
—*vt.* **1.** fasten or tie (something) with a rope. ¶*~ and tie someone's feet.* **2.** separate or enclose (a place) with a rope. ¶*~ off a place from.*②

rope-danc·er [róupdæ̀nsər / -dɑ̀ːnsə] *n.* Ⓒ a person who walks or dances on a rope high above the ground.
Ro·sa [róuzə] *n.* a woman's name.
ro·sa·ry [róuzəri] *n.* Ⓒ (pl. **-ries**) **1.** (*Catholic*) a string of beads for counting a series of prayers; a series of prayers thus counted on a rosary. ⇒fig. **2.** a rose garden.

[rosary 1.]

‡**rose**¹ [rouz] *n.* Ⓒ **1.** a sweet-smelling flower growing on a bush with thorny stems. ¶*No ~ without a thorn.*① **2.** Ⓤ a pink color. **3.** something shaped like a rose.
1) *a bed of* [*life's*] *roses,* very easy and pleasant conditions.
2) *gather* [*life's*] *roses,* seek the pleasures of life.
3) *It is not all roses.*, It is not always easy.
4) *under the rose,* in secret.
—*adj.* of a rose color; rosy. —*vt.* make (something) rosy.

‡**rose**² [rouz] *v.* pt. of **rise**.
ro·se·ate [róuziit] *adj.* **1.** of a rose color; rosy. **2.** hopeful; optimistic.
rose·bud [róuzbʌ̀d] *n.* Ⓒ the bud of a rose.
rose·bush [róuzbùʃ] *n.* Ⓒ a bush bearing roses.
rose color [⌐ ⌐⌐] *n.* a pink color.
rose-col·ored, *Brit.*, **-col·oured** [róuzkʌ̀lərd] *adj.* **1.** pink. **2.** hopeful; optimistic.
rose leaf [⌐ ⌐] *n.* a leaf of a rose bush.
rose·mar·y [róuzmɛ̀əri / -m(ə)ri] *n.* Ⓒ (pl. **-mar·ies**) an evergreen and sweet-smelling bush, the leaves of which are used for making perfume.

/②산기슭 **3.** 근본, 근저(根底); 원인; 근원 ¶③사물의 근본(진상)을 캐다 **4.** (數) 근(根) ¶④입방(평방)근 **5.** 어근(語根); 원형

🅟 1)철저히, 완전히 2)ⓐ뿌리박다 ⓑ 정착하다
—⑪ **1.** …을 뿌리박게 하다; 심다 **2.** …을 정착시키다; 움직이지 못하게 하다 ¶⑤공포로 그 자리에서 꼼짝도 못했다 **3.** …에 입각하다, 원인이 있다 ¶⑥사실에 입각하다/⑦그 일은 그의 게으름이 원인이다 **4.** …을 뿌리째 뽑다, 근절하다 —⑫ 뿌리박다; 정착하다

—⑬ [무우·고구마 따위의] 근채류(根菜類) [작물]
—⑬ 응원자
—⑬ 작은 뿌리, 곁뿌리
—⑬ 근경(根莖)

—⑬ **1.** 밧줄, 새끼, 로우프 **2.** 교수용 밧줄; 교수형 **3.** 끈 모양으로 이은 것 ¶① 진주 목걸이

🅟 1)…을 제멋대로 하게 하다 2)사정을 잘 알고 있다 3)의기양양하여

—⑪ **1.** …을 밧줄로 묶다 **2.** …을 밧줄로 간막이하다(두르다) ¶②…하지 않도록 어떤 장소에 새끼줄을 치다
—⑬ 밧줄 타는 곡예사

—⑬ 여자 이름
—⑬ **1.** (가톨릭) 염주, 묵주(알을 하나 하나 세면서 기도함); 로자리오의 기도 **2.** 장미원

—⑬ **1.** 장미꽃 ¶①(俚)가시 없는 장미는 없다; 세상엔 완전한 행복이란 없다 **2.** 장미꽃 **3.** 장미꽃 모양의 것

🅟 1)안락한 처지(지위) 2)환락을 쫓다 3)편하기만 한 것은 아니다 4)비밀히, 몰래

—⑬ 장미빛의 —⑪ …을 장미빛으로 하다
—⑬ **1.** 장미빛의 **2.** 유망한; 낙관적인
—⑬ 장미꽃 봉오리
—⑬ 장미나무(덤불)
—⑬ 장미빛, 유망
—⑪ **1.** 장미빛의 **2.** 유망한, 낙관적인

—⑬ 장미 잎사귀
—⑬ 로우즈메리(상록 관목)

ro·sette [rouzét] *n.* [C] **1.** a ribbon in the shape of a rose used as an ornament. **2.** a piece of stone or glass cut in the shape of a rose and used as an ornament.
—[名] 1. 리본의 장미 매듭 2. 장미 모양의 장식

rose water [ˊ ˌ–] *n.* a sweet-smelling water made from roses.
—[名] 장미 향수

rose window [ˊ ˌ–] *n.* an ornamental round window chiefly used in churches. ⇒fig.
—[名] 장미 꽃모양의 창, 원화창(圓花窓)

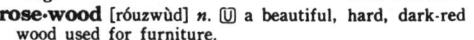

[rose window]

rose·wood [róuzwùd] *n.* [U] a beautiful, hard, dark-red wood used for furniture.
—[名] 자단(紫檀)

ros·i·ly [róuzili] *adv.* **1.** in a rosy manner; with a rosy color. **2.** cheerfully; optimistically.
—[副] 1. 장미빛으로 2. 쾌활하게; 낙관적으로

ros·in [rázin / rɔ́z-] *n.* [U] a solid substance obtained from the sticky juice of the pine tree. **—*vt.*** rub (something) with rosin.
—[名] 로진(송진에서 테레빈유를 증류하고 남은 찌꺼기) —[他] …을 로진으로 문지르다

ros·i·ness [róuzinis] *n.* [U] the state or quality of being rosy.
—[名] 장미빛; 유망; 낙관

Ross [rɔːs / rɔs] *n.* a man's name.
—[名] 남자 이름

ros·ter [rástər / róustə] *n.* [C] (*Military*) a list of officers and enlisted men available for duty; a list.
—[名] 《軍》 근무 당번표; 명부

ros·trum [rástrəm / rɔ́s-] *n.* [C] (pl. **-trums** or **-tra** [-trə]) a platform for public speaking; a stage. ¶*take the* ~.①
—[名] 설교단, 연단 ¶①등단하다

***ros·y** [róuzi] *adj.* (**ros·i·er, ros·i·est**) **1.** like a rose; rose-red; blushing. **2.** bright; cheerful; promising; optimistic. ¶*a* ~ *future* / ~ *views.*
—[形] 1. 장미 같은; 장미빛의; 홍안의 2. 밝은; 쾌활한; 유망한; 낙관적인

rot [rat / rɔt] *v.* (**rot·ted, rot·ting**) *vi.* decay; spoil; become corrupt. 《~ *off* (or *away, from*)》 **—*vt.*** cause (something) to decay; spoil. ¶*Dampness rots wood.* **—*n.*** [U] **1.** decay; rotten matter. **2.** certain diseases of plants; a liver disease of a sheep. **3.** (*Brit. slang*) nonsense; rubbish. **—*interj.*** an exclamation expressing disgust, contempt, etc. ¶*Rot!*①
—[自] 썩다, 부패하다; 타락하다 —[他] …을 썩이다; 못쓰게 만들다
—[名] 1. 부패; 부패물 2. 부패병, [양의] 디스토마병 3. 《英俗》 허튼소리 —[感] 시시하다! ¶①시시하다!

Ro·tar·i·an [routέəriən] *n.* [C] a member of a Rotary Club. **—*adj.*** of Rotary Clubs.
—[名] 로우터리 클럽의 회원 —[形] 로우터리 클럽의

ro·ta·ry [róutəri] *adj.* turning around; rotating. ¶*a* ~ *fan*① / *a* ~ *machine* (or *press*).② **—*n.*** (pl. **-ries**) **1.** [C] a rotary machine. **2.** 《*R*-》 =Rotary Club.
—[形] 회전하는 ¶①선풍기/②윤전기
—[名] 1. 윤전기

Rotary Club [ˊ-- ˌ] *n.* an association of business and professional men organized for social and charitable purposes.
—[名] 로우터리 클럽

ro·tate [róuteit / -ˊ] *vi.* turn on an axis; revolve; take turns. ¶*The earth rotates on its axis.*① **—*vt.*** cause (something) to turn on an axis; cause (something) to take turns or to happen in turns. ¶~ *crops.*②
—[自] 회전하다; 순환하다; 교대하다 ¶①지구는 지축으로 자전한다 —[他] …을 회전시키다; 교대시키다 ¶②윤작(輪作)하다

ro·ta·tion [routéiʃ(ə)n] *n.* [U][C] the act of rotating; the state of being rotated.
—[名] 회전; 순환; 교대

by (or ***in***) ***rotation,*** in turn; in regular succession.
[熟] 차례로; 윤번으로

ro·ta·to·ry [róutətɔ̀ːri / róutət(ə)ri, routéitə-] *adj.* rotary; rotating.
—[形] 회전하는; 순환하는; 교대하는

rote [rout] *n.* [U] a set, mechanical way of doing something.
—[名] 기계적 방법

by rote, by memory. ¶*learn by* ~.①
[熟] 기계적으로; 암기로 ¶①암기하다

***rot·ten** [rátn / rɔ́tn] *adj.* (~·**er**, ~·**est**) **1.** decayed; spoiled. **2.** corrupt. **3.** (*slang*) bad; disagreeable.
—[形] 1. 썩은, 부패한 2. 타락한 3. 《俗》 열등한; 불쾌한

rot·ten·ness [rátnnis / rɔ́t-] *n.* [U] the state of being rotten; decay; corruption.
—[名] 부패; 타락; 하등

ro·tund [routʌ́nd] *adj.* **1.** round; plump. **2.** (of a voice, speech, etc.) full-sounding; (of an expression, a style, etc.) exaggerated.
—[形] 1. 토실토실 살찐 2. 목소리가 낭랑한; [표현·문체 따위가] 과장된

ro·tun·di·ty [routʌ́nditi] *n.* [U] the state of being rotund; roundness.
—[名] 원형; 비만(肥滿); 낭랑함

rou·ble [rúːbl] *n.* [C] a Russian silver coin.
—[名] 루우블(소련의 은화)

rouge [ruːʒ] *n.* [U] red powder or paste used for coloring the cheeks and lips. **—*vi., vt.*** color (something) with rouge.
—[名] [화장용의] 연지, 루우즈
—[自][他] […에] 루우즈를 바르다

R

⁑rough [rʌf] *adj.* **1.** not smooth; not level; coarse. ↔ smooth ¶*~ hands / feel ~ / The road is ~.* **2.** violent; stormy. ¶*~ weather / The sea is ~.* **3.** not gentle; rude; vulgar. ¶*a ~ man / He is ~ in manner.* **4.** (of sounds) harsh; (of tastes) harsh or sharp. ¶*~ music / ~ wine.* **5.** not refined; natural; raw. ¶*~ ruby / a ~ oat*① */ ~ skin.*② **6.** not precise; not complete. ¶*a ~ guess / a ~ estimate*③ */ a ~ sketch.* **7.** (*colloq.*) difficult; severe. ¶*have a ~ time / You are ~ on him in saying so.*④

—[形] 1. 거친, 거칠거칠한; 울퉁불퉁한 2. [날씨가] 험악한, 폭풍우의 3. 난폭한 우악스러운; 거친; 버릇없는 4. 귀에 거슬리는; [맛이] 떫은 5. 가공하지 않은, 날림의 ¶①덜 빻은 호밀/②원피(原皮) 6. 대강의, 대충의 ¶③개산(概算) 7. 《口》 고된, 쓰라린; 엄한 ¶④그를 그렇게 말하는 것은 가혹하다

rough and ready, made in a hurry to use for a short time.

[熟] 임시변통으로 쓰는

—*adv.* roughly.

—[副] 거칠게; 난폭하게; 대충

—*n.* **1.** [U] that which is rough; a rough part of something. **2.** [U] a rough piece ground. **3.** [C] a rough person. **4.** [U] an unfinished or natural state; a rough sketch. **5.** [U] a difficult state. ¶*the ~ and the smooth.*⑤

—[名] 1. 거친 것, 거칠거칠한 것 2. 울퉁불퉁한 토지 3. 난폭자 4. 미완성, 미가공; 밑그림 5. 고생, 신고 ¶⑤인생의 영고성쇠

1) ***in the rough,*** ⓐ in an unfinished or natural state. ⓑ nearly. ⓒ (*colloq.*) in a difficult situation.
2) ***take the rough with the smooth,*** accept facts as they are; be prepared to meet the hardships of life.

[熟] 1)ⓐ미완성의, 미가공의 ⓑ대체로 ⓒ《口》난처하여 2)태평하게 있다; 인생의 고생을 태연히 맞이하다

—*vt.* **1.** make (something) rough. **2.** treat roughly. 《*~ up* something》 **3.** sketch roughly. 《*~ in* or *out* something》 **—*vi.*** become rough; behave roughly.

—[他] 1. …을 거칠거칠하게 하다; 헝클어뜨리다 2. …을 학대하다 3. …의 개요를 쓰다 —[自] 거칠거칠하게 되다; 거칠어지다

rough it, live without comforts or conveniences.

[熟] 불편한 생활을 참다

rough-and-read·y [rʌ́fənrédi] *adj.* rough or crude, but effective enough; hastily prepared.

—[形] 졸속주의의; 임시변통의; 아무렇게나 하는

rough-and-tum·ble [rʌ́fəntʌ́mbl] *adj.* violent and disorderly; disregarding all rules and formalities. **— *n.*** [C] a fight or struggle of this kind.

—[形] 불규칙한; 무모한 —[名] 혼전(混戰); 난투

rough·en [rʌ́fn] *vt., vi.* make (something) rough; become rough.

—[他][自] 거칠게 하다(되다)

rough-hew [rʌ́fhjúː] *vt.* (**-hewed, -hewn** or **-hewed**) cut or chop (stone, timber, etc.) roughly or without smoothing; shape or form roughly.

—[他] [돌·재목 따위]를 대충 자르다(다듬다); …을 날림으로 만들다

rough-hewn [rʌ́fhjúːn] *v.* pp. of **rough-hew.**
—*adj.* roughly shaped; rugged; unpolished.

—[形] 대충 다듬은; 교양 없는, 투박한

•rough·ly [rʌ́fli] *adv.* **1.** in a rough manner. **2.** approximately.

—[副] 1. 거칠게; 난폭하게 2. 대충, 대략

rough·ness [rʌ́fnis] *n.* [U] the state or quality of being rough; harshness; coarseness.

—[名] 거칢; 난폭; 교양 없음

rough·rid·er [rʌ́fràidər] *n.* [C] a person who is skilled in breaking in and riding rough wild horses.

—[名] 야생마 조마사(調馬師)

rough-spo·ken [rʌ́fspòuk(ə)n] *adj.* using rough, coarse language.

—[形] 말투가 거친

rou·lette [ru(ː)lét] *n.* **1.** [U] a gambling game played with a turning wheel and a ball. ⇒fig. **2.** [C] a small, toothed wheel for making rows of marks or dots.

—[名] 1. 루울렛 노름 2. 톱니바퀴 점선기(點線器)

〔roulette wheel〕

Rou·ma·ni·a [ru(ː)méiniə] *n.* =Rumania.

Rou·ma·ni·an [ru(ː)méiniən] *adj., n.* =Rumanian.

⁑round [raund] *adj.* **1.** shaped like a ball, ring, circle or cylinder; curved like part of a circle. ¶*a ~ apple / a ~ table / a ~ window / a ~ arch.*① **2.** nicely fat; plump. ¶*a ~ face.* **3.** moving in a circle. ¶*a ~ trip*② */ a ~ dance.*③ **4.** (of a voice) full, rich, and loud; sonorous; (of a style) flowing; (of a taste) rich and mellow. ¶*a ~ voice / a ~ style / a ~ wine.* **5.** full; complete. ¶*a ~ dozen / a ~ trick*④ */ a ~ angle.*⑤ **6.** pretty much; ample. ¶*a good ~ sum of money.* **7.** nearly correct; approximate. ¶*in ~ numbers.*⑥ **8.** frank; honest. ¶*a ~ oath / be ~ with others.*⑦ **9.** vigorous; brisk.

—[形] 1. 둥근; 구형(球形)의; 원통형의; 반원형의 ¶①반원 아아치 2. 포동포동 살찐 3. 한 바퀴 도는; 일주하는 ¶②일주 여행/③원무 4. [목소리가] 낭랑하게 울리는; [문체가] 유창한; 맛이 나는 5. 순전한; 완전한 ¶④순전한 속임수/⑤360° 6. 상당한; 꽤 많은 7. 개수(概數)의; 대강의 ¶⑥개수(概數)로 8. 솔직한, 정직한 ¶⑦…에게 솔직하게 말하다 9. 기운찬; 쾌속의

—*n.* [C] **1.** something round. ¶*this earthly ~*⑧ */ dance in a ~.* **2.** a circular course; a regular course. ¶*go*

—[名] 1. 원, 원형물, 고리; 공, 고리 모양의 것, 원통형의 것 ¶⑧지구 2. 일주,

*for a long ~ | a policeman on his rounds.*⑨ **3.** a series or succession of actions, events, duties, etc. ¶*a ~ of visits*⑩ | *one's daily ~*⑪ | *the ~ of the seasons.* **4.** a group of people. ¶*a ~ of students.* **5.** a part into which a fight or a game is divided. ¶*a fight of fifteen rounds.*⑫ **6.** (*Music*) a song sung by several persons beginning at different times; a dance which moves in a circle.

한 바퀴 돌기; 순회[구역] ¶⑨순찰중인 순경 **3.** 연속; 순환 ¶⑩순방(巡訪)/⑪나날의 일 **4.** 일단의 사람 **5.** 한 승부(시합) ¶⑫15회전 **6.** 윤창; 원무

go the round*[*s*] *of (=*be passed around*) *a place.*

[熟] [소문이] …에 퍼지다

—*adv.* =around.
1) ***round about,*** ⓐ in every direction around. ⓑ in or to the opposite direction.
2) ***round and round,*** many times around.

[熟] 1)ⓐ빙 돌아서; 둘레에 ⓑ반대 방향으로 2)몇 번이고

—*prep.* =around.
—*vt.* **1.** make (something) round. ¶~ *one's eyes.* **2.** complete. **3.** go around. ¶~ *a corner* | ~ *an island.*
—*vi.* **1.** become round. **2.** develop. 《~ *into* something》 ¶~ *into womanhood.*⑬ **3.** go around; turn around. ¶~ *on one's heels* | ~ *to the right.*
1) ***round off,*** ⓐ make (something) round. ⓑ complete.
2) ***round*** (=*make a sudden, usu. verbal attack*) ***on*** (or ***upon***) *someone.*
3) ***round out,*** ⓐ make or become round. ⓑ complete.
4) ***round up,*** ⓐ drive (cattle, etc.) together. ⓑ gather.

—[他] **1.** …을 둥글게 하다 **2.** …을 완성하다 **3.** …을 돌다, 일주하다
—[自] **1.** 둥글게 되다, 원형이 되다 **2.** 발달하다, 원숙해지다 ¶⑬여자다와지다 **3.** 순회하다; 돌다
[熟] 1)ⓐ…을 둥글게 하다 ⓑ…을 완성하다 2)…을 욕하다 3)ⓐ…을 둥글게 하다(되다) ⓑ…을 완성하다 4)ⓐ…을 몰아 모으다 ⓑ…을 모으다

round·a·bout [ráundəbàut] *adj.* not direct; not straightforward. ¶*in a ~ way.*① **—***n.* [C] **1.** an indirect way. **2.** (*Brit.*) a merry-go-round. **3.** (*Brit.*) a place where all traffic follows a circular, indirect course. **4.** a short jacket for boys.

—[形] 멀리 도는, 우회(迂回)하는 ¶① 멀리 돌아서 —[名] **1.** 에움길, 우회로 **2.** 회전목마 **3.** 환상(環狀) 교차점 **4.** 남아용 짧은 자켓

R

roun·del [ráundl] *n.* [C] **1.** something round; a small round ornament, shield, window, etc. **2.** a rondo.

—[名] **1.** 작은 원형물; 원형 문장(紋章); 원형의 방패, 작은 원창(圓窓) **2.** 론도

roun·de·lay [ráundilèi] *n.* [C] a short song in which one part is continually repeated.

—[名] 짧은 후렴이 있는 노래

round·er [ráundər] *n.* [C] **1.** a person who makes a round of calls. **2.** a tool which rounds a thing. **3.** 《*pl.*, used as *sing.*》 a game somewhat like baseball.

—[名] **1.** 순회자 **2.** 둥글게 하는 도구 **3.** 야구 비슷한 일종의 게임

Round·head [ráundhèd] *n.* [C] a member of the Parliament side in the English Civil War of the 17th century, so called from his close-cut hair.

—[名] 원두파(圓頭派) 의회 당원

round·house [ráundhàus] *n.* [C] **1.** a cabin on the after part of a ship's deck. **2.** a circular building in which locomotives are stored and repaired.

—[名] **1.** 후갑판의 선실 **2.** 원형 기관차고

round·ish [ráundiʃ] *adj.* rather round.

—[形] 둥그스름한

round·ly [ráundli] *adv.* **1.** in a round form. **2.** in plain words. **3.** fully; completely.

—[副] **1.** 원형으로 **2.** 솔직하게 **3.** 완전히

round-shoul·dered [ráundʃóuldərd] *adj.* having the shoulders bent forward.

—[形] 어깨가 둥근, 새우 등의

round table [ˊ ˊ-] *n.* a group of persons gathered together for an informal discussion; such a discussion.

—[名] 원탁을 둘러앉은 사람들; 원탁회의

round trip [ˊ ˊ] *n.* (*U.S.*) a trip to a place and back to the starting point. (cf. *Brit.* return trip)

—[名] 《美》 왕복 여행

round·up [ráundʌ̀p] *n.* [C] **1.** (*U.S.*) the act of driving cattle, etc. together. **2.** any act of gathering persons together.

—[名] **1.** 《美》 가축을 몰아 모으기 **2.** 사람을 모으기, 소집

* **rouse** [rauz] *vt.* **1.** waken; excite. ¶~ *oneself* | ~ *someone to action* | ~ *someone from sleep.* **2.** stir up; mix well. **3.** cause (an animal or a bird) to leave a hiding place. **—***vi.* awake from sleep; become active.

—[他] **1.** …의 눈을 뜨게 하다; …을 분기시키다 **2.** …을 휘젓다 **3.** [짐승]을 몰아내다 —[自] 눈을 뜨다; 분기하다

rout[1] [raut] *n.* **1.** [U] a noisy, disorderly crowd. **2.** [U][C] a disorderly flight of defeated army. ¶*put to ~.*① **—***vt.* make (an enemy) run away.

—[名] **1.** 폭도, 혼란된 군중 **2.** 패주 ¶① 패주시키다 —[他] [적]을 패주시키다

rout[2] [raut] *vt., vi.* dig up.

—[他][自] 파 일으키다

⁑ **route** [ru:t] *n.* [C] a road; a way; a course. ¶*an air ~*① | *take one's ~ to the destination*② | *en* [ã] *~.*③ **—***vt.* arrange the route for (something); send (something) by a certain route.

—[名] 길; 노정(路程); 항로 ¶①항공로/②목적지로 향해 나아가다/③도중에 —[他] …의 노정을 정하다; …을 발송하다

* **rou·tine** [ruːtíːn] *n.* **1.** [C] a regular way of doing something. ¶*an official* ~① | *the daily* ~ *of classes and homework*② | *the day's* ~.③ **2.** [U] the ordinary course. —*adj.* of a routine; regular.
—[名] 1. 날마다 되풀이되는 틀에 박힌 일, 일과 ¶①기계적인 일과/②수업과 숙제의 일과/③일과 2. 관례 —[形] 틀에 박힌

* **rove** [rouv] *vi.* wander about; go from place to place. —*vt.* wander over. —*n.* [C] the act of roving.
—[自] 헤매다; 배회하다 —[他] …을 배회하다 —[名] 배회

rov·er [róuvər] *n.* [C] **1.** a wanderer. **2.** (*archaic*) a pirate; a pirate ship.
—[名] 1. 배회자 2.《古》 해적; 해적선

‡ **row**¹ [rou] *n.* [C] a line of people, houses, seats, etc. standing side by side. ¶*a* ~ *of houses* | *in rows.*①
—[名] 열, 줄, 늘어선 집들(가로수·좌석) ¶①열을 이루어

‡ **row**² [rou] *vi.* move a boat by means of oars. —*vt.* **1.** propel (a boat) by means of oars. ¶~ *40 to the minute* | ~ *a fast stroke.*① **2.** carry (something) in a boat. **3.** perform (a race, etc.) by rowing. ¶~ *a race.* **row down,** overtake by rowing.
—*n.* [C] the act of using oars; a trip in a rowboat.
—[自] 배를 젓다 —[他] 1. [배]를 젓다 ¶①힘차게 젓다 2. …을 저어서 나르다 3. …을 저어서 경쟁하다
[熟] 저어서 쫓아가다
—[名] 젓기, 뱃놀이

row³ [rau] *n.* (*colloq.*) **1.** [U] loud noise. **2.** [C] a noisy quarrel. ¶*make* (or *kick up*) *a* ~.① —*vi.* (*colloq.*) quarrel noisily; make much noise.
—[名] 1.《口》 소동, 법석 2. 싸움, 말다툼 ¶①소동을 일으키다 —[自] 떠들다; 싸움을 하다

row·an [róuən, ráu-] *n.* [C] a shrub of the rose family; its red berry.
—[名] 산마가목; 그 붉은 열매

row·boat [róubòut] *n.* [C] a boat moved by means of oars.
—[名] [노로 젓는] 보우트

row·dy [ráudi] *adj.* (**-di·er, -di·est**) rough; noisy and rude. —*n.* [C] (pl. **-dies**) a rowdy person.
—[形] 난폭한, 시끄러운 —[名] 난폭자, 시끄러운 사람

row·dy·ish [ráudiiʃ] *adj.* rowdy; rough and disorderly.
—[形] 난폭한, 시끄러운

row·dy·ism [ráudiìz(ə)m] *n.* [U] rough, noisy behavior.
—[名] 난폭, 시끄러움

row·ing boat [róuiŋbòut] *n.* (*Brit.*) a rowboat.
—[名]《英》 [노로 젓는] 보우트

row·lock [rʌ́lək / rɔ́lək, rʌ́-] *n.* [C] a wooden or metal part on a boat to hold the oar; an oarlock. ⇒oarlock (fig.)
—[名] 노받이

Roy [rɔi] *n.* a man's name.
—[名] 남자 이름

‡ **roy·al** [rɔ́i(ə)l] *adj.* **1.** of a king or queen. ¶*a* ~ *palace*① | *a* ~ *crown*② | *a* ~ *prince* (*princess*).③ **2.** under the rule of a king or queen; having the rank of a king or queen. ¶*a* ~ *charter*④ | *the* ~ *forest.*⑤ **3.** fit for a king or queen; noble; majestic. ¶*behave with* ~ *dignity.* **4.** (*colloq.*) splendid; fine; excellent. ¶*be in* ~ *spirits.*⑥
—[形] 1. 왕(여왕)의 ¶①왕궁/②왕관/③왕자(왕녀) 2. 왕립의; 칙허(勅許)의; 왕위의 ¶④칙허장(勅許狀)/⑤왕실림(王室林) 3. 왕자(王者)다운; 고귀한; 위엄있는 4.《口》 멋들어진, 훌륭한 ¶⑥아주 원기왕성하다

roy·al·ist [rɔ́iəlist] *n.* [C] a supporter of a king or a royal government.
—[名] 왕당파; 왕당원

roy·al·ly [rɔ́iəli] *adv.* in a royal or majestic manner.
—[副] 왕답게; 장엄하게

roy·al·ty [rɔ́i(ə)lti] *n.* (pl. **-ties**) **1.** [U] the rank or power of a king or queen. ¶*a symbol of* ~. **2.** [C] 《usu. *pl.*》 a royal person; 《*collectively*》 royal persons. **3.** [U] royal quality; kingliness. **4.** [C] a payment to the owner of a copyright or patent.
—[名] 1. 왕위; 왕권 2. 왕족 3. 왕의 존엄성; 왕자의 위풍 4. 인세(印稅); 특허권 사용료

‡ **rub** [rʌb] *v.* (**rubbed, rub·bing**) *vt.* **1.** press (one thing) against another and move it back and forth, or up and down. ¶~ *one's hands with soap* | ~ *lotion on one's skin* | *The dog rubbed its head against his legs.*① **2.** clean or polish (something) by rubbing; wipe thoroughly. 《~ someone or something *dry, clean,* etc.》 ¶*I rubbed myself dry.*② **3.** make (something) sore by rubbing. ¶*My shoe is rubbing my heel.*③ —*vi.* **1.** move with pressure against something. ¶*The door rubbed on the floor.* **2.** keep going with difficulty; manage to exist. 《~ *along* (or *on, through*) something》 ¶~ *along through life*④ | ~ *through the world.*⑤
—[他] 1. …을 문지르다, 마찰하다 ¶①그 개는 머리를 그의 발에 비볐다 2. …을 닦다; 닦아 내다 ¶②나는 몸을 닦아 말렸다 3. …을 스쳐 다치다, 까다 ¶③구두에 발꿈치가 까지다 —[自] 1. 까지다; 마찰하다 2. 애써 나아가다; 그럭저럭 해나가다 ¶④이럭저럭 생활해 가다/⑤이럭저럭 세상을 살아가다

1) ***rub down,*** ⓐ give a massage to (someone). ⓑ polish, smooth, or wear down (something) by rubbing.
2) ***rub elbows*** (or ***shoulders***) ***with*** (=*meet and mix with*) *someone.*
[熟] 1)ⓐ…을 마사아지하다 ⓑ…을 닦다, 문지르다 2)…와 교제하다

—*n.* [C] **1.** an act of rubbing. ¶*give something a* ~.⑥ **2.** an obstacle; a difficulty. ¶*the rubs and worries of life*⑦ | *There's the* ~.⑧
—[名] 1. 마찰 ¶⑥…을 닦다 2. 장애, 곤란 ¶⑦인생의 고달픔/⑧그게 큰일이야

rub-a-dub [rʌ́bədʌ̀b] *n.* [C] the sound made by beating a drum; a loud noise.
—[名] 둥둥(북소리)

rubber

:rub·ber[1] [rΛ́bər] *n.* **1.** Ⓤ an elastic substance produced from the milky juice of certain trees; Ⓒ something made of this substance. ¶*crude ~*① / *natural ~*② / *synthetic ~*.③ **2.** (*pl.*) (*U.S.*) overshoes made of rubber. —*adj.* made of rubber. —*vt.* cover or coat (something) with rubber.
—图 1.고무; 고무 제품 ¶①생고무/②천연 고무/③인조 고무 2.(美) 고무 덧신 —图 고무로 만든 —他 …에 고무를 입히다

rub·ber[2] [rΛ́bər] *n.* (*the ~*) Ⓒ the winning of a series of two games out of three games in cards; the deciding game in such a series.
—图 3판 2승의 승부; 결승전

rub·ber·ize [rΛ́bəràiz] *vt.* cover or treat (something) with rubber.
—他 …에 고무를 입히다

• **rub·bish** [rΛ́biʃ] *n.* Ⓤ **1.** waste material; trash. **2.** worthless ideas; nonsense. ¶*Don't talk ~.* / *Oh, ~ !*
—图 1.쓰레기; 폐물 2:시시한 생각; 터무니없는 일

rub·bish·y [rΛ́biʃi] *adj.* like rubbish; worthless.
—形 쓰레기의,폐물의; 시시한

rub·ble [rΛ́bl] *n.* Ⓤ rough broken pieces of stone, rock, brick, etc.
—图 으스러진 돌, 자갈

ru·bi·cund [rúːbikΛnd / -kənd] *adj.* (of the face, etc.) reddish; ruddy.
—形 불그스름한, 불그레한

ru·ble [rúːbl] *n.* Ⓒ the unit of money in the Soviet Union.
—图 루우블 화폐

ru·bric [rúːbrik] *n.* Ⓒ **1.** the title of a chapter written or printed in red. **2.** a direction in a prayer book for conducting religious services.
—图 1.붉은 글씨, 주서(朱書) 2. 예배 규정

ru·by [rúːbi] *n.* (pl. **ru·bies**) **1.** Ⓒ a precious red stone. **2.** Ⓤ a deep, glowing red color. —*adj.* deep, glowing red.
—图 1.루우비, 홍옥(紅玉) 2.루우비빛, 진홍색
—形 루우비빛의, 진홍빛의

Ru·by [rúːbi] *n.* a woman's name.
—图 여자 이름

ruck·sack [rΛ́ksæk, rúk-] *n.* Ⓒ a kind of knapsack carried on the back by the straps.
—图 배낭, 룩색

ruc·tion [rΛ́kʃ(ə)n] *n.* Ⓒ (usu. *pl.*) (*colloq.*) trouble; a quarrel.
—图 (口) 소동, 법석; 싸움

rud·der [rΛ́dər] *n.* Ⓒ a flat piece at the back of a ship, boat, or an airplane used to change the course.
—图 [배의] 키; [비행기의] 방향타 (舵)

rud·di·ness [rΛ́dinis] *n.* Ⓤ the state of being ruddy.
—图 붉은 빛, 홍안

rud·dy [rΛ́di] *adj.* (-**di·er**, -**di·est**) red; having the color of good health.
—形 붉은; 혈색이 좋은

:rude [ruːd] *adj.* **1.** rough in manner; impolite. ¶*~ remarks.* **2.** violent; severe. **3.** primitive; uncivilized. **4.** roughly made or done; coarse; raw. ¶*~ cotton / ~ ore.* **5.** unskillful; rough. ¶*a ~ estimate.*
—形 1. 버릇없는, 실례가 되는 2. 난폭한; 격렬한 3.미개한; 교양없는 4. 조립한; 가공하지 않은 5. 솜씨없는; 대강의

ru·di·ment [rúːdimənt] *n.* Ⓒ (usu. *pl.*) **1.** one of the basic principles; the first or beginning of something. ¶*the rudiments of law*① / *learn the rudiments of radio.*② **2.** (of a plant or an animal) an imperfectly developed part or organ.
—图 1. 근본, 기초 원리; 초보 ¶①법학원론/②라디오의 초보를 배우다 2. [생물의] 퇴화한 기관(器官)

ru·di·men·ta·ry [rùːdiméntə(ə)ri] *adj.* **1.** elementary; beginning; basic. **2.** undeveloped.
—形 1. 기본의; 초보의 2. 미발달의

rue[1] [ruː] *vt.* regret; grieve. —*vi.* sorrow; feel sorrow.
—他 …을 후회하다 —自 슬퍼하다

rue[2] [ruː] *n.* Ⓤ a small evergreen shrub with yellow flowers and bitter-tasting leaves. ⇒N.B.
—图 운향(芸香)과의 약초 N.B. 원래 흥분제·자극제로 썼음

rue·ful [rúːf(u)l] *adj.* filled with regret; mournful; causing pity.
—形 후회하는; 슬퍼하고 있는; 불쌍한

rue·ful·ly [rúːfuli] *adv.* in a rueful manner; mournfully.
—副 후회하여, 슬픈 듯이

ruff [rΛf] *n.* Ⓒ **1.** a high, frilled collar worn in the 16th and 17th centuries. ⇒fig. **2.** a ring of feathers or fur like a collar around the neck of a bird or an animal.
—图 1. 주름 웃깃 2. [새·짐승의] 목깃, 목털

[ruff 1.]

ruf·fi·an [rΛ́fiən] *n.* Ⓒ a brutal or cruel person.
—图 악한; 건달

ruf·fi·an·ism [rΛ́fiəniz(ə)m] *n.* Ⓤ brutality; violence.
—图 흉악[성]; 잔인한 행위

ruf·fi·an·ly [rΛ́fiənli] *adj.* like a ruffian; brutal; violent.
—形 악한 같은; 흉악한

• **ruf·fle** [rΛ́fl] *vt.* **1.** fold (cloth, etc.) into ruffles; put ruffles on. **2.** wrinkle; ripple. **3.** make (feathers, etc.) stand up in a ruff. **4.** disturb; irritate. —*vi.* **1.** become wrinkled. **2.** become disturbed. —*n.* Ⓒ **1.** a
—他 1. …에 주름을 잡다 2. …에 구김살지게 하다; …을 물결 일게 하다 3. …을 어지럽히다, 성나게 하다 —自 1. 구겨지다 2. 성내다 —图 1. 주름장식

piece of cloth gathered into folds and used for trimming. **2.** a ruff of feathers or fur. **3.** a ripple. **4.** irritation; a disturbance.
2. 목털 3. 잔물결 4. 짜증; 소동

‡rug [rʌg] *n.* [C] **1.** a heavy mat for covering the floor. **2.** (chiefly *Brit.*) a piece of heavy cloth laid over the knees.
—[名] 1. 깔개, 융단 2.《英》 무릎을 덮는 담요

***Rug·by** [rʌ́gbi] *n.* **1.** a city in central England. **2.** a famous boy's school in that city. **3.** a form of football; Rugby football; rugger.
—[名] 1. 영국의 도시 2. 럭비교(校) 3. 럭비식 축구

‡rug·ged [rʌ́gid] *adj.* (sometimes **~·er, ~·est**) **1.** rough; uneven; steep and rocky. ↔smooth **2.** wrinkled. ¶*~ features.* **3.** rude; unpolished. ¶*~ manners.*① **4.** stern; harsh; severe. ¶*a ~ teacher / a ~ winter.*
—[名] 1. 울퉁불퉁한; 험준한, 바위투성이의 2. 주름살진 3. 세련되지 않은, 투박한 ¶①버릇없음 4. 엄격한; 쓰라린, 고된

rug·ger [rʌ́gər] *n.* [U] (*Brit. slang*) Rugby football.
—[名]《英俗》 럭비, 럭비식 축구

‡ru·in [rú:in / ruin] *n.* [U] **1.** destruction; downfall; decay; bankruptcy. ¶*the ~ of my hopes / The house is falling to ~. / He is on the brink of ~.*① */ He brought his country to ~.*② */ go* (or *come, fall*) *to ~.*③ **2.** 《often *pl.*》 the remains of a building, a wall, etc. destroyed or fallen into decay. ¶*the ruins of Rome*④ */ the ruins of a building.* **3.** 《usu. *sing.*》 a cause of ruin. ¶*Gambling was his ~.*⑤
—[名] 1. 파괴; 멸망; 황폐; 파산 ¶①그는 몰락 일보 직전에 있다/②그는 국가를 멸망시켰다/③멸망하다 2. 폐허 ¶④로마의 폐허 3. 파멸의 원인 ¶⑤그의 파멸의 원인은 노름이다

—*vt.* bring (someone or something) to ruin; destroy. ¶*~ someone's prospects*⑥ */ ~ oneself.*⑦ —*vi.* go or come to ruin.
—[他] …을 파멸시키다 ¶⑥…의 전도의 희망을 파괴하다/⑦패가망신하다
—[自] 파멸하다, 황폐하다

ru·in·a·tion [rù:inéiʃ(ə)n / rùi-] *n.* **1.** [U] ruin; downfall. **2.** [C] a cause of ruin.
—[名] 1. 파괴, 파멸; 영락(零落) 2. 파멸의 원인

ru·in·ous [rú:inəs / rúin-] *adj.* **1.** bringing ruin; destructive. **2.** fallen into ruins.
—[形] 1. 파멸적인 2. 황폐한

‡rule [ru:l] *n.* **1.** [C] a principle that must be kept by all; a regulation; a law. ¶*the rules of the game / the ~ of the air* (*the road*)① */ apply a ~*② */ break a ~ / follow* (or *observe*) *the ~.* **2.** [C] a usual way; a custom; a habit. ¶*I make it a ~* (or *It is a ~ with me*) *to take a walk in the park every morning.*③ **3.** [C] something common; a standard. **4.** [U] control; government. ¶*The islands are under direct ~ of the United States.*
—[名] 1. 법칙, 규칙; 규정 ¶①항공(교통)규칙/②규칙을 적용하다 2. 습관 ¶③나는 매일 아침 공원을 산책하기로 하고 있다 3. 통칙(通則); 표준 4. 지배; 통치

1) ***as a rule,*** usually.
2) ***by rule,*** according to rules.
[熟] 1)대체로, 일반적으로 2)규정대로

—*vt.* **1.** govern; control. ¶*~ one's country.* **2.** control (one's desires, etc.). ¶*~ one's appetite.* **3.** give a formal decision; determine. 《*~ that …*》 ¶*The judge ruled that he had no right to claim the property.*④ **4.** 《usu. in *passive*》 guide; have an influence over. ¶*be ruled by one's passions.* **5.** draw (a straight line) with a ruler; mark a straight line on (paper, etc.) with a ruler. ¶*~ lines on the sheet; ~ the sheet / He rules his paper neatly.* —*vi.* **1.** govern. 《*~ over* someone or something》 **2.** make a formal decision. ¶*The chairman has ruled on the question.* **3.** (of prices, etc.) have a certain general level; be current. ¶*The prices ~ high. / The crops ~ good.*⑤
—[他] 1. …을 지배하다, 통치하다 2. …을 억누르다 3. …을 규정하다; 판결하다 ¶④판사는 그 재산을 요구할 권리가 그에게 없다고 판결했다 4. …을 지도하다; 좌우하다 5. [선]을 자로 긋다; …에 괘선을 치다 —[自] 1. 지배하다, 통치하다 2. 판결하다; 판단하다 3. [시세 따위가] 대체로 …의 상태를 유지하다; 보합하다 ¶⑤작물은 대체로 양호하다

rule out (or ***off***), exclude.
[熟] …을 제외하다

‡rul·er [rú:lər] *n.* [C] **1.** a person who rules. **2.** a strip of wood, metal, etc. used in drawing lines or in measuring.
—[名] 1. 지배자, 통치자 2. 자

rul·ing [rú:liŋ] *adj.* **1.** governing. ¶*the ~ classes.* **2.** chief. **3.** general. ¶*the ~ price*① */ The ~ feeling of the students is in favor of their new teacher.* —*n.* [C] a decision by a judge; [U] the act of drawing a line.
—[形] 1. 지배하는, 통치하는 2. 유력한, 주된 3. 일반의, 평균의 ¶①시가(時價)
—[名] 판결; 선을 긋기

rum[1] [rʌm] *n.* [U] **1.** a strong alcoholic drink made from sugar cane. **2.** (*U.S.*) any alcoholic drink.
—[名] 1. 럼 술 2.《美》 술

rum[2] [rʌm] *adj.* (*Brit. slang*) odd; queer.
—[形]《英俗》 기묘한; 이상한

Ru·ma·ni·a [ru(:)méiniə] *n.* a country in south central Europe.
—[名] 루마니아

Ru·ma·ni·an [ru(:)méiniən] *adj.* of Rumania, its people or
—[形] 루마니아[사람·말]의

their language. —*n.* [C] a person of Rumania; [U] the language of Rumania.
—[名] 루마니아 사람; 루마니아 말

rum·ba [rʌ́mbə] *n.* [C] a light and quick dance of Cuban Negro origin; a piece of music for this dance.
—[名] 룸바; 그 곡

rum·ble [rʌ́mbl] *vi.* **1.** make a deep rolling sound. **2.** move or go with such a sound. ¶*The train rumbled on.* —*vt.* **1.** cause (something) to make such a sound. **2.** move (something) with such a sound. —*n.* [U][C] a deep rolling sound. ¶*the distant ~ of thunder.*
—[自] 1. 우르르 울리다 2. 덜거덕거리며 가다 —[他] 1. …을 우르르 울리다 2. 덜거덕거리며 가게 하다 —[名] 우르르 (덜거덕) 소리

ru·mi·nant [rú:minənt] *adj.* **1.** (of some grass-eating animals) eating food and then bringing it back from the stomach to chew it again. **2.** (of persons) often meditating; reflective. —*n.* [C] a grass-eating, ruminant animal.
—[形] 1. 반추(反芻)하는 2. 생각에 잠기는 —[名] 반추동물

ru·mi·nate [rú:minèit] *vi., vt.* **1.** chew one's food and bring it back from the stomach to chew it again. **2.** think about (something) deeply; meditate.
—[自][他] 1. 반추(反芻)하다 2. 심사숙고하다, 곰곰이 생각하다

ru·mi·na·tion [rù:minéiʃ(ə)n] *n.* [U] the act of ruminating.
—[名] 반추(反芻); 심사숙고; 묵상

ru·mi·na·tive [rú:minèitiv / -nətiv] *adj.* meditating often.
—[形] 곰곰이 생각하는, 묵상에 잠기는

rum·mage [rʌ́midʒ] *vt.* search thoroughly. —*vi.* make a thorough but disorderly search. —*n.* [U] **1.** the act of rummaging. **2.** things found by rummaging; odds and ends.
—[他] …을 샅샅이 뒤지다 —[自] 휘저어서 찾다 —[名] 1. 샅샅이 뒤지기 2. 잡동사니, 쓰레기

rummage sale, a sale of odds and ends.
[熟] 재고품 정리 판매

rum·my [rʌ́mi] *adj.* (**-mi·er, -mi·est**) =rum.[2]

* **ru·mor,** *Brit.* **-mour** [rú:mər] *n.* [C][U] a story that passes from person to person without any proof that it is true; gossip. ¶*start a ~*① / *Rumor says* (or *has it*) *that war will break out.*② —*vt.* tell or spread (something) by rumor. ¶*It is rumored that …*③
—[名] 소문, 풍설 ¶①소문을 내다/②전쟁이 일어날 것이라는 소문이다 —[他] …의 소문을 하다 ¶③…이라는 소문이다

rump [rʌmp] *n.* [C] the back part of an animal; a cut of meat from this part.
—[名] 엉덩이, [소의] 엉덩이 살

rum·ple [rʌ́mpl] *vt.* gather up (paper or cloth) in a disorderly way. —*n.* [C] a state of being rumpled.
—[他] …을 구기다 —[名] 구김살

rum·pus [rʌ́mpəs] *n.* [C] 《*sing.* only》 (*colloq.*) noise; uproar.
—[名] 《口》 소동

‡ **run** [rʌn] *v.* (**ran, run, run·ning**) *vi.* **1.** move with quick steps; move faster than in walking. **2.** hasten; rush. ¶*~ through one's work*① / *~ to catch the train.* **3.** take part in a race; offer oneself as a candidate in an election. ¶*~ in a race*② / *~ for President.*③ **4.** (of a train, a bus, a ship, etc.) start and arrive regularly. ¶*The buses ~ every five minutes.*④ / *Trains ~ very often between Seoul and Incheon* ⑤ **5.** move at a certain speed. ¶*~ at 60 miles an hour.* **6.** (of time) pass; go by. ¶*How fast the years ~ by!* **7.** (of a stream, etc.) flow along; (of a liquid) flow; be covered with a flow of a liquid; overflow. ¶*Rivers run into the sea.* / *A nose runs.*⑥ / *The floor ran with water.*⑦ **8.** melt and spread to other parts. ¶*The ink runs on this paper.*⑧ **9.** work; operate. ¶*This machine runs by electricity.* / *Things ~ smoothly.*⑨ **10.** (of fire, news, etc.) spread rapidly. ¶*Fire ran along the ground.* / *The rumor runs that he is sick.* **11.** (of thoughts, eyes, etc.) pass quickly. ¶*A thought ran through my mind.* / *His eyes ran over the room.* / *A cold shiver ran down his spine.*⑩ **12.** extend; stretch out. ¶*The road runs some miles by the sea.*⑪ **13.** continue. ¶*The play ran for a year.*⑫ / *The law runs for ten years.* **14.** become. 《*~ high, low,* etc.》 ¶*~ mad* / *~ big* / *~ strong* / *~ dry* / *~ short.*⑬ **15.** be written or expressed. ¶*So the story runs.* / *The letter runs as follows.* —*vt.* **1.** cause (someone or something) to run or move; work; operate. ¶*~ a horse to death*⑭ / *~ a steamer* / *~ a sewing ma-*
—[自] 1. 달리다, 뛰다 2. 서두르다, 돌진하다 ¶①일을 급히 해치우다 3. 경주에 나가다; 입후보하다 ¶②레이스에 출전하다/③대통령으로 입후보하다 4. 운행하다, 다니다 ¶④버스는 5분마다 다닌다/⑤서울·인천 사이는 기차가 많이 있다 5. 어떤 속도로 달리다 6. [시간이] 경과하다 7. [강 따위가] 흐르다; [액체가] 흐르다, 엎질러지다 ¶⑥콧물이 나오다/⑦마루에 물이 흘렀다 8. 녹아서 번지다, 스며 나오다 ¶⑧잉크는 종이에 번진다 9. 운전하다, 움직이다 ¶⑨만사가 잘돼 가다 10. 급히 퍼지다 11. [생각 따위가] 갑자기 떠오르다, 나타나다; 대충 훑어보다 ¶⑩그는 등골이 오싹했다 12. 뻗다, 미치다, 걸치다 ¶⑪도로는 해안에 수마일 뻗어 있다 13. 계속하다 ¶⑫그 연극은 1년간 공연되었다 14. …이 되다 ¶⑬부족해지다 15. …이라고 씌어 있다 —[他] 1. …을 달리게 하다; 움직이다; 운전하다; ¶⑭말을 너무 타서 죽이다 2. …에서 도망치다 ¶⑮망명하다 3. …을 몰아대다; 쫓다 4. 달려서 …을 하다, 달려서 [어떤 거리를] 가다 ¶⑯경주하다/⑰심부름을 하다 5. 달려서 …을 지나가다; [어떤 거리]를 달리다 ¶⑱주루(走壘)하다 6. …을 입후보시키다 ¶⑲…

chine. **2.** escape from (a place). ¶~ *one's country.*[16] **3.** drive (an animal); hunt; trace. **4.** do (something) by running or by moving. ¶~ *a race*[16] | ~ *errands*[17] **5.** run along (a road, etc.); go over (a distance) by running. ¶~ *the streets* | ~ *bases.*[18] **6.** support (someone) to be elected. ¶~ *someone for the Senate.*[19] **7.** cause (one's eyes, etc.) to pass quickly. ¶~ *one's eyes over a letter* | ~ *one's fingers over the keys of a piano.* **8.** drive; thrust. ¶~ *a thread through a needle's eye*[20] | ~ *one's hand into one's pocket.* **9.** cause (water, etc.) to flow. ¶~ *tears.* **10.** manage; conduct. ¶~ *a hotel* | ~ *a campaign.*[21] **11.** expose oneself to (danger, adventure, etc.) ¶~ *the risk of.* **12.** publish; print.

을 상원에 입후보시키다 **7.** 대충 …을 훑어보다 **8.** …을 꿰찌르다, 꿰뚫다 ¶⑳바늘귀에 실을 꿰다 **9.** …을 흘리다, 흐르게 하다 **10.** …을 경영하다; 지휘하다 ¶㉑정치 운동을 지휘하다 **11.** [위험 따위]를 초래하다; 무릅쓰다 **12** …을 발표하다, 게재하다

1) ***run across,*** meet (someone) by chance; find.
2) ***run after,*** follow and try to catch; pursue.
3) ***run against,*** ⓐ rush against; collide with (something). ⓑ meet (someone) by chance.
4) ***run at*** (=*attack*) *someone* or *something.*
5) ***run away,*** ⓐ escape; flee. ⓑ go away; leave home and go elsewhere.
6) ***run away with,*** ⓐ carry off; steal. ⓑ go away with (someone). ⓒ cause (someone) to lose self-control. ¶*Don't let your anger ~ away with you.*
7) ***run down,*** ⓐ (of a machine) stop operating. ⓑ catch (someone) after a long pursuit. ⓒ knock down; collide with (something). ⓓ speak ill of (someone). ⓔ ⟪in *passive*⟫ be in weak health.
8) ***run for it,*** (*colloq.*) run in order to escape or avoid something.
9) ***run in,*** ⓐ seize (someone) by authority of the law; arrest. ⓑ visit casually.
10) ***run into,*** ⓐ strike against (another car, etc.). ⓑ meet (someone) by chance. ⓒ pass into a certain condition. ¶~ *into danger* (*trouble*). ⓓ amount to (a certain degree). ⓔ follow; succeed.
11) ***run off,*** ⓐ run away. ⓑ flow away; cause (water, etc.) to flow away. ⓒ write or speak fluently.
12) ***run on,*** ⓐ (of written letters) be joined together. ⓑ continue.
13) ***run out,*** come to an end; become used up.
14) ***run out of*** (=*use up; have no more of*) *something.*
15) ***run over,*** ⓐ do again; repeat. ⓑ ride or drive over (someone). ⓒ overflow.
16) ***run through,*** ⓐ examine, review, etc. quickly. ⓑ pierce. ⓒ use up (something) carelessly or recklessly.
17) ***run to,*** ⓐ reach (an amount, a number, etc.). ⓑ have money for (something); (of money) be enough for (something).
18) ***run up,*** ⓐ increase; cause (something) to increase. ⓑ raise; hoist. ⓒ add up (a column of figures). ⓓ do (something) rapidly.
19) ***run upon,*** ⓐ strike. ⓑ (of thoughts, etc.) be concerned with (something). ⓒ meet (someone) by chance.

[熟] 1)…에 마주치다 2)…의 뒤를 쫓다 3)ⓐ…에 충돌하다 ⓑ마주치다 4)…을 습격하다 5)ⓐ도주하다; 탈주하다 ⓑ가출하다 6)ⓐ…을 가지고 도망치다; 훔치다 ⓑ…을 데리고 도망치다, …와 함께 도망가다 ⓒ[감정 따위]에 치우치다 7)ⓐ[기계 따위]가 서다, 멎다 ⓑ…을 몰아내다가 잡다 ⓒ쓰러뜨리다; 충돌하다 ⓓ…을 헐뜯다 ⓔ쇠약하다 8)⟪口⟫도망치다 9)ⓐ…을 체포하다, 구류하다 ⓑ…을 우연히 찾아가다 10)ⓐ…와 충돌하다 ⓑ뜻밖에 …와 마주치다 ⓒ[어떤 상태에] 빠지다 ⓓ…에 달하다 ⓔ…에 계속하다 11)ⓐ도망치다 ⓑ유출하다; …을 유출시키다 ⓒ막힘없이 쓰다(읽다) 12)ⓐ[글씨체가] 끊이지 않고 이어 나가다 ⓑ…을 계속하다 13)끝나다, 다되다 14)…을 다 써 버리다 15)ⓐ…을 복습하다; 되풀이하다 ⓑ[차가] …을 치다 ⓒ넘치다 16)ⓐ…을 대충 훑어보다 ⓑ…을 꿰뚫다 ⓒ…을 다 써 버리다 17)ⓐ[수량이] …에 달하다 ⓑ…의 자력이 있다; [돈이] …에 충분하다 18)ⓐ올라가다, 오르다; …을 올리다 ⓑ…을 게양하다 ⓒ[숫자를] 급히 보태다 ⓓ황급히 …하다 19)ⓐ…을 치다 ⓑ[생각이] …에 미치다 ⓒ…을 뜻밖에 만나다

—*n.* [C] **1.** the act of running; a running pace. ¶*at a ~*[22] | *take a ~.*[23] **2.** [U] capacity for running. ¶*There is no more ~ left in him.*[24] **3.** a quick trip. ¶*a ~ on the Continent.* **4.** the distance covered. ¶*a ~ of a mile* | *the train's ~ from Tokyo to Osaka.* **5.** continuation; succession. ¶*a ~ of good weather* | *The play had a long ~.*[25] **6.** free use. ¶*I give you the ~ of my car.*[26] **7.** the average sort. ¶*the common ~ of men.*[27] **8.** [C] (*Baseball*) a scoring point. ¶*score two runs.*

—[名] **1.** 달리기; 구보 ¶㉒구보로/㉓한바탕 달리다 **2.** 달리는 힘, 주력 ¶㉔그에게는 이제 달릴 힘이 없다 **3.** 여행 **4.** 주행 거리 **5.** 연속 ¶㉕그 연극은 장기 흥행을 했다 **6.** 사용의 자유 ¶㉖내 차를 마음대로 써도 좋다 **7.** 보통 정도 ㉗ ¶보통 사람 **8.** ⟪野球⟫ 득점, 1점

1) ***by the run,*** suddenly.
2) ***in the long run,*** finally.
3) ***on the run,*** ⓐ in flight. ⓑ continuously active.

[熟] 1)갑자기 2)결국, 드디어 3)ⓐ도주하여 ⓑ바빠서, 다망하여

R

run·a·bout [rʌ́nəbàut] *n.* [C] **1.** a person who runs about from one place to another. **2.** a light, open automobile; a light motorboat.
—[名] 1. 떠돌아다니는 사람 2. 소형 자동차; 소형 모우터 보우트

run·a·way [rʌ́nəwèi] *n.* **1.** [C] a person, horse, etc. that runs away or escapes. **2.** [U] the act of running away. —*adj.* escaping. ¶*a ~ horse.*①
—[名] 1. 도망자, 탈주자; 도망친 말 2. 도망, 탈주 —[形] 도망친 ¶①도망친 말

run-down [rʌ́ndàun] *adj.* **1.** tired; sick. **2.** that has stopped working.
—[形] 1. 지친; 건강을 해친 2. [기계가] 움직이지 않는, 것은

rune [ru:n] *n.* [C] **1.** any letter of an ancient alphabet which originated in North Europe. **2.** a magic sign.
—[名] 1. 루운 문자 2. 신비적인 기초

⁑rung[1] [rʌŋ] *v.* pt. and pp. of **ring**[2].

rung[2] [rʌŋ] *n.* [C] one of the steps of a ladder; a cross-piece set between the legs of a chair.
—[名] [사닥다리·의자 다리의] 가로장, 단(段)

ru·nic [rú:nik] *adj.* of or written in runes.
—[形] 루운 문자의(로 쓰어진)

run·let [rʌ́nlit] *n.* [C] a small stream.
—[名] 시내, 개울

run·nel [rʌ́nəl] *n.* [C] a small stream.
—[名] 시내, 개울

***run·ner** [rʌ́nər] *n.* [C] **1.** a person who runs or is running; a racer. **2.** a messenger. **3.** one of the long narrow pieces on which a sleigh slides; the blade of a skate. **4.** a slender, trailing branch that takes root at the end; a plant that spreads in this way, such as a strawberry. ⇒fig.
—[名] 1. 달리는 사람; 경쟁자; 경주 말 2. 사자(使者) 3. 썰매의 활주부; 스케이트의 날 4. 덩굴; 덩굴식물

〔runner 4.〕

⁑run·ning [rʌ́niŋ] *adj.* **1.** moving rapidly; flowing. **2.** going or carried on continuously; repeated continuously. ¶*five times ~.*① **3.** (of plants) creeping. **4.** current. —*n.* [U] something that runs or flows; the amount that runs or flows.
—[形] 1. 달리는, 흐르는 2. 잇따른, 연속적인 ¶①5회 계속하여 3. [식물이] 땅을 기는 4. 현재의, 목하의 —[名] 유출물; 유출량

in (out of) the running, in (out of) the competition; having a chance (no chance) to win.
[熟] 경주에 참가하여(참가하지 않고); 승산이 있는(없는)

running board [ˊ-ˋ] *n.* a board along the side of an automobile on which a person steps to get in or out.
—[名] [자동차 양쪽 문의] 발판

running hand [ˊ-ˋ] *n.* rapid handwriting.
—[名] 초서체

run-off [rʌ́nɔ̀:f / -ɔ̀f] *n.* **1.** [C] a final, deciding race, game, etc. **2.** [U] something that flows out.
—[名] 1. [동점자끼리의] 결승전 2. [빗물 따위] 흐르는 것

runt [rʌnt] *n.* [C] a small-sized animal, person, or plant.
—[名] 작은 동물(사람·식물)

run·way [rʌ́nwèi] *n.* [C] **1.** a track along which something runs or moves. **2.** a beaten way or path along which animals pass.
—[名] 1. 주로(走路), 활주로, 자동차길 2. [동물이] 다니는 길

ru·pee [ru:pí:] *n.* [C] a unit of money in India.
—[名] 루피(인도의 화폐 단위)

rup·ture [rʌ́ptʃər] *n.* **1.** [U][C] the act of bursting or breaking apart. ¶*the ~ of a blood vessel.* **2.** [U][C] an interruption of friendly relations. ¶*come to a ~.* **3.** [C] a hernia. —*vt.* **1.** break apart; burst. **2.** interrupt (a connection, a relation, etc.). **3.** cause a hernia in (someone). —*vi.* **1.** break. **2.** suffer or develop a hernia.
—[名] 1. 파열 2. 단절, 불화, 반목 3. 탈장(脫腸), 헤르니아 —[他] 1. …을 파열시키다 2. …을 불화하게 하다 3. …을 헤르니아에 걸리게 하다 —[自] 1. 째지다 2. 헤르니아에 걸리다

***ru·ral** [rúər(ə)l] *adj.* of the countryside. ↔urban ¶*a ~ area*① / *a ~ life* / *in ~ seclusion.*②
—[形] 전원의, 시골의 ¶①농촌지역/②외따로 떨어져서

ruse [ru:z] *n.* [C] a trick; a deceitful way of acting.
—[名] 계략; 책략

⁑rush[1] [rʌʃ] *vi.* **1.** move with speed; hurry; dash. ¶*~ at the enemy*① / *~ for a good seat* / *Policemen rushed to the spot of murder.* **2.** act swiftly without thinking enough. 《~ *into* something》 ¶*~ into debt*② / *~ to a conclusion.*③ **3.** go or come rapidly or suddenly. ¶*~ into one's mind*④ / *Blood rushed to her face.* **4.** pass rapidly. ¶*The years rushed by us.*⑤ —*vt.* **1.** cause (someone or something) to go or move swiftly; hurry. ¶*The teacher rushed the boy out of the room.* **2.** do swiftly. ¶*~ one's work.* **3.** send or carry swiftly. ¶*~ a message*⑥ / *~ a letter to the post office.* **4.** attack suddenly; get (something) by a sudden attack. ¶*~ a fort* / *~ a bridge.*
—[自] 1. 돌진하다; 돌격하다 ¶①적을 향해 돌격하다 2. 급히 하다; 앞뒤를 헤아리지 않게 하다 ¶②함부로 빚을 지다/③급히 결론을 내리다 3. 급히 나타나다 ¶④갑자기 마음에 떠오르다 4. 빨리 지나가다 ¶⑤세월이 자꾸 지나가다 —[他] 1. …을 돌진시키다; 재촉하다 2. …을 급히 하다 3. …을 급송하다; 급히 나르다 ¶⑥지급보(至急報)로 보내다 4. …을 급습하다

R

—*n.* [C] **1.** the act of rushing. ¶*a ~ of wind*⑦ | *He made a ~ for the door.* **2.** a state of being unusually busy or crowded; a hurry. ¶*a ~ of work*⑧ | *come home during the evening ~*⑨ | *His store has a great ~ of business.* **3.** a great or sudden demand. ⟪*~ on, for*⟫ ¶*a ~ for uranium.*

—[名] 1. 돌진; 돌격 ¶⑦한바탕의 돌풍 2. 몹시 바쁨, 분망; 서두름 ¶⑧산더미 같은 일/⑨붐비는 저녁때에 귀가하다 3. 큰 수요, 주문의 쇄도

with a rush, suddenly and forcefully.

[熟] 왈칵 한꺼번에

—*adj.* that must be done in a hurry; requiring haste; busy; crowded.

—[形] 급한; 바쁜; 쇄도하는

rush² [rʌʃ] *n.* **1.** [C] a plant with tall leaves that grows in or near water; [U] slender long stems of this plant, used for making chair seats, etc. **2.** [C] ⟪usu. in *negative*⟫ something of little or no value. ¶*do not care a ~.*①

—[名] 1. 골풀, 등심초 2. 하찮은 것 ¶①조금도 개의치 않다

rush·y [rʌ́ʃi] *adj.* (**rush·i·er, rush·i·est**) full or made of rushes; covered with rushes.

—[形] 골풀이 많은; 골풀로 만든

rusk [rʌsk] *n.* [C] a piece of bread or cake baked in an oven.

—[名] 화덕으로 누렇게 구운 빵

rus·set [rʌ́sit] *adj.* of reddish brown or yellowish-brown.

—[形] 적갈색의; 황갈색의

—*n.* **1.** [U] reddish brown; yellowish brown. **2.** [U] a rough, russet-colored cloth. **3.** [C] a winter apple with a rough, brownish skin.

—[名] 1. 적갈색; 황갈색 2. 적갈색의 나사천 3. 붉은 겨울 사과

⁑ **Rus·sia** [rʌ́ʃə] *n.* a country in eastern Europe and western and northern Asia; the Soviet Union; the Union of the Soviet Socialist Republics.

—[名] 러시아; 소비에트 연방

⁑ **Rus·sian** [rʌ́ʃ(ə)n] *adj.* of Russia, its people or their language. **—*n.*** [C] a native of Russia; [U] the language of Russian people.

—[形] 러시아의; 러시아 사람(말)의
—[名] 러시아 사람; 러시아 말

Rus·so-Jap·a·nese [rʌ́soudʒæ̀pəní:z] *adj.* Russian and Japanese.

—[形] 일본과 러시아의

* **rust** [rʌst] *n.* [U] **1.** the reddish-brown coating that forms on iron or steel when exposed to air or dampness. ¶*gather ~.*① **2.** a fungus which causes a plant disease with colored spots. **3.** a weakened state of mind.
—*vi.* become covered with rust; grow worthless because of idleness. **—*vt.*** cause (something) to rust.

—[名] 1. 녹 ¶①녹슬다 2. [식물의] 녹병 3. 무디어짐; 무위(無爲), 무활동 —[自] 녹슬다; 무디어지다, 쓸모없게 되다 —[他] …을 녹슬게 하다

* **rus·tic** [rʌ́stik] *adj.* **1.** of the countryside; rural. ↔urban **2.** simple; plain; rough; lacking refinement. **3.** made of rough, bark-covered branches or roots. ¶*a ~ bridge.*①
—*n.* [C] a country person. ▷**rus·ti·cal·ly** [-kəli] *adv.*

—[形] 1. 시골의 2. 단순한; 소박한 3. 야비한; 통나무로 만든 ¶①통나무 다리
—[名] 시골뜨기

rus·ti·cate [rʌ́stikèit] *vi.* go to the country; live in the country. **—*vt.*** **1.** send (something) to the country; make (someone) rustic; make (something) in the rustic style. **2.** (*Brit.*) send (a student) away from the university for a while as a punishment.

—[自] 시골로 가다; 시골에서 살다 —[他] 1. …을 시골로 보내다; 시골식으로 만들다 2. ⟪英⟫ …에게 정학(停學)을 명하다

rus·tic·i·ty [rʌstísiti] *n.* [U] **1.** the quality or state of being rustic; [C] rustic life. **2.** simplicity; ignorance.

—[名] 1. 시골투(티); 시골 생활 2. 소박; 순박; 조야(粗野)

rust·i·ness [rʌ́stinis] *n.* [U] the state of being rusty.

—[名] 녹슬어 있음

* **rus·tle** [rʌ́sl] *vi.* **1.** (of silk clothes, leaves, etc.) make a soft light sound. **2.** (*U.S. colloq.*) act or do with energy. ⟪*~ up*⟫ **3.** (*U.S. colloq.*) steal (cattle, etc.) **—*n.*** [C][U] a soft sound made by the wind, clothes, etc.

—[自] 1. 살랑살랑 소리내다 2. ⟪美口⟫ 활발하게 하다 3. ⟪美口⟫ [가축 따위를] 훔치다 —[名] 살랑살랑 소리

rus·tler [rʌ́slər] *n.* [C] **1.** (*U.S. colloq.*) an energetic person. **2.** (*U.S. colloq.*) a person who steals cattle, etc.

—[名] 1. ⟪美口⟫ 활동가, 활약가 2. ⟪美口⟫ 가축 도둑

rust·proof [rʌ́stprù:f] *adj.* resisting rust.

—[形] 녹슬지 않는

* **rust·y** [rʌ́sti] *adj.* (**rust·i·er, rust·i·est**) **1.** covered with rust. **2.** not working perfectly because of lack of use. **3.** colored like rust; faded.

—[形] 1. 녹슨 2. [사용하지 않아서] 무디어진 3. 녹빛의; 빛깔이 바랜

rut [rʌt] *n.* [C] **1.** a hollow track made by a wheel. **2.** a fixed way of acting or thinking. ¶*move in a ~.*①
—*vt.* (**rut·ted, rut·ting**) ⟪usu. in *passive*⟫ make a rut or ruts in (something). ¶*The road is rutted.*

—[名] 1. 바퀴 자국 2. 관례, 판에 박은 방식 ¶①틀에 박힌 대로만 하다 —[他] 에 바퀴 자국을 내다

Ruth [ru:θ] *n.* a woman's name.

—[名] 여자 이름

ruth·less [rú:θlis] *adj.* having no pity; merciless; cruel.

—[形] 무자비한; 무정한

rye [rai] *n.* [U] a plant producing a grain which can be made into a coarse dark bread; the grain of this plant.

—[名] 호밀, 쌀보리

S

S¹, s [es] *n.* Ⓒ (pl. **S's, Ss, s's, ss** [ésiz]) **1.** the 19th letter of the English alphabet. **2.** anything having the shape of an S.
—ⓝ 1. 영어 알파벳의 열 아홉째 글자 2. S자 형[의 것]

S² **1.** south, southern. **2.** (*Chemical*) sulfur. **3.** Saint. **4.** School. **5.** Saturday; Sunday. **6.** September.

s. (pl. **ss**) shilling; shillings.

Sab·bath [sǽbəθ] *n.* **1.** ⟪usu. *the* ~⟫ a day of the week for rest and services in honor of God, Saturday for Jews, Sunday for most Christians. **2.** Ⓒ (*s-*) a period of rest, peace, quiet, etc.
—ⓝ 1. 안식일(유대교는 토요일, 그리스도교는 일요일) 2. 휴식기간

sab·bat·i·cal [səbǽtik(ə)l] *adj.* **1.** of or like the Sabbath. **2.** of or for a rest from work.
—ⓐ 1. 안식일의(같은) 2. 안식의

sa·ber, *Brit.* **-bre** [séibər] *n.* Ⓒ a heavy sword with a curved blade used by cavalry soldiers. —*vt.* strike or kill (someone) with a saber.
—ⓝ 기병도(騎兵刀), 군도 —ⓥ …을 기병도로 베다(죽이다)

sa·ble [séibl] *n.* (pl. **-bles** or *collectively* **-ble**) **1.** Ⓒ a small flesheating animal covered with beautiful dark fur. ⇒fig. **2.** Ⓤ the fur of this animal. **3.** (*pl.*) mourning garments. —*adj.* **1.** made of sable (*n.* 2). **2.** (*poetic*) black; gloomy.
—ⓝ 1. 검은담비 2. 검은담비의 모피 3. 상복(喪服) —ⓐ 1. 검은담비 가죽의 2. 검은; 음침한

[sable 1.]

sab·ot [sǽbou, +U.S. -́] *n.* Ⓒ **1.** a shoe made out of a piece of wood. ⇒fig. **2.** a shoe with a wooden sole.
—ⓝ 1. 나막신 2. 바닥에 나무를 댄 신

sab·o·tage [sǽbətɑ:ʒ] *n.* Ⓤ **1.** the act of breaking the machinery by workmen as an attack on or a threat against an employer. **2.** damage to a nation's property by persons who act for the enemy. —*vt.* injure or attack (something) by sabotage.
—ⓝ 1. [노동쟁의에 있어서] 기계류의 파괴행위, 사보타지 2. [전시에 적의 앞잡이에 의한] 파괴 —ⓥ …에 대하여 사보타지를 일으키다, 일부러 파괴(공격)하다

[sabot 1.]

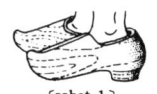

sa·bre [séibər] *n., v.* (*Brit.*) =saber.

sac [sæk] *n.* Ⓒ a baglike part of a plant or an animal, usu. for holding liquids. ⌈stance made from coal tar.⌉
—ⓝ [동식물의] 주머니 모양의 부분, 액낭(液囊)

sac·cha·rin [sǽkərin] *n.* Ⓤ a very sweet, white sub-
—ⓝ 사카린

sac·cha·rine [sǽkərin, -rài n / -rài n] *adj.* **1.** of saccharin. **2.** like sugar; very sweet.
—ⓐ 1. 사카린의 2. 설탕 같은; 달콤한

sac·er·do·tal [sæ̀sərdóutl] *adj.* **1.** of a priest. **2.** of the office or rank of a priest. ⌈American Indians.⌉
—ⓐ 1. 성직자의 2. 사제(司祭)[제도]의, 성직의

sa·chem [séitʃəm, +*Brit.* -tʃem] *n.* Ⓒ a chief among
—ⓝ [북미 토인의] 추장

sack¹ [sæk] *n.* Ⓒ **1.** a bag made of coarse cloth used for holding corn, coal, etc. **2.** any bag. **3.** the amount a bag holds. **4.** a loose jacket or dress for a woman or child. **5.** (*Brit. colloq.*) dismissal from employment. ***get*** (or ***have***) ***the sack,*** be dismissed.
—*vt.* **1.** put (something) into a sack. **2.** (*Brit. colloq.*) dismiss (someone) from his occupation.
—ⓝ 1. [삼베·즈크 따위의] 자루, 부대 2. [일반적으로] 자루 3. 한 부대의 분량 4. [부인·아동용의] 헐거운 웃옷 5. 《英口》 해고
숙 해고다하다, 퇴짜맞다
—ⓥ 1. …을 자루(부대)에 넣다 2. 《英口》 …을 해고하다

sack² [sæk] *n.* ⟪*the* ~⟫ the act of robbing violently in a town seized in war. —*vt.* rob violently after the capture of (a town, etc.). ⌈used for making sacks.⌉
—ⓝ [점령지의] 약탈 —ⓥ [도시 따위]를 약탈하다

sack·cloth [sǽkklɔ̀:θ / -klɔ̀(:)θ] *n.* Ⓤ the coarse cloth
—ⓝ 즈크, 자루 만드는 삼베

sack coat [́ ́] *n.* a man's short, loose-fitting coat usu. a part of a business suit. ⇒N.B.
—ⓝ 양복 저고리 N.B. 양복 상하는 sack suit

sack·ful [sǽkf(u)l] *n.* Ⓒ the amount that a sack can contain. ¶*a* ~ *of sugar.*① ⌈sacks; sackcloth.⌉
—ⓝ 한 자루분의 분량 ¶①설탕 한 자루

sack·ing [sǽkiŋ] *n.* Ⓤ the coarse cloth used for making
—ⓝ 자룻감, 즈크

sac·ra·ment [sǽkrəmənt] *n.* Ⓒ **1.** a solemn, religious
—ⓝ 1. 성례(聖禮), 성식(聖式) 2. 성찬

act or ceremony of the Christian church. **2.** 《often *the S-*》 the Lord's supper communion. ¶ *go to* (or *take, receive*) *the* ~.①

¶①성찬을 받다

sac·ra·men·tal [sæ̀krəméntl] *adj.* **1.** of or used in a sacrament. ¶ ~ *wine.*① **2.** sacred or holy. **—*n.*** [C] the act of crossing or of using holy water, oil, etc.

—[形] 1. 성례의, 성찬[식]의 ¶①성찬식용 포도주 2. 신성한 —[名] 준성사(準聖事)

‡ sa·cred [séikrid] *adj.* **1.** holy; belonging to God. ¶ ~ *history.*① **2.** of religion; religious. **3.** not to be violated. **4.** worthy of reverence. **5.** reverently given to someone. ¶ *a monument ~ to the memory of Lincoln.*

1) ***be sacred from,*** be protected against.
2) ***hold sacred,*** respect.

—[形] 1. 신성한; 신의 ¶①성서에 기록된 역사 2. 종교의, 종교적인 3. 침범할 수 없는 4. 존경할 만한 5. 바친

[熟] 1)…을 모면하다 2)…을 존중하다

‡ sac·ri·fice [sǽkrifàis] *n.* **1.** [U][C] the act of offering something to God. **2.** [C] a thing offered to God. **3.** [U][C] the act of giving up something valuable to gain something else. ¶ *a ~ hit.*① **4.** [C] the thing made a sacrifice to something else. **5.** [C] damage; loss.

1) ***at the sacrifice of,*** at the cost of.
2) ***fall a sacrifice*** (=*fall a victim*) ***to*** *someone.*
3) ***make a sacrifice to*** (=*pay sacrifice to*) *someone.*

—*vt.* **1.** offer (something) to God. **2.** give up (something) as a sacrifice. **3.** sell (something) at a loss. **—*vi.*** (*Baseball*) advance a runner by means of a sacrifice hit.

—[名] 1. 산 제물·희생을 바치기 2. 산 제물, 희생 3. 희생하기 ¶①희생타(犧牲打) 4. 희생 5. 손실

[熟] 1)…을 희생으로 하여 2)…의 희생이 되다 3)…을 위해 희생하다

—[他] 1. …을 산 제물로 바치다 2. …을 희생하다 3. …을 투매(投賣)하다 —[自] 희생타(犧牲打)하다

sac·ri·fi·cial [sæ̀krifíʃ(ə)l] *adj.* **1.** of a sacrifice. **2.** devoted to God as a sacrifice. **3.** selling at a loss.

—[形] 1. 희생의, 산 제물의 2. 신에게 바쳐진 3. 투매(投賣)의

sac·ri·lege [sǽkrilidʒ] *n.* [U] an intended violence or disrespect toward anyone or anything holy.

—[名] 신성모독

sac·ri·le·gious [sæ̀krilídʒəs] *adj.* of sacrilege; showing contempt or disregard for God or holy things.

—[形] 신성모독의

sac·ro·sanct [sǽkrousæ̀ŋ(k)t] *adj.* very sacred; set apart for a holy purpose.

—[形] 극히 신성한; 신성 불가침의

‡ sad [sæd] *adj.* (**sad·der, sad·dest**) **1.** not happy; sorrowful. **2.** causing sorrow or grief. **3.** dull in color; sober; dark. **4.** (*colloq.*) very bad; shameful.

1) ***in sad earnest,*** in all soberness; seriously.
2) ***make sad work of*** (=*be a failure in*) *something.*

—[形] 1. 슬픈, 쓸쓸한 2. 슬프게 하는, 괴롭히는 3. 칙칙한, 거무스름한 4. 심한, 통탄할

[熟] 1)진지하게, 진정으로 2)…에 실패하다

sad·den [sǽdn] *vt.* make (someone) mournful, melancholy, gloomy, etc. **—*vi.*** become sad.

—[他] …을 슬퍼하게 하다 —[自] 슬퍼지다

‡ sad·dle [sǽdl] *n.* [C] **1.** a seat for a rider on horseback or on a bicycle. **2.** anything like a saddle. **3.** a ridge between two mountains. **4.** a piece of meat including the backbone and ribs.

1) ***be in the saddle,*** ⓐ ride on horseback. ⓑ have a job. ⓒ have power.
2) ***lose the saddle,*** fall from a horse's back.
3) ***take*** (or ***get into***) ***the saddle,*** begin to ride on horseback.

—*vt.* **1.** place a saddle on (a horse's back). **2.** burden (someone) with responsibility.

—[名] 1. [말의] 안장, [자전거의] 안장 2. 안장 모양의 것 3. [두 봉우리 사이의] 안부(鞍部) 4. 등심 고기

[熟] 1)ⓐ말에 타다 ⓑ직업이 있다 ⓒ권력을 쥐고 있다 2)말에서 떨어지다 3)말에 타다

—[他] 1. …에 안장을 놓다(달다) 2. …에게 책임을 지우다

sad·dle·bag [sǽdlbæ̀g] *n.* [C] one of a pair of bags laid over a horse's back.

—[名] 안장에 다는 주머니

saddle horse [⌐–⌐] *n.* a horse fit for riding.

—[名] 승용 말

sad·dler [sǽdlər] *n.* [C] a person who makes and mends saddles, reins, etc.

—[名] 마구(馬具) 제조인

sad·ism [sǽdiz(ə)m] *n.* [U] abnormal sexual satisfaction gained by causing or watching cruelty.

—[名] 가학성 음란증(加虐性淫亂症)

‡ sad·ly [sǽdli] *adv.* in a sad manner; sorrowfully; mournfully.

—[副] 슬프게; 슬픈 듯이; 비참하게

*** sad·ness** [sǽdnis] *n.* [U] the state of being sad; great sorrow. ¶ *She had an air of ~ about her.*①

—[名] 슬픔 ¶①그녀는 어딘가 슬픈 표정을 짓고 있었다

‡ safe [seif] *adj.* **1.** free from danger; secure from harm. ¶ *put money in a ~ place.* **2.** not injured. ¶ *come* (*arrive, bring, keep*) ~ / *He came home ~ from the war.* **3.** sure; reliable; certain to be successful. ¶ *a ~ investment* / *a ~ guide*① / *a ~ first.*② **4.** no longer dangerous; securely held. ¶ *The murderer is ~ in prison.* **5.** cautious in avoiding danger; timid. ¶ *a ~ driver.* **6.** (*Baseball*) successful in reaching a base.

—[形] 1. 안전한; 해가 없는 2. 손상 없는; 무사한 3. 확실한, 틀림없는; 신뢰할 수 있는; 확실히 …하는 ¶①믿을 만한 안내인/②틀림없이 첫째가 될 사람 4. [붙잡혀서] 위험이 없는; 도망칠 염려가 없는 5. 조심성있는; 소심한 6. 《野球》 세이프의

safe-conduct

1) *be on the safe side*, do not take any risks.
2) *play safe*, be prudent or cautious.
—*n.* ⓒ **1.** a strong steel or iron box for money, jewels, etc. **2.** an air-cooled cupboard for food.

safe·con·duct [séifkʌ́ndʌkt / -kɔ́n-] *n.* **1.** Ⓤ a permission or accepted right to pass safely through a dangerous district, esp. in time of war. **2.** ⓒ a document granting this right; a pass.

safe·guard [séifgɑ̀:rd] *vt.* **1.** guard (someone); protect (someone or something). **2.** accompany (someone) in order to guard them; escort. —*n.* Ⓤⓒ **1.** the act of defending or guarding. **2.** the act of escorting.

safe·keep·ing [séifkí:piŋ] *n.* Ⓤ the act of keeping safe or defending; care. ¶*be in ~ with.*①

* **safe·ly** [séifli] *adv.* in a safe manner; securely.

: **safe·ty** [séifti] *n.* (pl. **-ties**) **1.** Ⓤ the state of being safe and sound. ¶*Safety First.* / *~ zone* / *There is ~ in numbers.*① **2.** ⓒ an apparatus or a device protecting *play for safety*, be careful. ⌊from danger.⌋

safety lamp [´-´] *n.* a miner's lamp in which the flame is protected from setting fire to explosive gases by a piece of wire gauze. ⇒fig.

safety match [´-´] *n.* a match which lights only when rubbed on the special surface of a match box. ⌈covering its point.⌉

safety pin [´-´] *n.* a bent pin with a guard

* **safety razor** [´-´-´] *n.* a razor with a [safety lamp] guard that prevents it from cutting the skin.

safety valve [´-´] *n.* **1.** a valve to control the pressure in a steam boiler. **2.** something that serves as an outlet for the release of strong emotion.

safety zone [´-´] *n.* an area in the street made to guard passengers getting on and off the streetcars, buses, etc.

saf·fron [sǽfr(ə)n] *n.* **1.** ⓒ a kind of plant with purple flowers. **2.** bright yellow. —*adj.* bright yellow colored.

sag [sæg] *vi.* (**sagged, sag·ging**) **1.** bend or sink down in the middle under weight, pressure, etc. **2.** become weak; become less firm. —*n.* ⓒ **1.** the act of sagging. **2.** the place of such sagging or sinking; a sunken place. ⌈heroic deeds.⌉

sa·ga [sɑ́:gə] *n.* ⓒ an old Norse legend or history of

sa·ga·cious [səgéiʃ(ə)s] *adj.* having a sharp intelligence; showing sound judgment.

sa·gac·i·ty [səgǽsiti] *n.* Ⓤ good judgment; sharpness of intellect; keenness of insight.

* **sage**¹ [seidʒ] *adj.* wise. —*n.* ⓒ a very wise man.

sage² [seidʒ] *n.* ⓒ **1.** a plant with dull green leaves used for giving flavor in cooking, etc. **2.** sagebrush.

sage·brush [séidʒbrʌ̀ʃ] *n.* ⓒ a weed or bushy plant common on the plains of the western United States.

sa·go [séigou] *n.* (pl. **-gos**) **1.** Ⓤ a powdered starch used in making pudding, etc. **2.** ⓒ a kind of palm tree from which this starch is made. ⌈Africa.⌉

Sa·har·a [səhéərə / -hɑ́:rə] *n.* the great desert in North

sa·hib [sɑ́:(h)ib] *n.* (without *an article*) sir; master. (used by people of India when they address European people.)

: **said** [sed] *v.* pt. and pp. of **say**.
—*adj.* named or spoken of before. ¶*the ~ person.*①

: **sail** [seil] *n.* **1.** ⓒ a large sheet of heavy cloth spread to catch the wind and make a ship move; Ⓤ (*collectively*) some or all of a ship's sails. ¶*hoist a ~*① / *shorten a ~.*② **2.** ⓒ a ship, esp. a sailing ship; (*collectively*)

熟 1)모험을 하지 않다 2)신중하게 행동하다
—名 1. 금고 2. 냉장고

—名 1. [특히 전시의] 안전 통행[권] 2. [안전이 보증된] 통행권

—動 1. …을 보호하다 2. …에 호위로서 동반하다 —名 1. 보호 2. 호위하기

—名 보관, 보호 ¶①…의 곳에 보관되어 있다

—副 안전하게; 확실히

—名 1. 안전, 무사 ¶①수가 많은 편이 안전하다 2. [총 따위의] 안전장치

熟 신중을 기하다
—名 [광산용의] 안전등

—名 안전 성냥

—名 안전 핀
—名 안전 면도

—名 1. [보일러의] 안전 밸브 2. [감정·정신력 따위의] 배출구

—名 안전지대

—名 1. 사프란 2. 선황색(鮮黃色)
—形 사프란 색의

—自 1. [줄 따위가] 꺼지다, 내려앉다; [다리·그물 따위가] 처지다; 구부러지다 2. [기운 따위가] 약해지다 —名 1. 늘어짐 2. [도로의] 꺼짐, 옴폭한 곳

—名 중세 북유럽의 전설; 무용담
—形 총명한; 영리한, 예민한, 민감한

—名 현명; 총명; 예민

—形 현명한 —名 현인
—名 1. 샐비어 2. 쑥의 일종

—名 [미국 서부산의] 쑥의 일종

—名 1. [사고야자로 만드는] 녹말 2. 사고야자

—名 사하라 사막
—名 각하, 선생, …님

—形 앞서(위에) 말한, ¶①본인
—名 1. 돛; 돛의 일부 또는 전부 ¶①돛을 올리다/②돛을 걷이다(좁히다) 2. 돛배; [총칭적으로] 배 ¶①10척으로 편성된 선대 3. 범주(帆走), 항해 4.

sailboat [1004] **sake**

ships. ¶*a fleet of 10 ~.*② **3.** Ⓤ a voyage on a boat with sails. ¶*go for a ~.* **4.** Ⓒ something like a sail in shape or purpose; an arm of a windmill.
1) *in full sail,* with all sails spread.
2) *set sail,* start a voyage; hoist a boat's sails.
3) *take in sail,* ⓐ reduce the amount of sail spread. ⓑ lower one's ambitions, etc.
4) *under sail,* with sails spread on one's way.
—*vi.* **1.** travel on a ship with sails; start a voyage. ¶*The steamer sailed on Monday.* / *The ship sailed from Kobe for America.* **2.** move along with dignity; go smoothly through the air, etc. as if sailing. ¶*She sailed into the room.*④ / *The airship sailed slowly.* —*vt.* **1.** pass over or travel (a body of water) on a ship. **2.** manage or direct (a ship or boat with sails, etc.).
   sail against the wind, ⓐ sail in a direction other than that of the wind. ⓑ work under difficulties or against opposition.
sail·boat [séilbòut] *n.* Ⓒ (*U.S.*) a boat moved forward by the wind blowing on sails. (cf. *Brit.* sailing boat)
sail·cloth [séilklɔ̀:θ / -klɔ̀(:)θ] *n.* Ⓤ canvas or other material for making sails.
sail·er [séilər] *n.* Ⓒ a sailboat; any kind of fast ship.
sail·ing [séiliŋ] *n.* Ⓤ the act of a person or thing that sails a boat.
   —*adj.* (of a sailboat) that sails; that moves or starts by the action of wind on sails.
sailing boat [≤ ⸺] *n. Brit.* =sailboat.
sailing ship [≤ ⸺] *n.* a large ship moved by sails.
sailing vessel [≤ ⸺] *n.* a sailboat; a sailing ship.
: sail·or [séilər] *n.* Ⓒ **1.** a person who sails; esp. one who works on a boat; one of the crew. ¶*a ~ before the mast*① / *a good (bad) ~.*② **2.** a member of seaman who is not an officer.
sail·or·ly [séilərli] *adj.* like a sailor; fit for a sailor.
: saint [seint] *n.* Ⓒ **1.** a holy and godly person. ¶*Young saints, old devils* (or *sinners*).① **2.** (usu. *pl.*) a dead man; a person who has gone to heaven. **3.** a person who is recognized as a saint by the Roman Catholic Church. **4.** a person who lives a pure life. —*adj.* holy; sacred. ¶*Saint Paul.*

Saint Ber·nard [sèintbərná:rd / sn(t)bə́:nəd] *n.* Ⓒ a large, powerful, intelligent dog, often trained to search for and rescue travelers lost in the snow. ⇒NB, fig.

[Saint Bernard]

saint·ed [séintid] *adj.* **1.** regarded as a saint. **2.** in heaven; dead. ¶*my ~ father.* **3.** pious; holy; sacred. **4.** looking a saintly.
saint·li·ness [séintlinis] *n.* Ⓤ the state or quality of being saintly.
saint·ly [séintli] *adj.* (-li·er, -li·est) like a saint; very sacred.
saith [seθ] *v.* (*archaic*) third person singular, present of say; says.
: sake [seik] *n.* Ⓤ cause; object; end; purpose; interest. ⇒USAGE ¶*for the ~ of peace*① / *art for art's ~.*②
1) *for any sake,* anyhow.
2) *for heaven's* (or *goodness', God's, mercy's, pity's*) *sake,* an exclamation making appeal for pity or expressing great surprise or dismay.
3) *for old sake's sake,* for the sake of old friendship.
4) *Sakes* [*alive*]*! (U. S. slang)* an exclamations of sur-

돛 모양의 것; 풍차의 날개

熟 1)돛을 모두 올리고 2)출범하다; [출범하기 위해] 돛을 올리다 ⓐ돛을 줄이다 ⓑ야심 따위를 누르다 4)돛을 펴고

—自 1. 범주(帆走)하다; 출범하다 2. 당당하게 나아가다; 공중 따위를 활주하다 ¶ⓓ그녀는 당당하게 방으로 들어왔다 —他 1. [바다 따위]를 항해하다; 항행하다 2. [배 따위]를 조종하다

熟 ⓐ바람에 거슬러서 나아가다 ⓑ곤란(반대)을 무릅쓰고 하다

—名 (美) 돛단배

—名 돛베, 범포(帆布), 즈크

—名 돛단배; 배
—名 범주(帆走)하기

—形 범주(帆走)하는, 출범의, 항해의

—名 돛단배
—名 돛단배
—名 돛단배; 범선

—名 1. 수부; 선원, 뱃사람 ¶①평수부 /②뱃멀미 안 하는(하는) 사람 2. 수병

—形 뱃사람 같은, 선원에 알맞은
—名 1. 성도(聖徒), 성인 ¶①젊었을 때의 신앙심은 믿을 수 없다 2. 저승에 간 사람, 천당에 올라간 사람 3. 사도(使徒), 교부(敎父), 교도 4. 성자(使徒)—形 신성한; 성(聖)…

—名 세인트버어나아드 개 NB 원래 Alps의 St. Bernard에 있는 수도원에서 눈속의 구조용으로 사육된 개

—形 1. 성도로 모셔진 2. 천국의, 하늘에 있는; 죽은 3. 신성한, 거룩한 4. 성도 같은

—名 성자다움; 거룩함
—形 성자다운; 거룩한

—名 동기, 목적, 이유, 이익 USAGE 보통 for the sake of; for sake's sake「…을 위하여」「…을 보아서」의 형으로 쓰임 ¶①평화를 위해서/②예술을 위한 예술
熟 1)하여튼 2)제발, 아무쪼록; 이건 놀랍다 3)옛정을 생각해서 4)(美俗) 이런!, 놀랐는걸!

Sakhalin — sally

prise or dismay. 「Japan, east of Siberia.」
Sak·ha·lin [sǽkəli:n / ㅅㅡㅡ] *n.* a Russian island north of
sa·laam [səlɑ́:m] *n.* ⓒ an Oriental, esp. Mohammedan, greeting which means "peace," made by placing the right hand on the forehead; a low bow.
sal·a·ble [séiləbl] *adj.* suitable or easy to be sold; marketable. ¶ *a ~ price.*① 「decent; not pure.」
sa·la·cious [səléiʃəs] *adj.* full of physical desire; not
‡**sal·ad** [sǽləd] *n.* 1. ⓤⓒ a cold dish of raw vegetables or fruit, usu. served with dressing, sometimes mixed with chopped cold meat, fish, etc. ¶ *a vegetable ~.* 2. ⓤ any plant used for such a dish or eaten raw.
sal·a·man·der [sǽləmændər] *n.* ⓒ
1. a lizard-like animal belonging to the frog family that lives either in water or on land. ⇒fig. 2. a reptile or lizard which supposedly lived in fire.

[salamander 1.]

sal·a·ried [sǽlərid] *adj.* accepting a salary; paid by salary. ¶ *a ~ man.*①
‡**sal·a·ry** [sǽləri] *n.* ⓒ (pl. **-ries**) a regular payment, usu. paid monthly. ¶ *get* (or *draw*) *a high ~.*①
‡**sale** [seil] *n.* 1. ⓤ the act of selling; ⓤⓒ the exchange of goods for an agreed price. ¶ *a ~ for cash*① / *a ~ on credit.*② 2. ⓤ the demand for goods; (often *pl.*) the amount sold. ¶ *a sales slip*③ / *be dull of ~.*④ 3. ⓒ the act of selling at reduced prices; a discounted sale; a clearing sale. ¶ *a bargain ~.*⑤ 4. ⓒ a public sale or auction.
1) *for* (or *on*) *sale*, available; that can be bought.
2) *not for sale*, not to be sold. ¶ *an article not for ~.*⑥
3) *put up something for sale*, offer something to sell.
sale·a·ble [séiləbl] *adj.* =salable
sales·clerk [séilzklə̀:rk / -klà:k] *n.* ⓒ a person employed to sell goods in a store.
sales·girl [séilzgə̀:rl] *n.* ⓒ a girl whose work is to sell goods in a store.
* **sales·man** [séilzmən] *n.* ⓒ (pl. **-men** [-mən]) a man who sells goods, esp. by traveling around. 「goods.」
sales·man·ship [séilzmənʃìp] *n.* ⓤ skill in selling
sales·wom·an [séilzwùmən] *n.* ⓒ (pl. **-women** [-wìmin]) a woman who sells goods or services, esp. in a store.
sa·li·ent [séiliənt] *adj.* 1. outstanding; prominent; striking. ¶ *a ~ feature.*① 2. projecting. 3. jumping; leaping; jetting. —*n.* ⓒ 1. a projecting angle. 2. the part of a battle line projecting toward the enemy.
sa·line *adj.* [séilain, -li:n / -lain →*n.*] 1. containing salt; salty. ¶ *a ~ lake.*① 2. of or like salt. —*n.* [Brit. səláin] 1. ⓒ a salt lake, marsh, etc. 2. ⓒ anything that contains salt; ⓤ a salty substance.
sa·li·va [səláivə] *n.* ⓤ the liquid in the mouth; spit; spittle. 「saliva. ¶ *~ glands.*①」
sal·i·var·y [sǽlivèri / -vər-] *adj.* of saliva; producing
sal·low [sǽlou] *adj.* (**-low·er, -low·est**) (of skin) of a pale, sickly yellow color. —*vt., vi.* make (something) yellowish; become yellowish.
* **sal·ly** [sǽli] *n.* ⓒ (pl. **-lies**) 1. a surprise attack by besieged troops. ¶ *make a ~.*① 2. the act of going to the outskirts or suburbs; an excursion. 3. an outburst of activity, feeling, etc. 4. a witty remark; a satirical remark. —*vi.* (**-lied**) 1. make a surprise attack from a defensive position. 2. go out suddenly. 3. go forth for an excursion, etc.

—名 사할린
—名 [회교도의] 이마에 손을 대고 하는 것; 인사, 절

—形 팔기 알맞은; [값이] 알맞은 ¶ ①알맞은 값
—形 호색적인, 음란한
—名 1. 샐러드, 생야채 요리 2. [특히 샌치 따위] 샐러드용 야채

—名 1. 도롱뇽 2. 불도마뱀 (불 속에 산다는 전설상의 괴물)

—形 봉급을 받는 ¶①봉급장이
—名 봉급 ¶①높은 봉급을 받다
—名 1. 판매; 매각, 매매, 거래 ¶①현금 거래/②외상 판매 2. 팔리기; 수요; 매상[고] ¶③매상 전표/④팔리지 않다 3. 매출; 재고 처분 대매출 ¶⑤염가판매, 특매 4. 공매; 경매

熟 1)팔려고 내놓은, 팔 것인 2)비매품인 ¶⑥비매품 3)…을 팔려고 내놓다

—名 점원, 판매원
—名 여점원, 여자 판매원

—名 판매원, 점원; 외무 판매원

—名 판매술; 외교적 수완
—名 여점원, 여자 판매원

—形 1. 현저한, 눈에 띄는 ¶①특징 2. 튀어나온 3. 뛰는, 분출하는 —名 1. 돌각(突角) 2. [전선(戰線) 따위의] 돌출부
—形 1. 염분을 함유한, 짠 ¶①염수호(鹽水湖) 2. 염분의, 염성의 —名 1. 염수호, 염소(鹽沼) 2. 함수물(含鹽物), 염류
—名 침, 타액
「腺」
—形 침의; 타액[분비]의 ¶①타선(唾)
—形 누르스름한, 혈색이 나쁜 —他自 […을] 누르스름한 빛깔로 하다(되다)

—名 1. 농성군(籠城軍)·비행기 따위의] 출격 ¶①출격하다 2. 소풍 3. 갑작스러운 행동; [감정 따위의] 폭발 4. 재담, 경구, 익살; 풍자 —自 1. 급습하다 2. 갑자기 떠나다 3. [소풍 따위를] 떠나다

Sal·ly [sǽli] *n.* a woman's name.
—[名] 여자 이름

* **salm·on** [sǽmən] *n.* [C] (pl. **-ons** or *collectively* **-on**) a large, edible fish with silvery scales and pink flesh. —*adj.* orange-pink; like the color of salmon flesh.
—[名] 연어
—[形] 연어 살빛의

sa·lon [səlάn / sǽlɔn] *n.* [C] **1.** a large room for receiving guests; a reception room. **2.** a reception held by a lady in Parisian society; a fashionable assembly of distinguished persons in such a room. **3.** a place used to show works of art; an art gallery. **4.** ⸨*the S-*⸩ an annual exhibition of art in Paris.
—[名] 1. 큰 호울, 객실 2. 파리의 상류 부인의 초대회; 명사들의 모임 3. 미술 전람회장 4. 살롱(파리의 현대 미술전람회)

* **sa·loon** [səlú:n] *n.* [C] **1.** (*U.S.*) a bar; (*Brit.*) a public house. **2.** a large room used for general, public purpose; a large living room or sitting room such as in a hotel; a hall. ¶*a dining* ~① / *a billiard* ~.②
—[名] 1. ⸨美⸩ 술집, 바아; ⸨英⸩ 고급 술집 2. [특별한 목적으로 쓰이는] 공개되는 방; 큰 호올 ¶①대식당/②당구장

‡ **salt** [sɔ:lt / sɔ(:)lt] *n.* [U] **1.** a white powder used in cooking, usu. found in sea water, etc.; anything like salt. ¶*Please pass me the* ~. **2.** [C] a chemical compound of any alkali with any acid; ⸨*pl.*⸩ any of various salts used as medicines. **3.** ⸨often *a* ~⸩ dry wit; that which gives liveliness or interest to anything. ¶*Adventure is the* ~ *of life.*①
—[名] 1. 소금, 식염; 소금 비슷한 것 2. [화학상의] 염(鹽); 약용염 3. 기지(機知); 자극 ¶①모험은 인생의 자극제이다

1) ***in salt,*** sprinkled with salt.
2) ***not worth one's salt,*** useless; worthless.
3) ***take a story, etc. with a grain*** (or ***pinch***) ***of salt,*** be doubtful in believing a story, etc.
4) ***the salt of the earth,*** those who help to make society good and wholesome; the really good people. ⇒[N.B.]

[熟] 1)소금을 뿌린; 소금에 절인 2)밥벌레의, 쓸모 없는 3)[이야기 따위]를 에누리하여 듣다 4)세상의 소금(부패·타락을 막는 건전한 사회층) [N.B.] 마태복음 5장 13절

—*adj.* **1.** containing salt; tasting of salt. ¶~ *breezes.* **2.** treated with salt. ¶~ *pork.*
—[形] 1. 소금기가 있는 2. 소금에 절인

—*vt.* **1.** season, treat, or preserve (something) with salt. ¶*salted meat.* **2.** make (a story, etc.) keen or biting. ¶*He salts his conversation with wit.*
—[他] 1. …에 소금을 뿌리다; …을 소금에 절이다 2. [이야기 따위]를 재미있게 하다

salt·cel·lar [sɔ́:ltsèlər / sɔ́(:)ltsèlə] *n.* [C] a small pot or dish containing salt, used on the table.
—[名] [식탁용] 소금병

salt·pe·ter, *Brit.* **-tre** [sɔ̀:ltpí:tər / sɔ́(:)ltpì:tə] *n.* [U] a white salty mineral used to make gunpowder and matches and to preserve meat.
—[名] 초석(硝石)

salt·y [sɔ́:lti / sɔ́(:)lti] *adj.* (**salt·i·er, salt·i·est**) **1.** containing or tasting of salt. **2.** keen; witty; sharp; biting.
—[形] 1. 소금기가 있는 2. 기지(機知)가 있는, 신랄한

sa·lu·bri·ous [səlú:briəs] *adj.* giving health; good for the health; healthful.
—[形] 건강에 좋은

sa·lu·bri·ty [səlú:briti] *n.* [U] the state of being salubrious.
—[名] 위생적임, 건강에 좋음

sal·u·tar·y [sǽljutèri / -t(ə)ri] *adj.* **1.** helpful; useful. **2.** good for the health.
—[形] 1. 유익한, 도움이 되는 2. 건강에 좋은

sal·u·ta·tion [sæ̀lju(:)téiʃ(ə)n] *n.* **1.** [U] the act of greeting; [C] an expression of greeting, goodwill, or welcome. **2.** the opening words of a letter, such as "Dear Sir" in a business letter.
—[名] 1. 인사; 인사말 2. [편지] 첫머리의 인사말

* **sa·lute** [səlú:t] *n.* [C] **1.** a gesture of respect, made esp. at meeting or parting; a greeting. **2.** an act of military, naval, or other official respect, done by raising a hand, lowering a flag or firing guns. ¶*a return* ~① / *a* ~ *of 21 guns*② / *take the* ~.③ —*vt.* **1.** greet (someone) with kind wishes, words, a kiss, a bow, etc.; greet. **2.** honor (someone) by raising a hand, lowering a flag, etc. ¶*The soldiers saluted the general.* —*vi.* make a salute.
—[名] 1. 인사, 절 2. [군대의] 경례; 받들어총; 축포 ¶①답례/②21발의 예포/③일동의 경례를 받다 —[他] 1. …을 따뜻하게 맞이하다; …에게 인사하다 2. …에 [거수 따위로] 경례하다
—[自] 인사(경례)하다

sal·vage [sǽlvidʒ] *n.* [U] **1.** the act of saving cargo or a ship after a wreck. ¶*a* ~ *boat*① / *in the* ~ *operation.*② **2.** the money or payment for rescuing a ship or cargo. **3.** the act of saving goods or property from fire, etc. ¶*a* ~ *corps.*③ **4.** the goods, cargo, or ship rescued in case of shipwreck, fire, etc. —*vt.* rescue (goods or property) from fire or shipwreck.
—[名] 1. 해난 구조; 선박(뱃짐)의 구출; [침몰선의] 인양작업 ¶①해난 구조선/②인양작업 중 2. 해난 구조료 3. [화재 때의] 구조 ¶③화재 구조반 4. 구출된 재화(선박) —[他] …을 구출하다

* **sal·va·tion** [sælvéiʃ(ə)n] *n.* **1.** [U] the act of saving; the
—[名] 1. 구조, 구제 2. 구제 수단, 구제자

Salvation Army

state of being saved. **2.** ⓒ that which makes safe or saves; a person who saves. **3.** Ⓤ the act of rescuing the spirit or soul; freedom from sin. ¶*work out one's own ~* ①
1) *be the salvation* (=become the rescuer) *of someone or something.*
2) *find salvation,* be converted.

3. 구원, 구세(救世) ¶①스스로 자기 영혼의 구제책을 강구하다
熟 1)···의 구원이 되다 2)개종(改宗)하다

Salvation Army [-ㅗ -ㅗ-], *the n.* a Christian organization which engages in mission work and helps the poor.
—名 구세군

salve¹ [sælv, sɑːv] *n.* **1.** Ⓤ a substance made from oil, rubbed on the skin to heal pain. **2.** Ⓤⓒ anything that makes less a pain of the spirit. —*vt.* **1.** put or rub salve on (wounds, etc.). **2.** calm; soothe.
—名 1. 고약, 연고(軟膏) 2. [마음의 고통을] 위로하는 것, 위안 —他 1. ···에 고약을 바르다 2. [고통]을 진정시키다, ···을 고치다

salve² [sælv] *vt.* salvage.
—他 ···을 구출하다

sal·ver [sǽlvər] *n.* ⓒ a tray of silver or other metal, used for carrying small things. [flowers.]
—名 [금속제의] 쟁반

sal·vi·a [sǽlviə] *n.* ⓒ a garden plant with bright red
—名 샐비어

sal·vo [sǽlvou] *n.* ⓒ (pl. **-voes** or **-vos**) **1.** the act of firing guns all at the same time. **2.** loud cheers or shouts from a crowd.
—名 1. 일제 연속사격 2. 박수갈채

Sa·mar·i·tan [səmǽritn] *n.* ⓒ **1.** a person of Samaria. **2.** a kind person who gives practical help to other persons in trouble. ¶*a good ~.* ① —*adj.* of Samaria or its people.
—名 1. 사마리아 사람 2. 인정 많은 사람 ¶①인정 많은 사람 —형 사마리아 [사람]의

‡**same** [seim] *adj.* **1.** (*the, this, that ~*) not another; not different; identical. ¶*In the ~ place as yesterday / This is the ~ watch that I lost.* **2.** (*the ~*) exactly alike in kind, amount, quality, etc.; similar; corresponding. ¶*Several women have on the ~ dress as you. | This is the ~ watch as I lost.*① ⇒ǀusageǀ *| It was colder at the ~ time last year.* **3.** (*the ~*) not changed in character, condition, etc. ¶*He is the ~ kind gentleman.*② **4.** (*the, this, that ~*) just mentioned before. ¶*That ~ boy was to become king.* [more of the ~.]
—*pron.* (*the ~*) the same thing. ¶*Please give me some one and the same,* absolutely the same.
—*adv.* (*the ~*) in the same way. ¶*I feel the ~ toward someone.*③
1) *all the same,* ⓐ yet; nevertheless. ¶*I shall go all the ~.* ⓑ of no difference.
2) *just the same,* ⓐ nevertheless. ⓑ in the same way.

—形 1. 동일한, 같은 2. 같은 분량(종류)의, 동등한; 아주 비슷한; 상당한 ¶①이것은 내가 잃어버린 것과 같은 형의 시계다 ǀusageǀ 보통 the same ···as는 "같은 종류의 것"을, the ··· same that는 "동일물"을 가리킴. 다만 생략형에는 언제나 as 3. [이전과] 변함없는, 여전한 ¶②그는 여전히 친절한 신사다 4. 앞서 말한
—代 동일한
熟 아주 똑같은
—副 똑같이 ¶③···에 대한 기분은 변함이 없다
熟 1)ⓐ그래도 여전히 ⓑ아무래도 좋은 2)ⓐ그래도 여전히 ⓑ같은 방법으로

same·ness [séimnis] *n.* Ⓤ the state of being the same; absence of variety or change.
—名 동일; 무변화, 단조로움

sam·o·var [sǽməvɑːr / sǽmouvɑ́ːr] *n.* ⓒ a metal pot used for boiling water to make tea in Russia. ⇒fig.
—名 러시아의 차 끓이는 주전자

sam·pan [sǽmpæn] *n.* ⓒ a small, flat-bottomed boat used in China which has one sail and one or more oars.
—名 삼판(三板)(중국의 밑이 평평한 작은 배)

·**sam·ple** [sǽmpl / sɑ́ːm-] *n.* ⓒ a part of something taken to show the kind or quality of the whole; an example. ¶*a ~ fair*① [samovar] *come up to ~.*② —*vt.* take (something) as a sample; test the quality of (something) by a sample.
—名 견본, 표본; 실례(實例) ¶①견본시(市) ②견본에 맞다 —他 ···의 견본을 뽑다; ···을 견본으로 시험하다

sam·pler [sǽmplər / sɑ́ːmplə] *n.* ⓒ **1.** a person who tests samples. **2.** a piece of cloth that shows one's skill in needlework. [and judge in Israel.]
—名 1. 견본 검사인 2. 자수 연습작품

Sam·son [sǽmsn] *n.* (in the Bible) a powerful hero
—名 삼손

san·a·to·ri·a [sæ̀nətɔ́ːriə] *n.* pl. of **sanatorium.**

san·a·to·ri·um [sæ̀nətɔ́ːriəm] *n.* ⓒ (pl. **-ri·ums** or **-ri·a**) a hospital, esp. one for people suffering from diseases of the lungs.
—名 [특히 결핵환자의] 요양소

san·a·to·ry [sǽnətɔ̀ːri / -t(ə)ri] *adj.* helpful to the health.
—形 건강에 좋은

sanc·ta [sǽŋ(k)tə] *n.* pl. of **sanctum.**

sanc·ti·fi·ca·tion [sæ̀ŋ(k)tifikéiʃ(ə)n] *n.* Ⓤ the act of
—名 신성하게 하기(되기), 신성화

sanctify

making something or someone holy; the state of being sanctified.

sanc·ti·fy [sǽŋ(k)tifài] *vt.* (**-fied**) **1.** make (someone or something) holy. **2.** set (someone or something) apart for some holy use. **3.** make (human beings) free from sin. 「love serving God and the church.」

sanc·ti·mo·ni·ous [sæ̀ŋ(k)timóuniəs] *adj.* pretending to

・**sanc·tion** [sǽŋ(k)ʃ(ə)n] *n.* Ⓤ **1.** formal permission or approval from the authorities; support. **2.** (usu. *pl.*) punishment of the country after it has broken an international law. **3.** punishment of a person for breaking the rules. —*vt.* permit (someone); approve (something).

sanc·ti·ty [sǽŋ(k)titi] *n.* (pl. **-ties**) **1.** Ⓤ the state of being very holy; holiness; sacredness. **2.** (*pl.*) holy duties or feelings.

sanc·tu·ar·y [sǽŋ(k)tʃuèri / -tjuəri] *n.* Ⓒ (pl. **-ries**) **1.** a holy place; a temple; a church. **2.** the holiest part of a temple or church. **3.** a special temple or church in which a person is protected from the power of the law; a place of protection. **4.** a place protecting birds or animals from hunters.

sanc·tum [sǽŋ(k)təm] *n.* Ⓒ (pl. **-tums** or **-ta**) **1.** a sacred place. **2.** a private room.

‡**sand** [sænd] *n.* Ⓤ **1.** the material made of broken stone found on the seashore, etc. **2.** (*pl.*) large area of sandy land; a seaside area composed mostly of sand; the desert. **3.** (usu. *pl.*) the sand of an hourglass.
1) ***build on sand,*** do meaningless or useless things.
2) ***make ropes of sand,*** try to do something impossible. 「useless things.」
3) ***plow*** (or ***sow***) ***the sands,*** do something in vain; do
—*vt.* scatter sand on (something); cover (something) with sand; mix (something) with sand; polish (something) with sand or sandpaper.

san·dal [sǽndl] *n.* Ⓒ **1.** a kind of shoe held to the foot by leather cords or straps, used by the ancient Greeks and Romans. **2.** in modern times, a light, topless shoe for children and women. **3.** a rubber overshoe with no heel.

san·dal·wood [sǽndlwùd] *n.* Ⓤ sweet-smelling wood used for making fans, etc. ¶*red ~.*①

sand·bag [sǽn(d)bæ̀g] *n.* Ⓒ a bag filled with sand. — *vt.* (**-bagged, -bag·ging**) protect (something) with sandbags; hit (someone) down with a sandbag.

sand·bank [sǽn(d)bæ̀ŋk] *n.* Ⓒ a bank of sand rising from the sea bed.

sand bar [´ ˋ] *n.* a shallow sandy ridge formed by the action of water currents.

sand·glass [sǽndglæ̀s / -glɑ̀ːs] *n.* Ⓒ an hourglass filled with sand, used to measure time. ⇨fig.

sand hill [´ ˋ] *n.* a hill of sand formed by the wind.

sand·man [sǽn(d)mæ̀n] *n.* Ⓒ (pl. **-men** [-mèn]) a fairy supposed to make children sleep by dropping sand into their eyes.

sand·pa·per [sǽn(d)pèipər] *n.* Ⓤ strong paper coated with sand, used for smoothing or polishing the surfaces of things. —*vt.* smooth or polish (something) with sandpaper.

[sandglass]

sand·pip·er [sǽn(d)pàipər] *n.* Ⓒ a small bird living on sandy shores.

sand pit [´ ˋ] *n.* a hole from which sand can be taken; a

[1008]

sand pit

—他 1. …을 신성하게 하다, 깨끗이 하다 2. …을 성별(聖別)하다 3. [인류] 의 죄를 깨끗이 하다

—형 신앙이 깊은 체하는

—名 1. 비준(批准), 허가, 인가; 찬성 2. [국제연합 따위가 국제법 위반국에 대하여 취하는] 제재 3. [규칙 위반에 대한] 처벌 —他 …을 허가하다, 인가하다, 시인하다

—名 1. 거룩함, 신성 2. 신성한 의무, 성 스런 감정

—名 1. 신성한 곳, 신전, 사원 2. 교회당 의 내진(內陣)(제단 둘레의 부분) 3. 성역(聖域)(중세에 법률의 힘이 미치지 않은 교회); 피난처 4. 금렵구(禁獵區)

—名 1. 신성한 곳 2. 사실(私室)

—名 1. 모래 2. 모래밭, 사장, 사막 3. 모래시계의 모래

熟 1) 어리석은 (헛된) 짓을 하다 2) 불가능한 일을 꾀하다 3) 헛수고하다, 무익한 짓을 하다

—他 …에 모래를 뿌리다; …을 모래로 덮다; …에 모래를 섞다; …을 모래로 닦다

—名 1. [고대·그리이스·로마인의] 샌들 2. [부인·아동용의] 샌들신 3. 운두가 낮은 덧신

—名 백단향(白檀香) ¶①자단(紫檀)

—名 모래 주머니 —他 …을 모래 주머니로 막다; 모래 주머니로 때려눕히다

—名 모래톱, 모래언덕

—名 모래톱(강어귀나 항구의 얕은 곳)

—名 모래시계

—名 모래언덕

—名 잠귀신(잘 시간이 되면 어린이의 눈에 모래를 넣어 잠들게 한다는 동화의 요정)

—名 사포(砂布) —他 …을 사포로 닦다

—名 도요새의 일종

—名 모래 파는 곳, 사갱(砂坑); [어린

sand·stone [sǽn(d)stòun] *n.* Ⓤ a kind of rock made mostly of sand. —명 사암(砂岩)

sand·storm [sǽn(d)stɔ̀:rm] *n.* Ⓒ a storm with clouds of sand blown by the wind in a desert or wasteland. —명 [사막의] 모래 폭풍

: **sand·wich** [sǽn(d)witʃ / sǽnwidʒ] *n.* Ⓒ **1.** the two slices of bread between which meat, etc. is inserted. **2.** anything formed like sandwich. ¶*ride* (or *sit*) ~.① —*vt.* put (something) in between two things. 《~ something *in*》
—명 1. 샌드위치 2. 샌드위치 모양의 것 ¶①두 사람 사이에 타다(앉다)
—타 …을 삽입하다, 사이에 끼우다

sandwich man [ˊ-ˋ] *n.* (pl. ~men [mèn]) a person carrying two advertising boards, one hanging before him and one behind his back.
—명 샌드위치맨(광고판을 앞뒤에 메고 다니는 사람)

• **sand·y** [sǽndi] *adj.* (**sand·i·er, sand·i·est**) **1.** of sand; covered with sand. **2.** (of hair, etc.) rather yellow-red.
—형 1. 모래의, 모래투성이의 2. [머리카락이] 엷은 갈색의

• **sane** [sein] *adj.* **1.** in a sound condition of mind. ↔insane **2.** having good sense and judgment; moderate. ▷**sane·ly** [-li] *adv.* —**sane·ness** [-nis] *n.*
—형 1. 제정신의 2. [사상 따위가] 온건한

San Fran·cis·co [sæ̀nfr(æ)nsískou] *n.* a large seaport in California.
—명 미국 California 주의 항구도시

sang [sæŋ] *v.* pt. of **sing**.

san·gui·nar·y [sǽŋgwinèri / -nəri] *adj.* **1.** with the shedding of blood; covered with blood. **2.** taking great pleasure in the shedding of blood; cruel.
—형 1. 유혈의; 피투성이의; 피비린내 나는 2. 살륙을 좋아하는, 잔인한

san·guine [sǽŋgwin] *adj.* **1.** hopeful; confident. **2.** of a healthy red color. **3.** having a passionate temperament. **4.** cruel. ▷**san·guine·ly** [-li] *adv.*
—형 1. 쾌활한; 자신에 찬 2. 혈색이 좋은 3. 다혈질의 4. 잔인한

san·i·tar·i·a [sæ̀nitέəriə] *n.* pl. of **sanitarium**.

san·i·tar·i·an [sæ̀nitέəriən] *n.* Ⓒ a person who is well acquainted with or who takes part in sanitary work. —*adj.* relating to health or preventing disease; sanitary.
—명 위생학자, 공중위생 개선가
—형 위생의, 공중위생의

san·i·tar·i·um [sæ̀nitέəriəm] *n.* (pl. -**i·ums** or -**i·a**) (*U.S.*) =sanatorium.

• **san·i·tar·y** [sǽnitèri / -t(ə)ri] *adj.* **1.** of or for health. ¶*a ~ inspector*① / ~ *science* / *The Sanitary Office.*② **2.** clean. —*n.* Ⓒ a public toilet; a water closet.
—형 1. [공중] 위생의 ¶①위생 검사관/②검역소 2. 위생적인, 청결한 —명 공중변소

san·i·ta·tion [sæ̀nitéiʃ(ə)n] *n.* Ⓤ the act of protecting health; the public facilities that protect health, such as drainage.
—명 공중위생; 위생 설비(하수 설비 따위)

san·i·ty [sǽniti] *n.* Ⓤ **1.** health of the mind. ↔insanity **2.** the soundness of judgment; moderateness.
—명 1. 제정신 2. [사상 따위의] 온전함

: **sank** [sæŋk] *v.* pt. of **sink**.

San·skrit, -scrit [sǽnskrit] *n.* the ancient literary language of India.
—명 산스크릿, 범어(梵語)

• **San·ta Claus** [sǽntəklɔ̀:z, +*Brit.* ˋ-ˊ] *n.* an old man with a white beard who visits houses giving children presents on Christmas Eve.
—명 산타 클로오스(어린이의 수호신 St. Nicholas를 이름)

San·ti·a·go [sæ̀ntiá:gou] *n.* the capital of Chile.
—명 칠레의 수도

• **sap**¹ [sæp] *n.* Ⓤ **1.** the liquid in a plant. **2.** vigor; vitality. **3.** the white part just inside the skin of a tree; sapwood.
—명 1. 수액(樹液) 2. 원기, 활력 3. [나무껍질 아래의] 백목질(白木質)

sap² [sæp] *v.* (**sapped, sap·ping**) *vt.* **1.** weaken (something) by digging under its foundation; use up. **2.** approach (the enemy) by digging a trench. —*vi.* dig a covered, protected trench; approach an enemy in this way. —*n.* Ⓒ a covered trench; the act of digging a trench.
—타 1. …의 아래를 파서 약하게 하다 2. [적]에 참호를 파서 접근하다 —자 참호를 파다; 참호를 파서 적에게 접근하다
—명 참호[를 파기]

sa·pi·ent [séipiənt] *adj.* wise. ▷**sa·pi·ent·ly** [-li] *adv.*
—형 현명한

sap·less [sǽplis] *adj.* **1.** (of a plant) without its natural juice; dry. **2.** without any active energy.
—형 1. 수액이 없는, 말라빠진 2. 활기 없는

sap·ling [sǽpliŋ] *n.* Ⓒ **1.** a young tree. **2.** a young man; a youth.
—명 1. 어린 나무 2. 젊은이, 풋나기

sap·phire [sǽfaiər] *n.* **1.** Ⓒ a deep blue, hard and clear jewel. **2.** Ⓤ the color of this jewel. —*adj.* deep blue.
—명 1. 사파이어 2. 사파이어 빛 —형 사파이어 빛의

sap·py [sǽpi] *adj.* (-**pi·er, -pi·est**) **1.** having much sap; juicy. **2.** full of vigor; lively. ▷**sap·pi·ness** [-nis] *n.*
—형 1. 수액이 많은 2. 활기에 찬

sap·wood [sǽpwùd] *n.* Ⓤ the soft, living part of wood just beneath the bark of a tree.
—명 백목질(白木質)

Sar·a·cen [sǽrəs(e)n] *n.* [C] an old name for an Arab. **—***adj.* of the Saracens; relating to the Saracens.
—[名] 사라센 사람 —[形] 사라센[사람]의; 사라센풍의

Sar·ah [séərə] *n.* a woman's name.
—[名] 여자 이름

sar·casm [sɑ́:rkæz(ə)m] *n.* [C] bitter, ironical words; [U] the act of using such words. ¶*in ~.*①
—[名] 빈정댐, 비꼼, 풍자; 빈정대기 ¶①비꼬아서

sar·cas·tic [sɑ:rkǽstik] *adj.* expressing sarcasm; mocking; ironical.
—[形] 비꼬는, 풍자적인

sar·cas·ti·cal·ly [sɑ:rkǽstik(ə)li] *adv.* in a sarcastic manner.
—[副] 비꼬아서

sar·dine [sɑ:rdí:n] *n.* [C] (pl. **-dines** or esp. *collectively* **-dine**) a small fish, usu. preserved in oil for use as food.
—[名] 정어리

packed like sardines, so closely crowded that it is almost impossible to move.
[熟] 빽빽이 들어찬

sar·don·ic [sɑ:rdɑ́nik / sɑ:dɔ́n-] *adj.* sneering; mocking; scornful; cynical.
—[形] 냉소하는, 비웃는, 비꼬는

sar·don·i·cal·ly [sɑ:rdɑ́nik(ə)li / -dɔ́n-] *adv.* in a sardonic manner; sneeringly.
—[副] 냉소하여

* **sash**[1] [sæʃ] *n.* [C] an ornamental, long, wide piece of ribbon worn around the waist or over one shoulder.
—[名] [부녀자용의] 띠; [어깨에 걸치는] 현장(懸章)

sash[2] [sæʃ] *n.* [C] the frame that holds the glass in a window or door. **—***vt.* furnish (windows) with sashes.
—[名] 창틀, 새시 —[他] [창]에 틀을 달다

‡ **sat** [sæt] *v.* pt. and pp. of **sit.**

Sat. Saturday.

* **sa·tan** [séit(ə)n] *n.* [C] a wicked spirit; the spirit of evil; ((*S-*)) the Devil.
—[名] 악령; 악마, 사탄

sa·tan·ic [seitǽnik / sət-] *adj.* of or like Satan; wicked; evil. ¶*a ~ smile.*
—[形] 사탄의, 악마의; 악마 같은; 흉악한

satch·el [sǽtʃ(ə)l] *n.* [C] a small cloth or leather bag for carrying books, clothes, etc.
—[名] 작은 가방; 손가방

sate[1] [seit] *vt.* satisfy (something) completely; weary (someone) with an excessive supply of something. ¶*be sated with food*① / *~ oneself with (something).*②
—[他] …을 배불리 먹이다; 물리게 하다 ¶①포식하다/②…에 물리다

sate[2] [sæt, seit] *v.* (*archaic*) pt. and pp. of **sit.**

sat·el·lite [sǽtəlàit] *n.* [C] **1.** a heavenly body that moves around a planet. ¶*an artificial* (or *an earth*) *~*① / *a ~ station.*② **2.** a follower of an important person; a steady attendant.
—[名] **1.** 위성 ¶①인공위성/②인공위성(우주선) 기지 **2.** 종자(從者), 추종자

sa·ti·a·ble [séiʃ(i)əbl] *adj.* that can be supplied with something too much; that can be satisfied.
—[形] 물리게 할 수 있는

sa·ti·ate [séiʃièit] *vt.* **1.** ((usu. in *passive*)) satisfy (the appetite, etc.) fully. **2.** make (someone) weary too much. ¶*be satiated with cake.*①
—[他] **1.** …을 만족시키다 **2.** …을 물리게 하다 ¶①케이크에 물리다

sa·ti·e·ty [sətáiəti] *n.* [U] the state of being satiated; a strong feeling of dislike because of overfullness. ¶*to ~.*①
—[名] 포식, 만끽 ¶①싫증날 만큼

sat·in [sǽt(i)n] *n.* [U] silk or rayon cloth with glossy surface. **—***adj.* **1.** of satin; made of satin. **2.** like satin; smooth and glossy.
—[名] 공단, 수자(繻子) —[形] **1.** 수자의 **2.** 수자 같은; 매끈매끈한; 광택이 있는

* **sat·ire** [sǽtaiər] *n.* **1.** [U] the use of bitter irony to attack an evil or foolish thing. ¶*~ on life.*① **2.** [C] a poem, essay, story, etc. used to attack in this manner; [U] a sarcastic piece of writing.
—[名] **1.** 풍자, 비꼼, 빈정댐 ¶①인생에 대한 풍자 **2.** 풍자시(문); 풍자 문학

sa·tir·ic [sətírik], **-i·cal** [-ik(ə)l] *adj.* of or like satire; ironical; sarcastic; cutting. ¶*a ~ man*① / *with a ~ smile.*②
—[形] 풍자의; 비꼬는, 풍자적인, 신랄한 ¶①풍자가/②빈정대는 웃음을 띠고

sa·tir·i·cal·ly [sətírik(ə)li] *adv.* in a satirical manner; sarcastically.
—[副] 비꼬아서, 풍자적으로

sat·i·rist [sǽtirist] *n.* [C] a person who is fond of indulging in satire; a person who writes satires.
—[名] 풍자[작]가, 잘 비꼬는 사람

sat·i·rize [sǽtiràiz] *vt.* denounce (someone) by means of satire; criticize (someone) satirically.
—[他] …을 풍자하다, 비꼬다

‡ **sat·is·fac·tion** [sæ̀tisfǽkʃ(ə)n] *n.* [U] **1.** the act of satisfying; the state of being satisfied; contentment. ¶*to the ~ of someone.*① **2.** [C] anything that makes persons feel satisfied. **3.** the act of paying back or getting even; compensation; reparation.
—[名] **1.** 만족시키기(하기); 만족 ¶①…에게 만족이 되도록 **2.** 만족스러운 일(것) **3.** 배상, 속죄, 청산

1) ***demand satisfaction,*** demand an apology; claim damages.
[熟] 1)사죄를 요구하다, 손해배상을 요

2) ***find satisfaction in*** (=*be contented with*) *something.* 3) ***give satisfaction to,*** ⓐ satisfy. ⓑ accept a challenge to duel. 4) ***in satisfaction of*** (=*in compensation for*) *something.* 5) ***to one's satisfaction,*** so that one is contented, pleased or convinced. ¶*She proved it to my ~.*②

구하다 2)…에 만족하다 3)ⓐ…을 만족시키다 ⓑ결투의 신청에 응하다 4)…의 대상(代償)으로서 5)만족할 만큼, 직성이 풀리도록 ¶②그녀는 그것을 나에게 충분히 납득시켰다

sat·is·fac·to·ri·ly [sæ̀tisfǽkt(ə)rili] *adv.* in a satisfactory manner.

—[副] 만족할 만큼, 말할나위 없이, 충분히

⁑ sat·is·fac·to·ry [sæ̀tisfǽkt(ə)ri] *adj.* giving contentment; fulfilling all needs or wishes; satisfying. ¶*a ~ answer*① / *The student's progress is ~.*②

—[形] 만족스러운, 말할나위 없는 ¶①나무랄 데 없는 대답/②그 학생의 진보는 만족할 만하다

⁑ sat·is·fy [sǽtisfài] *v.* (**-fied**) *vt.* **1.** give (someone) what he desires, needs, or demands; fulfill (desires, needs, etc.); content. ¶*~ a desire / ~ one's thirst / Even great wealth does not always ~ some people.* **2.** remove (a doubt, an anxiety, etc.); make (someone) believe; convince; persuade. ⟪~ someone *of*; ~ someone *that* ...⟫ ¶*~ one's fears / She satisfied herself of the truth of my report. / He satisfied her that he was innocent.* **3.** pay off; discharge. ¶*~ a creditor / ~ a claim for damage.*① —*vi.* give satisfaction.

—[他] **1.** …을 만족시키다;[욕구·필요·요구 따위]를 채우다; 만족시키다 **2.** [의심]을 풀다; [근심 따위]를 가라앉히다; …을 납득시키다, 이해하게 하다 **3.** …을 반제(返濟)하다;[의무]를 수행하다; …을 배상하다 ¶①손해에 대한 배상에 응하다 —[自] 만족을 주다

be satisfied that ..., no longer doubt that...

[熟] …을 확신하다

sat·u·rate [sǽtʃurèit] *vt.* **1.** soak fully; make (something) very wet. **2.** (*Chemistry*) cause (one substance) to combine with the greatest possible amount of another substance. ¶*a saturated solution.*①

—[他] **1.** …을 담그다, 함빡 적시다 **2.** …을 포화시키다 ¶①포화 용액

sat·u·ra·tion [sæ̀tʃuréiʃ(ə)n] *n.* [U] the act of saturating; the state of being saturated. ¶*~ point.*①

—[名] 침투; 포화 ¶①포화점

⁑ Sat·ur·day [sǽtərdi, -dèi] *n.* the seventh day of the week. ⇒[N.B.]

—[名] 토요일 [N.B.] Sat.로 줄임

Sat·urn [sǽtə(ː)rn] *n.* **1.** (in Roman mythology) the god of agriculture. ⇒[N.B.] **2.** the large planet, sixth from the sun, with a ring around it. ¶*Saturn's rings.*①

—[名] **1.** 농업의 신 [N.B.] 그리이스 신화의 Cronus에 해당 **2.** 토성(土星) ¶①토성환(環)

Sat·ur·na·li·a [sæ̀tə(ː)rnéiliə] *n.* (pl. **-li·a**) **1.** the ancient Roman festival of Saturn, held in December with wild noisy feasting. **2.** ⟪*s-*⟫ [C] a scene or period of unrestrained merrymaking.

—[名] **1.** 농신제(農神祭) **2.** 잔치 소동; 흥청거림, 흥청대는 기간

Sa·tur·ni·an [sətə́ːrniən / sætə́ː-] *adj.* **1.** of the Roman god Saturn. **2.** of the golden age when he reigned. **3.** successful; peaceful; happy. **4.** of the planet Saturn.

—[形] **1.** 농신(農神)의 **2.** 농신의 치세의, 황금시대의 **3.** 번영하는, 행복한 **4.** 토성의

sat·ur·nine [sǽtərnàin] *adj.* dark; saddened; not gay.

—[形] 음울한, 음산한

sat·yr [séitər, sǽt- / sǽtə-] *n.* [C] (in Greek mythology) a forest god, part man and part beast, a follower of Bacchus. ⇒fig.

—[名] 숲의 신(반인반수의 괴물)

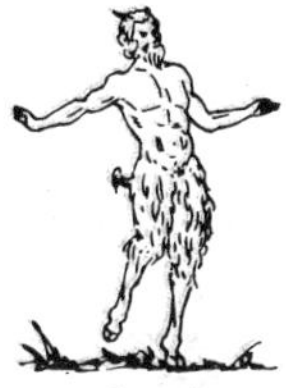
(satyr)

∗ sauce [sɔːs] *n.* **1.** [U] [C] a liquid served with food to improve the taste of the food. ¶*Hunger is the best ~.*① **2.** (*U.S.*) stewed and sweetened fruit. **3.** [C] something that increases interest. **4.** [U] (*slang*) impoliteness; impertinence; impudence. ¶*I don't want any of your ~!*②

—[名] **1.** 소오스 ¶①시장이 반찬 **2.** ⟪美⟫ 과실의 설탕조림 **3.** 맛·흥을 돋우는 것 **4.** ⟪俗⟫ 무례; 건방짐 ¶②건방진 소리 말아라

—*vt.* **1.** flavor or season (food) with sauce. **2.** (*colloq.*) be impudent to (someone).

—[他] **1.** …에 소오스를 치다 **2.** ⟪口⟫ 건방진 소리를 하다

sauce·boat [sɔ́ːsbòut] *n.* [C] a boat-shaped bowl in which sauce is served. ⇒fig.

—[名] 배 모양의 소오스 그릇

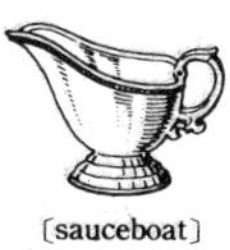
(sauceboat)

sauce·pan [sɔ́ːspæ̀n] *n.* [C] a small metal cooking pan with a handle.

—[名] 스튜우 남비

⁑ sau·cer [sɔ́ːsər] *n.* [C] **1.** a shallow dish to hold a cup. ¶*a cup and ~.* **2.** a small, round dish with a curved edge. **3.** something shallow and round like a saucer. ¶*a flying ~.*①

—[名] **1.** [컵·화분 따위의] 받침접시 **2.** 가장자리가 있는 받침접시 **3.** 받침접시 모양의 것 ¶①비행접시

sau·cer-eyed [sɔ́:sərὰid] *adj.* having large, round, wide-open eyes, usu. as a result of surprise.
—[形] 접시같이 둥근 눈을 한

sau·cy [sɔ́:si] *adj.* (**-ci·er, -ci·est**) **1.** impudent, rude. **2.** (of a ship) smart.
—[形] **1.** 건방진, 뻔뻔스러운 **2.** 날씬한, 멋있는

sauer·kraut [sáuərkràut] *n.* [U] finely-sliced cabbage, salted and allowed to get sour.
—[名] 소금에 절인 양배추

saun·ter [sɔ́:ntər, +*U.S.* sá:n-] *vi.* walk slowly and idly; stroll. ¶~ *through the park* / ~ *through life.*① —*n.* [C] a leisurely walk. ¶*take a morning* ~.
—[自] 산책하다, 어슬렁어슬렁하다 ¶①평생을 빈들빈들 지내다 —[名] 어슬렁거림, 산책

* **sau·sage** [sɔ́:sidʒ / sɔ́-] *n.* [U][C] ground pork, beef, or other meat cut small and put in a thin, tubelike skin.
—[名] 소시지

** **sav·age** [sǽvidʒ] *adj.* (usu. **-ag·er, -ag·est**) **1.** wild; uncivilized. **2.** cruel. —*n.* [C] **1.** a person of an uncivilized country. **2.** a brutal and cruel person.
—[形] **1.** 야만의, 미개한 **2.** 사나운, 잔인한 —[名] **1.** 미개인 **2.** 잔인한 사람

sav·age·ly [sǽvidʒli] *adv.* in a savage manner.
—[副] 야만적으로, 잔인하게

sav·age·ry [sǽvidʒ(ə)ri] *n.* (pl. **-ries**) [U] **1.** the state of being wild or uncivilized. **2.** the quality of being brutal; [C] a brutal fierce act.
—[名] **1.** 야만 상태; 미개한 상태 **2.** 잔인성, 야만[적인 행위]

sa·van·na -nah [səvǽnə] *n.* [C] a flat, treeless stretch of land, esp. in the parts of America.
—[名] [미국 남부의] 대초원

sa·vant [sævá:nt, sǽvənt] *n.* [C] a great scholar.
—[名] 대학자

** **save** [seiv] *vt.* **1.** bring or keep (someone or something) out of danger, harm, disaster, etc.; rescue; protect. 《~ something or someone *from*》 ¶~ *one's life* / ~ *one's skin*① / ~ *one's country* / ~ *someone from drowning.* **2.** keep (money) for future use; reserve. ¶~ *one's strength for tomorrow's work*② / *He saved 100 dollars.* **3.** make (trouble, work, expense, etc.) less; keep (something) from being spent or lost. ¶~ *work* / ~ *trouble* / ~ *oneself*③ / ~ *one's pains*④ / ~ *one's pocket*⑤ / ~ *one's carfare and walk* / *She saves her dress by wearing an apron.* / (*proverb*) *A stitch in time saves nine.*⑥ **4.** set (someone) free from sin. ¶~ *souls.* —*vi.* **1.** keep money for future use. **2.** avoid waste; be economical. **3.** keep someone or something from danger, harm, evil, etc. **4.** (of food) keep or be preserved. ¶*Fish saves best in a cold place.*
—[他] **1.** [위험 따위에서] …을 구하다, 지키다, 보호하다 ¶①상처 입지 않다 **2.** [돈 따위]를 모으다, 저축하다 ¶②내일의 일을 위해 힘을 여축하다 **3.** [경비·수고]를 덜다; …을 소중히 하다, 쓰지 않고 두다 ¶③몸을 아끼다/④헛수고를 하지 않다/⑤돈을 쓰지 않다; 남에게 돈을 쓰지 않게 하다/⑥《俚》오늘의 한 바늘이 내일의 아홉 바늘을 덜어 준다 **4.** …을 죄에서 구하다 —[自] **1.** 저축하다 **2.** 절약하다 **3.** 구조하다, 구해내다, 구제하다 **4.** [음식이] 오래가다

save up, keep money, etc. for future use.
[熟] 저축하다

—*prep.* (*archaic, poetic*) except; but. ¶*all* ~ *him.*
—[前] …을 제외하고

—*conj.* (*archaic*) except. 《~ *that …*》 ¶*I am well* ~ *that I have a cold.*
—[接] […임]을 제외하고는

1) ***save and except,*** except.
2) ***save for,*** except.
[熟] 1)…을 제외하고 2)…을 제외하면(하고)

sav·er [séivər] *n.* [C] a person or thing that saves. ¶*A vacuum cleaner is a* ~ *of time and labor.*
—[名] 구조자, 구제자, 절약가; 절약하는 것

** **sav·ing** [séiviŋ] *adj.* **1.** rescuing. **2.** economical; not wasteful. **3.** in reserve. ¶*a* ~ *clause.*① —*n.* [U] 《*pl.*》 money saved. —*prep.* **1.** except; excepting. **2.** in honor of someone; as a mark of respect for someone. ¶~ *your presence.* —*conj.* except.
—[形] **1.** 구조의 **2.** 절약하는 **3.** 보류하는 ¶①유보 조항, 단서 —[名] 저금 —[前] **1.** …외는, …을 제외하고 **2.** …에 경의를 표하여, 실례이지만 —[接] …을 제외하고는

sav·ings bank[séiviŋzbæ̀ŋk] *n.* a bank which receives small amounts of money and pays interest on them.
—[名] 저축은행

sav·ior, *Brit.* **-iour** [séivjər] *n.* **1.** [C] a person who rescues. **2.** 《*the S-*》 Christ.
—[名] **1.** 구조자 **2.** 구세주; 그리스도

sa·vor, *Brit.* **-vour** [séivər] *n.* **1.** [U] the quality of something that affects the sense of taste or smell. **2.** [C] a particular taste or smell; a flavor. **3.** [C] a distinctive quality. —*vi.* **1.** have a particular taste or smell. **2.** have a characteristic quality. **3.** having a touch of something. —*vt.* give a flavor to (something).
—[名] **1.** 맛; 향기 **2.** [특별한] 풍미, 향기 **3.** 특징; 흥미 —[自] **1.** 풍미(향기)가 있다 **2.** …의 [성질]이 있다 **3.** …의 기미가 있다 —[他] …에 맛(풍미)을 내다

sa·vor·y, *Brit.* **-vour·y** [séiv(ə)ri] *adj.* (**-vor·i·er, -vor·i·est,** *Brit.* **-vour·i·er, -vour·i·est**) **1.** pleasing in taste or smell; of a fine flavor. **2.** salty. ↔sweet —*n.* [C] (**-vor·ies** or *Brit.* **-vour·ies**) (*Brit.*) a highly seasoned dish served at the beginning or end of a dinner.
—[形] **1.** 맛이 좋은, 풍미 있는 **2.** 소금기가 있는, 짭짤한 —[名] 식전(후)에 나오는 짭짤한 요리; 입가심

⁑ saw[1] [sɔː] *n.* [C] a cutting tool made of a thin, steel blade with a row of sharp teeth along or around the edge. **—***v.* (**saw·ed, sawn** or **saw·ed**) *vt.* **1.** cut (something) with a saw. **2.** make (something) with a saw. ¶ *~ a log into boards.* **3.** make motions as if using a saw. **—***vi.* **1.** use a saw. **2.** be cut with a saw.
saw the air, move the arms as if sawing.

—[名] 톱 —[他] 1. …을 톱으로 켜다 2. 톱으로 …을 만들다 3. 톱질하듯이 손을 앞뒤로 움직이다 —[自] 1. 톱질하다 2. 톱으로 켜지다

[熟] 톱질하듯이 손을 앞뒤로 움직이다

saw[2] [sɔː] *n.* [C] a short, wise saying used for a long time by many people; a proverb; a saying.

—[名] 속담, 격언

⁑ saw[3] [sɔː] *v.* pt. of **see**.

saw·dust [sɔ́ːdʌst] *n.* [U] the small powdered pieces of wood which result from sawing.

—[名] 톱밥

saw·horse [sɔ́ːhɔ̀ːrs] *n.* [C] a frame for holding wood which is being sawn.

—[名] 톱질 모탕

sawn [sɔːn] *v.* pp. of **saw**.

saw·yer [sɔ́ːjər] *n.* [C] a person whose work is sawing wood.

—[名] 톱질꾼

Sax·on [sǽksn] *n.* **1.** [C] a member of any of several German tribes in what is now northwestern Germany. **2.** [U] the language of the Saxons. **—***adj.* of the Saxons.

—[名] 1. 색슨 사람 2. 색슨 말 —[形] 색슨 사람(말)의

sax·o·phone [sǽksəfòun] *n.* [C] a musical instrument consisting of a metal body with many keys and a reed mouthpiece. ⇒fig.

—[名] 색소폰

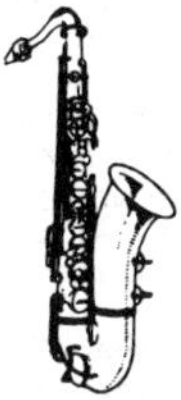

[saxophone]

⁑ say [sei] *v.* (**said**) *vt.* **1.** utter; speak. ⟪~ something *to* someone; ~ *that…*⟫ ¶ *~ yes*① | *~ [someone] nay*② | *~ a good word for someone*③ | *What did you ~?* | *He said to me, "Good night."* | *He said [that] he was hungry.* **2.** express (something) in words; declare (something) as one's opinion or decision. ⟪~ something *to* someone; ~ *what* or *who,* etc.; ~ *that…*⟫ ¶ *Say what you mean.*④ | *He says it is true.* **3.** ⟪often in *passive*⟫ report; state positively but without proof. ⟪~ *that…*; ~ *to do*⟫ ¶ *People* (or *They*) *~ that…* | *It is generally said that …* | *Don't believe everything people ~.* **4.** repeat; recite. ¶ *~ one's prayers.*⑤ **5.** ⟪*imperatively*⟫ select (something) as an example; assume (something) as true. ¶ *Anyone, let us ~ yourself, might have done it.*⑥ | *You may take a few of them, ~ a dozen.* **—***vi.* speak; relate; answer. ¶ *just as you ~*⑦ | *I cannot ~.*⑧ | *Say on!*⑨

—[他] 1. …을 말하다, 이야기하다 ¶①「예」하고 말하다; 승낙하다/②거절하다; …에게 아니라고 말하다/③…을 칭찬하다, 변호하다 2. …을 말로 표현하다; 주장하다, 판단하다, 결정하다 ¶④하고 싶은 말을 해봐라 3. [세상에서] …을 전하다, 소문내다, …이라고 하다 4. …외다, 암송하다 ¶⑤기도문을 외다 5. …이라고 가정하다; 예를 들면, 말하자면 ¶⑥누군가 예를 들면 너라도 그렇게 했을지 모른다
—[自] 말하다, 대답하다 ¶⑦네 말대로/⑧나는 모르겠다/⑨말을 계속해라

1) ***I say,*** an expression used to draw attention, open conversation, or express surprise.
2) ***say out,*** utter frankly.
3) ***that is to say,*** in other words.
4) ***to say nothing of,*** without mentioning.
5) ***What do you say to*** (=*How would you like*) *something?*
6) ***You don't say so.,*** (an expression indicating surprise)

[熟] 1)저어; 여보세요; 이건 놀랐다 2)솔직히 말하다 3)다른 말로는; 즉 4)…은 말할 것도 없이 5)…은 어떻겠읍니까? 6)설마!, 그럴까?

—*n.* [C] ⟪*sing.* only⟫ **1.** what one wants to say or has to say. ¶ *I have a ~ in the matter.* **2.** the chance or right to express an opinion, etc. ¶ *Let her have her ~.* **3.** ⟪*the ~*⟫ the power to decide. ¶ *have the ~.*⑩

—[名] 1. 하고 싶은 말, 할 말 2. 발언의 기회(권리) 3. 결정권 ¶⑩최종 결정권을 갖다

⁑ say·ing [séiiŋ] *n.* [C] **1.** something which is said; a statement. **2.** a proverb; a maxim.
1) ***go without saying,*** be needless to say; be evident.
2) ***There is no saying that …,*** It is impossible to say that …

—[名] 1. 말하기, 말 2. 속담

[熟] 1)…은 말할 것도 없이 2)…은 알 수 없다

scab [skæb] *n.* [C] **1.** a dry cover formed over a wound. **2.** [U] a skin disease of animals, esp. sheep. **3.** (*colloq.*) a worker who will not join a strike; a strikebreaker. **—***vi.* (**scabbed, scab·bing**) **1.** become covered with a scab. **2.** act or work as a scab.

—[名] 1. [상처의] 딱지 2. [양의] 개선(疥癬) 3. ⟪口⟫ 파업에 참가하지 않는 직공 —[自] 1. 딱지가 앉다 2. 파업을 깨뜨리다

S

scab·bard [skǽbərd] *n.* [C] a case for a sword.
—[名] 칼집

scab·by [skǽbi] *adj.* (**-bi·er, -bi·est**) covered with many scabs.
—[形] 딱지투성이의

scaf·fold [skǽfould] *n.* [C] **1.** a framework for holding workmen or materials during building, painting, repairing, etc. **2.** ⟪*the* ~⟫ a wooden platform for putting criminals to death by hanging.
1) ***go to*** (or ***mount***) ***the scaffold,*** be put to death; be killed.
2) ***send*** (or ***bring***) *someone* ***to the scaffold,*** put someone to death.
—[名] 1. [건축용의] 발판 2. 처형대, 교수대
[熟] 1)사형에 처해지다 2)…을 사형에 처하다

scaf·fold·ing [skǽfouldiŋ] *n.* **1.** [C] a scaffold; a system of scaffolds. **2.** [U] materials for making a scaffold.
—[名] 1. [건축용의] 발판, 비계; 발판의 구조 2. 발판 재료

scald [skɔːld] *vt.* **1.** burn (the hand, etc.) with boiling water, oil, steam, etc. ¶~ *oneself with boiling water.*① **2.** pour boiling water over (something). **3.** put (something) into boiling water. **4.** heat (water, oil, etc.) almost to the boiling point. —*vi.* have a burn.
—*n.* [C] a burn caused by boiling water, oil, steam, etc.
—[他] 1. …을 데게 하다 ¶①뜨거운 물에 데다 2. …에 끓는 물을 붓다 3. …을 비등점 가까이까지 끓이다 —[自] 데다
—[名] [액체·증기 따위에 의한] 화상

‡scale[1] [skeil] *n.* [C] **1.** a regular series of marks on a stick, dial, etc. used for measuring. **2.** an instrument with marks at regular distances for measuring, etc. **3.** an arrangement in a series from low to high; any graded system. ¶*sink in the* ~① / *high in the social* ~ / *a* ~ *of wages.*② **4.** the size of a picture, plan, model, etc. compared with the size of the thing itself. ¶*a* ~ *of one inch to a mile.* **5.** a relative size or degree. ¶*on a small* ~③ / *a building of a large* ~. **6.** a series of musical tones going up or down in a regular order. ¶*the major* (*minor*) ~.④
—[名] 1. 눈금, 척도 2. 자 3. 계급, 등급 ¶①사회적 지위가 내려가다/②임금률 4. 비율, 비례; 축척(縮尺) 5. 규모, 정도 ¶③소규모로 6. 음계 ¶④장(단)음계

—*vt.* **1.** climb, esp. by means of a ladder. ¶~ *a cliff.* **2.** make a drawing of (something) according to a scale; control. ¶~ *a house* / ~ *one's spending to one's income.*
scale down (***up***), reduce (increase) (something) by a certain proportion. ¶~ *down wages.*
—[他] 1. …을 [사닥다리로] 기어 올라가다 2. …을 비율로 나타내다, 축척하다; 비율에 따라 …을 정하다
[熟] …의 비율로 …을 감소(증가)시키다

‡scale[2] [skeil] *n.* [C] **1.** one of the two pans or dishes of a balance. **2.** ⟪*the* ~*s, a pair of* ~⟫ a balance for weighing; any form of weighing machine. ¶*weigh in the scales.*
1) ***hold the scales true*** (or ***even***), be fair in one's judgment.
2) ***turn the scale***[***s***], cause one of two sides to outweigh the other; reverse a situation.
3) ***turn*** (or ***tip***) ***the scales at*** (=*weigh*) *5 pounds, etc.*
—[名] 1. 저울의 접시 2. 천칭(天秤), 저울
[熟] 1)…을 공평하게 판정하다 2)형세를 역전하다 3)…의 무게가 있다

—*vt.* **1.** weigh (something) with scales. **2.** amount to (a certain weight). ¶*It scales 150 pounds.*
—[他] 1. …을 저울로 재다 2. …의 무게가 있다

***scale**[3] [skeil] *n.* [C] **1.** one of the small, thin, hard plates covering the bodies of some fish, snakes and insects. **2.** one of the small, thin flakes of dry, dead skin. **3.** ⟪without *an article*⟫ a coat of hard matter which forms inside boilers, etc. **4.** one of the tiny leaves covering a flower bud.
—[名] 1. [물고기·뱀 따위의] 비늘; 인편(鱗片) 2. 피부의 엷은 조각; [상처의] 딱지 3. [보일러 따위에 낀] 물때; 치석(齒石), 이똥 4. [식물의] 아린(芽鱗); 꼭지; 꼬투리

—*vt.* **1.** take away scales or a scale from (something). ¶~ *a fish.* **2.** cover (something) with scales. **3.** (*U.S.*) throw (a flat stone) so that it skips along the surface of water. —*vi.* **1.** come off in scales or flakes. ¶*The paint is scaling off the house.* **2.** (of a boiler, skin, etc.) form scales.
—[他] 1. …의 비늘을 벗기다 2. …을 비늘 따위로 덮다 3. [납작한 돌로] 물수제비를 뜨다 —[自] 1. [피부의 엷은 조각 따위가] 벗겨져 떨어지다 2. 물때가 앉다; 딱지가 생기다

scal·lop, scol- [skɑ́ləp, skǽl- / skɔ́l-] *n.* [C] **1.** a shellfish with two fan-shaped shells. ⇒fig. **2.** the muscle of this shellfish, valued as food. **3.** ⟪usu. *pl.*⟫ a curving ornamental edging of a dress. ⇒p. 1015 fig. —*vt.* **1.** bake (fish, oysters, etc.) with sauce, bread crumbs, etc. in a scallop shell or dish. **2.** decorate (the
—[名] 1. 가리비 2. 조가비살 3. 물결(부채꼴) 무늬의 가장자리 장식
—[他] 1. …을 조가비(작은 접시)에 넣어 굽다 2. …에 물결무늬(부채꼴) 장식을 달다

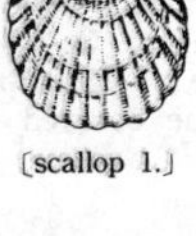
[scallop 1.]

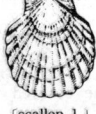

edge of dress, etc.) with scallops.

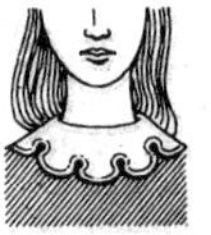
(scallop 3.)

scalp [skælp] *n.* [C] the skin and hair on the top of the head.
—[名] [머리털이 붙어 있는] 머리가죽
1) ***have the scalp of,*** defeat.
2) ***take scalps,*** tear off the enemies' scalps; win.
[熟] 1)…을 해치우다 2)적의 머리가죽을 벗기다, 이기다
—*vt.* tear off the scalp of (an enemy, etc.)
—[他] [적]의 머리가죽을 벗기다

scal·pel [skǽlp(ə)l] *n.* [C] a small knife used by surgeons.
—[名] 외과용 메스

scal·y [skéili] *adj.* (**scal·i·er, scal·i·est**) **1.** covered with scales. **2.** like scales. **3.** coming off in flakes.
—[形] **1.** 비늘이 있는 **2.** 비늘 모양의 **3.** 벗겨져 떨어지는

scamp [skæmp] *n.* [C] a rascal; a worthless fellow. —*vt.* do (work, etc.) carelessly and hastily; skimp.
—[名] 건달, 망나니 —[他] [일 따위]를 아무렇게나 하다

scam·per [skǽmpər] *vi.* **1.** run away quickly. **2.** run about playfully.
—[自] **1.** [동물·어린이가] 급히 도망치다 **2.** 뛰어 다니다
—*n.* [C] **1.** a quick run. **2.** a hurried trip.
—[名] **1.** 질주 **2.** 급한 여행

scan [skæn] *v.* (**scanned, scan·ning**) *vt.* **1.** watch (something) closely; examine the details of (something) carefully. **2.** glance at (something) quickly. **3.** divide (a line of poetry) into metrical feet. **4.** read or recite (a line of poetry) so as to show its rythmic structure. **5.** (*Electronics*) make a small beam of light pass over (a surface) rapidly in order to send or reproduce a picture.
—*vi.* **1.** examine the rhythmic structure of poetry. **2.** accord with the rules of meter. **3.** (*Electronics*) scan a surface.
—[他] **1.** …을 자세히 보다; 자세히 조사하다 **2.** …을 대충 훑어보다 **3.** …을 음각(音脚)으로 나누다 **4.** [시]를 운율을 붙여 읽다 **5.** […의 표면]을 주사(走査)하다 —[自] **1.** 시의 운율을 살피다 **2.** 운율의 규칙에 따르다 **3.** 화상(畫像)을 주사하다

* **scan·dal** [skǽndl] *n.* [U] **1.** [C][U] a shameful action or state that brings dishonor. **2.** disgrace. **3.** careless or wicked public talk about someone.
—[名] **1.** 추문; 부정 사건; 스캔들 **2.** 치욕, 창피 **3.** 중상(中傷)

scan·dal·ize, *Brit.* **-ise** [skǽnd(ə)làiz] *vt.* shock or offend (someone) by actions or opinions considered wrong or immoral.
—[他] …을 분개시키다, 망신시키다

scan·dal·mon·ger [skǽndlmʌ̀ŋgər] *n.* [C] a person who spreads scandal.
—[名] 남을 비방하고 다니는 사람, 험담가

scan·dal·ous [skǽnd(ə)ləs] *adj.* **1.** shameful; shocking. ¶~ *speech and behavior.*① **2.** tending to damage someone's reputation; speaking or spreading slander. ¶*a ~ rumor.*
—[形] **1.** 창피한, 부끄러운, 지독한 ¶① 괘씸한 언행 **2.** 욕설의; 중상적인

scan·dal·ous·ly [skǽnd(ə)ləsli] *adv.* in a scandalous manner; shamefully; terribly; blamably.
—[副] 괘씸하게, 창피하게, 지독히; 비난하여

Scan·di·na·via [skæ̀ndinéiviə] *n.* **1.** Norway, Sweden, Denmark and Iceland. **2.** the peninsula that consists of Norway and Sweden.
—[名] 스칸디나비아, 스칸디나비아 반도

Scan·di·na·vian [skæ̀ndinéiviən] *adj.* of Scandinavia; of Scandinavian people or languages. —*n.* **1.** [C] a person of the Scandinavian countries. **2.** [U] one or all of the languages of Scandinavia, including Norwegian, Swedish and Danish.
—[形] 스칸디나비아의, 스칸디나비아 사람(말)의 —[名] **1.** 스칸디나비아 사람 **2.** 스칸디나비아 말

scan·sion [skǽnʃ(ə)n] *n.* [U] the act of dividing lines of poetry according to the rhythm or meter.
—[名] 시를 운율에 맞춰 낭독하기

scant [skænt] *adj.* **1.** not enough in size or amount. **2.** barely enough.
—[形] **1.** 부족한, 모자라는 **2.** 간신히 자라가는
scant of, not having enough; be lacking in.
[熟] …이 충분하지 않다, 모자라다

scant·i·ly [skǽntili] *adv.* in a scanty manner; not sufficiently.
—[副] 불충분하게, 부족하여

scant·i·ness [skǽntinis] *n.* [U] the state of being scanty; shortage.
—[名] 불충분, 부족

* **scant·y** [skǽnti] *adj.* (**scant·i·er, scant·i·est**) **1.** not enough in amount. **2.** barely enough.
—[形] **1.** 부족한, 불충분한 **2.** 간신히 자라 가는

scape·goat [skéipgòut] *n.* [C] **1.** (in the Bible) a goat selected to bear the sins of the people and driven out into the wilderness. **2.** a person who bears all the blame for others who are guilty.
—[名] **1.** 속죄 염소(고대 유대에서 속죄일에 사람의 죄를 지워 황야에 버린 염소) **2.** 남의 대신 죄를 뒤집어쓰는 사람, 제물

scape·grace [skéipgrèis] *n.* [C] a worthless fellow; a rascal.
—[名] 말썽꾸러기, 밥벌레

S

* **scar** [skɑː*r*] *n.* [C] **1.** a mark left on the skin after a wound, burn, etc. has become well. **2.** any mark like a scar. **—*v.*** (**scarred, scar·ring**) *vt.* mark (something) with a scar. **—*vi.*** become well, forming a scar.
—[名] 1. 상처 자국 2. 흔적 —[他] …에 상처 자국을 남기다 —[自] 흉터가 남다

* **scarce** [skɛə*r*s] *adj.* difficult to get; not easily found; uncommon; rare. **—*adv.*** (*poetic*) =scarcely.
—[形] 입수하기 어려운; 좀처럼 없는, 드문; 진귀한

‡ **scarce·ly** [skɛ́ə*r*sli] *adv.* **1.** with difficulty; barely. ¶*There were ~ fifty people present.* **2.** hardly. ¶*I ~ know him.* **3.** certainly not. ¶*He can ~ have done that.*
1) ***scarcely ever,*** rarely.
2) ***scarcely...when*** (or ***before***), as soon as...
—[副] 1. 간신히, 겨우 2. 거의 …없다 3. 설마 …하지 않다
[熟] 1)좀처럼 2)…하자마자

scar·ci·ty [skɛ́ə*r*siti] *n.* [U] **1.** 《sometime *a ~*》 too small a supply. ¶*a ~ of food.*① **2.** rareness.
—[名] 1. 부족; 결핍 ¶①식량 부족 2. 품귀, 드묾

‡ **scare** [skɛə*r*] *vt.* **1.** strike (someone) with sudden fear; make (someone) afraid. ¶*He was scared by a sudden noise.* **2.** drive (someone or something) away by fear. 《~ someone *away* or *off*》 ¶*The boy scared the birds away.* **—*vi.*** be frightened; fill with fear.
—*n.* [C] a sudden fear; panic.
—[他] 1. …을 깜짝 놀라게 하다; 겁을 먹게 하다 2. …을 위협하여 쫓아버리다 —[自] 깜짝 놀라다, 겁을 먹다
—[名] 공포, 겁; 공황

scare·crow [skɛ́ə*r*kròu] *n.* [C] a figure of a man set up in a field to frighten birds away from crops.
—[名] 허수아비

* **scarf** [skɑː*r*f] *n.* [C] (pl. **scarfs** or **scarves**) **1.** a long piece of silk, wool, etc. worn about the neck or shoulders or over the head. **2.** a long strip of cloth used as a cover for furniture.
—[名] 1. 스카아프 2. [가구의] 겉보, 씌우개

* **scar·let** [skɑ́ː*r*lit] *n.* [U] a very bright red. **—*adj.*** of a bright red color.
—[名] 진홍색, 주홍색 —[形] 진홍색의

scarlet fever [´– ´–] *n.* a disease marked by a scarlet rash, a sore throat, and fever.
—[名] 성홍열(猩紅熱)

scarp [skɑː*r*p] *n.* [C] a sharp slope.
—[名] 가파른 비탈

scarves [skɑː*r*vz] *n.* (*Brit.*) pl. of **scarf**.

scath·ing [skéiðiŋ] *adj.* bitter; severe.
—[形] 격렬한; 통렬한

* **scat·ter** [skǽtə*r*] *vt.* **1.** throw (something) here and there. 《~ something *over* or *about*》 **2.** separate and drive (a mob, etc.) off in different directions. ¶*The police scattered the crowd.*① **—*vi.*** separate and go in different directions.
—[他] 1. …을 흩뿌리다 2. …을 흩뜨리다, 쫓아버리다, 해산시키다 ¶①경찰은 군중을 해산시켰다 —[自] 뿔뿔이 흩어지다

scat·tered [skǽtə*r*d] *adj.* lacking a proper relation; lying in all different directions.
—[形] 산산이 흩어진, 뿔뿔이 헤어진

scat·ter·ing [skǽtəriŋ] *adj.* distributed widely; spread out here and there.
—[形] 뿔뿔이 흩어진, 드문드문 있는

scav·enge [skǽvindʒ] *vt., vi.* clean up (a street, etc.).
—[他][自] …을 소제하다

scav·en·ger [skǽvindʒə*r*] *n.* [C] a person who cleans streets, taking away dirty things.
—[名] 도로 청소부

sce·nar·i·o [sinέəriòu, -nɑ́ːr- / sinɑ́ːriòu] *n.* [C] (pl. **-os**) **1.** an outline of a motion picture, giving the story of the scenes, direction for the actors, etc. **2.** an outline of any play.
—[名] 1. [영화의] 각본, 시나리오 2. 연극(영화·가극)의 줄거리

sce·nar·ist [sinέərist, -nɑ́ːr- / síːnərist] *n.* [C] a person who writes scenarios for motion pictures.
—[名] 영화의 각본 작가

‡ **scene** [siːn] *n.* [C] **1.** one of the parts into which an act of a play is divided. ¶*Act 1, ~ 2.*① **2.** the place or circumstances in which action of a play or story takes place. **3.** a painted background on the stage showing the place of action. **4.** a particular incident in a story, play or novel. **5.** a view; a landscape. **6.** the location of an actual event.
behind the scenes, behind the curtains; secretly.
—[名] 1. [극의] 장(場) ¶①제 1 막 제 2 장 2. 무대, 장소 3. 배경, 도구 설비 4. [특정의] 장면 5. 광경, 풍경 6. 현장
[熟] 무대 뒤에서, 남몰래

* **scen·er·y** [síːnəri] *n.* [U] 《*collectively*》 **1.** the general view of a landscape. **2.** the painted hangings, screens, etc. used on a stage to show the location.
—[名] 1. 풍경 2. 배경

sce·nic [síːnik, sén-] *adj.* **1.** having natural beauty; of natural scenery. **2.** of the stage or a play.
—[形] 1. 풍경의; 경치가 좋은 2. 무대의, 극의

* **scent** [sent] *n.* **1.** [C][U] smell; a sweet smell. ¶*the ~ of flowers.* **2.** [C] the sense of smell; the power to smell. ¶*Dogs have a keen ~.*① **3.** [C] 《*sing.* only》 the smell left
—[名] 1. 냄새, 향기 2. 후각(嗅覺) ¶①개는 날카로운 후각을 갖고 있다 3. [짐승이] 남긴 냄새; 흔적 ¶②강한 냄새

by an animal. ¶*a hot ~*② | *follow up the ~.*③ **4.** [U] perfume; liquid having a sweet smell. ¶*put ~ on one's handkerchief.*④ 자취/③[사냥개가 짐승의] 냄새자취를 따라 쫓아가다 4. 향수 ¶④손수건에 향수를 뿌리다

on the scent, successful in following someone in trying to discover a secret, etc. [熟] 단서를 잡고

—*vt.* **1.** smell at (something). **2.** get a slight suggestion of (something); try to catch (something) by using the sense of smell. **3.** spread the sweet smell of (something) around oneself; spray perfume on (something). **4.** be aware of (a secret etc.). —[他] 1. …을 냄새맡다 2. [짐승 따위]를 냄새로 찾다 3. …을 냄새나게 하다, …에 향수를 뿌리다 4. [비밀 따위]를 눈치채다

scent·less [séntlis] *adj.* having no smell. —[形] 향기 없는, 냄새 안 나는

scep·ter, *Brit.* **-tre** [séptər] *n.* [C] **1.** a stick held by a king as a sign of royal power. ⇒fig. **2.** 《*the ~*》 royal power; royal rank. ¶*lay down the ~.*① —[名] 1. [왕의] 홀(笏) 2. 왕권, 왕위 ¶①왕위에서 물러나다

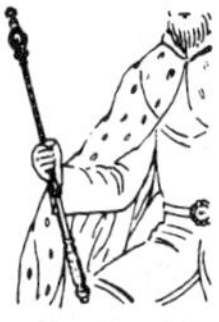
[scepter 1.]

scep·tered, *Brit.* **-tred** [séptərd] *adj.* having a scepter; having royal power or rank. —[形] 홀을 가진; 왕권이 있는

scep·tic [sképtik] *n., adj.* =skeptic.

scep·ti·cal [sképtik(ə)l] *adj.* =skeptical.

scep·ti·cism [sképtisìz(ə)m] *n.* =skepticism.

* **sched·ule** [skédʒu(ː)l / ʃédjuːl] *n.* [C] **1.** a list; a catalogue. **2.** a list of the times for the comings and goings of trains; a timetable; a program. ¶*a train ~*① | *behind ~*② | *leave for London on ~.*③ **3.** a. plan; a detailed statement. ¶*according to ~.*④ —*vt.* **1.** make a list of (something). **2.** make a plan of (something to be done at a certain time). ¶*I'm scheduled to meet him next Sunday.*⑤ | *The reception for the American girls is scheduled on* (or *for*) *Monday.* —[名] 1. 일람표, 목록 2. 시간표, 예정표 ¶①기차의 시간표/②늦어서/③예정대로 런던으로 출발하다 3. 계획, 명세서 ¶④계획대로 —[他] 1. …의 일람표를 만들다 2. …을 예정하다 ¶⑤다음 일요일에 그를 만날 예정이다

sche·mat·ic [ski(ː)mǽtik] *adj.* of a plan; shown in a figure drawn with lines. ▷**sche·mat·i·cal·ly** [-ik(ə)li] *adv.* —[形] 개요(槪要)의; 도해의

‡ **scheme** [skiːm] *n.* [C] **1.** a plan. ¶*lay down a ~*① | *carry out a ~.*② **2.** a secret and cunning plan to cheat someone; a plot. **3.** a system. ¶*an educational ~*③ | *the ~ of society.*④ **4.** an outline. ¶*the ~ of the novel.* —*vi., vt.* **1.** make a plan of (something). **2.** make a secret and cunning plan to cheat someone; plot. —[名] 1. 계획 ¶①계획을 세우다/②계획을 실행하다 2. 음모 3. 조직 ¶③교육 제도/④사회 조직 4. 대요(大要) —[自][他] 1. [···을] 계획하다 2. [···을] 꾸미다

schem·ing [skíːmiŋ] *adj.* full of tricks; cunning. —[形] 음모로 가득 찬; 계획적인

scher·zi [skέərtsi] *n.* pl. of **scherzo.**

scher·zo [skέərtsou] *n.* [C] (pl. **-zos** or **-zi**) a light, playful passage in music. —[名] 해학곡(활발하고 변덕스러운 기분의 악곡)

schism [síz(ə)m] *n.* [U][C] a divided state resulting from a difference of opinion in a church. —[名] [교회의] 분립, 분파; 종파 분립

schis·mat·ic [sizmǽtik] *adj.* of or causing a schism. —[形] 분리의, 교회 분립을 꾀하는

* **schol·ar** [skálər / skɔ́l-] *n.* [C] **1.** a person who has much expert knowledge; a learned person. **2.** a student; a pupil. **3.** a clever student receiving money from a school to help him continue his studies. —[名] 1. 학자 2. 학생, 생도 3. 장학금 수령자, 급비생

schol·ar·ly [skálərli / skɔ́ləli] *adj.* of a scholar; fit for a scholar; having much knowledge; fond of study. —[形] 학자의, 학자다운; 박식한; 학구적인

* **schol·ar·ship** [skálərʃìp / skɔ́lə-] *n.* **1.** [U] the knowledge gained by long study; much knowledge. **2.** [C] the special money given to clever students to help him continue his studies. —[名] 1. 학식, 학문, 박식 2. 급비(給費); 장학금

scho·las·tic [skəlǽstik] *adj.* **1.** relating to a school, student or teacher; of education. ¶*a ~ year*① | *~ attainments.*② **2.** like academic life. —[形] 1. 학교의, 교육의 ¶①학년/②학업성적 2. 학자풍의, 학자인 체하는

‡ **school**[1] [skuːl] *n.* [C] **1.** a place for teaching and learning; a schoolhouse or schoolroom. ¶*a primary ~* | *enter a ~*① | *keep a ~.*② **2.** 《*the ~, collectively*》 the complete group of pupils or teachers. ¶*the entire ~.* **3.** [U] 《usu. without *an article*》 the time of lessons; a —[名] 1. 학교; 교사(校舍); 교실 ¶①학교에 입학하다/②사립학교를 경영하다 2. 전교생; 교사와 학생 전체 3. 수업시간; 재학기간 ¶③수업 중이다, 취학 중이다/④재학 중이다/⑤통학하다

S

boy's or girl's school period or state. ¶~ *age* | ~ *days* ~ *hours* | *after* ~ | *be at* ~③ | *be in* ~④ | *go to* ~ | *attend* ~⑤ | *leave* ~⑥ | *School begins at 9 o'clock.* **4.** a division of a university occupied with one branch of learning. ¶*a medical* ~ | *a graduate* ~.⑦ **5.** the place or condition where a special sort of training is given ¶*the* ~ *of experience*⑧ | *bring up in a hard* ~. **6.** a group of thinkers or artists who have the same ideas; the principles, methods or characteristics of a group of thinkers or artists. ¶*the* ~ *of Plato*⑨ | *the Stoic* ~. —*vt.* educate (someone) at school; teach; train; discipline. ¶~ *a horse* | ~ *oneself to keep silent.*⑩
⑥퇴학하다 4. [대학의] 학부 ¶⑦대학원 5. 시련장, 수양장; 경우 ¶⑧경험이라는 고된 시련장 6. 학파; 유파(流派) ¶⑨플라톤 학파
—[他] …을 교육하다; 훈련하다; 참다; 가르치다 ¶⑩잠자코 있도록 가르치다

school² [sku:l] *n.* [C] a large group of the same kind of fish or sea animals swimming together. ¶*a* ~ *of fish.* —*vi.* (of fish, whales, etc.) swim in large numbers.
—[名] [물고기 따위의] 떼 —[自] [물고기 따위가] 떼를 짓다

school board [ˊ ˋ] *n.* (*U.S.*) a committee managing the public schools; (*Brit.*) a local education authority.
—[名] 《美》 교육 위원회; 《英》 학무 위원회

school·book [skú:lbùk] *n.* [C] a book used in schools; a textbook.
—[名] 교과서, 학습서

***school·boy** [skú:lbɔ̀i] *n.* [C] a boy studying in school.
—[名] 남학생

school days [ˊ ˋ] *n. pl.* the time of being at school.
—[名] 학창시절

school·fel·low [skú:lfèlou] *n.* [C] a companion at school.
—[名] 학우(學友)

***school·girl** [skú:lgə̀:*r*l] *n.* [C] a girl studying in school.
—[名] 여학생

***school·house** [skú:lhàus] *n.* [C] a building used for school.
—[名] 교사(校舍)

school·ing [skú:liŋ] *n.* [U] the education in school.
—[名] 학교 교육; [통신 교육의] 교실 수업

***school·mas·ter** [skú:lmæ̀stə*r* / -mɑ̀:stə] *n.* [C] a man teaching in school; a school principal.
—[名] 교원; 교장

school·mate [skú:lmèit] *n.* [C] a fellow at school.
—[名] 학우

school·mis·tress [skú:lmìstris] *n.* [C] a woman teaching in school; a woman school principal.
—[名] 여자 교원; 여교장

school·room [skú:lrù(:)m] *n.* [C] a classroom.
—[名] 교실

school·teach·er [skú:ltì:tʃə*r*] *n.* [C] a teacher in school.
—[名] 학교 교사

school·time [skú:ltaim] *n.* [C] **1.** the hours of teaching in school. **2.** school days.
—[名] 1. 수업시간 2. 학창시절

school·work [skú:lwə̀:*r*k] *n.* [U] the studies; the lessons.
—[名] 학업

school·yard [skú:ljɑ̀:*r*d] *n.* [C] a ground of a school.
—[名] 교정, 운동장

schoon·er [skú:nə*r*] *n.* [C] a small sailing boat with two or more masts. ⇒fig.
—[名] 스쿠우너 선(2, 3개 또는 4개의 돛대를 단 종범식(縱帆式) 범선)

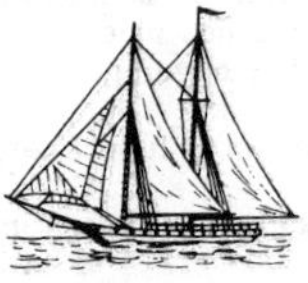
〔schooner〕

Schu·bert [ʃú:bə(:)*r*t], **Franz** *n.* (1797–1828) an Austrian composer.
—[名] 오스트리아의 작곡가

⁑**sci·ence** [sáiəns] *n.* **1.** [U] the study of all material things, observing and arranging them in a systematic law; the subjects relating to this study, such as biology, chemistry, and physics; [C] one of these subjects. ¶*Politics and economics are social sciences.*① **2.** [U] skill; technique. ¶*In judo,* ~ *is more important than strength.*②
—[名] 1. 과학; 자연과학 ¶①정치학과 경제학은 사회과학이다 2. 기술, 숙련 ¶②유도에서는 힘보다 기술이 중요하다

⁑**sci·en·tif·ic** [sàiəntífik] *adj.* **1.** of science. ¶*a* ~ *book.*① **2.** using or based on the methods and principles of science; accurate; systematic; skillful. ¶~ *method.*②
—[形] 1. 과학의 ¶①과학서적 2. 과학상의; 정확한; 계통이 선; 기술이 있는 ¶②과학적 방법

sci·en·tif·i·cal·ly [sàiəntífik(ə)li] *adv.* in a scientific manner; skillfully.
—[副] 과학적으로; 교묘하게

⁑**sci·en·tist** [sáiəntist] *n.* [C] a person who is learned in science, esp. natural science.
—[名] 과학자; [특히] 자연과학자

scim·i·tar, -ter [símitə*r*] *n.* [C] a short curved sword, used by Arabs and other Oriental people. ⇒fig.
—[名] [아라비아 사람들이 쓴] 초승달 모양의 칼

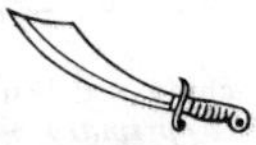
〔scimitar〕

scin·til·la [sintílə] *n.* [C] **1.** a spark; a glimmer. **2.** 《usu. in *negative*》 a small piece. ¶*There is not a* ~ *of evidence.*①
—[名] 1. 꽃불 2. 미량, 조금 ¶①증거는 조금도 없다

scin·til·late [síntilèit] *vi.* **1.** send out little sparks;
—[自] 1. 불꽃을 튀기다 2. [재치 따위

scintillation

shine suddenly. **2.** (of wit, intelligence, etc.) flash.
scin·til·la·tion [sìntiléiʃ(ə)n] *n.* Ⓤ the act of scintillating; a spark; Ⓒ a flash ǀof witǀ.
sci·on [sáiən] *n.* Ⓒ **1.** a slender shoot of a plant, used for attaching to another or for planting. **2.** a descendant, esp. of a noble or rich family.
* **scis·sors** [sízərz] *n. pl.* a cutting tool with two sharp blades which work towards each other.
scoff [skɔːf, skɑf / skɔf] *n.* Ⓒ the act of laughing at someone; an expression of contempt or scorn; an object of contempt or scorn. ¶*be the ~ of the world.*① —*vi., vt.* mock; sneer. 《*~ at* someone or something》 ¶*~ someone in one's heart* / *~ at a speaker.*②
scof·fing·ly [skɔ́ːfiŋli, skɑ́f- / skɔ́f-] *adv.* scornfully.
* **scold** [skould] *vi., vt.* blame (someone) with angry words; speak sharply and angrily to (someone). —*n.* Ⓒ a person who constantly finds fault with others; esp. a sharp-tongued, noisy woman.
scold·ing [skóuldiŋ] *n.* Ⓒ a sharp or severe rebuke. ¶*give a child a ~.*① —*adj.* (esp. of a woman) fault-finding; scolding constantly.
scol·lop [skɑ́ləp / skɔ́l-] *n., v.* =scallop.
sconce [skɑns / skɔns] *n.* Ⓒ a candlestick with a handle or an ornamental bracket fixed to a wall. ⇒fig.
scone [skoun, +*U.S.* skɑn, +*Brit.* skɔn] *n.* Ⓒ a soft, round, flat cake, usu. cooked quickly in a hot oven.
scoop [skuːp] *n.* Ⓒ **1.** a tool like a shovel, used for taking up or moving coal, grain, etc. **2.** any of several kitchen utensils to take up sugar, salt, flour etc.; [sconce] a large spoon. **3.** the amount obtained at one time by a scoop. **4.** the act of skimming. **5.** (*colloq.*) the act of obtaining striking news before any rival newspaper does; the news thus obtained.
—*vt.* **1.** take up (something) with a scoop; dig up. 《~ *out* or *up* something》 ¶*~ [out] a hole in the sand.* **2.** (*colloq.*) gather in (profits, etc.), as if by a scoop. **3.** get and publish (striking news) before a rival newspaper does. ⌈contains.⌉
scoop·ful [skúːpfùl] *n.* Ⓒ (pl. **-fuls**) the amount a scoop
scoot [skuːt] *vi.* (*colloq.*) run away swiftly; hurry off.
scoot·er [skúːtər] *n.* Ⓒ **1.** a child's toy vehicle with two wheels which a rider drives by pushing against the ground with one foot. ⇒fig. **2.** (*U.S.*) a small bicycle that moves by means of a motor. ⇒fig. —*vi.* move by scooter.

[scooter 1.]

* **scope** [skoup] *n.* Ⓤ **1.** the extent of understanding or knowledge. ¶*a man of wide ~* / *a book beyond the ~ of such a small child.* **2.** the area covered or reached by a study, plan, activity, etc.; extent. ¶*It is beyond the ~ of science.* **3.** room for free activity; opportunity; freedom. ¶*seek ~ for*① / *give full* (or *ample*) *~ for* (or *to*).②

* **scorch** [skɔːrtʃ] *vt.* **1.** burn slightly the surface of (something). ¶*a scorching day.*① **2.** wither (grass, etc.); dry up (something) by heat.

[scooter 2.]

scorch

가] 번득이다
—⊕ 불꽃을 튀기기, 불꽃, 섬광; [재치의] 번득임

—⊕ 1. [접목(接木)에 쓰는] 어린 가지, 움돋이 2. [특히 명문의] 자손

—⊕ 가위

—⊕ 조소; 웃음거리 ¶①세상의 웃음거리가 되다 —⾃ […을] 조소하다, 비웃다 ¶②연설자를 비웃다

—⓭ 냉소하여
—⾃⊕ […을] 꾸짖다; […에게] 잔소리하다 —⊕ 잔소리 심한 사람; [특히] 바가지 긁는 여자

—⊕ 꾸짖기; 잔소리 ¶①아이에게 잔소리하다 —⓭ 잔소리가 심한, 꾸짖는

—⊕ [벽 따위에 붙인] 돌출 촛대

—⊕ 호트케이크 같은 둥근 과자빵

—⊕ 1. [석탄 따위를 푸는] 작은 삽 2. [부엌용의] 주걱, 국자, 큰 숟가락 3. 한 번에 떠내는 양 4. 퍼내기 5. 특종기사로 다른 신문을 앞지르기; 특종기사

—⊕ 1. …을 푸다, 뜨다; 파다, 도려내다 2. 《口》 큰 돈을 벌다 3. [신문이 특종기사]를 내다

—⊕ 한 숟가락(주걱·삽)[의 분량]
—⾃ 《口》 뛰어가다, 달리다
—⊕ 1. [어린이의] 외발 스케이트 2. 모우터 스쿠우터 —⾃ 스쿠우터로 달리다

—⊕ 1. [지력 따위의] 범위; 지식의 한계 2. [연구·활동 따위의] 범위 3. [활동 따위의] 여지, 기회, 자유 ¶①…의 기회를 찾다/②…을 발휘할 충분한 기회를 주다

—⊕ 1. …을 그을리다, 눋게 하다 ¶①찌는 듯이 더운 날 2. …을 시들게 하다 3. …에게 욕설을 퍼붓다, 깎아 내리다 4. …을 질주시키다 —⾃ 눋다; [열

3. laugh at (someone) bitterly; abuse. **4.** drive (a car, etc.) very fast. **—*vi.*** **1.** burn slightly; wither by heat. ¶*scorched-earth policy* (or *tactics*).② **2.** run at full speed. **—*n.*** [C] **1.** a mark made by burning. **2.** a very fast ride.

때문에] 시들다 ¶②초토 작전 2. 질주하다

—[명] 1. 눋기 2. 질주

scorch·er [skɔ́:rtʃər] *n.* [C] **1.** a person or thing that scorches. **2.** (*colloq.*) a very hot day. **3.** a person who drives very fast.

—[명] 1. 눋게 하는 사람(것) 2.《口》 타는 듯이 더운 날 3. 질주자

‡score [skɔ:r] *n.* [C] **1.** a cut, mark, or line made with a sharp point. ¶*scores on rock.* **2.** the record of points made in a game, a test, etc. ¶*The baseball ~ was 6 to 1.* **3.** a debt; an amount or a sum owed. ⇒[N.B.] ¶*pay one's ~*① / (*proverb*) *Death pays all scores.*② **4.** (pl. **score**) a group or set of twenty things, people, etc.; (*pl.*) a great many. ¶*three ~ apples* / (*Bible*) *three ~ and ten*③ / *scores of people.*④ **5.** a point; a reason; an excuse. ¶*on that ~*⑤ / *be absent on the ~ of illness.*⑥ **6.** a copy of work of music showing separate parts for different instruments or voices.

1) ***go off at score,*** start vigorously.

2) ***pay off*** (or ***settle***) ***old scores,*** ⓐ get equal with (someone) for past wrongs or injuries. ⓑ pay out.

—*vt.* **1.** make cuts, marks, or lines in or on (something). ¶*~ mistakes in red ink.* **2.** get (a specified number of points) in a game or test; gain; achieve. ¶*~ a success* / *~ three points over one's opponent.* **3.** keep a record or an account of (something); mark a score of (something). ¶*He was appointed to ~ the basketball game.* **4.** (*U.S.*) grade or mark (an examination, a candidate, etc.). ¶*~ a test.* **5.** arrange (a piece of music). **—*vi.*** **1.** make a point; achieve a success; gain an advantage. ¶*Neither team scored.* **2.** keep a score.

1) ***score off,*** get an advantage over (someone); get the better of (someone) in an argument, etc.

2) ***score out,*** cancel (words, etc.) by drawing lines through or under.

—[명] 1. 새긴 금; 선(線); 흠; 벤 상처 2. [경기의] 득점; [시험 따위의] 득점 3. 빚, 계산, 셈 [N.B.] 옛날 선술집 따위에서 나무 따위에 분필로 표시한 데서 ¶①빚을 갚다/②《俚》죽으면 원한도 사라진다 4. 20, 20 개; 다수 ¶③[인생의] 70 년/④다수의 사람 5. 점, 이유 ¶⑤그 점에 관해서는/⑥병 때문에 쉬다 6. 악보, 총보(總譜)

[숙] 1)기운차게 시작하다 2)ⓐ…에 앙갚음하다 ⓑ반제(返濟)하다

—[타] 1. …에 새김눈을 내다; 기초를 하다; 줄을 그어 지우다 2. …을 득점하다; [성공 따위]를 획득하다 3. [득점 따위]를 기록하다; …을 계산하다 4. [시험 따위]를 채점하다 5. …의 음악을 만들다 —[자] 1. 득점하다; 성공하다; 이익을 얻다 2. 득점을 기록하다

[숙] 1)…을 해치우다; 의론 따위에서 지게 하다 2)[말 따위]를 줄을 그어 지우다

score·board [skɔ́:rbɔ̀:rd] *n.* [C] a board that shows the score in a game.

—[명] 득점 게시판; 스코어 보오드

score·book [skɔ́:rbùk] *n.* [C] a book in which the scores of the game are written and kept for reference.

—[명] 득점표, 득점 장부

scor·er [skɔ́:rər] *n.* [C] a person who keeps the score.

—[명] 채점자(계), 득점 기록계

‡scorn [skɔ:rn] *n.* **1.** [U] a feeling of strong dislike; contempt; disdain. ¶*have* (or *feel*) *scorn for someone*① / *hold someone in scorn.*② **2.** [C] a person or thing that is despised; an object of contempt.

—*vt.* show contempt for (someone); despise; reject. ¶*~ to take a bribe.*③

—[명] 1. 경멸 ¶①…에 경멸감을 품다/②…을 경멸하다 2. 경멸(조소)당하는 사람(것), 웃음거리

—[타] …을 경멸하다; 퇴짜놓다 ¶③뇌물을 거절하다

•scorn·ful [skɔ́:rnf(u)l] *adj.* showing disdain openly; full of contempt.

—[형] 경멸하는, 조소적인

scorn·ful·ly [skɔ́:rnfuli] *adv.* in a scornful manner; disrespectfully.

—[부] 경멸하여

scor·pi·on [skɔ́:rpiən] *n.* [C] **1.** a small animal having eight legs, two large claws and a tail with a poisonous sting. ⇒fig. **2.** an evil person. **3.** (*the S-*) the name given to a group of stars.

—[명] 1. 전갈(全蠍) 2. 뱃속 검은 사람 3. 전갈좌(座)

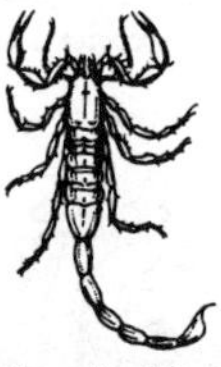

[scorpion 1.]

•Scot [skɑt / skɔt] *n.* [C] a person of Scotland; a Scotchman. ¶*Great Scot!*①

—[명] 스코틀랜드 사람 ¶①참!, 아차, 저런!

•Scotch [skɑtʃ / skɔtʃ] *adj.* of Scotland, its people or their language. ⇒[N.B.]

—*n.* **1.** (*the ~, collectively*) the people of Scotland. **2.** the language of Scotland. **3.** [U] a fine kind of whiskey made in Scotland.

—[형] 스코틀랜드[사람·말]의

—[명] 1. 스코틀랜드 사람 2. 스코틀랜드 말 3. 스코틀랜드산 위스키

Scotch·man [skɑ́tʃmən / skɔ́tʃ-] *n.* [C] (pl. **-men** [-mən])

—[명] 스코틀랜드 사람

a person of Scotland; a Scotsman.

Scotch·wom·an [skátʃwúmən / skɔ́tʃ-] *n.* [C] (pl. **-wom·en** [-wìmin]) a woman of Scotland.
—[名] 스코틀랜드 여자

scot-free [skátfríː / skɔ́t-] *adj.* completely free from harm, punishment, payment, etc.; unpunished; unharmed; safe. ¶*go* (or *get off*) ~.①
—[形] 처벌을 면한; 무사한; 지불 면제의 ¶①무사히 도망치다

⁑Scot·land [skátlənd / skɔ́t-] *n.* the northern part of Great Britain.
—[名] 스코틀랜드

Scotland Yard [⌐– ⌐] *n.* the headquarters of the London Police, esp. the department of criminal investigation. ⇒[N.B.]
—[名] 런던 경시청, [특히] 런던 경시청 수사과 [N.B.] 옛 소재지의 이름에서

Scots [skɑts / skɔts] *adj.* of Scotland; Scottish. —*n. pl.* **1.** 《*the* ~, *collectively*》 the people of Scotland. **2.** [U] the language or dialect of Scotland.
—[形] 스코틀랜드의 —[名] **1.** 스코틀랜드 사람 **2.** 스코틀랜드 말(사투리)

Scots·man [scátsmən / skɔ́ts-] *n.* (pl. **-men** [-mən]) =Scotchman.

Scots·wom·an [skátswùmən / skɔ́ts-] *n.* (pl. **-women** [-wìmin]) =Scotchwoman.

∗Scot·tish [skátiʃ / skɔ́t-] *adj., n.* =Scotch.

scoun·drel [skáundr(ə)l] *n.* [C] an evil man; a wicked man; a rascal.
—[名] 악당, 무뢰한

scour[1] [skáuər] *vt., vi.* **1.** polish (something) by hard rubbing; burnish. **2.** remove or wash off (dirt, grease, etc.) by hard rubbing or with water. 《~ something *away* (or *off, out*)》 ¶~ *the rust off.*① —*n.* [U] the act of scouring. ¶*give a dirty frying pan a good* ~.
—[他][自] **1.** [···을] 문질러 닦다; 윤나게 하다 **2.** [···을] 세게 문질러 닦아내다; 씻어내다 ¶①녹을 문질러 닦다
—[名] 씻어내기, 문질러 닦기

scour[2] [skáuər] *vt.* search for (someone or something) quickly and thoroughly; pursue thoroughly. ¶*We scoured the woods for the lost child.*① —*vi.* move swiftly, as if searching.
—[他] ···을 바삐 찾아 다니다; 샅샅이 찾다 ¶①우리는 숲을 샅샅이 뒤져 길 잃은 아이를 찾았다 —[自] 뛰어다니다

∗scourge [skəːrdʒ] *n.* [C] **1.** the act of whipping; a whip. **2.** a means of punishment; a cause of trouble, pain, misfortune, etc. —*vt.* strike or hit (someone) with a whip; punish severely; torment very much.
—[名] **1.** 채찍질; 회초리, 매 **2.** 벌; 고민거리 —[他] ···을 채찍질하다, 엄중히 처벌하다; ···을 크게 괴롭히다

scour·ings [skáuəriŋz] *n., pl.* **1.** dust or material rubbed off. **2.** the rubbish removed from grain.
—[名] **1.** [문질러 뗀] 먼지, 쓰레기 **2.** 곡식 부스러기

⁑scout [skaut] *n.* [C] **1.** a person, a ship, an airplane, etc. sent or used to obtain information about the enemy. **2.** the act of obtaining information about the enemy. **3.** a member of the Boy Scouts or Girl Scouts. **4.** (*colloq.*) a fellow. —*vi.* perform as a scout; search for something. ¶*He is out scouting.*①
—[名] **1.** 척후, 정찰병; 정찰함(기) **2.** 정찰하기 **3.** 소년단(소녀단)의 단원 **4.** 《口》 놈, 녀석 —[自] 수색(정찰)하다; 찾아다니다 ¶①그는 척후로 나가 있다

scout about (or ***around***), go from place to place, searching for (something); search about for (something).
[熟] 여러 곳을 찾아 다니다

scout·mas·ter [skáutmæ̀stər / -mɑ́ːstə] *n.* [C] a leader of a band of Boy Scouts.
—[名] 소년단 단장

scowl [skaul] *vi.* look displeased or angry; frown at someone heavily. 《~ *at* or *on* someone or something》 ¶*The man scowled at me.*① —*vt.* **1.** make (someone) do something by scowling. 《~ someone *down* or *away*; ~ someone *into* silence, etc.》 **2.** express (angry feelings, etc.) with a scowl.
—*n.* [C] a frowning face; a sulky face.
—[自] 얼굴을 찡그리다, 노려보다 ¶①그 남자는 나를 노려보았다 —[他] **1.** ···에게 얼굴을 찡그려 ···시키다 **2.** 얼굴을 찡그려 [분노의 감정 따위]를 나타내다
—[名] 찡그린 얼굴

scrab·ble [skræ̀bl] *vi.* **1.** scratch about with the hands or paws. **2.** write carelessly or hastily; scribble.
—[自] **1.** 뒤져서 찾다 **2.** 휘갈겨 쓰다

scrag [skræg] *n.* [C] **1.** a thin, skinny person or animal. **2.** [U] a lean, bony part of a sheep's neck, used for making soup. **3.** (*colloq.*) a neck. —*vt.* (**scragged, scrag·ging**) (*colloq.*) twist or wring the neck of (someone); put (someone) to death by hanging or strangling.
—[名] **1.** 말라빠진 사람(동물) **2.** 양의 목덜미 고기 **3.** 《口》 목 —[他] 《口》 ···의 목을 조르다; ···을 교수형에 처하다; 목을 졸라 죽이다

scrag·gy [skræ̀gi] *adj.* (**-gi·er, -gi·est**) **1.** thin; skinny; bony. **2.** (of rocks, etc.) ragged; rough.
—[形] **1.** 말라빠진 **2.** 울퉁불퉁한; 깔쭉깔쭉한

∗scram·ble [skræ̀mbl] *vi.* **1.** climb or move along with the hands and feet. 《~ *up* or *along* a wall, a cliff, etc.》 **2.** struggle or fight with others for something. —*vt.* **1.** collect (something) in a hurry; mix (something)
—[自] **1.** 기어오르다, 기다 **2.** 서로 빼앗다 —[他] **1.** ···을 급히 모으다; 휘젓다 **2.** [계란]을 휘저으며 요리하다, 휘지어 섞다

[S]

scrap

together. **2.** mix the whites and yolks of (eggs) together. —*n.* ⓒ **1.** the act of climbing a steep hill, etc. **2.** a hard or disorderly struggle.

* **scrap** [skræp] *n.* ⓒ **1.** a small or broken piece. **2.** a small piece of a book or something written; (*pl.*) pieces of paper, etc. that are cut from books, newspapers, etc. **3.** ((*collectively*)) wasted metal, such as pieces of iron. **4.** (*pl.*) the fat of an animal remaining after the oil has been taken away; (*pl.*) small pieces of food left after a meal.
  1) *do not care a scrap,* do not care or mind at all.
  2) *not a scrap,* not at all.
  —*vt.* (**scrapped, scrap·ping**) make (something) into scraps; throw (something) away as useless.

scrap·book [skrǽpbùk] *n.* ⓒ a book of blank pages for pasting and keeping clippings from newspapers, etc.

* **scrape** [skreip] *vt.* **1.** take off (something) by rubbing with a rough or sharp tool. ((~ something *off* (or *out, from*))) ¶ ~ *old paint from a door.* **2.** rub the surface of (something) with a rough or sharp tool; make (something) smooth or clean by rubbing with a rough or sharp tool. ¶ ~ *a ship's bottom* / ~ *one's plate*① / ~ *one's chin*② / *Scrape your muddy shoes.* **3.** injure or scratch (something) by scraping. ((~ one's knee, etc. *on* or *against*)) ¶ *I scraped my knee on a stone.* **4.** dig (a hole, etc.), esp. with the hands and nails. ¶ ~ *a hole in the ground.* —*vi.* **1.** rub anything with a hard object. **2.** produce a rough sound. **3.** succeed barely or manage with difficulty. ((~ *along* (or *by, through*) something)) ¶ ~ *through an examination.*③ **4.** make money slowly and with difficulty. **5.** draw back the foot when bowing. ¶*bow and* ~.④
  1) *scrape* [*up*] *an acquaintance with,* meet (someone) by making advances; get a chance to meet (someone) by pushing oneself into his company.
  2) *scrape out,* play (music) on a violin, etc. with rough sounds.
  3) *scrape up* (or *together*), gather or save (something).
  —*n.* **1.** ⓤⓒ the act or sound of scraping. **2.** ⓒ a difficult or unpleasant situation caused by one's bad behavior. ¶*He got into a* ~.⑤

scrap·er [skréipər] *n.* ⓒ **1.** a tool or an instrument for scraping. **2.** a door mat. ¶*wipe shoes on the* ~. **3.** a tool for leveling the ground. [of iron scraps.

scrap heap [^{ㅗㅅ}] *n.* a pile of useless articles; a pile

scrap·ing [skréipiŋ] *n.* (usu. *pl.*) something scraped.

scrap·py [skrǽpi] *adj.* (**-pi·er, -pi·est**) **1.** made up of scraps. **2.** consisting of fragments; disconnected.

: **scratch** [skrætʃ] *vt.* **1.** mark or cut the surface of (something) with something pointed or hard; break, cut, or mark (something) lightly by doing this. ¶ ~ *the varnish of a door* / *The cat scratched my hand.* / *She scratched her name on the post.* **2.** rub (the skin, etc.) lightly with the fingernails, etc. to stop an itch. ¶ ~ *one's nose.* **3.** make (a hole, etc.) by scratching. **4.** blot out or erase (writing, etc.); withdraw (a horse, a candidate, etc.) from a race or contest. ¶ ~ *a horse.* **5.** write in a hurry or poorly. ¶ ~ *one's signature.*
—*vi.* **1.** wound or dig with the nails or claws. ¶*Cats* ~. **2.** rub the skin, etc. lightly with the fingernails, etc. to stop an itch. **3.** (of a pen, etc.) make a bad sound. [get along somehow.
  1) *scratch along,* (*colloq.*) make a living by hard work;
  2) *scratch out* (or *off*), take out words, etc. by drawing

scratch

—㉠ 1. 기어오르기 2. 다투어 빼앗기

—㉠ 1. 작은 조각, 파편 2. 단편; 발췌, 오려낸 조각 3. 찌꺼기, 파쇠 4. 기름을 짜고 난 찌꺼기; 먹다 남은 것

㈜ 1) 조금도 개의치 않다 2) 조금도 …않다
—㉯ …을 쓰레기로 버리다, 폐기하다

—㉠ 스크랩북

—㉯ 1. …을 문질러 벗기다(메다), 깎다 2. …을 문지르다, 긁어내다; 닦다, 깨끗이 하다 ¶①먹어 치우다/②수염을 깎다 3. …을 할퀴다, 할퀴어 상처를 내다, 스쳐 벗기다 4. …을 파다, 긁어내다 —㉰ 1. 문지르다, 스치다 2. 삐걱거리다, 켜서 울리다 3. 이럭저럭 빠져나가다 ¶③시험에 이럭저럭 합격하다 4. 고생하여 돈을 모으다 5. [절을 할 때] 한쪽 발을 뒤로 빼다 ¶④절을 하며 발을 뒤로 빼다; 아첨하다

㈜ 1) …에 억지로 달라붙어 사귀다 2) 바이올린 따위를 켜서 연주하다 3) [고생하여] …을 긁어 모으다(저축하다)

—㉠ 1. 문지르기, 긁기; 문지르는(긁는) 소리 2. 고생; 궁지 ¶⑤그는 궁지에 빠졌다
—㉠ 1. 긁는(깎는) 도구 2. [구두의] 흙털개 3. 땅을 고르는 기계

—㉠ 쓰레기 더미, 파쇠 더미
—㉠ (깎아낸) 쓰레기, 부스러기
—㉯ 1. 부스러기의 2. 단편적인

—㉯ 1. …의 표면을 [날카로운 것으로] 긁다, 할퀴다; …을 할퀴다; …에 생채기를 내다 2. [손톱 따위로 가려운 곳을] 긁다 3. [구멍 따위]를 파다, 긁어내다 4. …을 지우다, 삭제하다; [경주말의 출장]을 취소하다; [후보자의 이름]을 취소하다 5. …을 휘갈겨 쓰다
—㉰ 1. 할퀴다; [동물이] 지면을 긁다 2. [가려운 데를] 긁다 3. [펜 따위가 종이에] 가치작거리다, 깔짝깔짝 소리 내다

㈜ 1) 이럭저럭 해나가다 2) …을 말소하다 3) 고생하여 …을 긁어 모으다

a line through.
3) ***scratch up*** (or ***together***), gather (something) with difficulty.
—*n.* [C] **1.** a mark, cut, or sound made by scratching. **2.** [U] the act of scratching. ¶*Dogs enjoy a good ~.*① **3.** a slight wound. ¶*It is only a ~.* **4.** the mark from which a race is started. **5.** a hurried piece of handwriting.

—[名] 1. 긁은 자국, 긁는 소리 2. 할퀴기 ¶①개는 몸을 긁기를 좋아한다 3. 생채기, 할퀸 상처 4. 출발선 5. 휘갈겨 쓰기

—*adj.* used for hasty writing, notes, etc. ¶*~ paper.*

—[形] 휘갈겨 쓰는

scratch·y [skrǽtʃi] *adj.* (**scratch·i·er, scratch·i·est**) **1.** (of writing, drawing, etc.) written or drawn hastily or carelessly. **2.** making the sound of scratching. ¶*a ~ pen.*① ▷**scratch·i·ly** [-li] *adv.* —**scratch·i·ness** [-nis] *n.*

—[形] 1. 휘갈겨 쓴(그린) 2. [펜이] 가치작거리는, 깔짝깔짝 소리내는 ¶①가치작거리는 펜

scrawl [skrɔːl] *vi., vt.* write or draw carelessly or hastily; make meaningless writing. ¶*~ all over the door.*

—[自][他] [···을] 휘갈겨 쓰다, 낙서하다

—*n.* [C] a bad, careless or meaningless handwriting; a letter written quickly and badly.

—[名] 휘갈겨 쓰기, 낙서; 휘갈겨 쓴 편지

scraw·ny [skrɔ́ːni] *adj.* (**-ni·er, -ni·est**) (*U.S.*) lean and bony.

—[形] 《美》 야윈, 뼈만 앙상한

* **scream** [skriːm] *vi.* **1.** make a loud, sharp cry from pain, strong emotion, etc. ¶*~ with laughter*① / *The baby screamed.* **2.** (of a bird, etc.) give a loud, sharp cry; (of wind, etc.) make a loud noise; give a whistle. —*vt.* say (something) with a loud sharp cry.

—[自] 1. 짹(빽)소리를 지르다 ¶①깔깔 웃다 2. [새 따위가] 날카로운 소리로 울다, [바람 따위가] 쌩쌩 불다(소리내다) —[他] ···을 [비명을 질러] 말하다

—*n.* [C] **1.** a loud, sharp cry; a shriek. **2.** something that is very funny.

—[名] 1. 절규, 날카로운 소리 2. 웃음을 자아내는 것, 웃음거리

screech [skriːtʃ] *n.* [C] a sharp, loud cry. —*vi., vt.* cry out (something) in a sharp, loud voice; make a harsh or shrill noise. ▷**screech·er** [-ər] *n.*

—[名] 날카로운 웃음소리, 삑삑소리 —[自][他] 찢는 듯한 소리로 외치다; 삐걱삐걱 소리나다(내다)

screech owl [⌐ ⌐] *n.* (*Brit.*) a sort of owl that cries out sharply in a high voice; (*U.S.*) a small owl with hornlike ear tufts of feathers.

—[名] 《英》 올빼미의 일종; 《美》 올빼미류의 부엉이

* **screen** [skriːn] *n.* [C] **1.** a covered frame or panels used to hide or protect. ¶*a folding ~.*① **2.** a window made of wire. **3.** a thing that divides or separates a room into parts, esp. in a church. **4.** a shelter; something that interrupts the view. ¶*under ~ of darkness.* **5.** the white surface on which a motion picture is projected. **6.** 《*the ~*》 the movies. **7.** a tool made of wire net and used to separate sand, coal, seeds, etc.

—[名] 1. 간막이, 병풍 ¶①병풍 2. [창에 끼우는] 쇠그물 3. [방의 특히 교회의] 간막이 4. 가로 막는 것 ¶②어둠을 틈타서 5. 스크리인, 영사막 6. 영화 7. [자갈 따위를 거르는] 큰 체

—*vt.* **1.** shelter; conceal, protect. 《~ something *from* view, etc.》 ¶*I screened my face with a handkerchief.* **2.** project (a motion picture) on a screen. **3.** photograph (a scene, etc.) by using a camera. **4.** adapt (a novel, story, etc.) in making a motion picture. **5.** separate (coal, sand, etc.) by using a screen.

—[他] 1. ···을 가로막다, 숨기다 2. ···을 영사하다 3. ···을 촬영하다 4. ···을 각색하다 5. 석탄 따위를 체질하다

* **screw** [skruː] *n.* [C] **1.** a nail of metal driven into wood, etc. by being turned around or twisted. ⇒fig. **2.** anything like a screw; a propeller of a ship or an airplane. **3.** a turn or motion of a screw. ¶*give a ~ to a cork.*① **4.** (*Brit. colloq.*) salary; wages.

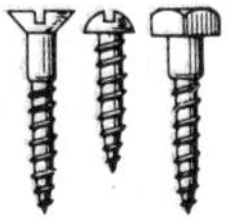
[screw 1.]

—[名] 1. 나사; 나사못 2. 나사 모양의 것; [선박·비행기의] 나선(螺旋) 추진기 3. [나사의] 한 바퀴 죄기(돌리기) ¶①코르크 마개를 한 바퀴 돌리다 4. 《英口》 급료

1) ***put the screw*** (or ***screws***) ***on,*** use one's power to force (someone) to do something.
2) ***There is a screw loose somewhere.,*** Something is wrong with a machine, an organization, etc.

[熟] 1)···하도록 압력을 가하다 2)어딘가 잘못된 데(고장)가 있다

—*vt.* **1.** press, force, fasten, or tighten (something) with a screw; apply a screw to (something). ¶*~ a lock on the door.* **2.** twist; wind. **3.** force; extract (something) by pressure. 《~ *out*; ~ something *out of*》 ¶*He screwed a dollar out of me.*② —*vi.* **1.** turn in the manner of a screw; move with twisting movements. **2.** be fitted for being put together or taken apart by a screw. ¶*The hatrack screwed on to the wall.*③

—[他] 1. ···을 나사로 죄다, ···에 나사못을 박다 2. ···을 비틀다, 꼬다 3. ···을 억지로 꺼내다 ¶②그는 나에게서 억지로 1달러를 빼앗았다 —[自] 1. 나사처럼 돌아가다, 비틀리다 2. 나사로 고정되다(분리되다) ¶③모자걸이는 나사못으로 벽에 고정되었다

1) ***screw up,*** twist (something) out of its natural shape. ¶*~ up one's mouth.*

[熟] 1)[얼굴 따위]를 찡그리다 2)용기를 불러 일으키다

screwdriver — scrutinize

2) **screw up one's courage**, overcome one's fear.

screw·driv·er [skrú:dràivər] *n.* ⓒ a tool used to turn a screw. —⊛ 나사돌리개

scrib·ble [skríbl] *vt., vi.* write hastily or carelessly; make meaningless or hard-to-read handwriting. ¶~ *a letter.*① —*n.* ⓒ something written carelessly and hastily; the meaningless or hard-to-read marks that are so written. —⊕ⓑ […을] 아무렇게나 쓰다, 휘갈겨 쓰다; 낙서하다 ¶①짧은 편지를 휘갈겨 쓰다 —⊛ 난필, 낙서

scrib·bler [skríblər] *n.* ⓒ a person who writes carelessly or hastily; an author of a low rank. —⊛ 난필가; 삼류 문인

scribe [skraib] *n.* ⓒ **1.** in former times, a person who copied writings as a professional; a person who writes letters, etc. for another as a job. **2.** in ancient times, a person who studied and taught Jewish Law. —⊛ 1. [주로 인쇄술이 없었던 시대의] 필기자; 대서인 2. 법학자

scrim·mage [skrímidʒ] *n.* ⓒ **1.** a confused struggle or fight. **2.** (*Rugby*) =scrummage. —*vi., vt.* **1.** take part in a confused struggle. **2.** (*Rugby*) =scrummage. —⊛ 1. 난투, 작은 전투 —⊛ 1. 난투를 벌이다

scrimp [skrimp] *vt.* cut down (expenses, etc.); use (something) less than enough. —*vi.* **1.** avoid useless expenses. **2.** be too economical in spending money or in the use of things. —⊕ [경비 따위]를 바짝 줄이다 —ⓑ 1. 절약하다 2. 인색하게 굴다

script [skript] *n.* **1.** Ⓤ handwriting; the style of writing. ¶~ *style.*① **2.** Ⓤ a kind of printing type imitating handwriting. **3.** ⓒ a manuscript of a play, an actor's part, etc.; a text used in broadcasting. ¶*a film* ~. —⊛ 1. 손으로 쓴 글; 필적 ¶①필기체 2. 스크립트(초서체 활자) 3. [영화의] 대본, 각본; [라디오 방송용의] 텍스트

scrip·tur·al [skríptʃ(u)r(ə)l] *adj.* of the Bible; based on the Bible. ▷**scrip·tur·al·ly** [-əli] *adv.* —⊕ 성서의, 성서의 가르침에 입각한

scrip·ture [skríptʃər] *n.* ⓒ **1.** (*S-*, *Holy S-*, *the S-s*) the Bible. **2.** the religious writings of any other religion. —⊛ 1. 성서 2. [그리스도교 이외의] 경전(經典), 성전

scroll [skroul] *n.* **1.** ⓒ a roll of paper or the skin of goats or sheep, used as a writing material, etc; a book written on such a roll. ⇒fig. **2.** Ⓤⓒ an ornamental design based on curving or coiled form.

[scroll 1.]

—⊛ 1. [종이나 양피지의] 두루마리 2. 소용돌이 무늬, 와형(渦形)

* **scrub**¹ [skrʌb] *v.* (**scrubbed, scrub·bing**) *vt.* wash or rub (something) hard. ¶~ *the windowpane clean.*① —*vi.* clean by rubbing hard. —*n.* ⓒ the act of cleaning by hard rubbing. —⊕ …을 박박 문지르다 (씻다, 닦다) ¶①창유리를 문질러서 닦다 —ⓑ 박박 문질러서 깨끗이 하다 —⊛ 박박 문질러 닦기

scrub² [skrʌb] *n.* **1.** Ⓤ (*collectively*) a shrub; [land with] trees or bushes that are of poor quality and small. **2.** ⓒ anything that is inferior or small in size. **3.** ⓒ a player of a second team as opposed to a regular team. —⊛ 1. 관목, 덤불; 잡목숲[이 있는 토지] 2. 작고 보잘것 없는 사람(것) 3. 후보 선수단의 선수

scrub·bing brush [skrʌ́biŋbrʌ̀ʃ] *n.* a brush used for washing. —⊛ 빨래솔, 수세미

scrub·by [skrʌ́bi] *adj.* (**-bi·er, -bi·est**) **1.** (of trees, animals, etc.) small or checked in growth. **2.** poor; shabby. —⊛ 1. 잘 자라지 못한 2. 볼품 없는

scruff [skrʌf] *n.* ⓒ (*usu. the* ~ *of the neck*) the back of the neck. —⊛ 목덜미

scrum [skrʌm] *n.* (*Brit. colloq.*) =scrummage.

scrum·mage [skrʌ́midʒ] *n.* ⓒ (*Rugby*) a play in which the forwards of the two teams make a compact mass around the ball. —*vi.* take part in a scrummage. —⊛ (럭비) 스크럼 —ⓑ 스크럼을 짜다

scru·ple [skrú:pl] *n.* **1.** ⓒ a unit of weight that equals 20 grains. **2.** Ⓤ (often *pl.*) a feeling of uneasiness, suspicion or hesitation in deciding; uneasiness of conscience. ¶*do a thing without* ~① / *have scruples about doing..*② —*vi.* hesitate because of conscience or a feeling. ((~ *to do*) ¶~ *to ask someone's help.*③ —⊛ 1. 스크루우플(약 무게의 단위) 2. 의혹, 망설임; 양심의 가책 ¶①태연히 …을 하다 ¶②…하는 것에 마음이 거리끼다 —ⓑ 망설이다; 마음이 거리끼다 ¶③도움을 청하기를 망설이다

scru·pu·lous [skrú:pjuləs] *adj.* **1.** cautious to follow one's sense of right or duty. ¶*with* ~ *honesty.*① **2.** paying attention to details; very careful. —⊕ 1. 양심적인, 성실한 2. 면밀한, 정확한; 세심한

scru·ti·nize [skrú:t(i)nàiz] *vt.* look at (someone) very carefully; study or examine closely. ¶~ *a machine.* —⊕ …을 자세히 바라보다, 세밀히 검사하다

scru·ti·ny [skrúːt(i)ni] *n.* (pl. **-nies**) **1.** [U] the act of staring at someone's face. **2.** [C] a careful examination.
—[名] 1. 자세히 바라보기 2. 정밀한 조사(검사)

scud [skʌd] *vi.* (**scud·ded, scud·ding**) run swiftly; move lightly over. ¶*Clouds are scudding across the sky.*① —*n.* **1.** [C] the act of moving swiftly. **2.** [U] clouds driven by the wind; [C] a shower.
—[自] 질주하다, 휙 스치고 지나가다 ¶①구름이 하늘을 날아간다 —[名] 1. 질주 2. 날아가는 구름; 소나기

scuff [skʌf] *vi.* walk without lifting the feet from the ground.
—[自] 발을 질질 끌며 걷다

scuf·fle [skʌ́fl] *vi.* struggle in a confused manner. —*n.* [C] a confused fight or struggle.
—[自] 맞붙어 싸우다, 난투하다 —[名] 격투

scull [skʌl] *n.* [C] **1.** an oar rowed from side to side at the end of a boat. ⇒fig. **2.** one of a pair of oars rowed with each oar in one hand. **3.** a racing boat with two sculls. ⇒fig. —*vt., vi.* row (a boat) with an oar or oars.
—[名] 1. [배 뒤에 달린] 고물노 2. 스컬, [한 쌍의 노의] 한 개 3. 두 개의 노로 젓는 경주용 보우트 —[他][自] 스컬로 젓다

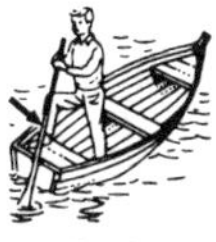
〔scull 1.〕

scul·ler·y [skʌ́ləri] *n.* [C] (pl. **-ler·ies**) (chiefly *Brit.*) a small room near a kitchen where dirty kettles, pots, etc. are cleaned.
—[名] 식기 씻는 곳(부엌에 딸린 작은 방)

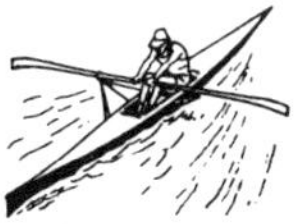
〔scull 3.〕

* **sculp·tor** [skʌ́lptə*r*] *n.* [C] an artist who carves or models figures in stone, wood, etc.
—[名] 조각가

sculp·tur·al [skʌ́lptʃ(ə)rəl] *adj.* of sculpture. ▷**sculp·tur·al·ly** [-i] *adv.*
—[形] 조각의

* **sculp·ture** [skʌ́lptʃə*r*] *n.* **1.** [U] the art of making figures in stone, wood, clay, etc. **2.** [C] a piece of such work; a figure formed by this art. —*vt.* cut (stone, wood, etc.) into figures.
—[名] 1. 조각[술] 2. 조각품 —[他] …을 조각하다

scum [skʌm] *n.* [U] **1.** the thin layer of foam or dirt on the top of some liquids. **2.** ⟪*collectively*⟫ a scrap; a worthless person.
—[名] 1. [발효할 때의] 뜬 찌꺼기, 더껑이, 거품 2. 찌꺼기; 인간의 쓰레기

scurf [skəː*r*f] *n.* [U] the small bits of dead skin on the surface of the head.
—[名] 비듬

scurf·y [skə́ː*r*fi] *adj.* (**scurf·i·er, scurf·i·est**) covered with scurf.
—[形] 비듬투성이의

scur·ril·i·ty [skəríliti, skʌr-] *n.* (pl. **-ties**) **1.** [U] the quality of being scurrilous. **2.** [C] a coarse, abusive remark.
—[名] 1. 상스러움, 천함 2. 독설

scur·ri·lous [skə́ːriləs / skʌ́r-] *adj.* using rough and vulgar abuse or jokes; vulgar in using language.
—[形] 입버릇 사나운; [말 따위가] 상스러운

scur·ry [skə́ːri / skʌ́r-] *vi.* (**-ried**) run with quick, short steps. —*n.* (pl. **-ries**) **1.** [C] a hurried movement; [U] the act or state of walking in such way. **2.** [C] a very light fall of snow.
—[自] 종종걸음으로 달리다 —[名] 1. 종종걸음, 허둥대기 2. 갑자기 오는 눈

scur·vy [skə́ː*r*vi] *n.* [U] a disease caused by the lack of fresh fruits and vegetables. —*adj.* (**-vi·er, -vi·est**) low and bad; mean. ¶*a ~ trick.*① ▷**scur·vi·ly** [-li] *adv.*
—[名] 괴혈병 —[形] 상스러운, 비열한 ¶①비열한 수단

scut [skʌt] *n.* [C] the short tail of a rabbit, etc.
—[名] [토끼 따위의] 짧은 꼬리

scut·tle[1] [skʌ́tl] *n.* [C] a bucket used to carry coal.
—[名] 석탄통

scut·tle[2] [skʌ́tl] *n.* [C] the act of running away at a quick pace. —*vi.* run away quickly with short steps; hurry off. ⟪~ *away, off*⟫
—[名] 급히 도망치기; 종종걸음 —[自] 허둥지둥 달리다(도망치다)

scut·tle[3] [skʌ́tl] *n.* [C] a small opening or window in a roof of a house, or in a deck or side of a ship. —*vt.* make a hole through (the bottom or sides) of a ship to sink it.
—[名] [지붕·벽 따위의] 뚜껑 있는 작은 창; 배의 해치의 입구 —[他] [배]에 구멍을 내어 가라앉히다

scythe [saið] *n.* [C] a cutting tool with a long, curved handle, used for mowing grass or grain. ⇒fig.
—[名] [자루가 긴] 풀 베는 낫

⁑ **sea** [siː] *n.* [C] **1.** a large body of salt water covering the earth; the ocean; any part of the ocean. **2.** the state of the sea. ¶*a calm ~.* **3.** a large, high wave. ¶*a heavy ~.*① **4.** anything like the sea in its greatness or depth; a large quantity. ¶*a ~ of flame.*②
—[名] 1. 바다 2. 바다의 상태 3. 큰 파도, 파랑 ¶①격랑(激浪) 4. 바다같이 넓고 깊은 것; 대량, 다량 ¶②불바다

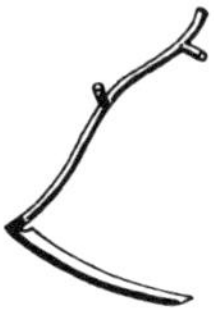
〔scythe〕

1) ***at sea,*** ⓐ in a ship on the sea. ⓑ not knowing what or how to do; bewildered.
2) ***go to sea; follow the sea,*** become a sailor.
[熟] 1)ⓐ바다 위에, 항해 중에 ⓑ오리무중에, 어찌할 바를 몰라 2)선원이 되다

sea anemone [ˊ -ˊ--] *n.* an animal shaped like a flower which has a tubelike body and lives in the sea.
—[名] 말미잘

sea bathing [ˊ ˋ-] *n.* the enjoyment of bathing in the sea.
—[名] 해수욕

sea·beach [ˊ ˋ] *n.* [C] a beach beside the sea.
—[名] 바닷가, 해안

sea·board [síːbɔ̀ːrd] *n.* [C] the land along the sea; the seacoast. ¶*the Pacific* ~.①
—[名] 연안, 연안지방 ¶①미국의 태평양 연안

sea boat [ˊ ˋ] *n.* a ship having the power to go out to the ocean.
—[名] 외양 항행선, 외항선

sea·borne [síːbɔ̀ːrn] *adj.* carried by ships.
—[形] 배로 운반된

sea breeze [ˊ ˋ] *n.* a wind blowing towards the land from the sea.
—[名] 해풍

sea calf [ˊ ˋ] *n.* a large animal living in the sea, hunted for its skin.
—[名] 바다표범

sea chart [ˊ ˋ] *n.* a map relating to the sea, used by sailors on a voyage.
—[名] 해도(海圖)

sea·coast [síːkòust] *n.* [C] the seashore.
—[名] 해안

sea dog [ˊ ˋ] *n.* **1.** an old, experienced sailor. **2.** =sea calf.
—[名] 노련한 선원

sea·far·er [síːfὲərər] *n.* [C] a sailor; a person who travels by sea.
—[名] 뱃사람; 항해자

sea·far·ing [síːfὲəriŋ] *adj.* living on the sea as a sailor; traveling by sea. **—*n.*** [U] the business of a sailor.
—[形] 항해의; 선원살이 —[名] 선원 생활; 항해

sea front [ˊ ˋ] *n.* the street of a town facing the sea.
—[名] 해안 도로

sea·girt [síːgə̀ːrt] *adj.* enclosed by the sea.
—[形] 바다로 둘러싸인

sea·go·ing [síːgòuiŋ] *adj.* (of a ship) made for crossing the ocean; (of a person) living as a sailor.
—[形] 원양 항해용의; 항해를 직업으로 하는

sea green [ˊ ˋ] *n.* the color of light bluish green.
—[名] 해록색(海綠色)의

sea gull [ˊ ˋ] *n.* a large bird that lives near the sea and feeds on fish.
—[名] 바다 갈매기

sea horse [ˊ ˋ] *n.* **1.** (in mythology) a sea animal, half horse and half fish. ⇒fig. **2.** a kind of small fish with a head like that of a horse.
—[名] 1. 해마(海馬) 2. 해상(海象)

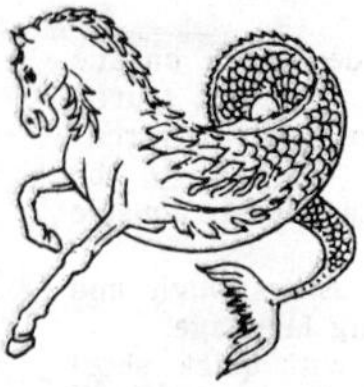
[sea horse 1.]

***seal¹** [siːl] *n.* [C] **1.** a design impressed on a piece of wax or other soft material to show ownership; a paper stamped with such a design. ¶*The government papers are stamped with the ~ of the United States.*① **2.** a piece of wax, metal, etc. stamped with a design and placed on a letter or package to close it. ¶*break the ~ of a letter.*② **3.** something that closes another thing tightly. **4.** a decorative stamp, such as a Christmas seal. **5.** something that makes safe. ¶*under the ~ of secrecy.*③
—[名] 1. 인장(印章), 도장; 날인된 서류 ¶①그 정부 문서에는 합중국의 인장이 찍혀 있다 2. 봉인(封印) ¶②편지를 개봉하다 3. 밀봉 4. 스탬프, 시일 5. 비밀 엄수의 약속, 확증 ¶③비밀 엄수의 약속으로

—*vt.* **1.** put a seal on (papers, etc.). **2.** fasten (a letter, etc.) with a seal. **3.** close tightly. **4.** give a mark to (something) to show that it is true. ¶*They sealed their bargain by shaking hands.*④ **5.** determine. ¶*His love sealed her fate.*
—[他] 1. …에 날인하다 2. …을 봉인하다 3. …을 밀봉하다 4. …을 확실한 것으로 하다, 증명하다 ¶④그들은 악수를 함으로써 그 계약을 확인했다 5. …을 결정하다

***seal²** [siːl] *n.* [C] (pl. **seals** or *collectively* **seal**) a large animal living in the sea in cold regions, hunted for its skin and oil; the fur of this animal.
—[名] 바다표범, 물개; 물개의 모피

sealed [siːld] *adj.* closed up tightly with a seal. ¶*a ~ book.*①
—[形] 밀봉한 ¶①내용비밀의 책, 비밀

sea legs [ˊ ˋ] *n. pl.* legs that get used to walking without loss of balance on a rolling ship.
—[名] 흔들리는 갑판 위를 비틀거리지 않고 걷는 걸음, 배에 익숙하기

find (or ***get***) ***one's sea legs*** [***on***]***,*** get used to the motion of a ship so that a person no longer feels sick.
[熟] [뱃멀미를 하지 않고] 갑판 위를 비틀거리지 않고 걸을 수 있다

seal·er¹ [síːlər] *n.* [C] **1.** a person who seals. **2.** an official who checks weights and measures.
—[名] 1. 날인자 2. 도량형 검사관

seal·er² [síːlər] *n.* [C] a man or ship that hunts seals.
—[名] 물개 사냥꾼(수렵선)

sea level [ˊ ˋ-] *n.* the surface of the sea. ¶*Mt. Halla*
—[名] [평균] 해면 ¶①한라산은 해발

S

*is 1,950 meters above ~.*①
1,950 미터이다

seal·ing wax [sí:liŋwæ̀ks] *n.* a kind of wax used to seal letters, packages, etc.
—[名] 봉랍(封蠟)(편지 봉하는 데나 병마개 따위에 씀)

sea lion [ˊ ˋ–] *n.* a large animal with a long body and flippers instead of feet, living in the North Pacific.
—[名] 강치

seal ring [ˊ ˋ] *n.* a kind of finger ring engraved with a picture, initials, etc.
—[名] 인발이 박힌 반지

seal·skin [sí:lskìn] *n.* [U] the skin of a seal; [C] a garment made of this skin.
—[名] 물개 가죽, 그것으로 만든 옷

* **seam** [si:m] *n.* [C] **1.** the line formed by sewing two pieces of cloth together; any line made by joining two edges of material. **2.** a mark like a seam, but made by cutting. ¶*the ~ of an old cut.*① **3.** a layer of a mineral in the earth.
—[名] 1. [천의] 솔기; 이음매 2. 상처 자국, 흉터 ¶①오래된 벤 자국 3. 광물의 층

—*vt.* **1.** sew (two pieces of cloth) together; join (two things) together. **2.** mark (a face, etc.) with lines like seams by cutting.
—[形] 1. …을 꿰매 붙이다, 이어 붙이다 2. …에 상처 자국(틈)을 내다, 흉터를 남기다

sea·man [sí:mən] *n.* [C] (pl. **-men** [-mən]) a sailor; (in the navy) a sailor who is below the rank of an officer.
—[名] 수부, 선원; 수병

sea·man·ship [sí:mənʃìp] *n.* [U] skill in controlling a ship.
—[名] 선박 조종술, 항해술

sea·mark [sí:mɑ̀:rk] *n.* [C] **1.** a landmark on shore, such as a lighthouse, used as a guide for a ship's course. **2.** a line on the shore showing the limit of the tide.
—[名] 1. 항로 표지(標識) 2. 해안선

sea mew [ˊ ˋ] *n.* a large sea bird; a sea gull.
—[名] 갈매기

seam·less [sí:mlis] *adj.* having no seam.
—[形] 솔기(이음매)가 없는

seam·stress [sí:mstris / sém-] *n.* [C] a woman who earns her living by sewing.
—[名] 침모, 여자 재봉사

seam·y [sí:mi] *adj.* (**seam·i·er, seam·i·est**) **1.** having seams. **2.** worse; unpleasant. ¶*the ~ side of life.*①
—[形] 1. 솔기가 있는 2. 이면의, 더러운 ¶①인생의 암흑면

sea·plane [sí:plèin] *n.* [C] an airplane designed to come down on and rise from water.
—[名] 수상 비행기

sea·port [sí:pɔ̀:rt] *n.* [C] a port for seagoing ships; a town with such a port.
—[名] 항구; 항구 도시

sea power [ˊ ˋ–] *n.* **1.** naval strength. **2.** a nation that has great naval strength.
—[名] 1. 해군력 2. 해군국

sear [siər] *vt.* **1.** burn the outside of (something). **2.** make (something) dry up. **3.** make (a mind, etc.) hard and insensible. —*adj.* dried; withered.
—[他] 1. …을 그슬리다 2. …을 시들게 하다, 말리다 3. …을 마비시키다 —[形] 시든

⁑ **search** [sə:rtʃ] *vt.* **1.** look for; try to find something hidden by looking over or going through (a place, etc.) carefully; carefully look in the clothing of (a prisoner, etc.) for something stolen. 《~ a place or someone *for*》 **2.** examine. ¶*~ one's memory.*①
—[他] 1. …을 찾다; 수색하여 찾다; [죄수 등]을 취조하다, 조사하다 2. [기억]을 더듬다, 살피다 ¶①기억을 더듬다

1) ***search into,*** examine.
2) ***search out,*** find (something) by searching.
[熟] 1)…을 조사하다 2)…을 찾아내다

—*n.* [U][C] the act of searching; an examination.
—[名] 찾기, 수색; 조사, 음미

in search of, looking for; trying to find.
[熟] …을 찾아서

search·ing [sə́:rtʃiŋ] *adj.* sharp; keen; severe; thorough.
—[形] 날카로운, 엄중한, 철저한

search·light [sə́:rtʃlàit] *n.* [C] a large, powerful, movable electric light used for seeking out airplanes or ships in time of war, etc.
—[名] 탐조등, 서어치라이트

sea rover [ˊ ˋ–] *n.* **1.** a pirate; a searobber. **2.** a pirate ship; a ship used by a pirate.
—[名] 1. 해적 2. 해적선

sea·scape [sí:skèip] *n.* **1.** [C] a picture of a scene on the sea. **2.** [U] the scenery on the sea. ↔landscape
—[名] 1. 바다 그림 2. 바다 경치

sea shell [ˊ ˋ] *n.* a shell of any shell-bearing animal living in the sea.
—[名] 조가비

* **sea·shore** [sí:ʃɔ̀:r] *n.* [C] a seacoast; the land at the edge of the sea; a beach.
—[名] 해안

sea·sick [sí:sìk] *adj.* suffering from sickness caused by the pitching and rolling of a boat. ¶*He easily gets ~.*①
—[形] 뱃멀미하는 ¶①그는 쉽게 뱃멀미한다

* **sea·side** [sí:sàid] *n.* [C] 《usu. *the ~*》 the land close to the sea. —*adj.* on or of the seashore. ¶*a ~ hotel.*
—[名] 해안 —[形] 해안의

⁑ **sea·son** [sí:zn] *n.* [C] **1.** one of the four parts of a year, such as spring and autumn. **2.** a part of the year
—[名] 1. 계절 2. 시절 ¶①건기(乾期) 3. …에 적합한 시기, 시이즌; 한창; 좋

having a special character. ¶*the dry ~*① / *the Christmas ~*. **3.** the time in a year suitable for a special purpose or activity; the right time to do something. ¶*the tourist ~*② / *the harvest ~*.③
은 기회 ¶②여행 시이즌/③수확기

1) ***in season,*** at the right time; timely. ↔out of season
2) ***in season and out of season,*** all the time.
[熟] 1)시기에 알맞은 2)시종

—*vt.* **1.** give a good taste to (food) with salt, sugar, etc. **2.** make (a story, etc.) more interesting. ¶*~ one's speech with wit.*④ **3.** make (something) less severe. ¶*~ anger*. **4.** bring (something) into good condition for use; mature. ¶*~ wine in a cask*⑤ / *~ timber.*⑥
—*vi.* become mature; come into good condition.
—[他] 1. …에 양념하다 2. …에 흥미를 돋구다 ¶④이야기에 재치를 가미하다 3. …을 부드럽게 하다 4. …을 쓰기 알맞게 만들다; 익히다 ¶⑤통 속에서 포도주를 익히다/⑥재목을 가공할 수 있는 상태로 만들다 —[自] 익다, 쓰기에 알맞게 되다

sea·son·a·ble [sí:z(ə)nəbl] *adj.* **1.** suitable to the season. **2.** occurring at the correct or proper time.
—[形] 1. 계절의, 계절에 알맞은 2. 시기가 적합한, 형편이 좋은

sea·son·a·bly [sí:z(ə)nəbli] *adv.* on a seasonable occasion; at the right time.
—[副] 시기에 알맞게, 좋은 시기에, 형편 좋게

sea·son·al [sí:z(ə)nl] *adj.* of the seasons; occurring only at a certain period of the year. ¶*~ disease*① / *~ change of climate.*②
—[形] 계절의; 어떤 계절에 국한되는 ¶①계절병/②계절의 변화

sea·soned [sí:znd] *adj.* ripe; dried; familiar.
—[形] 익은; 말린; 익숙한

sea·son·ing [sí:zniŋ] *n.* [C] something that gives food a better taste.
—[名] 조미료

season ticket [⌐– ⌐–] *n.* **1.** a ticket which allows its holder to attend a series of games, concerts. **2.** (*Brit.*) a ticket which allows its holder to travel between two stated stations for a certain period.
—[名] 1. [극장 따위의] 시이즌 통용 입장권 2. [탈것의] 정기 승차권

⁝ **seat** [si:t] *n.* [C] **1.** a thing used to sit on. ¶*have a ~*① / *give one's ~ to someone.*② **2.** a place in which one has a right to sit; the right to sit in that place. ¶*win one's ~ in a parliament.*③ **3.** the part of a chair, stool, bench, etc. on which someone sits. **4.** the part of the body on which one sits; the part of the clothes covering it. ¶*the ~ of his trousers.* **5.** the manner of sitting on a horse's back. **6.** something on which anything rests; a base. **7.** a place where something usu. is.
—[名] 1. 자리, 좌석 ¶①착석하다/②…에 자리를 양보하다 2. 의석, 의석권 ¶③의회에 의석을 얻다, 의원으로 당선되다 3. [의자 따위의] 앉는 자리 4. 엉덩이, [옷의] 엉덩이 부분 5. 말을 타는 자세 6. 대(台), 받침 7. 장소, 소재지

—*vt.* **1.** place (someone) on a seat. **2.** have seats for (a fixed number of people). ¶*This theater can ~ 1,000 people.*④ **3.** repair or place seats on (something).
—[他] 1. …을 착석시키다 2. …을 수용하다; …을 수용할 만한 좌석이 있다 ¶④이 영화관은 천 명 수용할 수 있다 3. …에 앉는 부분을 달다(갈다)

sea urchin [⌐ ⌐–] *n.* a small, round-shaped sea animal that has a thin shell covered with sharp spines.
—[名] 섬게

sea wall [⌐ ⌐] *n.* a wall or sea bank built to protect the shore against the damage of waves.
—[名] 호안 제방; 방파제

sea·ward [sí:wərd] *adj.* **1.** facing or directed toward the sea. **2.** (of wind) from the sea. **—*n.*** [U] 《*the ~*》 the direction toward the sea. **—*adv.*** toward the sea.
—[形] 1. 바다로 향한, 바다쪽으로의 2. 바다로부터의 —[名] 바다쪽 —[副] 바다쪽으로, 바다를 향하여

sea·wards [sí:wərdz] *adv.* =seaward.

sea·way [sí:wèi] *n.* [C] **1.** a route over the sea. **2.** a rough sea. ¶*in a ~*. **3.** [U] the forward motion of a ship through the waves. **4.** an inland waterway that is deep enough for large ships.
—[名] 1. 해로(海路), 항로 2. 거친 바다; 거친 파도 3. [배의] 전진, 항진(航進) 4. [내륙의] 수로(水路)

sea·weed [sí:wì:d] *n.* [U] [C] any plant growing in the sea.
—[名] 해초

sea·wor·thy [sí:wə̀:rði] *adj.* fit to sail on the sea; good for a sea trip. ¶*a ~ ship*.
—[形] 항해에 알맞은(견디는)

se·cede [si(:)sí:d] *vi.* withdraw from a political party, a church, etc. 《*~ from* something》
—[自] [정당·교회 따위에서] 탈퇴하다

se·ces·sion [siséʃ(ə)n] *n.* [U] [C] the act of seceding from a political party, etc.
—[名] [정당·교회에서의] 탈퇴; 분리

se·clude [siklú:d] *vt.* separate (someone) from others; keep (someone) away from others. ¶*~ oneself from society.*①
—[他] …을 떼어놓다; 격리하다 ¶①사회에서 은퇴하다

se·clud·ed [siklú:did] *adj.* set apart from others; isolated. ¶*a ~ life.*
—[形] 격리한; 은둔한

se·clu·sion [siklú:ʒ(ə)n] *n.* **1.** [U] the act of secluding; the state of being secluded; retirement. ¶*a policy of ~*① / *live in ~.*② **2.** [C] a secluded place.
—[名] 1. 은퇴; 한거(閑居) ¶①쇄국 정책/②은둔하다 2. 외딴 장소

⁝ **sec·ond**¹ [sék(ə)nd] *adj.* **1.** coming just after the first.
—[形] 1. 두 번째의 ¶①제 2 주자/②하

¶*the ~ runner*① / *every ~ day.*② **2.** next to the first in rank, quality, etc.; sub-. ¶*the ~ prize*③ / *the ~ city in England.* **3.** another; like the first one.
—*n.* [C] **1.** ⦅usu. *the ~*⦆ a person or thing next after the first in place, rank, etc. **2.** ⦅often *pl.*⦆ goods of the second grade. **3.** an assistant, esp. as in a boxing match.
—*vt.* **1.** act as an assistant to (someone). **2.** support; back up.

루 걸려 **2.** 2위의, 2등의; 부(副)의 ¶③ 2등상 **3.** 또 하나의; 아주 비슷한
—[名] **1.** 제 2위, 제 2위의 사람(것) **2.** 2급품 **3.** 조수; 시중꾼
—[他] **1.** …의 조수(시중꾼) 노릇을 하다 **2.** …을 후원하다, 지지하다

⁑ sec·ond[2] [sék(ə)nd] *n.* [C] (of time or degree) $^{1}/_{60}$ part of a minute; a moment; a short time.
—[名] 초(秒); 순식간

*** sec·ond·ar·y** [sék(ə)ndèri / -(ə)r-] *adj.* **1.** second in order, rank, value, place, time, etc. **2.** coming after the original. —*n.* [C] (pl. **-ar·ies**) something that is secondary.
—[形] **1.** 제 2위의, 2류의 **2.** 제 2차적인, 부(副)의 —[名] 2류의 것, 2차적인 것

secondary school [ˊ---ˋ] *n.* a school ranking between a primary school and a college or university.
—[名] 중등학교(우리나라의 중·고교를 합친 것)

sec·ond-best [sék(ə)ndbèst] *adj.* next to the best.
—[形] 두 번째로 좋은, 차선(次善)의

sec·ond-class [sék(ə)ndklǽs / -klɑ́:s] *adj.* **1.** of the class or grade next to the first. **2.** lower in quality; of inferior quality or grade. —*adv.* on a second-class ticket. ¶*travel ~.*①
—[形] **1.** 2등(류·급)의 **2.** 열등한; 별로 고급이 아닌 —[副] 2등으로 ¶① 2등으로 여행하다

⁑ sec·ond-hand [sék(ə)ndhǽnd] *adj.* **1.** not new; used by someone else. **2.** learned or heard from someone else; not original. **3.** of a store buying and selling used goods. —*adv.* **1.** after being used by someone else. **2.** indirectly.
—[形] **1.** 써서 낡은, 중고의 **2.** 간접의, 전해 들은 **3.** 고물상의 —[副] **1.** 중고품으로 **2.** 간접적으로, 전문(傳聞)으로

second hand [ˊ-ˋ] *n.* **1.** the hand of a clock which points to the seconds. **2.** a thing which has already been used.
—[名] **1.** 초침 **2.** 고물, 중고품

sec·ond·ly [sék(ə)ndli] *adv.* in the second place; in the place next to the best.
—[副] 두 번째로, 다음으로

sec·ond-rate [sék(ə)ndréit] *adj.* **1.** of the second rank. **2.** inferior.
—[形] **1.** 2류의 **2.** 열등한

*** se·cre·cy** [sí:krisi] *n.* [U] **1.** the state of being secret. **2.** the act or ability of keeping things secret.
1) ***in secrecy,*** secretly.
2) ***in the secrecy of*** *one's* ***heart,*** deep down in one's heart; truly; sincerely.
—[名] **1.** 비밀 **2.** 비밀을 지키는 습관·힘, 비밀주의
[熟] 1)비밀리 2)마음속으로는

⁑ se·cret [sí:krit] *adj.* **1.** kept from the sight or knowledge of others; not known. ¶*a ~ meeting.* **2.** hard to understand or discover. ¶*the ~ ways of God.*①
—*n.* **1.** [C] something hidden or unknown; a mystery. ¶*keep a ~.*② **2.** [U] a true way of doing something.
in secret, not openly; secretly.
—[形] **1.** 숨은; 알려지지 않은; 비밀의 **2.** 이해(발견)하기 곤란한; 헤아릴 수 없는 ¶①신의 불가사의한 섭리
—[名] **1.** 비밀; 신비 ¶②비밀을 지키다 **2.** 비결
[熟] 비밀리

sec·re·tar·i·al [sèkritέəriəl] *adj.* of a secretary.
—[形] 서기의; 비서의; 장관의

sec·re·tar·i·at, -i·ate [sèkritέəriət] *n.* **1.** [U] the position of a secretary. **2.** [C] ⦅*the ~*, often *collectively*⦆ the office or place where the secretarial staff works.
—[名] **1.** 서기(비서)의 직 **2.** 비서과

⁑ sec·re·tar·y [sékritèri / -tr-] *n.* [C] (pl. **-tar·ies**) **1.** a person employed to write letters, keep written records, etc. for a person or an organization. **2.** a government official in charge of a department. **3.** a desk with a set of drawers and book shelves. ⇒fig.
—[名] **1.** 서기; 비서 **2.** 장관, 국무위원 **3.** 책상

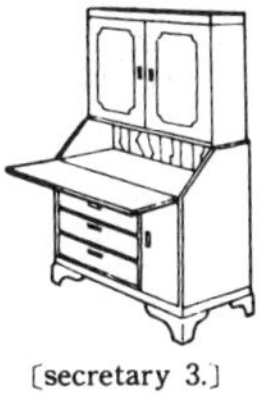
[secretary 3.]

se·crete [sikrí:t] *vt.* **1.** keep (a matter) secret; hide (something) from someone. **2.** (*Biology*) produce (a substance) in the body.
—[他] **1.** …을 비밀로 하다, 숨기다 **2.** …을 분비하다

se·cre·tion [sikrí:ʃ(ə)n] *n.* [U] **1.** the substance that is produced by an animal, etc. **2.** the act of producing a substance in the body. **3.** the act of hiding.
—[名] **1.** 분비물 **2.** 분비 작용 **3.** 숨기기

se·cre·tive [sikrí:tiv] *adj.* **1.** tending to keep things secret; of the principle of secrecy. **2.** causing secretion
—[形] **1.** 숨기는, 비밀주의의 **2.** 분비를 촉진하는

se·cre·to·ry [sikrí:təri] *adj.* of the action of secreting. —*n.* [C] (pl. **-ries**) a secreting organ of the body.
—[形] 분비하는 —[名] 분비 기관(器官)

sect [sekt] *n.* [C] a group of people having the same opinions, esp. about religion.
—[名] 종파, 분파, 당파

sec·tar·i·an [sektέəriən] *adj.* **1.** of a sect. **2.** strongly devoted to a particular sect. —*n.* [C] a person strongly devoted to a sect.
—[形] 1. 종파의, 학파의 2. 당파심이 강한 —[名] 당파심이 강한 사람

:sec·tion [sékʃ(ə)n] *n.* [C] **1.** the act of cutting off. **2.** a part divided or cut off. ¶*divide a cake into three sections.*① **3.** a division of a book. **4.** a district; an area distinctly limited. ¶*the farming* (*business*) ~.②
—[名] 1. 절개(切開), 절단 2. 부분; 단편(斷片) ¶①케이크를 세 쪽으로 나누다 3. [서적의] 절(節), 항 4. 지역, 구역 ¶②경작(상업)지구

sec·tion·al [sékʃ(ə)n(ə)l] *adj.* **1.** of or like a section. **2.** composed of parts joined together; made of sections.
—[形] 1. 구분의, 부문의; 부분의 2. 조립식의

sec·tor [séktər] *n.* **1.** [C] the part of a circle between two radii. **2.** a section of a battle-line.
—[名] 1. 부채꼴 2. 전투지구

sec·u·lar [sékjulər] *adj.* **1.** of this world's life; not religious or sacred. ¶~ *affairs*. **2.** lasting for a long period of time; immortal. —*n.* [C] a parish priest.
—[形] 1. 속인(俗人)의, 세속의, 비종교적인 2. 불후(不朽)의 —[名] 교구 목사

sec·u·lar·ize [sékjuləràiz] *vt.* **1.** make (something) worldly. **2.** remove (property, etc.) from the ownership of a church to that of the government.
—[他] 1. …을 세속화하다 2. …을 교회의 손에서 정부의 소유로 옮기다; 세속용으로 제공하다

:se·cure [sikjúər] *adj.* (**-cur·er, -cur·est**) **1.** free from fear or danger; safe; protected. ¶*feel* ~ / *This building is* ~ *from any earthquake.*① **2.** kept so as not to escape; in good keeping. ¶*keep a dog* ~. **3.** certain; sure. ¶*Our victory is* ~. **4.** firmly fixed; fastened.
—[形] 1. 안전한; 안심인; 위험이 없는 ¶①이 건물은 어떤 지진에도 안전하다 2. 도망칠 우려가 없는; 잘 보관된 3. 고정된

be secure (=*sure*) ***of something.***
[熟] …을 확신하다

—*vt.* **1.** make (something) safe from danger; protect. 《~ *against* something》 **2.** keep (someone) so that he can not escape. **3.** get; gain; obtain. **4.** make (something) sure. **5.** fix firmly; fasten.
—[他] 1. …을 안전하게 하다; 보호하다 2. …을 도망치지 못하게 하다 3. …을 획득하다 4. …을 보증하다 5. …을 단단히 잠그다, 걸쇠를 걸다

se·cure·ly [sikjúərli] *adv.* in a secure manner; firmly; tightly.
—[副] 안전하게, 단단히

:se·cu·ri·ty [sikjúəriti] *n.* (pl. **-ties**) **1.** [U] the state of being safe; freedom from danger or fear. **2.** [C] a thing which secures; a kind of protection. **3.** [C] a thing given as a pledge that a person will fulfill his duties. **4.** [C] a person who gives security for another. **5.** 《usu. *pl.*》 stocks and bonds.
—[名] 1. 안전; 안심 2. 보호물; 방위물 3. 담보물 4. 보증인 5. 증권

se·dan [sidǽn] *n.* [C] **1.** an automobile for four or more persons. **2.** =sedan chair.
—[名] 1. 세단형 자동차

sedan chair [⌐⌐ ⌐] *n.* a covered chair carried on poles by two men.
—[名] 가마

se·date [sidéit] *adj.* serious in mind or manner; calm; quiet.
—[形] 진지한, 차분한, 침착한

se·date·ly [sidéitli] *adv.* in a sedate manner; quietly; calmly.
—[副] 조용히, 침착하게, 진지하게

sed·a·tive [sédətiv] *n.* [C] a medicine that lessens pain or excitement. —*adj.* lessening pain or excitement; calming down.
—[名] 진정제 —[形] 진정시키는; 가라앉히는

sed·en·tar·y [sédntèri / -t(ə)ri] *adj.* **1.** being in the habit of sitting for a long time. **2.** required much sitting. ¶~ *work*. **3.** motionless. **4.** settled at one spot; not moving from one place to another.
—[形] 1. [늘] 앉아 있는 2. 앉아서 하는 3. 활발하지 못한; 비활동적인 4. 정착성의, 정주(定住)의

sedge [sedʒ] *n.* [C] a grasslike plant growing in wet places.
—[名] 사초속(屬)

sed·i·ment [sédimənt] *n.* [C] the matter setting at the bottom of a liquid.
—[名] 침전물

sed·i·men·ta·ry [sèdiméntəri] *adj.* **1.** of sediment. **2.** formed from sediment.
—[形] 1. 침전물의 2. 침전작용의

se·di·tion [sidíʃ(ə)n] *n.* [U] an action, speech, or piece of writing which arouses resistance against lawful authority.
—[名] 선동, 치안 방해

se·di·tious [sidíʃəs] *adj.* **1.** of sedition; likely to cause sedition. **2.** taking part in sedition.
—[形] 1. 치안 방해의, 선동의 2. 선동(동란)에 참가한

se·duce [sid(j)ú:s / -djú:s] *vt.* **1.** persuade (someone) to do wrong. **2.** lead (someone) away from the right way.
—[他] 1. …을 부추기다, 유혹하다 2. …을 타락시키다

se·duc·er [sid(j)ú:sər / -djú:sə] *n.* [C] a person who seduces, esp. a man who seduces a woman.
—[名] 유혹자; 색마, 호색가

se·duc·tion [sidʌ́kʃ(ə)n] *n.* **1.** [U] the act of seducing; the state of being seduced. **2.** 《usu. *pl.*》 a quality or nature of someone or something that seduces or attracts.
—[名] 1. 유혹, 부추김 2. 매력, 끌어당기는 것

se·duc·tive [sidʌ́ktiv] *adj.* very attractive; charming; tending to tempt. ¶*a ~ smile.*①
—[形] 매혹적인, 유혹하는 ¶①매혹적인 미소

sed·u·lous [sédʒuləs / -djul-] *adj.* diligent; hard-working; painstaking. ¶*a ~ student.* ▷**sed·u·lous·ly** [-li] *adv.*
—[形] 근면한; 정성(공)들인

‡**see**[1] [siː] *v.* (**saw, seen**) *vt.* **1.** perceive (something) by the eye; look at (something). 《~ someone *do* or *doing*》 ¶*What do you ~ above the hill? | I saw her dancing last night. |* (*proverb*) *Seeing is believing.* **2.** understand. 《~ *that* ...; ~ *how* or *what* ...》 ¶*I ~ what you mean.*① **3.** experience. ¶*~ life*② *| I have never seen such rudeness.*③ **4.** imagine; consider; think. ¶*I ~ things differently now.*④ **5.** meet. ¶*Very glad to ~ you.*⑤ **6.** visit. ¶*~ a play*⑥ *| I am seeing her tomorrow.*⑦ **7.** go with (someone); accompany. ¶*~ someone home*⑧ *| I saw my aunt to the station.* **8.** make sure; examine. **—*vi.*** **1.** have the power of sight. ¶*We cannot ~ without light.* **2.** understand; become aware. **3.** take care; be attentive. ¶*Go and ~ for yourself.*⑨
—[他] 1. …이 보이다; …을 보다 2. …을 이해하다, 깨닫다 ¶①네가 하려는 말을 알겠다 3. …을 경험하다 ¶②세상을 알다/③이런 무례한 일은 처음이다 4. …을 상상하다, 생각하다 ¶④지금은 생각이 다르다 5. …을 만나다 ¶⑤만나뵈어 반갑습니다 6. …을 방문하다 ¶⑥연극 구경을 하다/⑦내일 그녀를 만날 예정이다 7. …을 수반하다; …을 보살펴 주다 ¶⑧집까지 바래다 주다 8. …을 조심하다, 유의하다 —[自] 1. 보이다 2. 알다 3. 유의(주의)하다 ¶ 가서 확인해 보아라

1) ***see about,*** ⓐ take (something) into consideration. ⓑ take steps to do (something).
2) ***see after*** (=*take care of*) *something.*
3) ***see eye to eye,*** be in agreement; agree with each other.
4) ***see fit,*** think right. 《~ *to do*》
5) ***see into*** (=*examine*) *something.*
6) ***see off,*** accompany (someone) to the starting place of a journey.
7) ***see** someone **out,*** accompany someone to the door.
8) ***see** something **out,*** live, stay or wait until the end of something.
9) ***see over*** (=*look over; inspect*) *something.*
10) ***see*** [***to it***] ***that ...,*** take care that ...; make sure that ...
11) ***see through,*** ⓐ understand the real nature or purpose of (something). ⓑ carry out (something) to the end.
12) ***see** someone **through,*** continue to help someone in work, trouble, etc. until it is finished.
13) ***see to*** (=*attend to; take care of*) *something.*

[熟] 1)ⓐ…을 고려에 넣다 ⓑ…의 조치를 취하다 2)…을 돌보다, 시중들다 3)의견이 일치하다 4)[…하는 것이] 좋다고 생각하다 5)…을 조사하다 6)…을 전송하다 7)…을 문간까지 전송하다 8)…까지 살다; 해내다; 끝까지 지켜보다 9)…을 검사하다 10)…하도록 주선하다 11)ⓐ…의 진상을 간파하다 ⓑ…을 끝까지 해내다 12)…을 끝까지 도와주다 13)…에 마음을 쓰다

see[2] [siː] *n.* [C] the position or authority of a bishop; the district over which a bishop has authority.
—[名] 사교(司教)의 지위(권력·관구)

‡**seed** [siːd] *n.* [C] **1.** [C][U] a small object produced in a plant which itself grows into a young plant. **2.** (in the Bible) descendants. ¶*the ~ of Abraham.*① **3.** 《*pl.*》 a source or an origin of anything. ¶*seeds of discontent.*②
—[名] 1. 씨, 종자 2. 자손 ¶①아브라함의 자손(유대인) 3. 원인, 근원 ¶②불만의 씨

go (or ***run***) ***to seed,*** come to the end of usefulness, prosperity, etc.; become careless of one's appearance.
[熟] 꽃필 때가 지나다; 쇠퇴하다; 몸차림에 관심을 안 갖게 되다

—*vi.* produce seeds; shed seeds. **—*vt.*** **1.** sow seeds over (a garden, etc.). 《~ *down* the wheat, etc.; ~ a place *with* wheat, etc.》 **2.** remove the seeds from (fruit, etc.). ¶*~ a melon.* **3.** (esp. in tennis) separate good players from poor players to make a tournament more interesting.
—[自] 열매를 맺다, 씨가 생기다; 씨가 떨어지다 —[他] 1. …에 씨를 뿌리다 2. …에서 씨를 없애다 3. [강한 사람끼리 처음부터 마주치지 않도록] …의 대진을 미리 조정하다

seed·bed [síːdbèd] *n.* [C] a bed of fine soil where seeds are sown.
—[名] 묘상(苗床), 모판

seed·er [síːdər] *n.* [C] **1.** a person or thing that sows seeds. **2.** a device or machine that takes seeds out of fruit, etc.
—[名] 1. 씨를 뿌리는 사람; 파종기(機) 2. 씨 빼는 기구

seed·less [síːdlis] *adj.* having no seeds.
—[形] 씨가 없는

seed·ling [síːdliŋ] *n.* [C] a young plant or tree which has grown from a seed; a tree which is not yet three feet high.
—[名] 실생(實生), 묘목

seed·y [síːdi] *adj.* (**seed·i·er, seed·i·est**) **1.** full of seeds. **2.** (*colloq.*) worn out; shabby. **3.** (*colloq.*) not feeling well. ¶*I feel ~.*①
—[形] 1. 씨가 많은 2. 《口》 지쳐빠진; 초라한 3. 《口》 기분이 나쁜 ¶①나는 기분이 나쁘다

***see·ing** [síːiŋ] *conj.* in view of the fact that...; considering [that]; since. ¶*Seeing* [*that*] *she looks happy, the rumor*
—[名] …을 생각하여, …이므로

S

must be true.

‡ seek [si:k] *v.* (**sought**) *vt.* **1.** look or search for (something). 《~ *out* something》 ¶~ *a gold mine.* **2.** try to get or gain (help, advice, etc.). **3.** try to do (something); attempt. 《~ *to do*》 ¶*For many years they sought to overcome the difficulty.*① **4.** (*poetic*) go to (a place, etc.); visit. **—*vi.*** make a search. 《~ *after* or *for* someone or something》
1) ***be much to seek,*** be very rarely found.
2) ***seek someone's life,*** plot to kill someone.
3) ***seek out,*** find out; look for carefully.
4) ***seek through a place,*** etc., examine a place, etc. thoroughly.

—[他] 1. …을 찾다, 탐색하다 2. …을 얻으려고 하다, 구하다 3. …하려고 노력하다 ¶①여러 해에 걸쳐 그들은 그 곤란을 극복하려고 노력했다 4. …으로 가다
—[自] 수색하다
[熟] 1)극히 드물다 2)…을 죽이려고 하다 3)샅샅이 뒤지다, 찾아내다 4)…을 샅샅이 뒤지다

seek·er [sí:kər] *n.* [C] a person who tries to find something or to learn something; a person who tries to obtain something.
—[名] 수색자, 탐구자

‡ seem [si:m] *vi.* **1.** appear to be; look like. 《~ *to do*; ~ *that* …》 ¶*He seems* [*to be*] *deaf.*① / *She seems to have been ill.* **2.** appear to be true. 《~ *that* …》 ¶*It seems to me that you told a lie.*②
—[自] 1. …처럼 보이다(생각되다); …인 듯하다 ¶①그는 귀가 먼 것 같다 2. 진실(사실)인 듯하다 ¶②너는 거짓말을 하는 것 같다

seem·ing [sí:miŋ] *adj.* appearing to be; apparent. ¶*her ~ friendship.*
—[形] 외관상의; 그럴 듯한

seem·ing·ly [sí:miŋli] *adv.* in outward appearance; apparently. ¶*He was ~ satisfied with the result.*
—[副] 겉으로는, 표면상, 보기에

seem·ly [sí:mli] *adj.* (**-li·er, -li·est**) suitable; becoming; proper; decent.
—[形] 적당한, 알맞은, 품위있는

‡ seen [si:n] *v.* pp. of **see**[1].

seep [si:p] *vi.* (of liquid) leak through small holes slowly and gradually; ooze.
—[自] 새다; 스며나오다

se·er [sí(:)ər] *n.* [C] a person who foretells the future; a prophet.
—[名] 예언자; 선각자

see·saw [sí:sɔ̀:] *n.* [C] a board balanced at the middle, while the ends move up and down; [U] a game of children played on such a board; [U][C] any up-and-down movement. **—*vi.*** ride on a seesaw; move up and down. **—*adj.*** moving up and down or back and forth.
—[名] 시이소오, 시이소오 판; 시이소오 놀이; 상하 운동 —[自] 시이소오에 타다, 아래위로 움직이다, 동요하다
—[形] 아래위로 움직이는, 동요하는

S

seethe [si:ð] *vi., vt.* **1.** boil; stew. **2.** get violently agitated or excited. 《~ *with* something》
—[自][他] 1. 끓다, 비등하다; …을 끓이다 2. 소란해지다, 떠들다

seg·ment [ségmənt] *n.* [C] **1.** a part of a circle, sphere, etc. which is cut off by a line or plane. ⇒fig. **2.** a section; a division.
—[名] 1. 원·구(球)에서 절단한 궁형(弓形) 부분 2. 부분

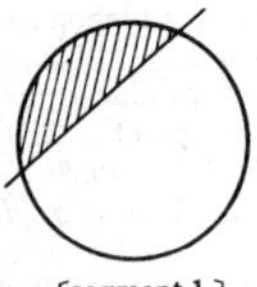
[segment 1.]

seg·men·ta·tion [sègmentéiʃ(ə)n] *n.* [U] the act of dividing into segments; the state of being divided into segments; (*Biology*) the act of forming many cells from a single cell.
—[名] 분열, 절단; 세포 분열

seg·re·gate [ségrigèit] *vt., vi.* separate (someone) from others; keep apart; become separated; isolate.
—[他][自] [···을] 분리하다; 격리하다

seg·re·ga·tion [sègrigéiʃ(ə)n] *n.* [U] the act of segregating; the state of being segregated; isolation; a separation of one race from other races. ↔integration
—[名] 분리, 격리; 인종적 구별, 인종 차별

Seine [sein]**, the** *n.* a river which flows through Paris and into the English Channel.
—[名] 세에느강

seis·mic [sáizmik, +*U.S.* sáis-] *adj.* of or caused by an earthquake.
—[形] 지진의; 지진에 의해 생기는

seis·mo·gram [sáizmougræ̀m, +*U.S.* sáis-] *n.* [C] a record which is made by a seismograph.
—[名] 지진도(圖)

seis·mo·graph [sáizməgræ̀f, sáis- / sáizməgrɑ̀:f] *n.* [C] an instrument which registers the vibrations of earthquakes.
—[名] 지진계

seis·mo·log·i·cal [sàizmoulɑ́dʒik(ə)l, sàis-/sàizmoulɔ́dʒ-] *adj.* of seismology.
—[形] 지진학의

seis·mol·o·gist [saizmɑ́lədʒist, sais- / saizmɔ́l-] *n* [C] a person who is especially trained in the science of earthquakes.
—[名] 지진학자

seis·mol·o·gy [saizmɑ́lədʒi, sais- / saizmɔ́l-] *n.* [U] the science or study of earthquakes.
—[名] 지진학

‡ seize [si:z] *vt.* **1.** hold or grip suddenly. ¶~ *someone's*
—[他] 1. …을 쥐다, 잡다 2. …을 붙들다

hand. **2.** catch (something) by force; capture. ¶ ~ *someone by the ear*① / *The robbers were seized by the police.* **3.** take possession of (something) by force or by authority. ¶ ~ *the enemy's castle.* **4.** understand. **—*vi.*** grasp; hold; catch. 《~ *on* or *upon* something》
1) ***seize hold of*** (=*grasp*) *something.*
2) ***seize on*** (or ***upon***), catch hold of (something) suddenly.

¶①…의 귀를 붙들다 **3.** …을 빼앗다; 몰수하다 **4.** …을 이해하다, 양해하다 —[自] 잡다; 붙들다
[熟] 1)…을 붙잡다 2)…을 쥐다, 붙잡다

sei·zure [síːʒər] *n.* **1.** [U] [C] the act of seizing; the state of being seized; capture. **2.** [C] a sudden attack of a disease, esp. a stroke.
—[名] **1.** 붙잡기, 포획; 차압, 압수; 강탈 **2.** [병의] 발작, [특히] 뇌일혈

⁑ sel·dom [séldəm] *adv.* not often; rarely. ¶*She is ~ cheerless.* / *I ~ go to the movies.*
1) ***not seldom,*** often.
2) ***seldom or never; very seldom,*** hardly ever. ¶*She ~ or never expresses her opinion.*①
—[副] 드물게, 좀처럼 …않다
[熟] 1)종종 2)좀처럼 …없다 ¶①그녀가 의견을 말하는 일은 좀처럼 없다

⁑ se·lect [silékt] *vt.* pick out or choose carefully. ¶*You must ~ good books for your children.* **—*adj.*** **1.** especially or carefully chosen as the best; choicest; of best quality. ¶ ~ *musicians.* **2.** (of a society, club, etc.) not easy to join; exclusive.
—[他] …을 고르다, 선택(선발)하다 —[形] **1.** 고른, 정선(精選)한, 일류의 **2.** 입회 조건이 까다로운

se·lect·ed [siléktid] *adj.* chosen or picked out as best.
—[形] 선발된, 정선된

*** se·lec·tion** [silékʃ(ə)n] *n.* **1.** [U] the act of selecting; the state of being selected; choice. **2.** [C] a person, thing or group selected. **3.** [U] (*Biology*) the process of selecting for the purpose of survival which is seen in animals and plants. ¶*natural ~.*①
—[名] **1.** 선택, 선발, 선정 **2.** 선택물, 정선물, 발췌(拔萃) **3.** 도태(淘汰) ¶①자연도태

se·lec·tive [siléktiv] *adj.* of selection; having the power to choose; selecting.
—[形] 선택의; 선택하는, 도태하는

⁑ self [self] *n.* (pl. **selves** [selvz]) **1.** [C] one's own character or personality. **2.** [U] personal interest or advantage.
—[名] **1.** 자기, 자아(自我), 자신 **2.** 사심, 사리(私利)

self- [self-] a word element meaning *of, by, to, in* or *for oneself.*
—「자기, 스스로」를 뜻하는 연결형

self-a·ban·doned [sélfəbǽndənd] *adj.* giving oneself up to bad ways.
—[形] 자포자기의

self-a·ban·don·ment [sélfəbǽndənmənt] *n.* [U] the state or condition of being self-abandoned.
—[名] 자포자기

self-a·base·ment [sélfəbéismənt] *n.* [U] the act of degrading or humbling oneself, as in rank, position, etc.
—[名] 자기 비하(卑下), 겸손

self-ab·sorbed [sélfəbsɔ́ːrbd] *adj.* giving one's whole mind, attention, etc. to oneself or to one's interests.
—[形] 자기의 생각에 잠기는, 자기 일에 몰두한

self-ab·sorp·tion [sélfəbsɔ́ːrpʃ(ə)n] *n.* [U] the state of being self-absorbed.
—[名] 자기 몰두, 열중

self-ac·cu·sa·tion [sèlfækjuzéiʃ(ə)n] *n.* [U] the act of accusing oneself.
—[名] 자책(自責)

self-act·ing [sélfǽktiŋ] *adj.* acting by itself; automatic.
—[形] 자동의

self-ad·just·ing [sélfədʒʌ́stiŋ] *adj.* able to adjust itself automatically.
—[形] 자동 조정의

self-as·sert·ing [sélfəsə́ːrtiŋ] *adj.* insisting on one's own claims, opinions, importance, etc.
—[形] 자기를 주장하는(내세우는)

self-as·ser·tion [sélfəsə́ːrʃ(ə)n] *n.* [U] the act of insisting on one's own claims, opinions, importance, etc.
—[名] 자기 주장

self-as·ser·tive [sélfəsə́ːrtiv] *adj.* =self-asserting.

self-as·sur·ance [sélfəʃúərəns] *n.* [U] confidence in oneself; self-confidence.
—[名] 자신(自信)

self-cen·tered, *Brit.* **-tred** [sélfséntərd] *adj.* interested only in one's own affairs; selfish.
—[形] 자기본위의, 이기적인

self-col·ored, *Brit.* **-oured** [sélfkʌ́lərd] *adj.* **1.** of a single color. **2.** of the natural color.
—[形] **1.** 단색(單色)의 **2.** 자연색의

self-com·mand [sélfkəmǽnd / -mάːnd] *n.* [U] control of one's own emotions and actions; self-control.
—[名] 극기, 자제, 침착

self-com·pla·cence [sélfkəmpléisns], **-cen·cy** [-s(ə)nsi] *n.* [U] the state of being satisfied with onself.
—[名] 자기만족

self-com·pla·cent [sélfkəmpléisnt] *adj.* satisfied or excessively pleased with oneself.
—[形] 자기만족의

self-con·ceit [sélfkənsíːt] *n.* [U] too much pride in one's own abilities; vanity.
—[名] 자부심, 허영심

self-con·ceit·ed [sélfkənsíːtid] *adj.* having too much self-conceit; vain.
—[形] 자부심이 강한, 허영의

S

• **self-con·fi·dence** [sélfkάnfid(ə)ns / -kɔ́n-] *n.* [U] belief in one's own self and ability. —[名] 자신, 자기 과신

self-con·fi·dent [sélfkάnfid(ə)nt / -kɔ́n-] *adj.* believing in oneself and one's own ability. —[形] 자신이 강한, 자기를 과신하고 있는

self-con·scious [sélfkάnʃəs / -kɔ́n-] *adj.* too much aware of one's appearance, manners, actions, etc. esp. in the presence of others; shy. ▷**self-con·scious·ness** [-nis] *n.* —[形] 자의식이 강한; 소심한; 수줍어하는

self-con·tained [sélfkəntéind] *adj.* **1.** (of a person) hardly ever talking; reserved. **2.** (of a thing) having all that is necessary; independent; (of a machine) complete in itself. —[形] 1. 말 수 적은; 터놓지 않는 2. 필요한 것이 모두 갖추어진; 독립한; [기계가] 자체로 완비된

self-con·tra·dic·tion [sélfkὰntrədíkʃ(ə)n / -kɔ̀n-] *n.* [U][C] the act or fact of contradicting oneself or itself. —[名] 자기모순

self-con·tra·dic·to·ry [sélfkὰntrədíkt(ə)ri / -kɔ̀n-] *adj.* contradicting oneself or itself; not consistent. —[形] 자기모순의

self-con·trol [sélfkəntróul] *n.* [U] control of one's own acts, desires, emotions, feelings, etc. —[名] 극기, 자제

self-de·fense, *Brit.* **-de·fence** [sélfdiféns] *n.* [U] the act of protecting one's own person, property, reputation, rights, etc. —[名] 자위(自衛), 정당방위

• **self-de·ni·al** [sélfdinái(ə)l] *n.* [U] refusal to enjoy oneself, often for the benefit of others; self-sacrifice. —[名] 극기, 금욕; 자기 희생

self-de·ny·ing [sélfdináiiŋ] *adj.* of self-denial; sacrificing oneself; unselfish. —[形] 극기의, 자제하는, 헌신적인

self-de·struc·tion [sélfdistrʌ́kʃ(ə)n] *n.* [U] the destruction of oneself or itself; self-ruin; suicide. —[名] 자멸, 자살

self-de·ter·mi·na·tion [sélfditə̀ːrminéiʃ(ə)n] *n.* [U] **1.** the act of making decisions by oneself. **2.** (of a nation) the act of people making decisions on the form of government without being influenced by other nations. —[名] 1. 자기 결정 2. 민족자결

S

self-de·vo·tion [sélfdivóuʃ(ə)n] *n.* [U] self-sacrifice; the act of giving up oneself to another person or other people. —[名] 자기 희생; 헌신

self-dis·ci·pline [sélfdísiplin] *n.* [U] the act of training oneself for the purpose of improving of one's abilities. —[名] 자기 훈련(수양)

self-ed·u·cat·ed [sélfédʒukèitid / -édju-] *adj.* educated by one's own efforts without going to school or being taught by a teacher; self-taught. —[形] 독학의

self-es·teem [sélfistíːm] *n.* [U] self-respect; too high an opinion of oneself. —[名] 자존, 자만, 자부심

self-ev·i·dent [sélfévid(ə)nt] *adj.* clear without any additional proof. —[形] 자명(自明)의, 뻔한

self-ex·am·i·na·tion [sélfegzæ̀minéiʃ(ə)n] *n.* [U] examination into one's own conduct, manners, motives, etc. —[名] 반성, 자성(自省)

self-ex·plan·a·to·ry [sélfiksplǽnətɔ̀ːri / -t(ə)ri] *adj.* clear in itself; self-evident. —[形] 자명의

self-fill·ing [sélffíliŋ] *adj.* able to fill itself. —[形] 자동 주입식의

self-gov·ern·ing [sélfgʌ́vərniŋ] *adj.* **1.** governing itself; independent. **2.** having self-control. —[形] 1. 자치의; 자립의 2. 자제(自制)의, 극기의

self-gov·ern·ment [sélfgʌ́vərnmənt] *n.* [U] **1.** government of a nation by its own people. **2.** self-control. —[名] 1. 자치 2. 자제, 극기

self-help [sélfhélp] *n.* [U] the act of doing something without help or guidance from others. —[名] 자립, 자조(自助), 독립독행(獨立獨行)

self-im·por·tance [sélfimpɔ́ːrt(ə)ns] *n.* [U] the state of having or showing too much pride in oneself. —[名] 자존, 자부심, 거만

self-im·por·tant [sélfimpɔ́ːrt(ə)nt] *adj.* having or showing too much pride in oneself. —[形] 자부심이 강한, 잘난 체하는, 거만한

self-im·posed [sélfimpóuzd] *adj.* (of a task, etc.) imposed on oneself by oneself; self-chosen. —[形] 스스로 과(課)한, 자신이 좋아서 하는

self-im·prove·ment [sélfimprúːvmənt] *n.* [U] improvement of one's mind, etc. by one's own efforts. —[名] 자기 개선, 수양

self-in·dul·gence [sélfindʌ́ldʒ(ə)ns] *n.* [U] the act of giving way to one's own desires, passions, etc.; the act of paying little attention to others' happiness, interests, etc. —[名] 제멋대로 하기, 방종

self-in·dul·gent [sélfindʌ́ldʒ(ə)nt] *adj.* characterized by self-indulgence. —[形] 제멋대로의, 방종한

self-interest [sélfínt(ə)rist] *n.* Ⓤ one's own interest or welfare; the act of thinking of one's own welfare; selfishness. ⌈ests, wishes, etc.⌉
— 图 사리(私利), 사욕; 이기주의

* **self·ish** [sélfiʃ] *adj.* chiefly thinking of one's own inter-
— 阌 이기주의의, 제멋대로의

self·less [sélflis] *adj.* not thinking of one's own profits; sacrificing one's own interests; unselfish. ⌈ishness.⌉
— 阌 이기심(욕심)이 없는; 자신을 돌보지 않는

self·love [sélflʌv] *n.* Ⓤ instinctive love of oneself; self-
— 图 [본능적인] 자애(自愛); 이기주의

self·made [sélfméid] *adj.* having succeeded without others' help; made by one's own ability or efforts.
— 阌 자력으로 출세한; 스스로 만든

self·mas·tery [sèlfmǽst(ə)ri / ‑máːs‑] *n.* Ⓤ self-control; self-command; self-possession. ⌈self; suicide.⌉
— 图 극기, 자제, 침착

self·mur·der [sélfmə́ːrdər] *n.* Ⓤ the act of killing one-
— 图 자살

self·o·pin·ion·at·ed [sèlfəpínjənèitid] *adj.* thinking or insisting too much that one is right.
— 阌 자부심이 강한; 고집이 센

self·pit·y [sélfpíti] *n.* Ⓤ pity for oneself.
— 图 자기 연민

self·por·trait [sélfpɔ́ːtrit, +*Brit.* ‑pɔ́ːtreit] *n.* Ⓒ a portrait of oneself painted, etc. by oneself.
— 图 자화상

self·pos·sessed [sélfpəzést] *adj.* (of the mind or behavior) being or showing calm; not excited.
— 阌 냉정한, 침착한

self·pos·ses·sion [sélfpəzéʃ(ə)n] *n.* Ⓤ the act or state of controlling one's mind, feelings, behavior, etc.
— 图 냉정, 침착

self·pres·er·va·tion [sélfprèzərv(ː)véiʃ(ə)n] *n.* Ⓤ the act of keeping oneself from danger, harm, destruction, etc.; the instinctive desire to do so.
— 图 자기 보존, 자위[본능]

self·re·al·i·za·tion [sélfrìːəlizéiʃ(ə)n / ‐‐‐‐‐‐] *n.* Ⓤ realization or development of one's abilities.
— 图 자기 실현

self·re·cord·ing [sélfrikɔ́ːrdiŋ] *adj.* making a record automatically.
— 阌 자동 기록의

self·re·gard [sélfrigáːrd] *n.* Ⓤ **1.** love of oneself; the act of paying attention to one's own interests. **2.** self-respect; respect for oneself. ⌈own abilities, etc.⌉
— 图 1. 자애(自愛), 이기(利己) 2. 자존 ⌈立獨行⌉

self·re·li·ance [sélfriláiəns] *n.* Ⓤ dependence on one's
— 图 자신의 힘을 믿기, 독립독행(獨)

self·re·li·ant [sélfriláiənt] *adj.* having or showing self-reliance. ⌈one's conscience.⌉
— 阌 자신의 힘을 믿는, 독립독행의

self·re·proach [sélfripróutʃ] *n.* Ⓤ blame of oneself by
— 图 자책, 양심의 가책, 후회

self·re·spect [sélfrispékt] *n.* Ⓤ pride in oneself; proper respect for oneself. ⌈self-respect.⌉
— 图 자존, 자중

self·re·spect·ing [sélfrispéktiŋ] *adj.* having or showing
— 阌 자존심이 있는, 자중하는

self·re·straint [sélfristréint] *n.* Ⓤ self-control; the act of controlling one's desires or passions by one's own will.
— 图 자제(自制)

self·right·eous [sélfráitʃəs] *adj.* thinking that one's own opinion or thought is superior to others'.
— 阌 독선적인, 스스로 옳다고 하는

self·sac·ri·fice [sélfsǽkrifàis] *n.* Ⓤ sacrifice of one's personal desires, life, etc. for the sake of others or one's duty.
— 图 자기 희생, 헌신

self·same [sélfséim] *adj.* the very same; identical.
— 阌 아주 똑같은

self·sat·is·fac·tion [sélfsæ̀tisfǽkʃ(ə)n] *n.* Ⓤ satisfaction or contentment with oneself.
— 图 자기만족, 자부

self·sat·is·fied [sélfsǽtisfàid] *adj.* satisfied or contented with oneself; complacent; vain.
— 阌 자기만족의, 혼자서 좋아하는

self·seek·er [sélfsíːkər] *n.* Ⓒ a selfish person; a person who always thinks about his own interests.
— 图 이기주의자, 독선적인 사람

self·seek·ing [sélfsíːkiŋ] *adj.* selfish.
— 阌 이기주의의, 독선적인

self·serv·ice [sélfsə́ːrvis] *n.* Ⓤ the act of serving oneself in a restaurant, a store, etc.
— 图 셀프 서어비스

self·start·er [sélfstáːrtər] *n.* Ⓒ an electric motor to start an engine automatically.
— 图 자동 시동기(始動機)

self·styled [sélfstáild] *adj.* using a name which one has given oneself; named by oneself.
— 阌 자칭의, 제멋대로의

self·suf·fi·cien·cy [sélfsəfíʃ(ə)nsi] *n.* Ⓤ the state of being self-sufficient.
— 图 자족(自足); 자부심

self·suf·fi·cient [sélfsəfíʃ(ə)nt] *adj.* **1.** able to supply one's needs by oneself. **2.** too proud of oneself; over-confident.
— 阌 1. 자급자족의, 자급할 수 있는 2. 자부심이 강한, 거만한

self-sup·port·ing [sélfsəpɔ́:rtiŋ] *adj.* earning money for one's own living expenses, etc.; getting along without help from others. —[형] 자활하는, 자급하는, 자립하는

self-sus·tain·ing [sélfsəstéiniŋ] *adj.* self-supporting; needing no outside help. —[형] 자활의, 자립의

self-taught [sélftɔ́:t] *adj.* taught by one's own efforts and without any help from others; self-educated. —[형] 독학의, 독습의

self-will [sélfwíl] *n.* [U] insistence that one should have one's own way; the state of not being obedient. —[명] 제멋대로임, 완고

self-willed [sélfwíld] *adj.* being inclined to have one's own way; showing self-will; stubborn. —[형] 제멋대로의, 외고집의

self-wind·ing [sélfwáindiŋ] *adj.* (of a clock, a watch, etc.) winding itself by a mechanism; wound automatically. —[형] [시계 태엽이] 자동으로 감기는

⁑**sell** [sel] *v.* (**sold**) *vt.* **1.** give (something) in exchange for money. ↔buy ¶*He sold the book for 1,000 won* / *I sold him the house.; I sold the house to him.* **2.** deal in (something). ¶*They ~ shoes at the store.*① **3.** betray. ¶*He sold his country for money.*② —*vi.* be sold. ¶*This book sells well.*③
1) ***sell off,*** sell all the stock of (goods, etc.) cheaply.
2) ***sell out,*** sell all the stock of (goods, etc.).
3) ***sell up,*** sell all a debtor's property in order to pay his creditor.

—[타] 1. …을 팔다 2. …을 장사하다 ¶①저 가게에서는 신을 팔고 있다 3. …을 배신(배반)하다 ¶②돈 때문에 그는 조국을 팔았다 —[자] 팔리다 ¶③이 책은 잘 팔린다
[숙] 1)싸게 …을 팔아 치우다 2)…을 다 팔아 버리다 3)…을 경매하다

***sell·er** [sélər] *n.* [C] **1.** a person who sells. ↔buyer **2.** a thing that sells. —[명] 1. 파는 사람, 판매인 2. 팔리는 것

sel·vage, -vedge [sélvidʒ] *n.* [C] an edge of cloth woven so as to prevent it from separating into thread. —[명] [피륙 양쪽의] 귀, 가장자리

selves [selvz] *n.* pl. of **self.**

se·man·tics [simǽntiks] *n. pl.* 《used as *sing.*》 the study of the meanings of words and their changes of meaning. —[명] 의미론; 어의학(語義學)

sem·a·phore [séməfɔ̀:r] *n.* [C] **1.** an apparatus for sending signals by mechanical arms, flags, lanterns, etc. used in railroad signaling. ⇒fig. **2.** a system of signaling by means of a flag held in each hand, used in the army. —*vt.* signal (messages, commands, etc.) by [a] semaphore. —[명] 1. [철도의] 완목(腕木) 신호기 2. [군대의] 수기(手旗) 신호 —[타] …을 신호[기]로 알리다

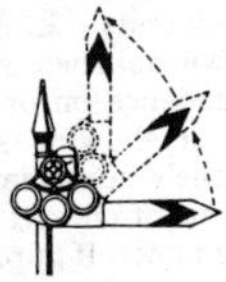
〔semaphore 1.〕

sem·blance [sémbləns] *n.* [C][U] **1.** an outward appearance; pretense. ¶*He has the ~ of a kind man.*① **2.** likeness; resemblance. ¶*have the ~ of ...* —[명] 1. 외형, 외관, 겉치레 ¶①그는 친절한 체한다 2. 비슷한 것; 상사(相似)

se·mes·ter [siméstər] *n.* [C] one of two terms of a school year. —[명] [1년 2학기제의] 1학기

sem·i- [semi-] a word element meaning *half, twice* or *partly.* —「절반」「2회」「다소」 따위의 뜻의 연결형

sem·i·an·nu·al [sèmiǽnjuəl] *adj.* happening every half year; lasting for half a year. —[형] 한 해 두 번의; 반년간의

sem·i·cir·cle [sémisə̀:rkl] *n.* [C] half a circle. —[명] 반원, 반원형

sem·i·cir·cu·lar [sèmisə́:rkjulər] *adj.* of a semicircle; having the form of a semicircle. —[형] 반원[형]의

sem·i·civ·i·lized [sémisívilàizd] *adj.* partly or somewhat civilized. —[형] 반문명의

***sem·i·co·lon** [sémikòulən] *n.* [C] a mark of punctuation (;) showing a more distinct separation than a comma, but not so distinctly as a period. —[명] 세미콜론

sem·i·de·tached [sémiditǽtʃt] *adj.* partly detached; (of a house) joined to other buildings by a common wall on one side. —[형] 절반쯤 떨어진; [집이] 간막이 벽으로 갈려 있는

sem·i·fi·nal [sémifáin(ə)l] *n.* [C] a match, round or contest just before the final one. —*adj.* of such a match, round, contest, etc. —[명] 준결승[전] —[형] 준결승[전]의

sem·i·flu·id [sémiflú:id] *adj.* not completely fluid. —*n.* [U][C] a substance which is neither completely solid nor fluid. —[형] 반유동체의 —[명] 반유동체

sem·i·month·ly [sémimʌ́nθli] *adj.* occurring or done twice a month. —*n.* [C] (pl. **-lies**) anything that is published twice a month. —*adv.* twice a month. —[형] 반달마다의, 월 2회의 —[명] 월 2회의 출판물 —[부] 월 2회, 반달마다

sem·i·nar [séminà:r] *n.* [C] **1.** a group of students in a —[명] 1. 연구 그루우프, 세미나아 2. 연

university doing research or advanced study under the direction of the teacher. **2.** a course or subject of study for such a group.
구 과정; 연구 과제, 연습(演習)

sem·i·nar·y [séminèri / -nəri] *n.* [C] (pl. **-nar·ies**) **1.** a school, esp. a private school for young women. **2.** a school which prepares or trains students to be priests.
—[名] 1. 학교; 특히 여학교 2. 신학교

sem·i·of·fi·cial [sémiəfíʃ(ə)l] *adj.* partly official; not entirely official.
—[形] 반관(半官)의

Sem·ite [sémait, +*Brit.* síːm-] *n.* [C] a member of one of the groups of people, including the Hebrews, Arabs, Phoenicians, and Assyrians who speak Semitic languages.
—[名] 셈 사람, 셈 말을 쓰는 종족

Se·mit·ic [simítik] *adj.* of the Semites or their languages. **—*n.*** [U] a group of languages which include Hebrew, Arabic, Phoenician, and Assyrian.
—[形] 셈 사람의; 셈 말의 —[名] 셈 말

sem·i·tone [sémitòun] *n.* [C] **1.** (*Music*) a tone which is half a tone different from another. **2.** an interval between these two tones.
—[名] 1. 《樂》 반음 2. 반음정

sem·i·trans·par·ent [sèmitrænspέərənt] *adj.* imperfectly transparent; translucent.
—[形] 반투명의

sem·i·trop·i·cal [sèmitrápik(ə)l / -trɔ́p-] *adj.* half tropical; subtropical.
—[形] 아열대의

⁑ sen·ate [sénit] *n.* [C] **1.** 《*the S-*》 the upper house of Congress in the United States, France, etc. **2.** the supreme legislative and governing body in ancient Rome.
—[名] 1. 상원 2. [고대 로마의] 원로원

⁑ sen·a·tor [sénitər] *n.* [C] a member of a senate.
—[名] 상원의원; 원로원 의원

sen·a·to·ri·al [sènitɔ́ːriəl] *adj.* **1.** of senators or a senate. **2.** (*U.S.*) entitled to elect a senator. ¶~ *district.*
—[形] 1. 상원(원로원)[의원]의 2. 《美》 상원의원 선거권이 있는

⁂ send [send] *v.* (**sent**) *vt.* **1.** cause (something or someone) to go from one place to another. ¶~ *a parcel by mail* / ~ *help at once* / ~ *someone to school.* **2.** throw; cast. ¶~ *a ball.* **3.** (of God) give; grant. ¶*God ~ him success!*① **4.** force (someone) to become; drive. ¶~ *someone mad.* **—*vi.*** send a message.
1) ***send for,*** ⓐ send a messenger asking (someone) to come; call. ¶~ *for a doctor.* ⓑ send a request or order for something. ¶~ *for a dozen copies of a book.*
2) ***send forth,*** give out.
3) ***send off,*** ⓐ send a piece of mail. ⓑ make (someone) go away. ⓒ see (someone) start or leave.
—[他] 1. …을 보내다; 가게 하다, 파견하다 2. …을 던지다 3. [신이] …을 주다; 수여하다 ¶①신이여 저 분에게 성공을 주옵소서 4. …으로 하다, 몰아쳐서 …하게 하다 —[自] 심부름 보내다; 편지를 부치다
[熟] 1)ⓐ…을 부르러 보내다 ⓑ…을 주문하다 2)…을 내다; 방출하다 3)ⓐ…을 발송하다 ⓑ…을 몰아내다 ⓒ…을 전송하다

send·er [séndər] *n.* [C] **1.** a person who sends. **2.** a device that sends, such as a transmitter in telegraphy.
—[名] 1. 발송인, 출하주(出荷主) 2. 발신기, 송신(송화)기

send-off [séndɔ̀ːf / -ɔ̀(ː)f, ⌐⌐] *n.* [C] a friendly demonstration for someone starting out on a journey.
—[名] 전송, 송별

se·nile [síːnail] *adj.* of old age; suffering from weakness caused by old age.
—[形] 고령의, 노쇠한; 노령에 의한

se·nil·i·ty [siníliti] *n.* [U] **1.** old age. **2.** bodily or mental weakness caused by old age.
—[名] 1. 고령; 노년 2. 노쇠

*** se·nior** [síːnjər] *adj.* **1.** older in years. **2.** the older (used after the name of a father when his son has the same name). **3.** higher in rank, standing, position, etc. **4.** (*U.S.*) of the final year of high school or college. **—*n.*** [C] **1.** a person who is older. **2.** a person who is higher in rank or position. **3.** a student in his final year of high school or college.
—[形] 1. 손위의, 연장(年長)의 2. [같은 이름의 부자 중] 아버지의, 연장의 3. 상위의, 상사의, 선임의 4. 최상급의, 최종학년의
—[名] 1. 연장자 2. 선배, 상사 3. 최상급생

se·nior·i·ty [siːnjɔ́ːriti, -njár- / -niɔ́r-] *n.* [U] the state or condition of being senior in age, rank, standing, etc.
—[名] 손위임, 고참, 선임 순위

Senr. Senior.

*** sen·sa·tion** [senséiʃ(ə)n] *n.* [C] [U] **1.** a feeling in one's body or mind. **2.** the state of being in great excitement. **3.** [C] a cause of such excitement.
—[名] 1. 느낌, 기분, 감각, 지각(知覺) 2. 감동, 대평판 3. 감동을 일으키는 것

sen·sa·tion·al [senséiʃ(ə)n(ə)l] *adj.* **1.** causing excitement; arousing excited feeling. **2.** giving news in such a way as to arouse great excitement; startling. **3.** of the senses.
—[形] 1. 세상을 떠들썩하게 하는 2. 선정적인, 충동을 주는 3. 감각의; 지각의

⁑ sense [sens] *n.* **1.** [C] the power to feel, see, hear, taste, etc. ¶*the five senses*① / *He has a keen ~ of smell.*②
—[名] 1. 감각, 지각 ¶①오관/②그는 냄새를 잘 맡는다 2. 사려, 분별 ¶③분별

senseless

2. ⓤ the power to understand or judge; judgment. ¶*a man of ~* ⓓ */ a ~ of guilt.* **3.** (*pl.*) the normal condition of mind; sanity. ¶*out of one's senses.*ⓓ **4.** ⓒ a meaning. ¶*in a ~*ⓓ */ the ~ of a word.*
1) ***have the sense to do***, be wise enough to do.
2) ***make sense***, can be understood easily.
3) ***take the sense of someone***, make sure of someone's opinion. —*vt.* feel. ¶*~ danger.*

sense·less [sénslis] *adj.* **1.** without feeling; unconscious. ¶*He was made ~ by a blow on the head.* **2.** stupid; foolish. ¶*Stop such a ~ argument.* **3.** meaningless.
1) ***fell senseless***, become unconscious.
2) ***knock senseless***, knock someone so as to make him unconscious.

sense organ [⌐ ⌐] *n.* any part of the body which receives sensations of heat, sound, color, smell, etc.

sen·si·bil·i·ty [sènsibíliti] *n.* **1.** ⓤ capacity to feel. **2.** sensitiveness; delicacy in the capacity for emotion.

* **sen·si·ble** [sénsibl] *adj.* **1.** able to feel; noticeable by the senses. ¶*a ~ rise in temperature.* **2.** having good judgment; reasonable. **3.** conscious; aware.

sen·si·bly [sénsibli] *adv.* **1.** in a sensible manner; remarkably. **2.** wisely.

* **sen·si·tive** [sénsitiv] *adj.* **1.** quick to receive impressions from external conditions. ¶*a ~ ear.* **2.** easily influenced. ¶*The photographic film is ~ to light.* **3.** easily hurt or damaged. ¶*~ to others' criticism.* **4.** of senses or sensations. ▷ **sen·si·tive·ness** [-nis] *n.*

sen·si·tiv·i·ty [sènsitíviti] *n.* ⓤ the state or quality of being sensitive. [sensitive to light.]

sen·si·tize [sénsitàiz] *vt.* (*Photography*) make (a film)

sen·so·ry [sénsəri] *adj.* of senses or sensations.

sen·su·al [sénʃuəl, +*Brit.* -sjuəl] *adj.* **1.** of the pleasure of the bodily senses; not mental or spiritual. **2.** given up to the pleasures of the body; lustful. [too sensual.]

sen·su·al·i·ty [sènʃuǽliti / -sju-] *n.* ⓤ the state of being

sen·su·ous [sénʃuəs, +*Brit.* -sju-] *adj.* appealing to the senses.

‡ **sent** [sent] *v.* pt. and pp. of **send**.

‡ **sen·tence** [séntəns] *n.* ⓒ **1.** (*Grammar*) a group of words that expresses a complete thought. **2.** (*Law*) judgment given on a prisoner by a court; punishment. ¶*His ~ was ten years in prison.*ⓓ **3.** (*archaic*) saying; proverb. —*vt.* pronounce a judgment on or decide a punishment for (a prisoner).

sen·ten·tious [sentén ʃəs] *adj.* **1.** full of proverbs. **2.** expressing much in few words.

sen·tient [sénʃ(ə)nt] *adj.* having the ability of feeling. —*n.* ⓒ a person or thing that is sentient.

‡ **sen·ti·ment** [séntimənt] *n.* ⓤⓒ **1.** an opinion based on one's feeling or emotion. **2.** feeling, esp. of pity or affection. ¶*appeal to his ~.* **3.** (often *pl.*) the thought which expresses one's feeling; one's personal opinion.
a man of sentiment, a man who is easily influenced by emotion rather than by reason.

sen·ti·men·tal [sèntiméntl] *adj.* **1.** easily moved to pity, love, sympathy, etc. **2.** appealing to one's emotions. **3.** of sentiment.

sen·ti·men·tal·ism [sèntimént(ə)lìz(ə)m] *n.* ⓤ **1.** the tendency or characteristic of being easily moved by emotion. **2.** sentimental speech or behavior.

sen·ti·men·tal·ist [sèntimént(ə)list] *n.* ⓒ a sentimental person; a person who is given to sentimentality.

sen·ti·men·tal·i·ty [sèntimentǽliti] *n.* (pl. **-ties**) **1.** ⓤ the quality of being sentimental. **2.** ⓒ a sentimental

sentimentality

있는 사람 **3.** 제정신 ¶ⓓ머리가 돌아 **4.** 의미 ¶⑤어떤 의미에서는

熟 1)…할 만한 분별이 있다 2)의미가 명백하다 3)…의 의향을 확인하다

—ⓥ …을 느끼다
—ⓐ 1. 무감각한, 무의식의, 인사불성의 2. 무분별한, 어리석은, 터무니없는 3. 무의미한

熟 1)기절하다 2)때려서 기절시키다

—ⓝ 감각 기관

—ⓝ 1. 감각[력]; 감도(感度) 2. 감수성, 민감, 다정다감

—ⓐ 1. 느낄(지각할) 수 있는 2. 사려 깊은, 현명한 3. 의식이 있는, 알고 있는

—ⓐⓓ 1. 지각할 수 있게, 현저하게 2. 현명하게, 재치있게

—ⓐ 1. 느끼기 쉬운, 민감한 2. 과민한, 영향받기 쉬운, 반응이 빠른 3. 신경질적인, 성마른, 노하기 쉬운 4. 감각의, 감수성의

—ⓝ 민감도; 감수성; 감동

—ⓥ …에 감광성(感光性)을 주다
—ⓐ 감각의, 지각의, 지각기관의
—ⓐ 1. 육체의, 육감(肉感)적인 2. 육욕에 빠진, 음탕한

—ⓝ 육욕에 빠짐, 호색
—ⓐ 감각에 호소하는, 감각적인

—ⓝ 1.《문법》문(文) 2.《法》판결, 선고, 형벌 ¶①그는 금고 10년의 형을 언도받았다 3.《古》금언, 격언, 속담
—ⓥ 판결을 내리다

—ⓐ 1. 금언(교훈) 같은 2. 간결하고 매서운, 의미심장한
—ⓐ 지각력이 있는 —ⓝ 감각이 있는 사람(것)

—ⓝ 1. 감정, 정, 정서 2. 다정다감, 감상 (感傷) 3. 의견, 감상(感想)

熟 감정가

—ⓐ 1. 감정에 움직이기 쉬운, 감상적인 2. 감정에 호소하는, 정서적이다 3. 감정의, 정서의

—ⓝ 1. 감정에 움직이기 쉬움, 감상벽 (感傷癖) 2. 감정적 언동

—ⓝ 감상가, 감정적인 사람

—ⓝ 1. 감상적임, 감상성 2. 감상적 특징 (언동·표현)

characteristic, manner, way of behavior, expression, etc.

sen·ti·nel [séntin(ə)l] *n.* [C] a person who keeps watch and guards. **—*vt.*** guard or watch over (an enemy, etc.). —[名] 보초, 감시인 —[他] …을 감시하다

sen·try [séntri] *n.* [C] (pl. **-tries**) a soldier who keeps watch and guards. —[名] 보초

Seoul [soul, +*U.S.* sá:ul] *n.* the capital of Korea. —[名] 서울

Sep. September.

se·pal [sí:p(ə)l, +*Brit.* sép-] *n.* [C] one of the little leaflike parts at the base of a flower which protect the bud. ⇒fig. —[名] 악편(萼片), 꽃받침

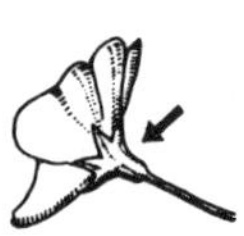

(sepal)

sep·a·ra·ble [sép(ə)rəbl] *adj.* that can be separated. —[形] 분리할 수 있는

‡ **sep·a·rate** *v.* [sép(ə)rèit →*adj.*] *vt.* **1.** divide. ¶ *The river separates the two states.*① **2.** keep (something or someone) apart. **3.** see the difference between (things); put (things) in different groups; distinguish. 《~ one thing *from* another》 **—*vi.*** become parted; be divided; branch. —[他] 1. …을 나누다, 분리하다 ¶①그 강으로 두 주(州)가 갈라져 있다 2. …을 떼어놓다, 절단하다 3. …을 구별하다; 분류하다 —[自] 갈라지다; 나뉘다

—*adj.* [sépərit] divided from others; not connected; alone. —[形] 분리한; 개개의

sep·a·rate·ly [sép(ə)ritli] *adv.* in a separate manner; one by one. —[副] 따로따로, 하나하나, 분리하여

* **sep·a·ra·tion** [sèpəréiʃ(ə)n] *n.* [U][C] **1.** the act of separating; the state of being separated. **2.** the act or state of a husband and wife living apart by order of a court of law or by agreement. —[名] 1. 분리; 이별; 이탈 2. [부부의] 별거

sep·a·ra·tist [sép(ə)rèitist, -rə- / sép(ə)rətist] *n.* [C] a member of a group, esp. a political or religious group, who wants separation and independence. —[名] 분리주의자, 독립주의자

sep·a·ra·tive [sépərèitiv, -rə- / sép(ə)rətiv] *adj.* inclined to separate; causing separation. —[形] 분리적인, 독립적인

sep·a·ra·tor [sépərèitər] *n.* [C] **1.** a person or thing that separates. **2.** a device used for separating the cream from milk, etc. —[名] 1. 분리하는 사람(것) 2. 분리기; 분할기

se·pi·a [sí:piə] *n.* [U] **1.** a dark brown paint made from the inky fluid of a cuttlefish. **2.** a dark-brown color. **—*adj.*** of a dark-brown color. —[名] 1. 오징어의 먹; 오징어 먹으로 만든 갈색 그림물감 2. 세피아빛 —[形] 세피아[빛깔]의

sep·sis [sépsis] *n.* [U] a disease caused by poisonous matter spreading in the blood vessels. —[名] 패혈증(敗血症)

Sept. September.

‡ **Sep·tem·ber** [septémbər] *n.* the ninth month of the year. —[名] 9월

sep·tic [séptik] *adj.* poisoned; of poisoning or decay. —[形] 병독(病毒)의; 부패의

sep·tu·a·ge·nar·i·an [sèptʃuədʒinέəriən / -tjuə-] *adj.* of the age of 70 years, or between 70 and 80 years old. —[形] 70세(대)의

—*n.* [C] a person of this age. —[名] 70세(대)의 사람

sep·ul·cher, *Brit.* **-chre** [sép(ə)lkər] *n.* [C] a tomb; a grave; a place of burial. —[名] 무덤

se·quel [sí:kw(ə)l] *n.* [C] **1.** something that follows or comes after; a continuation. **2.** a result. —[名] 1. 계속, 속편 2. 결과, 귀착점

se·quence [sí:kwəns] *n.* **1.** [U] the act of following; the coming of one thing after another. **2.** the order of sequence. ¶*alphabetical ~.*① **3.** [C] an event that follows. —[名] 1. 계속하기, 연속, 연발 2. 순서 ¶①알파벳순 3. 연속하여 일어나는 일(것)

1) ***in regular sequence,*** in good order.
2) ***in sequence,*** one after another.
3) ***sequence of tense,*** (*Grammar*) principles by which the tenses of subordinate clauses are made to suit those of principal clauses.

[熟] 1)정연하게, 순서바르게 2)차례로 3)《文法》 시제(時制)의 일치

se·quent [sí:kwənt] *adj.* **1.** coming after; following. **2.** following or happening as a result. —[形] 1. 차례로 계속되는 2. 결과로서 일어나는

se·quen·tial [sikwénʃ(ə)l] *adj.* sequent. —[形] 잇따라(결과로서) 일어나는

se·ques·ter [sikwéstər] *vt.* **1.** set apart; separate; withdraw (someone) from public view. ¶*~ oneself from the world.*① **2.** take away (property) for a time till legal claims are satisfied. **3.** take and control (the property of an enemy). —[他] 1. …을 격리시키다; 은퇴시키다 ¶①은거(隱居)하다 2. …을 차압하다; 압수하다 3. …을 몰수하다

se·quoi·a [sikwɔ́iə] *n.* [C] a very tall evergreen tree of California. —[名] 미국삼나무

se·ra [síərə] *n.* pl. of **serum.**

ser·aph [sérəf] *n.* [C] (pl. **-aphs** or **-a·phim**) an angel of the highest rank.
—[名] 최고 천사

se·raph·ic [serǽfik] *adj.* of or like a seraph.
—[形] 천사 같은

ser·a·phim [sérəfim] *n.* pl. of **seraph.**

Serb [səːrb] *n., adj.* =Serbian.

Ser·bi·a [sə́ːrbiə] *n.* a district in Yugoslavia, in former times a kingdom.
—[名] 세르비아

Ser·bi·an [sə́ːrbiən] *n.* **1.** [C] a person of Serbia. **2.** [U] the language of Serbia. —*adj.* of the Serbia or Serbian.
—[名] 1. 세르비아 사람 2. 세르비아 말 —[形] 세르비아[사람·말]의

sere [siər] *adj.* (*poetic*) dried up; withered.
—[形] 《詩》 말라빠진, 시든

ser·e·nade [sèrinéid] *n.* [C] a piece of music played or sung at night, esp. under a lady's window by someone who loves her; a piece of music suitable for this. —*vt., vi.* sing or play a serenade (for a lady).
—[名] 세레나아데, 소야곡 —[他][自] […에게] 세레나아데를 연주(노래)하다

* **se·rene** [siríːn] *adj.* (**-ren·er, -ren·est**) **1.** clear; bright. **2.** calm; peaceful.
—[形] 1. 청명한, 맑게 갠 2. 잔잔한, 조용한, 평화로운

se·rene·ly [siríːnli] *adv.* in a serene manner; calmly.
—[副] 청명하게, 침착하게

se·ren·i·ty [siréniti] *n.* [U][C] (pl. **-ties**) **1.** clearness; brightness. **2.** calmness; peacefulness.
—[名] 1. 청명, 화창 2. 평온, 침착

serf [səːrf] *n.* [C] (pl. **serfs**) in the Middle Ages, a person who belonged to the land and was usually sold with it.
—[名] 농노(農奴)

serf·dom [sə́ːrfdəm] *n.* [U] the condition or quality of being a serf.
—[名] 농노의 처지(신분)

serge [səːrdʒ] *n.* [U] a woolen material used for dresses, suits, etc.
—[名] 사아지(옷감의 일종)

* **ser·geant** [sɑ́ːrdʒ(ə)nt] *n.* [C] **1.** a non-commissioned officer in the army or marines ranking next above a corporal. **2.** a police officer of a minor rank.
—[名] 1. 상사, 중사 2. 경사(警査)

se·ri·al [síəriəl] *n.* [C] a story told in successive parts or numbers in a magazine or thus broadcast on television, etc. —*adj.* **1.** arranged in a series. ¶~ *numbers.*① **2.** published, broadcast, televised, etc. one following one another.
—[名] 연속물, 연재소설, 정기 출판물, 연속극 —[形] 1. 연속의 ¶①일련번호 2. 연속극의; 연재물의

se·ri·al·ly [síəriəli] *adv.* in a series.
—[副] 연속적으로, 연속물로서

ser·i·cul·tur·al [sèrikʌ́ltʃ(u)r(ə)l] *adj.* of sericulture.
—[形] 양잠의

ser·i·cul·ture [sérikʌltʃər] *n.* [U] the art or process of growing silkworms for the production of silk.
—[名] 양잠

ser·i·cul·tur·ist [sèrikʌ́ltʃ(ə)rist] *n.* [C] a person who is engaged in sericulture.
—[名] 양잠가, 양잠업자

⁑ **se·ries** [síəriːz] *n.* [C] (pl. **se·ries**) a number of similar things or events following one after another.
—[名] 연속된 것, 연속물; 연속

⁑ **se·ri·ous** [síəriəs] *adj.* **1.** grave; thoughtful; sincere; not joking. ¶*She was quite ~ about the matter.* **2.** requiring thought and attention. ¶*a ~ book.* **3.** important because it is dangerous. ¶*a ~ accident.*①
—[形] 1. 진지한, 진정인, 열심인 2. 중대한, 심각한 3. 얕보지 못할, 위험한, 위독한 ¶①중대 사건

⁑ **se·ri·ous·ly** [síəriəsli] *adv.* in a serious manner.
—[副] 진지하게, 진심으로, 위독하여

se·ri·ous·ness [síəriəsnis] *n.* [U] the state of being serious.
—[名] 진지함; 중대; 위독 상태

* **ser·mon** [sə́ːrmən] *n.* [C] **1.** a public speech on religion or religious matters, usu. given in a church. ¶*the Sermon on the Mount.*① **2.** any serious talk on morals, conduct, etc. **3.** a long, dull speech.
—[名] 1. 설교 ¶①산상 수훈(垂訓) 2. 교훈담 3. 지루한 이야기, 잔소리

* **ser·pent** [sə́ːrp(ə)nt] *n.* [C] **1.** a snake, esp. a big one. **2.** a sly, deceitful person.
—[名] 1. 뱀; 구렁이 2. 음험한 사람

ser·pen·tine [sə́ːrp(ə)ntàin] *adj.* **1.** snakelike; winding; twisting. **2.** deceitful; treacherous; sly.
—[形] 1. 뱀 모양의, 꾸불꾸불한, 나선형의 2. 음험한, 교활한

ser·rate [sérit, -eit] *adj.* having a toothed edge like a saw.
ser·rat·ed [séreitid / ─ˊ─] *adj.* =serrate.
—[形] 톱니 모양의, 톱니처럼 깔쭉깔쭉한

ser·ried [sérid] *adj.* crowded closely together.
—[形] 꽉 들어찬, 밀집한

se·rum [síərəm] *n.* [U][C] (pl. **-ra** or **-rums**) **1.** the pale yellow, watery part of the blood. **2.** such a fluid, taken from an animal that has been given a certain disease and then injected into a human body to help in fighting the same disease.
—[名] 1. 혈청(血淸); 혈장(血漿) 2. 면역 혈청

⁑ **ser·vant** [sə́ːrv(ə)nt] *n.* [C] **1.** a person employed to carry out household or personal duties. **2.** a person who
—[名] 1. 하인, 하녀 2. 관리, 공무원 3. 봉사자, 부하, 종복

works for the public. **3.** a person who is devoted to a certain belief.

⁝ serve [sə:rv] *vt.* **1.** work or do good for (someone or something); do one's duty for (someone). ¶*They served their country.* | *She serves me well.*① **2.** bring (food or drink) to someone. ¶*~ tea and cake.* **3.** take care of (someone) at table or in a shop. ¶*Is there no one to ~ me?*② **4.** treat. ¶*He served me very badly.* | *It serves you right.*③ **5.** be useful to (someone or something). ¶*That will ~ my purpose.*④ **—vi. 1.** work for another; do one's duties. ¶*~ as a soldier* | *~ in the kitchen.* **2.** suit; be useful. **3.** (in tennis, etc.) hit the ball to begin the play.
1) ***serve for*** (=*be used as*) *something.*
2) ***serve round,*** hand (food, etc.) to each in turn.
3) ***serve up,*** bring (food, drink, etc.) to a table.

—[他] 1. …을 위해서 일하다; 봉사하다 ¶①그녀는 나를 잘 돌봐 준다 2. [식사]를 차려내다 3. …을 돌봐 주다; …에게 시중들다 ¶②내 말을 들어줄 사람은 없는가? 4. …을 대우(보답)하다 ¶③네게는 그것이 당연한 보답이다, 꼴 좋게 됐다 5. …의 도움이 되다 ¶④그것은 내 목적에 맞는다 —[自] 1. 봉사하다; 근무하다 2. 목적에 맞다, 쓸모 있다 3. 서어브하다

[熟] 1)…으로서 쓸모가 있다 2)…을 차례로 도르다 3)…을 식탁으로 나르다

serv·er [sə́:rvər] *n.* [C] **1.** a person who serves. **2.** (of tennis, etc.) the player who puts the ball in play. **3.** a tray for dishes.

—[名] 1. 봉사자, 급사 2. 서어브하는 사람 3. 쟁반, 접시

⁝ serv·ice [sə́:rvis] *n.* **1.** [U] the work or kindness done for others; the duty required in one's business. ¶*be in ~*① | *He was of great ~ to me.*② **2.** [C][U] a system or means for public use. ¶*the telephone ~* | *There is good train ~.*③ **3.** [C][U] a religious meeting, ceremony, etc. ¶*a marriage ~.* **4.** [C] a set of dishes. **5.** [U] the act of serving at table. ¶*The ~ in this hotel is excellent.* **6.** [C][U] (in tennis, etc.) the act of serving a ball to begin the play.
1) ***at someone's service,*** ready to do what someone wants.
2) ***in active service; on active service,*** actually at work; be in a branch of the armed forces.
3) ***take service with*** (=*be employed; work for*) *someone.*
4) ***take someone into one's service,*** employ someone as one's servant or employee.

—[名] 1. 봉사; 근무, 업무 ¶①근무하고 있다/②그는 나에게 잘해 주었다 2. 공공(公共)의 편의 ¶③기차편이 좋다 3. 예배 [식]; 신을 섬김 4. 식기 한 벌 5. 시중들기 6. 서어브

[熟] 1)…의 뜻대로 2)현역의, 재직 중인 3)…을 섬기다, …에 근무하다 4)…을 사용인으로서 고용하다

serv·ice·a·ble [sə́:rvisəbl] *adj.* **1.** that can give good service; useful. **2.** that can stand long use; useful for a long time.

—[形] 1. 쓸모있는, 편리한 2. 오래가는, 질긴

service station [´-- ˌ-] *n.* a place selling gasoline, oil, etc. for cars.

—[名] 급유소, 주유소

ser·vi·ette [sə̀:rviét] *n.* [C] a napkin.

—[名] 냅킨

ser·vile [sə́:rvil / -vail] *adj.* like a slave; humble like a slave; lacking a spirit of self-respect. ¶*a ~ flatterer.*①

—[形] 노예의; 노예 근성의; 천한 ¶①야비한 아첨꾼

ser·vil·i·ty [sə:rvíliti] *n.* [U] manners like a slave; lack of self-respect; the state of being a slave.

—[名] 노예 근성, 비굴; 노예 상태

ser·vi·tude [sə́:rvit(j)ù:d / -tjù:d] *n.* [U] the state of being a slave; forced labor as a punishment.

—[名] 노예임; 고역(苦役)

ses·a·me [sésəmi] *n.* **1.** [C] a plant whose seeds have much oil and are used for food. **2.** [U] ⦅*collectively*⦆ the seeds.

—[名] 1. 참깨(식물) 2. 참개(열매)

• ses·sion [séʃ(ə)n] *n.* **1.** [U] a meeting of a law court, a council, a parliament, etc.; [C] a series of such meetings; [C] a period of such meetings. **2.** [C] (*U.S.*) a period of lessons and study; the hours of lessons.
in session, holding a meeting.

—[名] 1. [재판소의] 개정(開廷), [의회 따위의] 개회; [국회·의회 따위의] 회기 2. ⦅美⦆ 학기(보통 7개월); 수업시간

[熟] 회의 중[에, 의], 개회 중; 개정 중

⁝ set [set] *v.* (**set, set·ting**) *vt.* **1.** put (something) in a position; place. ⦅~ something *on* or *in*⦆ ¶*~ a vase on a table* | *~ a stake in the ground.* **2.** bring (something) into contact with something else; cause (something) to go, point, or face in a direction. ⦅~ something *to* or *on*⦆ ¶*~ a glass to one's lips; ~ one's lips to a glass* | *~ fire to a house; ~ a house on fire* | *~ one's face to the sun* | *~ one's horse toward home.* **3.** put (something) in the proper condition or place; regulate; make (something) ready for use. ¶*~ a watch* | *~ sails*① | *~ a trap* | *~ the table* | *~ one's watch by the radio.* **4.** appoint (someone) for certain duties. ¶*~ a guard at*

—[他] 1. …을 놓다, 두다, 앉히다 2. 갖다 대다; [불 따위]를 붙이다; [얼굴 따위]를 돌리다; …의 쪽으로 돌리다 3. [기계·기구] 따위를 조절하다; …을 준비하다 ¶①돛을 되다 4. …을 임무에 배치하다

S

set

the gate. **5.** bid or make (someone) do something; begin to apply (oneself) to a job, etc. (《~ someone *to do*》 ¶ ~ *a man to dig a well.* **6.** give a lesson, task, etc. to (a learner, etc.) to do; give (an example, a pattern, a lesson, etc.) to someone. ¶ ~ *someone a difficult problem* / ~ *someone an example;* ~ *an example to someone.* **7.** fix (a gem, etc.) in gold, etc.; fix (something) firmly in a frame. ¶ ~ *a diamond in gold* / ~ *the glass in the window.* **8.** sow or plant (seeds or plants). ¶ ~ *young plants.* **9.** put (someone or something) into some condition or relation. (《~ someone or something *doing*》 ¶ ~ *a prisoner free* / ~ *someone thinking*② / ~ *a machine going* / *Set your mind at rest.* **10.** direct and keep (one's hopes, heart, etc.) firmly on something. (《~ one's hopes, etc. *on* or *in*》 ¶ ~ *one's mind on going to church.*③ **11.** cause (something) to become firm or hard. ¶ ~ *the mortar* / ~ *a broken bone*④ / ~ *a color in dying* / ~ *one's teeth* / ~ *one's hair* / *have one's hair* ~⑤ / *He* ~ *his jaw.*⑥ **12.** fix (the price or value) of something. ¶ ~ *the value at £100.*⑦ **13.** fix (a time, date, etc.) for something; fix (boundaries or limits). ¶ ~ *a boundary* / ~ *the date* (*hour*) *for an interview* / ~ *a time limit.* **14.** place (a hen) on eggs; place (eggs) under a hen. **15.** write (words) to music; write (music) to words. ¶ ~ *a song to music.* **16.** compose (type); put (copy) into type.

—*vi.* **1.** (of the sun, moon, etc.) sink below the horizon. ¶ *The sun sets in the west.* **2.** (of a liquid, any soft substance, etc.) become hard or solid. ¶ *The jelly has* ~. **3.** (of a current, opinion, custom) have a definite motion, direction, or tendency. ¶ *The wind sets to the north.* **4.** (*U.S.*) (of clothes) fit. **5.** (of a hen) sit on eggs. **6.** (of flowers or plants) develop fruit. ¶ *The apples won't* ~ *this year.* **7.** (of a sporting dog) take a stiff attitude as a sign that birds, etc. are present.

1) *set about,* begin; start; take steps toward doing. ¶ ~ *about doing a piece of work.*
2) *set against,* ⓐ balance; compare. ⓑ make (someone) unfriendly with someone else.
3) *set apart,* ⓐ reserve. ⌈of no effect. ⓒ ignore.⌉
4) *set aside,* ⓐ reserve; save. ⓑ make (something)
5) *set at,* attack; make (a dog, etc.) attack something.
6) *set back,* ⓐ stop or reverse the progress of (something). ⓑ turn backwards. ⓒ cost.
7) *set before,* represent or explain (facts) to someone.
8) *set by,* reserve.
9) *set down,* ⓐ put (something) in writing or print. ⓑ let (passengers) get off. ⓒ regard; consider. (《~ *down as*》 ⓓ attribute. (《~ *down to*》 ¶ ~ *down one's success to luck.*
10) *set forth,* ⓐ start on a journey. ⓑ explain or state.
11) *set forward,* ⓐ promote. ⓑ present. ⓒ start.
12) *set in,* begin. ⓑ move or blow toward the shore.
13) *set off,* ⓐ serve as a contrast. ⓑ explode. ¶ ~ *off the fireworks.* ⓒ begin a journey. ⓓ start (someone) laughing or talking. ⌈attack, pursue, etc.⌉
14) *set on* (or *upon*), attack; cause (a dog, etc.) to
15) *set out,* ⓐ start to go. ⓑ spread (something) for
16) *set over,* control. ⌊display, sale, etc. ⓒ plant.⌋
17) *set to,* ⓐ begin (a piece of work). ⓑ begin fighting.
18) *set up,* ⓐ start in (business, etc.) ⓑ build; establish. ⓒ place (something) in an upright position. ⓓ raise (someone) in place, power, etc.
19) *set up for,* pretend to be.

5. …에게 …시키다 6. [문제·일 따위]를 과하다; [모범 따위]를 보이다 7. [보석 따위]를 박다; 틀에 끼우다 8. [씨·식물]을 뿌리다, 심다 9. …을 …의 상태로 하다 ¶ ②…을 생각하게 하다 10. [희망·마음]을 쏟다, 돌리다 11. ③교회에 다니기로 결심하다 11. …을 고정시키다, 굳히다, 고정하다 ¶ ④정골(整骨)하다/⑤머리를 세트하다/⑥그는 입을 꽉 다물었다 12. …에 값을 매기다 ¶ ⑦100 파운드로 값을 매기다 13. [날짜·시간]을 정하다; [경계 따위]를 설정하다 14. [닭]에게 알을 품게 하다 15. [곡]에 가사를 붙이다; [가사]에 곡을 붙이다, 작곡(편곡)하다 16. [활자]를 판으로 짜다; [원고]를 활자로 짜다

—*自* 1. [천체가] 지다, 가라앉다 2. [부드러운 것·액체가] 굳어지다, 분명한 모양이 되다 3. [흐름·의견 따위]가 뚜렷이 움직이다 4. [옷이 몸에] 맞다 5. [암탉이] 알을 품다 6. [꽃·식물이] 열매를 맺다 7. [사냥개가] 부동의 자세로 짐승을 가리키다

關 1) …을 시작하다 2) ⓐ…을 균형 시키다; …을 비교하다 ⓑ…의 사이를 나쁘게 하다 3) 따로 두다 4) ⓐ따로 두다; 저축하다 ⓑ…을 무효로 하다 ⓒ…을 무시하다 5) …에 덤벼들다; …을 부추기다 6) ⓐ…을 방해하다 ⓑ…을 퇴보시키다 ⓒ[값이] 들다 7) …을 진열하다; 설명하다 8) …을 저축해 두다 9) ⓐ…을 써 넣다 ⓑ[승객]을 내리다 ⓒ…으로 간주하다 ⓓ…의 탓으로 하다 10) ⓐ여행을 떠나다 ⓑ…을 설명하다 11) ⓐ…을 촉진하다 ⓑ…을 제출하다 ⓒ출발하다 12) ⓐ시작되다 ⓑ[조수 따위]가 육지 쪽으로 향하다 13) ⓐ…을 돋보이게 하다 ⓑ폭발시키다 ⓒ여행을 시작하다 ⓓ…을 웃기다, 이야기 시키다 14) …을 공격하다; …을 부추기다 15) ⓐ출발하다 ⓑ[물품 따위]를 펴(늘어) 놓다 ⓒ[묘목 따위]를 심다 16) …을 지배하다 17) ⓐ…을 시작하다 ⓑ싸우기 시작하다 18) ⓐ[장사 따위]를 시작하다 ⓑ…을 조립하다, 설치하다, 세우다 ⓒ…을 세우다 ⓓ[높은 지위에] …을 올리다 19) …인 체하다; …이라 자칭하다

setback [1043] **settle**

—*adj.* **1.** (of a smile, the eyes, a look, etc.) fixed; unmoving. ¶*a ~ smile.*① **2.** (of a purpose) intentional. **3.** (of a time or date) arranged in advance. ¶*at a ~ time.* **4.** formed; made; built. ¶*~ fireworks / a ~ scene.* **5.** (of a speech, prayer, etc.) formal; regular. ¶*a ~ speech / a ~ phrase.* **6.** (of a person, one's mind, etc.) fixed; obstinate. ((*~ on* or *upon*)) ¶*He is ~ on going today.* **7.** (of eggs, jelly, etc.) having set; solid. **8.** (of the weather) good and giving no sign of change. **9.** (of the sun, etc.) below the horizon.

—*n.* **1.** ⓒ a number of things of the same kind. ¶*a ~ of tools.* **2.** ⓒ a group of persons joined by common interests, etc. ¶*a literary ~.*① **3.** ⓒ a radio or television receiver. **4.** ((*the ~*)) form; shape. ¶*the ~ of one's shoulders.* **5.** ⓒ a group of games which count as a unit. ¶*a ~ of tennis.* **6.** Ⓤ (*poetic*) the setting of the sun. ↔rise **7.** ⓒ the place or stage of an action in a play, a movie, etc. **8.** Ⓤ ((*the ~*)) the direction of the wind or current; the tendency of opinion. ¶*the ~ of public opinion / the ~ of the wind.* **9.** ((*the ~*)) (of clothing) the way clothing fits or hangs. **10.** ⓒ a young shoot for planting.

make a dead set, attack strongly and violently.

set·back [sétbæk] *n.* ⓒ a stop or check to any progress or advancement.

set down [´ ´] *n.* bitter blame.

Seth [seθ] *n.* **1.** a man's name. **2.** (in the Bible) a son of Adam.

set-off [sétɔ̀:f / -ɔ̀(:)f] *n.* ⓒ **1.** something used to make someone or something look better; a decoration. **2.** a start.

set-out [sétàut] *n.* Ⓤ start; beginning.

set square [´ ´] *n.* a triangle with angles of 90°, 60° and 30°, or of 45°, 45°, and 90° used to draw lines.

set·tee [setí:] *n.* ⓒ a sofa or a long seat with a back and arms. ⇒fig.

set·ter [sétər] *n.* ⓒ a long-haired hunting dog.

set·ting [sétiŋ] *n.* **1.** ⓒ a frame or other thing in which something is set or fastened; a framework in which jewels are fixed. ¶*My pearl ring has a gold ~.* **2.** ⓒ the background of a story; the stage furniture, etc. of a play. **3.** Ⓤ music composed esp. to accompany a story or poem.

[settee]

‡**set·tle**¹ [sétl] *vi.* **1.** come to rest; stop. ((*~ on* something)) ¶*A bird settled on the branch.* **2.** make one's home in a new country or place; build up colonies. ¶*They settled in New York.* **3.** sink to the bottom; (of a liquid) become clear by the sinking of particles. ¶*Dust settled on the book.* **4.** (of a building, an earth, etc.) sink gradually. **5.** become calm or fixed. ¶*The weather has settled.* —*vt.* **1.** place or set (someone or something) in a fixed state, occupation, etc. ¶*~ oneself* [*down*] *in an easy chair*① */ ~ one's daughter by marriage.*② **2.** put (something) in order; arrange. ¶*~ one's affairs.*③ **3.** provide (a place) with settlers; bring (people) to live in a country. **4.** make (the nerves, etc.) calm or quiet. ¶*~ a disordered brain.* **5.** pay (a bill, etc.); fulfill. ¶*~ a bill.* **6.** bring (an argument, a doubt, etc.) to an end; adjust. ¶*~ a dispute.* **7.** cause (something) to sink to the bottom; make (a liquid) pure and clear. ⌈become quiet and peaceful.⌉

1) *settle down,* ⓐ live a more regular way of life. ⓑ

2) ***settle up,*** complete one's transactions; pay up.
3) ***settle upon*** (or ***on***) (=*agree on*) *the time, a price, etc.*
4) ***settle*** *property, etc.* ***upon*** (or ***on***), give property, etc. to (someone) by legal means.
5) ***settle with,*** ⓐ pay one's debts to (someone). ⓑ come to an agreement with (someone).

위가] 가라앉다; 차분해지다 2)정리하다; 지불하다 3)…을 정하다 4)[재산]을 …에게 양도하다 5)ⓐ…에 부채를 갚다 ⓑ…와 화해하다; 합의에 도달하다

set·tle² [sétl] *n.* [C] a long, wooden bench with arms and a high, straight back. ⇒fig.

—[名] 등받이가 높은 긴 의자

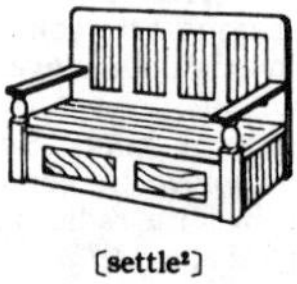
〔settle²〕

set·tled [sétld] *adj.* **1.** fastened or fixed firmly. **2.** placed on a sure basis.

—[形] 1. 고정한 2. 단단한, 뿌리깊은

⁑set·tle·ment [sétlmənt] *n.* **1.** [U] [C] the act of settling; the state of being settled; the act of bringing a quarrel to an end. ¶*come to a ~.*① **2.** [U] the establishment of one's life by marriage. **3.** [U] the process of colonizing; [C] a place where a number of people have gone to live. **4.** [U] [C] decision; the complete payment of a bill. **5.** [C] a group of persons living in a poor and crowded section of a large city for giving educational or recreational service to the people in that section; a building used for this purpose.

—[名] 1. 해결; 화해 ¶①해결하다 2. [결혼 따위에 의한] 생활 안정, 정주(定住) 3. 식민, 이민; 식민지 4. 결정; 청산 5. 인보(隣保) 사업단(빈민가에 정주하며 그 향상을 꾀하는 사회사업 단체); 인보관

***set·tler** [sétlər] *n.* [C] a person who settles in a new country; a colonist.

—[名] 이주자; 식민자

set·tling [sétliŋ] *n.* [U] **1.** the state of being fixed; the state of living in one place for a long time. **2.** the settlement of accounts; a decision.

—[名] 1. 고정; 정주 2. 결산; 결정

set·tlings [sétliŋz] *n. pl.* things which sink to the bottom of liquid.

—[名] 침전물, 찌끼

S

set·up [sétʌp] *n.* [C] organization; the way in which something is begun or done.

—[名] 기구(機構), 조직, 구성

⁑sev·en [sév(ə)n] *n.* **1.** [U] the number between six and eight; 7. **2.** [C] any group or set of seven persons or things. **3.** [C] anything shaped like 7. **—*adj.*** of 7.

—[名] 1. 일곱, 7 2. 일곱 사람; 일곱 개 3. 7의 기호, 7자형의 것 —[形] 일곱의

sev·en·fold [sév(ə)nfòuld] *adv.* seven times as much or as many.

—[副] 7배로; 일곱 겹으로

⁑sev·en·teen [sév(ə)ntíːn] *n.* **1.** [U] the number between sixteen and eighteen; 17. **2.** [C] any group or set of seventeen persons or things. **—*adj.*** of 17.

—[名] 1. 열 일곱, 17 2. 17개, 17명 —[形] 17의

⁑sev·en·teenth [sév(ə)ntíːnθ] *n.* **1.** (usu. *the* ~) the number 17; 17th. **2.** [C] one of 17 equal parts of anything. **—*adj.*** of the 17th.

—[名] 1. 제 17, 열 일곱 번째 2. 17분의 1 —[形] 열 일곱 번째의; 17분의 1의

⁑sev·enth [sév(ə)nθ] *n.* **1.** (usu. *the* ~) the number 7; 7th. **2.** [C] one of 7 equal parts of anything. **—*adj.*** of the 7th.

—[名] 1. 제 7, 제 7 번째 2. 7분의 1 —[形] 제 7[번째]의; 7분의 1의

seventh heaven [⌐– ⌐–] *n.* (usu. *the* ~) the highest part of heaven; a very happy condition.

—[名] 제 7천국; 최고천(最高天), 득의, 의기양양

sev·enth·ly [sév(ə)nθli] *adv.* in the seventh place.

—[副] 일곱 번째

⁑sev·en·ti·eth [sév(ə)ntiiθ] *n.* **1.** (usu. *the* ~) the number 70; 70th. **2.** [C] one of 70 equal parts of anything. **—*adj.*** of 70th.

—[名] 1. 제 70, 일흔 번째 2. 70분의 1 —[形] 일흔 번째의; 70분의 1의

⁑sev·en·ty [sév(ə)nti] *n.* [U] seven times ten; 70. **—*adj.*** of 70.

—[名] 70 —[形] 70의

sev·er [sévər] *vt.* **1.** cut apart; cut off; separate. **2.** break off (friendly relations). **—*vi.*** become divided.

—[他] 1. …을 절단하다 2. …을 불화하게 하다 —[自] 잘리다

⁑sev·er·al [sévr(ə)l] *adj.* **1.** some; three or more, but not many. **2.** separate; individual. ¶*They went their ~ ways.* **—*pron.*** several persons or things.

—[形] 1. 여럿의, 몇 개의 2. 따로따로의, 각자의; 여러가지의 —[代] 몇 사람, 몇 개

sev·er·al·ly [sévrəli] *adv.* separately; individually.

—[副] 각각, 따로따로

sev·er·ance [sévər(ə)ns] *n.* [U] the act of severing; the state of being severed; division; separation.

—[名] 절단, 분리, 단절

⁑se·vere [sivíər] *adj.* **1.** strict; stern. ¶*~ judgment.* **2.** serious; grave. ¶*a ~ look.* **3.** violent; sharp. ¶*a ~ cold.* **4.** extremely plain or simple. ¶*a dress of ~*

—[形] 1. 엄한, 용서없는 2. 진지한, 심각한 3. 가혹한, 통렬한 4. 간소한, 꾸밈없는

severely [1045] **shade**

style. 「plainly; simply.」
* **se·vere·ly** [sivíərli] *adv.* in a severe manner; violently;
se·ver·i·ty [sivériti] *n.* ⓤ **1.** strictness; sternness; harshness. **2.** seriousness. **3.** violence; sharpness. **4.** simplicity or plainness of style or taste.
‡ **sew** [sou] *v.* (**sewed, sewed** or **sewn**) *vt.* **1.** make (clothes) by means of making stitches. **2.** join or attach (something) to another thing by making stitches. **3.** close or repair (a wound, a tear, etc.) by means of making stitches. ——*vi.* work with needle and thread.
sew·age [sú(:)idʒ / s(j)ú(:)-] *n.* ⓤ waste water or matter carried away through a sewer.
sew·er¹ [sú(:)ər / s(j)ú(:)ə] *n.* ⓒ an underground pipe to carry off waste water, waste matter, etc.
sew·er² [sóuər] *n.* ⓒ a person or thing that sews.
sew·er·age [sú(:)əridʒ / sjúər-] *n.* ⓤ **1.** the system of sewers. **2.** removal of waste by sewers. **3.** sewage.
* **sew·ing** [sóuiŋ] *n.* **1.** ⓤ work with needle and thread. **2.** (*pl.*) thread for sewing. ——*adj.* to be used for sewing. 「stitches, etc.」
sewing machine [⌐ ⌐⌐] *n.* a machine for making
sewn [soun] *v.* pp. of **sew**.
* **sex** [seks] *n.* **1.** (*collectively*) one of the two groups into which creatures or plants are divided; male or female. ¶ *Men, boys, and bulls are all of the male* ~. **2.** ⓤⓒ the characteristics which distinguish any creature or plant as either male or female. **3.** ⓤ anything connected with sexual matters, esp. the instinct or attraction drawing one sex toward another.
sex·a·ge·nar·i·an [sèksədʒinéəriən] *adj.* of the age of 60 years, or between 60 and 70 years old. ——*n.* ⓒ a person in this age. 「a sense of sex.」
sex·less [sékslis] *adj.* **1.** having no sex. **2.** lacking in
sex·tant [sékst(ə)nt] *n.* ⓒ **1.** an instrument used by sailors for measuring the height of the sun or a star above the horizon in order to determine their positions at sea. ⇒fig. **2.** one sixth of a circle.
sex·ton [sékst(ə)n] *n.* ⓒ a man who takes care of a church and churchyard and who attends to burials.
sex·u·al [sékʃu(ə)l, +*Brit.* -ksju-] *adj.* [sextant 1.] **1.** of sex. **2.** having sex; either male or female. **3.** of the sexual appetite. **4.** of the sexual organs.
shab·bi·ly [ʃǽbili] *adv.* in a shabby manner.
shab·bi·ness [ʃǽbinis] *n.* ⓤ the state or quality of being shabby.
* **shab·by** [ʃǽbi] *adj.* (**-bi·er, -bi·est**) **1.** much worn; used too much. **2.** wearing worn clothes. **3.** mean; unfair.
shack [ʃæk] *n.* ⓒ (*U.S., Can.*) a very small, poor house; 「a hut.」
shack·le [ʃǽkl] *n.* ⓒ **1.** (usu. *pl.*) iron rings to fastened around a prisoner's ankle or wrist so as to stop him from escaping. ⇒fig. **2.** any device used to fasten or couple. **3.** anything that prevents freedom; restraint. ——*vt.* **1.** put shackles on (someone). **2.** fasten or couple (two things) together with a shackle. **3.** prevent; restrain. [shackles]
‡ **shade** [ʃeid] *n.* **1.** ⓤ a slight darkness or coolness made by something blocking the light; ⓒ a partly dark place. ¶ *light and* ~① / *under the* ~ *of a tree.*② **2.** (*the* ~*s*) the darkness of the evening or night. ¶ *the shades of*

——㉠ 엄하게, 맹렬하게, 간소하게
——㉠ 1. 격렬, 혹독, 통렬 2. 진지함, 엄숙, 중후(重厚) 3. 가혹함 4. 간소, 소박; 검소

——㉥ 1. [옷]을 꿰매다 2. …을 꿰매 붙이다 3. …을 꿰매 합치다

——㉠ 바느질을 하다
——㉠ 하수, 시궁창물

——㉠ 하수도

——㉠ 꿰매는 사람, 재봉사, 재봉틀
——㉠ 1. 하수 시설, 하수도 2. 하수 처리 3. 시궁창물, 오수
——㉠ 1. 바느질 2. 꿰매는 실 ——㉠ 재봉용의

——㉠ 재봉틀

——㉠ 1. 남자, 여자; 수컷, 암컷 2. 성(性) 성별 3. 성적요소, [특히] 성욕

——㉠ 60세의, 60대의 ——㉠ 60대의 사람, 60대의 사람
「성감각이 없는」
——㉠ 1. 남녀(자웅)의 구별이 없는 2.
——㉠ 1. 육분의(六分儀) 2. 원(圓)의 6분의 1

——㉠ 묘목파니, 무덤 파는 인부

——㉠ 1. 성의 2. 성이 있는, 남녀(자웅)의 3. 성욕의 4. 생식기의

——㉠ 초라하게
——㉠ 초라함, 비열, 인색

——㉠ 1. 입어서 낡은 2. 누더기를 입은, 초라한 3. 천한
——㉠ 《美·캐나다》 통나무집
——㉠ 1. 수갑, 족쇄 2. 잇는 것; [철도의] 연환(連環) 따위 3. 속박, 구속, 방해

——㉠ 1. …에 수갑(족쇄)을 채우다 2. …을 연환으로 잇다 3. …을 방해하다

——㉠ 1. 그늘, 응달 ¶①명암/②나뭇그늘에서 2. 땅거미, 어스름, 어둠 ¶③저녁의 어둠 3. 차양; 차일; 문장(門帳); 전등의 갓 4. 명암(농담)의 정도; 그림

*evening.*③ **3.** [C] something that shuts out light or brightness. ¶*the windows shades.* **4.** [C] a degree of color; the darker parts of a picture. ¶*all shades of blue.*④ **5.** 《*a* ~》 a slight degree, amount, or difference. ¶*a ~ to the right*⑤ | *a delicate ~ of meaning.*⑥ **6.** [C] a ghost; 《*the ~s*》 the world of the dead.

의] 색조 ¶④온갖 푸른 색조 5. 극소, 조금, 기미; 미묘한 차이 ¶⑤약간 오른쪽에/⑥미세한 의미의 차이 6. 유령; 저승, 명부(冥府)

cast (or ***throw, put***) *someone* or *something* ***into the shade,*** make someone or something obscure.

[熟] …을 눈에 띄지 않게 하다

—*vt.* **1.** keep (something) from light or heat; darken. ¶*The trees ~ the house.* **2.** make (parts of a picture, etc.) darker to give differences of brightness, etc. **—*vi.*** change little by little, esp. in color. 《~ *into* another color or quality》

—[他] 1. …을 [빛·열 따위에서] 가로막다; …을 어둡게 하다 2. [그림]에 음영(陰影)을 주다 —[自] 차츰 변화하다

shad·ing [ʃéidiŋ] *n.* **1.** [C] a slight difference in color or tone. **2.** [U] the representation of light or shade in a painting or drawing.

—[名] 1. 미세한 변화, 차이 2. 명암법

‡ **shad·ow** [ʃǽdou] *n.* [C] **1.** a dark form made on the ground, etc. by a thing that cuts off light. ¶*the ~ of a cloud* | *be afraid of one's ~*① | *May your ~ never grow less!*② **2.** [U] shade; darkness; the dark part of a place or picture; 《*the ~s*》 the darkness after sunset. ¶*the ~ of a tree* | *the shadows of evening.* **3.** sadness; gloom. ¶*the ~ of death* | *Trouble cast a ~ on my thoughts.* **4.** 《*a* ~, usu. in *negative*》 a small degree; a very slight sign. ¶*There is not a ~ of doubt.* **5.** a person who follows another about everywhere; a person who watches another. ¶*Trouble is a ~ to life.* **6.** a poor likeness of a former condition; an unreal thing. ¶*a ~ of one's former life.*③ **7.** a ghost. **8.** [U] protection. ¶*under the ~ of an angel's wings.*④

—[名] 1. [일정한 모양의] 그림자, 투영(投影) ¶①자기의 그림자를 무서워하다; 몹시 겁내다/②오래오래 건강하시기를 빕니다 2. 그늘, 어둑한 곳; [그림의] 음영, 암영; 어둠 3. 슬픔; 우울 4. 근소, 미세 5. 붙어 다니는 사람; 아첨장이; 미행자 6. [어떤 물건의] 그림자 같은 존재, 희미한 모습; 환영(幻影) ¶③왕년의 모습 7. 유령 8. 비호(庇護); 보호 ¶④천사의 날개에 보호되어

under (or ***in***) ***the shadow of** something,* very near to something.

[熟] …의 가까이에

—*vt.* **1.** send a shade or shadow upon (something or someone); protect (something) from light, heat, etc. ¶*Her face is shadowed from the light.* **2.** follow and watch closely. **3.** represent vaguely. 《~ *forth* or *out* something》

—[他] 1. …에 그림자를 던지다, …을 어둡게 하다; 가로막다 2. …을 미행하다 3. …을 넌지시 나타내다

shad·ow·y [ʃǽdoui] *adj.* **1.** filled with shadows. **2.** like a shadow; faint; dim. **3.** unreal, like a ghost.

—[形] 1. 그림자에 싸인 2. 그림자 같은; 희미한; 어두운 3. 환영(幻影)의

• **shad·y** [ʃéidi] *adj.* (**shad·i·er, shad·i·est**) **1.** sheltered from the light; shaded. ¶*walk along a ~ road.* **2.** giving shade. ¶*a ~ tree.* **3.** (*colloq.*) of doubtful character; questionable.

—[形] 1. 그늘진 2. 그늘을 이루는 3. 《口》 뒤가 구린, 수상쩍은

1) ***keep** something **shady,*** keep something out of sight.
2) ***on the shady side of*** (=*older than*) *forty, etc.*

[熟] 1)…을 비밀로 하다 2)[40]의 고개를 넘어서

• **shaft** [ʃæft / ʃɑ:ft] *n.* [C] **1.** the long stem or handle of an arrow or spear. **2.** an arrow; a spear. **3.** a beam of light; a ray. **4.** a bar supporting the part that turns in a machine or engine. **5.** (*Architecture*) the main part of a column. **6.** the pole of a carriage or wagon. **7.** a passage by which to enter an underground mine.

—[名] 1. 화살대, [창·도끼 따위의] 자루 2. 화살, 창 3. 전광, 광선 4. 굴대, 축(軸) 5. 《建》 기둥몸, 주신(柱身) 6. [수레의] 채, 끌채 7. 수갱(竪坑)

shag [ʃæg] *n.* [U] **1.** rough, matted hair. **2.** a kind of coarse tobacco. **3.** a long, rough nap of cloth. **4.** cloth having a long, rough nap.

—[名] 1. 거친 털, 조모(粗毛) 2. 독한 살담배의 일종 3. 보풀 4. 빳빳한 보풀이 있는 직물

shag·gy [ʃǽgi] *adj.* (**-gi·er, -gi·est**) covered with rough, uneven hair.

—[形] 텁수룩한, 털이 많은

sha·green [ʃəgrí:n, +*Brit.* ʃæ-] *n.* [U] a kind of untanned leather made from the skin of horses or asses.

—[名] [말·노새 따위의] 도톨도톨한 가죽

‡ **shake** [ʃeik] *v.* (**shook, shak·en**) *vt.* **1.** move (something or someone) rapidly from side to side or up and down. ¶*His rough steps shook the room.* **2.** bring, throw, or scatter (something) by a shaking movement. ¶*~ the snow from one's shoes.* **3.** make (someone) afraid; give a shock to (someone); weaken; disturb. ¶*~ one's decision* | *be shaken by* (or *with, at*) *the news*① | *Her lying*

—[他] 1. …을 흔들다, 흔들어 움직이다 2. …을 흔들어 …하다 3. …을 두려워하게 하다, 동요시키다, 놀라게 하다; …을 흔들흔들하게 하다 ¶①그 소식을 듣고 놀라다 4. [인사로서 남의 손]을 쥐다; …와 악수하다 5. …을 흔들다, 휘두르다 ¶②…에게 주먹을 휘두르다

shaken [1047] **shame**

shook my faith in her. **4.** take grip of (someone's hand); take grip of the hand of (someone) in greeting. ¶~ *hands with someone* / ~ *someone by the hand.* **5.** wave about. ¶~ *a handkerchief* / ~ *one's fist at someone.* **6.** mix; blend. ¶~ *milk before pouring it.* **7.** (*U.S. colloq.*) get rid of (someone or something). —*vi.* **1.** be shaken; tremble. ((~ *with* cold, etc.)) ¶~ *with fear.* **2.** become unsteady.
  1) *shake down,* ⓐ cause (fruit, etc.) to fall by shaking a tree, etc. ⓑ settle or become compact by shaking.
  2) *shake off,* get rid of (someone or something unwelcome).
  3) *shake up,* ⓐ mix (liquid, etc.) by shaking. ⓑ disturb; agitate.
—*n.* ⓒ **1.** the act of shaking. ¶*a ~ of the head.* **2.** a drink made by shaking quickly; a milk shake.
‡**shak·en** [ʃéik(ə)n] *v.* pp. of **shake**.
shak·er [ʃéikər] *n.* ⓒ **1.** a person who shakes. **2.** a container for pepper, salt, etc. from the top of which the contents are shaken out. **3.** a skaking device used in mixing or blending something. **4.** (*S-*) a member of a certain religious sect in the United States.
***Shake·speare, Shak-** [ʃéikspiər], **William** *n.* (1564-1616) England's greatest poet and dramatist.
Shake·spear·i·an, -sper- or **-spear·e·an, -sper·e·an** [ʃeikspíəriən] *adj.* of or suggestive of Shakespeare or the style of his works. —*n.* ⓒ a scholar who studies Shakespeare's works.
shake-up [ʃéikʌp] *n.* ⓒ **1.** a complete change in business, a department, etc. **2.** unrest; uproar.
shak·y [ʃéiki] *adj.* (**shak·i·er, shak·i·est**) **1.** shaking; not secure. **2.** uncertain; not to be relied on. **3.** not well; weak.
shale [ʃeil] *n.* ⓤ a kind of rock formed from clay or mud and easily split into thin sheets.
‡**shall** [ʃæl, ʃəl, ʃl] *auxil. v.* (**should**) **1.** ((used with *the first person* to express *simple future time*)) ¶*I ~ be seventeen years old next year.* / *Shall I be in time for the train?* / *He said he should be back by five.* **2.** (esp. *U.S.*) ((expressing *intention* to do something in *the future*)) be to; be determined to. ¶*I ~ come back home every day.* / *We ~ not go.* **3.** ((used with *the second and third person* to express *the speaker's will*)) have to; must; may. ¶*They ~ not pass.* / *He ~ die.* / *You ~ have this book.* **4.** ((used to ask *the intention* of *the second person*)) ¶*Shall I open the window?* / *When ~ he call on you?* **5.** (*literary*) ((used in *laws* with *all persons*)) ¶*Article 1. The Emperor ~ be the symbol of the State.*
***shal·low** [ʃǽlou] *adj.* **1.** not deep. **2.** lacking thought. —*n.* ⓒ ((sometimes *the ~s*)) a shallow place in the water.
shalt [ʃælt] *auxil. v.* (*archaic*) shall. ¶*Thou ~ not kill.*
sham [ʃæm] *n.* ⓒ **1.** fraud; pretence. ¶*The news was all ~.* **2.** imitation. —*v.* (**shammed, sham·ming**) *vt.* **1.** make an imitation of (something). **2.** pretend to be (ill, etc.). —*vi.* arrange a false appearance of something. —*adj.* pretended; not real. ¶*a ~ jewel.*
sham·ble [ʃǽmbl] *vi.* walk unsteadily. —*n.* ⓒ unsteady walking.
sham·bles [ʃǽmblz] *n. pl.* ((often used as *sing.*)) **1.** a house where animals are killed for food. **2.** a scene of great disorder or bloodshed.
‡**shame** [ʃeim] *n.* **1.** ⓤ a painful feeling which attacks a person when he has done something wrong. **2.** ⓤ disgrace; dishonor. **3.** ⓒ something which makes a

6. …을 쉬다 7. …을 뿌리쳐 버리다; [추적자]를 따돌리다 —自 1. 흔들리다, 진동하다; 덜덜 떨다 2. 흔들흔들하다; 비틀거리다

圈 1)ⓐ[나무에서 과일 따위]를 흔들어 떨어뜨리다 ⓑ흔들어서 꽉 채우다 2)…을 뿌리쳐 버리다 3)ⓐ…을 흔들어 쉬다 ⓑ…을 어지럽히다, 혼란케 하다 —名 1. 흔들기; 한 번 흔들기 2. 밀크 세이크

—名 1. 흔드는 사람 2. 진탕기(震盪器) 3. 교반기(攪拌器), 세이커 4. 세이커 교도

—名 영국의 시인・희곡작가

—形 셰익스피어[풍]의 —名 셰익스피어 학자(연구가)

—名 1. 대소동, 대정리, 개조 2. 동요, 큰 소동

—形 1. 떨리는, 흔들리는, 불안정한 2. 믿을 수 없는, 마음 놓을 수 없는, 불확실한 3. 병약한

—名 혈암(頁岩), 이판암(泥板岩)

—助 1. ((1인칭에 써서 단순 미래를 나타냄))…일 것이다 ¶①나는 기차시간에 댈 수 있을까요? 2. ((1인칭에 써서 예정・결정・의향을 나타냄))…의 작정이다; …일 것이다 3. ((2・3인칭에서 말하는 사람의 의사를 나타냄))…시키겠다. 4. ((의문문에서 1・3인칭에 써서 상대의 의사를 물음))…할까요 5. ((법률문 따위에서 모든 인칭에 써서))…한다, …이다

—形 1. 얕은 2. 천박한, 생각이 모자라는 —名 여울, 물이 얕은 곳
—助 shall 의 고형
—名 1. 속임수, 야바위, 가짜 2. 모조품, 가짜 —他 1. …의 모조품을 만들다 2. …인 체하다 —自 거짓 꾸미다 —形 속임수의, 가짜의

—自 휘청휘청 걷다 —名 휘청거림

—名 1. 도살장 2. 수라장, 유혈의 장면

—名 1. 부끄러움, 창피한 생각 2. 불명예, 치욕 3. 부끄러운 일

shamefaced [1048] **shark**

person ashamed.
1) *cannot do it for very shame,* too ashamed to do it.
2) *dead to* (or *past*) *shame,* without a sense of shame.
3) *be lost to shame,* have no sense of shame.
4) *put* (or *bring*) *someone to shame,* cause someone to be ashamed.
—*vt.* 1. cause (someone) to feel shame. 2. bring disgrace on (someone). 3. drive or force (someone) to do or not to do something because of his sense of shame.

shame·faced [ʃéimfèist] *adj.* shy; showing shame or embarrassment.

* **shame·ful** [ʃéimf(u)l] *adj.* causing shame; disgraceful.

shame·ful·ly [ʃéimf(u)li] *adv.* in a shameful manner; disgracefully.

shame·less [ʃéimlis] *adj.* without any sense of shame.

shame·less·ly [ʃéimlisli] *adv.* in a shameless manner.

sham·poo [ʃæmpú:] *vt.* wash (the hair). —*n.* 1. ⓤ the act of washing the hair. 2. ⓒ something used to wash the hair.

sham·rock [ʃǽmrɑk / -rɔk] *n.* ⓒ a kind of three-leaved plant of the clover family. ⇒fig.

shank [ʃæŋk] *n.* ⓒ 1. the part of a leg between the ankle and the knee in man and some animals. 2. the straight part of a tool, a plant, etc.

shan't [ʃænt / ʃɑ:nt] shall not.   [shamrock]

shan·ty [ʃǽnti] *n.* ⓒ (pl. **-ties**) a hut; a rude cabin.

shape [ʃeip] *n.* 1. ⓤⓒ the form or figure of a thing; an outward form or appearance; outline. ¶*clouds of different shapes.* 2. ⓤ definite form or pattern; orderly arrangement. ¶*put an idea into* ~① / *The new boat gradually took* ~.② 3. ⓤ (*U.S.*) condition; state. ¶*Everything was in bad* ~. 4. ⓒ a dimly-perceived form; ghost. 5. ⓤⓒ false appearance. ¶*a devil in human* ~. 6. ⓒ something used to give form.
1) *in any shape or form,* in any way; at all.
2) *lick into shape,* train; drill; make (something) perfect.
3) *out of shape,* ⓐ having lost its original shape or form. ⓑ in poor physical condition.
—*vt.* 1. give a definite form or character to (something or someone). ¶~ *a piece of wood into a statue* / ~ *a plan.* 2. direct (one's course). ¶~ *one's course in life.* 3. adapt (something) in shape; make (something) suitable. —*vi.* 1. take shape. 2. develop.

shape·less [ʃéiplis] *adj.* 1. without definite form or shape. 2. ill-formed.

shape·ly [ʃéipli] *adj.* well-shaped; well-balanced.

* **share** [ʃɛ́ər] *n.* 1. ⓒ a part of something belonging to one individual. 2. ⓤ a part of something given or belonging to one of a group of persons who own or undertake it together. 3. one of the equal proportions into which a company's capital stock is divided.
1) *bear* (or *take*) *one's share of,* pay or do what one should.
2) *take the lion's share,* take the largest amount of profits, etc.
—*vt.* 1. divide (something) into parts and distribute them. 2. have a share of (something); have (something) in common. (~ *something with*) —*vi.* give or receive a share. (~ *in something*)

share·hold·er [ʃɛ́ərhòuldər] *n.* ⓒ (*Brit.*) a person who owns shares of stock; a stockholder.

shark [ʃɑ:rk] *n.* ⓒ a large sharp-toothed fish found in warm seas.

熟 1)부끄러워서 …할 수 없다 2)창피한 줄 모르는 3)부끄러운 줄 모르는 4)…에 창피를 주다

— 타 1. …을 부끄러워하게 하다; …에 창피를 주다 2. …을 망신시키다 3. 창피하여 …하도록(하지 않도록) …시키다

— 형 부끄러워하는, 수줍은; 얌전한

— 형 부끄러운; 괘씸한; 추잡한

— 부 괘씸하게도, 창피하게도, 부끄럽게

— 형 창피한 줄 모르는, 외설스러운

— 부 창피한 줄 모르고, 뻔뻔스럽게

— 타 [머리]를 감다 —명 1. 세발(洗髮) 2. 세발용 세제(洗劑), 샴푸우

— 명 토끼풀의 일종

— 명 1. 정강이, 정강이 뼈; 다리 2. 축(軸); 자루; 줄기, 잎줄기

— 명 오두막집

— 명 1. [외면적인] 모양, 형상; 형체, 윤곽; 모습 2. 구체적 형태; 실현 ¶① 생각을 구체화하다/②새 보우트가 차츰 모양을 갖추게 되었다 3. (美) 상태, 형편 4. 희미한 물건의 모양; 유령 5. 꾸민 형체(모습) 6. [모양을 만들기 위한] 형(型), 나무골, 틀

熟 1)방법이야 어떻든 2)훈련하여 …을 상당한 것으로 만들다 3)ⓐ모양이 망가진 ⓑ[몸이] 탈이 난, 편찮은

— 타 1. …의 형체를 주다, 형상을 이루다, 구체화하다 2. [진로]를 …으로 돌리다 3. …을 적합시키다 — 자 1. 형체를 이루다 2. […이] 되다; 발달하다

— 형 1. 정형(定形)이 없는 2. 모양 없는, 보기 흉한

— 형 모양이 좋은, 맵시있는

— 명 1. 몫, 배당된 몫 2. 역할, 분담 3. 주식, 주(株)

熟 1)…의 할당된 몫을 치르다; 분담하다 2)제일 좋은 몫을 차지하다; 단물을 빨다

— 타 1. …을 분배하다 2. …을 분담하다, …의 몫을 갖다; …을 같이 쓰다

— 자 몫을 갖다(주다)

— 명 (英) 주주

— 명 상어

sharp

sharp [ʃɑːrp] *adj.* **1.** having a thin, cutting, keen edge or point. ↔blunt; dull ¶*a ~ knife*. **2.** having a point. ¶*a ~ nose | a ~ peak*. **3.** (of a curve, slope, etc.) sudden and abrupt. ¶*a ~ curve in the road*. **4.** (of an angle) narrow. **5.** (of a sound or voice) high; seeming to go through the head. ¶*a ~ cry*. **6.** (of an outline, etc.) distinct; clear. ¶*a ~ contrast*. **7.** (of the senses, intelligence, etc.) quickly aware of things; keen; clever. ¶*~ ears | a ~ boy*. **8.** intensely painful; intense; eager; (of air, etc.) very cold. ¶*a ~ pain | a ~ desire| a ~ morning*. **9.** (of a taste) acid; biting. **10.** violent; severe; fierce. ¶*a ~ remark | a ~ contest*. **11.** dishonest; quick to look after one's own advantage. ¶*a ~ gambler*. **12.** (of a fight, a walk, etc.) quick, violent; energetic. ¶*a ~ walk*. **13.** (in music) raised half a step in pitch. ↔flat
—*adv.* **1.** promptly; keenly; abruptly. ¶*turn ~ right*. **2.** punctually; exactly. ¶*Come at 5 o'clock ~*.
—*n.* ⓒ (in music) a tone one half step above a given tone; the symbol (#) indicating this.

sharp-cut [ʃáːrpkʌ̀t] *adj.* having a clear outline.
- **sharp-en** [ʃáːrp(ə)n] *vt.* make (something) sharp. —*vi.* become sharp. ¶*a pencil ~*.
sharp-en-er [ʃáːrpnər] *n.* ⓒ a person or thing that
sharp-er [ʃáːrpər] *n.* ⓒ a cheater; a gambler, esp. at cards.
sharp-eyed [ʃáːrpáid] *adj.* having keen sight; sharp-
sharp-ly [ʃáːrpli] *adv.* in a sharp manner. ⌊sighted.
sharp-ness [ʃáːrpnis] *n.* ⓤ the state of being sharp.
sharp-set [ʃáːrpsèt] *adj.* keen; very hungry; eager to dominate. ⌈good at shooting, esp. with a rifle.
sharp-shoot-er [ʃáːrpʃùːtər] *n.* ⓒ a person who is very
sharp-sight-ed [ʃáːrpsáitid] *adj.* having keen sight; sharp-eyed. ⌈mind.
sharp-wit-ted [ʃáːrpwítid] *adj.* having a quick, sharp
- **shat-ter** [ʃǽtər] *vt.* **1.** break or smash (something) into pieces. **2.** destroy; ruin; disturb greatly. —*vi.* be broken into pieces; be damaged.
- **shave** [ʃeiv] *v.* (**shaved, shaved** or **shav-en**) *vt.* **1.** remove hair from (the face, the legs, etc.) with a razor. **2.** cut off (hair, etc.) with a razor. **3.** cut (something) into thin slices. **4.** come or pass very close to (something). ¶*An arrow shaved my ear.* —*vi.* cut off hair or a beard with a razor. —*n.* ⓒ **1.** the act of cutting off with a razor. **2.** a thin slice. **3.** a device for shaving, scraping, etc.

shav-en [ʃéiv(ə)n] *v.* pp. of **shave**.
shav-er [ʃéivər] *n.* ⓒ **1.** a person who shaves. **2.** an instrument for shaving. ⌈cut off by a plane or knife.
shav-ing [ʃéiviŋ] *n.* ⓤ (often *pl.*) thin slices of wood
shawl [ʃɔːl] *n.* ⓒ a square or oblong piece of cloth worn over the shoulders by women.
she [ʃiː] *pron.* (pl. **they**) a girl, woman, or anything imagined as a female mentioned before. ⇒usage —*n.* ⓒ a woman; a female animal. ¶*Is the baby a he or a ~?*
she- [ʃiː] a word element meaning female.
sheaf [ʃiːf] *n.* ⓒ (pl. **sheaves**) a bundle of things of the same kind tied together. ¶*a ~ of wheat① | a ~ of arrows② | a ~ of papers③*.
- **shear** [ʃiər] *n.* ⓒ (usu. *pl.*) a large double-bladed instrument for cutting, such as scissors. ¶*a pgir of shears*.
—*v.* (**sheared, sheared** or **shorn**) *vt.* **1.** cut off (hair, wool, etc.) with shears or scissors. ¶*~ the sheep.①* **2.** (usu. in *passive*) deprive. ¶*be shorn of (something).②*

shear

—働 1. 날카로운; 예리한 2. 끝이 뾰족한 3. [길 따위] 갑자기 구부러지는; 가파른 4. [각도가] 예각의 5. [음·목소리가] 날카로운; 쩨지는 듯한 6. [윤곽 따위가] 명확한; 뚜렷한 7. [감각이] 예민한; 영리한, 똑똑한 8. [고통·욕망 따위가] 강렬한; [추위 따위가] 살을 에는 듯한, 매서운 9. [맛이] 자극적인; 신 10. 격렬한; 신랄한 11. 남을 속이는; 빈틈없는 12. [행동이] 민첩한; 활발한 13. 반음 높은

—働 1. 갑자기; 민속하게 2. 꼭, 정각에; 정확히
—❀ 《樂》 올림음; 올림표

—働 [윤곽이] 뚜렷한
—働 …을 예리하게 하다; 뾰족하게 하다 —❀ 날카로와지다, 뾰족해지다
—❀ 가는(깎는) 사람(것)
—❀ 사기꾼, 직업적인 도박자
—働 눈초리가 매서운, 눈치빠른
—働 날카롭게, 엄하게, 재빨리
—❀ 예리, 통렬, 영리, 교활
—働 날카로운; 굶주린; 갈망하는

—❀ 사격의 명수
—働 눈이 잘 보이는, 눈치빠른

—働 기지가 날카로운, 약삭빠른
—働 1. …을 부수다, 분쇄하다 2. …을 망쳐 놓다, 못쓰게 하다 —❀ 산산조각이 나다
—働 1. [얼굴·발 따위]를 면도하다 2. [머리·수염]을 밀다 3. …을 얇게 자르다, 대패질하다 4. …을 스치다 ¶①화살이 귀를 스쳤다 —❀ 1. 면도하기, 2. 엷은 조각 3. 면도 도구, 깎는 기구

—❀ 1. 면도하는(깎는) 사람, 이발사 2. 면도기; 깎는 도구
—❀ 깎아낸 부스러기, 대팻밥
—❀ 쇼올, 어깨걸이

—⑰ 그녀는(가) usage 인간이 아니더라도 여성으로 취급되는 「배·달·국가」 따위에도 쓰임 —❀ 여자; 암컷

—「여성」을 뜻하는 연결형
—❀ 다발 ¶①한 다발의 밀/②한 다발의 화살/③한 뭉치의 서류

—❀ 큰 가위

—働 1. [양털 따위]를 큰 가위로 깎다, 자르다 ¶①양털을 깎다 2. …을 벗겨내다 ¶②…을 빼앗기다 —自 가위질

sheath

—*vi.* cut with shears or scissors; cut off wool from sheep with shears or clippers.

sheath [ʃi:θ] *n.* ⓒ (pl. **sheaths** [ʃi:ðz]) **1.** a case or covering for a sword blade or knife. **2.** any protective covering. —⑲ 1.[칼 따위의] 집 2.[도구의] 덮개

sheathe [ʃi:ð] *vt.* **1.** put (a sword, etc.) into a sheath. ¶ *~ a sword.* **2.** protect (something) with a covering. —⑲ 1.[칼 따위]를 집어넣다 2. ····을 덮다

sheath·ing [ʃi:ðiŋ] *n.* **1.** Ⓤ the act of covering (something) with a sheath. **2.** a cover; a thing that protects something. ¶ *the copper ~.*① —⑲ 1.[칼]집에 넣기 2.덮개, 씌우개, 싸개 ¶①구리로 만든 덮개

sheaves [ʃi:vz] *n.* pl. of **sheaf**.

‡ **shed**¹ [ʃed] *vt.* **1.** cause (blood, tears, etc.) to flow or drop. ¶ *~ tears.*① **2.** throw off; cast or take off (leaves, hair, skin, etc.) by a natural process. **3.** give off (light, sound, etc.). ¶ *The sun sheds light.*② —*vi.* **1.** take off hair, skin, etc. by a natural process. **2.** (of leaves, seeds, etc.) drop off; fall out.
shed one's blood, sacrifice oneself; die. —⑲ 1.[피·눈물 따위]를 흘리다 ¶①눈물을 흘리다 2.[잎사귀·털 따위]를 탈락시키다, 벗다;[옷 따위]를 벗어 버리다 3.[광선 따위]를 발산하다, 내다 ¶②태양은 빛을 발산한다 —⑲ 1. 탈피하다, 탈모(脫毛)하다 2. 떨어지다 ▨ 희생이 되다; 죽다

* **shed**² [ʃed] *n.* ⓒ a small one-floor building for storing tools or supplies, for sheltering animals, etc.; an outhouse. ¶ *a bicycle ~*① / *a cattle ~.*② —⑲ 우리; 헛간, 창고 ¶①자전거 두는 곳/②외양간

she'd [ʃi:d] **1.** she had. **2.** she would.

sheen [ʃi:n] *n.* Ⓤ brightness, esp. that caused by a shining surface that reflects light; gloss. —⑲ 광택

sheen·y [ʃi:ni] *adj.* (**sheen·i·er, sheen·i·est**) having a sheen; bright; glossy. —⑲ 번쩍번쩍 빛나는

‡ **sheep** [ʃi:p] *n.* ⓒ (pl. **sheep**) **1.** a weak, cowardly animal with a thick coat of wool. **2.** a weak, cowardly person. **3.** ((*collectively*)) members of a church or religious community. **4.** Ⓤ sheepskin.
separate the sheep and (or *from*) *the goats,* distinguish the good from the bad. ⌈are kept.⌉ —⑲ 1. 양 2. 겁장이 3. 신자(信者), 교구민 4. 양피

▨ 선인과 악인을 구별하다

sheep-cote [ʃi:pkòut] *n.* ⓒ an enclosure where sheep —⑲ 양우리

sheep dog [´ ´] *n.* a dog trained to look after or protect sheep along with a shepherd. —⑲ 양 지키는 개

sheep·fold [ʃi:pfòuld] *n.* ⓒ a small enclosure or yard for sheep; a sheepcote. —⑲ 양우리

sheep·ish [ʃi:piʃ] *adj.* **1.** like a sheep; weak and cowardly the. **2.** somewhat silly. —⑲ 1. 양 같은; 소심한, 수줍어하는 2. 어리석은

sheep·skin [ʃi:pskìn] *n.* **1.** Ⓤ the skin of a sheep, usu. with the wool still on it, used for garments. **2.** Ⓤ leather or parchment made from the skin of sheep. **3.** ⓒ (*U. S. colloq.*) a graduation diploma. —⑲ 1. 양가죽 2. 양피지 3. [美口] 졸업증서

* **sheer** [ʃiər] *adj.* **1.** pure; unmixed. **2.** absolute; complete. ¶ *a ~ waste of time.*① **3.** very thin; that can be seen through. ¶ *~ curtain.* **4.** straight up and down; steep. ¶ *a ~ cliff.*② —*adv.* **1.** steeply; straight. ¶ *The rock rises ~ from the water.* **2.** completely. —⑲ 1.순수한 2.순전한, 완전한 ¶①완전한 시간 낭비 3.얇고 투명한 4.수직의 ¶②깎아지른 듯한 벼랑 —⑲ 1.수직으로 2.순전히, 완전히

‡ **sheet** [ʃi:t] *n.* ⓒ **1.** a large, thin piece of anything. **2.** a piece of cloth to cover a bed. **3.** a single piece of paper; a letter; a newspaper. **4.** a wide space or surface. ¶ *a ~ of flame (blood).*① **5.** a rope attached to a 1) *be between the sheets,* be in bed. ⌊sail.⌉ 2) *in sheets,* heavily. ¶ *The rain fell in sheets.* —*vt.* cover (a bed) with a sheet. —⑲ 1. 널빤지(종이) 모양의 것 2. 홑이불, 시이트 3. 한 장, 한 닢; 편지; 신문 4. 퍼진 면 ¶①불(피)바다 5. 돛자락 매는 밧줄 ▨ 1)잠자리에 들어 있다 2)격렬하게; 역수같이 —⑲ ···에 시이트를 깔다

sheet·ing [ʃi:tiŋ] *n.* Ⓤ **1.** ((*collectively*)) cotton or linen material for sheets. **2.** the act of making (something) into sheets. ⌈or plate.⌉ —⑲ 1. 시이트[감] 2. 판금(鐵板)으로 만들기

sheet iron [´ ´ ´] *n.* iron rolled, in the form of a sheet —⑲ [얇은] 철판

sheik, sheikh [ʃi:k, +*Brit.* ʃeik] *n.* ⓒ **1.** the chief of an Arab family, tribe, or village, used as a title of respect. **2.** a leader in Mohammedan countries. —⑲ 1. [아라비아의] 가장(家長), 족장 2. [회교도의] 교주(敎主)

* **shelf** [ʃelf] *n.* ⓒ (pl. **shelves**) **1.** a thin, flat piece placed on a wall for holding things. **2.** something like a —⑲ 1. 선반 2. 선반 모양의 것[사주(砂洲)·암붕(岩棚) 따위]

shelf.

be on the shelf, be out of use; be undesirable.
[熟] 사용되지 않다; 보류되다; 해고당하다

• **shell** [ʃel] *n.* [C] **1.** a hard outside covering on some animals, vegetables, or kinds of fruit. **2.** the skeleton of a building, a ship, etc. **3.** a very light racing boat. ⇒fig. **4.** a case holding gunpowder to be fired from a rifle, pistol, cannon, etc.
—[名] 1. 껍질; 깍지; 조가비; 껍데기; 외피 2. [건물·선박 따위의] 뼈대 3. 경기용 보우트 4. 탄피; 포탄

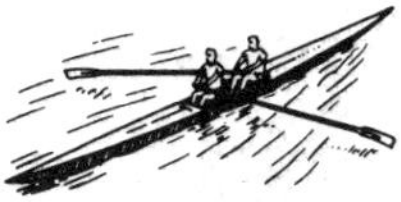

[shell 3.]

1) ***come out of one's shell,*** become sociable and less shy; talk in a familiar manner.
2) ***go*** (or ***retire***) ***into one's shell,*** become shy and less sociable.
[熟] 1)터놓고 말하다 2)마음을 터 놓지 않다

—*vt.* **1.** remove a shell from (something); take out (something) from a shell. ¶~ *nuts.* **2.** fire shells (*n.* 4) at (something). —*vi.* come out of a shell; (of a shell, etc.) fall; peel off.
—[他] 1. …의 껍데기를 벗기다, …을 껍데기 속에서 꺼내다 2. …을 포격하다
—[自] 껍데기에서 나오다; 끄투리가 벌어지다

shell out, (*colloq.*) pay out; hand over. ▷**shell·like** [-làik] *adj.*
[熟] ((口)) …을 남김없이 지불하다; 건네주다

⁑ **she'll** [ʃiːl] **1.** she will. **2.** she shall.

shel·lac [ʃəlǽk] *n.* [U] a sticky substance used in making varnish. —*vt.* (**-lacked, -lack·ing**) coat or cover (something) with shellac.
—[名] 셸락[lac을 정제(精製)한 와니스의 원료] —[他] …에 셸락을 칠하다

Shel·ley [ʃéli], **Percy Bysshe** *n.* (1792–1822) an English poet.
—[名] 영국의 시인

• **shell·fish** [ʃélfìʃ] *n.* [C] (pl. **-fish·es** or *collectively* **-fish**) a water animal with a shell, such as a lobster, a crab, or an oyster.
—[名] 조개·게·새우 따위의 총칭

shell shock [ˊ ˋ] *n.* (*Medicine*) a nervous or mental disorder resulting from the noise or strain of war.
—[名] ((醫)) 탄환 충격(폭탄의 파열 따위로 일어나는 기억력·시각의 상실증)

shell·y [ʃéli] *adj.* (**shell·i·er, shell·i·est**) **1.** having or covering with many shells. **2.** of or like a shell.
—[形] 1. 조가비가 많은, 조가비로 덮인 2. 조가비의

⁑ **shel·ter** [ʃéltər] *n.* **1.** [C] something that covers or protects from any danger; a safe place. **2.** [U] the state of being protected or covered; protection. ¶ *find* (or *take*) ~ *from a storm*① / *give* (or *provide*) ~ *to* (*someone*).② —*vt.* protect; cover. —*vi.* find shelter.
—[名] 1. 보호자; 피난처 2. 보호 ¶①폭풍우를 피하다/②…을 보호하다
—[他] …을 보호하다; 숨기다 —[自]피난하다

shelter (=*conceal*) *oneself* ***under*** *someone.*
[熟] …에 몸을 숨기다

shelve [ʃelv] *vt.* **1.** put (something) on a shelf. ¶~ *boxes.*① **2.** put off (problems, etc.) indefinitely; lay aside.
—[他] 1. …을 선반에 얹다 ¶①상자를 선반에 얹다 2. [문제 따위의 해결을] 연기하다

shelves [ʃelvz] *n.* pl. of **shelf**.

shelv·ing [ʃélviŋ] *n.* [U] **1.** material for shelves. **2.** ((*collectively*)) shelves.
—[名] 1. 선반의 재료 2. 선반

⁑ **shep·herd** [ʃépərd] *n.* [C] **1.** a person who looks after sheep. ¶*a shepherd's dog.*① **2.** a minister; a priest. ¶*the Good Shepherd.*② —*vt.* **1.** look after (sheep); take care of (someone). **2.** guide or direct. ¶~ *a group into a train.*③
—[名] 1. 양 치는 사람 ¶①양 치는 개 2. 목사 ¶②예수 그리스도 —[他] 1. [양]을 지키다 2. …을 인도하다 ¶③사람들을 인도하여 기차에 태우다

shep·herd·ess [ʃépərdis] *n.* [C] a female shepherd.
—[名] 양 치는 여자

sher·bet [ʃə́ːrbit] *n.* [U] a frozen dessert made of fruit juice, milk, whites of eggs, gelatin, etc.; an ice water with a fruit flavor.
—[名] 셔어벳(과즙에 계란 흰자위·우유·설탕 따위를 넣어 얼린 것); 셔어벳 수(水)

• **sher·iff** [ʃérif] *n.* **1.** (*U.S.*) the chief law officer in a county, elected by the people. **2.** (*Brit.*) an honorary official of a county or shire in England, usu. called High Sheriff.
—[名] 1. ((美)) [민선(民選)의] 지방 사법관; 군(郡) 보안관, 셰리프 2. ((英)) [임기 1년의 명예직인] 주(州)장관

sher·ry [ʃéri] *n.* [U] a strong wine, its color varies from light brown to dark brown, originally made in Spain.
—[名] 셰리 술

• **she's** [ʃiːz] **1.** she is. **2.** she has.

shew [ʃou] *vt., vi.* (**shewed, shewn**) (*Brit. archaic*) = show.

shib·bo·leth [ʃíbouliθ, -lèθ] *n.* [C] a test word; a catch word.
—[名] 시험삼아 물어보는 단어; [특수계급·단체의] 암호, 군호; 표어

shield — shiny

:shield [ʃi:ld] *n.* Ⓒ **1.** a piece of metal, wood, etc. carried on the arm by soldiers to protect the body in fighting. ⇒fig. **2.** a person or thing that protects; a protector. **3.** something shaped like a shield, such as a trophy. —*vt.* protect. (~ someone *from*)

:shift [ʃift] *vt.* **1.** move (something) from one place to another. ¶~ *a suitcase from one hand to another.* **2.** change. ¶~ *one's partner.*② **3.** get rid of (something). —*vi.* **1.** change. ¶*The wind shifted to the east.*② **2.** manage somehow; do with difficulty. ¶~ *with a small income.*③

[shield 1.]

—㉢ 1. 방패 2. 보호물(자) 3. 방패 모양 —㉺ …을 보호하다

—㉺ 1. …의 위치를 옮기다 2. …을 바꾸다, 변경하다 ¶①상대를 바꾸다 3. …을 치워 버리다 —㉡ 1. 바뀌다 ②풍향이 동쪽으로 바뀌었다 2. 여러가지로 해보다; 이럭저럭 둘러맞추다 ¶③적은 수입으로 그럭저럭 지내다

shift one's ground, change one's point of view in an argument.
—*n.* Ⓒ **1.** the act of shifting; change. ¶*a ~ of the tide.*④ **2.** the period during which work is regularly done. ¶*an eight-hour ~.* **3.** a group of people working at one time. ¶*a night (a day) ~.*⑤ **4.** ((often *pl.*)) plot; trick. ¶*the last shift[s].*⑥
make a shift, manage somehow.

圞 입장(주장)을 바꾸다

—㉢ 1. 변화; 전환; 바꾸어 놓기 ¶④조류의 변화 2. [교대제의] 근무 시간 3. 한 교대시간 동안에 일하는 노동자들 ¶⑤야간반(주간반) 4. 계획, 궁리, 묘안 ¶⑥최후의 수단
圞 그럭저럭 해나가다

shift·less [ʃíftlis] *adj.* lacking the will to accomplish something; lazy; incapable.

—㉺ 할 생각이 없는; 게으른; 무력한

shift·y [ʃífti] *adj.* (**shift·i·er, shift·i·est**) **1.** deceitful; tricky. **2.** not to be trusted; unreliable.

—㉺ 1. 잘 속이는 2. 믿을 수 없는

:shil·ling [ʃíliŋ] *n.* Ⓒ a British silver coin equal to twelve pence. ⇒N.B.

—㉢ 실링 N.B. 1파운드의 20분의 1로서 s.로 줄임

shil·ly-shal·ly [ʃíliʃæli] *n.* Ⓤ indecision in trifling things; hesitation. —*vi.* be slow to decide; hesitate. —*adj.* undecided; irresolute.

—㉢ 우유부단 —㉡ 망설이다 —㉺ 우유부단의; 우물쭈물하는

shim·mer [ʃímər] *vi.* shine with a wavering light; glimmer. ¶*The moonlight is shimmering on the sea.* —*n.* Ⓒ ((*sing.* only)) a faint, wavering light or gleam.

—㉡ 아른아른 빛나다 —㉢ 아른거리는 빛

shin [ʃin] *n.* Ⓒ the front part of the leg between the ankle and the knee. —*vt., vi.* (**shinned, shin·ning**) **1.** climb (a rope, tree, etc.) with hands and legs. (~ *up* something) **2.** kick (someone) in the shins. ¶~ *oneself against a chair.*①

—㉢ 정강이 —㉺㉡ 1. […에] 기어오르다 2. […의] 정강이를 차다 ¶①의자에 정강이를 부딪치다

shin·dy [ʃíndi] *n.* Ⓒ (pl. **-dies** [-diz]) (*colloq.*) a disturbance; an uproar.

—㉢ (口) 소동

:shine [ʃain] *vi.* (**shone** → *vt.*) **1.** give out or reflect light. ¶*The sun shines bright in the sky.* **2.** be bright. ¶*Her face shone with joy.* **3.** be best; be excellent. ¶*He shines in mathematics.*① —*vt.* (**shined**) cause (something) to reflect light; polish. ¶*I must have my shoes shined.*
—*n.* **1.** Ⓤ sunshine. **2.** Ⓤ bright weather. **3.** Ⓤ brightness; light; glow.

—㉡ 1. 빛나다; 빛을 반사하다 2. 멋있다, 환하다 3. 가장 뛰어나다, 탁월하다 ¶①그는 특히 수학에 뛰어났다 —㉺ …을 빛나게 하다; 닦다

—㉢ 1. 일광, 볕 2. 맑은 날씨 3. 빛남; 광택

shin·gle¹ [ʃíŋgl] *n.* Ⓒ **1.** a thin piece of wood, slate, etc. used in making roofs. **2.** (*U.S. colloq.*) a small signboard, esp. for a doctor's or lawyer's office. **3.** a kind of haircut for women. —*vt.* **1.** cover (a roof) with shingles. **2.** cut (a woman's hair) short.

—㉢ 1. 지붕 이는 널빤지 2. [의사·변호사 등의] 작은 간판 3. [여자의 뒷머리를] 바싹 치켜 깎기 —㉺ 1. …을 널빤지로 이다 2. [머리]를 치켜 깎다

shin·gle² [ʃíŋgl] *n.* Ⓒ (pl. **-gle**) (chiefly *Brit.*) small pebbles on a beach; a beach covered with shingle.

—㉢ [강가·바닷가의] 자갈, 조약돌; 자갈이 많은 해변

shin·gly [ʃíŋgli] *adj.* covered with small pebbles.

—㉺ 자갈이 많은

shin guard [⌃⌃] *n.* (in football, hockey, etc.) a heavy guard worn to protect the shins.

—㉢ [축구·하키 선수의] 정강이받이

shin·ing [ʃáiniŋ] *adj.* **1.** bright; reflecting light. **2.** remarkable. ▷**shin·ing·ly** [-li] *adv.*

—㉺ 1. 빛나는 2. 눈에 띄는, 탁월한

shin·y [ʃáini] *adj.* (**shin·i·er, shin·i·est**) **1.** bright; shining. **2.** polished. ¶~ *shoes.* **3.** glossy because of long wear. ¶*a ~ coat.*

—㉺ 1. 빛나는 2. 광택이 있는 3. 오래 입어서 번드르르한

‡ **ship** [ʃip] *n.* [C] **1.** a large sea-going boat. ¶*go to America by ~ | leave a ~ at Yokohama.* **2.** something like a ship in use or shape. ¶*an airship*① | *a spaceship.*②
—[名] 1. 배 2. 배 모양의 것 ¶①비행선 /②우주선

1) ***when one's ship comes home,*** when one gets money; when one's hopes have been realized.
2) ***on board a ship,*** into a ship; in a ship.
[熟] 1)돈을 벌면; 부자가 되면 2)배 안으로; 배 안에

—*vt.* **1.** carry (something) by ship; (*U.S.*) carry (something) by a ship, train, truck, etc.; send. **2.** employ (someone) for service on a ship. —*vi.* **1.** go on board a ship. **2.** take a job on a ship; be a sailor.
—[他] 1. …을 배로 나르다; 보내다 2. [선원]을 고용하다 —[自] 1. 배에 타다 2. 선원이 되다

ship·board [ʃípbɔ̀ːrd] *n.* [U] a ship.
—[名] 배

on shipboard, on a ship. ¶*go on ~.*①
[熟] 배 위에 ¶①승선하다

ship·build·er [ʃípbìldər] *n.* [C] a person who designs or builds ships.
—[名] 조선업자(기사)

ship·build·ing [ʃípbìldiŋ] *n.* [U] the construction of ships; the art of constructing ships. —*adj.* of shipbuilding.
—[名] 조선[술] —[形] 조선[술]의

ship canal [ˊ-ˋ] *n.* a canal through which a ship can pass.
—[名] 큰 배가 지날 수 있는 운하

ship chandler [ˊ ˋ-] *n.* (chiefly *Brit.*) a person who deals in supplies for ships.
—[名] 《주로 英》 선구상(船具商)

ship·load [ʃíplòud] *n.* [C] a full load or cargo for a ship.
—[名] 배 1척분의 적하량

ship·mas·ter [ʃípmæ̀stər / -mɑ̀ːstə] *n.* [C] the master, commander, or captain of a merchant ship.
—[名] 선장

ship·mate [ʃípmèit] *n.* [C] a fellow sailor on a ship.
—[名] 선원 동료

• **ship·ment** [ʃípmənt] *n.* **1.** [U] the act of loading goods into a ship. **2.** [C] goods transported at one time by a ship or by any means of transportation.
—[名] 1. 출하(出荷), 선적(船積) 2. 선적량, 적하

ship·own·er [ʃípòunər] *n.* [C] an owner of a ship or ships.
—[名] 선주

ship·per [ʃípər] *n.* [C] a person who sends goods by ship or by any means of transportation.
—[名] 하주(荷主)

• **ship·ping** [ʃípiŋ] *n.* [U] **1.** 《*collectively*》 all the ships of a port, a nation, a company, etc. **2.** the act or business of transporting goods.
—[名] 1. 선박 2. 선적; 해운[업]

ship·shape [ʃípʃèip] *adj.* having everything in good order; neat. —*adv.* in a shipshape manner.
—[形] 정연한 —[副] 정연히

ship·worm [ʃípwɔ̀ːrm] *n.* [C] a small animal with a soft and wormlike body which makes holes in the timbers of ships under the water.
—[名] 좀조개

ship·wreck [ʃíprèk] *n.* **1.** [U] the destruction or loss of a ship by an accident at sea. **2.** [C] a wrecked ship. **3.** [U] destruction; failure.
—[名] 1. 난파 2. 난파선 3. 파괴; 실패

make a shipwreck of (=*destroy* or *ruin*) *something.*
[熟] …을 멸망시키다

—*vt.* **1.** destroy (a ship) by shipwreck. **2.** destroy (something like a hope, happiness, etc.).
—[他] 1. …을 난파시키다 2. …을 파괴하다

ship·wright [ʃípràit] *n.* [C] a person who builds or repairs ships.
—[名] 배목수, 조선공(造船工)

ship·yard [ʃípjɑ̀ːrd] *n.* [C] a yard or place where ships are built or repaired.
—[名] 조선소

shire [ʃáiər] *n.* [C] a county in Great Britain.
—[名] [영국의] 주

shirk [ʃəːrk] *vt., vi.* avoid purposely; escape.
—[他][自] 피하다, 도망하다

shirk·er [ʃə́ːrkər] *n.* [C] a person who escapes doing works, etc.
—[名] 꾀부리는 사람

shirr [ʃəːr] *n.* [C] (*U.S.*) a gathered arrangement of cloth, etc. —*vt.* gather (cloth) on three or more parallel threads.
—[名] 《美》 주름 —[他] …에 주름을 잡다

‡ **shirt** [ʃəːrt] *n.* [C] a man's thin garment with sleeves and a collar, worn under a coat or jacket; the under-garment for the upper part of the body; a woman's blouse.
—[名] 와이샤쓰, 샤쓰; [부인용] 블라우스

shirt front [ˊ ˋ] *n.* the front of a man's shirt.
—[名] 와이샤쓰의 가슴

shirt·ing [ʃə́ːrtiŋ] *n.* [U] material for making shirts.
—[名] 샤쓰(와이샤쓰)감

shirt sleeve [ˊ ˋ] *n.* the sleeve of a shirt.
—[名] 와이샤쓰의 소매

shirt-sleeve [ʃə́ːrtslìːv] *adj.* (*colloq.*) informal; plain; rude.
—[形] 《口》 비공식의; 솔직한; 조잡한

shirt·waist [ʃə́ːrtwèist] *n.* [C] (*U.S.*) a woman's blouse with a collar and cuffs worn under a skirt.
—[名] 《美》 [여자용] 블라우스

• **shiv·er**¹ [ʃívər] *vi.* tremble with fear or cold. —*n.* [C]
—[自] [추위·공포 따위로] 떨다 —[名]

the act of trembling from cold or fear. ¶*give someone the shivers.*① ▷**shiv·er·er** [-rər] *n.*
떨림, 전율 ¶①남을 오싹하게 하다

shiv·er² [ʃívər] *n.* [C] ⦅usu. *pl.*⦆ a small piece. ¶*break into* (or *in*) *shivers.*① —*vt., vi.* break (something) into many small pieces.
—[名] 산산조각; 파편 ¶①산산조각이 되다 —[他][自] 산산이 부수다(부서지다)

shiv·er·y [ʃívəri] *adj.* inclined to shiver; causing shivers from cold or fear.
—[形] 떨리는; 후들후들하는

shoal¹ [ʃoul] *n.* [C] **1.** a shallow place in the water; a sandbank in a river or the sea. **2.** ⦅usu. *pl.*⦆ a hidden or unexpected danger. —*adj.* shallow. —*vi.* become shallow.
—[名] 1. 여울; 모래톱 2. 눈에 안 보이는 위험 —[形] 얕은 —[自] 얕아지다

shoal² [ʃoul] *n.* [C] a large number or mass, esp. of fish. ¶*a* ~ *of flying fish.*① **2.** ⦅usu. *pl.*⦆ a large crowd. ¶*shoals of students.*② —*vi.* crowd and swim together.
—[名] 1. [물고기의] 떼 ¶①날치의 떼 2. 다수, 무리 ¶②많은 학생 —[自] 떼 짓다

‡**shock¹** [ʃɑk / ʃɔk] *n.* **1.** [C] a sudden blow or shake. **2.** [C] a sudden great sorrow or surprise; [U] a condition of physical or mental weakness caused by a shock. ¶*The news gave a great* ~ *to me.*①
—[名] 1. 충돌; 진동 2. 충격; 쇽 ¶①그 뉴우스는 나에게 충격을 주었다

—*vt.* cause (someone) to feel horror, anger, disgust, etc. ¶*I was shocked to see the scene.*
—[他] …에게 충동을 주다; …을 깜짝 놀라게 하다; 분개시키다

shock² [ʃɑk / ʃɔk] *n.* [C] a pile of corn or a group of bundles of grain set up in a field to dry after the harvest.
—[名] 밀·호밀 따위의 가리; 옥수수의 단(다발)

shock³ [ʃɑk / ʃɔk] *n.* [C] ⦅usu. *a* ~ *of hair*⦆ a thick, untidy mass of hair.
—[名] 헝클어진 머리

shock·er [ʃákər / ʃɔ́kə] *n.* [C] a person or thing that gives a shock.
—[名] 오싹하게 하는(충격을 주는) 것; 기가 막힌 녀석

shock-head·ed [ʃákhèdid / ʃɔ́k-] *adj.* having a thick, untidy mass of hair.
—[形] 헝클어진 머리의

shock·ing [ʃákiŋ / ʃɔ́k-] *adj.* **1.** disgusting; unpleasant. **2.** causing horror or surprise. **3.** (*colloq.*) very bad.
—[形] 1. 괘씸한 2. 오싹하게 하는 3. ⦅口⦆ 형편없는, 조잡한

shock·ing·ly [ʃákiŋli / ʃɔ́k-] *adv.* as if giving a shock; extremely.
—[副] 오싹할 만큼; 지독하게

shod [ʃɑd / ʃɔd] *v.* pt. and pp. of **shoe**.

shod·dy [ʃádi / ʃɔ́di] *n.* (pl. **-dies**) **1.** [U][C] a cloth of wool of poor quality made from woolen waste, old rags, yarn, etc. **2.** [C] anything of poor quality which looks better than it really is. —*adj.* (**-di·er, -di·est**) **1.** made of shoddy. **2.** of poor quality; of poorer quality than it looks. ▷**shod·di·ness** [-nis] *n.*
—[名] 1. 재생한 털실(모직물) 2. 가짜, 보조품 —[形] 1. 재생 털실의 2. 겉만 번지르르한; 가짜의

‡**shoe** [ʃu:] *n.* [C] **1.** ⦅usu. *pl.*⦆ an outer covering for the foot usu. made of leather and having a thick or stiff sole at the heel. ⇒[N.B.] ¶*a pair of shoes*① / *put on* (or *take off*) *one's shoes.*② **2.** something in the shape of a shoe or used like a shoe; a U-shaped metal band fastened to a horse's hoof. **3.** the part of a brake pressing on a wheel to stop a car. **4.** a metal ring or cap for the protection of the end of a pole, stick, etc.
—[名] 1. 구두 [N.B.] 영국에서는 발목까지 오는 단화, 미국에서는 편상화도 포함하여 씀 ¶①구두 한 켤레/②구두를 신다(벗다) 2. 구두 모양의 것; 편자 3. 제동기, 브레이크 4. [지팡이 따위의] 마구리 쇠; 쇠테

1) ***another pair of shoes,*** quite a different thing or matter.
2) ***shake in one's shoes,*** shiver; be afraid.
3) ***stand in someone's shoes,*** take the place of someone.
[熟] 1)전혀 별개의 일 2)덜덜 떨다 3) …을 대신하다

—*vt.* (**shod**) **1.** fasten shoes on to (a horse). **2.** protect (the edge of a stick, etc. with metal).
—[他] 1. [말]에 편자를 박다 2. [지팡이 따위]의 끝에 쇠붙이를 달다

shoe·black [ʃú:blæ̀k] *n.* [C] (*Brit.*) a person who cleans and polishes the shoes of passers-by to earn money.
—[名] ⦅英⦆ 구두닦이

shoe·horn [ʃú:hɔ̀:rn] *n.* [C] a piece of metal, horn, or other material to get a foot into a shoe easily by making the shoe easier to slip on.
—[名] 구두주걱

shoe·lace [ʃú:lèis] *n.* [C] a string, cord, or leather strip used to fasten a shoe; a shoe string.
—[名] 구두끈

·**shoe·mak·er** [ʃú:mèikər] *n.* [C] a person who makes or repairs shoes.
—[名] 구두 직공(수선공)

shoe·string [ʃú:strìŋ] *n.* [C] a shoelace.
—[名] 구두끈

‡**shone** [ʃoun / ʃɔn] *v.* pt. and pp. of **shine**.

shoo [ʃu:] *interj.* a word used for driving or scaring away animals or birds. —*vt.* drive away (animals or birds) by crying "Shoo!"
—[感] 쉬이!, 쉿!(새 따위를 쫓을 때의 소리) —[他] [새 따위]를 쉬이하고 쫓아 버리다

‡ shook [ʃuk] *v.* pt. of **shake.**

‡ shoot [ʃu:t] *v.* (**shot**) *vt.* **1.** fire (a gun); let fly (an arrow). ¶ *~ an arrow* / *~ a gun at a target.* **2.** send (something) off quickly. ¶ *~ out one's hand*① / *~ a glance*② / *He shot question after question.*③ **3.** hit or kill (something) with a bullet or an arrow. ¶ *~ a bird.* **4.** send (something) forth with sudden force. ¶ *~ a ball at the goal.* **—*vi.*** **1.** fire a gun; let fly an arrow. **2.** move very fast; dash; rush. ¶ *A bird shot across the sky.*④ **3.** grow a fresh branch rapidly. ¶ *The plants are beginning to ~.*⑤ **4.** feel a sharp pain.
shoot straight, shoot with good aim; be a good shot.
—*n.* [C] **1.** the act of shooting. **2.** a new growth; a young branch. **3.** a shooting match; a hunt. **4.** a shooting distance or range.

—[他] 1. …을 쏘다, 발사하다; 사격하다 2. …을 재빨리 보내다 ¶①손을 쑥 내밀다/②흘깃 보다/③그는 질문을 연발했다 3. …을 쏘아 맞히다; 쏘아 떨어뜨리다 4. …을 내던지다, 돌진시키다 —[自] 1. 쏘다, 사격하다 2. 돌진하다 ¶④새 한 마리가 하늘을 휙 날아 갔다 3. 싹을 내는 ¶⑤식물은 싹을 내기 시작했다 4. 욱신욱신 아프다
[熟] 잘 쏘다, 명중하다
—[名] 1. 사격 2. 어린 싹(가지) 3. 사격 시합; 사냥 4. 사정 거리

shoot·er [ʃú:tər] *n.* [C] a person who shoots.
—[名] 사수(射手)

shoot·ing [ʃú:tiŋ] *n.* **1.** [U] the act of shooting. **2.** [C] (chiefly *Brit.*) a particular area rented in order to shoot game there; [U] the right of shooting in a particular area.
—[名] 1. 사격 2. 《英》 [총] 사냥터; 총렵권(銃獵權)

shooting box [∠-∸] *n.* (chiefly *Brit.*) a small house or lodge used during the shooting season.
—[名] 사격장

shooting range [∠-∸] *n.* a place used to practice shooting with rifles; a rifle range.
—[名] 사냥철에 사용하는 움막

shooting star [∠-∠] *n.* a falling star; a meteor.
—[名] 유성, 운석(隕石)

‡ shop [ʃɑp / ʃɔp] *n.* [C] **1.** a small store. ¶ *a fancy ~*① / *keep a ~.*② **2.** a place where things are made or repaired; a workshop. ¶ *a shoemaker's ~.*
1) ***set up shop,*** start a business or work.
2) ***shut up shop,*** close a shop; go out of business.
3) ***talk shop,*** talk about one's business.
—*vi.* (**shopped, shop·ping**) visit shops or stores to look at and buy goods. ¶ *go shopping.*

—[名] 1. 소매점, 가게 ¶①장신구 가게/②가게를 갖고 있다 2. 수리 공장; 제작소
[熟] 1)일을 시작하다 2)폐점하다, 일을 그만두다 3)자기 장사(전문) 이야기를 하다
—[自] 물건을 사러 가다

shop assistant [∠ -∸-] *n.* (*Brit.*) a person employed in a shop or store.
—[名] 《英》 점원

shop·boy [ʃɑ́pbɔ̀i / ʃɔ́p-] *n.* [C] (*Brit.*) a young clerk in a shop or store.
—[名] 《英》 남자 점원

shop·girl [ʃɑ́pgə̀:rl / ʃɔ́pgə̀:l] *n.* [C] (*Brit.*) a young girl who works in a shop or store. (cf. *U.S.* saleswoman, salesgirl)
—[名] 《英》 여점원

shop·hours [ʃɑ́pàuərz / ʃɔ́pàuəz] *n. pl.* the hours during which a store is open for business.
—[名] [상점의] 영업 시간

shop·keep·er [ʃɑ́pkì:pər / ʃɔ́pkì:pə] *n.* [C] (*Brit.*) an owner of a shop or store, usu. one that is not very big.
—[名] 《英》 가게 주인, 소매상인

shop·keep·ing [ʃɑ́pkì:piŋ / ʃɔ́p-] *n.* [U] (*Brit.*) the business of a shopkeeper.
—[名] 《英》 가게의 경영; 소매상

shop·lift·er [ʃɑ́plìftər / ʃɔ́plìftə] *n.* [C] a person who steals goods displayed in a shop or store.
—[名] 들치기꾼

shop·lift·ing [ʃɑ́plìftiŋ / ʃɔ́p-] *n.* [U] the act of stealing from a shop while pretending to buy.
—[名] 들치기

shop·man [ʃɑ́pmən / ʃɔ́p-] *n.* [C] (pl. **-men** [-mən]) **1.** (chiefly *Brit.*) a salesman in a shop or store; a clerk. **2.** a shopkeeper.
—[名] 1. 《英》 점원 2. 소매상인

shop·per [ʃɑ́pər / ʃɔ́pə] *n.* [C] a person who goes to shops to buy things.
—[名] 물건 사는 손님

shop-soiled [ʃɑ́psɔ̀ild / ʃɔ́p-] *adj.* shopworn.
—[形] 팔리지 않아 가게에 오래 묵은

shop·walk·er [ʃɑ́pwɔ̀:kər / ʃɔ́pwɔ̀:kə] *n.* [C] (*Brit.*) a person hired by a large store or shop to direct the customers or to control the shop assistants.
—[名] 《英》 판매장 감독

shop·win·dow [ʃɑ́pwìndou / ʃɔ́p-] *n.* [C] a show window; a window used for showing goods sold at a shop.
—[名] 가게의 진열창

shop·worn [ʃɑ́pwɔ̀:rn / ʃɔ́pwɔ̀:n] *adj.* (of goods) slightly dirty or damaged from having been displayed in a store.
—[形] 진열된 채 가게에서 오래 묵은

‡ shore[1] [ʃɔ:r] *n.* **1.** [C] the land on the edge of a sea, a lake, etc. ¶ *go on ~*① / *live on the ~.*② **2.** [U] land.
1) ***in shore,*** near or nearer the shore [on the water].
2) ***off shore,*** away from the shore.

—[名] 1. [바다·호수·강의] 기슭 ¶①상륙하다/②해안에 살다 2. 육지
[熟] 1)기슭 가까이에, 여울에 2)기슭을 떠나서, 앞바다에

S

shore² [ʃɔ:r] *n.* ⓒ a support which is placed against or beneath something like a ship, a building, a tree, etc. to hold it up. —*vt.* support (something) with a shore or shores. 《~ *up* something》 —ⓝ 지주(支柱) —ⓥ …을 지주로 받치다

shore·ward [ʃɔ́:rwərd] *adv., adj.* toward the shore. —ⓐⓓ 기슭 쪽으로(의)

shorn [ʃɔ:rn] *v.* pp. of **shear**.

‡short [ʃɔ:rt] *adj.* **1.** not long; not tall. ¶~ *legs* / *a ~ journey* / *a ~ man*. **2.** not enough; less than the right amount. ¶~ *weight*① / *The change was five cents ~*. **3.** so brief as to be almost rude. **4.** brief; concise.
1) *be short of* (=have not enough of) something.
2) *to make a long story short,* briefly speaking; in a few words.
—*adv.* **1.** suddenly; quickly; briefly. ¶*stop* ~. **2.** not to reach. ¶*jump* ~.①
1) *come short; fall short,* ⓐ be in sufficient. ⓑ fail
2) *cut short,* ⓐ cause (someone) to stop speaking. ¶*cut the speaker* ~. ⓑ cause (something) to end at
3) *run short,* use up; be used up.
—*n.* **1.** Ⓤ briefness; shortness. **2.** ⓒ anything short or brief. **3.** 《*the ~*》 the essential point. **4.** 《usu. *pl.*》 shortage. **5.** 《*pl.*》 short trousers; short pants. **6.** (*Baseball*) a shortstop.
1) *for short,* by way of making a name, etc. short.
2) *in short,* briefly speaking; in a few words.

—ⓐ 1. 짧은; 키가 작은 2. 불충분한; 부족한 ¶①중량 부족 3. 무뚝뚝한, 통명스러운 4. 간결한, 간단한

爋 1)…이 부족하다 2)간단히 말하면, 요는

—ⓐⓓ 1. 갑자기; 재빨리; 무뚝뚝하게 2. 미치지 못하여 ¶②뛰어넘지 못하다
爋 1)ⓐ…에 달하지 못하다; 부족하다 ⓑ실패하다 2)ⓐ…의 이야기를 가로막다 ⓑ…을 정지시키다 3)없어지다; 다되다

—ⓝ 1. 짧음; 간결 2. 짧은(간결한) 것 3. 요점 4. 부족 5. 반즈봉 6. 《野球》 유격수

爋 1)줄여서 2)간단히 말하면

short·age [ʃɔ́:rtidʒ] *n.* ⓤⓒ the state of being short or not enough; ⓒ the amount of lack or by which something is short. —ⓝ 부족; 부족액

short·cake [ʃɔ́:rtkèik] *n.* ⓤⓒ (*U.S.*) a kind of sweetened sponge cake with fruit and cream on it. —ⓝ 《美》 쇼오트 케이크

short circuit [⌐ ⌐] *n.* an abnormal circuit of electricity caused by the touching of two electric wires. —ⓝ 단락(短絡)

short·com·ing [ʃɔ́:rtkÀmiŋ] *n.* ⓒ 《often *pl.*》 a fault; a defect. —ⓝ 결점, 단점

short cut [⌐ ⌐] *n.* a shorter way; a quicker method to do something. —ⓝ 지름길

‧short·en [ʃɔ́:rtn] *vt.* **1.** make (something) short. ↔lengthen ¶*The new highway shortened the trip*.① **2.** make (a cake, etc.) crisp and flaky by adding butter, lard, etc. —*vi.* become short or less. ¶*The days ~ in the fall*.
—ⓥ 1. …을 짧게 하다 ¶①새로운 도로는 여행을 단축했다 2. [과자]를 바삭바삭하게 하다 —ⓥ 짧아지다, 감소하다

short·hand [ʃɔ́:rthænd] *n.* ⓤ a method of rapid writing in which symbols are used for words, phrases, etc.; stenography. ¶*write* [*in*] ~① / *a ~ writer*.② —*adj.* of or by shorthand. workmen.
—ⓝ 속기[법] ¶①속기하다/②속기자
—ⓐ 속기[법]의(에 의한)

short·hand·ed [ʃɔ́:rthǽndid] *adj.* not having enough —ⓐ 일손이 모자라는

short·horn [ʃɔ́:rthɔ:rn] *n.* ⓒ a kind of cattle with short horns, raised for beef. ing only a short time. —ⓝ 뿔이 짧은 소

short·lived [ʃɔ́:rtláivd, -lívd / -lívd] *adj.* living or last- —ⓐ 목숨이 짧은; 일시적인

‡short·ly [ʃɔ́:rtli] *adv.* **1.** very soon. ¶*The plane leaves* ~. **2.** briefly. ¶*to put it* ~① **3.** abruptly and rudely. —ⓐⓓ 1. 얼마 안 있어; 곧 2. 간단히 ¶①간단히 말하면 3. 무뚝뚝하게

short·ness [ʃɔ́:rtnis] *n.* ⓤ the state of being short. —ⓝ 짧음

shorts [ʃɔ:rts] *n. pl.* short trousers cut above the knee. —ⓝ 반즈봉

short·sight·ed [ʃɔ́:rtsáitid] *adj.* **1.** that cannot see things in the distance. **2.** not thinking clearly of the future. ¶*a ~ policy*.①
—ⓐ 1. 근시[안]의 2. 선견지명이 없는 ¶①근시안적 정책

short·stop [ʃɔ́:rtstàp / ʃɔ́:rtstɔ̀p] *n.* ⓒ (*Baseball*) a player between second and third base. —ⓝ 《野球》 유격수

short-tem·pered [ʃɔ́:rttémpərd] *adj.* easily becoming angry; having a quick temper. —ⓐ 성마른, 성급한

short wave [⌐ ⌐] *n.* (*Electricity*) a radio wave that is 60 meters or less in length. —ⓝ 《電》 단파

short-wind·ed [ʃɔ́:rtwíndid] *adj.* becoming breathless very quickly; very easily out of breath. —ⓐ 숨찬, 숨가쁜

⁑ **shot**[1] [ʃat / ʃɔt] *n.* [C] **1.** a ball for a gun or cannon; 《*collectively*》 small balls for a shotgun. ¶*a solid* ~① / *A* ~ *passed through the wall.*② **2.** the act of firing a gun or cannon. ¶*He fired five shots in rapid succession.*③ **3.** [U] the distance over which a shot can travel; a range. ¶*be within rifle* ~.④ **4.** an attempt to hit or do anything; a guess. **5.** a person who shoots.

1) ***have a shot for*** (=*try to catch*) *something.*
2) ***make a shot at*** (=*guess*) *something.*
3) ***not a shot in the locker,*** with no money available.

—[명] 1. 탄환; 포탄 ¶①실탄/②탄환은 벽을 꿰뚫었다 2. 발포 ¶③그는 연달아 5발을 쏘았다 3. 사정(射程) ¶④사정거리 안에 있다 4. 시도; 추측 5. 사수(射手)

[熟] 1)…을 시도해 보다 2) …을 어림짐작하다 3)빈털터리로

shot[2] [ʃat / ʃɔt] *v.* pt. and pp. of **shoot.**
—*adj.* woven so as to change color when moved or seen from different angles. ¶~ *silk.*

—[형] 보는 각도에 따라 빛깔이 달라지게 짠

shot·gun [ʃátgʌ̀n / ʃɔ́t-] *n.* [C] a gun for shooting many small shots at one time at short range.

—[명] 산탄총(散彈銃)

shot put [ˊ ˋ] *n.* a contest in which a heavy metal ball is thrown a long distance.

—[명] 투포환

⁑ **should** [ʃud, ʃəd, ʃd, ʃt] *auxil. v.* pt. of **shall. 1.** 《used to express something ***uncertain*** in ***an if-clause***》 ¶*If it* ~ *rain, what should I do?*① / *If any one* ~ *call, say I'm out.*② **2.** ought to; must. ¶*You* ~ *brush your teeth after each meal.*③ / *Why* ~ *I obey his orders?*④ **3.** 《used to express something that ***might have happened*** *but did not*》 ¶*You* ~ *not have said so.* / *If I had been you, I* ~ *have done it.*⑤ **4.** 《used to express ***a matter of course*** with ***verbs*** such as ***surprise, regret,*** and ***dislike***》 ¶*It is natural that she* ~ *refuse it.*⑥ / *I'm surprised that you* ~ *have been so lazy.*⑦ **5.** 《used after *what, who, how,* etc. expressing ***surprise,*** etc.》 ¶*Whom* ~ *I see but you?*⑧ **6.** 《used after ***the past tense*** of a verb expressing ***proposal, decision,*** or ***command***》 must. ¶*He insisted that the prisoners* ~ *be set free at once.*⑨ **7.** 《used to express ***strong probability*** or ***expectation***》 must; can. ¶*With an early start, they* ~ *be here by noon.*

1) ***lest one should do,*** [so] that one may not do; so as not to do. ¶*Study hard lest you* ~ *fail.*
2) ***should like*** (=*want*) ***to do.***

—[조] 1. 만일 …이라면 ¶①만일 비가 오면 어떻게 할까?/②만일 전화가 오면 외출했다고 해라 2. …하여야 한다; …하는 것이 당연하다 ¶③식사를 하고 나면 이를 닦아야 한다/④왜 그의 명령에 따라야 하는가? 3. …이었을 것이다; …해야 했다 ¶⑤만일 내가 너였더라면 그것을 했을 텐데 4. …하는 것은; …이라니 ¶⑥그녀가 그것을 하는 것은 당연하다/⑦네가 그렇게 게으르다니 놀랐다 5. …하다니 ¶⑧너를 만나다니? 6. …하여야 하다 ¶⑨그는 죄수들을 곧 석방해야 한다고 주장했다 7. …에 틀림없다; 꼭 …할 수 있다

[熟] 1)…하지 않도록 2)…하고 싶다

⁑ **shoul·der** [ʃóuldər] *n.* [C] **1.** the part of a human or an animal body where an arm or a foreleg joins the trunk. ¶*over one's* ~① / *He has broad shoulders.*② / *I patted him on the* ~.③ **2.** 《*pl.*》 the upper part of the back. **3.** anything shaped like a shoulder. ¶*the* ~ *of a mountain.*④

1) ***give the cold shoulder to*** (=*show dislike for; avoid*) ***someone.***
2) ***put one's shoulder to the wheel,*** set to work with a great effort.
3) ***rub shoulders*** (=*associate*) ***with someone.***
4) ***shift the blame on to other shoulders,*** make others take the blame.
5) ***shoulder to shoulder,*** close together; helping one another.
6) ***stand head and shoulder above*** (=***be very much*** *superior to*) *something.*

—*vt.* **1.** take (something) upon a shoulder. **2.** assume (something) as a responsibility. ¶*I'll* ~ *the expense.* **3.** push (something) aside with a shoulder.
—*vi.* push with a shoulder.
shoulder someone out of the way, push someone aside with a shoulder.

—[명] 1. 어깨 ¶①어깨너머로/②그는 어깨가 넓다/③그의 어깨를 가볍게 두드렸다 2. 어깻죽지 3. 튀어나온 부분 ¶④산등

[熟] 1)…을 쌀쌀하게 대하다 2)전력을 기울이다 3)…와 교제하다 4)남에게 책임을 전가하다 5)어깨를 나란히 하여; 서로 도와 가며 6)…보다 훨씬 뛰어나다

—[타] 1. …을 어깨에 메다 2. …을 떠맡다 3. …을 어깨로 밀어젖히다

—[자] 어깨로 밀어젖히고 나아가다
[熟] 어깨로 …을 밀어젖히다

shoulder blade [ˊ- ˋ] *n.* one of the pair of flat bones of the shoulder.

—[명] 견갑골(肩甲骨)

shoulder strap [ˊ- ˋ] *n.* **1.** a narrow strap worn over the shoulder to support a garment. **2.** a strip at the shoulder of an officer's uniform to show his rank.

—[명] 1. [즈봉·스커어트 따위의] 멜빵 2. [군인의] 견장(肩章)

• **should·n't** [ʃúdnt] should not.

shouldst [ʃudst] (*archaic*) =should.

S

shout [ʃaut] vi. call out loudly; speak loudly. ¶~ with (or for) joy① / ~ for a waiter② / ~ with a laugh.③ —vt. say (something) loudly. ¶~ one's orders.④
  shout down, prevent (someone) from speaking by shouting. ¶*The audience shouted the speaker down.*
  —n. ⓒ a loud and sudden cry or call. ¶*a ~ of joy.*
shout·ing [ʃáutiŋ] n. Ⓤ loud crying or cheering; shouts.
shove [ʃʌv] vt., vi. push roughly. ¶~ *across a crowd.*
  —n. ⓒ a push.
shov·el [ʃʌvl] n. ⓒ 1. a tool with a broad blade for digging, lifting or throwing coal, snow, grain, etc. 2. =shovelful. —vt. (-eled, -el·ing or Brit. -elled, el·ling) 1. take up, gather, or throw (something) with a shovel. 2. make (a way, etc.) with a shovel. ¶~ *a path.*①
shov·el·ful [ʃʌvlful] n. ⓒ the amount a shovel can hold.
show [ʃou] v. (showed, shown or showed) vt. 1. cause (something) to be seen; cause (someone) to see. ¶*Show [me] your ticket, please.* 2. guide; lead. ¶*He has shown me upstairs.*① 3. make (something) clear to someone; teach. (~ *that ...; ~ how or what ...; ~ someone to do*) ¶*Will you please ~ me the way to the station? / The fact shows that he is clever.*② / *Show me how you have done it.*③ 4. give; bestow; grant. ¶*He has shown me much kindness.*④ —vi. appear; be in sight; be visible.
  1) **show one's face**, appear.
  2) **show off**, ⓐ display. ⓑ try to attract other's attention. 「get out of the house.」
  3) **show someone the door**, (colloq.) order someone to
  4) **show up**, ⓐ cause (something) to be seen more clearly. ⓑ stand out clearly. ⓒ make (a secret, etc.) known to the public. ⓓ appear.
  —n. 1. Ⓤ the act of showing. 2. ⓒ a display; an exhibition; any public performance. ¶*a flower ~*⑤ / *a charity ~.*⑥ 3. Ⓤ (sometimes *a ~*) false appearance. ¶*by a ~ of honesty.*⑦ 4. ⓒ a chance, esp. one to show one's ability.
  for show, trying to attract others' attention.
show bill [~] n. an advertising poster, placard, etc.
show·boat [ʃóubòut] n. ⓒ a steamboat with a theater and carrying its own actors, dancers, etc.
show·case [ʃóukèis] n. ⓒ a case with glass sides to show and protect articles in stores, museums, etc.
show·down [ʃóudàun] n. ⓒ (colloq.) a full disclosure of facts, purposes, plans, etc.
show·er¹ [ʃáuər] n. ⓒ 1. a brief fall of rain. 2. something like a shower. 3. a party for giving presents to a future bride, etc. 4. a shower bath. —vi. 1. fall or pour in a shower. 2. take a shower bath. —vt. 1. make (something) wet with a shower. 2. give (something) in a large amount. 「strates.」
show·er² [ʃóuər] n. ⓒ a person who shows or demon-
shower bath [ʃáuərbæ̀θ / ʃáuəbɑ̀ːθ] n. a bath in which water pours down on the body like a shower; an apparatus for such a bath.
show·er·y [ʃáuəri] adj. 1. falling in showers. 2. abundant with showers. 3. of or like a shower.
show·i·ly [ʃóuili] adv. in a showy manner.
show·i·ness [ʃóuinis] n. Ⓤ the state of being showy.
show·ing [ʃóuiŋ] n. ⓒ (*sing.* only) the impression made by a person's appearance or actions, or by facts.
show·man [ʃóumən] n. ⓒ (pl. -men [-mən]) a person who presents shows or other entertainment.
show·man·ship [ʃóumənʃip] n. Ⓤ the skill or ability
shown [ʃoun] v. pp. of **show**. 「of a showman.」

—自 큰 소리로 외치다, 큰 소리로 말하다 ¶①환호하다/②큰 소리로 급사를 부르다/③큰 소리로 웃다 —他 …을 외치다, 고함치다 ¶④큰 소리로 명령하다
📖 고함쳐서 입 다물게 하다 「다」
—名 외침; 큰 소리
—名 외침; 환성
—他自 […을] 밀치다; 떼밀다
—名 밀치기
—名 1. 삽 —名 1. …을 삽으로 뜨다 (모으다, 던지다) 2. …을 삽으로 만들다 ¶①삽으로 길을 만들다

—名 한 삽 가득
—他 1. …을(에게) 보이다, 보여주다 2. …을 안내하다; 인도하다 ¶①그는 나를 2층으로 안내했다 3. …을 설명하다; 가르치다 ¶②그 사실로 그가 영리하다는 것을 알 수 있다/③그것을 어떻게 했는지 가르쳐다오 4. …을 주다 ¶④그는 내게 꽤 친절하게 해주었다
—自 나타나다, 보이다
📖 1)얼굴을 내밀다 2)ⓐ…을 진열하다 ⓑ남의 주목을 끌려고 하다 3)(口) …에게 나가라고 하다. 4)ⓐ…을 똑똑히 보이게 하다 ⓑ돋보이다 ⓒ…을 폭로하다 ⓓ나타나다, 오다

—名 1. 보이기 2. 전시; 전람회; 구경거리, 쇼우 ¶⑤화초 품평회/⑥자선 행 3. 겉치레, 시늉, 티; 외관 ¶⑦정직한 체하여 4. 기회

📖 여보란 듯이, 효과를 노려
—名 광고 삐라, 포스터
—名 연예선(演藝船)

—名 진열장, 쇼우케이스

—名 (口) [진상 따위의] 공개, 폭로

—名 1. 소나기 2. [총알 따위의] 빗발침 3. 신부에게 축하 선물을 주는 파아티 4. 샤우어 목욕 —自 1. 소나기가 오다 2. 샤우어 목욕을 하다 —他 1. …을 소나기로 적시다 2. …을 아낌없이 주다
—名 보이는 사람
—名 샤우어 목욕

—形 1. 소나기 같은 2. 소나기가 잦은 3. 소나기의
—副 화려하게, 번지르르하게
—名 화려함, 야함
—名 외관

—名 흥행사

—名 흥행사의 수완, 연예인 근성

show·room [ʃóurù(ː)m] *n.* [C] a room where things for sale are displayed. — [名] 진열실

show window [⌐ ⌐‿] *n.* a window in front of a store where things are displayed. — [名] 진열창

show·y [ʃóui] *adj.* (**show·i·er, show·i·est**) **1.** making a striking display. **2.** too bright and not in good taste. **3.** intended to attract attention. — [形] 1. 눈에 띄는 2. 번지르르한, 야한 3. 자랑삼아 보이는, 뽐내는

shrank [ʃræŋk] *v.* pt. of **shrink.**

shrap·nel [ʃrǽpn(ə)l] *n.* [C] (pl. **-nel**) a shell filled with bullets and powder, designed to burst in the air and scatter the bullets all over. — [名] 유산탄(榴散彈)

shred [ʃred] *n.* [C] **1.** a long, narrow piece torn or cut off; a fragment. **2.** a bit. — [名] 1. 한 조각, 나부랑이 2. 조금
tear into (or *in, to*) *shreds,* tear into pieces. [熟] 토막내다, 찢어발기다
—*vt., vi.* tear or cut (something) into pieces. — [他][自] 토막토막 자르다(잘리다, 찢어지다)

shrew [ʃruː] *n.* [C] **1.** a bad-tempered woman who constantly quarrels. **2.** a small animal like a mouse with a long nose and small eyes. — [名] 1. 바가지 긁는 여자 2. 뒤쥐

* **shrewd** [ʃruːd] *adj.* clever; sharp-witted; keen. ¶*a ~ guess*① / *He is a ~ businessman.* ▷**shrewd·ness** [-nis] *n.* — [形] 영리한, 빈틈없는 ¶①빈틈없는 추측

shrewd·ly [ʃrúːdli] *adv.* in a shrewd manner; cleverly or wisely. — [副] 빈틈없이

shrew·ish [ʃrúːiʃ] *adj.* sharp-tongued; bad-tempered. — [形] 입버릇 사나운; 심술궂은

* **shriek** [ʃriːk] *vi.* cry out in a loud and shrill voice; scream; utter a loud, sharp cry. ¶*~ with laughter*① / *~ with pain.* —*vt.* utter (something) with a shriek. —*n.* [C] a sharp scream; an outcry; a loud, shrill sound. — [自] 비명을 지르다; 째지는 듯한 소리를 내다 ¶①깔깔 웃다 — [他] …을 째지는 듯한 소리로 말하다 — [名] 비명; 째지는 듯한 소리

* **shrill** [ʃril] *adj.* having a high-pitched tone; uttered in a shrill tone. ¶*a ~ note*① / *the ~ cry of a hyena.* —*adv.* in a shrill tone. —*vt.* utter (something) in a sharp, shrill tone. —*vi.* cry in a sharp tone. — [形] 날카로운; 째는 듯한 ¶①째지는 듯한 음조 — [副] 째지는 듯한 소리로 — [他] …을 째지는 듯한 소리로 말하다 — [自] 째지는 듯한 소리로 외치다

shrimp [ʃrimp] *n.* [C] **1.** a small shellfish with a long tail, used for food. **2.** a small person; a person of little importance. — [名] 1. 작은 새우 2. 꼬마; 보잘것 없는 사람

* **shrine** [ʃrain] *n.* [C] **1.** a case or box to place holy things in. **2.** any sacred place of worship with a tomb or statue. **3.** a place made sacred for historic reasons. ¶*Mecca is a Moslem ~.*① —*vt.* enshrine. — [名] 1. 성물함(聖物函) 2. 성당, 사당, 묘(廟) 3. 전당(殿堂); 성지(聖地) ¶①메카는 회교도의 성지다 — [他] …을 안치하다, 모시다

* **shrink** [ʃriŋk] *v.* (**shrank** or **shrunk, shrunk** or **shrunk·en**) *vi.* **1.** become smaller, shorter or less. ¶*The sweater shrunk when it was washed.*① / *She shrunk with fear.*② **2.** draw back; withdraw. ¶*He shrank from the task.* —*vt.* make (something) smaller, shorter or less. — [自] 1. 오그라들다; 줄어들다; 적어지다 ¶①스웨터를 빨았더니 줄었다/②그녀는 무서워서 움츠렸다 2. 움찔하다; 겁내다 — [他] …을 줄이다
1) ***shrink*** [***back***] ***from*** (=*draw away from*) *something.*
2) ***shrink away,*** retreat; withdraw; become shortened.
[熟] 1) …을 피하다 2) 뒷걸음질치다; 위축하다, 겁내다

shrink·age [ʃríŋkidʒ] *n.* [U] the act of shrinking in size or amount. — [名] 수축; 감소

shriv·el [ʃrívl] *v.* (**-eled, -el·ing** or *Brit.* **-elled, -el·ling**) *vi.* shrink and wrinkle; dry up. ¶*His skin shriveled.* —*vt.* curl up (something) with heat, cold, age, etc. — [自] 주름지다; 오그라들다; 줄다 — [他] …을 오그라들게 하다

shroud [ʃraud] *n.* [C] **1.** a cloth sheet or dress used to wrap a dead body for burial. **2.** something that covers or conceals. **3.** (usu. *pl.*) a set of ropes from a mast to the sides of a ship for supporting the masts. ⇒fig. —*vt.* **1.** wrap (a dead body) in a shroud for burial. **2.** cover or conceal. — [名] 1. 수의(壽衣) 2. 싸는 것 3. [뱃전으로 연결된] 돛대 받침줄 — [他] 1. [시체]에 수의를 입히다 2. …을 싸다

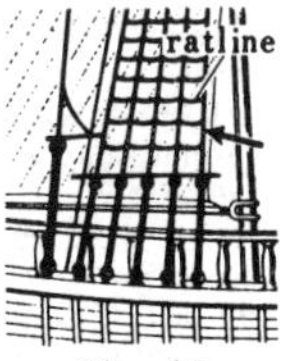

(shrouds)

* **shrub** [ʃrʌb] *n.* [C] a woody plant smaller than a tree. — [名] 관목, 덤불

shrub·ber·y [ʃrʌ́bəri] *n.* (pl. **-ber·ies**) **1.** [U] (*collectively*) a group of shrubs. **2.** [C] a place planted with shrubs. — [名] 1. 관목, 덤불 2. 관목숲

shrub·by [ʃrʌ́bi] *adj.* (**-bi·er, -bi·est**) **1.** abounding in shrubs. **2.** like a shrub. — [形] 1. 관목(덤불)이 많은 2. 관목 같은

S

shrug [ʃrʌg] *vt., vi.* (**shrugged, shrug·ging**) raise (one's shoulders) to show dislike, doubt, contempt, etc. —*n.* ⓒ the act of shrugging.
—㉠ [어깨를] 움츠리다 —㉡ 어깨를 움츠리기

shrunk [ʃrʌŋk] *v.* pt. and pp. of **shrink**.

shrunk·en [ʃrʌŋk(ə)n] *v.* pp. of **shrink**.
—*adj.* grown smaller, thinner or withered. ¶*a ~ face.*①
—㉠ 쭈글쭈글한 ¶①쭈글쭈글한 얼굴

* **shud·der** [ʃʌ́dər] *vi.* tremble with fear, cold, horror, etc. 《*~ at* or *to do* something》 ¶*I shuddered at the mere thought of it.*① —*n.* ⓒ a violent and sudden shake of the body. ¶*The sight gave me shudders.*②
—㉠ [추위·공포 따위로] 떨다 ¶① 그 생각만 해도 떨렸다 —㉡ 멸림 ¶② 그 광경을 보고 몸서리쳤다

shud·der·ing [ʃʌ́dəriŋ] *adj.* **1.** trembling with fear, cold, horror, etc. **2.** causing a shudder.
—㉠ 1. 떠는, 몸서리치는 2. 오싹하게 하는

shuf·fle [ʃʌ́fl] *vt.* **1.** drag (the feet) in walking or dancing. **2.** mix (the cards in a pack) to change the order. **3.** do (something) in a careless, clumsy or tricky manner. —*vi.* **1.** walk with dragging feet. **2.** mix the cards in a pack. **3.** act in a tricky way.
shuffle off (=*get rid of*) something.
—*n.* ⓒ **1.** the act of dragging the feet. **2.** the act of mixing cards. **3.** a trick. ▷**shuf·fler** [-ər] *n.*
—㉠ 1. [발]을 질질 끌다 2. [카아드]를 섞어 치다 3. …을 얼버무리다 —㉡ 1. 발을 질질 끌며 걷다 2. 카아드를 섞어 치다 3. 속이다, 얼버무리다
§…을 없애다, 회피하다
—㉡ 1. 발을 질질 끌며 걷기 2. 카아드를 섞어 치기 3. 속임수

* **shun** [ʃʌn] *vt.* (**shunned, shun·ning**) keep away from (something); avoid. ▷**shun·ner** [-ər] *n.*
—㉠ …을 피하다

shunt [ʃʌnt] *vt.* **1.** turn (something) aside. **2.** get rid of (something). **3.** switch (a train, etc.) from one track to another. —*vi.* **1.** move out of the way. **2.** (of a train, etc.) move from one track to another. —*n.* ⓒ **1.** the act of turning aside. **2.** a railroad switch.
—㉠ 1. …을 옆으로 돌리다(비키다) 2. …을 피하다 3. [기차 따위]를 다른 선로에 바꿔넣다; 대피시키다 —㉡ 1. 비키다 2. [기차가] 대피하다 —㉢ 1. 비키기 2. 전철기(轉轍器)

‡**shut** [ʃʌt] *v.* (**shut, shut·ting**) *vt.* **1.** close. ¶*He ~ the door with a loud bang.*① / *Keep your eyes ~.*② **2.** fold up. ¶*~ a screen.* **3.** keep out. ¶*Do not ~ the new boy of your games.*③ **4.** close in. ¶*She ~ her cat in the box.* —*vi.* become closed. ¶*The door won't ~.*④
1) *shut down*, stop working for a time.
2) *shut in*, keep (someone or something) from going out; confine.
3) *shut off*, stop the flow of (gas, water, etc.); turn off.
4) *shut out*, ⓐ keep (someone) from coming in. ⓑ (in baseball) prevent an opposing team from scoring.
5) *shut up*, ⓐ close completely. ⓑ shut in. ⓒ(*colloq.*) stop talking. ¶*Shut up!*⑤
—*adj.* closed.
—㉠ …을 닫다 ¶①그는 문을 쾅하고 닫았다/②눈을 감아라 2. …을 접다 3. …을 내쫓다 ¶③새로 온 소년을 너희들 놀이에서 내쫓지 말아라 4. …을 가둬넣다 —㉡ 닫히다 ¶④문이 닫히지 않는다
§ 1)휴업하다 2)…을 가둬넣다, 감금하다 3)…을 막다, 잠그다 4)ⓐ…을 내쫓다 ⓑ[野球]영패(零敗)시키다 5)ⓐ…을 꽉 닫다 ⓑ…을 감금하다 ⓒ(口)입 다물다
—㉢ 닫힌

* **shut·ter** [ʃʌ́tər] *n.* ⓒ **1.** a person or thing that shuts. **2.** a movable cover or screen for a window. **3.** (*Photography*) the part of a camera that covers the lens.
—㉡ 1. 닫는 사람(것) 2. 덧문, 겉창 3. (寫)셔터

shut·tle [ʃʌ́tl] *n.* ⓒ **1.** an instrument used to carry the thread from side to side in weaving. ⇨fig. **2.** a part of a sewing machine that holds and carries the lower thread. **3.** anything that moves back and forth regularly between two places; (*U.S.*) a shuttle train. ¶*a ~ bus*① / *~ service.*② —*vt., vi.* move back and forth between two places.

·bobbin

yarn

[shuttle 1.]

—㉡ 1. [베틀의] 북 2. [재봉틀의] 북 실통 3. 2점 사이를 왕복하는 것; (美) 근거리 왕복 열차 ¶①근거리 왕복 버스/②왕복 운행 —㉠㉡ [북처럼] 좌우로 움직이다; 왕복하다(시키다)

shut·tle·cock [ʃʌ́tlkàk / -kòk] *n.* ⓒ a cork stuck with feathers, used in the game of battledore and shuttlecock or in badminton. ¶*play battledore and ~.*①
—㉡ 제기 ¶①제기차기 놀이를 하다

shuttle train [´-´] *n.* a train that runs regularly back and forth over a short distance.
—㉡ 근거리 왕복 열차

* **shy**¹ [ʃai] *adj.* (**shy·er, shy·est** or **shi·er, shi·est**) **1.** uneasy in the presence of other people. 《*~ of, with*》 **2.** *fight shy of*, avoid. [easily frightened; timid.] —*vi.* (**shied**) start back suddenly. 《*~ at* something》 ¶*The horse shied at the passing car.*①
—㉢ 1. 암면, 수줍은 2. 잘 놀라는, 겁많은
§ …을 피하다
—㉡ 뛰어 물러나다 ¶①말이 지나가는 차에 놀라서 뒷걸음질했다

shy² [ʃai] *vt., vi.* (**shied**) throw. —*n.* ⓒ (pl. **shies**) **1.** a throw. **2.** (*colloq.*) a try; a trial.
—㉠㉡ […을] 던지다 —㉢ 1. 던지기 2. 시도

have a shy at, try to do (something).
[熟] …을 하려고 시도하다

Shy·lock [ʃáilɑk / -lɔk] *n.* the cruel Jewish moneylender in Shakespeare's play 'The Merchant of Venice.'
━[名] 샤일록

shy·ly [ʃáili] *adv.* in a shy manner.
━[副] 수줍어서; 겁내며

Si·am [saiǽm, ∠–] *n.* the former name of Thailand.
━[名] 샴(태국의 옛이름)

Si·a·mese [sàiəmíːz] *adj.* of Siam, its people, or their language. ¶*a ~ cat*① / *a ~ twins.*② ━*n.* **1.** [C] the people of Siam. **2.** [U] the language of Siam.
━[形] 샴[사람·말]의 ¶①샴 고양이/②샴 쌍둥이 ━[名] 1. 샴 사람 2. 샴 말

Si·be·ri·a [saibíəriə] *n.* a part of the Soviet Union, in northern Asia, extending from the Ural Mountains to the Pacific.
━[名] 시베리아

Si·be·ri·an [saibíəriən] *adj.* of Siberia. ¶*the ~ Railway.*① ━*n.* [C] a person of Siberia.
━[形] 시베리아의 ¶①시베리아 철도 ━[名] 시베리아 사람

sib·i·lant [síbilənt] *adj.* having a sound like that of steam in a radiator; of a hissing sound which is made by drawing out the sound of "s". ¶*~ sounds.*① ━*n.* [C] (*Phonetics*) a sibilant sound [s, z, ʃ, ʒ].
━[形] 쉬쉬 소리내는; 치찰음(齒擦音)의 ¶①치찰음 ━[名] 치찰음

sib·yl [síbil] *n.* [C] (in Greek and Roman mythology) one of several women who were believed to have powers of foretelling; a fortuneteller.
━[名] [고대 그리이스·로마의] 무당; 예언자

⁑**sick** [sik] *adj.* **1.** ill; in ill-health; 《as *predicative*》 being ill. ¶*~ people / He was taken ~.* **2.** 《as *predicative*》 (esp. *Brit.*) about to throw up food from the stomach. ¶*I feel ~ in the stomach.*① **3.** longing for. 《*~ for*》 ¶*He was ~ for a sight of home.*② **4.** tired; bored; much troubled or annoyed. 《*~ of*》 ¶*I am ~ of his talk.*③
━[形] 1. 병든; 몸이 편찮은 2.《英》구역질나는 ¶①아무래도 토할 것 같다 3. 그리워하는, 동경하는 ¶②그는 고향을 한 번 보고 싶어했다 4. 싫증나는, 짜증나는 ¶③그의 이야기엔 넌더리가 난다

sick at heart, very sad; affected by sorrow.
[熟] 슬픈

sick·bed [síkbèd] *n.* [C] a bed on which a sick person lies.
━[名] 병상, 병석

sick·en [sík(ə)n] *vi.* **1.** become ill. **2.** become tired of. 《*~ of* something》 **3.** feel sick or disgusted. ━*vt.* **1.** make (someone) ill. **2.** make (someone) feel sick or disgusted. **3.** make (someone) tired of something.
━[自] 1. 병이 나다 2. 싫어지다, 물리다 3. 욕지기나다 ━[他] 1. …을 병나게 하다 2. …에 구역질나게 하다 3. …을 넌더리나게 하다

sick·en·ing [sík(ə)niŋ] *adj.* making someone feel sick; disgusting. ▷**sick·en·ing·ly** [-li] *adv.*
━[形] 메스꺼워지는, 싫어지는

sick·ish [síkiʃ] *adj.* somewhat sick; somewhat sickening.
━[形] 좀 편찮은

sick·le [síkl] *n.* [C] a small tool consisting of a curved steel blade and a short handle for cutting grass, etc. ⇨fig.
━[名] 낫

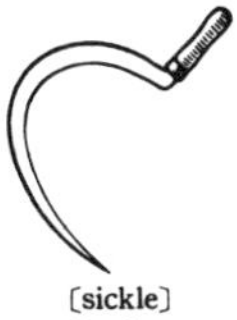
[sickle]

sick·ly [síkli] *adj.* (**-li·er, -li·est**) **1.** weak in health; often sick. ¶*a ~ child*① / *He has been ~ from birth.*② **2.** harmful to health. ¶*a ~ climate.*③ **3.** making someone feel sick; causing disgust. ¶*a ~ smell.*④ **4.** caused by illness; of sickness. ¶*Her face has a ~ color.*⑤
━[形] 1. 병약한 ¶①허약한 아이/②그는 나면서부터 병약하다 2. 건강에 나쁜 ¶③건강에 나쁜 기후 3. 구역질나게 하는 ¶④메스꺼운 냄새 4. 병자 같은, 창백한 ¶⑤그녀의 얼굴은 창백하다

***sick·ness** [síknis] *n.* [U] **1.** the state of being sick. **2.** the state of feeling sick.
━[名] 1. 병 2. 멀미, 구역질

sick·room [síkrù(ː)m] *n.* [C] a room where a sick person lies.
━[名] 병실

⁑**side** [said] *n.* [C] **1.** one of the surfaces of an object. ¶*the bright ~ of life*① / *Put down your name on both sides of the paper.* / *A box has six sides.*② **2.** an edge; one of the lines bounding an object. **3.** the position right or left of the center. **4.** a family line from the mother or the father. ¶*the maternal ~.*③ **5.** a group of people who hold the same opinion. ¶*our ~*④ / *I'm always on your ~.*⑤ **6.** a right or left part of the body between the shoulder and the hip.
━[名] 1. 측(側), 면, 쪽 ¶①인생의 밝은 면/②상자에는 6면이 있다 2. 가장자리; 가 3. 우측, 좌측 4. 혈통 ¶③어머니쪽 5. 편, 당, 파 ¶④우리 편/⑤나는 언제나 네 편이다 6. 옆구리

1) ***at*** (or ***by***) ***the side of,*** ⓐ beside; near to. ⓑ compared with.
2) ***on all sides,*** in every direction.
3) ***put*** *something* ***on*** (or ***to***) ***one side,*** set something apart or aside.
4) ***side by side,*** close together; beside each other.
5) ***take sides with*** (=*give support to*) *someone.*
[熟] 1)ⓐ…의 옆에; 가까이에 ⓑ…와 비교하여 2)사방팔방으로 3)…을 따로 두다, 치워 두다 4)나란히 5)…에 편들다

━*adj.* **1.** of, to, or from one side. ¶*a ~ step / a ~*
━[形] 1. 옆[으로, 에서]의; 측면의 2. 종

S

sideboard [1062] **sigh**

entrance. **2.** not so important; secondary. ¶~ *job.*① —*vi.* have the same opinion as someone; support someone. (~ *with someone*)
— 속적인; 부(副)의 ¶⑥부업 —自 […에] 편들다, 찬성하다

side·board [sáidbɔ̀ːrd] *n.* ⓒ a piece of furniture in a dining room for holding food, plates, etc.
—名 식기 선반

side·car [sáidkùːr] *n.* ⓒ a small car for a passenger or baggage attached to the side of a motorcycle.
—名 [오오토바이의] 사이드카아

side·light [sáidlàit] *n.* ⓒ **1.** a light that comes from the side. **2.** U information or knowledge about something that is interesting but not vital, and that is given by chance. **3.** a lamp or light on the side of a ship or car.
—名 1. 측광(側光) 2. 우연의 설명; 정보 3. [배·자동차의] 현등(舷燈), 측등(側燈)

side·line [sáidlàin] *n.* ⓒ **1.** a line limiting the area of the field in football, tennis, etc. **2.** one's second trade in addition to a main trade.
—名 1. [축구 따위의] 사이드라인, 측선(側線) 2. 부업

side·long [sáidlɔ̀(ː)ŋ / -lɔ̀ŋ] *adj.* to the side. ¶*cast a ~ glance upon someone.*① —*adv.* sideways. ¶*look ~ at someone.*
—형 옆의, 비스듬한 ¶①…을 곁눈으로 힐끗 보다 —부 옆으로; 비스듬히

si·de·re·al [saidíəriəl] *adj.* of the stars; measured by the apparent motion of fixed stars. ¶*a ~ revolution*① / *a ~ year.*②
—형 별의; 항성(恒星)의; 항성의 운동에 입각하여 측정한 ¶①항성 주기 /②항성년

side·slip [sáidslìp] *n.* ⓒ (of an airplane, a motorcar, etc.) a slip to one side. —*vt., vi.* slip to one side.
—名 [자동차·비행기의] 옆으로 미끄러짐 —自타 옆으로 미끄러지다

side·split·ting [sáidsplìtiŋ] *adj.* causing laughter; extremely funny.
—형 포복절도할, 허리가 끊어지게 우스운

side step [⌣⌢] *n.* **1.** a step to one side to avoid something. **2.** a step or stair attached to the side of a horse carriage; a footboard.
—名 1. 옆으로 비키기 2. [마차 따위 입구의] 옆발판

side·track [sáidtræ̀k] *n.* ⓒ (chiefly *U.S.*) a railroad track by the side of a main track. —*vt.* **1.** send (a train, etc.) from a main track to a sidetrack. **2.** set (something) aside; divert.
—名 (美) 대피선 —타 1. …을 대피선에 넣다 2. …을 피하다

side view [⌣⌢] *n.* a view from one side; a profile.
—名 측면도, 옆모습

• **side·walk** [sáidwɔ̀ːk] *n.* ⓒ (*U.S.*) a path beside a street or road for foot passengers.
—名 (美) 인도(人道), 보도

side·ward [sáidwərd] *adj., adv.* on or toward one side.
—형부 옆의(으로)

side·ways [sáidwèiz] *adv.* **1.** toward or from the side. **2.** with one side foremost. —*adj.* directed toward or from the side. ¶*a ~ glance.*①
—부 1. 옆으로(에서) 2. 비스듬하게 —형 옆의, 옆에서의 ¶①곁눈질

sid·ing [sáidiŋ] *n.* ⓒ a short railroad track by the side of a main track where a slow train can wait for a fast train to pass, etc.
—名 [철도의] 대피선

si·dle [sáidl] *vi.* move sideways towards someone in a shy or stealthy manner. (~ *along* or *up to someone*) —*n.* ⓒ an act of sidling.
—自 다가서다 —名 다가서기

• **siege** [siːdʒ] *n.* U ⓒ the act of surrounding a place by an army to force it to surrender. ¶*lay ~ to a town*① / *raise the ~ of the capital*② / *withstand a long ~.*③
—名 포위공격 ¶①도시를 포위하다/②수도에 대한 포위를 풀다/③장기간의 포위공격에 견디다

si·er·ra [siérə, +*Brit.* siǽrə] *n.* ⓒ a chain of mountains rising in jagged peaks like a saw.
—名 [톱니 모양의] 산맥

si·es·ta [siéstə] *n.* ⓒ a short sleep or rest taken at noon or in the afternoon, esp. in hot countries.
—名 [열대지방의] 낮잠

sieve [siv] *n.* ⓒ a frame with a wire net at the bottom, used for separating smaller pieces from larger ones.
—名 체

• **sift** [sift] *vt.* **1.** separate (smaller pieces) from larger ones with a sieve. (~ *something from*) **2.** scatter (something) through a sieve. **3.** examine (something) very carefully. ¶*Let us ~ the facts before we make a decision.*① —*vi.* come through a sieve.
—타 1. …을 체로 쳐서 거르다 2. 체질하여 떨어뜨리다 3. …을 정밀하게 조사하다 ¶①결론을 내리기 전에 사실을 규명하자

: **sigh** [sai] *vi.* **1.** let out a long, deep breath to show sorrow, relief, fatigue, etc. ¶*She sighed for grief in spite of herself.*① **2.** desire very earnestly. (~ *for something*) —*vt.* **1.** express (sorrow, relief, etc.) by a sigh. **2.** lament (something) sighing. —*n.* ⓒ a
—自 1. 한숨을 쉬다; 탄식하다 ¶①그녀는 자기도 모르게 탄식했다 2. 그리워하다 —타 1. …을 탄식으로 나타내다 2. …을 탄식하며 이야기하다 —名 한숨; 탄식 ¶②한숨을 쉬다/③크게

deep, audible breath from sorrow, relief, etc. ¶*draw a* ~② | *sigh a deep* ~.③ ▷**sigh·er** [-ər]

한숨쉬다

‡ **sight** [sait] *n.* [U] **1.** the power of seeing. ¶*lose one's* ~ | *He has good* ~.① **2.** ⦅sometimes *a* ~⦆ the act of seeing; the state of seeing or being seen. ¶*He ran away at the* ~ *of me.*② | *I know him only by* ~.③ | *I hate the* ~ *of her.*④ **3.** the range or field that one can see. ¶*The hill came in* ~. | (*proverb*) *Out of* ~, *out of mind.*⑤ **4.** [C] something worth seeing; a spectacle; ⦅*pl.*⦆ places worth seeing. ¶*The sunrise is a wonderful* ~. | *see* (or *do*) *the sights of Seoul*⑥ **5.** appearance. ¶*I lost* ~ *of him in the crowd.*⑦ **6.** [C] an instrument to help in aiming with a gun, etc. **7.** judgment; opinion. ¶*Do what's right in your* ~.⑧

—[名] 1. 시력, 시각 ¶①그는 시력이 좋다 2. 보기, 보이기 ¶②그는 나를 보자마자 도망쳤다/③나는 그를 그저 알고만 있을 뿐이다/④그녀는 보기도 싫다 3. 시야, 시계(視界) ¶⑤거자일익소(去者日益疎) 4. 광경, 경치; 구경거리; 명소(名所); 조망 ¶⑥서울 구경을 하다 5. 모습 ¶⑦군중 속에서 그를 잃었다 6. 조준 7. 판단, 견해 ¶⑧네 판단으로 옳은 일을 해라

1) ***at*** (or ***on***) ***sight,*** as soon as seen; at once.
2) ***catch*** (or ***get, take***) ***sight of*** (=*see*) *something.*

[熟] 1)보자마자; 곧 2)…을 보다

—*vt.* **1.** see. **2.** aim at (something). **3.** look at (something) carefully; examine. **—*vi.*** aim at something with a gun, etc.

—[他] 1. …을 보다 2. …에 조준을 맞추다, 겨냥하다 3. …을 관찰하다 —[自] 겨냥하다

sight·less [sáitlis] *adj.* blind; invisible; unseen.

—[形] 눈먼; 눈이 안 보이는

sight·ly [sáitli] *adj.* (**-li·er, -li·est**) **1.** pleasant to look at. **2.** (*U.S.*) commanding or giving a fine view.

—[形] 1. 보기 좋은, 아름다운 2. 조망(경치)이 좋은

sight·see·ing [sáitsì:iŋ] *n.* [U] the act of going around to see places and things of interest. ¶*go* ~.① **—*adj.*** of sightseeing. ¶*a* ~ *bus* (*party*).②

—[名] 관광 ¶①관광하러 가다 —[形] 관광의 ¶②관광버스(단)

sight·se·er [sáitsì:ər] *n.* [C] a person who goes sightseeing.

—[名] 관광객

‡ **sign** [sain] [C] **1.** a mark or letter that expresses some idea; a symbol. ¶*the plus* ~ | *the phonetic signs.*① **2.** anything that tells some fact; a proof; a token. ¶*a* ~ *of love*② | *Yawning is a* ~ *of sleepiness.*③ **3.** anything that tells of the future; an omen. ¶*the signs of the times*④ | *show signs of spring*⑤ | *Black clouds are signs of a storm.*⑥ **4.** a gesture or signal used instead of words. ¶*A nod of the head is a* ~ *of approval.*⑦

—[名] 1. 부호, 기호 ¶①발음 기호 2. 증거; 표적(表蹟) ¶②사랑의 표적/③하품은 졸린 증거다 3. 징조, 전조 ¶④시대의 추세/⑤봄의 징조가 나타나다/⑥검은 구름은 폭풍우의 전조다 4. 몸짓; 신호 ¶⑦머리를 끄덕이는 것은 찬성의 표시다

make the sign of the cross, trace the cross with the hand as a religious act.

[熟] 손가락으로 십자를 긋다

—*vt.* **1.** show (some idea, etc.) with a sign; signify. **2.** write one's name on (a paper, etc.) to show one's consent, etc. **3.** mark. **—*vi.*** make a sign or signal. ¶*I signed to him to come.*⑧

—[他] 1. …을 기호로 나타내다; 신호하다 2. …에 서명하다 3. …에 표를 하다 —[自] 서명하다; 신호하다 ¶⑧그에게 오라고 신호했다

sign away, write one's name to give up (a right, etc.).

[熟] 서명하여 …을 양도하다

‡ **sig·nal** [sígn(ə)l] *n.* [C] **1.** a gesture, look or sign giving information, notice of danger, etc; a mechanical device for giving such a message. **2.** anything which causes some other action. ⦅~ *for*⦆ **3.** a token; an indication. ¶*a* ~ *fire*① | *a* ~ *of danger*② | *make a* ~.③

—[名] 1. 신호; 신호기 2. 동기 3. 전조 ¶①봉화/②위험신호/③신호하다

—*vt., vi.* (**-naled, -nal·ing** or *Brit.* **-nalled, -nal·ling**) make (something) known by a signal; communicate by means of a signal. ⦅~ someone *to do*⦆ **—*adj.*** **1.** used as a signal or in signaling. **2.** remarkable; noteworthy.

—[他][自] 신호하다; [···을] 신호로 알리다 —[形] 1. 신호의 2. 현저한, 뛰어난

sig·nal·er, *Brit.* **-nal·ler** [sígnələr] *n.* [C] a person or thing that gives a signal.

—[名] 신호수; 신호기

sig·nal·ize [sígnəlàiz] *vt.* make (someone or something) remarkable or notable; indicate (something) particularly.

—[他] …을 두드러지게 하다; 이채를 띠게 하다

sig·nal·ly [sígnəli] *adv.* in a signal manner; remarkably.

—[副] 현저하게, 드드러지게

sig·nal·man [sígn(ə)lmən] *n.* [C] (pl. **-men** [-mən]) a person who signals or works with signals.

—[名] 신호수

sig·na·to·ry [sígnətɔ̀:ri / -t(ə)ri] *n.* [C] (pl. **-ries**) a person who has signed a document, esp. as a representative of a nation. **—*adj.*** having signed a document.

—[名] 서명자 —[形] 서명한, 조인한

• **sig·na·ture** [sígnətʃər] *n.* [C] **1.** the name of a person written by himself; the act of writing one's name. **2.** a mark at the beginning of a staff to show the key,

—[名] 1. 서명 2. [조(調)·박자의] 기호

S

time and pitch of music.

* **sign·board** [sáinbɔ̀:rd] *n.* [C] a board displaying a name, a notice, etc. esp. a painted one to show the name of an inn or a shop. —[名] 간판

sig·net [sígnit] *n.* [C] a small seal; an official seal. —[名] 인장, 인감; 관인

* **sig·nif·i·cance** [signífikəns] *n.* [U] the state or quality of being significant; meaning; importance. ¶*a word of great* ~① | *a matter of* ~② | *I could grasp the real* ~ *of his remark.*③ —[名] 의미[가 있음]; 의의(意義); 중요성 ¶①의미 심장한 말/②중요한 사항/③나는 그의 말의 참뜻을 이해할 수 없었다

* **sig·nif·i·cant** [signífikənt] *adj.* **1.** full or expressive of meaning. ¶*a* ~ *look* | *Her gesture is* ~ *of consent.*① **2.** important. ▷**sig·nif·i·cant·ly** [-li] *adv.* —[形] 1. 의미있는; 의미를 나타내는 ¶①그녀의 몸짓은 승낙의 뜻이다 2. 중요한

sig·ni·fi·ca·tion [sìgnifikéiʃ(ə)n] *n.* [C][U] the act of sìgnifying; a meaning or sense. —[名] 의의; 의미

* **sig·ni·fy** [sígnifài] *vt.* **(-fied) 1.** show (something) by a sign, a gesture, etc.; indicate. 《~ something *with*; ~ *that*...》 ¶~ *one's consent with a nod*① | *He signified that we might go out.* **2.** become a sign of (something); mean. ¶*What does it* ~*?*② **—*vi.*** 《usu. in *negative*》 be of importance. ¶*It does not* ~.③ —[他] 1. [말·신호 따위로] …을 나타내다 ¶①머리를 끄떡여 승낙의 뜻을 나타내다 2. …의 전조가 되다; …을 의미하다 ¶②그것은 뭐냐? —[自] 중요하다 ¶③대단한 것은 아니다

sign·post [sáinpòust] *n.* [C] a post having a sign, notice or direction on it for guidance or information. —[名] 광고 기둥; 도표(道標)

⁑ **si·lence** [sáiləns] *n.* [U] **1.** the state of being silent; stillness. ¶*There was* ~ *between them.*① | (*proverb*) *Speech is silver,* ~ *is golden.*② **2.** the state of being forgotten; absence of mention. ¶*pass into* ~.③ **—*vt.*** cause (someone) to be still. **—*interj.*** be silent! —[名] 1. 침묵; 정적 ¶①그들은 잠자코 있었다/②《俚》웅변은 은이요 침묵은 금이다 2. 망각; 묵살 ¶③잊혀지다 —[他] …을 침묵시키다 —[感] 조용히!, 쉬!

si·lenc·er [sáilənsər] *n.* [C] **1.** a person or thing that silences. **2.** a device that deadens the sound of an engine, a gun, etc. —[名] 1. 침묵시키는 사람(것) 2. 소음기(消音器); 방음 장치

⁑ **si·lent** [sáilənt] *adj.* **1.** saying little or nothing; mute. ¶*a* ~ *man* | *remain* (or *keep*) ~① | *I'll be* ~ *about her conduct.* **2.** not mentioned or spoken. ¶*His speech is* ~ *on the subject.*② **3.** making no noise; quiet. ¶~ *as the grave.*③ **4.** (*Phonetics*) written but not pronounced. ¶*The "l" in "palm" is a* ~ *letter.*④ —[形] 1. 침묵의, 말없는 ¶①잠자코 있다 2. 언급하지 않는; 공개하지 않는 ¶②그의 연설은 그 문제에 언급하지 않았다 3. 조용한 ¶③조용하기 짝이 없다 4. 《音聲》 발음하지 않는 ¶④ palm의 *l*은 묵자(默字)이다

si·lent·ly [sáiləntli] *adv.* in a silent manner; without making a sound; quietly. —[副] 조용히

sil·hou·ette [sìlu(:)ét] *n.* [C] a black outline portrait, esp. a profile; a dark figure of a person or thing against a light; a shadow. **—*vt.*** show (something) in outline. —[名] 반면영상(半面影像), 실루엣; 그림자 —[他] …을 실루엣으로 그리다; …의 그림자를 비추다

sil·i·ca [sílikə] *n.* [U][C] (*Chemistry*) a hard white or colorless substance used in making glass, etc. —[名] 《化》 규산(珪酸); 규토(珪土)

sil·i·cate [sílikit, -kèit] *n.* [U] (*Chemistry*) one of the compound containing silica. —[名] 《化》 규산염

sil·i·con [sílikən] *n.* [U] a brown, nonmetallic element found in a combined state in mineral and rocks. —[名] 규소(珪素)

⁑ **silk** [silk] *n.* [U] **1.** a fine thread obtained from silkworms. ¶*raw* ~.① **2.** a cloth made from this thread. **3.** 《*pl.*》 garments made of silk. ¶*be dressed in silks.*② **—*adj.*** of or like silk. —[名] 1. 명주; 명주실 ¶①생사(生絲) 2. 비단 3. 비단옷 ¶②비단옷을 입고 있다 —[形] 비단의; 비단 모양의

silk·en [sílk(ə)n] *adj.* **1.** (*archaic, poetic*) made of silk. **2.** like silk; soft and smooth; silky; glossy. —[形] 1. 《古·詩》 비단의 2. 비단 같은, 부드럽고 매끄러운, 광택 있는

silk·worm [sílkwə̀:rm] *n.* [C] a moth caterpillar that produces a strong silk fiber to form its cocoon. —[名] 누에

silk·y [sílki] *adj.* **(silk·i·er, silk·i·est)** of or like silk; fine and soft; glossy. —[形] 비단의(같은); 부드럽고 매끄러운; 윤나는

sill [sil] *n.* [C] a piece of wood or stone forming the bottom of a window or door. —[名] 문지방; 창문턱

sil·li·ness [sílinis] *n.* **1.** [U] the quality of being silly. **2.** [C] something silly; a silly act. —[名] 1. 어리석음 2. 어리석은 짓

⁑ **sil·ly** [síli] *adj.* **(-li·er, -li·est) 1.** foolish; having little sense or judgment. ¶*It would be* ~ *to die now.* **2.** (*archaic*) innocent. **—*n.*** [C] (pl. **-lies**) (*colloq.*) a silly person. —[形] 1. 어리석은; 사려 없는 2. 《古》 순진한, 철모르는 —[名] 《口》 바보; 천치

si·lo [sáilou] *n.* ⓒ (pl. **-los**) an airtight building or tower in which green food for animals is preserved. ⇨fig.

silt [silt] *n.* ⓤ mud or sand carried by moving water and left behind. —*vt., vi.* fill (something) or become filled with silt.

sil·van [sílvən] *adj.* =sylvan.

‡**sil·ver** [sílvər] *n.* ⓤ **1.** a soft, white, shining metal, used for making coins, dishes, etc. **2.** ((collectively)) things made of this metal; coins made of silver. ¶*table ~① / 200 dollars in ~.②* **3.** the color of silver.
—*adj.* **1.** made of silver. ¶*a ~ knife.③* **2.** having the color of silver. **3.** soft and clear in tune or voice. —*vt.* coat or cover (something) with silver or something like silver. —*vi.* become silver in color.

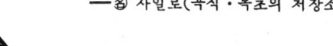
[silo]

sil·ver-gilt [sílvərgílt] *adj.* coated with silver or silver-leaf.

sil·ver-haired [sílvərhɛ́ərd] *adj.* having silvery-white or grey hair.

sil·vern [sílvərn] *adj.* (*archaic*) of or like silver.

silver plate [´-´] *n.* ((collectively)) tableware made of silver or coated with silver.

sil·ver-plat·ed [sílvərpléitid] *adj.* covered or coated with silver or a silverlike material.

silver screen [´-´] *n.* **1.** a screen on which motion pictures are shown. **2.** ((the ~, collectively)) motion pictures.

sil·ver-smith [sílvərsmìθ] *n.* ⓒ a person who makes silver articles.

sil·ver-tongued [sílvərtʌ́ŋd] *adj.* eloquent.

sil·ver·ware [sílvərwɛ̀ər] *n.* ⓤ ((collectively)) (*U.S.*) articles made of or plated with silver.

silver wedding [´-´ ´-´] *n.* the 25th anniversary of a wedding.

sil·ver·y [sílv(ə)ri] *adj.* **1.** like silver in color or appearance. ¶*~ moonlight.* **2.** (of a sound, a voice, etc.) soft and clear.

‡**sim·i·lar** [símilər] *adj.* **1.** almost alike; resembling. ((*~ to*)) ¶*In a ~ way① / Yours are very ~ to mine.②* **2.** (*Mathematics*) having the same shape, but not the same size.

sim·i·lar·i·ty [sìməlǽriti] *n.* (pl. **-ties**) **1.** ⓤ the state or quality of being similar; likeness. **2.** ⓒ a point or feature in which things are similar.

sim·i·lar·ly [símilərli] *adv.* in the same way; likewise.

sim·i·le [síməli] *n.* ⓒ an expression in which two different things or ideas are compared. ⇨N.B.

si·mil·i·tude [simílit(j)ùːd / -tjùːn] *n.* **1.** ⓤ the state or quality of being similar; similarity; resemblance. **2.** ⓒ a comparison.

sim·mer [símər] *vt.* boil (water, food, etc.) gently. —*vi.* **1.** make a low, humming sound while boiling gently. ¶*The kettle simmered on the gas range.* **2.** cook or keep at or just below the boiling point. **3.** (of anger, etc.) be about to burst out.
simmer down, become calm or cool.
—*n.* ⓒ ((sing. only)) the state of boiling gently or being near the point of bursting out.

Si·mon [sáimən] *n.* a man's name.

si·moom [simúːm], **-moon** [-múːn] *n.* ⓒ a hot, dry, desert wind with sand in Arabia, Syria, etc.

sim·per [símpər] *vi.* smile in a silly, self-conscious way.
—*n.* ⓒ a silly, self-conscious smile.

sim·per·ing·ly [símpəriŋli] *adv.* with a simper.

‡**sim·ple** [símpl] *adj.* (**-pler, -plest**) **1.** easy to do or un-

—ⓝ 사일로(곡식·목초의 저장소)

—ⓝ [강바닥의] 해감, 침적토(沈積土)
—ⓣⓘ […을] 진흙으로 막다

—ⓝ 1. 은 2. 은식기; 은 세공; 은화 ¶①식탁용 은그릇/②은화로 200 달러 3. 은빛
—ⓐ 1. 은의 ¶③은 나이프 2. 은빛의 3. [목소리 따위] 낭랑한; 맑은

—ⓣ …에 은 도금을 하다; 은을 바르다; …을 은빛으로 하다 —ⓘ 은빛이 되다

—ⓐ 은 도금의

—ⓐ 백발의, 은발의

—ⓐ 은의(같은)
—ⓝ 은 [도금] 식기류

—ⓐ 은 도금의

—ⓝ 1. 은막 2. 영화

—ⓝ 은 세공사
—ⓐ 웅변의
—ⓝ (美) 은 [도금] 식기

—ⓝ 은혼식
—ⓐ 1. 은 같은 2. 상쾌한

—ⓐ 1. 비슷한, 같은 모양의 ¶①마찬가지로/②네것은 내것과 비슷하다 2. (數) 닮은꼴의, 상사(相似)의

—ⓝ 1. 유사(類似) 2. 유사점(물)

—ⓐⓓ 마찬가지로
—ⓝ 직유(直喩) N.B. as brave as a lion 따위와 같은 예
—ⓝ 1. 유사 2. 예, 보기

—ⓣ [물·음식]을 부글부글 끓이다
—ⓘ 1. 부글부글 끓다 2. 막 끓으려 하고 있다 3. 당장이라도 폭발하려 하고 있다

ⓢ 냉정해지다, 식다
—ⓝ 당장 끓으려는 상태; 당장이라도 부아(웃음보)가 터져나려는 상태
—ⓝ 남자 이름
—ⓝ 열풍(아라비아 지방의 사막에 붊)

—ⓘ 선웃음을 웃다, 싱글싱글 웃다
—ⓝ 선웃음
—ⓐⓓ 선웃음으로, 싱글싱글

—ⓐ 1. 간단한; 쉬운 2. 소박한, 검소

derstand. ¶*a ~ question.* **2.** plain; not decorated. ¶*~ living.*① **3.** innocent; not affected. ¶*in a ~ manner.* **4.** honest; sincere. ¶*a ~ heart.*② **5.** easily deceived; foolish. **6.** humble; common. **7.** not mixed; mere. ¶*a ~ fact / pure and ~.*③
—*n.* [C] **1.** a foolish person. **2.** something simple. **3.** any plant for medical use; the medicine made from such a plant. ▷**sim·ple·ness** [-nis] *n.*

sim·ple-heart·ed [símplhá:rtid] *adj.* having a simple heart; sincere; frank.

sim·ple-mind·ed [símplmáindid] *adj.* easily deceived; stupid.

sim·ple·ton [símplt(ə)n] *n.* [C] a silly, stupid person who is easily deceived.

* **sim·plic·i·ty** [simplísiti] *n.* [U] the state of being simple.

sim·pli·fi·ca·tion [sìmplifikéiʃ(ə)n] *n.* **1.** [U] the act of simplifying; the state of being simplified. **2.** [C] something made simpler.

sim·pli·fy [símplifài] *vt.* (**-fied**) make (something) simpler or easier.

‡ **sim·ply** [símpli] *adv.* **1.** in a simple, plain manner. **2.** without ornament. ¶*a woman ~ dressed.*① **3.** foolishly. **4.** merely; completely. ¶*~ delicious.*

sim·u·la·cra [sìmjuléikrə] *n.* pl. of **simulacrum.**

sim·u·la·crum [sìmjuléikrəm] *n.* [C] (pl. **-cra** or **crums**) **1.** an image. **2.** something made in resemblance to a thing; a slight likeness.

sim·u·late [símjulèit] *vt.* **1.** pretend. **2.** look or act like (something). ▷**sim·u·la·tor** [-ər] *n.*

sim·u·la·tion [sìmjuléiʃ(ə)n] *n.* [U] the act of simulating.

si·mul·ta·ne·i·ty [sàim(ə)ltəní(:)iti, sìm-] *n.* [U] the quality of being simultaneous.

si·mul·ta·ne·ous [sàim(ə)ltéiniəs, sìmi-] *adj.* existing or occurring at the same time. ⟪*~ with*⟫ ¶*~ translation.*①

si·mul·ta·ne·ous·ly [sàim(ə)ltéiniəsli, sìm-] *adv.* at the same time; all at once.

‡ **sin** [sin] *n.* **1.** [U][C] the act of breaking God's laws. **2.** [C] an immoral act. ⟪*~ against*⟫ ¶*the original ~*① / *commit a ~.*② —*v.* (**sinned, sin·ning**) *vi.* break one of God's laws; do wrong or evil. ⟪*~ against* something⟫ —*vt.* commit (a wrong deed).

Si·nai [sáiniai, sáiniài / sáiniài] *n.* **1.** ⟪*Mount* or *Mt. ~*⟫ (in the Bible) the mountain where the law was given to Moses from God. **2.** a peninsula at the northern end of the Red Sea.

‡ **since** [sins] *prep.* from the time of; after. ¶*~ then*① / *I've not seen her ~ Monday.*
—*conj.* **1.** from the time when. ¶*Ten years have passed ~ he died.* **2.** because; seeing that. ¶*Since you say so, it must be true.*② —*adv.* **1.** from that time until now. ¶*ever ~*③ / *I have not heard from him ~.*④ **2.** before now; ago. ¶*It happened many years ~.* **3.** sometime after. ¶*He lived in Pusan at that time but has ~ moved away.*⑤

* **sin·cere** [sinsíər] *adj.* (usu. **-cer·er, -cer·est**) honest; faithful.

‡ **sin·cere·ly** [sinsíərli] *adv.* in a sincere manner; heartily.

* **sin·cer·i·ty** [sinsériti] *n.* [U] the state of being sincere; honesty.

si·ne·cure [sáinikjùər, síni-] *n.* [C] an office or position that is paid well and does not require much work or responsibility.

sin·ew [sínju:] *n.* [C] **1.** a tough piece of tissue that joins muscle to a bone. **2.** ⟪often *pl.*⟫ muscular strength; energy. **3.** ⟪*pl.*⟫ source of strength. —*vt.* strengthen; give (someone) power.

sin·ew·y [sínju(:)i] *adj.* **1.** having many sinews that join muscle to a bone. **2.** strong and vigorous.

한, 꾸밈없는 ¶①검소한 살림 **3.** 순진한 **4.** 정직한 ¶②정직한 마음 **5.** 속기 쉬운; 어리석은 **6.** [신분이] 천한 **7.** 순전한; 순수한 ¶③순전한
—[名] **1.** 바보 **2.** 단순한 것 **3.** 약초[로 만든 약]

—[形] 순진한, 정직한
—[形] 속기 쉬운, 어리석은
—[名] 바보
—[名] 간이(簡易); 순진; 검소; 소박
—[名] **1.** 간이화, 단순화 **2.** 단순화된 것
—[他] …을 간단하게 하다
—[副] **1.** 간단히 **2.** 꾸밈없이 ¶①소박한 몸차림의 부인 **3.** 어리석게 **4.** 단지, 다만, 전혀
—[名] **1.** 상(像) **2.** 가짜; 환영(幻影)
—[他] **1.** …을 가장하다 **2.** …인 체하다, …을 흉내내다
—[名] …인 체하기
—[名] 동시에 일어남; 동시성
—[形] 동시의 ¶①동시 통역
—[副] 동시에, 일제히
—[名] **1.** [종교·도덕상의] 죄 **2.** 과실, 위반 ¶①원죄(原罪)/②죄를 저지르다
—[自] [종교상의] 죄를 저지르다; 범하다
—[他] [죄를] 범하다
—[名] **1.** 시내 산(모세가 신에게서 십계를 받은 곳) **2.** 시나이 반도
—[前] …때부터, …이후, …이래 ¶①그때부터
—[接] **1.** …의 때부터, …이후 **2.** …이므로 ¶②네가 그렇게 말하니까 사실일게다 —[副] **1.** 그 이후 ¶③그후 쭉/④그후 그에게서 소식이 없다 **2.** 이전에 **3.** 그 후 ¶⑤그는 부산에 살고 있었는데 그 후 이사했다
—[形] 진실의, 성실한, 순수한
—[副] 마음으로부터, 정말로
—[名] 정직, 성실, 순수
—[名] 한직(閑職); 일도 책임도 대단치 않은 유급(有給)의 지위
—[名] **1.** 건(腱) **2.** 완력; 원기 **3.** 원동력 —[他] …을 기운내게 하다
—[形] **1.** 건질(腱質)의 **2.** 튼튼한, 건장한

sin·ful [sínf(u)l] *adj.* full of sin; immoral; wrong. ▷**sin·ful·ly** [-fuli] *adv.* —**sin·ful·ness** [-nis] *n.*
—[形] 죄가 있는

⁑ **sing** [siŋ] *v.* (**sang, sung**) *vi.* **1.** make musical sounds with the voice. ¶ ~ *in tune*① / ~ *in a low voice.* **2.** say words with musical tones. ¶ ~ *a ballad.*② **3.** make musical sounds, as do birds, the wind, etc. ¶ *Birds are singing.*③ **4.** tell or praise in verse or poetry. 《~ *of* something》 —*vt.* **1.** praise or tell of (someone or something) in song; chant. **2.** bring (someone) into a certain state by singing. ¶ ~ *a child to sleep.*④
—[自] 1. 노래하다 ¶①가락에 맞춰 노래하다 2. 가락을 붙여 부르다 ¶②민요를 부르다 3. 울다; 지저귀다 ¶③새가 지저귀고 있다 4. 시로 찬미하다 —[他] 1. …을 노래로 찬미하다; …을 노래 부르다 2. 노래로 [남]을 …하게 하다 ¶④노래로 아이를 재우다

singe [sindʒ] *v.* (**singe·ing** [síndʒiŋ]) *vt.* burn slightly; remove or take off (feathers, the feathery part of cloth, etc.) by slight burning. —*vi.* burn a little.
—[他] …을 그슬리다; [새털·천의 보풀 따위]를 그슬려 없애다 —[自] 그슬려지다
—*n.* [C] a slight burn or scorch on the surface of something.
—[名] 그슬림

⁑ **sing·er** [síŋər] *n.* [C] a person or bird that sings.
—[名] 가수; 지저귀는 새

Sin·gha·lese [sìŋgəlí:z, +*Brit.* sìŋhəl-] *adj.* of Ceylon, its native people, or their language. —*n.* (pl. **Sin·gha·lese**) [C] a person of Ceylon; [U] the language of Ceylon.
—[形] 실론[사람·말]의 —[名] 실론 사람; 실론 말

sing·ing [síŋiŋ] *n.* [U] **1.** the sound made by a person who sings; the act of the singer. **2.** the whistling sound of a bullet, etc.
—[名] 1. 노래; 창가 2. [화살·탄환 따위의] 윙윙 소리

⁑ **sin·gle** [síŋgl] *adj.* **1.** only one. ¶ *a ~ piece of chalk*① / *He would not move a ~ step from the place.*② **2.** (*Botany*) having only one ring of petals. ¶ *a ~ flower.*③ **3.** unmarried; for one person. ¶ *a ~ bed*④ / *a ~ man.*⑤ **4.** having only one on each side in a fight. ¶ [*a*] ~ *combat.*⑥ **5.** (*Brit.*) for only one course on a railway. ¶ *a ~ ticket.* **6.** sincere; honest. ¶ *a man of ~ meaning.* —*n.* [C] **1.** 《*pl.*》 (in tennis) a game played with one person on each side. **2.** (*Baseball*) a base hit. **3.** (*Brit.*) a one-way ticket. —*vt.* choose (someone or something) from others. 《~ *out* something》
—[形] 1. 단 하나의 ¶①분필 한 개/②그는 그 자리에서 한 발자국도 움직이지 않았다 2. 《植》 단판(單瓣)의 ¶③단판화 3. 독신의; 혼자 쓰는 ¶④1인용 침대/⑤독신자 4. 단식 시합의, 일대일의 ¶⑥일대일의 싸움 5. 《英》[차표가] 편도(片道)의 6. 성실한; 정직한 —[名] 1. [정구의] 단식 시합 2. 《野球》 단타(單打) 3. 편도 차표
—[他] …을 선발하다

sin·gle-breast·ed [síŋglbréstid] *adj.* (of a coat, etc.) having one line of buttons in the center of the breast.
—[形] [상의가] 싱글의, 단추가 외줄의

sin·gle-eyed [síŋgláid] *adj.* **1.** having only one eye. **2.** devoted to only one purpose; earnest.
—[形] 1. 단안(單眼)의, 애꾸의 2. 한눈팔지 않는

sin·gle-hand·ed [síŋglhǽndid] *adj., adv.* **1.** of or by only one hand. **2.** of or by only one person without any help from others. ▷**sin·gle-hand·ed·ly** [-li] *adv.*
—[形][副] 1. 한 손의(으로) 2. 단독의(으로)

sin·gle-heart·ed [síŋglhá:rtid] *adj.* having an honest, simple heart; faithful. ▷**sin·gle-heart·ed·ly** [-li] *adv.*
—[形] 성실한

sin·gle-mind·ed [síŋglmáindid] *adj.* devoted to one purpose; single-hearted; sincere.
—[形] 일편단심의; 성실한

sin·gle·ness [síŋglnis] *n.* [U] **1.** the state of being single. **2.** sincerity.
—[名] 1. 단일 2. 성실

sin·gle·stick [síŋglstìk] *n.* [C] a swordlike, wooden stick held in one hand, used in fencing; [U] fencing with such a stick.
—[名] 목검(木劍); 검술

sin·gly [síŋgli] *adv.* **1.** one by one; individually. **2.** by oneself; without others' help.
—[副] 1. 하나씩, 한 사람씩 2. 혼자서

sing·song [síŋsɔ̀:ŋ / -sɔ̀(:)ŋ] *n.* [C] a monotonous rising and falling tone. —*adj.* monotonous in tone or sound.
—[名] 단조로운 말투 —[形] 단조로운, 억양이 없는

* **sin·gu·lar** [síŋgjulər] *adj.* **1.** extraordinary; uncommon. ¶ *a story of ~ interest.*① **2.** strange; queer. ¶ *She is ~ in her looks.*② **3.** (*Grammar*) of one person or thing. ↔plural —*n.* [C] 《usu. *the* ~》 the singular number; the form of a word of the singular number.
—[形] 1. 보통이 아닌, 이상한 ¶①아주 재미있는 이야기 2. 기묘한 ¶②그녀는 외양이 기묘하다 3. 단수의 —[名] 《文法》 단수[형]

sin·gu·lar·i·ty [sìŋgjulǽriti] *n.* (pl. **-ties**) **1.** [U] the state of being singular; strangeness; a special quality. **2.** [C] something singular or peculiar.
—[名] 1. 단독; 기이함 2. 기묘한 것; 특성; 진귀한 것

sin·gu·lar·ly [síŋgjulərli] *adv.* strangely; particularly.
—[副] 기묘하게

sin·is·ter [sínistər] *adj.* **1.** suggesting the possibility of misfortune, disaster, etc. **2.** showing ill will or evil intentions. ¶ *a ~ look.*①
—[形] 1. 불길한 2. 악의를 품은 ¶①인상이 나쁜 얼굴

S

sink

sink [siŋk] v. (**sank** or **sunk**, **sunk** or **sunk·en**) vi. **1.** go downward little by little. ¶*The sun is sinking in the west.* | *The road sinks toward the lake.*① **2.** fall under water. ¶*The ship sank to the bottom of the sea.*② **3.** become lower than the usual level. ¶*The building sank into the ground.*③ / *The district is sinking.*④ **4.** become less in value, degree, etc. ¶~ *in price* / *The wind has sunk down.* / *My heart sank.*⑤ **5.** bend downward. **6.** soak. ——vt. **1.** cause (something) to sink. ¶*The ship was sunk by the storm.* **2.** make (value, degree, etc.) lower. **3.** dig. ¶~ *a well.* **4.** fix (a pole, etc.) firmly into the ground.
sink oneself, give up one's own interests and think of something or someone else.
——n. ⓒ a kitchen basin with a pipe to carry away water, used for washing dishes, pots, etc.

sink·er [síŋkər] n. ⓒ **1.** a person or thing that sinks. **2.** a weight to sink a fishing line or net. **3.** (*Baseball*) (*U.S. colloq.*) a ball that drops sharply downward when it reaches the batter.

sink·ing [síŋkiŋ] n. ⓤⓒ a feeling of collapse from weakness, fear, etc. ——*adj.* that sinks; dying.

sinking fund [´-´] n. a fund which is set aside periodically by a government, a corporation, etc. to pay a debt.

sin·less [sínlis] *adj.* free from sin; innocent.

sin·ner [sínər] n. ⓒ a person who commits sin or does wrong.

Si·no- [sáinou-, sínou-] a word element meaning *Chinese*.

Si·nol·o·gy [saináləʤi, sin-/sinɔ́l-, sainɔ́l-] n. ⓤ the study of Chinese literature, history, art, etc.

sin·u·ous [sínjuəs] *adj.* filled with curves or turns; bending; not frank or honest. ▷**sin·u·ous·ly** [-li] *adv.*

sip [sip] vt., vi. (**sipped**, **sip·ping**) drink (tea, coffee, etc.) slowly and only a very little at a time. ——n. ⓒ a very small mouthful of a drink. ¶*take a* ~.①

si·phon [sáif(ə)n] n. ⓒ **1.** a tube or pipe in the shape of U which carries liquid from one level to a lower level by air pressure. ⇒fig. **2.** a bottle with a tube through which the liquid, such as soda water, is forced by the pressure of the gas in it; a siphon bottle.

[siphon.]

sir [sə:r, sər] n. ⓒ **1.** a polite form of address used to a man. **2.** an ironic title. **3.** (*S-*) a title of a knight or baronet.

sire [sáiər] n. ⓒ **1.** a title of respect formerly used in addressing a king or a great noble. **2.** (*poetic*) a father; an ancestor. **3.** (of animals) the male parent. ↔dam

si·ren [sáiərin] n. ⓒ **1.** a sea nymph, part woman and part bird, who attracted sailors to destruction on the rocks by her singing. **2.** a beautiful or charming woman who deceives men. **3.** a device for producing a loud, shrill sound.

Sir·i·us [síriəs] n. the brightest star in the sky; the Dog Star.

sir·loin [sə́:rlɔin] n. ⓤⓒ the part of beef taken from the upper loin.

si·roc·co [sirákou / -rɔ́k-] n. ⓒ (pl. **-cos**) a hot, unpleasant wind which blows from Africa to south European countries.

sir·up [sírəp, +*U.S.* sə́:r-] n. =syrup.

sis [sis] n. ⓒ (*U.S. colloq.*) =sister.

sis·al [sáis(ə)l, +*U.S.* sís-] n. ⓤ a strong, white fiber of a kind of hemp used for making rope; sisal hemp.

sis·sy [sísi] n. ⓒ (pl. **-sies**) **1.** a sister. **2.** a man whose

behavior, interests, etc. are like those of a woman.
한) 사내

‡ **sis·ter** [sístər] *n.* [C] **1.** a girl or woman who has the same parents as another person. **2.** a girl or woman who is a very close friend to another. **3.** a woman who belongs to the same class, society, church, etc.
—[名] 1. 자매, 누이 2. 자매 같은 사람, 여자 친구 3. 여자 동급생, 여자 동지, 부인회원

sis·ter·hood [sístərhùd] *n.* **1.** [U] the state of being sisters. **2.** [C] an association of women with a common aim.
—[名] 1. 자매임 2. 부인단체, 부인회

sis·ter-in-law [sístərinlɔ̀ː] *n.* [C] (pl. **sis·ters-**) a sister of one's husband or wife; the wife of one's brother; the wife of the brother of one's husband or wife.
—[名] 시누이, 올케, 처형, 처제, 형수, 제수

sis·ter·ly [sístərli] *adj.* like a sister.
—[形] 자매 같은

‡ **sit** [sit] *v.* (**sat, sit·ting**) *vi.* **1.** rest on the lower part of the body; be seated; use a seat. ¶~ *on a chair.* **2.** (of a bird) come to rest on a branch, etc. 《~ *on* something》 ¶~ *on a bar.* **3.** be situated; lie. ¶*The village sits in a hollow.* **4.** hold a special position of the body for an artist, a photographer, etc.; (esp. *Brit.*) attempt to pass an examination. ¶~ *for a portrait.*① **5.** press or weigh. ¶~ *heavy on the stomach / Her duties ~ lightly on her shoulders.* **6.** (of a committee, Parliament, etc.) be at work. **7.** have a position as a member; have a seat officially. ¶~ *in Congress.* **8.** (of clothes) fit. ¶*Your coat does not ~ in the shoulders.* **9.** (of a bird) cover eggs so as to make young come out. —*vt.* **1.** cause (someone) to sit; seat. ¶*He sat her on his right.* **2.** ride (a horse). ¶*She sits her horse well.*
—[自] 1. 앉다; 착석하다 2. [새가] 앉다 3. 위치하다; 자리잡다 4. [초상화·촬영을 위해] 자세를 취하다, 앉다;《英》[시험]을 치르다 ¶①초상화를 그리게 하다 5. 누르다 6. [의회 따위가] 개원하다 7. 의원(위원)이 되다, 직위에 있다 8. [의복이] 어울리다 9. [새가] 알을 품다 —[他] 1. …을 앉히다 2. [말]에 타다

1) ***sit down,*** take a seat.
2) ***sit down under,*** accept (an insult, etc.) without complaint.
3) ***sit in,*** (*colloq.*) take part in (a conference, etc.).
4) ***sit on,*** meet in judgment on (a case, etc.); investigate.
5) ***sit out,*** [a] stay later than (another); stay until the end of (something). [b] remain seated during (a dance); refuse to participate in (something).
6) ***sit under,*** attend the sermons of (someone); study under (a teacher).
7) ***sit up,*** [a] not go to bed till late. [b] raise the body to an erect sitting position.

[熟] 1)앉다 2)[모욕 따위]를 달게 받다 3)《口》[회의 따위]에 참가하다 4)…에 관해 협의하다; …을 조사하다 5)[a][다른 손님보다도] 오래 머물다; …의 끝까지 있다 [b][무도회에서] 자리에 앉아 있다, 참가하지 않다 6)…의 설교를 듣다; [선생]에게 배우다 7)[a]자지 않고 일어나 있다 [b]일어나 앉다

sit-down strike [sítdaunstrài k] *n.* a strike in which the workers do not work at all but instead remain idle until their demands are satisfied.
—[名] 농성(연좌) 파업

• **site** [sait] *n.* [C] **1.** a piece of land to build a house on; the place where something is located. **2.** the place where something has happened.
—[名] 1. 집터, 대지 2. 유적, 위치

sit·ter [sítər] *n.* [C] **1.** a person who sits. **2.** a person who is hired to take care of a child or children while the parents are away, esp. in the evening; a baby sitter. **3.** a bird that sits on eggs in order to hatch them.
—[名] 1. 착석자 2. 아이보는 사람 3. 알을 품은 새

sit·ting [sítiŋ] *n.* [C] **1.** a session or meeting of a court, legislature, etc. **2.** a group of eggs on which a bird is sitting in order to hatch them.
—[名] 1. 개회, 개정(開廷), 회기 2. 한 번에 품는 알의 수

at a (or ***one***) ***sitting,*** without rest; all at once.
[熟] 단번에, 단숨에

• **sitting room** [ˊ– ˋ] *n.* a living room.
—[名] 거실, 안방

• **sit·u·at·ed** [sítʃuèitid, +*Brit.* -tju-] *adj.* located; placed. ¶*Tokyo is situated in the center of Japan.*
—[形] …에 위치하고 있는, …에 있는

‡ **sit·u·a·tion** [sìtʃuéiʃ(ə)n, +*Brit.* -tju-] *n.* [C] **1.** a place; a locality. **2.** a condition of being situated; a place or position of an object in relation to its environment. **3.** a condition; a case. **4.** a combination of circumstances; the state of affairs. ¶*a difficult ~ / the political ~.*① **5.** a place to work; a job.
—[名] 1. 장소, 위치 2. 상태, 위치, 입장 3. 경우, 처지 4. 사태, 국면 ¶①정국(政局) 5. 일자리, 취직자리

‡ **six** [siks] *n.* **1.** [U] the number between five and seven;
—[名] 1. 여섯 2. 6 명(개) 한 벌이 되는

sixfold

6. **2.** ⓒ (in volleyball, etc.) any group or set of six persons or things. **3.** ⓒ anything shaped like 6.
at sixes and sevens, in great confusion.
—*adj.* of 6.

six·fold [síksfòuld] *adj.* **1.** six times as much or as many. **2.** having six parts. —*adv.* six times as much or as many. ·「six feet tall.」
six-foot·er [síksfútər] *n.* ⓒ a person or thing that is
six·pence [síkspəns] *n.* **1.** ⓒ a small silver coin of Great Britain worth half a shilling. **2.** Ⓤ six British pennies.
six·pen·ny [síkspəni, +*U.S.* -pèni] *adj.* **1.** worth or costing sixpence. **2.** of little value.
six-shoot·er [síksʃúːtər] *n.* ⓒ a revolver which can fire six shots without reloading.
‡**six·teen** [síkstíːn] *n.* Ⓤ the number between fifteen and seventeen ; 16. —*adj.* of 16.
‡**six·teenth** [síkstíːnθ, -´-] *n.* **1.** (usu. *the ~*) the number 16; 16th. **2.** ⓒ one of the 16 equal parts of anything. —*adj.* of the 16th.
‡**sixth** [siksθ] *n.* **1.** (usu. *the ~*) the number 6; 6th. **2.** ⓒ one of six equal parts of anything. —*adj.* of the 6th.
‡**six·ti·eth** [síkstiiθ] *n.* **1.** (usu. *the ~*) the number 60; 60th. **2.** ⓒ one of 60 equal parts of anything. —*adj.* of the 60th.
six·ty [síksti] *n.* Ⓤ six times ten; 60. —*adj.* of 60.
siz·a·ble [sáizəbl] *adj.* rather large.
‡**size**¹ [saiz] *n.* **1.** Ⓤ the bigness or amount of a thing; scale; bulk. ¶*of natural ~ | the ~ of an industry*② / *of some ~*② *| take the ~ of*② *| the ~ of an apple | a crowd of considerable ~.* **2.** ⓒ one of a series of measures for articles. ¶*children's ~.* **3.** Ⓤ intellectual ability or force of character. ¶*a man of considerable of a size,* equal in size. [~.④]
—*vt.* **1.** arrange or separate (things) according to size. **2.** make (something) in a certain size.
size up, ⓐ measure the size of (something). ⓑ form an opinion or a judgement of (someone); conclude.
size² [saiz] *n.* Ⓤ special material made from glue, starch, etc., used for coating paper, cloth, etc. —*vt.* coat or treat (something) with size.
siz·zle [sízl] *vi.* make a hissing sound such as oil in a very hot frying pan does. —*n.* (*sing.* only) a hissing sound.
‡**skate** [skeit] *n.* ⓒ (usu. *pl.*) **1.** a frame with a steel blade fixed to a shoe so that a person wearing it can glide over ice. **2.** a plate with wheels for gliding over any smooth surface ; a roller skate. —*vi.* glide on skates.
skate over thin ice, deal with a problem which is very hard to solve.
skat·er [skéitər] *n.* ⓒ a person who skates.
skat·ing rink [skéitiŋriŋk] *n.* ⓒ **1.** a floor for roller skating. **2.** a smooth stretch of ice for skating.
skel·e·ton [skélitn] *n.* ⓒ **1.** the bony framework of a man or an animal. **2.** a very thin person or animal. **3.** the supporting framework of a buiding, a ship, etc. **4.** an outline or general idea for anything.
a skeleton in the cupboard (or *closet*), something that a family tries to keep secret because of shame.
skeleton key [-́--́] *n.* a key which is made to open many locks.
skep·tic [sképtik] *n.* ⓒ a person who cannot help questioning any fact or theory; a person who doubts the truth of a religious belief. —*adj.* =skeptical.

skeptic

것 3. 6 자형의 것
團 혼란하여
—영 of 6외, 6개의, 6명의
—働 1. 6배의 2. 여섯 겹의 —働 6배로
「6피이트의 것」
—영 키가 6피이트되는 사람(거인);
—영 1. 6펜스 은화 2. 6펜스

—働 1. 6펜스의 2. 하찮은 ; 싸구려의

—영 6연발 권총

—영 16 —働 16의

—영 1. 제 16, 열 여섯 번째 2. 16 분의 1
—働 제 16의 ; 열 여섯 번째의 ; 16 분의 1 의

—영 1. 제 6, 여섯 번째 2. 6분의 1 —働 여섯 번째의 ; 6분의 1의

—영 1. 제 60 ; 예순 번째 2. 60 분의 1
—働 제 60의, 예순 번째의 ; 60 분의 1 의

—영 60 —働 60 의
—働 꽤 큰
—영 1. [물건의] 크기, 양(量) ; 규모 ; 부피 ¶①사업의 규모/②꽤 큰/③…의 치수를 재다 2. 치수, 사이즈 3. 역량, 수완 ¶④역량이 상당한 사람

團 같은 크기의
—働 1. …의 크기의 차례로 분류하다 2. …을 어떤 크기로 만들다
團 ⓐ…의 치수를 재다 ⓑ[인물 따위]를 평가하다, 판단하다
—영 아교풀(종이·천에 먹여 먹·그림물감이 번지는 것을 막음)
—働 아교풀을 바르다
—働 지글거리다 —영 지글거리는 소리

—영 1. 스케이트 2. 로울러 스케이트
—働 스케이트를 타다

團 곤란한 문제를 다루다

—영 스케이트 타는 사람
—영 1. 로울러 스케이트장 2. 아이스 스케이트장
—영 1. 골격 ; 해골 2. 해골 같은 사람 ; 뼈와 가죽만 남은 사람 3. [배·가옥 따위의] 뼈대 4. 줄거리, 골자, 윤곽, 개략
團 남의 이목이 두려운 집안의 비밀

—영 맞쇠

—영 회의론자(懷疑論者) ; 종교적 회의론자

skep·ti·cal [sképtik(ə)l] *adj.* inclined to doubt the truth of any facts or theories; not believing anything easily. ―⑱ 의심 깊은, 회의적인

skep·ti·cism [sképtisìz(ə)m] *n.* ⓤ **1.** skeptical attitude. **2.** doubt or unbelief with regard to a religion. ―⑧ 1. 회의적인 태도 2. 종교적 회의

* **sketch** [sketʃ] *n.* ⓒ **1.** a drawing made simply and quickly. **2.** a rough draft; an outline. **3.** a short description, story, stage play, etc. ―*vt.* **1.** make a sketch of (something). **2.** explain (something) briefly and quickly. ―*vi.* make a sketch. ―⑧ 1. 스케치, 사생화, 밑그림 2. 초고, 초안, 약도; 줄거리, 개요 3. 소품(小品), 단편, 촌극 ―⑭ 1. …을 스케치하다 2. …을 개설(概說)하다 ―⑭ 스케치를 하다

sketch·book [skétʃbùk] *n.* ⓒ **1.** a book of drawing paper for sketches. **2.** a book of short stories, essays, etc. ―⑧ 1. 사생화첩 2. 소품집, 단편집, 수필집

sketch·y [skétʃi] *adj.* (**sketch·i·er, sketch·i·est**) **1.** like a sketch. **2.** showing only outlines; imperfect; done incompletely. ―⑱ 1. 스케치 같은 2. 줄거리만의, 대강의; 미완성의

skew [skju:] *adj.* **1.** slanting; twisted. **2.** not symmetrical. ―*n.* ⓒ a slant; a twist. ―*vt., vi.* give a slanting form to (something); twist; turn aside. ―⑱ 1. 비스듬한, 비뚠 2. 대칭적(對稱的)이 아닌 ―⑧ 비틀림, 비낌 ―⑭⑮ 비뚤어지[게 하]다

skew·er [skjú(:)ər] *n.* ⓒ a wooden or metal pin to hold meat together while cooking. ―*vt.* fasten (meat, fish, etc.) with or as if with a skewer. ―⑧ 꼬챙이, 산적 꼬챙이 ―⑭ …을 꼬챙이에 꿰다

: ski [ski:] *n.* ⓒ (pl. **skis** or **ski**) one of a pair of long, narrow pieces of wood, metal or plastic, to be fastened to the shoes for gliding over snow. ―*vi.* move over snow on skis. ―⑧ 스키이, 스키이 용구 ―⑭ 스키이로 활주하다, 스키이를 타다

skid [skid] *n.* ⓒ **1.** a frame, a rail, etc. on which heavy objects roll or slide. **2.** a piece of wood or metal used to prevent a wheel from going around. ―*v.* (**skid·ded, skid·ding**) *vi.* slip or slide sideways suddenly. ―*vt.* **1.** pull (something heavy) on a rail, a timber, etc. **2.** prevent (a wheel, etc.) from turning around by. ―⑧ 1. 활재(滑材), 침목(枕木) 2. [바퀴가] 굴러 내려가지 않도록 괴는 모탕, 제동기, 브레이크 ―⑭ 미끄러지다 ―⑭ 1. …을 활재 위에 놓고 끌다 2. [바퀴 따위가] 굴러 내려가지 않도록 모탕을 괴다

ski·er [skí:ər] *n.* ⓒ a person who skis. [means of a skid.] ―⑧ 스키이 타는 사람

skiff [skif] *n.* ⓒ a small light rowboat. ―⑧ 작은 보우트

ski jump [∠ ∠] *n.* **1.** a jump that is made by a skier. **2.** a place for jumping with skis. ―⑧ 1. 스키이 점프 2. 점프 경기장

* **skil·ful** [skílf(u)l] *adj.* (*Brit.*) =skillful.
skil·ful·ly [skílfuli] *adv.* (*Brit.*) =skillfully.
skil·ful·ness [skílf(u)lnis] *n.* (*Brit.*) =skillfulness.

: skill [skil] *n.* ⓤ the ability to do something very well as a result of long practice; cleverness.
have no skill in (=*be unable to do*) *something*.
―⑧ 숙련, 노련, 교묘, 솜씨, 재간
⑲ …에 서투르다

* **skilled** [skild] *adj.* **1.** able to do something well; trained; expert; skillful. **2.** requiring skill. ―⑱ 1. 숙련된, 교묘한, 노련한 2. 숙련(기술)을 필요로 하는

skil·let [skílit] *n.* ⓒ **1.** a small, shallow pan for frying; a frying pan. **2.** a long-handled saucepan. ―⑧ 1. 프라이팬 2. 자루가 긴 스튜우 냄비

* **skill·ful**, *Brit.* **skil-** [skílf(u)l] *adj.* having expert training; clever; experienced. ⌈of being skillful.⌉ ―⑱ 솜씨있는, 교묘한, 숙련된, 능숙한

skill·ful·ness, *Brit.* **skil-** [skílf(u)lnis] *n.* ⓤ the state ―⑧ 교묘, 숙련, 능숙

skill·ful·ly, *Brit.* **skil-** [skílfuli] *adv.* with skill. ―⑭ 교묘하게, 능숙하게

* **skim** [skim] *v.* (**skimmed, skim·ming**) *vt.* **1.** take off floating substances from the surface of (liquid); take up (something) from the surface of liquid. **2.** move or glide over or along (the surface). **3.** read (a book, etc.) quickly or carelessly. ―*vi.* **1.** pass or glide quickly over a surface. **2.** read quickly or carelessly.
1) *skim the cream* [*off milk*], take the best part off a thing.
2) *skim the surface*, deal with a thing superficially.
―*n.* ⓒ floating substances.
―⑭ 1. [액체]의 표면에 뜬 찌끼(더껑이)를 걷어내다; …을 액체의 표면에서 없애다 2. […의 표면]을 미끄러져 가다 3. [책]을 대충 읽다 ―⑭ 1. 표면을 미끄러지다 2. 대충 훑어보다

熟 1) 우유에서 크리임을 떠내다; 가장 좋은 부분을 가져가다 2) 피상적으로 다루다
―⑧ 뜬 찌끼, 더껑이

skim·mer [skímər] *n.* ⓒ **1.** a person who skims liquids; a thing used in skimming liquids. **2.** a kind of sea bird with long wings. ⌈already been taken away.⌉ ―⑧ 1. 더껑이를 걷어내는 도구(사람), 그물 국자 2. 갈매기류의 물새

skim milk [∠ ∠] *n.* milk from which the cream has ―⑧ 탈지유(脫脂乳)

skim·ming [skímiŋ] *n.* **1.** ⓤ the act of skimming milk, etc. **2.** ⓒ the cream obtained by skimming milk. ―⑧ 1. 더껑이를 걷어내기 2. 걷어낸 크리임

skimp [skimp] *vi.* be very economical. —*vt.* do not supply (something) enough of.
—[自] 인색하게 굴다 —[他] …을 인색하게 굴다

skimp·y [skímpi] *adj.* (**skimp·i·er, skimp·i·est**) not rich or large enough; narrow.
—[形] 빈약한; 야윈; 좁은

‡ **skin** [skin] *n.* [U][C] **1.** the outer cover of the body in persons and animals. **2.** a cover of an animal after it has been removed from the body. **3.** anything like a skin; the outer cover of a piece of fruit; bark. **4.** [C] a bag made of skin in which water, wine, etc. is kept.
—[名] 1.[인간·동물의] 피부, 살갗; 껍질 2.[동물의] 생가죽; 피혁; 가죽깔개 3.과일 껍질; 껍데기; [전체의] 외판(外板) 4.가죽 그릇; 가죽부대

1) ***by the skin of one's teeth,*** very narrowly; just barely.
2) ***jump*** (or ***fly***) ***out of one's skin,*** forget oneself because of joy, etc.
3) ***save one's skin,*** save one's life; avoid injury.
[熟] 1)간신히, 가까스로 2)[기쁨 따위로] 자신을 잊다 3)무사히 도망치다

—*v.* (**skinned, skin·ning**) *vt.* **1.** remove or strip the skin from (something). ¶~ *a rabbit.* **2.** cover (something) with skin. **3.** rub off a small piece of skin from (something). **4.** (*colloq.*) take something from (someone) by a dishonest act. 《~ someone *of* or *out of*》 —*vi.* become covered with skin.
—[他] 1.…의 가죽을 벗기다 2.…을 가죽으로 덮다 3.…을 스쳐 까다 4.《口》…에서 속여 빼앗다 —[自] 가죽으로 덮이다

skin-deep [skíndí:p] *adj.* **1.** on the surface of the skin. **2.** shallow; slight.
—[形] 1.가죽뿐인 2.피상적인, 천박한

skin diving [´ ` -] *n.* the sport of diving into the water with an aqualung.
—[名] 스킨다이빙

skin·ner [skínər] *n.* [C] a person who deals in skins, furs, etc.
—[名] 피혁상

skin·ny [skíni] *adj.* (**-ni·er, -ni·est**) very thin. ▷**skin·ni·ness** [-nis] *n.*
—[形] 말라빠진

* **skip** [skip] *v.* (**skipped, skip·ping**) *vi.* **1.** jump or spring lightly and quickly, as children do. **2.** hurry along in reading, omitting some parts of a book. **3.** jump lightly over a rope. **4.** (*colloq.*) run away rapidly and secretly. 《~ *out of* a place》 ¶~ *out of town.*① **5.** pass along rapidly. 《~ *over* a place》 —*vt.* **1.** jump lightly over (something). ¶~ *a fence.* **2.** omit (some parts of a book). ¶*She skipped difficult words in reading.*② **3.** fail to notice (something). **4.** (*colloq.*) leave (a place) rapidly and secretly. ¶*He skipped his home town one night.*
—[自] 1.[아이가] 뛰놀다, 뛰어다니다, 까불다 2.띄엄띄엄 읽다 3.줄넘기를 하다 4.《口》도망하다 ¶①읍에서 도망치다 5.급히 지나가다 —[他] 1.…을 뛰어넘다 2.…을 군데군데 빼고 읽다 ¶②그녀는 어려운 단어는 빼고 읽었다 3.…을 못 보고 넘기다, 알아보지 못하다 4.《口》…을 몰래 빠져나가다

—*n.* [C] a light, quick, gay and dancing jump.
—[名] 뛰기, 뛰놀기

skip·per[1] [skípər] *n.* [C] **1.** a captain of a small ship. **2.** a captain or leader of a cricket team, etc.
—[名] 1.[작은 상선·어선의] 선장 2.[크리켓 따위에서] 한쪽의 주장

skip·per[2] [skípər] *n.* [C] **1.** a person or an insect that skips. **2.** a butterfly that makes short, swift flights.
—[名] 1.뛰는 사람; 뛰는 벌레 2.팔랑나비

skir·mish [skə́:rmiʃ] *n.* [C] a slight and brief fight between small groups of soldiers. —*vi.* (of small groups of soldiers) quarrel and fight.
—[名] [부대 사이의] 소규모 전투, 접전 —[自] 소규모 접전을 벌이다; 충돌하다

‡ **skirt** [skə:rt] *n.* [C] **1.** a woman's or girl's outer garment hanging from the waist; the lower part of a coat, dress, etc. **2.** an edge; a border. **3.** 《*pl.*》 the suburbs; the outer part of a place. —*vt.* border (something); pass along the edge of (a place or a group of people).
—[名] 1.[여자] 스커어트; [일반적으로] 코우트 따위의 아랫자락 2.가장자리; 끝 3.교외, 변두리 —[他] …을 둘러싸다; …의 가장자리를 지나다

skit [skit] *n.* [C] a short humorous sketch, esp. used or performed on a stage.
—[名] 가벼운 풍자; 희문(戱文)

skit·tish [skítiʃ] *adj.* **1.** (of a horse, etc.) easily frightened. **2.** shy.
—[形] 1.[말 따위가] 잘 놀라는 2.암띤, 소심한, 마음 약한

skit·tles [skítl] *n. pl.* 《used as *sing.*》 a game in which a ball or disk is used to knock down ninepins. ⇒fig.
—[名] 구주희(九柱戲)

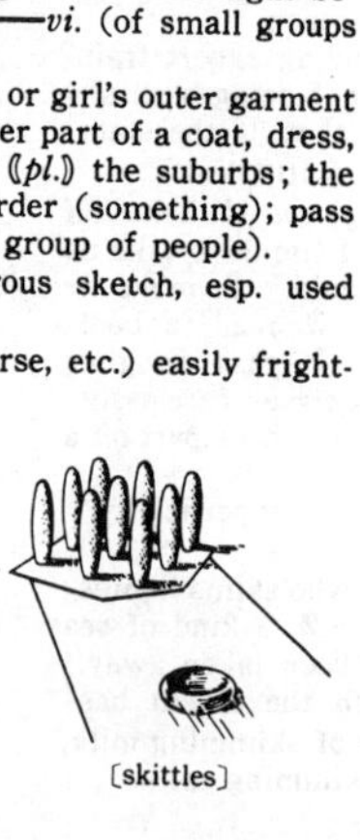
(skittles)

skulk [skʌlk] *vi.* hide to avoid duties, dangers etc. in a cowardly way; move stealthily with an evil purpose.
—[自] 살금살금 숨다, 살금살금 걷다, 숨어 다니다

* **skull** [skʌl] *n.* [C] the bones of the head; the head; the brain.
—[名] 두개골; 머리, 골통; 뇌

skull and crossbones

skull and cross·bones [skʌ́ləndkrɔ́sbòunz] *n.* a picture of a skull and two crossed thigh bones which was formerly used as a symbol of death on a pirate's flag. ―图 해골과 십자골(옛날은 해적기였으나 지금은 독약의 표지로 씀)

skull·cap [skʌ́lkæp] *n.* ⓒ a close-fitting cap, usu. used by an old man indoors. ―图 [실내에서 노인이 쓰는] 벨벳 두건

* **skunk** [skʌŋk] *n.* **1.** ⓒ a small black animal which gives off a very strong, unpleasant smell when frightened or attacked. ⇒fig. **2.** Ⓤ the fur of this animal. ―图 1. 스컹크 2. 스컹크의 모피

[skunk 1.]

‡ **sky** [skai] *n.* ⓒ (pl. **skies**) **1.** the space over the world where the clouds are. **2.** (*the* ~ or *the skies*) the place in heaven where God and His angels live. **3.** (often *pl.*) weather. *out of a clear sky*, suddenly; unexpectedly. ―图 1. 하늘, 창공 2. 천국, 천당 3. 날씨, 기후

憨 별안간, 난데없이

sky blue [´ ´] *n.* a light clear blue. ―图 하늘색

sky-high [skáihái] *adj., adv.* very high. ―形勳 아주 높은(높이)

sky·lark [skáilɑ̀ːrk] *n.* ⓒ a small bird known for its sweet song in early spring. ―图 종달새

sky·light [skáilàit] *n.* ⓒ a window in a roof or ceiling. ―图 [천장의] 채광창, 천창(天窓)

sky·line [skáilàin] *n.* ⓒ **1.** the line at which the sky seems to meet the earth; the horizon. **2.** the outline of mountains, trees, buildings, etc. against the sky. ―图 1. 지평선 2. [산 따위의] 하늘을 배경으로 하는 윤곽

sky·rock·et [skáirɑ̀kit / -rɔ̀k-] *n.* ⓒ a firework that rises rapidly high in the air. ―*vi.* rise suddenly and rapidly. ―图 공중폭발 불꽃 ―自 급격히 상승하다

sky·scrap·er [skáiskrèipər] *n.* ⓒ a very tall building. ―图 고층건물, 마천루

sky·ward [skáiwərd] *adj., adv.* toward the sky. ―形勳 하늘쪽의(으로)

sky·wards [skáiwərdz] *adv.* = skyward.

slab [slæb] *n.* ⓒ a flat and thick piece of wood, stone, etc.; a thick slice of bread, meat, etc. ―图 [재목·돌 따위의] 두꺼운 평판(平板); [빵·고기 따위의] 두꺼운 조각

slack [slæk] *adj.* **1.** loose; not tight. **2.** slow. **3.** not careful; lazy. **4.** not busy; not active; dull. ―*n.* ⓒ **1.** a part of a rope, a wire, etc. that is not stretched tight. **2.** a dull season in business. ―*vt., vi.* make (something) slack; become slack. ▷**slack·ness** [-nis] *n.* ―颪 1. 느슨한 2. 느린 3. 부주의한 4. 칠체한 ―图 1. 느슨함 2. 불황기 ―勳自 […을] 느슨하게 하다(되다); […을] 느리게 하다(되다); […을] 불황으로 하다(되다)

slack·en [slǽk(ə)n] *vi.* **1.** become less firm; become loose. **2.** become less active. **3.** become slower. ―*vt.* **1.** make (a rope, a wire, etc.) less firm. **2.** make (the speed, the pace, etc.) slower. ―自 1. 느슨해지다 2. 불황이 되다 3. 느리게 되다 ―勳 1. [로우프 따위를] 늦추다 2. [속도 따위를] 줄이다

slacks [slæks] *n. pl.* trousers; loose trousers for informal wear. ―图 여자용 바지, 슬랙스

slag [slæg] *n.* Ⓤ waste matter remaining when metal has been taken from a natural combination of minerals by melting. ―图 [광석을 녹일 때 생기는] 쇠똥, 광석 찌꺼

slain [slein] *v.* pp. of **slay**.

slake [sleik] *vt.* **1.** put out (a fire). **2.** satisfy (thirst or a desire). **3.** add water to (lime) in order to change its chemical nature. ―勳 1. [불]을 끄다 2. [갈증]을 풀다; [욕망]을 채우다 3. [석회]를 비화(沸化)하다

slam [slæm] *v.* (**slammed, slam·ming**) *vt.* **1.** close or shut violently and noisily. ¶*He slammed the door in anger.*① **2.** put or throw (something) with force and a loud noise. ⟪~ *a book, etc. on*⟫ ¶*He slammed down the cap on the table.*② ―*vi.* (of a door, a window, etc.) shut with a bang. ¶*In the strong wind, the door slammed.*③ ―*n.* ⓒ the noise of a door shutting violently; a bang. ¶*with a* ~. ―勳 1. …을 쾅하고 닫다 ¶①그는 화가 나서 문을 쾅하고 닫았다 2. …을 쿵하고 놓다 ¶②그는 모자를 테이블 위에 쾅하고 던졌다 ―自 [문 따위가] 쾅하고 닫히다 ¶③강풍으로 문이 쾅하고 닫혔다 ―图 쾅하고 닫히는 소리

slan·der [slǽndər / slɑ́ːndə] *n.* Ⓤⓒ a false report or statement about someone in order to harm him. ―*vt.* talk falsely about (someone) in order to hurt his character. ―图 중상, 비방; 험담 ―勳 …을 중상하다

slan·der·er [slǽnd(ə)rər / slɑ́ːnd(ə)rə] *n.* ⓒ a person who slanders. ―图 중상자(中傷者)

slan·der·ous [slǽnd(ə)rəs / slɑ́ːn-] *adj.* speaking or spreading slander. ▷**slan·der·ous·ly** [-li] *adv.* ―颪 중상적인, 명예를 훼손하는

* **slang** [slæŋ] *n.* Ⓤ **1.** words or phrases used in popular speech, but not regarded as formal language. **2.** the ―图 1. 속어 2. [어떤 사회의] 통용어; [도둑·죄인 등의] 은어

special language of a particular group of people.

slang·y [slǽŋi] *adj.* (**slang·i·er, slang·i·est**) of slang; full of slang; using slang.
—[形] 속어의, 속어가 많은, 속어를 쓰는

* **slant** [slænt / slɑːnt] *adj.* sloping. —*n.* [C] **1.** a slope. ¶*The mountain has a sharp ~.*① **2.** a way of looking at something; an opinion; a point of view. ¶*He has a new ~ on the novel.* —*vt.* give a slope to (something). —*vi.* be on a slope. ¶*The roof slants a bit.*②
—[形] 비스듬한, 기운 —[名] 1. 경사 ¶①그 산은 경사가 가파르다 2. 사물의 관점, 의견 —[他] …을 경사지게 하다 —[自] 기울다 ¶②지붕은 약간 경사졌다

slant·ing [slǽntiŋ / slɑ́ːn-] *adj.* with a sloping direction.
—[形] 경사진

slant·wise [slǽntwàiz / slɑ́ːnt-] *adv.* in a slanting manner.
—[副] 비스듬히, 기울어

* **slap** [slæp] *n.* [C] a blow with the open hand.
—[名] 손바닥으로 찰싹 때리기

a slap in (or *across*) *the face,* ⓐ a blow on the face with the open hand. ⓑ a refusal.
[熟] ⓐ손바닥으로 얼굴을 때리기 ⓑ거절

—*vt.* (**slapped, slap·ping**) **1.** hit (someone) with the open hand. **2.** throw (something) down with a noise.
—[他] 1. …을 [손바닥으로] 찰싹 때리다 2. …을 쾅하고 던지다

1) ***slap on,*** put (something) on quickly.
2) ***slap** someone **on the back,*** pat someone on the back in a friendly manner.
[熟] 1)재빨리 입다(쓰다) 2)[다정하게 남의] 등을 툭 치다

—*adv.* **1.** straight; directly. **2.** suddenly. ¶*When I turned the corner, I run ~ into him.*
—[副] 1. 찰싹; 똑바로 2. 느닷없이

slash [slæʃ] *vt.* **1.** cut (something) violently and aimlessly. **2.** cut slits in (a dress) in order to show the different material beneath. **3.** whip repeatedly. **4.** reduce (a budget, a salary, etc.) very much. **5.** criticize severely or unkindly.
—[他] 1. …을 깊이 베다, 난도질하다 2. [의복의 일부분을] 갈라놓다 3. …을 매질하다 4. 대폭적으로 줄이다 5. …을 혹평하다

—*n.* [C] a long cut; a sweeping stroke.
—[名] 깊은 상처; 일격

slat [slæt] *n.* [C] a thin, narrow strip of wood, metal, etc.
—[名] [나무·금속의] 가늘고 긴 얇은 판

* **slate** [sleit] *n.* **1.** [U] hard, blue-gray rock that easily splits into thin layers; [C] a thin plate of this rock, used for coating a roof. **2.** [U] dark, bluish gray. **3.** [C] (*U.S.*) a list of candidates for election.
—[名] 1. 석판(石板); [지붕을 이는 한 장의] 슬레이트 2. 회색 3. ((美)) 후보자 명부

—*vt.* **1.** cover (something) with slate. **2.** list (candidates) for election.
—[他] 1. …을 슬레이트로 이다 2. …을 후보자로서 기입하다

slate pencil [ˊ ˋ-] *n.* a pencil used for writing on a slate.
—[名] 석필(石筆)

slat·tern [slǽtərn] *n.* [C] a woman who is careless and lazy.
—[名] 체신머리 없는(행실 나쁜) 여자

slat·tern·ly [slǽtərnli] *adj.* (of a woman) careless and untidy.
—[形] 체신머리 없는, 행실 나쁜

slat·y [sléiti] *adj.* (**slat·i·er, salt·i·est**) of slate; slate-colored.
—[形] 슬레이트[질(質)]의, 석판 모양의, 회색의

* **slaugh·ter** [slɔ́ːtər] *n.* [U] **1.** the act of killing in great numbers; a massacre. **2.** the act of killing animals for food. —*vt.* kill (people) in great numbers cruelly; kill (animals) for food.
—[名] 1. 살륙, 학살 2. 도살 —[他] …을 살륙하다; 도살하다

slaugh·ter·er [slɔ́ːtərər] *n.* [C] a person who slaughters.
—[名] 살륙자; 도살자

slaugh·ter·house [slɔ́ːtərhàus] *n.* [C] a place where animals are killed for food; a place or scene of cruel fighting.
—[名] 도살장; 수라장

Slav [slɑːv, slæv] *n.* [C] a member of one of the races living in eastern Europe, such as Russians, Poles, Czechs, Slovaks, Bulgarians and Yugoslavs. —*adj.* of the Slavs and their languages.
—[名] 슬라브 민족 —[形] 슬라브 민족(말)의

‡ **slave** [sleiv] *n.* [C] **1.** a person who has no freedom because of being the property of another. **2.** a person who works very hard like a slave. **3.** a person who is given to some bad habit, desire, etc. —*vi.* work very hard like a slave.
—[名] 1. 노예 2. 노예처럼 일하는 사람 3. [욕망·악습 따위의] 탐닉자 —[自] [노예처럼] 악착같이 일하다

slave driver [ˊ ˋ-] *n.* **1.** an overseer of slaves. **2.** an employer who is unkind to his employees.
—[名] 1. 노예 감시인 2. 혹사하는 고용주

slave·hold·er [sléivhòuldər] *n.* [C] a person who owns slaves.
—[名] 노예 소유자

slave·hold·ing [sléivhòuldiŋ] *n.* [U] the act of owning slaves. —*adj.* having slaves.
—[名] 노예 소유 —[形] 노예 소유의

slav·er[1] [sléivər] *n.* [C] **1.** a dealer in slaves. **2.** a ship used in the slave trade.
—[名] 1. 노예 매매자 2. 노예 무역선

slav·er² [slǽvər, +*U.S.* sléiv-] *n.* [U] the liquid that runs from the mouth. **—*vi.*** let slaver flow from the mouth. **—*vt.*** wet (something) with slaver.
—[名] 군침 —[自] 군침을 흘리다 —[他] …을 침으로 더럽히다

***slav·er·y** [sléiv(ə)ri] *n.* [U] **1.** the custom of owning slaves. **2.** the state of being a slave. **3.** very hard work. **4.** the condition of being given to some bad habit or influence. ¶~ *to fashion.*
—[名] 1. 노예제도 2. 노예의 신분, 예속 3. 고역 4. 사로잡히기

slave trade [ˊ ˋ] *n.* the business of selling and buying slaves.
—[名] 노예 매매

Slav·ic [slǽvik, slɑ́:v-] *adj., n.* =Slavonic.

slav·ish [sléiviʃ] *adj.* of a slave; base; mean.
—[形] 노예의; 노예 근성의; 비굴한

Sla·von·ic [sləvɑ́nik / -vɔ́n-] *adj.* of the Slavs and their languages. **—*n.*** [U] the Slavic languages.
—[形] 슬라브족(말)의 —[名] 슬라브 말

slaw [slɔ:] *n.* [U] sliced cabbage served as salad.
—[名] 양배추 샐러드

***slay** [slei] *vt.* (**slew, slain**) kill violently.
—[他] …을 죽이다, 살해하다

slay·er [sléiər] *n.* [C] a person who kills or has killed a person.
—[名] 살해자

sled [sled] *n.* [C] a flat, low, wooden framework for carrying loads on snow or ice. ⇒fig. **—*vi., vt.*** (**sled·ded, sled·ding**) ride on a sled; carry (something) on a sled.
—[名] 썰매, 작은 썰매 —[自][他] 썰매로 가다; …을 썰매로 나르다

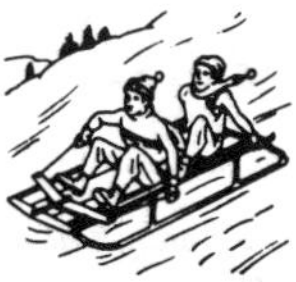
[sled]

sledge¹ [sledʒ] *n.* [C] a sled; a sleigh. **—*vi., vt.*** ride or carry (something) on a sledge.
—[名] 썰매 —[自][他] 썰매로 가다; …을 썰매로 나르다

sledge² [sledʒ] *n.* =sledge hammer.

sledge-ham·mer [slédʒhæ̀mər] *vt.* **1.** hit (something) with a sledge hammer. **2.** do great damage to (the enemy, etc.) **—*adj.*** powerful; crushing. ¶*a ~ blow.*①
—[他] 1. …을 큰 망치로 치다 2. …에 큰 타격을 주다 —[形] 파괴적인 ¶① 큰 타격

sledge hammer [ˊ ˋ-] *n.* a heavy hammer usu. used with both hands.
—[名] 큰 망치

sleek [sli:k] *adj.* **1.** smooth; glossy; neat. **2.** flattering in speech. **—*vt.*** make (something) smooth and glossy.
—[形] 1. 매끄러운 2. 구변 좋은 —[他] …을 매끄럽게 하다

‡sleep [sli:p] *n.* [U] **1.** the state of being not awake; (*a* ~) a period of sleeping. ¶*a sound ~ / fall* [*into*] *~*① */ go to ~*② */ put someone to ~.*③ **2.** a state like sleep; death. ¶*the ~ of death / the last ~*④ */ winter ~.*⑤
—[名] 1. 잠, 수면; 수면 기간 ¶①잠들다/②잠자다/③…을 재우다 2. 정지(靜止); 죽음 ¶④영면/⑤동면

—*v.* (**slept**) *vi.* **1.** be in a state of sleep; go to bed. ¶*~ well / ~ like a log*⑥ */ She slept twelve hours.* **2.** be motionless; be dead; be in a state like sleep. ¶*~ in the grave / The town slept.* **—*vt.* 1.** rest in (a kind of sleep). ⇒[usage] ¶*~ a sound sleep / ~ one's last sleep.*⑦ **2.** (of a hotel, etc.) have beds enough for (persons). ¶*This hut can ~ ten people.*
—[自] 1. 잠자다 ¶⑥푹 자다 2. 정지하다, 죽어 있다; 동면하고 있다 —[他] 1. 잠자다 [usage] 동족 목적어와 함께 쓰임 ¶⑦죽다 2. [호텔 따위에서] …을 숙박시키다

1) ***sleep away,*** ⓐ spend in one's sleep. ⓑ get rid of (a headache, etc.) by sleeping. ¶*~ away one's cares.*
2) ***sleep off,*** recover from (a headache, etc.) by sleeping.
3) ***sleep on*** (or ***upon***) ***a question,*** leave a decision until the next day.
[熟] 1)ⓐ잠자며 보내다 ⓑ[두통 따위]를 잠을 자서 고치다 2)[두통 따위]를 잠을 자서 고치다 3)[문제 따위]를 하룻밤 자면서 생각하다

sleep·er [slí:pər] *n.* [C] **1.** a person who sleeps. **2.** a horizontal beam. **3.** a sleeping car.
—[名] 1. 잠자는 사람 2. 침목(枕木) 3. 침대차

sleep·i·ly [slí:pili] *adv.* in a sleepy manner.
—[副] 졸리게, 졸린 듯이

sleep·i·ness [slí:pinis] *n.* [U] the condition of being sleepy.
—[名] 졸림

‡sleep·ing [slí:piŋ] *n.* [U] **1.** sleep. **2.** rest. **—*adj.* 1.** asleep. **2.** of or for sleep. ¶*a ~ bag.*
—[名] 1. 수면 2. 휴지(休止) —[形] 1. 자고 있는 2. 수면[용]의

‡sleeping car [ˊ- ˋ] *n.* a railway car with beds for passengers.
—[名] 침대차

sleeping sickness [ˊ- ˋ-] *n.* a disease of tropical Africa, causing fever, sleepiness, and usu. death.
—[名] 열대 아프리카의 기면병(嗜眠病)

sleep·less [slí:plis] *adj.* **1.** unable to sleep; not sleeping. **2.** restless; watchful.
—[形] 1. 잠 못 자는, 불면증의 2. 쉬지 않는, 방심하지 않는

sleep·walk·er [slí:pwɔ̀:kər] *n.* [C] a person who walks about while sleeping.
—[名] 몽유병자

***sleep·y** [slí:pi] *adj.* (**sleep·i·er, sleep·i·est**) **1.** inclined to sleep. ¶*a ~ face* **2.** (of a place, etc.) inactive; quiet. ¶*a ~ town.*
—[形] 1. 졸리는, 졸린 듯한; 멍하니 있는 2. 활기 없는; 조용한

sleep·y·head [slí:pihèd] *n.* [C] a person who looks half asleep; a sleepy person.
—[名] 잠꾸러기

S

sleet [sli:t] *n.* [U] snow or hail mixed with rain; frozen or partly-frozen rain. —*vi.* shower half-frozen rain.
—[名] 진눈깨비 —[自] 진눈깨비가 내리다

sleet·y [slí:ti] *adj.* (**sleet·i·er, sleet·i·est**) of sleet; with sleet falling.
—[形] 진눈깨비의(같은), 진눈깨비가 오는

⁑ **sleeve** [sli:v] *n.* [C] the part of a dress, coat, etc. that covers all or a part of the arm.
—[名] 소매

1) ***have something up one's sleeve,*** keep something secretly ready for use when needed.
2) ***laugh in*** (or ***up***) ***one's sleeve,*** be secretly amused.
3) ***wear one's heart on one's sleeve,*** show one's feeling openly.
[熟] 1)…을 언제라도 쓸 수 있도록 준비해 두다 2)뒷전에서 웃다(재미있어 하다) 3)감정을 드러내 보이다

sleeve·less [slí:vlis] *adj.* without sleeves.
—[形] 소매 없는

sleigh [slei] *n.* [C] a carriage for use on snow or ice. ⇒fig. —*vi., vt.* ride or carry (something) in a sleigh.
—[名] 썰매 —[自][他] 썰매에 타다(로 가다), …을 썰매로 나르다

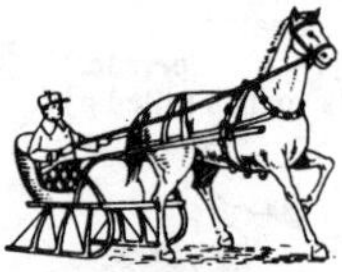
[sleigh]

sleigh·ing [sléiiŋ] *n.* [U] the act of riding in a sleigh.
—[名] 썰매에 타기

sleight [slait] *n.* [U] skill; a skillful trick.
—[名] 날랜 재주, 교묘; 간계(奸計)

sleight of hand, skill with the hands, esp. in performing tricks, as in magic; a trick thus performed; a magic trick.
[熟] [요술 따위의] 날랜 손재주; 요술

⁑ **slen·der** [sléndər] *adj.* **1.** long and thin; slim. ¶*He is ~ in build.*① **2.** not hopeful; weak; poor.
—[形] 1. 호리호리한 ¶①그는 체격이 호리호리하다 2. [희망 따위] 가냘픈; 약한; 빈약한

⁑ **slept** [slept] *v.* pt. and pp. of **sleep**.

sleuth·hound [slú:θhàund] *n.* [C] a large dog used for hunting escaped prisoners; a bloodhound; a detective.
—[名] 탐정견(犬), 사냥개; 탐정

• **slew¹** [slu:] *v.* pt. of **slay**.

slew² [slu:] *vi., vt.* turn; twist. 《~ *around* something》 —*n.* [C] the act of turning or twisting.
—[自][他] [수평으로] 돌다, [...을] 돌리다 —[名] [수평의] 회전

S

⁑ **slice** [slais] *n.* [C] **1.** a thin, flat piece cut from something. ¶*a ~ of bread.* **2.** a part; a portion; a share. **3.** a knife with a thin, broad blade. —*vt.* cut (something) into slices; cut off. 《~ *off* something》
—[名] 1. 얇은 조각, 한 조각 2. 일부분, 몫 3. 식칼, 생선 베는 식탁용 나이프 —[他] …을 얇게 베다(저미다), 깎아내다

slick [slik] *adj.* **1.** smooth; glossy. ¶*~ hair.* **2.** clever. **3.** cunning; sly; tricky. **4.** too smooth in speech. **5.** very slippery; easy to slip on. ¶*a street ~ with ice.* —*adv.* **1.** directly; straight. **2.** smoothly. **3.** cleverly. —*n.* [C] a smooth part of a road, etc.
—[形] 1. 매끄러운 2. 영리한 3. 교활한 4 구변 좋은 5. 미끌미끌한 —[副] 1. 똑바로; 정면으로 2. 매끄럽게 3. 영리하게 —[名] 매끄러운 부분

slick·er [slíkər] *n.* [C] (*U.S.*) **1.** a long, loose, waterproof coat. **2.** a tricky person.
—[名] 《美》 1. 길고 헐거운 우비 2. 교활한 사람

• **slid** [slid] *v.* pt. and pp. of **slide**.

• **slid·den** [slídn] *v.* pp. of **slide**.

⁑ **slide** [slaid] *v.* (**slid, slid** or **slid·den**) *vi.* **1.** move smoothly, as over ice; glide. **2.** move quietly and secretly. 《~ *into* a place, etc.》 **3.** fall gradually or unconsciously into a certain condition. 《~ *into* a bad habit, etc.》 **4.** (of time, etc.) pass quietly or gradually; slip away. —*vt.* **1.** cause (something) to move smoothly. **2.** put (something) in quietly.
—[自] 1. [얼음 위 따위를] 미끄러져 가다 2. 살금살금 걷다; 몰래 들어가다 3. [어떤 상태로] 모르는 사이에 빠지다 4. [시간 따위가] 모르는 사이에 지나가다, 경과하다
—[他] 1. …을 미끄러지게 하다 2. …을 슬쩍 넣다

1) ***let something slide,*** leave something as it is.
2) ***slide away,*** leave or go away quietly and secretly; pass away gradually.
3) ***slide over,*** pass over quickly. ¶*~ over a difficult problem.*①
[熟] 1)[사물]을 돼가는 대로 놔두다, 내버려 두다 2)몰래 떠나다, 모르는 사이에 지나가다 3)…을 간단히 해치우다 ¶①곤란한 문제를 쉽게 해결하다

—*n.* [C] **1.** the act of sliding. **2.** any smooth, slippery road or surface. **3.** a mass of earth, snow, etc., sliding down a steep slope; a landslide. **4.** a thin sheet of glass used for examining specimens under a microscope; slides with pictures used in magic lanterns.
—[名] 1. 활주, 미끄러져 들어가기 2. 미끄럼길, 활주장, 미끄럼대 3. 사태, 산사태 4. [현미경의] 검경판(檢鏡板), [환등의] 슬라이드

slide fastener [∠ ∠∸] *n.* a zipper.
—[名] 척

slid·er [sláidər] *n.* [C] **1.** a person who slides. **2.** (*Baseball*) a sharp ball that curves slightly in front of a batter.
—[名] 1. 미끄러지는 사람 2. 《野球》 슬라이더, 평곡구(平曲球), 활구(滑球)

slide rule [́ ̀] *n.* a device consisting of a ruler with a sliding scale, used for making rapid calculations.
—[名] 계산자, 활척(滑尺)

‡slight [slait] *adj.* **1.** not much; not important; small. ¶*a ~ rainfall.* **2.** slender; thin; not big. ¶*a ~ girl.* **3.** frail; not strong. ¶*a ~ cold / a ~ hope.*
—[形] 1. 적은, 사소한, 보잘것 없는 2. 가느다란, 호리호리한 3. 경미한, 취약(脆弱)한
—*n.* [C] an act of neglecting; an insult.
—[名] 경시, 경멸
put a slight upon (=*despise*) *someone.*
[熟] …을 경시하다
—*vt.* despise; have contempt for.
—[他] …을 얕보다, 모욕하다

‡slight·ly [sláitli] *adv.* **1.** in a slight manner. **2.** to a slight degree.
—[副] 1. 가느다랗게 2. 근소하게

∗slim [slim] *adj.* (**slim·mer, slim·mest**) **1.** slender; thin. **2.** not much; scant; small. **3.** sly; tricky. —*vt., vi.* make (something) or become thin.
—[形] 1. 가느다란, 약한; 얇은 2. 근소한 3. 교활한 —[他][自] 가느다랗게(얇게) 하다(되다), 야위다

slime [slaim] *n.* [U] **1.** soft, sticky mud. **2.** a sticky substance given off by the skin of snails, snakes, etc.
—[名] 1. 눈지렁이, 진흙 2. 점액(粘液), 끈적끈적한 것

slim·ly [slímli] *adv.* in a slim manner.
—[名] 가늘게; 호리호리하게; 조금

slim·y [slími] *adj.* (**slim·i·er, slim·i·est**) **1.** covered with slime. **2.** of or like slime. **3.** flattering; mean; unpleasant. ▷**slim·i·ly** [-li] *adv.*
—[形] 1. 진흙을 바른, 진흙투성이의 2. 끈적끈적한; 점착(粘着)하는 3. 아첨하는, 비열한

sling [sliŋ] *n.* [C] **1.** a strip of leather used for throwing a stone. **2.** a hanging loop of cloth fastened around the neck for supporting a wounded arm. **3.** any of several devices composed of ropes, chains, etc. for lifting or carrying heavy objects. ⇒fig. —*vt.* (**slung**) **1.** throw (a stone) by means of a sling. **2.** lift or carry (something) in a sling. **3.** hang (something) so that it swings.
—[名] 1. 투석기(投石器) 2. 어깨에 거는 붕대 3. 매다는 밧줄(사슬)
—[他] 1. 투석기로 [돌]을 날리다 2. …을 달아 올리다 3. …을 매달다

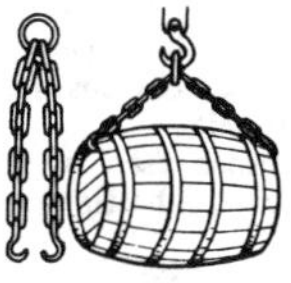
〔sling 3.〕

slink [sliŋk] *vi.* (**slunk**) move, walk or go in a secret or guilty manner.
—[自] 살금살금 걷다; 몰래 도망치다

‡slip¹ [slip] *v.* (**slipped, slip·ping**) *vi.* **1.** move out of position; slide accidentally and fall. ¶*The knife slipped and cut my hand.* **2.** lose one's footing; fall down. ¶*I slipped on the ice.* **3.** move or pass secretly and quickly; escape. ¶*He slipped away without a sound. / Time slips by* (or *away*). **4.** go or move smoothly, quietly, or quickly. ¶*~ along over the snow / ~ through the waves*① */ ~ into one's chair.*② **5.** make a mistake or an error. ¶*~ in one's grammar.* **6.** escape from one's memory. ¶*Her name slipped* [*from*] *my mind.* **7.** put a garment on or off easily. ¶*~ into* (*out of*) *a jacket.* —*vt.* **1.** cause (something) to slip, pass, or move quickly or easily. ¶*~ a ring on* [*to*] *one's finger*③ */ ~ one's coat on* (*off*). **2.** put or take quickly or secretly. ¶*~ a letter into one's pocket / She slipped a coin into the porter's hand.* **3.** escape from (someone or something) ¶*~ one's pursuers / ~ one's memory* (or *mind*). **4.** let (something) loose, go, or pass; miss. ¶*~ a hound*④ */ Don't ~ the chance.*
—[自] 1. [물건이] 미끄러지다, 미끄러져 떨어지다 2. [발이] 미끄러지다, 헛딛다 3. 슬쩍 가 버리다(들어가다); [시간이] 어느덧 지나가다 4. 미끄러지듯 나아가다(달리다, 움직이다) ¶①[배가] 파도를 헤치며 나아가다/②의자에 슬그머니 앉다 5. 깜박 실수하다 6. 잊어버리다 7. [옷을] 훌떡 벗다(입다) —[他] 1. …을 쑥 끼우다, 미끄러지게 하다 ¶③손가락에 반지를 쑥 끼우다 2. …을 슬쩍 넣다(꺼내다) 3. …에서 도망치다; [기억 따위]에서 사라지다 4. …을 놓치다, …을 못 보고 넘기다 ¶④사냥개를 풀어놓다
slip up, (*U.S. colloq.*) make a mistake.
[熟] 잘못하다, 실패하다
—*n.* [C] **1.** an act of slipping; a sudden slide. **2.** a small, unintentional mistake or error. ¶*a ~ of the tongue*⑤ */* (*proverb*) *There's many a ~ between the cup and the lip.*⑥ **3.** a woman's underdress; a loose cover for a cushion, a bed, etc. **4.** a smooth slope on which a ship is built or repaired; (*U.S.*) a place for a ship between two piers.
—[名] 1. 미끄름; 헛디뎌서 넘어지기 2. 간과(看過); 잘못 ¶⑤실언(失言)/⑥(俚)잔을 입에 가져가는 사이에도 실수는 얼마든지 있다 3. 부인용 속옷; 베갯잇 4. 조선대(造船臺); [부두의 돌제(突堤) 사이의] 정박소
give someone the slip, escape from someone.
[熟] …을 따돌리다

slip² [slip] *n.* [C] **1.** a long, thin piece of paper, wood, etc. **2.** a small branch, stem, or twig cut from a plant, used for planting. **3.** a young, thin person.
—[名] 1. 가느다란 종잇조각; 가는 나뭇조각 2. 접지(接枝) 3. 호리호리한 아이

slip·cov·er [slípkʌvər] *n.* [C] a cloth cover for a chair, a sofa, etc.
—[名] [의자 따위의] 덮개, 커버

slip knot [́ ̀] *n.* a knot made to slip along the string
—[名] 잡아당기면 쉬 풀리는 매듭

around which it is formed.

‡ slip·per [slípər] *n.* [C] a light, low shoe for house wear. —[名] 슬리퍼

*** slip·per·y** [slípəri] *adj.* (**-per·i·er, -per·i·est**) **1.** (of a road) likely to cause slipping because of slime or smoothness. **2.** that cannot be caught easily; not trustworthy. —[形] 1. [길 따위가] 미끄러운 2. 쉽게 잡을 수 없는; 믿을 수 없는

slip·shod [slípʃɑ̀d / -ʃɔ̀d] *adj.* **1.** wearing shoes worn down at the heels. **2.** rubbing the feet along the ground when walking. **3.** careless; untidy. —[形] 1. 뒤축이 닳은 신을 신은 2. 질질 끌며 걷는 3. 되는 대로의; 단정치 못한

slit [slit] *vt.* (**slit, slit·ting**) **1.** make a long cut or opening in (something). **2.** cut or tear (something) into long strips. **—*n.*** [C] a long, straight cut or opening. —[他] 1. …을 째어 가르다, …에 벤 자국을 내다 2. …을 가느다랗게 베다 —[名] 길게 베인 상처(자국)

slith·er [slíðər] *vi.* move with a sliding motion. —[自] 주르르 미끄러지다

sliv·er [slívər] *n.* [C] a long, thin piece of wood, glass, etc. **—*vt., vi.*** split or break (something) into slender fragments. —[名] [재목 따위의] 쪼개진 조각 —[他][自] […을] 길쭉하게 베다, 째다, 쪼개다; 째지다, 갈라지다

slob·ber [slɑ́bər / slɔ́bə] *vi.* **1.** let saliva flow out of the mouth; soil with saliva. **2.** talk sentimentally or emotionally. **—*vt.*** wet (something) with saliva. **—*n.*** [U] **1.** saliva. **2.** sentimental talk. —[自] 1. 침을 흘리다, 침으로 더러워지다 2. 넋두리를 늘어놓다 —[他] …을 침으로 더럽히다 —[名] 1. 침, 타액(唾液) 2. 넋두리

sloe [slou] *n.* [C] a shrub with a small, plumlike fruit; the fruit. —[名] 인목(橉木)[의 열매]

slog [slɑg / slɔg] *vt., vi.* (**slogged, slog·ging**) (in boxing, cricket, etc.) hit hard. **—*n.*** [C] a hard hit. —[他][自] [복싱·크리켓에서] 강타하다 —[名] 강타

slo·gan [slóugən] *n.* [C] **1.** a word or phrase used by a party or group as a motto. **2.** a war cry; a battle cry. —[名] 1. 슬로우건, 표어; 주의, 주장 2. 함성

sloop [slu:p] *n.* [C] a sailboat with a single mast. ⇒fig. —[名] 외돛대의 돛배, 슬루우프형의 배

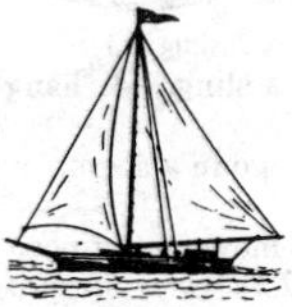

[sloop]

slop [slɑp / slɔp] *n.* **1.** [C] water or other liquid carelessly spilled or splashed about. **2.** 《often *pl.*》 dirty water from a kitchen. **3.** 《often *pl.*》 waste matter from a kitchen used as food for animals. **4.** 《often *pl.*》 weak, thin or poor liquid food. **—*vt.* 1.** soil (something) by letting liquid fall upon it. **2.** spill or splash (water). **—*vi.* 1.** spill or splash water. **2.** (of water) spill or splash out. **3.** walk or go through muddy water. —[名] 1. 쏟아진 물 2. 구정물 3. 부엌의 쓰레기, 구정물 4. 유동식(流動食)(죽 따위) —[他] 1. 물 따위를 엎질러서 …을 더럽히다 2. [물]을 쏟다 —[自] 1. 물을 엎지르다(튀기다) 2. [물이] 엎질러지다, 튀다 3. 진창 속을 걷다

slop basin [ˊ ˋˊ] *n.* a basin used to empty waste matter from teacups, etc, at table; a slop bowl. —[名] 물 버리는 그릇

‡ slope [sloup] *n.* **1.** [C] a slanting line or surface which goes upwards or downwards. **2.** [U][C] the amount or degree of a slope. **—*vt.*** cause (something) to go up or down at an angle. **—*vi.*** go up and down at an angle. —[名] 1. 경사, 사면, 비탈 2. 경사도, 구배(勾配) —[他] …을 경사지게 하다 —[自] 경사지다, 비탈지다

slop·py [slɑ́pi / slɔ́p-] *adj.* (**-pi·er, -pi·est**) **1.** wet; muddy. **2.** splashed or soiled with liquid. **3.** careless; untidy. ¶~ *clothes.* **4.** (*colloq.*) sentimental; silly. —[形] 1. 묽은; 진창의 2. 물을 엎지른 자국이 있는 3. 단정치 못한 4. 《口》 감상적(感傷的)인

slot [slɑt / slɔt] *n.* [C] a straight, narrow opening. ¶*a mail ~ in the door / a ~ for a penny.*① **—*vt.*** (**slot·ted, slot·ting**) make a slot or slots in (something). —[名] 홈; 갸름한 구멍 ¶①[자동 판매기의] 요금 넣는 구멍 —[他] …에 홈을 파다; 구멍을 내다

sloth [slouθ] *n.* **1.** [U] laziness; idleness. **2.** [C] a South American animal which is very slow in moving and which lives in trees, hanging upside down from the branches. ⇒fig. —[名] 1. 태만, 게으름 2. 게으름뱅이

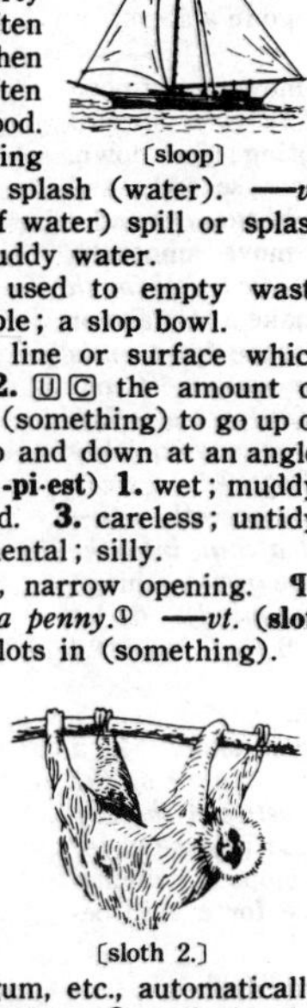

[sloth 2.]

sloth·ful [slóuθf(u)l] *adj.* lazy; idle. —[形] 게으른, 태만한, 나태한

slot machine [ˊ ˋˊ] *n.* **1.** a machine which sells peanuts, gum, etc., automatically when a coin is dropped into a slot. **2.** a device for gambling. —[名] 1. 자동 판매기 2. 자동 도박기

slouch [slautʃ] *vi.* **1.** walk, stand or sit with the head or shoulders bent forward. **2.** bend downward, like a halfdead plant. **—*vt.*** cause (something) to bend down- —[自] 1. 앞으로 수그리고 걷다(서다, 앉다) 2. 앞으로 숙이다, 구부리다 —[他] …을 꾸부리다, 수그리다 —[名] 1. 앞으

S

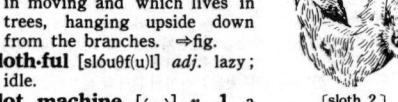

ward. —*n.* [C] **1.** an act or state of bending the head or shoulders downward. **2.** a lazy person.
로 수그림 2. 게으름뱅이

slouch·y [sláutʃi] *adj.* (**slouch·i·er, slouch·i·est**) slouching in an awkward manner; untidy.
—[形] 앞으로 수그린; 단정치 못한

slough[1] [slau →1.] *n.* [C] **1.** [*U.S.* slu:] a deep, muddy place; a marsh. **2.** a condition of helplessness; a hopeless situation.
—[名] 1. 수렁, 늪 2. 절망의 구렁텅이, 궁지

slough[2] [slʌf] *n.* [C] **1.** the old skin cast off by snakes and certain other animals. **2.** a layer of dead skin that drops off as a wound gets well. —*vi., vt.* drop off.
—[名] 1. [뱀 따위의] 허물 2. [헌데], 딱지 —[自][他] 허물벗다, …을 벗어 버리다

slov·en [slʌ́v(ə)n] *n.* [C] a person who is careless in his appearance, habits, etc.
—[名] 단정치 못한 사람

slov·en·li·ness [slʌ́v(ə)nlinis] *n.* [U] the state of being slovenly.
—[名] 단정치 못함, 지저분함

slov·en·ly [slʌ́v(ə)nli] *adj.* (**-li·er, -li·est**) untidy; careless in appearance, etc. —*adv.* in a slovenly manner.
—[形] 단정치 못한, 게으른, 지저분한
—[副] 지저분하게

‡**slow** [slou] *adj.* **1.** not quick in motion; not rapid; taking much time; not hurrying. ¶*a ~ journey / a ~ train / a ~ fire*① / *He is ~ to anger.*② / (*proverb*) *Slow and steady wins the race.*③ **2.** later than the correct time. ↔fast ¶*This watch is two minutes ~.* **3.** dull in mind; not clever. ¶*a rather ~ girl.* **4.** not interesting; dull; not active. ¶*a ~ game / a ~ town.*
—[形] 1. 느린, 더딘; 시간이 걸리는; 허둥대지 않는 ¶①약한 불/②그는 좀처럼 성을 안 낸다/③《俚》느려도 꾸준하면 이긴다 2. [시계가] 더디 가는 3. 둔한, 굼뜬 4. 재미없는; 지루한; 활기없는

—*adv.* in a slow manner. ¶*How ~ you read! / Do speak slower.*
—[副] 느리게, 더디게

—*vt.* make (something) slow or slower. —*vi.* become slow or slower.
—[他] …의 속도를 떨어뜨리다 —[自] 속도를 떨어뜨리다

slow down (or ***up***), make or become gradually slower.
[熟] [속력을] 떨어뜨리다, 떨어지다

‡**slow·ly** [slóuli] *adv.* not quickly.
—[副] 느리게, 천천히

slow·ness [slóunis] *n.* [U] the state or quality of being slow.
—[名] 느림, 더딤

sludge [slʌdʒ] *n.* [U] **1.** soft mud. **2.** solid matter that sinks to the bottom of water.
—[名] 1. 진창 2. 침전물

sludg·y [slʌ́dʒi] *adj.* (**sludg·i·er, sludg·i·est**) of soft mud; full of mud.
—[形] 진흙투성이의, 진창의

slue [slu:] *n.* =slough.[1]

slug[1] [slʌg] *n.* [C] **1.** an animal like a snail, but without a shell. **2.** a person or thing that moves slowly. **3.** a lump of metal. **4.** a small piece of lead or other metal for firing from a gun.
—[名] 1. 태괄충(胎括蟲) 2. 굼뜬 것(사람·동물·차) 3. 금속 덩어리 4. 작은 탄환

slug[2] [slʌg] *n.* [C] a hard hit or blow with a fist. —*vt.* (**slug·ged, slug·ging**) strike or hit (something) hard with a fist.
—[名] 강타 —[他] …을 강타하다

slug·gard [slʌ́gərd] *n.* [C] a person who is idle or lazy. —*adj.* idle; lazy.
—[名] 게으름뱅이 —[形] 게으른

slug·gish [slʌ́giʃ] *adj.* **1.** slow-moving. **2.** not active. **3.** idle; lazy. ▷**slug·gish·ly** [-li] *adv.* —**slug·gish·ness** [-nis] *n.*
—[形] 1. 느린 2. 둔한; 부진한, 활발치 못한 3. 게으른

sluice [slu:s] *n.* [C] **1.** an artificial channel for controlling the water of a river, a lake, etc. **2.** a gate or valve for opening and closing such a channel; a sluice gate. **3.** a device through which water is run for washing gold ore, etc. —*vt.* **1.** let out (water) by opening a sluice. **2.** wash (gold ore) with water flowing in a sluice. **3.** carry (something) in a sluice. —*vi.* run or flow in a sluice.
—[名] 1. 수로(水路); 방수로(放水路) 2. 수문 3. [광산의] 세광통(洗鑛樋)
—[他] 1. 수문을 열어 [물]을 방출하다 2. 홈통에 물을 흘려 [금광석(金鑛石)]을 씻다 3. …을 수로로 나르다 —[自] [물이 수로를] 흐르다

sluice gate [∠ ∠] *n.* a gate in an artificial passage for water, used to control its flow. ⇒fig.
—[名] 수문

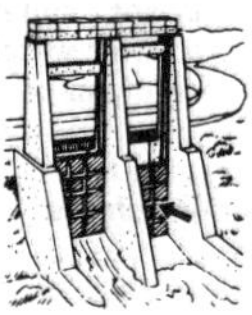
[sluice gate]

slum [slʌm] *n.* [C] (often *pl.*) a crowded part of a city or town where the houses are dirty and unhealthy.
—[名] 빈민가, 빈민굴

***slum·ber** [slʌ́mbər] *vi.* **1.** sleep. **2.** be in a state of rest, inactivity or sleeping. ¶*The volcano had slumbered for several years.*① —*vt.* spend (time) in sleep. —*n.* [U][C] **1.** sleep. **2.** the state of rest or inactivity.
—[自] 1. 자다, 선잠자다 2. 잠자는 것 같은 휴식상태에 있다 ¶①그 화산은 수년간 활동을 중지하고 있었다 —[他] 잠자며 [시간]을 보내다 —[名] 1. 잠 2. 잠과 같은 휴식상태

slum·ber·er [slʌ́mbərər] *n.* [C] a person who slumbers. —[名] 잠자는 사람

slum·ber·ous [slʌ́mb(ə)rəs] *adj.* causing sleep; sleepy. —[形] 졸음이 도는; 졸린

slum·brous [slʌ́mbrəs] *adj.* =slumberous.

slump [slʌmp] *vi.* drop or sink down suddenly and heavily. **—*n.*** [C] **1.** the act of sinking down. ¶*a ~ into mud.*① **2.** a sudden drop in prices or trade. ¶*Business is a ~ in Feb. and Aug.* **3.** loss of interest. —[自] 푹 빠지다 —[名] 1. 푹 빠지기 ¶①진창에 빠지기 2. [주가(株價) 따위의] 폭락, 부진 3. 흥미의 상실, 의기소침

slung [slʌŋ] *v.* pt. and pp. of **sling**.

slunk [slʌŋk] *v.* pt. and pp. of **slink**.

slur [slə:*r*] *vt.* (**slurred, slur·ring**) **1.** pass over (something) quickly and lightly. **2.** pronounce (a word) hastily and indistinctly when speaking. **3.** (*Music.*) sing or play (two tones) in a smooth or connected way. **—*n.*** [C] **1.** a hasty and indistinct pronunciation or way of pronunciation. ¶*talk with a ~.* **2.** (*Music*) a mark for two or more notes to be sung or played smoothly. ⇒fig. **3.** anything harmful to a person's reputation. —[他] 1. …을 재빨리 휙 지나가다; 못 보고 넘어가다 2. …을 똑똑치 않게 발음하다 3. [두 개의 음표]를 잇대어 노래(연주)하다 —[名] 1. 불명료한 발음 2. 《樂》 연결(선), 슬러 3. 오명, 치욕

[slur 2.]

slush [slʌʃ] *n.* [U] soft mud; melted snow. —[名] 진창; 녹은 눈

slush·y [slʌ́ʃi] *adj.* (**slush·i·er, slush·i·est**) of slush; full of slush. —[形] 진창의; 눈이 녹은

slut [slʌt] *n.* [C] a dirty, careless woman. —[名] 단정치 못한 여자

slut·tish [slʌ́tiʃ] *adj.* careless; untidy. —[形] 단정치 못한

* **sly** [slai] *adj.* (**sli·er** or **sly·er, sli·est** or **sly·est**) **1.** cunning; full of tricks; apt to behave secretly. **2.** playful in an annoying way. —[形] 1. 교활한, 엉큼한, 간교한 2. 장난꾸러기의

on (or ***upon***) ***the sly,*** secretly. [熟] 숨어서, 몰래

sly·ly [sláili] *adv.* in a sly manner; secretly. —[副] 교활하게, 몰래

smack[1] [smæk] *n.* [C] **1.** a slight taste or flavor. **2.** a bit; a slight appearance; a suggestion. ¶*a ~ of Europe.* **—*vi.*** have a taste; suggest. 《*~ of* something》 —[名] 1. 맛, 향기, 풍미 2. 조금, 기미, …다운 곳 —[自] …의 맛이 나다; 기미가 있다

smack[2] [smæk] *n.* [C] **1.** a quick, sharp noise made with the lips as a sign of enjoying food. **2.** a quick blow with a whip; the sound of hitting by the flat of the hand. **3.** a loud kiss. **—*vt.* 1.** make a sharp sound with (the lips) as a sign of enjoying food. **2.** hit (someone or something) loudly with the flat of the hand. —[名] 1. 입맛다시기 2. 채찍 소리, 찰싹 때리는 소리 3. 쪽하는 키스 —[他] 1. 쩝쩝 입맛을 다시다 2. …을 찰싹하고 때리다

smack[3] [smæk] *n.* [C] a small sailing boat with only one sail. —[名] 외돛대의 종범(縱帆) 어선

smack·ing [smǽkiŋ] *adj.* lively; sharp. —[形] 활기 있는, 격렬한

‡ **small** [smɔ:l] *adj.* **1.** little in size, degree, amount, etc; not large. ¶*a ~ child / ~ money / The loss is ~.*① **2.** of little worth or value; unimportant. ¶*a ~ mistake.*② **3.** narrow-minded; humble; mean. ¶*a ~ nature.* —[形] 1. 작은; 적은; 소규모의 ¶①손실은 적다 2. 중요하지 않은 ¶②사소한 잘못 3. 도량이 좁은; 비열한

1) ***in a small way,*** on a small scale.
2) ***no small,*** a great.
[熟] 1)소규모로 2)큰; 대단한

small arms [⌐ ⌐] *n. pl.* weapons that can be easily carried by a man, such as a rifle or a pistol. —[名] 휴대 병기(소총·권총류)

small change [⌐ ⌐] *n.* **1.** coins which have little value. **2.** a person or thing that is not important. —[名] 1. 잔돈 2. 시시한 사람(것)

small holder [⌐ ⌐–] *n.* (*Brit.*) a farmer who owns or rents a small piece of land for a farm. —[名] 소규모의 자작농

small holding [⌐ ⌐–] *n.* a small farm. —[名] 소규모의 자작농지

small hours [⌐ ⌐] *n. pl.* 《*the ~*》 the early hours of the morning just after midnight. —[名] 새벽 한 시부터 세 시까지

small letter [⌐ ⌐–] *n.* an ordinary letter; a letter which is not capital. —[名] 소문자

small-mind·ed [smɔ́:lmáindid] *adj.* narrow-minded; limited in one's view of life; mean. —[形] 도량이 좁은; 인색한

small·ness [smɔ́:lnis] *n.* [U] the state or quality of being small in size, quantity, etc; small-mindedness. —[名] 작음, 근소; 옹졸

small·pox [smɔ́:lpàks / -pɔ̀ks] *n.* [U] a dangerous, easily-spreading disease that causes spots on the skin. —[名] 천연두

‡ **smart** [smɑ:rt] *adj.* **1.** (of a blow or pain) severe; sharp. **2.** quick; lively. ¶*a ~ walk.* **3.** skillful; clever; intelligent. **4.** clever but dishonest. **5.** neat; well-dressed; —[形] 1. 날카로운, 격렬한; 찌르는 듯한 2. 빠른, 민첩한 3. 솜씨있는, 능숙한; 영리한 4. 건방진, 약은 5. 말쑥한, 맵시있

smarten [1081] **smirk**

fashionable. ¶*a ~ dress.*
—*vi.* **1.** feel a sharp pain on the surface of the skin. ¶*My face smarts with the cold wind.* **2.** suffer mental pain. —*n.* ⓒ **1.** a lively, sharp pain. **2.** severe suffering and sorrow. ⌈become smart.
smart·en [smɑ́rtn] *vt.* make (something) smart. —*vi.*
smart·ly [smɑ́rtli] *adv.* in a smart way.
* **smash** [smæʃ] *vt.* **1.** break (something) into pieces with violence. **2.** hit; give a blow to (something or someone). **3.** crush; ruin, esp. financially. **4.** (*Tennis*) hit (the ball) with a hard, fast, overhand stroke. —*vi.* **1.** be broken into many pieces. **2.** rush against or into something violently. 《*~ into* something》 ¶*The car smashed into the wall.* **3.** become ruined.
—*n.* ⓒ **1.** an act or a sound of breaking to pieces. **2.** a violent accident. **3.** a complete ruin in business. **4.** (*Tennis*) a hard, fast, overhand stroke.
go (or *come*) *to smash,* be ruined.
—*adv.* with a smash.
smash·ing [smǽʃiŋ] *adj.* so strong and powerful as to shatter or destroy something extraordinary.
smash-up [smǽʃʌp] *n.* ⓒ a violent accident between motor vehicles; a failure in business; a great misfortune.
smat·ter·er [smǽtərər] *n.* ⓒ a person with little knowledge of something. ⌈something.
smat·ter·ing [smǽt(ə)riŋ] *n.* 《*a ~*》 little knowledge of
smear [smiər] *vt.* **1.** spread or spoil (something) with anything dirty, sticky, or greasy. ¶*~ one's fingers with milk; ~ milk on one's fingers.* **2.** harm or injure the good reputation of (someone), esp. falsely. —*n.* ⓒ **1.** a dirty mark made by smearing. **2.** an act of harming a reputation. ⌈full of dirty spots.
smear·y [smíəri] *adj.* (**smear·i·er, smear·i·est**) smeared;
‡ **smell** [smel] *v.* (**smelled** or **smelt**) *vt.* get the odor of (something) through the nose. ¶*I ~ something burning.*
—*vi.* **1.** try to get an odor through the nose. 《*~ at* something》 ¶*~ at a flower.* **2.** have an odor. 《*~ of* something》 ¶*~ good (bad)*? | *He smells of fish.*
smell out, find out another's secret, etc.
—*n.* **1.** ⓤ the sense of smell. ¶*A dog has keen ~.* **2.** ⓤⓒ odor; scent. **3.** ⓒ 《*sing.* only》 an act of smelling.
smelt[1] [smelt] *vt.* melt (ore or metal) so as to separate the metal out of it; refine (impure metal) by melting.
‡ **smelt**[2] [smelt] *v.* pt. and pp. of **smell**.
smelt·er [sméltər] *n.* ⓒ a person who smelts ores or metals; a place where ores and metals are smelted.
‡ **smile** [smail] *vi.* **1.** show pleasure or happiness in the face. **2.** present a cheerful aspect. ¶*a smiling landscape.* **3.** look with favor; look pleasant. ¶*Fortune smiled on her future.* —*vt.* **1.** express (something) by smiling. **2.** change or affect (someone) by smiling. 《*~ someone into* or *out of*》 ¶*She smiled me out of my anger.* **3.** give (a smile). ⇒usage ⌈smiling.
1) *smile away,* drive or put away (tears, etc.) by
2) *smile on* (or *upon*), show favor to (someone); look on (someone) with approval. ⌈smiling face.
—*n.* ⓒ **1.** an act of smiling; an ironical smile. **2.** a
smil·ing [smáiliŋ] *adj.* showing smiles; looking pleasant; looking favorable. ▷**smil·ing·ly** [-li] *adv.*
smirch [smə:rtʃ] *vt.* make (something) dirty; dishonor. —*n.* ⓒ a dirty mark.
smirk [smə:rk] *n.* ⓒ an affected smile; a self-satisfied smile. —*vi.* smile in this way.

는; 유행의
—自 1. [피부가] 쓰리다 2. 피로와하다

—名 1. 쓰림, 아픔, 쑤심 2. 고뇌, 비통

—他 …을 말쑥하게 하다 —自 깨끗
—副 멋지게; 기민하게 ⌊해지다
—他 1. …을 산산이 부수다, 쪼개다 2. …을 때리다 3. …을 참패시키다; 파산시키다 4. [공]을 스매시하다 —自 1. 산산조각이 되다 2. 충돌하다 ¶①차는 벽에 충돌했다 3. 파산하다

—名 1. 분쇄[하는 소리] 2. 대충돌 3. 전멸, 파산 4. 《庭球》 스매시

熟 파산(파멸)하다
—副 꽝, 와지끈, 정면으로
—形 분쇄하는, 맹렬한

—名 분쇄; 대충돌; 실패; 파산; 재난

—名 [지식 따위]를 어설피 아는 사람

—名 어설피 아는 지식
—他 1. 기름 따위를 …에 문지르다, …을 [기름으로] 더럽히다 ¶①손가락을 밀크로 더럽히다 2. [명예 따위]를 더럽히다 —名 1. 더럼, 얼룩 2. [명예 따위를] 더럽히기

—形 더러워진, 얼룩투성이의
—他 …의 냄새를 맡다 ¶①무엇인가 타는 내가 난다 —自 1. 냄새 맡다 ¶②꽃의 향기를 맡다 2. 냄새가 나다 ¶③좋은(나쁜) 냄새가 나다/④그에게서는 생선 냄새가 난다
熟 [비밀 따위]를 알아내다
—名 1. 후각(嗅覺) 2. 냄새; 향기 3. 냄새맡기

—他 [금속]을 용해하다, 제련하다

—名 제련자, 제련소

—自 1. 미소하다, 방긋 웃다 2. 환하다 ¶①밝은 풍경 3. [운·기회가] 열리다, 트이다 ¶②그녀에게는 운이 틔었다
—他 1. …을 우으로 나타내다 2. 미소하여 …시키다 3. …한 웃음을 웃다 usage 동족 목적어와 함께 쓰임

熟 1)[눈물]을 웃음으로 없애다 2)…에 호의를 보이다; [운이] …에게 트이다
—名 1. 미소; 냉소, 조소 2. 웃는 얼굴
—形 미소하는; 환한; 호의적인

—他 …을 더럽히다; [남의 명예]를 더럽히다 —名 오점
—名 억지웃음, 능글맞은 웃음 —自 억지웃음을 웃다

smit [smit] *v.* pp. of **smite.**

* **smite** [smait] *vt.* (**smote, smit·ten** or **smit**) **1.** strike hard. **2.** destroy; kill. **3.** attack (someone or something) with force. ¶*The plague smote the entire country.*① **4.** move the feelings of (someone) with a strong feeling such as love, fear, or grief. **—*vi.*** come with force. 《~ *upon* something》 **—*n.*** [C] a heavy blow; trial.
—[他] 1. …을 세게 치다 2. …을 멸망시키다, 죽이다 3. [병 따위가] 덮치다 ¶①페스트가 온 나라를 덮쳤다 4. …의 양심을 가책하다, 괴롭히다 —[自] 치다, 강타하다 —[名] 강타; 시도

smith [smiθ] *n.* [C] a person who makes things of metal with a hammer and an anvil.
—[名] 대장장이, 금속 세공인

smith·y [smíθi, smíði] *n.* [C] (pl. **smith·ies**) a blacksmith's workshop.
—[名] 대장간

smit·ten [smítn] *v.* pp. of **smite.**

smock [smɑk / smɔk] *n.* [C] a long loose outer garment for protecting clothing. **—*vt.*** trim or ornament (a dress, a blouse, etc.) with smocking.
—[名] 겉옷, 작업복 —[他] …을 주름으로 장식하다

smock·ing [smɑ́kiŋ / smɔ́k-] *n.* [U] an ornamental gather for smocks, dresses, etc. ⇨fig.
—[名] 장식 주름

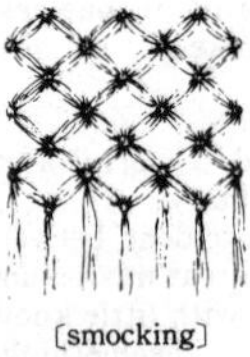
[smocking]

smog [smɑg, smɔ:g / smɔg] *n.* [U] a mixture of smoke and fog in the air, esp. over a city.
—[名] 연기 섞인 안개, 연무(煙霧)

: **smoke** [smouk] *n.* **1.** [U] cloud-like gas that rises when something burns. ¶*There is no ~ without fire.*① **2.** anything like smoke, such as vapor, fog, etc. **3.** 《*sing.* only》 the act of smoking. ¶***have a ~.***② **4.** [C] a cigar; a cigarette.
end in smoke, end in failure; have no solid result.
—*vt.* 1. dry (meat, fish, etc.) by smoke. **2.** breathe in and out the smoke of (tobacco). **3.** make (someone or something) by forcing in smoke. 《~ *out* something》 **—*vi.* 1.** give off smoke, esp. more than usual. **2.** give off something like smoke. **3.** breathe in and out the smoke of tobacco.
—[名] 1. 연기 ¶①불 안 땐 굴뚝에 연기 나랴? 2. 연기 모양의 것 3. 담배 한 대; 끽연 ¶②한 대 피우다 4. 엽궐련, 궐련
[熟] 실패로 끝나다, 헛수고가 되다
—[他] 1. …을 훈제(燻製)하다 2. [담배]를 피우다 3. …을 연기로 소독하다
—[自] 1. 연기를 피우다 2. 내다, 김이 나다 3. 담배 피우다

smoke-dried [smóukdràid] *adj.* dried in smoke.
—[形] 훈제(燻製)의

smoke·house [smóukhàus] *n.* [C] a place where meat, fish, etc., are smoked.
—[名] [육류의] 훈제장(실)

smoke·less [smóuklis] *adj.* producing or having no smoke.
—[形] 연기가 없는(안 나는)

smok·er [smóukər] *n.* [C] **1.** a person who smokes tobacco. **2.** a railway car, or a part of one, where a person may smoke.
—[名] 1. 끽연자 2. 끽연차

smoke screen [ˊ ˋ] *n.* a cloud of thick smoke for hiding ships, airplanes, etc. from the enemy.
—[名] 연막

smoke·stack [smóukstæ̀k] *n.* [C] a tall chimney of a factory, a ship, etc.
—[名] 기선의 굴뚝

smok·ing room [smóukiŋrù(:)m] *n.* a room for smoking or in which smoking is permitted.
—[名] 끽연실

smok·y [smóuki] *adj.* (**smok·i·er, smok·i·est**) **1.** giving off much smoke. **2.** full of smoke. **3.** like smoke in color, smell, etc.
—[形] 1. 연기나는, 내는 2. 연기가 많은 3. 연기빛의, [냄새가] 연기 같은

smol·der, *Brit.* **smoul-** [smóuldər] *vi.* **1.** burn or give out smoke slowly without any flame. **2.** (of feelings, etc.) exist in one's heart, though showing little outward sign. **—*n.*** [C] the state of burning slowly without any flame.
—[自] 1. 내다, 그을다 2. [감정이] 마음속에 쌓이다
—[名] 연기, 내는 불

: **smooth** [smu:ð] *adj.* **1.** not rough; having an even surface. **2.** gently and easily moving; without trouble. **3.** mild; calm. ¶*The sea is ~.* **4.** (of speech) flowing; fluent. ¶*a smooth-tongued man.*①
—*vt.* 1. make (something) flat or even; polish. **2.** make (something) easy or calm; regulate. **3.** refine. **—*vi.*** become smooth, calm, or quiet.
1) ***smooth away*** (=*get rid of*) *difficulties, etc.*
2) ***smooth down,*** make or become calm.
▷**smooth·ness** [-nis] *n.*
—[形] 1. 매끄러운; 평평한 2. 원활히 움직이는; 순조로운; [사물이] 술술 되어 가는 3. 순한, 온화한 4. 유창한 ¶①구변 좋은 사람
—[他] 1. …을 매끄럽게 하다; 닦다 2. …을 용이하게 하다; 원활히 하다 3. …을 세련되게 하다 —[自] 매끄러워지다; 온화해지다
[熟] 1) [곤란 따위]를 제거하다 2) 평온하게 하다(되다)

smooth-faced [smú:ðféist] *adj.* **1.** (of a face) having a smooth surface; beardless; clean-shaven. **2.** agreeable in speech and manners, but with little sincerity.
—[形] 1. 말끔히 면도한; 수염이 없는 2. 사근사근한; 위선적인

* **smooth·ly** [smú:ðli] *adv.* in a smooth manner; fluently.
—[副] 매끄럽게; 온화하게; 유창하게

smooth-spo·ken [smú:ðspóuk(ə)n] *adj.* speaking agreeably and pleasantly, but not sincerely.
—[形] 말주변이 있는, 구변 좋은

smooth-tongued [smú:ðtʌ́ŋd] *adj.* =smooth-spoken.

* **smote** [smout] *v.* pt. of **smite**.

smoth·er [smʌ́ðər] *vt.* **1.** make it difficult for (someone) to breathe; kill (someone) by stopping or preventing the breath. **2.** put out (a fire) by covering it thickly. **3.** conceal; (of feelings, etc.) suppress. **—*vi.*** have difficulty in breathing.
—[他] 1. …을 숨차게 하다, 질식시키다, 질식시켜 죽이다 2. [불]을 묻다, 덮어 끄다 3. …을 은폐하다; [감정 따위]를 억제하다 —[自] 질식하다

smoul·der [smóuldər] *v., n.* (*Brit.*) =smolder.

smudge [smʌdʒ] *n.* [C] **1.** a dirty mark; a spot. **2.** (chiefly *U.S.*) a smoldering fire for driving away insects, etc. **—*vt.* 1.** make dirty marks on (something). **2.** (chiefly *U.S.*) give out smoke to drive away insects from (a place). **—*vi.*** become dirty.
—[名] 1. 더럼, 얼룩 2. 《美》 모깃불 —[他] 1. …을 더럽히다 2. …에 모깃불을 놓다 —[自] 더러워지다

smudg·y [smʌ́dʒi] *adj.* (**smudg·i·er, smudg·i·est**) marked with smudges.
—[形] 더러워진, 그을은

smug [smʌg] *adj.* (**smug·ger, smug·gest**) very pleased with oneself; narrow-minded; self-satisfied.
—[形] 점잔빼는, 잘난 체하는

smug·gle [smʌ́gl] *vt.* bring (goods) into or take (goods) out of a country secretly, without paying custom duties; carry secretly. ¶*He tried to ~ his puppy into his bedroom.* **—*vi.*** import or export secretly.
—[他] …을 밀수출(밀수입)하다; 몰래 들여오다(내가다) —[自] 밀수입(밀수출)하다

smug·gler [smʌ́glər] *n.* [C] **1.** a person who smuggles. **2.** a ship used for smuggling.
—[名] 1. 밀수꾼 2. 밀수선

smut [smʌt] *n.* **1.** [C] a mass of dirt or a black substance in one smoke, etc; a dirty spot. **2.** [U] words or talk that cause a person to feel shame. **3.** [U] a disease of wheat in which the ears of grain are ruined.
—[名] 1. [검댕 따위의] 덩어리; 더럼 2. 음담패설 3. [보리의] 흑수병(黑穗病)

—*v.* (**smut·ted, smut·ting**) *vt.* make (something) dirty or black. **—*vi.*** become dirty or black; be attacked by the disease of smut.
—[他] …을 더럽히다 —[自] 더러워지다, 검게 되다; 흑수병에 걸리다

smut·ty [smʌ́ti] *adj.* (**-ti·er, -ti·est**) **1.** soiled with soot, dirt, etc. **2.** attacked by the plant disease of smut.
—[形] 1. 더러워진, 그을은 2. 흑수병에 걸린

snack [snæk] *n.* [C] **1.** a light meal taken in a hurry. **2.** something which is divided for a person; a share. ¶*go snacks.*①
—[名] 1. 경식사, 간단한 식사 2. 몫 ¶①몫으로 나누다

snag [snæg] *n.* [C] **1.** a tree hidden in a river. **2.** unexpected difficulties.
—[名] 1. 물에 잠긴 나무 2. 뜻밖의 장애

snail [sneil] *n.* [C] **1.** a small animal with a spiral shell on its back that crawls very slowly. ¶*at a snail's pace.*① **2.** a slow-moving person.
—[名] 1. 달팽이 ¶①느릿느릿 2. 굼뜬 사람

* **snake** [sneik] *n.* [C] **1.** a long, crawling animal without legs. ¶*have snakes in one's boots*① / *raise* (or *wake*) *snakes.*② **2.** an unsincere or double-faced person. **—*vi.*** move or wind like a snake.
—[名] 1. 뱀 ¶①곤드레만드레 취하다/②소동을 일으키다 2. 음흉한 사람 —[自] 뱀처럼 꿈틀꿈틀 움직이다

snake charmer [´ ⌣ ⌣] *n.* a person who controls snakes by music.
—[名] 뱀을 부리는 사람

snak·y [snéiki] *adj.* (**snak·i·er, snak·i·est**) **1.** of or like a snake. **2.** twisting; winding. **3.** untrustworthy.
—[形] 1. 뱀의(같은) 2. 꾸불꾸불한 3. 음험한

‡ **snap** [snæp] *v.* (**snapped, snap·ping**) *vi.* **1.** break suddenly with a sharp sound. ¶*The branch snapped under the heavy snows.* **2.** make a sharp, sudden sound. ¶*The wood snapped as it burned.*① **3.** be shut or opened with a sharp sound. ¶*The door snapped behind me.*② **4.** say sharply or angrily. **5.** move quickly. **—*vt.* 1.** break (something) suddenly and with a sharp sound. **2.** cause (something) to make a short, sharp sound. ¶*~ on* (*off*) *the switch.* **3.** bite suddenly. **4.** take a photograph of (something) instantly.
—[自] 1. 뚝 부러지다, 툭 끊어지다 2. 찰칵(탕)하고 소리나다 ¶①나무가 타면서 탕탕 소리났다 3. 탕하고 닫히다(열리다) ¶②문이 내 뒤에서 쾅하고 닫혔다 4. 딱딱거리다 5. 재빨리 움직이다 —[他] 1. …을 딱하고 꺾다; …이 쟁그렁하고 깨지다 2. …을 탕(찰깍)하고 소리내다 3. …을 물어뜯다 4. …의 스냅사진을 찍다.

—*n.* [C] **1.** an act of snapping. **2.** a sharp, short sound. ¶*shut a window with a ~.* **3.** a sudden bite. **4.** a fastener that closes with a snapping sound. **5.** a pho-
—[名] 1. 뚝하고 부러뜨리기 2. 탕(찰깍)하는 소리 3. 갑자기 물어뜯기 4. 찰깍하고 채워지는 멈춤쇠 5. 스냅사진

S

snappish

tograph taken instantly; a snapshot. **6.** weather which has suddenly changed. ¶*a cold ~.*① —*adj.* sudden; unexpected. ¶*a ~ decision.* —*adv.* with a sharp and sudden sound.

snap·pish [snǽpiʃ] *adj.* **1.** likely to bite. **2.** sharp in speech; apt to be irritated.

snap·py [snǽpi] *adj.* (**-pi·er, -pi·est**) **1.** apt to bite. **2.** (*colloq.*) lively; bright. **3.** irritable.

snap·shot [snǽpʃɑt / -ʃɔt] *n.* ⓒ **1.** a photograph taken quickly. **2.** a quick shot.

*** snare** [snɛər] *n.* ⓒ **1.** a trap, often made with a loop of cord or wire, for catching a small animal or bird. **2.** a thing which attracts or tempts. —*vt.* catch (a bird or an animal) with a snare.

*** snarl**¹ [snɑːrl] *vi.* **1.** (of a dog, etc.) make a low noise in the throat; show the teeth [with anger]. **2.** speak in a harsh, angry tone. (*~ at someone or something*) —*vt.* utter or say (something) in a rough, harsh voice. —*n.* ⓒ the act or sound of snarling.

snarl² [snɑːrl] *n.* ⓒ a knot; a tangle; a confused state. —*vt.* make (something) tangled or confused. —*vi.* become confused.

*** snatch** [snætʃ] *vt.* take (something) suddenly by force; get quickly. ¶*A man snatched the handbag from her hand and ran away.* | *He snatched off his hat.*① —*vi.* try to snatch. (*~ at something*) ¶*~ at a chance.* —*n.* ⓒ **1.** an act of snatching. **2.** (*often pl.*) a short time; a small amount; a piece; a bit. ¶*eat a ~*② | *short snatches of an essay* | *sleep in snatches.*③

sneak [sniːk] *vi.* **1.** come into or go out of a place; in a secret manner. **2.** act in a sly way. ¶*~ out of duty (danger).* —*vt.* **1.** carry, transfer, do, etc. (something) in a secret manner. **2.** (*colloq.*) steal. —*n.* ⓒ **1.** a cowardly, mean person. **2.** a person who tells about others' faults.

sneak·er [sníːkər] *n.* ⓒ **1.** a person who sneaks. **2.** (*pl.*) canvas shoes with soles of rubber or another light material.

sneak·ing [sníːkiŋ] *adj.* **1.** walking stealthily. **2.** mean; not open or frank. ▷**sneak·ing·ly** [-li] *adv.*

*** sneer** [sniər] *vi.* show scorn or contempt; laugh in scorn; speak ironical words. (*~ at something or someone*) —*vt.* speak to (someone) by sneering; affect (someone) in a certain condition by sneering. (*~ someone into* or *out of*) ¶*~ someone into silence.*① —*n.* ⓒ a scornful smile or remark.

sneer·ing·ly [sníəriŋli] *adv.* in a sneering way.

sneeze [sniːz] *n.* ⓒ a sudden burst of breath through the nose and mouth. —*vi.* make a sneeze.
not to be sneezed at, not to be despised.

snick·er [sníkər] *vi.* laugh in a half-suppressed way. —*n.* ⓒ such a laugh.

*** sniff** [snif] *vi.* **1.** draw air or breathe through the nose [to smell]. (*~ at something*) ¶*~ at the bottle of perfume.*① **2.** show a feeling of contempt. (*~ at someone or something*) —*vt.* **1.** make a sound while smelling (something). **2.** notice (danger, a trick, etc.) —*n.* ⓒ the act or sound of sniffing.

snif·fle [snifl] *vi.* make a sniffing sound again and again —*n.* ⓒ (*the ~s*) a loud sniffing sound; a slight cold in the nose.

snip [snip] *vt., vi.* (**snipped, snip·ping**) cut (something) by scissors with a short, quick motion. —*n.* ⓒ a single cut with scissors; a small piece [cut off].

snip

6. 날씨의 급변 ¶③갑작스러운 강추위
—❀ 갑작스러운; 예기치 못한
—❀ 푹하고; 탕하고
—❀ 1. 물려고 덤비는 2. 딱딱거리는, 성 잘 내는
—❀ 1. 물려고 덤비는 2. 원기 있는, 쾌활한 3. 성 잘 내는
—❀ 1. 스냅사진; 속사(速寫) 2. 속사(速射)
—❀ 1. 올가미, 덫 2. 유혹 —❀ …을 덫으로 잡다

—⃝ 1. 으르렁거리다; 이를 드러내고 덤비다 2. 고함치다, 고함쳐 말하다
—❀ …을 고함치다, 고함쳐 말하다
—❀ 으르렁거림, 서로 으르렁대기

—❀ 얽힘, 혼란 —❀ …을 얽히게 하다 —⃝ 얽히다

—❀ …을 잡아채다; 급히 벗다; 갑자기 얻다 ¶①그는 급히 모자를 벗었다 —⃝ 잡아채려고 하다; 덤벼들다

—❀ 1. 잡아채기, 강탈. 2. 잠깐, 한바탕 한 조각, 한 입 ¶②한 입 먹다/③ 잠깐잠깐씩 자다

—⃝ 1. 몰래 들어오다(나가다) 2. 교활하게(약게) 굴다 —❀ 1. …을 몰래 움직이다(하다) 2. [口] …을 훔치다 —❀ 1. 비열한 사람, 겁장이 2. 고자질꾼

—❀ 1. 엉큼한 짓을 하는 사람, 비열한 사람 2. 고무창을 댄 운동화

—❀ 1. 살금살금 걷는 2. 비열한; 비밀의

—❀ 비웃다, 코웃음치다; 빈정대다
—❀ …을 비웃으며 말하다; 조소하여 …시키다 ¶①조소하여 …을 입다물게 하다 —❀ 냉소, 조소; 욕지거리

—❀ 조소하여
—❀ 재채기
—⃝ 재채기하다
▨ 무시할 수 없는
—⃝ 킬킬 웃다
—❀ 킬킬 웃기

—⃝ 1. 콩콩거리며 냄새맡다, [소리를 내며] 코로 들이마시다 ¶①향수병의 냄새를 맡다 2. 코웃음치다 —❀ 1. 콩콩거리며 냄새맡다 2. [위험 따위]를 껌새채다, 눈치채다

—⃝ 콩콩거리며 냄새맡기; 코웃음
—⃝ 훌쩍훌쩍 울다
—❀ 훌쩍이며 울기; 코감기

—❀⃝ 싹독 자르다 —❀ 싹독 자르기, 가위질, 한 조각

snipe [snaip] *n.* [C] (pl. **snipe**) a bird with a long bill that lives in marshes. —*vi.* **1.** hunt this bird. **2.** shoot enemies from a hidden place. —*vt.* shoot (soldiers etc.) in this way.
—[名] 도요새 —[自] 1. 도요새 사냥을 하다 2. 저격(狙擊)하다 —[他] …을 저격하다

sniv·el [snívl] *vi.* (**-eled, -el·ing** or *Brit.* **-elled, -el·ling**) **1.** have liquid coming from the nose. **2.** cry with sniffling; complain. —*n.* [C] **1.** running liquid from the nose. **2.** a pretended grief.
—[自] 1. 코를 흘리다(훌쩍이다) 2. 훌쩍이며 울다; 불평하다 —[名] 1. 콧물 2. 건성으로 울며 슬픈 체하기

snob [snɑb / snɔb] *n.* [C] a person who too much admires persons of wealth or in a high position, and looks down on those below him.
—[名] 웃사람에게는 알랑거리고 아랫사람에게는 뻐기는 사람, 속물(俗物)

snob·ber·y [snɑ́bəri / snɔ́b-] *n.* [U] the character or state of being snobbish.
—[名] 속물근성

snob·bish [snɑ́biʃ / snɔ́b-] *adj.* of or like a snob.
—[形] 속물근성의, 신사인 체하는

snoop [snu:p] *vi.* (*colloq.*) move about secretly; search curiously. —*n.* [C] a person who snoops.
—[自] 《口》 기웃거리며 다니다 —[名] 기웃거리며 다니는 사람

snooze [snu:z] *vi.* have a short nap but not in bed; take a nap. —*n.* [C] a short nap not taken in bed.
—[自] 졸다 —[名] 선잠, 낮잠

snore [snɔ:*r*] *vi.* breathe noisily through the nose, or nose and mouth, while sleeping. —*n.* [C] the noisy sound made in snoring.
—[自] 코를 골다 —[名] 코고는 소리

snor·er [snɔ́:rər] *n.* [C] a person who habitually snores.
—[名] 코고는 사람

snort [snɔ:*r*t] *vi.* **1.** (of a horse) force the air out through the nose violently. **2.** express anger or contempt by making a harsh, noisy sound. —*vt.* talk or express (something) by a harsh, noisy sound. —*n.* [C] a harsh, noisy sound which results from breathing through the nose violently. ▷**snort·er** [-ər] *n.*
—[自] 1. [말이] 코를 울리다 2. [분노·경멸 따위를 나타내어] 코방귀를 뀌다 —[他] …을 씩씩거리며 말하다 —[名] 씩씩거리는 소리

snout [snaut] *n.* [C] **1.** (of a pig, a dog, etc.) the projecting part around nose. **2.** anything pointed like an animal's snout.
—[名] 1. [돼지·개 따위의] 코, 주둥이 2. 주둥이처럼 생긴 뾰족한 것

⁝ **snow** [snou] *n.* **1.** [U] small flakes of frozen water falling from the sky; [U][C] a fall of snow. **2.** 《often *pl.*》 a mass of snow on the ground. **3.** [U] something like snow in its whiteness, etc.; [U] (*poetic*) pure whiteness. —*vi.* drop from the sky in the form of snow; fall like snow. —*vt.* cover (something) with snow. ¶*be snowed in* (or *up, over*).①
—[名] 1. 눈; 강설 2. 적설(積雪) 3. 눈 모양의 것; 《詩》 설백(雪白) —[自] 눈이 내리다; 눈처럼 내리다 —[他] …을 눈으로 덮다 ¶①눈에 갇히다

snow·ball [snóubɔ̀:l] *n.* [C] a ball of snow packed for throwing. —*vi.* throw balls of snow.
—[名] 눈덩이, 눈뭉치 —[自] 눈덩이를 던지다

snow-bound [snóubàund] *adj.* shut in by a heavy fall of snow.
—[形] 눈에 갇힌

snow-capped [snóukæ̀pt] *adj.* covered with snow on the top.
—[形] 꼭대기가 눈으로 덮인

snow·drift [snóudrìft] *n.* [C] a heap of snow piled up by the wind.
—[名] 바람에 불려 쌓인 눈더미

snow·drop [snóudràp / -drɔ̀p] *n.* [C] a small plant with snow-white flowers which bloom in early spring.
—[名] 갈란투스, 아네모네

snow·fall [snóufɔ̀:l] *n.* [C][U] **1.** a fall of snow. **2.** the amount of snow which falls in a certain period.
—[名] 1. 강설 2. 강설량

snow-field [snóufì:ld] *n.* [C] a region always covered with snow.
—[名] 눈벌판

snow·flake [snóuflèik] *n.* [C] a small, white, featherlike crystal of snow.
—[名] 눈송이

snow line [⌐ ⌐] *n.* the line on mountains above which snow never melts.
—[名] 설선(雪線)

snow·man [snóumæ̀n] *n.* [C] (pl. **-men** [-mèn]) a human figure made of snow.
—[名] 눈사람

snow·plow, *Brit.* **-plough** [snóuplàu] *n.* [C] a machine for clearing away snow from railway tracks or roads.
—[名] 제설기(차)

snow·shoes [snóuʃù:z] *n. pl.* a pair of wooden frames with nets of leather, etc. for walking on deep and soft snow. ⇨fig.
—[名] 눈신, 설상화

⌊snowshoes⌋

snow·slide [snóuslàid] *n.* [C] a slide of snow down a steep slope [of a mountain].
—[名] 눈사태

snow·storm [snóustɔ̀:*r*m] *n.* [C] a heavy fall of snow with strong
—[名] 눈보라, 폭풍설

S

winds.

snow-white [snóu(h)wáit] *adj.* white as snow.
—[形] 눈처럼 흰, 순백의

snow·y [snóui] *adj.* (**snow·i·er, snow·i·est**) **1.** having much snow; covered with snow. **2.** white as snow. ¶*~ hair.* **3.** pure and clean.
—[形] 1. 눈이 많은; 눈으로 덮인 2. 눈처럼 흰 3. 깨끗한, 더럼이 없는

snub [snʌb] *vt.* (**snubbed, snub·bing**) **1.** treat (someone) coldly or scornfully. **2.** stop or check (a boat, a horse, etc.) suddenly.
—[他] 1. …을 쌀쌀하게 대하다, 푸대접하다 2. …을 갑자기 멈추다
—*adj.* (of the nose) short and turned up at the tip.
—[形] 들창코의
—*n.* [C] **1.** an example of cold, scornful or contemptuous treatment. **2.** a sudden check or stop.
—[名] 1. 냉대, 윽박지르기 2. 급정지, 갑자기 그만두기

snub-nosed [snʌ́bnòuzd] *adj.* with a snub nose.
—[形] 들창코의

snuff¹ [snʌf] *n.* [U] powdered tobacco to be taken into the nose by sniffing.
—[名] 코담배
—*vt.* draw in (something) through the nose; sniff.
—[他] …을 코로 들이쉬다, 냄새맡다
—*vi.* smell powdered tobacco.
—[自] 코담배를 냄새맡다

snuff² [snʌf] *n.* [C] the burnt part of a candlewick. —*vt.* **1.** cut off the snuff of (a candle). **2.** put out (a candle); extinguish.
—[名] 양초가 타서 까맣게 된 심지 —[他] 1. [양초의] 심지를 자르다 2. …을 끄다
snuff out, ⓐ put out (a candle). ⓑ bring (something) to an end suddenly; destroy. ⓒ suppress.
[熟] ⓐ[촛불]을 끄다 ⓑ…을 갑자기 끝나게 하다, 파괴하다 ⓒ억압하다

snuff·box [snʌ́fbàks / -bɔ̀ks] *n.* [C] a box for holding snuff.
—[名] 코담배통

snuff·ers [snʌ́fərz] *n. pl.* small tongs used for taking off burned wicks. ⇒fig.
—[名] [양초의] 심지 자르는 가위

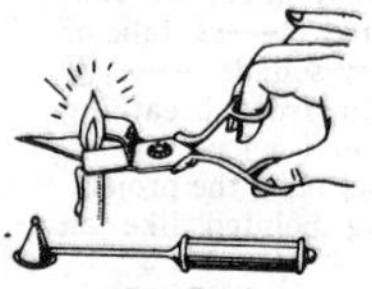
[snuffers]

snuf·fle [snʌ́fl] *vi.* **1.** breathe with a sound. **2.** speak or sing through the nose. —*vt.* utter (something) in a nasal tone.
—[自] 1. 소리를 내며 숨을 쉬다 2. 콧소리를 내다 —[他] …을 콧소리로 말하다
—*n.* [C] **1.** a noisy breathing through the nose. **2.** 《*the ~s*》 a nasal tone of voice; (of the nose) the state of being stuffed up.
—[名] 1. 소리를 내며 숨을 쉬기 2. 콧소리, 비음(鼻音); 코가 멤

* **snug** [snʌg] *adj.* (**snug·ger, snug·gest**) **1.** comfortable. **2.** neat; compact. ¶*a ~ little house.* **3.** not very much but enough. ¶*a ~ income.*
—[形] 1. 아늑한, 편안한 2. 아담한, 깔끔한, 꼭 맞는 3. 불편이 없는
as snug as a bug in a rug, very comfortable.
[熟] 아주 편안한(아늑한)
—*adv.* in a snug manner.
—[副] 아늑하게, 기분좋게
—*v.* (**snug·ged, snug·ging**) *vt.* make (something) comfortable and neat. —*vi.* lie comfortably.
—[他] …을 잘 정돈하다, 편안하게 하다
—[自] 편안하게 눕다

snug·gle [snʌ́gl] *vi.* come closer for warmth or from affection. 《*~ up to* someone; *~ in*》 —*vt.* draw or hold (someone) closely.
—[自] 곁에 다가붙다 —[他] …을 끌어안다

snug·ly [snʌ́gli] *adv.* in a snug manner.
—[副] 아늑하게, 단정하게

‡ **so** [sou] *adv.* **1.** in that way; in the condition shown; just as said. ¶*if ~ / Is that ~? / I don't think ~. / You will never do it ~.* **2.** 《often used after *a negative*》 to that extent; to the same extent or degree. ¶*He did not live ~ long. / He is not ~ great a man as you.* **3.** very; very much. ¶*I am ~ sleepy. / My teeth ache ~.* **4.** also. ¶*I was wrong, but ~ were you.* **5.** as a result; therefore. ¶*It was stormy, and ~ he did not come.* **6.** in a manner previously mentioned. ¶*The board fence is brown and has been ~ for some time.*①
—[副] 1. 그대로; 그 상태로; 그렇게; 그처럼 2. 그만큼, 그토록 3. 대단히, 아주, 정말로 4. …도 마찬가지로 5. 그런 까닭에, 그러므로, 그래서 6. 앞서 말한 상태로 ¶①갈색 판장은 얼맛동안 그 상태를 유지했다
—*conj.* **1.** therefore. ¶*It was late, ~ we went home.* **2.** (*U.S.*) in order that. ¶*Go away ~ I can rest.* ⇒ ***so that.***
—[接] 1. 그러므로, 때문에 2. 《美》 …하도록
—*pron.* **1.** 《used after *or*》 more or less. ¶*a pound or ~.*② **2.** what has been said or described. ¶*He is a poor writer and will remain ~.*③
—[代] 1. [이와 함께] …쯤, …정도, 약 ¶②1파운드 가량 2. 그렇게, 그처럼 ¶③그는 가난한 작가이다. 그리고 얼마동안 그렇게 계속될 것이다
—*interj.* 《used as a sign of *surprise, question,* or *approval*》 well; all right; Is that true?; How can that be. ¶*So! Late again! / "The train is late." "So?"*④
—[感] 그래, 저런, 여어, 됐다; 설마 ¶④「기차가 늦는다」「설마?」
1) ***and so on*** (or ***forth***), and more of the same sort;
[熟] 1) 따위, 등 2) …하도록 3) …할 만큼;

et cetera. ⌜*fast* ~ *as to be in time.*⌟
2) **so as to**, in order to; in such a way as to. ¶*Walk*
3) **so ... as to**, to such a degree that; in such a way that. ¶*He was* ~ *angry as to be unable to speak.*
4) **so that**, ⓐ in order that. ¶*We got up early* ~ *that we might catch the first train.* ⓑ therefore; with the result that. ¶*The dog ran slowly,* ~ *that he was easily caught.* ⓒ in such a way that. ¶*I stood* ~ *that my head did not appear.*⑤
5) **so ... [that]**, ⓐ to such a degree that. ¶*He was* ~ *angry that he could not speak a word.* ⓑ in order that. ¶*He studied* ~ *hard that he passed the entrance examination.* ⓒ in such a way that. ¶*It* ~ *happened that he was not at home.*⑤

* **soak** [souk] *vi.* **1.** become wet throughout. **2.** pass through pores, holes, etc. (~ *in* (or *through, out*) something) —*vt.* **1.** make (something) very wet. ¶*The heavy rain soaked the whole village.* **2.** make (something) soft or wet by leaving it in water. **3.** absorb. ¶*The sponge soaks up water.*
  soak oneself to (=*devote oneself*) **in something.**
  —*n.* ⓒ **1.** the act of soaking. **2.** the act of heavy drinking; a drunkard; a heavy drinker. **3.** a heavy rainfall.
so-and-so [sóuənsòu] *n.* ⓒ (pl. **-sos**) some person; such-and-such a person. ⌜used for washing.⌟
‡ **soap** [soup] *n.* ⓤ a substance made of fat and an alkali,
soap·box [sóupbɑ̀ks / -bɔ̀ks] *n.* ⓒ **1.** a large wooden box for soap. **2.** a box used as a platform by agitators or street speakers.
soap·suds [sóupsʌ̀dz] *n. pl.* foam made with soap and water.
soap·y [sóupi] *adj.* (**soap·i·er, soap·i·est**) **1.** of or like soap. **2.** covered with soap; full of soap.
* **soar** [sɔːr] *vi.* **1.** fly high; rise far above. ¶*The eagle soars through the sky.* **2.** (of one's spirit, hope, etc.) rise beyond what is usual. **3.** (of prices, etc.) rise higher rapidly.
‡ **sob** [sab / sɔb] *v.* (**sobbed, sob·bing**) *vi.* **1.** cry or weep with gasping short breaths. **2.** make such noises. —*vt.* speak (something) with tears and sobs. —*n.* ⓒ **1.** a tearful cry or word. **2.** a sound like that of the wind.
sob·bing [sábiŋ / sɔ́b-] *adj.* weeping with short, quick breaths. ⌜with tears.⌟
sob·bing·ly [sábiŋli / sɔ́b-] *adv.* in a sobbing manner;
‡ **so·ber** [sóubər] *adj.* (usu. ~**er**, ~**est**) **1.** not drunk. **2.** temperate by habit. **3.** serious; solemn. **4.** (of color) quiet; not gay. —*vt.* **1.** make (someone) sober. **2.** make (something) calm or quiet. —*vi.* become sober.
so·ber·ly [sóubərli] *adv.* in a sober manner.
so·ber-mind·ed [sóubərmáindid] *adj.* calm and quiet in mind.
so·bri·e·ty [soubráiəti] *n.* ⓤ **1.** the state of being sober; temperance. **2.** seriousness; quietness; calmness.
so·bri·quet, sou- [sóubrikèi] *n.* ⓒ a nickname.
* **so-called** [sóukɔ́ːld] *adj.* named or called so, but not truly so; called thus. ↪usage
soc·cer [sákər / sɔ́kə] *n.* ⓤ a form of football played between two teams of 11 players each with a ball that must not be touched with the hands.
so·cia·bil·i·ty [sòuʃəbíliti] *n.* ⓤ the quality of being sociable; social disposition; friendliness.
so·cia·ble [sóuʃəbl] *adj.* fond of company; companion-

…하도록 4)ⓐ…하도록, …할 수 있도록 ⓑ그러므로, 그 까닭에 ⓒ…하는 식으로 ¶ⓓ나는 얼굴이 보이지 않게 섰다 5)ⓐ아주 …하므로 …이다; …할 만큼 그렇게 …이다 ⓑ…하도록 …하다 ⓒ …할 만큼 …이다 ¶ⓕ공교롭게도 그는 집에 없었다

—ⓥ 1. 함빡 젖다 2. 스며들다, 배다; 스며나오다 —ⓣ 1. …을 함빡 적시다 2. …을 물에 담그다, 물에 담가 부드럽게 하다 3. …을 흡수하다

…에 몰두하다
—ⓝ 1. 적시기, 담그기; 스며들기; 흡수 2. 폭음(暴飲); 술주정뱅이 3. 억수, 큰비
—ⓝ 아무개

—ⓝ 비누
—ⓝ 1. 비누 상자 2. [가두 연설의 연단으로 쓰는] 빈 상자

—ⓝ 거품이 인 비눗물

—ⓐ 1. 비누의(같은) 2. 비누투성이의

—ⓥ 1. 높이 솟다; 날아 오르다, 우뚝 솟다 2. [희망·원기 따위가] 치솟다, 솟구치다 3. [물가가] 급등하다

—ⓥ 1. 흐느끼다; 목메어 울다 2. 흐느끼는 듯한 소리를 내다 —ⓣ …을 흐느끼면서 말하다 —ⓝ 1. 오열, 흐느낌 2. 흐느껴 우는 듯한 소리

—ⓐ 흐느껴 울고 있는

—ⓐⓓ 흐느껴 울면서
—ⓐ 1. 술마시지 않은 2. 금주의 3. 온건한, 진지한 4. [빛깔 따위] 차분한, 야하지 않은 —ⓣ 1. …의 술을 깨우다 2. …을 침착하게 하다 —ⓥ 술이 깨다
—ⓐⓓ 술을 안 마시고
—ⓐ 침착한

—ⓝ 1. 맑은 정신; 금주 2. 진지함; 냉정, 침착
—ⓝ 별명
—ⓐ 소위, 이른바 [usage] 보통 붙신·경멸의 뜻을 내포
—ⓝ 축구

—ⓝ 사교성, 상냥함, 사교에 능함

—ⓐ 사교적인, 교제에 능한, 상냥한, 우

able; friendly; not formal. —*n.* [U] (*U.S.*) an informal social gathering. ▷**so·cia·bly** [-bli] *adv.*
호적인 ―[名] 《美》 비공식 간담회

⁑ **so·cial** [sóuʃ(ə)l] *adj.* **1.** of human beings living together in a group; of the happiness and welfare of people. ¶*the ~ problem*① / *~ good.*② **2.** fond of company; friendly. **3.** (of animals) living in organized communities. **4.** of socialism.
―[形] 1. 사회의, 사회생활의 ¶①사회문제/②사회 복지 2. 사교적인, 교제에 능한 3. 사회생활을 하는, 군거(群居)의 4. 사회주의의

so·cial·ism [sóuʃəlìz(ə)m] *n.* [U] the theory of social organization in which the means of production and distribution are owned, managed and controlled by the government.
―[名] 사회주의

* **so·cial·ist** [sóuʃəlist] *n.* [C] a person who believes in socialism.
―[名] 사회주의자

so·cial·is·tic [ʃòuʃəlístik] *adj.* of socialism or socialists.
―[形] 사회주의[자]의

so·cial·i·za·tion [sòuʃəlizéiʃ(ə)n / -laiz-] *n.* [U] the act of socializing; the state of being socialized.
―[名] 사회로의 적합, 사회화, 사회주의화

so·cial·ize [sóuʃəlàiz] *vt.* **1.** make (someone) socia.. **2.** change or regulate (a country) according to socialism.
―[他] 1. …을 사교적으로 하다 2. …을 사회주의화하다

so·cial·ly [sóuʃəli] *adv.* in a social or friendly manner.
―[副] 사회적으로, 사교적으로

⁑ **so·ci·e·ty** [səsáiəti] *n.* (pl. **-ties**) **1.** [U] 《without *an article*》 persons living together, as a whole. **2.** [U] the upper class; people of high rank. **3.** [U] companionship. **4.** [C] a group of persons joined together for a common purpose. ¶*a literary ~.*
―[名] 1. 사회 2. 상류사회, 사교계[의 사람들] 3. 교제, 사교 4. 협회, 학회, 단체

so·ci·o·log·i·cal [sòusiəlάdʒik(ə)l, -ʃiə-] *adj.* of sociology.
―[形] 사회학[상]의

so·ci·ol·o·gist [sòusiάlədʒist, -ʃiάl- / -siɔ́l-] *n.* [C] a scholar of sociology.
―[名] 사회학자

so·ci·ol·o·gy [sòusiάlədʒi, -ʃiάl- / -siɔ́l-] *n.* [U] the science which studies the nature, development, and origin of human society; the science of the forms, institutions and functions of society.
―[名] 사회학

⁑ **sock** [sαk / sɔk] *n.* [C] (pl. **socks** or **sox**) 《usu. *pl.*》 a short stocking reaching halfway to the knee.
―[名] 짧은 양말

sock·er [sάkər / sɔ́kə] *n.* =soccer.

sock·et [sάkit / sɔ́k-] *n.* [C] a hollow or hole into which something fits. ¶*the ~ of the eye* / *an electric light ~.*
―[名] 꽂는(끼우는) 구멍, 소켓

Soc·ra·tes [sάkrətìːz / sɔ́k-] *n.* (469-399 B.C.) a philosopher of Athens.
―[名] 아테네의 철학가

So·crat·ic [soukrǽtik / sɔ-] *adj.* of Socrates and his philosophy. —*n.* [C] a followers of Socrates.
―[形] 소크라테스[학도]의 ―[名] 소크라테스 학도

sod [sαd / sɔd] *n.* [U] ground covered with grass; turf; [C] a piece of turf, usu. cut square. —*vt.* cover (a piece of ground, etc.) with sod.
―[名] 잔디밭; 잔디 ―[他] …에 잔디를 깔다, …을 잔디로 덮다

* **so·da** [sóudə] *n.* [U][C] **1.** a substance containing sodium. **2.** =soda water.
―[名] 1. 소오다, [중]탄산 소오다, 중조

soda fountain [ˊ- ˋ-] *n.* **1.** an apparatus for soda water, syrups, etc. **2.** (*U.S.*) a counter where soda water, soft drinks, ice cream, etc. are sold.
―[名] 1. 소오다수 그릇 2. 소오다수 판매장

⁑ **soda water** [ˊ- ˋ-] *n.* water containing gas to make it bubble and fizz.
―[名] 소오다수, 탄산수

sod·den [sάdn / sɔ́d-] *adj.* **1.** soaked and wet through. **2.** half-burnt. **3.** stupid or dull-looking because of drunkenness or fatigue.
―[形] 1. 함빡 젖은 2. 설구워진 3. [음주·피로로] 멍청한, 얼이 빠져 있는

so·di·um [sóudiəm] *n.* [U] a silver-white, metallic substance found in salt, soda. etc.
―[名] 나트륨, 소듐

* **so·fa** [sóufə] *n.* [C] a long padded couch with a back and two arms.
―[名] 소파, 긴 의자

⁑ **soft** [sɔːft / sɔft] *adj.* **1.** not hard; easily cut or shaped. ↔hard, tough ¶*a ~ bed* / *~ clay* / *Pure gold is ~.* **2.** (of cloth, etc.) smooth to the touch. ↔rough ¶*~ hair.* **3.** (of light, color, etc.) not bright or hard. ¶*a ~ color.* **4.** (of an outline; of lines in a picture, etc.) not sharp or clear. ¶*~ contours.* **5.** (of sound, etc.) not loud. ¶*a ~ voice.* **6.** (of the weather, air, etc.) mild; gentle; warm. ¶*~ air* / *a ~ climate.* **7.** (of persons) kind; weak. ¶*a ~ heart.* **8.** (of action, manner, speech, etc.) gentle; tender; quiet. ¶*a ~ manner.* **9.** not fit to endure hardships. ¶*~ muscles.* **10.** (*colloq.*)
―[形] 1. 부드러운; 연한 2. [의복 따위가] 보들보들한, 매끈매끈한 3. [색·광선이] 차분한, 거칠지 않은; 온화한 4. [윤곽·그림의 선 따위가] 부드러운 5. [음이] 낮은; 조용한 6. [날씨 따위가] 온화한, 상쾌한 7. [사람이] 친절한; 유약한 8. [태도·말·성질 따위가] 조용한, 온건한 9. 곤란에 견딜 수 없는 10. 《口》 [머리가] 모자라는; 어리석은 11. 《美》 알코홀을 함유하지 않은 12. 《音聲》 연음(軟音)의 (cent의 c, gen-

of weak intellect; silly. ¶ *I think he is a bit ~.* **11.** (*U.S.*) having no alcohol. **12.** (*Phonetics*) (of *c* and *g*) pronounced as in *cent* and *gentle* instead of as in *cake* or *get.* **13.** (of water) not containing certain minerals. ¶ ~ *water.*
tle의 g 따위) **13.** 연수(軟水)의

—*n.* [C] **1.** a soft part; something soft. **2.** a silly or weak person.
—[名] **1.** 부드러운 부분 **2.** 얼간이

—*adv.* in a soft manner; softly. ¶ *fall ~ / lie ~.*
—[副] 부드럽게, 조용히

⁑ soft·ball [sɔ́ːftbɔ̀ːl / sɔ́ft-] *n.* [U] a game similar to baseball but played with a larger and softer ball; [C] the ball used in this game.
—[名] 소프트 보올(10명이 하는 야구의 일종); 그 공

soft-boiled [sɔ́ːftbɔ́ild / sɔ́ft-] *adj.* (of eggs etc.) boiled only a short time so that the yolk does not become hard.
—[形] 반숙의

*** sof·ten** [sɔ́ːfn / sɔ́fn] *vt., vi.* make (something) soft or softer; become soft or softer. ¶ *Her gentle face softened his hard heart. / Lard softens in heat.*
—[他][自] [···을] 부드럽게 하다(되다), 누이다, 누그러지다

soft-head·ed [sɔ́ːfthédid / sɔ́ft-] *adj.* foolish; silly.
—[形] 어리석은

soft-heart·ed [sɔ́ːfthɑ́ːrtid / sɔ́fthɑ́ːt-] *adj.* gentle; tender-hearted.
—[形] 다정다감한; 인정이 있는

⁑ soft·ly [sɔ́ːftli / sɔ́ft-] *adv.* in a soft manner; kindly; quietly and calmly.
—[副] 부드럽게, 상냥하게, 관대하게, 조용히

soft·ness [sɔ́ːftnis / sɔ́ft-] *n.* [U] the state or quality of being soft; comfort; gentleness; mildness.
—[名] 부드러움; 온화; 유약, 온순, 관대

soft-spo·ken [sɔ́ftspóuk(ə)n] *adj.* talking or spoken in a gentle voice.
—[形] 말씨가 상냥한, 온화한

soft·wood [sɔ́ːftwùd / sɔ́ft-] *n.* **1.** [U] wood that is easy to cut. **2.** [C] any cone-bearing tree, such as the pine and spruce; [U] the wood of such a tree.
—[名] **1.** 연한 나무(재목) **2.** 침엽수(재목)

sog·gy [sɑ́gi / sɔ́g-] *adj.* (**-gi·er, -gi·est**) completely wet; soaked; damp and heavy.
—[形] 함빡 젖은, 축축한

⁑ soil¹ [sɔil] *n.* [U] **1.** earth; dirt. **2.** land; country. ¶ *one's native ~.*①
—[名] **1.** 흙, 토양 **2.** 나라, 토지 ¶①고향

*** soil²** [sɔil] *n.* [U] **1.** stain; dirt. **2.** manure used to enriching the earth. —*vt., vi.* **1.** make (something) dirty; become dirty. **2.** dishonor; corrupt morally. ¶ ~ *the family name.*
—[名] **1.** 오물; 오점, 얼룩 **2.** 똥, 거름 —[他][自] **1.** 더럽히다, 더러워지다 **2.** [명예를] 손상하다; 타락하다

soiled [sɔild] *adj.* not clean; dirty.
—[形] 더러워진

soi·ree, soi·rée [swɑ́ːrèi / ⌐–] *n.* [C] an evening party.
—[名] 야회(夜會)

so·journ *vi.* [sóudʒəːrn, –⌐ →*n.* / sɔ́dʒəːn] stay for a time.
—[自] [일시적으로] 체재하다, 기숙하다

—*n.* [*U.S.* ⌐–] [C] a short or temporary stay.
—[名] 체재, 체류

so·journ·er [sóudʒəːrnər / sɔ́dʒəːnə] *n.* [C] a person who sojourns.
—[名] 체재자, 기류자

Sol [sɑl / sɔl] *n.* **1.** the sun. **2.** the Roman god of the sun.
—[名] **1.** 태양 **2.** 태양신

sol·ace [sɑ́ləs / sɔ́l-] *n.* [U][C] comfort; consolation.
—[名] 위안

—*vt.* give relief, comfort, etc. to (someone); console.
—[他] ···을 위로하다

so·lar [sóulər] *adj.* **1.** of or having to do with the sun. **2.** coming from or produced by the sun; measured by the sun. ¶ ~ *energy / the ~ calendar.*①
—[形] **1.** 태양의(에 관한) **2.** 태양에서 생기는, 태양에 의해 측정한 ¶①태양력(曆)

so·lar·i·a [souléəriə] *n.* pl. of **solarium**.

so·lar·i·um [souléəriəm] *n.* [C] (pl. **-ums** or **-lar·i·a**) a room to enjoy the warmth and heat of the sun; a sunroom.
—[名] 일광욕실

⁑ sold [sould] *v.* pt. and pp. of **sell**.

sol·der [sɑ́dər] *n.* **1.** [U] a metal or an alloy used to join or mend metal surfaces. **2.** [C] anything that unites or joins firmly; a bond. —*vt.* join or fasten (something) with solder; unite; join.
—[名] **1.** 땜납 **2.** 결합시키는 것; 유대, 기반(羈絆) —[他] ···을 땜납으로 붙이다; 결합하다

sol·der·ing iron [sɑ́dəriŋàiərn] *n.* a tool for joining or fastening (metal plates, etc.) together with solder.
—[名] 땜질용 인두

*** sol·dier** [sóuldʒər] *n.* [C] **1.** a man who serves in an army; an enlisted man as distinguished from an officer. **2.** a man who is skilled and experienced in war. **3.** a great leader in any cause.
—[名] **1.** [육군] 군인; 병사, 병졸 **2.** [뛰어난] 무인(武人), 지휘관, 명장 **3.** [···의] 투사

1) ***a soldier of Christ*** (or ***the cross***), a missionary of Christianity.
2) ***a soldier of fortune,*** a person who is willing to serve in any army for money or adventure; an adventurer.
[熟] 1)그리스도교 전도자 2)[급료와 모험이 목적인] 용병(傭兵); 모험가

—*vi.* **1.** become a soldier. **2.** (*colloq.*) do not work hard; pretend to work.
—[自] **1.** 군인이 되다 **2.**《口》농땡이부리다; 일을 하는 체하다

sol·dier·like [sóuldʒərlàik] *adj.* =soldierly.

S

sol·dier·ly [sóuldʒərli] *adj.* like a soldier; suitable for a soldier. —[형] 군인다운, 군인에 알맞은

sol·dier·y [sóuldʒəri] *n.* 《*collectively*, often *a* ~》 soldiers. —[명] 군인, 군대

* **sole**[1] [soul] *adj.* **1.** one and only; unique. **2.** of or for only one person; exclusive. **3.** not married; single. —[형] 1. 유일한, 단독의 2. 독점적인 3. 미혼의, 독신의

sole[2] [soul] *n.* [C] **1.** the bottom of the foot, shoes, boots, etc. **2.** the lower part. —*vt.* put a sole on (shoes, etc.). —[명] 1. 발바닥; 신바닥, 구두창 2. [물건의] 밑바닥; 토대 —[타] [구두 따위]에 밑바닥을 대다

sol·e·cism [sálisìz(ə)m / sɔ́l-] *n.* [C] **1.** incorrect grammar or usage of a language. **2.** bad manners. —[명] 1. 문법 위반, 어법 위반, 파격(破格) 2. 버릇없음, 부적당

* **sole·ly** [sóulli] *adv.* in a sole manner; singly; only. —[부] 단독으로; 단지, 오로지

* **sol·emn** [sáləm / sɔ́l-] *adj.* (~·**er**, ~·**est**) **1.** serious; grave; sacred. **2.** dignified; formal; ceremonial. **3.** valuable; important. —[형] 1. 엄숙한, 신성한 2. 점잖은 체하는 3. 중요한, 중대한

so·lem·ni·ty [səlémniti] *n.* [U] (pl. **-ties**) **1.** the state of being solemn; great seriousness. **2.** 《often *pl.*》 a formal ceremony. —[명] 1. 엄숙, 장엄 2. 의식, 제전(祭典)

sol·em·ni·za·tion [sɑ̀ləmnizéiʃ(ə)n / sɔ̀ləmnai-] *n.* [U][C] the act of solemnizing; the state of being solemnized. —[명] 장엄하게 하기; 식을 올림

sol·em·nize [sáləmnàiz / sɔ́l-] *vt.* perform (something) with religious ceremonies; celebrate or perform (a marriage, etc.) in a proper manner. ¶~ *a wedding.* —[타] …을 장엄하게 하다; [결혼 따위]를 식을 올려 축하하다

sol·emn·ly [sáləmli / sɔ́l-] *adv.* in a solemn manner; gravely; seriously; formally. —[부] 엄숙하게, 장엄하게, 점잔빼어; 정식으로

sol-fa [sòulfá: / sɔ̀l-] *n.* [U] a system or way of singing using syllables corresponding to the notes of the scale. —[명] 도레미파 노래법

* **so·lic·it** [səlísit] *vt., vi.* ask for (something) earnestly; entreat and beg repeatedly; make appeals. 《~ someone *for*; ~ something *of* or *from*》 ¶~ *someone for money* / *We ~ favors from* (or *of*) *you.*① —[타][자] [… 을] 간청하다; 끈질기게 조르다 ¶①귀하의 애호를 바랍니다(상용문의 상투적 문구)

so·lic·i·ta·tion [səlìsitéiʃ(ə)n] *n.* [U][C] **1.** the act of soliciting; earnest request and appeal. **2.** the temptation of a street girl. —[명] 1. 간청, 권유 2. [매춘부의] 유혹, 유객(誘客)

so·lic·i·tor [səlísitər] *n.* [C] **1.** (*Brit.*) a lawyer. ⇒[N.B.] **2.** a person who entreats and appeals repeatedly; a person who seeks trade. —[명] 1. 《英》 변호사 [N.B.] 주로 재판 사무를 다룸 2. 간청자; 주문받는 사람

solicitor general [-´-- ´--] *n.* (pl. **solicitors ~**) **1.** (*Brit.*) a law officer who assists the attorney general. **2.** (*U.S.*) 《*S- G-*》 the chief law officer. —[명] 1. 《英》 법무차관 2. 《美》 주(州) 법무국장

so·lic·it·ous [səlísitəs] *adj.* **1.** anxious. 《~ *about* or *for*》 ¶*I am ~ for his future.* **2.** eagerly looking for (something); desirous. 《~ *of*; ~ *to do*》 —[형] 1. 염려하는, 근심하는 2. 열망하는, 열심인

so·lic·i·tude [səlísit(j)ù:d / -tjù:d] *n.* [U] anxiety; concern. —[명] 우려; 염려

‡ **sol·id** [sálid / sɔ́l-] *adj.* (~·**er**, ~·**est**) **1.** not a liquid or a gas; firm; hard. ¶*When water becomes ~, we call it ice.* **2.** without holes or spaces inside; filled with matter; thick. ¶*a ~ iron bar.* **3.** all of one material, color, or kind. ¶*a ~ color* / *a fork of ~ silver.* **4.** (of structures, furniture, etc.) strongly built; (of reasons, etc.) sound; with a sound financial position. ¶*a man of ~ build*① / *a ~ building.* **5.** reliable; of sound character. ¶*a man of ~ character.*② **6.** firmly united in support of something; united in a single opinion. ¶*a ~ vote of approval.* **7.** real; true; complete. ¶~ *comfort.* **8.** (*U.S. colloq.*) very friendly. ¶*be ~ with someone.* —[형] 1. 고체의, 고형의; 굳은 2. 속이 비지 않은; 충실한; 실속있는 3. 모두 동일한; [빛깔이] 한결같은, 고른 4. [건물·구조 따위가] 튼튼한; [이유 따위가] 합리적인; [재정적으로] 신용이 있는; 확실한 ¶①체격이 튼튼한 사람 5. 신뢰할 수 있는; [사람이] 착실한 ¶②신뢰할 수 있는 사람 6. 단결한, 만장일치의 7. 진짜의; 완전한 8. 《美口》 사이가 좋은

—*n.* [C] **1.** a body or substance that is not a liquid or a gas. **2.** a body that has length, breadth, and thickness. —[명] 1. 고체; 고형물 2. 입체

sol·i·dar·i·ty [sɑ̀lidǽriti / sɔ̀l-] *n.* [U] the unity or agreement of responsibilities, interests, purposes, etc. in a group. —[명] 협동 일치; 연대책임

so·lid·i·fi·ca·tion [səlìdifikéiʃ(ə)n] *n.* [U] the act of solidifying; the state of being solidified; unity. —[명] 응고, 고체화; 결속, 단결

so·lid·i·fy [səlídifài] *vt., vi.* (**-fied**) **1.** make (something) solid; become solid. **2.** make (people) unite; become —[타][자] 1. [… 을] 굳게 하다(되다), 응고시키다(하다) 2. [… 을] 결속시키다

firmly united. (하다)

so·lid·i·ty [səlíditi] *n.* [U] the state of being solid; firmness; sureness. —[名] 고체성; 충실; 확실함

so·lil·o·quize [səlíləkwàiz] *vi.* talk to oneself; utter a dramatic monologue on stage, etc. —[自] 혼잣말을 하다; 독백하다

so·lil·o·quy [səlíləkwi] *n.* (pl. **-quies**) **1.** [U] the act of speaking to oneself. **2.** [C] an act of speaking to the audience in a drama. —[名] 1. 혼잣말 2. 독백

sol·i·taire [sálitὲər / sɔ̀litέə] *n.* [C] **1.** a single gem, esp. a diamond, set by itself. **2.** [U] a game of cards played by one person alone. —[名] 1. [반지 따위에 단 하나 끼여 있는] 보석 2. 혼자 하는 카아드놀이

* **sol·i·tar·y** [sálitèri / sɔ́lit(ə)ri] *adj.* **1.** alone; living alone. ¶*a ~ cell.*① **2.** seldom visited. ¶*a ~ village* / *feel ~*② —*n.* [C] (pl. **-tar·ies**) a person who lives alone. —[形] 1. 혼자의 ¶①독방 2. 인적이 드문, 외딴 ¶②외롭게 느끼다 —[名] 혼자 사는 사람; 은자(隱者)

* **sol·i·tude** [sálit(j)ù:d / sɔ́litjù:d] *n.* **1.** [U] the state of being alone. **2.** [C] a lonely place. ¶*live in ~.*① —[名] 1. 고독; 혼자 삶 2. 외딴(쓸쓸한) 장소 ¶①단지 혼자서 살다

so·lo [sóulou] *n.* [C] (pl. **-los** or **-li**) **1.** a piece of music played or sung by one person. ¶*a piano ~.*① **2.** anything done by one person. —*adj.* done by one person alone. ¶*a ~ flight.* —*vi.* (**-loed, -lo·ing**) perform by oneself; make a solo flight in an airplane. —[名] 1. 독창(주)곡 ¶①피아노 독주 2. [무용·비행 따위] 단독으로 하는 것 —[形] 혼자서 하는; 단독의 —[自] 혼자서 하다; 단독비행하다

so·lo·ist [sóulouist] *n.* [C] (*Music*) a person who performs a solo. —[名] 독주자, 독창자

Sol·o·mon [sáləmən / sɔ́l-] *n.* **1.** (in the Bible) a king of Israel in the 10th century B.C. who was famous for his wisdom and the great temple he built. **2.** [C] a very wise man like Solomon. —[名] 1. 기원전 10세기의 이스라엘 왕 2. 현인(賢人)

sol·stice [sálstis / sɔ́l-] *n.* [C] either of the two points in the sun's path at which the sun is at its greatest distance from the celestial equator. ¶*the summer ~*① / *the winter ~.*② —[名] [태양의] 지점(至點) ¶①하지/②동지

sol·u·bil·i·ty [sàljubíliti / sɔ̀l-] *n.* [U] the quality of being soluble. —[名] 용해성; 해결할 수 있음

sol·u·ble [sáljubl / sɔ́l-] *adj.* **1.** that can be dissolved in a liquid. ¶*Sugar is readily ~ in water.*① **2.** that can be solved or explained. —[形] 1. 녹는 ¶①설탕은 물에 곧 녹는다 2. [문제 따위가] 해결할 수 있는

⁑ **so·lu·tion** [səlú:ʃ(ə)n] *n.* **1.** [U] the act of solving a problem; [C] an answer to a problem. ¶*They cannot find a ~ of* (or *for, to*) *the difficulty.*① **2.** [U] the act of dissolving a substance into a liquid; the state of being dissolved. ¶*chemical ~.*② **3.** [U][C] a liquid or some other mixture formed by dissolving. ¶*a ~ of salt.*③ —[名] 1. [문제 따위의] 해결; 해답 ¶①그들은 그 곤란에 대한 해결책을 못 찾고 있다 2. 용해 ¶②화학적 용해 3. 용액 ¶③식염 용액

solv·a·ble [sálvəbl / sɔ́l-] *adj.* that can be solved or dissolved. —[形] 풀 수 있는; 분해할 수 있는

⁑ **solve** [sálv / sɔ́lv] *vt.* find the answer to or explanation of (a problem, a puzzle, etc). —[他] [문제 따위]를 풀다, 해결하다

sol·ven·cy [sálv(ə)nsi / sɔ́l-] *n.* [U] the ability to pay one's debts. —[名] 지불 능력; 자력(資力)

sol·vent [sálv(ə)nt / sɔ́l-] *adj.* **1.** able to pay one's debts. **2.** able to dissolve some other substance. **3.** able to weaken a feeling, emotion, etc. ¶*the ~ power of laughter.*① —*n.* [C] a substance that can dissolve some other substance. —[形] 1. 지불(변제) 능력이 있는 2. 용해력이 있는 3. [마음 따위를] 누그러뜨리는 ¶①사람의 마음을 누그러뜨리는 웃음의 힘 —[名] 용제(溶劑)

som·ber, *Brit.* **-bre** [sámbər / sɔ́mbə] *adj.* **1.** dark and dull. ¶*a ~ sky.*① **2.** tending to make someone feel sad and gloomy; melancholy. ¶*a ~ expression*② / *The outlook is ~ indeed.*③ —[形] 1. 어두컴컴한 ¶①어두운 하늘 2. 우울한 ¶②음울한 표정/③앞길은 정말 암담하다

som·bre·ro [sambréərou / səm-] *n.* [C] (pl. **-ros**) a hat, usu. made of felt and with a broad brim, worn esp. in Spain, Latin America, etc. ⇒fig. —[名] [남미에서 쓰는] 챙 넓은 펠트 모자

[sombrero]

⁑ **some** [sʌm / səm] *adj.* **1.** a certain amount or number of; a few. ¶*~ money* / *for ~ time* / *Will you have ~ tea?*① **2.** not known; a certain. ¶*~ experienced person.* **3.** (*U.S. colloq.*) a pretty large amount of; rather important. ¶*~ scholar*② / *It took ~ patience to persuade him* —[形] 1. 어떤 양(量)(수)의 ¶①차를 드시겠소? 2. 어떤, 누군가의, 무엇인가의 3. 상당한 ¶②상당한 학자/③그에게 그 계획을 단념시키는 데에 상당한 인내가 필요했다 4. 약… ¶④약 20마일 떨어져 있다

S

*to give up the plan.*③ **4.** 《with *numerals*》 about. ¶~ *20 miles off.*④

—*pron.* **1.** persons or things whose names are not known. ¶*Some say one thing and others another.*⑤ / *Some are silver and* ~ [*are*] *gold.*⑥ **2.** a certain amount or number. ¶*I have just drunk* ~.⑦ / *He took away* ~ *of it.* —*adv.* **1.** (*colloq.*) somewhat; to some extent; rather. ¶*He is* ~ *better today.*⑧ **2.** (*U.S. colloq.*) good deal; to a great extent. ¶*He seemed tired* ~.

—[代] 1. 어떤 사람들; 어떤 것 ¶⑤사람에 따라 말하는 것이 다르다/⑥어떤 것은 은이고 어떤 것은 금이다 2. 약간, 다소 ¶⑦약간 술을 마셨다 —[副] 1. 얼마간, 다소 ¶⑧그는 오늘은 다소 낫다 2. 상당히, 꽤

⁝ **some·body** [sʌ́mbɑ̀di, -bʌ̀di / -bədi] *pron.* a person unknown; someone. ¶*Somebody will find it.*① / *I want* ~ *to help me.* —*n.* [C] (pl. **-bod·ies**) a person of importance. ¶*He thinks himself to be* [*a*] ~.②

—[代] 누군가, 어떤 사람 ¶①누군가 그것을 찾아낼 게다 —[名] 상당한 인물 ¶②그는 자기가 위대한 사람인 줄 알고 있다

⁝ **some·how** [sʌ́mhàu] *adv.* in one way or another; in some way not known or stated. ¶*I must finish this work* ~.① / *Somehow I don't like him.*

somehow or other, in one way or another.

—[副] 어떻게 해서든지, 어찌된 일인지 ¶①나는 어떻게 해서든 이 일을 끝내야 한다

[熟] 그럭저럭

⁝ **some·one** [sʌ́mwʌ̀n, -wən / -wʌ̀n] *pron.* somebody.

—[代] 누군가, 어떤 사람

som·er·sault [sʌ́mərsɔ̀:lt] *n.* [C] an acrobatic leap or dive in which one turns the heels over the head while in the air. ¶*a double* ~① / *turn a* ~.② —*vi.* perform a somersault.

—[名] 공중제비 ¶①연속 두 번의 공중제비/②공중제비하다 —[自] 공중제비를 하다

som·er·set [sʌ́mərsèt, +*Brit.* -sit] *n., v.* =somersault.

⁝ **some·thing** [sʌ́mθiŋ] *pron.* **1.** a thing not clearly pointed out; some thing. ¶~ *important* / *Give me* ~ *else.*① / *There is* ~ *in it.*② / *I have* ~ *to do with the matter.* **2.** a certain amount; a portion; a part. ¶*He has* ~ *of the painter in him.*③

—[代] 1. 어떤 것 ¶①무엇인가 딴 것을 주시오/②거기에도 일리가 있다 2. 다소; 부분 ¶③그는 화가의 소질이 얼마간 있다

—*n.* [C] an important thing or person. ¶*He thinks* ~ *of himself.; He thinks himself* ~.④

—*adv.* 《followed by *like*》 **1.** in some degree; somewhat; rather. ¶*He looks* ~ *like his father.*⑤ **2.** about; nearly.

—[名] 중요한 것(사람) ¶④그는 자신을 상당한 사람으로 알고 있다

—[副] 1. 어느 정도; 어딘가 ¶⑤그는 어딘가 아버지를 닮았다 2. 약…, 대략

⁝ **some·time** [sʌ́mtàim] *adv.* **1.** at a time not exactly known or decided; at an indefinite future time. ¶~ *during the night*① / ~ *or other.*② **2.** (*archaic*) formerly. ¶*He was* ~ *Mayor of Pusan*③ —*adj.* former. ¶*the* ~ *professor at Harvard University.*④

—[副] 1. 언젠가 ¶①언젠가 밤중에/②조만간 2. 이전 ¶③그는 이전에 부산시장이었다 —[形] 전의 ¶④전(前)하아버드 대학 교수

⁝ **some·times** [sʌ́mtàimz] *adv.* now and then; from time to time.

—[副] 때때로

some·way [sʌ́mwèi] *adv.* in some way; somehow.

—[副] 어떻게든지 해서

⁝ **some·what** [sʌ́m(h)wɑ̀t, -(h)wʌ̀t / -(h)wɔ̀t] *adv.* to a certain extent or degree. ¶*He was* ~ *puzzled.*① —*pron.* some part or amount. ¶*He is* ~ *of a musician.*②

—[副] 얼마간, 다소 ¶①그는 다소 어리둥절했다 —[代] 어느 정도 ¶②그는 음악가다운 데가 있다

⁝ **some·where** [sʌ́m(h)wɛ̀ər] *adv.* **1.** in or to one place or another. ¶*He lives* ~ *about here.* / *You'll find the quotation* ~ *in Shakespeare.*① **2.** at some point in time, amount, degree, etc. ¶*It happened* ~ *about three.*②

—[副] 1. 어딘가에 ¶①셰익스피어의 어딘가에 그 인용문이 있다 2. 언젠가, 얼마만큼 ¶②3시경의 일이었다

som·nam·bu·lism [sɑmnǽmbjulìz(ə)m / sɔ́m-] *n.* [U] sleepwalking; the act or state of walking while one sleeps.

—[名] 몽유병

som·nam·bu·list [sɑmnǽmbjulist / sɔ́m-] *n.* [C] a sleepwalker.

—[名] 몽유병자

som·no·lence [sɑ́mnələns / sɔ́m-] *n.* [U] sleepiness; drowsiness.

—[名] 졸림

som·no·lent [sɑ́mnələnt / sɔ́m-] *adj.* **1.** sleepy or drowsy. **2.** causing someone to sleep.

—[形] 1. 졸리는 2. 졸음이 오게 하는

⁝ **son** [sʌn] *n.* [C] **1.** a male child in relation to his parent or parents. ↔daughter ¶*the eldest* ~.① **2.** a male descendent. ¶*the sons of Adam.*② **3.** a native of a country. **4.** anything regarded as the product of a particular nation, age, civilization, etc. **5.** a friendly term of address to a boy.

—[名] 1. 아들 ¶①장남 2. [남자] 자손 ¶②아담의 자손(인류를 이름) 3. 국민 4. …의 아들 5. 젊은이, 친구

so·na·ta [sənɑ́:tə] *n.* [C] a type of musical composition in three or four movements, usu. for the piano.

—[名] 소나타, 주명곡(奏鳴曲)

⁝ **song** [sɔ(:)ŋ / sɔŋ] *n.* **1.** [C] a piece of music composed to be sung. **2.** [U] the act of singing; music produced by

—[名] 1. 노래, 가곡 2. 노래하기, 가창(歌唱) 3. 새의 지저귀는 소리 4. [노래하

the human voice. **3.** [U] the sounds like singing produced by a bird. **4.** [C] a piece of poetry suitable to be set to music. **5.** [C] (*colloq.*) a trifle; a low price.

기에 알맞은] 짧은 시 5.《口》 사소한 일; 싼값

1) ***for a song,*** for very little money.
2) ***nothing to make a song about,*** (*colloq.*) of no importance.
3) ***song and dance,*** (*U.S. colloq.*) talk or explanation that is pointless.

[熟] 1)헐값으로 2)《口》아주 사소한 것 3)《口》요령부득의 이야기, 꾸며대는 핑계

song·bird [sɔ́(:)ŋbə̀:rd / sɔ́ŋbə̀:d] *n.* [C] a singing bird such as a canary, nightingale, or lark. —[名] 우는 새, 명금(鳴禽)

song·book [sɔ́(:)ŋbùk / sɔ́ŋ-] *n.* [C] a book containing a number of songs. —[名] 가곡집, 노래책

song·ful [sɔ́(:)ŋf(u)l / sɔ́ŋ-] *adj.* **1.** melodious. **2.** full of song. —[形] 1. 가락이 좋은 2. 노래가 많은, 잘 노래하는

song·ster [sɔ́(:)ŋstər / sɔ́ŋstə] *n.* [C] **1.** a person who sings; a singer. **2.** a songbird. **3.** a person who writes songs or poems. —[名] 1. 가수 2. 우는 새 3. 시인

song·stress [sɔ́(:)ŋstris / sɔ́ŋ-] *n.* [C] a female songster. —[名] 여자 가수, 시인, 지저귀는 새

song thrush [⌐ ⌐] *n.* a European songbird. —[名] 지빠귀의 일종

son-in-law [sʌ́ninlɔ̀:] *n.* [C] (pl. **sons-**) the husband of one's daughter. —[名] 사위, 양자

son·net [sɑ́nit / sɔ́n-] *n.* [C] a poem of fourteen lines expressing a single theme or idea. —[名] 14 행시, 소네트

son·ny [sʌ́ni] *n.* [C] (pl. **-nies**) a pet name or a familiar way to call a little boy; a young son. —[名] [부르는 말로] 야아, 아가

so·nor·i·ty [sənɔ́:riti, +*U.S.* -nɑ́r- / -nɔ́r-] *n.* [U] the state of being sonorous. —[名] 울려퍼짐

so·no·rous [sounɔ́:rəs] *adj.* **1.** giving a full, deep or loud sound. ¶*a ~ voice*① / *a ~ bell.*② **2.** (of speech or writing) making a deep impression. —[形] 1. 울려퍼지는, 우렁찬 ¶①우렁찬 목소리/②울려퍼지는 종 2. 쩡쩡 울리는, 낭랑한

⁑soon [su:n] *adv.* **1.** in a short time; before long. ¶*He will ~ be back.* **2.** early. ¶*Winter has come rather ~ this year.*① **3.** quickly; at once. ¶*Soon got, ~ gone.*② —[副] 1. 곧, 멀지않아 2. 빨리 ¶①올해는 겨울이 좀 일찍 왔다 3. 재빨리 ¶②쉽게 얻은 것은 쉽게 나간다

1) ***as soon as,*** at once; immediately.
2) ***no sooner...than,*** hardly...when; scarcely...before. ¶*He has no sooner seen me than he ran away.*
3) ***sooner or later,*** some day; at some unknown time.
4) ***would sooner...than ~,*** would rather...than ~. ¶*I would sooner sleep than do it.*③

[熟] 1)…하자마자 2)…하자마자 3)조만간; 늦건 이르건 4)…하기보다는 오히려 …하고 싶다 ¶③그것을 하느니 자는 편이 낫다

soot [sut] *n.* [U] a soft, black substance produced as part of the smoke when coal, wood, oil, etc. are burned. —*vt.* cover (something) with soot. ▷**soot·less** [-lis] *adj.* —[名] 검댕, 매연(煤煙) —[他] …을 검댕투성이로 만들다

***soothe** [su:ð] *vt.* (**soothed, sooth·ing**) **1.** make (someone) calm or quiet. ¶*The babysitter soothed the crying child.*① **2.** make (pain) less severe. ▷**sooth·er** [-ər] *n.* —[他] 1. …을 달래다 ¶①아이 보는 사람은 우는 아이를 달랬다 2. [고통 따위]를 누그러뜨리다

sooth·ing·ly [sú:ðiŋli] *adv.* in a soothing manner. —[副] 위로하여

sooth·say·er [sú:θsèiər] *n.* [C] a person who tells what will happen. —[名] 점장이

sooth·say·ing [sú:θsèiiŋ] *n.* [U] the act of foretelling future events. —[名] 점

soot·y [súti] *adj.* (**soot·i·er, soot·i·est**) **1.** covered or stained with soot. **2.** of or like soot. **3.** dark-brown. —[形] 1. 그을은 2. 검댕의(같은) 3. 거무튀튀한, 검댕빛의

sop [sɑp / sɔp] *n.* [C] **1.** a piece of bread dipped or soaked in milk, soup, etc. **2.** something given to someone to soothe him. **3.** a person or thing thoroughly soaked. —[名] 1. [우유·수우프 따위에 적셔 먹는] 빵조각 2. 뇌물 3. 함빡 젖은 것

—*v.* (**sopped, sop·ping**) *vt.* **1.** dip; soak. ¶*~ bread in milk.* **2.** take up (water) by absorbing; wipe. **3.** wet (something) thoroughly; drench. —*vi.* soak; become drenched. —[他] 1. …을 적시다 2. …을 빨아들이다 3. …을 함빡 젖게 하다 —[自] 배다; 함빡 젖다

soph·ism [sɑ́fiz(ə)m / sɔ́f-] *n.* [U] a clever but misleading argument or form of reasoning; [C] a false argument. —[名] 궤변

soph·ist [sɑ́fist / sɔ́f-] *n.* [C] **1.** one of a group of teachers in ancient Greece who taught rhetoric, politics, philosophy, etc. and used sophisms. **2.** a person who uses sophisms. —[名] 1. 고대 그리이스의 철학·수사학(修辭學)의 교사 2. 궤변가

so·phis·ti·cal [səfístik(ə)l] *adj.* **1.** clever but unsound and misleading. **2.** using a false argument. —[形] 1. 궤변의 2. 궤변을 부리는

so·phis·ti·cate *v.* [səfístikèit, →*n.*] *vt.* **1.** use sophistical —[他] 1. …에 궤변을 부리다; …을 궤변

arguments about (something); mislead (someone). **2.** spoil the natural simplicity of (someone); change (a text) without authority. **3.** make (wine, tobacco, etc.) impure by mixture. —*vi.* use sophistry.
—*n.* [+*U.S.* -kit] [C] a sophisticated person.
으로 속이다 2.…을 세파에 물들게 하다;[원작]을 멋대로 바꾸다 3.…에 섞음질을 하여 질을 떨어뜨리다 —[自] 궤변을 부리다 —[名] 세파에 물든 사람

so·phis·ti·cat·ed [səfístikèitid] *adj.* **1.** lacking in natural simplicity; wise in worldly ways. **2.** misleading. **3.** not in a natural state.
—[形] 1. 굴러먹은, 세상물정을 아는 2. 속임수의 3. 불순물을 섞은

so·phis·ti·ca·tion [səfìstikéiʃ(ə)n] *n.* [U] the act of sophisticating; the state or quality of being sophisticated.
—[名] 궤변을 부리기; 가짜; 세상에 물들기

soph·ist·ry [sáfistri / sɔ́f-] *n.* (pl. **-ries**) **1.** [U] clever and unsound reasoning; [C] a particular argument on false reasoning. **2.** [U] the art, skill, or learning of the sophists of ancient Greece.
—[名] 1. 궤변, 억지 이론 2. 고대 그리이스의 궤변법

soph·o·more [sáf(ə)mɔ̀:*r* / sɔ́fəmɔ̀:] *n.* [C] (*U.S.*) a second-year student of a university, college or high school.
—[名] 《美》 [대학·고교의] 2년생

so·po·rif·ic [sàpəríf ik / sɔ̀p-] *adj.* **1.** causing sleep. **2.** sleepy. —*n.* [C] something, esp. a drug, that causes sleep.
—[形] 1. 졸음이 오게 하는; 최면의 2. 졸리운 —[名] 수면제

sop·py [sápi / sɔ́p-] *adj.* (**-pi·er, -pi·est**) **1.** very wet; rainy. **2.** (*Brit. colloq.*) too sentimental.
—[形] 1. 함빡 젖은; 축축한 2. 《口》 감상적(感傷的)인; 눈물이 많은

so·pran·o [səprǽnou / -prá:-] *n.* (pl. **-pran·os**) **1.** [U] the highest singing voice of a woman or boy. **2.** [C] a singer with this voice. **3.** [U] a part of music for such a voice. —*adj.* of the soprano.
—[名] 1. 소프라노, 최고음 2. 소프라노 가수 3. 최고음부 —[形] 소프라노의

sor·cer·er [sɔ́:*r*s(ə)rə*r*] *n.* [C] a person who practices magic through the aid of evil spirits; a magician.
—[名] 마술사, 마법사

sor·cer·ess [sɔ́:*r*s(ə)ris] *n.* [C] a woman sorcerer.
—[名] 여자 마술사

sor·cer·y [sɔ́:*r*s(ə)ri] *n.* [U] magic performed through the aid of evil spirits; witchcraft.
—[名] 마법, 마술

sor·did [sɔ́:*r*did] *adj.* **1.** dirty. ¶*live in a place with ~ surroundings.*① **2.** morally mean or low; degraded. ¶*a ~ quarrel*② / *~ desires.*
—[形] 1. 누추한, 지저분한 ¶①누추한 곳에 살다 2. 비열한; 상스러운 ②¶ 치사한 싸움

⁑ sore [sɔ:*r*] *adj.* (**sor·er, sor·est**) **1.** painful when touched; feeling pain from a wound, a bruise, etc. ¶*~ eyes*① / *have a ~ throat.*② **2.** filled with sadness or sorrow; distressed. ¶*a ~ heart*③ / *She is ~ at heart.*④ **3.** (*colloq.*) easily offended; inclined to feel injured or hurt. 《*~ about, over*》 ¶*feel ~ about something*⑤ / *He got ~ over such an innocent remark.* **4.** severe; intense.
—[形] 1. 조금만 건드려도 아픈; 진무른, 헐은 ¶①진무른 눈/②목이 아프다 2. 비탄에 잠긴 ¶③슬픈 마음/④그녀는 비탄에 잠겨 있다 3. 《口》 성 잘 내는; 느끼기 쉬운; 상처받기 쉬운 ¶⑤…을 성내다 4. 심한; 격렬한

1) ***like a bear with a sore head,*** bad-tempered.
2) ***a sight for sore eyes,*** something pleasant to see.
[熟] 1)기분이 언짢은 2)보기만 해도 즐거운 것

—*n.* [C] **1.** a painful or diseased spot on one's skin. **2.** a cause of pain, grief, irritation, etc. ¶*Time does not always cure old sores.* —*adv.* severely; sorely.
—[名] 1. 건드리면 아픈 곳; 상처 2. 고통거리; 묵은 상처 —[副] 몹시

sore·ly [sɔ́:*r*li] *adv.* **1.** painfully; severely. **2.** extremely; very much. ¶*I feel ~ inclined to go.*①
—[副] 1. 아프게; 심하게 2. 몹시 ¶① 가고 싶어서 못 견디겠다

sore·ness [sɔ́:*r*nis] *n.* [U] the state of being sore; painfulness; offense. ¶*There was some ~ between them.*
—[名] 욱신욱신 아픔; 화, 성; 불화

so·ror·i·ty [sərɔ́:riti, +*U.S.* -rár- / -rɔ́r-] *n.* [C] (pl. **-ties**) (*U.S.*) a club or society of women at many colleges.
—[名] 《美》 대학 내의 여학생 사교클럽

sor·rel¹ [sɔ́:r(ə)l, sár- / sɔ́r-] *n.* [C] any of several plants with sour-tasting leaves used in salads.
—[名] 참소리쟁이; 수영류; 괭이밥

sor·rel² [sɔ́:r(ə)l, +*U.S.* sár- / sɔ́r-] *adj.* reddish-brown.
—*n.* [C] a reddish-brown horse.
—[形] 밤색의 —[名] 밤색의 말

⁑ sor·row [sárou / sɔ́r-] *n.* [U] **1.** sadness; grief. ¶*feel ~ for someone's dishonor*① / *be in great ~.*② / *to one's ~.*③ **2.** regret. 《*~ at, for, over*》 ¶*She expressed ~ at her mistake.*④ **3.** [U][C] 《often *pl.*》 a cause of grief, disappointment, regret, etc; a misfortune. ¶*the Man of Sorrows.*⑤ / *I have had many sorrows.*⑥ —*vi.* feel or show sadness. ¶*~ at* (or *for, over*) *a misfortune.*⑦
▷**sor·row·er** [-ər] *n.* —**sor·row·less** [-lis] *adj.*
—[名] 1. 슬픔 ¶①남의 불명예를 슬퍼하다/②몹시 슬퍼하고 있다/③슬픈 일은 2. 후회 ¶④그녀는 잘못을 후회했다 3. 불행; 고생 ¶⑤그리스도/⑥나는 슬픈 일을 많이 겪었다 —[自] 슬퍼하다 ¶⑦불행을 슬퍼하다

• sor·row·ful [sárouf(u)l, sɔ́:r- / sɔ́r-] *adj.* **1.** full of sadness;
—[形] 1. 슬픈 2. 슬픔을 자아내는 ¶①

showing sadness; sad. **2.** causing or feeling sadness. ¶*a ~ sight.*①
애처로운 광경

sor·row·ful·ly [sάroufuli, sɔ́:r- / sɔ́r-] *adv.* in a sorrowful manner; with sorrow.
—[副] 슬퍼하여

⁑ sor·ry [sάri, sɔ́:- / sɔ́ri] *adj.* (**-ri·er, -ri·est**) **1.** ⦅as *predicative*⦆ feeling regret for something. ¶*I'm ~ to trouble you.*① **2.** ⦅as *predicative*⦆ feeling pity or sad for someone. ¶*I'm ~ to hear it.*② | *I'm ~ you are ill.* **3.** poor; worthless. ¶*a ~ excuse.* **4.** sad; miserable. ¶*She lived in a ~ place.*
—[形] 1. 서운한, 유감스러운, 애석한 ¶①폐를 끼쳐 죄송합니다 2. 가엾게 여기는, 불쌍한 ¶②그것을 들으니 참 안됐읍니다 3. 서투른; 가치없는 4. 슬픈; 비참한

⁑ sort [sɔ:rt] *n.* [C] **1.** a kind; a class; a type. ¶*this ~ of* [*a*] *person*① | *What ~ of friends do you have?* **2.** a quality; a character; a nature. ¶*He is a good ~.*②
1) ***in some sort,*** to a certain extent.
2) ***out of sorts,*** not feeling well; out of order. ¶*I am a little out of sorts today.*
—*vt.* arrange (things) according to the class of each; classify; select. ⦅~ *over* or *out* things⦆
—[名] 1. 종류; 부류 ¶①이런 부류의 사람 2. 품질; 성질; 성미 ¶②그는 성질이 괜찮다
[熟] 1)어느 정도 2)기분이 언짢은
—[他] …을 분류하다; 고르다

sor·tie [sɔ́:rti(:)] *n.* [C] **1.** a sudden attack by troops who are themselves surrounded. **2.** a single flight of an aircraft to attack the enemy.
—[名] 1. [포위군에 대한] 출격 2. 단기(單機) 출격

SOS [ésòués] *n.* [C] (pl. **SOS's** [-iz]) a call for help, usu. sent by radio in an emergency.
—[名] 조난[무전]신호

so-so [sóusòu] *adj.* (*colloq.*) neither very good nor very bad; not so good; passable.
—[形] ⦅口⦆ 대단치 않은, 그저 그만한

sot [sαt / sɔt] *n.* [C] a person in the habit of heavy drinking; a habitual drunkard.
—[名] 주정뱅이

sot·tish [sάtiʃ / sɔ́t-] *adj.* of or like a sot; given to heavy drinking.
—[形] 주정뱅이의

sot·to vo·ce [sάtouvóutʃi / sɔ́t-] *adj.* in a low voice which cannot be overheard.
—[副] 낮은 목소리로

sough [sau, sʌf] *vi.* make a low, murmuring sound.
—*n.* [C] a low, murmuring sound.
—[自] [바람이] 쏴쏴(휘휘) 불다
—[名] 휘휘(쏴쏴)하는 소리

⁑ sought [sɔ:t] *v.* pt. and pp. of **seek**.

⁑ soul [soul] *n.* **1.** [C] man's spirit. ¶*The ~ is believed to exist forever.* **2.** [U] life; essential part. ¶*Brevity is the ~ of wit.*① **3.** [U] a human being; a man. ¶*Not a ~ was to be seen.*② | *Poor ~!*③ **4.** [C] the spirit of a dead person.
1) ***have no soul,*** lack passion.
2) ***keep soul and body together,*** manage to live.
3) ***upon my soul,*** by God; surely.
—[名] 1. 정신, 혼(魂) 2. 생명; 정수(精髓) ¶①간결은 기지(機知)의 정수이다 3. 인간 ¶②사람 하나 안 보였다/③불쌍한 녀석! 4. 영혼; 망령
[熟] 1)정열이 없다 2)살림을 꾸려가다 3)맹세코; 확실히

soul·ful [sóulf(u)l] *adj.* full of or showing deep feeling or emotion.
—[形] 감정을 담은; 정열적인

soul·less [sóullis] *adj.* having no soul; without deep feeling or emotion; cruel. ▷**soul·less·ly** [-li] *adv.*
—[形] 영혼이 없는; 무정한

⁑ sound¹ [saund] *adj.* **1.** healthy; without any bad point. ¶*A ~ mind in a ~ body.*① | *a ~ piece of fruit.* **2.** correct; right; reasonable. ¶*a ~ judgment.* **3.** complete; deep. ¶*a ~ sleep.* **4.** safe; reliable. ¶*a ~ business.* **5.** legal; lawful. —*adv.* soundly. ¶*sleep ~.*
—[形] 1. 건전한; 완전한 ¶①건전한 정신은 건전한 신체에 깃든다 2. 올바른, 정당한 3. 충분한; 깊은 4. 안전한; 견실한 5. 합법적인; 공식의 —[副] 깊이

⁑ sound² [saund] *n.* **1.** [U][C] what is heard. ¶*Not a ~ was heard.*① **2.** [C] tone. **3.** [U] noise. **4.** [C] a meaning; an impression. ¶*This sentence has a strange ~.*② **5.** [U] the distance something can be heard. ¶*within the ~ of the whistle.*
—*vi.* **1.** make sounds. ¶*The buzzer sounds.* **2.** give a certain impression to someone's ear. ¶*The music sounds well.*③ **3.** appear; seem. ¶*His story sounds like a fiction.*④ | *The plan sounds wonderful.*⑤ —*vt.* **1.** cause (something) to make a noise. ¶*~ a bell* | *~ a horn.*⑥ **2.** examine (something) by hitting and making it sound. ¶*~ someone's breast.*
—[名] 1. 소리, 음향 ¶①소리 하나 들리지 않았다 2. 음조 3. 소음 4. 의미; 느낌 ¶②이 문장은 이상한 느낌이 든다 5. 들리는 거리
—[自] 1. 소리를 내다; 울리다 2. …에게 들리다 ¶③그 음악은 듣기 좋다 3. 보이다, 여겨지다 ¶④그의 이야기는 지어낸 것 같다/⑤그 계획은 멋있을 것 같다 —[他] 1. …을 울리다; 소리를 내게 하다 ¶⑥경적을 울리다 2. …을 타진하다

sound³ [saund] *vt.* **1.** measure the depth of (water) by lowering a weight attached to the end of a line. **2.** try to find someone's feelings, opinion, etc.; examine. ¶*~ someone's opinion.*① —*vi.* **1.** measure the depth of water. **2.** go to the bottom; dive deeply into water.
—[他] 1. [측연(測鉛)으로] …의 깊이를 조사하다 2. …의 의중을 떠보다 ¶①남의 의견을 타진하다 —[自] 1. 수심을 재다 2. 바닥에 닿다; 물 밑으로 잠수하다

S

sound[4] [saund] *n.* [C] **1.** a long stretch of water joining two large areas of water or lying between the mainland and an island. **2.** an air bag of a fish.
—[名] 1. 해협 2. [물고기의] 부레

sound film [ˊ ˋ] *n.* a motion picture film with a sound track on one edge.
—[名] 발성영화

sound·ing[1] [sáundiŋ] *adj.* **1.** making a sound; noisy. **2.** high-sounding but meaningless. ¶ ~ *oratory*① / *a ~ promise.*②
—[形] 1. 울리는 2. 과장된 ¶①과장된 연설/②알맹이 없는 약속

sound·ing[2] [sáundiŋ] *n.* [C] **1.** 《often *pl.*》 the act of measuring the depth of water by lowering a weight attached to a line. **2.** 《*pl.*》 the depth of water measured in this way.
—[名] 1. 수심 측량 2. 수심

sound·less [sáundlis] *adj.* **1.** having no sound; perfectly quiet. **2.** (of the depth of water) that cannot be measured. ▷**sound·less·ly** [-li] *adv.*
—[形] 1. 소리없는 2. [깊이를] 잴 수 없는, 아주 깊은

sound·ly [sáundli] *adv.* **1.** in a sound manner; healthily. **2.** without being awakened; deeply. ¶*sleep ~.* **3.** completely; thoroughly.
—[副] 1. 건전하게 2. [잠 따위] 깊이, 푹 3. 호되게

sound·ness [sáundnis] *n.* [U] the state or quality of being sound.
—[名] 건전

sound·proof [sáundprùːf] *adj.* not allowing sound to pass through. **—***vt.* make (something) soundproof.
—[形] 방음(防音)의 —[他] …에 방음장치를 하다

sound track [ˊ ˋ] *n.* a sound record along one side of a motion picture film.
—[名] [발성영화의 필름 가장자리에 있는] 녹음대(錄音帶)

sound waves [ˊ ˋ] *n.* vibrating waves which produce sounds when they strike the hearing organs.
—[名] 음파

⁑ **soup** [suːp] *n.* [U] a liquid food made by boiling meat, bones, vegetables, fish, etc. in water, milk etc.
—[名] 수우프

in the soup, in trouble. ¶*He left many persons in the ~.*①
[熟] 곤경에 빠져 ¶①그는 많은 사람들을 곤경에 빠뜨렸다

• **sour** [sáuər] *adj.* **1.** having a taste like vinegar or green fruit; (of milk, etc.) spoiled. ¶ ~ *milk*① / *Green fruit is ~.*② **2.** bad-tempered; disagreeable. ¶*make a ~ face.*③ **3.** (of soil) sterile; unproductive.
—[形] 1. 신, 시어진 ¶①시어진 우유/②익지 않은 과일은 시다 2. 심술궂은, 불쾌한 ¶③언짢은 표정을 짓다 3. 불모의

1) ***be sour on,*** (*U.S. colloq.*) dislike (something), esp. after one has previously liked it.
2) ***sour grapes,*** the act of pretending to scorn something one cannot have but would like to.
[熟] 1)《美》…이 싫어지다 2)지기 싫어 허세부리기

—*vt., vi.* **1.** make (something) sour; become sour. **2.** make (someone) bad-tempered; become bad-tempered. **—***n.* something sour.
—[他][自] 1. [···을] 시게 하다(되다) 2. 기분이 언짢게 하다(되다) —[名] 시큼한 것

⁑ **source** [sɔːrs] *n.* [C] **1.** the beginning of a stream or river. ¶*the sources of the Thames*① / *The river takes its ~ from the lake.*② **2.** a place from which something comes; a cause. ¶*historical sources*③ / *I have heard it from a reliable ~.*④
—[名] 1. 원천, 수원지 ¶①테임즈강의 원천/②그 강의 원천은 호수이다 2. 출처; 원인 ¶③사료(史料)/④나는 그것을 확실한 소식통에서 들었다

sour·ly [sáuərli] *adv.* in a sour manner; with bad temper.
—[副] 시큼하게; 기분이 언짢게

sour·ness [sáuərnis] *n.* [U] the state or quality of being sour.
—[名] 심, 시큼함; 기분이 언짢음

souse [saus] *n.* [U] **1.** liquid used for pickling. **2.** [U] something preserved in salt pickle. **3.** [C] the act of plunging into water. ¶*I got a thorough ~ in the thunderstorm.*① **—***vt., vi.* **1.** pickle. **2.** make (someone) or become wet to the skin.
—[名] 1. 간국, 간물 2. 소금에 절인 것 3. 함빡 젖음 ¶①뇌우(雷雨)로 함빡 젖었다 —[他][自] 1. [···을] 소금에 절이다 2. [···을] 함빡 적시다(젖다)

⁑ **south** [sauθ] *n.* **1.** 《usu. *the ~*》 one of the four points of the compass; the direction opposite to the north. **2.** the area or part to the south. ¶*in* (*on, to*) *the ~ of Seoul.*①
—[名] 1. 남쪽 2. 남부; 남국 ¶①서울 남부에(남쪽에 접하여, 남쪽에)

—*adj.* of or from the south. ¶*the ~ wind.*② **—***adv.* towards, in or from the south. ¶*sail ~ / The wind is blowing ~.*③
—[形] 남쪽의 ¶②남풍 —[副] 남쪽에(으로, 에서) ¶③바람은 남쪽에서 불고 있다

South America [ˊ ˊˋˋ] *n.* a continent southeast of North America.
—[名] 남미

South American [ˊ ˊˋˋ] *adj.* of South America or its people. **—***n.* a person of South America.
—[形] 남미의, 남미 사람의 —[名] 남미 사람

South Carolina [ˊ ˋˋˊˋ] *n.* a state in the southeastern part of the United States, on the Atlantic coast.
—[名] 남캐롤라이나 주 [N.B.] S.C.로 줄임. 수도는 Columiba

* **south·east** [sàuθíːst, *Nautical* sàuíːst] *n.* ⦅usu. *the* ~⦆ the point of compass halfway between south and east; a place situated in this direction. —*adj.* of, in, at, from, or towards the southeast. —*adv.* in, from, or towards the southeast.
—[名] 동남; 동남 지방 —[形] 동남의(에서의, 으로의) —[副] 동남에(으로, 에서)

south·east·er [sàuθíːstər] *n.* [C] a wind or storm coming from the southeast.
—[名] 동남풍

south·east·er·ly [sàuθíːstərli] *adv., adj.* toward or from the southeast.
—[副][形] 동남으로[의]; 동남에서[의]

south·east·ern [sàuθíːstərn] *adj.* of the southeast; from, toward or situated in the southeast.
—[形] 동남의; 동남에서의(으로의), 동남에 있는

south·er·ly [sʌ́ðərli] *adv., adj.* in, toward or from the south.
—[副][形] 남쪽의(으로[의], 에서[의])

⁑ **south·ern** [sʌ́ðərn] *adj.* of, in, toward, from or situated in the south. ¶*the ~ aspect*① / *the Southern States.*②
—[形] 남쪽의(으로의, 에서의, 에 있는) ¶①남향/②남부 제주(諸州)

south·ern·er [sʌ́ðərnər] *n.* [C] **1.** a person who lives in or comes from the south. **2.** ⦅*S*-⦆ a person of the south part of the United States.
—[名] 1. 남국 사람 2. 남부 제주의 사람

Southern Hemisphere [ˊ-- ˊ---] *n.* the half of the earth that is south of the equator.
—[名] 남반구

south·ern·most [sʌ́ðərnmòust] *adj.* most southern; situated farthest to the south.
—[形] 가장 남쪽의

South Pole [ˊ ˊ] *n.* the southernmost end of the earth, in the Antarctic region.
—[名] 남극

* **south·ward** [sáuθwərd] *adj., adv.* toward the south. ¶*sail* ~ ① —*n.* ⦅usu. *the* ~⦆ the south.
—[形][副] 남쪽의[으로] ¶①남쪽으로 항행하다 —[名] 남방; 남부

* **south·wards** [sáuθwərdz] *adv.* =southward.

* **south·west** [sáuθwést, *Nautical* souwést] *n.* ⦅usu. *the* ~⦆ the point of the compass halfway between south and west; a place in this direction. —*adj.* of, in, at, from, or towards the southwest. —*adv.* in, from, or towards the southwest.
—[名] 서남, 서남 지방
—[形] 서남의(에서의, 으로의) —[副] 서남방에(에서, 으로)

south·west·er [sàuθwéstər] *n.* [C] **1.** a strong wind or storm from the southwest. **2.** a waterproof hat with a broad brim, worn by seamen. ⇒fig.
—[名] 1. 강한 서남풍 2. [선원 등이 폭풍우 때 쓰는] 방수(防水) 모자

[southwester 2.]

south·west·er·ly [sàuθwéstərli] *adj.* from or toward the southwest.
—[形] 서남에서의; 서남으로의

sou·ve·nir [sùːvəníər / súːv(ə)nìə] *n.* [C] something that reminds a person of some person, place, event, etc.
—[名] 기념품, 유물; 선물

* **sov·er·eign** [sάvrin / sɔ́v-] *n.* [C] **1.** a ruler; a monarch; a king or queen. **2.** a state having independent power. **3.** a British gold coin equal to one pound. —*adj.* **1.** having absolute power. ¶*a ~ prince*① / *~ power.*② **2.** having independent power. ¶*a ~ state.*③ **3.** best; greatest. ¶*the ~ good*④ / *Character is of ~ importance.*⑤ **4.** very effective. ¶*a ~ remedy.*⑥
—[名] 1. 원수(元首) 2. 독립국 3. 영국의 1파운드 금화 —[形] 1. 주권이 있는 ¶①군주/②주권 2. 독립의 ¶③독립국 3. 최상의 ¶④지상선(至上善)/⑤인격은 가장 중요하다 4. 특효가 있는 ¶⑥특효약

sov·er·eign·ty [sάvr(i)nti / sɔ́v-] *n.* **1.** [U] the chief ruling power or authority; the power that a state holds over other states. ¶*popular ~.*① **2.** [C] a sovereign state.
—[名] 1. 주권; 통치권 ¶①재민(在民) 주권 2. 독립국

* **so·vi·et** [sóuvièt / sóuviət] *n.* **1.** [C] a council in Soviet Union. **2.** ⦅*the S*-⦆ the largest country in the world, in both eastern Europe and western Asia. ⇒[N.B.] —*adj.* **1.** of a soviet. **2.** ⦅*S*-⦆ of the Soviet Union.
—[名] 1. [소련의] 회의 2. 소련 [N.B.] 정식명은 The Union of Soviet Socialist Republics, 약어 U.S.S.R
—[形] 1. 회의의 2. 소련의

⁑ **sow**¹ [sou] *vt., vi.* (**sowed, sown** [soun] or **sowed**) **1.** throw and spread (seed) on the earth; plant (seed) in the earth. ¶*~ the field with barley; ~ barley in the field.*① **2.** spread. ¶*a sky sown with stars.*②
—[他][自] 1. [씨를] 뿌리다 ¶①밭에 보리를 뿌리다 2. [소문 따위를] 퍼뜨리다 ¶②별이 총총히 박힌 하늘

sow² [sau] *n.* [C] a female pig.
—[名] 암돼지

sow·er [sóuər] *n.* [C] **1.** a person or thing that sows. **2.** a person who spreads news, gossip, etc. among people.
—[名] 1. 씨를 뿌리는 사람(기계) 2. 유포자(流布者)

⁑ **sown** [soun] *v.* pp. of **sow**.

sox [sɑks / sɔks] *n.* pl. of **sock**.

soy [sɔi] *n.* [U] a salty sauce made from soybeans used in the Orient, for fish and other dishes.
—[名] 간장

S

soy·bean [sɔ́ibìːn] *n.* [C] a plant grown, esp. in China and Japan; its seed, used in making flour, soy, or oil.
—[명] 콩, 대두

spa [spɑː] *n.* [C] **1.** a mineral spring. **2.** a place which has such a mineral spring.
—[명] 1. 광천(鑛泉) 2. 온천장

⁑ space [speis] *n.* **1.** [U] the unlimited room extending in all directions. ¶~ *and time.* **2.** [U] the region outside the earth's atmosphere in which are the moon, sun, and stars. **3.** [U][C] a limited area or distance. ¶*an open ~ | take up ~*① *| for the ~ of a mile.*② **4.** [C] a length of time. ¶*for the ~ of one year.* **5.** [C] (*Music*) a degree or open place between the lines of the staff. **6.** [C] (*Printing*) a blank interval between words; a thin piece of metal used to make this.
—[명] 1. 공간 2. 우주 3. [일정한] 공간, 장소; 거리; 간격 ¶①장소를 차지하다/②1 마일의 거리에 걸쳐 4. [시간의] 사이, 기간, 동안 5. 《樂》 [보표의] 선간(線間) 6. 《印刷》 단어 사이의 공간; 공목(空木), 인테르

—vt. 1. arrange (something) at intervals. **2.** (*Printing*) separate (words, lines, etc.) by spaces.
—[타] 1. …을 사이에 두고 배치하다 2. 《印刷》 글(행) 사이를 떼다

space capsule [ˊ ˋ–] *n.* a container for space travel in which a man rides.
—[명] 우주 캡슈울

space flight [ˊ ˋ] *n.* a flight of a manned or unmanned vehicle through space.
—[명] 우주 비행

space man [ˊ –] *n.* (pl. **-men** [mən]) an astronaut.
—[명] 우주 비행사

space medicine [ˊ ˋ––] *n.* a branch of medicine dealing with the effects on man during space flight.
—[명] 우주 의학

space science [ˊ ˋ–] *n.* a branch of study dealing with the facts or truths of space travel.
—[명] 우주 과학

space·ship [spéisʃìp] *n.* [C] something driven by rockets to carry men and things from the earth through space to the moon or planets.
—[명] 우주선

space suit [ˊ ˋ] *n.* a sealed suit worn by a spaceman.
—[명] 우주복

spac·ing [spéisiŋ] *n.* [U] the act of arranging spaces; [C] the spaces thus arranged.
—[명] 간격을 두기; 공간, 간격

• spa·cious [spéiʃəs] *adj.* **1.** having much space; vast. ¶*a ~ plain.*① **2.** broad in view, etc. ¶*the ~ times of Queen Elizabeth.*
—[형] 1. 널따란 ¶①널따란 평원 2. 견해가 넓은, 스케일이 큰

⁑ spade¹ [speid] *n.* [C] a tool which has a broad blade of iron and a long handle used for turning over the earth.
—[명] 가래, 삽

call a spade a spade, speak plainly.
[熟] …을 솔직히 말하다

—vt. dig (a garden, etc.) with a spade.
—[타] [정원 따위]를 삽으로 파다

spade² [speid] *n.* [C] a black figure like a pointed spade; 《*pl.*》 one of the four suits of playing cards marked with such figures.
—[명] [카아드의] 스페이드; 스페이드 한 벌

spade·ful [spéidfúl] *n.* [C] the amount that a spade can hold.
—[명] 한 삽

spade·work [spéidwə̀ːrk] *n.* [U] hard necessary work on which more advanced work is to be based.
—[명] 힘드는 기초 공작(준비·연구)

spa·ghet·ti [spəgéti] *n.* [U] food made from flour in long, slender pieces.
—[명] 스파게티

• Spain [spein] *n.* a country in southwest Europe. ⇒[N.B.]
—[명] 스페인 [N.B.] 수도 Madrid

• span¹ [spæn] *n.* [C] **1.** the distance between the tips of a man's little finger and thumb when extended (usu. nine inches). **2.** a short period of time; a short distance. ¶*Our life is but a short ~.*① **3.** the full extent in space or time. ¶*the ~ of one's arms.* **4.** the distance between the supports of an arch, a bridge, etc.; the full length of the wings of an airplane.
—[명] 1. 한 뼘(엄지손가락과 새끼손가락 사이의 길이); 보통 9 인치 2. 짧은 기간(거리) ¶①인생은 수유에 불과하다 3. 전장(全長); 전기간 4. 경간(徑間); 홍예문·교량 따위의 지주(支柱) 사이의 길이; 비행기의 날개 길이

—vt. (**spanned, span·ning**) **1.** measure (something) by the spread of a hand. **2.** (of a bridge, etc.) extend or stretch over or across (something). ¶~ *a river with a bridge.* **3.** extend over (a period of time).
—[타] 1. …의 치수를 손가락으로 재다 2. [다리 따위가] …에 걸치다 3. [시간이] …에 미치다

span² [spæn] *n.* [C] (*U.S.*) a pair of horses or other animals harnessed together to pull a cart.
—[명] 《美》 한 멍에를 멘 한 쌍의 말(소)

span³ [spæn] *v.* (*archaic*) pt. of **spin**.

span·gle [spǽŋgl] *n.* [C] a small metal disk sewn on a dress for ornament; any small piece of shining metal used for decoration. ¶*a gold ~.*① **—vt.** decorate (something) with spangles.
—[명] 반짝이는 금속 조각 장식 ¶①[크리스마스의] 금빛 장식 —[타] …에 반짝이는 금속 장식을 달다

• Span·iard [spǽnjərd] *n.* [C] a person of Spain.
—[명] 스페인 사람

span·iel [spǽnjəl] *n.* ⓒ a medium-sized dog with long, silky hair and hanging ears. —ⓝ 스파니엘 개

Span·ish [spǽniʃ] *adj.* of Spain, its people or their language. —*n.* ⓤ the language of Spain; ((*the* ~, *collectively*)) the people of Spain. ¶~ *America*① / ~ *American* / *the* ~ *Armada*.② —ⓗ 스페인[사람·말]의 —ⓝ 스페인 말; 스페인 사람 ¶①스페인 말을 쓰는 중남미/②스페인의 무적함대

spank [spæŋk] *vt.* punish (someone) by striking him with the open hand, a slipper, etc. —*n.* ⓒ a blow with the open hand, a slipper, etc. —ⓗ 벌로서 …을 손바닥·슬리퍼로 찰싹 때리다 —ⓝ 찰싹 때리기

spank·ing [spǽŋkiŋ] *adj.* **1.** moving rapidly; blowing strongly. ¶*a* ~ *trot*① / *a* ~ *breeze*.② **2.** (*colloq.*) unusually fine, large, strong, vigorous, etc. —ⓗ 1. 활발한; 강한 ¶①활발한 빠른 걸음/②강한 바람 2.《口》멋진

span·ner [spǽnər] *n.* (*Brit.*) a tool for tightening or turning a nut, a bolt, etc. —ⓝ《英》스패너

spar¹ [spɑːr] *n.* ⓒ **1.** a pole of a ship, used to support and stretch the sails of a ship. **2.** a main part of the framework of an airplane wing. —*vt.* (**sparred, spar·ring**) provide (a ship) with spars. —ⓝ 1. [돛대 따위의] 둥근 기둥 2. [비행기 날개의] 골조(骨造), 익형(翼桁) —ⓗ [배]에 둥근 재목을 달다

spar² [spɑːr] *vi.* (**sparred, spar·ring**) **1.** fight with the arms and fists; box. ¶*a sparring partner*① / ~ *at someone*.② **2.** (*colloq.*) talk to someone violently in trying to prove something. —*n.* ⓒ the act of sparring. —ⓗ 1. 권투를 하다 ¶①연습 상대가 돼주는 권투선수/②…에게 치고 덤비다 2. 말다툼하다 —ⓝ 권투 시합; 말다툼

:spare [spɛər] *vt.* **1.** use (something) in an economical way. ¶~ *oneself*① / *Spare the rod and spoil the child.*② **2.** do without (something); afford to give. ¶*I have no time to* ~ *for it.* / *Can you* ~ *me a pencil?*; *Can you* ~ *a pencil for me?*③ **3.** save (someone) from killing, punishing, etc.; show mercy to (someone); avoid harming or destroying (something). ¶*The prisoner was spared.* **4.** save or protect (someone) from strain, discomfort, etc. —*vi.* **1.** live economically. **2.** show mercy; forgive.
—*adj.* **1.** free for other uses; extra. ¶~ *time* / *a* ~ *room.* **2.** (of a person) thin. ¶*a* ~ *man.* **3.** (of a meal, etc.) poor; small. —*n.* ⓒ something which is spare or extra. —ⓗ 1. …을 절약하다; 인색하게 쓰다 ¶①수고를 아끼다/②매를 아끼면 자식을 망친다 2. …없이 지내다;…을 나누어 주다 ¶③나에게 연필을 한 자루 나누어 주겠나? 3. …의 목숨을 살려주다;…에게 자비를 베풀다; 위해를 가하지 않다 4.[남]을 …시키지(끼치지) 않다 —ⓥ 1. 절약(검약)하다 2. 용서하다
—ⓗ 1. 여분의; 예비의 2. 야윈, 마른 3. 빈약한, 모자라는 —ⓝ 예비품; 여분의 것

spar·ing [spɛ́əriŋ] *adj.* economical in money. ¶*a* ~ *use of* …① —ⓗ 절약하는, 아끼는 ¶①…의 절약

spar·ing·ly [spɛ́əriŋli] *adv.* economically. —ⓥ 절약하여; 모자라게

* **spark** [spɑːrk] *n.* ⓒ **1.** a small particle of burning matter thrown off by something burning; any flash or gleam. ¶*a* ~ *of light*① / *Burning wood throws off sparks.*② **2.** a sign of life. ¶*the* ~ *of life.*③ **3.** ((*a* ~, chiefly in *negative*)) a small amount. ¶*She hasn't a* ~ *of interest in the plan.*④ **4.** a flash of light produced by an electrical discharge. —*vi.* give off sparks. —ⓝ 1. 불꽃; 섬광; 번득임; 반짝임 ¶①섬광/②불타는 나무가 불꽃을 낸다 2. 생기, 활기 ¶③생기 3. 다소, 조금 ¶④그녀는 그 계획에는 조금도 흥미를 갖고 있지 않다 4.[전기]스파크 —ⓥ 불꽃이 튀다; 스파크하다

* **spar·kle** [spɑ́ːrkl] *n.* ⓒ a little spark; a flash of light. —*vi.* **1.** give off little sparks; flash. ¶*The diamond sparkled.*① / *The woman's eyes sparkled with delight.* **2.** produce bubbles. ¶*The beer sparkles.* —ⓝ 불꽃, 불똥; 섬광 —ⓥ 1. 불꽃을 튀기다; 번득이다 ¶①다이아몬드가 번쩍번쩍 빛났다 2. 거품 일다

:spar·row [spǽrou] *n.* ⓒ a small, common, brownish-grey bird found in most parts of the world. —ⓝ 참새

sparse [spɑːrs] *adj.* thinly spread or scattered. ↔dense —ⓗ 드문드문한, 희박한

sparse·ly [spɑ́ːrsli] *adv.* in a sparse manner. —ⓥ 드문드문하게, 희박하게

sparse·ness [spɑ́ːrsnis] *n.* ⓤ the state of being sparse. —ⓝ 희박

Spar·ta [spɑ́ːrtə] *n.* an ancient city in Greece, famous for its strict and hard training. —ⓝ 스파르타

Spar·tan [spɑ́ːrtən] *adj.* **1.** of Sparta or its people. **2.** like the Spartans; brave; highly-trained. ¶~ *training.*① —*n.* ⓒ **1.** a person of Sparta. **2.** a person who has Spartan characteristics. —ⓗ 1. 스파르타[사람]의 2. 스파르타식의; 용감한, 엄격한 ¶①스파르타식 교육 —ⓝ 1. 스파르타 사람 2. 용감하고 강직한 사람

spasm [spǽz(ə)m] *n.* ⓒ a sudden, abnormal tightening of a muscle; a sudden, violent feeling or shock. ¶*The* ~ *passed off.*① / *I had a* ~ *of laughing at his words.*② —ⓝ 경련; 발작 ¶①경련이 멎었다/②그의 말을 듣고 포복절도했다

spas·mod·ic [spæzmádik / -mɔ́d-] *adj.* characterized by spasms; happening suddenly and violently.

spas·mod·i·cal·ly [spæzmádik(ə)li / -mɔ́d-] *adv.* in a spasmodic manner.

*** spat**[1] [spæt] *v.* pt. and pp. of **spit**.[1]

spat[2] [spæt] *n.* ⓒ (usu. *pl.*) a short cloth covering for the upper part of the boot or shoe and the ankle. ⇒fig.

spate [speit] *n.* ⓒ (*Brit.*) a sudden downpour of rain; a flood.

spa·tial [spéiʃ(ə)l] *adj.* of space; existing in space.

[spat²]

spat·ter [spǽtər] *vt.* splash (water, mud, etc.) in all directions. ¶*The car spattered us with mud.*① —*vi.* fall in drops. ¶*Rain is spattering on the pavement.* —*n.* ⓒ 1. a light splash. 2. the sound of spattering.

spawn [spɔːn] *n.* Ⓤ 1. the eggs of fish, frogs or other water creatures. 2. the threadlike thing from which mushroom grows. —*vi., vt.* lay or produce (eggs) in large numbers.

⁑ speak [spiːk] *v.* (**spoke, spok·en** or *archaic* **spake, spoke**) *vi.*① 1. say words; talk. ¶*~ clearly | generally speaking*① *| ~ under one's breath.*② 2. make a speech. ¶*~ in public.* 3. talk together; discuss. (*~ about* something) 4. express an idea, a feeling, etc.; tell. ¶*Action speaks louder than words.*③ 5. (of guns, musical instruments, etc.) sound. ¶*The organ spoke.* —*vt.* 1. use (a language) in speaking. ¶*She can ~ French.* 2. make (something) known; express. ¶*Her smile spoke a warm welcome.*

1) *so to speak,* speaking in general terms; as it were.
2) *speak for,* ⓐ represent; speak in behalf of (someone). ⓑ recommend. ⓒ (*U.S.*) reserve.
3) *speak for oneself,* express one's own view only.
4) *speak one's mind,* say frankly what one thinks.
5) *speak of,* mention. ⌈and clearly.⌉
6) *speak out* (or *up*), ⓐ say openly. ⓑ speak loudly
7) *speak well* (*ill*) *of* (=*práise* (*bláme*)) something or someone.

*** speak·er** [spíːkər] *n.* ⓒ 1. a person who speaks. 2. a person who makes effective speeches in public. ¶*He is no ~.*① 3. (*the S-*) the chairman of a lawmaking body, such as the House of Commons. ¶*the Speaker of the House; the Speaker of Parliament.*②

speak·ing [spíːkiŋ] *adj.* 1. allowing speech. 2. seem to speak; very expressive; vivid. ¶*a ~ proof.*

speaking trumpet [ˊ‒ ‒ˋ] *n.* an instrument like a trumpet used to make louder the sound of the human voice.

speaking tube [ˊ‒ ˋ] *n.* a tube or pipe through which a voice can be sent from one part of a building to another.

*** spear** [spiər] *n.* ⓒ a weapon consisting of a long, slender stick with a sharp-pointed metal head. ¶*catch a fish with a ~.*① —*vt.* strike (something) with a spear.

spear·head [spíərhèd] *n.* ⓒ 1. the point of a spear. 2. a person or thing that comes first in an attack, an undertaking, etc.

spear·man [spíərmən] *n.* ⓒ (pl. **-men** [-mən]) a man, esp. a soldier, armed with a spear.

⁑ spe·cial [spéʃ(ə)l] *adj.* 1. distinct from others; particular in kind. ¶*receive ~ care*① *| Speech is a ~ attribute of man.* 2. made for a particular purpose; specialized; extra. ¶*a ~ tool | a ~ train | a ~ correspondent*② *| a*

— 刑 경련의; 발작적인

— 剛 경련적으로; 발작적으로

— 名 짧은 각반

— 名 (英) 큰비; 홍수

— 刑 공간의

— 他 [물·진흙 따위]를 튀기다 ¶①자동차가 우리에게 진흙을 튀겼다
— 自 후드득후드득 내리다
— 名 1. 튐, 튀긴 것 2. 후드득 소리

— 名 1. [물고기·개구리 따위의] 알 2. 균사(菌絲) — 自 他 [물고기 따위가] 알을 낳다

— 自 1. 말하다, 지껄이다 ¶①대체로 말하면/②소곤소곤 이야기하다 2. 연설하다 3. 담화하다 4. 사상·의견 따위를 전하다; 표현하다 ¶③행동은 말보다 똑똑히 의미를 전한다 5. [대포·악기 따위가] 울리다 — 他 1. [국어]로 말하다, 지껄이다 2. …을 이야기하다, 전하다

關 1)말하자면 2)ⓐ…을 대표하여 말하다, 대변하다 ⓑ…을 권하다 ⓒ(美)…을 예약하다 3)자기 견해만 말하다 4)자기 생각을 까놓고 말하다 5)…을 언급하다 6)ⓐ거리낌없이 말하다 ⓑ큰소리로 말하다 7)…의 일을 좋게(나쁘게) 말하다

— 名 1. 말하는 사람 2. 연설자 ¶①그는 연설이 서투르다 3. [하원] 의장 ¶②하원 의장

— 刑 1. 이야기를 하는 사이의 2. 말을 할 듯한, 생생한
— 名 확성기, 메가폰

— 名 통화관(通話管)

— 名 창; 작살 ¶①작살로 물고기를 잡다 — 他 …을 창으로 찌르다

— 名 1. 창끝 2. 선봉, 돌격 선두

— 名 창병(槍兵)

— 刑 1. 특별한; 특수한; 독특한 ¶①특별한 보살핌을 받다 2. 특별한 목적을 위한; 전문의, 전공의; 임시로 마련된 ¶②특파원/③전문 병원 3. 개인의

~ *hospital*① | ~ *study*. **3.** private. ¶*my* ~ *chair* | *It is her* ~ *business*. **4.** unusual; distinguished; exceptional; (of friends) close; intimate. ¶*a* ~ *holiday*.
4. 예외의; 특이한; [친구가] 특히 친한

—*n.* [C] **1.** a special thing or person. **2.** a special train. **3.** a special edition of a newspaper.
—[名] 1. 특별한 사람(것) 2. 특별 열차 3. [신문의] 특별판

special delivery [ˊ- -ˊ--] *n.* (*U.S.*) a kind of mail delivered, for an extra fee, sooner than regular mail. (cf. *Brit.* express delivery)
—[名] 《美》 속달[우편]

spe·cial·ism [spéʃ(ə)lìz(ə)m] *n.* [U][C] a devotion to a particular branch of study or work.
—[名] 전문, 전공

* **spe·cial·ist** [spéʃ(ə)list] *n.* [C] a person who is devoted in a particular field of study, business, medicine, etc. ¶*an eye* ~① | *a* ~ *in diseases of the heart.*②
—[名] 전문가, 전문 의사 ¶①안과 전문의(醫)/②심장병 전문의

spe·ci·al·i·ty [spèʃiǽliti] *n.* [C] (pl. **-ties**) **1.** a special quality or characteristic of a person or thing. **2.** a special point; a particular; a detail. **3.** a special or particular field of study, business, etc. **4.** a special product.
—[名] 1. 특색 2. 상세 3. 전문; 전공 4. 특산품; 특제품

spe·cial·i·za·tion [spèʃəlizéiʃ(ə)n, -ʃəlai-] *n.* [U] the act of specializing; the state of being specialized.
—[名] 특수화, 전문화

* **spe·cial·ize** [spéʃəlàiz] *vt.* make (something) special; direct (something) to a particular object. —*vi.* follow some particular branch of work, study, etc. 《~ *in* something》 ¶*He specializes in chemistry.*①
—[他] …을 특수화하다; …을 전문화하다 —[自] 전공하다 ¶①그는 화학 전공이다

* **spe·cial·ly** [spéʃ(ə)li] *adv.* especially; particularly; for a special purpose. ¶*I came here* ~ *to see you.*①
—[副] 특히; 일부러 ¶①너를 만나러 일부러 왔다

spe·cial·ty [spéʃ(ə)lti] *n.* [C] (pl. **-ties**) **1.** a special branch of work or study. **2.** a special quality or characteristic. **3.** an article to which special attention is given.
—[名] 1. 전문 2. 특성 3. 특제품

spe·cie [spíːʃi(ː)] *n.* [U] money in coins; metal money. ↔paper money ¶*a* ~ *bank.*①
—[名] 정금(正金), 정화(正貨) ¶①정금은행(正金銀行)

* **spe·cies** [spíːʃi(ː)z] *n.* (pl. **-cies**) **1.** a group of animals or plants of the same general kind with important common characteristics; a kind. ¶*butterflies of many* ~① | *"The Origin of Species"*② | *The* ~ *are very numerous.*③ **2.** bread and wine used in the Mass.
—[名] 1. 종(種); 종류 ¶①각종의 나비/②「종의 기원」/③그 종류는 아주 많다 2. 미사용의 포도주

* **spe·cif·ic** [spisífik] *adj.* **1.** particular. ¶*for a* ~ *purpose.*① **2.** of species. ¶*the* ~ *name of an animal.*② **3.** having a special effect in curing a certain disease. ¶*a* ~ *medicine.*③ **4.** definite; precise. ¶*a* ~ *statement.*④ —*n.* [C] **1.** any specific quality. **2.** a cure for a certain disease.
—[形] 1. 특정의 ¶①특정의 목적으로 2. 종(種)의 ¶②어떤 동물의 종 이름 3. 특효가 있는 ¶③특효약 4. 명확한, 상세한 ¶④상세한 진실 —[名] 1. 특성 2. 특효약

spe·cif·i·cal·ly [spisífik(ə)li] *adv.* definitely; particularly.
—[副] 명확히, 특별히

spec·i·fi·ca·tion [spès(i)fikéiʃ(ə)n] *n.* [U] **1.** the act of stating in detail. **2.** 《*pl.*》 a detailed description of requirements to carry out some work or plan.
—[名] 1. 상술(詳述) 2. 명세서, 내역

specific gravity [-ˊ- ˊ--] *n.* (*Physics*) the ratio between the weight of a certain substance and that of another substance, esp. water in the same volume.
—[名] 《理》 비중(比重)

spec·i·fy [spésifài] *vt.* (**-fied**) mention or describe (something) in detail; state fully and clearly. ¶~ *the persons concerned*① | ~ *reasons for one's failure.*②
—[他] …을 자세히 적다(쓰다) ¶①관계자의 이름을 명기하다/②실패의 이유를 명기하다

* **spec·i·men** [spésimin] *n.* [C] a part of something, or one of a group of something which represents the whole; a sample. ¶~ *pages*① | *an insect* ~② | *a stuffed* ~.③
—[名] 견본; 표본 ¶①[책의] 내용 견본/②곤충의 표본/③박제(剝製) 표본

spe·cious [spíːʃəs] *adj.* seeming good or correct, but not really so. ¶*a* ~ *argument.*①
—[形] 외양뿐인, 그럴듯한 ¶①그럴듯한 의론

spe·cious·ly [spíːʃəsli] *adv.* in a specious manner; plausibly.
—[副] 그럴듯하게

spe·cious·ness [spíːʃəsnis] *n.* [U] the state or quality of being specious.
—[名] 그럴듯함

* **speck** [spek] *n.* [C] **1.** a small spot on something. **2.** a very tiny thing. ¶*I don't like it a* ~.① —*vt.* 《usu. in *passive*》 mark (something) with spots.
—[名] 1. 작은 얼룩, 오점 2. 작은 알갱이(조각) ¶①나는 전혀 마음에 안 든다 —[他] …에 얼룩(반점)을 찍다

speck·le [spékl] *n.* [C] a small spot or mark on some-
—[名] 작은 반점, 얼룩 ¶①흰 반점이

S

thing. ¶*a gray dog with white speckles.*① —*vt.* ⦅usu. in *passive*⦆ mark (something) with speckles.
있는 회색 강아지 —[他] …에 작은 반점을 찍다

speck·less [spéklis] *adj.* having no spot; without a speck; clean.
—[形] 반점이 없는, 오점이 없는

***spec·ta·cle** [spéktəkl] *n.* [C] **1.** something impressive to look at; a public show. ¶*a charming* ~① / *He was a sad ~ in his rags.*② **2.** ⦅*pl.*⦆ a pair of eyeglasses to help a person to see. ¶*a man in* ~.③
—[名] 1. 광경; 구경거리 ¶①아름다운 광경/②누더기를 입고 있는 그를 보기란 불쌍했다 2. 안경 ¶③안경을 쓴 사내

spec·ta·cled [spéktəkld] *adj.* **1.** wearing spectacles. **2.** having markings like spectacles in form. ¶*a ~ bear.*①
—[形] 1. 안경을 쓴 2. 안경 모양의 무늬가 있는 ¶①[남미산] 안경곰

spec·tac·u·lar [spektǽkjulər] *adj.* **1.** of a spectacle or show. **2.** making a wonderful show. ¶*in a ~ fashion*① / *do ~ things.*②
—[形] 1. 구경거리가 될 만한 2. 장관(壯觀)인 ¶①화려하게/②눈부신 일을 하다

***spec·ta·tor** [spékteitər / spektéitə] *n.* [C] a person who looks on at some event; an observer. ¶*a crowd of spectators at a game*① / *remain a ~ / sit as a ~.*②
—[名] 구경꾼; 방관자 ¶①시합의 많은 관중/②방관하다

spec·ter, *Brit.* **-tre** [spéktər] *n.* [C] a ghost.
—[名] 유령

spec·tra [spéktrə] *n.* pl. of **spectrum**.

spec·tral [spéktr(ə)l] *adj.* **1.** of or like a ghost. **2.** of the spectrum. ¶~ *colors*① / ~ *analysis.*②
—[形] 1. 유령의(같은) 2. 스펙트럼의 ¶①무지개의 일곱 가지 색/②스펙트럼 분석

spec·tre [spéktər] *n.* (*Brit.*) =specter.

spec·tro·gram [spéktrougræ̀m] *n.* [C] a photograph of a spectrum.
—[名] 분광(分光) 사진, 스펙트럼 사진

spec·tro·graph [spéktrougræ̀f, +*Brit.* -grɑ̀:f] *n.* [C] an instrument for photographing spectra.
—[名] 분광 사진기

spec·tro·scope [spéktrəskòup] *n.* [C] an instrument for making spectra from any source.
—[名] 분광기

spec·trum [spéktrəm] *n.* [C] (pl. **-tra** or **-trums**) the band of colors formed when light passes through a prism, a water drop, etc.
—[名] 스펙트럼, 분광

S

spec·u·late [spékjulèit] *vi.* **1.** consider a subject carefully; meditate. ⦅~ *about* or *on* something⦆ ¶~ *on the origin of the universe.*① **2.** buy or sell stock, land, etc. with the hope of profiting by a change in the price. ¶~ *in stocks* (or *shares*).②
—[自] 1. 사색하다 ¶①우주의 기원에 대해서 사색하다 2. 투기하다 ¶②증권에 손을 대다

***spec·u·la·tion** [spèkjuléiʃ(ə)n] *n.* **1.** [U] meditation; consideration. ¶*be much given to* ~.① **2.** [C] an opinion or a conclusion reached by such meditation. **3.** [U] the act of buying or selling stocks, land, etc. when there is a large risk, but with the hope of making large profits. ¶*on* ~② / *engage in* ~.③
—[名] 1. 사색 ¶①사색에 잠겨 있다 2. 사색에서 얻는 의견(결론) 3. 투기 ¶②투기로/③투기하다

spec·u·la·tive [spékjulèitiv / -kjulə-] *adj.* **1.** thoughtful; theoretical; not practical. **2.** of commercial or financial speculation. ▷**spec·u·la·tive·ly** [-li] *adv.*
—[形] 1. 사색적인; 이론상의, 공론(空論)의 2. 투기적인

spec·u·la·tor [spékjulèitər] *n.* [C] **1.** (in business) a person who is engaged in financial speculation. **2.** a person who buys tickets in advance to sell them later at a higher price; a ticket speculator. **3.** a person who devotes himself to mental speculation.
—[名] 1. 투기업자; 협잡꾼 2. 암표 장수 3. 사색가, 이론가

⁑**sped** [sped] *v.* pt. and pp. of **speed**.

⁑**speech** [spi:tʃ] *n.* **1.** [U] language. **2.** [U] the act of speaking. ¶*Speech is silvern, silence is golden.*① **3.** [U] the manner of speaking. ¶*a clear* ~② / *be slow of* ~.③ **4.** [U] the power of speaking. ¶*lose one's* ~.④ **5.** [C] a talk given in public; an address. ¶*an opening* ~⑤ / *make a* ~. **6.** [U] (*Grammar*) narration. ¶*direct* (*indirect*) ~.⑥
—[名] 1. 언어 2. 이야기, 지껄이기 ¶①웅변은 은이요 침묵은 금이다 3. 말씨, 말투 ¶②똑똑한 말씨/③말투가 느리다 4. 말을 하는 능력 ¶④말을 못하게 되다 5. 연설 ¶⑤개회사 6. ⦅文法⦆ 화법 ¶⑥직접(간접)화법

speech day [´ ˌ] *n.* (*Brit.*) the last day of the school year, when prizes and oral exercises are given. (cf. *U. S.* commencement)
—[名] ⦅英⦆ 졸업식, 졸업일

speech·i·fy [spí:tʃifài] *vi.* (**-fied**) make a long, dull speech.
—[自] 연설하다

speech·less [spí:tʃlis] *adj.* **1.** unable to speak; silent. ¶*He was ~ with surprise.*① / *I stood ~ with fear.* **2.** that cannot be expressed in words. ¶*a ~ grief.*
—[形] 1. 말을 못하는 ¶①그는 놀라서 말도 할 수 없었다 2. 말로 표현할 수 없는

⁑**speed** [spi:d] *n.* **1.** [U] swift or quick movement. ¶*with*
—[名] 1. 빠른 움직임; 신속한 동작 ¶

great ~① / *More haste, less* ~.② **2.** [U][C] the rate of motion or progress. ¶*at a* ~ *of fifty miles an hour* / [*at*] *full* ~; (*U.S.*) *at top* ~; *at the top of one's* ~.③
—*v.* (**sped** or **speed·ed**) *vi.* **1.** go fast; move quickly. ¶*He sped along the street.* **2.** drive a car more rapidly than is safe or allowed by law. **3.** (*archaic*) live; get on. —*vt.* **1.** cause (something) to move, go, or pass quickly. **2.** cause (something) to succeed or prosper.
1) ***God speed you!,*** ((said at *parting*)) It is my hope that God will take care of you.
2) ***speed up,*** go faster; cause (something) to go more quickly. ¶*Speed up the work.*④

①황급히/②급하면 돌아가라 **2.** 속도, 속력 ¶③전속력으로
—[自] **1.** 급히 가다 **2.** 스피이드를 위반하다 **3.** 해나가다, 살아가다 —[他] **1.** …을 서두르게 하다, 촉진하다; …의 속력을 높이다 **2.** …을 성공(번영)시키다
[熟] 1)행운을 빌겠읍니다 2)빨라지다; …의 속도를 빨리하다 ¶④일을 좀더 빨리 해라

speed·i·ly [spíːdili] *adv.* with speed; soon.
—[副] 빨리, 곧

speed limit [⌐ ⌐-] *n.* the fastest speed permitted by law.
—[名] [허용된] 최고 속도

speed·om·e·ter [spi(ː)dάmitər / -ɔ́mitə] *n.* [C] an instrument attached to an automobile or other vehicle to measure its speed.
—[名] 속도계

speed·way [spíːdwèi] *n.* [C] (*U.S.*) **1.** a road or highway for high-speed traffic. **2.** a track for automobile races.
—[名] **1.** 고속 자동차 도로 **2.** 자동차 경주장

∗**speed·y** [spíːdi] *adj.* (**speed·i·er, speed·i·est**) **1.** fast; rapid. ¶*a* ~ *flight*① / ~ *progress.*② **2.** without delay; prompt. ¶*a* ~ *answer.*③ ▷**speed·i·ness** [-nis] *n.*
—[形] **1.** 신속한, 빠른 ¶①재빠른 도주/②장족의 진보 **2.** 즉각의 ¶③즉답

⁑**spell**[1] [spel] *v.* (**spelled** or **spelt**) *vt.* **1.** write or say the letters of (a word) in correct order. ¶*How do you* ~ *your name?* **2.** make up or form (a word). ¶*O-n-e spells 'one.'*① **3.** mean. ¶*Delay spells danger.*② —*vi.* form words with letters. ¶*We learn to* ~ *in school.*
spell out, read each word with difficulty
—[他] **1.** [낱말]을 철자하다 **2.** [철자가 낱말]을 만들다 ¶① O-n-e로 쓰고 「원」이라 읽는다 **3.** …을 의미하다 ¶②지연은 위험을 뜻한다 —[自] 글자를 철자하다
[熟] 한자 한자 애써 읽다

∗**spell**[2] [spel] *n.* [C] **1.** a word or words which are supposed to have magic power. ¶*be bound by a* ~① / *cast a* ~ *on someone.*② **2.** charm; fascination. ¶*be under the* ~ *of her beauty.*③
—[名] **1.** 주문(呪文), 진언(眞言) ¶①주문에 묶여 있다/②마법을 걸다 **2.** 매력 ¶③그녀의 아름다움에 매혹되어 있다

∗**spell**[3] [spel] *n.* [C] **1.** a period of work. ¶*a* ~ *of work.*① **2.** a turn at work in place of another. ¶*a* ~ *of eight hours*② / *have a spell.*③ **3.** a period of a specified sort of weather. ¶*a long* ~ *of fine weather.*④ **4.** (*U.S.*) a period of some illness. —*vt.* work in place of (another). ¶*I'll* ~ *you at driving.*⑤
—[名] **1.** 한바탕의 일 ¶①한바탕의 일 **2.** [일의] 교대 ¶②여덟 시간 근무(교대)/③교대하다 **3.** [날씨의] 한동안 ¶④계속되는 좋은 날씨 **4.** 기분이 나쁜 때 —[他] …와 교대하다 ¶⑤운전을 교대해 주겠다

spell·bound [spélbàund] *adj.* held by a spell; too attracted to move; fascinated. ¶*listen* ~.①
—[形] 주문에 묶인; 매혹된 ¶①홀린 듯이 듣다

spell·er [spélər] *n.* [C] **1.** a person who spells words. **2.** (*U.S.*) a spelling book.
—[名] **1.** 철자하는 사람 **2.** ((美)) 철자 교과서

∗**spell·ing** [spéliŋ] *n.* [C] the way in which a word is spelled. ¶*He is poor at* ~.① / *a* ~ *bee.*②
—[名] 철자법 ¶①그는 철자를 잘 못한다/②철자법 경쟁

spelling book [⌐- ⌐] *n.* a book used to practice spelling.
—[名] 철자 교과서

spelt [spelt] *v.* pt. and pp. of **spell**[1].

⁑**spend** [spend] *v.* (**spent**) *vt.* **1.** pay out (money, etc.). ¶*I spent ten dollars today.* **2.** give (labor, time, etc.) for some purpose. ¶*Don't* ~ *much time on that lesson.* **3.** use up; exhaust; wear out (oneself or itself). ¶*The storm has spent itself.*① **4.** pass (time, days, etc.) in a particular manner, place, etc. ¶~ *a sleepless night.* —*vi.* pay out money.
—[他] **1.** [돈 따위]를 쓰다, 소비하다 **2.** [어떤 목적에 노력·시간 따위]를 쓰다, 바치다 **3.** …을 다 쓰다; 지치게(약하게) 하다 ¶①폭풍은 가라앉았다 **4.** [시간]을 보내다 —[自] 돈을 쓰다

spen·der [spéndər] *n.* [C] **1.** a person who spends. **2.** a person who wastes money.
—[名] **1.** 쓰는 사람 **2.** 낭비가

spend·thrift [spéndθrìft] *n.* [C] a person who spends money carelessly and foolishly. —*adj.* wasteful; extravagant.
—[名] 돈 씀씀이가 헤픈 사람, 낭비가 —[形] 돈을 헤프게 쓰는, 사치스러운

⁑**spent** [spent] *v.* pt. and pp. of **spend**.
—*adj.* tired out; used up; without any more power or energy. ¶*a well-spent life*① / *a* ~ *battery.*②
—[形] 지쳐빠진; 다 써 버린; 소비된 ¶①유익하게 보낸 일생/②다 쓴 전지

sperm [spəːrm] *n.* [U] the generative fluid of a male animal.
—[名] 정액(精液)

sperm oil [⌐ ⌐] *n.* a yellowish oil taken from the sperm whale.
—[名] 경유(鯨油)

S

sperm whale [´-´] *n.* a large square-headed whale. —영 향유고래

* **sphere** [sfiər] *n.* Ⓒ **1.** a round body like a ball; a globe. **2.** one of the stars or planets; a heavenly body. **3.** a globe representing the earth or its surface. **4.** the extent of knowledge, influence, activity, etc.; a scope; a range. ¶*a ~ of influence*① / *remain in one's ~.*② **5.** social order or rank. **6.** (*pl., collectively*) (*poetic*) all the stars in the sky; the sky; the heavens. —영 1.구(球) 2.천체 3.지구의(儀) 4.범위,영역 ¶①세력 범위/②자기의 본분을 지키다 5.지위 6.하늘

spher·i·cal [sférik(ə)l] *adj.* of a sphere; having a form like a sphere. ¶*a ~ body*① / *~ geometry.*② —영 구[형]의; 구[면]의 ¶①구체(球體)/②구면(球面) 기하학

sphin·ges [sfíndʒi:z] *n.* pl. of **sphinx.**

sphinx [sfiŋks] *n.* (pl. **sphinx·es** or **sphin·ges**). **1.** (*the S-*) in Greek mythology) a monster with the head of a woman and the body of a winged lion. **2.** (*the S-*) a huge statue in Egypt with a human head and a lion's body. **3.** Ⓒ a mysterious person. —영 1.스핑크스 2.[이집트에 있는] 스핑크스 석상 3.수수께끼 같은 사람

* **spice** [spais] *n.* Ⓤ **1.** a substance with a strong flavor added to food, such as pepper, nutmeg, cloves, and ginger; (*collectively*) such substances. **2.** (often *a ~*) a slight trace or suggestion. (*~ of*) ¶*a ~ of humor*① / *the ~ of life.*② —영 1.양념, 조미료, 향료 2. …한 기미, 정취(情趣) ¶①우스움/②생활의 정감(情感)

—*vt.* **1.** put spice in (something). (*~ something with*) ¶*~ with ginger.*③ **2.** give interest or flavor to (something). ¶*~ one's speech with humorous anecdotes.*④ —태 1. …에 양념을 넣다 ¶③새앙으로 양념을 하다 2. …에 흥미(맛·재미)를 곁들이다 ¶④익살스런 유우머로 연설을 재미있게 하다

spick-and-span [spík(ə)n(d)spǽn] *adj.* entirely new; neat and clean. ¶*She keeps her home ~.*① —영 아주 새로운, 산뜻한 ¶①그녀는 집을 깨끗이 해둔다

spic·y [spáisi] *adj.* (**spic·i·er, spic·i·est**) **1.** flavored with spice; having the flavor of a spice. **2.** witty; lively. ¶*~ criticism.*① —영 1. 양념을 넣은 2. 흥취있는, 짜릿한 ¶①호된 비평

* **spi·der** [spáidər] *n.* Ⓒ one of a number of small eight-legged animals, many of which spin webs to catch insects for food. —영 거미

spi·der·y [spáidəri] *adj.* **1.** like a spider or a spider's web. **2.** long and thin like a spider's legs. **3.** full of spiders. —영 1.거미[줄] 같은 2.거미의 발 같은 3.거미가 많은

spig·ot [spígət] *n.* Ⓒ **1.** a small plug or peg used to stop the flow of liquid through the hole of a cask, a barrel, etc. **2.** (*U.S.*) a faucet. —영 1.[통 따위의] 마개 2.(美) 물꼭지, 물주둥이

spike [spaik] *n.* Ⓒ **1.** a large, heavy nail; a sharp-pointed rod, bar, etc. at the top of a wall. **2.** sharp-pointed metal pieces on the sole of a shoe. **3.** an ear of corn; a long, pointed flower cluster on a stem. —영 1.큰대못; 담장에 박는 큰 못 2.[경기용 구두 밑창에 박는] 뾰족한 징, 스파이크 3.[보리 따위의] 이삭; 수상화(穗狀花)

—*vt.* **1.** fasten (something) with spikes; pierce (something) with a spike. ¶*spiked shoes.*① **2.** make (a cannon, a gun, etc.) useless by driving a spike into its opening. ¶*~ someone's gun.*② **3.** make (a plan, etc.) useless or ineffective. —태 1. …을 큰 못으로 박아 놓이다; …에 스파이크를 박다 ¶①스파이크화(靴) 2.화문전(火門栓)을 들어박다 ¶②대포의 화문전(火門栓)을 들어박다; 계획을 좌절시키다 3.[계획 따위]를 소용없게 만들다

spik·y [spáiki] *adj.* (**spik·i·er, spik·i·est**) **1.** shaped like a spike; having spikes. **2.** (of a person, etc.) difficult to handle. —영 1. 끝이 뾰족한; 못투성이의 2.다루기 힘든

* **spill**¹ [spil] *v.* (**spilt** or **spilled**) *vt.* **1.** cause (liquid, powder, etc.) to fall or flow out. ¶(*proverb*) *It is no use crying over spilt milk.*① **2.** (*colloq.*) throw out (someone or something) from a horse or vehicle. (*~ someone or something from*) **3.** (*Nautical*) let wind out of (a sail) —*vi.* overflow; flow out. —태 1. …을 엎지르다 ¶①(俚) 엎지른 물은 다시 담을 수 없다 2.(口)[말안장·차에서] …을 내팽개치다 3.(海)[돛에서] 바람이 새게 하다 —자 엎질러지다

—*n.* Ⓒ a fall from a horse or vehicle. —영 [말안장·차 따위에서] 떨어지기

spill² [spil] *n.* Ⓒ a thin piece of wood or paper to light candles, pipes, etc. —영 엷은 나무조각; [불붙이는] 종잇조각, 불쏘시개

spilt [spilt] *v.* pt. and pp. of **spill.**

* **spin** [spin] *v.* (**spun** or *archaic* **span, spun, spin·ning**) *vt.* **1.** draw out and twist (cotton, wool, etc.) into threads. (*~ something into or out of*) ¶*~ cotton into yarn*① / *~ thread out of cotton.*② **2.** make (a web, a cocoon, etc.) by giving out thread from the body. ¶*A* —태 1. …을 잣다 ¶①솜을 자아 실을 만들다/②솜에서 실을 잣다 2.[거미·누에 따위가] 실을 내다 ¶③거미는 거미줄을 친다 3. …을 [장황하게] 이

*spider spins a web.*③ **3.** tell (a story, etc.) **4.** cause (something) to turn around swiftly. ¶*~ a top.*④ **—*vi.*** **1.** spin thread; turn around swiftly. **2.** move along swiftly. **3.** feel dizzy. ¶*My head spins.*⑤
1) ***spin a yarn,*** tell a story at full length.
2) ***spin out,*** make (something) long.
—*n.* **1.** [C][U] swift turning motion. ¶*fall in ~.*⑥ **2.** [C] a swift movement; a short drive or ride.

야기하다 4. …을 돌리다 ¶④팽이를 돌리다 —[自] 1. 잣다; 빙글빙글 돌다 2. 질주하다 3. 현기증이 나다 ¶⑤머리가 어지럽다
[熟] 1)장황하게 이야기하다 2)…을 질질 끌다, 길게 늘이다
—[名] 1. 회전 ¶⑥빙글빙글 돌면서 떨어지다 2. 질주; 한바탕 달리기

spin·ach [spínitʃ / -nidʒ] ***n.*** [U] a common vegetable with green leaves which can be cooked and eaten.
—[名] 시금치

spi·nal [spáinl] ***adj.*** of the spine or backbone.
—[形] 등뼈의

spin·dle [spíndl] ***n.*** [C] **1.** a long, thin rod or pin used in spinning to twist and wind the thread. **2.** a rod or pin about which something turns; an axle. **—*vi.*** grow long and thin.
—[名] 1. 방추(紡錘), 북 2. 축(軸), 굴대 —[自] 길쭉해지다

spin·dle-leg·ged [spíndllègd, +*U.S.* -gid] ***adj.*** having long, slender legs.
—[形] 가늘고 긴 다리의

spin·dle·legs [spíndllègz] ***n. pl.*** **1.** long, slender legs; **2.** ⟪used as *sing.*⟫ (*colloq.*) a person who has long, slender legs.
—[名] 1. 가늘고 긴 다리 2. 다리가 가늘고 긴 사람

spin·dle-shanked [spíndlʃæŋkt] ***adj.*** =spindle-legged.

spin·dly [spíndli] ***adj.*** (**-dli·er, -dli·est**) long and thin.
—[形] 가늘고 긴

spine [spain] ***n.*** [C] **1.** the backbone. **2.** the back of a book, with the title and the author's name on it. **3.** a sharp-pointed part sticking out from a plant, an animal, etc.; a thorn.
—[名] 1. 등뼈 2. 책의 등 3. [고슴도치·선인장 따위의] 바늘, 가시

spine·less [spáinlis] ***adj.*** **1.** having no spine. **2.** having no courage, energy or determination; irresolute.
—[形] 1. 등뼈가 없는 2. 우유부단한

spin·et [spínit, +*Brit.* spinét] ***n.*** [C] a musical instrument like a piano. ⇒[N.B.]
—[名] 스피넷 [N.B.] 16—18세기에 쓰인 피아노의 전신

spin·ner [spínər] ***n.*** [C] a person who spins; a machine for spinning cotton, wool, etc.
—[名] 방적공(紡績工)(기)

spinning wheel [∠–∸] ***n.*** a machine with a spindle driven by a large wheel, once used for spinning yarn. ⇒fig.
—[名] 물레

[spinning wheel]

spin·ster [spínstər] ***n.*** [C] **1.** a woman who spins yarn. **2.** an unmarried woman; esp. an elderly woman who has not married.
—[名] 1. 물레질하는 여자 2. 미혼 여자, 노처녀

spin·y [spáini] ***adj.*** (**spin·i·er, spin·i·est**) **1.** covered with or full of spines. **2.** full of difficulties.
—[形] 1. 가시투성이의 2. 곤란한

spi·ral [spáiər(ə)l] ***adj.*** winding around a point in a widening coil; coiled. ¶*a ~ staircase*① / *a ~ spring.*② **—*n.*** [C] a winding coil around a point in increasingly larger circles; anything that has a spiral shape. **—*vt., vi.*** (**-raled, -ral·ing** or *Brit.* **-ralled, -ral·ling**) move in a spiral course; form into a spiral. ▷**spi·ral·ly** [-rəli] ***adv.***
—[形] 소용돌이 모양의, 나선형의 ¶①나선 계단/②나선(螺旋) 용수철 —[名] 나선, 와선(渦線) —[他][自] […을] 나선형으로 움직이다; 나선형으로 하다(되다)

spire[1] [spáiər] ***n.*** [C] **1.** the pointed top of a steeple. **2.** something shaped like a spire. ¶*the rocky spires of a mountain.*① **—*vi.*** **1.** point upward. **2.** shoot up. **—*vt.*** **1.** furnish (something) with a spire. **2.** cause (a plant, etc.) to shoot up.
—[名] 1. 뾰족탑, 첨탑 2. 첨탑 모양의 ¶①뾰족한 바위 봉우리 —[自] 뾰족이 나오다 3. 싹을 내다 —[他] 1. …에 첨탑을 달다 2. …을 싹트게 하다

spire[2] [spáiər] ***n.*** [C] a spiral; a single coil or turn in a spiral.
—[名] 나선(螺線); 소용돌이

‡ **spir·it** [spírit] ***n.*** **1.** [U] soul; mind; intelligence. ¶*develop the ~.*① **2.** [U] the part of man that lasts forever. ¶*the immortality of the ~*② / *the* [*Holy*] *Spirit.*③ **3.** [C] a ghost; a fairy. **4.** [U] courage; power of mind. ¶*a man of ~*④ / *He shows great ~.* **5.** ⟪usu. *pl.*⟫ temper; way of feeling. ¶*in good spirits*⑤ / *out of spirits*⑥ / *lose one's spirits.*⑦ **6.** ⟪often *a ~*⟫ nature; mood. ¶*public ~*⑧ / *say something in a kind ~.*⑨ **7.** ⟪usu. *pl.*⟫ alcohol; strong alcoholic drinks.
—*vt.* **1.** take away (someone) in secret, as if by magic.
—[名] 1. 정신; 마음 ¶①마음을 계발(啓發)하다 2. 혼; 영혼 ¶②영혼의 불멸/③성령(聖靈) 3. 유령; 요정 4. 용기; 원기 ¶④용기있는 사람 5. 기분, 마음 ¶⑤원기왕성하여, 기분이 좋아/⑥풀이 죽어서/⑦낙심하다 6. 기질, 마음가짐 ¶⑧공공심/⑨…을 친절심에서 말하다 7. 알코올; 독한 술
—[他] 1. …을 유괴하다; 감쪽같이 채가

(~ *away* or *off* someone) **2.** encourage. (~ *up* someone) ¶~ *up someone with alcohol.*⑩
다 2. …을 기운내게 하다 ¶⑩…을 술로 기운을 돋우다

spir·it·ed [spíritid] *adj.* **1.** full of life or energy; lively. ¶*a ~ old man.*① **2.** (in *compounds*) having a particular character or mood. ¶*high-spirited / low-spirited.*
—[形] 1. 힘찬, 활발한 ¶①정정한 노인 2. …한 정신을 가진, …한 기분의

spirit lamp [´– ˋ] *n.* a lamp in which alcohol is burnt.
—[名] 알코홀 남포

spir·it·less [spíritlis] *adj.* lacking spirit or courage; not lively.
—[形] 기운 없는

spirit level [´– – ˋ–] *n.* a glass tube containing alcohol used to find out whether a surface is level shown by an air-bubble.
—[名] 알코홀 수준기(水準器)

* **spir·i·tu·al** [spíritʃuəl, +*Brit.* -tju-] *adj.* **1.** of the spirit or mind. ↔material ¶~ *awakening.*① **2.** of religion or sacred things; holy. ¶*the ~ life*② / ~ *songs.*③
—*n.* [C] (*U.S.*) a religious song or hymn sung by the Negroes of the South.
—[形] 1. 정신의, 영적(靈的)인 ¶①정신적 각성 2. 신앙의; 신성한 ¶②신앙생활/③성가(聖歌)
—[名] 《美》 흑인 영가

spir·i·tu·al·ism [spíritʃuəliz(ə)m, +*Brit.* -tju-] *n.* [U] **1.** the belief that spirits of the dead can talk with living people through a special person. **2.** the philosophical doctrine that spirit alone is real. ↔materialism
—[名] 1. 심령 현상을 믿기, 심령론 2. 유심론(唯心論)

spir·i·tu·al·ist [spíritʃuəlist, +*Brit.* -tju-] *n.* [C] a person who believes in spiritualism.
—[名] 심령론자; 유심론자

spir·i·tu·al·i·ty [spìritʃuǽliti, +*Brit.* -tju-] *n.* (pl. **-ties**) **1.** [U] the state or quality of being spiritual. **2.** (usu. *pl.*) the right, income, or property of a church or a clergyman.
—[名] 1. 정신적임 2. 교회(성직자)의 권리(수입·재산)

spir·i·tu·al·ize [spíritʃuəlàiz, +*Brit.* -tju-] *vt.* **1.** make (something) spiritual or pure. **2.** interpret or understand spiritually. ↔literalize
—[他] 1. …을 정신적으로 하다; 고상하게 하다 2. …을 정신적인 의미로 해석(이해)하다

spir·it·u·al·ly [spirítʃuəli, +*Brit.* -tju-] *adv.* in a spiritual manner.
—[副] 정신적으로

spir·i·tu·ous [spíritʃuəs, +*Brit.* -tju-] *adj.* **1.** containing much alcohol. **2.** distilled. ↔fermented
—[形] 1. 알코홀 성분을 함유한 2. 증류한

spi·rom·e·ter [spàiərámitər / -rɔ́mitə] *n.* [C] an instrument for measuring the breathing capacity of the lungs.
—[名] 폐활량계(肺活量計)

spirt [spəːrt] *v., n.* =spurt.

spir·y [spáiəri] *adj.* shaped like a spire; abounding in spires.
—[形] 뾰족탑 모양의; 뾰족탑이 많은

* **spit**¹ [spit] *v.* (**spat** or *archaic* **spit, spit·ting**) *vt.* **1.** throw out (saliva, blood, etc.) from the mouth. (~ *forth* (or *out, up*) something) ¶~ *blood.* **2.** throw out or utter (an oath, etc.) violently. (~ *out* curses, etc.) —*vi.* **1.** throw out saliva from the mouth. ¶~ *in someone's face*① / *No spitting.*② **2.** (of a cat, etc.) make an angry, hissing sound. **3.** rain slightly or briefly.
—[他] 1. [침·피 따위]를 토하다 2. [욕설 따위]를 내뱉다 —[自] 1. 침을 뱉다 ¶①…의 얼굴에 침을 뱉다/②침을 뱉지 마시오(게시문) 2. [고양이 따위가 성이 나서] 으르렁거리다 3. [비가] 후드득후드득 내리다

—*n.* [U] **1.** saliva. **2.** [C] the act or sound of spitting. **3.** [C] a light or brief rain.
—[名] 1. 침 2. 침을 뱉기(뱉는 소리) 3. 후드득거리는 비

spit² [spit] *n.* [C] **1.** a long, pointed rod or bar to hold meat for roasting. **2.** a narrow point of land extending into the water. —*vt.* (**spit·ted, spit·ting**) pierce (something) with a spit.
—[名] 1. [고기 굽는] 쇠꼬챙이 2. 모래톱; 갑(岬) —[他] …을 쇠꼬챙이에 꿰다

⁑ **spite** [spait] *n.* [U] ill-will; (*a* ~) hatred toward someone. ¶*from* (or *out of, in*) ~① / *bear someone a ~; have a ~ against someone.*②
—[名] 악의; 원한 ¶①화풀이로/②…에 대하여 원한을 품다

in spite of, notwithstanding; although. ¶*In ~ of his misfortune, he is quite cheerful.*③
[熟] …에도 불구하고 ¶③불행에도 불구하고 그는 쾌활하다

—*vt.* show ill-will to (someone); injure.
—[他] …에게 심술부리다

spite·ful [spáitf(u)l] *adj.* full of ill will; desiring to annoy or injure. ¶~ *words.*
—[形] 심술궂은

spit·fire [spítfàiər] *n.* [C] a quick-tempered person, esp. a woman.
—[名] 성미 급한 사람(특히 여자)

spit·tle [spítl] *n.* [U] saliva, esp. when spit out.
—[名] [특히 뱉은] 침

spit·toon [spitúːn] *n.* [C] a container like a jar to spit into.
—[名] 타구(唾具)

* **splash** [splæʃ] *vt.* **1.** cause (water, mud, etc.) to fly about. (~ something *with* (or *about, on, over*)) ¶~ *a dress with mud; ~ mud on a dress.*① **2.** make (something) wet with mud, water, etc. **3.** make (one's way,
—[他] 1. [물·진흙 따위]를 튀기다 ¶①옷에 진흙을 튀기다 2. 철버덕거리며 …하다 ¶②철버덕거리며 개울을 건너가다

etc.) by splashing. ¶ ~ *one's way across a stream.*②
—*vi.* **1.** (of a liquid) fly about. **2.** fall or move with splashes or splashing noises. 《~ *across* (or *along, with, into*) something》 ¶*He splashed into the dirty water.*
—[自] 1. [물 따위가] 튀다 2. 첨벙하고 떨어지다; 철버덕거리며 가다
—*n.* [C] **1.** the act or sound of splashing. ¶*with a* ~. **2.** a spot or mark of liquid splashed.
—[名] 1. 튀김, 철버덕[거리는 소리] 2. 튄 얼룩
make a splash, ⓐ make a sound of splashing. ⓑ attract the attention of others.
[熟] ⓐ첨벙하고 소리내다 ⓑ세상을 떠들썩하게 하다

splash·board [splǽʃbɔ̀ːrd] *n.* [C] a screen or guard on a vehicle for protecting from splashes made by the turning wheels.
—[名] [자동차 따위의] 진흙받이

splash·y [splǽʃi] *adj.* (**splash·i·er, splash·i·est**) **1.** making a splash. **2.** full of splashes or spots.
—[形] 1. 튀는 2. 흙물(얼룩)투성이의

spleen [spliːn] *n.* **1.** [C] an organ at the left of the stomach which changes the structure of the blood. **2.** [U] ill nature; bad temper; melancholy.
—[名] 1. 비장(脾臟), 지라 2. 심술, 울화, 우울, 의기소침

‡ **splen·did** [spléndid] *adj.* **1.** magnificent; glorious. ¶*a ~ sunset glow.* **2.** worthy of praise; fine. ¶*a ~ achievement.* **3.** (*colloq.*) very good; excellent.
—[形] 1. 훌륭한, 화려한 2. 장한, 눈부신 3. 《口》 멋진, 썩 좋은

splen·did·ly [spléndidli] *adv.* in a splendid manner.
—[副] 화려하게, 훌륭하게

* **splen·dor,** *Brit.* **-dour** [spléndər] *n.* [U] **1.** brilliance; brightness. ¶*the ~ of the jewel.*① **2.** magnificence; impressiveness. ¶*the ~ of the building*② / *live in ~.*③
—[名] 1. 광휘, 빛남 ¶①보석의 광채 2. 훌륭함, 장려(壯麗) ¶②건물의 웅장함/③호화롭게 살다

sple·net·ic [splinétik] *adj.* **1.** of the spleen. **2.** bad-tempered; impatient. —*n.* [C] a person who gets angry easily.
—[形] 1. 비장(지라)의 2. 심기가 사나운, 성마른 —[名] 성미 까다로운 사람

splen·ic [splénik, splíː-] *adj.* of [the] spleen.
—[形] 비장의

splice [splais] *vt.* **1.** join (ropes, etc.) together by weaving the untwisted ends into each other. ⇒fig. **2.** join (pieces of wood or metal) together by fastening in an overlapping position. ⇒fig. **3.** (*colloq.*) marry. —*n.* [C] a union of ropes or pieces of wood, etc. made by splicing.
—[他] 1. [두 가닥의 끈]의 끝을 풀어서 꼬아 잇다 2. …을 겹쳐 잇다 3. 《口》 …을 결혼시키다 —[名] 꼬아 잇기, 겹쳐 잇기

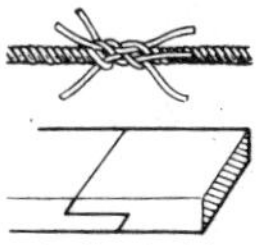
[splice 1., 2.]

splint [splint] *n.* [C] **1.** a piece of wood, metal, etc. for holding a broken bones etc. in the right position. **2.** a thin strip of wood used to make a basket, a chair, etc.
—[名] 1. [접골 치료용] 부목(副木) 2. 엷은 널조각

splin·ter [splíntər] *n.* [C] a thin, sharp piece of broken glass, wood, metal, etc.; a fragment. ¶*a ~ of a bullet*①/ *in* (or *into*) *splinters.*② —*vt., vi.* break (something) into splinters.
—[名] [나무·유리 따위의]부서진 조각, 파편 ¶①탄환의 파편/②산산조각으로 —[他][自] 쪼개다, 쪼개지다; 찢다, 찢어지다

splin·ter·y [splíntəri] *adj.* **1.** of or like a splinter. **2.** apt to break into splinters. **3.** full of splinters; sharp-edged.
—[形] 1. 열편(裂片)의(같은) 2. 찢어지기 쉬운 3. 깔쭉깔쭉한

* **split** [split] *v.* (**split, split·ting**) *vt.* **1.** break (something) from top to bottom; tear violently. ¶ ~ *a stick into two.*① **2.** cause (a group, a party, etc.) to separate. **3.** divide (something) into parts. ¶ ~ *the candy with him* (*among ourselves*).② —*vi.* **1.** be broken in parts; separate. ¶ ~ *in half* / *The party ~ into two groups.*③ **2.** ache violently. ¶*My head is splitting.*④
—[他] 1. …을 세로로 쪼개다; 찢다, 째다 ¶①막대기를 둘로 쪼개다 2. …을 분열시키다 3. …을 나누다 ¶②그와 (우리들끼리) 케이크를 나누다 —[自] 1. 찢어지다, 쪼개지다; 나뉘다, 분열하다 ¶③당은 둘로 분열되었다 2. 몹시 아프다 ¶④머리가 쪼개질 것 같다
—*n.* [C] **1.** an act or a result of splitting. ¶*a ~ in a board.* **2.** a piece split off; a crack. **3.** a special group in a party; a division. ¶*a ~ in the class.*
—[名] 1. 찢어지기, 찢기; 쪼개진 틈 2. 파편 3. 분파, 당파
—*adj.* broken from top to bottom.
—[形] 세로로 쪼개진, 찢어진

split·ting [splítiŋ] *adj.* (of a headache) very severe. ¶*a ~ headache.*①
—[形] 빠개지는 것 같은 ¶①빠개질 것 같은 두통

splotch [splatʃ / splɔtʃ] *n.* [C] a large, irregular spot; a dirty mark.
—[名] 반점(斑點), 얼룩

splut·ter [splʌ́tər] *vi.* speak in a hasty, confused manner; make a sputtering or hissing sound. —*vt.* speak (something) in a hasty, confused manner. —*n.* [U][C] the sound or act of spluttering.
—[自] 침을 튀기며 말하다; 바지직바지직 소리나다 —[他] …을 침을 튀기며 말하다 —[名] 침을 튀기며 말하기

‡ **spoil** [spɔil] *v.* (**spoiled** or **spoilt**) *vt.* **1.** make (something) bad and useless; damage. ¶*a watch spoilt by the damp-*
—[他] 1. …을 못쓰게 만들다; 손상하다 2. …의 가치(흥미)를 줄이다 ¶①비가

S

spoilt [1108] **spoon-fed**

ness / *A spot of ink spoiled her clothes.* **2.** make (something) less valuable, interesting, etc. ¶*The rain spoiled the picnic.*① **3.** cause (someone) to be lazy or weak in his character by too much kindness. ¶(*proverb*) *Spare the rod and ~ the child.*② —*vi.* become useless; decay; rot. ¶*Meat easily spoils if not kept cold.*
—*n.* Ⓤ **1.** (often *pl.*) a thing which is taken from other by violence; stolen goods. **2.** (usu. *pl.*) profits got by means of one's political power.

—名 1. 약탈품, 전리품, 장물(贓物) 2. 관직에 따른 이득, 이권

spoilt [spɔilt] *v.* pt. and pp. of **spoil**.

spoke¹ [spouk] *n.* Ⓒ **1.** one of the bars extending from the center of a wheel to the rim. **2.** a stick or bar to stop the wheels from turning.

—名 1. [바퀴의] 살 2. 바퀴 멈춤대

spoke² [spouk] *v.* pt. of **speak**.

spo·ken [spóuk(ə)n] *v.* pp. of **speak**.
—*adj.* **1.** oral; told. ↔written **2.** speaking in a certain way. ¶*smooth-spoken.*①

—形 1. 구두(口頭)의 2. 말주변이 …한 ¶①말주변이 좋은

spokes·man [spóuksmən] *n.* Ⓒ (pl. **-men** [-mən]) a person who speaks for others; a representative.

—名 대변인, 대변자

spo·li·a·tion [spòuliéiʃ(ə)n] *n.* Ⓤ robbery of neutral ships at sea in wartime.

—名 약탈

* **sponge** [spʌndʒ] *n.* **1.** Ⓒ a kind of sea animal having a soft, yellow, fiberlike skeleton; Ⓤ Ⓒ [a piece of] its light skeleton used for washing and cleaning. **2.** Ⓤ Ⓒ something like this soft skeleton. **3.** Ⓒ (*colloq.*) a person who lives at the expense of others.
  1) ***pass the sponge over*** (=*agree to forget*) *something.*
  2) ***throw up*** (or ***in***) ***the sponge,*** admit defeat.

—名 1. 해면(海綿) 동물; 해면 2. 해면 모양의 것 3.《口》기식자(寄食者), 식객

熟 1)…을 잊어버리다 2) 항복하다

—*vt.* wipe or absorb (something) with a sponge. ¶*~ down dust.* —*vi.* **1.** gather sponges. **2.** live at the expense of others. (*~ on* or *upon someone or something*)

—他 …을 해면으로 닦다(빨아 올리다) —自 1. 해면을 채집하다 2. 기식하다, 뜯어먹고 살다

sponge cake [´-´] *n.* a soft, light cake made of flour, sugar, eggs, etc.

—名 카스텔라

spong·er [spʌ́ndʒər] *n.* Ⓒ **1.** a person or ship that gathers sponges. **2.** (*colloq.*) a person who lives at the expense of others.

—名 1. 해면 채집선(자) 2. 기식자, 식객

spon·gy [spʌ́ndʒi] *adj.* (**-gi·er, -gi·est**) of or like a sponge.

—形 해면 모양의(같은)

spon·sor [spɑ́nsər / spɔ́nsə] *n.* Ⓒ **1.** a person who is responsible for another. (*~ for*) **2.** a person who answers for a child at his baptism; a godparent. ¶*stand ~ to someone.*① **3.** a person who supports another. **4.** a person, a company, etc. that pays the cost of radio or television programs as an advertisement. 「*program.*②
—*vt.* act as sponsor for (something). ¶*~ a television*

—名 1. 보증인 2. 대부(代父), 대모 ¶① …의 대부가 되다 3. 후원자 4. 광고주, 스폰서

—他 …을 보증하다; 후원하다; …의 스폰서가 되다 ¶②텔레비전 프로를 제공하다

spon·ta·ne·i·ty [spɑ̀ntəníːiti / spɔ̀n-] *n.* Ⓤ the state or quality of being spontaneous; a spontaneous nature.

—名 자발성(自發性); 자연발생

spon·ta·ne·ous [spɑntéiniəs / spɔn-] *adj.* happening naturally; arising from a natural impulse; not planned.

—形 자발적인; 무의식적인; 자연스러운

spon·ta·ne·ous·ly [spɑntéiniəsli / spɔn-] *adv.* in a spontaneous manner; naturally.

—副 자발적으로; 자연히

spoof [spuːf] *n.* Ⓤ Ⓒ (*colloq.*) a mischievous trick or joke. —*vt.* trick jokingly.

—名《口》장난으로 속이기 —他 …을 속이다

spook [spuːk] *n.* Ⓒ (*colloq.*) a ghost.

—名《口》유령

spool [spuːl] *n.* Ⓒ a hollow reel of wood or metal on which thread, wire, etc. is wound. —*vt.* wind (thread, wire, etc.) on a spool.

—名 실감개, 실패 —他 …을 실패에 감다

spoon [spuːn] *n.* Ⓒ **1.** a small, shallow bowl with a long handle, used in lifting, serving or eating food. **2.** something like a spoon in its shape. 「*rich.*」
be born with a silver spoon in one's mouth, be born
—*vt.* take up (something) with a spoon. ¶*~ up soup.*①

—名 1. 숟가락 2. 숟가락 모양의 것

熟 부잣집에 태어나다
—他 숟가락으로 뜨다 ¶①수우프를 숟가락으로 뜨다

spoon-fed [spúːnfèd] *adj.* **1.** (of a child, a patient, etc.)

—形 1. 숟가락으로 떠 먹이는 2. 지나

spoon·ful [spúːnf(u)l] *n.* ⓒ the amount that a spoon can [hold.]
—名 숟가락 가득

spo·rad·ic [spərǽdik] *adj.* **1.** happening occasionally; seen apart or widely separated from others. **2.** (of a disease) appearing or occurring in single cases.
—形 1. 때때로 일어나는; 산재(散在)하는 2. 특발성(特發性)의

spo·rad·i·cal·ly [spərǽdik(ə)li] *adv.* in a sporadic manner; separately. [new plant or animal.]
—副 산발적으로; 우발적으로

spore [spɔːr] *n.* ⓒ a very small cell that grows into a
—名 아포(芽胞); 생식세포

:sport [spɔːrt] *n.* ⓒ **1.** a form of game or way of playing, esp. outdoor. ¶*athletic sports* / *Baseball is a favorite ~ for those boys.* **2.** (*pl.*) a meeting for athletic contests. **3.** Ⓤ fun; amusement. ¶*It is great ~ to drive.* **4.** a thing played with. ¶*be the ~ of circumstances.* **5.** an animal or a plant that shows a sudden variation from the normal type. **6.** (*colloq.*) a sportsman. **7.** (*U.S.*) a gambler. **8.** (*U.S. colloq.*) a gay, showy, good-humored person.
1) *in* (or *for*) *sport*, as a joke.
2) *make sport of* (=*laugh at*) *something* or *someone*.
—*vi.* **1.** engage in a sport. **2.** play; make a joke or jest. **3.** become suddenly different from the normal type. —*vt.* show off; display.
—名 1. 운동, 경기 ¶①운동 경기 2. 운동회, 경기회 3. 오락, 농담 ¶②자동차를 모는 것은 아주 재미있다 4. 농락당하는 것, 웃음거리 ¶③환경에 농락되다 5. 돌연변이의 동물(식물) 6. (口) 운동가 7. (美) 도박사 8. (美口) 맵시꾼

慣 1)농담으로 2)…을 놀리다
—自 1. 운동을 하다 2. 까불다, 장난치다 3. 돌연변이를 일으키다 —他 …을 자랑삼아 보이다

sport·ing [spɔ́ːrtiŋ] *adj.* **1.** of or interested in sports. **2.** having the characteristics of a sportsman; fair. ¶*~ spirit.* **3.** interested in gambling; willing to take risks.
—形 1. 운동의(을 좋아하는) 2. 운동가다운; 정정당당한 3. 도박적인

spor·tive [spɔ́ːrtiv] *adj.* playful; merry.
—形 놀기 좋아하는; 쾌활한

spor·tive·ly [spɔ́ːrtivli] *adv.* playfully; merrily.
—副 까불며, 쾌활하게

sports [spɔːrts] *adj.* of sport or sports. ¶*~ clothes.*
—形 스포오츠의; 운동의

:sports·man [spɔ́ːrtsmən] *n.* ⓒ (pl. **-men** [-mən]) **1.** a person who takes part in sports. **2.** a person who plays fair and does not complain even if he loses.
—名 1. 운동가 2. 정정당당하게 하는 사람

sports·man·like [spɔ́ːrtsmənlàik] *adj.* like a sportsman.
—形 운동가다운

sports·man·ship [spɔ́ːrtsmənʃip] *n.* Ⓤ **1.** qualities and behavior of a sportsman; fair play. **2.** skill in sports.
—名 1. 운동정신; 정정당당한 시합 태도 2. 운동의 솜씨(기량)

sports·wom·an [spɔ́ːrtswùmən] *n.* ⓒ (pl. **-women** [-wìmin]) a woman who takes part in sports.
—名 여자 운동가

sport·y [spɔ́ːrti] *adj* (**sport·i·er, sport·i·est**) (*colloq.*) **1.** sportsmanlike. **2.** gay or showy in dress, appearance, etc. ▷**sport·i·ness** [-nis] *n.*
—形 (口) 1. 운동가다운 2. [복장 따위] 화려한

:spot [spɑt / spɔt] *n.* ⓒ **1.** a dirty mark; a stain; a small [round] mark, differing in color, etc. from the rest. ¶*a ~ of ink* / *a ~ on the sun* / *His tie is red with white spots.* **2.** a moral stain on a good character, reputation or name. ¶*His character is without a ~.* **3.** a place; a location. ¶*I found a nice ~ to play.* **4.** (*Brit. colloq.*) a small amount. ¶*a ~ of whisky.*
1) *in a spot*, in trouble.
2) *on the spot*, ⓐ at once; immediately. ¶*decide on the ~.* ⓑ at the very place; there.
—*v.* (**spot·ted, spot·ting**) *vt.* **1.** make spots on (something); stain. ¶*~ a dress.* **2.** stain (one's character or reputation); injure. **3.** see; recognize; discover (an exact position). ¶*Can you ~ your friend in the crowd?* **4.** place (someone or something) in a certain spot.
—*vi.* become spotted; make a spot.
—*adj.* **1.** on hand; ready. ¶*a ~ answer.* **2.** (of advertisements or announcements) made between regular radio or television programs. [*a ~ reputation.*]
—名 1. 얼룩; 더럼; 점 ¶①태양 흑점 2. [인격의] 오점, 흠 ¶②그의 인격에는 흠이 하나도 없다 3. 지점; 장소 4. 《英口》 소량

慣 1)곤경에 빠져 2)ⓐ즉석에서 ⓑ현장에서

—他 1. …을 얼룩지게 하다, …을 더럽히다 2. [명성] 을 해치다, …을 손상하다 3. …을 찾아내다; 간파하다; [소재]를 알아내다 4. …을 두다, 배치하다
—自 더러워지다, 얼룩지다
—形 1. 즉석의 2. [광고 따위] 정규 프로 사이에 삽입된

spot·less [spɑ́tlis / spɔ́t-] *adj.* having no spot; pure.
—形 오점이 없는; 깨끗한

spot·light [spɑ́tlàit / spɔ́t-] *n.* ⓒ **1.** a strong beam of light focused upon a person or thing on the stage. **2.** public attention. [spots. **2.** stained.]
—名 1. [무대에 투사(投射)하는] 스폿라이트 2. 세상의 주목

spot·ted [spɑ́tid / spɔ́t-] *adj.* **1.** marked or covered with [진]
—形 1. 얼룩진, 반점이 있는 2. 더러워

spot·ty [spáti / spɔ́t-] *adj.* (**-ti·er, -ti·est**) **1.** having spots; spotted. **2.** irregular or uneven in quality. ¶*a ~ piece of work.*①
—[形] 1. 반점이 있는 2. 한결같지 않은, 고르지 않은 ¶①일관성이 없는 작품

spouse [spauz, +*U.S.* spaus] *n.* [C] a partner in marriage; a husband or wife.
—[名] 배우자

spout [spaut] *vt.* **1.** throw out (a liquid) in a jet or stream with force. ¶*A whale spouts water.*① **2.** say (something) in a self-important way. **—*vi.*** **1.** come out in a jet or stream. 《~ *from* or *out of* something》 **2.** speak in a self-important manner.
—[他] 1. …을 뿜어내다, 분출시키다 ¶①고래는 물을 뿜어낸다 2. …을 청산유수로 말하다 —[自] 1. 뿜어나오다 2. 청산유수로 말하다

—*n.* [C] **1.** a projecting tube, nozzle, pipe, etc. through which a liquid flows out. **2.** a stream or jet of liquid. ***up the spout,*** ⓐ in pawn. ⓑ hard up; in trouble.
—[名] 1. [주전자 따위의] 주둥이, 입 2. 분수; 분출
[熟] ⓐ저당잡혀 ⓑ난처하여

sprain [sprein] *vt.* injure (a joint or muscle) by a sudden twist. ¶~ *one's ankle.*① **—*n.*** [C] an injury to a muscle or joint caused by a bad twist or wrench.
—[他] [근육·관절 따위를] 삐다, 접질리다 ¶①발목을 삐다 —[名] 삠, 접질림

‡ **sprang** [spræŋ] *v.* pt. of **spring**.

sprawl [sprɔːl] *vi.* **1.** lie or sit with the limbs spread out. **2.** crawl along. **3.** spread out irregularly. **—*vt.*** spread out (something) in an ungraceful manner. **—*n.*** [U] the act of sprawling.
—[自] 1. [큰 대(大)자로] 드러눕다 2. 기어다니다 3. 모양없이 퍼지다 —[他] …을 큰 대자로(모양없이) 뻗게 하다 —[名] 큰 대자로 드러눕기

* **spray**[1] [sprei] *n.* **1.** [U] fine waterdrops going through the air. ¶*the ~ of a waterfall.*① **2.** [U][C] a liquid, esp. a medicine, used in a spray machine. **3.** [C] an instrument for scattering fine waterdrops or vapor. **—*vt.*** **1.** apply fine drops of liquid to (something). ¶~ *mosquitoes.*② **2.** scatter (a liquid) in fine drops.
—[名] 1. 물보라 ¶①폭포의 물안개 2. 분무액(噴霧液) 3. 분무기 —[他] 1. …에게 액체를 뿌리다 ¶②모기에 약을 뿌리다 2. …을 안개 모양으로 뿜어나오게 하다

spray[2] [sprei] *n.* [C] **1.** a small branch or piece of a plant with its leaves, flowers or berries. **2.** an ornament like this.
—[名] 1. [잎·꽃·열매 따위에 붙은] 잔가지 2. 잔가지 무늬

‡ **spread** [spred] *v.* (**spread**) *vt.* **1.** cover the surface of (something) with a thin substance; put (a thin substance) so as to cover. 《~ something *on* or *with*》 ¶~ *butter on toast;* ~ *toast with butter.* **2.** open (something rolled or folded); open out; extend or stretch (the limbs, etc.). 《~ something *with* or *on*; ~ something *to do*》 ¶~ *a tablecloth on the table;* ~ *the table with a tablecloth* / *The eagle ~ its wings.* / *She ~ the wet blanket to dry.* **3.** make (news, etc.) widely known to many people; communicate; extend (something) in all directions; scatter. ¶~ *disease* / ~ *knowledge.* **4.** set (a table, etc.) for a meal. 《~ something *on* or *with*》 ¶~ *the table* [*with dishes*]; ~ *dishes on the table.*
—[他] 1. …의 거죽에 바르다; …을 …으로 덮다 2. …을 펴다, 열다; [손가락·팔 따위]를 벌리다 3. [보도·질병 따위]를 퍼뜨리다; 보급시키다 4. [식탁]을 차리다; [음식]을 늘어놓다

—*vi.* **1.** extend over an area; expand. ¶*The desert spreads for miles and miles.* **2.** (of news, disease, etc.) become widely known, suffered, etc.; scatter. ¶*Rumors ~ quickly.* **3.** be placed as a thin substance.
—[自] 1. 펼쳐지다, 미치다; 전개되다 2. [보도·질병 따위가] 퍼지다; 흩어지다 3. 늘어나다

—*n.* [C] **1.** the act of spreading; growth; expansion. ¶*the ~ of a bird's wings* / *the ~ of education.* **2.** width; extent. ¶*The sail has a ~ of 60 feet.* **3.** a cloth covering for a bed, table, etc. **4.** (*colloq.*) a meal; a feast. **5.** (*U.S.*) a soft food for spreading on bread, etc. such as jam.
—[名] 1. 펼치기, 퍼지기; 보급; 분포 2. 범위; 퍼짐 3. 식탁보, 책상보, 침대보 4. 《口》 맛있는 음식, 식사; 연회 5. 《美》 [버터·잼 따위] 빵 따위에 바르는 것

spree [spriː] *n.* [C] **1.** merry-making; a gay time. **2.** a period of drinking.
—[名] 1. 흥청대기 2. 술잔치

* **sprig** [sprig] *n.* [C] **1.** a small branch. **2.** an ornament or design in the form of a spray. **3.** a young man.
—[名] 1. 잔가지 2. 잔가지 무늬 3. 젊은이

spright·ly [spráitli] *adj.* (**-li·er, -li·est**) lively; gay. ¶*a ~ kitten.*
—[形] 쾌활한, 명랑한

‡ **spring** [spriŋ] *v.* (**sprang** or **sprung, sprung**) *vi.* **1.** leap; jump; rise up suddenly. ¶~ *to one's feet*① / ~ *out of bed* / ~ *up from one's seat.*② **2.** arise; grow; come from some source. 《~ *from* something》 ¶~ *from seeds* / *The water springs from the ground.* / *The family springs from* (or *of*) *ancient kings.* **3.** arise, come, or appear suddenly. ¶~ *out of the darkness*③ / ~ *into fame*④ /
—[自] 1. 뛰다; 껑충 뛰다 ¶①갑자기 일어서다/②자리에서 벌떡 일어나다 2. [물 따위가] 솟아나오다; 싹을 내다; 생기다; [귀족 등의] 출신이다 3. [갑자기] 생기다, 일어나다, 출현하다 ¶③어둠 속에서 불쑥 나오다/④일약 유명해지다 4. 되튀다 ¶⑤가지가 되튕겼다

A light breeze has sprung up. | *A strange thought sprang in my mind.* **4.** move back as a reaction. ¶*The branch sprang back.*⑤ **5.** (of wood) become bent or cracked. —*vt.* **1.** cause (something) to spring; jump over or across (something). ¶~ *a fence* | ~ *a horse.* **2.** release the spring of (something). ¶~ *a trap.* **3.** explode. ¶~ *a mine.* **4.** produce or do unexpectedly and suddenly. 《~ something *on*》 ¶~ *a surprise on someone.*⑥ **5.** cause (wood) to bend or crack. ¶~ *a beam.*

5. [널빤지 따위가] 휘다, 쪼개지다 —[他] 1. …을 뛰게 하다, 뛰어 넘다 2. …의 용수철을 되튀게 하다 3. …을 폭발시키다 4. …을 갑자기 꺼내다(말하기 시작하다) ¶⑥갑자기 …을 깜짝 놀라게 하다 5. [널빤지 따위]를 휘게 하다

—*n.* [C] **1.** the act of springing; a leap or jump. ¶*He made a* ~ *at me.*⑦ **2.** a coil of wire that returns to its first shape after being pulled or bent. ¶*It works by [means of] a* ~. **3.** [U] elastic quality or energy. **4.** [C] a place where water or natural oil comes to the surface of the ground; a natural well. **5.** [C] a source or origin; a cause of action. **6.** [U][C] the first season of the year; the season between winter and summer; youth. ¶*the* ~ *of life.*⑧

—[名] 1. 뛰기; 튀기; 도약 ¶⑦그는 나에게 덤벼들었다 2. 용수철, 태엽 3. 되튀기, 탄력성 4. 샘; 수원(水源), 원천 5. 근원; 동기 6. 봄; 젊음 ¶⑧인생의 봄

—*adj.* of or in spring; of a spring. ¶*a* ~ *rain* | *a* ~ *bed.*

—[形] 봄의; 용수철(태엽)의

spring·board [spríŋbɔ̀:rd] *n.* [C] **1.** a springy board used in jumping, etc. to get added height or spring. **2.** a diving board.

—[名] 1. 도약판, 뜀틀 2. [수영의] 도약판

spring·tide [spríŋtàid] *n.* =springtime.

spring tide [⌐⌐] *n.* the tide at its greatest height, occurring at each new moon and full moon.

—[名] 대조(大潮), 한사리

spring·time [spríŋtàim] *n.* [U] the season of spring.

—[名] 봄

spring·y [spríŋi] *adj.* (**spring·i·er, spring·i·est**) **1.** that springs; elastic. **2.** full of springs of water.

—[形] 1. 용수철이 있는; 탄력이 있는 2. 샘이 많은

* **sprin·kle** [spríŋkl] *vt.* **1.** scatter (water, powder, etc.) in small drops or tiny bits. **2.** scatter small drops or tiny bits on or over (something). 《~ something *on* (or *over, with*)》 ¶~ *salt on a dish*① | ~ *the dusty street with water.*② —*vi.* **1.** scatter in drops or tiny bits. **2.** rain lightly.

—[他] 1. …을 흩뿌리다 2. …에 뿌리다 ¶①요리에 소금을 뿌리다/②먼지가 이는 거리에 물을 뿌리다 —[自] 1. 뿌려지다 2. 부슬비가 내리다

—*n.* [C] **1.** the act of sprinkling. **2.** a light shower of liquid. **3.** a small amount of something.

—[名] 1. 뿌리기 2. 부슬비 3. 조금, 소량

sprin·kler [spríŋklər] *n.* [C] **1.** a person who sprinkles. **2.** a device or a vehicle for sprinkling water, etc.

—[名] 1. 뿌리는 사람 2. 살수차, 살수기

sprin·kling [spríŋkliŋ] *n.* [C] **1.** a small quantity of liquid, etc. that falls in scattered drops. **2.** a small number of people. ¶*a* ~ *of students in the audience.*①

—[名] 1. 소량; 부슬부슬 내리기 2. 소수 ¶①청중 속에 간혹 있는 학생들

sprint [sprint] *n.* [C] a short race at full speed. ¶*a* ~ *race.* —*vi.* run a short distance at full speed.

—[名] 단거리 경주 —[自] [단거리를] 전속력으로 달리다

sprint·er [spríntər] *n.* [C] a person who takes part in a sprint race.

—[名] 단거리 경주 선수, 스프린터

sprite [sprait] *n.* [C] a fairy; an elf.

—[名] 요정(妖精)

sprock·et [sprákit / sprɔ́k-] *n.* [C] **1.** a tooth-like projection on the outer rim of a wheel arranged so as to fit into the links of a chain. **2.** a wheel with such teeth. ⇒fig.

—[名] 1. 사슬 물개 2. 톱니바퀴

[sprocket 2.]

sprout [spraut] *n.* [C] **1.** a bud. **2.** 《*pl.*》 Brussels sprouts. —*vi.* start to grow; send out new shoots. —*vt.* cause (a bud) to grow.

—[名] 1. 싹, 새싹 2. 싹눈 양배추
—[自] 싹트다; 솟아나기 시작하다
—[他] …을 싹트게 하다

spruce[1] [spru:s] *n.* **1.** [C] an evergreen tree with cones and short, needle-shaped leaves. **2.** [U] the wood of this tree.

—[名] 1. 가문비나무속(屬)의 교목, 전나무 2. 전나무 재목

spruce[2] [spru:s] *adj.* (**spruc·er, spruc·est**) neat; tidy; smart. —*vt.* make something spruce. ¶~ *up the room.* —*vi.* (*colloq.*) make oneself neat.

—[形] 조촐한, 깨끔한; 맵시있는
—[他] …을 깨끗이 하다 —[自] 깨끗해지다

⁑ **sprung** [sprʌŋ] *v.* pt. and pp. of **spring**.

spume [spju:m] *n.* [U] foam; froth. —*vi., vt.* foam; froth.

—[名] 거품 —[自][他] [···을] 거품일[게 하]다

S

: **spun** [spʌn] v. pt. and pp. of **spin**.
· **spur** [spəːr] n. ⓒ **1.** a pointed metal instrument fitted to a rider's boot heel for urging on a horse. ⇒fig. **2.** anything that urges on; a stimulus. ¶*put spurs to.*① **3.** anything like a spur, as a sharp spine on a rooster's leg, etc. ⇒fig. **4.** a mountain peak. **5.** a short branch railroad track.

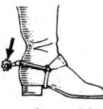
[spur 1.]

[spur 3.]

1) *on the spur of the moment*, suddenly, without thought.
2) *win one's spurs*, win honor and fame.
3) *with whip and spur*, at once.
—v. (**spurred, spur·ring**) vt. **1.** prick (a horse) with a spur or spurs. **2.** urge on. ¶*Ambition spurred him to succeed.*② **3.** provide (a boot) with a spur. —vi. spur a horse.

spu·ri·ous [spjúəriəs] adj. **1.** not genuine; false. ¶*a ~ bank note.*① **2.** of a child whose parents were not married; illegitimate.

spurn [spəːrn] vt. **1.** kick away. ¶*~ the ground.*① **2.** drive (something) away roughly. ¶*He spurned the beggar from his door.* **3.** reject or treat (someone) with contempt.

spurt [spəːrt] vi. **1.** flow forth suddenly in a stream or jet. ¶*~ out in streams*① / *Blood spurted from the wound.*② **2.** show a sudden burst of energy. —vt. cause (something) to flow forth. —n. ⓒ **1.** a sudden flowing forth of (liquid, fire, etc.). ¶*a ~ of flames.*③ **2.** a short outburst of energy. ¶*make a ~*④ / *put a ~ on.*

sput·ter [spʌ́tər] vi. **1.** spit out drops of saliva when speaking angrily or excitedly. **2.** make a noise like sputtering. **3.** talk in an excited manner. —vt. throw out (bits or drops) suddenly.
—n. ⓤ **1.** ⓒ the act of sputtering. **2.** a sputtering noise. **3.** an excited and hasty remark, etc.

: **spy** [spai] n. ⓒ (pl. **spies**) **1.** a person who is employed to keep a secret watch on others. **2.** a person who secretly enters an enemy's land to get information about it. ¶*a ~ ring*① / *on a ~ mission.*②
—v. (**spied, spy·ing**) vt. **1.** watch (someone or something) secretly and carefully. **2.** catch sight of (someone or something); discover (someone or something) by careful and secret examination. —vi. **1.** watch secretly and carefully. ¶*~ into someone's actions.*③ **2.** act as a spy. ¶*~ for the enemy.*④

spy·glass [spáiglæs / -glɑ̀ːs] n. ⓒ a small telescope.

sq. square.

squab·ble [skwábl / skwɔ́b-] n. ⓒ a noisy quarrel about some unimportant matter. —vi. quarrel noisily about some unimportant matter.

squad [skwɑd / skwɔd] n. ⓒ **1.** a small number of soldiers grouped for drill or work. **2.** a small group of people working together. ¶*a ~ car*① / *a ~ of police.*②

squad·ron [skwádr(ə)n / skwɔ́d-] n. ⓒ **1.** a body of soldiers on horses, usu. containing from 120 to 200 men. **2.** a unit of airplanes under one command. **3.** a group of warships. **4.** any organized group.

squal·id [skwálid / skwɔ́l-] adj. very dirty, poor and neglected. ¶*a ~ life*① / *a ~ slum.* [dirtily; meanly.]

squal·id·ly [skwálidli / skwɔ́l-] adv. in a squalid manner;

squall¹ [skwɔːl] n. ⓒ **1.** a sudden, violent windstorm with rain or snow. **2.** (colloq.) a piece of trouble.

squall² [skwɔːl] vi., vt. cry out loudly; scream violently.

—名 1. 박차(拍車) 2. 자극 ¶①…에 박차를 가하다 3. 박차 모양의 돌기물 4. 산의 돌출부 5. [철도의] 지선(支線)

圖 1)충동적으로 2)공을 세우다 3)곧, 즉시
—他 1. 박차를 가하여 [말]을 나아가게 하다 2. …을 자극하다, 격려하다 ¶②야심이 그를 성공으로 몰았다 —自 말에 박차를 가하다

—形 1. 가짜의; 눈속임의 ¶①위조 지폐 2. 사생아의

—他 1. …을 차다 ¶①뛰다 2. 쫓아내다 3. …을 퇴짜놓다, 코방귀 뀌다

—自 1. 분출하다 ¶①뿜어져 흘러나오다/②피가 상처에서 뿜어나오다 2. 갑자기 온힘을 다 내다. —他 …을 분출시키다 —名 1. 분출 ¶③불길의 솟아오름. 2. 격발(激發); 역주(力走) ¶④역주하다

—自 1. 침을 튀기다 2. 바지직바지직 소리가 나다 3. 침을 튀기며 말하다 —他 …을 뿜어내다, 분출하다 —名 1. 침 따위를 튀기기; 침을 튀기며 말하기 2. 바지직바지직 소리 3. 다급한 말

—名 1. 탐정 2. 스파이, 간첩 ¶①간첩단/②간첩의 임무를 띠고

—他 1. …을 탐정(정찰)하다 2. …을 찾아내다; 냄새맡다 —自 1. 탐정하다 ¶③…의 행동을 몰래 조사하다 2. 스파이 노릇을 하다

—名 소형 망원경

—名 사소한 싸움(말다툼) —自 사소한 일로 싸움(말다툼)하다

—名 1. 반(班), 분대 2. 일단 ¶①순찰차/②일단의 경관

—名 1. 기병 대대 2. 비행 중대 3. 소함대 4. 단체

—形 더러운; 치사스러운 ¶①비참한 생활

—副 지저분하게; 상스럽게

—名 1. 돌풍, 스코올 2. (口) 소동

—自他 큰 소리로 울다; 고함치다

squally

—*n.* ⓤ a loud cry or scream.
squall·y [skwɔ́:li] *adj.* (**squall·i·er, squall·i·est**) **1.** of a squall; having many squalls. **2.** threatening.
squal·or [skwálər / skwɔ́lə] *n.* ⓤ the state of being squalid; miserable and dirty conditions.
squan·der [skwándər / skwɔ́ndə] *vt.* spend (money, time, etc.) wastefully and foolishly.
: square [skwɛər] *n.* ⓒ **1.** a figure having 4 equal sides and 4 right angles; anything having this form. **2.** an area in a city bounded by four streets; (*U.S.*) the length of the side of such an area. ¶*Go two squares north.* **3.** a large open place, often a park, in a city. ¶*Times Square / Red Square.* **4.** an instrument, L-shaped or T-shaped, used for drawing or measuring right angles. **5.** the answer when a number is multiplied by itself. ¶*bring to a ~ / 36 is the ~ of 6.*
 on the square, honest; trustworthy.
 —*adj.* **1.** having 4 equal sides and 4 equal angles. ¶*a ~ box.* **2.** of the form of a right angle. ¶*a ~ corner.* **3.** like a square. ¶*a ~ jaw / ~ shoulders.* **4.** even; balanced; having all accounts settled. ¶*make accounts ~.*① **5.** fair or honest; clear; direct; in good order. ¶*a ~ deal / a ~ refusal*② */ get things ~.*③ **6.** (*colloq.*) satisfying; full. ¶*a ~ meal.* **7.** multiplied by itself. ¶*a ~ mile.* ⌈honestly.⌉
 —*adv.* **1.** so as to be in a square form. **2.** frankly;
 —*vt.* **1.** make (something) square; form (something) into a right angle. ¶*~ the edge of a board.* **2.** bring (something) near the form of a right angle. ¶*~ one's shoulders.* **3.** make (something) straight or level. **4.** make (something) even; settle; pay (a bill). ¶*~ accounts.* **5.** adapt; fit. (*~ something by or with*) ¶*~ one's theory with the facts.* **6.** multiply (a number or quantity) by itself. ¶*5 squared is 25.* —*vi.* **1.** make square. **2.** fit; agree. (*~ with something*) ¶*His statement does not ~ with the facts.*
 1) *square the circle,* ⓐ try to construct a square exactly equal in area to a given circle. ⓑ try to do something impossible.
 2) *square up,* ⓐ prepare to fight. ⓑ pay debts or bills.
square dance [´-´] *n.* a dance consisting of a series of set steps for a group of couples.
square·ly [skwɛ́ərli] *adv.* **1.** in a square form; in a right angle. **2.** directly. **3.** honestly.
square·ness [skwɛ́ərnis] *n.* ⓤ **1.** the state of being square. **2.** sincerity; honesty.
squash¹ [skwɑʃ / skwɔʃ] *vt.* **1.** crush (something) into pulp. **2.** stop (something) by force; suppress. ¶*The police quickly squashed the riot.*① **3.** (*colloq.*) make (someone) silent with a crushing argument. —*vi.* **1.** crush. ¶*The fruit will ~ if it is badly packed.*② **2.** fall or move with a squashing sound. **3.** force one's way. (*~ into something*)
 —*n.* ⓒ **1.** something crushed. **2.** a squashing sound. ¶*go to ~.* **3.** a crowd. **4.** ⓤ (*Brit.*) a drink made from the juice of crushed fruit and soda water.
squash² [skwɑʃ / skwɔʃ] *n.* ⓒ (pl. **squash**) a large fruit which is green outside and yellow inside, used as a vegetable.
squash·y [skwɑ́ʃi / skwɔ́ʃi] *adj.* (**squash·i·er, squash·i·est**) **1.** easily crushed. **2.** soft and wet; muddy.
squat [skwɑt / skwɔt] *vi.* (**squat·ted** or **squat, squat·ting**) **1.** sit on one's heels; sit on the ground or floor with one's legs drawn in close to the body. ¶*A cat squats*

squat

—ⓝ 비명
—ⓐ 1.질풍의; 폭풍의 2.폭풍이 일 듯한
—ⓝ 더러움; 치사함

—ⓥ …을 낭비하다, 헛되게 쓰다

—ⓝ 1.정방형, 네모진 물건 2.[거리로 사면이 둘러싸인] 한 구획; 《美》그 한 쪽의 거리 3.거리의 네모꼴의 광장 4.[L자·T자형의] 자, 곱자 5.제곱, 자승; 평방

關 정직하게; 공명하게
—ⓐ 1.정방형의, 네모지 2.직각의 3.각을 이룬, 모가 난 4.평등한; 반반의, 셈이 끝난 ¶①대차(貸借)를 결제하다 5.공정한; 정직한; 단호한; 정돈된 ¶②단호한 거절/③물건을 정돈하다 6. 《口》실속있는, 알찬; 충분한 7.평방의, 제곱의

—ⓐ 1.직각(4각)으로 2.솔직하게, 정직하게
—ⓥ 1.…을 정방형(4각)으로 하다, 직각으로 하다 2.…을 모나게 하다 3.…을 똑바로 하다 4.…을 반반으로 하다; …을 청산하다 5.…을 적합시키다, 일치시키다 6.…을 제곱하다 —ⓥ 1.직각을 이루다 2.일치하다

關 1)ⓐ원을 4각으로 하다 ⓑ불가능한 일을 시도하다 2)ⓐ…싸울 자세를 취하다 ⓑ…을 청산하다

—ⓝ 스퀘어 댄스

—ⓐ 1.4각으로 2.정면으로 3.정직하게
—ⓝ 1.4각 2.정직

—ⓥ 1.…을 으깨다 2.…을 진압하다 ¶①경찰은 곧 폭동을 진압했다 3.《口》 꼭소리 못하게 하다
—ⓥ 1.짓이겨지다 ¶②과일은 잘못 꾸리면 으깨진다 2.철썩 떨어지다 3.비집고 들어가다
—ⓝ 1.으깨진 것 2.철썩 떨어지는 소리 3.군중 4.《英》소오다수에 과즙을 넣은 음료
—ⓝ 호박

—ⓐ 1.뭉크러지기 쉬운 2.흐물흐물한

—ⓥ 1.웅크리다; [동물이] 몸을 엎드리다 ¶①고양이는 점프하기 전에 몸을 웅크린다 2.타인의 토지 또는 공유지에

*before jumping.*① **2.** settle on another's land without permission; settle on a piece of public land to get possession of it. **—*adj.*** **1.** sitting; bending down. **2.** short and thick. **—*n.*** [C] the act of squatting.
무단히 입주하다 —[形] 1. 웅크린, 쪼그리고 앉은 2. 땅딸막한 —[名] 웅크리기

squat·ter [skwátər / skwɔ́tə] *n.* [C] **1.** a person or animal that sits or bends down. **2.** a person who settles on land without permission; a person who settles on a piece of public land to get possession of it.
—[名] 1. 웅크리는 사람(동물) 2. [남의 토지 · 공유지의] 무단 입주자

squaw [skwɔː] *n.* [C] **1.** an American Indian woman or wife. **2.** (*colloq.*) a woman or wife.
—[名] 1. [북미 토인의] 여자; 아내 2. 《口》 여자, 아내

squawk [skwɔːk] *vi.* (of a hen or duck) make a short, loud cry. **—*n.*** [C] a short, loud cry.
—[自] 꺼억꺼억 울다 —[名] 꺼억꺼억 우는 소리

squeak [skwiːk] *vi.* make a short, high sound. ¶*Shoes* ~. **—*n.*** [C] **1.** the short, high cry of a mouse, etc. **2.** 《always with *narrow*》 a narrow escape.
—[自] 찍찍 울다; 삐걱거리다 —[名] 1. 쥐의 울음소리; 삐걱거리는 소리 2. 위기일발

squeak·y [skwíːki] *adj.* (**squeak·i·er, squeak·i·est**) making short, high sounds.
—[形] 찍찍(삑삑) 우는; 삐걱거리는

squeal [skwiːl] *vt., vi.* **1.** make a long, high cry or sound. ¶*The pig squealed in pain.*① **2.** (*colloq.*) act as an informer, esp. to the police to betray someone.
—[他][自] 1. 깩깩거리다; 비명을 지르다 ¶①돼지는 아파서 비명을 질렀다 2. 《口》[…을] 밀고하다

squeam·ish [skwíːmiʃ] *adj.* **1.** easily shocked; very sensitive. **2.** easily made sick.
—[形] 1. 신경질의 2. 토하기 잘하는

* **squeeze** [skwiːz] *vt.* **1.** get (juice, water, etc.) by pressure. ¶~ *a lemon* / ~ *juice from a lemon*① / ~ *water from a wet towel.* **2.** press (something) hard; hold (someone or something) tightly. ¶*be squeezed to death*② / ~ *someone's hand.* **3.** get (something) by force or effort. ¶~ *a confession from someone*③ / ~ *money from someone.* **4.** pack (something) tightly. ¶~ *oneself into*④ / ~ *things into a box.* **—*vi.*** **1.** produce the result of pressure. **2.** move or force one's way. 《~ *through* (or *in, out*) a place》 ¶~ *through a crowd.*⑤ **—*n.*** [C] 《usu. *sing.*》 **1.** the act of squeezing. **2.** a firm friendly pressure of another's hand; a tight hold in the arms. **3.** a crowd.
—[他] 1. …을 압착하다, 짜다 ¶①레몬에서 즙을 짜내다 2. …을 눌러 찌그러뜨리다; 꽉 쥐다 ¶②압사하다 3. …을 압박하다; …에게 억지로 입을 열게 하다 ¶③…에게 억지로 자백시키다 4. …을 밀어넣다 ¶④…에 억지로 밀고 들어가다 —[自] 1. 짜지다 2. 밀고 나아가다 ¶⑤군중 사이를 비집고 나아가다
—[名] 1. 짜기 2. 꽉 쥐기; 꼭 껴안기 3. 붐빔, 혼잡

squeeze play [⌐ ⌐] *n.* (*Baseball*) a play to get one score while the batter tries to bunt.
—[名] 《野球》 스퀴이즈 플레이

squeez·er [skwíːzər] *n.* [C] **1.** a person who squeezes. **2.** an instrument to squeeze fruit for juice.
—[名] 1. 압착자, 착취자 2. 압착기

squelch [skweltʃ] *vt.* **1.** crush (something) by stamping upon it. **2.** cause (someone) to become silent by criticizing him. **—*vi.*** make a splashing sound when walking in mud. **—*n.*** [C] **1.** a crushing sound. **2.** the act of crushing. **3.** a crushing answer or argument.
—[他] 1. …을 눌러 찌그러뜨리다, 진압하다 2. …을 말문이 막히게 하다 —[自] 철벅철벅 소리내다 —[名] 1. 철벅거리는 소리 2. 눌러 찌그러뜨리기 3. 말문을 막기

squib [skwib] *n.* [C] **1.** a small firework that gives off sparks white burning and explodes with a loud noise. **2.** a short, witty attack in speech or writing.
—[名] 1. 폭죽 2. 풍자

squid [skwid] *n.* [C] (pl. **squids** or *collectively* **squid**) a kind of small cuttlefish.
—[名] [각종의] 오징어

squint [skwint] *adj.* with each eye looking in a different direction. **—*n.*** [C] **1.** the state of being squint. ¶*She has a bad* ~.① **2.** a sidelong glance. **3.** a quick glance. **—*vi.*** **1.** be squint. **2.** look with eyes half closed. **3.** take a glance. 《~ *at* something》 ▷**squint·er** [-ər] *n.*
—[形] 사시(斜視)의, 사팔눈의 —[名] 1. 사시 ¶①그녀는 심한 사팔뜨기다 2. 곁눈질 3. 한눈 —[自] 1. 사팔뜨기다 2. 눈을 가늘게 뜨고 보다 3. 흘깃 보다

squint-eyed [skwíntàid] *adj.* with each eye looking in a different direction.
—[形] 사팔뜨기의, 사시의

* **squire** [skwaiər] *n.* [C] **1.** (*Brit.*) the chief landowner of some district. **2.** (*U.S.*) a justice of the peace. **3.** (*History*) a young person who attended a knight.
—[名] 1. 《英》 지주 2. 《美》 치안판사 3. 《史》 기사의 종자(從者)

* **squir·rel** [skwə́ːr(ə)l / skwír(ə)l] *n.* [C] a small leaping animal with a large bushy tail, usu. gray or brown, which lives in trees.
—[名] 다람쥐

squirt [skwəːrt] *vi.* flow forth in a stream out of a tube, etc. **—*vt.*** force out (liquid) out of a small opening.
—[自] 뿜어나오다 —[他] [물]을 분출시키다 ¶①물총에서 물이 뿜어나오다

S

¶~ *water from a water pistol.*① —*n.* [C] **1.** a stream or jet of liquid. **2.** any device for squirting a liquid.
—[명] 1. 분출 2. 액체를 뿜어나오게 하는 장치

Sr. **1.** senior. **2.** Sir.

S.S. steamship.

***St.** **1.** Street. **2.** Saint.

***stab** [stæb] *v.* (**stabbed, stab·bing**) *vt.* **1.** wound (someone) with a sharp pointed weapon. ¶~ *someone with a dagger;* ~ *a dagger into someone.*① **2.** hurt (the feelings, etc.) sharply and deeply. ¶~ *someone's name.*② —*vi.* **1.** wound with a stab. (~ *at* someone) **2.** (of pain) give a sensation as if stabbed by a sharp weapon. —*n.* [C] **1.** a thrust or blow with a sharp weapon; a wound made by such a way. **2.** a painful sensation.
—[타] 1. …을 찌르다 ¶①남을 단검으로 찌르다 2. [감정 따위]에 깊은 상처를 입히다 ¶②명성에 상처를 입히다 —[자] 1. 찌르다 2. 찌르듯이 아프다 —[명] 1. 찌르기; 자상(刺傷) 2. 정신적인 아픔, 양심의 가책

stab·ber [stǽbər] *n.* [C] **1.** a person who stabs someone else. **2.** an instrument used for stabbing.
—[명] 1. 자객(刺客) 2. 찌르는 것

***sta·bil·i·ty** [stəbíliti] *n.* [U] the state of being stable; firmness.
—[명] 안정; 착실

sta·bi·li·za·tion [stèibilizéiʃ(ə)n / -lai-] *n.* [U] the act of stabilizing; the state of being stabilized.
—[명] 안정

sta·bi·lize [stéibilàiz] *vt.* **1.** make (something) firm, steady or dependable. ¶~ *prices.*① **2.** keep the balance of (an airplane, etc.) by automatic devices.
—[타] 1. …을 안정시키다 ¶①물가를 안정시키다 2. [비행기 따위]의 안정을 유지하다

sta·bi·liz·er [stéibilàizər] *n.* [C] **1.** a person or thing that stabilizes something. **2.** a device for keeping the balance of an airplane, a ship, etc.
—[명] 1. 안정시키는 사람(것) 2. 안정장치

⁑**sta·ble**¹ [stéibl] *adj.* **1.** fixed; firm; not easily moved. ¶~ *foundations.*① **2.** firm in character; unwavering. ¶~ *opinions.*② ▷**sta·bly** [-bli] *adv.*
—[명] 1. 튼튼한, 단단한; 안정된 ¶①단단한 토대 2. 착실한 ¶②착실한 의견

***sta·ble**² [stéibl] *n.* [C] **1.** a house in which horses are kept. **2.** a group of horses kept in such a building. —*vt., vi.* put (horses) in a stable.
—[명] 1. 마굿간 2. [어떤 마굿간에 속하는 전부의] 말 —[타][자] [말을] 마굿간에 넣다

sta·ble·boy [stéiblbɔ̀i] *n.* [C] a boy who works in a stable.
—[명] [소년] 마부

sta·ble·man [stéiblmən] *n.* [C] (pl. **-men** [-mən]) a man who works in a stable.
—[명] 마부, 마굿간지기

stac·ca·to [stəkɑ́:tou] *adj.* (*Music*) disconnected; with breaks between successive tones. ¶*a* ~ *mark.*① —*adv.* in a staccato manner.
—[형] 단주적(斷奏的)인, 스타카토의 ¶①단음부(斷音符) —[부] 단주적으로

stack [stæk] *n.* [C] **1.** a large pile of hay, straw, etc. **2.** an orderly pile of anything. ¶*a* ~ *of books.*① **3.** (usu. *pl.*) a set of bookcases in a library. **4.** a chimney of a steamer. **5.** rifles arranged with their openings together in the form of a pyramid. —*vt.* arrange (something) in a stack; heap or pile up. ¶~ *hay.*②
—[명] 1. [건초·밀짚 따위의] 더미, 낟가리 2. …의 더미 ¶①책더미 3. 서가(書架) 4. [기선 따위의] 굴뚝 5. 세워 놓은 총들 —[타] …을 겹쳐 쌓다 ¶②건초를 쌓다

sta·di·a [stéidiə] *n.* pl. of **stadium**.

***sta·di·um** [stéidiəm] *n.* [C] (pl. **-di·ums** or **-di·a**) **1.** a running track for foot races in ancient Greece with seats for spectators all around it. **2.** a similar modern sports field.
—[명] 1. [고대 그리이스의] 도보 경주장 2. [현대의] 경기장

⁑**staff** [stæf / stɑ:f] *n.* [C] (pl. **staffs** or **staves** [steivz]) **1.** (*collectively*) (in the army) a group of officers as advisers. ¶*the general* ~① / *a* ~ *officer.*② **2.** (*collectively*) a group of persons working as one unit. ¶*the editorial* ~③ / *the medical* ~ *of a hospital.*④ **3.** a stick; a rod; a pole. ¶*a flag* ~.⑤ **4.** a support. ¶*Bread is the* ~ *of life.*⑥ **5.** (*Music*) the five lines with the spaces between them on which music is written. —*vt.* provide a staff for (an office).
—[명] 1. 참모 ¶①참모 본부/②참모 장교 2. 직원, 부원 ¶③편집부원/④병원의 의사 3. 지팡이, 막대기, 장대 ¶⑤깃대 4. 의지가 되는 것 5. (樂) 보표(譜表) —[타] …에 직원[등]을 두다

stag [stæg] *n.* [C] **1.** a grown-up male deer. **2.** a male of various kind of animals. **3.** (*U.S. colloq.*) a man who goes to a social gathering unaccompanied by a lady. ¶*a* ~ *party.*①
—[명] 1. 수사슴 2. [각종 동물의] 수컷 3. [무도회 따위에] 여자의 동반 없이 가는 사람 ¶①남자들만의 파아티

⁑**stage** [steidʒ] *n.* [C] **1.** a high platform in a theater on which a play is acted, etc. ¶*a* ~ *effect*① / *put on the* ~.② **2.** (*the* ~) the profession of an actor. ¶*go on the* ~.③ **3.** (*the* ~) the drama. ¶*the medieval* ~.④ **4.** a scene or
—[명] 1. [극장의] 무대 ¶①무대 효과/②상연하다 2. 배우업; 연극계 ¶③배우가 되다 3. 연극 ¶④중세의 연극 4. [활동의] 무대; [전쟁 따위가 일어

S

place of action. **5.** a period in a development. ¶*an early ~ of civilization.*⑤ **6.** a stoppingplace on a journey; the distance between two stoppingplaces. **7.** a stagecoach. **8.** a wooden frame put up around a building which is being built. **—*vt., vi.*** put (a play) on the stage. ▷**stage·like** [-làik] *adj.*

났던] 장소 5. [발달 따위의] 단계, 시기 ¶⑤문명의 초기 6. [여행 도중의] 역; 여정(旅程) 7. 역마차 8. [건축용의] 발판, 비계 —[他][自] [극을] 상연하다

stage·coach [stéidʒkòutʃ] *n.* [C] a large coach, drawn by horses, formerly used for carrying passengers over a regular route. ⇒fig.

—[名] 역마차

[stagecoach]

stage fright [ˊ ˋ] *n.* the nervous fear felt by an actor or speaker when appearing before an audience.

—[名] 무대에 처음 나설 때의 두려움

∗**stag·ger** [stǽgər] *vi.* **1.** walk back and forth or weave from side to side unsteadily. ¶*~ down the street.*① **2.** hesitate. ¶*~ under the severe gunfire.*② **—*vt.* 1.** cause (someone) to move back and forth or from side to side. ¶*The boxer was staggered by the blow.*③ **2.** make (someone) hesitate. ¶*~ someone's resolution.*④ **3.** shock or surprise very much. ¶*I was staggered by the news.*⑤ **4.** arrange (something) so that it does not happen at the same time as (another thing).
—*n.* [C] **1.** an unsteady movement. **2.** ⦅*the ~s*, used as *sing.*⦆ a nervous disease of horses, cattle, etc. that causes them to stagger or fall suddenly. ⇒[N.B.]

—[自] 1. 비틀거리다 ¶①비틀거리며 길을 가다 2. 망설이다 ¶②심한 포화에 주저하다
—[他] 1. …을 비틀거리게 하다 ¶③그 권투 선수는 일격에 비틀거렸다 2. …을 흔들리게 하다 ¶④결심이 흔들리게 하다 3. …을 깜짝 놀라게 하다 ¶⑤그 뉴우스에 깜짝 놀랐다 4. …을 시간차를 두다
—[名] 1. 비틀거림 2. 훈도병(暈倒病)

stag·nan·cy [stǽgnənsi] *n.* [U] the state of being stagnant.

—[名] 침체; 불경기

stag·nant [stǽgnənt] *adj.* **1.** motionless; not flowing; foul or stale from standing still. ¶*~ air / a ~ pool.*① **2.** not active; dull. ¶*a ~ economy / a ~ brain.*②

—[形] 1. 괴어 있는 ¶①괴어 있는 물웅덩이 2. 활발치 못한, 침체한 ¶②둔한 머리

stag·nant·ly [stǽgnəntli] *adv.* in a stagnant manner.

—[副] 괴어서; 부진하여

stag·nate [stǽgneit] *vi.* be or become stagnant. **—*vt.*** make (something) stagnant.

—[自] 흐르지 않다, 괴다; 침체하다, 불경기가 되다 —[他] …을 침체시키다

stag·na·tion [stægnéiʃ(ə)n] *n.* [U] the act of stagnating; the state of being stagnant. ¶*fall into ~.*①

—[名] 굄, 침체; 불경기 ¶①불경기가 되다

stag·y [stéidʒi] *adj.* (**stag·i·er, stag·i·est**) **1.** of the stage. **2.** theatrical or artificial in speech, manner, etc.

—[形] 1. 무대의 2. 연극조의; 과장된, 일부러 꾸민

staid [steid] *adj.* settled and steady; sober; quiet. ¶*~ behavior.* ▷**staid·ness** [-nis] *n.* —**staid·ly** [-li] *adv.*

—[形] 침착한, 착실한; 진지한

∗**stain** [stein] *vt.* **1.** make a blot on (something). ¶*a stained shirt.* **2.** spoil (one's reputation, character, etc.) by disgrace. **3.** put color on or in (something). ¶*stained glass.*① **—*vi.*** take a stain; become stained.
—*n.* [C] **1.** a dirty spot. ¶*an ink ~.*② **2.** a moral defect; dishonor. ¶*without a ~ on one's character.*③ **3.** [U] a color given to wood, glass, wall paper, etc.; the coloring matter for this.

—[他] 1. …을 더럽히다, …에 얼룩지게 하다 2. [명성 따위]를 더럽히다, 손상하다 3. …에 착색하다 ¶①착색 유리
—[自] 더러워지다 —[名] 1. 얼룩 ¶②잉크의 얼룩 2. 오점 ¶③성격에 흠이라고는 없는 3. 착색; 물감, 염료, 착색제

∗**stain·less** [stéinlis] *adj.* **1.** without a stain. **2.** not easily stained or discolored. ¶*~ steel.*

—[形] 1. 더럼이 없는 2. 잘 더러워지지 않는; 변색하지 않는

⁑**stair** [stɛər] *n.* [C] **1.** any one of a set of steps for going from one level to another. **2.** ⦅usu. *pl.*⦆ a set of such steps. ¶*winding stairs*① */ go up the stairs.*②

—[名] 1. 계단의 한 단 2. 계단 ¶①나선계단/②계단을 오르다

∗**stair·case** [stɛ́ərkèis] *n.* [C] a set of stairs with a supporting framework and a handrail.

—[名] 계단

stair·way [stɛ́ərwèi] *n.* [C] (chiefly *U.S.*) a staircase.

⁑**stake**[1] [steik] *n.* [C] **1.** a stick or post sharpened at one end for driving into the ground. ¶*drive in a ~.*① **2.** the post to which people were tied and burned to death in olden times. ¶*be condemned to the ~.*②
—*vt.* 1. fasten (something) to a stake. ¶*~ a horse.* **2.** (*U.S.*) mark (the ground) with stakes.
pull up stakes, (*U.S.*) move away.

—[名] 1. 말뚝, 막대기 ¶①말뚝을 박다 2. 화형주(火刑柱) ¶②화형의 선고를 받다
—[他] 1. …을 말뚝에 묶다 2. 《美》 …을 말뚝으로 구획하다
[熟] 《美》 떠나가다

stake[2] [steik] *n.* [C] **1.** ⦅usu. *pl.*⦆ money risked; some-

—[名] 1. 내기에 건 돈(물건) 2. 배당, 상

thing which is staked. **2.** ((often *pl.*)) the prize or reward in a contest or race. **3.** a share or interest in property. ¶*have a ~ in an undertaking.*①
금 3. 이해관계 ¶①사업에 이해관계가 있다

—*vt.* risk (money, one's life, etc.) on some event. ¶*I ~ my reputation on his honesty.*②
—[他] …을 걸다 ¶②명예를 걸고 그가 정직함을 보증한다

at stake, ⓐ risked. ⓑ in danger.
[熟] ⓐ성패를 건 ⓑ위태로운

sta·lac·tite [stəlǽktait / stǽlək-] *n.* [C] a formation of limestone shaped like an icicle, hanging from the roof of a cave. ⇒fig.
—[名] 종유석(鐘乳石)

sta·lag·mite [stəlǽgmait / stǽləg-] *n.* [C] a formation of limestone shaped like a cone, forming on the floor of a cave. ⇒fig.
—[名] 석순(石筍)

[stalactite, stalagmite]

*** stale** [steil] *adj.* **1.** not new; having no taste; dried out. ¶*~ beer*① / *~ bread.*② **2.** not interesting because of constant use. ¶*a ~ joke.* **3.** out of condition because of too much activity. ¶*He has become ~ through overtraining.*
—[形] 1. 신선하지 않은; 김이 빠진; 말라빠진 ¶①김 빠진 맥주/②말라빠진 빵 2. 케케묵은 3. 피폐한; 생기없는

—*vt., vi.* make or become stale.
—[他][自] 신선한 맛을 없애다(이 없어지다)

stale·mate [stéilmèit / ´ˋ] *n.* [C] **1.** (in chess) a position in which no move can be made without placing the king in check. **2.** a position in which any further action is impossible; a deadlock. —*vt.* put (something) in such a position.
—[名] 1. 쌍방의 수가 모두 막힘 2. 막다른 골목, 궁지 —[他] …의 수가 막히게 하다; …을 궁지에 몰아넣다

*** stalk¹** [stɔːk] *n.* [C] **1.** the stem of a plant, a leaf, a flower or a piece of fruit. **2.** any support like a stem.
—[名] 1. 줄기, 대, 엽병(葉柄) 2. 가느다란 버팀대

*** stalk²** [stɔːk] *vt.* follow or approach (an animal or person) secretly. ¶*The hunter stalked the deer.* —*vi.* **1.** walk in a stiff, proud manner. **2.** approach silently and secretly. —*n.* [U] the act of stalking.
—[他] …에 몰래 다가가다 —[自] 1. 당당하게 걷다 2. 몰래 다가가다 —[名] 몰래 접근하기, 활보

stalk·ing-horse [stɔ́ːkiŋhɔ̀ːrs] *n.* [C] **1.** a horse or figure of a horse behind which a hunter hides in approaching game. **2.** anything put forward to hide one's plans, etc.
—[名] 1. 숨는 말 (사냥꾼이 그 뒤에 숨어서 짐승에 접근함) 2. 위장, 구실

*** stall** [stɔːl] *n.* [C] **1.** a place for an animal in a stable. **2.** a table or booth on which things are displayed for sale. ¶*a street ~.*① **3.** a seat near the stage or screen, esp. one separated from others. **4.** a fixed seat in the choir of a church for the clergy.
—[名] 1. [마굿간·외양간의] 한 간막이 2. 매점, 노점 ¶①노점 3. [영화관·극장 따위의] 1층 특등석 4. [교회의] 성가대석

—*vt.* **1.** keep (an animal) in a stall, esp. for fattening. **2.** cause (a vehicle, etc.) to stick fast in mud, snow, etc.; unintentionally cause (a vehicle's engine) to come to a standstill. —*vi.* **1.** stick fast in mud; come to a standstill. ¶*The car stalled on the hill.* **2.** (of an airplane) loose flying speed and fall. **3.** (of an animal) live in a stall.
—[他] 1. …을 간막이에 넣어 두다 2. [말·마차 따위]를 눈이나 진흙 속에 빠지게 하다, …을 오도가도 못하게 하다 —[自] 1. 진흙에 묻히다; 오도가도 못하게 되다 2. 실속(失速)하다 3. 간막이 속에 들어가 있다

stal·lion [stǽljən] *n.* [C] a male horse kept for breeding.
—[名] 종마(種馬)

stal·wart [stɔ́ːlwərt] *adj.* **1.** strongly built; brave. ¶*a ~ soldier.* **2.** firm and reliable. ¶*They are always my ~ friends.*① —*n.* [C] a brave, reliable person.
—[形] 1. 건장한, 용감한 2. 든든한, 믿을 수 있는 ¶①그들은 내가 언제나 믿을 수 있는 친구들이다 —[名] 의지가 되는 사람

sta·men [stéimən, +*Brit.* -men] *n.* [C] the part of a flower bearing pollen.
—[名] 수술, 웅예(雄蕊)

stam·i·na [stǽminə] *n.* [U] the physical strength to work hard and long.
—[名] 정력; 지구력, 스태미너

*** stam·mer** [stǽmər] *vi.* repeat the same sound several times before uttering a word; hesitate in speaking.
—[自] 말을 더듬다, 더듬으며 말하다

—*vt.* utter (something) in this manner. ¶*stammer out an excuse.*① —*n.* [C] the act of stammering.
—[他] …을 더듬으며 말하다 ¶①더듬으며 핑계를 대다 —[名] 더듬기

stam·mer·er [stǽmərər] *n.* [C] a person who stammers.
—[名] 말더듬이

stam·mer·ing·ly [stǽməriŋli] *adv.* in a stammering manner.
—[副] 더듬으며

stamp [stæmp] *n.* [C] **1.** an instrument for pressing some mark on paper, etc; a mark pressed by this. ¶*a rubber ~ / These articles bear the ~ of the maker.*① **2.** a small piece of printed paper, put on letters or docu-
—[名] 1. 도장, 스탬프; 검인 ¶①이들 상품에는 메이커의 도장이 찍혀 있다 2. 인지; 우표 3. 표적; 자국; 특징 ¶②그의 얼굴에는 고생한 자국이 있다

S

stampede [1118] **stand**

ments to show that a fee has been paid; a postage stamp. **3.** anything that shows the truth; an impression; a sign; a characteristic. ¶*His face bears the ~ of suffering.*② **4.** (*sing.* only) a kind; a form. ¶*men of the same ~.* **5.** the act of stamping one's foot.
— *vt.* **1.** press a mark on (something); press (a mark) on something. ¶*This document is stamped with his seal.*③ / *~ one's name on a document.* **2.** put a stamp on (a letter, etc.). **3.** put (one's foot) down with force. ¶*~ one's foot with anger.* **4.** destroy or crush (something) by stamping one's foot; tread. ¶*~ the flower bed / ~ the grass flat.*④ **5.** make a deep impression on (someone). ¶*The deed is stamped on my momory.*⑤
— *vi.* put one's foot down with force.

stam·pede [stæmpíːd] *n.* ⓒ **1.** a sudden, wild running away of a herd of frightened animals. **2.** any sudden, excited rush by a large group.
— *vi.* move together in panic. — *vt.* cause (something) to run away suddenly and wildly.

stance [stæns] *n.* ⓒ a position of a player's feet in a golf, baseball, etc. when hitting a ball.

stanch¹ [stɔːntʃ, staːntʃ / staːntʃ] *vt.* stop or check the flow of (blood, etc.); stop the flow of blood from (a wound). — *vi.* (of blood, etc.) stop flowing.

stanch² [stɔːntʃ, staːntʃ / staːntʃ] *adj.* **1.** firm and reliable; strong. ¶*a ~ defense.* **2.** loyal; trustworthy. ¶*a ~ friend.*

stan·chion [stænʃ(ə)n, -tʃ(ə)n / stáːnʃ(ə)n] *n.* ⓒ an upright bar, post, beam or support in a window, a wall, etc.

stand [stænd] *v.* (**stood**) *vi.* **1.** take or keep an erect position on the feet. ¶*~ straight*① */ ~ at ease*② */ Please ~* **2.** (of a person or thing) be in an erect position. ¶*~ still / The building still stood after the earthquake.* **3.** be placed; be situated. ¶*The vase stands over there. / My house stands on a hill.* **4.** be kept in a certain position or condition. ¶*~ smoking / ~ amazed / The door stood open. / He stands ready for anything.*③ **5.** be still in force; be unchanged. ¶*The rule stands.* **6.** be of a certain height; be at a certain point on a scale; occupy a certain place in a series of things. ¶*~ five feet [tall] in one's socks*④ */ The thermometer stands at 37°.*⑤ */ She stands second in her class.* **7.** (of a person, etc.) stop; gather and stay. ¶*Stand where you are. / The tears stood in her eyes.*⑥ **8.** (chiefly *Brit.*) become a political candidate. **9.** (*Nautical*) hold a course at sea. — *vt.* **1.** place (something or someone) in an upright position or in a certain position. ¶*~ a dictionary on end / ~ a desk in the corner / ~ a boy in front of a blackboard.* **2.** endure; bear. ¶*~ great heat / This book will ~ the test of time.*⑦ **3.** (*colloq.*) pay for or bear the cost of something.
1) ***stand a chance,*** have a chance.
2) ***stand by,*** ⓐ help; support. ⓑ be ready to act. ⓒ keep (a promise, etc.)
3) ***stand for,*** ⓐ mean; represent. ⓑ take the place of (something). ⓒ take the side of (something). ⓓ (*colloq.*) endure. ⌈something) at a distance.⌉
4) ***stand off,*** remain at a distance; keep (someone or
5) ***stand on,*** ⓐ insist on. ⓑ depend on.
6) ***stand out,*** ⓐ be noticeable; attract special attention.
7) ***stand over,*** be postponed. ⌊ⓑ continue to endure.⌋
8) ***stand up,*** ⓐ get to one's feet. ⓑ endure; last.
9) ***stand up for,*** defend; support; take the side of (something).

4. 종류 5. 발을 구르기

— ⓣ 1. …에 도장을 찍다;[도장]을 누르다 ¶③이 서류에는 그의 도장이 있다 2. …에 우표(인지)를 붙이다 3. [발]을 구르다, 쿵쿵거리다 4. …을 짓밟다, 밟아 짓이기다 ¶④꽃을 짓밟다 5. …에게 깊은 인상을 주다 ¶⑤그의 행위는 내 기억에 깊은 감명을 주었다
— ⓘ 발을 구르다

— ⓝ 1. [가축 떼가] 놀라서 우르르 도망치기 2. 앞을 다투어 달아나기

— ⓘ 우르르 도망치다 — ⓣ …을 일제히 도망치게 하다

— ⓝ 타자의 발의 위치; 스탠스

— ⓣ [피의 흐름]을 멈추다; [상처]를 지혈(止血)하다 — ⓘ 피가 멎다

— ⓐ 1. 굳은; 튼튼한 2. 성실한, 신뢰할 수 있는

— ⓝ 지주(支柱), 간막이 막대

— ⓘ 1. 서다, 일어서다; 선 자세로 있다 ¶①똑바로 서다/②쉬어의 자세로 서다 2. [사람・물건이] 서 있다 3. 위치하다, 있다 4. […의] 상태(입장)에 있다 ¶③그는 어떤 일에 대해서도 준비가 되어 있다 5. 유효하다; 그대로의 상태로 있다 6. [높이가] …이다; [온도가] …도이다; [등급이] …이다 ¶④키는 구두를 벗고 5피이트다/⑤온도계는 37°로 되어 있다 7. 멈춰 서다; 정지해 있다 ¶⑥그녀의 눈에 눈물이 괴어 있었다 8. 입후보하다 9. 어떤 방향으로 나아가다 — ⓣ 1. …을 세우다, 어떤 위치에 두다 2. …을 참다, …에 견디다 ¶⑦이 책은 시대의 시련을 견디고 후세까지 남을 것이다 3. (口) …의 대가(代價)를 치르다, …을 한턱 내다

圖 1)가망이 있다 2)ⓐ …을 원조하다; …에 편들다 ⓑ 대기하다 ⓒ(약속 따위)를 지키다 3)ⓐ …을 나타내다, 의미하다 ⓑ …의 대신이 되다 ⓒ …을 지지하다, …에 편들다 ⓓ …을 참다 4)접근하지 않다; 멀리하고 있다, 경원하다 5)ⓐ …을 주장하다, 굳게 지키다 ⓑ …에 의각하다 6)ⓐ 눈에 띄다; 탁월하다 ⓑ 끝까지 버티다 7)연기하다(되다) 8)ⓐ 기립하다 ⓑ …을 견디다, 지속하다 9)…을 옹호하다; …에 편들다 10)…에 용감히 맞서다

10) ***stand up to,*** resist boldly and bravely.

—*n.* [C] **1.** a stop. ¶*come to a* ~⑧ / *bring* (*something*) *to a* ~.⑨ **2.** an attitude; a position supported with regard to something. ¶*one's* ~ *toward the matter* / *take one's* ~ *on something.*⑩ **3.** a place where a person or thing stands. ¶*The guard took his* ~ *near the door.* **4.** an outdoor counter where things are sold. ¶*a newsstand* / *a popcorn* ~. **5.** a small table or frame to put things on or in. ¶*a music* ~⑪ / *a hat* ~. **6.** a raised platform, as for a speaker. **7.** a set of sloping outdoor seats on which people sit to see games, etc. **8.** a place where taxis or public vehicles may wait. **9.** (of an army, etc.) a stop made in defending one's territory; resistance. ¶*make a last* ~ *against the enemy.* **10.** (*U.S.*) a witness box. **11.** (*U.S.*) a group of growing trees.

—[名] 1. 정지(停止, 靜止) ¶⑧멈춰서다/⑨…을 멈춰 세우다 2. 태도; 입장; 생각 ¶⑩…에 대한 자기의 입장을 주장하다 3. 위치 4. 매점; 노점 5. [물건을 올려놓는] 대(臺), …걸이 ¶⑪악보대 6. 연단 7. 관람석, 스탠드 8. [택시 따위의] 주차장 9. 저항; 방어 10. 《美》 [법정의] 증인석 11. 《美》 수목, 입목(立木)

:stand·ard [stǽndərd] [C] **1.** a flag; a banner. ¶*under a* ~ *of*① / *raise the* ~ *of revolt.*② **2.** any state, degree or level taken as a desirable one or as a basis of comparison; a model. ¶*the* ~ *of living*③ / *come up to the* ~.④ **3.** an authorized measure of weight, length, quality, etc. **4.** (*Brit.*) a grade in an elementary school. **5.** anything upright used as a support.

—[名] 1. 깃발, 기 ¶①…의 깃발 하래/②반기(反旗)를 들다 2. 표준, 규격 ¶③생활 수준/④표준에 달하다 3. [도량형의] 원기(原器) 4. [국민학교의] 학년 5. 똑바른 지주(支柱)

—*adj.* used or generally recognized as an authority or model. ¶~ *English*⑤ / *the* ~ *time.*⑥

—[形] 표준의; 권위 있는 ¶⑤표준 영어/⑥표준시

stand·ard-bear·er [stǽndərdbɛ̀ərər] *n.* [C] **1.** a soldier who carries a standard or flag. **2.** the leader of a movement, political party, etc.

—[名] 1. 기수(旗手) 2. 주창자

stand·ard·i·za·tion [stæ̀ndərdizéiʃ(ə)n / -əːdai-] *n.* [U] the act of standardizing; the state of being standardized.

—[名] 표준화, 통일

stand·ard·ize [stǽndərdàiz] *vt.* make (something) standard in size weight, quality, etc. ¶*These parts are standardized by KIS.*①

—[他] …을 표준에. 맞추다; 규격화하다 ¶①이들 부분품은 한국 공업 규격에 맞는다

stand-by [stǽn(d)bài] *n.* [C] **1.** (pl. **-bys**) a person or thing that can always be relied upon. **2.** a signal for a boat or ship to wait nearby.

—[名] 1. 의지가 되는 사람(것) 2. 대기 신호

stand-in [stǽndìn] *n.* [C] **1.** (*U.S. colloq.*) a position of favor. **2.** (*U.S.*) a person who works as a substitute for a motion picture actor or actress in dangerous scenes, etc. **3.** any substitute.

—[名] 1. 《美口》 총애, 연줄 2. 《美》 대역(代役) 3. 대리, 대용, 대신

***stand·ing** [stǽndiŋ] *adj.* **1.** not movable; established. ¶*a* ~ *army* / *a* ~ *color.*① **2.** not flowing. ¶~ *water.*

—[形] 1. 고정된, 상비(常備)의 ¶①바래지 않는 빛깔 2. 흐르지 않는

—*n.* **1.** [U][C] position; rank. ¶*people of high* ~. **2.** [U] duration. ¶*a custom of long* ~.

—[名] 1. 지위, 입장, 신분 2. 계속

stand-off·ish [stǽndɔ̀ːfiʃ / -ɔ̀f-] *adj.* **1.** standing apart. **2.** not friendly.

—[形] 1. 멀어져 있는 2. 서름서름한

stand·point [stǽn(d)pɔ̀int] *n.* [C] a position or point at which one stands to consider or judge something; a point of view. ¶*from an educational* ~.①

—[名] 견지; 관점 ¶①교육적인 견지에서

stand·still [stǽn(d)stìl] *n.* [C][U] a complete stop. ¶*be at a* ~.①

—[名] 정지 ¶①정돈상태에 있다

stand-up [stǽndʌ̀p] *adj.* **1.** standing upright. ↔turn-down ¶*a* ~ *collar.*① **2.** done or taken while standing. ¶*a* ~ *meal.*②

—[形] 1. 서 있는 ¶①꼿꼿한 깃 2. 선 채로 하는 ¶②서서 먹기

stank [stæŋk] *v.* pt. of **stink**.

***stan·za** [stǽnzə] *n.* [C] a group of four or more lines forming a unit or a section of a poem.

—[名] [시의] 절(節), 연(聯)

sta·ple¹ [stéipl] *n.* [C] **1.** a U-shaped piece of metal used to hold hooks. **2.** a similar piece of thin wire used to hold papers together. —*vt.* fasten (something) with a staple. ¶~ *the papers together.*①

—[名] 1. U자형 꺾쇠 2. 멈치쇠, 꺾쇠 —[他] …에 멈치쇠를 달다; …을 꺾쇠로 묶다 ¶①서류를 철하다

sta·ple² [stéipl] *n.* **1.** [C] the chief or most important product of a place. **2.** [C] the chief element or part. **3.** [U] raw material. **4.** [U] the fiber of wool, cotton, etc. ¶*wool of fine* ~.① —*adj.* principal; chief. ¶~ *food*② / *the* ~ *industries of our country.*③

—[名] 1. 주요 산물 2. 주요소(主要素) 3. 원료 4. 섬유 ¶①고급 양모 —[形] 주요한 ¶②주식(主食)/③우리나라의 주요산업

staple fiber, *Brit.* **-bre** [⌐- ⌐-] *n.* fiber produced by

—[名] 인조섬유, 스프

stapler [1120] **start**

artificial means. 「papers with wire staples.」
sta·pler [stéiplər] n. ⓒ a device for fastening together
star [stɑ:r] n. ⓒ **1.** any of the heavenly bodies, which is seen in the night sky, esp. a self-luminous one. ¶*the morning (the evening) ~*① */ a falling ~*. **2.** a figure with five or six points. ¶*the Stars and Stripes.*② **3.** a leading player or actor. ¶*a ~ player /a movie ~*. **4.** fate; fortune. ¶ *He was born under a lucky ~.*③ */ thank (or bless) one's lucky ~*.
—v. (**starred, star·ring**) vi. **1.** act as a leading actor or player. **·2.** shine like a star. —vt. **1.** put a starmark on (something); decorate (something) with stars. **2.** make a star of (someone); act as a star in (a movie, etc.).
star·board [stá:rbərd, -bɔ̀:rd] n. Ⓤ the right side of a ship as one faces the bow. ↔port —adj. on the right side of a ship. —vt. turn (the helm) to the right side.
starch [stɑ:rtʃ] n. Ⓤ **1.** a white, tasteless food substance found in nearly all plants, but esp. in grain and potatoes. **2.** a powdered form of this substance used for stiffening cloth, etc. when mixed with water.
—vt. stiffen (cloth, etc.) with starch.
starch·y [stá:rtʃi] adj. (**starch·i·er, starch·i·est**) **1.** of or like starch; containing starch. **2.** stiffened with starch. **3.** (colloq.) stiff and formal in manner.
star·dom [stá:rdəm] n. Ⓤ **1.** the status or position of a star. **2.** (collectively) a body of professional stars.
stare [stɛər] vi. look with the eyes wide open. ¶*~ with surprise.*① —vt. look at (someone or something) steadily or fixedly. ¶*~ someone up and down*.
—n. ⓒ a long fixed look or gaze.
star·fish [stá:rfìʃ] n. ⓒ (pl. **-fish**) a sea animal with a star-shaped body.
star·ing [stéəriŋ] adj. striking or too bright in colors.
stark [stɑ:rk] adj. **1.** stiff; rigid. ¶*a ~ and cold corpse.*① **2.** complete; absolute. ¶*~ madness*. —adv. completely. ¶*~ naked*. ▷**stark·ly** [-li] adv.
star·less [stá:rlis] adj. without stars or starlight.
star·light [stá:rlàit] n. Ⓤ light given by the stars.
star·like [stá:rlàik] adj. like a star in shape or brilliance.
star·ling [stá:rliŋ] n. ⓒ a bird about the size of a robin which makes its nest near buildings. 「*night.*①
star·lit [stá:rlìt] adj. lighted by the stars. ¶*a ~*
star·red [stɑ:rd] adj. **1.** decorated or marked with stars. **2.** considered to be influenced by the stars. ¶*illstarred*.
star·ry [stá:ri] adj. (**-ri·er, -ri·est**) **1.** of stars; starshaped. **2.** containing many stars. ¶*a ~ sky.*① **3.** shining bright like stars. ¶*~ eyes.*②
star-span·gled [stá:rspæ̀ŋgld] adj. with many stars here and there. ¶*The Star-Spangled Banner.*
start [stɑ:rt] vi. **1.** begin. ¶*~ in life*① */ ~ on an enterprise*② */ ~ off at one's work.*③ **2.** begin to move. ¶*The engine won't ~.*④ **3.** begin to go somewhere. ¶*~ from Seoul for Pusan / He started on a journey.* **4.** arise. ¶*The fire started in the kitchen.*⑤ **5.** jump with a sudden fear; be amazed. ¶*They started at the sound of a rifle shot.* —vt. **1.** begin. (*~ to do*; *~ doing*) ¶*~ dinner / It started to rain; It started raining.*⑥ **2.** cause (something) to begin, to arise, to move, etc. ¶*~ a fire* / *~ an engine.* **3.** make (someone) begin; cause. (*~ someone doing*) ¶*The news started her crying.*⑦ **4.** help (someone) to begin his career.
to start with, in the first place; firstly.
—n. ⓒ **1.** an act of starting; a starting point. ¶*make*

—ⓢ 종이 철하는 기구, 스테이플러
—ⓢ 1. 별, 항성(恒星) ¶①샛별(개밥바라기) 2. 별 모양의 것; 별표 ¶②성조기 3. 인기 있는 사람, 스타아 4. 운명 ¶③그는 행운의 별을 타고났다

—ⓢ 1. 주연배우 노릇을 하다 2. 별처럼 반짝이다 —㉸ 1. …에 별표를 달다; …을 성장(星章)으로 꾸미다 2. …을 스타아(주역)로 하다; …에 주연하다
—ⓢ 우현(右舷) —㉸ 우현의(에서)
—㉸ [키]를 우현으로 돌리다

—ⓢ 1. 전분, 녹말 2. [풀을 만드는] 녹말, 풀

—㉸ …을 풀로 붙이다
—㉶ 1. 전분[질]의 2. 풀을 먹인 3. 거북살스러운

—ⓢ 1. 스타아의 신분 2. 스타아들

—㉠ 눈을 크게(동그랗게) 뜨고 보다, 응시하다 ¶①놀라서 눈을 크게 뜨다
—㉸ 을 빤히 바라보다
—ⓢ 응시
—ⓢ 불가사리

—㉶ [빛깔이] 야한
—㉶ 1. 굳어버린, 빳빳해진 ¶①차갑고 굳은 시체 2. 진짜의, 순수한 —㉺ 완전히
—㉶ 별이 없는
—ⓢ 별빛
—㉶ 별 모양의; 별처럼 빛나는
—ⓢ 찌르레기

—㉶ 별빛의 ¶①별빛 밝은 밤
—㉶ 1. 별로 장식한; 별표가 있는 2. …의 별을 타고난
—㉶ 1. 별의; 별 모양의 2. 별이 많은 ¶①별빛 밝은 하늘 3. 반짝반짝 빛나는 ¶②빛나는 눈동자
—㉶ 별을 점점이 박은 ¶①성조기

—㉠ 1. 시작하다 ¶①인생을 시작하다/②사업을 시작하다/③일에 착수하다 2. 움직이기 시작하다 ¶④엔진이 걸리지 않는다 3. 출발하다 4. 일어나다 ¶⑤불은 부엌에서 일어났다 5. [놀람·공포로] 움찔하다 —㉸ 1. …을 시작하다 ¶⑥비가 내리기 시작했다 2. …을 시작시키다; 일으키다; 움직이다 3. …에게 시키다 ¶⑦그 소식을 듣고 그녀는 울기 시작했다 4. …을 세상에 내보내다; [장사 따위를] 시작하게 하다

🅡 우선 먼저
—ⓢ 1. 출발; 출발점 2. 뛰어 일어남

an early start | take one's ~ in life. **2.** a sudden movement or shock. ¶*jump up with a ~.*
놀람, 움찔함

⁑ star·tle [stá:rtl] *vt.* cause (someone or something) to start or move suddenly; frighten. ¶*We were very much startled by the news.*① —*n.* [C] **1.** a shock or surprise. **2.** something which gives a shock or surprise.
—[他] …을 깜짝 놀라게 하다 ¶①그 소식을 듣고 깜짝 놀랐다 —[名] **1.** 놀람 **2.** 놀라게 하는 것

*** star·tling** [stá:rtliŋ] *adj.* surprising; alarming. ¶~ *news.*
—[形] 놀랄 만한

star·va·tion [sta:rvéiʃ(ə)n] *n.* [U] the state of being starved; death caused by lack of food. ¶~ *wages.*①
—[名] 굶주림, 기아; 아사(餓死) ¶①기아 임금

⁑ starve [sta:rv] *vi.* **1.** suffer or die from a lack of food. **2.** (*colloq.*) feel very hungry. **3.** have a strong desire or need. 《~ *for* something》 ¶~ *for friendship.*① —*vt.* cause (a person or an animal) to suffer or die from lack of food or something needed. ¶~ *oneself.*②
—[自] **1.** 굶주리다; 굶어 죽다 **2.** 몹시 배고프다 **3.** 갈망하다; 열망하다 ¶①우정을 갈망하다 —[他] …을 굶기다, 굶어 죽게 하다 ¶②굶어 죽다; 단식하다

starve·ling [stá:rvliŋ] *adj.* starving; hungry-looking. —*n.* [C] a thin, weak person or animal suffering from lack of food.
—[形] 굶주린 —[名] 굶주려 야윈 사람(동물)

⁑ state [steit] *n.* [C] **1.** 《usu. *sing.*》 the condition in which a person or thing is. ¶*the ~ of affairs* (or *things*)① | *one's ~ of health | in a ~ of confusion*② | *The world is in a terrible ~.* **2.** 《usu. *sing.*》 a particular mental condition; a condition of anxiety, distress, etc. ¶*in quite a ~*③ | *What a ~ you are in!*④ **3.** 《often *the S-*》 the whole body of people under one government; a nation. ¶*affairs of ~*⑤ | *the Department of* [*the*] *State; the State Department.*⑥ **4.** 《often *S-*》 one of the main political and geographical units that are joined to form a nation; one of the United States. ¶*the fifty States of the United States.* **5.** [U] one's position in life; rank. ¶*persons of every ~ of life.*⑦ **6.** [U] style of living, esp. of a high-placed person; luxury and splendor; dignity. ¶*live in ~*⑧ | *keep one's ~.*⑨
—[名] **1.** 상태; 형세; 사정 ¶①상황; 사정/②혼란 상태에 있는 **2.** 정신 상태; 흥분 상태 ¶③아주 흥분하여/④그게 무슨 꼴이냐! **3.** 국가; 나라 ¶⑤국사(國事)/⑥국무성 **4.** [특히 미국 등의] 주(州) **5.** 지위; 신분 ¶⑦온갖 계급의 사람들 **6.** [특히 높은 신분의] 생활 양식; 호화스러움; 위엄 ¶⑧호화로운 생활을 하다/⑨위엄을 부리다; 젠체하고 있다

—*adj.* **1.** used for occasions of ceremony; formal. ¶*a ~ call.*⑩ **2.** of a country. ¶*a ~ prisoner*⑪ | *~ papers*⑫ | *a ~ policy.* **3.** 《usu. *S-*》 of a State. ¶*a State Bank | State University.*⑬
—[形] **1.** 의식용의, 공식의 ¶⑩공식 방문 **2.** 국가의, 나라의 ¶⑪중죄인, 국사범/⑫공문서 **3.** 주(州)의 ¶⑬주립대학

—*vt.* **1.** express (a fact, an opinion, etc.) in words; say. 《~ *that…*; ~ *what…*; ~ someone *to do*》 ¶*Each states his position. | It is stated that …*⑭ **2.** place in a certain position; settle; fix.
—[他] **1.** [사실·의견 따위]를 말하다, 진술하다 ¶⑭…이라는 이야기다 **2.** [날짜 따위]를 정하다

state·craft [stéitkræ̀ft / -krà:ft] *n.* [U] the art or skill of managing public affairs; statesmanship.
—[名] 정치; 경륜(經綸), 정치 수완

stat·ed [stéitid] *adj.* fixed or settled beforehand. ¶*at a ~ time.*①
—[形] 정해진 ¶①정해진 시간에

State·house [stéithàus] *n.* (*U.S.*) the capitol of a State.
—[名] 《美》 주(州)의사당

state·less [stéitlis] *adj.* without a state or nationality.
—[形] 국적이 없는

*** state·ly** [stéitli] *adj.* (**-li·er, -li·est**) having a grand or dignified manner or appearance; majestic.
—[形] 위엄있는; 당당한

⁑ state·ment [stéitmənt] *n.* [U][C] **1.** the act of expressing an opinion, a fact, a belief, etc, in words; something stated. ¶*a written ~.*① **2.** a report of a financial condition.
—[名] **1.** 진술; 성명 ¶①성명서 **2.** 결산서; 영업 보고서

state·room [stéitrù(:)m] *n.* [C] **1.** a private room or cabin on a ship. **2.** (*U.S.*) a private compartment on a railroad train.
—[名] **1.** [배의] 특등실 **2.** [기차의] 특별실

*** states·man** [stéitsmən] *n.* [C] (pl. **-men** [-mən]) a person with experience in the management of public affairs and the art of government.
—[名] 정치가

states·man·like [stéitsmənlàik] *adj.* having the qualities of a good statesman.
—[形] 정치가다운, 정치가에 알맞은

states·man·ship [stéitsmənʃìp] *n.* [U] the qualities or methods of a statesman; skill in managing public or national affairs.
—[名] 정치적 수완

stat·ic [stǽtik] *adj.* **1.** standing still; not moving. **2.** of static or atmospheric electricity. —*n.* [U] static or
—[形] **1.** 정적(靜的)인 **2.** 정전기의; 공전(空電)의 —[名] 정전기, 공전

S

stat·ics [stætiks] *n. pl.* ((used as *sing.*)) the branch of mechanics dealing with bodies at rest or with forces that balance one another.
— 名 정력학(靜力學)

‡ **sta·tion** [stéiʃ(ə)n] *n.* ⓒ **1.** a place where trains, buses, etc. stop to pick up or set down passengers; the building connected with this place. ¶*a bus ~ | a railway ~.* **2.** a building or place used for some particular official work; a military post; a naval base. ¶*a police ~*① *| a gas ~ | a military ~ abroad | a naval ~.*② **3.** an assigned location or place. ¶*take up one's ~.*③ **4.** Ⓤ ⓒ one's social position; rank; a high position. ¶*a man of* [*high*] *~.*④ **5.** a place for sending out or receiving programs, etc. by radio or television.
—*vt.* place (someone) in a certain post, position, rank or situation. (*~ someone at*) ¶*~ a guard at the gate.*
— 名 **1.** 역, 정거장; 역사(驛舍). [관청 따위의] 서(署), 국, 소(所); [군대 따위의] 주둔지; [함대의] 경비 구역 ¶①경찰서/②군항 **3.** [지정 또는 임명된] 위치, 부서 ¶③부서에 자리잡다 **4.** 신분; 지위; 높은 지위 ¶④높은 지위의 사람 **5.** 방송국

— 動 ⋯을 배치하다; 부서에 배치하다

station agent [⌞⌞ ⌞⌞] *n.* (*U.S.*) a stationmaster.
— 名 (美) 역장

sta·tion·ar·y [stéiʃ(ə)nèri / -əri] *adj.* **1.** not moving. **2.** settled; fixed in a certain position. ¶*a ~ crane*① */ ~ troops.*② **3.** unchanging in condition, number, etc. ¶*a ~ population.*③
— 形 **1.** 움직이지 않는, 고정된 **2.** 주둔한, 정주(定住)해 있는 ¶①고정 기중기/②주둔군 **3.** 변동이 없는 ¶③변동 없는 인구

sta·tion·er [stéiʃ(ə)nər] *n.* ⓒ a person who sells writing goods.
— 名 문방구상

sta·tion·er·y [stéiʃ(ə)nèri / -əri] *n.* Ⓤ (*collectively*) writing goods, such as papers, pens, pencils, inks, envelopes, etc.
— 名 문방구

sta·tion·mas·ter [stéiʃ(ə)nmæstər / -mɑ̀:stə] *n.* ⓒ a person in charge of the operation of a railroad station; a station agent.
— 名 역장

stat·ist [stéitist] *n.* =statistician.

sta·tis·ti·cal [stətístik(ə)l] *adj.* of or based on statistics. ¶*a ~ table.*①
— 形 통계[상]의 ¶①통계표

stat·is·ti·cian [stæ̀tistíʃ(ə)n] *n.* ⓒ an expert or a specialist in statistics.
— 名 통계자; 통계학자

* **sta·tis·tics** [stətístiks] *n. pl.* **1.** facts or data shown by numbers. ¶*~ of population.*① **2.** ((used as *sing.*)) the science of gathering and classifying such facts and data.
— 名 **1.** 통계 ¶①인구 통계 **2.** 통계학

stat·u·ar·y [stætʃuèri / -tjuəri] *n.* Ⓤ **1.** (*collectively*) statues. **2.** the art of making statues. —*adj.* of or suitable for statues.
— 名 **1.** 조상(彫像) **2.** 조상술 — 形 조상의

‡ **stat·ue** [stætʃu:] *n.* ⓒ the image of a person or an animal carved in stone, etc. or cast in metal.
— 名 상(像), 조상(彫像)

stat·u·esque [stæ̀tʃuésk / -tju-] *adj.* like a statue in dignity, formal grace or beauty.
— 形 조상(彫像) 같은; 조상처럼 위엄이 있는 (우아한, 아름다운)

stat·u·ette [stæ̀tʃuét / -tju-] *n.* ⓒ a small statue.
— 名 작은 상(像)

* **stat·ure** [stætʃər] *n.* Ⓤ **1.** the height of a person or an animal. **2.** physical or mental worth or development.
— 名 **1.** 키, 신장 **2.** [심적·도덕적인] 능력, 성장

sta·tus [stéitəs, +*U.S.* stǽt-] *n.* Ⓤ **1.** the position, state, or rank of a person in relation to others. ¶*his ~ among novelists.*① **2.** (*Law*) legal position.
— 名 **1.** 지위 ¶①소설가 가운데서의 그의 지위 **2.** 신분

* **stat·ute** [stætʃu:t, +*Brit.* -tju:t] *n.* ⓒ **1.** a law passed by a legislative body. **2.** an established rule.
— 名 **1.** 성문물, 법령 **2.** 규칙

statute law [⌞⌞ ⌞] *n.* a law established by a legislative body.
— 名 성문물

stat·u·to·ry [stætʃutɔ̀:ri / -tjut(ə)ri] *adj.* of a statute; fixed or established by statute. ¶*a ~ offense.*①
— 形 법정(法定)의, 법령의(에 입각하는) ¶①법에 위배되는 죄

staunch [stɔ:ntʃ, stɑ:ntʃ] *v., adj.* =stanch.¹,²

stave [steiv] *n.* ⓒ **1.** one of the curved, narrow pieces of wood which form the sides of a tub, a barrel, etc. ⇒fig. **2.** a heavy stick or staff. **3.** (*Music*) five lines with spaces between them for writing music. **4.** a verse or stanza of a poem.

[stave 1.]

—*v.* (**staved** or **stove**) *vt.* **1.** break a hole through the side of (a barrel, a boat, etc.); break (something). ¶*~*

— 名 **1.** 통보 **2.** 막대기 **3.** (樂) 보표(譜表) **4.** 시의 일절

— 動 **1.** [통 따위에] 구멍을 뚫다; ⋯을 부수다 ¶①⋯을 산산이 부수다 **2.** ⋯에 통널을 붙이다

staves

to pieces.① **2.** furnish (something) with staves. —vi. become smashed or broken.

staves [steivz] *n.* **1.** pl. of **staff**. **2.** pl. of **stave**.

stay¹ [stei] *vi.* **1.** remain in one place; wait. ¶~ [at] home① / ~ out② / ~ away③ / Stay here until I return. **2.** live for a while as a guest or visitor. ¶~ overnight④ / I stayed at my uncle's. **3.** remain; continue to be. ¶Prices ~ high. / The door stayed closed. / The weather stayed fine. **4.** endure; last. ¶~ to the last. —vt. **1.** stop the progress of (something); check. ¶~ one's steps⑤ / ~ the spread of disease. **2.** satisfy (hunger, thirst, etc.) for a time. ¶~ one's hunger. **3.** put off; delay. ¶~ judgment. **4.** remain in the same place or condition through or during (a period of time). ¶~ the course / She decided to ~ the week out.
—*n.* **1.** ⓒ The act or time of staying; a visit. **2.** Ⓤⓒ a delay; a stop. ¶a two year's ~ of execution.⑥

stay² [stei] *n.* ⓒ **1.** a support or prop to steady something. **2.** a strong rope or wire to support a mast of a ship. **3.** someone that supports. ¶He is the chief ~ of his family.① **4.** (*pl.*) (*Brit.*) a corset. —*vt.* support (something) with a rope, wire, etc.

stay-at-home [stéiəthòum] *adj.* (*colloq.*) staying mostly at home. —*n.* ⓒ a person who stays at home and will not go out or travel.

stead [sted] *n.* Ⓤ **1.** the place or position which another person or thing has or might have. ¶He died in my ~.① **2.** advantage; use.
stand in good stead, be useful.

* **stead·fast** [stédfæst, -fəst, / stédfəst] *adj.* steady; fixed firmly; unchanging. ¶a ~ faith.①

stead·fast·ly [stédfæstli, -fəst-] *adv.* in a steadfast manner.

‡ **stead·i·ly** [stédili] *adv.* in a steady manner; firmly; continuously.

stead·i·ness [stédinis] *n.* Ⓤ the state of being steady.

‡ **stead·y** [stédi] *adj.* (**stead·i·er, stead·i·est**) **1.** fixed; firm. ¶a ~ chair / a ~ gaze② / a ~ step. **2.** not changing in mind; constant. ¶~ friendship (love). **3.** regular; uniform. ¶a ~ wind / (*proverb*) Slow and ~ wins the race.② **4.** having good habits; serious.
—*vt.* **1.** make or keep (something) steady. **2.** make (something) constant. —*vi.* become steady.

* **steak** [steik] *n.* Ⓤⓒ **1.** a thick slice of meat or fish cut for broiling or frying. **2.** beefsteak.

‡ **steal** [sti:l] *v.* (**stole, stol·en**) *vt.* **1.** take (another's property) without permission or right. ¶He had his watch stolen.① **2.** gain or do (something) secretly. ¶~ a kiss / ~ a ride on a train.② **3.** (*Baseball*) gain a base) without the aid of a hit. —*vi.* **1.** commit an act of stealing. ¶Thou shalt not ~.③ **2.** move quietly or secretly; come or go without notice. ¶She stole softly out of (into) the room. / The years stole by.④ / The winter has stolen upon us.⑤ | thing./

stealth [stelθ] *n.* Ⓤ secret or sly means of doing some-

stealth·i·ly [stélθili] *adv.* secretly; slyly.

stealth·y [stélθi] *adj.* (**stealth·i·er, stealth·i·est**) done secretly or cautiously. ¶a ~ glance① / ~ footsteps.②

‡ **steam** [sti:m] *n.* Ⓤ **1.** the vapor that rises from boiling water. ¶give off ~.① **2.** (*colloq.*) energy.
1) *at full steam,* at full speed.
2) *get up steam,* ⓐ begin to put forth one's strength or energy. ⓑ get excited.
3) *let* (or *blow*) *off steam,* express strong feelings.

steam

—自 부서지다

—自 1.[장소에] 머무르다; 기다리다 ¶①[외출하지 않고] 집에 있다/②밖에 나가 있다/③집을 비우다; 결석하다 2.체재하다, 묵다 ¶④일박하다 3.…인 채로 있다 4.견디다, 계속하다 —他 1.…을 멈추다; 막다, 방해하다 ¶⑤정지하다 2.일시적으로 [굶주림 따위]를 만족시키다 3.…을 연기하다, 유예하다 4.…의 끝까지 머무르다(지속하다)

—名 1.체재, 체재 기간 2.연기, 중지 ¶⑥형의 집행유예 2년
—名 1.지주(支柱) 2.[돛대 따위를 버티는] 지색(支索) 3.의지가 되는 것 ¶①그는 집안의 기둥이다 4.(英) 코르셋 —他 …을 지색으로 받치다

—形 (口) 집에만 틀어박혀 있는, 나가기 싫어하는 —名 구들직장

—名 1.대신 ¶①그는 나 대신 죽었다 2.도움, 이익

熟 쓸모가 있다
—形 확고한 ¶①부동의 신념

—副 확고하게, 단호하게

—副 착실히; 끊임없이

—名 착실, 부동(不動); 한결같음
—形 1.확고한 ¶①응시 2.[마음이] 견고한, 불변의 3.규칙적이; 착실한, 건실한 ¶②(느려도 꾸준하면 이긴다 4.진지한
—他 1.…을 견고하게 하다, 확고하게 하다 2.…을 일정하게 하다, 건실하게 하다 —自 견고해지다
—名 1.[고기·생선의] 두껍게 저민 살 2.비이프스테이크

—他 1.…을 훔치다 ¶①그는 시계를 도둑맞았다 2.…을 몰래 입수하다(행하다) ¶②[기차에] 무임승차하다 3.(野球) 도루(盜壘)하다 —自 1.도둑질을 하다 ¶③도둑질을 말라 2.몰래 들어가다, 몰래 가다; 모르는 사이에 오다 ¶④세월은 모르는 사이에 지나갔다/⑤어느 사이엔가 겨울이 되었다

—名 몰래 하기
—副 몰래, 비밀히
—形 몰래 하는, 은밀한 ¶①훔쳐 보기/②살금살금 걷는 발소리

—名 1.증기, 김 ¶①증기를 방출하다 2.기운, 원기
熟 1)전속력으로 2)ⓐ기운내다 ⓑ흥분하다 3)울분을 풀다

steamboat   [1124]   steer

—*vt.* expose (something) to steam; soften (something) by steam. ¶~ *potatoes.*② —*vi.* **1.** give off steam. ¶*The kettle is steaming.*③ **2.** move by the power of steam. ¶*The train steamed into the station.*④ **3.** rise in the form of vapor or steam.
  steam up, ⓐ become covered with vapor. ⓑ use one's energy. ⓒ make (someone) excited or angry.
—他 …을 찌다 ¶②감자를 찌다 —自 1. 김을 내다 ¶③주전자가 김을 내고 있다 2. 증기로 달리다 ¶④기차는 역에 들어왔다 3. 증발하다
steam up, ⓐ증기로 흐려지다 ⓑ기운을 내다 ⓒ…을 흥분시키다, 화나게 하다

* **steam·boat** [stíːmbòut] *n.* ⓒ a boat driven by steam. —名 [소형] 기선, 증기선
  steam boiler [´ `] *n.* a boiler in which water is boiled to make steam. —名 증기 솥, 보일러
  steam engine [´ `] *n.* an engine operated by the ⌈pressure of steam.⌉ —名 증기기관
: **steam·er** [stíːmər] *n.* ⓒ **1.** a steamship or steamboat. **2.** an engine operated by steam. **3.** a container in which food is steamed.
—名 1. 기선 2. 증기기관 3. [요리용] 시루, 찌는 도구

  steam·ing [stíːmiŋ] *adj.* giving off steam; very hot. ¶~ *coffee.* —*adv.* to a steaming degree. ¶*be ~ hot.*
—形 김을 내는; 몹시 뜨거운 —副 김을 낼 만큼

  steam roller [´ `] *n.* a heavy roller driven by steam, used for leveling roads.
—名 증기 로울러

: **steam·ship** [stíːmʃìp] *n.* ⓒ a ship driven by steam power. ⇒NB. ¶*the S.S. Titanic*① / *a ~ company.*
—名 기선 NB S.S., SS로 줄임 ¶① 타이태닉 호

  steam·y [stíːmi] *adj.* (**steam·i·er, steam·i·est**) **1.** of or like steam. **2.** covered or filled with steam. **3.** giving off steam. ⌈or a spirited horse.⌉
—形 1. 증기의(같은) 2. 증기가 자욱한 3. 김이 나는

* **steed** [stiːd] *n.* ⓒ (*poetic*) a horse, esp. a riding horse
—名 (詩) 승용 말, 군마

: **steel** [stiːl] *n.* ⓤ **1.** a compound of iron with carbon and other elements. ¶*hard ~.*① **2.** something made from steel. ¶*cold ~.*② **3.** great, steellike hardness. ¶*a grip of ~*③ / *a heart of ~.*④ —*adj.* made of or like steel. ¶*a ~ pen*⑤ / *a ~ mill.*⑥ —*vt.* **1.** cover (something) with steel. **2.** make (something) hard, strong or firm. ¶*~ one's heart against someone.*⑦
—名 1. 강철, 강(鋼) ¶①경강(硬鋼) 2. 강철제의 물건 ¶②칼붙이 3. 견고함 ¶③굳게 쥐기/④냉혹한 마음 —形 강철의 ¶⑤강철 펜/⑥강철 공장 —他 1. …에 강철을 쐬우다 2. …을 굳게 하다 ¶⑦…에 대하여 마음을 굳게 먹다

  steel-clad [stíːlklæ̀d] *adj.* covered with armor.
—갑옷을 입은

  steel·works [stíːlwə̀ːrks] *n. pl.* (used as *pl.* and *sing.*) a place where steel is manufactured; a steel mill.
—名 강철 공장

  steel·y [stíːli] *adj.* (**steel·i·er, steel·i·est**) **1.** of or made of steel. **2.** like or suggesting steel; hard and strong; merciless.
—形 1. 강철의, 강철로 만든 2. 강철 같은; 굳은; 무정한

  steel·yard [stíːljɑ̀ːrd, -jərd / stíːljɑ̀ːd] *n.* ⓒ a scale for weighing with arms or unequal length.
—名 대저울

: **steep**¹ [stiːp] *adj.* **1.** having a sharp slope or incline. ¶*a ~ hill.*① **2.** (*colloq.*) (of prices) unreasonable; very high. ¶*His demand is a bit ~.*② —*n.* ⓒ a steep slope; a precipice. ¶*the rugged steeps of the mountain.*③
—形 1. 험준한 ¶①가파른 언덕 2. 터무니없는 ¶②그의 요구는 좀 무리하다 —名 가파른 비탈; 벼랑 ¶③산의 가파른 비탈

  steep² [stiːp] *vt.* **1.** soak (something) in a liquid. ¶*~ the vegetables in water.*① **2.** wet or fill thoroughly. ¶*be steeped in crime*② / *~ oneself in reading books.*③ —*n.* ⓤ the act of steeping; ⓒ a liquid to soak something in. ¶*in ~.*④ ⌈steeper or become so.⌉
—他 1. [물·액체 따위에] …을 담그다 ¶①야채를 물에 담그다 2. …을 깊이 스며(배어)들게 하다 ¶②악에 물들어 있다/③독서에 몰두하다 —名 담그기; 담그는 액체 ¶④담가서

  steep·en [stíːp(ə)n] *vt., vi.* make (something) steep or
—他自 가파르게 하다(되다)

* **stee·ple** [stíːpl] *n.* ⓒ a high tower above the roof of a church, usu. capped with a spire. ⇒fig.
—名 뾰족탑, 첨탑

  stee·ple·chase [stíːpltʃèis] *n.* ⓒ a horse race across country obstructed with ditches, hedges, walls, etc.
—名 야외 횡단 경마, 장애 경마

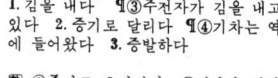
[steeple]

: **steer**¹ [stiər] *vt.* **1.** direct or guide the course of (a ship, an automobile, etc.). ¶*~ a ship.* **2.** direct; control. ¶*He steered our efforts to success.*① —*vi.* direct a ship, an automobile, etc.; follow a course. ¶*~ toward* (or *for*) *harbor.*②
—他 1. [배·자동차 따위를] 조종하다 2. …을 이끌다, 나아가게 하다 ¶①그는 우리의 노력을 성공으로 이끌었다 —自 키를 잡다; 나아가다 ¶②항구를 향해 키를 잡다

  steer clear of (=*avoid*) *someone* or *something.*
熟 …을 피하다

  steer² [stiər] *n.* ⓒ a young ox ⇒NB.; a male beef
—名 수송아지 NB 보통 두 살에서

cattle.
네 살까지의 소; 식용우(牛)

steer·age [stíəridʒ] *n.* **1.** 《usu. *the* ~, *sing.* only》 the section of a ship occupied by passengers traveling at the lowest fare. ¶*a* ~ *passenger*① / *travel* ~.② **2.** [U] [C] the act of steering.
—[名] 1. 3 등 선실 ¶① 3 등 선객/②[배의] 3 등으로 하다 2. 조타(操舵)

steer·ing wheel [stíəriŋ(h)wìːl] *n.* a wheel to turn a ship's rudder or to guide a motorcar.
—[名] 타륜(舵輪), [차의] 핸들

steers·man [stíərzmən] *n.* [C] (pl. **-men** [-mən]) a person who steers a vessel.
—[名] 키잡이, 타수(舵手)

stel·lar [stélər] *adj.* of or like a star.
—[形] 별의(같은)

‡stem[1] [stem] *n.* [C] **1.** the main part of a plant that holds a flower, a leaf, a branch, etc. **2.** something like a stem of a plant. **3.** the bow or front end of a boat. **4.** a branch of a family. —*vt.* pluck the stem from (a leaf, etc.). —*vi.* (*U.S.*) spring or develop. 《~ *from* or *out of* something》 ¶~ *from a noble family.*①
—[名] 1. [초목의] 줄기, 대; 엽병(葉柄) 2. 줄기 비슷한 것 3. 선수, 이물 4. 가계(家系) —[他] [잎 따위에서] 줄기를 떼어내다 —[自] 《美》 생기다 ¶①명문 출신이다

‡stem[2] [stem] *vt.* (**stemmed, stem·ming**) **1.** make progress or headway against (the wind, etc.). ¶~ *the tide.*① **2.** stop or check. ¶~ *the flow of water.*
—[他] 1. [바람 따위]에 거슬러서 나아가다 ¶①조류에 거슬러 나아가다 2. 막다, 저지하다

stench [stentʃ] *n.* [U] a very bad smell or odor.
—[名] 악취, 고약한 냄새

sten·cil [sténsl] *n.* [C] a thin sheet of metal, paper, etc. with letters or designs cut through it. ¶~ *paper*① / *a* ~ *pen.*② —*vt.* (**-ciled -cil·ing** or *Brit.* **-cilled, -cil·ling**) make copies of (something) by using a stencil.
—[名] 형지(型紙); 원지 ¶①등사판 원지/②[등사판용] 철필 —[他] …을 등사하다

sten·o·graph [sténougræf, +*Brit.* -grɑːf] *n.* [C] **1.** an act of writing in shorthand. **2.** a keyboard instrument used for printing shorthand symbols. **3.** a symbol for shorthand. —*vt.* write (something) in shorthand.
—[名] 1. 속기 2. 속기 타자기 3. 속기 문자 —[他] …을 속기하다

ste·nog·ra·pher [stenágrəfər / -nɔ́grəfə] *n.* [C] a person who is a specialist in stenography.
—[名] 속기자

sten·o·graph·ic [stènougrǽfik] *adj.* of stenography; written in shorthand.
—[形] 속기[술]의

ste·nog·ra·phy [stenágrəfi / -nɔ́g-] *n.* [U] a method of writing rapidly using simplified symbols; the act of writing in such symbols; shorthand.
—[名] 속기[술]

sten·to·ri·an [stentɔ́ːriən] *adj.* (of a voice) very loud.
—[形] 큰 소리의

‡step [step] *n.* [C] **1.** one movement of the leg in walking or running. ¶*take two steps forward* / *Watch* (or *Mind*) *your* ~!① **2.** the distance covered by one such movement; a short distance. ¶*His house is only a few steps from the station.* / *I'm too tired to walk a* ~ *farther.*② **3.** a sound or mark made by the foot in walking, etc. ¶*Steps were heard approaching.* /*The police found the burglar's steps in the snow.* **4.** [U] [C] the manner of walking; pace, esp. in marching; a regular movement of the feet in dancing. ¶*a light* ~③ / *in* (*out of*) ~④ / *a waltz* ~. **5.** one of the parts of a stair or ladder; 《*pl.*》 a flight of stairs. ¶*a doorstep*⑤ / *cut steps in the rock.*⑥ **6.** a degree in grade or rank; an advance that forms one of a series. ¶*He got his* ~.⑦ / *A sergeant is one* ~ *above a corporal.* **7.** an act or a measure done for some purpose. ¶*a bold* ~⑧ / *take steps*⑨ / *the first* ~ *in our work.* **8.** an interval in music; a tone.
—[名] 1. 걸음, 한 걸음 ¶①발밑을 조심해라 2. 1 보의 간격(보통 3 피이트); 한 발자국; 근거리 ¶②너무 지쳐서 한 걸음도 못 옮기겠다 3. 발소리; 발자국 4. 걸음걸이, 발걸음; 보조; [댄스의] 스텝 ¶③가벼운 발걸음/④보조를 맞추어(흩뜨려) 5. 단(段), 디딤대; 계급 ¶⑤[현관의] 층층대/⑥바위에 발판을 새기다 6. 단계; 계급; 승진, 승급 ¶⑦그는 승진했다 7. 수단; 조치 ¶⑧대담한 조치/⑨수단을 강구하다, 조치를 취하다 8. 음정(音程)

1) ***in step,*** at the same pace with another person or thing.
2) ***keep step with*** (=*move at the same pace as*) *someone.*
3) ***out of step,*** having a different pace with another person or thing.
4) ***step by step,*** gradually; slowly.

[熟] 1)보조를 맞추어; 조화하여 2)…와 보조를 맞추다 3)보조를 흩뜨려 4)한 걸음 한걸음; 조금씩 착실히

—*vi.* **1.** go, come, or move by one or more steps; walk a short distance. ¶~ *forward* (*backward*) / *Step this way, please.*⑩ **2.** press the foot on something. 《~ *on* something》 ¶~ *on a worm.* —*vt.* **1.** take (a step, a stride, etc.) ¶~ *two paces.* **2.** measure (a distance) by steps. ⇒***step off.*** **3.** perform the steps of (a dance).
—[自] 1. 걷다, 가다 ¶⑩이리로 오시오 2. 밟다, 디디다 —[他] 1. 걸음을 걷다 2. …을 걸어서 재다 3. [춤]을 추다

1) ***step aside,*** make way for others.
2) ***step down,*** ⓐ retire from (a position of authority). ⓑ reduce (an electric current, etc.).
3) ***step in,*** ⓐ enter. ¶ *~ in a house.* ⓑ come or be between.
4) ***step off,*** (*U.S.*) measure (a distance) by steps.
5) ***step out,*** ⓐ start to walk with long strides. ⓑ (*U.S.*) go out to have a good time.
6) ***step up,*** increase; speed up. ¶ *~ up sales.*

[熟] 1)비켜 서다 2)ⓐ[직위]를 그만두다 ⓑ[전압]을 내리다 3)ⓐ…에 들어가다 ⓑ…의 사이에 끼어들다 4)《美》…을 걸어서 재다 5)ⓐ큰 걸음으로 걷기 시작하다 ⓑ《美》놀러 나가다 6)…을 늘리다, 촉진하다

step·broth·er [stépbrʌ̀ðər] *n.* [C] a son of one's stepfather or stepmother by a former marriage. —[名] 의형제, 이복형제

step·child [stéptʃàild] *n.* [C] (pl. **-chil·dren** [-tʃíldr(ə)n]) a child of one's husband or wife by a former marriage. —[名] 의붓자식

step·daugh·ter [stépdɔ̀ːtər] *n.* [C] a daughter of one's husband or wife by a former marriage. —[名] 의붓딸

step-down [stépdàun] *adj.* converting an electric current from a higher to a lower voltage. —[形] 전압을 내리는

step·fa·ther [stépfɑ̀ːðər] *n.* [C] a man married to one's mother after the death or divorce of one's own father. —[名] 의붓아버지, 의부

Ste·phen [stíːv(ə)n] *n.* a man's name. —[名] 남자 이름

step·lad·der [stéplæ̀dər] *n.* [C] a short portable ladder with flat steps and, often, folding legs. ⇒fig. —[名] 발판 사다다리

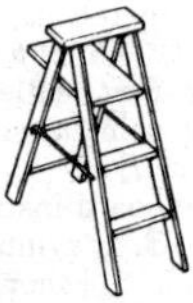

〔stepladder〕

step·moth·er [stépmʌ̀ðər] *n.* [C] a woman married to one's father after the death or divorce of one's own mother. —[名] 의붓어머니, 의모

step·par·ent [steppɛ̀ər(ə)nt, +*U.S.* -pæ̀r-, -pɛ̀ər(ə)nt] *n.* [C] a stepfather or stepmother. —[名] 의붓어버이

steppe [step] *n.* [C] a vast, grassy plain without trees; 《*The Steppes*》 the vast, treeless Russian grasslands. —[名] 대초원; 스텝(시베리아의 대초원)

step·ping stone [stépiŋstòun] *n.* **1.** one of a line of stones placed in a shallow stream, soft turf, etc. **2.** something used as a means of advancing or rising. 《~ *to*》 ¶ *a ~ to victory.*① —[名] **1.** 디딤돌, 징검다리 돌 **2.** [어떤 목적의 달성을 위한] 수단 ¶①승리의 수단

step·sis·ter [stépsìstər] *n.* [C] a daughter of one's stepfather or stepmother by a former marriage. —[名] 의붓자매

step·son [stépsʌn] *n.* [C] a son of one's husband or wife by a former marriage. —[名] 의붓아들

ster·e·o·phon·ic [stèrioufánik, stìəriou- / -fóun-, stìəriə-] *adj.* of or giving sound reproduction through two or more channels at the same time. —[形] 입체음향의, 스테레오의

ster·e·o·scope [stériəskòup, +*Brit.* stíər-] *n.* [C] an instrument through which two pictures of the same scene appear to be one which has depth. —[名] 입체경(鏡)

ster·e·o·type [stérioutàip, stíər-] *n.* [C] **1.** a printing metal plate made by casting comrosed type in a mold; the process of making such m.tal plates. **2.** a fixed expression. —*vt.* **1.** print (something) from a stereotype. **2.** give a settled form to (something). —[名] **1.** 연판(鉛版), 스테로판; 연판 제조 **2.** 상투적 문구 —[他] **1.** …을 연판으로 인쇄하다 **2.** …을 틀에 박히게 하다

ster·ile [stéril / stérail] *adj.* **1.** unable to produce offsprings. ¶ *a ~ cow.*① **2.** not fertile; barren. ↔fertile ¶ *a wild stretch of ~ land.*② **3.** free from any living germs. ¶ *Surgical knives are always kept ~.*③ **4.** unsuccessful; useless. ¶ *~ hopes.* **5.** lacking interest, emotion, imagination, etc. ¶ *a ~ lecture.* —[形] **1.** 불임(不姙)의 ¶①새끼를 못 낳는 소 **2.** 불모의, 메마른 ¶②광막한 불모지 **3.** 살균한 ¶③메스는 늘 살균해 둔다 **4.** 성과가 없는; 쓸모없는 **5.** 흥미없는, 멋없는

ste·ril·i·ty [stəríliti / ster-] *n.* [U] the state or quality of being sterile; barrenness. —[名] 불임; 불모; 무미건조

ster·i·li·za·tion [stèrilizéiʃ(ə)n / -laiz-] *n.* [U] the act of sterilizing; the state of being sterilized. —[名] 살균 소독; 불임화(不姙化)

ster·i·lize [stérilàiz] *vt.* **1.** free (something) from living germs. ¶ *~ water by boiling.*① **2.** deprive (an animal) of reproductive power. —[他] **1.** …을 살균(소독)하다 ¶①물을 끓여 살균하다 **2.** …을 불임이 되게 하다

ster·ling [stə́ːrliŋ] *adj.* **1.** of British money. ⇒[N.B.] ¶ *£500s.; £500 stg.* **2.** of real value; excellent. ¶ ~ —[形] **1.** 영화(英貨)의 [N.B.] s., stg.로 줄여 파운드 다음에 붙임 **2.** 진정(眞

*worth*① / *a* ~ *character.* —*n.* [U] British money.
正)한 ¶①진가(眞價) —[名] 영화(英貨)

‡ **stern**¹ [stəːrn] *adj.* **1.** severe; strict. ¶*a* ~ *teacher*① / *a* ~ *command.*② **2.** firm; hard. ¶*a* ~ *resolve.*
—[形] 1. 엄격한 ¶①엄격한 교사/②엄명 2. 단호한

stern² [stəːrn] *n.* [C] the back part of a ship. ↔bow ¶*from stem to* ~.①
—[名] 선미(船尾), 고물 ¶①배의 구석구석까지

stern·ly [stə́ːrnli] *adv.* in a stern manner; severely; strictly.
—[副] 엄하게, 엄격하게

steth·o·scope [stéθəskòup] *n.* [C] an instrument used by doctors for listening to heartbeats.
—[名] 청진기

ste·ve·dore [stíːvidɔ̀ːr] *n.* [C] a person who carries packages onto or off a ship.
—[名] 부두 하역 인부

* **stew** [st(j)uː / stjuː] *vt., vi.* **1.** boil slowly. ¶~ *meat and vegetables.* **2.** (*colloq.*) worry.
—[他][自] 1. [···을] 뭉근한 불에 끓이다(찌다) 2. 애타게 하다; 애태우다

let someone stew in his own juice, do not help someone out of difficulty.
[熟] 제멋대로 하게 내버려두다

—*n.* **1.** [C][U] a stewed dish made of meat and vegetables. **2.** [C] (*colloq.*) a state of worry; a difficulty.
—[名] 1. 스튜우 2.《口》근심

* **stew·ard** [st(j)úːərd / stjuəd] *n.* [C] **1.** a man to manage the household affairs of his master's family. **2.** a waiter on a ship or train, at a club, etc.
—[名] 1. 집사, 간사 2. 급사

stew·ard·ess [st(j)úːərdis / stjúəd-] *n.* [C] a waitress on a ship, an airplane, etc.
—[名] 여급사, 스튜어디스

stew·pan [st(j)úːpæ̀n / stjúː-] *n.* [C] a pan used for making stew.
—[名] 스튜우 남비

‡ **stick**¹ [stik] *n.* [C] **1.** a piece of wood cut or broken from a tree; a long, narrow piece of wood. **2.** something like a stick in shape or use; a walking stick; a hockey stick. ¶*a* ~ *of candy.* **3.** (*colloq.*) a dull or stupid person. ¶*He is a* ~.
—[名] 1. 나뭇가지, 마른 가지; 막대기 2. 막대기 모양의 것; 지팡이, 스틱; [하키의] 스틱 3.《口》얼간이, 등신

‡ **stick**² [stik] *v.* (**stuck**) *vt.* **1.** push (a pointed thing) into someone or something; thrust or pierce (something or someone) with a pointed thing. 《~ something *into* or *through*; ~ something or someone *with*》 ¶~ *a fork into a potato* / ~ *a knife into one's belly.* **2.** fix or fasten (something) by or on a point. 《~ something *on* or *in*》 ¶~ *a flower in a buttonhole.*① **3.** fix or attach (something) with paste glue, etc. 《~ something *on* or *to*》 ¶~ *a stamp on a letter* / ~ *a notice to a door.*② **4.** put or thrust (something) in a place or position. 《~ something *into, out of, in*》 ¶~ *a letter in one's pocket* / *Don't* ~ *your head out of the train window.*③ **5.** 《usu. in *passive*》 bring (something) to a stop. 《~ something *in*》 ¶*The car was stuck in the mud.*④ —*vi.* **1.** be thrust. 《~ *in* something》 ¶*A splinter stuck in his leg.* **2.** become attached or fastened. 《~ *to* something》 ¶*The glue stuck to his fingers.* **3.** keep close; hold fast. 《~ *to* something》 ¶*The boy stuck to his mother's heels.*⑤ **4.** become motionless; stay. ¶~ *at home* / *The horse stuck on the hill.* **5.** be fixed; be unable to go farther. ¶*The door has stuck.*⑥ / *Our car stuck in the mud.* **6.** be in trouble; be puzzled.
—[他] 1. ···에 [바늘 따위 예리한 것]을 찌르다; [예리한 것으로] ···을 찌르다, 찔러 넣다, 꿰뚫다, 찔러 죽이다 2. ···을 찔러서 달다, 장식하다 ¶①꽃을 단추구멍에 끼우다 3. ···을 붙이다, 고착시키다 ¶②문에 게시문을 붙이다 4. ···을 두다, 놓다, 끼워 넣다 ¶③기차의 창밖으로 얼굴을 내밀지 말라 5. ···을 옴쭉 못하게 하다 ¶④자동차는 진흙에 빠져 꼼짝 못했다 —[自] 1. 꽂히다 2. 들러붙다, 붙여져 있다 3. 들러붙어 있다, 붙어서 떨어지지 않다 ¶⑤그 소년은 어머니 뒤에 붙어 있었다 4. 멎다, 머무르다 5. 막히다, 멎어서 움직이지 않다 ¶⑥문이 열리지 않는다 6. 난처해지다, 당황하다

1) *stick at,* ⓐ keep hard at (one's job, etc.). ⓑ hesitate or stop for (something). ¶*She'll* ~ *at nothing.*⑦
2) *stick out,* ⓐ thrust out; stand out. ¶~ *out one's tongue.* ⓑ be plainly apparent.
3) *stick to,* ⓐ keep on with; continue with (one's work, etc.). ¶~ *to one's task.* ⓑ be faithful to; be true to; keep. ¶~ *to one's agreement.*⑧
4) *stick up,* be or make (something) upright. ¶~ *up a post.*
5) *stick up for,* support (someone) in an argument; defend.

[熟] 1)ⓐ···을 꾸준히 하다 ⓑ···을 망설이다 ¶⑦그녀는 아무 일에나 망설이지 않을 것이다 2)ⓐ내밀다, 삐져나오다 ⓑ눈에 띄게 드러나다 3)ⓐ···에 집착하다; 버티다; 계속하다 ⓑ···에 충실하다; 떨어지지 않다 ¶⑧약속을 지키다 4)곧추 서다, 곧추 세우다 5)···을 지지하다, 변호하다; 지키다

stick·er [stíkər] *n.* [C] **1.** a person or thing that sticks. **2.** (*U.S.*) a gummed label.
—[名] 1. 붙이는 사람(것) 2. 풀 묻힌 레테르

stick·ing plaster [stíkiŋplæ̀stər / -plɑ̀ːstə] *n.* a sticky tape of cloth for covering and closing slight wounds.
—[名] 반창고

stick-in-the-mud [stík(i)nðəmʌ̀d] *n.* [C] (*colloq.*) a person
—[名]《口》구식 사람

stickler

who resists progress or change.
stick·ler [stíklər] *n.* ⓒ a person who worries or is concerned about small matters. —㊄ 하찮은 일에 구애되는 사람; 잔소리꾼
stick·y [stíki] *adj.* (**stick·i·er, stick·i·est**) **1.** that sticks. ¶*The paste left my fingers ~.*① **2.** (*colloq.*) (of weather) unpleasantly hot and wet. ▷**stick·i·ly** [-li] *adv.* —**stick·i·ness** [-nis] *n.* —㊇ 1.끈적끈적한 ¶①풀이 손가락에 남아 끈적거렸다 2.《口》몹시 무더운
‡**stiff** [stif] *adj.* **1.** not easily bent; firm; rigid. ¶*a ~ collar.* **2.** not able to move without pain; hard to move or operate. ¶*~ hinges | have a ~ neck.* **3.** formal; cold in one's manner. ¶*a ~ bow | a ~ manner.* **4.** difficult; hard. ¶*a ~ examination.* **5.** not yielding or giving way; obstinate. ¶*He is very ~ about it.* **6.** (of winds, currents, etc.) strong; (of alcoholic drinks) very strong; (of a penalty, etc.) severe. ¶*a ~ gale | a ~ fine.* **7.** not flowing easily; thick and heavy. ¶*a ~ varnish.* —㊇ 1.구부리기 힘든;딱딱한,굳은 2.[관절 따위가] 아파서 움직이지 않는, 술을 움직이지 않는 3.격식을 차린, 서글서글한 4.어려운 5.양보하지 않는, 완고한 6.[바람·조류 따위가] 강한; 알코올분이 강한; [형벌이] 가혹한, 엄한 7.묽지 않은,걸쭉한
stiff·en [stíf(ə)n] *vt., vi.* make (something) stiff; become stiff. ¶*She stiffened the sheets with starch.*① —㊄㊈ 굳게 하다(되다) ¶①그녀는 시이트를 빳빳하게 풀먹였다
·**stiff·ly** [stífli] *adv.* in a stiff manner. —㊄ 딱딱하게; 완고하게
stiff·ness [stífnis] *n.* Ⓤ the state or quality of being stiff. —㊇ 굳음
sti·fle [stáifl] *vt.* **1.** prevent (someone) from breathing. ¶*The large crowds in the train stifled me.*① **2.** put out. ¶*~ a fire.* **3.** hold back or stop. ¶*~ tears | ~ a yawn.* —*vi.* become unable to breathe freely. —㊄ 1.…을 질식시키다 ¶①기차는 아주 붐벼서 숨이 막힐 것 같았다 2. …을 끄다 3.…을 누르다 —㊈ 숨막히다
sti·fling [stáifliŋ] *adj.* in a condition where it is difficult to breathe. ¶*be ~ hot.*① —㊇ 숨막힐 것 같은; 답답한 ¶①숨이 막힐 것처럼 덥다
stig·ma [stígmə] *n.* ⓒ (pl. **-mas** or **-ma·ta**) **1.** a mark of shame or dishonor. **2.** a burnt sign on a slave or criminal in olden days. **3.** the upper part of a flower. —㊇ 1.오명 2.낙인 3.[꽃의] 암술머리
stig·ma·ta [stígmətə] *n. pl.* of **stigma**.
stig·ma·tize [stígmətàiz] *vt.* **1.** mark (someone) as shameful. **2.** put a burnt sign on (a slave, etc.). —㊄ 1.…에 오명을 씌우다 2.…에게 낙인을 찍다
stile [stail] *n.* ⓒ a step or steps for getting over a fence. ⇒fig. —㊇ 가축은 못 넘으나 사람은 넘게 만든 울타리 층계
sti·let·to [stilétou] *n.* ⓒ (pl. **-tos** or **-toes**) **1.** a small weapon shaped like a knife. **2.** a tool for making small holes in cloth. [stile] —㊇ 1.작은 검 2.[자수용] 구멍 내는 바늘
‡**still**¹ [stil] *adj.* **1.** quiet; making no sound; silent. ¶*a ~ evening.* **2.** having no motion; without movement; (of water) calm. ¶*Please stand ~. |(proverb) Still waters run deep.* **3.** (of sounds) soft; low. ¶*(Bible) a (or the) ~ small voice.*① —*adv.* **1.** up to this or that time; now, as before; as yet. ¶*The baby is ~ asleep. | She will ~ be here tomorrow.* **2.** (used with a *comparative*) even; (used *intensively*) yet. ¶*He is tall enough, but his brother is ~ taller.* **3.** (used *conjunctively*) however; in spite of that. ¶*He is a good man, ~ I don't like him.*
—*vt.* make (something) quiet, silent, or calm. ¶*~ a crying baby | ~ one's desire.* —*vi.* become still.
—*n.* ⓒ **1.** (*poetic*) silence. **2.** a single photograph from the series that form a motion picture film. —㊇ 1.조용한; 소리 안 나는; 묵묵한 2.움직이지 않는,정지한; [수면이] 잔잔한 3.목소리가 낮은,부드러운 ¶①조용하고 작은 목소리(신·양심의 속삭임) —㊄ 1.아직도, 상금, 지금도 2.더욱, 더 한층 3.그래도, 역시

—㊄ …을 고요하게 하다, 달래다; 누그러뜨리다 —㊈ 조용해지다, 잔잔해지다 —㊇ 1.《詩》고요; 침묵 2.스틸 사진
still² [stil] *n.* ⓒ an apparatus used for making whisky or brandy. —㊇ [알코올류의] 증류기
still·born [stílbɔ̀ːrn] *adj.* dead when born. —㊇ 사산(死産)의
still life [⌐ ⌐] *n.* a picture representing only lifeless objects, such as flowers, furniture, and books. —㊇ 정물화(靜物畵)
·**still·ness** [stílnis] *n.* Ⓤ silence. —㊇ 고요, 정적
stilt·ed [stíltid] *adj.* **1.** raised on stilts. **2.** too formal; not natural. —㊇ 1.죽마(竹馬)에 탄 2.과장된
stilts [stilts] *n. pl.* a pair of wooden poles for walking above the ground. ¶*walk on ~.*① —㊇ 죽마 ¶①죽마를 타고 걷다
stim·u·lant [stímjulənt] *n.* ⓒ some drink or medicine that gives power and excitement to the body. ¶*Alcoholic drinks and coffee are stimulants.*① —㊇ [몸에 작용하는 음식물·약 따위의] 자극물 ¶①알콜 음료와 코오피는 자극물이다

* **stim·u·late** [stímjulèit] *vt.* excite or encourage (someone) to action; quicken the activity of (some bodily function). ¶*Wine stimulates a sick person.* / *Praise stimulates students to work hard.*①
—[他] …을 자극하다; 기운내게 하다 ¶①칭찬을 하면 학생들은 더욱 열심히 공부한다

stim·u·lat·ing [stímjulèitiŋ] *adj.* exciting mental or physical activity.
—[形] 자극하는; 기운내게 하는

stim·u·la·tion [stìmjuléiʃ(ə)n] *n.* [U] the act of stimulating; the state of being stimulated.
—[名] 자극; 격려

stim·u·la·tive [stímjulèitiv, +*Brit.* -lətiv] *adj.* having power to stimulate someone.
—[形] 자극하는; 자극적인; 격려하는

stim·u·lat·or [stímjulèitər] *n.* [C] a person or thing that stimulates.
—[名] 자극자(물)

stim·u·li [stímjulài] *n.* pl. of **stimulus.**

stim·u·lus [stímjuləs] *n.* [C] (pl. **-li**) **1.** something that urges someone to action. **2.** =stimulant.
—[名] 1. [정신에 작용하는] 자극; 자극물

‡ **sting** [stiŋ] *n.* [C] **1.** a sharp, pointed organ in some insects, animals, and plants which often contains poison. **2.** the wound or pain caused by a sting; the act of stinging. **3.** [C][U] any sharp, sudden pain of mind or body; wounding quality or capacity. ¶*a jest with a ~ in it*① / *the stings of conscience.*
—[名] 1. [곤충의] 독아(毒芽), 바늘; [식물의] 가시 2. 찔린 상처; 찔린 아픔; 찌르기 3. [일반적으로] 찌르는 듯한 아픔; 심한 고통; 자극; 찌르는 힘 ¶①신랄한 농담

—*v.* (**stung**) *vt.* **1.** wound or pierce (someone or something) with a sting. ¶*A bee stung her cheek.* **2.** give a sharp physical or emotional pain to (someone). ¶*His remark stung my pride.* **3.** excite (someone) to act. 《~ someone *into* or *to*》 ¶*He was stung into action.*
—*vi.* **1.** prick with a sting; have a sting. ¶*The rosebush stings.* **2.** feel a mental or physical pain.
—[他] 1. [바늘로] …을 찌르다 2. …을 찌르듯이 아프게 하다, 욱신욱신 쑤시게 하다 3. …을 자극하여 …시키다 —[自] 1. 찌르다, 가시가 있다 2. 욱신욱신 아프다; [후회 따위로] 마음이 괴롭다

stin·gy [stíndʒi] *adj.* (**-gi·er, -gi·est**) mean in giving or spending money. ▷**stin·gi·ly** [-li] *adv.*
—[形] 인색한

stink [stiŋk] *v.* (**stank** or **stunk, stunk**) *vi.* give off a bad smell. —*vt.* drive or force (someone) out by means of a bad smell. 《~ *out* something》 —*n.* [C] a very bad smell.
—[自] 악취를 내다 —[他] …을 악취로 쫓아내다 —[名] 악취

stint [stint] *vt.* spend or give not enough of (something); limit (something) within a certain amount or number.
—[他] …을 바짝 줄이다, 주기 싫어하다
—*n.* **1.** [U] a limit. **2.** [C] a limited amount of work.
—[名] 1. 제한 2. 할당된 일

sti·pend [stáipend] *n.* [C] a fixed payment for work.
—[名] 봉급

sti·pen·di·ar·y [staipéndièri / -diəri] *adj.* receiving a stipend. —*n.* [C] (pl. **-ar·ies**) a person who receives a stipend.
—[形] 봉급을 받는 —[名] 봉급장이

stip·u·late [stípjulèit] *vt.* arrange (a matter) as a part of an agreement.
—[他] …을 약정하다; 계약의 조건으로서 요구하다

stip·u·la·tion [stìpjuléiʃ(ə)n] *n.* [U][C] the act of stipulating; [C] something that is stipulated.
—[名] 약정, 규정, 조항

‡ **stir** [stəːr] *v.* (**stirred, stir·ring**) *vt.* **1.** move; shake. ¶*The tide stirs the boat.* **2.** mix (a liquid, etc.) by moving it around with a spoon, etc. ¶*~ coffee with a spoon* / *~ sugar into one's coffee.* **3.** cause (someone or something) to act, feel, or think; excite. 《~ someone *to* an act; ~ someone *to do*》 ¶*~ one's interest* / *The news stirred him to action.*① —*vi.* **1.** be active; be in motion; move little. ¶*Nobody is stirring in the house.* **2.** be mixed. ¶*This dough stirs hard.*② **3.** become excited; begin to develop. ¶*Pity stirred in her heart.*
—[他] 1. …을 [조금] 움직이다, 흔들다 2. [액체 따위]를 휘젓다, 저어서 섞다 3. [사람의 감정·상상 따위를] 움직이다, …을 선동하다 ¶①그 소식을 듣고 그는 행동을 개시했다 —[自] 1. 활동하고 있다; 일어나 있다; [조금] 움직이다 2. 휘저어지다 ¶②이 반죽은 반죽하기가 힘들다 3. [감정 따위가] 일어나다

stir up, ⓐ mix (a liquid, etc.). ⓑ cause (something) to rise by stirring; cause; excite. ¶*~ up trouble.*
[熟] ⓐ…을 잘 젓다 ⓑ…을 뒤섞다; 야기하다; 선동하다

—*n.* **1.** [C] a very small motion. ¶*There was not a ~ in the audience.* **2.** [U][C] the state of excitement; general or public interest. ¶*make a ~*③ / *His behavior caused a great ~.* **3.** [U][C] the act of stirring a liquid, etc.
—[名] 1. 조금 움직이기 2. 흥분, 큰 소동 ¶③큰 소동을 벌이다 3. 뒤섞기

stir·ring [stə́ːriŋ] *adj.* **1.** moving; exciting. ¶*a ~ speech*① / *a ~ event.* **2.** full of action. ¶*~ times*② / *a ~ city.*
—[形] 1. 감동시키는; 고무하는 ¶①남의 마음을 고무하는 연설 2. 활발한 ¶②시끄러운 세상

stir·rup [stə́ːrəp / stírəp] *n.* [C] one of a pair of supports for a horse rider's feet.
—[名] 등자(鐙子)

* **stitch** [stitʃ] *n.* [C] **1.** a complete movement of the threaded needle in sewing or knitting. ¶(*proverb*) *A ~*
—[名] 1. 한 바늘, 한 뜸, 한 코 ¶①제때의 한 바늘은 나중의 아홉 바늘의 수

*in time saves nine.*① **2.** a loop or knot made by a stitch. **3.** a method of taking stitches. **4.** ⟪*sing.* only⟫ a sudden, sharp pain. **—***vt.* join, mend or fasten (something) with stitches. **—***vi.* make stitches; sew.

고를 던다 **2.** 솔기 **3.** 꿰매는 법 **4.** 심한 아픔 **—**[他] …을 꿰매 붙이다 **—**[自] 바느질하다

⁑ **stock** [stɑk / stɔk] *n.* **1.** [U] [C] a store of things for use or sale. ¶*in (out of)* ~① / *have a small ~ on hand* / *have a great ~ of knowledge*② / *His store has a large ~ of goods.* **2.** [U] cattle or other farm animals. **3.** [C] a trunk or stem of a tree or plant. **4.** [U] family line as having certain qualities; birth; race; a group of related languages. ¶*the languages of German ~* / *He comes of a noble ~.*③ **5.** [C] a part of a thing used as its support, handle, or base. ¶*the ~ of a rifle.*④ **6.** [U] raw material; liquid in which bones, meat, etc. have been cooked, used for making soup, etc. ¶*paper ~*⑤ / *soup ~.* **7.** [C] [U] capital or shares of a business company; ⟪*the ~s*⟫ (*Brit.*) money lent to the government at fixed interest. ¶*bank stocks* / *She has money in stocks.*⑥ **8.** [C] a sweet-smelling garden flower. **9.** ⟪*pl.*⟫ the frame on which a ship is built. ¶*off the stocks* / *on the stocks.* **10.** ⟪*pl.*⟫ a frame used for punishment. ⇒fig.

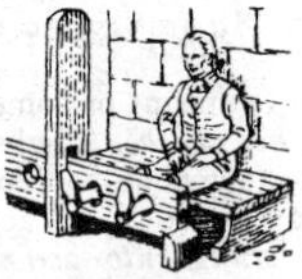
[stocks 10.]

—[名] **1.** 저장, 저축, 재고(在庫); 재고품 ¶①재고가 있는(없는)/②풍부한 지식이 있다 **2.** 가축 **3.** 줄기 **4.** 가계(家系); 혈통; [언어의] 어계(語系) ¶③그는 고귀한 가문 출신이다 **5.** [도구의] 자루, 대(臺) ¶④총개머리판 **6.** 원료; 수우프 거리 ¶⑤제지 원료 **7.** 주식; 영업 자본; 공채(公債) ¶⑥그녀는 돈을 공채로 갖고 있다 **8.** 자라난화(紫羅欄花) **9.** 조선대(造船臺) **10.** 족쇄, 차꼬, 수갑, 효수대

1) ***on the stocks,*** (of a plan, etc.) in progress.
2) ***take stock,*** check the quantity of goods on hand.
3) ***take*** (or ***put***) ***stock in*** (=*trust; have faith in*) *something.* ¶*I take little ~ in what she says.*⑦

[熟] 1)[계획 따위가] 진행중인 2)재고를 조사하다 3)…을 신용하다 ¶⑦그녀의 말은 전혀 신용하지 않는다

—*vt.* **1.** supply; store up. ⟪~ a place *with* something⟫ ¶*~ a store with goods*⑧ / *~ the lake with fish.*⑨ **2.** keep (something) regularly for use or for sale. ¶*He does not ~ that kind of food.* **3.** furnish (a farm) with cattle, etc.; sow (land) with seed, etc.

—[他] **1.** …을 사들이다; 저장하다 ¶⑧가게에 물건을 사들이다/⑨호수에 물고기를 방류(放流)하다 **2.** …을 저장해 두다 **3.** …에 가축을 넣다; …에 씨 따위를 뿌리다

—*adj.* **1.** kept on hand regularly; standard. ¶*~ sizes.* **2.** in common use; ordinary. ¶*a ~ joke* / *a ~ phrase.*

—[形] **1.** 수중에 있는, 재고의; 표준의 **2.** 흔해빠진, 케케묵은, 진부한

stock·ade [stɑkéid / stɔk-] *n.* [C] a strong fence used as a defense or enclosure for cattle, etc.
—[名] 방어용 말뚝 울타리

stock·bro·ker [stɑ́kbròukər / stɔ́kbròukə] *n.* [C] a person who buys and sells stocks and bonds for others.
—[名] 주식 중매인(仲買人)

stock·bro·king [stɑ́kbròukiŋ / stɔ́k-] *n.* [U] the business or work of a stockbroker.
—[名] 주식 매매

stock exchange [´ –´–] *n.* a place where stocks and bonds are bought and sold.
—[名] 주식(증권) 거래소

stock farm [´ ´] *n.* a farm for raising animals for sale.
—[名] 목축장

stock·hold·er [stɑ́khòuldər / stɔ́khòuldə] *n.* [C] (*U.S.*) a person who holds stocks or shares in a company. (cf. *Brit.* shareholder)
—[名] ⟪美⟫ 주주

⁑ **stock·ing** [stɑ́kiŋ / stɔ́k-] *n.* [C] ⟪usu. *pl.*⟫ a close-fitting covering for the foot and leg. ¶*in one's stockings.*①
—[名] 양말 ¶①[신을 벗고] 양말바람으로

stock in trade [´ – ´] *n.* **1.** a stock of goods for sale at a store. **2.** a workman's tools or materials for carrying on a trade. **3.** one's means for any purpose.
—[名] **1.** 재고품 **2.** 장사 도구 **3.** 상투 수단

stock market [´ ´–] *n.* **1.** a stock exchange. **2.** the business in such a place. **3.** the prices of stocks and bonds.
—[名] **1.** 주식(증권) 거래소(시장) **2.** 증권 거래 **3.** 증권 시세

stock·pile [stɑ́kpàil / stɔ́k-] *n.* [C] a supply of raw material, goods, etc. held in reserve for use when needed. **—***vt., vi.* keep a stockpile.
—[名] [원료의] 축적 **—**[他][自] [원료를] 축적하다

stock rais·ing [stɑ́krèiziŋ / stɔ́k-] *n.* the act or business of raising livestock.
—[名] 목축[업]

stock-still [stɑ́kstíl / stɔ́k-] *adj.* entirely motionless.
—[形] 움직이지 않는

stock·tak·ing [stɑ́ktèikiŋ / stɔ́k-] *n.* [U] periodical check of the quantity of goods in a store.
—[名] 재고 조사

stock·y [stɑ́ki / stɔ́ki] *adj.* (**stock·i·er, stock·i·est**) short,
—[形] 땅딸막한 ¶①그는 땅딸보다

stout and strong. ¶*He is ~ in build.*①

stock·yard [stákjɑ̀:rd / stɔ́kjɑ̀:d] *n.* [C] a place where cattle are kept before being sent to market or killed.
—[名] 가축 수용장(收容場)

stodg·y [stádʒi / stɔ́dʒi] *adj.* (**stodg·i·er, stodg·i·est**) **1.** (of food) heavy. **2.** (of a book, talk, etc.) dull and uninteresting. **3.** short and fat. ¶*a ~ person.*
—[形] 1. 소화가 잘 안 되는, 되직한 2. 재미없는 3. 땅딸막한

Sto·ic [stóuik] *adj.* **1.** of the philosophy of the Stoics or their philosophy. **2.** ⦅*s*-⦆ stoical.
—[形] 1. 스토아 철학[파]의 2. 금욕주의의

—*n.* [C] **1.** a member of a school of philosophy founded by Zeno, who believed that man should be free from all passion. **2.** ⦅*s*-⦆ a person who is always calm and shows indifference to his passion, etc.
—[名] 1. 스토아 철학자 2. 금욕주의자

sto·i·cal [stóuik(ə)l] *adj.* self-controlled; indifferent to joy, pleasure, passion, etc.
—[形] 금욕의; 냉정한

sto·i·cal·ly [stóuik(ə)li] *adv.* in a stoic manner.
—[副] 금욕적으로; 냉정하게

Sto·i·cism [stóuisìz(ə)m] *n.* [U] **1.** the philosophy of the Stoics. **2.** ⦅*s*-⦆ self-control; indifference to pleasure and pain.
—[名] 1. 스토아 철학(주의) 2. 극기(克己); 냉정

stoke [stouk] *vt., vi.* **1.** put (fuel) on a fire; attend to (a fire). **2.** (*colloq.*) eat.
—[他][自] 1. 불을 때다, 화부 노릇을 하다 2. …을 먹다

‡ **stole**[1] [stoul] *v.* pt. of **steal**.

stole[2] [stoul] *n.* [C] **1.** a long strip of silk, etc. worn around the neck by a priest. **2.** a woman's scarf of cloth or fur worn over the shoulders.
—[名] 1. 스톨라(목사 어깨에 걸치는 것) 2. 여자 스카아프의 일종

‡ **sto·len** [stóul(ə)n] *v.* pp. of **steal**.

stol·id [stálid / stɔ́l-] *adj.* not easily excited; dull; showing no emotion or feeling.
—[形] 둔감한, 무신경의

sto·lid·i·ty [stəlíditi, +*Brit.* stɔl-] *n.* [U] the state or quality of being stolid.
—[名] 둔감, 무신경

stol·id·ly [stálidli / stɔ́l-] *adv.* in a stolid manner; dully; impassively.
—[副] 멍하니, 무신경하게

stol·id·ness [stálidnis / stɔ́l-] *n.* [U] stolidity.
—[名] 멍하니 있음, 무신경

‡ **stom·ach** [stʌ́mək] *n.* **1.** [C] a baglike part of the body where food is swallowed and digested; the part of the body containing the stomach. ¶*put the ~ out of order*① / *lie on one's stomach*② / *My ~ rises at it.*③ **2.** [U] appetite. **3.** [U] desire; inclination. ¶*He has no ~ for fighting.*④
—[名] 1. 위; 배 ¶①배탈이 나다/②엎드리다/③그것을 보면 메스꺼워진다 2. 식욕 3. 욕망; 기호(嗜好); 기분 ¶④그에게는 싸울 마음이 없다

—*vt.* **1.** be able to eat (food); digest (food). **2.** ⦅mostly in *negative*⦆ bear. ¶*He could not ~ such an insult.*⑤
—[他] 1. …을 먹을 수 있다, 소화하다 2. 참다 ¶⑤그는 그런 모욕을 참을 수 없었다

stom·ach·ache [stʌ́məkèik] *n.* [U][C] pain in the stomach ¶*have a ~.*①
—[名] 복통 ¶①배가 아프다

sto·mach·ic [stoumǽkik] *adj.* **1.** of the stomach. **2.** good for the stomach or appetite. —*n.* [C] medicine for the stomach.
—[形] 1. 위(胃)의 2. 위에 좋은; 식욕을 돋우는 —[名] 건위제(健胃劑); 소화제

‡ **stone** [stoun] *n.* **1.** [U][C] a small piece of rock larger than a grain sand; a hard mineral material found in the earth. ¶*throw a ~ at a dog* / *a heart of ~*① / (*proverb*) *A rolling ~ gathers no moss.*② **2.** [U] a piece of rock shaped and used for a particular purpose. ¶*a paving ~.* **3.** [C] a precious stone; a jewel. ¶*The ring is set with five stones.* **4.** [C] a hard seed of a piece of fruit. **5.** [C] a hard mass formed inside the body in certain diseases. **6.** (pl. **stone**) an English unit of weight, usu. 14 pounds.
—[名] 1. 돌, 작은 돌 ¶①돌처럼 무정한 마음/②⦅俚⦆굴러다니는 돌에는 이끼가 안 낀다 2. 석재(石材) 3. 보석 4. [과실의] 씨, 핵(核) 5. 결석(結石) 6. 스토운(보통 14 파운드의 중량 단위)

1) ***kill two birds with one stone,*** (*proverb*) accomplish two purposes with one action.
2) ***leave no stone unturned,*** use every possible means.
3) ***within a stone's throw*** (or ***cast***)***,*** within a very short distance.
[熟] 1)일거양득을 하다 2)온갖 수단을 다 쓰다 3)아주 가까이에

—*vt.* **1.** throw stones at (someone or something). ¶*~ someone to death.*③ **2.** take seeds out of (fruit). ¶*~ cherries.* **3.** pave or face (something) with stone.
—[他] 1. …에 돌을 던지다 ¶③…에 돌을 던져 죽이다 2. [과일]의 씨를 빼다 3. …에 돌을 깔다

—*adj.* made of stone. ¶*a ~ bridge.*
—[形] 돌의, 돌로 만든

Stone Age [ˊ ˋ] *n.* a prehistoric period when stone was used for tools and weapons.
—[名] 석기시대

stone·blind [stóunbláind] *adj.* completely blind.
—[形] 아주 눈이 먼

S

stone·cut·ter [stóunkʌtər] *n.* [C] **1.** a person who is engaged in cutting or carving stone. **2.** a machine for cutting stone.
—[名] 1. 석공(石工) 2. 돌 뜨는 기계

stone-dead [stóundéd] *adj.* completely dead.
—[形] 완전히 죽은

stone-deaf [stóundéf] *adj.* completely deaf.
—[形] 아주 귀먹은

stone fruit [´ ˋ] *n.* any fruit containing a hard core inside a soft layer of pulp.
—[名] [복숭아 따위] 핵과(核果)

Stone·henge [stóunhèndʒ / ´ ˋ] *n.* a prehistoric, ruined stone structure on Salisbury Plain in England.
—[名] 환열석주(環列石柱)(석기시대 후기의 거대한 돌기둥들)

stone·less [stóunlis] *adj.* **1.** without stones. **2.** without hard seeds.
—[形] 1. 돌이 없는 2. 씨가 없는

stone·ma·son [stóunmèisn] *n.* [C] a person who cuts stone for use in making walls, buildings, etc.
—[名] 석공

stone pit [´ ˋ] *n.* a place where stone is got out by cutting or blasting; a quarry.
—[名] 채석장

stone·ware [stóunwὲər] *n.* [U] a kind of pottery used for earthen pipes, jars, etc. which is rough and hard, but covered with a shining surface.
—[名] 석기

stone·work [stóunwə̀:rk] *n.* [U] **1.** the art of working in stone. **2.** the part of a building made or built in stone.
—[名] 1. 돌 세공 2. 석조물

* **ston·y** [stóuni] *adj.* (**ston·i·er, ston·i·est**) **1.** covered with stones; full of stones. ¶*a ~ path.* **2.** hard like stone; cold or cruel. ¶*a ~ heart.*① **3.** having hard seeds. ¶*a ~ fruit.*② **4.** showing no feeling; rigid.
—[形] 1. 돌을 깐, 돌이 많은 2. 굳은; 냉혹한 ¶①냉혹한 마음 3. 굳은 씨가 있는, 핵이 있는 ¶②핵과 4. 무표정한

ston·y-heart·ed [stóunihá:rtid] *adj.* showing no feeling; having no pity.
—[形] 냉혹한

‡ **stood** [stud] *v.* pt. and pp. of **stand.**

‡ **stool** [stu:l] *n.* [C] **1.** a seat without back or arms. ⇒fig. **2.** a rest for the feet or knees. ⇒fig. **3.** an article or a place used as a toilet. **4.** the waste matter from the bowels. **5.** a pole to which a bird is fastened as a trick. **6.** a root of a tree that sends out shoots.
—[名] 1. 의자, 걸상 2. 발판, 무릎 기대는 대 3. 변기; 변소 4. 변(便) 5. 새어리의 홰 6. [움이 돋는] 등걸, 뿌리

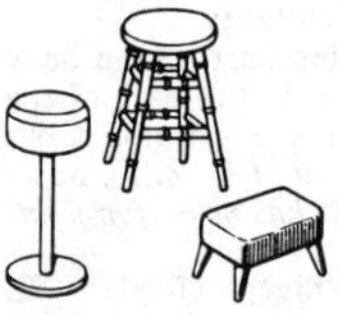
[stool 1., 2.]

fall between two stools, lose an opportunity by hesitating between two courses.
[熟] 양다리 걸치다가 모두 실패하다

‡ **stoop** [stu:p] *vi.* **1.** bend the upper part of the body down and forward. ¶*~ to pick up a stone.*① **2.** carry the head and shoulders habitually bent forward. **3.** lower or disgrace oneself. ¶*~ to meanness.*② —*vt.* bend (the head, the shoulders, etc.) forward.
—[自] 1. 꾸부리다 ¶①몸을 꾸부려 돌을 줍다 2. 곱사등이다 3. 몸을 굽혀(품위를 떨어뜨려) …하다 ¶②비열한 짓을 하다 —[他] [머리·어깨 등]을 꾸부리다

—*n.* [C] ⦅usu. *sing.*⦆ **1.** the act or position of stooping. **2.** the act of lowering oneself.
—[名] 1. 꾸부리기 2. 굴종; 품위를 떨어뜨리기

‡ **stop** [stɑp / stɔp] *v.* (**stopped, stop·ping**) *vt.* **1.** cause (something or someone) to cease to move or act. ¶*She stopped her car at the red light.* **2.** prevent; check. ⦅~ someone or something *from doing*⦆ ¶*~ a speaker*① | *~ a fight*② | *Nothing will ~ me from going.*③ | *She stopped the water from running by turning off the faucet.* | *The snow has stopped all traffic.* **3.** bring (doing something) to an end; cease. ⦅*~ doing*⦆ ¶*~ running* | *~ smoking* | *Stop that nonsense!*④ **4.** fill (a hole, a crack, etc.); close or obstruct (a passageway, etc.); block. ⦅~ [*up*] a hole, etc. *in* or *with.* ⇒***stop up***⦆ ¶*~ a wound*⑤ | *~ one's ears*⑥ | *~* [*up*] *a leak in a dike* | *~ a bottle with a cork* | *A big, fat man with packages stopped the passage.* | *Dead leaves stopped* [*up*] *the drain.* **5.** cut off; hold back (some regular payment). ¶*~ supplies*⑦ | *~ one's wages.*
—[他] 1. [움직이고 있는 것을] 멈추다, 세우다 2. …을 방해하다, 억제하다, 저지하다 ¶①연사의 말을 중지시키다/②싸움을 말리다/③내가 가는 길을 막을 자는 없으리라 3. …을 그만두다, 그치다, 하지 않게 되다, 정지하다 ¶④시시한 소리는 집어치워라 4. [구멍 따위]를 막다; [통행 장소]를 막다, 차단하다 ¶⑤상처의 피를 멎게 하다/⑥귀를 막다 5. …을 중단(중지)하다 ¶⑦공급을 중단하다

—*vi.* **1.** cease from moving or from doing something; come to rest; pause. ⦅*~ to do*⦆ ¶*~ to smoke*⑧ | *~ to*
—[自] 1. [움직이고 있는 것이] 멎다, 서다, 멈춰 서다 ¶⑧담배를 피우기 위해

rest | *The train stops at all stations.* **2.** come to an end; cease. ¶*The rain has stopped.* **3.** stay; visit. ⟪~ *at* a place, etc.⟫ ¶~ *at a hotel.*

서다 2. 그치다, 그만두다 3. 묵다, 체재하다

1) ***stop by,*** drop in.
2) ***stop off,*** make a brief stay at a place while on a journey.
3) ***stop over,*** (*U.S.*) stop for a short period at a certain place in the course of a longer trip.
4) ***stop up,*** block; close.

[熟] 1)들르다 2)도중하차하다 3)⟪美⟫도중하차하다; 잠깐 체재하다 4)…을 막다, 메우다

—*n.* [C] **1.** the act of stopping; the state of being stopped. ¶*without a ~*⑨ | *be at a ~*⑩ | *come to a ~*⑪ | *We must find some way of putting a ~ to that noise.*⑫ **2.** a place where a bus, a train, etc. stops. ¶*the bus ~.* **3.** a short visit; a stay. ¶*We made a three-day ~ in Osaka.* **4.** a thing that stops, such as a plug, a stopper, etc. **5.** (chiefly *Brit.*) any of the marks of punctuation which act to conclude a sentence or an independent part of a sentence, such as a semicolon (;), a question mark (?), etc. but esp. a period. ¶*a full ~.* **6.** a key or device that controls the pitch of a musical instrument, esp. an organ.

—[名] 1. 정지, 휴지(休止), 중지 ¶⑨쉬지 않고, 끊임없이/⑩정지해(쉬고) 있다/⑪서다, 끝나다/⑫그 소음을 없애는 방법을 찾아내야 한다 2. 정거장, 정류장 3. 체재, 숙박 4. 마개, 메움 5. ⟪英⟫ 구둣점; 종지부 6. [오르간 따위의] 음전(音栓)

stop·cock [stápkàk / stɔ́pkɔ̀k] ***n.*** [C] a valve that opens and closes a pipe carrying a liquid or gas; a faucet.

—[名] 마개

stop·gap [stápgæ̀p / stɔ́p-] ***n.*** [C] a thing for taking the place of something else, usu. temporarily. **—*adj.*** serving as a stopgap.

—[名] 구멍 메우개; 임시변통 —[形] 구멍을 메우는; 임시변통의

stop·o·ver [stápòuvər / stɔ́pòuvə] ***n.*** [C] (*U.S.*) **1.** a brief stop or stay in the course of a journey. **2.** a train ticket permitting such a trip.

—[名] ⟪美⟫ 1. [여행 중의] 일시 체류; 도중하차 2. 도중 하차표

stop·page [stápidʒ / stɔ́p-] ***n.*** [U][C] the act of stopping; the state of being stopped.

—[名] 정지, 두절; 멈추기, 멎기

stop·per [stápər / stɔ́pə] ***n.*** [C] a plug or cork to close a bottle, a pipe, etc. **—*vt.*** close (a bottle, pipe, etc.) with a stopper.

—[名] 마개 —[他] …에 마개를 하다

stop watch [⌐⌐] ***n.*** a watch that can be stopped or started to measure the exact duration of an event.

—[名] [경기용] 스톱워치

* **stor·age** [stɔ́:ridʒ] ***n.*** **1.** [U] the act of storing goods; the state of being stored. ¶*put the fish in cold ~.*① **2.** [C] a place for storing goods. **3.** [U] the price for storing goods.

—[名] 1. 저장 ¶①생선을 냉동 저장하다 2. 저장소 3. 보관료

‡ **store** [stɔ:r] ***n.*** [C] **1.** a supply for future use; a reserve. ¶*a ~ of food.* **2.** ⟪usu. *a ~*⟫ a large amount. ¶*have a ~* (or *stores*) *of knowledge*① | *have a ~ of energy.* **3.** ⟪*pl.*⟫ a supply of goods needed for some special purpose. ¶*ship's stores.*② **4.** (chiefly *U.S.*) a shop. **5.** ⟪*pl.* or *S-s*⟫ (*Brit.*) a large shop which sells all kinds of things. (cf. *U.S.* department store) **6.** (*Brit.*) a place where goods are kept.

—[名] 1. 저장, 저축; 준비 2. 다량 ¶①많은 지식을 갖고 있다 3. [선박 따위의] 비품, 필수품 ¶②선박 용품 4. ⟪美⟫ 가게, 상점 5. ⟪英⟫ 백화점 6. ⟪英⟫ 창고

1) ***in store,*** ⓐ kept for future use. ¶*There is sufficient food in ~ for next year.*③ ⓑ waiting.
2) ***set store by,*** value highly.

[熟] 1)ⓐ저장하여, 준비하여 ¶③내년에 쓸 식량이 충분히 준비돼 있다 ⓑ기다리기 2)…을 중시하다

—*vt.* **1.** keep (something) for future use; lay up. ⇒ ***store up.*** **2.** ⟪esp. in *passive*⟫ supply; fill (something) with supplies. ⟪~ something *with*⟫ ¶~ *the ship with fresh water*④ | *a mind stored with knowledge.* **3.** put (something) in a place used for preserving. ⟪~ something *in*⟫ ¶~ *goods in the cellar.*

—[他] 1. …을 저장하다, 축적하다 2. …에 공급하다, 준비하다 ¶④배에 신선한 물을 공급하다 3. …을 창고 따위에 보관하다

store up, keep (something) for future use. ¶~ *up fuel for the winter*⑤ | ~ *up knowledge.*

[熟] …을 저장하다 ¶⑤겨울의 연료를 저장하다

store·house [stɔ́:rhàus] ***n.*** [C] (pl. **-hous·es** [-hàuziz]) a place for keeping goods; anything similar to such a place. ¶*He is a ~ of information.*①

—[名] 창고; 보관소 ¶①그는 꽤 박식하다

store·keep·er [stɔ́:rkì:pər] ***n.*** [C] (*U.S.*) a person who is in charge of a store. (cf. *Brit.* shopkeeper)

—[名] ⟪美⟫ 소매 상인; 가게 주인

store·room [stɔ́:rù(:)m] ***n.*** [C] a room for keeping goods.

—[名] 저장실

* **sto·rey** [stɔ́:ri] *n.* [C] (*Brit.*) a story of a building.
—[名] 《英》 [건물의] 층

sto·ried[1] [stɔ́:rid] *adj.* **1.** famous in story or history. **2.** decorated with designs showing happenings in history or story.
—[形] 1. 이야기(역사)로 유명한 2. 역사적 그림(조각)으로 장식된

sto·ried[2] [stɔ́:rid] *adj.* having stories or floors. ¶*a two-storied house.*①
—[形] …층의 ¶① 2 층집

stork [stɔ:*r*k] *n.* [C] a large bird with long legs and a long bill.
—[名] 황새

⁑ **storm** [stɔ:*r*m] *n.* [C] **1.** a strong wind with heavy rain, snow, etc. ¶*A ~ is gathering.*① / *The ~ has broken out.*② **2.** anything like a storm; a violent outburst. ¶*a ~ of bullets*③ / *a ~ of cheers.*④ **3.** [U] a violent attack. ¶*the castle taken by ~.*
—[名] 1. 폭풍[우] ¶①폭풍이 다가오고 있다/②폭풍이 멎었다 2. …의 빗발; [격정의] 발작 ¶③빗발 같은 탄환/④갈채의 폭풍 3. 급습, 강습

a storm in a teacup, great excitement over something unimportant.
[熟] 사소한 파란, 헛소동

—*vi.* **1.** blow, rain, snow, etc. violently. **2.** shout loudly and angrily. 《~ *at* something》 **—*vt.*** attack (an enemy) violently.
—[自] 1. [날씨가] 험악해지다 2. 마구 야단치다 —[他] [적]을 강습하다

storm·beat·en [stɔ́:*r*mbì:tn] *adj.* damaged by a storm.
—[形] 폭풍우가 휩쓴

storm·bound [stɔ́:*r*mbàund] *adj.* separated from others, stopped or delayed by storms.
—[形] 폭풍우 때문에 고립(정지·지연)된

storm center [⌐ ⌐–] *n.* **1.** the center of a storm. **2.** the center of trouble.
—[名] 1. 폭풍우의 중심 2. 소동의 중심

storm cloud [⌐ ⌐] *n.* **1.** a heavy cloud showing the coming of a storm. **2.** a sign of some coming trouble.
—[名] 1. 비구름 2. 동란의 징조

* **storm·y** [stɔ́:*r*mi] *adj.* (**storm·i·er, storm·i·est**) **1.** of a storm; likely to have storms. ¶*~ weather.* **2.** showing violent emotion. ¶*a ~ life.*①
—[形] 1. 폭풍우의; 폭풍우가 일 듯한 2. 격정적인 ¶①파란만장의 일생

⁑ **sto·ry**[1] [stɔ́:ri] *n.* [C] (pl. **-ries**) **1.** anything told or written of an event; a report. ¶*a newspaper ~ of a traffic accident* / *Tell me the ~ of how he got such a large sum of money.*① **2.** a tale of fiction. ¶*the ~ of Cinderella.* **3.** anything acted or said by someone during his life; an anecdote. ¶*a woman with a ~.*② **4.** an outline of a novel or play. **5.** (*colloq.*) a lie.
—[名] 1. [사실의] 이야기, 전말; 보고, 보도 ¶①그가 어떻게 그런 큰 돈을 얻었는지 이야기해 주시오 2. 가공의 이야기 3. 이력; 일화 ¶②과거가 있는 여자 4. 줄거리 5. 《口》 거짓말

to make a long story short, in short.
[熟] 요약해서 말하자면

* **sto·ry**[2], *Brit.* **-rey** [stɔ́:ri] *n.* [C] (pl. **-ries** or *Brit.* **-reys**) any level of a building; a floor. ¶*a one-story house* / *the first-story.*①
—[名] 층 ¶①《美》1 층; 《英》 2 층

sto·ry·tell·er [stɔ́:ritèlə*r*] *n.* [C] **1.** a person who tells or writes stories. **2.** (*colloq.*) a person who tells a lie.
—[名] 1. 이야기하는 사람; 야담가, 소설가 2. 《口》 거짓말장이

⁑ **stout** [staut] *adj.* **1.** strong; tough. **2.** brave; stubborn. **3.** bulky; fat. **—*n.*** [U] a dark, strong beer.
—[形] 1. 튼튼한 2. 용감한; 완강한 3. 뚱뚱한 —[名] 흑맥주

stout-heart·ed [stáuthá:*r*tid] *adj.* brave; fearless.
—[形] 용감한

stout·ly [stáutli] *adv.* bravely; firmly.
—[副] 용감하게; 완강하게

stout·ness [stáutnis] *n.* [U] the state or quality of being stout.
—[名] 튼튼함; 용감; 뚱뚱함

⁑ **stove**[1] [stouv] *n.* [C] a device for heating and cooking, which uses coal, wood, gas, etc.
—[名] 스토우브, 난로, 요리용 솥

stove[2] [stouv] *v.* pt. and pp. of **stave**.

stow [stou] *vt.* pack (something) carefully or closely. 《~ a place *with*》
—[他] …을 챙겨넣다, 잔뜩 채워넣다

stow away, hide on a ship or train, etc. without paying or secretly.
[熟] 밀항하다

stow·a·way [stóuəwèi] *n.* [C] a person who hides on a ship, a train, etc. secretly.
—[名] 밀항자

strad·dle [strǽdl] *vi.* **1.** stand, sit, or walk with the legs wide apart. **2.** (*colloq.*) support both sides of a question; not stand on a certain side decisively. **—*vt.*** stand or sit with the legs wide apart on or across (something). **—*n.*** [C] the act of straddling.
—[自] 1. 가랑이를 벌리고 서다(앉다, 걷다) 2. 애매한 태도를 취하다 —[他] …에 걸터앉다 —[名] 두 다리로 버티기; 걸터앉기

strag·gle [strǽgl] *vi.* **1.** wander away from the main group. **2.** (of hair, etc.) hang down in an irregular manner. **3.** occur here and there.
—[自] 1. [대열에서] 이탈하여 헤매다, 낙오하다 2. 얽히다 3. 산재(散在)하다

strag·gler [strǽglə*r*] *n.* [C] a person or thing that straggles.
—[名] 낙오자, 패잔병, 부랑자

strag·gling [strǽgliŋ] *adj.* **1.** wandered away from the main group. **2.** hanging down irregularly. **3.** occurring
—[形] 1. 낙오한; [가지 따위] 뻗어나간 2. 헝클어진 3. 뿔뿔이 흩어진; 산재한

or existing here and there.

⁑ **straight** [streit] *adj.* **1.** not bent or curved; not twisted; direct. ¶*a ~ line*① / *a ~ back*② / *~ hair.* **2.** level; upright; vertical. ¶*put a picture ~.*③ **3.** honest, sincere; frank. ¶*a ~ answer* / *~ talk.*④ **4.** in good order or condition; right or correct. ¶*keep a room ~* / *His accounts are ~.* **5.** reliable. ¶*a ~ piece of information.* **6.** not mixed with anyting else; not changed. ¶*~ whisky.* **7.** continuous. ¶*win five ~ victories.*⑤
—*adv.* **1.** in a straight line; directly. ¶*shoot ~* / *walk ~.* **2.** upright. ¶*stand ~.* **3.** in the shortest way. ¶*go ~ home.* **4.** at once; without loss of time. **5.** frankly; honestly. ¶*I told it ~.* **6.** continuously.

—[形] **1.** 똑바른, 일직선의 ¶①직선/②똑바른 등 **2.** 수평의; 곧추 선, 수직의 ¶③그림을 똑바로 걸다 **3.** 정직한, 진지한; 솔직한 ¶④직언(直言) **4.** 정돈된; 올바른 **5.** 신뢰할 수 있는 **6.** 불순물을 섞지 않은; 순수한 **7.** 연속된 ¶⑤연승하다 —[副] **1.** 똑바로, 일직선으로 **2.** 곧추 서서 **3.** 직접, 빗나가지 않고 **4.** 곧, 당장 **5.** 정직하게; 솔직히 **6.** 연속하여

1) ***come straight to the point,*** explain clearly and directly.
2) ***straight away*** (or ***off***)***,*** at once.

[熟] 1)바로 요점을 이야기하다 2)곧, 당장

—*n.* ⟪*the ~*⟫ a straight line; a straight part of a race track just before the goal. ¶*on the ~*⑥ / *be out of the ~.*⑦

—[名] 직선; 직선 코오스 ¶⑥똑바로/⑦꾸부러져 있다

straight·a·way [stréitəwèi] *n.* [C] a straight course. —*adj.* in a straight course.

—[名] 직선 코오스 —[形] 일직선의

* **straight·en** [stréitn] *vt., vi.* **1.** make (something) straight; become straight. ¶*~ a path.*① **2.** put (something) in order.

—[他][自] **1.** 똑바로 하다(되다) ¶①길을 똑바로 하다 **2.** …을 정돈하다

straighten out, ⓐ make (something) straight. ⓑ make (something) clear; put (something) in order.

[熟] ⓐ…을 똑바로 하다 ⓑ…을 청산하다; 정돈하다

straight·for·ward [strèitfɔ́:rwərd] *adj.* **1.** going in a direct course or manner. **2.** honest; simple.

—[形] **1.** 똑바른 **2.** 정직한

* **straight·way** [stréitwèi] *adv.* at once; without delay.

—[副] 당장, 즉각

⁑ **strain**[1] [strein] *vt.* **1.** pull or stretch (something) as much as possible. ¶*~ a rope.* **2.** put (one's powers, etc.) to the fullest possible use. ¶*~ one's ears*① / *~ one's nerves* / *~ oneself.*② **3.** hurt or weaken (a muscle or another part of the body) by using it too much or wrongly. ¶*~ the ankle* / *I strained my eyes* [*by reading*]. **4.** stretch (the meaning, etc.) beyond the proper limit. ¶*~ the laws.* **5.** make excessive demands on (someone's patience, friendship, etc.). ¶*~ someone's generosity.* **6.** make (liquid) pure or get (solids) from liquid matter by using a cloth or wire net. ¶*~ coffee* / *~ seeds from lemon juice.* **7.** hold tightly. ¶*~ a child to one's breast.* —*vi.* **1.** pull hard. ⟪*~ at* something⟫ ¶*~ at a rope.* **2.** make a great physical or mental effort. **3.** make liquid pure by using a cloth or net.

—[他] **1.** …을 [팽팽하게] 당기다, 죄다 **2.** …을 긴장시키다, 힘껏 일하게 하다 ¶①귀를 기울이다/②힘껏 노력하다 **3.** …을 너무 써서 약화(손상)시키다; 삐다 **4.** [의미 따위]를 곡해하다, 억지로 갖다붙이다 **5.** …을 이용하다, 강요하다 **6.** …을 거르다, 걸러서 …을 없애다 **7.** …을 꽉 껴안다 —[自] **1.** 잡아당기다 **2.** 긴장하다, 몹시 애쓰다 **3.** 거르다

—*n.* **1.** [U][C] the act of straining; the state of being strained. ¶*The rope will bear the ~.* **2.** [U][C] violent effort; tiredness caused by such effort. ¶*He became ill under the ~ of overwork.* **3.** [C] an injury or a damage caused by straining. ¶*a ~ in the arm.*③

—[名] **1.** 잡아당기기 **2.** 심한 노력; 과로 **3.** [근육 따위의] 삠, 염좌(捻挫) ¶③팔을 삐기

strain[2] [strein] *n.* **1.** [C][U] family line; race; breed. ¶*come of* [*a*] *noble ~.* **2.** [C][U] a marked quality that runs through personality, a family or a race. ¶*He has a ~ of cruelty in his character.* **3.** [C] ⟪often *pl.*⟫ a part of a piece of music; a melody; a song. **4.** [C] the manner or style of writing or speaking. ¶*a ~ of humor.*

—[名] **1.** 가계(家系); 종족 **2.** 기질; 유전적 성질 **3.** 가곡, 선율, 가락 **4.** 문체, 말투

strained [streind] *adj.* **1.** (of a rope, etc.) drawn tightly; being in a high state of tension. **2.** not natural.

—[形] **1.** 팽팽한; 긴장한 **2.** 부자연스러운

strain·er [stréinər] *n.* [C] **1.** a person or thing that strains. **2.** (in making coffee, tea, etc.) a kitchen instrument with a net for separating the liquid. ⇒fig.

—[名] **1.** 잡아당기는 사람(것) **2.** 여과기(濾過器), 거르는 그물

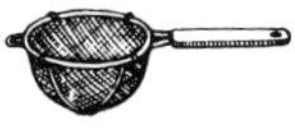

[strainer 2.]

* **strait** [streit] *n.* [C] **1.** a narrow channel joining two large bodies of water. ⇒[usage] **2.**

—[名] **1.** 해협 [usage] 지명에 붙이는 경우는 보통 복수로 씀 **2.** 곤란; 궁핍

《often *pl.*》 difficulties; need. —*adj.* (*archaic*) narrow. —[形] 좁은

strait·en [stréitn] *vt.* 《chiefly used as *pp.*》 put (someone) into financial difficulties. ¶*be in straitened circumstances.*① —[他] …을 곤궁하게 하다 ¶①쪼들리고 있다

strand¹ [strænd] *n.* [C] (*poetic*) a shore. —*vi., vt.* **1.** drive or run ashore. **2.** bring or be left in a difficult state because of lack of money, etc. —[名] 기슭, 해안 —[自][他] 1. [···을] 좌초하다(시키다) 2. [···이] 궁지에 빠지다(빠지게 하다)

strand² [strænd] *n.* [C] one of the threads, wires, etc. forming a rope. —[名] [밧줄의] 외가닥, 끈 실

⁑ **strange** [streindʒ] *adj.* **1.** not familiar; not known, seen, or heard of before. ¶*a ~ face* | *The place was ~ to me.* **2.** odd; unusual; queer. ¶*a ~ occurrence* | *~ clothes* | *It is ~ that you should think so.* **3.** not at home; out of place; not accustomed. ¶*He is still ~ to his job.*① | *The poor girl felt ~ in my house.* | *I'm quite ~ here.*② —[形] 1. 알지 못 하는; 보지(듣지) 못한 2. 이상한; 별난 3. 생소한; 미숙한 ¶①그는 아직 그의 일에 생소하다/②나는 이곳은 전혀 처음입니다

* **strange·ly** [stréindʒli] *adv.* in a strange manner. —[副] 이상하게도, 별나게

strange·ness [stréindʒnis] *n.* [U] the state or quality of being strange; unfamiliarity. —[名] 기묘; 이상함; 미지(未知)

⁑ **stran·ger** [stréindʒər] *n.* [C] **1.** a person whom one does not know; a person from another place or another country. ¶*He is a ~ to us.* **2.** a person or thing new to a place; a person not used to something. 《~ *to*》 —[名] 1. 낯선 사람; 외국인 2. 문외한; 미숙한 사람

stran·gle [strǽŋgl] *vt.* **1.** kill (a living thing) by pressing the throat. **2.** cause (someone or something) difficulty in breathing; suppress; keep under control. ▷**stran·gler** [-ər] *n.* —[他] 1. ···을 목졸라 죽이다 2. ···을 억압하다, 묵살하다

stran·gu·late [strǽŋgjulèit] *vt.* **1.** kill (someone or something) by pressing the throat. **2.** press (a tube of a body) to stop the circulation of air, liquid, etc. —[他] 1. ···을 목졸라 죽이다 2. [체액의 유동을] 괄약(括約)하다

stran·gu·la·tion [stræ̀ŋgjuléiʃ(ə)n] *n.* [U] the act of strangulating; the state of being strangulated. —[名] 교살(絞殺)

* **strap** [stræp] *n.* [C] **1.** a narrow strip of leather, etc. to hold things together; a strip of leather, etc. for a standing person to hold for support. ¶*hang on to a ~.*① **2.** a strip of leather for sharpening razors. —*vt.* (**strapped, strap·ping**) **1.** fasten (something) with a strap. **2.** beat (someone) with a strap. **3.** sharpen (a razor) on a strap. —[名] 1. 가죽끈, 끈, [전차 따위의] 손잡이 ¶①손잡이에 매달리다 2. 혁지(革砥) —[他] 1. ···을 가죽끈으로 묶다 2. ···을 가죽끈으로 때리다 3. ···을 혁지로 갈다

strap·ping [strǽpiŋ] *adj.* (*colloq.*) tall and strong. —[形] 《口》 기골이 장대한

stra·ta [stréitə, +*U.S.* -rǽt-, +*Brit.* -rɑ́:t-] *n.* pl. of **stratum**.

strat·a·gem [strǽtidʒəm] *n.* [U][C] **1.** a trick or scheme to deceive an enemy in war. **2.** any trick. —[名] 1. 전략 2. 계략, 술책

stra·te·gic [strətí:dʒik], **-gi·cal** [-dʒik(ə)l] *adj.* **1.** of or based on strategy. **2.** important in strategy. —[形] 1. 전략[상]의, 계략의 2. 전략상 중요한

stra·te·gi·cal·ly [strətí:dʒik(ə)li] *adv.* in a strategic manner. —[副] 전략상

strat·e·gist [strǽtidʒist] *n.* [C] a person who is skilled in strategy. —[名] 전략가

strat·e·gy [strǽtidʒi] *n.* [U] **1.** the art or science of military movement in war. **2.** skill in managing or planning. —[名] 1. 용병학(用兵學) 2. 전략, 전술, 병법

stra·ti [stréitai] *n.* pl. of **stratus**.

strat·i·fy [strǽtifài] *vt., vi.* (**-fied**) form into layers. ¶*stratified rock.*① —[他][自] 층을 이루다 ¶①성층암(成層岩)

strat·o·sphere [strǽtousfìər] *n.* [C] the highest part of the atmosphere above the earth. —[名] 성층권

stra·tum [stréitəm, +*U.S.* -rǽt-, +*Brit.* -rɑ́:t-] *n.* [C] (pl. **-ta** or **-tums**) **1.** a layer of rock or earth. **2.** a rank in society. —[名] 1. 지층 2. 계급

stra·tus [stréitəs] *n.* [C] (pl. **stra·ti**) a low layer of gray clouds spreading widely. —[名] 층운(層雲)

⁑ **straw** [strɔ:] *n.* [U][C] the stalk of grain; cut and dried stalks of grain used for making hats, etc. —[名] 짚, 밀짚

a man of straw, a person who looks important, but actually has little power and acts in obedience to others. [熟] 간판으로 내세운 사람, 실권 없는 허수아비

*** straw·ber·ry** [strɔ́ːbèri / -b(ə)ri] *n.* [C] (pl. **-ries**) a small red fruit of a low-growing plant; this plant; a red color of or like that of this fruit.
—[名] 양딸기; 딸기빛

straw·board [strɔ́ːbɔ̀ːrd] *n.* [U] a thick, stiff paper made from straw and used for boxes, etc.
—[名] [밀짚] 마분지

straw color [ˊ ˊ-] *n.* the color of straw; pale yellow.
—[名] 밀짚 빛깔, 담황색

‡ straw·hat [strɔ́ːhæ̀t] *n.* [C] a hat made of straws.
—[名] 맥고모자

straw·y [strɔ́ːi] *adj.* (**straw·i·er, straw·i·est**) of or like straw; made of straw.
—[形] 밀짚의(같은); 밀짚으로 만든

*** stray** [strei] *vi.* **1.** lose one's way; wander. ¶*His dog has strayed off somewhere.*① **2.** turn aside from strict morality. **3.** depart temporarily from the main subject in talking or thinking about something.
—[自] 1. 길을 잃다 ¶①그 개는 길을 잃고 어디론가 가 버렸다 2. 정도(正道)에서 벗어나다, 죄를 범하다 3. [이야기·생각 따위가] 빗나가다
—*n.* [C] a person or domestic animal that has strayed.
—[名] 길 잃은 사람(가축); 미아(迷兒)
—*adj.* **1.** wandering; lost. ¶*a ~ dog.* **2.** happening occasionally; not frequently; isolated; occasional.
—[形] 1. 길을 잃은, 헤매는 2. 이따금의; 간혹 나타나는

*** streak** [striːk] *n.* [C] **1.** a long, narrow mark; a stripe. ¶*a ~ of lightning.*① **2.** a layer of something. ¶*streaks of fat in meat.*② **3.** a tendency in behavior, etc.; a trace. ¶*He does not have a ~ of humor.*③ —*vt.* mark (something) with streaks. —*vi.* **1.** become streaked. **2.** (*colloq.*) move at a high speed; go fast.
—[名] 1. 줄무늬, 줄, 선 ¶①한 줄기의 번개 2. 층 ¶②고기의 비계층 3. 경향, 기미, …한 점 ¶③그는 전혀 유우머를 모른다 —[他] …에 줄[무늬]을 넣다 —[自] 1. 줄[무늬]로 되다 2. 전속력으로 가다

streak·y [stríːki] *adj.* (**streak·i·er, streak·i·est**) marked with streaks; occurring in or as streaks.
—[形] 줄[무늬]이 있는, 줄[무늬]로 된

‡ stream [striːm] *n.* [C] **1.** a flow or current of water; running water; a brook. ¶*up (down) the ~*① */ with (against) the ~.*② **2.** a flow of liquid, gas, etc. ¶*a ~ of tears (air, light).* **3.** a continuous flow; a succession. ¶*a ~ of cars (persons, words) / in a ~; in streams.*③ **4.** a general direction; a tendency; a current [of the times].
—[名] 1. 흐름; 흐름의 방향; 시내, 개울 ¶①상(하)류에/②흐름을 따라(에 거슬러서) 2. [액체·유동체의] 흐름, 유출 3. 끊임없는 흐름 ¶③계속 4. 경향; 풍조; 형세
—*vi.* **1.** flow like a stream. ¶*Tears ~ down her cheeks. / Headlights streamed across the pavement.* **2.** move continuously like a stream. ¶*People streamed out of the concert hall.* **3.** (of a flag, etc.) move up and down; (of hair) wave. —*vt.* **1.** cause (liquid, gas, etc.) to flow. ¶*The wound streamed blood.* **2.** cause (a flag, hair, etc.) to wave.
—[自] 1. 흐르다, 흘러나오다 2. 쉴새없이 계속되다 3. [깃발 따위]가 나부끼다; [머리카락이] 치렁치렁 처지다 —[他] 1. …을 흘리다, 흘러나오게 하다 2. …을 나부끼게 하다

stream·er [stríːmər] *n.* [C] **1.** a long, narrow flag. **2.** any long, narrow, flowing strip. **3.** (*U. S.*) a newspaper headline that extends across the full page.
—[名] 1. 기드림, 장기(長旗) 2. 가느다란 리본(천) 3. 《美》 [신문의] 톱 전단(全段)에 걸친 표제

stream·line [stríːmlàin] *n.* [C] **1.** a course of water, air, etc. that finds the least resistance in flowing. **2.** a shape offering the least resistance to a current of air, etc.
—[名] 1. 유선(流線) 2. 유선형
—*adj.* having a shape or an outline designed to offer the least resistance to air or water. ¶*a ~ form (car).*①
—[形] 유선형의 ¶①유선형(유선형 자동차)
—*vt.* **1.** make (something) into a streamline form. **2.** change (a process of work, etc.) to make it more efficient.
—[他] 1. …을 유선형으로 하다 2. [일 따위] 합리화(능률화)하다

stream·lined [stríːmlàind] *adj.* **1.** having a streamline form. **2.** arranged or designed to gain the greatest efficiency. ¶*a ~ office.* **3.** up-to-date; modernized.
—[形] 1. 유선형의 2. [근대적으로] 능률화한 3. 최신식의

‡ street [striːt] *n.* [C] a public road in a city, a town, or a village, usu. with buildings on one or on both sides. ¶*a main (side) ~*① */ The hospital is located on Lincoln Street.*② */ I met her on the ~.*③
—[名] 거리, 가도, 한길 ¶①대로(옆골목)/②병원은 링컨가(街)에 있다/③거리에서 그녀를 만났다
not in the same street with, not able to be compared with; being no match for.
[熟] …와 비교가 안 되는

street Arab [ˊ ˊ-] *n.* a homeless or neglected child who roams in the streets.
—[名] 집 없는 아이, 부랑아

‡ street·car [stríːtkàːr] *n.* [C] (*U. S.*) a public vehicle that runs regularly along rails in a street. (cf. *Brit.* tramcar)
—[名] 《美》 전차

street·light [strí:tlàit] *n.* [C] a light for illuminating a street, usu. supported by a post.
—[名] 가로등

street railway [ˊ ˊ–] *n.* a company operating street-cars or buses.
—[名] 시가 전차·버스 회사

⁑ **strength** [streŋ(k)θ] *n.* [U] **1.** the quality or state of being physically strong; power; force. ¶*a man of* ~.① **2.** mental, intellectual or moral power. **3.** strong point. ↔weak point ¶*French is her* ~.② **4.** power to resist or endure; toughness. ¶*the* ~ *of a rope.* **5.** force as measured by the number of soldiers, warships, etc. ¶*military* ~③ | *in full* ~.④ **6.** degree of concentration or intensity. ¶*the* ~ *of poison gas.*
on the strength of, relying on; influenced or encouraged by.
—[名] 1. 힘, 체력 ¶①힘이 센 사람 2. [지성·성격 따위의] 강함 3. 강점, 장점 ¶②프랑스어를 할 수 있는 것이 그녀의 강점이다 4. [물건의] 내구력; 튼튼함 5. 병력, 군대, 다수 ¶③병력/④전원이 모여서 6. 강도(强度); 농도
[熟] …을 믿고, …에 영향(격려)되어

* **strength·en** [stréŋ(k)θ(ə)n] *vt.* make (someone or something) strong or stronger. —*vi.* become or grow stronger.
—[他] …을 강하게 하다, 강화하다
—[自] 강해지다

stren·u·ous [strénjuəs] *adj.* **1.** requiring great effort or energy. **2.** very eager; zealous.
—[形] 1. 분투적인; 노력이 필요한 2. 열심인, 열렬한

stren·u·ous·ly [strénjuəsli] *adv.* in a strenuous manner.
—[副] 분발하여; 열심히

strep·to·my·cin [strèptoumáisin] *n.* [U] a drug obtained from a certain soil and used against various diseases, esp. tuberculosis.
—[名] 스트렙토마이신

* **stress** [stres] *n.* **1.** [U] tension; pressure; strain. **2.** [U] pressing condition; urgency. **3.** [U] [C] accent given to a speech sound or to a music note. **4.** [U] [C] emphasis; importance. —*vt.* **1.** put stress, pressure, tension, etc. on (something). **2.** give stress or accent to (something). **3.** emphasize.
—[名] 1. 강제, 압박 2. 긴장, 긴급 3. 강세(强勢), 악센트 4. 강조, 중점 —[他] 1. …을 강제하다; …에 압력을 가하다 2. …을 강하게 발음하다 3. …을 강조하다

⁑ **stretch** [stretʃ] *vt.* **1.** draw (something) out to a greater length or width; draw (something) tight; expand. ¶~ *a rope tight* | ~ *trousers*① | ~ *a rubber band* | ~ *the violin string.* **2.** extend (oneself, the body, limbs, wings, etc.) to the full length; straighten out. ¶~ *one's arms.* **3.** extend (the law, the truth, etc.) beyond its proper limits; exaggerate. ¶~ *a rule* | ~ *facts.* **4.** strain (a muscle, etc.) to the utmost. —*vi.* **1.** extend one's limbs fully. ¶~ *out on the sofa.* **2.** (of rubber, etc.) become longer or wider under use, pressure, etc. ¶*Rubber stretches.* **3.** extend; spread; last. ¶*The road stretches away.*② | *The war stretched over three years.*
—[他] 1. …을 잡아당기다, 팽팽하게 하다; …을 펴다, 깔다 ¶①즈봉의 주름을 펴다 2. [신체·손발·날개 따위]를 한껏 펴다, 뻗다 3. [법률·진리 따위]를 확대 해석하다, 곡해하다 4. [근육 따위]를 극도로 긴장시키다 —[自] 1. 신체를 펴다 2. [고무 따위가] 늘어나다 3. 퍼지다; 뻗다; 계속하다 ¶②[도로가] 멀리까지 뻗어 있다

—*n.* [C] **1.** the act of stretching; the state of being stretched. **2.** a continuous line, surface, or period. ¶*a* ~ *of flat land* | *He works ten hours at a* ~.③ **3.** tension; exaggeration; abuse. ¶*a* ~ *of* [*the*] *imagination.* **4.** the straight section of the race course, esp. before the goal. **5.** a short walk.
—[名] 1. 뻗기, 펴기 2. 범위, 퍼짐; 계속되는 시간 ¶③그는 계속해서 10 시간 일을 한다 3. 긴장; 과장; 남용 4. [경기장의] 직선 코오스 5. 산책

stretch·er [strétʃər] *n.* [C] **1.** a person or thing that stretches. **2.** a frame with canvas for carrying the sick, wounded or dead; a litter.
—[名] 1. 뻗는(펴는, 펼치는) 사람(것), 신장구(伸張具) 2. 들것

strew [stru:] *vt.* (**strewed, strewed** or **strewn**) **1.** scatter; sprinkle. **2.** cover the surface of (something) with anything scattered or sprinkled. ¶~ *the road with sand.*
—[他] 1. …을 흩뿌리다 2. …에 흩뿌리다; 뿌리다

strewn [stru:n] *v.* pp. of **strew.**

⁑ **strick·en** [strík(ə)n] *v.* (*archaic*) pp. of **strike.**
—*adj.* **1.** struck; wounded. **2.** hit or attacked by diseases, sorrow, etc.
—[形] 1. 맞은, 다친 2. 병에 걸린, 상처를 입은, 괴로와하는

* **strict** [strikt] *adj.* **1.** not allowing to turn away from standards or rules; severe; stern. ¶~ *orders* | *a* ~ *observer of rules* | *He is very* ~ *with his pupils.*① **2.** accurate; precise. ¶*in the* ~ *sense.*② **3.** perfect; absolute. ¶*in* ~ *privacy.* ▷**strict·ness** [-nis] *n.*
—[形] 1. 엄한, 엄격한; 엄중한 ¶①그는 학생들에게 무척 엄하다 2. 정밀한, 정확한 ¶②엄밀히 말하면 3. 완전한, 순수한; 절대의

* **strict·ly** [stríktli] *adv.* in a strict manner; precisely.
—[副] 엄격히, 정확히

stric·ture [stríktʃər] *n.* [C] (usu. *pl.*) a harsh or severe criticism. ¶~ *on* (or *upon*) *somebody.*
—[名] 비난, 혹평

*** strid·den** [strídn] *v.* pp. of **stride.**

*** stride** [straid] *v.* (**strode, strid·den**) *vi.* **1.** walk with long steps. **2.** pass over in one long step. 《~ *across* or *over* something》 ¶~ *across* (or *over*) *a brook.* **—***vt.* **1.** pass over (a ditch, etc.) in one step. **2.** sit or stand across (a fence, etc.) with the legs widely separated.

—[自] 1. 성큼성큼 걷다 2. 타고 넘다 —[他] 1. …을 타고 넘다 2. …에 걸터앉다(서다)

—*n.* [C] **1.** a long step. **2.** the length of one long step.

1) ***at a stride,*** with one long step.
2) (*U.S.*) ***hit one's stride;*** (*Brit.*) ***get into one's stride,*** reach one's normal speed or rate of activity.
3) ***make great*** (or ***rapid***) ***strides,*** make great progress. 《~ *in* something》
4) ***take something in one's stride,*** do something easily; not be affected by bad news, etc.

—[名] 1. 큰 걸음 2. 한 걸음의 폭
[熟] 1)한 걸음에 2)본궤도에 오르다 3)[…에] 장족의 진보를 하다 4)[사물]을 쉽게 해치우다, …에 조금도 동요하지 않다

stri·dent [stráid(ə)nt] *adj.* (of a sound) loud and rough; creaking. **▷stri·dent·ly** [-li] *adv.*

—[形] 삐걱거리는; 귀에 거슬리는

*** strife** [straif] *n.* [U][C] a conflict; a fight; a struggle. ¶*domestic* ~.①

—[名] 싸움, 다툼; 불화 ¶①가정 불화

‡ strike [straik] *v.* (**struck, struck** or *archaic* **strick·en**) *vt.* **1.** give a blow to (someone or something); deliver (a blow); hit. ¶~ *someone in the face* | *He struck me on the head.* | *Lightning struck the barn.*① **2.** thrust; pierce. 《~ a knife, etc. *into*》 ¶~*a knife into someone's heart.* **3.** bring (one thing) into contact with another; come into contact with (something) suddenly. ¶*A car struck the wall.* | *He struck his foot against a stone.*② | *We struck our heads together.* **4.** find; discover luckily. ¶~ *gold* | ~ *a short cut.*③ **5.** (of an idea or a thought) occur suddenly. ¶*A bright idea struck him.* **6.** affect the feelings of (someone); impress; influence. ¶*He was struck with her beauty.*④ | *How does the news ~ you?*⑤ **7.** put (terror, etc.) into someone's heart, etc.; put (someone) into a certain condition suddenly. ¶~ *terror into someone's heart* | ~ *someone blind.*⑥ **8.** (of illness, disaster, etc.) attack suddenly and violently. ¶*The plague struck the small town.* **9.** set (a match) on fire by rubbing it. ¶*He struck a match.* **10.** make (a coin, a medal, etc.) by stamping. ¶~ *a coin.* **11.** (of a clock) sound (the time). ¶*The clock struck ten.* **12.** lower; take down (a sail, a flag, a tent, etc.). **13.** remove; cancel. ¶*I'll ~ these items off the list.* **14.** assume (an attitude or a pose). ¶*She struck a pose.* **15.** touch (keys, etc.) so as to produce a musical sound. ¶~ *a chord.*⑦ **16.** calculate. ¶*He struck a balance.* **17.** agree on or conclude (a bargain, etc.). ¶*We have struck an agreement.*⑧ **—***vi.* **1.** give a blow; aim a blow. ¶*I struck at the ball, but missed.* **2.** be in contact with something; hit. ¶*The ship struck against a rock.* **3.** attack. ¶*The enemy struck at daybreak.* **4.** (of a match) be set on fire by rubbing. ¶*These matches won't ~.*⑨ **5.** (of a clock) sound the time. ¶*The clock is striking.* **6.** cease from work until certain demands are met. ¶*The workers struck.* **7.** direct one's course; proceed; advance. ¶*He struck northward.* | ~ *through the wood.*⑩ **8.** thrust through. ¶*The light struck through the cloud.*⑪ **9.** take down a flag, esp. as a sign of giving up the fight.

—[他] 1. …에 타격을 주다; [타격]을 가하다; …을 치다 ¶①헛간에 벼락이 떨어졌다 2. [나이프 따위]를 찌르다 3. …을 부딪치다; …에 충돌하다 ¶②그는 발을 돌에 부딪쳤다 4. …에 마주치다; …을 우연히 발견하다 ¶③우연히 지름길을 찾다 5. [생각 따위가] …의 마음에 떠오르다 6. [남]의 마음을 치다, [남]에게 감명을 주다 ¶④그녀의 아름다움에 끌렸다/⑤그 뉴우스를 어떻게 생각하느냐? 7. [공포 따위]를 마음에 주다; [남]을 갑자기 …으로 하다 ¶⑥남을 갑자기 장님으로 만들다 8. [병 따위가] 갑자기 …을 엄습하다 9. [성냥]을 켜다 10. [화폐 따위]를 주조하다 11. [시계가 시간]을 치다 12. [돛·깃발 따위]를 내리다; [천막]을 접다, 걷다 13. …을 제거하다, 취소하다 14. [태도]를 취하다 15. …을 울리다 ¶⑦화음을 연주하다 16. …을 결산하다 17. [계약 따위]를 확정짓다 ¶⑧계약을 확정짓다 —[自] 1. 치다, 때리다 2. 부딪치다, 충돌하다 3. 공격하다 4. [성냥이] 켜지다 ¶⑨이 성냥은 잘 켜지지 않는다 5. [시계 따위가 시간을] 치다 6. 파업을 하다 7. 나아가다, 향하다 ¶⑩숲속을 나아가다 8. 꿰뚫다, 스며들다 ¶⑪빛이 구름 사이를 뚫고 지나갔다 9. 깃발을 내리고 항복하다

1) ***strike aside,*** turn aside (a weapon, a blow, etc.).
2) ***strike down,*** knock down; kill.
3) ***strike home,*** give an effective blow.
4) ***strike in,*** interrupt.
5) ***strike into,*** start suddenly.
6) ***strike it rich,*** (*U.S.*) ⓐ discover rich oil by boring. ⓑ become rich suddenly.
7) ***strike off,*** ⓐ cut off (the head, etc.). ¶~ *off some-*

[熟] 1)[창 끝]을 받아넘기다, 피하다 2)…을 때려 눕히다; 죽이다 3)급소를 찌르다 4)…에 말참견하다 5)갑자기 …하기 시작하다 6)[美] ⓐ석유를 발견하다 ⓑ뜻밖의 큰 성공을 거두다 7)ⓐ[목 따위]를 쳐서 떨어뜨리다 ⓑ…을 삭제하다 ⓒ…을 인쇄하다 ⓓ옆으로 빗나가다 8)ⓐ…을 발명하다, 꾸며

S

strike-out [1140] **stringently**

one's head. ⓑ remove (an item, a name, etc.) from a record. ¶*I struck his name off the register.* ⓒ print (copies). ⓓ go in another way.
8) ***strike out,*** ⓐ invent or contrive (a plan, a theory, etc.). ⓑ remove (something) from a record. ⓒ start in the direction of a certain place. ⓓ (in baseball) be put out or put (a batter) out by pitching three strikes.
9) ***strike up,*** ⓐ begin playing, singing, etc. ¶*The brass band struck up.* ⓑ begin (a friendship, etc.).
—*n.* ⓒ **1.** a blow. **2.** a new or unexpected discovery of rich oil, gold, etc.; great success. **3.** ⓒⓊ a general refusal of workmen to work. ¶*go on ~ / The workers are on ~.* **4.** (*Baseball*) a nice pitched ball which a batter misses or hits foul. **5.** (*Bowling*) the act of knocking down all the pins with one ball.

⁑ **strike-out** [stráikàut] *n.* ⓒ (*Baseball*) an out made by a batter to whom three strikes have been pitched.

strik·er [stráikər] *n.* ⓒ **1.** a person or thing that strikes. **2.** a worker on strike. **3.** (*U.S. Army*) a soldier acting as an officer's servant.

⁑ **strik·ing** [stráikiŋ] *adj.* **1.** hitting. **2.** attracting attention; attractive; remarkable. ¶*She is a lady of ~ beauty.* **3.** being on strike.

strik·ing·ly [stráikiŋli] *adv.* attractively; remarkably.

⁑ **string** [striŋ] *n.* ⓒ **1.** ⓒ a thick thread; a fine cord; a very thin rope. ⇒N.B. ¶*a piece of ~.* **2.** ⓤⓒ anything used for tying or binding. ¶*a shoe ~.* **3.** a set of things arranged on a cord. ¶*She wore a ~ of pearls around her neck.*① **4.** a slender cord for musical instruments, bows, etc. ¶*the strings of a guitar.* **5.** a number of things in a line; a row; a series. ¶*a ~ of lies*② */ A ~ of cars sped by.* **6.** (*the ~s*) musical instruments such as violins, cellos, etc. **7.** a fiber of a plant. **8.** (*pl.*) (*U.S. colloq.*) a condition attached to an offer, etc. ¶*accept an offer with a ~ attached to it.* 「one's control.」
1) *have someone on a string,* have someone under
2) *have two strings to one's bow,* have an alternative way of doing or getting something.
3) *pull strings,* use one's personal influence with someone secretly to gain advantage.
—*v.* (**strung**) *vt.* **1.** put or thread (something) on a string. ¶*~ pearls on a thread.* **2.** provide (something) with strings. ¶*~ a tennis racket / He strung his bow.* **3.** tune the strings of (a musical instrument) by tightening, etc. **4.** ((often in *passive*)) make (someone) tense or excited. ¶*A runner is strung up before a race.* **5.** remove the strings or fibers from (beans, etc.). ¶*She strung the beans.* **6.** arrange (something) in a row. **7.** stretch; extend. ¶*~ a cable.* 「along in a line.」
—*vi.* **1.** form into a string; become stringy. **2.** move
1) *string along,* (*colloq.*) fool.
2) *string along with* (=*follow faithfully*) *someone.*
3) *string out,* (*U.S. colloq.*) prolong; extend.
4) *string up,* (*colloq.*) kill (someone) by hanging.

stringed [striŋd] *adj.* **1.** (of musical instruments) having strings. **2.** produced by strings.

strin·gen·cy [stríndʒ(ə)nsi] *n.* Ⓤ **1.** strictness; severity. ¶*the ~ of the rules.* **2.** scarcity, esp. of money. ¶ *monetary ~.* **3.** convincing force of reasoning.

strin·gent [stríndʒ(ə)nt] *adj.* **1.** strict; rigid. ¶*~ rules.* **2.** short in loan or investment money; tight. ¶*The money market is ~.* **3.** convincing. ¶*a ~ argument.*

strin·gent·ly [stríndʒ(ə)ntli] *adv.* in a stringent manner.

내다 ⓑ …을 삭제하다 ⓒ […을] 향하여 나아가기 시작하다 ⓓ(野球) 삼진(三振)당하다; …을 삼진시키다 9)ⓐ …을 연주(노래)하기 시작하다 ⓑ[교제 따위]를 시작하다

—ⓝ **1.** 치기, 때리기, 타격 **2.** [석유·금광 따위의] 발견; 대성공 **3.** 파업 **4.** 《野球》스트라이크 **5.** 《보올링》스트라이크

—ⓝ 《野球》삼진(三振)

—ⓝ **1.** 치는 사람(것), 타자 **2.** 파업 참가자 **3.** 《美軍》당번병

—ⓐ **1.** 치는, 공격하는 **2.** 눈에 띄는, 주의를 끄는 **3.** 파업 중인

—ⓐ 눈에 띄게, 현저하게

—ⓝ **1.** 끈, 실 N.B. cord 보다 가늘고 thread 보다 굵음 **2.** [묶는] 끈 **3.** 실을 꿴 것; 한 줄에 이은 것 ¶①그녀는 목에 진주목걸이를 달고 있다 **4.** [악기·활의] 현(絃) **5.** 한 줄, 일렬; 연속 ¶②잇따른 거짓말 **6.** 현악기 **7.** [식물의] 섬유 **8.** 부대(附帶) 조건, 단서(但書)

熟 1)[남]을 조종하다 2)예비책을 마련해 두다, 양다리 걸치다 3)[남]을 조종하다, 흑막이 되다

—ⓥ **1.** …을 실에 꿰다; 주렁주렁 달다 **2.** …에 현을 달다. [라켓의] 줄(거트)을 매다 **3.** [악기의] 현을 죄다 **4.** [남]의 기분을 긴장시키다, 흥분시키다 **5.** [콩 따위]의 줄기를 없애다 **6.** …을 줄지어 늘어놓다 **7.** [밧줄 따위]를 매다 —ⓥⓘ **1.** 실이 되다, 실 모양으로 되다 **2.** 줄지어 나아가다

熟 1)(口)[남]을 놀리다 2)[남]에게 충실히 따르다 3)(美口)…을 잡아늘이다, 연장하다 4)(口)…을 목졸라 죽이다

—ⓐ **1.** 현이 있는 **2.** 현악기에 의한

—ⓝ **1.** 엄중, 엄격 **2.** [금융 따위의] 경색(梗塞) **3.** [학설 따위의] 설득력, 박력

—ⓐ **1.** 엄중한; 엄격한 **2.** 금융 경색의, 돈이 잘 안 도는 **3.** 설득력이 있는

—ⓐ 엄중히; 절박하여

string·y [stríŋi] *adj.* (**string·i·er, string·i·est**) **1.** like a string or strings. ¶*be overgrown with ~ weeds.* **2.** full of strings; having hard fibers; tough. ¶*a ~ piece of meat.* **3.** having good muscular development. ¶*a ~ youth.* ▷**string·i·ness** [-nis] *n.*

—[形] 1. 실(끈) 같은 2. 섬유질의, 힘줄이 많은 3. 근골(筋骨)이 건장한

⁑ **strip**[1] [strip] *v.* (**stripped** or *rarely* **stript, strip·ping**) *vt.* **1.** take off the covering of (something). ⟪~ something *from* or *of*⟫; undress ⟪~ someone *of*⟫. ¶*~ the bark from the oak; ~ the oak of its bark.*① **2.** take away or clear out (furniture, etc.) from a house, etc. **3.** rob; take away honors, titles, possessions, etc. away from (someone or something). ⟪~ someone or something *of*⟫ ¶*~ someone of all his honors.*② | *He stripped me of all my belongings.* **4.** break the thread of (a gear, bolt, etc.). **5.** draw the last milk from (a cow). —*vi.* **1.** undress. **2.** separate; come off. ¶*Bananas ~ easily.* **3.** lose the thread of a screw, etc.

—[他] 1. [껍질 따위]를 벗기다; …을 벌거벗기다 ¶①떡갈나무의 껍질을 벗기다 2. [비품 따위]를 떼어 내다 3. …에서 빼앗다, 강탈하다; [남]에게서 명예·직함 따위를 박탈하다 ¶②…에서 온갖 명예를 박탈하다 4. [나사의 이]를 닳게 하다 5. [젖소]의 젖을 죄어 짜다 —[自] 1. 옷을 벗다, 벌거벗다 2. 벗겨지다 3. [나사의] 이가 닳다

⁑ **strip**[2] [strip] *n.* [C] **1.** a long, narrow, flat piece of cloth, land, tape, etc. ¶*a comic ~*① | *He bought a ~ of land along the coast.* **2.** a place for airplanes to take off and land; an airstrip.

—[名] 1. [천·판자·토지 따위의] 조각, 가느다란 한 조각 ¶①연속 만화 2. 활주로

* **stripe** [straip] *n.* [C] **1.** a long, narrow band. ¶*A zebra has stripes.* **2.** ⟪*pl.*⟫ a number of pieces of braid sewn on a uniform showing rank, length of service, etc. ¶*The soldier had three stripes on his sleeve.* **3.** a blow with a whip; a welt. **4.** kind; type. ¶*He is a scholar of quite a different ~.* | *They are people of the same ~.*

—[名] 1. 줄, 줄무늬 2. 수장(袖章), 견장(肩章) 3. 채찍질; 채찍질 자국 4. 형(型), 종류

—*vt.* mark (something) with stripes.

—[他] …에 줄[무늬]을 달다

striped [straipt] *adj.* having stripes.

—[形] 줄이 있는, 줄무늬가 있는

strip·ling [stríplìŋ] *n.* [C] a youth just passing from boyhood to manhood.

—[名] 애송이, 젊은이

* **strive** [straiv] *vi.* (**strove, striv·en**) **1.** make great efforts; try hard. ¶*He strives for success.* | *I ~ to convince him.* **2.** struggle; fight. ¶*They strove against tyranny.*

—[自] 1. 노력하다, 애쓰다 2. 싸우다, 다투다

striv·en [strívn] *v.* pp. of **strive**.

strode [stroud] *v.* pt. of **stride**.

⁑ **stroke**[1] [strouk] *n.* [C] **1.** the act of striking with a hammer, a weapon, etc.; a blow. ¶*The tree was hit by a ~ of lightning.*① | (*proverb*) *Little strokes fell great oaks.*② **2.** the sound of a striking clock. ¶*They arrived there at the ~ of seven.*③ **3.** a beat of the heart. **4.** a mark or movement made by a pen, a brush, etc. ¶*He writes with a thick ~.*④ **5.** a vigorous effort or attempt to accomplish something. ¶*a bold ~ for freedom* | *He refused to do a ~ of work.* **6.** any particularly successful, brilliant effort or its achievement. ¶*a ~ of genius.* **7.** a way of swimming; a single movement of the arms, hands, oars, etc. ¶*He swims the breast ~.*⑤ | *The boat is gaining at every ~.*⑥ **8.** a sudden action or event. ¶*He made a fortune by a ~ of good luck.*⑦ **9.** a sudden attack of disease. ¶*He had a ~ of paralysis.* **10.** the rower who leads the rate of rowing.

—[名] 1. 치기, 타격, 일격 ¶①그 나무는 벼락을 맞았다/②〔俚〕티끌 모아 태산 2. 시계 치는 소리 ¶③그들은 7시를 칠 때에 그곳에 도착했다 3. 심장의 고동 4. [펜·붓 따위의] 한 번 쓰기, 한 획 ¶④그는 굵은 필체로 쓴다 5. 목적 달성을 위한 노력, 시도 6. 수완, 공적, 업적 7. 팔·손 따위의 한 번 놀리기 ¶⑤그는 평영으로 헤엄친다/⑥보우트는 한 번 저을 때마다 전진하고 있다 8. 갑작스러운 행위, 뜻밖의 일 ¶⑦그는 뜻밖의 행운으로 재산을 모았다 9. 발작 10. 보우트의 정조수(整調手)

1) ***at a stroke,*** at a blow; at one time.
2) ***keep stroke,*** make strokes or row in rhythm.

[熟] 1)일격에; 곧 당장 2)박자에 맞추어 노를 젓다

—*vt.* act as a stroke for (a boat). ¶*Who stroked your crew?* ▷**strok·er** [-ər] *n.*

—[他] [보우트]의 정조수(整調手) 노릇을 하다

⁑ **stroke**[2] [strouk] *vt.* rub (something) gently with the hand. ¶*~ one's kitten.* —*n.* [C] a soft, repeated movement of the hand, etc. in one direction.

—[他] …을 쓰다듬다, 어루만지다 —[名] 쓰다듬기, 어루만지기

* **stroll** [stroul] *vi.* walk about in a leisurely manner; wander from place to place. ¶*Let's ~ up toward the cabin.* —*vt.* walk leisurely along or through (a place). ¶*We strolled the broad avenue.* —*n.* [C] a leisurely walk. ¶*go for a ~.*

—[自] 한가로이 거닐다, 산책하다 —[他] …을 이리저리 거닐다; …을 산책하다 —[名] 산책, 거닐기

stroll·er [stróulər] *n.* [C] **1.** a wanderer. **2.** a strolling actor or performer. **3.** a light carriage in which very small children sit. ⇒fig.
—[名] 1. 방랑자 2. 순회 연예인(흥행사) 3. 유모차

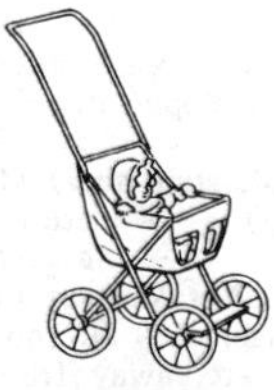
[stroller 3.]

⁑ **strong** [strɔːŋ / strɔŋ] *adj.* **1.** having physical power; tough; in good health; sound. ¶*a ~ boxer* / *a ~ dog* / *I feel stronger today.* **2.** having great mental or moral power; intellectually powerful; firm. ¶*~ nerves*① / *a ~ faith* / *a ~ brain*② / *a ~ imagination*③ / *He is a man of ~ will.* **3.** not easily broken or damaged. ¶*~ cloth* / *a ~ fort.* **4.** producing a great effect; able or tending to persuade or convince. ¶*~ evidence*④ / *He made a ~ speech.* / *He took ~ measures.*⑤ **5.** great in numbers and wealth; having influence; sufficient. ¶*a ~ nation* / *an army 200,000 ~.*⑥ **6.** having a large amount or proportion of the essential quality. ¶*~ colors* / *a ~ voice* / *He likes ~ coffee.* **7.** affecting one of the senses powerfully; intense. ¶*a ~ light* / *a ~ odor* / *a ~ flavor.* **8.** deeply earnest; passionate. ¶*a man of ~ affections and ~ dislikes.*⑦ **9.** (of the wind, the tide, etc.) blowing or moving forcefully. ¶*a ~ wind* / *a ~ tide.* **10.** (*colloq.*) having special ability. 《*~ in*》 ¶*He is ~ in physics.*⑧ **11.** (*Commercial*) rising to higher prices. ¶*The silk market is very ~.*⑨ **12.** (*Grammar*) (of verbs) forming the variation of tense by a change of vowel within the root of the word; irregular. ⇒[N.B.]
—[形] 1. 힘센, 기운이 있는; 건강한, 튼튼한 2. [정신력·신념 따위가] 강한; [지력이] 강한 ¶①강인한 신경/②강한 지력/③강한 상상력 3. 쉽게 깨지지(부서지지, 줄지) 않는 4. [의론·증거 따위가] 유력한, 박력있는; [수단 따위가] 강경한 ¶④유력한 증거/⑤그는 강경 수단을 취했다 5. 다수의, 유력한, 세력이 있는; …의 병력의 ¶⑥병력 20만의 군대 6. [성분 따위] 강한, 강도(強度)의 7. [감각에 대한 자극이] 강한 8. 열심인, 열렬한 ¶⑦가리는 것이 많은 사람 9. [바람 따위가] 세찬, 강한 10. 《口》 잘하는; 유능한 ¶⑧그는 물리를 잘한다 11. 《商》 강세(強勢)의, 등귀하는 ¶⑨비단의 시세는 꽤 강세를 보이고 있다 12. 《文法》 강변화의, 불규칙 변화의 [N.B.] give, gave, given 따위

—*adv.* powerfully; strongly.
—[副] 강하게, 격렬하게, 강력하게

go strong, (*colloq.*) continue in good health. ¶*He is going ~.*
[熟] 《口》 건강하다

strong·box [strɔ́ːŋbɑ̀ks / strɔ́ŋbɔ̀ks] *n.* [C] a strongly-made box to hold money, jewels, etc.
—[名] 금고, 귀중품 상자

strong·hold [strɔ́ːŋhòuld / strɔ́ŋ-] *n.* [C] **1.** a place or building which is built to stand against the attack of enemies; a fortress; a safe place of refuge. **2.** a central place of support for a certain idea or cause.
—[名] 1. 요새, 성채; 안전한 장소 2. 중심점

⁑ **strong·ly** [strɔ́ːŋli / strɔ́ŋ-] *adv.* in a strong manner; severely; with force. ¶*I ~ advised him to go.*
—[副] 강하게, 세게

strong-minded [strɔ́ːŋmáindid / strɔ́ŋ-] *adj.* having a strong mind; determined. ¶*I need a ~ boy.*
—[形] 단호한, 결단력이 있는

stron·ti·um [strɑ́nʃiəm / strɔ́n-, -tiəm, -ʃiəm] *n.* [U] a hard chemical element resembling calcium, found only in combination.
—[名] 스트론튬

strop [strɑp / strɔp] *n.* [C] a leather strip used for sharpening razors. —*vt.* (**stropped, strop·ping**) sharpen (a razor) on a strop.
—[名] 면도의 혁지(革砥) —[他] …을 혁지로 갈다

* **strove** [strouv] *v.* pt. of **strive.**

⁑ **struck** [strʌk] *v.* pt. and pp. of **strike.**
—*adj.* closed or affected by a labor strike.
—[形] 파업으로 문을 닫은

struc·tur·al [strʌ́ktʃ(u)r(ə)l] *adj.* **1.** of or relating to structure. ¶*Structural changes were made to the city hall.* **2.** used in building. ▷**struc·tur·al·ly** [-i] *adv.*
—[形] 1. 구조상의, 건축 구조상의 2. 건축용의

⁑ **struc·ture** [strʌ́ktʃər] *n.* **1.** [U] the manner of building. ¶*The ~ of airplanes has been greatly improved.* **2.** [U] the form or arrangement of all the parts or elements. ¶*the ~ of a play* / *Good sentence ~ is necessary in excellent prose.* **3.** [C] something built; a building.
—[名] 1. 건조, 구축(構築)[술] 2. 구조, 뼈대, 조직 3. 건조물

⁑ **strug·gle** [strʌ́gl] *vi.* **1.** make great efforts to escape from a grasp, danger, etc.; contend. 《*~ against* or *with something*》 ¶*Animals ~ to survive.* / *The small boat struggled against the violent current of the river.*① **2.** fight eagerly against difficulties; strive; labor. ¶*He struggled to overcome his bad habits.*② **3.** make one's way with great efforts. ¶*~ through a crowd.*
—[自] 1. 싸우다, 격투하다, 몸부림치다, 버둥거리다 ¶①작은 보우트는 강의 격류와 싸우고 있었다 2. 열심히 노력하다, 분투하다 ¶②그는 악습을 극복하기 위해 노력했다 3. 밀어젖히고 나아가다

—*n.* [C] **1.** a great effort; a hard piece of work. ¶*a ~ for existence.* **2.** a fight. ¶*a ~ to escape.*
—[名] 1. 노력, 고투; 중노동 2. 싸움, 투쟁

strug·gler [strʌ́glər] *n.* [C] a person who struggles.
—[名] 몸부림치는 사람; 노력가

strum [strʌm] *vt., vi.* (**strummed, strum·ming**) play on (a guitar, etc.) unskillfully or carelessly. ¶*~ on the piano | He used to ~ a banjo.* —*n.* [C] ⦅*sing.* only⦆ an act or a sound of strumming.
—[他][自] …을 서투르게(아무렇게나) 켜다 —[名] 악기를 켜기(켜는 소리)

* **strung** [strʌŋ] *v.* pt. and pp. of **string**.

strut[1] [strʌt] *vi.* (**strut·ted, strut·ting**) walk in a vain, proud or self-satisfied manner. ¶*The bully strutted around the room.*① —*n.* [C] a strutting walk.
—[自] 뽐내며 걷다 ¶①개구장이는 뽐내며 방 안을 걸어다녔다 —[名] 뽐내는 걸음걸이

strut[2] [strʌt] *n.* [C] a piece of wood or metal used in a framework for resisting pressure. —*vt.* (**strut·ted, strut·ting**) support (something) with struts.
—[名] 지주(支柱), 버팀대 —[他] …을 지주로 받치다

stub [stʌb] *n.* [C] **1.** the short remaining part of a tree after it has been cut down; a stock. **2.** (of a cigarette, a pencil, etc.) any short remaining piece. **3.** the part of a check, bill, ticket, etc. kept as a record. **4.** a pen with a short and not sharp point. —*vt.* (**stubbed, stub·bing**) strike (one's toe or foot) against something hard.
—[名] 1. [나무] 그루터기 2. 쓰다 남은 토막 3. [어음 책 따위의] 부본(副本) 4. 뭉툭해진 펜촉 —[他] [발]을 부딪치다

stub·ble [stʌ́bl] *n.* [C] **1.** the short remaining piece of grain left standing after the harvest. **2.** a short growth of beard. ¶*He had three days' ~ on his chin.*
—[名] 1. 벼·보리 따위의 그루터기 2. 짧고 억센 수염

* **stub·born** [stʌ́bərn] *adj.* **1.** fixed in an opinion, etc.; determined; obstinate; firm. ¶*~ resistance | He is as ~ as a mule.*① **2.** hard to treat, manage or handle.
—[形] 1. 단호한, 불굴의, 완고한 ¶①그는 정말로 고집이 세다 2. 다루기 어려운

stub·born·ly [stʌ́bərnli] *adv.* in a stubborn manner.
—[副] 완고하게

stub·born·ness [stʌ́bərnnis] *n.* [U] the state or quality of being stubborn.
—[名] 고집, 불굴, 완고함

stub·by [stʌ́bi] *adj.* (**-bi·er, -bi·est**) **1.** short, thick, and stiff. ¶*The old man has ~ fingers. | He wore a ~ beard.* **2.** covered with stubble[s].
—[形] 1. 땅딸막한, 짧고 굵은 2. 그루터기투성이의

stuc·co [stʌ́kou] *n.* [U][C] (pl. **-cos** or **-coes**) a kind of plaster used for covering walls, etc. —*vt.* cover (something) with stucco.
—[名] 치장 벽토 —[他] …에 치장 벽토를 칠하다

* **stuck** [stʌk] *v.* pt. and pp. of **stick**.

stuck-up [stʌ́kʌ́p] *adj.* (*colloq.*) very pleased with oneself; conceited.
—[形] 거만한, 건방진

stud[1] [stʌd] *n.* [C] **1.** a large-headed nail, knob, etc. projecting from a surface. ¶*He wore a belt with silver studs.* **2.** a kind of small button used as a fastener. ⇒fig. **3.** an upright piece in walls to which other pieces of wood are nailed. —*vt.* (**stud·ded, stud·ding**) **1.** decorate or set (something) with studs. **2.** set thickly. **3.** be scattered over (a place, etc.).

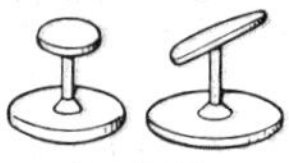
[stud[1] 2.]

—[名] 1. 장식용 못(징) 2. 장식 단추 3. 샛기둥 —[他] 1. …을 못(징)으로 장식하다 2. …을 점점이 박다, 산재(散在)시키다 3. …에 흩어지다

stud[2] [stʌd] *n.* [C] **1.** a group of horses kept for breeding, racing, etc. **2.** the place where such horses are kept. **3.** (*U.S.*) a studhorse.
—[名] 1. 말떼 2. 말의 사육장 3. 종마(種馬)

‡ **stu·dent** [st(j)úːd(ə)nt / stjúː-] *n.* [C] **1.** a person who studies. ¶*a ~ of folklore.*① **2.** a person who studies at a school, a college, etc. ¶*a college ~.*
—[名] 1. 연구가, 학자 ¶①민화(民話)의 연구가 2. 학생, 생도

stud·horse [stʌ́dhɔ̀ːrs] *n.* [C] a male horse kept for breeding purposes; a stallion.
—[名] 종마(種馬)

* **stud·ied** [stʌ́did] *adj.* **1.** carefully planned. ¶*It's a well-studied plot.* **2.** done on purpose; calculated.
—[形] 1. 연구를 쌓은 2. 일부러의, 고의의

* **stu·di·o** [st(j)úːdiou / stjúː-] *n.* [C] (pl. **-di·os**) **1.** the workroom of an artist. **2.** a place where motion pictures are made. **3.** a place where a radio or television program is broadcast or recorded.
—[名] 1. 작업장 2. 촬영소 3. 방송실; 녹음실, 녹화실

stu·di·ous [st(j)úːdiəs / stjúː-] *adj.* **1.** fond of study. **2.** thoughtful; zealous. ¶*make a ~ effort.*
—[形] 1. 학문을 좋아하는, 학구적인 2. 신중한, 공을 들인; 열심인

stu·di·ous·ly [st(j)úːdiəsli / stjúː-] *adv.* in a studious manner; thoughtfully.
—[副] 일부러; 열심히

S

‡ stud·y [stʌ́di] *n.* (pl. **stud·ies**) **1.** [U] effort to learn by reading, thinking, etc. **2.** [C] ⟪often *pl.*⟫ the act or process of pursuing some branch of knowledge; a careful examination. ¶*the ~ of modern languages*① / *He made a ~ of certain plants.*② **3.** [C] a branch or department of learning. ¶*the ~ of medicine* / *Of all my studies I like English best.* **4.** [C] ⟪*sing.* only⟫ something deserving to be examined. ¶*His character is a perfect ~.*③ **5.** [C] a room used for reading and writing. ¶*He is reading in his ~.* **6.** ⟪often *one's ~* or *pl.*⟫ education. ¶*Don't stop your studies.*④ **7.** [C] an earnest effort. ¶*Her constant ~ is to do her duty well.*⑤ **8.** [C] a sketch for a picture, a story, etc.; a piece of music for practice. **9.** [C] ⟪*sing.* only⟫ deep thought; meditation. ¶*be in deep ~*⑥ / *He is in a brown ~.*⑦

—[名] 1. 공부, 면학(勉學) 2. 연구, 학문, 조사 ¶①현대어의 연구/②그는 어떤 식물의 연구를 했다 3. 학과; 연구 제목 4. 연구 가치가 있는 것; 구경거리 ¶③그의 성격은 정말 연구해 볼 만하다 5. 서재, 공부방 6. 학업 ¶④학업을 중단하지 말라 7. 노력, 수고 ¶⑤그녀는 의무를 다하는 일에 끊임없는 노력을 하고 있다 8. 습작; 연습곡 9. 깊은 생각, 명상 ¶⑥깊은 생각에 잠겨 있다/⑦그는 멍하니 생각에 잠겨 있다

—*v.* (**stud·ied**) *vt.* **1.** seek knowledge of (a subject) by study. ¶*He studies history of America.* **2.** consider or examine carefully; look at (something) carefully. ¶*I'll ~ this problem.*⑧ / *He studied her face.* **3.** think out; plan. ¶*He studied ways to escape from the island.* **4.** learn (something) by heart. **5.** try hard; think about (something) carefully. ⟪*~ to do*⟫ ¶*~ one's own interest*⑨ / *We must ~ to do right.* **—***vi.* **1.** seek knowledge. ¶*~ hard* / *~ to become a lawyer.* **2.** be a student. **3.** think deeply; meditate.

—[他] 1. …을 공부하다, 연구하다 2. …을 주의하여 보다; …을 조사하다 ¶⑧이 문제를 충분히 조사하겠다 3. …을 궁리해내다; …을 계획하다 4. …을 외다, 암기하다 5. …을 하려고 뜻하다, …을 고려하다 ¶⑨사리(私利)를 꾀하다
—[自] 1. 공부하다, 배우다 2. 제자가 되다 3. 생각에 잠기다

‡ stuff [stʌf] *n.* **1.** [U] [C] the material out of which something is made; any material. **2.** [U] the quality or character of a person, a matter, etc.; basic elements. ¶*the ~ of democracy* / *He has good ~ in him.*① **3.** [U] personal belongings; goods. ¶*green ~* / *household ~*② / *He left his ~ in the room.*③ **4.** [U] cloth, esp. woollen cloth. **5.** [U] a worthless collection; worthless ideas, writings, etc. ¶*a lot of ~ and nonsense.*④

—[名] 1. 재료, 원료 2. 소질, 요소 ¶①그는 좋은 소질을 갖고 있다 3. 소지품; 것 ¶②가구/③그는 방에 소지품을 남기고 왔다 4. 직물, 피륙, [특히] 모직물 5. 잡동사니; 헛소리; 졸작(拙作) ¶④쓸데없이 많은 허튼소리

—*vt.* **1.** fill or pack closely. ⟪~ something *into* or *with*⟫ ¶*~ potatoes into a bag; ~ a bag with potatoes.* **2.** fill the skin of (a dead animal, bird, etc.) so as to keep its natural form and appearance. ¶*a stuffed lion.* **3.** fill (a chicken, a turkey, etc.) with seasoned bread crumbs, etc. **4.** fill (one's stomach) with food. ¶*~ oneself.*⑤ **5.** stop up (a crack, a hole, etc.); block. **—***vi.* eat too much.

—[他] 1. …을 채워넣다 2. …을 박제(剝製)로 만들다 3. [요리용 새 따위]에 속을 넣다 4. [뱃속]에 잔뜩 틀어넣다 ¶⑤과식하다 5. [구멍 따위]를 채워 넣다 —[自] 게걸스럽게 먹다

stuff·ing [stʌ́fiŋ] *n.* **1.** [U] the material with which a mat, a cushion, a pillow, etc. is packed. ¶*the ~ of a pillow.* **2.** [U] [C] a seasoned mixture of bread, chopped meat, etc. put into a chicken, a turkey, etc. before cooking.

—[名] 1. [베개·이불 따위의] 속감, 짚, 털, 깃털 2. [요리용 새 따위의] 속에 넣는 빵부스러기

stuff·y [stʌ́fi] *adj.* (**stuff·i·er, stuff·i·est**) **1.** lacking fresh air; close. ¶*a ~ room.* **2.** causing difficult breathing. **3.** dull; not interesting. ¶*a ~ conversation.* **4.** (*colloq.*) opposed to change; conservative. ▷**stuff·i·ness** [-nis] *n.*

—[形] 1. 통풍이 잘 안 되는 2. 숨이 막힐 듯한 3. 시시한, 싫증나는 4. 케케묵은, 딱딱한

stul·ti·fy [stʌ́ltifài] *vt.* (**-fied**) **1.** cause (someone) to appear foolish. ¶*Drudgery can ~ the mind.* **2.** make (something) worthless or useless.

—[他] 1. …을 바보로 보이게 하다 2. …을 쓸모없게 하다, 무효로 하다

*** stum·ble** [stʌ́mbl] *vi.* **1.** fall or trip in walking, running, etc. ¶*~ over a stub*① / *He stumbled downstairs.* **2.** walk unsteadily. ¶*The man stumbled along the road.* **3.** hesitate; speak or act in a hesitating manner. **4.** do wrong; make a mistake. **5.** find or happen on something by chance. ⟪*~ on* or *upon* something⟫
—*n.* [C] **1.** an act of tripping. **2.** a mistake; an error.

—[自] 1. 비트적거리다, [걸려] 넘어지다 ¶①그루터기에 걸려 넘어지다 2. 비틀비틀 걷다 3. 망설이다, 말을 더듬다 4. 실패하다, 잘못하다 5. 우연히 발견하다, 마주치다
—[名] 1. 걸려 넘어짐, 비틀거림 2. 실패, 실수

stumbling block [stʌ́mbliŋblὰk / -blɔ̀k] *n.* **1.** an obstacle. **2.** anything causing difficulty.

—[名] 1. 방해물 2. 장애

*** stump** [stʌmp] *n.* [C] **1.** the part of a tree or plant left after it has been cut down. **2.** the part of an arm, a leg, a tooth, etc. left after the rest has been removed.

—[名] 1. 그루터기 2. 부러진 이뿌리; 손·발의 절단하고 남은 부분; [물건의] 쓰다 남은 것 3. 의족(義足) 4. 정견발

stumper

3. a wooden leg. **4.** a platform from which a political speech is made. ¶ *go on the ~.*① **5.** a heavy step; the sound of such a step. **6.** (in cricket) one of the sticks which are put upright in the ground.
—*vt.* **1.** remove stumps from (land). **2.** puzzle; confuse. ¶ *Your question stumps me.* **3.** travel over (a district) making political speeches. —*vi.* **1.** walk heavily with noisy steps. **2.** go about making political speeches.

stump·er [stʌ́mpər] *n.* ⓒ **1.** a person or thing that stumps. **2.** an extremely difficult problem, task, etc. **3.** a person who goes about making political speeches.

stump·y [stʌ́mpi] *adj.* (**stump·i·er, stump·i·est**) **1.** short and thick. **2.** having many stumps. ¶ *a ~ field.*

stun [stʌn] *vt.* (**stunned, stun·ning**) **1.** make (someone) unconscious, as by a blow; knock senseless. ¶ *I was stunned by the blow.* **2.** daze; shock.

• **stung** [stʌŋ] *v.* pt. and pp. of **sting**.

stunk [stʌŋk] *v.* pt. and pp. of **stink**.

stun·ning [stʌ́niŋ] *adj.* **1.** that stuns; shocking. ¶ *deliver a ~ blow.* **2.** (*colloq.*) very attractive; good-looking; remarkable. ¶ *a ~ beauty.* ▷ **stun·ning·ly** [-li] *adv.*

stunt¹ [stʌnt] *vt.* check (someone or something) in growth. ¶ *Lack of water stunted these potted plants.* —*n.* ⓤⓒ the act of stunting.

stunt² [stʌnt] *n.* ⓒ (*colloq.*) something done to show skill or boldness; a striking performance or feat. ¶ *He will perform a flying ~.* —*vt., vi.* perform a stunt with (something).

stu·pe·fac·tion [st(j)u:pifǽkʃ(ə)n / stjù:-] *n.* ⓤ the act of stupefying; the state of being stupefied; a dazed or senseless condition; amazement.

stu·pe·fy [st(j)ú:pifài / stjú:-] *vt.* (**-fied**) **1.** make (someone) stupid or senseless. **2.** astonish. ¶ *They were stupefied by the accident.* ▷ **stu·pe·fi·er** [-ər] *n.*

stu·pen·dous [st(j)u(:)péndəs / stju:-] *adj.* amazing, esp. because of great size; marvelous. ▷ **stu·pen·dous·ly** [-li] *adv.* —**stu·pen·dous·ness** [-nis] *n.*

• **stu·pid** [st(j)ú:pid / stjú:-] *adj.* (**~·er, ~·est**) **1.** dull; foolish; not intelligent. ↔ wise ¶ *a ~ boy / a ~ mistake.* **2.** not interesting. ¶ *What a ~ book!* **3.** senseless.

stu·pid·i·ty [st(j)u:píditi / stju:-] *n.* (pl. **-ties**) **1.** ⓤ foolishness. **2.** ⓒ (*pl.*) a foolish act, idea, etc.

stu·pid·ly [st(j)ú:pidli / stjú:pə-] *adv.* in a stupid manner.

stu·por [st(j)ú:pər / stjú:pə] *n.* ⓒⓤ **1.** a condition in which someone is nearly unconscious; a loss of the power to feel. **2.** the state of being amazed.

• **stur·dy** [stə́:rdi] *adj.* (**-di·er, -di·est**) **1.** strong; stout. **2.** firm.

stur·geon [stə́:rdʒ(ə)n] *n.* (pl. **-geons** or *collectively* **-geon**) a large edible fish. ⇒ fig.

stut·ter [stʌ́tər] *vi.* repeat the same sound because one has difficulty in speaking; stammer. —*vt.* repeat (a sound) with difficulty. —*n.* ⓒ the act of stuttering.

[sturgeon]

sty¹ [stai] *n.* ⓒ (pl. **sties**) **1.** a place where pigs are kept. **2.** a dirty place. ⌜the edge of the eyelid.⌉

sty², **stye** [stai] *n.* ⓒ (pl. **styes** or **sties**) a swelling on

‡ **style** [stail] *n.* **1.** ⓤⓒ fashion. ¶ *in (out of) ~*① */ the latest styles from Paris.* **2.** ⓤ manner or method of doing or making something. ¶ *in fine ~*② */ the modern ~ of living.* **3.** ⓒⓤ a distinctive manner of writ-

style

표용 그루터기 연단 ¶①선거 연설을 하고 다니다 5. 무거운 발걸음; 그와 같은 발소리 6. [크리켓의] 기둥

—㉰ 1. [토지]에서 그루터기를 뽑다 2. [남]을 괴롭히다, 난처하게 하다 3. [어떤 지방]을 유세하다 —㉲ 1. 쿵쿵 걷다 2. 유세하다

—㉯ 1. 당황케 하는 사람(것) 2. 난문, 난제 3. 정치(선거) 연설가

—㉯ 1. 땅딸막한 2. 그루터기투성이의

—㉰ 1. [때려서] …을 기절시키다 2. …을 멍하게 만들다, …의 간담을 서늘하게 하다

—㉯ 1. 기절시키는; 간담을 서늘하게 하는 2. 〔口〕아주 매력적인; 아름다운; 멋진
—㉯ …의 발육을 방해하다

—㉯ 발육의 저해(저지)
—㉯ 〔口〕묘기, 아슬아슬한 재주 —㉰ ㉲ […에서] 아슬아슬한 재주를 부리다

—㉯ 마비[시키기]; 의식 불명[의 상태]; 깜짝 놀람

—㉰ 1. …을 마비시키다, 멍하게 만들다 2. …을 깜짝 놀라게 하다

—㉯ 놀랄 만한; 터무니없는; 거대한; 멋들어진

—㉯ 1. 머리가 둔한, 바보의 2. 시시한, 재미없는 3. 감각이 없는, 마비된

—㉯ 1. 어리석음, 우둔 2. 어리석은 짓 (생각)
—㉯ 어리석게

—㉯ 1. 실신(失神); 무감각; 인사불성 2. 아연실색; 깜짝 놀람

—㉯ 1. 힘센; 튼튼한 2. 불굴의

—㉯ 철갑상어

—㉲ 말더듬다 —㉰ …을 더듬더듬 말하다 —㉯ 더듬기

—㉯ 1. 돼지우리 2. 지저분한 곳

—㉯ 다래끼, 맥립종(麥粒腫)
—㉯ 1. 유행, 스타일 ¶①유행하는(유행에 뒤진) 2. 하는 방법; 양식 ¶②훌륭하게, 화려하게 3. 문체; 말투 4. [예술 작품의] 유파, 양식 ¶③고디식

stylebook

ing or speaking. ¶*a concise ~ / an easy ~*. **4.** ⓒⓊ a characteristic manner of expression. ¶*the Gothic ~ of architecture.*④ **5.** an elegant or distinguished manner of living or way of acting. ¶*He has no ~ about him.*④ **6.** Ⓤ kind; sort. ¶*What ~ man is he?* **7.** ⓒ a person's full title; a trade name. **8.** ⓒ a pointed instrument used in ancient times for writing on wax; a stylus.
— *vt.* give a title to (someone); name; call.

style·book [stáilbùk] *n.* ⓒ **1.** a book on various fashions in dress. **2.** a book for printers, in which rules of punctuation, capitalization, etc. are shown.

sty·li [stáilai] *n.* pl. of **stylus**.

styl·ish [stáiliʃ] *adj.* very modern; fashionable.

styl·ist [stáilist] ⓒ **1.** a writer who has a good style. **2.** a designer of interior decorations, clothes, etc.

sty·lis·tic [stailístik] *adj.* of or about style.

sty·lis·ti·cal·ly [stailístik(ə)li] *adv.* with regard to style.

sty·lus [stáiləs] *n.* ⓒ (pl. **-li** or **-lus·es**) **1.** a pointed instrument for writing on wax. **2.** a needle used in playing phonograph records.

sty·mie [stáimi] *n.* ⓒ **1.** (*Golf*) obstruction by the opponent's ball lying between the player and the hole. **2.** an obstacle. — *vt.* hinder.

Styx [stiks] *n.* (in Greek mythology) a river across which the souls of the dead were transported.

sua·sion [swéiʒ(ə)n] *n.* Ⓤ persuasion.

suave [swɑːv] *adj.* agreeable; polite.

suave·ly [swɑ́ːvli] *adv.* agreeably; politely.

sua·vi·ty [swɑ́ːviti] *n.* Ⓤ agreeable quality; politeness.

sub- [sʌb-, səb-] *pref.* **1.** under; below: *subway* (= underground railway). **2.** again; further: *sublet* (= let again). **3.** near; nearly: *subarctic* (= near the arctic region). **4.** slightly: *subacid* (= slightly acid). **5.** assistant: *subeditor* (= subordinate editor).

sub·al·tern [səbɔ́ːltərn / sʌ́blt(ə)n] *n.* ⓒ (*Brit.*) an army officer ranking below a captain. — *adj.* **1.** subordinate. **2.** ranking below a captain.

sub·com·mit·tee [sʌ́bkəmìti] *n.* ⓒ a small committee chosen from a larger committee.

sub·con·scious [sʌbkɑ́nʃəs / -kɔ́n-] *adj.* existing in the mind but not felt. — *n.* Ⓤ (*the ~*) the mental activity of which the individual is not aware.

sub·con·scious·ly [sʌbkɑ́nʃəsli / -kɔ́n-] *adv.* in a subconscious.

sub·con·tract [sʌbkɑ́ntrækt / -kɔ́n- ‖ →*v.*] *n.* ⓒ a contract which is made to supplement a primary or previous contract. — *v.* [sʌ̀bkəntrǽkt] *vt.* make a subcontract for (something). — *vi.* make a subcontract.

sub·cu·ta·ne·ous [sʌ̀bkju(ː)téiniəs] *adj.* under the skin. ¶*~ injection.*①

sub·di·vide [sʌ̀bdiváid] *vt.* divide (what has already been divided) into even smaller parts. — *vi.* become separated into smaller parts.

sub·di·vi·sion [sʌ́bdivìʒ(ə)n] *n.* **1.** ⓒ a part subdivided, esp. a piece of land near a city subdivided into many lots for houses. **2.** Ⓤ the act of subdividing.

sub·du·al [səbd(j)úː(ː)əl / -djúː(ː)əl] *n.* Ⓤ the act of subduing.

* **sub·due** [səbd(j)úː / -djúː] *vt.* **1.** conquer; overcome. ¶*~ nature.* **2.** soften. ¶*subdued light.*

sub·head [sʌ́bhèd] *n.* ⓒ a title or heading of a subdivision.

sub·head·ing [sʌ́bhèdiŋ] *n.* = subhead.

‡ **sub·ject** [sʌ́bdʒikt →*vt.*] *n.* ⓒ **1.** a person who is under the power or control of another or of a certain gov-

subject

건축 5. 기품, 품위; 고상함 ¶④그에게는 품위가 없다 6. 종류 7. [사람의 정식의] 칭호; [상사 따위의] 상호 8. [고대인이 쓰던] 첨필(尖筆), 철필

— ⓗ …을 부르다, 일컫다

— ⓢ 1. [복장의] 스타일 북 2. [인쇄업자의] 구둣점·활자 견본책, 인쇄 편람

— ⓟ 현대식의, 멋진
— ⓢ 1. 명문가, 문장가 2. [실내 장식·의복의] 디자이너
— ⓟ 문체 [상]의
— ⓐ 문체상
— ⓢ 1. 철필, 첨필 2. 레코오드의 바늘

— ⓢ 1. (골프) 방해구(球) 2. 방해물
— ⓗ …을 방해하다

— ⓢ 삼도천(三途川)

— ⓢ 설득
— ⓟ 기분좋은, 은근한
— ⓐ 기분좋게, 은근하게
— ⓢ 기분좋음, 은근함
—(接頭) 1. 아래의 2. 다시, 게다가 3. 아(亞)… 4. 약간, 조금, 약(弱)… 5. 부(副)…

— ⓢ 육군 중위, 소위 — ⓟ 1. 부(副)의, 하위의 2. 중위·소위의

— ⓢ 분과 위원회

— ⓟ 잠재의식의 — ⓢ 잠재의식
「하여」
— ⓐ 잠재의식적으로, 희미하게 의식
— ⓢ 하청, 하청 계약 — ⓗ …의 하청을 하다 — ⓘ 하청을 맡다

— ⓟ 피하(皮下)의 ¶①피하주사

— ⓗ …을 다시 나누다; 세분하다 — ⓘ 다시 나뉘다; 세분되다

— ⓢ 1. 세분된 것; 건축 대지로 구획한 토지 2. 재분할

— ⓢ 정복

— ⓗ 1. …을 정복하다 2. …을 누그러뜨리다
— ⓢ 작은 표제

— ⓢ 1. 신민, 신하, 부하 ¶①영국[왕]의 신민, 영국민 2. 주제(主題), 문제, 제

ernment. ¶*a British* ~.① **2.** a topic treated or chosen in conversation, study, writing, painting, etc.; a theme. ¶*a* ~ *of conversation* / *the* ~ *in hand*② / *Let's change the* ~. **3.** a course of study taught in a school, a college, etc. ¶*an elective* (*a required*) ~.③ **4.** (*Grammar*) the noun or pronoun governing a verb. **5.** a cause or motive. 《~ *for, of*》 ¶*a* ~ *of ridicule*④ / *a* ~ *of complaint.* **6.** a person or animal on whom an experiment is performed; a dead body used for experimentation. **7.** (*Philosophy*) the thinking and feeling mind or ego; substance.

목, 화제; [음악의] 주제 ¶②당면 문제 3. 학과, 과목 ¶③선택(필수) 과목 4.《文法》 주어, 주부(主部) 5. …의 씨, 원인 ¶④조소의 대상, 웃음거리 6. [의학 따위의] 피(被)실험자; 해부 시체 7. 주관, 자아(自我); [행위의] 주체

—*adj.* **1.** under the power of another. 《~ *to*》 ¶~ *nations* / *Everything is* ~ *to the laws of nature.*⑤ **2.** apt to suffer frequently; likely to have. 《~ *to*》 ¶*be* ~ *to damage* / *She is* ~ *to colds.* / *The prices are* ~ *to change.* **3.** dependent on; on the condition of. 《~ *to*》 ¶*a plan* ~ *to your approval.*⑥

—[形] 1. 복종하는, 종속의, 지배를 받는 ¶⑤만물은 자연의 법칙에 지배된다 2. 받기 쉬운, …이 되기 쉬운, …을 입는 3. …이라는 조건이 붙은 ¶⑥귀하의 승인이 필요한 계획

—*vt.* [səbdʒékt] **1.** bring (someone or something) under control. 《~ someone or something *to*》 ¶~ *a neighboring country to one's rule.* **2.** expose; cause (someone) to experience or endure. 《~ someone or something *to*》 ¶~ *oneself to insult*⑦ / ~ *a prisoner to torture.*⑧ **3.** submit. 《~ something *to*》

—[他] 1. …을 복종시키다, 지배하에 두다 2. …에 노출시키다; …에게 …을 받게(입게) 하다 ¶⑦모욕을 당하다/⑧죄수를 고문하다 3. …을 제출하다

sub·jec·tion [səbdʒékʃ(ə)n] *n.* [U] **1.** the act of conquering. **2.** the state of being under the control of some power.
—[名] 1. 정복 2. 복종, 종속

sub·jec·tive [səbdʒéktiv] *adj.* existing only in the mind of someone; personal. ↔objective
—[形] 주관적인; 개인적인

sub·jec·tive·ly [səbdʒéktivli] *adv.* in a subjective manner.
—[副] 주관적으로

sub·jec·tiv·i·ty [sʌbdʒektíviti] *n.* [U] a subjective quality.
—[名] 주관성

subject matter [⌐- ∸-] *n.* something thought about, discussed, etc.
—[名] 주제(主題), 논제(論題)

sub·join [səbdʒɔ́in / sʌ́b-] *vt.* add (something) at the end of something written or said.
—[他] …을 추가하다

sub·ju·gate [sʌ́bdʒugèit] *vt.* conquer; subdue.
—[他] …을 정복하다

sub·ju·ga·tion [sʌ̀bdʒugéiʃ(ə)n] *n.* [U] conquest.
—[名] 정복

* **sub·junc·tive** [səbdʒʌ́ŋ(k)tiv] *n.* 《*the* ~》 (*Grammar*) the mood of a verb which expresses a state or action, not as a fact, but as something imagined. **—*adj.*** of this mood.
—[名] 《文法》 가정법 —[形] 가정법의

sub·let [sʌblét] *vt.* rent to another (something that has already been rent to oneself).
—[他] …을 전대(轉貸)하다

sub·li·mate *v.* [sʌ́blimèit →*adj.*] *vt.* make pure; elevate. —*vi.* become pure; become elevated. —*adj.* [-mit, -mèit] purified; sublimated.
—[他] …을 순수하게 하다, 고상하게 하다 —[自] 순화(純化)하다, 승화(昇華)하다 —[形] 순화한; 승화한

sub·li·ma·tion [sʌ̀bliméiʃ(ə)n] *n.* [U] the act of sublimating.
—[名] 순화; 승화

* **sub·lime** [səbláim] *adj.* noble; lofty. ¶*a* ~ *beauty.*
—[形] 숭고한; 장엄한

sub·lime·ly [səbláimli] *adv.* in a sublime manner.
—[副] 숭고하게; 고상하게

sub·lim·i·ty [səblímiti] *n.* (pl. **-ties**) **1.** [U] the state of being sublime. **2.** [C] 《often *pl.*》 someone or something sublime.
—[名] 1. 숭고; 웅대 2. 숭고한 사람(것)

* **sub·ma·rine** *n.* [sʌ́bmərì:n / ∸-⌐ ‖ →*v., adj.*] [C] a warship that can move under water. **—*adj., vt.*** [∸-⌐] *adj.* living. being or growing under water. ¶~ *plants.* **—*vt.*** (*colloq.*) attack (the enemy) by means of a submarine.
—[名] 잠수함 —[形] 수중의, 해저의 —[他] …을 잠수함으로 공격하다

sub·merge [səbmə́:rdʒ] *vt.* put (something) under water; cover (something) with water. ¶*The waves submerged the boat.* —*vi.* sink under water; go under water.
—[他] …을 물속에 가라앉히다; 물에 잠그다 —[自] 가라앉다; 잠수하다

sub·mer·gence [səbmə́:rdʒ(ə)ns] *n.* [U] the act of submerging; the state of being submerged.
—[名] 침수; 잠수; 침몰

sub·mer·sion [səbmə́:rʒ(ə)n / -mə:ʃ(ə)n] *n.* =submergence.

sub·mis·sion [səbmíʃ(ə)n] *n.* [U] **1.** the act of yielding to the power or authority of another. **2.** obedience; humbleness.
—[名] 1. 굴복, 복종 2. 온순; 온화, 겸손

sub·mis·sive [səbmísiv] *adj.* unresisting; obedient.
—[形] 굴종하는, 유순한

sub·mis·sive·ly [səbmísivli] *adv.* in a submissive man-
—[副] 유순하게, 온순하게

ner; obediently.
: **sub·mit** [səbmít] v. (-**mit·ted, -mit·ting**) vt. 1. 《reflexively》 place (oneself) under the control of another. 《~ oneself to》 2. offer (something) for consideration.
—vi. yield; give way. —⑩ 1. …을 복종시키다 2. …을 제출하다; 심의에 붙이다
—⑪ 굴복하다

sub·nor·mal [sʌbnɔ́ːrm(ə)l] adj. below normal.
—n. ⓒ a subnormal person. —⑫ 보통 이하의
—⑬ 저능한 사람

* **sub·or·di·nate** [səbɔ́ːrd(i)nit →v.] adj. 1. lower in rank, value, importance, etc. 2. under the control of others; dependent. —n. ⓒ a person who is below another in rank. —vt. [-nèit] place (something) in a lower rank; make secondary. —⑫ 1. 하위의; 다음가는 2. 종속하는
—⑬ 부하, 아랫사람 —⑩ …을 종속시키다; 하위에 두다

sub·or·di·na·tion [səbɔ̀ːrd(i)néiʃ(ə)n] n. ⓤ 1. the act of subordinating; the state of being subordinated. 2. submission to authority; obedience. —⑬ 1. 하위에 두기(있음); 하위 2. 종속; 복종

sub·or·di·na·tive [səbɔ́ːrd(i)nèitiv / səbɔ́ːdinətiv] adj. subordinate; secondary. —⑫ 종속적인

* **sub·scribe** [səbskráiv] vt. 1. give (money) to some good purpose. ¶~ money to a charity. 2. promise to buy (something). 3. sign one's name to (a document).
—vi. 1. give money. 《~ to something》 ¶~ to a charity.
2. arrange to take a newspaper, a magazine, etc. 3. show agreement. 4. sign one's name. ¶~ to a document. —⑩ 1. …을 기부하다 2. …을 예약하다 3. …에 서명하다
—⑪ 1. 기부하다 2. 구독(購讀)을 예약하다 3. 찬성하다 4. 서명하다

* **sub·scrip·tion** [səbskrípʃ(ə)n] n. ⓤ 1. the act of subscribing. 2. a sum of money subscribed; a contribution or donation. ¶by ~① / raise a ~.② —⑬ 1. 기부; 예약 2. 기부금; 예약금
¶①예약으로/②기부금을 모집하다

sub·se·quence [sʌ́bsikwəns] n. ⓤ the state of being subsequent; a subsequent event or occurrence. —⑬ 뒤; 뒤이어 일어남; 결과

* **sub·se·quent** [sʌ́bsikwənt] adj. coming later; following.
sub·se·quent·ly [sʌ́bsikwəntli] adv. afterward; later. —⑫ 그 후에 일어나는; 뒤의
—⑪ 그 뒤에; 뒤이어

sub·serve [səbsə́ːrv] vt. be of help or use to (something); assist. ⌈ing of use. 2. servility.⌉ —⑩ …에 쓸모가 있다, …을 돕다

sub·ser·vi·ence [səbsə́ːrviəns] n. ⓤ 1. the state of be-
sub·ser·vi·ent [səbsə́ːrviənt] adj. useful. 《~ to》 2. very obedient, like a slave; servile. —⑬ 1. 쓸모 있음 2. 노예근성, 비굴
—⑬ 1. 쓸모 있는 2. 예속적인; 비굴한

sub·side [səbsáid] vi. 1. fall to the bottom; sink gradually. 2. become calm; abate. ¶The storm subsided. —⑪ 1. 내려앉다; 가라앉다 2. 진정되다, 가라앉다

sub·sid·ence [səbsáid(ə)ns, sʌ́bsid-] n. ⓤ the act of subsiding; a downward movement of the ground. —⑬ 진정; [지반(地盤)의] 함몰

sub·sid·i·ar·y [səbsídièri / -iəri] adj. 1. supplementary; assistant. 2. secondary. 3. being given money by a government or another company. —n. ⓒ (pl. **-ar·ies**) 1. 《usu. pl.》 a person or thing that assists. 2. a company most of whose stock is held by another company. —⑫ 1. 보조의 2. 종속적인 3. 보조금을 받는 —⑬ 1. 보조자(물) 2. 자(子)(종속)회사

sub·si·dize [sʌ́bsidàiz] vt. assist (a company, etc.) by giving money. —⑩ [회사 따위]에 보조금을 주다

sub·si·dy [sʌ́bsidi] n. ⓒ (pl. **-dies**) a sum of money given by a government to an enterprise, etc. as help. —⑬ 보조금; 장려금

sub·sist [səbsíst] vi. 1. continue to be; remain in existence; exist. ¶Superstitions still~in many countries.①
2. maintain life; live. 《~ on or by something》 ¶We ~ on rice. —vt. feed. —⑪ 1. 존재하다, 존속하다 ¶①미신은 아직도 많은 나라에 존재한다 2. 살아가다 —⑩ …에 먹을 것을 주다

sub·sist·ence [səbsíst(ə)ns] n. ⓤ 1. existence. 2. means of living; livelihood. ⌈under the soil.⌉ —⑬ 1. 존재 2. 살림, 생계

sub·soil [sʌ́bsɔ̀il] n. ⓤ the layer of earth that lies just⌋ —⑬ 밑흙, 하층토(下層土)

: **sub·stance** [sʌ́bst(ə)ns] n. ⓤ 1. ⓒ the material of which a thing consists; matter. ¶Wood is a solid ~.
2. the real and essential part of a thing; the essence.
3. the chief point of a speech or a book. ¶the ~ of his speech. 4. wealth. ¶a man of ~.①
in substance, ⓐ mainly. ⓑ really; in fact. —⑬ 1. 물질, 물체; 요소, 재료 2. 실체, 본질; 요지; 대의(大意) 4. 자산 ¶①자산가

🔲 ⓐ대체로 ⓑ실제로

* **sub·stan·tial** [səbstǽnʃ(ə)l] adj. 1. really existing; actual. 2. made of a good substance; solid; strong. ¶a ~ building. 3. of real worth; important; considerable. —⑫ 1. 실재(實在)의 2. 견실한, 튼튼한 3. 가치 있는, 중요한, 상당한 ¶①상당한 금액 4. 본질적인 5. 풍부한

¶*a ~ sum of money.*① **4.** essential. **5.** wealthy.

sub·stan·ti·al·i·ty [səbstæ̀nʃiǽliti] *n.* [U] the state of being substantial; real existence; solidity; real worth.
—[名] 실재, 실체; 견고; 진가(眞價)

sub·stan·tial·ly [səbstǽnʃəli] *adv.* essentially; really; mainly; strongly.
—[副] 실질상, 참으로; 대체로; 튼튼하게

sub·stan·ti·ate [səbstǽnʃièit] *vt.* **1.** prove (something) to be true by showing evidence. ¶*~ a rumor.* **2.** give substantial existence to (something); make (something) real.
—[他] 1. …을 입증하다 2. …을 실체화하다

sub·stan·ti·a·tion [səbstæ̀nʃiéiʃ(ə)n] *n.* [U] the act of substantiating; the state of being substantiated; proof; embodiment.
—[名] 입증; 실체화

sub·stan·tive [sʌ́bst(ə)ntiv] *n.* [C] (*Grammar*) a noun; a word or a group of words used as a noun. —*adj.* **1.** (*Grammar*) showing existence; used as a noun. **2.** independent. **3.** real.
—[名] 《文法》 명사, 명사 상당어[구] —[形] 1.《文法》 존재를 나타내는 2. 자립의 3. 실재의

sub·sta·tion [sʌ́bstèiʃ(ə)n] *n.* [C] a branch station.
—[名] 지서(支署), 분국(分局)

:sub·sti·tute [sʌ́bstit(j)ù:t / -tjù:t] *n.* [C] a thing used instead of another; a person taking the place of another. —*vt.* use or place (something) in place of another. 《~ something *for*》 ¶*They substituted Mr. Smith for him.*① —*vi.* take the place of another.
—[名] 대리, 대용품 —[他] …으로 바꾸다, …을 대신 쓰다 ¶①그들은 그 사람 대신 스미드씨를 썼다 —[自] 대리하다

sub·sti·tu·tion [sʌ̀bstit(j)ú:ʃ(ə)n / -tjú:ʃ-] *n.* [U][C] the act of substituting; the state of being substituted.
—[名] 대리, 대용

sub·stra·ta [sʌ́bstréitə, -rǽtə / sʌbstrɑ́:tə] *n.* pl. of **sub·stra·tum.**

sub·stra·tum [sʌbstréitəm, -rǽ- / sʌ́bstrɑ́:-] *n.* [C] (pl. **-stra·ta** or **-stra·tums**) **1.** the layer lying below another. **2.** a basis; a foundation.
—[名] 1. 하층 2. 토대, 기초

sub·struc·ture [sʌ́bstrʌ̀ktʃər, +*U.S.* ––́–] *n.* [C] a structure which forms the foundation of a building; foundation.
—[名] 기초

sub·ter·fuge [sʌ́btərfjù:dʒ] *n.* [C] a trick or an excuse to escape from a difficulty, blame, etc.
—[名] [곤란·비난을 피하는] 핑계, 구실

sub·ter·ra·ne·an [sʌ̀btəréiniən] *adj.* under the earth; underground; hidden.
—[形] 지하의; 숨은

sub·ter·ra·ne·ous [sʌ̀btəréiniəs] *adj.* =subterranean.

sub·ti·tle [sʌ́btàitl] *n.* [C] **1.** an additional title of a book, etc. **2.** printed explanatory words in motion pictures.
—[名] 1. 작은 표제; 부제(副題) 2. 설명자막

·sub·tle [sʌ́tl] *adj.* (**sub·tler, sub·tlest**) **1.** delicate; faint; mysterious. **2.** clever; keen. **3.** cunning; sly.
—[形] 1. 미묘한; 희미한; 신비스러운 2. 민감한 3. 교활한

sub·tle·ty [sʌ́tlti] *n.* (pl. **-ties**) **1.** [U] the quality of being subtle. **2.** [C] something subtle.
—[名] 1. 미묘, 예민, 교묘, 음험 2. 미묘한 것

sub·tly [sʌ́tli] *adv.* in a subtle manner.
—[副] 미묘하게; 예민하게; 교활하게

sub·tract [səbtrǽkt] *vt.* take away; deduct. ↔add ¶*Subtract 2 from 5, and you have 3.*
—[他] …을 빼다, 감하다

·sub·trac·tion [səbtrǽkʃ(ə)n] *n.* [U][C] the act of subtracting.
—[名] 공제; 뺄셈

sub·trop·i·cal [sʌ̀btrɑ́pik(ə)l / -trɔ́p-] *adj.* of the regions bordering on the tropics; nearly tropical.
—[形] 아열대(亞熱帶)의

:sub·urb [sʌ́bə:rb] *n.* [C] 《usu. *pl.*》 a district on the outskirts of a large city.
—[名] 교외

sub·ur·ban [səbə́:rb(ə)n] *adj.* of the suburbs.
—[形] 교외의

sub·ur·bi·a [səbə́:rbiə] *n.* [U] 《*collectively*》 **1.** suburbs. **2.** people living in the suburbs.
—[名] 1. 교외 2. 교외 거주자

sub·ven·tion [səbvénʃ(ə)n] *n.* [C] money given by a government to help or support a study, an undertaking, etc.; subsidy.
—[名] 보조금; 조성금(助成金)

sub·ver·sion [səbvə́:rʒ(ə)n, -ʃ(ə)n / -və́:ʃ(ə)n] *n.* [U] the act of subverting; the state of being subverted; overthrow; ruin.
—[名] 전복, 타도, 파괴

sub·ver·sive [səbvə́:rsiv] *adj.* tending to subvert or overthrow; liable to cause ruin; destructive.
—[形] 전복하는, 타도하는, 파괴하는

sub·vert [səbvə́:rt] *vt.* overthrow; destroy; ruin.
—[他] …을 뒤엎다, 타도(파괴)하다

:sub·way [sʌ́bwèi] *n.* [C] **1.** (*U.S.*) an underground rail-
—[名] 1.《美》 지하철 2.《英》 지하도

succeed

way. **2.** (*Brit.*) an underground passage.

‡ **suc·ceed** [səksíːd] *vi.* **1.** do well; have success. (~ *in* something; ~ *in doing*) ⇒N.B. ↔fail ¶~ *in the examination* / ~ *as an artist.* **2.** be next to take an office, a position, a rank, etc.; follow; become heir. (~ *to* something) ¶~ *to the throne* / *He succeeded to his father's estate.*① ⇒N.B. ―*vt.* **1.** come after and take the place of (someone). (~ *someone as* or *in*) ¶*Elizabeth succeeded Mary as Queen.* / *He succeeded his father in his estate.* **2.** follow (something) in order or time. ¶*Night succeeds day.* / *A great calm succeeded the storm.*

‡ **suc·cess** [səksés] *n.* **1.** U C the act of succeeding; a favorable result; good fortune; triumph. ↔failure **2.** C a person or thing that succeeds.
make a success of (=*succeed in*) *something*.

‡ **suc·cess·ful** [səksésf(u)l] *adj.* having a favorable result; having achieved success.

• **suc·cess·ful·ly** [səksésfuli] *adv.* with success.

• **suc·ces·sion** [səkséʃ(ə)n] *n.* **1.** C the coming of one thing or person after another; a series. ¶*I had a ~ of colds.*① **2.** U the act or right of succeeding to a position, property, etc. ¶*the ~ to the throne.*②
in succession, one after another.

• **suc·ces·sive** [səksésiv] *adj.* coming one after another.

suc·ces·sive·ly [səksésivli] *adv.* one after another.

• **suc·ces·sor** [səksésər] *n.* C a person who succeeds or follows another. [clearly expressed in few words.]

suc·cinct [səksíŋ(k)t] *adj.* (sometimes ~*er*, ~*est*)

suc·cinct·ly [səksíŋ(k)tli] *adv.* in a succinct manner.

suc·cinct·ness [səksíŋ(k)tnis] *n.* U the state of being succinct.

suc·cor, *Brit.* **-cour** [sʌ́kər] *n.* **1.** U help. **2.** C a person or thing that helps. ―*vt.* help (someone in difficulty).

suc·cu·lence [sʌ́kjuləns] *n.* U juiciness.

suc·cu·lent [sʌ́kjulənt] *adj.* full of juice. ¶*a ~ fruit.*

suc·cumb [səkʌ́m] *vi.* **1.** be conquered by a person or thing and obey. **2.** yield to disease; die.

‡ **such** [sʌtʃ, sətʃ] *adj.* (the order with *a* or *an* is *such a*, not *a such*) **1.** (showing a particular person or thing already or to be mentioned or meant) of that kind, degree, or quality. ¶~ *a man* / (*proverb*) *Such master, ~ man.*① / *Such luxury was unfamiliar to her.* **2.** (with *as*) of the same kind, degree, or quality. ¶*children ~ as these* / *There are few ~ towns as this.* / *He is a great scientist ~ as we all admire.*② **3.** (with *that*) of the kind, degree, or quality [that]. ¶*He had ~ a fright that he could not speak.* / *She had ~ a fever that she almost died.*③ **4.** so great, so much, so good, etc. ¶~ *a good man* / ~ *a wonderful time.*
―*pron.* **1.** this or that kind of person or thing. ¶*Such was his real intention.*④ **2.** (with *as*) those people who. ¶*Such as have erred must be punished.* **3.** this thing, these circumstances, etc. ¶*If ~ is the case, I will go.*⑤
1) *as such,* ⓐ as being what has been mentioned. ⓑ
2) *such and such,* some; [a] certain. ⌊in itself.⌋

such·like [sʌ́tʃlàik] *adj.* of such a kind. ―*pron.* persons or things of such a kind.

• **suck** [sʌk] *vt.* **1.** draw (liquid) into the mouth by the action of the lips and tongue; draw the liquid from (something). (~ *something from* (or *out of, through*)) ¶~ *an orange* / ~ *the milk from the bottle.* **2.** draw (moisture, air, etc.) by any process resembling this; absorb. (~ *something from*) ¶*Plants ~ moisture from the earth.* **3.** keep (candy, one's thumb, etc.) in the

suck

―自 1. 성공하다 N.B. 명사형은 succcess 2. 뒤잇다; 뒤를 잇다, 후임이 되다; 상속하다 ¶①그는 아버지의 재산을 상속했다 N.B. 명사형은 succession ―他 1. …의 뒤를 잇다; [지위·재산 따위]를 상속하다 2. …에 잇따르다; …의 뒤에 오다, …에 뒤이어 일어나다

―名 1. 성공, 행운, 승리 2. 성공자, 성공한 것

熟 …을 성공하다
―形 성공한, 결과가 좋은

―副 성공적으로, 운좋게
―名 1. 연속; 뒤이어 일어남 ¶①계속 감기가 들었다 2. 계승; 상속[권] ¶②왕위 계승

熟 잇따라, 연속하여
―形 연속하는, 잇따르는
―副 잇따라, 차례로
―名 계승자

―形 문체가 간결한
―副 간결하게
―名 간결; 간명(簡明)

―名 1. 원조; 구원 2. 구조자(물) ―他 …을 돕다, 구원하다

―名 즙(물기)이 많음
―形 1. 즙이 많은
―自 1. 지다, 굴복하다 2. 병으로 쓰러지다, 죽다

―形 1. 그러한; 이와 같은, 그 같은 ¶①(俚)그 주인에 그 머슴 2. [···같은] 그러한 ¶②그는 우리 모두가 존경하는 그러한 과학자이다 3. …만큼의; 대단히 …한 ¶③그녀는 거의 죽을 뻔한 정도로 열이 높았었다 4. 아주 좋은, 대단한, 멋진, 지독한

―代 1. 이런 사람(것·일) ¶④그의 참뜻은 그런 것이었다 2. 그런 사람들 3. 이런 일; 사정 ¶⑤사정이 그렇다면 내가 가겠다
熟 1)ⓐ그런 것으로서 ⓑ그 자체로서는 2)그렇고 그런, 어떤
―形 이와 같은 ―代 이런 사람(것)

―他 1. …을 빨다, 홀짝거리다 2. …을 흡수하다, 빨아 올리다 3. [손가락 따위]를 핥다, 빨다 4. [지식]을 흡수하다; [이익]을 얻다 ¶①…에서 이익을 보다 ―自 1. 젖을 빨다; 홀짝거리다, 빨다 2. 빠는 소리를 내다

mouth, pushing the tongue against it but not biting. **4.** gain or take in (knowledge, profit, etc.). ¶*~ advantage out of something.*① **—*vi.*** **1.** draw milk from a breast or bottle into the mouth; draw something by sucking. **2.** make the sound of sucking.
—*n.* **1.** [U] the act of sucking; the sound or force of sucking. ¶*give ~ to a baby.*② **2.** [C] a small drink; what is sucked at one time. ¶*take a ~ at something.*③
—[名] 1. 빨기; 젖을 빨기; 빠는 소리; 빠는 힘 ¶②어린아이에게 젖을 먹이다 2. 한 번 빨기; 한 번 홀짝거리기 ¶③…을 한 번 빨다

suck·er [sʌ́kər] *n.* [C] **1.** a person or thing that sucks; a baby or young animal. **2.** a disc-shaped organ of some animals used for sucking or holding to a surface.
—[名] 1. 빠는 사람(것); [젖을 떼지 않은] 어린아이(짐승) 2. [문어 따위의] 흡반(吸盤)

suck·ing [sʌ́kiŋ] *adj.* being in the state of drinking milk.
—[形] 젖이 안 떨어진

suck·le [sʌ́kl] *vt.* feed (a baby) with milk; bring up.
—[他] …에 젖을 먹이다, …을 기르다

suck·ling [sʌ́kliŋ] *n.* [C] a baby or young animal fed with milk.
—[名] 젖먹이, 젖먹이 짐승

suc·tion [sʌ́kʃ(ə)n] *n.* [U] the act of sucking. ¶*a ~ pump.*
—[名] 흡수, 흡인, 빨기

‡ **sud·den** [sʌ́dn] *adj.* unexpected; quick; rapid. ¶*his ~ death.*① **—*n.*** [U] the state of being sudden.
1) ***all of a sudden,*** suddenly.
2) ***on a sudden,*** suddenly.
—[形] 갑작스러운, 불시의 ¶①그의 급사 —[名] 갑작스러움
[熟] 1)갑자기, 불시에 2)갑자기, 불시에

‡ **sud·den·ly** [sʌ́dnli] *adv.* in a sudden manner.
—[副] 갑자기, 불시에

suds [sʌdz] *n. pl.* soapy water; small round balls of soapy water.
—[名] 비눗물, 비누거품

sue [su: / s(j)u:] *vt.* **1.** make a claim against (someone) in a court of law. ¶*~ a man for damages.*① **2.** beg. 《~ someone *for*》 **—*vi.*** **1.** make a claim in a court of law. 《~ *for* something》 ¶*~ for damages.* **2.** beg; ask. 《~ *for* something》 ¶*~ for mercy.*
—[他] 1. …을 고소하다 ¶①손해 배상으로 남을 고소하다 2. …을 간청하다, 구하다 —[自] 1. 고소하다 2. 간청하다; 구하다

Sue [su: / s(j)u:] *n.* a nickname for Susan or Susanna.
—[名] Susan, Susanna 의 애칭

suede [sweid] *n.* [U] a kind of soft, tanned leather.
—[名] 스웨드 가죽

Su·ez [sú(:)ez, -ˊ / s(j)ú(:)iz] *n.* the narrow neck of land between Asia and Africa.
—[名] 수에즈 운하

Suez Canal [ˊ-- -ˊ], **the** *n.* the canal across Suez.
—[名] 수에즈 운하

‡ **suf·fer** [sʌ́fər] *vt.* **1.** have, feel, or experience (pain, hardship, discomfort, grief, etc.). ¶*~ loss / ~ punishment.*① **2.** 《usu. in *negative*》 allow; permit; endure. ¶*I'll not ~ such conduct.*② / *These trees cannot ~ a cold winter.* **—*vi.*** **1.** feel pain, grief, etc. 《~ *from* something》 ¶*~ from a fever*③ / *Japan is suffering from overpopulation.* **2.** experience harm, damage, loss, etc.; be punished. 《~ *from* something》
—[他] 1. [고통·손해 따위]를 입다, 받다 ¶①벌을 받다 2. …을 참다, 용서하다 ¶②그런 행위는 용서할 수 없다 —[自] 1. 괴로와하다, 앓다 ¶③열병에 걸리다 2. 해를 입다, 손해를 보다; 벌을 받다

suf·fer·a·ble [sʌ́f(ə)rəbl] *adj.* bearable.
—[形] 참을 수 있다

suf·fer·ance [sʌ́f(ə)r(ə)ns] *n.* [U] the power to bear.
on sufferance, allowed, but not really supported.
—[名] 허용력, 인내력
[熟] 묵인 아래, 눈감아 주어

suf·fer·er [sʌ́f(ə)rər] *n.* [C] a person who suffers.
—[名] 고통을 받는 사람, 환자

* **suf·fer·ing** [sʌ́f(ə)riŋ] *n.* **1.** [U] pain. **2.** 《often *pl.*》 something that is suffered by someone.
—[名] 1. 괴로움 2. 고통, 고생

* **suf·fice** [səfáis, +*U.S.* -fáiz] *vi.* be enough. **—*vt.*** satisfy.
—[自] 자라다, 충분히 있다 —[他] …을 만족시키다

suf·fi·cien·cy [səfíʃ(ə)nsi] *n.* [U] 《usu. *a ~*》 an amount which is enough.
—[名] 충분한 분량

‡ **suf·fi·cient** [səfíʃ(ə)nt] *adj.* enough. ¶*a ~ dinner for us.*
—[名] 충분한

* **suf·fi·cient·ly** [səfíʃ(ə)ntli] *adv.* enough.
—[副] 충분하게

* **suf·fix** *n.* [sʌ́fiks →*v.*] [C] (*Grammar*) an addition placed at the end of a word. **—*vt.*** [-ˊ] add (-ly, -ness, etc.) as a suffix.
—[名] 《文法》 접미사 —[他] …을 접미사로서 붙이다

suf·fo·cate [sʌ́fəkèit] *vt.* kill (someone) by stopping the breath; make it difficult for (someone) to breathe. **—*vi.*** be difficult to breathe.
—[他] …을 질식[사]시키다 —[自] 질식하다

suf·fo·ca·tion [sʌ̀fəkéiʃ(ə)n] *n.* [U] the act of suffocating.
—[名] 질식

suf·frage [sʌ́fridʒ] *n.* **1.** [C] a vote in favor of someone or something. **2.** [U] the right to vote.
—[名] 1. [찬성] 투표 2. 투표권, 선거권

suf·fuse [səfjú:z] *vt.* spread all over; cover.
be suffused with, be full of.
—[他] …을 덮다
[熟] …이 가득차 있다

suf·fu·sion [səfjú:ʒ(ə)n] *n.* [U] the act of suffusing; the state of being full.
—[名] 가득 채우기; 충만

sugar — sulfur

‡ **sug·ar** [ʃúgər] *n.* ⓤⓒ a sweet white powder used in cooking. —*vt.* 1. make (something) sweet by mixing sugar. 2. make (someone or something) pleasant.
—ⓝ 설탕 —ⓥ 1. …을 설탕으로 달게 하다 2. …에 알랑거리다, 기분좋게 하다

sugar beet [⌞-⌞] *n.* a kind of plant from which sugar is made.
—ⓝ 사탕무우, 첨채(甜菜)

sugar candy [⌞-⌞-] *n.* a kind of candy made by boiling pure sugar.
—ⓝ 얼음사탕

sugar cane [⌞-⌞] *n.* a tall grass from which sugar is obtained.
—ⓝ 사탕수수

sug·ar·y [ʃúgəri] *adj.* sweet like sugar.
—ⓝ 설탕처럼 단

‡ **sug·gest** [sədʒést, +U.S. səgdʒést] *vt.* 1. recall (an idea) to the mind of a person. (~ something *to*) ¶*Winter suggests skating and skiing.*① 2. offer (a plan) for consideration. ¶*Tom suggested that we go to a coffee shop.*② (~ something *to*; ~ *that*…; ~ *doing*) 3. hint; show (something) in an indirect way. (~ something *to*; ~ *that*…; ~ *doing*)
—ⓥ 1. …을 연상시키다 ¶①겨울은 스케이트나 스키를 연상시킨다 2. …을 제안하다 ¶②톰은 다방에 가자고 제안했다 3. …을 암시하다, 넌지시 비치다

• **sug·ges·tion** [sədʒéstʃ(ə)n, +U.S. səgdʒés-] *n.* 1. ⓤ the act of recalling an idea to the mind of a person; ⓒ an idea brought to the mind by a natural connection. 2. ⓤ the act of offering a plan; ⓒ a plan, an idea, etc. that is offered. 3. ⓤ the act of showing something in an indirect way; ⓒ a hint.
—ⓝ 1. 연상시키기; 연상 2. 제안하기; 제안된 것 3. 암시

sug·ges·tive [sədʒéstiv, +U.S. səgdʒés-] *adj.* suggesting.
—ⓐ 암시적인, 연상시키는

sug·ges·tive·ly [sədʒéstivli, +U.S. səgdʒés-] *adv.* with a suggestion.
—ⓥ 암시적으로

su·i·cid·al [sù:isáidl / s(j)ù(:)i-] *adj.* of suicide; causing suicide.
—ⓐ 자살의; 자살적인

• **su·i·cide** [sú:isàid / s(j)ú(:)i-] *n.* 1. ⓤⓒ the act of killing oneself. 2. ⓒ a person who kills himself.
—ⓝ 1. 자살행위 2. 자살자

‡ **suit** [su:t / s(j)u:t] *n.* 1. ⓒ a set of clothes worn together, as a jacket and either trousers or a skirt. 2. ⓒ a claim or question to be settled by a court of law; an action taken to a court of law. ¶*start a ~ to cover damages*① / *bring (or institute) a ~ against someone.*② 3. ⓒ one of the four sets (spades, hearts, diamonds, and clubs) of playing cards. 4. ⓤⓒ an act of asking or requesting, esp. for marriage made by men. ¶*make ~ to someone*③ / *press (or push) one's ~.*④
follow suit, ⓐ follow the example of another. ⓑ play a card of the same suit as that led.
—*vt.* 1. make (someone or something) suitable; fit. (~ something *to*; ~ someone *for doing*; ~ *to do*) ¶*~ one's action to one's word* / *He is not suited for teaching.*; *He is not suited to be a teacher.* 2. (used in *passive*) look well on (someone or something). ¶*This necktie does not ~ me.* 3. be convenient for (someone); satisfy; please. (~ *to do*) ¶*~ oneself*⑤ / *The climate suits me.* / *Would it ~ you to come tomorrow?* / *It's impossible to ~ everyone.*⑥
—ⓝ 1. [한 벌의] 옷 2. 고소, 소송 ¶①손해배상 소송을 제기하다/②…을 고소하다 3. [트럼프 패의] 한 벌, 짝패 4. 청원, 소망, [특히] 구혼 ¶③…에 청원하다/④탄원하다; 줄기차게 구애하다

熟 ⓐ남이 하는 대로 하다 ⓑ[카아드 놀이에서] 먼저 낸 패와 같은 종류의 패를 내다

—ⓥ 1. …을 적합시키다, 맞추다 2. [의복 따위가] …에 어울리다 3. …에게 형편이 좋다; …의 마음에 들다 ¶⑤마음대로 하다/⑥모든 사람의 마음에 들게 할 수는 없다 —ⓥ 적합하다, 어울리다

suit·a·bil·i·ty [sù:təbíliti / s(j)ù:-] *n.* ⓤ the state of being suitable.
—ⓝ 적합, 적당, 어울림

• **suit·a·ble** [sú:təbl / s(j)ú:-] *adj.* proper; well-fitting. (~ *for* or *to* someone or something)
—ⓐ 어울리는, 적당한

suit·a·bly [sú:təbli / s(j)ú:-] *adv.* in a suitable manner.
—ⓥ 적당하게, 어울리게

• **suit·case** [sú:tkèis / s(j)ú:t-] *n.* ⓒ a flat traveling case for carrying clothes.
—ⓝ 수우트케이스

suite [swi:t →2] *n.* ⓒ 1. a number of things making a set or series. 2. [+U.S. su:t] a set of furniture for one room. 3. (*Music*) several instrumental movements or pieces composed as a group. 4. a group of servants; a staff.
—ⓝ 1. 한 벌, 일조 2. 가구 한 벌 3. (樂) 조곡(組曲) 4. 수행원

suit·or [sú:tər / s(j)ú:tə] *n.* ⓒ 1. a man who asks a woman to marry him. 2. a person who brings a case into a law court. 3. a person who makes a request.
—ⓝ 1. 구혼자 2. 원고(原告) 3. 청원자

sul·fate, *Brit.* **-phate** [sʌ́lfeit] *n.* ⓤⓒ (*Chemistry*) any salt of sulfuric acid.
—ⓝ (化) 황산염

• **sul·fur**, *Brit.* **-phur** [sʌ́lfər] *n.* ⓤ (*Chemistry*) a yellow
—ⓝ (化) 유황 —ⓐ 유황색의

material burning with a blue flame and producing a sharp smell. —*adj.* greenish-yellow.

sul·fu·re·ous, *Brit.* **-phu-** [sʌlfjúəriəs] *adj.* of or containing sulfur; like sulfur; sulfurous.
—[形] 유황의, 유황을 함유하는, 유황 모양의

sul·fu·ric, *Brit.* **-phu-** [sʌlfjúərik] *adj.* containing or of sulfur.
—[形] 유황을 함유한; 유황의

sul·fur·ous, *Brit.* **-phur-** [sʌ́lfərəs, -fjur-] *adj.* of or containing sulfur; sulfureous.
—[形] 유황의, 유황을 함유하는

sulk [sʌlk] *vi.* keep silent in an ill-humored state; be sullen. —*n.* 《usu. *pl.*》 a sulky state.
—[自] 실쭉하다 —[名] 실쭉하기, 뿌루퉁함

sulk·i·ly [sʌ́lkili] *adv.* in a sullen mood.
—[副] 실쭉하여, 삐져서

sulk·i·ness [sʌ́lkinis] *n.* [U] the state of being sulky; sullenness; displeasure.
—[名] 실쭉함, 부루퉁함

sulk·y [sʌ́lki] *adj.* (**sulk·i·er, sulk·i·est**) in a bad humor; sullen. —*n.* [C] (pl. **sulk·ies**) a light two-wheeled carriage for one person. ⇒fig.
—[形] 뿌루퉁한 —[名] 1인승 2륜 경마차

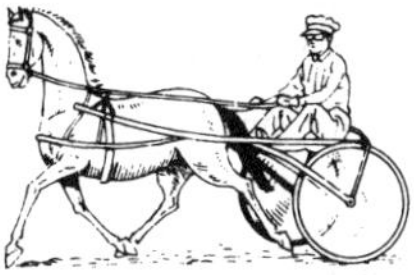

〔sulky〕

∗ **sul·len** [sʌ́lin] *adj.* **1.** silent; showing bad humor. **2.** gloomy; dismal.
—[形] 1. 실쭉한, 뿌루퉁한 2. 음산한, 음울한

sul·len·ly [sʌ́linli] *adv.* in a sullen mood.
—[副] 실쭉하여

sul·len·ness [sʌ́linnis] *n.* [U] the state of being sullen.
—[名] 실쭉함, 뚱함

sul·ly [sʌ́li] *vt.* (**-lied**) make (something) dirty; cause the loss of (respect, etc.).
—[他] …을 더럽히다;[명성 따위]를 더럽히다

sul·phate [sʌ́lfeit] *n.* (*Brit.*) =sulfate.

∗ **sul·phur** [sʌ́lfər] *n.* (*Brit.*) =sulfur.

sul·phu·re·ous [sʌlfjúəriəs] *adj.* (*Brit.*) =sulfureous.

sul·phu·ric [sʌlfjúərik] *adj.* (*Brit.*) =sulfuric.

sul·phur·ous [sʌ́lfərəs, -fjur-] *adj.* (*Brit.*) =sulfurous.

sul·tan [sʌ́lt(ə)n] *n.* [C] **1.** a Mohammedan ruler. **2.** 《*the S-*》 the former emperor of Turkey.
—[名] 1. 회교국 군주 2. [옛날의] 터어키 황제

sul·tan·a [sʌltǽnə / -tά:nə] *n.* [C] the wife of a sultan.
—[名] 회교국 왕비

sul·tan·ate [sʌ́ltənèit, +*Brit.* -tənit] *n.* [U] the position of a sultan; [C] the territory of a sultan.
—[名] 설탄의 지위(영토)

sul·try [sʌ́ltri] *adj.* (**-tri·er, -tri·est**) (of weather, etc.) hot and moist.
—[形] 무더운

⁑ **sum** [sʌm] *n.* [C] **1.** the result of adding two or more numbers or quantities; the total numbers or quantities. **2.** an amount of money. **3.** a problem in arithmetic; 《*pl.*》 calculation. ¶*do sums.*① **4.** 《*the* ~》 the main points; a summary.
—[名] 1. 화(和); 총계, 합계 2. 금액 3. 산수 문제; 계산 ¶①계산하다 4. 대의, 개요

in sum, in short.
[熟] 요는

—*v.* (**summed, sum·ming**) *vt.* **1.** add together; total. 《~ *up*》 **2.** express the main points of (something). 《~ *up*》 —*vi.* make a summary.
—[他] 1. …을 합계(총계)하다 2. …을 요약하다 —[自] 요약하다

to sum up, in short; to speak briefly.
[熟] 요약하면

sum·ma·rize [sʌ́mərὰiz] *vt.* sum up; speak briefly.
—[他] …을 요약하다

∗ **sum·ma·ry** [sʌ́məri] *n.* [C] (pl. **-ries**) a brief statement giving only the main points. —*adj.* **1.** brief. ¶*a* ~ *account.* **2.** done without delay. ¶*a* ~ *punishment.*
—[他] 적요(摘要), 개요 —[形] 1. 간략한 2. 즉결의

⁑ **sum·mer** [sʌ́mər] *n.* [U][C] 《usu. ~ or *the* ~》 **1.** the hottest season of the year, between spring and autumn. **2.** 《usu. *the* ~》 a period of the finest development. —*adj.* in or like summer. —*vi.* pass the summer.
—[名] 1. 여름 2. 장년기, 한창때 —[形] 여름의 —[自] 여름을 치내다

sum·mer·time [sʌ́mərtὰim] *n.* [U] the season of summer.
—[名] 여름철

summer time [⌐- ⌐] *n.* (*Brit.*) the system of time in summer, when the clocks are advanced one hour; daylight-saving time.
—[名] 《英》 하계 일광 절약시간

∗ **sum·mit** [sʌ́mit] *n.* [C] **1.** the top; the highest point. **2.** (of government, etc.) the highest members of the government, the staff, etc.
—[名] 1. 꼭대기, 정상; 정점 2. [정부 따위의] 최고 수뇌진

⁑ **sum·mon** [sʌ́mən] *vt.* **1.** order (someone) to come [to court]. **2.** arouse; gather together. ¶~ *one's courage.*
—[他] 1. …을 소환하다, 부르다 2. [용기 따위]를 불러 일으키다

sum·mons [sʌ́mənz] *n.* [C] (pl. ~·**es** [-iz]) **1.** the act of
—[名] 1. 소환; 소집; 불러내기 2. 소환

S

ordering (someone) to come [to court]. **2.** a message containing such an order. **—***vt.* (*colloq.*) summon (someone) to court.
장 **—**[他] …을 소환하다

sump·tu·ar·y [sʌ́m(p)tʃuèri / -tju(ə)ri] *adj.* of or about saving money or expenses.
—[形] 절약의; 사치를 금하는

sump·tu·ous [sʌ́m(p)tʃuəs] *adj.* costly; magnificent.
—[形] 사치스러운; 화려한

⁑sun [sʌn] *n.* **1.** [C] 《usu. *the* ~》 the brightest heavenly body, around which the earth and the other planets move. **2.** [U] 《often *the* ~》 the light and heat of the sun; sunshine. ¶*lay at full length in the* ~① / *take the* ~.② **3.** [C] a fixed star around which planets move. **4.** [C] one's best days; glory. ¶*hail the rising* ~.③
—[名] **1.** 해, 태양 **2.** 일광, 양지 ¶①양지에 드러눕다/②햇볕을 쬐다 **3.** [위성을 가진] 항성(恒星) **4.** 전성[기], 한창[때] ¶③신흥세력에 아첨하다

1) ***a place in the sun,*** an advantageous position; a position of success.
2) ***see the sun,*** be alive.
3) ***under the sun,*** on earth.
[熟] 1)좋은 환경, 양지바른 곳 2)살아 있다 3)이 세상에

—*v.* (**sunned, sun·ning**) *vt.* expose (something) to the sun. **—***vi.* expose oneself to the sun.
—[他] …을 햇볕에 쬐다 **—**[自] 일광욕하다, 햇볕을 쬐다

Sun. Sunday.

sun bath [ˊ ˋ] *n.* an exposure of the body to sunshine.
—[名] 일광욕

⁑sun·beam [sʌ́nbìːm] *n.* [C] a ray of sunlight.
—[名] 햇볕, 일광

sun·bon·net [sʌ́nbànit / -bɔ̀n-] *n.* [C] a bonnet with a wide brim to shade the face. ⇒fig.
—[名] [부인·유아의] 햇볕 가리는 모자

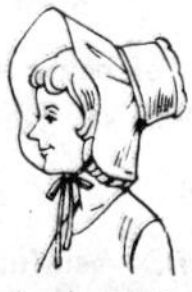
[sunbonnet]

sun·burn [sʌ́nbəːrn] *n.* [C][U] a reddening the skin, caused by excessive exposure to the sun. **—***v.* (**-burned** or **-burnt**) *vi.* become burned by the sun.
—[名] 볕에 탐 **—**[自] 볕에 타다

—*vt.* (of the sun) burn the skin of (someone).
—[他] …을 볕에 타게 하다

sun·burned [sʌ́nbəːrnd] *adj.* made dark by exposure to the sun.
—[形] 햇볕에 탄

sun·burnt [sʌ́nbəːrnt] *v.* pt. and pp. of **sunburn**. **—***adj.* =sunburned.

sun·dae [sʌ́ndi, -dei / -dei] *n.* [C] ice cream with syrup and fruit, etc. placed on top.
—[名] 과즙을 넣은 아이스크리임의 일종

⁑Sun·day [sʌ́ndi, -dei] *n.* the first day of the week; (among Christians) the day of rest and worship. ⇒[N.B.]
—[名] 일요일; 안식일, 주일 [N.B.] Sun.으로 줄임

Sunday school [ˊ- ˋ] *n.* a school held on Sunday for studying religion and the Bible.
—[名] 주일학교

sun·der [sʌ́ndər] *vt.* (*archaic* or *poetic*) divide; separate.
—[他] 《古·詩》 …을 나누다, 베다

sun·dew [sʌ́nd(j)ùː / -djùː] *n.* [C] a plant with sticky hairs growing in a marsh.
—[名] 끈끈이주걱, 끈끈이귀개

sun·di·al [sʌ́ndài(ə)l] *n.* [C] an instrument that shows the time by position of the shadow thrown by sunlight. ⇒fig.
—[名] 해시계

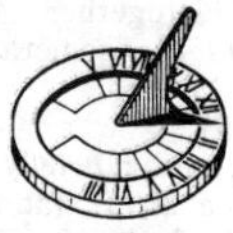
[sundial]

sun·down [sʌ́ndàun] *n.* [C] sunset.
—[名] 일몰

sun-dried [sʌ́ndràid] *adj.* dried by the sun.
—[形] 볕에 말린

sun·dry [sʌ́ndri] *adj.* various. **—***n.* [C] (pl. **-dries**) 《usu. *pl.*》 various small articles; groceries.
—[形] 여러가지의 **—**[名] 잡화, 잡동사니

all and sundry, everybody.
[熟] 각자 모두

sun·flow·er [sʌ́nflàuər] *n.* [C] a tall plant with large yellow flowers.
—[名] 해바라기

⁑sung [sʌŋ] *v.* pp. of **sing**.

sun·glass·es [sʌ́nglæ̀siz / -glɑ̀ːs-] *n. pl.* spectacles with colored glass to protect the eyes from the sun.
—[名] [햇빛을 가리는] 색안경

⁑sunk [sʌŋk] *v.* pp. and pt. of **sink**.

***sunk·en** [sʌ́ŋk(ə)n] *v.* pp. of **sink**.
—*adj.* **1.** sunk. **2.** (of eyes, cheeks, etc.) fallen; hollow.
—[形] **1.** 가라앉은 **2.** [눈·뺨 따위가] 움푹한, 푹 팬

sun lamp [ˊ ˋ] *n.* an electric lamp which gives off ultraviolet rays.
—[名] 태양등(자외선을 방사함)

sun·less [sʌ́nlis] *adj.* without sunlight; dark.
—[形] 볕이 들지 않는; 어두운

***sun·light** [sʌ́nlàit] *n.* [U] the light of the sun.
—[名] 햇볕

sun·lit [sʌ́nlìt] *adj.* lighted by the sun.
—[形] 볕이 드는

sun·ni·ly [sʌ́nili] *adv.* with much sunlight; merrily.
—[副] 양지바르게; 명랑하게

sunny [1155] **superfluous**

- **sun·ny** [sʌ́ni] *adj.* (-ni·er, -ni·est) 1. having much sunlight. ¶*a ~ garden.*① 2. cheerful; bright. ¶*look on the ~ side of things.*② —㉠ 1. 양지바른 ¶①양지바른 정원 2. 명랑한, 밝은 ¶②사물을 낙관하다
- **sun·proof** [sʌ́nprùːf] *adj.* not allowing the rays of the sun to pass through something; not affected by the rays of the sun. —㉠ 햇볕이 통하지 못하는; 내광성(耐光性)의
- **sun·rise** [sʌ́nràiz] *n.* Ⓤ the rising of the sun; the time [when the sun rises. ↔sunset] —㉢ 해돋이; 일출 시각
- **sun·room** [sʌ́nrùː(ː)m] *n.* Ⓒ a room with many windows to let in sunlight; a sun parlor. —㉢ 일광욕실
- **sun·set** [sʌ́nsèt] *n.* Ⓤ the setting of the sun; the time when the sun sets. ↔sunrise —㉢ 일몰; 일몰 시각
  sun·shade [sʌ́nʃèid] *n.* Ⓒ 1. a parasol. 2. a window covering to shade a room from the rays of the sun. —㉢ 1. 양산 2. 차양
- **sun·shine** [sʌ́nʃàin] *n.* Ⓤ 1. the light or rays of the sun. ¶*in the ~.*① 2. fine weather. 3. brightness; cheerfulness. ¶*Her smile is always full of ~.*② —㉢ 1. 햇볕 ¶①햇볕에[서] 2. 맑은 날씨 3. 쾌활, 명랑 ¶②그녀의 웃음은 언제나 명랑하다
  sun·shin·y [sʌ́nʃàini] *adj.* of or full of sunshine. —㉢ 양지바른, 갠
  sun·spot [sʌ́nspɑ̀t / -spɔ̀t] *n.* Ⓒ a dark point on the sun. —㉢ 태양의 흑점
  sun·stroke [sʌ́nstròuk] *n.* Ⓤ a sudden illness caused by exposure of the heat of the sun. ¶*take* (or *be affected by*) *~.*① —㉢ 일사병(日射病) ¶①일사병에 걸리다
  sun·ward [sʌ́nwərd] *adv.* toward the sun. —*adj.* fac- [ing the sun.] —㉠ 태양쪽으로 —㉠ 태양쪽으로의
  sun·wards [sʌ́nwərdz] *adv., adj.* =sunward
  sup¹ [sʌp] *v.* (**supped, sup·ping**) *vi.* eat supper. ¶*~ on bread.* —*vt.* give a supper to (someone). —㉢ 저녁을 먹다 —㉠ …에 저녁을 주다
  sup² [sʌp] *vi., vt.* (**supped, sup·ping**) take a little (liquid or liquid food) into the mouth at a time. —*n.* Ⓒ a little mouthful of liquid; a sip. —㉢㉠ […을] 홀짝홀짝 마시다 —㉢ 한 번 마시기, 한 모금
  su·per- [súːpər / s(j)úːpə-] *pref.* above; more than. —(接頭) 위; 이상; 초(超); 과(過)
  su·per·a·bun·dance [sùːp(ə)rəbʌ́ndəns / s(j)ùː-] *n.* Ⓤ Ⓒ an amount more than is usual or needed. —㉢ 과잉, 여분
  su·per·a·bun·dant [sùːp(ə)rəbʌ́ndənt / s(j)ùː-] *adj.* more than is usual or needed. [further.] —㉠ 과잉의, 여분의
  su·per·add [sùːpəræd / s(j)úːp-] *vt.* add (something) —㉠ …을 다시 보태다
  su·per·an·nu·ate [sùːpərǽnjuèit / s(j)úːp-] *vt.* cause (someone) to leave a school or a place of employment because he is too weak or too old. —㉠ …을 병약(病弱)하여(노령으로) 퇴학(퇴직)시키다
  su·per·an·nu·a·tion [sùːpəræ̀njuéiʃ(ə)n / s(j)úːp-] *n.* 1. Ⓤ the act of superannuating; the state of being superannuated. 2. Ⓒ money given to someone who leaves his work because of old age. —㉢ 1. 노령 퇴직 2. 퇴직금; 은급, 연금(年金)
  su·perb [supə́ːrb / s(j)u(ː)pə́ːb] *adj.* (sometimes ~·er, ~·est) very grand and beautiful. [manner.] —㉠ 멋들어진, 훌륭한
  su·perb·ly [supə́ːrbli / s(j)u(ː)pə́ːb-] *adv.* in a superb —㉠ 당당하게, 훌륭히
  su·per·car·go [súːpərkɑ̀ːrgou / s(j)úːpəkɑ̀ːgou] *n.* Ⓒ (pl. -**goes** or -**gos**) an officer on a merchant ship who has charge of the goods carried on the ship. —㉢ [상선에서 화주를 대리하는] 화물 관리인
  su·per·cil·i·ous [sùːpərsíliəs / s(j)úː-pəsíliəs] *adj.* proud; treating others as if they were not so good as oneself. —㉠ 거만한, 건방진
  su·per·em·i·nent [sùːpəréminənt / s(j)úː-] *adj.* having higher rank, character, etc. [excellent.] —㉠ 탁월한, 뛰어난
  su·per·ex·cel·lent [sùːpəréks(ə)lənt / s(j)úː-] *adj.* very —㉠ 아주 우수한, 무상의
  su·per·fi·cial [sùːpərfíʃ(ə)l / s(j)úːpə-] *adj.* on the surface only; not deep; shallow. ↔profound —㉠ 표면의; 천박한, 피상적인
  su·per·fi·ci·al·i·ty [sùːpərfìʃiǽliti / s(j)úːpə-] *n.* Ⓤ the state or quality of being superficial. —㉢ 표면적인, 천박, 피상적임
  su·per·fi·cial·ly [sùːpərfíʃəli / s(j)úːpə-] *adv.* in a superficial manner; not thoroughly. —㉠ 표면적으로, 천박하게, 피상적으로
  su·per·fine [sùːpərfáin / s(j)úːpə-] *adj.* very fine. —㉠ 극상의, 최상의
  su·per·flu·i·ty [sùːpərflúː(ː)iti / s(j)úːpə-] *n.* (pl. -**ties**) 1. Ⓤ a greater amount than is needed. 2. (usu. *pl.*) something not needed. —㉢ 1. 여분, 과잉, 과다 2. 여분의 것
  su·per·flu·ous [su(ː)pə́ːrfluəs / s(j)u(ː)pə́ː-] *adj.* more than is needed; excessive; needless. —㉠ 여분의; 불필요한

su·per·flu·ous·ly [su(:)pə́:rfluəsli / s(j)u(:)pə́:-] *adv.* in a superfluous manner; excessively; needlessly. —[副] 여분으로, 불필요하게

su·per·hu·man [sù:pər(h)jú:mən / s(j)ù:pəhjú:-] *adj.* above or beyond what is human; supernatural; divine. —[形] 초인적인; 사람의 짓이 아닌, 신의 솜씨인

su·per·in·tend [sù:p(ə)rinténd / s(j)ù:-] *vt.* watch, direct, or manage (work, an institution, or workers). —[他] …을 감독하다, 관리하다

su·per·in·tend·ence [sù:p(ə)rinténdəns / s(j)ù:-] *n.* [U] guidance and direction; management. —[名] 감독, 관리, 지휘

* **su·per·in·tend·ent** [sù:p(ə)rinténdənt / s(j)ù:-] *n.* [C] a person who watches, directs, or manages others. —[名] 감독자, 관리자

⁑ **su·pe·ri·or** [supíəriər / s(j)u:-] *adj.* **1.** higher or better in quality, value, rank, etc. 《~ *to*》 ↔inferior ¶~ *knowledge*① / *be* ~ *to temptation.*② **2.** proud. ¶*with a* ~ *air*③ —*n.* [C] **1.** a person who is superior. **2.** the head of a religious house. —[形] 1. 뛰어난, 우월한 ¶①뛰어난 지식/②유혹에 지지 않다 2. 거만한 ¶③잘난 듯이 —[名] 1. 뛰어난 사람, 우월한 사람, 상관, 선배 2. 수도원장

su·pe·ri·or·i·ty [supìəriɔ́:riti, -ári- / s(j)u:pìəriɔ́r-] *n.* [U] the state or quality of being superior. ↔inferiority —[名] 우월, 탁월, 뛰어남

* **su·per·la·tive** [supə́:rlətiv, s(j)u:pə́:-] *adj.* **1.** better than all others. **2.** (*Grammar*) expressing the highest degree of an adjective and adverb. —[形] 1. 최상의 비길데 없는 2. 《文法》 최상급의

—*n.* **1.** 《*the* ~》 (*Grammar*) the form of the highest degree of an adjective or adverb. **2.** [C] a word or words expressing this degree. **3.** [C] a very good person or thing. —[名] 1. 《文法》 최상급 2. 최상급의 단어 3. 최상급의 사람(것)

su·per·man [sú:pərmæ̀n / s(j)ú:pə-] *n.* [C] (pl. **-men** [-mèn]) a person who is more than human in ability. —[名] 초인(超人)

super·market [sú:pərmà:rkit / sjú:pəmà:-] *n.* [C] a large self-service store. —[名] 수우퍼마아켓

su·per·nal [su(:)pə́:rnl / s(j)u(:)-] *adj.* heavenly; divine. —[形] 하늘 위에 있는; 신의

su·per·nat·u·ral [sù:pərnǽtʃ(u)rəl / s(j)ù(:)-] *adj.* above or beyond what is natural; not explained by the laws of nature; heavenly; divine. —*n.* 《*the* ~》 something which is supernatural. —[形] 초자연의; 불가사의한; 신의 솜씨인 —[名] 초자연력, 신비

su·per·nu·mer·ar·y [sù:pərn(j)ú:m(ə)rèri / s(j)ù:pənjú:m(ə)rəri] *adj.* more than the usual or necessary number. —*n.* [C] (**-ar·ies**) a supernumerary person or thing. —[形] 정원 외의, 여분의 —[名] 여분의 인원(것)

su·per·pose [sù:pərpóuz / s(j)ù:pə-] *vt.* place (something) above or on something else. —[他] …을 겹쳐놓다, 위에 놓다

su·per·po·si·tion [sù:pərpəzíʃ(ə)n / s(j)ù:pə-] *n.* [U] the act of superposing; the state of being superposed. —[名] [물건을] 포개기, 겹쳐놓기

su·per·scrip·tion [sù:pərskrípʃ(ə)n / s(j)ù:pə-] *n.* [C] **1.** the act of writing one's name, etc. on or outside of something. **2.** a name, address, etc. written on or outside a letter, a parcel, etc. —[名] 1. 위에 쓰기 2. 표제, 제목, 주소 성명

su·per·sede [sù:pərsí:d / s(j)ù(:)pə-] *vt.* take the place of (someone or something); cause (something) to be set aside. ¶~ *an old car with a new one.*① —[他] …에 대신 들어서다, …을 바꾸다 ¶①헌 차를 새 차와 바꾸다

su·per·ses·sion [sù:pərséʃ(ə)n / s(j)ù(:)pə-] *n.* [U] the act of superseding; the state of being superseded. —[名] 폐기, 대용, 경질

su·per·son·ic [sù:pərsánik / s(j)ú:pəsɔ́n-] *adj.* faster than sound. —[形] 초음속의

* **su·per·sti·tion** [sù:pərstíʃ(ə)n, / s(j)ù:pə-] *n.* [U] an unreasoning fear or belief in something unknown or mysterious. —[名] 미신

su·per·sti·tious [sù:pərstíʃəs / s(j)ù:pə-] *adj.* of or full of superstition; caused by superstition. —[形] 미신적인, 미신에 홀린

su·per·struc·ture [sú:pərstrʌ̀ktʃər / s(j)ú:pəstrʌ̀ktʃə] *n.* **1.** [U] anything built on something else. **2.** [U] the part of a building above the ground. **3.** [C] the part of a ship above the main deck. ↔substructure —[名] 1. 상부 건축 2. [기초 위의] 건축, 건물 3. [배의] 주갑판 위의 부분

su·per·tax [sú:pərtæ̀ks / s(j)ú:pə-] *n.* [U][C] a tax in addition to the normal income tax. —[名] 부가 소득세, 부가세

su·per·vene [sù:pərví:n / s(j)ù(:)pə-] *vi.* happen while something else is happening; happen as something ad- —[自] 병발(併發)하다; 부수하여 일어나다

su·per·ven·tion [sùːpərvénʃ(ə)n / s(j)uː·pə-] *n.* **1.** ⓤ the act of supervening. **2.** ⓒ a supervening event.
—ⓝ 1. 부가, 추가 2. 잇따라 일어나는 사건, 병발 사건

su·per·vise [súːpərvàiz / s(j)úː·pə-] *vt.* watch over (persons, machines, etc.) to see that they work properly.
—ⓥ …을 감독하다, 관리하다

su·per·vi·sion [sùːpərvíʒ(ə)n / s(j)uː·(ː)pə-] *n.* ⓤ the act of supervising; oversight.
—ⓝ 관리, 감독

su·per·vi·sor [súːpərvàizər / s(j)úː·pə-] *n.* ⓒ a person ⌈who supervises.⌉
—ⓝ 감독자, 관리인

su·per·vi·so·ry [sùːpərváiz(ə)ri / s(j)ùː(ː)pə-] *adj.* of a supervisor or supervision. ⌈prone ⌈ lazy; idle.⌉
—ⓐ 감독(관리)자의, 감독(관리)의

su·pine [suːpáin / s(j)uː-] *adj.* **1.** lying on the back. ↔
—ⓐ 1. 발딱 드러누운 2. 게으른

sup·per [sʌ́pər] *n.* ⓤⓒ the last meal of the day; the evening meal. ¶*at* ~① / *have* (or *eat, take*) ~.②
—ⓝ 만찬, 저녁 ¶①저녁 때에/②저녁을 먹다

sup·plant [səplǽnt / -pláːnt] *vt.* **1.** take the place of (something or someone); replace. ¶*Airplanes have supplanted trains.*① **2.** take the place of (another) by unfair methods or force. ¶*plot to* ~ *the king.*②
—ⓥ 1. …에 대신 들어앉다, 대신하다 ¶①비행기에 기차가 밀려났다 2. …을 밀어젖히다 ¶②왕위를 빼앗으려고 꾸미다

sup·ple [sʌ́pl] *adj.* (**-pler, -plest**) **1.** easily bent. ¶~ *leather* / ~ *movement.*① **2.** adaptable to different ideas, circumstances, etc. ¶*a* ~ *mind.* —*vt.* make (something or someone) supple. —*vi.* grow or become supple.
—ⓐ 1. 유연한 ¶①경쾌한 동작 2. 유순한; 순응성이 있는 —ⓥ …을 유연하게 하다 —ⓥ 유연해지다

sup·ple·ment *n.* [sʌ́plimənt →.] ⓒ **1.** something added to complete a thing. **2.** an added part of a newspaper, a magazine, or a book. —*vt.* [-mènt] complete; add to (something). ⌈is lacking; additional.⌉
—ⓝ 1. 보유(補遺), 증보, 추가 2. [신문·잡지의] 부록; [책의] 보유 —ⓥ …을 보충하다, 증보하다, 추가하다

sup·ple·men·tal [sʌ̀pliméntl] *adj.* added to supply what
sup·ple·men·ta·ry [sʌ̀plimént(ə)ri] *adj.* =supplemental.
—ⓐ 보충의; 추가의

sup·pli·ant [sʌ́pliənt] *adj.* asking humbly and earnestly.
—*n.* ⓒ a person who begs for a favor.
—ⓐ 간청하는, 탄원하는
—ⓝ 탄원자, 간청자

sup·pli·cate [sʌ́plikèit] *vt.* beg or pray to (someone) for something humbly and earnestly. ⟨~ *someone to do* or *for*⟩ ¶~ *one's master for mercy.*① ⌈plicating.⌉
—ⓥ …을 탄원하다 ¶①주인에게 자비를 빌다

sup·pli·ca·tion [sʌ̀plikéiʃ(ə)n] *n.* ⓤ the act of sup-
—ⓝ 탄원, 간청, 기원

sup·pli·ca·to·ry [sʌ́plikətɔ̀ːri / -t(ə)ri] *adj.* supplicating.
—ⓐ 탄원의, 기원의

sup·pli·er [səpláiər] *n.* ⓒ a person who supplies.
—ⓝ 공급자, 보충자

sup·ply [səplái] *vt.* (**-plied**) **1.** give (something needed or wanted); fill the needs of (something or someone). ⟨~ *someone* or *something with*; ~ *something for*⟩ ¶~ *a city with electricity* / *We supplied food and clothes for the sufferers.* **2.** furnish (a loss, a lack, a need, etc.); satisfy (a need). ¶~ *the demand* / ~ *the need.* —*n.* (*pl.* **-plies**) **1.** ⓤ the act of supplying. ¶~ *and demand.* **2.** ⓒ something supplied; an amount wanted. ¶*have a good* (or *a large*) ~ *of.*① **3.** (usu. *pl.*) the amount of daily necessaries required; a store of food used in an army, etc. **4.** ⓒ (often *pl.*) money allowed for the expenses of a government.
—ⓥ 1. [필수품]을 공급하다; …에 대주다, 지급하다 2. [부족 따위]를 보충하다; [필요]를 충족시키다

—ⓝ 1. 공급; 보충 2. 공급품; 재고품; 공급량 ¶①…을 많이 갖고 있다 3. 생활 필수품;[군대의] 양식 4. [국회가 인정한] 세출

sup·port [səpɔ́ːrt] *vt.* **1.** keep (something) from falling, sinking, slipping, etc.; hold up; carry the weight of (something). ¶*The foundation supports a house.* / *She supported her chin on her hand.*① **2.** give hope or courage to (someone); comfort; carry on; maintain. ¶~ *life* **3.** supply (someone) with food, clothes, etc.; provide money for (someone or something). ¶~ *a family* / ~ *a school*② / *He has a wife and a child to* ~.③ **4.** be actively in favor of (a policy, a claim, etc.); back up. **5.** (of facts, etc.) show proof for (a theory, etc.). ¶*His theory is supported by facts.* **6.** endure; bear. ¶*I can't* ~ *your insults any more.*
—*n.* **1.** ⓤ the act of supporting; the state of being supported; means of providing; help. ¶*give* ~ *to a roof*④ / *He can stand without* ~. / *His income was not sufficient for the* ~ *of his family.* / *I need his* ~. **2.** ⓒ a person or thing that supports; a proof. ¶*Place it on*
—ⓥ 1. …을 버티다, 받치다; …의 무게에 견디다 ¶①그녀는 손으로 턱을 받쳤다 2. …에 기운나게 하다, …을 격려하다;[생명 따위]를 유지하다 3. …을 부양하다;[재정적으로 남·사업 따위]를 원조하다 ¶②학교를 원조하다/③그에게는 부양해야 할 아내와 한 자식이 있다 4. [정책 따위]를 지지하다; …을 지원하다 5. [사실 따위가] …을 입증하다 6. …을 참다

—ⓝ 1. 버팀; 지지; 부양; 원조 ¶④지붕을 받치다 2. 지지물; 지지자; 증거 ¶⑤그것을 기둥으로 받쳐라

a ~.④ **3.** [C] an actor who assists others in a play.
3. 조연자(助演者)

sup·port·a·ble [səpɔ́:rtəbl] *adj.* that can be supported; bearable.
—[형] 지탱할 수 있는, 지지받을 수 있는, 부양(원조)할 수 있는

* **sup·port·er** [səpɔ́:rtər] *n.* [C] a person or thing that supports.
—[명] 지지자(물), 부양자

‡ **sup·pose** [səpóuz] *vt.* **1.** take (something) as true for the sake of argument; consider (something) as possible; expect. 《~ *that* ...; ~ something *to do*》 ¶*Let's ~ that the rumor is true. / I ~ I'll see you at the meeting.*① **2.** imagine; think; believe. 《~ *that* ...; ~ someone or something *to do*》 ¶*I ~ he'll come. / What do you ~ he'll do?*② **3.** 《in *imperative* or *participle*》 if; consider (something) as a proposal or suggestion. ¶*Suppose* (or *Supposing*) *he saw you, he would be very glad.* **4.** (of a theory or result) require (something) as a condition. ¶*Democracy supposes free elections.*③ **5.** 《in *passive*》 require; expect; desire. 《~ *to do*》 ¶*She is supposed to arrive on the two o'clock train.*④
—[타] 1. …라 가정하다; …을 기대하다 ¶①모임에서 너를 만날 수 있을 게다 2. …이라 상상하다, 추측하다, 생각하다 ¶②그가 무얼 하리라고 생각하느냐? 3. …이라면; …이라 하더라도; …이라면 어떨까 4. [이론 따위가] …을 포함하다 ¶③민주주의는 당연히 자유 선거가 예기된다 5. …을 기대하다 ¶④그녀는 두 시 기차로 도착하게 돼 있다

* **sup·posed** [səpóuzd] *adj.* believed to exist; considered as possible; assumed.
—[형] 가정상의, 상상상의; 상상된

sup·pos·ed·ly [səpóuzidli] *adv.* according to what is or was supposed.
—[부] 상상으로, 아마

sup·pos·ing [səpóuziŋ] *conj.* if; assuming; in the event that. ¶*Supposing* [*that*] *it is true, what would happen?*①
—[접] 만일 …이라면 ¶①만일 정말이라면 어떻게 되느냐?

sup·po·si·tion [sʌ̀pəzíʃ(ə)n] *n.* **1.** [U] the act of supposing. **2.** [C] something supposed.
—[명] 1. 상상, 추정, 상정(想定) 2. 가정, 가설

sup·po·si·tion·al [sʌ̀pəzíʃənl] *adj.* of or based on supposition.
—[형] 상상상(想像上)의

* **sup·press** [səprés] *vt.* **1.** put down (someone or something) by force; put an end to (something). **2.** hold back; prevent (something) from being known. **3.** stop the publication of (a book, etc.).
—[타] 1. …을 억압하다, 진압하다 2. …을 억제하다; [하품 따위]를 억누르다; [증거 따위]를 감추다 3. …의 발행을 금지하다

sup·press·i·ble [səprésibl] *adj.* that can be suppressed.
—[형] 억제(억압)할 수 있는

sup·pres·sion [səpréʃ(ə)n] *n.* [U] the act of suppressing; the state of being suppressed.
—[명] 억압, 억제, 감추기, 발매 금지

sup·pu·rate [sʌ́pju(ə)rèit] *vi.* (of a poisoned wound) produce a yellow-white liquid.
—[자] 곪다, 화농하다

sup·pu·ra·tion [sʌ̀pju(ə)réiʃ(ə)n] *n.* [U] **1.** the state or condition of suppurating. **2.** the liquid which comes out of a poisoned wound; pus.
—[명] 1. 화농 2. 고름

su·prem·a·cy [supréməsi, s(j)u-] *n.* [U] **1.** the state of being supreme. **2.** the highest rank or power.
—[명] 1. 최고, 지상(至上) 2. 주권, 최상권

‡ **su·preme** [su(:)prí:m / s(j)u(:)-] *adj.* highest in power or rank; greatest or best possible. ¶~ *power / the ~ commander*① */ at the ~ moment* (or *hour*).②
—[형] 최고의, 최상의, 지상의, 궁극의, 더할 나위 없는 ¶①최고 사령관/②가장 중요한 때에

Supreme Court [-ˊ ˊ] *n.* the highest court in the United States; a similar court in other countries.
—[명] 대법원, 대심원, 최고 재판소

su·preme·ly [su(:)prí:mli / s(j)u(:)-] *adv.* in or with a supreme manner.
—[부] 최상으로, 더할 나위 없이

Supreme Soviet [-ˊ ˊ--], **the** *n.* the parliament of the Soviet Union.
—[명] 최고 소비에트, 소련방 최고회의

sur- [sʌr, sər] *pref.* =super-.

sur·charge *n.* [sə́:rtʃɑ̀:rdʒ →*v.*] **1.** [C] money to be paid in addition to what has been paid already; an extra charge. **2.** [U] an additional or excessive load. —*vt.* [ˊˊ] **1.** charge too much; overcharge. **2.** overload.
—[명] 1. 특별[부가] 요금 2. 과중, 과도하게 쌓기 —[타] 1. …에 부당한 대금을 청구하다 2. …에 과도하게 쌓다

‡ **sure** [ʃuər, +*Brit.* ʃɔ:] *adj.* **1.** 《in *predicative*》 convinced; having a good reason for belief. 《~ *of*; ~ *that* ...》 ¶*Are you ~ of success?; Are you ~* [*that*] *you will succeed? / I'm ~ he is honest.* **2.** 《in *predicative*》 without fail; never missing. 《~ *of*; ~ *to do*》 ¶*He is ~ to succeed. / It's ~ to rain.*① **3.** certain; reliable; safe. ¶*a ~ friend / a ~ method*② */ a ~ way to victory.*③
—[형] 1. 확신하는; 자신이 있는 2. 꼭 …하는, 반드시 …하는 ¶①틀림없이 비가 온다 3. 확실한; 신뢰할 수 있는; 안전한 ¶②확실한 방법/③승리를 얻는 확실한 길

—*adv.* (*U.S. colloq.*) 《expressing *agreement*》 certainly.
—[부] 《美口》 확실히; 좋고말고

1) ***for sure,*** certainly.
2) ***make sure,*** make certain.
3) ***to be sure,*** certainly.
[숙] 1)확실히 2)확인하다 3)확실히

‡ **sure·ly** [ʃúərli] *adv.* in a sure manner; certainly; un-
—[부] 확실히, 안전하게, 꼭, 반드시 ¶①

doubtedly; without fail. ¶*slowly but ~.*①
더디더라도 확실히

sure·ness [ʃúərnis] *n.* [U] the state of being sure.
—[名] 확실, 정확, 안전

sure·ty [ʃúərti, +*U.S.* ʃúriti] *n.* [C] (pl. **-ties**) a person who promises to be responsible for another.
—[名] 보증인

surf [səːrf] *n.* [U] the breaking waves of the sea.
—[名] 바닷가에 부딪치는 파도

‡ **sur·face** [sə́ːrfis] *n.* [C] the outside of anything; any face or side of something; the outward appearance. ¶*below* (or *beneath*) *the ~*① / *on the ~.*②
—*adj.* of, on, or at the surface.
—*vt.* put a surface on (something); make (something) smooth. 《~ something *with*》 ¶*~ a table with paint.*③
—*vi.* come up to the surface from below.
—[名] 표면; 겉, 외면; 외부; 외관, 외양, 겉보기 ¶①내면으로는, 속으로는/②표면상, 겉보기는
—[形] 표면의, 외관의, 피상적인
—[他] …에 표면을 대다; …을 포장(鋪裝)하다, 평평하게 하다 ¶③테이블에 페인트를 칠하다 —[自] 수면으로 떠오르다

surf·board [sə́ːrfbɔ̀ːrd] *n.* [C] a long, narrow board used for riding incoming ocean waves.
—[名] 파도 타기용의 널빤지

sur·feit [sə́ːrfit] *n.* [U] excess in eating or drinking; the feeling of fullness or sickness resulting from such excess. —*vt.* overfeed. 《~ someone *with*》 ¶*~ oneself with fruit*① / *be surfeited with pleasure.*
—[名] 과식, 과음; 만복, 식상(食傷) —[他] …에게 과식하게 하다, …을 물리게 하다 ¶①과일을 너무 먹다

surf·rid·ing [sə́ːrfràidiŋ] *n.* [U] the act or sport of riding on a surfboard. ⇒fig.
—[名] 파도타기[놀이]

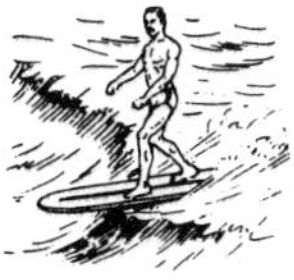
(surfriding)

* **surge** [səːrdʒ] *n.* [C] **1.** a large wave. **2.** a strong and sudden rising motion, feeling, etc. —*vi.* move up and down like waves; rush like a large wave. ¶*surging crowds*① / *A great wave of emotion surged over us.*
—[名] 1. 큰 파도, 물 너울 2. 동요; 격동, 파동 —[自] 물결치다; [파도처럼] 밀려오다 ¶①노도처럼 밀려오는 군중

* **sur·geon** [sə́ːrdʒ(ə)n] *n.* [C] a doctor who performs operations.
—[名] 외과 의사

sur·ger·y [sə́ːrdʒ(ə)ri] *n.* (pl. **-ger·ies**) **1.** [U] the art and science of medical operations. **2.** [C] an office or operating room of a surgeon. **3.** (*Brit.*) [C] a doctor's office.
—[名] 1. 외과, 외과술 2. 외과 진료실; 수술실 3.《英》[외과] 병원

sur·gi·cal [sə́ːrdʒik(ə)l] *adj.* of surgery or surgeons, used in surgery.
—[形] 외과의, 외과 의사의; 외과 수술[용]의

sur·ly [sə́ːrli] *adj.* (sometimes **-li·er, -li·est**) ill-humored; bad-tempered and unfriendly.
—[形] 심술궂은; 무뚝뚝한, 통명스러운

sur·mise *v.* [səːrmáiz → *n.*] *vt., vi.* guess; suppose. —*n.* [´–, –´] [U] a guess or thought based on something not evident.
—[他][自] …을 추측하다, 생각하다 —[名] 추측, 억측

sur·mount [sə(ː)rmáunt] *vt.* **1.** get over (a difficulty); overcome. **2.** climb over (a hill, etc.). **3.** stand or lie on top of (something).
—[他] 1. [곤란]을 이겨내다, 극복하다 2. [산]을 타고 넘다, 올라가다 3. …의 위에 있다(솟다, 놓다)

sur·mount·a·ble [sə(ː)rmáuntəbl] *adj.* that can be overcome.
—[形] 극복(타파)할 수 있는

sur·name [sə́ːrnèim] *n.* [C] **1.** a family name; a last name. ↔Christian name; first name **2.** a name added to the real name. —*vt.* give an added name to (someone); call (someone) by his surname.
—[名] 1. 성(姓) 2. 별명, 이명(異名) —[他]…에 별명을 붙이다, …을 성(별명)으로 부르다

* **sur·pass** [sə(ː)rpǽs / sə(ː)páːs] *vt.* **1.** be better or bigger than (someone or something). ¶*~ someone in ability.* **2.** go beyond; exceed. ¶*~ oneself.*①
—[他] 1. …보다 뛰어나다, 낫다 2. …을 초월(능가)하다 ¶①자기 능력 이상의 일을 하다

sur·plice [sə́ːrplis] *n.* [C] a loose white garment with broad sleeves worn by a priest. ⇒fig.
—[名] [목사가 성직복 위에 입는] 흰옷

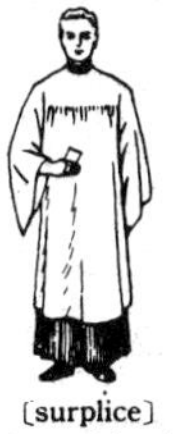
(surplice)

sur·plus [sə́ːrpləs, +*U.S.* -plʌ̀s] *n.* [U][C] an amount above what is needed; a remainder; excess. ↔deficit —*adj.* more than is needed. ¶*~ population.*①
—[名] 잉여, 나머지, 초과액 —[形] 과잉의 ¶①과잉 인구

‡ **sur·prise** [sərpráiz] *vt.* **1.** cause (someone) to feel wonder or astonishment; startle; shock. ¶*His sudden fury surprised me.* / *Her behavior surprised us.*① / *I was surprised at the news.* / *I'm surprised that you still remain here.*② **2.** catch or attack suddenly and unexpectedly. ¶*~ an enemy* / *~ a thief.* **3.** startle
—[他] 1. [남]을 놀라게 하다 ¶①우리들은 그녀의 행동에 놀랐다/②아직 여기 남아 있었다니 놀랐다 2. …을 급습(기습)하다, …을 불시에 공격하다 3. [남]을 놀라게 하여 …시키다; …을 드러나게 하다 ¶③놀라게 하여 사실을 말하게 하다/④그를 놀라게 하여 비밀

and cause (someone) to say or to do something that he has not intended; bring (something) to light by such means. 《~ someone *into*》 ¶~ *someone into telling the truth*③ / *He surprised me into confusion.* / *I surprised the secret out of him.*④
을 알아냈다

—*n.* **1.** [U] the feeling caused by something sudden or unexpected. ¶*show no* ~ / *with a look of* ~ / *in* ~ / *to one's* ~ / *It was a great* ~ *to me.* **2.** [C] something sudden or unexpected. ¶*Here is a small* ~ *for you.* **3.** [U] the act of attacking or catching suddenly or unexpectedly. ¶*be caught by* ~.
—[명] **1.** 놀람, 경악 **2.** 뜻밖의 일, 놀랄 만한 일 **3.** 기습, 급습

***take** someone or something **by surprise**,* ⓐ catch or attack suddenly. ¶*He took me by* ~. ⓑ surprise.
[숙] ⓐ…을 기습하다, 기습하여 붙잡다 ⓑ…을 놀라게 하다

sur·prised [sərpráizd] *adj.* showing or feeling surprise.
—[형] 놀란

sur·prised·ly [sərpráiz(i)dli] *adv.* in a surprised manner.
—[부] 놀라서, 깜짝 놀라

* **sur·pris·ing** [sərpráiziŋ] *adj.* causing surprise.
—[형] 놀랄 만한, 의외의, 이상한

sur·pris·ing·ly [sərpráiziŋli] *adv.* in a surprising manner; to a surprising degree.
—[부] 놀라서; 뜻밖에, 놀랄 만큼

* **sur·ren·der** [səréndər] *vt.* give (something) up to someone or something; give (oneself) up to something; yield. ¶~ *a city to the enemy*① / ~ *oneself to despair.*② —*vi.* yield. ¶~ *to the enemy.*③ —*n.* [U][C] the act of surrendering.
—[타] …을 넘겨주다, 포기하다; [몸]을 맡기다 ¶①도시를 적에게 넘겨주다/②절망에 빠지다 —[자] 항복하다 ¶③적에게 항복하다 —[명] 인도, 포기, 항복

sur·rep·ti·tious [sə̀:rəptíʃəs / sʌ̀r-] *adj.* done secretly; secret.
—[형] 비밀의, 은밀한

sur·rep·ti·tious·ly [sə̀:rəptíʃəsli / sʌ̀r-] *adv.* in a surreptitious manner; secretly.
—[부] 은밀히, 몰래

: **sur·round** [səráund] *vt.* enclose (someone or something) on all sides. ¶*A high wall surrounds the city.*① / *Korea is surrounded with* (or *by*) *the sea on three sides.*②
—[타] …을 둘러싸다, 포위하다 ¶①높은 절벽이 그 도시를 둘러싸고 있다/②한국은 삼면이 바다로 둘러싸여 있다

S

* **sur·round·ings** [səráundiŋz] *n. pl.* all the conditions that surround someone. ¶*home* ~①
—[명] 주위, 환경 ¶①가정환경

sur·tax [sə́:rtæ̀ks] *n.* [U][C] (*U.S.*) a tax added to the normal income tax. (cf. *Brit.* supertax)
—[명] 《美》 부가세

sur·veil·lance [sə:rvéiləns] *n.* [U] careful watch.
—[명] 감시, 망보기

: **sur·vey** *vt.* [sə(:)rvéi →*n.*] **1.** look at (something) carefully; examine generally. ¶~ *the scene from the hill*①/ ~ *the history of science.*② **2.** measure.
—[타] **1.** …을 주의깊게 보다, 조망(眺望)하다; 개관(概觀)하다 ¶①언덕에서 경치를 내려다보다/②과학의 역사를 살피다 **2.** …을 측량하다

—*n.* [sə́:rvei, sə(:)véi] [C] **1.** the act of surveying; a general examination. **2.** the act of measuring land carefully.
—[명] **1.** 주의깊게 보기; 개관 **2.** 측량

sur·vey·ing [sə(:)rvéiiŋ] *n.* [U] the act of measuring land.
—[명] 측량

sur·vey·or [sə(:)rvéiər] *n.* [C] a person who measures land.
—[명] 측량 기사

sur·viv·al [sərváiv(ə)l] *n.* **1.** [U] the act or state of surviving. **2.** [C] =survivor.
—[명] **1.** 살아 남음, 잔존(殘存)

* **sur·vive** [sərváiv] *vt.* live longer than (others); live beyond some dangerous experience. ¶~ *one's children*① / ~ *a storm.* —*vi.* remain alive or in existence. ¶~ *to our time*② / ~ *for two years.*
—[타] …보다 오래 살다; …의 뒤에도 아직 살아 있다 ¶①자식보다 오래 살다 —[자] 살아남다, 잔존하다 ¶②오늘날까지 살아남다

sur·vi·vor [sərváivər] *n.* [C] a person or thing that remains alive.
—[명] 잔존자(물)

Su·san [sú:zn], **Su·san·na[h]** [su(:)zǽnə] *n.* a woman's name. ⇒[N.B.]
—[명] 여자 이름 [N.B.] 애칭 Sue

sus·cep·ti·bil·i·ty [səsèptəbíləti] *n.* [U] the quality of being susceptible.
—[명] 감수성, 느끼기 쉬움

sus·cep·ti·ble [səséptəbl] *adj.* **1.** easily affected by feelings, emotions, diseases, etc.; very sensitive. 《~ *to*》 ¶*be* ~ *to influenza.*① **2.** allowing; admitting. 《~ *of*》 ¶*facts not susceptible of proof.*②
—[형] **1.** 느끼기 쉬운, 민감한 ¶①독감에 걸리기 쉽다 **2.** …을 허용하는, 가능한 ¶②증거를 댈 수 없는 사실

: **sus·pect** *vt.* [səspékt →*n., adj.*] **1.** imagine or believe (something) to exist. ¶~ *danger.*① **2.** think likely; suppose. 《~ someone *to be*; ~ *that…*》 ¶*I* ~ *him* [*to be*] *mad.*; *I* ~ *that he is mad.* **3.** doubt the truth of (something); doubt. ¶*I* ~ *her motives.* / *I suspected the picture of being a fake.*② **4.** believe (someone) to be guilty, but without proof. 《~ someone *of*》 ¶*They* ~ *him of murder.* / *He is suspected of stealing.*③
—[타] **1.** […의 존재]를 알아채다, 낌새채다 ¶①위험을 알아채다 **2.** …이 아닌가 하고 생각하다; …이라고 생각(상상)하다 **3.** [사물이 정말인지 아닌지]를 의심하다, 미심쩍어 하다; …을 믿지 않다 ¶②나는 그 그림이 가짜라고 의심했다 **4.** …에게 혐의(의심)를 두다 ¶③그는 도둑질의 혐의를 쓰고 있다

suspend

—*n.* [sʌ́spekt] ⓒ a person suspected, esp. of a crime; a person suspected of having or spreading a disease. ¶*The policeman arrested one ~ for the murder.*
—*adj.* [sʌ́spekt] (as *predicative*) suspected; questionable. ¶*The man's honesty is ~.*

* **sus·pend** [səspénd] *vt.* **1.** hang. (*~ something from*) ¶*~ a lamp from the ceiling.* **2.** stop (something) for a while. ¶*~ business.* **3.** (chiefly in *passive*) put (a balloon, smoke, etc.) in place, as if hanging. ¶*The oil is suspended in the water. / The smoke was suspended in the air.* **4.** keep (something) undecided.

sus·pend·ers [səspéndərz] *n. pl.* **1.** (*U.S.*) bands worn by men to keep up their trousers. ⇒ NB. **2.** (*Brit.*) bands worn to keep up the stockings.

sus·pense [səspéns] *n.* Ⓤ **1.** the state of being uncertain; doubt. **2.** the state of being undecided.

sus·pen·sion [səspénʃ(ə)n] *n.* Ⓤ the act of suspending; the state of being suspended; stop; an undecided state.

sus·pen·sive [səspénsiv] *adj.* stopping; undecided.

‡ **sus·pi·cion** [səspíʃ(ə)n] *n.* **1.** Ⓤⓒ the act of suspecting; the feeling that something is bad, wrong, etc. ¶*hold someone in ~; cast ~ on someone / I had a ~ that I was being followed.* **2.** (usu. *a ~*) a very small amount; a slight taste. ¶*a ~ of whisky.*

* **sus·pi·cious** [səspíʃəs] *adj.* **1.** showing doubt; likely to think badly of others. (*~ of*) ¶*a ~ glance / He is ~ of you.* **2.** causing doubt; questionable.

sus·pi·cious·ly [səspíʃəsli] *adv.* in a suspicious manner.

* **sus·tain** [səstéin] *vt.* **1.** support; hold up. ¶*~ the arch.* **2.** experience. ¶*~ a loss.* **3.** bear; endure. ¶*~ a shock.* **4.** support (oneself, one's family, etc.); keep alive; continue. ¶*~ a family.* **5.** admit; allow; uphold.

sus·te·nance [sʌ́stinəns] *n.* Ⓤ the act of sustaining; food.

Su·tra, su·tra [súːtrə] *n.* Ⓒ a holy writing of the Buddhist religion.

su·ture [súːtʃər / s(j)úːtʃə] *n.* Ⓤ the act of sewing up a wound; Ⓒ a seam formed by such a way.

su·ze·rain [súːzərèin, +*U.S.* -rin, +*Brit.* sjúː-] *n.* Ⓒ a ruler; a state controlling another state politically.

su·ze·rain·ty [súːzərèinti, +*U.S.* -rin-, +*Brit.* sjúː-] *n.* Ⓤ the position or power of a suzerain.

SW, S.W., s.w. southwest.

swab [swɔb / swɔb] *n.* Ⓒ **1.** a mop for cleaning decks, floors, etc. **2.** a piece of cotton for cleaning some part of the body. —*vt.* (**swabbed, swab·bing**) clean (something) with a swab. ¶*~ down the decks.*

swad·dle [swádl / swɔ́dl] *vt.* wrap (a baby) with clothes. —*n.* Ⓒ the cloth used for swaddling.

swad·dling clothes [swádliŋklòuðz / swɔ́d-] *n. pl.* many clothes wrapped around a newborn baby; baby clothes.

swag·ger [swǽgər] *vi.* **1.** walk in a proud, self-satisfied way. **2.** talk or act in such a way. —*n.* Ⓒ the act of swaggering.

swain [swein] *n.* Ⓒ (*archaic, poetic*) a male lover.

‡ **swal·low**¹ [swálou / swɔ́l-] *vt.* **1.** take (food, etc.) down the throat into the stomach. **2.** take (something) in; use up; conceal (something) from sight. ¶*Expenses ~ up earnings. / He was swallowed up in the mist.* **3.** believe easily. **4.** bear quietly. ¶*~ a yawn.* **5.** take back (words, etc.). ¶*~ words said in anger.*
—*n.* **1.** Ⓤ the act of swallowing. **2.** Ⓒ the amount swallowed at one time. ¶*take a ~ of water.*

* **swal·low**² [swálou / swɔ́l-] *n.* Ⓒ a bird with long, pointed wings and a forked tail.

swallow

—ⓝ 용의자, 혐의자

—ⓐ 의심스러운

—ⓥ 1. …을 매달다, 걸다 2. …을 중지하다 ¶①영업을 중지하다 3. …을 뜨게 하다 ¶②기구가 물에 떠 있다 / ③연기가 공중에서 감돌고 있었다 4. …을 보류하다, 미결로 남겨두다

—ⓝ 1. (美) 바지의 멜빵 NB 영국에서는 braces라 함 2. (英) 양말 대님

—ⓝ 1. 염려, 불안 2. 미결, 미정(상태)

—ⓝ 매달기, 부유(浮遊); 중지; 미결(정)

—ⓐ 중지의, 정지의; 결단이 안 서는

—ⓝ 1. 혐의, 의심 ¶①…을 의심하다 / ②미행하는 것 같은 생각이 들었다 2. 소량, 조금, 기미 ¶③아주 소량의 위스키

—ⓐ 1. 의심하는 듯한 ¶①의심스러운 눈초리 / ②그는 너를 의심하고 있다 2. 의심스러운

—ⓐ 의심깊게, 수상쩍게

—ⓥ 1. …을 떠받치다 2. …을 입다, 경험하다 3. …에 견디다, 참다 4. …을 유지하다, 지속하다 5. …을 인정하다, 지지하다

—ⓝ 지지; 지속; 생계; 음식

—ⓝ [불교의] 경전

—ⓝ [상처의] 봉합(縫合); 상처의 꿰맨 자리

—ⓝ 영주(領主), 종주(宗主); 종주국

—ⓝ 종주권; 영주의 지위(권력)

—ⓝ 1. 자루 달린 걸레 2. 소독면(消毒綿) —ⓥ …을 걸레로 소제하다, 훔치다 ¶갑판을 걸레로 소제하다

—ⓥ [갓난애]를 포대기로 싸다
—ⓝ 포대기, 강보

—ⓝ 강보, 두렁이

—ⓥ 1. 뽐내며 걷다 2. 뻐기다, 으스대다 —ⓝ 뽐내며 걷기, 허풍, 자랑

—ⓝ (古·詩) 애인
—ⓥ 1. …을 삼키다 2. …을 흡수하다; 다 써 버리다; 싸다, 덮다 ¶①경비가 수입을 몽땅 써 버리다 3. …을 곧이 곧대로 듣다 4. …을 참다 ¶②하품을 꾹 참다 5. …을 취소하다

—ⓝ 1. 삼키기, 마시기 2. 한 모금
—ⓝ 제비

swal·low·tail [swálouteìl / swɔ́l-] *n.* [C] **1.** a swallow's tail. **2.** =swallow-tailed coat.
—[名] 1. 제비 꼬리

swal·low-tailed coat [swálouteìldkóut / swɔ́l-] *n.* a man's formal coat with a forked tail like a swallow's.
—[名] 연미복

swam [swæm] *v.* pt. of **swim**.

swamp [swamp / swɔmp] *n.* [U] [C] a piece of soft, very wet land. **—*vt.*** **1.** fill (something) with water and sink (it). **2.** ⟪usu. in *passive*⟫ cover or swallow up (something or someone) completely; make (someone) helpless; overwhelm. ¶*be swamped with invitations.*①
—[名] 습지, 수렁, 늪 —[他] 1. …을 물에 잠겨 침몰시키다 2. …을 압도하다, 궁지에 빠뜨리다 ¶①초대공세(招待攻勢)를 받다

swamp·y [swámpi / swɔ́mpi] *adj.* (**swamp·i·er, swamp·i·est**) of or like a swamp.
—[形] 수렁의, 늪 같은

swan [swan / swɔn] *n.* [C] a large, beautiful water bird with a long neck.
—[名] 백조

swank [swæŋk] *n.* [U] a proud outward show; proud action; smartness. **—*vi.*** show off.
—[名] 자랑, 허세; 멋짐 —[自] 자랑하다

swank·y [swǽŋki] *adj.* (**swank·i·er, swank·i·est**) stylish; smart.
—[形] 멋진, 화려한

swan song [⌐⌐] *n.* **1.** (in legends) the song supposed to be sung by a dying swan. **2.** a person's last work before death.
—[名] 1. [전설에서] 백조가 임종 때 부른다는 아름다운 노래 2. 최후의 작품, 절필(絶筆), 마지막 업적

swap [swap / swɔp] *vt., vi.* (**swapped, swap·ping**) (*colloq.*) exchange. **—*n.*** [C] an exchange.
—[他][自] [···을] 교환하다 —[名] 교환, 바꾸기

sward [swɔːrd] *n.* [U] grassy land; lawn.
—[名] 풀밭, 잔디

swarm[1] [swɔːrm] *n.* [C] **1.** a large crowd of bees or birds. ⟪~ *of*⟫ ¶*a ~ of bees | in a ~.*① **2.** a large crowd of persons. ⟪~ *of*⟫ ¶*swarms of children.* **—*vi.*** move about in great numbers; be crowded. ¶*~ into a theater | ~ with flies.* **—*vt.*** crowd.
—[名] 1. [벌·새 따위의] 우글거리는 무리 ¶①떼를 지어 2. 떼, 군중 —[自] 떼짓다, 우글거리다 —[他] …에 떼지어 모이다

swarm[2] [swɔːrm] *vi., vt.* climb. ⟪~ *up* a tree, etc.⟫
—[自][他] [나무 따위에] 기어오르다

swarth·y [swɔ́ːrði, -θi] *adj.* (**swarth·i·er, swarth·i·est**) dark-skinned; dark.
—[形] [얼굴이] 거무스름한

swash [swaʃ / swɔʃ] *vi., vt.* dash (water, etc.) with a splashing sound; splash. ¶*~ against the cliff.* **—*n.*** [U] [C] a swashing sound or action.
—[自][他] [물 따위가] 튀기는 소리를 내다, 찰싹 부딪치다 —[名] 철썩하고 부딪치는 소리(부딪치기)

swash·buck·ler [swáʃbʌklər / swɔ́ʃbʌklə] *n.* [C] a person, esp. a soldier, who speaks proudly and noisily.
—[名] 허세부리는 사람

swash·buck·ling [swáʃbʌkliŋ / swɔ́ʃ-] *adj.* speaking in a proud, noisy, self-satisfied manner.
—[形] 허세부리는

swas·ti·ka [swástikə / swɔ́s-] *n.* [C] **1.** a symbol supposed to bring good fortune. **2.** the symbol of the followers of Hitler in Germany. ⇒fig.
—[名] 1. 만자(卍字) 2. 독일의 나찌스당의 상징

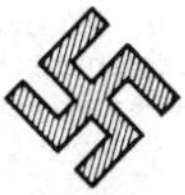
[swastika 2.]

swat [swat / swɔt] *vt.* (**swat·ted, swat·ting**) hit or strike (a fly, etc.) with a sharp, quick blow. **—*n.*** [U] [C] (colloq.) a sharp or quick blow.
—[他] …을 찰싹 때리다 —[名] ⟪口⟫ 찰싹 때리기

swath [swɔːθ, +*U.S.* swaθ] *n.* [C] (pl. **swaths** [swɔːðz]) a line of cut grass in a field.
—[名] 한 줄로 벤 풀

swathe [sweið, +*U.S.* swaːð] *vt.* bind (a wound, etc.) with a long piece of cloth; wrap; enclose. **—*n.*** [C] a bandage.
—[他] …을 붕대로 감다, 감다, 싸다 —[名] 붕대

sway [swei] *vt.* **1.** swing (something) back and forth; move (something) from side to side. ¶*~ oneself.*① **2.** make (someone's mind) lean to one side. ¶*~ many votes.*② **3.** have an effect on (someone); control. **—*vi.*** **1.** move or swing from side to side. **2.** lean to one side. **—*n.*** **1.** [U] [C] the act of swaying. **2.** [U] control.
—[他] 1. …을 흔들다, 동요시키다 ¶①몸을 흔들다 2. [마음 따위]를 한쪽으로 기울게 하다 ¶②많은 표를 좌우하다 3. …을 지배하다, 통치하다 —[自] 1. 흔들리다, 동요하다 2. 한쪽으로 기울다 —[名] 1. 동요, 진동 2. 지배, 통치

swear [swεər] *v.* (**swore, sworn**) *vi.* **1.** make a serious statement, with an appeal to God as witness. ⟪~ *to* something⟫ ¶*~ by* (or *on*) *the Bible*① | *~ against someone*② | *I will ~ to it.*③ **2.** use bad language against someone; utter curses. ⟪~ *at* someone⟫ ¶*He swore at his friend.*④ **—*vt.*** **1.** say (something) seriously in the name of God. ⟪~ *to do*; ~ *that…*⟫ ¶*~ eternal friendship*⑤ | *I ~ to love her as long as I live.* | *He*
—[自] 1. 맹세하다, 선서하다, 증언하다 ¶①성서에 손을 얹고 선서하다/②…에 불리한 증언을 하다/③나는 그것을 서약한다 2. 욕설을 하다 ¶④그는 친구에게 욕을 퍼부었다 —[他] 1. …을 신에게 맹세하다, 선서하다 ¶⑤영원의 우정을 맹세하다 2. …을 단언하다 3. …에 서약시키다, 선서시키다

swears that he is innocent. **2.** declare. **3.** cause (someone) to make a promise.

1) ***swear by,*** ⓐ name (someone or something) as a witness. ¶*I ~ by God that…*⑥ ⓑ have great faith in (someone or something).
2) ***swear in,*** induct (someone) into an office by oath.
3) ***swear off,*** declare or take an oath to give up. ¶*Father swore off smoking.*⑦
4) ***swear to,*** say (something) with an oath; guarantee. ¶*~ to his faithfulness.*⑧

[熟] 1)ⓐ…을 걸고 맹세하다 ¶⑥신을 걸고 …을 맹세하다 ⓑ…을 깊이 신뢰하다 2)…을 [선서하고] 취임시키다 3)맹세하고 …을 그만두다 ¶⑦아버지는 맹세를 하고 담배를 끊었다 4)…을 증언하다 ¶⑧그의 성실을 증언하다

* **sweat** [swet] *n.* **1.** [U] the liquid coming through the skin when it is hot; sweat-like drops forming on the surface of a thing. ¶*nightly sweats*① / *~ on a pipe* / *Sweat ran from the man's brow.* **2.** [C] the act of sweating; the condition of sweating. ¶*A ~ will do you good.*② **3.** [C] ⦅usu. *sing.*⦆ (*colloq.*) a piece of hard work.

—[名] **1.** 땀; 물방울 ¶①도한(盜汗) **2.** 땀이 나기, 땀흘리기, 발한(發汗) ¶②한바탕 땀을 흘리면 좋을 게다 **3.** 힘드는 일

in a cold sweat, greatly frightened and having a chilly feeling; in a state of acute fear or anxiety.

[熟] 식은 땀을 흘리고; 몹시 근심하여, 무서워하여

—*v.* (**sweat** or **sweat·ed**) *vi.* **1.** give off sweat. ¶*~ with fear*③. **2.** come out in drops; become damp on the outside of a thing. ¶*A glass of cold water sweats.* **3.** (*colloq.*) work very hard. ¶*~ [away] at one's job.*④ —*vt.* **1.** cause (someone or something) to sweat. ¶*~ a horse.* **2.** (*U.S.*) make (something) wet with sweat. ¶*~ one's shirt.* **3.** cause (someone) to work hard for very low wages.

—[自] **1.** 땀을 흘리다 ¶③무서워서 땀이 나다 **2.** 물방울이 되어 나오다; 물기가 맺히다 **3.** ⦅口⦆ 열심히 일하다 ¶④땀을 흘리며 일하다 —[他] **1.** …에게 땀흘리게 하다 **2.** …을 땀투성이로 하다 **3.** …을 싼 임금으로 혹사하다

sweat out (or ***away***), get rid of (a cold, etc.) by sweating.

[熟] 땀을 흘려 …을 없애다

sweat·er [swétər] *n.* [C] **1.** a person who sweats. **2.** a woollen garment for the upper part of the body. **3.** an employer who underpays his workers.

—[名] **1.** 땀흘리는 사람 **2.** 스웨터 **3.** 싼 임금으로 노동자를 혹사하는 고용주

sweat·shop [swétʃɑ̀p / -ʃɔ̀p] *n.* [C] a workshop or factory where workers are employed at low wages under bad working conditions.

—[名] 착취 공장(저임금·악조건으로 노동자를 혹사하는 공장)

sweat·y [swéti] *adj.* (**sweat·i·er, sweat·i·est**) **1.** covered with sweat; causing sweat; sweating. **2.** laborious.

—[形] **1.** 땀이 나는, 땀투성이의, 땀에 젖은 **2.** 힘드는

Swede [swi:d] *n.* [C] a person of Sweden.

—[名] 스웨덴 사람

Swe·den [swí:dn] *n.* a country in northern Europe on the Scandinavian peninsula. ⇨[N.B.]

—[名] 스웨덴 [N.B.] 수도 Stockholm

Swe·dish [swí:diʃ] *adj.* of Sweden, its people or their language. —*n.* **1.** [U] the language of Sweden. **2.** ⦅*the* ~⦆ the people of Sweden.

—[形] 스웨덴[사람·말]의 —[名] **1.** 스웨덴 말 **2.** 스웨덴 사람

‡ **sweep** [swi:p] *v.* (**swept**) *vt.* **1.** clean (a floor, a room, etc.) with a broom, a brush, etc.; clean off (dust, etc.) by using a broom, etc. ¶*~ a room* / *~ the dust off a coat* / *~ the room clean.* **2.** drive or carry (something) away, off or down with a violent force; clean away. ¶*~ off the snow*① / *~ the seas*② / *~ all obstacles from one's path* / *The flood swept away the bridge.*③ **3.** pass over or through (a region, etc.) quickly. ¶*An epidemic swept the country.*④ **4.** pass over or across (something) with a swift and steady movement. ¶*Her fingers swept the strings of the harp.* / *Her eyes swept the faces in the hall.*⑤ **5.** trail upon (something). ¶*Her dress swept the floor.* —*vi.* **1.** clean with a broom, etc. ¶(*proverb*) *A new broom sweeps clean.*⑥ **2.** (of news, disease, etc.) pass with speed and force. ¶*The troops swept past.* / *A hurricane swept over the whole region.* **3.** move in a swift, proud, stately manner. ¶*~ into a room.*⑦ **4.** move or extend in a long, curving course. ¶*The shore sweeps to the north for miles.*

—[他] **1.** …을 소제하다, 쓸다; [먼지 따위]를 털다 **2.** …을 일소하다, 밀어(씻어) 내리다, 불어 날리다 ¶①눈을 불어 날리다/②소해(掃海)하다, 해상의 적을 일소하다/③홍수로 다리가 떠내려 갔다 **3.** [장소]를 휙 지나가다 ¶④전염병이 온 나라를 휩쓸었다 **4.** …을 한눈에 보다; 쓰다듬다 ¶⑤그녀는 호올에 있는 사람들의 얼굴을 휘둘러 보았다 **5.** [옷이] …에 자락을 끌다 —[自] **1.** 소제하다 ¶⑥⦅俚⦆비는 새것일수록 더 잘 쓸어진다(신임자는 일을 잘한다) **2.** 휙 지나가다, 습격하다 **3.** 뽐내며(당당하게) 걷다 ¶⑦뽐내며 방으로 들어오다 **4.** 널리 퍼지다(미치다, 계속되다)

—*n.* [C] **1.** an act of sweeping. **2.** a long sweeping motion; a stroke or blow. ¶*a ~ of the oars.*⑧ **3.** a steady, driving motion; a smooth, flowing motion. ¶*the ~ of the wind* / *the ~ of verse.*⑨ **4.** [U] a wide expanse; extent. ¶*a ~ of meadow*⑩ / *with* (*beyond*) *the*

—[名] **1.** 쓸기, 소제 **2.** 한 번 흔들기(휘두르기, 젓기) ¶⑧노를 한 번 젓기 **3.** 불어 날리기, 떠내려 보내기; 매끄러운 움직임 ¶⑨시의 유창한 흐름 **4.** 범위, 퍼짐 ¶⑩널따란 목장 **5.** 만곡(彎曲),

S

~ *of the eye.* **5.** a curve; a curving line; a great curve of a road, etc. **6.** a long pole, attached to a post, used to raise or lower a bucket in a well. **7.** a big victory. **8.** a person who sweeps chimneys, streets, etc.
곡선; 꾸불꾸불한 길 6. 반동식 두레박의 대 7. 큰 승리 8. 굴뚝 소제부, 청소부

make a clean sweep of, get rid of (something) completely and thoroughly.
[熟] …을 깨끗이 일소하다

sweep·er [swíːpər] *n.* [C] a person or device that sweeps.
—[名] 청소부, 소제기

* **sweep·ing** [swíːpiŋ] *adj.* of a wide range or extent; complete. ¶*a ~ glance*① / *a ~ victory.*② **—n.** ((*pl.*)) dust; scraps; rubbish.
—[形] 광범위한, 완전한 ¶①흘긋 둘러보기/②압승 —[名] 먼지, 쓰레기

sweep·ing·ly [swíːpiŋli] *adv.* in a sweeping manner.
—[副] 일소하여, 간추려서

⁑ sweet [swiːt] *adj.* **1.** having a taste like sugar or honey. ↔bitter, sour ¶*Sugar is ~.* **2.** having a pleasant smell; (of sounds) pleasant. ¶*~ herbs / a ~ sound.* **3.** fresh; not sour or salted. ¶*~ air / ~ milk.* **4.** gentle; kind; mild. ¶*a ~ temper / That is very ~ of you.*① **5.** pleasant; delightful. ¶*a ~ sleep.* **6.** (*colloq.*) charming; lovely. ¶*a ~ little girl.*
—[形] 1. 단, 달콤한 2. 향기가 좋은; [소리가] 듣기 좋은 3. 신선한; 신(짠)맛이 없는 4. 친절한, 상냥한; 얌전한 ¶①참 친절도 하십니다 5. 기분이 좋은; 유쾌한 6. ((口)) 애교가 있는, 귀여운

have a sweet tooth, be fond of very sweet food.
[熟] 단 것을 매우 좋아하다

—n. [C] **1.** [U] a sweet taste or smell. **2.** (chiefly *Brit.*) a candy. **3.** (*Brit.*) ((*pl.*)) the dessert course of a meal, such as puddings, ice cream or jellies. **4.** ((*pl.*)) pleasures; delights. ¶*the sweets of victory.*②
—[名] 1. 감미, 단맛 2. 사탕과자; 캔디 3. 식후에 나오는 달콤한 요리 4. 유쾌; 쾌락 ¶②승리의 기쁨

sweet·bread [swíːtbrèd] *n.* [C] an inner part of the body of a calf, a lamb etc., used as food.
—[名] 송아지·새끼 양 따위의 지라

sweet corn [ˊ ˋ] *n.* a kind of Indian corn with a sweetish flavor, eaten in its unripe state; green corn.
—[名] 사탕 옥수수

sweet·en [swíːtn] *vt., vi.* **1.** make (something) sweet; become sweet. **2.** make (something or someone) agreeable or pleasant, or become so.
—[他][自] 1. [···을] 달게 하다(되다) 2. [···을] 기분좋게 하다(되다), 유쾌하게 하다(되다)

sweet·en·ing [swíːtniŋ] *n.* [U] the process of making something sweet; [C] something that sweetens.
—[名] 달게 하기, 감미료

* **sweet·heart** [swíːthàːrt] *n.* [C] a lover, esp. a girl or woman who is in love.
—[名] 연인, 애인

sweet·ish [swíːtiʃ] *adj.* rather sweet.
—[形] 좀 달콤한; 귀여운

* **sweet·ly** [swíːtli] *adv.* in a sweet manner; agreeably; comfortably; pleasantly.
—[副] 달게, 귀엽게, 기분좋게, 즐겁게

sweet·meats [swíːtmìːts] *n. pl.* candy; bonbons.
—[名] 캔디; 봉봉[과자]

* **sweet·ness** [swíːtnis] *n.* [U] the quality or state of being sweet.
—[名] 달콤함, 단 맛, 유쾌, 부드러움, 귀여움

sweet oil [ˊ ˋ] *n.* an oil obtained from olives; olive oil.
—[名] 올리브유(油)

sweet pea [ˊ ˋ] *n.* a kind of plant with sweet-smelling flowers; the flower of this plant.
—[名] 사향연리초, 스위트피이

sweet pepper [ˊ ˋˊ] *n.* a kind of pepper plant bearing a mild fruit; its fruit; the green pepper.
—[名] 사자고추[의 열매]

sweet potato [ˊ ˋˊˋ] *n.* a plant that produces edible, sweet, thick yellow or reddish roots.
—[名] 고구마

sweet-scent·ed [swíːtsèntid] *adj.* having a pleasant smell.
—[形] 냄새 좋은, 향기로운

sweet shop [ˊ ˋ] *n.* (*Brit.*) a shop which sells candies, etc. ⇒[N.B.]
—[名] 과자가게 [N.B.] 미국에서는 candy store라고 함

sweet-tem·pered [swíːttémpərd] *adj.* having a gentle nature; good-natured.
—[形] 마음씨 고운

⁑ swell [swel] *v.* (**swelled, swelled** or **swol·len**) *vi.* **1.** increase in size, volume, or force; grow bigger. ¶*Buds~*①/ *A balloon began to ~. / The river has swollen with melted snow.* **2.** increase in number, degree, or quantity. ¶*Her savings swelled as she continued to work hard.* **3.** become rough with waves; be higher or thicker in a particular place; stick out. ¶*The cask swells in the middle. / The sea is swelling.*② **4.** (of a sound) become louder. **5.** become filled with pride, grief, or some other strong feelings. ¶*~ with pride / His heart swelled with pity.*③ **—vt.** **1.** cause (something) to increase in size, volume, force, etc. ¶*Wind swells the sail. / The rain will ~ the river.* **2.** fill (someone) with pride or
—[自] 1. 부풀다, 커지다; 부어오르다; [물이] 붇다 ¶①봉오리가 부푼다 2. [수량이] 증대하다, 증가하다 3. 파도치다; 삐죽 나오다, [땅이] 높아지다 ¶②바다가 파도치고 있다 4. [소리가] 높아지다 5. 자랑하다, 뽐내다; [감정이] 북받쳐 오르다 ¶③불쌍한 생각으로 그의 가슴은 벅찼다 —[他] 1. …을 부풀게 하다, 크게 하다; 증대하다, 증가하다 2. …의 감정으로 가슴 벅차게 하다 ¶④의기양양해지다

some other strong feelings. ¶*be swollen with pride.*④
—*n.* **1.** [U][C] the act of swelling; the state of being swollen. ¶*a rapid ~ in the population.* **2.** [C] a part that swells out. ¶*the ~ of a belly.* **3.** [C] a gradual rise in the height of the ground; a large, unbroken wave. **4.** [U] a swelling tone or sound. ¶*the ~ of the violin's tone.* **5.** [C] (*colloq.*) a well-dressed or socially important person.
—[名] 1. [모양·수량·정도 따위의] 증대, 늘어남 2. 부푼 부분 3. [토지의] 융기(隆起); 큰 파도 4. [음·목소리의] 높아짐 5. 〔口〕 명사(名士), 맵시꾼

—*adj.* (*colloq.*) first-rate; well-dressed.
—[形] 〔口〕 일류의; 멋장이의

swell·ing [swéliŋ] *n.* **1.** [U] increase; growth. **2.** [C] a swollen part of the body.
—[名] 1. 팽창, 증대 2. 부어오름, 종기

swel·ter [swéltər] *vi.* suffer from the heat; feel very hot; sweat. ¶*under the sweltering sky.*① —*vt.* cause (someone) to swelter. —*n.* [U] the condition of being very hot.
—[自] 더위먹다, 땀투성이가 되다 ¶①염천 아래에서 —[他] …을 더위먹게 하다 —[名] 폭서, 무더위

⁑swept [swept] *v.* pt. and pp. of **sweep**.

swerve [swəːrv] *vi., vt.* curve or cause (something) to turn aside from a straight line. ¶*The car swerved from the road.*① —*n.* [C] the act of swerving; something that swerves.
—[自][他] 빗나가다, 벗어나다; …을 빗나가게 하다 ¶①차는 도로에서 벗어났다 —[名] 빗나감, 벗어남, 벗어난 것

⁑swift [swift] *adj.* able to move very fast; rapid in acting; quick; speedy; prompt. 《~ *to do*》 ↔slow ¶~ *to act.*① —*adv.* quickly; rapidly. —*n.* [C] a small bird somewhat like a swallow.
—[形] 빠른, 곧 …하는; 민속한, 당장의 ¶①곧 행동하다 —[副] 빨리, 신속하게 —[名] 칼새

Swift [swift], **Jonathan** *n.* (1667–1745) a British writer. ⇨[N.B.]
—[名] 영국의 소설가 [N.B.] *Gulliver's Travel* 의 저자

⁑swift·ly [swíftli] *adv.* in a swift manner; quickly; rapidly.
—[副] 재빨리, 신속하게

swig [swig] *n.* [C] (*colloq.*) a big drink drunk without breathing. ¶*take a quick ~ of beer.*① —*vt., vi.* (**swigged, swig·ging**) drink heartily; gulp.
—[名] 벌떡벌떡 마시기 ¶①맥주를 꿀떡꿀떡 들이키다 —[他][自] [···을] 벌떡벌떡 마시다

swill [swil] *n.* **1.** [C] kitchen rubbish; pigs' food. **2.** [U] a deep drink. —*vt., vi.* **1.** drink too much. **2.** wash out (something); rinse.
—[名] 1. 밥찌꺼기 2. 통음(痛飮) —[他][自] 1. [···을] 통음하다 2. [···을] 헹구다

⁑swim [swim] *v.* (**swam, swum, swim·ming**) *vi.* **1.** move in the water by moving the hands and feet; cross a river, etc. by swimming. ¶~ *about*① / ~ *across a river* / ~ *on one's back*② / ~ *against the current* / *go to* ~; *go swimming* / ~ *hand over hand.*③ **2.** float. ¶*a leaf swimming down the river.* **3.** go smoothly; glide. ¶*She swam into the room.* **4.** be dizzy. ¶*My head swims.*④ —*vt.* **1.** move in or across (a river, etc.) by swimming. **2.** cause (someone) to swim or float.
—[自] 1. 헤엄치다, 수영하다, 헤엄쳐 건너다 ¶①헤엄쳐 다니다/②드러누워서 헤엄치다/③크로올로 헤엄치다 2. 뜨다 3. 미끄러지듯이 가다 4. 현기증이 나다 ¶④머리가 어지럽다 —[他] 1. …을 헤엄치다, 헤엄쳐 건너다 2. …을 헤엄치게 하다, 뜨게 하다

—*n.* **1.** [C] the act of swimming. **2.** 《*the* ~》 the current of affairs. ¶*be in* (*out of*) *the* ~ [*of things*].⑤
—[名] 1. 수영, 헤엄 2. 대세, 시대조류 ¶⑤실정에 밝다(어둡다)

swimming bath [⌐–⌐] *n.* a pool for swimming in, usu. indoors.
—[名] [보통] 실내 수영장

swim·ming·ly [swímiŋli] *adv.* with great ease; smoothly; easily.
—[副] 막힘없이, 쉽사리

swimming pool [⌐–⌐] *n.* an artificial pool for swimming in.
—[名] 수영장

swimming suit [⌐–⌐] *n.* a garment worn while swimming; a bathing suit.
—[名] 수영복

swin·dle [swíndl] *vt., vi.* get (something) by deceiving; cheat. ¶~*a person out of money;* ~ *money out of a person.*① —*n.* [C] an act of swindling; a cheat.
—[他][自] [···을] 속여 빼앗다;속이다 ¶①…에게서 돈을 편취하다 —[名] 사기, 협잡, 편취

swin·dler [swíndlər] *n.* [C] a person who swindles.
—[名] 사기꾼

swine [swain] *n.* [C] (pl. **swine**) **1.** a pig. **2.** a very greedy, dishonest or immoral person.
—[名] 1. 돼지 2. 탐욕한 사내, 비열한 사람

swine·herd [swáinhəːrd] *n.* [C] a person who looks after pigs.
—[名] 양돈업자, 돼지치는 사람

⁑swing [swiŋ] *v.* (**swung**) *vi.* **1.** move forward and back, esp. with a regular motion, like a thing hanging from a string. ¶*She swung her arms as she walked.* **2.** move in a curve; turn. ¶~ *round on one's heel*① / ~ *round the bend in the road* / *The door swung open.*② **3.** walk quickly and rhythmically, moving the arms to and fro. ¶*The boys went swinging down the road.*③ **4.** hang down; (*colloq.*) be executed by hanging. ¶~ *from*
—[自] 1. 흔들리다, 진동하다 2. 회전하다, 빙그르르 돌다 ¶①뒤꿈치로 빙그르르 돌다/②문이 빙그르르 열렸다 3. [팔 따위를 흔들면서] 기운차게 걷다 ¶③소년들이 기운차게 길을 걸어갔다 4. 매달리다; 교수형에 처해지다 5. 그네에 타다

S

a branch. **5.** go back and forth in a swing (*n.* 3.). **—*vt.*** **1.** cause (something) to sway back and forth, esp. with a regular motion. ¶~ *one's legs.*④ **2.** cause (something grasped) to move in a circle or a part of a circle. ¶*The batter swung the bat at the ball.* **3.** cause (someone) to go back and forth in a swing. ¶~ *a child.* **4.** cause (something) to hang. ¶~ *a hammock* **5.** cause (something) to turn around. ¶~ *a car.* **6.** (*U.S. colloq.*) manage or handle (something) successfully. ¶*Will she be able to* ~ *it?*

—[他] 1. …을 흔들다, 동요시키다 ¶④발을 흔들흔들하다 2. [쥔 것]을 휘두르다 3. …을 [그네 따위로] 흔들다 4. …을 매달다, 걸다 5. 빙그르르 …의 방향을 바꾸다 6. 《美》 …을 잘 처리하다

—*n.* **1.** [U][C] the act or manner of swinging; the amount of swinging. ¶*the* ~ *of the pendulum* / *give it a* ~. **2.** [C] a free, easy motion, esp. in marching or walking. ¶*walk with a* ~.⑤ **3.** [C] a seat hung from ropes in which one may sit and swing; the act of moving thus. ¶*my turn for a* ~. **4.** [U] freedom of action. ¶*give full* (or *free*) ~ *to him.*⑥ **5.** [U][C] the rhythmic beat of music or poetry.

—[名] 1. 진동, 동요; 휘두르기; 흔드는 법; 진폭(振幅) 2. 기운찬 걸음걸이; 활개치고 걷기 ¶⑤활기있게 걷다 3. 그네[에 타기] 4. 자유 활동; 제멋대로임 ¶⑥그를 자유로 활동시키다 5. [시·음악의] 리듬, 음률, 가락

in full swing, fully operating or proceeding.

[熟] 한창인; 잘 돼가는

swinge·ing [swíndʒiŋ] *adj.* (*colloq.*) very forcible or powerful; very huge; very good.

—[形] 《口》 강한, 심한; 거대한, 엄청난

swing·ing [swíŋiŋ] *adj.* **1.** moving from side to side. **2.** vigorous; lively. **3.** (*colloq.*) excellent.

—[形] 1. 흔들리는 2. 활기있는, 기운찬 3. 《口》 훌륭한

swin·ish [swáiniʃ] *adj.* like a pig; disgusting; mean.

—[形] 돼지 같은; 탐욕한; 상스러운;

swipe [swaip] *n.* [C] (*colloq.*) (in cricket, etc.) a hard blow. **—*vi., vt.*** **1.** (*colloq.*) hit hard. **2.** (*colloq.*) snatch away; steal.

—[名] 《口》 강타 —[自][他] 1. 《口》 [···을] 세게 때리다 2. 《口》 날치기하다, 훔치다

swirl [swəːrl] *n.* [C] **1.** a circular motion of water or the like. **2.** a twist; a curl. ¶*a* ~ *of hair.* **—*vi.*** move quickly with a circular motion; feel dizzy.

—[名] 1. 소용돌이 2. 소용돌이꼴[의 것]
—[自] 소용돌이치다; [머리가] 어지럽다

swish [swiʃ] *vi.* (of a whip, wings, etc.) make a light, hissing sound by cutting through the air. **—*vt.*** **1.** beat (something) with a whip; whip. **2.** cause (something) to swish. **—*n.*** [C] a swishing movement or sound.

—[自] 휙휙 소리나다(내다) —[他] 1. …을 채찍으로 때리다 2. …을 휙휙 울리다 —[名] 채찍을 한 번 휘두르기, 휙하는 소리

Swiss** [swis] *n.* [C] (pl. **Swiss**) a person of Switzerland; 《*the* ~, *collectively*》 the people of Switzerland. **—*adj. of Switzerland, its people, or its culture.

—[名] 스위스 사람 —[形] 스위스의, 스위스 사람의, 스위스 문화의

***switch** [switʃ] *n.* [C] **1.** a long, thin, slender shoot or branch. **2.** a very thin stick used in whipping; a blow with a whip. **3.** a device for turning an electric current on and off. **4.** (*U.S.*) a set of movable rails for turning a train from one track to another. ⇒[N.B.] **5.** a bunch of dead hair used in hair dressing. **6.** a sudden or complete change. ¶*His sudden death caused a* ~ *in the program.*①

—[名] 1. 낭창낭창한 가지 2. 채찍, 회초리; 채찍질 3. [전기의] 스위치, 개폐기(開閉器) 4. [철도의] 전철기(轉轍器) [N.B.] 영국에서는 points라 함 5. [여자가 머리에 넣는] 다리 6. 전환, 변경 ¶①그의 급사로 계획이 변경됐다

—*vt.* **1.** beat (someone or something) with a switch. ¶*He switched the dog with a small stick.* **2.** swing or move (something) back and forth or up and down like a whip. ¶*The horse switched her tail.* **3.** turn (a train) from one track to another. ¶~ *a train from one track to another.*② **4.** (chiefly *U.S.*) direct (thoughts, talk, etc.) to some other subject; change. **5.** (*U.S. colloq.*) exchange. ¶~ *seats at the movie.* **6.** turn on or off (an electric light or current). ¶~ *the radio on* (*off*).

—[他] 1. …을 채찍질하다 2. [회초리·꼬리] 따위를 흔들다, 휘두르다 3. [열차를] 전철하다 4. 《美》 [화제 따위]를 바꾸다; …을 전환하다 5. 《美口》 …을 교환하다, 바꾸다 6. [전기]의 스위치를 움직이다

—*vi.* change. ¶*The wind switched to the south.*

—[自] 바뀌다

switch on (***off***), turn on (off) (an electric light or an electric current, etc.) using a switch; turn on (off) a radio, a television set, etc. ¶~ *on* (*off*) *the radio.*

[熟] …의 스위치를 넣다(끊다); [라디오·텔레비전 따위]를 켜다(끄다)

switch·back [swítʃbæk] *n.* [C] a railroad which runs up and down steep slopes; a railroad which runs in a zigzag manner.

—[名] 전향선(轉向線) (Z자형의 산악 철도선)

switch·board [swítʃbɔːrd] *n.* [C] a board or panel with switches and plugs for connecting electric lines, esp. telephone lines.

—[名] [전력·전등 따위의] 배전반(配電盤), [전화의] 교환기

switch·man [swítʃmən] *n.* ⓒ (pl. **-men** [-mən]) a man who operates railroad switches. —몡 [철도의] 전철수

Switz·er·land [swíts(ə)rlənd/swíts(ə)-] *n.* a small country in central Europe. ⇒N.B. —몡 스위스 N.B. 수도 Bern

swiv·el [swívl] *n.* ⓒ a coupling device which allows two parts to turn freely. ⇒fig. —*vt., vi.* (**-eled, -el·ing** or *Brit.* **-elled, -el·ling**) turn (something) around freely; revolve. —몡 회전 쇠고리 —타재 […을] 선회시키다(하다), 회전시키다(하다)

swivel chair [⌐⌐] *n.* a chair which turns around on its base. [swivel] —몡 회전의자

swol·len [swóul(ə)n] *v.* pp. of **swell**. —*adj.* increased in size or volume; puffed up. —재 부푼, 부어오른

swoon [swu:n] *n.* ⓒ a sudden loss of all feeling caused by illness or shock; a faint. ¶*fall into a ~.*① —*vi.* fall senseless; faint. —몡 기절, 졸도 ¶①기절하다 —재 기절하다, 졸도하다

swoop [swu:p] *vi.* suddenly descend through the air, esp. to attack something. 《~ *down* or *upon* something》 ¶*The eagle swooped down* [*up*]*on the hare.*① —*vt.* carry (something) off suddenly; snatch. 《~ *up* something》 —재 하늘에서 내리덮치다, 습격하다 ¶①독수리가 하늘에서 그 토끼를 향해 내리덮쳤다 —타 갑자기 …을 잡아채다

—*n.* ⓒ the act of swooping; a sudden attack. —몡 급습, 불시의 습격

swop [swɑp / swɔp] *v.* (**swopped, swop·ping**), *n.* =**swap**.

: sword [sɔːrd] *n.* **1.** ⓒ a long, cutting weapon used by a soldier. ¶*draw a ~*① / *put up* (or *sheathe*) *a ~.*② **2.** 《*the ~*》 military power; war. ¶*appeal to the ~*③ / (*proverb*) *The pen is mightier than the ~.*④
1) *at sword's points* [*with each other*], very unfriendly; ready to quarrel.
2) *cross swords*, ⓐ fight. ⓑ argue violently.
3) *put to the sword*, kill (someone) with a sword.
4) *the sword of justice*, the power of the law.
—몡 1. 검(劍), 칼 ¶①칼을 뽑다/②칼을 칼집에 넣다 2. 무력; 전쟁 ¶③무력에 호소하다/④《俚》문(文)은 무(武)보다 강하다
관 1)불화하여, 적대하여 2)ⓐ…와 싸우다 ⓑ격론(激論)을 벌이다 3)…을 죽이다 4)사법권

sword belt [⌐ ⌐] *n.* a belt from which a sword is hung. —몡 칼띠

sword dance [⌐ ⌐] *n.* a dance using swords. —몡 칼춤, 검무(劍舞)

sword·fish [sɔ́ːrdfìʃ] *n.* ⓒ (pl. **-fish·es** or collectively **-fish**) a very large salt-water edible fish with a sword-like point. ⌈sword; fencing.⌉ —몡 황새치

sword·play [sɔ́ːrdplèi] *n.* ⓤ the act or art of using a —몡 검술, 펜싱

swords·man [sɔ́ːrdzmən] *n.* ⓒ (pl. **-men** [-mən]) **1.** a person skilled in the use of a sword. **2.** a person who uses a sword. —몡 1. 검객, 검사 2. 군인, 무사

swore [swɔːr] *v.* pt. of **swear**.

sworn [swɔːrn] *v.* pp. of **swear**. —*adj.* declared; promised in the name of God. ¶~ *brothers*① / ~ *enemies.*② —재 맹세한 ¶①형제의 의를 맺은 친구/②불구대천의 원수

swum [swʌm] *v.* pp. of **swim**.

swung [swʌŋ] *v.* pt. and pp. of **swing**.

syc·a·more [síkəmɔ̀ːr] *n.* ⓒ **1.** a kind of fig tree. **2.** a kind of maple tree; the sycamore maple. —몡 1. 무화과나무의 일종 2. 큰단풍나무

syc·o·phant [síkəfənt] *n.* ⓒ a person who tries to win favor by flattering. —몡 아첨꾼

Syd·ney [sídni] *n.* the largest city and most important seaport in Australia. —몡 시드니

syl·la·bi [síləbài] *n.* pl. of **syllabus**.

syl·lab·ic [siláebik] *adj.* **1.** of or in syllables. **2.** pronounced syllable by syllable. —재 1. 음절의, 음절을 이루는 2. 음절마다 발음하는

syl·lab·i·cate [siláebikèit] *vt.* divide (a word, etc.) into syllables. ⌈words into syllables.⌉ —타 [단어]를 음절로 나누다

syl·lab·i·ca·tion [siláebikéiʃ(ə)n] *n.* ⓤ the division of —몡 음절로 나누기, 분절법

syl·la·ble [síləbl] *n.* ⓒ **1.** a·part of a word pronounced as a unit. **2.** the smallest unit of speech. ¶*I never uttered a ~.*① —몡 1. 음절 2. 한 마디 ¶①그는 한마디도 말을 하지 않았다

syl·la·bus [síləbəs] *n.* ⓒ (pl. **-bus·es** or **-bi**) **1.** a brief statement of a course of study. **2.** a written list of subjects to be studied. —몡 1. [강의의] 적요(摘要), 대요 2. 교수 세목(細目)

syl·lo·gism [síləd͡ʒìz(ə)m] *n.* [U][C] a form of reasoning consisting of two statements and a conclusion.
—[名] 삼단논법

sylph [silf] *n.* [C] **1.** a fairy of the air. **2.** a slender, graceful girl.
—[名] 1. 공기의 정(精) 2. 호리호리한 미녀

syl·van [sílvən] *adj.* of or consisting of the woods or trees; wooded.
—[形] 삼림의, 수목이 우거진

Syl·vi·a [sílviə] *n.* a woman's name.
—[名] 여자 이름

* **sym·bol** [símb(ə)l] *n.* [C] a sign; something that represents or stands for something else.
—[名] 부호, 기호, 상징, 표상

sym·bol·ic [simbálik / -bɔ́l-], **-cal** [-k(ə)l] *adj.* **1.** used as a symbol; of a symbol. **2.** expressed by a symbol.
—[形] 1. 부호(기호)의, 상징적인 2. 부호(기호)로 나타낸

sym·bol·ism [símb(ə)lìz(ə)m] *n.* [U] **1.** the use of symbols to express ideas. **2.** an artistic or literary movement in which symbols are emphasized; the theory or practice of using symbols.
—[名] 1. 부호(기호) 사용, 부호(기호)로 나타내기 2. 상징주의

sym·bol·ize [símb(ə)làiz] *vt.* be a symbol of (something); represent (something) by a symbol. ***—vi.*** use symbols.
—[他] …의 상징이다, …을 상징하다, 부호(기호)로 나타내다 —[自] 부호(기호)를 쓰다

* **sym·met·ri·cal** [simétrik(ə)l] *adj.* having symmetry; well-proportioned.
—[形] 대칭적(對稱的)인, 균형이 잡힌

sym·met·ri·cal·ly [simétrik(ə)li] *adv.* in a symmetrical manner.
—[副] 대칭적으로, 균형있게

sym·me·trize [símitràiz] *vt.* make (something) symmetrical.
—[他] …을 대칭적으로 하다, …의 균형을 잡히게 하다

* **sym·me·try** [símitri] *n.* [U] **1.** similarity of form or arrangement on the opposite sides of a line or plane. **2.** well-balanced form or arrangement of parts.
—[名] 1. 대칭 2. 균형, 균정(均整), 조화

* **sym·pa·thet·ic** [sìmpəθétik] *adj.* **1.** sharing the feelings of another; showing kind feelings toward others. **2.** well-suited.
—[形] 1. 동감하는, 공명하는, 동정하는, 인정있는, 꼭맞는 2. 성미에 맞는

sym·pa·thet·i·cal·ly [sìmpəθétik(ə)li] *adv.* in a sympathetic manner.
—[副] 동정하여, 인정있게

* **sym·pa·thize** [símpəθàiz] *vi.* **1.** share the feelings of another. ¶~ *with someone in his view*① / ~ *with someone's desire.* **2.** feel or show sympathy toward others. ¶~ *with someone in his grief.*②
—[自] 1. 동감하다, 동의하다, 공명하다 ¶①…의 견해에 동의하다 2. 동정하다 ¶②…와 슬픔을 함께하다

sym·pa·thiz·er [símpəθàizər] *n.* [C] a person who sympathizes.
—[名] 동정자, 지지자, 공명자

‡ **sym·pa·thy** [símpəθi] *n.* **1.** [U] sameness of feeling; the state of sharing another's feeling. **2.** [U][C] the ability to share sorrow or trouble with another person. **3.** [U] the feeling of pity.
—[名] 1. 동감, 공명 2. 동정, 인정 3. 연민

sym·phon·ic [simfánik / -fɔ́n-] *adj.* (*Music*) of or having the nature of a symphony.
—[形] 《樂》 교향악의, 교향악적인

sym·pho·ny [símfəni] *n.* [C] **(-nies) 1.** (*Music*) a piece of music for an orchestra. ¶*a ~ orchestra.*① **2.** a pleasant harmony of sounds.
—[名] 1. 《樂》 교향곡(악), 심포니 ¶① 교향악단 2. 조화, 화음

sym·po·si·um [simpóuziəm] *n.* [C] (pl. **-ums** or **-si·a** [-ziə]) **1.** a collection of writing by different writers on one subject. **2.** a meeting for the discussion of one subject.
—[名] 1. [하나의 문제에 관한] 논문집 2. 심포지움, 토론회

* **symp·tom** [sím(p)təm] *n.* [C] a sign; an indication. ¶*a ~ of cancer.*①
—[名] 징후, 징조 ¶①암의 징후

symp·to·mat·ic [sìm(p)təmǽtik] *adj.* of symptoms; signifying; indicative.
—[形] 징후를 나타내는, 징후의, …을 나타내는

syn·a·gogue [sínəgàg / -gɔ̀g] *n.* [C] **1.** an assembly of Jews for religious purposes. **2.** a building for Jewish worship.
—[名] 1. 유대인 집회 2. 유대 교회

syn·chro·nism [síŋkrənìz(ə)m] *n.* [U] **1.** the state of being synchronous. **2.** the arrangement of historical events or persons in order of time.
—[名] 1. 동시성, 동시 발생, 동기(同期) 2. [역사적 사건·인물의] 연대별 배열

syn·chro·nize [síŋkrənàiz] *vi.* happen at the same time. ***—vt.*** **1.** cause (something) to happen at the same time. **2.** arrange (historical events or persons) according to dates. **3.** make (something) agree in time.
—[自] 동시에 일어나다 —[他] 1. …을 동시로 하다, …에 동시성을 지니게 하다 2. …을 발생 연대순으로 배열하다 3. …의 시간을 맞추다

syn·chro·nous [síŋkrənəs] *adj.* happening at the same time.
—[形] 동시의; 동기의

syn·co·pate [síŋkəpèit] *vt.* **1.** (*Grammar*) shorten (a word) by taking letters or sounds from the middle. ⇒[N.B.] **2.** (*Music*) begin (a tone) from the unaccented beat and hold it into an accented one.
—[他] 1. [낱말]의 가운데 음절을 생략하다 [N.B.] over를 o'er로 하는 따위 2. 《樂》 …을 절분(切分)하다

syn·co·pa·tion [sìŋkəpéiʃ(ə)n] *n.* Ⓤ the act of syncopating; the state of being syncopated.
—名 [낱말의] 생략, 중략; [음의] 절분, 싱코페이션

syn·di·cate *n.* [síndikit →*v.*] Ⓒ **1.** persons or companies united in carrying out some plan, usu. needing a large amount of money. **2.** an organization which supplies special articles, pictures, etc. to newspapers, etc.
—*vt.* [-kèit] **1.** combine (companies) into a syndicate. **2.** publish (articles, etc.) through a syndicate.
—名 1. 신디케이트, 기업 연합 2. 신문 잡지 연맹
—他 1. …을 신디케이트 조직으로 하다 2. …을 신디케이트를 통해 발표하다

syn·od [sínəd] *n.* Ⓒ a meeting of officers of a church; an assembly; a council.
—名 종교 회의; 회의

syn·o·nym [sínənim] *n.* Ⓒ a word having the same or almost the same meaning as another word. ↔antonym
—名 동의어, 유어(類語)

syn·on·y·mous [sinónimə s / -nɔ́n-] *adj.* having the same or almost the same meaning.
—形 같은 뜻의, 유사한

syn·op·ses [sinápsi:z / -nɔ́p-] *n.* pl. of **synopsis**.

syn·op·sis [sinápsis / -nɔ́p-] *n.* Ⓒ (pl. **-ses**) a short statement outlining a subject, a book, etc. [or outline.]
—名 줄거리, 개요

syn·op·tic [sinάptik / -nɔ́p-] *adj.* giving a general view
—形 개요의, 개괄적인

syn·op·ti·cal·ly [sinάptik(ə)li / -nɔ́p-] *adv.* in a synoptical manner; in outline; as a summary. [rules of syntax.]
—副 개괄적으로

syn·tac·ti·cal·ly [sintǽktik(ə)li] *adv.* according to the
—副 문장론적으로, 문장 구성상

syn·tax [síntæks] *n.* Ⓤ **1.** sentence structure. **2.** the arrangement of words. **3.** the branch of grammar dealing with this.
—名 1. 문장 구조, 구문(構文) 2. 어구 배열 3. 구문법, 통어론(統語論); 문장론

syn·the·ses [sínθisi:z] *n.* pl. of **synthesis**.

syn·the·sis [sínθisis] *n.* (pl. **-ses**) **1.** Ⓤ the combination of parts or elements so as to form a whole. ↔analysis **2.** Ⓒ a whole formed by combining parts. **3.** Ⓤ the formation of a chemical compound substance.
—名 1. 종합, 합성 2. 종합체 3. 합성

syn·thet·ic [sinθétik] *adj.* **1.** of synthesis. ↔analytic **2.** (*Chemistry*) produced artificially, chiefly by chemical reactions. ¶*a ~ rubber.*① [ner; through synthesis.]
—形 1. 종합의, 합성적인 2. 합성의, 인조의 ¶①인조 고무

syn·thet·i·cal·ly [sinθétik(ə)li] *adv.* in a synthetic man-
—副 종합적으로, 합성적으로

syph·i·lis [sífilis] *n.* Ⓤ a dangerous disease which finally
—名 매독

sy·phon [sáif(ə)n] *n.* =siphon. [affects the brain.]

Syr·i·a [síriə] *n.* a country in western Asia. ⇒N.B.
—名 시리아 N.B. 수도 Damascus

Syr·i·an [síriən] *n.* Ⓒ the people of Syria; Ⓤ the language of Syria. —*adj.* of Syria or Syrians.
—名 시리아 사람, 시리아 말 —形 시리아[사람·말]의

sy·ringe [sírindʒ, -´] *n.* Ⓒ a device for injecting medical liquid, etc. into a body. —*vt.* clean or inject (something) by using a syringe.
—名 주사기, 세척기(洗滌器) —他 …을 주사기로 주사하다, 세척기로 세척하다

syr·up, sir- [sírəp, +*U.S.* sə́:-] *n.* Ⓤ very sweet liquid made from sugar or fruit juices.
—名 시럽, 당밀(糖蜜)

: sys·tem [sístim] *n.* Ⓒ **1.** a group of things, ideas, etc. forming a whole which operates or mo ̄ in harmony. ¶*a mountain ~*① / *the social ~.*② **2.** a classified and arranged group of facts, principles, rules, etc. in a certain field of study. **3.** (*the ~* or *one's ~*) the human body as a whole. **4.** a group of bodily organs having the same function. ¶*the digestive ~.*④ **5.** (*this ~*) the universe. **6.** a plan or method of putting things into classes or groups.
—名 1. 조직, 계통 ¶①산계(山系)/② 사회조직 2. [학문적] 체계 3. 신체 4. [신체 기관의] 계통 ¶③소화[기] 계통 5. 우주 6. 분류법

• **sys·tem·at·ic** [sìstimǽtik] *adj.* **1.** according to a system; orderly; methodical. ¶*a ~ method.*① **2.** having a plan. **3.** of putting things into classes; classifying.
—形 1. 조직적인; 계통적인; 질서 있는 ¶①조직적 방법 2. 계획적인 3. 분류식인

sys·tem·at·i·cal·ly [sìstimǽtik(ə)li] *adv.* according to a system; in a systematic manner.
—副 계통적으로, 조직적으로, 정연히, 계획적으로, 분류적으로

sys·tem·a·ti·za·tion [sìstimətizéiʃ(ə)n / -taizéiʃ(ə)n] *n.* Ⓤ the act of systematizing; the state of being systematized.
—名 계통을 세우기, 조직화, 분류

sys·tem·a·tize [sístimətàiz] *vt.* put (something) into a system; arrange (something) according to a system.
—他 …을 조직화하다, 계통을 세우다, 체계를 세우다, 분류하다

sys·tem·ic [sistémik] *adj.* **1.** of a system. **2.** of or affecting the body as a whole. ¶*a ~ disease.*①
—形 1. 계통의, 조직의 2. 온몸의, 온몸에 걸친 ¶①전신병

T

T, t [tiː] *n.* ⓒ (pl. **T's, t's, Ts, ts** [tiːz]) **1.** the 20th letter of the English alphabet. **2.** an object shaped like T.
 1) *cross the t's*, pay careful attention to very minute points.
 2) *to a T*, exactly; perfectly.

tab [tæb] *n.* ⓒ **1.** a small piece of cloth attached to a coat, etc. used for hanging it up, etc. **2.** any small piece of cloth or paper attached to the edge of a larger piece. **3.** (*colloq.*) account.
 keep a tab (or *tabs*) *on*, (*colloq.*) ⓐ keep an account of (income, outgo, etc.). ⓑ keep (someone or something) under observation.

tab·by [tǽbi] *n.* (pl. **-bies**) **1.** ⓒ a brown or gray cat with black stripes; a female cat. **2.** ⓒ an old woman who gossips unkindly.

tab·er·nac·le [tǽbə(ː)rnæ̀kl] *n.* ⓒ **1.** a tent or hut used as a house for a while. **2.** the human body considered as the place where the soul exists. **3.** (*the T-*) a Jewish temple; a place of worship.

‡**ta·ble** [téibl] *n.* ⓒ **1.** a piece of furniture having a smooth, flat top and legs. ¶ *lay* (or *set, spread*) *the ~.* **2.** (*sing.* only) the food served at a table. ¶ *keep a good ~.* **3.** (*collectively*) the people seated at a table to eat, talk, etc. ¶ *amuse the whole ~.* **4.** a flat surface; a high area of flat land. **5.** a thin, flat piece of wood, stone, metal, etc.; a tablet. **6.** a list; an orderly arrangement of facts, information, figures, etc. ¶ *a ~ of contents* / *a ~ of interest* / *a ~ of weights and measures.*
 1) *at table*, having a meal.
 2) *turn the tables*, reverse a situation.
 —*vt.* **1.** put (cards, etc.) on a table. **2.** (*Parliament*) (*U. S.*) postpone a decision on (a proposal, etc.) indefinitely. **3.** make a list of (something)

tab·leau [tǽblou, +*U.S.* -́] *n.* ⓒ (pl. **-leaus** or **-leaux**) **1.** a representation of a well-known picture, statue, scene, etc. by living persons posing and dressed in costume. **2.** a picture.

tab·leaux [tǽblouz, +*U.S.* -́] *n.* pl. of **tableau**.

ta·ble·cloth [téiblklɔ̀ːθ / -klɔ̀(ː)θ] *n.* ⓒ a cloth for covering a table.

ta·ble d'hôte [tæ̀bldóut] *n.* ⓒ (pl. **ta·bles d'hôte** [tǽblzdóut / tɑ́ːblz-]) a meal served at a fixed time and price at a hotel or restaurant. ↔ à la carte

ta·ble·land [téibllæ̀nd] *n.* ⓒ a high plain; a plateau.

***ta·ble·spoon** [téiblspùːn] *n.* ⓒ **1.** a large spoon used to prepare and serve food. **2.** the amount such a spoon will hold; a tablespoonful. [tablespoon will hold.]

ta·ble·spoon·ful · [téiblspuːnfùl] *n.* ⓒ the amount a

***tab·let** [tǽblit] *n.* ⓒ **1.** a small flat sheet of stone, wood, etc., used to write on; a stone or metal plate with letters carved on it. ¶ *an ancestral ~* / *a memorial ~.* **2.** a number of sheets of writing paper fixed together at one end. **3.** a small, flat piece of medicine.

table talk [-́ -́] *n.* conversation at meals.

table tennis [-́ -́-] *n.* an indoor sport played on a table with small bats and a celluloid ball; ping-pong.

ta·ble·ware [téiblwɛ̀ər] *n.* Ⓤ dishes, knives, spoons, forks, etc. used to set a table or to serve food and drink.

—명 1. 알파벳의 스무 번째 글자 2. T 자형의 것
숙 1)세심한 주의를 기울이다 2)정확히, 꼭

—명 1. [의복 따위의] 옷걸이 끈(천) 2. 부속된 부분 3. (口) 계산

숙 ⓐ…을 기장(記帳)하다 ⓑ…을 감독하다

—명 1. 얼룩 고양이; 암코양이 2. 수다스럽고 심술궂은 노파

—명 1. 임시 오두막집 2. [영혼이 머무르는] 신체 3. 유대 신전(神殿); 예배당

—명 1. 테이블; 식탁 ¶①상을 차리다 2. 식탁에 차린 요리; 음식물 ¶②늘 잘 먹다(호식하다) 3. 식탁에 앉은 사람들; 일좌(一座) 4. 평면; 대지(臺地) 5. 널빤지, 석판(石板); 금속판; 서판(書板) 6. [각종의] 표; 일람표; 목록 ¶③책의 목차/④이율표

숙 1)식사 중 2)형세를 일변시키다; 역습하다
—타 1. …을 탁상에 놓다 2. (美) [의안 따위를] 묵살하다 3. …의 표를 만들다
—명 1. 활인화(活人畫) 2. 그림

—명 테이블보

—명 정식(定食)

—명 고원, 대지(臺地)
—명 1. [식탁용] 큰 숟가락 2. 큰 숟가락 가득[의 분량]

—명 큰 숟가락 하나 가득
—명 1. 서판(書板); 작은 패(牌) ¶① 위패(位牌)/②기념패 2. 메모지, 편지지 3. 정제(錠劑)

—명 식탁에서의 잡담
—명 탁구, 핑퐁

—명 탁상 식기류

tab·loid [tǽblɔid] *n.* ⓒ **1.** a tablet of medicine. **2.** a small daily newspaper with many photographs. *in tabloid form,* condensed.
— 名 1. 정제 2. 타블로이드판 신문
熟 요약되어

ta·boo [təbúː] *n.* ⓒⓊ (*pl.* **-boos**) (esp. among primitive races) the state of being prohibited to use, to speak of, etc. by social force. —*adj.* forbidden or prohibited by social force. ¶ ~ *words.* —*vt.* forbid to do (something) by taboo.
— 名 타부우, 금기(禁忌); 금제(禁制), 금지 — 形 금제로 되어 있는 — 他 …을 금지하다

ta·bor, *Brit.* **-bour** [téibər] *n.* ⓒ a small drum.
— 名 작은 북

tab·u·lar [tǽbjulər] *adj.* **1.** having a flat, tablelike surface. **2.** arranged in a list. ¶*in* ~ *form.*①
— 形 1. 평판(平板)[모양]의 2. 표의, 표로 만든 ¶①표로 만든

tab·u·late *vt.* [tǽbjulèit →*adj.*] arrange (facts, numbers, etc.) in lists. —*adj.* [tǽbjəlit, -leit / -bju-] having a flat surface.
— 他 ¶①을 표로 만들다 — 形 평면의, 평판 모양의

tab·u·la·tion [tæ̀bjuléiʃ(ə)n] *n.* Ⓤ arrangement in lists.
— 名 표로 만들기

tac·it [tǽsit] *adj.* silent; not spoken; understood without being said. ¶*a* ~ *agreement*① / ~ *consent.*②
— 形 무언의; 암묵적(暗默的)인 ¶① 무언의 양해 / ② 묵낙(默諾)

tac·it·ly [tǽsitli] *adv.* in a tacit manner.
— 副 묵묵히; 암암리에

tac·i·turn [tǽsitə̀ːrn] *adj.* speaking very little; not liking to talk. ↔talkative ⌈of being taciturn.⌉
— 形 말수 적은, 과묵한

tac·i·tur·ni·ty [tæ̀sitə́ːrniti] *n.* Ⓤ the state or quality⌉
— 名 무언, 과묵

tack [tæk] *n.* ⓒ **1.** a short nail with a broad, flat head. **2.** (*pl.*) long, loose stitch. **3.** a course of action. ¶*change one's ~.* **4.** the action of sailing a zigzag course against the wind. ⌈(right) course.⌉
1) *be on the wrong (right) tack,* be in the wrong
2) *come* (or *get*) *down to [brass] tacks,* deal with the most important facts.
3) *on the port (starboard) tack,* with the wind on the port (starboard) side.
—*vt.* **1.** fasten (something) with tacks. **2.** stitch (something) loosely together. —*vi.* **1.** sail in a zigzag course against the wind. **2.** change one's course.
— 名 1. 납작한 못, 압정 2. 시침질, 홈질, 가봉 3. 침로(針路); 방침 4. [요트의] 갈짓자로 나아가기
熟 1)방침이 틀리다(틀리지 않다) 2) 3)좌(우)현에 바람을 받고

— 他 1. …을 압정으로 고정시키다 2. …을 가봉하다 — 自 1. 갈짓자로 항행하다 2. 방침(침로)을 바꾸다

• **tack·le** [tǽkl] *n.* **1.** ⓒⓊ a set of ropes and wheels for moving heavy weights, sails, etc. ⇨*fig.* **2.** Ⓤ all the things needed for a play or task; gear. ¶*fishing ~.*① **3.** ⓒ (*Football*) the act of tackling. —*vt.* **1.** try to solve (a problem); try to do (a piece of work, etc.). **2.** (*Football*) seize and stop (an opponent ball-carrier). —*vi.* (*Football*) seize and pull down or stop an opponent ball-carrier. ⌈in a difficult situation.⌉
[tackle 1.]
— 名 1. 활차 장치 2. 도구, 용구 ¶①낚시 도구 3. 〈蹴球〉 태클 — 他 1. …에 달려들다, …을 시도하다 2. 〈蹴球〉 태클하다 — 自 〈蹴球〉 태클하다

tact [tækt] *n.* Ⓤ ability to deal wisely with others, esp.⌉
— 名 재치, 눈치, 약삭빠름

tact·ful [tǽktf(u)l] *adj.* having or showing tact.
— 形 약삭빠른, 재치있는

tac·ti·cal [tǽktik(ə)l] *adj.* of tactics; showing skill in tactics. ▷**tac·ti·cal·ly** [-kəli] *adv.*
— 形 전술의, 전술적이다; 책략에 능한

tac·ti·cian [tæktíʃ(ə)n] *n.* ⓒ an expert in tactics.
— 名 전술가, 책략가

tac·tics [tǽktiks] *n. pl.* **1.** (usu. used as *sing.*) the art or science of arranging and using military and naval forces during a battle. **2.** (used as *pl.*) any skillful methods used to gain an end.
— 名 1. 전술, 병법 2. 책략, 술책

tac·tile [tǽkti(l) / -tail] *adj.* of or having the sense of touch; that can be felt by touch. ¶*a* ~ *organ.*①
— 形 촉각의, 촉각이 있는; 만져서 알 수 있는 ¶①촉각 기관

tact·less [tǽktlis] *adj.* not having or showing tact.
— 形 재치없는, 요령없는

tad·pole [tǽdpòul] *n.* ⓒ a young frog when it first comes out of its egg.
— 名 올챙이

taff·rail [tǽfrèil] *n.* ⓒ a rail around the ship's stern.
— 名 선미(船尾)의 난간

taf·fy [tǽfi] *n.* Ⓤⓒ (*pl.* **-fies**) (*U. S.*) a candy made of sugar, butter and nuts; toffee.
— 名 땅콩을 넣은 캔디, 태피

tag¹ [tæg] *n.* ⓒ **1.** a piece of cardboard, paper, etc. attached to something to show what it is or where it is to be sent. **2.** a small hanging piece; a metal point at
— 名 1. 꼬리표, 짐표 2. 늘어진 것(리본 따위); 끈 끝의 쇠붙이 3. 상투적 문구

the end of a string. **3.** a phrase or sentence often quoted. **—v.** (**tagged, tag·ging**) *vt.* **1.** fix a tag to (something). **2.** (*colloq.*) follow closely. **—*vi.*** (*colloq.*) follow closely.

—[他] 1. …에 꼬리표를 달다 2. 〔口〕 …에 붙어 다니다 —[自] 붙어 다니다

tag² [tæg] *n.* [U] a children's game in which one runs after and tries to touch another. **—*vt.*** (**tagged, tag·ging**) touch or tap (someone) with the hand.

—[名] 술래잡기 —[他] [술래잡기에서 술래가] …을 붙잡다

⁑**tail** [teil] *n.* [C] **1.** the movable part at the end of the body of an animal, bird, or fish. **2.** something like a tail in its shape; a long braid of hair. ¶*the ~ of a comet.* **3.** the end or last part of anything; back or rear. ¶*the ~ of a procession*① | *the ~ of one's eye*② | *the ~ of a storm.*③ **4.** 《*pl.*》 the reverse side of a coin. ↔heads **5.** 《*pl.*》 (*colloq.*) a tail coat

—[名] 1. [짐승 · 새 · 물고기 따위의] 꼬리, 꽁지 2. 꼬리 모양의 것; 땋아늘인 머리 3. 끄트머리; 말미(末尾); 끝 ¶①행렬의 후부 / ②눈초리 / ③폭풍우의 잔재 4. [돈 던지기에서] 동전의 뒷면 5. 《口》 연미복

1) ***keep tails up,*** be in good spirits.
2) ***turn tail,*** run away from danger, difficulty, trouble, etc.
3) ***twist** someone's **tail,*** cause someone to feel pain; torment.
4) ***with the*** (or *one's*) ***tail between the*** (or *one's*) ***legs,*** utterly defeated and frightened.

[熟] 1)원기 왕성하다 2)[홱 돌아서서] 내빼다 3)…을 못살게 굴다 4)주눅이 들어, 겁에 질려

—*vt.* **1.** provide (a coat, etc.) with a tail. **2.** connect (something) at the end. **3.** remove a tail from (something). **4.** (*colloq.*) follow (someone) closely and secretly. ¶*~ a thief.* **—*vi.*** **1.** follow as a tail. 《*~ along* or *behind* something or someone》 **2.** grow less. **3.** (*colloq.*) follow closely behind. 《*~ after* someone》

—[他] 1. …에 꼬리를 달다 2. …을 [꼬리 부분에서] 연결하다 3. …의 꼬리를 자르다 4. …을 미행하다 —[自] 1. 꼬리처럼되다 2. 차츰 작아지다(사라지다) 3. 뒤따라가다

tail coat [⏑ ⏑] *n.* a man's coat with long tails in the back, usu. worn on formal occasions.

—[名] 연미복

tail·less [téillis] *adj.* without a tail.

—[形] 꼬리 없는

tail·light [téillàit] *n.* [C] a light at the back end of a vehicle.

—[名] 미등(尾燈)

⁑**tai·lor** [téilər] *n.* [C] a person whose business is to make or repair clothes. ¶*sit ~ fashion*① | *The ~ makes the man.*② **—*vt.*** make (clothes) by a tailor's work.

—[名] 양복 짓는 사람 ¶①책상다리를 하고 앉다/②옷이 날개다 —[他] [옷]을 짓다, 재단하다

tai·lored [téilərd] *adj.* (usu. of a woman's dress) simple and well-fitting.

—[形] [보통 부인복이] 몸에 꼭 맞는

tai·lor-made [téilərmèid] *adj.* **1.** tailored. **2.** custom-made; made-to-order.

—[形] 1. 몸에 꼭 맞는 2. 마춤 옷의

taint [teint] *n.* **1.** [C] a spot or stain; a trace of something bad, impure, or corrupt. ¶*a ~ of insanity.* **2.** [U] infection; corruption. **—*vt.*** give a taint to (something); spoil. **—*vi.*** become tainted.

—[名] 1. 더럼, 오점; [나쁜 것의] 형적, 기미 2. 감염; 부패, 타락 —[他] …을 더럽히다, 부패시키다 —[自] 더러워지다, 부패하다

⁑**take** [teik] *v.* (**took, tak·en**) *vt.* **1.** grasp; hold; embrace. ¶*She took me by the hand.* **2.** get possession of (something); catch; seize; capture. ¶*~ the enemy's fort.*① **3.** gain; obtain; earn. ¶*~ a degree*② | *~ first place* | *~ 200 dollars a week.* **4.** rent; hire. ¶*~ a house at the seaside.* **5.** buy or receive (a newspaper, etc.) regularly by paying for it. ¶*She takes two pints of milk daily.* **6.** receive or accept willingly. ¶*~ presents.* **7.** remove; subtract; steal. ¶*~ 7 from 12* | *Cancer took her husband.*③ **8.** suffer an attack of (a disease, etc.) ¶*~ cold* | *be taken with a violent pain.* **9.** choose; select. ¶*~ the shorter way* | *~ a line from Milton.* **10.** make use of (something). ¶*You should ~ every opportunity.*④ **11.** eat; drink; swallow. ¶*~ breakfast* | *~ a deep breath.* **12.** lead. 《~ someone or something *to*》 ¶*This road takes you to the park.* **13.** carry. ¶*~ letters to the post office* | *She took him some flowers.* **14.** require; need; spend. ⇒[usage] ¶*The baggage takes much room.*⑤ | *It took them many years to make this.* **15.** please; attract; charm. ¶*~ one's fancy*⑥ | *She was taken with the painting on sight.*⑦ **16.** travel by (a bus, train, etc.). ¶*~ a plane to Osaka.* **17.** undergo; endure. ¶*~ punishment*⑧ | *~ an examination.* **18.** photograph. ¶*She takes a good picture.* **19.** have (something) in mind; feel. ¶*~ pride in my work* | *~ pleasure in painting.* **20.** do; perform; execute. ¶~

—[他] 1. …을 [손에] 잡다; 쥐다; 품다 2. …을 손에 넣다; 붙잡다; 포박하다 ¶①적의 요새를 점령하다 3. …을 얻다; 획득하다; 벌다 ¶②학위를 따다 4. …을 임차(賃借)하다 5. …을 구독하다; 받다 6. …을 받다, 받아들이다 7. …을 제거하다; 가져가 버리다; 훔치다 ¶③암으로 그녀는 남편을 잃었다 8. [병]에 걸리다, 감염하다 9. …을 선택하다 10. …을 이용하다 ¶④모든 기회는 이용해야 한다 11. [음식]을 먹다; 마시다; 숨쉬다 12. …을 데리고 가다; 이끌다 13. …을 가지고 가다, 휴대하다 14. …을 필요로 하다 [usage] 때로 it를 주어로 취함 ¶⑤이 짐은 장소를 많이 차지한다 15. [마음]을 끌다; 기쁘게 하다 ¶⑥마음에 들다/⑦그녀는 그 그림을 보고 마음이 끌렸다 16. …을 타고 가다 17. …에 따르다; …을 받아들이다; 감수하다 ¶⑧벌을 받다 18. [사진]을 찍다; 촬영하다 19. …을 느끼다 20. [어떤 동작]을 하다 21. …에 적다; 적어 두다 22. …을 재다; 확인하다 ¶⑨키를 재다 23. …이라고 생각하다, 여기다; 해석하다 ¶⑩어떤 일을 나쁘게(좋게) 생각하다/⑪사람들을 있는 그대

a leap | *~ care* | *~ exercise.* **21.** write down. ¶*The students took notes on the lecture.* **22.** find out (something) by inquiry, measurement, etc. ¶*~ one's measure.*⑨ **23.** regard; consider; assume as a fact; understand. 《~ something *as*》 ¶*~ something easy* | *~ something ill (well)*⑩ | *~ people as they are*⑪ | *How do you ~ his remarks?* **24.** surprise or attack esp. suddenly; strike. ¶*~ the enemy in the rear*⑫ | *The blow took him on the nose.* **25.** adopt; employ; admit. ¶*~ a lodger* | *~ a woman.*⑬ **26.** enjoy; indulge in (a nap, etc.) ¶*~ one's ease* | *~ a holiday.* **—*vi.*** **1.** get possession; catch. **2.** have effect. ¶*The vaccination took.* **3.** (of a plant) take root. **4.** become popular. ¶*That book took well.* **5.** (*U.S.*) (*colloq.*) become ill or sick. **6.** be photographed in a specified way. ¶*She always takes well.*⑭ **7.** take away; detract. 《~ *from* enjoyment, etc.》

로 생각하다 **24.** …을 [갑자기] 놀라게 하다; 습격하다; 치다 ¶⑫적의 배후를 습격하다 **25.** …을 맞이하다 ¶⑬아내를 맞이하다 **26.** [휴식 따위]를 취하다(즐기다) **—**[自] **1.** 취하다, 획득하다 **2.** [우두가] 앉다; [약이] 듣다 **3.** 뿌리박다 **4.** 인기를 얻다 **5.** 《口》 [병이] 되다, 옮다 **6.** [사진이] 찍히다 ¶⑭그녀는 언제나 사진이 잘 된다 **7.** 빼다; 빠지다

1) ***take after,*** ⓐ resemble; look like. ⓑ run after; pursue.
2) ***take back,*** ⓐ regain possession. ⓑ withdraw.
3) ***take down,*** ⓐ write down. ⓑ lower (someone) in power, pride, etc. ⓒ pull down (a building, etc.) piece by piece. ⓓ swallow (food) with difficulty.
4) ***take*** (=*mistake*) *someone* ***for*** *another person.*
5) ***take in,*** ⓐ receive; admit. ¶***~ in*** *boarders.* ⓑ visit; attend. ⓒ include. ⓓ cheat; deceive. ⓔ understand.
6) ***take it out of,*** (*colloq.*) exhaust; tire (someone) greatly.
7) ***take off,*** ⓐ remove (clothes, etc.). ⓑ leave; go out. ⓒ (of an airplane) depart. ⓓ (*colloq.*) imitate. ⓔ draw away; subtract.
8) ***take on,*** ⓐ employ. ⓑ undertake. ⓒ accept (a challenge, etc.). ⓓ (*colloq.*) show violent emotion.
9) ***take out,*** ⓐ remove. ⓑ (*colloq.*) accompany; escort. ⓒ obtain (a license, etc.).
10) ***take to,*** ⓐ become fond of. ⓑ go to or escape to (a place). ⓒ devote oneself to. ⓓ fall into the habit of using (something).
11) ***take up,*** ⓐ lift; raise; pick up. ⓑ begin; begin (something interrupted). ¶*~ up a story.* ⓒ shorten. ⓓ arrest. ⓔ absorb (liquid). ⓕ occupy (place or time). ⓖ study.
12) ***take up*** (=*become friendly*) ***with*** *someone.*

[熟] 1)ⓐ…을 닮다 ⓑ…의 뒤를 쫓다 2)ⓐ되찾다 ⓑ철회하다 3)ⓐ…을 쓰다, 적다 ⓑ…에게 창피를 주다 ⓒ…을 부수다 ⓓ…을 삼키다 4)…을 …이라고 잘못 생각하다 5)ⓐ…을 받아들이다; 수용하다 ⓑ…을 방문하다 ⓒ…을 포괄하다 ⓓ…을 속이다 ⓔ…을 이해하다 6)《口》…을 지치게 하다 7)…을 벗다 ⓐ가 버리다 ⓑ출발(이륙)하다 ⓒ《口》흉내내다 ⓓ…을 에누리하다, 빼다 8)ⓐ…을 고용하다 ⓑ…을 떠맡다 ⓒ…와 싸우다 ⓓ《口》흥분하다 9)ⓐ…을 꺼내다 ⓑ《口》…에 시중들다 ⓒ…을 출원(出願)하다 10)ⓐ…을 좋아하게 되다 ⓑ…으로 가다 ⓒ…에 전렴하다 ⓓ…이 습관이 되다 11)ⓐ…을 들어 올리다; 태워주다 ⓑ…을 시작하다; [중단된 이야기 따위]의 뒤를 잇다 ⓒ…을 줄이다, 짧게 하다 ⓓ…을 체포하다 ⓔ…을 빨아 올리다; 흡수하다 ⓕ…을 차지하다 ⓖ공부하다; 이수(履修)하다 12)…와 사이가 좋아지다

—*n.* [C] **1.** the quantity of fish ¶*a large ~ of fish.* **2.** the act or process of taking. **3.** (*U.S.*) an amount taken or received in payment.

—[名] **1.** 어획량 **2.** 받기, 취(取)하기 **3.** 《美》 매상고; 이익

take-in [téikìn] *n.* [C] (*colloq.*) cheating; trickery.

—[名] 《口》 협잡, 사기

:tak·en [téik(ə)n] *v.* pp. of **take**.

take-off [téikɔ̀ːf / -ɔ̀f] *n.* [C] **1.** (*colloq.*) an amusing imitation; a caricature. **2.** the place at which the feet leave the ground in jumping; the place where an airplane leaves the ground. **3.** the act or process of taking off.

—[名] **1.** 《口》 흉내; 만화 **2.** 도약점(跳躍點); 이륙점 **3.** 도약; 이륙

tak·ing [téikiŋ] *adj.* **1.** attractive; pleasing. **2.** infectious. **—*n.*** [C] **1.** something taken. **2.** 《*pl.*》 earnings; receipts. **3.** (*colloq.*) perplexity; a state of agitation. ¶*in a great ~.*①

—[形] **1.** 매력이 있는; 애교가 있는 **2.** 전염하는 **—**[名] **1.** 포획물 **2.** 소득; 매상고 **3.** 《口》 난처함; 소동 ¶①몹시 조바심하여

talc [tælk] *n.* [U] a soft, smooth mineral, used to make face powder, etc.

—[名] 활석(滑石)

tal·cum [tǽlkəm] *n.* [U] **1.** talc. **2.** powder for the body and face made from talc; talcum powder.

—[名] **1.** 활석 **2.** 화장분

:tale [teil] *n.* [C] **1.** a story. ¶*a fairy ~* | *tell one's ~*① | *His ~ is told.*② **2.** 《*pl.*》 a piece of gossip or scandal; a falsehood; a lie. ¶*old wives' tales*③ **3.** (*archaic*) count; total. ¶*The ~ is complete.*
1) ***tell its own tale,*** explain itself.
2) ***tell tales,*** tell someone else's secrets; gossip.

—[名] **1.** 이야기 ¶①신세타령을 하다/②그는 이제 글렀다 **2.** 고자질; 험담; 거짓말 ¶③터무니없는 이야기 **3.** 《古》 계산; 총계
[熟] 1)설명을 들을 것도 없이 명백하다 2)고자질하다

T

tale·bear·er [téilbɛ̀ərər] *n.* ⓒ a person who gossips or tells secrets. —名 고자질군, 밀고자

*tal·ent [tǽlənt] *n.* **1.** ⓒⓊ ability to do something well. (~ *for*) ¶*a man of ~*① / *He has a ~ for writing.* **2.** (*collectively*) people who have talent. ¶*all the ~ of the country.*② [abilities to lie idle.] *hide one's talents in a napkin,* allow one's gifts and —名 1. [특수한] 재능, 재주 ¶①재능 (才人) 2. 재능있는 사람들, 인재, 인재 ¶② 한 나라의 인재

熟 [자기의] 재능을 썩이다

tal·ent·ed [tǽləntid] *adj.* having talent; gifted. —形 재능 있는, 유능한

tal·ent·less [tǽlntlis] *adj.* without talent. —形 재능이 없는, 무능한

tale·tell·er [téiltèlər] *n.* ⓒ a storyteller; a talebearer. —名 이야기하는 사람; 고자질군

tal·is·man [tǽlismən / -liz-] *n.* ⓒ (pl. **-mans**) a stone, ring, etc. engraved with figures, supposed to have magic power and to bring good luck; a charm. —名 부적, 호신부(護身符)

‡talk [tɔːk] *vi.* **1.** express ideas by spoken words; communicate. ¶*~ sensible (big, tall)*① / *~ by signs* / *Her baby can't ~ yet.* **2.** have a conversation; consult. ¶*~ to another* / *You should ~ with your adviser.* / *What are you talking about?* **3.** chatter; gossip. ¶*~ behind one's back.* **4.** make sounds that suggest speech. ¶*The kettles were talking.*② —*vt.* **1.** express (something) in speech; discuss. ¶*~ nonsense* / *~ business.*③ **2.** use (a certain language) in speaking. ¶*~ French.* **3.** bring (someone) into a certain state by talking; persuade. (*~ someone to do; ~ someone into or out of doing*) ¶*~ oneself hoarse*④ / *~ a child to sleep.*

—自 1. 말하다; 이야기하다; 지껄이다 ¶①그럴 듯한(터무니없는) 이야기를 하다 2. 서로 이야기하다; 담화하다;의 논하다 3. 수다떨다, 소문 이야기를 하 다 4. 지껄이는 듯한 소리를 내다 ¶② 주전자가 소리를 내며 끓고 있었다 — 他 1. …을 이야기하다, 말하다 ¶③장 사(전문) 이야기를 하다 2. [외국어]를 말하다, 쓰다 3. 이야기하여 …에게 … 시키다 ¶④너무 지껄여서 목이 쉬다

1) *talk someone around* (or *Brit.* **round**), persuade.
2) *talk at,* (*U. S.*) say something critical of (someone) in his presence but to a third person.
3) *talk back,* answer in an impolite manner.
4) *talk down,* make (someone) silent by talking loudly and effectively.
5) *talk down to,* talk to (someone) in a rude manner.
6) *talk of,* take (something) as a topic of conversation; discuss. ¶*Talk of the devil, and he is sure to appear.*
7) *talk out,* talk until conversation is exhausted.
8) *talk over,* ⓐ persuade. ⓑ discuss.
9) *talk up,* ⓐ speak clearly and openly. ⓑ praise. ⓒ speak to (someone) to promote his interest.

熟 1) …을 설득하다 2) (美) …에 빗대 어 말하다 3) 말대꾸하다, 말을 되받다 4) …을 말로 꼼짝 못하게 하다 5) …을 깔보고 말하다, …에게 무례한 말씨를 쓰다 6) …의 일을 이야기하다; 소문 이야기를 하다 7) 철저하게 말하다 8) ⓐ …을 설득하다 ⓑ …을 논하다 9) ⓐ 큰 소리로 똑똑히 말하다 ⓑ …을 칭찬 하다 ⓒ …을 흥미있게 이야기하다

—*n.* **1.** Ⓤⓒ the act of talking; conversation; idle chatter; spoken words. ¶*big ~*⑤ / *end in ~.*⑥ **2.** ⓒ an informal speech; an address. ¶*give a ~ on a problem.* **3.** Ⓤ rumor; gossip; the subject of gossip or conversation. ¶*the ~ of the town.* **4.** a meeting for discussion; a conference. **5.** Ⓤ the way of talking.

—名 1. 이야기, 담화, 좌담 ¶⑤호언장 담 /⑥말만으로 끝나다 2. [약식의] 강 화(講話); 연설 3. 소문, 평판; 화제, 이 야깃거리 4. 회의, 회담 5. 말투, 말씨

talk·a·tive [tɔ́ːkətiv] *adj.* fond of talking. ↔taciturn —形 수다스러운, 이야기하기 좋아하는

talk·er [tɔ́ːkər] *n.* ⓒ a person who talks; a talkative person. [↔silent film] —名 이야기하는 사람; 수다장이

‡talk·ie [tɔ́ːki] *n.* (often *pl.*) (*colloq.*) a talking picture. —名 (口) 발성 영화

talk·ing [tɔ́ːkiŋ] *adj.* that talks; talkative. —*n.* Ⓤ discussion; conversation. [buke.] —形 말을 하는; 수다스러운 —名 담 화, 수다

talk·ing-to [tɔ́ːkiŋtùː] *n.* ⓒ (**-tos**) (*colloq.*) a severe re- —名 (口) 잔소리, 꾸지람

‡tall [tɔːl] *adj.* **1.** high; higher than the average. ↔short ¶*a ~ man.* **2.** of a certain height. ¶*I am five feet ~.* **3.** (*colloq.*) impossible or almost impossible to believe. ¶*a ~ price*① / *a ~ order*② / *a ~ tale.*③ —形 1. 키가 큰 2. 키(높이)가 …의 3. (口) 터무니없는; 과장된 ¶①터무니 없는 값/② 되지도 않을 말/③허풍

tal·low [tǽlou] *n.* Ⓤ the fat from animals, such as sheep, cows, etc. used to make candles and soap. —*adj.* made of tallow. ¶*a ~ candle.*① [color in the face.] —名 수지(獸脂) —形 수지로 만든 ¶ ①수지 양초

tal·low-faced [tǽloufèist] *adj.* having a pale, unhealthy —形 얼굴이 창백한

tal·ly [tǽli] *n.* ⓒ (pl. **-lies**) **1.** a stick on which scores are recorded to show the amount of a payment. **2.** anything used as a record for an account. **3.** a cut mark made on a tally. **4.** an account; the score. ¶*a ~ of a game.* —*vt.* **1.** mark (a score) on a tally; —名 1. 할부(割符), 부모(符木), 부신 (符信) 2. 계산서 3. [할부의] 새긴 눈 금 4. 계산; 득점 —他 1. [할부에] 을 새기다; …을 기록하다; 계산하다

talon [1175] **tank**

record; count up. **2.** make (two things) agree or correspond. —*vi.* agree; correspond. (*~ with something*)
tal·on [tǽlən] *n.* ⓒ ((usu. *pl.*)) a claw of a bird such as eagle or an hawk.
tam·a·ble [téiməbl] *adj.* that can be tamed.
tam·a·risk [tǽmərìsk] *n.* ⓒ a small evergreen tree with slender, feathery branches.
tam·bou·rine [tæ̀mbərí:n] *n.* ⓒ a small drum with several pairs of metal disks used in some dances.
* **tame** [teim] *adj.* **1.** changed from a wild state to a harmless and gentle state; gentle; harmless. ¶*a ~ bird* / *~ cats.*① **2.** without spirit; dull; not interesting. —*vt.* make (an animal) gentle and harmless. —*vi.* become gentle and harmless.
tame·a·ble [téiməbl] *adj.* =tamable.
tame·ly [téimli] *adv.* in a tame manner.
tame·ness [téimnis] *n.* Ⓤ the state or quality of being [tame.]
tam-o'-shan·ter [tǽməʃæ̀ntər / tæ̀məʃǽntə] *n.* ⓒ a Scotch cap with a loose, round top like a beret. ⇒N.B., fig.
tamp [tæmp] *vt.* **1.** pack down (the earth) by a series of blows or taps. **2.** fill (a hole) with mud, etc.
tam·per [tǽmpər] *vi.* change dishonestly; change in a wrong way so as to cause damage. (*~ with something*) ¶ *~ with a written paper*① / *~ with a machine.*②
* **tan** [tæn] *v.* (**tanned, tan·ning**) *vt.* **1.** turn (the skin of an animal) into leather with a special liquid. **2.** (of the sun) make (a person's skin) brown. —*vi.* **1.** be made into leather. **2.** become brown by the sun. —*n.* Ⓤ a yellowish-brown color; a brown color given to a person's skin by the sun. —*adj.* yellowish-brown.
tan·dem [tǽndəm] *adv.* (of two horses) one behind another. —*n.* ⓒ **1.** a pair of horses which pull a carriage arranged one behind the other; such a carriage. **2.** a bicycle with two seats, one behind the other. ⇒fig. —*adj.* arranged tandem. [tandem 2.]
tang¹ [tæŋ] *n.* ⓒ **1.** the part of a knife, etc. that is connected with the handle. **2.** a strong taste; a sharp [smell.]
tang² [tæŋ] *n.* ⓒ a sharp ringing sound.
tan·gent [tǽndʒ(ə)nt] *adj.* touching; (*Geometry*) touching a curve at one point only.
—*n.* ⓒ (*Geometry*) a tangent line.
fly (or *go*) *off at a tangent,* change suddenly from one line of thought or action to another.
tan·ge·rine [tæ̀ndʒərí:n] *n.* ⓒ a small orange with a thick, loose skin.
tan·gi·bil·i·ty [tæ̀ndʒibíliti] *n.* Ⓤ the quality or state that can be touched; clearness. [actual.]
tan·gi·ble [tǽndʒəbl] *adj.* **1.** touchable. **2.** real; clear;
tan·gle [tǽŋgl] *vt.* **1.** twist (threads, etc.) in a confused mass. **2.** confuse; make (something) difficult to understand. —*vi.* become tangled. —*n.* ⓒ a tangled mass; a confused state. ¶*be in a ~* / *traffic ~*.
tan·go [tǽŋgou] *n.* ⓒ (pl. **-gos**) a slow dance for two persons originally from South America; music for this dance.
* **tank** [tæŋk] *n.* ⓒ **1.** a large metal container for holding a liquid or gas. ¶*a ~ car*① / *a ~ ship.*② **2.** a heavy fighting motor-car carrying guns, used in battle.

2. …을 부합시키다 —⃞自 부합하다, 일치하다
—⃞名 [맹금(猛禽)의] 발톱

—⃞名 길들일 수 있는
—⃞名 위성류(渭城柳)

—⃞名 탬버린

—⃞名 1. 길든 ¶①집고양이 2. 유순한; 무기력한; 시시한; 재미없는 —⃞他 [동물]을 길들이다 —⃞自 [동물이] 길들다

—⃞名 길들여서, 유순하게
—⃞名 길듦; 유순
—⃞名 베레에 형 모자 N.B. tam 이라고도 함

—⃞他 1. [흙 따위]를 다져 굳히다 2. [남포 구멍]에 진흙 따위를 틀어막다

—⃞自 함부로 고치다; 만지작거리다 ¶①서류를 함부로 고치다/②기계를 만지작거려 망가뜨리다

—⃞他 1. [가죽]을 무두질하다 2. [피부]를 볕에 태우다 —⃞自 1. 무두질 가죽이 되다 2. [피부가] 햇볕에 타다 —⃞名 황갈색; 햇볕에 탐 —⃞形 황갈색의

—⃞副 [두 마리의 말을] 세로로 한 줄로 매어
—⃞名 1. 세로로 맨 두 마리의 [말이 끄는 마차] 2. 2인승 자전거

—⃞形 두 마리를 맨, 2인승의
—⃞名 1. [칼 따위의] 슴베 2. 얼얼한 맛, 독한 냄새
—⃞名 강한 음향
—⃞形 접하는, 《幾》 접선(接線)의

—⃞名 《幾》 접선
熟 [이야기 따위가] 갑자기 옆길로 나가다
—⃞名 탄지르 오렌지

—⃞名 만져서 알 수 있음; 명백

—⃞形 1. 만질 수 있는 2. 명백한; 현실의
—⃞他 1. …을 엉키게 하다, 얽히게 하다 2. …을 당황하게 하다 —⃞自 엉키다, 얽히다; 당황하다 —⃞名 엉킴; 분규

—⃞名 탕고[춤]; 그 곡

—⃞名 1. [물·기름·가스 따위의] 탱크 ¶①유조차(油槽車)(물차) / ②유조선 2. 전차(戰車), 탱크

tankard [1176] tarantella

tank·ard [tǽŋkərd] *n.* ⓒ a large cup with one handle used for drinking beer. ⇒fig.
—ⓝ 큰 컵

tank·er [tǽŋkər] *n.* ⓒ a ship with tanks for carrying oil.
—ⓝ 유조선

tan·ner [tǽnər] *n.* ⓒ a person whose business is to make leather by tanning the skins of animals.
—ⓝ 무두질 직공, 제혁 업자(製革業者)

tan·ner·y [tǽnəri] *n.* ⓒ (pl. **-ner·ies**) a place where the skin of animals are tanned.
—ⓝ 피혁공장

[tankard]

tan·nic [tǽnik] *adj.* of or found in tannic acid.
—ⓐ 타닌의

tannic acid [⌐ ⌐] *n.* a strong acid found in tea, etc.
—ⓝ 타닌산(酸)

tan·nin [tǽnin] *n.* =tannic acid.

tan·ta·lize [tǽntəlàiz] *vt.* trouble (someone) by exciting hopes or fears which will not be realized.
—ⓥ …을 애타게 만들다

Tan·ta·lus [tǽntələs] *n.* (in Greek mythology) a son
tan·ta·mount [tǽntəmàunt] *adj.* equal. of Zeus.
—ⓝ 탄탈루스
—ⓐ 동등한

tan·trum [tǽntrəm] *n.* ⓒ a fit of bad temper.
—ⓝ 짜증, 화

* **tap**¹ [tæp] *v.* (**tapped, tap·ping**) *vt.* strike or touch lightly. ¶ ~ *someone on the shoulder*① / ~ *one's stick against the window.* —*vi.* strike light blows. —*n.* ⓒ a light blow; the sound made by it.
—ⓥ …을 가볍게 치다, 톡톡 두드리다 ¶①남의 어깨를 톡톡 치다 —ⓝ 톡톡 두드리다 —ⓝ 경타(輕打), 가볍게 치는 소리

tap² [tæp] *n.* ⓒ 1. a pipe or hole of a cask through which liquor is drawn; a cock. ¶ *turn on (off) a ~.*① 2. (*Electricity*) a point where connection is made.
on tap, ⓐ (of liquor) kept in a cask with a tap and ready to be drawn off. ⓑ (*colloq.*) ready for use.
—*vt.* (**tapped, tap·ping**) put a tap on (a cask); let out (liquor) by drawing a tap. feet, toes, or heels.
—ⓝ 1. [술통의] 꼭지, 주둥이, 마개 ¶①마개를 따다(열다) 2. 탭[도선(導線)의 접촉점]
熟 ⓐ[술을] 언제든지 마개를 따서 마실 수 있는 ⓑ준비가 된
—ⓥ …에 주둥이를 달다; [술통]의 마개를 빼고 술을 따르다

tap dance [⌐ ⌐] *n.* a dance with taps (tap¹ *n.*) of the
—ⓝ 탭댄스

* **tape** [teip] *n.* 1. ⓤⓒ a long, narrow strip of cloth, paper or metal used to tie something; material in the form of a narrow strip. 2. ⓤⓒ tape of paper on which telegraph messages are recorded. 3. ⓒ a tape measure.
—ⓝ 1. 납작한 끈, 테이프 2. 전신 수신기 3. 줄자, 권척(卷尺)

tape·line [téiplàin] *n.* =tape measure.

tape measure [⌐ ⌐⌐] *n.* a long narrow strip of cloth, paper, metal, etc. used for measuring length.
—ⓝ 줄자

* **ta·per** [téipər] *n.* ⓒ a long, slender candle. —*adj.* becoming smaller toward one end. —*vi.* become gradually smaller toward one end. —*vt.* make (something) gradually smaller toward one end.
—ⓝ 가느다란 양초 —ⓐ 끝이 가느다란 —ⓥ 끝이 가느다래지다 —ⓥ …을 끝을 가느다랗게 하다

* **tape recorder** [⌐ ⌐⌐⌐] *n.* an electrical machine for recording and playing back sound on magnetic tape.
—ⓝ 테이프 녹음기

tap·es·try [tǽpistri] *n.* ⓤⓒ (pl. **-tries**) cloth with pictures or designs woven in it, used to decorate a room.
—ⓝ 수단(繡緞)

tape·worm [téipwə̀:rm] *n.* ⓒ a long, flat worm that lives in the bowels of man and other animals.
—ⓝ 촌충

tap·i·o·ca [tæ̀pióukə] *n.* ⓤ a starchy food obtained from the root of the cassava plant and used for puddings, etc.
—ⓝ 타피오카(식용 녹말의 일종)

ta·pir [téipər] *n.* ⓒ a large pig-like animal with a long nose in Central and South America. ⇒fig.
—ⓝ 맥(貊)

[tapir]

tap·room [tǽprù(:)m] *n.* ⓒ a room where alcoholic drinks are served; a barroom.
—ⓝ 술집

tap·root [tǽprù:t, +*U.S.* -rùt] *n.* ⓒ the main root of a plant.
—ⓝ 직근(直根)

* **tar**¹ [tɑ:r] *n.* ⓤ a thick, black, oily substance obtained from wood, coal, etc. ¶ *coal* ~.① —*vt.* (**tarred, tar·ring**) cover (something) with tar. faults.
1) *be tarred with the same brush,* have the same
2) *tar and feather,* cover (someone) with heated tar and feathers as a punishment.
—ⓝ 타르 ¶①코울타르 —ⓥ …에 타르를 칠하다
熟 1)똑같은 결점을 갖고 있다 2)사람의 몸에 타르를 칠하고 그 위에 깃털을 꽂다[옛날 미국 흑인의 사형(私刑)]

tar·an·tel·la [tæ̀rəntélə] *n.* ⓒ a dance of southern Italy
—ⓝ 타란빌라[춤; 곡]

in which two persons turn round quickly; music for this dance.

tar·di·ly [tá:rdili] *adv.* slowly; late.
—[副] 느릿느릿

tar·di·ness [tá:rdinis] *n.* [U] the quality or condition of being tardy.
—[名] 느림, 지각

tar·dy [tá:rdi] *adj.* (**-di·er, -di·est**) slow; late; not on time.
—[形] 느린, 더딘; 지각한

tare[1] [tεər] *n.* **1.** [C] any of the plants of the bean family grown as food for cattle. **2.** 《*pl.*》 (in the Bible) a weed which is poisonous.
—[名] 1. 들완두 2. [성경에서] 독초

tare[2] [tεər] *n.* [U] the weight of the container, wrapper, truck, etc. —*vt.* mark the tare of (a container, etc.).
—[名] 포장(용기·트럭 따위)의 중량
—[他] …의 포장(용기)의 무게를 달다

***tar·get** [tá:rgit] *n.* [C] **1.** a mark to shoot at. ¶*a ~ area.*① **2.** an object of scorn, criticism, attack, etc.
—[名] 1. 표적, 과녁, 목표 ¶①[폭격의] 목표지구 2. […의] 대상

***tar·iff** [tǽrif] *n.* [C] **1.** a list or system of taxes on exports or imports; a tax of this kind, or its rate. **2.** any list or scale of prices.
—[名] 1. 관세, 세율표; 관세율 2. [철도·여관 따위의] 요금표

tarn [tɑ:rn] *n.* [C] a small lake in the mountains.
—[名] 산 속의 작은 호수

tar·nish [tá:rniʃ] *vt.* make (something) lose its shine or brightness; stain; disgrace. ¶*~ one's fame.* —*vi.* lose shine or brightness. —*n.* **1.** [U] the loss of luster or brightness. **2.** [C] [U] a stain.
—[他] …을 흐리게 하다, 녹슬게 하다; 더럽히다 —[名] 1. 흐림, 더럼, 변색 2. 녹; 오점

ta·ro [tá:rou] *n.* [C] (**-ros**) a tropical plant with a starchy root, grown for food; the root of this plant.
—[名] 타로 토란

tar·pau·lin [tɑ:rpɔ́:lin] *n.* **1.** [U] strong waterproof canvas. **2.** [C] a sailor's hat or coat made of this cloth.
—[名] 1. 타르를 칠한 방수포(防水布) 2. [선원의] 방수모; 방수 외투

tar·ry[1] [tǽri] *vi.* (**-ried**) **1.** be late; delay. **2.** live in a place for a time; stay. **3.** wait.
—[自] 1. 늦어지다, 지체하다 2. 체재하다, 머무르다 3. 기다리다

tar·ry[2] [tá:ri] *adj.* (**-ri·er, -ri·est**) of or like tar; covered with tar.
—[形] 타르의; 타르를 칠한

tart[1] [tɑ:rt] *adj.* **1.** sharp to the taste; sour. **2.** sharp. ▷**tart·ly** [-li] *adv.* —**tart·ness** [-nis] *n.*
—[形] 1. 신, 시큼한 2. 신랄한

tart[2] [tɑ:rt] *n.* [C] **1.** (*Brit.*) a fruit pie. **2.** (*U.S.*) a pie filled with fruit or jam and open at the top.
—[名] 1. (英) 과일 파이 2. [속이 보이는] 작은 파이

tar·tan[1] [tá:rt(ə)n] *n.* **1.** [U] checked woolen cloth worn esp. in the Scottish Highlands. **2.** [C] any tartan pattern or design. —*adj.* of or like tartan.
—[名] 1. 바둑판 무늬의 모직물 2. 바둑판 무늬 —[形] 바둑판 무늬의

tar·tar [tá:rtər] *n.* [U] **1.** an acid substance found on the inside of wine casks while the wine is being made. ¶*cream of ~.*① **2.** a hard substance found on the teeth.
—[名] 1. 주석(酒石) ¶①주석영(酒石英) 2. 치석(齒石)

Tar·tar [tá:rtər] *n.* **1.** [C] a member of a group of peoples including Turks, Cossacks, etc. **2.** [U] any of their languages. **3.** [C] 《usu. *t-*》 a savage or bad-tempered person.
—[名] 1. 타타르 사람 2. 타타르 말 3. 포악한 사람

catch a tartar, attack a very strong person.
[熟] 처치곤란한 상대를 만나다

—*adj.* of a Tartar or Tartans.
—[形] 타타르 사람의

tar·tar·ic [tɑ:rtǽrik] *adj.* of tartar. ¶*~ acid.*①
—[形] 주석(酒石)의 ¶①주석산

Tar·ta·rus [tá:rtərəs] *n.* (in Greek mythology) a place of punishment below Hades; Hell.
—[名] 지옥의 한없이 깊은 못; 지옥

Tar·ta·ry [tá:rtəri] *n.* a vast region of central and western Siberia and southern Russia.
—[名] 타타르 [지방]

‡task [tæsk / tɑ:sk] *n.* [C] a piece of work to be done. ¶*home ~*① / *be at one's ~*② / *set someone to a ~* / *take a ~ upon oneself.*
—[名] 일, 과업, 직무 ¶①숙제/②일을 하고 있다

take (or ***call, bring***) ***someone to task for,*** blame someone for.
[熟] …으로 남을 나무라다(꾸짖다)

—*vt.* **1.** give a task to (someone). **2.** burden; strain.
—[他] 1. …에게 일을 맡기다 2. …을 괴롭히다; 혹사(酷使)하다

task force [∠ ∠] *n.* a military unit organized for a special purpose.
—[名] 기동부대, 특수임무 부대

task·mas·ter [tǽskmæstər / tá:skmɑ̀:stə] *n.* [C] a person who gives tasks to others.
—[名] 감독, 십장

tas·sel [tǽs(ə)l] *n.* [C] a hanging ornament made of a tuft of threads or cords of silk, wool, etc.; the hanging flower or head of certain plants. —*v.* **-seled, -sel·ing** or *Brit.* **-selled, -sel·ling**) *vt.* **1.** put tassels on (something). **2.** take tassels from (corn, etc.). —*vi.* grow tassels.
—[名] 술, 장식 술; 총상화서(總狀花序); [옥수수의] 수염 —[他] 1. …에 술[장식]을 달다 2. [옥수수의] 수염을 뜯다 —[自] [옥수수의] 수염이 나오다; 술이 되다

tas·seled, *Brit.* **-selled** [tǽs(ə)ld] *adj.* having a tassel or tassels.
—[形] 술이 달린; 술장식이 있는

‡taste [teist] *vt.* **1.** test the flavor of (something) by the tongue; 《in *negative*》 eat or drink a little. ¶*I have*
—[他] 1. …을 맛보다, 먹다, 마시다 ¶① 오늘은 아무 것도 먹지 않았다 2. …을

tasteful [1178] **tax**

*tasted no food today.*① **2.** experience. ¶~ *great sorrow.* —*vi.* **1.** have a certain flavor. ¶*This orange tastes sour.*② **2.** have the sense of taste.
—*n.* ⓒ **1.** ⟨*the ~*⟩ the feeling which is gotten by the tongue; flavor. ¶*be sour to the ~*③ **2.** ⟨*sing.* only⟩ a small amount put into the mouth; a mouthful. **3.** Ⓤ the ability to judge what is beautiful and excellent; the manner or style that shows such ability. ¶*show ~ in fine arts.* **4.** Ⓤⓒ liking; fondness. ⟨*~ for*⟩ ¶*have a ~ for traveling* / ⟨*proverb*⟩ *There is no accounting for tastes.*④

1) *in bad* (or *poor*) *taste,* showing lack of a sense of beauty, excellence, etc.
2) *in good* (or *excellent*) *taste,* showing a sense of beauty, excellence, etc.
3) *in taste,* in good taste.
4) *leave a bad taste in the mouth,* cause a bad impression or a feeling.
5) *to taste,* to the amount desired.
6) *to one's taste,* agreeable or pleasing to one.

taste·ful [téistf(u)l] *adj.* having or showing good taste.
taste·ful·ly [téistfuli] *adv.* in a tasteful manner.
taste·less [téistlis] *adv.* **1.** without taste or flavor. **2.** lacking good taste; in poor taste.
taste·less·ly [téistlisli] *adv.* in a tasteless manner.
tast·y [téisti] *adj.* (**tast·i·er, tast·i·est**) ⟨*colloq.*⟩ **1.** tasting good. **2.** having or showing good taste. ▷ **tast·i·ly** [-li] *adv.* —**tast·i·ness** [-nis] *n.*
Ta·tar [táːtər] *n., adj.* =Tartar.
Ta·ta·ry [táːtəri] *n.* =Tartary.
tat·ter [tǽtər] *n.* ⓒ **1.** a torn piece. **2.** ⟨usu. *pl.*⟩ torn or ragged clothes. ¶*be in tatters*① / *tear to tatters.*② —*vt.* tear or wear (something) to pieces; make ragged. —*vi.* become ragged.
tat·ter·de·mal·ion [tætərdiméiliən / -dəm-, -mǽl-] *n.* ⓒ a person in tattered clothes.
tat·tered [tǽtərd] *adj.* **1.** ragged. **2.** wearing ragged clothes.
tat·tle [tǽtl] *vi.* talk idly; tell tales; gossip. —*vt.* reveal (a secret); utter (something) idly. —*n.* Ⓤ idle talk; gossip.
tat·tler [tǽtlər] *n.* ⓒ a person who tattles.
tat·too¹ [tætúː / tətúː] *n.* ⓒ ⟨pl. **-toos**⟩ **1.** ⟨*sing.* only⟩ a signal on a bugle, drum, etc. calling soldiers, etc. back to their quarters at night. **2.** a continuous beating or tapping.
tat·too² [tætúː] *n.* ⓒ ⟨pl. **-toos**⟩ a design marked on the skin by pricking and then rubbing in dye. —*vt.* mark (the skin) with tattoos.
‡taught [tɔːt] *v.* pt. and pp. of **teach**.
taunt [tɔːnt, +*U.S.* tɑːnt] *vt.* **1.** mock; reproach. ¶*~ someone with cowardice.* **2.** drive (someone) by taunting. —*n.* ⓒ a scornful remark; gibe.
taut [tɔːt] *adj.* **1.** (of a rope etc.) tightly stretched. **2.** in good condition; tidy. [tautology.]
tau·to·log·i·cal [tɔ̀ːtəládʒik(ə)l / -lɔ́dʒ-] *adj.* of or using
tau·tol·o·gy [tɔːtálədʒi / -tɔ́l-] *n.* Ⓤ the act of saying the same thing over again in different words; useless repetition.
*** tav·ern** [tǽvərn] ⓒ *n.* **1.** a place where alcoholic drinks are sold and drunk. **2.** an inn. [gaudy.]
taw·dry [tɔ́ːdri] *adj.* (**-dri·er, -dri·est**) showy and cheap;
taw·ny [tɔ́ːni] *adj.* (**-ni·er, -ni·est**) brownish yellow.
‡tax [tæks] *n.* **1.** Ⓤⓒ money paid by people to the government for public purposes. ¶*free of ~*① / *lay* (or

경험하다 —㉠ 1. […의] 맛이 나다 ¶②이 귤은 시다 2. 맛을 알다

—⊛ 1. 미각; 맛 ¶③맛이 시다 2. 입, 한 모금 3. 심미안, 감식력; [말씨·태도 따위의] 멋 4. 기호(嗜好) ¶④ ⟨俚⟩외를 거꾸로 먹어도 제멋이다

圝 1)나쁜 취미로; 양식에서 벗어나 2)좋은 취미로 3) 4)뒷맛이 나쁘게 5) 기호에 따라서 6)마음에 들어

—㊗ 취미가 고상한; 눈이 높은
—㊹ ⊙이러게, 품위있게
—㊗ 1. 맛이 없는 2. 풍류가 없는; 상스러운
—㊹ 맛없게; 무미건조하게
—㊗ ⟨口⟩ 1. 맛있는 2. 고상한, 풍류가 있는

—㊗ 1. 헝겊조각, 넝마 2. 누더기옷 ¶ ①누더기가 되어 있다/②발기발기 찢다 —㊹ 너덜너덜하게 찢다 —㉠ 누더기가 되다
—㊗ 누더기옷을 입은 사람

—㊗ 1. 누덕누덕한 2. 누더기를 입은
—㉠ 잡담을 하다; 고자질하다 —㊹ [비밀]을 누설하다 —㊗ 잡담, 수다

—㊗ 잡담 잘하는 사람, 수다쟁이
—㊗ 1. 귀영(歸營) 나팔(북) 2. 둥둥 연달아 치기

—㊗ 문신(文身) —㊹ …에 문신을 하다

—㊹ 1. 조소하다; 욕설을 퍼붓다 2. …을 조소하여 도발하다 —㊗ 비웃음, 냉소
—㊗ 1. 팽팽하게 친 2. 정돈된, 말쑥한

—㊗ 동의어(유어) 중복의, 중복의
—㊗ 동의어(유어) 반복; 중복; 쓸데없는 반복

—㊗ 1. 선술집 2. 여인숙

—㊗ 값 싸고 번지르르한, 야한
—㊗ 황갈색의
—㊗ 1. 세금 ¶①세금 없이/②…에 금을 부과하다/③부가세/④사업(소득)

levy) *a ~ on* (or *upon*) *something*② / *an additional ~*③ / *business* (*income*) *~*④ / *national* (*local*) *taxes*⑤ / *a succession ~*.⑥ **2.** ⟪*sing.* only⟫ a burden; strain.
—*vt.* **1.** put a tax on (income, property, etc.). **2.** lay a heavy burden on (someone). **3.** reprove; accuse. ¶*~ someone with a fault.*⑦

세/⑤국(지방)세/⑥상속세 **2.** 무거운 짐, 부담
—[他] **1.** …에 세금을 부과하다 **2.** …에 부담을 지우다 **3.** …을 나무라다, 책망하다 ¶⑦남의 과실을 책망하다

tax·a·ble [tǽksəbl] *adj.* that can be taxed.
—[形] 과세할 수 있는, 유세의

* **tax·a·tion** [tækséiʃ(ə)n] *n.* [U] **1.** the act or system of taxing. ¶*progressive ~*① / *the ~ office*② / *be subject to ~.*③ **2.** the amount of money imposed as a tax.
—[名] **1.** 과세, 세제(稅制); 징세 ¶①누진과세/②세무서/③과세되다 **2.** 세액

* **tax·i** [tǽksi] *n.* [C] a taxicab. —*vi.* (**tax·ied, tax·i·ing** or **tax·y·ing**) **1.** ride in a taxi. **2.** (of an airplane) run along the ground or on the surface of the water just before rising or after landing.
—[名] 택시 —[自] **1.** 택시로 가다 **2.** 활주하다

tax·i·cab [tǽksikæ̀b] *n.* [C] a car for hire that goes about the streets looking for customers.
—[名] 택시

tax·i·me·ter [tǽksimìːtər] *n.* [C] a small machine fitted to a taxicab that shows the fare to be paid.
—[名] [택시의] 요금 표시기

tax·pay·er [tǽkspèiər] *n.* [C] a person who pays a tax.
—[名] 납세자

⁝ **tea** [tiː] *n.* **1.** [C] a low tree of eastern Asia, cultivated for its leaves. **2.** [U] the dried leaves of this plant; the drink made by pouring boiling water on the leaves. ¶*black ~*① / *green ~*② / *make ~.*③ **3.** [U] any of the drinks resembling tea. **4.** [U][C] (chiefly *Brit.*) a light meal in the late afternoon at which tea is served. **5.** [U][C] an afternoon reception at which tea is served.
—[名] **1.** 차나무 **2.** 차 잎사귀; 차; 홍차 ¶①홍차/②녹차/③차를 달이다 **3.** [홍차 비슷한] 음료 **4.** ⟪주로 英⟫ 오후의 간식(다과회) **5.** 오후의 초대

⁝ **teach** [tiːtʃ] *v.* (**taught**) *vt.* **1.** give knowledge or lessons to (someone); instruct. ⟪~someone *to do* or *that* …⟫ ¶*~ English* / *~ a girl English; ~ English to a girl* / (*U.S.*) *~ school*① / *Experience taught me what poverty was.*② / *This accident has taught me to be careful in crossing the street.* **2.** show how to do (something); train. ⟪~ someone [*how*] *to do*; ~ someone *how* …⟫ ¶*~ a dog to beg*③ / *~ a boy how to swim* / *~ the ear to distinguish sounds.*④ —*vi.* **1.** give lessons or instruction. **2.** be a teacher. ¶*The widow teaches for a living.*⑤
—[他] **1.** [⋯에게] ⋯을 가르치다 ¶①⟪美⟫ 학교의 교사 노릇을 하다/②경험으로 가난이 어떤 것인지 알았다 **2.** ⋯에게[⋯의 방법을] 가르치다; ⋯을 훈련시키다; 길들이다 ¶③개에게 앞발을 들고 서는 법을 가르치다/④음을 분간할 수 있도록 귀를 훈련하다 —[自] **1.** 가르치다 **2.** 교사 노릇을 하다 ¶⑤그 미망인은 생활을 위해 교사 노릇을 하고 있다.

teach·a·ble [tíːtʃəbl] *adj.* **1.** that can be taught. ¶*a ~ boy.* **2.** that can be used for teaching.
—[形] **1.** 가르침을 받을 수 있는 **2.** [교재 따위가] 가르칠 수 있는

⁝ **teach·er** [tíːtʃər] *n.* [C] a person who teaches. ¶*a ~ of English*① / *be one's own ~.*②
—[名] 교사 ¶①영어 선생/②독학하다

⁝ **teach·ing** [tíːtʃiŋ] *n.* [U] **1.** the act or profession of a teacher. **2.** ⟪usu. *pl.*⟫ something that is taught.
—[名] **1.** 가르치기, 교수, 수업 **2.** 가르침, 교훈, 교리(敎理)

tea·cup [tíːkʌ̀p] *n.* [C] a cup for tea. ¶*a storm* (or *a tempest*) *in a ~.*①
—[名] 찻잔 ¶①내분(內紛)

tea·house [tíːhàus] *n.* [C] (**-hous·es** [hàuziz]) a restaurant in China or Japan where tea is served.
—[名] 찻집, 다방

teak [tiːk] *n.* **1.** [C] a large East Indian tree with very hard wood. **2.** [U] the wood of this tree, used for shipbuilding, making fine furniture, etc.
—[名] **1.** 티이크나무 **2.** 티이크 재목

tea·ket·tle [tíːkètl] *n.* [C] a kettle for boiling water to make tea.
—[名] 차탕관, 주전자

⁝ **team** [tiːm] *n.* [C] **1.** a group of people acting together. ¶*a baseball ~* / *a ~ race*① / *~ spirit.*② **2.** two or more horses, oxen, etc. harnessed together to pull a cart. ¶*a ~ of horses.* —*vt.* **1.** join (someone or something) together in a team. **2.** transport (animals, etc.) with a team. —*vi.* drive a team.
team up (=*work together*) *with others.*
—[名] **1.** 한 패의 사람들, 티임 ¶①단체 경주/②단체 정신 **2.** 한 수레에 맨 가축들 —[他] **1.** ⋯을 한 수레에 매다 **2.** [가축을] 한 줄에 매어 나르다 —[自] 가축을 한데 매어 부리다
[熟] ⋯와 협동(협력)하다

team·mate [tíːmmèit] *n.* [C] a fellow member of a team.
—[名] 같은 티임의 사람

team·ster [tíːmstər] *n.* [C] **1.** a driver of a team of horses or other animals. **2.** (*U.S.*) a driver of a truck.
—[名] **1.** 한 떼의 가축을 부리는 사람 **2.** ⟪美⟫ 트럭 운전수

team·work [tíːmwə̀ːrk] *n.* [U] the activity of a number of people working together in a team.
—[名] 공동작업, 티임워크

tea party [∠ ∠–] *n.* a social gathering at an afternoon tea.
—[名] [오후의] 다과회

T

tea·pot [tí:pàt / -pɔ̀t] *n.* [C] a vessel with a spout and handle for making and serving tea. —[名] 찻주전자, 찻병

⁑**tear**[1] [tɛər] *v.* (**tore, torn**) *vt.* **1.** break (paper, cloth, etc.) by pulling it apart; rip. ¶*~ up a letter* / *She has torn her dress in pieces.* **2.** pull violently away; drag off. 《~ something *from*》 ¶*~ off a leaf from the calendar.* / *She tore the baby from its mother's breast.*① **3.** wound (something) by tearing; make (a cut, hole, etc.) by tearing. ¶*He tore his hand on a nail.*② / *~ a hole in one's dress.* **4.** cause deep sorrow or pain in (someone's heart); 《usu. in *passive*》 ruin the peace of (something). ¶*~ the heart* / *My heart was torn by grief.* / *a country torn by a civil war.*③ **—*vi.*** **1.** become torn. ¶*This paper tears easily.* **2.** (*colloq.*) move violently or hurriedly; rush. ¶*A car came tearing along the street.*④ / *He tore off without saying good-bye.*
—[他] 1. …을 찢다; 째다 2. …을 잡아떼다; 억지로 떼어내다 ¶①그녀는 갓난아이를 어머니의 가슴에서 떼어냈다 3. …을 잡아째어 상처를 내다; 째서 [구멍 따위]를 내다 ¶②그는 못에 손을 다쳤다 4. [마음·가슴 따위]를 괴롭히다; …의 평화를 깨뜨리다 ¶③내란으로 어지러워진 나라 —[自] 1. 찢어지다, 째지다 2. 《口》 돌진하다, 질주하다 ¶④차가 거리를 질주해 왔다

—*n.* [C] **1.** an act of tearing. **2.** a cut or hole made by tearing. ¶*a big ~ in her dress.* **3.** rush; rage. —[名] 1. 잡아째기; 쥐어뜯기 2. 째진 틈 3. 돌진; 격분

⁑**tear**[2] [tiər] *n.* [C] **1.** 《often *pl.*》 a drop of salty water coming from the eye; teardrop. ¶*in tears* / *shed tears*①/ *burst into tears*② / *Tears stood in her eyes.*③ **2.** something like a tear. **3.** 《*pl.*》 grief; sorrow. —[名] 1. 눈물 ¶①눈물을 흘리다/②왈칵 울음을 터뜨리다/③그녀는 눈물을 글썽거리고 있었다 2. 눈물 비슷한 것 3. 비탄, 슬픔; 비애

tear·drop [tíərdràp / -drɔ̀p] *n.* [C] a tear. —[名] 눈물, 눈물 방울

tear·ful [tíərf(u)l] *adj.* **1.** full of tears. **2.** causing tears; sad. —[形] 1. 눈물어린; 걸핏하면 우는 2. 슬픈

tear·ful·ly [tíərfuli] *adv.* in a tearful manner. —[副] 눈물을 흘리며

tear gas [ˊ ˋ] *n.* a gas that causes tears and blindness. —[名] 최루(催淚)가스

tear·ing [tέəriŋ] *adj.* (*colloq.*) violent; raging. —[形] 《口》 맹렬한, 심한

tear·less [tíərlis] *adj.* without tears; not weeping. —[形] 눈물 없는, 눈물을 흘리지 않는

tea·room [tí:rù(:)m] *n.* [C] a room or shop where tea, coffee, light lunches, etc. are served. —[名] 다방, 끽다실

∗**tease** [ti:z] *vt.* **1.** trouble playfully. **2.** beg. 《~ someone *for* or *to do*》 ¶*The little boy teased his father to tell an interesting story.* **3.** comb (wool, etc.); roughen the surface of (cloth). —[他] 1. …을 못살게 굴다, 놀리다 2. …에게 조르다, 졸라대다 3. [양털 따위]를 빗다; [나사(羅紗)]의 보풀을 세우다

tea·sel [tí:zl] *n.* [C] a plant with stiff flower heads; one of these dried flower heads. **—*vt.*** (**-seled, -sel·ing** or *Brit.* **-selled, -sel·ling**) roughen the surface of (cloth) with teasels. —[名] 산토끼꽃; 그 열매(그 가시는 모직물의 보풀을 세우는 데 씀) —[他] [모직물의] 보풀을 세우다

teas·er [tí:zər] *n.* [C] a person who teases. —[名] 놀리는(못살게 구는) 사람

⁑**tea·spoon** [tí:spù:n] *n.* [C] a small spoon used to stir tea or coffee. —[名] 차숟가락

tea·spoon·ful [tí:spu:nfùl] *n.* [C] a quantity as much as a teaspoon will hold. —[名] 차숟가락 하나 가득

teat [ti:t] *n.* [C] the part of a breast through which milk is drawn. —[名] 젖꼭지

tea table [ˊ ˋ–] *n.* a small table used in serving tea for several people. —[名] 차 탁자

tea-things [tí:θìŋz] *n. pl.* a tea-set. —[名] 차 도구

tea·time [tí:tàim] *n.* [U] the time at which tea is taken in the afternoon. —[名] [오후의] 차 마시는 시간

tea tray [ˊ ˋ] *n.* a tray on which tea-things are placed. —[名] 차 쟁반

tea wagon [ˊ ˋ–] *n.* a small tea table on wheels. ⇒fig. —[名] 차 도구 운반대

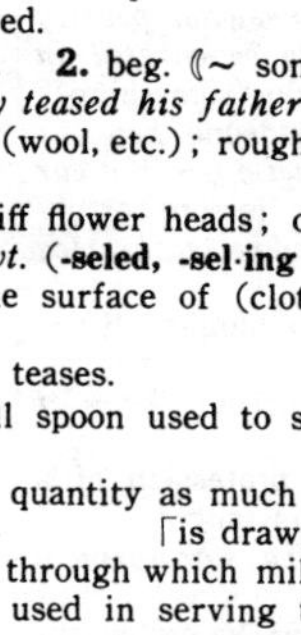
(tea wagon)

tea·zel [tí:zl] *n., vt.* =teasel.

tech·nic [téknik] *n.* **1.** =technique. **2.** 《usu. *pl.*》 the science dealing with mechanical or industrial arts. **3.** 《*pl.*》 technical terms. —[名] 2. 공예[학] 3. 술어, 전문어

∗**tech·ni·cal** [téknik(ə)l] *adj.* **1.** of a particular science or technique. ¶*a ~ book*① / *~ terms.*② **2.** of mechanical or industrial arts. ¶*a ~ school.*③ —[形] 1. 전문의, 전문적인; 학술[상]의; 기술의 ¶①전문 서적/②전문어, 술어 2. 공예의, 공업의 ¶③공업 학교

tech·ni·cal·i·ty [tèknikǽliti] *n.* **1.** [U] the state or quality of being technical. **2.** [C] 《often *pl.*》 a technical detail, expression, term, etc. —[名] 1. 전문적임 2. 전문적 사항, 전문적 표현, 전문어

tech·ni·cal·ly [téknikəli] *adv.* in a technical manner; in technical terms. —[副] 전문적으로, 기술적으로; 술어로

technician [1181] telephotograph

tech·ni·cian [tekníʃ(ə)n] *n.* ⓒ a person skilled in the technicalities of a subject. — 图 전문가, 기술자

Tech·ni·col·or [téknikʌ̀lər] *n.* Ⓤ (*Trademark*) a special process by which many three-color photographs are combined in one film. — 图 〔商標〕 테크니컬러

* **tech·nique** [tekníːk] *n.* Ⓤ technical skill in art, music, etc.; ⓒ a special method or system used to complete something. — 图 기교, 기술; 수법, 기법, 예풍(藝風), 연주법

tech·no·log·i·cal [tèknəládʒik(ə)l / -lɔ́dʒ-] *adj.* of technology. ▷**tech·no·log·i·cal·ly** [-i] *adv.* — 囮 과학 기술의, 공예[학]상의

tech·nol·o·gy [teknálədʒi / -nɔ́l-] *n.* Ⓤ **1.** the science of industrial arts. **2.** technical terms used in an art, science, etc. — 图 1. 과학 기술; 공예[학] 2. [과학·예술 따위의] 전문어, 술어

Ted [ted] *n.* a nickname for Edward or Theodore. — 图 Edward, Theodore 의 애칭

Ted·dy [tédi] *n.* =Ted.

teddy bear [´-ˌ-] *n.* a child's toy bear. — 图 장난감 곰

* **te·di·ous** [tíːdiəs, -dʒəs / -djəs] *adj.* tiresome. — 囮 지루한
  ▷**te·di·ous·ly** [-li] *adv.*
te·di·ous·ness [tíːdiəsnis, -dʒəs- / -djəs-] *n.* Ⓤ the quality of being tedious. — 图 지루함
te·di·um [tíːdiəm / -djəm] *n.* Ⓤ tediousness; tiresomeness. — 图 지루함

tee [tiː] *n.* ⓒ the mark aimed at in some games; (*Golf*) the place where a player starts in playing each hole. — 图 목표; 〔골프〕구좌(球座), 티이
—*vt., vi.* put (a golf ball) on a tee. — 囲圓 [공을] 티이 위에 올려놓다

teem [tiːm] *vi.* be full; be abundant. (*~ in* or *with* something) ¶*The sea teems with fish. | Monkeys ~ in the forest.* — 圓 충만하다, 풍부하다

teem·ing [tíːmiŋ] *adj.* full; abundant. — 囮 풍부한, 우글우글하게 많은

teen-age [tíːnèidʒ] *adj.* in one's teens. — 囮 10 대의

* **teen-ag·er** [tíːnèidʒər] *n.* ⓒ a teen-age person. — 图 10 대의 소년(소녀)

* **teens** [tiːnz] *n. pl.* the years of one's life from 13 to 19. ¶*in his late ~* ① — 图 10 대 ¶① 19 세의 나이에

tee·pee [tíːpiː] *n.* =tepee.

tee·ter [tíːtər] *n.* ⓒ (*U.S.*) a seesaw. — 图 〔美〕 시이소오

:**teeth** [tiːθ] *n. pl.* of **tooth**.

teethe [tiːð] *vi.* (of a baby) grow teeth. — 圓 젖니가 나다

teeth·ing [tíːðiŋ] *n.* Ⓤ the process or period of growing teeth. — 图 젖니의 발생, 젖니의 발생기

tee·to·tal [tiːtóutl] *adj.* drinking no alcoholic drinks. — 囮 절대 금주의

tee·to·tal·er [tiːtóutlər] *n.* ⓒ a person who drinks no alcoholic drinks. — 图 절대 금주자

Te·he·ran, Te·hran [tèhərǽn, -ráːn, tìːə-, téiə- / tiərɑ́ːn] *n.* the capital of Iran. — 图 테헤란

tel. 1. telephone. **2.** telegraph.

tel·e·cast [télikæ̀st / -kὰːst] *vt., vi.* broadcast (a program) by television. —*n.* ⓒ a television broadcast. — 囲圓 텔레비전으로 방송하다 — 图 텔레비전 방송

:**tel·e·gram** [téligræ̀m] *n.* ⓒ a message sent by telegraph. ¶*a ~ form* ① *| by ~* ② *| send a ~ to* (*someone*). ③ — 图 전보 ¶①전보용지/②전신(전보)으로/③…에 전보를 치다

:**tel·e·graph** [téligræ̀f / -grὰːf] *n.* ⓒ an apparatus or a method for sending messages by electricity; a telegram. ¶*a ~ office* (or *station*)① *| a ~ slip* ② *| by ~* ③ —*vt.* send (a message) by telegraph; send a telegram to (someone). ¶*~ news.* —*vi.* send a telegram. — 图 전신기; 전신; 전보 ¶①전신국/②전보용지/③전신(전보)로 —囲 [메시지]를 타전하다, …에게 전보를 치다 —圓 타전하다

tel·eg·ra·pher [tilégrəfər, te-] *n.* ⓒ a person who sends and receives telegraphic messages. ¶*a ~ message.* — 图 전신기사

tel·e·graph·ic [tèligrǽfik] *adj.* of or by the telegraph. — 囮 전신기의; 전신(전보)의

tel·eg·ra·phy [tilégrəfi, tel-] *n.* Ⓤ the process or art of sending messages by telegraph. — 图 전신[술]

:**tel·e·phone** [télifòun] *n.* ⓒⓊ an instrument or method for sending sound or speech over a distance by electricity. ¶*a public ~* ① *| a ~ directory* (or *book*)② *| a ~ set* ③ *| by ~* ④ *| call someone on the ~.* ⑤ — 图 전화[기] ¶①공중 전화/②전화번호부/③전화기/④전화로/⑤…에게 전화를 걸다

tel·e·pho·to [télifòutou / ˌ-ˈ-ˌ-] *adj.* of or for a telephotograph. ¶*a ~ lens.* —*n.* ⓒ a telephotograph. — 囮 망원 사진의; 전송 사진의 — 图 망원 사진, 전송 사진

tel·e·pho·to·graph [tèlifóutəgræ̀f / -grὰːf] *n.* ⓒ a photograph taken with a telephoto lens which makes far objects seem close; a photograph sent by telegraphy. —*vt., vi.* take (photographs) with a telephoto lens; send (photographs) by telegraphy. — 图 망원 사진; 전송 사진 —囲圓 망원 렌즈로 촬영하다; [사진을] 전송하다

* **tel·e·scope** [télisk̀oup] *n.* [C] an instrument with lenses which makes distant objects appear nearer and larger. ¶*an astronomical* ~.① —*vi.* slide into one another. —*vt.* **1.** make (two things) slide into one another; shorten. **2.** force (two things) into one another. ¶*The crashed cars were telescoped.*②

—[名] 망원경 ¶①천체 망원경 —[自] 서로 끼워지다, 포개지다 —[他] 1. …을 끼워넣다; 단축하다 2. …을 서로 끼워지게 하다 ¶①충돌한 차가 포개졌다

tel·e·scop·ic [tèliskápic / -skɔ́p-] *adj.* **1.** of a telescope; seen by means of a telescope; visible only through a telescope. **2.** consisting of sections which slide one inside another.

—[形] 1. 망원경의; 망원경으로 본; 망원경으로밖에 안 보이는 2. 포개어 끼우는 식의; 신축 자재의

tel·e·type [télitàip] *n.* [C] a telegraphic device that sends and receives signals like a typewriter; ⟪*T*-⟫ the trademark for this. —*vt.* send (a message) by teletype.

—[名] 텔레타이프, 전신 인자기(電信印字機); 그 상표명 —[他] [메시지]를 타이프로 보내다

tel·e·vise [télivàiz] *vt.* send or receive (a program, etc.) by television.

—[他] [프로 따위]를 텔레비전으로 방송(수상)하다

‡**tel·e·vi·sion** [télivìʒ(ə)n] *n.* [U] the process of sending and receiving images by electric waves to a distant place; [C] a television receiving set. ¶*a* ~ *set*① / *on* ~.②

—[名] 텔레비전 ¶①텔레비전 수상기/②텔레비전으로(에)

‡**tell** [tel] *v.* (**told**) *vt.* **1.** express (something) in words; make (something) known; say; narrate. ⟪~ *how* or *what* ...; ~ *that* ...⟫ ¶~ *a lie* (*the truth*) / ~ *someone a secret* / *I can't* ~ *how happy I am.* / *Tell me all you know.* / *I told her that he had been ill in bed.* / *I will* ~ *you what.*① / *I will* ~ *you.*② / *I will* ~ *you what to do.* **2.** reveal; show; disclose. ¶*His face told his joy.* **3.** order; command. ⟪~ someone *to do*⟫ ¶*I* ~ *her to come at once.* **4.** ⟪with *can* or *be able to*⟫ distinguish; recognize; know. ⟪~ one thing *from* another; ~ *how* or *what* ...⟫ ¶*I can't* ~ *George from his twin brother.*③ / *I couldn't* ~ *what to do.* **5.** count. ¶~ *sheep*④ —*vi.* **1.** give a story or report. ⟪~ *about* or *of* something⟫ ¶*He told about his trip.* **2.** give evidence. ¶*His ragged clothes tell of his poverty.*⑤ **3.** make secrets known. ¶*He promised not to tell.* **4.** produce a result; be effective. ⟪~ *on* (or *upon*, *about*, *against*) something⟫ ¶*Every shot told.*⑥ / *The hard work is telling on him.*⑦

1) ***all told***, in all; counting all.
2) ***tell off***, (*colloq.*) scold.
3) ***tell the world***, (*colloq.*) announce openly.

—[他] 1. …을 말하다, 이야기하다; 알리다, 전하다 ¶①저어 말이야(할 얘기가 있다)/②사실을 말하겠다 2. …을 나타내다 3. …을 명령하다 4. …을 식별하다, 분간하다; 알다 ¶③나는 조오지와 그의 쌍동이 형제를 분간 못한다 5. …을 세다 ¶④양을 세다 —[自] 1. 말하다, 보고하다 2. 증명하다; 알리다 ¶⑤그의 누더기옷을 보면 그의 가난을 알 수 있다 3. 비밀을 누설하다; 고자질하다; 4. 효력을 나타내다; 영향을 주다; 작용하다 ¶⑥탄환은 모두 명중했다/⑦중노동은 그의 몸에 영향을 주고 있다

[熟] 1)모두 합해서; 총계 2)…을 꾸짖다, …에게 잔소리를 하다 3)공언하다

tell·er [télər] *n.* [C] **1.** a person who tells a story; a narrator. **2.** a person who counts, pays out, and receives money; a clerk in a bank. ¶*a deposit* ~① / *a paying* (*a receiving*) ~.②

—[名] 1. 이야기하는 사람 2. 계산하는 사람; [은행의] 출납계 ¶①예금계/②지출(출납)계

tell·ing [téliŋ] *adj.* having effect or force; striking.

—[形] 효과가 있는, 잘 듣는; 현저한

tell·ing·ly [téliŋli] *adv.* in a telling manner.

—[副] 유효하게, 강력하게

tell·tale [téltèil] *n.* [C] **1.** a person who tells tales; a person who reveals secrets. **2.** an outward look that reveals a secret. **3.** an indicator. —*adj.* revealing secrets, hidden feelings, etc.

—[名] 1. 고자질꾼; 남의 비밀을 지껄이는 사람 2. 내막을 폭로하는 것 3. 자동표시기 —[形] 내정을 폭로하는

te·mer·i·ty [timériti] *n.* [U] rashness; boldness.

—[名] 무모함, 뻔뻔스러움

‡**tem·per** [témpər] *n.* [U][C] **1.** one's natural way of feeling; disposition; mood. ¶*a sweet* (*hot, quick, short*) ~ / *get out of* ~; *lose one's* ~.① **2.** anger; irritation; passion. ¶*be in a* ~② / *get into* (or *in*) *a* ~ / *show* ~. —*vt.* **1.** make (something) less extreme; soften; moderate. ¶~ *one's grief* / ~ *strong drink with water* / ~ *justice with mercy.* **2.** change the quality of (iron, etc.). ¶*He tempered the steel by heating and sudden cooling.* **3.** (*Music*) tune or moderate (a piano, violin, etc.). —*vi.* become soft and tempered.

—[名] 1. 기질; 성미; 성질; 기분; 심기 ¶①버럭 화를 내다 2. 노기; 울화 ¶②화가 나 있다

—[他] 1. …을 누이다; 조절(조화·완화)하다; 억누르다 2. [강철 따위]를 불리다 3. ⟪樂⟫ [악기]를 조율하다 —[自] 부드러워지다; 누그러지다; [쇠 따위가] 불리다

tem·per·a [témpərə] *n.* **1.** [U] a technique of painting in which the whites of egg are used instead of oil. **2.** [C] a painting made by this technique.

—[名] 1. 템페라 화법(畫法) 2. 템페라화

* **tem·per·a·ment** [témp(ə)rəmənt] *n.* [U][C] one's nature

—[名] 기질; 성질 ¶①우울한 성질/②

or disposition. ¶*a melancholic ~*① / *an artistic ~*.② — 예술가 기질

tem·per·a·men·tal [tèmp(ə)rəméntl] *adj.* **1.** of or caused by temperament. **2.** easily excited; moody. —[形] 1. 기질상의, 기분의 2. 성 잘 내는; 변덕스러운

tem·per·a·men·tal·ly [tèmp(ə)rméntəli] *adv.* excitedly; moodily. —[副] 기질상, 흥분하기 쉽게; 변덕스럽게

* **tem·per·ance** [témp(ə)r(ə)ns] *n.* [U] **1.** the state of being not extreme in action, speech, etc. **2.** the state of using alcoholic drinks not at all or not too much. ¶*a ~ hotel*① / *a ~ movement* (*league, society*).② —[名] 1. 절제; 중용(中庸) 2. 절주, 금주 ¶①술을 팔지 않는 여관/②금주 운동(동맹·회)

* **tem·per·ate** [témp(ə)rit] *adj.* **1.** self-controlled; moderate. **2.** using alcoholic drinks not at all or not too much. **3.** neither hot nor cold. ¶*the Temperate Zones.*① —[形] 1. 절제있는, 온건한 2. 절주의 3. 따뜻한 ¶①온대

⁑ **tem·per·a·ture** [témp(ə)ritʃər] *n.* [U][C] **1.** the degree of heat or cold measured by a thermometer. **2.** the degree of heat of the human body. ¶*take one's ~*① / *a ~ chart.*② **3.** an excess of this heat above normal; fever. ¶*have a ~*.③ —[名] 1. 온도 2. 체온 ¶①체온을 재다/②체온표 3. 고열 ¶③열이 있다

* **tem·pest** [témpist] *n.* [C] **1.** a violent storm. **2.** a violent disturbance. ¶*a ~ of weeping.*① —[名] 1. 폭풍우 2. 야단법석 ¶①아우성, 울부짖음

tem·pes·tu·ous [tempéstʃuəs / -tju-] *adj.* **1.** stormy. **2.** violent. —[形] 1. 폭풍우의 2. 격렬한

tem·pi [témpi:] *n.* pl. of **tempo.**

tem·ple[1] [témpl] *n.* [C] **1.** a building used for the worship of a god or gods. ¶*the Temple of Apollo*① / *the Haein Temple*② / *a ~ of music.*③ **2.** a building for Christian public worship. —[名] 1. 신전(神殿), 사원 ¶①아폴로 신전/②해인사/③음악의 전당 2. [그리스도교의] 교회당

⁑ **tem·ple**[2] [témpl] *n.* [C] 《usu. *pl.*》 the flat part on either side of the forehead. —[名] 관자놀이

tem·po [témpou] *n.* [C] (pl. **-pos** or **-pi**) **1.** (*Music*) the time or rate at which music is played. **2.** the rate or pattern of activity. —[名] 1. 《樂》 속도, 템포 2. 빠르기

tem·po·ral [témp(ə)rəl] *adj.* **1.** of this world; of this life. **2.** of time. ↔spatial **3.** lasting for a short time; temporary. ↔eternal **4.** (*Grammar*) expressing time; of verbal tense —[形] 1. 이승의; 속세의 2. 시간의 3. 일시적인 4. 《文法》 시간을 나타내는

tem·po·rar·i·ly [témp(ə)rèrili / -rəri-] *adv.* for a short time. —[副] 일시적으로, 잠시

* **tem·po·rar·y** [témp(ə)rèri / -rəri] *adj.* lasting for a short time only. ¶*~ account* (*business*)① / *a ~ job.* —[形] 일시적인, 덧없는; 임시의 ¶①가계정(假計定)(영업)

tem·po·rize [témpəràiz] *vi.* **1.** adjust oneself to the time or occasion. **2.** delay a decision or action so as to gain time or to avoid argument. ▷**tem·po·riz·er** [-ər] *n.* —[自] 1. 시국에 따르다 2. 형세를 관망하다; 우물쭈물하다

* **tempt** [tem(p)t] *vt.* persuade; try to persuade. 《~ some-one *to do*》; appeal strongly; attract. ¶*~ someone to sin*① / *~ one's appetite.* —[他] …을 유혹하다; 매혹하다; …할 마음이 나게 하다 ¶①남을 꾀어 죄를 저지르게 하다

tempt Providence, take a great risk. [熟] 큰 모험을 하다

* **temp·ta·tion** [tem(p)téiʃ(ə)n] *n.* **1.** [U] the act of tempting; the state of being tempted. ¶*fall into ~*① / *lead someone into ~*.② **2.** [C] something that tempts. —[名] 1. 유혹 ¶①유혹에 빠지다/②남을 유혹에 빠뜨리다 2. 유혹물

tempt·er [tém(p)tər] *n.* **1.** [C] a person who tempts. **2.** 《*the T-*》 Satan; the Devil. —[名] 1. 유혹자 2. 악마

tempt·ing·ly [tém(p)tiŋli] *adv.* alluringly; attractively. —[副] 유혹하듯이

⁑ **ten** [ten] *n.* **1.** the number between nine and eleven; 10. ¶*~ to one.*① **2.** a group or set of ten persons or things. —*adj.* of ten. ¶*I'd ~ times rather do* (*something*).② —[名] 1. 열, 10 ¶①십중팔구 2. 10명(개) 한 티임(벌) —[形] 10의 ¶②…하는 편이 훨씬 낫다

ten·a·ble [ténəbl] *adj.* that can be defended or maintained. —[形] 방어(유지)할 수 있는

te·na·cious [tinéiʃəs] *adj.* **1.** holding fast; persistent. ¶*~ efforts* / *a ~ grip.* **2.** that can remember. —[形] 1. 집요한; 고집하는, 끈질긴 2. 기억이 확실한

te·na·cious·ly [tinéiʃəsli] *adv.* in a tenacious manner. —[副] 끈질기게, 집요하게

te·nac·i·ty [tinǽsiti] *n.* [U] the state of being tenacious. —[名] 완강; 고집; 끈질김

ten·an·cy [ténənsi] *n.* (pl. **-cies**) **1.** [U] the act of renting land, a house, etc.; the condition of being a tenant. **2.** [C] a property occupied by a tenant. —[名] 1. [토지·집 따위의] 차용(借用) 2. 차지(借地), 셋집

* **ten·ant** [ténənt] *n.* [C] **1.** a person who pays rent for the use of land, a building, etc. ¶*a ~ farmer*① / *a ~ right.*② **2.** an occupant; a dweller. ¶*tenants of the grave.*③ —*vt.* occupy (land, a house, etc.) as a tenant. —[名] 1. 차용자, 소작인, 세든 사람 ¶①소작인/②차지권 2. 거주자 ¶③무덤의 주민, 죽은 사람 —[他] [토지·집 따위]를 차용하다; 거주하다

T

ten·ant·less [ténəntlis] *adj.* without a tenant; unoccupied.
—[形] 차용인(거주자)이 없는

ten·ant·ry [ténəntri] *n.* **1.** 《*collectively*》 all the tenants on an estate. **2.** [U] tenancy.
—[名] 1. 차지인, 세든 사람 2. [토지·가옥의] 차용

Ten Commandments [ˊ -ˊ-], **the** *n.* (in the Bible) the ten rules of living and worship given to Moses by God on Mount Sinai.
—[名] 모세의 십계

‡tend[1] [tend] *vi.* **1.** be apt; incline. 《~ *to do*; ~ *to* or *toward* something》 ¶*He tends to follow the opinions of others.* | *He tends towards conservatism.*① **2.** proceed; go; be directed. 《~ *to* or *toward* a place》 ¶*This road tends north.*② | ~ *to the same conclusion.*
—[自] 1. …하기 쉽다; …의 경향이 있다 ¶①그는 보수주의의 경향이 있다 2. 향하다, 향하여 가다 ¶②이 길은 북쪽으로 가는 길이다

‡tend[2] [tend] *vt.* look after; attend to; watch over (something). ¶~ *the sick*① | ~ *a store*② | *The shepherd tends his flock.* —*vi.* wait on. 《~ *on* someone》; (*colloq.*) pay attention. 《~ *to* something》 ¶~ *to one's own affairs.*
—[他] …을 돌보다, 간호하다, 지키다 ¶①환자를 보살피다/②가게를 지키다 —[自] 시중들다; 주의하다

***tend·en·cy** [téndənsi] *n.* [C] (pl. **-cies**) an inclination; a trend ¶*a* ~ *to drink too much* | *a* ~ *to improvement.*①
—[名] 경향; 풍조; 성질; 취향 ¶①나아지는 경향

ten·den·tious [tendénʃəs] *adj.* (of a speech, piece of writing, etc.) having a special effect or aim.
—[形] [발언·문서 따위] 특별한 의도가 있는

‡ten·der[1] [téndər] *adj.* (**~·er, ~·est**) **1.** soft; not hard or tough. ¶~ *meat.* **2.** easily hurt; weak; feeble. ¶*a* ~ *skin.* **3.** too young to be strong enough; immature. ¶*of* ~ *age* (*years*) | ~ *buds.* **4.** sensitive; delicate. ¶*a* ~ *conscience* (*heart*). **5.** feeling pain quickly; sore. ¶~ *teeth* | *a* ~ *spot.* **6.** mild; light. ¶~ *colors* | ~ *green.*① **7.** gentle. ¶*a* ~ *touch of one's hand.* **8.** requiring careful handling. ¶~ *questions* | *a* ~ *situation.* **9.** kind; loving. ¶*the* ~ *emotions* (*passion, sentiment*) | *a* ~ *smile.*
—[形] 1. 부드러운 2. 상처 입기 쉬운; 약한; 부서지기 쉬운 3. 젊은; 미숙한 4. 민감한; 예민한 5. 만지면 아픈 6. [빛깔·광선이] 부드러운, 약한 ¶①신록 7. 다정한, 상냥한, 온화한 8. 신중해야 하는 9. 친절한; 사랑하는

***ten·der**[2] [téndər] *vt.* **1.** present; offer. ¶~ *someone a reception*① | ~ *one's services*② | ~ *thanks for something.* **2.** offer (money, goods, etc.) to pay a debt, etc.
—*n.* **1.** [C] something offered; an offer; a bid. **2.** [U] anything that one cannot refuse to receive when offered in payment for a debt. ¶*legal* ~.③
—[他] 1. …을 내밀다; 제출하다; 신청하다 ¶①…의 환영회를 열다/②봉사하겠다고 나서다 2. …을 지불하다 —[名] 1. 제출, 제의; 입찰; 제공물 2. [수령을 거부할 수 없는] 변제(辨濟) 물건 ¶③법화(法貨)

ten·der[3] [téndər] *n.* [C] **1.** a person who takes care of someone. **2.** a small boat used for carrying goods and passengers between a large ship and the land. **3.** a small railroad car containing coal and water, attached behind a locomotive.
—[名] 1. 돌보는 사람, 간호인, 감시인 2. 거룻배 3. [기관차의] 탄수차(炭水車)

‡ten·der-heart·ed [téndərhá:rtid] *adj.* having a tender heart; sympathetic; kindly.
—[形] 상냥한, 다정다감한

ten·der·loin [téndərlɔ̀in] *n.* [U][C] the tenderest part of a loin of beef, pork, etc.
—[名] [소·돼지 따위의] 허리의 연한 살

***ten·der·ly** [téndərli] *adv.* in a tender manner; with tenderness; gently.
—[副] 다정하게, 상냥하게, 부드럽게

***ten·der·ness** [téndərnis] *n.* [U] the state of being tender.
—[名] 부드러움, 상냥함, 민감, 친절

ten·don [téndən] *n.* [C] a tough, thick cord that attaches a muscle to a bone; a sinew.
—[名] 건(腱)

ten·dril [téndril] *n.* [C] a thin curling part of a climbing plant that attaches itself to something and makes the plant able to climb. ⇒fig.
—[名] [식물의] 권수(卷鬚), 덩굴

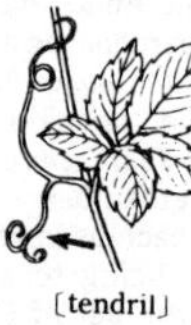
[tendril]

ten·e·ment [ténimənt] *n.* [C] **1.** a house or part of a house rented by a tenant; a dwelling house. ¶*the soul's* ~.① **2.** (*Law*) any kind of permanent property rented from another. **3.** =tenement house.
—[名] 1. 셋집; 가옥 ¶①영혼이 머무는 곳, 육체 2. 《法》 보유 재산, 차지(借地), 셋집

tenement house [ˊ-- ˋ] *n.* a building divided into cheap apartments.
—[名] 아파트, 공동 주택

ten·et [ténit / tí:net] *n.* [C] a firm belief; a principle; a doctrine.
—[名] 주의; 교리(敎理)

ten·fold [ténfòuld] *adj., adv.* ten times as many or as much.
—[形][副] 10배의(로)

Tenn. Tennessee.
Ten·nes·se·an [tènisíːən] *n.* ⓒ a person of Tennessee. —*adj.* of Tennessee.
Ten·nes·see [tènəsíː] *n.* a south central State of the United States. ⇒N.B.
‡**ten·nis** [ténis] *n.* Ⓤ a game for two or two pairs of persons played by hitting a ball back and forth over a net with a racket. ¶ a ~ ball① / a ~ court② / ~ sets.③
ten·on [ténən] *n.* ⓒ the end of a board shaped to be inserted into a hole in another so as to hold the two together. —*vt.* joint (two boards) by tenon and hole; make a tenon in (a board).
ten·or¹ [ténər] *n.* ⓒ 1. the general tendency or course. 2. the general meaning; the drift.
ten·or² [ténər] *n.* (*Music*) 1. Ⓤ the highest men's voice; 2. ⓒ (*the* ~) the part in a song taken by this voice. 2. ⓒ a man who sings such a part; ⓒ an instrument which plays it.
ten·pins [ténpinz] *n. pl.* (*U.S.*) (used as *sing.*) a bowling game played with ten pins and a ball; ⓒ the pins used for this game. ⇒ N.B, fig.
‡**tense**¹ [tens] *adj.* tightly stretched; strained. ↔lax, loose ¶ a ~ cord① / ~ nerves.②
tense² [tens] *n.* ⓒ (usu. *the* ~) (*Grammar*) the form of a verb showing the time of an action or state. ¶ the past ~① / the present ~.②

[tenpins]

tense·ly [ténsli] *adv.* in a tense manner.
tense·ness [ténsnis] *n.* Ⓤ the state of being tense.
ten·sile [téns(ə)l / ténsail] *adj.* 1. that can be stretched without breaking. 2. of or relating to tension. ¶ ~ force① / ~ strength.②
•**ten·sion** [ténʃ(ə)n] *n.* Ⓤ 1. the act of stretching or straining; the state of being tightly stretched or strained. 2. mental strain; ill relation between persons, countries, etc. ¶ ~ of feeling.① 3. voltage. ¶ a high-tension wire② / a high-tension current.③ [by poles and ropes.
‡**tent** [tent] *n.* ⓒ a cloth shelter for camping supported
ten·ta·cle [téntəkl] *n.* ⓒ a long, slender organ growing around the mouth of a certain animal, used to touch and feel; a sensitive, hairlike growth on the head of an insect or the leaves of a certain plant.
en·ta·tive [téntətiv] *adj.* made or done as a trial. ¶ a ~ theory① / a ~ plan.② ▷**ten·ta·tive·ly** [-li] *adv.* —**ten·ta·tive·ness** [-nis] *n.*
‡**tenth** [tenθ] *n.* 1. (usu. *the* ~) number 10; 10th. 2. ⓒ one of 10 equal parts of anything. —*adj.* of 10th.
ten·u·ous [ténjuəs] *adj.* thin; slender; not dense; having slight importance. ▷**ten·u·ous·ly** [-li] *adv.* —**ten·u·ous·ness** [-nis] *n.*
ten·ure [ténjər / ténjuə] *n.* Ⓤ the act or right of holding land, buildings, etc.; Ⓤ the condition on which something is held; ⓒ the period during which something is held.
tep·id [tépid] *adj.* a little warm; not showing strong feeling. ¶ ~ water① / a ~ reception.② ▷**tep·id·ness** [-nis] *n.*
te·pid·i·ty [tepíditi] *n.* Ⓤ the state of being tepid.
ter·cen·te·nar·y [təːrséntinèri, tə̀ːrsenténəri / tə̀ːsentíːnəri] *adj.* of a period of 300 years. —*n.* ⓒ (pl. **-naries**) a period of 300 years; a 300th anniversary.

—⊛ 테네시 주의 사람 —⊛ 테네시 주의
—⊛ 테네시 주 N.B. Tenn.으로 줄임. 수도 Nashville
—⊛ 테니스,정구 ¶①테니스 공/②테니스 코오트/③정구 도구

—⊛ [목공의] 장부 —⊛ …을 장부로 만들다; …에 장부를 만들다

—⊛ 1.진로; 방침 2.취지, 주지(主旨); 대의(大意)
—⊛ (樂) 1. 테너, 차중음(次中音) 2. 테너 가수; 테너 악기

—⊛ (美) 십주희(十柱戱); 십주희용의 기둥(한 개는 a tenpin) N.B. 영국의 ninepins 에 해당

—⊛ 팽팽한;긴장한 ¶①팽팽한 밧줄/②긴장된 신경

—⊛ [동사의] 시제(時制), 시상(時相) ¶①과거 시제/②현재 시제

—⊛ 팽팽하게, 긴장하여
—⊛ 긴장[상태]
—⊛ 1.잡아늘일 수 있는 2.장력(張力)의 ¶①장력/②장력 강도, 항(抗)장력
—⊛ 1.긴장 2.[정신적인] 긴장, [정세 따위의] 절박 ¶①긴장된 감정 3.전압 ¶②고압선/③고압 전류

—⊛ 텐트, 천막
—⊛ [강장(腔腸) 동물 따위의] 촉수(觸手),[곤충의] 촉각,[식물의] 촉사(觸絲),촉모(觸毛)

—⊛ 임시의; 시험적인 ¶①가설/②시안(試案)

—⊛ 1.열 번째; 10번 2.10 분의 1
—⊛ 열 번째의; 10분의 1의
—⊛ 얇은; 가느다란, 희박한; 보잘것없는

—⊛ [부동산의] 보유[권]; 보유 조건; 보유 기간

—⊛ 미지근한; 열의 없는 ¶①미지근한 물/②열의 없는 환영

—⊛ 미지근함; 열의가 없음
—⊛ 300 년[간]의 —⊛ 300 년; 300 년제(祭)

:term [tə:rm] *n.* [C] **1.** a fixed or limited period of time. ¶*a ~ of office.*① **2.** a date for payment. ¶ *~ day.* **3.** a part of a school year. ¶*keep a ~.*② **4.** a word or phrase, esp. one expressing a special meaning or idea in some science, art, etc. ¶*medical terms.* **5.** ⦅*pl.*⦆ a way of speaking; mode of expression. ¶*in plain terms*③ / *in high terms.*④ **6.** ⦅*pl.*⦆ mutual relationships among or between persons; friendly relations. ¶*on good terms with someone / be on speaking terms with someone*⑤ / *They are not on terms.*⑥ **7.** conditions. ¶*on even terms*⑦ / *set terms.*⑧
— [名] 1. 기간 ¶①임기 2. 지불 기일 3. 학기 ¶②1학기 동안 출석하다 4. 말, 언어; 전문어, 용어 5. 말씨; 표현 ¶③쉬운 말로/④칭찬의 말로 6. 관계, 친한 사이 ¶⑤…와 말을 하는(서로 방문하는) 사이다/⑥그들은 사이가 좋지 않다 7. 조건 ¶⑦대등한 조건으로/⑧조건을 달다

1) ***bring** someone **to terms,*** force someone to surrender; cause someone to accept conditions.
2) ***come to terms with*** (=*reach an agreement with; yield to*) *someone.*
3) ***in terms of,*** ⓐ in the language of. ⓑ by means of. ⓒ from the standpoint of. ⓓ concerning.
[熟] 1)…을 항복시키다; 승낙시키다 2)…와 타협이 되다; …에 굴복하다 3) ⓐ…의 말로 ⓑ…에 의하여 ⓒ…의 견지에서 ⓓ…에 관하여

—*vt.* call (something) by a term; give a name to (something). ¶*Her life may be termed happy.*⑨
— [他] …이라고 부르다; …을 …이라고 이름짓다 ¶⑨그녀의 일생은 행복하다고 할 수 있을 것이다.

ter·ma·gant [tə́:rməgənt] *n.* [C] a noisy, scolding woman. —*adj.* quarrelsome; scolding.
— [名] 입심사나운 여자 — [形] 입심사나운

ter·mi·na·ble [tə́:rminəbl] *adj.* that can be ended [after a certain time]. ▷**ter·mi·na·bly** [-i] *adv.*
— [形] 기한이 있는, 유한의

ter·mi·nal [tə́:rmin(ə)l] *adj.* **1.** forming the end. ¶*the ~ station.*① **2.** coming at the end of a certain time. ¶*a ~ examination.*② —*n.* [C] **1.** an end; a limit. **2.** (*U.S.*) the end of a railroad line; the last station. (cf. *Brit.* terminus)
— [形] 1. 끝의, 종점의 ¶①종착역 2. ⦅美⦆ 학기의; 학기마다의; 정기적인 ¶②학기말 시험 — [名] 1. 말단; 종말 2. 종점; 종착역

ter·mi·nal·ly [tə́:rminəli] *adv.* at the end; every term.
— [副] 말단에; 정기적으로

ter·mi·nate [tə́:rminèit] *vt.* **1.** bring (something) to an end; finish. **2.** limit; bound. —*vi.* come to an end; end. ⦅~ *at,* (or *in, with*) something⦆ ▷**ter·mi·na·tor** [-ər] *n.*
— [他] 1. …을 끝나게 하다 2. [장소 따위]를 제한(한정)하다 — [自] 끝나다

ter·mi·na·tion [tə̀:rminéiʃ(ə)n] *n.* [U] [C] the state of being terminated; the end; the conclusion.
— [名] 종료, 종결, 결말

ter·mi·ni [tə́:rminài] *n.* pl. of **terminus.**

ter·mi·nol·o·gy [tə̀:rminálədʒi / tə̀:minɔ́l-] *n.* [U] ⦅*collectively*⦆ the special or technical words used in science, art, etc.
— [名] 술어, [전문] 용어

ter·mi·nus [tə́:rminəs] *n.* [C] (pl. **-mi·ni** or **-nus·es**) **1.** a limit; an end; a goal. **2.** (*Brit.*) a station or town at the end of a railway or bus line, etc. (cf. *U.S.* terminal)
— [名] 1. 종점, 끝, 목적지 2. ⦅英⦆ 종착역; 종점 도시

ter·mite [tə́:rmait] *n.* [C] a white ant.
— [名] 흰 개미

tern [tə:rn] *n.* [C] a sea-bird like a gull, but more slender, smaller, and faster.
— [名] 제비 갈매기

ter·race [térəs] *n.* [C] **1.** an outdoor space touching a house like a balcony. **2.** a flat, raised piece of land made in the side of a hill. **3.** a street along the side or top of a slope; a row of houses on such a street.
— [名] 1. 테라스 2. 단구(段丘); 대지(臺地) 3. 높은 지대의 거리(집들)

ter·ra cot·ta [térəkátə / -kɔ́tə] *n.* **1.** hard baked earth of a brownish-red color, used for making vases, ornamental figures, etc. **2.** a brownish-red color.
— [名] 1. 테라코타, 진흙을 구워 만든 토기 2. 적갈색

ter·ra fir·ma [térəfə́:rmə] *n.* [U] dry land.
— [名] 육지

ter·rain [teréin, térein / térein] *n.* [C] a stretch of land, esp. when considered from a military point of view.
— [名] [군사상에서 본] 지형, 지세

ter·ra·pin [térəpin] *n.* [C] a turtle used for food, found in fresh water of North America.
— [名] [북미산의] 식용 거북

ter·res·tri·al [tiréstriəl] *adj.* **1.** of the earth; of land. ¶*a ~ globe*① / *the ~ ball.*② **2.** worldly.
— [形] 1. 지구[상]의; 육지[상]의 ¶①지구의(儀)/②지구 2. 현세의

:ter·ri·ble [téribl] *adj.* **1.** dreadful; causing terror. ¶*a ~ look / a ~ fire / be ~ in anger.*① **2.** severe; hard to bear; causing extreme discomfort. **3.** (*colloq.*) very bad. ▷**ter·ri·ble·ness** [-nis] *n.*
— [形] 1. 무서운 ¶①성나면 무섭다 2. 지독한; 몹시 불쾌한 3. ⦅口⦆ 아주 나쁜

:ter·ri·bly [téribli] *adv.* in a terrible manner; (*colloq.*) extremely.
— [副] 무섭게; ⦅口⦆ 매우, 몹시

ter·ri·er [tériər] *n.* [C] an active, intelligent, courageous dog, usu. of a small size, such as a Scotch terrier or a fox-terrier.
—[名] 테리어

＊**ter·rif·ic** [tərífik] *adj.* causing terror; terrible; (*colloq.*) extreme; very great.
—[形] 무서운; 무시무시한

＊**ter·ri·fy** [térifài] *vt.* (**-fied**) fill (someone) with great fear; frighten very much. 《~ someone *at* or *with*; ~ someone *into doing*》 ¶*be terrified out of one's senses*① / *You ~ me.*②
—[他] …을 무서워하게 하다, 놀라게 하다 ¶①놀라서 혼비백산하다/②아이 깜짝이야

ter·ri·to·ri·al [tèritɔ́:riəl] *adj.* **1.** of territory; of land. ¶~ *rights* / ~ *expansion*① / ~ *air*② / ~ *waters.*③ **2.** local; of a particular district.
—[形] 1. 영토의 ¶①영토의 확장/②영공/③영해 2. 지방의; 특정 지방의

＊＊**ter·ri·to·ry** [téritɔ̀:ri / -təri] *n.* (pl. **-ries**) **1.** [U][C] the land and waters which a state or government controls. ¶*Once India was British* ~. **2.** [U][C] a large area of land; a part of a country. **3.** [C] the facts belonging to science or learning. **4.** [C] the area where a salesman sells. **5.** 《*T-*》 (*U. S.*) a district of the country not admitted as a State.
—[名] 1. 영토 2. 지역; 지방 3. [과학·학문 따위의] 영역, 분야 4. [외판원 등의] 담당 구역, 세력권 5. [미국의] 준주(準州)

＊＊**ter·ror** [térər] *n.* **1.** [U][C] great fear; a thing or person that causes great fear. ¶*a novel of* ~① / *have a holy* ~ *of*② / *strike* ~ *into someone's heart*③ / *He was a* ~ *to all.* **2.** [C] (*colloq.*) a thing or person that causes much trouble and unpleasantness.
—[名] 1. [심한] 공포, 놀람; 공포심을 일으키는 것 ¶①괴기 소설/②…을 몹시 무서워하다/③남을 공포에 떨게 하다 2. 《口》 골칫거리, 매우 성가신 것(사람)

ter·ror·ism [térərìz(ə)m] *n.* [U] the state of terror; politics that governs by the use of terror.
—[名] 공포상태; 공포정치; 테러행위

ter·ror·ist [térərist] *n.* [C] a person who uses terrorism.
—[名] 공포정치가, 테러분자

ter·ror·ize [térəràiz] *vt.* fill (someone) with terror; rule or dominate (a nation, etc.) by means of terror.
—[他] …을 무서워하게 하다; 공포정책으로 지배하다

ter·ror-strick·en [térərstrìk(ə)n] *adj.* stricken or overwhelmed by terror; terrified.
—[形] 공포에 질린

ter·ror-struck [térərstrʌ̀k] *adj.* struck with great fear.
—[形] 공포에 질린

terse [tə:rs] *adj.* (of speech, style, or speakers) elegantly brief and to the point. ¶*a* ~ *letter.* ▷**terse·ness** [-nis] *n.*
—[形] 간결한, 요령있는

terse·ly [tə́:rsli] *adv.* in a terse manner.
—[副] 간결하게

ter·ti·ar·y [tə́:rʃièri, / tə́:ʃəri] *adj.* **1.** of the third rank or order; third. **2.** 《*T*~》 (*Geology*) of the Tertiary. —*n.* 《*the T* ~》 (*Geology*) the third period in the formation of rocks.
—[形] 1. 제 3 의 2. 제 3 기(紀)의
—[名] 제 3 기

tes·sel·late *vt.* [tésilèit] pave (floors, pavements, etc.) with small blocks in a mosaic pattern.
—[他] …을 모자이크 무늬로 깔다; 모자이크식으로 포장하다

＊＊＊**test** [test] *n.* [C] **1.** an examination; trial. ¶*a* ~ *pilot* / *a* ~ *for color blindness*① / *put to the* ~② / *give a* ~ *in English.*③ **2.** means of trial; touchstone. ¶*Poverty is a* ~ *of character.* **3.** a standard to judge the quality of a thing by. ¶*a sure* ~ *of education.* **4.** (*Chemistry*) an analysis; the substance used in the analysis.
—[名] 1. 시험; 검사; 테스트 ¶①색맹 검사/②시험하다/③영어 시험을 치르게 하다 2. 시험 수단; 시금석(試金石) 3. [판단의] 기준 4. 《化》 분석; 시약(試藥)

—*vt.* **1.** examine; try. ¶~ *a wall for cracks.*④ **2.** analyze; examine the quality of (something). ¶~ *ore for gold* / ~ *a solution by litmus paper.*
—[他] 1. …을 시험하다; 시도하다 ¶④벽의 갈라진 틈을 검사하다 2. …을 분석하다

＊**tes·ta·ment** [téstəmənt] *n.* [C] **1.** (*Law*) a written document in which a person declares what to do with his property after his death; a will. ⇒[N.B.] **2.** 《*the T-*》 either of the two main parts of the Bible; (*colloq.*) the New Testament. ¶*the Old* (*New*) *Testament.*①
—[名] 1. 《法》 유언, 유서 [N.B.] 보통 one's last will and testament라 함 2. 신약(또는 구약) 성서; 《口》 신약 성서 ¶①구(신)약 성서

tes·tate [tésteit / -tit] *adj.* having made and left a will at death. —*n.* [C] a person who has died leaving a will.
—[形] 유언을 남긴 —[名] 유언을 남기고 죽은 사람

test·er [téstər] *n.* [C] a person or thing that tests.
—[名] 시험하는 사람; 시험기(器)

＊**tes·ti·fy** [téstifài] *v.* (**-fied**) *vi.* bear witness; give evidence. 《~ *to* something》 ¶*This fact testifies to his innocence.*① / ~ *on behalf of someone.*② —*vt.* bear witness to; give evidence of (something); profess. 《~ *that*...》. ¶*This fact testifies that he is innocent.*
—[自] 입증하다; 증언하다 ¶①이 사실이 그의 무죄를 증명한다/②남에게 유리하게 증언하다 —[他] …을 증명하다; 증언하다; 언명하다

tes·ti·ly [téstili] *adv.* in a testy manner.
—[副] 성미 급하게, 퉁명스럽게

tes·ti·mo·ni·al [tèstimóuniəl] *n.* [C] **1.** a letter telling
—[名] 1. 증명서; 추천장 2. 감사장; 기

T

the character, ability, etc., of a person, or the value of a thing. **2.** a gift showing esteem, thankfulness, etc.
념품

* **tes·ti·mo·ny** [téstimòuni / -mə-] *n.* (pl. **-nies**) **1.** [U] the statement by a witness on oath. ¶ ***produce ~ of*** (or ***to***) ***the fact***① | ***call someone in ~.***② **2.** [U][C] anything that shows or make clear; outward proof.
1) ***bear testimony to,*** affirm.
2) ***in testimony of,*** as evidence or proof of.
—[名] 1. 증명; 증언 ¶①그 사실의 증거를 제출하다/②…을 증인으로 소환하다 2. 증명이 되는 것
[熟] 1)입증하다 2)…의 증거로서

test pilot [ˊ ˊ-] *n.* a pilot who tests new or experimental airplanes.
—[名] 시험 비행사

test tube [ˊ ˊ] *n.* a thin glass tube, closed at one end, used in chemical tests.
—[名] 시험관(管)

tes·ty [tésti] *adj.* (**-ti·er, -ti·est**) quick-tempered; irritable; impatient. ▷**tes·ti·ly** [téstili] *adv.* —**tes·ti·ness** [-nis] *n.*
—[形] 성 잘 내는; 성급한

tet·a·nus [tétənəs] *n.* [U] a serious nerve disease causing stiffness of the muscles and even death.
—[名] 파상풍(破傷風)

teth·er [téðər] *n.* **1.** [C] a rope or chain to tie cattle. **2.** [U] the range of one's ability, endurance, resources, etc. ¶ ***at the end of one's ~***① | ***beyond one's ~.***②
—*vt.* fasten (cattle, etc.) with a tether.
—[名] 1. [가축 매는] 밧줄, 사슬 2. 범위, 한계 ¶①참지 못할 지경에 이르러/②힘에 부치는
—[他] …을 밧줄로 매다

Teu·ton [t(j)ú:t(ə)n / tjú:t(ə)n] *n.* [C] **1.** a member of the group of people including the Germans, Dutch, Anglo-Saxons and Scandinavians. **2.** a German.
—[名] 1. 튜우튼 사람 2. 독일인

Teu·ton·ic [t(j)u:tánik / tju:tɔ́n-] *adj.* **1.** of the Teutons or their languages. **2.** German. —*n.* [U] the Teutonic languages; Germanic.
—[形] 1. 튜우튼 사람(민족·말)의 2. 독일인(어)의 —[名] 튜우튼(게르만) 말

Tex·as [téksəs] *n.* a southern State of the United States, on the gulf of Mexico. ⇒[N.B.]
—[名] 텍사스 주 [N.B.] Tex.로 줄임. 수도 Austin

⁑ text [tekst] *n.* **1.** [U] the main body of a book or printed page. **2.** [C] the original words of a writer. **3.** [C] a short passage in the Bible used as the subject of a sermon, etc. **4.** [C] a subject of a discussion; a theme. **5.** [C] a textbook. ▷**text·less** [-lis] *adj.*
—[名] 1. 본문 2. 원문 3. [설교 따위에 인용한] 성서의 원구(原句) 4. 화제; 논제 5. 교과서

⁑ text·book [tékstbùk] *n.* [C] a book used in schools and colleges.
—[名] 교과서

tex·tile [tékst(i)l, -tail / tékstail] *adj.* **1.** of weaving. ¶ ***~ industry.***① **2.** woven. ¶ ***~ fabrics.***② **3.** that can be woven. —*n.* [C] (usu. *pl.*) **1.** woven fabric. **2.** textile material.
—[形] 1. 직물의 ¶①직물 공업 2. 방직된 ¶②직물 3. 방직할 수 있는 —[名] 1. 직물 2. 직물의 원료

tex·tu·al [tékstʃuəl / -tju-] *adj.* of the text; based on the text. ¶ ***a ~ error.***①
—[形] 본문의, 원문대로의 ¶①원문의 잘못

tex·ture [tékstʃər] *n.* [C][U] **1.** the character of the woven fabrics resulting from the quality or arrangement of the thread. ¶ ***a loose*** (***fine***) ***~.***① **2.** the arrangement of the parts; structure. **3.** the quality of the surface.
—[名] 1. [피륙의] 짜임새; 바탕 ¶①결이 거친(고운) 피륙 2. 조직; 구조 3. 결, 촉감

Th. Thursday.

Thai [tai, +*U.S.* tá:i:] *n.* **1.** [U] a branch of the Indo-Chinese languages; the language of Thailand. **2.** [C] a member of a group of Thai-speaking people; the people of Thailand. —*adj.* of Thailand.
—[名] 1. 타이 말; 샴 말 2. 타이 사람
—[形] 타이 사람의, 타이 말의

Thai·land [táilæ̀nd] *n.* a country in southeastern Asia, between Burma and Malaya. ⇒[N.B.]
—[名] 타일란드 [N.B.] 옛이름 Siam. 수도 Bangkok

Thai·land·er [táilæ̀ndər] *n.* [C] a person of Thailand.
—[名] 타일란드 사람

* **Thames** [temz], **the** *n.* a river in southern England.
—[名] 템즈 강

⁑ than [ðən, ðæn] *conj.* **1.** (used after *comparative adjectives, adverbs,* and such other word, as *other, otherwise* and *else*) in comparison with (or that...). ¶ ***I know you better ~*** [***I know***] ***him.*** | ***I love her more ~ he*** [***loves her*** (or ***does***)]. | ***It's less cold in March ~ in February.***① **2.** (used after *soon, rather,* etc.) if...at all; if one should have to... ¶ ***I would rather*** [***sooner***] ***starve to death ~ steal.***② **3.** (used after some *adverbs* and *adjectives,* such as *else, other,* and *otherwise*) except; besides. ¶ ***We had no choice other ~ this.*** | ***No other ~ his parents can help him.***③ | ***She did nothing else ~ sob.***④ | ***She is otherwise ~ he thought.***⑤
—[接] 1. …보다도; …에 비하여 ¶①3월은 2월만큼 춥지 않다 2. …하느니 오히려; 하기보다는 차라리 ¶②도둑질을 하느니 차라리 굶어죽는 게 낫다 3. …밖의; …이외에는 ¶③부모 이외에 그를 도울 사람은 없다/④그녀는 그저 흐느껴 울 뿐이었다/⑤그녀는 그가 생각한 그런 사람이 아니다

—*prep.* (usu. in the phrase *than whom*) in relation
—[前] …보다도 ¶⑥여기에 내 아들이

to; compared to. ¶*She is a girl ~ whom I can imagine no one prettier.* | *Here is my son ~ whom a better does not exist.*⑥

있지만 나에게는 얘보다 좋은 사람이 없다

⁑**thank** [θæŋk] *n.* [C] 《*pl.*》 gratitude; an expression of gratitude. ¶*express one's thanks* | *give* (or *return*) *thanks to someone.*

—[名] 감사; 감사의 말

thanks to, owing to; as the result of; because of.

[熟] …의 덕택으로, …이 원인으로

—*vt.* **1.** express gratitude to (someone). 《~someone *for*》 ¶*Thank you for the beautiful pearl necklace.* | *Thank you for nothing.*① | *No, ~ you.*② **2.** ask; demand. 《~someone *to do*》 ¶*I will ~ you to open the door.*③ | *I will ~ you to be a little more polite.*

—[他] **1.** …에게 감사하다; 사의를 표하다 ¶①내 걱정 말게/②아니 괜찮습니다 **2.** …에게 …하여 주기를 바라다 ¶③문을 좀 열어 주시오

have only *oneself* ***to thank*** (=be responsible) ***for*** *something.* ¶*He has only himself to ~ for his failure.*④

[熟] …은 자신의 탓이다 ¶④그의 실패는 자업자득이다

***thank·ful** [θǽŋkf(u)l] *adj.* feeling or expressing thanks; grateful. 《~ *to* someone *for*…; ~ *to do*; ~ *that*》 ¶*I am ~ to you for your favors.*① | *I am ~ to see you.*

—[形] 고마운; 아주 기쁜 ¶①신세를 져서 고맙게 여깁니다

thank·ful·ly [θǽŋkfuli] *adv.* with thanks; gratefully.

—[副] 감사하여

thank·ful·ness [θǽŋkf(u)lnis] *n.* [U] the state of being thankful; gratitude.

—[名] 감사, 사은

thank·less [θǽŋklis] *adj.* **1.** not feeling or expressing thanks; not grateful. **2.** not leading to be rewarded with thanks; unprofitable. ▷**thank·less·ness** [-nis] *n.*

—[形] **1.** 은혜를 모르는, 배은망덕한 **2.** 감사할 가치 없는; 생색 안 나는

thank·less·ly [θǽŋklisli] *adv.* in a thankless manner.

—[副] 감사할 줄 모르고; 은혜를 모르고

***thanks·giv·ing** [θæ̀ŋksgíviŋ / ⌐⌐–] *n.* **1.** [U] the expression of gratitude, esp. to God. **2.** [C] a prayer expressing thanks to God. **3.** 《*T-*》 Thanksgiving Day.

—[名] **1.** [특히 신에 대한] 감사 **2.** 감사기도 **3.** 감사절

Thanksgiving Day [⌐⌐–⌐] *n.* (*U.S.*) a national holiday for giving thanks to God, on the fourth Thursday in November.

—[名] 《美》 감사절

⁑**that** [ðæt] *adj.* (pl. **those**) **1.** already told or pointed out; the. ¶*The wind blew ~ night.* | *In those days they worked very hard.* **2.** which is at a distance. ¶*You see ~ tower.* | *What is ~ noise?* **3.** 《in contrast with *this*》 the other; another; farther of two or more. ¶*This car is mine and ~ one is hers.*

—[形] **1.** 그, 저; 예(例)의 **2.** 저쪽의 **3.** 또 한쪽의, 저편의

T

—*adv.* to that extent; to such a degree; so. ¶*The little girl can't walk ~ far.* | *He has done only ~ much.*①

—[副] 그만큼; 그렇게 ¶①그는 그만큼밖에 하지 않았다

—*pron.* (pl. **those**) **1.** the person or thing already known or understood. ¶*After ~ his attitude changed.* | *That will do.*② | *Her manner was ~ of a lady.*③ **2.** 《in contrast with *this*》 the farther of two or more things; one of two or more persons or things. ¶*Which do you like better, this or ~?* **3.** a person or thing which is at a distance. ¶*Can you see ~?* **4.** 《in contrast with *this*》 the former. ¶*Virtue and vice before you; this leads to misery, and ~ to peace.*④ **5.** [ðæt, ðət] 《as an *antecedent* to a *relative pronoun*》 ¶*What was ~ he said?*⑤ | (*proverb*) *Heaven helps those who help themselves.*⑥

—[他] **1.** 저것; 저 일 ¶②그것으로 좋다(됐다)/③그녀 태도는 숙녀의 태도이다 **2.** 다른 쪽; 또 한쪽 **3.** 저것; 저쪽의 것 **4.** 전자(前者) ¶④덕과 악덕이 우리 앞에 있다, 후자는 불행으로 전자는 평화로 인도한다 **5.** […하는 바의] 일, 것 ¶⑤그가 한 말은 무엇이었읍니까? /⑥《俚》하늘은 스스로 돕는 자를 돕는다

1) ***and all that,*** and what not; etc.
2) ***at that,*** (*colloq.*) besides; further more; even so.
3) ***for all that,*** in spite of that.
4) ***in that,*** because.
5) ***that is*** (***to say***), namely. ⇨[N.B.]
6) ***That's right,*** (*Brit.*) Yes, just so.; (*U.S.*) Hear, hear.
7) ***That's that,*** (*colloq.*) That is finished or decided.

[熟] 1)및 … 따위 2)《口》게다가, 더구나; 그 위에; 그렇다고는 하나 3)그럼에도 불구하고 4)…의 이유로 5)즉 [N.B.] i.e.로 줄임 6)《英》됐다, 좋다; 《美》옳소, 옳소! 7)《口》그것으로 끝이다(결정됐다)

—*rel. pron.* **1.** who; whom; which. ⇨[usage] ¶*the greatest writer ~ has ever lived* | *the girl ~ you met yesterday.* **2.** 《in place of a *relative adverb*》 when; where. ¶*the last time ~ I saw her* | *This is the place ~ I was born.* **3.** 《*It is…that…*》 ¶*It is Shakespeare ~ I like best.* | *It is you ~ are in the wrong.*⑦

—《關代》 **1.** …하는 바의 [usage] 목적절을 이끄는 경우, 특히 구어(口語)일 때는 흔히 생략됨 **2.** …라는 바의 [날·시간·장소] **3.** …라는 것은 ¶⑦틀린 것은 바로 너다

—*conj.* [ðæt, ðət] **1.** 《used to introduce a *noun clause*》

—[接] **1.** …이라는 것, 한다는 것 ¶⑧그

¶*That you would fail was certain.* | *It is certain ~ our team will win.* | *I have no doubt ~ he will succeed.*⑧ **2.** 《used to introduce an *adverb clause*》 ⓐ 《expressing *purpose*》 ¶*I hurried ~* (or *so ~*; *in order ~*) *I might be in time.* ⓑ 《expressing *result*》 ¶*I was so tired ~ I could not go on any farther.* | *The news gave her such a shock ~ her face turned white.* ⓒ 《expressing *cause* or *reason*》 ¶*I am sorry ~ I cannot help you.* | *If I scold you, it is ~ I want you to be a good boy.*⑨ **3.** 《used to introduce a sentence expressing *desire, surprise,* or other *strong emotion*》 ¶*That he should do such a thing!*⑩ | *O ~ I were in Rome now!*⑪ **4.** 《emphasizing *an adverb* [*phrase*]》 ¶*It was yesterday ~ I met him.* | *It's much to be regretted ~ he died.*⑫

1) ***now that,*** since; because.
2) ***seeing that,*** since; because.

가 성공하리라는 것은 의심치 않는다 **2.** ⓐ…하도록,…하기 위하여 ⓐ그러므로; 따라서 ⓒ…이므로,…때문에 ¶⑨내가 너를 야단치더라도 그것은 네가 착한 아이가 되기를 바라기 때문이다 **3.** …이 되도록; …이라면 좋겠는데; …이라니 ¶⑩그가 그런 일을 하다니/⑪아아 내가 지금 로마에 있다면 **4.** …이라는 것은 ¶⑫그가 죽었다는 것은 유감이다

[熟] 1)…이므로; …이니까 2)…이므로

thatch [θætʃ] *n.* **1.** [C] a roof or covering made of straw, reeds, palm-leaves, etc. **2.** [U] the material used as a roof or covering. **3.** [U] (*colloq.*) the hair of the head. **—*vt.*** cover or roof (a house, etc.) with thatch.

—[名] **1.** 초가 지붕 **2.** 이엉,지붕 이는 재료 **3.** 머리카락

—[他] [지붕]을 이엉으로 이다

* **that's** [ðæts] that is.

* **thaw** [θɔː] *vi.* **1.** (of ice, snow or anything frozen) melt; become water. ¶*It is thawing.*① **2.** grow warm enough to melt ice and snow. **3.** become friendly. **—*vt.*** cause (the ice) to melt; cause (someone) to be friendly.
—*n.* [C] 《usu. *sing.*》 the state of the weather when ice or snow is melting.

—[自] **1.** 녹다 ¶①서리(눈·얼음)가 녹는다 **2.** [눈이 녹을 만큼] 따뜻해지다 **3.** 누그러지다 —[他] …을 녹이다; 누그러지게 하다
—[名] 눈석임,해빙; 봄날씨

⁝ **the** [ðiː, ðə, *before vowels* ði] *def. art.* **1.** already known or understood; obvious without relating; that. ¶*Please open ~ window.* | *The girl I met yesterday was my niece.* **2.** unique; only one; sole. ¶*~ sun* | *~ world* | *~ Bible* | *~ winter* | *~ south* | *~ highest tower in Korea.* **3.** (of a part of the body) one's. ¶*take someone by ~ hand.*① **4.** 《in names of diseases》 ¶*~ blues*② | *have ~ measles.*③ **5.** whole of class or species of; every; any. ¶*The dog is a faithful animal.*④ | *The pen is mightier than ~ sword.* **6.** such; so; enough. ¶*He was not ~ man to betray her.*⑤ | *He had ~ kindness to show me the way.* **7.** typical; real; true. ¶*He is ~ man.*⑥ | *This is ~ life.* **8.** best. ¶*Beer is ~ drink for hot weaher.* | *This is ~ hotel in this town.* **9.** per; a. ¶*5 dollars ~ pound* | *so much ~ hour.*⑦ **10.** 《used before *proper nouns*》 ¶*~ United States* [*of America*] | *~ Himalayas* | *~ Mississippi* | *~ Pacific Ocean* | *~ Suez Canal* | *~ Bay of Wonsan* | *~ White House* | *~ Jeil Bank* | *~ Enterprice* | *The New York Times.* **11.** 《used before a *title* and *family name*》 ¶*Alfred ~ Great*⑧ | *~ Duke of Wellington*⑨ | *~ Napoleons*⑩ **12.** 《used before *adjective* to make *nouns*》 ¶*~ young* | *~ living and ~ dead*⑪ | *~ beautiful*⑫
—*adv.* 《used with the *comparative degree*》 by so much; that much; to that extent. ¶*The higher we go up in the air, ~ colder it becomes.* | *I take a walk every morning and feel ~ better for it.*

—《定冠詞》 **1.** 그; 예(例)의 **2.** 단 하나의; 독특한 **3.** 사람의 ¶①남의 손을 잡다 **4.** 《병명에 붙여서》 ¶②우울증/③홍역에 걸리다 **5.** 모든 ¶④개란 충성스런 동물이다 **6.** …하는 그러한 ¶⑤그는 그녀를 배반할 그런 남자가 아니다 **7.** 전형적인; 참된 ¶⑥그야말로 정말 사내다 **8.** 가장 좋은 **9.** …에 대하여 ¶⑦한 시간에 대하여 그만큼 **10.** 《고유명사에 붙여》 **11.** 《칭호·집안 이름에 붙여》 ¶⑧알프렛 대왕/⑨웰링턴 공작/⑩나폴레옹 가(家) **12.** 《형용사에 붙여》 ¶⑪산 자와 죽은 자/⑫미(美)

—[副] 한층,오히려; …하면 할수록; 그만큼

⁝ **the·a·ter,** *Brit.* **-tre** [θí(ː)ətər / θíətə] *n.* [C] **1.** a place where plays are acted; a place where motion pictures are shown. ⇒[N.B.] **2.** 《*the ~*》 the drama; the dramatic art. ¶*the modern ~*① | *go to the ~.*② **3.** a hall or room with seats like a theater, used for lectures in a university, etc. **4.** a place of important action.

—[名] **1.** 극장;영화관 [N.B.] 미국에서 극장명으로서는 가끔 theatre를 씀 **2.** 극,연극 ¶①현대극/②연극 관람하러 가다 **3.** 계단식 강단,계단 교실 **4.** 활동의 장소,무대

the·at·ri·cal [θiǽtrik(ə)l] *adj.* of a theater; of the drama; (of words or action) better for the theater than for real life; not natural. **—*n.*** 《*pl.*》 dramatic performances, esp. by amateurs.

—[形] 극장의; 극의; 연극조의; 부자연한 —[名] 소인극(素人劇)

the·at·ri·cal·ly [θiǽtrik(ə)li] *adv.* in a theatrical manner. —ⓑ 연극적으로, 연극조로
thee [ði:] *pron.* (*archaic*) objective case of **thy.**
theft [θeft] *n.* Ⓤ (sometimes *a* ~) the act of stealing. ¶*commit a* ~.① —⓷ 도둑질, 절도 ¶①도둑질을 하다
their [ðɛər] *pron.* the possessive case of **they.** —⓹ 그들의
theirs [ðɛərz] *pron.* possessive form of **they**; the one or ones belonging to them. ¶*a favorite picture of* ~ / *The land is* ~. / *Our car is older than* ~.① —⓹ 그들의 것 ¶①우리 차는 그들의 것보다 헌 것이다
the·ism [θíːiz(ə)m] *n.* Ⓤ belief in a god or gods; belief in one God, the creator and ruler of the universe. —⓷ 유신론(有神論); 일신교(一神敎)
the·ist [θíːist] *n.* Ⓒ a believer in theism. ↔atheist —⓷ 유신론자
them [ðem, ðəm] *pron.* the objective case of **they.** —⓹ 그들을(에게)
* **theme** [θiːm] *n.* Ⓒ **1.** the topic or subject of a speech, essay, etc. **2.** (esp. *U.S.*) a short essay on a certain subject. **3.** (*Music*) the chief melody in a piece of music; a theme song. —⓷ 1. 데에마, 화제, 논제 2.(美) 과제작문 3.(樂) 주제, 주(主)선율; 데에마 음악
them·selves [ð(ə)msélvz] *pron.* the emphatic or reflexive form of **they** or **them.** ¶*They hid* ~. —⓹ 그들 자신[이, 을, 에게]
then [ðen] *adv.* **1.** at that time in the future or in the past. ¶*She was a little girl* ~.① / *Things will be different* ~.② **2.** soon afterward; after that. ¶*She shut the door and* ~ *burst into tears.* **3.** besides. ¶*I like to walk, and* ~ *it's good for the health.*③ **4.** in that case; therefore. ¶*He isn't here. Where is he,* ~ ? —⓷ 1.그 때 ¶①그 무렵 그녀는 아직 소녀였다/②그 때에는 사태가 달라져 있을 것이다 2.그리고서[곧]; 다음에는 3.게다가, 더구나 ¶③나는 걷기를 좋아한다, 게다가 걷는 것은 건강에 좋다 4.그렇다면; 그런 까닭으로
—*adj.* of that time; existing at that time. —⓹ 당시의; 그 때의
—*n.* Ⓤ that time. ¶*before (by, since, till)* ~ / *from* ~ *on*① / *up to* (or *till*) ~. —⓷ 그 때 ¶①그때 이래
1) *but then,* but on the other hand.
2) *every now and then,* sometimes.
3) *now then,* I say.; listen to me.; at any rate.
4) *then and there,* at once.
5) *What then?* What would happen in that case?
熟 1)그러나 한편; 그렇다면 2)이따금 3)이봐이봐; 이봐 그런데; 자 그러면 4)당장에 5)그렇다면 어떻게 될까?
* **thence** [ðens] *adv.* **1.** from that place. ¶*She departed* ~. **2.** for that reason or source; therefore. ¶*You are young, and* ~ *romantic.* **3.** from then. ¶*a week* ~. —⓷ 1.거기서부터 2.그 까닭에 3.그 때부터
thence·forth [ðènsfɔ́ːrθ / ðénsfɔ̀ːθ] *adv.* from that time on; thereafter. [that time on; thenceforth.] —⓷ 그 때부터
thence·for·ward [ðènsfɔ́ːrwərd / ðénsfɔ̀ːwəd] *adv.* from —⓷ 그 때부터
the·oc·ra·cy [θi:ákrəsi / -ɔ́k-] *n.* (pl. **-cies**) Ⓤ a form of polity in which people claim to be governed by a God.; Ⓤ government by priests; Ⓒ a country governed in this way. —⓷ 신정(神政); 신권(神權) 정치; 신정국(神政國)
the·o·crat·ic [θìːəkrǽtik / θìək-] *adj.* of theocracy; having a theocracy. [for measuring angles.] —⓹ 신정(神政)의
the·od·o·lite [θi:ádəlàit / θiɔ́də-] *n.* Ⓒ an instrument —⓷ [측량용] 경위의(經緯儀)
the·o·lo·gian [θìːəlóudʒən / -dʒiən, θìəlóudʒiən] *n.* Ⓒ a person who is skilled in theology. —⓷ 신학자
the·o·log·i·cal [θìːəládʒik(ə)l / θìəlɔ́dʒi-] *adj.* of theology. —⓹ 신학[상]의, 신학적인
the·ol·o·gy [θi:álədʒi / θiɔ́lə-] *n.* Ⓤ the systematic study of God and His relations to man and the universe; the science of religion. —⓷ 신학
the·o·rem [θíːərəm / θíə-] *n.* Ⓒ a statement, proposition, or rule that can be proved to be true by logical reasoning. —⓷ 법칙, 정리(定理)
the·o·ret·ic [θìːərétik / θìə-], **-i·cal** [-ik(ə)l] *adj.* based on theory, not practical or based on experience. ↔empirical —⓹ 이론[상]의
the·o·ret·i·cal·ly [θìːərétikəli / θìə-] *adv.* in a theoretical manner ; according to theory. —⓹ 이론상, 이론적으로
the·o·rist [θíːərist / θíə-] *n.* Ⓒ a person who forms theories. —⓷ 이론가; 공론가(空論家)
the·o·rize [θíːəràiz / θíə-] *vi.* form theories. —⓻ 이론을 세우다
* **the·o·ry** [θíːəri / θíə-] *n.* (pl. **-ries**) Ⓒ **1.** the general and fundamental principles of an art, science, etc. ↔practice ¶*It is not so easy in practice as in* ~. **2.** a reasoned supposition put forward to explain facts or events. ¶*the* ~ *of evolution.*① **3.** a peculiar opinion; an idea. —⓷ 1.[실지에 대한] 이론 2.학설, 논(論) ¶①진화론 3.지론(持論), 의견; 생각

ther·a·peu·tic [θèrəpjú:tik] *adj.* of the treatment of disease; curative. ▷**ther·a·peu·ti·cal·ly** [-k(ə)li] *adv.*
—[形] 치료[상]의

ther·a·peu·tics [θèrəpjú:tiks] *n. pl.* ⦅used as *sing.*⦆ the branch of medicine that deals with the treatment and cure of diseases.
—[名] 치료학

ther·a·py [θérəpi] *n.* [U] the treatment aimed at curing diseases.
—[名] 요법(療法)

⁑**there** [ðɛər] *adv.* **1.** in that place; to or toward that place. ↔here ¶*here and ~ / go ~ / He was not ~. / We shall stay ~ all summer. / The boy ~ is my nephew.*① **2.** at that point. ¶*There we can't agree with him.*② */ There I am wrong.* **3.** ⦅used to call *attention*⦆ Hear!; Listen! ¶*There she goes! / There goes the whistle! / There you are!*③ **4.** ⦅used in sentences in which the verb comes before the subject⦆ ¶*There came to the city a stranger. / There is a dictionary on the desk. / There remains for you to work hard.*④
—[副] 1. 그곳(저기)에서, 저리로 ¶①저기 있는 소년은 내 조카다 2. 그 점에서; 거기에서 ¶②그 점에서 우리는 그와 의견이 다르다 3. 저것 봐, 들어 봐 ¶③그것 보라니까; 그래 그거다 4. ⦅주어의 앞에 동사가 오는 문장에 써서⦆ ¶④이제는 네가 열심히 공부할 일만 남았다

1) ***all there,*** alert; wide-awake; not mad.
2) ***get there,*** (*slang*) succeed.
3) ***get there and back,*** go to that place and come back again.
4) ***over there,*** at a far or farther place.
5) ***then and there,*** at that particular time and place.

[熟] 1)방심 않는, 빈틈없는 2)⦅俗⦆성공하다 3)왕복하다 4)저쪽에 5)그때, 그 자리에서

—*pron.* that place or point. ¶*from (near, up to) ~.*
—[代] 그곳; 저기

—*interj.* ⦅used to express *satisfaction, comfort,* etc.⦆ ¶*There, ~, don't worry about that! / There now!*⑤
—[感] 그래그래; 그만그만; 잘한다 ¶⑤자 어때!

there·a·bout [ðɛ́ərəbàut], **-bouts** [-bàuts] *adv.* near that place, time, number, etc.; nearly.
—[副] 그 근처에; 그 무렵에; 대략 …, …정도

***there·af·ter** [ðɛ̀ərǽftər / -ɑ́:ftə] *adv.* after that; afterward; subsequently.
—[副] 그 후는; 그때 이래

***there·by** [ðɛ̀ərbái] *adv.* by that means; in that connection.
—[副] 그것에 의하여; 그것에 관하여

⁑**there·fore** [ðɛ́ərfɔ̀:r] *adv.* for that reason; on that account; accordingly.
—[副] 그 까닭에; 그 결과

there·from [ðɛ̀ərfrɑ́m / ðɛ̀əfrɔ́m] *adv.* from this; from that; from it.
—[副] 거기서부터; 그것으로부터

there·in [ðɛ̀ərín] *adv.* in that place; in it; in that respect.
—[副] 그 속에, 그곳에, 그 점에서

***there·of** [ðɛ̀ərɑ́v / ðɛ̀ərɔ́v] *adv.* **1.** of that; of it. **2.** from that; from it.
—[副] 1. 그것을 2. 그것에서부터

⁑**there's** [ðɛərz] there is; there has.

there·to [ðɛ̀ərtú:] *adv.* to that; to it; in addition to that.
—[副] 거기에; 그 위에 또, 게다가

***there·up·on** [ðɛ̀ərəpɑ́n / -əpɔ́n] *adv.* on that; on it; soon after that; for that reason.
—[副] 그 위에; 그러자 곧; 그 까닭에

ther·mal [θə́:rm(ə)l] *adj.* of heat; warm; hot.
—[形] 열(熱)의, 온도의; 따뜻한, 뜨거운

***ther·mom·e·ter** [θərmɑ́mitər / -mɔ́mitə] *n.* [C] an instrument for measuring temperature. ¶*a Centigrade ~*① */ a Fahrenheit ~.*②
—[名] 한란계, 온도계 ¶①섭씨 온도계 / ②화씨 온도계

ther·mos bottle [θə́:rməsbɑ̀tl / θə́:mɔsbɔ̀tl] *n.* a bottle for keeping water or other liquid hot or cold.
—[名] 마법병, 진공 보온병

ther·mo·stat [θə́:rməstæ̀t] *n.* [C] a device which controls the temperature automatically.
—[名] 온도 조절 장치

the·sau·ri [θisɔ́:rai] *n.* pl. of **thesaurus.**

the·sau·rus [θisɔ́:rəs] *n.* [C] (pl. **-sau·ri** or **~es**) **1.** a place where treasures are kept. **2.** a collection of much information and knowledge, such as a dictionary, encyclopedia, etc.
—[名] 1. 보고(寶庫) 2. 지식의 보고, 보전(寶典)

⁑**these** [ði:z] *adj., pron.* pl. of **this.**

the·ses [θí:si:z] *n.* pl. of **thesis.**

the·sis [θí:sis] *n.* [U][C] (pl. **the·ses**) **1.** a written essay written in order to get a university degree. **2.** a statement of an idea to be proved.
—[名] 1. [학위·졸업의] 논문 2. 명제(命題)

thews [θju:z] *n. pl.* muscles; strength of a body.
—[名] 근육; 체력

⁑**they** [ðei] *pron.* **1.** pl. of **he, she,** or **it. 2.** people in general. ¶*They grow rice in this part of the country. / They say that she will marry.*
—[代] 1. 그들은(이) 2. 사람들

***they'd** [ðeid] they had; they would.

***they'll** [ðeil] they will; they shall.

***they're** [ðéiər] they are.

***they've** [ðeiv] they have.

⁑**thick** [θik] *adj.* **1.** having much space from one surface
—[形] 1. 두꺼운 2. 두께가 …의 3. 굵은

thicken

to another; not thin. ↔thin ¶*~ cloth | a ~ board.* **2.** from one surface to another. ¶*a board 4 inches ~.* **3.** having a large diameter in relation to length. ¶*a ~ pipe (finger, neck, trunk)* **4.** compact. ¶*~ hair | a ~ wood (forest).* **5.** full; abundant; crowded. ¶*a bus ~ with child | the air ~ with rain.*① **6.** dense; heavy. ¶*a ~ fog | a ~ syrup.* **7.** not clear. ¶*The air was ~ with smoke.*② *| The river looked ~ after the rain. | The weather was ~.*③ **8.** husky; hoarse. ¶*a ~ voice.* **9.** slow in understanding; stupid; dull. ¶*have a ~ head.* **10.** (*colloq.*) (as *predicative*) intimate; very friendly. ¶*He and I are very ~.*
—*adv.* thickly; heavily.´ ¶*Snow falls ~ and fast.*④
—*n.* Ⓤ (*the ~*) the thickest part; the most active part. ¶*the ~ of the town.*
1) *in the thick of,* in the midst of.
2) *through thick and thin,* under any conditions; steadfastly; resolutely.

thick·en [θík(ə)n] *vt., vi.* make or become thick or thick-
thick·et [θíkit] *n.* Ⓒ a thick growth of small trees.
thick-head·ed [θíkhèdid] *adj.* a little foolish; slow in understanding or learning. ▷**thick-head·ed·ness** [-nis] *n.*
thick·ly [θíkli] *adv.* **1.** in a thick manner. **2.** in great numbers; very often.
• **thick·ness** [θíknis] *n.* **1.** Ⓤ the state or quality of being thick. **2.** Ⓤ Ⓒ the distance between the opposite outside parts of a book, tree, etc. ¶*The large dictionary is three inches in ~.*① **3.** Ⓒ a layer. ¶*two thicknesses of cloth.*②
thick-set [θíksét] *adj.* **1.** closely planted. **2.** having a short, stout body.
thick-skinned [θíkskínd] *adj.* having a thick skin; not sensitive to other people's bad opinion of oneself.
: thief [θi:f] *n.* Ⓒ (pl. **thieves**) a person who steals.
thieve [θi:v] *vt., vi.* steal.
thieves [θi:vz] *n.* pl. of thief. [a thief.
thiev·ish [θí:viʃ] *adj.* having the habit of stealing; like
• **thigh** [θai] *n.* Ⓒ the thick part of the leg between the hip and the knee.
thigh-bone [θáibòun] *n.* Ⓒ the bone of the thigh.
thim·ble [θímbl] *n.* Ⓒ a small cap of metal, celluloid, etc. used to protect the finger when pushing the needle in sewing. ⇒Ⓝ.Ⓑ, fig.
: thin [θin] *adj.* (**thin·ner, thin·nest**) **1.** having little space from one surface to another. ¶*~ paper (clothes).* **2.** having a small diameter in relation to length. ¶*a ~ thread | ~ fingers.* **3.** having little flesh; slender; [thimble] slim. ¶*~ in face | She is ~.* **4.** not close together; scattered; scanty. ¶*a ~ audience (meeting)*① *| a ~ population.* **5.** not dense; watery. ¶*~ beer | ~ milk (soup).* **6.** weak; poor; faint. ¶*the ~ sunlight*
—*vt.* make (something) thin. ¶*The war thinned [down] the population. | ~ [out] flowers.*③ —*vi.* become thin. ¶*My hair is thinning.* [vowel) =your.
• **thine** [ðain] *pron.* (*archaic*) **1.** =yours. **2.** (before *a*
: thing [θiŋ] *n.* Ⓒ **1.** all that exist; any material object. ¶*a living ~ | Put these things in the bag.* **2.** all that can be thought or imagined, such as a fact, an idea, an opinion, and an act. ¶*It is a good ~ to think so.* **3.** an event; an affair; a matter. ¶*things Korean*① *| A strange ~ has happened. | This is the ~ in question.*② **4.** a fellow; a person. ¶*a little ~.* **5.** (often *pl.*) the state of affairs; circumstances. ¶*Things are going well.*③ **6.** (*pl.*) things that belong to someone; someone's

thing

4. 우거진, 무성한; 빽빽한 **5.** 가득찬; 붐비는 ¶①비를 머금은 공기 **6.** 진한, 걸쭉한 **7.** 선명치 않은; 흐린, 탁한 ¶②공기는 연기로 자욱했다/③날씨가 흐렸다 **8.** [목소리가] 쉰 **9.** 둔한; 우둔한 **10.** 《口》친한; 사이가 좋은

—⒜ 두껍게; 진하게; 빈번히; 숱하게
¶④눈은 평평 쏟아지고 있다

—⒩ 가장 굵은(두꺼운, 우거진, 밀집한) 부분; 사람이 붐비는 곳
圀 1)…이 한창일 때에 2)만난을 무릅쓰고

—⒣⒤ 두껍게 하다(되다)
—⒩ 관목숲, 덤불
—⒜ 머리가 둔한

—⒜ 1. 두껍게; 진하게 빽빽이 2. 줄기차게; 빈번히
—⒩ 1. 농도; 밀도; 밀집; 빈번함 2. 두께, 굵기 ¶①그 큰 사전의 두께는 3인치다 3. 층, 겹 ¶②두 겹의 천

—⒜ 1. 무성한 2. 땅딸막한
—⒜ 껍질(피부)이 두꺼운, 둔감한

—⒩ 도둑
—⒣⒤ 훔치다

—⒜ 도벽(盜癖)이 있는; 도둑 같은
—⒩ 넓적다리

—⒩ 대퇴골
—⒩ [재봉용의] 끝무 Ⓝ.Ⓑ. 모자 모양으로 생겼음

—⒜ 1. 얇은 2. 가느다란 3. 호리호리한, 야윈 4. 드문드문 있는; 출석자가 적은 ¶①얼마 안 되는 청중(한산한 모임) 5. 묽은, 맹물 같은 6. 약한; 희미한

—⒣ …을 얇게(묽게) 하다; 가늘게 하다 ¶②꽃을 솎다 —⒤ 야위다; 얇아지다; 드문드문해지다

—⒩ 1. 물체, 물건, 것 2. 생각할 수 있는 것; 사물 3. 사건; 일 ¶①한국의 풍물/②이것이 문제되고 있는 일이다 4. 사람, 녀석 5. 형세; 상황; 사태 ¶③사태는 호전돼 가고 있다 6. 소지품; 재산 ¶④나는 차 속에 소지품을 두고 내렸다 7. 의복; 외출복 ¶⑤옷을 벗다 8. 도구 9. 어울리는 일 ¶⑥여자를 빤히 바라다보는 것은 좋지 않다

belongings. ¶*I have left my things in the car.*④ **7.** ⦅*pl.*⦆ clothes; outdoor clothes. ¶*take off one's things.*⑤ **8.** ⦅*pl.*⦆ instruments; tools. ¶*kitchen things.* **9.** ⦅*the* ~⦆ what is fitting. ¶*It is not the ~ to stare at women.*⑥

1) ***above all things,*** more than anything else; above all.
2) ...***and things,*** (*colloq.*) and the like.
3) [*the*] ***first thing,*** before anything else.
4) ***for one thing,*** as one reason. ¶*For one ~, I am busy.*⑦
5) ***know a thing or two,*** be experienced or wise.
6) ***make a good thing of*** (=*profit by*) *something.*

[熟] 1)무엇보다도, 우선 먼저; 그 중에서도 2)⦅口⦆…따위 3)우선 첫째로 4)한 가지 이유로서 ¶⑦우선 틈이 없다 5)경험이 있다; 빈틈이 없다 6)…으로 이익을 얻다

:think [θiŋk] *v.* (**thought**) *vt.* **1.** form or have (an idea, an opinion, etc.) in mind. ¶*~ happy thoughts.* **2.** imagine. ⦅*~ how* or *what* [*to do*]...⦆ ¶*I can't ~ how you do it.*① **3.** judge; regard. ⦅*~ that...*⦆ ¶*I ~* [*that*] *she will come.* | *They thought him* [*to be*] *mad.* **4.** intend; expect. ⦅*~ that...*; *~ to do*⦆ ¶*I ~ I'll start tomorrow.* | *He did not ~ to meet her at such a place.*② **5.** call (something) to mind; remember. ¶*He was thinking what to do next.*③ **6.** understand. ¶*I can't ~ why she wept yesterday.* **7.** feel (something) in one's mind. ¶*The boy was thinking how strange the man was.* **—*vi.*** **1.** have an opinion. **2.** use one's mind hard to understand something; reflect; meditate. ¶*~ in English* | *Think before you speak.*

—[타] 1.…을 생각하다; 마음에 품다 2.…을 상상하다 ¶①네가 그것을 어떻게 할지 상상도 못하겠다 3.…이라고 생각하다; …이라고 간주하다 4.[…할] 작정이다; …이라고 예상하다 ¶②그는 그녀를 그런 장소에서 만나리라고는 생각도 못했었다 5.…을 생각해내다 ¶③그는 다음에 할 일을 생각해내고 있었다 6.…을 이해하다 7.…을 마음으로 느끼다 —[자] 1.생각하다 2.숙고하다

1) ***think about,*** ⓐ consider. ¶*His proposal needs to be thought about very carefully.*④ ⓑ have an opinion about (something). ¶*Tell me what you ~ about this novel.* ⓒ be interested in; give one's mind to (something). ¶*She thinks about nothing but clothes.*⑤
2) ***think aloud,*** speak one's thoughts as they come into one's mind.
3) ***think better of,*** change one's opinion of (something) after thinking again.
4) ***think of,*** ⓐ call (something) to mind. ¶*I cannot ~ of his name.* ⓑ have (an idea) in mind. ¶*In those days space travel had not been thought of.*⑥ ⓒ intend; plan. ¶*~ of going to Hawaii.* ⓓ have an opinion of (something). ⓔ consider.
5) ***think out,*** think about (something) to the end.
6) ***think over,*** reflect; consider.
7) ***think through,*** think about (something) until one gets a conclusion.
8) ***think to oneself,*** speak to oneself; consider secretly in one's mind.
9) ***think twice,*** think again before acting; hesitate.

[熟] 1)ⓐ숙고하다 ¶④그의 제의는 신중히 고려해 볼 필요가 있다 ⓑ…에 대해 의견을 갖다 ⓒ…에 관심을 갖다; …에 유의하다 ¶⑤그녀는 의복 이외에는 관심이 없다 2)중얼거리며 생각하다 3)…을 재고하다; 고쳐 생각하다 4)ⓐ…을 기억해 내다 ⓑ…한 생각을 품다 ¶⑥당시에는 우주 생각 따위는 엄두도 못했다 ⓒ…할 작정이다 ⓓ…에 대하여 의견을 갖다 ⓔ숙고하다 5)…을 끝까지 생각하다 6)…을 숙고하다 7)…의 결론을 내리다 8)혼자서 생각하다 9)재고하다; 망설이다

think·a·ble [θíŋkəbl] *adj.* that can be thought.
—[형] 생각(상상)할 수 있는

think·er [θíŋkər] *n.* [C] a person who thinks.
—[명] 생각하는 사람, 사상가

·think·ing [θíŋkiŋ] *adj.* that thinks; that can think; thoughtful. **—*n.*** [U] thought; way of thought. ¶*to my ~.*①
—[형] 생각하는, 사색력이 있는 —[명] 사고(思考), 사색 ¶①내 생각으로는

thin·ly [θínli] *adv.* in a thin manner; in small numbers.
—[부] 얇게, 가늘게, 드물게

thin·ness [θínnis] *n.* [U] the state of being thin.
—[명] 얇음, 희박

:third [θə:rd] *n.* **1.** ⦅usu. *the* ~⦆ number 3; 3rd. ¶*Henry the Third.*① **2.** [C] one of 3 equal parts of anything. **—*adj.*** of 3rd.
—[명] 1.제 3, 세 번째 ¶①헨리 3세 2. 3분의 1 —[형] 제 3의, 세 번째의, 3분의 1의

third-class [θə́:rdklǽs / -klá:s] *adj.* of the third class; less good than the first and second class. **—*adv.*** by third class.
—[형] 3등의, 하등의, 열등한 —[부] 3등으로

third·ly [θə́:rdli] *adv.* in the third place.
—[부] 세 번째로, 제 3으로

·third-rate [θə́:rdréit] *adj.* of the third rate; inferior.
—[형] 3류의; 하등의; 열등한

:thirst [θə:rst] *n.* [U] ⦅often *a* ~⦆ **1.** a painful feeling caused by need of something to drink; a desire for drink. **2.** a strong desire for anything. ⦅*~ for, after, of*⦆ ¶*a ~ for knowledge.*
—[명] 1.목마름, 갈증 2.열망, 갈망

—*vi.* **1.** feel thirst. **2.** have a strong desire. ⦅*~ after* or *for* something⦆ ¶*~ for fame.*
—[자] 1.목이 마르다 2.열망하다

thirst·i·ly [θə́:rstili] *adv.* **1.** with thirst. **2.** eagerly. —[副] 1. 목말라서 2. 열망하여

: **thirst·y** [θə́:rsti] *adj.* (**thirst·i·er, thirst·i·est**) **1.** feeling thirst. **2.** dry. **3.** having a strong desire. —[形] 1. 목마른 2. 건조한 3. 열망하는

⋮ **thir·teen** [θə́:rtí:n] *n.* [C] the number between twelve and fourteen; 13. —*adj.* of 13. —[名] 13 —[形] 13의

thir·teenth [θə́:rtí:nθ] *n.* **1.** 《usu. *the* ~》 the number 13; 13th. **2.** [C] one of 13 equal parts of anything. —*adj.* of the 13th. —[名] 1. 13 번째 2. 13 분의 1 —[形] 13 번째의; 13 분의 1 의

: **thir·ti·eth** [θə́:rtiiθ] *n.* **1.** 《usu. *the* ~》 the number 30; 30th. **2.** [C] one of 30 equal parts of anything. —*adj.* of the 30th. —[名] 1. 30 번째 2. 30 분의 1 —[形] 30 번째의; 30 분의 1 의

⋮ **thir·ty** [θə́:rti] *n.* [U] three times 10; 30. —*adj.* of 30. —[名] 30 —[形] 30 의

⋮ **this** [ðis] *adj.* (pl. **these**) **1.** which is near in time or space, or which has just been mentioned. ¶ *~ month (year) / ~ day week.*① **2.** 《in contrast with *that*》 which is here; nearer of two or more. ¶ *This car is better than that one.* —[形] 1. 이; 지금의, 현재의; 다음의 ¶ ①내주(또는 전주)의 오늘 2. [that 와 상관적으로 써서]이, 이쪽에 있는

—*pron.* (pl. **these**) **1.** the thing or person near in time or space. ¶ *~ time / Who is ~? / This is Sunday.* **2.** the fact or idea about to be mentioned or which has just been mentioned. ¶ *Do it like ~.*② */ Answer me ~.* **3.** 《in contrast with *that*》 the thing or person here; the nearer of two or more things. ¶ *This is newer than that.* **4.** 《in contrast with *that*》 the latter. ¶ *Work and play are both necessary to health; ~ gives us rest, and that gives us energy.* —[代] 1. 이것, 이 사람, 이 일 2. 다음 일 ¶②이와 같이(지금부터 말하는 것처럼) 해라 3. 이것, 이쪽 4. 후자(後者)

—*adv.* to this extent; so. ¶ *~ big (early, much, far).* —[副] 이것만큼, 이 정도까지

for all this, in spite of this. [熟] 이럼에도 불구하고

this·tle [θísl] *n.* [C] a plant with a prickly stalk and leaves, and usu. with purple flowers. —[名] 엉겅퀴

this·tle·down [θísldàun] *n.* [C] a soft, feathery substance part on thistle seeds. —[名] 엉겅퀴 씨의 관모(冠毛)

* **thith·er** [θíðər, ðíðər] *adv.* (*archaic*) to that place; in that direction. —[副] 《古》 저기에; 저쪽에

* **tho,** *Brit.* **tho'** [ðou] *conj., adv.* =though.

thong [θɔ:ŋ / θɔŋ] *n.* [C] a narrow strip of leather. —[名] 가죽끈

tho·ra·ces [θɔ́:rəsì:z] *n.* pl. of **thorax.**

tho·rax [θɔ́:ræks] *n.* [C] (pl. **-rax·es** or **-ra·ces**) **1.** (of the human body) the chest. **2.** (of insects) the middle of the three main sections of the body. —[名] 1. [인간의] 가슴; 흉부 2. [곤충의] 흉부

* **thorn** [θɔ:rn] *n.* [C] **1.** a sharp point on the stem of a plant; a prickle. **2.** a plant that has thorns on it. **3.** a source of trouble. —[名] 1. 가시 2. 가시가 있는 식물 3. 고민거리

thorn·y [θɔ́:rni] *adj.* (**thorn·i·er, thorn·i·est**) **1.** with thorns; full of thorns. **2.** troublesome. ¶ *a ~ path.*① —[形] 1. 가시가 있는; 가시투성이의 2. 곤란한 ¶①가시밭길

* **thor·ough** [θə́:rou / θʌ́rə] *adj.* complete; absolute; accurate; careful. ¶ *It wants a ~ change.* —[形] 완전한; 절대적인; 용의주도한; 주의 깊은

thor·ough·bred [θə́:roubrèd / θʌ́rə-] *adj.* **1.** (of an animal) pure-bred. **2.** (of persons) noble; of good birth and breeding. —*n.* [C] **1.** a thoroughbred animal, esp. a horse. **2.** a well-bred person. —[形] 1. 순혈종(純血種)의 2. 고귀한, 고상한; 우아한 —[名] 1. 순혈종의 동물 2. 가문이 좋은 사람

thor·ough·fare [θə́:roufὲər / θʌ́rəfὲə] *n.* [C] a street, road, or passage open at both ends. —[名] 한길, 공로; 통로

No thoroughfare, people are forbidden to go through (this street). [熟] 통행금지

thor·ough·go·ing [θə́:rougòuiŋ / θʌ́rə--] *adj.* thorough; complete. —[形] 철저한; 완전한

: **thor·ough·ly** [θə́:rouli / θʌ́rə-] *adv.* fully; completely. —[副] 철저하게; 완전히

thor·ough·ness [θə́:rounis / θʌ́rə-] *n.* [U] completeness. —[名] 완전; 철저

⋮ **those** [ðouz] *adj., pron.* pl. of **that.**

* **thou** [ðau] *pron.* (pl. **ye** or **you**) (*archaic, poetic*) you. —[代] 그대

⋮ **though** [ðou] *conj.* **1.** in spite of the fact that; although. ¶ *Though [he is] rich, he works very hard.* **2.** yet; still; nevertheless; however. ¶ *She is better, ~ not yet cured.* —[接] 1. …이지만 2. …이라고는 하나; 과연 …이기는 해도

thought

—*adv.* ((placed at the end of a sentence)) however ; all
1) *as though,* as if. [the same.
2) *even though,* even if. ¶*I shall go even ~ it snows.*
3) *what though,* what does it matter if.

thought [θɔ:t] *v.* pt. and pp. of *think*.
—*n.* Ⓤ **1.** the act or process of thinking ; the working of the mind. **2.** the power of thinking, imagining, reasoning, etc. **3.** Ⓒ that which a person thinks ; a product of thinking, such as an idea, or an opinion. **4.** care ; consideration ; concern. **5.** a way of thinking characteristic of a period, nation, etc. ¶*modern ~.*
1) *have no thought* (=*have no intention*) *of doing.*
2) *on second thought*[*s*], after thinking again.
3) *take thought for* (=*worry about*) *something.*

thought·ful [θɔ́:tf(u)l] *adj.* **1.** full of thought. **2.** kind. (*~ of*) ¶*He is ~ of his friends.* [**2.** kindly.

thought·ful·ly [θɔ́:tfuli] *adv.* **1.** in a thoughtful manner.

thought·ful·ness [θɔ́:tfulnis] *n.* Ⓤ **1.** the state of being thoughtful. **2.** kindness. [**2.** unkind

thought·less [θɔ́:tlis] *adj.* **1.** without thought ; careless.

thou·sand [θáuz(ə)nd] *n.* Ⓒ **1.** ten hundred ; 1,000. **2.** (*pl.*) a large number. (*~ of*) ¶*thousands of books.*
—*adj.* **1.** of 1,000. **2.** indefinitely many.

thou·sand·fold [θáuz(ə)ndfòuld] *adj.* a thousand times as much or as many. —*adv.* a thousand times.

thou·sandth [θáuz(ə)ndθ] *n.* **1.** ((usu. *the ~*)) number 1,000 ; 1,000th. **2.** Ⓒ one of the 1,000 equal parts of anything.
—*adj.* of a thousandth. [being a slave.

thrall·dom, thral·dom [θrɔ́:ldəm] *n.* Ⓤ the state of

thrash [θræʃ] *vt.* **1.** separate (grain) from its straw, husks, etc. ; thresh. **2.** beat (someone) in punishment. **3.** defeat (someone) completely or mercilessly.
—*vi.* **1.** move violently ; toss about. **2.** separate grain from its straw, husks, etc. ; thresh. **3.** sail against a *thrash over,* go over again. [strong wind.

thrash·er [θrǽʃər] *n.* Ⓒ **1.** a person or thing that thrashes. **2.** a large shark.

thread [θred] *n.* Ⓒ **1.** Ⓤ Ⓒ the fine, twisted fiber of cotton, flax, wool, silk, etc. **2.** something like a thread. ¶*a ~ of smoke.* **3.** something that connects the parts of anything. ¶*the ~ of argument.* **4.** the spiral ridge of a screw. ⇒fig.
1) *hang by a thread,* be in a dangerous state.
2) *have not a dry thread,* be wet through.
3) *the thread of life,* the length of life. [thread 4.]
—*vt.* **1.** pass a thread through (a needle, beads, etc.). **2.** make (one's way) through. —*vi.* move in a thread-like course. ▷**thread·like** [-làik] *adj.*

thread·bare [θrédbèər] *adj.* **1.** (of clothes) so much worn out that the threads are seen ; shabby. **2.** (of persons) wearing threadbare clothes. **3.** worn-out ; old.

threat [θret] *n.* Ⓒ **1.** a sign or warning of evil or trouble to come. ¶*There's a ~ of rain.* **2.** a saying that someone will be hurt or punished ; a menace.

threat·en [θrétn] *vt.* **1.** make a threat against (someone). ((*~ someone with* ; *~ to do*)) ¶*~ someone with punishment* / *~ to kill someone.* **2.** give a sign of (evil or trouble to come). ¶*The clouds ~ storm.* **3.** be a cause of danger to (something). ¶*The fever threatens the city.* —*vi.* **1.** make a threat. **2.** be likely to come.

threat·en·ing [θrétniŋ] *adj.* making a threat ; showing a sign of possible evil or trouble. [—*adj.* of three.

three [θri:] *n.* Ⓒ the number between two and four.

three

—圖 그래도, 그러나 ; 하긴
熟 1)마치 …인 것처럼 2)비록 …일지라도 3)…인들 무슨 상관인가

—名 1. 사고(思考), 생각 2. 사고력, 상상력 3. 의견, 생각 4. 근심, 염려 ; 관심 5. 사상 ; 사조(思潮)

熟 1)…할 생각은 없다 2)다시 생각하여 3)…을 걱정하다

—形 1. 사려깊은 2. 동정심이 있는, 인정이 깊은
—副 1. 생각 깊게 2. 친절히
—名 1. 사려깊음 2. 인정이 있음

—形 1. 지각 없는 2. 인정 없는
—名 1. 1,000 2. 무수, 수천 —形 1. 1,000의 2. 다수의

—形 1,000 배의 —副 1,000 배로

—名 1. 1,000 번째 2. 1,000 분의 1
—形 1,000 번째의 ; 1,000 분의 1의

—名 노예의 신분
—名 1. …을 탈곡(脫穀)하다 2. …을 치다, 채찍질하다 3. …을 여지없이 패배시키다
—名 1. 딩굴다 2. 도리깨질하다 3. 강풍에 거슬러 항행하다
熟 되풀이하다
—名 1. 타작하는 사람 ; 탈곡기 ; 매질하는 사람 2. 환도상어
—名 1. [무명·비단·양모·아마(亞麻) 따위의] 실, 섬유 2. 실처럼 가는 것 ¶①란 줄기의 연기 3. [이야기 따위의] 줄거리 ¶②의론의 줄거리 4. 나삿니

熟 1)위험한 상태에 있다 2)함빡 젖다 3)수명

—動 1. …에 실을 꿰다 2. …을 누비듯이 빠져나가다 —自 누비듯이 나아가다

—形 1. [의복이] 해져 실밥이 보이는 2. [사람이] 해진 옷을 입고 있는 3. 케케묵은, 진부한
—名 1. …할 듯한 기세 ; 형세 2. 위협, 협박

—他 1. …을 으르다, 협박하다 ¶①처벌하겠다고 위협하다 2. …의 염려가 있다 ¶②저 구름으로는 폭풍우가 될 듯하다 3. …을 위협하다 —自 1. 협박하다, 위협하다 2. …할 듯하다

—形 위협적인 ; 험악한

—名 3, 셋 —形 3의 ; 3개의

three·fold [θríːfòuld] *adj.* having three times as much or as many. **—*adv.*** three times as much or as many.
— [形] 3배의; 세 겹의 — [副] 3배로; 세 겹으로

three·pence [θríp(ə)ns, θrép- / θrép(ə)ns, θríp-] *n.* [U] three pence; [C] a coin of this value.
— [名] 3펜스; 3펜스 화폐

three·pen·ny [θríp(ə)ni, θrép- / θrépəni, θríp-] *adj.* **1.** of three pence. **2.** of little worth; cheap.
— [形] 1. 3펜스 2. 보잘것 없는; 싸구려의

three·score [θríːskɔ́ːr] *adj.* three times twenty; sixty.
— [形] 20의 3배의; 60의

thresh [θreʃ] *v.* =thrash.

thresh·er [θréʃər] *n.* [C] =thrasher.

* **thresh·old** [θréʃould, θréʃhould] *n.* [C] **1.** the piece of stone or wood under a door; a doorway. **2.** a beginning point.
— [名] 1. 문지방; 입구 2. 출발점; 발단(發端)

⁑ **threw** [θruː] *v.* pt. of **throw**.

* **thrice** [θrais] *adv.* three times.
— [副] 3회; 세 번

thrift [θrift] *n.* [U] the act of saving money; economy.
— [名] 절약; 경제

thrift·i·ly [θríftili] *adv.* in a thrifty manner; economically.
— [副] 절약하여

thrift·less [θríftlis] *adj.* without thrift; wasteful.
— [形] 절약하지 않는; 낭비하는

thrift·y [θrífti] *adj.* (**thrift·i·er, thrift·i·est**) **1.** careful about spending money or resources; saving; economical. **2.** growing thickly; prosperous. ▷**thrift·i·ness** [-nis] *n.*
— [形] 1. 절약하는, 검소한 2. 번영하는

* **thrill** [θril] *n.* [C] an example of intense excitement or emotion; [U] the act of trembling or shaking. **—*vt.*** cause intense excitement to (someone); cause (someone) to tremble. **—*vi.*** be deeply excited; tremble.
— [名] 오싹오싹함, 드릴, 전율; 떨림 — [他] …을 오싹오싹하게 하다; 떨리게 하다 — [自] 오싹해지다; 떨리다

thrill·er [θrílər] *n.* [C] something that arouses intense excitement; a mystery story, play or film, etc.
— [名] 드릴을 주는 것; [소설·극·영화의] 드릴러물(物)

* **thrive** [θraiv] *vi.* (**throve** or **thrived, thrived** or **thriv·en**) grow rich or well; prosper; succeed.
— [自] 번영하다, 무성해지다; 성공하다

thriv·en [θrív(ə)n] *v.* pp. of **thrive**.

thro', thro [θruː] *adv., prep.* =through.

⁑ **throat** [θrout] *n.* [C] **1.** the front part of the neck; the passage through it. **2.** a narrow passage.
1) ***at the top of one's throat,*** as loudly as possible.
2) ***clear one's throat,*** hem; cough.
3) ***cut one another's throat,*** destroy or hurt one another.
4) ***cut one's own throat,*** destroy or hurt oneself.
5) ***jump down someone's throat,*** attack someone suddenly.
6) ***stick in one's throat,*** be difficult to say or express.
7) ***thrust*** (or ***force, push, ram***) *something down someone's* ***throat,*** force someone to agree to something.
— [名] 1. 목구멍; 기관(氣管) 2. 좁은 통로
[熟] 1)목청껏 2)헛기침을 하다 3)서로 망할 짓을 하다 4)자멸하다 5)…을 갑자기 공격하다 6)말 따위가 하기 거북하다 7)…에게 …을 억지로 승낙시키다

throb [θrɑb / θrɔb] *vi.* (**throbbed, throb·bing**) **1.** (of the heart and pulse) beat rapidly or strongly. **2.** tremble; quiver; vibrate. **—*n.*** [C] (of the heart and pulse) a rapid or strong beating; a regular beating.
— [自] 1. 고동하다; 두근거리다 2. 진동하다 — [名] 동계(動悸); 고동

throe [θrou] *n.* (*usu. pl.*) **1.** a sharp pain. **2.** the pains of childbirth; a violent or desperate struggle; anguish.
in the throes of, struggling desperately with. ¶ *He is in the throes of stomachache.*①
— [名] 1. 격통, 심한 고통 2. 진통; 고투
[熟] …으로 몹시 괴로와하여 ¶①그는 복통으로 몹시 괴로와하고 있다

* **throne** [θroun] *n.* [C] the seat, power, or authority of a king, queen, bishop, etc. **—*vt.*** place (someone) on a throne.
— [名] 왕좌; 옥좌; 왕권 — [他] …을 왕위에 앉히다

* **throng** [θrɔːŋ / θrɔŋ] *n.* [C] a great number of people gathered at a place; a crowd. **—*vt.*** fill (a place) with a crowd. **—*vi.*** crowd together.
— [名] 군중 — [他] …에 모여들다 — [自] 모여들다; 밀어닥치다

thros·tle [θrɑ́sl / θrɔ́sl] *n.* (*Brit.*) [C] a kind of thrush; the song thrush.
— [名] (英) 지빠귀의 일종

throt·tle [θrɑ́tl / θrɔ́tl] *n.* [C] **1.** (*Machinery*) a valve controlling the flow of steam, gas, etc. to an engine. **2.** (*rare*) a throat.
—*vt.* **1.** make (someone) unable to breathe by pressing the throat. **2.** (*Machinery*) control the flow of steam, gas, etc. to an engine by means of a throttle valve.
— [名] 1. (機) 절기판(節汽瓣) 2. (稀) 목구멍
— [他] 1. …의 목을 조르다 2. …을 절기판(節汽瓣)으로 조절하다

⁑ **through** [θruː] *prep.* **1.** from one end to the other end of; from one side to the other side of. ¶ *The road runs ~ the village.* **2.** (of time) from the beginning to the
— [前] 1. …을 통하여(꿰뚫어); …의 끝에서 끝까지 2. …내내; …의 처음부터 끝까지 ¶①하루 종일 3. …의 여

T

end of. ¶ ~ *the day.*① **3.** (of place) among; over the whole surface of; all over. ¶ *The rumor spread ~ the town.* **4.** by way of; by means of. ¶ *go out ~ the window*② | *I heard of you ~ your sister.* | *He became rich ~ hard work.* **5.** on account of; by reason of. ¶ *run away ~ fear.* **6.** finished with; past. ¶ *go ~ the work.* **7.** (*U.S.*) to the end of. ¶ *from 1970 ~ 1975.*

기저기에, 도처에; …의 구석구석에 4. …을 지나서; …에 의하여 ¶②창을 통해 밖으로 나가다 5. …때문에; …의 나머지 6. 끝나서; 통과하여 7. 《美》 [… 에서] …까지 쭉

—*adv.* **1.** from end to end; from side to side. ¶ *shoot a wall ~.* **2.** from the beginning to the end; to a conclusion. ¶ *read a book ~* | *see it ~.*③ **3.** all the way. ¶ *We talked the whole night ~.* **4.** finished. ¶ *I'm almost ~* **5.** completely; thoroughly. ¶ *She was wet ~.*

—[副] 1. 통하여; 꿰뚫어 2. 처음부터 끝까지 ¶③그것을 끝까지 보다 3. 쭉, 쉬지 않고 4. 끝내고 5. 완전히, 철저하게

—*adj.* **1.** passing from one end to the other. ¶ *no ~ street.* **2.** traveling to the destination without stops; going all the way without change of line. ¶ *a ~ ticket.*④

—[形] 1. 지나갈 수 있는 2. 통과하는; 직통의 ¶④직행 차표

1) ***be through*** (=*have finished*) ***with*** *something* or *someone.* (*colloq.*) ¶ *I will be ~ with this book.*
2) ***through and through,*** completely; thoroughly.

[熟] 1)…을 끝내다 2)완전히; 철저하게

•through·out [θru:áut] *prep.* in every part of; all the way through; during. ¶ *It is easily found ~ Japan.*

—[前] …의 도처에; …동안 내내

—*adv.* in every part; everywhere; from beginning to end. ¶ *She knows it ~.*

—[副] 모조리; 전부; 도처에; 시종

throve [θrouv] *v.* pt. of **thrive.**

⁑throw [θrou] *v.* (**threw, thrown**) *vt.* **1.** cause (something) to move through the air with force, esp. with a motion of the arm; cast; hurl. 《~ something *at* or *to*》 ¶ ~ *stones at a dog* | *I threw the ball to him.; I threw him the ball.* **2.** cause (something or someone) to fall to the ground or floor. ¶ ~ *a wrestler* | *The horse threw the rider.* **3.** send; direct; project. ¶ ~ *a kiss* | ~ *a glance at someone* | ~ *a shadow on the wall.* **4.** move or send rapidly. ¶ ~ *troops into battle.* **5.** put hurriedly. 《~ something *on* or *over*》 ¶ ~ *a cloak over one's shoulders* | ~ *a hat on.* **6.** put (something or someone) in a certain state or position. 《~ something or someone *into* or *out of*》 ¶ ~ *oneself into the arms of* | ~ *men out of work.* **7.** (*U.S. colloq.*) let an opponent win (a race, game, etc.), often in return money. **8.** cast (dice); make (a specified cast) of dice. —*vi.* cast, fling, or hurl something.

—[他] 1. [공·돌 따위]를 힘차게 던지다 2. …을 던지다, 내동댕이치다 3. [그림자 따위]를 던지다, 투사(投射)하다 4. …을 갑자기 움직이다 5. 급히 [옷 따위]를 걸치다 6. [어떤 상태 따위에] …을 던지다; 빠지게 하다 7. …에게 일부러 져 주다 8. [주사위]를 던지다; [주사위를] 던져서 …이 나오게 하다 —[自] 던지다; 투구하다

1) ***throw about,*** ⓐ wave violently. ⓑ waste; scatter.
2) ***throw away,*** ⓐ waste. ⓑ get rid of (something).
3) ***throw back,*** ⓐ delay. ⓑ reflect (light, etc.). ⓒ show characteristics inherited from a remote ancestor.
4) ***throw cold water on*** (=*discourage*) *one's idea, etc.*
5) ***throw in,*** ⓐ interject (a remark). ⓑ add extra.
6) ***throw off,*** ⓐ cast off (clothes). ⓑ write or speak quickly.
7) ***throw on,*** put on (a garment) carelessly or hastily.
8) ***throw oneself at*** (=*try very hard to get the friendship or love of*) *someone.*
9) ***throw*** *oneself* ***into*** (=*work very hard at*) *something.*
10) ***throw*** *oneself* (=*be dependent*) ***on*** *someone.*
11) ***throw open,*** open suddenly or completely.
12) ***throw out,*** ⓐ reject. ⓑ get rid of (something). ⓒ utter.
13) ***throw over,*** desert; abandon.
14) ***throw together,*** make or construct carelessly or hastily.
15) ***throw up,*** ⓐ abandon (a job). ⓑ construct rapidly. ⓒ lift up. ⓓ (*colloq.*) vomit.

[熟] 1)ⓐ…을 휘두르다 ⓑ…을 낭비하다 2)ⓐ…을 낭비하다 ⓑ…을 버리다 3)ⓐ…을 지연시키다 ⓑ…을 반사하다 ⓒ[생물 따위가] 조상의 성질로 되돌아 가다 4)[계획 따위]에 찬물을 끼얹다 5)ⓐ…을 끼워넣다 ⓑ…을 덤으로 붙이다 6)ⓐ[옷]을 벗어 버리다 ⓑ[시 따위]를 즉석에서 짓다 7)[옷]을 급히 입다 8)…의 우정(사랑)을 얻으려고 애쓰다 9)…에 몸을 던지다, 본격적으로 덤벼들다 10)…을 기대하다, …에 의지하다 11)…을 홱 열다 12)ⓐ…을 버리다 ⓑ부결하다 ⓒ말하다 13)…을 버리다; 파기하다 14)…을 급히 만들다(짓다) 15)ⓐ…을 사직하다 ⓑ…을 급히 만들다 ⓒ…을 밀어 올리다 ⓓ《口》…을 게우다

—*n.* [C] **1.** the action or an instance of throwing. ¶ *a straight ~.*① **2.** the distance a thing is or can be thrown. **3.** a cast of dice or the number cast. **4.** (*colloq.*) a venture; risk. **5.** (*U.S.*) a light blanket for a bed, etc.

—[名] 1. 던지기; 던짐 ¶①직구 2. 던져서 닿는 거리 3. 주사위를 흔들기; 흔들어서 나온 주사위의 끗수 4. 《口》 모험; 운수 5. 《美》 침대보, 덮개

a stone's throw, a short distance.

[熟] 돌을 던져서 닿는 거리

thrown [θroun] *v.* pp. of throw.
thru [θru:] *prep., adv.* (chiefly *U.S.*) =through.
thrum [θrʌm] *v.* (**thrummed, thrum·ming**) *vi.* play on a guitar, banjo, etc. carelessly or idly. —*vt.* **1.** play carelessly or idly. **2.** tap (a table) with the fingers. —*n.* ⓒ the sound made by thrumming. —自 현악기를 통겨서 울리다 —他 **1.**[현악기]를 통겨 울리다 **2.**[테이블]을 똑똑 두드리다 —⓼ 퉁겨 울리는 소리
thrush [θrʌʃ] *n.* ⓒ a bird which sings in a very sweet voice. —⓼ 지빠귀
:thrust [θrʌst] *v.* (**thrust**) *vt.* **1.** push (something or someone) with force; shove. ¶~ *a paper into one's pocket.* **2.** pierce; stab. 《~ *a pointed weapon, etc. into* or *through*》 ¶~ *a sword into his back.* **3.** force (someone) into some condition. 《~ *oneself into*》 ¶*He* ~ *himself into danger.* **4.** impose. 《~ *something on* or *upon*》. **5.** force (a way) by pushing. ¶*He* ~ *his way through the crowd.* **6.** put in (a question, etc.) while another person is speaking. **7.** extend (a branch, etc.) into some place. —*vi.* **1.** push against something. **2.** make a stab. ¶*She* ~ *at him with a dagger.* **3.** force one's way. 《~ *through* or *into a crowd, etc.*》 **4.** extend.
 1) *thrust one's nose into* (=*interfere in*) someone else's affairs.
 2) *thrust oneself forward,* draw attention to oneself.
—*n.* ⓒ **1.** a sudden push; a stab. ¶*a* ~ *with a knife.* **2.** a driving force, one esp. one produced by a jet engine, a propeller, or a rocket.
—他 **1.** …을 세게 밀다, 밀어 내다 **2.** …을 찌르다, 찔러 넣다 **3.** …을 억지로 어떤 상태에 두다 **4.** …을 강요하다 **5.** …을 밀어젖히고 나아가다 **6.** …에 옆에서 말참견하다 **7.**[가지 따위]를 펴다 —自 **1.** 밀다. 찌르다; 찌르려고 달려들다 **3.** 밀어젖히고 나아가다 **4.**[가지 따위를] 뻗치다

鬪 **1)** …에 간섭하다, 남의 일에 간섭하다 **2)** 주제넘게 나서다
—⓼ **1.** 갑자기 밀기; 찌르기 **2.**[프로펠러·제트 추진 따위의] 추진력

thud [θʌd] *n.* ⓒ a heavy sound made by something falling. —*v.* (**thud·ded, thud·ding**) *vi.* make a heavy sound. —*vt.* beat (something) with a heavy sound.
—⓼ 쿵 떨어지는 소리 —自 쿵하는 소리를 내다 —他 …을 쾅하고 치다

thug [θʌg] *n.* ⓒ a professional murderer; a dangerous, lawless fellow.
—⓼ 직업적 살인자, 자객; 악한

*•**thumb** [θʌm] *n.* ⓒ the shortest and thickest finger of the hand; the part of a glove covering the thumb.
 1) *all thumbs,* very unskillful in work.
 2) *thumbs down up,* a sign of no.
 3) *under the thumb of,* under the power of.
—*vt.* **1.** turn over (a book) with the thumb. **2.** rub or dirty (something) with the thumb. **3.** (of a hitchhiker) ask for (a ride) by signaling with the thumb.
—⓼ 엄지손가락; 장갑의 엄지손가락

鬪 **1)**손재주가 없는 **2)**불찬성[의 신호] **3)**…에 좌지우지되어
—他 **1.** 엄지손가락으로 [책장]을 넘기다 **2.** …을 엄지손가락으로 더럽히다 **3.** 엄지손가락으로 태워 달라고 신호하다

thumb·nail [θʌ́mnèil] *n.* ⓒ **1.** the nail of the thumb. **2.** something very small or small. —*adj.* of the size of a thumbnail; very short or small.
—⓼ **1.** 엄지 손톱 **2.** 매우 짧은 것 —⓹ 엄지 크기의; 아주 짧은

thumb nut [´ ´] *n.* a nut that has a head that can be turned easily by a thumb and a finger. ⇒fig.
—⓼ 나비날개 모양의 암나사

thumb·screw [θʌ́mskrù:] *n.* ⓒ a nail-shaped piece of metal that has a head that can be turned easily by a thumb and a finger. ⇒fig.
[thumb nut]
—⓼ 나비날개 모양의 암나사

thumb·tack [θʌ́mtæ̀k] *n.* ⓒ a pin used to fasten paper, cloth, etc. on a wall with the thumb.
—⓼ 제도용 압핀

[thumbscrew]

*•**thump** [θʌmp] *vt.* strike (something) with a heavy thing. ¶~ *the desk with fist.*① —*vi.* **1.** strike heavily. **2.** walk with heavy steps. **3.** (of the heart) beat violently. ¶~ *with excitement.* —*n.* ⓒ a heavy knock; a sound made by a thump. ▷**thump·er** [-ər] *n.*
—他 …을 막하고 때리다 ¶①책상을 주먹으로 쾅 치다 —自 **1.** 막하고 때리다 **2.** 쿵쿵 걷다 **3.**[가슴이] 두근거리다 —⓼ 막하고 때리기, 막하는 소리

:thun·der [θʌ́ndər] *n.* **1.** Ⓤ the loud noise which is heard in the sky as a result of the passage of lightning. **2.** (usu. *pl.*) a loud noise like thunder.
 steal someone's thunder, use another's idea without his permission; prevent someone from appearing at his best by using his idea, etc. first.
—*vi.* **1.** 《using *it* as the subject》 give forth thunder.
—⓼ **1.** 우뢰 **2.** 우뢰 같은 소리

鬪 남의 생각을 가로채다; …의 기선 (機先)을 제하다
—自 **1.** 우뢰가 울리다 **2.** 우뢰 같은 소

2. make a loud noise like thunder. **3.** shout out. —*vt.* shout out at (someone).
리를 내다 3. 고함지르다 —[他] …을 고함치다

thun·der·bolt [θʌ́ndərbòult] *n.* [C] **1.** a flash of lightning with the noise of thunder. **2.** something terrible that happens suddenly.
—[名] 1. 번개, 벼락 2. 예기치 못한 재난

thun·der·clap [θʌ́ndərklæ̀p] *n.* [C] **1.** a loud noise of thunder. **2.** something unexpected.
—[名] 1. 천둥소리 2. 청천의 벽력

thun·der·cloud [θʌ́ndərklàud] *n.* [C] a dark cloud that brings thunder.
—[名] 뇌운(雷雲)

thun·der·head [θʌ́ndərhèd] *n.* [C] one of the white masses of cloud which often develop into thunderclouds.
—[名] 뭉게구름, 뇌적운(雷積雲)

thun·der·ous [θʌ́nd(ə)rəs] *adj.* of thunder; like thunder.
—[形] 우뢰의; 우뢰 같은

thun·der·storm [θʌ́ndərstɔ̀ːrm] *n.* [C] a storm with thunder and lightning.
—[名] 뇌우

thun·der·struck [θʌ́ndərstrʌ̀k] *adj.* **1.** struck by a thunderbolt. **2.** very surprised.
—[形] 1. 벼락맞은 2. 깜짝 놀란

Thurs., Thur. Thursday.

‡Thurs·day [θə́ːrzdi, -dei] *n.* the fifth day of this week. ⇒[N.B.]
—[名] 목요일 [N.B.] Thurs. 또는 Thur.로 줄임

‡thus [ðʌs] *adv.* in this way; to this degree; for the reason; so.
—[副] 이와같이; 이제까지; 그러므로

thus far, so far; to this point.
[熟] 지금까지는

thwack [θwæk] *vt.* strike (something) sharply with something flat. —*n.* [C] a sharp blow with something flat.
—[他] …을 찰싹 때리다 —[名] 찰싹 때리기

thwart [θwɔːrt] *vt.* do not agree with (someone); oppose; prevent. 《~ someone *from doing*》 —*n.* [C] a rower's seat across a boat. ⇒fig. —*adj.* lying across. —*adv.* across.
—[他] …에 반대하다; …을 방해하다 —[名] 보우트의 노젓는 사람의 좌석 —[形] 옆의 —[副] 옆으로

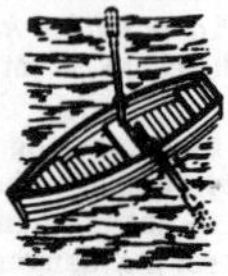
〔thwart〕

•thy [ðai] *pron.* (*archaic*) =your.

thyme [taim] *n.* [C] a small plant with leaves which are used to give a good taste to food.
—[名] 백리향(百里香)

thy·roid [θáirɔid, +*Brit.* θáiə-] *n.* [C] a small gland in the neck which produces a liquid to control the growth of the body. —*adj.* of the thyroid.
—[名] 갑상선(甲狀腺) —[形] 갑상선의

•thy·self [ðaisélf] *pron.* (*archaic*) =yourself.

ti·ar·a [tiǽrə / tiɑ́ːrə] *n.* [C] **1.** a head ornament worn by women. **2.** the crown of the Pope. **3.** a head dress worn by ancient Persians.
—[名] 1. 부인의 머리 장식 2. 로마 교황의 삼중관(三重冠) 3. 고대 페르시아 사람의 관

Ti·bet [tibét] *n.* a country in central Asia, now a part of China. ⇒[N.B.]
—[名] 티베트 [N.B.] Thibet로도 씀

Ti·bet·an [tibét(ə)n] *adj.* of or belonging to Tibet. —*n.* **1.** [C] a person of Tibet. **2.** [U] the language of Tibet.
—[形] 티베트[사람·말]의 —[名] 1. 티베트 사람 2. 티베트 말

•tick¹ [tik] *n.* [C] **1.** a sound made by a clock, watch, etc. **2.** (*Brit. colloq.*) a moment. **3.** a check mark(✓); a dot.
—[名] 1. [시계 따위의] 똑딱똑딱[소리] 2.《英口》순간 3. 체크 표; 점(點)

to the tick, very correctly; very punctual.
[熟] 아주 정확히; 꼭

—*vi.* make a tick. —*vt.* **1.** announce (time) by ticking sounds. **2.** mark (something) with a tick. 《~ *off* something》
—[自] 똑딱똑딱 소리를 내다 —[他] 1. [시간]을 알리다 2. …에 표를 하다; …에 체크하다

tick² [tik] *n.* [C] a small insect that sucks the blood of man and other animals.
—[名] 진드기

tick³ [tik] *n.* [C] a covering of a mattress or pillow.
—[名] 이불잇; 베갯잇

tick·er [tíkər] *n.* [C] **1.** a person or thing that ticks. **2.** a telegraphic instrument that records market reports on a paper tape. **3.** (*colloq.*) a clock; the heart.
—[名] 1. 장부를 다는 사람; 똑딱똑딱 소리내는 것 2. 증권시세 표시기 3. 《口》시계; 심장

‡tick·et [tíkit] *n.* [C] **1.** a small piece of paper that gives its owner a certain right, as to ride on a train. **2.** a small card showing the price of goods in a shop. **3.** (*U.S.*) a list of candidates to be voted upon.
—[名] 1. 표, 입장권 2. 정찰(正札), 정가표 3.《美》후보자 명부

That's the ticket, (*colloq.*) That's the proper thing.; That's right.
[熟]《口》그것이 좋다; 맞다

—*vt.* put a ticket on (something).
—[他] …에 정찰을 달다

tick·ing [tíkiŋ] *n.* [U] a strong cloth for covering a mattress or pillow.
—[名] 이불감; 이불잇; 베갯잇

•tick·le [tíkl] *vt.* **1.** touch (someone) lightly to cause a thrill, laughter, etc. **2.** please; amuse. —*vi.* have
—[他] 1. …을 간질이다 2. …을 기쁘게 하다 —[自] 간지럽다 —[名] 간지럼

a tingling feeling. —*n.* [C] a tickling feeling.

tick·lish [tíkliʃ] *adj.* **1.** of a nature to be easily moved by tickling. **2.** difficult to handle; delicate; apt to get angry. ¶*He is ~ on that matter.* ▷**tick·lish·ly** [-li] *adv.*
—[形] 1. 간지러운 2. 다루기 힘든, 괴까다로운; 성 잘 내는

tick·tack [tíktæ̀k] *n.* [C] a light sound repeating regularly; the sound of the heart or a clock.
—[名] 규칙바르게 똑딱거리는 소리; 심장의 고동; 시계 소리

tick·tock [tíktɑ̀k / -tɔ́k] *n.* [C] the sound made by a clock.
—[名] 시계의 똑딱거리는 소리

tid·al [táidl] *adj.* of tides; affected by tides.
—[形] 조수의; 조수의 작용을 받는

tidal wave [⌐– ⌐] *n.* **1.** a very large ocean wave caused by an earthquake or a heavy wind. **2.** a great movement.
—[名] 1. 해일(海溢) 2. 큰 변동

tid·bit [tídbìt] *n.* [C] (*U.S.*) **1.** a delicious bit of food. **2.** a pleasing bit of news.
—[名] 《口》 1. 맛있는 것 한 입 2. 재미있는 토막 뉴우스

‡tide [taid] *n.* **1.** [C] [U] the regular rise and fall of the ocean caused by the pull of the moon and the sun. **2.** [C] anything that rises and falls like the tide; a current. ¶*There is a ~ in the affairs of men.* **3.** [U] (*archaic*) a season; a period. ¶(*proverb*) *Time and ~ wait for no man.*①
—[名] 1. 조수; 조수의 간만; 조류 2. 풍조; 홍망, 성쇠 3. 《口》 계절; 때 ¶ ①《俚》세월은 사람을 기다리지 않는다

turn the tide, change the course from one extreme to another.
[熟] 형세를 일변시키다

—*vi.* flow as the tide does; flow with the tide. —*vt.* carry (something) along as the tide does.
—[自] 조수처럼 흐르다; 조수에 밀려가다 —[他] …을 조수처럼 날라가다

tide over, ⓐ overcome. ⓑ assist or manage (someone) in time of difficulty.
[熟] ⓐ…을 극복하다 ⓑ…을 잘 처리하다

ti·di·ly [táidili] *adv.* in a tidy manner; with tidiness.
—[副] 깨끗하게

ti·di·ness [táidinis] *n.* [U] the state of being tidy.
—[名] 정연함, 말쑥함

***ti·dings** [táidiŋz] *n. pl.* 《used as *sing.* or *pl.*》 news; information.
—[名] 통지, 기별; 소식

ti·dy [táidi] *adj.* (**-di·er, -di·est**) **1.** neat; in good order. **2.** (*colloq.*) fairly good; considerable. —*vt.* (**-di·ed**) put (something) in order. 《~ *up* something》 —*n.* [C] (pl. **-dies**) **1.** a cover for the arm or back of a chair. **2.** a box-like container for keeping things tidy.
—[形] 1. 깨끗한; 단정한 2. 《口》 꽤 좋은; 상당한 —[他] …을 깨끗이 정리하다 —[名] 1. 의자의 등씌우개 2. 자질구레한 물건을 넣는 통

‡tie [tai] *v.* (ppr. **ty·ing**) *vt.* **1.** bind, fasten, or attach (something) with a string, rope, etc. ¶*~ a package / ~ a dog to a tree.* **2.** make (a knot or bow) in a cord, etc.; secure (a cord, etc.) by a knot or bow. ¶*~ a knot / ~ one's shoelaces.* **3.** fasten or connect firmly. **4.** restrict; limit. 《~ someone *to*》 ¶*~ someone to a bad condition / I am tied to my work.; My work ties me.* **5.** equal (the score of an opponent) in a contest; equal the score of (an opponent). ¶*~ one's competitor / His team tied mine.* —*vi.* **1.** form a bow or knot. ¶*That doesn't ~ well.* **2.** be equal in a contest. ¶*The two teams tied. / Our team tied with his.*
—[他] 1. [끈 따위로] …을 매다, 묶다 2. [끈]을 매다, [매듭]을 만들다 3. [일반적으로] …을 단단히 매다 4. …을 속박(구속)하다 5. [경기에서] …와 동점이 되다 —[自] 1. 매이다, 묶이다 2. [경기에서] 동점이 되다

1) ***tie down,*** restrict; limit.
2) ***tie in,*** ⓐ connect or be connected. ⓑ be in agreement.
3) ***tie up,*** ⓐ fasten (someone or something) with a rope, string, etc. ⓑ delay; stop. ⓒ engage; occupy.
[熟] 1)…을 제한(구속)하다 2)ⓐ접합하다 ⓑ꼭 일치하다 3)ⓐ…을 굳게(단단히) 묶다 ⓑ[교통]을 방해하다; 정체(停滯)시키다 ⓒ구속하다

—*n.* [C] **1.** a rope, cord, or string that is used to tie; a necktie; a shoelace. **2.** a knot; an ornamental knot. **3.** something that unites; a link; a bond; 《often *pl.*》 obligation; burden. ¶*political ties / Her children were a great ~ to the widow.* **4.** a state of equality in a contest. ¶*The game ended in a ~.* **5.** a beam holding together a structure ⇒fig.; (*U.S.*) one of the beams to which the rails of a railroad are fastened. ⇒fig.
—[名] 1. [묶는 데 쓰는] 끈, 새끼, 밧줄; 넥타이; 구두끈 2. 매듭, 장식 매듭 3. [일반적으로] 매는 것; 인연; 기반(羈絆); 귀찮은 장애물 4. [경기의] 동점 5. 이음 나무(재목); [철도의] 침목

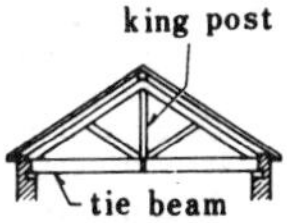

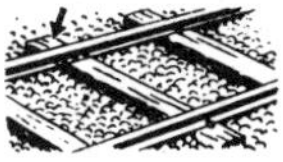
[tie 5.]

tie·pin [táipìn] *n.* [C] a pin for fastening the necktie.
—[名] 넥타이핀

tier¹ [tiər] *n.* [C] one of a series rows arranged one above
—[名] [관람석 따위의] 단(段), 층 —[自]

T

and behind another. —*vi.* raise in tiers. —*vt.* arrange (something) in tiers.
층층으로 되어 있다 —[他] …을 층층으로 쌓다

tier[2] [táiər] *n.* [C] a person or thing that ties.
—[名] 매는 사람(것)

tie-up [táiʌp] *n.* [C] **1.** a stopping of work or action caused by a strike of the employees or an accident. **2.** (*colloq.*) connection; relation.
—[名] 1.정지; 휴업 2.《口》 관계; 제휴; 협력

tiff [tif] *n.* [C] **1.** a little quarrel. **2.** ill temper.
—[名] 1.사소한 말다툼 2.언짢음

tif·fin [tífin] *n.* [C] (*Brit.*) lunch. —*vi.* eat lunch.
—[名] 《英》 점심 —[自] 점심을 먹다

⁑**ti·ger** [táigər] *n.* [C] a large, fierce animal of the cat family. ▷**ti·ger·like** [-làik] *adj.*
—[名] 범,호랑이

tiger lily [ˊ-ˋ-] *n.* a lily with orange flowers spotted with black.
—[名] 참나리

⁑**tight** [tait] *adj.* **1.** stretched; tense. ↔slack ¶*a ~ rope.* **2.** firm; knotted; closed; compact; firmly or closely fixed in place. ¶*a ~ knot.* **3.** close; fitting [too] closely. ↔loose ¶*~ shoes | feel ~ around the waist.* **4.** 《esp. in *compounds*》 not letting water, air or gas in or out. ¶*a ~ ship (roof) | watertight shoes.* **5.** (of a situation) difficult or dangerous to deal with; severe; strict. ¶*be in a ~ place (corner, spot)*① | *He kept ~ control over his pupils.* **6.** (of a commodity) difficult to obtain; (of money) scarce. ¶*Money will be ~ next year.* **7.** (*colloq.*) stingy.
—[形] 1.팽팽하게 친 2.단단히 맨; 꽉 들어찬; 단단히 고정된 3.[옷 따위가 몸에] 꼭 맞는; 너무 꼭 끼는 4.빈틈이 없는; [공기·물 따위가] 새지 않는 5.[입장 따위가] 난처한; 어려운 ¶① 꼼짝달싹 못하다 6.[상품이] 구하기 힘든; 돈이 딸리는 7.《口》 인색한

—*adv.* tightly; firmly. ¶*She kept her mouth ~ shut.*
—[副] 단단히,꼭,꽉

1) ***hold tight,*** grasp firmly; hold strongly to (something).
2) ***sit tight,*** ⓐ stay where one is. ⓑ stick to one's position.
[熟] 1)…을 단단히 잡다 2)ⓐ…에 꼼짝 않고 앉아 있다 ⓑ자기의 입장을 고수하다

—*n.* 《*pl.*》 a tightly-fitting garment worn by acrobats, dancers, etc.
—[名] 타이트(댄서 등의 몸에 꼭 끼는 옷)

***tight·en** [táitn] *vi.* become tight. —*vt.* make (something) tight.
—[自] 꽉 죄다 —[他] …을 꽉 죄다

***tight·ly** [táitli] *adv.* in a tight manner.
—[副] 단단히

tight·ness [táitnis] *n.* [U] the state of being tight.
—[名] 견고,긴장,거북함

tight·rope [táitròup] *n.* [C] a tightly-stretched rope or wire on which acrobats walk or move.
—[名] [줄타기의] 팽팽히 맨 밧줄

***ti·gress** [táigris] *n.* [C] a female tiger.
—[名] 암범

Ti·gris [táigris], **the** *n.* a river in southwestern Asia.
—[名] 티그리스 강

tike [taik] *n.* =tyke.

til·de [tíldə / tild, tíldi] *n.* [C] a mark used on some letters to show a nasal sound, such as ñ and ã.
—[名] 비음(鼻音)을 나타내기 위해 a 나 n의 위에 붙이는 기호(~)

***tile** [tail] *n.* [C] **1.** a thin piece of baked clay for covering roofs, floors, etc. **2.** (*colloq.*) a high silk hat. —*vt.* cover (roofs, floors, etc.) with tiles.
—[名] 1.타일; 기와 2.실크햇 —[他]…에 타일을 붙이다,[지붕 따위]를 기와로 이다

⁑**till**[1] [til] *prep.* up to the time of. ¶*I waited for him ~ seven.* —*conj.* up to the time when. ¶*Wait ~ he comes back.*
—[前] …까지 —[接] …까지

till[2] [til] *vt.* prepare (land) for growing crops; cultivate.
—[他] [토지]를 갈다

till[3] [til] *n.* [C] a money drawer in a shop.
—[名] [계산대의] 돈궤,돈서랍

till·age [tílidʒ] *n.* [U] **1.** the act of tilling; cultivation. **2.** tilled land.
—[名] 1.경작 2.경작지

till·er [tílər] *n.* [C] a handle or bar for turning the rudder of a boat.
—[名] 키의 손잡이

***tilt** [tilt] *vi.* **1.** lean; slope. **2.** fight with a spear on horseback. **3.** make an attack. 《~ *at* something》. —*vt.* **1.** cause (something) to lean; raise (something) at one end. **2.** attack (someone) with a spear.
—[自] 1.기울다,경사지다 2.말 타고 창으로 싸우다 3.공격하다 —[他] 1.…을 기울이다 2.…을 창으로 공격하다

tilt at a windmill, make a useless attack at an unreal enemy.
[熟] 가공의 적과 싸우다

—*n.* [C] **1.** a slope. **2.** a fight on horseback with spears. **3.** a quarrel.
—[名] 1.경사 2.마상 창시합 3.말다툼

[*at*] ***full tilt,*** at full speed.
[熟] 전속력으로

tilth [tilθ] *n.* **1.** [U] the act of tilling. **2.** tilled land.
—[名] 1.경작 2.경작지

⁑**tim·ber** [tímbər] *n.* [U] **1.** wood before it is ready for building and making things. **2.** [C] a large piece of wood used for house-building. **3.** [C] woodland from which timber is taken. **4.** [U] (*U.S.*) personality; quality. —*vt.* support (something) with timber.
—[名] 1.재목 2.가옥 건축용 목재 3.삼림지,숲 4.《美》 성격 —[他] …을 목재로 버티다

tim·bered [tímbərd] *adj.* **1.** made of timber. **2.** covered with growing trees.
—[形] 1.목재로 만든 2.입목(立木)이 있는; 나무로 둘러싸인

tim·bre [tímbər, tǽm- / tέ:(m)br, tǽmbə] *n.* [U] the special quality of the sound of a voice or musical instrument that makes it different from others.

—[名] 음색

time [taim] *n.* [U] **1.** 《without *an article*》 the concept of past, present, and future, taken separately or as a whole. ¶*~ and space*① | (*proverb*) *Time flies like an arrow.* **2.** [C] 《usu. *a ~*》 a length of time. ¶*a short ~ | for a ~.* **3.** [U][C] an appointed, fit, or proper time for something to happen. 《*~ to do*》 ¶*It is ~ to go home. | There is a ~ for everything.*② **4.** [C] an occasion; a portion of time in which an action or event is repeated; the point when something occurs. ¶*next ~ | at all times*③ *| At that ~ she was away from home.* **5.** some particular hour in the day; a system of measuring the passage of time. ¶*by this ~*④ *| keep good ~ | Greenwich ~ | What ~ is it?* **6.** leisure or spare time. 《*~ to do*; *~ for*》 ¶*I have little ~ to play.; I have little ~ for playing.* **7.** 《usu. *pl.*》 a particular period; age; epoch; era; 《*the ~*》 the present time. ¶*in modern times | the times of Queen Elizabeth | He was no longer a professor at that college in my ~.* **8.** 《often *pl.*》 one's experience during a certain time; conditions of life at present or a certain period. ¶*hard times*⑤ *| have a good (bad) ~ [of it].*⑥ **9.** a particular part of a year, day, etc.; season. ¶*Christmas ~ | dinner ~.* **10.** [C] the state of being multiplied by a number. ¶*She has three times as many books as I have*⑦. *| Four times six is twenty-four.* **11.** lifetime; time of death. ¶*His ~ has come.*⑧ **12.** the rate of speed in marching, driving, etc. **13.** (*Music*) tempo or rhythm; the length of a note or rest. ¶*beat ~ | keep ~ with something.*⑨ **14.** the period occupied by one's work; rate of pay, esp. reckoned by the hour. **15.** a signal for the end or suspension of play in a game; the period in which a game is played.

—[名] **1.** 때, 시간, 세월 ¶①시간과 공간 **2.** 기간 **3.** [···에 알맞은 또는 정해진] 시간, 시기; 기회 ¶②무슨 일에나 시기란 것이 있다 **4.** [···하는(한)] 때, 마다; ···번, ···회 ¶③언제나 **5.** 시각; 표준시 ¶④이때까지, 지금쯤은 **6.** 여유; 여가 **7.** 시대, 연대; 현대 **8.** 경기; 시세(時勢), 경험[하는 시간] ¶⑤불경기/⑥유쾌한 때를 지내다(혼이 나다) **9.** 계절; 시절; 특정의 시간 **10.** ···번, ···회, ···배 ¶⑦그녀는 나보다 책을 세 배나 갖고 있다 **11.** 일생; 사기(死期) ¶⑧그의 죽을 때가 왔다 **12.** 행진 속도; 운전 속도 **13**《樂》 박자, 속도, 리듬 ¶⑨···에 박자를 맞추다 **14.** 근무 시간; 시간급(給) **15.** [시작 또는 중지의] 신호; 소요 시간

1) ***against time,*** trying to finish in a given time; as fast as possible.
2) ***all the time,*** continuously; throughout a specified period.
3) ***at no time,*** never.
4) ***at one time,*** ⓐ formerly. ⓑ at the same time.
5) ***at the same time,*** ⓐ however; nevertheless. ⓑ in the same period.
6) ***at times,*** now and then; sometimes.
7) ***behind the times,*** old-fashioned.
8) ***for the time being,*** for the present time.
9) ***from time to time,*** now and then; occasionally.
10) ***gain time,*** ⓐ (of a watch) go too fast. ⓑ save time.
11) ***in good time,*** ⓐ at the proper time. ⓑ quickly.
12) ***in no time,*** almost at once; very quickly.
13) ***in time,*** ⓐ early enough; in the future; eventually. ⓑ in the correct tempo.
14) ***lose time,*** go at too slow a rate.
15) ***make time,*** go fast to recover lost time.
16) ***many a time,*** many times; again and again.
17) ***on time,*** at the appointed time; punctual[ly].
18) ***out of time,*** ⓐ not at the usual time. ⓑ not in the proper rhythm.
19) ***pass the time of day,*** exchange brief words of greeting.
20) ***take one's time,*** be slow in doing something.
21) ***time after time,*** again and again; repeatedly; continually.
22) ***time of life,*** [a person's] age.
23) ***time out of mind,*** from time immemorial; since long long ago.

[熟] 1)정한 시간에 대려고; 전속력으로 2)그 동안 줄곧; 시종; 언제나 3)일찌기 ···않다 4)ⓐ전에 ⓑ동시에 5)ⓐ그래도 역시 ⓑ동시에 6)때때로 7)시대에 뒤진 8)당분간 9)때때로 10)ⓐ[시계가] 더 가다 ⓑ시간 여유를 얻다 11)ⓐ마침 좋은 때에 ⓑ즉시 12)당장 13)ⓐ멀지않아; 결국 ⓑ박자를 맞추어 14)우물우물하다 15)서두르다; 지체된 시간을 돌이키다 16)가끔 17)제시간에 18)ⓐ제철이 아닌 ⓑ박자가 안 맞는 19)인사를 주고받다 20)서두르지 않다 21)재삼재사 22)[사람의] 나이 23)먼 옛날[부터]

—*vt.* **1.** choose the moment or occassion for (some-

—[他] **1.** ···의 좋은 기회를 노리다 **2.** ···

T

time-honored [1204] **tinker**

thing) 《~ something *to do*》 ¶*We timed our visit to suit her convenience.* **2.** arrange or set the time of (something); adjust (a watch). ¶*Time your watch. with mine.* **3.** record the time of (something). ¶*~ a race.* **4.** cause (something) to agree in rhythm. ¶*~ one's steps to the music.* —*vi.* keep or beat time.
—*adj.* **1.** of time. **2.** designed to explode, open, etc. at a fixed time. **3.** based on installment payments.

time-hon·ored, *Brit.* **-hon·oured** [táimɑ̀nərd / -ɔ̀nəd] *adj.* old; continued over a long period.

time·keep·er [táimkìːpər] *n.* ⓒ **1.** a watch; a clock. **2.** a person who records the period when workmen work.

time·less [táimlis] *adj.* **1.** never ending. **2.** restricted to no special time.

time·ly [táimli] *adj.* (**-li·er, -li·est**) at the right time. ▷ **time·li·ness** [-nis] *n.* 「time; a watch; a clock.」

time·piece [táimpìːs] *n.* ⓒ anything that records the

tim·er [táimər] *n.* ⓒ **1.** a person who records time. **2.** a device for recording time; a stop watch. **3.** an instrument for controlling machinery at a fixed time.

time·sav·ing [táimsèiviŋ] *adj.* reducing the time needed to do something

time·serv·er [táimsə́ːrvər] *n.* ⓒ a person who easily varies his opinions for his own selfish purposes.

time·ta·ble [táimtèibl] *n.* ⓒ a list of times at which trains, buses, ships, etc. are due to arrive and leave.

time·work [táimwə̀ːrk] *n.* Ⓤ work paid for by the hour.

time·worn [táimwɔ̀ːrn] *adj.* worn-out by long use or existence. 「the same. ⇒N.B.」

time zone [⌐ ⌐] *n.* an area where the standard time is

• **tim·id** [tímid] *adj.* (**-id·er, -id·est**) lacking in courage; easily frightened; shy. 「shyness.」

ti·mid·i·ty [timíditi] *n.* Ⓤ the state of being timid;

tim·id·ly [tímidli] *adv.* in a timid manner.

tim·or·ous [tímərəs] *adj.* very timid; easily frightened; fearful. ▷ **tim·or·ous·ly** [-li] *adv.*

tim·o·thy [tíməθi] *n.* ⓒ a kind of grass used for hay.

: **tin** [tin] *n.* Ⓤ **1.** a soft, silvery-white, metallic element. **2.** thin plate of iron or steel covered with tin; ⓒ (*Brit.*) a container made of tin. (cf. *U.S.* can) **3.** (*slang*) money. —*adj.* made of tin. —*vt.* **1.** cover (something) with tin. **2.** keep (something) in a tin can.

tinc·ture [tíŋktʃər] *n.* **1.** Ⓤ a medicinal solution in alcohol. **2.** ⓒ a color **3.** ⓒ a slight trace or flavor 《~ *of*》 ¶*a ~ of garlic*①. —*vt.* **1.** color; tinge **2.** give a trace to (something); 《~ something *with*》

tin·der [tíndər] *n.* Ⓤ very inflammable material that catches fire easily from a spark.

tin·der·box [tíndərbɑ̀ks / -dɔ̀bɔks] *n.* ⓒ a box for keeping tinder, flint and steel.

tine [tain] *n.* ⓒ a sharp projecting point. 「goods.」

tin foil [⌐ ⌐] *n.* a very thin sheet of tin for wrapping

tinge [tindʒ] *vt.* **1.** color slightly. 《~ something *with*》 ¶*The sunrise tinged the clouds with pink.* **2.** give a flavor to (something); affect slightly 《~ something *with*》 ¶*Melancholy tinged his words.* —*n.* ⓒ **1.** a slight color; a tint. **2.** a small amount; a trace; a touch.

tin·gle [tíŋgl] *vi.* have a pricking feeling; feel stirred with excitement or emotion. —*n.* Ⓤ a tingling condition; a pricking feeling; an excited emotion.

tink·er [tíŋkər] *n.* ⓒ **1.** a person who repairs kettles, pans, etc. **2.** an unskilled worker; a person who makes unskilled repairs. **3.** a person who does all kinds of small repairing.

의 시간을 정하다; [시계]를 맞추다 3. [경쟁 따위]의 시간을 재다; 시계를 맞추다 4. …을 박자에 맞추다 —⃝自 박자를 맞추다

—⃝形 1. 시간의, 시간에 관한 2. 시한(時限)의 3. 월부의

—⃝形 1. 옛날부터의

—⃝名 1. 시계 2. 시간 기록계

—⃝形 1. 영구적인 2. 부정기(不定期)의

—⃝形 마침 좋은 때의

—⃝名 계시기(計時器); 시계

—⃝名 1. 시간 기록계 2. 스톱워치 3. 시간 조절 장치

—⃝形 시간 절약의

—⃝名 기회주의자

—⃝名 시간표

—⃝名 시간제 노동
—⃝形 낡아빠진

—⃝名 시간대(帶) N.B. time belt라고
—⃝形 겁 많은; 수줍어하는 도 함

—⃝名 겁; 소심
—⃝副 겁내어; 소심하게
—⃝形 매우 겁이 많은

—⃝名 큰조아제비(목초)
—⃝名 1. 주석(朱錫) 2. 생철; (英) 생철 깡통, 통조림 3. (俗) 금전 —⃝形 주석 으로 만든 —⃝他 1. …에 주석을 입히다 2. …을 통조림으로 만들다

—⃝名 1. 정기제(丁幾劑) 2. 빛깔; 색소 3. 기미, …한 티 ¶①마늘 냄새 —⃝他 1. …을 착색하다 2. …에 …의 색채를 주다

—⃝名 부싯깃

—⃝名 부싯깃통

—⃝名 [사슴 뿔 따위의] 가지, 가랑이
—⃝名 석박(錫箔), 은종이
—⃝他 1. …을 엷게 착색하다 2. …을 곁들이다; …의 기미(티)를 띠게 하다 —⃝名 1. 색조 2. 아주 조금, 기미; …한 티

—⃝自 욱신 쑤시다; 얼얼하다; 두근거리다 —⃝名 욱신 쑤심, 얼얼함

—⃝名 1. 땜장이 2. 서투른 수선공 3. 조그마한 수선은 무엇이나 하는 사람

tinned —*vi., vt.* **1.** work as a tinker. **2.** repair roughly or clumsily. (*~ with* (or *at, up*) something). ―自他 1. 땜장이 노릇을 하다 2. […을] 서투르게 수선하다

tinned [tind] *adj.* **1.** covered with tin. **2.** (*Brit.*) (of food, etc.) kept in a can. ¶*~ fruit* (*beans, beef*). ―形 1. 주석(생철)을 입힌 2. 《英》통조림의

tin·ny [tíni] *adj.* (**-ni·er, -ni·est**) of or containing tin; (of sound or looks) like tin; (of food) having the taste of tin. ―形 주석의; 주석을 함유하는; 주석 같은; 생철 냄새가 나는

tin opener [⸗ ⸗] *n.* (*Brit.*) a device for opening a tin. (cf. *U. S.* a can opener) ―名 《英》깡통따개

tin plate [⸗ ⸗] *n.* a thin sheet of iron or steel covered with tin. ―名 생철

tin·sel [tíns(ə)l] *n.* Ⓤ **1.** a thin piece of glittering metal used for decoration. **2.** something showy but of little value. ―*vt.* (**-seled, -sel·ing** or *Brit.* **-selled, -sel·ling**) decorate (something) with tinsel. ―*adj.* of or like tinsel; showy but of little value. ―名 1. 반짝반짝하는 금속 조각 2. 번지르르한 싸구려 물건 ―他 …을 번쩍거리는 물건으로 장식하다 ―形 번쩍거리는; 겉만 번지르르한

tin·smith [tínsmiθ] *n.* Ⓒ a person who works with tin. ―名 생철 직공

・**tint** [tint] *n.* Ⓒ **1.** a variety of color or hue. ¶*several tints of yellow.* **2.** a faint color. ―*vt.* color slightly. ―名 1. 색조 2. 엷은 빛깔 ―他 …을 엷게 착색하다

tin·ware [tínwɛ̀ər] *n.* Ⓤ articles made of tin plate. ―名 생철 제품

‡**ti·ny** [táini] *adj.* (**-ni·er, -ni·est**) very small; minute. ―形 아주 작은

-tion [-ʃ(ə)n] *suf.* **1.** act of : *revolution* (=act of revolving) **2.** state of : *starvation* (=state of being starved) **3.** result of : *determination* (=result of determining) ―《接尾》1. 행위를 나타냄 2. 상태를 나타냄 3. 결과를 나타냄

‡**tip**¹ [tip] *n.* Ⓒ **1.** the pointed or thinner end of anything. ¶*walk on the tips of one's toes.*① **2.** a small piece put on the end of something. **3.** the top; the summit.
  1) *from tip to toe,* through and through; completely.
  2) *have something at* (or *on*) *the tip of one's tongue,* be just going to say something.
  3) *to the tips of one's fingers,* completely.
―*vt.* (**tipped, tip·ping**) **1.** furnish (something) with a point. **2.** cover the point of (something) (*~ something with*) ¶*~ an arrow with stone.* ―名 1. 끝; 첨단 ¶①발끝으로 걷다 2. 첨단에 붙이는 것 3. [산 따위의] 정상; 꼭대기

熟 1)철두철미 2)입밖에 낼 뻔하다 3)완전히

―他 1. …에 끝을 달다 2. …의 끝을 장식하다

・**tip**² [tip] *v.* (**tipped, tip·ping**) *vt.* **1.** cause (something) to incline. ¶*~ a table.* **2.** take off (one's hat) in salutation. (*~ one's hat to someone.*) **3.** (*Brit.*) empty (the contents) by tipping. ―*vi.* become inclined.
tip over, cause (something) to overturn; become overturned; upset. ¶*~ over a glass of water.*
―他 1. …을 기울이다 2. [모자]를 조금 들어 인사를 하다 3. [그릇을 쓰러뜨려] 속을 비우다 ―自 기울다

熟 …을 뒤집어엎다; 뒤집히다

・**tip**³ [tip] *n.* Ⓒ **1.** a small present of money given to a waiter, porter, etc. for services done. **2.** a friendly hint or suggestion ; a piece of secret or private information. ―*v.* (**tipped, tip·ping**) *vt.* **1.** give a small present of money to (someone). ¶*~ a waitress five shillings.* **2.** give secret information to (someone). ¶*~ a winner.* ―*vi.* give a tip. ―名 1. 팁, 행하(行下) 2. 조언, 힌트; 비밀정보; 예상 ―他 1. …에게 팁을 주다 2. …에게 비밀정보 따위를 슬며시 알리다 ―自 팁을 주다

tip someone off, (*colloq.*) give secret information to someone; warn. 熟 …에게 비밀정보를 알리다; 경고를 주다

tip⁴ [tip] *vt.* (**tipped, tip·ping**) **1.** strike lightly. **2.** (*Baseball, Cricket*) strike (a ball) a glancing blow. ―*n.* Ⓒ a light, glancing stroke. ―他 1. …을 가볍게 치다 2. [野球・크리켓] [공]을 팁하다, 끝을 깎아 치다 ―名 팁

tip·ple [típl] *vi., vt.* drink (strong liquor) little by little but repeatedly. ―*n.* Ⓤ [a kind of] strong liquor. ―自他 [독한 술을] 홀짝홀짝 마시다 ―名 독한 술

tip·sy [típsi] *adj.* (**-si·er, -si·est**) slightly drunk. ―形 얼근히 취한

tip·toe [típtòu] *n.* Ⓒ the end of a toe. ―名 발끝
on tiptoe[s], ⓐ on one's toes. ⓑ eagerly. ⓒ stealthily; secretly. ―*vi.* walk on the toes. ―*adv.* on the toes; stealthily. 熟 ⓐ발끝으로 ⓑ열심히 ⓒ몰래 ―自 발끝으로 걷다 ―副 발끝으로; 몰래

tip·top [típtɑ̀p / -tɔ̀p] *n.* Ⓒ the highest point. ―*adj.* of the very best; very fine; first-rate. ―*adv.* (*colloq.*) quite satisfactorily. ―名 절정 ―形 극상의 ―副 《口》말할 나위 없이

ti·rade [táireid, tiréid / táiréid, tiréid] *n.* Ⓒ a long, scolding speech. ―名 [공격적인] 장광설

‡**tire**¹ [táiər] *vt.* **1.** make (someone) weary. ¶*Walking soon tires me.*① **2.** make (someone) lose interest or patience. (*~ someone with*) ¶*He always tires me with his old stories.*② ―*vi.* **1.** become weary. (*~ with*) ―他 1. …을 지치게 하다 ¶①나는 걸으면 곧 지친다 2. …을 싫증나게 하다, 물리게 하다 ¶②그는 언제나 옛이야기로 나를 싫증나게 한다 ―自 1. 지

something》 ¶ *The old woman soon tires with walking.*③ **2.** lose interest or patience. 《~ *of* something》 ¶ *She'll ~ of the work.* *tire out,* make (someone) very tired. ¶ *He is tired out.*

치다 ¶①그 노부인은 걸으면 곧 피로해진다 2. 싫증나다, 물리다

[熟] …을 기진맥진하게 만들다

⁑ tire[2] [táiər] *n.* [C] a hoop of rubber or iron around the rim of a wheel. **—***vt.* furnish (something) with a tire. ⇒[N.B.]

—[名] [쇠·고무의] 타이어 —[他] 타이어를 …에 달다 [N.B.] tyre 로도 씀

⁑ tired [táiərd] *adj.* (sometimes **~·er, ~·est**) **1.** physically weary. 《~ *with*》 ¶ *He was ~ with the long walk.* **2.** mentally weary. 《~ *of*》 ¶ *I am ~ of reading.*

—[形] 1. 지친, 피로한 2. 싫증난

tired·ness [táiərdnis] *n.* [U] the state of being tired.

—[名] 피로; 권태

tire·less [táiərlis] *adj.* that does not grow tired; that does not stop. ¶ *a ~ worker / ~ efforts.*①

—[形] 지치지 않는, 참을성 있는; 끊임없는 ¶①줄기찬 노력

tire·less·ly [táiərlisli] *adv.* without growing tired.

—[副] 지칠 줄 모르고; 물리지 않고

tire·less·ness [táiərlisnis] *n.* [U] the state or quality of being tireless.

—[名] 지칠 줄 모름; 물리지 않음

· tire·some [táiərsəm] *adj.* **1.** irritating; troublesome. ¶ *a ~ child / It's very ~, but it can't be helped.* **2.** boring; dull. ▷**tire·some·ly** [-li] *adv.* —**tire·some·ness** [-nis] *n.*

—[形] 1. 속상하는; 성가신, 귀찮은 2. 넌더리나는

ti·ro [táiərou] *n.* [C] (pl. **-ros**) a beginner.

—[名] 초심자, 풋나기

· 'tis [tiz] it is.

· tis·sue [tíʃuː] *n.* **1.** [U][C] the groups of cells forming the parts of animals or plants. ¶ *the nervous ~.*① **2.** [U][C] a thin woven cloth. **3.** [C] a connected series or mass. ¶ *a ~ of lies.*②

—[名] 1. [생물의] 조직 ¶①신경조직 2. 얇은 직물 3. 연속, 뒤범벅 ¶②거짓말투성이

tissue paper [⌐– ⌐–] *n.* very thin, soft paper for wrapping fine articles or for toilet use, etc.

—[名] 박엽지(薄葉紙)

tit[1] [tit] *n.* =titmouse.

tit[2] [tit] *n.* [C] the part of the breast from which milk is given.

—[名] 젖꼭지

Ti·tan [táit(ə)n] *n.* (in Greek mythology) one of the giant gods who ruled the world before the Olympian gods.

—[名] 타이탄 신(神)

Ti·tan·ic [taitǽnik] *adj.* **1.** of or like the Titans. **2.** 《often *t-*》 large in size, in strong, in power, etc.

—[形] 1. 타이탄 신의(같은) 2. 거대한; 힘센

tit·bit [títbìt] *n.* =tidbit

tit·il·late [títilèit] *vt.* **1.** touch (someone) lightly to cause him to laugh. **2.** excite (someone) pleasantly or agreeably.

—[他] 1. …을 간질이다 2. …의 흥미를 돋우다

tit·il·la·tion [tìtiléiʃ(ə)n] *n.* [U] the act of titillating; the state of being titillated.

—[名] 간질이기; 흥을 돋우기

⁑ ti·tle [táitl] *n.* [C] **1.** the name of a book, picture, poem, film, etc. ¶ *the ~ of a chapter*① / *publish a book under the ~ of.*② **2.** the signification of a person's rank or profession, such as Doctor or Lady, usu. placed before a person's name. ¶ *the man of ~.*③ **3.** a claim or right. 《*~to, in, of*》 **4.** [U] the legal right of ownership. ¶ *~ to property.*④ **5.** championship. ¶ *defend the ~ / lose the ~.*

—*vt.* give a title to (someone or something).

—[名] 1. 책 이름, 제목; [영화의] 자막(字幕) ¶①장(章)의 제목/②…이라는 이름의 책을 출판하다 2. 직함, 칭호 ¶③직함이 있는 사람 3. [요구해야 할 정당한] 권리, [권리 따위를 주장할 수 있는] 자격 4. 소유권 ¶④재산의 소유권 5. 선수권

—[他]…에 칭호를 주다; [책 따위]에 제목을 붙이다

ti·tled [táitld] *adj.* having a title.

—[形] 직함이 있는

title deed [⌐– ⌐] *n.* a document showing a person's ownership of land.

—[名] 부동산 권리 증서

title page [⌐– ⌐] *n.* the front page of a book containing the title, the author's name, the publisher, etc. of the book.

—[名] [서적의] 안표지, 표제지(表題紙)

tit·mice [títmàis] *n.* pl. of **titmouse**.

tit·mouse [títmàus] *n.* [C] (pl.**-mice**) any one of a number of small song-birds with dull-colored feathers.

—[名] 박새과의 각종 새

tit·ter [títər] *vi.* laugh in a partly suppressed way.

—[自] 킬킬 웃다

tit·tle [titl] *n.* 《*a ~*, in *negative*》 a very small amount. ¶ *There is not a ~ of truth in his words.*①

—[名] 아주 조금 ¶①그의 말에는 진실이라곤 조금도 없다

tit·tle-tat·tle [títltæ̀tl] *n.* [U] gossip; chatter.

—[名] 잡담; 수다

tit·u·lar [títʃulər / títjulə] *adj.* **1.** having a title. **2.** of a title. **3.** existing in name only. ¶ *a ~ leader.*

—[形] 1. 직함이 있는 2. 표제의 3. 유명무실한

⁑ to [tu(ː), tə] *prep.* **1.** toward; in the direction of. ¶ *from east ~ west / He went ~ the left. / The station is ~ the south of the park.*① **2.** as far as. ¶ *go ~ New York.*

—[前] 1. …쪽으로 ¶①역은 공원 남쪽에 있다 2. …의 지점까지 3. …의 시점(時點)까지 ¶②5시 15분 전/③오늘

3. before; until. ¶*a quarter ~ five*② | *~ this day.*③ **4.** for the purpose of; for. ¶*They came ~ our rescue.* | *drink ~ one's health.* **5.** until it becomes the state of; causing or resulting in. ¶*The house was burnt ~ ashes.*④ | *To my disappointment, my son failed in the entrance examination.* **6.** in agreement (or harmony) with. ¶*This job is not ~ my taste.* **7.** accompanied by; along with. ¶*They danced ~ the music.*⑤ **8.** compared with. ¶*three shillings ~ the pound* | *prefer beer ~ whisky*⑥ | *We often compare life ~ a voyage.* **9.** of; belonging to. ¶*a daughter ~ the Queen* | *a key ~ the room.*⑦ **10.** on; against. ¶*She is deeply attached ~ her friend's brother.*⑧ | *stick ~ one's opinion* | *apply varnish ~ the surface.* **11.** 《introducing the *direct object*》 ¶*He gave the book ~ the girl.* **12.** 《used with the *infinitive form* of verbs》 ¶*I want ~ do it.* | *It is necessary for him ~ do it at once.* | *I've nothing ~ eat.* | *I studied ~ pass the exam.* | *These oranges are fit ~ eat.* | *I am very happy ~ meet you.* | *She grew up ~ be an actress.*⑨ | *to speak frankly.*⑩

까지 **4.** …을 위하여; …의 목적으로 **5.** …이 될 때까지; …한 것은 ¶④그 집은 불타서 재가 되었다 **6.** …에 맞는 **7.** …에 맞추어 ¶⑤그들은 음악에 맞추어 춤췄다 **8.** …와 비교하여; 대응시켜 ¶⑥위스키보다 맥주를 좋아하다 **9.** …의; …에 속하는 ¶⑦방의 열쇠 **10.** …으로; …에 ¶⑧그녀는 친구 오빠한테 깊이 관심을 두고 있다 **11.** 《간접 목적어의 대용구를 만듦》 **12.** 《부정사를 이끎》 …하는 것; …하기 위한; …하기 위하여 ¶⑨그녀는 자라서 여배우가 됐다/⑩솔직히 말하면

—*adv.* forward; in the usual position, esp. a still or close one. ¶*Is the door ~?*⑪ | *Your hat is on the wrong side ~.*⑫
to and fro, back and forth.

—[부] 앞쪽으로; 여느때의 상태로 ¶⑪문은 닫혔는가?/⑫넌 모자를 돌려 쓰고 있구나
[熟] 여기저기에

***toad** [toud] *n.* [C] a small frog-like animal with a rough skin, living on land rather than in water. —[명] 두꺼비

toad·y [tóudi] *n.* [C] (pl. **toad·ies**) a person who flatters a rich or powerful person. —[명] 아첨꾼, 알랑쇠

toast** [toust] *n.* [U] a slice of bread made brown on both sides by heat. **—*vt. **1.** make (bread, etc.) brown by heating it. **2.** (*colloq.*) warm (oneself) thoroughly before the fire. **—*vi.*** **1.** (of bread, etc.) become brown by heat. **2.** drink to someone's health or success.
—[명] 구운 빵, 토우스트 —[타] **1.** [빵 따위]를 누르스름하게 굽다 **2.** 《口》 불에 쬐다 —[자] **1.** [빵 따위가] 누르스름하게 구워지다 **2.** 축배를 들다

toast·er [tóustər] *n.* [C] **1.** a person who toasts bread, etc. **2.** an instrument for toasting bread. —[명] **1.** 빵을 굽는 사람 **2.** 빵 굽는 기구, 토우스터

toast·mas·ter [tóustmæstər / -mɑːstə] *n.* [C] **1.** a person who proposes drinking to someone's health or success. **2.** a person who acts as the chairman at a dinner. —[명] **1.** 축배의 말을 하는 사람 **2.** [연회의] 사회자

‡**to·bac·co** [təbǽkou] *n.* (pl. **-cos** or **-coes**) [U] a plant with large leaves which are dried and used for smoking; the dried leaves of this plant ¶*a ~ pipe.*① —[명] 담배; [파이프용의] 살담배 ¶①파이프

to·bac·co·nist [təbǽkənist] *n.* [C] a person who sells tobacco and other smoking supplies. —[명] 담배장수

-to·be [-təbíː] *suf.* in the future: *a minister-to-be* (=a minister in the future). —《接尾》 미래의 …, 이제부터 되려고 하는 …

to·bog·gan [təbɑ́gən / -bɔ́g-] *n.* [C] a long, narrow, flat sled made of thin board which carries four or more persons, used for sliding down a snow-covered hill. ⇒fig **—*vi.*** **1.** slide down a snow-covered hill on a tobbogan. **2.** (*U.S. colloq.*) fall sharply and rapidly in price, value, etc.
—[명] 터보건 썰매 —[자] **1.** 터보건 썰매로 언덕을 미끄러져 내려가다 **2.** [물가 따위가] 폭락하다

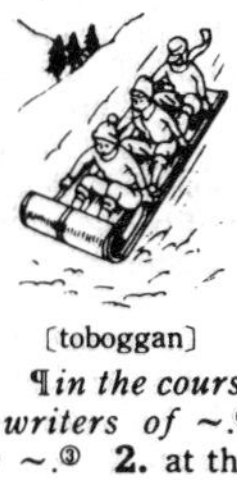
〔toboggan〕

toc·sin [tɑ́ksin / tɔ́k-] *n.* [C] an alarm bell; the sound of an alarm bell. —[명] 경종(警鐘); 경종 소리

‡**to·day, to-day** [tədéi] *n.* [U] **1.** this day. ¶*in the course of ~.*① **2.** the present time. ¶*the writers of ~.*② **—*adv.*** **1.** on this day. ¶*It is Monday ~.*③ **2.** at the present time.
—[명] **1.** 오늘 ¶①오늘 안에 **2.** 현대, 오늘날 ¶②현대의 작가 —[부] **1.** 오늘은 월요일이다 **2.** 오늘날은

tod·dle [tɑ́dl / tɔ́dl] *vi.* walk with short, unsteady steps like a baby. —[자] 아장아장 걷다

tod·dler [tɑ́dlər / tɔ́dlə] *n.* [C] a child that has just learnt to walk. —[명] 아장아장 걷기 시작한 갓난아이

tod·dy [tɑ́di / tɔ́di] *n.* [U][C] (pl. **-dies**) a drink made of whisky, brandy, etc., plus hot water, sugar, and spices. —[명] 토디(양주에 뜨거운 물을 부어 설탕과 레몬을 탄 음료)

‡**toe** [tou] *n.* [C] **1.** one of the five separate parts at the end —[명] **1.** 발가락 **2.** [신·양말의] 발끝

T

toffee

of a foot. **2.** the front part of any foot covering, such as of a shoe or stocking.
1) *from top to toe,* from head to foot.
2) *on one's toe,* ready to act.
3) *tread on someone's toe,* hurt someone's feelings.
—*vt.* touch (someone) with the toe.
toe the line, ⓐ stand on the starting line of a race with the toes touching it. ⓑ (*colloq.*) obey orders, rules, etc. exactly.

tof·fee [tɔ́:fi, táfi / tɔ́fi] *n.* Ⓤ Ⓒ (usu. *Brit.*) a hard candy made of boiled sugar and butter. ⇒ NB.

tog [tag / tɔg] *n.* (usu. *pl.*) (*colloq.*) clothes. —*vt.* (**togged, tog·ging**) dress (someone) carefully and smartly. (*~ out, up* someone)

to·ga [tóugə] *n.* Ⓒ (pl. **-gas** or **-gae**) a loose outer dress worn by ancient Romans.
to·gae [tóudʒi] *n.* pl. of **toga**. ⇨fig.

‡ **to·geth·er** [təɡéðər] *adv.* **1.** with each other; in company. ¶ *go about ~.*① **2.** into one body or place. ¶ *call the people ~*② / *sew pieces ~.* **3.** at the same time. ¶ *shout ~.*③ **4.** in succession. ¶ *study for hours ~.*
together with, along with.

tog·gle [tágl / tɔ́gl] *n.* Ⓒ a metal pin, bolt, or rod for putting through a loop of rope or the link of a chain to prevent slipping. [toga]

toil¹ [tɔil] *n.* Ⓤ hard work. ¶ *with ~ and moil.*①
—*vi.* **1.** work hard. (*~ at* something) ¶ *~ at the knitting.* **2.** move with difficulty and effort.

toil² [tɔil] *n.* (usu. *pl.*) (*archaic*) a snare.

• **toi·let** [tɔ́ilit] *n.* Ⓒ **1.** the act or process of dressing, bathing, washing, arranging the hair or clothes, etc. ¶ *a brief ~*① / *~ articles.*② **2.** (*U. S. colloq.*) a bathroom; a water closet. ¶ *~ paper.*③

toil·some [tɔ́ilsəm] *adj.* requiring toil; laborious.
toil·worn [tɔ́ilwɔ̀:rn] *adj.* worn out by toil.

• **to·ken** [tóuk(ə)n] *n.* **1.** Ⓒ a sign or symbol of some fact, feeling, etc.; a mark that proves some fact. ¶ *A four-leaf clover is a ~ of good luck.*① **2.** something kept as a reminder; a memorial thing. **3.** a piece of metal used instead of money.
1) *as a token of; in token of,* as a sign of. ⌜more.⌝
2) *by the same token; by that token,* more; further-
—*adj.* serving as a token; slight and not real. ¶ *a ~ resistance.*②

‡ **told** [tould] *v.* pt. and pp. of **tell**.

tol·er·a·ble [tálərəbl / tɔ́l-] *adj.* **1.** that can be endured. ¶ *The pain was bad, but it was tolerable.*① **2.** fairly good; not bad. ¶ *His drawing was ~.*② ▷ **tol·er·a·ble·ness** [-nis] *n.* ⌜fairly.⌝

tol·er·a·bly [tálərəbli / tɔ́l-] *adv.* to a tolerable degree;

tol·er·ance [tálərəns / tɔ́l-] *n.* Ⓤ state of being, or hope to be, tolerant of other's opinions or customs; the act of tolerating.

tol·er·ant [tálərənt / tɔ́l-] *adj.* willing to allow other people's beliefs, opinions or actions which are different from one's own. (*~ of*) ▷ **tol·er·ant·ly** [-li] *adv.*

tol·er·ate [tálərèit / tɔ́l-] *vt.* allow (something) to exist against one's own liking; bear; endure. ¶ *We must ~ other people's ideas.*①

tol·er·a·tion [tàləréiʃ(ə)n / tɔ̀l-] *n.* Ⓤ **1.** tolerance. **2.** allowance of religions which are different from the officially recognized religion.

• **toll**¹ [toul] *vt.* ring (a bell) slowly and with a single stroke at regular intervals. ¶ *~ someone's death.*①

toll

圏 1)머리 꼭대기에서 발끝까지 2)준비를 갖추고 3)…의 감정을 해치다
—他 …을 발끝으로 건드리다
圏 ⓐ (경주 따위에서) 출발선에 발끝을 대고 서다 ⓑ (口)명령에 따르다

—名 당과(糖果)의 일종 NB 북미에서는 taffy로 씀

—名 (口) 의복 —他 …에게 입히다

—名 고대 로마시민이 입던 헐거운 옷

—副 1. 함께 ¶① 함께 떠나다 2. 함께 (만나게) 되도록 ¶② 사람들을 불러모으다 3. 동시에 ¶③ 모두 일제히 외치다 4. 계속

圏 …와 함께
—名 [딴 밧줄을 걸어매는] 비녀장

—名 수고, 노고 ¶① 고생고생 일하여
—自 1. 애써 일하다 2. 터벅터벅 애써 나아가다
—名 (古) 올가미
—名 1. 화장 ¶① 간단한 화장 /② 화장품 2. 욕실; 세면소; 변소 ¶③ 휴지

—形 힘드는
—形 지쳐빠진
—名 1. 표; 상징; 증거 ¶① 네 잎 클로우버는 행운의 상징이다 2. 기념품; 유물 3. 대용 화폐

圏 1)…의 표시(증거)로 2)게다가, 그 위에
—形 보증으로서 받는; 명목뿐인 ¶② 명목뿐의 반항

—形 1. 참을 수 있는 ¶① 아픔은 심했지만 참을 수 없을 정도는 아니었다 2. 상당한 ¶② 그의 그림은 꽤 잘됐다

—副 꽤, 상당히
—名 관용; 포용력

—形 관대한

—他 …을 관대히 다루다; …을 참다 ¶① 우리는 다른 사람들의 의견을 잘 들어야 한다
—名 1. 관용 2. 신앙의 자유

—他 [만종(挽鐘) 따위를] 천천히 치다 ¶① 남의 죽음을 종을 울려 알리다

toll

—*vi.* ring or sound in this way. ¶ *The bell tolled three.*② —*n.* (usu. in *sing.*) the sound of a tolling bell.
toll² [toul] *n.* ⓒ **1.** the fee paid for using something or passing through some place. ¶ *pay a ~.*① **2.** a charge for a long-distance telephone call. ¶ *a ~ call.* —*vi.* collect tolls.
toll bar [⌒ ⌒] *n.* a bar or gate across a road where toll is taken. [passage.]
toll bridge [⌒ ⌒] *n.* a bridge at which toll is paid for
toll·gate [tóulgèit] *n.* ⓒ a gate on a road or bridge where toll is taken.
toll·house [tóulhàus] *n.* ⓒ (pl. **-hous·es** [-hauziz]) a house at a tollgate where the tollkeepers live.
toll·keep·er [tóulki:pər] *n.* ⓒ a person who collects tolls.
Tom [tam / tɔm] *n.* a nickname for Thomas.
tom·a·hawk [táməhɔ̀:k / tɔ́m-] *n.* ⓒ a kind of light ax or hatchet used by North American Indians as a weapon and a tool. ⇒fig.
  1) *bury* (or *lay aside*) *the tomahawk*, stop fighting.
  2) *take up* (or *dig up*) *the tomahawk*, begin fighting.
—*vt.* strike, kill, or cut (something) with a tomahawk.

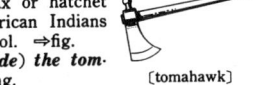
[tomahawk]

‡**to·ma·to** [təméitou / -má:-] *n.* (pl. **-toes**) ⓒ **1.** a plant with yellow flowers, hairy leaves and red, juicy fruit which are eaten. **2.** a fruit of this plant.
•**tomb** [tu:m] *n.* **1.** ⓒ a grave for a dead body. **2.** (*the ~*). death. —*vt.* bury (a dead body). [a boy.]
tom·boy [támbɔ̀i / tɔ́m-] *n.* ⓒ a girl who behaves like
tomb·stone [tú:mstòun] *n.* ⓒ a stone or monument over a grave, usu. bearing at least the name and dates of birth and death of the dead person.
tom·cat [támkæ̀t / tɔ́m-] *n.* ⓒ a male cat.
tome [toum] *n.* ⓒ a book; a large, heavy book.
tom·fool [támfú:l / tɔ́m-] *n.* ⓒ a silly, stupid person.
tom·fool·er·y [tàmfú:ləri / tɔ̀m-] *n.* (pl. **-er·ies**) Ⓤⓒ silly and stupid behavior; nonsense.
Tom·my [támi / tɔ́mi] *n.* a nickname for Thomas.
‡**to·mor·row** [təmɔ́:rou, -már- / təmɔ́rou] *n.* Ⓤ **1.** the day after today. ¶ *the day after ~*① */ Tomorrow never comes.*② **2.** the near future. ¶ *~ week.* —*adv.* on the day after today.
tom-tom [támtàm / tɔ́mtɔ̀m] *n.* ⓒ an Indian drum, usu. beaten with the hands. ⇒fig. —*vi.* beat this drum.
‡**ton** [tʌn] *n.* ⓒ **1.** a unit of weight. **2.** a unit of the internal capacity of ships. ¶ *capacity ~*① */ shipping ~*② **3.** a unit of volume of freight.
ton·al [tóun(ə)l] *adj.* of tone.
•**tone** [toun] *n.* **1.** ⓒ the quality of sound; intonation. ¶ *sweet tones of a harp.* **2.** [tom-tom] the manner of speaking or writing. ¶ *speak in an angry ~.*① **3.** the general character; mental attitude; spirit. ¶ *the ~ of the school*② */ A ~ of refinement prevails in her room.*③ **4.** the general effect of color or light; tint; hue; shade. ¶ *a light ~ of blue* / *a vivid* (*dull, cool*) *~.* **5.** Ⓤ normal healthy condition.
—*vi.* harmonize. (*~ in* [*with*] *something*). ¶ *The hat tones in well with her coat.* —*vt.* give a tone to; change the tone of (a sound). ¶ *Sorrow toned her voice.*
tongs [tɔ:ŋz / tɔŋz] *n. pl.* a tool with two arms, joined by a hinge, used for holding things. ¶ *a pair of ~.*①
‡**tongue** [tʌŋ] *n.* ⓒ **1.** the movable organ in the mouth

tongue

—⾃ 천천히 울리다 ¶②종이 세 번 울렸다 —❀ 종소리
—❀ 1.사용료; 통행료 ¶①통행료를 내다 2.장거리 전화료 —⾃ 통행세를 징수하다

—❀ [통행세를 징수하는 곳의] 도로 차단봉
— 통행세를 받는 다리
—❀ 통행세 징수소

—❀ 통행세 징수소

—❀ 통행세 징수인
— Thomas 의 애칭
—❀ [북미 토인의] 전부(戰斧), 전투용 도끼

圖 1)정전하다, 친선을 맺다 2)싸움을 개시하다, 선전(宣戰)하다

—⾍ …을 도끼로 치다(죽이다, 자르다)
—❀ 1.토마토나무 2.토마토

—❀ 1.무덤 2.죽음 —⾍ …을 매장하다
—❀ 말괄량이
—❀ 묘석, 묘비

—❀ 수코양이
—❀ 책, 큰 책
—❀ 멍텅구리, 바보
—❀ 바보짓

— Thomas 의 애칭
—❀ 1.내일 ¶①모레/② 내일이 있다고 믿지 말아라 2.가까운 장래 —⾏ 내일[은, 에]

—❀ [인도·아프리카 토인의] 북 —⾃ 북을 치다

—❀ 1.중량의 단위 2.배의 용적 단위; 군함의 배수(排水)톤 ¶①화물의 적재톤/②적재톤 3.화물의 체적 단위, 적재톤

—⼀ 음조의
—❀ 1.음색; 억양 2.어조, 논조, 말투 ¶①성난 말투로 말하다 3.경향; 기풍, 기품 ¶②교풍(校風)/③그녀의 방에는 우아한 기품이 가득차 있었다 4.색채 효과; 색조, 명암도 5.[정신·신체의] 상태; 건강상태

—⾃ 조화하다 —⾍ …의 음조를 주다(바꾸다); 색조를 주다

—❀ 집게, 부젓가락 ¶①부젓가락

—❀ 1.혀 2.말씨 ¶①달변(達辯)/②

used for licking, tasting, and talking. **2.** the manner of speaking. ¶*an eloquent ~*① | *a flattering ~*② | *a sharp ~*③ | *a slip of the ~.*④ **3.** a language. ¶*the Greek ~*⑤ | *one's mother ~.*⑥ **4.** anything like a tongue in shape, movement, or use. **5.** a vibrating reed in a musical instrument.
1) ***give tongue,*** (of people) shout with a loud voice; (of hounds) begin to bark.
2) ***have a ready tongue,*** speak fluently.
3) ***have** one's **tongue in** one's **cheek,*** speak ironically or insincerely.
4) ***hold** one's **tongue,*** keep silent.
5) ***lose** one's **tongue,*** cannot speak for a moment.

아첨의 말/③욕설/④실언 **3.** 국어 ¶⑤그리이스어/⑥모국어 **4.** 혀 모양의 물건 **5.** 관악기의 혀

[熟] 1)[사람이] 고함치듯이 말하다;[사냥개가] 짖다 2)구변이 좋다 3)빈정대며 말하다 4)잠자코 있다 5)부끄러움 따위로 말을 못하다

tongue·less [tʌ́ŋlis] *adj.* **1.** having no tongue. **2.** not speaking.
—[形] **1.** 혀가 없는 **2.** 말이 없는

tongue-tied [tʌ́ŋtàid] *adj.* **1.** not able to speak clearly because of some defect of the tongue. **2.** not able to speak because of amazement, embarrassment, shyness, fear, etc.
—[形] **1.** 혀짜래기의 **2.** [놀라서] 말문이 막힌

ton·ic [tánik / tɔ́nik] *n.* [C] **1.** a medicine that gives strength and energy. ¶*a hair ~.*① **2.** (*Music*) the keynote of a scale. —*adj.* **1.** giving vigor and strength. ¶*a ~ medicine.*② **2.** (*Music*) of a keynote or tone.
—[名] **1.** 강장제 ¶①양모제 **2.**《樂》 주음(主音) —[形] **1.** 튼튼하게 하는 ¶②강장제 **2.**《樂》 주음의

: **to·night, to-night** [tənáit] *n.* [U] the night of today. —*adv.* on or during this night.
—[名] 오늘밤 —[副] 오늘밤[은, 에]

ton·nage [tʌ́nidʒ] *n.* [U] **1.** the carrying capacity of a ship, measured in tons. **2.** the total amount of shipping in tons. **3.** duty or tax laid on ships according to the cargo carried.
—[名] **1.** [선박의] 용적 톤수 **2.** [선박의] 총톤수 **3.** [배·적하(積荷)의] 톤세(稅)

ton·sil [táns(i)l / tɔ́n-] *n.* [C] one of a pair of oval-shaped masses of tissue on the sides of the throat.
—[名] 편도선

ton·sil·lar [tánsilər / tɔ́nsilə] *adj.* of the tonsils.
—[形] 편도선의

ton·sure [tánʃər / tɔ́nʃə, -ʃuə] *n.* **1.** [U] the act of shaving the head to become a priest; the state of being shaven in this way. **2.** [C] the part of the head shaved in this way. —*vt.* shave the head of (someone)
—[名] **1.** 체발(剃髮), 승문(僧門)에 들어가기 **2.** 머리를 박박 민 부분
—[他] …의 머리를 박박 밀다

: **too** [tu:] *adv.* **1.** also; moreover. ¶*She is kind, and pretty ~.* | *He can speak English and German, ~.* **2.** excessive; more than enough. ¶*It is ~ beautiful for words.*① | *We cannot be ~ careful.*② | *The problem is ~ difficult for me to solve.* | *It is never ~ late to mend.*③ **3.** (*colloq.*) very; so. ¶*She is ~ happy.* | *He is not ~ well today.*④
1) ***but** (or **only**) **too,*** ⓐ to be regretted that .... ¶*It is but ~ true.* ⓑ extremely.
2) ***none too,*** not at all.

—[副] **1.** 또한; 게다가 **2.** 지나치게; 너무하는 ¶①형용할 수 없을 만큼 아름답다/②아무리 조심하더라도 지나치다고 할 수 없다/③고치는 데에 늦었다는 법은 없다 **3.** 몹시, 매우, 무척 ¶④별로 기분이 좋지 않다

[熟] 1)ⓐ유감이지만 …이다 ⓑ지나치게 2)조금도 …이 아니다

: **took** [tuk] *v.* pt. of **take**.

: **tool** [tu:l] *n.* [C] **1.** an instrument used with the hands in doing work. ¶*a machine ~*① | *a set of carpenter's tools.*② **2.** anything used as a tool. ¶*literary tools.*③ **3.** a person used by another to work, esp. dishonestly. —*vt.* shape or form (something) with a tool.
—[名] **1.** 도구 ¶①기계 공구/②한 벌의 목수 도구 **2.** [일반적으로] 용구(用具) ¶③문방구 **3.** 앞잡이
—[他] …을 도구로 제작하다

toot [tu:t] *vt.* cause (a horn, whistle, etc.) to sound. —*vi.* give a short, sharp sound on a horn. —*n.* [C] an act or sound of tooting. ▷**toot·er** [-ər] *n.*
—[他] [휘파람·나팔 따위]를 불다 —[自] 울리다 —[名] [휘파람·나팔 따위를] 불기, 부는 소리

: **tooth** [tu:θ] *n.* (pl. **teeth**) [C] **1.** one of the hard, bony growths in the jaws, used for biting and chewing. ¶*a decayed ~*① | *a false ~.*② **2.** something like a tooth, as of comb, saw or rake.
1) ***cast** something **in** one's **teeth,*** reproach someone for something.
2) ***draw** someone's **teeth,*** deprive someone of the cause of his complaints.
3) ***escape by the skin of** one's **teeth,*** escape narrowly.
4) ***in the teeth of,*** straight against; in spite of.
5) ***lie in** one's **teeth,*** tell a black lie.
6) ***set** one's **teeth,*** make up one's mind.
7) ***show** one's **teeth,*** show anger or hostility.

—[名] **1.** 이(齒) ¶①충치/②의치 **2.** 이 모양의 것

[熟] 1)[…의 일로] …을 나무라다 2)…의 불평의 원인을 없애다 3)아슬아슬하게 도망치다 4)…의 면전에서 5)새빨간 거짓말을 하다 6)결심을 굳히다 7)위협하다, 성내다 8)완전히 9)필사적으로, 전력을 다하여

toothache [1211] **topping**

8) **to the teeth,** fully.
9) **tooth and nail,** with all one's force.
tooth·ache [túːèik] *n.* ⓒⓊ an ache in a tooth. —똉 치통
tooth·brush [túːθbrʌʃ] *n.* ⓒ a small brush for cleaning the teeth.　　　「V-shaped cut. ¶a ~ *wheel.*① —똉 칫솔
toothed [túːθt, túːðd] *adj.* **1.** having teeth. **2.** having a —똉 1.이가 있는 2.톱니 모양의 ¶
tooth·less [túːθlis] *adj.* having no teeth.　　　「teeth. —똉 이가 없는　　　└①톱니바퀴
tooth·paste [túːθpèist] *n.* Ⓤ a paste for cleaning the —똉 치약
tooth·pick [túːθpìk] *n.* ⓒ a small, pointed piece of wood used for cleaning the teeth. —똉 이쑤시개
tooth powder [⌐ ⌐⌐] *n.* Ⓤ powder for cleaning the teeth. —똉 치마분(齒磨粉)
tooth·some [túːθsəm] *adj.* pleasing to the taste; delicious. —똉 맛있는
too·tle [túːtl] *v.*, *n.* =toot.　　　└cious.
:top¹ [tap / tɔp] *n.* ⓒ **1.** the highest point or part; the upper end or surface. ¶*the* ~ *of a hill* (*mountain, tree*). **2.** the highest rank or place. ¶*sit at the* ~ *of the table*① / *He is* [*at*] *the* ~ *of his class.* **3.** the highest degree or extent. ¶*run at the* ~ *of one's speed* / *cry* (or *shout*) *at the* ~ *of one's voice.* **4.** (usu. *pl.*) the part of a food plant above ground. ¶*radish* (*carrot*) *tops.* **5.** a covering; a lid. ¶*the bottle* ~. —똉 1.정상; 꼭대기, 최상부 2.최고위; 수석 ¶①식탁의 상좌에 앉다 3. 절정; 극한 4.[무우 따위의] 땅 위의 부분 5.마개, 뚜껑

1) *from top to bottom* (or *toe, tail*), completely.
2) *on top,* successful; above.
3) *on top of* (=*in addition to*) *something.*
4) *top and tail,* the whole; completely.
5) *the top of the tree* (*ladder*), the highest position in a profession.　　　「~ *secret.*①

🌑 1)완전히; 머리 끝에서 발끝까지 2) 성공하여; …의 위에 3)…에 더하여 4) 전체; 완전히 5)최고의 지위; 제 1인자

—*adj.* greatest; highest. ¶*at* ~ *speed* / *the* ~ *boy* / *a* —똉 최고의; 맨 위의 ¶①극비
—*v.* (**top·ped, top·ping**) *vt.* **1.** put a top on; be the top of (something). ¶*a church topped with* (or *by*) *a spire*② / *the mountain topped with snow.* **2.** be better, larger, taller, stronger, etc. than (someone); surpass; outdo. ¶*He tops us all at chess.* / *He tops his father by four inches.*③ **3.** reach the top of (a hill, etc.) ¶*We topped the mountain toward noon.* **4.** rise above (something). ¶*The moon topped the horizon.* —똉 1.…에 씌우다; …의 꼭대기를 덮다 ¶②첨탑이 꼭대기에 있는 교회 2.…을 능가하다; …보다 낫다 ¶③그는 아버지보다 4인치나 더 크다 3.…의 꼭대기에 이르다 4.…의 위에 오르다

1) *top off,* complete; end.
2) *top up,* fill up (a partly empty container).

🌑 1)마무리하다; 끝내다 2)더 부어서 [그릇에] 가득 채우다

* **top**² [tap / tɔp] *n.* ⓒ a child's toy shaped like a cone with a point on which it spins. —똉 팽이
to·paz [tóupæz] *n.* Ⓤⓒ a mineral, usu. yellow in color but sometimes blue or green, used as a gem. —똉 황옥(黃玉)
top boots [⌐ ⌐] *n. pl.* a kind of riding boot reaching almost up to the knee. —똉 승마 구두의 일종
top·coat [tápkòut / tɔ́p-] *n.* ⓒ a light-weight over coat. —똉 가벼운 외투
top·er [tóupər] *n.* ⓒ a person who drinks alcoholic liquor in large amounts; a drunkard. —똉 주정뱅이
top hat [⌐⌐ / ⌐⌐] *n.* a man's tall silk hat. —똉 실크햇
top-heav·y [tápèvi / tɔ́phèvi] *adj.* having the top much heavier than the base. —똉 머리가 큰, 불안정한
:top·ic [tápik / tɔ́p-] *n.* ⓒ a subject for conversation, discussion, writing, etc. —똉 화제, 논제, 제목
top·mast [tápmæst / tɔ́pmɑ̀ːst] *n.* ⓒ the second section of a mast above the deck of a ship.　「very top. —똉 중간 돛대
top·most [tápmòust / tɔ́p-, -məst] *adj.* highest; at the —똉 최고의
to·pog·ra·pher [təpágrəfər / -pɔ́g-] *n.* ⓒ **1.** a person who is skilled in topography. **2.** a person who accurately describes a place or area. —똉 1.지형 학자 2.지지(地誌) 작자
to·pog·ra·phy [təpágrəfi / -pɔ́grəfə] *n.* Ⓤ **1.** the science of making a map or showing the surface features of a place or region. **2.** the surface of a place or region. —똉 1.지형학 2.지세(地勢)
top·per [tápər / tɔ́pə] *n.* ⓒ **1.** (*colloq.*) a person or thing that is first-rate. **2.** a woman's short topcoat. —똉 1.(口) 뛰어난 사람(물건), 제 1급의 인물 2.[부인용] 털거운 겉옷
top·ping [tápiŋ / tɔ́p-] *adj.* **1.** that is at the top in —똉 1.우뚝 솟은; 뛰어난 2.멋들어진,

topple / **torture**

top·ple [tápl / tɔ́pl] *vi., vt.* **1.** become unsteady; cause (something) to be unsteady. **2.** turn over; cause (something) to turn over. ((~ *down* or *over something*))
—自他 1. 흔들흔들하다; 흔들리게 하다 2. 비틀거려 쓰러지다

top·rank·ing [tɔ́præŋkiŋ / tɔ́p-] *adj.* (*U.S. colloq.*) highest in rank, quality, etc.
—형 《美口》 일류의, 최고의

top·sail [tɔ́psèil, *Nautical* -sl / tɔ́psl] *n.* ⓒ (*Nautical*) the second sail above the lowermost sail on a mast.
—명 가운데 돛

top·sy·tur·vy [tɑ́psitə́:rvi / tɔ́psitə́:vi] *adv., adj.* **1.** in a confused condition or in disorder. **2.** upside down.
—*n.* Ⓤ the state of confusion or disorder.
—부형 1. 뒤죽박죽으로(의) 2. 거꾸로[의] —명 전도(轉倒); 뒤죽박죽; 혼란상태

toque [touk] *n.* ⓒ a woman's small hat without a brim. ⇒fig.
—명 챙이 좁은 부인모

torch [tɔ:rtʃ] *n.* ⓒ **1.** a light made by burning wood, flax, etc. and carried by hand. **2.** (*Brit.*) a flashlight. **3.** something regarded as the source of enlightenment, inspiration, etc. ¶the ~ of learning.① *carry a torch for* (=be in love with) ⌜someone.⌝
—명 1. 횃불 2. 회중전등 3. [지식·문화의] 빛 ¶①학문의 빛
關 …을 사랑하고 있다

torch·bear·er [tɔ́:rtʃbɛ̀ərər] *n.* ⓒ **1.** a person who carries a torch. **2.** a person who is a leader in a movement, a campaign, a crusade, etc. [toque]
—명 1. 횃불을 든 사람 2. [개혁 운동 따위의] 선구자; 계몽가

torch·light [tɔ́:rtʃlàit] *n.* Ⓤ the light which a torch gives off.
—명 횃불빛

tore [tɔ:r] *v.* pt. of *tear*.

tor·e·a·dor [tɔ́:riədɔ̀:r / tɔ́riədɔ̀:] *n.* ⓒ a bullfighter on horseback in Spain.
—명 [스페인의] 기마 투우사

tor·ment *n.* [tɔ́:rmənt →v.] **1.** Ⓤ great mental or physical pain. **2.** ⓒ a cause of suffering, anxiety, or pain.
—*vt.* [tɔ:rmént] cause pain to (someone) mentally or physically. ⌜thing that torments others.⌝
—명 1. [정신적·육체적] 고민, 고통 2. 고민거리
—타 …을 괴롭히다

tor·men·tor, -ment·er [tɔ:rméntər] *n.* ⓒ a person or
—명 괴롭히는 사람; 괴롭히는 것

torn [tɔ:rn] *v.* pp. of *tear*.

tor·na·do [tɔ:rnéidou] *n.* ⓒ (pl. **-does** or **-dos**) a violent, whirling wind that destroys everything in its course.
—명 선풍, 회오리바람

tor·pe·do [tɔ:rpí:dou] *n.* ⓒ (pl. **-does**) a large, cigar-shaped missile which goes underwater by its own power, used for blowing up enemy ships; a similar explosive weapon discharged by aircraft.
—명 어뢰, 수뢰(水雷); 공뢰(空雷)

tor·pid [tɔ́:rpid] *adj.* **1.** (of animals) not moving or feeling; dormant. **2.** dull; inactive. ⌜ness.⌝
—형 1. 움직이지 않는; 동면한 2. 활발치 못한; 둔한

tor·por [tɔ́:rpər] *n.* Ⓤ torpid condition; dullness; numb-
—명 동면; 불활발; 무감각

tor·rent [tɔ́:r(ə)nt, tɑr- / tɔ́r-] *n.* ⓒ **1.** a violent, rapid stream. **2.** (*pl.*) a violent flow of rain, words, etc. ¶*a* ~ *of abuse*① / *torrents of rain*② / *in torrents*.
—명 1. 분류, 격류 2. 억수[같은 비]; [질문 따위의] 연발 ¶①욕설의 연발/②억수같이 내리는 비

tor·ren·tial [tɔ:rénʃ(ə)l, tɑr- / tɔr-] *adj.* of or like a torrent; violent. ⌜of the sun; extremely hot.⌝
—형 분류 같은; 맹렬한

tor·rid [tɔ́:rid, tɑ́r- / tɔ́r-] *adj.* dried by the scorching heat
—형 바싹 마른; 염열(炎熱)의

tor·si [tɔ́:rsi:] *n.* pl. of *torso*. ⌜of being twisted.⌝

tor·sion [tɔ́:rʃ(ə)n] *n.* Ⓤ the act of twisting; the state
—명 비틀림, 뒤틀림

tor·so [tɔ́:rsou] *n.* ⓒ (pl. **-sos** or **si**) **1.** the upper part of the human body without the head or the limbs. **2.** a headless and limbless statue of the human trunk.
—명 1. [인체의] 허리 2. 토로소[머리·손발이 없는 조상(彫像)]

tor·toise [tɔ́:rtəs] *n.* ⓒ (pl. **-tois·es** or **-toise**) a turtle, esp. one that lives on land.
—명 [특히 육지에 사는] 거북

tortoise shell [⌐ ⌐] *n.* the hard shell, with yellow and brown spots, of a turtle or tortoise, used for combs and ornaments. ⌜ing. **2.** crooked in mind.⌝
—명 귀갑(龜甲)

tor·tu·ous [tɔ́:rtʃuəs / tɔ́:tjuəs] *adj.* **1.** twisting; wind-
—형 1. 뒤틀린 2. 올바르지 못한

tor·ture [tɔ́:rtʃər] *n.* **1.** Ⓤ the act of causing severe pain to someone in order to make him do something, usu. confess. ¶*put someone to* [*the*] ~.① **2.** (*pl.*) extreme pain.
—*vt.* **1.** cause extreme pain or agony to (someone).
—명 1. 고문 ¶①…을 고문하다 2. 고통
—타 1. …을 고문하다 2. [남의 말]을

《~ someone *with* or *by*》 **2.** twist or distort (another's words, etc.) ▷**tor·tur·er** [-tʃərər] *n.*
곡해하다, 억지로 둘러대다

To·ry [tɔ́:ri] *n.* [C] (pl. **-ries**) **1.** (*Brit. History*) a member of the political party that supported the royal power. ⇒[N.B.] **2.** (*U.S. History*) an American who favored the British during the American Revolution. **3.** 《*t-*》 a conservative person.
—[名] 1.《英史》 토오리 당원 [N.B.] 현존하지는 않으나 보수당(the Conservative Party)원을 가리키는 일도 있음 2.《美史》 영국파 3. 보수주의자

To·ry·ism [tɔ́:riìz(ə)m] *n.* [U] the doctrines or beliefs of a Tory.
—[名] 보수(왕당)주의

: toss [tɔ:s / tɔs] *vt.* **1.** throw (something) up lightly into the air; pitch. 《~ something *to* (or *into, aside*)》 ¶*~ a coin to a beggar; ~ a beggar a coin* | *The horse tossed its rider.* **2.** raise or throw up suddenly. ¶*The girl tossed her head scornfully.*① **3.** cause (something or someone) to move up and down or from side to side continuously or fitfully. ¶*The boat was tossed by waves.* | *The trees tossed their branches in the wind.* **4.** throw (a coin, etc.) into the air to decide something by the way it falls. ¶*I'll ~ you for who goes first.* **5.** disturb; agitate. ¶*She was tossed by jealousy.* —*vi.* **1.** throw oneself from side to side. ¶*~ [about] in one's bed all night.*② **2.** move restlessly or violently. **3.** throw a coin.
—[他] 1. …을 가볍게(휙) 던지다;[테니스에서 공]을 위로 올리다 2. 홱 [머리 따위]를 쳐들다(세우다)(경멸·항의·무관심의 몸짓) ¶①그 소녀는 비웃듯이 머리를 홱 돌렸다 3. …을 흔들어 움직이다; [몸]을 돌아 눕다 4. [동전]을 던져 사물을 결정하다 5. [마음]을 동요시키다, 어지럽히다 —[自] 1. 돌아눕다 ¶②밤새도록 자리 속에서 엎치락뒤치락하다 2. 흔들리다 3. 동전 던지기를 하다

1) ***toss off,*** ⓐ do or make quickly and easily. ⓑ drink all at once.
2) ***toss up,*** throw a coin to decide between two alternatives.
[熟] 1)ⓐ손쉽게 해치우다 ⓑ[술]을 단숨에 들이켜다 2)동전을 던져 앞뒤 어느 쪽이 나오느냐에 따라 결정하다

—*n.* [C] **1.** the act of tossing; a throw. **2.** the act of tossing a coin to decide something. ¶*win* (*lose*) *the ~.* **3.** the distance to which something is or can be tossed.
—[名] 1. 던져 올리기 2. 돈 던지기 3. 물건이 던져지는 거리

take a toss, (*Brit.*) be thrown by a horse.
[熟] 《英》 말에서 떨어지다

toss-up [tɔ́:sʌ̀p / tɔ́s-] *n.* [C] **1.** the act of tossing a coin to decide something. **2.** (*colloq.*) an even chance.
—[名] 1. 돈 던지기 2.《口》 반반의 가망

tot [tɑt / tɔt] *n.* [C] **1.** a small child. **2.** (*Brit.*) a small glass of alcoholic liquor.
—[名] 1. 어린아이 2.《英》 [술의] 한 모금

: to·tal [tóutl] *adj.* **1.** whole; entire. ¶*the sum ~*① | *the ~ amount.*② **2.** complete. ¶*a ~ eclipse*③ | *a ~ loss.*④ —*n.* [C] the whole sum or amount. ¶*grand ~.*⑤ —*vt., vi.* (**-taled, -tal·ing** or esp. *Brit.* **-talled, -tal·ling**) **1.** add up. **2.** amount to 《~ *to* or *up to*》 ¶*My expenses totaled ¥50,000.* | *The visitors totaled 250.*⑥
—[形] 1. 전체의 ¶①총액/②총량 2. 완전한 ¶③개기식(皆旣蝕)/④전손(全損) —[名] 총계 ¶⑤총계
—[他][自] 1. …을 합계하다 2. 총계 …이 되다 ¶⑥방문객은 모두 250명이었다

to·tal·i·tar·i·an [toutæ̀litέəriən / ⌐--⌐--, --⌐⌐--] *adj.* of totalitarianism. —*n.* [C] a person who believes in and supports totalitarianism.
—[形] 전체주의의 —[名] 전체주의자

to·tal·i·tar·i·an·ism [toutæ̀litέəriənìz(ə)m / ⌐--⌐---, --⌐⌐----] *n.* [U] the doctrine that everything should be used just for the good of a country under a government controlled by one political party.
—[名] 전체주의

to·tal·i·ty [toutǽliti] *n.* (pl. **-ties**) **1.** [U] the state or quality of being total. **2.** [U][C] the total amount or number.
—[名] 1. 전체 2. 총계; 총액

to·tal·ize [tóut(ə)làiz] *vt.* add (accounts, etc.) together; make a total of (bills, etc.)
—[他] …을 합계하다

• to·tal·ly [tóut(ə)li] *adv.* completely; entirely. ¶*The man is ~ blind.*①
—[副] 완전히 ¶①그는 완전한 장님이다

to·tem [tóutəm] *n.* [C] **1.** an animal or object believed by primitive American Indians to be closely related by blood to their tribe and family. **2.** a carved or painted image of a totem.
—[名] 1. 토템(미개인, 특히 북미 토인 사이에서 세습적으로 씨족의 상징으로서 숭배하는 자연물 또는 짐승) 2. 토템상(像)

totem pole [⌐- ⌐] *n.* a post carved and painted with totems, erected in front of their houses by several tribes of American Indians. ⇒fig.
—[名] 토템 기둥, 장승

[totem pole]

tot·ter [tɑ́tər / tɔ́tə] *vi.* (of persons) stand unsteadily; walk with weak, unsteady steps; stagger; (of buildings, etc.) shake as if about to fall down.
—[自] 비틀거리다; 쓰러지려고 하다; 흔들흔들하다

tou·can [túːkæn, tuːkάːn / túːkən, -kæn, -kɑːn] *n.* ⓒ a noisy, bright-colored bird with a very large bill, found in tropical America. ⇒fig.

[toucan]

‡ touch [tʌtʃ] *vt.* **1.** put the hand or some other part of the body in contact with (something) to feel it; come into contact with and perceive (something). 《~ something or someone *to* (or *on, with*)》 ¶ ~ *someone on the head* / ~ *it with a stick* / *Don't* ~ *the wet paint.* **2.** be in or come into contact with (something). ¶ *The sun touched the horizon.* / *Your sleeve is touching the butter.* **3.** play on (a musical instrument); strike lightly or gently; tap. ¶ ~ *the keys of the piano* / ~ *a bell* / ~ *a horse with a whip.* **4.** attain; reach. ¶ ~ *the ceiling* / *The temperature touched 65 degrees.* **5.** 《used in *negative*》 compare with; equal. 《~ someone *in* or *for*》 ¶ *My skill at tennis doesn't* ~ *yours.* / *Nobody can* ~ *her in English conversation.* **6.** adjoin; border on (something). ¶ *The state touches the lake.* **7.** 《usu. used in *negative* or *interrogative*》 eat; taste. ¶ *He never touches alcohol.*① / *He did not* ~ *his lunch.* **8.** concern; relate to; mention, esp. in a casual way. ¶ ~ *various topics during the conversation* / *The problem touches you.*② **9.** injure, wound, or affect slightly. ¶ *The heavy rain touched the flowers.*③ / *The child was hardly touched by the fall.* / *Water won't* ~ *that stain.*④ **10.** move; affect emotionally; arouse an emotion of sympathy, gratitude, etc. in (someone); make (someone) angry or pain. ¶ *The scene touched him to the heart.* / *His story touched her to tears.* / *He is touched with joy.*

— *vi.* be in contact. ¶ *The two hands touched.*

1) **touch at,** (of a ship) call at (a harbor).
2) **touch down,** (of an airplane) land usu. briefly.
3) **touch off,** ⓐ set off; cause (something) to explode; ignite. ⓑ represent exactly.
4) **touch** (*someone*) **to the quick,** injure deeply the feelings of (someone).
5) **touch up,** modify; improve or finish (a painting, etc.) by making slight changes.
6) **touch [up]on,** ⓐ come near to (something). · ⓑ mention (a subject) briefly. ⓒ relate to (something).

— *n.* ⓒ **1.** Ⓤ the act of touching; the state or fact of being touched; ⓒ a contact; a gentle stroke, tap, etc. ¶ *give someone a* ~ / *I felt a* ~ *on my left shoulder.* **2.** the sense by which things are felt. ¶ *soft to the* ~⑤ / *have a keen* ~. **3.** a close relation of communication, agreement, sympathy, etc; harmony. **4.** a very small amount, degree, etc.; a trace. ¶ *a* ~ *of red* / *a* ~ *of winter in the air.* **5.** a slight attack of illness. ¶ *My son is in bed with a* ~ *of a cold.* **6.** a delicate stroke with a brush in painting; a slight change in or addition to a painting, story, or other work. ¶ *finishing touches.*⑥ **7.** (*Music*) the manner of playing. ¶ *The pianist has an excellent* ~.

1) *a near touch,* a narrow escape.
2) *get in touch* (=*communicate*) *with someone.*
3) *keep in touch* (=*remain in communication*) *with someone.*
4) *lose touch* (=*fail to maintain communication*) *with [someone.]*
5) *out of touch* (=*not in communication*) *with someone.*

touch-and-go [tʌ́tʃən(d)góu] *adj.* involving risk; extremely uncertain. ¶ *a* ~ *business.*①

— ⓝ [열대 남미산의] 큰부리새

— ⓥ 1. [손·손가락 따위를] …에 대다, 만지다; …을 건드리다 2. [물건이] …에 닿다, 접촉하다 3. [악기를] 연주하다; …을 가볍게 두드리다(밀다) 4. …에 달하다; 미치다 5. …에 필적하다 6. …에 인접하다, …와 경계를 접하다 7. [음식 따위에] 손대다, 먹어치우다 ¶ ① 그는 술을 입에 대지 않는다 8. …에 관계하다; 언급하다 ¶ ② 그 문제는 너에게 관계가 있다 9. …을 손상하다, 해치다; …에 작용하다, 영향하다 ¶ ③ 폭우로 꽃이 망가졌다 / ④ 물로는 그 얼룩이 빠지지 않을 것이다 10. …을 감동시키다; …에 동정(감사 따위)의 마음이 일게 하다; …을 성나게 하다

— ⓥ 닿다, 접촉하다, 만지다

쭉 1) [배가] …에 기항하다 2) [비행기가] 착륙하다 3) ⓐ …을 발사하다, 폭발시키다 ⓑ …을 정확히 나타내다 4) …을 성나게 하다 5) …을 수정하다, 마무리하다 6) ⓐ …에 접근하다 ⓑ [문제]에 대하여 간단히 언급하다 ⓒ …에 관계하다

— ⓝ 1. 만지기, 닿기, 접촉; 경타(輕打) 2. 촉감, 감촉 ¶ ⑤ 촉감이 부드럽다 3. [정신적인] 접촉, 교제, 연락; 조화 4. 소량, 기미 5. [가벼운] 병, 탈 6. [그림 따위의] 한 번 붓을 대기, 필치; 마무리; 솜씨 ¶ ⑥ [그림·소설 따위의] 마무리 7. 《樂》 연주 솜씨; 촉건법 (觸鍵法)

쭉 1) 구사일생 2) …와 접촉하다 3) …와 접촉(연락)을 갖다 4) …와의 접촉을 잃다 5) …와 접촉하지 않고

— ⓐ 일촉즉발의; 몹시 불안한 ¶ ① 위험한 일

touch·ing [tʌ́tʃiŋ] *adj.* arousing the emotions or feelings of sympathy. **—*prep.*** in regard to; concerning.
—[形] 감동시키는; 애처로운 —[前] …에 관하여

touch·stone [tʌ́tʃstòun] *n.* [C] **1.** a kind of black stone used to test the purity of gold or silver. **2.** a test for deciding the qualities or value of a thing; a standard.
—[名] 1. 시금석(試金石) 2. 사물의 진가(眞價)를 알아보는 방법; 표준

touch·y [tʌ́tʃi] *adj.* (**touch·i·er, touch·i·est**) easily offended; irritable; too sensitive. ▷**touch·i·ly** [-li] *adv.*
—[形] 성 잘 내는; 성급한; 과민한

* **tough** [tʌf] *adj.* **1.** hard to break, cut or bend; sticky. ¶~ *leather*① / ~ *clay.*② **2.** able to endure hardship or suffering; strong; stubborn. **3.** difficult; (*colloq.*) unpleasant. ¶*a* ~ *job.* **4.** (*colloq.*) violent.
—*n.* [C] (*U.S.*) a violent, brutal person; a ruffian.
—[形] 1. 굳은; 끈기있는 ¶①굳은 가죽/②끈기있는 점토 2. 끈질긴; 튼튼한; 완고한 3. 곤란한; 불쾌한 4.《口》 무법의 —[名] 건달, 깡패

tough·en [tʌ́fn] *vi., vt.* become or make tough.
—[自][他] 굳게 하다(되다)

tough·ness [tʌ́fnis] *n.* [U] the quality of being tough.
—[名] 튼튼함; 완고

* **tour** [tuər] *n.* [C] **1.** a long journey for sightseeing or inspection or on business. ¶*go on a* ~① / *a* ~ *of observation.*② **2.** a short journey; an excursion. ¶*an educational* ~③ / *He has gone on a walking* ~.④
—*vi.* go on a tour. 《~ *about* or *through* a place》 **—*vt.*** go on a tour through (a place). ¶~ *Canada.*
—[名] 1. 관광 여행 ¶①유람 여행을 떠나다/②시찰 여행 2. 짧은 여행; 소풍 ¶③수학여행/④그는 도보여행을 갔다
—[自] 유람 여행하다; 여행하다
—[他] …을 여행하다

* **tour·ist** [túərist] *n.* [C] a person who travels in many places just for pleasure. ¶*a* ~ *bureau*① / *a* ~ *party.*②
—[名] 관광객 ¶①관광 협회/②관광단

* **tour·na·ment** [túərnəmənt] *n.* [C] **1.** a series of contests to determine a championship. ¶*a tennis* ~. **2.** (in the Middle Ages) a contest between armed knights with blunt weapons and on horseback.
—[名] 1. 패자는 떨어져 나가는 시합 2. [중세의] 무장 마상(馬上)시합

tour·ney [túərni] *n.* [C] a tournament in the Middle Ages.
—[名] [중세의] 무장 마상시합

tou·sle [táuzl] *vt.* put (the hair) into disorder; make (the hair) untidy. **—*n.*** [U] an untidy mass of hair; [U][C] a disordered condition.
—[他] [머리]를 흐트러뜨리다; 헝클다 —[名] 헝클어진 머리; 난잡

tow[1] [tou] *vt.* **1.** pull or drag (a boat, etc.) by a rope or line. **2.** pull or drag (something) behind.
—*n.* 1. [U] the act of towing; the state of being towed. ¶*a boat in* ~. **2.** [C] something pulled by a rope or line. **3.** [C] the rope or line used in towing.
have (or ***take***) ***in tow,*** ⓐ pull (a boat) by a rope. ⓑ have (someone) under one's charge.
—[他] 1. [배]를 밧줄로 끌다 2. …을 끌고 가다
—[名] 1. 밧줄로 끌기; 밧줄로 끌려가기 2. 밧줄에 끌리는 것 3. 끄는 밧줄
[熟] ⓐ[배]를 밧줄로 끌다 ⓑ…을 보살피다

tow[2] [tou] *n.* [U] the short, rough, broken fibers of flax or hemp.
—[名] 삼부스러기; 거친 삼실

tow·age [tóuidʒ] *n.* [U] **1.** the act of towing; the state of being towed. **2.** the charge for towing.
—[名] 1. [배 따위를] 끌기, 견인 2. 배 끄는 요금

‡ **to·ward** [təwɔ́ːrd, tu-, tɔ́ːrd, twɔ́ːrd] *prep.* **1.** in the direction of. ¶*go* ~ *the beach.* **2.** facing. ¶*My house looks* ~ *the sea.* / *She wept with her back* ~ *me.* **3.** (of time) near; just before. ¶*He came back* ~ *midnight* (*morning*). **4.** as regards; concerning. ¶*What is your attitude* ~ *marriage?* **5.** for the purpose of. ¶*She is saving* ~ *her old age.* **6.** about; nearly as much (many) as. ¶*She was* ~ *thirty.*
—[前] 1. [운동이] …쪽으로, …을 향하여 2. [위치가] …쪽을 향하여 3. [시간]이 …가까이, …무렵 4. [관계가] …에 관하여는, …에 대하여 5. [목적이] …을 위하여 6. [수량이] …쯤, …정도

‡ **to·wards** [təwɔ́ːrdz, tuwɔ́ːrdz, tɔːrdz, twɔːrdz] *prep.* =toward.

tow·boat [tóubòut] *n.* [C] a boat for towing; a tugboat.
—[名] 예인선(曳引船)

‡ **tow·el** [táu(ə)l] *n.* [C] a piece of cloth or paper used for wiping and drying something wet. ¶*a bath* ~① / *wring a* ~.② **—*vt., vi.*** (**-eled, -el·ing** or *Brit.* **-elled, -el·ling**) wipe or dry with a towel.
—[名] 수건, 타월 ¶①목욕 타월/②수건을 짜다 —[他][自] …을 타월로 닦다(문지르다)

towel rack [⌐-⌐] *n.* a wooden frame to hang towels on.
—[名] 타월걸이

tow·el·ing, *Brit.* **-el·ling** [táuəliŋ] *n.* [U] material for making towels.
—[名] 타월감(천)

‡ **tow·er** [táuər] *n.* [C] **1.** a high structure standing alone or forming a part of another building. ¶*a bell* ~ / *the* (or *a*) ~ *of ivory.*① **2.** 《*the T* ~》 the Tower of London. **3.** a fortress; a protector.
a tower of strength, a reliable person.
—*vi.* rise to a great height like a tower.
tower above, be superior to; rise far above.
—[名] 1. 탑 ¶①상아탑 2. 런던탑 3. 요새; 옹호자
[熟] 의지가 되는 사람
—[自] 우뚝 솟다; 뛰어나다
[熟] …보다 월등히 뛰어나다

tow·ered [táuərd] *adj.* having a tower.
—[形] 탑이 있는

tow·er·ing [táuəriŋ] *adj.* **1.** rising very high; lofty. **2.** very great. **3.** very violent. ¶*in a ~ rage.*①
—[形] **1.** 높이 솟은 **2.** 큰, 높은 **3.** 격렬한 ¶①몹시 성이 나서

towing line [ˊ-ˋ] *n.* =towline.

towing path [ˊ-ˋ] *n.* =towpath.

tow·line [tóulàin] *n.* [C] a rope, chain, etc. used in towing.
—[名] 끄는 밧줄

⁑town [taun] *n.* [C] **1.** a group of houses and buildings larger than a village and smaller than a city. ¶[*one's*] *home* (or *native*) ~① **2.** 《*the ~*》 the people of a town. **3.** the business or shopping center. **4.** the city as opposed to the country. ¶*~ life.* **5.** 《without *article*》 (*Brit.*) London. ¶*come to ~.*②
—[名] **1.** 읍(邑), 도회 ¶①고향 **2.** 읍민, 시민 **3.** 도심; 상업지구 **4.** [교외에 대한] 도회 **5.** 런던 ¶②런던으로 나가다

town council [ˊ ˊ-] *n.* the governing body of a town.
—[名] 읍의회; 시의회

town councilor [ˊ ˊ--] *n.* a member of the town council.
—[名] 읍(시)의회 의원

town hall [ˊ ˊ] *n.* a building in a town which contains the public offices and often, a hall for public meetings.
—[名] 시청, 시 공회당; 시의회 의사당

town house [ˊ ˋ] *n.* a house in town owned by a person who has another house in the country.
—[名] 읍에 있는 저택

town·i·fied [táunifàid] *adj.* of a town; of town life. ↔countrified
—[形] 도회의; 도회풍의

towns·folk [táunzfòuk] *n. pl.* people living in a town.
—[名] 읍민, 시민

towns·man [táunzmən] *n.* [C] (pl. **-men** [-mən]) **1.** a person living in a town. **2.** a person living in his own town; people in the same town.
—[名] **1.** 읍민 **2.** 읍내의 사람

towns·peo·ple [táunzpì:pl] *n. pl.* =townsfolk.

tow·path [tóupæ̀θ / -pà:θ] *n.* [C] a path along a canal or river used for towing boats by men, horses, etc.
—[名] 배를 끄는 길

tox·ic [táksik / tɔ́k-] *adj.* poisonous; of a poison. ¶*~ symptoms*① / *~ smoke.*②
—[形] 독(毒)의 ¶①중독 증상/②독가스

tox·in [táksin / tɔ́k-] *n.* [C] any poison natually produced in a plant or animal.
—[名] 독소

⁑toy [tɔi] *n.* [C] **1.** a plaything for a child. ¶*a ~ dog.*① **2.** something of little value.
—[名] **1.** 장난감 ¶①강아지 **2.** 시시한 것

make a toy of (=***amuse oneself by***; ***play with***) something.
[熟] …을 가지고 장난하다

—*vi.* handle or treat something in a half-hearted way; play; trifle. 《*~ with* something》
—[自] 가지고 놀다; 장난하다

toy·shop [tɔ́iʃàp / -ʃɔ̀p] *n.* [C] a store where toys are sold.
—[名] 장난감 가게

⁑trace [treis] *n.* [C] **1.** 《often *pl.*》 a visible mark, sign, piece of evidence, etc., left by a person, thing or event. ¶*the traces of an ancient civilization*① / *Sorrow had left its traces on her face.*② **2.** a footprint or beaten path left by people, animals or vehicles. ¶*follow up a ~.*③ **3.** a very small amount or quantity. ¶*a ~ of fear.*④ **4.** a drawing or sketch of something.
—[名] **1.** 형적(形跡); 증거 ¶①고대 문명의 유적/②슬픔이 그녀의 얼굴에 자국을 남겼다 **2.** 자국; 발자국 ¶③자국을 남기다 **3.** 조금, 소량 ¶④약간의 공포의 빛 **4.** 선(線); 도형

—*vt.* **1.** follow a trail or footprint of (something). ¶*A policeman traced a thief.* **2.** find out; follow the course of (something) by going backward. ¶*We cannot ~ any letter of that date.*⑤ **3.** copy (a drawing, etc.) by following the lines. **—*vi.*** go back to [the past].
—[他] **1.** …의 자국을 내다 **2.** …을 발견하다; 더듬다 ¶①그 날짜의 편지는 찾을 수 없었다 **3.** …을 선으로 그리다 —[自] [옛날로] 거슬러 올라가다

trac·er [tréisər] *n.* [C] **1.** a person who traces or searches for something lost. **2.** an instrument for tracing drawings, designs, etc. **3.** (*U.S.*) an inquiry for a missing letter, package, etc. **4.** (*Military*) a bullet that is shot up in the air leaving behind a trail of smoke or fire.
—[名] **1.** 추적자; 분실물 수색계 **2.** 철필; [재봉용] 트레이서 **3.** [분실 우편물의] 수사 조회장(狀) **4.** 《軍》 예광탄; 발연탄(發煙彈)

trac·er·y [tréisəri] *n.* [U][C] (pl. **-er·ies**) an ornament or design based on lines, as in a Gothic window. ⇒fig.
—[名] [창 위의] 장식 무늬

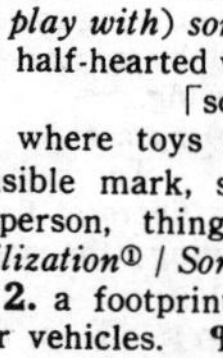
〔tracery〕

tra·che·a [tréikiə / trəkí(:)ə] *n.* [C] (pl. **-as** or **-ae**) an air tube at the back of the mouth, leading to the lungs.
—[名] 기관(氣管)

tra·che·ae [tréikì:i:] *n.* pl. of **trachea**.

tra·cho·ma [trəkóumə] *n.* [U] (*Medicine*) a disease of the inner eyelids.
—[名] 트라홈, 트라코마

trac·ing [tréisiŋ] *n.* [U] **1.** the act of a person who traces. **2.** a copy of
—[名] **1.** 투사(透寫); 복사 **2.** 투사도

a picture, map, design, etc. made by tracing the lines on thin, transparent paper. ¶ ~ *cloth*① / ~ *paper*.②

¶①투사포(布)/②투사지, 트레이싱 페이퍼

:track [træk] *n.* [C] **1.** a trace; a mark left by a foot, wheel, etc. ¶*follow up a* ~.① **2.** a path; a trodden path or trail taken by persons, animals or vehicles. ¶*the* ~ *of a bird*.② **3.** a course for races; (*U.S.*) running or hurdling events performed on a track. ¶*a* ~ *meet*.③ **4.** metal rails on which trains or streetcars run.

—[名] 1. 지나간 자국 ¶①자국을 따라가다 2. 통로; [밟아 다져진] 오솔길 ¶②새의 통로 3. 트랙; 《美》 트랙 경기 ¶③육상 경기회 4. 궤도

1) ***the beaten track,*** the ordinary routine of action.
2) ***cover one's track[s],*** keep one's movements or plans secret.
3) ***keep track of*** (*U.S.*) (=*follow the course of; keep in touch with*) *something.*
4) ***leave the track,*** (*U.S.*) (of a train, etc.) run off the rails.
5) ***lose track of*** (*U.S.*) (=*lose sight or knowledge of*) *something.*
6) ***make tracks,*** (*colloq.*) go very fast.
7) ***off the track,*** away from the subject, objective, etc.
8) ***on the track of*** (=*in search of*) *something.*

[熟] 1)세상의 상도(常道) 2)행동(계획)을 비밀로 하다 3)《美》에 따라가다; …을 놓치지 않다 4)《美》탈선하다 5)《美》…을 따라가다 놓치다; …의 소식이 끊기다 6)《口》급히 가다 7)탈선하여; 정도(正道)에서 벗어나 8)…을 추적하여

—*vt.* **1.** follow (someone or something) by means of footprints, marks, etc. left on the ground. **2.** draw or pull (a ship) from a shore.

—[他] 1. …을 추적하다 2. 배를 끌다

track·less [trǽklis] *adj.* **1.** without a track, path, etc. ¶*a* ~ *waste.* **2.** having no rails; not running on rails.

—[形] 1. 발자국이 없는; 인적미답의 2. 궤도가 없는

·tract¹ [trækt] *n.* [C] **1.** an expanse of land. ¶*a* ~ *of country*① / *an immense* ~ *of land*.② **2.** (*poetic*) a period of time. **3.** (***Anatomy***) a system of bodily organs serving a particular function.

—[名] 1. 광대한 지역 ¶①한 지방/②광대한 토지 2. 《詩》 기간 3. 《解》 관(管), 계(系), 도(道)

tract² [trækt] *n.* [C] a little pamphlet, esp. about religion.

—[名] [특히 종교문제의] 소책자

trac·ta·ble [trǽktəbl] *adj.* **1.** easily controlled or trained. ¶*a* ~ *child*.① **2.** easily made into various shapes.

—[形] 1. 다루기 쉬운 ¶①다루기 쉬운 아이 2. 세공(細工)하기 쉬운

trac·tion [trǽkʃ(ə)n] *n.* [U] **1.** the act of pulling or drawing along a surface, road, railroad, etc.; the state of being pulled. **2.** the power used for pulling. **3.** friction.

—[名] 1. 끌기; 끌리기 2. 견인력(牽引力) 3. 마찰, 수축(收縮)

·trac·tor [trǽktər] *n.* [C] a heavy vehicle for pulling wagons, plows, etc.

—[名] 견인차, 트랙터

:trade [treid] *n.* **1.** [U] the act of buying, selling or exchanging goods; commerce. ¶*foreign* ~① / *free* ~.② **2.** [C] an occupation by which a person earns his living, esp. skilled work. ¶*Jack of all trades*③ / *He is a barber by* ~.④ / (*proverb*) *Everyone to his* ~.⑤ **3.** [U] 《*collectively*》 all the people engaged in the same kind of work or business. ¶*the publishing* ~.⑥

—[名] 1. 상거래; 무역 ¶①외국 무역/②자유 무역 2. [특히 숙련을 요하는] 직업, 가업(家業) ¶③무엇이나 수선하는 사람; 무엇이나 파는 사람/④그의 직업은 이발사다/⑤《俚》장사에는 제각기 전문이 있는 법 3. 동업자 ¶⑥출판업자

—*vt.* buy and sell (goods).

—[他] …을 매매하다

1) ***trade in,*** give (one's used automobile, etc.) as part payment for something.
2) ***trade on*** (=*make use of*) *something.*

[熟] 1)중고품에 웃돈을 얹어주고 …을 사다 2)…을 이용하다

trade·mark [tréidmà:rk / -má:k] *n.* [C] a mark, picture, name, or design used by a manufacturer to distinguish his goods from the goods of others. ¶*a registered* ~.①

—[名] 상표 ¶①등록상표

trade name [⌐ ⌐] *n.* **1.** a name given by a manufacturer or dealer to articles that he sells. **2.** the business name of a company.

—[名] 1. 상품명 2. [상점의] 상호, 옥호

·trad·er [tréidər] *n.* [C] **1.** a person engaged in trade. **2.** a ship used in trade.

—[名] 1. 상인; 무역업자 2. 무역선, 상선

trades·man [tréidzmən] *n.* [C] (pl.**-men** [-mən]) **1.** a shopkeeper. **2.** a person skilled in a certain craft; a craftsman.

—[名] 1. 소매상인 2. 직공

trades·peo·ple [tréidzpì:pl] *n. pl.* storekeepers.

—[名] 상인; 소매인

trades union [⌐ ⌐-] *n.* (*Brit.*) trade union.

—[名] 노동조합

trade union [⌐ ⌐-] *n.* an association of workers in a particular trade for mutual aid and for the protection of their rights; a labor union.

—[名] 노동조합

trade unionism [⌐ ⌐--] *n.* the principles, system, or theory of trade unions.

—[名] 노동조합의 주의(조직·이론)

trade wind [⌐ ⌐] *n.* a wind which blows continuously towards the equator from the northeast on the north

—[名] 무역풍

tradition [1218] **training**

and from the southeast on the south.

tra‧di‧tion [trədíʃ(ə)n] *n.* ⓤⓒ the act of handing down beliefs, customs, tales, practices, etc. from generation to generation; things handed down in this way. —⑬ 구비(口碑); 전설; 관습

tra‧di‧tion‧al [trədíʃ(ə)n(ə)l] *adj.* of, based on, or handed down by tradition; customary. —⑬ 전설의; 전통적인

tra‧di‧tion‧ar‧y [trədíʃənèri / -ʃənəri] *adj.* =traditional.

: traf‧fic [trǽfik] *n.* ⓤ 1. trade; the act of buying and selling goods. 2. the movement of people, cars, ships, etc. from place to place. ¶*heávy ~*① / *a ~ cónstable*② / *~ vólume.*③ —*vi.* (**-ficked, -fick‧ing**) buy and sell goods; deal in goods. (*~ in* something *with*) —⑬ 1. 매매, 무역 2. [사람·수레의] 통행, 교통 ¶①격심한 교통량/②교통순경/③교통량 —⑪ 무역하다; 거래하다

traf‧ficked [trǽfikt] *v.* pt. and pp. of **traffic**.
traf‧fick‧ing [trǽfikiŋ] *v.* ppr. of **traffic**.

tra‧ge‧di‧an [trədʒí:diən] *n.* ⓒ 1. an actor in tragedy. 2. a writer of tragedies. —⑬ 1. 비극 배우 2. 비극 작자

‧trag‧e‧dy [trǽdʒidi] *n.* (pl. **-dies**) 1. ⓤ a drama which has an unhappy ending. ↔comedy 2. ⓒ a play of this kind of drama. 3. ⓤ the act of writing this kind of drama. 4. ⓒ a very sad or dreadful event in real life. —⑬ 1. [극의 종류로서의] 비극 2. [하나의] 비극 작품 3. 비극의 창작 4. 비극적 사건

‧trag‧ic [trǽdʒik] *adj.* of or like tragedy; very sad. —⑪ 비극의, 비극적인, 비참한
trag‧i‧cal [trǽdʒik(ə)l] *adj.* =tragic.
trag‧i‧cal‧ly [trǽdʒik(ə)li] *adv.* in a tragic manner. —⑪ 비극적으로; 비참하게

trag‧i‧com‧e‧dy [trædʒikámidi / trædʒikɔ́m-] *n.* ⓤⓒ (pl. **-dies**) a play which contains both tragic and comic elements; a real event or situation like this. —⑬ 비극적 희극[작품]

trag‧i‧com‧ic [trædʒikámik / trædʒikɔ́m-] *adj.* of tragicomedy. —⑪ 희비극 같은

: trail [treil] *n.* ⓒ 1. a mark, footprint, etc. left by a person or animal; a smell left by an animal on the ground. ¶*off the trails*① / *on the ~ of someone*② / *a ~ of blood*③. 2. a path or track made by treading through woods or wilderness. 3. a stream of dust, smoke, light, etc. that is made behind something that has passed. —*vt.* 1. pull (something) behind oneself along the ground, floor, etc. ¶*The woman trailed her dress through the mud.*④ 2. follow the track left by (something). ¶*The cat trailed the mouse.* 3. (*U.S.*) make (a path, track) by treading down grass, glants, etc. —⑬ 1. 지나간 자국; [짐승의] 냄새 자국 ¶①냄새 자국을 잃고; 길을 잃어/②...을 추적하여/③핏자국 2. [황야·산속의] 길 3. [구름·연기 따위의] 나부낌; [유성 따위의] 꼬리; 늘어진 머리 —⑪ 1. ...을 질질 끌다 ¶④그 부인은 드레스를 진탕에 질질 끌고 있었다 2. ...의 뒤를 쫓다 3. 밟아서 [길]을 내다

trail‧er [tréilər] *n.* ⓒ 1. a person or animal that follows another secretly. 2. a vine or plant creeping along the ground or over walls. 3. a wagon, cart, etc. pulled along behind by another automobile, truck, etc. —⑬ 1. 추적자 2. 덩굴 식물 3. [자동차 따위의] 트레일러

: train [trein] *vt.* 1. teach; bring up; instruct. (*~ someone to do*) ¶*~ a boy to obey* (or *to obedience*)① / *She is training her daughter as a doctor.* 2. make (someone) do often so as to be skillful; practise; drill. ¶*~ dancers* / *~ a boy to play the piano.*② 3. aim; direct. (*~ something on* or *upon*) ¶*~ a camera on the scene.* 4. cause (animals or plants) to grow in a certain way. ¶*~ vines around a post.* —*vi.* prepare for something by practice. (*~ for* or *on* something) —⑪ 1. ...을 교육하다, 훈련하다 ¶①소년에게 복종하도록 가르치다 2. ...을 길들이다; 가르치다; 단련하다 ¶②소년에게 피아노를 가르치다 3. ...을 겨누다, 조준하다 4. ...을 좋아하는 모양으로 가꾸다 —⑪ 훈련을 받다; 연습하다

—*n.* ⓒ 1. a line of railroad car. ¶*a passenger ~* / *go by ~* / *an express ~* / *a through ~*③ / *take the 8 : 30 (a.m.) ~ to the city.* 2. a group of followers; a procession. ¶*the princess and her ~* / *a funeral ~.* 3. a group of things happening one after another. ¶*a ~ of events* (thought)④ / *a long ~ of misfortunes.* 4. something that trails. ¶*the ~ of her gown* / *the ~ of a comet* / *the ~ of a peacock.* —⑬ 1. 열차 ¶③직행 열차 2. 수행원, 따라다니는 사람들 3. [사건의] 연속 ¶④계속 일어나는 사건(떠오르는 생각) 4. 옷자락; [길게 끌리는] 꼬리

‧train‧er [tréinər] *n.* ⓒ a person who trains people for sports contests, animals for races, etc. —⑬ 훈련시키는 사람; 조마사(調馬師)

train ferry [⌃ ⌄⌄] *n.* a ferryboat to carry a railway train. —⑬ 열차 연락선

: train‧ing [tréiniŋ] *n.* ⓤ 1. the act of instructing or exer- —⑬ 1. 훈련, 연습 ¶①연습을 시작하

cising. ¶*go into ~.*① **2.** good condition kept by such instruction or exercise. ¶*be in ~.*② **3.** the act of controlling plants to grow them in a desirable shape.
다 2. [연습에 있어서의] 컨디션 ¶②컨디션이 좋다 3. [심은 나무 따위의] 가꾸기

train·man [tréinmən] *n.* [C] (pl. **-men** [-mən]) (*U.S.*) a person employed to work on a train, esp. a brakeman.
—[名] 《美》 열차 승무원, 제동수(制動手)

trait [treit / trei, treit] *n.* [C] a characteristic. ¶*English traits*① / *a ~ of humor.*②
—[名] 특성, 특색 ¶①영국의 국민성/②유우머의 맛

* **trai·tor** [tréitər] *n.* [C] a person who betrays his country, friends, etc. 《~ *to*》
—[名] 반역자

trai·tor·ous [tréitərəs] *adj.* of a traitor.
—[形] 반역의

trai·tor·ous·ly [tréitərəsli] *adv.* in a traitorous way.
—[副] 반역하여

trai·tress [tréitris] *n.* [C] a woman traitor.
—[名] 여성의 반역자

tra·jec·to·ry [trədʒéktɔ̀:ri / trǽdʒiktəri] *n.* [C] (pl. **-ries**) the curved path of something shot through space, such as a rocket or comet.
—[名] [방사체(放射體)의] 탄도

* **tram** [træm] *n.* [C] **1.** (*Brit.*) a tramcar; a streetcar. ¶*go by ~.*① **2.** a tramline. —*vt., vi.* (**trammed, tram·ming**) travel or carry by tram.
—[名] 1. 《英》 시가 전차 ¶①전차로 가다 2. 전차 선로 —[他][自] 전차로 가다; …을 전차로 나르다

tram·car [trǽmkà:r] *n.* [C] (*Brit.*) a streetcar.
—[名] 시가 전차

tram·line [trǽmlàin] *n.* [C] (*Brit.*) a streetcar line.
—[名] 전차 선로

tram·mel [trǽm(ə)l] *n.* [C] **1.** 《*pl.*》 anything that checks and stops free action, movement, etc. ¶*the trammels of etiquette.*① **2.** a net for catching fish or birds. **3.** a hook for holding pots, kettles, etc. over a fire.
—[名] 1. 구속; 방해 ¶①귀찮은 예법 2. [물고기·새를 잡는] 그물 3. 자재(自在) 갈고리

—*vt.* (**-meled, -mel·ing** or *Brit.* **-melled, mel·ling**) prevent the free movement of (someone).
—[他] …을 방해하다

* **tramp** [træmp] *vt., vi.* **1.** walk heavily. **2.** travel about on foot; go on foot. ¶*~ it*① / *We heard soldiers tramping by.* —*n.* [C] **1.** the act of tramping. **2.** the sound of heavy steps. **3.** a person who travels about on foot; a wanderer. ¶*look like a ~*② / *on* [*the*] *~.*③ **4.** a freight ship that runs irregularly between ports to pick up cargo. ▷**tramp·er** [-ər] *n.*
—[他][自] 1. [힘차게] 쿵쿵 걷다 2. 도보 여행을 하다; 걸어가다 ¶①터벅터벅 걷다 —[名] 1. 쿵쿵 걷기 2. 쿵쿵 걷는 소리 3. 도보 여행자; 부랑자 ¶②지저분한 차림을 하고 있다/③방랑하여 4. 부정기 화물선

* **tram·ple** [trǽmpl] *vi.* walk heavily and noisily. —*vt.* press (something) down heavily and roughly with the feet.
trample on, treat cruelly.
—[自] 쿵쿵 걷다; 밟다 —[他] 짓밟다
[熟] 심하게 다루다

trance [træns / trɑ:ns] *n.* [C] **1.** an unconscious state like sleep; a deep sleep produced by illness. **2.** an dreamy state. ▷**trance·like** [-làik] *adj.*
—[名] 1. 인사불성; 혼수상태 2. 황홀, 무아경

* **tran·quil** [trǽŋkwil] *adj.* (**-quil·er, -quil·est** or *Brit.* **-quil·ler, -quil·lest**) calm; peaceful; quiet. ¶*live a ~ life.*①
—[形] 잔잔한, 차분한; 조용한 ¶①평안하게 살다

tran·quil·li·ty, -quil·i- [træŋkwíliti] *n.* [U] the state of being tranquil; calmness.
—[名] 평온, 잔잔함, 침착

tran·quil·lize, -quil·ize [trǽŋkwilàiz] *vt., vi.* make (something) or become calm and peaceful.
—[他][自] …을 조용하게 하다(되다), 마음을 가라앉히다, 침착해지다

tran·quil·liz·er, -quil·ize- [trǽŋkwilàizər] *n.* [C] **1.** a person or thing that tranquilizes. **2.** a medicine that controls a person's anxiety, fear, etc.
—[名] 1. 가라앉히는 사람(것) 2. 진정제

trans- [trænz-, træns- / trɑ:nz-, trɑ:ns-] *pref.* **1.** across: *transcontinental* (=across the continent). **2.** on the other side of: *transatlantic.* (=lying on the other side of the Atlantic). **3.** into a different state, quality, etc.: *transform* (=change into something else).
—《接頭》 1. 가로질러 2. 다른 쪽에 3. 다른 상태(장소)로

trans·act [trænzǽkt, træns- / trɑ:ns-] *vt.* conduct; manage; perform (business). ¶*He transacts business with several stores in Seoul.*① —*vi.* do business 《~ *with* something》
—[他] …을 집행하다; [사무 따위]를 처리하다 ¶①그는 서울의 여러 가게와 거래하고 있다 —[自] 거래하다

trans·ac·tion [trænzǽkʃ(ə)n, træns- / trɑ:n-] *n.* **1.** [U] the act of transacting; the state of being transacted. **2.** [C] something transacted; a business deal. **3.** 《*pl.*》 the published records of what was done at the meetings of a society, a club, etc.
—[名] 1. [사무의] 처리 2. 상거래; 매매 3. 의사록; 보고서

trans·al·pine [trænsǽlpin / trænzǽlpain] *adj.* beyond the Alps as seen from Italy; passing through the Alps.
—[名] 알프스 저편의; 알프스 횡단의

tran·scend [trænsénd] *vt.* go or rise beyond the limits
—[他] [한계·범위]를 초월하다; 능가

T

of; be superior to (something). ¶~ *words.*① — 하다 ¶①말로 표현할 수 없다

tran·scend·ence [trænséndəns] *n.* [U] the state or quality of being transcendent. —[名] 초월; 탁월

tran·scend·en·cy [trænséndənsi] *n.* =transcendence.

tran·scend·ent [trænséndənt] *adj.* much more excellent than others in quality or extent. —*n.* [C] a person or thing that is transcendent. ▷**tran·scend·ent·ly** [-li] *adv.* —[形] 탁월한 —[名] 탁월한 사람(것)

tran·scen·den·tal [trӕnsendéntl] *adj.* **1.** =transcendent. **2.** beyond human knowledge, experience, or thought. **3.** supernatural. —[形] 2. [경험·지식을] 초월한 3. 초자연의

tran·scribe [trænskráib] *vt.* **1.** copy (something) by writing or typewriting. **2.** arrange (music) for an instrument, voice, etc. **3.** make a recording of (something) for broadcasting. ▷**tran·scrib·er** [-ər] *n.* —[他] 1. …을 베껴 쓰다 2. …을 편곡하다 3. …을 녹음하다

tran·script [trǽnskript] *n.* [C] a written, printed, or typewritten copy; a reproduction of another document. —[名] 사본(寫本); 등본

tran·scrip·tion [trænskrípʃ(ə)n] *n.* **1.** [U] the act of transcribing. **2.** [C] a copy. **3.** [C][U] the act of recording or broadcasting a phonograph record, a play, etc. —[名] 1. 전사(轉寫) 2. 사본 3. [라디오의] 녹음[방송]

:trans·fer [trænsfə́:r →*n.*] *v.* (**-ferred, -fer·ring**) *vt.* **1.** carry or remove (something) from one place or person to another. **2.** give over the possession of (something). ⦅~ something *to*⦆. **3.** copy or imprint (a drawing, design, etc.) on one surface from another. —*vi.* **1.** change from one train, bus, etc. to another. **2.** change from one place or position to another. —[他] 1. …을 움직이다(옮기다) 2. [재산 따위]를 양도하다 3. [그림 따위]를 전사하다 —[自] 1. 바꿔 타다 2. 옮다; 전임(轉任)하다

—*n.* [trǽnsfə(:)r] **1.** [U][C] the act of transferring; the state of being transferred. **2.** [C] (*U.S.*) a place for changing trains, buses, etc. **3.** (*U.S.*) a ticket allowing a person to change a train, bus, etc. **4.** [U] the act of giving over a right or possession from one person to another. **5.** [C] a picture, design, pattern, etc. that is imprinted from a surface to another. —[名] 1. 이전, 이동 2. ⦅美⦆ 바꿔타는 장소 3. ⦅美⦆ 바꿔타는 차표 4. [재산·권리의] 양도 5. 옮겨 그린 그림(무늬)

trans·fer·a·ble [trænsfə́:rəbl] *adj.* that can be transferred. —[形] 옮길 수 있는; 전사(양도)할 수 있는

trans·fer·ence [trænsfə́:rəns / trǽnsf(ə)r(ə)ns] *n.* [U] the act of transferring; the state of being transferred. —[名] 이전; 양도

trans·fig·u·ra·tion [trӕnsfigjəréiʃ(ə)n / -gju-] *n.* **1.** [U][C] the act of transfiguring; the state of being transfigured. **2.** ⦅*the T-*⦆ the supernatural change in appearance of Christ recorded in the New Testament. —[名] 1. 변모(變貌) 2. [그리스도의] 변모

trans·fig·ure [trænsfígjər / -fígə] *vt.* **1.** change (something) in appearance. **2.** make (something) bright and beautiful. ¶*a face transfigured with happiness.* —[他] 1. …의 모습을 바꾸다 2. [얼굴 따위]를 [기쁨으로] 빛나게 하다

trans·fix [trænsfíks] *vt.* **1.** make a hole through (something) with a sharp-pointed tool. ⦅~ something *with*⦆ ¶~ *a bird with an arrow.*① **2.** make (someone) motionless with surprise, terror, etc. —[他] 1. …을 찌르다 ¶①새를 화살로 쏘아 꿎다 2. …을 오금을 못쓰게 하다

·trans·form [trænsfɔ́:rm] *vt.* **1.** change (something or someone) in form or appearance. ¶*A caterpillar is transformed into a butterfly.*① **2.** change (something or someone) in nature; change (something) from one form of energy to another. ¶*Heat transforms ice into water.* **3.** change (someone) in character or personality. ¶*He was transformed into another man.*② —[他] 1. …의 외양을 현저하게 바꾸다 ¶①모충(毛虫)은 나비가 된다 2. …의 성질·기능을 바꾸다; …의 에너지를 변환(變換)하다 3. …을 딴 사람으로 만들다 ¶②그는 딴 사람이 되었다

trans·for·ma·tion [trӕnsfərméiʃ(ə)n] *n.* [U][C] the act of transforming; the state of being transformed. —[名] 변형; 변질

trans·form·er [trænsfɔ́:rmər] *n.* [C] **1.** a person or thing that transforms something. **2.** a device for changing the current of electrical voltage. —[名] 1. 변화시키는 사람(것) 2. 변압기

trans·fuse [trænsfjú:z] *vt.* **1.** transfer (water, etc.) from one glass into another. **2.** transfer (blood) from one person into another. —[他] 1. [액체]를 부어 옮기다 2. …을 수혈(輸血)하다

trans·fu·sion [trænsfjú:ʒ(ə)n] *n.* [U][C] the act of transfusing. —[名] 부어 넣기; 수혈

trans·gress [trænsgrés, trænz-] *vt., vi.* **1.** break a law —[他][自] 1. [법규 따위를] 어기다; [도

or rule; break moral or religious principles. **2.** go without control; go beyond (any limit).
덕적인 죄를] 범하다 2. [한계를] 넘다

trans·gres·sion [trænsgréʃ(ə)n, trænz-] *n.* [U] [C] the act of transgressing.
—[名] 위반; [종교·도덕상의] 죄

trans·gres·sor [trænsgrésər, trænz-] *n.* [C] a person who transgresses; a sinner.
—[名] 위반자; [종교·도덕상의] 죄인

tran·sient [trǽnʃ(ə)nt / -ziənt] *adj.* not lasting; temporary. ¶*the ~ affairs of this life.*① —*n.* [C] (*U.S.*) a visitor who stays for a short time.
—[形] 일시적인; 짧은 ¶①덧없는 인생 —[名] 《美》 잠시 머무르는 손님

tran·sient·ly [trǽnʃ(ə)ntli / trǽnziənt-] *adv.* for a moment; for a short time; briefly.
—[副] 일시적으로; 덧없이

tran·sis·tor [trænzístər] *n.* [C] **1.** a small electronic device for controlling the current, used in portable radios, etc. **2.** (*colloq.*) a radio with transistors in it.
—[名] 1. 트랜지스터[게르마늄을 이용한 증폭(增幅) 장치] 2. 《口》 트랜지스터 라디오

trans·it [trǽnsit, trǽnz-] *n.* [U] **1.** the act of passing or carrying across or through; the state of being passed or carried across or through. ¶*allow two days for the ~ of the lake*① / *~ duty*② / *overland ~.*③ **2.** =a transit compass.
—[名] 1. 통과; 수송 ¶①호수를 통과하는 데 이틀이 걸리다/②통행세/③육상 수송로

transit compass [⌐– ⌐–] *n.* an instrument with a telescope for measuring horizontal angles.
—[名] [토지 측량용] 전경의(轉鏡儀)

tran·si·tion [trænzíʃ(ə)n / trænsíʒ(ə)n] *n.* [U] [C] the change or movement from one place, period, state, etc., to another. ¶*the ~ from boyhood to manhood*① / *a ~ period.*②
—[名] 변이(變移), 변천; 과도기 ¶①어린이에서 어른으로 되기/②과도기

tran·si·tion·al [trænzíʃən(ə)l / trænsíʒən-] *adj.* of transition.
—[形] 과도기의

* **tran·si·tive** [trǽnsitiv] *adj.* (*Grammar*) taking a direct object. ¶*a ~ verb.* —*n.* [C] a transitive verb.
—[形] 타동사의 —[名] 타동사

tran·si·to·ry [trǽnsitɔ̀:ri / -t(ə)ri] *adj.* passing or changing quickly; lasting only a short time.
—[形] 일시적인; 덧없는

* **trans·late** [trænsléit, trænz-] *vt.* **1.** change (a language) into another language. ¶*~ English into Japanese*① / *~ word for word.*② **2.** change the state, position, or form of (something). ¶*~ promises (emotion) into action*③ **3.** explain the meaning of (something); interpret. —*vi.* **1.** put something written or spoken from one language into another. **2.** be able to be translated. ¶*This novel translates well.*④ ▷**trans·lat·a·ble** [-əbl] *adj.*
—[他] 1. …을 번역하다 ¶①영어를 한국어로 번역하다/②축어역(逐語譯)을 하다 2. …을 변형하다 ¶③약속을 행동으로 옮기다(감동을 행동으로 나타내다) 3. …을 해석(설명)하다 —[自] 1. 번역하다 2. 번역할 수 있다 ¶④이 소설은 번역이 잘 된다

* **trans·la·tion** [trænsléiʃ(ə)n, trænz-] *n.* **1.** [U] the act of translating; the state of being translated. ¶*literal ~.*① **2.** [C] something translated, esp. of a literary work.
—[名] 1. 번역; 변형 ¶①직역(直譯) 2. 번역물

trans·la·tor [trænsléitər, trænz-] *n.* [C] a person who translates books, speeches, etc.
—[名] 번역자; 통역

trans·lit·er·ate [trænslítərèit / trænz-] *vt.* change (words, letters, etc.) into symbols of another alphabet or language that represent the same sounds.
—[他] …을 음역(音譯)하다; [다른 나라의 해당 문자]로 고쳐 쓰다

trans·lu·cence [trænslú:səns, trænz-] *n.* [U] the state or quality of being translucent.
—[名] 반투명

trans·lu·cent [trænslú:snt / trænz-] *adj.* letting the light pass through, but not transparent.
—[形] 반투명의

trans·mi·gra·tion [trænsmaigréiʃ(ə)n / trænz-] *n.* [U] **1.** the act of moving from one place or country to another. **2.** the passage of a soul at death into a new body or a new life.
—[名] 1. 이주 2. [힌두교 따위의] 전생(轉生), 윤회(輪廻)

trans·mis·sion [trænsmíʃ(ə)n / trænz-] *n.* [U] **1.** the act of transmitting; the state of being transmitted. **2.** the broadcasting of radio waves from a transmitting station to a receiving station. **3.** [C] the part of an automobile which transmits power from the engine to the driving wheels.
—[名] 1. 전달; 양도 2. 송신 3. [자동차의] 전동(傳動) 장치

trans·mit [trænsmít, trænz-] *vt.* (**-mit·ted, -mit·ting**) **1.** send ¶*~ the parcel by train.*① **2.** hand down (something) from parents to children. ¶*~ the title from father to son.*② **3.** spread (disease) to others. **4.** pass on (news, information, etc.). **5.** cause or allow (light,
—[他] 1. …을 보내다 ¶①기차로 소하물을 보내다 2. [자손]에게 전하다 ¶②아버지로부터 아들에게 소유권을 전하다 3. [질병 따위]를 옮기다, 전염시키다 4. …을 전하다 5. [열·전기 따

heat, electricity, etc.) to pass through. **6.** send out (signals, a voice, etc.) by radio. ¶~ *news by wire.*

위]를 전도(傳導)하다, 통하다 6.[전파·신호 따위]를 보내다

trans·mit·ter [trænsmítər, trænz-] *n.* [C] **1.** a person or thing that transmits. **2.** a device for sending out signals, messages, a voice, etc., such as the mouthpiece of a telephone or a radio set.

—[名] 1.회송자(回送者); 전달자; 전도물 2.송신기

trans·mu·ta·tion [trӕnsmjuːtéiʃ(ə)n, trӕnz-] *n.* [U] the act of transmuting; the state of being transmuted.

—[名] 변형; 변질

trans·mute [trænsmjúːt, trænz-] *vt.* change (something) into another form, nature or substance; transform.

—[他] …을 변화시키다; 변형(변질)시키다

trans·o·ce·an·ic [trӕnsouʃiǽnik, trӕnz-] *adj.* **1.** crossing the ocean. **2.** located on the other side of the ocean.

—[形] 1.대양 횡단의 2.대양 건너편의

tran·som [trǽnsəm] *n.* [C] **1.** a small hinged window above a door or other window; a transom window. **2.** a horizontal crossbar across the top of a window or door.

—[名] 1.[문짝 위의] 채광창(採光窓) 2.문틀(문짝과 그 위의 채광창 사이를 막은 가로장)

trans·pa·cif·ic [trӕnspəsífik] *adj.* **1.** crossing the Pacific. **2.** located on the other side of the Pacific.

—[形] 1.태평양 횡단의 2.태평양 저편의

trans·par·en·cy [trænspέərənsi] *n.* **1.** [U] the state or quality of being transparent. **2.** [C] something transparent; a picture, design, etc. on glass made visible when light shines through.

—[名] 1.투명[도] 2.투명한 것; 투명화(畫)

* **trans·par·ent** [trænspέərənt] *adj.* **1.** so clear or thin that objects on the other side can be seen. ¶~ *colors.*① **2.** frank. **3.** easy to recognize or find out.

—[形] 1.투명한; 비치는 ¶①투명 그림물감 2.솔직한 3.명백한

trans·par·ent·ly [trænspέərəntli] *adv.* in a transparent manner.

—[副] 투명하게; 명백하게

tran·spi·ra·tion [trӕnspiréiʃ(ə)n] *n.* [U] the act or process of transpiring.

—[名] 증발

tran·spire [trænspáiər] *vi.* **1.** send out vapor, moisture, etc. through the surface or the pores of the skin, etc. **2.** pass through the surface, pores, etc. **3.** become known. **4.** (*colloq.*) happen. —*vt.* send out (vapor, moisture, etc.) through the surface.

—[自] 1.수증기(냄새)를 발산하다 2.발산하다, 증발하다 3.[비밀 따위가] 누설되다 4.《口》 일어나다 —[他] [수증기·냄새 따위]를 발산(배출)하다

T

trans·plant [trænsplǽnt / -pláːnt] *vt.* **1.** take (a plant) from one place and plant it in another place. **2.** move (people) from one place to another. ¶~ *to another country.* **3.** (*Medicine*) transfer (an organ or tissue) from one part of the body to another or from one body to another.

—[他] 1.…을 이식(移植)하다 2.…을 이주시키다 3.《醫》 [기관(器官)조직]을 이식하다, 식피(植皮)하다

trans·plan·ta·tion [trӕnsplæntéiʃ(ə)n / -plɑːn-] *n.* [U][C] **1.** the act of transplanting; the state of being transplanted. **2.** a transplanted plant, person, etc.

—[名] 1.이식 2.이식한 식물; 이민

‡ **trans·port** *vt.* [trænspɔ́ːrt →*n.*] **1.** carry or move (something) from one place to another. **2.** send (a criminal) away from a country; exile. **3.** 《usu. in *passive*》 carry away (someone) by strong emotion or feeling. —*n.* [trǽnspɔːrt] **1.** [U] the act of transporting. **2.** [C] a ship or plane for carrying troops, passengers, military stores, etc. **3.** [C] an exiled criminal. **4.** [U] a strong feeling or emotion. ¶*He cried out in a* ~ *of rage.*① ▷**trans·port·er** [-ər] *n.*

—[他] 1.…을 수송하다 2.[죄인]을 해외로 추방하다 3.…을 열중케 하다 —[名] 1.수송 2.수송선 3.유형수(流刑囚) 4.열중, 격정 ¶①그는 미칠 듯이 성이 나서 외쳤다

* **trans·por·ta·tion** [trӕnspərtéiʃ(ə)n / -pɔː-] *n.* [U] **1.** the act of transporting; the state of being transported. **2.** (*Brit.*) the act of sending away a criminal. **3.** (*U. S.*) means or cost of transporting. **4.** [C] (*U. S.*) tickets for travel or transport.

—[名] 1.수송 2.《英》 유형 3.《美》 수송기관; 수송료 4.《美》 차표, 비행기표

trans·pose [trænspóuz] *vt.* **1.** change the place or order of (something). **2.** (*Mathematics*) bring (a term) from one side of an equation to the other. **3.** (*Music*) perform or write (a musical composion) in a different key.

—[他] 1.[…의 위치·순서]를 바꿔 놓다 2.《數》 …을 이항(移項)하다 3.《樂》 이조(移調)하다

trans·po·si·tion [trӕnspəzíʃ(ə)n] *n.* [U][C] the act of transposing; the state of being transposed.

—[名] [위치 따위의] 전환, 전위(轉位)

trans·ship [trænsʃíp] *vt.* move (passengers, things, etc.) from one ship, train, etc. to another.

—[他] [승객·화물]을 다른 배·열차 따위로 옮기다

trans·ship·ment [trænsʃípmənt] *n.* [U] the act of transshipping.
—[名] 옮겨 태우기, 옮겨 싣기

trans·verse [trænsvə́:rs / trǽnzvə:s] *adj.* placed across or in a cross direction; crosswise. ¶*a ~ section.*①
—[形] 가로의; 횡단한 ¶①횡단면

⁑**trap**[1] [træp] *n.* [C] **1.** an instrument for catching animals ⇒fig.; a snare; a trick for deceiving a person. ¶*lay* (or *set*) *a ~ for a fox*① / *walk* (or *fall*) *into a ~.*② **2.** a machine to throw clay disks into the air as rifle targets. **3.** an S- or U- shaped pipe for preventing the escape of gas or bad smells. ⇒fig.
—[名] 1. 올가미, 덫; 계략; 책략 ¶①여우를 잡으려고 덫을 놓다/②덫에 걸리다 2. [클레이 사격용의] 표적 발사 장치 3. 방취용(防臭用) U자관

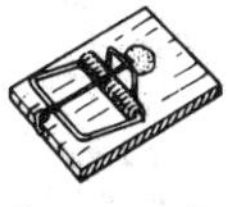
〔mouse trap〕

—*v.* (**trapped, trap·ping**) *vt.* **1.** catch (an animal) in a trap; set with traps ¶*~ a rabbit* / *~ the wood.* **2.** cheat; deceive. ¶*~ someone into a confession.*③ —*vi.* set traps. ⟪*~ for* animals⟫ ¶*~ for rabbits.*
—[他] 1. …을 덫으로 잡다; …에 덫을 놓다 2. …을 계략에 빠뜨리다 ¶③남을 계략에 빠뜨려 자백시키다 —[自] 덫을 놓다

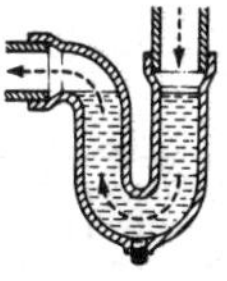
〔trap 3.〕

trap[2] [træp] *n.* [C] ⟪usu. *pl.*⟫ (*colloq.*) personal belongings; baggage.
—[名] ⟪口⟫ 휴대품, 소지품

trap door [⌐ ⌐] *n.* a hinged or sliding door in a floor, roof, etc.
—[名] 치켜올리는 문, 뚜껑문, 들창

tra·peze [trəpí:z] *n.* [C] a swinging horizontal bar hung by two ropes, used in gymnastics, circus performances, etc.
—[名] 그네

trap·per [trǽpər] *n.* [C] a person who traps animals, esp. for their furs.
—[名] 덫으로 새·짐승을 잡는 사람

trap·pings [trǽpiŋz] *n. pl.* **1.** ornamental harness or covering for a horse. **2.** ceremonial dress of an ornamental character.
—[名] 1. [의식용] 마구(馬具), 말 장식 2. 예복

trash [træʃ] *n.* **1.** [U] broken or torn parts. **2.** [U] worthless things; rubbish. **3.** [U] worthless or foolish talk, ideas, or writing. **4.** [U] poor literature, art, or music. **5.** ⟪*collectively*⟫ worthless people.
—[名] 1. 꺾인(찢어진) 부스러기 2. 쓰레기 3. 시시한 이야기(생각) 4. [문학·미술·음악 따위의] 태작(駄作) 5. 건달

trash·y [trǽʃi] *adj.* (**trash·i·er, trash·i·est**) of or like trash; having no value; useless.
—[形] 쓰레기의; 시시한, 쓸모없는

trav·ail [trǽveil] *n.* [U] **1.** the pains endured in childbirth. **2.** severe agony. —*vi.* **1.** suffer the pains of childbirth. **2.** work hard; toil.
—[名] 1. 진통 2. 노고, 수고 —[自] 1. 진통이 일어나다 2. 애쓰다

⁑**trav·el** [trǽvl] *v.* (**-eled, -el·ing** or *Brit.* **-elled, -el·ling**) *vi.* **1.** go from one place to another over a long distance; make a trip. ¶*~ abroad*① / *~ round the world* / *~ second-class to London by air*② / *~* [*for*] *six months* / *~ for a company* / *~ in jewelry.*③ **2.** move or pass from one point to another. ⟪*~ over* something⟫ ¶*Her mind traveled over her past happy days.* / *His eyes traveled over the scene.* **3.** move; run; walk. ¶*The moon travels round the earth.* —*vt.* make a journey through (a place); pass across (a place). ¶*~ England from end to end.*
—[自] 1. 여행하다 ¶①해외 여행하다/②런던까지 비행기의 2등으로 가다/③보석 행상을 하다 2. 차례차례 생각해 내다; 차례로 훑어보다 3. 이동하다; 달리다; 가다 —[他] …을 여행하다

—*n.* **1.** [U] the act of traveling; ⟪*pl.*⟫ journeys abroad. **2.** ⟪usu. *pl.*⟫ a book about travels and experiences. ¶"*Gulliver's Travels*" / *I am fond of reading travels.*
—[名] 1. 여행[하기]; [해외] 여행 2. 여행기, 기행(紀行)

trav·eled, *Brit.* **-elled** [trǽvld] *adj.* **1.** having experienced many journeys; having visited many lands. **2.** (of roads, etc.) used frequently by travelers.
—[形] 1. 널리 여행한; 각지를 돌아다니고 있는 2. [길 따위가] 길손(왕래)이 많은

⁑**trav·el·er,** *Brit.* **-el·ler** [trǽvlər] *n.* [C] **1.** a person who travels. **2.** a traveling salesman; a commercial traveler.
—[名] 1. 여행자, 길손 2. 출장 판매원; 외무원

trav·e·log, *Brit.* **-logue** [trǽvəlɔ̀:g, -lɑ̀g / -lɔ̀g] *n.* [C] a lecture or talk on travel with the aid of pictures, a motion picture, etc.
—[名] [슬라이드·영화 따위를 사용해서 하는] 여행담

⁎**trav·erse** [trǽvə(:)rs] *vt.* **1.** pass across, over, on, or through (a place); travel across. ¶*The ship traversed the Pacific Ocean in nine days.* **2.** extend across or over (a place). ¶*A bridge traverses the river.*① **3.**
—[他] 1. …을 가로지르다; 횡단하다 2. …의 위로 뻗다; 걸리다 ¶①강에 다리가 놓여 있다 3. …을 전반적으로(상세히) 논하다 4. …에 반대하다 —[自]

T

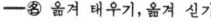

discuss thoroughly. **4.** oppose. ¶~ *one's opinion.* —*vi.* pass along or go across something. —*n.* [C] **1.** the act of crossing. **2.** anything that lies between two things; an obstacle; opposition.
가로질러 가다 —[名] 1. 횡단 2. 개재물; 방해; 반대

trav·es·ty [trǽvisti] *n.* [C] (pl. **-ties**) any treatment that makes a serious work seem ridiculous; a ridiculous imitation or translation of a serious work. —*vt.* (**-tied**) make (a serious work) ridiculous.
—[名] [진지한 작품을] 우스꽝스럽게 고치기; 우습게 고친 작품, 희화(戲畫) —[他] [진지한 작품]을 우스꽝스럽게 고치다

trawl [trɔːl] *n.* [C] **1.** a long line with buoys and short lines with hooks attached at intervals. **2.** a strong bag-like fishing net dragged behind a boat along the bottom of the sea. —*vt., vi.* fish or catch (fish) with a trawl.
—[名] 1. 트로올 그물 2. 저인망(底引網) —[他][自] 트로올 어업을 하다

trawl·er [trɔ́ːlər] *n.* [C] **1.** a boat used for trawling. **2.** a person who works on such a boat.
—[名] 1. 트로올 어선 2. 트로올선 어부

trawl·net [trɔ́ːlnèt] *n.* =trawl.

***tray** [trei] *n.* [C] a flat piece of wood, glass, etc., with a raised rim, used for carrying or holding things.
—[名] 쟁반; 접시

***treach·er·ous** [trétʃ(ə)rəs] *adj.* **1.** deceiving; disloyal. **2.** not reliable in spite of appearance. ¶~ *weather.*
—[形] 1. 배신하는; 불충한 2. 믿을 수 없는

***treach·er·y** [trétʃ(ə)ri] *n.* (pl. **-er·ies**) [U][C] the act of treason; the state of being treacherous; deceit.
—[名] [국가에 대한] 배신; 반역

trea·cle [tríːkl] *n.* [U] (*U.S.*) dark, thick syrup produced in refining sugar; molasses.
—[名] 《美》 당밀

***tread** [tred] *v.* (**trod, trod·den** or **trod**) *vi.* **1.** walk; go. **2.** set one's foot. 《~ *on* or *upon* something》 —*vt.* **1.** step or walk on or along (a place). ¶~ *the ground.* **2.** press (something) under the feet; step on (something) to crush it. ¶~ *out the juice of the grapes.* **3.** win a victory over (something); conquer; oppress. ¶~ *down a sad feeling* (*the fire*).
—[自] 1. 걷다, 가다 2. 밟다, 짓밟다 —[他] 1. …을 걷다, 가다, 지나다 2. …을 짓밟다, 밟아 뭉개다; …을 밟아서 …하다 3. …을 정복하다, 억누르다

1) ***tread on air,*** feel very happy and gay.
2) ***tread on someone's toes*** [***corns***], make someone angry.
3) ***tread the deck,*** become a sailor.

[熟] 1)기뻐서 어쩔 줄 모르다 2)[남]을 성나게 하다 3)뱃사람이 되다

—*n.* [C] **1.** the act, sound, or way of treading. ¶*walk with an airy* ~.① **2.** the flat upper surface of a stair. **3.** the part of a boat or shoe which touches the ground; the part of a tire of a wheel that touches the ground.
—[名] 1. 걷기, 밟기; 발소리; 걸음걸이 ¶①경쾌한 걸음으로 걷다 2. [계단의] 디딤판 3. 바닥, 신발 창; 지면에 닿는 부분

trea·dle [trédl] *n.* [C] a level or pedal on which the foot presses to operate a machine. ⇒fig. —*vi.* operate a treadle.
—[名] [자전거·재봉틀 따위의] 페달, 발판 —[自] 페달을 밟다

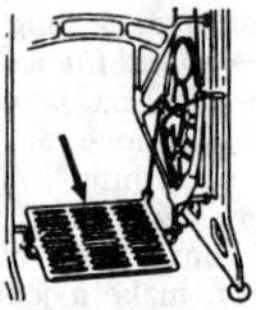
[treadle]

tread·mill [trédmìl] *n.* [C] **1.** a wheel that is turned round by a person or animal treading on a moving, endless belt. **2.** a monotonous and tiresome routine of work or activity.
—[名] 1. 밟아서 돌리는 수레 2. 단조로운 일

***trea·son** [tríːzn] *n.* [U] an attempt to overthrow a government in some illegal way. ¶*high* ~.①
—[名] 반역[죄] ¶①대역죄

trea·son·a·ble [tríːz(ə)nəbl] *adj.* of treason.
—[形] 반역의

trea·son·ous [tríːz(ə)nəs] *adj.* treasonable.
—[形] 반역의

‡**treas·ure** [tréʒər] *n.* **1.** [U][C] a store of money, jewels, precious metals, etc. ¶*a store of hidden* ~.① **2.** [C] a person or thing highly valued. —*vt.* **1.** store or save up (something) for future use. **2.** value (something) highly. ¶*This is the child she treasured.*
—[名] 1. [금전·금은·보석 따위의] 재보(財寶) ¶①미발견의 많은 재화 2. 가장 사랑하는 것; 귀중품 —[他] 1. …을 저장하다 2. …을 소중히 하다

treasure house [∠-∠] *n.* **1.** a building or room where treasure is stored. **2.** a place where many valuable things can be found. ¶*a* ~ *of knowledge.*①
—[名] 1. 보물창고; 광 2. 보고(寶庫) ¶①지식의 보고

***treas·ur·er** [tréʒərər] *n.* [C] a person in charge of receiving and paying out money.
—[名] 회계원; 출납계원

treas·ure-trove [tréʒərtròuv] *n.* [U] (*Law*) treasure found hidden, the owner of which is unknown.
—[名] 《法》 소유자 불명의 발굴물

***treas·ur·y** [tréʒəri] *n.* (pl. **-ur·ies**) [C] **1.** a place where
—[名] 1. 보고(寶庫) 2. 공고(公庫); 국

treasure or money is kept; a treasure house. **2.** 《often *the T-*》 a place where public funds are kept. **3.** the funds of an organization. **4.** 《*the T ~*》 the department of the government that manages a nation's money.
고 **3.** 자금; 기금 **4.** 재무성

:treat [tri:t] *vt.* **1.** act or behave toward (someone). ¶*~ one's friends with respect | He treats his children well. | He treats me as a child.* **2.** regard; consider. ¶*Don't ~ it too seriously. | I treated his words as a joke.* **3.** give medical care to (someone). ¶*~ him for his illness | ~ his tooth.* **4.** entertain (someone) with food, drink, or amusement. 《~ someone *to*》 ¶*~ her to a box at the opera | She treated herself to a dinner at a Chinese restaurant.*① **5.** deal with (something) as the subject of art or literature; discuss; express. ¶*The writer treated his subject realistically.* **6.** give a certain effect to (something) in order to get a certain result. ¶*~ a metal with acid.*② **—*vi.*** **1.** deal with a subject in speech or writing. 《~ *of* something》 ¶*His lecture treated of life and youth.* **2.** discuss; negotiate. ¶*~ with them for peace.* **3.** pay the expense of food, entertainment, etc. for others. ¶*It is your turn to ~ now.*③
—[他] **1.** …을 다루다, 대우하다 **2.** …이라고 간주하다, 여기다 **3.** …을 치료하다 **4.** …에 한턱 내다; 대접하다 ¶①그녀는 큰 마음 먹고 점심으로 중화요리를 먹었다 **5.** …을 논하다; …을 [테에마로] 다루다 **6.** …을 처리하다; …에 작용시키다 ¶②금속을 산으로 처리하다 —[自] **1.** 논하다; [테에마로서] 다루다 **2.** 논의하다; 교섭하다 **3.** 한턱 쓰다 ¶③이번엔 네가 한턱 쓸 차례다

—*n.* [C] **1.** the act of entertaining; a gift of food, drink, or entertainment. ¶*This is my ~.*④ **2.** a delight; anything that gives great pleasure.
—[名] **1.** 한턱 내기; 대접; 접대 ¶④이것은 내가 내는 것이다 **2.** 뜻밖의 기쁨

trea·tise [trí:tis / -tiz] *n.* [C] a formal and systematic book or essay written on a particular subject. 《~ *on*》
—[名] 논문

:treat·ment [trí:tmənt] *n.* [U][C] **1.** the act or way of treating. **2.** a kind of medical or surgical care. ¶*surgical ~*① *| a new ~ for polio.*②
—[名] **1.** 다루기, 대우 **2.** 치료[법] ¶①외과 요법/②소아마비의 새 치료법

***trea·ty** [trí:ti] *n.* (pl. **-ties**) [C] a formal agreement between nations about peace, trade, etc. ¶*conclude* (or *enter into*) *a ~*① *| denounce a ~.*②
—[名] 조약 ¶①조약을 체결하다/②조약을 파기하다

tre·ble [trébl] *adj.* **1.** three times. **2.** (*Music*) of the highest instrumental or vocal part. **3.** high-pitched; shrill. **—*n.*** [C] **1.** the highest part in music. **2.** a voice or an instrument taking the highest part; soprano. **—*vt., vi.*** make (something) or become three times as many or much.
—[形] **1.** 3배의 **2.** 《樂》 최고음부의 **3.** 째지는 듯한 —[名] **1.** 최고음[부] **2.** 고음부의 음·악기; 소프라노
—[他][自] 3배로 하다(되다)

tre·bly [trébli] *adv.* three times.
—[副] 3배로

:tree [tri:] *n.* [C] **1.** a large plant with a woody trunk, branches. and leaves. ⇒[N.B.] **2.** any shrub, bush, etc. resembling a tree in form or size. **3.** a piece of wood used for a certain purpose. ¶*a shoe ~.*① **4.** something like a tree. ¶*a family ~*②.
—[名] **1.** 나무, 교목(喬木) [N.B.] 관목은 bush, shrub **2.** 수목, 입목(立木) **3.** 목제의 물건 ¶①구두골 **4.** 나무 같은 것 ¶②계도(系圖), 가계도(家系圖)

—*vt.* **1.** drive (something) up a tree. **2.** (*colloq.*) put (someone) into a difficult situation.
—[他] **1.** …을 나무 위로 쫓다 **2.** …을 궁지에 몰아넣다

tree fern [ˊ ˋ] *n.* a large fern with a stem like a trunk.
—[名] 목생(木生) 양치류

tree·less [trí:lis] *adj.* having no trees.
—[形] 나무가 없는

tree trunk [ˊ ˋ] *n.* the main stem of a tree.
—[名] 나무 줄기

trek [trek] *vi.* (**trekked, trek·king**) **1.** go on a long journey by ox wagon. **2.** travel slowly or with difficulty.
—[自] **1.** 달구지로 여행하다 **2.** 느릿느릿 힘드는 여행을 하다

—*n.* [C] a long journey, esp. by ox wagon.
—[名] [소 달구지] 여행

trel·lis [trélis] *n.* [C] a light frame of wood or metal used for supporting growing vines or as a garden screen.
—[名] 격자(格子) 울타리; 격자(창 따위에 붙임)

—*vt.* **1.** support (vines) on a trellis. ¶*~ a climbing rose.* **2.** provide (a window) with a trellis.
—[他] **1.** …을 격자 시렁으로 떠받치다 **2.** [창]에 격자를 달다

:trem·ble [trémbl] *vi.* **1.** shake with fear, cold, etc. ¶*Her voice trembled with anger* (*for fear*)*. | He trembled at his father's voice.*① **2.** move gently; quake. ¶*The leaves were trembling in the breeze.* **3.** feel great fear or anxiety. 《~ *for* something; ~ *to do*》 ¶*I trembled to think what had become of her.*②
—[自] **1.** 바들바들 떨다 ¶①그는 아버지의 목소리를 듣고 떨었다 **2.** 조용히 흔들리다, 산들거리다 **3.** 조바심하다; 마음졸이다 ¶②그녀가 어떻게 되었는지 생각하면 조바심이 났다

—*n.* [C] the act or state of trembling.
—[名] 떨림; 전율; 흔들림

be all of a tremble, (*colloq.*) tremble all over.
[熟] 온몸이 부들부들 떨리다

trem·bling [trémbliŋ] *n.* [U] the state of trembling. —*adj.* that trembles; shaking or shivering.
—[名] 떨림; 전율 —[形] 떨리는, 전율하는

:tre·men·dous [triméndəs] *adj.* **1.** terrible; very important. ¶*a ~ catastrophe*① / *a ~ responsibility.*② **2.** (*colloq.*) very great; amazing. ¶*a ~ difference*③ / *with a ~ effort.*④ ▷**tre·men·dous·ly** [-li] *adv.*
—[形] 1. 무서운; 중대한 ¶①무서운 천지이변/②중대한 책임 2. 거대한, 대단한 ¶③엄청난 차이/④굉장히 애써서

trem·o·lo [tréməlou] *n.* (pl. **-los**) [C] (*Music*) a trembling tone produced by the rapid repetition of the same tone in singing or playing an instrument.
—[名] 《樂》 트레몰로, 전음(顫音)

trem·or [trémər] *n.* [C] **1.** a shivering or trembling of the voice, leaves, etc. **2.** a shrinking of courage; the state of being excited; a thrill of emotion.
—[名] 1. [잎사귀 · 목소리 따위의] 떨림 2. 겁; 오싹하는 느낌

trem·u·lous [trémjuləs] *adj.* **1.** trembling or quivering. ¶*a voice ~ with fear.*① **2.** cowardly; nervous.
—[形] 1. 떨리는 ¶①무서워서 떨리는 소리 2. 겁 많은

trem·u·lous·ly [trémjuləsli] *adv.* tremblingly; timidly.
—[副] 떨려서; 후들후들 떨며

•trench [trentʃ] *n.* [C] **1.** a long, narrow ditch dug in the earth to protect soldiers in a battle field. **2.** a deep ditch. —*vt.* **1.** surround (something) with a trench. **2.** dig a trench in (some place). **3.** cultivate. —*vi.* dig a trench.
—[名] 1. 참호 2. 도랑 —[他] 1. 을 참호로 두르다 2. …에 참호(도랑)를 파다 3. (토지)를 경작하다 —[自] 참호(도랑)를 파다

trench·ant [tréntʃ(ə)nt] *adj.* **1.** biting; keen. ¶*~ wit.* **2.** clear; distinct.
—[形] 1. 통렬한 2. 간결한; 명확한

trench·er[1] [tréntʃər] *n.* [C] a person who digs trenches.
—[名] 도랑(참호)을 파는 사람

trench·er[2] [tréntʃər] *n.* [C] a wooden plate for serving meat.
—[名] 나무 접시

•trend [trend] *n.* [C] **1.** the general tendency. ¶*the ~ of public opinion*① / *the ~ of time.*② **2.** the direction of a road, river, mountains, etc. ¶*The hills have a western ~.*③ —*vi.* **1.** turn, bend, or run in a certain direction. ¶*The road trends to the north.*④ **2.** have a general tendency. ¶*Prices are trending upward.*
—[名] 1. 경향 ¶①여론의 경향/②시대의 추세 2. [도로 · 하천 따위의] 방향 ¶③이 산맥은 서쪽으로 뻗어 있다 —[自] 1. […으로] 향하다, 기울다 ¶④그 길은 북쪽을 향해 있다 2. […의] 경향이 있다

tres·pass [tréspəs] *vi.* **1.** go on someone's land without permission. 《~ *on* or *upon* some place》 ¶*~ on someone's land*① / *No trespassing.*② **2.** commit an offense; do wrong; sin. 《~ *against* something》 ¶*~ against the law.*③ **3.** take too much of someone's time, privacy, attention, etc. ¶*~ on someone's right.*④ —*n.* [U] [C] the act of going on someone's land or property unlawfully.
—[自] 1. [남의 토지에] 침입하다; 침해하다 ¶①…의 토지에 침입하다/②들어가지 마시오 2. …을 어기다 ¶③법률을 어기다 3. [남의 권리를] 침해하다; [시간을] 방해하다 ¶④남의 권리를 침해하다 —[名] 침입

tres·pass·er [tréspəsər] *n.* [C] a person who trespasses.
—[名] 침입자; 침해자

tress [tres] *n.* [C] a curl or lock of hair.
—[名] [머리칼의] 한 다발

tres·tle [trésl] *n.* [C] **1.** a movable frame with two pairs of spreading legs used to support a platform, table tap, etc. ⇒fig. **2.** a rigid framework for supporting a bridge across a gap.
—[名] 1. 말 모양의 다리가 달린 가대(架臺); 발판 2. 교각(橋脚); 구각(構脚)

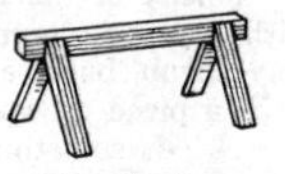
〔trestle 1.〕

trestle bridge [ˊ-- ˋ] *n.* a bridge supported by trestles. ⇒fig.
—[名] 구각교(構脚橋)

tri- [trai-] *prefix.* **1.** having three: *tricycle* (=a three-wheeled vehicle). **2.** three times; into three parts: *trisect* (=divide into three equal part). **3.** once in three; every third: *triweekly* (=every three weeks).
—《接頭》 1. 세 개의 2. 3배의; 3등분의 3. 3…마다

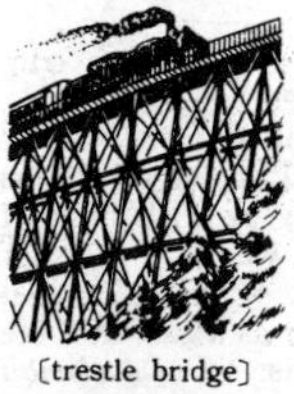
〔trestle bridge〕

tri·ad [tráiæd / -əd] *n.* [C] a group of three persons or things.
—[名] 세 개 한 벌의 것

:trial [tráiəl] *n.* [C] **1.** a test. ¶*the ~ of a new car*① / *by way of ~*② / *~ and error.*③ **2.** the state of being tested. **3.** a hardship or trouble that tries one's endurance. ¶*stand the ~.*④ **4.** the inquiry into or decision on a case in a court of law. ¶*bring a person to ~.*
—[名] 1. 해보기; 시험 ¶①새 차 시험/②시험삼아/③시행 착오 2. 시험받기 3. 시련; 골칫거리 ¶④시련에 견디다 4. 재판, 공판

on trial, in order to test; when tested; under judicial examination or inquiry.
[熟] 시험삼아; 시험 중인; 공판 중인

—*adj.* of a trial. ¶*a ~ trip* / *a ~ cruise.*
—[形] 시험의

tri·an·gle [tráiæŋgl] *n.* [C] **1.** a figure with three sides
—[名] 1. 삼각형; 삼각자 2. 《樂》 트라이

T

and angles; a triangular instrument used in drawing figures. **2.** (*Music*) a triangular musical instrument made of steel and played by being struck with a metal rod.
앵글

tri·an·gu·lar [traiǽŋgjulər] *adj.* **1.** having the shape of a triangle. **2.** of three persons, parties, parts, etc. ¶~ *treaty.*①
—[形] 1. 삼각의 2. 3 자간의, 3 당(黨) 사이의 ¶① 3 국 조약

trib·al [tráibəl] *adj.* of a tribe.
—[形] 종족의

⁑tribe [traib] *n.* [C] **1.** a group of primitive people living under one chief. ¶*a ~ of Indians*① / *a cannibal ~.*② **2.** a group of people who have the same habits, interests, occupation, etc. ¶*a ~ of politicians.*③ **3.** (*Biology*) a group, class or kind of animals or plants.
—[名] 1. 종족 ¶①인디언의 한 종족/②식인종 2. 패거리, 동아리 ¶③정치꾼들 3. 《生》 족(族)

tribes·man [tráibzmən] *n.* [C] (pl. **-men** [-mən]) a member of a tribe.
—[名] 같은 종족의 일원

trib·u·la·tion [trìbjuléiʃ(ə)n] *n.* [U] [C] great suffering or trouble; distress.
—[名] 고난, 재난, 고통; 시련

tri·bu·nal [traibjú:n(ə)l, tri-] *n.* [C] **1.** a court of justice. **2.** the seat in the court where the judge sits.
—[名] 1. 법정 2. 판사석

trib·une [tríbju:n] *n.* [C] **1.** (*History*) an ancient Roman official elected by the people to protect their rights and liberties. **2.** a defender of the rights and liberties of the people. ⇒[N.B.]
—[名] 1. 《史》 [고대 로마의] 호민관(護民官) 2. 인민의 권리를 지키는 것 [N.B.] 신문 이름으로 쓰이는 일이 많음

***trib·u·tar·y** [tríbjutèri / -t(ə)ri] *n.* [C] (pl. **-tar·ies**) **1.** a nation that pays tribute to a superior, more powerful one. **2.** a stream flowing into a larger one.
—[名] 1. 속국 2. 지류

—*adj.* **1.** paying tribute to another nation. ¶*a ~ state.*① **2.** flowing into a larger stream. ¶*a ~ stream.*②
—[形] 1. 종속하는 ¶①속국 2. 지류의 ¶②지류

***trib·ute** [tríbju:t] *n.* [U] [C] **1.** money paid by a nation to a superior, more powerful nation in return for peace or safety. **2.** a gift, words, etc. given to show respect, praise, honor, etc. ¶*a ~ of praise*① / *pay* [*a*] *~ to the memory of the founder.*②
—[名] 1. 공물(貢物) 2. [존경·감사 따위를 위해] 바치는 것 ¶①찬사/②창립자를 기념하여 경의를 표하다

trice [trais] *n.* [C] an instant; a moment.
—[名] 순간

⁑trick [trik] *n.* [C] **1.** an act done in order to deceive or cheat; an illusion. ¶*His illness proved a ~ to avoid school.* / *a ~ of eyesight*① / *tricks of memory.*② **2.** a mischievous action. ¶*tricks of fortune.* **3.** habit. ¶*He has a ~ of stroking his nose.* **4.** the best way of doing something. ¶*the tricks of the trade.* **5.** a kind of magic. ¶*a card ~.*
—[名] 1. 계략; 속임수; 착각 ¶① 환각/②착각 2. 장난 3. 버릇 4. 비결, 요령 5. 요술

do (or ***turn***) ***the trick,*** (*colloq.*) get the desired result or effect.
[熟] 《口》 잘 해내다; 목적을 달성하다

—*vt.* cheat; deceive. ¶*~ someone out of his money.*③
—[他] …을 속이다 ¶③속여서 돈을 빼앗다

trick up (or ***out***), dress up; adorn.
[熟] 모양내다, 멋부리다

trick·er·y [tríkəri] *n.* [U] the act of cheating; the practice of playing tricks.
—[名] 협잡, 사기; 간책(奸策)

trick·le [tríkl] *vi.* **1.** flow slowly in a small or thin stream or fall in drops. 《~ *down* something》 ¶*Tears trickled down her cheeks.* **2.** come or go slowly and irregularly. ¶*Subscriptions are trickling in.*① —*vt.* cause (liquid) to flow in a small, thin stream.
—[自] 1. 졸졸 흐르다; 똑똑 떨어지다 2. 드문드문 오다(가다) ¶①예약이 조금씩 들어오고 있다 —[他] …을 똑똑 떨어지게 하다

—*n.* [C] a small stream or drop.
—[名] 똑똑 떨어짐; 실개천

trick·ster [tríkstər] *n.* [C] a person who cheats or deceives.
—[名] 사기꾼

trick·y [tríki] *adj.* (**trick·i·er, trick·i·est**) **1.** (of persons) apt to play tricks; unreliable. **2.** difficult to handle or understand. ¶*a ~ problem.*① **3.** (of work, etc.) skilled; complicated; intricate. ¶*a ~ lamp.*②
—[形] 1. 교활한 2. 힘드는 ¶①어려운 문제 3. 정교한 ¶②정교한 남포

tri·col·or [tráikʌ̀lər / tríkələ] *adj.* having three colors.
—*n.* [C] a flag of three colors, esp. the flag of France.
—[形] 3색의 —[名] 3색기; 프랑스 국기

***tri·cy·cle** [tráisikl] *n.* [C] a vehicle with three wheels moved by pedals.
—[名] 3륜차

tri·dent [tráid(ə)nt] *n.* [C] (*Mythology*) a three-pointed spear used by the sea god Neptune.
—[名] 《神話》 삼지창(三枝槍)(바다의 신 Neptune의 제해권의 상징)

⁑tried [traid] *adj.* tested and proved; reliable. ¶*~ and true.*
—[形] 시험이 끝난; 확실한

***tri·fle** [tráifl] *n.* [C] **1.** 《often *pl.*》 something of little
—[名] 1. 보잘것 없는 것 ¶①그런 하찮

trifler [1228] **tripartite**

value or importance ¶*Don't worry over such trifles.*① **2.** (*a* ~) a small amount or degree, as of money. ¶*The house was sold for a* ~.② ― *vi.* talk, act, or handle insincerely or lightly; play with something. (~ *with* someone or something) ¶*a man not to be trifled with*③ / ~ *with one's moustache.* ― *vt.* waste. (~ *away* time, money, etc.) ¶*He trifled away the whole afternoon by the lake.*④

― 은 일로 걱정하지 말라 2. 소량; 조금의 돈 ¶②그 집은 얼마 안 되는 돈에 팔렸다
― 国 장난치다; 놀리다; 만지작거리다 ¶③만만하게 다룰 수 없는 사내 ―他 …을 낭비하다 ¶④그는 호수 옆에서 빈둘빈둘 오후를 지냈다

tri·fler [tráiflər] *n.* ⓒ a person who talks and acts insincerely, esp. one who wastes away time.

―名 농담하는 사람; 게으름뱅이

*** tri·fling** [tráifliŋ] *adj.* of little importance or value; small in amount. ¶*a* ~ *error*① / *a* ~ *character.*②

―形 보잘것 없는; 근소한 ¶①사소한 잘못/②보잘것 없는 사람

trig·ger [trígər] *n.* ⓒ a small lever to fire a gun by pulling it back with the finger.

―名 방아쇠

trig·o·nom·e·try [trìgənámitri / -nɔ́m-] *n.* Ⓤ a branch of mathematics dealing with the relations between the sides and angles of triangles.

―名 삼각법

trill [tril] *vt., vi.* **1.** sing or speak in a shaking voice. **2.** pronounce (a sound or word) with a trill. ― *n.* ⓒ **1.** a shaking sound or voice. **2.** a pronunciation made by a rapid vibration of the tongue.

―他自 1. [목소리를] 떨다;전음(顫音)으로 노래하다 2. 혀를 굴려서 발음하다 ―名 1. 떨리는 목소리 2. 혀를 굴려서 내는 발음(r 따위)

tril·lion [tríljən] *n.* ⓒ **1.** (*U.S.*) a thousand billions. **2.** (*Brit.*) a million billions. ― *adj.* amounting to a trillion.

―名 1. (美) 1 조(兆); 백만의 제곱 2. (英) 백만의 세제곱 ―形 백만의 제곱 (세제곱)의

tril·o·gy [tríləʤi] *n.* ⓒ (pl. **-gies**) a set of three plays, novels, musical compositions, etc. that makes a completely related series though each part has its own unity.

―名 3 부작, 3 부곡

‡ **trim** [trim] *v.* (**trimmed, trim·ming**) *vt.* **1.** cut off the edge of (something) neatly. ¶~ *one's nails* / ~ *a hedge.* **2.** put (something) into shape; make (something) ready for use. ¶~ *the lumber.* **3.** decorate; dress. (~ *oneself*) ¶~ *the dress with lace* / *The girl trimmed herself up.* **4.** clip; cut. ¶~ *dead branches off the tree.* ― *vi.* change one's opinions to suit other people. ― *n.* Ⓤ **1.** good order or condition. ¶*in good* (*proper*) ~. **2.** decoration. **3.** preparation. [*condition.*] ― *adj.* (**trim·mer, trim·mest**) orderly; neat; in good

―他 1. …을 가지런히 깎다 2. …을 깎아서 모양을 갖추다; 쓸 수 있도록 준비하다 3. …을 장식하다; …으로 꾸미다; 가장하다; …을 준비시키다 4. …을 잘라내다 ―自 남에게 맞추어 의견을 바꾸다
―名 1. 정돈; [좋은] 컨디션 2. 장식 3. 준비
―形 단정한; 정비된

trim·e·ter [trímitər] *n.* ⓒ a poetry having three metrical feet in each line. ― *adj.* having three metrical feet.

―名 [시구(詩句)의] 3 보격(步格) ―形 3 보격의

trim·ly [trímli] *adv.* in a trim manner.

―副 말쑥하게

trim·ming [trímiŋ] *n.* Ⓤ **1.** the act of a person who trims. **2.** (*pl.*) decoration, esp. of clothes. ¶*the trimmings on a hat.*① **3.** (*pl.*) additions to a meal.

―名 1. 정돈, 손질 2. [의복 따위의] 장식 ¶①모자 장식 3. [요리 따위의] 고명, 곁들여서 나오는 반찬

Trin·i·ty [tríniti] *n.* **1.** (*Religion*) the union of Father, Son, and Holy Ghost in one God. **2.** (*t-*) ⓒ a group of three persons or things.

―名 1. 삼위일체 2. 3 인조; 세 개 한 벌

trin·ket [tríŋkit] *n.* ⓒ **1.** a small ornament, jewel, etc. **2.** something of little value.

―名 1. 장신구(裝身具) 2. 보잘것 없는 것

tri·o [tríːou / tríː(ː)ou] *n.* ⓒ **1.** (*Music*) a composition for three players; a group of three singers or players. **2.** a group of three persons or things.

―名 1. (樂) 3 중주(곡); 3 중주단 2. 3 인조; 세 개 한 벌

‡ **trip** [trip] *n.* ⓒ **1.** a journey, usu. short and esp. for pleasure. ¶*make a* ~ *to Pusan* / *a round* ~.① **2.** light, quick step. **3.** stumble; slip; mistake. ― *v.* (**tripped, trip·ping**) *vi.* **1.** run with short steps; skip. ¶*The boy came tripping down.* **2.** stumble; slip. ¶*The little boy tripped over the stone.*② **3.** make a mistake. (~ *on* something) ¶~ *on a difficult problem.* ― *vt.* **1.** cause (someone) to stumble and fall; overthrow. ¶*The frozen road tripped him.* **2.** cause (someone) to make a mistake. ¶*I was tripped by the question.* **3.** perform (a dance) lightly.

―名 1. [짧은] 여행 ¶①일주 여행 2. 가벼운 발걸음 3. 헛디딤, 실족; 과실
―自 1. 경쾌한 발걸음으로 걷다; 달리다 2. 걸려 넘어지다; 미끄러져 넘어지다 ¶②그 아이는 돌에 걸려 넘어졌다 3. 틀리다 ―他 1. …을 걸려 넘어지게 하다; 나동그라지게 하다 2. …을 실패시키다 3. …을 경쾌하게 춤추다

tri·par·tite [traipáːrtait] *adj.* of or divided into three parts; made or shared between three parties.

―形 셋으로 나뉜, 3 부로 이루어진; 3 자간의

tri·ple [trípl] *adj.* **1.** three times as much or as many. **2.** consisting of three parts. ¶*~ alliance.*① **—*vi., vt.*** **1.** become or make (something) three times as much or as many. **2.** (*Baseball*) make a three-base hit.
—[形] 1. 3배의 2. 3부로 이루어지는 ¶①3국 동맹 —[自][他] 1. 3배로 하다(되다) 2.《野球》 3루타를 치다

tri·plet [tríplit] *n.* [C] **1.** a set of three things. **2.** one of three children born at a single birth.
—[名] 1. 세 개 한 벌의 것 2. 세쌍동이의 한 사람

triple time [⌐– ⌐] *n.* (*Music*) time or rhythm which has three beats to the measure.
—[名]《樂》 3박자

tri·plex [trípleks, trái-] *adj.* triple; threefold. **—*n.*** [C] (*Music*) triple time.
—[形] 세 겹의; 3부로 이루어지는 —[名] 3박자

trip·li·cate [tríplikit →*vt.*] *adj.* threefold; made in three copies. **—*n.*** [C] one of the same three copies. **—*vt.*** [tríplikèit] **1.** make (something) threefold. **2.** make three copies of (something).
—[形] 세 겹의; 세 통의 —[名] 세 통의 서류(세 개 한 벌)의 하나 —[他] 1. …을 세 배(겹)로 하다 2. …을 세 통 작성하다

tri·pod [tráipɑd / -pɔd] *n.* [C] a stand, support, table, etc. with three legs. ¶*a photographic ~.*① **—*adj.*** having three legs. ¶*~ race.*②
—[名] 삼각대(三脚臺), [사진기용의] 삼각 ¶①사진기의 삼각 —[形] 삼각의 ¶②2인 3각

trip·per [trípər] *n.* [C] (*Brit.*) a traveler.
—[名] 여행자; 유람객

trip·ping [trípiŋ] *adj.* walking with light and quick steps.
—[形] 발걸음이 가벼운

trite [trait] *adj.* worn out by too much use; commonplace.
—[形] 케케묵은; 흔해빠진

:tri·umph [tráiəmf] *n.* **1.** [U][C] the state of being victorious; a victory; a success. ¶*shouts of ~.*① **2.** [U] joy over victory or success. ¶*be full of ~.*② **3.** [C] a parade in celebration of a victory in ancient Rome.
—[名] 1. 승리; 성공 ¶①승리의 외침 2. 승리감, 성공의 기쁨 ¶②의기양양하다 3. [고대 로마의] 개선식

in triumph, triumphantly.
[熟] 의기양양하게

—*vi.* gain a victory or success; feel joy over victory or success. (*~ over* someone or something)
—[自] 승리를 얻다; 성공하다; 이겨서 뽐내다

tri·um·phal [traiʌ́mf(ə)l] *adj.* **1.** of a triumph. **2.** celebrating a triumph or victory. ¶*a ~ arch*① / *a ~ feast.*②
—[形] 1. 개선의 2. 승리를 축하하는 ¶①개선문/②승리의 축연

***tri·um·phant** [traiʌ́mfənt] *adj.* **1.** having gained a victory or success; victorious. ¶*the ~ progress of knowledge.*① **2.** showing joy over victory or success. ¶*~ cries.*②
—[形] 1. 승리(성공)를 얻은 ¶①눈부신 지식의 진전 2. 이겨서 뽐내는 ¶②승리의 함성

tri·um·phant·ly [taiʌ́mfəntli] *adv.* in a triumphant manner; victoriously; rejoicingly.
—[副] 이겨서 뽐내어; 의기양양하게

***triv·i·al** [tríviəl] *adj.* not important; of little value. ¶*~ round of daily life.*① ▷**triv·i·al·ly** [-i] *adv.*
—[形] 사소한; 보잘것 없는 ¶①평범한 일상생활

triv·i·al·i·ty [trìviǽliti] *n.* (pl. **-ties**) **1.** [U] the state of being trivial. **2.** [C] something that has little importance and value.
—[名] 1. 하찮음 2. 하찮은 것

***trod** [trɑd / trɔd] *v.* pt. and pp. of **tread.**

trod·den [trɑ́dn / trɔ́dn] *v.* pp. of **tread.**

trog·lo·dyte [trɑ́glədàit / trɔ́g-] *n.* [C] **1.** an ancient man who lived in a cave. **2.** a person living alone.
—[名] 1. 혈거인(穴居人) 2. 속세를 등진 사람

troi·ka [trɔ́ikə] *n.* [C] (in Russia) a wagon drawn by three horses.
—[名] 트로이카

Tro·jan [tróudʒ(ə)n] *n.* [C] a person of Troy. **—*adj.*** of Troy or Trojan.
—[名] 트로이 사람 —[形] 트로이[사람]의

troll [troul] *vt., vi.* **1.** sing the different parts of the same melody in succession. **2.** sing merrily. ▷**troll·er** [-ər] *n.*
—[他][自] 1. 윤창하다 2. 명랑하게 노래하다

trol·ley [trɑ́li / trɔ́li] *n.* [C] **1.** (*U.S.*) a trolley bus. **2.** (*Brit.*) a hand-cart. **3.** a small wheel at the end of a pole on a trolley bus, streetcar, etc. ⇒fig.
—[名] 1.《美》 트롤리 버스 2.《英》 손수레 3. [트롤리 버스·전차 따위의 채끝의] 촉륜(觸輪)

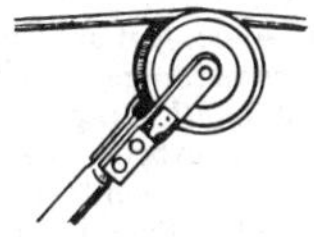
[trolley 3.]

trolley bus [⌐– ⌐] *n.* a bus driven by electric current taken from overhead wires. ⇒fig.
—[名] 트롤리 버스, 무궤도 전차

trolley car [⌐– ⌐] *n.* (*U.S.*) an electric streetcar.
—[名]《美》 [시가] 전차

trom·bone [trɑmbóun, trɑ́mboun / trɔmbóun] *n.* [C] a long brass musical instrument with a U-shaped tube. ⇒p. 1230 fig.
—[名] 트롬본

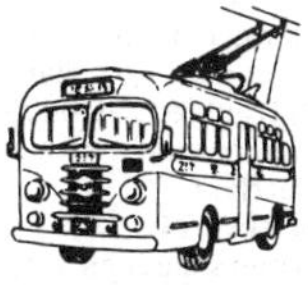
[trolley bus]

:troop [tru:p] *n.* [C] **1.** a large group of persons or animals. ¶*a ~ of boys.*① **2.** (*pl.*) soldiers. ¶*send*
—[名] 1. [사람·새·짐승의] 떼 ¶①일단의 소년 2. 군대 ¶②군대를 전선으

*troops to the front.*② —*vi.* **1.** gather in crowds. 《~ *up, together*》 ¶*Children trooped together around the pretty dog.*③ **2.** move in or out in large numbers. ¶*People came trooping out of the theater.*④

로 보내다 —[自] 1. 떼짓다 ¶③아이들은 귀여운 개의 주위로 몰려들었다 2. 떼지어 들어가다(나오다) ¶④사람이 극장에서 떼지어 나왔다

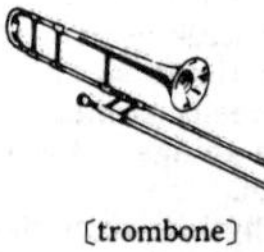

(trombone)

troop·er [trú:pər] *n.* [C] **1.** a soldier on a horse. **2.** (*Brit.*) a troopship.

—[名] 1. 기병 2. 《英》 수송선

troop·ship [trú:pʃìp] *n.* [C] a ship for carrying military troops.

—[名] 수송선

* **tro·phy** [tróufi] *n.* [C] (pl. **-phies**) **1.** a prize given to a winner in a contest, such as a silver cup. **2.** something taken from the enemy in war as a memorial of victory. ¶*a ~ of war.*①

—[名] 1. 우승배, 우승 상품 2. 전리품 ¶①전리품

trop·ic [trápik / trɔ́p-] *n.* [C] **1.** either of two imaginary circles around the earth parallel to the equator. ¶*the Tropic of Cancer*① / *the Tropic of Capricorn.*② **2.** 《*the ~s*》 the hottest region on the earth, between the Tropic of Cancer and the Tropic of Capricorn.

—[名] 1. 회귀선(回歸線) ¶①북회귀선 /②남회귀선 2. 열대[지방]

* **trop·i·cal** [trápik(ə)l / trɔ́p-] *adj.* of the tropics.

—[形] 열대의

* **trot** [trɑt / trɔt] *v.* (**trot·ted, trot·ting**) *vi.* **1.** (of a horse) go at a pace faster than a walk. **2.** go at a quick pace; hurry; run with short steps. ¶*We must be trotting off home.*① —*vt.* **1.** cause (a horse) to trot. **2.** go along (a road, etc.) by trotting. ¶*~ a winding path.* —*n.* [C] **1.** 《*sing.* only》 the motion of a trotting horse. **2.** the quick walk or run of a person. **3.** busy, quick movement.
on the trot, busy.

—[自] 1. [말이] 속보로 나아가다 2. [사람이] 총총걸음으로 걷다; 바쁘게 달리다 ¶①이젠 집에 가 봐야 한다 —[他] 1. [말]을 속보로 달리게 하다 2. …을 빠른 걸음으로 가다 —[名] 1. [말의] 속보 2. [사람의] 빠른 걸음, 총총걸음 3. 바쁜 일
[熟] 바쁜

trou·ba·dour [trú:bədɔ̀:r / -dùə, -dɔ:] *n.* [C] one of the poets or singers who were popular in France, Spain, and Italy from the 11th to the 13th centuries.

—[名] [11세기에서 13세기까지 프랑스·이탈리아에서 세력을 차지한] 음유(吟遊) 서정시인

⁝ **trou·ble** [trʌ́bl] *n.* **1.** [U][C] anxiety; worry; difficulty. ¶*That will get him into ~.* / *give someone so much ~.*① **2.** 《often *pl.*》 disturbance; social or political unrest. ¶*domestic troubles* / *labor troubles*② / *political troubles.* **3.** [U][C] disease; illness. ¶*suffer from mental ~.* **4.** [U] inconvenience; effort; labor; pain. ¶*We must always take the ~ to consult a dictionary.* **5.** [C] a person or thing that causes trouble. ¶*I always find it a great ~ to get up early in the morning.*③

—[名] 1. 근심[거리]; 고민; 고뇌 ¶①…에게 큰 폐를 끼치다 2. 분쟁; 분규; 쟁의 ¶②노동 쟁의 3. 병, 탈 4. 불편; 수고, 번거로움 5. 말썽꾼; 고생의 원인 ¶③아침 일찍 일어나는 것이 언제나 고통거리다

1) ***ask*** (or ***look***) ***for trouble,*** (*colloq.*) show lack of caution.
2) ***get into trouble,*** do something that will bring trouble.

[熟] 1)《口》경솔한 짓을 하다 2)문제를 일으키다

—*vt.* **1.** cause trouble to (someone). ¶*What troubles me most is that I am weak.* / *I'm troubled with a bad cold.* / *He is troubled about his only daughter.* **2.** give trouble to (someone). ¶*I'm sorry to ~ you so much, but ...* / *May I ~ you for some money?*④ / *I do not ~ myself about* (or *with*) *such things.*⑤ —*vi.* feel anxious; worry; bother. 《*~ to do*; *~ about* something》 ⇒[N.B.] ¶*Don't ~ to write.*⑥ / *Don't ~ about small things.*

—[他] 1. …을 괴롭히다, 근심시키다 2. …에 폐를 끼치다, 번거로움을 주다 ¶④돈을 좀 꾸어 주시겠소?/⑤그런 일로 걱정하지는 않는다 —[自] 애쓰다; 근심하다; 일부러 …하다 [N.B.] 특히 부정문·의문문으로 쓰임 ¶⑥일부러 편지를 안 써도 좋다

trou·bled [trʌ́bld] *adj.* **1.** stormy; disturbed. ¶*a ~ sea.*① **2.** worried. ¶*a ~ look.*
fish in troubled waters, gain an advantage in the midst of confusion.

—[形] 1. 거친, 어수선한 ¶①거친 바다 2. 근심스러운
[熟] 혼란을 틈타 한몫 보다

trou·ble·mak·er [trʌ́blmèikər] *n.* [C] a person who causes trouble or difficulties for others.

—[名] 말썽꾸러기

* **trou·ble·some** [trʌ́blsəm] *adj.* causing trouble or difficulties. ¶*this ~ world*① / *a ~ job.*

—[形] 성가신, 번거로운 ¶①골치아픈 이 세상

trou·blous [trʌ́bləs] *adj.* (*archaic*) troubled; troublesome.

—[形] 《古》 거친; 어지러운

trough [trɔ:f / trɔf] *n.* [C] a wooden container used to keep water or food for horses or cattle.

—[名] 여물통, 구유

trounce [trauns] *vt.* beat (someone) severely.

—[他] …을 치다

troupe [tru:p] *n.* [C] a group of performers such as actors, singers, or acrobats.

—[名] [배우 등의] 일좌(一座)

* **trou·sers** [tráuzərz] *n. pl.* two-legged outer clothing covering the body from the waist to the ankles or knees.
—[名] 즈봉

trous·seau [trú:sou, -ˊ] *n.* [C] (pl. **-seaux** or **-seaus**) the clothes, jewelry, personal things, etc. of a bride.
—[名] 혼수감, 혼수 의장(衣裝)

trous·seaux [trú:souz, -ˊ] *n.* pl. of **trousseau.**

* **trout** [traut] *n.* [C] (pl. **trouts** or *collectively* **trout**) a food fish living in clear freshwater, belonging to the salmon family.
—[名] 송어

trow·el [tráu(ə)l] *n.* [C] **1.** a tool with a thin, flat blade of wood or metal used for spreading or smoothing mortar. **2.** a tool used to take small plants from one place to another.
—[名] 1. [미장이·석수가 쓰는] 흙손 2. [원예용의] 모종삽

Troy [trɔi] *n.* an ancient city in northwestern Asia Minor.
—[名] 트로이

troy weight [ˊ ˋ] *n.* a system of weight used for precious metals, gems, etc.
—[名] 트로이식 형량(衡量), 금형(金衡)

tru·an·cy [trú:ənsi] *n.* [U][C] (pl. **-cies**) the act of being absent from school without any proper reason.
—[名] [학생의] 농뗑이짓, 무단결석

tru·ant [trú:ənt] *n.* [C] **1.** a child who stays away from school without any proper reason or without permission. ¶*play* ~.① **2.** a person who neglects his duty. **—*adj.*** being absent from school without any proper reason or without permission.
—[名] 1. [학교의] 무단결석자 ¶①무단결석하다 2. 게으름뱅이 —[形] 게으름 피우는, 무단결석하는

truce [tru:s] *n.* [C][U] **1.** a temporary peace in a war made possible by mutual agreement. ¶*a ~ talk*① / *make a ~*② / *a flag of ~.*③ **2.** a pause or rest from trouble, pain, etc.
—[名] 1. 휴전 ¶①휴전회담/②휴전하다/③휴전의 백기 2. [곤란·고통의] 휴지(休止), 중단

⁑ **truck**¹ [trʌk] *n.* [C] **1.** (*U.S.*) a large, strong vehicle for carrying heavy loads. **2.** a small cart with two wheels used for carrying luggage. **3.** (*Brit.*) an open railroad freight car.
—[名] 1. 《美》 화물 자동차 2. 손수레 3. 《英》 무개 화차

truck² [trʌk] *n.* [U] **1.** exchange; barter. ¶~ *system.*① **2.** (*U.S.*) vegetables cultivated for sale in a market. **—*vt., vi.*** exchange (goods) for other goods.
—[名] 1. 물물교환 ¶①물품 임금제 2. 시장에 낼 야채; 채소류 —[他][自] 물물교환하다

truck farm [ˊ ˋ] *n.* (*U.S.*) a farm where vegetables are grown to be sold in a market.
—[名] 《美》 시장에 내려고 재배하는 채소밭

truc·u·lence [trʌ́kjuləns, trú:k-] *n.* [U] the state or quality of being truculent.
—[名] 사나운 느낌; 잔인

truc·u·lent [trʌ́kjulənt, trú:k-] *adj.* very fierce and cruel; ready to fight.
—[形] 흉악한; 잔인한

trudge [trʌdʒ] *vt., vi.* walk wearily and laboriously. **—*n.*** [C] a long, wearying walk.
—[他][自] 터벅터벅 걷다 —[名] 터벅터벅 걷기

⁑ **true** [tru:] *adj.* **1.** according to fact; correct. ↔false ¶*the ~ meaning* / *a ~ story.* **2.** real; genuine. ¶~ *kindness* / ~ *gold* / ~ *love.* **3.** exact; accurate; right. 《~ *to*》 ¶~ *to life*① / ~ *to time*② / ~ *to nature*③ / *hold* ~.④ **4.** faithful; loyal; sincere. 《~ *to*》 ¶~ *to one's principles* / *True to his words, he came to see me.*⑤
—[形] 1. 정말의; 참다운 2. 진짜의 3. 확실한; 정확한 ¶①실물 그대로의/②시간에 정확히/③박진(迫眞)의/④들어맞다 4. 성실한, 충실한 ¶⑤약속대로 그는 나를 만나러 왔다

come true, become real; happen as expected.
[熟] 실현하다; 정말로 일어나다

—*adv.* truly; exactly; accurately. ¶*aim ~* / *Please tell me ~.* / *speak ~* / *ring ~.*⑥
—[副] 정말로; 정확히 ¶⑥정말처럼 들리다

true blue [ˊ ˊ] *n.* **1.** a fast blue color. **2.** a person faithful to a party or principle.
—[名] 1. [바래지 않는] 남빛 2. [주의 따위에] 충실한 사람

true-blue [trú:blú:] *adj.* very loyal; faithful.
—[形] [주의 따위에] 충실한

true·bred [trú:bréd] *adj.* **1.** thoroughbred. **2.** wellbred.
—[形] 1. 순혈종(純血種)의 2. 가정교육이 좋은

true-heart·ed [trú:há:rtid] *adj.* true and faithful; honest.
—[形] 성실한

tru·ism [trú:iz(ə)m] *n.* [C] a statement that is clearly true and well known.
—[名] 자명한 이치, 공리(公理)

⁑ **tru·ly** [trú:li] *adv.* **1.** indeed. ¶*a ~ surprising report* / *I can ~ say.*① **2.** sincerely. ¶*serve ~*② / *speak ~.* **3.** correctly; really. ¶*It is ~ said that time is money.*
—[副] 1. 정말로 ¶①정말로 그렇다 2. 정직하게 ¶②성실하게 섬기다 3. 올바르게; 진실하게

trump [trʌmp] *n.* [C] **1.** any playing card of a suit that is temporarily ranked higher than any other suit. ¶*play a ~.*① **2.** (*colloq.*) a good, reliable person.
—[名] 1. [카아드의] 으뜸패 ¶①으뜸패(비책)를 내놓다 2. 〔口〕 믿음직한 사람

trump card [ˊ ˋ] *n.* a trump.
—[名] 으뜸패

trump·er·y [trʌ́mp(ə)ri] *n.* [U][C] (pl. **-er·ies**) something
—[名] 겉만 번지르르한 것 —[形] 겉만

T

showy but worthless. —*adj.* good in appearance but without value. ¶*This clothing is very ~.*①

번지르르한 ¶①이 옷은 정말 허울뿐이다

∗**trum·pet** [trʌ́mpit] *n.* [C] **1.** a musical instrument with a curved brass tube, keys, a bell-shaped mouth, etc. producing a powerful tone. **2.** something like a trumpet in shape or sound. ¶*an ear ~.*①

—[名] 1. 트럼펫 2. 트럼펫 비슷한 것 ¶①보청기

blow one's own trumpet, boast of oneself.

[熟] 자화자찬하다

—*vi.* **1.** blow a trumpet. **2.** (of an elephant) make a sound like a trumpet. —*vt.* announce (something) in a loud voice. ¶*~ someone's fame abroad.*

—[自] 1. 나팔을 불다 2. [코끼리가 코로] 울부짖다 —[他] …을 큰 소리로 퍼뜨리다

trum·pet·er [trʌ́mpitər] *n.* [C] a person who blows a trumpet; a soldier who blows a trumpet as a signal.

—[名] 트럼펫 연주자; 나팔수

trumpet lily [∠– ∠–] *n.* a lily that has long trumpet-like flowers.

—[名] 흰백합

trun·cate [trʌ́ŋkeit] *vt.* **1.** cut off the top of (something). **2.** shorten (a sentence) by cutting off some parts of it. ▷**trun·ca·tion** [trʌŋkéiʃ(ə)n] *n.*

—[他] 1. [수목 따위의] 꼭대기를 자르다 2. [문장 따위]를 잘라 줄이다

trun·cheon [trʌ́ntʃ(ə)n] *n.* [C] (chiefly *Brit.*) a short, thick stick used as a policeman's baton. (cf. *U.S.* night stick)

—[名] 《英》 경찰봉, 경봉(警棒)

trun·dle [trʌ́ndl] *vt.* cause (something heavy) to roll along. —*vi.* roll along. —*n.* [C] **1.** the act or state of rolling. **2.** a small wheel for supporting or carrying something heavy. **3.** a low bed on wheels; a trundle bed.

—[他] [무거운 것]을 굴리면서 가다 —[自] 구르다 —[名] 1. 굴러가기 2. [침대·피아노 따위의] 작은 바퀴; 각륜(脚輪) 3. 각륜이 있는 침대

⁑**trunk** [trʌŋk] *n.* [C] **1.** the main stem of a tree. **2.** the body of a man or an animal, apart from the head and limbs. **3.** the main part of anything; a trunk line. **4.** a large box or chest to hold or carry clothes or personal belongings. **5.** the large nose of an elephant. **6.** 《*pl.*》 very short trousers worn by athletes, swimmers, etc. **7.** (*U.S. colloq.*) the compartment of an automobile for holding baggage, etc. (cf. *Brit.* boot)

—[名] 1. [나무의] 줄기 2. [동물의] 동체 3. 주요부; 간선(幹線); 본선 4. [여행용의] 큰 가방 5. 코끼리의 코 6. [스포오츠용] 짧은 바지 7. 《美口》 [자동차 뒤의] 짐 싣는 곳

trunk line [∠∠] *n.* the main line of a railroad, canal, long distance telephone exchange, etc.

—[名] [철도·운하·장거리 전신 따위의] 간선, 본선

trunk road [∠∠] *n.* a main road.

—[名] 간선도로

truss [trʌs] *vt.* **1.** tie (something) into a bundle. **2.** bind the wings of (a fowl) to the body before cooking. **3.** bind (a person's arms) to the body. 《*~ up* something》 **4.** support (a roof, bridge, etc.) with a framework.

—[他] 1. …을 다발로 만들다 2. [요리할 때에 새의 날개와 몸뚱이]를 한데 묶다 3. [사람의 두 팔]을 옆구리에 동이다 4. [지붕 따위]를 형구(桁構)로 버티다

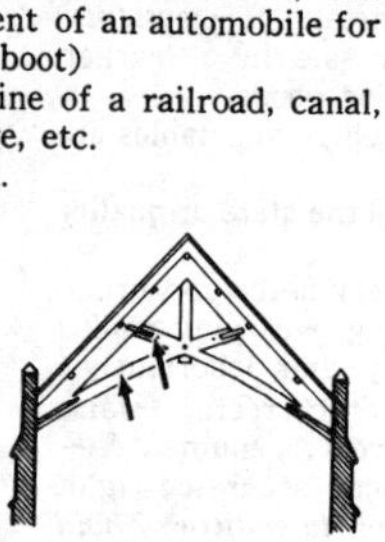

[truss 3.]

—*n.* [C] **1.** a bundle of hay or straw. **2.** a cluster of flowers. **3.** (*Architecture*) a framework of wood or metal supporting a roof or bridge. ⇒fig.

—[名] 1. [짚 따위의] 한 다발 2. [꽃의] 한 송이 3. 《建》 트러스, 형구(桁構)

⁑**trust** [trʌst] *n.* **1.** [U] firm belief in other's honesty, ability, etc. ¶*have* (or *put, place, repose*) *~ in someone.*① **2.** [C] a person or thing firmly believed in. ¶*She is our sole ~.* | *Our ~ is in God.*② **3.** [U] charge; duty; responsibility. ¶*hold something in ~*③ | *leave something in ~.*④ **4.** [U] business credit. ¶*buy things on* (or *upon*) *~.*⑤

—[名] 1. 신용; 신뢰 ¶①…을 신뢰하다 2. 신뢰할 수 있는 것 ¶②우리들이 신뢰하는 것은 신이다 3. 신탁; 책임; 의무 ¶③…을 보관하다/④…을 위탁하다 4. 신용 대부; 외상 ¶⑤외상으로 사다

—*vt.* **1.** rely on; have faith in (someone or something). 《~ someone *in*》 ¶*I cannot ~ your account.* **2.** sell things to (someone) on the condition of future payment; give credit to (someone). 《~ someone *for*》 ¶*Will you ~ me till next Friday?*⑥ | *He trusted me for the camera.* **3.** put (something) into another's care; entrust. 《~ something *to*; ~ someone *with*》 ¶*in ~* | *~ my typewriter to him* | *~ him with my watch.* **4.** tell a secret to (someone); confide. **5.** allow without fear. 《~ someone *to do*》 ¶*She didn't ~ her little boy out of her sight.*⑦ | *He could ~ the man to do the work.* **6.** hope;

—[他] 1. …을 신용(신뢰)하다 2. …에게 외상으로 팔다; 신용 대부하다 ¶⑥내주 금요일까지 외상으로 주시겠소? 3. …에게 맡기다, 신탁하다 4. 비밀 따위를 …에게 터놓다 5. 안심하고 …시켜 두다 ¶⑦그녀의 어린 아들은 눈만 떼면 안심할 수가 없다 6. 기대(희망)하다; …을 확신하다, 믿다 ¶⑧너를 도울 수 있으리라 믿는다 —[自] 신용하다; 신뢰하다

trust company

expect; believe. (~ *that* ... ; ~ *to do*) ¶*I ~ that she will soon feel better.* / *I ~ to be able to help you.*② —*vi.* have faith. (~ *in* (or *on, to*) *something*) ¶*I ~ in God.*

trust company [´ ˰´] *n.* a company that takes charge of the money or property of others. ⌈trust.⌉ —몡 신탁회사

trust deed [´ ´] *n.* a deed that transfers property in⌋ —몡 신탁증서

trus·tee [trʌstíː] *n.* ⓒ a person or firm who is responsible for the property of another person or company. —몡 수탁인(受託人); 보관인

trus·tee·ship [trʌstíːʃip] *n.* ⓤ **1.** the position or function of a trustee. **2.** the administrative control of some region, colony, etc. granted to another country by the United Nations. —몡 1. 수탁인의 권능 2. [국제연합의] 신탁통치

trust·ful [trʌ́stf(u)l] *adj.* ready to believe; full of confidence; trusting. ▷**trust·ful·ly** [-fuli] *adv.* —**trust·ful·ness** [-nis] *n.* ⌈other people; trustful.⌉ —몡 믿는; 신뢰하는

trust·ing [trʌ́stiŋ] *adj.* that trusts; apt to believe in⌋ —몡 믿는; 믿기 쉬운

trust·wor·thy [trʌ́stwə̀ːrði] *adj.* that can be relied on; worthy of trust; reliable. —몡 신용(신뢰)할 수 있는

trust·y [trʌ́sti] *adj.* (**trust·i·er, trust·i·est**) reliable; trustworthy. ¶*a ~ servant.*① —*n.* ⓒ (pl. **trust·i·es**) **1.** a trusty person. **2.** a prisoner considered to be trustworthy and so given special privileges. ▷**trust·i·ly** [-li] *adv.* —**trust·i·ness** [-nis] *n.* —몡 신뢰할 수 있는 ¶①믿을 만한 하인 —몡 1. 신뢰할 수 있는 사람 2. 모범수(囚)

‡**truth** [truːθ] *n.* (pl. **truths** [truːðz, +*Brit.* truːθs]) **1.** ⓤ the quality or state of being real or according to fact. **2.** ⓒ an established fact or principle; that which is true. ¶*Tell me the whole ~.*① / *To tell the ~, he is not honest.*② / *scientific truths.*③ **3.** sincerity.
in truth, in fact. —몡 1. 진리; 진실 2. 사실; 진상 ¶①진상을 전부 말해 다오/②사실을 말하면 그는 정직하지 못하다/③과학적 사실 3. 성실

圈 정말은; 실제는

truth·ful [trúːθf(u)l] *adj.* **1.** telling the truth habitually. **2.** according to reality; true. ¶*a ~ nature.*① —몡 1. 정직한, 거짓말을 안 하는 2. 정말의 ¶①거짓말을 안 하는 성질

truth·ful·ly [trúːθfuli] *adv.* with truth or honesty; in a truthful manner. ⌈of being truthful.⌉ —몡 성실히, 올바르게

truth·ful·ness [trúːθf(u)lnis] *n.* ⓤ the state or quality —몡 정직; 성실; 진실

‡**try** [trai] *v.* (**tried**) *vt.* **1.** attempt; endeavor. (~ *to do*) ¶*~ one's best* / *Try to get it finished by tomorrow.* / *She tried hard to keep back her tears.*① **2.** test. ¶*~ a new suit on*② / *Please ~ me for the job.*③ / *I tried the door to find out whether it was locked.*④ **3.** afflict; put (something) to a severe test; strain. ¶*His patience (courage) was severely tried.*⑤ / *Reading tries my eyes.* / *The waitress tries my patience.*⑥ **4.** examine and judge (something or someone) in a law court. (~ *someone for a crime*) ¶*~ a case* / *~ someone for election law violation* / *The prisoner was tried for murder.* —*vi.* make an effort; attempt; endeavor. (~ *at* (or *for, after*) *something*) ¶*~ for a post (after a position)* / *Try harder next time.* / *Try and be punctual.* —*n.* ⓒ (pl. **tries**) **1.** an attempt; an effort. ¶*have a ~ to catch it.* **2.** (*Rugby*) the act of putting the ball on the ground beyond the opponents' goal line. —몡 1. …을 하려고 노력하다; 해보다 ¶①그녀는 눈물을 참으려고 애썼다 2. …을 시험하다; 시험삼아 해보다 ¶②새 옷을 입어 보다/③시험삼아 내게 그 일을 시켜 보시오/④문이 잠겼는지 알아보려고 열어보았다 3. …을 피롭히다, 시련을 겪게 하다 ¶⑤그는 큰 인내(용기)가 필요했다/⑥그 여급에게는 참을 수가 없다 4. …을 심리(재판)하다 —몡 시도하다; 노력하다

—몡 1. 시도; 노력 2. (럭비) 트라이

·**try·ing** [tráiiŋ] *adj.* very annoying and difficult; painful. —몡 몹시 고된; 피로운

tsar [zɑːr, tsɑːr] *n.* ⓒ the title of the emperor of Russia; czar. —몡 러시아 황제의 칭호

T-shirt [tíːʃəːrt] *n.* ⓒ an undershirt for a man or boy with short sleeves and a round collarless neckline. —몡 티이샤쓰(목이 둥근 반소매 샤쓰)

Tu. Tuesday.

·**tub** [tʌb] *n.* ⓒ **1.** a large open container of wood or metal, used to hold water for washing, etc. **2.** a bathtub. **3.** a small cask for holding butter or lard. **4.** the amount contained in a tub. ¶*a ~ of water.* **5.** (*Brit. colloq.*) a bath. ¶*a hot ~.*① —몡 1. 물통, 함지 2. 목욕통, 욕조(浴槽) 3. 버터(라아드)통 4. 통(함지) 가득한 분량 5. (英) 목욕 ¶①뜨거운 목욕

tu·ba [t(j)úːbə / tjúː-] *n.* ⓒ a large brass wind instru- —몡 튜우바

ment that produces deep tones.

:tube [t(j)u:b / tju:b] *n.* [C] **1.** a long pipe of metal, glass, rubber, etc. ¶*a test* ~.① **2.** an enclosed hollow container made of thin metal, with a screw cap at the end, used for holding toothpaste, paint, etc. **3.** (*Brit.*) an underground railway; a subway. **4.** (*U.S.*) a bulb containing a vacuum and used in X-rays, radios, etc.
—[名] 1. 관(管) ¶①시험관 2. 튜우브 3.《英》지하철 4.《美》진공관

tu·ber [t(j)ú:bər / tjú:bə] *n.* [C] a thick round part of an underground stem bearing buds or eyes from which new plants grow.
—[名] 구근(球根); 괴경(塊莖)

tu·ber·cu·lar [t(j)u(:)bə́:rkjulər / tju(:)bə́:kjulə] *adj.* of tuberculosis.
—[形] 결핵[성]의

tu·ber·cu·lin [t(j)u(:)bə́:rkjulin / tju(:)bə́:k-] *n.* [U] a liquid made from the germ causing tuberculosis, used as a test of the presence of tuberculosis by being injected under the skin.
—[名] 투베르클린 주사액

tu·ber·cu·lo·sis [t(j)u(:)bə̀:rkjulóusis / tjubə̀:kju-] *n.* [U] a disease affecting various parts of the body, esp. the lungs.
—[名] 결핵

tu·ber·cu·lous [t(j)u(:)bə́:rkjuləs / tju(:)bə́:-] *adj.* of tuberculosis; tubercular.
—[形] 결핵[성]의

·tuck [tʌk] *vt.* **1.** push the edge of (something) into a narrow space. ¶*The bird tucks its head under its wings when it sleeps.* **2.** gather up (a dress) into a fold. **3.** fold (sleeves, etc.) tightly. ¶~ *up one's sleeves.*① —*vi.* **1.** draw together into folds. **2.** sew an end of dress so as to make it shorter.
—[他] 1. …을 끼워넣다 2. [옷]에 주름을 만들다, 접어 올리고 호다 3. [소매 따위]를 걷어 올리다 ¶①소매를 걷어 올리다 —[自] 1. 주름을 만들다 2. 접어 올리고 호다

—*n.* [C] cloth folded for ornament or to make a dress shorter.
—[名] 주름 겹단; 접어올려 시친 단

Tu·dor [t(j)ú:dər / tjú:də] *n.* the name of a royal family in England.
—[名] 튜우더 왕가

Tues. Tuesday.

:Tues·day [t(j)ú:zdí, -dei / tjú:z-] *n.* the third day of the week. ⇒[N.B.]
—[名] 화요일 [N.B.] Tues. 또는 Tu. 로 줄임

tuft [tʌft] *n.* [C] **1.** a small bunch of feathers, grass, hair, threads, etc. held together at the base. **2.** a group of plants or trees. ¶*a* ~ *of grass.*①
—[名] 1. [풀·깃털·털 따위의] 술, 타래, 뭉치 2. 덤불, 나무숲 ¶①한 다발의 풀

tuft·ed [tʌ́ftid] *adj.* **1.** decorated with a tuft. **2.** forming a tuft.
—[形] 1. 술을 단 2. 술 모양의

·tug [tʌg] *vt, vi.* (**tugged, tug·ging**) pull with force. ¶*The child tugged at his mother's hand.* / ~ *the cart out of the mire.* —*n.* [C] **1.** the act of pulling hard. ¶*The baby gave a* ~ *at Mary's hair.*① **2.** a tugboat.
—[他][自] [···을] 힘을 주어 당기다 —[名] 1. 세게 당기기 ¶①갓난아이는 메리의 머리카락을 홱 당겼다 2. 예인선(曳引船)

tug·boat [tʌ́gbòut] *n.* [C] a small, powerful boat used to pull large ships.
—[名] 예인선

tu·i·tion [t(j)u(:)íʃ(ə)n / tju(:)íʃ(ə)n] *n.* [U] **1.** teaching. **2.** the payment for teaching.
—[名] 교수, 수업; 수업료

:tu·lip [t(j)ú:lip / tjú:-] *n.* [C] a plant that has a brilliant-colored flower shaped like a cup; its flower.
—[名] 튜울립

tulip tree [ˊ-ˌ ˋ] *n.* a tall tree in North America which has tuliplike flowers and wood which is used in making furniture.
—[名] 튜울립 나무(북미산 목련과의 교목)

:tum·ble [tʌ́mbl] *vi.* **1.** fall down suddenly and violently by losing one's footing or support. ¶~ *down the stairs*① / ~ *into the room.*② **2.** roll about. ¶*He tumbled restlessly in his bed.*③ **3.** turn in an acrobatic way. —*vt.* **1.** cause (something or someone) to fall down suddenly and violently. **2.** throw down. 《~ something *out of* or *over*》
—[自] 1. 구르다, 쓰러지다 ¶①계단에서 굴러 떨어지다/②방으로 굴듯이 들어가다 2. 뒹굴다, 몸부림치다 ¶③그는 침대 안에서 몸부림쳤다 3. 공중제비하다 —[他] 1. …을 굴리다 2. …을 내던지다

—*n.* [C] **1.** an act of falling down suddenly. **2.** a skillful acrobatic act. **3.** a confused heap of things. ¶*Things are all in a tumble.*④
—[名] 1. 전도(轉倒) 2. 공중제비 3. 혼란, 뒤죽박죽 ¶④모두가 뒤죽박죽이다

tum·ble-down [tʌ́mbldàun] *adj.* ready to fall down; in a state of ruin.
—[形] 무너질 듯한; 황폐한

tum·bler [tʌ́mblər] *n.* [C] **1.** a person who performs tricks of jumping and falling; an acrobat. **2.** a drinking glass without a foot.
—[名] 1. 곡예사 2. [밑이 판판한] 큰 컵

tu·mid [t(j)ú:mid / tjú:-] *adj.* **1.** swollen. **2.** using many fine words but little meaning.
—[形] 1. 부어오른 2. 미사여구를 늘어놓은

tu·mor [t(j)ú:mər / tjú:mə] *n.* [C] a swelling part of the body.
—[名] 종기, 종양(腫瘍)

tu·mu·li [t(j)ú:mjulài / tjú:-] *n.* pl. of **tumulus**.

tu·mult [t(j)ú:mʌlt / tjú:-] *n.* ⓒ **1.** noise and confusion caused by great excitement. ¶*a great ~*①/ *make a ~.*② **2.** excitement; agitation of mind and emotion. ¶*in a ~ of feeling.*③
— ⓝ 1. 소동, 법석 ¶①큰 소동/②소동을 벌이다 2. 흥분; [마음의] 격동 ¶③마음이 산란하여

tu·mul·tu·ous [t(j)u(:)mʌltʃuəs / tju(:)mʌltjuəs] *adj.* full of tumult; excited; confused; stormy. ¶*a ~ meeting*①/ *~ passion.*② ▷**tu·mul·tu·ous·ness** [-nis] *n.*
— ⓐ 시끄러운; 흥분한; 혼란된; 폭풍우 같은 ¶①혼란된 모임/②폭풍 같은 격정

tu·mul·tu·ous·ly [t(j)u(:)mʌltʃuəsli / tju(:)mʌltju-] *adv.* in a tumultuous way; noisily; with agitation.
— ⓓ 시끄럽게; 마음이 산란하여

tu·mu·lus [t(j)ú:mjuləs / tjú(:)-] *n.* ⓒ (pl. **-lus·es** or **-li**) an ancient mound of earth over a grave.
— ⓝ 고분(古墳)

tu·na [tú:nə] *n.* ⓒ (pl. **-nas** or *collectively* **-na**) (*U.S.*) a very large fish caught for food in warm seas. (cf. *Brit.* tunny)
— ⓝ 《美》 다랑어, 참치

tun·dra [tʌ́ndrə, +*U.S.* tún-] *n.* ⓒ a vast, frozen plain in the northern part of Canada, Russia, etc.
— ⓝ 툰드라[지대], 동토대(凍土帶)

:**tune** [t(j)u:n / tju:n] *n.* **1.** ⓒ a melody. ¶*sing a merry ~*①/ *dance to a ~.* **2.** ⓤ the state of having the correct musical pitch. ¶*sing in ~*②/ *This piano is out of ~.*③ **3.** ⓤ the state of harmonious adjustment. ¶*He is in ~ with his friends.*④
—*vt.* adjust (one musical instrument's sound) to another, standard sound. ¶*~ up a violin*⑤/ *~ the piano.*
tune in, adjust a radio receiver to a particular frequency to receive a broadcast.
— ⓝ 1. 곡조, 가곡 ¶①즐거운 곡을 노래하다 2. 바른 가락 ¶②바른 가락으로 노래하다/③이 피아노의 음조는 틀린다 3. 조화 ¶④그는 친구들과 기분이 맞는다
— ⓥ [가락]을 맞추다 ¶⑤바이올린의 음조를 맞추다
🔲 [라디오의] 주파수를 맞추다

tune·ful [t(j)ú:nf(u)l / tju:n-] *adj.* full of melody; musical.
— ⓐ 가락이 맞는; 음악적인

tune·less [t(j)ú:nlis / tjú:n-] *adj.* not melodious; not musical.
— ⓐ 가락이 안 맞는

tun·er [t(j)ú:nər / tjú:nə] *n.* ⓒ a person who adjusts musical instruments to some standard state of harmony.
— ⓝ [악기의] 조율사(調律師)

tung·sten [tʌ́ŋstən] *n.* ⓤ a hard, heavy, metallic element used in making steel and for electric-lamp filaments.
— ⓝ 텅스텐

tu·nic [t(j)ú:nik / tjú:-] *n.* ⓒ **1.** a shirt-like garment worn by the ancient Greeks and Romans. ⇒fig. **2.** (*Brit.*) a short coat worn by soldiers or policemen. **3.** a woman's long jacket, usu. reaching below the hips.
— ⓝ 1. [고대 로마인이 입던] 가운 같은 겉옷 2. 《英》 약식 군복의 웃옷 3. [허리까지 내려오는] 부인용 웃옷

tuning fork [´- `-] *n.* a small steel instrument which gives a fixed tone when struck.
— ⓝ 음차(音叉)

[tunic 1.]

:**tun·nel** [tʌ́n(ə)l] *n.* ⓒ an underground passageway for a railroad, etc. —*vt., vi.* (**-neled, -nel·ing** or *Brit.* **-nelled, -nel·ling**) make a tunnel. ¶*~ a hill.*①
— ⓝ 터널, 굴 — ⓥⓝ 터널을 파다 ①언덕에 터널을 파다

tun·ny [tʌ́ni] *n.* ⓒ (pl. **-nies** or *collectively* **-ny**) (*Brit.*) the tuna; a large sea fish caught for food and sport. (cf. *U.S.* tuna)
— ⓝ 《英》 다랑어, 참치

tup·pence [tʌ́pəns] *n.* (*Brit. colloq.*) =twopence.

tur·ban [tə́:rbən] *n.* ⓒ **1.** a scarf to wind about the head, chiefly worn by men in India or in Mohammedan countries. **2.** a woman's hat shaped like this turban.
— ⓝ 1. 터어반 2. 터어반 같은 모자

tur·baned [tə́:rbənd] *adj.* wearing a turban.
— ⓐ 터어반을 쓴

tur·bid [tə́:rbid] *adj.* **1.** (of water, etc.) muddy; (of clouds, smoke, etc.) thick. ¶*a ~ river.*① **2.** confused; not clear. ¶*~ thought.*②
— ⓐ 1. 흐린, 탁한; 자욱한 ¶①탁한 강 2. 혼란한 ¶②혼란된 생각

tur·bine [tə́:rbin] *n.* ⓒ a kind of engine or motor operated by the force of water, steam, or air falling on the rim of a wheel.
— ⓝ 터어빈(수력이나 증기력으로 회전하는 일종의 원동기)

tur·bo·jet [tə́:rboudʒèt / tə́:boudʒét] *n.* ⓒ a jet engine that has a turbine-driven air compressor.
— ⓝ 터어보제트식 추진기관

tur·bu·lence [tə́:rbjuləns] *n.* ⓤ the state of being turbulent; disorder; confusion.
— ⓝ 동란; 혼란

tur·bu·lent [tə́:rbjulənt] *adj.* violently agitated or disturbed; not easy to control; disorderly. ¶*a ~ mob.*①
— ⓐ 미쳐서 날뛰는; 난폭한 ¶①소란한 군중

tu·reen [t(j)u:rí:n / tərí:n] *n.* [C] a large, deep dish with a lid for holding soup on a table. ⇒fig.
—[名] 뚜껑이 있는 움푹한 수우프 접시

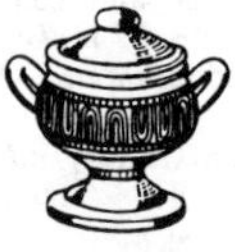
[tureen]

• **turf** [tə:rf] *n.* (pl. **turfs** or **turves**) **1.** [U] ⦅*collectively*⦆ short and thick grass with the earth under it; [C] a piece of this; sod. **2.** a solid mass of partly rotted plants and moss found in a marsh, used as fuel; peat. **3.** ⦅*the* ~⦆ a track for horse racing; horse racing.
—[名] 1. 잔디; 잔디밭; 옮겨심기 위해 떠낸 잔디 2. 이탄(泥炭) 3. 경마장; 경마용 말

tur·gid [tɔ́:rdʒid] *adj.* **1.** swollen. **2.** full of fine but unimportant words or expressions.
—[形] 1. 부어오른 2. 미사여구를 늘어놓은

tur·gid·i·ty [tə:rdʒíditi] *n.* [U] the state or quality of being turgid.
—[名] 부어오름; 과장

Turk [tə:rk] *n.* [C] a person of Turkey.
—[名] 터어키 사람

⁑ **tur·key** [tɔ́:rki] *n.* [C] a large domestic bird, the flesh of which is used for food; [U] its flesh.
—[名] 칠면조; 칠면조 고기

talk turkey, (*colloq.*) talk frankly and roughly.
[熟] ⦅口⦆솔직히 말하다

Tur·key [tɔ́:rki] *n.* a country in Asia Minor.
—[名] 터어키

Turk·ish [tɔ́:rkiʃ] *adj.* of Turkey; of the Turks or their language. **—*n.*** [U] the language of the Turks.
—[形] 터어키[사람・말]의
—[名] 터어키 말

tur·moil [tɔ́:rmɔil] *n.* [U] confusion; disturbance.
—[名] 소동; 혼란

⁑ **turn** [tə:rn] *vt.* **1.** cause (something) to move round a point; rotate. ¶ ~ *a handle.* **2.** change the position or sides of (something); cause (something) to become upside down; reverse. ¶ ~ [*over*] *the pages of a book*① / *She turned her collar up.*② / ~ *down the corner of a page* / ~ *a suit inside out.*③ **3.** change the direction of (one's eyes, face, etc.); direct; aim. ⦅~ *to* (or *toward, on*) something⦆ ¶ ~ *one's attention to someone* / ~ *one's eyes around* / ~ *one's course to the west.* **4.** change the nature or state of (something); make; translate. ¶ ~ *love to hate* / *The sound turned him pale.* / *Turn this passage into Japanese.* **5.** cause (someone) to go away; send; drive. ¶ *She always turns* [*away*] *beggars from her door.* / ~ *him adrift in the world.*④ **6.** go beyond; reach and pass. ¶ ~ [*the age of*] *eighty* / *It has just turned two.*⑤ **7.** go around (a corner). **8.** think about (something) carefully; consider. ⦅~ something *over*⦆ ¶ *We have turned this problem over and over.* **—*vi.*** **1.** move in a circle. ¶ *The moon turns round the earth.* **2.** change a course or direction of movement. ¶ ~ *around the corner to the left* / *This road turns at that points.* / *He turned when she called* [*to*] *him.*⑥ **3.** depend. ⦅~ *on* or *to* something⦆ ¶ *The success of the excursion turns on the weather.* / *She has no one but you to* ~ *to.*⑦ **4.** become changed in nature or condition. ⦅~ *into* something else⦆ ¶ ~ *red* / *Milk turns sour.* / *Water turns into ice.* **5.** (of leaves) change the color. ¶ *The leaves are turning.* **6.** change one's feelings, attitude, etc. ⦅~ *against* someone⦆ ¶ *He turned against his sweetheart.*
—[他] 1. …을 회전시키다; 돌리다 2. …을 뒤집어 엎다 ¶①책의 페이지를 넘기다/②그녀는 옷깃을 세웠다/③옷을 뒤집다 3. [방향・위치]를 바꾸다, …의 쪽으로 돌리다 4. [···의 모양・성질・마음]을 바꾸다; 번역하다 5. …을 쫓아버리다; 가게 하다 ¶④그를 세상에 내동댕이치다 6. …을 넘다 ¶⑤두 시가 좀 지났다 7. [모퉁이]를 돌다 8. …을 숙고하다 —[自] 1. 돌다 2. 방향을 바꾸다, 구부러지다 ¶⑥그녀가 부르자 그는 뒤돌아 보았다 3. …에 달려 있다; 의지하다 ¶⑦그녀에게는 너밖에 의지할 사람이 없다 4. …이 되다; 바뀌다 5. [나뭇잎이] 변색하다 6. 태도 따위를 바꾸다

1) ***turn about,*** look back.
2) ***turn away,*** dismiss; reject.
3) ***turn down,*** ⓐ reject. ¶ ~ *down the scheme.* ⓑ make less; reduce.
4) ***turn in,*** ⓐ (*colloq.*) go to bed. ⓑ (chiefly *U.S.*) hand over. ¶ ~ *in the report to the committee.* ⓒ return. ⓓ exchange. ¶ ~ *in an old car for a new one.* ⓔ enter.
5) ***turn loose,*** set free.
6) ***turn off,*** ⓐ stop the flow of (liquid or gas). ⓑ put out; dismiss.
7) ***turn on,*** ⓐ start the flow of (liquid or gas). ⓑ attack.
8) ***turn out,*** ⓐ drive (someone) out; expel; dismiss. ⓑ produce. ⓒ prove to be. ¶ *Her story turned out* [*to be*] *false.*

[熟] 1) 뒤돌아보다 2)해고하다, 추방하다 3)ⓐ각하하다; 거절하다 ⓑ작게(적게) 하다 4)ⓐ⦅口⦆취침하다 ⓑ⦅美⦆넘겨주다; 제출하다 ⓒ되돌리다, 돌려주다 ⓓ교환하다 ⓔ들어가다 5)해방하다 6)ⓐ마개를 틀어 …을 멈추다 ⓑ몰아내다; 해고하다 7)ⓐ마개를 틀어 …을 나오게 하다 ⓑ공격하다 8)ⓐ…을 쫓아내다; 추방하다; 해고하다 ⓑ…을 생산하다 ⓒ…임이 판명되다 9)ⓐ…을 넘겨주다; 제출하다 ⓑ[돈]을 벌어서 쓰다; 다루다 ¶⑧우리 회사는 작년에 100만 달러를 올렸다 ⓒ…을

9) ***turn over,*** ⓐ hand over. ⓑ (of money) get and use; handle. ¶*Our firm turned over a million dollars last year.*⑧ ⓒ think about (something).
10) ***turn up,*** ⓐ (*collóq.*) arrive; come. ⓑ (*Brit.*) find. ⓒ appear; come to light; happen.

잘 생각하다 10)ⓐ《口》도착하다; 오다 ⓑ《英》찾아내다 ⓒ나타나다; 분명해지다; 일어나다

—*n.* [C] **1.** the act of moving around; rotation. ¶*the ~ of a wheel.* **2.** a change of state or movement. ¶*take a ~*⑨ | *at the ~ of the century* | *a ~ of the wrist.*⑩ **3.** a curve; a bend. ¶*a ~ in the path.* **4.** a characteristic; a talent. ¶*be of a humorous ~*⑪ | *have a special ~ for music.* **5.** one's time or chance for doing something. ¶*It is your ~ to sing.* **6.** 《*a ~*》 an act; a spell of work. ¶*a good ~* | *take a ~ of work.* **7.** a short walk for exercise or pleasure. ¶*take a ~ in the garden.* **8.** form; style. ¶*I like the ~ of his sentences.*

—[名] 1. 회전 2. 변화; 전환 ¶⑨바뀌다/⑩손목의 비틀림 3. 굽은 곳, 모퉁이 4. 성격; 재능 ¶⑪유우머가 있는 성격이다 5. 차례 6. 행위; 한바탕의 일 7. 산책 8. 표현; 문체

1) ***at every turn,*** very often; every time; without exception.
2) ***by turns,*** one after another.
3) ***in turn,*** in proper order.
4) ***on the turn,*** about to turn or change.
5) ***out of turn,*** not in proper order.
6) ***take turns,*** do one after another in order; rotate.

[熟] 1)늘, 언제나; 예외없이 2)번갈아 3)차례로 4)바뀌는 고비에서 5)순서 없이 6)…을 교대로 하다

turn·coat [tə́ːrnkòut] *n.* [C] a person who gives up his former party or principles.

—[名] 배신자, 변절자

turn·down [tə́ːrndàun] *adj.* having the upper part folded or doubled down.

—[形] [옷깃을] 접어 젖힌

turn·er [tə́ːrnər] *n.* [C] a person or thing that turns, esp. a person who operates a machine to shape articles of wood, metal, etc.

—[名] [물건을] 돌리는 사람(것), 회전하는 사람(것); 녹로(轆轤) 세공사

turn·er·y [tə́ːrnəri] *n.* **1.** [C] a place where a turner works. **2.** [U] the art or product of a turner.

—[名] 1. 선반 공장 2. 녹로 세공

∗**turn·ing** [tə́ːrniŋ] *n.* **1.** [U] [C] the act of a person or thing that turns. **2.** a place where a road turns or branches off. ¶*Take the second ~ to the right.*

—[名] 1. 회전 2. 도는 모퉁이

turning point [∠- ∠] *n.* **1.** a place where something moving changes its direction. **2.** a time when a big change happens; a decisive moment. ¶*the ~ of one's life.*①

—[名] 1. 전환점 2. 전환기; 전기(轉機), 위기 ¶①생애의 전환기

tur·nip [tə́ːrnip] *n.* [C] a plant with a large, edible, round root.

—[名] 순무우

turn·key [tə́ːrnkìː] *n.* [C] a person who keeps keys of prison doors; a jailer.

—[名] 간수, 교도관

turn·out [tə́ːrnàut] *n.* [C] **1.** a group of people gathered for a special purpose. **2.** the amount produced; output. **3.** a carriage with its horses and attendants. **4.** (*Brit.*) a labor strike. **5.** (*U.S.*) the way in which a person is dressed and equipped.

—[名] 1. 사람의 모임, 출석자 2. 산출량, 생산고 3. 마차와 시중꾼 일행 4.《英》 동맹파업 5.《美》 몸치장, 옷차림

turn·o·ver [tə́ːrnòuvər] *n.* [U] **1.** the act of turning over. **2.** the total amount of money handled in a business during a given period.

—[名] 1. 전복, 뒤집힘 2. [일정 기간의] 총매상고

turn·pike [tə́ːrnpàik] *n.* [C] **1.** a gate where tolls are paid. **2.** a toll road.

—[名] 1. 통행세 징수소 2. 유료 도로

turn·stile [tə́ːrnstàil] *n.* [C] a post with horizontal cross bars that turn, used at entrances for making persons pass one by one; a similar mechanical device, as at a subway entrance. ⇨fig.

—[名] [십자형으로 된] 회전식 문

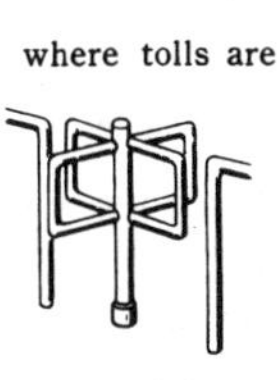
〔turnstile〕

turn·ta·ble [tə́ːrntèibl] *n.* **1.** [C] a round platform that turns, used for turning locomotives or cars around. ⇨fig. **2.** a similar platform for turning phonograph records.

—[名] 1. [철도의] 전차대(轉車臺) 2. [축음기의] 회전반

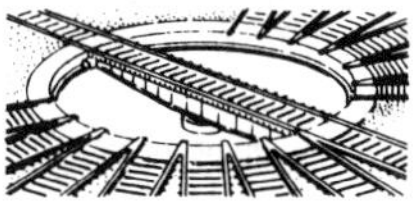
〔turntable 1.〕

tur·pen·tine [tə́ːrp(ə)ntàin] *n.* [U] a sticky, light-colored oil obtained from pine trees, used in paint and varnish.

—[名] 테레빈[유(油)]

T

tur·pi·tude [tə́:rpit(j)ù:d / tə́:pitjù:d] *n.* Ⓤ wickedness; baseness.

—ⓝ 사악(邪惡); 비열

tur·quoise [tə́:rkɔiz, -kwɔiz / tə́:kwɑ:z] *n.* Ⓤ **1.** a blue or greenish-blue precious stone. **2.** the color of this stone.

—ⓝ 1. 터어키옥(玉) 2. 청록색, 하늘빛

tur·ret [tə́:rit, túrit / tʌ́rit] *n.* Ⓒ **1.** a small tower added to the corner of a building or large tower. ⇒fig. **2.** a low, round, turning structure on a warship, tank, fort, etc. from which guns are fired.

—ⓝ 1. 작은 탑 2. [군함·전차·요새 따위의] 포탑

tur·ret·ed [tə́:ritid, túritid / tʌ́ritid] *adj.* having a turret or turrets.

—ⓐ 작은 탑(포탑)이 있는

tur·tle [tə́:rtl] *n.* Ⓒ a sea animal with a hard shell around its soft body.

—ⓝ 바다거북

tur·tle·dove [tə́:rtldʌ̀v] *n.* Ⓒ a kind of small European dove with a long tail, noted for its affection toward its mate.

[turret 1.]

—ⓝ 산비둘기

turtle shell [⌒ ⌒] *n.* tortoise shell.

—ⓝ 귀갑(龜甲)

tusk [tʌsk] *n.* Ⓒ a long, pointed tooth projecting from the mouths of some animals, such as elephants and wild boars. ⇒N.B. 「worm that produces it.」

—ⓝ [코끼리·산돼지·바다짐승 따위의] 엄니 N.B. 독사·맹수의 엄니는= fang

tus·sah [tʌ́sə] *n.* **1.** Ⓤ coarse, tough silk. **2.** Ⓒ the silk.

—ⓝ 1. 멧누에고치 실 2. 멧누에

tus·sle [tʌ́sl] *n.* Ⓒ a rough struggle. —*vi.* struggle roughly. (~ *with* someone)

—ⓝ 드잡이, 격투 —ⓥ 드잡이하다

tus·sock [tʌ́sək] *n.* Ⓒ a thick tuft or bunch of growing 「grass, twigs, etc.」

—ⓝ 풀숲, 덤불

tus·sore [tʌ́sɔ:r / tʌ́sə, -sɔ:] *n.* =tussah.

tut [tʌt] *interj.* an exclamation showing impatience, rebuke, annoyance, or contempt.

—ⓘ [짜증·경멸·비난을 나타내어] 쳇!, 쯧!

tu·te·lage [t(j)ú:tilidʒ / tjú:-] *n.* Ⓤ **1.** protection. **2.** the state of being under a tutor or guardian. **3.** teaching.

—ⓝ 1. 보호; 후견(後見) 2. 보호를 받음 3. 지도

tu·te·lar·y [t(j)ú:tilèri / tjú:tiləri] *adj.* **1.** serving as a protector or guardian. ¶*a ~ angel.*① **2.** of a protector or guardian.

—ⓐ 1. 수호하는 ¶①수호 천사 2. 수호의; 후견의

* **tu·tor** [t(j)ú:tər / tjú:tə] *n.* Ⓒ **1.** a private teacher. **2.** (*Brit.*) an officer in charge of the studies of undergraduates in universities or colleges, esp. at Oxford and Cambridge. **3.** (*U.S.*) a teacher ranked lower than an instructor in some universities and colleges. —*vt.* teach privately.

—ⓝ 1. 가정교사 2. (英) [개인적으로 연구를 지도하는] 지도교수 3. (美) 대학강사 —ⓥ …에 개인적으로 지도하다

—*vi.* act as a tutor. 「*the ~ system.*」

—ⓥ 가정교사를 하다

tu·to·ri·al [t(j)u:tɔ́:riəl / tju(:)-] *adj.* of a tutor. ¶~ *classes*」

—ⓐ 가정교사의; 개인지도의

tux·e·do, Tux·e·do [tʌksí:dou] *n.* Ⓒ (pl. **-dos** or **-does**) (*U.S.*) a man's black coat for evening wear with no TV television. 「tails; a dinner jacket.」

—ⓝ 턱시이도우

twad·dle [twádl / twɔ́dl] *n.* Ⓤ silly, tiresome talk or writing. —*vi.* talk or write in a silly or tiresome way.

—ⓝ 실없는 소리; 태작(駄作) —ⓥ 실없는 소리를 하다(쓰다)

twain [twein] *n., adj.* (*poetic*) =two.

twang [twæŋ] *n.* Ⓒ **1.** a sharp, quick, ringing sound of the string of a musical instrument, etc. **2.** a nasal tone of voice. —*vt.* cause (something) to make a sharp, ringing sound. —*vi.* **1.** make a sharp, ringing sound.

—ⓝ 1. [현(絃) 따위 퉁겼을 때의] 날카로운 진동음 2. 콧소리 —ⓥ …팅(윙)하고 울리다 —ⓥ 1. 팅하고 울리다 2. 콧소리를 내다

* **'twas** [twɑz / twɔz, twəz] it was. 「**2.** utter a nasal sound.」

tweak [twi:k] *vt.* pinch and twist (the nose, ears, etc.) suddenly and sharply with the fingers.

—ⓥ …을 꼬집다

—*n.* Ⓒ a sudden and sharp pinch and twist.

—ⓝ 꼬집기, 비틀기

tweed [twi:d] *n.* Ⓤ **1.** a soft woolen cloth with a rough surface, usu. made from two or more colors of yarn. **2.** (*pl.*) clothes made of tweed.

—ⓝ 1. 트위이드 2. 트위이드감의 옷

'tween [twi:n] *prep.* (*poetic*) =between.

tweet [twi:t] *n.* Ⓒ the chirping sound of a young bird. —*vi.* utter a tweet.

—ⓝ [새의] 지저귀 —ⓥ [새가] 짹짹 지저귀다

tweez·ers [twí:zərz] *n. pl.* a small instrument for pulling out hairs or picking up very small things.

—ⓝ 족집게, 핀셋

⁑ **twelfth** [twelfθ] *n.* **1.** ⦅usu. *the* ~⦆ number 12; 12th. **2.** [C] one of 12 equal parts of anything. —*adj.* of a 12th.
—[名] 1. 제 12 2. 12 분의 1 —[形] 제 12 의; 12 분의 1 의

⁑ **twelve** [twelv] *n.* **1.** [U] the number between eleven and thirteen; 12. **2.** [C] any group or set of twelve persons or things.
—[名] 1. 12, 열 둘 2. 12 개; 12 명

the Twelve Apostles, twelve persons chosen by Christ to preach the gospel to all the world.
[熟] 그리스도의 12 사도

—*adj.* of 12.
—[形] 12 의; 12 개의; 12 명의

twelve·month [twélvmʌ̀nθ] *n.* [C] (chiefly *Brit.*) twelve months; a year. ¶*this day* ~.①
—[名] 1년 ¶① 1년 후의 오늘

⁑ **twen·ti·eth** [twéntiiθ] *n.* **1.** ⦅usu. *the* ~⦆ number 20; 20th. **2.** [C] one of 20 equal parts of anything. —*adj.* of a 20th.
—[名] 1. 제 20 2. 20 분의 1 —[形] 제 20 의: 20 분의 1 의

⁑ **twen·ty** [twénti] *n.* [U] two times ten; 20. —*adj.* of 20.
—[名] 스물, 20 —[形] 20 의

'twere [twəːr, twər] =it were.

⁑ **twice** [twais] *adv.* **1.** two times. ¶*wash one's face ~ a day.* **2.** doubly. ¶*I want twice as much.*
—[副] 1. 두 번 2. 2 배

twice-told [twáistóuld] *adj.* **1.** told twice. **2.** told many times before; common and not fresh. ¶~ *tales.*
—[形] 1. 두 번 말한 2. 몇 번이나 말한; 케케묵은

twid·dle [twídl] *vt.* turn (something) a round idly; twirl. ¶~ *one's thumbs.* —*vi.* play idly. ⦅~ *with* something⦆
—[他] …을 만지작거리다 —[自] 만지작거리다; 가지고 장난하다

* **twig** [twig] *n.* [C] a small, slender branch of a tree or shrub.
—[名] 작은 가지

⁑ **twi·light** [twáilàit] *n.* [U] **1.** the faint light from the sky before sunrise or after sunset. ¶*morning ~ / evening ~.* **2.** any faint light. **3.** the period after or before full development.
—[名] 1. 해뜨기 전 또는 해지기 전의 땅거미, 어스레함 2. 희미한 빛 3. 여명기

—*adj.* **1.** of twilight. **2.** done during twilight. ¶*a ~ baseball game.*①
—[形] 1. 어스레한; 황혼의 2. 땅거미 속에서 행하여진 ¶①어둑어둑할 때 한 게임

twill [twil] *n.* [U] a strong cloth that shows parallel diagonal lines on the surface.
—[名] 능직(綾織)

'twill [twil] it will.

twilled [twild] *adj.* woven in diagonal lines.
—[形] 이랑지게 짠, 능직(綾織)의

* **twin** [twin] *n.* [C] **1.** one of two children or animals born at a single birth. **2.** one of two persons or things looking exactly like each other in appearance, shape, etc.
—[名] 1. 쌍동이 중의 한 사람 2. 아주 비슷한 것의 한 쪽, 쌍으로 된 것의 하나

—*adj.* **1.** born at a single birth. ¶~ *brothers.*① **2.** of two things separated but similar. ¶~ *beds.*
—[形] 1. 쌍동이의 ¶①쌍동이 형제 2. 한 쌍의

* **twine** [twain] *n.* [U][C] **1.** a strong, twisted thread or string of two or more strands. **2.** the act of twisting; the state of being twisted. —*vt.* twist. ¶~ *garlands.*① —*vi.* wind round. ⦅~ *about* or *round* something⦆ ¶*The snake twined around an apple tree.*②
—[名] 1. 꼰 실 2. 꼬아 합치기; 얽힘 —[他] …을 꼬다; 짜다 ¶①화환을 엮다 —[自] 감기다 ¶②뱀이 사과나무에 감겨 있었다

twinge [twindʒ] *n.* [C] a sudden, sharp pain in body or mind. ¶*a ~ of rheumatism / a ~ of conscience.*① —*vi.* feel a sudden sharp pain. —*vt.* cause such pain in (something).
—[名] 찌르는 듯한 아픔; 가책 ¶①양심의 가책 —[自] 찌르는 듯한 아픔(가책)을 느끼다 —[他] …을 아프게 하다

* **twin·kle** [twíŋkl] *vi.* **1.** shine with a flickering light. ¶*Stars ~.*① **2.** (of eyes) become bright. ¶*His eyes twinkled.* **3.** move quickly and lightly. ¶*The dancer's feet twinkled.* —*vt.* light flickeringly. —*n.* [U][C] **1.** a flickering light. **2.** a wink of the eye. ¶*in a ~.*②
—[自] 반짝이다 ¶①별이 반짝인다 2. [눈이] 반짝 빛나다 3. 어른거리다 —[他] …을 반짝반짝 빛나게 하다 —[名] 1. 반짝임 2. [눈을] 깜빡임 ¶②순식간에

twin·kling [twíŋkliŋ] *n.* [U][C] **1.** ⦅*sing.* only⦆ an instant. ¶*in a ~; in the ~ of an eye.*① **2.** a rapid flash or sparkle. ¶*the ~ of the stars.*
—[名] 1. 순간 ¶①순식간에 2. 반짝임

twirl [twəːrl] *vt.* **1.** turn (something) around rapidly. ¶~ *a cane.*① **2.** twiddle. ¶~ *one's moustache.* —*vi.* revolve rapidly. —*n.* [C] the act of twirling; the state of being twirled.
—[他] 1. …을 빙글빙글 돌리다 ¶①지팡이를 휘두르다 2. …을 만지작거리다 —[自] 빙글빙글 돌리다 —[名] 회전; 만지작거리기

⁑ **twist** [twist] *vt.* **1.** join (two or more threads, etc.) by winding one around another; make (a rope, etc.) in this way; intertwine. ¶~ *together threads into a rope / ~ a rope.* **2.** coil (something) about something else. ¶~ *a tape around a stick.* **3.** turn two ends of (some-
—[他] 1. [새끼 따위]를 꼬다, 뜨다; 꼬아서 …을 만들다 2. …을 감다 3. …을 비틀다; 짜다 ¶①철사를 비틀어 끊다 4. …을 누비고 나아가다 5. …을 삐다 6. [얼굴]을 찡그리다, 찌푸리다 ¶②그

thing) in opposite directions. ¶~ *a wet towel* / ~ *off a piece of wire.*① **4.** make (one's way) often changing from one direction to another. ¶~ *one's way through the crowd.* **5.** injure the muscle of (a part of the body) by twisting; wrench. ¶~ *one's ankle.* **6.** make (one's face) out of shape; give an ugly expression to (one's face); distort. ¶*Her face was twisted with pain.*② **7.** pull suddenly. ¶*The man twisted the letter out of her hand.* **8.** change the original meaning of (something); represent wrongly. ¶*They twisted her words into a hundred meanings.*③ —*vi.* **1.** be joined by winding one around another; be intertwined. **2.** wind or coil around something. **3.** (of a road, etc.) curve; wind. ¶*The path twists up the hillside.*④ **4.** go or move by often changing from one direction to another. ¶*They twisted through the crowd.* **5.** be injured in the muscle by twisting.
—*n.* [C] **1.** the act of twisting; the state of being twisted. ¶*a* ~ *in a rope* / *give a* ~.⑤ **2.** something made by twisting. ¶*a* ~ *of bread.*⑥ **3.** a sharp turn. ¶*a road with many twists.* **4.** an eccentric characteristic. ¶*His behavior shows his mental* ~.

녀의 얼굴은 고통으로 일그러졌다 7. …을 홱 당기다 8. [의미]를 외곡(歪曲)하다; 곡해하다 ¶③그들은 그녀의 말을 수백 가지로 달리 해석했다 —[自] 1. 꼬이다, 비틀리다 2. 감기다 3. [길 따위가] 구불구불 나아가다 ¶④길이 구불구불하게 언덕으로 통하고 있다 4. 요리조리 뚫고 나아가다 5. 삐다

—[名] 1. 꼼; 비틀림 ¶⑤ 꼬다, 비틀다 2. 꼰 실, 새끼 ¶⑥비비 꼰 빵 3. 굽이, 만곡(彎曲) 4. 부정, 부정직; 편협

twitch [twitʃ] *vt.* **1.** pull (something) with a quick, sharp movement. ¶~ *the table cloth from the table.*① **2.** move (a part of the body) with a sudden movement. ¶~ *one's fingers.*② —*vi.* **1.** pull suddenly. **2.** move suddenly in a quick manner. ¶*His face twitched with pain.* —*n.* [C] **1.** a sudden pull. **2.** a quick, sudden movement of a muscle.

—[他] 1. …을 홱 잡아당기다 ¶①식탁에서 식탁보를 홱 당겨 치우다 2. [몸]을 팔딱팔딱 움직이다 ¶②손가락을 까딱거리다 —[自] 1. 홱 잡아당기다 2. 팔딱팔딱 움직이다 —[名] 1. 홱 잡아당기기 2. 경련

twit·ter [twítər] *n.* [C] **1.** a sharp sound made by a bird. **2.** an act of laughing voicelessly; a giggle. **3.** an excited and restless condition. —*vt., vi.* **1.** (of a bird) sing. **2.** giggle; laugh voicelessly. **3.** tremble from excitement.

—[名] 1. [새의] 지저귐 2. 킬킬 웃음 3. 흥분, 떨림 —[他][自] 1. 지저귀다 2. 킬킬 웃다 3. [흥분하여] 부들부들 떨다

T

'twixt [twikst] *prep.* (*poetic*) between.

⁝ **two** [tu:] *n.* **1.** [U] the number between one and three; 2. ¶*a day or* ~.① **2.** [C] any set of two persons or things. ¶*by twos and threes*② / ~ *by* ~.③ **3.** [C] anything shaped like 2. —*adj.* of two.

—[名] 1. 둘, 2 ¶① 하루 이틀 2. 두 개; 두 사람 ¶②삼삼오오/③둘씩 3. 2자형의 것 —[形] 둘의; 두 개의; 두 사람의

two-edged [tú:édʒd] *adj.* **1.** having two cutting edges. **2.** having two different meanings.

—[形] 1. 쌍날의 2. 두 가지 뜻이 있는

two-faced [tú:fèist] *adj.* **1.** having two faces. **2.** ready to deceive others.

—[形] 1. 두 면이 있는 2. 위선적인

two·fold [tú:fòuld] *adj.* double; made of two parts. —*adv.* doubly.

—[形] 두 배(겹)의 —[副] 두 배(겹)로

two-hand·ed [tù:hǽndid] *adj.* **1.** having two hands. **2.** for use by two persons. **3.** needing two persons to operate.

—[形] 1. 두 손이 있는 2. 2인용의 3. 두 사람이 하는

two-masted [tù:mǽstid / -mɑ́:stid] *adj.* having two masts.

—[形] 쌍돛대의

two·pence [tʌ́pəns] *n.* [U] (*Brit.*) the sum of two pennies.

—[名] 《英》 2펜스

two·pen·ny [tʌ́pəni] *adj.* **1.** worth twopence. **2.** of little value; worthless.

—[形] 1. 2펜스의 2. 보잘것 없는

two-seat·er [tú:sí:tər] *n.* [C] a car or an airplane furnished with two seats.

—[名] 2인승 자동차(비행기)

two-step [tú:stèp] *n.* [C] a kind of dance in $^2/_4$ time; music for this dance.

—[名] 사교 댄스의 일종; 그 곡

two-storied [tú:stɔ́:rid] *adj.* having two stories or floors.

—[形] 2층집의

'twould [twud] it would.

ty·coon [taikú:n] *n.* [C] **1.** (*U.S. colloq.*) a wealthy, powerful businessman. **2.** the title formerly given to the Shogun of Japan.

—[名] 1. 《美口》 [실업계의] 거물 2. 대군(大君) [일본의 막부(幕府)의 쇼우군(將軍)에 대한 외국인의 호칭]

⁝ **ty·ing** [táiiŋ] *v.* ppr. of **tie**.

tyke [taik] *n.* =tike.

tym·pa·na [tímpənə] *n.* pl. of **tym·pa·num**

tym·pa·num [tímpənəm] *n.* [C] (pl. **-nums** or **-na**) **1.** the middle ear. **2.** the eardrum; thin skin in the ear which helps in hearing sounds.

—[名] 1. 중이(中耳) 2. 고막

type [taip] *n.* [C] **1.** a class, kind, or group having common characteristics. ¶*different types of hats*① / *He is of a poetic ~.*② **2.** a person or thing representing the characteristics, qualities, etc. of a kind, class, group, etc. **3.** a piece of metal or wood with a letter on its surface; ⦅*collectively*⦆ a set of such pieces. **4.** a printed letter, figure, design, etc. on either side of a coin or medal.
—[名] 1. 형(型), 타이프 ¶①틀린 형의 모자/②그는 시인형이다 2. 전형(典型), 견본 3. [인쇄] 활자 4. [화폐·메달 따위의] 앞뒤의 문자

—*vt., vi.* **1.** write or print (something) with a typewriter. **2.** become a model for (something).
—[他][自] 1. 타자기로 치다 2. 표본(전형)이 되다

type·script [táipskrìpt] [C] *n.* a typewritten copy.
—[名] 타자기로 친 원고

type·set·ter [táipsètər] [C] *n.* a person or machine that sets type.
—[名] 식자공(植字工); 식자기

type·set·ting [táipsètiŋ] *n.* [U] the act of setting type. ¶*a ~ machine.*①
—[名] 식자 ¶①자동 식자기

type·write [táipràit] *vt., vi.* (**-wrote, -writ·ten**) write or print with a typewriter.
—[他][自] 타자기로 치다

***type·writ·er** [táipràitər] *n.* [C] **1.** a machine for printing letters on paper by means of keys which are operated by the fingers. **2.** a typist.
—[名] 1. 타자기 2. 타자수

type·writ·ing [táipràitiŋ] *n.* [U] the act or art of using a typewriter; work done by such an act.
—[名] 타자기로 치기; 타자술; 타자기로 한 일

type·writ·ten [táiprìtn] *v.* pp. of **typewrite**
—*adj.* printed by a typewriter.
—[形] 타자기로 친

type·wrote [táipròut] *v.* pt. of **typewrite**.

ty·phoid [táifɔid] *n.* [U] a serious illness carried by dirty water or food, common in hot countries. —*adj.* of typhoid.
—[名] 장티푸스 —[形] 장티푸스의

***ty·phoon** [taifú:n] *n.* [C] a violent storm occurring in the western Pacific area.
—[名] 태풍

ty·phus [táifəs] *n.* [U] a serious disease which is carried to man by lice and other insects and which causes red spots on the skin.
—[名] 발진티푸스

***typ·i·cal** [típik(ə)l] *adj.* representing the characteristics, qualities, etc., of a kind, group, class, etc. ¶*a ~ example*① / *a man ~ of his class.*②
—[形] 전형적인; 대표적인 ¶①전형적인 일례/②그 계급을 대표하는 사람

typ·i·cal·ly [típik(ə)li] *adv.* in a typical way; to a typical degree.
—[副] 전형적으로

typ·i·fi·ca·tion [tìpifikéiʃ(ə)n] *n.* [U][C] the act of typifying; the state of being typified.
—[名] 대표, 상징

typ·i·fy [típifài] *vt.* represent (the characteristics, qualities, etc.) of a kind, class, etc. ¶*He typifies the pioneer.*①
—[他] …의 전형이 되다; …을 대표하다 ¶①그는 전형적인 개척자다

typ·ing [táipiŋ] *n.* [U] the act of printing by a typewriter; the art of using a typewriter.
—[名] 타이프를 치기; 타이프라이터 사용법

***typ·ist** [táipist] *n.* [C] a person who works with a typewriter, esp. one who does it as an occupation.
—[名] 타이피스트

ty·po·graph·ic [tàipəgrǽfik], **-i·cal** [-ik(ə)l] *adj.* of typography or printing.
—[形] [활판] 인쇄[술]의

ty·pog·ra·phy [taipágrəfi / -pɔ́g-] *n.* [U] **1.** the art of printing. **2.** the style or arrangement of printing.
—[名] 1. 인쇄술 2. 활자 조판체재

ty·ran·ni·cal [tirǽnik(ə)l], **-nic** [-nik] *adj.* of or like a tyrant; cruel; oppressive.
—[形] 폭군의, 전제적인; 압제의

ty·ran·ni·cal·ly [tirǽnikəli] *adv.* in a tyrannical manner; cruelly.
—[副] 압제적으로, 포학하게

tyr·an·nize [tírənàiz] *vt., vi.* rule as a tyrant with power and cruelty; oppress. ⦅~ *over* a nation⦆
—[他][自] 포학한 정치를 하다; 압제하다

***tyr·an·ny** [tírəni] *n.* (pl. **-nies**) [U][C] **1.** the cruel and oppressive exercise of power. **2.** [C] a tyrannical act. **3.** government by a cruel, absolute ruler.
—[名] 1. 압제 2. 포학한 행위 3. 전제정치

***ty·rant** [táiərənt] *n.* [C] a cruel, oppressive, and unjust ruler or person.
—[名] 폭군; 전제자

***tyre** [táiər] *n.* (*Brit.*) =tire.

ty·ro [táiərou] *n.* (pl. **-ros**) =tiro.

Ty·rol [tírɑl / tír(ə)l, tiróul] *n.* a region in the Alps partly in western Austria and partly in Italy and Germany.
—[名] 티롤

tzar [zɑ:r, tsɑ:r / zɑ:] *n.* =czar

U

U, u [ju:] *n.* [C] (pl. **U's, Us', u's, us** [ju:z]) **1.** the 21st letter of the English alphabet. **2.** something shaped like the letter U. ¶*a U tube.*①
—[名] 1. 영어 알파벳의 스물한번째 글자 2. U자형의 것 ¶①U자관(管)

u·biq·ui·tous [ju(:)bíkwitəs] *adj.* existing or appearing everywhere at the same time.
—[形] 편재(遍在)하는, 도처에 있는

u·biq·ui·ty [ju(:)bíkwiti] *n.* [U] the state of being ubiquitous.
—[名] 편재

U bolt [ˊ ˋ] *n.* a U-shaped bolt with threads and a nut at each end. ⇒fig.
—[名] U[자형] 볼트

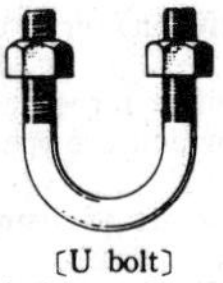
[U bolt]

ud·der [ʌ́dər] *n.* [C] (of a cow, a goat, etc.) the part of the body from which the milk comes.
—[名] [소·염소 따위의] 젖통

ugh [u:x, ʌx, uh] *interj.* an exclamation expressing horror, disgust, etc.
—[感] 억(공포·혐오 따위의 소리)

ug·li·ness [ʌ́glinis] *n.* [U] the state of being ugly.
—[名] 보기 흉함; 추악

⁑**ug·ly** [ʌ́gli] *adj.* (**-li·er, -li·est**) **1.** not pleasant to look at. ↔beautiful ¶*an ~ face* **2.** bad; disagreeable. ¶*~ news / an ~ rumor.*① **3.** threatening; dangerous. ¶*an ~ wound / The sky has an ~ look.*② **4.** (*U.S. colloq.*) ill-natured; bad-tempered.
—[形] 1. 보기 흉한, 못생긴 2. 나쁜, 불쾌한 ¶①나쁜 소문 3. 험악한; 위험한 ¶②날씨가 험악하다 4. 《美口》 까다로운; 심술궂은

u·ku·le·le [jù:kəléili] *n.* [C] a four-stringed guitar-shaped instrument of Hawaiian origin.
—[名] 우쿨레레

ul·cer [ʌ́lsər] *n.* [C] **1.** an open sore that discharges pus. **2.** a morally bad influence.
—[名] 1. 궤양 2. 폐해, 악폐

ul·cer·ate [ʌ́lsərèit] *vt., vi.* cause (the stomach, etc.) to have an ulcer; have or form an ulcer.
—[他][自] …에 궤양이 생기게 하다(생기다)

ul·cer·a·tion [ʌ̀lsəréiʃ(ə)n] *n.* [U] the act of ulcerating; the state of being ulcerated; an ulcer or group of ulcers.
—[名] 궤양[형성]

ul·cer·ous [ʌ́ls(ə)rəs] *adj.* of ulcers; having ulcers.
—[形] 궤양성의, 궤양에 걸린

ult. ultimo.

ul·te·ri·or [ʌltíəriər] *adj.* **1.** on the farther side. **2.** beyond what is expressed; hidden. ¶*~ plans.* **3.** later; future.
—[形] 1. 저쪽의 2. 밝히지 않는; 이면의 3. 뒤의; 장래의

ul·ti·ma·ta [ʌ̀ltiméitə] *n.* pl. of **ultimatum**.

•**ul·ti·mate** [ʌ́ltimit] *adj.* **1.** coming at the end; final. **2.** fundamental; basic. **3.** farthest. ¶*the ~ end of the globe.*①
—[形] 1. 최후의; 최종적인 2. 근본적인; 근본의 3. 가장 먼 ¶①지구의 끝

ul·ti·mate·ly [ʌ́ltimitli] *adv.* finally; in the end.
—[副] 마지막에, 결국은

ul·ti·ma·tum [ʌ̀ltiméitəm] *n.* [C] (pl. **-tums** or **-ma·ta**) a final condition or terms offered with threats.
—[名] 마지막 말; 최후 통첩

ul·ti·mo [ʌ́ltimòu] *adv.* in the last month. ⇒[N.B.] ¶*your letter received on the 10th ult.*
—[副] 지난달에 [N.B.] ult.로 줄임

ul·tra [ʌ́ltrə] *adj.* extreme. **—*n.*** [C] a person who has extreme opinions or who urges extreme measures.
—[形] 극단적인; 과격한 —[名] 과격론자; 급진론자

ul·tra- [ʌ́ltrə-] a word element meaning *beyond what is usual.*
— 「극단적으로」「초(超)…」「과(過)…」의 뜻의 연결형

ul·tra·ma·rine [ʌ̀ltrəmərí:n] *n.* [U] a bright, pure blue color. **—*adj.*** **1.** of a bright pure, blue color. **2.** beyond the sea; from overseas. ¶*~ provinces.*
—[名] 군청(群青) —[形] 1. 군청색의 2. 바다 저편의, 해외의

ul·tra·red [ʌ̀ltrəréd] *adj.* =infrared.

ul·tra·vi·o·let [ʌ̀ltrəváiəlit] *adj.* of the invisible part of the spectrum just beyond the violet. ¶*~ rays.*
—[形] 자외[선]의

U·lys·ses [ju(:)lísi:z] *n.* the hero of Homer's 'Odyssey'.
—[名] 율리시이즈

um·ber [ʌ́mbər] *n.* [U] a brown earth used as coloring matter; a brown or dark brown. **—*adj.*** of brown or dark brown.
—[名] 엄버(황갈색의 천연 광물 안료); 짙은 갈색 —[形] 짙은 갈색의

um·brage [ʌ́mbridʒ] *n.* [U] **1.** offense; displeasure. ¶*give ~ to someone*① */ take ~ at someone.*② **2.** all the
—[名] 1. 분개, 억울함; 불쾌 ¶①…을 화나게 하다/②…에 화내다 2. 나뭇잎;

leaves of a tree; (*poetic*) shade; shadow.
그늘, 응달

‡ **um·brel·la** [ʌmbrélə] *n.* [C] a light, folding frame covered with cloth, used as a protection against rain or sun.
—[名] 우산; 양산

um·pire [ʌ́mpaiər] *n.* [C] a person chosen to settle disputes; a person who rules on the plays in a game; a judge. —*vi., vt.* act as an umpire.
—[名] 중재자; 심판원 —[自][他] 심판하다

un, 'un [ən] *pron.* [C] (*colloq.*) one. ¶*He's a good ~.*
—[代] 《口》 놈, 것

un- [ʌn-] *pref.* **1.** 《before *adjectives* and *adverbs*》 not: *uninteresting* (=not interesting). **2.** 《before *nouns*》 lack of: *unhappiness* (=lack of happiness). **3.** 《before *verbs*》 do the opposite of: *unfold* (=do the opposite of folding).
—《接頭》 **1.** 부정을 나타냄 **2.** 결여 · 반대 **3.** 반대의 행위를 나타냄

UN, U. N. United Nations.

un·a·bashed [ʌ̀nəbǽʃt] *adj.* not ashamed.
—[形] 얼굴을 붉히지 않는

un·a·bat·ed [ʌ̀nəbéitid / ⌐ ⌐–-] *adj.* in full force; as violent as before.
—[形] 줄지 않는, 약해지지 않는

‡ **un·a·ble** [ʌnéibl] *adj.* not able; incapable. ¶*The baby was ~ to walk yet.* ↔able
—[形] 할 수 없는

un·a·bridged [ʌ̀nəbrídʒd] *adj.* not shortened; complete.
—[形] 생략할 수 없는; 완전한

un·ac·com·pa·nied [ʌ̀nəkʌ́mpənid] *adj.* **1.** not accompanied. **2.** (in music) without any instrument to support the main music.
—[形] **1.** 동행이 없는 **2.** (樂) 무반주의

un·ac·count·a·ble [ʌ̀nəkáuntəbl] *adj.* **1.** that can not be accounted for; strange. **2.** not responsible.
—[形] **1.** 설명할 수 없는; 기묘한 **2.** 책임 없는

un·ac·cus·tomed [ʌ̀nəkʌ́stəmd] *adj.* **1.** not accustomed. 《~ *to*》 **2.** not familiar; strange.
—[形] **1.** 익숙하지 않은 **2.** 낯선, 보지 못한; 기묘한

un·a·dorned [ʌ̀nədɔ́:rnd] *adj.* not adorned; simple.
—[形] 장식 없는; 간소한; 소박한

un·ad·vised [ʌ̀nədváizd] *adj.* **1.** done without due consideration; unwise. **2.** not advised.
—[形] **1.** 무분별한, 경솔한 **2.** 충고를 받지 않은

un·ad·vis·ed·ly [ʌ̀nədváizidli] *adv.* in an unadvised manner.
—[副] **1.** 무분별하게, 경솔하게

un·af·fect·ed [ʌ̀nəféktid →2.] *adj.* **1.** without pretense; simple; sincere; natural. ¶*He stared at me in ~ astonishment.* **2.** [*Brit.* ⌐– ⌐–] not affected; not influenced.
—[形] **1.** 젠체하지 않는; 소박한; 성실한; 자연스러운 **2.** 영향을 받지 않은

un·aid·ed [ʌnéidid] *adj.* not aided; without help.
—[形] 도움이 없는

u·na·nim·i·ty [jù:nənímiti] *n.* [U] complete agreement or unity.
—[名] 만장일치, 전원 합의

u·nan·i·mous [ju(:)nǽniməs] *adj.* being of one opinion or mind; showing complete agreement. ¶*a ~ agreement.*
—[形] 만장일치의, 이구동성의

* **u·nan·i·mous·ly** [ju(:)nǽniməsli] *adv.* in a unanimous manner; with complete agreement.
—[副] 이의 없이, 만장일치로

un·an·swered [ʌnǽnsərd / -á:nsəd] *adj.* **1.** not replied to. **2.** not proved wrong or mistaken. **3.** not returned.
—[形] **1.** 대답이 없는 **2.** 반박을 안 받는 **3.** 보답 없는

un·ap·proach·a·ble [ʌ̀nəpróutʃəbl] *adj.* that cannot be approached; very hard to approach; without an equal.
—[形] 가까이하기 힘든; 무적의

un·arm [ʌná:rm] *vt., vi.* take away weapons or means of attack. ¶*~someone of his weapon.*①
—[他][自] 무장을 해제하다 ¶①…에서 무기를 빼앗다

un·armed [ʌná:rmd] *adj.* not armed; without weapons; disarmed.
—[形] 무장하지 않은; 무기 없는

un·asked [ʌnǽskt / -á:skt] *adj.* not asked for.
—[形] 부탁받지 않은; 찾는 이 없는

un·as·sail·a·ble [ʌ̀nəséiləbl] *adj.* that can not be attacked.
—[形] 공격할 수 없는

un·as·sum·ing [ʌ̀nəsú:miŋ / -s(j)ú:m-] *adj.* unaffected; modest. ▷**un·as·sum·ing·ly** [-li] *adv.*
—[形] 젠체하지 않는; 겸손한

un·a·vail·a·ble [ʌ̀nəvéiləbl] *adj.* not available.
—[形] 쓸모없는; 이용할 수 없는

un·a·vail·ing [ʌ̀nəvéiliŋ] *adj.* without effect; useless. ▷**un·a·vail·ing·ly** [-li] *adv.*
—[形] 효과 없는; 무익한

un·a·void·a·ble [ʌ̀nəvɔ́idəbl] *adj.* that can not be escaped.
—[形] 피할 수 없는; 부득이한

* **un·a·ware** [ʌ̀nəwɛ́ər] *adj.* not aware; not knowing. ¶*He was ~ of the danger.* / *I was ~ that war was near.*
—[形] 알아채지 못하는; 모르는

un·a·wares [ʌ̀nəwɛ́ərz] *adv.* without being aware; by surprise; unintentionally.
—[副] 모르고, 불시에

un·bal·anced [ʌnbǽlənst] *adj.* not balanced; disordered in mind.
—[形] 균형을 잃은; 착란한

un·bar [ʌnbá:r] *vt.* (**-barred, -bar·ring**) remove the bars from (something); unlock.
—[他] …의 가로장을 떼다, 빗장을 벗기다

un·bear·a·ble [ʌnbɛ́ərəbl] *adj.* not bearable; impossible to endure. ▷**un·bear·a·ble·ness** [-nis] *n.*
—[形] 참을 수 없는; 견딜 수 없는

un·bear·a·bly [ʌnbɛ́ərəbli] *adv.* in an unbearable manner.
—[副] 참을 수 없을 만큼

U

un·beat·en [ʌnbí:tn] *adj.* **1.** not struck. **2.** not defeated. **3.** not trodden. ¶*an ~ track.* —[形] **1.** 매맞지 않은 **2.** 져 본 일이 없는 **3.** 밟아 다지지 않은

un·be·com·ing [ʌ̀nbikʌ́miŋ] *adj.* not becoming, not suitable; improper. —[形] 어울리지 않는; 부적당한; 예의에 어긋난

un·be·lief [ʌ̀nbilí:f] *n.* [U] lack of belief; lack of belief in God. —[名] 의심, 의혹; 신을 믿지 않음

un·be·liev·a·ble [ʌ̀nbilí:vəbl] *adj.* not believable; that can not be believed or trusted. —[形] 믿기 어려운

un·be·liev·er [ʌ̀nbilí:vər] *n.* [C] a person who does not believe; a person who does not believe in God. —[名] 믿지 않는 사람; 회의(懷疑)하는 사람

un·bend [ʌnbénd] *v.* (**-bent** or **-bend·ed**) *vt.* **1.** make (something bent) straight. **2.** relax. ¶~ *oneself.* —*vi.* become straight; become relaxed. —[他] **1.** …을 곧게 하다 **2.** …을 편하게 하다 —[自] 곧게 되다, 긴장을 풀고 쉬다

un·bend·ing [ʌnbéndiŋ] *adj.* not bending; stiff; firm. —*n.* [U] relaxation. —[形] 구부러지지 않는; 굳은; 고집 센 —[名] 몸을 편하게 하기; 기분풀이

un·bent [ʌnbént] pt. and pp. of **unbend**.

un·bi·ased, -assed [ʌnbáiəst] *adj.* not prejudiced; fair. —[形] 편견없는; 공평한

un·bid·den [ʌnbídn] *adj.* **1.** not commanded. **2.** not invited. —[形] **1.** 명령받지 않은 **2.** 초대받지 않은

un·blessed, -blest [ʌnblést] *adj.* not blessed; unhappy; miserable; not holy. —[形] 축복받지 못한; 불행한; 신성하지 않은

un·blush·ing [ʌnblʌ́ʃiŋ] *adj.* not blushing; shameless. —[形] 얼굴을 붉히지 않는

un·bod·ied [ʌnbádid / -bɔ́did] *adj.* having no body; formless. —[形] 육체에서 떠난; 무형의

un·born [ʌnbɔ́:rn] *adj.* not yet born; of the future. —[形] 아직 태어나지 않은; 장래의

un·bos·om [ʌnbúzəm] *vt.* reveal; confess. ¶~ *oneself.* —[他] …을 털어놓다; 고백하다

un·bound·ed [ʌnbáundid] *adj.* not limited; boundless. —[形] 한계 없는; 무한의

un·bri·dled [ʌnbráidld] *adj.* not having a bridle on; not controlled. —[形] 말굴레가 없는; 구속받지 않은

un·bro·ken [ʌnbróuk(ə)n] *adj.* **1.** not broken; whole. **2.** not interrupted; continuous. ¶*She had seven hours of ~ sleep.* **3.** not beaten. ¶*an ~ record.* **4.** not tamed. —[形] **1.** 부서지지 않은; 완전한 **2.** 방해받지 않은; 계속되는 **3.** 깨뜨릴 수 없는 **4.** 길들지 않은

un·buck·le [ʌnbʌ́kl] *vt.* unfasten the buckle or buckles of (something). —[他] …의 죔쇠를 끄르다

un·bur·den [ʌnbə́:rdn] *vt.* remove a load from (something); relieve (one's mind or heart) by talking. —[他] …에서 짐을 내리다; [마음]의 무거운 짐을 덜다

un·but·ton [ʌnbʌ́tn] *vt.* unfasten the button or buttons of (something). —[他] …의 단추를 끄르다

un·called-for [ʌnkɔ́:ldfɔ̀:r] *adj.* not required or desired; not necessary; out of place. —[形] 쓸데없는, 불필요한; 부당한

un·can·ny [ʌnkǽni] *adj.* (**-ni·er, -ni·est**) strange; mysterious. —[形] 무시무시한; 신비한

un·cared-for [ʌ́nkɛ́ərdfɔ̀:r] *adj.* not looked after; neglected. —[形] 돌보는 사람 없는; 내팽개친

un·ceas·ing [ʌnsí:siŋ] *adj.* without stop; continuous. ▷**un·ceas·ing·ly** [-li] *adv.* —[形] 끊임없는; 연속된

un·cer·e·mo·ni·ous [ʌ̀nserimóuniəs] *adj.* informal; lacking in polite behavior. —[形] 격식을 안 차리는; 허물없는; 실례되는

un·cer·e·mo·ni·ous·ly [ʌ̀nserimóuniəsli] *adv.* in an unceremonious manner. —[副] 격식을 차리지 않고; 버릇없이

* **un·cer·tain** [ʌnsə́:rtn] *adj.* **1.** doubtful; not sure. 《~ *of*》 ¶*I am ~ of success. / It is ~ how long I shall stay.* **2.** often changing; not reliable. ¶~ *weather.* —[形] **1.** 의심스러운; 불확실한 **2.** 변하기 쉬운; 기대할 수 없는

un·cer·tain·ty [ʌnsə́:rtnti] *n.* (*pl.* **-ties**) **1.** [U] lack of certainty; doubt. **2.** [C] something uncertain. —[名] **1.** 불확실; 불확정; 의심 **2.** 미덥지 못한 것

un·change·a·ble [ʌntʃéindʒəbl] *adj.* impossible or unlikely to be changed. —[形] 변하지 않는, 불변의

un·changed [ʌntʃéindʒd] *adj.* not changed. —[形] 변화없는

un·chart·ed [ʌntʃá:rtid] *adj.* not mapped; not marked on a chart. —[形] 해도(지도)에 없는; 해도(지도)에 표시되지 않은

un·chris·tian [ʌnkrístʃ(ə)n, +*Brit.* ʌ́nkrístjən] *adj.* not Christian; unworthy of Christians. —[形] 그리스도 교도가 아닌; 그리스도 교도답지 않은

un·civ·il [ʌnsív(i)l] *adj.* **1.** not civil; impolite. **2.** not civilized. —[形] **1.** 예의를 모르는; 버릇없는 **2.** 야만의

un·civ·i·lized [ʌnsívilàizd] *adj.* not civilized; savage; barbarous. —[形] 미개한; 야만의

un·clasp [ʌnklǽsp / -klá:sp] *vt.* unfasten; release (something) from a clasp or grasp. ¶~ *a pistol.* —*vi.* become unfastened; open. —[他] …의 걸쇠를 벗기다; [손에 쥐고 있던 것]을 놓다 —[自] 벗겨지다; 열리다

: **un·cle** [ʌ́ŋkl] *n.* [C] **1.** the brother of one's father or —[名] **1.** 아저씨, 백부, 숙부 **2.** 이모부, 고

mother. **2.** the husband of one's aunt. **3.** (*colloq.*) an elderly man. **4.** (*slang*) a pawnbroker.
모부 **3.** [아무에게나 부르는 말로] 아저씨 **4.** 《口》 전당포 주인

Uncle Sam [ˊ- ˊ] *n.* the government or people of the United States.
—[名] 미국 정부, 미국민

un·close [ʌnklóuz] *vt., vi.* open; disclose.
—[他][自] [···을] 열다; 드러내다

un·coil [ʌnkɔ́il] *vt.* unwind. —*vi.* become loose.
—[他] ···을 풀다 —[自] 풀리다

* **un·com·fort·a·ble** [ʌnkʌ́mfərtəbl] *adj.* not comfortable; uneasy; disagreeable. ▷**un·com·fort·a·ble·ness** [-nis] *n.*
—[形] 기분이 언짢은; 불안한; 불쾌한

* **un·com·mon** [ʌnkámən / -kɔ́m-] *adj.* unusual; rare; remarkable. ▷**un·com·mon·ness** [-nis] *n.*
—[形] 좀처럼 없는, 진귀한; 비범한

un·com·mon·ly [ʌnkámənli / -kɔ́m-] *adv.* not common; unusually; remarkably.
—[副] 드물게; 보통 아니게; 멋지게

un·com·pro·mis·ing [ʌ̀nkámprəmàiziŋ / -kɔ́m-] *adj.* firm; determined.
—[形] 타협하지 않는, 완고한

un·con·cern [ʌ̀nkənsə́:rn] *n.* [U] lack of concern or interest.
—[名] 무관심; 냉담

un·con·cerned [ʌ̀nkənsə́:rnd] *adj.* not concerned; not interested.
—[形] 무관심한; 태연한; 근심하지 않는

un·con·cern·ed·ly [ʌ̀nkənsə́:rn(i)dli] *adv.* in an unconcerned manner; indifferently.
—[副] 태연히, 개의치 않고

un·con·di·tion·al [ʌ̀nkəndíʃən(ə)l] *adj.* without conditions; absolute.
—[形] 무조건의; 절대적인

un·con·quer·a·ble [ʌnkáŋkərəbl / -kɔ́ŋ-] *adj.* that can not be conquered.
—[形] 정복할 수 없는

un·con·scion·a·ble [ʌnkánʃ(ə)nəbl / -kɔ́n-] *adj.* not guided or controlled by conscience; unreasonable.
—[形] 비양심적인; 무도한; 불합리한

* **un·con·scious** [ʌnkánʃəs / -kɔ́n-] *adj.* **1.** not conscious; not clearly perceived to exist. **2.** not aware. 《~ *of*》 ¶*He was ~ of his guilt.* / *I am ~ of having said so.*① **3.** not deliberate; not intended.
—[形] **1.** 무의식의; 의식불명의 **2.** 모르는 ¶①그렇게 말한 기억이 없다 **3.** 고의가 아닌

the unconscious, one's unconscious thoughts, desires, fears, etc.
[熟] [사상·욕망·공포 따위의] 잠재의식

un·con·scious·ly [ʌnkánʃəsli / -kɔ́n-] *adv.* in an unconscious manner.
—[副] 무의식적으로, 자기도 모르게

un·con·sti·tu·tion·al [ʌ̀nkanstit(j)ú:ʃən(ə)l / -kɔnstitjú:-] *adj.* contrary to the constitution.
—[形] 헌법 위반의

un·cork [ʌnkɔ́:rk] *vt.* pull a cork from (something).
—[他] ···의 코르크 마개를 뽑다

un·cou·ple [ʌnkʌ́pl] *vt.* loose (dogs, etc.) from a leash or couple; unfasten.
—[他] [개 따위]를 가죽끈에서 끄르다; ···을 풀다

un·couth [ʌnkú:θ] *adj.* **1.** not skillful; lacking in polish and grace. **2.** strange; not known or familiar. ▷**un·couth·ness** [-nis] *n.*
—[形] **1.** 미숙한; 세련되지 못한, 투박한 **2.** 이상한; 미지의; 친숙하지 않은

* **un·cov·er** [ʌnkʌ́vər] *vt.* **1.** remove the top or cover from (something); take the hat or cap from (one's head). **2.** expose; reveal. —*vi.* take off the hat or cap out of respect.
—[他] **1.** ···의 뚜껑(덮개)을 벗기다; ···에서 모자를 벗다 **2.** ···을 폭로하다; 털어놓다 —[自] 탈모하다

unc·tion [ʌ́ŋkʃ(ə)n] *n.* [U] **1.** the act of rubbing with oil at a religious ceremony; the oil used for this. **2.** the oil used to heal wounds.
—[名] [성별(聖別)의 표시인] 도유(塗油) **2.** 바르는 기름; 고약, 연고

un·cul·ti·vat·ed [ʌnkʌ́ltivèitid] *adj.* **1.** not cultivated. **2.** not developed. **3.** uncivilized.
—[形] **1.** 개간되지 않은 **2.** 육성(배양)되지 않은 **3.** 교양 없는

un·daunt·ed [ʌndɔ́:ntid] *adj.* not afraid; bold.
—[形] 겁내지 않는, 용감한

un·de·ceive [ʌ̀ndisí:v] *vt.* free (someone) from deception, mistake, or a belief for which there is no foundation.
—[他] ···의 미몽(迷夢)을 깨우치다, ···에게 진실을 깨닫게 하다

un·de·cid·ed [ʌ̀ndisáidid] *adj.* not decided; not having made up one's mind.
—[形] 미결정의; 우유부단한

un·de·fined [ʌ̀ndifáind] *adj.* not described or explained exactly; indefinite.
—[形] 정의(定義)가 안 내려진; 막연한

un·de·ni·a·ble [ʌ̀ndináiəbl] *adj.* that can not be denied; unquestionable; excellent.
—[形] 부정할 수 없는, 말할 나위 없는

un·de·ni·a·bly [ʌ̀ndináiəbli] *adv.* beyond denial; certainly.
—[副] 부정할 수 없게; 명백히

⁝ **un·der** [ʌ́ndər] *prep.* **1.** situated below; beneath. ¶*Tired, they rested ~ a tree.* / *They sang in the open air ~ the moon.* **2.** in a position lower than the surface of; covered by; sheltered by. ¶*the water ~ the ground*① / *~ heavy blankets* / *~ cover of darkness.*② **3.** less or below in number, amount, quality, etc. than. ¶*He looks to be ~ forty.* / *I bought this hat for ~ £2.* **4.** subject to the control, influence, instruction, etc. of. ¶*~ the*
—[前] **1.** ···의 아래에; ···의 기슭에 **2.** ···의 표면 밑에; ···에 덮여(가리어져) ¶①지하수/②어둠을 틈타서 **3.** [수량 따위가] ···이하의, 미만의 **4.** ···의 지배하에, 영향 밑에서, 지도하에서

U

leadership of two statesmen | *He studied* ~ *a noted scientist.* | *He was an officer* ~ *Napoleon.*③ **5.** during the time or rule of. ¶ *Under this sovereign, the country became the theater of a long war.*④ **6.** subjected to the effort or action of; in the process of. ¶ *a building* ~ *construction*⑤ | *a question* ~ *discussion* | *be* ~ *medical treatment.*⑥ **7.** according to; bound by. ¶ ~ *oath*⑦ | ~ *the terms of the contract.* **8.** suffering the effect of. ¶ ~ *an anesthetic.* **9.** because of. ¶ ~ *the circumstances.* **10.** represented by. ¶ ~ *a false name.*⑧ **11.** beneath in classification. ¶ ~ *this subject.*

¶③그는 나폴레옹 휘하의 군인이었다 **5.** …의 사이, …시대에(의) ¶④이 국왕의 치세 중에 그 나라는 오랜 전쟁의 무대가 되었다 **6.** …을 받아; 진행중으로(의) ¶⑤건축 중인 건물/⑥치료를 받고 있다 **7.** …에 따라서; …에 얽매여 ¶⑦선서를 하고 **8.** [약 따위가] 효과가 있어 **9.** …때문에 **10.** …의 아래 [숨어] ¶⑧가명으로 **11.** [분류 따위에] 속하여

—*adv.* in or to a lower position or state; below. ¶ *A cork floated, but a stone went* ~.

—[副] 아래에, 종속하여; 이하로

—*adj.* lower in position, rank, amount, or degree. ¶ *the* ~ *lip* | *the* ~ *surface of a leaf.*

—[形] 하부의

un·der·brush [ʌ́ndərbrʌ̀ʃ] *n.* [U] bushes or small trees growing beneath large trees in a forest.

—[名] [큰 나무 밑의] 잔풀, 덤불

un·der·clothes [ʌ́ndərklòuz, -klòuðz] *n. pl.* underwear; clothes worn under a suit or dress.

—[名] 속옷, 내의

un·der·cloth·ing [ʌ́ndərklòuðiŋ] *n.* [U] underclothes.

—[名] 속옷, 내의

un·der·cov·er [ʌ̀ndərkʌ́vər / ʌ́ndəkʌ̀və] *adj.* working or done in secret.

—[形] 비밀리에 행해진, 비밀의

un·der·cur·rent [ʌ́ndərkə̀:r(ə)nt / ʌ́ndəkʌ̀r(ə)nt] *n.* [C] a current of water flowing beneath the surface; a hidden or underlying tendency of feeling or opinion.

—[名] 저류(底流), 암류; 속마음

un·der·cut [ʌ̀ndərkʌ́t →*n.*] *vt.* (**-cut, -cut·ting**) **1.** cut away (something) from below or beneath. **2.** offer (goods, etc.) at a lower price than one's competitors. **3.** (in games) hit (a golf ball, etc.) so that it rises high and comes to rest without rolling far. —*n.* [⌐–⌐] **1.** [C] a cut made underneath. **2.** [U] the tenderloin or fillet of beef. —*adj.* cut away underneath.

—[他] **1.** …의 밑을 잘라내다 **2.** …을 싸게 팔다 **3.** [공]을 쳐올리다
—[名] **1.** 밑을 잘라내기 **2.** [소·돼지의] 허릿살 —[形] 밑을 잘라낸

under·de·vel·oped [ʌ̀ndərdivéləpt] *adj.* not yet fully developed.

—[形] 발육부전의; 현상 부족의

un·der·dog [ʌ́ndərdɔ̀:g / ʌ́ndədɔ̀g] *n.* [C] a loser or probable loser in a contest or struggle.

—[名] 패배자, 패배가 예상되는 사람

un·der·done [ʌ̀ndərdʌ́n] *adj.* not cooked enough.

—[形] 설구워진, 설익은

un·der·es·ti·mate *vt.* [ʌ̀ndəréstimèit →*n.*] estimate (something) below the actual value, amount, etc. ↔overestimate —*n.* [-mit, -mèit] [C] an estimate that is too low.

—[他] …을 싸게 평가하다; 너무 얕보다 —[名] 싼 견적; 과소평가

un·der·ex·po·sure [ʌ̀nd(ə)rikspóuʒər] *n.* [U] [C] exposure to the light for too short a time; an underexposed film or plate. ↔overexposure

—[名] [필름 따위의] 노출부족; 노출부족의 필름

un·der·fed [ʌ̀ndərféd] *v.* pt. and pp. of **underfeed**.
—*adj.* given insufficient food; not properly nourished.

—[形] 음식이 불충분한; 영양불량의

un·der·feed [ʌ̀ndərfí:d] *vt.* (**-fed**) feed too little.

—[他] …에게 음식을 충분히 주지 않다

un·der·foot [ʌ̀ndərfút] *adv.* beneath the feet; (*U. S.*) in the way.

—[副] 발 밑에, 짓밟아; 《美》 방해가 되어

un·der·gar·ment [ʌ́ndərgɑ̀:rmənt] *n.* [C] an article of underwear.

—[名] 속옷, 내의

* **un·der·go** [ʌ̀ndərgóu] *vt.* (**-went, -gone**) experience; be subjected to; endure; suffer. ¶ ~ *an operation.*①

—[他] …을 경험하다; 받다; 참다; 입다 ¶①수술을 받다

un·der·gone [ʌ̀ndərgɔ́:n / ʌ̀ndəgɔ́n] *v.* pp. of **undergo**.

un·der·grad·u·ate [ʌ̀ndərgrǽdʒuit / -djuit] *n.* [C] a university student who has not yet received a degree. ↔postgraduate. —*adj.* of or for undergraduates.

—[名] 대학의 재학생 —[形] [재학 중인] 대학생의

* **un·der·ground** *adj.* [ʌ́ndərgráund →*adv.*] **1.** beneath the surface of the earth. **2.** secret. —*n.* [C] 《usu. *the* ~》 (*Brit.*) a subway. —*adv.* [ʌ̀ndərgráund] beneath the surface of the ground; secretly. ¶ *go* ~.①

—[形] **1.** 지하의 **2.** 비밀의 —[名] 지하철 —[副] 지하에; 비밀히 ¶①지하로 들어가다(잠입하다)

un·der·growth [ʌ́ndərgròuθ] *n.* [U] low bushes or shrubs in a wood or forest; underbrush.

—[名] [큰 나무 밑의] 잔풀; 덤불

un·der·hand [ʌ́ndərhæ̀nd] *adj.* **1.** (of a ball) thrown with the hand kept below the level of the shoulder. **2.** not

—[形] **1.** [공을 어깨] 밑으로 던지는 **2.** 비밀의; 교활한

underhanded [1247] **understand**

open; secret; dishonest. —*adv.* **1.** with the hand below the shoulder. **2.** secretly.
—⦿ 1. 밑으로 먼저서 2. 비밀히

un·der·hand·ed [ʌ̀ndərhǽndid] *adj.* secret; lacking the required number of workers, etc.
—⦿ 비밀의; 일손이 모자라는

un·der·laid [ʌ̀ndərléid] *v.* pt. and pp. of **underlay**.
un·der·lain [ʌ̀ndərléin] *v.* pp. of **underlie**.
un·der·lay [ʌ̀ndərléi] *vt.* (**-laid**) lay (something) under something else.
—⦿ …을 […의] 아래에 깔다

un·der·lie [ʌ̀ndərlái] *vt.* (**-lay, -lain, -ly·ing**) lie or be beneath; be at the basis of (something).
—⦿ …의 밑에 있다; …의 기초가 되다

un·der·line *vt.* [ʌ̀ndərláin → *n.*] draw a line beneath (a word, words, etc.); emphasize. —*n.* [ʌ́ndərlàin] ⓒ a line underneath; an underscore.
—⦿ …의 밑에 줄을 긋다; …을 강조하다 —⦾ 밑줄

un·der·ling [ʌ́ndərliŋ] *n.* ⓒ a person of a lower rank or position; a subordinate.
—⦾ 하급직원, 부하, 아랫사람

un·der·mine [ʌ̀ndərmáin] *vt.* **1.** dig beneath; make a tunnel under (a wall, etc.). **2.** work against (something) secretly. **3.** weaken.
—⦿ 1. …의 아래를 파다; 아래에 갱도를 파다 2. …을 몰래 손상시키다 3. …을 약하게 하다

un·der·most [ʌ́ndərmòust] *adj.* lowest.
—⦾ 최하의, 최저의

*** un·der·neath** [ʌ̀ndərníːθ] *adv., prep.* beneath; below.
—⦿⦾ …의 아래에; 낮게

un·der·nour·ished [ʌ̀ndərnə́ːriʃt / ʌ̀ndənʌ́riʃt] *adj.* not sufficiently nourished.
—⦾ 영양불량의

un·der·pay [ʌ̀ndərpéi / ⌐-⌐] *vt.* (**-paid**) pay insufficiently.
—⦿ …에 충분한 요금(급료)을 주지 않다

un·der·pin [ʌ̀ndərpín] *vt.* support or strengthen (something) from beneath.
—⦿ …을 밑에서 버티다

un·der·rate [ʌ̀ndərréit] *vt.* place too low a value or estimate upon (something); underestimate.
—⦿ …을 싸게(낮게) 평가하다; 경시하다

un·der·score *vt.* [ʌ̀ndərskɔ́ːr → *n.*] underline. —*n.* [ʌ́ndərskɔ̀ːr] ⓒ an underscored line.
—⦿ …의 밑에 줄을 긋다 —⦾ 밑줄

un·der·sea *adj.* [ʌ́ndərsìː → *adv.*] beneath the surface of the sea. —*adv.* [ʌ̀ndərsíː] underseas.
—⦿ 바다 밑의, 해저의 —⦿ 바다 밑에(으로), 해저에(로)

un·der·seas [ʌ̀ndərsíːz] *adv.* beneath the surface of the sea.
—⦿ 바다 밑에(으로), 해저에(로)

un·der·sec·re·tar·y [ʌ̀ndərsékritéri / -t(ə)ri] *n.* ⓒ (pl. **-tar·ies**) an assistant secretary.
—⦾ 차관(次官)

un·der·sell [ʌ̀ndərsél / ⌐-⌐] *vt.* (**-sold**) sell goods at a lower price than (a competitors').
—⦿ …을 보다 싸게 팔다

un·der·shirt [ʌ́ndərʃə̀ːrt] *n.* ⓒ a shirt worn next to the skin under other clothing.
—⦾ 속옷

un·der·shot [ʌ́ndərʃɑ̀t / ʌ́ndəʃɔ̀t] *adj.* **1.** (of a water wheel) driven by water passing beneath. ⇒fig. **2.** having the lower jaw projecting beyond the upper.
—⦿ 1. 밑으로 흐르는 물로 움직이는 2. 아래턱이 튀어나온

un·der·side [ʌ́ndərsàid] *n.* ⓒ an under or lower side.
—⦾ 하면, 아래쪽

un·der·sign [ʌ̀ndərsáin, ⌐-⌐] *vt.* [undershot wheel] sign one's name at the end of (a letter, a document, etc.).
—⦿ [편지·문서 따위]의 끝에 서명하다

un·der·sized [ʌ́ndərsáizd] *adj.* smaller than the usual size.
—⦿ 보통보다 작은, 꼬마의

un·der·stand [ʌ̀ndərstǽnd] *v.* (**-stood**) *vt.* **1.** get the meaning of (something). (~ someone's *doing*; ~ *what* ...) ¶*Do you* ~ *me?; Do you* ~ *what I say? / I can't* ~ *your doing that; I can't* ~ *why you did (or do) that.* **2.** have knowledge of (something); know well. ¶*I* ~ *a good deal of what is going on around me.*① */ I* ~ *you are not satisfied.*② **3.** accept (something) as a fact; interpret; assume; believe. (~ *that*...) ¶*I* ~ *her to be happy; I* ~ *that she is happy.*③ **4.** get (something) as information; hear or learn. (~ *that*...) ¶*I* ~ *that you are going to marry Mary.* **5.** (in passive) supply (a word, idea, etc.) in the mind. ¶*In the sentence "Come here," the subject "you" is understood.* —*vi.* **1.** be able to get the meaning; comprehend. ¶*She is slow to* ~. **2.** hear; be informed.
—⦿ 1. …[의 의미]를 이해하다; …을 알다 2. …의 지식이 있다; …을 잘 알고 있다 ¶①내 주위에서 어떤 일이 일어나고 있는지는 거의 다 알고 있다/②네가 불만인 것도 안다 3. …을 해석하다, 추정하다, 생각하다 ¶③그녀가 행복하다고 생각하고 있다 4. …을 듣다, 들어서 알고 있다 5. [어구(語句) 따위]를 보충하여 생각하다; 생략하다
—⊜ 1. 알다, 이해하다 2. 들어서 알고 있다

understandable [1248] **undo**

*make oneself **understood**,* make one's meaning clear. ¶*I failed to make myself understood in English.*

un·der·stand·a·ble [ʌndərstǽndəbl] *adj.* that can be understood. —형 이해할 수 있는

un·der·stand·a·bly [ʌndərstǽndəbli] *adv.* so as to be understandable; in an understandable manner; naturally. —부 이해할 수 있게

:**un·der·stand·ing** [ʌndərstǽndiŋ] *n.* **1.** Ⓤ knowledge; comprehension. **2.** Ⓤ the power to think and learn; intelligence. ¶*a man of* ~. **3.** Ⓒ (*sing.* only) mutual agreement. ¶*come to an* ~ *with*① / *have* (or *keep*) *an* —*adj.* able to understand; intelligent. ⌊~ *with.*②
—명 1.지식;이해, 양해 2.이해력;지력(知力) 3.상호간의 이해, 일치 ¶①…와 양해가 성립되다/②…와 의사가 소통하고 있다
—형 이해심이 있는, 분별 있는

un·der·state [ʌndərstéit / ´--´] *vt.* state too weakly; tell less than the truth about (something).
—타 …을 가볍게 말하다; 적게(줄여서) 말하다

un·der·state·ment [ʌndərstéitmənt / ´--´-] *n.* **1.** Ⓤ the act of understating. **2.** Ⓒ a statement that is too weak or moderate.
—명 1.줄여서 이야기하기 2.삼가서 하는 말

:**un·der·stood** [ʌndərstúd] *v.* pt. and pp. of **understand.**

un·der·take [ʌndərtéik] *vt.* (-**took**, -**ta·ken**) **1.** take (something) upon oneself; attempt. ¶~ *a new enterprise.* **2.** contract to do (so.nething); promise. ¶~ *to do.* ¶~ *to be here.* **3.** affirm; guarantee. ¶~ *that*…
—타 1. …을 맡다; …에 착수하다 2. …을 약속하다 3. …을 보증하다

un·der·tak·er *n.* **1.** Ⓒ [ʌndərtéikər →2.] a person who undertakes something. **2.** [´--´-] a person who makes a business of preparing the dead for burial and of taking charge of funerals.
—명 1.인수인;청부업자;기업가 2.장의사 업자

un·der·tak·ing *n.* [ʌndərtéikiŋ →3.] **1.** Ⓒ something undertaken; a task; an enterprise. **2.** Ⓒ a promise; a guarantee. **3.** [´--´-] Ⓤ the business of preparing the dead for burial and taking charge of funerals.
—명 1.맡기;청부;기업 2.약속;보증 3.장의사업

un·der·tone [ʌndərtòun] *n.* Ⓒ **1.** a low or very quiet tone. **2.** a subdued color. **3.** an underlying quality.
—명 1.낮은 소리, 작은 소리 2.엷은 색깔 3.잠재적 성질, 저류(底流)

un·der·took [ʌndərtúk] *v.* pt. of **undertake.**

un·der·val·ue [ʌndərvǽlju(ː)] *vt.* value too low; regard (something) too lightly.
—타 …의 값을 싸게 보다, …을 과소 평가하다;경시하다

un·der·vest [ʌ́ndərvèst] *n.* Ⓤ (*Brit.*) an undershirt. —명 속샤쓰

un·der·wear [ʌ́ndəwɛ̀ər] *n.* Ⓤ underclothing. —명 속옷

un·der·went [ʌndərwént] *v.* pt. of **undergo.**

un·der·world [ʌ́ndərwə̀ːrld] *n.* Ⓒ (*usu. the* ~) **1.** the earth. **2.** the world of the dead; Hades. **3.** the lower, degraded, or criminal part of society. **4.** the opposite side of the earth.
—명 1.지구 2.저승, 지옥; 하계(下界) 3.사회의 최하층[민], 범죄 사회 4.지구의 뒤쪽

un·der·write [ʌndərráit] *v.* (-**wrote**, -**writ·ten**) *vt.* **1.** (usu. in *passive*) write (something) under other written matter; sign one's name to (a document, etc.). **2.** insure (property) against loss. **3.** agree to buy (an issue of stocks, bonds, etc.). —*vi.* act as an underwriter.
—타 1. …을 […의] 밑에 쓰다; 서명하다 2. …에 보험을 들다; 보증하다 3. [사채(社債) 따위]의 구입을 승낙하다 —자 보험업자

un·der·writ·er [ʌ́ndəràitər] *n.* Ⓒ **1.** a person who underwrites insurance. **2.** a person who underwrites issues of stocks, bonds, etc.
—명 1.[해상]보험 업자 2.[증권·공채 따위의] 인수인

un·der·writ·ten [ʌndərítn] *v.* pp. of **underwrite.**

un·der·wrote [ʌndəróut] *v.* pt. of **underwrite.**

un·de·sir·a·ble [ʌndizáiərəbl] *adj.* not desirable; disagreeable. —*n.* Ⓒ an undesirable person or thing.
—형 달갑지 않은; 불쾌한
—명 달갑지 않은 사람(것)

un·de·vel·oped [ʌndivéləpt] *adj.* not fully grown. —형 발전되지 않은, 미달의

• **un·did** [ʌndíd] *v.* pt. of **undo.** ⌊trained.⌋
—형 훈련되지 않은; 미숙한

un·dis·ci·plined [ʌndísiplind] *adj.* not disciplined; un-
—형 변장하지 않은 2. 숨기지 않은 공공연한

un·dis·guised [ʌndisgáizd] *adj.* **1.** not disguised. **2.** unconcealed; open. ⌊doubted.⌋

un·dis·put·ed [ʌndispjúːtid] *adj.* not disputed; not
—형 다툴 나위 없는; 의심없는

un·dis·turbed [ʌndistə́ːrbd] *adj.* not disturbed; calm.
—형 방해받지 않은, 어지러지지 않은

un·di·vid·ed [ʌndiváidid] *adj.* not divided; whole; continuous.
—형 나누지 않은; 완전한; 연속된

• **un·do** [ʌndúː] *vt.* (-**did**, -**done**) **1.** do away with; cause (something) to be as if it had never been done.
—타 1. …을 취소하다, 원상태로 되돌리다 ¶①엎지른 물은 다시 담을 수

¶ *What's done cannot be undone.*① **2.** unfasten; loosen. ¶ *~ a parcel.*② **3.** bring (something or someone) to ruin. ¶ *His laziness will ~ him sooner or later.*
없다 2. …을 벗기다; 늦추다; 풀다 ¶ ②짐을 풀다 3. …을 파멸시키다

un·done[1] [ʌndʌ́n] *v.* pp. of **undo**. —*adj.* **1.** not tied; ruined. **2.** destroyed. ¶ *I am ~!*①
—[形] 1. 풀린; 몰락한 2. 파멸한 ¶① 이젠 다 틀렸다

un·done[2] [ʌndʌ́n] *adj.* not done; not finished.
—[形] 하지 않은; 미완성의

un·doubt·ed [ʌndáutid] *adj.* not to be doubted; certain.
—[形] 의심할 여지 없는; 확실한

* **un·doubt·ed·ly** [ʌndáutidli] *adv.* beyond doubt; certainly.
—[副] 의심할 여지 없이; 확실히

un·dreamed-of [ʌndríːmdɔ̀v / -drémtɔ̀v], **un·dreamt-of** [ʌndrémtɑv / -ɔv] *adj.* unimagined; not thought of.
—[形] 꿈에도 생각 못한, 예상 밖의

un·dress *v., n.* [ʌndrés / ⌐⌐ → *adj.*] *vt.* take off the clothing of (someone); strip. ¶ *~ oneself.*① —*vi.* take off one's clothes. —*n.* [U] loose, informal dress; ordinary clothes. —*adj.* [*Brit.* ⌐⌐] of informal or ordinary clothes.
—[他] …의 옷을 벗기다 ¶①옷을 벗다 —[自] 옷을 벗다 —[名] 약복(略服), 평상복 —[形] 약복의, 평상복의

un·due [ʌnd(j)úː / -djúː] *adj.* **1.** excessive. ¶ *an ~ fondness for liquor.*① **2.** not right; not fitting; improper. ¶ *an ~ claim.*②
—[形] 1. 지나친 ¶①술을 지나치게 좋아함 2. 부당한; 부적당한 ¶②부당한 요구

un·du·late *v.* [ʌ́ndʒulèit → *adj.* / -dju-] *vi.* **1.** move in waves. **2.** have a wavy form or surface. —*vt.* **1.** cause (something) to move in waves. **2.** give a wavy form or surface to (something). —*adj.* [*U.S.* ʌ́ndʒulit, -lèit] wavy.
—[自] 1. 파동하다, 물결치다 2. 파도 모양이 되다, 굽이치다 —[他] 1. …을 물결치게 하다, 물결일게 하다 2. …을 파도 모양으로 하다 —[形] 파도 같은, 파도 모양의

un·du·la·tion [ʌ̀ndʒuléiʃ(ə)n / -dju-] *n.* **1.** [U] wave-like motion or form. **2.** [C] one of a number of wave-like curves or slopes.
—[名] 1. 파동; 물결 모양; 기복 2. 굽이침

un·du·ly [ʌnd(j)úːli / -djúː-] *adv.* **1.** excessively. **2.** improperly.
—[副] 1. 지나치게 2. 부당하게

un·dy·ing [ʌndáiiŋ] *adj.* immortal; eternal.
—[形] 죽지 않는, 불멸의; 영원의

un·earned [ʌnə́ːrnd] *adj.* **1.** not earned by work. ¶ *an ~ income.* **2.** not deserved.
—[形] 1. 애쓰지 않고 얻은 2. 어울리지 않는

un·earth [ʌnə́ːrθ] *vt.* **1.** dig up. **2.** bring (something) to light; discover.
—[他] 1. …을 발굴하다 2. …을 세상에 알리다

un·earth·ly [ʌnə́ːrθli] *adj.* **1.** not of this world; supernatural. **2.** strange; mysterious; ghostly. **3.** (*colloq.*) fantastic.
—[形] 1. 이 세상 것 같지 않은, 초자연적인 2. 기묘한; 무시무시한 3. 《口》 터무니없는

un·eas·i·ly [ʌníːzili] *adv.* in an uneasy manner; anxiously; uncomfortably; awkwardly.
—[副] 불안한 듯이; 불쾌한 듯이; 거북하게

un·eas·i·ness [ʌníːzinis] *n.* [U] the quality or state of being uneasy.
—[名] 근심; 불안; 불쾌

* **un·eas·y** [ʌníːzi] *adj.* (-**eas·i·er**, -**eas·i·est**) **1.** anxious; restless; worried. ¶ *I feel ~ about my health.* **2.** not comfortable. ¶ *I feel ~ in tight clothes.* **3.** not easy in manner; awkward.
—[形] 1. 근심되는; 불안한 2. 편하지 않은, 거북한 3. 어색한, 딱딱한

un·em·ployed [ʌ̀nemplɔ́id] *adj.* not employed; not being used; idle. —*n.* (*the ~, collectively*) all the people out of work.
—[形] 일이 없는, 실업한; 이용되지 않는; 한가로운 —[名] 실업자

* **un·em·ploy·ment** [ʌ̀nemplɔ́imənt] *n.* [U] the state of being out of work. ¶ *an ~ benefit*① / *~ insurance.*②
—[名] 실업, 실직; 실업 상태 ¶①실업수당/②실업 보험

* **un·e·qual** [ʌníːkw(ə)l] *adj.* **1.** not of the same size, strength, amount, etc. **2.** not balanced. **3.** not even; not regular. **4.** not enough; not adequate. ¶ *be ~ to the task.*①
—[形] 1. 같지 않은 2. 균형이 맞지 않는 3. 한결같지 않은; 고르지 않은 4. 불충분한; 부적당한 ¶①그 일을 감당 못하다

un·e·quiv·o·cal [ʌ̀nikwívək(ə)l] *adj.* not equivocal; plain; clear.
—[形] 애매하지 않은; 명백한

un·err·ing [ʌnə́ːriŋ] *adj.* making no mistakes; without error; accurate.
—[形] 잘못이 없는, 정확한; 틀림없는

UNESCO [ju(ː)néskou] *n.* the United Nations Educational, Scientific, and Cultural Organization.
—[名] 국제연합 교육·과학·문화기구

un·ex·am·pled [ʌ̀negzǽmpld / -egzɑ́ːm-] *adj.* having no parallel or similar case; without precedent.
—[形] 유례없는; 전례가 없는

un·ex·cep·tion·a·ble [ʌ̀neksépʃ(ə)n(ə)bl] *adj.* beyond criticism; wholly admirable.
—[形] 흠잡을 데 없는, 훌륭한

* **un·ex·pect·ed** [ʌ̀nekspéktid] *adj.* not expected; sudden.
—[形] 예기치 않은; 뜻밖의

* **un·ex·pect·ed·ly** [ʌ̀nekspéktidli] *adv.* in a way that is not expected; suddenly.
—[副] 뜻밖에; 갑자기

un·fail·ing [ʌnféiliŋ] *adj.* **1.** not failing. **2.** never running short; always present.. **3.** reliable; certain.
—[形] 1. 잘못이 없는 2. 끊임없는 3. 확실한, 의지가 되는

U

un·fair [ʌnfέər] *adj.* not fair; unjust; not honest. ▷**un·fair·ly** [-li] *adv.* —**un·fair·ness** [-nis] *n.*
—[형] 불공평한, 부정(不正)의; 정직하지 않은

un·faith·ful [ʌnféiθf(u)l] *adj.* **1.** not faithful; untrue. **2.** not accurate or exact.
—[형] 1. 불성실한; 불신의 2. 부정확한

un·fal·ter·ing [ʌnfɔ́:lt(ə)riŋ] *adj.* not wavering or hesitating.
—[형] 비틀거리지 않는; 망설이지 않는

un·fa·mil·iar [ʌ̀nfəmíljər] *adj.* not familiar; not acquainted. ¶*I am ~ with this job.; This job is ~ to me.*
—[형] 친하지 않은, 잘 모르는; 익숙치 못한

un·fas·ten [ʌnfǽsn / -fá:sn] *vt.* untie; loosen.
—[타] …을 풀다; 벗기다, 늦추다

un·fath·om·a·ble [ʌnfǽðəməbl] *adj.* too deep to measure; impossible to understand.
—[형] 잴 수 없는, 불가해한; 심원한

un·fath·omed [ʌnfǽðəmd] *adj.* not measured; not understood; not solved.
—[형] 잴 수 없는; 미해결의

un·fa·vor·a·ble, *Brit.* **-vour-** [ʌnféiv(ə)rəbl] *adj.* not favorable; disadvantageous. ¶*an ~ wind.*①
—[형] 계제가 나쁜; 불리한 ¶①역풍

un·feel·ing [ʌnfí:liŋ] *adj.* not able to feel; hard-hearted; cruel.
—[형] 감각이 없는; 무정한; 잔인한

un·feigned [ʌnféind] *adj.* real; sincere.
—[형] 진실의; 성실한

un·fin·ished [ʌnfíniʃt] *adj.* **1.** not finished; not complete. **2.** not polished; rough.
—[형] 1. 미완성의 2. 세련되지 않은

un·fit [ʌnfít] *adj.* (**-fit·ter, -fit·test**) not suitable; not fit; not qualified. —*vt.* (**-fit·ted, -fit·ting**) make (someone or something) unfit. 《~ someone *for*; ~ someone *to do*》 ¶*His age unfits him for such work.*①
—[형] 부적당한; 적임(適任)이 아닌 —[타] …을 부적당하게 하다; 자격이 없게 하다 ¶①그의 나이로는 그런 일은 부적당하다

un·flinch·ing [ʌnflíntʃiŋ] *adj.* not flinching, yielding or shrinking; firm.
—[형] 굽히지 않는, 겁없는; 단호한

***un·fold** [ʌnfóuld] *vt.* **1.** open the folds of; open and spread out (something). **2.** reveal; show; explain. —*vi.* become unfolded.
—[타] 1. …을 펴다, 펼치다 2. …을 나타내다, 밝히다; 표명하다 —[자] 펴지다, 열리다

un·fore·seen [ʌ̀nfɔ:rsí:n] *adj.* not known beforehand; unexpected.
—[형] 미리 알지 못한, 뜻밖의

***un·for·tu·nate** [ʌnfɔ́:rtʃnit] *adj.* **1.** not fortunate; not lucky. **2.** not suitable. —*n.* [C] an unfortunate person.
—[형] 1. 불행한; 불운의 2. 부적당한 —[명] 불행한 사람

***un·for·tu·nate·ly** [ʌnfɔ́:rtʃnitli] *adv.* in an unfortunate manner.
—[부] 불행하게[도], 불운하게[도]

un·found·ed [ʌnfáundid] *adj.* not founded on fact; without reason; untrue. ¶*an ~ rumor.*①
—[형] 근거없는; 사실무근의 ¶①근거없는 소문

un·fre·quent·ed [ʌ̀nfrikwéntid] *adj.* seldom visited; lonely.
—[형] 인적이 드문; 좀처럼 사람이 오지 않는

un·friend·ly [ʌnfréndli] *adj.* **1.** not friendly. **2.** not favorable. ▷**un·friend·li·ness** [-nis] *n.*
—[형] 1. 우정이 없는, 불친절한 2. 계제 나쁜

un·fruit·ful [ʌnfrú:tf(u)l] *adj.* not fruitful; not productive.
—[형] 열매를 맺지 않는; 쓸데없는

un·furl [ʌnfɔ́:rl] *vt., vi.* spread out; unfold.
—[타][자] …을 펼치다, 펴지다

un·gain·ly [ʌngéinli] *adj.* (**-li·er, -li·est**) clumsy; awkward.
—[형] 꼴사나운, 몰골스러운

un·god·ly [ʌngádli / -gɔ́d-] *adj.* (**-li·er, -li·est**) **1.** not religious; wicked; sinful. **2.** (*colloq.*) shocking; dreadful.
—[형] 1. 신앙심 없는; 죄 많은 2. 《口》 심한, 지독한

***un·grate·ful** [ʌngréitf(u)l] *adj.* **1.** not grateful. **2.** unpleasant.
—[형] 1. 은혜를 모르는 2. 불쾌한

un·ground·ed [ʌngráundid] *adj.* without foundation or reason; baseless; unfounded.
—[형] 근거없는, 사실무근의

un·guard·ed [ʌngá:rdid] *adj.* **1.** not guarded. **2.** careless. ¶*in an ~ moment.*①
—[형] 1. 무방비의 2. 부주의한 ¶①방심한 틈을 타서

un·hand [ʌnhǽnd] *vt.* take the hands from (something); let (something) go.
—[타] …을 손에서 놓다; …에서 손을 놓다

un·hap·pi·ly [ʌnhǽpili] *adv.* **1.** not happily; unfortunately. **2.** unsuitably.
—[부] 1. 불행하게 2. 부적당하게

****un·hap·py** [ʌnhǽpi] *adj.* (**-pi·er, -pi·est**) **1.** unfortunate; unlucky. **2.** sad; sorrowful. **3.** not suitable.
—[형] 1. 불운한 2. 불행한, 비참한 3. 적절하지 않은

un·har·ness [ʌnhá:rnis] *vt.* **1.** take harness or gear off from (a horse, etc.). **2.** take off armor from (a knight, etc.); disarm.
—[타] 1. [말]에서 마구(馬具)를 벗기다 2. …의 갑옷을 벗게 하다; 무장을 해제시키다

un·health·ful [ʌnhélθf(u)l] *adj.* bad for the health.
—[형] 건강에 나쁜, 건강하지 않은

un·health·y [ʌnhélθi] *adj.* (**-health·i·er, -health·i·est**) **1.** not in good health; sickly. **2.** not good for the health; harmful to the health. **3.** indicating poor health. ¶*an ~ complexion.*①
—[형] 1. 병약한, 건강하지 않은 2. 건강에 해로운 3. 건강하지 않아 보이는 ¶①건강치 못한 안색

un·heard [ʌnhɔ́:rd / ʌ́nhɔ́:d] *adj.* **1.** not perceived by the ear; not heard. **2.** not given a hearing or audience. **3.** not heard of before.
—[형] 1. 들리지 않는 2. 변명을 들어 주지 않는, 귀담아 들어 주지 않는 3. 아직 들어 보지 못한

un·heard-of [ʌnhɔ́:rdàv / -hɔ́:dɔ̀v] *adj.* not heard of before; unknown.
—[형] 전대미문의; 전례 없는

un·heed·ed [ʌnhí:did] *adj.* not paid attention; not heed-
—[형] 주의하는 이 없는; 돌보지 않는

un·hinge [ʌnhíndʒ] *vt.* **1.** remove (something) from the hinges; remove the hinges from (something). **2.** throw (the mind, etc.) into confusion. **3.** detach.
— ⓣ 1. …에서 경첩을 떼다 2. …을 혼란시키다, 난처하게 하다 3. …을 떼어 놓다

un·ho·ly [ʌnhóuli] *adj.* (**-li·er, -li·est**) **1.** not holy; godless; wicked. **2.** (*colloq.*) dreadful; fearful. ⌈back.⌉
— ⓐ 1. 신성하지 않은; 신앙심 없는; 사악한 2. (口) 심한; 무서운

un·horse [ʌnhɔ́ːrs] *vt.* throw (a rider) from a horse's
— ⓣ …을 말에서 떨어뜨리다

un·hurt [ʌnhə́ːrt / ʌ́nhəːrt] *adj.* not hurt; not injured.
— ⓐ 부상하지 않은; 다치지 않은

u·ni·corn [júːnikɔ̀ːrn] *n.* Ⓒ an imaginary horselike animal with a horn on its forehead. ⇒fig.
— ⓝ 일각수(一角獸)

un·i·den·ti·fied [ʌ̀naidéntifàid] *adj.* not identified.
— ⓐ 미확인의, 신원 미상의

u·ni·fi·ca·tion [jùːnifikéiʃ(ə)n] *n.* Ⓤ the act of unifying; the state of being unified.
— ⓝ 통일, 단일화

ː u·ni·form [júːnifɔ̀ːrm] *adj.* **1.** always the same; not changing. **2.** all alike; like one another. ¶ *be ~ in shape*① */ be ~ with.*② — *n.* Ⓒ Ⓤ a special kind of clothing worn by a member of a group. ¶ *in [full] ~*③ */ out of ~.*④
[unicorn]
— ⓐ 1. 불변의, 일정한 2. 동일한; 한결같은 ¶①모양이 한결같다/②…와 동일하다 — ⓝ 제복; 군복 ¶③제복을 입고/④평상복으로

— *vt.* **1.** clothe (someone) in or supply (someone) with a uniform. **2.** make (things) uniform.
— ⓣ 1. …에 제복을 입히다 2. …을 한결같게 하다

u·ni·formed [júːnifɔ̀ːrmd] *adj.* wearing a uniform.
— ⓐ 제복을 입은

u·ni·form·i·ty [jùːnifɔ́ːrmiti] *n.* Ⓤ the state of being uniform; sameness.
— ⓝ 동일; 한결같음; 일정; 불변

u·ni·form·ly [júːnifɔ̀ːrmli] *adv.* in a uniform manner.
— ⓐ 한결같이, 균등하게, 일률적으로

u·ni·fy [júːnifài] *vt.* (**-fied**) make (things) into one.
— ⓣ …을 한몸으로 하다

u·ni·lat·er·al [jùːnilǽt(ə)r(ə)l] *adj.* **1.** one-sided; of, occurring, on or affecting one side only. **2.** (*Law*) done by or obligating one side only.
— ⓐ 1. 한쪽의; 한쪽만의 2. 《法》편무(片務)의, 일방적인

un·im·peach·a·ble [ʌ̀nimpíːtʃəbl] *adj.* not impeachable; blameless. ⌈not made use of.⌉
— 비난의 여지가 없는, 흠잡을 데 없는

un·im·proved [ʌ̀nimprúːvd] *adj.* **1.** not improved. **2.**
— ⓐ 1. 개량되지 않은 2. 이용되지 않은

un·in·tend·ed [ʌ̀nintɛ́ndid] *adj.* not intended.
— ⓐ 고의가 아닌

un·in·ter·est·ed [ʌ̀nínt(ə)ristid] *adj.* **1.** not having interests. **2.** not interested; paying no attention.
— ⓐ 1. 이해관계가 없는 2. 무관심한

un·in·ter·est·ing [ʌ̀nínt(ə)ristiŋ] *adj.* not interesting.
— ⓐ 흥미없는, 재미없는

ː un·ion [júːnjən] *n.* Ⓒ **1.** Ⓤ the act of uniting two or more things into one whole; the state of being united. ¶ *Union is strength.*① */ in ~.*② **2.** a league or an association formed to protect and promote a common interest. ¶ *a trade ~*③ */ a labor ~.*④ **3.** a group of people, states, etc. united for some purpose. **4.** (*the U-*) the United States of America. **5.** a device for joining together parts of a machine, etc.
— ⓝ 1. 결합, 연합, 합병 ¶①단결은 힘이다/②화합하여 2. 동맹; 조합 ¶③동업자 조합/④노동조합 3. 연합국가, 연방 4. 아메리카 합중국 5. 접합(接合)장치

union flag [´ ´] *n.* the union jack.
— ⓝ 영국 국기

un·ion·ism [júːnjənìzm] *n.* Ⓤ **1.** the principle of union. **2.** the system or principles of labor unions.
— ⓝ 1. 연합주의; 조합주의 2. 노동조합 주의

un·ion·ist [júːnjənist] *n.* Ⓒ **1.** a person who believes in unionism. **2.** a member of a labor union.
— ⓝ 1. 연합주의자 2. 노동조합원

union jack [´ ´], **the** *n.* (sometimes *U- J-*) the British national flag. ⇒fig.
— ⓝ 영국 국기

* **u·nique** [juː(ː)níːk] *adj.* **1.** having no like or equal; different from all others. ⇒ usage **2.** (*colloq.*) rare; unusual.
— ⓐ 1. 유일한, 비길 데 없는 [usage] 원칙적으로 비교급·최상급이 없음 2. 진귀한

u·ni·son [júːnisn, -zn] *n.* Ⓤ **1.** agreement; harmony. **2.** a passage of music in which all performers sing or play the same part.

[the union jack]
— ⓝ 1. 조화, 일치 2. 제창(齊唱), 제주(齊奏)

* **u·nit** [júːnit] *n.* Ⓒ **1.** a single thing or person. **2.** a group of things or persons considered as one part of
— ⓝ 1. 한 개, 한 사람, 개체 2. 구성단위; 일단, 일 부대 ¶①가족은 사회의

a whole. ¶*The family is the ~ of society.*① **3.** (*Mathematics*) the smallest whole number; one. **4.** a fixed amount or quantity taken as a standard of measurement. ¶*The meter is a ~ of length.*
구성단위이다 **3.**《數》 최소 완전수 **4.** 단위

ː u·nite [ju(ː)náit] *vt.* **1.** join together; combine (two or more) so as to make one. ¶*~ two families by marriage* | (*proverb*) *United we stand, divided we fall.*① **2.** have or show (qualities, etc.) in combination. ¶*She unites beauty and intelligence.*② **—*vi.*** **1.** become joined or combined together; become one. ¶*All the choirs will ~ in singing the refrain.* **2.** act together, as for a purpose. ¶*People or societies who ~ for some purpose form a union.*③
—[他] **1.** …을 하나로 합치다, 결합하다 ¶①《俚》뭉치면 살고 헤어지면 죽는다 **2.** [성질 따위]를 겸비하다 ¶②그녀는 재색을 겸비하고 있다 —[自] **1.** 결합하다; 하나로 합쳐지다 **2.** [목적 따위에서] 행동을 함께 하다 ¶③어떤 목적을 위해 한몸이 될 사람들이나 모임은 조합을 만든다

ː u·nit·ed [ju(ː)náitid] *adj.* joined together; joined in spirit; in harmony.
—[形] 결합한, 연합한; [정신적으로] 일치한, 화합한

United Kingdom [-ˊ- ˊ-], **the** *n.* [the Kingdom of] Great Britain and Northern Ireland.
—[名] 연합왕국

United Nations [-ˊ- ˊ-], **the** *n.* an international organization formed to promote international peace, security, and cooperation.
—[名] 국제연합

United States [-ˊ- ˊ], **the** *n.* the United States of America.
—[名] 아메리카 합중국

ː United States of America [-ˊ- ˊ - -ˊ--], **the** *n.* a country in North America made up of 50 States and the District of Columbia.
—[名] 아메리카 합중국

· u·ni·ty [júːniti] *n.* (pl. **-ties**) [U] **1.** the state of being united; oneness. **2.** harmony; agreement. ¶*live in ~ with all neighbors.* **3.** [C] (*Mathematics*) the numeral one.
—[名] **1.** 단일, 통일; 통일체, 개체 **2.** 일치; 화합, 조화 **3.**《數》 1

Univ. University.

ː u·ni·ver·sal [jùːnivə́ːrs(ə)l] *adj.* **1.** belonging to or done by everyone; of or for all; of the universe. **2.** existing everywhere; general. ↔particular ¶*~ rules.*① **3.** adaptable to any use. **—*n.*** [C] **1.** (*Logic*) a universal proposition. **2.** (*Philosophy*) a general concept.
—[形] **1.** 만인의; 우주의; 전세계의 **2.** 보편적인; 일반적인 ¶①일반 법칙 **3.** 만능의 —[名] **1.**《論》 전칭(全稱) 명제 **2.**《哲》 일반 개념

u·ni·ver·sal·i·ty [jùːnivəːrsǽliti] *n.* [U] the state of being universal.
—[名] 일반성, 보편성

· u·ni·ver·sal·ly [jùːnivə́ːrs(ə)li] *adv.* without exception; everywhere.
—[副] 일반적으로; 예외없이, 도처에

· u·ni·verse [júːnivə̀ːrs] *n.* [C] 《*the ~*》 the whole system of existing things; the cosmos; the world.
—[名] 우주; 전세계; 전인류

ː u·ni·ver·si·ty [jùːnivə́ːrs(i)ti] *n.* [C] (pl. **-ties**) an institution for learning of the highest grade, usu. divided into schools.
—[名] 종합 대학교, 대학

· un·just [ʌndʒʌ́st] *adj.* not just; unfair. ▷**un·just·ly** [-li] *adv.* —**un·just·ness** [-nis] *n.*
—[形] 부정(不正)의; 불공평한

un·kempt [ʌnkémpt] *adj.* **1.** untidy; neglected. **2.** not combed.
—[形] **1.** 단정치 못한 **2.** 빗질하지 않은

un·kind [ʌnkáind] *adj.* not kind; cruel.
—[形] 불친절한; 매정한

un·kind·ness [ʌnkáindnis] *n.* [U] the state of being unkind.
—[名] 불친절, 매정, 몰인정

ː un·known [ʌnnóun] *adj.* not known; not familiar; not discovered. **—*n.*** 《*the ~*》 **1.** an unknown person or thing. **2.** an unknown quantity.
—[形] 미지의; 무명의; 미발견의 —[名] **1.** 미지의 사람(것) **2.** 미지수

un·lace [ʌnléis] *vt.* undo the laces of (something). ¶*~ a shoe.*
—[他] …의 끈을 끄르다

· un·law·ful [ʌnlɔ́ːf(u)l] *adj.* against the law; illegal.
—[形] 불법의; 위법의

un·law·ful·ly. [ʌnlɔ́ːfuli] *adv.* in an unlawful manner; illegally.
—[副] 불법적으로, 부정하게

un·learn [ʌnlə́ːrn / ʌ́nlə́ːn] *vt.* (**-learned** or **-learnt**) forget (something learned).
—[他] …을 잊다

un·learn·ed [ʌnlə́ːrnid / ʌ́nlə́ːnid ∥ →*adj.* 2.] *v.* pt. and pp. of **unlearn**.
—*adj.* **1.** not educated; ignorant. **2.** [ʌnlə́ːrnt] not learned; known without being learned.
—[形] **1.** 학문이 없는, 무식한 **2.** 배우지 않은; 배우지 않고도 알고 있는

un·learnt [ʌnlə́ːrnt / ʌ́nlə́ːnt] *v.* pt. and pp. of **unlearn**. **—*adj.*** =unlearned.

un·leash [ʌnlíːʃ] *vt.* free (something) from a leash; release (something) from control.
—[他] …의 가죽끈을 풀다; …을 해방하다

un·leav·ened [ʌnlév(ə)nd] *adj.* (of bread) made without yeast.
—[形] 이이스트를 넣지 않은

ː un·less [ənlés] *conj.* if not. ¶*Unless you work harder, you will fail.*
unless and until, until.
—[接] 만일 …이 아니면
[熟] …까지

U

un·let·tered [ʌnlétərd / ʌ́nlétəd] *adj.* not educated; not able to read or write.
—[형] 교육받지 못한; 읽고 쓸 줄 모르는

• **un·like** [ʌnláik] *adj.* not like; different. —*prep.* different from.
—[형] 비슷하지 않은 —[전] …와 달라서

un·like·ly [ʌnláikli] *adj.* **1.** not likely to happen. ¶*It is ~ to rain.* **2.** not likely to succeed. ¶*an ~ plan.*
—[형] 1. 있음직하지 않은 2. 성공할 것 같지 않은

un·load [ʌnlóud] *vt.* **1.** remove (a load, a cargo, etc.); take the load from (a car, a ship, etc.). ¶*~ a ship.* **2.** remove power, shot, etc. from (a gun, etc.). **3.** relieve (someone or something) from care or trouble. ¶*~ one's mind.* —*vi.* discharge a cargo.
—[타] 1. [짐]을 내리다, 부리다; …에서 짐을 내리다 2. [총]에서 탄환 따위를 빼다 3. …에서 마음의 무거운 짐을 내리다 —[자] 짐을 내리다

• **un·lock** [ʌnlák / -lɔ́k] *vt.* **1.** open the lock of (a door, a box, etc.); open (anything firmly closed). **2.** make (something) clear; reveal. —*vi.* become unlocked.
—[타] 1. …의 자물쇠를 열다; …을 열다 2. …을 터놓고 말하다 —[자] [자물쇠가] 열리다

un·looked-for [ʌnlúktfɔ̀:r] *adj.* unexpected.
—[형] 의외의; 예기치 않은

un·loose [ʌnlú:s] *vt.* let loose; release.
—[타] …을 풀다, 늦추다; 해방하다

• **un·luck·y** [ʌnlʌ́ki] *adj.* (**-luck·i·er, -luck·i·est**) not lucky; unfortunate. ▷**un·luck·i·ly** [-li] *adv.*
—[형] 불운한, 불행한

un·man [ʌnmǽn] *vt.* (**-manned, -man·ning**) deprive (someone) of the qualities of a man; make (someone) weak. ▷**un·man·ly** [-li] *adv.*
—[타] …의 사내다움을 잃게 하다; 나약하게 하다

un·man·ner·ly [ʌnmǽnərli] *adj.* having bad manners; rude. —*adv.* in an unmannerly way; rudely.
—[형] 버릇없는 —[부] 버릇없이

un·mask [ʌnmǽsk / -má:sk] *vt.* **1.** remove a mask or disguise from (someone). **2.** show the true nature of (someone or something). —*vi.* **1.** take off a mask or disguise. **2.** appear in one's true character.
—[타] 1. …의 가면을 벗기다 2. …의 정체를 폭로하다 —[자] 1. 가면을 벗다 2. 정체를 나타내다

un·matched [ʌnmǽtʃt] *adj.* not matched or equaled.
—[형] 상대가 없는, 대항할 수 없는

un·mean·ing [ʌnmí:niŋ] *adj.* without meaning or sense.
—[형] 무의미한, 시시한

un·meas·ured [ʌnméʒərd] *adj.* **1.** not measured or limited. **2.** excessive.
—[형] 1. 잴 수 없는; 무한의 2. 과도한

un·men·tion·a·ble [ʌnménʃ(ə)nəbl] *adj.* not fit to be spoken about.
—[형] 입에 담을 수 없는

un·mis·tak·a·ble [ʌ̀nmistéikəbl] *adj.* that can not be mistaken; clear; evident.
—[형] 틀릴 여지가 없는; 명백한

un·mit·i·gat·ed [ʌnmítigèitid] *adj.* not softened or lessened; absolute.
—[형] 누그러지지 않은, 줄지 않는, 절대의

un·moved [ʌnmú:vd] *adj.* **1.** not moved; firm. **2.** not disturbed; indifferent.
—[형] 1. 부동의, 확고한 2. 태연한

un·named [ʌ̀nnéimd] *adj.* **1.** without a name; nameless. **2.** not indicated or mentioned by name.
—[형] 1. 이름없는, 무명의 2. 이름이 밝혀지지 않은

• **un·nat·u·ral** [ʌnnǽtʃ(ə)r(ə)l] *adj.* **1.** not natural. **2.** lacking human emotion; cruel.
—[형] 1. 부자연스러운 2. 몰인정한; 잔인한

un·nat·u·ral·ly [ʌnnǽtʃ(ə)rəli] *adv.* in an unnatural manner.
—[부] 부자연하게, 몰인정하게, 잔인하게

• **un·nec·es·sar·y** [ʌnnésisèri / -s(ə)ri] *adj.* not necessary; needless. ▷**un·nec·es·sar·i·ly** [-li] *adv.*
—[형] 불필요한; 쓸데 없는

un·nerve [ʌnnə́:rv] *vt.* deprive (someone) of courage or self-control.
—[타] …의 용기를 잃게 하다; …을 당황하게 하다

• **un·no·ticed** [ʌnnóutist] *adj.* not noticed.
—[형] 눈에 뜨지 못한

un·num·bered [ʌnnʌ́mbərd / ʌ́nnʌ́mbəd] *adj.* **1.** not counted. **2.** too many to be counted.
—[형] 1. 세지 않은 2. 무수한

un·oc·cu·pied [ʌnákjupàid / -ɔ́k-] *adj.* (of a house, etc.) not occupied; vacant; (of persons) not engaged in any job; idle.
—[형] 점유되지 않은; 비어 있는; 한가한

un·pack [ʌnpǽk] *vt.* **1.** take (something) out of a package, a trunk, etc. **2.** open and take out the contents of (a package, etc.). —*vi.* take out the contents of a package, a trunk, etc.
—[타] 1. [짐을 풀고] …을 꺼내다 2. [짐]을 풀다 —[자] 짐을 풀다

un·paid [ʌnpéid] *adj.* not paid.
—[형] 지불하지 않은, 미납의; 급료 없는

un·par·al·leled [ʌnpǽrəlèld] *adj.* having no equal; unrivaled.
—[형] 비길데 없는; 견줄데 없는

• **un·pleas·ant** [ʌnpléznt] *adj.* not pleasant; disagreeable.
—[형] 불쾌한; 싫은

un·pop·u·lar [ʌnpápjulər / -pɔ́pjulə] *adj.* not generally liked or approved; not popular.
—[형] 인망(인기)이 없는; 평판이 나쁜

un·pop·u·lar·i·ty [ʌ̀npapjulǽriti / -pɔ̀p-] *n.* [U] the state of being unpopular.
—[명] 인망(인기)이 없음

un·prac·ticed, *Brit.* **-tised** [ʌnprǽktist] *adj.* **1.** not practiced. **2.** not skilled.
—[형] 1. 실행되지 않은 2. 미숙한, 서투른

un·prec·e·dent·ed [ʌnprésidèntid / -d(ə)ntid] *adj.* having no precedent; never known before.
—[형] 전례 없는; 공전(空前)의

U

un·pre·pared [ʌnpripɛ́ərd] *adj.* not ready; not equipped. —[형] 준비가 없는; 뜻밖의

un·pre·tend·ing [ʌnpriténdiŋ] *adj.* unassuming; modest. —[형] 젠체하지 않는; 겸허한

un·prin·ci·pled [ʌnprínsipld] *adj.* lacking good moral principles. —[형] 부도덕한; 절조없는

un·pro·voked [ʌ̀nprəvóukt] *adj.* without provocation. —[형] 자극되지 않은; 까닭없는

un·qual·i·fied [ʌnkwálifàid / -kwɔ́l-] *adj.* **1.** lacking the proper qualifications. **2.** not limited or modified. **3.** complete; absolute. —[형] **1.** 자격 없는; 부적당한 **2.** 무제한의 **3.** 완전한; 절대적인

un·ques·tion·a·ble [ʌnkwéstʃ(ə)nəbl] *adj.* beyond question or doubt; certain. —[형] 의심할 여지 없는; 확실한

un·ques·tioned [ʌnkwéstʃ(ə)nd] *adj.* not questioned; not disputed; undoubted. —[형] 질문(조사)받지 않은; 반대할 수 없는; 의심없는

un·rav·el [ʌnrǽv(ə)l] *v.* (**-eled, -el·ing** or *Brit.* **-elled, -el·ling**) *vt.* **1.** undo (something woven, tangled, etc.). **2.** solve. —*vi.* become unraveled. —[타] **1.** [엉킨 실]을 풀다 **2.** …을 해명하다 —[자] 풀리다

un·re·al [ʌnrí:əl / -ríəl] *adj.* not real; imaginary; fanciful. —[형] 실재(實在)하지 않는; 비현실적인; 가공의

un·rea·son·a·ble [ʌnrí:znəbl] *adj.* **1.** not reasonable. **2.** not moderate; excessive. —[형] **1.** 이성이 없는; 무분별한 **2.** 터무니없는

un·rea·son·a·bly [ʌnrí:znəbli] *adv.* in an unreasonable manner. —[부] 무분별하게; 부당하게; 터무니없이

un·rea·son·ing [ʌnrí:zniŋ] *adj.* not reasoning. —[형] 도리를 모르는

un·re·flect·ing [ʌnrifléktiŋ] *adj.* **1.** not reflecting the light. **2.** unthinking; thoughtless. —[형] **1.** 빛을 반사하지 않는 **2.** 반성하지 않는; 무분별한

un·re·gard·ed [ʌ̀nrigá:rdid] *adj.* disregarded; neglected. —[형] 주목되지 않는; 무시된

un·re·lent·ing [ʌ̀nriléntiŋ] *adj.* showing no mercy; cruel. ▷**un·re·lent·ing·ly** [-li] *adv.* —[형] 용서없는; 냉혹한

un·re·mit·ting [ʌ̀nrimítiŋ] *adj.* without stopping; not slackening; persistent. —[형] 쉴 사이 없는; 참을성 있는

un·re·quit·ed [ʌ̀nrikwáitid] *adj.* not returned or rewarded. —[형] 보답받지 못하는; 보수를 받지 않는

un·rest [ʌnrést] *n.* [U] uneasiness; restlessness. —[명] 불온, 불안; 근심

un·rid·dle [ʌnrídl] *vt.* solve (a riddle, etc.). —[타] …의 수수께끼를 풀다

un·ri·valed, *Brit.* **-valled** [ʌnráiv(ə)ld] *adj.* having no rival; matchless. —[형] 경쟁자 없는; 비길데 없는; 무쌍의

un·roll [ʌnróul] *vt.* open or spread out (something rolled); display; uncoil. —*vi.* become unrolled. —[타] [말아 둔 것]을 풀다, 펴다; 보이다 —[자] 풀리다, 펴지다

un·ruf·fled [ʌnrʌ́fld] *adj.* not disturbed; calm. —[형] 떠들어대지 않는; 조용한

un·ru·ly [ʌnrú:li] *adj.* (**-rul·i·er, -rul·i·est**) hard to control; lawless. —[형] 고분고분하지 않은; 버릇없는

un·sad·dle [ʌnsǽdl] *vt.* **1.** take the saddle off (a horse, etc.). **2.** cause (someone) to fall from a horse. —*vi.* take the saddle off a horse, etc. —[타] **1.** [말 따위]의 안장을 벗기다 **2.** …을 낙마시키다 —[자] 말의 안장을 벗기다

un·said [ʌnséd] *v.* pt. and pp. of **unsay**.
—*adj.* not said or spoken. —[형] 말하지 않은

un·sat·is·fac·to·ry [ʌ̀nsætisfǽkt(ə)ri / ∸∸-∸∸-] *adj.* not satisfactory. —[형] 만족스럽지 못한, 불충분한

un·sat·is·fied [ʌnsǽtisfàid] *adj.* not satisfied. —[형] 만족한

un·sa·vor·y, *Brit.* **-vour-** [ʌnséiv(ə)ri] *adj.* **1.** without flavor; tasteless. **2.** unpleasant in taste or smell. **3.** morally bad; disgusting. —[형] **1.** 맛없는 **2.** 맛(냄새)이 역겨운 **3.** [도덕적으로] 불미스러운

un·say [ʌ̀nséi] *vt.* (**-said**) take back (something said); recall. —[타] [앞서의 말]을 취소하다

un·scathed [ʌnskéiðd] *adj.* not harmed. —[형] 상처 없는, 다치지 않은

un·sci·en·tif·ic [ʌ̀nsàiəntífik] *adj.* not scientific. —[형] 과학적이 아닌, 비과학적인

un·screw [ʌ̀nskrú:] *vt.* **1.** remove a screw or screws from (something). **2.** take out or loosen (something) by turning it. —*vi.* become unscrewed. —[타] **1.** …의 나사를 빼다 **2.** …을 돌려서 뽑다(늦추다) —[자] 나사가 빠지다

un·scru·pu·lous [ʌnskrú:pjuləs] *adj.* without moral principles; without conscience. —[형] 부도덕한; 파렴치한; 양심 없는

un·seal [ʌnsí:l] *vt.* **1.** break or remove the seal of (a letter, etc.). **2.** open (something tightly shut or sealed). —[타] **1.** …을 개봉하다, [봉한 것]을 뜯다 **2.** …을 열다

un·sea·son·a·ble [ʌnsí:znəbl] *adj.* **1.** not suitable to the season. **2.** coming at the wrong time; untimely. —[형] **1.** 철(시절)에 맞지 않는 **2.** 때를 얻지 못한

un·seat [ʌnsí:t] *vt.* **1.** throw (a rider) from a saddle. **2.** remove (someone) from an official position. —[타] **1.** …을 낙마시키다 **2.** …을 퇴직시키다; …의 의석을 박탈하다

un·seem·ly [ʌnsí:mli] *adj.* not seemly; not proper. —[형] 보기 흉한; 부적당한
—*adv.* in an unsuitable manner; improperly. —[부] 보기 흉하게, 꼴사납게

un·seen [ʌnsí:n] *adj.* not seen; not visible; unobserved. ¶*the* ~.① —[형] 눈에 보이지 않는; 본 일이 없는 ¶①영계(靈界)

* **un·self·ish** [ʌnsélfiʃ] *adj.* not selfish; generous. —[형] 이기적이 아닌; 욕심 없는

un·set·tle [ʌnsétl] *vt.* make (something) unstable; make (someone) uneasy; disturb. —*vi.* become unstable. —[타] …을 동요시키다; 어지럽히다; 불안하게 하다 —[자] 동요하다

un·set·tled [ʌnsétld] *adj.* **1.** not determined or decided. **2.** changeable; uncertain. **3.** not inhabited by settlers. **4.** disturbed; disordered. —[형] 1. 결정되지 않은 2. 일정치 않은, 변하기 쉬운 3. 정주자(定住者)가 없는 4. 무질서한

un·shak·en [ʌnʃéik(ə)n] *adj.* not shaken; firm. —[형] 흔들리지 않는; 단호한

un·sheathe [ʌnʃí:ð] *vt.* draw (a sword, a knife, etc.) from a sheath. —[타] [칼 따위]를 칼집에서 뽑다

un·shod [ʌnʃád / -ʃɔ́d] *adj.* without shoes. —[형] 신을 신지 않은

un·sight·ly [ʌ̀nsáitli] *adj.* (**-li·er, -li·est**) not pleasant to look at; ugly. —[형] 보기 흉한; 추한

un·skilled [ʌnskíld] *adj.* **1.** not skilled. **2.** not requiring skill. —[형] 1. 미숙한 2. 숙련을 필요로 하지 않는

un·skill·ful, *Brit.* **-skil-** [ʌ̀nskílf(u)l] *adj.* without skill; awkward; clumsy. —[형] 서투른; 솜씨 없는

un·so·phis·ti·cat·ed [ʌ̀nsəfístikèitid] *adj.* not sophisticated; simple; genuine. —[형] 굴어먹지 않은, 순박한; 순수한

un·sought [ʌnsɔ́:t] *adj.* not looked for; not sought. —[형] 찾지 않는; 원하지 않는

un·spar·ing [ʌnspέəriŋ] *adj.* **1.** very generous. **2.** not merciful; severe. —[형] 1. 인색하지 않은 2. 용서없는

un·speak·a·ble [ʌnspí:kəbl] *adj.* **1.** that cannot be expressed in words. **2.** too bad to be mentioned. —[형] 1. 말로 표현할 수 없는 2. 입에 담기도 싫은, 언어도단의

un·sta·ble [ʌnstéibl] *adj.* not stable, fixed, or constant; unsteady. —[형] 불안정한; 흔들흔들하는; 변하기 쉬운

un·stead·y [ʌnstédi] *adj.* (**-stead·i·er, -stead·i·est**) not steady; likely to change. —[형] 불안정한; 변하기 쉬운

un·string [ʌnstríŋ] *vt.* (**-strung**) **1.** remove or loosen the string or strings of (something). **2.** remove (beads, etc.) from a string. **3.** make (someone) weak or nervous. —[타] 1. …의 줄을 풀다(늦추다) 2. [구슬 따위]를 실에서 뽑아 내다 3. …을 약하게 하다, 자제력을 잃게 하다

un·strung [ʌnstrʌ́ŋ] *v.* pt. and pp. of **unstring**. —*adj.* **1.** having the strings loosened. **2.** nervous. —[형] 1. 줄이 느슨해진 2. 자제력을 잃은

un·stud·ied [ʌnstʌ́did] *adj.* **1.** not got by study; natural. **2.** not having knowledge; unlearned. —[형] 1. 자연히 알게 된; 자연스러운 2. 배우지 않은; 모르는

un·suc·cess·ful [ʌ̀nsəksésf(u)l / ⌐-⌐] *adj.* not successful. —[형] 성공하지 못한; 실패한

un·suit·a·ble [ʌnsú:təbl / -s(j)ú:t-] *adj.* not suitable; inappropriate. —[형] 부적당한; 어울리지 않는

un·sus·pect·ed [ʌ̀nsəspéktid] *adj.* **1.** not suspected. **2.** not imagined to be existent. —[형] 1. 의심받지 않는 2. 있을성 싶지 않은

un·taught [ʌ̀ntɔ́:t] *v.* pt. and pp. of **unteach**. —*adj.* **1.** not taught or educated; ignorant. **2.** (of knowledge) got without being taught. —[형] 1. 배우지 못한; 무식한 2. 배우지 않고도 알고 있는

un·teach [ʌ̀ntí:tʃ] *vt.* (**-taught**) **1.** cause to forget (something learned). **2.** teach the opposite of (something previously taught). —[타] 1. [배운 것]을 잊게 하다 2. [배운 것]과 반대로 가르치다

un·ten·a·ble [ʌnténəbl / -tén-, ʌ́ntí:n-] *adj.* that cannot be defended or maintained. —[형] 지킬 수 없는, 유지하기 힘드는

un·think·a·ble [ʌnθíŋkəbl] *adj.* that cannot be thought of; incredible; unlikely. —[형] 생각할 수 없는; 상상도 할 수 없는

un·think·ing [ʌ̀nθíŋkiŋ] *adj.* thoughtless; careless. —[형] 생각(지각) 없는; 부주의한

un·thought-of [ʌnθɔ́:tàv / -ɔ̀v] *adj.* not previously imagined or considered. —[형] 생각도 못한; 뜻밖의

un·ti·dy [ʌntáidi] *adj.* (**-di·er, -di·est**) not in good order; not neat. —[형] 단정치 못한; 게으른

un·tie [ʌ̀ntái] *vt.* **1.** unfasten or loosen (something knotted or tied). **2.** free (someone) from fastening or restraint. **3.** resolve. —*vi.* become unfastened. —[타] 1. …을 풀다 2. …을 개방하다 3. …을 해결하다 —[자] 풀리다

‡ **un·til** [əntíl] *prep.* up to the time of; before. ¶*He will stay here ~ next Sunday.* —*conj.* up to the time when; before; to the point that. ¶*Until he came back, none of them went out. / Wait here ~ I come back.* ⇨[usage] —[전] …까지 —[접] …할 때까지[쪽]; …할수록 [usage] till 보다도 문어적(文語的). 주문 앞의 구·절을 이끄는 일이 많음

un·time·ly [ʌntáimli] *adj.* **1.** not at the right moment. **2.** happening too soon or before the usual time. —*adv.* **1.** inopportunely. **2.** too soon; prematurely. —[형] 1. 때아닌; 때를 못 만난 2. 너무 이른, 시기상조의 —[부] 1. 때아닌 때에 2. 너무 이르게

un·tir·ing [ʌntáiəriŋ] *adj.* not growing tired; tireless. —[형] 지칠 줄 모르는; 꾸준한

un·ti·tled [ʌ́ntáitld] *adj.* having no title. —[형] 칭호가 없는; 표제가 없는

* **un·to** [ʌ́ntu; *before consonants often* ʌ́ntə] *prep.* (*archaic, poetic*) to. —[전] 《古·詩》 …으로, …의 쪽으로

un·told [ʌntóuld] *adj.* **1.** not told; not expressed. **2.** countless; very great. ¶*~ wealth.* —[형] 1. 이야기하지 않은; 밝혀지지 않은 2. 무수한; 막대한

un·touch·a·ble [ʌntʌ́tʃəbl] *adj.* **1.** that can not or should not to be touched. **2.** out of reach. **—*n.*** [C] a person of the lowest caste in India.
—[形] 1. 손댈 수 없는 2. 손이 닿지 않는 —[名] 불가촉천민(不可觸賤民)

un·touched [ʌntʌ́tʃt] *adj.* not touched or affected.
—[形] 손대지 않은; 감동되지 않은

un·to·ward [ʌntɔ́:rd / -tóuəd] *adj.* **1.** hard to manage or deal with; willful. **2.** inconvenient; unfortunate. ¶~ *circumstances*① / *an ~ wind.*②
—[形] 1. 고집 센; 외고집의 2. 계제가 나쁜; 운이 나쁜 ¶①역경/②역풍

un·trained [ʌntréind] *adj.* without training or education.
—[形] 훈련받지 않은; 연습을 쌓지 않은

un·tried [ʌntráid / ⏑⏑] *adj.* not tried; not tested.
—[形] 시도되지 않은; 시험해 보지 않은

un·trod [ʌntrɑ́d / -trɔ́d], **-trod·den** [-trɑ́dn / -trɔ́dn] *adj.* never been stepped on by human beings.
—[形] 인적 미답의

un·true [ʌntrú:] *adj.* **1.** not true; false. **2.** not faithful. **3.** not agreeing with a standard or rule.
—[形] 1. 진실이 아닌 2. 충실하지 않은 3. 표준에 맞지 않는

un·truth [ʌntrú:θ] *n.* **1.** [U] lack of truth; falsity. **2.** [C] an untrue statement; a lie.
—[名] 1. 허위, 진실이 아님 2. 거짓말

un·truth·ful [ʌntrú:θf(u)l] *adj.* **1.** not truthful. **2.** likely to tell lies.
—[形] 1. 거짓의 2. 거짓말을 하는, 거짓말장이의

un·tu·tored [ʌnt(j)ú:tərd / ʌ́ntjú:təd] *adj.* **1.** not taught. **2.** unsophisticated; simple.
—[形] 1. 교육을 받지 않은 2. 소박한

un·used [ʌnjú:zd / ⏑⏑→2.] *adj.* **1.** not used. **2.** [*Brit.* ʌ́njú:st] not accustomed. ¶*be ~ to labor.*
—[形] 1. 사용되지 않는; 쓰인 일이 없는 2. 익숙치 않은

‡**un·u·su·al** [ʌnjú:ʒuəl] *adj.* not usual; not common; rare; strange.
—[形] 보통이 아닌; 이상한; 진귀한

***un·u·su·al·ly** [ʌnjú:ʒuəli] *adv.* in an unusual manner; uncommonly; rarely; extremely.
—[副] 이상하게; 희귀하게; 대단히; 유별나게

un·ut·ter·a·ble [ʌnʌ́t(ə)rəbl] *adj.* that cannot be put into words; indescribable.
—[形] 말로 형언할 수 없는, 이루 말할 수 없는

un·var·nished [ʌnvɑ́:rniʃt] *adj.* **1.** not varnished. **2.** unadorned; plain; simple.
—[形] 1. 와니스를 칠하지 않은 2. 꾸미지 않은

un·veil [ʌnvéil] *vt.* remove a veil or covering from (something); disclose; reveal. **—*vi.*** take off a veil or covering; reveal oneself.
—[他] …의 베일(덮개)을 벗기다; …을 터놓다 —[自] 베일을 벗다; 정체를 나타내다

un·wa·ver·ing [ʌnwéiv(ə)riŋ] *adj.* fixed; steadfast.
—[形] 동요하지 않는; 확고한

un·wea·ried [ʌnwíərid] *adj.* **1.** not weary; not tired. **2.** never growing weary; tireless.
—[形] 1. 피로하지 않은 2. 물리지 않는; 꾸준한

***un·wel·come** [ʌnwélkəm] *adj.* not welcome; not pleasing.
—[形] 환영받지 못하는; 반갑지 않은

un·well [ʌnwél] *adj.* not well; sick.
—[形] 몸이 편치 않은

un·wield·y [ʌnwí:ldi] *adj.* (**-wield·i·er, -wield·i·est**) difficult to move or manage.
—[形] 다루기 힘든; 움직이기 힘든

***un·will·ing** [ʌnwíliŋ] *adj.* not willing; reluctant. ¶*willing or ~*① / *She is ~ to come.*
—[形] 마음내키지 않는; 마지못해 하는 ¶①싫든 좋든

un·wind [ʌnwáind] *vt.* (**-wound**) wind off (something wound); uncoil. **—*vi.*** become unwound; relax.
—[他] [감긴 것]을 풀다; 되감다 —[自] 되감기다, 풀리다

un·wise [ʌnwáiz] *adj.* lacking good judgment; foolish.
—[形] 지혜 없는; 어리석은

un·wit·ting [ʌnwítiŋ] *adj.* not knowing; unconscious.
—[形] 모르는; 무의식의

un·wit·ting·ly [ʌnwítiŋli] *adv.* unconsciously.
—[副] 모르는 사이에, 무의식적으로

un·wont·ed [ʌnwóuntid, +*U.S.* -wɔ́:nt-] *adj.* unusual; not accustomed.
—[形] 보통이 아닌; 익숙치 않은

***un·wor·thy** [ʌnwɔ́:rði] *adj.* (**-thi·er, -thi·est**) **1.** not worthy; worthless. ¶*an ~ man.* **2.** not deserving. ¶*He is ~ of confidence.* **3.** not suitable; shameful.
—[形] 1. 가치없는 2. [···할] 값어치 없는 3. 어울리지 않는; 창피한

un·wound [ʌnwáund] *v.* pt. and pp. of **unwind**.

un·writ·ten [ʌnrítn] *adj.* **1.** not expressed in writing. ¶*an ~ law.* **2.** without writing; blank.
—[形] 1. 씌어져 있지 않은; 불문(不文)의 2. 백지의; 빈칸의

‡**up** [ʌp] *adv.* ↔down **1.** from a lower to a higher place; in the direction opposite to down. ¶~ *in the sky*① / *She has pulled ~ her stockings.* **2.** in or into a standing or upright position; on one's feet; out of bed. ¶*Stand straight ~.*② / *She gets ~ early in the morning.* **3.** above the horizon, ground, or level. ¶*The sun is ~.*③ / *The corn is ~.* **4.** to a higher rank or social condition. ¶*go ~ in the world.*④ **5.** to a higher amount, value, price, volume, etc. ¶*Prices have gone ~.* / *Speak ~, so that I can hear you.* **6.** into view, notice, or consideration; well informed. ¶*The question came ~ for discussion.*⑤ / *Your name's ~ in the village.* **7.** into
—[副] 1. 위로, 위쪽으로, 올려서 ¶①하늘에, 공중에 2. 똑바로; 일어나서 ¶②똑바로 서라 3. 지평선 위에, 지상에 ¶③해가 떴다 4. [사회적 지위 따위가] 올라가 ¶④출세하다 5. [가치·값이] 올라, 비싸, 높게; [분량이] 늘어나 6. [주목·논제·고려 따위]에 올라 ¶⑤그 문제는 토의에 올려졌다 7. 활동적으로; 흥분하여 ¶⑥무기를 들고 일어서다 8. 완전히, 다하여 [usage] 동사와 함께 쓰임. 의미 없이 쓰이는 일도 있음 ¶⑦파이프에 불을 붙이다/⑧나는

U

activity; into an excited state. ¶*be ~ in arms*⑥ | *Her temper is ~.* **8.** completely. ⇒[usage] ¶*light ~ one's pipe*⑦ | *He drank it ~.* | *I am completely used ~.*⑧ **9.** over; at an end. ¶*Your time is ~.*⑨ | *The rain is letting ~.* **10.** to a place or in the direction that is looked on as more important; near. ¶*come ~ from the country* | *go ~ to Tokyo* | *A lady came ~ to me and asked the time.* **11.** from an earlier to a later period. ¶*~ from youth* | *bring ~ a child.*⑩ **12.** so as to be even with in time, degree, condition, space, etc.; not behind. ¶*keep ~ with the times*⑪ | *catch ~ with a friend.* **13.** in a safe place; aside; in reserve. ¶*lay ~ money* | *put ~ fruit.* **14.** (*Sports, Games*) ahead of an opponent with regard to points, etc. ¶*We are two games ~.* **15.** (in tennis, etc.) each. ¶*The score is three ~.* **16.** (in baseball) at bat.

기진맥진했다 **9.** …이 끝나 ¶⑨시간이 다 됐다 **10.** [도회 따위 중심지·말하는 사람]의 쪽에 **11.** 성장하여; 커져서 ¶⑩아이를 기르다 **12.** …에 쫓아가서; …을 유지하여; 늦지 않도록 ¶⑪시대에 따라가다 **13.** 간수하여; 옆에 **14.** 《競技》 …점 이겨서 **15.** 각각 **16.** [야구에서] 타석에 돌어서서

—*prep.* ↔down **1.** to or at a higher place on or along. ¶*climb ~ a tree.* **2.** farther along. ¶*walk ~ a street.* **3.** toward the beginning of a river, etc., toward or in the inner or upper part of a country, etc. ¶*sail ~ the Hudson.* **4.** at or near the top of. ¶*Her house is ~ the hill.*

—[前] **1.** …의 위쪽에(으로) **2.** …을 따라서 **3.** 강 상류에; [나라]의 안쪽에 **4.** …의 꼭대기 쪽에

1) ***be up against,*** be faced with. ¶*be ~ against serious trouble.*
2) ***be up against it,*** be in difficulty.
3) ***It's all up with ...,*** There is no more hope for ... ¶*It's all ~ with me now.*
4) ***up and about*** (or ***around***), recovered (from sickness) and able to walk about.
5) ***up and doing,*** active, busy. ¶*If you really want to find work, you must be ~ and doing.*⑫
6) ***up for,*** being considered for an elective office, etc.
7) ***up on*** (or ***in***), informed about; expert in. ¶*be well ~ in history.*
8) ***up to,*** ⓐ doing; in process of doing. ¶*He is ~ to no good.*⑬ ⓑ dependent upon the decision of; resting on as a duty. ¶*That's ~ to you.* ⓒ equal to; able to do. ¶*He is not ~ to the job.*⑭ ⓓ until; as far as; as much as. ¶*~ to date*⑮ | *count ~ to ten* | *~ to this time.*
9) ***What's up?,*** What's the matter?; What's happening?

[熟] 1)…에 당면해 있다 2)곤란에 빠져 있다 3)…은 가망이 없다 4)[환자가] 의자에서 일어나서 5)열심히 일하여; 바쁘게 ¶⑫네가 정말 일거리를 찾는다면 열심히 돌아다녀야 한다 6)[선거 따위]에 입후보하여 7)…에 정통하여 8)ⓐ…에 종사하여 ¶⑬무엇인가 나쁜 짓을 하고 있다 ⓑ…의 결정에 따라; [책임으로서] …에게 걸려 있는 ⓒ…할 수가 있어서, …을 할 수 있는 ¶⑭그는 그 일을 할 수 없다; 그 일에 적합하지 않다 ⓓ…까지; …에 달하여 ¶⑮오늘날까지 9)어찌된 일이냐?

—*adj.* going or directed up. ¶*the ~ train.*

—[形] 위로 향한, 상행(上行)의

—*n.* [C] an upward movement; 《usu. *pl.*》 a rise in fortune.

—[名] 상승; 번영

ups and downs, rises and falls; the times of good fortune and bad fortune. ¶*the ups and downs of life.*

[熟] 오르내림, 기복, [인생의] 흥망성쇠

—*v.* (**upped** or **up, up·ping**) (*colloq.*) ***vt.*** **1.** raise; increase. ¶*~ prices.* **2.** put or take up. **—*vi.*** get up; jump up.

—[他] 《口》 **1.** …을 높이다, 올리다 **2.** …을 들어 올리다, 집어 올리다 —[自] 일어나다(서다)

up-and-down [ʌ́pəndáun] *adj.* alternately rising and falling; varying.

—[形] 오르내리는; 변동하는

up·braid [ʌpbréid] *vt.* scold severely; blame; criticise. **—*vi.*** speak with reproach.

—[他] …을 나무라다; 책망하다
—[自] 잔소리하다

up·bring·ing [ʌ́pbrìŋiŋ] *n.* [U] the training and education received during childhood; bringing-up.

—[名] 양육, 교육, 훈육

up·coun·try *n., adj.* [ʌ́pkʌntri / ⌐⌐– → *adv.*] *n.* 《*the ~*》 the interior of a country. **—*adj.*** interior; inland. **—*adv.*** [ʌ́pkʌntri / –⌐–] toward or in the interior of a country.

—[名] 내륙, 오지(奧地) —[形] 내륙의, 오지의 —[副] 내륙으로, 오지로

up·grade *adj., adv., vt.* [ʌ́pgréid → *n.*] *adj., adv.* uphill. **—*vt.*** raise (something) to a higher grade. **—*n.*** [ʌ́pgrèid] [C] an upward slope or incline. ¶*on the ~.*

—[形][副] 오르막길의(에서) —[他] …의 등급을 올리다, 승격시키다 —[名] 오르막길, 치받이

up·heav·al [ʌphíːv(ə)l] *n.* **1.** [C] a movement or an act of rising up from below; the state of being raised up, esp. in an earthquake. **2.** [U][C] a sudden great and violent change in circumstances.

—[名] **1.** 밀어 올리기; 들어 올리기; 지진에 의한 융기(隆起) **2.** 큰 변동,, 격변; 동란

up·heave [ʌphíːv] *v.* (**-heaved** or **-hove**) *vt.* raise (something) from beneath; lift up; heave up. **—*vi.*** rise.

—[他] …을 들어올리다, 밀어올리다
—[自] 받쳐 올라가다; 융기하다

U

up·held [ʌphéld] *v.* pt. and pp. of **uphold**.

up·hill [ʌ́phíl] *adj.* **1.** up the slope of a hill; rising; ascending. ↔downhill ¶*an ~ road* / *The road is ~.*① **2.** difficult. ¶*an ~ task.* **—*adv.*** upward. —[形] 1. 치받이의; 올라가는 ¶①그 길은 치받이다 2. 어려운, 힘드는 —[副] 언덕 위로

***up·hold** [ʌphóuld] *vt.* (**-held**) **1.** keep (something) from falling; support. **2.** give moral or spiritual support or encouragement to (someone). **3.** approve; confirm. —[他] 1. …을 들어 올리다; 버티다 2. …을 지지하다, 격려하다 3. …에 찬성하다; …을 확인하다

up·hold·er [ʌphóuldər] *n.* [C] a person who upholds; a supporter. —[名] 지지자; 후원자

up·hol·ster [ʌphóulstər] *vt.* **1.** furnish (a room, etc.) with curtains, carpets, etc. **2.** provide (furniture, etc.) with cushions, springs, coverings, etc. —[他] 1. [방]을 장식하다 2. [의자 따위에] 속·용수철·커버 따위를 대다

up·hol·ster·y [ʌphóulst(ə)ri] *n.* [U] **1.** ⟪*collectively*⟫ the material used in upholstering. **2.** the business of upholstering. —[名] 1. 가구류, 실내 장식품 2. 실내 장식업; 가구업

up·hove [ʌphóuv] *v.* pt. and pp. of **upheave**.

up·keep [ʌ́pkìːp] *n.* [U] **1.** the act of keeping something in good order; maintenance. **2.** the cost of maintenance. —[名] 1. 유지 2. 유지비

up·land [ʌ́plənd] *n.* [C] a high area. **—*adj.*** of or in high land. —[名] 고지(高地), 대지(臺地), 고원 —[形] 고지의

up·lift *vt.* [ʌ̀plíft → *n.*] **1.** lift up; raise. **2.** raise socially or morally. **—*n.*** [⌐ ⌐] **1.** [C] the act of lifting up. **2.** [U] social or moral improvement. —[他] 1. …을 들어 올리다; 높이다 2. …을 향상시키다 —[名] 1. 들어 올리기 2. 향상, 고양(高揚)

⁑**up·on** [əpán, əpɔ́ːn / əpɔ́n] *prep.* =on. ¶*~ my word*① / *depend ~ it*② / *once ~ a time.*③ —[前] ¶①맹세코/ ②틀림없이/ ③먼 옛날에

⁑**up·per** [ʌ́pər] *adj.* **1.** higher. ¶*the ~ deck*① / *the ~ lip.* **2.** farther from the sea. ¶*the ~ course of a river.*② **3.** higher in rank, office, etc. ¶*the ~ classes.*③ **—*n.*** ⟪usu. *pl.*⟫ the part of a shoe or boot above the sole. —[形] 1. 상부의, 위쪽의 ¶①상갑판 2. 오지(奧地)의 ¶②강의 상류 3. 상위의 ¶③상류계급 —[名] 구두의 윗부분

on one's uppers, (*colloq.*) wearing worn-out shoes; very poor. [熟] ⟪口⟫ 다 닳은 구두를 신은; 아주 가난한

up·per-class [ʌ́pərklǽs / ʌ́pəklɑ́ːs] *adj.* **1.** of the upper class. **2.** of the junior and senior classes in a high school, college, etc. —[形] 1. 상류계급의 2. 상급 학년의

up·per·cut [ʌ́pərkʌ̀t] *n.* [C] (in boxing) a swinging blow directed upwards. **—*vt.*** (**-cut, -cut·ting**) hit (someone) with an uppercut. —[名] [권투의] 어퍼커트 —[他] …에게 어퍼커트를 먹이다

Upper House [⌐ ⌐], **the** *n.* the smaller and less representative branch of a legislature; (*Brit.*) the House of Lords; (*U.S.*) the Senate. ↔Lower House —[名] 상원

up·per·most [ʌ́pərmòust] *adj.* highest; topmost. **—*adv.*** in the highest place; first. —[形] 최상의, 최고의 —[副] 최상으로, 최고로; 최초로

up·pish [ʌ́piʃ] *adj.* (*colloq.*) somewhat arrogant or conceited. —[形] 거만한, 건방진

up·raise [ʌpréiz] *vt.* raise up; lift. —[他] …을 들어 올리다

up·rear [ʌpríər] *vt.* rear up; raise; bring up. —[他] …을 일으키다; 키우다, 기르다

⁑**up·right** [ʌ́pràit, ⌐⌐] *adj.* **1.** standing erect; vertical. **2.** just; honest; honorable. **—*adv.*** in an erect position. ¶*set a pole ~.* **—*n.*** **1.** [U] the state of being upright. ¶*be out of ~.*① **2.** [C] something upright. **3.** [C] an upright piano. —[形] 1. 똑바른, 곧추 선; 수직의 2. 바른; 정직한; 고결한 —[副] 똑바로 —[名] 1. 똑바른 상태 ¶①기울어져 있다 2. 곧추 선 물건 3. 수형(竪型) 피아노

up·right·ness [ʌ́pràitnis] *n.* [U] justness; honesty. —[名] 결백; 정직

upright piano [⌐⌐ ⌐⌐] *n.* a piano with vertical strings. —[名] 수형(竪型) 피아노

up·rise *vi.* [ʌpráiz → *n.*] (**-rose, -ris·en**) **1.** get up; rise. **2.** increase in volume, size, etc. **3.** rise into view. **4.** rise in revolt. **—*n.*** [ʌ́pràiz] [C] **1.** the act of rising up. **2.** an upward slope. —[自] 1. 일어나다; 올라가다; 오르다; 똑바로 되다 2. [분량이] 늘다; 커지다 3. 출현하다 4. 폭동을 일으키다 —[名] 1. 상승 2. 치받이

up·ris·en [ʌprízn] *v.* pp. of **uprise**.

up·ris·ing [ʌpráiziŋ, ⌐⌐⌐] *n.* [C] **1.** an upward slope. **2.** a revolt. —[名] 1. 치받이 2. 반란, 폭동

up·roar [ʌ́prɔ̀ːr] *n.* [U] ⟪sometimes *an ~*⟫ **1.** a noisy disturbance. ¶*in* [*an*] *~.*① **2.** a loud noise. —[名] 1. 대소동 ¶①몹시 소란하여 2. 소음

up·roar·i·ous [ʌprɔ́ːriəs] *adj.* making an uproar; very noisy; confused. —[形] 시끄러운; 혼란된

up·root [ʌprúːt, +*U.S.* -rút] *vt.* **1.** tear up (a plant, etc.) —[他] 1. …을 뿌리째 뽑다; 근절시키다;

up·rose [ʌpróuz] *v.* pt. of uprise.

up·set *v.* [ʌpsét →*n., adj.*] (**up·set, -set·ting**) *vt.* **1.** turn over. ¶ *A child has ~ his glass of milk.* **2.** overthrow. ¶ *~ the government.* **3.** (*U.S.*) defeat unexpectedly. **4.** throw (something) out of order; disturb greatly. ¶ *Don't ~ his plans now.* **5.** disturb mentally. ¶ *My mother was very much ~ when my brother failed in the examination.* **6.** make (someone) sick. ¶ *~ someone's stomach* / *The raw fish I had last night ~ me.* —*vi.* be disturbed or turned over; be distressed. —*n.* [⌣́⌣́] ⓒ the act of upsetting; the state of being upset; (*U.S.*) a totally unexpected defeat; a disorder. ¶ *nervous and emotional upsets.* 〔**2.** overturned.〕 —*adj.* [⌣́⌣́ / ⌣⌣́] **1.** mentally or physically disturbed.

up·shot [ʌ́pʃɑt / -ʃɔt] *n.* ⓒ (*the ~*) the conclusion; the result.

up·side [ʌ́psàid] *n.* (*the ~*) the upper side or part.

up·side-down [ʌ́psai(d)dáun] *adj., adv.* with the top part at the bottom.

up·stage [ʌ́pstéidʒ] *adj.* at the back of the stage. —*adv.* toward or at the back of the stage.

up·stairs [ʌ́pstéərz] *adv.* up the stairs; on an upper floor. ↔downstairs —*adj.* on an upper floor. —*n. pl.* (usu. used as *sing.*) an upper story or stories.

up·stand·ing [ʌpstǽndiŋ] *adj.* standing upright; honorable.

up·start [ʌ́pstɑ̀ːrt] *n.* ⓒ a person who has suddenly risen to wealth or power; a conceited person. —*adj.* suddenly risen to wealth or power; conceited.

up·stream [ʌ́pstríːm] *adv., adj.* against the current of a stream. ↔downstream

up-to-date [ʌ́ptədéit] *adj.* **1.** extending to or including the present time. **2.** of the present time; of the newest sort.

up-to-the-min·ute [ʌ́ptəðəmínit] *adj.* modern; latest.

up·town [ʌ́ptáun] ↔downtown *adv.* in or toward the upper part of a town or city. —*adj.* of or in the upper part of a town or city. —*n.* ⓤⓒ the upper part of a town or city.

up·turn *vt.* [ʌptə́ːrn →*n.*] turn up. —*n.* [ʌ́ptə̀ːrn] ⓒ an upward turn; a change for the better.

up·ward [ʌ́pwərd] *adj.* moving toward a higher place; in a higher position. ↔downward ¶ *an ~ glance* ① / *an ~ tendency.* ② —*adv.* toward a higher place; toward a higher rank, amount, etc.; above; more. ¶ *from his youth ~* ③ / *children of six years and ~.* ④

upward of, more than.

up·wards [ʌ́pwərdz] *adv.* =upward.

u·ra·ni·um [juəréiniəm] *n.* ⓤ a heavy, white, radioactive metallic element.

ur·ban [ə́ːrbən] *adj.* of or in a city or town. ↔rural

ur·bane [əːrbéin] *adj.* polite; refined; elegant.

ur·ban·i·ty [əːrbǽniti] *n.* (*pl.* **-ties**) **1.** ⓤ the state of being urbane; politeness; refinement. **2.** (*pl.*) polite manners.

ur·ban·i·za·tion [əːrbənizéiʃ(ə)n / əːbənai-] *n.* ⓤ the act of urbanizing; the state of being urbanized.

ur·ban·ize, *Brit.* **-ise** [ə́ːrbənàiz] *vt.* change (the character of a rural district) into an urban one.

ur·chin [ə́ːrtʃin] *n.* ⓒ **1.** a mischievous small boy. **2.** a poor, ragged child. 〔urine of mammals.〕

u·re·a [júəriə] *n.* ⓤ the main substance found in the

urge [ə:rdʒ] *vt.* **1.** drive (something) with force. **2.** try to influence (someone) by arguments. ⟪~ someone to do⟫ ¶*Please don't ~ me to eat more.*① **3.** speak one's opinion about (something) strongly and earnestly; argue earnestly. ⟪~ something *upon*; ~ *that*...⟫
—*n.* ⓒⓤ a driving force or impulse.

ur·gen·cy [ə́:rdʒ(ə)nsi] *n.* ⓤ **1.** the quality or state of being urgent; need for action. **2.** the act of urging.

• **ur·gent** [ə́:rdʒ(ə)nt] *adj.* **1.** calling for immediate action or attention; pressing. ¶*on ~ business* | *be in ~ need of.*① **2.** insistent. ⌜**2.** insistently.⌝

ur·gent·ly [ə́:rdʒ(ə)ntli] *adv.* **1.** in an urgent manner.⌟

u·ri·nar·y [júərinèri / júərinəri] *adj.* of urine.

u·rine [júərin] *n.* ⓤ the fluid formed in the kidneys and eliminated from the body as waste.

urn [ə:rn] *n.* ⓒ **1.** a vase with a foot or pedestal, esp. a large one for holding the ashes of the dead. ⇒fig. **2.** a large metal container in which tea or coffee is made and kept hot. ⇒fig.

‡ **us** [ʌs, əs, s] *pron.* the objective case of **we.**

[urn 1.]

‡ **U. S. A.** the United States of America.

us·a·ble [júːzəbl] *adj.* able or fit to be used.

us·age [júːsidʒ, júːzidʒ] *n.* **1.** ⓤ the act or way of using. ¶*ill-usage.*① **2.** ⓤⓒ the customary way of using words. ¶*American ~.* **3.** ⓤⓒ a long-continued practice; habit; custom.

[urn 2.]

‡ **use** *v.* [juːz → *n.*] *vt.* **1.** put (something) into action or service; employ. ¶*~ tools* | *The spining-wheel was used by early American settlers.* **2.** exercise; practice. ¶*~ care*① | *~ one's brains* | *~ one's common sense.*② **3.** conduct oneself toward (someone); treat. ¶*~ someone well (ill).*③ **4.** expend; consume. ¶*We ~ much coal every day.* **5.** employ (something) habitually. ¶*She often used anodyne for a headache.*④ | *He can ~ Russian.* **6.** use (someone) selfishly for one's own purpose. ¶*He was always using his younger sister.* —*vi.* be accustomed. ⟪~ *to do*⟫ ⇒**used**²
use up, consume completely. ¶*All the gasoline is used up.*
—*n.* [juːs] ⓤ **1.** the act of using; the way of using. ¶*He made frequent ~ of quotations from the Bible.* | *It can be enriched or spoiled by its ~.*① **2.** the right or permission to use. ¶*He gave us the ~ of his name.* **3.** the power, ability, or opportunity to use. ¶*She lost the ~ of her left eye.* **4.** ⓒⓤ the need, purpose, or reason to use; practical worth; usefulness. ¶*It's no ~ crying.*② **5.** ⓤⓒ custom; habit; practice.
 1) **have no use for,** (colloq.) dislike strongly.
 2) **in use,** being used. ¶*The compass was already in ⌝ use.⌟*
 3) **make use of,** use.
 4) **out of use,** no longer used.
 5) **put to use,** make use of.

‡ **used**¹ [juːzd →2.] *adj.* **1.** secondhand. **2.** [juːst] accustomed. ⟪~ *to doing*⟫ ¶*You'll soon get ~ to getting up early.* | *I am ~ to his scolding.*

‡ **used**² [juːst] *vi.* was accustomed. ⟪~ *to do*⟫ ¶*I ~ to drive a Buick.* | *There ~ to be a tall tree here.*

use·ful [júːsf(u)l] *adj.* of use; helpful; serviceable. ↔**useless** ¶*make oneself generally ~.*①

—ⓣ 1. …을 몰다, 몰아대다 2. …을 전하다; 격려하다; 재촉하다 ¶①이제 더 먹지 못하겠읍니다 3. …을 주장하다, 역설하다

—ⓝ 충동, 자극
—ⓝ 1. 절박, 급박; 긴급 2. 강요, 역설

—ⓐ 1. 긴급한; 절박한 ¶①…의 필요가 긴박한 처지에 있다 2. 강요하다, 끈질기게 조르다

—ⓐ 1. 긴급하게 2. 끈질기게
—ⓐ 오줌의
—ⓝ 소변, 오줌

—ⓝ 1. 단지, 항아리; 유골 단지; 무덤 2. 코오피 주전자

—ⓟ 우리를(에게)

—ⓐ 사용할 수 있는; 편리한

—ⓝ 1. 사용[법] ¶①혹사(酷使) 2. 어법(語法); [언어의] 관용법 3. 관습, 관례; 습관

—ⓣ 1. …을 쓰다, 사용하다, 이용하다 2. …을 행사하다, 써먹다 ¶①주의하다 /②상식을 써먹다 3. …을 다루다, 대우하다 ¶③…을 친절하게 대하다(학대하다) 4. …을 소비하다 5. …을 습관적으로 쓰다 ¶④그녀는 두통에 진통제를 상용했다 6. …을 이기적인 목적을 위해 이용하다 —ⓘ …하는 것이 예사(습관)이다

🟦 …을 다 써 버리다
—ⓝ 1. 쓰기; 사용, 사용법 ¶⑤쓰기에 따라서 그것은 좋게도 되고 나쁘게도 된다 2. 사용권(허가) 3. 사용권(능력) 4. 사용의 필요, 용도, 쓸 곳; 쓸모있음 ¶⑥울어도 소용없다 5. 습관, 관습

🟦 1) …은 아주 싫다 2) 쓰여져있다 3) …을 사용(이용)하다 4) 쓰이지 않게 되어 5) …을 쓰다

—ⓐ 1. 써서 낡은 2. …에 익숙한

—ⓘ …하는 것이 보통이었다, 늘 …했다

—ⓐ 쓸모있는, 유익한, 유용한 ¶①여러모로 도움을 주다

use·ful·ly [jú:sfuli] *adv.* in a useful manner. —(副) 쓸모있게, 유익하게

use·ful·ness [jú:sf(u)lnis] *n.* Ⓤ the state of being useful. —(名) 쓸모있음, 유익

⁑**use·less** [jú:slis] *adj.* of no use; worthless. ↔useful —(形) 쓸모없는, 무익한

use·less·ly [jú:slisli] *adv.* in a useless manner. —(副) 쓸모없이, 무익하게

use·less·ness [jú:slisnis] *n.* Ⓤ the state of being useless. —(名) 무익, 쓸모없음

U-shaped [jú:ʃèipt] *adj.* having the shape of the letter U. —(形) U자형의

ush·er [ʌ́ʃər] *n.* Ⓒ a person who shows people to their seats in a church, a theater, etc. —*vt.* escort; conduct. —(名) 안내인 —(他) …을 안내하다; 호위하다; 선도(先導)하다

U.S.S.R., USSR the Union of Soviet Socialist Republics.

⁑**u·su·al** [jú:ʒuəl] *adj.* ordinary; customary. ¶*as is ~ with him*① / *He got up earlier than ~.* —(形) 보통의; 통상의; 여느때의 ¶① 그는 언제나 그렇지만

as usual, in the usual manner. (熟) 평소와 같이, 여느때처럼

⁑**u·su·al·ly** [jú:ʒuəli] *adv.* according to what is usual; customarily. —(副) 보통, 통상적으로

u·su·rer [jú:ʒ(ə)rər] *n.* Ⓒ a person who lends money at an excessively high rate of interest. —(名) 고리대금 업자

u·su·ri·ous [ju:zjúəriəs] *adj.* **1.** taking extremely high interest for the use of money. **2.** of usury. —(形) 1. 고리의, 높은 이자를 받아 먹는 2. 고리대금 업자의

u·surp [ju:zə́:rp] *vt.* take possession of (power, position, authority, etc.) by force or unjust means. —*vi.* commit usurpation. 《*~ upon* or *on power, position,* etc.》 —(他) [권력 · 지위 따위]를 빼앗다; 강탈하다 —(自) 침해하다

u·sur·pa·tion [jù:zə:rpéiʃ(ə)n] *n.* ⓊⒸ the act of usurping. —(名) 강탈, 횡령

u·su·ry [jú:ʒuri] *n.* Ⓤ **1.** the act of lending money at an excessively high rate of interest. **2.** a very high rate of interest. —(名) 1. 고리대금 2. 비싼 이자

u·ten·sil [ju(:)téns(i)l] *n.* Ⓒ an instrument or tool used in cooking, housework, etc. ¶*farming utensils*① / *kitchen utensils.*② —(名) 도구, 기구, 용구 ¶①농기구/②부엌 도구

u·ter·i [jú:tərài] *n.* pl. of **uterus.**

u·ter·us [jú:tərəs] *n.* Ⓒ (pl. **-ter·i**) the womb. —(名) 자궁

u·til·i·tar·i·an [ju:tìlitɛ́əriən] *adj.* **1.** of utility. **2.** of utilitarians or their ideas. —*n.* Ⓒ a person who believes in utilitarianism. —(形) 1. 공리적(功利的)인 2. 공리주의[자]의, 공리설의 —(名) 공리주의자

u·til·i·tar·i·an·ism [ju:tìlitɛ́əriənìz(ə)m] *n.* Ⓤ **1.** the doctrine or belief that the purpose of all action should be to bring about the greatest happiness of the greatest number of people. **2.** the doctrine or belief that anything is good when it is useful. —(名) 1. 공리설(주의) 2. 실용주의

•**u·til·i·ty** [ju(:)tíliti] *n.* (pl. **-ties**) **1.** Ⓤ the quality or state of being suitable for use; usefulness. **2.** 《usu. *pl.*》 a useful thing. **3.** Ⓒ (*U.S.*) an organization that performs public service to a community. —(名) 1. 쓸모있음, 유익함, 효용 2. 쓸모있는 것 3. 공익 사업

u·ti·li·za·tion [jù:tilizéiʃ(ə)n / -tilai-] *n.* Ⓤ the act of utilizing; the state of being utilized. —(名) 이용

•**u·ti·lize** [jú:tilàiz] *vt.* use (something) for a practical purpose; make use of (something). —(他) …을 이용하다; 쓸모있게 하다

•**ut·most** [ʌ́tmòust] *adj.* **1.** most distant; farthest. ¶*to the ~ ends of the earth.*① **2.** of the highest degree; greatest. ¶*with the ~ pleasure.* —*n.* 《*the ~* or *one's ~*》 the most that is possible; extreme limit or degree. ¶*at the ~*② / *do one's ~*③ / *to the ~.*④ —(形) 1. 가장 먼 ¶①지구의 끝까지 2. 최대의, 최고의 —(名) 최대한, 최고도 ¶②기껏/③전력을 다하다/④극도로, 극력

•**U·to·pi·a** [ju:tóupiə] *n.* **1.** an imaginary island described in 'Utopia' by Sir Thomas More. **2.** Ⓒ 《often *u-*》 an ideal place or state. —(名) 1. 유토피아 2. 이상향

•**U·to·pi·an** [ju:tóupiən] *adj.* **1.** of or like Utopia. **2.** 《often *u-*》 idealistic; visionary. —*n.* Ⓒ **1.** a person of Utopia. **2.** 《often *u-*》 an idealist. —(形) 1. 유토피아의(같은) 2. 이상적인; 몽상적인 —(名) 1. 유토피아의 주민 2. 이상가

•**ut·ter**¹ [ʌ́tər] *adj.* complete; entire; absolute. ¶*~ darkness.* —(形) 완전한, 전적인; 철저한

•**ut·ter**² [ʌ́tər] *vt.* **1.** speak; express. ¶*~ one's feelings.* **2.** give out. ¶*~ a sigh.* **3.** put (bad checks or money) into circulation. —(他) 1. …을 말하다; 말로 표현하다 2. …을 입밖에 내다 3. [위조지폐] 따위를 사용하다

•**ut·ter·ance** [ʌ́t(ə)r(ə)ns] *n.* **1.** Ⓤ the act of uttering; expression in words. **2.** Ⓤ 《sometimes *an ~*》 a way of —(名) 1. 입밖에 내기; 발언 2. 말씨; 어조 3. 말

speaking. **3.** [C] something uttered; a spoken word.

* **ut·ter·ly** [ʌ́tərli] *adv.* completely; absolutely.
—[副] 전혀, 완전히

ut·ter·most [ʌ́tərmòust] *adj., n.* ([U] ⟪*the* ~⟫) utmost. ¶*to the ~ of one's power.*①
—[形][名] 최대한[의], 최고[의] ¶①될 수 있는 한

u·vu·la [jú:vjulə] *n.* [C] (pl. **-las** or **-lae**) a small piece of flesh hanging at the back of the throat.
—[名] 목젖, 현옹수(懸壅垂)

u·vu·lae [jú:vjulì:] *n.* pl. of **uvula.**

V

V, v [vi:] *n.* [C] (pl. **V's, Vs, v's, vs** [vi:z]) **1.** the 22nd letter of the English alphabet. **2.** something shaped like the letter V. ¶*the V sign.* **3.** the Roman number for five.
—[名] 1. 영어 자모의 스물 두째 글자 2. V자형[의 것] 3. [로마자의] 5

v. 1. velocity. **2.** verb. **3.** volt.

Va. Virginia.

va·can·cy [véik(ə)nsi] *n.* (pl. **-cies**) **1.** [U] the state of being vacant; emptiness. **2.** [C] an unoccupied post or position. **3.** [C] an unoccupied room for rent.
—[名] 1. 텅 빔, 공허 2. 결원, 빈 자리, 공석 3. [세놓을] 빈 방

* **va·cant** [véik(ə)nt] *adj.* **1.** unoccupied; empty. ¶*a ~ room* / *look into ~ space.* **2.** without thought or expression; thoughtless. ¶*a ~ look* / *look with ~ eyes.*① **3.** unengaged; leisure. ¶*~ hours.*
1) ***be vacant of*** (=*be wanting in*) *something.*
2) ***fall vacant,*** become unoccupied.
—[形] 1. 사람이 살고 있지 않는, 비어 있는, 공허한 2. 멍하니(우두커니) 있는 ¶①멍하니 보다 3. 일이 없는, 한가한
[熟] 1)…이 없다, 결핍되어 있다 2)[방·지위 따위가] 비다, 공석이 되다

va·cant·ly [véik(ə)ntli] *adv.* in a vacant manner; absent-mindedly.
—[副] 멍하니, 우두커니, 넋을 잃고

va·cate [véikeit / vəkéit] *vt.* leave (a room, a post, etc.) empty or unoccupied. —*vi.* give up a house, an office, a position, etc.
—[他] …을 비우다, 공허하게 하다, 철수하다, [직위 따위]를 사퇴하다
—[自] 물러가다, 철수하다; 사직하다

‡ **va·ca·tion** [veikéiʃ(ə)n, vək- / vək-] *n.* **1.** [C][U] a period of time for recreation and rest from work. ¶*the summer ~.* **2.** [U] the act of vacating; resignation. ¶*the ~ of his position.* —*vi.* (*U.S.*) take or spend a vacation.
—[名] 1. 휴가 2. [집·지위 따위를] 비우기, 명도(明渡), 철수; 사직, 퇴임
—[自] ⟪美⟫ 휴가를 얻다(보내다)

va·ca·tion·ist [veikéiʃ(ə)nist, vək- / vək-] *n.* [C] (*U.S.*) a person who is taking a vacation. (cf. *Brit.* holidayer)
—[名] ⟪美⟫ 휴가를 얻고 있는 사람

vac·ci·nate [vǽks(i)nèit] *vt.* give (someone) vaccine or some other preventive injection to protect him from smallpox or from a severe attack of any other disease.
—[他] …에게 종두를 놓다, 예방주사를 놓다

vac·ci·na·tion [vӕks(i)néiʃ(ə)n] *n.* [C][U] the act of vaccinating.
—[名] 왁찐 주사, 종두

vac·cine [vǽksi:n, +*U.S.* -ˊ] *n.* [U][C] **1.** the germs obtained from cowpox, used to protect a person from smallpox. **2.** any preparation of disease germs used in vaccination.
—[名] 1. 우두종(牛痘種) 2. 왁찐

vac·il·late [vǽsilèit] *vi.* **1.** swing to and fro; move to and fro. **2.** be undecided in opinion or purpose.
—[自] 1. 흔들리다, 흔들흔들하다 2. [마음]이 동요하다

vac·il·la·tion [vӕsiléiʃ(ə)n] *n.* [U][C] **1.** the act of vacillating. **2.** unsteadiness of mind or opinion.
—[名] 1. 진동 2. 갈팡질팡함, 우유부단

va·cu·a [vǽkjuə] *n.* pl. of **vacuum.**

va·cu·i·ty [vӕkjú(:)iti] *n.* (pl. **-ties**) **1.** [U] emptiness. **2.** ⟪usu. *pl.*⟫ something foolish or absurd.
—[名] 1. 공허, 진공(眞空) 2. 허황된 일

vac·u·ous [vǽkjuəs] *adj.* **1.** containing nothing; empty. **2.** unintelligent; foolish.
—[形] 1. 텅 빈, 공허한 2. 현명하지 못한; 어리석은

vac·u·um [vǽkjuəm] *n.* [C] (pl. **-ums** or **va·cu·a**) **1.** a space completely empty, without even air. **2.** a machine used for cleaning; a vacuum cleaner.
—[名] 1. 진공(眞空) 2. 진공 소제기

vacuum bottle [ˊ-- ˋ-] *n.* a glass container with a double wall to keep liquids hot or cold.
—[名] 진공병, 마법병

vacuum cleaner [ˊ-- ˋ-] *n.* a machine used for cleaning carpets, etc. by the act of sucking.
—[名] 진공 소제기

vacuum tube [ˊ-- ˋ] *n.* a tube from which all the air
—[名] 진공관

V

has been removed, used in radio sets to control the flow of electric currents.

va·de me·cum [véidimí:kəm] *n.* **1.** a useful thing which a person carries about with him. **2.** a guide book; a handbook. —[名] 1. 휴대용 필수품 2. 편람(便覽)

vag·a·bond [vǽgəbɑ̀nd / -bɔ̀nd] *n.* [C] **1.** a person who wanders from place to place without purpose. **2.** a bad, dishonest person. —*adj.* **1.** moving about without purpose. **2.** valueless; useless. —[名] 1. 방랑자, 유랑객 2. 망나니, 건달 —[形] 1. 방랑(유랑)하는 2. 쓸모없는, 보잘것 없는

va·gar·i·ous [vəgɛ́əriəs] *adj.* capricious; fanciful. —[形] 변덕스러운; 엉뚱한, 별난

va·gar·y [vəgɛ́əri, véigəri] *n.* [C] (pl. **-gar·ies**) a strange and fanciful notion; a passing fancy; a sudden fancy. —[名] 엉뚱한 생각; 일시적 기분, 변덕

va·gran·cy [véigr(ə)nsi] *n.* [U] the act of wandering from place to place without purpose. —[名] 방랑, 유랑

va·grant [véigr(ə)nt] *n.* [C] a person who wanders about, having no home. —*adj.* **1.** wandering about; unsettled. **2.** of a vagrant. —[名] 방랑자, 부랑자 —[形] 1. 떠도는, 정처없이 방랑하는 2. 방랑자(부랑자)의

***vague** [veig] *adj.* not clear; indistinct. —[形] 분명치 않은; 모호한

***vague·ly** [véigli] *adv.* in a vague manner. —[副] 막연히, 모호하게, 흐리멍덩하게

‡**vain** [vein] *adj.* **1.** having a high opinion or admiration of oneself; boastful; self-satisfied. ¶*She is a nice girl, but inclined to be ~.* **2.** useless; without success. ¶*They made a ~ search for him.*① **3.** empty; valueless. ¶*~ delights*② / *~ words.* —[形] 1. 자부심이 강한 2. 쓸모없는, 소용없는; 아무 보람없는 ¶①그들은 그를 찾았으나 허사였다 3. 공허한; 실질적 가치가 없는 ¶②허황된 기쁨

in vain, without success; to no purpose. ¶*All my efforts were in ~.* [熟] 헛되이, 보람없이

vain·glo·ri·ous [vèinglɔ́:riəs] *adj.* extremely proud; vain. —[形] 자부심이 강한, 허영심이 강한

vain·glo·ry [vèinglɔ́:ri] *n.* [U] **1.** excessive or boastful vanity. **2.** unworthy or empty show. —[名] 1. 허영; 자만; 자부심 2. 허영, 허식

vain·ly [véinli] *adv.* **1.** without success; in vain; uselessly. **2.** conceitedly. —[副] 1. 헛되이, 공연히; 무익하게 2. 자만하여, 잘난 체하여

val·ance [vǽləns] *n.* [C] **1.** a short curtain hanging over the top of a window. ⇒fig. **2.** a short curtain around a bedstead. ⇒fig. —[名] 1. 휘장 2. 침대 밑의 짧은 커어튼

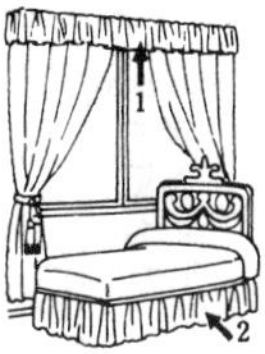

〔valance 1., 2.〕

***vale** [veil] *n.* [C] (*poetic*) a valley. —[名] 《詩》 골짜기

val·e·dic·tion [væ̀lidíkʃ(ə)n] *n.* [C] **1.** the act of saying farewell. **2.** the words uttered in parting. —[名] 1. 작별, 고별 2. 작별의 말, 고별사

val·e·dic·to·ry [væ̀lidíkt(ə)ri] *n.* [C] (pl. **-ries**) an address of farewell, esp. at the ceremony of graduation from school. —*adj.* said or done at farewell. —[名] [특히 졸업식의] 고별 연설 —[形] 고별의

val·en·tine [vǽləntàin] *n.* [C] **1.** a card or gift sent on Saint Valentine's Day, February 14. **2.** a sweetheart chosen on this day. —[名] 1. 성(聖)발렌타인 축제일에 보내는 사랑의 카아드나 선물 2. 이날에 고른 애인(연인)

va·le·ri·an [vəlíəriən] *n.* **1.** [C] a strong smelling plant with white or pink flowers. **2.** [U] a drug made from the root of the valerian plant. —[名] 1. 쥐오줌풀 2. 쥐오줌풀의 말린 뿌리에서 채취한 진정제

val·et [vǽlit, -lei] *n.* [C] **1.** a manservant who takes care of clothes, rooms, etc. **2.** a servant who cleans and presses clothes, shines shoes, etc. in a hotel. —*vt.* serve (someone) as a valet. —[名] 1. 시종, 종자(從者) 2. 호텔의 보이 —[他] …의 시종 노릇을 하다

val·e·tu·di·nar·i·an [væ̀lit(j)ù(:)dinɛ́əriən / -tjù(:)d-] *adj.* **1.** in poor health; sickly. **2.** worrying or thinking too much about one's health. —*n.* [C] a valetudinarian person. —[形] 1. 병든, 병약한 2. 건강을 너무 염려하는 —[名] 병약자; 건강을 너무 염려하는 사람

***val·iant** [vǽliənt] *adj.* without fear; full of courage; brave. ¶*~ deeds / ~ soldiers.* —[形] 1. 씩씩한, 용감한

val·id [vǽlid] *adj.* ↔invalid **1.** based on or supported by fact; sound. **2.** having legal effect. —[形] 1. 근거가 확실한 2. 법적으로 유효한

val·i·date [vǽlidèit] *vt.* **1.** give (something) legal power. **2.** make (something) certain by verifying facts; confirm. —[他] 1. …에 법적 효과를 주다 2. …을 확인하다

va·lid·i·ty [vəlíditi] *n.* [U] **1.** the state of being valid. **2.** effectiveness. —[名] 1. 정당함; 확실함 2. 효력, 유효성

va·lise [vəlí:s, +*Brit.* -lí:z] *n.* [C] a traveling bag. —[名] 여행 가방

‡val·ley [vǽli] *n.* [C] **1.** a narrow, low strip of land between hills, etc. **2.** a wide district along a river. ¶*the ~ of the Nile.*
—[名] 1. 골짜기, 계곡 2. [큰 강의] 유역

***val·or,** *Brit.* **-our** [vǽlər] *n.* [U] the state of being brave; fearlessness.
—[名] 용기, 무용(武勇)

val·or·ous [vǽlərəs] *adj.* courageous; brave.
—[形] 용감한, 씩씩한

‡val·u·a·ble [vǽljuəbl] *adj.* **1.** having value; of great value. **2.** costing much. **—*n.*** (usu. *pl.*) something of great value.
—[形] 1. 가치있는, 가치가 높은 2. 값비싼 —[名] 값진 물건

val·u·a·tion [væ̀ljuéiʃ(ə)n] *n.* **1.** [U] the act of judging the value of something. **2.** [C] the estimated value or price.
—[名] 1. 평가, 가격 사정 2. 평가액

‡val·ue [vǽlju:] *n.* [U][C] **1.** [U] worth; usefulness; relative worth; real worth. ¶*anything of real ~*① */ one's sense of values*② */ the values of classical learning / the question of the ~ of fresh air / It has ~ if used regularly.*③ **2.** amount of money or other goods for which a thing may be exchanged; price; fair return. ¶*the nominal ~ / face ~ / the market ~ of a house / get full ~ for one's money.*④ **3.** esteem; regard; importance. ¶*His opinions was of ~ to us. / I set a high ~ on my time.* **4.** exact meaning. ¶*the true ~ of a word.* **5.** power to buy. ¶*the ~ of money.* **6.** degree of lightness and darkness in painting. ¶*This is used for color values.* **7.** (*Mathematics*) the amount of which a sign is representative.
—[名] 1. 가치, 값; 유용성; 상대적인 가치; 진가 ¶①참된 가치가 있는 것/②가치관/③규칙적으로 사용되면 가치가 있다 2. [금전적] 가치, 가격; 대가 ¶④치른 돈에 대하여 충분히 가치있는 물건을 받다 3. 높은 평가; 존중 4. [문장 속의 말의] 정확한 의미 5. 구독력(購讀力) 6. [그림의] 명암의 도(度) 7. [기호 따위가 표시하는] 수치(數値)

—*vt.* **1.** estimate the worth of (something); put a price on (something). ¶*The insurer valued the insured items.* **2.** think highly of (something); esteem. ¶*~ his judgment highly.*
—[他] 1. …을 평가하다; …에 가격을 매기다 2. …을 존중하다; 높이 평가하다

val·ued [vǽlju(:)d] *adj.* **1.** highly estimated or determined. **2.** highly esteemed or considered.
—[形] 1. 높이 평가된 2. 존중된

***val·ue·less** [vǽlju(:)lis] *adj.* of no worth; worthless.
—[形] 가치(값어치) 없는; 하찮은, 보잘것 없는

***valve** [vælv] *n.* [C] **1.** a part of a blood vessel or other device which prevents a backward flow. **2.** a part of a device which shuts and opens the passage. ⇒fig. **3.** either of the shells of a shellfish.
—[名] 1. 판(瓣), 판막(瓣膜) 2. 개폐판(開閉瓣), 밸브 3. 조개껍데기, 조가비

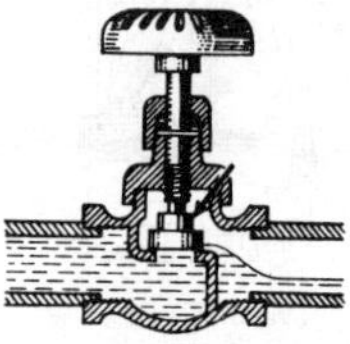
(valve 2.)

vamp¹ [væmp] *n.* [C] **1.** the upper front part of a shoe or boot. **2.** anything added to an old thing to make it look new. **—*vt.*** **1.** repair (a shoe) with a vamp. **2.** make (an old thing) look new; repair. (~ *up* something)
—[名] 1. [구두의] 등가죽 2. 기운 것, 새것처럼 보이게 덧댄 것
—[他] 1. [구두]에 등가죽을 대다 2. [헌 것]을 새것처럼 보이게 하다; 깁다, 수선하다

vamp² [væmp] *vi.* make love just to get money or please one's vanity. **—*n.*** [C] (*U.S. colloq.*) a woman who vamps; a vampire.
—[自] 남자를 후리다(등쳐먹다) —[名] 요부, 탕녀

vam·pire [vǽmpaiər] *n.* [C] **1.** a ghost supposed to leave its grave and suck the blood of sleeping people. **2.** a person who preys on others. **3.** a woman who ruins the man she tempts; a vamp. **4.** one of various bats that suck blood.
—[名] 1. 흡혈귀 2. 남의 고혈을 빨아먹는 착취자 3. 요부 4. 흡혈 박쥐

‡van¹ [væn] *n.* [C] (often *the ~*) the front part of an army or marching group; a vanguard.
—[名] 전위(前衛); 선봉, 선구자; 선두

1) ***in the van of,*** in advance of.
2) ***lead the van of,*** take the lead.
[熟] 1) …의 선두에 서서 2) …의 선구자가 되다

van² [væn] *n.* [C] **1.** a large covered truck. **2.** (*Brit.*) a closed railroad baggage car.
—[名] 1. 포장 달린 대형 트럭 2. 유개화차

van·dal [vǽnd(ə)l] *n.* [C] **1.** a person who destroys a work of art or another beautiful thing. **2.** (*V-*) a member of a Germanic tribe which invaded Spain and North Africa and captured Rome in 455 A.D.
—[名] 1. 예술·자연미 따위의 파괴자 2. 반달 사람(455년에 스페인과 북아프리카에 침입하여 로마를 약탈한 게르만의 한 종족)

van·dal·ism [vǽnd(ə)lìz(ə)m] *n.* [U] the act of damaging beautiful things.
—[名] 예술 파괴 행위

vane [vein] *n.* [C] **1.** a device to show the direction of the wind; a weathercock. ⇒fig. **2.** a flat leaf of a windmill; a propeller of a ship.
—[名] 1. 바람개비, 풍향계(風向計) 2. [풍차의] 날개; [배의] 프로펠러

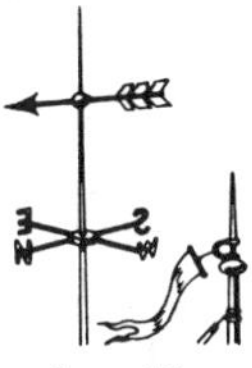
〔vane 1.〕

van·guard [vǽngɑ̀:rd] *n.* [C] **1.** the front part of an army or marching group. ↔rear guard **2.** 《*collectively*》 the leaders of a political movement, an artistic movement, etc.
—[名] 1. 선두, 전위 2. 선도자, 선구자

va·nil·la [vənílə] *n.* [C] **1.** [U] a flavoring essence used in candy, etc. **2.** the tropical plant, the beans of which are used in making this flavoring. **3.** the bean itself.
—[名] 1. 바닐라 향료 2. 바닐라(열대산의 덩굴 식물) 3. 바닐라 열매

⁑ **van·ish** [vǽniʃ] *vi.* **1.** go out of sight; disappear. **2.** cease to exist.
—[自] 1. 보이지 않게 되다, 자취를 감추다 2. 없어지다, 소멸하다

van·ish·ing cream [vǽniʃiŋkrì:m] *n.* a kind of cream which is absorbed quickly, used to apply to the face.
—[名] 바니싱 크리임[화장용 크리임]

vanishing point [´-- ˋ] *n.* (*Painting*) the point where receding parallel lines seem to meet each other.
—[名] [투시화법(透視畫法)의] 소점(消點)

* **van·i·ty** [vǽniti] *n.* (pl. **-ties**) **1.** [U] too much pride in one's looks, ability, etc. **2.** [U] the state or quality of being valueless. **3.** [C] anything of no real worth.
—[名] 1. 허영[심]; 자만[심], 자부[심] 2. 헛됨, 덧없음 3. 허무한(헛된) 사물

vanity case [´-- ˋ] *n.* a case containing various kinds of cosmetics.
—[名] 화장도구 상자, 화장품 케이스

van·quish [vǽŋkwiʃ, +*U.S.* vǽn-] *vt.* defeat thoroughly; conquer.
—[他] …에 이겨내다, 극복하다

van·tage [vǽntidʒ / vɑ́:n-] *n.* [U] **1.** a better position or condition; advantage. **2.** (in tennis) the first point scored after deuce.
—[名] 1. 유리한 입장(상태) 2. 《庭球》 듀우스 후의 1점의 득점

vantage ground [´- ˋ] *n.* a favorable position.
—[名] 유리한 지위

vap·id [vǽpid] *adj.* without flavor; not interesting; not active. ¶*a ~ speech / run ~*.①
—[形] 김빠진; 흥미없는, 싱거운; 활기없는 ¶①김빠지다, 맥빠지다

* **va·por,** *Brit.* **-pour** [véipər] [U][C] **1.** steam coming from boiling water; moisture in the air that can be seen. **2.** a gas formed from a substance which is usu. in a liquid or a solid form.
—[名] 1. 김; 수증기 2. 증기, 기화(氣化) 물질

va·por·i·za·tion [vèipərizéiʃ(ə)n / -raiz-] *n.* [U] the act of vaporizing; the state of being vaporized.
—[名] 증발, 기화(氣化)

va·por·ize [véipəràiz] *vt.* change (liquid, etc.) into vapor. —*vi.* be changed into vapor.
—[他] …을 수증기가 되게 하다, 증발시키다 —[自] 증기로 되다, 증발하다

va·por·i·zer [véipəràizər] *n.* [C] a device for vaporizing; an atomizer.
—[名] 기화기(氣化器); 분무기

va·por·ous [véipərəs] *adj.* **1.** covered or hidden by mist; filled with vapor. **2.** like vapor. **3.** lacking real worth; useless.
—[形] 1. 안개에 뒤덮인, 안개 자욱한; 수증기가 많은 2. 증기 같은 3. 실질이 없는, 쓸모없는

vapor trail [´- ˋ] *n.* a cloud formed from the vapor of an airplane.
—[名] 비행운(雲)

va·por·y, *Brit.* **-pour-** [véipəri] *adj.* =vaporous.

var·i·a·bil·i·ty [vὲəriəbíliti] *n.* [U] the state of being variable.
—[名] 변하기 쉬움, 가변성(可變性)

var·i·a·ble [vέəriəbl] *adj.* **1.** changeable; likely to change; not certain. ¶*~ weather*① / *a man of ~ temper.*② **2.** that can be changed. ¶*a ~ condenser.*③ **3.** varying from the strict biological type.
—*n.* [C] a thing or quantity that varies.
—[形] 1. 변하기 쉬운; 일정치 않은 ¶①변덕스러운 날씨/②변덕스러운 사람 2. 변화시킬 수 있는 ¶③가변(可變) 콘덴서 3. 변종(變種)의 —[名] 변화하는 것, 변수(變數)

var·i·ance [vέəriəns] *n.* [U] **1.** difference in opinion, etc.; disagreement. **2.** variation; change.
—[名] 1. 불일치, 상이(相異) 2. 변화, 변동

var·i·ant [vέəriənt] *adj.* **1.** different. ¶*~ type.* **2.** changeable. —*n.* [C] **1.** a varying form. **2.** a different form of pronouncing or spelling a certain word.
—[形] 1. 틀리는, 상이한 2. 변하기 쉬운, 변덕스러운 —[名] 1. 변형 2. 전화(轉化)

* **var·i·a·tion** [vὲəriéiʃ(ə)n] *n.* **1.** [U][C] a change in condition, degree, etc. **2.** [U][C] the amount of change. **3.** [C] a changed form. **4.** [C] (*Music*) the act of repeating a single tune or theme with changes; a series of such repetition.
—[名] 1. 변화, 변동, 변경 2. 변화량 3. 변화형, 변형 4. 《樂》 변주; 변주곡

var·i·col·ored, *Brit.* **-oured** [vέərikʌ̀lərd] *adj.* of or having many different colors.
—[形] 잡색의, 얼룩덜룩한

* **var·ied** [vέərid] *adj.* of different sorts; having various kinds.
—[形] 가지가지의, 가지각색의; 다채로운

var·ie·gat·ed [vέəri(ə)gèitid, +*U. S.* vέərə-] *adj.* different in appearance; marked with various colors; having many different things.
—[형] 다채로운, 변화가 풍부한

‡**va·ri·e·ty** [vəráiəti] *n.* (pl. **-ties**) **1.** [U] the state of being different; lack of sameness; change. **2.** [C] a collection of many different things. **3.** [C] a kind; a sort. **4.** [U] a performance consisting of several different kinds of acts; vaudeville.
—[명] **1.** 변화가 풍부함, 다양성 **2.** 잡동사니, 잡다함 **3.** 종류 **4.** 버라이어티 쇼우(다채로운 연예 프로)

var·i·o·rum [vèərió:rəm] *n.* [C] a book with the comments and notes of many editors or critics. **—*adj.*** of a variorum.
—[명] 여러 대가의 주를 단 책, 집주본(集注本) —[형] 여러 대가의 주가 있는

‡**var·i·ous** [vέəriəs] *adj.* of different kinds; not alike; different; several; many.
—[형] 변화가 풍부한, 다수의, 여러가지의, 가지각색의

var·i·ous·ly [vέəriəsli] *adv.* in many ways; in various manners.
—[부] 여러가지로, 다채롭게

var·nish [vá:rniʃ] *n.* [U][C] **1.** a liquid used to give a smooth surface to wood, cloth, etc. **2.** false appearance; outside show.
—[명] **1.** 와니스, 니스 **2.** 거죽만의 꾸밈, 겉치레

—*vt.* **1.** put varnish on the surface of (something). **2.** hide (something) under a false appearance.
—[타] **1.** …에 니스를 칠하다 **2.** …을 속이다, 눈가림하다, 분식(粉飾)하다

var·si·ty [vá:rs(i)ti] *n.* [C] (pl. **-ties**) **1.** the most important team playing a sport in a university or college. **2.** (chiefly *Brit. colloq.*) a university.
—[명] **1.** 대학의 대표 티임 **2.** 《英口》 대학

‡**var·y** [vέəri] *v.* (**var·ied**) *vt.* make (something) different; give variety to (something); change. **—*vi.*** become different; differ; change.
—[타] …을 바꾸다, …에 변화를 주다 —[자] 변화하다, 달라지다

‡**vase** [veis, veiz / vɑ:z] *n.* [C] an ornamental vessel used for holding flowers.
—[명] 꽃병, 화병

Vas·e·line, vas- [vǽsilì:n] *n.* [U] [a trade name for] a kind of grease.
—[명] 와셀린

vas·sal [vǽs(ə)l] *n.* [C] **1.** a person who receives land and protection in return for doing certain duties. **2.** a servant.
—[명] **1.** [봉건시대의] 가신(家臣), 봉신(封臣) **2.** 하인, 종복

vas·sal·age [vǽs(ə)lidʒ] *n.* [U] **1.** the state of being a vassal. **2.** feudal homage; loyalty. **3.** the ruled land controlled by a vassal.
—[명] **1.** 가신(家臣)임, 종속적 지위 **2.** 충성 **3.** 봉신(封臣)의 영토, 봉토(封土)

‡**vast** [væst / vɑ:st] *adj.* very large; great; huge. ¶*a ~ crowd of people.*
—[형] 굉장한, 광대한, 거대한

vast·ly [vǽstli / vá:st-] *adv.* very greatly; to a vast extent or degree.
—[부] 크게, 광대하게; 무한히

vast·ness [vǽstnis / vá:st-] *n.* [U] the state of being vast.
—[명] 광대, 막대, 거대

vat [væt] *n.* [C] a large container for liquid; a tank.
—[명] [술 따위를 넣는] 큰 통

Vat·i·can [vǽtikən], **the** *n.* **1.** the palace of the Pope in Rome. **2.** the authority of the Pope; the papal government.
—[명] **1.** 바티칸 궁전 **2.** 교황권, 교황정치

Vatican City [∠–– ∠–], **the** *n.* an independent state in Rome ruled by the Pope.
—[명] 바티칸시(市)

vaude·ville [vɔ́:d(ə)vil vóud-] *n.* [U] **1.** (*Brit.*) a light musical comedy. **2.** (*U. S.*) a performance consisting of different kinds of acts; variety.
—[명] **1.** 《英》 경음악극 **2.** 《美》 버라이어티 쇼우, 다채로운 연예 프로

vault**[1] [vɔ:lt] *n.* [C] **1.** an arched roof or ceiling. **2.** an underground storehouse. **3.** a tomb. **4.** a room in a bank for keeping valuable things. **—*vt. cover (something) with a vault.
—[명] **1.** 둥근 지붕 **2.** 지하 저장실 **3.** 무덤 **4.** 귀중품 저장실 —[타] …에 둥근 천장을 달다

vault[2] [vɔ:lt] *vi., vt.* leap or jump over (something) with the aid of hands or a pole. **—*n.*** [C] a jump or leap made in this way.
—[자][타] 뛰다, 도약하다, [···을] 뛰어넘다 —[명] 뛰기, 도약

vault·ing [vɔ́:ltiŋ] *n.* [U] **1.** a vaulted building. **2.** (*collectively*) an arched roof or ceiling.
—[명] **1.** 둥근 천장의 건축물 **2.** 둥근 천장

vaulting horse [∠– ∸] *n.* a wooden horse used for jumping over in gymnastics.
—[명] [도약용·체조용] 목마

vaunt [vɔ:nt, +*U. S.* vɑ:nt] *vi., vt.* show off; boast of (something). **—*n.*** [U][C] vain display; boasting.
—[자][타] 자랑하다 —[명] 자랑

veal [vi:l] *n.* [U] the meat of a calf.
—[명] 송아지 고기

veer [viər] *vi.* change direction. **—*vt.*** change the direction of (a ship, etc.).
—[자] 방향이 바뀌다 —[타] …의 방향을 바꾸다

Ve·ga [ví:gə] *n.* a star of the first magnitude in the Lyra constellation; the weaving girl star.
—[명] 베가성(星), 직녀성

‡ **veg·e·ta·ble** [védʒ(i)təbl] *n.* [C] **1.** a plant or a part of a plant used for food. **2.** a plant. **—*adj.*** **1.** of or like a plant. **2.** made of vegetables.
—[名] 1. 야채, 채소 2. 식물 —[形] 1. 식물의(같은) 2. 식물에서 채취한, 식물로 만든, 식물성의

veg·e·tar·i·an·ism [vèdʒitέəriənìz(ə)m] *n.* [U] the principle of eating vegetables only.
—[名] 채식주의

veg·e·tate [védʒitèit] *vi.* **1.** grow like plants. **2.** live in an idle or monotonous way.
—[自] 1. 식물처럼 성장하다 2. 무미건조한 생활을 하다, 무위도식하다

* **veg·e·ta·tion** [vèdʒitéiʃ(ə)n] *n.* [U] **1.** ⟪*collectively*⟫ plants. **2.** the act of vegetating; the growth of plants.
—[名] 1. 식물 2. 식물의 성장(발육)

veg·e·ta·tive [védʒitèitiv, +*Brit.* -tətiv] *adj.* **1.** growing like plants. **2.** of plants. **3.** able to grow plants. ¶~ *soil.* **4.** not moving; quiet; inactive.
—[形] 1. 식물처럼 성장하는 2. 식물의 3. 식물을 성장시키는 4. 활발치 못한, 정적(靜的)인

ve·he·mence [víːiməns] *n.* [U] the state of being vehement; rough force; violence.
—[名] 열렬함; 격렬; 맹렬

ve·he·ment [víːimənt] *adj.* **1.** having passion; having strong feelings; passionate. ¶*a ~ desire.*① **2.** full of force; very forceful; violent. ¶*~heat.*②
—[形] 1. 열렬한, 열정적인, 열의가 있는 ¶①열렬한 욕망 2. 맹렬한; 격렬한 ¶②맹렬한 열

ve·he·ment·ly [víːiməntli] *adv.* in a vehement manner; passionately; violently.
—[副] 열렬히; 맹렬히

* **ve·hi·cle** [víːikl] *n.* [C] **1.** anything used for carrying passengers or goods, esp. on land. **2.** a means of conveying ideas, information, etc.
—[名] 1. 탈것, 차, 차량 2. 전달 수단, 매체(媒體)

‡ **veil** [veil] *n.* [C] **1.** a piece of cloth worn over the head, the face or the shoulders. **2.** anything that covers. ¶*a ~ of mist.*
1) ***beyond the veil,*** beyond this world.
2) ***draw a*** (or ***the***) ***veil over,*** cover; conceal.
3) ***take the veil,*** become a nun.
—*vt.* cover (something) with a veil.
—[名] 1. 베일, 너울, 면사포 2. 덮어 가리는 것, 포장, 휘장, 장막
[熟] 1)저승에 2)…을 덮어 가리다 3)수녀가 되다
—[他] …을 베일로 가리다

veil·ing [véiliŋ] *n.* [U] cloth used for making veils.
—[名] 베일용 천

‡ **vein** [vein] *n.* [C] **1.** one of the blood vessels which carries the blood to the heart. ↔artery **2.** one of the branching lines on a leaf or the wing of an insect. **3.** a crack or seam in rock filled with other material. **4.** a long thin mark of a different color in wood or marble. **5.** ⟪*sing.* only⟫ a state of mind or feeling; a mood.
—*vt.* mark (something) with lines like veins.
—[名] 1. 정맥(靜脈) 2. 엽맥(葉脈), 시맥(翅脈) 3. 광맥, 암맥(岩脈) 4. 나뭇결, [나무·대리석 따위의] 줄무늬 5. 기질; 기분
—[他] …에 맥(脈) 같은 줄무늬를 넣다

veld, veldt [velt, +*U.S.* felt] *n.* [C] an open grassland in South Africa.
—[名] 남아프리카의 초원

vel·lum [véləm] *n.* [U] **1.** fine parchment for writing or for binding books. **2.** a kind of writing paper made in imitation of this.
—[名] 1. 고급 피지(皮紙) 2. 모조 피지

ve·loc·i·pede [vilásipìːd / -lɔ́s-] *n.* [C] **1.** a small vehicle with three wheels for children. **2.** a bicycle.
—[名] 1. [어린이용] 세발자전거 2. [옛날의] 자전거

ve·loc·i·ty [vilás(i)ti / -lɔ́s-] *n.* [U][C] (pl. **-ties**) **1.** the quickness of motion; speed. **2.** the rate of motion. ¶*at a ~ of 2 miles a minute.*①
—[名] 1. 빠름, 빠르기 2. 속도, 속력 ¶①분속(分速) 2 마일로

ve·lour, -lours [vəlúər] *n.* [U] cloth made of silk, wool or cotten woven like velvet.
—[名] 벨루어(명주·털·무명으로 벨벳처럼 짠 천)

‡ **vel·vet** [vélvit] *n.* [U] **1.** cloth with a thick, soft pile made of silk. **2.** something made like velvet. **—*adj.*** **1.** made of velvet. **2.** like velvet.
—[名] 1. 벨벳, 우단 2. 벨벳 비슷한 것
—[形] 1. 벨벳으로 만든 2. 벨벳 같은

vel·vet·een [vèlvitíːn] *n.* [U] cotton cloth like velvet.
—[名] 모조 벨벳, 면(綿)벨벳

vel·vet·y [vélviti] *adj.* soft and smooth like velvet.
—[形] 벨벳 같은, 벨벳처럼 부드러운

ve·nal [víːnl] *adj.* **1.** willing to work only for money; willing to get money unfairly. ¶*~ conduct*① / *a ~ politician.*② **2.** influenced by unfair money.
—[形] 1. 뇌물(금전)로 좌우할 수 있는, 매수할 수 있는 ¶①타산적 행위/②돈에 따라 움직이는 정치가 2. 매수된

ve·nal·i·ty [viːnǽliti] *n.* [U] the state of being venal.
—[名] 돈으로 좌우됨; 돈에 따라 움직임

ve·na·tion [viːnéiʃ(ə)n] *n.* [U] **1.** a pattern of veins in a leaf or in an insect's wing. **2.** ⟪*collectively*⟫ the veins of such a pattern.
—[名] 1. 도맥(導脈)·시맥(翅脈)의 분포상태 2. 엽맥(葉脈), 시맥

vend [vend] *vt.* sell.
—[他] …을 팔다, 판매하다

vend·er, -or [véndər] *n.* [C] **1.** a person who sells something. ¶*a peanut ~.* **2.** a vending machine.
—[名] 1. 파는 사람, 행상인 2. 자동 판매기

vending machine [⌐-- -⌐] *n.* a machine from which a person gets something by putting in a coin or coins.
—[名] 자동 판매기

V

ve·neer [viníər] *n.* **1.** [U] [C] a thin layer of fine wood or other material used to surface a substance of poorer quality. ⇒[N.B.] **2.** [C] the outside appearance.
—*vt.* **1.** cover (something) with a veneer. **2.** make (something cheap or mean) look bright and beautiful.
—[名] 1. [합판용] 얇은 판자, 장식용 판자 [N.B.] 한국에서 말하는 「베니어 판자」는 plywood라 함 2. 겉치레, 허식
—[他] 1. …에 장식용 판자를 대다 2. …의 거죽을 꾸미다, 겉치장하다

ven·er·a·ble [vén(ə)rəbl] *adj.* deserving and receiving respect because of age, character, etc. ¶*a ~ oak*① / *a ~ priest.*②
—[形] 존경(공경)할 만한 ¶①고색창연한 오우크나무/②덕망 높은 성직자

ven·er·ate [vénərèit] *vt.* look upon (someone) with respect.
—[他] …을 존경하다; 숭배(숭상)하다

ven·er·a·tion [vènəréiʃ(ən] *n.* [U] deep respect.
—[名] 존경, 숭배

venge·ance [véndʒ(ə)ns] *n.* [U] [C] punishment in return for a wrong; the return of evil for evil.
1) ***exact a vengeance from*** (*someone*) ***for,*** take revenge on someone, esp. for murder.
2) ***with a vengeance,*** ⓐ with great force and energy; violently. ⓑ much more than wanted; very.
—[名] 보복, 복수, 원수 갚음
[熟] 1)남에게 …의 복수를 하다 2)ⓐ난폭하게, 거칠게; 심하게 ⓑ극도로; 몹시

venge·ful [véndʒf(u)l] *adj.* full of a strong wish for revenge; revengeful.
—[形] 앙심을 먹은; 복수심을 품은

ve·ni·al [ví:niəl] *adj.* that can be excused; deserving pardon; that can be pardoned.
—[形] 크게 탓할 것 없는, 별로 나쁘지 않은, 용서할 만한

ven·i·son [vénizn, +*U.S.* -sn, +*Brit.* vénzn] *n.* [U] the meat of deer.
—[名] 사슴 고기

ven·om [vénəm] *n.* [U] **1.** the poisonous liquid of snakes, etc. **2.** strong desire to do harm to others; ill will.
—[名] 1. 독, 독액 2. 악의

ven·om·ous [vénəməs] *adj.* **1.** containing poison. ¶*a ~ serpent.*① **2.** desiring to do harm to others.
—[形] 1. 독이 있는 ¶①독사 2. 악의에 찬

vent [vent] *n.* [C] **1.** a small hole or opening for the passage of air, smoke, etc. ¶*the ~ of a chimney.* **2.** the act of letting out, esp. in speech; expression. ¶*give ~ to one's anger* / *His passion found ~ in writing.*① **3.** a finger hole in a musical instrument.
—*vt.* **1.** express (one's feelings) freely in words or actions; utter. ¶*He vented his anger on his children.* **2.** make (smoke, etc.) escape through a hole; make a vent in (something). ¶*The chimney vented the smoke.*
—[名] 1. [공기·액체 따위가 통하는] 구멍, 빠져나가는(새는) 구멍 2. [감정 따위의] 배출구 ¶①그의 정열은 저작에서 그 배출구를 찾았다 3. 악기의 손가락 대는 구멍
—[他] 1. [감정 따위]를 자유로이 표현하다, 발하다, 토하다, 배출하다 2. [연기 따위]를 내다; …에 구멍을 내다

***ven·ti·late** [véntilèit] *vt.* **1.** bring fresh air in and drive stale air out of (a room, etc.). **2.** make (blood, etc.) pure by supplying fresh air. **3.** make (something) known openly. **4.** supply (a room, etc.) with a vent.
—[他] 1. …의 환기(換氣)를 하다 2. …을 신선한 공기로 정화하다 3. …을 공표하다, 세상에 묻다 4. …에 환기구멍을 내다(마련하다)

***ven·ti·la·tion** [vèntiléiʃ(ə)n] *n.* [U] **1.** the act of ventilating. **2.** the means of ventilating.
—[名] 1. 환기, 통풍 2. 환기장치

***ven·ti·la·tor** [véntilèitər] *n.* [C] a device for changing or supplying air.
—[名] 환기장치

ven·tral [véntrəl] *adj.* **1.** of the belly. **2.** of or on the surface of the belly.
—[形] 1. 배의, 복부의 2. 표면에 있는

ven·tril·o·quism [ventríləkwìz(ə)m] *n.* [U] the art of speaking in which the voice seems to come from some other person than the speaker.
—[名] 복화술(腹話術)

ven·tril·o·quist [ventríləkwist] *n.* [C] a person who is skilled in the art of ventiloquism.
—[名] 복화술사(腹話術師)

ven·ture [véntʃər] *n.* **1.** [U] [C] a risky course of action; a risky piece of business; risk; chance; luck. **2.** [C] a business enterprise. ¶*He lost his first ~ in oil stock.*
at a venture, by chance; at random; at a guess.
—*vt.* **1.** expose (something) to danger, risk, or chance; risk. ¶*~ money in speculations.* **2.** dare to say or do. 《*~ to do*》 ¶*~ a guess* / *He ventured a critical comment.* / *He ventures to say what he believes.* —*vi.* take a risk; dare to do or go something dangerous. ¶*He ventured from his hiding place.*①
—[名] 1. 모험; 위험한 일 2. 투기, 투기사업
[熟] 모험적으로, 운수에 맡기고, 되어가는 대로
—[他] 1. …을 위험스럽게 하다; …에 내걸다, 내맡기다 2. 과감히 …하다, …을 과감하게 표명하다 —[自] 위험을 무릅쓰다; 위험을 무릅쓰고 가다 ¶①그는 은신처에서 위험을 무릅쓰고 나갔다

ven·ture·some [véntʃərsəm] *adj.* **1.** willing to take risks; daring. **2.** dangerous; risky.
—[形] 1. 모험을 좋아하는, 대담한, 물불을 가리지 않는 2. 위험한

Ve·nus [ví:nəs] *n.* **1.** (in Roman mythology) the goddess of love and beauty. **2.** a very beautiful woman. **3.** the most brilliant planet, second in order from the sun.
—[名] 1. 비이너스(로마신화의 사랑과 미의 여신) 2. 미녀 3. 금성(金星)

ve·ra·cious [veréiʃəs] *adj.* **1.** always telling the truth;
—[形] 1. 성실한, 정직한 2. 옳은, 진실한

truthful. **2.** true.

ve·rac·i·ty [vərǽsiti] *n.* [U] **1.** the state of being truthful. **2.** something which is true. **3.** exactness; the state of having no mistakes.
—[名] 1. 성실, 정직 2. 진실 3. 정확, 확실

ve·ran·da, -dah [vərǽndə] *n.* [C] a long, open porch with a roof.
—[名] 베란다

:**verb** [və:rb] *n.* [C] (*Grammar*) a word that expresses an action, a state of being, or a condition.
—[名] 《文法》 동사

ver·bal [və́:rb(ə)l] *adj.* **1.** of or consisting of words. ¶ *~ expression.*① **2.** expressed by spoken words; not written. **3.** word for word; literal. ¶*a ~ translation.*② **4.** (*Grammar*) of or derived from a verb.
—*n.* [C] (*Grammar*) an infinitive, gerund or participle.
—[形] 1. 말의, 언어의 ¶①언어·표현 2. 말로 나타내는, 구두(口頭)의 3. 문자 그대로의, 축어적(逐語的)인 ¶②축어역, 직역 4.《文法》 동사의; 동사에서 나온 —[名] 《文法》 준(準)동사

verbal noun [⌐–⌐] *n.* a noun derived from a verb, formed by adding *-ing* at the end of a verb or *to* before a verb; a gerund or infinitive.
—[名] 동명사; 부정사(不定詞) 명사용법

ver·bal·ly [və́:rbəli] *adv.* **1.** in words. **2.** by spoken words. **3.** word for word. **4.** in words only. **5.** as a verb.
—[副] 1. 말로, 언어로 2. 구두로 3. 축어적(逐語的)으로 4. 말만으로는, 언어상으로는 5. 동사로서

ver·ba·tim [və:rbéitim] *adv., adj.* word for word; literal[ly].
—[副][形] 축어적으로; 축어적인; 문자 그대로의

ver·be·na [və(:)rbí:nə] *n.* [C] a garden plant with a mass of small flowers in various colors and with various smells. ⇒fig.
—[名] 버어베나속(屬)의 식물

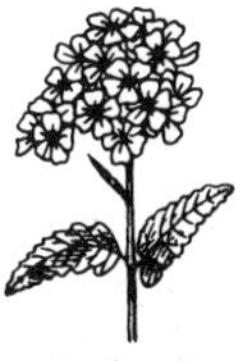
〔verbena〕

ver·bi·age [və́:rbiidʒ] *n.* [U] the use of too many words.
—[名] 다변(多辯), 쓸데없는 말이 많음

ver·bose [və:rbóus] *adj.* expressed in or using too many words; wordy.
—[形] 말 수가 많은, 말 많은, 용장(冗長)한

ver·bos·i·ty [və:rbásiti / və:bɔ́s-] *n.* [U] the state of being verbose.
—[名] 말 많음, 다변, 용장

ver·dant [və́:rd(ə)nt] *adj.* **1.** covered with grass or leaves; fresh and green. **2.** fresh and not experienced. ¶*in one's ~ youth.*①
—[形] 1. 초록에 뒤덮인; 신록의 2. 순진한, 천진한, 미숙한 ¶①순진한 청년시대에

ver·dict [və́:rdikt] *n.* [C] **1.** the judgment made by a jury in a law court. **2.** the act of making up one's mind.
—[名] 1.《法》평결(評決) 2. 결의(決意), 결단

ver·di·gris [və́:rdigrì(:)s] *n.* [U] the green, poisonous compound formed on brass, bronze or copper which has been kept for a long time without being cleaned.
—[名] 녹청(綠靑)

ver·dure [və́:rdʒər] *n.* [U] **1.** greenness; freshness. **2.** fresh green grass or growing plants.
—[名] 1. 초록, 신록 2. 푸른 초목

ver·dur·ous [və́:rdʒ(ə)rəs] *adj.* fresh and green.
—[形] 싱싱한 초록빛의, 푸릇푸릇한

verge [və:rdʒ] *n.* [C] **1.** an edge. **2.** a limit; a border.
—*vi.* **1.** become near to something; approach. 《~ *to* something》 **2.** tend; incline. 《~ *to* or *toward* something》
—[名] 1. 가장자리, 가, 변두리 2. 경계, 한계 —[自] 1. 가까와지다, 접근하다 2. 향하다, 기울다

ver·ger [və́:rdʒər] *n.* [C] **1.** a person who takes charge of a church; a sexton. **2.** a person who carries the rod symbolic of his position or rank before a bishop, etc.
—[名] 1. 교회지기, 성당지기 2. 권표(權標) 받드는 사람

ver·i·fi·ca·tion [vèrifikéiʃ(ə)n] *n.* [U] **1.** the act of proving the truth of a fact. **2.** a statement made in order to prove something.
—[名] 1. 입증; 증명 2. 증언

ver·i·fy [vérifài] *vt.* (**-fied**) **1.** prove the truth of (something); confirm. **2.** test the exactness of (something).
—[他] 1. …을 실증하다, 확인하다 2. …을 확실하게 하다, 맞추어 보다, 대조하다

ver·i·ly [vérili] *adv.* truly; in truth; really.
—[副] 진실로, 사실로, 참으로

ver·i·si·mil·i·tude [vèrisimílit(j)ù:d / -tjù:d] *n.* [U] **1.** the state of being likely or probable; likelihood. **2.** something which seems to be true.
—[名] 1. 있음직함, 정말 같음 2. 정말같이 보이는 일

ver·i·ta·ble [véritəbl] *adj.* actual; real; genuine.
—[形] 사실인, 진정한, 정말인; 진짜인

ver·i·ty [vériti] *n.* **1.** [U] the state or quality of being true; reality. **2.** [C] something taken as fundamentally and essentially true.
—[名] 1. 진실, 진실성 2. 진리

ver·mi·cel·li [və̀:rmiséli, +*U.S.* -tʃéli] *n.* [U] food like macaroni and spaghetti, but thinner and longer than them.
—[名] 베르미첼리(스파게티 · 마카로니보다 가는 것)

ver·mi·cide [və́:rmisàid] *n.* [C] any drug that kills worms, esp. those that live in the bowels.
—[名] 살충제; 회충약, 구충제

ver·mi·form [və́:rmifɔ̀:rm] *adj.* shaped like a worm.
—[形] 벌레 모양의

ver·mil·ion [vərmíljən] *n.* [U] **1.** a bright red color. **2.**
—[名] 1. 주색(朱色) 2. 주(朱), 진사(辰

a material making a bright-red color. —*adj*. bright red.
ver·min [vɚ́ːrmin] *n*. ⓤ (*collectively*, usu. used as *pl*.) harmful and unpleasant insects, small animals, or people.
ver·min·ous [vɚ́ːrminəs] *adj*. 1. troubled by harmful insects or animals. 2. caused by vermin. 3. like vermin; harmful; poisonous.
Ver·mont [vəːrmɑ́nt / vəːmɔ́nt] *n*. a State of the northeastern United States; a part of New England. →N.B.
ver·mouth [vərmúːθ / vɚ́ːməθ] *n*. ⓤ a kind of white wine flavored with various strong-smelling plants.
ver·nac·u·lar [vərnǽkjulər] *n*. ⓒ 1. a native language; the language used by the people of a certain district. 2. informal language spoken every day. 3. technical terms. —*adj*. 1. used by the people in a certain place; native. ¶ *a ~ disease*.① 2. of the native language.
ver·nal [vɚ́ːrnl] *adj*. 1. of or like spring. ¶*the ~ bloom / ~ weather*. 2. having the looks of youth; fresh.
ver·ni·er [vɚ́ːrniər] *n*. ⓒ a small, movable scale attached to a larger, fixed scale and used for measuring fractional parts or divisions.
ve·ron·i·ca [virɑ́nikə / -rɔ́n-] *n*. ⓒ 1. a shrub with blue, pink or white flowers. 2. a cloth on which Christ's face is drawn.
Ver·sailles [vɛərsái, +*U.S.* -séilz] *n*. 1. a city near Paris. 2. a large palace in this city.
ver·sa·tile [vɚ́ːrsət(i)l / vɚ́ːsətàil] *adj*. that can do many things well. ⌜satile.⌝
ver·sa·til·i·ty [vɚ̀ːrsətíliti] *n*. ⓤ the state of being ver-⌟
‡ **verse** [vəːrs] *n*. ⓒ 1. a single line of poetry. 2. a group of lines of poetry; a stanza. 3. ⓤ a literary composition with rhythm; poetry. 4. a short, numbered division of a chapter in the Bible.
* **versed** [vəːrst] *adj*. having experience; well practiced; skillful. ¶*She is well ~ in speaking*.①
ver·si·fi·ca·tion [vɚ̀ːrsifikéiʃ(ə)n] *n*. ⓤ 1. the act of making verses. 2. the art or method of making verses. 3. the form or pattern of poetry. ⌜a poet.⌝
ver·si·fi·er [vɚ́ːrsifàiər] *n*. ⓒ a person who makes verse;⌟
ver·si·fy [vɚ́ːrsifài] *vt*. (-**fied**) 1. write poetry about (something). 2. translate (prose) into poetry. —*vi*. tell in poetry.
* **ver·sion** [vɚ́ːrʒ(ə)n, -ʃ(ə)n] *n*. ⓒ 1. a translation from one language to another. ¶*the Authorized Version*① / *the Revised Version*.② 2. a particular remark; a statement; a description. ¶*my ~ of the affair*.③
ver·sus [vɚ́ːrsəs] *prep*. against. ¶*Oxford ~ Cambridge*.
ver·te·brate [vɚ́ːrtibrit, -brèit] *n*. ⓒ an animal having a backbone, such as fishes, birds, and mammals. —*adj*. having a backbone. ¶*a ~ animal*.①
* **ver·ti·cal** [vɚ́ːrtik(ə)l] *adj*. straight up and down; upright; erect. ↔horizontal —*n*. (*the ~*) a vertical line, plane, position, etc. ⌜right angles; uprightly.⌝
ver·ti·cal·ly [vɚ́ːrtik(ə)li] *adv*. in a vertical position; at⌟
ver·tig·i·nes [vəːrtídʒinìːz] *n*. pl. of vertigo.
ver·tig·i·nous [vəːrtídʒinəs] *adj*. 1. turning round and round; rotating. 2. of vertigo; dizzy. 3. changeable; unstable.
ver·ti·go [vɚ́ːrtigòu] *n*. ⓤ the feeling as if one's head were turning around; dizziness.
verve [vəːrv] *n*. ⓤ a strong feeling of animation; active strength or energy; force; spirit.
‡ **ver·y** [véri] *adv*. 1. in a high degree; greatly; extremely. ¶*~ wet / a ~ wet day / ~ thoughtfully planned*① / *~ much troubled / ~ well received / ~ well stated / ~ re-*

⒝) —⒜ 주[홍]색의
—⒝ 해충; 해로운 짐승; [사회에 해독을 끼치는] 못된 자, 망나니
—⒜ 1. 해충(해로운 짐승)이 들끓는, 2. 해충(해로운 짐승)으로 말미암아 일어난 3. 해충(해로운 짐승) 같은;유해한
—⒝ 미국 동북부의 주 usage Vt.로 줄여 씀.수도는 Montpelier
—⒝ 베르뭇 술(약초로 향미를 낸 백포도주)
—⒝ 1. 자기 나라 말, 자국어; 지방 사투리, 방언 2. 일상 쓰는 저속한 말 3. 전문어, 직업어
—⒜ 1. 모국의, 자기 나라의 ¶①풍토병 2. 자국어의
—⒜ 1. 봄의, 봄 같은 2. 청춘의; 생기에 찬
—⒝ 부척(副尺), 유표척(遊標尺)[주척 눈금의 단수(端數)를 재기 위하여 주척에 따라 왔다갔다하게 만든 보조척]
—⒝ 1. 꼬리풀속(屬)의 식물 2. 그리스도의 얼굴을 그린 천
—⒝ 1. 베르사이유(파리 근교의 도시) 2. 베르사이유 궁전
—⒜ 재주 많은, 다예(多藝)한, 다재한
—⒝ 다예, 다재
—⒝ 1. 시의 1행 2. 시의 1절 3. 시, 운문 4. 성서의 절(節)

—⒜ 경험이 있는; 숙달된, 정통한 ¶①그녀는 이야기 솜씨가 있다
—⒝ 1. 작시(作詩), 시작(詩作) 2. 작시법 3. 시형(詩形)

—⒝ 시인; 작시가
—⒝ 1. …의 시를 쓰다 2. [산문]을 시로 고치다 —⒜ 시로 말하다

—⒝ 1. 번역[서], 번역문, 역문(譯文) ¶①흠정역(欽定譯) 성서/②개역 성서 2. 설명; 의견 ¶③그 사건에 대한 나의 의견
—⒠ …대(對) N.B. v., vs.로 줄여 씀
—⒝ 척추 동물 —⒜ 척추가 있는 ¶①척추 동물

—⒜ 곧추 선, 수직의, 세로의 —⒝ 수직의 것, 수직선(면), 수직한 위치

—⒠ 수직으로, 직립하여

—⒜ 1. 빙글빙글 도는; 선회하는 2. 어지러운, 현기증나는 3. 변화가 심한, 불안정한
—⒝ 현기증

—⒝ 열정; 활기; 힘; 기력; 열의(熱意)
—⒠ 1. 몹시, 매우, 대단히, 퍽 ¶①매우 치밀하게 계획된 usage 감정을 나타내는 피동형으로는 much를 쓰는 것이

spectfully yours / *a ~ pleasing voice* / *~ much annoyed* ⇒[usage] / *It is not ~ warm today.*② **2.** ((with *a superlative, my, your, his, own, etc.*)) absolutely; really. ¶*my ~ own* / *He drank it to the ~ last drop.*
원칙이지만, 《口》에서는 very를 쓰는 일이 많음/②오늘은 별로 따뜻한 날씨가 아니다 2. 아주, 참으로

—*adj.* (**ver·i·er, ver·i·est**) **1.** real; true. ¶*in ~ truth*③/ *her ~ son.* **2.** ((as an *intensive,* placed after *the, this, that, my, your, his*)) same; precise; actual; absolute. ¶ *at the ~ moment* / *On the ~ day she was married, she* had *an accident.*④ **3.** ((as an *intensive*)) even; mere. ¶*The ~ thought of war makes me shudder.*
—[形] 1. 참된, 참말의, 진정한, 진실의 ¶③정말로, 진실로 2. 바로 그, 다름 아닌, 문자 그대로의, 틀림없는 ¶④결혼한 바로 그날에 그녀는 사고를 만났다 3. …조차도, …까지도

ves·per [véspər] *n.* [U] **1.** ((*V-*)) the evening star; Hesperus. **2.** ((usu. *pl.*)) an evening prayer or church service. —*adj.* of evening.
—[名] 1. 개밥바라기 2. 저녁 기도 —[形] 저녁의, 해질 무렵의

* **ves·sel** [vésl] *n.* [C] **1.** a hollow container for liquids. **2.** a tube in a body carrying blood or other liquids. **3.** a large boat; ship.
—[名] 1. 그릇, 용기(容器) 2. 관(管) 3. 배(보우트보다 큰 배)

* **vest** [vest] *n.* [C] **1.** a short, sleeveless garment worn by men under the coat. **2.** a similar garment worn by women. **3.** (*Brit.*) an undershirt.
—*vt.* **1.** put clothes on (someone). **2.** give power, rights, authority, etc. to (someone). **3.** put (power, authority, etc.) into the care or possession of someone.
—*vi.* **1.** put on garments. **2.** pass to someone.
—[名] 1. 조끼 2. 베스트(부인용 조끼) 3. 《英》 속옷, 내의
—[他] 1. …에 옷을 입히다 2. [남]에게 권력 따위를 주다 3. [권력 따위]를 남에게 주다 —[自] 1. 옷을 입다 2. 남에게 귀속하다

Ves·ta [véstə] *n.* **1.** (in Roman mythology) the goddess of the hearth. **2.** [C] ((*v-*)) a kind of short wax match.
—[名] 1. [로마 신화의] 베스타 여신 2. 밀랍 성냥

ves·tal [véstl] *n.* [C] **1.** a girl serving Vesta; a vestal virgin. **2.** an unmarried woman; a virgin. **3.** a nun. —*adj.* **1.** of Vesta. **2.** pure; virgin.
—[名] 1. 베스타 여신의 시중을 든 처녀 2. 처녀 3. 수녀 —[形] 1. 베스타 여신의 2. 순결한, 처녀의

vest·ed [véstid] *adj.* **1.** (*Law*) fixed; settled. **2.** dressed in robes, esp. in church garments.
—[形] 1. 《法》 기득(既得)의, 기정(既定)의 2. 제복(祭服)을 입은, 법의를 입은

ves·ti·bule [véstibjù:l] *n.* [C] **1.** a hall between the outer and inner doors; an entrance hall. **2.** (*U. S.*) the enclosed space at the end of a railway passenger car.
—[名] 1. 현관; 현관의 호올 2. 《美》 객차의 입구에 있는 작은 방, 연랑(連廊)

ves·tige [véstidʒ] *n.* [C] **1.** a mark made by something which has passed; a trace. **2.** (*Biology*) a part or an organ that is no longer useful.
—[名] 1. 자취, 흔적 2. 퇴화한 기관, 흔적기관

ves·tig·i·al [vestídʒiəl] *adj.* of a vestige.
—[形] 흔적의, 자국으로 남은; 퇴화한

vest·ment [véstmənt] *n.* [C] **1.** any article of dress or clothing. **2.** a robe or garment worn by a clergyman in a ceremony.
—[名] 1. 옷, 의복 2. 제복(祭服), 법의(法衣)

vest-pock·et [véstpɑ̀kit / -pɔ̀k-] *adj.* that can be put into a pocket of a vest; very tiny; small-sized.
—[形] 호주머니에 들어갈 만한; 작은; 소형의

ves·try [véstri] *n.* [C] (pl. **-tries**) **1.** a room in a church where vestments are kept. **2.** a room in a church used for Sunday School, prayer meetings, etc. **3.** a meeting of the people of a parish on church business.
—[名] 1. 제복실(祭服室) 2. 예배실 3. 교구회(教區會)

ves·ture [véstʃər] *n.* [U] [C] **1.** garments; clothes. **2.** anything that covers or protects.
—[名] 1. 옷, 의복 2. 가리개, 씌우개

vet [vet] *n.* [C] (*colloq.*) a veterinarian.
—[名] 《口》 수의(獸醫)

vetch [vetʃ] *n.* [C] a plant of the pea family grown as food for cattle.
—[名] 살갈퀴속(屬)의 식물(가축의 먹이)

* **vet·er·an** [vét(ə)rən] *n.* [C] **1.** a person who has had much experience in war. **2.** a person who has done military service. **3.** a person who has had much experience in some profession or position.
—*adj.* **1.** having much experience in war. **2.** experienced; long-trained.
—[名] 1. 고참병, 노병(老兵) 2. 퇴역 군인 3. 노련가, 고참
—[形] 1. 전쟁 경험이 많은 2. 노련한

vet·er·i·nar·i·an [vèt(ə)rinɛ́əriən] *n.* [C] a doctor who treats animals.
—[名] 수의(獸醫)

vet·er·i·nar·y [vét(ə)rinèri / -n(ə)ri] *adj.* concerning the medical or surgical treatment of animals. —*n.* [C] (pl. **-nar·ies**) a veterinarian.
—[形] 수의의 —[名] 수의

ve·to [ví:tou] *n.* [C] (pl. **-toes**) **1.** the right of a president, etc. to refuse bills and so prevent them from becoming law. **2.** the use of this right. **3.** refusal of consent or agreement; prohibition. *put a veto on,* refuse.
—[名] 1. 거부권, 부인권(否認權) 2. 거부권 행사, 거부, 부인 3. 금지, 금제(禁制) [熟] …을 거부하다, …에 거부권을 행사하다

—*adj.* of a veto. — [形] 거부[권]의, 부인하는

—*vt.* **1.** refuse (bills) by a veto. **2.** forbid someone to consent to (something); prohibit. — [他] 1. …을 거부하다 2. …을 금지하다

∗**vex** [veks] *vt.* **1.** make (someone) angry, esp. by a worthless idea; annoy; irritate. **2.** disturb; trouble. — [他] 1. …을 성가시게 굴다, 짜증나게 굴다, 괴롭히다 2. …을 소란스럽게 하다

vex·a·tion [vekséiʃ(ə)n] *n.* **1.** [U] the act of vexing; the state of being vexed. **2.** [C] a thing which annoys. — [名] 1. 짜증나게 하기; 짜증, 화남 2. 고민거리, 화나는 일

vex·a·tious [vekséiʃəs] *adj.* causing vexation; worrying. — [形] 화나는, 성가신, 짜증나는

v.i., vi. intransitive verb.

vi·a [váiə] *prep.* by way of. ¶*He returned home ~ America.* — [前] …경유로, …을 거쳐서

vi·a·duct [váiədʌkt] *n.* [C] a bridge built to carry a road or railway over a valley. — [名] 고가교(高架橋), 육교

vi·al [vái(ə)l] *n.* [C] a small glass bottle for holding medicines; a bottle. — [名] 약병, 작은 유리병

vi·and [váiənd] *n.* [C] **1.** an article of food. **2.** (*pl.*) food; provisions. — [名] 1. 식품 2. 음식물, 식료품

vi·brant [váibr(ə)nt] *adj.* **1.** moving rapidly to and fro; vibrating. **2.** continuing to sound; ringing. — [形] 1. 진동하는; 떠는 2. 울려퍼지는

∗**vi·brate** [váibreit / -ˊ] *vi.* **1.** move quickly back and forth; tremble; shake. **2.** have an exciting feeling. — [自] 1. 진동하다; 떨다, 떨리다 2. 전율(戰慄)하다

—*vt.* **1.** make (something or someone) swing. **2.** give an exciting feeling to (someone). — [他] 1. …을 뒤흔들다 2. …을 전율케 하다

vi·bra·tion [vaibréiʃ(ə)n] *n.* [U][C] a quick movement to and fro. — [名] 떪, 떨림; 진동

vic·ar [víkər] *n.* [C] **1.** a person performing the service in a church of an English parish. **2.** a clergyman in a parish of the Protestant Episcopal Church. **3.** a clergyman representing the Pope or a bishop of a Roman Catholic church. **4.** a person who acts in place of another. — [名] 1. 교구 목사 2. 회당(會堂) 목사, 전도 목사 3. 교황 대리 4. 대리인

vic·ar·age [víkəridʒ] *n.* [C] the house of a vicar. — [名] 목사관(館)

vi·car·i·ous [vaikέəriəs, vi-] *adj.* **1.** acting for another. **2.** done or suffered for another. **3.** felt by sympathizing with another's experience. — [形] 1. 대리하는, 대리의, 대신의 2. 대신하여 받는 3. 동감하는

‡**vice**[1] [vais] *n.* [U][C] **1.** a bad habit or tendency. **2.** evil conduct; wickedness. **3.** a bad habit or fault of a horse, a dog, etc. — [名] 1. 악습, 악폐 2. 악덕, 비행; 사악 3. [말·개의] 나쁜 버릇, 악벽, 결점

vice[2] [vais] *n.* (esp. *Brit.*) =vise.

vice- *pref.* **1.** in place of. **2.** lower in rank. — 《接頭》 1. …대리[의] 2. 차(次)…, 부(副)…

vice-ad·mi·ral [váisǽdm(ə)r(ə)l] *n.* [C] a naval officer next below an admiral in rank. — [名] 해군 중장

vice·ge·rent [vaisdʒíər(ə)nt, +*Brit.* -dʒér-] *n.* [C] a person appointed by a ruler, etc. to exercise his power and authority. — [名] 대리인

vice-gov·er·nor [váisgʌ́vənər] *n.* [C] an officer next below a governor in rank. — [名] 부총독; 부지사

vice-pres·i·dent [váisprézid(ə)nt] *n.* [C] an officer ranked next below a president. — [名] 부통령, 부회장, 부사장, 부교장

vice·roy [váisrɔi] *n.* [C] a person who rules a country, province or colony as representative of a king or queen. — [名] 태수(太守); 총독

vi·ce ver·sa [váisivə́:rsə] *adv.* the other way round; conversely. ¶*He distrusts her, and ~.* — [副] 반대로, 거꾸로도 또한 마찬가지

∗**vi·cin·i·ty** [visíniti] *n.* [U] **1.** the state of being near; nearness. **2.** the surrounding area; the neighborhood. — [名] 1. 가까움 2. 근처

∗**vi·cious** [víʃəs] *adj.* **1.** evil; wicked. ¶*a ~ companion*① / *lead a ~ life.*② **2.** full of faults; not correct. ¶*a ~ pronunciation.*③ **3.** full of malice or ill will; spiteful. ¶*~ remarks.*④ **4.** (*colloq.*) extremely unpleasant. ¶*a ~ headache.*⑤ ▷**vi·cious·ly** [-li] *adv.* —**vi·cious·ness** [-nis] *n.* — [形] 1. 악덕의 ¶①악우(惡友)/②타락한 생활을 보내다 2. 결점이 있는 ¶③틀린 발음 3. 악의에 찬 ¶④악의에 찬 말 4. 《口》 아주 심한, 지독한 ¶⑤심한 두통

vi·cis·si·tude [visísit(j)ù:d / -tjù:d] *n.* [C] 《usu. *pl.*》 a change in circumstances, conditions, etc. — [名] 변천, 변이(變移); 영고성쇠

∗**vic·tim** [víktim] *n.* [C] **1.** a living being killed as a sacrifice to some god. **2.** a person or an animal injured or killed in some accident, misfortune, etc. — [名] 1. 산제물, 희생 2. 희생자; 피해자

vic·tim·ize [víktimàiz] *vt.* **1.** make (someone) a victim of someone or something else. **2.** cause (someone) to suffer. **3.** cheat. — [他] 1. …을 희생(제물)으로 하다 2. …을 괴롭히다 3. …을 속이다

∗**vic·tor** [víktər] *n.* [C] a winner; a conqueror. —*adj.* of a victor; victorious. — [名] 승리자 —[形] 승리자의

Vic·tor [víktər] ***n.*** a man's name.
—[名] 남자 이름

Vic·to·ri·a [viktɔ́:riə] ***n.*** **1.** a woman's name. **2.** the queen of England from 1837 to 1901.
—[名] 1.여자 이름 2.빅토리아 여왕(1837~1910년까지 재위한 영국여왕)

Vic·to·ri·an [viktɔ́:riən] ***adj.*** **1.** of the time of Queen Victoria. **2.** showing characteristics of the people who lived in the Victorian period. **—*n.*** [C] any of the writers of the Victorian age.
—[形] 1.빅토리아 여왕 시대의 2.빅토리아 왕조풍의 —[名] 빅토리아 여왕 시대의 작가

* **vic·to·ri·ous** [viktɔ́:riəs] ***adj.*** having won a victory in battle or contest; of victory. ¶*a ~ battle*① | *come out ~*.② ▷**vic·to·ri·ous·ly** [-li] ***adv.***
—[形] 전쟁에서 승리한; 승리의 ¶①승전/②이기다, 승리하다

⁑ **vic·to·ry** [víkt(ə)ri] ***n.*** [U][C] (pl. **-ries**) success in any contest, battle, etc. ↔defeat
—[名] 승리

vict·ual [vítl] ***n.*** 《usu. *pl.*》 (*colloq.*) food. **—*v.*** **(-ualed, -ual·ing** or *Brit.* **-ualled, -ual·ling)** ***vt.*** provide (someone) with food. **—*vi.*** take on a supply of food.
—[名] 《口》 음식물 —[他] …에 음식물을 공급하다 —[自] 음식물을 공급하다

vict·ual·er, *Brit.* **-ual·ler** [vítlər] ***n.*** [C] **1.** a person who supplies food to a ship, an army, etc. **2.** (*Brit.*) an innkeeper licensed to sell alcohol.
—[名] 1.식료품 공급자 2.《英》 여인숙 주인

vi·de·li·cet [vidélisit / -dí:lisèt] ***adv.*** that is to say; namely. ⇒[N.B.]
—[副] 즉 [N.B.] 보통 viz.로 줄여 쓰며, 「namely라 읽음」

vid·eo [vídiòu] ***adj.*** **1.** of television. **2.** of the picture on television. ↔audio **—*n.*** [U] television.
—[形] 1.텔레비전의 2.[텔레비전] 영상(映像)의 —[名] 텔레비전

vie [vai] ***vi.*** **(vied, vy·ing)** strive with someone for superiority; compete. 《~ *with* someone》
—[自] 경쟁하다, 우열을 겨루다

Vi·en·na [viénə] ***n.*** the capital of Austria, on the Danube. ⇒[N.B.]
—[名] 비인 [N.B.] 오스트리아의 수도이며, 독일명은 Wien

Vi·en·nese [vìəní:z] ***n.*** a person of Vienna. **—*adj.*** of Vienna or the Viennese people.
—[名] 비인 사람 —[形] 비인[사람]의

Vi·et·nam, Vi·et·Nam [viétná:m, -nǽm] ***n.*** a country in southeastern Asia, formerly a part of French Indo-China. ⇒[N.B.]
—[名] 베트남 [N.B.] South Vietnam(수도 Saigon)과 North Vietnam(수도 Hanoi)으로 분할

⁑ **view** [vju:] ***n.*** [C] **1.** the act of seeing; a look. ¶*Magellan's first ~ of the Pacific.* **2.** [U] the power of seeing; the range of the eye. ¶*The ship soon came into ~.*① **3.** that which is seen; a scene. ¶*From the road I had a good ~ of the sea.*② **4.** a picture of some scene, esp. of a landscape. **5.** the way of looking at a matter; an opinion; a thought; a judgment; mental examination. ¶*He spoke his views on the election.* | *What is your ~ of life after death?*③ **6.** a purpose; an intention; a prospect; an expectation. ¶*a definite plan in ~.* **7.** a mental picture; an idea.
—[名] 1.보기; 관찰 2.시력; 보이는 범위, 시야 ¶①배가 곧 시야에 들어왔다 3.보이는 것; 경치, 광경 ¶②길에서 바다가 잘 보였다 4.풍경화; 풍경 사진 5.사물의 관점; 의견; 생각, 견해; 판단; 고찰 ¶③사후의 생명에 대한 당신의 견해는 어떠하십니까? 6.목적; 의도; 기대 7.심적(心的) 인상; 착상

1) ***in view,*** ⓐ in sight. ⓑ under consideration. ⓒ as a purpose; as an expectation.
2) ***in view of,*** ⓐ in sight of. ⓑ considering; because of. ¶*in ~ of the grave situation.*
3) ***on view,*** open for people to see; on display.
4) ***with a view to,*** for the purpose of. 《~ *doing*》 ¶*He works hard with a ~ to winning a scholarship.*
[熟] 1)ⓐ보여서 ⓑ고려중 ⓒ피하여; 기대하여 2)ⓐ보이는 곳에 ⓑ…을 고려하여; …할 생각으로 3)전시하여, 진열하여 4)…할 목적으로

—*vt.* **1.** look at (something) carefully; see; examine. ¶*Columbus first viewed land on October 12.* **2.** consider; regard; form an opinion about (something). ¶*The proposal was viewed favorably.*④
—[他] 1.[특히 주의하여] …을 보다; 조사하다 2.…이라고 간주하다; …을 생각하다, …의 견해를 취하다 ¶④그 제안은 찬성으로 간주되었다(호의적으로 검토되었다)

view·find·er [vjú:fàindər] ***n.*** [C] a device attached to a camera for selecting view to photograph.
—[名] [사진에서 피사체(被寫體)의 위치를 보는] 파인더

view·less [vjú:lis] ***adj.*** **1.** not able to be seen; invisible. **2.** (*U.S.*) having no view or opinion. **3.** offering no view.
—[形] 1.보이지 않는 2.《美》 의견이 없는, 무정견(無定見)한 3.조망이 나쁜

* **view·point** [vjú:pɔ̀int] ***n.*** [C] a place from which someone looks at something; a way of looking at something; a point of view. ¶*Consider it from another ~.*①
—[名] 견지; 견해; 관점 ¶①다른 관점에서 생각해 보시오

vig·il [vídʒil] ***n.*** **1.** [U] the act of staying awake all night for some purpose. ¶*keep ~ over a sick person.*① **2.** 《usu. *pl.*》 a religious service, prayers, etc. on the night before a festival.
—[名] 1.불침번, 철야 ¶①철야로 환자를 간호하다 2.축제 전날 밤의 철야기도

vig·i·lance [vídʒiləns] ***n.*** [U] the state of being vigilant; watchfulness.
—[名] 불침번; 경계, 조심

vig·i·lant [vídʒilənt] *adj.* watchful to prevent or avoid possible danger; keenly watchful. ¶*keep a ~ guard.*① ▷**vig·i·lant·ly** [-li] *adv.*
—[형] 주의깊은, 경계를 게을리하지 않는 ¶①주의깊게 감시하다

vi·gnette [vinjét] *n.* [C] **1.** a decorative design on the title page of a book. **2.** a literary description in words. **3.** a drawing, etc. in which figures shade off gradually at the edge.
—[명] 1. [책의 제목 페이지의] 장식 무늬 2. 소품문(小品文) 3. 비넷(배경을 흐릿하게 한 그림)

* **vig·or,** *Brit.* **-our** [vígər] *n.* [U] mental or physical strength; energy or force. ¶*He is full of ~.*①
—[명] 원기, 정력, 기력, 활력 ¶①그는 원기왕성하다

* **vig·or·ous** [víg(ə)rəs] *adj.* of vigor or strength; energetic; lively. ¶*a ~ style*① | *a ~ young man.*②
—[형] 정력적인, 기운찬, 힘센 ¶①힘찬 문체/②혈기왕성한 청년

vig·or·ous·ly [víg(ə)rəsli] *adv.* in a vigorous manner; actively; powerfully.
—[부] 원기있게, 힘차게, 활발하게

Vi·king [váikiŋ] *n.* one of the Scandinavian pirates who made raids upon the coasts of Europe from the 8th to the 10th centuries.
—[명] 바이킹(8—10세기에 유럽 해안을 약탈하던 북유럽 해적)

* **vile** [vail] *adj.* **1.** wicked; disgraceful. **2.** (*colloq.*) extremely bad. ▷**vile·ly** [-li] *adv.* —**vile·ness** [-nis] *n.*
—[형] 1. 나쁜, 사악한; 지긋지긋한 2. 《口》 지독한, 형편없는

vil·i·fy [vílifài] *vt.* (**-fied**) speak evil of (someone). ▷**vil·i·fi·er** [-ər] *n.*
—[타] …의 험담을 하다, 헐뜯다, 비방하다

vil·la [vílə] *n.* [C] a large elegant house in the country or the suburbs.
—[명] 교외의 저택; 별장

‡ **vil·lage** [vílidʒ] *n.* [C] **1.** a group of houses in the country, smaller than a town. **2.** 《*the ~, collectively*》 the people of a village.
—[명] 1. 마을, 촌락 2. 마을 사람들

vil·lag·er [vílidʒər] *n.* [C] a person who lives in a village.
—[명] 마을 사람, 촌민

vil·lain [vílən → 3.] *n.* [C] **1.** a wicked person. **2.** the enemy of the hero in a play. **3.** [+vílin] (*History*) a villein.
—[명] 1. 악한, 악인 2. 악인역, 악역 3. 《史》 농노(農奴)

vil·lain·ous [vílənəs] *adj.* **1.** very wicked; evil. **2.** (*colloq.*) extremely bad or unpleasant.
—[형] 1. 극악한, 악랄한 2. 《口》 몹시 나쁜, 형편없는, 지독한

vil·lain·y [víləni] *n.* (pl. **-lain·ies**) [U] **1.** the state of being villainous. **2.** 《*pl.*》 a very wicked act; a crime.
—[명] 1. 극악, 흉악, 비도(非道) 2. 나쁜 짓, 악행

vil·lein [vílin] *n.* [C] (*History*) a class of half-free peasants under the feudal system in the Middle Ages.
—[명] 《史》 농노(農奴)

Vin·cent [víns(ə)nt] *n.* a man's name.
—[명] 남자 이름

Vin·ci [víntʃi(:)], **Leonarde da** *n.* (1452–1519) an Italian painter, sculptor, architect and scientist.
—[명] 이탈리아의 화가・조각가・건축가・과학자

vin·di·cate [víndikèit] *vt.* **1.** defend (something) from unjust criticism or opposition. **2.** prove and establish the truth of (something).
—[타] 1. …을 옹호하다 2. …을 입증하다, 증명하다, 확립하다

vin·di·ca·tion [vìndikéiʃ(ə)n] *n.* [U] [C] **1.** proof and establishment of right or innocence. **2.** a successful defense against unjust criticism, opposition, etc. ¶*in ~ of.*①
—[명] 1. 입증, 증명, 확립 2. 변호 ¶①…을 변호하여

vin·dic·tive [vindíktiv] *adj.* full of a desire for revenge; bearing a feeling to revenge.
—[형] 복수심이 있는; 앙심을 품은

‡ **vine** [vain] *n.* [C] **1.** a grape plant; a grapevine. **2.** a plant with a long stem that climbs on a wall, a tree, or another support.
—[명] 1. 포도나무 2. 덩굴 식물, 덩굴

* **vin·e·gar** [vínigər] *n.* [U] a sour liquid used in flavoring or pickling food.
—[명] 초, 식초

vine·yard [vínjərd] *n.* [C] a place where grapevines are grown.
—[명] 포도밭, 포도원

vi·nous [váinəs] *adj.* **1.** of or like wine. **2.** affected by wine.
—[형] 1. 포도주의(같은) 2. 포도주로 기운차린

vin·tage [víntidʒ] *n.* **1.** [C] an year's production of grapes. **2.** [C] the act of gathering grapes for wine. **3.** [C] the season for gathering grapes. **4.** [U] [C] wine made at some particular time. ¶*the ~ of 1870*① | *~ wine.*②
—[명] 1. 포도의 수확고 2. 포도의 수확 3. 포도의 수확기 4. 우량 포도주 ¶①1870년에 양조한 포도주/②우량 포도주

vint·ner [víntnər] *n.* [C] (*Brit.*) a wine dealer.
—[명] 《英》 포도주 상인

vi·nyl [váin(i)l, vín-] *n.* [U] (*Chemistry*) a radical which is obtained from ethylene and which is used to form resins and plastics.
—[명] 《化》 비닐[기(基)]

vi·ol [váiəl] *n.* [C] a musical instrument of the Middle Ages, with six strings and played with a bow.
—[명] 비올[중세의 6현(絃) 현악기로서 활로 켬]

vi·o·la [vióulə, +*U.S.* vai-] *n.* [C] a musical instrument like a violin but a little larger and deeper in tone.
—[명] 비올라(violin 비슷하나 좀 더 큰 현악기)

• **vi·o·late** [váiəlèit] *vt.* **1.** break (an agreement, a law, a rule, etc.). **2.** treat (something holy) with lack of respect. ¶ *~ the church.*① **3.** disturb; interrupt. ¶ *~ another's privacy.* **4.** use force against (a woman); rape.
—[他] 1. [규칙 따위]를 어기다, …을 위반하다 2. …을 더럽히다 ¶①교회를 모독하다 3. …을 방해하다 4. …에 폭행을 가하다

vi·o·la·tion [vàiəléiʃ(ə)n] *n.* [U] [C] **1.** the act of breaking (an agreement, a law, a rule, etc.). **2.** treatment with lack of respect. **3.** interruption; disturbance. **4.** rape.
—[名] 1. 위반, 위배 2. [신성함을] 더럽히기, 모독 3. 방해, 침해 4. 폭행

vi·o·la·tor [váiəlèitər] *n.* [C] a person who violates.
—[名] 위반자; 방해자; 폭행자

‡ **vi·o·lence** [váiələns] *n.* [U] **1.** great strength in action; intensity. ¶ *the ~ of the wind.*① **2.** furious or harmful action; injury. ¶ *die by ~*② / *do ~ to.*③
—[名] 1. 격렬함, 맹렬함 ¶①바람의 맹위 2. 난폭, 폭행 ¶②폭력으로 피살되다/③…에게 폭력을 가하다

‡ **vi·o·lent** [váiələnt] *adj.* **1.** severe; forceful. ¶ *a ~ dislike*① / *a ~ storm.*② **2.** resulting from the use of force, strong feeling, action, etc. ¶ *~ deeds*③ / *a ~ death.*④
—[形] 1. 격렬한, 맹렬한, 심한 ¶①심한 혐오, 질색/②맹렬한 폭풍우 2. 난폭한; 폭력에 의한 ¶③폭행/④변사, 횡사

• **vi·o·lent·ly** [váiələntli] *adv.* in a violent manner.
—[副] 격렬하게, 맹렬히, 지독히

‡ **vi·o·let** [váiəlit] *n.* **1.** [C] a small, low plant with purple, blue or white flowers; its flower. **2.** [U] the color of the common violet. —*adj.* of the violet color.
—[名] 1. 제비꽃 2. 보랏빛 —[形] 보랏빛의

‡ **vi·o·lin** [vàiəlín] *n.* [C] a musical instrument with four strings and played with a bow.
—[名] 바이올린, 제금(提琴)

vi·o·lin·ist [vàiəlínist] *n.* [C] a person who plays the violin.
—[名] 바이올린 연주자, 제금가

vi·o·lon·cel·list [vìələntʃélist, vàiələn-] *n.* [C] a person who plays the violoncello; a cellist.
—[名] 첼로 연주자, 첼리스트

vi·o·lon·cel·lo [vìələntʃélou, vàiələn-] *n.* [C] (pl. **-los**) a musical instrument with four strings, larger than and tuned below the viola; a cello.
—[名] 첼로[6현(絃)의 현악기]

vi·per [váipər] *n.* [C] **1.** any of several kinds of poisonous snakes. **2.** an evil and treacherous person.
—[名] 1. 독사, 살무사 2. 악인, 음흉한 사람

vi·ra·go [viréigou, +*Brit.* -rá:-] *n.* [C] (pl. **-goes** or **-gos**) a bad-tempered woman who always shouts and scolds.
—[名] 잔소리 심한(바가지 긁는) 여자

vir·gin [və́:rdʒin] *n.* **1.** [C] a pure and chaste woman; a maiden. **2.** 《*the V-*》 the Virgin Mary. —*adj.* **1.** of or suited to a virgin; chaste and pure. ¶ *~ modesty.*① **2.** fresh; new; untouched. ¶ *a ~ forest*② / *a ~ voyage.*
—[名] 1. 처녀 2. 성모(동정녀) 마리아 —[形] 1. 처녀의; 처녀다운 ¶①처녀 같은 얌전함 2. 처음인; 더럽혀지지 않은; 손대지 않은, 밟힌 일이 없는 ¶②처녀림

vir·gin·al [və́:rdʒinl] *adj.* of or like a virgin; pure and chaste. ¶ *~ bloom*① / *~ generation.*②
—[名] 처녀의(같은); 순결한 ¶①한창 때의 처녀/②단성(처녀) 생식

Vir·gin·ia [və(:)rdʒíniə] *n.* **1.** a woman's name. **2.** a State in the southeastern part of the United States. ⇒[N.B.]
—[名] 1. 여자 이름 2. 미국 동남부의 주 [N.B.] Va., Virg.로 줄여 씀. 수도는 Richmond

Virginia creeper [-ˊ- ˊ-] *n.* a woody vine with large leaves, greenish flowers and blue-black berries, also called the American ivy.
—[名] 아메리카담쟁이

vir·gin·i·ty [və(:)rdʒíniti] *n.* [U] the state of being a virgin; maidenhood.
—[名] 처녀임, 처녀성, 순결

Virgin Mary [ˊ- ˊ-], **the** *n.* the mother of Christ.
—[名] 성모(동정녀) 마리아

vir·ile [víril, / -rail] *adj.* **1.** of a man; manly. **2.** strong; forceful.
—[形] 1. 남자의; 장정의; 남자다운, 남성적인 2. 힘센, 꿋꿋한

vi·ril·i·ty [viríliti] *n.* [U] the state or quality of being virile.
—[名] 남자다움, 남성적임, 힘셈, 강건

vir·tu·al [və́:rtʃuəl] *adj.* really so in effect, though not so in name. ¶ *That was their ~ defeat.*①
—[形] 사실상의 ¶①그것은 그들의 사실상의 패배였다

vir·tu·al·ly [və́:rtʃuəli] *adv.* almost. ¶ *He is ~ dead.*①
—[副] 사실상, 실질적으로 ¶①그는 죽은 거나 다름없다

‡ **vir·tue** [və́:rtʃu:, +*Brit.* və́:tju:] *n.* ↔vice **1.** [U] moral excellence in general; goodness. ¶ *~ and vice* / *a man of ~.* **2.** [C] a particular moral excellence. ¶ *Faith, hope and charity are three Christian virtues.*① **3.** [C] a good quality; a merit; a value. ¶ *Taciturnity is sometimes a ~.*② **4.** [U] (of a medicine, etc.) power to do good. ¶ *There is little ~ in that remedy.*③ **5.** [U] the state of being chaste or pure. ¶ *a woman of ~* / *a lady of easy ~.*④
—[名] 1. 도덕적인 탁월, 덕, 선(善) 2. 어떤 구체적인 덕성, 미덕 ¶①믿음·소망·사랑은 기독교의 세 가지 덕이다 3. 미점; 장점 ¶②침묵도 때로는 미점이다 4. 효력, 효험 ¶③그 치료법은 효험이 없다 5. 정절(貞節); 순결 ¶④바람둥이 여자

by (or **in**) **virtue** (=*by the authority, force,* or *fact of something.*)
[熟] …의 힘으로, …에 의하여

vir·tu·o·si [və̀:rtʃuóusi / və̀:tjuóuzi] *n.* pl. of **virtuoso**.

vir·tu·o·so [və̀:rtʃuóusou / və̀:tjuóuzou] *n.* [C] (pl. **-sos** or **-si**) **1.** a person with great interest or skill in art; a collector of art objects or curios. **2.** a person with
—[名] 1. 미술 애호가; 골동품 전문가 2. [예술의] 대가, 음악의 대가

V

great skill in some fine art, esp. in playing a musical instrument.

* **vir·tu·ous** [vəː́rtʃuəs] *adj.* **1.** having or showing moral excellence. **2.** chaste; pure. ▷**vir·tu·ous·ly** [-li] *adv.* —**vir·tu·ous·ness** [-nis] *n.*
—[形] 1. 덕망이 높은, 고결한 2. 정숙한, 순결한

vir·u·lence [vír(j)uləns] *n.* [U] the state or quality of being virulent; hostility.
—[名] 독성; 증오

vir·u·lent [vír(j)ulənt] *adj.* **1.** very poisonous; deadly. **2.** bitterly hostile; malicious. ¶~ *abuse.*① ▷**vir·u·lent·ly** [-li] *adv.*
—[形] 1. 독성의, 유독한; 치명적인 2. 독살스러운; 악의를 품은 ¶①독살스러운 욕지거리, 독설

vi·rus [váiərəs] *n.* [C] **1.** any of a group of living things, smaller than bacteria, which cause various diseases. **2.** a poison produced in the body by a disease. **3.** something which poisons the mind or the character.
—[名] 1. 바이러스, 비루스(박테리아보다 작은 병원체) 2. 병독 3. 해독

vi·sa [víːzə] *n.* [C] a signature on a passport by a representative of a country showing that it has been examined and approved so that a person can enter that country. **—*vt.*** **1.** put a visa on (a passport). **2.** give a visa to (someone).
—[名] [여권 따위의] 이서(裏書), 사증(査證), 비자
—[他] 1. [여권]에 이서(사증)하다 2. …에 비자를 발급하다

vis·age [vízidʒ] *n.* [C] the face [of a person].
—[名] 얼굴, 용모

vis-a-vis [vìːzəvíː, +*Brit.* -zɑː-] *adv., adj.* face to face. ¶*sit ~ in a train.* **—*prep.*** **1.** face to face with. **2.** in relation to. **—*n.*** [C] a person who is face to face with another.
—[副][形] 마주보고(본), 마주 대하고(대한) —[前] 1. …와 마주 대한 2. …에 관하여 —[名] 마주 보고(대하고) 있는 사람

vis·cer·a [vísərə] *n. pl.* (sing. **viscus**) the inside organs of the body.
—[名] 내장, 창자

vis·cid [vísid] *adj.* thick and sticky like a syrup or glue; viscous.
—[形] 끈적끈적한, 흐물흐물한, 점착성의

vis·cose [vískous] *n.* [U] a kind of cellulose used in making rayon thread, fabrics and cellophane.
—[名] 비스코우스(인조 견사나 셀로판을 만드는 데 쓰는 셀룰로우스)

vis·cos·i·ty [viskɑ́siti / -kɔ́s-] *n.* [U] the state or quality of being viscous.
—[名] 점질(粘質); 점성(粘性)

vis·count [váikàunt] *n.* [C] a nobleman next below an earl in rank.
—[名] 자작(子爵)

vis·count·ess [váikàuntis] *n.* [C] the wife of a viscount.
—[名] 자작 부인

vis·cous [vískəs] *adj.* thick and sticky like syrup.
—[形] 끈적거리는, 점착성이 있는

vis·cus [vískəs] *n.* sing. of **viscera**.

vise [vais] *n.* [C] (*U.S.*) a tool with two jaws to hold objects firmly while work is being done on them. (cf. esp. *Brit.* vice) ⇒fig.
—[名] 《美》 바이스

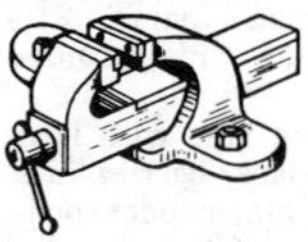
[vise]

vi·sé [víːzei] *n., v.* (**vi·séed, vi·sé·ing**) =visa.

vis·i·bil·i·ty [vìzibíliti] *n.* [U] **1.** the state or quality of being visible. **2.** the degree of things being able to be seen at a given distance, with a certain atmosphere, etc.
—[名] 1. 눈에 보이는 일(상태) 2. 시계(視界), 시거(視距); 가시도(可視度)

* **vis·i·ble** [vízibl] *adj.* **1.** able to be seen. ↔invisible ¶*the ~.*① **2.** apparent. ¶*with ~ impatience.*
—[形] 1. 눈에 보이는 ¶①물질 2. 명백한, 분명한

vis·i·bly [vízibli] *adv.* to a visible extent; plainly.
—[副] 눈에 보여(보이게); 뚜렷이, 명백히

⁑ **vi·sion** [víʒ(ə)n] *n.* **1.** [U] power of seeing; the sense of sight. ¶*poor ~*① / *the field of ~.*② **2.** [C] something which can be seen; sight. ¶*a lovely ~.*③ **3.** [C] something seen in imagination, a dream, etc. ¶*romantic visions of youth.*④ **4.** [U] foresight; imagination. ¶*a man of ~.* **—*vt.*** see (something) in a vision.
—[名] 1. 시력; 시각 ¶①약한 시력/②시야 2. 눈에 보이는 것 ¶③사랑스러운 자태 3. 공상 ¶④청년 시절의 걷잡을 수 없는 공상 4. 선견[지명]; 통찰력
—[他] …을 환상으로 보다

vi·sion·ar·y [víʒ(ə)nèri / -nəri] *adj.* **1.** of or seen in a vision; not real; imaginary. ¶*a ~ castle*① / *a ~ plan.*② **2.** having a tendency to see visions; dreamy. ¶*a ~ boy.* **—*n.*** [C] an impractical person; an idealist.
—[形] 1. 환상의; 비현실적인 ¶①가공의 성/②꿈 같은 계획 2. 환상에 잠기는; 공상적인
—[名] 공상가, 몽상가

⁑ **vis·it** [vízit] *vt.* **1.** go or come to see (someone) socially for a short time; call on (someone). ¶*A friend of mine visited me.* / *Father visited my uncle in* [*the*] *hospital.* **2.** be a guest of (someone). ¶*He is visiting his aunt in the country for a week.* **3.** go to see (a place). ¶*He visited Nara for the first time.* **4.** inspect; call on
—[他] 1. [사교적으로] …을 방문하다, 찾아가다 2. …의 손님이 되다 3. …을 구경하러 가다, 참배하다 4. [직무상] …을 시찰하러 가다; …을 왕진하다 ¶①환자를 왕진하다 5. 재난 따위가 [남]에게 닥치다, [남]을 엄습하다, 괴롭히

visitant [1277] **vituperative**

(a sick person) officially. ¶~ *a factory* / ~ *the sick*.① **5.** cause great pain or trouble to (someone); attack; come upon (someone). ¶*She was visited by a series of misfortunes.*② / *She was visited by a strange notion.*③ / (*Bible*) *The sins of the fathers are visited upon the children.* —*vi.* make a visit; be a guest.
—*n.* ⓒ a social or business call; a short stay. ¶*a periodic office* ~④ / *He would pay a* ~.
vis·it·ant [vízit(ə)nt] *n.* ⓒ **1.** a temporary guest; a visitor. **2.** a migratory bird. —*adj.* visiting.
vis·it·a·tion [vìzitéiʃ(ə)n] *n.* ⓒ **1.** the act of visiting. **2.** an official visit for inspection or examination. **3.** a reward or punishment by God.
visiting card [⌣⌣ ⌣] *n.* a calling card.
: vis·i·tor [vízitər] *n.* ⓒ a person who makes a visit.
vi·sor, -zor [váizər] *n.* ⓒ **1.** the movable front part of a helmet that protects the face. ⇒fig. **2.** (*U. S.*) the brim of a cap.
vis·ta [vístə] *n.* ⓒ **1.** a view through a long, narrow opening; a passage with trees framing such a view. **2.** a mental view of a series of events in the past or future. ¶*the vistas of one's future*.① [visor 1.]
vis·u·al [víʒuəl] *adj.* **1.** of sight. ¶*the* ~ *nerve*① / *the* ~ *sense*.② **2.** that can be seen; visible. ¶*a* ~ *field*.③
visual aids [⌣⌣ ⌣] *n. pl.* something used in helping learning through the sense of sight, such as motion pictures and charts.
vis·u·al·ize [víʒuəlàiz] *vt.* **1.** make (something) visible. **2.** form a mental picture of (something). —*vi.* form a clear mental image of something.
• **vi·tal** [váitl] *adj.* **1.** of life. ¶~ *energies*.① **2.** necessary to life. ¶~ *organs*. **3.** very important; essential. **4.** causing death or ruin; affecting life; fatal. ¶*a* ~ *wound*.② **5.** full of life or energy; vivid.
vital capacity [⌣⌣ ⌣⌣⌣] *n.* the breathing capacity of the lungs; lung capacity.
vi·tal·i·ty [vaitǽliti] *n.* Ⓤ **1.** power to keep on living; vital force. **2.** strength or liveliness of mind. **3.** strength to endure.
vi·tal·ize [váitəlàiz] *vt.* give life or vigor to (something).
▷ **vi·tal·i·za·tion** [vàitəlizéiʃ(ə)n, -lai-] *n.*
vi·tal·ly [váitəli] *adv.* to a vital degree.
vi·tals [váitlz] *n. pl.* **1.** the organs of the body necessary to life. **2.** the essential parts of anything.
vital sta·tis·tics [⌣⌣ ⌣⌣⌣] *n. pl.* statistics dealing with births, marriages, and deaths in a certain area.
• **vi·ta·min** [váitəmin, +*Brit*. vít-] *n.* ⓒ any of certain substances contained in natural food and necessary for health and the growth of the body.
vi·ti·ate [víʃièit] *vt.* **1.** make (something) impure and faulty; spoil. ¶*vitiated air*.① **2.** weaken morally. ▷ **vi·ti·a·tion** [vìʃiéiʃ(ə)n] *n.*
vit·re·ous [vítriəs] *adj.* **1.** of or like glass. **2.** made [of glass.]
vit·ri·ol [vítriəl] *n.* Ⓤ **1.** (*Chemistry*) any salt of sulfuric acid. ¶*blue* ~.① **2.** sulfuric acid. **3.** sharp, severe speech or criticism.
vi·tu·per·ate [vait(j)úːpərèit / vitjúː-] *vt.* blame (someone) in abusive words; find fault with (someone).
vi·tu·per·a·tion [vaitjùːpəréiʃ(ə)n, vi-, +*U. S.* -túː-] *n.* Ⓤ the act of vituperating; bitter and severe words.
vi·tu·per·a·tive [vait(j)úːpərèitiv, vitjúːpərətiv, vai-] *adj.* having the nature of vituperation; abusive.

다 ¶②그녀는 잇달아 불행을 만났다/ ③그녀는 해괴한 생각에 사로잡히고 말았다 —*自* 방문하다; 체류하다, [손님으로] 묵다

—*名* 방문, 문안; 짧은 체류 ¶④[회사·병원 따위의] 정기적 방문

—*名* 1. 방문객, 손님 2. 철새, 후조
—*形* 방문하는
—*名* 1. 방문, 왕방, 내방 2. 순시, 순찰 3. 하늘의 보답, 천혜(天惠); 천벌

—*名* 명함
—*名* 방문객; 시찰원
—*名* 1. [투구의] 면갑(面甲) 2. [모자의] 챙

—*名* 1. [양쪽에 가로수·건물 따위가 죽 늘어선] 좁고 긴 조망 2. 추억; 예상 ¶①장래의 전망

—*形* 1. 시각의 ¶①시(視)신경/②시각 2. 눈에 보이는 ¶③시계(視界)
—*名* 시각 교육 기구

—*他* 1. …을 눈에 보이도록 하다 2. …을 마음속에 그리다 —*自* 마음속에 선하게 그리다
—*形* 1. 생명의 ¶①생명력 2. 생명유지에 필요한 3. 매우 중요한 4. 생사에 관계되는, 치명적인 ¶②치명상 5. 생기에 찬, 활력이 넘치는
—*名* 폐활량(肺活量)

—*名* 1. 생명력 2. 생기, 활기 3. 지속력, 존속력

—*他* …에 생명(활력)을 주다

—*副* 치명적으로
—*名* 1. 생명 유지에 필요한 기관 2. 급소

—*名* 인구동태 통계

—*名* 비타민, 영양소

—*他* 1. …을 더럽히다 ¶①오염된 공기 2. …을 타락시키다

—*形* 1. 유리의(같은) 2. 유리로 만든
—*名* 1. (化) 황산염(黃酸鹽) ¶①황산동 2. 황산 3. 통렬한 풍자, 신랄한 비평

—*他* …을 꾸짖다; …에게 욕지거리를 하다
—*名* 꾸짖음; 독설, 욕지거리

—*形* 욕지거리하는, 악담하는

vi·va [víːvə] *interj.* long live [someone]! [liveliness.] —❷ 만세!

vi·va·ce [viváːtʃei / -tʃi] *adv.* (*Music*) with spirit and —❺ (樂) 쾌활하게, 활발히

vi·va·cious [vivéiʃəs, vai-] *adj.* lively; high spirited. ▷**vi·va·cious·ly** [-li] *adv.* —**vi·va·cious·ness** [-nis] *n.* —❸ 활기있는, 활발한

vi·vac·i·ty [vivǽsiti, vai-] *n.* Ⓤ high spirits; liveliness. —❷ 쾌활, 활발; 명랑

vi·va vo·ce [váivəvóusi] *adv.* by the mouth; orally. —❺ 구두(口頭)로

* **viv·id** [vívid] *adj.* **1.** full of life; active. **2.** realistic. ¶*a ~ description.*① **3.** (of color) bright; brilliant. ↔ dull ¶*~ green.* —❸ 1. 발랄한, 팔팔한 2. 생생한, 여실한 ¶①생생한 묘사 3. [빛깔이] 밝은, 선명한

viv·id·ly [vívidli] *adv.* **1.** actively; in a lively manner. **2.** brilliantly; distinctly. [ing vivid.] —❺ 1. 발랄하게, 팔팔하게 2. 선명하게

viv·id·ness [vívidnis] *n.* Ⓤ the state or quality of be- —❷ 발랄; 선명

viv·i·fy [vívifài] *vt.* (-fied) give life to (someone); make (something) vivid. ▷**viv·i·fi·ca·tion** [vìvifikéiʃ(ə)n] *n.* —❹ …에 생기를 불어넣다; …을 활기띠게 하다

vi·vip·a·rous [vaivípərəs, +*Brit.* viv-] *adj.* bringing forth living young instead of laying eggs. ↔oviparous —❸ 태생(胎生)의

viv·i·sect [vívisèkt, ⸗⸗́] *vt.* cut up the living body of (an animal, etc.) for scientific study. —*vi.* practice vivisection. —❹ …을 생체(生體)해부하다 —❺ 생체해부하다

viv·i·sec·tion [vìvisékʃ(ə)n] *n.* Ⓤ Ⓒ an operation done on living animals for scientific study. —❷ 생체해부

vix·en [víksn] *n.* Ⓒ **1.** a female fox. **2.** a bad-tempered, quarrelsome woman. —❷ 1. 암여우 2. 입심사납고 심술궂은 여자

viz. [néimli] videlicet. —❷ 즉

vi·zier [vizíər, ⸗́⸗] *n.* Ⓒ a high official in a Moslem coun- **vi·zor** [váizər, víz-] *n.* =visor. [try, esp. a state minister.] —❷ [회교국의] 고관, 대신

* **vo·cab·u·lar·y** [voukǽbjulèri / -əri] *n.* (pl. **-lar·ies**) **1.** Ⓤ a list of words arranged in alphabetical order and with their meanings. **2.** Ⓤ Ⓒ (*collectively*) all the words used by a group, a person, etc. —❷ 1. 어구집(語句集), 어해(語解), 단어표 2. 어휘, 용어수, 용어 범위

vo·cal [vóuk(ə)l] *adj.* **1.** of the voice. ¶*~ music.*① **2.** uttered with the voice. ¶*a ~ message.*② **3.** full of sound; inclined to speak freely. **4.** (*Phonetics*) voiced. —*n.* Ⓒ a vocal sound; a vowel. —❸ 1. 목소리의, 음성의 ¶①성악 2. 구두(口頭)의, 말로 하는 ¶②구두 전달 3. 소리내는, 울리는; 시끄러운 4. 유성음의 —❷ 목소리; 모음 [(音聲) 유성음의]

vocal cords [⸗ ⸗] *n. pl.* two pairs of thin skinlike objects in the throat which vibrate to produce sound. —❷ 성대(聲帶)

vo·cal·ist [vóukəlist] *n.* Ⓒ a singer. —❷ 성악가

vo·ca·tion [voukéiʃ(ə)n] *n.* **1.** Ⓤ a call or summons by a god. **2.** Ⓤ special fitness or natural ability for a particular kind of work. ¶*~ for literature.*① **3.** Ⓒ a profession; an occupation. [bureau.②] —❷ 1. 신의 부르심 2. 적성(適性), 천분(天分), 소질; 천직, 사명 ¶①문학의 재능 3. 직업

vo·ca·tion·al [voukéiʃ(ə)n(ə)l] *adj.* of a vocation. ¶*a ~* —❸ 직업의 ¶①직업 상담소

voc·a·tive [vákətiv / vɔ́k-] *adj.* (*Grammar*) showing a person or thing addressed. ¶*the ~ case.*① —❸ 〈文法〉호격(呼格)의 ¶①호격

vo·cif·er·ate [vousífərèit] *vi., vt.* cry out with a loud voice; shout. [erating; a loud cry.] —⾃❹ 큰 소리로 외치다

vo·cif·er·a·tion [vousìfəréiʃ(ə)n] *n.* Ⓤ the act of vocif- —❷ 고함, 외침

vo·cif·er·ous [vousíf(ə)rəs] *adj.* speaking out noisily; loud and noisy. ▷**vo·cif·er·ous·ly** [-li] *adv.* —**vo·cif·er·ous·ness** [-nis] *n.* [made from rye, potatoes, etc.] —❸ 큰 소리로 외치는

vod·ka [vádkə / vɔ́d-] *n.* Ⓤ a Russian alcoholic drink —❷ 워트카(호밀·감자 따위로 만든 러시아의 독한 술)

vogue [voug] *n.* Ⓒ **1.** the fashion of the time. ¶*out of ~*① / *This kind of shirt is in ~ now.* **2.** popularity. ¶*His lectures have a great ~.*② —❷ 1. 유행 ¶①유행이 지나서, 유행하지 않게 되어 2. 인기, 호평 ¶②그의 강의는 대단한 인기가 있다

‡ **voice** [vɔis] *n.* **1.** Ⓤ Ⓒ the sound coming from the mouth, esp. from the human mouth, in speaking, etc. ¶*in low voices*① / *a soft ~* / *I lost my ~.*② **2.** Ⓒ a sound suggesting voice or speech. ¶*the voices of the birds* / *He loved to listen to the voices of nature.*③ **3.** Ⓤ an expressed opinion, choice, or wish. ¶*the ~ of the majority* / *His ~ was for (against) the plan.*④ **4.** Ⓤ the right to express an opinion or choice; a vote. ¶*He has no ~ in this matter.* **5.** Ⓒ anything resembling human speech. ¶(*proverb*) *The people's ~ is the ~ of God.*⑤ **6.** Ⓒ a part of a piece of music produced by —❷ 1. 목소리, 음성 ¶①낮은 목소리로 / ②나는 갑자기 말이 나오지 않았다 / 사람 목소리 같은 소리 ¶③그는 자연의 소리를 듣기를 좋아했다 3. [표명된] 의견, 선택, 의향 ¶④그의 의견은 그 계획에 찬성(반대)이었다 4. 발언권, 투표권 5. 사람의 말에 비유한 목소리 ¶⑤(俚)백성의 소리는 신의 소리다 6. [성악의] 성부; 성부(聲部) 이 노래는 몇 가지 성부에 의해 불려진다 7. 가수 8. 〈文法〉[동사의] 태(態), 상

one kind of singer or instrument. ¶*a soprano ~* / *The song is sung by several voices.*⑥ **7.** ⓒ a singer. **8.** ⓒ (*Grammar*) ((usu. *the ~*)) a form of the verb indicating whether the subject is passive or active. **9.** Ⓤ a sound produced by the vocal organs.　⌜givings.⌝
1) *give voice to,* express. ¶*They gave ~ to their mis-*
2) *in voice,* in good condition for singing or talking.
3) *raise one's voice,* speak loudly.
4) *with one voice,* unanimously.
— *vt.* **1.** give expression to (something); speak; report. **2.** make (sound) with the vocal cords, not with the breath. **3.** regulate the tones of (an organ, etc.)
voiced [vɔist] *adj.* **1.** having a voice; having a special kind of or tone of voice. ¶*a sweet-voiced girl.*① **2.** expressed by the voice. **3.** (*Phonetics*) spoken with the aid of the vocal cords.
voice·less [vɔ́islis] *adj.* **1.** having no voice; unable to utter words. **2.** (*Phonetics*) spoken without the aid of the vocal cords. ¶*a ~ sound.*①
* **void** [vɔid] *adj.* **1.** empty. ¶*a ~ house.*① **2.** lacking; wanting. ¶*He is ~ of learning.*② **3.** (*Law*) without legal force or effect. 　⌜emptiness.⌝
— *n.* **1.** ⓒ an empty space. **2.** Ⓤ a feeling of loss or
— *vt.* **1.** make (something) of no effect. **2.** discharge.
voile [vɔil] *n.* ⓒ a very thin dress material of silk,
vol. volume. 　⌞wool, etc.⌟
vol·a·tile [vάlət(i)l / vɔ́lətàil] *adj.* **1.** changing into gaseous form quickly and easily. ¶*~ oils.*① **2.** changeable in mood or interest.
vol·a·til·i·ty [vὰlətíliti / vɔ̀l-] *n.* Ⓤ volatile quality; an example of being volatile.
vol·a·til·ize [vάlətilàiz / vɔ́l-] *vt.* cause (some liquid) to become vapor. — *vi.* change into vapor.
vol·can·ic [vɑlkǽnik / vɔl-] *adj.* **1.** of a volcano; produced by a volcano. ¶*~ activity*① / *~ ashes.*② **2.** violent like a volcano. ¶*a ~ character.*③
* **vol·ca·no** [vɑlkéinou / vɔl-] *n.* ⓒ (pl. **-noes** or **-nos**) a mountain with an opening or some openings through which steam, ashes, and liquid rock are forced out.
vole [voul] *n.* ⓒ a small ratlike animal with a short tail, living in the fields.
vo·li·tion [voulíʃ(ə)n] *n.* Ⓤ **1.** the act of exercising one's will. ¶*by one's own ~.* **2.** the power of willing.
vo·li·tion·al [voulíʃ(ə)n(ə)l] *adj.* of volition. ¶*~ power.*①
vol·ley [vάli / vɔ́li] *n.* ⓒ **1.** the act of throwing many bullets, arrows, etc. at one time. **2.** (in sports) the act of striking the ball back before it touches the ground.
— *vt., vi.* **1.** discharge many things at one time. **2.** (in sports) strike a ball before it touches the ground.
vol·ley·ball [vάlibɔ̀ːl / vɔ́li-] *n.* **1.** Ⓤ a game in which two teams try to hit a large ball back and forth over a high net with the hands, without letting the ball touch the ground. **2.** ⓒ a ball used in this game.
volt [voult] *n.* ⓒ the unit of electromotive force.
volt·age [vóultidʒ] *n.* Ⓤ electromotive force as measured in volts.
vol·ta·ic [vɑltéiik / vɔl-] *adj.* producing an electric current by chemical action; of an electric current.
volt·me·ter [vóultmìːtər] *n.* ⓒ an instrument for measuring electromotive force.
vol·u·bil·i·ty [vὰljubíliti / vɔ̀l-] *n.* Ⓤ the state or quality of being voluble.
vol·u·ble [vάljubl / vɔ́l-] *adj.* **1.** talking too much; talkative. **2.** talking with a rapid flow of words; fluent.

(相) 9. 유성음, 탁음

圈 1)…을 입밖에 내다, 표명하다 2)목소리의 상태가 좋다 3)큰 소리로(음성을 높여) 말하다 4)이구동성으로, 일제히

—働 1. …을 말로 나타내다, 표명(언명)하다 2. …을 유성음으로 하다 3. [풍금 따위]를 조정하다

—働 1. 유성의, 목소리가 …한 ¶①목소리가 고운 소녀 2. 목소리로 나타낸 3.《音聲》성대를 떨어 울려서 내는 목소리의, 유성음의

—働 1. 소리가 없는, 무언의 2.《音聲》무성[음]의 ¶①무성음

—働 1. 빈, 공허한 ¶①빈 집 2. …이 없는, 결핍된 ¶②그는 학식이 없다 3. (法) [법적으로] 무효의
—㉢ 1. 빈 곳 2. 공허　⌜설하다⌝
—働 1. …을 무효로 하다 2. …을 배
—㉢ 보일(명주·양털 따위로 만든 얇은 직물)

—働 1. 휘발성의 ¶①휘발유 2. 변덕스러운

—㉢ 휘발성; 변덕

—働 …을 휘발(증발)시키다 —㉣ 휘발(증발)하다

—働 1. 화산의, 화산 활동에 의해 생긴 ¶①화산 활동/②화산 재 2. 격렬한, 폭발성의 ¶③격렬한 성격

—㉢ 화산

—㉢ 들쥐

—㉢ 1. 결단, 의지의 작용 2. 결단력, 의지의 힘
—働 의지의 ¶①의지력
—㉢ 1. 일제사격 2. 발리(공이 땅에 떨어지기 전에 되치기)

—働㉣ 1. 일제사격하다 2. 발리를 하다

—㉢ 1. 배구 2. 배구 공

—㉢ 볼트(전압의 실용 단위)
—㉢ 볼트 수

—働 기전력(起電力)이 있는; 유전기(流電氣)의
—㉢ 전압계, 전량계

—㉢ 다변(多辯), 요설(饒舌)

—働 1. 말을 많이 지껄이는, 다변의 2. 변설이 유창한

:vol·ume [válju:m / vɔ́lju(:)m] *n.* **1.** [C] a number of printed sheets bound together; a book. **2.** one of the books in a set or series. ⇒[N.B.] ¶*a novel in three volumes* / *Volume Two of the novel.*① **3.** [C] a large amount. ¶*volumes of smoke.*② **4.** [U] the amount of space occupied by a liquid, a gas, etc. **5.** [U] the amount of sound.

—[名] 1. 책, 서적 2. 한 권(卷) [N.B.] vol. (복수는 vols.)로 줄여 씀 ¶①소설의 제 2 권 3. 대량, 다량 ¶②뭉게뭉게 올라가는 연기 4. 분량, 용적 5. 음량(音量)

vo·lu·mi·nous [vəlú:minəs / -ljú:-] *adj.* **1.** consisting of many volumes. ¶*a ~ library.*① **2.** large in quantity or size. ¶*~ correspondence*② / *a ~ robe.*

—[形] 1. 권 수가 많은, 여러 권으로 된, 대부수(大部數)의 ¶①다량의 장서 2. 부피가 큰 ¶②방대한 [양의] 통신

vol·un·tar·i·ly [válәntèrili / vɔ́lәnt(ә)r-] *adv.* by one's own free will; without compulsion; freely.

—[副] 자유의사로, 자발적으로

***vol·un·tar·y** [válәntèri / vɔ́lәnt(ә)ri] *adj.* **1.** done of one's own free will; not ordered or compelled. ↔involuntary ¶*a ~ army.*① **2.** done on purpose; not accidental.

—[形] 1. 자발적인; 지원(志願)의 ¶①의용군 2. 고의(故意)의

—*n.* [C] **1.** anything done of one's own will. **2.** an organ solo played at a church service.

—[名] 1. 자발적으로 한 일 2. 오르간 독주

***vol·un·teer** [vàlәntíәr / vɔ̀lәntíә] *n.* [C] a person who enters into any service, esp. a military service or one in some other way dangerous, of his own free will.

—[名] 지원자, 지원병

—*vt.* offer (one's service, etc.) willingly. ¶*~ one's opinion* / *~ to do the work.* —*vi.* work as a volunteer.

—[他] …을 자진해서(자발적으로) 제의하다 —[自] 자진해서(자발적으로) 하다

—*adj.* **1.** of a volunteer or volunteers. **2.** made up of volunteers. ¶*a ~ corps.*①

—[形] 1. 지원자의 2. 지원자에 의해 구성되는 ¶①의용군

vo·lup·tu·ar·y [vәlʌ́ptʃuèri / -tʃuәri, tjuә-] *n.* [C] (pl. **-ar·ies**) a person devoted to luxurious or sensual pleasures.

—[名] 주색에 빠진 사람

vo·lup·tu·ous [vәlʌ́ptʃuәs] *adj.* **1.** devoted to the pleasures of the senses. **2.** full of or suggesting sensual delights and pleasures.

—[形] 1. 주색에 빠진 2. 육감적인, 도발적인

vo·lute [voulú:t / -l(j)ú:t, vɔl-] *n.* [C] **1.** a spiral ornament in architecture used in Ionic and Corinthian capitals. ⇒fig. **2.** a turn of a spiral shell.

—[名] 1. [건축물의] 소용돌이꼴[의 장식] 2. [권패(卷貝)의] 소용돌이

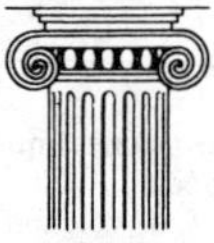

[volute 1.]

vom·it [vámit / vɔ́m-] *vi.* throw up the contents of the stomach through the mouth. —*vt.* **1.** throw up (something eaten) from the stomach. **2.** throw out (something) with force. ¶*The chimney is vomiting* [*forth*] *smoke.*

—[自] 토하다, 게우다 —[他] 1. …을 토하다 2. …을 내뿜다, 분출하다

—*n.* [U] **1.** the act of vomiting. **2.** something vomited from the stomach. **3.** rough or cruel words in speech or writing.

—[名] 1. 토하기, 구토 2. 토한 것 3. 상스러운 말, 폭언

vo·ra·cious [vouréiʃәs, vɔ:-] *adj.* **1.** greedy in eating; eager to eat much. **2.** very eager to do something.

—[形] 1. 게걸스럽게 먹는 2. 탐욕스러운

vo·ra·cious·ly [vouréiʃәsli / vɔ:-] *adv.* in a voracious manner.

—[副] 게걸스럽게; 탐욕스럽게

vo·rac·i·ty [vourǽsiti / vɔ(:)-] *n.* [U] the state or quality of being voracious.

—[名] 대식(大食); 탐욕

vor·tex [vɔ́:rteks] *n.* [C] (pl. **-tex·es** or **-ti·ces**) **1.** a whirling liquid or gas that sucks in everything near it. **2.** anything that seems to swallow up everything into it.

—[名] 1. 소용돌이 2. [사회적인] 소용돌이

vor·ti·ces [vɔ́:rtisi:z] *n.* pl. of **vortex**.

vo·ta·ress [vóut(ә)ris] *n.* [C] a woman votary.

—[名] votary의 여성형

vo·ta·ry [vóutәri] *n.* [C] (pl. **-ries**) **1.** a person bound by vows to a religious life. **2.** a person devoted to something; a devotee. ¶*a ~ of music.*①

—[名] 1. 신에게 봉사하는 사람, 신앙인, 신자 2. 열렬한 애호가, 심취자 ¶①음악 애호가

:vote [vout] *n.* [C] **1.** a formal expression of will or opinion in regard to some question. ¶*an open* (*a secret*) *~* / *put a bill* (*a question*) *to the ~*① / *take a ~ on a bill*② / *come* (or *go, proceed*) *to the ~*③ / *It was decided by ~.* **2.** the method by which such a choice is expressed, such as by written ballot, by voice, or by a show of hands; a ballot. ¶*cast a ~ for* (*against*)…④ / *give one's ~ to* (or *for*)…⑤ **3.** the right to express such a choice or wish. ¶*I have no ~ in this matter.*⑥ **4.** something expressed by a majority. ¶*a ~ of censure*⑦ / *a ~ of thanks.*⑧ **5.** ((*collectively*)) the entire

—[名] 1. [의안 따위에 대한] 찬반 표사, 표결 ¶①법안(문제)을 표결에 붙이다 /②법안을 표결하다/③표결에 붙여지다 2. 투표[의 한 표] ¶④…에 찬성(반대)표를 던지다/⑤…에 투표하다 3. 투표권 ¶⑥나는 이 문제에 대해서는 의결권(투표권)이 없다 4. [표결된] 결의 사항 ¶⑦불신임 결의(투표)/⑧감사 결의 5. 투표 총수, 득표 ¶⑨다수의 득표

voter [1281] **vying**

number of such expressions. ¶*a large ~.*①
—*vi.* express one's wish or choice by a vote; cast a vote. ¶*~ for (against) a measure.*② —*vt.* **1.** decide, or establish (something) by a vote. ¶*~ a reform | ~ someone into (out of) office.*③ **2.** (*colloq.*) declare (something) by general consent. ¶*They voted the new play a success.* **3.** suggest or propose. ¶*I ~ that we go.*
vote down, vote against; defeat (something) by a vote.

- **vot·er** [vóutər] *n.* ⓒ a person who votes or who has a legal right to vote; an elector. ¶*a casting ~.*①

vot·ing [vóutiŋ] *n.* Ⓤ the act of casting a vote.

vo·tive [vóutiv] *adj.* given in accordance with a vow or promise.

vouch [vautʃ] *vi.* guarantee; be responsible. (*~ for* 「something」)

vouch·er [váutʃər] *n.* ⓒ **1.** a person who gives a guarantee for something. **2.** a written paper showing that a sum of money has been paid, etc.

vouch·safe [vautʃséif] *vt.* **1.** give something in a gracious manner or out of pity. ¶*Can you ~ me a visit?*① **2.** do something in a kind or polite way.

: **vow** [vau] *n.* ⓒ **1.** an earnest promise to God; a pledge of love and faithfulness. **2.** the content of a vow.
be under a vow, bind oneself by a vow.
—*vt.* **1.** make a vow to do (something). **2.** declare earnestly and firmly.

vow·el [váu(ə)l] *n.* ⓒ **1.** (*Phonetics*) a simple vocal sound with the mouth and lips partly open. ↔consonant **2.** a letter representing such a sound, such as a, e, i, o and u.

: **voy·age** [vɔ́iidʒ, +*Brit.* vɔidʒ] *n.* ⓒ a journey by sea or by air. ¶*a ~ around the world | Bon ~ [bɔ̃ŋvwɑjɑːʒ]*① */ on the ~.* —*vt., vi.* travel by sea or by air.

voy·ag·er [vɔ́iidʒər] *n.* ⓒ a person who makes a voyage.

vs. versus.

V-shaped [víːʃeipt] *adj.* having the shape of the letter 「V」

v.t., vt. transitive verb.

vul·can·ite [vʌ́lkənàit] *n.* Ⓤ a hard, black substance, also called ebonite, used for making combs, etc.

vul·can·ize [vʌ́lkənaiz] *vt.* treat (rubber) with sulfur to make it more elastic and harder.

- **vul·gar** [vʌ́lgər] *adj.* **1.** belonging to the common people; common. ¶*~ life.*① **2.** showing a lack of culture, refinement, taste, etc. ↔refined ¶*~ manners.*②

vul·gar·ism [vʌ́lgəriz(ə)m] *n.* **1.** ⓒ a word or an expression used only in coarse speech. **2.** Ⓤ vulgarity.

vul·gar·i·ty [vʌlgǽriti] *n.* (pl. **-ties**) **1.** Ⓤ the state or quality of being vulgar. **2.** (*pl.*) vulgar actions, habits, speech, writing, etc.

vul·gar·ize [vʌ́lgəraiz] *vt.* make (something) vulgar.

Vul·gate [vʌ́lgeit, -git]**, the** *n.* the Latin translation of the Bible made in the 4th century A.D., long used by the Roman Catholic Church.

vul·ner·a·bil·i·ty [vʌ̀ln(ə)rəbíliti] *n.* Ⓤ the state or quality of being vulnerable.

vul·ner·a·ble [vʌ́ln(ə)rəbl] *adj.* **1.** that can be injured or wounded. **2.** open to injury or criticism. ¶*a ~ point*① */ be ~ to ridicule.*② ▷**vul·ner·a·bly** [-i] *adv.*

vul·ture [vʌ́ltʃər] *n.* ⓒ a large bird [vulture] of prey with a bald head that eats the flesh of dead animals. ⇒fig.

vy·ing [váiiŋ] *v.* ppr. of vie.

—⾃ 투표하다, 선거하다 ¶⑩의 안에 대하여 찬성(반대) 투표하다 —⽫ 1. …을 투표하여 결정하다, 가결하다 ¶①[남]을 직위에 선출하다(투표하여 해임하다) 2. [세상이] …이라고 간주하다, 인정하다 3. …을 제안하다

圀 …을 부정(부결)하다

—⿰ 투표자, 선거인 ¶①결정 투표자 (의장 등)

—⿰ 투표, 선거, 투표권 행사

—⿰ 기원(祈願)의; 봉납한, 봉헌의

—⾃ 보증하다; 보증인이 되다

—⿰ 1. 보증인 2. [금전 지불 관계의] 증빙서, 영수증

—⽫ 1. …을 주다, 허락하다 ¶①방문을 허락해 주시겠읍니까? 2. 친절하게도 …하다

—⿰ 1. 맹세; 서약 2. 서약의 내용(취지)

圀 맹세하다, 서약하다

—⽫ 1. …하겠다고 맹세(서약)하다 2. …을 단언(확언)하다

—⿰ 1.《音聲》모음 2. 모음자(字)

—⿰ 항해, 항행; 항공 여행 ¶①여행중 안녕히 —⽫⾃ 항해하다; 항공 여행을 하다

—⿰ 항해(항공) 여행자

—⿰ V자형의
—⿰ 타동사
—⿰ 에보나이트, 경질(硬質) 고무

—⽫ [고무]를 경화(硬化)하다

—⿰ 1. 일반 민중의, 서민의 ¶①서민 생활 2. 천한, 저속(야비)한 ¶②야비한 거동(예절)

—⿰ 1. 상말, 비어(卑語) 2. 속악, 야비

—⿰ 1. 속악, 야비 2. 야비한 언행

—⽫ …을 속되게(저속하게) 하다
—⿰ [가톨릭 교회 공인의] 라틴어역(譯) 성서

—⿰ 비난을 받기 쉬움; 약점

—⽫ 1. 상처입기 쉬운 2. 비난받기 쉬운 ¶①약점/②웃음거리가 되기 쉽다

—⿰ 콘도르, 독수리

W

W, w [dʌ́blju(ː)] *n.* ⓒ (pl. **W's, Ws, w's, ws** [dʌ́blju(ː)z])
 1. the 23rd letter of the English alphabet. 2. something having the form of W.
W. 1. Watt. 2. west.

wab·ble [wábl / wɔ́bl] *vi., v.* =wobble.

wad [wad / wɔd] *n.* ⓒ 1. a small mass of soft material, used to stop up an opening or to keep things in place. 2. a pile of paper money. ¶ *a ~ of bills.*① 3. a plug to hold powder and shot in place in a gun.
 —*vt.* (**wad·ded, wad·ding**) 1. make (something) into a small mass. 2. stuff (something) with a wad.

wad·ding [wádiŋ / wɔ́d-] *n.* Ⓤ a soft material for packing, stuffing, etc.

wad·dle [wádl / wɔ́dl] *vi.* walk with short steps and a swaying motion. —*n.* ⓒ (*sing.* only) the act of waddling.

* **wade** [weid] *vi.* 1. walk through water, mud, sand, etc. that hinders progress. 2. make one's way with effort or difficulty. —*vt.* cross or pass through (a stream, etc.) by wading. —*n.* Ⓤ the act of wading.

wad·er [wéidər] *n.* 1. ⓒ a person who wades. 2. ⓒ a long-legged bird that wades about in water in search of food. 3. (*pl.*) (*Brit.*) high waterproof boots.

wa·fer [wéifər] *n.* Ⓤ 1. a thin, flat biscuit or cake. 2. a small piece of colored paper for fastening or sealing.

waf·fle [wáfl / wɔ́fl] *n.* ⓒ a flat cake baked between two hinged metal plates.

waft [wæft, waːft / waːft] *vt.* carry (something) lightly over water or through air. ¶ *The breeze wafted the scent of roses.*① —*vi.* float smoothly on the water or through the air. —*n.* ⓒ 1. the act of wafting; the state of being wafted. 2. a breath or gust of wind. 3. a waving movement.

* **wag**¹ [wæg] *v.* (**wagged, wag·ging**) *vt.* cause (something) to move from side to side or up and down rapidly. ¶ *The dog wagged its tail.*① —*vi.* move from side to side or up and down rapidly. —*n.* ⓒ the act of wagging. ¶ *show disagreement by a ~ of the head.*②

wag² [wæg] *n.* ⓒ a person who is fond of making jokes.

wage [weidʒ] *n.* (usu. *pl.*) 1. (sometimes used as *sing.*) money paid for work. ¶ *a living ~*① */ a ~ increase.*② 2. (used as *sing.*) something given as a reward. ¶ *The wages of sin is death.*③ —*vt.* carry on or engage in (something). ▷**wage·less** [-lis] *adj.*

wage earner [⌐ ⌐ ⌐] *n.* a person who works for wages.

wag·ger·y [wǽgəri] *n.* (pl. **-ger·ies**) 1. Ⓤ the action or spirit of a humorous person. 2. ⓒ a joke.

wag·gish [wǽgiʃ] *adj.* 1. fond of playing jokes. 2. humorous or comical.

wag·on, *Brit.* **wag·gon** [wǽgən] *n.* ⓒ 1. a four-wheeled vehicle drawn by horses and used to carry loads. ⇒ fig. 2. (*Brit.*) an open railroad freight car. ⇒ p. 1283 fig.

wag·on·er, *Brit.* **wag·gon·er** [wǽgənər] *n.* ⓒ a person who drives a wagon.

[wagon 1.]

—⊛ 1. 영어 자모의 스물 세째 글자 2. W 자형의 물건

—⊛ 1.[솜·종이 따위의] 작은 덩어리(뭉치) 2. 지폐 뭉치 ¶①지폐 뭉치 3.[탄알의 화약을 고정시키는] 충전물

—⑪ 1. …을 작은 덩어리(뭉치)로 만들다 2.[충전물로] …에 메워(채워)넣다
—⊛ 채우는(메우는) 물건, 충전물; 메우는 솜

—⾃ 어기적어기적(비틀비틀) 걷다
—⊛ 어기적어기적 걷기

—⾃ 1. [개울·진창길 따위를] 걸어서 건너다 2. 애써(힘들여) 나아가다 —⑪ …을 걸어서 건너다 —⊛ 걸어서 건너기

—⊛ 1. 걸어서 건너는 사람 2. 섭금류(涉禽類)의 새 3.(英)[얕은 물에서 신는] 방수 장화

—⊛ 1. 웨이퍼스(얇고 납작한 비스킷·과자) 2. 봉랍지(封緘紙)

—⊛ 와플(두 짝의 철판 사이에 끼워서 구운 납작한 과자)

—⑪ …을 떠돌게 하다, 부동(浮動)시키다; 날려서 보내다 ¶①미풍에 장미의 향기가 풍겨 왔다 —⾃ 떠돌다, 표류(부동)하다 —⊛ 1. 부동;떠돌기, 표류 2. 한 차례의 바람 3.[새의] 날개치기, 퍼덕임

—⑪ …을 상하(좌우)로 흔들다 ¶①개가 꼬리를 흔들었다 —⾃ 흔들리다
—⊛ 흔들기, 흔들어 움직이기 ¶②머리를 옆으로 저어 불만의 뜻을 나타내다

—⊛ 익살꾸러기, 까불이

—⊛ 1. 임금, 노임, 급료 ¶①생활을 유지할 수 있는 임금/②임금 인상 2. [죄 따위의] 보상, 대가(代價) ¶③죄의 보상은 죽음이다 —⑪ [전쟁 따위를] 행하다, 수행하다

—⊛ 임금 생활자, 임금 노동자

—⊛ 1. 우스꽝스러운 짓, 익살 2. 농담, 장난

—⑪ 1. 장난 좋아하는 2. 익살맞은, 우스꽝스러운

—⊛ 1. 짐마차 2.(英) 무개(無蓋)화차

—⊛ 짐마차의 마부

wag·on·ette [wæ̀gənét] *n.* [C] a light, open carriage with side-seats facing each other.
—[名] 좌석이 마주앉게 된 유람 마차

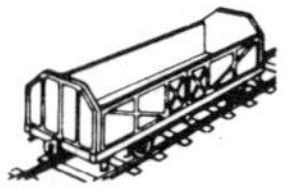
〔wagon 2.〕

waif [weif] *n.* [C] (pl. **waifs**) **1.** a person without a home. **2.** a lost animal; a lost child.
—[名] 1. 방랑자, 떠돌이, 부랑자 2. 임자 없는 동물; 길 잃은(집 없는) 아이

* **wail** [weil] *vi.* **1.** cry loud in grief or pain. ¶*The baby wailed for hours.*① **2.** make a sound like a cry. ¶*The wind wailed in the woods.*
—*n.* [C] **1.** a long, loud cry of pain or grief. **2.** a sound like a cry.
—[自] 1. 슬퍼서(아파서) 울다 ¶①아기가 몇 시간 동안 울었다 2. [우는 듯이] 구슬프게 울리다
—[名] 1. 울부짖는 소리, 울부짖음 2. [울음소리 같은] 구슬픈 소리

wain·scot [wéinskət, +*U.S.* -skɑt] *n.* [U] a wooden lining on the walls of a room. —*vt., vi.* (**-scot·ed, -scot·ing** or *Brit.* **-scot·ted, -scot·ting**) line (a wall) with wood.
—[名] [방의 안벽에 대는] 널, 벽판(壁板) —[他][自] 벽판을 붙이다(대다)

⁑ **waist** [weist] *n.* [C] **1.** the part of the body between the ribs and the hips. **2.** a garment or the part of a garment covering the waist. **3.** the middle part of a ship.
—[名] 1. 허리 2. 옷의 허리 부분; 조끼 3. [배의] 중부 갑판

waist·band [wésbənd, wéistbæ̀nd / wéistbæ̀nd] *n.* [C] a band around the waist on trousers or a skirt.
—[名] 허리띠

waist·coat [wéskət, wéistkòut / wéistkout] *n.* [C] (*Brit.*) a man's vest.
—[名] 《英》 조끼

waist·line [wéistlàin] *n.* [C] **1.** a line around the waist. **2.** the narrow part of a woman's dress. **3.** the line where the waist and skirt of a dress meet.
—[名] 1. 허리의 [잘룩한] 선 2. 부인복의 웨이스트(잘룩한 부분) 3. 부인복의 허리와 스커어트가 접합하는 선

⁑ **wait** [weit] *vi.* **1.** stay or remain until someone comes or something happens. 《~ *for* someone or something; ~ *to do*》. ¶*~ and see*① / *~ around* (or *Brit. about*)② / *keep someone waiting*③ / *I have been waiting to hear from you.* / (*proverb*) *Time and tide ~ for no man.*④ **2.** be in readiness. ¶*Boys, dinner's waiting for you.* **3.** remain neglected for a time; be delayed. ¶*He says it cannot ~.*⑤ **4.** be or act as a waiter, esp. at table. 《~ *on* or *upon* someone》 ¶*~ on* (or *Brit. at*) *table*[*s*].⑥
—*vt.* **1.** wait for (something). ¶*~ one's chance* / *~ one's turn.*⑦ **2.** delay or put off (a meal). ¶*Don't ~ supper for me.*
1) ***wait on*** (*or* ***upon***), ⓐ visit (someone, esp. a superior) formally. ⓑ attend or follow.
2) ***wait table,*** serve at table.
3) ***wait up*** (=*put off going to bed*) ***for*** *someone or something.*
—*n.* **1.** [C] the act or time of waiting. ¶*It was a long ~ before we found a taxi.* **2.** (esp. *Brit.*) 《*the ~s*》 persons going from door to door at Christmas singing songs.
lie in wait (=*hide and wait*) ***for*** *someone or something.*
—[自] 1. 기다리다, 대기(기대)하다 ¶①일이 되어가는 것을 두고 보다/②서성거리며 기다리다/③남을 기다리게 하다/④《俚》세월은 사람을 기다리지 않는다 2. 준비가 되어 있다, [때가 오기만을] 기다리고 있다 3. 늦어지다, 지연되다 ¶⑤그는 그것은 뒤로 미룰 수 없다고 말한다 4. 시중들다, 섬기다 ¶⑥식탁 시중을 들다
—[他] 1. …을 기다리다 ¶⑦차례를 기다리다 2. [식사]를 미루다, 지연시키다
[熟] 1)ⓐ…을 방문하다 ⓑ…을 모시고 가다, 수행하다 2)식탁의 시중을 들다 3)[자지 않고] …을 기다리다
—[名] 1. 기다리기, 대기; 기다리는 시간 2. 《英》 크리스마스날 밤에 집집마다 돌아다니며 노래를 부르는 성가대
[熟] …을 숨어서 기다리다, 매복하다

* **wait·er** [wéitər] *n.* [C] **1.** a person who serves at table in a hotel or restaurant. **2.** a tray for carrying dishes.
—[名] 1. 급사, 웨이터 2. [급사가 음식을 나르는] 쟁반

* **wait·ing** [wéitiŋ] *adj.* serving. ¶*a ~ man*① / *a ~ maid.*②
—*n.* [U] the act of serving someone. ¶*in ~.*③
—[形] 시중드는, 섬기는 ¶①시종, 하인/②시녀, 몸종
—[名] 시중들기, 섬기기 ¶③모시고, 섬기고

waiting room [⌐-⌐] *n.* a room at a railroad station, etc. where people wait for trains, etc.
—[名] 대기실, 대합실

wait·ress [wéitris] *n.* [C] a woman who serves at table in a hotel or restaurant.
—[名] 여급사, 여급, 웨이트리스

waive [weiv] *vt.* **1.** give up (a right, a chance, etc.). **2.** put (something) off until later.
—[他] 1. [권리 따위]를 포기하다 2. …을 [당분간] 보류하다; 연기하다

⁑ **wake**[1] [weik] *v.* (**waked** or **woke, waked**) *vi.* **1.** stay awake. ¶*in one's waking hours.* **2.** stop sleeping. **3.** become active or alive. —*vt.* **1.** cause (someone) to stop sleeping. **2.** make (someone or something) alive or active.
—*n.* [C] the act of watching; an all-night watch over a dead body before burial.
—[自] 1. 깨어 있다, 자지 않고 있다 2. 눈을 뜨다, 잠이 깨다, 일어나다 3. 활기띠다 —[他] 1. …을 깨우다 2. …을 활기띠게 하다
—[名] 감시; 밤샘, 철야, 경야(經夜)

wake[2] [weik] *n.* [C] the trail left behind a moving ship.
—[名] 배 지나간 자국, 항적(航跡)

wake·ful [wéikf(u)l] *adj.* **1.** free from sleepiness; unable to sleep. ¶*a ~ night.*① **2.** wide-awake. ¶*a ~ watch.*②
—[形] 1. 잠이 안 오는, 졸리지 않는 ¶①잠 안 오는 밤 2. 자지 않고 있는, 깨어 있는, 자지 않는 ¶②불침번

⁑ **wak·en** [wéik(ə)n] *v.* =wake.[1]

W

wale [weil] *n.* [C] **1.** a streak made on the skin by a stick or whip. **2.** a raised line made in the weave of cloth. **—***vt.* **1.** mark (the skin) with wales. **2.** make (cloth) with wales.

—[名] 1. 채찍 자국 2. [직물의] 이랑 —[他] 1. …에 채찍 자국을 내다 2. [천]을 이랑지게 하다

Wales [weilz] *n.* a division of Great Britain west of England; the land of the Welsh. ¶*The Prince of ~.*①

—[名] [영국의] 웨일즈 지방 ¶①영국의 황태자

⁝ walk [wɔːk] *vi.* **1.** go or travel on foot at a moderate pace; go about on foot for the purpose of exercise or pleasure. ¶*~ about*① / *~ up and down*② / *I would rather ~ than ride.* **2.** (of a ghost) go about on the earth. ¶*The ghost walks on such a dark night.* **3.** (*Baseball*) advance to first base after four balls have been pitched. **—***vt.* **1.** go over (some place) on foot. ¶*~ the streets at night.* **2.** cause (a person or an animal) to walk. ¶*~ the horse.* **3.** accompany or lead (someone) on foot. ¶*I'll ~ you to the station.* **4.** (*Baseball*) advance (a batter) to first base by pitching four balls.

—[自] 1. 걷다; 산책하다 ¶①거닐다, 산책하다/②이리저리 거닐다 2. [유령이] 나오다, 나돌아 다니다 3. 《野球》 4구로 1루에 진출하다 —[他] 1. …을 걷다 2. …을 걷게 하다, 걸리다 3. 걸어서 [남]을 따라가다; [남]을 데리고 가다 4. 《野球》 [타자]를 4구로 1루에 진출시키다

1) ***walk away from,*** ⓐ go far ahead. ⓑ beat (one's enemy, etc.) easily in a contest.
2) ***walk away*** (or ***off***) ***with,*** ⓐ steal. ⓑ win or gain.
3) ***walk off,*** ⓐ leave, esp. without saying good-bye. ⓑ get rid of (something) by walking. ¶*I usually ~ off my sleepiness.*③
4) ***walk over,*** win easily.

[熟] 1)ⓐ…을 훨씬 앞서 가다 ⓑ[경쟁에서] …에게 낙승하다 2)ⓐ…을 가지고 도망치다 ⓑ…을 쟁취(획득)하다, [상 따위]를 타다 3)ⓐ물러가다, 가 버리다 ⓑ걸어서 …을 없애다(쫓아버리다) ¶③나는 늘 산책하여 졸음을 쫓는다 4)…에게 낙승하다

—*n.* [C] **1.** the act of walking, esp. a little journey on foot for exercise or pleasure. ¶*take* (or *go for*) *a ~*④ / *take someone for a ~.* **2.** a distance walked. ¶*It is a ten-minute ~ to the station.* **3.** a manner of walking. ¶*He had a ~ like a duck.* **4.** a path for walking. **5.** (of a horse) a slow pace. ¶*go at a ~.*⑤ **6.** (*Baseball*) an advance to first base as a result of four balls.

—[名] 1. 걷기, 걸음, 보행; 산책; 도보여행 ¶④산책하다 2. 보행 거리 3. 걸음걸이, 걸음새 4. 산책길, 보도(步道) 5. [말 따위의] 보통 걸음 ¶⑤보통 걸음으로 가다 6. 《野球》 [타자가] 4구로 1루에 진출하기

walk of life, an occupation; a rank in society.

[熟] 직업; 지위, 계급

walk·ing stick [⌐–⌐] *n.* (*Brit.*) a stick carried when a person takes a walk; a cane.

—[名] 《英》 지팡이

walk·out [wɔ́ːkàut] *n.* [C] (*U.S. colloq.*) a strike of workmen.

—[名] 《美口》 동맹파업, 스트라이크

walk·o·ver [wɔ́ːkòuvər] *n.* [C] (*colloq*) an easy victory.

—[名] 쉽게 이기기, 낙승

⁝ wall [wɔːl] *n.* [C] **1.** the side of a building; a fence built of wood, brick, etc. ¶*a blank ~*① / *a wooden ~*② / *within four walls*③ / *lean against the ~* / *be at bay against the ~*④ / *There is a map on the ~.* / (*proverb*) *Walls have ears.*⑤ **2.** 《usu. *pl.*》 a defensive wall of a town, a city, etc. ¶*town walls* / *the Great Wall of China.*⑥ **3.** something like a wall. ¶*a ~ of water* / *a ~ of suspicion.*⑦ **4.** 《otfen *pl.*》 the inside surface of a vessel, etc. ¶*the walls of the heart*⑧ / *the walls of a vessel.*⑨

—[名] 1. 벽; 담 ¶①장식이 없는 벽/②판장/③방 안에서; 비밀히/④쫓기어서 벽에 등을 대고 서 있다/⑤《俚》벽에도 귀가 있다(낮말은 새가 듣고 밤 말은 쥐가 듣는다) 2. 성벽 ¶⑥만리장성 3. 벽 같은 것, 장벽 ¶⑦의심의 장벽 4. 안벽, 안쪽 ¶⑧흉벽(胸壁)/⑨그릇의 안쪽 면

1) ***drive*** (or ***push***) ***someone to the wall,*** force someone into a difficult situation.
2) ***give someone the wall,*** allow someone to pass.
3) ***go to the wall,*** ⓐ suffer defeat. ⓑ fail in business.
4) ***run one's head against a wall,*** try to do something impossible.
5) ***see through*** (or ***into***) ***a brick wall,*** have a wonderful insight.
6) ***with one's back to the wall,*** in a position where escape is impossible.

[熟] 1)[남]을 궁지에 몰아넣다 2)[남]에게 길을 양보하다(비켜주다) 3)ⓐ지다, 패배하다 ⓑ사업에 실패하다 4)불가능한 일을 시도하다 5)날카로운 통찰력이 있다 6)궁지에 몰려서

—*vt.* **1.** divide, enclose, or protect (something) with a wall. ¶*The city was walled before the war.* **2.** close up (an opening) with a wall. ¶*~ up a window.*⑩

—[他] 1. …을 벽으로 간막이하다; 벽(담)으로 둘러싸다; …을 성벽으로 방어하다 2. …을 벽으로 막다 ¶⑩창을 벽으로 막다

*** wal·let** [wálit, wɔ́ːl- / wɔ́lit] *n.* [C] **1.** a leather case for holding paper money, cards, etc. in one's pocket. **2.** (*archaic*) a bag for food and light articles for a journey.

—[名] 1. 지갑 2. 《古》 여행용 자루, 전대, 바랑

wall·flow·er [wɔ́ːlflàuər] *n.* [C] **1.** (*colloq.*) a woman who sits by the wall at a dance because she has no partner. **2.** a plant with yellow or red flowers that have a sweet smell.

—[名] 1. 《口》 무도회에서 상대자가 없는 여자 2. 향꽃장대(노랑 또는 빨강 꽃이 피는 향기로운 식물)

wal·low [wálou / wɔ́l-] *vi.* **1.** roll about (in mud, a dirty

—[自] 1. [진창·물속에서] 데굴데굴 굴

water, etc.) **2.** indulge oneself with pleasures or enjoyment. ¶~ *in luxury.* —*n.* [C] **1.** the act of wallowing. **2.** a muddy place where animals wallow.
다, 뒹굴다 2. [쾌락 따위에] 빠지다, 탐닉하다 —[名] 1. [데굴데굴] 뒹굴기 2. [물소 따위가 뒹구는] 수렁, 소택지

wall·pa·per [wɔ́:lpèipər] *n.* [U] paper used for pasting on walls. —*vt.* cover (something) with wallpaper.
—[名] 벽지, 도배지 —[他] …에 벽지를 바르다, 도배하다

Wall Street [ˊ ˋ] *n.* **1.** a street in New York which is the location of the chief American financial center. **2.** the money market of the United States.
—[名] 1. 월가(街)(뉴욕시에 있는 미국 재정의 중심지) 2. 미국 금융 시장(금융계)

* **wal·nut** [wɔ́:lnʌt, -nət] *n.* [C] a hard-shelled nut that may be eaten; its tree; [U] the wood of this tree.
—[名] 호도; 호도나무; 호도나무 목재

wal·rus [wɔ́:lrəs] *n.* [C] (pl. **-rus·es** or *collectively* **-rus**) a large sea animal of the Arctic regions which is valued for its tusks and skin. ⇒fig.
—[名] 해마(海馬)

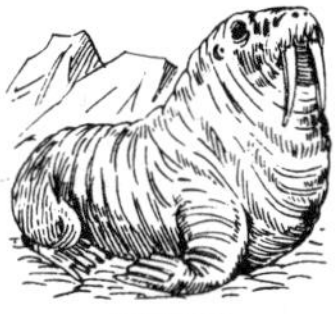
[walrus]

waltz [wɔ:l(t)s] *n.* [C] a smooth, graceful dance in triple rhythm for couples; the music for it. —*vi.* dance a waltz.
—[名] 왈츠; 왈츠곡, 원무곡 —[自] 왈츠를 추다

wan [wan / wɔn] *adj.* (**wan·ner, wan·nest**) **1.** pale. ¶*a* ~ *complexion*① **2.** looking tired and weak. ¶*with a* ~ *smile.*② ▷**wan·ly** [-li] *adv.* —**wan·ness** [-nis] *n.*
—[形] 1. 창백한 ¶①창백한 안색 2. 가냘픈, 힘없는, 파리한 ¶②가냘픈 미소로

* **wand** [wand / wɔnd] *n.* [C] a slender stick or a rod for a magician or a conductor.
—[名] [마법의] 지팡이, 요술지팡이; 지휘봉

⁑ **wan·der** [wándər / wɔ́ndə] *vi.* **1.** move aimlessly here and there. ¶~ *about the world.* **2.** stray; lose one's way. **3.** go astray in thought and speech. ¶*He is wandering in his head.*① / *The speaker began to* ~ *from the subject.*② —*vt.* (*poetic*) roam through (a place, etc.) without any particular purpose.
—[自] 1. [정처없이] 돌아다니다, 헤매다 2. 길을 잃다 3. 생각이 종잡을 수 없게 되다, 이야기가 본론에서 빗나가다 ¶①그는 머리가 이상하다/②연사는 본론에서 벗어난 이야기를 지껄이기 시작했다 —[他] 《詩》 …을 돌아다니다, 방랑하다

wan·der·er [wándərər / wɔ́ndərə] *n.* [C] a person who wanders.
—[名] 방랑자

wane [wein] *vi.* **1.** (of the moon) become smaller. ↔wax **2.** decline in strength, importance, influence, etc. —*n.* 《*the* ~》 **1.** a gradual decrease in strength, importance, influence, etc. **2.** the decrease in the size of the visible face of the moon.
—[自] 1. [달이] 이지러지다 2. [힘·명성 따위가] 쇠퇴하다

⁑ **want** [want, wɔ:nt / wɔnt] *vt.* **1.** wish, desire. 《~ *to do;* ~ someone *to do;* ~ someone *doing;* ~ something *done*》 ¶*I* ~ *to go there.* / *I* ~ *you to try it.*① / *I don't* ~ *you making a fool of me.* / *I* ~ *this work finished promptly.* **2.** (esp. *Brit.*) require; need; ought. 《~ *to do;* ~ *doing*》 ⇒[USAGE] ¶*I* ~ *more money.* / *You don't* ~ *to be rude.*② / *The trousers* ~ *pressing.*③ / *Do you* ~ *him?* **3.** lack. ¶*The book wants a page.* / *It wants five minutes to* (or *of*) *nine.*④ **4.** wish to see or speak to (someone). ¶*Father wants you.* / *He is wanted by the police.* —*vi.* have a need; be lacking; be in a state of poverty. 《~ *for* something》 ¶*He shall* ~ *for nothing.*⑤ —*n.* [U] **1.** lack; shortage. ¶*for* ~ *of*⑥ / *suffer from* ~ *of food* / *The plants died from* ~ *of water.* **2.** poverty. ¶*the bitterness of* ~.⑦ **3.** need. ¶*Are you in* ~ *of money?* **4.** [C] 《usu. *pl.*》 something needed or desired. ¶*a man of few wants.*⑧
—[他] 1. …을 바라다, 원하다, 탐내다 ¶①네가 그것을 해주기 바란다 2. …을 필요로 하다; …할 필요가 있다; …해야 한다 [USAGE] 이 뜻으로는 보통 be wanting in을 씀 ¶②예의없이 굴어서는 안 된다/③바지는 프레스를 해야 되겠다 3. …이 결여되어 있다, …이 부족하다, 모자라다 ¶④9시 5분 전이다 4. …에게 볼일이 있다, …을 만나고 싶다 —[自] 필요로 하다; 결핍되다; 궁하다, 옹색하다 ¶⑤그에게는 아무 부족함이 없도록 하겠다 —[名] 1. 결핍, 부족 ¶⑥…의 부족으로 2. 가난, 빈곤, 궁핍 ¶⑦가난의 쓰라림 3. 필요 4. 필요품, 필수품, 탐나는 것 ¶⑧욕심이 적은 사람

* **want·ing** [wántiŋ, wɔ́:nt- / wɔ́nt-] *adj.* **1.** lacking or absent. 《~ *in*》 ¶*He is a bit* ~ *in politeness.*① **2.** not up to standard. —*prep.* without. ¶*a month* ~ *two days.*
—[形] 1. 결핍된; …이 없는; 모자라는 ¶①그는 다소 예의가 없다 2. 표준에 미달된 —[前] …이 없는; 결핍되어서

wan·ton [wántən / wɔ́nt-] *adj.* **1.** playful. ¶*a* ~ *child.* **2.** not moral. **3.** heartless; cruel. **4.** not controlled; unrestrained. —*n.* [C] a wanton person.
—[形] 1. 장난기가 있는; 변덕스러운 2. 음탕한, 부정한 3. 무자비한 4. 규율이 없는, 방종한 —[名] 바람둥이, 난봉꾼

⁑ **war** [wɔ:r] *n.* **1.** [C] a fight with armed force between nations or between parties within a nation; [U] the state created by such a fight. ↔peace ¶*a civil* ~① / *a hot* (*a cold*) ~② / *World War II*③ ⇒[N.B.] / *in times of* ~ /
—[名] 1. 전쟁; 전쟁 상태 ¶①내란/②열(냉)전/③2차 세계대전 [N.B.] world war two로 읽음/④…와 교전중이다/⑤…에 대해 선전포고를 하다/⑥…에

W

*be at ~ with*④ / *declare ~ against* (or *on*)⑤ / *make ~ upon*⑥ / *go to ~*.⑦ **2.** [C] a conflict; fighting. ¶*a ~ of nerves*⑧ / *a ~ of words.*⑨ **3.** [U] the art or science of fighting. ¶*~ with* (or *against*) *evil.*

전쟁을 걸다, …와 개전하다/⑦전쟁하다, 무력에 호소하다 **2.** 싸움, 투쟁 ¶⑧신경전/⑨설전(舌戰), 논쟁 **3.** 전술

—vi. (**warred, war·ring**) make war; fight or struggle.

—[自] 전쟁하다, 싸우다

war·ble [wɔ́ːrbl] *vt., vi.* sing melodiously with trills. **—n.** [C] the act of warbling; a bird's song.

—[他][自] 지저귀듯이 노래하다; 지저귀다
—[名] 지저귐

war·bler [wɔ́ːrblər] *n.* [C] **1.** a person or bird that warbles. **2.** any one of several small, brightly-colored singing birds.

—[名] **1.** 지저귀듯이 노래하는 사람; 지저귀는 새 **2.** 휘파람새과에 속하는 빛깔이 아름다운 새

war cry [´ ´] *n.* a word or cry shouted in battle to create or sustain spirit.

—[名] 전투의 함성

* **ward** [wɔːrd] *n.* [C] **1.** [U] the act of guarding; the state of being guarded. **2.** a young person under the care of a court or guardian. **3.** a division of a city. **4.** a division of a hospital or prison. ¶*an isolation ~.*①

—[名] **1.** 보호, 감시, 감독 **2.** 피(被)후견인, 피보호자 **3.** [도시의] 구(區) **4.** 구획; 병실; 감방 ¶①격리 병실(병동)

—vt. 1. (*archaic*) guard. **2.** turn aside. 《*~ off* something》 ¶*He shook his head as if to ~ off sleep.*

—[他] **1.** …을 지키다, 보호하다 **2.** …을 격퇴하다, 물리치다, 막다

ward·en [wɔ́ːrdn] *n.* [C] **1.** a person in charge of something; a guardian. **2.** (*U. S.*) the head keeper of a prison. **3.** (*Brit.*) the head of certain colleges, schools, etc. **4.** a public official.

—[名] **1.** 지키는 사람, 감시인 **2.**《美》[교도소의] 간수장 **3.**《英》학장 **4.** [각종 관공서의] 기관장

ward·er [wɔ́ːrdər] *n.* [C] a prison-keeper; a watchman.

—[名] 간수; 감시인, 파수꾼

ward·robe [wɔ́ːrdròub] *n.* **1.** [C] a piece of furniture for storing clothes. **2.** 《*collectively*》 all of one's clothes.

—[名] **1.** 옷장, 양복장 **2.** 의상, 의류

ward·room [wɔ́ːrdrù(ː)m] *n.* [C] a room in a warship used by all the commissioned officers.

—[名] 사관실

* **ware** [wɛər] *n.* **1.** 《usu. *pl.*》 articles for sale. ¶*praise one's own wares.*① **2.** [U] 《in *compounds*》 manufactured articles. ¶*iron ~*② / *table ~.*③

—[名] **1.** 상품 ¶①자화자찬하다 **2.** 세공품, 제품 ¶②철기(鐵器)/③식기

ware·house [wɛ́ərhàus] *n.* [C] a building where goods are kept.

—[名] 창고

* **war·fare** [wɔ́ːrfɛ̀ər] *n.* [U] the act or process of making war; the state of being at war. ¶*air ~.*①

—[名] 교전; 투쟁 ¶①공중전

war·i·ly [wɛ́ərili] *adv.* cautiously.

—[副] 방심치 않고, 주의하여

war·i·ness [wɛ́ərinis] *n.* [U] the state of being cautious. ¶*The cat and dog eyed each other with ~.*①

—[名] 조심, 주의; 경계 ¶①고양이와 개는 서로 경계하여 노려보았다

war·like [wɔ́ːrlàik] *adj.* **1.** of war. ¶*~ preparations.*① **2.** fond of war; quick to fight.

—[形] **1.** 전쟁의, 전쟁에 관한 ¶①전비(戰備), 전쟁준비 **2.** 호전적인; 도전적인

⁑ **warm** [wɔːrm] *adj.* **1.** not cold, but pleasantly hot. ↔cool ¶*It's ~ today.* / *She wears ~ clothing.* **2.** having bodily heat. ¶*I am ~ from exercise.*① **3.** hearty; sincere. ¶*a ~ friend* / *~ thanks.* **4.** enthusiastic; lively; excited. ¶*a ~ temperament* / *a ~ argument* / *get* (or *grow*) *~.*② **5.** (of colors) suggesting warmth. ↔cool ¶*Red, yellow, and orange are called ~ colors.*

—[形] **1.** 따뜻한, 따스한, 포근한, 온난한; 다소 더운 **2.** [몸이] 뜨거운, 더운 ¶①운동을 하였더니 덥다 **3.** 동정심(인정) 있는; 진심에서의 **4.** 열심인, 열렬한; 활발한; 흥분한 ¶②흥분하다 **5.** [색깔이] 따뜻한 느낌을 주는

—vt. 1. make (someone or something) warm; heat. ¶*~ oneself at the fire.*③ **2.** inspire or fill (someone) with kindly emotions. ¶*The sight of the baby warmed the killer.*④ **3.** make (someone or something) enthusiastic, lively, excited, etc. **—vi. 1.** become warm. **2.** become kindly. 《*~ to* or *toward* someone or something》 ¶*My heart warms to him.* **3.** become enthusiastic, lively, excited, etc.

—[他] **1.** …을 데우다, 따뜻하게 하다 ¶③불을 쬐다 **2.** [남의] 기분을 따뜻하게(부드럽게) 하다 ¶④그 아기를 보고 살인자는 부드러운 기분을 느꼈다 **3.** …을 열중시키다; 활발하게 하다; 흥분시키다 —[自] **1.** 따뜻해지다 **2.** 동정(호의)을 보내다 **3.** 열중하다; 흥분하다

warm up, ⓐ become warmer; heat (food) again after cooking it once. ¶*~ up the milk.* ⓑ prepare for a game by practice beforehand.

[熟] ⓐ따뜻해(더워)지다; …을 다시 데우다 ⓑ시합 전에 준비운동을 하다

—n. 《usu. *a ~*》 the act of warming. ¶*have* (or *get, take*) *a ~.*⑤

—[名] 따뜻하게 하기, 따뜻해지기 ¶⑤따뜻해지다

warm-blood·ed [wɔ́ːrmblʌ́did] *adj.* **1.** having warm blood. ¶*~ animals.*① **2.** having much feeling.

—[形] **1.** 온혈(溫血)의 ¶①온혈 동물 **2.** 격하기 쉬운, 열정적인

warm·er [wɔ́ːrmər] *n.* [C] a device for making something warm.

—[名] 가온(加溫) 장치, 가온기

warm·heart·ed [wɔ́ːrmhɑ́ːrtid] *adj.* having a warm heart; sympathetic; friendly.

—[形] 마음이 온화한, 마음씨 고운; 친절한

* **warm·ly** [wɔ́ːrmli] *adv.* in a warm manner.

—[副] 따뜻하게; 친절히; 열심히

⁑ **warmth** [wɔːrmθ] *n.* [U] **1.** the state of being warm;

—[名] **1.** 따뜻함, 온난 **2.** 열심; 흥분 **3.** 온

W

moderate heat. **2.** enthusiasm. **3.** warm feeling.
warm-up [wɔ́:rmʌ̀p] *n.* ⓤⓒ the act of practicing before going into a game, race, etc.
: **warn** [wɔːrn] *vt.* **1.** make (someone) aware of possible danger. **2.** give a notice to (someone).
* **warn·ing** [wɔ́ːrniŋ] *n.* **1.** ⓒ something that warns. **2.** ⓤ a notice given in advance.
* **warp** [wɔːrp] *n.* ⓒ **1.** the lengthwise thread in a piece of cloth. ↔woof **2.** a bend or twist. ¶*Dampness gave the board a bad ~.*① **3.** a mental twist. —*vt., vi.* make or become bent or twisted; twist mentally. ¶*Prejudice warps our judgment.*②
* **war·rant** [wɔ́:rənt, wɑ́r- / wɔ́r-] *n.* **1.** ⓤ a good and sufficient reason for belief; a guarantee. ¶*without a ~*① / *What ~ have you to say such a thing?*② **2.** ⓒ a document giving someone a legal right to do something. ¶*a search ~.*③ **3.** ⓒ something which gives a right; authority; justification. —*vt.* **1.** justify. ¶*The crime warranted severe punishment.* **2.** guarantee.
war·ran·tee [wɔ̀(:)rəntíː, wɑ̀r- / wɔ̀rəntíː] *n.* ⓒ a person to whom a warranty is made.
war·ran·ter, -tor [wɔ́:rəntər, wɑ́r- / wɔ́rəntə] *n.* ⓒ a person who warrants.
war·ran·ty [wɔ́:rənti, wɑ́r- / wɔ́r-] *n.* ⓒ (pl. **-ties**) **1.** a reasonable ground. **2.** (*Law*) a guarantee, usu. in written or printed form.
war·ren [wɑ́rən, wɑ́r- / wɔ́:r-] *n.* ⓒ **1.** a place for raising rabbits. **2.** a crowded district.
: **war·ri·or** [wɔ́:riər, wɑ́r- / wɔ́riə] *n.* ⓒ a soldier.
war·ship [wɔ́:rʃip] *n.* ⓒ a ship armed for war.
wart [wɔːrt] *n.* ⓒ a small hard lump on the skin or on a plant stem.
war·time [wɔ́:rtàim] *n.* ⓤ the period during which a war continues. ↔peacetime
war·y [wɛ́əri] *adj.* (**war·i·er war·i·est**) habitually on guard; careful. ¶*The old farmer was ~ of city folk.*①
: **was** [waz, wəz / wɔz, wəz] *v.* pt. of **is** or **am**.
: **wash** [waʃ, wɔːʃ / wɔʃ] *vt.* **1.** clean (one's body, clothes, etc.), usu. with water. ¶*~ one's hands*① / *oneself*② / *Wash your hands clean before eating.* **2.** remove (spots, stains, etc.) by washing. 《~ *away* (or *off, out*) something》 ¶*~ off stains from a coat.* **3.** free from (sin, guilt, etc.); purify (the soul). 《~ *away* something》 ¶*~ away one's sin.*③ **4.** of the sea, a river, waves, etc.) flow through, over, or against (something) ¶*The waves washed the shore.* **5.** make (something) wet. ¶*The flowers were washed with dew.* **6.** remove or carry away (something) by the action of water, etc. 《~ something *away*》 ¶*The bridge was washed away by the flood.* **7.** wear (something) by flowing over it; make or form (a channel, etc.). ¶*Water washed a channel.*④ **8.** cover (something) with a thin coat of metal or of paint. 《~ something *with* gold, white, etc.》
—*vi.* **1.** wash one's hands, face, etc.; wash oneself. ¶*You must ~ before dinner.* **2.** wash clothes. **3.** be able to stand washing without damage. ¶*This cloth won't ~.*⑤ **4.** beat or flow with a lapping sound. 《~ *against* (or *over, along*) something》 **5.** be removed or carried by the action of water. 《~ *away* or *out* something》
 1) ***wash down***, ⓐ clean by washing. ⓑ help the chewing or swallowing of (a food) by drinking water, etc.
 2) ***wash up***, ⓐ wash one's face and hands. ⓑ (*Brit.*) wash (dishes, etc.) after meals.
—*n.* **1.** ⓒⓤ (usu. *a ~*) the act of washing. ¶*have*

정, 동정심
—ⓝ [시합 전의] 가벼운 준비운동
—ⓥ **1.** …에 조심시키다; 경고하다 **2.** …에 예고(통고)하다
—ⓝ **1.** 경고, 주의; 전조(前兆) **2.** 예고
—ⓝ **1.** 날실 **2.** [재목 따위의] 휨, 굽음, 비뚤림 ¶①습기로 널빤지가 휘었다 **3.** 마음보가 비뚤림 —ⓥⓥ 휘게(굽게) 하다, 뒤틀리게 하다; ¶②편견은 판단을 비뚤어지게 한다
—ⓝ **1.** 정당한 이유, 보증, 근거 ¶①정당한 이유없이/②무슨 근거로 그런 말을 하는가? **2.** 영장, 위임장 ¶③수색영장 **3.** 권한, 권능 —ⓥ **1.** …을 정당화하다 **2.** …을 보증하다

—ⓝ 피(被)보증인

—ⓝ 보증인

—ⓝ **1.** 정당한 이유 **2.** 《法》 보증; 담보

—ⓝ **1.** 토끼 사육장 **2.** 많은 사람들이 붐비는 지역
—ⓝ 군인, 병사; 전사, 무사
—ⓝ 군함
—ⓝ 사마귀; [나무의] 혹, 옹이

—ⓝ 전시(戰時)

—ⓥ 조심성있는; 신중한 ¶①그 늙은 농부는 도시 사람들에게 방심치 않았
—ⓥ **1.** [몸·옷 따위]를 씻다, 세탁하다, 세척하다 ¶①손을 씻[으러 가]다, [완곡하게] 변소에 가다/②몸[얼굴]을 씻다, 목욕하다 **2.** [얼룩·더럼 따위]를 씻어내다 **3.** [죄 따위]를 면하다; 씻다 ¶③죄를 씻다 **4.** [바닷물 따위가]…을 씻다, …에 밀려 오다 **5.** …을 적시다, 젖게 하다 **6.** …을 떠[밀려]내려가게 하다, [물이] …을 운반하다 **7.** …을 파다, 침식하다, [물이 해협 따위]를 만들다 ¶④수세(水勢)로 도랑이 생겼다 **8.** …에 도금하다; [그림물감]을 엷게 칠하다
—ⓥ **1.** 손[얼굴]을 씻다, 세수하다; 몸을 씻다, 목욕하다 **2.** 세탁하다, 빨래하다 **3.** 세탁이 잘 되다, [천이 상하지 않고] 때가 잘 지다 ¶⑤이 천은 때가 잘 안 진다 **4.** [물결이] 철썩철썩 밀려오다, 기슭을 씻다 **5.** [물에] 밀려 내려가다, 떠내려가다; 침식되다

圞 1)ⓐ…을 씻어 내리다 ⓑ[음료·음식]을 [목에] 흘려 넣다 2)ⓐ세수하다 ⓑ《英》[식기 따위]를 씻어 치우다, 설겆이를 하다
—ⓝ **1.** 씻기, 세탁, 세척 ¶⑥씻다, 세탁

(or *get*) *a* ~⑥ / *give something a good* ~.⑦ **2.** 《*collectively*》 clothes, etc. to be washed or being washed; (*Brit.*) the process of washing at a laundry. ¶*She is hanging out the* ~.⑧ / *He sends clothes to the* ~ *once a week.*⑨ **3.** [C] 《*the* ~》 the movement or flow of water; the sound of this. **4.** [C] a liquid for washing eyes, hair, etc. **5.** [U] weak liquid or food. ¶*This soup is mere* ~. **6.** [U] waste liquid containing waste food from the kitchen. **7.** [U] 《*the* ~》 the disturbed water left behind a moving ship, etc.; disturbed air behind a moving airplane. **8.** [U] a thin coat of gold, silver, etc. laid on something. **9.** [U] 《usu. *the* ~》 the matter that is carried and deposited by flowing water.
하다/⑦물건을 잘 빨다(씻다) **2.** 세탁물, 빨랫감; 《英》 세탁소에서의 세탁 ¶⑧그녀는 빨래를 널고 있다/⑨그는 1주일에 한 번 옷을 세탁소에 보낸다 **3.** [물결의] 밀려옴; 밀려오는 소리 **4.** 세척제, 화장수, 세제 **5.** 물기 많은 음식물 **6.** 부엌 설겆이대의 음식 찌기 **7.** [배 지나간 뒤의] 물결의 굽이침; [비행기가 지나간 뒤의] 기류의 소용돌이 **8.** [금속 따위의] 얇은 도금박(箔) **9.** [흐르는 물에 밀려온] 개흙, 침전물

—*adj.* (*U.S.*) washable. ¶*a* ~ *dress.* —[形] 《美》 세탁이 잘 되는

wash·a·ble [wɑ́ʃəbl, wɔ́:ʃ- / wɔ́ʃ-] *adj.* that can be washed. ¶~ *cloth* / *a* ~ *ink spot.*① —[形] 세탁할 수 있는, 세탁이 잘 되는 ¶①빨아서 지울 수 있는 잉크 얼룩

wash·ba·sin [wɑ́ʃbèisn, wɔ́:ʃ- / wɔ́ʃ-] *n.* [C] (*Brit.*) a washbowl. —[名] 《英》 세면기, 세수 대야

wash·board [wɑ́ʃbɔ̀:rd, wɔ́(:)ʃ- / wɔ́ʃbɔ̀:d] *n.* [C] a board with ridges used for rubbing the dirt out of clothes. —[名] 빨래판

wash·bowl [wɑ́ʃbòul, wɔ́:ʃ- / wɔ́ʃ-] *n.* [C] (*U.S.*) a bowl or basin for washing one's hands and face, etc. —[名] 《美》 세수 대야

wash·cloth [wɑ́ʃklɔ̀:θ, wɔ́:ʃklɑ̀θ / wɔ́ʃklɔ̀(:)θ] *n.* [C] (*U.S.*) a small cloth for washing the face and body. —[名] 《美》 세수 수건

washed-out [wɑ́ʃtáut, wɔ́(:)ʃt- / wɔ́ʃ-] *adj.* **1.** faded during washing. **2.** (*colloq.*) quite tired; tiredlooking. —[形] **1.** 빨아서 바랜, 색이 바랜 **2.** 《口》 지친, 기진맥진한; 기운없는

wash·er [wɑ́ʃər, wɔ́:ʃ- / wɔ́ʃə] *n.* [C] **1.** a person who washes. **2.** a washing machine. **3.** a flat ring of metal, leather, rubber, etc. used to give tightness to a joint. ⇒fig. —[名] **1.** 씻는 사람, 세탁인 **2.** 세탁기 **3.** [쇠·가죽·고무로 된] 나사받이

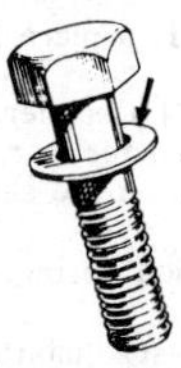
[washer 3.]

wash·er·man [wɑ́ʃərmən, wɔ́:ʃ- / wɔ́ʃə-] *n.* [C] (pl. **-men** [-mən]) a person who washes for money. —[名] 세탁업자, 세탁인

wash·er·wom·an [wɑ́ʃərwùmən / wɔ́ʃə-] *n.* [C] (pl. **-wom·en** [-wìmin]) a woman who washes for money. —[名] [직업적인] 세탁부(婦)

* **wash·ing** [wɑ́ʃiŋ, wɔ́:ʃ- / wɔ́ʃ-] *n.* 《*collectively*》 clothes to be washed or in process of being washed. —[名] 세탁물, 빨랫감

washing machine [ˊ-- -ˊ-] *n.* a machine for washing clothes, etc. —[名] 세탁기

⁑ **Wash·ing·ton** [wɑ́ʃiŋtən, wɔ́:ʃ- / wɔ́ʃ-] *n.* **1.** the capital of the United States. **2.** a State in the northwestern part of the United States. ⇒[N.B.] **3. George** (1732–99) the first President of the United States. —[名] **1.** 와싱턴시(미국의 수도) **2.** 와싱턴주 [N.B.] Wash.로 줄여 씀. 주도(州都)는 Olympia **3.** 와싱턴(미국의 초대 대통령)

wash·stand [wɑ́ʃstæ̀nd, wɔ́:ʃ- / wɔ́ʃ-] *n.* [C] a stand for supporting a basin, pitcher, etc. for washing the hands and face. —[名] 세면대

wash·tub [wɑ́ʃtʌ̀b, wɔ́:ʃ- / wɔ́ʃ-] *n.* [C] a large wooden tub for washing clothes. —[名] 빨래 통(나무로 만든 큰 것)

⁑ **was·n't** [wɑ́znt / wɔ́z-] =was not.

wasp [wasp / wɔsp] *n.* [C] a flying insect with a powerful sting and a slender body of black and yellow stripes. —[名] 말벌, 나나니벌

wasp·ish [wɑ́spiʃ / wɔ́sp-] *adj.* **1.** like a wasp. **2.** easily angered; bad-tempered; irritable. **3.** full of ill-will. —[形] **1.** 말벌 같은 **2.** 성 잘 내는, 성깔진 **3.** 심술궂은

was·sail [wɑ́səl, wɑ́seil / wɔ́seil] *n.* [C] (*archaic*) a drinking party. —*vi.* **1.** take part in a wassail. **2.** drink to the health of someone. —[名] 《古》 술잔치, 주연 —[自] **1.** 주연에 참석하다 **2.** 축배를 들다

wast [wɑst, wəst / wɔst, wəst] *vi.* (*archaic*) =were.

wast·age [wéistidʒ] *n.* **1.** [U] loss by use; decay; waste. **2.** [C] the amount wasted. —[名] **1.** 소모, 손실 **2.** 소모량(액)

⁑ **waste** [weist] *adj.* **1.** not cultivated; not inhabited; wild; barren. ¶~ *land* / *lie* ~.① **2.** of no value; useless; more than being necessary. ¶~ *paper.* —[形] **1.** 미개의; 사람이 살지 않는; 황폐한; 불모의 ¶①황폐해 있다 **2.** 무가치한; 쓸모없는; 남아도는, 여분의

lay waste, destroy completely; make (something) desolate. [熟] …을 황폐시키다

—*vt.* **1.** spend uselessly or carelessly. ¶*Don't* ~ *your* —[他] **1.** …을 낭비하다 **2.** …을 황폐시

wastebasket [1289] **water**

time and money. **2.** destroy; ruin. ¶*World War III will ~ the whole world.*③ **3.** wear away gradually; make (someone or something) weak or feeble. ¶*His body was wasted by a long illness.* —*vi.* **1.** become weak; lose strength. ¶*He wasted away through a long illness.* **2.** be used up gradually; be used badly.
—*n.* **1.** Ⓤ Ⓒ the act of wasting; the state of being wasted. ¶*a ~ of time.* **2.** Ⓒ a piece of waste land; an unbroken expanse. ¶*a ~ of waters*④ / *There are many wastes in this country.* **3.** Ⓤ gradual destruction or decay. **4.** Ⓤ waste material. ⌈spoiled.⌉
run (or *go*) *to waste,* be wasted; become useless or
waste·bas·ket [wéistbæ̀skit / -bɑ̀:s-] *n.* Ⓒ a basket for wastepaper; a wastepaper basket.
waste·ful [wéistf(u)l] *adj.* using or spending more than is necessary. ¶*He is ~ of his parents' money.*
waste·ful·ly [wéistfuli] *adv.* in a wasteful manner.
waste·ful·ness [wéistf(u)lnis] *n.* Ⓤ the act of causing waste; the state of being wasteful. ⌈as useless.⌉
waste·pa·per [wéistpèipər] *n.* Ⓤ paper thrown away
waste pipe [ˊˊ] *n.* a pipe to carry off waste water.
: **watch** [wɑtʃ / wɔtʃ] *n.* **1.** Ⓒ a small clock for the pocket or the wrist. ¶*a ~ and chain.*① **2.** Ⓤ the act of keeping the eyes on something; guard. ¶*be on the ~ for*② / *keep ~.*③ **3.** Ⓒ an act of keeping awake for some special purpose. ¶*a mother's ~ over a sick baby.* **4.** Ⓒ a person or a group of persons on guard, esp. at night. ¶*place a ~.* **5.** Ⓒ (*Nautical*) a period (usu. four hours) of duty of a ship's crew; a part (usu. a half) of a crew on duty during such a period. ¶*be on (off) ~.*④
—*vi.* **1.** look carefully; observe; be careful; wait carefully. (*~ to do* something; *~ for* something) ¶*He watched to see what would happen.*⑤ / *I watched for the chance to kill him.* **2.** keep awake; look at someone or something carefully, without sleeping. ¶*~ with a sick person.* **3.** keep guard. ¶*I asked him to ~.* —*vt.* **1.** look at; observe; direct the attention upon (someone or something). (*~ someone or something do* (or *doing*); *~ how* (or *what,* etc.)...) ¶*~ television* / *~ the house burning* / *I watched the girl cry.* / *He watched how the flower opened.* **2.** guard; tend. ¶*She watched the poor old man.* **3.** wait carefully for (someone or something). ¶*~ one's time.*⑥
1) *watch out,* be careful; look out.
2) *watch over,* guard; tend.
watch·dog [wɑ́tʃdɔ̀:g, -dɑ̀g / wɔ́tʃdɔ̀g] *n.* Ⓒ a dog for guarding a building, property, etc.
watch·er [wɑ́tʃər / wɔ́tʃə] *n.* Ⓒ a person who watches.
watch·ful [wɑ́tʃf(u)l / wɔ́tʃf-] *adj.* watching carefully; alert; wide-awake.
watch glass [ˊˊ] *n.* Ⓒ (*Brit.*) a cover of glass for a watch. (cf. *U. S.* crystal) ⌈to a watch.⌉
watch guard [ˊˊ] *n.* Ⓒ a chain, a cord, etc. attached
watch·mak·er [wɑ́tʃmèikər / wɔ́tʃmèikə] *n.* Ⓒ a person who makes or repairs watches. ⌈guard.⌉
watch·man [wɑ́tʃmən / wɔ́tʃ-] *n.* Ⓒ (pl. *-men* [-mən]) a
watch·tow·er [wɑ́tʃtàuər / wɔ́tʃtàuə] *n.* Ⓒ a tower from which a guard keeps watch.
watch·word [wɑ́tʃwə̀:rd / wɔ́tʃwə̀:d] *n.* Ⓒ **1.** a secret word known only among a limited number of people; a password. **2.** a motto; a slogan.
: **wa·ter** [wɔ́:tər, +*U.S.* wɑ́t-] *n.* **1.** Ⓤ the commonest liquid; the liquid which fills rivers, seas, etc. ¶*hot ~*① / *hard* (*soft*) *~*② / *sea ~*③ / *No living things can live with-*

키다 ¶③제 3 차 세계대전은 전(全)세계를 황폐시킬 것이다 **3.** …을 소모시키다, 쇠약케 하다
—ⓐ 써서 점점 없어지다(줄다), 낭비되다

—ⓝ **1.** 닒ᆼ비 **2.** 황무지; 광활(廣闊) ¶④광막한 대해 **3.** 소모, 쇠약 **4.** 페물, 쓰레기

᷾ 페물이 되다, 못쓰게(쓸모없게) 되다
—ⓝ 휴지통

—ⓐ 낭비하는, 비경제적인, 헛된

—ⓐ 비경제적으로, 헛되이
—ⓝ 낭비, 불경제

—ⓝ 휴지, 파지
—ⓝ 배수관(排水管)

—ⓝ **1.** 회중(손목)시계 ¶①사슬 달린 회중시계 **2.** 주의, 조심, 경계; 망보기, 감시 ¶②…을 경계하다/③망보다, 감시하다 **3.** 불침번 **4.** 파수꾼, 감시인 **5.** (海) 당직 시간; 당직자 ¶④당직(비번)이다

—ⓐ **1.** 지켜보다, 주목(주시)하다; 대기하다, 기다리다 ¶⑤그는 무슨 일이 일어날까 하고 가만히 지켜보았다 **2.** 자지 않고 있다, 불침번을 서다 **3.** 망보다, 감시하다 —ⓥ **1.** …을 보다, 지켜보다, …에 주의하다 **2.** …을 망보다(감시하다); …을 간호하다 **3.** …을 기다리다 ¶⑥시기를 엿보다

᷾ 1) …을 조심하다; …을 경계하다 2) …을 돌보다(보살피다), 간호하다
—ⓝ 집 지키는 개

—ⓝ 파수꾼, 감시인; 간호인
—ⓐ 주의깊은; 조심하는; 마음을 놓지 않는, 방심않는
—ⓝ (英) 회중시계의 유리 뚜껑

—ⓝ 회중시계의 사슬(줄)
—ⓝ 시계 제조(수리)인

—ⓝ 경비원, 감시원; 야경꾼
—ⓝ 망루(望樓), 망대

—ⓝ **1.** 암호, 군호 **2.** 표어, 모토

—ⓝ **1.** 물 ¶①뜨거운 물/②경(연)수/③바닷물, 해수 **2.** 강[물], 호수[물], 바다[물] ¶④한국 수역/⑤해상에서/⑥

out ~. **2.** [C] 《often *pl.*》 a body of water, as a river, lake, sea, etc. ¶*the Korean waters*④ | *on the waters*⑤ | *cross the waters.*⑥ **3.** [U] the state of the tide. ¶*high* (*low*) ~⑦ **4.** [U] the water used for drinking. ¶*I want a glass of* ~. **5.** 《*pl.*》 the water which contains minerals. ¶*table waters*⑧ | *drink* (or *take*) *the waters.*⑨ **6.** [U] a liquid that contains water. ¶*rose* ~⑩ | *soda* ~. **7.** [U] the liquid like water which comes out from the body of animals. ¶*make* (or *pass*) ~⑪ | *Water runs from her eyes.*⑫

바다를 건너다 **3.** 조수 ¶⑦만(간)조 **4.** 음료수 **5.** 광천수(鑛泉水) ¶⑧식탁용 광천수/⑨광천수를 마시다; 온천을 하[여 병을 고치]다 **6.** 용액 ¶⑩장미향수 **7.** [눈물·땀·오줌 따위] 분비액 ¶⑪오줌을 누다/⑫눈물이 그녀의 눈에서 흘러내린다

1) ***above water,*** out of difficulty; free from debt.
2) ***by water,*** by boat or ship.
3) ***get into hot water,*** get into trouble.
4) ***hold water,*** ⓐ contain water safely. ⓑ be logical.
5) ***in deep water[s],*** in great difficulty.
6) ***in smooth water,*** in the state of no longer having difficulties.
7) ***like water,*** freely; generously; wastefully. ¶*She spends her money like water.*⑬
8) ***of the first water,*** of the finest quality.
9) ***throw cold water on,*** discourage.
10) ***written in water,*** soon forgotten.

[熟] 1)곤란을 벗어나; 빚지지 않고 2)수로(水路)로 3)곤경에 빠지다 4)ⓐ물이 새지 않다 ⓑ이치에 맞다 5)곤경에 빠져서 6)곤경을 넘기고, 순조롭게 7)아낌없이, 물같이 헤프게 ¶⑬그녀는 돈을 물쓰듯 한다 8)일류의, 최고급품의 9)…에 찬물을 끼얹다, 흥을 깨뜨리다, 트집을 잡다 10)곧 잊혀지는; 덧없는

—*vt.* **1.** give water to or pour water on (something); make (something) wet with water. ¶~ *flowers* | ~ *the road.*⑭ **2.** supply (something) with water; give water to a horse, etc. to drink. ¶~ *the horses* | *Seoul was not well watered last summer.*⑮ **3.** add water to and so weaken (something). 《~ *down* something》 ¶~ *milk.* —*vi.* **1.** (of an animal) drink water. **2.** (of a ship) take in a supply of water. **3.** fill with tears. ¶*His eyes watered in the smoke.*
water down, add water to; weaken the force or effect of (something).

—[他] **1.** …에 물을 주다, 물을 뿌리다(끼얹다); …을 적시다 ¶⑭길에 물을 뿌리다 **2.** …에 급수(給水)하다; …에게 물을 먹이다 ¶⑮작년 여름 서울은 물기근이었다 **3.** …을 물로 묽게 하다; …에 물을 타다 —[自] **1.** 물을 마시다(먹다) **2.** 급수 받다 **3.** 눈물이 나오다(그득하다)
[熟] …을 물로 묽게 하다; …의 효과를 약하게 하다

water bird [´- `] *n.* a bird that swims in or lives near water, such as a duck or a swan. —[名] 물새

water bottle [´- `-] *n.* a bottle for holding water. —[名] 물병; 수통

water buffalo [´- `--] *n.* (pl. **-loes, -los** or *collectively* **-lo**) a buffalo of Asia and the Philippines. —[名] 물소

water clock [´- `] *n.* an instrument to measure time by the fall or flow of water. —[名] 물시계

water closet [´- `-] *n.* a toilet flushed by water. —[名] [수세식] 변소

wa·ter·col·or [wɔ́:tərkʌ̀lər, +*U.S.* wάt-] *n.* **1.** 《usu. *pl.*》 a paint which is mixed with water instead of oil. **2.** [C] a painting or picture made with water colors. —[名] **1.** [수채화용] 그림물감 **2.** 수채화

wa·ter·course [wɔ́:tərkɔ̀:rs, +*U.S.* wάt-] *n.* [C] **1.** a stream of water; a river. **2.** a channel for water. —[名] **1.** 물줄기, 강 **2.** 수로(水路); 운하

***wa·ter·fall** [wɔ́:tərfɔ̀:l, +*U.S.* wάt-] *n.* [C] a stream of water falling from a high place; a cataract. —[名] 폭포

wa·ter·fowl [wɔ́:tərfàul, +*U.S.* wάt-] *n.* [C] (pl. **-fowls** or *collectively* **-fowl**) a water bird; 《*collectively*》 water birds. —[名] 물새

water front [´- `] *n.* the part of a city near a river, lake, or sea. —[名] 강(호수·바다)가에 접한 거리, 해안(강변)통

water gauge [´- `] *n.* a device for showing the height of water in a tank, boiler, etc. —[名] 수면계(水面計)

water glass [´- `] *n.* **1.** a drinking glass; a tumbler. **2.** an instrument with a glass bottom for looking at things in water. —[名] **1.** 물 마시는 컵 **2.** [물 속을 들여다보는] 상자 모양의 수중 안경

wa·ter·ing place [wɔ́:təriŋpleis, +*U.S.* wάt-] *n.* **1.** a place where animals or persons come to drink water. **2.** a seaside or lakeside place for recreation. **3.** a place with springs for recreation. —[名] **1.** 물 마시는 곳 **2.** 해변(호숫가)의 휴양지 **3.** 온천장

water lily [´- `-] *n.* a water plant with broad, flat, floating leaves and beautiful, sweet-smelling flowers. —[名] 수련(睡蓮)

water line [´- `] *n.* the line along which the surface of the water touches the side of a ship. —[名] 흘수선(吃水線)

wa·ter-logged [wɔ́:tərlɔ̀gd, +*U.S.* wάt-, -lὰgd] *adj.* com- —[形] [목재 따위가] 물이 밴, 물에 잠

pletely soaked with water; so filled with water as to be unable or almost unable to float. — 진; [배 따위가] 침수한

Wa·ter·loo [wɔ́:tərlù:, wát- / wɔ̀:təlú:] *n.* the village in Belgium where Napoleon was defeated. — [名] 나폴레옹이 패전한 벨기에의 한 마을

water main [ˊ– ˋ] *n.* a main pipe for carrying water. — [名] 수도 본관(本管)

wa·ter·man [wɔ́:tərmən, +*U.S.* wát-] *n.* [C] (pl. **-men** [-mən]) a boatman; an oarsman. — [名] 나룻배 사공; 노젓는 사람

wa·ter·mark [wɔ́:tərmà:rk, +*U.S.* wát-] *n.* [C] **1.** a faintly visible design made in some kinds of paper. **2.** a mark which shows the height of the rise of water. — [名] **1.** 종이의 내비치는 무늬 **2.** 수위표(水位標)

wa·ter·mel·on [wɔ́:tərmèlən, +*U.S.* wát-] *n.* [C] a large melon with a juicy, pink, or red pulp; the plant on which this melon grows. — [名] 수박

water mill [ˊ– ˋ] *n.* a mill whose machinery is driven by water. — [名] 물방아, 물레방아

water plant [ˊ– ˋ] *n.* any plant which grows in water; an aquatic plant. — [名] 수초(水草)

water polo [ˊ– ˋ–] *n.* a ball game played in a swimming pool by two teams of seven swimmers each. — [名] 수구(水球)

water power [ˊ– ˋ–] *n.* power produced by flowing or falling water; hydraulic power. — [名] 수력(水力)

wa·ter·proof [wɔ́:tərprù:f, +*U.S.* wát-] *adj.* not allowing water to pass through. **—*n.*** (pl. **-proofs**) [U] waterproof cloth; [C] a raincoat. — [形] 방수의, 내수(耐水)의 —[名] 방수포, 방수복

wa·ter·shed [wɔ́:tərʃéd, +*U.S.* wát-] *n.* [C] **1.** a dividing line between areas drained by different river systems. **2.** a region drained by a single river system. — [名] **1.** 분수계(分水界)(선) **2.** 유역(流域)

wa·ter·side [wɔ́:tərsàid, +*U.S.* wát-] *n.* [C] the land along a river, a lake, the sea, etc. — [名] 물가(강변·호숫가·바닷가 따위)

water ski [wɔ́:tərskì:, +*U.S.* wát-] *n.* a kind of ski used to glide over water. — [名] 수상 스키이

water·skin [wɔ́:tərskìn, +*U.S.* wát-] *n.* [C] a skin bag for carrying water. — [名] 물을 길어 나르는 가죽 부대

wa·ter·spout [wɔ́:tərspàut, +*U.S.* wát-] *n.* [C] **1.** a whirlwind over the sea. **2.** a pipe for carrying away rain water. — [名] **1.** [물의] 소용돌이, 물기둥 **2.** 홈통 구멍, 배수구

water table [ˊ– ˋ–] *n.* the level below which the ground is saturated with water. — [名] 지하수면

wa·ter·tight [wɔ́:tərtàit, +*U.S.* wát-] *adj.* **1.** so closely made that water cannot pass in. **2.** (of a plan, etc.) so clear that there cannot be any misunderstanding. — [形] **1.** 물이 새지 않는, 방수의 **2.** [계획·의론 따위가] 조금도 빈틈(허술한 데)이 없는, 물샐틈 없는, 완벽한

water tower [ˊ– ˋ–] *n.* a tower for holding water; an apparatus for extinguishing a fire in a tall building by throwing water. — [名] 급수탑, 방수탑(放水塔); 소방용 분수탑

water vapor [ˊ– ˋ–] *n.* water in a gaseous state. — [名] [비등점 이하의] 수증기

wa·ter·way [wɔ́:tərwèi, +*U.S.* wát-] *n.* [C] **1.** a river, a canal, etc. where a ship can go. **2.** a channel for water. — [名] **1.** 수로(水路), 항로 **2.** 운하

water wheel [ˊ– ˋ–] *n.* a wheel turned by water. — [名] 물레바퀴, 수차(水車)

wa·ter·works [wɔ́:tərwə̀:rks, +*U.S.* wát-] *n. pl.* ⦅often used as *sing.*⦆ a system for supplying a city or town with water. — [名] 수도, 급수 설비

wa·ter·worn [wɔ́:tərwɔ̀:rn, +*U.S.* wát-] *adj.* made smooth or worn by the action of water. — [形] 물의 작용으로 닳아서 동글동글해진

wa·ter·y [wɔ́:t(ə)ri, +*U.S.* wát-] *adj.* **1.** of or like water. **2.** (of food) containing too much water. ¶~ *soup.* **3.** tearful. ¶~ *eyes.* **4.** (of a color) weak; pale. ¶*a* ~ *green.* **5.** (of the weather) likely to rain. — [形] **1.** 물의, 물 같은 **2.** 물기가 많은, 싱거운, 맛없는 **3.** 눈물어린, 눈물이 글썽한 **4.** [빛깔이] 연한, 흐릿한 **5.** 비가 올 듯한

watt [wat / wɔt] *n.* [C] a unit of electric power. — [名] 와트(전력의 단위)

watt·hour [wátàuər / wɔ́tàuə] *n.* [C] the unit of electric energy, equal to one watt maintained for one hour. — [名] 와트시(時)

wat·tle [wátl / wɔ́t-] *n.* [C] **1.** a framework of twigs and sticks woven together. **2.** a fence made of interwoven twigs and sticks. **3.** the folds of loose red flesh hanging from the throat of a bird such as a turkey. **4.** the acacia in Australia. **—*vt.*** make (a fence, framework, etc.) by interweaving twigs and sticks. — [名] **1.** 나뭇가지를 엮어서 만든 세공 **2.** 울바자 **3.** [칠면조 따위의] 늘어진 군살 **4.** 오스트레일리아산 아카시아나무 —[他] 나뭇가지를 엮어서[울바자·광주리 따위]를 만들다

⁑**wave** [weiv] *n.* [C] **1.** an up and down and rolling movement on the surface of water. ¶*The waves will run* — [名] **1.** 파도, 물결 ¶①물결이 높아질 것이다 **2.** 바다 **3.** 물결 같은 움직임, 굽

*high.*① **2.** 《*the* ~》 (*poetic*) the sea. **3.** a movement like a wave. ¶*attack in waves*② | *a ~ of prosperity*③ | *a cold ~.*④ **4.** an increase or a rush of feelings. ¶*a ~ of enthusiasm.*⑤ **5.** a curve like a wave in the hair, in cloth, etc; a curl. ¶*She has a beautiful ~ in her hair.* **6.** a wave-like movement of electric current, sound, heat, etc. ¶*short* (*long, medium*) *waves* | *sound waves.* **7.** an act of moving up and down, etc.; a sign made with a wave of the hand, a flag, etc.

이침 ¶②파도처럼 밀려오다/③호경기(好景氣)의 물결/④한파(寒波) 4.[감정]의 고조 ¶⑤열광의 고조 5.[머리털·천의] 웨이브, 물결 모양 6.파동, 전파, 음파 7.흔들기; [손 따위를 흔드는] 신호

—*vi.* **1.** move up and down and roll; swing. ¶*A flag waves in the breeze.*⑥ **2.** have curves or waves. ¶*The road waves along the valley.* | *His hair waves naturally.* **3.** make a signal by waving a hand, etc. ¶*~ in farewell.*⑦ **—*vt.*** **1.** cause (something) to move like a wave; swing. ¶*~ a handkerchief.* **2.** make a signal to (someone) by waving a hand, etc.; express (something) by waving a hand, etc. ¶*~ someone on* (*away* or *off*)⑧ | *~ a goodbye to someone.* **3.** give a curving form to (something). ¶*I have my hair waved.*⑨
wave aside, set aside (objections, etc.).

—[自] 1.물결치다, 흔들리다 ¶⑥기가 바람에 펄럭이다 2.굽이치다, 물결무늬를 이루다 3.손 따위를 흔들어 신호하다 ¶⑦손을 흔들어 작별 인사를 하다 —[他] 1.…을 흔들어 움직이다;…을 흔들리게 하다 2.손 따위를 흔들어 …에게 신호하다,…을 손으로 신호하다 ¶⑧손을 흔들어 전진하게 하다(쫓아버리다) 3.…에 물결 무늬를 내다 ¶⑨내 머리를 웨이브로 하게 했다
[熟] …을 물리치다

wave length [ˊ ˋ] *n.* (*Physics*) the distance from a point on one wave to the corresponding point of the next.

—[名] 《理》 파장(波長)

wa·ver** [wéivər] *vi.* **1.** tremble; flicker. **2.** begin to give way; fail. ¶*The line of troops wavered.* **3.** hesitate; be undecided. **—*n. [U] hesitation.

—[自] 1.흔들리다, 펄럭이다 2.무너지기 시작하다; 굴복하다, 패배하다 3.망설이다, 결심이 흔들리다 —[名] 망설임

wav·y [wéivi] *adj.* (**wav·i·er, wav·i·est**) **1.** moving like waves. **2.** having waves. ¶*~ hair.*

—[形] 1.흔들리며 움직이는, 파동하는 2.물결 모양의, 굽이치는, 기복이 있는

‡wax¹ [wæks] *n.* [U] **1.** a sticky, yellowish substance of a honeycomb. **2.** any mineral or vegetable substance like this. **—*vt.*** cover or polish (floors, furniture, etc.) with wax (*n.* 2). **—*adj.*** made of wax.

—[名] 1.밀랍(蜜蠟) 2.밀, 밀 같은 물질(파라핀 따위); 목랍 —[他] …에 밀을 바르다(먹이다);…을 밀로 닦다 —[形] 밀랍으로 만든

wax² [wæks] *vi.* (**waxed, waxed** or *poetic* **wax·en, wax·ing**) **1.** (esp. of the moon) grow bigger or greater; increase in number or size. ↔wane **2.** gradually become. ¶*The party waxed gay.*
wax and wane, (esp. of the moon) grow bigger and then smaller.

—[自] 1.[달 따위가] 차다, 점점 커지다; 늘다 2.차차 …이 되다
[熟] [달이] 찼다이울었다하다

waxed [wækst] *adj.* covered or polished by wax.

—[形] 밀랍을 바른; 밀랍으로 닦은

wax·en [wæks(ə)n] *adj.* **1.** of wax; made of wax. **2.** like wax; smooth, pale or soft like wax.

—[形] 1.밀랍의, 밀랍으로 만든 2.밀랍 모양의, 밀랍 같은

wax·work [wækswəːrk] *n.* [U] **1.** statues made of wax. **2.** 《*pl.*, used as *sing.*》 an exhibition of such statues.

—[名] 1.밀랍 세공, 밀랍 인형 2.밀랍 세공의 진열[장]

wax·y [wæksi] *adj.* (**wax·i·er, wax·i·est**) [made] of wax; like wax.

—[形] 밀랍의, 밀랍으로 만든; 밀랍 같은

‡way¹ [wei] *n.* [C] **1.** a means used to go from one place to another; a path; a street. ¶*a rough ~* | *lead the ~*① | *make one's ~*② | *lose the* (or *one's*) *~*③ | *keep* (or *hold*) *one's ~*④ | (*proverb*) *The longest ~ round is the shortest ~ home.*⑤ **2.** travel or movement along a route. ¶*on the* (or *one's*) *~ home*⑥ | *go on one's ~.*⑦ **3.** distance. ¶*a long ~ off*⑧ | *He has come quite a ~.*⑨ **4.** direction. ¶*this ~ and that*⑩ | *Step this ~, please.* **5.** a method; a manner; a means. ¶*in this ~*⑪ | *to one's ~ of thinking*⑫ | *There is no two ways about it.*⑬ | *This is the ~ of doing it* (or *to do it*). | *The ~ I looked around, they must have thought I was crazy.* **6.** a habit or custom; a style. ¶*He has a ~ of thinking things over.*⑭ | *This is the ~ of the world.* **7.** [U] progress; advance. ¶*make one's* [*own*] *~*⑮ | *make one's ~ home*⑯ | *fight* (*push*) *one's ~*⑰ | *force one's ~.*⑱ **8.** respect; point. ¶*in a* (or *one*) *~.*⑲ **9.** a state; a condition. ¶*be in a bad ~*⑳ | *live in a small ~.*㉑ **10.** [U] one's wish or will. ¶*want one's ~*㉒ | *have* (or *get*) *one's ~.*㉓ **11.** range or scope of experience; occupation. ¶*be in the*

—[名] 1.길, 도로, 통로 ¶①앞장서서 길을 안내하다/②나아가다/③길을 잃다/④길을 잃지 않다/⑤《俚》급할수록 돌아가라 2.가는 도중, 노중(路中) ¶⑥귀로에/⑦여행을 계속하다 3.거리, 노정(路程) ¶⑧훨씬 멀리에/⑨그는 원로에 찾아왔다 4.방향 ¶⑩이리저리로 5.방법, 방식, 수단 ¶⑪이렇게, 이런식으로/⑫…의 생각으로는/⑬물론 그렇다, 두말할 나위가 없다 6.버릇, 습관; 관습 ¶⑭그는 일을 끝까지 생각하는 버릇이 있다 7.진행, 진보 ¶⑮나아가다; 번영하다/⑯귀로에 오르다/⑰싸워서(밀어젖히고) 나아가다/⑱억지로 나아가다 8.[…의] 점(點) ¶⑲어느 점에서는; 다소, 얼마간 9.상태, 형편 ¶⑳형편이 좋지 않다, 신통치 않다/㉑조촐하게 살다 10.희망, 의사 ¶㉒자기 의사를 관철시키려고 하다/㉓뜻대로 하다, 제멋대로 하다 11.[경험의] 범위;

W

way 〔1293〕 **weakness**

bakery ~ / *Such things have never come in my ~.*²⁴
1) ***by the way***, ⓐ on the way. ⓑ incidentally.
2) ***by way of***, ⓐ through; via. ⓑ for the purpose of. ⓒ as a means of or as a method.
3) ***feel one's way***, proceed with great caution.
4) ***gather way***, (of a ship) gain speed.
5) ***get*** (or ***have***) ***one's*** [***own***] ***way***, get or do what one wants.
6) ***give way***, ⓐ break down. ⓑ withdraw; yield.
7) ***go out of the*** (or ***one's***) ***way***, ⓐ make a special effort. ⓑ lose one's way.
8) ***go one's own way***, act independently or as one wishes.
9) ***go*** [***one's***] ***way***, start; leave.
10) ***have it both ways***, benefit by each of two contrary possibilities.
11) ***lose way***, (of a ship) lose speed; slow down.
12) ***make the best of one's way***, go as fast as possible.
13) ***make way*** (=*clear* or *prepare the way*) ***for someone***.
14) ***out of the way***, ⓐ in a position to so as not to hinder. ⓑ not on the right or usual route.
15) ***pave the way*** (=*prepare*) ***for something***.
16) ***put someone out of the way***, kill someone.
17) ***see one's way clear***, find (something) to be possible.
18) ***stand in the way of*** (=*be an obstacle to*) *something*.
19) ***take one's way to***, go to.
20) ***under way***, moving; making progress.
21) ***ways and means***, devices and resources for doing something.

way² [wei] *adv.* (*U.S. colloq.*) away; far; much. ¶~ *down the road.*①

way·far·er [wéifɛ̀ərər] *n.* ⓒ a traveler, esp. on foot.
way·far·ing [wéifɛ̀əriŋ] *adj.* of a wayfarer; traveling.
—*n.* Ⓤ the act of traveling, esp. on foot.
way·laid [wèiléid] *v.* pt. and pp. of **waylay**.
way·lay [wèiléi] *vt.* (**-laid**) lie in wait for (someone) to rob, kill, etc. him; attack (someone) on a street, etc.
way·side [wéisàid] *n.* ⓒ the edge of a road or path. —*adj.* on or along the side of a road.
way·ward [wéiwərd] *adj.* **1.** disobedient. **2.** not steady; irregular.
way·ward·ness [wéiwərdnis] *n.* Ⓤ the quality or state of being wayward.
way·worn [wéiwɔ̀:rn] *adj.* tired with traveling.
w. c., W. C. water closet.

we [wi:] *pron.* (sing. **I**) **1.** the first person plural of the personal pronoun; the group of people including the speaker or writer. **2.** the pronoun used by an author, editor, king, etc. instead of I. ⇒N.B.

weak [wi:k] *adj.* **1.** not strong; lacking in bodily strength; easily broken under pressure or strain. ¶ *a ~ bridge* / *a ~ point* (or *side*)① / *a ~ heart* / *~ health* / *the weaker vessel.*② **2.** lacking in mental power, judgment, etc.; foolish. ¶ *~ compliance*③ / *a ~ mind*④ / *a ~ will.* **3.** not good at; lacking skill. ¶ *be ~ in English.* **4.** not containing the usual amount of the main element; watery. ¶ *~ tea.* **5.** lacking in power, force, etc.; not able to rule well. ¶ *a ~ king*⑤ / *a ~ law.*

weak·en [wí:k(ə)n] *vt.* make (someone or something) weak or less strong. —*vi.* become weak or less strong.
weak-kneed [wí:kní:d] *adj.* **1.** having weak knees. **2.** of a weak will; yielding easily.
weak·ling [wí:kliŋ] *n.* ⓒ a weak person. —*adj.* weak.
weak·ly [wí:kli] *adj.* (**-li·er, -li·est**) weak; sickly. —*adv.* in a weak manner.
weak-mind·ed [wí:kmáindid] *adj.* **1.** of or showing a weak mind; feeble-minded. **2.** lacking mental firmness.
weak·ness [wí:knis] *n.* **1.** Ⓤ the quality or state of being weak. **2.** ⓒ a weak point. **3.** ⓒ (*a ~*) a special

직업 ¶㉔그런 일을 여태껏 경험해 본 적이 없다

圏 1)ⓐ도중에 ⓑ그런데…, 그리고 참 … 2)ⓐ…을 지나서, …경유로 ⓑ…을 위해서, …하려고 ⓒ…으로서 3)길을 더듬어서 나아가다 4)속력을 내다 5)바라던 것을 얻다; 뜻대로 되다 6)ⓐ무너지다, 꺾이다, 깨지다 ⓑ물러가다, 후퇴하다; 양보하다 7)ⓐ일부러 …하다 ⓑ길을 잃다 8)자기 나름대로 행하다, 제멋대로 하다 9)출발하다, 떠나가다 10)양다리 걸치다 11)속력을 줄이다 12)될 수 있는 대로 빨리 가다 13)…을 위하여 길을 열어주다 14)ⓐ방해가 되지 않는 곳에 ⓑ상도(常道)를 벗어나서 15)…의 준비를 하다 16)[남]을 죽이다 17)…할 수 있을 것같이 생각되다 18)…의 방해가 되다 19)…으로 가다 20)진행 중인; 행해 중인 21)수단과 재원(財源)

—ⓐ 《美口》 저 멀리, 아득히; 훨씬 ¶ ① 그 길을 한참 간 곳에
—ⓝ 나그네, 도보 여행자
—ⓐ 나그네의; 도보 여행의 —ⓝ 도보 여행, 나그넷길

—ⓥ …을 숨어서 기다리다, 매복하다, 요격(邀擊)하다
—ⓝ 길가, 노변 —ⓐ 길가의, 노변의

—ⓐ 1. 말을 안 듣는, 제멋대로 하려고 하는, 외고집의 2. 변덕스러운; 불규칙한
—ⓝ 제멋대로 하기, 외고집; 변덕
—ⓐ 여행에 지친, 노독에 걸린

—ⓟ 1. 우리[들], 저희[들] 2. 필자; 짐(朕) N.B. editorial 'we', royal 'we'라 함

—ⓐ 1. 약한, 연약한, 허약한; 가냘픈 ¶①약점/②여자, 여성 2. 결단력 없는; 우둔한 ¶③마지못해 하는 승낙/④지능(低能) 3. 서투른; 졸렬한 4. 묽은, 멀건; 물기가 많은, 싱거운 5. 무력한; 지배력이 없는 ¶⑤무력한 왕

—ⓥ …을 약하게 하다, 무르게 하다, …의 힘을 빼다 —ⓥ 약해지다
—ⓐ 1. 무릎에 힘이 없는 2. 우유부단한, 의지가 약한; 쉽게 굴복하는
—ⓝ 허약한 사람, 약골 —ⓐ 약한
—ⓐ 약한, 병약한 —ⓐ 약하게, 가냘프게, 숫대없이
—ⓐ 1. 저능한 2. 마음이 약한, 우유부단한
—ⓝ 1. 약함, 역부족(力不足), 허약, 우유부단 2. 약점, 결점 3. 썩 좋아하는

liking. ¶*Girls have a ~ for sweets.* — 것, 사족을 못 쓰는 것

weal [wiːl] *n.* [U] well-being; happiness. ¶*in ~ and woe.*① — —[名] 복지, 복리, 행복 ¶①행복에나 재난에나

⁑wealth [welθ] *n.* **1.** [U] a large amount of money or property; riches. **2.** [C] 《usu. *sing*》 abundance of anything. ¶*a ~ of experience.* — —[名] 1. 부(富), 재산 2. [물건의] 풍부, 막대함

⁑wealth·y [wélθi] *adj.* (**wealth·i·er, wealth·i·est**) rich; abundant. — —[形] 부유한, 넉넉한, 풍부한, 많은

wean [wiːn] *vt.* **1.** accustom (a child or young animal) to take food different from its mother's milk. **2.** cause (someone) to turn away from a habit or an interest. 《~ someone *away* or *from*》 ¶*~ someone from drinking and smoking.*① — —[他] 1. …을 젖을 떼다, 이유(離乳)시키다 2. …을 서서히 떼어버리다, …와 관계를 끊게 하다 ¶①금주금연(禁酒禁煙)시키다

⁑weap·on [wépən] *n.* [C] anything used in fighting, such as swords, arrows, guns, teeth, horns, etc. — —[名] 무기, 병기

⁑wear [wɛər] *v.* (**wore, worn**) *vt.* **1.** have or put (something) on the body. ¶*~ a hat / ~ a pair of glasses / She always wears green.*① **2.** arrange (hair, etc.) in a special way. ¶*~ one's hair waved / ~ a mustache.*② **3.** (of looks) have or show. ¶*~ a smile / ~ a discontented look.* **4.** bear. ¶*~ one's honors.*③ **5.** damage or waste (something) by constant or hard use; bring (something) to a certain state by using it. ¶*I wore my coat to rags.* **6.** make (a hole, etc.) by rubbing, flowing, etc. ¶(*proverb*) *Constant dropping wears the stone.*④ **7.** tire or exhaust. —*vi.* **1.** become damaged or wasted by constant use; become exhausted. ¶*The cloth has worn thin.* **2.** endure continued use; last. ¶*~ well / This cloth wears for years.* **3.** come to a certain state. ¶*My hope wore thin.* **4.** (of time) pass away gradually.

—[他] 1. …을 몸에 걸치고 있다, 입고 있다, 신고 있다, 쓰고(끼고, 띠고) 있다 ¶①그녀는 항상 초록빛 옷을 입고 있다 2. [머리 따위]를 [어떤 모양으로] 기르고 있다 ¶②콧수염을 기르고 있다 3. [표정]을 나타내다 4. …을 마음에 간직하고 있다 ¶③명예를 유지하다 5. …을 닳게 하다, 써서 낡게 하다, …을 너무 써서 어떤 상태가 되게 하다 6. [마찰하거나 하여 구멍 따위]를 파다 ¶④《俚》물방울도 돌에 구멍을 판다 7. …을 피로케 하다 —[自] 1. 닳아 없어지다, 마멸되다; 지치다 2. 사용에 견디다, 오래 가다 3. [점점] …의 상태가 되다 4. [시간이] 점점 지나가다, 경과하다

1) ***wear away,*** ⓐ waste or become thin by use. ⓑ (of time) pass, spend.
2) ***wear down,*** ⓐ waste or become thin by use. ⓑ break down by constant attack.
3) ***wear off,*** ⓐ waste or become thin by use. ⓑ pass away gradually. ¶*Her toothache wore off at last.*
4) ***wear on,*** (of time) pass slowly and gradually.
5) ***wear out,*** ⓐ make or become useless by use. ⓑ tire out. ⓒ waste gradually.

[熟] 1)ⓐ…을 닳아 없애다(없어지다) ⓑ[시간이]지나다, [때]를 보내다 2)ⓑ…을 닳게 하다(닳다) ⓑ끈덕지게 버틴 끝에 이기다 3)ⓐ…을 닳려 없애다(없어지다) ⓑ…이 점점 없어지다 4)[때가] 서서히 지나다 5)ⓐ…을 닳아 떨어지[게 하]다 ⓑ…을 지치게 하다 ⓒ…을 점점 써서 없애다

—*n.* [U] **1.** the act of putting clothes on. ¶*clothes for everyday ~.*⑤ **2.** things worn on body; clothing. ¶*men's ~.* **3.** the fashion of dress. ¶*in general ~.*⑥ **4.** the ability to endure. ¶*There is plenty of ~ in your hat yet.*⑦ **5.** damage from use. ¶*~ and tear.*⑧ — —[名] 1. 착용 ¶⑤평상복(平常服) 2. 옷, 의복 3. [옷의] 유행 ¶⑥유행하여 4. 사용에 견디는 힘, 오래 감 ¶⑦너의 모자는 아직 상당히 오래 쓸 수 있다 5. 닳아서 없어짐, 마멸 ¶⑧마멸, 마손, 마모

***wea·ri·ly** [wíərili] *adv.* in an weary manner. — —[副] 지쳐서, 싫증이 나서

wea·ri·ness [wíərinis] *n.* [U] the weary state or feeling. — —[名] 피로, 권태, 싫증

wea·ri·some [wíərisəm] *adj.* causing fatigue; tedious. — —[形] 지치게 하는, 물리게(싫증나게) 하는

⁑wea·ry [wíəri] *adj.* (**-ri·er, -ri·est**) **1.** tired. ¶*be ~ after hard work.* **2.** causing tiredness. ¶*a ~ journey.* —*vt.* make (someone) weary or bored. —*vi.* become weary; be bored. — —[形] 1. 지친, 피로한 2. 싫증나게 하는, 물리게 하는, 지루한 —[他] …을 지치게(지루하게) 하다 —[自] 지치다; 싫증(진력)나다

wea·sel [wíːzl] *n.* [C] a small, active animal which feeds on birds, eggs, mice, etc. — —[名] 족제비

⁑weath·er [wéðər] *n.* [U] **1.** the general condition of a place at a certain time with respect to sun, wind, temperature, cloudiness, etc. ¶*good (bad, fine, wet, hot, windy) ~ / in all weathers*① */ make good (bad) ~*② */ ~ permitting*③ */ How is the ~?* **2.** windy, rainy, or stormy weather. ¶*under stress of ~*④ */ for protection against the ~*⑤ */ We were exposed to the ~.*⑥

—[名] 1. 날씨, 일기, 기상 ¶①어떠한 날씨에도/②좋은(궂은) 날씨를 만나다/③날씨가 좋으면 2. 비바람, 폭풍우, 험악한 날씨 ¶④폭풍우(악천후) 때문에/⑤풍우에 대비하여/⑥우리는 비바람을 만났다

under the weather, (*colloq.*) ⓐ not feeling well; ill. ⓑ somewhat drunk. — [熟] 《口》ⓐ몸이 불편하여, 병이 나서 ⓑ술에 좀 취하여

—*vt.* **1.** expose (something) to the weather. ¶*~ timber.*⑦ **2.** wear away, discolor, etc. (something) by such exposure. **3.** slope (a roof, etc.) in order to throw off rain, etc. **4.** come through (a storm or something difficult) successfully. ¶*~ a storm (a crisis).* —*vi.* be affected or discolored by exposure to the weather.

—[他] 1. …을 비바람·햇볕에 맞게 하다 ¶⑦목재를 볕에 말리다 2. …을 풍화(風化)시키다 3. [비 따위가 흘러내리도록 지붕 따위]를 경사지게 하다 4. [폭풍우·곤란]을 극복하다 —[自] 풍화하다

W

—*adj.* windward.
—[形] 바람 불어오는 쪽의

weath·er-beat·en [wéðərbìːtn] *adj.* **1.** worn by the sun, wind, and rain. **2.** (of skin) bearing marks which are due to exposure to the sun.
—[形] 1. 풍우에 시달린(손상된) 2. [살갗이] 햇볕에 탄

Weather Bureau [ˊ- ˋ-] *n.* the bureau of the United States Department of Commerce responsible for recording and forecasting the weather.
—[名] 기상국(氣象局)

weath·er·cock [wéðərkàk / wéðəkɔ̀k] *n.* [C] a device, esp. in the shape of a cock, to show the direction of the wind. ⇒fig.
—[名] 닭 모양의 풍향계(風向計)

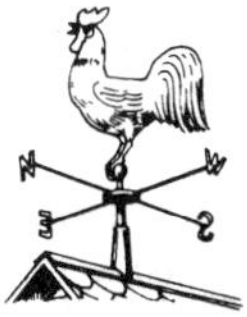
[weathercock]

weather forecast [ˊ- ˋ-] *n.* a statement about the weather for the future.
—[名] 일기예보

weath·er·glass [wéðərglæ̀s / wéðəglɑ̀ːs] *n.* [C] an instrument for showing changes in the weather; a barometer.
—[名] 청우계; 기압계

weath·er·ing [wéðəriŋ] *n.* [U] destructive force of air, frost, snow, water, etc. esp. on rock.
—[名] 풍화[작용]

weath·er·man [wéðərmæ̀n] *n.* [C] (pl. **-men** [-mèn]) (*colloq.*) a person who records and forecasts the weather.
—[名] 《口》 일기 예보자, 관상대 직원

weather map [ˊ- ˋ] *n.* a map in which various weather conditions at a particular time are shown.
—[名] 천기도, 기상도

weather vane [ˊ- ˋ] *n.* =weathercock.

⁑weave [wiːv] *v.* (**wove, wov·en** or **wove**) *vt.* **1.** form (threads or strips) into a fabric, etc.; make (cloth) out of threads. **2.** unite or entwine (details, incidents, etc.) into a story, poem, etc. —*vi.* **1.** make something by interlacing. **2.** move from side to side or in and out.
—[他] 1. [피륙]을 짜다, 뜨다 2. …을 꾸미다, 엮어 만들다 —[自] 1. 뜨개질하다; 피륙을 짜다 2. 누비듯이 나아가다
—*n.* [C] a method, manner, or pattern of weaving.
—[名] 짜는 법, 뜨는(뜨개질하는) 법

weav·er [wíːvər] *n.* [C] a person who weaves.
—[名] 짜는 사람, 뜨개질하는 사람

***web** [web] *n.* [C] **1.** a network of threads made by a spider. **2.** a whole piece of cloth woven at one time. **3.** the skin joining the toes of ducks, beavers, etc.
—[名] 1. 거미줄(집) 2. 직물, 피륙; 한 베틀분의 천 3. 물갈퀴, 오리발

webbed [webd] *adj.* **1.** having a web; formed like a web. **2.** having fingers or toes joined by webs (*n.* 3).
—[形] 1. 거미줄을 친; 거미줄 모양의 2. 물갈퀴가 있는

web·foot [wébfùt] *n.* [C] (pl. **-feet**) **1.** a foot whose toes are joined by a web. **2.** a bird or animal with webfeet.
—[名] 1. 물갈퀴 발 2. 물갈퀴 발을 가진 새(짐승)

wed [wed] *vt.* (**wed·ded, wed·ded** or **wed, wed·ding**) **1.** marry. **2.** join; unite. —*vi.* marry.
—[他] 1. …와 결혼하다 2. …을 결합하다 —[自] 결혼하다
be wedded to one's work, be extremely devoted to one's work.
[熟] 일에 몰두(전렴)하다

we'd [wiːd] =we would; we had; we should.

Wed. Wednesday.

wed·ded [wédid] *adj.* **1.** married. **2.** devoted.
—[形] 1. 결혼한 2. 몰두한

⁑wed·ding [wédiŋ] *n.* [C] **1.** a marriage ceremony. **2.** a marriage anniversary. ¶*silver* ~① / *golden* ~.②
—[名] 1. 결혼식 2. 결혼 기념일 ¶①은혼식/②금혼식

wedding cake [ˊ- ˋ] *n.* a large cake for a wedding ceremony.
—[名] 웨딩 케이크(결혼식용 과자)

wedding march [ˊ- ˋ] *n.* march played during a wedding ceremony.
—[名] 결혼 행진곡

wedding ring [ˊ- ˋ] *n.* a ring which is put on a bride's finger at a wedding ceremony.
—[名] 결혼 반지

***wedge** [wedʒ] *n.* [C] **1.** a piece of wood or metal, thick at one side and thin at the other, used for splitting a log, a rock, etc. ⇒fig. **2.** anything like a wedge.
—[名] 1. 쐐기 2. 쐐기 모양의 물건

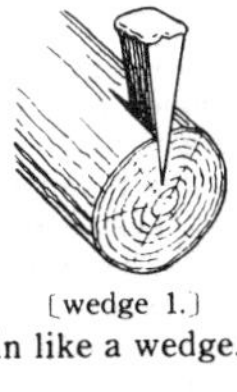
[wedge 1.]

the thin end of the wedge, a small change that is likely to lead to a further, serious change.
[熟] 보기에는 사소하나 장차 중대한 결과를 가져오는 일
—*vt.* **1.** split (something) by the use of a wedge. **2.** use a wedge for fastening (something). **3.** force (something) in like a wedge. ¶*wedge oneself in.*①
—[他] 1. …을 쐐기로 쪼개다 2. …을 쐐기로 고정시키다 3. …을 [쐐기처럼] 박아넣다 ¶①…에 비집고 들어가다

wed·lock [wédlɑk / -lɔk] *n.* [U] the state of being married; marriage; married life.
—[名] 혼인, 결혼생활

⁑Wednes·day [wénzdi, -dei] *n.* the fourth day of the week. ⇒[N.B.]
—[名] 수요일 [N.B.] W., Wed.로 줄여 씀

W

* **wee** [wi:] *adj.* (**we·er, we·est**) very small; tiny.
—[形] 아주 작은

* **weed** [wi:d] *n.* [C] **1.** ⟪usu. *pl.*⟫ a wild, useless plant which grows without cultivation. **2.** ⟪*the* ~⟫ (*colloq.*) tobacco. —*vt.* **1.** remove weeds out of (a garden, etc.). **2.** remove (weeds). **3.** take out (something useless or harmful). —*vi.* remove weeds.
—[名] 1. 잡초 2. ⟪口⟫ 담배
—[他] 1. …의 잡초를 뽑다, 제초하다 2. [잡초]를 없애다 3. …을 제거하다, 일소하다 —[自] 잡초를 뽑다(없애다)

weed·er [wí:dər] *n.* [C] a person who weeds; a tool for weeding.
—[名] 풀 뽑는 사람, 제초기

weed·y [wí:di] *adj.* (**weed·i·er, weed·i·est**) **1.** full of weeds. **2.** growing quickly like weeds. **3.** thin and tall like weeds.
—[形] 1. 잡초가 많은(우거진) 2. 잡초처럼 빨리 자라는 3. 호리호리한

* **week** [wi:k] *n.* [C] **1.** a period of seven days. **2.** the six working days of the week.
1) ***week after week,*** each week.
2) ***week in, week out,*** week after week.
3) ***a week of Sundays; a week of weeks,*** (*colloq.*) a long time.
—[名] 1. 주, 1주간(7일간) 2. 일요일 이외의 6일간, 취업일
[熟] 1)매주 2)매주매주, 주마다 3)⟪口⟫ 오랫동안

week·day [wí:kdèi] *n.* [C] any day of the week except Sunday.
—[名] 주일(週日), 일요일 이외의 날, 평일, 취업일

* **week·end** [wí:kènd, ⸗⸗] *n.* [C] the time from Friday night or Saturday afternoon to Monday morning. —*adj.* of a weekend. —*vi.* spend a weekend.
—[名] 주말 —[形] 주말의 —[自] 주말을 보내다

* **week·ly** [wí:kli] *adj.* **1.** of a week; every week; lasting a week. **2.** done once a week. —*adv.* every week; once a week. —*n.* [C] (pl. **-lies**) ⟪usu. *pl.*⟫ a newspaper or magazine published once a week.
—[形] 1. 1주간의, 매주의; 1주일분의 2. 1주일에 한 번의 —[副] 매주, 1주일에 한 번씩, 매주마다 —[名] 주간신문(잡지)

* **weep** [wi:p] *v.* (**wept**) *vi.* **1.** express grief, sorrow or other strong emotion by shedding tears; shed tears; cry. **2.** let fall drops of water or another liquid; drip. **3.** send forth water or another liquid. —*vt.* **1.** weep for (someone or something). **2.** shed (tears). **3.** send forth (water or another liquid). **4.** bring (someone or something) to a desired condition by weeping.
1) ***weep oneself out,*** weep as much as one wants to.
2) ***weep out,*** talk while crying.
—[自] 1. 울다, 눈물을 흘리다 2. [물방울 따위를] 떨어뜨리다 3. [물방울 따위를] 스며나오게 하다, 나오다 —[他] 1. …을 울며 슬퍼하다 2. [눈물]을 흘리다 3. [물 따위]를 스며나오게 하다, 뿜어내다 4. 울어서 …시키다(하게 하다)
[熟] 1)실컷 울다 2)울면서 말하다

wee·vil [wí:v(i)l] *n.* [C] a small beetle with a hard shell which destroys cotton, grain, fruit, etc.
—[名] 바구미과(科)의 곤충

weft [weft] *n.* [C] the threads that cross from side across the warp in a piece of cloth, etc.
—[名] [피륙의] 씨실

* **weigh** [wei] *vt.* **1.** determine the weight of (something) by means of a scale or balance; balance (something) in the hand in order to estimate its weight. ⟪~ something *in* or *on*⟫ ¶ ~ *oneself on the scales*① | *I weighed the stone in my hands.* | ~ *eggs on a scale.* **2.** consider carefully; consider (something) in order to make a choice. ¶ ~ *one's words*② | ~ *one plan against another.*③ **3.** press down; burden. ⟪~ something *down*⟫. ¶*Fruits* ~ *the branch down.* | *He is weighed down with cares.*④ **4.** (*Nautical*) lift (an anchor). ¶ ~ *anchor.* —*vi.* **1.** have a certain weight. ¶*He weighs 60 pounds.* | *How much do you* ~? **2.** have importance. ⟪~ *with* someone⟫. ¶*His opinion doesn't* ~ *with me.*⑤ **3.** be a burden. ⟪~ *on* or *upon* one's mind, etc.⟫ ¶*Many troubles weighed on* (or *upon*) *his mind.*⑥
1) ***weigh down,*** ⓐ cause (something) to bend under a load. ⓑ bring (someone) under emotional stress.
2) ***weigh in,*** weigh (a boxer) before a fight.
3) ***weigh out,*** measure out (something) by weighing.
—[他] 1. …을 저울에 달다, …의 무게를 재다; 손으로 …의 무게를 달아 보다 ¶①저울로 체중을 재다 2. …을 숙고하다; [비교]고찰하다 ¶②잘 생각해서 말하다/③계획을 비교 고찰하다 3. …을 압박하다, 내리누르다 ¶④그는 걱정거리로 짓눌려 있다 4. [닻]을 올리다 —[自] 1. 무게가 [얼마] 나가다 2. 무게를 지니다, 중요시되다 ¶⑤그의 의견 따위는 별것 아니다 3. 압박하다 ¶⑥여러가지 성가신 일들이 그의 마음을 짓누르고 있었다
[熟] 1)ⓐ…을 무게로 내려앉게 하다 ⓑ…을 짓누르다, 내리누르다 2)[권투선수 등]을 시합 전에 체중검사하다 3)…을 저울로 달아서 나누다

* **weight** [weit] *n.* **1.** [U] the amount of heaviness; the amount something or someone weighs. ¶*sell by* ~ | *under the* ~ *of*① | *gain* (*lose*) ~② | *give short* ~③ | *pull one's* ~④ | *What is your* ~? **2.** [U] the force with which a body is pulled toward the center of the earth; gravity. **3.** [C] ⟪often *a* ~ or *the* ~⟫ a burden. ¶*a* ~ *of care* | *a* ~ *on one's mind* | *the* ~ *of years*⑤ | *That is a great* ~ *off my mind.*⑥ **4.** [U] influence; importance. ¶*a man*
—[名] 1. 무게, 중량; 체중 ¶①…의 무게에 눌려/②체중이 늘다(줄다)/③무게를 속이다/④자기의 역할(소임)을 다하다 2. 중력 3. 무거운 짐, 부담 ¶⑤나이의 부담/⑥그것으로 마음의 부담이 많이 줄어든다 4. 영향력; 중요함 ¶⑦그의 의견은 한국에서 중요시되고 있다/⑧…에게 중요하다 5. 무거운 것; 저

W

of ~ / *of no* ~ / *His opinion carries* ~ *in Korea.*⑦/ *have* ~ *with*⑧ / *give* ~ *to.* **5.** [C] a heavy object; a piece of metal used on a balance or scale in weighing. ¶*an ounce* ~.⑨ **6.** a system of units for expressing weight; a unit of mass or weight. ¶*a table of weights and measures.*⑩

울추; 문진(文鎭) ¶⑨1 온스의 저울추 6. 무게를 재는 단위; 형법(衡法) ¶⑩ 도량형법

1) ***pull*** *one's* ***weight,*** do one's part or share of work. 2) ***put on weight,*** grow fat; become heavier.

[熟] 1)자기의 소임을 다하다 2)체중이 늘다, 살찌다

—*vt.* **1.** add weight to (something); make (something) heavy or heavier. 《~ something *with* stone, etc.》 **2.** burden. ¶*He weights himself with care.*

—[他] 1. …에 무게를 더하다; …을 무겁게 하다 2. …에 무거운 짐(부담)을 지우다; …을 압박하다(괴롭히다)

weight·y [wéiti] *adj.* (**weight·i·er, weight·i·est**) **1.** heavy. **2.** important; influential; convincing. ¶*a* ~ *argument.* **3.** burdensome. ¶~ *responsibility.*

—[形] 1. 무거운 2. 유력한, 남을 수긍시키는 힘을 지닌 3. 견디기 어려운, 고생스러운

weir [wiər] *n.* [C] **1.** a dam in a river. **2.** a fence set in a river to catch fish.

—[名] 1. [강의] 둑, 댐 2. [고기잡이용] 어살

weird [wiərd] *adj.* **1.** of destiny or fate. **2.** strange; mysterious. **3.** (*colloq.*) curious; funny; odd.

—[形] 1. 운명의, 숙명의 2. 불가사의한 3. 《口》 기묘한, 별난

⁑ **wel·come** [wélkəm] *adj.* **1.** (of a person) gladly received. ¶*a* ~ *guest* / *make someone* ~① / *You are* ~.② ⇒[N.B.] **2.** permitted gladly to use or enjoy. 《~ *to;* ~ *to do*》 ¶*You are* ~ *to any book in my library.* / *You are* ~ *to pick the flowers.* **3.** (of events, circumstances, etc.) agreeable. ¶~ *news* / *as* ~ *as flowers in May.*

—[形] 1. [사람이] 환영받는 ¶①남을 환대하나/②잘 오셨읍니다 [N.B.] 미국에서는 사례의 말에 응답하여 「별 말씀을」의 뜻 2. 마음대로 쓸 수 있는; 마음대로 …해도 좋은 3. 반가운, 기쁜

—*n.* [C] a kindly greeting or reception. ¶*a hearty* ~ / *bid someone* ~ / *say* ~ *to someone* / *wear out one's* ~.③

—[名] 환영, 환영의 말(인사) ¶③귀찮게 방문하여(오래 앉아 있어서) 미움을 받다

—*vt.* say welcome to (someone); receive (someone or something) with pleasure. ¶~ *one's criticism* / *He was warmly welcomed.*

—[他] …을 환영하다; 반가이 맞아 들이다; 기쁘게 받다

—*interj.* an expression of kind greeting. ¶*Welcome to Japan!* / *Welcome home!*

—[感] 어서 오십시오, 잘 오셨읍니다

weld [weld] *vt.* **1.** join (two pieces of metal) by heating their edges to the melting point and then pressing them together. **2.** unite closely. **—*vi.*** be welded; be able to be welded. **—*n.*** **1.** [U] the act of welding; the state of being welded. **2.** [C] a welded joint.

—[他] 1. [금속]을 용접하다 2. …을 밀착(결합)시키다 —[自] 용접하다, 용접되다 —[名] 1. 용접 2. 용접점, 접합점

* **wel·fare** [wélfɛ̀ər] *n.* [U] the state of having good health, happiness, prosperity, etc.

—[名] 행복, 복지, 번영

welfare state [ˊ-ˋ] *n.* a state in which the government aims to insure the welfare of its people through National Insurance, free medical treatment, old-age pensions, etc.

—[名] 복지국가

welfare work [ˊ-ˋ] *n.* an organized effort made for the welfare of a community or group.

—[名] 복지(후생) 사업

⁑ **well**[1] [wel] *n.* [C] **1.** a deep hole made in the ground to get oil, water, etc. ¶*an oil* ~. **2.** a natural spring or fountain of water. **3.** a source of much knowledge, etc. ¶*My father is a* ~ *of information.*① **4.** something like a well in shape or use; a stairwell.

—[名] 1. 우물 2. 샘 3. [지식 따위의] 원천, 근원 ¶①나의 아버지는 지식의 원천이다 4. 우물(샘) 모양의 오목한 곳; 층계의 뚫린 공간

—*vi.* come forth; spring. ¶*Tears welled* [*up*] *from* (or *in*) *her eyes.*

—[自] 샘솟다, 용솟음쳐 나오다; 분출하다

⁑ **well**[2] [wel] *adv.* (**bet·ter, best**) **1.** in a desirable, satisfactory manner. ¶*Things are going* ~. **2.** in a good, proper, or friendly manner. ¶*He spoke* ~ *of you.* / *You did* ~ *to refuse.*① **3.** skillfully; excellently. ¶*speak English* ~ / *This is* ~ *said.*② / *Well done!*③ **4.** 《*may* ~》 with reason; in justice; probably. ¶*You may* ~ *say so.*④ / *It may* ~ *be true.*⑤ **5.** fully; thoroughly; clearly. ¶*shake* ~ *before opening* / *Think* ~ *before you act.* / *You know* ~ *what I mean.* **6.** to a considerable degree or extent. ¶*That man is* ~ *past sixty.*⑥ / *My study is* ~ *advanced.* **7.** closely; personally. ¶*I know him* ~. **8.** in a successful manner; richly. ¶*do oneself* ~⑦ / *They lived* ~ *here.*

—[副] 1. 잘, 바람직하게, 만족하게 2. 정당하게, 알맞게, 적절히; 친절히 ¶①거절하기 잘 했다 3. 솜씨있게; 훌륭히 ¶②암 그렇지, 옳은 말이다/③잘했다! 4. 일리가 있어; 지당하게; 아마 ¶④네가 그렇게 말하는 것도 무리가 아니다/⑤그것은 아마 사실일걸 5. 충분히; 분명히, 똑똑히 6. 꽤, 상당히 ¶⑥저 사람은 60이 훨씬 넘었다 7. 친하게, 가깝게 8. 유복하게, 부유하게 ¶⑦유복하게 지내다

1) ***as well,*** ⓐ in addition; besides. ⓑ equally.

[熟] 1)ⓐ…도 또; 게다가 ⓑ마찬가지로

W

2) ***as well as***, ⓐ in addition to. ¶*He gave me clothes as ~ as money.* ⓑ equally as. ¶*I know him as ~ as I know myself.*
3) ***do well*** (=*be wise*) ***to*** *do.*
4) ***may as well*** (=*had better*) *do.* ¶*We may as ~ go at once.*
5) ***stand well with*** (=*please*) *someone.*

2)ⓐ…도 또 ⓑ…와 만찬가지로, …와 꼭같이 3)…하는 것이 좋다 4)…하는 편이 좋다 5)[남]의 마음에 들다

—*adj.* (**bet·ter, best**) ⦅as *predicative*⦆ **1.** in good health; sound. ¶*look ~ / a ~ man.*⑧ ⇒[N.B.] / *I am not feeling very ~ today.* **2.** in a good condition. ¶*All's ~ [with us]. / It is all very ~, but…*⑨ **3.** proper; suitable; fortunate. ¶*He is ~ enough as a teacher. / It is just as ~ to be careful.*⑩ / *It is ~ that you came.*

—[形] 1.건강한, 튼튼한 ¶⑧몸이 튼튼한 사람 [N.B.] 미식 용법 2.더할 나위 없는 ¶⑨그것은 아주 더할 나위 없이 좋지만… 3.적당한; 알맞은 ¶⑩주의하는 것이 좋다

—*interj.* **1.** ⦅expressing *surprise, relief, expectation, etc.*⦆ ¶*Well, to be sure!*⑪ / *Well, then?* **2.** used to continue one's speech. ¶*Well, as I was saying, …*

—[感] 1.어머나!, 저런!, 나 원!, 그럼 ¶⑪어머나, 놀랐네! 2.그래서, 그리고, 그런데

***we'll** [wi:l] =we shall; we will.

well-advised [wélədváizd] *adj.* thoughtful; careful; wise.
—[形] 사려(분별) 있는, 신중한; 현명한

well-ap·point·ed [wéləpɔ́intid] *adj.* with very good equipment or furnishings.
—[形] 준비가 잘 갖추어진, 설비가 좋은

well-bal·anced [wélbǽlənst] *adj.* **1.** properly balanced. **2.** with common sense; sensible.
—[形] 1.균형이 잘 잡힌 2.제정신의; 상식이 있는

well-be·haved [wélbihéivd] *adj.* having or showing good manners; behaving well.
—[形] 품행이 단정한, 행실이 좋은

well-be·ing [wélbí:iŋ] *n.* [U] health and happiness; welfare.
—[名] 행복, 복지, 복리

well·born [wélbɔ́:rn] *adj.* born of a good family.
—[形] 태생(가문)이 좋은

well-bred [wélbréd] *adj.* **1.** showing good breeding in manners; polite. **2.** (of animals) of good stock or birth.
—[形] 1.좋은 가문에서 자란, 예절 바른 2.혈통이 좋은, 좋은 품종의

well-con·duct·ed [wélkəndʌ́ktid] *adj.* having good manners.
—[形] 행실이 좋은, 예절 바른

well-con·nect·ed [wélkənéktid] *adj.* having good or important relatives.
—[形] 집안이 좋은, 연줄이 좋은

well-de·fined [wéldifáind] *adj.* clearly stated or described.
—[形] 윤곽이 뚜렷한; 명확하게 정의를 내린

well-dis·posed [wéldispóuzd] *adj.* **1.** rightly or suitably placed. **2.** having a favorable or kind nature.
—[形] 1.적절히 배치(배열)한 2.마음씨가 고운

well-fa·vored [wélféivərd] *adj.* having good looks; attractive; beautiful.
—[形] 잘 생긴, 예쁜, 미모의

well-found·ed [wélfáundid] *adj.* based on facts or good reasons; not imaginative.
—[形] 근거가 충분한

well-ground·ed [wélgráundid] *adj.* **1.** with a good knowledge of the basic principles of a subject. **2.** based on facts or good reasons.
—[形] 1.기본 교육(훈련)을 받은 2.근거가 충분한

well·head [wélhèd] *n.* [C] a source of water; a fountainhead; a source.
—[名] 수원(水源), 샘; 원천, 근원

well-in·formed [wélinfɔ́:rmd] *adj.* with wide knowledge and information about various subjects.
—[形] 견문이 넓은, 아는 것이 많은

well-in·ten·tioned [wélintén∫(ə)nd] *adj.* coming from a good will or good intentions.
—[形] 선의의, 선의로 한

well-kept [wélképt] *adj.* kept with good care.
—[形] 잘 간수된, 손질이 잘된

well-knit [wélnít] *adj.* **1.** (of the body) firmly or strongly made. **2.** carefully or closely joined or related.
—[形] 1.골격이 잘 짜인, 건강한 2.튼튼히 결합된

⁑**well-known** [wélnóun] *adj.* **1.** widely known; famous. **2.** familiar.
—[形] 1.유명한, 잘 알려진 2.친한

well-man·nered [wélmǽnərd] *adj.* having good manners; polite.
—[形] 예절 바른, 얌전한, 점잖은

well-mean·ing [wélmí:niŋ] *adj.* having good intentions.
—[形] 선의의, 호의에서 한

well-meant [wélmént] *adj.* said or done with good intentions.
—[形] 선의로 한

well-nigh [wélnái] *adv.* very nearly; almost.
—[副] 거의

well-off [wélɔ́:f / -ɔ́(:)f] *adj.* in good or favorable conditions; rich; wealthy. ↔badly-off ⇒[usage]
—[形] 유복한, 잘 사는 [usage] 주로 서술적으로 씀

well-read [wélréd] *adj.* having wide knowledge through reading.
—[形] 많이 읽은, 박식한

well-reg·u·lat·ed [wélrégjulèitid] *adj.* in good order.
—[形] 잘 정돈된, 규칙이 잘 선

well-round·ed [wélráundid] *adj.* well-balanced.
—[形] 균형이 잘 잡힌

well-spo·ken [wélspóuk(ə)n] *adj.* **1.** speaking fittingly and pleasingly in a refined manner. **2.** properly or aptly spoken.
—[形] 1.말을 잘 하는, 말씨가 점잖은(세련된) 2.용어가 적절한

W

well-spring [wélspriŋ] *n.* ⓒ **1.** the source of a stream; a fountainhead. **2.** the source of an abundant supply of anything; a source.
—名 1. 수원(水源), 샘 2. 자원, 원천

well-timed [wéltáimd] *adj.* timely.
—形 시기가 좋은, 때를 잘 맞춘

well-to-do [wéltədú:] *adj.* fairly rich; prosperous.
—形 아무 부족함이 없는, 유복한

well-turned [wéltə́:rnd] *adj.* (of a phrase, etc.) expressed to the point; graceful.
—形 교묘히 (적절히) 표현된

well-wish·er [wélwìʃər] *n.* ⓒ a person who wishes the happiness of another person or persons.
—名 남의 행복을 비는 사람, 호의를 보이는 사람

well-worn [wélwɔ́:rn] *adj.* **1.** much used. **2.** stale.
—形 1. 써서 낡은 2. 진부한

Welsh [welʃ, +U.S. weltʃ] *n.* **1.** the people of Wales. **2.** the language spoken in Wales. —*adj.* of Wales or Welsh. [-mən]) a person of Wales.
—名 1. 웨일즈 사람 2. 웨일즈 말 — 形 웨일즈[사람·말]의

Welsh·man [wélʃmən, +U.S. wéltʃ-] *n.* ⓒ (pl. **-men**)
—名 웨일즈 사람

wel·ter [wéltər] *vi.* **1.** roll about. **2.** be soaked or bathed in mud, dirty water, etc. —*n.* Ⓤ **1.** (of waves) the act of rolling. **2.** confusion.
—自 1. 뒹굴다, 구르다, 굴러다니다 2. [수렁·진창 따위에] 빠지다, 잠기다
—名 1. [파도 따위의] 굽이침 2. 혼란

wel·ter·weight [wéltərwèit] *n.* ⓒ a boxer or wrestler having a weight between that of a lightweight and a middleweight.
—名 웰터급 선수

wen [wen] *n.* ⓒ a harmless growth on the skin.
—名 [머리 따위의] 종기, 혹

wench [wentʃ] *n.* ⓒ a girl or a young woman; a country girl. [—*vt.* direct; continue.]
—名 소녀, 처녀; 시골 처녀

wend [wend] *v.* (**wended** or *archaic* **went**) *vi.* go; travel.
—自 가다, 전진하다 —他 [걸음]을 향하게 하다, …을 속행하다

‡went [went] *v.* pt. of **go**.

‡wept [wept] *v.* pt. and pp. of **weep**.

‡were [wə:r, wər] *v.*, *auxil. v.* pt. of **are**.
  1) *as it were,* so to speak.
  2) *were it not for,* without.
  3) *were to,* if…should.
—⑩⑩ are의 과거형
熟 1)즉, 말하자면 2)만약 …이 없다면 3)만약 …이라면

‡we're [wiər] =we are.

‡were·n't [wə:rnt] =were not.

wert [wə:rt] (*archaic*) (used with *thou*) =were.

‡west [west] *n.* (usu. *the* ~) **1.** one of the main points of the compass; the direction of the sunset. **2.** the area or section to the west. **3.** (*the W-*) the western part of the United States. [toward the west.] —*adj.* situated in the west; coming from the west; —*adv.* toward, in or from the west.
—名 1. 서쪽 2. 서양 3.《美》서부 지방
—形 서쪽에 있는, 서쪽에서 오는, 서향 (西向)의
—副 서쪽으로(에, 에서)

west·er·ly [wéstərli] *adj.*, *adv.* of, toward, in or from the west. ¶*a ~ wind*①／*The wind blows ~.*
—形副 서쪽의, 서쪽으로부터[의], 서쪽으로(의) ¶①서풍

‡west·ern [wéstərn] *adj.* of, toward, from or in the west.
—形 서쪽의, 서쪽으로부터의, 서부의

west·ern·i·za·tion [wèstərnizéiʃ(ə)n / -naiz-] *n.* Ⓤ the act of westernizing.
—名 서구화

west·ern·ize [wéstərnàiz] *vt.* introduce (the idea, habits or things) of Western civilization.
—他 [사고방식·습관]을 서구화하다

west·ern·most [wéstərnmòust] *adj.* farthest west.
—形 가장 서쪽의, 극서(極西)의

West·min·ster [wés(t)mìnstər] *n.* **1.** the part of London where Westminster Abbey and the Houses of Parliament are located. **2.** the Houses of Parliament.
  at Westminster, at the Diet.
—名 1. 웨스트민스터(런던 중앙의 자치구) 2. 영국 국회 의사당
熟《英》의회에서

West Virginia [-́-́-] *n.* the eastern state of the United States. ⇒N.B.
—名 미국 동부의 주 N.B. W.Va.로 줄여 씀. 수도는 Charleston

• **west·ward** [wéstwərd] *adj.*, *adv.* toward the west.
—形副 서쪽을 향한, 서향의; 서쪽으로

west·wards [wéstwərdz] *adv.* =westward.

‡wet [wet] *adj.* (**wet·ter, wet·test**) **1.** covered with water or another liquid; damp. ¶*The grass is ~ with dew.* **2.** (of paint, ink, etc.) not yet dry. ¶*Wet Paint.*② **3.** rainy. ¶*a ~ day*③ *~ or fine.*② [soaked.] *wet through; wet to the skin,* with one's clothes —*v.* (**wet·ted** or *U.S.* **wet, wet·ting**) *vt.* make (something) wet. ¶*~ the bed.*③ —*vi.* become wet. —*n.* **1.** Ⓤ (often *the* ~) liquid which wets something; water; wetness. **2.** (usu. *the* ~) rain or rainy
—形 1.젖은, 축축한, 습기있는 2.[페인트 따위가] 아직 마르지 않은 ¶①페인트 주의 3.비가 오는, 비가 많이 내리는 ¶②비가 오거나 맑게 개거나
熟 흠뻑(함빡) 젖어서
—他 …을 적시다, 젖게 하다 ¶③자다가 오줌 싸다 —自 젖다
—名 1.수분; 물; 습기, 물기 2.비, 우천(雨天)

weather. ¶*He walked in the ~ with her.*

weth·er [wéðər] *n.* [C] a male sheep.
—[名] [거세한] 양

* **we've** [wiːv] =we have.

whack [(h)wæk] *n.* [C] (*colloq.*) a sharp, noisy blow. —*vt.* strike (someone or something) with a sharp blow.
—[名] ⦅口⦆ 찰싹 때리기, 강타 —[他] …을 찰싹 때리다

whale[1] [(h)weil] *n.* [C] **1.** a huge animal which lives in the sea. **2.** a person or thing that is very large.
—[名] 1. 고래 2. 몹시 큰 사람(것)

a whale of, exceedingly much of.
[熟] 다수(다량)의

—*vi.* hunt whales.
—[自] 고래잡이에 종사하다

whale·boat [(h)wéilbòut] *n.* [C] a long and narrow row-boat formerly used in catching whales.
—[名] 노로 젓는 보우트의 일종

whale·bone [(h)wéilbòun] *n.* [C] **1.** an elastic, horny substance in the upper jaw of certain whales. **2.** a thing made of whalebone.
—[名] 1. 고래 수염(뼈) 2. 고래 수염으로 만든 물건

whal·er [(h)wéilər] *n.* [C] **1.** a person who hunts whales. **2.** a ship used in hunting whales.
—[名] 1. 포경자 2. 포경선

whang [(h)wæŋ] *vt.* strike (something) with a heavy blow. —*n.* [C] a sharp, heavy blow.
—[他] …을 찰싹 때리다, 강타하다
—[名] 찰싹 때리기, 강타

* **wharf** [(h)wɔːrf] *n.* (pl. **wharves** [(h)wɔːvz] or **wharfs**) a platform built on the shore where a ship can load or unload; a pier; a quay.
—[名] 부두, 선창

wharf·age [(h)wɔ́ːrfidʒ] *n.* [U] **1.** the use of a wharf. **2.** the charge made for the use of a wharf.
—[名] 1. 부두 사용 2. 부두 사용료

‡ **what** [(h)wɑt, (h)wʌt / (h)wɔt] *adj.* **1.** ⦅*interrogative adjective*⦆ which; which kind of, etc. ¶*What news?*① / *What ship is that?* / *I know ~ books you will need.* **2.** ⦅in *exclamations*⦆ how greatly, etc. ¶*What an idea!*② / *What a fine day* [*it is*]! / *What splendid ships* [*they are*]! **3.** ⦅*relative adjective*⦆ the … that; as much (many) as; any … that. ¶*I will give you ~ help I can.* / *He has sold ~ books he had.* / *Wear ~ clothes you please.*
—[形] 1. 무슨; 무엇이라고 하는; 어떠한 ¶①무슨 색다른 일이라도 있나? 2. 얼마나, 어쩌면 [그다지도] ¶②얼마나 멋진 생각인가! 3. [···하는] 바의 그; [···하는] 만큼의; [···하는] 어떠한

—*pron.* **1.** ⦅*interrogative pronoun*⦆ what thing; what things. ¶*What has happened?* / *What is his name?* / *What is he?*③ / *What is he like?* / *What is the price?* / *What about it?* / *I was at a loss ~ to do.* / *What do you say to…?*④ / *What next?*⑤ / *Well, ~ of it?*⑥ / *What though* (or *if*) *we are poor?*⑦ / *Do you know ~ it is?* **2.** ⦅in *exclamations*⦆ how much; what a large amount. ¶*What, do you really mean it?*⑧ **3.** ⦅*relative pronoun*⦆ that which; those which. ¶*I don't understand ~ he says.* / *What I say is true.* / *He lost his money and, ~ was worse, his life.*⑨ **4.** anything that; whatever. ¶*Do ~ you please.* **5.** the kind of thing or person that; such. ¶*She is not ~ she was.*
—[代] 1. 무엇, 어떤 것, 무슨 일 ¶③그는 무엇을 하는 사람인가?/④…하는 것이 어떤가?/⑤다음은 무엇인가?/⑥그래 그것이 어떻다는 말인가?/⑦설사 우리가 가난한들 어떠냐? 2. 무엇, 얼마나 ¶⑧뭐라고? 그것이 진심으로 하는 말인가? 3. [···하는] 바의 것(일) ¶⑨그는 돈을 잃은 데다가 더욱 불행하게도 목숨까지 잃었다 4. [···하는 것] 무엇이든지 5. ···와 같은 것(사람)

1) ***and what not,*** and other things of all sorts; and so forth.
2) ***I know what.,*** I have an idea.
3) ***no matter what…,*** in spite of anything that…
4) ***what for,*** why.
5) ***what if,*** what is (or will be) the result if…? ¶*What if we were to try?*⑩
6) ***what's what,*** (*colloq.*) the true state of affairs; truth.
[熟] 1)…기타 여러가지, …따위 2)옳지, 좋은 수가 있다 3)무엇이라 할지라도 4)왜, 무엇 때문에 5)…하면 어떨까요 ¶⑩해본다고 하면 어떻게 될까? 6) ⦅口⦆진실한 일(것); 진상

—*adv.* how; how much; partly. ¶*What is he better for it?* /*What he has suffered!*
—[副] 어떻게; 얼마만큼, 얼마나; 얼마간, 어느 정도

what with, because of. ¶*What with money and ~ with promises, I bribed him.*⑪
[熟] …의 이유로 ¶⑪돈이랑 약속으로 그를 매수했다

—*conj.* (*colloq.*) as much as; as many as. ¶*I helped him ~ I could.*⑫
—[接] ⦅口⦆ …만큼 ¶⑫할 수 있는 만큼은 도와주었다

but what, (*colloq.*) that … not. ¶*There was not a day but ~ it rained.*
[熟] …아니하는 [바의]

—*interj.* ⦅*as an exclamation* to show *surprise, anger, liking, etc.*⦆ ¶*What!, rain again?*
—[感] 뭐?, 뭣이라고!

what·e'er [(h)wɑtέər, (h)wʌt- / (h)wɔt-] *pron., adj.* (*poetic*) =whatever.

‡ **what·ev·er** [(h)wɑtévər, (h)wʌt- / (h)wɔtévə] *pron.* **1.** anything that. ¶*You shall have ~ you like.*① **2.** no matter what. ¶*Do it ~ happens.* / *Whatever it is, it is all right.* **3.** (*colloq.*) ⦅in *interrogative*, a strong form of
—[代] 1. 무엇이든지 ¶①네가 좋아하는 것은 무엇이라도 주겠다 2. 아무리 …이라도, 어떤 것이 …일지라도 3. 도대체 무엇이(을) ¶②도대체 무슨 일이 일

what》 what in the world. ¶ *Whatever has happened?*② —*adj.* **1.** of no matter what type, degree, etc. ¶ *Whatever orders he gives are obeyed.* / *You may have ~ help you want.* **2.** being what or who it may be. ¶ *Whatever task it may be, you should not slight it.*③ **3.** 《in *negative* or *interrogative*, used after *no* or *any*》 of any kind; at all. ¶ *There is no doubt ~.* / *Is there any chance ~?*

어났나? —[形] 1. 어떠한 …이라도 2. 설사(비록) …이라도 ¶③어떠한 일이라 할지라도 소홀히 해서는 안 된다 3. 아무런 …도, 추호의 …도

what·not [(h)wátnàt, (h)wʌ́t- / (h)wɔ́tnɔ̀t] *n.* [C] a set of shelves for books, small ornaments, etc. ⇒fig. —[名] 장식 선반

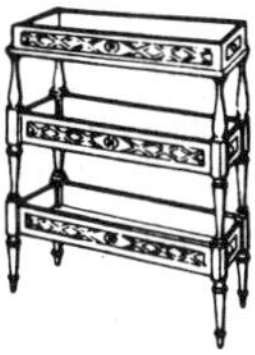
〔whatnot〕

***what's** [(h)wats, (h)wʌts / (h)wɔts] = what is.

what·so·e'er [(h)wàtsouέər, (h)wʌ̀t- / (h)wɔ̀t-] *pron., adj.* (*poetic*) =whatsoever.

***what·so·ev·er** [(h)wàtsouévər, (h)wʌ̀t- / (h)wɔ̀tsouévə] *pron., adj.* =whatever.

⁝wheat [(h)wi:t] *n.* [U] the grain from which flour is made; the plant on which this grain grows. —[名] 밀, 소맥(小麥)

wheat·en [(h)wí:tn] *adj.* made of wheat. —[形] 밀로 만든

whee·dle [(h)wí:dl] *vt.* **1.** influence (someone) by flattery; coax. **2.** get (something) by flattery. —[他] 1. …을 감언으로 꾀다 2. …을 감언으로 속이다, 속여서 빼앗다

⁝wheel [(h)wi:l] *n.* [C] **1.** a round frame turning on a central axis or axle. **2.** a vehicle or machine with a wheel or wheels as an essential part; (*colloq.*) a bicycle. ¶ *a steering ~*① / *a spinning ~.*② **3.** a round, movable part of a machine. **4.** a movement like the turning of a wheel. **5.** 《usu. *pl.*》 the propelling or driving force. —[名] 1. 바퀴, 차바퀴 2. 바퀴가 달린 것; 자전거 ¶①[배의] 타륜(舵輪)/②물레[바퀴] 3. 회전 부분 4. 윤전(輪轉), 선회 운동 5. 원동력, 추진력, 지배력

1) ***be at the wheel,*** ⓐ take the steering wheel. ⓑ be in control.
2) ***wheel of fortune,*** Fortune's wheel; the ups and downs of life; fate.
3) ***wheels within wheels,*** complicated circumstances.

[熟] 1)ⓐ타륜을 잡다 ⓑ지배력이 있다, 지배권을 잡고 있다 2)운명, 흥망성쇠 3)[연달아 일어나는] 복잡한 사정

—*vt.* **1.** carry or move (something) on wheels. **2.** cause (a line of soldiers) to turn around like a wheel. **3.** provide (something) with wheels. —*vi.* **1.** (of a line of soldiers) turn around like a wheel. **2.** (*colloq.*) ride a bicycle. —[他] 1. …을 차로 나르다 2. [대열]을 선회시키다 3. …에 차바퀴를 달다 —[自] 1. [대열이] 선회하다 2. 자전거에 타다

wheel·bar·row [(h)wí:lbæ̀rou] *n.* [C] a vehicle with one wheel and two handles pushed by hand. ⇒fig. —[名] 외바퀴 손수레

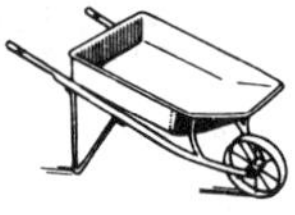
〔wheelbarrow〕

wheel chair [⌐ ⌐] *n.* a chair with wheels used by a person who can't walk. ⇒fig. —[名] 환자용 바퀴 달린 의자

wheeled [(h)wi:ld] *adj.* with wheels. —[形] 차바퀴가 달린

wheel·wright [(h)wí:lràit] *n.* [C] a person who makes or repairs vehicles. —[名] 수레바퀴[를 만드는] 목수

wheeze [(h)wi:z] *vi.* **1.** breathe hard and noisily. **2.** make a sound like this. —*vt.* say (something) with a wheezing sound. —*n.* [C] **1.** noisy breathing; the sound of this. **2.** (of jokes) old or familiar words. —[自] 1. [숨차서] 씨근거리다 2. 씩씩소리를 내다 —[他] 씨근거리며 …을 말하다 —[名] 1. 씩씩거리는 호흡; 씩씩하는 소리 2. 케케묵은 익살(재담)

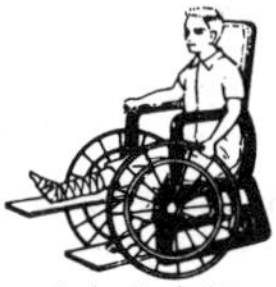
〔wheel chair〕

wheez·y [(h)wí:zi] *adj.* (**wheez·i·er, wheez·i·est**) making noises in breathing. —[形] 씩씩거리는

whelp [(h)welp] *n.* [C] **1.** the young of a dog, lion, fox, etc. **2.** an unpleasant, worthless young man. —*vt., vi.* (of animals) give birth (to young). —[名] 1. 강아지, [사자·여우·호랑이 따위의] 새끼 2. 개구장이, 버릇없이 자란 젊은이 —[他][自] [새끼]를 낳다

⁝when [(h)wen] *adj.* **1.** 《*interrogative adverb*》 at what time. ¶ *When did you see her last?* / *Tell me ~ to start.*① **2.** 《*relative adverb*》 at or on which; and then; just then. ¶ *I don't know the time ~ he will arrive.* / *We were about to start, ~ it began to rain.*② —[副] 1. 언제 ¶①언제 출발하려는지 말해 다오 2. […할] 때의; …하자 그때에 ¶②우리가 막 떠나려던 참에 비가 내리기 시작했다

W

whence [1302] **whet**

—*conj.* **1.** at, during, or after the time that. ¶ ~ due℗ / ~ speaking / ~ ready / You may leave ~ you have finished your task. **2.** every time that. ¶ She cries ~ you criticize her. / When he goes out, he takes his dog with him. **3.** although; though. ¶ She walks ~ she might ride. **4.** if. ¶ I'll give it to you ~ you say, 'Please.' **5.** being what time it may be. ¶ Die ~ you will, I will be with you.℗
—*pron.* what time; which time. ¶ Since ~ has she been ill? / Till ~ can you stay?℗ [where.℗]
—*n.* ((the ~)) the time or moment. ¶ [the] ~ and [the]

: **whence** [(h)wens] *adv.* **1.** from what place; from where. ↔*whither* **2.** from what reason ..why. **3.** from which.
—*pron.* **1.** where. **2.** from where.

: **when·ev·er** [(h)wenévər] *conj., adv.* **1.** at any time; at whatever time. **2.** when in the world.

: **where** [(h)ɛər] *adv.* **1.** ((*interrogative adverb*)) at or in what place; to or toward what place; in what respect; from what place or source. ¶ Where are you going? / Where do I come into the matter?℗ / Where do you live? / Where did you get your information? **2.** ((*relative adverb*)) in or to which; and there. ¶ This is the house ~ I was born. / He went to Paris, ~ he stayed for a week.℗
—*conj.* at, in, or to the place or situation in which. ¶ You may go ~ you like. / Leave the book ~ he can get it. / (*proverb*) Where there's a will, there's a way.℗
—*pron.* **1.** ((*interrogative pronoun*)) what place. ¶ Where are you going 'to]? / Where do you come from? **2.** ((*relative pronoun*)) the place at, in or to which. ¶ This is the place ~ he comes from. / This is ~ I live. / He came up to ~ we were.℗ [whens.℗]
—*n.* Ⓤ ((the ~)) the place. ¶ the wheres and the

where·a·bouts [(h)wέərəbàuts / -́-́] *adv.* at or near what place; where. —*n.* ((one's ~ or the ~, used as *sing.*)) the place where a person or thing is.

* **where·as** [(h)wɛərǽz] *conj.* **1.** considering that; since. **2.** on the contrary; while; but.

* **where·by** [(h)wɛərbái] *adv.* **1.** by what; why; how. ¶ Whereby did he escape? **2.** by which. ¶ This is the only way ~ we live.

: **where·fore** [(h)wέərfɔ̀ːr] *adv.* **1.** for what reason; why. ¶ Wherefore does she cry? **2.** for which reason. ¶ the reason ~ she cries.℗ —*n.* ((the ~s)) the reason.

where·in [(h)wɛərín] *adv.* **1.** in what; in what point. ¶ Wherein am I wrong?℗ **2.** in which. ¶ the room ~ she was murdered.

where·of [(h)wɛəráv, -ʌ́v / -ɔ́v] *adv.* **1.** of what. ¶ Whereof does he talk? **2.** of which; of whom. ¶ the matter ~ he talks.℗

where·on [(h)wɛərán, -ɔ́ːn / (h)wɛərɔ́n] *adv.* **1.** on what; to whom. ¶ Whereon do you rely? **2.** on which. ¶ a person ~ we depend.℗

where·to [(h)wɛərtúː] *adv.* **1.** to what place; where; for what. ¶ Whereto did you go yesterday? / Whereto are we to work?℗ **2.** to which. ¶ the address ~ the letter is to be sent.℗

where·up·on [(h)wɛərəpán, -pɔ́ːn / (h)wέərəpɔ́n] *adv.* at which; after which. ¶..., ~ we ate lunch.℗

: **wher·ev·er** [(h)wɛərévər] *adv.* **1.** in whatever place; to any place. **2.** (*colloq.*) where.

where·with [(h)wɛərwíð, +*U.S.* -wíθ] *adv.* **1.** with what. ¶ Wherewith did you make this? **2.** with which.

whet [(h)wet] *vt.* (**whet·ted, whet·ting**) **1.** sharpen. **2.**

cause (one's appetite, etc.) to increase. **—***n.* **1.** [U] the act of sharpening. **2.** [C] an appetizer, like wine.

⁝ **wheth·er** [(h)wéðər] *conj.* **1.** ((introducing *an indirect question*)) if it be the case or fact that… ⇒[usage] ¶*I don't know ~ it is true or not.*① | *I asked him ~ he would come.* | *I don't know ~ to laugh or to cry.* | *I wonder ~ he will go himself.* **2.** in either case that… ¶*You must do it ~ you like it or not.*

whether or no, in either case.

whet·stone [(h)wétstòun] *n.* [C] a stone for sharpening knives or blades.

whew [(h)wju: / hju:] *interj.* an exclamation of surprise, disgust, etc.

whey [(h)wei] *n.* [U] the thin, watery part of milk that is separated from the curds in making cheese.

⁝ **which** [(h)witʃ] *adj.* **1.** ((*interrogative adjective*)) being what one or ones out of a group. ¶*Which book is yours?* | *Which one do you mean?* | *Which subject do you like best?* **2.** ((*relative adjective*)) whatever. ¶*Run ~ way you will, you won't escape.* **3.** ((*relative adjective*)) that. ¶*We went to Rome, at ~ place we parted.*①

—*pron.* **1.** ((*interrogative pronoun*)) what one or ones. ¶*Which do you like better, an apple or an orange?* | *Which do you like best?* | *Which of these umbrellas is yours?* | *Can you tell ~ is ~?*② **2.** ((*relative pronoun*)) that; and this or these. ⇒[usage] ¶*This is the house ~ my father lived in.* | *He is rich; ~ no other people know.* | *He said he had no brother; ~ was a lie.* | *My parents intended me for a doctor; ~ I did not like.*③ **3.** ((*relative pronoun*)) the one that; any that. ¶*Tell me ~ you prefer.* | *You may take ~ you like.*

* **which·ev·er** [(h)wìtʃévər] *pron., adj.* **1.** anything that. ¶*You may have ~ you want.* **2.** no matter which. ¶*Whichever course you take, you'll be pleased.*

whiff [(h)wif] *n.* [C] **1.** a slight breath; a puff. **2.** a faint smell. **—***vt., vi.* **1.** blow lightly; puff. **2.** smell faintly.

Whig [(h)wig] *n.* [C] **1.** a member of the Whig Party, a former political party of Great Britain. **2.** an American who supported the War of Independence against England.

⁝ **while** [(h)wail] *n.* [C] a space of time; a period. ¶*after a ~*① | *all the (that, this) ~*② | *at whiles*③ | *between whiles*④ | *for a ~* | *in a little ~*⑤ | *Don't keep me waiting a long ~.*⑥

once in a while, occasionally; sometimes.

—*conj.* **1.** during or in the time that. ¶*While [I am] in New York, I often visit my aunt.* | (*proverb*) *Make hay ~ the sun shines.*⑦ **2.** at the same time that; although. ¶*While they don't agree, they continue to be friends.* **3.** (*colloq.*) whereas; and. ¶*Wise men seek after truth, ~ fools despise it.*⑧ | *His father is a doctor, and his mother is a doctress, ~ he is a medical student.*

—*vt.* spend or pass (time) idly. ¶*~ away the time fishing.*

whim [(h)wim] *n.* [C] a sudden fancy.

whim·per [(h)wímpər] *vi.* cry with a low, broken voice. **—***vt.* say (something) with a whimper. **—***n.* [C] a low, feeble cry or sound.

whim·si·cal [(h)wímzik(ə)l] *adj.* **1.** full of whims. **2.** fanciful; odd.

whim·sy [(h)wímzi] *n.* [C] (pl. **-sies**) a whim; an odd fancy.

whine [(h)wain] *vi.* **1.** make a low, complaining cry. **2.** complain in a childish way. **—***vt.* say (something) with a whine. **—***n.* [C] **1.** a low, complaining cry or sound. **2.** a childish complaint.

시키다, 돋구다 —[名] 1. 갈기, 벼리기, 연마 2. 식욕을 돋구는 것, 반주

—[接] 1. …인지 어떤지 [usage] whether ~ or …의 형식으로 쓰는 일이 많음 ¶①그것이 사실인지 아닌지 모르겠다 2. …이든 [아니든]

[熟] 1)어떻든, 여하간

—[名] 숫돌

—[感] 아휴, 에구(놀람·실망 따위의 소리)

—[名] 우유의 수분, 유장(乳漿)

—[形] 1. 어느쪽의, 어느 2. 어떠한 …이라도 3. 그리고 이; 그리고 이[것]들의 ¶①우리는 로마까지 가서 거기서 헤어졌다

—[代] 1. 어느쪽[의 것, 사람] ¶②어느 것이 어느 것인지 분간할 수 있느냐? 2. …하는 바의; 그리고 그것은(을) [usage] 선행사가 사람인 경우 현재는 쓰이지 않음 ¶③나의 부모는 나를 의사를 시키려고 하였으나 나는 싫었다 3. …하는 바의 것(일); …하는 어느 것이라도

—[代][形] 1. 어느 것이든 2. 어느 쪽이든

—[名] 1. 한 번 불기 2. 냄새 —[他][自] 1. 가볍게 불다 2. 냄새가 풍기다

—[名] 1. 휘그당원(영국의 예전 정당) 2. ((美)) 독립당원

—[名] 동안, 시간 ¶①잠시 후 /②그 동안 쭉, 시종/③때때로, 이따금/④가끔, 틈틈이/⑤이윽고, 곧/⑥오래 기다리지 않도록 해주게

[熟] 때때로, 이따금

—[接] 1. …하는 동안(사이) ¶⑦((俚))해가 있는 동안에 풀을 말려라; 좋은 기회를 놓치지 말라 2. …인데, 그런데 3. ((口)) …에 반하여; 그리고 ¶⑧현자는 진리를 구하지만 우자는 이것을 업신여긴다

—[他] [시간]을 빈둥빈둥 보내다

—[名] 변덕, 일시적 기분

—[自] 훌쩍훌쩍(흐느껴) 울다 —[他] …을 우는 소리로 말하다 「소리

—[名] 흐느껴 울기; 코를 킁킁거리는

—[形] 1. 변덕스러운 2. 별난, 묘한, 기이한

—[名] 변덕, 일시적 기분; 기발한 생각

—[自] 1. 처량한 목소리를 내다 2. 투정하다, 투덜대다 —[他] 처량한 목소리로 …이라고 말하다 —[名] 1. 처량한 목소리; 코를 킁킁거리는 소리 2. 투정, 불평

W

whin·ny [(h)wíni] *n.* [C] (pl. **-nies**) the sound which a horse makes; a neigh. —*vi.* (**-nied**) (of a horse) make such sound.

—[名] [말의] 울음소리, 히힝소리 —[自] 히힝하고 울다

‡ **whip** [(h)wip] *v.* (**whipped** or +*U.S.* **whipt, whip·ping**) *vt.* **1.** strike (a person or an animal) with a lash, rod, etc.; beat. ¶～ *a cow.* **2.** force or urge by whipping. ¶～ *a slave to work* | ～ *manners into a child*① | ～ *a fault out of a child.*② **3.** (*colloq.*) defeat. **4.** beat (something) in a manner like whipping. ¶*The rain whipped our tin roof.*③ **5.** move, pull or seize (something) quickly and suddenly. ¶～ *off one's coat* | ～ *out a knife.*④ **6.** beat (eggs, cream, etc.) with a beater, a mixer, etc. ¶*whipped cream.* **7.** fish (a stream) with a rod and line. **8.** bind (a rope, etc.) with a cord, etc. **9.** sew over (a seam). —*vi.* **1.** move, go or pass quickly and suddenly. **2.** wave up and down. ¶*The flags whipped in the wind.*

—[他] **1.** …을 채찍질하다 **2.** …을 채찍질하여 시키다 ¶①아이를 매질하여 버릇을 가르치다/②아이를 매질하여 결점을 고치게 하다 **3.** (口) …을 지우다, 패배시키다 **4.** …을 채찍질하듯이 때리다 ¶③비가 우리의 함석 지붕을 두들겼다 **5.** …을 갑자기 움직이다; 잡아채다; 거머쥐다; 홱 꺼내다 ¶④나이프를 홱 꺼내다 **6.** …을 휘저어 거품 일게 하다 **7.** …에서 낚시질하다 **8.** …을 끈으로 둘둘 감다 **9.** …을 감치다 —[自] **1.** 갑자기 움직이다; 돌진하다 **2.** 펄럭이다, 나부끼다

1) ***whip around,*** turn around suddenly and swiftly.
2) ***whip up,*** ⓐ make (a horse) run faster by whipping. ⓑ prepare quickly. ⓒ rouse; excite.

[熟] 1)휙 뒤돌아보다 2)ⓐ채찍질하여 …을 더 빨리 달리게 하다 ⓑ…을 서둘러 준비하다 ⓒ…을 자극하다

—*n.* [C] **1.** an instrument for striking or beating, such as a rod with a lash. **2.** a person who uses a whip; a driver. ¶*I am no* ～. **3.** a dessert made of fruit, sugar, and whipped cream or the whipped whites of eggs. **4.** a manager of a political party.

—[名] **1.** 채찍 **2.** 채찍질하는 사람, 마부 **3.** 크리임·계란 따위를 휘저어 섞어서 거품을 일게 한 식후의 과자 **4.** [당의] 원내 총무

whip·lash [hwíplæʃ] *n.* **1.** [C] the lash for a whip. **2.** [U] a neck injury caused by a sudden stopping of a car.

—[名] **1.** 채찍끈 **2.** 자동차가 갑자기 멈추는 바람에 생긴 목의 상처

whir, whirr [(h)wəːr] *vi.* (**whirred, whir·ring**) move quickly with a humming sound. —*n.* [C] (usu. *sing.*) the sound made by moving things rapidly.

—[自] 핑하고 날아가다; 윙윙 돌다
—[名] 핑하는 소리; 윙윙 도는 소리

‡ **whirl** [(h)wəːrl] *vi.* **1.** turn around and around. **2.** move swiftly. **3.** feel dizzy. —*vt.* **1.** cause (something) to turn around and around. **2.** carry (something) quickly. —*n.* [C] **1.** a circular motion. **2.** (of water) a quick act of spinning around. **3.** confusion.

—[自] **1.** 빙빙 돌다 **2.** 급히 가다 **3.** 현기증나다 —[他] **1.** …을 빙빙 돌리다 **2.** …을 신속히 운반하다 —[名] **1.** 회전, 선회 **2.** 소용돌이 **3.** 혼란

whirl·pool [(h)wə́ːrlpùːl] *n.* [C] (of water) the act of spinning rapidly and violently.

—[名] 소용돌이.

whirl·wind [(h)wə́ːrlwìnd] *n.* [C] a current of air circling violently with a spiral motion.

—[名] 회오리바람, 선풍(旋風)

whirr [(h)wəːr] *vi., n.* =whir.

whisk [(h)wisk] *n.* [C] **1.** a small brush or broom. **2.** a sudden, quick motion. **3.** a quick motion of brushing. **4.** an instrument for whipping eggs, cream, etc.
—*vt.* **1.** sweep; brush. **2.** take or carry off suddenly. **3.** beat (eggs, creams, etc.) into a froth.

—[名] **1.** 작은 비; 솔 **2.** 날랜 동작, 휙 움직이기 **3.** 가볍게 톡 털기, 쓱 쓸기 **4.** 거품 일게 하는 기구 —[他] **1.** …을 털다, 털어 없애다 **2.** …을 휙 가져(데려)가다 **3.** …을 거품 일게 하다

whisk·er [(h)wískər] *n.* [C] (usu. *pl.*) **1.** hair growing on the side of a man's face. **2.** long hair growing near the mouth of a cat, a rat, etc.

—[名] **1.** 구레나룻 **2.** [고양이 따위의] 수염

• **whis·key, -ky** [(h)wíski] *n.* [U] a strong alcoholic drink made from various grains, esp. rye and barley.

—[名] 위스키(독한 양주의 일종)

• **whis·per** [(h)wíspər] *vi.* **1.** speak in a very soft and low voice. **2.** talk secretly or privately. **3.** make a soft, rustling sound like a whisper. —*vt.* **1.** say (something) very softly. **2.** tell (something) secretly. —*n.* [C] **1.** a very soft and low voice. **2.** a soft, faint, rustling sound. **3.** a hint; a rumor.

—[自] **1.** 속삭이다 **2.** 수군거리다, 밀담하다 **3.** 살랑살랑(솔솔) 불다, 졸졸 흐르다 —[他] **1.** …을 작은 목소리로 말하다 **2.** …을 몰래 수군거리다
—[名] **1.** 속삭임, 속삭이는 목소리 **2.** 속삭이는 듯한 소리 **3.** 힌트; 소문, 풍문

‡ **whis·tle** [(h)wísl] *vi.* **1.** make a shrill sound by forcing the breath between the teeth or rounded lips. **2.** make any similar sound. ¶*The wind whistles.*① —*vt.* call or signal (something) by a whistling.

—[自] **1.** 휘파람을 불다 **2.** 휘파람 소리 같은 소리를 내다 ¶①바람이 휭휭 불다 —[他] 휘파람으로 …을 부르다(신호하다)

whistle for, ⓐ call (someone or something) by a whistle. ⓑ fail to get (something).

[熟] ⓐ…을 휘파람으로 부르다 ⓑ…을 구하려 해도 구하지 못하다

—*n.* [C] **1.** a shrill sound made by whistling. **2.** an instrument for producing such a sound.

—[名] **1.** 휘파람 **2.** 피리, 기적, 경적, 호각

1) ***not worth the whistle,*** valueless.
2) ***pay for one's whistle,*** pay too much money for something worthless.

[熟] 1)전혀 무익한 2)무가치한 것을 비싸게 사다

whit [(h)wit] *n.* [C] the least bit.

—[名] 미소(微少), 극소, 아주 조금

not (or ***never***) ***a whit,*** not at all; not in the least.

[熟] 조금도 …않다

⁝ **white** [(h)wait] *adj.* **1.** of the color of snow or pure milk ↔black; of no color. ¶ *~ clouds / as ~ as milk* (or *chalk*) */ ~ hands*① */ ~ light.*② **2.** of a light or pale color. ¶ *~ wine / She turned ~ at the news. / be in ~ terror*③ */ Her face went ~.* **3.** of a silver color; gray; covered with snow; blank. ¶ *a ~ metal*④ */ a ~ Christmas / a ~ page.* **4.** without a stain; pure; innocent; harmless. ¶ *a ~ lie / My father made his name ~ again.*⑤ **5.** having a light-colored skin. ¶ *the ~ race.* **6.** (of wine) light yellow.

—[形] 1. 흰, 하얀, 백색의; 무색의 ¶①[일하지 않은] 하얀 손; 결백 /②대낮의 햇빛, 백일광; 편견 없는 판단 2. 빛깔이 엷은, 흰빛이 도는, 창백한 ¶③공포로 창백해지다 3. 은빛의; 눈에 덮인; 백지의 ¶④가짜(모조) 은 4. 오점이 없는; 순진한, 천진한; 해독이 없는, 무해한 ¶⑤나의 아버지는 누명을 벗었다 5. 백색인종의 6. 호박색(琥珀色)의

1) ***bleed someone white,*** take all the money from someone.
2) ***white coffee,*** coffee mixed with milk or cream.

[熟] 1)[남]의 자산을 탕진하다 2)크리임(밀크)을 탄 코오피

—*n.* **1.** [U] white color. **2.** [U] the state of being white; innocence. **3.** [C] white coloring material. ¶ *A grain or two of ~ fell on the surface of the desk.* **4.** [U] white cloth; (usu. *pl.*) white garments. ¶ *a woman in ~.* **5.** [C] a white person. ¶ *White only.*⑥ **6.** the white part of something, such as an eye or an egg.

—[名] 1. 흰 빛, 백색 2. 순진, 천진, 무해(無害) 3. 흰(백색) 그림물감 4. 흰 옷, 백의(白衣), 흰 천; 흰 천으로 만든 것 5. 백인 ¶⑥백인 전용 6. [눈의] 흰자위; [달걀의] 흰자위

white·cap [(h)wáitkæ̀p] *n.* [C] (usu. *pl.*) the ridge of a wave as it breaks into foam.

—[名] 흰 거품이 이는 파도

white clover [ˊ ˊˋ] *n.* a kind of clover with white flowers.

—[名] 흰 클로우버(토끼풀)

white-col·lar [(h)wáitkɑ̀lər] *adj.* of a person who is engaged in business or professional work. ¶ *a ~worker.*①

—[形] 두뇌 노동자의 ¶①두뇌 노동자

White·hall [(h)wáithɔ́:l, ˊˋ] *n.* **1.** a street in London where there are many important government offices. **2.** the British government.

—[名] 1. 런던의 관청가(街) 2. 영국 정부

white-hot [(h)wáithɑ́t / -hɔ́t] *adj.* **1.** very hot; white with heat. **2.** very excited or angry.

—[形] 1. 몹시 뜨거운, 백열(白熱)의 2. 백열된; 몹시 흥분한; 격분한

White House, [ˊˋ] **the** *n.* the official residence of the President of the United States, in Washington, D. C.

—[名] 백악관(미국 대통령 관저)

white-liv·ered [(h)wáitlívərd] *adj.* cowardly.

—[形] 겁 많은, 비겁한

whit·en [(h)wáitn] *vt.* make (something) white. —*vi* become white.

—[他] …을 희게 칠하다; 표백하다
—[自] 하얘지다, 하얗게 되다

white·ness [(h)wáitnis] *n.* [U] **1.** the state of being white. **2.** cleanliness; purity.

—[名] 1. 흼, 순백 2. 순결, 결백

white paper [ˊ ˊˋ] *n.* a report issued by the British Government to give information; a similar report issued by any government.

—[名] [영국의] 백서(白書); [일반적으로] 백서

white·wash [(h)wáitwɑ̀ʃ, -wɔ̀:ʃ / -wɔ̀ʃ] *n.* [U] a substance for whitening walls, fences, etc. —*vt.* **1.** whiten (walls, fences, etc.) with whitewash. **2.** cover up or hide the mistakes of (someone).

—[名] 백색도료 —[他] 1. …에 백색 도료를 칠하다 2. …을 호도(糊塗)하다, …의 실패를 감추다

* **whith·er** [(h)wíðər] *adv.* (*poetic*) **1.** to what place. ↔whence ¶ *Whither are you going?* **2.** to which place; where. ¶ *the shore ~ we landed.*① **3.** to whatever place, point, etc.; wherever. ¶ *Go ~ you will.*②

—[副] 《詩》 1. 어디에, 어디로 2. 그곳에 ¶①우리들이 상륙한 해안 3. 어디든지 ¶②어디든지 가고 싶은 곳으로 가거라

whit·ing [(h)wáitiŋ] *n.* **1.** [U] white chalk. **2.** [C] (pl. **-ings** or *collectively* **-ing**) a small sea fish for food.

—[名] 1. 백악(白堊) 2. 작은 대구의 일종

whit·ish [(h)wáitiʃ] *adj.* somewhat white.

—[形] 좀 흰, 희읍스름한

Whit·sun [(h)wítsn] *adj.* of Whitsunday.

—[形] 성령 강림제의

Whit·sun·day [(h)wítsʌ́ndi, -sndèi] *n.* the seventh Sunday after Easter.

—[名] 성령 강림제(부활제 후 일곱 번째 일요일)

Whit·sun·tide [(h)wítsntàid] *n.* the week that begins with Whitsunday, esp. the first three days of that week.

—[名] 성령 강림절(성령 강림제부터 1주일간, 특히 처음 3일간)

whit·tle [(h)wítl] *vt.* **1.** cut (a piece of wood) with a knife; cut away. **2.** reduce (something) little by little.

—[他] 1. 나이프로 …을 깎다; 베어(잘라)내다 2. …을 조금씩 줄이다

whiz, whizz [(h)wiz] *n.* [C] a hissing sound made by something which moves quickly through the air. —*vi.* (**whizzed, whizz·ing**) make a hissing sound; move with a hissing sound. ¶ *An arrow whizzed over his head.*①

—[名] 윙, 핑(화살·총알 따위가 날아가는 소리) —[自] 핑 소리나다; 윙 날아가다 ¶①화살이 그의 머리 위를 윙하고 날아갔다

W

who [hu:→2.] *pron.* **1.** (*interrogative pronoun*) what or which person[s]. ¶*Who says so?* / *"Who is he?" "He is Mr. Smith."* / *He may be the best source of information as to ~ was where at what time.* / *It was a question of ~ had taken the money.* / *I don't know ~ to give it to.*① **2.** [hu:, u] (*relative pronoun*) [the persons] that; and he; any person that. ¶*the man ~ came here yesterday* / *There is somebody at the door* [~] *wants to see you.* / (*proverb*) *Who steals my purse steals trash.*② / *I lived with Mr. A, ~ taught me English.*

who·dun·it [hu:dʌ́nit] *n.* ⓒ (*colloq.*) a story, motion picture or drama that deals with crime and its detection.

- **who·ev·er** [hu(:)évər] *pron.* **1.** any person that. ¶*Whoever wants the treasure shall have it.* **2.** no matter who. ¶*Whoever tries it, he will never succeed.*①

whole [houl] *adj.* **1.** (*the or one's ~*) containing all-parts; full; entire. ↔partial ¶*the ~ country* / *the ~ world* / *the ~ truth* / *with one's ~ heart*① / *put one's ~ heart and soul into something.*② **2.** complete; not divided. ¶*a ~ day* / *for five ~ days.* **3.** not broken; not injured; sound. ¶*with a ~ skin.*③
a whole lot of, (*colloq.*) a lot of; a great deal of.
—*n.* ⓒ **1.** (*the ~*) the entire amount, extent, or sum. ↔part ¶*the ~ of one's property* / *the ~ and the parts.*④ **2.** a thing complete in itself; a unity.
1) *as a whole,* as a complete unit.
2) *on* (or *upon*) *the whole,* in general.

whole-heart-ed [hóulhá:rtid] *adj.* full of sincerity; hearty and cordial.

whole·sale [hóulsèil] *adj.* **1.** selling in large quantities. **2.** having a large scale. —*adv.* in large quantities. —*n.* Ⓤ the sale of goods in large quantities. —*vt.* sell (goods) in large quantities. ↔retail

- **whole·some** [hóulsəm] *adj.* **1.** good for the health; healthful. **2.** good for the mind; sound.

who'll [hu:l] =who will; who shall.

- **whol·ly** [hóul(l)i] *adv.* entirely; completely.

whom [hu:m] *pron.* the objective case of **who. 1.** (*interrogative pronoun*) what person. ¶*Whom are you looking for?*① **2.** (*relative pronoun*) that person. ¶*I visited my uncle ~ I had not seen for years.*②

whom·ev·er [hu:mévər] *pron.* the objective case of **whoever.** ⌈of **whosoever.**⌉

whom·so·ev·er [hù:msouévər] *pron.* the objective case

whoop [hu:p, +*U.S.* hwu:p] *n.* ⓒ **1.** a loud cry. **2.** the cry of an owl, a crane, etc. **3.** a gasping cough.
not care a whoop, not care at all.
—*vi.* **1.** shout loudly. **2.** make a whooping noise like an owl, a crane, etc.
whoop it up, (*colloq.*) make much noise, usu. joyfully.

whop·per [(h)wápər / (h)wɔ́pə] *n.* ⓒ (*colloq.*) **1.** something very large. **2.** a big lie.

whop·ping [(h)wápiŋ / (h)wɔ́p-] *n.* ⓤⓒ **1.** the act of beating with a stick. **2.** defeat. —*adj.* (*colloq.*) very or unusually large. —*adv.* very; extraordinarily.

whorl [(h)wə:rl] *n.* ⓒ **1.** one turn of a spiral shell. **2.** a circle of leaves, petals, flowers, etc. around a part of a stem.

who's [hu:z] who is; who has.

whose [hu:z] *pron.* the possessive case of **who** and **which. 1.** (*interrogative pronoun*) of whom. ¶*Whose pencil is this?* **2.** (*relative pronoun*) of which. ¶*An orphan is a child ~ parents are dead.* **3.** the one possessed by someone. ¶*Whose is this pencil?*

who·so·ev·er [hù:souévər] *pron.* =whoever.

—㈹ 1. 누구, 어느(어떤) 사람 ¶①그것을 누구에게 줘야 할지 모르겠다 2. …하는 [사람]; 그리고 그 사람은; …하는 사람은 누구든지 ¶②(俚)내 지갑을 훔치는 자는 쓰레기를 훔치는 것과 같다; 돈은 도난당해도 아깝지 않다

—㈜ (口) 추리소설(영화·극), 탐정물

—㈹ 1. 누구든지 2. 누가 …하든지 ¶① 누가 하든 결코 성공치 못할 것이다

—㉠ 1. 모든, 전체의, 전(全)… ¶①충심으로/②…에 온갖 심혈을 기울이다 2. 꼬박…; 만(滿)…, 꼭 3. 아무 홈 없는, 완전한, 온전한 ¶③아무 다친데 없이, 무사히

㊀ (口) 많은
—㈜ 1. 전체, 전부 ¶④전체와 부분 2. 완전한 것; 통일체

㊀ 1)전체로서, 총괄하여 2)전체적으로 보아서, 대체로

—㉠ 진심(성의)어린; 전심전력의

—㉠ 1. 도매의 2. 대규모의 —㉮ 도매로; 대규모로 —㈜ 도매 —㉨ [상품]을 도매하다

—㉠ 1. 건강에 좋은; 건강한 2. 건전한

—㉮ 전혀, 완전히, 전적으로
—㈹ 1. 누구를 ¶①누구를 찾느냐? 2. 그 사람을 ¶②나는 몇 년 동안 만나지 못한 아저씨를 방문했다

—㈜ 1. 어어(야아)[하고 부르는 소리] 2. 부엉부엉 우는 소리 3. 씨근거리는 [숨]소리 ㊀ 조금도 개의치 않다
—㉨ 1. 외치다, 소리치다 2. 부엉부엉 울다
㊀ (口) 큰 소리를 지르며 떠들어대다
—㈜ (口) 1. 엄청나게 큰 것 2. 허풍, 엄청난 거짓말
—㈜ 1. 매질, 태형(答刑) 2. 패배 —㉠ 엄청나게(굉장히) 큰 —㉮ 굉장히; 엄청나게
—㈜ 1. 권패(卷貝)의 한 나층(螺層), 나선부(部) 2. [식물의] 윤생체(輪生體)
—㈹ 1. 누구의; 어느 것의 2. 그의 3. 누구의 것

why [(h)wai→*interj.*] *adv.* **1.** (*interrogative adverb*) for what reason or purpose. ¶*Why did you do it? / Why so?*① */ Do you know ~ he was absent?* **2.** (*relative adverb*) because of or on account of which; for which. ¶*That is [the reason] ~ I cannot go. / I know ~ you were scolded.* ⇒usage
——*n.* ⓒ (pl. **whys**) the reason. ¶*the whys and wherefores*② */ None of your whys!*③
——*interj.* [wai] (expressing *surprise, protest*, etc., or introducing *a new idea*) ¶*Why, it is surely Tom. / Why, of course I know. / Why, yes, I think so.*

wick [wik] *n.* Ⓤⓒ a cord of woven fibers in a candle or oil lamp that draws up melted fat or oil.

wick·ed [wíkid] *adj.* **1.** bad; evil; sinful. **2.** mischievous. **3.** harmful; dangerous.

wick·ed·ness [wíkidnis] *n.* Ⓤ **1.** the state or quality of being wicked. **2.** ⓒ a wicked act.

wick·er [wíkər] *n.* ⓒ Ⓤ **1.** an easily bent twig or branch. **2.** baskets, furniture, etc. made of such twigs woven together. ——*adj.* made of wicker.

wick·et [wíkit] *n.* ⓒ **1.** a small gate or door. **2.** a small window or opening, such as in a bank. **3.** (in cricket) a set of three sticks between which one side tries to bowl the ball. ——*fig.*

wick·et-keep·er [wíkitkì:pər] *n.* ⓒ (in cricket) the player who stands just behind the wicket.

[wicket keeper] [wicket 3.]

wide [waid] *adj.* **1.** extending over a large area; broad. ↔narrow ¶*a ~ cloth / at ~ intervals.*① **2.** having a certain distance from side to side. ¶*How ~ it is? / It is 5 feet ~.* **3.** vast; extensive; spacious. ¶*Suddenly there opened a ~ field.*② **4.** open to the full; loose. ¶*with one's eyes ~ with terror*③ */ ~ knickerbockers.*④ **5.** of great scope or range. **6.** far from a certain point. ¶*be ~ of the truth.*⑤
——*adv.* **1.** to a great distance from side to side. ¶*wander far and ~.* **2.** to the full extent; fully. ¶*with eyes ~ open.* **3.** far from the point aimed at. ¶*speak ~ of the mark*⑥ */ He is shooting ~. / His blow went ~.*

wide-a·wake [wáidəwéik] *adj.* **1.** awake and with eyes open wide. **2.** watchful; prudent.

wide-eyed [wáidáid] *adj.* with the eyes open wide.

wide·ly [wáidli] *adv.* to a great extent. ¶*He is ~ known.*

wid·en [wáidn] *vt.* make (something) wider. ——*vi.* become wider.

wide-open [wáidóup(ə)n] *adj.* opening widely.

wide·spread [wáidspréd] *adj.* **1.** opened or spread to full extent. ¶*a bird's ~ wings.* **2.** spread over a large area; very common. ¶*a ~ superstition.*①

wid·ow [wídou] *n.* ⓒ a woman whose husband is dead.
——*vt.* make (a woman) a widow.

wid·ow·er [wídouər] *n.* ⓒ a man whose wife is dead.

wid·ow·hood [wídouhùd] *n.* Ⓤ the state of being a widow.

width [widθ, witθ] *n.* Ⓤ **1.** the size of something from side to side. **2.** the state of being wide. **3.** ⓒ something of a certain width. ¶*join two widths of paper.*①

wield [wi:ld] *vt.* **1.** use (a tool, etc.) with the hands. **2.** rule over.

wie·ner [wí:nər] *n.* Ⓤⓒ sausage made of pork and [beef mixed together.]

wife [waif] *n.* ⓒ (pl. **wives** [waivz]) **1.** a married woman. *take a woman to wife,* marry. **2.** a woman.
wife-like [wáiflàik] *adj.* like or suitable to a wife.
wife-ly [wáifli] *adj.* (-li-er, -li-est) of or like a wife.
wig [wig] *n.* ⓒ a covering of hair for the head. ¶*wear*
wigged [wigd] *adj.* wearing a wig. ⌊*a* ~.⌋
wig-gle [wígl] *vi., vt.* move with short, quick movements. ¶*Stop wiggling your feet.*①
Get a wiggle on [*you*]*!,* (*U. S. colloq.*) hurry.
wig-wag [wígwæg] *vi., vt.* (**-wagged, -wag-ging**) **1.** move back and forth or to and fro. **2.** signal by moving flags or flashing lights.
—*n.* Ⓤ the act of signaling by flags or lights.
wig-wam [wígwɑm / -wæm] *n.* ⓒ a hut used by American Indians.
wild [waild] *adj.* **1.** (of animals or plants) not trained or produced by man; living or growing in a natural state. ¶~ *flowers* / *grow* ~① / *The lion is a* ~ *animal.* **2.** not civilized; savage; (of land) waste; with few or no inhabitants. ¶*a* ~ *tribe* / *a* ~ *land.* **3.** violent; stormy; rough. ¶*a* ~ *sea* / *a* ~ *weather.* **4.** not obeying; lawless; not controlled. ¶*a* ~ *fellow* / *a* ~ *temper* / ~ *youth.* **5.** not orderly; disturbed. ¶~ *hair.* **6.** crazy; greatly excited; very eager; (*colloq.*) very angry. ¶~ *rage* / *be* ~ *about*② / ~ *with excitement* / *be* ~ *to go*③ / *be* ~ *for revenge* / *drive someone* ~.⑥ ~ **7.** reckless; missing the aim. ¶*a* ~ *plan* / *a* ~ *pitch*⑤ / *a* ~ *shot.*⑥
run wild, be without control or limitation.
—*adv.* in a wild manner; without aim. ¶*shoot* ~.
—*n.* ⓒ (*pl.* or *the* ~) an area far from the dwellings of men; a desert.
wild boar [´ ´] *n.* a wild hog.
wild-cat [wáil(d)kæt] *n.* ⓒ **1.** a savage and wild animal like a cat. **2.** an ill-natured person. **3.** a reckless or unsafe business. —*adj.* **1.** wild; reckless. **2.** illegal; not authorized. ⌊poems, novels and plays.⌋
Wilde [waild], **Oscar** *n.* (1856-1900) a British writer of
wil·der·ness [wíldərnis] *n.* ⓒ (*sing.* only) a place without people living in it; a wild place.
wild·fire [wáildfàiər] *n.* Ⓤ **1.** a substance which catches fire easily and is hard to put out. **2.** anything which spreads rapidly. ⌊and pheasants.⌋
wild·fowl [wáildfàul] *n.* ⓒ hunting birds, such as ducks
wild goose [´ ´] *n.* any goose that is not cultivated.
wild·ly [wáildli] *adv.* **1.** with a wild nature; violently. **2.** recklessly; not thoughtfully. ⌊wild.⌋
wild·ness [wáildnis] *n.* Ⓤ the state or quality of being
wile [wail] *n.* ⓒ (*usu. pl.*) a cunning trick. —*vt.* get (someone) to do something in a cunning way. (~ *someone from something,* ~ *someone into doing*)
Wil·fred [wílfrid] *n.* a man's name.
wil·ful [wílf(u)l] *adj.* (*Brit.*) =willful.
wil·ful·ly [wílfuli] *adv.* (*Brit.*) ==willfully.
will [wil, wəl, əl, l] *auxil. v.* (**would**) **1.** be going to; be about to. ⇨usage ¶*You* ~ *succeed.* / *It'll be fine tomorrow.* / *Will he be at home tomorrow?* / *When* ~ *this train get to Osaka?* **2.** be determined to. ¶*I* ~ *write to him at once.* / *Will you come for a walk this evening?* **3.** (*expressing a firm resolution*) ¶*You* ~ *have your own way.*① / *I* ~ *be obeyed.*② **4.** do usu. or often; be accustomed to. ¶*He* ~ *sit there for hours.* **5.** be willing to; wish to. ¶*This door* ~ *not open.*① / *Ask him if he* ~ *have some money.* **6.** be apt or inclined to. ¶*Boys* ~ *be boys.*① / *Accidents* ~ *happen.* / *Murder* ~ *out.*③ **7.** (expressing *probability, expectation, etc.*)

—ⓝ 1. 아내, 처 2. 여자
熟 …을 아내로 맞이하다, 장가가다
—ⓐ 아내다운, 아내로서 어울리는
—ⓐ 아내의, 아내다운
—ⓝ 가발(假髮)
—ⓐ 가발을 쓴
—自他 [꼬리 따위를] 흔들다, [방정맞게] 떨다 ¶①방정맞게 발을 떨지 마라
熟 [美口] 서둘러라!, 빨리 해라!
—自他 1. 흔들다; 기를 흔들다 2. [수기(手旗) 따위로] 신호하다 —ⓝ [수기·등불 따위에 의한] 신호

—ⓝ 북미 토인의 오두막

—ⓐ 1. 사람의 손으로 기르지(가꾸지) 않은, 들에서 자란, 야생의; 길들이지 않은, 사나운 ¶①야생이다 2. 미개한; 야만의; 황폐(荒廢)한 3. [바람 따위가] 격렬한, 거친, 사나운 4. 난폭한; 제멋대로의, 방종한 5. 혼란한, 난잡한; 어질러진 6. 미친 듯한, 광기의; 몹시 흥분한; 열중한; [口] 격분한 ¶②열중해 있다 /③몹시 가고 싶어하고 있다 /④몸을 열중케 하다 7. 무모한; 얼토당토않은, 엉뚱한 ¶⑤폭투(暴投) /⑥난사(亂射)

熟 난폭해지다
—ⓐ 난폭하게; 되는 대로, 닥치는 대로
—ⓝ 황무지, 황야, 미개지
—ⓐ 야생의 돼지, 산돼지
—ⓝ 1. 삵쾡이 2. [삵쾡이처럼] 심술사나운 사람 3. 무모한 기업 —ⓐ 1. 무모한, 앞뒤를 헤아리지 않는 2. 비(非)합법적인

—ⓝ 영국의 시인·소설가·극작가
—ⓝ 황무지, 황야, 널따란 곳

—ⓝ 1. 연소제(燃燒劑) 2. 금방 퍼지는 것(일)

—ⓝ [오리·꿩 따위의] 엽조(獵鳥)
—ⓝ 기러기
—ⓐ 1. 야성적으로, 난폭하게 2. 무모하게, 함부로
—ⓝ 야성; 야생; 난폭; 방탕, 방종
—ⓝ 농간, 책략, 간계 —ⓐ …을 속이다, 속여서 …시키다

—ⓝ 남자 이름

—ⓐ 1. …일 것이다 USAGE 평서문(平叙文)에서는 2인칭·3인칭에 쓰며, 1인칭은 shall. 단, (美)에서는 I(we)이 단순미래에 쓰임. ②의문문에서는 3인칭에 쓰임 2. …하겠다, …할 작정이다 3. 아무렇게든 (꼭) …하다 ¶①너는 어디까지나 너의 뜻대로 하는구나 /②내가 하라는 대로 해야 한다 4. 곧잘 …하다, …하기를 잘한다 5. 기꺼이 …하다; …을 바라다 ¶③이 문은 암만해도 잘 열리지 않는다 6. …하기가 쉽다, …하는 경향이 있다 ¶④아이들은 [역시]

¶*This'll be our train, I fancy.* | *I suppose this ~ be the Tower of London.* **8.** be required to. ¶*You ~ do it at once.* **9.** can; be able to. ¶*The flower ~ live without water for two weeks.*

아이들이다/⑤못된 짓은 발각되는 법이다 7. 아마 …일 것이다 8. …이 필요할 것이다 9. …할 수 있다

—*n.* ⟪*sing.* only⟫ **1.** [C] ⟪*the ~*⟫ the mental power by which a person can decide how to act. ¶*the freedom of the ~.* **2.** [U] [C] the mental power by which a person can control himself; strong intention. ¶*have a strong (a weak) ~*⑥ | *He has no ~ of his own.* | *He must always have his ~.* | *(proverb) The ~ is as good as the deed.*⑦ | *(proverb) Where there's a ~, there's a way.*⑧ **3.** [C] enthusiasm. ¶*He works with a ~.* **4.** [C] a wish; a desire; a pleasure. ¶*against one's ~*⑨ | *have one's ~*⑩ | *the ~ to fight.* **5.** [U] manner or feeling towards others. ¶*show good (ill) ~.*⑪ **6.** [C] a written statement showing what is to be done with a person's money and goods after his death. ¶*make one's ~.*

—[名] 1. 의지 2. 의지력; 결의(決意) ¶⑥의지가 강하다(약하다) / ⑦⟪俚⟫무슨 일에나 뜻이 중요하다 / ⑧⟪俚⟫뜻이 있는 곳에 길이 있다 (하려고 하면 방법은 있는 법이다) 3. 열의, 열성 4. 바람; 소망; 욕망 ¶⑨본의 아니게/⑩뜻을 관철하다, 소망을 이루다 5. 의도, 의향 ¶⑪호의(악의)를 보이다 6. 유언, 유서

1) **at will; at** *one's* [**own sweet**] **will,** at one's pleasure.
2) **do the will** (=*obey the wish or command*) **of** *someone.*

[熟] 1)뜻대로, 임의로 2)…의 희망(명령)대로 하다

—*vt.* **1.** determine; decide. ⟪*~ to do; ~ that…*⟫ ¶*The girl willed to be honest.* **2.** influence or control (someone) by exercising the will. ¶*He willed himself into contentment.*⑫ **3.** leave (money, etc.) by means of a will (*n.* 6.). ¶*He willed his money to a school.* —*vi.* **1.** exercise the will (*n.* 1.). **2.** wish; desire.

—[他] 1. …을 의지로 결정하다, 결의하다 2. [남]에게 의지의 힘으로 …시키다 ¶⑫그는 굳이 만족했다 3. …을 유증(遺贈)하다, 유언하다 —[自] 1. 의지를 행사(발동)하다 2. 바라다, 원하다

will·ful, *Brit.* **wil-** [wílf(u)l] *adj.* **1.** done on purpose. **2.** determined to have one's own way; stubborn.

—[形] 1. 고의적인 2. 제멋대로의, 외고집의

will·ful·ly, *Brit.* **wil-** [wílfuli] *adv.* in a willful manner.

—[副] 고의로; 제멋대로

will·ful·ness, *Brit.* **wil-** [wílf(u)lnis] *n.* [U] the state or quality of being willful.

—[名] 고의; 완고, 외고집

⁑ **will·ing** [wíliŋ] *adj.* **1.** cheerfully; ready. ⟪*~ to do*⟫ ¶*She is ~ to join us.*① **2.** given or done readily or gladly. ¶*~ assistance.*

—[形] 1. 기꺼이 …하는, 자진해서 …하는 ¶①그녀는 기꺼이 우리와 어울렸다 2. 자발적인, 자유 의사의

* **will·ing·ly** [wíliŋli] *adv.* in a willing manner.

—[副] 기꺼이, 쾌히, 자발적으로

will·ing·ness [wíliŋnis] *n.* [U] the state or quality of being willing.

—[名] 자진해서 행하기, 자발성

will-o'-the-wisp [wíləð(ə)wísp] *n.* [C] **1.** a light seen moving at night over wet or marshy places. **2.** a thing that misleads or deceives.

—[名] 1. 도깨비불 2. 사람을 홀리는 것

* **wil·low** [wílou] *n.* [C] a tree with easily bent branches.

—[名] 버들

wil·low·y [wíloui] *adj.* **1.** like a willow; easily bent; graceful. **2.** full of willows.

—[形] 1. 버들 같은; 나긋나긋한 2. 버들이 많은

* **wilt**¹ [wilt] *vi.* (of a plant) become dry and lifeless; lose freshness; wither; (of a person) become weak or faint. —*vt.* cause (a plant, a person, etc.) to wilt.

—[自] 시들다; 생기를 잃다; 약해지다 —[他] …을 시들게 하다; 약하게 하다

wilt² [wilt] *auxil. v.* (*archaic*) =will. ⇒[N.B.]

—[助] [N.B.] 주어는 thou

wil·y [wáili] *adj.* (**wil·i·er, wil·i·est**) full of tricks.

—[形] 꾀가 많은, 책략이 많은, 교활한

wim·ple [wímpl] *n.* [C] a cloth for covering the head and chin, worn by nuns, etc. —*vt.* cover or muffle (something) with a wimple. —*vi.* ripple.

—[名] [수녀 등이 쓰는] 베일 —[他] …을 베일로 싸다(가리다) —[自] 잔물결이 일다, 파문이 일다

⁑ **win** [win] *v.* (**won, win·ning**) *vt.* **1.** be successful in (a game, a battle, etc.). ↔lose ¶*~ a game.* **2.** gain (a prize, fame, love, etc.). ¶*~ one's bread*① | *~ someone's heart*② | *The book won him fame.* **3.** succeed in reaching (a place, etc.) by great effort. ¶*~ the summit.* **4.** persuade. ¶*We won him to consent.*③ | *He won her over to his side.*④ —*vi.* **1.** gain a victory. ¶*~ by a boat's length* | *~ against someone* | *~ over an opposing team.* **2.** succeed, after a struggle, in reaching a certain state or place. ¶*~ home* | *~ to shore.*

—[他] 1. [경기·전쟁 따위]에 이기다 2. [상품·명성 따위]를 얻다, 타다, 획득하다 ¶①양식을 벌다/②남의 사랑을 얻는 데 성공하다 3. [곤란을 배제하고] …에 도달하다, 이르다 4. …을 설득하다 ¶③우리는 그를 설득하여 승낙시켰다/④그는 그녀를 자기 편에 끌어 넣었다 —[自] 1. 이기다 2. 도달하다

1) **win free** (or **clear, loose**), make one's way through; escape by successful effort.
2) **win out** (or **through**), ⓐ make one's way through. ⓑ succeed.

[熟] 1)빠져나가다, 자유로와지다 2)ⓐ빠져나가다 ⓑ성공하다 3)싸움에 이기

3) ***win the day*** (or ***the field***), gain a victory.
4) ***win one's way,*** ⓐ go with great effort. ⓑ succeed in life by effort.
—*n.* [C] (*colloq.*) a victory; success.

wince [wins] *vi.* draw back suddenly because of fear, pain, etc. —*n.* [C] an act of suddenly drawing back; flinching.

winch [wintʃ] *n.* [C] a machine for lifting or pulling by means of a rope or chain wound on a roller. ⇒fig.

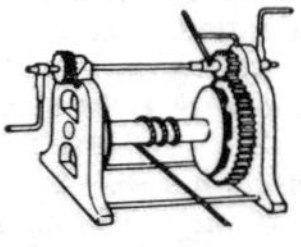
[winch]

⁑ **wind**[1] [wind, *poetic* waind] *n.* **1.** [C] [U] a current of air; air moved by a fan, etc.; a strong wind; a storm. ¶*a gentle ~ | a strong ~ | a wet ~*① *| a fair (contrary) ~*② *| ~ and rain*③ *| a gust of ~ | the ~ of the passing train | against the ~*④ *| like the ~*⑤ *| with the ~*⑥ *| The ~ rises (falls). | There is a high ~. | before the ~*⑦ *|* *in* (or *into*) *the ~*⑧ *| off the ~*⑨ *| on* (or *upon*) *the ~*⑩ *| to the ~*⑪ *| up* (*down*) *the ~*⑫ **2.** [U] a smell carried by the wind; a hint; a rumor. ¶*keep the ~*⑬ *| get* (or *take*) *~*⑭ *| get* (or *have*) *~ of.*⑮ **3.** [U] breath; the power of breathing. ¶*broken ~*⑯ *| second ~*⑰ *| get* (or *recover*) *one's ~ | I have lost my ~.* **4.** [U] empty talk; nonsense. ¶*His speech is always only ~.* **5.** ⦅*the ~*⦆ ⦅*collectively*⦆ the wind instruments; ⦅*the ~s*⦆ the members of an orchestra who play the wind instruments.
1) ***between wind and water,*** ⓐ close to the water line of a ship. ⓑ in a dangerous spot.
2) ***cast*** (or ***fling***) (fears, modesty, etc.) ***to the winds,*** neglect; take no thought of.
3) ***the four winds,*** all sides; all directions.
4) ***in the teeth of the wind; in the wind's eye,*** against the wind.
5) ***in the wind,*** happening or about to happen secretly.
6) ***know how the wind blows*** (or ***lies***), know what the state of affairs, public opinion, etc. is.
7) ***sail close to the wind,*** ⓐ sail nearly against the wind. ⓑ do something that is almost dishonest, indecent, etc.
8) ***take the wind out of*** *someone's* ***sails,*** do or say what someone else was going to do or say; interrupt someone in his conversation, usu. while boasting.
—*vt.* **1.** expose (something) to the wind. **2.** follow the smell of (something). ¶*~ a plot | The hound winded the fox.* **3.** cause (someone) to be out of breath. ¶*I was quite winded by the climb.* **4.** rest (a horse, etc.) to allow recovery of breath.

wind[2] [waind] *vt.* (**wound**) blow (a horn, etc.).

W

⁑ **wind**[3] [waind] *v.* (**wound**) *vt.* **1.** form (a thread, cord, etc.) into a ball by rolling; coil (something) around something else; twist together. ¶*~ string into a ball | ~ a bandage around one's finger.* **2.** tighten the spring of (a watch, etc.) by turning some part of it. ¶*~ up a watch.*① **3.** turn. ¶*~ a handle.*② **4.** raise (something) by winding. ¶*~ water from a well.*③ **5.** wrap closely. ¶*~ a shawl around a baby.* **6.** make (one's way) in a frequent bending course. ¶*Our bus wound its way.* —*vi.* **1.** go or move in a curving or zigzagging manner. ¶*The road winds among the hills.* **2.** twist or turn around something. ⦅*~ about* or *around* something⦆ ¶*The flag winds around the flagpole.* **3.** undergo winding. ¶*a clock which winds with a key.*④
1) ***wind off,*** unwind.
2) ***wind*** *someone* ***round*** *one's* ***fingers,*** make someone do what one pleases.
3) ***wind up,*** ⓐ coil round and round. ⓑ bring or come

다, 승리를 거두다 4)ⓐ애써 나아가다 ⓑ노력하여 성공하다
—[名] 승리; 성공
—[自] 움츠리다, 꽁무니를 빼다, 주춤하다 —[名] 주춤하기, 움츠리기, 위축
—[名] 윈치, 권양기(卷揚機)
—[名] 1. 바람; [인위적인] 바람; 강풍; 폭풍 ¶①비를 머금은 바람 /②순(역)풍/③비바람, 풍우/④바람에 거슬러서/⑤바람처럼 [빠르게] / ⑥바람과 함께, 바람 부는 대로/⑦바람을 따라서, 순풍에/⑧바람 불어오는 쪽으로 / ⑨순풍을 받고/⑩바람을 타고/⑪바람을 안고/⑫바람을 거슬러(바람 부는 쪽으로) 2. [바람에 실려오는] 향기, 냄새; 예감; 소문 ¶⑬냄새 자취를 잃지 않도록 하다/⑭소문으로 전해지다/⑮[…소문]을 알아채다, 눈치채다 3. 숨, 호흡[력] ¶⑯가쁜 숨, 헐떡거림/⑰[숨차다가 회복된] 정상적인 호흡 4. 빈말, 허튼소리 5. 관악기; 관악기 연주자들

[熟] 1)ⓐ[배의] 흘수선부(吃水線部)에 ⓑ급소에 2)…을 무시하다; 버리고 돌보지 않다 3)사방팔방에 4)바람에 거슬러서 5)몰래(비밀리에) 행하여져서, 일어날 것 같은 6)바람이 부는 방향(여론의 방향)을 알다 7)ⓐ거의 바람에 역행하여 나아가다 ⓑ거의 부정직(부도덕)하게 세상을 살아나가다 8)…을 앞지르다; 기선을 제하다; 남의 말을 가로채다(방해하다)

—[他] 1. …을 바람에 쐬다 2. …을 알아채다(낌새채다) 3. [남을] 숨차게 하다 4. [말 따위에게] 숨을 돌리게 하다

—[他] [뿔나팔 따위]를 불다
—[他] 1. …을 감다; …을 휘감다 2. [시계의 태엽 따위]를 감다 ¶①시계의 태엽을 감다 3. …을 돌리다 ¶②핸들(손잡이)을 돌리다 4. …을 감아 올리다 ¶③[고패 장치로] 우물에서 물을 길어 올리다 5. …으로 꼭 싸다, 둥치다 6. [길 따위]를 꾸불꾸불 나아가다 —[自] 1. 꾸불꾸불 나아가다, 꼬불꼬불하다 2. 감기다; 휘감기다 3. [시계 태엽이] 감기다 ¶④열쇠 같은 것으로 태엽을 감는 시계

[熟] 1)감긴 것을 풀다 2)…을 손아귀에 넣고 마음대로 부려먹다 3)ⓐ…을 둘둘 감다 ⓑ…을 결말짓다; …을 그만

to an end; conclude. ⓒ (*Baseball*) swing the arm before pitching.
두다; 끝맺다 ⓒ《野球》[투수가] 투구하기 전에 팔을 휘두르다

—*n.* [C] **1.** a turn; a curve; a bend. ¶*out of* ~.⑤ **2.** a single turn of something wound.
—[名] 1. 굽음, 굴곡; 굽이침 ¶⑤굽어 있지 않은 2. 한 번 돌리기, 한 번 감기

wind·bag [wín(d)bæ̀g] *n.* [C] (*colloq.*) a person who talks much but does not say anything of importance.
—[名] 《口》 수다장이, 공론가, 허풍장이

wind-blown [wíndblòun] *adj.* blown by the wind.
—[形] 바람에 날린

wind-borne [wíndbɔ̀:rn] *adj.* (of seed, pollen, etc.) carried by the wind.
—[形] 바람으로 운반된; 풍매(風媒)의

wind·break [wíndbrèik] *n.* [C] a shelter or protection from the wind, such as a row of trees or a walls.
—[名] 바람막이, 방풍림(防風林), 방풍벽

wind·break·er [wíndbrèikər] *n.* [C] a jacket for outdoor wear, made of wool, leather, etc.
—[名] 스포오츠용 자켓의 일종

wind·fall [wín(d)fɔ̀:l] *n.* [C] **1.** a piece of fruit fallen from the tree because of the wind. **2.** good luck; a gain, esp. of money, etc., that is unexpected.
—[名] 1. 바람으로 떨어진 과일 2. 행운; 뜻밖의 횡재, 굴러든 복

wind gauge [´ ˋ] *n.* an instrument for measuring the speed and force of the wind.
—[名] 풍력계(風力計)

wind·ing sheet [wáindiŋʃì:t] *n.* a cloth for wrapping a dead person.
—[名] 수의(壽衣)

wind instrument [´ ˋ-–] *n.* a musical instrument played by blowing air into it.
—[名] 관악기

wind·lass [wíndləs] *n.* [C] a machine for lifting or pulling; a winch. ⇨ fig.
—[名] 권양기(捲揚機), 윈치

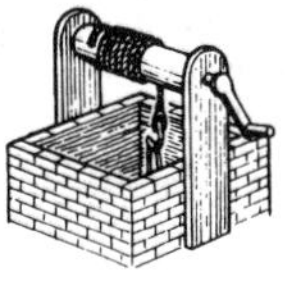
(windlass)

wind·less [wíndlis] *adj.* **1.** without wind. **2.** out of breath.
—[形] 1. 바람이 없는(잔), 고요한, 잔잔한 2. 숨이 찬

* **wind·mill** [wín(d)mìl] *n.* [C] a mill or machine for grinding operated by wind.
—[名] 풍차

⁝ **win·dow** [wíndou] *n.* [C] **1.** an opening in a wall, roof, etc. in order to let in air or light, usu. covered with glass. **2.** the framework, panes of glass, etc. filling such an opening.
—[名] 1. 창, 창구(窓口) 2. 창틀, 창유리

have all one's goods in the front window, be merely superficial.
[熟] 겉치레뿐이다, 허울뿐이다

window box [´- ˋ] *n.* a box for growing plants put under a window.
—[名] 창 밑 따위에 놓는 화초 가꾸는 상자

window dressing [´- ˋ-] *n.* **1.** the decoration or display of a store window. **2.** the act of intending to give a misleadingly favorable impression.
—[名] 1. 창문 장식, 진열장 장식[법] 2. 체면(걸)치레

window envelope [´- ˋ--] *n.* an envelope which has paraffin paper or a similar transparent section on its front so that we can read the address on the letter inside.
—[名] 창문 봉투(주소·성명을 쓴 부분이 보이게 파라핀 따위 투명한 종이를 붙인 봉투)

win·dow·pane [wíndoupèin] *n.* [C] a panel of glass in a window.
—[名] 창유리, 판유리

window seat [´- ˋ] *n.* a bench which is built into the wall of a room, beneath a window. ⇨fig.
—[名] 창 밑에 장치된 걸상

window-shop [wíndouʃàp / -ʃɔ̀p] *vi.* (**-shopped, -shop·ping**) look at the displays of goods in store windows without buying.
—[自] [사지는 않고] 진열장을 들여다보며 다니다

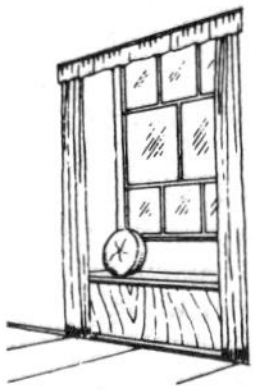
(window seat)

wind·screen [wín(d)skrì:n] *n.* [C] (*Brit.*) =windshield.

wind·shield [wín(d)ʃì:ld] *n.* [C] (*U.S.*) a sheet of glass at the front of a car, etc. to protect people from wind, rain, etc. (cf. *Brit.* windscreen)
—[名] 《美》 [자동차 앞쪽의] 바람막이 유리

wind·storm [wíndstɔ̀:rm] *n.* [C] a storm, a hurricane, etc., often without rain.
—[名] 폭풍

wind-up [wáindʌ̀p] *n.* [C] **1.** end; conclusion. **2.** (*Baseball*) preparatory arm movements of a pitcher before pitching.
—[名] 1. 종결, 결말 2. 예비 운동

wind·ward [wíndwərd] *adj.* on the side from which the wind blows. —*adv.* towards the direction from which the wind blows. —*n.* [U] the side from which
—[形] 바람 불어오는 쪽의 —[副] 바람 불어오는 쪽으로 —[名] 바람 불어오는 쪽

the wind blows. ⌈a better position than.
to the windward of, towards the place which is in⌋ [熟] …보다 유리한 쪽으로

wind·y [wíndi] *adj.* (**wind·i·er, wind·i·est**) **1.** having much wind. ¶*a ~ season.* **2.** exposed to the wind. ¶*the ~ side of the building.* **3.** talking too much or emptily. ¶*a ~ speech.* **4.** producing gas in the stomach, etc. —[形] 1. 바람이 부는 2. 바람을 세게 맞는(받는) 3. 수다스러운; 말뿐인 4. 뱃속에 가스가 괴는

⁑**wine** [wain] *n.* [U] **1.** alcoholic drink made from the juice of grapes. **2.** a similar drink made from other fruits or plants. **3.** the color of red wine. —[名] 1. 포도주 2. 과실주 3. 포도주 빛

1) ***be in wine,*** be drunk.
2) ***new wine in old bottles,*** something new which is expressed in old forms. ⌈health.
3) ***take wine with someone,*** drink to each other's⌋

[熟] 1)술에 취해 있다 2)낡은 가죽 부대에 담은 새 술(낡은 형식으로는 다룰 수 없는 새 주의) 3)건배하다

wine·glass [wáinglæ̀s / -glɑ̀:s] *n.* [C] a glass used for drinking wine. —[名] 포도주 잔

⌈juice from grapes.
wine press [⌐ ⌐] *n.* a machine used for pressing the⌋ —[名] 포도주 짜는 기구

wine·skin [wáinskìn] *n.* [C] a container made of the skin of a goat, hog, etc., used for holding wine. —[名] 포도주 넣는 가죽 부대

⁑**wing** [wiŋ] *n.* [C] **1.** the part of a bird, insect, etc. by which it flies. **2.** one of the main supporting surfaces of an airplane. **3.** the vane of a windwill. **4.** a part of a building projecting from the main part. **5.** the stage platform in a theater. **6.** (in the army or navy) the extreme right or left of the main force. **7.** a part of a political party. —[名] 1. 날개, 날갯죽지 2. 비행기의 날개 3. 풍차의 날개 4. 건물의 물림(퇴) 5. 무대의 양 옆 6. 군대의 좌우익(翼) 7. 당파(정당의 주의상의 좌우익)

1) ***add wings to,*** promote.
2) ***on the wing,*** in flight.
3) ***on the wings of the wind,*** swiftly.
4) ***take wing,*** fly away.
5) ***under the wing of,*** under the protection of.

[熟] 1)…을 촉진하다 2)비행 중인 3)신속하게, 날래게 4)날아가다 5)…의 보호 아래

—*vt.* **1.** supply (something) with wings. **2.** cause (an arrow, etc.) to fly. ¶*~ an arrow at the mark.* **3.** fly across, over or through (something). **4.** hurt (a bird or person) in the wings or arms. ¶*The poor bird was badly winged.* —*vi.* fly. ¶*The year wings away like an arrow.* —[他] 1. …에 날개를 달다 2. …을 날[수 있]게 하다 3. …을 날다 4. …의 날개(팔)에 상처를 입히다 —[自] 날다

wing chair [⌐ ⌐] *n.* a chair with winglike sides. —[名] 등 부분이 날개 모양으로 된 안락의자

winged [wiŋd, *poetic* wíŋgid] *adj.* **1.** having wings. **2.** swift. **3.** having the wings damaged or hurt. —[形] 1. 날개가 있는 2. 신속한, 날랜 3. 날개에 부상을 입은

wing·less [wíŋlis] *adj.* without wings; unable to fly. —[形] 날개가 없는; 날 수 없는

wing·spread [wíŋsprèd] *n.* [U] the distance between the tips of the spread wings of a plane or bird. —[名] 날개의 폭(길이)

***wink** [wiŋk] *vt.* **1.** close and open (one or both eyes) quickly. **2.** move or remove (something) by winking. —*vi.* **1.** close and open one or both eyes quickly. **2.** give a hint or signal by doing so. **3.** pretend not to see. ¶*~ at someone's mistake.* **4.** (of the stars) twinkle. —*n.* [C] **1.** the act of winking. **2.** a very short time; an instant. ¶*in a ~ / do not get a ~ of sleep.* —[他] 1. [눈]을 깜박거리다 2. …을 눈짓하여 치워버리다(제거하다) —[自] 1. 눈을 깜짝이다 2. 눈짓하다 3. 보고도 못본 체하다 4. [별이] 반짝이다 —[名] 1. 눈을 깜박거림; 눈짓, 윙크 2. 일순간, 눈 깜박할 사이

get the winks, receive a signal by winking. [熟] 눈짓(신호)을 받다

***win·ner** [wínər] *n.* [C] a person or thing that wins. —[名] 승리자; [경마에서] 이긴 말; 수상자(작품)

***win·ning** [wíniŋ] *adj.* **1.** victorious; successful. ¶*the ~ team.* **2.** attractive; charming. ¶*a ~ personality.* —*n.* **1.** [U][C] victory; the act of gaining. **2.** ⟪*pl.*⟫ money which one has won. —[形] 1. 이긴, 승리의 2. 애교있는, 매력있는 —[名] 1. 승리; 획득 2. 상금, 상품

winning post [⌐- ⌐] *n.* the goal of a race. —[名] 결승점

win·now [wínou] *vt.* **1.** blow off or drive away the strawlike bits from (grain). **2.** sort out; separate. —*vi.* blow off the strawlike bits from grain. —[他] 1. …의 겨를 까부르다 2. …을 골라내다, 추리다 —[自] 곡물의 겨를 까부르다

win·now·er [wínouər] *n.* [C] **1.** a person who winnows. **2.** a machine for winnowing grain, etc. —[名] 1. 곡물의 겨를 까부르는 사람 2. 풍구

win·some [wínsəm] *adj.* charming; attractive; cheerful. —[形] 매력있는, 애교있는; 쾌활한

⁑**win·ter** [wíntər] *n.* **1.** [U][C] the coldest season of the year. **2.** [C] (*poetic*) the last period of a man's life; a —[名] 1. 겨울 2. ⟪詩⟫ 만년, 노령; 감퇴(쇠퇴)기

W

period suggesting decline, gloom, etc.
—*adj.* **1.** of winter; used in winter. **2.** (of fruit and vegetables) of a kind that may be kept for use during the winter.
—[形] 1. 겨울의; 겨울에 쓰는 2. 겨울 동안 저장할 수 있는

—*vi.* pass the winter. ¶*Frogs ~ in the ground.* —*vt.* keep (cattle, etc.) during the cold season.
—[自] 겨울을 보내다(나다), 월동하다
—[他] [가축]을 겨울 동안 기르다

win·try [wíntri] *adj.* (**-tri·er, -tri·est**) **1.** of or like winter. ¶*a ~ sky.* **2.** cold and not friendly. ¶*a ~ greeting.*①
—[形] 1. 겨울의, 추운, 쓸쓸한, 황량한 2. 냉담한, 쌀쌀한 ¶①냉담한 인사

‡**wipe** [waip] *vt.* **1.** rub (something) with a cloth or some soft material in order to clean or dry; remove (something) by wiping. 《*~ away* (or *off, out, up*)》 ¶*~ one's eye; ~ one's tears away*① / *~ up spilt milk* / *~ dishes clean.* **2.** rub (a cloth, etc.) over something.
—[他] 1. …을 씻다; …을 닦아내다, 훔쳐 없애다 ¶①눈물을 닦다 2. [천 따위]를 문지르다

wipe out, ⓐ remove (something) by wiping. ⓑ clean the inside of (something). ⓒ destroy completely.
[熟] ⓐ…을 닦아내다, 지워없애다 ⓑ…의 속을 훔치다 ⓒ…을 일소(一掃)하다

—*n.* [C] the act of wiping. ¶*Give my glasses a ~.*
—[名] 닦기, 훔치기, 씻기

wip·er [wáipər] *n.* [C] **1.** a person who wipes. **2.** a thing used for wiping. ¶*a windshield ~ on a car.*
—[名] 1. 닦는(훔치는, 씻는) 사람 2. 행주, 수건, 걸레

‡**wire** [wáiər] *n.* **1.** [U] metal drawn out into a very long, thin thread; [C] a piece of this. ¶*barbed ~*① / *telephone wires*② / *a live* [laiv] *wire.*③ **2.** [U] telegraph; (*colloq.*) [C] a telegram. ¶*by ~* / *send a ~ home.*④
—[名] 1. 철사; 전선(電線); [악기의] 현(絃) ¶①가시 철사, 철조망/②전화선/③전기가 통하고 있는 철사; 활동가 2. 전신; 전보 ¶④집에 전보를 치다

1) ***get under the wire,*** manage to enter or achieve barely on time.
2) ***pull*** [***the***] ***wires,*** control affairs through secret influence.
[熟] 1)겨우 마감시간에 대다, 간신히 제시간에 해내다 2)막후(이면)에서 조종하다

—*vt.* **1.** fasten, connect, bind, or string (something) with a wire or wires. ¶*He wired firewood together.* **2.** supply (a house, etc.) with a system of wires for electricity. **3.** catch (birds, etc.) with wire. **4.** (*colloq.*) telegraph. 《~ someone *to do* or *that* …; ~ *that* …; ~ something *to*》 ¶*He wired us to get it ready by next Monday.*⑤ —*vi.* (*colloq.*) send a telegram. ¶*He wired for me to come.*
—[他] 1. …을 철사로 고정시키다(잡아매다, 잇다) 2. …에 전선을 끌다 3. [새 따위]를 철망으로 잡다 4. 《口》 …에(의) 전보를 치다 ¶⑤그는 우리들에게 요다음 월요일까지 그것을 끝마쳐 놓으라고 전보를 보내왔다 —[自] 《口》 전보를 치다

wire cutter [∠ ∠–] *n.* 《usu. *pl.*》 a tool for cutting wire. ¶*a pair of wire cutters.*
—[名] 철사 끊는 기구

wire-haired [wáiərhɛ̀ərd] *adj.* (of a dog) with coarse, stiff hair.
—[形] [개의] 털이 뻣뻣한

•**wire·less** [wáiərlis] *adj.* **1.** without wires. ¶*~ telegraphy.* **2.** (*Brit.*) of or by radio. —*n.* [U] wireless telegraph or telephone; a telegram; 《*the ~*》 (*Brit.*) radio. —*vt.* (*Brit.*) send (messages) by radio.
—[形] 1. 무선[전신]의 2. 라디오의(방송에 의한) —[名] 무선전신(전화); 전보; 라디오 [방송]
—[他] …을 라디오로 방송하다

wire·pull·er [wáiərpùlər] *n.* [C] **1.** a person who pulls wires, as in moving dolls, etc. **2.** a person who uses secret means to gain his purpose.
—[名] 1. 꼭둑각시를 놀리는 사람 2. 흑막의 인물, 막후(배후) 조종자

wire rope [∠ ∠] *n.* a rope made of twisted wires.
—[名] 쇠 밧줄, 와이어로우프

wir·ing [wáiəriŋ] *n.* [U] a system of wires for electric currents, etc.
—[名] 배선(配線) 조직

wir·y [wáiəri] *adj.* (**wir·i·er, wir·i·est**) **1.** of shape like wire. **2.** made of wire. **3.** strong.
—[形] 1. 철사 모양의 2. 철사로 만든 3. 강인한, 튼튼한, 억센

Wis·con·sin [wiskάns(i)n / -kɔ́n-] *n.* a north central State of the United States. ⇒[N.B.]
—[名] 미국 중북부의 주 [N.B.] Wis[c]. 로 줄여 씀. 수도는 Madison

Wis·con·sin·ite [wiskάns(i)nàit / -kɔ́n-] *n.* [C] a person of Wisconsin.
—[名] 위스콘신 주의 주민

‡**wis·dom** [wízd(ə)m] *n.* [U] **1.** the quality of being wise; good judgment and common sense. **2.** learning; knowledge gained by study. **3.** wise words; a maxim.
—[名] 1. 지혜; 분별 2. 학식; 지식 3. 금언, 명언

wisdom tooth [∠– ∸] *n.* the back tooth on either side of the human jaw.
—[名] 사랑니

‡**wise**¹ [waiz] *adj.* **1.** having or showing good judgment. ↔foolish ¶*a ~ man* / *a ~ saw*① / *He is wiser than he looks.* **2.** learned. ¶*be ~ in the law.*② **3.** 《usu. *wiser*》 having knowledge of. ¶*Nobody will be the wiser.*③ / *Who will be the wiser?*④
—[形] 1. 현명한, 사려[분별]있는 ¶①금언, 격언 2. 박식한, 박학의 ¶②법률에 조예가 깊다 3. 아는, 알고 있는 ¶③아무도 모를 것이다/④누가 알겠는가? (아무도 모른다)

1) ***be*** (***get***) ***wise to,*** (*U.S. colloq.*) be (become) aware of (something).
2) ***none the wiser; no wiser than before; as wise as before,*** knowing no more than before.
[熟] 1)《美口》 …을 알고 있다(알다) 2) 여전히 모르는 3)《美口》[남]에게 …을 알려주다

W

3) ***put someone wise to*** (or ***on***), (*U.S. colloq.*) inform someone about (something).

wise[2] [waiz] *n.* Ⓒ ⦅*sing.* only⦆ (*archaic*) manner; way; fashion. ¶*in some* ~① / *in this* ~② / *in no* ~.③

—[名] 《古》 방법, 방식, 식 ¶①어느 정도. 어딘가/②이와 같이/③조금도 …않는

wise·ly [wáizli] *adv.* in a wise manner.

—[副] 현명하게, 빈틈없이

⁑**wish** [wiʃ] *vt.* **1.** want. ⦅~ *to do;* ~ someone *to do;* ~ someone or something *done*⦆ ¶*I* ~ *to read Aesop's Fables.* / *I wished to have come.*① / *I* ~ *you to go at once.* / *I* ~ *the promise kept.* **2.** have or express a desire that…; be anxious that… ⦅~ *that…*⦆ ⇒[usage] ¶*I* ~ *I were a bird.* / *I* ~ *I were there.* / *I* ~ *I had been there.*② / *I* ~ [*that*] *it would rain.* **3.** express a desire to or for (someone). ¶*I* ~ *myself at home.*③ / *He wishes nobody ill.* **4.** express a desire with respect to the fortune, etc. of (someone); give a certain greeting to (someone). ¶*I* ~ *you joy.*④ / *I* ~ *you a Happy New Year.*⑤ **5.** request or order. ⦅~ someone *to do*⦆ ¶*I* ~ *you to do it.* —*vi.* have a desire; hope. ⦅~ *for* something⦆ ¶*I would not* ~ *for anything better.*⑥ / *We are apt to* ~ *for what we can't have.*

—[他] 1. …을 바라다, 원하다, …하고 싶다 ¶①오고 싶었으나 올 수 없었다 2. [실현 불가능한 일]을 바라다, …이었으면 하고 생각하다 [usage] that는 생략되는 것이 보통 ¶② 거기 있고 싶었다 3. [남이] …이었으면 좋겠다고 생각하다 ¶③나는 집에 있었으면 했다 4. [남]에게 …을 빌다, 기원하다; …을 말하다 ¶④축하합니다/⑤새해 복 많이 받으시오 5. …을 요구하다 —[自] 바라다, 원하다 ¶⑥이 이상의 것은 바라지 않겠다

—*n.* **1.** Ⓒ Ⓤ a desire: longing. ¶*with every good* ~⑦ / *with best wishes*⑧ / *have a great* ~ *to do* / *Please send your parents my best wishes.*⑨ / *We obtained results to our wishes.*⑩ **2.** Ⓒ something wished for. ¶*He has got his* ~. / *You shall have your all wishes.*

—[名] 1. 바람, 소망, 희망 ¶⑦마음으로부터의 호의를 가지고/⑧행복을 빌며/⑨부모님께 안부 전해 주십시오/⑩결과는 우리가 바라던 대로 되었다 2. 바라는 것

wish·ful [wíʃf(u)l] *adj.* **1.** having or showing a wish. ⦅~ *for*⦆. ¶*be* ~ *for happier days*① / *be* ~ *to do something.*② **2.** desirous. ¶~ *eyes.*

—[形] 1. 갈망하는 ¶①보다 더 행복한 날이 있기를 바라다/②…을 하고 싶어하다 2. 욕망을 나타내는, 탐내는

wisp [wisp] *n.* Ⓒ (of grass, etc.) a small bundle; a handful; (of hair, etc.) a small amount.

—[名] [풀 따위의] 작은 다발(단), 한 줌; [머리 따위의] 숱, 성김

wist [wist] *v.* pt. and pp. of **wit**.

wis·tar·i·a [wistέəriə], **wis·te·ri·a** [wistíəriə] *n.* Ⓒ a climbing tree with purple flowers.

—[名] 등나무속(屬)

wist·ful [wístf(u)l] *adj.* longing; melancholy. ¶*in a* ~ *mood*① / *cast a* ~ *glance at something.*

—[形] 탐나는 듯한, 부러운 듯한, 동경하는; 생각에 잠긴 ¶①생각에 잠기어

⁑**wit** [wit] *n.* **1.** Ⓤ the ability to say clever and amusing things. ¶*a man of* ~.① **2.** Ⓒ a person with such power. **3.** Ⓒ ⦅often *pl.*⦆ intelligence; understanding. ¶*have quick wits*② / *out of one's wits*③ / *in wits.*④

—[名] 1. 기지, 재치 ¶①재치(기지) 있는 사람 2. 재주꾼, 재사 3. 이해력, 분별 ¶②이해력이 빠르다/③제 정신을 잃고/④제 정신으로

1) ***at one's wit's end,*** at a loss; not knowing what to do or say.
2) ***have*** (or ***keep***) *one's* ***wits about*** *one,* be observant and careful.
3) ***out of*** *one's* ***wits,*** mad.

[熟] 1)어찌 할 바를 몰라 2)제 정신을 잃고, 미쳐서

—*vt., vi.* (**wist, wit·ting**) (*archaic*) know. ⇒[usage]
to wit, that is to say.

—[他][自] 알다, 알고 있다 [usage] 지금은 다음 성구로만 쓰임
[熟] 즉, 말하자면

·**witch** [witʃ] *n.* Ⓒ a woman who has magic power; an ugly old woman; (*colloq.*) a charming young woman. ↔wizard ¶*a white* ~① / *a* ~ *doctor.*② —*vt.* exert magic power toward (someone); charm.

—[名] 마녀; 마귀할멈; 《口》 매력있는 여자 ¶①선(善)마녀/②[특히 아프리카 토인의] 요술사 —[他]…에 마술을 걸다; …을 홀리게 하다, 매혹하다

witch·craft [wítʃkræ̀ft / -krɑ̀:ft] *n.* Ⓤ magic.

—[名] 마법, 마력

witch·er·y [wítʃəri] *n.* Ⓤ magic; charm.

—[名] 마법, 매력

witch·ing [wítʃiŋ] *adj.* magical; charming.

—[形] 마력을 가진; 매혹적인

⁑**with** [wið, wiθ] *prep.* **1.** accompanied by; in the company of. ¶*walk* ~ *one's friend* / *In the great war they fought* ~ *the French against the Germans.* **2.** in some particular relation to. ¶*have dealings* ~① / *I have nothing to do* ~ *that affair.*② **3.** of the same opinion, belief, etc. as; in support of. ¶*in harmony* ~③ / *vote* ~ *the party* / *I feel* ~ *you.*④ / *I am entirely* ~ *you in this.*⑤ **4.** concerning; in regard to. ¶*What do you want* ~ *me.*⑥ / *What is the matter* ~ *you?*⑦ / *It is usual* ~ *him.*⑧ **5.** in proportion to. ¶*compare* ~ / *grow wise* ~ *age.*⑨ **6.** having; possessing; wearing. ¶*a lady* ~ *golden*

—[前] 1. …와 함께, …와 더불어 2. …와 관계하여 ¶①…와 거래관계가 있다/②나는 그 사건과는 아무 관계가 없다 3. …에 찬성하여; …을 지지하여 ¶③…와 조화하여/④너와 동감이다/⑤나는 이 점에 대해서는 전적으로 너와 동감이다 4. …에 관하여 ¶⑥나에게 무슨 볼일이 있는가?/⑦무슨 일인가?/⑧그에게는 그것이 보통이다 5. …와 비교하여, …에 따라서 ¶⑨나이를 먹음에 따라 현명해지다 6. …을 가지고;

*hair | a man ~ ten thousand dollars a year.*⑩ **7.** in keeping or in care of. ¶*I will leave the children ~ my grandmother.* **8.** because of; as a result of. ¶*bent ~ age | eyes dim ~ tears.* **9.** notwithstanding; in spite of. ⇒***with all*** **10.** by means of; by the use of. ¶*cut ~ a knife | I have not a pen to write ~.*⑪ *| I've got no money to buy it ~. | I filled the glass ~ water. | The garden is enclosed ~ a fence.* **11.** (of manner) using or showing. ¶*~ ease*⑫ *| ~ care*⑬ *| ~ courage*⑭ *| ~ an ugly smile on his face.* **12.** at the same time as; during. ¶*contemporary ~*⑮ *| rise ~ the sun.*⑯ **13.** (of separation) from. ¶*part ~ a friend | He differed ~ me.* **14.** against. ¶*fight ~ | He argued ~ his wife.*

with all, in spite of. ¶*With all his efforts, he failed. | With all his faults, I like him.*

with·al [wiðɔ́:l, +*U.S.* wiθ-] *adv.* (*archaic*) besides; still; at the same time; nevertheless. ¶*He was wise and handsome, and rich ~.* **—*prep.*** with. ⇒[usage] ¶*He has nothing to fill his belly ~.*

* **with·draw** [wiðdrɔ́:, wiθ-] *v.* (**-drew, -drawn**) *vt.* pull back; take back; draw (money, etc.) back. ⦅~ something *from*⦆ ¶*~ money from the bank.* **—*vi.*** leave; go away. ¶*~ from someone's presence.*①

with·draw·al [wiðdrɔ́:əl, wiθ-] *n.* [U] [C] the act of withdrawing; the state of being withdrawn. ¶*a ~ from a room | a ~ of money from the bank.*①

with·drawn [wiðdrɔ́:n, wiθ-] *v.* pp. of **withdraw**.

with·drew [wiðdrú:, +*U.S.* wiθ-] *v.* pt. of **withdraw**.

withe [wiθ, wið, waið] *n.* [C] an easily bent stick.

* **with·er** [wíðər] *vi.* dry up and fade. ¶*The grass withered in the hot sun.* **—*vt.*** **1.** cause (something) to dry up and fade. **2.** cause (someone) to feel ashamed or to lose vigor. ¶*~ someone with an angry glance.*①

with·held [wiðhéld, wiθ-] *v.* pt. and pp. of **withhold**.

with·hold [wiðhóuld, wiθ-] *vt.* (**-held**) keep or hold (something) back; keep (someone) from action.

⁑ **with·in** [wiðín] *adv.* **1.** in the inner part; inside. ¶*It is green without, but yellow ~.* **2.** at home; indoors. ¶*He is ~. | go ~.* **3.** in the mind or conscience.

—*prep.* **1.** in the inner part of; inside of; in. ¶*~ the room | ~ doors.*① **2.** in the limits, range, or scope of; not beyond. ¶*~ hearing*② *| ~ ten minutes | ~ a stone's throw*③ *| Live ~ your income.*④ *| They live ~ a few miles of Paris. | Is the shelf ~ your reach?*

—*n.* [U] the inside. ¶*Their actions are seen from ~.*

⁑ **with·out** [wiðáut, +*U.S.* wiθ-] *prep.* **1.** outside of; beyond. ¶*~ doors.*① **2.** not having; lacking in. ¶*~ leave*② *| ~ number*③ *| ~ reserve*④ *| ~ a single word spoken | do ~*⑤ *| It goes ~ saying that ...*⑥

—*adv.* outside. ¶*within and ~ | He is waiting ~.*

—*conj.* (*slang*) unless.

* **with·stand** [wiðstǽnd, wiθ-] *vt.* (**-stood**) oppose; resist; endure.

with·stood [wiðstúd, wiθ-] *v.* pt. and pp. of **withstand**.

with·y [wíði, +*U.S.* -θi] *n.* (pl. **with·ies**) =withe.

wit·less [wítlis] *adj.* without sense; foolish.

⁑ **wit·ness** [wítnis] *n.* [U] evidence; [C] a person who actually saw an event; anything that is used as evidence. ¶*in ~ of ...*① *| be my ~ that...*② *| give ~ on behalf of ...*③ *| bear someone ~*④ *| call* (or *take*) *someone to ~.*⑤

1) ***bear witness to*** (or ***of***)***,*** give evidence about (something).
2) ***with a witness,*** without a doubt.

—*vt.* **1.** be present and see (an event, etc.). **2.** give evidence of (an event, etc.). ¶*He witnessed that it was the driver's fault.* **3.** sign (a paper) as a wit-

…을 소유하고 있는 ¶⑩연수(年收) 1만 달러의 사람 7. …을 보관하여, …의 수중에 8. … 때문에, 탓으로 9. …에도 불구하고 10. …에 의하여; …으로써, …을 써서 ¶⑪쓸 펜이 없다 11. [상태 · 태도가] …하여 ¶⑫쉽게, 수월하게/⑬주의(조심)하여 / ⑭용감하게 12. …와 동시에 ¶⑮…와 같은 시대의 /⑯해가 뜨는 것과 동시에 일어나다 13. …와 떨어져서 14. …에 반대하여

[熟] …에도 불구하고

—[副] 《古》 그 위에, 게다가; 여전히; 동시에 —[前] …으로[써], …을 가지고 [usage] 항상 문장 끝이나 낱말 끝에 옴

—[他] …을 움츠리다, 뒤로 물리다; 철수시키다, 되돌리다 —[自] 물러나다, 가버리다, 떠나다 ¶①남이 있는 곳에서 물러가다

—[名] 움츠림, 물러남; 거두어들임, 회수 ¶①은행에서 돈을 찾아내기

—[名] [장작 따위를 묶는] 등 넝쿨, 실버들 가지

—[自] 시들다, 말라죽다 —[他] 1. …을 시들게 하다, 말라죽게 하다 2. …을 위축시키다; 좌절시키다, 맥 못추게 하다 ¶①남을 노려보아 기를 죽이다

—[他] …을 보류하다; [남]을 억제하다, 억누르다

—[副] 1. 안(속)에, 내부에 2. 집안에, 실내에 3. 마음 속에, 심중에

—[前] 1. …의 안(속)에, …의 내부에 ¶①실내에 2. …의 범위내에서; …을 넘지 않는 ¶②[부르면] 들리는 곳에/③돌을 던지면 닿는 곳에/④수입의 한도내에서 생활하라

—[名] 안, 속, 내부

—[前] 1. …의 밖에[서] ¶①옥외에서 2. …이 없는, 없이 ¶②무단히, 함부로/③무수한/④서슴지 않고/⑤…없이 해내다(지내다)/⑥…은 말할 나위도 없다

—[副] …밖에, 밖은, 밖에서, 밖으로

—[接] …하지 않고서는, 하지 않으면

—[他] …에 반항하다, 견디다

—[形] 지혜(재치 · 분별)없는; 어리석은

—[名] 증거; 목격자, 증거물 ¶①…의 증거로/②…을 맹세코 단언하다/③…을 위하여 증언하다/④[남]의 증인이 되다, …의 증언을 하다/⑤…을 증인으로 내세우다

[熟] 1) …을 입증하다 2) 명백히, 의심할 바 없이

—[他] 1. …을 목격하다 2. …을 입증하다 3. …에 서명하다

W

ness. **—**_vi._ give or serve as evidence. 《~ _for_ or _against_ someone ; ~ _to_ something》 ¶~ _to someone's reputation_① | _Witness Heaven!_②
—[自] 입증하다 ¶①…의 명성을 증명하다/②하늘이여 굽어살피소서 !

wit·ti·ly [wítili] _adv._ in a witty manner.
—[副] 재치있게, 임기응변으로, 익살스럽게

wit·ting·ly [wítiŋli] _adv._ intentionally ; knowingly.
—[副] 일부러, 고의로 ; 알면서

wit·ty [wíti] _adj._ (**-ti·er, -ti·est**) clever and amusing in speech.
—[形] 재치있는, 기지가 풍부한

⁑**wives** [waivz] _n._ pl. of **wife**.

wiz·ard [wízərd] _n._ [C] a man who has magic power. ↔witch
—[名] 마법사

wiz·ened [wíznd] _adj._ dried up ; faded.
—[形] 시든, 말라붙은, 쇠퇴한

wob·ble [wábl / wɔ́bl] _vi., vt._ move unsteadily ; often change one's opinion. **—**_n._ [C] the act of wobbling ; [U] the state of being wobbly.
—[自][他] 흔들흔들하다, 동요하다 ; 변덕부리다 ; …을 흔들리게 하다 —[名] 흔들리기, 동요

wob·bly [wábli / wɔ́b-] _adj._ (**-bli·er, -bli·est**) unsteady ; shaky.
—[形] 흔들흔들하는, 불안정한, 주견 없는

***woe** [wou] _n._ [U] deep grief. ¶_in weal and_ ~① | _a tale of_ ~.
—[名] 슬픔, 비애 ¶①행·불행간에

woe·be·gone [wóubigɔ̀:n / -gɔ̀n] _adj._ looking very sad.
—[形] 슬픔(수심)에 잠긴

woe·ful [wóuf(u)l] _adj._ sorrowful ; pitiful. ▷**woe·ful·ly** [-fuli]
—[形] 슬픈, 비참한

⁑**woke** [wouk] _v._ pt. and pp. of **wake**.

wold [would] _n._ [U][C] a gently sloping, treeless region ; an open, uncultivated region.
—[名] 황야, 황무지

⁑**wolf** [wulf] _n._ [C] (pl. **wolves**) **1.** a wild animal like a dog. **2.** a cruel, greedy person. ¶(_Bible_) _a ~ in sheep's clothing; a ~ in a lamb's skin_①|_have a ~ in the stomach._②
—[名] 1. 이리, 늑대 2. 탐욕스러운 사람, 잔인한 사람 ¶①《聖》위선자/②몹시 시장하다, 허기지다

1) _**cry wolf,**_ raise a false alarm.
2) _**keep the wolf from the door,**_ get just enough food or money to live on.
[熟] 1)거짓 경보를 전하다(이솝 이야기에서) 2)기갈을 면하다, 요기하다

—_vt._ eat (food) quickly and greedily.
—[他] …을 게걸스럽게 먹다

wolf·hound [wúlfhàund] _n._ [C] a large dog formerly used for hunting wolves.
—[名] 늑대 사냥에 쓰던 큰 개

wolf·ish [wúlfiʃ] _adj._ like a wolf ; cruel ; greedy.
—[形] 늑대 같은 ; 잔인한 ; 욕심사나운

***wolves** [wulvz] _n._ pl. of **wolf**.

⁑**wom·an** [wúmən] _n._ [C] (pl. **wom·en**) **1.** a grown-up human female. ¶_a married_ ~. **2.** [U] 《_collectively_》 the female sex. ¶_Frailty, thy name is_ ~.① **3.** 《_the_ ~》 womanly qualities. ¶_There is little of the ~ in her._②
—[名] 1. [성숙한] 여자, 여인, 부인 2. [일반적으로] 여자, 여성 ¶①약한 자여, 너의 이름은 여자니라 3. 여자다움 ¶②그녀에게는 여자다운 데가 없다

wom·an·hood [wúmənhùd] _n._ **1.** [U] the condition of being a woman. **2.** 《_collectively_》 women.
—[名] 1. 여자다움 2. [일반적으로] 여성, 부인

wom·an·ish [wúməniʃ] _adj._ like a woman ; weak.
—[形] 여자다운, 여자 같은 ; 연약한

wom·an·kind [wúmənkàind] _n._ [U] 《_collectively_》 women ; the female sex.
—[名] 부인, 여성

wom·an·like [wúmənlàik] _adj._ womanly; like a woman.
—[形] 여자다운, 여자 같은

wom·an·ly [wúmənli] _adj._ (**-li·er, -li·est**) **1.** like a woman. **2.** suitable for a woman.
—[形] 1. 여자다운, 여자 같은 2. 여성에게 알맞은(어울리는)

womb [wu:m] _n._ [C] the organ in the female body in which the young are grown till birth. ¶_a fruit of the_ ~① | _in the ~ of time._②
—[名] 자궁(子宮) ¶①아이, 아기/②장차 일어날

⁑**wom·en** [wímin] _n._ pl. of **woman**.

wom·en·folk [wíminfòuk] _n. pl._ women as a group.
—[名] 부인, 여성들

⁑**won** [wʌn] _v._ pt. and pp. of **win**.

⁑**won·der** [wʌ́ndər] _n._ **1.** [U] an emotion or feeling of surprise, awe, admiration, etc. excited by something strange or unexpected. ¶_be filled with ~ | be lost in_ ~.① **2.** [C] a person, thing, or event that excites surprise and admiration ; a miracle. ¶_the seven wonders of the world_② | _a nine day's_ ~③ | _for a_ ~④ | _to a_ ~⑤ | _do_ (or _work_) _wonders_⑥ | _He failed, and no_ ~.⑦ | _It is a ~ [that] he was alive._; _The ~ is that he was alive._⑧ | _[It is] no ~ [that] he didn't want to go._ | _What ~ [that] he didn't come?_⑨
—[名] 1. 경탄, 경이(驚異), 놀라움 ¶①경탄하다 2. 경이적인 인물, 불가사의한 사람(일·사건) ; 기적 ¶②세계의 일곱가지 불가사의/③한때의 소문/④이상스럽게도/⑤놀랄 만큼/⑥기적을 행하다/⑦그가 실패한 데 대해 이상할 것은 없다/⑧이상하게도 그는 살아 있었다/⑨그가 오지 않은 것이 뭐가 이상한가 ?

—_vi._ be filled with wonder ; marvel. 《~ _at_ someone or something ; ~ _to do_》 ¶_I ~ at you._⑩ | _I ~ to see you here._ **—**_vt._ **1.** be surprised. 《~ _that_...》 ¶_I ~ that he did not ask you about it._ **2.** want to know. 《~ _how_ (or _what_, etc.) _to do_; ~ _how_ (or _what_, etc.)...》
—[自] 이상하게 생각하다, 놀라다 ¶⑩너에게는 놀랐다(기가 막히네) —[他] 1. …을 이상하게 여기다, …에 놀라다 2. …일까[하고 생각하다] ¶⑪좀 도와주실 수 있을는지요

W

¶*I ~ whether* (or *if*) *I might ask you to help me.*⑪ / *I ~ who he is.*

‡ **won·der·ful** [wʌ́ndərf(u)l] *adj.* astonishing; amazing; marvelous. ▷**won·der·ful·ly** [-fuli] *adv.*
—[形] 놀랄 만한, 놀라운; 훌륭한; 이상한, 불가사의한

won·der·land [wʌ́ndərlæ̀nd] *n.* [C] a land full of wonders; a fairyland.
—[名] 이상한 나라, 요정(妖精)의 나라, 선경(仙境)

won·der·ment [wʌ́ndərmənt] *n.* [U] a feeling or state of wonder; surprise.
—[名] 경탄, 경이(驚異), 놀라움

won·der·struck [wʌ́ndərstrʌ̀k] *adj.* struck with wonder; feeling surprise.
—[形] 놀라움에 질린, 깜짝 놀란, 아연실색한

* **won·drous** [wʌ́ndrəs] *adj.* wonderful. —*adv.* wonderfully.
—[形] 놀랄 만한, 신기한, 이상한 —[副] 놀랄 만큼

* **wont** [wount, +*U.S.* wʌnt, wɔ:nt] *adj.* accustomed. ⟪~ *to do*⟫ ¶*as he was ~ to say.* —*n.* [U] custom; habit.
—[形] …에 익숙한, …하는 것이 보통인 —[名] 습관, 습성

‡ **won't** [wount, +*U.S.* wʌnt] will not.

wont·ed [wóuntid, +*U.S.* wɔ:nt-] *adj.* accustomed; usual. ¶*He won every game with his ~ ease.*①
—[形] 습관이 된; 늘 …하는 ¶①일상의 침착성으로 전(全)경기에 이겼다

* **woo** [wu:] *vt.* **1.** try to gain the love of (someone). **2.** try to get.
—[他] 1. …에게 구애(구혼)하다 2. …을 추구(追求)하다; …에게 조르다

‡ **wood** [wud] *n.* **1.** [C] ⟪often *pl.*⟫ a land covered with trees, etc.; a forest. **2.** [U] trees cut up for making something; timber; lumber.
1) ***cannot see the wood*[*s*] *for the tree,*** cannot see the whole because of too many details.
2) ***out of the wood,*** out of danger; clear of difficulties.
—[名] 1. 숲, 삼림 2. 목재; 목질(木質); 재목
[熟] 1)나무만 보고 숲은 못 보다; 작은 것에 사로잡혀 대국(大局)을 내다보지 못하다 2)위험을 모면하여

wood alcohol [⌐ ⌐--] *n.* methyl alcohol.
—[名] 메틸 알코올, 목정(木精)

wood block [⌐ ⌐] *n.* **1.** a block of wood. **2.** a piece of wood on which figures are carved.
—[名] 1. 나무 벽돌 2. 목판(木版), 판목(版木)

wood carving [⌐ ⌐-] *n.* the art of carving objects by hand from wood.
—[名] 목각(木刻), 목조(木彫), 목재 조각

wood·chuck [wúdtʃʌ̀k] *n.* [C] a brown animal of the rat family; a North American marmot.
—[名] 마아못의 일종(북미산 쥐과의 동물)

wood·cock [wúdkɑ̀k / -kɔ̀k] *n.* [C] (pl. **-cocks** or *collectively* **-cock**) a small brown game bird. ⇒fig.
—[名] 누른 도요

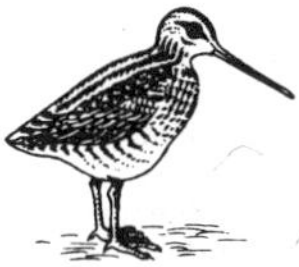
〔woodcock〕

wood·craft [wúdkræ̀ft / -krɑ̀:ft] *n.* [U] skill or knowledge in anything concerning forests or woods.
—[名] 삼림(森林) 기술; 삼림의 지식

wood·cut [wúdkʌ̀t] *n.* [C] a piece of wood cut so as to print a picture; a picture printed from such a block.
—[名] 목판[화]

wood·cut·ter [wúdkʌ̀tər] *n.* [C] a person who cuts down trees; a person who makes woodcuts.
—[名] 나무꾼; 목판[조각]사

wood·ed [wúdid] *adj.* covered with trees.
—[形] 나무가 무성한, 숲이 많은

‡ **wood·en** [wúdn] *adj.* **1.** made of wood. **2.** lifeless; dull. **3.** not skillful.
—[形] 1. 나무로 만든, 목제(목조)의 2. 활기 없는; 우둔한 3. 서투른, 어색한

wood engraver [⌐ -⌐-] *n.* a person who cuts a design on wood for printing.
—[名] 목판사(木版師), 목각사(木刻師)

wood engraving [⌐ -⌐-] *n.* the art or process of cutting designs on wood for printing.
—[名] 목판, 목조각(木彫刻)

wood·en·head·ed [wúdnhèdid] *adj.* dull; foolish.
—[形] 우둔한, 멍청한, 어리석은

wood·land *n.* [wúdlæ̀nd, -lənd / -lənd ‖ → *adj.*] [U] a piece of land covered with trees; forest. —*adj.* [-lə̀nd] of woods.
—[名] 삼림지(森林地) —[形] 삼림지의, 숲의

wood·man [wúdmən] *n.* [C] (pl. **-men** [-mən]) **1.** a woodcutter. **2.** a person who lives in the woods. **3.** a person who takes care of forests.
—[名] 1. 나무꾼 2. 숲에서 사는 사람, 산(山)사람 3. 삼림 감독관, 산지기

wood·peck·er [wúdpèkər] *n.* [C] a brightly-colored bird which makes holes in trees in order to get insects to eat.
—[名] 딱다구리

wood pulp [⌐ ⌐] *n.* a pulp made from wood and from which paper is made.
—[名] 목재 펄프

woods·man [wúdzmən] *n.* (pl. **-men** [-mən]) =woodman

wood·wind [wúdwìnd] *n.* [C] **1.** ⟪*pl.*⟫ the wind instruments of an orchestra, esp. those made of wood. **2.** any of these wind instruments. ¶*a ~ instrument.*
—[名] 1. 목관악기류(부) 2. 목관악기

wood·work [wúdwə̀:rk] *n.* [U] the wooden parts of a
—[名] 목조부; 나무 세공, 목공물

W

house; work done in or with wood.

wood·y [wúdi] *adj.* (**wood·i·er, wood·i·est**) having many trees; like wood.
—[형] 나무가 많은; 나무 같은, 목질의

woo·er [wú(:)ər] *n.* [C] a person who woos.
—[명] 구애자, 구혼자

woof [wuf, wu:f / wu:f] *n.* [U] the cross threads in cloth. ↔warp
—[명] [피륙의] 씨실

wool [wul] *n.* [U] **1.** the soft hair of sheep, etc. **2.** cloth made of wool.
1) ***all wool and a yard wide,*** genuine; admirable.
2) ***draw the wool over** someone's **eyes,*** deceive.
—[명] **1.** 양모, 털실 **2.** 모직물, 나사(羅紗)
[熟] 1)흠잡을 데 없는, 순수한; 훌륭한 2)[남의 눈을] 속이다

wool·en, *Brit.* **wool·len** [wúlin] *adj.* made of wool; of wool. ¶ ~ *cloth.*① —*n.* [U] [C] material made from wool.
—[형] 모직의, 양털의, 양모로 만든 ¶①나사(羅紗) —[명] 모직물, 나사

wool·gath·er·ing [wúlgæð(ə)riŋ] *n.* [U] absent-mindedness. —*adj.* absent-minded.
—[명] 방심 —[형] 방심한, 넋나간, 멍청한

wool·ly, wool·y [wúli] *adj.* (**wool·[l]i·er, wool·[l]i·est**) like wool; covered with wool, etc. —*n.* [C] a sweater; [U] something made from wool.
—[형] 털 같은, 털이 많은 —[명] 스웨터; 양모 제품

word [wə:rd] *n.* **1.** [C] a sound or series of sounds, or a letter or group of letters, used as a unit of language. ¶*words and phrases.*① **2.** [C] 《usu. *pl.*》 a speech; a thing said; a remark. ¶*a man of few* (*many*) *words*② / *big words*③ / *good* (or *fair*) *words*④ / *a ~ in* (*out of*) *season*⑤ / *I want to have a ~ with you.* **3.** [C] 《usu. *pl.*》 a quarrel. ¶*hot words*⑥ / *have words with*⑦ / *come to* [*high*] *words.*⑧ **4.** [U] 《usu. without *an article*》 news; information. ¶*bring ~*⑨ / *get ~ from* / *send ~* / *leave ~.*⑩ **5.** [U] 《*sing.* only, *one's ~*》 a promise; an assurance. ¶*a man of his ~*⑪ / *give* (or *pass*) *one's ~*⑫ / *keep* (*break*) *one's ~* / *On my ~ of honor, I'll get it.*⑬ **6.** [U] an order or a command; 《*the ~*》 a password; a watchword. ¶*give the ~ to fire*⑭ / *give the ~*⑮ / *Sharp's the ~!*⑯
1) ***at a*** (or ***one***) ***word,*** immediately.
2) ***be as good as** one's **word,*** hold to one's promises.
3) ***by word of mouth,*** by speech; orally.
4) ***eat** one's **words,*** take back one's statement.
5) ***have no words for,*** be unable to describe.
6) ***have the last word,*** make the final remark in an argument; win an argument.
7) ***in a*** (or ***one***) ***word,*** in short; briefly.
8) ***in so many words,*** precisely; literally.
9) ***my word upon it,*** on my honor.
10) ***on*** (or ***with***) ***the word,*** as soon as something is said.
11) ***say*** (or ***put in***) ***a good word for,*** speak favorably of (something); commend.
12) ***take** someone **at his word,*** take someone's statement to be literally true.
13) ***upon my word,*** ⓐ on my honor. ⓑ 《an exclamation of *surprise, irritation, etc.*》 indeed!
14) ***word for word,*** literally.
—*vt.* express (something) in words. ¶ ~ *one's ideas clearly.*
—[명] **1.** 낱말, 단어; 말 ¶①단어와 숙어 **2.** 말, 이야기, 담화; 한 마디[의 말] ¶②말 수 적은(수다스러운) 사람/③호언장담/④듣기 좋은(알랑거리는) 말/⑤때에 맞는(안 맞는) 말 **3.** 말다툼, 언쟁 ¶⑥논쟁/⑦…와 말다툼하다/⑧말이 격해지다, 말다툼이 되다 **4.** 알림, 기별, 소식, 전언(傳言) ¶⑨소식을 전하다/⑩전할 말을 남기다 **5.** 약속 ¶⑪약속을 지키는 사람/⑫약속하다/⑬명예를 걸고 그것을 얻고야 말겠다 **6.** 명령, 지시; 암호말, 군호 ¶⑭발포 명령을 내리다/⑮군호를 말하다/⑯서둘러라!
[熟] 1)즉시, 당장에 2)약속을 이행하다 3)구두(口頭)로 4)식언하다, 먼저 한 말을 번복하다 5)…을 무어라 표현할 말이 없다 6)결정적인(남이 꼼짝못할) 말을 하다 7)한 마디로 말해서, 요는 8)똑똑히, 간결하게 9)확실히, 맹세코 10)말하기가 무섭게, 즉각 11)…을 추천하다 12)…이 하는 말을 그대로 믿다 13)ⓐ맹세코 ⓑ이런, 이것 참! 14)한마디 한마디, 축어적(逐語的)으로
—[타] …을 말로 나타내다(표현하다)

word·book [wə́:rdbùk] *n.* [C] a dictionary; a list of words.
—[명] 사전; 단어집

word·ing [wə́:rdiŋ] *n.* [U] a way of expressing a thought; choice of words.
—[명] 표현법, 어법, 말씨

word·less [wə́:rdlis] *adj.* speechless; without words.
—[형] 무언의, 말 없는

word·y [wə́:rdi] *adj.* (**word·i·er, word·i·est**) of words; using too many words. ¶ ~ *warfare.*①
—[형] 말의; 말 많은, 장황한 ¶①설전(舌戰), 논쟁

wore [wɔ:r] *v.* pt. of **wear.**

work [wə:rk] *n.* **1.** [U] bodily or mental effort to do something; labor; toil. ¶*a good day's ~*① / *hard ~* / *~ of time*② / (*proverb*) *All ~ and no play makes Jack a dull boy.* **2.** [U] something to be done or made; a task. ¶*I have a lot of ~ to do.* **3.** [U] employment; occupation; trade. ¶*look for ~.* **4.** [U] 《*collectively*》 that which is produced by effort or activity. **5.** [C] a
—[명] **1.** 일, 작업, 노동 ¶①하루 꼬박의 일거리/②시간이 걸리는 일 **2.** [하여야 할] 일, 과업, 임무 **3.** 업, 직업, 생업; 장사 **4.** 세공물 **5.** 작품, 저작(著作) ¶③미술품/④셰익스피어 전집 **6.** 공장, 제작소 ¶⑤유리 공장 **7.** [시계 따위]의 기계 장치 **8.** 행위, 소행, 짓 ¶⑥이것은

W

product of the intellect or the imagination. ¶*a ~ of art*③ | *the works of Shakespeare.*④ **6.** ((usu. *pl.*, often used as *sing.*)) a place where work is done; a factory. ¶*a glass works.*⑤ **7.** [C] ((usu. *pl.*)) the working parts of a watch, etc. **8.** [C] ((often *pl.*)) an act; a deed. ¶*This is the ~ of the enemy.*⑥ **9.** [U] manner of working; workmanship. ¶*unskillful ~.*

적의 소행이다 9. 일하는 방식; 일솜씨

1) ***all in the*** (or ***a***) ***day's work,*** normal; what is usual.
2) ***at work,*** working. ¶*She is hard at ~.*
3) ***fall*** (or ***get, set, go***) ***to work,*** begin to work.
4) ***have one's work cut out for one,*** have as much a task as one can do; have very much to do.
5) ***in*** (***out of***) ***work,*** having (not having) a job.
6) ***make short*** (or ***quick***) ***work of,*** finish quickly.

[熟] 1)당연한 [일] 2)일을 하여 3)일에 착수하다 4)할 일이 태산같이 많다 5)직업이 있어(실직하여) 6)…을 재빨리 해치우다

—*v.* (**worked** or *archaic* **wrought**) *vi.* **1.** do work; labor. ¶*~ hard* | *~ at a desk* | *~ for the public good.*⑦ **2.** be employed. ¶*~ in a factory.* **3.** (of a machine, a bodily organ, etc.) operate; act. ¶*The electric bell won't ~.*⑧ **4.** (of a plan, etc.) be successful or effective; achieve the desired result. ¶*The medicine works like magic.*⑨ **5.** move slowly and with difficulty; gradually become. ¶*Her elbow had worked through the sleeve.*⑩ | *The wind has worked around.*⑪ **6.** move in agitation. ¶*His face worked violently.* **7.** (of yeast or a liquid) undergo a slow chemical change. ¶*Yeast makes beer ~.* **8.** have an effect or influence. ((*~ on* or *upon* someone or something)) **—*vt.*** **1.** cause (a machine, etc.) to operate; cause (a person, horse, etc.) to labor. ¶*~ a pump* | *~ one's servants unmercifully.* **2.** operate; manage. ¶*~ a farm.* **3.** solve. ¶*~ a problem.* **4.** form; shape; knit. ¶*He worked the clay into a pretty vase.* **5.** bring about; accomplish. ¶*~ one's will.*⑫ **6.** achieve (something) by effort or work. ¶*~ one's way* (or *passage*)⑬ | *~ one's way through college.*⑭ **7.** excite, move, or stir (someone's feelings). ¶*~ someone into rage*⑮ | *~ oneself into a temper.*⑯ **8.** carry on one's occupation in, through, or along (a region, etc.). ¶*The salesman works the East Coast.*

—[自] 1. 일하다, 노동하다 ¶⑦공익을 위해서 일하다 2. 종사하고(근무하고) 있다 3. [기계·기관 따위가] 움직이다, 작용(가동)하다 ¶⑧초인종이 울리지 않는다 4. [계획 따위가] 잘 되어 가다, [효력이] 듣다 ¶⑨그 약은 신통하게 잘 듣는다 5. [노력하여] 가아가다; 점점 …이 되다 ¶⑩그녀의 팔꿈치가 소매를 간신히 빠져나갔다/⑪바람 방향이 바뀌었다 6. [얼굴·마음 따위가] 동요하다; 실룩거리다 7. 발효하다 8. 영향(효력)이 있다 —[他] 1. …을 움직이다; …을 작용시키다 2. …을 경영하다 3. …을 풀다, 해결하다 4. …을 만들다; …을 [어떤 모양으로] 하다; …을 뜨다, 짜다 5. …을 가져오다, 초래하다; 성취하다 ¶⑫뜻을 성취하다 6. 노력하여(애써서) …을 얻다, …을 나아가다 ¶⑬애써서(고생하여) 나아가다/⑭고학하여 대학을 나오다 7. …을 흥분시키다, 자극하다 ¶⑮…을 성나게 하다/⑯격분(격노)하다 8. [땅]을 작업장으로 만들다

1) ***work at,*** apply oneself to (something); study.
2) ***work away*** (or ***on***)***,*** continue to work.
3) ***work in,*** insert; gradually mix into (something).
4) ***work off,*** get rid of; dispose of (something).
5) ***work on*** (or ***upon***)***,*** ⓐ try to persuade. ⓑ influence.
6) ***work out,*** ⓐ calculate. ⓑ solve. ⓒ bring about by work. ⓓ exhaust through working. ⓔ plan out; develop. ⓕ be calculated. ⓖ accomplish; get the result.
7) ***work up,*** ⓐ build up (something) gradually by effort. ⓑ excite. ⓒ elaborate. ⓓ advance; rise. ((*~ to* a place, etc.)) ⓔ develop; prepare.

[熟] 1)…에 종사하다; …을 공부하다 2)일을 계속하다, 부지런히 일하다 3)…을 삽입하다; …에 서서히 섞이다 4)…을 없애다, 제거하다; 해치우다, 처치하다 5)ⓐ설득하다 ⓑ…을 감화하다, …에 영향을 미치다 6)ⓐ산출(算出)하다 ⓑ풀다, 해결하다 ⓒ노력하여 이루다 ⓓ다 파 버리다, 다 파서 동나게 하다 ⓔ계획을 세우다 ⓕ산정(算定)되다 ⓖ…을 달성하다; …으로 되다, 끝나다 7) ⓐ차차 이루다 ⓑ…을 흥분시키다 ⓒ공들여 만들다 ⓓ…으로 나아가다 ⓔ…을 발전시키다; 준비하다

work·a·ble [wə́ːrkəbl] *adj.* that can be worked or operated.

—[形] 움직일 수 있는, 실행할 수 있는

work·a·day [wə́ːrkədèi] *adj* **1.** of working days. **2.** ordinary; practical.

—[形] 1. 일하는 날의 2. 평범한; 실제적인

work·bench [wə́ːrkbèntʃ] *n.* [C] a table at which work is done.

—[名] 작업대(臺), 세공대

work·book [wə́ːrkbùk] *n.* [C] **1.** a book with questions and answers which students use to study. **2.** a book that contains the rules for doing certain work.

—[名] 1. 학습장, 연습장, 수련장 2. [일 따위의] 규칙서, 사무 규정

work·day [wə́ːrkdèi] *n.* [C] a day for work; a day on which work is done.

—[名] 일하는 날, 근무(작업)일, 평일

work·er [wə́ːrkər] *n.* [C] **1.** a person who works; a person who works for wages; a laborer. **2.** (*Zoology*) ants, bees, etc. that work for their colony.

—[名] 1. 일하는 사람(것), 노동자 2. 《動》 일벌; 일개미

work·house [wə́ːrkhàus] *n.* [C] **1.** (*U.S.*) a kind of prison where criminal boys and girls are confined and made to work in order to reform them. **2.** (*Brit.*) a

—[名] 1. 《美》 감화원, 교화원, 교도소 2. 《英》 구빈원(救貧院)

place for homeless poor people.

‡ **work·ing** [wə́:rkiŋ] *n.* **1.** [U][C] operation; action. **2.** 《usu. *pl.*》 parts of a mine, quarry, etc. where work is done. **—***adj.* that works. ¶*a ~ committee*① / *~ expenses*② / *a ~ plan* / *~ knowledge.*③

—[名] 1. 작업, 운전, 작용, 활동 2. [광산의] 채광장, 작업장, 현장 —[形] 일하는, 노동의, 운전의 ¶①운영 위원회/②경영비/③실용적 지식

working day [⌐– ⌐] *n.* a day on which work is done; the part of a day during which work is done.

—[名] 작업일, 하루의 노동(근무)시간

working-day [wə́:rkiŋdèi] *adj.* =workaday.

working drawing [⌐– ⌐–] *n.* a drawing for guiding workmen in making a machine, etc.

—[名] 시공도(施工圖), 공작도

work·ing·man [wə́:rkiŋmæ̀n] *n.* [C] (pl. **-men** [-mèn]) a person who works, esp. with his hands; a laborer.

—[名] 노동자, 직공, 일꾼

‡ **work·man** [wə́:rkmən] *n.* [C] (pl. **-men** [-mən]) a worker; a laborer; a person who is skilled in his trade; a craftsman. ¶*a good ~*① / *a workman's train.*②

—[名] 직공, 일꾼, 기술이 있는 직공 ¶①숙련공/②[노동자의] 조조할인 열차

work·man·like [wə́:rkmənlàik] *adj.* well-made; skillful.

—[形] 훌륭하게 만든, 솜씨있는, 능숙한

work·man·ship [wə́:rkmənʃip] *n.* [U] the art or skill of a worker; skill; the quality of something made; the work which is done.

—[名] 솜씨, 기술; 완성된 품(효과); 세공, 만들어진 것

work·out [wə́:rkàut] *n.* [C] (*U.S. colloq.*) an exercise; a trial; a test.

—[名] 《美口》 [예비]연습, 시험

work·room [wə́:rkrù(:)m] *n.* [C] a room where work is done.

—[名] 작업실

work·shop [wə́:rkʃɑ̀p / wə́:kʃɔ̀p] *n.* [C] a shop or building where work is done.

—[名] 작업장, 공장

‡ **world** [wə:rld] *n.* [C] **1.** 《usu. *the ~*, used as *sing.*》 the earth; the universe; a star or planet. ¶*the whole ~* / *all the ~* / *the world's fastest airplane* / *sail round the ~.* **2.** 《*the ~*》 human life on earth. ¶*another ~; a better ~*① / *this ~ and the next ~*② / *the ~ to come.* **3.** 《*the ~*》 human life and experience; human society in general. ¶*a man of the ~*③ / *as the ~ goes*④ / *How is the ~ using you?*⑤ / *The ~ goes very well with me.*⑥ **4.** 《usu. *the ~*, used as *sing.*》 the earth and its people; mankind; the public; worldly people; everybody. ¶*The whole ~ knows it.* / *He showed the ~ that he was not a fool.* **5.** any sphere of interest or activity. ¶*the fashionable ~*⑦ / *the movie ~*⑧ / *the great ~*⑨ / *the literary ~; the ~ of letters.*⑩ **6.** a division of things belonging to the earth. ¶*the animal (the vegetable, the mineral) ~.* **7.** 《*W-*》 some part of the earth. ¶*the New (the Old) World.*⑪ **8.** 《often *pl.*》 a large amount. ¶*a ~ of waters.*⑫

—[名] 1. 세계, 지구; 천지, 우주, 만물; 별, 천체 2. 현세; 이 세상 ¶①내세, 저승/②현세와 내세 3. 세상, 세상일; 인간세상 ¶③세상사에 정통한 사람/④세상에서 흔히 말하듯이/⑤어떻게 지내십니까?/⑥무사히 지내고 있읍니다 4. 세상 사람; 인류; 세인(世人); 속인(俗人) 5. …사회, 사교 ¶⑦유행계/⑧영화계/⑨상류 사회/⑩문단 6. [자연계의] …계 7. [지구의] 어떤 지방 ¶⑪신(구)세계 8. 다량, 다수 ¶⑫대양(大洋)

1) ***be all the world to,*** be everything to (someone); be very important to (someone).
2) ***begin the world,*** start one's career.
3) ***bring a child into the world,*** give birth to a child.
4) ***come into the world,*** be born.
5) ***for all the world,*** ⓐ exactly. ⓑ for any consideration. ¶*Don't kill oneself for all the ~.*⑬
6) ***in the world,*** ⓐ on earth. ⓑ at all.
7) ***not for the world,*** not on any account; not for any reason.
8) ***out of this*** (or ***the***) ***world,*** exceptionally fine.
9) [***the***] ***world without end,*** forever.

[熟] 1)…에게는 귀중한 보물이다 2)세상(사회)에 나오다 3)[아이]를 낳다 4)태어나다 5)ⓐ확실히, 틀림없이 ⓑ무슨 일이 있더라도 ¶⑬어떠한 일이 있더라도 자살은 하지 마라 6)ⓐ도대체 ⓑ전혀 7)결코 …아니다(않다) 8)아주 훌륭한 9)영원히

world-famous [wə́:rldféiməs] *adj.* famous all over the world.

—[形] 세상에 이름난, 세계적으로 유명한

world language [⌐ ⌐–] *n.* a language that is spoken in various parts of the world.

—[名] 세계어, 국제어

world·ling [wə́:rldliŋ] *n.* [C] a worldly person.

—[名] 속물(俗物)

• **world·ly** [wə́:rldli] *adj.* (**-li·er, -li·est**) of this world; devoted to the things of this world. ¶*~ affairs*① / *~ goods*② / *~ wisdom.*③ ▷**world·li·ness** [-nis] *n.*

—[形] 이 세상의, 속세의, 세속적인, 범속(凡俗)한 ¶①세속 일, 속사(俗事)/②재화(財貨), 재산/③처세하는 재간

world·ly-mind·ed [wə́:rldlimáindid] *adj.* caring much for worldly pleasures, interests, etc.

—[形] 세속적 명리를 쫓는

world-wide [wə́:rldwáid] *adj.* spread all over the world.

—[形] 세계에 널리 알려진

‡ **worm** [wə:rm] *n.* [C] **1.** a small, slender, soft-bodied, animal. ¶*become food for worms*① / (*proverb*) *A ~* (or

—[名] 1. 벌레, 지렁이, 구더기 ¶①죽다/②[俚]지렁이도 밟으면 꿈틀한다 2. 벌

*Even a ~) will turn.*② **2.** a person who is useless, mean, etc. like a worm. ¶*I am a ~ today.*③ / *He is a little ~.* **3.** something that injures someone slowly. ¶*the ~ of conscience.*④ **4.** a screw; the spiral of a screw.
레 같은 인간, 비열한(卑劣漢)/③오늘은 기운이 없다 3. 고통의 씨(원인) ¶④양심의 가책 4. 나사; 나사의 나선

—*vt.* **1.** move (one's way, etc.) like a worm. ¶*~ one's way out of a crowd*⑤ / *~ one's way* (or *oneself*) *through the bushes* / *~ oneself into favor.*⑥ **2.** obtain (information, etc.) by slow and indirect means. ¶*~ a secret out of someone.* **—*vi.*** move like a worm.
—[他] 1. …을 천천히 나아가게 하다 ¶⑤군중 속에서 비집고 나오다/⑥조금씩 조금씩 호감을 사다 2. [정보 따위]를 슬금슬금 알아내다 —[自] 기어가듯이 나아가다

worm-eat·en [wə́ːrmìːtn] *adj.* **1.** full of holes caused by worms. **2.** out-of-date.
—[形] 1. 벌레 먹은, 좀 먹은 2. 낡아빠진

worm gear [ˊ ˋ] *n.* a wheel with teeth on its edges to enable it to move with a worm; a worm wheel. ⇒fig.
—[名] 워엄 톱니바퀴 [장치]

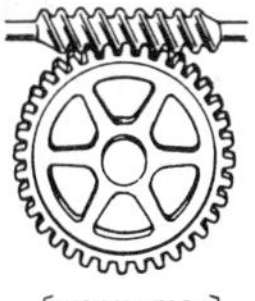
[worm gear]

worm wheel [ˊ ˋ] *n.* =worm gear.

worm·wood [wə́ːrmwùd] *n.* [U] **1.** a kind of plant used in medicine, etc. **2.** something bitter or extremely unpleasant.
—[名] 1. 향쑥 2. 고민, 고뇌

worm·y [wə́ːrmi] *adj.* (**worm·i·er, worm·i·est**) **1.** eaten or damaged by worms. **2.** full of worms; like a worm.
—[形] 1. 벌레 붙은, 벌레(좀) 먹은 2. 벌레가 들끓는; 벌레 같은

‡**worn** [wɔːrn] *v.* pp. of **wear**.
—*adj.* **1.** damaged by long wear, etc. **2.** tired.
—[形] 1. 해진, 닳아진 2. 지친, 피로한

worn-out [wɔ́ːrnáut] *adj.* **1.** used until no longer serviceable. **2.** thoroughly tired.
—[形] 1. 써서 다 낡은, 해진, 닳아빠진 2. 지친, 녹초가 된

‡**wor·ry** [wə́ːri / wʌ́ri] *v.* (**-ried**) *vt.* **1.** bother; trouble; make (someone) anxious. 《~ someone *to do*》 ¶*~ oneself*① / *~ a problem out*② / *get* (*be*) *worried*③ / *look worried*④ / *~ someone with perpetual questions* / *There's really nothing to be worried about.* **2.** (of a dog, etc.) seize and shake (something) with the teeth. **—*vi.*** be troubled, anxious, or uneasy. 《~ *about* something; ~ *doing*; ~ *that...*》 ¶*Don't ~ about it.* / (*U.S. colloq.*) *I should ~.*⑤
—[他] 1. …을 성가시게 굴다, 괴롭히다; …을 걱정시키다 ¶①걱정하다, 근심하다/②문제를 끝까지 생각해내다/③고민하다(고민하고 있다)/④난처한 얼굴을 하다 2. [개 따위가] …을 물고 뒤흔들다 —[自] 고민하다, 걱정하다 ¶⑤《美口》[폐가 되기는커녕] 조금도 상관없다

worry along (or ***through***), manage to get on in spite of difficulties.
[熟] 고생하면서 그럭저럭 해나가다(지내다)

—*n.* (pl. **-ries**) **1.** [U] anxiety; uneasiness. **2.** [C] 《usu. *pl.*》 a cause of anxiety; a trouble.
—[名] 1. 근심, 걱정, 고민 2. 걱정거리

‡**worse** [wəːrs] *adj.* compar. of **bad** and **ill**. **1.** bad in a greater degree; less good. ¶*the ~ for drink* (*wear*)① / *so much the ~*② / *and what is ~; to make matters ~*③ / *be ~ than useless*④ / *It got ~ and ~.* **2.** 《as *predicative*》 in a less good state of health; more ill. ¶*He grew rapidly ~.* **3.** 《as *predicative*》 in a less good condition.
—[形] 1. 더[한층] 나쁜, 더욱 나쁜 ¶①취하여(입어서 해뜨려)/②그만큼 오히려 나쁜/③더욱 더 곤란한 것은/④유해무익하다 2. 건강이 먼저보다도 더 나쁜 3. [형편이] 더욱 더 어렵게 된

—*adv.* compar. of **badly** and **ill.** **1.** more badly. ¶*sing ~ than before.* **2.** to a worse degree. ¶*It is blowing ~ than before.*
—[副] 1. 더욱 나쁘게 2. 한층 더 심하게

1) ***be worse off,*** be more badly situated.
2) ***none the worse,*** no less.
[熟] 1)[살림]형편이 더욱 더 어렵다 2) 역시, 그럼에도 불구하고

—*n.* [U] that which is worse; 《*the ~*》 a worse state. ¶*a change for the ~*⑤ / *for better or ~*⑥ / *do ~* / *have the ~*⑦ / *put someone to the ~*⑧ / *I have ~ to tell.; Worse remains to tell.*⑨
—[名] 더욱 나쁜 것; 더욱 나쁜 편, 불리; 패배 ¶⑤악화/⑥좋건 궂건/⑦패배하다/⑧…을 지우다/⑨더 나쁜 일이 있네

‡**wor·ship** [wə́ːrʃip] *n.* [U] **1.** respect, honor, etc. paid to God or another religious object. **2.** ceremonies in honor of God. ¶*public ~.* **3.** great or excessive admiration.
—[名] 1. 신을 참배하기, 예배 2. 예배식 3. 숭배, 존경

—*v.* (**-shiped, -ship·ing** or *Brit.* **-shipped, -ship·ping**) *vt.* **1.** pay great honor or respect to (God, etc.). **2.** consider (someone or something) very precious; adore. **—*vi.*** take part in worship; attend church service.
—[他] 1. [신]을 참배하다, 예배하다 2. …을 숭배하다, 존경하다 —[自] 예배하다, 예배에 나가다

‡**worst** [wəːrst] *adj.* (superl. of **bad** and **ill**) bad to the
—[形] 가장 나쁜, 최악의

worsted highest degree; least good. ¶*the ~ frost for fifty years.* —*adv.* (*the superlative* of badly and ill) most badly. ¶*~ of all.*①
—*n.* Ⓤ that which is worst; the worst state or part. ¶*be prepared for the ~ | do one's ~*② *| speak the ~ of someone*③ *| The ~ of it is that ...*④
1) *give someone the worst of it,* defeat.
2) *if* [*the*] *worst comes to* [*the*] *worst,* if the worst happens. [*aspects*) *of something.*|
3) *make the worst* (=consider only the least favorable
—*vt.* defeat; beat. ¶*be worsted.*⑤

wor·sted [wústid] *n.* Ⓤ **1.** fine, twisted woolen thread. **2.** cloth made from worsted. —*adj.* made of worsted.

worth [wə:rθ] *adj.* (as *predicative*) **1.** having a certain value or price. ¶*It is not ~ a penny.* **2.** deserving or worthy of. ¶*a task ~ the trouble | not ~ the salt*① *| It is ~ seeing. | It is ~ while reading* (or *to read*) *this book.*② **3.** having property amounting to. ¶*He is ~ a million.*③ *| He died ~ a million.*
1) *for all one is worth,* to the extent of one's power.
2) *put in one's two cents worth,* give one's own opinion.
—*n.* Ⓤ **1.** value; merit; virtue; excellence. ¶*of* [*great*] *~*④ */ of little* (*no*) *~ | a man of ~.*⑤ **2.** the amount of something that may be had for a given sum. ¶*a shilling's ~ of fruit | twenty dollars' ~ of halves.*⑥

* **worth·less** [wə́:rθlis] *adj.* without worth; useless; valueless. [tance, etc.; worth time and trouble.|
worth·while [wə́:rθ(h)wáil] *adj.* of true value, impor-

: **wor·thy** [wə́:rði] *adj.* (*-thi·er, -thi·est*) **1.** having worth or excellence; respectable. ¶*a ~ man.* **2.** deserving; praiseworthy. ¶*a poet ~ of the name.*① —*n.* Ⓒ (pl. *-thies*) an excellent or important person.

: **would** [wud, wəd, (ə)d] *auxil. v.* pt. of **will.** **1.** (expressing the future in indirect narration) ¶*I said he ~ succeed.* **2.** (expressing *condition*) ¶*If I had a chance, I ~ try. | You ~ do so if you could. | If he had been there, he ~ have seen it.*② **3.** (expressing *past habitual action*) used to. ¶*When I was young, I ~ often go there.* ⇒ USAGE **4.** (expressing *a wish*) ⇒ USAGE ¶*Would to God that... | Would that I were young again.*② **5.** (expressing *a polite request*) ¶*Would you kindly show me the way?*③ **6.** (expressing *intention* or *determination*) wished to; be willing to; be determined to. ¶*I ~ rather not accept your offer. | I ~ fain do it.*④ */ I ~ like to go.*

would-be [wúdbì:] *adj.* wishing or aiming to be; intended to be. ¶*a ~ poet.*

* **would·n't** [wúdnt] would not.

: **wound**¹ [wu:nd] *n.* **1.** Ⓒ a cut, hurt or an injury to the body. ¶*a mortal* (or *fatal*) *~.*① **2.** Ⓤ a hurt or an injury to someone's feelings or reputation. ¶*a ~ to someone's pride.*② —*vt.* **1.** injure (someone) by force. ¶*be wounded in the arm.* **2.** hurt the feelings of (someone). ¶*willing to ~.*③

wound² [waund] *v.* pt. and pp. of **wind.**²,³

wove [wouv] *v.* pt. and pp. of **weave.**

wo·ven [wóuv(ə)n] *v.* pp. of **weave.**

wrack [ræk] *n.* Ⓤ **1.** ruin; destruction. **2.** wreckage. **3.** the sea plants thrown up on the shore.

wraith [reiθ] *n.* Ⓒ the spirit of a person supposed to appear just before or after his death.

wran·gle [rǽŋgl] *vi.* argue or quarrel noisily. —*n.* Ⓒ a noisy argument or quarrel.

wran·gler [rǽŋglər] *n.* Ⓒ **1.** a person who wrangles.

—働 가장 나쁘게 ¶①무엇보다도 나쁜 것은, 가장 곤란한 것은

—솅 최악의 것(사태) ¶②될 수 있는 한의 몹쓸 짓을 하다/③…을 헐뜯다, 비방하다/④가장 나쁜(곤란한) 것은 …이다

图 1)…을 지우다 2)만일(최악)의 경우에는 3)…을 최악으로 생각하다, 아주 큰일 난 것처럼 생각하다
—働 …을 지우다 ¶⑤지다

—솅 1. 소모사(梳毛絲); 털실 2. 모직물 —働 소모사로 만든; 털실로 만든

—働 1. …의 가치가 있는, 값어치가 있는 2. …할 만한 가치가 있는, …하기에 족한 ¶①먹고 살아갈 말한 일거리가 없는/②이 책은 읽을 만한 가치가 있다 3. 재산이 …만큼의, …만큼의 재산이 있는 ¶③그는 백만장자다

图 1)전력을 다하여 2)자기의 의견을 말하여
—솅 1. 가치; 진가 ¶④대단히 가치가 있는/⑤훌륭한 사람 2. …어치, …에 상당하는 만큼 ¶⑥ 20 달러분의 50 센트 은화

—働 가치가 없는, 하찮은, 쓸모없는
[당한」
—働 할 보람이 있는, 가치가 있는, 상
—働 1. 가치가 있는, 훌륭한 2. …하기에 족한, …에 어울리는 ¶①시인다운 시인 —솅 훌륭한 사람, 명사

—줄 1. …을 것이다 2. [만약 …이라면] …할 것이다 ¶①그가 만약 거기 있었더라면 그것을 보았을 텐데 3. 늘 …하였다 USAGE 보통 과거의 불규칙적 습관에는 would를, 규칙적 습관에는 used to 를 씀 4. …이라면 좋겠는데 USAGE 때로 I를 생략함 ¶②내가 다시 젊어진다면 좋겠는데 5. …해 주시겠읍니까? ¶③그 길을 가르쳐 주시겠읍니까? 6. …할 생각(작정)이다(이 없다) ¶④기꺼이 그것을 하겠다

—働 …이 되고 싶어하는, …연(然)하는, 자칭의 ¶①자칭 시인

—솅 1. 상처, 부상, 다친 데 ¶①치명상 2. [감정을] 상함, 고충, 모욕, 타격 ¶②자존심을 손상시키는 것
—働 1. …에게 상처를 입히다 2. …의 감정을 해치다, 손상시키다/¶③악의가 있는

—솅 1. 파멸, 멸망 2. 난파 3. 파도에 밀려 올라온 해초

—솅 생령(生靈), 사령(死靈), 망령, 유령

—톱 언쟁하다, 말다툼하다
—솅 언쟁, 논쟁; 말다툼

—솅 1. 논쟁(언쟁)자 2. 〈英〉 Cam-

wrap

2. (*Brit.*) a student in the highest class in mathematics at Cambridge University.
bridge 대학의 수학학위 시험의 우등생

:**wrap** [ræp] *vt.* (**wrapped** or **wrapt, wrap·ping**) **1.** cover or envelop (something) by winding or folding something else around it. ¶ ~ *oneself up in a cloak.*① **2.** wind or fold (something) as a covering. ¶*She wrapped her shawl around her neck.* **3.** cover; hide.
—*n.* ⓒ (often *pl.*) an outer covering.
— 他 1. …을 싸다, 두르다 ¶①외투를 입다 2. …을 감다, 걸치다 3. 씌우개에 싸다, 감추다, 숨기다
— 图 싸개, 덮개, 목도리, 외투

wrap·per [rǽpər] *n.* ⓒ **1.** a person or thing that wraps; a covering; a cover. **2.** a woman's loose gown worn indoors. ⌜grapes of ~.①⌝
— 图 1. 싸는 사람(것); 포장지; [잡지 따위의] 커버 2. [여자용] 실내복, 화장옷

* **wrath** [ræθ, rɑ:θ / rɔ:(:)θ] *n.* Ⓤ very great anger. ¶*the*⌐ ⌐의 분노⌐
— 图 격노, 분노 ¶①분노의 포도; 신

wrath·ful [rǽθf(u)l, rɑ́:θ- / rɔ́:(:)θ-] *adj.* very angry.
— 图 노발대발한, 격노한, 격분한

wreak [ri:k] *vt.* bring (one's idea one's anger, etc.) into effect; give expression to (one's feelings, etc.).
— 他 …을 실행에 옮기다; [감정 따위]를 나타내다

* **wreath** [ri:θ] *n.* ⓒ **1.** a circle of leaves and flowers. **2.** something like a ring or curl.
— 图 1. 화환(花環) 2. 고리, 소용돌이

wreathe [ri:ð] *vt.* **1.** make (something) into a circle. **2.** decorate (something) with, or as, a wreath. **3.** envelop. **4.** make a ring around (something or someone); wind. ¶*The snake wreathed itself around the branch.*① —*vi.* **1.** (of branches, etc.) get twisted. **2.** take the form of a wreath; move in coils.
— 他 1. …을 고리(화환)로 만들다 2. …을 화환으로(처럼) 장식하다 3. 싸다 4. …을 휘감다, 감다 ¶①뱀이 나뭇가지를 휘감았다 — 自 1. 휘감기다, 뒤얽히다 2. 고리로 되다

:**wreck** [rek] *n.* **1.** Ⓤ damage or ruin of a ship, a building, etc. caused by wind, a storm, etc. **2.** ⓒ remains of anything, esp. of a ship, that has been destroyed or much injured.
—*vt.* cause the wreck of (something); destroy; ruin.
—*vi.* be wrecked; suffer damage, ruin, etc.
— 图 1. 난파, 파괴, 파멸 2. 난파선, 파괴물, 잔해(殘骸)
— 他 …을 난파시키다, 부수다, 파괴시키다 — 自 난파하다, 파멸하다

wreck·age [rékidʒ] *n.* Ⓤ **1.** the act of wrecking; the state of being wrecked. **2.** the remains of anything that has been wrecked.
— 图 1. 난파, 파괴 2. 잔해(殘骸)

wreck·er [rékər] *n.* ⓒ **1.** a person or thing that wrecks; a person who steals cargo, etc. from wrecked ships. **2.** a person, ship, etc. that is employed to recover cargo from wrecked ships, etc. **3.** a person, car, boat, etc. that removes wrecks.
— 图 1. 난파시키는 사람(것); 파괴하는 사람(것); 난파선 약탈자 2. 난파선 구조자(선) 3. 구난 작업자(차)

wrench [rentʃ] *n.* ⓒ **1.** a sudden, violent twist or pull. **2.** an injury caused by such a pull. ¶*give a ~ to one's ankle.*① **3.** the pain or grief of parting. **4.** (chiefly *U. S.*) a tool for turning nuts, bolts, etc. (cf. *Brit.* spanner) ⇒fig.
—*vt.* **1.** pull (something) suddenly and with force. ¶ ~ *fruit off a branch.*② **2.** injure (an ankle, etc.) in this way.

[wrench 4.]

— 图 1. 비틀기, 뒤틀기 2. 삠, 염좌(捻挫) ¶①발목을 삐다 3. 이별의 슬픔, 쓰라림, 고통 4. 《美》 나사돌리개, 렌치, 스패너
— 他 1. …을 비틀다, 비틀어 떼다 ¶②나뭇가지에서 과일을 비틀어 따다 2. …을 삐다, 염좌하다

wrest [rest] *vt.* twist or turn (something) by force; pull or take (something) away violently. ¶ ~ *a gun from a gangster.*① —*n.* ⓒ the act of wresting; a twist.
— 他 …을 비틀다; 비틀어 떼다, 잡아 떼다 ¶①갱한테서 총을 낚아채다
— 图 비틀기, 뒤틀기

wres·tle [résl] *vi.* **1.** struggle with someone to throw him to the ground. **2.** struggle; try hard. 《 ~ *with* or *against* someone or something》 ¶ ~ *with God.*①
—*n.* **1.** ⓒ a wrestling match. **2.** Ⓤ a hard struggle.
— 图 1. 레슬링을 하다, 격투하다, 맞붙어 싸우다 2. 싸우다, 고투하다; 애를 쓰다 ¶①열심히 기도하다
— 图 1. 레슬링, 씨름 2. 분투, 고투

wres·tler [réslər] *n.* ⓒ a person who wrestles, esp. in regular matches.
— 图 레슬링 선수, 씨름꾼, 장사

wres·tling [réslin] *n.* Ⓤ a sport in which opponents struggle and try to throw each other to the ground.
— 图 레슬링, 씨름

wretch [retʃ] *n.* ⓒ a sad, poor person; a bad, shameless person. ⌜mean.⌐
— 图 불쌍한(비참한) 사람; 철면피한 사람, 비열한(漢)

* **wretch·ed** [rétʃid] *adj.* **1.** miserable; unhappy. **2.**
— 图 1. 비참한, 불행한, 불쌍한 2. 비열⌐ ⌐한⌐

wrig·gle [rígl] *vi.* **1.** twist and turn; move like a snake. **2.** proceed by tricks or shifty means. ¶ ~ *out of the difficulty.* —*vt.* cause (something) to wriggle. —*n.*
— 自 1. 꿈틀거리다, 몸부림치다; 꿈틀대며 나아가다 2. 요리조리 빠져나가다
— 他 …을 꿈틀거리게 하다 — 图 꿈틀

[C] the act or motion of twisting.
거림, 몸부림

wright [rait] *n.* [C] 《usu. in *combinations*》 a person who makes something. ¶*a cartwright*① / *a playwright.*②
—[名] 장색(匠色), 장인, 제조인, 작자 ¶①수레 목수/②극작가

* **wring** [riŋ] *vt.* (**wrung**) **1.** squeeze or twist hard. ¶~ *a cloth dry.* **2.** force (something) out by twisting or by force. ¶~ *money out of someone.*① **3.** give pain to (someone). —*n.* [C] the act of wringing.
—[他] 1. …을 비틀다, 짜다 2. …을 짜내다, 착취하다 ¶①…에게서 돈을 읽어내다 3. …을 괴롭히다 —[名] 짜기, 비틀기

wring·er [ríŋər] *n.* [C] a person or thing that wrings; a machine for squeezing wet clothes.
—[名] 짜는 사람, 짜는 기계

* **wrin·kle** [ríŋkl] *n.* [C] a small fold on a surface. —*vt.* make wrinkles in (something). —*vi.* become wrinkled.
—[名] 주름[살] —[他]…에 주름지게 하다, …을 주름잡다 —[自] 주름지다

⁑ **wrist** [rist] *n.* [C] the joint connecting the arm and the hand.
—[名] 손목

wrist·band [rís(t)bæ̀nd] *n.* [C] the part of a sleeve fitting around the wrist.
—[名] 소매끝, 소맷부리

wrist watch [ˊ ˋ] *n.* a watch worn on the wrist.
—[名] 팔목(손목) 시계

writ[1] [rit] *n.* [C] **1.** (*archaic*) something written. ¶*the Holy Writ.*① **2.** a written order from a law court. ¶*serve a ~ on someone*② / *a ~ of attachment.*③
—[名] 1. 《古》 써 넣은 것, 문서 ¶①성서 2. 영장(令狀) ¶②…에게 영장을 발부하다/③차압 영장

⁑ **write** [rait] *v.* (**wrote, written**) *vi.* **1.** form words or letters with a pen or pencil. ¶ *He cannot read or ~.* / *She writes well.*① **2.** compose books or other literary matter. 《~ *on* (or *of, about*) something》 ¶~ *for a living*② / *He is writing for "Life".*③ **3.** write a letter or letters. ¶~ *home* / *He wrote to me for money.* —*vt.* **1.** form (words, etc.) on a surface. ¶~ *Chinese characters*④ / ~ *a letter in ink* / *He writes himself "Colonel."*⑤ **2.** express; put down in writing. 《~ *that* …》 **3.** produce (a literary or musical composition). ¶*He wrote many books.* / *Beethoven wrote nine symphonies.*⑥ **4.** send a letter to (someone). 《~ *that*…; ~ someone *to do*; ~ someone *that*…; ~ someone *how* (or *what*, etc.) …》 ¶*He wrote me the news.* / *He wrote his mother to come up to town.*⑦ **5.** 《usu. in *passive*》 show clear signs of (something). ¶*Honesty is written on his face.*⑧
—[自] 1. 글씨를 쓰다 ¶①그녀는 글씨는 잘 쓴다 2. 책을 집필하다, 저술하다 ¶②문필을 업으로 하다/③그는 라이프지에 집필하고 있다 3 편지를 쓰다 —[他] 1. [글씨 따위]를 쓰다 ¶④한자를 쓰다/⑤그는 자기를 「대령」이라고 쓰고 있다 2. …이라고 기입하다, 적다 3. [책 따위]를 저술하다; 작곡하다 ¶⑥베에토오벤은 9개의 교향곡을 작곡했다 4. …에게 편지를 쓰다 ¶⑦그는 어머니에게 상경하라고 편지를 썼다 5. …을 뚜렷이 나타내다 ¶⑧정직하다는 것이 그의 얼굴에 나타나 있다

1) ***write down,*** ⓐ make a note of (something); record. ⓑ put a lower value on (something).
2) ***write off,*** ⓐ compose quickly and easily. ⓑ cancel.
3) ***write out,*** write (something) in full.
4) ***write up,*** ⓐ praise (something or someone) in writing. ⓑ write (something) in detail.
[熟] 1)ⓐ…을 써(적어) 두다 ⓑ…을 지상(紙上)에서 헐뜯다(혹평하다); 기술(記述)하다 2)ⓐ…을 술술 쓰다 ⓑ…을 장부에서 지워 버리다 3)…을 모조리 쓰다 4)ⓐ…을 칭찬하여 쓰다 ⓑ…을 자세히 쓰다

⁑ **writ·er** [ráitər] *n.* [C] a person who writes; a person whose occupation is writing; an author.
—[名] 쓰는 사람, 필생, 서기; 작가

writhe [raið] *vi.* **1.** twist and turn about in pain. ¶~ *with a toothache.* **2.** suffer from mental distress.
—[自] 1. 몸부림치다, 괴로와서 딩굴다 2. 고민하다, 번민하다

⁑ **writ·ing** [ráitiŋ] *n.* [U] **1.** anything that is written. **2.** handwriting; penmanship. **3.** the profession of a writer. **4.** [C] 《*pl.*》 literary works. **5.** literary style.
—[名] 1. 쓴 것, 서류, 문서 2. 서법(書法), 필적 3. 문필업, 저술업 4. 저작, 저서, 작품 5. 문체

W

writing desk [ˊ-ˋ] *n.* a desk for writing at.
—[名] 글 쓰는 책상, 사자대(寫字臺)

writing ink [ˊ-ˋ] *n.* ink for writing.
—[名] 필기용 잉크

writing paper [ˊ-ˋ-] *n.* paper for witing on.
—[名] 글 쓰는 용지

⁑ **writ·ten** [rítn] *v.* pp. of **write**.

⁑ **wrong** [rɔːŋ / rɔŋ] *adj.* ↔right **1.** not morally right; sinful. ¶*It is ~ to steal.* **2.** not correct or true; not proper or suitable. ¶*the ~ answer* / *take the ~ way (direction)*① / *Sorry, ~ number.*② **3.** 《in *predicative*》 out of order. ¶*My watch is ~.* / *Something is ~ with the engine.* **4.** that should be worn or kept inward or under; back. ¶*She put her sock on ~ side out.*③
—[形] 1. [도덕상] 나쁜, 옳지 않은 2. 틀린, 그릇된; 부적당한 ¶①길(방향)을 잘못 들다(잘못 잡다) / ②[전화에서] 잘못 걸렸읍니다(번호가 틀렸읍니다) 3. 탈난, 고장난 4. 역(逆)의, 반대쪽의 ¶③그녀는 양말을 뒤집어 신었다

1) ***get hold of the wrong end of the stick,*** misunderstand.
2) ***on the wrong side of,*** older than.
[熟] 1) 오해하다 2)[나이가] …살을 넘어서

—*adv.* in a wrong manner; not rightly. ¶*answer ~* / *do a thing ~*④ / *guess ~.*
—[副] 나쁘게; 잘못하여, 틀려서; 거꾸로, 반대로; 고장나서 ¶④일을 그르치다(잘못하다)

1) ***get*** *someone* ***in wrong,*** (*U.S. colloq.*) bring someone into disfavor.
[熟] 1)《美口》남을 미움받게 하다 2)잘

2) ***get it wrong,*** ⓐ miscalculate. ⓑ misunderstand.
3) ***go wrong,*** ⓐ take the wrong path; go astray. ⓑ fail.
—*n.* **1.** [U] that which is wrong; [C] a wrong action. ¶*do* ~⑤ / *distinguish* (or *know*) *between right and* ~. **2.** [U] injustice; harm; ill-treatment; [C] an instance of this. ¶*suffer* ~⑥ / *do someone* ~; *do* ~ *to someone.*⑦
1) ***in the wrong,*** wrong. ¶*I was quite in the* ~.
2) ***put someone in the wrong,*** make someone appear responsible for a mistake, etc.
—*vt.* **1.** do wrong to (someone); injure. **2.** dishonor; judge unfairly. ¶*You wronged him by thinking he took your book.*

못 계산하다, 계산이 틀리다 ⓑ오해하다 3)ⓐ길을 잘못 들다, 길을 잃다, 타락하다 ⓑ실패하다
—[名] 1. 부정, 악, 죄; 나쁜 짓 ¶⑤나쁜 짓을 하다 2. 부당, 불법; 학대; 해(害) ¶⑥부당한 취급을 받다/⑦…을 학대하다; 오해하다
[熟] 1)잘못하여, 그릇된, 부정으로 2)잘못을 …의 탓으로 하다
—[他] 1. …을 학대하다; …에게 해를 끼치다 2. …을 불명예스럽게 하다; 오해하다

wrong·do·er [rɔ́:ŋdù(:)ər / rɔ́ŋdú(:)ə] *n.* [C] a person who does wrong. —[名] 못된 짓을 하는 사람, 비행자(非行者), 가해자

wrong·do·ing [rɔ́:ŋdù(:)iŋ / rɔ́ŋ-] *n.* [U] the act of doing wrong; evil actions; sin. —[名] 못된 짓 하기; 악행, 비행; 죄

wrong·ful [rɔ́:ŋf(u)l / rɔ́ŋ-] *adj.* wrong; evil; unjust; unlawful. —[形] 부정한; 해로운; 불법의, 부당한

wrong-head·ed [rɔ́:ŋhédid / rɔ́ŋ-] *adj.* hard to change in opinions, esp. in wrong opinions. —[形] 완고한, 외고집의; 생각이 그릇된

wrong·ly [rɔ́:ŋli / rɔ́ŋ-] *adv.* unjustly; unlawfully. —[副] 나쁘게, 사악하게; 부정하게; 불법으로, 그릇되게

⁑ **wrote** [rout] *v.* pt. of **write.**

* **wrought** [rɔ:t] *v.* pt. and pp. of **work.**
—*adj.* worked; fashioned; did; done. ¶*highly* ~.① —[形] 세공한, 만든, 가공한 ¶①정교(精巧)한

wrought iron [⊿ ⊿-] *n.* a kind of iron that is hard and yet soft enough to be hammered into shape. —[名] 연철(鍊鐵), 단철(鍛鐵)

wrought-up [rɔ́:tʌ́p] *adj.* greatly excited; disturbed. —[形] 흥분한; 초조한

wrung [rʌŋ] *v.* pt. and pp. of **wring.**

wry [rai] *adj.* (**wri·er, wri·est** or **wry·er, wry·est**) twisted. —[形] 뒤틀린, 비틀어진

Wy., Wyo. Wyoming.

Wy·o·ming [waióumiŋ] *n.* a northwestern State of the United States. ⇒[N.B.] —[名] 미국 서북부의 주 [N.B.] Wy., Wyo.로 줄여 씀. 수도는 Cheyenne

X

X, x [eks] *n.* [C] (pl. **X's, Xs, x's, xs** [éksiz]) **1.** the twenty-fourth letter of the English alphabet. **2.** the Roman number 10. **3.** a term for an unknown quantity, etc. —[名] 1. 영어 알파벳의 스물 네째 글자 2. 로마숫자의 10 3. 미지수의 부호, 미지의 것

Xmas [krísməs] *n.* =Christmas.

* **X ray** [⊿ ⊿] *n.* **1.** 《usu. *pl.*》 a Roentgen ray. **2.** a photograph made by means of X rays. —[名] 1. X선 2. X선 사진

* **X-ray** [éksrèi, +*Brit.* ⊿⊿] *vt.* use X rays to examine (something); examine or treat (someone) with X rays. —*adj.* of X rays. —[他] X선으로…을 조사하다, 치료하다 —[形] X선의

xy·lo·phone [záiləfòun, zílə-] *n.* [C] a musical instrument made of pieces of wood, each giving a different note when struck ⇒fig. —[名] 실로폰, 목금(木琴)

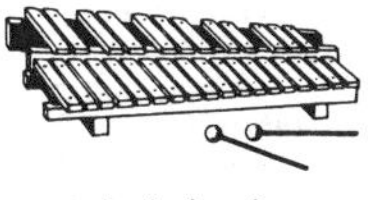

〔xylophone〕

Y

Y, y [wai] *n.* [C] (pl. **Y's, Ys, y's, ys** [waiz]) **1.** the twenty-fifth letter of the English alphabet. **2.** the usual symbol for a second unknown quantity. **3.** something shaped like the letter Y. —[名] 1. 영어 알파벳의 스물 다섯째 글자 2. 제 2 미지수 3. Y자형의 것

⁑ **yacht** [jɑt / jɔt] *n.* [C] a boat for pleasure or racing. —*vi.* sail or race in a yacht. —[名] 요트 —[自] 요트에 타다, 요트를 달리다

Y

yachts·man [játsmən / jɔ́ts-] *n.* [C] (pl. **-men** [-mən]) a person who sails or owns a yacht.
—[名] 요트 조종자(소유자)

yak [jæk] *n.* [C] an animal like a cow, but with longer hair. ⇒[N.B.], fig.
—[名] 야크, 이우(犛牛) [N.B.] 티베트산 들소

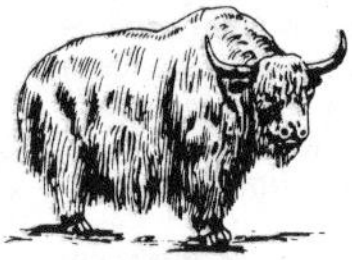
〔yak〕

yam [jæm] *n.* [C] **1.** a root grown for food in warm countries. **2.** (*U.S.*) a kind of sweet potato.
—[名] **1.** 마 **2.** 《美》 고구마

* **Yan·kee** [jǽŋki] *n.* [C] **1.** a person of New England. **2.** a person of the United States. —*adj.* of or like Yankees.
—[名] **1.** 뉴잉글랜드 사람 **2.** 미국인, 양키 —[形] 양키의, 양키류의

Yan·kee·ism [jǽŋkiìz(ə)m] *n.* [U] **1.** a Yankee's nature and special quality. **2.** a particular Yankee word or expression.
—[名] **1.** 양키식, 양키 기질 **2.** 미국 사투리, 미어(美語)

yap [jæp] *n.* [C] **1.** a short, sharp noise which a dog makes when very excited. **2.** (*slang*) noisy or foolish talk. —*vi.* (**yapped, yap·ping**) make a yap.
—[名] **1.** [시끄럽게] 짖는 소리 **2.** 《俗》 시끄러운 수다 —[自] 시끄럽게 짖어대다; 시끄럽게 잔소리하다

⁝ **yard**[1] [jɑːrd] *n.* [C] **1.** a small piece of ground near a house. **2.** a space in which some particular business is carried on. ⇒[N.B.] —*vt.* put (animals, etc.) into a yard.
—[名] **1.** 뜰, 안마당, 둘러싸인 땅 **2.** 작업장, 공장 [N.B.] 흔히 합성어를 만듦(보기; brickyard) —[他] …을 우리에 넣다

⁝ **yard**[2] [jɑːrd] *n.* [C] **1.** a unit of length equal to three feet. ⇒[N.B.] **2.** a pole to which a sail is fixed on a ship.
—[名] **1.** 야아드 [N.B.] yd.로 줄임 **2.** 돛가름대, 활대

yard measure [ˊ ˋˋ] *n.* a stick, tape, etc. used for measuring.
—[名] 야아드 자(줄자 또는 대자)

yard·stick [jáːrdstìk] *n.* [C] a wooden or metal stick one yard long, used for measuring.
—[名] [나무·금속제의] 야아드 자

* **yarn** [jɑːrn] *n.* **1.** [U] a spun thread used for weaving, knitting and rope-making. **2.** [C] (*colloq.*) a tale or story which is hard to believe.
—[名] **1.** 방사(紡絲), 밧줄을 드리기 위해 꼰 실, 뜨개실 **2.** 《口》 [미덥지 않은] 이야기, 여행담

yar·row [jǽrou] *n.* [C] a plant with small pink or white flowers with a strong smell and with finely-divided leaves.
—[名] 서양가새풀

yaw [jɔː] *vi.* (of a ship or an airplane) go unsteadily and leave the right course. —*n.* [C] the act of yawing.
—[自] 침로(針路)를 벗어나다 —[名] 침로를 벗어나기, 편주(偏走)

* **yawn** [jɔːn] *vi.* open the mouth wide because one is tired or sleepy. —*vt.* say (something) with a yawn. —*n.* [C] the act of yawning. ¶*give a* ~.①
—[自] 하품을 하다 —[他] 하품을 하면서 …을 말하다 —[名] 하품 ¶①하품을 하다

yd. yard.

yds. yards.

* **ye** [jiː] *pron. pl.* (*archaic*) you. ¶*Oh, ~ gods!*① ⇒[N.B.]
—[代] 《古》 그대는(가) ¶①오오 신들이여 [N.B.] 단수형 thou

* **yea** [jei] *adv.* (*archaic*) **1.** yes; indeed. ↔nay **2.** moreover. —*n.* [C] an expression of agreement.
—[副] 《古》 **1.** 예, 그렇다, 실은 **2.** 그 위에 —[名] 긍정, 찬성

⁝ **year** [jiər, +*Brit.* jəː] *n.* [C] **1.** the period from January 1 to December 31; twelve months. ¶*this* (*last, next*) ~① / *a common* (*a leap*) ~② / *for years*③ / *in the 45th ~ of Christ*④ / *It has been years since he left his country.*⑤ **2.** the part of a year given to a certain kind of activity. ¶*the school ~ / the fiscal ~.*⑥ **3.** 《usu. *pl.*》 age; time of life. ¶*a man of years*⑦ / *She is seventy years old.*⑧ / *You don't look your years.*⑨
1) ***all the year round;*** (*U.S.*) ***the year round,*** throughout the year.
2) ***from year to year; year after*** (or ***by***) ***year;*** every year; each year.
3) ***year in, year out,*** every year; going on year after year.
—[名] **1.** 해, 연(年) ¶①금년(작년·내년)/②평년(윤년)/③몇년 동안이나/④서기 45년에/⑤그는 고국을 떠난 지 여러 해 됐다 **2.** 연도; 학년 ¶⑥회계연도 **3.** 나이, 연령 ¶⑦노인/⑧그녀는 70세이다/⑨너는 네 나이로 안 보인다
[熟] 1)일년 내내 2)해마다, 매년 3)해마다, 쉴새없이

year·ling [jíərliŋ, +*Brit.* jə́ː-] *n.* [C] an animal between one and two years old. —*adj.* one year old.
—[名] 만 한 살의 동물; 한 살된 말 —[形] 한 살된, 1년이 지난

year·long [jíərlɔ̀ːŋ, +*Brit.* jə́ː-] *adj.* lasting for a year.
—[形] 1년에 걸친, 1년 계속되는

* **year·ly** [jíərli, +*Brit.* jə́-] *adj.* happening each or every year; done once a year. —*adv.* every year; once a year; annually.
—[形] 매년의, 1년 1회의 —[副] 매년, 한 해 한 번

* **yearn** [jəːrn] *vi.* **1.** desire greatly. ¶~ *for* (or *after*) *home.*① **2.** feel pity. 《~ *for* someone》
—[自] **1.** 동경하다, 그리워하다 ¶①고향을 그리워하다 **2.** 동정하다

yearn·ing [jə́ːrniŋ] *n.* [U] strong desire; deep longing.
—[名] 동경, 사모, 열망

yeast [jiːst] *n.* **1.** [U] the yellow material used to make
—[名] **1.** 효모, 누룩, 이이스트 **2.** 거품

Y

yeasty

beer and bread. **2.** ⓒ small round balls of liquid filled with air, etc.; foam.

yeast·y [jí:sti] *adj.* (**yeast·i·er, yeast·i·est**) **1.** of, like, or containing yeast. **2.** of or forming yeast; foamy.

—㉠ 1. 효모의(같은) 2. 발효하는; 거품이 이는

yell [jel] *vi.* cry out loudly. ¶~ *with pain*① / ~ *with laughter.*② —*vt.* say (something) by yelling. ¶~ *out an order.*③ —*n.* ⓒ **1.** a loud voice. **2.** (*U.S.*) a special shout given by students at a football game, etc.

—㉤ 외치다; 고함치다 ¶①아파서 울부짖다/②폭소하다 —㉦ 외쳐서 …을 말하다 ¶③큰 소리로 명령하다 —㉡ 1. 외침소리 2.《美》[축구 경기의] 응원의 외침소리

yel·low [jélou] *adj.* (~·**er**, ~·**est**) **1.** of the color like that of gold, butter or a ripe lemon. ¶*a* ~ *ribbon* / *the* ~ *race*① / ~ *fever.*② **2.** (*colloq.*) cowardly; untrustworthy. ¶*He is* ~. **3.** jealous; envious. ¶~ *looks.*③ **4.** (of a newspaper, etc.) sensational. ¶~ *journals.*④ —*n.* **1.** Ⓤ the color yellow. **2.** Ⓤ yellow paint or dye. **3.** ⓒ something having a yellow color; the yellow part of an egg. —*vi.* become yellow. —*vt.* make (something) yellow.

—㉠ 1. 노란, 황색의 ¶①황색인종/②황열병 2. 비겁한, 소심한 3. 질투심 많은 ¶③질투에 찬 눈 4.선정적인 ¶④선정적인 신문
—㉡ 1. 황색 2. 황색 안료(물감) 3. 황색의 것; 노른자위 —㉤ 황색이 되다, 노래지다 —㉦ …을 노랗게 하다

yel·low·ish [jélouiʃ] *adj.* rather yellow.

—㉠ 누르스름한, 누른 빛을 띤

yel·low·y [jéloui] *adj.* rather yellow.

—㉠ 황색의, 누르스름한

yelp [jelp] *n.* ⓒ a sudden sharp cry of a dog when hurt. —*vi.* give such a cry; utter a yelp. [→N.B.]

—㉡ [개의 성난] 짖는 소리 —㉤ 짖다, 고함을 지르다

yen [jen] *n.* ⓒ (pl. **yen**) the unit of money in Japan.

—㉡ 엔(圓) N.B. ¥로 줄임

yeo·man [jóumən] *n.* ⓒ (pl. **-men** [-mən]) **1.** (*Brit.*) (in olden days) a small landowner; (nowadays) a farmer who owns his farm. **2.** (*U. S. Navy*) a petty officer with clerical duties.

—㉡ 1.《口》자작농; [중산] 농민, 소지주 2.《美海軍》서기(書記) 하사관

yeo·man·ry [jóumənri] *n.* **1.** (*collectively*) yeomen. **2.** (*Brit.*) special soldiers who fight on horseback and who are normally farmers.

—㉡ 1. 소지주들, 자작농 2.《英》의용 농기병(대)

yes [jes] *adv.* ↔no **1.** (expressing *agreement, consent* or *affirmation*) just so; it is so; as you say. ¶"*Can you swim?*" "*Yes, I can.*" / "*Isn't it snowing?*" "*Yes, it is.*"① ⇒USAGE **2.** and what is more; in addition; moreover. ¶*His lecture was good,* ~, *very good.* **3.** (used in a rising tone and expressing *doubt, interest*, etc.) Is it so?; Indeed? ¶"*He made a large profit.*" "*Yes?*"
—*n.* ⓒ (pl. **yes·es**) an answer that agrees or consents; an affirmative reply or vote. ¶2 *yeses and 3 noes*.

—㉣ 1.예; 예,그렇습니다 ¶①「눈이 안 오지요?」「아니오,오고 있읍니다」 USAGE 질문형식이 어떻든 대답이 긍정이면 yes로 대답한다 2. 아니(그 위에), 더구나 3. 그래요?, 정말?

—㉡ 긍정・승낙의 말; 찬성, 찬성 투표

yes man [⌐⌐] *n.* (*slang*) a person who always agrees with his superior, officer, etc. ↔no man

—㉡《俗》웃사람에게 맹목적으로 복종하는 사람

yes·ter·day [jéstərdi, -dèi] *n.* Ⓤ **1.** the day before today. ¶*yesterday's paper* / *the day before* ~① / *a week* [*from*] ~.② **2.** (usu. *pl.*) the past; the recent past.
—*adv.* on the day before today; recently.

—㉡ 1. 어제 ¶①그저께/②전주의 오늘 2. 과거, 요즈음 —㉣ 어제[는], 작금

yet [jet] *adv.* **1.** (in *negative*) up to the present time; so far. ¶*The work is not* ~ *done.* / *It was not* ~ *dark.* / "*Have you seen it?*" "*Not* ~."① / *Don't start* ~. **2.** (in *affirmative*) still; even now. ¶*She is sick* ~. / *There is* ~ *a chance for success.*② **3.** (often with *compar.*) in addition; still; moreover. ¶*more and more*③ / *You must study* ~ *harder*. **4.** (in *interrogative*) by this time. ¶*Has she gone* ~?④ ⇒USAGE **5.** some future day; sometime; eventually. ¶*He will win the championship* ~.⑤ **6.** nevertheless; for all that. ¶*She is pretty,* ~ *unwise.* [*hard.*
1) **and yet**, but. ¶*I am tired, and* ~ *I must work*
2) **as yet**, until now. ¶~ *nor* ~ *write.*
3) **nor yet**, even as much as; either. ¶*He can't read*
—*conj.* but still; nevertheless; however. ¶*She is not rich,* ~ *she looks happy.* [*dark green leaves.*

—㉣ 1. 아직[…이 아니다], 지금껏[…않다] ¶①「그것을 봤느냐?」「아직 못 봤다」 2. 여전히, 지금도 ¶②아직 성공할 기회는 있다 3. 게다가, 또 그 위에 ¶③더욱, 아직도 4. 벌써 ¶④그 여자는 벌써 갔느냐? USAGE yet 대신 already를 쓰면 놀람・뜻밖의 기분을 나타냄 5. 언젠가는, 멀지 않아 ¶⑤그는 언젠가는 우승할 것이다 6. 그러나, …이지만

圈 1)그러나 2)지금까지로서는 3)…도 또한 …이 아니다
—㉠ 그럼에도 불구하고

yew [ju:] *n.* ⓒ a large, cone-bearing, evergreen tree with

—㉡ 서양주목(朱木)

yield [ji:ld] *vt.* **1.** produce; bring forth. ¶*The farms* ~

—㉦ 1. …을 낳다, 출산하다 ¶①그 두

rice and wheat. | *The investment yielded rich profits.*① **2.** give away (something) to force; give up; surrender. 《~ oneself or something [*up*] *to*》 ¶ *~ a town to the enemy* | *She yielded herself* [*up*] *to temptation.*② **3.** give consent; grant; permit. ¶ *~ consent*③ | *~ possession*④ | *~ precedence to someone*⑤ | *~ the point in an argument.*⑥ **—*vi.*** **1.** produce. ¶ *The apple tree yields well.*⑦ **2.** give away; surrender. 《~ *to* something or someone》 ¶ *~ to none*⑧ | *~ to pleasure.*

자는 많은 이익을 가져왔다 2.[압박되어] …을 양도하다, 포기하다, …에 굴복하다 ¶②그녀는 유혹에 졌다 3. …을 동의하다, 허가하다 ¶③승낙하다/④소유권을 양도하다/⑤…에게 차례를 양보하다/⑥논점을 양보하다 —[自] 1.[작물이] 산출되다, 나다 ¶⑦그 사과나무는 잘 열린다 2. 굴복하다, 양보하다, 지다 ¶⑧아무에게도 지지 않다

1) ***yield the palm to*** (=*be exceeded by*) *someone.*
2) ***yield up the life*** (or ***ghost, soul, breath, spirit***), die.

[熟] 1)…에게 지다 2)죽다

—*n.* [C] the amount yielded; something yielded; products. ¶ *The yields of the farm have increased recently.*

[名] 산출액(고); 수확

yield·ing [jíːldiŋ] *adj.* soft; easily bent. ¶ *a ~ disposition.*

—[形] 구부러지기 쉬운; 영향받기 쉬운

Y.M.C.A., YMCA Young Men's Christian Association.

—《略》 그리스도교 청년회

yo·del, -dle [jóudl] *n.* [C] a song sung by quickly changing from a high to a low note, as the Swiss in the mountains do.

—[名] 요우들

* **yoke** [jouk] *n.* [C] **1.** a wooden frame to fasten a pair of oxen together. ⇒fig. **2.** 《used as *sing.* and *pl.*》 a pair of oxen working together under a yoke. **3.** something like a yoke in shape or use; a frame fitting over the shoulders for carrying pairs of pails. **4.** a part of a garment fitted about the neck and shoulders or about the hip for supporting the gathered parts. ⇒fig. **5.** something that connects or unites; a bond; a tie. ¶ *the ~ of love* (*brotherhood*).① **6.** 《usu. *the ~*》 rule; power; the state of being a slave. ¶ *endure the ~*② | *cast* (or *shake, throw*) *off the ~*③ | *submit to someone's ~.*④

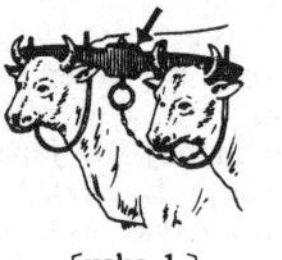

〔yoke 1.〕

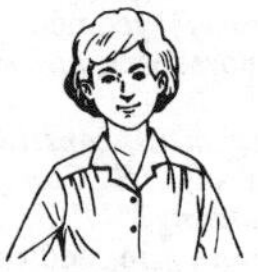

〔yoke 4.〕

—[名] 1. 멍에 2.[멍에를 멘] 한 쌍의 소 3. 멍에 모양의 것; [두 끝에 통을 매달고 메는] 목도 4. 요우크(의복의 어깨 또는 허리 부분) 5. 속박, 기반(羈絆) ¶①애정(형제)의 기반 6. 지배, 권력; 굴종 ¶②남의 지배를 받다/③속박을 벗어나다/④…의 지배에 복종하다

1) ***pass*** (or ***come***) ***under the yoke,*** yield; surrender; be conquered 「in; defeat.
2) ***send someone under the yoke,*** make someone give

[熟] 1)굴복하다 2)…을 굴복시키다

—*vt.* put a yoke on (someone or something); join or link together; unite. **—*vi.*** be joined together.

—[他] …에 멍에를 메우다; …을 잇다, 붙들어매다 —[自] 결합하다, 매어지다

yolk [jouk, +*U.S.* joulk] *n.* [U] [C] the yellow part of an egg.

—[名] 노른자위

* **yon** [jɑn / jɔn] *adj., adv.* (*archaic, dialect*)=yonder.

‡ **yon·der** [jɑ́ndər / jɔ́ndə] *adj.* situated at a distance, but in sight. ¶ *~ group of trees.* **—*adv.*** over there.

—[形] 저쪽의, 저곳의 —[副] 저쪽에, 저곳에

yore [jɔːr] *n.* [U] (*archaic*) a time long ago.

—[名] 《古》 옛날

‡ **you** [ju, jə, juː] *pron.* (pl. **you**) **1.** the person or persons spoken to. ¶ *~ and I* | *The dog will do ~ no harm.*① **2.** one; anyone. ¶ *You never can tell it.*

—[代] 1. 당신[들]은(이), 너[희들]을(에게) ¶①개는 너에게 아무 해도 안 끼친다 2. 누구나

* **you'd** [juːd] you had; you would.

* **you'll** [juːl] you will; you shall.

‡ **young** [jʌŋ] *adj.* ↔old **1.** in the early period of life or growth; not old. ¶ *the ~*① ⇒[usage] | *a ~ girl* | *in one's young*[*er*] *days*② | *When ~, he learned how to fly.*③ **2.** having the looks or qualities of youth; youthful; vigorous; fresh. ¶ *~ passion* (*ambitions*) | *He is ~ in heart.*④ | *She is ~ for her age.*⑤ **3.** (of a period, time, etc.) in an early state; not far advanced. ¶ *a ~ wine* (*moon*) | *The night was still ~ when they parted.*⑥ **4.** (of countries) recently established; newly born; new. ¶ *a ~ nation in Africa.* **5.** the younger of two persons in a family having the same name; junior. ¶ *the young*[*er*] *Sam*⑦ | [*the*] *~ Mrs. Johnson.*⑧ **6.** without much experience or practice; inexperienced. ¶ *He is still ~ at* (or

—[形] 1. 젊은, 어린 ¶①젊은이들 [usage] 형용사에 the를 붙인 명사 용법/②젊었을 때에는/③그는 젊었을 때 비행기 조종술을 배웠다 2. 한창 젊은, 씩씩한, 발랄한 ¶④그는 마음이 젊다/⑤그녀는 나이에 비해 젊다 3.[시일 따위가] 아직 얼마 안 되는, 이른 ¶⑥그들이 헤어졌을 때의 밤은 아직 일렀다 4. 역사가 얕은, 신흥의, 새로운 5.[부모·형제 등과 구별하여] 손아래의 ¶⑦어린 샘(아들인 샘)/⑧존슨씨 집의 젊은 마님 6. 경험이 없는, 미숙한 ¶⑨그는 이 일에 아직 미숙하다

Y

in) *this work.*①　「heart.」
1) one's **young man** (or *woman*), (*colloq.*) one's sweet-
2) **young and old,** [all] the young people and old people.　「*fox and her* ~.」
— *n.* Ⓤ (*collectively*) the offspring of an animal. ¶*a with young,* (of a female) with child; pregnant.
young blood [⌣ ⌣] *n.* **1.** youthful strength, energy, etc. **2.** (*collectively*) young people.
young·ish [jʌ́niʃ] *adj.* rather young.
* **young·ster** [jʌ́ŋstər] *n.* Ⓒ **1.** a young person; a lad. **2.** a child. **3.** a young animal.
‡ **your** [jɔːr, juər, jər] *pron.* (possessive form of **you**) of you; belonging to you.
* **you're** [jɔːr, juər] you are.
‡ **yours** [jɔːrz, juərz] *pron.* a possessive form of **you**.
‡ **your·self** [jɔːrsélf, juər-, jər-] *pron.* (pl. **-selves**) **1.** a reflexive and emphatic form of **you**. **2.** your normal physical or mental condition.
‡ **your·selves** [jɔːrsélvz, juər-, jər-] *pron.* pl. of **yourself**.
‡ **youth** [juːθ] *n.* (pl. **youths** [juːðz]) **1.** Ⓤ the state of being young. ¶*the secret of keeping one's* ~. **2.** the early part of life. ¶*in the days of his* ~.① **3.** Ⓒ a young man. ¶*a promising* ~.② **4.** Ⓤ (*collectively*) young men and women. **5.** Ⓤ an early or first stage of development. ¶*during the* ~ *of this country*.
* **youth·ful** [júːθfəl] *adj.* young; of or suitable for youth.
* **you've** [juːv] you have.
yowl [jaul] *n.* Ⓒ a long, sad cry. — *vi.* make such a cry.
Yu·ca·tan [jùːkətǽn, +*Brit*. -táːn] *n.* a narrow neck of land in southeast Mexico.
yuc·ca [jʌ́kə] *n.* Ⓒ a plant of the lily family. ⇒fig.
yule, Yule [juːl] *n.* Ⓤ Christmas.
yule log [⌣ ⌣] *n.* a huge log burned on Christmas Eve.
yule·tide [júːltàid] *n.* Ⓤ the Christmas season.
Y.W.C.A., YWCA Young Women's Christian Association.　[yucca]

Z

Z, z [ziː / zed] *n.* Ⓒ (pl. **Z's, Zs, z's, zs** [ziːz / zedz]) **1.** the twenty-sixth and last letter of the English alphabet. ¶*from A to Z*.① **2.** something shaped like the letter Z.
* **zeal** [ziːl] *n.* Ⓤ eargerness; earnestness. ¶*with* ~.①
zeal·ot [zélət] *n.* Ⓒ a person who is too eager and fixed in his beliefs.　「zealot; too great zeal.」
zeal·ot·ry [zélətri] *n.* Ⓤ the actions or emotions of a
* **zeal·ous** [zéləs] *adj.* eager; earnest. ((~ *for* or *to do*))
zeal·ous·ly [zéləsli] *adv.* in a zealous manner.
ze·bra [zíːbrə, +*Brit*. zéb-] *n.* Ⓒ an African animal like a horse but with black and white lines on the body.
ze·nith [zíːniθ / zé-] *n.* Ⓒ ((usu. *the* ~ or *one's* ~, used as *sing.*)) **1.** the part of the sky just above one's head. ↔nadir **2.** the highest point; the top.
zeph·yr [zéfər] *n.* **1.** Ⓒ the west wind; a gentle wind; a breeze. **2.** Ⓤ a kind of fine woolen material.
‡ **ze·ro** [zíərou] *n.* (pl. **-ros** or **-roes**) **1.** Ⓒ 0; nothing. **2.** Ⓤ the point marked 0 on a scale, from which read-

ings begin in either direction. ¶*three degrees below ~.*① **3.** [U] the lowest point. ¶*His courage was at ~.*② — 텅이 ¶②그는 풀이 죽었다

zest [zest] *n.* [U] **1.** something added to give a sharp and pleasant taste. ¶*give* (or *add*) *~ to something.*① **2.** keenness; eagerness. ¶*with ~.*② — [名] 1. 향미, 풍미를 곁들이는 것 ¶①…에 묘미를 더하다 2. 열심 ¶②강한 흥미를 갖고, 열심히

Zeus [zu:s / zju:s] *n.* (in Greek mythology) the ruler of the gods. — [名] 제우스신

zig·zag [zígzæ̀g] *adj.* (of a line) shaped like the letter Z; having short, sharp turns. **—*n.*** [C] one of such turns; a zigzag line. **—*vi.*** (**-zagged, -zag·ging**) follow a zigzag course. — [形] Z자형의, 지그재그의 —[名] Z자형, 번개꼴 —[自] Z자형으로 나아가다, 지그재그로 나아가다

zinc [ziŋk] *n.* [U] a white metal used to protect iron from the wet. **—*vt.*** (**zincked** or **zinced** [ziŋkt], **zinck·ing** or **zinc·ing**) coat or cover (something) with zinc. — [名] 아연 —[他] 아연을 입히다

zincked [ziŋkt] *v.* pt. and pp. of **zinc.**

zinck·ing [ziŋkiŋ] *v.* ppr. of **zinc.**

zin·ni·a [zíniə] *n.* [C] a garden plant with large, showy flowers. — [名] 백일초(百日草), 지니아

Zi·on [záiən] *n.* **1.** a hill in Jerusalem. **2.** ⟪*collectively*⟫ the Jewish people. **3.** heaven. **4.** the Christian church. — [名] 1. 시온산 2. 유대인 3. 천국 4. 그리스도 교회

Zi·on·ism [záiənìz(ə)m] *n.* [U] a plan or movement to establish a national home for the Jews in Palestine. — [名] 시온주의

Zi·on·ist [záiənist] *n.* [C] a person who approves of Zionism. — [名] 시온주의자

zip [zip] *n.* **1.** [C] the sound made by an object passing quickly through the air. **2.** [U] (*colloq.*) energy. **—*vi.*** (**zipped, zip·ping**) make a zip; (*colloq.*) act quickly. — [名] 1. [탄환 따위의] 핑핑하는 소리 2. ⟪口⟫ 정력 —[自] 핑하고 소리내다; ⟪口⟫ 힘차게 하다

zip·per [zípər] *n.* [C] a sliding fastener. — [名] 지퍼, 척

zo·di·ac [zóudiæ̀k] *n.* [C] ⟪*the* ~⟫ an imaginary belt of sky, followed by the sun, the moon, and planets; a plan of part of the sky divided into twelve equal parts showing the places of certain stars. ¶*the signs of the ~.*① ⇒fig. — [名] 황도대(黃道帶); 12궁(宮) ¶①황도 12궁

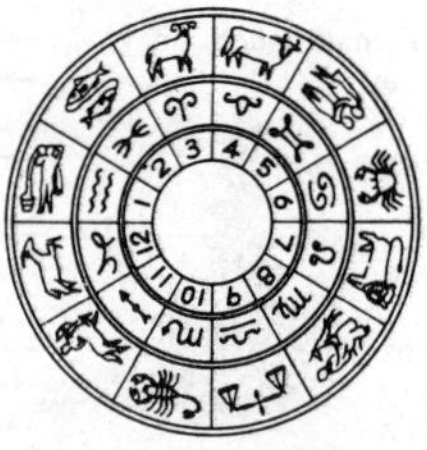

[the signs of the Zodiac]

zone** [zoun] *n.* [C] **1.** a belt; an area that is set off or differentiated from other areas in some respect. ¶*a safety ~*① / *a school ~*② / *the Frigid Zone*③ / *the Temperate Zone.*④ **2.** (*U.S.*) a particular area of a country or a city in which certain postal and telephone rates are charged. **—*vt. divide or separate (a place, etc.) into zones. — [名] 1. 띠; 지대, 지구 ¶①안전지대/②교육지구/③한대/④온대 2. [우편·전차 따위의] 동일 요금 지구 —[他] …을 지역으로 나누다; [동일 요금의] 우편구로 나누다

‡zoo [zu:] *n.* [C] a place where living animals are kept for the public to see. — [名] 동물원

zo·o·log·i·cal [zòuəlάdʒik(ə)l / -lɔ́dʒ-] *adj.* of [the study of] animal life. — [形] 동물[학상]의

zoological garden [ˌ–ˊ–– ˊ–] *n.* a zoo. — [名] 동물원

zo·ol·o·gist [zouάlədʒist / -ɔ́l-] *n.* [C] a student or a specialist who is skilled in zoology. — [名] 동물학자

zo·ol·o·gy [zouάlədʒi / -ɔ́l-] *n.* [U] the study of animals, as their ways of living, etc. — [名] 동물학

zoom [zu:m] *n.* [U] **1.** a sudden upward flight. **2.** a deep, low sound. **—*vi.*** **1.** (of an airplane) climb for a short time at a very steep angle. **2.** make a deep, low sound. — [名] 1. 급상승 2. 윙윙거리는 소리 —[自] 1. [비행기가] 급각도로 상승하다 2. 윙윙거리다

Zo·ro·as·ter [zóurouæ̀stər / zɔ̀rouǽstə] *n.* a founder of the ancient Persian religion. — [名] 조로아스터

Zu·rich, Zü·rich [zúərik, +*Brit.* zjúə-] *n.* a city in northern Switzerland. — [名] 스위스 북부의 도시

● 附錄

- ABBREVIATIONS(略語) /1333
- 重要引用句와 俗談/1354
- 외어 두면 편리한 會話文型/1359
- Language of Flowers(꽃말) /1370
- 符號와 數·數式 읽는 법/1376
- Presidents of the United States /1378
- Vice Presidents of the United States /1379
- The Declaration of Independence /1380
- States of the United States /1382
- Independent States of the World /1384
- Major Rivers of the World /1387
- Major Mountain Peaks of the World /1391
- Oceans and Seas of the World /1396
- 不規則動詞表/1397

ABBREVIATIONS

A

A, in *chemistry,* argon.
A., Academy; acre; America; American; angstrom unit; April; Artillery.
a., about; acre; acres; active; adjective; alto; ampere; anonymous; answer.
A.A., Associate in Arts.
AAA, Agricultural Adjustment Administration.
A.A.A., Amateur Athletic Association; American Automobile Association; Automobile Association of America.
A.A.A.L., American Academy of Arts and Letters.
A.A.A.S., American Academy of Arts and Sciences; American Association for the Advancement of Science.
A.A.E., American Association of Engineers.
A.A.S., American Academy of Sciences; (*Academiae Americanae Socius*), Fellow of the American Academy.
A.A.U., Amateur Athletic Union.
A.A.U.P., American Association of University Professors; Association of American University Presses.
A.A.U.W., American Association of University Women.
ab., about.
A.B. (*Artium Baccalaureus*), Bachelor of Arts.
A.B., a.b., able-bodied (seaman).
A.B.A., American Bankers Association; American Bar Association.
abb., abbess; abbot.
abbr., abbrev., abbreviated; abbreviation.
A.B.C., ABC, American Broadcasting Company.
abr., abridge; abridged; abridgment.
abs., absent; absolute; abstract.
Ac, in *chemistry,* actinium.
A/C, a/c, in *bookkeeping,* account; account current.
A.C., Air Corps; Armored Corps; Army Corps; (*Ante Christum*), before Christ.
A.C., a.c., in *electricity,* alternating current.
acad., academic; academy.
acc., acceptance; accompanied; according; account; accountant.
acct., account.
A.C.S., American Chemical Society; American College of Surgeons.
A/cs pay., accounts payable.
A/cs rec., accounts receivable.
act., active.
actg., acting.
ad., adverb; advertisement.
A.D. (*Anno Domini*), in the year of the Lord.
a.d., after date.
A.D.A., American Dental Association; Americans for Democratic Action.
A.D.C., aide-de-camp.
ad inf. (*ad infinitum*), endlessly; forever; without limit.
ad int. (*ad interim*), in the meantime.
adj., adjective; adjourned; adjudged.
Adjt., Adjutant.
ad-lib (*ad libitum*), to improvise; extemporize.
Adm., Admiral; Admiralty.
adm., administrator.
adv., adverb; adverbial; advertisement.
ad val. (*ad valorem*), according to value.
advt., advertisement.
AEC, Atomic Energy Commission.
A.E.F., American Expeditionary Force (or Forces).
AF, Air Force.
Af., Afr., Africa; African.
A.F., a.f., audio frequency.
A.F.A.M., Ancient Free and Accepted Masons.
AFL–CIO, American Federation of Labor and Congress of Industrial Organizations.
aft., afternoon.
Ag (*argentum*), in *chemistry,* silver.
A.G., Adjutant General; Attorney General.
agcy., agency.
agr., agric., agricultural; agriculture; agriculturist.
agt., agent.

A.I.C., American Institute of Chemists.
AID, Agency for International Development.
A.I.E.E., American Institute of Electrical Engineers.
A.I.G.A., American Institute of Graphic Arts.
A.I.M.E., American Institute of Mining Engineers; Associate of the Institute of Mechanical Engineers.
Al, in *chemistry,* aluminum.
A.L., American League; American Legion.
Ala., Alabama.
A.L.A., American Library Association.
Alas., Alaska.
Ald., Aldm., Alderman.
alg., algebra.
A.L.P., American Labor Party.
alt., alternate; alternating; altitude; alto.
Alta., Alberta.
alum., aluminum.
AM, A.M., amplitude modulation.
Am, in *chemistry,* americium.
Am., America; American.
A.M. (*anno mundi*), in the year of the world; (*Artium Magister*), Master of Arts.
A.M., a.m. (*ante meridiem*), before noon.
A.M.A., American Management Association; American Medical Association.
Amb., Ambassador.
Amer., America; American.
amp., amperage; ampere; amperes.
amt., amount.
an., anonymous; (*anno*), in the year.
anal., analogous; analogy; analysis.
anat., anatomical; anatomist; anatomy.
ANC, Army Nurse Corps.
anc., ancient; anciently.
and., andante.
ann., annual; annuity.
anon., anonymous.
ans., answer.
ant., antiquity; antiquities; antonym.
anthrop., anthropol., anthropological; anthropology.
antiq., antiqu., antiquarian; antiquities; antiquity.
AP, A.P., accounts payable; Associated Press.

Ap., Apostle; April.
APO, Army Post Office.
Apoc., Apocalypse; Apocrypha; Apocryphal.
app., appended; appendix; appointed; apprentice.
appar., apparently.
approx., approximate; approximately.
Apr., April.
Apt., apt., apartment.
Ar., Arabic; Aramaic.
a.r. (*anno regni*), in the year of the reign.
A.R.A., American Railway Association; Associate of the Royal Academy.
Arab., Arabian; Arabic.
ARC, American Red Cross.
Arch., Archbishop.
arch., archaic; archipelago; architect; architectural; architecture.
archaeol., archaeology.
Archd., Archdeacon; Archduke.
A.R.C.S., Associate of the Royal College of Science; Associate of Royal College of Surgeons.
Arg., Argentina; Argentine.
arith., arithmetic; arithmetical.
Ariz., Arizona.
Ark., Arkansas.
Arm., Armenian; Armoric.
arr., arranged; arrangements; arrival; arrives.
art., article; artificial; artillery; artist.
arty., artillery.
A.R.U., American Railway Union.
As, in *chemistry,* arsenic.
As., Asia; Asian; Asiatic.
A.S., Academy of Science; Air Service; Anglo-Saxon.
a.s., assistant secretary.
A.S.A., Acoustical Society of America; American Standards Association; American Statistical Association.
ASC, Army Service Corps.
ASCAP, American Society of Composers, Authors, and Publishers.
A.S.P.C.A., American Society for Prevention of Cruelty to Animals.
ass., assistant; association; assorted.
ASSC, Air Service Signal Corps.
assn., association.

assoc., associate; associated; association.
asst., assistant.
Assyr., Assyrian.
astr., astron., astronomer; astronomical; astronomy.
astrol., astrologer; astrological; astrology.
At, in *chemistry,* astatine.
at., atmosphere; atomic; attorney.
Atl., Atlantic.
atm., atmosphere; atmospheric.
at. no., atomic number.
ATS, Army Transport Service.
att., attorney.
atty., attorney.
Atty. Gen., Attorney General.
at. wt., atomic weight.
Au (*aurum*), in *chemistry,* gold.
aud., auditor.
Aug., August.
Aust., Austria; Austria-Hungary; Austrian.
auth., author; authoress; authorized.
Auth. Ver., A.V., Authorized Version (of the Bible).
aux., auxil., auxiliary.
a/v, ad valorem, according to value.
av., average; avoirdupois.
A.V.C., American Veterans Committee.
avdp., avoirdupois.
Ave., Av., Avenue.
avoir., avoirdupois.
AVS, Army Veterinary Service.
A.W.O.L., a.w.o.l., absent or (absence) without leave.

B

B, in *chemistry,* boron.
B., in *medicine,* bacillus; Bible; Boston; British; Brotherhood.
B., b., bachelor; battery; bay; bicuspid; bolivar; book; born; brother.
Ba, in *chemistry,* barium.
B.A. (*Baccalaureus Artium*), Bachelor of Arts.
bact., bacteriology.
B.Ag., B.Agr., Bachelor of Agriculture.
bal., balance; balancing.
bank., banking.
Bap., Bapt., Baptist.
bar., barometer; barrel; barrister.

B.Ar., B.Arch., Bachelor of Architecture.
B.A.S., B.A.Sc., Bachelor of Agricultural Science; Bachelor of Applied Science.
bat., batt., battalion; battery.
B.B., Blue Book.
B.B.A., Bachelor of Business Administration.
B.B.C., British Broadcasting Corporation.
bbl., barrel or barrels.
B.C., Bachelor of Chemistry; Bachelor of Commerce; before Christ; British Columbia.
BCC, bcc, blind carbon copy.
B.C.E., Bachelor of Chemical Engineering; Bachelor of Civil Engineering.
B.C.L., Bachelor of Civil Law.
B.C.S., Bachelor of Chemical Science.
bd., board; bond; bound; bundle.
B/D, bank draft; bills discounted.
B.D., Bachelor of Divinity; bills discounted.
bd.ft., board feet; board foot.
bdl., bundle.
bds., boards; bundles.
B.D.S., Bachelor of Dental Surgery.
Be, in *chemistry,* beryllium.
B.E., Bachelor of Education; Bachelor of Engineering; Bank of England; Board of Education.
B.E., B/E, b.e., bill of exchange.
B.E.E., Bachelor of Electrical Engineering.
bef., before.
B.E.F., British Expeditionary Force.
Bel., Belg., Belgian; Belgium.
bet., between.
bf, b.f., in *printing,* boldface.
B/F, in *bookkeeping,* brought forward.
B.F., Bachelor of Finance; Bachelor of Forestry.
B.F.A., Bachelor of Fine Arts.
bg., bag.
Bi, in *chemistry,* bismuth.
Bib., Bible; Biblical.
bibliog., bibliography.
bicarb., sodium bicarbonate; baking soda.
biog., biographer; biographical; biography.
biol., biological; biologist; biology.
Bk, in *chemistry,* berkelium.
bk., bank; block; book.

bkg., banking.
bkkpg., bookkeeping.
bkpt., bankrupt.
bkt., basket; bracket.
B/L, b.l., bill of lading.
bl., bale; bales; barrel; barrels; black.
B.L., Bachelor of Laws; Bachelor of Letters.
bldg., building.
B.Lit., B.Litt. (*Baccalaureus Lit[t]erarum*), Bachelor of Letters; Bachelor of Literature.
B.LL. (*Baccalaureus Legum*), Bachelor of Laws.
BLS, Bureau of Labor Statistics.
B.L.S., Bachelor of Library Science.
Blvd., Boulevard.
B.M. (*Baccalaureus Medicinae*), Bachelor of Medicine; (*Baccalaureus Musicae*), Bachelor of Music.
B.M.A., British Medical Association.
B.M.E., Bachelor of Mechanical Engineering; Bachelor of Mining Engineering.
B.Mus., Bachelor of Music.
B.N., bank note.
B/O, in *bookkeeping*, brought over.
B.O., Board of Ordnance; body odor.
b.o., back order; bad order; box office; branch office; broker's order; buyer's option.
Bol., Bolivia; Bolivian.
bor., boron; borough.
bot., botanical; botanist; botany; bottle.
B.O.T., Board of Trade.
bp., birthplace; bishop.
B.P. (*Baccalaureus Pharmaciae*), Bachelor of Pharmacy; (*Baccalaureus Philosophiae*), Bachelor of Philosophy.
b.p., below proof; boiling point.
b.p., B/P, bill of parcels; bills payable.
B. pay., bills payable.
B.P.E., Bachelor of Physical Education.
B.P.O.E., Benevolent and Protective Order of Elks.
Br, in *chemistry*, bromine.
Br., Britain; British.
br., branch; brig; bronze; brother.
b.r., B/R, B. Rec., b. rec., bills receivable.

Braz., Brazil; Brazilian.
B.R.C.S., British Red Cross Society.
Brig. Gen., Brigadier General.
Brit., Britain; Britannia; British.
bro., brother.
bros., brothers.
B.S., Bachelor of Science; Bachelor of Surgery; British Standard.
b.s., balance sheet.
b.s., B/S, bill of sale.
B.S.A., Boy Scouts of America.
B.Sc. (*Baccalaureus Scientiae*), Bachelor of Science.
B.S.Ed., Bachelor of Science in Education.
bskt., basket.
Bs/L, bills of lading.
B.S.P., Bachelor of Science in Pharmacy.
B.T., B.Th. (*Baccalaureus Theologiae*), Bachelor of Theology.
B.T.U., Btu, B.t.u., British thermal unit (or units).
bu., bureau; bushel; bushels.
bul., bull., bulletin.
Bulg., Bulgaria; Bulgarian.
B.W.I., British West Indies.
bx., box; boxes.
bx., boxes.
Bz., benzene.

C

C, in *chemistry*, carbon.
C., Catholic; Congress; Conservative; Corps; Court.
C., c., capacity; carbon; carton; case; cent or cents; centigrade; centimeter; century; chapter; circa; copy; copyright; corps; cost; cubic; hundredweight.
Ca, in *chemistry*, calcium.
ca., cathode; centiare; circa (about).
C/A, capital accountant; credit account; current account.
C.A., Central America; Coast Artillery; Court of Appeal.
C.A., c.a., chartered accountant; chief accountant; commercial agent; consular agent; controller of accounts.
CAA, Civil Aeronautics Authority.

CAB, Civil Aeronautics Board.
C.A.F., c.a.f., cost and freight; cost, assurance, and freight.
Cal., California; large calorie (or calories).
cal., calendar; caliber; small calorie (or calories).
Calif., California.
Can., Canada; Canadian.
cap., capital; capitalize; captain.
caps., capitals (capital letters).
Capt., Captain.
car., carat; carats.
Card., Cardinal.
CARE, Co-operative for American Remittances to Europe, Inc.
cat., catalogue; catechism.
Cath., Catholic; (*also* **cath.**), cathedral.
cav., cavalier; cavalry.
C/B, c.b., cashbook.
C.B.S., CBS, Columbia Broadcasting System.
cc., chapters.
cc., c.c., carbon copy; cubic centimeter; cubic centimeters.
C.C., c.c., carbon copy; cashier's check; chief clerk; circuit court; city council; civil court; county clerk; county commissioner; county council; county court.
C.C.A., Chief Clerk of the Admiralty; Circuit Court of Appeals; County Court of Appeals.
CCC, Commodity Credit Corporation.
ccm., centimeters.
C.C.P., Court of Common Pleas.
C.C.R., Commission on Civil Rights.
Cd, in *chemistry*, cadmium.
c.d., cash discount.
Ce, in *chemistry*, cerium.
C.E., Chemical Engineer; Chief Engineer; Church of England; Civil Engineer.
C.E.F., Canadian Expeditionary Force (or Forces).
cen., central; century.
cent., centigrade; centimeter; central; century.
cert., certif., certificate.
Cf, in *chemistry*, californium.

cf. (*confer*), compare.
c/f, in *bookkeeping*, carried forward.
C.F., c.f., cost and freight.
C.F.I., c.f.i., cost, freight, and insurance.
cg., centigram; centigrams.
C.G., Coast Guard; Consul General.
ch., chapter; chief; child; church.
c.h., courthouse; customhouse.
chap., chaplain; chapter.
Ch.E., Chem. E., Chemical Engineer.
chem., chemical; chemist; chemistry.
chg., charge.
chgd., charged.
chgs., charges.
Chin., China; Chinese.
chm., chmn., chairman.
Chr., Christ; Christian.
Chron., Chronicles.
chron., chronol., chronological; chronology.
chs., chapters.
CIA, Central Intelligence Agency.
C.I.C., Commander in Chief.
C.I.F., c.i.f., cost, insurance, and freight.
CIO. C.I.O., Congress of Industrial Organizations.
cit., citation; cited; citizen.
civ., civil; civilian.
ck., cask; check.
Cl, in *chemistry*, chlorine.
cl., centiliter; centiliters; claim; class; clause; clearance; clerk; cloth.
c.l., carload; carload lots; civil law.
C.L.D., Doctor of Civil Law.
clk., clerk; clock.
Cm, in *chemistry*, curium.
cm., centimeter; centimeters.
cml., commercial.
C/N, circular note; credit note.
Co, in *chemistry*, cobalt.
C/O, cash order.
c/o, c.o., care of; carried over.
Co., co., company; county.
C.O., Commanding Officer; Conscientious Objector.
coad., coadjutor.
C.O.D., c.o.d., cash on delivery; collect on delivery.
C. of S., Chief of Staff.

Col., Colombia; Colombian; Colonel; Colorado; Colossians.
col., collected; collector; college; colonial; colony; color; colored; column.
coll., colleague; collect; collection; collective; collector; college; colloquial.
collab., collaboration; collaborator.
collat., collateral; collaterally.
colloq., colloquial; colloquialism; colloquially.
Colo., Colorado.
Com., Commander; Commission; Commissioner; Committee; Commodore; Communist.
com., comedy; commentary; commerce; commercial; common; commonly; commune; communication; community.
comb., combination.
comdg., commanding.
Comdr., Commander.
Comdt., Commandant.
comm., commander; commentary; commerce; commission; committee; communication.
comp., companion; comparative; compare; compiled; compiler; composer; composition; compound; compounded.
Comr., Commissioner.
con., concerto; conclusion; connection; consolidate; consul.
conc., concentrate; concentrated; concentration; concerning.
Confed., Confederate.
Cong., Congregational; Congregationalist; Congress; Congressional.
conj., conjugation; conjunction; conjunctive.
Conn., Connecticut.
cons., Cons., constable; constitution. nant; constitution; construction.
cons., Cons., constable; constitution.
Cont., Continental.
cont., containing; contents; continent; continue; continued; contra; contract.
contemp., contemporary.
contr., contract; contracted; contraction; contralto; contrary; contrasted; control; controller.
contrib., contributor.

co-op., coöp., coop., co-operative.
cop., copper; copyrighted.
Cor., Corinthians; Coroner.
cor., corner; coroner; correct; corrected; correction; correspondence; correspondent; corresponding.
Corp., Corporal.
corp., corpn., corporation.
corr., corrected; correspond; correspondence; correspondent; corrupt; corrupted; corruption.
cos, cosine.
Cos., cos., companies; counties.
cp., compare.
C.P., Chief Patriarch; Command Post; Common Pleas; Common Prayer; Communist Party.
c.p., candle power; chemically pure.
C.P.A., c.p.a., Certified Public Accountant.
C.P.H., Certificate in Public Health.
Cpl., Corporal.
C.P.O., Chief Petty Officer.
CPS, Certified Professional Secretary.
Cr, in *chemistry,* chromium.
cr., credit; creditor; creek; crown.
C.R., Costa Rica.
crim., criminal.
crit., critical; criticism; criticized.
cryst., crystalline; crystallography.
Cs, in *chemistry,* cesium.
C.S., Christian Science; Christian Scientist.
C.S., c.s., capital stock; civil service.
CSC, Civil Service Commission.
csk., cask.
C.S.T., Central Standard Time.
Ct., Connecticut; Count.
ct., cent; certificate; county; court.
c.t., certified teacher; commercial traveler.
ctf., certificate.
ctg., cartage.
ctr., center.
cts., cents.
Cu (*cuprum*), in *chemistry,* copper.
cu., cub., cubic.
cu. cm., cubic centimeter; cubic centimeters.
cur., currency; current (of the present day, week, month, or year).

CWA, Civil Works Administration.
cwt., hundredweight.
cyl., cylinder.
C.Z., Canal Zone.

D

D., December; Democrat; Democratic; Duchess; Duke; Dutch.
d., date; daughter; day; days; dead; degree; delete; density; deputy; deserter; diameter; died; dime; director; dividend; dollar; dorsai; dose.
da., daughter; day; days.
D.A., District Attorney.
Dan., Danish.
d. and s., demand and supply.
D.A.R., Daughters of the American Revolution.
D.Arch., Doctor of Architecture.
D.A.V., Disabled American Veterans.
db, decibel.
d.b., daybook.
dbl., double.
D.C., in *music, da capo;* Dental Corps; District of Columbia; Doctor of Chiropractic.
D.C., d.c., direct current.
D.C.L., Doctor of Civil Law.
D.Cn.L., Doctor of Canon Law.
D.C.S., Deputy Clerk of Sessions; Doctor of Christian Science; Doctor of Commercial Science.
dd, d/d, delivered.
D.D. (*Divinitatis Doctor*), Doctor of Divinity.
D.D., D/D, demand draft.
D.D.S., Doctor of Dental Surgery.
D.D.Sc., Doctor of Dental Science.
DDT, dichlorodiphenyltrichloroethane.
D.E., D.Eng., Doctor of Engineering.
deb., debenture.
Dec., December.
dec., deceased; decimeter; declaration; declension; declination; decrease.
decl., declension.
def., defendant; defense; deferred; defined; definite; definition.
deg., degree; degrees.
Del., Delaware.
del., delegate; delete.

Dem., Democrat; Democratic.
Den., Denmark.
dent., dental; dentist; dentistry.
dep., department; departs; departure; deponent; deposed; deposit; deputy.
dept., department; deponent; deputy.
der., deriv., derivation; derivative; derived.
Deut., Deuteronomy.
D.F.C., Distinguished Flying Cross.
di., dia., diameter.
diag., diagonal; diagram.
dial., dialect; dialectal; dialectic; dialectical.
diam., diameter.
dict., dictated (by); dictator; dictionary.
dif., diff., difference; different.
dig., digest.
dil., dilute.
dim., dimension; (*also* **dimin.**), diminuendo; diminutive.
dis., distance; distant; distribute.
disc., discount; discovered; discoverer.
dist., discount; distance; distant; distinguish; district.
Div., Divinity.
div., diversion; divide; dividend; divine; division; divisor; divorced.
DL, day letter.
D/L, demand loan.
DLF, Development Loan Fund.
D.Lit., D.Litt. (*Doctor Lit[t]erarum*), Doctor of Letters; Doctor of Literature.
D.L.S., Doctor of Library Science.
D.Mus., Doctor of Music.
D.N.B., Dictionary of National Biography.
D/O, d.o., delivery order.
do., ditto.
D.O., District Office; Doctor of Optometry; Doctor of Osteopathy.
dol., dollar.
dols., dollars.
dom., domestic; dominion.
Dom. Rep., Dominican Republic.
doz., dozen; dozens.
D.P., displaced person.
dpt., department; deponent.
D.P.W., Department of Public Works.

Dr., Doctor.
dr., debit; debtor; dram; drams; drawer.
d.r., dead reckoning; deposit receipt.
D.S., D.Sc., Doctor of Science.
D.S.C., Distinguished Service Cross.
D.S.M., Distinguished Service Medal.
D.S.O., District Staff Officer.
D.S.T., Daylight Saving Time.
d.t., delirium tremens; double time.
D.Th., D. Theol., Doctor of Theology.
dup., duplicate.
D.V.M., Doctor of Veterinary Medicine.
D.V.S., Doctor of Veterinary Surgery.
Dy, in *chemistry,* dysprosium.
dz., dozen; dozens.

E

E, in *chemistry,* einsteinium.
E, E., e, e., east; eastern.
E., Earl; Easter; English.
E., e., earth; eastern; engineer; engineering.
ea., each.
E. A., in *psychology,* educational age.
E. & O.E., e. & o.e., errors and omissions excepted.
E.C., Engineering Corps; Established Church.
eccl., eccles., ecclesiastical.
Eccles., Eccl., Ecclesiastes.
Ecclus., Ecclesiasticus.
econ., economic; economics; economy.
ed., edited; edition; editor.
Ed.B., Bachelor of Education.
Ed.D., Doctor of Education.
Ed.M., Master of Education.
educ., education; educational; educator.
E.E., Early English; Electrical Engineering.
e.e., errors excepted.
E.E.C., European Economic Community.
Eg., Egypt; Egyptian.
e.g. (*exempli gratia*), for example.
e.h.p., effective horsepower.
E.I., East India; East Indian; East Indies.
elec., elect., electric; electrical; electricity.
elem., element; elementary; elements.
Eliz., Elizabethan.

E.M.F., e.m.f., EMF, emf, electromotive force.
Emp., Emperor; Empire; Empress.
enc., enclosed; enclosure; encyclopedia.
Eng., England; English.
eng., engine; engineer; engineering; engraved; engraver; engraving.
enl., enlarge; enlarged; enlisted.
Ens., Ensign.
Eph., Ephes., Ephesians.
eq., equal; equalizer; equation; equator; equivalent.
Er, in *chemistry,* erbium.
Esk., Eskimo.
ESP, E.S.P., extrasensory perception.
esp., especially.
Esq., Esqr., Esquire.
est., established; estimated.
E.S.T., Eastern Standard Time.
Esth., Esther.
E.T.A., Estimated Time of Arrival.
et al. (*et alibi*), and elsewhere; (*et alii*), and others.
etc., &c, et cetera.
E.T.D., Estimated Time of Departure.
Eu, in *chemistry,* europium.
Eur., Europe; European.
Ex., Exod., Exodus.
ex., examined; example; except; excepted; exception; exchange; executive; export; extra; extract.
exam., examination.
Exc., Excellency.
exc., excellent; except; excepted; exception; exchange.
exch., exchange; exchequer.
exec., executive; executor.
exp., expenses; export; exported; express.
ext., extension; external; extinct; extra.
Ez., Ezr., Ezra.
Ezek., Ezekiel.

F

F, in *chemistry,* fluorine.
F., Fahrenheit; February; Fellow; France; French; Friday.
F., f., farad; farthing; father; fathom; feet; feminine; fine; fluid; folio; folios;

following; foot; form; in *music,* forte; franc; francs; from.

f.a., fire alarm; freight agent.

FAA, Federal Aviation Agency.

F.A.A.A.S., Fellow of the American Academy of Arts and Sciences; Fellow of the American Association for the Advancement of Science.

fac., facsimile.

Fah., Fahr., Fahrenheit.

F.A.M., Free and Accepted Masons.

FAO, Food and Agriculture Organization (UN).

f.a.s., free alongside ship.

f.b., freight bill.

FBI, F.B.I., Federal Bureau of Investigation; Federation of British Industries.

f.c., in *printing,* follow copy.

FCA, Farm Credit Administration.

FCC, Federal Communications Commission.

F.D., Fire Department.

FDA, Food and Drug Administration.

FDIC, Federal Deposit Insurance Corporation.

Fe (*ferrum*), in *chemistry,* iron.

Feb., February.

Fed., Federal; Federation.

fem., feminine.

FEPC, Fair Employment Practices Committee.

feud., feudal; feudalism.

ff., folios; following (pages); in *music,* fortissimo.

FFCA, Federal Farm Credit Administration.

FFMC, Federal Farm Mortgage Corporation.

F.F.V., First Families of Virginia.

FHA, Federal Housing Administration.

FHLBB, Federal Home Loan Bank Board.

fict., fiction.

fig., figurative; figuratively; figure; figures.

Fin., Finland; Finnish.

fin., finance; financial.

Finn., Finnish.

fl., floor; flourished; flower; fluid.

Fla., Flor., Florida.

fl. oz., fluid ounce; fluid ounces.

FM, frequency modulation.

Fm, in *chemistry,* fermium.

fm., fathom; from.

F.M., Field Marshall; Foreign Missions.

F.O., Foreign Office.

F.O.B., f.o.b., free on board.

F.O.E., Fraternal Order of Eagles.

fol., folio; following.

for., foreign; forestry.

F.O.R., f.o.r., free on rail.

fp., F.P., f.p., foot-pound; foot-pounds.

F.P., f.p., in *insurance,* fire policy; floating policy; fully paid.

f.p., fp, fp., freezing point.

FPC, Federal Power Commission.

FPO, Fleet Post Office.

FR, full-rate cable.

Fr, in *chemistry,* francium.

Fr., Father; France; *Frau;* French; Friar; Friday.

fr., fragment; franc; francs; frequent; from.

FRB, Federal Reserve Bank; Federal Reserve Board.

freq., frequent; frequently.

Fri., Friday.

frt., freight.

FSA, Farm Security Administration; Federal Security Agency.

FSCC, Federal Surplus Commodities Corporation.

FSR, F.S.R., Field Service Regulations.

ft., feet; foot; fortification.

FTC, Federal Trade Commission.

fth., fthm., fathom.

ft-lb, foot-pound.

fut., future.

F.Y.I., for your information.

G

G., German; Germany; specific gravity.

G., g., gauge; gold; grain; gram; grams; grand; guide; guinea; guineas; gulf.

g., gender; general; genitive.

Ga, in *chemistry,* gallium.

Ga., Gaelic; Gallic; Georgia.

G.A., General Agent; General Assembly.

G.A., G/A, g.a. in *insurance,* general average.

gal., gallon; gallons.
G.A.R., Grand Army of the Republic.
gaz., gazette; gazetteer.
G.B., Great Britain.
g-cal., gram calorie; gram calories.
G.C.D., **g.c.d**, greatest common divisor.
G.C.F., **g.c.f**, greatest common factor.
G.C.L.H., Grand Cross of the Legion of Honor.
G.C.M., **g.c.m.**, greatest common measure.
Gd, in *chemistry*, gadolinium.
gds., goods.
Ge, in *chemistry*, germanium.
Gen., General; Genesis; Geneva.
gen., gender; genera; general; generally; generator; generic; genitive; genus.
geneal., genealogy.
genl., general.
Gent., **gent.**, gentleman; gentlemen.
geog., geographer; geographical; geography.
geol., geologic; geological; geologist; geology.
geom., geometric; geometrical; geometrician; geometry.
Ger., German; Germany.
ger., gerund.
G.F.T.U., General Federation of Trade Unions.
g.gr., great gross.
GHQ, General Headquarters.
gi., gill; gills.
Gk., Greek.
gl., glass; gloss.
gloss., glossary.
gm., gram; grams.
G.M., general manager; Grand Master.
Gmc., Germanic.
G.M.T., Greenwich mean time.
GNP, gross national product.
G.O., **g.o.**, general office; general order.
G.O.P., Grand Old Party (Republican Party).
Goth., **goth.**, Gothic.
Gov., **gov.**, government; governor.
Gov. Gen., Governor General.
govt., **Govt.**, government.
G.P., **g.p.**, general practitioner.
G.P.O., General Post Office; (*also* **GPO**), Government Printing Office.
Gr., Grecian; Greece; Greek.
gr., grade; grain or grains; gram or grams; grammar; great; gross; group.
grad., graduate; graduated.
gram., grammar; grammarian; grammatical.
Gr. Brit., **Gr. Br.**, Great Britain.
gro., gross.
G.S.A., Girl Scouts of America.
GSC, General Staff Corps.
gt., gilt; great.
Gt. Brit., **Gt. Br.**, Great Britain.
guar., guaranteed.
Guat., Guatemala; Guatemalan.

H

H, in *physics*, henry; in *chemistry*, hydrogen.
H., **h.**, harbor; hard; hardness; height; hence; high; hour; hours; hundred; husband.
ha., hectare; hectares.
Hab., Habakkuk.
Hag., Haggai.
Hal., halogen.
Hb, hemoglobin.
H.B.M., His (or Her) Britannic Majesty.
H.C., House of Commons.
H.C.F., **h.c.f.**, highest common factor.
h.c.l., **h.c. of l.**, high cost of living.
hd., head.
hdqrs., headquarters.
HE, **H.E.**, high explosive.
He, in *chemistry*, helium.
H.E., His Eminence; His Excellency.
Heb., Hebrew; Hebrews.
Hf, in *chemistry*, hafnium.
hf., half.
H.F., high frequency.
Hg (*hydrargyrum*), in *chemistry*, mercury.
H.G., His (or Her) Grace; Home Guard.
hgt., height.
H.H., His (or Her) Highness; His Holiness.
H.I., Hawaiian Islands.
H.I.H., His (or Her) Imperial Highness.

hist., historian; historical; history.
H.L., House of Lords.
H.M.S., His (or Her) Majesty's Service, Ship, or Steamer.
Ho, in *chemistry*, holmium.
H.O., head office.
HOLC, Home Owners' Loan Corporation.
Hon., hon., honorable; honorary.
Hond., Honduran; Honduras.
hor., horizon; horizontal.
Hos., Hosea.
hosp., hospital.
H.P., HP, h.p., hp, high pressure; horsepower.
H.Q., Hq., headquarters.
hr., hour; hours.
H.R., Home Rule; House of Representatives.
H.R.H., His (or Her) Royal Highness.
hrs., hours.
ht., heat; height; heights.
hts., heights.
hund., hundred; hundreds.
Hung., Hungarian; Hungary.
hyd., hydraulics; hydrostatics.
hyp., hypotenuse; hypothesis; hypothetical.

I

I, in *chemistry*, iodine.
I., Idaho; Independent; Iowa.
I., i., island; islands; isle; isles.
i., incisor; interest; intransitive.
Ia., Iowa.
i.a. (*in absentia*), in absence; absent.
I.A.M., International Association of Machinists.
ib., ibid. (*ibidem*), in the same place.
IBM, I.B.M., International Business Machines.
ICBM, intercontinental ballistic missile.
ICC, Interstate Commerce Commission.
Ice., Icel., Iceland; Icelandic.
Id., Idaho.
id. (*idem*), the same.
I.D., Intelligence Department.
Ida., Idaho.
IDP, integrated data processing.

i.e. (*id est*), that is.
I.F.S., Irish Free State.
I.G., Inspector General.
ign., ignition; (*ignotus*), unknown.
I.L.G.W.U., ILGWU, International Ladies' Garment Workers Union.
Ill., Illinois.
ill., illus., illust., illustrated; illustration.
ILO, International Labor Organization.
imp., imperative; imperfect; imperial; impersonal; import; imported; importer; imprimatur; imprint.
imper., impv., imperative.
imperf., impf., imperfect.
impers., impersonal.
In, in *chemistry*, indium.
in., inch or inches.
inc., inclosure; included; including; inclusive; income; incorporated; increase.
incl., inclosure; including; inclusive.
incog., incognito.
incorp., incor., incorporated.
Ind., India; Indian; Indiana; Indies.
ind., independent; index; indicative; industrial.
indef., indefinite.
indic., indicating; indicative; indicator.
individ., individual.
Inf., inf., infantry.
inf., infinitive; information; (*infra*), below.
infin., infinitive.
init., initial.
ins., inches; inscribed; insulated; insurance.
insp., inspector.
Inst., Institute; Institution.
inst., instant (the present month); instrumental; installment.
instr., instructor; instrument; instrumental.
int., interest; interim; interior; interjection; internal; international; intransitive.
inter., interrogation.
interj., interjection.
interrog., interrogation; interrogative.
intr., intransitive.
in trans. (*in transitu*), on the way.
Int. Rev., Internal Revenue.

introd., intro., introduction; introductory.
inv., invented; inventor; invoice.
invt., inventory.
Io., Iowa.
I.O.F., Independent Order of Foresters.
Ion., Ionic.
I.O.O.F., Independent Order of Odd Fellows.
I.O.R.M., Improved Order of Red Men.
IOU, I.O.U., I owe you.
IPA, International Phonetic Alphabet; International Phonetic Association.
IQ, I.Q., intelligence quotient.
Ir, in *chemistry*, iridium.
Ir., Ireland; Irish.
Iran., Iranian.
Ire., Ireland.
IRS, Internal Revenue Service.
Is., Isa., Isaiah.
is., isl., island; isle.
Ital., It., Italian; Italic; Italy.
ital., it., italic; italics.
I.W.W., Industrial Workers of the World.

J

J, in *physics*, joule.
J., James; Judge; Justice.
Ja., James; January.
J/A, j/a, joint account.
J.A., Joint Agent; Judge Advocate.
J.A.G., Judge Advocate General.
Jam., Jamaica.
Jan., January.
Jap., Japan; Japanese.
Jas., James.
J.C., Jesus Christ.
jct., junction.
J.D. (*Jurum Doctor*), Doctor of Laws.
Jer., Jeremiah; Jeremy.
Jew., Jewish.
j.g., jg, junior grade.
Josh., Joshua.
jour., journal; journeyman.
J.P., Justice of the Peace.
Jr., jr., junior.
Jud., Judges; Judith.
Judg., Judges.
Jul., July.
jus., justice.
J.W.V., Jewish War Veterans.

K

K (*kalium*), in *chemistry*, potassium.
K., k., in *electricity*, capacity; karat; kilo; kilogram; king; knight; kopeck or kopecks; krona; krone; kronen; kroner; kronor; in *nautical usage*, knot.
Kan., Kans., Kas., Kansas.
kc., kilocycle; kilocycles.
K.C., King's Counsel; Knight (or Knights) of Columbus.
K.D., in *commerce*, knocked down (not assembled).
Ken., Kentucky.
kg., keg; kegs; kilogram; kilograms.
Ki., Kings (book of the Bible).
kilo., kilogram; kilometer.
kilom., kilometer.
K.K.K., KKK, Ku Klux Klan.
kl., kiloliter; kiloliters.
km., kilometer or kilometers; kingdom.
K.O., KO, k.o., in *boxing*, knockout.
K. of C., Knight (or Knights) of Columbus.
K. of P., Knight (or Knights) of Pythias.
KP, K.P., kitchen police.
Kr, in *chemistry*, krypton.
kr., kreutzer; krona; krone; kronen; kroner; kronor.
kt., carat.
K.T., Knight (or Knights) Templar.
kw., kilowatt.
kwh., K.W.H., kw-h, kw-hr, kilowatt-hour.
Ky., Kentucky.

L

L., Latin.
L., l., lady; lake; land; latitude; law; leaf; league; left; length; liberal; (*libra*), pound; (*librae*), pounds; line; link; lira; lire; liter; liters; lord; low.
La, in *chemistry*, lanthanum.
La., Louisiana.
L.A., Legislative Assembly; Los Angeles.
Lab., Laborite; Labrador.
lab., laboratory.
Lam., Lamentations.
lang., language.

Lat., Latin.
lat., latitude.
lb. (*libra*), pound; (*librae*), pounds.
L.B. (*Litterarum Baccalaureus*), Bachelor of Letters; Bachelor of Literature.
lbs., pounds.
L/C, l/c, letter of credit.
l.c., in *printing*, lower case.
L.C.D., l.c.d., lowest (or least) common denominator.
L.C.F., l.c.f., lowest (or least) common factor.
L.C.L., l.c.l., in *commerce*, less than carload lot.
L.C.M., l.c.m., lowest (or least) common multiple.
lect., lecture; lecturer.
leg., legal; legend; legislative; legislature.
Lev., Levit., Leviticus.
lex., lexicon.
L.F., low frequency.
lgth., length.
lg. tn., long ton.
L.H.D. (*Litterarum Humaniorum Doctor*), Doctor of Humanities.
Li, in *chemistry*, lithium.
L.I., Light Infantry; Long Island.
Lib., Liberal; Liberia.
lib., librarian; library.
Lieut., Lieutenant.
lin., lineal; linear.
lit., liter or liters; literal; literally; literary; literature.
Litt.B. (*Litterarum Baccalaureus*), Bachelor of Letters; Bachelor of Literature.
Litt.D. (*Litterarum Doctor*), Doctor of Letters; Doctor of Literature.
ll., lines.
LL.B. (*Legum Baccalaureus*), Bachelor of Laws.
LL.D. (*Legum Doctor*), Doctor of Laws.
loc. cit. (*loco citato*), in the place cited.
log, logarithm.
log., logic.
long., longitude.
L.O.O.M., Loyal Order of Moose.
L.R., Lloyd's Register.
L.S. (*locus sigilli*), place of the seal.
LT, letter telegram.
Lt., Lieutenant.

l.t., long ton.
Lt. Col., Lieutenant Colonel.
Lt. Comdr., Lt.-Comm., Lieutenant Commander.
Ltd., ltd., limited.
Lt. Gen., Lieutenant General.
Lt. Gov., Lieutenant Governor.
Lu, in *chemistry*, lutetium.
Luth., Lutheran.
Lux., Luxemburg.
lv., leave; leaves.
Lw, in *chemistry*, lawrencium.

M

M., Manitoba; Marshal; Master; Medieval; Monday; Monsieur.
M., m., majesty; male; manual; married; masculine; medicine; medium; meridian; (*meridies*), noon; meter; meters; middle; mile; miles; mill; mills; minim; minute; minutes; month; moon; morning; mountain.
M.A. (*Magister Artium*), Master of Arts.
Mac., Macc., Maccabees.
mach., machine; machinery; machinist.
Maj., Major.
Maj. Gen., Major General.
Mal., Malachi; Malay; Malayan.
Man., Manit., Manitoba.
manuf., manufac., manufacture; manufacturer; manufacturing.
Mar., March.
mar., marine; maritime; married.
marg., margin; marginal.
masc., masculine.
Mass., Massachusetts.
math., mathematical; mathematician; mathematics.
Matt., Matthew.
max., maximum.
M.B.A., Master of Business Administration.
M.B.S., MBS, Mutual Broadcasting System.
M.B.S., M.B.Sc., Master of Business Science.
M.C., Master of Ceremonies; Medical Corps; Member of Congress; Member of Council.

Md., Maryland.
M.D. (*Medicinae Doctor*), Doctor of Medicine; Medical Department.
Mdlle., Mademoiselle.
Mdm., Madam.
Mdme., Madame.
M.D.S., Master of Dental Surgery.
mdse., merchandise.
Me., Maine.
M.E., Mechanical Engineer; Methodist Episcopal; Middle English; Military Engineer; Mining Engineer.
meas., measure.
mech., mechanical; mechanics; mechanism.
med., median; medical; medicine; medieval; medium.
Medit., Mediterranean.
mem., member; memoir; memoranda; memorandum; memorial.
Messrs., Messieurs.
met., metaphor; metaphysical; metropolitan.
metal., metallurgical; metallurgy.
Meth., Methodist.
Mex., Mexican; Mexico.
M.F.A., Master of Fine Arts.
mfd., manufactured.
mfg., manufacturing.
mfr., manufacture; manufacturer.
Mg, in *chemistry*, magnesium.
mg., milligram; milligrams.
Mgr., Manager; Monseigneur; Monsignor.
M.H.R., Member of the House of Representatives.
mi., mile; miles; mill; mills; minute; minor.
M.I., Military Intelligence; Mounted Infantry.
Mic., Micah.
Mich., Michigan.
mid., middle; midshipman.
mil., military; militia.
min., mineralogy; minimum; mining; minister; minor; minute; minutes.
Minn., Minnesota.
misc., miscellaneous; miscellany.
Miss., Mississippi.
mkt., market.
ml., mail; milliliter; milliliters.
Mlle., Mademoiselle.
Mlles., Mademoiselles.
M.L.S., Master of Library Science.
MM., Messieurs.
mm. (*millia*), thousands; millimeter; millimeters.
Mme., Madame.
Mmes., Mesdames.
Mn, in *chemistry*, manganese.
Mo, in *chemistry*, molybdenum.
Mo., Missouri; Monday.
mo., month.
M.O., mo., money order.
mod., moderate; modern.
Mon., Monastery; Monday; Monsignor.
Mont., Montana.
Mor., Morocco.
mos., months.
MP, M.P., Military Police.
M.P., Member of Parliament; Metropolitan Police; Mounted Police.
M.P., m.p., melting point.
mph, m.p.h., miles per hour.
Mr., Mister.
Mrs., Mistress.
MS., ms., manuscript.
M.S., M.Sc., Master of Science.
Msgr., Monsignor.
M.Sgt., M/Sgt, Master Sergeant.
MSS, mss., manuscripts.
M.S.T., Mountain Standard Time.
Mt., mt., mount; mountain.
mtg., meeting; mortgage.
mtn., mountain.
mts., mountains.
mun., municipal.
mus., museum; music; musical; musician.
mut., mutilated; mutual.
Mv, in *chemistry*, mendelevium.
myth., mythol., mythological; mythology.

N

N, in *chemistry*, nitrogen.
N, N., n, n., north; northern.
N., National; Nationalist; Norse; November.
N., n., nail; name; (*natus*), born; navy; neuter; new; nominative; noon; northern; noun.
n., nephew; net; note; number.

Na (*natrium*), in *chemistry*, sodium.
n/a, in *banking*, no account.
N.A., National Academy; National Army; North America.
N.A.A.C.P., NAACP, National Association for the Advancement of Colored People.
Nah., Nahum.
N.A.M., NAM, National Association of Manufacturers.
N.A.S., National Academy of Sciences.
NASA, National Aeronautics and Space Administration.
nat. (*natus*), born; national; native; natural; naturalist.
natl., national.
NATO, North Atlantic Treaty Organization.
naut., nautical.
Nb, in *chemistry*, niobium.
N.B., New Brunswick.
N.B., n.b. (*nota bene*), note well.
N.B.C., NBC, National Broadcasting Company.
N.C., North Carolina.
NCO, noncommissioned officer.
Nd, in *chemistry*, neodymium.
N.D., n.d., no date.
N.D., N. Dak., North Dakota.
Ne, in *chemistry*, neon.
N.E., Naval Engineer; New England.
N.E.A., National Education Association.
Neb., Nebr., Nebraska.
N.E.D., New English Dictionary (the Oxford English Dictionary).
neg., negative.
Neh., Nehemiah.
Neth., Netherlands.
neut., neuter.
Nev., Nevada.
Newf., N.F., Nfd., Nfld., Newfoundland.
New M., New Mexico.
N.F., n/f, in *banking*, no funds.
N.G., National Guard.
N.G., n.g., no good.
N.H., New Hampshire.
Ni, in *chemistry*, nickel.
NIRA, N.I.R.A., National Industrial Recovery Act.
N.J., New Jersey.
NL, night letter.

NLRB, National Labor Relations Board.
N.M., N. Mex., New Mexico.
N.M.U., NMU, National Maritime Union.
NNE, N.N.E., n.n.e., north-northeast.
NNW, N. N. W., n.n.w., north-northwest.
No, in *chemistry*, nobelium.
No., Noah; north; northern.
No., no., number.
nom., nominative.
NOMA, National Office Management Association.
Nor., Norman; North; Norway; Norwegian.
Nov., November.
Np, in *chemistry*, neptunium.
N.P., n.p., new paragraph; Notary Public.
NRA, National Recovery Administration.
N.S., New Series; New Style; Nova Scotia.
N/S, n/s, N.S.F., in *banking*, not sufficient funds.
NSA, National Secretaries Association; National Security Agency; National Shipping Authority.
N.S.P.C.A., National Society for the Prevention of Cruelty to Animals.
NT., N.T., New Testament.
nt. wt., net weight.
Num., Numb., Numbers (book of the Bible).
num., number; numeral; numerals.
N.Y., New York.
N.Y.C., New York Central; New York City.
N.Z., N. Zeal., New Zealand.

O

O, in *physics*, ohm; in *chemistry*, oxygen.
O., Ocean; October; Ohio; Ontario; Oregon.
o., off; only; order.
OAS, Organization of American States.
Ob., Obad., Obadiah.
obj., object; objection; objective.
Obs., obs., observatory; obsolete.
occas., occasion; occasional; occasionally.
Oct., October.
oct., octavo.
O.D., Doctor of Optometry; Officer of the Day; overdraft; overdrawn.

OE., O.E., Old English.
O.E., o.e., omissions excepted.
O.E.D., OED, Oxford English Dictionary.
OEO, Office of Economic Opportunity.
off., office; officer; official.
O.K., OK, o.k., approval; approved.
Okla., Oklahoma.
Ont., Ontario.
op., opera; operation; opposite; opus.
O.P., o.p., out of print.
op. cit. (*opere citato*), in the work cited.
opt., optician; optics; optional.
Or., Oregon; Oriental.
o.r., owner's risk.
orch., orchestra.
ord., ordained; order; ordinal; ordinance; ordinary; ordnance.
Ore., Oreg., Oregon.
org., organic; organization; organized.
orig., origin; original; originally.
Os, in *chemistry*, osmium.
O.S., Old Series; Old Style; ordinary seaman.
o.s., out of stock.
OSS, Office of Strategic Services.
O.T., OT, OT., Old Testament.
Ox., Oxf., Oxford.
oz., ounce.
ozs., ounces.

P

P, in *chemistry*, phosphorus; in *mechanics*, power, pressure.
P., p., pastor; post; power; president; pressure; priest; prince.
p., page; participle; past; penny; per; in *music*, piano; pint; pipe; population.
Pa, in *chemistry*, protactinium.
Pa., Pennsylvania.
P.A., Passenger Agent; public address (system); Purchasing Agent.
Pac., Pacif., Pacific.
Pan., Panama; Panamanian.
par., paragraph; parallel; parenthesis.
Para., Paraguay; Paraguayan.
paren., parenthesis.
Parl., Parliament; Parliamentary.
part., participial; participle; particular.
pass., passenger; passive; passim.
pat., patent; patented; pattern.
path., pathol., pathological; pathology.
Pat. Off., Patent Office.
pat. pend., patent pending.
Pb (*plumbum*), in *chemistry*, lead.
PBX, P.B.X., Private Branch Exchange.
P/C, p/c, petty cash; prices current.
pc., piece; prices.
p.c., per cent; postal card; post card.
pct., per cent.
Pd, in *chemistry*, palladium.
pd., paid.
P.D., Police Department; postal district; (*also* **p.d.**), per diem.
P.E., Presiding Elder; probable error; Protestant Episcopal.
Penn., Penna., Pennsylvania.
Per., Pers., Persia; Persian.
per., period; person.
perf., perfect; perforated.
pers., person; personal; personally.
pert., pertaining.
Peruv., Peruvian.
Pet., Peter.
pf., perfect; pianoforte; preferred.
Pfc., Private First Class.
pfd., preferred.
Pg., Portugal; Portuguese.
Phar., Pharm., pharmaceutical; pharmacy.
Ph.D. (*Philosophiae Doctor*), Doctor of Philosophy.
Phil., Philippians; Philippine.
phil., philosophy.
phot., photog., photograph; photographer; photographic; photography.
PHS, P.H.S., Public Health Service.
phys., physical; physician; physics; physiological; physiology.
P.I., Philippine Islands.
pk., pack; park; peak; peck.
pkg., package; packages.
pl., place; plate; plural.
plup., plupf., pluperfect.
Pm, in *chemistry*, promethium.
pm., premium.
P.M., Paymaster; Postmaster; Prime Minister.
P.M., p.m. (*post meridiem*), after noon.

p.m. (*post-mortem*), after death.
pmk., postmark.
P/N, p.n., promissory note.
Po, in *chemistry*, polonium.
P.O., p.o., petty officer; postal order; post office.
POD, Post Office Department.
poet., poetic; poetry.
Pol., Poland; Polish.
pol., polit., political; politics.
POM, Personal Opinion Message.
pop., popular; popularly; population.
Port., Portugal; Portuguese.
pos., positive; possessive.
poss., possession; possessive; possibly.
pp., pages; past participle.
P.P., p.p., parcel post; past participle; postpaid.
ppd., prepaid.
ppr., p. pr., present participle.
P.P.S., p.p.s. (*post postscriptum*), an additional postscript.
P.Q., previous question; Province of Quebec.
Pr, in *chemistry*, praseodymium.
pr., pair; power; preferred (stock); present; price; pronoun.
P.R., Puerto Rico; proportional representation; public relations.
pred., predicate.
pref., preface; prefatory; preference; preferred; prefix.
prelim., preliminary.
prep., preparatory; preposition.
Pres., Presbyterian; President.
pres., present; presidency.
prim., primary; primitive.
prin., principal; principally; principle.
priv., private; privative.
prob., probable; probably; problem.
Prof., Professor.
pron., pronoun; pronunciation.
prop., properly; property.
Prot., Protestant.
Prov., Provençal; Proverbs; Province.
Prus., Prussia; Prussian.
PS, P.S., p.s., postscript.
Ps., Psa., Psalm; Psalms.
ps., pieces; pseudonym.

P.S., passenger steamer; permanent secretary; Privy Seal; Public School.
pseud., pseudonym.
P.SS., postscripts.
P.S.T., Pacific Standard Time.
psych., psychological; psychology.
Pt, in *chemistry*, platinum.
pt., part; payment; pint; point.
p.t., past tense; pro tempore.
P.T.A., Parent–Teacher Association.
Pu, in *chemistry*, plutonium.
pub., public; publication; published; publisher; publishing.
Pvt., Private.
PWA, P.W.A., Public Works Administration.
PX, post exchange.

Q

Q., Quebec; Queen; Question.
q , quart; quarter; quarterly; quarto; quasi; queen; question; quintal; quire; quotient.
q.e. (*quod est*), which is.
Q.E.D. (*quod erat demonstrandum*), which was to be proved.
Q.M., Quartermaster.
qr., quarter; quire.
qrs., quarters.
qt., quantity; quart.
qto., quarto.
qts., quarts.
qu., quart; quarter; quarterly; queen; question.
quart., quarterly.
Que., Quebec.
quot., quotation.
q.v. (*quantum vis*), as much as you will; (*quod vide*), which see.
qy., query.

R

R, in *chemistry*, radical.
R., Radical; Republic; Republican.
R., r., rabbi; radius; railroad; railway; (*Regina*), queen; (*Rex*), king; right; river; road; ruble; rupee.
r., range; rare; received; residence; retired; rises; rod; rods; rubber.

RA, Regular Army.
Ra, in *chemistry*, radium.
rad., radial; radical; radius.
R.A.F., RAF, Royal Air Force.
Rb, in *chemistry*, rubidium.
R.C., Red Cross; Roman Catholic.
R.C.Ch., Roman Catholic Church.
rcd., received.
R.C.M.P., Royal Canadian Mounted Police.
R.C.P., Royal College of Physicians.
R.C.S., Royal College of Surgeons.
R/D, R.D., in *banking*, refer to drawer.
Rd., rd., road; rod; round.
R.D., Rural Delivery.
Re, in *chemistry*, rhenium.
R.E., real estate; Reformed Episcopal.
REA, R.E.A., Railway Express Agency; Rural Electrification Administration.
rec., receipt; received; recipe; record; recorded.
recd., rec'd., received.
Rec. Sec., rec. sec., recording secretary.
ref., referee; reference; referred; reformed.
Ref. Ch., Reformed Church.
refl., reflection; reflex; reflexive.
reg., regent; regiment; region; register; registered; registrar; regular; regulation.
Rep., Representative; Republic; Republican.
rep., repeat; report; reported; reporter.
res., research; reserve; residence; resides; resistance; resolution.
ret., retired; returned.
Rev., Revelation; Reverend.
rev., revenue; reverse; review; revise; revised; revision; revolution; revolving.
RFC, Reconstruction Finance Corporation.
RFD, R.F.D., Rural Free Delivery.
Rh, in *chemistry*, rhodium.
R.I., Rhode Island.
R.I.P. (*requiescat in pace*), may he (or she) rest in peace.
riv., river.
RM., r.m., reichsmark.
rm., ream; room.
rms., reams; rooms.

Rn. in *chemistry*, radon.
R.N., registered nurse; Royal Navy.
Rom., Roman; Romance; Romans.
Rom. Cath., Roman Catholic.
ROTC, Reserve Officers' Training Corps.
RP, reply paid.
r.p.m., revolutions per minute.
r.p.s., revolutions per second.
rpt., report.
R.R., railroad; Right Reverend.
Rs., reis; rupees.
R.S., Recording Secretary; Reformed Spelling.
RSV, R.S.V., Revised Standard Version (of the Bible).
R.S.V.P., r.s.v.p. (*répondez s'il vous plait*), please reply.
rt., right.
Ru, in *chemistry*, ruthenium.
Rum., Rumania; Rumanian.
Rus., Russ., Russia; Russian.
Ry., Railways.

S

S, in *chemistry*, sulfur.
S., S., s., s., south; southern.
S., Sabbath; Saturday; Saxon; Senate; September; *Signor*; Socialist; Sunday.
S., s., saint; school; society.
s., second; seconds; section; see; series; shilling; shillings; sign; silver; singular; son; steamer; substantive.
S.A., Salvation Army; South Africa; South America; South Australia.
SAC, Strategic Air Command.
S. Afr., South Africa; South African.
Salv., Salvador.
Sam., Saml., Sam'l., Samuel.
S. Am., S. Amer., South America; South American.
Sans., Sansk., Sanskrit.
Sask., Saskatchewan.
Sat., Saturday; Saturn.
Sb (*stibium*), in *chemistry*, antimony.
SBA, Small Business Administration.
Sc, in *chemistry*, scandium.
Sc., Scotch; Scots; Scottish.
sc., scale; scene; screw; scruple.
SC, Signal Corps; Staff Corps.

S.C., South Carolina; Supreme Court.
s.c., in *printing*, small capitals.
sch., school; schooner.
sci., science; scientific.
Scot., Scotch; Scotland; Scottish.
S/D, sight draft.
S.D., S. Dak., South Dakota.
Se, in *chemistry*, selenium.
SEATO, Southeast Asia Treaty Organization.
SEC, Securities and Exchange Commission.
sec., secant; second or seconds; secondary; secretary; section or sections; sector; security.
secy., sec'y., secretary.
sem., semicolon.
Sen., sen., Senate; Senator; senior.
Sep., Sept., September; Septuagint.
ser., series; sermon.
S.F., Sinking Fund.
s.g., specific gravity.
sgd., signed.
Sgt., sgt., Sergeant.
Shak., Shakespeare.
Si, in *chemistry*, silicon.
Sib., Siberia; Siberian.
Sic., Sicilian; Sicily.
Sig., sig., signal; signature; *Signor; Signore; Signori.*
Sig.na, *Signorina.*
Sig.ra, *Signora.*
sing., singular.
S.J., Society of Jesus.
Skr., Skrt., Skt., Sanskrit.
Slav., Slavic; Slavonian; Slavonic.
Sm, in *chemistry*, samarium.
Sn (*stannum*), in *chemistry*, tin.
So., South; southern.
Soc., Socialist; Society.
sociol., sociological; sociology.
sol., soluble; solution.
SOP, S.O.P., standard (or standing) operating procedure.
S O S, international distress signal.
Sp., Spain; Spaniard; Spanish.
sp., special; species; specific; spelling.
S.P., SP, Shore Patrol; Submarine Patrol.
Span., Spaniard; Spanish.

S.P.C.A., Society for Prevention of Cruelty to Animals.
S.P.C.C., Society for Prevention of Cruelty to Children.
spec., special; specifically; specification.
specif., specifically.
sp. gr., specific gravity.
spt., seaport.
Sq., sq., square.
Sr, in *chemistry*, strontium.
Sr., Senior; *Señor;* Sir.
Sra., *Señora.*
S.R.O., standing room only.
Srta., *Señorita.*
S.S., SS, S/S, steamship.
St., Saint; Strait; Street.
s.t., short ton.
Sta., Santa; Station.
ster., stg., sterling.
sub., substitute; substitutes; suburb; suburban.
subj., subject; subjective; subjunctive.
Sun., Sunday.
sup., superior; superlative; supplement; supplementary; supply; (*supra*), above; supreme.
Supt., supt., Superintendent.
surg., surgeon; surgery; surgical.
Sw., Swed., Sweden; Swedish.
syn., synonym; synonymous; synonymy.
Syr., Syria; Syriac; Syrian.
syst., system.

T

T., tablespoon; tablespoons; Testament; Tuesday; Turkish.
T., t., tenor; territorial; territory; ton; tons; (*tomus*), volume.
t., teaspoon; teaspoons; telephone; temperature; tense; time; tone; town; township; transitive; troy.
Ta, in *chemistry*, tantalum.
tan, tan., tangent.
Tasm., Tasmania.
TB, T.B., tb., t.b., tuberculosis.
Tb, in *chemistry*, terbium.
tbs., tbsp., tablespoon; tablespoons.
Tc, in *chemistry*, technetium.
Te, in *chemistry*, tellurium.
tech., technical; technically; technology.

tel., telegram; telegraph; telegraphic; telephone.
temp., temperature; temporary.
Tenn., Tennessee.
ter., terr., terrace; territory.
Test., Testament.
Teut., Teuton; Teutonic.
Tex., Texas.
Th, in *chemistry,* thorium.
Th., Thursday.
theol., theologian; theological; theology.
Thess., Thessalonians.
Thur., Thurs., Thursday.
Ti, in *chemistry,* titanium.
Tim., Timothy.
Tl, in *chemistry,* thallium.
Tm, in *chemistry,* thulium.
tn., ton; tons.
TNT, T.N.T., trinitrotoluene.
topog., topographical; topography.
tp., township.
t.p., title page.
tr., trace; transitive; translated; translation; translator; transpose; treasurer.
trans., transactions; transitive; translated; translation; translator; transportation; transpose.
transl., translated; translation.
treas., treasurer; treasury.
trig., trigon., trigonometric; trigonometry.
tsp., teaspoon; teaspoons.
Tu., Tues., Tuesday.
Turk., Turkey; Turkish.
TV, T.V., television.
TVA, Tennessee Valley Authority.
twp., township.
TWX, Teletypewriter Exchange Service.

U

U, in *chemistry,* uranium.
U., Uncle; Union; University.
U., u., upper.
U.A.W., UAW, United Automobile, Aerospace, and Agricultural Implement Workers of America.
U.C., Upper Canada.
u.c, in *printing,* upper case.
UFO, unidentified flying object.
UHF, ultrahigh frequency.
U.K., United Kingdom.
Ukr., Ukraine.
UL, Underwriters' Laboratories.
ult., ultimate; ultimately; ultimo.
UMT, Universal Military Training.
UMW, U.M.W., United Mine Workers of America.
UN, U.N., United Nations.
UNESCO, United Nations Educational, Scientific, and Cultural Organization.
UNICEF, United Nations Children's Fund.
Unit., Unitarian.
Univ., Universalist; University.
univ., universal; universally.
UPI, United Press International.
Uru., Uruguay; Uruguayan.
U.S., US, United States.
U.S.A., USA, United States of America; United States Army.
USAF, United States Air Force.
USCG, United States Coast Guard.
USIA, United States Information Agency.
USIS, United States Information Service.
U.S.M., United States Mail; United States Marines; United States Mint.
USMA, United States Military Academy.
USMC, United States Marine Corps.
USN, United States Navy.
USNA, United States Naval Academy.
USNG, United States National Guard.
USNR, United States Naval Reserve.
USO, U.S.O., United Service Organizations.
U.S.P., U.S. Pharm., United States Pharmacopoeia.
U.S.S., United States Senate; United States Ship; United States Steamer; United States Steamship.
U.S.S.R., USSR, Union of Soviet Socialist Republics.
Ut., Utah.

V

V, in *chemistry,* vanadium.
V, v, vector; velocity; volt; volts.
v., verb; verse; version; versus; (*vide*), see; village; violin; voice; voltage; volume.
VA, Veterans' Administration.

Va., Virginia.
var., variant; variation; variety; various.
vb., verb; verbal.
V.C., Vice-Chairman; Vice-Chancellor; Victoria Cross.
V.D., venereal disease.
Venez., Venezuela; Venezuelan.
vet., veteran; veterinarian; veterinary.
V.F.W., VFW, Veterans of Foreign Wars.
V.I., Virgin Islands.
v.i., intransitive verb; (*vide infra*), see below.
Vic., Vict., Victoria.
V.I.P., VIP, very important person.
VISTA, Volunteers in Service to America.
viz. (*videlicet*), namely; that is.
vocab., vocabulary.
vol., volcanic; volcano; volume.
vols., volumes.
V.P., Vice-President.
V. Rev., Very Reverend.
vs., versus.
Vt., Vermont.
v.t., transitive verb.
Vul., Vulg., Vulgate.
vv., verses; violins.
v.v., vice versa.

W

W, in *chemistry*, tungsten; watt; watts; west; western; (*wolfram*).
W., Wales; Wednesday; Welsh; West; Western.
W., w., warehouse; watt; watts; weight; west; western; width.
W., week; weeks; wide; wife; with; won.
WAC, Women's Army Corps.
Wash., Washington.
WAVES, Women Accepted for Volunteer Emergency Service (Women's Reserve, USNR).
W.B., W/B, waybill.
W.C.T.U., Woman's Christian Temperance Union.
Wed., Wednesday.
w.f., wf, in *printing*, wrong font.
WFTU, W.F.T.U., World Federation of Trade Unions.
WHO, World Health Organization (UN).
W.I., West Indian; West Indies.
Wis., Wisc., Wisconsin.
wk., week; work.
wkly., weekly.
w.l., wave length.
WO, War Office; Warrant Officer.
wt., weight.
W.Va., West Virginia.
Wyo., Wy., Wyoming.

XYZ

x, in *mathematics*, an unknown quantity; a sign of multiplication.
Xe, in *chemistry*, xenon.
Y, in *chemistry*, yttrium.
Y., Young Men's Christian Association.
y., yard; yards; year; years.
Yb, in *chemistry*, ytterbium.
yd., yard; yards.
Y.M.C.A., Young Men's Christian Association.
Y.M.Cath.A., Young Men's Catholic Association.
Y.M.H.A., Young Men's Hebrew Association.
yr., year; younger; your.
yrs., years; yours.
Y.W.C.A., Young Women's Christian Association.
Y.W.H.A., Young Women's Hebrew Association.
Z., in *chemistry*, atomic number; in *astronomy*, zenith distance.
Z., z., zone.
Zech., Zechariah.
Zeph., Zephaniah.
ZIP, Zoning Improvement Plan.
Zn, in *chemistry*, zinc.
zool., zoological; zoology.
Zr, in *chemistry*, zirconium.

重要引用句와 俗談

A bird in the hand is worth two in the bush.

A burnt child dreads the fire.
A drowning man will catch at a straw.

A friend in need is a friend indeed.
A good beginning is half the battle.
A good beginning makes a good ending.
A little learning is a dangerous thing.
　—Alexander Pope(1688~1744):
　　　　　　　　　　　　Essay on Criticism
All is not gold that glitters.
All work and no play makes Jack a dull boy.

A man is known by the company he keeps.
A rolling stone gathers no moss.
Art is long, and time is fleeting.
　—Henry Wadsworth Longfellow(1807~1882):
　　　　　　　　　　　　A Psalm of Life
Ask, and it shall be given you; seek, and ye shall find; knock, and it shall be opened unto you.　　　　　　—*Bible, Matthew*
A stitch in time saves nine.

Beauty is truth, truth beauty.
　　　　　　—John Keats(1795~1821):
　　　　　　　　　　　Ode on a Grecian Urn
Behind the clouds is the sun still shining.
　—Henry Wadsworth Longfellow(1807~1882):
　　　　　　　　　　　　　The Rainy Day
Be it ever so humble, there's no place like home.
　　　　　　—J.H. Payne(1792~1852):
　　　　　　　　　　　　Home, Sweet Home.
Better late than never.

Birds of a feather flock together.
Bitters do good to the stomach.
Blood is thicker than water.
Care killed the cat.
Conscience makes cowards of us all.
　—William Shakespeare(1564~1616): *Hamlet*
Cut your coat according to your cloth.
Danger comes soonest when it is despised.
Do as you would be done by.
Dust thou art, and unto dust thou shalt return.
　　　　　　　　　　　　　—*Bible, Genesis*

— 내 집 병아리가 남의 집 금송아지보다 낫다.
— 국에 덴 놈 물 보고도 분다.
— 물에 빠진 사람은 지푸라기라도 잡는다.
— 아쉬울 때 돕는 친구가 참된 친구다.
— 시작이 좋으면 절반은 성공.
— 시작이 좋으면 결과도 좋다.
— 반풍수 집안 망친다.

— 번쩍이는 것이 모두 금은 아니다.
— 일만 알고 놀 줄 모르면 사람이 둔해진다.
— 친구를 보면 그 사람을 알 수 있다.
— 구르는 돌에는 이끼가 끼지 않는다.
— 예술은 길고, 세월은 유수와 같다.

— 구하라, 그러면 너희에게 주실 것이요, 찾으라, 그러면 찾을 것이요, 문을 두드리라, 그러면 열릴 것이다.
— 때 맞추어 손질하면 열 배의 일손을 덜게 된다.
— 미(美)는 진리요, 진리는 미다.

— 구름 뒤쪽에는 언제나 태양이 빛나고 있다.

— 가난하고 험해도 내 집보다 나은 곳은 세상에 없다.

— 늦게라도 하는 것이 아주 않는 것보다는 낫다.

— 유유상종(類類相從).
— 입에 쓴 약이 몸에는 좋다.
— 피는 물보다 진하다.
— 근심 걱정은 피를 마르게 한다.
— 양심은 사람을 비겁하게 한다.

— 분수에 맞춰서 살림을 꾸려라.
— 설마가 사람 죽인다.
— 대접받고 싶은 대로 남에게 베풀어라.
— 너는 흙이니 흙으로 돌아갈 것이니라.

East and West, Home is best.
East is East, and West is West, and never the twain shall meet.
　　　　　—Rudyard Kipling(1864—1936):
　　　　　　　　The Ballad of East and West
Enter ye in at the strait gate; for wide is the gate, and broad is the way, that leadeth to destruction, and many there be which go in thereat.　　　　　—*Bible, Matthew*
Even Homer nods at times.
Everybody's business is nobody's business.
Every man has his fault.
　　　　　—William Shakespeare(1564〜1616):
　　　　　　　　　　　　Timon of Athens
Every man is the architect of his own fortune.

First come, first served.
Fools rush in where angels fear to tread.
　　　　　—Alexander Pope(1688〜1744):
　　　　　　　　　　　Essay on Criticism
Frailty, thy name is woman!
　　　　　—William Shakespeare(1564—1616): *Hamlet*
Good company on the road is the shortest cut.
　　　　　—Olivre Goldsmith(1728〜1774):
　　　　　　　　　　　Vicar of Wakefield
Handsome is that handsome does.
Haste makes (*or* is) waste.
Heaven helps those who help themselves.
Health is better than wealth.
He knows most who speaks least.

History repeats itself.
Honesty is the best policy.
I come to bury Caesar, not to praise him. The evil that man do lives after them; The good is oft interred with their bones.
　　　　　—William Shakespeare(1564〜1616):
　　　　　　　　　　　　Julius Caesar
If Winter comes, can Spring be far behind?
　　　　　—Percy B. Shelly (1792〜1822):
　　　　　　　　　　Ode to the West Wind
Ignorance is bliss.
Ill news travels fast.
In the sweat of the face shalt thy eat bread.
　　　　　　　　　　　—*Bible, Genesis*
It is a long lane that has no turning.

It is an ill wind that blows nobody good.

—동쪽 서쪽 하여도 내 집이 제일.
—동쪽은 동쪽, 서쪽은 서쪽, 둘을 결코 맞닿지 않으리라.

—좁은 문으로 들어가라. 멸망으로 인도하는 문은 크고 그 길이 넓어 그리로 들어가는 자가 많으니라.

—항우도 낙상할 적이 있다.
—공동책임은 무책임.
—사람은 누구나 결점이 있다.

—사람은 누구나 자기 운명의 건설자이다.
—먼저 온 자가 먼저 차지한다.
—천사가 밟기 두려워하는 곳에 어리석은 자들은 몰려든다.

—약한 자여, 그대 이름은 여자이니라.

—좋은 길동무는 가장 가까운 지름길이다.

—외모보다는 마음씨.
—서두르면 일을 망친다.
—하늘은 스스로 돕는 자를 돕는다.
—재산보다 건강.
—말수 적은 사람이 많이 아는 사람이다.

—역사는 돌고 돈다.
—정직은 가장 좋은 정책이다.
—나는 시이저를 장사지내기 위하여 왔으며, 그를 칭찬하기 위해 오지는 않았다. 사람의 악행은 그가 죽은 뒤에도 살고, 선행은 때때로 그의 뼈와 함께 묻혀 버리고 만다.

—겨울이 오면 봄도 멀지 않으리.

—모르는 게 약.
—나쁜 소식은 발이 빠르다.
—네 얼굴에 땀이 흘려야 빵을 먹을지니라.
—굽이 없는 길은 없다(쥐구멍에도 볕들 날이 있다)
—손해 보는 사람 있으면 이득보는 사람도 있다.

It is a wise father that knows his own child.　—William Shakespeare(1564~1616) *The Merchant of Venice* ―제 자식을 제대로 아는 아버지는 드물다.

It is comparison that makes men happy or miserable. ―사람의 행복과 불행은 비교에서 비롯된다.

It is more blessed to give than to receive. —*Bible, the Acts* ―받는 것보다 주는 것이 더 복되니라.

It is never too late to mend. —Charles Reade(1814~1884): *Title of Novel* ―고치기가 너무 늦었다는 일은 없다.

It is no use crying over spilt milk. ―엎질러진 물

It never rains but it pours. ―왔다 하면 억수로 쏟아진다(禍不單行).

Jack of all trades and master of none. ―팔방미인에 명인 없다.

Let sleeping dogs lie. ―긁어부스럼을 만들지 마라.

Light gains make heavy purses. —Francis Bacon(1561~1626): *Essays* ―적은 수입이 무거운 지갑을 만든다 (티끌 모아 태산).

Light suppers make long life. ―모자란 듯 먹는 것이 장수(長壽)의 비결.

Like father, like son. ―그 아버지에 그 아들.

Little brooks make great rivers. ―티끌 모아 태산.

Look before you leap. ―구멍 보아 가며 말뚝 깎아라.

Love your enemies, bless them that curse you. —*Bible, Matthew* ―너희 원수를 사랑하며 너희를 핍박하는 자를 위하여 기도하라.

Make hay while the sun shines. ―햇볕이 쬐는 동안에 풀을 말려라.

Man is the lord of creation. ―사람은 만물의 영장.

Marry in haste, and repent at leisure. ―결혼을 서두르면 나중에 후회한다.

Men in great place are thrice servants—servants of the monarch or state, servants of fame and servants of business. —Francis Bacon(1561~1626): *Essays* ―높은 자리에 앉은 사람은 삼중의 머슴――임금 혹은 나라의 머슴이요, 명예의 머슴이요, 일의 머슴이다.

Misfortunes never come singly. ―설상가상, 화불단행.

Money makes the mare [to] go. ―돈만 있으면 귀신도 부릴 수 있다.

Necessity hath no law. —Oliver Cromwell(1653~1698): *Speech to Parliament* ―필요 앞엔 법이 없다.

Necessity is the mother of invention. ―필요는 발명의 어머니.

Never put off till tomorrow what you can do today. —Lord Chesterfield(1693~1773): *Letter to His Son* ―오늘 할 수 있는 일을 내일로 밀지 마라.

Never too old to learn. ―배우기에 너무 늙은 나이는 없다.

No gains without pains. ―고생 없이 소득 없다.

No news is good news. ―무소식이 희소식.

Not every man is born with a silver spoon in his mouth. ―사람마다 누구나 유복한 가정에 태어나는 것은 아니다.

Of two evils choose the lesser. ―어차피 고생일 바엔 덜한 길을 택하라.

One man's meat is another man's poison. ―한 사람에게 약되는 것은 다른 사람에게는 독.

One swallow does not make a summer. ―제비 한 마리가 왔다고 여름이 되는 것은 아니다(속단은 금물).

Out of sight, out of mind.	—안 보이게 되면은 마음에서도 사라져 간다.
Out of the frying-pan into the fire.	—늑대를 피해 가서 호랑이를 만난다.
Penny wise, pound foolish.	—약은 개 밤눈 어둡다.
People will [wíl] talk.	—사람이란 말을 하게 마련.
Practice makes perfect.	—일에 숙달하려면 연습이 제일.
Pride goes before a fall.	—오만한 자는 오래 가지 못한다.
Render therefore unto Caesar the things which are Caesar's and to God that are God's ——Bible, Matthew	—그런즉, 가이사의 것은 가이사에게, 하나님의 것은 하나님께 바치라.
Rome was not built in a day.	—로마는 하루에 이루어지지 않았다 (大器晩成).
Saying and doing are two things.	—말하는 것과 실천하는 것은 별개 문제다.
See Naples and die.	—나폴리를 보고 죽어라.
Slow and steady wins the race. ——David Lloyd(1625~1691): *Fables*	—느려도 꾸준히 하면 경주에 이긴다. (느릿느릿 걸어도 황소 걸음)
So many men, so many minds.	—사람의 마음은 백인 백색.
Sound mind in sound body.	—건전한 육체에 건전한 정신.
Spare the rod and spoil the child.	—매를 아끼면 아이를 버린다.
Speech is silver: silence is golden.	—웅변은 은, 침묵은 금.
Still waters run deep.	—깊은 물은 조용히 흐른다.
Strike the iron while it is hot.	—쇠뿔은 단김에 빼렸다 (勿失好機).
Talk of the devil, and he will appear.	—호랑이도 제 말하면 온다.
The Child is father of the Man. ——William Wordsworth(1770~1850): *My Heart Leaps Up*	—어린이는 어른의 아버지.
The early bird catches the worm.	—일찍 일어나는 새가 벌레를 잡는다.
The grape are sour.	—저 포도는 시다(제 힘 모자라 못해 놓고 남의 탓으로 돌린다).
The more haste, the less speed.	—바쁠수록 천천히.
The nearer the church, the farther from God.	—교회 가까이에 살수록 하나님에게서 멀어진다.
The pen is mightier than the sword. ——Bulwer-Lytton(1803~1873): *Richelieu*	—붓은 칼보다 강하다.
There are more things in heavenand earth than are dreamt of in your philosophy. ——William Shakespeare(1564~1616):*Hamlet*	—이 천지간에는 소위 철학으로는 몽상도 할 수 없는 일들이 얼마든지 있다.
There is no accounting for tastes.	—오이를 꼭지부터 먹는 것도 제 멋.
There is no new things under the sun.	—해 아래 새로운 것은 없다.
There is no royal road to learning.	—학문에는 왕도가 없다.
There is no rule without exceptions.	—예외 없는 규칙은 없다.
There is no wool so white but a dyer can make it black.	—근묵자흑 (近墨者黑).
The style is the man himself. ——George de Buffon(1707~1788): *Discourse on Style*	—글은 사람이다.
Time and tide wait for no man.	—세월은 사람을 기다리지 않는다.
To be, or not to be: that is the question: whether 'tis nobler in the mind to suffer the slings and arrows of outrageous fortune, or to take	—살 것인가, 죽을 것인가, 그것이 문제로다. 잔인한 운명의 돌팔매와 화살을 마음속으로 참고 견디는 게 의로운

arms against a sea of troubles, and by opposing end them?
　　—William Shakespeare(1564～1616): *Hamlet*
To see is to believe. /Seeing is believing.
Too many cooks spoil the broth.

Translators, traitors.
Tread on a worm and it will turn.
Truth is stranger than fiction.
Two heads are better than one.
　　　　　　　　　　—Homer: *Iliad*
Walls have ears.
Whatever is worth doing at all is worth doing well.
　　—Lord Chesterfield(1694～1773):
　　　　　　　　　　Letter to His Son
What cannot be cured must be endured.

What is done can't be undone.
　　—William Shakespeare(1564～1616): *Macbeth*
When in Rome, do as the Romans do.
When the cat is away, the mouse will play.
Where there is a will, there is a way.
Where there is smoke, there is fire.
You cannot eat your cake and have it.

You may take a horse to the water, but you can't make him drink.
Youth comes but once in a lifetime.
　　—Henry Wadsworth Longfellow(1807～1882):
　　　　　　　　　　Hyperion
Whom the gods love, die young.
　　　　—Lord Byron(1788～1824): *Don Juan*

가, 아니면 고난의 바다를 향해 창칼을 들고 덤벼, 이를 쳐 없애는 게 의로운가.
—백문이 불여일견.
—사공이 많으면 배가 산으로 올라간다.
—번역자는 반역자.
—지렁이도 밟으면 꿈틀거린다.
—사실은 소설보다 기이하다.
—백지장도 맞들면 낫다.

—벽에도 귀가 있다.
—할 가치가 있는 일은 무엇이나 잘해낼 가치가 있다.

—고칠 수 없는 것은 참고 견딜 수밖에 없다.
—저질러진 일을 취소할 수는 없다.

—입향순속(入鄕循俗).
—고양이가 없어지면 쥐가 놀아난다.
—뜻이 있는 곳에 길이 있다.
—불 안 뗀 굴뚝에 연기 날까.
—먹어버린 케이크를 갖고 있을 수는 없다.
—말을 물가로 끌고 갈 수는 있어도 물을 먹일 수는 없다.
—청춘은 일생에 단 한번뿐이다.

—가인박명(佳人薄命).

외어 두면 편리한 會話文型

what, why, where, who, whose, whom, how 와 같은 의문사로 시작되는 의문문
회화에서 자주 쓰이는 말이기 때문에, 이 문형과 대답하는 방법을 잘 익혀 두면 편리하다.

What

1. *What*'s this? (*What* is this?)/ It's a novel. ─이것은 무엇입니까?/소설입니다.
2. *What* are Rotarians?/ They are members of the Rotary Club. ─「로오터리안즈」란 무엇입니까?/로오터리 클럽의 회원입니다.
3. *What* was the name of the inn?/It was Changmi-jang. ─숙소의 이름은 무엇이었던가요?/「장미장」이었읍니다.
4. *What* will be the rate for one night?/It will be fifteen hundred won. ─하룻저녁 (숙박료가) 얼마입니까?/1,500원이겠지요.
5. *What* happened?/A terrible thing happened. ─무슨 일이 있었읍니까?/무서운 일이 있었읍니다.
6. *What* will happen next?/Nothing will happen. ─다음엔 또 무슨 일이 일어날까요?/아무 일도 안 일어나겠지요.
7. *What* has gone wrong?/The battery has. ─무엇이 고장났어요?/바테리가(고장났읍니다).
8. *What* has not arrived?/The package has not. ─무엇이 도착하지 않았나요?/소포입니다.
9. *What* do you know about New Mexico?/ I know nothing (about it). ─뉴우 멕시코주에 대해서, 무엇을 알고 계십니까?/아무것도 모릅니다.
10. *What* have you done with my pen?/ I have borrowed it. ─내 펜은 어쨌지?/내가 빌려 갔어.
11. *What* did they do for you?/ They put me up overnight. ─그 사람들은 자네를 위해서 무엇을 했나?/하룻저녁 재워 주었어.
12. *What* is made here?/ Nylon is. ─여기서 무엇을 만들고 계십니까?/나일론을 만들고 있읍니다.
13. *What* was broken by the cat?/ The new vase was. ─고양이가 무엇을 깨뜨렸나?/새 꽃병을(깨뜨렸어).
14. *What* is going on?/ We are dancing ─무얼 하고 있어?/춤을 추고 있지.

　　　　A dance is.라고 대답하는 것이 종래의 문법에 맞는 표현이겠지만, "We are dancing."이라고 하는 편이 회화다운 표현이다.

15. *What*'s being done about it?/ Nothing (is). ─그것과 관련해서 어떤 일이 일어나고 있지?/아무것도(안 일어나고 있어).

Where

16. *Where* is your mother?/ She is upstairs. ─자네 어머니는 어디 계신가?/이층에(계십니다).
17. *Where* are the students?/ They are in the gym. ─학생들은 어디 있지?/체육관에 있읍니다.
18. *Where* will you be?/ I'll be downstairs. ─자넨 어디 있겠나?/아래층에(있겠읍니다).
19. *Where* did you go last night?/ I went to the bowling center. ─어젯밤엔 어디 갔었나?/보울링장에 갔었읍니다.
20. *Where* have you been?/ I've been to London. ─어딜 다녀왔나?/런던에 다녀왔읍니다.

21. *Where* had you been when I saw you last night?/ I had been to the movies.
—어젯밤 자네를 만났을 때, 어딜 다녀왔나?/ 영화 구경하러 다녀왔읍니다.

22. *Where* were you last Thursday?/ I was home.
—지난 목요일에는 어디 있었나?/ 집에 있었읍니다.

Why

23. *Why* am I left out?/ Because you are too young.
—왜 전 안 데리고 가지요?/ 넌 너무 어리니까.
24. *Why* are you blue?/ Because I'm broke.
—왜 우울해 있지?/ 파산했어.
25. *Why* is he happy?/ Because he is free again.
—왜 그 사람이 좋아하지?/ 또 다시 자유로운 몸이 됐으니까.
26. *Why* are they locked up?/ Because they are drunk.
—왜 그녀석들이 감금됐지?/ 만취했었기 때문이야.
27. *Why* was I left behind?/ Because you were late.
—왜 나를 안 데리고 갔지?/ 자네가 늦었기 때문이야.
28. *Why* were you absent?/ Because my mother was ill.
—왜 안 왔지?/ 어머니가 병환이 나셨기 때문이야.
29. *Why* was she so tired?/ Because she did a lot of washing today.
—왜 그 여자는 그렇게 지쳤지?/ 오늘 빨래를 많이 했기 때문이야.
30. *Why* were they angry?/ Because they were refused admission.
—왜 저 사람들이 화를 냈지?/ 입장을 거절당했거든.
31. *Why* am I not included?/ Because you are not a regular member.
—어째서 나를 넣어 주지 않지요?/ 당신은 정회원이 아니기 때문이지요.
32. *Why* weren't you promoted?/ Because the boss doesn't like me.
—어째서 당신은 승진을 안 했지요?/ 사장이 나를 싫어하기 때문이지요.
33. *Why* weren't we invited?/ Because the room was too small.
—왜 우리들은 초대하지 않았을까요?/ 방이 너무 작기 때문이지요.
34. *Why* wasn't she paid?/ Because she didn't do her part.
—왜 그 여자는 돈을 못 받았지?/ 자기 맡은 일을 하지 않았기 때문이지요.
35. *Why* have you come so early?/ Because I wanted a good seat.
—왜 그렇게 일찍 왔지요?/ 좋은 자리를 차지하려고요.
36. *Why* has she left you?/ Because she has found someone else.
—왜 그 여자는 자네한테서 떠났지?/ 달리 좋은 사람을 발견했기 때문이야.
37. *Why* haven't you been studying?/ Because the game was so exciting.
—왜 공부는 안 했니?/ 시합이 너무 재미있어서 그랬어요.
38. *Why* did you tell a lie?/ Because I was afraid.
—왜 거짓말을 했니?/ 겁이 나서 그랬어요.
39. *Why* didn't you turn in the purse to the police?/ Because the amount was so small.
—어째서 지갑을 경찰에 갖다주지 않았지?/ 돈이 너무 조금 들었기 때문이었어요.

When

40. *When* will you pay me?/ I will pay you tomorrow.
—언제 지불하겠소?/ 내일 지불하겠어요.
41. *When* did you come home last night?/ I came home at midnight.
—어젯밤엔 언제 집에 돌아왔지요?/ 한밤중에 왔어요.
42. *When* did they get married?/ They got married last March.
—저 사람들은 언제 결혼했지요?/ 지난 3월에 했어요.
43. *When* will I get a raise?/ Wait till next spring.
—언제 제 봉급을 올려 주시겠읍니까?/ 내년 봄까지 기다려 주게.

44. *When* were you last promoted?/ It was a year ago. —마지막 승진한 것이 언제였나?/ 1년 전이었읍니다.
45. *When* will this ship arrive in Pusan?/ She will arrive in Pusan at noon. —이 배는 부산에 언제 도착합니까?/정오에 도착하겠지요.

Who

46. *Who* are you?/ I'm Detective Drake. —누구시지요?/드레이크 탐정입니다.
47. *Who* is that lady?/ She is Mrs. Mason. —저 부인은 누구시지요?/메이슨 부인입니다.
48. *Who* won?/ The Los Angeles Dodgers. —누가 이겼지요?/로스앤질리스 더저어스예요.
49. *Who*'s been in my room?/ I have. —누가 내 방에 있었지?/제가요.
50. *Who* will help me eat this pie?/ I will. —누가 내 파이를 먹어 줄래?/내가 먹어 주지.

51. *Who* was killed in the accident?/ The driver and one passenger (were). —누가 사고로 죽었나?/운전수하고 승객 한 사람이요.
52. *Who* was not paid?/ I was not. —급료를 못 받은 사람은 누구였지?/저였어요.

요즈음에는 whom을 who로 말들을 하게 되었다. 다음 예문 중의 who는 본래 whom의 뜻이었음을 알아 둘 것.

53. *Who* am I going out with?/ You are going out with the boss's brother. —저는 누구하고 함께 갑니까?/자네는 사장 동생하고 함께 가는 걸세.
54. *Who* are you fighting with?/ I'm fighting with Terry. —누구하고 싸움하고 있는 거야?/테리하고 싸움하고 있어.
55. *Who* is this package for?/ It's for you. —이 보따리는 누구한테 줄 거지?/자네한테(줄 거야).

56. *Who* did you beat?/ We beat New York. —어떤 티임을 물리쳤나?/누우요오크 티임을 물리쳤지.
57. *Who* were you out with yesterday?/ I was out with my girl friend. —어저께는 누구하고 외출했었나?/거얼프렌드하고 외출했었지.
58. *Who* do I thank for this present?/ Thank Mr. Kim. —이 선물 감사하다고 누구한테 인사해야 할까요?/김씨한테(하면 돼).

Whose

59. *Whose* son are you?/ I'm a son of Chang-ho Kim. —당신은 누구의 자제분이십니까?/김창호의 아들입니다.
60. *Whose* pen is this?/ That's John's —이 펜은 누구 것입니까?/존의 것입니다.
61. *Whose* watch was that?/ It was my uncle's. —그것은 누구의 시계였지요?/제 아저씨의 것이었읍니다.
62. *Whose* address are you looking for?/ I'm looking for Mrs. Reynolds'. —누구의 주소를 찾고 계신가요?/레이놀즈 부인의 주소를 찾고 있읍니다.
63. *Whose* turn for nightwatch was it?/ It was Myeong-gi Yi's. —야경은 누구 차례였나?/이 형기 차례였지요.
64. *Whose* neck will it be next?/ Nobody can tell. —다음엔 누구 모가지가 달아날까?/아무도 모르지.

How

65. *How* are you?/ I'm fine, thank you. —안녕하십니까?/예, 감사합니다.
66. *How*'s your mother?/ She's fine. —어머니께서도 안녕하십니까?/예, 안녕하십니다.

67. *How* was the movie?/ It was very good. —영화는 어땠어?/ 매우 재미있었어.
68. *How* do you do?/ How do you do? —안녕하십니까?/ 안녕하십니까?
69. *How* do you do it?/ Turn it to the right. —당신이라면 어떻게 하시겠소?/ 오른쪽으로 꼬부리십시오.
70. *How* did you win his heart?/ Through his stomach. —어떻게 해서 그 사람의 마음을 사로잡았나?/ 맛있는 음식을 먹였지.
71. *How* did you know I was here?/ Your sister told me. —내가 여기 있는 것을 어떻게 알았나?/ 자네 누이가 말해 주더군.
72. *How* do we get to the subway?/ Go through that gate. —지하철에 가려면 어떻게 갑니까?/ 그 문으로 들어가십시오.
73. *How* can I thank you?/ It was nothing. —뭐라고 인사를 드려야 할지?/ 천만에요.
74. *How* can you do such a thing to me?/ I didn't mean it. —자네는 어쩌서 나한테 그런 일을 하나?/그렇게 하려고 한 것은 아닙니다.
75. *How* may I repay you?/ I'll ask you a favor someday. —어떻게 인사를 드려야(은혜를 갚아야) 하나요?/ 후일 내가 부탁할 일이 있겠죠, 뭐.

How much와 How many

76. *How much* is this?/ It's 200 won. —얼맙니까?/ 200원입니다.
77. *How much* was it?/ It was two dollars. —얼마였읍니까?/ 2 달러였읍니다.
78. *How much* do I owe you?/ You owe me one thousand won. —자네한테 얼마를 빌렸지?/ 1,000원 빌렸지.
79. *How much* did it cost you?/ It cost me ten thousand won. —그건 얼마나 들었나?/ 10,000원 들었어.
80. *How much* does it mean to you?/ It means everything to me. —그건 자네한테 어느정도의 가치가 있나?/ 나한테는 무엇보다도 중요해.
81. *How much* money do you have on yóu?/ I have only two thousand won on me. —돈은 얼마나 가지고 계십니까?/ 2,000원뿐입니다.
82. *How much* water does this jar hold?/ It holds about four glasses of water. —이 항아리에 물이 얼마큼 들어 있읍니까?/ 네 컵 정도 들어 있읍니다.
83. *How much* gas (gasoline) will she take?/ She will take 10 gallons. —가솔린을 얼마나 소비하나요?/ 10 갈론 소비할 겁니다.

84. *How many* eggs do you want?/ I want two. —계란이 얼마나 필요하십니까?/ 두 개요.
85. *How many* rooms do you have in your apartment?/ We have only two rooms in our apartment. —당신 아파아트에는 방이 몇 개 있읍니까?/ 두 개밖에 없읍니다.
86. *Hom many* ships can you see?/ I can see one, two, three, four, five——five ships. —배가 몇 척이 보입니까?/ 하나, 둘, 셋, 넷, 다섯——다섯 척이 보입니다.
87. *How many* (cubes of) sugar do you want in your coffee?/ Give me two. —커피에 각설탕을 몇 개 넣을까요?/ 두 개 넣어 주십시오.
88. *How many* glasses of milk do you drink every day?/ I drink three glasses (of milk) every day. —매일 우유를 몇 컵이나 드십니까?/ 매일 세 컵 마십니다.
89. *How many* miles from here to Inchon?/ It's about 20 miles. —여기서 인천까지 몇 마일입니까?/ 약 20마일입니다.
90. *How many* hours will it take?/ It will take 2 hours. —몇 시간 걸립니까?/ 두 시간 걸릴 겁니다.

How와 형용사가 들어 있는 문형

91. *How old* are you?/ I'm seven.
92. *How old* were you last year?/ I was six.
93. *How old* will you be on your next birthday?/ I'll be eight.
94. *How far* is it from Seoul to Pusan?/ It's only about 300 miles.
95. *How hard* is it raining?/ It's raining cats and dogs.
96. *How tall* is he?/ He's about 1.75 meters tall, or 6 feet and 8 inches tall.
97. *How high* is Mt. Han-ra?/ It's 1,950 meters high.
98. *How soon* will you return the money?/ I will return it to you in one week.

—몇 살이지?/ 일곱 살이에요.
—작년엔 몇 살이었지?/ 여섯 살.
—다음 생일에는 몇 살이 되지?/ 여덟 살요.
—서울에서 부산까지는 거리가 얼마나 됩니까?/ 약 300마일입니다.
—어느 정도로 비가 오고 있읍니까?/ 억수같이 쏟아지고 있읍니다.
—그 사람의 키는 얼마나 됩니까?/ 1미터 75, 그러니까 6피이트 8인치입니다.
—한라산의 높이는 얼마나 됩니까?/ 1,950미터입니다.
—돈은 언제 갚으시겠읍니까?/ 1주일 후에 갚겠읍니다.

관계대명사가 들어 있는 문형

좀 긴 문장에는 what, which, that가 관계대명사로서 들어 있는 일이 많다. 다음은 그 일 반적인 예들이다.

Who (또는 Whom)

99. The man *who* is speaking to Mr. Choe is Mr. Pak.
100. I am going to see the doctor *who* lives near the river.
101. You are just the person *whom* I wanted to see.

—최선생에게 말하고 있는 사람은 박선생입니다.
—강 근처에 살고 있는 의사한테 가는 길입니다.
—당신이야말로 내가 만나고 싶었던 분이야.

이 경우의 whom은 종종 생략된다. 즉, You are just the person I wanted to see.

102. I saw your cousin yesterday, *who* is leaving for France soon.
103. My uncle, *who* works in a department store, is looking for an interpreter.
104. Mr. and Mrs. Finch, *whom* I am corresponding with, were my American "parents."

—어제 당신 사촌을 만났지요. 곧 프랑스로 떠나신다는군요.
—백화점에서 일하고 있는 아저씨가 통역을 구하고 있읍니다.
—나와 편지 왕래가 있는 핀치부부는, 내가 미국에 있을 때 부모님으로 모시던 분입니다.

Which

105. Where is the book *which* I ordered?
106. Give me the envelope *which* he brought.
107. The bus, *which* goes to Suwon, stops here.
108. The school, *which* he built, bears his name.

—내가 주문한 책은 어디 있읍니까?
—그 사람이 가져온 봉투를 주십시오.
—수원행 버스는 여기서 섭니다.
—그 사람이 세운 학교에, 그 사람의 이름을 붙였읍니다.

사람한테는 which를 사용하지 않지만 that는 who, whom, which 대신으로 두루 쓰일 수 있다. 따라서, 위 문장은 모두 that로 말해도 된다.

That

109. I hear *that* you are going to America.
110. Do you think *that* Mr. Yi will show up?
111. Do you know *that* there was an earth-

—미국에 가신다지요?
—이군이 나타날 것 같읍니까?
—어저께 캘리포오니어주에 지진이 일

quake in California yesterday? — 어났던 사실을 알고 계십니까?
112. He said *that* he would leave the hotel at three o'clock. — 그는 세 시에 호텔을 나오겠다고 했읍니다.
113. I feel *that* you should stay in bed. — 당신은 좀더 주무셔야겠어요.
114. I believe *that* Mr. John is looking for you. — 존씨가 당신을 찾고 있을 겁니다.
115. I suggest *that* you take a hot bath. — 당신은 더운 물에 목욕을 하는 게 좋을 것 같아요.
116. I propose *that* we go back. — 저는, 모두 돌아가실 것을 제안합니다.
117. I advise *that* you keep out of this. — 이 일에서 손을 떼도록 충고합니다.

that가 이렇게 쓰일 때는, 발음이 약해지는 것이 보통이다.
[비교] That's my car. [ðæts]/That house looks old. [ðæt]
It's funny that he isn't here. [ðət]

118. I am sorry *that* I am late. — 늦어서 죄송합니다.
119. I am sorry *that* you can't go with us. — 자네가 우리와 함께 가지 않는다니 섭섭하군.
120. *That* he wears heavy glasses is an important point. — 그 사람이 돗수 높은 안경을 끼고 있다는 사실이 중요해.
121. *That* you know him well makes a big difference. — 당신이 그이를 잘 알고 있다는 것이 큰 차이점입니다.
122. The fact *that* you know his brother makes a big difference. — 당신이 그 사람의 동생을 알고 있다는 사실이 큰 차이를 이루고 있읍니다.

두 가지를 비교하는 문형

123. Blood is *thicker than* water. — 피는 물보다 진하다.
124. You are *taller than* I. — 너는 나보다 키가 크다.
125. I like tea *better than* coffee. — 나는 커피보다 홍차를 좋아해.
126. You can reach him *faster than* I can. — 자네는 나보다 먼저 그 사람한테 연락할 수 있어.
127. You'll get there *faster* by walking *than* by car. — 자네는 자동차로 가는 것보다 걸어서 가는 편이 빨리 도착할 거야.
128. This is a *better* book *than* the one you have. — 이것은 자네 것보다 더 좋은 책이야.

최상급을 나타내는 문형

129. This is *the largest* table in the room. — 이것이 방에서 제일 큰 테이블입니다.
130. Today is *the longest* day of the year. — 오늘은 일년 중 가장 해가 긴 날입니다.
131. You are *the best* student in the class. — 자네는 클라스에서 가장 훌륭한 학생이야.
132. She is *the most* popular girl in town. — 그 여자는 마을에서 가장 인기 있는 아가씨야.
133. Mt. Paektu is *the highest* among all the mountains in Korea. — 백두산은 한국에서 가장 높은 산입니다.
134. Alaska is *the largest* state and Texas is *the* second *largest* in America. — 알라스카는 미국에서 가장 큰 주이고, 텍사스는 두번째로 큰 주입니다.
135. Green is the color I like *the best*. — 초록색은 내가 제일 좋아하는 빛깔이다.
136. Please give him my *best* wishes. — 그분에게 안부 전해 주십시오.
137. May *the best* man win! — 훌륭한 사람이 승리하기를!

138. Sangho is *the oldest* of his five sons. —상호는 그 사람의 다섯 아들 중에서 맏이입니다.

There is와 그 유형

There는 본래 장소를 나타내는 부사이지만, 그런 이론에 구애되지 말고 입버릇이 될 때까지 연습해 두면, 매우 편리하다.

139. *There is* a red cottage on the hill. —언덕 위에 빨간 오두막이 있읍니다.
140. *There are* pine trees around it. —그 주위에는 소나무가 있읍니다.
141. *There was* an old man living in it. —거기서 노인 한 분이 살고 있었읍니다.
142. *There were* many cats living with him. —그분은 여러 마리의 고양이를 데리고 있었읍니다.
143. *There has been* a mystery about the man's death. —그 사람의 죽음에 대해서는 불가사의한 점이 있읍니다.
144. *There have been* many explanations about it. —거기 대해서는 여러가지 이야기가 있읍니다.
145. *There will be* many more. —앞으로 더욱 많이 있겠지요.

There is와 의문사의 결합

146. *What's there* in that bag?/ There are marbles in it. —그 주머니 속엔 무엇이 있냐?/ 공깃돌이 있어요.
147. *How many* marbles *are there* in it?/ There are about twenty-five marbles in it. —공깃돌이 몇 개 들어 있냐?/ 스물 다섯 개쯤 들어 있어요.
148. *Why is there* so much dust in Seoul?/ Because they are digging up the street all the time. —서울엔 왜 먼지가 이렇게도 많습니까?/ 길을 자꾸만 파헤치기 때문입니다.

이것은 영문을 몰라서 물어보는 것이다. 이와같이, 몰라서 물어볼 경우에는 단수로 질문한다.

149. *What was* there to see?/ There was an exhibition game. —뭐 볼 만한 것이 있었읍니까?/ 모범시합이 있었읍니다.
150. *Why was there* so much noise?/ Children was playing. —왜 그렇게 시끄러웠읍니까?/ 아이들이 놀고 있었어요.
151. *Why were there* so many people?/ They were watching a house on fire. —사람들이 왜 그렇게 많았지요?/ 불구경이 있었읍니다.

접속사가 있는 문형

접속사에는, (1)단어와 단어를 연결하는 것, (2) 문절(文節)을 연결하는 것이 있다.

(1) 단어를 연결하는 것

And

152. I want sugar *and* cream in my coffee. — 커피에 설탕과 크리임을 넣어 주십시오.
153. I have been to Taegu *and* Pusan. —대구와 부산에 다녀왔읍니다.
154. Will you *and* your sister come to our home for dinner on Wednesday? —수요일에, 자네와 자네 누이동생이 우리집에서 저녁을 같이하지 않겠나?
155. This is a race between my will power *and* my stamina. —이것은 내 정력과 인내력의 경쟁이야.
156. This is the funniest *and* truest book of them all. —이것은 전체의 책 중에서 가장 재미있고도 진리가 담긴 책입니다.
157. Seoul is big *and* modern. —서울은 크고도 현대적입니다.
158. She is lovely *and* modest. —그 여자는 귀엽고도 얌전합니다.
159. She works hard *and* long. —그 여자는 열심히 오랫동안 일합니다.

160. She washes *and* irons every day. —그 여자는 매일 빨래하고 다림질합니다.
161. She dresses beautifully *and* correctly. —그 여자는 옷매무새가 좋고 단정합니다.
162. Mr. *and* Mrs. Lawman live modesty *and* piously. —로오만씨 부부는 겸손하고 경건한 생활을 합니다.
163. When *and* how did you get home? —언제 어떻게 집에 오셨읍니까?
164. He gave me a dollar *and* twenty-five cents. —그 사람이 1달러 25센트를 주었읍니다.

Or
165. Do you want water *or* something? —물이나 뭘 드릴까요?
166. Are you a man *or* a mouse? —당신은 그러고도 남자요?
167. You *or* I must go. —자네가 가든지 내가 가든지 해야겠어.
168. Is it a boy *or* a girl? —아들이야, 딸이야?
169. Which do you want, pork *or* beef? —돼지고기로 하실까요, 쇠고기로 하실까요?
170. Which do you like better, him *or* me? —저이가 좋습니까, 제가 좋습니까?
171. How are you traveling, by train *or* by plane? —기차로 여행하십니까, 비행기로 여행하십니까?
172. Are you coming *or* going? —오시는 겁니까, 가시는 겁니까?
173. Is this Wednesday *or* Thursday? —오늘이 수요일이요, 목요일이요?
174. We'll go rain *or* shine. —비가 오든 날이 개든 갑시다.
175. He'll be back in two *or* three minutes. —이삼 분 후에는 돌아오겠지요.

문절(文節)을 접속하는 것
And
176. Go straight ahead, *and* you will find it. —곧장 가시면 거기 있읍니다.
177. Come tomorrow, *and* you will have a job. —내일 오시면 일거리가 있읍니다.
178. You are a doctor, *and* I am a lawyer. —당신은 의사고 나는 변호사입니다.

Or
179. Give me liberty *or* give me death. —자유 아니면 죽음을 달라.
180. Hurry up, *or* you will be late. —서둘지 않으면 늦는다.
181. I will see you tomorrow *or* send you a message. —내일 뵙거나 아니면 편지를 올리겠읍니다.

Either … or
182. You must either pay me now *or* pay interest. —오늘 지불해 주시지 않으면 이자를 주십시오.
183. Will you either come in *or* leave? —들어오거나 나가거나 해 주십시오.

Whether … or
184. I don't care whether you stay home *or* go out. —자네가 집에 있든 나가든 난 몰라.
185. We'll go whether it rains *or* not. —비가 오건 말건 갑시다.

For
186. I am not going out, *for* it's raining. —비가 오기 때문에 난 안 가겠어.
187. I threw it away, *for* it was broken. —망가져서 내버렸어.

회화에서는 because를 for 대신에 사용하는 경우가 많다. 다음을 참조할 것.

Because
188. I cannot do it, *because* it's illegal. —그건 불법행위이기 때문에 난 못하겠어.
189. *Because* you lied to me, I am not going —자네는 나한테 거짓말을 했기 때문

to trust you. 에, 이젠 자벨 안 믿겠어.

As
190. *As* I was tired, I went to bed right away. ─저는 피로했기 때문에 곧 잤어요.
191. I've forgotten all about it, *as* I was busy. ─저는 바빴기 때문에 완전히 잊어버렸읍니다.
192. *As* I was about to leave the house, the phone rang. ─집을 막 나오려고 하는데 전화가 왔어요.
193. *As* a child I used to listen to his stories. ─어렸을 때, 늘 그 사람이 해주는 얘기를 들었지요.
194. I did *as* I was told. ─들은 대로 했어요.
195. When in Rome, do *as* the Romans do. ─입향순속(入鄕循俗).

But
196. I'm busy now, *but* I can see you later. ─지금은 바쁘니까, 다음에 만납시다.
197. I asked you to come right away, *but* you didn't. ─자네보고 곧 오라고 했는데, 오지 않았네.

Since
198. *Since* you are going downtown anyway, will you get me some stamps? ─하여튼, 시내에 가면 우표를 좀 사다 주게나.
199. Where have you been *since* I saw you last? ─요전에 자네를 만난 후에 어디 가 있었나?
200. How long is it *since* you arrived? ─자네가 도착한 지 얼마나 되었나?

When
201. *When* you see him, tell him to phone me. ─그 사람을 만나거든, 나한테 전화해 달라고 말해 주게.
202. *When* I eat out, I eat light. ─나는 외식할 때에는 간단히 먹어.
203. *When* you do something, do it well. ─뭘 할 때에는 잘 해.
204. *When* I speak to you, please look at me. ─내가 말할 때에는 나를 쳐다 봐 주시오.

Whenever
205. *Whenever* I travel alone, I get indigestion. ─혼자 여행할 때는 언제나 소화가 잘 안 돼.
206. Come and see me *whenever* you can. ─형편이 닿는 대로 언제든 만나러 오게.

Where
207. *Where* you go, I'll go. ─당신이 가는 곳이라면 어디든지 따라가겠어요.
208. *Where* there's a will, there's a way. ─뜻이 있는 곳에 길이 있다.

Wherever
209. *Wherever* you go in Seoul, you'll see school children on excursions. ─서울 어디를 가시든지, 당신은 수학여행 온 학생들을 보시게 될 겁니다.
210. *Wherever* there's an opening, something is being planted. ─공터란 공터에는 무슨 나무건 심어져 있다.

While
211. *While* you were away, Mr. Chang came to see us. ─자네가 외출중에, 장군이 우릴 만나러 왔어.
212. This is pure entertainment, *while* that is gambling. ─그건 도박이지만, 이건 순수한 오락이야.

So that
213. I came early *so that* I could help you. ─당신을 도우려고 일찍 왔읍니다.
214. He studied English *so that* he could go ─그 사람은 무역업에 종사하려고 영

into import and export business.

So … that
215. He came home *so* tired *that* I put him to bed at once.
—너무 피곤해서 돌아왔기 때문에, 곧 재웠읍니다.
216. It was raining *so* hard *that* we cancelled the tour.
—비가 너무 심하게 오고 있었기 때문에, 여행을 중지했읍니다.

In order that
217. We put the sign up *in order that* no one could misunderstand the rule.
—규칙을 잘못 아는 사람이 없도록 게시를 했읍니다.
218. The students were divided up into small groups *in order that* everyone would have a chance to practice English conversation with an instructor.
—모두들 선생님과 영어회화를 할 기회를 가질 수 있도록 학생들을 작은 그루우프로 나누었읍니다.

Unless
219. *Unless* you return it right away, they'll charge you extra.
—곧 반환하지 않으면, 그 사람들한테 추가요금을 물어야 합니다.
220. Don't come *unless* I call you.
—부르지 않으면 오지 마십시오.
221. Come anyway *unless* I phone you to the contrary.
—오지 말라는 전화를 하지 않는 한, 하여튼 오십시오.

to+동사가 들어 있는 문장
222. I'd like *to speak* to you.
—당신과 얘기하고 싶어요.
223. I want *to sit* down.
—앉고 싶군요.
224. Will you come *to see* me soon?
—근일 내로 오시지 않겠어요?
225. My sister went to Europe *to study* social work.
—제 누이는 사회사업에 관해서 공부하려고 유럽에 갔읍니다.
226. What are you going *to do?*
—자넨 뭘 하려고 하나?
227. I am *to keep* an eye on you.
—나는 자네를 감시하고 있어야 해.

It is … to ∼
228. *It's* good *to* see you again.
—또 만나게 되어서 반갑습니다.
229. *It's* good *to* have seen you again.
—또 만나게 되어서 반갑습니다.
230. *It was* wrong *to* go there.
—거기 가는 건 좋지 않았어.
231. *Is it* all right *to* open this?
—이걸 열어도 좋습니까?
232. *Isn't it* wrong *to* call up people late at night?
—밤 늦게 남한테 전화 거는 건 나쁘지요?
233. *Will it be* all right *to* leave my baggage here?
—짐을 여기 놓고 가도 괜찮을까요?

It is too … to ∼
234. *It's* too late *to* go.
—가기에는 너무 늦었다.
235. *It's* too hot *to* go out.
—외출하기에는 너무 덥다.
236. *Is it* too early *to* get up?
—일어나기엔 너무 이를까?
237. *It's* too good *to* be true.
—꿈이야, 생시야?

동명사가 들어 있는 문장
238. *Seeing* is *believing*.
—백문이 불여일견.
239. Do you enjoy *traveling?*
—여행을 좋아하십니까?
240. I enjoyed *meeting* you all.
—여러분들을 만나게 돼서 기뻤읍니다.
241. Will you stop *talking* so loud?
—그렇게 큰 소리로 말하지 마십시오.
242. I cannot help *liking* him.
—그이를 좋아하지 않고는 못 배기겠다.
243. Not *telling* the truth is as bad as *lying*.
—진실을 말하지 않는 것은 거짓말을 하는 것처럼 나쁘다.

244. Do you like *being* alone?
245. *Being* young does not always mean *being* immature.
246. I will give you 100 won for *being* a good boy.

―혼자 계시기를 좋아하십니까?
―젊다고 해서 반드시 미숙한 것은 아니다.
―착한 일 하면 100원 주마.

Go+동사ing 가 있는 문장

247. Let's *go swimming*.
248. I am going to *go shopping* in a few minutes.
249. Will you *go* mountain-*climbing* with us?
250. How do you like to go *hunting* next fall?
251. Did you go *comping* last summer?
252. We *went fishing* a week ago.

―수영하러 갑시다.
―곧 물건 사러 가겠읍니다.
―우리와 함께 등산 가시겠읍니까?
―내년 가을에 사냥하러 가실까요?
―작년 여름에 캠프하러 갔었읍니까?
―우리는 일주일 전에 낚시질하러 갔었읍니다.

Language of Flowers 꽃말

acacia	friendship	아카시아	우정
acanthus	the fine arts	어캔더스	미술
	artifice		기교
aconite	misanthropy	바곳	염세
almond	stupidity	감복숭아	둔감
	indiscretion		경솔
aloe	grief	노회(蘆薈)	비애
	religious superstition		미신
amaranth	immortality	애머랜드	불멸
anemone	sickness	아네모네	병(病)
	expectation		예상
	withered hopes		시들어버린 희망
	forsaken		배반당한
apple	temptation	사과	유혹
apple blossom	preference	사과꽃	선택
apricot blossom	doubt	살구꽃	의혹
arbutus	Thee only do I love.	소귀나무	당신만을 사랑해
ash tree	grandeur	서양물푸레나무	장대(壯大)
aspen tree	lamentation	포플라	슬픔
	fear		두려움
aster	variety	과꽃	다방면
	after-thought		뒤늦은 생각
autumnal leaves	melancholy	단풍잎	우울
azalea	temperance	진달래	절제
bay tree	glory	월계수	영광
beech tree	prosperity	너도밤나무	번영
begonia	deformity	베고니아	불구
bellflower	gratitude	초롱꽃	감사
	constancy		절조
birch	meekness	자작나무	온순
bluebottle	delicacy	달구지국화	우아
broom	humility	금작화(金雀花)	겸손
	neatness		청순
buttercup	riches	애기미나리아재비	부(富)
cabbage	profit	양배추	이윤
cactus	grandeur	선인장	장대(壯大)
	warmth		온정
camellia	unpretending excellence	동백	겸손한 우월
carnation	Alas! for my poor heart.	카아네이션	오오, 이 가엾은 마음을 위하여.
	disdain		경멸
catchfly	snare	끈끈이대나물	함정
cedar	strength	삼목	힘
cedar leaf	I live for thee.	삼목잎	그대 위해 산다오.
cherry blossom	spiritual beauty	벚꽃	정신적인 아름다움
	insincerity		불성실

chestnut tree	Do me justice.	밤나무	공평히 해 주시오.
chrysanthemum, red	I love.	국화(빨강)	나는 사랑해.
chrysanthemum, white	truth	국화(하양)	진실
chrysanthemum, yellow	slighted love	국화(노랑)	무시당한 사랑
cineraria	always delightful	시네라리아	언제나 즐거움
clematis	mental beauty	클레머티스	마음의 아름다움
	artifice		기교
clover, four-leaved	Be mine.	클로우버(네 잎)	내것이 돼 주오.
clover, red	industry	클로우버(빨강)	근면
clover, white	Think of me.	클로우버(하양)	나를 생각해 주오.
	promise		약속
columbine	folly	매발톱꽃	어리석음
convolvulus	bonds	메꽃, 나팔꽃	유대(紐帶)
corn	riches	옥수수	부유
cowslip	pensiveness	눈동이나물	생각에 잠김
	winning grace		마음을 사로잡는 애교
	youthful beauty		젊음의 아름다움
crocus	Abuse not.	크로커스	배반하지 마시오.
	impatience		성급
cyclamen	diffidence	시클라멘	망설임
daffodil	regard	나팔수선화	존중
	unrequited love		짝사랑
dahlia	instability	다알리아	불안
	pomp		호화
daisy	innocence	데이지	순진
dandelion	rustic oracle	민들레	순박한 예언
dead leaves	sadness	가랑잎	비애
elder	zealousness	양딱총나무	열심
elm	dignity	느룹나무	위엄
evening primrose	silent love	달맞이꽃	무언의 사랑
everlasting	never-ceasing remembrance	떡쑥	잊지 않는 기억
fennel	worthy of praise	회양풀	찬양의 가치 있는
	strength		힘
fern	fascination	양치류	매혹
	magic		마법
	sincerity		성실
fig	argument	무화과	변론
fig tree	prolific	무화과나무	다산(多産)
fir	time	전나무	때, 시간
flax	domestic industry	아마(亞麻)	가내공업
	fate		운명
	I feel your kindness.		나는 당신의 친절함을 알고 있소.
forget-me-not	true love	물망초	진실한 사랑
foxglove	insincerity	더기탈리스	불성실
geranium	deceit	양아욱	기만
golden rod	precaution	메역취	경계

gooseberry	anticipation	구즈베리	예상
grape	charity	포도	자선
grass	submission	포아풀	순종
	utility		효용(効用)
hawthorn	hope	산사나무	희망
hazel	reconciliation	개암나무	화해
heath	solitude	히이드	고독
hemlock	You will be my death.	독당근	너는 나를 죽이리라.
hemp	fate	삼(대마)	운명
holly	foresight	호랑가시나무	선견(先見)
hollyhock	ambition	접시꽃	큰 희망
	fecundity		다산(多產)
honeysuckle	generous and devoted affection	인동덩굴	돈 잘 쓰는 정열
horse chestnut	luxury	마로니에	사치
hortensia	You are cold.	자양화	당신은 냉정하오.
humble plant	despondency	함수초	의기소침
hyacinth	sport	히아신스	경기
	game		승부
Indian cress	warlike trophy	한련	전리품
Iris	message	붓꽃	편지
ivy	friendship	담쟁이덩굴	우정
	fidelity		성실
	marriage		결혼
Japanese lilies	You cannot deceive me.	일본백합	나는 속지 않는다오.
jasmine	amiability	재스민	애교
jonquil	I desire a return of affection.	노랑수선화	나는 애정의 댓가를 바라오.
Judas tree	unbelief	박태기나무	불신
	betrayal		배반
luniper	succour	노간주나무	구조
	protection		보호
larch	audacity	낙엽송	대담
larkspur	lightness	참제비고깔	가벼움
	levity		경솔
laurel	glory	월계수	영광
lemon	zest	레몬	좋은 맛
lemon blossoms	fidelity in love	레몬꽃	애정에 대한 성실
lettuce	cold-heartedness	상치	냉담
lichen	dejection	이끼	낙심
	solitude		고독
lilac, field	humility	라일락(벌판의)	겸손
lilac, purple	first emotion of love	라일락(자주)	사랑의 첫감격
lilac, white	youthful innocence	라일락(하양)	젊은이의 순진함
lily, white	purity	백합(하양)	순결
	sweetness		좋은 맛
lily, yellow	falsehood	백합(노랑)	거짓말
	gaiety		즐거움
lily of the valley	return of happiness	은방울꽃	행복이 돌아옴
	unconscious sweetness		무의식적인 미(美)
linden	conjugal love	참피나무	부부의 사랑

liverwort	confidence	우산이끼	신뢰
lotus flower	estranged love	연꽃	헤어진 사랑
lotus leaf	recantation	연잎	취소
madder	calumny	꼭두서니	중상(中傷)
magnolia	love of nature magnificence	목련	자연의 사랑 장려(壯麗)
mallow	mildness	당아욱	유화(柔和)
mandrake	horror	흰독말풀	공포
maple	reserve	단풍	장래에 대한 계획
marigold	grief	금잔화	슬픔
milfoil	war	서양톱풀	전쟁
milkwort	hermitage	애기풀	은둔
mint	virtue	박하	도덕
mistletoe	I surmount difficulties.	겨우살이	나는 곤란을 극복한다.
monkshood	A deadly foe is near.	바곳	강적이 가까이 있다.
morning glory	affection	나팔꽃	거짓 꾸밈
moss	maternal love	이끼	모성애
mushroom	suspicion I can't entirely trust you.	버섯	혐의 당신은 믿을 수 없어요.
musk plant	weakness	사향물파리아재비	연약
mustard seed	indifference	겨자씨	무관심
myrrh	gladness	몰약(沒藥)	기쁨
myrtle	love	도금양(桃金孃)	사랑
narcissus	egotism	수선화	자기중심주의
nettle	You are spiteful.	쐐기풀	당신은 짓궂어요.
night convolvulus	night	박꽃	밤
oak leaves	bravery	참나무잎	용감
oak tree	hospitality	참나무	후한 대접
oleander	Beware.	서양협죽도	조심하라.
olive	peace	올리브	평화
orange flower	chastity	오렌지꽃	정조
orange tree	generosity	오렌지나무	관대
orchid	belle	난초	미인
palm	victory	야자, 종려	승리
pansy	thoughts	팬지	생각
parsley	festivity	파아슬리	환락
pasque flower	You have no claims.	일본할미꽃	당신에겐 권리가 없어요.
pea	lasting pleasure	완두	영원한 쾌락
pear	affection	배	애정
peartree	comfort	배나무	안락
peony	shame bashfulness	작약	수치 수줍음
persimmon	Bury me amid Nature's beauties.	감	나를 자연의 아름다움속에 묻어 주오.
pine	pity	소나무	동정
pineapple	You are perfect.	파인애플	당신은 완전해요.
pink	boldness	패랭이꽃	대담
pink, red, double	pure and ardent love	패랭이꽃(빨강,겹)	순결한 정열

pink, white	ingeniousness talent	패랭이꽃(하양)	영리 재능
plum-tree	fidelity	오얏나무	성실
pomegranate	foolishness	석류	우둔
poplar, black	courage	포플라(짙은 것)	용기
poplar, white	time	포플라(하양)	때, 시간
poppy, red	consolation	양귀비(빨강)	위안
poppy, white	sleep	양귀비(하양)	수면
potato	benevolence	감자	자애
primrose	early youth and sadness	앵초(櫻草)	청춘과 슬픔
reed	complaisance music	갈대	공손함 음악
rhododendron	danger Beware.	석남화	위험 조심하시오.
rhubard	advice	장군풀	충고
rose	love	장미	사랑
rose, deep red	bashful shame	장미(진홍)	수줍음
rose, single	simplicity	장미(홑)	순박
rose, white	I am worthy of you.	장미(하양)	나는 당신과 잘 어울립니다.
rose, yellow	decrease of love jealousy	장미(노랑)	애정의 감소 질투
rosebud, red	pure and lovely	장미봉오리(빨강)	순결하고 사랑스런
rosebud, white	girlhood	장미봉오리(하양)	소녀시절
rush	docility	골풀	순종
saffron	Beware of excess.	사프란	지나친 것을 조심하시오.
St. John's wort	superstition	물레나물	미신
saxifrage	affection	범의 귀	애정
sensitive plant	sensibility	함수초	민감
shepherd's-purse	I offer you my all.	냉이	내 모든 것을 당신에게 바치오.
snowdrop	hope	눈꽃	희망
sorrel	affection	소루쟁이	애정
speedwell	female fidelity	꼬리풀	여자의 성실
spindle tree	Your charms are engraven on my heart.	화살나무	당신의 매력은 내 마음에 파고드오.
stock	lasting beauty	자라난화(紫羅爛花)	영원한 아름다움
stonecrop	tranquillity	꿩의비름	평온
strawberry blossom	foresight	딸기꽃	선견(先見)
sultan, white	sweetness	도깨비부채(하양)	달콤함
sultan, yellow	contempt	도깨비부채(노랑)	경멸
sumach	splendour	옻나무	화려
sunflower, dwarf	adoration	해바라기(작은)	동경
sunflower, tall	haughtiness	해바라기(큰)	오만
sweet pea	delicate pleasure	스위이트피이	격이 높은 쾌락
tamarisk	crime	위성류(渭城柳)	죄악
thistle	austerity independence	엉겅퀴	엄격 독립
trumpet flower	fame	능소화(凌霄花)	명예
tulip, red	declaration of love	튜울립(빨강)	사랑의 선언

English	Meaning	한국어	뜻
tulip, variegated	beautiful eyes	튜울립(얼룩얼룩한)	아름다운 눈
tulip, yellow	hopeless love	튜울립(노랑)	가망없는 사랑
turnip	charity	순무	자선
vervain	enchantment	마편초	매력
vine	intoxication	포도나무	도취
violet, blue	faithfulness	제비꽃(파랑)	성실
violet, sweet	modesty	향제비꽃	겸손
violet, yellow	rural happiness	제비꽃(노랑)	전원의 행복
walnut	intellect	호두	지력(知力)
	stratagem		책략(策略)
water-lily	purity of heart	수련	마음의 순결
water-melon	bulkiness	수박	부피가 늘어 남
weeping willow	mourning	수양버들	애도
wheat stalk	riches	밀짚	부유
whin	anger	가시금작화	노여움
wisteria	Welcome, fair stranger.	등나무	어서 오십시오, 아름다운 나그네여.
woodbine	fraternal love	인동덩굴	형제의 사랑
wood sorrel	joy	괭이밥	기쁨
	maternal tenderness		어머니의 사랑
yew	sorrow	주목(朱木)	슬픔

符号와 数·数式 읽는법

(A) 符　　　号

1. 語学記号
- **Period, Full stop** 마침표, 종지부
- , **Comma** 쉬는표, 휴식부
- : **Colon** 그침표, 중지부
- ; **Semicolon** 머무름표, 정류부
- ── **Dash** 말바꿈표, 환언표
  - ¶It was cold──bitter cold.
- ? **Interrogation mark, Question mark** 물음표, 의문부
  - ¶Do you see the clock?
- ! **Exclamation mark** 느낌표
  - ¶How tall he is!
- ' **Apostrophe** 어포스트로피
  - ¶I'll (=I will) go there.
- - **Hyphen** 붙임표, 접합부
  - ¶kind-hearted 친절한
- " ", ' ' **Quotation mark** 따옴표, 인용부
  - ¶"I am looking for you," she said.
- ( ) **Parentheses** 손톱묶음
- 《 》 **Double parentheses** 겹손톱묶음
- { } **Braces** 활짱묶음
- [ ] **Brackets** 꺾쇠묶음
- … **Ellipsis** 말없음표, 무언표
  - ¶"What? Oh…I didn't mean…"
- * **Asterisk** 별표
- † **Dagger** 칼표
- § **Section mark** 마디표
- ¶ **Paragraph** 단락표

2. 商用記号
- £ **Pound** 파운드
- **s., /** **Shilling** 실링
  - ¶3/2=three shillings & twopence
- **d.** **Penny, Pence** 페니, 펜스
  - [*denarius, denarii* 의 약어]
  - ¶£3. 4s. 5d.=three pounds four shillings five pence
- **$, $** **Dollar** 달러
  - ¶I bought it for $10.60 (=ten dollars and sixty cents).
- ¢ **Cent** 센트　¶75¢
- ₩ **Won** 원　¶₩100
- **lb.** **Pound in weight** 파운드
  - [*libra(e)* 의 약어]
- **oz.** **Ounce** 온스
- **c/o** 전교(転交) [care of 의 약어]
  - ¶c/o Mr. Yang 양 선생 전교
- **P.S.** 추신 [postscript 의 약어]
- **I.O.U., IOU** 차용증 [=I owe you.]
  - ¶IOU £20　20파운드 차용

3. 数学記号
- ° **Degree** 도(度)
- ' **Minute** 분
- " **Second** 초
  - ¶20°30′40″　20도 30분 40초
- Σ **Sum** 총화
- ∫ **Integral** 적분
- *f*, φ **Function** 관수(関数)　¶*f(x)*
- ∽ **Similar** 상사
- ∞ **Infinity** 무한대
- ∴ **Therefore, Hence** 그러므로
- ∵ **Because, Since** 왜냐하면
- % **Per cent** 퍼센트
- **c.c.** **Cubic centimeter**
- μ **Micron** 미크론

4. 電気記号
- **Hz** **Hertz** 주파수
- Ω **Ohm** 오옴

5. 略語
- **cf.** compare, confer 비교하라, 참고하라
- **e.g.** For example 예를 들면
  - [*exempli gratia* 의 약어]
- **etc., &c.** and so forth; and so on; and the rest …따위 [=*et cetera*]
  - [둘 이상을 열거할 경우에는 comma를 찍어서 사용] ¶A, B, C, etc.
- **&** and 그리고 [=*and per se and*]
- **ibid., ib.** in the same place 같은 곳에
  - [*ibidem* 의 약어]
- **vs., v.** against 대(対) [*versus* 의 약어]
- **pp.** Pages 페이지　¶pp. 10~16
- **ll.** lines　¶ll. 1~3
- **No.** Number …호(번)
- **vol.** volume …권
- **ult.** 지난달의 [*ultimo* 의 약어]
- **prox.** 내달의 [*proximo* 의 약어]
- **i.e.** that is 즉, 곧 [*id est* 의 약어]
- **O.K., OK** all correct 좋다
- **viz.** namely 즉, 곧 [*videlicet* 의 약어]

(B) 数 와 数 式

1. 数 字
0 zero, nought, cipher
78 seventy-eight
4961 four thousand, nine hundred [and] sixty-one; forty-nine hundred [and] sixty-one
10,000 ten thousand
200,000 two hundred thousand
3,000,000 three million
4,000,000,000 (*U.S.*) four billion; (*Brit.*) four milliard; four thousand million
6,324,859 six million, three hundred [and] twenty-four thousand, eight hundred [and] fifty-nine

2. 数 式
$2+3=5$ Two and (*or* plus) three are (*or* is, make[s], equal[s]) five.
$8-6=2$ Six from eight leaves two. Eight minus six equals two.
$2\times3=6$ Two times three is six. Two multiplied by three is (*or* equals) six.
$6\div3=2$ Three into six goes twice. Six divided by three makes two.
$a=b$ A equals b. A is identical with b.
$3^2=9$ The square of three is nine.
$3^3=27$ The cube of three is twenty-seven. Three cubed is twenty-seven.
$A=b^3$ A is b cube.
$a^2-b^2=(a+b)(a-b)$ A square minus b square equals parenthesis a plus b parenthesis times parenthesis a minus b parenthesis.
$(a+b)^2=a^2+2ab+b^2$ The square of the sum of a plus b equals a square plus two ab plus b square.
$\sqrt{4}=2$ The square root of four is two.
$\sqrt{a}$ square root of a
$\sqrt[3]{b}$ cube root of b
$\sqrt[m]{n}$ m root of n

3. 小数 分数
0.01 nought point nought one
0.12 nought point one two
2.1 two point one; two and one-tenth
$1/2$ a half, one-half
$1/3$ a third, one-third
$1/4$ a quarter, one-fourth
$3/7$ three-sevenths
$8\,2/5$ eight and two-fifths
$\dfrac{210}{365}$ two hundred [and] ten over three hundred [and] sixty-five
$\dfrac{c}{a+b}$ c over a plus b

4. 月日 年号
1969 nineteen sixty-nine
1800 eighteen hundred
1602 sixteen two, sixteen O two.
520 B.C. five twenty B.C.
July 14 (*U.S.*) July the fourteenth, July fourteen
10 April (*Brit.*) the tenth of April
9/12/69 nine twelve sixty-nine (*U.S.*) December nine 1969; (*Brit.*) nine December 1969.
May 1 19— May the first nineteen hundred and something

5. 기타
page 125 page one twenty-five
pp. 12~31 pages twelve to thirty-one
Chapter III chapter three; the third chapter
Lesson 24 lesson twenty-four; the twenty-fourth lesson
Elizabeth II Elizabeth the Second
World War I world war one; the first world war
Room 216 room two sixteen
Room 102 room one-O-two
Matt. iii. 5 Matthew, chapter three, verse five
***Hamlet*, IV. v. 23** Hamlet, act four, scene five, line twenty-three

Presidents of the United States

Name	Born	Died	Birthplace	Residence	Religious Affiliation	Party	Dates in Office	Wife's Name	Wife's Dates	Children
1. GEORGE WASHINGTON	Feb. 22, 1732	Dec. 14, 1799	Westmoreland Co., Va.	Va.	Episcopalian	Fed.	1789–1797	MARTHA DANDRIDGE CUSTIS	1732–1802	0
2. JOHN ADAMS	Oct. 30, 1735	July 4, 1826	Quincy, Mass.	Mass.	Unitarian	Fed.*	1797–1801	ABIGAIL SMITH	1744–1818	5
3. THOMAS JEFFERSON	Apr. 13, 1743	July 4, 1826	Shadwell, Va.	Va.	Episcopalian	Rep.*	1801–1809	MARTHA WAYLES SKELTON	1748–1782	6
4. JAMES MADISON	Mar. 16, 1751	June 28, 1836	Port Conway, Va.	Va.	Episcopalian	Rep.*	1809–1817	DOLLY PAYNE TODD	1768–1849	0
5. JAMES MONROE	Apr. 28, 1758	July 4, 1831	Westmoreland Co., Va.	Va.	Episcopalian	Rep.*	1817–1825	ELIZABETH KORTWRIGHT	1768–1830	2
6. JOHN QUINCY ADAMS	July 11, 1767	Feb. 23, 1848	Quincy, Mass.	Mass.	Unitarian	Rep.*	1825–1829	LOUISE CATHERINE JOHNSON	1775–1852	4
7. ANDREW JACKSON	Mar. 15, 1767	June 8, 1845	New Lancaster Co., S.C.	Tenn.	Presbyterian	Dem.	1829–1837	RACHEL DONELSON ROBARDS	1767–1828	0
8. MARTIN VAN BUREN	Dec. 5, 1782	July 24, 1862	Kinderhook, N.Y.	N.Y.	Reformed Dutch	Dem.	1837–1841	HANNAH HOES	1783–1819	4
9. WILLIAM HENRY HARRISON†	Feb. 9, 1773	Apr. 4, 1841	Berkeley, Va.	Ohio	Episcopalian	Whig	1841	ANNA SYMMES	1775–1864	10
10. JOHN TYLER	Mar. 29, 1790	Jan. 18, 1862	Greenway, Va.	Va.	Episcopalian	Whig	1841–1845	[1] LETITIA CHRISTIAN	1790–1842	7
								[2] JULIA GARDINER	1820–1889	7
11. JAMES KNOX POLK	Nov. 2, 1795	June 15, 1849	Mecklenburg Co., N.C.	Tenn.	Methodist	Dem.	1845–1849	SARAH CHILDRESS	1803–1891	0
12. ZACHARY TAYLOR†	Nov. 24, 1784	July 9, 1850	Orange Co., Va.	La.	Episcopalian	Whig	1849–1850	MARGARET SMITH	1788–1852	6
13. MILLARD FILLMORE	Jan. 7, 1800	Mar. 8, 1874	Cayuga Co., N.Y.	N.Y.	Unitarian	Whig	1850–1853	[1] ABIGAIL POWERS	1798–1853	2
								[2] CAROLINE CARMICHAEL McINTOSH	1813–1881	0
14. FRANKLIN PIERCE	Nov. 23, 1804	Oct. 8, 1869	Hillsboro, N.H.	N.H.	Episcopalian	Dem.	1853–1857	JANE MEANS APPLETON	1806–1863	3
15. JAMES BUCHANAN	Apr. 23, 1791	June 1, 1868	Mercersburg, Pa.	Pa.	Presbyterian	Dem.	1857–1861	none		
16. ABRAHAM LINCOLN†	Feb. 12, 1809	Apr. 15, 1865	Hardin Co., Ky.	Ill.	Nonmember	Rep.‡	1861–1865	MARY TODD	1818–1882	4
17. ANDREW JOHNSON	Dec. 29, 1808	July 31, 1875	Raleigh, N.C.	Tenn.	Nonmember	Dem.‡	1865–1869	ELIZA McCARDLE	1810–1876	5
18. ULYSSES SIMPSON GRANT	Apr. 27, 1822	July 23, 1885	Pt. Pleasant, Ohio	Ill.	Methodist	Rep.	1869–1877	JULIA DENT	1826–1902	4
19. RUTHERFORD BIRCHARD HAYES	Oct. 4, 1822	Jan. 17, 1893	Delaware, Ohio	Ohio	Nonmember	Rep.	1877–1881	LUCY WARD WEBB	1831–1889	8
20. JAMES ABRAM GARFIELD†	Nov. 19, 1831	Sept. 19, 1881	Orange, Ohio	Ohio	Disciples of Christ	Rep.	1881	LUCRETIA RUDOLPH	1832–1918	7
21. CHESTER ALAN ARTHUR	Oct. 5, 1830	Nov. 18, 1886	Fairfield, Vt.	N.Y.	Episcopalian	Rep.	1881–1885	ELLEN LEWIS HERNDON	1837–1880	3
22. GROVER CLEVELAND	Mar. 18, 1837	June 24, 1908	Caldwell, N.J.	N.Y.	Presbyterian	Dem.	1885–1889	FRANCES FOLSOM	1864–1947	5
23. BENJAMIN HARRISON	Aug. 20, 1833	Mar. 13, 1901	North Bend, Ohio	Ind.	Presbyterian	Rep.	1889–1893	[1] CAROLINE LAVINIA SCOTT	1832–1892	2
								[2] MARY SCOTT LORD DIMMOCK	1858–1948	1
24. GROVER CLEVELAND	See number 22			Ohio	Methodist	Dem.	1893–1897			
25. WILLIAM McKINLEY†	Jan. 29, 1843	Sept. 6, 1901	Niles, Ohio	Ohio	Methodist	Rep.	1897–1901	IDA SAXTON	1847–1907	2
26. THEODORE ROOSEVELT	Oct. 27, 1858	Jan. 6, 1919	New York, N.Y.	N.Y.	Reformed Dutch	Rep.	1901–1909	[1] ALICE HATHAWAY LEE	1861–1884	1
								[2] EDITH KERMIT CAROW	1861–1948	5
27. WILLIAM HOWARD TAFT	Sept. 15, 1857	Mar. 8, 1930	Cincinnati, Ohio	Ohio	Unitarian	Rep.	1909–1913	HELEN HERRON	1861–1943	3
28. WOODROW WILSON	Dec. 28, 1856	Feb. 3, 1924	Staunton, Va.	N.J.	Presbyterian	Dem.	1913–1921	[1] ELLEN LOUISE AXSON	1860–1914	3
								[2] EDITH BOLLING GALT	1872–1961	0
29. WARREN GAMALIEL HARDING†	Nov. 2, 1865	Aug. 2, 1923	Bloomington Grove, Ohio	Ohio	Baptist	Rep.	1921–1923	FLORENCE KLING DE WOLFE	1860–1924	0
30. CALVIN COOLIDGE	July 4, 1872	Jan. 5, 1933	Plymouth, Vt.	Mass.	Congregational	Rep.	1923–1929	GRACE A. GOODHUE	1879–1957	2
31. HERBERT CLARK HOOVER	Aug. 10, 1874	Oct. 20, 1964	West Branch, Iowa	Calif.	Society of Friends	Rep.	1929–1933	LOU HENRY	1875–1944	2
32. FRANKLIN DELANO ROOSEVELT†	Jan. 30, 1882	Apr. 12, 1945	Hyde Park, N.Y.	N.Y.	Episcopalian	Dem.	1933–1945	ANNA ELEANOR ROOSEVELT	1884–1962	6
33. HARRY S TRUMAN	May 8, 1884		Lamar, Mo.	Mo.	Baptist	Dem.	1945–1953	ELIZABETH VIRGINIA WALLACE	1885–	1
34. DWIGHT DAVID EISENHOWER	Oct. 14, 1890		Denison, Tex.	Tex.	Presbyterian	Rep.	1953–1961	MAMIE GENEVA DOUD	1896–	2
35. JOHN FITZGERALD KENNEDY†	May 29, 1917	Nov. 22, 1963	Brookline, Mass.	Mass.	Roman Catholic	Dem.	1961–1963	JACQUELINE BOUVIER	1929–	3
36. LYNDON BAINES JOHNSON	Aug. 27, 1908		Johnson City, Tex.	Tex.	Disciples of Christ	Dem.	1963–1969	CLAUDIA ALTA TAYLOR	1912–	2
37. RICHARD MILHOUS NIXON	Jan. 9, 1913		Yorba Linda, Calif.	N.Y.	Society of Friends	Rep.	1969–	THELMA PATRICIA RYAN	1913–	2

*Now the Democratic Party   †Died in office   ‡Elected on the Union party ticket

Vice Presidents of the United States [1379]

Name	Born	Died	Birthplace	Residence	Party	Dates in Office	Wife's Name	Children
1. JOHN ADAMS	Oct. 30, 1735	July 4, 1826	Quincy, Mass.	Mass.	Fed.	1789–1797	ABIGAIL SMITH	5
2. THOMAS JEFFERSON	Apr. 13, 1743	July 4, 1826	Shadwell, Va.	Va.	Rep.	1797–1801	MARTHA WAYLES SKELTON	6
3. AARON BURR	Feb. 6, 1756	Sept. 14, 1836	Newark, N.J.	N.Y.	Rep.	1801–1805	THEODOSIA BARTOW PREVOST	1
4. GEORGE CLINTON†	July 26, 1739	Apr. 20, 1812	Ulster Co., N.Y.	N.Y.	Rep.	1805–1812	CORNELIA TAPPEN	6
5. ELBRIDGE GERRY†	July 17, 1744	Nov. 23, 1814	Marblehead, Mass.	Mass.	Rep.	1813–1814	ANN THOMPSON	7
6. DANIEL D. TOMPKINS	June 21, 1774	June 11, 1825	Scarsdale, N.Y.	N.Y.	Rep.	1817–1825	HANNAH MINTHORNE	7
7. JOHN C. CALHOUN	Mar. 18, 1782	Mar. 31, 1850	Abbeville, S.C.	S.C.	Rep.	1825–1832	FLORIDE CALHOUN	9
8. MARTIN VAN BUREN	Dec. 5, 1782	July 24, 1862	Kinderhook, N.Y.	N.Y.	Dem.	1833–1837	HANNAH HOES	4
9. RICHARD M. JOHNSON	Oct. 17, 1781	Nov. 19, 1850	Louisville, Ky.	Ky.	Dem.	1837–1841	none	0
10. JOHN TYLER*	Mar. 29, 1790	Jan. 18, 1862	Greenway, Va.	Va.	Whig	1841	[1] LETITIA CHRISTIAN [2] JULIA GARDINER	0,7
11. GEORGE M. DALLAS	July 10, 1792	Dec. 31, 1864	Philadelphia, Pa.	Pa.	Dem.	1845–1849	SOPHIA NICKLIN	7
12. MILLARD FILLMORE*	Jan. 7, 1800	Mar. 8, 1874	Cayuga Co., N.Y.	N.Y.	Whig	1849–1850	[1] ABIGAIL POWERS [2] CAROLINE CARMICHAEL MCINTOSH	2,0
13. WILLIAM R. KING†	Apr. 7, 1786	Apr. 18, 1853	Sampson Co., N.C.	Ala.	Dem.	1853	none	0
14. JOHN C. BRECKINRIDGE	Jan. 21, 1821	May 17, 1875	Lexington, Ky.	Ky.	Dem.	1857–1861	MARY C. BURCH	0
15. HANNIBAL HAMLIN	Aug. 27, 1809	July 4, 1891	Paris, Me.	Me.	Rep.	1861–1865	[1] SARAH JANE EMERY [2] ELLEN VESTA EMERY	0,1
16. ANDREW JOHNSON*	Dec. 29, 1808	July 31, 1875	Raleigh, N.C.	Tenn.	Dem.‡	1865	ELIZA MCCARDLE	5
17. SCHUYLER COLFAX	Mar. 23, 1823	Jan. 13, 1885	New York, N.Y.	Ind.	Rep.	1869–1873	[1] EVELYN CLARK [2] ELLEN W. WADE	0,0
18. HENRY WILSON†	Feb. 16, 1812	Nov. 22, 1875	Farmington, N.H.	Mass.	Rep.	1873–1875	HARRIET MALVINA HOWE	1
19. WILLIAM A. WHEELER	June 30, 1819	June 4, 1887	Malone, N.Y.	N.Y.	Rep.	1877–1881	MARY KING	0
20. CHESTER A. ARTHUR*	Oct. 5, 1830	Nov. 18, 1886	Fairfield, Vt.	N.Y.	Rep.	1881	ELLEN LEWIS HERNDON	3
21. THOMAS A. HENDRICKS†	Sept. 7, 1819	Nov. 25, 1885	Muskingham Co., Ohio	Ind.	Dem.	1885	ELIZA C. MARGAN	1
22. LEVI P. MORTON	May 16, 1824	May 16, 1920	Shoreham, Vt.	N.Y.	Rep.	1889–1893	[1] LUCY YOUNG KIMBALL [2] ANNA LIVINGSTON READ STREET	0,5
23. ADLAI E. STEVENSON	Oct. 23, 1835	June 15, 1914	Christian Co., Ky.	Ill.	Dem.	1893–1897	LETITIA GREEN	1
24. GARRET A. HOBART†	June 3, 1844	Nov. 21, 1899	Long Branch, N.J.	N.J.	Rep.	1897–1899	JENNIE TUTTLE	2
25. THEODORE ROOSEVELT*	Oct. 27, 1858	Jan. 6, 1919	New York, N.Y.	N.Y.	Rep.	1901	[1] ALICE HATHAWAY LEE [2] EDITH KERMIT CAROW	1,5
26. CHARLES W. FAIRBANKS	May 11, 1852	June 4, 1918	Unionville Centre, Ohio	Ind.	Rep.	1905–1909	CORNELIA COLE	5
27. JAMES S. SHERMAN†	Oct. 24, 1855	Oct. 30, 1912	Utica, N.Y.	N.Y.	Rep.	1909–1912	CARRIE BABCOCK	3
28. THOMAS R. MARSHALL	Mar. 14, 1854	June 1, 1925	N. Manchester, Ind.	Ind.	Dem.	1913–1921	LOIS I. KIMSEY	0
29. CALVIN COOLIDGE*	July 4, 1872	Jan. 5, 1933	Plymouth, Vt.	Mass.	Rep.	1921–1923	GRACE A. GOODHUE	2
30. CHARLES G. DAWES	Aug. 27, 1865	Apr. 23, 1951	Marietta, Ohio	Ill.	Rep.	1925–1929	CARO D. BLYMER	4
31. CHARLES CURTIS	Jan. 25, 1860	Feb. 8, 1936	Topeka, Kan.	Kan.	Rep.	1929–1933	ANNA E. BAIRD	3
32. JOHN NANCE GARNER	Nov. 22, 1868	Nov. 7, 1967	Red River Co., Tex.	Tex.	Dem.	1933–1941	ETTIE RHEINER	1
33. HENRY AGARD WALLACE	Oct. 7, 1888	Nov. 18, 1965	Adair Co., Iowa	Iowa	Dem.	1941–1945	ILO BROWNE	3
34. HARRY S TRUMAN*	May 8, 1884		Lamar, Mo.	Mo.	Dem.	1945	ELIZABETH VIRGINIA WALLACE	1
35. ALBEN W. BARKLEY	Nov. 24, 1877	Apr. 30, 1956	Graves Co., Ky.	Ky.	Dem.	1949–1953	[1] DOROTHY BROWER [2] JANE HADLEY	3,0
36. RICHARD M. NIXON	Jan. 9, 1913		Yorba Linda, Calif.	Calif.	Rep.	1953–1961	THELMA PATRICIA RYAN	2
37. LYNDON B. JOHNSON*	Aug. 27, 1908		Johnson City, Tex.	Tex.	Dem.	1961–1963	CLAUDIA ALTA TAYLOR	2
38. HUBERT H. HUMPHREY	May 27, 1911		Wallace, S. Dak.	Minn.	Dem.	1965–1969	MURIEL FAY BUCK	4
39. SPIRO T. AGNEW	Nov. 9, 1918		Baltimore, Md.	Md.	Rep.	1969–	ELINOR ISOBEL JUDEFIND	4

*Succeeded to Presidency †Died in office ‡Elected on the Union party ticket

The Declaration of Independence

In CONGRESS, July 4, 1776.
A DECLARATION by the REPRESENTATIVES of the UNITED STATES OF AMERICA,
In GENERAL CONGRESS assembled.

WHEN in the Course of human Events, it becomes necessary for one People to dissolve the Political Bands which have connected them with another, and to assume among the Powers of the Earth, the separate and equal Station to which the Laws of Nature and of Nature's God entitle them, a decent Respect to the Opinions of Mankind requires that they should declare the causes which impel them to the Separation.

We hold these Truths to be self-evident, that all Men are created equal, that they are endowed by their Creator with certain unalienable Rights, that among these are Life, Liberty, and the Pursuit of Happiness—That to secure these Rights, Governments are instituted among Men, deriving their just Powers from the Consent of the Governed, that whenever any Form of Government becomes destructive of these Ends, it is the Right of the People to alter or to abolish it, and to institute new Government, laying its Foundation on such Principles, and organizing its Powers in such Form, as to them shall seem most likely to effect their Safety and Happiness. Prudence, indeed, will dictate that Governments long established should not be changed for light and transient Causes; and accordingly all Experience hath shewn, that Mankind are more disposed to suffer, while Evils are sufferable, than to right themselves by abolishing the Forms to which they are accustomed. But when a long Train of Abuses and Usurpations, pursuing invariably the same Object, evinces a Design to reduce them under absolute Despotism, it is their Right, it is their Duty, to throw off such Government, and to provide new Guards for their future Security. Such has been the patient Sufferance of these Colonies; and such is now the Necessity which constrains them to alter their former Systems of Government. The History of the present King of Great-Britain is a History of repeated Injuries and Usurpations, all having in direct Object the Establishment of an absolute Tyranny over these States. To prove this, let Facts be submitted to a candid World.

He has refused his Assent to Laws, the most wholesome and necessary for the public Good.

He has forbidden his Governors to pass Laws of immediate and pressing Importance, unless suspended in their Operation till his Assent should be obtained; and when so suspended, he has utterly neglected to attend to them.

He has refused to pass other Laws for the Accommodation of large Districts of People, unless those People would relinquish the Right of Representation in the Legislature, a Right inestimable to them, and formidable to Tyrants only.

He has called together Legislative Bodies at Places unusual, uncomfortable, and distant from the Depository of their public Records, for the sole Purpose of fatiguing them into Compliance with his Measures.

He has dissolved Representative Houses repeatedly, for opposing with manly Firmness his Invasions on the Rights of the People.

He has refused for a long Time, after such Dissolutions, to cause others to be elected; whereby the Legislative Powers, incapable of Annihilation, have returned to the People at large for their exercise; the State remaining in the mean time exposed to all the Dangers of Invasion from without, and Convulsions within.

He has endeavoured to prevent the Population of these States; for that Purpose obstructing the Laws for Naturalization of Foreigners; refusing to pass others to encourage their Migrations hither, and raising the Conditions of new Appropriations of Lands.

He has obstructed the Administration of Justice, by refusing his Assent to Laws for establishing Judiciary Powers.

He has made Judges dependent on his Will alone, for the Tenure of their Offices, and the Amount and Payment of their Salaries.

He has erected a Multitude of new Offices, and sent hither Swarms of Officers to harrass our People, and eat out their Substance.

He has kept among us, in Times of Peace, Standing Armies, without the consent of our Legislatures.

He has affected to render the Military independent of and superior to the Civil Power.

He has combined with others to subject us to a Jurisdiction foreign to our Constitution, and unacknowledged by our Laws; giving his Assent to their Acts of pretended Legislation:

For quartering large Bodies of Armed Troops among us:

For protecting them, by a mock Trial, from Punishment for any Murders which they should commit on the Inhabitants of these States:

For cutting off our Trade with all Parts of the World:

For imposing Taxes on us without our Consent:

For depriving us, in many Cases, of the Benefits of Trial by Jury:

For transporting us beyond Seas to be tried for pretended Offences:

For abolishing the free System of English Laws in a neighbouring Province, establishing therein an arbitrary Government, and enlarging its Boundaries, so as to render it at once an Example and fit Instrument for introducing the same absolute Rule into these Colonies:

For taking away our Charters, abolishing our most valuable Laws, and altering fundamentally the Forms of our Governments:

For suspending our own Legislatures, and declaring themselves invested with Power to legislate for us in all Cases whatsoever.

He has abdicated Government here, by declaring us out of his Protection and waging War against us.

He has plundered our Seas, ravaged our Coasts, burnt our Towns, and destroyed the Lives of our People.

He is, at this Time, transporting large Armies of foreign Mercenaries to compleat the Works of Death,

Desolation, and Tyranny, already begun with circumstances of Cruelty and Perfidy, scarcely paralleled in the most barbarous Ages, and totally unworthy the Head of a civilized Nation.

HE has constrained our fellow Citizens taken Captive on the high Seas to bear Arms against their Country, to become the Executioners of their Friends and Brethren, or to fall themselves by their Hands.

HE has excited domestic Insurrections amongst us, and has endeavoured to bring on the Inhabitants of our Frontiers, the merciless Indian Savages, whose known Rule of Warfare, is an undistinguished Destruction, of all Ages, Sexes and Conditions.

IN every stage of these Oppressions we have Petitioned for Redress in the most humble Terms: Our repeated Petitions have been answered only by repeated Injury. A Prince, whose Character is thus marked by every act which may define a Tyrant, is unfit to be the Ruler of a free People.

NOR have we been wanting in Attentions to our British Brethren. We have warned them from Time to Time of Attempts by their Legislature to extend an unwarrantable Jurisdiction over us. We have reminded them of the Circumstances of our Emigration and Settlement here. We have appealed to their native Justice and Magnanimity, and we have conjured them by the Ties of our common Kindred to disavow these Usurpations, which, would inevitably interrupt our Connections and Correspondence. They too have been deaf to the Voice of Justice and of Consanguinity. We must, therefore, acquiesce in the Necessity, which denounces our Separation, and hold them, as we hold the rest of Mankind, Enemies in War, in Peace, Friends.

WE, therefore, the Representatives of the UNITED STATES OF AMERICA, in GENERAL CONGRESS, Assembled, appealing to the Supreme Judge of the World for the Rectitude of our Intentions, do, in the Name, and by Authority of the good People of these Colonies, solemnly Publish and Declare, That these United Colonies are, and of Right ought to be, FREE AND INDEPENDENT STATES; that they are absolved from all Allegiance to the British Crown, and that all political Connection between them and the State of Great-Britain, is and ought to be totally dissolved; and that as FREE AND INDEPENDENT STATES, they have full Power to levy War, conclude Peace, contract Alliances, establish Commerce, and to do all other Acts and Things which INDEPENDENT STATES may of right do. And for the support of this Declaration, with a firm Reliance on the Protection of divine Providence, we mutually pledge to each other our Lives, our Fortunes, and our sacred Honor.

Signed by ORDER AND IN BEHALF *of the* CONGRESS,
JOHN HANCOCK, PRESIDENT.

ATTEST.
CHARLES THOMSON, SECRETARY.

States of the United States

State	Population 1960 Census	Total Area Sq. Miles	Land Area Only Sq. Miles	Population per Sq. Mile	Capital
Alabama	3,266,740	51,609	51,060	64.0	Montgomery
Alaska	226,167	586,400	571,065	0.4	Juneau
Arizona	1,302,161	113,909	113,575	11.5	Phoenix
Arkansas	1,786,272	53,103	52,499	34.0	Little Rock
California	15,717,204	158,693	156,573	100.4	Sacramento
Colorado	1,753,947	104,247	103,884	16.9	Denver
Connecticut	2,535,234	5,009	4,899	517.5	Hartford
Delaware	446,292	2,057	1,978	225.6	Dover
Dist. of Columbia	763,957	69	61	12,523.9	(Washington)·
Florida	4,951,560	58,560	54,252	91.3	Tallahassee
Georgia	3,943,116	58,876	58,274	67.7	Atlanta
Hawaii	632,772	6,454	6,415	98.6	Honolulu
Idaho	667,191	83,557	82,708	8.1	Boise
Illinois	10,081,158	56,400	55,930	180.3	Springfield
Indiana	4,662,498	36,291	36,185	128.9	Indianapolis
Iowa	2,757,537	56,280	56,032	49.2	Des Moines
Kansas	2,178,611	82,276	82,048	26.6	Topeka
Kentucky	3,038,156	40,395	39,863	76.2	Frankfort
Louisiana	3,257,022	48,522	45,106	72.2	Baton Rouge
Maine	969,265	33,215	31,012	31.3	Augusta
Maryland	3,100,689	10,577	9,874	314.0	Annapolis
Massachusetts	5,148,578	8,257	7,867	654.5	Boston
Michigan	7,823,194	58,216	57,019	137.2	Lansing
Minnesota	3,413,864	84,068	80,009	42.7	St. Paul
Mississippi	2,178,141	47,716	47,223	46.1	Jackson
Missouri	4,319,813	69,674	69,138	62.5	Jefferson City
Montana	674,767	147,138	145,736	4.6	Helena
Nebraska	1,411,330	77,237	76,612	18.4	Lincoln
Nevada	285,278	110,540	109,788	2.6	Carson City
New Hampshire	606,921	9,304	9,014	67.3	Concord
New Jersey	6,066,782	7,836	7,521	806.7	Trenton
New Mexico	951,023	121,666	121,510	7.8	Santa Fe
New York	16,782,304	49,576	47,939	350.1	Albany
North Carolina	4,556,155	52,712	49,067	92.9	Raleigh
North Dakota	632,446	70,665	69,457	9.1	Bismarck
Ohio	9,706,397	41,222	40,972	236.9	Columbus
Oklahoma	2,328,284	69,919	68,887	33.8	Oklahoma City
Oregon	1,768,687	96,981	96,248	18.4	Salem
Pennsylvania	11,319,366	45,333	45,007	251.5	Harrisburg
Rhode Island	859,488	1,214	1,058	812.4	Providence
South Carolina	2,382,594	31,055	30,272	78.7	Columbia
South Dakota	680,514	77,047	76,378	8.9	Pierre
Tennessee	3,567,089	42,246	41,762	85.4	Nashville
Texas	9,579,677	267,339	262,840	36.5	Austin
Utah	890,627	84,916	82,339	10.8	Salt Lake City
Vermont	389,881	9,609	9,276	42.0	Montpelier
Virginia	3,966,949	40,815	39,838	99.6	Richmond
Washington	2,853,214	68,192	66,709	42.8	Olympia
West Virginia	1,860,421	24,181	24,079	77.3	Charleston
Wisconsin	3,951,777	56,154	54,705	72.2	Madison
Wyoming	330,066	97,914	97,411	3.4	Cheyenne

States of the United States

Noun for Inhabitant	State Nickname	State Flower	Largest City
Alabamian	Cotton State	Camellia	Birmingham
Alaskan	Mainland State	Forget-me-not	Anchorage
Arizonan	Apache State	Giant Cactus	Phoenix
Arkansan	Bear State	Apple Blossom	Little Rock
Californian	Golden State	Golden Poppy	Los Angeles
Coloradan	Centennial State	Columbine	Denver
Nutmegger	Nutmeg State	Mountain Laurel	Hartford
Delawarean	Diamond State	Peach Blossom	Wilmington
Washingtonian	—	American Beauty Rose	Washington
Floridian	Everglade State	Orange Blossom	Miami
Georgian	Empire State of the South	Cherokee Rose	Atlanta
Hawaiian	Aloha State	Hibiscus	Honolulu
Idahoan	Gem State	Lewis Mockorange	Boise
Illinoisan	Prairie State	Butterfly Violet	Chicago
Hoosier	Hoosier State	Peony	Indianapolis
Iowan	Hawkeye State	Wild Prairie Rose	Des Moines
Kansan	Sunflower State	Sunflower	Wichita
Kentuckian	Bluegrass State	Goldenrod	Louisville
Louisianian	Pelican State	Magnolia Grandiflora	New Orleans
Downeaster	Pine Tree State	Pine Cone and Tassel	Portland
Marylander	Old Line State	Black-eyed Susan	Baltimore
Bay Stater	Bay State	Trailing Arbutus	Boston
Michigander	Wolverine State	Apple Blossom	Detroit
Minnesotan	Gopher State	Moccasin Flower	Minneapolis
Mississippian	Magnolia State	Magnolia	Jackson
Missourian	Bullion State	Hawthorn	St. Louis
Montanan	Treasure State	Bitterroot Lewisia	Great Falls
Nebraskan	Cornhusker State	Goldenrod	Omaha
Nevadan	Silver State	Sagebrush	Las Vegas
New Hampshirite	Granite State	Purple Lilac	Manchester
New Jerseyite	Garden State	Purple Violet	Newark
New Mexican	Sunshine State	Yucca	Albuquerque
New Yorker	Empire State	Rose	New York
North Carolinian	Old North State	Dogwood	Charlotte
North Dakotan	Flickertail State	Prairie Rose	Fargo
Ohioan	Buckeye State	Scarlet Carnation	Cleveland
Oklahoman	Sooner State	Mistletoe	Oklahoma City
Oregonian	Sunset State	Oregon Grape	Portland.
Pennsylvanian	Keystone State	Mountain Laurel	Philadelphia
Rhode Islander	Little Rhody	Violet	Providence
South Carolinian	Palmetto State	Carolina Jessamine	Columbia
South Dakotan	Sunshine State	Pasque	Sioux Falls
Tennessean	Volunteer State	Iris	Memphis
Texan	Lone-Star State	Bluebonnet	Houston
Utahn	Mormon State	Blue Spruce	Salt Lake City
Vermonter	Green Mountain State	Red Clover	Burlington
Virginian	Old Dominion State	American Dogwood	Norfolk
Washingtonian	Evergreen State	Rhododendron	Seattle
West Virginian	Panhandle State	Rosebay Rhododendron	Charleston
Wisconsinite	Badger State	Butterfly Violet	Milwaukee
Wyomingite	Equality State	Indian Paintbrush	Cheyenne

Independent States of the World

Short Form	Long Form	Population (000)	Area in Sq. Mi. (000)	Capital
Afghanistan	Kingdom of Afghanistan	13,150	250	Kabul
Albania	People's Republic of Albania	1,507	11	Tirana
Algeria	Democratic and Popular Republic of Algeria	9,925	919	Algiers
Andorra	—	7	(191)	Andorra
Argentina	Argentine Republic	20,959	1,084	Buenos Aires
Australia	Commonwealth of Australia	10,508	2,975	Canberra
Austria	Federal Republic of Austria	7,060	32	Vienna
Belgium	Kingdom of Belgium	9,229	12	Brussels
Bhutan	Kingdom of Bhutan	660	19	Thimbu
Bolivia	Republic of Bolivia	3,416	404	La Paz
Brazil	United States of Brazil	66,302	3,286	Brasilia
Bulgaria	People's Republic of Bulgaria	7,614	43	Sofia
Burma	Union of Burma	20,662	262	Rangoon
Burundi	Kingdom of Burundi	2,213	11	Usumbura
Cambodia	Kingdom of Cambodia	4,845	70	Phnom penh
Cameroon	Federal Republic of Cameroon	3,225	183	Yaounde
Canada	Dominion of Canada	18,238	3,690	Ottawa
—	Central African Republic	1,177	238	Bangui
Ceylon	Dominion of Ceylon	10,625	25	Colombo
Chad	Republic of Chad	2,730	501	Fort-Lamy
Chile	Republic of Chile	8,515	286	Santiago
China (mainland)	People's Republic of China	646,530	3,692	Peking
China (Taiwan)	Republic of China	12,180	14	Taipei
Colombia	Republic of Colombia	14,447	440	Bogotá
Congo	Republic of Congo (Brazzaville)	780	132	Brazzaville
—	Democratic Republic of the Congo (Léopoldville)	13,653	905	Leopoldville
Costa Rica	Republic of Costa Rica	1,199	19	San Jose
Cuba	Republic of Cuba	6,743	44	Havana
Cyprus	Republic of Cyprus	562	4	Nicosia
Czechoslovakia	Czechoslovak Socialist Republic	13,951	49	Prague
Dahomey	Republic of Dahomey	1,719	44	Porto Novo
Denmark	Kingdom of Denmark	4,585	17	Copenhagen
—	Dominican Republic	3,014	19	Santo Domingo
East Germany	German Democratic Republic	17,286	42	Berlin (East)
Ecuador	Republic of Ecuador	4,116	105	Quito
El Salvador	Republic of El Salvador	2,824	13	San Salvador
Ethiopia	Empire of Ethiopia	21,462	409	Addis Ababa
Finland	Republic of Finland	4,600	130	Helsinki
France	French Republic	46,520	213	Paris
Gabon	Gabon Republic	403	102	Libreville
Gambia, The	—	290	4	Bathurst
Germany	See East Germany, West Germany			
Ghana	Republic of Ghana	6,691	92	Accra
Greece	Kingdom of Greece	8,350	50	Athens
Guatemala	Republic of Guatemala	3,759	42	Guatemala City
Guinea	Republic of Guinea	2,727	97	Conakry
Haiti	Republic of Haiti	3,505	11	Port-au-Prince
Honduras	Republic of Honduras	1,885	43	Tegucigalpa
Hungary	Hungarian People's Republic	10,119	36	Budapest
Iceland	Republic of Iceland	189	40	Reykjavik
India	Republic of India	439,073	1,247	New Delhi
Indonesia	Republic of Indonesia	97,085	580	Djakarta
Iran	Empire of Iran	22,860	635	Teheran
Iraq	Republic of Iraq	8,262	172	Baghdad
Ireland	Irish Republic or Republic of Ireland	2,818	27	Dublin
Israel	State of Israel	2,430	8	Jerusalem
Italy	Italian Republic	50,464	116	Rome

Independent States of the World

Short Form	Long Form	Population (000)	Area in Sq. Mi. (000)	Capital
Ivory Coast	Republic of Ivory Coast	3,800	128	Abidjan
Jamaica	—	1,607	4	Kingston
Japan	—	93,406	142	Tokyo
Jordan	Hashemite Kingdom of Jordan	1,860	37	Amman
Kenya	Republic of Kenya	6,551	223	Nairobi
Korea	See North Korea, South Korea			
Kuwait	State of Kuwait	468	8	Kuwait
Laos	Kingdom of Laos	1,760	92	Vientiane
Lebanon	Republic of Lebanon	2,200	4	Beirut
Liberia	Republic of Liberia	1,250	43	Monrovia
Libya	United Kingdom of Libya	1,559	679	Benghazi Tripoli
Liechtenstein	Principality of Liechtenstein	16	(65)	Vaduz
Luxembourg	Grand Duchy of Luxembourg	313	1	Luxembourg
Madagascar	Malagasy Republic	5,298	228	Tananarive
Malawi	—	2,600	49	Zomba
Malaysia	—	8,487	126	Kuala Lumpur
Mali	Republic of Mali	4,200	464	Bamako
Malta	—	329	(121)	Valletta
Mauritania	Islamic Republic of Mauritania	730	418	Nouakchott
Mexico	United Mexican States	34,626	760	Mexico City
Monaco	Principality of Monaco	22	(0.5)	Monaco
Mongolia	Mongolian People's Republic	910	600	Ulan Bator
Morocco	Kingdom of Morocco	11,626	172	Rabat
Muscat and Oman	Sultanate of Muscat and Oman and Dependencies	550	82	Muscat
Nepal	Kingdom of Nepal	9,044	54	Katmandu
Netherlands	Kingdom of the Netherlands	11,417	13	Amsterdam
New Zealand	Dominion of New Zealand	2,594	103	Wellington
Nicaragua	Republic of Nicaragua	1,450	57	Managua
Niger	Republic of Niger	2,850	459	Niamey
Nigeria	Federation of Nigeria	34,296	360	Lagos
North Korea	Democratic People's Republic of Korea	9,770	50	Pyongyang
North Vietnam	Democratic Republic of Vietnam[4]	14,900	60	Hanoi
Norway	Kingdom of Norway	3,540	125	Oslo
Pakistan	Republic of Pakistan	93,812	365	Rawalpindi
Panama	Republic of Panama	1,067	29	Panama (city)
Paraguay	Republic of Paraguay	1,817	157	Asunción
Peru	Republic of Peru	10,364	496	Lima
Philippines	Republic of the Philippines	27,088	115	Manila
Poland	Polish People's Republic	30,940	121	Warsaw
Portugal	Republic of Portugal	9,130	35	Lisbon
Rumania	Rumanian People's Republic	18,927	92	Bucharest
Rwanda	Republic of Rwanda	2,634	10	Kigali
San Marino	Republic of San Marino	15	(38)	San Marino
Saudi Arabia	Kingdom of Saudi Arabia	6,036	600	Riyadh
Senegal	Republic of Senegal	3,400	76	Dakar
Sierra Leone	—	2,180	28	Freetown
Singapore	—	1,634	(220)	Singapore
Somalia	Somali Republic	1,990	246	Mogadiscio
South Africa	Republic of South Africa	15,983	472	Pretoria
South Korea	Republic of Korea	24,944	37	Seoul
South Vietnam	Republic of Vietnam	13,960	66	Saigon
Soviet Union	Union of Soviet Socialist Republics	214,400	8,650	Moscow
Spain	(The) Spanish State	31,077	195	Madrid
Sudan	Republic of the Sudan	11,615	967	Khartoum
Sweden	Kingdom of Sweden	7,777	173	Stockholm
Switzerland	Swiss Confederation	5,429	16	Bern
Syria	Syrian Arab Republic	5,180	71	Damascus
Taiwan	See China			
Tanzania	United Republic of Tanzania	10,179	363	Dar es Salaam

Short Form	Long Form	Population (000)	Area in Sq. Mi. (000)	Capital
Thailand	Kingdom of Thailand	22,718	198	Bangkok
Togo	Republic of Togo	1,424	22	Lomé
Trinidad and Tobago	—	765	2	Port-o1-Spain
Tunisia	Republic of Tunisia	3,954	48	Tunis
Turkey	Republic of Turkey	31,391	296	Ankara
Uganda	—	7,190	94	Kampala
—	United Arab Republic (Egypt)	26,059	386	Cairo
United Kingdom	United Kingdom of Great Britain and Northern Ireland	52,720	93	London
United States	United States of America	179,323	3,680	Washington
Upper Volta	Republic of Upper Volta	3,472	106	Ouagadougou
Uruguay	Oriental Republic of Uruguay	2,803	72	Montevideo
Vatican City	State of the Vatican City	1	(0.2)	Vatican City
Venezuela	Republic of Venezuela	7,533	352	Caracas
Vietnam	See North Vietnam, South Vietnam			
Western Samoa	The Independent State of Western Samoa	110	1	Apia
West Germany	Federal Republic of Germany	57,588	95	Bonn
Yemen	Yemen Arab Republic	4,500	75	San'a
Yugoslavia	Socialist Federal Republic of Yugoslavia	19,065	99	Belgrade
Zambia	Republic of Zambia	2,360	288	Lusaka

Major Rivers of the World

River	Countries of Transit	Outflow	Length in Miles
Nile	Uganda-Sudan-United Arab Republic	Mediterranean	4,000
Missouri-Mississippi	United States	Gulf of Mexico	3,988
Amazon	Peru-Brazil	Atlantic	3,900
Yangtze	China	East China Sea	3,200
Congo	Democratic Republic of the Congo-Republic of Congo	Atlantic	3,000
Lena	Soviet Union	Arctic Ocean	2,800
Yenisei	Soviet Union	Arctic Ocean	2,800
Hwang Ho	China	Gulf of Chihli	2,800
Missouri	United States	Mississippi River	2,723
Amur	China-Soviet Union	Tartary Strait	2,700
Mekong	China-Burma-Thailand-Laos-Cambodia	South China Sea	2,600
Niger	Guinea-Mali-Niger-Dahomey-Nigeria	Gulf of Guinea	2,600
Mackenzie	Canada	Beaufort Sea	2,525
Ob	Soviet Union	Gulf of Ob	2,500
Mississippi	United States	Gulf of Mexico	2,470
Parana	Brazil-Paraguay-Argentina	Rio de la Plata	2,450
Volga	Soviet Union	Caspian Sea	2,325
Madeira	Brazil	Amazon River	2,100
Purus	Brazil	Amazon River	2,000
Yukon	Canada-United States	Bering Sea	2,000
Indus	Pakistan (West)	Arabian Sea	1,900
Irtish	Soviet Union	Ob River	1,840
Rio Grande	United States-Mexico	Gulf of Mexico	1,800
São Francisco	Brazil	Atlantic	1,800
Japura	Colombia-Brazil	Amazon River	1,750
Salween	China-Burma	Bay of Bengal	1,750
Danube	West Germany-Austria-Czechoslovakia-Hungary-Yugoslavia-Rumania-Bulgaria-Soviet Union	Black Sea	1,725
Euphrates	Turkey-Syria-Iraq	Persian Gulf	1,700
Brahmaputra	China-India-Pakistan (East)	Bay of Bengal	1,700
Tocantins	Brazil	Para River	1,700
Zambezi	Angola-Zambia Southern Rhodesia-Mozambique	Indian Ocean	1,650
Orinoco	Venezuela-Colombia	Atlantic	1,600
Ganges	India	Bay of Bengal	1,550
Aldan	Soviet Union	Lena River	1,500
Paraguay	Brazil-Paraguay-Argentina	Paraná River	1,500
Arkansas	United States	Mississippi River	1,450
Colorado	United States-Mexico	Gulf of California	1,450
Amu Darya	Soviet Union	Aral Sea	1,400

Major Rivers of the World

River	Countries of Transit	Outflow	Length in Miles
Dnieper	Soviet Union	Black Sea	1,400
Negro	Colombia-Brazil	Amazon River	1,400
Ural	Soviet Union	Caspian Sea	1,400
Orange	Lesotho-South Africa-South-West Africa	Atlantic	1,300
Syr Darya	Soviet Union	Aral Sea	1,300
Xingú	Brazil	Amazon River	1,300
Irrawaddy	Burma	Bay of Bengal	1,250
Si	China	South China Sea	1,250
Columbia	Canada-United States	Pacific	1,215
Saskatchewan	Canada	Lake Winnipeg	1,205
Kama	Soviet Union	Volga	1,200
Don	Soviet Union	Sea of Azov	1,200
Juruá	Peru-Brazil	Amazon	1,200
Murray	Australia	Indian Ocean	1,200
Red	United States	Mississippi River	1,200
Salado	Argentina	Paraná River	1,200
Ucayali	Peru	Amazon River	1,200
Darling	Australia	Murray River	1,160
Angara	Soviet Union	Yenisei River	1,151
Tigris	Turkey-Syria-Iraq	Euphrates River	1,150
Araguaya	Brazil	Tocantins River	1,100
Pechora	Soviet Union	Arctic Ocean	1,100
Magdalena	Colombia	Caribbean Sea	1,060
Peace	Canada	Slave River	1,050
Snake	United States	Columbia River	1,038
Churchill	Canada	Hudson Bay	1,000
Kolyma	Soviet Union	Arctic Ocean	1,000
Marañón	Peru	Amazon	1,000
Pilcomayo	Bolivia-Argentina-Paraguay	Paraguay River	1,000
Senegal	Mali-Mauritania-Senegal	Atlantic	1,000
Ohio	United States	Mississippi	981
Uruguay	Brazil-Argentina-Uruguay	Rio de la Plata	981
Oka	Soviet Union	Volga River	950
Rio Theodore Roosevelt	Brazil	Madeira River	950
Canadian	United States	Arkansas River	906
Godavari	India	Bay of Bengal	900
Parnahiba	Brazil	Atlantic	900
Dniester	Soviet Union	Black Sea	875
Brazos	United States	Gulf of Mexico	870
Colorado (Texas)	United States	Gulf of Mexico	840
Rhine	Switzerland-West Germany-France-Netherlands	North Sea	820
Narbada	India	Arabian Sea	800
Sungari	China	Amur River	800
Tisza	Hungary-Yugoslavia	Danube River	800
Tobol	Soviet Union	Irtish River	800
Athabaska	Canada	Lake Athabaska	765
St. Lawrence	United States-Canada	Gulf of St. Lawrence	760
Pecos	United States	Rio Grande	735
Green	United States	Colorado River	730
Elbe	Czechoslovakia-East Germany-West		

Major Rivers of the World

River	Countries of Transit	Outflow	Length in Miles
	Germany	North Sea	725
James	United States	Missouri River	710
Negro	Argentina	Atlantic	700
Fraser	Canada	Pacific	695
White	United States	Mississippi River	690
Cumberland	United States	Ohio River	687
Ottawa	Canada	St. Lawrence River	685
Yellowstone	United States	Missouri River	671
Tennessee	United States	Ohio River	652
Donets	Soviet Union	Don River	650
Vistula	Poland	Baltic Sea	650
Dvina	Soviet Union	Baltic Sea	640
Gila	United States	Colorado River	630
Loire	France	Atlantic	625
Milk	United States	Missouri River	624
North Platte	United States	Platte River	618
Albany	Canada	Hudson Bay	610
Back	Canada	Arctic Ocean	605
Ouachita	United States	Red River	605
Cimarron	United States	Arkansas River	600
Meuse	France-Belgium-Netherlands	North Sea	575
Tagus	Spain-Portugal	Atlantic	566
Little Missouri	United States	Missouri River	560
Oder	Poland-East Germany	Baltic Sea	550
Red (of the North)	United States-Canada	Lake Winnipeg	545
Smoky Hill	United States	Kansas River	540
Bug, Southern	Soviet Union	Dnieper Bay	530
Des Moines	United States	Mississippi	530
Tombigbee	United States	Mobile River	525
Rhone	Switzerland-France	Mediterranean	504
Cheyenne	United States	Missouri River	500
Gambia	Guinea-Senegal-The Gambia	Atlantic	500
Osage	United States	Missouri River	500
Pearl	United States	Gulf of Mexico	485
Seine	France	English Channel	480
Wabash	United States	Ohio River	475
Dvina, North	Soviet Union	White Sea	470
Ebro	Spain	Mediterranean	470
Neosho	United States	Arkansas River	460
Bug, Western	Soviet Union-Poland	Vistula River	450
Drava	Austria-Yugoslavia-Hungary	Danube River	450
Susquehanna	United States	Chesapeake Bay	444
Pee Dee	United States	Atlantic	435
Niobrara	United States	Missouri River	431
Wisconsin	United States	Mississippi River	430
St. Francis	United States	Mississippi River	425
South Platte	United States	Platte River	424
Republican	United States	Kansas River	422
Salmon	United States	Snake River	420
Po	Italy	Adriatic Sea	418
St. Johns	United States-Canada	Bay of Fundy	418
Sabine	United States	Gulf of Mexico	403
Kootenay	Canada-United States	Columbia River	400
Mures	Rumania-Hungary	Tisza River	400

Major Rivers of the World

River	Countries of Transit	Outflow	Length in Miles
Nelson	Canada	Hudson Bay	400
Sacramento	United States	San Francisco Bay	382
Roanoke	United States	Albemarle Sound	380
Powder	United States	Yellowstone River	375
Green (Kentucky)	United States	Ohio River	360
San Juan	United States	Colorado River	360
Trinity	United States	Galveston Bay	360
Garonne	France	Gironde	350
San Joaquin	United States	San Francisco Bay	350
James (Virginia)	United States	Chesapeake Bay	340
Nueces	United States	Corpus Christi Bay	338
Big Horn	United States	Yellowstone River	336
Minnesota	United States	Mississippi River	332
Big Black	United States	Mississippi River	330
Cedar	United States	Iowa River	329
Allegheny	United States	Ohio River	325
Marne	France	Seine River	325
St. Maurice	Canada	St. Lawrence River	325
Alabama	United States	Mobile River	315
Savannah	United States	Atlantic	314
Platte	United States	Missouri River	310
Hudson	United States	New York Bay	306
Tallahatchie	United States	Yazoo River	301
Little Colorado	United States	Colorado River	300
Rock	United States	Mississippi River	300
Weser	West Germany	North Sea	300
Delaware	United States	Delaware Bay	296
Iowa	United States	Mississippi River	291
Humboldt	United States	Humboldt Sink	290
Potomac	United States	Chesapeake Bay	287
Coosa	United States	Alabama River	286
John Day	United States	Columbia River	281
Black	United States	White River	280
Neches	United States	Sabine Lake	280
St. Johns	United States	Atlantic	276
Illinois	United States	Mississippi River	273
Tallapoosa	United States	Alabama River	268
Flint	United States	Apalachicola River	265
Grand	United States	Lake Michigan	260
Neuse	United States	Pamlico Sound	260
Kentucky	United States	Ohio River	259
New	United States	Kanawha River	255
Deschutes	United States	Columbia River	250
Klamath	United States	Pacific	250
Owyhee	United States	Snake River	250
Tiber	Italy	Mediterranean	244
Shannon	Ireland	Atlantic	240
Thames	United Kingdom	North Sea	209
Jordan	Lebanon-Israel-Jordan	Dead Sea	200
Río de la Plata	Argentina-Uruguay	Atlantic	185
Saguenay	Canada	St. Lawrence River	125

Major Mountain Peaks of the World

Name	Country	Range or Location	Altitude
Everest	Nepal-Tibet	Himalaya Mountains	29,028
K² (Godwin Austen)	Kashmir	Karakoram Range	28,250
Kanchenjunga	Nepal-Sikkim	Himalaya Mountains	28,146
Makalu	Nepal-Tibet	Himalaya Mountains	27,790
Dhaulagiri	Nepal	Himalaya Mountains	26,826
Nanga Parbat	Kashmir	Himalaya Mountains	26,660
Annapurna	Nepal	Himalaya Mountains	26,503
Gasherbrum	Kashmir	Karakoram Range	26,470
Gosainthan	Tibet	Himalaya Mountains	26,291
Nanda Devi	India	Himalaya Mountains	25,661
Rakaposhi	Kashmir	Karakoram Range	25,560
Kamet	India	Himalaya Mountains	25,447
Ulugh Muztagh	Tibet	Kunlun Mountains	25,340
Tirich Mir	Pakistan	Hindu Kush	25,230
Muz Tagh Ata	China	Muz Tagh Ata Mountains	24,757
Mount Communism (Stalin Peak)	Soviet Union	Pamir-Alay Mountains	24,590
Pobeda Peak	China-Soviet Union	Tien Shan	24,407
Aconcagua	Argentina	Andes	22,834
Siniolchu	Sikkim	Himalaya Mountains	22,600
Ojos del Salado	Argentina-Chile	Andes	22,572
Tupungato	Argentina-Chile	Andes	22,300
Pissis	Argentina	Andes	22,241
Mercedario	Argentina	Andes	22,210
Huascarán	Peru	Andes	22,205
Llullaillaco	Argentina-Chile	Andes	22,057
Yerupaja	Peru	Andes	21,758
Incahuasi	Argentina-Chile	Andes	21,719
Ancohuma	Bolivia	Andes	21,490
Illampu	Bolivia	Andes	21,276
Chimborazo	Ecuador	Andes	20,702
McKinley	United States	Alaska Range	20,300
Logan	Canada	St. Elias Range	19,850
Cotopaxi	Ecuador	Andes	19,498
North Peak	United States	Alaska Range	19,370
Kilimanjaro	Tanzania	Northern Tanzania	19,321
El Misti	Peru	Andes	19,200
Cristóbal Colón	Colombia	Sierra Nevada de Santa Marta	18,947
Huila	Colombia	Cordillera Central	18,700
Demavend	Iran	Elburz Mountains	18,606
Orizaba	Mexico	Sierra Madre Oriental	18,546
Elbrus	Soviet Union	Caucasus Mountains	18,465
St. Elias	Canada-United States	St. Elias Range	18,008
Popocatepetl	Mexico	Altiplano de Mexico	17,887
Ixtaccihuatl	Mexico	Altiplano de Mexico	17,342
Foraker	United States	Alaska Range	17,280
Dykh-Tau	Soviet Union	Caucasus Mountains	17,054
Kenya	Kenya	Central Kenya	17,040
Shkhara Tau	Soviet Union	Caucasus Mountains	17,040
Mt. Stanley	Congo-Uganda	Ruwenzori (Mts. of the Moon)	16,790

Mountain Peaks of the World

Name	Country	Range or Location	Altitude
Ararat	Turkey	Armenia	16,945
Kazbek	Soviet Union	Caucasus Mountains	16,541
La Columna	Venezuela	Andes	16,410
Carstensz	Indonesia	Nassau Mountains, West Irian	16,404
Blackburn	United States	Wrangell Mountains	16,140
Klyuchevskaya	Soviet Union	Kamchatka Peninsula	15,912
Mont Blanc	France	Alps	15,781
Wilhelmina	Indonesia	Orange Mountains, West Irian	15,584
Wilhelm	Australia	Bismarck Range, Territory of New Guinea	15,400
Tabun Bogdo (Khuitun)	Mongolia	Altai Mountains	15,266
Monte Rosa (Dufourspitze)	Italy-Switzerland	Pennine Alps	15,217
Ras Dashan	Ethiopia	Simyen Mountains	15,160
Weisshorn	Switzerland	Alps	14,804
Matterhorn	Switzerland	Alps	14,780
Kirkpatrick	(Antarctica)	Queen Alexandra Range	14,600
Whitney	United States	Sierra Nevadas	14,495
Elbert	United States	Sawatch Range, Rocky Mountains	14,431
Harvard	United States	Sawatch Range, Rocky Mountains	14,420
Massive	United States	Sawatch Range, Rocky Mountains	14,418
Rainier	United States	Cascade Range	14,408
Blanca Peak	United States	Sangre de Cristo Mountains, Rocky Mountains	14,390
Williamson	United States	Sierra Nevadas	14,375
Uncompahgre Peak	United States	San Juan Mountains, Rocky Mountains	14,301
Grays Peak	United States	Front Range, Rocky Mountains	14,274
Markham	(Antarctica)	Queen Elizabeth Range	14,270
Evans	United States	Central Colorado, Rocky Mountains	14,260
Longs Peak	United States	Rocky Mountain National Park	14,255
Nevada de Colima	Mexico	Jalisco	14,235
Shasta	United States	Sierra Nevadas	14,161
Pikes Peak	United States	Central Colorado, Rocky Mountains	14,108
Wade	(Antarctica)	Queen Maude Range	14,070
Finsteraarhorn	Switzerland	Alps	14,026
Humphreys	United States	Sierra Nevadas	13,972
Tsasata Bogdo Uula	Mongolia	Altai Mountains	13,865
Tajumulco	Guatemala	Sierra Madre	13,816
Gannett Peak	United States	Wind River Range	13,785
Mauna Kea	United States	Island of Hawaii	13,784
Grand Teton	United States	Teton Range	13,766
Mauna Loa	United States	Island of Hawaii	13,680
Jungfrau	Switzerland	Alps	13,668

Mountain Peaks of the World

Name	Country	Range or Location	Altitude
Toubkal, Djebel	Morocco	Atlas Mountains	13,665
Kings Peak	United States	Uinta Mountains	13,498
Kinabalu	Malaysia	Crocker Range, Sabah	13,455
Bangeta	Australia	Bismarck Range, Territory of New Guinea	13,454
Cameroon	Cameroon	West Cameroon	13,370
Lister	(Antarctica)	Royal Society Range	13,350
Waddington	Canada	Coast Mountains	13,260
Victoria	Australia	Owen Stanley Range, Territory of New Guinea	13,240
Erebus	(Antarctica)	Ross Island	13,202
Cloud Peak	United States	Big Horn Mountains	13,175
Wheeler Peak	United States	Snake Range	13,160
Frîdtjof Nansen (Franz Josef)	(Antarctica)	Queen Maùd Range	13,150
Boundary Peak	United States	White Mountains (Calif.-Nev.)	13,145
Robson	Canada	Canadian Rockies	12,972
Niitaka (Morrison)	Taiwan	Niitaka Range	12,956
Chirripó Grande	Costa Rica	Cordillera de Talamanca	12,861
Granite Peak	United States	South Central Montana	12,799
Humphreys Peak	United States	San Francisco Mountains (Ariz.)	12,670
Borah Peak	United States	Lost River Range	12,662
Kerintji	Indonesia	Barisan Mountains, Sumatra	12,467
Gross Glockner	Austria	Tyrolian Alps	12,461
Fuji	Japan	Central Honshu Island	12,395
Cook	New Zealand	Southern Alps	12,349
Rindjani	Indonesia	Lombok Island	12,224
Pico de Tenerife	Spain	Canary Islands	12,192
Gunnbjörn	Greenland	Gunnbjörn Mountains	12,139
Mahameru	Indonesia	Java	12,060
San Gorgonio	United States	San Bernardino Mountains	11,485
Munku Sardik	Mongolia-Soviet Union	Sayan Mountains	11,447
Thabana Ntlenyana	Lesotho	Drakensberg Mountains	11,425
Mulhacén	Spain	Sierra Nevadas	11,411
Rantemario	Indonesia	Celebes	11,286
Hood	United States	Cascade Range	11,253
Emi Koussi	Chad	Tibesti Mountains	11,201
Pico de Néthou	Spain	Pyrenees	11,165
Chiriquí	Panama	Talamanca Mountains	11,070
Humphreys	United States	Yellowstone National Park	11,019
Mont aux Sources	South Africa	Drakensberg Mountains	10,822
Etna	Italy	Eastern Sicily	10,758
Lassen Peak	United States	Sierra Nevadas	10,465
Trujillo (Tina)	Dominican Republic	Cordillera Central	10,200
Balbi	Solomon Islands	Emperor Range, Bougainville I.	10,171

Mountain Peaks of the World

Name	Country	Range or Location	Altitude
Qurnet es Saluda	Lebanon	Lebanon Mountains	10,125
Piton des Neiges	Réunion	Center of Réunion Island	10,069
Haleakala	United States	Island of Maui	10,032
Jebel Sham	Muscat and Oman	Jebel Akdar	9,900
Zugspitze	West Germany	Bavarian Alps	9,738
Olympus	Greece	Between Thessaly and Macedonia	9,730
Apo	Philippines	Mindanao	9,690
Pulog	Philippines	Luzon	9,689
Musala (Stalin Peak)	Bulgaria	Rhodope Mountains	9,597
Corno	Italy	Apennines	9,585
Tahat	Algeria	Ahaggar Mountains	9,574
Maromokotro	Madagascar	Tsaratanana Massif	9,468
Pico da Bandeira	Brazil	Brazilian Highlands	9,462
Santa Isabel	Fernando Po	Fernando Po Island	9,449
Triglav	Yugoslavia	Julian Alps	9,393
Cano	Cape Verde Islands	Fogo Island	9,281
Hermon	Lebanon-Syria	Anti-Lebanon Mountains	9,232
Ruapehu	New Zealand	Central North Island	9,175
Cinto	France	Corsica	8,891
Anai Mudi	India	Western Ghats	8,841
Massif de la Selle	Haiti	La Selle Mountains	8,793
Guadalupe Peak	United States	Sacramento Mountains (Texas)	8,751
Gerlachovka (Stalin Peak)	Czechoslovakia	Carpathian Mountains	8,737
Gabel Katherina	United Arab Republic	Sinai Peninsula	8,664
Angka Peak (Inthanon Peak)	Thailand	Thanon Tong Chai Range	8,452
Kwanmo (Kanbo)	Korea	Pai Tou Shan (northern Korea)	8,337
Negoi	Rumania	Transylvanian Alps	8,320
Pidurutalagala	Ceylon	Central Ceylon	8,294
Paricutín	Mexico	Altiplano de Mexico	8,200
Ida	Greece	Crete	8,193
Galdhöppigen	Norway	Dovre Fjell	8,097
Parnassus	Greece	Central Greece	8,068
Olympus	United States	Olympic Mountains	7,954
Santa Ana (Izalco)	El Salvador	Sierra Madre	7,825
Orohena	French Polynesia	Tahiti	7,618
Pico	Portugal	Azores	7,611
The Father (Ulawan)	Bismarck Archipelago	New Britain Island	7,546
Blue Mountain Peak	Jamaica	Blue Mountains	7,520
Asahi-dake	Japan	Hokkaido	7,513
Kosciusko	Australia	Australian Alps	7,316
Harney Peak	United States	Black Hills	7,242
Gunong Tahan	Malaysia	Kelantan and Pahang States	7,186
Monte Cimone	Italy	Apennines	7,096
Kebnekaise	Sweden	Kjölen Range	7,005

Mountain Peaks of the World

Name	Country	Range or Location	Altitude
Öraefajökull	Iceland	Vatna Jökull	6,952
Mitchell	United States	Appalachian Mountains	6,684
Clingman's Dome	United States	Great Smoky Mountains	6,642
Pico de São Tomé	St. Thomas and Principe	St. Thomas Island	6,640
Bogong	Australia	Australian Alps	6,516
Pico de Turquino	Cuba	Sierra Maestra	6,500
Olympus (Troodos)	Cyprus	Olympus Mountains	6,406
Washington	United States	White Mountains (New Hampshire)	6,293
Narodnaya (Naroda)	Soviet Union	Ural Mountains	6,184
Mauga Silisili	Western Samoa	Savaii Island	6,094
Panié	New Caledonia	Northeast New Caledonia	5,412
Marcy	United States	Adirondack Mountains	5,344
Round Mountain	Australia	New England Range	5,300
Bartle Frere	Australia	Atherton Plateau	5,287
Katahdin	United States	Central Maine	5,273
Great Barrington	Australia	Liverpool Range	5,200
Kawaikini	United States	Kauai Island, Hawaii	5,170
Hekla	Iceland	Southern Iceland	4,747
Pelée	Martinique	Northern Martinique Island	4,428
Ben Nevis	United Kingdom	Western Scotland	4,406
Mansfield	United States	Green Mountains	4,393
Haltia	Finland	Northwest Finland	4,343
Victoria	Fiji Islands	Viti Levu	4,341
Kilauea	United States	Island of Hawaii	4,040
Kaala Peak	United States	Island of Oahu, Hawaii	4,030
Jebel Jarmaq	Israel	Central Highlands	3,963
Vesuvius	Italy	Naples Area	3,900
Snowdon	United Kingdom	Northwest Wales	3,560
Carrantouhill	Republic of Ireland	Macgillycuddy's Reeks	3,414
Kekes	Hungary	Matra Mountains	3,330
Scafell Pike	United Kingdom	Cumbrians (Lake District)	3,210
Stromboli	Italy	Lipari Islands	3,040
Krakatau	Indonesia	Island in Sunda Strait	2,667
Carmel	Israel	Northwest Israel	1,818

Oceans and Seas of the World

Ocean or Sea	Area in Sq. Mi.	Location
Pacific Ocean	70,000,000	
Atlantic Ocean	31,530,000	
Indian Ocean	28,357,000	
Arctic Ocean	5,540,000	
Mediterranean Sea	1,145,000	Between Europe, Africa, and Asia
South China Sea	895,000	Part of North Pacific, off coast of Southeast Asia
Bering Sea	878,000	Part of North Pacific, between northern North America and northern Asia
Caribbean Sea	750,000	Between Central America, West Indies, and South America
Gulf of Mexico	700,000	Arm of North Atlantic, off southeast coast of North America
Sea of Okhotsk	582,000	Arm of North Pacific, off east coast of Asia
East China Sea	480,000	Part of North Pacific, off east coast of Asia
Yellow Sea	480,000	Part of North Pacific, off east coast of Asia
Sea of Japan	405,000	Arm of North Pacific, between Asia mainland and Japanese Isles
Hudson Bay	400,000	Northern North America
Andaman Sea	308,000	Part of Bay of Bengal (Indian Ocean), off south coast of Asia
North Sea	201,000	Arm of North Atlantic, off coast of Northwest Europe
Red Sea	170,000	Arm of Indian Ocean, between northern Africa and Arabian Peninsula
Black Sea	164,000	Southeast Europe-Southwest Asia
Baltic Sea	160,000	Northern Europe
Persian Gulf	92,200	Between Iran and Arabian Peninsula
Gulf of St. Lawrence	92,000	Arm of North Atlantic, between mainland of southeast Canada and Newfoundland
Gulf of California	62,600	Arm of North Pacific, between west coast of Mexico and peninsula of Lower California

不規則動詞表

(고딕체는 중요 단어, 이탤릭체는 고어)

原　　形	過　　去	過　去　分　詞
A abide (머물다, 거주하다)	abode, abided	abode, abided
arise (일어나다, 발생하다)	**arose**	**arisen** [ərízn]
awake (잠에서 깨다)	**awoke**	**awaked, awoke**
B backbite (뒤에서 욕하다)	backbit	backbitten, backbit
backslide (타락하다)	backslid	backslid, backslidden
be (am, is, are) (있다)	**was, were**	**been**
bear (운반하다, 버티다)	**bore**	**born, borne**
beat (치다, 때리다)	**beat**	**beaten, beat**
become (…가 되다)	**became**	**become**
befall (일어나다, 생기다)	befell	befallen
beget (생기게 하다)	begot	begotten, begot
begin (시작하다, 시작되다)	**began**	**begun**
behold (보다)	beheld	beheld
bend (굽다, 굽히다)	**bent**	**bent**
bereave (빼앗다)	bereaved, bereft	bereaved, bereft
beseech (탄원하다)	besought	besought
beset (포위하다, 괴롭히다)	beset	beset
bespeak (예약하다)	bespoke	bespoken, bespoke
bestrew (흩뿌리다)	bestrewed	bestrewed, bestrewn
bestride (걸터앉다)	bestrode, bestrid	bestridden, bestrid
bet (내기하다)	bet, betted	bet, betted
betake (호소하다, 해보다)	betook	betaken
bethink (생각하다)	bethought	bethought
bid (명하다)	**bade, bad**	**bidden, bid**
bide (기다리다, 살다)	bided, bode	bided
bind (묶다)	**bound**	**bound**
bite (물다, 물어 끊다)	**bit**	**bitten, bit**
bleed (출혈하다)	bled	bled
bless (은혜를 주다)	**blessed, blest** [blest]	**blessed, blest** [blest]
blow (불다)	**blew**	**blown**
break (깨뜨리다, 깨지다)	**broke**	**broken**
breed (키우다)	bred	bred
bring (가져오다)	**brought**	**brought**
broadcast (방송하다)	broadcast, broadcasted	broadcast, broadcasted
build (건축하다)	**built**	**built**
burn (타다, 태우다)	**burnt, burned**	**burnt, burned**
burst (과열하다, 터지다)	**burst**	**burst**
buy (사다)	**bought**	**bought**
C **can** (…할 수 있다)	**could** [kud]	───
cast (던지다)	**cast**	**cast**
catch (잡다)	**caught** [kɔːt]	**caught** [kɔːt]
chide (꾸짖다)	chided, chid	chided, chidden, chid
choose (선택하다, 뽑다)	**chose**	**chosen**
cleave (찢다, 찢어지다)	clove, cleft	cloven, cleft

原　　　形	過　去	過去分詞
cling (들러붙다)	clung	clung
clothe (옷을 입히다)	**clothed,** *clad*	**clothed,** *clad*
come (오다)	came	come
cost (…의 비용이 들다)	cost	cost
creep (기다, 포복하다)	crept	crept
curse (저주하다)	cursed, *curst*	cursed, *curst*
cut (끊다, 자르다)	cut	cut
D　dare (감히 …하다)	dared, *durst*	dared
deal (분배하다, 나누어 주다)	dealt	dealt
dig (파다)	dug	dug
do (하다)	did	done
draw (끌다, 그리다)	drew	drawn
dream (꿈을 꾸다)	dreamt, dreamed [dremt]	dreamt, dreamed [dremt]
drink (마시다)	drank	drunk
drive (운전하다)	drove	driven [drívn]
drop (떨어뜨리다, 떨어지다)	dropped, dropt	dropped, dropt
dwell (살다)	dwelt, dwelled	dwelt, dwelled
E　eat (먹다)	ate	eaten
F　fall (떨어지다)	fell	fallen
feed (음식을 주다)	fed	fed
feel (느끼다)	felt	felt
fight (싸우다)	fought	fought
find (발견하다)	found	found
flee (달아나다)	fled	fled
fling (던지다)	flung	flung
fly (날다)	flew	flown
forbear (억제하다, 삼가다)	forbore	forborne
forbid (금하다)	forbade, forbad	forbidden, forbid
forecast (예보하다)	forecast, forecasted	forecast, forecasted
forego (…없이 지내다)	forewent	foregone
foreknow (미리 알다)	foreknew	foreknown
foresee (예견하다, 미리 알다)	foresaw	foreseen
foretell (예고하다)	foretold	foretold
forget (잊어버리다)	forgot	forgotten, forgot
forgive (용서하다)	forgave	forgiven
forsake (저버리다, 내버리다)	forsook	forsaken
forswear (맹세코 그만두다)	forswore	forsworn
freeze (얼다, 얼리다)	froze	frozen
G　gainsay (부정하다)	gainsaid	gainsaid
get (얻다)	got	got, (*U.S., archaic*) gotten
gild (금을 입히다)	gilded, gilt	gilded, gilt
gird (졸라매다)	girded, girt	girded, girt
give (주다)	gave	given
go (가다)	went	gone
grave (새기다, 조각하다)	graved	graved, graven
grind (갈다, 가루로 만들다)	ground	ground
grow (자라다)	grew	grown
H　hang (매달다, 걸다)	hung, hanged	hung, hanged

原　　形	過　去	過　去　分　詞
have (has) (가지다)	**had**	**had**
hear (듣다)	**heard**	**heard**
heave (들어올리다)	heaved, hove	heaved, hove
hew (베어 넘기다)	hewed	hewn, hewed
hide (숨기다, 숨다)	**hid**	**hidden**
hit (치다, 때리다)	**hit**	**hit**
hold (붙잡다)	**held**	**held**
hurt (상처내다)	**hurt**	**hurt**
I inlay (끼워넣다)	inlaid	inlaid
inset (끼워넣다)	inset	inset
K **keep** (지키다)	**kept**	**kept**
kneel (무릎 꿇다)	knelt	knelt
knit (짜다, 뜨다)	knit, knitted	knit, knitted
know (알다)	**knew**	**known**
L lade (짐을 쌓다, 싣다)	laded	laded, laden
lay (놓다, 눕다)	**laid**	**laid**
lead (이끌다)	**led**	**led**
lean (기대다, 의지하다)	**leaned,** (*Brit.*) **leant**	**leaned,** (*Brit.*) **leant**
leap (껑충 뛰다)	**leaped, leapt**	**leaped, leapt**
learn (배우다)	**learned, learnt**	**learned, learnt**
leave (떠나다)	**left**	**left**
lend (빌려주다)	**lent**	**lent**
let (…시키다)	**let**	**let**
lie (눕다)	**lay**	**lain**
light (불을 붙이다, 내리다)	**lit, lighted**	**lit, lighted**
lose (잃다)	**lost**	**lost**
M **make** (만들다)	**made**	**made**
may (…인지도 모르다)	**might**	―
mean (뜻하다)	**meant**	**meant**
meet (만나다)	**met**	**met**
melt (녹다, 녹이다)	melted	melted, molten
methinks (…라고 생각되다)	methought	―
misgive (걱정을 끼치다)	misgave	misgiven
mislay (잘못 두다, 놓고 있다)	mislaid	mislaid
mislead (잘못 인도하다)	misled	misled
misread (잘못 읽다)	misread [misréd]	misread [misréd]
misspell (철자를 잘못 적다)	misspelled, misspelt	misspelled, misspelt
misspend (낭비하다)	misspent	misspent
mistake (틀리다)	**mistook**	**mistaken**
misunderstand (오해하다)	misunderstood	misunderstood
mow (풀 따위를 베다)	mowed	mowed, mown
must (…하지 않으면 안 되다)	**must**	―
O outdo (보다 낫다, 능가하다)	outdid	outdone
outgrow (…보다 커지다)	outgrew	outgrown
outrun (…보다 빨리 달리다)	outran	outrun
outshine (…보다 강하게 빛나다)	outshone	outshone
outspread (넓히다, 넓어지다)	outspread	outspread
outwear (…보다 오래 가다)	outwore	outworn
overcast (어둡게 하다)	overcast	overcast

不規則動詞表

原　　　　形	過　　　去	過　去　分　詞
overcome (…에 이겨내다)	overcame	overcome
overdo (지나치게 하다)	overdid	overdone
overdraw (너무 당기다)	overdrew	overdrawn
overeat (너무 먹다)	overate	overeaten
overfeed (너무 먹이다)	overfed	overfed
overgrow (널리 퍼지다)	overgrew	overgrown
overhang (…위에 걸다)	overhung	overhung
overhear (귓결에 듣다)	overheard	overheard
overlay (…에 들씌우다)	overlaid	overlaid
overleap (…을 뛰어넘다)	overleaped, overleapt	overleaped, overleapt
override (…을 무시하다)	overrode	overridden
overrun (전반에 걸쳐 퍼지다)	overran	overrun
overset (뒤집다, 뒤집히다)	overset	overset
overshoot (넘겨 쏘다)	overshot	overshot
oversleep (너무 자다)	overslept	overslept
overspread (퍼지다)	overspread	overspread
overtake (좇아가다)	overtook	overtaken
overthrow (뒤집어 엎다)	overthrew	overthrown
overwork (지나치게 일하다)	overworked, overwrought	overworked, overwrought
P　partake (참가하다, 함께하다)	partook	partaken
pay (지불하다)	**paid**	**paid**
pen (쓰다, 적다)	penned	penned
prove (증명하다)	proved	proved, (U.S. archaic.) proven
put (놓다)	**put**	**put**
Q　quit (그만두다)	quitted, quit	quitted, quit
R　**read** [ri:d] (읽다)	**read** [red]	**read** [red]
rebuild (재건하다)	rebuilt	rebuilt
recast (고쳐 만들다)	recast	recast
relay (다시 놓다)	relaid	relaid
rend (째다, 찢다)	rent	rent
repay (반제하다, 되지불하다)	repaid	repaid
reread (되읽다)	reread	reread
resell (되팔다)	resold	resold
reset (다시 놓다, 고쳐 놓다)	reset	reset
retake (다시 잡다)	retook	retaken
retell (되풀이 말하다)	retold	retold
rewrite (고쳐 쓰다)	rewrote	rewritten
rid (해방하다, 면하게 하다)	rid, ridded	rid, ridded
ride (타다)	**rode**	**ridden**
ring (울리다)	**rang** [ræŋ]	**rung** [rʌŋ]
rise (오르다, 올리다)	**rose**	**risen** [rízn]
rive [raiv] (찢다, 쪼개다)	rived	riven [rívn], rived
run [rʌn] (달리다)	**ran** [ræn]	**run** [rʌn]
S　saw (톱질하다)	sawed	sawn, sawed
say (말하다)	**said**	**said**
see (보다, 보이다)	**saw**	**seen**
seek (구하다, 찾다)	**sought** [sɔ:t]	**sought** [sɔ:t]
sell (팔다)	sold	sold

原　　　　　形	過　　去	過　去　分　詞
send (보내다)	**sent**	**sent**
set (놓다)	**set**	**set**
sew [sou] (꿰매다)	**sewed**	**sewn, sewed**
shake (흔들다, 흔들리다)	**shook** [ʃuk]	**shaken**
shall (…일 것이다)	**should** [ʃud]	—
shave (면도하다)	shaved	shaved, shaven
shear- (양털 따위를 깎다)	sheared	sheared, shorn
shed (흘리다)	**shed**	**shed**
shine (빛나게 하다)	**shone**	**shone**
[註] 구두를 닦는 경우에는	shined,	shined
shoe (**구두를 신기다**)	shod	shod
shoot (반사하다)	**shot**	**shot**
show (보이다, 보게 하다)	**showed**	**shown, showed**
shrink (오그라들다)	shrank, (*rare*) shrunk	shrunk, (*rare*) shrunken
shut (닫다)	**shut**	**shut**
sing (노래하다)	**sang**	**sung**
sink (가라앉다, 가라앉히다)	**sank, sunk**	**sunk, sunken**
sit (앉다)	**sat**	**sat**
slay (살해하다)	slew	slain
sleep (자다)	**slept**	**slept**
slide (미끄러지다)	slid	slid, slidden
sling (투석기로 돌을 던지다)	slung	slung
slink (살그머니 걷다)	slunk	slunk
slit (베어 가르다)	slit	slit
smell (냄새 나다)	**smelled, smelt**	**smelled, smelt**
smite (세게 때리다)	smote	smitten
sow (씨를 뿌리다)	**sowed**	**sown, sowed**
speak (이야기하다)	**spoke**	**spoken**
speed (서두르다)	**sped, speeded**	**sped, speeded**
spell (철자하다)	**spelled, spelt**	**spelled, spelt**
spend (사용하다)	**spent**	**spent**
spill (엎지르다, 엎질러지다)	spilt, spilled	spilt, spilled
spin (잣다, 방적하다)	spun, span	spun
spit (뱉다)	spat	spat
split (쪼개다, 쪼개지다)	split	split
spoil (망쳐 놓다)	**spoiled, spoilt**	**spoiled, spoilt**
spread (펴다, 퍼지다)	**spread**	**spread**
spring (뛰다, 튀게 하다)	**sprang, sprung**	**sprung**
squat (웅크리다, 쭈그리다)	squatted, squat	squatted, squat
stand (일어나다, 일으키다)	**stood**	**stood**
stave (통에 널을 붙이다)	staved, stove	staved, stove
steal (훔치다)	**stole**	**stolen**
stick (찌르다)	stuck	stuck
sting (찌르다)	stung	stung
stink (고약한 냄새가 나다)	stank, stunk	stunk
strew (흩뿌리다)	strewed	strewed, strewn
stride (큰 걸음으로 걷다)	strode	stridden
strike (때리다, 치다)	**struck**	**struck, stricken**
string (끈이나 실로 묶다)	strung	strung

不規則動詞表

原　形	過　去	過去分詞
strive (노력하다)	strove	striven [strívn]
sunburn (볕볕에 그을리다)	sunburned, sunburnt	sunburned, sunburnt
swear (신에게 맹세하다)	**swore**	**sworn**
sweat [swet] (땀을 흘리게 하다)	sweat, sweated	sweat, sweated
sweep (쓸다, 소제하다)	**swept**	**swept**
swell (부풀다, 부풀리다)	**swelled**	**swollen, swelled**
swim (헤엄치다)	**swam**	**swum**
swing (흔들리다, 흔들다)	**swung**	**swung**
T **take** (잡다, 쥐다)	**took**	**taken**
teach (가르치다)	**taught**	**taught**
tear [tɛər] (찢다)	**tore**	**torn**
telecast (텔레비방송하다)	telecast, telecasted	telecast, telecasted
tell (말하다)	**told**	**told**
think (생각하다)	**thought**	**thought**
thrive (번영하다)	throve, thrived	thrived, thriven [θrívn]
throw (던지다)	**threw**	**thrown**
thrust (누르다)	**thrust**	**thrust**
tread (걷다, 밟다)	trod	trodden, trod
U unbend (곧게 펴다)	unbent	unbent
unbind (풀다)	unbound	unbound
underbid (보다 싼 값을 붙이다)	underbid	underbid
undercut (…의 밑을 자르다)	undercut	undercut
undergo (경험하다)	underwent	undergone
undersell (보다 싸게 팔다)	undersold	undersold
understand (이해하다)	**understood**	**understood**
undertake (떠맡다)	undertook	undertaken
undo (원상태로 돌리다)	undid	undone
unsay (취소하다)	unsaid	unsaid
unwind (풀다, 풀리다)	unwound	unwound
upset (뒤집어 엎다)	upset	upset
W **wake** (잠깨다, 일어나다)	**waked, woke**	**waked,** (*rare*) **woken**
waylay (매복하다)	waylaid	waylaid
wear (입고 있다)	**wore**	**worn**
weave (짜다, 뜨다)	**wove**	**woven, wove**
wed (결혼하다)	wedded, (*rare*) wed	wedded, (*rare*) wed
weep (울다)	**wept**	**wept**
will (…일 것이다)	**would** [wud]	──
win (이기다)	**won**	**won**
wind [waind] (굽이치다)	**wound** [waund]	**wound** [waund]
withdraw (움츠리다, 물러나다)	**withdrew**	**withdrawn**
withhold (보류하다, 억누르다)	withheld	withheld
withstand (저항하다)	withstood	withstood
work (일하다, 공부하다)	**worked,** (usu. *archaic*) **wrought** [rɔːt]	**worked,** (usu. *archaic*) **wrought** [rɔːt]
wring (짜다, 비틀다)	**wrung**	**wrung**
write (글씨를 쓰다)	**wrote**	**written**